PENGUIN REFERENCE

THE PENGUIN GUIDE TO COMPACT DISCS

Edward Greenfield, until his retirement, in 1993, was for forty years on the staff of the *Guardian*, succeeding Neville Cardus as Music Critic in 1975. He still contributes regularly to the record column which he founded in 1954. At the end of 1960 he joined the reviewing panel of *Gramophone*, specializing in operatic and orchestral issues. He is a regular broadcaster on music and records for the BBC, not just on Radios 3 and 4 but also on the BBC World Service, latterly with his weekly programme, *The Greenfield Collection*. In 1958 he published a monograph on the operas of Puccini. More recently he has written studies on the recorded work of Joan Sutherland and André Previn. He has been a regular juror on International Record awards and has appeared with such artists as Dame Elisabeth Schwarzkopf, Dame Joan Sutherland and Sir Georg Solti in public interviews. In October 1993 he was given a *Gramophone* Award for Special Achievement and in June 1994 received the OBE for services to music and journalism.

Robert Layton studied at Oxford with Edmund Rubbra for composition and with Egon Wellesz for the history of music. He spent two years in Sweden at the universities of Uppsala and Stockholm. He joined the BBC Music Division in 1959 and was responsible for Music Talks, including such pro-grammes as *Interpretations on Record*. He contributed 'A Quarterly Retrospect' to *Gramophone* magazine for thirty-four years and writes for the *BBC Music Magazine, International Record Review* and other journals. His books include studies of the Swedish composer Berwald and of Sibelius, as well as a monograph on the Dvořák symphonies and concertos for the *BBC Music Guides*, of which he was General Editor for many years. His prize-winning translation of Erik Tawaststjerna's definitive five-volume study of Sibelius was completed in 1998. In 1987 he was awarded the Sibelius Medal and in the following year made a Knight of the Order of the White Rose of Finland for his services to Finnish music. His other books include *Grieg: An Illustrated Life* and he has edited the *Guide to the Symphony* and the *Guide to the Concerto* (OUP). In 2001, at a ceremony to mark the Swedish presidency of the European Union, he was made a Knight of the Royal Order of the Polar Star.

Ivan March is a former professional musician. He studied at Trinity College of Music, London, and at the Royal Manchester College. After service in the Central Band of the RAF, he played the horn professionally for the BBC and travelled with the Carl Rosa and D'Oyly Carte opera companies. He is a well-known lecturer, journalist and personality in the world of recorded music and acts as consultant to Squires Gate Music Ltd, an international mail order source for classical CDs (www.lprl.demon.co.uk). As a journalist he has contributed to a number of record-reviewing magazines, but now reviews solely for *Gramophone*.

THE PENGUIN GUIDE
TO COMPACT DISCS
2002 *Edition*

IVAN MARCH,
EDWARD GREENFIELD and
ROBERT LAYTON

Edited by Ivan March
Assistant Editor: Paul Chaikowsky

PENGUIN BOOKS

PENGUIN BOOKS

Published by the Penguin Group
Penguin Books Ltd, 80 Strand, London WC2R 0RL, England
Penguin Putnam Inc., 375 Hudson Street, New York, New York 10014, USA
Penguin Books Australia Ltd, Ringwood, Victoria, Australia
Penguin Books Canada Ltd, 10 Alcorn Avenue, Toronto, Ontario, Canada M4V 3B2
Penguin Books India (P) Ltd, 11, Community Centre, Panchsheel Park, New Delhi – 110 017, India
Penguin Books (NZ) Ltd, Private Bag 102902, NSMC, Auckland, New Zealand
Penguin Books (South Africa) (Pty) Ltd, 5 Watkins Street, Denver Ext 4, Johannesburg 2094, South Africa

Penguin Books Ltd, Registered Offices: 80 Strand, London WC2R 0RL, England

This edition first published 2001
1

Set in 8.25/9.6 pt PostScript Adobe Minion
Typeset, from material supplied, by Rowland Phototypesetting Ltd, Bury St Edmunds, Suffolk
Made and printed in Great Britain by William Clowes (Beccles) Ltd, Beccles and London

CONTENTS

FOREWORD

The first complete *Penguin Guide to Compact Discs* of the new millennium covers in considerable depth, and with many thousands of listings and reviews, the whole range of our musical heritage – over nine centuries. And that means not only the widest possible choice of recordings within the standard repertoire, but the continuing discovery of huge amounts of unknown but immensely rewarding music, some new, some old. Many more composers have joined our roster, who hitherto have been regarded as just historical figures, or whose names are not familiar at all.

While Byzantine liturgical music, reaching back to the fourth century, is still part of the lives of millions of Eastern Orthodox Christians whose native language is Greek, the first music to be written down and preserved dates from 670, and from the ninth century onwards a primitive musical shorthand was achieved to record Byzantine chant (which was to evolve into Gregorian chant). But unfortunately that does not supply enough information for modern scholars to reconstruct the melismatic flow accurately. The earliest notation sufficiently detailed to indicate both the pitch of the notes and the intervals between them did not appear until late in the twelfth century, when primitive polyphony began to be organized into a musical style called 'Organum'. Our composer entries include two key names of early composers dating from that period. If you look up Leonin (*c.* 1163–90), who developed written two-part vocal organa, and his successor, Magister Perotinus (*c.* 1160–1225), who extended the part-writing to include three- and four-part vocal lines, you will have discovered the very beginnings of Western written music – which found its initial source and inspiration in the Christian church.

The scope of vocal and instrumental music expanded greatly in the centuries that followed, but opera did not really arrive until the very beginning of the seventeenth, and it was in the eighteenth that the symphony orchestra developed from an accompanying ensemble to become a fully fledged entity in its own right. We are fortunate that during those six centuries of expansion and development, and afterwards, all over Europe music libraries stored countless manuscripts of both secular and liturgical music. Much of it is only just being rediscovered and only a very small proportion of it is being performed live. And while forgotten manuscripts are immensely valuable to scholars, and much sought after by performing musicians, their full value is only realized when they are *heard*.

Although concert programmes and the repertoire of opera houses are becoming more adventurous, live performances can hardly begin to delve deeply enough into this musical treasure trove. But the compact disc *can* and *does*, thanks to the remarkable enterprise of singers and musicians who devote much of their time to making recordings, and the comparable enterprise of the record companies (especially the smaller and medium-sized ones), who are willing to finance the flood of CDs that has recently resulted. And much that has been hitherto forgotten is being revealed in our pages as genuine treasure. (Remember that Hermann Scherchen reintroduced Vivaldi's *Four Seasons* to the world – on 78 shellac discs – only as recently as 1948!)

CDs have never been better value. Apart from the many Duos and Doubles (two discs for the price of one), there are now far more super-bargain discs than ever before, for both EMI's new Encore label and Warner's Apex series have joined the lowest price-range, of which Naxos was the pioneer and is still market-leader.

But this book, as ever, is about excellence in recorded music, irrespective of cost. Our current survey evaluates many thousands of the very finest CD performances currently available. They have survived in the catalogue, or been reissued, because their excellence is recognized. Specialist historical labels like Biddulph and Testament have licensed earlier recordings from the majors, and taken great care to ensure that the original mono quality is not degraded by the CD analogue-to-digital transfers. And more recently Naxos have begun making inexpensive reissues of historical recordings, especially opera, which are out of copyright. But standing head and shoulders above all other such enterprises is the 'Dutton Lab.' series. Mike Dutton is the supreme magician of CD remastering, and his results are sometimes little short of miraculous.

The most significant change in performance styles of our own time is the return to the use of authentic original instruments for early music. Together with conjectural attempts to simulate period playing-techniques, the immediate effect on the sound of baroque music in particular has been unparalleled. In the last few years period performances have matured. Intonation has improved and the curious linear squeezing in the place of vibrato has all but abated. Moreover, modern-instrument performances have learned much from period-instrument practices, and the difference between the two styles has greatly narrowed. So we are getting the best of both worlds.

England has a great tradition of cathedral-trained male and latterly female choristers who have grouped together to take advantage of the new interest in early music. So arrived the Clerk's Group under Edward Wickham, the Clerkes of Oxenford, under Davis Wulstan, and (most economically on Naxos) the versatile Oxford Camerata directed by Jeremy Summerly. The Cardinall's Musick directed by Andrew Carwood, have already given us a complete survey of the music of Robert Fayrfax and are up to Volume 6 of a projected complete recording of all the music of Byrd; the Chapelle du Roi under Alistair Dixon have embarked on a comprehensive coverage of Tallis's music, and have now reached their fourth CD; while the King's Consort under Robert

King are recording all Vivaldi's vocal music, and have just reached Volume 6. Among many distinguished soloists, Emma Kirkby, with her delightfully fresh soprano voice, has become Queen of the Baroque, and was chosen to record the recently rediscovered *Gloria* of Handel.

But by far the greater part of our survey is the continual reassessment of major recordings of the standard orchestral, instrumental and vocal repertoire. The range of alternatives is now astonishing. While there are certain particularly distinguished and uniquely successful CDs, which tend to trump all the opposition by their musical perceptions and special insights, in most cases there is no longer such a thing as a 'best' recording, although some are better than others. While recordings and reissues new to the present volume – immediately recognizable by the prefix (N) before the catalogue number – are usually still discussed in some depth, what we have tried to do in the current revision is to pare each earlier review down to its essentials, so that the reader can choose his or her priorities in making an assessment, and deciding which recording to purchase.

Ivan March, Editor

THE COMING OF DVD

Like many readers and record collectors we were initially resistant to the concept of DVD. We were very content with just the music and, even in the world of opera, happy to listen to the singers, and use our imagination to picture the action. With orchestral, and especially chamber and instrumental, music a visual image seemed quite superfluous. But it is not so.

One's first experience of a really outstanding DVD is quite traumatic. Like the coming of stereo sound, or the silent background of a compact disc, this medium brings an added immediacy to the musical experience – and not only in the world of opera and ballet. Providing one can link one's reproducing equipment to a good TV set, placing the stereo speakers either side, one can often experience a remarkable added degree of communication with the performers and, through them, the music. Not only is the picture quality remarkably real and tangible, but the sound is too. The violin timbre as one watches Sir Georg Solti conduct the opening *Prelude* to the Decca DVD of *La traviata* is more real and tangible than on CD, and one can really feel that his hand movements are directly responsible for the musical results.

In the concert hall one is even more aware of the magnetism reaching out from the conductor to his players. Karajan's DVD of Bach's *Magnificat* has remarkable intensity, even though his movements are minimal, and (as R.L. has noted in his review below) Karajan's digital DG recording of Dvořák's *New World Symphony*, with the Vienna Philharmonic Orchestra, to which we awarded **(*) in its CD format, is unquestionably a *** issue on DVD. The slow movement, in particular, seems quite inspired, and has wonderful tonal subtlety and great refinement.

There are other instances, of course, where the realism of communication can have the opposite effect, making one more aware of an artist's self-awareness. But in most instances the listening experience and indeed the sound are both nearer to the experience of live music-making than an audio recording, and as such cherishable. Operas all have subtitles, but these can be omitted at will, as can the picture; for one would surely sometimes want to listen without the visual images. DVDs are here to stay and our next guide will be entitled *The Penguin Guide to Compact discs and DVDs*. Meanwhile a handpicked selection of current DVDs is discussed separately at the end of our CD composer listings.

INTRODUCTION

As in previous editions, the object of *The Penguin Guide to Compact Discs* is to give the serious collector a comprehensive survey of the finest recordings of permanent music on CD, irrespective of price. As many records are issued almost simultaneously on both sides of the Atlantic and use identical international catalogue numbers, this *Guide* should be found to be equally useful in the UK and the USA, as it will in Australia, Canada and New Zealand. The internationalization of repertoire and numbers now applies to almost all CDs issued by the major international companies and also by the smaller ones. Many European labels are imported in their original formats, into both Britain and the USA. Those CDs that are available only in Britain can be easily obtained by overseas collectors via the Web address given on page xvii.

We feel that it is a strength of our basic style to let our own conveyed pleasure and admiration (or otherwise) for the merits of an individual recording come over directly to the reader, even if this produces a certain ambivalence in the matter of such a final choice. Where there is disagreement between us (and this rarely happens), readers will find an indication of our different reactions in the text.

We have considered (and rejected) the use of initials against individual reviews, since this is essentially a team project. The occasions for disagreement generally concern matters of aesthetics – in the matter of recording balance for instance, where a contrived effect may trouble some ears more than others, or in the matter of style, where the difference between robustness and refinement of approach appeals differently to listening sensibilities rather than involving a question of artistic integrity. But over the years our views seem to have grown closer together rather than having diverged; perhaps we are getting mellower, but we are seldom ready to offer strong disagreement following the enthusiastic reception by one of the team of a controversial recording, providing the results are creatively stimulating. As performance standards have advanced, our perceptions of the advantages and disadvantages of performances of early music on original (as against modern) instruments seem fairly evenly balanced.

EVALUATION

Most major recordings issued today are of a high technical standard and offer performances of a quality at least as high as is experienced in the concert hall. In adopting a star system for the evaluation of records, we have decided to make use of from one to three stars. Brackets around one or more of the stars indicate some reservations about a recording's rating, and readers are advised to refer to the text. Brackets around all the stars usually indicate a basic

qualification: for instance, a mono recording of a performance of artistic interest, where some allowances may have to be made for the sound quality even though the recording may have been digitally remastered. Our evaluation system may be summarized as follows:

*** an outstanding performance and recording in every way

** a good performance and recording of today's normal high standard

* a fair or somewhat routine performance, reasonably well performed or recorded

Our evaluation is normally applied to the record as a whole, unless there are two main works or groups of works, and by different composers. In this case, each is dealt with separately in its appropriate place.

ROSETTES

To certain special records we have awarded a Rosette: ✿.

Unlike our general evaluations, in which we have tried to be consistent, a Rosette is a quite individual compliment by a member of the reviewing team to a recorded performance which, he finds, shows special illumination, magic, spiritual quality or even outstanding production values that place it in a very special class. Occasionally a Rosette has been awarded for an issue that seems to us to offer extraordinary value for money, but that presupposes that the performance or performances are outstanding too. The choice is essentially a personal one (although often it represents a shared view) and in some cases it is applied to an issue where certain reservations must also be mentioned in the text of the review. The Rosette symbol is placed before the usual evaluation and the record number. It is quite small – we do not mean to imply an 'Academy Award' but a personal token of appreciation for something uniquely valuable. We hope that, once the reader has discovered and perhaps acquired a 'rosetted' CD, its special qualities will soon become apparent. There are, of course, more of them now, for our survey has become a distillation of the excellence of CDs issued and reissued over a considerable time span.

DIGITAL RECORDINGS

Nearly all new compact discs are recorded digitally, but an increasingly large number of digitally remastered, reissued analogue recordings are now appearing, and we think it important to include a clear indication of the difference:

All listed CDs are digital *unless* the inclusion of (ADD) in the titling indicates analogue-to-digital remastering.

The indication ADD/Dig. (or Dig./ADD) applies to a compilation where recordings come from mixed sources.

LISTINGS AND PRICE RANGES

Our listing of each recording assumes that it is in the premium-price category, unless it indicates otherwise, as follows:

(M) medium-priced label
(B) bargain-priced label
(BB) super-bargain label

See below for differences in price structures between the UK and the USA.

LAYOUT OF TEXT

We have aimed to make our style as simple as possible. So immediately after the evaluation and before the catalogue number the record make is given, sometimes in abbreviated form. In the case of a set of two or more CDs, the number of units involved is given in brackets after the catalogue number.

AMERICAN CATALOGUE NUMBERS

The numbers which follow in square brackets are US catalogue numbers, if they are different from UK catalogue numbers (and this applies in particular to EMI's 'Great Recordings of the Century', which have a different number on each side of the Atlantic). RCA has moved now over to completely identical numbers, although a few earlier issues have an alphabetical prefix in the UK which is not used in the USA. Where a record is available in the USA but *not* the UK, *it will appear in square brackets only*, and that applies especially to some Mercury CDs. But EMI's American label, 'Red Line Classics', is now available in the UK to special order.

There are certain other small differences to be remembered by American readers. For instance, EMI use extra digits for their British compact discs; thus the British number CDM7 63351-2 becomes CDM 63351 in the USA (the -2 is the European indication that this is a compact disc). Prefixes can alter too. The British EMI forte and double forte CZS5 68583-2 becomes CDFB 68583 in the USA; and Virgin Classics VBD5 61469-2 becomes CDVB 61469. We have taken care to check catalogue information as far as is possible, but as all the editorial work has been done in England there is always the possibility of error; American readers are therefore invited, when ordering records locally, to take the precaution of giving their dealer the fullest information about the music and recordings they want.

The indications (M), (B) and (BB) immediately before the starring of a disc refer primarily to the British CD, as pricing systems are not always identical on both sides of the Atlantic. When CDs are imported by specialist distributors into the USA, this again usually involves a price difference. When mid-priced CDs on the smaller labels are imported into the USA, they often move up to the premium-price range. American readers are advised to check the current *Schwann* catalogue and to consult their local record store.

ABBREVIATIONS

To save space we have adopted a number of standard abbreviations in listing record companies, orchestras and performing groups (a list is provided below), and the titles of works are often shortened, especially where they are listed several times. Artists' forenames are usually omitted if they are not absolutely necessary for identification purposes. Also we have not usually listed the contents of operatic highlights and collections.

We have followed common practice in the use of the original language for titles where it seems sensible. In most cases, English is used for orchestral and instrumental music, and the original language for vocal music and opera. There are exceptions, however; for instance, the Johann Strauss discography uses the German language in the interests of consistency.

ORDER OF MUSIC

The order of music under each composer's name broadly follows the following system: orchestral music, including concertos and symphonies; chamber music; solo instrumental music (in some cases with keyboard and organ music separated); vocal and choral music; opera; vocal collections; miscellaneous collections. Within each group our listing follows an alphabetical sequence, and couplings within a single composer's output are *usually* discussed together instead of separately with cross-references. Occasionally (and inevitably because of this alphabetical approach), different recordings of a given work can become separated when a record is listed and discussed under the first work of its alphabetical sequence. The editor feels that alphabetical consistency is essential if the reader is to learn to find his or her way about.

CATALOGUE NUMBERS

Enormous care has gone into the checking of CD catalogue numbers and contents to ensure that all details are correct, but the editor and publishers cannot be held responsible for any mistakes that may have crept in despite all our zealous checking. When ordering CDs, readers are urged to provide their record-dealer with full details of the music and performers, as well as the catalogue number.

DELETIONS

Compact discs regularly succumb to the deletions axe, and many are likely to disappear during the lifetime of this book. Sometimes copies may still be found in specialist shops, and there remains the compensatory fact that most really important and desirable recordings are eventually reissued, often costing less! As we go to press, EMI have issued a fairly extensive deletions list. Where important recordings have been withdrawn, we have mentioned this in the text at the end of reviews. Most are likely to reappear. Also, for the moment, the Tactus label has no UK distributor.

Universal Classics have an import service for certain CDs which are not carried in their UK inventory, and these CDs are indicated with the abbreviation IMS. A small extra charge is made for these discs, which may have to be obtained from Germany or Holland. Of the smaller companies, both CRD and Gimell are currently repackaging and reissuing their catalogues. Not all their discs are currently available, and readers will need to persist in ordering until they come to hand. Many will remain unobtainable into 2002.

COVERAGE

As the output of major and minor labels continues to expand, it is obviously impossible for us to mention every CD that is available within the covers of a single book; this is recognized as a practical limitation if we are to update our survey regularly. Indeed, we have now to be very selective in choosing the discs to be included, and some good recordings inevitably fall by the wayside. There is generally a reason for omissions, and usually it is connected with the lack of ready availablity. However, we do welcome suggestions from readers about such omissions if they seem to be of special interest, although we cannot guarantee to include them in a future survey!

ACKNOWLEDGEMENTS

Our thanks are due to our Penguin copy editor, Helen Williams, especially for her work during the final assembly of all the material for this book. Paul Chaikowsky, as Assistant Editor, contributed to the titling – never an easy task; he also helped with retrieval of earlier reviews (connected with reissues). Our team of Penguin proof-readers have once again proved themselves indispensable. Grateful thanks also go to all those readers who write to us to point out factual errors and to remind us of important recordings which have escaped our notice.

FUTURE EDITIONS OF THE PENGUIN GUIDE

As will seem obvious, the 2002 Edition of *The Penguin Guide* has reached the point where it can no longer expand further in a single volume. Even now (following the procedure of the 1999 Edition) Concerts and Recitals have had to be carried forward to the 2002/3 *Yearbook*, which has in effect become the second stage of our bi-annual survey.

As we plan our next main *Guide*, to be published two years from now, it may well prove impossible to contain the entire composer listings and reviews in one book – even allowing for deletions (which may be extensive). We are considering three possible alternatives, and we should welcome your views as a reader, as to which is most acceptable.

While *all* new issues and reissues will be included in every instance:

(i) the composer survey could be cut back to cover only the top recommendations with the standard repertoire and the most worthwhile issues from the edge of the repertoire. This would mean that many desirable recordings which are not among the very top choices would be omitted from the book, and instead placed on a web site; or

(ii) the composer survey could fully cover *all* important recordings of the major composers, while minor composers (Spohr is a good example) would be carried forward to be given a similarly comprehensive coverage in the *Yearbook* which would be expanded and still include all subsequent new issues, plus Collections and DVDs; or

(iii) the obvious third alternative, which is to publish the Guide in *two separate volumes*, the first containing composers A–M, the second containing composers N-Z, plus Collections. DVDS would be included in both volumes. But we feel that many potential readers would not want to invest in *either* of these complementary volumes because each would be incomplete without the other.

We should much appreciate your comments – by letter please, not e-mail, to the following address:

Ivan March, c/o Penguin Press Commissioning Editorial, Penguin Books Ltd, 80 Strand, London WC2R ORL, U.K.

Ivan March, Editor

THE AMERICAN SCENE

CDs are much less expensive in the USA than they are in Great Britain, and because of this (so we are told) many bargain recordings available in Britain are not brought into the USA by their manufacturers. This applies especially to the Universal group, so that Decca Eclipse, DG Classikon and Philips Virtuoso labels have to be imported by the major US record stores and mail order outlets. What this means is that while almost any recording mentioned in these pages will be available in the USA, sometimes it will cost more than the buyer might reasonably expect.

Duos and Doubles, where available, remain at two discs for the cost of one premium-priced CD in both countries, and here US collectors have a price advantage. However, according to *Schwann*, many excellent lower-priced discs are not issued in the USA. Where a recording is of extra special interest, American collectors can obtain it readily by mail order from Britain, through the Website address given on page xvii. However, it will inevitably cost more than it would domestically.

From your many letters, and from visiting record stores in the USA, we know that our *Penguin Guide* is read, enjoyed and used as a tool by collectors on both sides of the Atlantic. We also know that some transatlantic readers feel that our reviews are too frequently oriented towards European and British recordings and performances. In concentrating on records which have common parlance in both Europe and the USA, we obviously give preference to the output of international companies, and in assessing both performers and performances we are concerned with only one factor: musical excellence. In a 400-year-old musical culture centred in Europe, it is not surprising that a great number of the finest interpreters should have been Europeans, and many of them have enjoyed recording in London, where there are four first-class symphony orchestras and many smaller groups at their disposal, supported by recording producers and engineers of the highest calibre. The early-music period-instrument revolution is also presently centred in London, which seems to add another bias, which is not of our making.

However, the continuing re-emergence of earlier recordings by major American recording orchestras and artists is slowly redressing the balance. Our performance coverage in the present volume – helped by the huge proportion of reissued older records – certainly reflects the American achievement, past and present and particularly the 1930s to 1960s. Then Koussevitzky was in Boston; Frederick Stock and, after him, Fritz Reiner were in Chicago; Mitropoulos, Bruno Walter and Bernstein directed the New York Philharmonic in its heyday; Stokowski and Ormandy were in Philadelphia; and George Szell was creating astonishing standards of orchestral virtuosity in Cleveland. At the same time, Heifetz and Horowitz, Piatigorsky, Rubinstein and Isaac Stern were carrying all before them in the instrumental field. With the current phenomenal improvements in transferring technology, we hope that increasing numbers of the recordings made by these great names from the past will enjoy the attention of the wider public.

PRICE DIFFERENCES IN THE UK AND USA

Retail prices are not fixed in either country, and various stores may offer even better deals at times, so our price structure must be taken as a guideline only. Premium-priced CDs cost on average approximately the same number of dollars in the USA as they do pounds in the UK. The Vanguard CD label (except for the 8000 Series, which retails at around $15) is now mid-price in both the USA and the UK. Harmonia Mundi's Musique d'Abord label (prefix HMA) is described as budget – which it is in the UK – but the American list-price is $9.98. Duos and Doubles, Delos Doubles, Double Deccas, double fortes, Dyads, Finlandia 'Meet the Composer', Chandos 2-for-1 sets, BMG/RCA 'twofers', and Warner Classics Ultimas where available (although they cost less west of the Atlantic) are two-for-the-cost-of-one premium-priced disc the world over. CDCFPD and the Virgin Classics 2 x 1 Doubles are two-for-the-price-of-one mid-priced CDs.

OTHER COMPARABLE PRICES IN THE UK AND USA

Here are comparative details of the other price-ranges (note that sets are multiples of the prices quoted):

(M) Mid-priced series
Includes: Avid; Chandos (Collect; Enchant); Classic fM (UK only); CPO/EMI Operas (UK only); CRD; Decca/London including Classic Sound, Legends, and Opera Gala; DG (including Originals); Dutton CDLX Epoch CDLX; CDCLP (UK only); EMI (Classics, British music series, and Great Recordings of the Century); Erato/Warner (UK), Erato/WEA (USA); DHM; Harmonia Mundi Musique d'Abord (USA), Suite; Mercury; Oiseau-Lyre; Philips; RCA Gold Seal and Living Stereo; RCA Melodiya; Revelation; Sony; Teldec/Warner (UK), Teldec/WEA (USA); Unicorn UKCD; Vanguard; Virgin.

> UK: under £10; more usually £9
> USA: under $13; usually under $12

(B) Bargain-priced series
Includes: Calliope Approche (UK only); CfP; Debut; Decca Eclipse (UK only); DG Classikon (UK only); Dutton CDAX; CDBP; CDEA; CDK; CDLX (UK only); Eminence (UK only); Harmonia Mundi Musique d'Abord (UK only); Solo; HMP; Hyperion Helios, Naxos Opera; Philips Virtuoso (UK only); Sony Essential Classics.

> UK: £5.50–£7
> USA: under $7

(BB) Super-bargain series
Includes: Arte Nova; Arts; ASV Quicksilva (UK only); some CPO (UK only); DHM Baroque Esprit; EMI Encore; Naxos; Universal Belart; RCA Navigator (UK only); Warner Apex.

> UK: £5; some (including Navigator) cost slightly less
> USA: $5–$6

THE AUSTRALIAN SCENE

We have been fortunate in obtaining for review some recordings from the Australian branch of Universal Classics (responsible for the three key labels Decca, DG and Philips), which have been making a series of local issues of Decca, DG and Philips repertoire of considerable interest, mostly not otherwise available. These are bargain issues in Australia, but because of import costs are more expensive in the UK and USA. All these Universal Australian CDs can be purchased via the Australian website:

www.buywell.com

Residents of the UK should be able to obtain them from: Seaford Music, 24 Pevensey Road, Eastbourne, East Sussex, BN 21 3HP (Tel. 01323 732553)

AN INTERNATIONAL MAIL-ORDER SOURCE FOR RECORDINGS IN THE UK

Readers are urged to support a local dealer who is prepared and able to give a proper service, and to remember that obtaining many CDs involves expertise and perseverance. However, in recent years many specialist sources have disappeared and for that reason, if any difficulty is experienced in obtaining the CDs you want, we suggest the following mail-order alternative, which offers competitive discounts in the UK but also operates world-wide. Through this service, advice on choice of recordings from the Editor of *The Penguin Guide to Bargain Compact Discs* is always readily available to mail-order customers:

Squires Gate Music Centre Ltd (PG Dept)
Rear, 13 St Andrew's Road South
St Annes on Sea
Lancashire FY8 1SX
UK
Tel.: (+44) (0) 1253 782588; Fax: (+44) (0) 1253 782985
Website address: www.lprl.demon.co.uk
E-mail address: sales@lprl.demon.co.uk

This organization can supply any recording available in Britain and patiently extends compact-disc orders until they finally come to hand. A full guarantee of safe delivery is made on any order undertaken. Please write or fax for further details, or make a trial credit-card order, by fax, e-mail or telephone.

❂ THE ROSETTE SERVICE

Squires Gate also offers a try-before-you-buy weekly loan service (within the UK only) so that customers can try out rosetted recordings at home, plus a hand-picked group of recommended key-repertoire CDs, for a small charge, without any obligation to purchase. If a CD is subsequently purchased, it will be discounted and the trial charge waived. Full details sent on request. It is hoped that DVDs may be added to this service in 2001/2002.

Squires Gate Music Centre also offers a simple bi-monthly mailing, listing a hand-picked selection of current new and reissued CDs, chosen by the Editor of the *Penguin Guide*, Ivan March. Regular customers of Squires Gate Music Centre Ltd, both domestic and overseas, receive the bulletin as available, and it is sent automatically with their purchases.

ABBREVIATIONS

ADD	Analogue to Digital remastered	LCP	London Classical Players
AAM	Academy of Ancient Music	LMP	London Mozart Players
Ac.	Academy, Academic	LOP	Lamoureux Orchestra of Paris
Amb. S.	Ambrosian Singers	LPO	London Philharmonic Orchestra
Ara.	Arabesque	LSO	London Symphony Orchestra
arr.	arranged, arrangement	(M)	mid-price CD
ASMF	Academy of St Martin-in-the-Fields	Mer.	Meridian
(B)	bargain-price CD	Met.	Metropolitan
(BB)	super-bargain-price CD	min.	minor
Bar.	Baroque	MoC	Ministry of Culture
Bav.	Bavarian	movt	movement
BBC	British Broadcasting Corporation	(N)	new listing and review for this edition
BPO	Berlin Philharmonic Orchestra	N.	North, Northern
BRT	Belgian Radio & Television (Brussels)	nar.	narrated
Cal.	Calliope	Nat.	National
Cap.	Cappriccio	Nim.	Nimbus
CBSO	City of Birmingham Symphony Orchestra	NY	New York
CfP	Classics for Pleasure	O	Orchestra, Orchestre
Ch.	Choir; Chorale; Chorus	OAE	Orchestra of the Age of Enlightenment
Chan.	Chandos	O-L	Oiseau-Lyre
CO	Chamber Orchestra	Op.	Opera (in performance listings); opus
COE	Chamber Orchestra of Europe		(in music titles)
Col. Mus. Ant.	Musica Antiqua, Cologne	orch.	orchestrated
Coll.	Collegium	ORR	Orchestre Révolutionnaire et
Coll. Aur.	Collegium Aureum		Romantique
Coll. Voc.	Collegium Vocale	ORTF	L'Orchestre de la Radio et Télévision
Concg. O	Royal Concertgebouw Orchestra of		Française
	Amsterdam	Ph.	Philips
cond.	conductor, conducted	Phd.	Philadelphia
Cons.	Consort	Philh.	Philharmonia
DG	Deutsche Grammophon	PO	Philharmonic Orchestra
DHM	Deutsche Harmonia Mundi	Qt	Quartet
Dig.	digital recording	R.	Radio
E.	England, English	Ref.	Référence
E. Bar. Sol.	English Baroque Soloists	RLPO	Royal Liverpool Philharmonic Orchestra
ECCO	European Community Chamber	ROHCG	Royal Opera House, Covent Garden
	Orchestra	RPO	Royal Philharmonic Orchestra
ECO	English Chamber Orchestra	RSNO	Royal Scottish National Orchestra
ENO	English National Opera Company	RSO	Radio Symphony Orchestra
Ens.	Ensemble	RTE	Radio Television Eireann
ESO	English Symphony Orchestra	S.	South
Fr.	French	SCO	Scottish Chamber Orchestra
GO	Gewandhaus Orchestra	Sinf.	Sinfonietta
Häns.	Hänssler	SNO	Scottish National Orchestra
HM	Harmonia Mundi	SO	Symphony Orchestra
Hung.	Hungaroton	Soc.	Society
Hyp.	Hyperion	Sol. Ven.	I Solisti Veneti
IMS	Import Music Service (Polygram – UK	SRO	Suisse Romande Orchestra
	only)	Sup.	Supraphon
L.	London	trans.	transcription, transcribed
LA	Los Angeles	V.	Vienna
LCO	London Chamber Orchestra	V/D	Video Director

Van.	Vanguard
VCM	Vienna Concentus Musicus
VPO	Vienna Philharmonic Orchestra
VSO	Vienna Symphony Orchestra
W.	West
WNO	Welsh National Opera Company

ABEL, Carl Friedrich (1723–87)

6 Symphonies, Op. 7.

**(*) Chan. 8648. Cantilena, Shepherd.

The six *Symphonies* of Op. 7 speak much the same language as J. C. Bach or early Mozart. The performances are not the last word in elegance but they are both lively and enjoyable, as well as being well recorded.

ABRIL, Anton Garcia (born 1933)

Concierto Mudéjar.

*** Analekta Fleur de lys FL 2 3049. Boucher, Amati Ens., Dessaints – TORROBA: *Sonatina*, etc. ***

The *Concerto* by the Aragonese composer Anton Abril is attractively idiomatic, and the haunting central *Andante* clearly draws on slow movements by predecessors Castelnuovo-Tedesco and Rodrigo. The dancing zapateado finale is also highly individual. The performance is superb in all respects. The recording too is truthful, warm and pleasing. Highly recommended.

ACHRON, Joseph (1886–1943)

Children's Suite (for violin & piano; arr. Heifetz); *Hebrew Melody, Op. 33; Hebrew Lullaby, Op. 35; Prelude, Op. 13; Sonata for Violin & Piano, Op. 29; Stimmungen, Op. 32; Suite (No. 1) en style ancien, Op. 21; Les Sylphides, Op. 18.*

(BB) **(*) ASV CDQS 6235. Kramer, Over.

Joseph Achron was a prolific composer with a hundred or so works to his credit. Judging from the *Violin Sonata No. 1* (1910), he was a writer of quality with a good feeling for large-scale structures. It is obvious from the sonata alone that Achron is a far from negligible composer. Miriam Kramer and Simon Over prove accomplished advocates, though Kramer's tone is not particularly big and, from hearing her play live, one knows that the rather close microphones do not do it full justice. Worth investigating, just the same.

ADAM, Adolphe (1803–56)

Le Corsaire (ballet): complete.

*** Decca (IMS) 430 286-2 (2). ECO, Bonynge.

Le Corsaire is agreeably colourful and amiably melodic, but has little of the distinction of *Giselle*. Bonynge conducts it with finesse, warmth and drama, and the recording is out of Decca's top drawer.

Le Diable à quatre (ballet): complete.

(M) *** Decca (IMS) 444 111-2. LSO, Bonynge – MASSENET: *La Navarraise: Nocturne,* etc.; BIZET: *Don Procopio: Entr'acte to Act II;* GOUNOD: *Le Tribut de Zamora, Act III: Danse grecque.* ***

Adam's *Le Diable à quatre* was recorded in a vintage period (1964) and produces Decca's top ballet quality, with glowing horns and woodwind and wonderfully vivid detail. Richard Bonynge points the elegant writing for the strings seductively. Moreover, for this reissue Decca have found five equally winning *entr'actes* from their vaults. Bonynge clearly relishes all these items and presents them with characteristic polish and spontaneity.

Giselle (ballet): complete.

(B) *** Double Decca 452 185-2 (2) . ROHCG O, Bonynge.

Giselle (older European score).

(BB) *** Naxos 8.550755/6. Slovak RSO, Mogrelia.

(M) **(*) Mercury (ADD) (IMS) 434 365-2 (2). LSO, Fistoulari – OFFENBACH: *Gaîté parisienne;* Johann STRAUSS: *Graduation Ball.* *

Giselle (1841) is the first of the great classical ballet scores. Andrew Mogrelia's complete recording uses the normal performing edition. The orchestral playing has grace, elegance and plenty of life: the brass are not ashamed of the melodrama. The recording is resonantly full and warm in ambience, yet well detailed.

Bonynge's performance on Decca restores Adam's original and is that bit more strongly characterized, while the Decca sound has a slightly sharper and brighter profile. That remains first choice (at Double Decca price) but the Naxos set costs slightly less.

Fistoulari was a great ballet conductor and the LSO play superbly for him: there is drama in plenty, while in the gentle, lyrical music his magical touch consistently beguiles the ear. The CD transfer is very successful and the early stereo sounds remarkably modern. The snag is that the quite logical Offenbach and Johann Strauss fill-ups were among Mercury's least successful Minneapolis recordings.

La Jolie Fille de Gand (complete ballet).

(N) *** Marco 8.223772-73 (2). Queensland SO, Mogrelia.

Like Auber, Adam had the knack of writing catchy little tunes which stick in the mind – ideal for the ballet music which this composer wrote so fluently. With *La Jolie Fille de Gand*, written in 1842, one year after *Giselle*, Adam was exploring the possibilities of new orchestral colour – cornets and an ophicleide were specified in the overture (not used here), while the finale features an unexpected and dramatic organ entry. Adam may not plumb the depths of emotional feeling, but he was able to convey atmosphere and characterization through the subtle use of orchestral colour. On top form, he could turn the most simple of phrases into something quite exquisite, and there are many such felicities sprinkled throughout this score. If in terms of recording and performance it doesn't quite come up to the level of Bonynge's classic recording of *Le Diable à quatre* (Decca), it is still very good indeed. An essential purchase for all balletomanes, or those who simply love sophisticated light music.

OPERA

Le Toréador (complete).

*** Decca 455 664-2. Jo, Tremont, Aler, WNO, Bonynge.

Richard Bonynge gives this delightful cross between opera and operetta just the sparkle and lift needed, with excellent WNO forces vividly recorded. Adam here offers the frothiest score, full of zest, crowned by a great coloratura show-piece, the variations on *Ah vous dirai-je maman* ('Twinkle twinkle, little star'). That inspires Sumi Jo to a dazzling performance, with John Aler as the flautist–lover and Michel Tremont as the old toreador–husband equally idiomatic. Spectacular sound, with the copious spoken dialogue well co-ordinated.

ADAMS, John (born 1947)

(i) *The Chairman Dances;* (ii; iii) *Chamber Symphony;* (i) *Christian Zeal and Activity; Common Tones in Simple Time;* (iv; v; vi) *Violin Concerto;* (vii; vi) *El Dorado;* (viii; iii; ix) *Eros Piano;* (viii; iii) *Fearful Symmetries;* (i) 2 *Fanfares for Orchestra: Tromba lontana; Short Ride in a Fast Machine;* (ii; iii; x) *Gnarly Buttons;* (ii; iii) *Grand Pianola Music;* (i) *Harmonielehre;* (xi) *Hoodoo Zephyr;* (vii; vi) *Lollapalooza;* (viii; iii) *Shaker Loops;* (vii; vi) *Slonimsky's Earbox.* Instrumental music: (xii) *John's Book of Alleged Dances.* Vocal music: (xiii) *Harmonium;* (xiv; viii; iii) *The Wound Dresser;* (xv; viii; iii) arr. of 5 *Songs* by Charles Ives. Opera: (xvi; vi) *The Death of Klinghoffer:* highlights. (xvii; iii) *I Was Looking at the Ceiling and I Then Saw the Sky;* (xviii) *Nixon in China:* excerpts.

(M)*** None. 7559 79453-2 (10). (i) San Francisco SO, De Waart; (ii) L. Sinfonietta; (iii) composer; (iv) Kremer; (v) LSO; (vi) Nagano; (vii) Hallé O; (viii) O of St Luke's; (ix) with Crossley; (x) with Collins; (xi) composer (synthesizer); (xii) Kronos Qt; (xiii) San Francisco Ch. & SO; (xiv) with Sylvan; (xv) with Upshaw; (xvi) Lyon Opera Ch. & O; (xvii) instrumental ens.; (xviii) Ch. & O of St Luke's, De Waart.

This impressive ten-CD box, with many of the performances directed by the composer himself (who is an excellent and persuasive advocate), gives an impressive survey of the achievement of John Adams. As Simon Rattle has aptly commented: 'In almost all of his best pieces, there's a mixture of ecstasy and sadness – the catharsis at the end of *Harmonium*, or the still, sad, personal last Act of *Nixon in China*, or the middle movement of the *Violin Concerto*. It has an immense sadness and depth at the centre of it.'

The obvious point of entry is *Grand Pianola Music*, scored for two pianos (John Alley and Shelagh Sutherland) and three female voices, as well as orchestra. The finale, *On the Dominant Divide*, seems custom-made for the Last Night of the Proms, with its 'flag-waving, gaudy tune, rocking back and forth between the pianos, amid ever increasing cascades of B flat major arpeggios'. But you might also begin with the early *Shaker Loops* with its tremolandos and trills, or the *Short Ride in a Fast Machine*. Many of the other works here are discussed below.

But much else is new to the catalogue, including the throbbing *Common Tones in Simple Time* ('a pastoral with pulse') and the infernally rhythmic *Lollapalooza*, dedicated to Simon Rattle. The title of the even more explosive *Slonimsky's Earbox*, so obviously Stravinsky-orientated, also celebrates another Russian, the author of a *Thesaurus of Scales and Melodic Patterns*, whose influence Adams also acknowledges. By contrast *Eros Piano* is a ruminative soliloquy, with distinct echoes of Messiaen. *Christian Zeal and Activity*, the earliest work here, which has an Ivesian flavour, exists as a framework for an actual revivalist sermon, taken from a radio broadcast.

Perhaps even more remarkable is *Hoodoo Zephyr*, a work for synthesizer, inspired by travel in the deserts of California and Nevada, heard in 'a wash of harmonies that shimmer and oscillate like objects at midday on the broiling floor of a desert sink'. Finally, the orchestration of five famous Ives song-settings should not be forgotten, especially *At the River*, so beautifully sung by Dawn Upshaw.

The set is extensively documented and handsomely packaged, but the lack of track information with each individual disc, and the complicated layout of the booklet, means that they are not easy to use together.

(i) *Chamber Concerto; Shaker Loops* (chamber version). (ii) *Phrygian Gates.*

*** RCA 09026 68674-2. (i) Ens. Modern, Edwards; (ii) Kretzschmar.

Even more than the composer's own version, Sian Edward's performance of the *Chamber Concerto* creates a dazzling wildness, with the polyphonic tapestries of the outer movements catching both the Stravinskian rhythmic influences in the one and the composer's vernacular jazzy leverage on the other. The string septet version of *Shaker Loops* is just as compelling as the version for string orchestra. Herman Kretzschmar's bravura performance of the piano work *Phrygian Gates* holds the listener's attention throughout its gradual shifts of mood and elliptical metamorphoses, but Gloria Cheng-Cochran (see below) is more imaginative in her tonal shading. Excellent recording throughout.

Chamber Symphony; Grand Pianola Music.

*** None. 7559 79219-2. L. Sinf., composer.

This Elektra coupling combines the *Grand Pianola Music* with a piece that is initially more intractable, the *Chamber Symphony*, written for 15 instruments and inspired by Schoenberg's Opus 9 (the choice of instrumentation is both comparable and different). It is surely given a definitive performance here. In the composer's hands *Grand Pianola Music* projects with overwhelmingly thrilling impact and, with extensive and illuminating notes from John Adams himself, this is a key issue in the Adams discography.

Violin Concerto.

*** Telarc CD 80494. McDuffie, Houston SO, Eschenbach – GLASS: *Violin Concerto.* ***

(i) *Violin Concerto;* (ii) *Shaker Loops.*

*** None. 7559 79360-2. (i) Kremer, LSO, Nagano; (ii) O of St Luke's, composer.

Robert McDuffie's performance of the Adams *Violin Concerto* may not have the dazzling projection of Kremer's account on Nonesuch, but it is splendidly played and infinitely better balanced, so that the brilliance of the solo playing in the outer movements is in proper perspective with the orchestra, and the great *Chaconne* which forms the central slow movement is no less movingly evocative. Moreover, the apt Glass coupling, equally well played, is a much better choice for coupling than the familiar *Shaker Loops*.

Gidon Kremer's account of the fiendishly demanding solo part is dazzling. The performance is superb, and the dream-like *Chaconne* offers aural and spiritual balm; but with the soloist closely balanced not all listeners will find it easy to last out the bravura battering provided by the 15-minute opening movement. *Shaker Loops*, however, tends to trump previous versions.

(i) *El Dorado*; (ii) *Berceuse élégiaque* (arrangement for chamber orchestra of Busoni's *Cradle Song of the Man at His Mother's Coffin*). *The Black Gondola* (orchestration of Liszt's *La Lugubre Gondola*).

*** None. 7559 79359-2. (i) Hallé O, Nagano; (ii) L. Sinf., composer.

El Dorado is a diptych of paired orchestral canvases, inspired (in 1991) by two giant paintings. Adams tells us: the first part is 'a musical embodiment of aggressive growth, beginning in a pre-dawn forest and culminating thirteen minutes later in a vast crescendo of brutal force'; the second, *Soledades*, is 'a landscape without man, the governing form a grand arch'. The two arrangements confirm Adams's skill as an imaginative orchestrator. *La Lugubre Gondola* is expanded and transformed into a darkly sensuous tone-painting of the gondola gliding through sluggish Venetian waters, carrying a coffin. John Adams is a splendid advocate of his own music and Nagano's Hallé version of the major work is equally committed and compelling.

Fearful Symmetries; (i) *The Wound Dresser*.

*** None. 7559 79218-2. O of St Luke's, Composer; (i) with Sylvan.

Fearful Symmetries, to use the composer's own words, 'is cut from the same cloth as *Grand Pianola Music*, although it is more choreographic in feeling'. In certain ways following on from Ives's *Central Park in the Dark*, 'it resembles one of those Soho night clubs with a heavy bouncer at the door; it mixes the weight and bravura of a big band with a glittering synthetic sheen of techno pop (samples and synthesizer) and the facility and finesse of a symphony orchestra'. The syncopations are increasingly dominant and after a section where the colours become more muted, even Ravelian, there is a wild climax, before the mood finally quietens. The composer's performance is most exhilarating.

The Wound Dresser is a very moving, elegiac setting (for baritone and orchestra) of Walt Whitman's poem, recalling the author's terrible experiences as a medic during the American Civil War. It is most touchingly sung by Sanford Sylvan and, partly but not entirely because of the music's delicacy of texture, every word is clear.

(i) *Gnarly Buttons*. (ii) *John's Book of Alleged Dances*.

*** None. 7559 79465-2. (i) Collins, L. Sinf., composer; (ii) Kronos Qt.

The clarinet was the composer's own instrument, and his concertante work, *Gnarly Buttons* is autobiographical and fashioned in three sections. *The Perilous Shore* twists and turns as it proceeds on its relatively intimate journey. *Hoe Down (Mad Cow)* is even more intricately energetic but ends nostalgically to make way for *Put Your Loving Arms Around Me*, a touchingly 'simple song, quiet and tender upfront'. The work was written for Michael Collins, who gives a haunting performance which the composer describes as ideal. *John's Book of Alleged Dances* (alleged 'because the steps for them have yet to be invented') opens and closes with a catchy rhythmic ostinato: 'vehicular music, following the streetcar tracks out into the fog and ultimately to the beach' and the composer's two-room cottage. Even the graceful Pavane, *She's So Fine*, eventually gathers impetus, but the *Habanera* is seductive and the slithering scales of *Alligator's Escalator* provide further bizarre contrast. The composer's minimalist imagination knows no bounds, and the Kronos players respond with much bravura to his kaleidoscopic ideas. The witty documentation from Adams himself is a delight.

Harmonielehre; The Chairman Dances; (i) *2 Fanfares: Tromba lontana; Short Ride in a Fast Machine.*

*** EMI CDC5 55051-2. CBSO, Rattle; (i) with Holland, Warren.

Harmonielehre is an extraordinary, large-scale (39-minute) work in three parts. *The Chairman Dances* his foxtrot for a full 13 minutes, with unabated energy. The *Two Fanfares* mystically and hauntingly pay their respects to Ives as well as to Copland, while the *Short* (exhilarating) *Ride in a Fast Machine* has an agreeably unstoppable momentum. The performances bring the most persuasive advocacy, and the excellent recording is clear, vivid and spacious.

Shaker Loops.

⏺ (M) *** Virgin VM5 61851-2. LCO, Warren-Green – GLASS: *Company*, etc.; REICH: *8 Lines*; HEATH: *Frontier.* ***
(B) *** Ph. (ADD) 412 214-2. San Francisco SO, De Waart – REICH: *Variations for Winds, Strings & Keyboards.* ***

The inspired performance by Christopher Warren-Green and his London Concert Orchestra is full of imaginative intensity, and understandably it received the composer's imprimatur. Outstandingly vivid recording.

The alternative San Francisco version is also first rate and very well recorded, even if the coupling is less generous.

PIANO MUSIC

China Gates; Phrygian Gates.

*** Telarc CD 80513. Cheng-Cochran – RILEY: *Heavenly Ladder, Book 7*, etc. ***

The miniature, *China Gates*, has moments of charm somehow reminiscent of Liadov, and some may feel its briefness to be an asset. Gloria Cheng-Cochran makes a very

good case for *Phrygian Gates*, which is (in the words of
the composer) 'a 26-minute tour of half the cycle of keys,
modulating by a circle of fifths rather than stepwise'. The
performance here is impressive in its control of mood and
Cheng-Cochran's veiled timbre in the music's reflective sections is seductively warm. Excellent recording. An important
disc for those interested in minimalism.

CHORAL MUSIC

Harmonium.

*** Telarc CD 80363. Atlanta Ch. & SO, Shaw –
RACHMANINOV: *The Bells*. ***

Harmonium is a setting of three poems. John Donne's curiously oblique 'Negative Love' opens the piece, with the
orchestra lapping evocatively round the chorus. The other
two poems are by Emily Dickinson. Robert Shaw's performance is very impressive and the Telarc recording is suitably
atmospheric and spectacular in its spaciousness and amplitude in the closing *Wild Nights*. Coupled with Rachmaninov,
this easily displaces the earlier, San Francisco version under
Edo de Waart (ECM 821 465-2), which had no coupling at
all.

OPERA

The Death of Klinghoffer (complete).

*** None. 7559 79281-2 (2). Nadler, Sylvan, Maddalena,
Friedman, Hammons, Felty, E. Op. Ch., Op. de Lyon,
Nagano.

The Death of Klinghoffer is far closer to a dramatic oratorio
than to an opera. Kent Nagano conducts Lyon Opéra forces
with the original singers who directly inspired the composer.
The story is based on the age-old conflict between Palestin-
ians and Jews. The closing scene brings the bitter concluding
lament of Klinghoffer's wife, Marilyn. The mezzo Sheila
Nadler rises to the challenge superbly, and the baritone
Sanford Sylvan is comparably sensitive as Klinghoffer himself, well matched by James Maddalena as the Captain, an
Evangelist-like commentator, and by Thomas Hammons
and Janice Felty in multiple roles. The recorded sound is
excellent, but the booklet reproduces an unrevised version
of the libretto.

I Was Looking at the Ceiling and Then I Saw the Sky.

**(*) None. 7559 79473-2. De Haas, Mazzie, McDonald,
McElroy, Muenz, Teek, Yang, composer.

Inspired by the 1994 California earthquake, using for its title
a quotation from one of the survivors, this theatre-piece is
an intriguing amalgam of opera and musical. It starts with
persistent ostinatos in Adams's early minimalist style, then
launches into melodic lines echoing pop and jazz. The dramatic point is lessened on the disc when no linking dialogue
is included, but the mixture is undemanding and agreeable,
often moving. Even so, it can hardly compare in its impact
with Adams's mainstream operas. Conducted by the

composer, the performance with a characterful line-up of
singers is persuasively idiomatic. Vivid, upfront sound.

Nixon in China: (highlights).

(M) *** None. 7559 79436-9. Sylvan, Craney, Maddalena,
St Luke's Ch. & O, De Waart.

It seemed an extraordinary idea to create an opera out of
President Richard Nixon's greatest political gamble (which
actually paid off): his 1972 visit to China to establish a
friendly relationship with the Communist regime and its
leader, Chou En-Lai; but those who saw the recent ENO
production will have discovered how grippingly it works in
the theatre. The complete recording is available only in the
USA (Nonesuch 9177) but this set of highlights gives a good
idea of Adams's score. His special brand of minimalism
works magnetically, and the music itself has a lyrical melodic
flow absent from most post-Britten operas. The choral music
is especially telling, and Chou's banquet speech/aria is
memorable, as is his wife's stirring soliloquy which closes
the selection. The singing is generally excellent, as is the
recording. A full translation is included.

ADDINSELL, Richard (1904–77)

(i) **Film music:** *Blithe Spirit (Waltz Theme)*. (ii) *The Day
Will Dawn (Tea-time Music)*. *Greengage Summer: Suite*.
(ii) *Highly Dangerous: Theme*. *The Lion Has Wings:
Cavalry of the Clouds (March)*. *Out of the Clouds: Theme*.
The Passionate Friends: Lover's Moon. *Sea Devils
(Prologue)*. *Under Capricorn: Theme*. **Radio themes:**
Britain to America: March of the United Nations.
(ii) *Journey into Romance: Invocation for Piano &
Orchestra*. *Warsaw Concerto*.

(M) *** ASV CDWHL 2108. Royal Ballet Sinfonia, Alwyn; with
(i) Jones; (ii) Lawson.

Richard Addinsell had the precious gift of melody. He
needed others to help with arrangements and scoring, and
it is good that Roy Douglas here receives belated recognition
for his work in fashioning Addinsell's musical ideas and
cleverly scoring them as a Rachmaninov pastiche for the
justly famous *Warsaw Concerto*. But there are many other
good things here, and Philip Lane's cleverly fashioned suite
from the film *The Greengage Summer* brims over with delightful ideas. Douglas Gamley assisted the composer in this
instance, and other credits include Leonard Isaac and Ron
Goodwin (who scored the *Cavalry of the Clouds* march).
When trifles like the *Tea-time Music* from *The Day Will
Dawn* and the delicious *Waltz* from *Blithe Spirit* are played
with such affection and polish under the understanding
Kenneth Alwyn, their gentle spirit is life-enhancing. The
Warsaw Concerto is treated as a miniature masterpiece and
given a performance which is as dramatic as it is heart-
warming. Martin Jones is the splendid soloist, and Peter
Lawson contributes equally sensitively to the several other
concertante numbers. The recording is first class in every
way. Not to be missed.

Film Music: Blithe Spirit: Prelude & Waltz. Encore: Miniature Overture. Fire Over England: Suite. Parisienne – 1885. The Passionate Friends: Suite. Scrooge: Suite. Southern Rhapsody; South Riding: Prelude. Waltz of the Toreadors: March & Waltz. WRNS March (arr. Douglas).

(M) **(*) ASV CDWHL 2115. Royal Ballet O, Alwyn.

Richard Addinsell's distinct melodic gift is heard at its best here in his early score for *Fire Over England* (1937) and, more especially, in the suite of music from *Scrooge* (the definitive 1951 version with Alistair Sim). As the *Waltz* for *Blithe Spirit* and the brief *March* for *Waltz of the Toreadors* show, there are some deft inventions elsewhere, but their composer needed help from others to realize them orchestrally. All this music is slight but it is very well played by the Royal Ballet Orchestra, affectionately and stylishly conducted by Kenneth Alwyn, and very well recorded.

Film and theatre music: Fire Over England: Suite. Goodbye Mr Chips: Theme. Journey to Romance: Invocation. The Prince and the Showgirl: selection. Ring round the Moon: Invitation Waltz. (i) *A Tale of Two Cities: Theme. Tom Brown's Schooldays: Overture.* (ii) *Trespass: Festival (beguine). The Isle of Apples;* (ii) *Smokey Mountain Concerto;* (i) *Tune in G.*

**(*) Marco 8.223732. BBC Concert O, Alwyn, with (i) Elms; (ii) Martin.

Kenneth Alwyn has pieced a good deal of the material together here where original scores are lost, notably in the 'Overture' from the film music for *Tom Brown's Schooldays* and the charming introductory sequence for *Goodbye Mr Chips*. The *Invitation Waltz* for Christopher Fry's translation, *Ring round the Moon*, of Jean Anouilh's *L'Invitation au château* is quite haunting, as is the gentle idyll, *The Isle of Apples*, and the simple *Tune in G* with its piano embroidery. These pieces, like the *Smokey Mountain Concerto*, were independent compositions. Alwyn and the BBC Concert Orchestra are thoroughly at home in this repertoire and they present it all freshly, the recording bright but with rather a brash sonority.

Warsaw Concerto (orch. & arr. Roy Douglas).

(B) *** Ph. 411 123-2. Dichter, Philh. O, Marriner (with Concert ***).

(M) *** Decca 430 726-2. Ortiz, RPO, Atzmon – GERSHWIN: *Rhapsody* **(*); GOTTSCHALK: *Grand Fantasia* ***; LISZT: *Hungarian Fantasia* *** (with LITOLFF: *Scherzo* ***).

Richard Addinsell's pastiche miniature concerto, written for the film *Dangerous Moonlight* in 1942, is perfectly crafted; moreover it has a truly memorable main theme. It is beautifully played here, with Marriner revealing the most engaging orchestral detail. The sound is first rate and the Virtuoso reissue has an attractive new livery.

The alternative from Cristina Ortiz is a warmly romantic account, spacious in conception. If the couplings are suitable, this is a rewarding collection, more substantial than Dichter's. The recording is first class.

ADÈS, Thomas (born 1971)

(i–ii) *Asyla, Op. 17;* (i; iii) *. . . But All Shall Be Well, Op. 10;* (iii–iv) *Chamber Symphony for 15 Players, Op. 2;* (iii–v) *Concerto Conciso for Piano & Chamber Orchestra, Op. 18;* (i; iii) *These Premises are Alarmed, Op. 18.*

*** EMI CDC5 56818-2. (i) CBSO; (ii) cond. Rattle; (iii) cond. composer; (iv) Birmingham Contemporary Music Group; (v) with composer (piano).

Rattle's superbly compelling account of *Asyla* (plural of 'asylum') confirms that this is Adès's major orchestral work so far, one which will surely join the repertoire. The *Chamber Symphony* is extraordinarily intricate in its rhythmic ideas, developing ear-tickling colouristic patterns. The *Concerto Conciso* has the solo piano well integrated into the instrumental group, where rhythms are free and jazzy, but it brings a calm central chaconne before the closing 'Brawl'. *These Premises are Alarmed* is a brief, witty apoplexy, designed as a brilliant orchestral showpiece for the Hallé Orchestra. Balance is restored in *. . . But All Shall be Well*, the title coming from *Little Gidding*, the last of T. S. Eliot's *Four Quartets*. Remarkable music, splendidly played and most vividly and atmospherically recorded.

(i) *Living Toys, Op. 9;* (ii) *Arcadiana, Op. 12;* (iii) *The Origin of the Harp, Op. 13;* (iv) *Sonata da caccia, Op. 11;* (v) *Anthem: Gefriolsae me, Op. 3b.*

(B) *** EMI CDZ5 72271-2. (i) L. Sinfonia, Stenz; (ii) Endellion Qt; (iii) Marsh, Robson, Richards, Busbridge, Knight, Boyd, Hopkins, Watkins, Tunnell, Benjafield, cond. composer; (iv) Niesemann, Clark, composer; (v) King's College, Cambridge, Ch., Cleobury; Quinney.

Thomas Adès's hushed, deeply devotional anthem, which he wrote in 1990 for King's College Choir, is relatively conventional harmonically, but it is still most original while, conversely, *Living Toys* is a brilliant and colourful sequence of eight movements inspired by the naïvely heroic ambitions of a Spanish child. *Arcadiana* is Adès's first string quartet, regularly exploiting original timbres and textures and paying tribute, most movingly, to Elgar's *Nimrod*. The *Sonata da caccia* is a trio for baroque oboe, horn and harpsichord which in its neo-classicism rises well clear of pastiche. The *Origin of the Harp* is an evocation of a symbolic Victorian painting for trios of clarinets, violas and cellos, plus percussion. Excellent performances and recording. Whatever he does, Adès cannot help creating original sounds.

Powder Her Face (opera; complete).

*** EMI CDC5 56649-2 (2). Gomez, Anderson, Morris, Bryson, Almeida Ens., composer.

For his first opera Adès presents what might be described as a cabaret opera. He bases it on the life of the notorious Duchess of Argyll, toast of smart London society in the 1930s, seen in a sequence of flashbacks from the scene in 1990 when, in final penury, she is evicted from her penthouse suite at the Dorchester Hotel. Flashy and superficial, she yet emerges as a pathetic, often ridiculous yet finally touching figure, with Adès's music regularly echoing the popular music of the 1930s grotesquely distorted. With voices over-lapping, words are not always clear but the progress of the plot is never obscured, and the result is both offbeat and attractive. Under the composer's energetic direction, with the original cast powerfully headed by Jill Gomez as the Duchess, the recording can be warmly recommended, with colourful chamber textures vividly caught.

ADORNO, Theodor (1903–69)

String Quartet; 2 Pieces for String Quartet, Op. 2; 6 Studies for String Quartet.

(BB) *** CPO 999 341-2. Leipzig Qt – EISLER: *Prelude & Fugue on B-A-C-H*, etc. ***

Adorno's *Six Studies* show an awareness of Schoenberg's musical language. There are many imaginative touches both here and in the *String Quartet* of the following year. Neither is negligible, even if neither possesses a significantly personal voice. Berg exerted some influence on the *Two Pieces for String Quartet*, Op. 2. The performances and recordings qualify for a three-star rating – though the music itself is another matter! But at its new budget price this is worth trying.

AGRICOLA, Alexander (c. 1446–1506)

Songs: *Adieu m'amour* (3 versions); *A la mignonne de fortune; Allez, regretez; Ay je rien fet; Cecus non in dicat de coloribus; De tous bien plaine* (3 versions); *Et qui la dira; Fortuna desperata; Guarde vostre visage* (3 versions); *J'ay beau huer; S'il vous plaist; Soit loing ou pres; Sonnes muses melodieusement.*

(BB) *** Naxos 8.553840. Unicorn Ens., Posch.

Agricola's music is expressive, but its structure and polyphony are quite complex, his polyphonic style nearer to Ockeghem than to Josquin, while his musical personality is less individual than either. Nevertheless, these secular love songs (sung in medieval French) are full of interest, the more so as they are often presented with a mixed consort of voices and instruments sharing the polyphony, with close blending of the whole ensemble. The piece which gives the disc its title, the sombre *Fortuna desperata*, makes a powerfully sonorous conclusion. The presentation is scholarly, direct and appealing, the recording excellent, and the documentation could hardly be bettered, with full translations included.

AHO, Kalevi (born 1949)

(i) *Violin Concerto; Hiljaisuus (Silence); Symphony No. 1.*

*** BIS CD 396. (i) Gräsbeck; Lahti SO, Vänskä.

Aho's *First Symphony* betokens an impressive musical personality at work. *Silence* is an imaginative piece. It is related to (and was conceived as an introduction to) the post-expressionist and more 'radical' and trendy *Violin Concerto*;

it is a work of considerable resource and imaginative intensity. Good performances and recording.

Symphonies Nos. 2; 7 (Insect Symphony).

*** BIS CD 936. Lahti SO, Vänskä.

The *Second Symphony* is a powerfully conceived and cogently argued work in one movement, predominantly fugal in texture, indebted to the world of Shostakovich and Bartók. The *Seventh Symphony* derives its material from an opera, *Insect Life* (based on a play by Karel Čapek). Aho decided to refashion its ideas in symphonic form. Each of the six movements is programmatic with titles like *Fox-Trot and Tango of the Butterflies*, *The Dung Beetles* and so on. It is more of a symphonic suite than a symphony but is scored imaginatively and with flair. Impeccable performances and extremely fine recording.

CHAMBER MUSIC

(i) *Bassoon Quintet;* (ii) *Quintet for Alto Saxophone, Bassoon, Viola, Cello & Double Bass.*

*** BIS CD 866. (i) Sinfonia Lahti Chamber Ens.

The *Bassoon Quintet* shows great understanding of the instruments though it has its longueurs. The *Quintet for Alto Saxophone, Bassoon, Viola, Cello and Double Bass* – an unusual combination but one rich in tonal variety – is the more concentrated of the two and leaves no doubt as to Aho's instrumental resource and imagination in writing for this ensemble. Virtuoso performances and natural, vivid recording.

Oboe Quintet (for flute, oboe, violin, viola and cello); 7 Inventions & Postlude for Oboe & Cello.

(N) *** BIS CD 1036. Sinfonia Lahti Chamber Ens.

It is quite obvious from the *Oboe Quintet* that Aho has a special feeling for the oboe, and he writes for it with individuality and feeling. The *Quintet* comes from 1973, when Aho was in his mid-20s, and draws the listener into its world from the first bar. There is a strong feeling for nature, and the melodic invention is fresh, even if interest is not sustained consistently over the piece's 30-minute span. The *Quintet for Flute, Oboe, Violin, Viola and Cello* was written in 1977, when Aho was 28, and is far more concentrated than the overlong *Bassoon Quintet* from the same year. Like the more recent *Inventions and Postlude* this music is well worth investigating and both performances and recording are of a high quality.

AKSES, Necil Kâzim (1908–99)

Violin Concerto.

(N) *** CPO 999 799-2. Askin, NDR RO, Hannover, Gökman.

Necil Akses is a key figure among the first generation of twentieth-century Turkish composers who turned to the West for their musical training. He studied in Vienna and Prague and on his return to Turkey he joined with Hindemith to help create the Ankara State Conservatory, where as professor of composition and (uncontaminated by serialism) he had considerable influence on the younger generation. As an accomplished violinist – he was a pupil of Suk – it is not surprising that his 1969 *Concerto* provides an impressively diverse, predominantly melodic solo role.

It is in two movements, sub-divided into four, with the first section longer than the other three combined. It opens with a powerfully rumbustious toccata-like tutti (laced with tam tam and percussion) which all but submerges the soloist. But the movement's lyricism soon predominates, even through bold rhythmic orchestral interruptions, and leads to a long cadenza, which in turn moves without a break into the hauntingly doleful slow movement.

The wild *Scherzo* is almost a tarantella; then the melting *Adagio* theme returns nostalgically, to take the listener to a second even more movingly ruminative cadenza, before being interrupted by the rumbustious return of the introductary tutti.

This live performance is passionately committed, and if Cihat Askin's timbre is small, his technique is fully up to the work's musical and technical demands. Apart from the balance problem at the opening, the recording is spaciously convincing. But the disc plays for only 45 minutes, and it was a pity that CPO could not have added Akses's *Ballad* or *Concerto for Orchestra*, or the *Poem for Cello and Orchestra*.

ALAIN, Jehan (1911–40)

Complete organ music

Andante; Aria; Ballade; Berceuse sur deux notes qui cornent; Choral cistercien; Choral dorien; Choral phrygien; Climat; 3 Danses; 2 Danses à Agni Yavishta; Grave; Monodie; Premier Fantaisie; Deuxième Fantaisie; Intermezzo; Le Jardin suspendu; Lamento; Litanies; Petite pièce; Postlude pour l'office des Complies; Premier Prélude; Deuxième Prélude; Prélude et fugue; Suite; Variations sur l'hymne 'Lucis Creator'; Variations sur un thème de Clément Jannequin.

(B) *** Erato Ultima 3984 26996-2 (2). Alain (Valtrin-Callinet-Schwenkedel organ of Basilique Saint-Christophe, Belfort, France).

(BB) *** Naxos 8.553632/3. Lebrun (Cavaillé-Coll organ of the Church of Saint-Antoine des Quinze-Vingts, Paris).

Andante; Aria; Ballade; Berceuse sur deux notes qui cornent; Chant donné; Choral cistercien; Choral dorien; Choral phrygien; Climat; Complainte à la mode ancienne; 3 Danses; 2 Danses à Agni Yavishta; Grave; Monodie; Premier Fantaisie; Deuxième Fantaisie; Fantasmagorie (1st version); Fugue en mode de fa; Intermezzo; Le Jardin suspendu; De Jules Lemaître; Lamento; Litanies; 3 Minutes; Petite pièce; Postlude pour l'office des Complies; Premier Prélude; Deuxième Prélude; Prélude et fugue; Suite; Variations sur l'hymne 'Lucis Creator'; Variations sur un thème de Clément Jannequin; Verset-vhoral.

(N) ● Erato 8573 80214-2; 8573 85773-2 (available separately). Alain (organs of Basilique Saint-Ferjeux à Besançon, l'Eglise

de la Madeleine, Paris, l'Abbaye de Valloires, D'Albert Alain Romainmôtier in Switzerland).

The reissue of Marie-Claire Alain's outstanding 1972 set on an Erato Ultima Double upstages the Naxos discs, fine as they are. The composer was her brother and she plays his music with extraordinary dedication and concentration. In her hands, pieces like *Le Jardin suspendu* and the *Postlude pour l'office des Complies* are hauntingly mystic in atmosphere, and the three *Chorals* have a palpable inner radiance. The chosen organ is ideal for her purposes and she conjures a marvellous range of bright colours from it. The opening of the *Première Fantaisie* brings a riveting burst of luminescence.

However Marie-Claire has since re-recorded the Alain's organ output digitally, chosing four different organs. The greater proportion of the music (including the famous *Litanies* which opens the first disc arrestingly) was recorded in Besançon, and the remainder is divided between three other superb-sounding organs, one of which is Swiss. Mme Alain has taken the opportunity to include some ten other short pieces, one or two of which (such as the *Chant donné*) are little more than exercises, but others are of more interest notably her final item, the bizarre *Fantasmagorie*. This she tells us in the extensive notes 'should be regarded as a huge joke'. It has different key signatures for each hand, and yet another change for the pedals. The registration too is very eccentric, yet the piece hangs together remarkably well. The performances throughout are seemingly spontaneous and characteristically full of insights. Undoubtedly this new set must now take pride of place, although for those with limited budgets the earlier set is offered at a very attractive price and remains highly recommendable.

Eric Lebrun is completely attuned to Alain's sound-world and his Cavaillé-Coll organ is ideal. These alternative Naxos performances are thoroughly recommendable and at the price make a real bargain.

Prière pour nous autres charnels.

*** Chan. 9504. Hill, Davies, BBC PO, Y. P. Tortelier – DUTILLEUX: *Violin Concerto*, etc. ***

Jehan Alain composed this short but beautiful setting of a prayer by Péguy for two soloists and organ; it is a moving piece, modal yet rich in its musical language, and it makes an admirable makeweight to the Dutilleux works.

ALBÉNIZ, Isaac (1860–1909)

Concierto fantástico; Rapsodia española (both for piano and orchestra).

(N) (BB) *** Warner Apex 8573 89223-2 Heisser, Lausanne CO, López-Cobos – FALLA: *Nights in the Gardens of Spain*; TURINA: *Rapsodia sinfónica*. ***

This most enjoyable collection of Spanish concertante piano works serves to introduce Apex, a new super-bargain label from Warner Classics. Both the *Concierto fantástico* and the *Rapsodia española* (the latter colourfully orchestrated by George Ensecu) are given sparkling, idiomatic performances by Jean-François Heisser and the excellent Lausanne

Chamber Orchestra under López-Cobos. The *Rapsodia* swaggers along at its close, not unlike Chabrier's *España*. The *Concierto* is a more romantic work, no less attractively scored, full of charm with delightfully nostalgic lyrical ideas contrasting with sparkling display passages for the keyboard. It is admirably played, the recording is excellent, and so are the couplings. Thoroughly recommended.

Iberia (Books I–IV) complete (orch. Arbós and Surinach).

(M) **(*) Telarc 2CD-80470. Cincinnati SO, López-Cobos.

Jesús López-Cobos is thoroughly at home in this repertory, and the Cincinnati orchestra responds to his flexible rubato very persuasively; the Mediterranean atmosphere is agreeably sultry, with some lovely warm Cincinnati string-playing. The rhythms too are often nicely bounced, but the playing, though warmly committed, could ideally be more gutsy. The Telarc recording is sumptuous, but at times one longs for more transparent and subtle textures – and indeed for a little more glitter. The set comes with two discs costing the same as one premium-priced CD, but with an overall timing of only 82 minutes.

Iberia (Books I–IV) complete (orch. Breiner).

(N) (BB) *(*) Naxos 8.553023. Moscow SO, Golovschin.

Peter Breiner's orchestration of *Iberia* does not match Arbós's suite in gaudiness of Mediterranean colour, neither does the playing of the Moscow Orchestra under Golvschin seem very idiomatic. They are obviously too far north and east to relish fully the balmy atmosphere and glitter of this music. The recording too lacks the necessary brilliance and sparkle.

Iberia (suite; orch. Arbós).

*** Chan. 8904. Philh. O, Y. P. Tortelier – FALLA: *Three-Cornered Hat.* ***

The Philharmonia's response brings glowing woodwind colours and seductive string-phrasing, well projected by the warmly resonant recording.

(i) *Iberia* (suite; orch. Arbós); *Navarra* (completed De Sévérec); (ii; iv) *Rapsodia española* (arr. Halffter); (iii; iv) *Suite española* (orch. Frühbeck de Burgos).

(B) *** Double Decca ADD/Dig. 433 905-2 (2). (i) SRO, Ansermet; (ii) De Larrocha, LPO; (iii) New Philh. O; (iv) Frühbeck de Burgos – TURINA: *Danzas fantásticas*, etc. (with GRANADOS: *Goyescas: Intermezzo; Danza española No. 5*; SARASATE: *Aires gitanos*. Ricci, LSO, Gamba ***).

This collection restores to the catalogue Ansermet's early stereo version of the Arbós orchestral suite from *Ibéria*, and the 1960 Geneva sound is still remarkably full and vivid. Ansermet's natural spontaneity combines meticulous care with colouring and balance. The Sarasate *Aires gitanos* from Ricci, with Gamba and the LSO, played with genuine panache, date from the same recording period and are no less vivid. The Granados encores are very successful too.

Rapsodia española (arr. Halfter).

(B) *** Decca 448 243-2. De Larrocha, LPO, Frühbeck de

Burgos – RODRIGO: *Concierto de Aranjuez* etc.; TURINA: *Rapsodia sinfónica.* ***

Alicia de Larrocha's performance is both evocative and dazzling, and she is given splendid support by Frühbeck de Burgos and brilliant Decca sound.

Suite española (arr. Frühbeck de Burgos).

(M) *** Decca (ADD) 448 601-2. New Philh. O, Frühbeck de Burgos – FALLA: *El amor brujo* (with GRANADOS: *Goyescas: Intermezzo* ***).

Albéniz's early *Suite española* offers light music of the best kind, colourful, tuneful, exotically scored and providing orchestra and recording engineers alike with a chance to show their paces, the sound bright and glittering, and fully worthy of reissue in Decca's Classic Sound series.

GUITAR MUSIC

Cantos de España: Córdoba, Op. 232/4. España (6 Hojas de Album), Op. 165. Iberia (excerpts): *El Puerto; Evocación; El Abaicín; Triana; Zambra Granadina. Mallorca (Barcarola), Op. 202; Suite española: Aragón.*

**(*) Channel CCS 10397. Peter and Zoltán Katona.

The Katona twins are a highly talented duo and they find plenty of colour and atmosphere in this familiar piano repertoire, very effectively transcribed. The recording too is warm and pleasing, although the resonance blunts the upper range just a little. A most attractive recital just the same.

Cantos de España: Córdoba, Op. 232/4; Mallorca (Barcarola), Op. 202; Piezás características: Zambra Granadina; Torre Bermeja, Op. 92/7, 12; Suite española: Granada; Sevilla; Cádiz; Asturias, Op. 47/1, 3–5.

*** Sony SK 36679. Williams.

Some of Albéniz's more colourful miniatures are here, and John Williams plays them most evocatively.

Cantos de España: Córdoba, Op. 232/4; Mallorca (Barcarola), Op. 202. Suite española: Granada; Cataluña; Sevilla; Cádiz, Op. 47/1–4.

🔹 (BB) *** RCA Navigator 74321 17903-2. Bream – GRANADOS: *Collection*; RODRIGO: *3 Piezas españolas.* *** 🔹

🔹 (BB) *** RCA 74321 68016-2. Bream – GRANADOS; MALATS; PUJOL: *Collection.* *** 🔹

Julian Bream is in superb form in this splendid recital, vividly recorded in the pleasingly warm acoustic of Wardour Chapel, near his home in Wiltshire. The playing itself has wonderfully communicative rhythmic feeling and great subtlety of colour, and its spontaneity increases the impression that one is experiencing a 'live' recital. The performance of the haunting *Córdoba* is unforgettable.

Suite española, Op. 47 (extended suite, arr. Barrueco).

(M) *** EMI CDM5 66574-2. Barrueco – TURINA: *Guitar music.* ***

Manuel Barrueco's playing combines warmth with a pleasing

intimacy and a natural, relaxed sense of spontaneity. The more famous evocations, *Castilla*, *Granada* and the closing *Sevilla*, are subtle in nuance and colour, while the vibrant *Asturias* brings a haunting, improvisational feeling in its calm middle section. The recording is beautifully judged, not over-projected.

PIANO MUSIC

Azulejos; Cantos de España (Preludio (Asturias); Oriental; Bajo la palmera (Cuba); Córdoba; Seguidillas (Castilla)). Malagueña; Mallorca (Barcarola); La Vega; Zambra Granadina; Zaragoza.

(M) *** EMI (ADD) CDM7 64523-2. De Larrocha.

Dating from 1959, this recital is a stimulating example of the younger Alicia de Larrocha playing with enormous dash and a glowing palette – the famous *Córdoba* is full of atmospheric poetry, helped by the warm bass resonance of the recording.

Cantos de España; Suite española.

(B) *** Double Decca ADD/Dig. 433 923-2 (2). De Larrocha – GRANADOS: *Allegro de concierto*, etc. ***

This makes a most rewarding bonus for the coupled Granados collection, and Alicia de Larrocha's playing is imbued with many subtle changes of colour and has refreshing vitality.

Iberia (complete).

(N) ** Chan. 9860. Nicholas Unwin.

Nicolas Unwin's recording is the first to place all four books of *Iberia* on a single CD, just short of 80 minutes in length. But his performance is far from being a primary choice. Very well recorded, he plays most musically throughout, and his rubato is convincing as is shown immediately in his poetic response to the opening *Evocation*. But as one travels on through this very Spanish scenery it becomes increasingly apparent that he cannot match Alicia de Larrocha in fully capturing the music's idiomatic atmosphere and Mediterranean colouring.

Iberia (complete); *Alhambra* (suite): *La vega; Azulejos: Prelude; Navarra* (both completed Jones). *6 Hojas de Album, Op. 165: Tango. Suite española, Op. 47.*

(BB) *** Nim. NI 5595/8 (4). Jones – GRANADOS: *Allegro de concierto*, etc. ***

Martin Jones penetrates the ethos of these pieces with a natural feeling for their Spanish atmosphere and he offers completions of both *Navarra* and the composer's very last, ruminative piece, *Azulejos*. His pianism is brilliantly coloured, rhythmically charismatic and often quite magical in its gentle evocation. This is apparent from the very opening of *Iberia*, which Jones's poetic sensibility illuminates and holds convincingly together. The series of descriptive vignettes of the *Suite española* is given a new dimension by the lilting freshness and subtlety of this remarkable playing. The recording is wholly natural, the ambience warm but not too resonant. This would be highly recommended even if it cost far more.

Iberia; Navarra; Suite española.

✹ *** Decca 417 887-2. De Larrocha.

On her digital Decca version, Alicia de Larrocha brings an altogether beguiling charm and character to these rewarding miniature tone-poems and makes light of their sometimes fiendish technical difficulties. The recording is among the most successful of piano sounds Decca has achieved.

Iberia (complete); *Suite española* (excerpts): *Granada; Cataluña; Sevilla; Cádiz; Aragon; Navarra. Pavana capricho, Op. 12; España (6 Hojas de Album): Tango* (only); *Recuerdos de viaje: Rumores de la caleta; Puerta de Tierra.*

(M) *** EMI (ADD) CMS7 64504-2 (2). De Larrocha.

The EMI set offers de Larrocha's earliest (1962) stereo recording of Albéniz's great piano suite, *Iberia*. The younger de Larrocha is far tougher, more daring, more fiery and, if anything, even more warmly expressive than she was later. The EMI discs include the haunting *Tango*, deliciously done, the most celebrated of all Albéniz's music; but the sound is not quite as fine as on the Decca sets.

Iberia (complete); *Navarra. 6 Hojas de Album, Op. 165: Malagueña; Tango. Pavana capricho, Op. 12. Recuerdos de viaje, Op. 71: Puerta de Tierra; Rumores de la caleta (Malagueña).*

(B) *** Double Decca (ADD) 433 926-2 (2). De Larrocha – FALLA: *Fantasia bética*, etc. ***

Iberia (complete); *Navarra.*

(B) *** Double Decca (ADD) 448 191-2 (2). De Larrocha – GRANADOS: *Goyescas.* *** ✹

Alicia de Larrocha's second analogue set of *Iberia* was made in 1972, a decade after her earliest stereo version for Hispavox. As in that version, she plays with full-blooded temperament and fire, both here and in *Navarra*. The piano recording is excellent in its realism, and the Double Decca reissue coupled with Granados's *Goyescas* makes a formidable bargain, for – on both artistic and technical merits – *Iberia* loses little ground to her later digital set which has rather more subtlety.

The other Double Decca, offering more of Albéniz's colourful genre-pieces, played with comparable understanding (and coupled with Falla), makes an alternative collection.

DG's début for the young Spanish pianist José María Pinzolas comes at mid-price (459 430-2). His control of keyboard colour is impressive but his rubato is not entirely convincing. He is well recorded.

OPERA

Merlin (complete).

(N) *** Decca 467 096-2 (2). Alvarez, Domingo, Henschel, Martinez, Spanish Nat. Ch., Madrid Comunidad Ch., Madrid SO, Eusebio.

Who would have expected the Spaniard, Isaac Albéniz, to write (in English) this grand opera based on the Arthurian legend, the first of a projected trilogy? He was prompted to do so by the British banker and would-be librettist, Francis Burdett-Money-Coutts, with Launcelot and Guinevere to follow in a *Ring*-cycle equivalent. Yet here is a richly enjoyable piece, sumptuously romantic, bearing little relationship to the nationalistic piano works on which Albéniz's reputation rests.

Though Wagnerian echoes abound in the plot, with Merlin a Wotan-equivalent and Arthur a cross between Siegfried and Siegmund (pulling out Excalibur from a block of marble as the climax of Act I), the idiom is more directly diatonic than Wagner's, less chromatic. What matters is the purposefulness of the writing, echoing no one. Anyone with a sweet tooth will love it (despite the absurdities of the libretto), thanks also to a passionate performance under Jose de Eusebio, spectacularly well recorded. Domingo makes a noble King Arthur, while Carlos Alvarez as Merlin uses his firm, dark baritone with an incisiveness and expressive range worthy of a Wotan.

In the two women's roles, both evil, the American sopranos, Jane Henschel as Morgan-le-Fay and Ana Maria Martinez as Nivian, Merlin's treacherous slave, both characterize well, with rich, warm voices. Christopher Maltman is a suitably sinister Mordred, and outstanding among the others is the young tenor, Angel Rodriguez, as Gawain. Chorus and orchestra are outstanding too, intensifying the score's evocative beauty.

ALBÉNIZ, Mateo de (c. 1755–1831)

Sonata in D.

(B) *** Double Decca (ADD) 433 920-2 (2). De Larrocha – GRANADOS: *Escenas románticas*, etc; SOLER: *Sonatas.* ***

Mateo Albéniz was a Basque church musician who is remembered mainly for this brief one-movement *Sonata* with its obvious homage to Domenico Scarlatti. It has great character and is beautifully played and recorded.

ALBERT, Eugen d' (1864–1932)

Piano Concertos Nos. 1 in B min., Op. 2; 2 in E, Op. 12.

*** Hyp. CDA 66747. Lane, BBC Scottish SO, Francis.

The *Piano Concerto No. 1 in B minor* (1884) is the more ambitious of the two works, written in a style half-way between Liszt and Rachmaninov, with a rather extraordinary fugal outburst towards the end of the work. Piers Lane plays with delicacy and virtuosity and is well supported by the BBC Scottish Symphony Orchestra. The *Piano Concerto No. 2 in E major* is a one-movement piece, though in four sections, following the style of Liszt's concertos. The recording is expertly balanced by Tony Kime.

Piano Sonata in F sharp min., Op. 10; 8 Klavierstücke, Op. 5; Klavierstücke, Op. 16/2–3; 5 schliche Klavierstücke 9 (Capriolen), Op. 32; Serenata.

*** Hyp. CDA 66945. Lane.

Eugene d'Albert's solo keyboard music inhabits the worlds of Brahms and Liszt, but there is much that can lay claim to a quiet individuality. Piers Lane plays it with total commitment. No want of virtuosity and dedication here, and very good recorded sound.

Die Abreise.

(M) **(*) CPO/EMI (ADD) CPO 999 558-2. Prey, Moser, Schreier, Philh. Hung. O, Kulka.

Eugen d'Albert wrote this charming one-acter, *Die Abreise* ('The Departure'), in 1898, five years before his most celebrated opera, *Tiefland*. Gilfen, bored with his wife Luise, plans to depart on a journey, but the machinations of his friend Trott alert him to the dangers, and it is Trott who departs. With delicate orchestral writing, it tells the story deftly in 20 brief sections of melodic conversation – though there are no separate tracks after the overture, and their absence makes it harder to follow the synopsis which is provided instead of a libretto. Nevertheless this is a first-rate, highly enjoyable performance, recorded in 1978 with three outstanding and characterful soloists. Warm, clear, EMI sound.

Tiefland (complete).

** Berlin Classics 0091082 (2). Kuhse, Gutstein, Rönisch, Hoppe, Adam, Dresden State Opera Ch. & O, Schmitz.

The Berlin Classics version, good though it is, is no match for the deleted RCA set, under Zanotelli, also recorded in 1963. The sound is dim and relatively distant, and the Dresden casting is generally weaker.

Die Toten Augen (complete).

*** CPO 999 692-2 (2). Schellenberger, Gjevang, Walker, Orth, Chalker, Odinius, Bär, Dresden PO Ch. & O, Weikert.

Die Toten Augen ('The Dead Eyes') is a luscious piece set at the time of Christ. The central action is framed by a Prelude and Postlude in which a shepherd (beautifully sung here by the tenor, Lothar Odinius), meets another symbolic character, the Reaper (the celebrated Olaf Bär), and goes off in search of a lost sheep. The central action, much more realistic, is then compressed into a single Act, telling of a Roman official, Arcesius, whose wife, Myrtocle, is blind. She is cured by the intervention (offstage) of Christ but, as predicted by Christ, the gift of sight proves a curse, bringing the disruption of her marriage and the murder of the handsome Galba whom she initially mistakes for her husband. In her love for Arcesius she opts to be blind again, with her 'dead eyes'.

The evocative pastoral sweetness of the Prelude and Postlude is set against the ripe German *verismo* style of the central action. It could easily be a sickly story, but d'Albert with rich orchestration and surging melody carries it off impressively. This live recording of a concert performance, well recorded, offers a persuasive account of the piece, with Dagmar Schellenberger powerful as Myrtocle, well matched by the fine mezzo, Anne Gjevang, as Mary of Magdala. A rarity to recommend to those with a sweet tooth.

ALBERT, Stephen (1941–92)

Cello Concerto.

*** Sony SK 57961. Ma, Baltimore SO, Zinman – BARTOK: *Viola Concerto;* BLOCH: *Schelomo.* ***

Stephen Albert's *Cello Concerto* (1989–90) was written for Yo-Yo Ma. The idiom is both tonal and distinctive. Ma and the Baltimore orchestra give a passionately committed account of it and are superbly recorded.

ALBICASTRO, Henricus

(1661–*c.* 1730)

Concerti à 4, Op. 7/2 & 12; Violin Sonata with Continuo (La follia), Op. 9/12; Trio Sonatas, Op. 8/9 & 11; (i) Motet: Coelestes angelici chori

(B) *** HM HMA 1905208. Ens. 415, Banchini; (i) with De Mey.

Swiss-born Henrico Albicastro's *La follia* variations are a shade conventional but, like the *Trio Sonatas,* are pleasingly assured and easily inventive. The two *Concerti* are even more striking in character, the *Allegros* vivacious and neatly imitative and the *Grave* slow movements rather fine. But the best work here is the cantata, which has both melodic appeal and genuine emotional eloquence. It is quite beautifully sung by Guy de Mey (and a translation is provided). Chiara Banchini and Ensemble 415 are on excellent form throughout, and the whole concert is very well recorded.

ALBINONI, Tomaso (1671–1751)

Adagio in G min. for Organ & Strings (arr. Giazotto).

(M) *** Sony (ADD) SMK 60161. La Grande Ecurie et la Chambre du Roy, Malgoire (with Concert, *'Music of the Baroque',* ECO, Leppard). ***

(M) *** DG (ADD) 449 724-2. BPO, Karajan – RESPIGHI: *Ancient airs* etc. ***

Malgoire and his authentic string group (with a sonorously balanced organ contribution) give an impressively dignified account of a justly attractive piece that can too readily sound inflated. This comes as the final item in a generous concert of Baroque lollipops.

Karajan's view is stately and measured, and the Berlin Philharmonic strings respond with dignity and sumptuous tone. The anachronism of Giazotto's arrangement is obviously relished.

(i) *12 Concerti a cinque, Op. 5;* (ii) *12 Concerti a cinque, Op. 7.*

(B) **(*) Ph. Duo (ADD) 464 052-2 (2). (i) Carmirelli, I Musici; (ii) Wätzig, Abel, Klinge, Berlin CO, Negri.

Philips have recoupled I Musici's Op. 5 with Negri's Op. 7, which meets strong competition. The playing in Berlin combines vitality and polish, but the balance is rather forward: the effect is vivid but the dynamic contrast is reduced.

Negri's direction, with its strong, incisive rhythms, also lacks something in flexibility and resilience.

12 Concerti a cinque, Op. 7; Sonatas for Strings a cinque: in D & G min., Op. 2/5–6.

*** Ph. (ADD) 432 115-2 (2). Holliger, Bourgue, I Musici.

Albinoni's Op. 7 consists of four each of solo oboe concertos, double oboe concertos and concertos for strings, with continuo. This recording by Heinz Holliger and Maurice Bourgue and I Musici is comparatively robust in using modern instruments, but it is eminently stylish, the effect sunny and lively by turns. The digital recording is fresh and naturally balanced. The two *String Sonatas* from Op. 2 are particularly attractive works, and here the recording is slightly closer.

Concerti a cinque, Op. 7/1–6; Oboe Concertos in G; G min.; G.

**(*) Tactus TC 670103. Pollastri, Bensi, Sinf. Perusina.

Here, besides the familiar first six concertos (for one or two oboes) of Op. 7, we are offered three more unpublished works preserved in German libraries. The *G minor Concerto* is quite a find, with an unusually wide-ranging solo part and a brief *Adagio,* accompanied pizzicato throughout. The second of the two *G major* works is also one of the composer's best. The two soloists here play their period instruments with expert bonhomie; the strings are athletic but a bit raw on top. There are odd moments when intonation is suspect, but these are few and will not worry all listeners. The recording is forward, with good ambience.

12 Concerti a cinque, Op. 7; 12 Concerti a cinque, Op. 9; Sinfonia for Strings.

*** Chan. 0602 (*Op. 7/1, 2, 4 & 5; Op. 9/1, 3, 4 & 6; Sinfonia*); 0579 (*Op. 7/3, 6, 9 & 12; Op. 9/2, 5, 8 & 11*) 0610 (*Op. 7/7, 8, 10 & 11; Op. 9/7, 10 & 12*). Robson, Latham, Coll. Musicum 90, Standage.

(BB) *** Naxos 8.553002 (*Op. 7/1–3, 6 & 8; Sinfonia*); 8.550735 (*Op. 7/4, 5, 6, 11 & 12; Op. 9/12*); 8.550739 (*Op. 9/2, 3, 5, 8, 9 & 11*). Camden, Girdwood, Alty, L. Virtuosi, Georgiadis.

Anthony Robson plays all eight solo concertos from Op. 7 and Op. 9 using a period oboe. His tone is most appealing and his phrasing and musicianship are second to none. Simon Standage provides alert accompaniments, also using original instruments, and creates bright, athletic string-timbres. Catherine Latham joins him to complete the Collegium Musicum sets of Opp. 7 and 9, including the works for strings. The artistic results are very lively and refreshing, although the balance is rather close.

The London Virtuosi use modern instruments, but their playing is fresh and refined and the digital recording is natural and beautifully balanced. The calibre of Anthony Camden's solo contribution is readily shown in slow movements, matched by Georgiadis's rapt, sensitive accompaniments. On the first disc Camden's excellent colleague is Julia Girdwood, but for the two other collections Alison Alty takes over, and the partnership seems even more felicitous with the two instruments blended quite perfectly. Also included is a *Sinfonia* arranged by Camden as a *Sinfonia concertante.* This series can be strongly recommended on all counts.

(i) *Concerti a cinque, Op. 7/2–3, 5–6, 8–9, 11–12;*
(ii) *Adagio in G min.* (arr. Giazotto).

(B) *** DG (ADD) 439 509-2. (i) Holliger, Elhorst, Bern
  Camerata; (ii) Lucerne Festival Strings, Baumgartner.

The playing of Heinz Holliger, Hans Elhorst and the Bern Camerata is refined, persuasive and vital, and the CD could hardly be more truthful or better detailed. This famous *Adagio* (in a perfectly acceptable performance under Baumgartner) has been added to tempt a wider public. Let us hope it does so.

Oboe Concertos, Op. 7/3, 6, 9 & 12; Op. 9/2, 5, 8 & 11.

*** Unicorn DKPCD 9088. Francis, L. Harpsichord Ens.

Those looking for a selection of *Oboe Concertos* from both Op. 7 and Op. 9 will find that Sarah Francis is an immensely stylish and gifted soloist. She is accompanied with warmth and grace, and the recording is first class, transparent yet full and naturally balanced.

Concerti a cinque, Op. 9/1–12.

*** O-L 458 129-2 (2). De Bruine, Bernardi, Manze, AAM,
  Hogwood.

(i) *Concerti a cinque, Op. 9/1–12;* (ii) *Adagio in G min.* for
Organ & Strings (arr. Giazotto).

(B) *** Ph. Duo (ADD) 456 333-2 (2). (i) Ayo, Holliger,
  Bourgue; (i–ii) Garatti (harpsichord or organ); I Musici.

Hogwood offers a separate complete set of Albinoni's splendid Op. 9 on original instruments, although the ear would hardly guess. String textures are smooth and pure, without a hint of acerbity, and only the lightness and transparency confirm the authenticity. To tell the truth, the undoubted intimacy of effect is just a little cosy, and if you want something more athletic you must turn to Anthony Robson with Simon Standage's Collegium Musicum 90 on Chandos, in which the concertos of Op. 7 and Op. 9 are intermingled (see above). However, the solo oboe playing of Frank de Bruine is very fine indeed. The lovely *Adagio* of *No. 11 in F* (for solo violin) is very like a Handel aria, and here Andrew Manze is delightfully sweet-timbred. The *Double Oboe Concertos* also bring some splendidly nimble teamwork, and altogether this is a most enjoyable set.

  The Philips Duo I Musici alternative on modern instruments is played with much finesse and style, which comment also applies to the famous *Adagio.* Ayo, Holliger and Bourgue are on top form throughout, and so are the Philips engineers.

Concerti a cinque, Op. 9/2, 5, 8, & 11.

(N) (BB) *** Virgin 2 x 1 VBD5 61878-2 (2). De Vries,
  Amsterdam Alma Musica, Van Asperen – TELEMANN:
  Oboe Concertos; Sonatas. ***

Hans de Vries plays a baroque oboe, made by Gottlob Crone in Leipzig around 1735, and produces a most appealing timbre, while his technique is remarkably assured and true. There is one cavil: the solo balance seems a shade too

forward, even though the interaction with the strings (which are well in the picture) is effectively managed. Bob van Asperen's accompaniments are as alert and stylish as the solo playing and this 2 x 1 bargain reissue comes in tandem with some equally fine performances of Telemann.

12 Concerti, Op. 10.

(B) *** Erato Ultima (ADD) 0630 18943-2 (2). Toso,
  Carmignola, Sol. Ven., Scimone.

Four of the Op. 10 set are violin concertos (Nos. 6, 8, 10 and 12) and three are *concerti grossi* with a small concertino group (Nos. 2, 3 and 4), while the remainder are without soloists and have non-fugal last movements. They radiate simple vitality, a love of life and a youthful exuberance that belies the composer's age. The playing is warm and musical, and the recording is made in an ample acoustic. Some may prefer more sharply etched detail, but the resonant string-timbres are immaculately transferred to CD.

Concertos for (solo) Organ in B flat & F (arr. from Op. 2);
Flute Sonatas, Op. 4/2 & 6; Op. 6/6 & 7; Oboe Sonata,
Op. 6/2; Recorder Sonata, Op. 6/5.

*** Mer. CDE 84400. Badinage (with BACH: (Organ) *Fugue
  in C, BWV 946,* after *Op. 1/12).*

A lightweight but pleasing programme with some particularly deft playing on a slightly watery-sounding baroque flute (a copy of an eighteenth-century instrument) and some very agreeable organ interludes. These are all transcriptions, mostly from violin sonatas. Although it seems likely that Op. 4 is wrongly attributed to Albinoni, the music itself is very agreeable. Good, natural sound.

CHAMBER MUSIC

6 Sonate da chiesa, Op. 4; 12 Trattenimenti armonici per
camera, Op. 6.

*** Hyp. CDA 66831/2. Locatelli Trio.

The set of 'Church' sonatas, showing the composer at his most lyrically appealing, contrasts with Op. 6. *Trattenimento* indicates 'Entertainment', suggesting a more secular style; and certainly the allegros of Op. 6 are strikingly lively and infectiously dance-like in character. The slow movements are often more formal, though never dull. The performances, using original instruments, are of high quality, well paced, sensitive and fresh, and the recording is well balanced and vivid.

Trio Sonatas, Op. 1/1–12.

(N) *** CPO 999 770-2. Parnassi Musici.

Albinoni's *Trio Sonatas, Op. 1* are not only important musically – they make delightful listening – but also historically. For although the four-movement *sonata da chiesa* format (slow–fast–slow–fast) was established by Corelli in the 1680s, it appeared exclusively in Albinoni's Op. 1, with six of these trio sonatas in the major and six in the minor keys. They are through-composed, i.e. all four movements are based on the same musical material. But Albinoni's variety of invention is inexhaustible, with touchingly expressive slow movements and many individual and often sprightly allegros, although the opening movements of the last two sonatas are especially striking. No. 11 opens with a doleful fugatto; No. 12 is built on a ground bass. The period-instrument performances here are first class in every way and they are excellently recorded.

VOCAL MUSIC

12 Cantatas, Op. 4.

*** Etcetera KTC 2027 (2). Schlick or Ragin, Selo, Shaw.

Albinoni's twelve *Cantatas*, Op. 4, are characteristic pastoral works of their period, lightweight but with plenty of charm; they are written alternately for soprano and alto, with the even-numbered works given to the latter voice. On the whole, the most poignant music is allotted to the soprano voice and the excellent Barbara Schlick responds appealingly, but both soloists rise to the occasion. The continuo too is first class, with Nicolas Selo's beautifully focused and crisply rhythmic cello contribution a particular pleasure. The recording is excellent. Full translations are provided.

Il nascimento dell'Aurora (festa pastorale; complete).

(B) **(*) Erato 4509 96374-2 (2). Anderson, Zimmermann, Klare, Browne, Yamaj, Sol. Ven., Scimone.

Written as a court celebration, *Il nascimento dell'Aurora* makes a substantial and attractive two-hour stage-entertainment. This well-balanced live recording, made in Vicenza, Italy, puts forward a persuasive case despite some roughness in the choral singing (which is particularly distracting in the first chorus) and some intrusive audience applause. Soloists are first rate and the orchestra generally stylish. The CD transfer is excellently managed. With full libretto and translation included, this is well worth exploring.

ALFVÉN, Hugo (1872–1960)

A Legend of the Skerries, Op. 20; Swedish Rhapsodies Nos. 1 (Midsummer Vigil), Op. 19; 2 (Uppsala Rhapsody), Op. 24; 3 (Dala Rhapsody), Op. 47; King Gustav II Adolf, Op. 49: Adagio.

*** Chan. 9313. Iceland SO, Sakari.

Midsummer Vigil, Alfvén's masterpiece, is quintessential Sweden, and so too is the affecting *Elegy* from the incidental music to Ludwig Nordström's play about *Gustav II Adolf*. Petri Sakari produces musically satisfying results, and this useful anthology can be warmly recommended. The Chandos sound is excellent.

Symphony No. 1 in F min., Op. 7; Andante religioso; Drapa (Ballad for Large Orchestra); Uppsala Rhapsody, Op. 24.

*** BIS CD 395. Stockholm PO, Järvi.

Järvi's version of the *First Symphony* is superior both artistically and technically and leaves the listener persuaded as to its merits. The *Uppsala Rhapsody* is based on student songs, but it is pretty thin stuff and the *Andante religioso* is rather

let down by its sugary closing pages. *Drapa* opens with some fanfares, full of sequential clichés and with a certain naïve pomp and splendour that verges on bombast.

Symphony No. 2 in D, Op. 11; Swedish Rhapsody No. 1 (Midsummer Vigil).

*** BIS CD 385. Stockholm PO, Järvi.

Like those of its predecessor, the ideas of the *Second Symphony* are pleasing though they do not possess a particularly individual stamp. On the whole, Järvi is very persuasive in the symphony and gives a delightful performance of the popular *Midsummer Vigil*.

Symphony No. 3 in E, Op. 23; Legend of the Skerries, Op. 20; Swedish Rhapsody No. 3 (Dala Rhapsody), Op. 47.

(BB) **(*) Naxos 8.553729. RSNO, Willén.

Symphony No. 3 in E, Op. 23; The Prodigal Son: Suite; Swedish Rhapsody No. 3 (Dala Rhapsody), Op. 47.

*** BIS CD 455. Royal Stockholm PO, Järvi.

Neeme Järvi's BIS CD is every bit as fine as its companions and, in addition to the *Third Symphony* and the *Dalarapsodi*, brings the perennially popular suite from *The Prodigal Son*. Excellent playing and recording of real quality. It is to be preferred to its Scottish alternative in terms of performance and certainly as far as the recorded sound is concerned.

The sensitive, well-prepared performance by the Scottish players under Niklas Willén also serves the symphony well. Moreover it comes with equally good accounts of the *Dalarapsodi* and the *Legend of the Skerries*. The Naxos disc is well worth its modest outlay.

(i) Symphony No. 4 (Havsbandet – From the Outermost Skerries), Op. 29; Legend of the Skerries, Op. 20.

*** BIS CD 505. Royal Stockholm PO, Järvi, (i) with Högman, Ahnsjö.

Alfvén's *Fourth Symphony* is perhaps his most ambitious work. There is a romantic programme relating to the emotions of two young lovers whose wordless melisma is heard to excellent effect in this very fine recording. However, although Alfvén's scoring is eminently resourceful, the results are conventionally voluptuous rather than ethereal. The performance is sensitive and persuasive; the recording has a natural perspective and admirable detail.

Symphony No. 5 in A min.; The Mountain King (Bergakungen): Suite; Gustav II Adolf: Elegy.

*** BIS CD 585. Royal Stockholm PO, Järvi.

The *Fifth Symphony* is a late work; it draws freely on ideas from the ballet, *The Mountain King*, whose suite completes this CD. The first movement is by far the best. The second movement has some beautiful ideas, but the last two movements are really rather feeble. *The Mountain King* is an inventive and attractive score; and both works, as well as the touching *Elegy* from the music to *Gustav II Adolf*, could hardly be presented more persuasively. The engineering is absolutely first class.

Choral music: Collection of Part-songs.

*** BIS CD 633. Ahnsjö, Alin, Orphei Drängar Ch., Sund.

Some of the part-songs Alfvén composed for the Orphei Drängar (Sons of Orpheus) are collected here and are sung to the highest standards of tonal virtuosity. Recommended with enthusiasm even to those who find the symphonies inflated and self-indulgent.

ALKAN, Charles-Valentin (1813–88)

Concerti da çamera Nos. 1 in A min.; 2 in C sharp min. Op. 10/1–2.

*** Hyp. CDA 66717. Hamelin, BBC Scottish SO, Brabbins –
   HENSELT: *Piano Concerto*, etc. ***

These are early pieces, miniature concertos of no mean interest and individuality. Elegantly played by Marc-André Hamelin and the BBC Scottish Symphony under Martyn Brabbins, they make an excellent foil for the Henselt *F minor Concerto.*

Piano Concerto, Op. 39 (orch. Klindworth); *Concerti da camera Nos. 1 in A min.; 2 in C sharp min.; 3 in C sharp min.* (reconstructed Hugh Macdonald).

(BB) *** Naxos 8.553702. Feofanov, Razumovsky SO,
   Stankovsky.

Alkan's Op. 39 consists of twelve *Études*, of which Nos. 8–10 comprise the *Concerto for Piano.* However, the first movement was orchestrated by the conductor and pianist, Karl Klindworth. Alkan's work is only the core from which the rather long work developed. Feofanov does a heroic job in the Klindworth and shows a sympathy with Alkan that the Slovak-based Razumovsky orchestra and Robert Stankovsky obviously share. Good recording makes this well worth anybody's money.

Barcarolle; Gigue, Op. 24; Marche, Op. 37/1; Nocturne No. 2, Op. 57/1; Saltarelle, Op. 23; Scherzo diabolico, Op. 39/3; Sonatine, Op. 61.

(B) *** HM (ADD) HMA 190 927. Ringeissen.

Bernard Ringeissen could be more flamboyant, but he is fully equal to the cruel technical demands of this music. The recording, from the beginning of the 1970s, is first class.

Barcarolle, Op. 65/6; 12 Studies in Minor Keys, Op. 39/4–7 (Symphonie), 12 (Le Festin d'Esope); Grande sonate, Op. 33: 2nd movt (Quasi Faust) only.

(M) *** RCA 09026 63310 2. Lewenthal – LISZT:
   Hexameron. ***

Raymond Lewenthal made a speciality of Alkan, first by editing his music, then by performing it and also by writing his biography. Lewenthal's passion for this music leaps out at you in these exciting performances, and the recording, dating from the mid-1960s, is excellent. Liszt's *Hexameron* is an excellent bonus, and these recordings are worthy of RCA's High Performance label.

12 Etudes in the Minor Keys, Op. 39/1–12. Etudes, Op. 3/5: Allegro barbaro. Chants: Assez vivement, Op. 38/1; Barcarolle, Op. 65/6. Esquisses: La staccatissimo; Les Cloches; Les Soupirs; En songe, Op. 63/2, 4, 11 & 48. Les Mois: Gros temps, Op. 74 (Suite 1: No. 2). Nocturne in B, Op. 22; Preludes: La Chanson de la folle au bord de la mer; Le Temps qui n'est plus; J'étais endormie, mais mon coeur veillait, Op. 31/8, 12–13.

*** ASV CDDCS 227 (2). Gibbons.

Alkan's music is almost exclusively for the keyboard, but it rarely finds its way into the modern concert-hall – not surprisingly, given its fiendish, hair-raising difficulties and (to be fair) uneven quality. Jack Gibbons has obviously inherited the mantle of Ronald Smith, to whom his notes pay homage, and he rises to the challenge these pieces present with triumphant virtuosity. Good sound, too.

12 Etudes in the Minor Keys: Symphony for Piano, Op. 39/ 4–7; Alleluia, Op. 25; Salut cendre du pauvre! Op. 45; Super flumina Babylonis, Op. 52; Souvenirs: 3 Morceaux dans le genre pathétique, Op. 15.

(N) *** Hyp. CDA 67218. Hamelin.

The *Symphony for Piano* comprises four movements (Nos. 4–7) from the *Douze études dans les tons mineurs* which Alkan published in 1857. There have been remarkable recordings in the past from those champions of Alkan, Ronald Smith and Raymond Lewenthal – and we remain greatly impressed by Jack Gibbons's virtuosity on ASV (see above). The *Symphony* and the other pieces here must sound effortless, just as a great dancer must seem weightless, and Marc-André Hamelin makes light of its many difficulties. He displays not only a transcendental virtuosity but a great poetic feeling in such pieces as the remarkable *Salut, cendre du pauvre!* Superb playing and very good recording – and noteworthy not for its dazzling virtuosity but its refined music-making.

Grande sonate (Les Quatre Âges), Op. 33; Barcarolle; Le Festin d'Esope; Sonatine, Op. 61.

*** Hyp. CDA 66794. Hamelin.

Under studio conditions Marc-André Hamelin records works by Alkan with breathtaking virtuosity. Alkan's *Grande sonate* over its four massive movements represents the hero at various ages, with the second, *Quasi-Faust*, the key one. The *Sonatine*, the most approachable of Alkan's major works, is done just as dazzlingly, with the hauntingly poetic *Barcarolle* and the swaggering *Festin d'Esope* as valuable makeweights.

25 Preludes, Op. 31.

*** Decca (IMS) 433 055-2. Mustonen – SHOSTAKOVICH: *24 Preludes.* ***

The *Preludes* are more poetic than barnstorming and they date from 1847. They go through all the major and minor keys, returning to C major in No. 25. The young Finnish pianist Olli Mustonen plays them supremely well. The recording is absolutely first class. Strongly recommended.

ALLEGRI, Gregorio (1582–1652)

Miserere.

*** Gimell (ADD) CDGIM 339. Tallis Scholars, Phillips –
  MUNDY: *Vox patris caelestis;* PALESTRINA: *Missa Papae
  Marcelli.* ***

(M) *** Decca (ADD) 466 373-2. King's College Ch., Willcocks
  – PALESTRINA: *Collection.* ***

Mozart was so impressed by Allegri's *Miserere* when he heard
it in the Sistine Chapel (which originally claimed exclusive
rights to its performance) that he wrote the music out from
memory so that it could be performed elsewhere. On the
much-praised Gimell version, the soaring treble solo is taken
by a girl, Alison Stamp, and her memorable contribution is
enhanced by the recording itself.

The famous 1963 King's performance of Allegri's *Miserere*,
with its equally arresting treble solo so beautifully and securely sung by Roy Goodman, is now reissued, impressively
remastered in Decca's Legends series – coupled with Palestrina at mid-price.

ALMEIDA, Francisco António de
(*c.* 1702–55)

Motets: *Beatus vir; O quam suavis.*

(M) *** DG 453 182-2. Smith, Magali, Schwartz, Serafim,
  Gulbenkian Chamber Ch. & O, Corboz – CARVALHO: *Te
  Deum;* SEIXAS: *Adebat Vincentius* etc.; TEIXEIRA:
  Gaudate, astra. ***

These two beautiful (and beautifully sung) motets confirm
the Portuguese baroque composer, Francisco António de
Almeida, as a composer of individuality. *Beatus vir* makes
considerable florid demands on both soprano and tenor
soloists, ending with an expansive *Amen* from the chorus.
The recording is in every way excellent, fresh and clear
within a warm acoustic.

La Giuditta (oratorio).

(B) *** HM HMA 901411/12. Lootens, Congiu, Hill, Köhler,
  Concerto Köln, Jacobs.

Here is a superb oratorio (based on the story from the
Apocrypha of Judith's deception of Holofernes) by a virtually unknown Portuguese composer. His music keeps reminding one of Handel at his finest. Almeida is surely lucky
that René Jacobs has assembled such a fine cast, with Lena
Lootens singing freshly and appealingly as Giuditta, Martyn
Hill a generally fine Holofernes (though perhaps not an
entirely convincing seducer) and Alex Köhler most impressive of all as Ozia, Commander of Bethulia. The work is
brimful of melody. The orchestral writing, using flutes,
oboes, horns (which come through spectacularly) and
strings, shows a true feeling for the orchestral palette and
the way it can be used to sharpen and colour the narrative.
Jacobs directs a performance that springs vividly to life, and
everything about this production, including the recording,
is first class. With excellent documentation this is very highly
recommended.

ALONSO-CRESPO, Eduardo
(born 1956)

Juana, la loca (overture and ballet music); *Putzi: Mephisto*
(waltz); *Yubarta:* overture.

*** Ocean OR101. Cincinnati CO, composer – GALBRAITH:
  Piano Concerto No. 1. ***

The Argentinian-born Alonso-Crespo writes colourfully in
a style which absorbs Latin-American rhythms and which
clearly reflects eclectic lyrical influences from his adopted
North American homeland, not least from Copland. There
is no shortage of melody. His operetta *Putzi* mixes Lisztian
biography with the Faust legend and the *Mephisto Waltz* is
used as a springboard for a rather charming pastiche. The
Cincinnati Chamber Orchestra responds to the composer's
direction with considerable aplomb, and the recording is
excellent.

ALWYN, William (1905–85)

(i) *Autumn Legend* (for cor anglais); (ii) *Lyra Angelica*
(concerto for harp); (iii) *Pastoral Fantasia* (for viola);
Tragic Interlude.

*** Chan. 9065. (i) Daniel; (ii) Masters; (iii) Tees; City of L.
  Sinfonia, Hickox.

Autumn Legend (1954) is a highly atmospheric tone-poem,
very Sibelian in feeling. So too is the *Pastoral Fantasia*,
yet the piece has its own developing individuality. A fine
performance, with Stephen Tees highly sympathetic to the
music's fluid poetic line. The *Tragic Interlude* is a powerful
lament for the dead of wars past. But the highlight of the
disc is the *Lyra Angelica*, a radiantly beautiful, extended
piece (just over half an hour in length) inspired by the
metaphysical poet Giles Fletcher's 'Christ's victorie and triumph'. The performance here is very moving, and the
recording has great richness of string-tone and a delicately
balanced harp texture. Rachel Masters's contribution is distinguished. This is the record to start with for those beginning to explore the music of this highly rewarding composer.

*Concerti Grossi Nos. 1 in B flat for Chamber Orchestra; 2
in G for String Orchestra; 3 for Woodwind, Brass & Strings;*
(i) *Oboe Concerto.*

*** Chan. 8866. (i) Daniel; City of L. Sinfonia, Hickox.

The improvisatory feeling and the changing moods of the
Oboe Concerto are beautifully caught by Nicholas Daniel,
with Hickox and the Sinfonia players providing admirable
support. They then turn to the more extrovert and strongly
contrasted *Concerti Grossi*, the first a miniature concerto for
orchestra, the second in the ripest tradition of English string
writing. The third is a fine *in memoriam* for Sir Henry Wood.
Excellent Chandos sound.

(i) *Piano Concerto No. 1. Symphony No. 1.*

*** Chan. 9155. (i) Shelley; LSO, Hickox.

Hickox's performance of the *First Symphony* is most compelling. The *First Piano Concerto* is also a flamboyant piece, in

a single movement. Howard Shelley is a splendid soloist, fully up to the rhetoric and touching the listener when the passion subsides, creating a haunting stillness at the very end. Again splendid recording.

(i) *Piano Concerto No. 2; Sinfonietta for Strings; Symphony No. 5 (Hydriotaphia).*

*** Chan. 9196. (i) Shelley; LSO, Hickox.

The *Piano Concerto No. 2* opens boldly and expansively and is romantically rhetorical, with sweeping use of the strings. The imaginative *Andante* is its highlight, but the jazzy 'fuoco' finale with its calm central section is overlong (13 minutes). Howard Shelley plays with brilliance and much sensitivity, and Alwyn admirers will be glad to have the work available on record, even if it is flawed.

The cogent *Fifth Symphony* has its dense argument distilled into one movement with four sub-sections, and the work is dedicated to the memory of physician/philosopher Sir Thomas Browne (1605–82), whose writings were always on the composer's bedside table. The string writing of the *Sinfonietta for Strings* is very much in the English tradition and is hauntingly atmospheric. Hickox is consistently sympathetic, with the structure of the symphony held in a strong grip.

(i) *Piano Concertos Nos. 1–2. Elizabethan Dances; Overture to a Masque.*

(N) *** Chan. 9935. (i) Shelley; LSO, Hickox.

The two piano concertos also now come coupled together with the *Elizabethan Dances* and *Overture to a Masque* to fill out the disc generously. No doubt Chandos plan also to recouple the symphonies.

(i) *Violin Concerto. Symphony No. 3.*

*** Chan. 9187. (i) Mordkovitch; LSO, Hickox.

The *Violin Concerto* – so sympathetically played here by Lydia Mordkovitch – is discursive but has moments of intense beauty, especially at the rapt closing section of the first movement, where Mordkovitch plays exquisitely. Hickox's reading of the *Third Symphony* is very convincing, while the LSO again respond to a symphony that is strongly conceived, powerfully argued, consistently inventive and impressively laid out. The expansive Chandos recording suits both works admirably.

4 Elizabethan Dances; Derby Day Overture; Festival March; The Magic Island; Sinfonietta for Strings.

*** Lyrita (ADD) SRCS 229. LPO, composer.

Alwyn's *Elizabethan Dances* are extrovert and tuneful in the Malcolm Arnold tradition (if not quite so ebullient in orchestration). Alwyn is no less successful in *Derby Day* and he is both poetic and romantically expansive in the Shakespearean evocation of *The Magic Island*. In the *Festival March*, while acknowledging his debt to Elgar and Walton, he brings an individual, restrained *nobilmente* to the main lyrical tune. But the most important work here is the *Sinfonietta for Strings*. The Lyrita recordings were made between 1972 and 1979 and show the usual engineering flair which distinguishes all reissues on this label.

Film scores: *The Fallen Idol; The History of Mr Polly; Odd Man Out; The Rake's Progress: Calypso* (all restored and arr. Palmer).

*** Chan. 9243. LSO, Hickox.

Unfortunately, all Alwyn's major film-scores were inadvertently destroyed at Pinewood Studios, and Christopher Palmer has had to return to the composer's sketches for these recordings. The result is impressive. *Odd Man Out* (about the IRA) has the most compellingly poignant music, but the lightweight *History of Mr Polly* is charming and *The Fallen Idol* sophisticated in its delineation of action and character. The orchestral playing is both warmly committed and polished, and the recording is out of Chandos's top drawer.

Symphonies Nos. 1–4; 5 (Hydriotaphia); Sinfonietta for Strings.

*** Chan. 9429 (3). LSO, Hickox.

William Alwyn's five symphonies plus the expansive *Sinfonietta for Strings* are given outstanding performances from the LSO under Hickox to match the composer's own in natural understanding. The Chandos recordings are consistently up to the high standard of the house, and this set can be commended without reservation.

Symphonies Nos. 1; 4.

*** Lyrita (ADD) SRCD 227. LPO, composer.

The first of Alwyn's symphonies dates from 1950 and is a work of considerable power and maturity. Its gestures offer obvious echoes of the film-scores of which Alwyn is so consummate a master. The LPO responds splendidly to the composer's direction, and the Lyrita analogue recording has fine presence, body and clarity.

Symphony No. 2; Derby Day Overture; Fanfare for a Joyful Occasion; The Magic Island; Overture to a Masque.

*** Chan. 9093. LSO, Hickox.

Hickox's account of the Sibelian *Second Symphony* is very fine, and the Chandos digital recording provides full and expansive sound for brass and strings and a natural concert-hall balance. *The Magic Island* is a fine piece, inspired by *The Tempest*, and Hickox's account is beautifully played. The pithy *Derby Day Overture* has plenty of energy here, but the *Overture to a Masque* with its 'pipe and tabor' Elizabethan flavour is comparatively slight. The brilliant *Fanfare* ends the concert spectacularly.

Symphony No. 3 – see under *Violin Concerto*

Symphony No. 4; Elizabethan Dances; Festival March.

*** Chan. 8902. LSO, Hickox.

Richard Hickox's conception of the *Fourth* is marginally more spacious than the composer's own – as the timings of the outer movements demonstrate. Yet he has a masterly grip on the score. The *Elizabethan Suite* doesn't bridge the opposing styles of the times of the queens Elizabeth I and II too convincingly, but there is a graceful waltz, an engaging mock-morris dance and a pleasing pavane.

CHAMBER MUSIC

Concerto for Flute & 8 Wind Instruments; Music for 3 Players; Naiades Fantasy (Sonata for Flute & Harp); Suite for Oboe & Harp; Trio for Flute, Cello & Piano.

*** Chan. 9152. Haffner Wind Ens. of L., Daniel, with Jones, Drake.

Alwyn's *Concerto for Flute and Eight Wind Instruments* is richly textured, yet the consistent inner movement fascinates the ear. The charmingly pastoral *Suite for Oboe and Harp* is most delectably played by Nicholas Daniel (oboe) and Ieuan Jones (harp). The *Naiades Fantasy for Flute and Harp* is a chimerical piece in six movements. The final work is an equally attractive two-movement *Trio*. The Haffner Wind Ensemble are very impressive, both individually as solo personalities and as a team. The recording is admirably balanced and very realistic.

Crépuscule for Solo Harp; Divertimento for Solo Flute; Clarinet Sonata; Flute Sonata; Oboe Sonata; Sonata Impromptu for Violin & Viola.

*** Chan. 9197. L. Haffner Wind Ens. (members), Daniel; Drake.

The *Oboe Sonata* is an inspired work; it is beautifully played here by Nicholas Daniel and Julius Drake. The *Clarinet Sonata* is a fantasy piece in which Joy Farrall combines extrovert freedom with a more thoughtful reserve, yet with wild excursions into the upper tessitura. By contrast the solo *Divertimento* for flute (the responsive Kate Hill) is neo-classical. The *Crépuscule* for solo harp (Ieuan Jones) is a quiet evocation of a cold, clear and frosty Christmas Eve. The *Sonata for Flute and Piano* and the *Sonata Impromptu for Violin and Viola* are no less striking. Overall, this programme is consistently rewarding and the recording is very real and immediate.

(i) Rhapsody for Piano Quartet. String Quartet No. 3; String Trio.

*** Chan. 8440. (i) Willison; Qt of London.

The *Third Quartet* is the most important work on this record; like its two predecessors, it is a concentrated and thoughtful piece of very considerable substance, elegiac in feeling. The playing of the Quartet of London throughout (and of David Willison in the *Rhapsody*) is both committed and persuasive. The recording brings the musicians vividly into one's living-room.

String Quartets Nos. 1 in D min.; 2 (Spring Waters).

**(*) Chan. 9219. Qt of London.

Both quartets are works of substance. The *First* has a probing, deeply felt first movement, a dancing, gossamer *Scherzo* and a profound, yearning *Andante*. Its companion comes 20 years later and derives its subtitle, *Spring Waters*, from Turgenev. Both works are well played and the performances are obviously felt and thoroughly committed. The digital

recording sounds admirably natural, but the playing time is too short for a full-priced record (45 minutes).

Fantasy-Waltzes; 12 Preludes.

**(*) Chan. 8399. Ogdon.

The *Fantasy-Waltzes* are highly attractive and are excellently played by John Ogdon, who is also responsible for a perceptive insert-note. The *Twelve Preludes* are equally fluent and inventive pieces that ought to be better known and well repay investigation. However, this reissue is expensive.

Fantasy-Waltzes; Green Hills; Movements; Night Thoughts; Sonata alla toccata.

(N) *** Chan. 9825. Milford.

Julian Milford plays the engaging *Fantasy-Waltzes* quite as persuasively as John Ogdon, his rubato particularly felicitous. He is given state-of-the-art recording. The *Sonata alla toccata*, too, is a most attractive work, with a single theme permeating all three movements. The vivacious finale is further enlivened with touches of syncopation, but ends with a very positive statement of the dominating chorale. The more turbulent *Movements* might be regarded as another sonata. It was the composer's first key work for the piano after a nervous breakdown, and is dedicated to his wife, Mary. The second movement uses a 'tone row' but remains thoroughly accessible, while the *Devil's Reel* of the finale is in essence another formidable toccata laced with angular syncopations. After this the nostalgic *Night Thoughts* and the memorably tranquil *Green Hills* come as balm.

VOCAL MUSIC

(i) Invocations; (ii) A Leave-Taking (Song-cycles).

*** Chan. 9220. (i) Gomez, Constable; (ii) Rolfe Johnson, Johnson.

Alwyn shows a keen ear for matching word-movement in music with a free *arioso* style. Notable in the tenor cycle *A Leave-Taking* is *The Ocean Wood*, subtly evocative in its sea inspirations. The soprano cycle is almost equally distinguished, leading to a beautiful *Invocation to the Queen of Moonlight* which suits Jill Gomez's sensuous high soprano perfectly. Excellent performances, not least from the accompanists, and first-rate recording.

Miss Julie (opera; complete).

*** Lyrita (ADD) SRCD 2218 (2). Gomez, Luxon, Jones, Mitchinson, Philh. O, Tausky.

Alwyn's operatic gestures are big and, though the melodies hardly match Puccini's, the score is rich and confident, passionately performed by the Philharmonia under Tausky's direction. Jill Gomez sings ravishingly as Miss Julie and Benjamin Luxon gives a most convincing characterization of the manservant lover, with roughness a part of the mixture. Della Jones's mezzo is not contrasted enough with the heroine's soprano but she sings warmly, and it is good to have as powerful a tenor as John Mitchinson in the incidental role of Ulrik. The 1983 Lyrita recording is well up to standard, beautifully clear as well as full, and it projects the narrative evocatively and involvingly.

ANDERSON, Leroy (1908–75)

Belle of the Ball; Blue Tango; Chicken Reel; China Doll; Fiddle-Faddle; The First Day of Spring; The Girl in Satin; Horse and Buggy; Jazz Legato; Jazz Pizzicato; The Phantom Regiment; Plink, Plank, Plunk!; Promenade; Saraband; Scottish Suite: The Bluebells of Scotland. Serenata; Sleigh Ride; Song of the Bells; Summer Skies; The Syncopated Clock; The Typewriter; The Waltzing Cat. Arr. of HANDEL: *Song of Jupiter.*

(M) *** Mercury (ADD) 432 013-2. Eastman-Rochester Pops O, or O, Fennell.

(i) *Carol Suite:* excerpts. *A Christmas Festival. Goldilocks: Pirate Dance.* (ii) *Irish Suite. Bugler's Holiday; Forgotten Dreams; Penny-Whistle Song; Sandpaper Ballet; Trumpeter's Lullaby.*

(M) *** Mercury (ADD) [434 376-2]. (i) London Pops O; (ii) Eastman-Rochester Pops O, Fennell – COATES: *Four ways,* etc. **(*)

The reissue of Frederick Fennell's Mercury performances is most welcome; they have a witty precision that is most attractive. The second disc includes the *Irish Suite*, one of Anderson's more ambitious enterprises. Its highlight is a clever arrangement of *The Minstrel Boy* in the form of a haunting little funeral march, advancing and retreating. Fennell also includes some arrangements of notable Christmas carols; and the vintage, rather dry and studio-ish recording suits the bright precision of the playing.

D'ANGLEBERT, Jean-Henri
(1635–91)

Pièces de clavecin (complete).

(N) *** O-L 458 588-2 (2). Rousset (harpsichord).

Jean-Henry D'Anglebert comes from the generation immediately following Chambonnières, whom he succeeded as 'Ordinaire de la musique de la chambre du roi'. It was D'Anglebert who expanded and built on the expressive world of Chambonnières and Louis Couperin. Through his position at Versailles, D'Anglebert was more closely in touch with Lully, many of whose arias he transcribed. In his scholarly notes Christophe Rousset argues the case for D'Anglebert as the key figure in the French music of his time, paving the way for Couperin-le-Grand and Rameau. He sees his output as constituting 'un fleuron de la musique française' and he also plays it with a jewelled clarity and sparkle. No one has recorded all this repertoire before and no one is better suited by temperament or in his understanding of style to offer it as persuasively. Rousset uses a Ruckers of 1624 which was modified at the turn of the seventeenth and eighteenth centuries to extend its compass. Tuned in meantone with a = 392, it is in the Musée d'Unterlinden at Colmar in Alsace, where these beautiful recordings were made. No one with an interest in Couperin or the keyboard music before Bach should overlook this magisterial survey.

ANGULO, Eduardo (born 1954)

Guitar Concerto No. 2 (El Alevín).

*** Guild GMCD 7176. Jiménez, Bournemouth Sinf., Frazor – RODRIGO: *Concierto de Aranjuez;* VILLA-LOBOS: *Guitar concerto.* ***

Angulo's *Concerto* has much in common with its famous Spanish coupling, with the slow movement at first pensive, then full-bloodedly romantic. The finale sparkles with Mexican dance-rhythms, gaudy and gentle by turns. Rafael Jiménez is a highly sensitive and brilliant soloist and Terence Frazor and the Bournemouth Sinfonietta accompany him with both understanding and gusto. This is a work of considerable popular appeal, and it is recorded very persuasively here.

ANTHEIL, George (1900–1959)

Symphonies Nos. 1 (Zingareska); 6 (after Delacroix); Archipelago.

(N) *** CPO 999 604-2. Frankfurt RSO, Wolff.

This CPO coupling of Antheil's first and last symphonies is very welcome, showing the marked contrast between the style of his time in Paris – when he associated with such fellow artists as Joyce, Hemingway, Pound and Picasso – and his later style, influenced by Soviet composers. The gypsy echoes suggested by the title for No. 1, *Zingareska,* are minimal. Far more important are the echoes of early Stravinsky, occasionally mixed with Gershwin, with the finale bringing direct imitations of passages from both *Petrushka* and *The Rite of Spring*. Though it is an attractive, at times brilliant work, the three-movement *Symphony No. 6* is more consistent, with the central slow movement languorously beautiful in its echoes of Satie's *Gymnopédies*, and with the Soviet-style ostinatos of the outer movements crisply and urgently controlled, helped by brilliant sound, enhanced by sumptuous orchestration. The Rumba, *Archipelago,* dazzlingly scored, makes a delightfully colourful supplement.

Symphony No. 4, '1942'.

(*) Everest EVC 9039. LSO, Sir Eugene Goossens – COPLAND: *Statements for Orchestra.* *

(N) (M) (***) Cala mono CACD 0528. NBC SO, Stokowski – BUTTERWORTH: *Shropshire Lad* **; VAUGHAN WILLIAMS: *Symphony No. 4.*(***)

Symphonies Nos. 4; 6 (after Delacroix); Concert Overture: McConkey's Ferry.

(N) (BB) **(*) Naxos 8.559033. NSO of Ukraine Nat. SO, Kuchar.

There are influences of the composer's east-European background in this symphony, which is probably his best. The performance, from a famous advocate of contemporary music, could not be more convincing, and the Everest stereo (from 1959) entirely belies its age. This music is not deep but it communicates readily, and one's only real complaint is that this excellently remastered reissue should have been offered less expensively – the disc plays for only 49 minutes.

In February 1944, Stokowski – temporarily replacing Toscanini with the NBC Symphony – conducted a radio performance of the *Fourth Symphony*. Dating from 1942, it relies greatly on march rhythms and persistant ostinatos, often in support of Prokofiev-like melodies; though the radio sound is limited in dynamic as well as frequency range, the clarity and weight are more than enough to convey the power, urgency and dramatic incisiveness of Stokowski's performance, with full and rich string sound very different from that under Toscanini. With the two English works for coupling, it makes an attractive and revealing disc.

The Naxos issue pairs what are probably Antheil's two most colourful symphonies. They are vividly recorded, with the Ukraine Orchestra sounding very idiomatic in Antheil's jazzy syncopations even while they relish the many echoes of Prokofiev and Shostakovich. Both these symphonies were written in Antheil's productive period in the 1940s, when for a while he was a war correspondent. Though the playing is not as polished as in rival versions, this is well worth considering, with the Concert Overture *McConkey's Ferry*, dating from the same period, a lively and attractive supplement.

ANTILL, John (1904–86)

Corroboree (ballet suite).

(*) Everest EVC 9007. LSO, Sir Eugene Goossens – GINASTERA: *Estancia*, etc. *; VILLA-LOBOS: *Little Train of the Caipira*. **(*)

The ballet-score, *Corroboree*, is based on an Aboriginal dance-ceremony. Its primitivism generates imaginatively exotic invention, very colourfully scored, to include an enticing *Dance to the Evening Star*, a strongly rhythmic *Rain Dance* and a boisterously frantic *Closing Fire Ceremony*. The performance here generates plenty of energy and, if the recording is over-resonant, it is immensely vivid.

ARBEAU, Thoinot (1520–1595)

Orchésographie (French popular dances).

(B) *** HM (ADD) HMA 1901052. Broadside Band, Barlow (with PLAYFORD: *English Dancing Master: 6 Dances* ***).

Unlike Praetorius, Arbeau was not himself a composer, and his collection of sixteenth-century dances, mostly galliards and branles, was part of a dissertation on dancing and its importance for the cultivated members of society, male and female alike. The tunes themselves are presented simply, giving the melody line only. One or two are familiar (*Ding dong merrily on high* appears as a branle), but all have plenty of character. The composer does offer some advice on instrumentation, but much editing and conjecture are required if they are to be brought fully to life. This the Broadside Band do admirably, and Jeremy Barlow's choice

of instrumentation is consistently ear-tickling. The performances are full of life and the recording excellent. By way of contrast Barlow offers half-a-dozen dances from John Playford's very similar collection, *The English Dancing Master*, which are equally personable and entertaining.

The New York Renaissance Band (Arabesque Z 6514) also uses a simple instrumental group. However, at times one feels the musicians could have been more daring, and this is a much less attractive disc than its Harmonia Mundi competitor.

ARENSKY, Anton (1861–1906)

Piano Concerto in F min., Op. 2; Fantasia on Russian Folksongs, Op. 48.

*** Hyp. CDA 66624. Coombs, BBC Scottish SO, Maksymiuk – BORTKIEWICZ: *Concerto*. ***

Arensky's *Piano Concerto in F minor* is an endearing piece, highly Chopinesque in feeling and with some very appealing ideas. Stephen Coombs is an artist of great sensitivity and effortless virtuosity, and he makes out the best possible case for both the *Concerto* and the much shorter *Fantasia on Russian Folksongs*. Good orchestral support and recording.

Violin Concerto in A min., Op. 54.

*** Chan. 9528. Trostiansky, I Musici de Montréal, Turovsky – GLAZUNOV: *Concerto ballata* etc. ***
**(*) Globe GLO 5174. Lubotsky, Estonian Nat. SO, Volmer – RIMSKY-KORSAKOV: *Concert Fantasy;* TCHAIKOVSKY: *Violin concerto.* **(*)

The *Violin Concerto in A minor* is a delightful piece that deserves to be every bit as popular as, say, the Glazunov. The concerto is beautifully played by Alexander Trostiansky. He has refinement, musicianship and impeccable taste. He is perhaps balanced rather too reticently, but the case for this concerto is made very persuasively by orchestra and engineers alike.

Mark Lubotsky's fine recording is also one of the best we have had since Aaron Rosand's dazzling Luxembourg Radio account from the early 1970s. Like that, it is coupled with the Rimsky-Korsakov *Concert Fantasy*. Good orchestral playing under Arvo Volmer and naturally balanced sound.

Egyptian Nights, Op. 50.

**(*) Marco 8.225028. Moscow SO, Yablonsky.

Egyptian Nights was composed in 1900 for Fokine and is based on Pushkin, albeit very loosely. The music cultivates a certain pallid exoticism with dances for Egyptian girls and, although the invention is not top-drawer, it is often endearing. Arensky was a master of the orchestra, and the ballet, which runs for 50 minutes, is certainly pleasing. Decent playing and recording.

Variations on a Theme of Tchaikovsky, Op. 35a.

(B) *** EMI double forte CZS5 69361 (2). LSO, Barbirolli – RIMSKY-KORSAKOV: *Scheherazade;* ** GLAZUNOV: *The Seasons*, etc. ***

These delightful variations, arguably Arensky's best-known

work, originally formed the slow movement of the *Second String Quartet in A minor*, composed in 1894, a year after Tchaikovsky's death, and subsequently arranged for full strings. Sir John Barbirolli's recording, made in the Kingsway Hall in 1965 and first published in harness with the Tchaikovsky *Serenade for Strings*, is warm and spacious. The playing of the LSO under this endearing conductor is suitably affectionate. It comes as part of a quite attractive two-CD Russian music package, let down a little by Svetlanov's rather idiosyncratic *Scheherazade*.

CHAMBER MUSIC

Piano Trio No. 1 in D min., Op. 32.

(M) *** CRD (ADD) 3409. Brown, Nash Ens. –
 RIMSKY-KORSAKOV: *Quintet.* ***
*** Chan. 8477. Borodin Trio – GLINKA: *Trio.* ***

Arensky's *D minor Piano Trio* is delightful. The account by members of the Nash Ensemble is first class in every way, capturing the Slav melancholy of the *Elegia*, while in the delightful *Scherzo* Ian Brown is both delicate and nimble-fingered. The warm, resonant 1982 analogue recording has transferred naturally to CD.

The Borodins, too, give a lively and full-blooded account of the *Trio*. The *Scherzo* comes off well, and the whole does justice to the Borodins' genial playing.

Piano Trios Nos. 1 in D min., Op. 32; 2 in F min., Op. 73.

*** Ph. (IMS) 442 127-2. Beaux Arts Trio.

The Beaux Arts offers the logical coupling and is a first recommendation now: lively playing, full of engagement and sparkle, and very well recorded.

String Quartet No. 2 in A min., Op. 35.

*** Hyp. CDA 66648. Raphael Ens. – TCHAIKOVSKY:
 Souvenir de Florence. ***

The *A minor Quartet* is unusual in being for only one violin and two cellos. The second movement is a set of variations on Tchaikovsky's *Legend* from the *Children's Songs*, Op. 54. It is marvellously played by members of the Raphael Ensemble though the recording is a bit close, placing the listener in the front row of the hall.

PIANO MUSIC

Arabesques (suite), *Op. 67; Essais dur des rhymes oubliées, Op. 28/1–6; 12 Etudes, Op. 74; 3 Morceaux, Op. 42; 12 Préludes, Op. 63.*

(N) *** Olympia OCD 692. Goldstone.

It is good to have a representative and generous collection of Arensky's piano music, so persuasively presented, even if (unlike his chamber and orchestral music) there is an almost total absence of any real Russian flavour, apart from at times a certain nostagia. The survey is comprehensive: the six *Essais dur des rhymes oubliées* were written in the composer's early thirties and are as fresh as they are diverse, the twelve *Preludes* date from around 1902, the *Arabesques* (brief, attrac-

tive vignettes) followed a year later and the *Etudes* came in 1905, a year before his death.

There are occasional hints of Arensky's pupil, Rachmaninov (notably in the last three *Preludes*), but for the most part the music is in a received idiom combining influences from the German School, notably Schumann and Mendelssohn, but also with reminders of Chopin. The rippling figuration in the right hand with the melody emerging in the left, heard in the opening *Prelude in A minor* and the cascading style of the *D major Etude* (No. 5) are characteristic, but Arensky uses a fairly wide range of pianistic devices and his invention is consistently pleasing.

The second of the three *Morceaux* (which close the recital) is like a song without words, and the last skips along delightfully. In short these pieces, though lightweight, are full of charm, which is fully captured by Anthony Goldstone, whose playing never suggests triviality. The recording is excellent, fairly closely observed within an ecclesiastical ambience.

Suites for 2 Pianos Nos. 1–4.

*** Hyp. CDA 66755. Coombs, Munro.

All the music here is endearingly fresh. The *Polonaise* which ends the *First Suite* would not disgrace a ballet by Tchaikovsky. *Suite No. 2*, written four years later, is subtitled *Silhouettes*, and each of its five movements represents a different character, *Le Savant* ('The Scholar'), *La Coquette*, and so on. *Suite No. 3* is a set of nine variations and is the most brilliant and pianistically resourceful of all four. *Suite No. 4* is hardly less beguiling than its companions. Two pianos are difficult to record and the recording, though too resonant, reproduces them very truthfully. Altogether delightful music and captivating playing.

ARMSTRONG, Thomas (1898–1994)

(iv) *Fantasy Quintet;* (iii, iv) *Friends Departed;* (iii) *Never Weather-beaten Sail; O Mortal Folk;* (ii–iv) *A Passer-by;* (iii) *She Is Not Fair to Outward View;* (iv) *Sinfonietta;* (iii) *Sweet Day; With Margerain Gentle.*

*** Chan. 9657. (i) Watson; (ii) Varcoe; (iii) L. Philh. Ch.;
 (iv) LPO, Daniel.

As a distinguished academic Sir Thomas Armstrong was a key figure in British musical life. In their echoes of English choral music from Parry to Vaughan Williams, and Holst by way of Delius, both *A Passer-by* (with baritone soloist) and *Friends Departed* (with soprano) have an immediate impact, passionate not academic. The *Fantasy Quintet* and the *Sinfonietta* are even more sensuous yet amiable pieces, and the six part-songs are beautifully written too. Paul Daniel is a most persuasive advocate in the big pieces, and the recording is warm and atmospheric.

ARNE, Thomas (1710–78)

Keyboard Concertos (played as listed): *Harpsichord Concertos: in C; in G min.; Organ Concertos: in B flat; in G; Piano Concertos: in A; in B flat.*

*** Hyp. CDA 66509. Nicholson, Parley of Instruments,
Holman.

The six keyboard concertos of Arne date from different
periods in his career and have a wide variety of movement-
structures. Holman varies the solo instrument according to
the character of each work, with the earliest, *No. 2 in G
major*, given on the organ, but the next oldest, *No. 5 in G
minor*, played on the harpsichord, when the Scarlattian
cross-hands writing is better suited to that instrument. As a
sampler, try the delectable *No. 3 in A*, given here on a
gentle-toned fortepiano. Exhilarating performances, the instrumental balances perfectly managed, achieving clarity
without exaggeration.

*Organ Concertos Nos. 1 in C; 2 in G; 3 in A; 4 in B flat; 5 in
G min.; 6 in B flat.*

**(*) Chan. 8604/5 (2). Bevan Williams, Cantilena, Shepherd.

Though Arne's concertos are simpler in style and construction than those of Handel, their invention is consistently
fresh. The performances here have admirable style and spirit,
and the recording is ideally balanced – the organ seems
perfectly chosen for this consistently engaging music. A
recommendable set in every respect, except for the playing
time (only 86 minutes).

Trio Sonatas Nos. 1–7 (complete).

(N) *** Chan. 0666. Collegium Musicum 90 (Standage,
Comberti, Coe, Parle).

Arne's seven *Trio Sonatas* (an unusual number for a published set) date from 1757. Unusually in four movements
(alternating slow and fast tempi), but framed by two five-
movement works, they epitomise the new galant manner of
the pre-classical period: the part-writing and the discourse
amiable, the mildly contrapuntal element in the writing
never seeming to predominate in determining the music's
style. Where there is a *Gigg* finale there is a flavour of an
English country dance, but the slow movements have a
comparatively rich expressive character to give the music
substance. For instance the noble opening Siciliana of the
five-movement No. 7 is nicely balanced by the closing *Gigg*
and fairly brisk Minuet finale. Excellent period-instrument
performances, spirited and appropriately genial, truthfully
balanced and recorded.

*Cymon and Iphigenia; Frolic and Free (cantatas); Jenny;
The Lover's Recantation; The Morning (cantata); Sigh no
More, Ladies; Thou Soft Flowing Avon; What Tho' His
Guilt.*

*** Hyp. CDA 66237. Kirkby, Morton, Parley of Instruments,
Goodman.

The present collection admirably shows the ingenuous simplicity of Arne's vocal writing, very much in the mid-
eighteenth-century English pastoral school with its 'Hey
down derrys'. Excellent, warm recording, with the voices
naturally projected. A most entertaining concert.

STAGE WORKS

Alfred (An English Masque).

*** DHM 75605 51314-2. Smith, Brandes, Daniels,
MacDougall, Philh. Ch. & Bar. O, McGegan.

Just as Elgar's *Coronation Ode* of 1902 spawned 'Land of
hope and glory', so Arne's English masque *Alfred* of 160
years earlier introduced 'Rule, Britannia', if in a slightly
different form from what we hear on the Last Night of the
Proms, with tenor and soprano soloists in alternation. First
heard in London in 1745, the year of the Jacobite uprising,
this story of King Alfred defying the Danes involves 27
musical numbers, with simple, tuneful songs for the rustic
characters and more elaborate arias for the royals. Nicholas
McGegan in this brilliant American recording directs his
period forces in fresh, resilient performances, with the
counter-tenor David Daniels outstanding among the
soloists.

Artaxerxes (complete).

*** Hyp. CDA 67051/2. Robson, Bott, Partridge, Spence,
Edgar-Wilson, Hyde, Parley of Instruments, Goodman.

This sparkling, lively performance impressively explains why
Arne's opera was such a success when it was first produced
at Covent Garden. The one number that has latterly become
popular – thanks largely to Joan Sutherland's brilliant
recording – is *The soldier tir'd*, but that dazzling climactic
number is only one of Mandane's formidable solos, whether
expressive or vehement. Catherine Bott gives a masterly
performance, with the counter-tenor Christopher Robson
also impressive in the castrato title-role, and with Ian Partridge pure-toned and incisive in the role of the villain,
Artabanes, even if his sweet tenor hardly conveys evil. With
the mezzo-soprano Patricia Spence taking the castrato role
of Arbaces, the others are first rate too. On two very well-
filled CDs, the set owes much of its success to the inspired
direction of Roy Goodman. The reconstruction of the score
has been achieved most capably by Peter Holman, who
contributes an excellent note.

ARNOLD, Malcolm (born 1921)

*Anniversary Overture; Beckus the Dandipratt Overture;
Flourish for Orchestra, Op. 112; Peterloo Overture, Op. 97;
Philharmonic Concerto; Symphony for Strings, Op. 13;
Water Music, Op. 82b.*

*** Conifer 75605 51298-2. BBC Concert O, Handley.

The short *Anniversary Overture* was written to accompany a
Hong Kong fireworks display: it is boisterous and tuneful.
The *Flourish for Orchestra* has a fine *nobilmente* tune framed
by Waltonian brass, with bells thrown in for good measure.
The *Symphony for Strings* (another early work) is a real find.
First performed in 1947, it has a characteristically jaunty
theme in the first movement, but for the most part its
atmosphere is unexpectedly plangent. The three-movement
Water Music, originally scored for wind alone, is heard
here in a later orchestral version, and its vivid scoring and

colourful ideas have much in common with the *English Dances*, especially the jubilant finale. The *Peterloo Overture* is comparatively familiar, but the *Philharmonic Concerto* is seldom heard. It was written in 1976 for the American bicentennial celebrations, reflecting on the loss of life in the War of Independence, with a confident closing *Chaconne* to convey the ongoing strength of the New World. Overall, this makes a most satisfying programme. Splendidly played and recorded, it was a happy idea to open with *Beckus the Dandipratt*, which first established the composer's reputation.

Overture: *Beckus the Dandipratt, Op. 5; Commonwealth Christmas, Op. 64; The Fair Field, Op. 110; The Smoke, Op. 21; A Sussex Overture.*

*** Ref. RR 48CD. LPO, composer.

This collection of overtures valuably fills in gaps in the Arnold discography, notably *Beckus the Dandipratt*, his very first orchestral work. Arnold at 70 is perhaps a less exhilarating conductor than in his earlier recordings, but only *The Fair Field* (celebrating the Croydon Fairfield Halls) lacks something in effervescence. *The Smoke* brings a contrasting sultry atmosphere in its central section and the Prokofievian *Sussex Overture* is jauntily full of good spirits, as is the exuberant *Commonwealth Christmas Overture*, with its injection of West Indian popular music, complete with steel band evocations. The LPO playing is strikingly alert throughout and the recording suitably brilliant.

Clarinet Concertos Nos. 1, Op. 20; 2, Op. 115; Divertimento for Flute, Oboe & Clarinet, Op. 37; Fantasy for B flat Clarinet, Op. 87; Clarinet Sonatina, Op. 29; 3 Shanties for Wind Quintet.

*** ASV CDDCA 922. Johnson, Martin, Kelly, Briggs, Cohen, Martineau; ECO, Bolton.

With the characterful Emma Johnson as the central figure in all five works, this makes a delightful collection of what is labelled as Arnold's 'Complete Works for Clarinet'. Above all, these performances bring out the fun in Arnold's music, his bluff sense of humour set alongside a vein of warm lyricism matched by few of his contemporaries.

(i) *Flute Concertos Nos. 1–2; (ii) Serenade for Small Orchestra; (iii) 5 Pieces for Violin & Piano; (iv) Children's Suite.*

*** Koch 3-7607-2. (i) Still, New Zealand CO, Braithwaite; (ii) San Diego CO, Barra; (iii) St Clair Trio (members); (iv) Frith.

This is a delightful performance of the *Serenade* (both witty and ironic) by Donald Barra and the San Diego Chamber Orchestra. Alexa Still gives memorable accounts of the two *Flute Concertos*, full of dazzling virtuosity, while the central soliloquy of No. 1 is utterly haunting. For a sampler of this ever-stimulating composer, writing with equal skill in four different formats, the present collection is hard to beat.

(i) *Flute Concerto, Op. 45; (ii) Oboe Concerto, Op. 39. Sinfoniettas Nos. 1, Op. 48; 2, Op. 65; 3, Op. 81.*

(BB) *** Arte Nova 74321 46503-2. (i) Pyne; (ii) Messiter; L. Festival O, Pople.

This is the identical programme of three *Sinfoniettas* plus concertos which Ross Pople recorded earlier for Hyperion with his London Festival Orchestra. In between he has radically rethought his interpretations, often choosing quite different speeds, sometimes faster (as in the *Sinfonietta No. 1*), sometimes much slower (as in the first movements of the other two *Sinfoniettas*). The changes in whichever direction generally bring lighter textures and manner, with Anna Pyne a more warmly expressive flute soloist than her predecessor, and the oboist Malcolm Messiter lighter than before. Very well recorded, at super-bargain price it makes an excellent issue, bringing together charming, beautifully crafted works that are far too little heard in the concert-hall.

Guitar Concerto, Op. 67.

(M) *** RCA (ADD) 09026 61598-2. Bream, Melos Ens., composer – BENNETT: *Concerto;* RODRIGO: *Concierto de Aranjuez.* ***

*** EMI CDC7 54661-2. Bream, CBSO (members), Rattle – RODRIGO: *Concierto de Aranjuez;* TAKEMITSU: *To the Edge of Dream.* ***

There are few guitar concertos to match the effectiveness of this jazz-inflected piece, written in 1957 for Julian Bream, whose first recording, made two years later with the composer directing the Melos Ensemble, is surely definitive. It was recorded by Decca engineers, so the balance is exemplary.

Bream's second recording, with Rattle, is also very successful indeed and gains from the modern, digital sound, which is vividly focused. As with the earlier version, the work is recorded in its original chamber scoring, which is especially effective in the infectious finale.

4 Cornish Dances, Op. 91; 8 English Dances, Set 1, Op. 27; Set 2, Op. 33; 4 Irish Dances, Op. 126; 4 Scottish Dances, Op. 59; 4 Welsh Dances, Op. 138.

(BB) *** Naxos 8.553526. Queensland SO, Penny.

The advantage this Naxos disc enjoys over its competitors – to say nothing of its price – is the inclusion of the four *Welsh Dances*, the last to be written and closer in mood to the *Cornish* and *Irish Dances* than to the cheerful ebullience of the masterly *English Dances* of 1950–51. They remain perennial favourites, and Andrew Penny and the Queensland orchestra present them with their colours gleaming. These performances have the composer's imprimatur (he was present at the recording sessions) and can be cordially recommended. The Naxos sound might be thought a shade over-resonant, but it does not lack brilliance.

Film music: *The Bridge on the River Kwai* (suite for large orchestra); *Hobson's Choice* (orchestral suite); *The Inn of the Sixth Happiness* (suite); *The Sound Barrier* (rhapsody), Op. 38; *Whistle Down the Wind* (small suite for small orchestra).

*** Chan. 9100. LSO, Hickox.

Malcolm Arnold wrote over 100 film scores, and it was the music for *The Bridge on the River Kwai* which (as the composer has acknowledged) put his name before the wider public. All this music is superbly played by Hickox and the LSO (who obviously relish the often virtuoso instrumental scoring), and the recording is as lavish as anyone could wish – very much in the Chandos demonstration bracket.

Film music: *David Copperfield; The Roots of Heaven.*

(N) *** Marco 8.225167. Moscow SO, Stromberg.

As usual on the Marco Polo label, sterling work has been done in reconstructing these scores (this time by John Morgan). *The Roots of Heaven* (1958), about a white man in central Africa who dedicates himself to prevent the slaughtering of elephants, has resonance today. Arnold provides us with a rumbustious 5-minute Overture, which presents various themes colourfully and imaginatively. The score is imbued with a fair share of exotic local colour: the oboes and percussion in *Fort Lamy* sounds suitably jungly. There are good examples of his heroic, romantic and humorous styles throughout, and one is always impressed by his imaginative tonal palate.

David Copperfield was written for a much later (1970) TV adaptation of the Dickens' famous story. The nostalgia is superbly caught in such numbers as *The Return to Yarmouth*. Dickens's characters are well drawn too, and the *Love for Dora* is heartfelt; indeed the melancholy vein which runs through this score leaves a potent after-effect. Both scores are consistently enjoyable and this is a fine disc in every way, even if the *David Copperfield* suite is even more haunting on Gamba's Chandos collection. The sleeve notes are remarkably helpful and informative.

Film music: *Machines for Brass, Percussion & Strings, Op. 30.* Overture: *The Roots of Heaven.* Arr. & where necessary orch. Philip Lane: (i) *Ballad for Piano & Orchestra* (from *Stolen Face*); *The Captain's Paradise: Postcard from the Med; David Copperfield* (suite); *No Love for Johnnie* (suite); *Trapeze* (suite). Arr. Christopher Palmer: *The Belles of St Trinian's: Exploits for Orchestra* (comedy suite). *Fantasy on Christmas Carols* from *The Holly and the Ivy.* (ii) *Scherzetto for Clarinet & Orchestra* from *You Know What Sailors Are.*

*** Chan. 9851. BBC PO, Gamba; with (i) Dyson; (ii) Bradbury.

Malcolm Arnold made his name with the general public in the cinema, providing scores for over a hundred films in a period of twenty years. Almost all the music here comes from the 1950s, and it brims over with memorable ideas, clothed in the glowing colours of Arnold's individual orchestral palette. The suite arranged by Philip Lane from *Trapeze* is a typical example of Arnold's ready flow of invention, including a swinging tune for the horns in the *Prelude*, a delectable blues for saxophone and guitar, an exuberant circus march and a characteristically lugubrious *Elephant Waltz* for a pair of tubas, while the closing sequence features an accordion to set the Parisian scene. The suite from *David Copperfield* opens with a typical melodic sweep, followed by a whimsical moto perpetuo representing the Micawbers. This features a solo clarinet, and Christopher Palmer has arranged another witty clarinet scherzetto from an equally capricious theme used in *You Know What Sailors Are*. The

concertante ballad for piano and orchestra, arranged by Philip Lane from *Stolen Face*, is rather discursive, but the *Overture* from *The Roots of Heaven* (especially written for the film's New York première) opens with a large-screen flamboyant flourish, followed by more catchy syncopation and a lilting waltz tune. Tender romantic melody comes in *No Love for Johnnie*, while *The Belles of St Trinian's* (the composer's favourite film) brings an audacious sparkle. If *The Holly and the Ivy* offers a rather overfamiliar collection of carols, for the most part not very enterprisingly scored, Arnold's jaunty samba from *The Captain's Paradise*, in which Alec Guiness starred in the bigamous title role, makes a splendid finale. Rumon Gamba and the excellent BBC Philharmonic provide plenty of infectious zest and a sometimes bitter-sweet lyricism, and the recording is of top Chandos quality. If you enjoy film music, it doesn't come any better than this.

The Sound Barrier (rhapsody) after film score, *Op. 38.*

(M) *** ASV CDWHL 2058. RPO, Alwyn – BAX: *Malta G.C.* etc. ***

Malcolm Arnold's *Rhapsody*, adapted in 1952 from his film score, shows the composer at his most characteristically inventive. Kenneth Alwyn and the RPO clearly relish the virtuosity demanded of them, and the recording is equally brilliant.

Symphonies Nos. 1, Op. 22; 2, Op. 40.

*** Chan. 9335. LSO, Hickox.

(BB) **(*) Naxos 8.553406. Nat. SO of Ireland, Penny.

Richard Hickox takes naturally to the Malcolm Arnold idiom and he is particularly impressive in the two slow movements, which are full of atmosphere, vividly coloured and strongly felt. The rumbustious finale of No. 2 brings a splendid release of tension, and the LSO response is powerful and thoroughly committed throughout. The recording is well up to the high standard we expect from this label. A first-rate coupling.

Andrew Penny in his Naxos version matches Hickox closely, but the National Orchestra of Ireland cannot command the richness of sonority of the LSO and in the poignant *Lento* of the *Second*, with its plangent funeral march, Hickox's more spacious tempo is profoundly moving.Yet the composer was present at these sessions and the slow movement of the *Second Symphony* communicates strongly in the Dublin performance. The Naxos recording is excellent, but the Chandos is very much in the demonstration bracket.

Symphonies Nos. (i) *2, Op. 40;* (ii) *5, Op. 74;* (i) *Peterloo Overture, Op. 97.*

(M) *** EMI (ADD) CDM5 66324-2. (i) Bournemouth SO, Groves; (ii) CBSO, composer.

The recoupling of two of Arnold's most impressive symphonies can be warmly welcomed; both recordings date from the 1970s. The composer secures an outstanding response from the Birmingham orchestra; in many ways his performance has not been surpassed, particularly in the expressive power of the slow movement. Groves in Bournemouth is equally dedicated, and this is one of his finest recordings. The CD transfer is outstandingly successful, and the overture makes a highly effective encore. Splendid value at mid-price.

Symphony No. 3, Op. 63.

**(*) Everest (ADD) EVC 9001. LPO, composer – VAUGHAN WILLIAMS: *Symphony No. 9.* **(*)

Arnold made his first recording of the *Third Symphony* at Walthamstow in the late 1950s. In the outer movements the performance has a certain chimerical, spontaneous quality that balances out the deeper feelings beneath the music's surface. The result is uncommonly fresh, even if Hickox's later recording has more gravitas. The early stereo is remarkably spacious and the brass writing is given fine sonority, though the violins are less full-bodied than we would expect today.

Symphonies Nos. 3, Op. 63; 4, Op. 71.

*** Chan. 9290. LSO, Hickox.

(BB) *** Naxos 8.553739. Nat. SO of Ireland, Penny.

Arnold's *Third Symphony* is notable for the long, expressively austere string-melody in the opening movement and the desolation of its *Lento* slow movement, both played with great expressive intensity under Hickox. The first movement of the *Fourth Symphony* is dominated by one of those entirely winning, Arnoldian lyrical tunes, even though there is jagged dissonance in the central episode. The slow movement brings another long-breathed, almost Mahlerian, melodic flow, and the finale has its bizarre – indeed raucous – moments, including a curious march sequence. Richard Hickox has the work's full measure, and the Chandos recording is superb, full of colour and atmosphere.

Andrew Penny and his Dublin orchestra also give finely played and spontaneous performances that can readily stand alongside the full-price competition, and this Naxos record understandably has the composer's imprimatur. The recording, if not as rich as the Chandos, is of high quality, atmospheric and with the orchestral colours emerging vividly; the special percussion effects in the exuberantly fugal finale of the *Fourth* are also very telling.

Symphony No. 5, Op. 74; The Belles of St Trinians (comedy suite); Divertimento No. 2, Op. 75; Machines (symphonic study); Solitaire: Sarabande & Polka.

**(*) Classico CLASSCD 294. Munich PO, Bostock.

Symphonies Nos. 5; 6, Op. 95.

*** Chan. 9385. LSO, Hickox.

(N) (BB) *** Naxos 8.552000. Nat. SO of Ireland, Penny.

Arnold's *Fifth Symphony* is a consciously elegiac work, written in memory of friends who died young. While the first movement brings moments of valedictory evocation in Hickox's hands, it is also dramatically vibrant, and the *Andante* has a certain restrained warmth of feeling to balance the jocularly brash Scherzo and finale. The disconsolate *Sixth Symphony* is a good deal less comfortable than the *Fifth*, but Hickox handles the powerfully menacing climax of the *Lento* quite superbly, gripping the listener in the

music's bleak despair, which then suddenly evaporates with the arrival of the joyous, syncopated brass fanfares of the rondo finale. In both symphonies the committed response of the LSO, together with the richly expansive Chandos recording, increases the weight and power.

Andrew Penny draws fine, concentrated playing from the National Symphony Orchestra of Ireland, with brass and percussion in particular brilliantly caught. As a bargain version this wins the highest recommendation, yet go to the Chandos version coupling the same two symphonies and you get performances that are not just more polished, weightier and even more richly recorded, but are more overtly emotional.

Arnold's *Fifth Symphony* is also idiomatically played in Munich by the excellent resident symphony orchestra, conducted by Douglas Bostock. It is an impressive performance, with the slow movement treated elegiacally and the characteristic whimsical zest of the Scherzo brightly caught, while the richly melodic reprise of the main theme of the slow movement in the finale has real ardour. Even so, Hickox's outstanding reading on Chandos is emotionally more gripping, with the closing section a deeply moving threnody. The finale, too, has just that bit more sharpness of articulation and the return of the great Arnoldian melody at the close has *nobilmente* as well as passion. Bostock is at his finest in three of the four other works included, which are all first recordings. The *Divertimento* is a colourful triptych, with a lively *Chaconne* for finale, and there is much uninhibited fun in the early *St Trinian's* film-score, in which the Munich orchestra let their hair down and obviously enjoy themselves. The touching *Sarabande* from *Solitaire* (one of Arnold's most beautiful tunes) and the audacious *Polka* are equally persuasive. *Machines* is forceful but needs just that bit more bite and propulsion.

Symphonies Nos. 7–9; (i) Oboe Concerto.

(N) (B) *** Chan. 9967 (2). BBC PO, Gamba; (i) with Galloway.

Symphonies Nos. 7, Op. 113; 8, Op.124.

(N) (BB) *** Naxos 8.552001. Irish Nat SO, Penny.

Andrew Penny and the Irish National Symphony Orchestra round off their fine cycle of the nine Arnold symphonies for Naxos with these two most troubled and challenging works, reflecting the darkest period of the composer's life. Not that these are depressing, for as a creative genius Arnold translates his emotions into symphonic structures at once imaginative and original. The darkness is relieved both by the characteristic colourfulness of Arnold's orchestration (with a battery of percussion prominent in No. 7), and also by the wealth of thematic material, demonstrating the vitality of the composer's imagination through his worst trials.

The Chandos coupling of Nos. 7, 8 and 9 comes in a two-for-the-price-of-one package, bringing weightier performances, generally more urgent than those on Naxos, helped by richer, fuller recording. It makes an excellent option for those who want all three symphonies, with the *Oboe Concerto* as a brilliantly played bonus. Yet Penny and the Irish Orchestra gain from the extra clarity of the Naxos recording, full and open, with dramatic contrasts sharply terraced.

Symphony No. 9, Op. 128.

(BB) *** Naxos 8.553540. Nat. SO of Ireland, Penny.

This superb first Naxos recording arrived to confirm the *Ninth Symphony* as a fitting culmination to Arnold's symphonic series. The baldness of the arguments, with two-part writing the general rule, might initially be thought disconcerting. But the music consistently speaks in a true Arnoldian accent, culminating in the long slow finale, almost as long as the other three movements together, registering a mood of tragedy and disillusion. The symphony ends quietly on a major triad, a firm D major chord, a mere sop towards granting release. The other three movements are just as direct, built on instantly memorable material. As to Penny's performance, this is not just concentrated and consistently committed but warmly resonant, with the Dublin strings sounding glorious and the woodwind and brass consistently brilliant. The recording is rich and firmly focused.

CHAMBER MUSIC

Divertimento for Flute, Oboe & Clarinet, Op. 37; Duo for Flute & Viola, Op. 10; Flute Sonata, Op. 121; Oboe Quartet, Op. 61; Quintet for Flute, Violin, Viola, Horn & Piano, Op. 7; 3 Shanties for Wind Quintet, Op. 4.

(N) (B) *** Hyp. Helios CDH 55073. Nash Ens.

Duo for 2 Cellos, Op. 85; Piano Trio, Op. 54; Viola Sonata No. 1, Op. 17; Violin Sonatas Nos. 1, Op. 15; 2, Op. 43; Pieces for Violin & Piano, Op. 54.

(N) (B) *** Hyp. Helios CDH 55071. Nash Ens.

Clarinet Sonatina, Op. 29; Fantasies for Wind, Opp. 86–90; Flute Sonatina, Op. 19; Oboe Sonatina, Op. 28; Recorder Sonatina, Op. 41; Trio for Flute, Bassoon & Piano, Op. 6.

(N) (B) *** Hyp. Helios CDH 55072. Nash Ens.

All the pieces on the first disc show conspicuous resource in the handling of the instruments. The second disc includes two *Violin Sonatas* which are cool, civilized and intelligent. The *Piano Trio* of 1956 has a powerful sense of direction. The third listing concentrates on the wind music. This is perhaps more for admirers of Arnold's music than for the generality of collectors. The playing is brilliant and sympathetic throughout all three discs and the recording first rate; good value at bargain price.

String Quartets Nos. 1, Op. 23; 2, Op. 118.

(N) *** Chan. 9112. McCapra Qt.

String Quartets Nos. 1–2; Phantasy (Vita abundans) for String Quartet; Quintet for Flute, Violin, Viola, Horn & Bassoon, Op. 7.

(N) *** Guild GMCD 7216. Ceruti Ens.

Malcom Arnold's two *String Quartets* were written twenty-six years apart. The *First*, an early work (and not without influences from Bartók), dates from 1949; the *Second*

came in 1974, the year after the *Seventh Symphony*. Both are enigmatic, but like all Arnold's finest music thoroughly worth coming to terms with, for all their stylistic and musical ambiguities and contradictions.

The *Andante* of the *First* is full of angst, coming after a first movement full of strange devices – glissandos, harmonics, sharply repeated notes – and an equally bizarre scherzo; the finale has a wry whimsicality. All four movements are thematically interrelated.

The *Second* opens with intensely felt scalic writing, yet the movement's coda produces one of Arnold's most reassuring and haunting warm bluesy melodies; in the second movement an improvisatory solo violin passage leads into a bizarre Celtic jig. The slow movement is permeated with a desperate yearning melancholy, yet the equally passionate close of the finale is life-assertive.

The *Phantasy (Vita abundans)* was written in 1941 for a chamber music competition and came second. The prizewinner, Ruth Gipps, declared that it should have won. In six sections, all drawing on its recurring lyrical opening theme, it teems with 'abundant life', and it is remarkable that it has remained unheard until this arrival of the splendidly alive performance on the present Guild CD.

The first movement of the engaging *Quintet* (dating from 1944, but revised in 1960) makes a delightful foil and is typical of the jocular, popular Arnold. The mood of the slow movement is more uneasy, but the lyrical melodic charm of the finale with its syncopated rhythmic touches is totally winning. The performances of all four works by members of the London Ceruti Ensemble are dedicated and full of spontaneous, often deeply passionate feeling, and the recording has splendid presence and realism.

The McCapra Quartet are hardly less impressive on Chandos; indeed, theirs were the premier recordings of the two quartets. These young players are right inside the music, their ensemble is if anything even more polished than the Ceruti group. Moreover, the Chandos sound is outstanding in its smooth realism. But they only offer the two quartets, and with a playing time of only 46 minutes, the Chandos disc is completely upstaged by the Guild CD, which plays for over 70!

PIANO MUSIC

Allegro in E min.; 2 Bagatelles, Op. 18; 8 Children's Pieces, Op. 36; Children's Suite, Op. 16; 3 Fantasies; 3 Pieces (1937); 2 Pieces (1941); 3 Pieces (1943); Prelude; Serenade in G; Sonata; Variations on a Ukrainian Folksong, Op. 9.

*** Koch 3-7162-2. Frith.

This splendid disc spans Malcolm Arnold's almost unknown piano output, from his earliest pieces (including the *Allegro in E minor*) to the *Three Fantasies* of 1986, terse in structure and much more ambivalent in expressive mood. The *Sonata* (1942) is succinct and strongly argued. The *Variations on a Ukrainian Theme* (1948) makes a bold contrast, its complexities demonstrating the composer imaginatively stretched. The two groups of short pieces for children are very much in the spirit of Elgar's nursery music. The more sombrely coloured *Ballades* provide further contrast. Benjamin Frith is clearly at home in all this music, to make a thoroughly rewarding 72-minute recital, and the piano recording is very fine indeed.

ARRIAGA, Juan (1806–26)

Symphony in D; Overture: Los esclavos felices.

*** Hyp. CDA 66800. SCO, Mackerras – VORISEK: *Symphony in D*. ***

The *Overture*, which comes before the *Symphony*, is a real charmer, almost Schubertian, but also very much in the style of Rossini, complete with crescendo. The *Symphony* could scarcely be played with more character, and the somewhat resonant but very well-balanced recording does not cloud detail. Highly recommended.

String Quartets Nos. 1 in D min.; 2 in A; 3 in E flat.

(N) *** MDG 603 0236–2. Voces Qt.

(M) **(*) CRD 33123 (2). Chilingirian Qt – WIKMANSON: *String Quartet No. 2*. ***

**(*) Ph. (IMS) 446 092-2. Guarneri Qt.

These three *Quartets* are marvellous works of great warmth and spontaneity that can hold their own in the most exalted company. It is barely credible that a boy still in his teens could have produced them.

The Romanian Voces Quartet is completely at home in this engaging music and gives warmly refined, polished performances of all three works, full of elegance and spirit. All three slow movements are beautifully played, with just the right degree of gravitas. The spring-like freshness of the first movement of the *Second Quartet* is particularly attractive, and the *Theme and Variations* that follows is most winningly done. The recording is warm and naturally balanced in an attractively warm acoustic.

The Chilingirians play with both conviction and feeling, but they involve a pair of CDs (admittedly with an interesting coupling).

The Guarneri Quartet, although too upfront as a recording, play the *Adagio* of the *D minor Quartet* very beautifully, and the *Theme and Variations* of the *A major* work is hardly less appealing. Their playing throughout is immaculate in ensemble yet has both warmth and ardour. But the newest version on MDG takes pride of place.

ATTERBERG, Kurt (1887–1974)

Symphonies Nos. 1 in B min., Op. 3; 4 in G min. (Sinfonia piccola), Op. 14.

*** CPO 999639-2. Frankfurt RSO, Rasilainen.

Atterberg's *First Symphony* is naturally derivative, but none the worse for that. The *Fourth (Sinfonia piccola)* of 1918 is distinctly folksy but enjoyable, particularly in this committed performance. Anyone coming to these symphonies for the first time will find these performances well played and with the advantage of superior recorded sound.

Symphonies Nos. 3 in D, Op. 10 (Västkustsbilder); 6 in C, Op. 31.

(N) *** CPO 999640-2. Hanover RSO, Rasilainen.

The *Third (West Coast Pictures)* and the *Sixth* (the so-called *Dollar* symphony, since it won the composer $10,000 in the 1928 Schubert Centenary Competition) are representative of the best in Atterberg's symphonic output. Although the (deleted) Dutton Laboratories transfer of the pioneering recordings made by Sir Thomas Beecham in 1929 sounds astonishingly good, readers will want a more modern version, and this issue fills the bill admirably. It maintains the high artistic and technical standards that Ari Rasilainen set in his earlier CPO recording of Nos. 1 and 4.

Symphony No. 6 in C, Op. 31; Ballad Without Words, Op. 56; A Värmland Rhapsody, Op. 36.

** BIS CD 553. Norrköping SO, Hirokami.

Atterberg's *Sixth Symphony* is a colourful and inventive score which deserves wide popularity. *A Värmland Rhapsody* is, appropriately enough, strongly folkloric. The *Ballad Without Words* has many imaginative touches. The Norrköping orchestra includes many sensitive players but the string-tone lacks weight and opulence. The recording is very clean.

Symphonies Nos. 7 (Sinfonia romantica), Op. 45; 8, Op. 48.

(N) *** CPO 999 641-2 SWR SO Stuttgart, Rasilainen
** Sterling CDS 1026-2. Malmö SO, Jurowski.

Ari Rasilainen and the Sudwestfunk Orchestra of Stuttgart give a very good account of both symphonies, which is more persuasive than Jurowski – though there is not a great deal in it. The CPO recording is excellent.

No. 7 is the more impressive of the two. It draws on (or, in this instance, rescues) material from an earlier opera. It is romantic in feeling, a protest against the modernity of the times. The *Eighth* is less successful, even if the slow movement has some characteristically beautiful ideas. The finale is insufferably folksy. Good playing from the Malmö orchestra and well-detailed recording.

AUBER, Daniel (1782–1871)

Overtures: The Bronze Horse; Fra Diavolo; Masaniello.

☸ (M) *** Mercury (ADD) 434 309-2. Detroit SO, Paray – SUPPE: *Overtures*. ***

Dazzling performances, full of verve and style, which will surely never be surpassed. The present recordings, made in the suitably resonant acoustic of Detroit's Old Orchestra Hall, show Mercury engineering (1959 vintage) at its very finest.

Le Dieu et la Bayadère: Overture & ballet music; L'Enfant prodigue: Overture; Jenny Bell: Overture; La Muette de Portici: Ballet music; Le Premier jour de Bonheur: Overture; La Sirène: Overture. Vendôme en Espagne: Boléro & Air pour le second ballet.

(N) **(*) Sterling CDS 1039-2. Gothenburg Op. O, Andersson.

Though not all of this music shows Auber at his best, it is

all thoroughly entertaining and almost all of it is unknown. Auber had the knack of writing catchy tunes, and with piquant orchestration, splashes of local colour, bacchanals and waltzes, and wit in plenty, one understands how this composer was such a success during the nineteenth century. The performance and recordings are very good, though they just miss the sheer exhilaration that Paul Paray and his Mercury team brought to this repertoire. This disc will bring much pleasure to those who respond to the repertoire.

(i) *Le Domino noir* (complete); *Gustave III ou Le Bal masqué* (Overture & ballet music)

✪ *** Decca 440 646-2 (2) (i) Jo, Vernet, Ford, Power, Bastin, Olmeda, Cachemaille, L. Voices; ECO, Bonynge.

For *Le Domino noir* Auber was inspired to write a sparkling score, full of delightful invention. The opening number directly anticipates the celebrated duet in Delibes's *Lakmé*, and other numbers bring clear anticipations of Gounod's *Faust* and of Verdi's *Il trovatore*, not to mention Gilbert and Sullivan. Three accompanied recitatives, written by Tchaikovsky for a planned performance in St Petersburg, are used very effectively in Act II. Bonynge makes the ideal advocate, moulding melodies, springing rhythms and aerating textures to make the music sparkle from first to last. The playing of the ECO is outstanding. Sumi Jo takes on a role leading her into dazzling coloratura. Bruce Ford as the hero and Patrick Power as his friend, Juliano, sing stylishly in well-contrasted tenor tones, while Isabelle Vernet is excellent as Brigitte. Martine Olmeda and Jules Bastin are both characterful in servant roles. The recording is among Decca's most vivid. On the second disc, after Act III, the fill-up aptly comes from another colourful but more serious opera of Auber, the one which, translated into Italian, prompted Verdi's *Ballo in maschera*.

OPERA

Fra Diavolo (complete; in Italian).

**(*) Fonit 3984 27266-2 (2). Serra, Dupuy, Raffanti, Portella, Cambridge University Chamber Ch., Martina Franca Festival O, Zedda.

While the deleted EMI recording offers the French text truncated, as the published score is incomplete, here Alberto Zedda in this live festival performance offers the first recording of the Italian version, with all the material preserved and with accompanied recitatives by Auber in place of dialogue. The result is substantially longer and dramatically more convincing. Though the live recording, close and rather dry, brings odd balances and stage noises with occasional rough ensemble, the result is lively and involving, bringing out the winning lyricism of Auber's writing. In the title-role Dano Raffanti characterizes well, using a ringing tenor with flair and only occasional coarseness, relishing the challenge of the big arias. Luciana Serra has a touch of acid at the top of the voice, but this is a bright, agile soprano who brings out the charm in the role of the country-girl, Zerlina. Nelson Portella and Martine Dupuy, clear and firm, are well

contrasted as the English Milord and Lady Pamela. An Italian libretto is provided but no translation.

AUBERT, Jacques (1689–1753)

Concerts de Simphonies for Violins, Flutes & Oboes: Suites: Nos. 2 in D; 5 in F; Concertos for 4 Violins, Cello & Bass Continuo: in D & G min., Op. 17/1 & 6; in E min. (Le Carillon), Op. 26/4.

*** Chan. 0577. Coll. Mus. 90, Standage.

Aubert was a contemporary of Rameau and Leclair; he possessed much of the former's melodic flair and feeling for orchestral colour and shared the latter's interest in extending violin technique. The leader (here the inestimable Simon Standage) has most of the bravura; the other violin soloists are subservient, and sometimes the cello joins the solo team. The orchestral concertos are neatly scored and full of attractive ideas. The performances here are polished, refreshingly alive and invigorating, and the recording is first class. Well worth investigating.

AUFSCHNAITER, Benedikt Anton (1665–1742)

Concors Discordia: Serenades Nos. 1–6.

*** CPO 999 457-2. L'Orfeo Bar. O, Gaigg.

These six *Serenades* are in essence elegant orchestral suites in the French style. Originally scored for strings alone, the composer commended the use of oboes or shawms, and bassoons, if 'among your musicians a few do a fine job of playing them'. So Michi Gaigg has taken him at his word and also included a recorder, to double up the string parts. They are given vigorous, polished performances. Although the somewhat edgy attack the Orfeo violins bring to allegros seems a shade over-enthusiastic, the ear soon adjusts when the contrasting dance movements are so graceful and amiable, and the wind playing is excellent. The recording too is warm and the acoustic unconfined.

AULIN, Tor (1866–1914)

Violin Concerto No. 3 in C min., Op. 4.

(BB) **(*) Naxos 8.554287. Ringborg, Swedish CO, Willén – BERWALD: *Violin Concerto*; STENHAMMAR: *2 Sentimental Romances.* **(*)

Tor Aulin's *Concerto* is a pleasing, well-crafted piece in the Brahms mould, and well worth reviving. A good performance with well-balanced recorded sound in a warm acoustic.

AURIC, Georges (1899–1983)

L'Eventail de Jeanne (complete ballet, including music by Delannoy, Ferroud, Ibert, Milhaud, Poulenc, Ravel, Roland-Manuel, Roussel, Florent Schmitt). *Les Mariés de la Tour Eiffel* (complete ballet, including music by Honegger, Milhaud, Poulenc, Tailleferre).

⚙ *** Chan. 8356. Philh. O, Simon.

A carefree spirit and captivating wit run through both these composite works; in fact these pieces are full of imagination and fun. Geoffrey Simon and the Philharmonia Orchestra give a very good account of themselves and the Chandos recording is little short of spectacular.

Film scores: Suites from: *Caesar and Cleopatra; Dead of Night; Father Brown; Hue and Cry (Overture); The Innocents; It Always Rains on Sunday; The Lavender Hill Mob; Moulin Rouge; Passport to Pimlico; The Titfield Thunderbolt.*

*** Chan. 8774. BBC PO, Gamba.

It is remarkable that a French composer should have provided the film-scores for some of the most famous Ealing comedies, so British in every other respect. But Auric's delicacy of orchestral touch and his feeling for atmosphere (together with his easy melodic gift) made him a perfect choice after his first flamboyant venture with Rank's *Caesar and Cleopatra.* From the witty railway music of *The Titfield Thunderbolt* and the distinct menace of *Dead of Night,* Auric moved easily to the buoyantly spirited *Passport to Pimlico.* But it was *Moulin Rouge* that gave Auric his popular hit, with a charming Parisian waltz song (delicately sung here by Mary Carewe) that was understandably to be a remarkable commercial success. Most of the excerpts are short vignettes but they make enjoyable listening when so well played and recorded.

Film scores: Suite: *Du Rififi Chez les Hommes. Macao, l'enfer du Jeu; Le Salaire de la Peur* (excerpts); *La Symphonie Pastorale*: Suite, with *Valse et Tango.*

(N) *** Marco 8.225136. Slovak Rad. SO, Adriano.

Auric's distinctive language is apparent from the first few seconds on this CD. His style is symphonic, with elements of popular songs (such as the *Valse* and *Tango,* which are heard on a gramophone in *La Symphonie Pastorale*), and all with gallic flair. *Macao* is largely reconstructed from music that written for, but not used in, the final edit of the film (including an exotic piece entitled *Chinoiserie*). Auric mixes melodrama and comedy with equal sophistication, and these varied suites stand up remarkably well on their own, which is important as most readers will not have seen the films to which they owe their existence.

Auric's imaginative scoring for a large orchestra is always ear-catching: the use of saxophone, high strings and bass drum at the beginning of *Du rififi chez les hommes,* for example, or the eerie *Etude sombre* of *Macao,* which sounds a little like Rachmaninov's *Isle of the Dead.*

Much background work was involved in making this recording possible by Adriano, for which many will be grateful – not least in his fascinating and lucid notes. The orchestra plays very well, the sound is atmospheric, and the CD presentation cannot be faulted.

Film scores (suites): *Orphée; Les Parents terribles; Ruy Blas; Thomas L'Imposteur.*

*** Marco 8.225066. Slovak RSO, Adriano.

Jean Cocteau considered Auric 'his' composer, and the music recorded here was for films that were either directed by Cocteau or for which he was the screenwriter. The elements of fantasy and imagination that marked *Orphée* are reflected in the music: though scored for a large orchestra, it has a classical restraint and is most haunting throughout. Also included is Auric's arrangement of *Eurydice's Lament* from Gluck's opera – a lovely, piquant bonus. For *Les Parents terribles* Auric dispenses with the strings and uses a large wind band, percussion, and piano: a short *'image musicale'* has been assembled for this recording. *Thomas L'Imposteur* starts off in military style and includes a wistful waltz for Clémence and Henriette. For the swashbuckler *Ruy Blas* Auric had to compose straightforward and colourful music, which gave him plenty of scope for his own distinct brand of orchestration. Adriano has done sterling work on assembling these suites and securing first-class playing from the orchestra, and the recording is good too.

Overture.

(M) *** Mercury [434 335-2]. LSO, Dorati – FETLER: *Contrasts;* FRANCAIX: *Piano Concertino;* MILHAUD: *Le Boeuf sur le toit;* SATIE: *Parade.* ***

Georges Auric's breezy *Overture* is irrepressibly high-spirited and its melodic freshness and Dorati's vivacious performance help to dispel the impression that it is a shade too long for its content. Vividly clear and transparent sound from near the end of the Mercury vintage era: 1965.

AVISON, Charles (1709–70)

12 Concerti grossi after Scarlatti.

(B) *** Ph. Duo (IMS) (ADD) 438 806-2 (2). ASMF, Marriner.
**(*) Hyp. CDA 66891/2. Brandenburg Consort, Goodman.

Marriner and the ASMF pioneered a complete recording of these works by the Newcastle-upon-Tyne composer, Charles Avison, which he ingeniously based on the keyboard sonatas of Domenico Scarlatti, and this fine set, with Iona Brown leading the solo group, has much grace and style. It makes a fine bargain on a Philips Duo two-discs-for-the-price-of-one.

Those seeking a period-instrument performance will find Roy Goodman's version has plenty of vitality. Fast movements fizz spiritedly, but the linear style of the slower movements, though not lacking expressive feeling, is altogether less smooth, and these performances are essentially for those totally converted to the authentic movement. The recording is excellent.

BABADZHANIAN, Arno Harutyuni (1921–83)

Heroic Ballade; Nocturne.

*** ASV CDDCA 984. Babakhanian, Armenian PO, Tjeknavorian – TJEKNAVORIAN: *Piano Concerto.* ***

Babadzhanian won a Stalin Prize for the *Heroic Ballade* but,
after a flamboyant opening, it turns out to be a rather
engaging set of concertante variations. The writing is eclectic
(mixing Armenian influences with Rachmaninov and
water), returning to populist flamboyance at the close, but
not before giving the soloist a chance to be poetically expressive. The performance is excellent, the recording vivid.

(i–iii) *Piano Trio in F sharp min.; (ii–iii) Violin Sonata in
B flat min. (Piano) (i) Impromptu.*

*** Marco 8.225030. (i) Kuyumjian; (ii) Kavafian;
  (iii) Bagratuni.

Both major works here show a strong lyrical impulse, plenty
of ideas, recognizably Armenian in colouring, and an ability
to create a cogent whole out of a loosely structured form.
The volatile *Violin Sonata* (1959) has plenty of energy, but
even the vibrant, syncopated finale gives way to a hauntingly
nostalgic closing section – reminiscent of Shostakovich. The
Piano Trio opens with a grave, sustained *Largo* (whose theme
is to dominate the work) and it develops a passionate impetus of a very Russian kind. The catchy, syncopated finale
has the energetic rhythmic drive we recognize in Khachaturian's better music, balanced by a warmly flowing secondary
theme on the cello. The engaging *Impromptu* for piano acts
as a cantabile encore. The performances here are fierily
passionate, but the players relax naturally into tenderness
whenever needed. The recording is bright, full and well
balanced.

THE BACH FAMILY, including Johann Sebastian

George Christoph(1642–97) Johann Christoph(1642–1703)
Johann Michael(1648–94) Johann Bernhard(1676–1749)
Johann Sebastian(1685–1750) Johann Lorenz(1695–1773)
Wilhelm Friedmann(1710–84) Johann Ernst(1722–77)

'In the name of Bach': J. B. BACH: *Ouverture in D:
Passepieds I & II; La Joye.* W. F. BACH: *Adagio & Fugue in
D min., F.65. Duet for 2 Flutes in E min., F.54.* J. C. BACH:
Quartet in G for Violin, 2 Cellos & Fortepiano, Op.2. J. E.
BACH: *Violin Sonata in F. Lieder from Sammlung
auserlesener, F.1: Der Affe und die Schäferin; Der Hund;
Die ungleichen Freunde; Die Unzufriedenheit.* G. C. BACH:
Geburstagskantate: Sie wie fein und lieblich ist es'.

*** Channel CCS 9095. Florilegium; with (i) Bott; (ii) J. Podger,
  R. Evans, M. McCarthy.

Florilegium provides here a diverting collection of variously
scored instrumental and vocal works to show the extraordinary talents inherent in the genes of the Bach family, not
only those of the sons of Johann Sebastian, but also of
his predecessors, cousins, uncles and nephews. The fine
Fortepiano Quartet by J. C. Bach is by no means the most
interesting work. The programme opens with an engaging
bravura cantata by Georg Christoph, robust and jolly. It is
sung with aplomb. The excerpts from Johann Bernhard's
Ouverture show him to be a distinct musical personality, as
do the works of Johann Ernst. His well-crafted *Violin Sonata*

brings closely interwoven part-writing and a slightly quirky
central *Arioso*. This is very fresh but is expressively plain
compared with his charming vocal fables about animals,
characterfully sung by Catherine Bott. But the highlight of
the concert is the lovely *Adagio* and busy *Fugue* of Wilhelm
Friedmann, who is emerging more and more as a major
figure. The serenely sustained interplay is a little like a
Brandenburg of J. S. B. Performances are full of life and
sensitivity, and the recording is warm and naturally balanced. The one minus point is that German texts only are
provided, without translations.

BACH, Carl Philipp Emanuel (1714–88)

*Cello Concertos: in A min., Wq.170, H.432; in B flat,
Wq.171, H.436; in A, Wq.172, H.439.*

⚫ *** BIS CD 807. Suzuki, Bach Collegium, Japan.
(BB) **(*) Naxos 8.553298. Hugh, Bournemouth Sinf., Studt.

(i) *Cello Concertos: in A min., Wq.170, H.432; in B flat,
Wq.171, H.436; in A, Wq.172, H. 436; Hamburg Sinfonias,
Wq.183/1–4; Sinfonia in B min., Wq.182/5.*

(BB) *** Virgin 2 x 1 VBD5 61794-2 (2). OAE, Leonhardt;
  (i) with Bylsma.

These concertos also have alternative versions for both keyboard and flute, but they suit the cello admirably. Hidemi
Suzuki creates a dashing flow of energy in the orchestral
ritornellos of outer movements, and the Bach Collegium
play with great zest and commitment. In slow movements
Suzuki's eloquent phrasing, warmth of feeling and breadth
of tone are totally compelling, a cello line of heart-stopping
intensity. The recording is splendid.

Bylsma's expressive intensity communicates strongly
without ever taking the music outside its boundaries of
sensibility, and these artists convey their commitment to
this music persuasively. The allegros are full of life, and
the slow movements are most eloquent, particularly the
hauntingly volatile *Largo con sordini* of Wq.172. The *Hamburg Sinfonias* (for woodwind and strings) are striking works,
notable for their refreshing originality. Gustav Leonhardt's
account of this second set is the one to have if you want
them on period instruments. A splendid bargain recommendation, although the BIS recording of the three *Cello Concertos* by Hidemi Suzuki is special.

Tim Hugh on Naxos is altogether more reticent, but he
plays with a persuasive lyrical warmth and Richard Studt's
accompaniments are crisp and stylish. The effect is spontaneous, the recording is vividly natural, and these modern-
instrument performances are alive and enjoyable in their
less extrovert way.

(i) *Cello Concerto in A min., Wq 170; (ii) Keyboard
Concerto in C, Wq. 20. Sinfonias: in G, Wq. 173; in E min.,
Wq. 178; in E flat, Wq. 179.*

(N) *** HM HMC 901711. (i) Bruns; (ii) Alpermann; Berlin
  Akademie für Alte Musik.

The explosive vitality of the playing of the period-instrument
group, the Berlin Akademie für Alte Musik, certainly does
not miss the quixotic volatility of C. P. E. Bach's symphonic

writing. The wildly abrupt mood changes and dynamic contrasts are heard at their most intense in the *Sinfonia in E flat*, Wq. 179 (1757), which opens the programme here, yet that same work has a jocular hunting finale, and there are similar contrasts and surprises in Wq. 178. The *G major Sinfonia*, Wq. 173, is much earlier, but already shows the same unpredictability, and also has a touchingly simple central *Andante*.

The emotionally charged *Adagio* of the *Harpsichord Concerto* is far more searching, contrasting with the exuberant finale, and no one could complain of a lack of rhythmic energy in the outer movements of the more familiar *A minor Cello Concerto*. In short, with a pair of equally fine soloists, and committedly vigorous and alert playing from the orchestra, this extremely generous 79-minute concert provides an ideal introduction to this remarkably original and individual composer. The recording is excellent and the balance places the soloists truthfully in relation to the main string group.

Cello Concerto (No. 2) in B flat, Wq.171.

*** Teldec 9031 77311-2. Rostropovich, Saint Paul CO, Wolff – TARTINI; VIVALDI: *Concertos.* ***

The present transcription is played with commanding eloquence and authority not only by Rostropovich but the fine Saint Paul orchestra. They produce great warmth along with the transparency of texture to which period-instrument ensembles aspire. The couplings too are well worth having. An excellently focused and fresh recording from 1993.

Ton Koopman Edition

Flute Concertos: in D min., Wq.22, H.425; in B flat, Wq.167. H.435; in A, Wq.168, H.428 (with Hünteler; 0630 16183-2).

Flute Concertos in A min., Wq.166, H.431; in G, Wq.169, H.445 (with Hünteler); *Double Harpsichord Concerto in F, Wq.46, H.408* (with Koopman, Mathot; 0630 16184-2).

Oboe Concertos: in B flat, Wq.164, H.466; in E flat, Wq.165, H.468; Sonata for Oboe & Continuo in G min., Wq.135, H.549 (with Ebbinge; 0630 16182-2).

Double Concerto for Harpsichord & Fortepiano in E flat, Wq.43, H.479 (with Koopman, Mathot); *4 Hamburg Sinfonias, Wq.183/1–4, H.663-6* (0630 16181-2).

Koopman Edition (as above).

(M) *** Erato (ADD) 0630 16180-2 (4). Soloists, Amsterdam Bar. O, Koopman.

If you want all the music in Koopman's collection, these well-recorded performances can certainly be recommended. Konrad Hünteler is a nimble and expressive player and is fully responsive to the *A major Concerto*, Wq.168, while the sprightly *Allegretto* which opens the B flat major, Wq.167, is pleasingly vivacious. The spirited and delightful *Concerto for Harpsichord and Fortepiano* and the *F major Double Harpsichord Concerto* are persuasively presented and the recording is deftly balanced. The two *Oboe Concertos* are very appealing in their wide range of mood in Ku Ebbinge's hands. Koopman and his talented Amsterdam players (like their soloists) use period instruments and, while they tend to favour relatively relaxed speeds in the four *Hamburg Sinfonias*, the music-making is very enjoyable in its easy-sounding spontaneity. At present these discs are not available separately, but the Erato Ultima below acts as a splendid sampler.

Flute Concertos in A min., Wq.166, H.431; G, Wq.169, H.445; Double Concerto for Harpsichord & Fortepiano in E flat, Wq.47, H.479; Double Harpsichord Concerto in F, Wq.46, H.408; 4 Hamburg Sinfonias, Wq. 183/1–4, H.663/ 6.

(N) (B) *** Erato Ultima 8573 88050-2 (2). Soloists, Amsterdam Bar. O, Koopman.

This Erato Ultima coverage offers what might be regarded as the pick of the Koopman Edition, including as it does two of the most attractive flute concertos, as well as the delectable duet concerto for harpsichord and fortepiano – one of Carl Philipp's most diverting and rewarding works – alongside the four *Hamburg Sinphonias*.

Flute Concertos: in D min., Wq.22; in A min., Wq.166; in B flat, Wq.167; in A, Wq.168; in G, Wq.169.

*** Cap. 10 104 (Wq.22, 166, 168); 10 105 (Wq.167, 169). Haupf, C. P. E. Bach CO, Haenchen.

Eckart Haupf gives lively, cleanly articulated performances of these concertos, written for the court of Frederick the Great, well supported by the strong, full-bodied and vigorous accompaniments of the C. P. E. Bach Chamber Orchestra under Hartmut Haenchen. Full, atmospheric recording from East German engineers.

Flute Concertos: in D min., Wq. 22; in A, Wq. 168; in G, Wq. 169.

(N) *** Hyp. CDA 67226. Brown, Brandenburg Consort, Goodman.

Rachel Brown's timbre is small and transluscent, but she plays spiritedly and her cleanly articulated roulades are well balanced against Goodman's often aggressively dynamic accompaniments. It is impossible not to respond to such exuberance, and in slow movements the orchestral textures are fined down to support the appealingly gentle flute line. Excellent recording, resonant but clear.

Flute Concerto in D min., Wq.22.

(BB) **(*) ASV (ADD) CDQS 6012. Dingfelder, ECO, Mackerras – HOFFMEISTER: *Concertos Nos. 6 & 9.* **(*)

Those who are interested in the Hoffmeister coupling will find Ingrid Dingfelder's playing both spirited and stylish.

(i) *Flute Concertos: in A min., Wq.166; in B flat, Wq.167; in A, Wq.168; in G, Wq.169; (ii–iii) Oboe Concertos: in B flat, Wq.164; in E flat, Wq.165; (ii; iv–v) Solo in G min., for Oboe & Continuo; (v) Solo in G for Harp, Wq.139.*

(B) **(*) Ph. (ADD) Duo 442 592-2 (2). (i) Nicolet, Netherlands CO, Zinman; (ii) Holliger; (iii) ECO, Leppard; (iv) Jucker; (v) Holliger.

Nicolet uses a modern instrument and plays very well, but the effect with a rather heavy string accompaniment (partly the result of the acoustic) makes less of the music than the rival versions on Capriccio. But those are at full price, and the Philips Duo set offers a great deal more music. Ursula Holliger's accounts of the *Oboe Concertos* are masterly. In addition to the excellence of the support from the ECO under Leppard, the Philips engineering is distinguished. The bonuses for oboe and continuo (in this instance harp and cello) and Ursula Holliger's harp *Solo* also add to the attractions of this very generous set.

Complete solo harpsichord concertos

Harpsichord Concertos: Nos. 1 in A min.; 2 in E flat; 3 in G, Wq.1–3 (H.403–5) (**(*) BIS CD 707); Nos. 4 in G ; 7 in A; 12 in F, Wq.4, 7 & 12 (H.406, 410 & 415) (**(*) BIS CD 708); Nos. 6 in G min.; 8 in A; 18 in D, Wq.6, 8 & 18 (H.409, 411 & 421) (**(*) BIS CD 767); Nos. 9 in G; 13 in D; 17 in D min., Wq.9, 13 & 17 (H.412, 416 & 420) (**(*) BIS CD 768).

Spányi (harpsichord), Concerto Armonico, Szüts.

This is an ongoing project in which Miklós Spányi is planning to record all 52 keyboard concertos which Carl Philipp Emanuel wrote between 1733 and 1788, most of which date from the early years of his musical life at the court of Frederick the Great in Berlin. From the very beginning his style moves away from the baroque concerto principles of Vivaldi and Handel to a more clearly defined and always engaging dialogue between the soloist and ensemble, making a direct path to the piano concertos of Mozart.

The early works are scored simply for strings and, although not without surprises, are free from the idiosyncrasies which the composer subsequently developed; instead they concentrate on display; lyrical lines often faintly pre-echo early Mozart, while allegros radiate energy. Miklós Spányi has chosen to play the early concertos on a harpsichord with a strong personality: a modern copy by Michael Walker of a 1734 Haas whose original maker lived in Hamburg. It is very well balanced with a period-instrument string-group (6;2;1;1), which is probably larger than the ensemble the composer would have expected, and the resonance of the recording (made in a Budapest church) also militates against a really intimate effect. But the playing has animation and elegance, and the soloist effectively improvises his own cadenzas at the recording sessions, which increases the sense of spontaneity. So, with spirited and sympathetic accompaniments one can readily warm to music-making that is polished and always alive, if not perhaps in the last resort distinctive.

In the first movements of both the *G major* and *D major Concertos*, Wq.9 and 13, Bach establishes a pioneering principle of sonata form. The closing section of the opening movement of the *G major* (1742) repeats the material of the opening section, but moving from the dominant key, to which the first section has modulated, back to the tonic. Spányi introduces a highly suitable fortepiano (built by Hemel after a 1749 Freiburg) for the *D major Concerto*, Wq.13, which offers contrast of colour and dynamic in the finale, where the string tuttis are so vigorously forthright. All these performances are impressive.

Keyboard Concertos No. 5 in C min., H. 407; 35 in E flat, H. 446; Sonatinas in D, H. 449; in G, H. 451.

(N) *** BIS CD 868. Spányi (tangent piano), Concerto Armonico, Szüts.

The two concertos here are both among Carl Philipp's most striking works. H.407 opens with a sombre minor key ritornello for strings, followed by a central lively *Arioso*; the Minuet finale with its dolorous cantilena is curiously reminiscent of Gluck in its colouring by the flutes. H. 446 is scored for braying horns as well as strings and is altogether more extrovert. The three-movement concertante *Sonatina in G* again includes flutes, opening with a *Larghetto*, and closing with a *Polacca* (with horns). However the highlight of the disc is the six-movement *Sonatina in D* in which Bach uses an unusual new format interchanging *Andante ed arioso* ritornelli for flutes and strings (in which the soloist participates) with delicate solo keyboard fantasias. The finale is vigorous and fully scored. Spányi is inspired to give of his best throughout this collection, especially in the solo fantasias, and the accompaniments are also full of character. This is one of the most stimulating discs in the series so far.

Keyboard Concertos: Nos. 11 in D; 14 in E; 19 in A, (H.414, 417 & 422) (**(*) BIS CD 785); Nos. 15 in E min.; 25 in B flat; 32 in G min. (H.418, 442 & 492) (**(*) BIS CD 786); Nos. 24 in E min.; 28 in B flat; 29 in A, (H. 428, 434 & 437) **(*) BIS CD 857).

Spányi (fortepiano or tangent piano), Concerto Armonico, Szüts.

For the present issues in Miklós Spányi's ongoing series he turns to the fortepiano (or the slightly more ambitious tangent piano). The *D major Concerto* (H.414), which opens BIS 785, immediately brings an aural surprise in its spectacular and rhythmic use of trumpet and drum parts in the outer movements which here, within a reverberant acoustic, serve to dwarf the fortepiano! On the other hand, the opening ritornello of the *A major* (H.422) recalls Bach's *Brandenburg Concerto No. 6*. The three concertos on BIS CD 786 are well contrasted. The *A major Concerto* (H.437) which opens the third collection has a darkly memorable slow movement; this and the *B flat major* work (H.434) are perhaps better known in alternative versions for cello and flute, yet they are very effective on the fortepiano, even if here the balance is less than ideal, with the rather beefy string-textures given added gruffness of attack by the period instruments.

Harpsichord Concertos: in E, Wq.14; in G, Wq.43.

(M) *** CRD (ADD) 3311. Pinnock, E. Concert – J. C. BACH (arr. MOZART): *Harpsichord Concerto.* ***

The *E major Harpsichord Concerto* is one of the most ambitious that C. P. E. Bach left us. Trevor Pinnock and his English Concert (using original instruments) give admirable performances, nicely balancing the claims of modern ears and total authenticity. First-rate recording and a fascinating coupling.

Double Concerto for Harpsichord & Fortepiano in E flat.

(N) (BB) *** Teldec (ADD) 0630 12326-2. Uittenbosch, Antonietti, Leonhardt Cons. – J. C. BACH: *Sinfonia Concertante in F*; W. F. BACH: *Double Concerto for 2 Harpsichords*. **(*)

(i) *Double Concerto in E flat for Harpsichord & Fortepiano, Wq.47;* **(ii)** *Double Concerto in F, for 2 Harpsichords, Wq.46;* **(i)** *Sonatina for 2 Harpsichords & Orchestra in D, Wq.109.*

(BB) *** DHM (ADD) 05472 77410-2. (i) Kelley, Van Immersel (fortepiano or harpsichord); (ii) Curtis, Leonhardt; Coll. Aur., Maier.

The spirited and delightful *E flat Concerto for Harpsichord and Fortepiano* comes from Bach's last year. It has a chirpily inviting opening theme and is given a wholly persuasive account by Kelley and van Immersel, with the solo instruments naturally balanced and a warm acoustic assisting a lively, authentic accompaniment. The *Sonatina for 2 Harpsichords and Orchestra* is ambitiously scored for three trumpets, two each of flutes, oboes and horns, bassoon and strings. The first movement (of two) is characteristically quirky and diverse. There are surprises, too, towards the end of the second, which is a Minuet with variations. The *F major Concerto*, scored for strings with the addition of two horns, is still thoroughly representative of this composer, with a memorable *Largo* slow movement. It is also very well played and, at its very economical price, this is a reissue not to be missed.

A hardly less attractive account of the Concerto for Harpsichord and Fortepiano also comes on Teldec in a similar price-range. The orchestral balance is somewhat better here and the fortepiano has a slightly bolder, more tangible image. The interplay between the two soloists is felicitous, and choice between the two performances must depend on couplings.

Oboe Concertos: in B flat, Wq.164; in E flat, Wq.165.

*** Ph. 454 450-2. Holliger, Camerata Bern – J. S. BACH: *Oboe d'amore Concerto etc.* ***

Oboe Concertos: in B flat, Wq.164; in E flat, Wq.165; **(Unaccompanied)** *Oboe Sonata in A min., Wq.132.*

(BB) **(*) Naxos 8.550556. Kiss, Ferenc Erkel CO – MARCELLO: *Concerto*. **(*)

Heinz Holliger's stylishly appealing accounts of these two delightful concertos tend to sweep the board, the more so as the accompaniments from the Camerata Bern, led by Thomas Zehetmair, have all the lightness of touch one expects from period-instrument performances, yet with an added fullness of timbre. The Philips recording is beautifully balanced.

József Kiss's playing is sensitive and musical, if without quite the individuality of Holliger, but he is very well accompanied and beautifully recorded. The solo *Sonata* is also worth having on disc, although one might have liked more dynamic light and shade here. But with an enjoyable Marcello coupling, this is well worth its modest cost.

Berlin Sinfonias: in C; in F, Wq.174/5; in E min.; in E flat, Wq.178/9; in F, Wq.181.

*** Cap. 10 103. C. P. E. Bach CO, Haenchen.

The playing of Haenchen's excellent C. P. E. Bach group is alert and vigorous, with airy textures and attractively sprung rhythms. Modern instruments are used in the best possible way. Excellent sound.

6 Hamburg Sinfonias, Wq.182/1–6.

(BB) *** Naxos 8.553285. Capella Istropolitana, Benda.

The six *Hamburg String Sinfonias* are magnificent examples of Bach's later style when, after the years at the Berlin court, he had greater freedom in Hamburg. They are particularly striking in their unexpected twists of imagination, and they contain some of his most inspired and original ideas. Using modern instruments at higher modern pitch, Benda directs light, well-sprung accounts. With more varied textures and tonal contrasts than in most period performances, Benda's have extra light and shade. The darkly chromatic slow movement of No. 3, for example, has a hushed mystery rarely caught. The excellent sound is full and open, as well as immediate. This makes an excellent bargain recommendation.

(i) *6 Hamburg Sinfonias, Wq.182/1–6; Berlin Sinfonias: in C, Wq.174; in D, Wq.176;* **(ii)** *Quartets for Flute, Viola, Fortepiano and* **(optional)** *Cello: Nos. 1 in A min.; 2 in D; 3 in G, Wq.93–5.* **(iii) (Keyboard)** *Fantasy in C, Wq.59/6.*

(B) *** O-L (ADD) Double 455 715-2 (2). (i) AAM, Hogwood; (ii) McGegan, Mackintosh, Pleeth, Hogwood; (iii) Hogwood.

Christopher Hogwood continually has one responding as to new music, not least in the dark, bare slow movements. The two *Berlin Symphonies* with wind make refreshing listening. The three *Quartets* are all beautifully fashioned, civilized pieces with many of the expressive devices familiar from this composer. Although the works were designated by Bach as *Quartets*, no bass part survives. In these Oiseau-Lyre performances the cello line is added judiciously where it seems useful to reinforce the texture. Hogwood uses a fortepiano rather than harpsichord and makes a good case for doing so (with documentary support in the notes). The playing overall is absolutely first rate; the recording is most naturally balanced and could hardly be bettered. Moreover the keyboard *Fantasia in C* is a most remarkable work – it is roughly contemporary with Mozart's *C minor Fantasy* and is more than just a bonus. It is splendidly played by Hogwood. Altogether this is one of the most stimulating of Hogwood's Oiseau-Lyre Doubles.

4 Hamburg Sinfonias, Wq.183/1–4.

(BB) **(*) Naxos 8.553289. Salzburg CO, Lee – W. F. BACH: *Sinfonia in F.* **(*)

The Naxos Salzburg versions are freshly played, the results spick and span, with polished playing from strings and woodwind alike. Obviously Yoon K. Lee knows about period-performance styles and, though modern instruments are used here, textures are clear and clean. While there is plenty of dramatic contrast, the expressive music seems just a shade cool. But the results are certainly stimulating, and this disc is worth its modest cost.

CHAMBER AND INSTRUMENTAL MUSIC

Duo for 2 Clarinets (Adagio & Allegro), H.636; 6 Sonatas for Pianoforte, Clarinet & Bassoon, H.516–521; Flute Sonatas (for flute and harpsichord): in E, H.506; in C, H.573; Oboe Sonata (for oboe and continuo) in G min., H.549; Pastorale for Oboe, Bassoon & Continuo.

*** CPO 999 508-2. Fiati con Tasto, Cologne.

This delightfully diverse cross-section of Carl Philipp Emanuel's chamber music for wind instruments could hardly be bettered as a source of exploration. The use of period instruments is expert, and the *Flute Sonatas* are engagingly perky and given attractively sprightly performances by Karl Kaiser, while Alfredo Bernadini's plaintive oboe timbre is as affecting in the sonatas as it is in the gentle *Pastorale* (a siciliano), in duet with a doleful bassoon. The felicitous interplay of the six *Sonatas for Fortepiano, Clarinet and Bassoon* at times anticipates Mozart, and Harald Hoelden's fortepiano contribution here is as nicely judged as his harpsichord playing in the flute sonatas. The recording is very natural and gives a vivid projection to one and all.

Duo for Flute & Violin in E min., Wq.140; 12 Short Pieces for 2 Flutes, 2 Violins & Continuo, Wq.81; Sonata for Flute & Continuo in G (Hamburg Sonata), Wq.133; Trios for Flute, Violin & Continuo: in B min., Wq.143; in C, Wq.147; (i) Cantata: Phyllis and Thirsis, Wq.232.

(BB) *** DHM ADD/Dig. 05472 77435-2. Soloists, Les Adieux, Schola Cantorum Basiliensis.

A wholly engaging anthology. The dozen pieces for two flutes, two violins and continuo deftly vary textures, and the result is most attractive when the authentic timbres are so fresh. The following *Hamburg Flute Sonata* needs to be played separately because there is a pitch change as it begins; but it is the *Trio Sonatas* which form the kernel of the concert, and they each have touchingly nostalgic *Adagios* to contrast with their bright outer movements. The programme ends with a miniature (7-minute) pastoral cantata, *Phyllis and Thirsis*, obviously selected because it includes obbligatos for two flutes. Both soloists (Nigel Rogers and Rosmarie Hofmann) rise to the occasion. Excellent recording – a real bargain.

Flute Sonatas: in C, Wq.73; in D, Wq.83; in E, Wq.84; in G, Wq.85; in G, Wq.86.

(BB) **(*) ASV CDQS 6205. Hyde-Smith, Dodd (harpsichord).

The ASV performances have plenty of life and feeling and, though the recording is resonant and the flute is close-miked, the effect is very spirited. The collection includes one of the least predictable of these works, Wq.73 (*in C major*), written in 1745, with its striking *Allegro di molto* opening movement, alongside Wq.84 (in *E major*) of four years later, which has an equally remarkable central *Adagio di molto*.

Flute Sonatas: in G, Wq.86; in C, Wq.87; in E min., Wq.124; in D, Wq.129; (Solo) Flute Sonata in A min., Wq.132; (i) 12 2- & 3-part kleine Stücke for 2 Flutes, Wq.82.

*** ASV CDGAU 161. Hadden, Carolan; Headly; (i) Walker.

The most striking work here is the unaccompanied *Flute Sonata in A minor*, written in 1747, an improvisatory work of characteristic originality written for Frederick the Great, who, Bach said, 'could not play it'. Nancy Hadden certainly can (using a copy of a Dresden period transverse flute). The twelve *Little Pieces* (1770) alternate trio and duo format and are very jolly and entertaining until the expressively wilting closing *Andante*. Bach favoured the clavichord rather than the harpsichord as appropriate in duo sonatas, and Lucy Carolan proves a fine partner; and the balance is equally well judged in the works with additional viola da gamba. This is all most engaging music, and it is admirably presented here in a concert running for 74 minutes.

Flute Sonatas: in E min., Wq.124; in G; in A min.; in D, Wq.127–9; in G, Wq.133; in G, Wq.134.

*** Cap. 10 101. Haupf, Pank, Thalheim.

Six more of the composer's eleven flute sonatas in fresh, lively performances, well recorded, ending with one written in Bach's Hamburg period, two years before he died, altogether lighter and more conventionally classical, presenting an interesting perspective on the rest.

Oboe Sonata in G min., Wq.135.

(BB) **(*) DHM 05472 77440-2. Piguet, Tilney – J. S. BACH: Oboe Sonatas **(*); W. F. BACH: Polonaise in E flat. ***

C. P. E. Bach's 'Hoboe solo', as it is described on the manuscript, was probably written around 1740. Although always spirited, it is the expressive quality of the writing which makes this sonata so individual, especially in the finale. The performance is polished and responsive, but the resonant yet forward recording does reduce the effective dynamic range.

Quartet in D for Flute, Viola, Cello & Fortepiano, Wq.94; (Unaccompanied) Flute Sonata in A min., Wq.132: Sonata in G min. for Viola da gamba & Harpsichord, Wq.88: Larghetto. Trio Sonatas: in C for Flute, Violin & Continuo, Wq.147; in C min. for 2 Violins & Continuo (Sanguineus & Melancholicus), Wq.161.

⊕ *** Channel CCS 11197. Florilegium.

A wholly delightful collection. Ashley Solomon's exquisite flute-playing dominates the *D major Quartet*, and the balance with Neal Peres da Costa's delicate fortepiano is quite perfect, registering subtle nuances of dynamic contrast. The *Larghetto* for viola da gamba and harpsichord then makes a melancholy interlude, before Bach's highly imaginative dialogue between Sanguine and Melancholy brings quixotic changes of mood and tempo, even in the central *Adagio*, where Sanguineus eventually wins and makes way for a lighthearted finale. The haunting solo *Flute Sonata* is recorded at a lower pitch to suit the period instrument used; the timbre has an almost alto sonority. Finally comes the diverting *Trio Sonata in C major*, which brings winningly imitative interchanges between flute and violin, particularly exuberant in the finale. The recording balance could hardly be bettered.

Sinfonia a tre voci in D; 12 Variations on La Folia, Wq.118/9; Trio Sonatas: in B flat, Wq.158; in C min. (Sanguineus & Melancholicus), Wq.161/1; Viola da gamba Sonata in D, Wq.137.

*** Hyp. CDA 66239. Purcell Qt.

The *Variations on La Folia* are fresh and inventive, particularly in Robert Woolley's hands, but the remaining pieces are hardly less rewarding. The Purcell Quartet play with sensitivity and seem well attuned to the particularly individual sensibility of this composer. The Hyperion recording is well balanced, faithful and present.

Viola da gamba Sonatas (for viola da gamba and continuo): in G min., Wq.88; in C & D, Wq.136/7; Harpsichord Sonatas in A min. (Württemberg No. 1), Wq.49/1; in E (Prussian No. 3), Wq.48/3.

(B) ******* HM HMA 1901410. L. Bar. (Medlam, Hunt, Egarr).

Carl Philipp Emanuel wrote his sonatas for viola da gamba during a period when all over Europe the instrument was being replaced by the cello. The solo line lies comparatively high and Charles Medlam achieves an impressively full singing cantilena. Of the three works the *G minor* is particularly fine, and it is very beautifully played. So are the splendid keyboard sonatas, where the level of invention is more immediately striking than in the two other gamba works. They are played with eloquence and spirit by Richard Egarr. The recording throughout is most naturally balanced, and at such a modest price this is a reissue which should not be missed by admirers of this highly individual composer.

KEYBOARD MUSIC

6 Easy Keyboard Sonatas, Nos. 1 in C; 2 in B flat; 3 in A min., Wq. 53/1–3; Keyboard Sonatas: in B flat & G, Wq. 62/16 & 19.

(N) ****** BIS CD 964. Spányi (clavichord).

6 Easy Keyboard Sonatas, Nos. 4 in B min.; 5 in C; 6 in F, Wq. 53/4–6; Keyboard Sonatas: in G min. & C, Wq. 62/18 & 20.

(N) ****** BIS CD 978. Spányi (clavichord).

Miklós Spányi is also recording all the *Sonatas* (previous releases have appeared on BIS 879, 882, and 963) and chooses a clavichord for his performances (a copy of a German instrument from about 1770). Its sound is comparatively full and robust (take care not to set the volume level too high). His playing is alive and sympathetic, but not everyone will respond to the eccentric little pauses with which he interrupts the melodic flow, especially in slow movements.

Keyboard Sonatas for Harpsichord: in E min., Wq.62/12, H.66; in E min., Wq.65/5, H.13; in B flat., Wq.65/20, H.51; for Fortepiano: in B flat, Wq.65/44, K H.211; in C, Wq.65/47, H.248; in G, Wq.65/48, H.280.

**(*) Metronome MET CD 1032. Cerasi (harpsichord or fortepiano).

In the *Harpsichord Sonatas*, the resonance of the recording does not help Carole Cerasi, but her very free musical line often brings a fussy effect. The opening *Allemande* of the *E minor Sonata*, Wq.62/12, is an obvious example of her very free rubato, and the lively closing *Gigue* too, marvellously articulated as it is, needs a cleaner outline, with the decorations less boldly done.

In the works played on the fortepiano it is the impulsiveness of Cerasi's approach that is daunting, with sudden *forte* accents and forward surges, especially well demonstrated in the finale of the *G major*, Wq.65/48. The preceding *Adagio* is more successful, but even here she seems determined to prove that C. P. E. Bach's music is quixotically temperamental.

Keyboard Sonatas: in B flat, Wq.62/16; in G, Wq.65/22; in E min., Wq.65/30; in A, Wq.65/37; in G, Wq.65/48; in A, Wq.70/1; Rondo in E flat, Wq.61/1.

(BB) ******* Naxos 8.5536450. Chaplin (piano).

François Chaplin plays these works freshly and confidently on the modern piano rather than on the clavichord (or harpsichord) which the composer would have expected, and he makes no attempt to imitate those instruments. The result demonstrates how forward-looking these sonatas are, especially the appealingly expressive slow movements of the later works. The closing *Rondo* of 1786 is particularly successful in using the piano's fuller sonority.

6 Prussian Sonatas, Wq.48 (H.24–9).

(N) (BB) ******* Teldec (ADD) 8573 85561-2. Van Asperen (harpsichord).

Bach's six Prussian Sonatas were written between 1740 and 1742; they immediately demonstrate the formal and expressive adventurousness which characterizes so much of his music, and were much admired by Haydn. Bob van Asperen uses a fine reproduction of a Dulcken harpsichord, and his approach throughout has a welcome rhythmic freedom, a fine sense of line and an appropriate intensity of feeeling when required. Although (as recorded) his range of dynamic might have been wider, if the volume control is judiciously set the effect brings both realism and a natural presence. Highly recommendable.

ORGAN MUSIC

Organ Sonatas: in F; A min.; D; G min., Wq.70/3–6; Fantasia & Fugue in C min., Wq.119/7; Fugue in D min.; Prelude in D, Wq.70/7; 6 Variations.

**(*) Mer. CDE 84313. Gifford (Organ of the Chapel of Hull University).

Carl Philipp Emanuel's organ music is a far cry from the magisterial polyphony of his father's output. The *Prelude in D major* opens grandly, but its imitative passage-work is simplicity itself and rather jolly. However, while the four lightweight *Sonatas* make no great technical demands on the performer, they are engaging enough when freshly presented, as here, with a lively, 'orchestral' palette. The *Variations* are in much the same style. The chapel organ at Hull University has bright, glowing reeds and Gerald Gifford's playing is persuasive.

VOCAL MUSIC

Anbetung dem Erbarmer (Easter Cantata) Wq.243; Auf schicke dich recht feierlich (Christmas Cantata), Wq.249; Heilig, Wq.217; Klopstocks Morgengesang am Schöpfungsfeste, Wq.239.

*** Cap. 10 208. Schlick, Lins, Prégardien, Elliott, Varcoe, Schwarz, Rheinische Kantorei, Kleine Konzert, Max.

Klopstocks Morgengesang am Schöpfungsfeste ('Klopstock's morning song on the celebration of creation') is a work of many beauties and is well performed by these artists. *Anbetung dem Erbarmer* ('Worship of the merciful') is another late work, full of modulatory surprises. *Auf schicke dich recht feierlich* ('Up, be reconciled') and *Heilig* ('Holy') (1779) are Christmas works. A record of unusual interest, very well performed and naturally recorded.

(i) *Die Auferstehung und Himmelfahrt Jesu (The Resurrection and Ascension of Jesus), Wq.240;* (ii) *Gott hat den Herrn auferweckt (Easter Cantata), Wq.244.*

*** Cap. 10 206/7 (2). (i) Schlick, Lins, Prégardien; (ii) Elliott, Varcoe, Schwarz; Rheinische Kantorei, Kleine Konzert, Max.

Carl Philipp Emanuel numbered *Die Auferstehung und Himmelfahrt Jesu* among his finest works. This two-CD set offers good solo singing and generally very good playing; the choral singing for the most part is respectable without being distinguished. Impressive music which no one with an interest in this composer should pass over.

Magnificat, Wq.215.

(B) *** Double Decca 458 370-2 (2). Palmer, Watts, Tear, Roberts, King's College Ch., ASMF, Ledger – J. S. BACH: *Magnificat;* A. SCARLATTI: *St Cecilia Mass.* ***

With vividly atmospheric recording, the performance under Philip Ledger comes electrically to life, with choir, soloists and orchestra all in splendid form. Indeed the solo singing (notably the lovely contribution of Felicity Palmer) is striking for its stylish expressive feeling. Aptly coupled with Johann Sebastian's earlier setting, and now also with Alessandro Scarlatti's splendid *St Cecilia Mass* added, this Double Decca can be strongly recommended.

The alternative Deutsche Harmonia Mundi recording is enjoyable too, even if the period-instrument playing at the introduction is robustly enthusiastic rather than immaculately tuned. Elly Ameling is outstanding among the soloists. Nevertheless, joined to one of Bach's finest cello concertos, expressively and resonantly played by Angelica May, this is still a bargain (DHM 05472 77473-2).

BACH, Johann Christian (1735–82)

Bassoon Concerto in E flat; Flute Concerto in D; Oboe Concerto No. 1 in F.

*** CPO 999 346-2. Ward, Brown, Robson, Hanover Band, Halstead.

Bassoon Concerto in B flat; Flute Concerto in G; Oboe Concerto No. 2 in F.

*** CPO 999 347. Ward, Brown, Robson, Hanover Band, Halstead.

These six early concertos had an obvious influence on Mozart's wind concertos, and if you enjoy the Mozart works you will surely enjoy those by J. C. Bach. The *First Oboe Concerto* on the first disc is another version of the *G major* work for flute on the companion CD. The so-described *D major Flute Concerto* is a joining of two separate movements taken from independent manuscripts – and how well they work together! The *Bassoon Concerto in E flat* is an alternative version of the *Sinfonia Concertante* in the same key for two violins and cello included below (on CPO 999 348). The *Bassoon Concerto in B flat,* is an even more winning piece, with a dignified *Adagio* set against a delectably frivolous finale. The six concertos are played with much felicity by Jeremy Ward, Rachael Brown and Anthony Robson respectively, and Anthony Halstead's accompaniments are a model of elegance. The recording is full and natural. Most enjoyable.

Harpsichord Concertos, Op. 1/1–6.

*** CPO 999 299-2. Halstead, Hanover Band.

Bach composed three sets of *Clavier Concertos*, each comprising six works. Those wanting a set of Op. 1 on period instruments could hardly better this CPO disc. These are all simple two-movement works, except for No. 4 with its wistful central *Andante* and No. 6 which closes with variations on *God Save the King*. The performances are sprightly and perfectly in scale and the balance quite excelllent.

5 Berlin Harpsichord Concertos: in B flat; F min.; D min., E & G. Concerto in F min. (attrib.).

*** CPO 999 393-2 & 999 462-2 (available separately). Halstead, Hanover Band.

Bach's early Berlin concertos (from the 1750s) in these splendid performances from Anthony Halstead, directing the Hanover Band from the keyboard, are appealingly fluent, full of flair and vitality. Slow movements are deeply expressive and outer movements bustle vigorously. The *F minor* is the best known of the set and it is splendidly played here; however the *Poco adagio* of the *G major* is in some ways the most searching of all, when the concentration of the hushed pianissimo playing is so compelling. The attributed *F minor Concerto* may or may not be by J. C. B. Its outer movements certainly have a fine energetic thrust. The recordings throughout are in the demonstration bracket.

Clavier Concertos, Op. 1/1–6; Op. 7/1–6.

(B) *** Ph. (ADD) (IMS) Duo 438 712-2 (2). Haebler (fortepiano), V. Capella Ac., Melkus.

(i) *Clavier Concertos, Op. 13/1–6;* (ii) *6 Sinfonias, Op. 3.*

(B) *** Ph. (ADD) Duo 456 064-2 (2). (i) Haebler (fortepiano), V. Capella Ac., Melkus; (ii) ASMF, Marriner.

It would be difficult to find a more suitable or persuasive advocate than Ingrid Haebler, who is accompanied excellently and recorded most truthfully. There is some delightful invention here, and it is difficult to imagine it being better presented.

The coupled *Sinfonias* are beguilingly played by the Academy of St Martin-in-the-Fields under Sir Neville Marriner, and beautifully recorded. Erik Smith, who has edited them, describes them as 'in essence Italian overtures, though with an unusual wealth of singing melody'.

Clavier Concertos, Op. 7/1–6.

*** CPO 999 600-2. Halstead, Hanover Band.

Anthony Halstead has recorded Opus 7 in chamber form with just an accompanying string trio. His solo playing is every bit as persuasive as Haebler's and the result is delightfully intimate. No. 5 in *E flat*, the finest of the set, surely anticipates Mozart from the very opening onwards; it has a touchingly expressive slow movement in C minor and a dancing finale; the disc is worth having for this performance alone. With recording of the highest quality, this is one of the most attractive CDs so far in Halstead's Hanover Band series.

Clavier Concertos, Op. 13/1–3; Concerto in E flat.

*** CPO 999 601-2. Halstead (piano), Hanover Band.

Bach's Op. 13 appeared in 1777 and shows him still developing in ideas and orchestration. These are most enjoyable concertos and are played here with great freshness by Halstead. The *Concerto in E flat* is almost identical with the *Sinfonia Concertante* in the same key, but in the present version the soloist has a strongly dominant role.

Clavier Concertos, Op. 13/4–6; Op. 14 in E flat.

(N) *** CPO 999 691-2. Halstead (piano), Hanover Band.

The remaining three concertos of Op. 13 are just as attractive as their earlier companions with the *Andante* of Op.13/4 particularly engaging. The two other works only have a pair of movements, the second in each case an elegant minuet. Op. 14 is more ambitious, although it may have been written earlier. The first movement is characterized by the frequent use of 'scotch rhythmic snaps' and the finale demands considerable virtuosity from the soloist, readily forthcoming here. Halstead used a Broadwood pianoforte and accompanies himself brightly and gracefully.

Harpsichord Concerto in D (arr. by Mozart as K.107/1).

(M) *** CRD 3311. Pinnock, E. Concert – C. P. E. BACH: *Harpsichord Concertos*. ***

It seemed more sensible to list this work here as it tends to get lost in the Mozartian discography. In the early 1770s the teenage Mozart turned three sonatas by J. C. Bach into keyboard concertos, adding accompaniments and ritornellos as well as cadenzas. The first of the group makes an excellent coupling for the two fine C. P. E. Bach concertos.

Sinfonia Concertante in C for Flute, Oboe, Violin, Cello & Orchestra; Sinfonia in G min., Op. 6/6; Sinfonia for

Double Orchestra in E flat, Op. 18/1; Sinfonia in D, Op. 18/4; Overture: Adriano in Siria.

**(*) Chan. 0540. AAM, Standage.

The *Sinfonia Concertante* is perhaps the most conventional piece here, but it has a memorable finale. The *G minor Sinfonia* shows J. C. Bach's imagination at full stretch, lively and intense. Excellent, well-played 'authentic' performances, but the characteristic Chandos resonance prevents the crispest focus.

Sinfonia Concertante in F for Oboe, Cello & Orchestra, T.VIII/6.

(N) (BB) **(*) Teldec 0630 12326-2. Schaeftlein, Bylsma, Leonhardt Cons. – C. P. E. BACH: *Double Concerto for Harpsichord & Fortepiano* ***; W. F. BACH: *Double Concerto for 2 Harpsichords.* **(*)

The *Sinfonia Concertante in F* is a pleasing but not distinctive work in two movements, given a good rather than a distinctive performance.

Sinfonia Concertante in A for Violin, Cello & Orchestra; Grand Overture in E flat.

(*) Sony MK 39964. Ma, Zukerman, St Paul CO – BOCCHERINI: *Cello Concerto* (arr. Grützmacher). *

Generally this is an enjoyable pairing and the playing of the soloists in the *Sinfonia Concertante* establishes a fine musical interplay, although the cadenza is over-elaborated. Good sound, with excellent stereo effects.

Sinfonias Concertantes: in A for Violin, Cello & Orchestra, SC 3; in E flat for 2 Violins, 2 Violas, Cello & Orchestra (MSC E flat 1); in E flat for 2 Clarinets, Bassoon & Orchestra (MSC E flat 4); in G for 2 Violins, Cello & Orchestra, SC 1.

(BB) *** ASV CDQS 6138. London Festival O, Pople.

The performances here are eminently vital and enthusiastic, and the recording is very bright and present. This is an invigorating disc which can be recommended strongly, especially at super-bargain price.

Sinfonias Concertantes: in E flat for 2 Violins, Oboe & Orchestra; in E flat & in G for 2 Violins, Cello & Orchestra.

**(*) CPO 999 348-2. Hanover Band, Halstead.

Sinfonias Concertantes: in B flat for Violin, Cello & Orchestra; in D for 2 Violins & Orchestra; in F for Oboe, Bassoon & Orchestra.

*** CPO 999 347-2. Hanover Band, Halstead.

Sinfonias Concertantes: in A for Violin & Cello; in E for 2 Violins, Cello, Flute & Orchestra; in E flat for 2 Clarinets, Bassoon, 2 Horns & Flute. Flute Concerto in D; Andante.

*** CPO 999 538-2. Hanover Band, Halstead.

Johann Christian Bach might well be regarded as the true father of the sinfonia concertante, for (among others, including Karl Stamitz) he wrote over a dozen of them for various solo instruments, and they are of a consistently higher musical quality than those of most of his contemporaries. Even so, these works have rather long (some might feel too long) orchestral ritornellos with which each first movement opens. The solo writing is always effective; the orchestration (with flutes, horns, clarinets) adds to the interest of tuttis and colours slow movements. Finales are usually robust minuets.

The piquant oboe solo in the *Andante* of the *E flat* work on the first disc is ear-catching; the two works for violins and cello are more uneven. The *B flat Concerto* on the second disc has an ambitious opening *Allegro maestoso* (almost Mozartian), which leads to a *Larghetto* dominated by a melancholy violin cantilena. The third disc opens with one of Bach's very finest works: in *E major*, with four soloists. The *E flat* work for woodwind has charmingly interwoven solo parts against a busy orchestral backing. The two-movement *A major* work for violin and cello again shows Bach's invention at its most elegantly appealing. With the inclusion of the recently discovered slow movement for the *Flute Concerto in D major* (see above, on CPO 999 346-2), this (third) disc offers the most rewarding collection of the three listed above. Throughout, the performances have warmth and proper finish and refinement; the balance and recording are excellent and the effect is undoubtedly authentic.

Sinfonias, Op. 3/1–6.

*** CPO 999268-2. Hanover Band, Halstead.

This excellent CPO disc offers a lively group of six symphonies (or overtures), each in three brief movements, all excellent examples of a fast-developing genre, offering arguments both pithy and imaginative, with the vigorous finales particularly enjoyable. Though the strings of the Hanover Band under Anthony Halstead are on the abrasive side, performances are fresh and alert.

Sinfonia (Huberty), Op. 6/1; Sinfonias (Markardt), Op. 8/ 2–4; Symphony in C (Venier No. 46; 2 versions); Symphony in F.

*** CPO 999 382-2. Hanover Band, Halstead.

J. C. Bach's most successful symphonies were often available from more than one publisher. The Huberty edition of Op. 6/1 includes an added Minuet and trio (with an agreeable horn duet), an interpolation from the hand of an unknown composer. The three Op. 8 *Sinfonias* are lively but comparatively conventional and are most appealing for their elegant slow movements. However, none is without interest and Op. 8/4 is the finest. Halstead offers two versions of the work in *C major*, described as No. 46 by its Parisian publisher. The splendid first movement is common to both; the other movements are quite different in each edition. The *Symphony in F* is recorded from manuscript. Its restless development certainly anticipates Mozart, and the *Andante* (for flute and strings) is quite delightful. Altogether a splendid collection, made the more so by the vitality and elegance of the playing. The recording is first class, the stereo detail particularly striking.

Sinfonia in G min. Op. 6/6.

*** Cap. 10 283. Concerto Köln – C. P. E. BACH: *Harpsichord Concerto*; J. C. F. BACH: *Sinfonias*; W. F. BACH: *Sinfonia*, etc. ***

This remarkable symphony, written in 1770 when Johann Christian was at the height of his fame, is altogether darker than is usual with this most gracious and genial of composers, and the Concerto Köln discover greater dramatic intensity in it than do most ensembles. It is recorded as excellently as it is played.

6 Sinfonias, Op. 6; 6 Sinfonias, Op. 9; 6 Sinfonias, Op. 18; Overture, La calamità de cuori.

(B) *** Ph. (ADD) (IMS) Duo 442 275-2 (2). Netherlands CO, Zinman.

David Zinman secures good, lively playing from the Netherlanders, and few (except dedicated authenticists) will quarrel with the results. A case could be made for giving some of the outer movements less elegance and greater weight. But if sometimes one feels that Zinman is too brisk, any newer versions using original instruments are likely to be brisker!

Sinfonias, Op. 9/1–2 (standard & original versions); Op. 9/ 3; in E flat, Sieber collection, No. 2.

*** CPO 999 487-2. Hanover Band, Halstead.

The Hanover Band are in their element in Op. 9, with crisp, dynamic allegros, and making the most of the sensuous element in slow movements, notably the delectable melody of No. 2. No. 3 has a galant central *Andante*, winningly scored, and a brief, whirlwind finale. Halstead then gives us the opportunity of hearing the first two symphonies in different versions. These rediscovered original scores feature clarinets and a bassoon (in the place of oboes) which colour the music quite differently. The additional *Sinfonia in E flat* is again heard here in its original scoring, making full use of clarinet duetting. With such lively, personable playing and excellent recording, this is one of the best of the Halstead series so far.

Sinfonias, Op. 9/1–4; Sinfonia Concertante in A for Violin & Cello; Sinfonia Concertante in E flat, for 2 Violins, Oboe & Orchestra.

(BB) **(*) Naxos 8.553085. Camerata Budapest, Gmür.

This disc is of interest, not so much for the symphonies as for the two *Sinfonias Concertantes*, which are beautifully played, with stylish and appealing contributions from the soloists, all drawn from the orchestra. The solo writing in the *A major Sinfonia Concertante* is quite elaborate, and in the *Andante* of the *E flat* work there is a surprise when the two solo violins introduce Gluck's *Che farò senza Euridice*, which is then taken up by the oboe. The second of the Op. 9 symphonies has a real lollipop *Andante con sordini*, presented over a pizzicato accompaniment. The balance is excellent.

6 Sinfonias (Grand Overtures), Op. 18.

(BB) **(*) Naxos 8.553367. Failoni O, Gmür.

Hanspeter Gmür and the Failoni Orchestra give warm and graceful accounts of Op. 18. The spirited allegros are slightly cushioned by the resonance, but slow movements are phrased very musically (particularly the lovely, almost Handelian melody of Op. 18/2, which also has a fine oboe solo from László Párkányi).

CHAMBER MUSIC

Flute Quartets (for 2 flutes, viola and cello), Op. 19/1–4.

** CPO 999 579-2. Camerata Köln.

Bach's Op. 19 *Flute Quartets* are elegant enough, but the scoring for two flutes means that the wind timbres, even using period instruments, tend to overwhelm the strings and the ear easily tires of the unvarying texture. The performances here are refined and polished.

6 Sonatas for the Harpsichord or Pianoforte with an Accompaniment for the Violin or Flute, Op. 16.

(N) (BB)**(*) CPO 999 494-2. Salzburger Hofmusik.

These atttractive galant sonatas (from 1779) are given period performances with plenty of life. They are played alternately on the violin, by Christine Busch, whose timbre is rather thin and edgy, and flute (Karl Kaiser), where the smoothness of sound is nigh perfect. In both cases the balance cannot be faulted and Wolfgang Brunner's contribution (on a most pleasing Viennese fortepiano) is first class throughout. The music itself is lightweight, spontaneously spirited and tuneful. A fair bargain.

KEYBOARD MUSIC

6 Sonatas for Harpsichord or Fortepiano, Op. 5; arr. of Haydn's Symphony No. 53 (Impériale).

(N) (BB) ** CPO 999 530-2. Heeren (fortepiano).

The six *Sonatas*, Op. 5, are comparatively simplistic works in two (or, more often, three) movements. Harold Heeren plays them straightforwardly but does not make them sound distinctive. He is faithfully recorded. The attribution of the arrangement of the Haydn symphony carries a fair degree of doubt; but this disc is inexpensive.

VOCAL MUSIC

Endimione (Serenata).

*(*) DHM 05472 77525-2 (2). Jezovšek, Monoyios, Waschinski, Hering, Cologne Vocal Ens., Capella Coloniensis, Weil.

Described as a serenata, *Endimione*, first heard in London in 1772, is an opera in all but name. It is less extended than the Handel operas which were popular in London a generation earlier, though the lively opening overture is a formidable piece. The dozen arias and concluding duet to Act I plus two choruses offer much delightful music, and it is a pity that the performance is flawed. The Capella Coloniensis favours an unreconstructed period style, rather abrasive in its string-tone, not helped by the curiously focused recording, which is slightly disembodied. Nor are the soloists ideal, though Ann Monoyios as the nymph Nice stands out for the silvery beauty of her singing. Vasiljka

Jezovšek is lighter and brighter if not so secure, while the counter-tenor, Jorg Waschinski, as Amore is rather fluttery, as is the tenor, Jorg Hering, as Endimione, not helped by the recording.

(i; ii) *Laudate pueri Dominum* (Vesper psalm); (i) *Salve regina* (antiphon); (ii) *Si nocte tenebrosa* (motet).

(N) *** CPO 999 718-2. (i) Kirkby; (ii) Schäfer; Orfeo Bar. O, Gaigg.

Johann Christian became a Roman Catholic in the late 1770s and his church music was all composed to Latin texts. The lyrical melodic flow has an unmistakeable operatic feel to its line and the delightful interchanges between the soloists in the opening and closing sections of the *Laudate pueri Dominum* is very reminiscent of Mozart in the opera house. The solos are no less expressive and spirited and the felicitous scoring (especially the use of horns and flutes at the opening of the *Gloria Patri*) is most winning).

Both the solo works are very attractive too. The extended *Salve regina* opens with a long sustained single-note crescendo which Emma Kirkby sings very beautifully, and she navigates brilliantly the sparkling bravura of the second section, *Ad te clamatus*, before the melting *Ad te suspiramus*. Bach's setting offers memorably melodic writing, and a moving response to the words. The solo motet, *Si nocte tenebrosa*, tells how a traveller on a gloomy night might comfort himself with a song, but closes with a supplication to the Virgin. Its wide range of mood is splendidly caught by the pleasing tenor voice of Markus Schäfer. Michi Gaigg's accompaniments are stylish and very well played, and the recording is first class. A collection which reveals an unexpected further dimension to the music of Johann Christian, and can also be cordially recommended for the pleasure it brings.

BACH, Johann Christoph Friedrich
(1732–95)

Sinfonias: in D min.; E flat, Wfv 1/3 & 10.

*** Cap. 10 283. Concerto Köln – C. P. E. BACH: *Harpsichord Concerto;* J. C. BACH: *Sinfonia;* W. F. BACH: *Sinfonia,* etc. ***

Both works recorded here are elegantly written and are well worth investigating. The playing of the Concerto Köln is enthusiastic, sprightly and sensitive, and they are excellently recorded.

Musikalisches Vielerley: Cello Sonata in A.

*** Sony SK 45945. Bylsma, Van Asperen – J. S. BACH: *Viola da gamba Sonatas Nos. 1–3.*

This *Sonata* is a work of considerable musical interest, and it is here played imaginatively by Anner Bylsma, using a piccolo cello, and by Bob van Asperen on a 'trunk' or chamber organ. Excellently recorded.

BACH, Johann Michael (1745–1820)

Friedens (Peace) Cantata: Jehova, Vater der Wesen;
Advent cantata: Mache dich auf, werde licht; Christmas
cantata: Das Volk, so im Finstern wandelt; Other cantatas:
Herr, wie sind deine Werke so gross und viel; Wie lieblich
sind auf den Bergen die Füss der Boten.

(N) *** CPO 999671-2. Schmithüsen, Crook, Schwarz, Mertens
& soloists, Rheinische Kantorei, Kleine Konzert, Max.

Johann Michael Bach the younger was a member of the
Hessian Bach family, an early branch off the family tree. He
was of the generation of Johann Sebastian's grandchildren,
but a direct relationship to J.S.B. cannot surely be determined. Yet the family genes are strong, for he was a most
talented composer and musician, and one who travelled
widely (it seems likely that he even crossed the Atlantic to
America). His ambitious *Peace Cantata* was first performed
in 1815 and obviously celebrates the end of the Napoleonic
wars. It is a remarkable work, with the orchestra opening
with a long powerful crescendo before the opening bass
recitative evokes the horrors of battle. Then a series of
engaging solos and choruses celebrates the spirit of peace
and the omnipotence of God. The other four cantatas are
equally inventive; each includes a major aria for one of the
soloists, often of striking expressive beauty. The music is
full of attractive melody and uses the orchestral palette,
woodwind and (especially) horns, to provide colourful
accompaniments. One is continually being reminded of
Haydn's *Creation* and *Seasons*, notably in the charming
soprano/tenor duet of the *Peace Cantata* ('Now the spirit of
peace whispers'), the closing bass aria ('Fill the temple,
merry songs') of the Advent cantata, and the lilting pastoral
opening chorus 'How lovely are the mountains' of the *Cantata for the Fourth Sunday in Advent*. With a splendid team
of soloists, all in fine voice, an excellent chorus, and lively
orchestral detail this CD is very highly recommended. You
cannot fail to enjoy it; even if the sound is a bit over-resonant,
the overall balance is good.

BACH, Johann Sebastian (1685–1750)

The Art of Fugue, BWV 1080.

**(*) Opus 111 30-191. Concerto Italiano, Alessandrini.

The Art of Fugue, BWV 1080; A Musical Offering, BWV
1079.

(B) *** Ph. (ADD) Duo 442 556-2 (2). ASMF, Marriner.
(N) (B) **(*) Double Decca (ADD) 467 267-2 (2) Stuttgart CO,
Münchinger.

How to perform *The Art of Fugue* has always presented
problems, since Bach's own indications are so sparse. Sir
Neville Marriner in the edition he prepared with Andrew
Davis has varied the textures most intelligently, giving a fair
proportion of the fugues and canons to keyboard instruments, organ as well as harpsichord. Marriner's style of
performance is profoundly satisfying, with finely judged
tempi, unmannered phrasing and resilient rhythms, and the
1974 recording is admirably refined. Similarly, in the *Musical*

Offering Marriner uses his own edition and instrumentation:
strings with three solo violins, solo viola and a solo cello;
flute, organ and harpsichord. The performance here is of
high quality, though some of the playing is a trifle bland. It
is excellently recorded and is among the most successful
accounts of the work.

Rinaldo Alessandrini's approach to *The Art of Fugue* is to
seek out its underlying expressive and colouristic possibilities. So, after opening with strings, he scores each of the
contrapuncti for different groups of wind and/or stringed
instruments, allotting only the four *Canons* to the harpsichord. The result has distinctive aural appeal, especially as
the work proceeds, with *Contrapuncti 12* and *13* engagingly
colourful dialogues involving flute, oboe da caccia, violin,
viola, bassoon, cello and harpsichord. Alessandrini's solution may not be conventional but the playing (on baroque
instruments) is full of life and easy to enjoy. The recording
is clear, within a pleasing ambience.

Münchinger's Stuttgart performances also have much to
offer. *The Art of Fugue* has no lack of momentum and its
essential sobriety has a cumulative power when the playing
itself is so responsive. The instrumentation generally allots
the fugues to the strings and the canons to the solo woodwind, varied with solo strings. After the incomplete quadruple fugue, Münchinger rounds off the work with the
chorale prelude, *Wenn wir in höchsten Nöten sein*, BWV
668a, in principal quite wrong but moving in practice. *The
Musical Offering*, although somewhat more relaxed, also
brings playing of genuine breadth and eloquence, particularly in the *Trio Sonata*. The canons are grouped together
and come off well, and the performance has many of the
fine qualities that distinguished Münchinger's Bach. The
recordings were made a decade apart (in the mid-1960s and
1970s) but are of vintage quality, with warmth and excellent
presence and detail.

Brandenburg Concertos Nos. 1–6, BWV 1046–51.

***Teldec 4509 98442-2 (2). Il Giardino Armonico, Antonini.
(B) *** Hyp. Dyad CDD 22001 (2). Brandenburg Consort,
Goodman.
*** DG 410 500/1-2. E. Concert, Pinnock.
*** Sony S2K 66289 (2). Tafelmusik, Lamon.
(BB) *** Virgin VBD5 61552-2 (2). OAE.
*** Telarc CD 80368 (*Nos. 1–3*), CD 80354 (*Nos. 4–6*) (2).
Boston Bar., Pearlman.
(B) *** EMI double forte CZS5 69749-2 (2). Polish CO,
Maksymiuk (with CORELLI: *Concerto grosso, Op. 6/8;*
MANFREDINI: *Concerto grosso, Op. 3/12;* TORELLI:
Concerto a quattro, Op. 8/6; LOCATELLI: *Concerto grosso,*
Op. 1/8 ***).
(N) (M) **(*) Astrée ES 9948 (2). Concert des Nations,
Capella Reial de Catalunya, Savall.
(N) **(*) BIS CD 1151/2 (with additional early version of first
movement of No. 5). Bach Collegium, Japan, Suzuki.

Brandenburg Concertos Nos. 1–6; Double Violin Concerto,
BWV 1043; Concerto for Violin & Oboe, BWV 1060.

(N) (B) *** Ph. Duo ADD/Dig. 468 549-2 (2). ASMF, Marriner.

The various competing versions of the *Brandenburg Concertos* offer excellence in every price range. The exhilarating

set from the Milanese period-instrument group, Il Giardino Armonico, directed by Giovanni Antonini, is among the finest. Tempi seem perfectly judged, buoyantly brisk but never exaggeratedly so. The playing is alive and joyful; slow movements have expressive warmth and serenity. The wind and brass soloists are first rate, the recorder, flute and oboe sounds are equally characterful, and the strings are bright and clean and without edge; the recording is both warm and freshly transparent so that one can hear the harpsichord coming through quite naturally. A splendid achievement.

Marriner's 1980 ASMF set has long been highly regarded by us as a leading contender for a performance on modern instruments. Above all, these performances communicate warmth and enjoyment. In three of the concertos Marriner introduces such distinguished soloists as Henryk Szering (who also contributes to the two additional duet concertos featuring the violin), Jean-Pierre Rampal and Michala Petri, adding individuality without breaking the consistency of beautifully sprung performances. George Malcolm is an ideal continuo player. With superb playing, well-chosen speeds and refined analogue recording this inexpensive Duo reissue could well be first choice for those not insisting on the use of period instruments.

Pinnock's DG set, played on original instruments, also shows him to be an outstanding advocate of authentic performance, with sounds that are clear and refreshing but not too abrasive. However, the set now seems expensive. The recordings are alternatively available on three mid-priced CDs (423 492-2), coupled with the *Orchestral Suites*, but the latter are somewhat controversial, bringing a distinct loss of breadth and grandeur.

However, Roy Goodman's excellent Hyperion set of the *Brandenburgs* is on a Dyad, with two discs offered for the price of one. The stylish, lively playing is another attractive example of authenticity, lacking something in polish but none in spirit, with the last three concertos especially fresh. Characterization is strong, and slow movements are often appealingly expressive. Tempi of outer movements are very brisk but often bring the lightest rhythmic touch. Very good sound.

Tafelmusik seldom disappoint, and their set of *Brandenburgs* is enjoyably robust and spontaneous, with the horn soloists in No. 1 playing mid-eighteenth-century hand horns with lustily extrovert vigour and bravura, so that one does not mind that intonation is not always exact. Crispian Steele-Perkins, the trumpet soloist in No. 2, plays with remarkable sophistication. Tempi are brisk but never hurried, and slow movements relax warmly as they should, with bulges in phrasing fairly minimal. The recording is excellent.

With the direction shared among four violinists – Monica Huggett, Catherine Mackintosh, Alison Bury and Elizabeth Wallfisch – the Orchestra of the Age of Enlightenment brings all the advantages of light, clear textures and no sense of haste, even when a movement is taken faster than has become traditional.

Martin Pearlman sets attractively lively and spirited tempi in outer movements, yet slow movements are not pressed on but are allowed space to expand. Solo playing is excellent, although Friedemann Immer's trumpet does have a few moments of ungainliness in No. 2. The *Sixth Concerto* is

played with one instrument to a part and uses violas da gamba. Not quite a first choice but, with first-class Telarc sound and a feeling that the players are enjoying themselves, this is well worth considering.

If you enjoy brisk tempi, the Polish set is another first-class example of a stylish account on modern instruments. The orchestra is augmented with English recorder soloists, who are obviously enjoying themselves, as does the trumpeter, who is called to flights of virtuosity in No. 2. No. 5 has a first-class contribution from the solo harpsichord player, Wladyslaw Klosiewicz. The analogue sound is very good, full and clear and very well balanced. What makes the set doubly attractive at its very modest price is the inclusion of a 1984 collection of key *Concerti grossi* by Corelli, Manfredini, Torelli and Locatelli, each with a beautiful *Pastoral* slow movement to make a Christmas connection. They are played and recorded very beautifully.

Savall's period-instrument set of the *Brandenburgs* is engagingly fresh. Textures are clear and often translucent, allegros are spirited but never rushed, tempi are well judged (No. 3 is just right), and slow movements are warmly expressive yet in perfect style. There is some breathtaking bravura from the hand horns in No. 1, especially in the closing *Polacca & Trio*, but Friedmann Immer's slightly throttled trumpet sounds in No. 2 are less appealing. At other times, ensemble and intonation are not without flaw, but there is no edginess from the strings, and the spontaneous vitality of this playing carries the day. Not a first choice but an enjoyable one when the sound is so pleasing.

Suzuki's long-awaited set of the *Brandenburgs* with his Bach Collegium of Japan proves to be a partial disappointment. Of course there is much fine playing from woodwind soloists and the strings (especially in the finale of No. 3), and Suzuki's own harpsichord contribution, notably in Nos. 4 and 5, is pretty dazzling, with the excellent balance ensuring that he does not dominate the texture too much. Tempi are comparatively relaxed and the overall atmosphere is sunny. But unfortunately the brass players let the side down. The horns are clumsy in the first movement of No. 1 and the trumpet playing of Toshio Shimasda in No. 2, using a specially designed coiled trumpet, sounds strained. He uses lip-pressure instead of valves or ' tone-holes' to ' bend' the upper partials to achieve accurate intonation, and some listeners may find the result slightly uncomfortable; others might relish the extra tension.

Alas, Jean-François Paillard's new digital set with his own Chamber Orchestra is a non-starter. His easygoing style has been bypassed by musical history. Fine playing, of course; but one needs more sparkle than this (RCA 74321 49184-2).

Boult recorded his lively set of *Brandenburgs* at the beginning of the 1970s; with fine solo playing and excellent recording, there is a place for this individual set (especially at super-bargain price), which is clearly preferable to other 'big orchestra' versions by Karajan and Klemperer (Royal DCL 705692 (2)).

(i) *Brandenburg Concertos Nos. 1–6*; (ii) *Flute Concerto in G min.* (from BWV 1056); *Double Concerto for Violin, Oboe & Strings in D min.* (from BWV 1060).

(B) *** Double Decca (ADD) 443 847-2 (2). (i) ECO, Britten;
(ii) ASMF, Marriner.

(i) *Brandenburg Concertos Nos. 1–6;* (ii) *Violin Concerto No. 1 in A min., BWV 1042.*

(B) *** Penguin/Decca (ADD) 466 209-2 (*Nos. 1–4*); 460 627-2 (*Nos. 5–6*). (i) ECO, Britten; (ii) Grumiaux, Solistes Romandes, Gerecz.

Britten made his recordings in the Maltings concert-hall in 1968. The result is a fairly ample sound that in its way goes well with Britten's interpretations. There is some lack of textural delicacy in the slow movements of Nos. 1, 2, 4 and 6; but the bubbling high spirits of the outer movements are hard to resist, and the harpsichordist, Philip Ledger, follows the pattern he had set in live Britten performances, with Britten-inspired extra elaborations a continual delight. As a makeweight for the Double Decca reissue, two more of Marriner's stylish performances of reconstructions of Bach's harpsichord concertos for alternative instruments have been added. First-class (originally Argo) recording, too.

Penguin Classics complete their set of *Brandenburgs* with Arthur Grumiaux's outstandingly fine version of the *A minor Violin Concerto*. Douglas Adams provides a personal commentary. But the Double Decca is less expensive.

Brandenburg Concertos Nos. 1–6; (i) Oboe Concertos: in A (from BWV 1055); in D min. (from BWV 1059); in F (from BWV 1053).

(M) **(*) DG (ADD) 445 578-2 (2). COE, (i) with Boyd.

A spirit of fun infects the COE version of the *Brandenburg Concertos*. Using modern instruments, these are among the happiest performances ever, marked by easily bouncing rhythms and warmly affectionate – but never sentimental – slow movements. Unfortunately, the first movement of No. 1 – the movement which many will sample first – takes relaxation too far, becoming almost ragged; conversely, the first movement of No. 6 is uncharacteristically rigid. Otherwise these performances, well recorded, give pure joy. The three *Oboe Concertos* are reconstructed from keyboard concertos and cantata movements. The soloist, Douglas Boyd, principal oboe of the COE from its foundation, directs his colleagues in delectable performances. First-rate sound.

Brandenburg Concertos Nos. 1–3; (i) Violin Concertos Nos. 1 in A min.; 2 in E, BWV 1041–2.

(M) *** Ph. (ADD) 442 386-2. ECO, Leppard; (i) with Grumiaux.

Brandenburg Concertos Nos. 4–6; (i) Triple Concerto in A min. for Violin, Flute & Harpsichord, BWV 1044.

(M) *** Ph. (ADD) 442 387-2. ECO, Leppard; (i) with Grumiaux, Garcia, Adeney.

Brandenburg Concertos Nos. 1–6, BWV 1046–51; (i) Violin Concertos Nos. 1 in A min.; 2 in E; (i–ii) Double Violin Concerto in D min., BWV 1041–3.

(BB) *** Virgin 2 x 1 VBD5 61403-2 (2). Scottish Ens., Rees; with (i) Rees; (ii) Murdoch.

Brandenburg Concertos Nos. 1–6, BWV 1046–51; Brandenburg Concerto No. 5 (early version), BWV 1050a;

Triple Concerto in A min. for Flute, Violin & Harpsichord, BWV 1044.

(M) *** Virgin VCD5 45255-2 (2). La Stravaganza, Hamburg, Rampe.

The La Stravaganza *Brandenburgs* are immensely vigorous and stimulating. Overall, the tempi must be among the fastest on record (disconcertingly so upon first hearing) and the throaty hand-horn playing in the outer movements of No. 1 brings the most extraordinary virtuosity – while the intonation is remarkably accurate. The buoyant outer movements of No. 2 are just as spirited. The strings in No. 3 play with enormous zest, particularly in the finale. Yet throughout, slow movements bring the warmest expressive feeling. No. 5 is offered not only in the 1719 version we know so well but also in an earlier chamber version, probably written in Carlsbad a year earlier, when Bach had only five players at his disposal. It is refreshingly light-textured. The *Triple Concerto* is played with comparable spirit and finesse. Outstandingly realistic recording.

The Jonathan Rees modern-instrument Scottish *Brandenburgs* are in every way competitive. Directed with much spirit, they are freshly played, with warm, clear recording and excellent internal balance. The tempi seem very apt when the players so convey their enjoyment and the sound has such a pleasing bloom. Rees then becomes the principal soloist in equally warm, buoyant performances of the *Violin Concertos*, with Jane Murdoch matching his stylishness in the *Double Concerto*.

The exhilaration of the mid-1970s Leppard set also brings much to enjoy, and the soloists include John Wilbraham's trumpet in No. 2 and a piquant recorder contribution from David Munrow in No. 4. The remastered sound is fresh and full. Grumiaux's accounts of the two solo concertos come from 1964, but the playing from one of the most musical soloists of our time is extremely satisfying; it has a purity of line and an expressive response that communicate very positively, and Leppard's stylish accompaniments have striking buoyancy. The *Triple Concerto* (recorded two decades later) has plenty of vitality, too; although the balance is a little contrived, the effect is certainly vivid.

Brandenburg Concertos Nos. 1–6; A Musical Offering, BWV 1079.

(M) *** Virgin Dig./ADD VED5 61154–2 (2). Linde Consort, Linde.

Quite apart from the considerable bonus of the *Musical Offering*, many will prefer the Linde version of the *Brandenburgs*, for the 1981 EMI recording is rather fuller than Pinnock's DG Archiv sound, with the strings very slightly less immediate. In *Brandenburg No. 3* there is a distinct gain in body and warmth, and No. 6 (also for strings alone) again brings a slightly more ample texture, without loss of inner definition. In the *Musical Offering* (recorded a year earlier) Linde is as stylish and accomplished as any of his rivals, and he and his six colleagues offer the preferred version of this work, using original instruments. They are again warmly as well as clearly recorded; indeed the analogue-to-digital transfer is particularly natural, and this set offers remarkable value.

Complete solo and multiple concertos

(i) *Harpsichord Concertos Nos. 1 in D min.; 2 in E; 3 in D; 4 in A; 5 in F min.; 6 in F; 7 in G min., BWV 1052–8;* (ii) *Double Harpsichord Concertos: Nos. 1 in C min.; 2 in C; 3 in C min., BWV 1060–2;* (i–iii) *Triple Harpsichord Concertos Nos. 1 in D min.; 2 in C, BWV 1063–4;* (i–iv) *Quadruple Harpsichord Concerto in A min., BWV 1065;* (i; v–vi) *Triple Concerto for Flute, Violin & Harpsichord, BWV 1044;* (vi–vii) *Double Concerto for Oboe & Violin in C min., BWV 1060;* (vii) *Oboe d'amore Concerto in A, BWV 1055;* (vi) *Violin Concertos Nos. 1 in A min.; 2 in E; (vi; viii) Double Violin Concerto in D min., BWV 1041–3.*

(B) *** DG ADD/Dig. 463 725-2 (5). E. Concert, Pinnock, with
 (i) Pinnock; (ii) Gilbert; (iii) Mortensen; (iv) Kraemer;
 (v) Beznosiuk; (vi) Standage; (vii) Reichenberg;
 (viii) Wilcock.

Pinnock's performances of the Bach *Harpsichord concertos* first appeared in 1981 and have dominated the catalogue ever since. In the solo concertos he plays with real panache, his scholarship tempered with excellent musicianship. Pacing is brisk but, to today's ears, used to period performances, the effect is convincing when the playing is so spontaneous, and the analogue sound is bright and clear.

The double, triple and quadruple concertos are digital, and the combination of period instruments and playing of determined vigour certainly makes a bold effect. There is a little more edge on the strings and everything is clearly laid out and forwardly projected. Outer movements emphasize the bravura of Bach's conceptions and, if slow movements could at times be more relaxed, those ears prepared to accept a hint of aggressiveness in the energetic musical flow will find these recordings as stimulating now as when they first appeared.

The transcribed concertos for flute, violin and harpsichord, for oboe and violin, and for oboe d'amore are equally persuasive, both vigorous and warm, with consistently resilient rhythms, while the violin concertos are equally welcome. Rhythms are again crisp and lifted at nicely chosen speeds – not too fast for slow movements – and the solo playing here, led by Simon Standage, is very stylish. Altogether this makes an impressive bargain package in DG's Collectors' Edition, thoroughly recommendable to anyone wanting to obtain all this music economically, both in terms of shelf space and financial outlay.

Complete harpsichord concertos

Concerto No. 1, BWV 1052; Double Concerto No. 2, BWV 1061; Triple Concerto for Flute, Violin & Harpsichord, BWV 1044 (*** Chan. 0641); *Concertos Nos. 2 & 7, BWV 1053 & 1058; Triple Concerto No. 2, BWV 1064; Quadruple Concerto, BWV 1065* (*** Chan. 0611); *Concertos Nos. 3 & 5, BWV 1054 & 1056; Double Concerto, BWV 1062. Brandenburg Concerto No. 5 in D* (*** Chan. 0595); *Concertos Nos. 4 & 6, BWV 1055 & 1057; Double Concerto No. 1, BWV 1060; Triple Concerto, BWV 1063* (*** Chan. 0636).

Woolley; Scott; Beckett; Nicholson; Toll; Preston; Mackintosh; Cummings; Purcell Qt.

The special feature of the complete set on the Chandos Chaconne label is that the accompaniment is played on period instruments, with one instrument to each part. The warm ambience ensures that the result is not at all thin; indeed the allegros sound striking, firm and full, and of course the balance with the harpsichord or harpsichords is just about ideal. The playing is of high quality, rhythmically fresh and pleasing.

The *Double Concerto in C*, BWV 1061, brings a particularly successful solo interplay in the fugal finale, while in the *Double Concerto in C minor* the interchange of the slow movement is very appealing. The *Quadruple Concerto* works splendidly, with the harpsichords sounding vigorously robust without jangle. The *Fifth Brandenburg Concerto* is an engagingly lithe and sprightly version of what was apparently Bach's very first concerto featuring a solo keyboard instrument. In the *Triple Concerto for Flute, Violin and Harpsichord* the lovely slow movement is exquisitely registered here. Taken as a whole, this set is very successful indeed, with the focus of multiple harpsichords clean and pleasing to the ear. The vitality and finesse of the playing give it claims to be placed alongside the Pinnock and Rousset versions, and in terms of recorded sound it is unsurpassed.

(i) *Harpsichord Concertos Nos. 1; 3; 5, BWV 1052, 1054, 1056;* (ii) *Violin Concerto No. 2, BWV 1042.*

*** O/L 448 178-2. (i) Rousset; (ii) Schröder; AAM, Hogwood.

(i) *Harpsichord Concertos Nos. 2; 4; 7, BWV 1053, 1055, 1058;* (ii) *Violin Concerto No. 1 in A min., BWV 1041.*

*** O/L 443 326-2. (i) Rousset; (ii) Schröder, AAM, Hogwood.

Rousset's performances of the Harpsichord Concertos are very fine, the effect warmer, softer-grained than with Pinnock (although the harpsichord is not so sharply focused). Neat ornamentation and plenty of flair from Rousset, ample vigour and vitality from the string group, and the slow movement of the F minor is beautifully played. Jaap Schröder's accounts of the solo violin concertos are also first class, with expressive slow movements and no unwanted edge to the violin timbre.

Other recordings

(i) *Harpsichord Concertos Nos. 1–8, BWV 1052–9;* (i–ii) *Double Harpsichord Concertos Nos. 1–3, BWV 1060–2;* (i; iii) *Triple Harpsichord Concertos Nos. 1–2, BWV 1063–4; Quadruple Harpsichord Concerto in A min., BWV 1065.* Solo pieces: (i) *Fantasia & Fugue in A min., BWV 904; Italian Concerto in F, BWV 971.*

(M) **(*) Virgin VBD5 61716-2 (4). (i) Van Asperen;
 (ii) Leonhardt; (iii) Klapprott, Bussi, Lohff; Melante Amsterdam.

Like Robert Woolley, above, Bob van Asperen favours an accompaniment with one instrument to each part, basically using a string quartet, with a double bass added in BWV

1052–4, a pair of recorders in BWV 1057, violone and oboe in BWV 1059. But even more than in the Chandos performances, one has an intimate sense of chamber music-making. Van Asperen's solo contribution is consistently nimble and has an appealingly graceful delicacy, and for the most part the accompaniments from the Melante Amsterdam are lightly etched in, although sometimes in slow movements the bass seems just a little heavy and the *Andante* of BWV 1058 could be more imaginative. The recording balance is excellent. However, when one turns to the *Double Concertos*, where Gustav Leonhardt takes over the leading keyboard role, the effect is more robustly vigorous, and this applies equally to the *Triple* and *Quadruple Concertos*. By their side, one feels a certain paleness about the solo concertos, even if they have no lack of character or style. But many collectors may find van Asperen's intimate approach exactly to their taste.

Clavier Concertos Nos. 1–7, BWV 1052–8.

*** Decca 425 676-2 (2). Schiff (piano), COE.

(BB) *** Naxos 8.550422 (*Nos. 1–3*); 8.550423 (*Nos. 4–7*).
   Chang (piano), Camerata Cassovia, Stankovsky.

As in his solo Bach records, Schiff's control of colour and articulation never seeks to present merely a harpsichord imitation, and his shaping of Bach's lovely slow movements brings fine sustained lines and a subtle variety of touch. He directs the Chamber Orchestra of Europe from the keyboard and chooses spirited, uncontroversial tempi for allegros, at the same time providing decoration that always adds to the joy and sparkle of the music-making.

   Hae-won Chang is a highly sympathetic Bach exponent, playing flexibly yet with strong rhythmic feeling, decorating nimbly and not fussily. Robert Stankovsky directs freshly resilient accompaniments; and both artists understand the need for a subtle gradation of light and shade. The digital recording, made in the House of Arts, Košice, is first class, with the piano balanced not too far forward. A fine super-bargain alternative.

Clavier Concertos Nos. 1, 2, & 4, BWV 1052–3 & 1054.

(N) *** Sony SK 89245. Perahia (piano), ASMF.

While only the first disc has been issued so far, it seems certain that Murray Perahia's new set of the Bach keyboard concertos is set to sweep the board. The performances are totally pianistic, with Perahia's lightness of rhythmic touch in allegros, and deliciously crisp ornamentation, communicating an exhilarating sense of joy. Slow movements are warmly expressive, helped by the elegant fullness of the Academy strings. Yet many individual touches, and the widest range of pianistic dynamic, create a continuing subtlety of colour and feeling. Beautifully balanced recording too. In short, the effect here is to put aside any consideration of period 'authenticity' and instead give this wonderfully life-enhancing music an ageless universality.

Clavier Concertos Nos. 1, 5 & 7, BWV 1052, 1056 & 1058; in D min. (reconstructed from Cantata No. 35 by Turek), BWV 1059.

(N) **(*) VAI 1192-2 (2). Turek (piano), Turek Bach Players –
   MOZART: *Piano Concerto No. 24.* **(*)

These are live performances caught on the wing in 1984 and most successfully recorded. Tempi of the allegros are slow (characteristically so for this period of the soloist's career) and the orchestral ensemble is less rhythmically crisp than we would expect today, but Turek's own solo articulation is characteristically ear-catching. The famous slow movement of the *F minor* (No. 5) is played with a direct simplicity, but the *Andante* of *No. 7 in G minor* brings a long orchestral decrescendo, which is overtly romantic, yet serves to introduce the soloist very effectively. For all one's reservations Turek is always magnetic when playing Bach, and her reconstruction of the *D minor Concerto* draws on the *Sinfonia* of *Cantata No. 35*, transferring part of the oboe solo to the violin, and using the alto aria *Geist und Seele wird verwirret* for the siciliano slow movement.

Harpsichord Concerto No. 3 in D, BWV 1054; Concerto for Violin & Oboe in C min., BWV 1060; Violin Concertos: in D min., BWV 1052; in G min., BWV 1056.

*** Virgin VC5 45361-2. Ciomei, Biondi, Bernadini, Europe Galante.

In the hands of such fine players, these four works, all familiar and all reconstructed from other concertos, make a rewarding collection, casting new light on the music, when the performances are so freshly and warmly played (on period instruments) and beautifully recorded. The *Double Concerto for Violin and Oboe* is a highlight, for Alfredo Bernadini's baroque oboe has a most appealing timbre and the balance with the violin is felicitous. Fabio Biondi, playing spiritedly and with easy virtuosity, then makes a good case for the two transcribed *Violin Concertos* (arranged from keyboard concertos), and his expressive line in the two slow movements is also memorable.

Harp Concertos (transcribed Zabaleta) from (Solo) Organ Concertos (after Vivaldi): in G, BWV 973; in C, BWV 976; in F, BWV 978.

(N) (B) ** DG (ADD) 469 544-2. Zabaleta, Kuentz CO, Kuentz
   – HANDEL: *Harp Concertos.* **(*)

These are Zabaleta's own concertante arrangements for harp and strings of Bach's organ transcriptions of three Vivaldi violin concertos (Opus 3/3 & 12, and Opus 7/2). The performances are engagingly refined and intimate, but the result is a little too romantically comfortable to be truly Vivaldian. The sound is excellent.

Oboe d'amore Concertos: in D, BWV 1053; in A, BWV 1055; Oboe Concertos: in G min., BWV 1056; in D min., BWV 1059; Double Concerto in C min. for Oboe & Violin, BWV 1060.

(BB) *** Naxos 8.554602. Hommel, Cologne CO, Müller-Brühl.

Christian Hommel's outstanding performances of concertos for oboe and oboe d'amore, all of them reconstructions of other works, are lively and sensitive; the recording, with the soloist balanced well in front, is excellent. A most enjoyable disc.

Oboe d'amore Concerto in D, BWV 1068; Sinfonia from Cantata No. 156; Canonic Trio in F, BWV 1040.

*** Ph. 454 450-2. Holliger, Camerata Bern – C. P. E. BACH: *Oboe Concertos.* ***

The *Oboe d'amore Concerto* is better known in its harpsichord version, but Holliger is a highly convincing advocate and he plays the lovely cantilena from the cantata exquisitely. The brief *Canonic Trio* is hardly less pleasing and the recording is admirably natural.

(i–iii) Violin Concertos Nos. 1–2; (i–ii; iv) Double Violin Concerto, BWV 1041–3; (i) Partita No. 2, BWV 1004: Chaconne.

✿ (M) (***) EMI mono CDH5 67201-2. (i) Menuhin; (ii) O Symphonique de Paris (iii) cond. Enescu; (iv) with Enescu (violin), cond. Monteux.

Menuhin's 78-r.p.m. recording of the *Double Concerto*, with Georges Enescu his partner (and teacher) and Monteux conducting, is legendary for its rapport and simple expressive beauty. It was recorded in Paris in 1932, the same year that Menuhin recorded the Elgar in London. The two solo concertos – with Enescu on the rostrum – followed in 1933 and 1936. They are hardly less remarkable, with a wonderful purity of line and natural expressive feeling. All these records were made when Menuhin was between sixteen and nineteen years of age and show (as did the Elgar in a quite different way) his unique instinctive musical vision, which came from within rather than from outside influences. The famous *Partita* is hardly less impressive (see below). In the concertos, the orchestral string-sound is dry, the violins unflattered, but this expert remastering by Andrew Walter makes the very most of the original 78s and, so moving is the slow movement of the *Double Concerto*, one quite forgets its early provenance. A Bach recording that should be in every collection.

(i) Violin Concertos Nos. 1–2; (ii) Double Violin Concerto, BWV 1041–3; (iii) Double Concerto for Violin & Oboe in C min., BWV 1060.

✿ (M) *** Ph. (ADD) 420 700-2. Grumiaux, with (ii) Krebbers, (iii) Holliger; (i–ii) Les Solistes Romandes, Gerecz; (iii) New Philh. O, de Waart.

(N) *** EMI CDC5 57091-2. Kennedy, BPO; with (i) Stabrawa ; (ii) Mayer.

(B) *** Nim. NI 1735(3). Shumsky, Scottish CO; with (ii) Tunnell; (iii) Miller – MOZART: *Concertos 4 & 5; Sonatas.* ***

(M) *** Classic fM 75605 57008-2. Hattori, with (ii) Clark, (iii) Williams; SCO, Hattori.

Arthur Grumiaux is joined in the *Double Concerto* by Hermann Krebbers. The result is an outstanding success. The way Grumiaux responds to the challenge of working with another great artist comes over equally clearly in the concerto with oboe, reconstructed from the *Double Harpsichord Concerto in C minor*. Grumiaux's performances of the two solo concertos are equally satisfying.

The maverick Kennedy and the centrally traditional Berlin Philharmonic may make curious partners in Bach, but these are positive, robust readings, marked by fast and fierce speeds in outer movements. Happily, there are none of the idiosyncrasies of Kennedy's version of Vivaldi's *Four Seasons*, and though he discreetly persuades the Berliners to adopt a few ideas from period performance, he is happiest when indulging in warmly expressive slow movements, taken at relatively expansive speeds. His soloist partners – Albrecht Mayer in the work with oboe, Daniel Stabrawa in the sublime *Double Violin Concerto* – make an excellent match.

One has only to sample the simple beauty of Shumsky's playing in the *Andante* of the *A minor Violin Concerto* to be won over to his dedicated Bach style, which is not quite as pure as Grumiaux's but is seductive in its simplicity of line and tonal beauty. John Tunnell makes highly musical exchanges with him in the *Double Violin Concerto*, and Robin Miller is a no less appealing partner in the work for violin and oboe.

The Classic fM disc is also outstanding, offering not just performances which stand high among versions using modern instruments, but full, immediate recording. Joji Hattori, winner of the Menuhin International Competition in 1989, plays with a tone both sweet and pure, flawless in intonation and immaculate in crisply alert passage-work. As director, he draws from the orchestra playing both clear and well sprung, with the clarity enhanced by the recording, and he is well matched by both his duet partners.

Violin Concertos Nos. 1–2; (i) Double Concerto; (ii) Triple Concerto for Flute, Violin & Harpsichord, BWV 1044.

(B) *** DG 463 014-2. Standage, E. Concert, Pinnock; with (i) Wilcock; (ii) Beznosiuk, Pinnock.

This collection of violin concertos, played on original instruments, is welcome back into the catalogue. Rhythms are crisp and lifted at nicely chosen speeds – not too fast for slow movements – and the solo playing is very stylish. The *Triple Concerto* is also very successful. The only snag is the edge on violin timbre which will not please all ears.

(i) Violin Concertos Nos. 1–2; (ii) Double Violin Concerto, BWV 1041–3; (iii) Double Concerto for Violin & Oboe, BWV 1060. (iv) Orchestral Suites Nos. 1–3, BWV 1066–8.

(BB) *** EMI Seraphim (ADD) CES5 68517-2 (2). (i–iii) Y. Menuhin; (ii) Ferras; (iii) L. Goossens; (iv) Schaffer; Bath Festival CO, Menuhin.

Menuhin's stereo set of the *Violin Concertos* date from 1960 and, played as they are here, both the solo concertos take flight, for their balance of warmth, humanity and classical sympathy is very appealing. In the *Double Violin Concerto* Ferras matches his timbre beautifully to that of Menuhin and the duet is a real partnership, with the slow movement especially fine. Leon Goossens makes a ravishing contribution to the *Adagio* of the *Concerto for Violin and Oboe*, the only slight snag being that the oboe is too backwardly balanced in the outer movements. To complete this attractive Menuhin/Bach package, we are offered three of the four *Orchestral Suites*, where Menuhin finds an admirable balance between freshness and warmth, conveying the music's spirit and breadth without inflation. The current remastering brings sound which is quite full, yet clear. The documentation – or lack of it – is no credit to the famous old EMI trademark, but the music-making is of the highest order.

(i) *Violin Concertos Nos. 1 in A min.; 2 in E*; (ii) *Double Violin Concerto, BWV 1041–3*; (iii) *Orchestral Suite No. 4 in D, BWV 1068*.

(B) **(*) DG 449 844-2. (i–ii) D. Oistrakh, RPO, Goossens; (ii) with I. Oistrakh; (iii) Munich Bach O, Richter.

David Oistrakh's playing is peerless and can be ranked alongside the Grumiaux versions. In the *Double Concerto* father and son are suitably contrasted in timbre, and the performance of the great slow movement is Elysian. The 1961 recording hardly sounds dated. Richter's account of the *Fourth Orchestral Suite* is rhythmically unstylish in the matter of double-dotting but is otherwise alert – less heavy than we had remembered.

Violin Concerto No. 2 in E, BWV 1042.

**(*) Simax PSC 1159. Tellefsen, Oslo Festival Strings, Berglund – SHOSTAKOVICH: *Violin Concerto No. 1*. **(*)
(N) (M) *(*) BBC (ADD) BBCL 4050-2. Menuhin, ECO, Malcolm – BRAHMS: *Double Concerto*. MENDELSSOHN: *Violin Concerto*. *(*)

Arve Tellefsen has never enjoyed the international exposure to which his gifts entitle him, but he is a fine musician who plays with great spirit, and he is well recorded too. Good, stylish playing that should enjoy wide appeal.

Menuhin's BBC version of the *E major Concerto* was recorded at the Aldeburgh Festival in 1963. It is conducted well by George Malcolm and played decently, although Menuhin is nowhere near his best.

(i) *Violin Concertos: No. 2 in E*; (ii) *in G min.* (from *BWV 1056*); (i; ii) *Double Violin Concerto, BWV 1043*.

(N) (BB) *** EMI Encore CDE5 74720-2. (i) Perlman; (ii) Zukerman, ECO, Barenboim.

This CD serves to launch Encore, a new super-budget label from EMI, dignified with the Angel logo, which goes back to the earliest days of the Gramophone Company, even before the famous HMV trademark was adopted. The first issue is auspicious. Perlman and Zukerman, with their friend and colleague Barenboim are inspired to give a magic performance of the great *Double Concerto*, one in which their artistry is beautifully matched in all its intensity. The slow movement in particular has rarely sounded more ravishing on record. Perlman is also most impressive in the slow movement of the *E major* solo *Concerto*, but neither he nor Zukerman in the *G minor Concerto* (arranged from the *F minor Harpsichord Concerto* with its sublime *Arioso* slow movement) is quite so inspired without the challenge of the other. None the less, with fine accompaniments from the ECO this is a Bach bargain to cherish.

Double Violin Concerto in D min., BWV 1043.

(M) *** RCA (ADD) 09026 63531-2. Heifetz, Friedman, London New SO, Sargent – BRAHMS: *Double Concerto*; MOZART: *Sinfonia Concertante, K.364*. ***

It is good to have Heifetz's 1961 stereo recording of the

Double Concerto as a worthy successor to Menuhin's two versions. Sargent's tempi in the outer movements are brisk, but are none the worse for that, and the Elysian dialogue of the slow movement, with Heifetz's pupil Erick Friedman a natural partner, is hardly less inspired and much better recorded.

(i) *Double Violin Concerto, BWV 1043*. *Suite No. 3, BWV 1068: Air* (arr. Wilhelmj). (Unaccompanied) *Violin Sonata No. 1 in G min., BWV 1001: Adagio*.

(M) (***) Biddulph mono LAB 056-7[id.]. Arnold Rosé, (i) with Alma Rosé, O – BEETHOVEN: *String Quartets Nos. 4, 10 & 14*. (***)

Arnold Rosé's sonata-partner was Bruno Walter and his brother-in-law was Mahler. His daughter, Alma, with whom he is heard in a 1931 recording of the Bach *D minor Double Concerto*, perished in Auschwitz. Interesting though these recordings are, the principal musical rewards in the set come from the three Beethoven quartets with which they are coupled.

A Musical Offering, BWV 1079 (see also above under *Art of Fugue*, *Brandenburgs*, and below under Chamber Music).

(BB) **(*) Naxos 8.553286. Capella Istropolitana, Benda.

Christian Benda uses a small chamber orchestra. Strings alone, with a minimum of vibrato, play the framing *Ricercars*. The first group of canons add in flute, oboe and bassoon; in the second group, the stringed instruments predominate. A harpsichord joins in the first, and the cor anglais and bassoon dolorously share the last (common) solution of the four offered alternative proposals for solving Bach's so-called 'puzzle canon'. The *Trio Sonata*, at the centre, is given a pleasing performance, expressive and lively, and overall this seems a thoroughly musical interpretation of a work about which any performance is conjectural. The recording is excellent, clear yet with a pleasing bloom, and the result, if a little didactic at times, is undoubtedly fresh.

Orchestral Suites Nos. 1–4, BWV 1066–9.

(M) *** Decca (ADD) 430 378-2. ASMF, Marriner.

Orchestral Suites Nos. 1–4; (i) *Double Harpsichord Concertos Nos. 1 & 3*.

(B) *** Double Decca 458 069-2 (2). AAM, Hogwood; (i) with Rousset, Hogwood.

Orchestral Suites Nos. 1–4; *Violin Concerto Movement in D, BWV 1045*; *Sinfonias from Cantatas Nos. 29; 42; 209*.

(B) *** Hyp. Dyad CDD 22002 (2). Brandenburg Cons., Goodman.

Orchestral Suites Nos. 1–4. *Sinfonias from Cantatas Nos. 42; 174 & Easter Oratorio, BWV 249*; (i) *Cantata No. 118: Chorus: Ich liebe den Höchsten von ganzem Gemüte*.

*** DG 439 780-2 (2). E. Concert, Pinnock; (i) with Ch.

With sound rather warmer and string-tone sweeter, Trevor Pinnock and the English Concert improve on their readings of 16 years earlier. In the dance movements of the *Suite No. 2* Lisa Beznosiuk takes her flute solos faster and more brilliantly than her predecessor, Stephen Preston, but otherwise speeds are generally a fraction broader in all four *Suites*, with allegros more jauntily sprung and phrasing a degree more espressivo. Above all, the great *Air* of *Suite No. 3* sounds far warmer, persuasively phrased on multiple violins instead of on a single, acid-toned instrument. The fill-ups are brief but make a fascinating bonus, winningly performed.

Hogwood's set of the Bach orchestral *Suites* illustrates how the Academy of Ancient Music has developed in refinement and purity of sound, modifying earlier abrasiveness without losing period-instrument freshness. That comes out in the famous *Air* from *Suite No. 3* where, with multiple violins and an avoidance of the old squeezed style, the tone is sweet even with little or no vibrato – a movement which in the old Pinnock version on DG Archiv, for example, sounds very sour. *Allegros* tend to be on the fast side but are well sprung, not breathless. The *Concertos for 2 Harpsichords*, added for the mid-priced reissue, are imaginatively played by Christopher Hogwood and Christophe Rousset. Hogwood aficionados need not hesitate.

Roy Goodman directs brisk and stylish readings of the four Bach *Orchestral Suites*, which are aptly supplemented by four *Sinfonias*, each following a suite in the same key. Though in the *Suites* Goodman in his eagerness occasionally chooses too breathless a tempo for fast movements, the lightness of rhythm and the crispness of ensemble are consistently persuasive, with textures cleanly caught in excellent, full-bodied sound. These are among the finest versions on a long list, with Rachael Brown an exceptionally warm-toned flautist in No. 2. Goodman, like Pinnock, observes all repeats, making the opening overtures longer than usual.

Marriner's 1970 recording of the Bach *Suites* with the ASMF comes on a single CD (77 minutes 48 seconds) and the remastering of the fine (originally Argo) recording is fresh and vivid. The playing throughout is expressive, without being romantic, and always buoyant and vigorous. A fine bargain for those not insisting on original instruments; there is nothing remotely unstylish here.

The Orchestra of the Age of Enlightenment play warmly, but dotted rhythms are too often lacking in the necessary lift. Lisa Beznosiuk is the able soloist in the *Second Suite*, but overall, Brüggen's set is a disappointment (Philips 442 151-2).

Pinnock's earlier, analogue recording of the *Suites* (now neatly fitted on to a single CD), dates from 1979, when period-instrument performances were still full of stylistic excesses, and the unprepared listener could find the bright edge on the squeezed vibratoless string-timbres disconcerting (DG 463 013-2).

(Orchestral) Suites Nos. 1–4, BWV 1066–9 (transcribed for guitar quartet by Amaral or Gloeden).

(N) *** Delos DE 3254 Brazilian Guitar Quartet.

The baroque era and the music of Bach in particular was a watershed for transcribing music from one set of instruments to another, so there is no absence of precedent for what seems a very audacious modern arrangement of the four orchestral suites for guitar quartet (made by two members of this Brazilian group). The result is astonishingly successful, with the four instruments perfectly integrated in ensemble, while contrapuntal detail emerges clearly within a pleasingly warm ambience.

The playing itself is expert, choice of tempi is relaxed but seems unerringly apt and these players never sentimentalize: the famous *Air* from the *Third Suite* (placed first on the CD) is most appealing, as is the *Sarabande* of the *Second*. The rhythms of following *Bourrées* are engagingly crisp, as is the ensuing *Polonaise and Double*. One misses the flute most in the *Badinerie*, but this too remains bright and attractive. More surprisingly, it is the lesser-known *First* and *Third* *Suites* which are given the most refreshing new presentation by the well-lifted rhythms of the playing here. The expert and communicative music-making is very enjoyable throughout, making this more than just a disc for guitar-specialists.

Collection

(i) *Brandenburg Concerto No. 5. Orchestral Suite No. 2* (for flute and strings); *Partita in A min.* (for unaccompanied flute), *BWV 1013; Trio Sonata in G, BWV 1038.*

⚫ (N) EMI CDC5 57111-2. Pahud; Kussmaul; Faust; Schornsheim; (i) Berlin Bar. Sol., Kussmaul.

At first sight, this looks like a rather arbitrary collection, but Emmanuel Pahud is a superb artist and the delicacy of his flute playing lights up everything he touches. The solo *Partita* is a model of linear subtlety and his colleagues play with comparable taste and style in the *Trio Sonata*. The famous *Badinerie* of the *Orchestral Suite No. 2* is exquisitely articulated and the finale of *Brandenburg No. 5* as light as thistledown, while earlier in the same work the harpsichord solo from Christine Schornsheim has similar finesse. The orchestral contribution is wonderfully buoyant and totally free from rhythmic and textural heaviness, the sound itself warm yet completely transparent. In short this superbly balanced and recorded CD is not to be missed, even if (inevitably) it brings duplication.

CHAMBER MUSIC

The Art of Fugue, BWV 1080.

(N) *** Hyp. CDA 67138. Delmé Qt.

**(*) ECM 1652. Keller Qt.

(N) ** MDG 619 0989-2. Calefax Reed Quintet.

Until relatively recently *The Art of Fugue* was thought of as purely theoretical and not designed for performance. Its earliest recordings were made on stringed instruments; one was an arrangement for string quartet by the American composer Roy Harris that included Tovey playing his completion of the final unfinished contrapunctus on the piano; another featured a string orchestra conducted by Hermann Diener. From the early 1950s the view that it was intended for the keyboard gained ground. However, Robert Simpson believed that it is 'essential that the four parts retain their identity throughout', and that 'the quartet is the ideal medium for conveying the beauty of four-part counterpoint with perfect clarity and sensitivity'. As the tessitura lies too low to perform the piece in D minor, Simpson has transposed the whole sequence into G minor. Incidentally, he includes Tovey's completion of *Contrapunctus XIV*, although the listener can play it without the conjectural ending if preferred. The Delmé Quartet, who have recorded ten of Simpson's own quartets, play with great dedication. Excellent recording.

The Hungarian Keller Quartet gives the impression of using a fair degree of vibrato, and this brings a more expressive style, so that the cello solo which opens Contrapunctus 3 is almost a lament. There is plenty of variety of both mood and tempo. Nevertheless keyboard versions delineate the part-writing more pointedly. The recording is full and naturally balanced.

The five players of the Calefax Quintet play many more than five instruments, including oboe d'amore, cor anglais, basset horn, bass clarinet, soprano and alto saxophones. The palette of colours they produce often gives an exotic tinge to Bach's contrapuntal exploration, although lively rhythms and sensible tempi prevent the results from being too eccentric. Nevertheless this version is obviously aimed at the listener for whom variety of colour is essential to approach Bach's polyphony agreeably.

Goebel's Cologne Musica Antiqua performance has genuine vitality, but the bite on the string-tone, and also the expressive bulges which at times are exaggerated, will pose a listening problem for some listeners (DG 463 027-2).

(Unaccompanied) *Cello Suites Nos. 1–6, BWV 1007–12.*

⚙ *** EMI CDS5 55363-2 (2). Rostropovich.
(BB) *** EMI double forte CZS5 74179-2 (2). Schiff.
(B) *** Double Decca 466 253-2 (2). Harrell.
(M) *** DG (ADD) 449 711-2 (2). Fournier.
(M) *** Sony S2K 63203 (2). Ma.
*** Virgin VCD5 45086-2 (2). Kirshbaum.
(B) *** Ph. (ADD) Duo 442 293-2 (2); or 422 494-2 (*Nos. 1, 4 & 6*); 422 495-2 (*Nos. 2–3 & 5*) Gendron.
(M) (***) EMI mono CHS7 61027-2 (2). Casals.

Rostropovich verbally characterizes each one of the series: 'No. 1, lightness; No. 2, sorrow and intensity; No. 3, brilliance; No. 4, majesty and opacity; No. 5, darkness; and No. 6, sunlight'. True to his word, more than usual he draws distinctions between each, also reflecting the point that the structure of each suite grows in complexity. The results are both moving and strong, with the sound of the cello, as recorded in a warm acoustic, full and powerful, making one hear the music afresh, with pianissimo repeats magically achieved.

Heinrich Schiff is straighter but no less concentrated in feeling. Strong and positive, producing a consistent flow of beautiful tone at whatever dynamic level, he here establishes his individual artistry very clearly, his rhythmic pointing a delight. He is treated to an excellent recording, with the cello given fine bloom against a warm but intimate acoustic. This is now an outstanding bargain as a double forte.

Harrell's comparative spareness and restraint contrast strongly with Rostropovich's more extrovert manner, but rarely if ever is the former guilty of understatement. The simple dedication of the playing, combined with cleanness of attack and purity of tone, brings natural, unforced inten-

sity, and in many ways these readings might be compared with Milstein's DG set of the *Unaccompanied Violin Sonatas*. One might disagree with the occasional tempo, but the overall command is unassailable. The recording quality, forward and real yet aptly intimate in acoustic, suits the performances admirably.

Fournier's richly phrased and warm-toned performances carry an impressive musical conviction. He can be profound and he can lift rhythms infectiously in dance movements, but above all he conveys the feeling that this is music to be enjoyed. This recording has been remastered splendidly and now has even greater presence and realism.

Yo-Yo Ma's playing has a characteristic rhythmic freedom and favours the widest range of dynamic. The improvisatory effect is seemingly spontaneous and these performances are very compelling indeed, for Ma seems right inside every bar of the music. The first-class recording is very real and natural, with the warm acoustic never blurring the focus.

Ralph Kirshbaum's 'authentic' set of the Bach *Cello Suites* is also very fine. He plays a Domenico Montagnana Venetian cello of 1729 and gives it a warmly vivid personality. Articulation in the dance movements is clear; expressive playing is without bulges and does not shirk a degree of vibrato. The performances have intensity, dedication, spontaneity and an intimate thoughtfulness which is genuinely moving.

No one artist holds all the secrets in this repertoire, but few succeed in producing such consistent beauty of tone as Maurice Gendron, with the digital remastering firming up an excellent and truthful analogue recording. His phrasing is unfailingly musical, and these readings with their restraint and fine judgement command admiration. At Philips's Duo price, they can be given a warm welcome back to the catalogue. As can be seen, these performances are also available on two separate bargain CDs, costing about the same as the Duo.

It was Casals who restored these pieces to the repertory after long decades of neglect. Some of the playing is far from flawless; passage-work is rushed or articulation uneven, and he is often wayward. But he brought to the *Cello Suites* insights that remain unrivalled. Casals brings one closer to this music than do most of his rivals. The EMI sound is inevitably dated but still comes over well in this transfer.

(Unaccompanied) *Cello Suites Nos. 1–6, BWV 1007–12;*
(i) *Viola da gamba Sonatas Nos. 1–2, BWV 1027–8.*

(M) **(*) Mercury (IMS) 432 756-2 (2). Starker, (i) with Sebök.

Janos Starker's performances come from 1963 and 1965 and are of great integrity and dedication, without having quite the same electric communication of his earlier mono recording. The two *Viola da gamba Sonatas* are not ideally balanced and favour György Sebök's piano, though there is no question of his artistry.

(Unaccompanied) *Cello Suite No. 1 in G, BWV 1007.*

(M) (***) EMI mono CDM5 67008-2. Casals – BEETHOVEN: *Cello Sonata No. 3;* BRAHMS: *Cello Sonata No. 2.* (***)

The *G major Suite* was recorded in 1938, and nobility shines through every bar. Of course this is available with the other suites, but duplication is worthwhile for the sake of its companions.

A Musical Offering, BWV 1079.

*** HM 05472 77307-2. Barthold, Sigiswald & Wieland Kuijken, Kohnen.

(N)(B) **(*) H.M. (ADD) HMA 1951260. Moroney, Cook, See, Holloway, Ter Linden.

The Kuijkens give a virtually ideal chamber account of the *Musical Offering*. With four period instruments taking individual parts, the polyphony is absolutely clear yet, because of the warm acoustic, never clinical. After the harpsichord plays the opening *Ricercar a 3*, the group joins together for the *Canon perpetua* on the King's theme, and again for the *Ricercar a 6*, the *Trio Sonata* and the closing *Canon perpetua*. The recording is most natural.

The Harmonia Mundi version makes a possible if somewhat less varied alternative. The introductory *Ricercar* and first group of *Canons* are presented clearly but not pedantically on one or two harpsichords, and the sensitively played *Trio Sonata* follows, given added colour by using flute, violin and continuo. The *Canon perpetua* is then heard on the same combination, and for the all remaining *Canons*, except one, Moroney returns to his harpsichord(s). Good recording, truthfully transferred.

Reinhard Goebel with his Musica Antiqua Köln places the *Canons* (which are finely done) together and successfully follows them with the *Trio Sonatas*. However, these sonatas are the musical centre-piece of the work and Goebel's reading is too mannered and self-conscious (particularly in the slow movement) to carry a strong recommendation (DG 463 026-2).

Flute Sonatas Nos. 1–6, BWV 1030–35.

(BB) *** ASV CDQS 6108. Bennett, Malcolm, Evans.

Flute Sonatas Nos. 1–6, BWV 1030–35; in G min., BWV 1020; Partita in A min. (for solo flute), BWV 1013.

(M) *** CRD (ADD) 3314/5 (2). Preston, Pinnock, Savall.

Flute Sonatas Nos. 1–6, BWV 1030–5; BWV 1020; Partita, BWV 1013; Trio Sonatas, BWV 1038–9; Suite, BWV 997.

(M)**(*) Häns. CD 92.121 (2). Gérard, Azzaloni, Blumenthal, Forchert, Formisano, Kleiner.

Flute Sonatas Nos. 1–2; 4–6, BWV 1030–31; 1033–5; in G min., BWV 1020.

*** RCA 09026 62555-2. Galway, Cunningham, Moll.

Flute Sonata No. 3, BWV 1032; Partita in A min. (for solo flute), BWV 1013; A Musical Offering, BWV 1079: Trio Sonata in C min.; Trio Sonatas Nos. 3 & 4 in G, BWV 1038–9.

*** RCA 09026 68182-2. Galway, Huggett, Cunningham, Moll.

Flute Sonatas Nos. 1, 4, & 6, BWV 1030, 1033 & 1035; Trio Sonata (for 2 flutes & continuo), BWV 1039; (Solo) Flute Partita, BWV 1013.

(N) **(*) MDG 309 0932-2. Kaiser, Musica Alta Ripa.

Flute Sonatas Nos. 2, 3, & 5, BWV 1031–2 & 1034; in C min., BWV 1079 (from Musical Offering); Trio Sonata (for flute, violin & continuo), BWV 1038.

(N) **(*) MDG 309 0931-2. Kaiser, Musica Alta Ripa.

Two of these *Sonatas*, BWV 1031 and 1033, are unauthenticated, but they still contain attractive music. Using an authentic one-key instrument, Stephen Preston plays all six with a rare delicacy. Throughout, the continuo playing, led by Trevor Pinnock, is of the highest standard and this is a clear first choice for this repertoire. This set now comes handsomely repackaged in a box.

William Bennett uses a modern flute, and in the first three sonatas he and George Malcolm manage without the nicety of including a viola da gamba in the continuo. In *Sonatas Nos. 4–6* the two players are joined by Michael Evans and the bass is subtly but tangibly reinforced and filled out, though the balance remains just as impressive. The playing, as might be expected of these artists, has superb character: it is strong in personality yet does not lack finesse. Bennett himself has made the reconstruction of the first movement of BWV 1032. A first class bargain alternative.

James Galway has now progressed to using period instrumentalists as partners. He is a superb artist (witness the unsurpassed account of the *Solo Partita*) and his line in slow movements is exquisite. Vibrato is sparing and the flute timbre is refined, if obviously richer than an eighteenth-century instrument. The balance in the *Trio Sonatas* (which are full of life) is first class, but in the works with continuo Galway tends to dominate the sound-picture aurally as well as musically. But who will grumble when he plays so beautifully, and his companions give excellent support.

Jean-Claude Gérard is a fine player, but it seems curious that all this repertoire should have been recorded (in 1999) with piano instead of harpsichord, and using a bassoon continuo. This is all very musical and pleasing enough in its way, but is hardly a first choice.

Karl Kaiser is a thoroughly musical and accomplished soloist and the members of Musica Alta Ripa all play period instruments very smoothly. Their performances are stylishly pleasing, if at times perhaps a little bland. Twice they use a fortepiano rather than a harpsichord (BWV 1035 and 1079), but with good effect. The set is well balanced and truthfully recorded, but would not be a first choice.

Flute Sonatas Nos. 1, BWV 1030; 3, BWV 1032; 5, BWV 1034; 6, BWV 1035.

(M) *** HM HMT 790065. Beaucoudray, Christie.

(N) (BB) **(*) H.M. HCX 3957024. See, Maroney (harpsichord), Springfels.

Flute Sonatas Nos. 1, 4, 5, & 6; (Solo) Partita, BWV 1013.

(N) **(*) Channel CCS 15798. Solomon, Charlston.

Those looking for period performances will surely be delighted with the Harmonia Mundi disc. Marc Beaucoudray makes the most delightful sounds on his baroque flute (not in the least watery), and the balance with William Christie's (Dowd) harpsichord could not be improved upon. They play beautifully together, with great sensitivity and a true sense of baroque style; the result is altogether captivating. The acoustic, too, is ideally judged.

The *American Capital Times* describes the See/Marony performances as 'wickedly charming'. Janet See's baroque flute has a warm yet watery timbre which is rather appealing, as is her lyrical phrasing, while she is chipper and lively in the allegros. Moroney's support is impeccable and Mary Springfield adds the viola da gamba part very neatly in the two latter works. The balance is excellent and this is certainly refreshing, but the disc is upstaged by Marc Beaucoudray and William Christie, who offer the same music at mid-price.

Ashley Solomon's solo playing is always flexible and spontaneous in feeling (especially in the Solo *Partita*) and Terry Charlston makes up an impressive partnership. They too are well recorded, but the snag here is that the close microphones mean that every time Solomon takes a breath it is all too audible, which could be a problem for some listeners.

(i) *Partita for Solo Flute in A min., BWV 1013*; (i–ii) *Flute Sonata in A, BWV 1032*; (iii; ii) *Viola da gamba Sonata in G*; (iv–v) *Violin Sonata No. 1 in B min., BWV 1014*; (iv; ii–iii) *Violin Sonata in G, BWV 1021.*

(B) *** DG 463 025-3. (i) Hazelzet; (ii) Bouman; (iii) Ter Linden, (iv) Goebel; (v) Hill.

In the works for flute, Wilbert Hazelzet plays with a gentle authority and sensitivity that are most persuasive, and he and his accomplished partner, Henk Bouman, also bring unobtrusive virtuosity to the allegros. The Goebel/Hill partnership in the *Violin Sonatas* give vigorous performances, pleasantly abrasive in violin-tone, bringing dance-based movements in particular vividly to life. Slow movements do not lack expressive feeling, and the sound is first rate.

Music for lute-harpsichord

Suites Nos. 1–2, BWV 996–7; 3 (Prelude, Fugue & Allegro in E flat), BWV 998; Fantasias & Fugues: in B flat, BWV 907; in D, BWV 928; Prelude & Fantasia in C min., BWV 921–1121; Prelude in C min., BWV 999.

*** Häns. CD 92-109. Hill.

Bach's effects, as listed in his posthumous estate, included two Lauten Werk (lute-harpsichords), and it is thought that some of the music now included in the repertoire of lutenists and guitar players was intended for this instrument. Indeed, the *Suite in E minor*, BWV 996, has the inscription 'Lautenwerck' on its title-page. But the instrument itself is obsolete. We know that it had one, two or three keyboards, used gut strings plucked simultaneously by several jacks and quills, and reputedly possessed an uncannily effective lute stop. So the present instrument, built by Keith Hill in Manchester, Michigan, USA, has had to be reconstructed conjecturally from descriptions of instruments in use in Bach's time. It features only one manual, authentically uses damperless jacks; an ingenious jack-slide, worked by a pedal, replaces the multiple system yet still allows some of the effect of multi-plucking. Robert Hill is a vivid and lively exponent of this experimental instrument; but, perversely, the works which come off best are the *Fantasias and Fugues* which are less directly associated with the lute. The recording could hardly be better managed, but the resonant, undamped sound means that there is less delicacy of texture than

with performances of the three *Suites* on lute or guitar. A fascinating collection none the less.

Music for lute and guitar

Sonatas for Solo Guitar (trans. from *Unaccompanied Violin Sonatas Nos. 1 in G min.; 2 in A min.; 3 in C, BWV 1001, 1003 & 1005*, arr. Barrueco).

*** EMI CDC5 56416-2. Barrueco (guitar).

Manuel Barrueco's guitar transcriptions of Bach's three *Sonatas for Unaccompanied Violin* are astonishingly successful. He makes them entirely his own, and such is the magnetism of this playing that, while under his spell, one almost forgets their original provenance. In short, Barrueco is a true Bach player, and these performances are a joy to the ear, for the guitar is beautifully recorded.

Lute Suites (arranged for guitar) *Nos. 1–3, BWV 995–7; Prelude in C min.; Fugue in G min., BWV 999–1000.*

(B) *** Sony (ADD) SBK 62972. Williams (guitar).
(M) ** DG 463 022-2. Yepes (lute).

Lute Suite No. 4, BWV 1006a; Prelude, Fugue & Allegro in E flat, BWV 998. (Unaccompanied) Cello Suite No. 3, BWV 1009: Bourrées Nos. 1–2. (i) arr. guitar and organ: *Cantata No. 140: Chorale: Wachet Auf!; Fugue à la gigue in G, BWV 877; Italian Concerto, BWV 971: Allegro. Trio Sonata No. 6 in G, BWV 530; Violin Sonata No. 4, BWV 1017: Adagio.*

(B) **(*) Sony ADD/Dig. SBK 62973 (2). Williams (guitar); (i) with Hurford (organ).

John Williams shows a natural response to Bach, and his performances of the four *Lute Suites* are among his finest records. The first of these two discs can be recommended unreservedly: the flair of his playing, with its rhythmic vitality and sense of colour, is always telling. The second disc opens with a most winning account of the *Fourth Suite* which includes a famous and catchy *Gavotte en Rondeau*, beloved of all guitarists from Segovia onwards. The transcriptions of the *Bourrées* from the *Cello Suite* are effective enough; but not all listeners will care for the rest of the programme of rather contrived duets for guitar and organ (an unlikely combination).

Yepes uses a baroque lute, and he plays very musically. However, guitar players do not always take easily to the lute, which employs a wholly different technique, and this playing does not have the same degree of lively communication as Yepes's earlier recordings of Bach on the guitar.

(i) *Lute Suites Nos. 1–2, BWV 996–7*; (ii) *Trio Sonatas Nos. 1, BWV 525; 5, BWV 529* (ed. Bream).

(M) *** RCA 09026 61603-2. Bream (i) (guitar); (ii) (lute), Malcolm.

The two *Lute Suites* are played with great subtlety and mastery on the guitar; the *Trio Sonatas* were originally written for organ; here they are heard on lute and harpsichord and are elegantly played and cleanly recorded within a convincing ambience: the effect is pleasingly transparent and intimate.

(i) *Oboe Sonatas in G min., BWV 1020; BWV 1030b. Fugue on a Theme of Albinoni in B min., BWV 951.*

(BB) **(*) DHM 05472 77440-2. Piguet, Tilney – C. P. E. BACH: *Oboe Sonata* **(*); W. F. BACH: *Polonaise in E flat.* ***

As can be seen above and below, these two sonatas are better known in their versions for violin (BWV 1020) and flute (BWV 1030). But they are certainly pleasing on the baroque oboe. Michel Piguet's timbre is appealing, although the close microphones (one can hear the player take a breath) mean a reduction in the effective dynamic range. The *Fugue* is used as a central interlude and seems to have been recorded at a different time, since the pitch is fractionally different; however, there are sufficiently long pauses to make this relatively unimportant.

6 (organ) Trio Sonatas: Nos. 1 in B flat; 2 in E min.; 3 in G min.; 4 in E min.; 5 in F; 6 in C, BWV 525–30.

*** Hyp. CDA 666843. King's Consort, King.

Bach's *Organ Sonatas* readily invite transcription, and Robert King makes a good case for presenting them in such arrangements as are offered here, all retaining the original keys. The baroque oboe and oboe d'amore suit Bach's invention especially well and the resulting ranges of colour are very appealing, giving this music a completely new dimension. The playing is joyous and light-hearted and always warm in spirit. First-class recording, too.

6 (organ) Trio Sonatas (arr. Boothby for 2 violins, viola da gamba and harpsichord), BWV 525–30.

(N) ** Chan. 0504. Purcell Qt.

Robert Boothby's simple arrangement for strings would seem the most obvious way to tackle these works instrumentally, but in the event the Purcell Quartet make a less attractive case for them than either of their competitors. Their relaxed playing is musical enough but is curiously lacking in sparkle and intensity.

Trio Sonatas Nos. 1–6, BWV 525–30 (arr. for 2 Lautenwerke).

*** Lyr. LEMS 8045. Leopard, Paul.

Shawn Leopard and John Paul make a good case for performing these works on a pair of keyboard instruments, modern reconstructions made following an eighteenth-century specification by Jacob Adlung. They were both built by Anden Houben, using gut strings, primarily double-strung. The one with a single keyboard is slightly brighter than its companion with a double keyboard, and their sound has something in common with both the lute and the clavichord, although with greater amplitude. (Both are pictured on the CD insert).

The performances here are highly musical and fluent and very well recorded, not too forwardly and in a very pleasing acoustic. The intimate result certainly bears out Carragan's contention that the counterpoint is cleaner and more audible than when the music is heard on the organ. A thoroughly worthwhile issue for the special Bach year which includes a

fascinating essay by Anden Houben on the problems of building these instruments.

Viola da gamba Sonatas Nos. 1–3, BWV 1027–9.

(N) (M) *** Alia Vox AV 9812. Savall, Koopman (with *Sonata in C, BWV 529*).

(M) *** Häns. CD 92.124. Peri (viola da gamba), Behringer (harpsichord).

*** DG 415 471-2. Maisky (cello), Argerich (piano).

*** Sony MK 37794. Ma (cello), Cooper (harpsichord).

(i) *Viola da gamba Sonatas Nos. 1–3. Preludes & Fugues: in D, BWV 850; in G, BWV 860; in G min., BWV 861.*

*** Signum SIGCD 024. (i) Crum (viola da gamba); Cummings (harpsichord).

Jordi Savall and Ton Koopman's new set completely supersedes their earlier performance on Virgin. There is a depth of expressive feeling here combined with an intimate rapport between the two players that gives an effect of eavesdropping on live music-making of the highest calibre. The recording is resonant but full, firm and cleanly focused. A clear first choice.

A fine alternative set comes from Alison Crum and Laurence Cummings. Here the harpsichord is very much in the picture, boldly played, with plenty of life and vigour, by Cummings. But Crum's firmly focused gamba is never eclipsed. Moreover, Cummings offers sparkling performances of three keyboard *Preludes and Fugues* as a bonus.

The performances on Hänssler are also warmly sympathetic and alive. Hilde Peri's tone is full – not edgy – and the balance with Michael Behringer's excellently articulated harpsichord-playing is good, the harpsichord a shade backward but still coming through in a warm but not clouding acoustic. A good mid-price alternative.

Mischa Maisky is a highly expressive cellist and he opts for the piano – successfully, for Martha Argerich is a Bach player of the first order. In fact the sonority of the cello and the modern piano seems a happier marriage than the compromise Ma and Cooper adopt.

Yo-Yo Ma plays with great eloquence and natural feeling. His tone is warm and refined and his technical command remains, as ever, irreproachable. Kenneth Cooper is a splendid partner.

(Unaccompanied) *Violin Sonatas Nos. 1–3, BWV 1001, 1003 & 1005; Violin Partitas Nos. 1–3, BWV 1002, 1004 & 1006.*

🏵 *** EMI CDS7 49483-2 (2). Perlman.

(M) *** DG (ADD) 457 701-2 (2). Milstein.

(M) (***) EMI mono EMI CHS5 67197-2 (2). Menuhin.

*** Testament SBT 2090 (2). Haendel.

(B) *** Ph. (ADD) Duo 438 736-2 (2). Grumiaux.

(B) *** DG (ADD) Double 453 004-2 (2). Szeryng.

(M) (***) Sony mono MP2K 46721 (2). Szeryng.

(B) **(*) EMI (ADD) double forte CZS5 73644-2 (2). Suk.

**(*) Channel CCS 12198 & 14498. Podger.

(BB) ** Arte Nova 74321 67501-2 (2). Gähler (Bach bow).

The range of tone in Perlman's playing adds to the power of these performances, infectiously rhythmic in dance movements but conveying the intensity of live performance in the great slow movements in hushed playing of great refinement. Some may still seek a greater sense of struggle conveyed in order to bring out the full depth of the writing, but the sense of spontaneity, of the player's own enjoyment of the music, makes this set a unique, revelatory experience.

Milstein's set from the mid-1970s remains among the most satisfying of all versions. Every phrase is beautifully shaped, there is a highly developed feeling for line, and these performances have an aristocratic poise and a classical finesse which are very satisfying.

It was the eighteen-year-old Yehudi Menuhin to whom (between 1934 and 1936) HMV entrusted the very first complete recording of the *Unaccompanied Sonatas* and *Partitas* and the young musician's remarkable accomplishment more than repaid the company's faith in him. The great *Chaconne* from BWV 1004 is one of most thrilling performances ever put on disc. Elsewhere, the rich, vibrant tone and direct approach (with no swooning or lingering) must have astonished listeners of the time. The microphone is obviously very close, but the secure bowing can take such a scrutiny: the violin image is a little dry, yet is remarkably real and immediate.

Though Ida Haendel's speeds are exceptionally broad, her playing is magnetic, making one welcome her decision to observe all repeats. She takes a full 18 minutes over the great *Chaconne* of the *D minor Partita* but the strong, steady pacing means that the build-up is all the more powerful, with counterpoint clearly defined, helped by vividly immediate recording.

Arthur Grumiaux strikes just the right balance between expressive feeling and purity of style. Some may prefer a rhythmically freer, more charismatic approach, but Grumiaux's readings of all six works are the product of superlative technique and a refined musical intellect.

Henryk Szeryng's tone has never before been caught on record with such leonine fullness and beauty. The technical mastery and polish are quite remarkable, his intonation flawless. These performances are rhythmically free and full of subtle touches.

Szeryng's earlier set was recorded in mono in the mid-1960s. The recording is equally real and present and the performances are just as fresh, never identical but following the same general pattern of interpretation; yet when one comes to the famous *Chaconne* of the *D minor Partita* there is no question that the earlier account is seemingly more spontaneous.

Josef Suk is a superb artist – but his playing, although technically immaculate, is curiously self-conscious. There seems a tendency to over-inflate the music with broad tempi, and these are not the searching performances one expects in this repertoire.

Rachel Podger uses a period instrument, but her technique and intonation are secure, her tone is full and clean without scratchiness or edge. Only in slow movements is there a minor reservation about the linear style, with moments of minor tonal swelling slightly disturbing the phrasing. There is much to praise in this artist's simplicity of approach, and she is beautifully recorded, but in the last resort this cannot quite compete with the very finest versions.

Playing with a curved bow, Rudolf Gähler easily solves the problem of how to play the many chords in this greatest of all unaccompanied violin music. Gähler attacks the notes simultaneously, making them genuine chords. He opts for a modern-style instrument, used with a fair degree of vibrato. His intonation is firm and true, which adds to the beauty of the performance. Interpretatively he takes a direct view, avoiding expressive mannerisms. But his heavy accenting and bold, continuously full timbre (sounding almost like a pair of unison instruments) are unable to offer enough subtlety of dynamic or variety of tone for these performances to be really satisfying.

Monica Huggett plays her period instrument with skill and accuracy but fails to communicate the inner world of this music. The result is curiously literal and uninvolving (Virgin VCD5 45205-2).

Sitkovetsky has a beautiful tone and his polished fluency is technically and musically admirable. But everything is too easy-going, there is no sense of grip, of difficulties being surmounted, of a strong forward pulse (Hänssler 92.119).

(Unaccompanied) *Violin Sonatas Nos. 1–3; Violin Partitas Nos. 1–3; (i) Violin Sonatas Nos. 3–4, BWV 1016–17.*

(N)(M) ******(*) Ph. (ADD) 464 673-2 (2). Grumiaux ; (i) with Sartori (harpsichord).

Grumiaux's set of the solo *Sonatas* and *Partitas* are available economically on a Philips Duo (see above). His musical authority and purity of intonation impress every bit as much as they did in 1960 when they were made, and the sound has a striking realism. There is an aristocratic quality to Grumiaux's playing as well as a natural unforced vitality, Here these performances are offered as one of Philips's '50 Great Recordings' at mid-price with two of the *Sonatas for Violin and Harpsichord* thrown in for good measure. But these were Grumiaux's earlier recordings with Egida Giordani Sartori, which, though his own playing is peerless, were less spontaneous in effect than his later set with Jaccottet (see below).

(Unaccompanied) *Violin Sonatas Nos. 1–3; Violin Partitas Nos. 1–3; (i; ii) Violin Sonata No. 3, BWV 1016 (2 versions).*

(N)(BB) **(***)** Naxos mono 8.110918 & 8.110964. Y. Menuhin with alternatively H. Menuhin or Landowska).

Menuhin's early recordings of the solo *Violin Sonatas* and *Partitas* are also available on Naxos. Ward Marston's transfers are expert, but the sound is not quite so smooth as that transferred by the EMI engineers (who had access to the original masters), and there is slightly more background noise. However the inclusion of Menuhin's two recordings made in 1938 and 1944 respectively, of the *E major Violin and Harpsichord Sonata* makes a fascinating comparison, the performance with Landowska's harpsichord slower and heavier in style (especially the *Adagio*) than the fresher version with his sister Hepzihbah on the piano.

(Unaccompanied) *Violin Partitas Nos. 2, BWV 1004 (complete); 3 (Minuets I & II only), BWV 1006; Violin Sonatas Nos. 1, BWV 1001; 3, BWV 1005 (complete);*

(i) *English Suite No. 3 in E, BWV 808: Sarabande; Gavottes Nos. I & II.*

(M) (***) EMI mono CDH7 64494-2. Heifetz, (i) with Sándor.

Heifetz's Bach was by no means romantic, but his chimerical bowing produces more variety of timbre and subtlety of dynamic shading than would have been likely or possible in Bach's time, while the great *Chaconne* has wonderful detail without losing strength. Such is the spontaneity of effect that the result gives enormous pleasure. The transfer is bright but truthful.

Violin Sonatas (for violin & harpsichord) *Nos. 1–6, BWV 1014–19.*

(N) *** Naxos 8.554614 (Nos. 1–4); 8.554783 (Nos. 5–6 & alternative movements for BWV 1019). Van Dael, Van Asperen.

(N) *** Opus OPS 30-127/8. Biondi, Alessandrini.

Violin Sonatas Nos. 1–6, BWV 1014–19; 1019a; Sonatas for Violin & Continuo, BWV 1020–24.

❀ (B) *** Ph. (ADD) Duo 454 011-2 (2). Grumiaux, Jaccottet, Mermoud (in BWV 1021 & 1023).

Violin Sonatas (for violin and harpsichord) *Nos. 1–6, BWV 1014–19; Sonatas for Violin & Continuo, BWV 1021, 1023 & 1024; Fugue in G min., BWV 1021.*

(M) **(*) Hyp. Dyad CDD 22025 (2). Huggett, Nicholson.

Violin & Harpsichord Sonatas Nos. 1–6, BWV 1014–19; (i) *Sonatas for Violin & Continuo, BWV 1021 & BWV 1023.*

*** Chan. 0603 (2). Mackintosh, Cole; (i) with Ward Clarke.

(BB) **(*) Virgin VBD5 61650-2 (2) [id]. Holloway, Moroney, Sheppard.

Violin Sonatas (for violin & harpsichord); *Nos. 1–6, BWV 1014–19; 1019a; Cantabile from 1019a* (2nd version); *Sonatas for Violin & Continuo, BWV 1021 & 1023.*

(N) *** Channel Classics CCS 14798 (2). Podger, Pinnock; (with Manson in BWV 1021 & 1023).

Violin Sonatas (for violin and harpsichord) *Nos. 1–6, BWV 1014–19, with alternative version of BWV 1019; Sonatas for Violin & Continuo, BWV 1021, 1023 & 1024; Toccata & Fugue in D min., BWV 565* (arr. Manze for solo violin).

**(*) HM HMU 907250.51 (2). Manze, Egarr, Ter Linden.

The Bach *Sonatas for Violin and Harpsichord* and for *Violin and Continuo* are marvellously played, with all the beauty of tone and line for which Grumiaux is renowned; they have great vitality, too. His admirable partner is Christiane Jaccottet, and in BWV 1021 and 1023 Philippe Mermoud (cello) joins the continuo. There is endless treasure to be discovered here, particularly when the music-making is so serenely communicative.

Catherine Mackintosh uses a baroque violin, but her timbre is full, her lyrical line flows with an affecting sensitivity. Articulation in allegros is exhilaratingly crisp and clean, and both players express their joy in the music. Maggie Cole's persuasive contribution is well in the picture, and the balance between violin and double-manual harpsichord could hardly be managed more adroitly. In Bach's two *Sonatas for Violin and Continuo* Jennifer Ward Clarke's cello contribution adds to the interest and sonority of the music. Our special allegiance to the Grumiaux performances of the same music on modern instruments remains undiminished, and their Philips Duo costs half as much as the Chandos set. But these new interpretations are very stimulating.

Two fine new period-instrument versions also go to the top of the list, one from Naxos, the other from Opus. They are both beautifully played and recorded, the balance of Fabio Biondi and Rinaldo Alessandrini rather more forward, which gives Biondi a slightly bolder profile and a touch more edge to his rather fuller timbre. Both violinists have equally positive relationships with their distinguished keyboard partners In the opening *Adagio* of the very first sonata Lucy van Dael and Bob van Asperen are slower, more reflective than their rivals, and again in the *Dolce* which opens BWV 1015 Van Dael, with her gentler timbre, is very beguiling. Yet it is a case of swings and roundabouts, for Biondi is especially appealing in his phrasing of the *Andante* of BWV 1015 and in the finale his brisk momentum is exhilarating (he despatches this *Presto* in 3'49 against Van Dael's 4'33). Both partnerships play the seraphic opening *Largo* of BWV 1018 very beautifully, but here Biondi is more extrovert and ardent, Van Deal characteristically contemplative. Each of these sets gives very great pleasure and satisfaction, but the second Naxos disc scores by including four alternative movements for BWV 1019, including a memorable B minor *Adagio*, heard against a chromatic descending bass line, and a jolly *Gavotte* (which also appears in the *Sixth Partita* in the first part of Bach's *Clavierübung*).

On the Hyperion Dyad, Monica Huggett often plays exquisitely, as she does in the opening *Dolce* of *No. 2 in A major.* Clearly these marvellous works strike a chord in her sensibility, and she also gives a remarkably spirited display of bravura. One simply has to come to terms with her characteristic timbre, with its thinness (some would say edginess) on top. Yet in the dancing allegros she brings out all the music's joy. The violin is beautifully balanced with Paul Nicholson's sensitive harpsichord backing, and where appropriate, Richard Tunnicliffe's busy cello.

The performances by Rachel Podger and Trevor Pinnock also carry the highest recommendation, even though the balance places the violin a fraction too near the microphones. This is immediately noticeable with the brightness of timbre of the opening allegro of BWV 1019, which begins the first disc and may trouble some ears. A period violin playing forte in its upper range needs no spotlight, and although the balance is excellent in the quieter slow movements, in some of the livelier movements the harpsichord detail is slightly masked by the violin, which is a pity for Trevor Pinnock's contribution is very distinguished. So too is the playing of Rachel Podger, always very stylish and warmly phrased. While BWV 1022 and 1024 are omitted, the inclusion of the fine extended *Cantabile* which Bach added to BWV 1019 in 1725 is a distinct asset. Apart from the balance, the recording acoustic is pleasing, but this set should be sampled before purchase.

Andrew Manze is nothing if not individual. Fast movements sparkle vivaciously. Slow movements are often played *sotto voce*, creating a withdrawn, almost unearthly sense of repose which is perhaps not quite what Bach intended, but is still very affecting. The balance with the harpsichord or continuo is excellent, yet it is Manze who dominates. For some reason a gamba is also added to the first, B minor Sonata, BWV 1014, and it is curiously intrusive. But the highlight of the collection is Manze's breathtaking paraphrase for solo violin of Bach's famous organ Toccata and Fugue in D minor, BWV 565. Here Manze's timbre is sweet and full, whereas elsewhere at times it seems unnecessarily meagre, with touches of edginess.

John Holloway too has long experience in the early-music field. His undoubted sensitivity, ability and good taste have won him a wide following, but some will find the actual sound he makes unpleasing: it is vinegary and at times downright ugly. Both Davitt Moroney and Susan Sheppard give excellent support, and the recording cannot be faulted in its clarity and presence.

As in his set of the Solo Violin Sonatas and Partitas, Sitkovetsky plays with great fluency and finish. But his use of vibrato and indulgently relaxed, lyrical manner are out of style. Robert Hill gives him fine support, but this cannot compete with Grumiaux (Hänssler 92.122).

KEYBOARD MUSIC

The Art of Fugue, BWV 1080; (i) A Musical Offering, BWV 1079; The Well-Tempered Clavier (48 Preludes & Fugues), BWV 846–93.

(M) *** HM HMX 2908084/90. Moroney (harpsichord);
    (i) with Cook, See, Holloway, Ter Linden.

If you want all these works played on the harpsichord, and that a modern instrument built in 1980, this Harmonia Mundi mid-priced box is worth considering, for Davitt Moroney has imagination as well as scholarship. His Art of Fugue commands not only the intellectual side of the work but also the aesthetic; his musicianship is second to none, and he is eminently well served by the engineers. The Musical Offering is also very much dominated by one or two harpsichords, although Moroney is joined by flute and violin in the trio sonata and the violin also shares the second of the six regal canons. Again the recording is well balanced and natural. In the Well-Tempered Clavier the balance is rather close, the harpsichord image full-bodied and clear. Moroney's considered approach is satisfying in its way. Stylistically, it will suit those who like a thoughtful, unostentatious approach to Bach, yet one that does not lack rhythmic resilience or vitality.

The Art of Fugue, BWV 1080 (see also string quartet and orchestral versions).

*** Häns CD 92.134 (2). Hill (harpsichord).
*** HM (ADD) HMC 901169/70. Moroney (harpsichord).
*** MusicMasters 1612 67173-2. Feltsman.

The Art of Fugue, BWV 1080; Partita No. 2 in C min., BWV 826.

(N) (M) **(*) OPS 52-9116/17. Sokolov (piano).

Robert Hill lays out Bach's fugal progression in front of the listener with admirable clarity and concern for the contra-

puntal detail, and he varies tempi with excellent judgement to keep the music continually alive. In the Duet Fugue he is joined by Michael Behringer. As an appendix he offers four contrapuncti and the Augmented Canon in Contrary Motion from Bach's early draft (BWV 1080a). The harpsichord itself has a fine, strong personality and is recorded in a warm acoustic which yet never blurs the interplay of the part-writing.

Davitt Moroney's account commands not only the intellectual side of the work but also the aesthetic, and his musicianship is second to none.

Although he begins gently, Vladimir Feltsman's articulation is at times bold, although it is never hard-edged. He intersperses the canons individually within the body of the work and makes the very most of dynamic contrast. Yet he can be thoughtfully meditative. Feltsman's interpretation is well thought out and thoroughly convincing. He is very well recorded but offers no coupling.

Sokolov's Art of Fugue is entirely pianistic. He is neither pedgogic nor didactic, but his linear clarity is admirable. He uses a wide range of dynamic and one can hear the fullest polyphonic detail, yet the music's underlying expressive character emerges readily. The nineteen Contrapuncti are played in order, ending – at the beginning of the second disc – with the unfinished No. 19, presented very slowly. He then groups the Canons together and closes the work with a deliberate rallentando. The C minor Partita makes a lively and characterful encore.

The Art of Fugue, BWV 1080 (version for two harpsichords).

(M) *** Erato 0630 16173-2. Koopman, Mathot (harpsichords).

Ton Koopman chooses a pair of instruments made by Willem Kroesbergen of Utrecht, himself leading with a copy of a Rückers, while his colleague, Tini Mathot, uses another modern copy, but of a Couchet. The partnership works well: pacing is well judged and contrapuntal detail is clear, yet within a not too dry acoustic. The approach is didactic, but by no means rigid.

(i) The Art of Fugue, BWV 1080; (ii) Applicato in C, BWV 994; Aria & 10 Variations in the Italian Style; Chorale: Joy and Peace, BWV 512; Fantasia in G min., BWV 917; Invention in C, BWV 772 & 772a (1720 & 1723 versions); Italian Concerto, BWV 971; Marches: in D & E flat, BWV Anh. 122 & 127; Musette in D, BWV Anh. 126; 2 Minuets in G, BWV Anh. 115–16; Polonaise in F, BWV Anh. 117a; Prelude & Fugue in A min., BWV 895; Suite in F, BWV 623 (incomplete). (TELEMANN): Suite in A, BWV 824 (wrongly attributed to J. S. B.).

(B) *** Sony Dig./ADD SB2K 63231. (i) Rosen; (ii) Tureck (piano).

Charles Rosen's superb account of The Art of Fugue is one of the great achievements of Bach keyboard recording. Rosen justifies his choice of a modern piano by his manner of playing, neutralizing any unwanted romantic overtones. The authority of his performance is remarkable and the depth of thought that lies behind the playing creates a satisfying sense of architecture. The 1967 recording is firm and clear, just right for such an exposition, and this performance has total mastery.

Tureck makes a perfect foil for Rosen in offering an essentially lightweight programme, mainly of short keyboard vignettes in which we can hear Bach relaxing and enjoying himself. One of the highlights of the recital is the *Aria in the Italian Style*, followed by ten crisply diverting variations. Tureck's playing not only shows the utmost felicity but also sensitive control of dynamic contrast. The 1981 digital recording is rather forward but not shallow; the *Italian Concerto* dates from 1979 and the sound is more clattery, less well focused. But this set is not to be missed by anyone who enjoys hearing Bach on the piano, and it is a great bargain.

Capriccio in E in Honour of Johann Christoph Bach, BWV 993; Capriccio on the Departure of a Beloved Brother, BWV 992; Chromatic Fantasia & Fugue, BWV 903; Fantasia & Fugues: in A min., BWV 944; in C min., BWV 906; Fantasias: in A min., BWV 922; in G min., BWV 917; Fantasia on a Rondeau in C min., BWV 918; Prelude in C min., BWV 921; Fantasia & Fugue in A min., BWV 944; Fugue on a Theme in A on a Theme of Albinoni, BWV 950; Prelude & Fugue on a Theme by Albinoni, BWV 923/951.

(N) *** BIS CD 1037. Suzuki (harpsichord).

Suzuki uses a modern Dutch copy after an enlarged 2-manual Ruckers harpsichord to spectacular effect. He opens with a dazzling bravura account of the *Chromatic fantasia*, and is equally impressive later in his brilliant articulation of the Albinoni *Prelude* and the engaging *C minor Prelude*, BWV 921 (which is marked *Harpeggiando – Prestissimo*). Yet the fugues are given aptly judged tempi, never rushed. The two *Capriccii*, both dedicated to Bach's brothers, are delightfully presented and the illustrative detail of BWV 992 genially realised, while BWV 993 is a lively but light-hearted *Toccata*. The rest of this varied programme is played with comparable flair and all of it is very well recorded. In short this is a very winning and often exciting collection, and if you are looking for keyboard virtuosity you won't be disappointed here.

Chromatic Fantasia & Fugue, BWV 903; 4 Duets, BWV 802–5; English Suites Nos. 1–6, BWV 806–11; Goldberg Variations, BWV 988; 2- & 3-Part Inventions, BWV 772a–786; French Suites Nos. 1–6, BWV 812–17; Partitas Nos. 1–6, BWV 825–30; Partita in B min., BWV 831; Well-Tempered Clavier, Books I–II, Preludes & Fugues Nos. 1–48, BWV 846–93.

(B) *** Decca 452 279-2 (12). Schiff (piano).

András Schiff recorded Bach's major keyboard works for Decca over a decade between 1982 and 1991. He makes no apologies for the range of dynamic and colour that the modern keyboard can command and of which Bach can have had no inkling. Yet Schiff's playing is so stylish, his expressive phrasing and rubato so natural, the presentation so spontaneous, that the critical listener is disarmed and is encouraged to sit back and simply enjoy the music. The Decca recording, natural and not too resonant, is surely ideal for such repertoire.

Chromatic Fantasia & Fugue, BWV 903; Goldberg Variations, BWV 988; Italian Concerto, BWV 971; Partita No. 1 in B flat, BWV 825; Prelude, Fugue & Allegro, BWV 998; Toccata, Adagio & Fugue, BWV 916.

(BB) *** Virgin 2 x 1 VBD5 61555-2 (2). Cole (harpsichord).

Maggie Cole plays the *Goldberg Variations* on a copy by Andrew Warlick of a harpsichord by J. C. Goujon of 1749. She is recorded with great clarity; as so often, the playback level needs to be reduced if a truthful and realistic effect is to be made. Her playing is completely straightforward and she holds the listener's interest throughout. The remaining items make up her first solo recital, and very good it is too. She uses a Rückers harpsichord of 1612 from the Royal Collection, tuned in unequal temperament. Again her playing is splendidly unfussy, free from interpretative mannerisms and not bound by rigid rhythms; her virtuosity in the *Chromatic Fantasia & Fugue* seems effortless and unforced, and there is an agreeable naturalness about the whole recital. The recording is thoroughly faithful and the acoustic lively, if small.

Chromatic Fantasia & Fugue in D min., BWV 903; 4 Duets, BWV 802–5; Italian Concerto in F, BWV 971; Partita in B min., BWV 831.

✪ *** O-L 433 054-2. Rousset (harpsichord).

(N)(BB) **(*) Warner Apex 8573 89224-2. Ross (harpsichord).

Christophe Rousset's playing combines the selfless authority and scholarly dedication of such artists as Leonhardt and Gilbert with the flair and imagination of younger players, and all the performances here have a taste and musical vitality that reward the listener.

Scott Ross's account of the Chromatic Fantasia has less flair than Rousset's. Some may respond to its breadth, emphasized by the full-bodied resonant harpsichord image. These are undoubtedly fine performances, considered, in excellent style, but at times seemingly a little didactic. They are rewarding, but not a first choice in this repertoire, even at budget price.

Concertos (for solo harpsichord) after Vivaldi, Nos. 1 in D (after Op. 3/9), BWV 972; 2 in C (after Op. 7/2), BWV 973; 4 in G min. (after Op. 4/6), BWV 975; 5 in C (after Op. 3/12), BWV 976; 7 in F (after Op. 3/3), BWV 978; 9 in G (after Op. 4/1), BWV 980; Italian Concerto, BWV 971.

✪ *** Erato 3984 25504-2. Baumont (harpsichord).

In Olivier Baumont's hands, Bach's transcriptions sound splendid on the harpsichord, full of vitality and vividly coloured. Baumont plays a modern French copy of a German harpsichord 'from the School of Silbermann' of 1735, and it has a particularly effective range of dynamic. The *Italian Concerto* is offered as an encore, and how eloquently Baumont plays the slow movement. This collection is very enjoyable indeed.

English Suites Nos. 1–6, BWV 806–11.

*** Sony SK 60276 (*Nos. 1, 3 & 6*); SK 60277 (*Nos. 2, 4 & 5*). Perahia (piano).

*** Decca 421 640-2 (2). Schiff (piano).

(B) *** Sony (ADD) S2BK 62949. Leonhardt (harpsichord).

As can be seen, Murray Perahia recorded the *English Suites* in two groups, a year apart, in La Chaux-de-Fonds, Switzerland, in July 1997 and 1998. In his hands the forward flow is a living thing in itself, and the listener is always made conscious of the richness of the underlying harmony, especially in the *Sarabandes*, which are played very beautifully indeed. The lighter dance movements have a refreshing lightness of articulation, with the decoration made to seem integral. Perahia's mastery is such that, while this is personalized Bach, using a full range of pianistic colour with a disarming naturalness, there is never any suggestion of self-awareness.

Schiff is straightforward, finely articulated, rhythmically supple and vital. Ornamentation is stylishly and sensibly observed. Everything is very alive, without being in the least over-projected or exaggerated in any way. The Decca recording is altogether natural and present.

Leonhardt uses a Skrowroneck harpsichord, vividly recorded, and if the volume level is set back a little the effect is very convincing. Leonhardt combines scholarship and artistry. The music flows freshly and expansively, even if he is not equally inspired in every movement. He is inconsistent in the matter of repeats, sometimes observing them throughout, sometimes not. But this is well worth its modest price.

English Suites Nos. 1–6, BWV 806–11; French Suites Nos. 1–6, BWV 812–17; Partitas Nos. 1–6, BWV 825–30.

(M) *** HM (ADD) HMX 2908078.83 (6). Gilbert (harpsichord).

In the *English Suites* and *Partitas*, Kenneth Gilbert uses a Couchet-Taskin of 1788 and is given first-class recording. In the *French Suites* he uses a 1636 Rückers, rebuilt by Hemsch, and again the engineering is well judged so that the effect is clear and robust, the balance forward but not excessively so. Gilbert's playing in the *English* and *French Suites* has a fine sense of style, the rubato flowing naturally and never self-conscious. He is inconsistent in the matter of repeats in the former, but that will not worry most collectors. Tempi are well judged, ornamentation is discreet, and there is no doubting the excellence of these performances which, in terms of scholarship and artistry, have much to recommend them. Overall this box is good value.

French Suites Nos. 1–6, BWV 812–17.

*** Erato 0630 16172-2. Koopman (harpsichord).

*** DG 445 840-2. Gavrilov (piano).

(B) **(*) Sony (ADD) SBK 60717. Leonhardt (harpsichord).

French Suites Nos. 1–6, BWV 812–17 (including 3 additional movements); 18 Little Preludes, BWV 924–8; 930; 933–43; 999; Prelude & Fugue in A min., BWV 894; Sonata in D min., BWV 964.

*** Hyp. CDA 67121/2. Hewitt (piano).

French Suites Nos. 1–6; Italian Concerto in F, BWV 971; Partita in B min., BWV 831.

*** Decca 433 313-2 (2). Schiff (piano).

(i) *French Suites Nos. 1–6*; (ii) *English Suite No. 3 in G min., BWV 808; Italian Concerto in F, BWV 971.*

(B) **(*) EMI double forte CZS5 69479-2 (2). (i) Gavrilov (piano); (ii) Bunin (piano).

French Suites Nos. 1–6, BWV 812–17; Suites in A min., BWV 818a; in E flat, BWV 819a.

(BB) *** Virgin 2 x 1 VBD5 61653-2 (2). Moroney (harpsichord).

(B) *** Double Decca 466 736-2 (2). Hogwood (with *Allemande, BWV 819a*).

Like Hogwood before him, Davitt Moroney plays two further suites, which are almost certainly authentic as they were included in a manuscript copy of the complete set made by Bach's pupil, Heinrich Nikolas Gerber, in 1725. For good measure Moroney also adds a recently discovered second *Gavotte* belonging to the original version of the *Suite No. 4 in E flat*. On artistic grounds too, these performances are very highly recommendable. Ornamentation may be individual, as is the addition of little *galanteries*, but the expressive content (notably in the *Sarabandes*) and the flexible spontaneity of his playing continually communicate a sense of 'live' music-making. Pacing is admirable and all repeats are included. He plays a modern harpsichord by John Phillips after Rückers/Taskin, and the recording gives him a nice presence in a well-judged acoustic. It is a pity that the accompanying notes have been truncated, but in all other respects the present reissue makes a splendid bargain.

Christopher Hogwood uses two harpsichords, a Rückers of 1646, enlarged and modified by Taskin in 1780, and a 1749 instrument, basically the work of Jean-Jacques Goujon and slightly modified by Jacques Joachim Swanen in 1784. They are magnificent creatures and Hogwood coaxes superb sounds from them: his playing is expressive, and the relentless sense of onward momentum that disfigures so many harpsichordists (though not Moroney) is pleasingly absent. These performances have both style and character and can be recommended with some enthusiasm alongside Davitt Moroney; however, the Virgin set has the advantage of a modest price.

András Schiff gives highly rewarding performances of just Nos. 1–6, his expressive style entirely without personal indulgence, his freedom in slow movements seemingly improvisatory and spontaneous, and his faster dance movements an unqualified delight. The *Partita in B minor* is slightly more severe in style than the rest of the programme. As with the rest of his series, the Decca recording is appealingly realistic and an ideal acoustic has been chosen.

Ton Koopman fits the six best-known *French Suites* on to a single 70-minute CD. He uses a copy of a Rückers to admirable effect, and these performances are stimulatingly rhythmic, exciting and thoughtful by turns. The *Fifth Suite* is especially spontaneous. The effect of the recording – not too closely balanced – is vivid and realistic. Ornaments are nicely handled and there is not a trace of pedantry here. A first choice for those not wanting the extra suites offered by Hogwood.

On DG, Andrei Gavrilov conveys the enormous inner vitality of these suites and makes this music vibrant. Such is the conviction he conveys that, while he is playing, one feels there is no other way to play this music and no other instrument to play it on. Very good sound.

Angela Hewitt's playing is informed by an intelligence and musicianship that are refreshing. Whether in the *Preludes*, written for Wilhelm Friedemann, or the suites themselves, she displays an imaginative vitality of a high order. The recorded sound is very natural.

Leonhardt uses a Rubio, modelled on a Taskin, and it sounds well, the recording only a shade close. The playing is generally flexible; perhaps the rhythmic French style is over-assertive at times, but the livelier dance-movements, like the famous *Gavotte* in BWV 816, have plenty of character. Good value at bargain price, but not a primary choice.

Gavrilov's earlier 1984 set of the *French Suites* is full of interesting things, and there is some sophisticated (not to say masterly) pianism. There is an element of the self-conscious here, but there is also much that is felicitous. To fill up the pair of discs, Stanislav Bunin's performances of the *Third English Suite* and the *Italian Concerto*, recorded six years later, have been added. His style is bold and direct, less flexible than Gavrilov's approach but totally unselfconscious. Both artists receive excellent recording.

Goldberg Variations, BWV 988.

*** O-L 444 866-2. Rousset (harpsichord).

*** Hyp. CDA 67305. Hewitt (piano).

(M) *** Penguin/Decca 466 214-2. Schiff (piano).

❀ *** VAI (ADD) VAIA 1029. Tureck (piano).

(N) *** Sony SK 89243. Perahia (piano).

*** DG (ADD) (IMS) 415 130-2. Pinnock (harpsichord).

*** Häns. CD 92.112 (2). Koroliov (piano).

(B) *** HMA 1951240. Gilbert (harpsichord).

(M) *** DG Double 459 599-2. Tureck (piano).

(M) *** DG 439 978-2. Kempff (piano).

(N) **(*) Opus OPS 30-84. Hantal (harpsichord).

(N) **(*) Delos DE 3279. Vínikour (harpsichord).

(M) *(**) Sony (ADD) SMK 64126. Gould (piano).

Goldberg Variations, BWV 988; Chromatic Fantasia & Fugue in D min., BWV 903; Italian Concerto, BWV 971.

(M) (**(*)) EMI mono CDH5 67200-2. Landowska (harpsichord).

Goldberg Variations, BWV 988; Fantasia in C min., BWV 906; Fantasia & Fugue in F min., BWV 904; Italian Concerto, BWV 971.

(M) **(*) DG 439 465-2. Kirkpatrick (harpsichord).

Goldberg Variations; Fughetta in C min., BWV 961; Preludes & Fugues: in A min., BWV 895; D min., BWV 899; E min., BWV 900; F, BWV 901; G, BWV 902.

**(*) Mer. CDA 84291. Cload (piano).

Goldberg Variations; Well-Tempered Clavier: Fugues in E, BWV 878; F sharp min., BWV 883.

(M) (**(*)) Sony mono SMK 52594 (1955 recording). Gould (piano).

Christophe Rousset takes his place fairly easily at the top of the list. He plays a 1751 Hemsch, which is superbly recorded within a generous but not too resonant acoustic, so that the harpsichord is very real and believable. His performance opens with an appealingly thoughtful account of the *Aria*, and the variations which follow are strong in character and

consistently imaginative in presentation. A playing time of 77 minutes ensures that repeats can be fully observed, and the playing has great freshness and spontaneity.

Angela Hewitt's performance is totally pianistic, involving the widest range of dynamic contrast, variety of touch and colour. It is imbued with what she calls 'the joyous tone that is characteristic of so much of this work'. She rightly regards the 'black pearl' Variation 25 as 'the greatest of all' and fully reveals its gentle, celestial beauty. After the bold *Quodlibet*, the return of the *Aria* on a magical half-tone reminds one of Tureck – and there can be no higher praise. The Hyperion recording is first class in every way.

András Schiff's set can also receive the most enthusiastic advocacy. His recording carries the imprimatur of no less an authority than George Malcolm, and Schiff's much-admired dexterity and musicianship will go far in persuading sceptics that this not only can but does give profound satisfaction in the hands of a perceptive artist. The part-writing emerges with splendid definition and subtlety. Schiff performs with a keen sense of enjoyment of the piano's colour and sonority – and devoid of vocal obbligato. The Decca recording is excellent in every way, clean and realistic.

Rosalyn Tureck's recording is very special indeed – there is no other record of Bach played on the piano quite as compelling as this, and for I. M. it would be a desert island disc.

Murray Perahia's set is even more personalised than Rosalyn Tureck's VAI version, essentially thoughtful and intimate, often introvert, even ruminative, but with moments of high drama. Some might prefer a more direct, less individualised approach, but Perahia's involvement and dedication are present in every bar of Bach's music, with continual contrasts of pianistic colour and dynamic, yet always with superbly clean articulation (sample Variation 14 – wonderfully crisp and clear).

In his personal note Perahia tells us that he regards Variations 24 ('a calming pastoral canon') followed by the famous Variation 25, the 'turning point' of Bach's structure. 'The semitonal intensity of this darkly chromatic piece' is presented as a threnody to imply 'a programmatic description of the Crucifixion'. He then sets off very swiftly in Variation 26, with a sense of release 'like a soul in flight' to suggest a 'programmatic analysis of the Resurrection'.

The closing variations are seen as an apotheosis: 'Variation 28 with its very high register and shimmering trills is all transcendence; Variation 29 brings these trills back to earth'; Variation 30 (the *Quodlibet*) brings the climax, and with the restatement of the *Aria*, the 'noble, radiant lines bring the music to rest'. The piano recording is wonderfully true and this performance justly won a *Gramophone* award.

Trevor Pinnock retains repeats in more than half the variations – which seems a good compromise, in that variety is maintained yet there is no necessity for an additional disc. The playing is eminently vital and intelligent, with alert, finely articulated rhythm. The recording is very truthful and vivid.

Evgeni Koroliov opens the *Aria* rather deliberately, but the performance immediately takes wing and his playing spontaneously gathers excitement as he proceeds. Though there is less variety of dynamic than with Hewitt, his splendidly clear articulation is a joy in itself, and the shaping of each individual variation is compelling. The digital dexterity is remarkable. There is also at times some vocalization, but it is less intrusive than Glenn Gould's. The bold style of the pianism is caught by the clear, forward recording.

Kenneth Gilbert uses a recent copy of a Rückers-Taskin, and it makes a very pleasing sound. His is an aristocratic reading: he avoids excessive display and there is a quiet, cultured quality about his playing that is very persuasive. An essentially introspective account, recorded in a rather less lively acoustic than is Pinnock, but he is a thoughtful and thought-provoking player which makes this an excellent bargain recommendation.

Rosalyn Tureck's newest, digital version of the *Goldberg* is overflowing with her characteristic insights and is beautifully recorded. She has spread herself to two CDs to include repeats; each disc plays for about 45 minutes, but the two are offered for the price of one. The key to this latest reading is her statement, printed inside the jewel case: 'I play as a life experience'. But her earlier stereo version has a sense of being carried along and aloft by Bach's musical inspiration, with quicksilver fluidity, so that detail is observed *en passant* rather than being deliberated upon.

Wanda Landowska (in 1933) not only rediscovered and reintroduced Bach's complete *Goldberg Variations* to the European musical public, but soon afterwards made its first recording, and this is it. She plays a large two-manual Pleyel and at times gives it a grand presence, but for the most part her playing is quite restrained, delicate in nuance, and often thoughtfully expressive. At other times her virtuosity is very compelling. One must remember that she had to choose her own tempi, for there was no precedent. She is not only convincing but also leads the ear forward most spontaneously. The *Italian Concerto* is understandably more robust, while the *Chromatic Fantasia* shows just how fleet her fingers could be. The remastered recording sounds very well indeed, although the problem of slight 'wow' on sustained passages is not solved. But one readily adjusts when the playing is so magnetic.

Kempff's version is not for purists, but it has a special magic of its own. Ornaments are ignored altogether in the outlining of the theme and the instances of anachronisms of style are too numerous to mention. Yet for all that, the sheer musicianship exhibited by this great artist fascinates and his playing is consistently refreshing. The 1969 recording is very natural.

Pierre Hantal studied with Gustav Leonhardt, so his credentials are impressive. His account of the *Goldberg Variations* has received much praise: 'a happy conjunction of heart and mind' suggested the review in *Gramophone*. The playing is certainly infectiously buoyant and full of life, but his direct manner of presentation and reprise of the *Aria* is borne out by his response to the *'Black Pearl' Adagio*, where we feel more expressive flexibility would have been in order. His harpsichord, a Dutch copy of an early eighteenth-century Mietke, is a fine instrument and splendidly recorded.

Jory Vínikour uses an American copy of a 1624 Ruckers, which is recorded clearly and cleanly in an attractive acoustic. His playing is alive and has plenty of character; ornamentation is judiciously judged. His inclusion of repeats and choice of tempi means this performance, at 85 minutes 39 seconds, runs to a second disc, but the two are offered for the cost of one. There is no doubt of the calibre of this playing, but there are a few idiosyncrasies and moments of thoughtful deliberation (Variation 16 for instance) which do not carry the music forward as strongly as with some performances.

Glenn Gould's stereo version of the *Goldberg Variations* was one of the last records he made. In his earlier record he made no repeats; now he repeats a section of almost half of them and also joins some pairs together (6 with 7 and 9 with 10, for example). Yet, even apart from his vocalise, he does a number of weird things – fierce staccatos, brutal accents, and so on – that inhibit one from suggesting this as a first recommendation even among piano versions. It is certainly a unique version, and with Gould nothing is either dull or predictable. The recording is, as usual with this artist, inclined to be dry and forward, which aids clarity. This also comes on a Super Audio CD for which a special player is required (SS 37779).

Gould's famous (1955) mono recording enjoyed cult status in its day, and its return will occasion rejoicing among his admirers. He observes no repeats and in terms of sheer keyboard wizardry commands admiration, even if you do not respond to the results. There is too much that is wilful and eccentric for this to be a straightforward recommendation, but it is a remarkable performance nevertheless.

Ralph Kirkpatrick is at his best in this work, providing light and subtle registration. The playing is lively when it should be, controlled and steady in the slow, stately, contrapuntal variations. He is a scholarly rather than an intuitive player and his thoughts are rarely without interest. Though not a first choice, this version includes three extra items in which he uses his modern Neupert harpsichord to good effect, while sounding more pedantic, particularly in the *Italian Concerto*.

Julia Cload observes the repeats in the opening *Aria* but not elsewhere; she therefore finds room for the *'Little' Preludes and Fugues*, which she plays appealingly and fluently. Her account of the *Goldberg Variations* is strong and thoughtful, not as inspirational as Tureck's; but some may like its directness of manner. The piano is well recorded, but the ear needs to adjust to the 'empty studio' acoustic.

Andrei Gavrilov is a player of astonishing keyboard prowess and there is much that will prompt admiration for both his integrity and articulation. All the same, he makes heavy weather of some of the variations and is, more importantly, handicapped by a less than glamorous recording. There is not enough space round the sound and the instrument is balanced too closely (DG 463 019-2).

15 2-Part Inventions, BWV 772–86; 15 3-Part Inventions, BWV 787–801.

*** BIS CD 1009. Suzuki (harpsichord).
*** Cap. 10 210 (with *6 Little Preludes, BWV 933–8*). Koopman (harpsichord).
**(*) Decca 411 974-2. Schiff (piano).

15 2-Part Inventions; 15 3-Part Inventions; Ornamented versions: *2-Part Invention No. 1 in C, BWV 772a; 3-Part*

Inventions Nos. 4–5, 7, 9, 11 & 13, BWV 790–91, 793, 795, 797 & 799.

**(*) Astrée E 8603. Verlet (harpsichord).

Masaaki Suzuki plays with perception and skill. These *Inventions* can sound dry, but not in his hands. His response is naturally spontaneous, fresh and alive, never didactic and rigid. Suzuki is one of the finest Bach exponents of our time and he is truthfully recorded.

Ton Koopman scores over rivals in offering the *Six Little Preludes* in addition to the two sets of *Inventions*, and he plays with spontaneity and sparkle.

András Schiff's playing is (for this repertoire) rather generous with rubato and other expressive touches but elegant in the articulation of the part-writing. Such is his musicianship and pianistic sensitivity, however, that the overall results are likely to persuade most listeners. The recording is excellent.

Blandine Verlet uses a 1624 Rückers which seems quite ideal for this repertoire. She plays with great spirit and the imitation between the parts is admirably clear. Her passage-work is never inflexible and, when the writing is comparatively expressive, her minor hesitations in the flow prevent any sense of rigidity; this is more striking in the *Three-Part* pieces. Having played through both sets, she then offers a selection with judicious ornamentation, strikingly effective in the very first of the *Two-Part Inventions*.

Klavierbüchlein for W. F. Bach.

**(*) Häns. CD 92.137-2 (2). Payne (harpsichord, clavichord, organ).

Joseph Payne combines organ, harpsichord and clavichord to survey the 63 miniatures which form Bach's *Klavierbüchlein*. Like the companion notebook for Anna Magdalena, it provides fascinating insights into Bach's composing process for, after a series of engaging musical fragments, Bach features early versions of a number of the *Preludes* from the *Well-Tempered Clavier*, of which the shorter version of the famous *C major Prelude*, BWV 846, is notable. These are presented with pleasing simplicity and vitality. Later a series of *Preambulums* and *Fantasias* turn out to be the *Two-* and *Three-Part Inventions*, and here Payne's linear style is a little fussy. But he is generally a fine advocate. The use of three different instruments introduces an appealing variety of colour.

Partitas Nos. 1–6, BWV 825–30.

*** O-L 440 217-2 (2). Rousset (harpsichord).
(N) ● (B) *** Nimbus 5673/4 . Roberts (piano)
*** Häns. CD 92.115 (2). Pinnock (harpsichord).
*** Hyp. CDA 67191/2. Hewitt (piano).
*** Signum SIGD 012. Carolan (harpsichord).
*** Chan. 0618 (2). Woolley (harpsichord).
*** Decca 411 732-2 (2). Schiff (piano).
(BB) *** Erato (ADD) Ultima 3984 18167-2 (2). Ross (harpsichord).
(M) *** Virgin VED5 61292-2 (2). Leonhardt (harpsichord).

Partitas Nos. 1–6, BWV 825–30; Partita in B min. (Overture in the French Style), BWV 831.

(B) *** Ph. (ADD) (IMS) Duo 442 559-2 (2). Verlet (harpsichord).

Christophe Rousset is an artist who wears his elegance and erudition lightly. The playing has complete naturalness and is obviously the product of a vital musical imagination. This must now be the first recommendation on the harpsichord in this repertoire.

However, the *Partitas* are more often today heard on the piano and the splendid new set from Bernard Roberts shows why. As the opening *Preambulum* of No. 1 immediately demonstrates, his clear clean articulation is a constant joy, and the dance movements are delightfully played. Yet the beautiful extended *Allemande* of No. 4 and the later *Sarabande* have a simple expressive depth which is totally disarming. Throughout, Roberts's playing reveals new facets of these many-faceted works, at times lighthearted but with un underlying profundity that is fully realized here. The Nimbus recording is first class in every way, beautifully focused, with just the right degree of resonance in an ideal acoustic.

Trevor Pinnock has recorded the six *Partitas* before for DG, but this new set is even finer. He uses a superb American copy of a Hemsch made by David Way in Stonington, Connecticut (with a particularly effective mute stop). As before, he plays these works with a keen sense of enjoyment and projects the music with enormous panache. The harpsichord is superbly recorded and given fine presence in a spaciously resonant acoustic, although the sound may seem a fraction over-resonant to some ears. Nevertheless, playing of this calibre is impossible to resist and this can be recommended alongside Rousset.

Those wanting a set on the piano can also safely turn to Angela Hewitt. Her performances are fluent, deeply musical and, while expressively flexible, less personally wayward than Schiff in the *Sarabandes*, which she still plays very sensitively. The Hyperion recording is first class.

Lucy Carolan's playing, too, is as full of life as it is of imaginative touches. She is both commanding and scholarly, and her ready virtuosity and keen articulation are exhilarating. Yet her touch can also be appealingly delicate. To add variety of colour, she uses a pair of harpsichords, both copies of early instruments. *Partitas Nos. 1, 3* and 6 are played on a copy of a Mietke, and *Partitas 2, 4* and 5 on a copy of a Goermans-Taskin instrument. Both are excellently recorded.

Robert Woolley's performances are also pleasingly fresh and musical, flowing naturally and spontaneously and with lively rhythmic feeling. He uses a particularly attractive harpsichord, a copy of a Mietke, an instrument of a kind that Bach would have known. It is beautifully recorded within a pleasing open acoustic.

Schiff is a most persuasive advocate of Bach on the piano. Though few will cavil at his treatment of fast movements, some may find him a degree wayward in slow movements, though the freshness of his rubato and the sparkle of his ornamentation are always winning. The sound is outstandingly fine.

Blandine Verlet's Philips Duo set is not only inexpensive, it is the only set of the *Partitas* to include the later *Overture in the French Style*, BWV 831, which is played with much character. Indeed, the performances throughout are direct and spontaneous, thoughtful and strongly characterized. Not an out-and-out first choice, but in its price range Verlet can certainly be strongly recommended.

Scott Ross's set of the *Partitas* dates from 1989. He uses an unidentified but attractive instrument which is recorded with both warmth and clarity. He plays with enjoyable style and panache, and despite one or two minor points (in the *B flat Gigue* not every note speaks evenly and at times greater rhythmic freedom would be welcome), his readings are eminently competitive reissued as an Ultima Double. They make a good bargain alternative to Verlet.

Gustav Leonhardt's set was recorded (in 1986) on a Dowd. In terms of sheer sound it is among the most satisfactory versions available, and in terms of style it combines elegance, spontaneity and authority. In many respects it is musically among the most satisfying of current sets, save for the fact that Leonhardt observes no repeats.

Partitas Nos. 2 in C min., BWV 826; 4 in D, BWV 828; 5 in G, BWV 829.

*** None. 7559 79483-2. Goode (piano).

It is a pity that Richard Goode's recording is incomplete, for the performances are both stylish and appealing. The crisp rhythmic control is arresting, as is the use of pianistic light and shade. Rhythms are lifted and, with piano tone that is clear but never too dry, this is very stimulating.

8 Preludes for W. F. Bach, BWV 924–31; 6 Little Preludes, BWV 933–8; 5 Preludes, BWV 939–43; Prelude, BWV 999; Prelude, Fugue & Allegro in E flat, BWV 998; Preludes & Fughettas: in F & G, BWV 901–2; Fantasia in C min., BWV 906; Fantasia & Fugue in A min., BWV 904.

(M) **(*) DG (IMS) 447 278-2. Gilbert (harpsichord).

Splendid artistry from this scholar-player; he is predictably stylish and authoritative. He uses a harpsichord by a Flemish maker, Jan Couchet, enlarged by Blanchet in 1759 and by Taskin in 1778, overhauled by Hubert Bédard. Even played at the lowest setting, the sound seems a bit unrelieved and overbright. The excellence of the playing, however, is not in question.

Toccatas: in F sharp min.; C min.; D; D min.; E min.; G min.; G; BWV 910–16.

*** Lyr. LEMS 8041. Troeger (clavichord).
(M) **(*) Sony SM2K 52612 (2). Gould (piano).

Bach's *Toccatas* are usually played on the harpsichord, organ or piano. But hearing them played so fluently and musically on the more intimate clavichord makes for an enjoyable diversity, and Richard Troeger certainly phrases and articulates with character. The recording engineer has not been tempted to put his microphones too close, and his comment that 'the clavichord is a quiet instrument, but it can fill a room with extraordinary resonance' is borne out here, yet the instrument's essential intimacy is retained.

The seven *Toccatas* offer some of Glenn Gould's finest Bach playing. They are often quite complex in structure but Gould has their full measure. The recording balance is close

and rather dry but truthful and with rather more bloom than in previous incarnations. The one overriding snag is the vocalise.

The Well-Tempered Clavier (48 Preludes & Fugues), BWV 846–93 (complete).

(BB) ***Virgin VBD 561711-2 (4). Van Asperen (harpsichord).
⊛ *** Hyp. CDA 67301/2 (Book I); CDA 67303/4 (Book II). Hewitt (piano).
(B) *** Nim. NI 5608/11 (4). Roberts (piano).
*** DG 413 439-2 (4). Gilbert (harpsichord).
*** Decca 414 388-2 (2) (Book I); 417 236-2 (2) (Book II). Schiff (piano).
*** Olympia OCD 703 ABCD (4). Nikolayeva (piano).
(N) (M) *** DG (ADD) 463 601-2 (2) (Book I); 463 623-2 (2) (Book II). Kirkpatrick (clavichord).
(B) *** HM HMA 1901285/8 (4). Moroney (harpsichord).
*** Ongaku 024-113 (2) (Book I); 024-115 (2) (Book II). Schepkin (piano).
*** ECM 835246-2 (2) (Book I); ECM 847936-2 (2) (Book II). Jarrett (piano or harpsichord).
(N) (BB) (***) Naxos mono 8.110651/2 (Book I); 8.110653/4 (Book II). Fischer (piano).
(M) (***) EMI mono CHS5 67214-2 (3). Fischer (piano).
(**(*)) DG mono 463 305-2 (4). Tureck (piano).

Collectors wanting a complete modern harpsichord version of the '48' will surely now choose the reissued mid-price 1989 Virgin Veritas set from Bob van Asperen. A pupil of Gustav Leonhardt, his account enshrines many of the finest of his master's qualities and outshines most of his rivals on CD. His playing is marked by consistent vitality, elegance and concentration: he plays every note as if he means it and is refreshingly unmetronomic without being too free. He plays a 1728 harpsichord by Christian Zell from the Hamburg Museum, which the engineers capture vividly. The acoustic is less resonant than with Gilbert on DG, which is an advantage, and with its price advantage van Asperen's set is very recommendable indeed.

Angela Hewitt uses all the resources of the modern piano to turn these preludes and fugues into ongoing concert music of great variety and interest. Her range of timbre and dynamic is wide, her articulation can be bold, lightweight or gently searching (as, for instance, in BWV 849). But every bar is imaginatively alive and her thoughtful expressiveness is never self-aware, nor does it obscure the clarity of the part-writing. An inspirational set, most naturally recorded.

Bernard Roberts's Nimbus survey is plainer than Angela Hewitt's Hyperion version, which is daringly adventurous in the use of dynamic rise and fall, and in exploring the full range of colour and feeling that is possible with a modern piano. But that is not to suggest that Roberts is unimaginative; indeed, his survey is full of individual touches and insights. Speeds feel undistractingly right throughout and, as in his comparable set of the Beethoven piano sonatas for Nimbus, Roberts refuses to divert attention away from the composer's argument with idiosyncratic gestures. That goes with the deepest concentration, bringing out the full power as well as the beauty, with counterpoint consistently clarified. To confirm the recommendation, the four discs come as a bargain offer, and this is the version, superbly recorded, which for many will be a first choice.

Gilbert's set of the '48' supplants nearly all existing harpsichord versions, with readings that are resilient and individual yet totally unmannered, although some might feel that the acoustic is just a shade too resonant.

Schiff often takes a very individual view of particular preludes and fugues, but his unexpected readings regularly win one over long before the end. Consistently he translates this music into pianistic terms, and his voyage of discovery through this supreme keyboard collection is the more riveting as the piano is an easier instrument to listen to over long periods. First-rate sound.

Tatiana Nikolayeva's set is also totally pianistic, using a wide range of dynamic and articulation, sometimes lightly staccato, at others crisp and bold or more gently sustained. She is at once authoritative yet, like Schiff, highly individual in her approach to each prelude and fugue. She is clearly moved by the music and at times her inspirational, soft-grained manner reminds one of Kempff. Whatever she does, she does not forget the composer and is never self-aware to the point of agogic distortion of line. She is beautifully recorded; a true, full, clear piano-sound.

It was a bold decision of Ralph Kirkpatrick to pioneer on the clavichord (in the mid-1960s). Some of the preludes and fugues seem better suited to this instrument. Yet this does not seem a problem for Kirkpatrick, whose expressive powers are never in doubt; nor is his scholarship or musicianship, and he fully realizes the possibilities inherent in the use of his gentler instrument, which is very finely recorded, the sound admirably remastered for this undoubtedly fascinating and rewarding Originals reissue. These are comparatively sober performances in the matter of registration, but there is no doubting Kirkpatrick's grip, or his ability to show a remarkable variety of mood and tone on his more limited instrument.

Davitt Moroney uses a modern harpsichord (built in 1980) which has a full-bodied yet cleanly focused image but which is rather too closely balanced. Yet the effect is certainly tangible and realistic, the perspective convincing. His thoughtful, considered approach is satisfying in its way, stylistically impeccable, although the playing is less concentrated than with Gilbert yet does not lack rhythmic resilience.

Sergey Schepkin immediately creates a more sharply focused, clearer style of articulation, still essentially pianistic but with the extra bite of a 'plucked' keyboard instrument underlying his presentation. He is comparatively chimerical, and attractively so, with tempi in the preludes (though not always the fugues) often faster than with his colleagues. Book II is, if anything, even more stimulating than Book I. American collectors in particular need not hesitate to invest in both volumes. Schepkin's approach is bolder, more vibrant than that of Angela Hewitt, yet the range and variety of the playing is comparable, showing a constantly individual grasp of the essence of Bach's inspiration. The piano is recorded forwardly and truthfully.

Keith Jarrett offers Book I on a modern piano, and we like it very much for its dedication, simplicity and integrity. In its way it is quite the equal of Schiff's recording. There is

no attempt at any excessive indulgence in keyboard colour, and the recording is very satisfying in its natural sonority. On the face of it, it seems a rather odd idea to revert to the harpsichord for Book II and, if his reasoning does not completely persuade us, his qualities of musicianship do. He is a highly intelligent and musical player whose readings and precise articulation can hold their own against the current competition.

Edwin Fischer's was the first ever '48' to be put on shellac 78's, being recorded in 1933–6. Fischer has often been spoken of as an artist of intellect but his approach here is neither remote nor cool. Moreover, he produces a beauty of sound and a sense of line that is an unfailing source of musical wisdom and nourishment. Whereas the earlier EMI transfers (CHS7 63188-2) were economically laid out on three mid-priced CDs, each accommodating close on 80 minutes, Naxos has issued each Book on a pair of super-bargain discs, so the saving in cost is less than it might have been. However, these new Naxos transfers are very impressive, the piano sound surprisingly full and pleasing, distinctly preferable to the EMI CDs. The mastery and subtlety of Fischer's Bach playing needs no re-stating for it has still never been surpassed. An indispensable part of any Bach library.

Rosalyn Tureck's classic recording, magnetic and concentrated, was made in New York in the early 1950s. The dry mono sound and limited dynamic range tend to exaggerate the muscularity of the playing, but the tonal contrasts are still brought out strongly, at times echoing in sharp staccato a harpsichord sound. Tureck's Bach is always special; even so, it is disconcerting to find her adopting such idiosyncratically slow speeds for some of the most formidable fugues of Book II. And to reissue such a set at full price seems an extraordinary gesture on DG's part.

Daniel Chorzempa quite arbitrarily divides Book I of Bach's '48' between clavichord and harpsichord and more controversially allots four preludes and fugues to a Dutch cabinet organ. In Book II the fortepiano joins the other instruments and is allotted half a dozen items against the organ's three. Chorzempa's style is on the whole fairly didactic, although always musically considered. This is not for everyone, but it's certainly a new approach (Philips 446 690-2).

The Well-Tempered Clavier, Book I, Preludes & Fugues Nos. 1–24, BWV 846–69.

*** BIS CD 813/4. Suzuki (harpsichord).
*** Mer. CDE 84384/5-2. Cload (piano).

Suzuki offers only Book I so far, but already he lays claim to being first choice for a harpsichord version of the '48'. His two-manual instrument (by Willem Kroesbergen of Utrecht after an enlarged Rückers) has a fine personality and is splendidly recorded. His pacing is admirably judged, his flexibility never sounds mannered and he brings Bach's great keyboard odyssey fully to life at every turn. A most satisfying achievement.

Julia Cload's new set also promises well, her pianistic style at times comparatively gentle (witness the opening prelude) but her control of dynamic follows Bach's underlying harmonic progressions very subtly. She can be both poetically reserved then suddenly extrovert and sparkling, and always remains faithful to the letter and spirit of this great work.

The Well-Tempered Clavier, Book I, excerpts: Preludes & Fugues Nos. 1–3; 5–17; 21–22.

(B) *** DG (ADD) 463 020-2. Kempff (piano).

Cool, clear and compelling, Kempff's performances from Book I of the '48' convey pianistic poetry as well as dedication to Bach. A splendid recital, with excellent sound, showing a great artist relaxed and enjoying himself. And so do we.

KEYBOARD RECITAL COLLECTIONS
Rosalyn Tureck recitals

'Bach and Tureck at Home' (a birthday offering):
(i) *Adagio in G, BWV 968; Aria & 10 Variations in the Italian Style, BWV 989; Capriccio on the Departure of a Beloved Brother, BWV 992; Chromatic Fantasia & Fugue, BWV 903; Fantasia, Adagio & Fugue in D, BWV 912; The Well-Tempered Clavier, Book I: Prelude & Fugue in B flat, BWV 866.* (ii) *English Suite No. 3 in G min., BWV 808; Italian Concerto, BWV 971; Sonata in D min., BWV 964 (trans. from Unaccompanied Violin Sonata No. 2 in A min., BWV 1003); Well-Tempered Clavier, Book I: Preludes & Fugues: in C min.; in C, BWV 847–8; Book II: Preludes & Fugues in C sharp, BWV 872; in G, BWV 884.* (iii) *Goldberg Variations, BWV 988;* (iv) *Partitas Nos. 1 in B flat, BWV 825; 2 in C min., BWV 826; 6 in E min., BWV 830.*

⚫ *** (i) VAIA 1041; (ii) VAIA 1051; (iii) VAIA 1029; (iv) VAIA 1040 (available separately). Tureck (piano).

Rosalyn Tureck's Bach playing is legendary, and the performances here show that her keyboard command and fluent sense of Bach style are as remarkable as ever. Tureck uses a wide dynamic and expressive range with consummate artistry, her decoration always adds to the musical effect, and she makes us feel that Bach's keyboard music could be played in no other way than this – the hallmark of a great artist.

English Suite No. 3, BWV 808; 6 Preludes, BWV 933/938, Sonata in D min., BWV 964 (arr. of Unaccompanied Violin Sonata, BWV 1003). Well-Tempered Clavier: Preludes & fugues: BWV 855, 880 & 849.

(***) VAI mono VAIA 1085. Tureck (piano).

Recorded (on 78s) at a live event in New York in 1948, this Bach recital shows the young Tureck to be intimately discerning and already completely at home on the piano in Bach's keyboard world. She plays very intimately and the recording is confined, but her thoughtfulness is magnetic throughout and one soon forgets the limited upper range of the sound. Unfortunately, the notes tell the collector little or nothing about the music.

Chromatic Fantasia & Fugue, BWV 903; Italian Concerto, BWV 971; Well-Tempered Clavier, Book I: Preludes & Fugues: BWV 850, 858, 866, 848. Book II: Preludes &

Fugues: BWV 871–2, 884–5, 903. Encore: Goldberg Variations: Variation No. 29.

*** VAI (ADD) VAIA 1139. Tureck (harpsichord).

This was recorded live in 1981 at the Metropolitan Museum of Art, New York. The balance is very close but the sharp focus of the instrument suits Tureck's amazingly clean articulation. She opens with five *Preludes and Fugues* from Book II of the *Well-Tempered Clavier*; then, after a dazzling account of the *Chromatic Fantasia* and a reflective fugue, she moves back to give us four *Preludes and Fugues* from Book I which bring the most remarkable bravura articulation; the fugues, however, unfold precisely. Then comes a buoyant *Italian Concerto* with a touchingly thoughtful central Andante. The ear soon adjusts to the dry, close, slighty tinkly harpsichord image.

Adagio in G, BWV 968; Aria & 10 Variations in the Italian Style, BWV 989; Capriccio on the Departure of a Beloved Brother, BWV 992; Chromatic Fantasia & Fugue, BWV 903; Partita No. 2 in C min., BWV 826; Prelude in E flat min., BWV 853; Musette in D (S. Anh. 126).

**(*) VAI VAIA 1131. Tureck (piano).

There is a slight element of disappointment about Tureck's 1995 Russian recital. She does not seem always to relax here as much as usual and, although the *Chromatic Fantasia* is very commanding indeed and the *Partita* is full of characteristic insights, the bold, truthful, but closely observed digital sound seems at times to bring an element of didacticism to her presentation. However, Tureck's full charisma returns in the closing *Prelude* and *Musette*, which are most movingly played. The documentation concentrates on the occasion and says little about the music.

Other keyboard collections

Capriccio in E, BWV 993; Capriccio on the Departure of a Beloved Brother, BWV 992; 4 Duets, BWV 802–5; Partita in B min., BWV 831.

(N)*** Hyp. CDA 67306. Hewitt (piano).

This enticing collection once again confirms Angela Hewitt's reputation for playing Bach on the piano with a distinction comparable to that of Rosalyn Tureck in the five decades before her. Her striking sense of keyboard colour is shown in the *'Departure' Capriccio*, especially the *Adagissimo*, and, together with an imaginatively wide variety of touch, makes the four *Duets* (so called on account of their two-part counterpoint) unusually diverse, like a suite. The gentle interchanges of No. 3 are particularly captivating. The so-called *Italian Concerto* is subtitled 'Concerto nach Italienischen Gusto', and the vibrant buoyancy of the outer movements readily reflects that feeling, while the central *Andante* is blissful. As for the famous *B minor Partita* (or *French Overture*), the sparklingly rhythmic dance movements make a perfect setting for the lovely central *Sarabande*. Hewitt is most naturally recorded and provides her own excellent notes.

Capriccio on the Departure of a Beloved Brother, BWV 992; Chaconne in D min. (from Partita No. 2 for Violin,

BWV 1004); *Choral Preludes: BWV 645; BWV 659; BWV 639; from Cantata No. 147; Chromatic Fantasia & Fugue, BWV 903; 4 Duets, BWV 802–5; Fantasia in C min., BWV 906. Fugue in G min., BWV 578; Inventions & Sinfonias, BWV 772-801. Italian Concerto, BWV 971. Siciliano in G min., (from Flute Sonata, BWV 1031); Toccata & Fugue in D min., BWV 565.*

**(*) Olympia (i) Dig./ADD OCD 627 (3). Nikolayeva.

As is well known, it was Tatiana Nikolayeva's Bach playing that inspired Shostakovich to compose his *24 Preludes and Fugues*; and this collection of her Bach performances, recorded at various times, gives a fairly representative picture of her artistry. Her Bach is commanding, old-fashioned perhaps, but undoubtedly masterly. She has poise, authority and an expressive quality that shines through. The sound, as one might expect, is variable in quality.

Chorale Preludes: BWV 639; BWV 659 (both arr. Busoni); Chromatic Fantasia & Fugue, BWV 903; Fantasia & Fugue in A min., BWV 904; Italian Concerto, BWV 971; Fantasia in A min., BWV 922.

(M) *** Ph. 442 400-2. Brendel (piano).

Brendel's performances are of the old school, with no attempt to strive after harpsichord effects, and with every piece creating a sound-world of its own. The *Italian Concerto* is particularly imposing, with a finely sustained sense of line and beautifully articulated rhythms. The recording is in every way truthful and present, bringing the grand piano very much into the living-room before one's very eyes. Masterly.

Chromatic Fantasia & Fugue in D min., BWV 903; Fantasia in C min., BWV 908; Fugue in A min., BWV 944; Italian Concerto in F, BWV 971; Suites: in C min. (arr. from Lute suite, BWV 995); in E flat (arr. from Cello Suite No. 4, BWV 1010); Toccatas: in D, BWV 912; in D min., BWV 913.

(B) ** Sony SB2K 60375. Leonhardt (harpsichord).

A good example of Leonhardt's playing from the late 1970s. He uses a highly suitable, early eighteenth-century instrument made by Christian Zell, and is well balanced and recorded. But the two arranged suites are the least attractive performances here and all the rest could have been easily fitted on to a single CD. The pair of *Toccatas* is very successful, as on the whole is the *Italian Concerto*, while the *Chromatic Fantasia* shows him at his most digitally dextrous.

Chromatic Fantasia & Fugue in D min., BWV 903; French Suite No. 5 in G, BWV 816; Italian Concerto, BWV 971; A Musical Offering, BWV 1079: Ricercar; Toccata in G, BWV 916.

(M) *** Erato 0630 16171-2. Koopman (harpsichord).

Ton Koopman is at his liveliest here, particularly in the brilliant *Chromatic Fantasia*. The *French Suite*, bright and brisk except for the thoughtful *Loure*, has plenty of character, and the *Italian Concerto* comes off equally vividly, helped by the clean projection of the Dutch harpsichord, built by Willem Kroesbergen of Utrecht.

Chromatic Fantasia & Fugue, BWV 903; Italian Concerto, BWV 971; Toccatas in C min. & D, BWV 911–12; Well-Tempered Clavier: Prelude & Fugue No. 5 in D, BWV 850;
(i) *Double Clavier Concerto in C, BWV 1061.*

(M) (**(*)) EMI mono CDH5 67210-2. Artur Schnabel (piano);
(i) with Karl Ulrich Schnabel, LSO, Boult.

These pioneering recordings are nearly all from the 1930s. Schnabel's playing has a magnetism and authority which made a strong case for playing Bach on the piano, even if the timbre is dry and bony. The *Chromatic Fantasia* is magnetically wayward, as is the excerpt from the *Well-Tempered Clavier*; the *Italian Concerto* is strongly characterized. The most impressively poised playing comes in the two *Toccatas* and the *Double Concerto*, where Artur and Karl Ulrich Schnabel are in total rapport; the two pianists seem to be making music together in a different dimension from Boult's positive, crisply efficient accompaniment, which is not flattered by the scratchy string-sound.

Chromatic Fantasia & Fugue, BWV 903; Partitas: Nos. 1 in B flat, BWV 825; in B min., BWV 831; Toccata in D min., BWV 913.

(B) **(*) DG ADD/Dig. 463 018-2. Pinnock (harpsichord).

Trevor Pinnock's stylistic sensibility is matched by his technical expertise, and there is no doubt that his explosive burst of bravura at the opening of the *Chromatic Fantasia* is exciting. Sometimes his approach seems too literal, but at others he allows himself more expressive latitude, notably so in the *B minor Partita*. The playing is always rhythmically alive, but the close recording of the harpsichord and the high level combine to create a somewhat unrelenting dynamic level, and the harpsichord timbre is metallic.

4 Duets, BWV 802/4; English Suite No. 6, BWV 811; Italian Concerto, BWV 971; Toccata in C min., BWV 911.

(B) *** DG 463 021-2. Hewitt (piano).

In both the *Italian Concerto* and the *English Suite*, Angela Hewitt's playing is enormously alive and stimulating. She plays with vital imaginative resource, totally free from any idiosyncrasy or affectation. The piano is beautifully captured on this recording, with fresh, lifelike sound and vivid presence.

English Suite No. 2 in A min., BWV 807; Partita No. 2 in C min., BWV 826; Toccata in C min., BWV 911.

(M) *** DG (ADD) 463 604-2 (2). Argerich (piano).

Martha Argerich's playing provides a genuinely musical experience: alive, keenly rhythmic, but also wonderfully flexible and rich in colour. There is an intellectual musical vitality here that is refreshing. She is very well recorded indeed, even if the measure (50 minutes) is not especially generous.

Keyboard transcriptions

Transcriptions (arr. Busoni): Chorales: Ich ruf' zu dir, Herr Jesu Christ, BWV 639; Nun freut euch, lieben

Christen, BWV 734: Nun komm, der Heiden Heiland, BWV 659; Wachet auf, ruft uns die stimme, BWV 645.

⚙ *** Sony SK 66511. Perahia – LISZT: *Concert Paraphrases*; MENDELSSOHN: *Songs Without Words*. ***

Murray Perahia knows how to make the piano sing as do few of his contemporaries, and how to control pace. His pianism is impeccable in its polish and naturalness of flow, and there is a wonderful bloom about the sound he produces.

Transcriptions by Ferruccio Busoni: Partita No. 2 (for unaccompanied violin): Chaconne, BWV 1004. (Organ) Chorale preludes: Durch Adam's Fall ist ganz verderbt, BWV 637; Durch Adam's Fall ist ganz verderbt, BWV 705; Herr Gott, nun schleuss den Himmel auf, BWV 617; Ich ruf zu dir, Herr Jesu Christ, BWV 639; In der ist Freude, BWV 615; Jesus Christus, unser Heiland, BWV 665; Komm', Gott, Schöpfer, heiliger Geist, BWV 667; Nun komm, der Heiden Heiland, BWV 659; Nun freut euch, liebe Christen g'mein, BWV 734; Wachet auf, ruft uns die Stimme, BWV 645; Toccata in C, BWV 564.

(N) *** Decca 467 358-2. Paik.

An artist of great sensibility who commands great beauty of tone colour, Kun-Woo Paik has made a strong impression in Liszt and Ravel and in this impressively recorded recital of Busoni transcriptions proves no less eloquent as a Bach interpreter. The *C major Toccata*, which opens the disc, is exhilarating and the *A minor Adagio* is played with great poetry and limpidity. This is distinguished piano playing by any standard and the famous *Chaconne* transcription gives much delight. Realistic and truthful if occasionally slightly bottom-heavy sound.

ORGAN MUSIC
Complete organ music

Helmut Walcha DG Archiv Series

The Art of Fugue, BWV 1080 (with Contrapuntus No. 18, completed Walcha); Allabreve, BWV 589; Chorale Settings: BWV 645–50 (Schübler Chorales), 651–64, 653b, 665–68a, 700, 709, 727, 733, 734, 736; Canonic Variations on 'Vom Himmel hoch', BWV 769; Canzona, BWV 588; Chorale Partita (Sei gegrüsset), BWV 768; Clavier-Übung, Part III (Organ Mass): Prelude & Fugue, BWV 552 & Chorale Settings, BWV 669–89; 4 Duets BWV 802–5; Fantasias: BWV 562, 572; Fantasias & Fugues, BWV 537, 542; Fugues: BWV 552/2, 578; Fugues on Themes by Legrenzi & Corelli, BWV 574, 579. Orgelbüchlein, BWV 599–644; Pastorale, BWV 590; Passacaglia & Fugue, BWV 582; Preludes & Fugues: BWV 531–6, 539, 541, 543–8, 550, 551; Toccatas & Fugues: BWV 538, 540, 564; Toccata, Adagio & Fugue, BWV 565; Trio Sonatas Nos. 1–6, BWV 525–30.

(B) **(*) DG (ADD) 463 712-2 (12). Walcha (organs at St Laurenskerk, Alkmaar, Netherlands, and Saint-Pierre-le-Jeune, Strasburg).

Helmut Walcha's pioneering stereo series was recorded between 1959 and 1971. Even if by today's standards Walcha's

Bach style seems very relaxed and sometimes lacking in internal tension, his carefully calculated interpretations create a genuine sense of organic unity and a deeply musical sense of line and phrase, which gains from felicitous registration using highly suitable organs, splendidly recorded.

In his distinguished version of *The Art of Fugue* the registration is admirably varied, yet with the contrasts in register and timbre heightened by the spatial effect of the stereo. The *Toccatas and Fugues* certainly do not lack bravura, and typical of Walcha's playing at its most monumental is the gigantic triptych of the *Toccata, Adagio and Fugue*, a rigorous test of any organist's technique. It is a work which Walcha comes through with flying colours, and the *Chorale Partita, Sei gegrüsset* is another expansive piece that comes off very successfully.

The *Preludes and Fugues* with their dignified tempi, although seldom flamboyant, are dedicated performances which allow every detail to come through, with the E flat work, BWV 552, especially impressive in its combination of majesty and clarity. Among the shorter, more colourful pieces the silvery arpeggios of the *Fantasia in G*, BWV 572, bring a fine example of perceptive registration, and in Walcha's hands the *Trio Sonatas* are not treated lightly but are used to reflect the contrapuntal and formal mastery of Bach's middle period.

Chorale Partita: Sei gegrüsset, BWV 768; Prelude & Fugue in E flat, BWV 552; 6 Schübler Chorales, BWV 646–50; Toccata & Fugue in D min., BWV 565; Trio Sonata No. 1 in E flat, BWV 525.

(M) **(*) DG (ADD) stereo/mono 457 704-2. Walcha (St Laurenskerk organ, Alkmaar).

DG have, on the whole, chosen well for a programme of 'Originals' to demonstrate Walcha's Bach style. Even if modern ears may find Walcha's approach rather slow and heavy, the performance of the famous *D minor Toccata and Fugue*, although comparatively unflamboyant, is not dull. The *Trio Sonata* is engagingly registered, as are the steadily presented *Schübler Chorales*. The last four of these are mono, but the ear hardly registers the difference because of the high quality of DG's recording.

Fantasia in G, BWV 572; Fantasia & Fugue in G min., BWV 542; Preludes & Fugues, BWV 536, 545 & 548; Toccata & Fugue in F, BWV 540.

(B) ** DG (ADD) 463 017-2. Walcha (organ).

All these performances represent the older, more circumspect German school of Bach playing which is essentially didactic, structurally impeccable, and with every detail laid out clearly before the listener. The famous Alkmaar organ is well focused in an excellent recording.

Lionel Rogg Complete Harmonia Mundi Series

Disc 1: (Early) *Preludes & Fugues, BWV 531–5, 539, 549–50; Fugues, BWV 575–9.*

Disc 2: *Toccatas & Fugues, BWV 538, 540, 566; Toccata, Adagio & Fugue, BWV 564.*

Disc 3: *Allabreve, BWV 586; Canzone, BWV 588; Chorale Partitas, BWV 766–8; Pastorale, BWV 590.*

Discs 4 & 5: *Orgelbüchlein, BWV 599–644; Chorales, BWV 653b, 720, 727, 734, 736–7.*

Disc 6: *Passacaglia & Fugue, BWV 582; Fantasias & Fugues, BWV 537, 542; Fantasias, BWV 562, 567; Chorale Fughettas BWV 696–9; 701, 703–4.*

Disc 7 & 8: *18 Leipzig Chorale Preludes, BWV 651–68; Chorale Preludes, BWV 690–1, 695, 706, 709–13, 714, 717–18, 731, 738, 740.*

Disc 9: *Trio Sonatas Nos. 1–6, BWV 525–30; Trio, BWV 583.*

Discs 10, 11 & 12: *Prelude, BWV 552; German Organ Mass, BWV 669/688; Fugue, BWV 552; 6 Schübler Chorales, BWV 645–650; Later Preludes & Fugues, BWV 536, 541, 543–8.*

(M) **(*) HM HMX 290772/83 (12). Lionel Rogg (Silbermann organ, Arlesheim).

Fantasias & Fugues: in C min., BWV 537; in G min., BWV 542; Passacaglia & Fugue in C min., BWV 582; 6 Schübler Chorales, BWV 645–650; Toccata & Fugue in C min., BWV 565.

(M) **(*) HM (ADD) HMX 295771 (from above). Lionel Rogg (Silbermann organ, Arlesheim).

Lionel Rogg made three surveys of Bach's organ music and this is the second, originally published in 1970. He followed on in the footsteps of DG's Walcha series, maintaining some of its scholarly sobriety yet clearly making progress towards the more volatile Bach style which was to transform the approach to Bach's organ music later in that decade. Aficionados will be glad to see that Rogg's complete set, as listed above, is available on CD; others will be content with the set of excerpts on a single disc.

The organ at Arlesheim is certainly a magnificent instrument but it is not quite as clear-textured (as recorded) as the Zurich organ on which Rogg recorded his previous series in the 1960s, issued on LP on the Bach and Oryx labels.

These big, expansive works admirably suited Rogg's measured style with its stateliness and gravity, and the performance has a cumulative effect, without ever being pressed forward. The famous *D minor Toccata and Fugue* also sounds well but it needs rather more flair and flamboyance. The two *Preludes and Fugues*, too, could use rather more variety of approach, although the concentration is in no doubt. The *Schübler Chorales* are the highlight of the recital and demonstrate Rogg's ready tapestry of baroque colouring, yet the cantus firmus always remains clear.

Wolfgang Rübsam Complete Philips Series

Volume I, Disc 1: *Fantasia, BWV 572; Preludes & Fugues, BWV 531–2; 535, 541, 544–5, 549–50; Toccata & Fugue in D min., BWV 565 (438 172-2).*

Disc 2: *Fugues, BWV 577–8; Fugue on a Theme of Corelli, BWV 579; Prelude, BWV 568; Preludes & Fugues, BWV 533–4; 536; 543; 546–7; Toccata & Fugue in D min. (Dorian), BWV 538 (438 173-2).*

Disc 3: *Canzona in D min., BWV 588; Preludes & Fugues, BWV 537, 539–40, 542, 548; Prelude, Adagio-trio; Fantasia & Fugue (without BWV No.) (438 174-2).*

Disc 4: *Allabreve in D, BWV 589; Fantasias: in C min. (without BWV No.); in C min., BWV 562; Fugues, BWV 575, 581; Passacaglia in C min., BWV 582; Pedal-exercitium, BWV 598; Toccata, BWV 564; Toccata & Fugue in E, BWV 566; Trios, BWV 583, 586, 1027a (438 175-2).*

Disc 5: *Fantasia in G, BWV 571; Trio Sonatas for 2 Keyboards & Pedal, BWV 525–9 (438 177-2).*

Disc 6: *Trio Sonata No. 6, BWV 530; Chorales, BWV 691a, 717, 725; Chorale Partitas, BWV 766–7; 770; Chorale Preludes, 745, 747 (438 178-2).*

Disc 7: *Canonic Variations on 'Vom Himmel hoch', BWV 768; Chorale Partita on 'Sei gegrüsset, Jesu gütig', BWV 768; Chorale Variations on 'Allein Gott in der Höh' sei Ehr', BWV 771; Chorale: 'Wie schön leuch't uns der Morgenstern', BWV 739; Fugue in C min. (Theme Legrenzianum, elaboratum cum subjecto pedaliter), BWV 574; Pastorale in D, BWV 590 (438 179-2).*

Disc 8: *Orgelbüchlein: Chorales, BWV 599–644 (438 180-2).*

Volume II, Disc 9: *Chorales, BWV 653b; O Lamm Gottes unschuldig (without BWV No.); Chorale Preludes, BWV 748–50, 754, 756, 759; Fuga sopra il magnificat, BWV 733; 6 Schübler Chorales, BWV 645–50; Clavier-Übung, Part 3: German Organ Mass (beginning): Prelude in E flat, BWV 552, & Chorale Preludes, BWV 669–74 (438 182-2).*

Disc 10: *Clavier-Übung, Part 3: German Organ Mass (cont.); Chorale Preludes, BWV 675–89; Fugue in E flat, BWV 552; Duets 1–4, BWV 802–5 (438 183-2).*

Disc 11: *6 Concertos after Various Composers, BWV 592–7; Leipzig Chorales Nos. 1–3, BWV 651–3 (438 184-2).*

Disc 12: *18 Leipzig Chorales, Nos. 4–18 (438 185-2).*

Disc 13: *Chorales & Chorale Preludes, BWV 690, 692–4, 700, 703, 710, 715, 719, 722, 724, 729, 732, 734, 738, 746, 751, 755, 757–8, 763; Chorale Fugues & Fughettas, BWV 699, 701–2, 716; Fantasia super 'Valet will ich dir geben', BWV 735; Fantasia in C, BWV 570; Fugues, BWV 570 & BWV 576; Kleines harmonisches Labyrinth, BWV 591; Prelude in C, BWV 567; Prelude & Fugue in A min., BWV 551; Trio in G min., BWV 584 (438 187-2).*

Disc 14: *Chorales & Chorale Preludes, BWV 691, 695, 705–9, 711–12, 714, 718, 720, 723, 726, 730, 740–44, 752, 765; Chorale fantasia, BWV 713; Chorale Fughettas, BWV 696–8, 704 (438 188-2).*

Disc 15: *Aria in F, BWV 587; Chorales & Chorale Preludes, BWV 721, 760–62, 727–8, 731, 736–7; Fantasia con imitazione, BWV 563; Fantasia & Fugue in A min., BWV 561; Fugue in D, BWV 580; Prelude in A min., BWV 569; Trio in C min., BWV 585; The Art of Fugue, BWV 1080* (beginning): *Contrapunctus 1–5* (438 189-2).

Disc 16: *The Art of Fugue* (conclusion): *Contrapunctus 6–11; Canon all'ottava; Fua a 3 soggetti. Chorale: 'Wenn wir in Höchsten Nöten sein', BWV 668a* (438 190-2).

(B) *** Ph. 456 080-2 (16). Wolfgang Rübsam (organs of Frauenfeld & Freiburg).

Wolfgang Rübsam's magnificent survey of Bach's organ music was made at the beginning of the 1970s. The bulk of the music was recorded on the fine instrument at St Nikolaus in Frauenfeld, Switzerland; for the chorale preludes and a few miscellaneous works, Rübsam turned to the Belgian Hockhois organ at Freiburg Münster. Sonically the results are highly stimulating, offering the widest range of colour, a rich overall blend, without clouding of detail and with plenty of support from the pedals. The *Trio Sonatas* are especially attractive in both their luminous palette and their liveliness. The six solo *Concertos*, based on music of others, are comparably successful, although here Rübsam adopts extreme tempi, with adagios very measured against sprightly allegros. But the key to the success of any Bach survey must lie with the way the performer approaches the large-scale concert pieces, notably the *Preludes and Fugues* and *Toccatas and Fugues*, and in these works Rübsam is consistently vital, and his registration often tickles the ear. The famous *Toccata, Adagio and Fugue*, BWV 564, is very well judged, while the *Passacaglia in C minor*, BWV 582, has a convincing forward momentum and plenty of imaginative detail. The *Art of Fugue* is placed at the end; a suitable postlude is provided with a complete version of the *Chorale*, BWV 668a. Rübsam's distinguished and consistently enjoyable survey anticipated the advance in style pioneered by Peter Hurford, while the remastered Philips analogue recording is often of comparable demonstration quality – a very major achievement. Again however, these discs are not available separately, but the Duo below acts as a fair sampler.

Chorale Preludes, BWV 599, 608, 615, 622, 625, 635–7, 639, 645, 650, 653b, 654, 659, 721, 730–1; Concerto No. 2, BWV 593; Fugue, BWV 579; Passacaglia & fugue, BWV 582; Preludes & Fugues, BWV 542 & 552 (St Anne); Toccata, Adagio & Fugue, BWV 564; Toccatas & Fugues: in D min., BWV 538 & 565; Trio, BWV 1027a; Trio Sonata No. 1, BWV 525.

(N) (B) **(*) Ph. Duo (ADD) 464 988-2. Rübsam (from above).

The present selection is well made and demonstrates Rübsam's fine Bach playing in varied repertoire, from the perceptively registered *Choral Preludes* and the engaging *Trio Sonata* to the larger-scale epic works. The CD transfer, however, seems lighter in the bass than on the original recordings, and this gives the pedals rather less weight and power than in the complete set.

Peter Hurford Complete Decca Series

Disc 1: *Preludes & Fugues, BWV 531–2, 548–50; Toccatas & Fugues, BWV 540, 565* (444 411-2).

Disc 2: *Fantasias & Fugues, BWV 542, 561; Kleines harmonisches Labyrinth, BWV 591; Preludes & Fugues, BWV 533, 551; Toccata, Adagio & Fugue, BWV 564; Toccata & Fugue, BWV 538; Trio, BWV 585* (444 412-2).

Disc 3: *Fantasias, BWV 562, 572; Fantasia & Fugue, BWV 537; Fugues, BWV 575–7, 579, 581; Passacaglia & Fugue, BWV 582; Pedal-exercitium, BWV 598; Prelude & Fugue, BWV 535; Trio, BWV 583* (444 413-2).

Disc 4: *Clavier-Übung, Part 3* (beginning): *German Organ Mass (Prelude & Fugue in E flat, BWV 552, & Chorale Preludes, BWV 669–71, 676, 678, 680, 682, 684, 686, 688)* (444 414-2).

Disc 5: *Clavier-Übung, Part 3* (conclusion): *Chorale Preludes, BWV 672–5, 677, 679, 681, 683, 685, 687, 689; 24 Kirnberger Chorale Preludes, BWV 690–713* (444 415-2).

Disc 6: *6 Trio Sonatas, BWV 525–30* (444 416-2).

Disc 7: *Canonic Variations: Vom Himmel hoch, BWV 769; Chorale Partitas: Christ, du bist der helle Tag; O Gott, du frommer Gott; Sei gegrüsset, Jesu gütig, BWV 766–8; Chorale variations: Ach, was soll ich Sünder machen, BWV 770* (444 417-2).

Disc 8: *Chorale Preludes, BWV 730–40; Schübler Chorale Preludes, BWV 645–50; Chorale variations: Allein Gott in der Höh' sei Ehr, BWV 771* (444 418-2).

Disc 9: *Chorale Preludes, BWV 726–9; Concertos Nos. 1–6, BWV 592–7* (444 419-2).

Disc 10: *Arnstadt Chorale Preludes, BWV 714, 719, 742 & 1090–1117* (from Yale manuscript, copied Neumeister) (444 420-2).

Disc 11: *Arnstadt Chorale Preludes, BWV 957, 1118–20* (from Yale manuscript, copied Neumeister); *Leipzig Chorale Preludes, BWV 651–62* (444 421-2).

Disc 12: *Leipzig Chorale Preludes, BWV 663–8. Chorale Preludes, BWV 714–25* (444 422-2).

Disc 13: *Allabreve in D, BWV 589; Fugue, BWV 580; Prelude, BWV 568; Preludes & Fugues, BWV 534, 536, 539, 541; 8 Short Preludes & Fugues, BWV 553–60; Trios, BWV 584 & 586* (444 423-2).

Disc 14: *Aria in F, BWV 587; Canzona in D min., BWV 588; Fantasia, BWV 571; Fugues, BWV 574 & 578; Pastorale, BWV 590; Preludes, BWV 567 & 569; Preludes & Fugues, BWV 546–7* (444 424-2).

Disc 15: *Fantasia, BWV 563; Musical Offering: Ricercare, BWV 1079/5. Preludes & Fugues, BWV 535a* (incomplete),

543–5; *Prelude, Trio & Fugue, BWV 545b; Toccata & Fugue in E, BWV 566; Trio, BWV 1027a* (444 425-2).

Disc 16: *Chorale Preludes Nos. 1–41 (Orgelbüchlein), BWV 599–639* (444 426-2).

Disc 17: *Chorale Preludes Nos. 42–6 (Orgelbüchlein), BWV 640–44. Chorale Preludes, BWV 620a, BWV 741–8, BWV 751–2, BWV 754–5, BWV 757–63, BWV 765, BWV Anh. 55; Fugue in G min., BWV 131a* (444 427-2).

(B) *** Decca ADD/Dig. 444 410-2 (17). Peter Hurford (organs of Ratzeburg Cathedral, Germany; Church of Our Lady of Sorrows, Toronto, Canada; New College Chapel, Oxford; Knox Grammar School Chapel, Sydney, Australia; Eton College, Windsor; Stiftskirche, Melk, Austria; Augustinerkirche, Vienna, Austria; All Souls Unitarian Church, Washington, DC, USA; Domkirche, St Pölten, Austria; St Catharine's College Chapel, Cambridge).

With the exception of the 35 *Arnstadt Chorale Preludes*, as copied by Neumeister – discovered quite recently in the Music Library of Yale University – which were added in 1986, Peter Hurford recorded his unique survey of Bach's organ music for Decca's Argo label over a period of eight years, 1974–82. Following the example of Bach himself, who was renowned for trying out organs, Hurford uses ten different organs, moving from Ratzeburg in Germany to Toronto in Canada, back home to New College, Oxford, then to Sydney, Australia, and so on. Each organ is caught superbly by the recording engineers, and the registration features a range of baroque colour that is almost orchestral in its diversity. The digital recording of the Vienna Bach organ chosen for the *Neumeister Chorales* is particularly beautiful.

It was Peter Hurford's achievement, following after Wolfgang Rübsam, to influence a complete change in approach to this repertoire, moving away from an enduring and essentially pedagogic, German tradition (shown at its best by organists like Helmut Walcha on DG Archiv). Vigour and energy are the keynotes of his approach to the large-scale works and, without losing their majesty, he never lets the fugal momentum get bogged down by the the music's weight and scale. We hear Bach's organ writing with new ears, its human vitality revealed alongside its extraordinary architecture. The set is supported with very good notes by Clifford Bartlett which are both scholarly and readable; full specifications of all the organs used are included. The recordings are splendidly transferred to CD and and while newer digital surveys are now appearing, from Kevin Bowyer, Christopher Herrick, Simon Preston and Ton Koopman among others, this set of 17 bargain-price CDs remains a cornerstone among available recordings of this repertoire. Apart from the selection below the discs unfortunately are not available separately.

Chorale Preludes, BWV 727, 729–30, 734, 659, 645 & 694; Fantasias: in C min., BWV 562; in G, BWV 572; Fantasias & Fugues: in C min., BWV 537; in G min., BWV 542; Passacaglia & Fugue in C min., BWV 582; Preludes & Fugues, BWV 543, 532 & (St Anne) BWV 552; Toccata, Adagio & Fugue in C, BWV 564; Toccatas & Fugues in D min. (Dorian), BWV 538; BWV 565.

(B) *** Double Decca (ADD) 443 485-2 (2). Hurford (various organs).

A generous 146-minute collection of major Bach organ works, taken from Peter Hurford's complete survey (see above), brings two separate recitals, each framed by major concert pieces, with the beautifully played chorales used in between the large-scale pieces to add contrast. The current bright transfers seem to have added an extra sharpness of outline to the sound of some of the big set-pieces, but this is something which will be more noticeable on some reproducers than on others, and the various organs are caught with fine realism and plenty of depth.

Marie-Claire Alain Erato Series

(M) **(*) Erato/Warner 4509 96358-2 (14). Marie-Claire Alain.

Marie-Claire Alain's series has much to offer the lover of Bach's organ music, and she plays to excellent effect on some splendid instruments. But competition is strong, and for most collectors a choice from among the separate issues, all at mid-price, would seem more sensible.

Volume 1: *Leipzig Chorale Preludes, BWV 653–4, 658 & 662–4; Preludes & Fugues: in B min., BWV 544; in E min., BWV 548.*

(M) **(*) Erato 4509 96718-2. Alain (organ of Martinikerk, Groningen).

The results here are not entirely satisfactory, for the engineers obtain a rich, weighty sound as in the opening *E minor Prelude and Fugue*, but the resonance makes the result rather opaque, which does not enable Alain to clarify detail. The fugue, however, is measured and powerful. This whole programme bears out her comments about tempi, which are essentially relaxed.

Volume 2: *Orgelbüchlein: Chorale Preludes, BWV 618–32; Prelude & Fugue in G min., BWV 535; Toccatas & Fugues: in D min. (Dorian), BWV 538; in C, BWV 566.*

(M) **(*) Erato 4509 96719-2. Alain (organ of Freiburg Cathedral).

Volume 2 was recorded on the early eighteenth-century Silbermann organ at Freiburg, and the sound is immediately more vivid and clear. The opening *Dorian Toccata in D minor* is brightly registered and lively and, if the fugue is unhurried, the tension is well sustained. The *C major Toccata*, however, is one of the finest performances in the cycle. Alain presents the earlier chorales from the *Orgelbüchlein* gently and persuasively, although she does not always make the cantus firmus stand out.

Volume 3: *Allabreve, BWV 589; Canzona, BWV 588; Fugues: BWV 575 & 577; Fugue sopra 'Meine Seele erhebet den Herren'; Kirnberger Chorale Preludes, BWV 694 & 710; Kleines harmonisches Labyrinth, BWV 591; Partita sopra 'O Gott, du frommer Gott', BWV 767; Preludes & Fugues: BWV 539, 545 & 551.*

(M) **(*) Erato 4509 96720-2. Alain (organ of Freiburg Cathedral).

Alain uses the fullest sonority for her weighty presentation of the opening *Prelude and Fugue in C*. However, the following *Fugue à la gigue* is impossibly slow and heavy. Alain is much more impressive in the *D minor Fugue*, BWV 539, which is cleanly pointed and rhythmically positive. The splendid virtuoso *Fugue in C minor* (which reminds one of the more famous *D minor*, BWV 565) is fluent and quite dramatic at the end, while in the fugue, based on the *Magnificat*, Alain uses the pedals impressively to build a most powerful climax. The *Kleines harmonisches Labyrinth* has sounded more original in other hands, but here the registration is certainly interesting.

Volume 4: *Chorale Preludes: BWV 711, 714–18, 722, 724–32, 734, 737–9 & 765; Fantasia in B min., BWV 563; Preludes & Fugues: in C, BWV 531; in E min., BWV 533.*

(M) **(*) Erato 4509 96721-2. Alain (organ of Georgenkirche, Rötha).

The Silbermann organ at Rötha proves ideal for this repertoire, and it stimulates Marie-Claire Alain to some of her most spontaneous performances so far in this variable series. After a robust *Prelude and Fugue in E minor*, Alain is at her most chimerical in the Christmas Chorale, *Nun freut euch, lieben Christen g'mein*, with the registration like tinkling bells, and *In dulci jubilo* is very grand indeed. Alain clearly revels in the elaborate passage on the pedals which opens the *Prelude in C*, BWV 531, and even conveys exuberance, while the fugue is equally alive and vivid. The contrapuntally grand *Herr Gott, dich loben wir* ends the recital massively, and here one feels Alain could have moved the music on a bit.

Volume 5: *Chorale Preludes: BWV 690–91, 695, 700, 706, 709, 712 & 721; Fantasia ('Jesu, meine Freude'), BWV 713; Fugue (on a Theme of Corelli), BWV 579; Kirnberger Chorale Preludes for Christmas, BWV 696–704; Partita sopra 'Christ, der du bist der helle Tag', BWV 766; Preludes & Fugues: BWV 537 & 549.*

(M) **(*) Erato 4509 96722-2. Alain (organ of Georgenkirche, Rötha).

Alain opens Volume 5 with the early *Prelude and Fugue in C minor* (1703–4) using the Rötha organ's pedals to bravura effect, following with a fairly spontaneous account of the jolly fugue. The first chorale, *Herr Jesus Christ, dich zu uns wend*, BWV 709, is full of gleaming sunshine, while *Erbarm' dich mein O Herre Gott* brings that dedicated feeling of repose which Alain manages so well. The *Partita sopra 'Christ, der du bist der helle Tag'* brings six variations and Alain finds an orchestral range of colour for them, with a gigue movement finally leading to a majestic close.

Volume 6: *Canonic Variations: Vom Himmel hoch, BWV 769; Chorale Preludes: BWV 669–79; Clavier-Übung, Part 3: German Organ Mass: Prelude in E flat, BWV 552; Prelude & Fugue in C, BWV 547.*

(M) **(*) Erato 4509 96723-2. Alain (organ of Martinikerk, Groningen).

If the *C major Fugue*, BWV 547, proceeds on its way somewhat remorselessly, the *Canonic Variations* bring out the very best in Marie-Claire Alain, and the opening presen-

tation, in which the Christmas Chorale cantus firmus subtly creeps through the flowing decorative lines is managed very cunningly, while the intricate contrapuntal writing remains clear throughout, and the chorales which follow have plenty of variety in presentation and mood.

Volume 7: *Chorale Preludes, BWV 655 & 668; Clavier-Übung, Part 3: German Organ Mass: Chorale Preludes, BWV 680–89; 4 Duets, BWV 802–5; Fugue in E flat, BWV 552.*

(M) *** Erato 4509 96724-2. Alain (organ of Martinikerk, Groningen).

This is repertoire which finds Alain at her very finest, for her performances of the Chorales clearly identify with their spiritual implications. Splendid recording: this can be strongly recommended.

Volume 8: *Chorale Preludes: Orgelbüchlein Nos. 35–46, BWV 633–44; Fantasia in C, BWV 570; Partita sopra 'Sei gegrüsset, Jesu gütig', BWV 768; Preludes & Fugues, BWV 534 & 546.*

(M) **(*) Erato 4509 96725-2. Alain (organ of St Laurentskerk, Alkmaar).

Alain's opening *Prelude and Fugue in C minor* is rather stoic, though it is certainly a powerful utterance. The dozen chorale preludes from the *Orgelbüchlein* bring the usual simplicity and variety, but it is the partita on *'Sei gegrüsset, Jesu gütig'* which really excites Alain's imagination – not surprisingly, as it is one of Bach's very finest sets of keyboard variations, which reaches a stunning apotheosis here. The recording dates from 1990.

Volume 9: *Chorale Preludes: Orgelbüchlein Nos. 1–19, BWV 599–617; BWV 735; Fantasias: in C min., BWV 562; in G, BWV 572; Fugue on a Theme of Legrenzi in C min., BWV 574.*

(M) **(*) Erato 4509 96742-2. Alain (organ of St Laurentskerk, Alkmaar).

The *Très vitement* opening of the *G major Fantasia* is always appealing, and Alain plays it perkily enough, then returning to her full-bodied style for the *Gravement–lentement*, which she takes very literally. The first of the Orgelbüchlein chorales included here, *Nunn komm' der Heiden Heiland*, BWV 599, is also very fully orchestrated, but in *Gottes Sohn ist kommen*, BWV 600, the balance between decoration and chorale is felicitous. The host of ascending and descending angels in BWV 606 is evocatively pictured, but it is in a quietly reflective piece like *Das alte Jahr vergangen ist*, BWV 614, that Alain is at her finest.

Volume 10: *Leipzig Chorale Preludes: BWV 651–2, 656–7, 659–61, 665–7; Prelude & Fugue in D, BWV 532; Trio in D min., BWV 583.*

(M) **(*) Erato 4509 96743-2. Alain (organ of St Laurentskerk, Alkmaar).

There is no denying the grandeur of Alain's opening *D major Prelude*, BWV 532, and the fugue is ebullient. The *Trio in D minor* provides a comparatively lightweight transition to a further extended grouping of Bach's splendid Leipzig Chorales, including three different settings of *Nun komm der Heiden Heiland*, and two each of *Komm, heiliger Geist* and *Jesus Christus, unser Heiland*. They definitely suit the panoply of colour possible with the Alkmaar organ, and Alain is generally very persuasive.

Volume 11: *Concertos* (for solo organ): *Nos. 1 in G* (after ERNST); *2 in A min.* (after VIVALDI: *Concerto, Op. 3/8*); *3 in C* (after VIVALDI: *Concerto, Op. 7/11*); *4 in C* (after ERNST); *5 in D min.* (after VIVALDI: *Concerto, Op. 3/11*), *BWV 592–6; Aria, BWV 587; Chorale Prelude, BWV 653b; Preludes & Fugues, BWV 536 & 550; Trio in G min., BWV 584.*

(M) *** Erato 4509 96744-2. Alain (organ of St Martin, Masevaux).

This splendid Müller organ with its bright, sunny reeds sounds just right for Bach's vivacious Vivaldi transcriptions. The works by Johann Ernst are also most rewarding. Alain's tempi are apt; allegros are not raced, but they are certainly infectious. The *Aria in F* is a Couperin transcription (from *Les Nations*). The two *Preludes and Fugues* are also comparatively lightweight, although still first-class Bach, from the early Weimar period. They are given attractively lively performances. A splendid disc and an ideal sampler to show this artist at her most perceptive.

Volume 12: *Pastorale, BWV 590; Prelude (Fantasia) & Fugue, BWV 542; Prelude & Fugue, BWV 543; Toccatas, BWV 564–5; Toccata & Fugue in F, BWV 540.*

⊛ (M) *** Erato 4509 96745-2. Alain (organs of St Bavokerk, Haarlem; Jakobijnkerk, Leeuwarden).

Using a pair of magnificent Dutch organs, Marie-Claire Alain here surveys an ideally chosen group of Bach's organ works on the largest scale, and she is not found wanting. The pedal solo in the *Toccata in F* is spectacular indeed, if muddied a little by the resonance, while the *Fantasia and Fugue in G minor*, BWV 542, is particularly imposing, with the fugue given a thrilling impetus. The famous *Toccata and Fugue in D minor* is again a shade resonant – there have been clearer-focused versions – but the performance certainly does not lack panache. The *Prelude and Fugue in A minor*, too, has unquestioned flair, while the *Toccata, Adagio and Fugue in C* is very commanding indeed. This performance climaxes a recital of the very highest calibre, superbly recorded.

Volume 13: *6 Trio Sonatas, BWV 525–30.*

(M) **(*)Erato 4509 96746-2. Alain (organ of Aa Kerk, Groningen).

Marie-Claire Alain decided to use the 'other' (Schnitger) organ in Groningen for the *Trio Sonatas* and to our ears the organ sounds very good indeed. Alain plays these Italianate works with considerable flair, and she is particularly appealing in slow movements. Just occasionally the running passages of the outer movements seem almost too mellifluous, but for the most part these are fresh and highly enjoyable performances that do justice to this splendid old instrument.

Volume 14: *Adagio (& Allegro), BWV 1027; Chorale Prelude, BWV 720; Fugue in G min., BWV 578; Passacaglia & Fugue in C min., BWV 582; Preludes, BWV 568–9; Prelude & Fugue, BWV 541; Ricercare a 6, BWV 1079; 6 Schübler Chorale Preludes, BWV 645–50.*

(M) **(*) Erato 4509 96747-2. Alain (organ of Stiftskirche, Goslar).

The famous *Schübler Chorales* are the highlight of Marie-Claire Alain's final volume. They are particularly imaginative and pleasing. Alain takes the famous *Passacaglia in C minor* very spaciously, and here she does not quite generate a high enough degree of tension to carry it at such a slow speed. The *Fugue in G minor* is a little didactic, too – although again very effectively registered. On the other hand, the *Prelude and Fugue in G major* and the *Prelude in G major* are both fine performances.

Kevin Bowyer Nimbus Series

Volume 1: *Chorale Preludes, BWV 1099 & 721; Concerto in G (after Prince Johann Ernst), BWV 592; Fantasia & Fugue in G min., BWV 542; Trio Sonata No. 1, BWV 525.*

*** Nim. NI 5280. Bowyer (Marcussen organ of Sct. Hans Kirke, Odense, Denmark).

Volume 2: *Chorale Preludes: BWV 720, 697 & 722, 751 & 729, 738; Fugue (Gigue) in G, BWV 577; Preludes & Fugues, BWV 532 & 541; Trio Sonata No. 5, BWV 529.*

*** Nim. NI 5289. Bowyer.

Volume 3: *Chorale Partita: Sei gegrüsset, Jesu gütig, BWV 768; Concerto in D min. after Vivaldi, BWV 596; Preludes & Fugues, BWV 534 & 543.*

**(*) Nim. NI 5290. Bowyer.

Volume 4: *Fantasia & imitatio, BWV 563; Fugue in C min., BWV 575; 2 Fugues on Themes of Albinoni, BWV 950–51; 8 Short Preludes & Fugues, BWV 553–60; Toccatas: in G min., BWV 915; in G, BWV 916.*

⊛ *** Nim. NI 5377. Bowyer.

Volume 5: *Aria in F (after Couperin), BWV 587; Concerto in A min. (after Vivaldi), BWV 593; Fugue in G, BWV 576; Prelude & Fugue, BWV 539; Toccata & Fugue in F, BWV 540.*

*** Nim. NI 5400. Bowyer.

Volume 6: *Chorale Partita 'Wenn wir in höchsten Nöten sein', BWV Anh. 78; Fantasias super 'Valet will ich dir geben', BWV 735–6; Preludes & Fugues, BWV 533 & 535; Toccata in E, BWV 566; Toccata, Adagio & Fugue in C, BWV 564; Trio in G min., BWV 584; Trio Sonata No. 6, BWV 630.*

*** Nim. NI 5423. Bowyer.

Volume 7: *Orgelbüchlein: Chorales & Chorale Preludes Nos. 1–46, BWV 599–644.*

**(*) Nim. NI 5457/8. Bowyer; Fynske Chamber Ch., Joensen.

Volume 8: *Chorale Preludes, BWV 653, 709 & 726, 731, 765; (4 Neumeister Chorales): BWV 1098, 1106, 1115–16. Concerto in F (after Vivaldi's Concerto, Op. 3/3); Fantasia & Fugue in C min., BWV 537; Fugue on a Theme by*

Legrenzi, *BWV 574; Preludes & Fugues, BWV 531, 544, 547 & 895* (attrib.); *6 Schübler Chorales, BWV 645–50; Toccata & Fugue in D min. (Dorian), BWV 538; Trio Sonata in G, BWV 1039/1027a.*

(B) *** Nim. Double NI 5500/1. Bowyer.

Volume 9: *Clavier-Übung. Part 3: German Organ Mass: Prelude in E, BWV 552; Chorale Preludes, BWV 669–89; 4 Duets, BWV 802–5; Fugue in E flat (St Anne), BWV 552. Concerto in G* (after VIVALDI: *Violin Concerto in G), BWV 973; Fugue in G min., BWV 578; Passacaglia & Fugue in C min., BWV 582.*

✹ (B) *** Nim. Double NI 5561/2. Bowyer.

Volume 10: *Leipzig Chorale Preludes Nos. 1–18, BWV 651–668a; 4 Early Chorale Settings, BWV 1104, 1108–4; 1199; Concerto No. 3 in C (after Vivaldi, Op. 3/11, RV 565); Fugue in A min., BWV 949.*

(B) *** Nim. Double NI 5573/4 (2). Bowyer.

Volume 11: *Canonic Variations on 'Vom Himmel hoch', BWV 769; Chorale Preludes, BWV 690–91, 698, 702, 733, 743, 756; BWV Anh. 55, 60 & 70; 8 Chorale Preludes from the Neumeister Collection* (Yale manuscript), *BWV 957, 1092, 1096; 1111–13, 1117–18; Fugue in B min. on a Theme of Corelli, BWV 579; Preludes & Fugues, BWV 943 & 953; BWV 546; (Wedge), BWV 548; Toccatas: in C min., BWV 911; in E min., BWV 914; Trios in B min.* (arr. from *BWV 570); in D min., BWV 583.*

(B) *** Nim. Double NI 5606/7 (2). Bowyer.

Volume 12: *Allabreve, BWV 589; Aria variata, BWV 989; Chorales, BWV 700–701; 710; 1090; Fantasias: (Concerto), BWV 571; in G, BWV 572; Fuga chromatisch bearbeitet, BWV An.44; Fugue in G min., BWV 131a; Kleines harmonisches Labyrinthe, BWV 591; Partita on Allein Gott in der Höh' sei Ehr, BWV 771; Preludes & Fugues, BWV 545 & 550; Toccata in F sharp min., BWV 918; Trio Sonatas Nos. 3–4, BWV 527–8.*

(N) (B) **(*) Nim. NI 5647/8. Bowyer (Marcussen organ as above).

Kevin Bowyer is another of the younger generation of organists who is embarking on a complete Bach survey, but he has chosen to produce a series of carefully planned recitals, using the same Danish organ throughout, rather than grouping works together in their respective genres. Characteristically, the Nimbus engineeers produce a sound-image with plenty of ambience, with glowing, colourful pipings and throaty reeds, the effect often expansively grand.

The first volume in the series sets the pattern by framing a collection of lighter pieces and chorale preludes with two ambitious major works. Bowyer's opening *Toccata and Fugue in D minor* is second to none, the toccata strong yet improvisational in feeling; then, after a solemn cadence, the fugue is vividly brilliant with a powerful apotheosis. The sound is magnificently rich in colour.

Volume 2, a predominantly cheerful programme, brings more examples of Bowyer's lively rhythmic style and the appealing colours and husky reeds of this fine Danish organ. Volume 3 seems slightly less successful overall than some of Bowyer's collections, with a rather easy-going approach

to the *Sei gegrüsset Variations*, and the Vivaldi concerto, too, is not as sprightly as it might be. The framing *Preludes and Fugues* are powerful and vigorous, especially the closing *A minor*, but the recording seems fractionally brighter than usual and the reeds just a trifle grainy.

Volume 4 is much more stimulating, opening with the brilliantly flamboyant *Toccata in G minor* which, after its thoughtful centrepiece, encapsulates a bouncing, minor-key version of the '*Gigue' Fugue*. This is played marvellously, yet the highlight of the recital is surely the set of *Short Preludes and Fugues, BWV 553–60*. Finally the three-part Weimar *G minor Toccata* closes the programme with sprightly, dancing 6/8 exuberance. There are few more invigorating Bach organ recitals than this.

Volume 5 begins with Bach's arrangement of Vivaldi, the *Concerto in A minor* opening jauntily, and almost immediately brings some engaging fluting in the glowing registration, as does the brightly extrovert *Fugue in G*. The colouring of the chorale preludes is nicely varied. The *Prelude and Fugue in D minor* has an improvisational thoughtfulness, while the closing Weimar *Toccata and Fugue in F* is vigorously articulated and suitably resplendent and weighty.

Volume 6 is another well-planned and highly successful collection. The powerful *Toccata, Adagio and Fugue in C* makes an arresting opener and Bowyer's virtuosity in the two contrasted Fantasias on '*Valet will ich dir geben*' is matched in the two often flamboyant *Preludes and Fugues* which are among Bach's most interesting (and exciting). Then the flowing variants on the very attractive chorale, '*Wenn wir in höchsten Nöten sein*', make a perfect contrast before the powerful *Toccata in E*, which demands more and more bravura as it proceeds to its majestic denouement.

Volume 7 is a double and presents the *Orgelbüchlein* with each organ chorale prelude immediately preceded by the sung chorale. While that is a good plan, its drawback is that there are no separate cues on the pair of CDs for each organ entry. The Danish choir sing admirably, but the choral focus is not as uniformly smooth as with the Amsterdam group on Koopman's set of the *Leipzig* and *Schübler Chorales*.

Comparing Kevin Bowyer's performances of the *Orgelbüchlein* directly with Christopher Herrick's versions (which in general we find more satisfying) reveals an astonishing difference of sound and characterization. The Danish organ has much more plangent reeds and Bowyer's performances are less warmly mellifluous, more dramatic. Yet those who like a lively presentation will find this set very much to their taste, for Bowyer's tempi are usually brisker than Herrick's. He is recorded very vividly.

As with the previous single discs, the two recitals which are paired together in the second Nimbus double (Volume 8) are meant to be listened to separately. Both are highly enjoyable and bring plenty of contrast. On the first, after the vigorous *Fugue in C minor, BWV 574*, the arrangement of Vivaldi's concerto from *L'estro armonico* for manuals only (no pedals) works extremely well, with the rich blending of colours in the *Largo* well contrasted with the framing allegros. Bowyer's choice of chorales is also intended to give maximum contrast, and sometimes he plays them in pairs to show Bach's imaginatively varied treatments of the same cantus firmus.

The *Trio Sonata in G* is a conjectural reconstruction, but a very successful one. The *Preludes and Fugues* have plenty of life and vigour. Bowyer also opens the famous first *Schübler Chorale* with a bouncing rhythmic lift, and he is equally enticing in his brilliant registration of the buoyant closing chorale of the set, *Kommst du nun, Jesu*, BWV 650. The recital ends with a superbly exuberant account of the *Dorian Toccata and Fugue in D minor* which here proves quite as exciting as its more famous companion in the same key (BWV 565).

Volume 9 centres on Bach's so-called *German Organ Mass*, and this account is unsurpassed on CD. After the powerful introductory *Prelude*, Bach presents each chorale in two contrasting versions, the first elaborate, then a simpler setting without pedals (although occasionally this order is reversed). Bowyer's imagination is inspired to use all the resources of the splendid organ to emphasize the contrapuntal and stylistic differences and to create the widest variety of mood. Bowyer gives the four deceptively simple *Duets* sparkling registrations to make a foil for the weighty power of the closing *St Anne's Fugue*, which holds the listener from the first bar to the last. Bowyer then continues his recital with a captivating account of Bach's transcription of one of Vivaldi's liveliest violin concertos, and he ends with a superbly eloquent performance of the great *Passacaglia and Fugue in C minor*.

As ever here, Bowyer's registration is consistently imaginative in Volume 10, and he conveys the devotional mood of the gentler pieces unsanctimoniously. The rock-like opening *Fantasia on 'Komm, Heiliger Geist'* is followed by a gentler, more meditative setting of the same chorale with the following *An Wasserflüssen Babylon* sublimely peaceful. The intricate texture of *Von Gott will ich nicht lassen* is splendidly clear, and the contrasts of the three settings of *Nun komm der Heiden Heiland* are made most effectively. Similarly the three versions of both *Allein Gott in der Höh' sei Ehr* and *Jesus Christus, unser Heiland* are comparably resourceful. The final chorale, *Vor deinen Thron tret ich*, is beautifully evoked. The life-assertive *Fugue in A minor*, a jaunty early work, is then followed by four more simple chorales, only recently discovered (also from Bach's youth), and the recital ends with an ebullient account of Bach's enthusiastic transcription of a familiar Vivaldi concerto.

Volume 11 is prefaced by a pair of Bach's mightiest fugues, the E minor work organically whole, with the opening music of the fugue recapitulated without alteration at the close, the C minor with the two parts less integrated – the prelude tempestuous, the fugue more sombre but reaching a powerful culmination. In between come a series of more lightly registered pieces (even the *Canonic Variations*). The second recital is framed by a pair of virtuoso *Toccatas* which Bowyer, recognizing as harpsichord originals, plays fluently and registers appropriately. Then come the simple early *Neumeister Chorales*, where the organ's full colour palette is indulged. The *Prelude* and *Fugue in C* act as an intermission. The recording, like the playing, is of very high quality.

As with previous recent issues, Volume 12 consists of two separate recitals, each including a *Trio Sonata* and items which are almost certainly not authentic Bach. The attractive *Fantasia* which opens the first disc and the ebullient *G major*

Prelude and Fugue which begins the second are highlights, but there is a good deal of slow music here, and in spite of Bowyer's colourful registration (as in the *Kleines harmonisches Labyrinthe* and the *Aria variata in A minor*, one would have liked more lively pieces and overall this is not one of his most stimulating sets. Christopher Herrick, for instance, is more ear-tickling in the extended but simple variations on *Allein Gott* which are unlikely to be by Bach. The *Fantasia and Fugue in C minor*, BWV 562 certainly is, as it exists in autograph, but it is incomplete and ends frustratingly in mid-air. Excellent recording, as usual in this series.

Christopher Herrick Hyperion Series

Trio Sonatas Nos. 1–6, BWV 525–30.

*** Hyp. CDA 66390. Herrick (Metzler organ of St Nicholas Church, Bremgarten, Switzerland).

Christopher Herrick, favouring a series of Swiss organs, is very much of the new generation of organists, giving equal precedence to momentum and vitality and colourful registration, alongside a feeling for the musical architecture. These performances of the *Trio Sonatas* may be comparatively relaxed but the playing has plenty of lift, and he produces colours in slow movements to charm the ear, with the lyrical lines flowing. He has chosen an instrument well suited to this repertoire and he is in full command of its palette, with registration suited to the character of each movement and articulation that is precise without pedantry. The Hyperion recording, too, cannot be faulted, and even the order of works is chosen to make the most of their variety of style.

Passacaglia in C min., BWV 582; Toccatas & Fugues: in D min. (Dorian), BWV 538; in D min., BWV 565; in F, BWV 540; Toccata, Adagio & Fugue in C, BWV 564.

*** Hyp. CDA 66434. Herrick (Metzler organ of Stadtkirche, Zofingen, Switzerland).

These are all powerfully structured yet attractively lively performances. The forward thrust is consistently impressive: the famous *D minor* work certainly sparkles yet does not lack power, while the *Fugue in C major*, which follows on after the *Toccata and Adagio*, BWV 564, is not too heavy. Similarly the *Passacaglia in C minor* has gravitas without seeming too sombre and is glowingly decorated. The recording has fine spectacle and realism.

Canonic Variations: Vom Himmel hoch, BWV 769; Chorale Partitas: Christ, der du bist der helle Tag, BWV 766; O Gott, du frommer Gott, BWV 767; Sei gegrüsset, Jesu gütig, BWV 767–8; Ach, was soll ich Sünder machen, BWV 770.

*** Hyp. CDA 66455. Herrick (organ of St Nicholas Church, Bremgarten, Switzerland).

There is certainly no lack of momentum here, and in Herrick's hands the splendid Metzler organ at Bremgarten illuminates Bach's intricate divisions with a wide colouristic range. He always keeps the music moving and in the *Chorale Partitas* this is to advantage. Certainly the recording does the organ justice in vivid palette and truthful balance, and the music-making is consistently alive.

Orgelbüchlein: Chorale Preludes Nos. 1–46, BWV 599–644.

*** Hyp. CDA 66756. Herrick (Metzler organ of Stadtkirche, Rheinfelden, Switzerland).

Herrick's *Orgelbüchlein* is in every way recommendable, and these performances can stand among the finest in the catalogue. The Swiss Metzler organ seems just right for these relatively simple yet sometimes florid pieces: it has a wide palette and an equal range of sonorities. The effect is never plangent, yet Herrick readily keeps the cantus firmus in front of the listener without exaggeration. His tempi invariably seem apt and his approach is obviously aware of the word-meaning of each chorale and its expressive implications. The recording is beautiful, smooth yet clear.

Fantasias: in C min., BWV 562; in G, BWV 572; in C min., BWV 537; in G min., BWV 542; Preludes & Fugues: BWV 536, 543–7, 532, (Wedge) 548, (St Anne) 552, 534 & 541.

*** Hyp. CDA 66791/2. Herrick (organ of Jesuits' Church, Lucerne).

Among all the individual mixed recitals, this very imposing two-disc set centres on some of the most powerfully structured and intellectually cogent of all Bach's major organ works. Herrick offers a presentation which is obviously built on a background of careful preparation, with a spontaneously vivid presentation that is as emotionally compelling as it is authoritative, with each fugue moving on to a gripping apotheosis. The chosen Swiss instrument seems ideal for the repertoire and it is superbly recorded, giving weight, amplitude and clarity in equal measure.

'The Italian Connection': Concertos (for solo organ) Nos. 1, BWV 592 (after ERNST); 2–3, BWV 593–4 (both after VIVALDI); 4, BWV 595 (after ERNST); 5, BWV 596 (after VIVALDI); Fugue on a Theme of Corelli, BWV 579; Fugue on a Theme of Legrenzi in C min., BWV 574.

**(*) Hyp. CDA 66813. Herrick (organ of St Peter and St Paul, Villmergen, Switzerland).

This is somewhat disappointing. The Metzler organ Herrick uses for these concerto transcriptions has a splendid range of colour – witness the delightful palette of the *Largo e spiccato* of Vivaldi's *D minor Concerto*. But in the allegros he is not helped by the lack of bite in the reeds, although the spirited finale of that same *D minor Concerto* still sounds splendid. The Corelli *Fugue*, on the other hand, tends to jog along and the *Concerto Movement in C major* for Johann Ernst is quite heavy going.

19 Kirnberger Chorales, BWV 690–91, 694–713; 18 Leipzig Chorales, BWV 651–68; 6 Schübler Chorales, BWV 645–50.

*** Hyp. CDA 67071/2. Herrick (Metzler organ of Jesuitenkirche, Lucerne, Switzerland).

Herrick bounces along joyfully in the first two *Schübler Chorales* which open this collection, and how beautifully he brings out the cantus firmus in No. 4 (*Meine Seele erhebt den Herren*). The 18 *Leipzig Chorales* offer considerable variety, with four texts bringing several contrasted settings

of the same cantus firmus. Here at times Herrick is more withdrawn, even sombre, but the particularly fine *Kirnberger Chorales* are played and registered splendidly. They are all individual settings, which Herrick places in groups where the sources indicate Advent and Christmas, Easter and so on. As with the other recitals in this series, the Lucerne organ is beautifully recorded.

'Miniatures': Allabreve in D, BWV 589; Canzona in D min., BWV 588; Couperin Aria in F, BWV 587; 4 Duets, BWV 802/5; Fantasias: in A min., BWV 561; in C, BWV 570; Fantasia con imitatione in B min., BWV 563; Fugues, BWV 575–6 & 578; Fugue alla giga, BWV 577; Musical Offering: 3- & 6-part Ricercares in C min., BWV 1079; Pastorale in F, BWV 590; Preludes, BWV 551, 569 & 568; Preludes & Fugues, BWV 533, 535, 539 (Fiddle Fugue), 549a, 550 & 569; Toccata in E, BWV 566; Trios: in D min., BWV 583; in C min. (Fasch), BWV 585; in G (Telemann), BWV 586; in G, BWV 1027a.

*** Hyp. CDA 67211/2. Herrick (Metzler organ of Stadtkirche, Rheinfelden, Switzerland).

This is a curious mixture. Not all of these pieces are short (the *Pastorale* – a most attractive performance – is in four movements) and many of the *Preludes and Fugues*, although not extended, are very considerable works and make a strong impression here. The very opening *Allabreve* is commanding, as is the *Toccata in E major* with its weighty pedals. Of course the engaging *Gigue Fugue*, the *Couperin Aria* and the *Telemann Trio* (all delightfully registered) are lightweight and serve well as interludes within the more substantial fare. But the set proves an attractive way of gathering up some of Bach's less obvious masterpieces, and they are all splendidly played, and recorded on a fine Swiss organ.

Clavier-Übung, Part 3: Prelude & Fugue in E flat, BWV 552; Chorale Preludes, BWV 669–89. Chorale Preludes, Fantasias & Fughettas, BWV 672–5; 677, 679, 681, 683, 685, 687, 715–18, 720–22, 724–36, 738–40.

**(*) Hyp. CDA 67213/4. Herrick (Metzler main and choir organs of Stadtkirche, Zofingen, Switzerland).

Unlike other recitalists, Herrick does not present Part 3 of Bach's *Clavier-Übung*, the so-called 'German Organ Mass', as a complete entity. He has already given us the four *Duets* in the collection of 'Miniatures' above, so here (on the first disc) he frames just the ten large-scale chorale settings with the mighty *E flat St Anne Prelude and Fugue*, using the church's large main organ. Then, on the second CD, he turns to the beautiful single-manual choir organ for the remaining ten lightweight chorales. In principle this works well enough, but it robs the listener of the added stimulation of hearing Bach's simple and elaborate settings of the same chorale side by side. Herrick's performances are well up to standard, but we are inclined to choose Kevin Bowyer's version of Part 3 of the *Clavier-Übung*, which presents the music in the normal published sequence.

'Organ Cornucopia': Chorale Preludes, BWV 723, 741, 743, 747, 753–5, 758 (4 verses), 762, 764–5; BWV Anh. 55; Concertos: in G, BWV 571; in E flat, BWV 597; Fantasia in

C, BWV 575; Fugues: in C, BWV 946; in C min., BWV 562; in D, BWV 580; Kleines harmonisches Labyrinth, BWV 591; Pedal-exercitium, BWV 598; Prelude & Fugue in C, BWV 531; Prelude in C, BWV 567; Trio in G min., BWV 584.

*** Hyp. CDA 67139. Herrick (Metzler organ of Pfarrkirche, St Michael, Kaisten, Switzerland).

This organ in Kaisten has the strongest personality, and Herrick's registration for the chorales is strikingly rich in colour. *O Vater, allmächtiger Gott*, BWV 758, is given in four verses, with the pedals reserved for the final verse. The *Pedal-exercitium* brings an arresting opportunity for virtuoso footwork and, of the two solo Concertos, BWV 571 in G also features the pedals strongly, with a descending bass-scale in its *Chaconne* finale which is remarkably gripping here. The strangely named and musically intangible *Kleines harmonisches Labyrinth* brings a further contrast near the end of this otherwise boldly presented recital which holds the listener from beginning to end.

36 Neumeister Chorales.

*** Hyp. CDA 67215. Herrick (Metzler organ of the Stadtkirche, Zofingen, Switzerland).

The original manuscript for the *Neumeister Chorales* was a comparatively recent discovery, found in a collection at Yale University. The music itself has plenty of variety, and Bach's imagination in this field was inexhaustible, and Herrick is a very persuasive advocate on this fine Swiss organ. The music is admirably paced, and always spontaneously alive, while detail remains clear.

Attributions: *15 Chorale Preludes, BWV 692–3, 744–6, 748–52, 756–7, 759, 760–61, 763; Chorale Partita, Allein Gott in der Höh' sei Ehr; Fugue in G, BWV 581; BWV 8 Little Preludes & Fugues, BWV 553–60.*

(N) *** Hyp. CDA 67263. Herrick (Metzler organ of Pfarrkirche St Michael, Kaisten, Switzerland).

As one knows from the 'Haydn' quartet, Op. 3/5, with its famous *Serenade*, now known to be composed by Hoffstetter, attributions usually make attractive listing, whoever composed them. So it is with the Eight Little Preludes & Fugues where the basic material is so striking, although scholars feel that the working out is not felicitous enough for J.S.B.

Yet the opening of *No. 1* is instantly commanding, the *Fugue* of *No. 2* and the *Prelude* of *No. 4* are attractively jaunty, *No. 6* opens grandly and the *Prelude* of *No. 8* brings a splendid excusion on the pedals which Herrick obviously relishes, followed by an equally appealling *Fugue*. Herrick effectively instersperses these works with the fifteen simple chorale settings, where his pacing and registration are so apt that these too are very diverting. Try the utterly different pair of settings of *Vater unser in Himmelreich*, BWV 749 and 750 or the engaging *In dulci jubilo*, BWV 751.

Herrick is perhaps at his finest in the always imaginative registration of the seventeen variations which make up the *Chorale Partita, Allein Gott*. As Stephen Westrop comments in the excellent notes which accompany this disc: 'Whoever the composer was, the work employs most of the techniques for varying chorales and displays unbounded energy and

invention'. The Swiss Metzler organ Herrick plays has a splendid palette, and is superbly recorded. Bach or not, this is a most rewarding recital, very highly recommended.

Ton Koopman Complete Teldec Series

Volume 1: *Canzona in D min., BWV 588; Fantasias, BWV 562, 570 & 572; Fantasia & Fugue in G min., BWV 542; Fugue in G min., BWV 578; Passacaglia in C min., BWV 582; Preludes & Fugues, BWV 531, 543–4.*

*** Teldec 4509 94458-2. Koopman (Rudolph Garrels organ, Grote Kerk, Maassluis).

Ton Koopman gets his Teldec series off to a good start by choosing a superb early eighteenth-century Netherlands organ at Maassluis – weighty, yet with a glowing upper register. He opens with a richly upholstered *Fantasia in G minor* and yet he gives a nice lift to all the fugues, which are aptly paced, his contrasts between prelude and fugue in each instance perceptively judged. The *Canzona* is effectively subdued, but the flamboyant *Prelude in C*, BWV 531, and lighter, more buoyant *G major Fantasia* are splendidly done. The programme ends with a massive yet very clearly detailed account of the masterly *Passacaglia in C minor*, which progresses powerfully, yet never sounds leaden. A splendid disc.

Volume 2: *18 Leipzig Chorale Preludes, with Chorales, BWV 651–68; 6 Schübler Chorale Preludes with Chorales, BWV 645–50.*

*** Teldec 4509 94459-2 (2). Koopman (Müller organ of Grote Kerk) with Amsterdam Baroque Ch.

For Volume 2, Ton Koopman presents two major sets of organ chorale preludes, together with the vocal chorales on which they are based. These chorales are sung simply and very beautifully by the Amsterdam Baroque Choir, and the appropriate organ work follows. In the case of the famous *Schübler* set, with which he begins, there are (in all but *Kommst du nun, Jesu, vom Himmel herunter*, BWV 650) two different vocal chorales for each of the organ pieces, which here are played as concert pieces. The *Leipzig Chorales* are played and registered very simply, so that the organ variants still carry the (usually) serene character of each hymn-like vocal setting. Both organ and choir are recorded most naturally.

Volume 3: *6 Trio Sonatas, BWV 525–30.*

*** Teldec 4509 94460-2. Koopman (Arp Schnitger organ of St Jacobi-Kirche, Hamburg).

These are engagingly sunny performances of beguiling music, Bach at his most light-hearted. There may be more ebullient accounts available on disc but none with more charm. The bright, mellow sounds he conjures from this Hamburg organ are a constant pleasure and his joy in the music comes over directly to the listener.

Volume 4: *Preludes & Fugues, BWV 532, 566; Toccata, Adagio & Fugue in D min., BWV 564; Toccatas & Fugues: in F, BWV 540; in D min. (Dorian), BWV 538; in D min., BWV 565.*

⚙ *** Teldec 4509 98443-2. Koopman (Arp Schnitger organ of St Jacobi-Kirche, Hamburg).

A magnificent record. What is so remarkable is the way Koopman uses the very same Arp Schnitger organ as for the *Trio Sonatas* above, yet seems to create an entirely new sound-world for these great, flamboyant masterpieces. The *Prelude in E major* is overwhelmingly massive and, while the fugue bounces along, the work's finale is powerfully expansive. Koopman revels in the nimble pedal-work of the *F major Toccata*, while the bravura scales for both keyboard and pedals at the opening of the *Toccata in C* are quite riveting; he then follows with a beautifully registered (and neatly ornamented) *Adagio* and buoyantly jolly *Fugue*. He opens the most famous of all Bach organ *Toccatas – in D minor* – with a repeated trill on the opening phrase and then, with his bravura swirls of notes, creates gripping tension which is finally resolved only at the work's overwhelming cadential apotheosis. The recording is superb, and happily in almost all cases where the music is in more than one section, each is separately cued.

Volume 5: *Clavier-Übung, Part 3: German Organ Mass (Prelude & Fugue in E flat, BWV 532; Chorale Preludes, BWV 669–89; 4 Duets, BWV 802–5). Canonic Variations on Vom Himmel hoch, BWV 769a.*

**(*) Teldec 4509 98464-2 (2). Koopman (organ of Dom St Marien, Freiberg).

The so-called 'German Organ Mass' is not easy to bring off. Koopman sets a serene mood for the earlier *Kyrie* chorales but is soon extending his palette, and he is especially impressive when he comes to contrast the two settings of *Allein Gott in der Höh' sei Ehr* with its following brief fughetta. The arrival of *Wir glauben all an einen Gott* makes an arrestingly powerful contrast. Later, Koopman's presentation again becomes more sober. The ambitious *Canonic Variations on 'Vom Himmel hoch'* make a fine pendant, and the recording is well up to standard. But overall we would not prefer Koopman's version of the *Clavier-Übung* Part 3 to Kevin Bowyer's Nimbus account.

Volume 6: *Allabreve in D, BWV 589; Fantasia & Fugue in C min., BWV 537; Fugue in C min., BWV 575; Prelude in A min., BWV 569; Preludes & Fugues, BWV 533, 535, 546, 550 & 549.*

*** Teldec 0630 13155-2. Koopman (Christian Muller organ, Waalse Kerk, Amsterdam).

The florid *Prelude in G*, amiable *Prelude in A minor*, busy *Prelude and Fugue in G minor*, BWV 535, and the more virtuosic *Prelude in G*, BWV 550, are all vividly played and the imitation is well observed in the *Fugue in E min.*, BWV 533, after the bravura flourishes of its lively prelude. But Koopman opens imposingly with the *C minor Prelude* and its solemn fugue, BWV 546; then he provides contrast with the following separate *Fugue* in the same key. We stay in C minor for BWV 549, with its opening pedal solo, which reappears in the fugue; then aptly the closing Leipzig *Fantasia*, BWV 537, returns once more to this key. It begins over a pedal and has a fugue which is full of interest.

Volume 7: *Pastorale in F, BWV 590; Fugue in G, BWV 577; Pedal-exercitium in G min., BWV 598; Preludes & Fugues, BWV 534, 539, 541, 545 & 547; Trio in D min., BWV 583.*

**(*) Teldec 0630 17647-2. Koopman (Christian Muller organ, Waalse Kerk, Amsterdam).

For the *Prelude and Fugue in C*, BWV 545, which opens this recital, Koopman uses the authentic earlier three-movement format (Bach borrowed the slow central movement from his *Trio Sonata*, BWV 529). It works very well; but then Koopman disappoints with a very laid-back account of the *Gigue Fugue*, lacking rhythmic buoyancy. The *Trio in D minor* is a gentle piece, followed by the vigorous *Pedal-exercitium*, for which – as Bach left it unfinished – Koopman improvises his own ending. The *Prelude and Fugue in G*, BWV 541, is another most attractive performance, and the *D minor* work, BWV 539, makes a suitable contrast, before the more floridly ambitious work in F minor. Then comes the engaging lightweight four-movement *Pastoral* before the catchy closing *Prelude and Fugue in C major* work, with its scalic main subject, a splendid example of Bach's mature style. This is a very well-planned recital, and it is a pity it is slightly let down by BWV 577.

Volume 8: *Orgelbüchlein: Choral Preludes Nos. 1–46, BWV 599–644.*

*** Teldec 3984 21466-2. Koopman (Riepp Dreifaltigkeitsorgel, Basilika of Sts Alexander and Theodor, Ottobeuren).

Ton Koopman revels in the kaleidoscopic colour combinations possible with this splendid eighteenth-century organ at what was once the Benedictine Abbey at Ottobeuren. He varies dynamics imaginatively from piece to piece, interchanging intimacy with an occasional burst of splendour, and decorating the cantus firmus of the gentler pieces with affectionate subtlety. A mysterious, almost blurred effect surrounds *In dulci jubilo* and *Jesu meine Freude* with an acoustic halo, compared with a bright regal trumpety mixture for *Helft mir Gotts Güte preisen* and *Heut triumphieret Gottes Sohn*. There are already several fine sets of these delightful miniature chorales from other organists, but Koopman's certainly ranks with the very best. The recording is flawless.

Volume 9: *Chorale Partitas (partite diverse): (i) Ach, was soll ich Sünder machen, BWV 770; Christ der du bist der helle Tag, BWV 766; (ii) O Gott, du frommer Gott, BWV 767; Sei gegrüsset, Jesu gütig, BWV 678; Chorale Preludes, BWV 690-91, 705-8, 728-9 & 764; Schmück Dich, O liebe Seele.*

*** Teldec 3984 24829-2. Koopman ((i) Riepp Dreifaltigkeitsorgel; (ii) Heilig-Geist-Orgel, Sts Alexander & Theodor, Ottobeuren).

For one of the finest CDs of his series Koopman has again sought out the magnificent pair of Rieppe/Silbermann organs in Ottobeuren (named after the Trinity and Holy Ghost respectively) on which to play four of Bach's large-scale *Chorale Partitas* in which the diverse variants have the widest range of styles and invite a rich palette of colour. He also chooses two sets of chorale preludes as interludes. The first group, beginning with *In dulci jubilo*, BWV 729, is boldly and fully registered, the second, beginning with *Liebster Jesu,* BWV 706, is more intimate and spiritual in feeling. The performances are of the highest order. Superb recording.

Volume 10: *Breikopf (Kirnberger) Chorales, BWV 694, 695a, 696–704, 709, 711–13, 715–18, 720–22, 724–7, 730–33, 735–6, 738–41, 743, 747, 749–50, 754–8, 762–5, 1085, BWV Anh. 49–50, 58; Other Chorales: Auf meinen lieben Gott (2 versions); Herr Christ, der einzig Gottes Sohn; Ich ruf zu Dir, Herr Jesu Christ; Komm, heilger Geist, erfüll die Herzen (all BWV deest).*

*** Teldec 3984 24828-2 (2). Koopman (Hans Heinrich Bader organ of St Walburgiskerk, Zutphen).

This is a convenient grouping of Bach's miscellaneous chorale preludes, simple chorale fantasias and fughettas which are named after one of Bach's pupils with whom their collection was associated: Johann Kirnberger.

The *manueliter* chorales were written for small organs without pedals, while the *pedaliter* pieces are more ambitious, written for larger church organs. Koopman creates his own order of performance, effectively alternating simpler and more elaborate settings. He also uses the widest possible range of registration, from piquant interplays as on the engaging opening *Allein Gott in der Höh' sei Ehr,* BWV 711, to a richer treatment of the same chorale, BWV 717. Indeed he often places different settings of the same chorale in juxtaposition to diverting effect. The polyphonic detail is very clear, with the cantus firmus always easily discernible, and this splendid organ with its vivid palette seems an ideal choice for such a programme.

Simon Preston DG Series

Disc 1: *Trio Sonatas Nos. 1–6, BWV 525–30* (Klais organ, St Katharina, Blankenberg).

Disc 2: *Fantasia & Fugue, BWV 537; Preludes & Fugues BWV 531, 533–5, 535a, 536, 539, 541; Toccata & Fugue (Dorian), BWV 538* (Marcussen organ, Tonbridge School Chapel).

Disc 3: *Fantasia & Fugue, BWV 542; Pedal-exercitium, BWV 598; Preludes & Fugues BWV 543–6; Toccata & Fugue, BW 540* (Tonbridge School organ, & Sauer organ, St Peter, Waltrop).

Disc 4: *Fantasias, BWV 562, con imitazione, BWV 563; Preludes & Fugues, BWV 547–51; Toccata, Adagio & Fugue, BWV 564* (Klais organ, St John's, Smith Square, London, & organ of St Peter, Waltrop).

Disc 5: *Fantasias, BWV 570 & 572; Pastorale, BWV 590; Preludes, BWV 568, pro organo pleno, BWV 569; Prelude & Fugue, BWV 532; Toccatas & Fugues, BWV 565–6* (Klais organ, Kreuzbergkirche, & organ of St John's, Smith Square).

Disc 6: *Allabreve, BWV 589; Aria, BWV 587; Canzona, BWV 588; Fugues, on a Theme of Legrenzi, BWV 574, BWV 575, 577–8, on a Theme of Corelli, BWV 579; Passacaglia &*

Fugue, BWV 582; Trios, BWV 586–7 (organs of St John's, Smith Square, & St Peter, Waltrop)

Disc 7: (Solo) *Concertos Nos. 1–5, BWV 592–6* (Marcussen organ, Lübeck Cathedral).

Disc 8: *Orgelbüchlein: Chorale Preludes Nos. 1–45, BWV 599–644* (organ of Klosterkirke, Sorø).

Disc 9: *6 Schübler Chorales, BWV 645–50; Leipzig Chorale Preludes Nos. 1–18, BWV 651–8* (Metzler organ of Trinity College, Cambridge).

Disc 10: *Leipzig Chorale Preludes Nos. 19–36, BWV 659–67; Clavier-Übung, Part 3: Organ Mass: Prelude (St Anne), BWV 552; Chorale Preludes, BWV 669–74* (organs of Trinity College, Cambridge, & Nidaros Domkirke, Trondheim).

Disc 11: *Clavier-Übung, Part 3: Organ Mass (cont.): Chorale Preludes, BWV 575–689; 4 Duets, BWV 802–5; Fugue (St Anne), BWV 552* (organ of Nidaros Domkirke, Trondheim).

Disc 12: *Kirnberger Chorales, BWV 690–713; Chorale Preludes, BWV 714–18, 720* (Anderson organ of Frue Kirke, Nyborg, & organ of Klosterkirke, Sorø).

Disc 13: *Chorale Preludes, BWV 721–4, 726–39, 741, 753, 764, BWV Anh. II/55; O Lamm Gottes* (without BWV number) (organ of Klosterkirke, Sorø).

Disc 14: *Chorale Partitas, BWV 766–8, 770; Canonic Variations, BWV 769* (Klais organ of Kreuzbergkirche, Bonn, & organ of Klosterkirke, Sorø).

(N)(B) *** DG 469 420-2 (14). Preston (various organs as listed above).

Simon Preston's survey was recorded over more than a decade from 1987 onwards, beginning with the solo *Concertos,* which set the standard for the entire series. These performances are first class in every way, and the recording of the Lübeck organ admirably clear, yet with an attractively resonant ambience. The *Chorale Partitas* that followed are lucid and beautifully registered, as is the single disc which gathers together all 45 chorales of the *Orgelbüchlein,* persuasively presented. Indeed Preston is at his most individual in this repertoire.

The first of the famous *Schübler Chorales,* which can often sound jerky, is smoothly articulated, and throughout the six the cantus firmus emerges clearly and firmly, the registration otherwise refined. Here and in the *Leipzig Chorales,* Preston, often favouring a degree of reticence, has chosen the comparatively mellow Metzler organ at Trinity College, Cambridge, while for the Kirnberger collection and other settings he has preferred the somewhat more characterful, reedier instrument at Sorø Abbey, Denmark. This is shown most strikingly in the registration of the famous *Ein' feste Burg, BWV 720,* while the organ's full panoply of colour is flamboyantly demonstrated in *Allein Gott in der Höh' sei Ehr, BWV 715.*

Preston revels in the extrovert brilliance of the early

Weimar *Preludes and Fugues* (and indeed also the *'Dorian' Toccata*) with their elaborately virtuoso use of the pedals, but relishes also the more mature, tightly structured works, which he plays with genuine panache. (Here the organ at St John's, Smith Square, shows its paces, especially in the excitingly played C minor and G major works, BWV 549 and 550).

The most ambitious structures like the *Passacaglia and Fugue in C minor* and the *Toccata, Adagio and Fugue in C minor* have an impressive sense of purpose and architecture, and the justly celebrated *D minor Toccata and Fugue, BWV 565*, played on the magnificent Sauer organ in Waltrop, has all the necessary panache. It is followed by the ebullient *Fantasia and Fugue in G minor*, an equally outstanding example of Preston's bravura.

Another highlight of the series is the (1993) set of *Trio Sonatas*. The sounds of the Blankenburg organ are sheer delight, with glowing colours in slow movements, while the reeds bring a touch more baroque bite to add character to the allegros, where Preston is always infectiously buoyant. The recording is in the demonstration bracket, but then the sound is state-of-the-art throughout. Part 3 of the *Clavier-Übung*, the so-called 'German Organ Mass', is split over two discs.

Some but by no means all of the repertoire has been issued on separate recital discs (see below), including a few works not included here, such as the *Eight Little Preludes and Fugues*, which are wrongly attributed to Bach. But apart from these omissions the whole series now appears in a DG bargain box, with the various genres sensibly grouped together. The performances are consistently alive and distinguished, and the choice of organs ear-ticklingly perceptive. Good notes, although the analysis of the music itself is general rather than detailed.

Simon Preston DG Series – Earlier Recitals

Allabreve, BWV 589; Aria in F, BWV 586 (transcription of Couperin); *Fantasias: in C, BWV 570; in G, BWV 571; Fantasia & Fugue in A min., BWV 561; Fugues: in C min., on a Theme by Legrenzi; in G, BWV 576; Fugue in B min. on a Theme of Corelli, BWV 579; Preludes, BWV 567–70; Kleines harmonisches Labyrinth, BWV 591; Preludes & Fugues, BWV 551 & 549; Trio in C min. (Fasch), BWV 585.*

**(*) DG (IMS) 453 541-2. Preston (Klais organ, St John's, Smith Square).

This is Simon Preston's equivalent of Christopher Herrick's collection of miniatures. Not all the music is of equal interest, but it gives Preston a chance to show the wide range of colour of the rebuilt St John's organ, with which he is personally associated, notably the strange *Kleines harmonisches Labyrinth*, while the *Prelude and Fugue in C minor* displays the full weight of this magnificent instrument. The reeds are bright, quite like a continental organ, although the effect is slightly more mellow; however, Bach's polyphony is always clearly yet not clinically defined.

Canzona, BWV 588; Fantasia con imitazione, BWV 563; Fugue all giga, BWV 577; Preludes & Fugues, BWV 548–50;

8 Short Preludes & Fugues, BWV 553–60; Toccata & Fugue in E, BWV 566.

***** DG 449 212-2. Preston.

This imposing recital includes music from Bach's Buxtehude-influenced early years, two fine *Preludes and Fugues* from his Leipzig period, very impressively played, and some enjoyable music which was probably not written by Bach at all. The *Gigue Fugue* is irresistible just the same, and the lightweight *Short Preludes and Fugues* are very agreeable listening. No 8, BWV 560, brings an astonishing burst of virtuosity from Preston in a bravura passage on the pedals. The recording is first class.

Concertos (for solo organ) *Nos. 1 in G* (after ERNST); *2 in A min.; 3 in C* (both after VIVALDI); *4 in C* (after ERNST); *5 in D min.* (after VIVALDI), *BWV 592–6.*

*** DG 423 087-2. Preston (organ of Lübeck Cathedral).

It was Prince Johann Ernst who introduced Bach to the Italian string concertos; these are Bach's arrangements, with the music for the most part left with little alteration or embellishment. The two Ernst works show a lively and inventive if not original musicianship. The performances are first class and the recording admirably lucid and clear, yet with an attractively resonant ambience.

Fantasia & Fugue in G min., BWV 542; Passacaglia & Fugue in C min., BWV 582; 6 Schübler Chorales, BWV 645–50; Toccata, Adagio & Fugue in C, BWV 564; Toccata & Fugue in F, BWV 540.

✿ *** DG 435 381-2. Preston (Sauer organ in St Peter's, Waltrop, near Dortmund).

Preston's recital at St Peter's, Waltrop, is a magnificent demonstration of the splendour and power of Bach's more ambitious organ statements, admirably contrasted with music which is inherently less weighty, if no less inspired. The engaging *Schübler Chorales* are used to provide contrast at the centre of the 71-minute recital, and Preston chooses a lighter, more pointed style than usual. The Sauer organ in Waltrop is a modern instrument (1984) that is ideal for baroque repertoire, and Bach in particular. There is an enormous reserve of power in the pedals, and the richer sonorities elsewhere bring no attendant clouding. This is one of the very finest Bach collections of the digital CD era.

Other organ music

33 Arnstadt Chorale Preludes (from Yale manuscript).

(B) *** HM HMA 1905158. Payne (organ of St Paul's, Brookline, Mass.).

Joseph Payne collects the complete set together on a single CD. Now reissued on Harmonia Mundi's budget Musique d'Abord label, this is even more attractive.

The Art of Fugue, BWV 1080.

(N) *** BIS CD1034. Hans Fagius (organ of Garnisons Kirke, Copenhagen).

The approach of the Swedish organist Hans Fagius is refreshingly straightforward and unaffected. Here he plays a Danish organ, a reconstruction from 1995 of an instrument made in 1724 by Lambert Daniel Kastens, a pupil of Arp Schnitger. He has the advantage of a first-class recording, as one would expect from this label and the producer–engineer Ingo Petry. This version has a lot going for it, quite apart from the sound, and those who like their Bach plain and unadorned will find it well worth considering.

Concertos (for solo organ) Nos. 1–5; 6 in E flat (arr. of concerto by an unnamed composer), BWV 592–7; Trio in C min (after FASCH), BWV 585; Trio in G (after TELEMANN), BWV 586; Aria in F (from COUPERIN: Les Nations), BWV 587).

(B) *** Naxos 8.550936. Rübsam (Flenthrop organ of St Mark's Cathedral, Seattle, Washington).

Whereas Wolfgang Rübsam's new ongoing re-recording of Bach's organ music for Naxos has proved at times disappointingly heavy-going, this is a strikingly successful exception. Moreover it is very comprehensive in including the rarely played 'anonymous' concerto transcription, BWV 597. This is a most engaging piece, particularly the jaunty closing section, and it is nicely registered, as are the other individual movements here, by Couperin, Fasch and Telemann. Rübsam's tempi for allegros remain buoyant throughout and the playing is always seemingly spontaneous. The recording is in the demonstration class.

38 Neumeister Chorales; 17 Rinck Chorales; 5 Rudorff Chorales.

(BB) ** Arte Nova 74321 31680-2 (3). Krumbach (Silbermann organ of Benedictine Monastery, Maurmünster in Elsass).

This three-disc Arte Nova set offers 38 recently discovered *Neumeister Chorales* (which have also been recorded, even more successfully, by Christopher Herrick). It also includes 17 from the legacy of Christian Heinrich Rinck (1770–1846), court organist at Darmstadt, plus five more settings from the Rudorff collection, held in the Leipzig music library, which are also thought to belong to the same early period (i.e. 1703–4). Wilhelm Krumbach is not as imaginative a player as Herrick, but he uses a characterful organ and presents the chorales simply and, where appropriate, robustly, with an expansive panoply of colour. He is well recorded and this inexpensive set is well worth its modest cost.

Orgelbüchlein: Chorale Preludes, Nos. 1–46, BWV 599–644.

(N) (B) *** H.M. (ADD) HMX 2951215. Saorgin (organ of Saint-Pierre de Luxeuil).
**(*) Häns. CD 92.094. Zerer (organ of Martinkerk, Groningen).

Orgelbüchlein: 19 Chorale Preludes for Advent, Christmas, New Year and the Purification, BWV 599–617; Fantasia in C, BWV 570; Fugue on a Theme of Corelli, BWV 579; Preludes & Fugues, BWV 531 & 534; Prelude in G, BWV 568.

(B) *** Naxos 8.553031. Rübsam (Flenthrop organ of Duke Chapel, Duke University, Durham, USA).

Orgelbüchlein: 27 Chorale Preludes for Passiontide; Easter; Pentecost; and expressing Faith, BWV 618–44; Fantasia in C, BWV 570; Fugue in B min., BWV 579; Preludes & Fugues, BWV 531 & 534; Prelude in G, BWV 568.

(B) *** Naxos 8.553032. Rübsam (Flenthrop organ of Duke Chapel, Duke University, Durham, USA).

The *Orgelbüchlein* (or 'Little Organ Book') includes 46 chorale preludes for the church year, written by Bach partly at Weimar and concluded later at Cöthen. Rübsam's presentation here is very well planned, with preludes and fugues acting as introductions and postludes to the eight groupings, each of which centres on one of the key periods of the Church calendar. Rübsam finds great variety for his presentation of each chorale. The Christmas section is preceded by the flamboyant and joyous *Prelude and Fugue in C*, with its resounding pedals, and the first recital is rounded off with a characteristically spacious account of the imposing *F minor Prelude and Fugue*, BWV 534. The Easter Chorales are more robust, while the four Pentecost Chorales are touchingly contemplative. There is infinite variety of mood and colour in the last group, opening with a piece symbolizing the ten commandments and showing Bach reflecting on various aspects of the Christian faith. The introduction of the closing *Prelude and Fugue in D minor*, BWV 539, is grave and dignified, but the fugue itself is optimistic and vital, ending the concert satisfyingly. The Duke University Chapel organ is a magnificent instrument, and the recording is superb throughout.

Wolfgang Zerer's set of the *Orgelbüchlein* is of high quality, both in its colouristic range and in its contrasts of mood and tempi. He can be vigorous and flamboyant when required (as in *In dir ist Freude*, BWV 615) but for the most part his presentation is intimate – and effectively so, though he opens up the registration to use the full organ when needed. An enjoyable set, but we are inclined to prefer Rübsam's Naxos set.

However, the best buy of all would appear to be René Saorgin's perceptively registered survey on an attractive French organ, with lively reeds, recorded in 1983 and excellently transferred to CD. Saorgin ensures that the *cantus firmus* of each chorale wherever possible emerges clearly, often standing out from its background decoration.

6 Trio Sonatas, BWV 525–30 (see also arrangements under Chamber Music, above).

(M) **(*) DG (IMS) 447 277-2. Koopman (organ of Waalse Kerk, Amsterdam).

Ton Koopman's earlier DG set comes from 1982 and is very well recorded on a highly suitable Dutch organ. The opening of the very first sonata promises well, with a buoyant rhythmic lift; the central *Adagio* is nicely coloured and the finale spirited. The *Adagio e dolce* of *No. 3 in D minor* again shows an apt choice of colouring but the finale (marked *Vivace*) tends to jog along, and the similarly indicated opening movement of No. 6 is also relaxed. Other versions of these works are that bit more spirited but not more glowing, and this is certainly enjoyable.

Organ recitals

Allabreve in D, BWV 589; Chorale Prelude: Ach Gott und Herr, BWV 714; Preludes & Fugues, BWV 532, 553–60; Toccata & Fugue in D min., BWV 565.

*** Mer. (ADD) ECD 84081. Sanger (organ of St Catharine's College, Cambridge).

The organ at St Catharine's College, Cambridge, was completely rebuilt in 1978–9. The result is a great success, and its reedy clarity and brightness of timbre are especially suitable for Bach. David Sanger's playing throughout is thoughtful and well structured; registration shows an excellent sense of colour without being flamboyant.

Canzona in D min., BWV 588; Fantasie in G, BWV 572; Passacaglia & Fugue in C min., BWV 582; 6 Schübler Chorales, BWV 645–50; Toccatas & Fugues in F, BWV 540; in D min., BWV 565.

(B) **(*) DG 439 477-2. Koopman (various organs).

Ton Koopman uses two different organs here, principally that of the Grote Kerk, Maassluis, but the *Schübler Chorales* are recorded on that of the Waalse Kerk, Amsterdam. The recital opens with the famous *Toccata and Fugue in D minor*, BWV 565, and Koopman (as is his wont) introduces decoration into the opening flourishes. The performance has an excitingly paced fugue and is superbly recorded. Contrast is provided by the *Canzona in D minor*, a slow and rather solemn contrapuntal exercise. The recital ends with the mighty *Passacaglia and Fugue in C minor*, BWV 582.

Chorale Preludes, BWV 721, 727, 622 & 680; Fugue in B min. on a Theme of Corelli, BWV 579; Passacaglia & Fugue in C min., BWV 582; Pastorale in F, BWV 590; Toccata & Fugue in D min., BWV 565.

(B) *** EMI CD-EMX 2218. Hurford (organ of Martinkerk, Groningen, Holland).

Having left his complete Decca Bach series long behind him, Peter Hurford here sets off on his travels again to record a familiar programme on a remarkably fine Groningen organ. Perhaps the most famous *Toccata and Fugue* is a fraction less flamboyant than before, and several of the chorale preludes are very relaxed and thoughtful. The *Pastorale*, too, is fairly static. But in the closing *Passacaglia and Fugue* he demonstrates how he can hold and build tension when setting off at a very measured pace. What a masterpiece this is! The EMI engineers do him proud.

(i) Pastorale in F, BWV 590; Passacaglia in C min., BWV 582; 6 Schübler Chorales, BWV 645–50; (ii) Toccata, Adagio & Fugue in C, BWV 564; (i) Toccatas & Fugues: in D min. (Dorian), BWV 538; (ii) in D min., BWV 565.

(B) *** DG ADD/Dig. 463 016-2. (i) Koopman; (ii) Preston (various organs).

This collection is divided between Simon Preston, on top form in his two contributions, and Ton Koopman, who has the lion's share and uses two different organs. The *Schübler Chorales* are recorded on the organ of the Waalse Kerk, Amsterdam, whose reeds are livelier, underscored by the emphatically rhythmic style of the playing. Excellent contrast is provided by the *Pastorale*, where the registration features the organ's flute stops piquantly. The other performances are well structured and alive, if sometimes rather considered in feeling. Excellent recording throughout.

VOCAL MUSIC

Complete Cantatas: Hänssler Series with Gächinger Kantorei, Bach-Collegium Stuttgart, Helmuth Rilling

Cantatas Nos. (i–ii) 1: Wie schön leuchtet uns der Morgerstern; (iii) 2: Ach Gott, vom Himmel; (ii; iv) 3: Ach Gott, wie manches Herzeleid.

**(*) Häns. (ADD) CD 92.001; with (i) Nielsen, Kraus; (ii) Huttenlocher; (iii) Watts, Baldin, Heldwein; (iv) Augér, Schreckenbach, Harder.

Cantatas Nos. 4: Christ lag in Todesbanden; 5: Wo soll ich fliehen hin; 6: Bleib bei uns, denn es will Abend werden.

**(*) Häns. (ADD) CD 92.002; with Wiens, Augér, Watkinson, Schreier, Baldin, Kraus, Schöne, Heldwein.

Cantatas Nos. 7: Christ unser Herr zum Jordan kam; 8: Liebster Gott, wann werd ich sterben; 9: Es ist das Heil uns kommen her.

**(*) Häns. (ADD) CD 92.003; with Augér, Sonntag, Watts, Schreckenbach, Kraus, Schöne, Huttenlocher.

Cantatas Nos. 10: Meine Seel' erhebt den Herren; 12: Weinen, Klagen, Sorgen, Zagen; 13: Meine Seufzer, meine Tränen.

**(*) Häns. (ADD) CD 92.004; with Augér, Neubauer, Watts, Watkinson, Baldin, Kraus, Schöne, Heldwein.

Cantatas Nos. 14: Wär Gott nicht mit uns diese Zeit; 16: Herr Gott, dich loben wir; 17: Wer Dank opfert, der preiset mich; 18: Gleichwie der Regen und Schnee vom Himmel fällt.

**(*) Häns. (ADD) CD 92.005; with Laki, Augér, Csapò, Schreckenbach, Schnaut, Baldin, Schreier, Kraus, Huttenlocher, Heldwein, Schöne, Württemberg CO.

Cantatas Nos. 19: Es erhub sich ein Streit; 20: O Ewigkeit, du Donnerwort.

**(*) Häns. (ADD) CD 92.006; with Rondelli, Kessler, Gohl, Kraus, Altmeyer, Nimsgern, Schöne, Frankfurter Kantorei.

Cantatas Nos. 21: Ich hatte viel Bekümmernis; 20: Jesus nahm zu sich die Zwölfe.

**(*) Häns. (ADD) CD 92.007; with Augér, Amini, Watts, Hagerman, Kraus, Robinson, Schöne, Anderson, Indiana University Chamber Singers.

Cantatas Nos. 23: Du wahrer Gott und Davids Sohn; 24: Ein ungefärbt Gemüte; 25: Es ich nichts Gesundes an meinem Leibe; 26: Ach wie flüchtig, ach wie nightig.

*** Häns. (ADD) CD 92.008; with Augér, Watts, Soffel, Baldin, Kraus, Tüller, Heldwein.

Cantatas Nos. 27: Wer weiss, wie nahe mir mein Ende; 28: Gottlob! Nun geht das Jahr zu Ende; 29: Wir danken dir, Gott.

*** Häns. (ADD) CD 92.009; with Wiens, Augér, Watts, Sonntag, Schreckenbach, Graff, Harder, Baldin, Kraus, Tüller, Heldwein, Huttenlocher.

Cantatas Nos. 30: Freue dich, erlöste Schar; 31: Der Himmel lacht! Die Erde jubilieret.

*** Häns. (ADD) CD 92.0010; with Cuccaro, Augér, Georg, Baldin, Kraus, Huttenlocher, Schöne.

Cantatas Nos. 32: Liebster Jesu, mein Verlangen; 33: Allein zu dir, Herr Jesu Christ; 34: O ewiges Feuer, O Ursprung der Liebe.

*** Häns. (ADD) CD 92.0011; with Augér, Watts, Lang, Kraus, Heldwein, Huttenlocher, Schöne.

Cantatas Nos. 35: Geist und Seele wird verwirret; 36: Schwingt freudig euch empor; 37: Wer da gläubet und getauft wird.

*** Häns. (ADD) CD 92.0012; with Augér, Hamari, Schreckenbach, Watkinson, Kraus, Heldwein, Huttenlocher.

Cantatas Nos. 38: Aus tiefer Not schrei ich zu dir; 39: Brich dem Hungrigen dein Brot; 40: Darzu ist erschienen der Sohn Gottes.

*** Häns. (ADD) CD 92.0013; with Augér, Watts, Schreckenbach, Gohl, Harder, Kraus, Huttenlocher, Nimsgern.

Cantatas Nos. 41: Jesu, nun sei gepreiset; 42: Am Abend aber desselbigen Sabbats.

*** Häns. (ADD) CD 92.0014; with Donath, Augér, Hoeffgen, Hamari, Kraus, Nimsgern, Huttenlocher, Nimsgern.

Cantatas Nos. 43: Gott fähret auf mit Jauchzen; 44: Sie werden euch in den Bann tun; 45: Es ist dir gesagt, Mensch, was gut ist.

*** Häns. (ADD) CD 92.0015; with Augér, Hamari, Watts, Harder, Baldin, Huttenlocher, Schöne.

Cantatas Nos. 46: Schauet doch und sehet, ob irgendein Schmerz sei; 47: Wer sich selbst erhöhet, der soll erniedriget wernen; 48: Ich elender Mensch, wer wird mich erlösen.

*** Häns. (ADD) CD 92.0016; with Augér, Watts, Hoeffgen, Kraus, Baldin, Huttenlocher, Schöne.

Cantatas Nos. 49: Ich geh und suche mit Verlangen; 50: Nun ist das Heil und die Kraft; 51: Jauchzett Gott in allen Landen; 52: Falsche Welt, dir trau ich nicht.

*** Häns. (ADD) CD 92.0017; with Augér, Huttenlocher.

Cantatas Nos. 54: Widerstehe doch der Sünde; 55: Ich armer Mensch, ich Sündenknecht; 56: Ich will den Kreuzstab gerne tragen; 57: Selig ist der Mann.

*** Häns. (ADD) CD 92.0018; with Augér, Hamari, Kraus, Fischer-Dieskau, Heldwein.

Cantatas Nos. 58: Ach Gott, wie manches Herzleid; 59: Wer mich liebet, der wird mein Wort halten; 60: O Ewigkeit, du Donnerwort; 61: Nun komm, der Heiden Heiland.

*** Häns. (ADD) CD 92.0019; with Reichelt, Augér, Donath, Watts, Kraus, Schöne, Tüller.

Cantatas Nos. 62: Nun komm, der Heiden Heiland; 63: Christen, ätzet diesen Tag; 64: Sehet, welch eine Liebes hat uns der Vater erzeiget.

**(*) Häns. (ADD) CD 92.020 with Nielsen, Augér, Watts, Hamari, Laurich, Murray, Baldin, Kraus, Huttenlocher, Heldwein, Schöne.

Cantatas Nos. 65: Sie werden aus Saba alle kommen; 66: Erfreut euch, ihr Herzen; 67: Halt im Gedächtnis Jesum Christ.

**(*) Häns. (ADD) CD 92.021 with Schreckenbach, Mitsui, Murray, Kraus, Huttenlocher, Heldwein.

Cantatas Nos. 68: Also hat Gott die Welt geliebet; 69: Lobe den Herrn, meine Seele; 70: Wachet! betet! betet! wachet!

**(*) Häns. (ADD) CD 92.022 with Augér, Donath, Hamari, Gohl, Kraus, Harder, Huttenlocher, Schöne, Nimsgern.

Cantatas Nos. 71: Gott ist mein König; 72: Alles nur nach Gottes Willen; 73: Herr, wie du willst, so schicks mit mir; 74: Wer mich liebet, der wird mein Wort halten.

**(*) Häns. (ADD) CD 92.023 with Grae, Augér, Schreiber, Donath, Gardow, Schwarz, Schreckenbach, Laurich, Senger, Kraus, Harder, Tuller, Huttenlocher, Schöne.

Cantatas Nos. 75: Die Elenden sollen essen; 76: Die Himmel erzählen die Ehre Gottes.

**(*) Häns. (ADD) CD 92.024; with Reichelt, Augér, Gohl, Hamari, Watts, Kraus, Baldin, Kunz, Nimsgern.

Cantatas Nos. 77: Du sollst Gott, deinen Herren, lieben; 78: Jesu, der du meine Seele; 79: Gott der Herr ist Sonn, und Schild.

**(*) Häns. CD (ADD) 92.025; with Donath, Augér, Hamari, Watkinson, Kraus, Baldin, Schöne, Huttenlocher.

Cantatas Nos. 80: Ein feste Burg ist unser Gott; 81: Jesus schläft, was soll ich hoffen?; 82: Ich habe genug.

**(*) Häns. (ADD) CD 92.026; with Augér, Schreckenbach, Hamari, Harder, Kraus, Huttenlocher, Nimsgern, Württemberg CO.

Cantatas Nos. 83: Erfreute Zeit im neuen Bunde; 84: Ich bin vergnügt mit meinem Glücke; 85: Ich bin ein Guter Hirt; 86: Wahrlich, wahrlich, ich sage euch.

**(*) Häns. (ADD) CD 92.027; with Augér, Watts, Schreckenbach, Kraus, Heldwein, Württemberg CO.

Cantatas Nos. 87: Bisher habt ich nichts gebeten in meinem Namen; 88: Siehe, ich will viel Fischer aussenden; 89: Was soll ich aus dir machen, Ephraim; 90: Es reisset euch ein schrecklich Ende.

**(*) Häns. (ADD) CD 92.028; with Reichelt, Augér, Hamari, Gohl, Watts, Baldin, Kraus, Heldwein, Schöne, Huttenlocher, Nimsgern.

Cantatas Nos. 91: Gelobet seist du, Jesu Christ; 92: Ich habe in Gottes Herz und Sinn; 93: Wer nur den lieben Gott lässt walten.

**(*) Häns. (ADD) CD 92.029; with Donath, Augér, Watts, Schreckenbach, Murray, Hamari, Baldin, Kraus, Huttenlocher, Heldwein, Schöne, Nimsgern, Württemberg CO.

Cantatas Nos. 94: Was frag, ich nach der Welt; 95: Christus, der ist mein Leben; 96: Herr Christ, der ein'ge Gottessohn.

**(*) Häns. (ADD) CD 92.030; with Donath, Augér, Paaske,

Höffgen, Baldin, Kraus, Kunz, Heldwein, Schöne, Nimsgern.

Cantatas Nos. 97: In allen meinen Taten; 98: Was Gott tut, das ist wohlgetan; 99: Was Gott tut, das ist wohlgetan.

**(*) Häns. (ADD) CD 92.031; with Donath, Augér, Gardow, Hamari, Watts, Kraus, Harder, Heldwein, Huttenlocher, Bröcheler.

Cantatas Nos. 100: Was Gott tut, das ist wohlgetan; 101: Nimm von uns, Herr, du treuer Gott; 102: Herr, deine Augen schen nach, dem Glauben.

**(*) Häns. (ADD) CD 92.032; with Augér, Hamari, Watts, Randova, Kraus, Baldin, Equiluz, Huttenlocher, Bröcheler, Schöne.

Cantatas Nos. 103: Ihr werdet weinen und heulen; 104: Du Hirte Israel, höre; 105: Herr, gehe nicht ins Gericht mit deinem Knecht.

**(*) Häns. (ADD) CD 92.033; with Augér, Soffel, Watts, Schreier, Kraus, Heldwein, Schöne.

Cantatas Nos. 106: Gottes Zeit ist die allerbeste Zeit; 107: Was willst du dich betrüben; 108: Es ist euch gut, dass ich hingehe.

**(*) Häns. (ADD) CD 92.034; with Csapo, Augér, Schwarz, Watkinson, Kraus, Baldin, Schreier, Schöne, Bröcheler, Huttenlocher.

Cantatas Nos. 109: Ich glaube, lieber Herr; 110: Unser Mund sei voll Lachens; 111: Was mein Gott will, das g'scheh allzeit.

**(*) Häns. (ADD) CD 92.035; with Graf, Augér, Schreckenbach, Gardow, Watts, Equiluz, Baldin, Harder, Schöne, Huttenlocher.

Cantatas Nos. 112: Das Herr ist mein getreuer Hirtl; 113: Herr Jesu Christ, du höchstes Gut; 114: Ach, lieben Christen, seid Getrost.

**(*) Häns. (ADD) CD 92.036; with Nielsen, Augér, Schnaut, Schreckenbach, Hamari, Baldin, Kraus, Equiluz, Heldwein, Tüller, Schöne.

Cantatas Nos. 115: Mache dich, mein Geist, bereit; 116: Du Friedefürst, Herr Jesu Christ; 117: Dei Lob' und Ehr dem höchsten Gut.

**(*) Häns. (ADD) CD 92.037; with Augér, Watts, Georg, Harder, Kraus, Schöne, Huttelocher, Schmidt.

Cantatas Nos. 119: Preise Jerusalem, den Herrn; 120, Gott, man lobet dich in der Stille; 121: Christum wir sollen loben schon.

**(*) Häns. (ADD) CD 92.038; with Augér, Donath, Murray, Laurich, Soffel, Kraus, Schöne.

Cantatas Nos. 122: Das neugeborne Kindelein; 123: Liebster Immanuel, Herzog der Frommen; 124: Meinen Jesum lass ich nicht; 125: Mit Fried und Freud ich fahr dahin.

**(*) Häns. (ADD) CD 92.039; with Augér, Donath, Watts, Hoffgen, Kraus, Balden, Equiluz, Tüller, Huttenlocher, Schöne.

Cantatas Nos. 126: Erhalt uns, Herr, bei deinem Wort; 127: Herr Jesu Christ, wahr' Mensch und Gott; 128: Auf Christi Himmelfahrt allein; 129: Gelobet sei der Herr, mein Gott.

**(*) Häns. (ADD) CD 92.040; with Augér, Watts, Schreckenbach, Kraus, Harder, Balden, Huttenlocher, Schöne.

Cantatas Nos. 130: Herr Gott, dich loben alle wir; 131: Aus der Tiefen rufe ich, Herr, zu dir; 132: Bereitet die Wege, bereitet die Bahn.

**(*) Häns. (ADD) CD 92.041; with Graf, Augér, Schnaut, Watts, Kraus, Equiluz, Schöne.

Cantatas Nos. 133: Ich freue mich in dir; 134: Ein Herz, das seinen Jesum lebend weiss; 135: Ach Herr, mich armen Sünder.

**(*) Häns. (ADD) CD 92.042; with Augér, Soffel, Watts, Baldin, Kraus, Huttenlocher.

Cantatas Nos. 136: Erforsche mich, Gott, und erfahre mein Herz; 137: Lobe den Herren, den mächtigen König der Ehren; 138: Warum betrübst du dich, mein Herz; 139: Wohl dem, der sich auf seinen Gott.

**(*) Häns. (ADD) CD 92.043; with Augér, Nielsen, Watts, Schreckenbach, Bollen, Equiluz, Kraus, Baldin, Tüller, Huttenlocher.

Cantatas Nos. 140: Wachet auf, ruft uns die Stimme; 143: Lobe den Herrn, meine Seele; 144: Nimm, was dein ist, und gehe him; 145: Ich lebe, mein Herze, zu deinem Ergötzen.

**(*) Häns. (ADD) CD 92.044; with Augér, Cszapò, Cuccaro, Watts, Baldin, Kraus, Huttenlocher, Schöne, Schmidt, Frankfurter Kantorei, Württemberg CO.

Cantatas Nos. 146: Wir müssen durch viel Trübsal; Herz und Mund und Tat und Leben.

**(*) Häns. (ADD) CD 92.045; with Augér, Donath, Watts, Hoeffgen, Equiluz, Schöne, Frankfurter Kantorei.

Cantatas Nos. 148: Bringet dem Herrn Ehre seines Namens; 149: Man singet mit Freuden vom Sieg; 150: Nach dir, Herr, verlanget mich; 151: Süsser Trost, mein Jesus kömmt.

**(*) Häns. (ADD) CD 92.046; with Augér, Schreiber, Gamo-Yamamoto, Watts, Georg, Jetter, Laurich, Equiluz, Baldin, Maus, Kraus, Huttenlocher, Kunz, Frankfurter Kantorei.

Cantatas Nos. 152: Tritt auf die Glaubensbahn; 153: Schau, lieber Gott, wie meine Feind; 154: Mein Liebster Jesus ist verloren; 155: Mein Gott, wie lang, ach lange.

**(*) Häns. (ADD) CD 92.047; with Augér, Reichelt, Murray, Lerer, Kraus, Baldin, Melzer, Schöne, Heldwein, Kunz.

Cantatas Nos. 156: Ich stehe mit einem Fuss im Grabe; 157: Ich lasse dich nicht, du segnest mich denn; 158: Der Friede sei mit dir; 159: Sehet, wir gehn hinauf gen Jerusalem.

**(*) Häns. (ADD) CD 92.048; with Laurich, Hamari, Equiluz, Kraus, Baldin, Schöne, Huttenlocher, Figuralchor der Gedächtniskirche.

Cantatas Nos. 161: Komm, du susse Todesstunde; 162: Ach! ich sehe, itzt, da ich zur Hochzeit gehe; 163: Nur jedem das Seine; 164: Ihr, die ihr euch von Christo nennet.

**(*) Häns. (ADD) CD 92.049; with Augér, Wiens, Laurich, Rogers, Watts, Hamari, Kraus, Equiluz, Harder, Schöne, Tüller, Heldwein, Frankfurter Kantorei.

Cantatas Nos. 165: O heiliges Geist und Wasserbad; 166:

Wo gehest du hin; 167: Ihr Menschen, rühmet Gottes Lieb; 168: Tue Rechnung! Donnerwort.

(N) **(*) Häns. (ADD) CD 92.050. Augér, Graf, Burns, Rogers, Watts, Gardow, Gohl, Equiluz, Baldin, Krauss, Altmeyer, Schöne, Tüller, Nimsgern, Gedächinger Kantorei, Frankfurt Kantorei, Stuttgart Bach Coll., Rilling.

Cantatas Nos. 169: Gott soll allein mein Herze haben; 170: Vergnügte Rühe! beliebt Seelenlust; 171 Gott, wie dein Name, so ist auch dein Ruhm.

(N) **(*) Häns. (ADD) CD 92.051. Augér, Watkinson, Baldin, Heldwein, Gedächinger Kantorei, Württemberg CO, Stuttgart Bach Coll., Rilling.

Cantatas Nos. 172: Eschallet, ihr Lieder; 173: Erhöltes Fleisch und Blut; 174: Ich liebe den Höchsten von ganzem Gemüte; 175: Er rufet seine Schlafen mit Namen.

(N) **(*) Häns. (ADD) CD 92.052. Csapo, Beckman, Soffel, Watts, Hamari, Watkinson, Baldin, Krauss, Schreier, Schöne, Tüller, Huttenlocher, Gedächinger Kantorei, Frankfurt Kantorei, Stuttgart Bach Coll., Württemberg CO, Rilling.

Cantatas Nos. 176: Es ist ein trotzig und verzagt Ding; 177: Ich ruf zu dir, Herr Jesu Christ; 178: Wo Gott der Herr nicht bei uns hält.

(N) **(*) Häns. (ADD) CD 92.053. Nielsen, Augér, Watkinson, Hamari, Schreckenbach, Schreier, Equiluz, Baldin, Heldwein, Schöne, Gedächinger Kantorei, Stuttgart Bach Coll., Rilling.

Cantatas Nos. 179: Siehe zu dass deine Gottesfurcht nicht Heuchelei sei; 180: Schmücke dich, O liebe Seele; 181: Leichtgesinnte Flattergeister.

(N) **(*) Häns. (ADD) CD 92.054. Augér, Watkinson, Schnaut, Schreckenbach, Equiluz, Kraus, Schöne, Heldwein, Tüller, Gedächinger Kantorei, Stuttgart Bach Coll., Rilling.

Cantatas Nos. 182: Himmelskönig, sei willkommen; 183: Sie werden euch in den Bann tun; 184: Erwünschtes Freudenlicht.

(N) **(*) Häns. (ADD) CD 92.055. Augér, Soffel, Hamari, Schnaut, Baldin, Schreier, Kraus, Huttenlocher, Heldwein, Tüller, Gedächinger Kantorei, Stuttgart Bach Coll., Rilling.

Cantatas Nos. 185: Barmherziges Herze der ewigen Liebe; 186: Ärgre dich, O Seele, nicht; 187: Es wartet alles aud dich.

(N) **(*) Häns. (ADD) CD 92.056. Augér, Friesenhausen, Laurich, Watts, Baldin, Equiluz, Huttenlocher, Schöne, Gedächinger Kantorei, Frankfurt Kantorei, Stuttgart Bach Coll., Rilling.

Cantatas Nos. 188: Ich habe meine Zuversicht; 190: Singet dem Herrn ein neues Lied; 191: Gloria in excelsis Deo; 192: Nun danket alle Gott.

(N) **(*) Häns. (ADD) CD 92.057. Augér, Gamo-Yamamoto, Donath, Hamari, Watts, Baldin, Equiluz, Kraus, Heldwein, Tüller, Gedächinger Kantorei, Württemberg CO, Stuttgart Bach Coll., Rilling.

Cantatas Nos. 193: Ihr Tore zu Zion; 194: Höchsterwünschtes Freudenfest.

(N) **(*) Häns. (ADD) CD 92.058. Augér, Hamari, Kraus, Watts, Heldwein, Gedächinger Kantorei, Stuttgart Bach Coll., Rilling.

Cantatas Nos. 195: Dem Gerechten muss das Licht; 196: Der Herr denket an uns; 197: Gott ist unsre Zuversicht.

(N) **(*) Häns. (ADD) CD 92.059. Inhoue-Heller, Soffel, Cuccaro, Graf, Georg, Pfaff, Baldin, Schmidt, Tüller, Huttenlocher, Gedächinger Kantorei, Württemberg CO, Stuttgart Bach Coll., Rilling.

Cantatas Nos. 198: Lass, Fürstin! lass noch einen Strahl; 199: Mein Herz schwimmt im Blut; 200: Bekennen will ich seinen Namen.

(N) **(*) Häns. (ADD) CD 92.060. Augér, Schreckenbach, George, Baldin, Huttenlocher, Gedächinger Kantorei, Württemberg CO, Stuttgart Bach Coll., Rilling.

Secular Cantatas

Cantata No. 201: Geschwinde, ihr wirbelnden Winde (The Contest between Phoebus and Pan).

**(*) Häns. (ADD) CD 98.162; with Rubens, Danz, Odinius, Taylor, Goerne, Henschel.

Cantatas Nos. 202: Weichet nur, betrübte Schatten; 203: Amore traditore; 204: Ich bin in mir vergnügt.

**(*) Häns. (ADD) CD 92.062; with Rubens, Henschel, Behringer.

Cantata No. 205: Der zufriedengestellte Aeolus; Quodlibet, BWV 524.

(N) **(*) Häns. CD 92.063. Rubens, Naff, Danz, Genz, Ullmann, Schmidtt, Gedächinger Kantorei, Stuttgart Bach Coll., Rilling.

Cantatas Nos. 206: Schleicht, spielende Wellen und murmelt Gelinde; 207: Vereinigte Zwietracht der wechselnden Saitern; 207a: Auf, schmetternde Töne der muntern Trompeten.

(N) **(*) Häns. CD 92.064. Schäfer, Petersen, Danz, Olsen, Ullmann, Volle, Häger, Gedächinger Kantorei, Stuttgart Bach Coll., Rilling.

Cantatas Nos. 207a: Auf, schmetternde Töne der muntern Trompeten; 212 (Peasant Cantata).

**(*) Häns. (ADD) CD 98.163; with Schäfer, Danz, Olsen, Quasthoff, Volle.

Cantatas Nos. 208: Was mir behagt, ist nur die muntre Jagd (Hunt Cantata); 209: Non sà che sia dolore.

**(*) Häns. CD 92.065; with Rubens, Schäfer, Taylor, Quasthoff.

Cantatas Nos. 208: Was mir behagt, ist nur die muntre Jagd (Hunt); 211: Schweigt stille, plaudert nicht (Coffee).

**(*) Häns. (ADD) CD 98.161; with Rubens, Schäfer, Kirchner, Taylor, Goerne, Quasthoff.

Cantatas Nos. 210: O holder Tag, erwünschte Zeit (Wedding Cantata); 211: Schweigt stille, plaudert nicht (Coffee Cantata).

**(*) Häns. CD 92.066 with Rubens, Schäfer, Taylor, Quasthoff.

Cantatas Nos. 212: Mer hahn en neue Oberkeet (Peasant Cantata); 213: Herkules auf dem Schweidewege (Hercules at the Crossroads).

(N) **(*) Häns. CD 92.067. Schäfer, Rubens, Danz, Ullmann, Quasthoff, Schmidtt, Gedächinger Kantorei, Stuttgart Bach Coll., Rilling.

Cantatas Nos. 214: Tönet, ihr Pauken! Erschallet, Trompeten; 215: Preise dein Glücke, gesegnetes Sachsen.

(N) Häns. **(*) CD 92.068. Rubens, Danz, Ullmann, Schäfer, Schmidtt, Henschell, Gedächinger Kantorei, Stuttgart Bach Coll., Rilling.

Helmut Rilling has spent a lifetime performing, recording and re-recording Bach, and Hänssler have now completed assembling his cantata cycle. As a glance at the above will show, the cantatas themselves run to some 68 discs. Each is available separately, attractively packaged. The series has never enjoyed the same exposure as the Leonhardt-Harnoncourt cycle, which was performed on period instruments and included the scores in its LP format, in most cases taken from the *Neue Bach Gesamtausgabe*. No doubt Rilling was not helped by the somewhat haphazard availability of his ongoing set, some of which appeared originally as single LPs and others in multiple LP sets. He recorded the secular cantatas in the mid to late 1960s with some fine singers, but Hänssler have replaced these with new accounts recorded in the late 1990s.

For those who generally favour modern as opposed to period instruments and women singers as opposed to boys, this set will be a godsend. There is no question as to the excellence and distinction of many of Rilling's soloists, which feature a number of famous Bach specialists of the last quarter of a century. There are over 20 different sopranos, among then Christine Schäfer, Edith Mathis, and the late lamented and much loved Arlene Augér performing at her peak in the period 1979–84. The two dozen mezzos and contraltos include Marga Höffgen, Helen Watts, and Doris Soffel. Among the men are Peter Schreier, Fischer-Dieskau, Kurt Equiluz, Matthias Goerne, Andreas Schmidt and Jakob Stämpfli, as well as Siegmund Nimsgern and Philippe Huttenlocher.

As we indicated in discussing earlier issues the choral singing is variable, but it rarely falls below an acceptable standard. Rilling has proved a pragmatist in matters of historical performance practice; he adopts brisk tempos and light accents at times, but allows himself considerable expressive and agogic freedom. It is not easy to make a summary recommendation among the modern instrument versions, though Rilling's performances are often (but not always) freer than the periodically stiff Karl Richter series that rightly enjoyed such renommé in the 1960s.

Rilling's treatment of recitatives has attracted some criticism, and there are some occasions when he too is a little rigid (albeit less so than Richter can be). If one can generalise in these matters Richter often has the advantage of the cleaner recording (much of his DG Archiv series used the Herkulesaal in Munich), and the Stuttgart choral sound is at times rather opaque. However, those who prefer the warmer sound of modern instruments will welcome this Hänssler set, and generally speaking the instrumentalists are

of a high quality. Readers who want a complete set should note that the Rilling is comprehensive. The quality of both performances and recordings are variable, but it must be said that Rilling's Hänssler survey rarely falls below a certain standard, and it is sometimes first rate. All in all we have derived much satisfaction in either making or renewing our acquaintance with his cycle, which will suit many collectors in search of a scholarly yet intelligently aware approach with a traditional sound. Documentation and transfers are eminently satisfactory, but alas, the series has now reverted to premium price.

Complete Cantatas Brilliant Series, Netherlands Bach Collegium, Leusink

Volume I: *Cantatas Nos. 16; 33; 37; 42; 56; 61; 72; 80; 82; 97; 113; 132; 133; 170.*

(N) (BB) ** Brill. 99363 (5). Holton, Buwalda, Van Der Meel, Schock, Ramselaar, Holland Boys' Ch., Netherlands Bach Collegium, Leusink.

Volume II: *Cantatas Nos. 22; 23; 44; 54; 57; 85; 86; 92; 98; 111; 114; 135; 155; 159; 165; 167; 188.*

(N) (BB) ** Brill. 99364 (5). Holton, Buwalda, Van Der Meel, Schock, Ramselaar, Holland Boys' Ch., Netherlands Bach Collegium, Leusink.

Volume III: *Cantatas Nos. 17; 35; 87; 90; 99; 106; 117; 123; 153; 161; 168; 172; 173; 182; 199.*

(N) (BB) ** Brill. 99367 (5). Holton, Strijk, Buwalda, Van Der Meel, Schock, Ramselaar, Holland Boys' Ch., Netherlands Bach Collegium, Leusink.

Volume IV: *Cantatas Nos. 7; 13; 45; 69; 81; 102; 116; 122; 130; 138; 144; 149; 150; 169; 196.*

(N) (BB) ** Brill. 99368 (5). Holton, Strijk, Buwalda, Van Der Meel, Schock, Ramselaar, Holland Boys' Ch., Netherlands Bach Collegium, Leusink.

Volume V: *Cantatas Nos. 6; 26; 27; 46; 55; 94; 96; 107; 115; 139; 156; 163; 164; 178; 179.*

(N) (BB) ** Brill. 99370 (5). Holton, Strijk, Buwalda, Van Der Meel, Schock, Beekman, Ramselaar, Holland Boys' Ch., Netherlands Bach Collegium, Leusink.

Volume VI: *Cantatas Nos. 2; 3; 8; 60; 62; 78; 93; 103; 128; 145; 151; 154; 171; 185; 186; 192.*

(N) (BB) ** Brill. 99371 (5). Holton, Strijk, Buwalda, Van Der Meel, Schock, Beekman, Ramselaar, Holland Boys' Ch., Netherlands Bach Collegium, Leusink.

Volume VII: *Cantatas Nos. 9; 36; 47; 73; 91; 110; 121; 125; 129; 152; 157; 166; 184; 198.*

(N) (BB) ** Brill. 99373 (5). Holton, Strijk, Buwalda, Van Der Meel, Schock, Ramselaar, Holland Boys' Ch., Netherlands Bach Collegium, Leusink.

Volume VIII: *Cantatas Nos. 18 ;30; 40; 49; 79; 84; 88; 89; 100; 108; 136; 140; 176; 187; 194.*

(N) (BB) ** Brill. 99374 (5). Holton, Strijk, Buwalda, Van Der Meel, Schock, Ramselaar, Holland Boys' Ch., Netherlands Bach Collegium, Leusink.

Secular Cantatas: *Cantatas Nos. 36c; 201; 202; 203; 204; 205; 206; 207; 208; 209; 210; 211; 212; 213; 214; 215.*

(N) (BB) **(*) Brill. 99366 (8). Mathis, Augér, Popp, Watkinson, Hamari, Schreier, Adam, Lorenz, Berlin Soloists and CO, Schreier.

On the newly established Brilliant label we have another complete survey of the Bach cantatas that is so economically priced as to make Naxos seem in the luxury price bracket. 15 or 16 cantatas for just under £10 per set, or roughly 60 pence per cantata, is a different proposition from the full-price sets which can be over £5 per cantata. Of course one should not assess this repertoire purely in these terms; once a year or so has passed it is quality rather than cost which will determine whether you return to these recordings. A substantial number of these performances were recorded in the last four months of 1999 and to accomplish such a venture in so short a time, rather than the many years taken by Karl Richter, Harnoncourt/Leonhardt and Rilling, is in itself no mean feat. Others were recorded early in 2000, and the secular cantatas, conducted by Peter Schreier and licensed from Edel UK, come from the late 1970s and early 1980s and are of an altogether higher calibre. The Leusink accounts are uneven and in some respects a hit-and-miss affair. Although some of the performances sound distinctly underprepared there is a great deal of enthusiasm and dedication in Pieter Jan Leusink's enterprise. Some of the performances sound like run-throughs, rather more rough than ready, but others have an eminently acceptable standard of singing and playing; BWV 188, *Ich habe meine Zuversicht*, is remarkably accomplished and features the fine tenor Nico van der Meel. Elsewhere there is some uneven solo singing, uncertain in execution and at times intonation, and certain cantatas do not come off at all well; BWV 198 (*Lass Fürstin, lass noch einen Strahl*) is rather insensitive, and there are more refined and thoughtful accounts for instance of BWV 112 and 106 (*Gottes Zeit ist die allerbeste Zeit*). However, more of Leusink's performances will give pleasure than not. The Holland Boys are robust and fresh voiced, and although the instrumental contributions need more polish and rehearsal, there is a straightforward no-nonsense approach that is welcome. The sound, if again variable, is perfectly acceptable. It is very difficult to give a star rating to these discs. They lack the polish and distinction of the best of the cantata series (by Suzuki, Rilling, Koopman, or Gardiner) but are often far from negligible, even when judged by the highest standards, as in BWV 56, *Ich will den Kreuzstab*, which features Bas Ramselaar's first-rate bass performance. Those who live in university or cathedral cities with a strong musical tradition will know what to expect and will find these performances congenial. They are not slick or glamorous, but at this price they fill a valuable need.

Complete Cantatas: Harnoncourt/Leonhardt Teldec Series

Cantatas Nos. 1–14; 16–52; 54–69; 69a; 70–117; 119–40; 143–59; 161–88; 192; 194–9 (complete).

(B) **(*) Teldec ADD/Dig. 4509 91765-2 (60). Treble soloists from V. Boys' & Regensburg Choirs, Esswood, Equiluz, Van Altena, Van Egmond, Hampson, Nimsgern, Van der Meer, Jacobs, Iconomou, Holl, Immler, King's College, Cambridge, Ch., V. Boys' Ch., Tölz Boys' Ch., Ch. Viennensis, Ghent Coll. Voc., VCM, Harnoncourt; Leonhardt Cons., Leonhardt.

Cantatas Nos. 1–14; 16–19

(M) *** Teldec (ADD) 4509 91755-2 (6)).

Cantatas Nos. 20–36

(M) *** Teldec (ADD) 4509 91756-2 (6).

Cantatas Nos. 37–52; 54; 55–60

(M) *** Teldec (ADD) 4509 91757-2 (6).

Cantatas Nos. 61–9; 69a; 70–78

(M) **(*) Teldec (ADD) 4509 91758-2 (6).

Cantatas Nos. 79–99

(M) **(*) Teldec (ADD) 4509 91759-2 (6).

Cantatas Nos. 100–113

(M) *** Teldec (ADD) 4509 91760-2 (6).

Cantatas Nos. 119–37

(M) **(*) Teldec (ADD) 4509 91761-2 (6).

Cantatas Nos. 138–40; 143–59; 161–2

(M) **(*) Teldec ADD/Dig. 4509 91762-2 (6).

Cantatas Nos. 163–82

(M) **(*) Teldec (ADD) 4509 91763-2 (6).

Cantatas Nos. 183–8; 192; 194–9

(M) **(*) Teldec (ADD) 4509 91764-2 (6).

This pioneering Teldec project, a recording of most – but not all – of Bach's cantatas, is offered in two alternative choices: as a 60-CD box (with more music on each disc) at bargain price or as a series of ten separate collections, each of six CDs, at mid-price.

The recordings got off to a very good start but, later in the project, various flaws of intonation, and sometimes a feeling that the ensemble would have benefited from more rehearsal, plus occasionally sluggish direction, slightly undermined the overall excellence. However, the authentic character of the performances is in no doubt. Boys replace women not only in the choruses but also as soloists (which brings occasional minor lapses of security), and the size of the forces is confined to what we know Bach himself would have expected. The simplicity of the approach brings its own merits, for the imperfect yet otherworldly quality of some of the treble soloists refreshingly focuses the listener's attention on the music itself. Less appealing is the quality of the violins, which eschew vibrato and, it would sometimes seem, any kind of timbre! Generally speaking, there is a certain want of rhythmic freedom and some expressive caution. Rhythmic accents are underlined with some regularity and the grandeur of Bach's inspiration is at times lost to view. Nevertheless there is much glorious music here which, to do justice to Harnoncourt and Leonhardt, usually emerges freshly to give the listener much musical nourishment. The CD transfers are first class. The acoustic is usually not too dry – and not too ecclesiastical, either – and the projection is realistic.

Complete Cantatas: Koopman Erato Series with Amsterdam Baroque Choir & Orchestra

Volume I: *Cantatas Nos. 4 (with Appendix: Chorus: Sie nun wieder zufrieden); 31; 71; 106 (Actus tragicus); 131; 150; 185; 196 (Wedding Cantata).*

**(*) Erato 4509 98536-2 (3); with Schlick, Wessel, De Mey, Mertens.

Volume II: *Cantatas Nos. 12; 18 (with Appendix); 61; 132; 152; 172; 182 (with Appendix); 199; 203: Amore traditore. Quodlibet, BWV 524.*

**(*) Erato 0630 12598-2 (3); with Schlick, Wessel, Prégardien, Mertens.

Koopman favours an intimate approach to choruses – namely one voice to a part – which seems to rob this repertory of some of the sheer majesty and breadth. Moreover, unlike Leonhardt–Harnoncourt, Koopman opts for female soloists rather than boys, as would have been the case in Bach's day, and he favours mixed rather than solely male choirs. For many this will be a plus point – and it is good news for fans of Barbara Schlick who is pretty well everywhere. Also, and again unlike Leonhardt–Harnoncourt, he goes for a higher than normal pitch – a semitone above present-day pitch which, as Christoph Wolff's notes point out, is what Bach used in Mühlhausen and Weimar, brightening the sonority quite a lot. The singing in virtually all the cantatas is pretty impressive and the instrumental playing is of a high order of accomplishment. Moreover Koopman offers the collector variants and alternative versions, which will again be an undoubted plus.

Volume III: *Cantatas Nos. 22–3; 54; 63 (2 versions); 155; 161; 162 (2 versions); 163; 165; 208 (Hunt).*

**(*) Erato 0630 14336-2 (3); with Schlick, Stam, Holton, Bongers, Von Magnus, Scholl, Agnew.

Koopman's survey is proceeding on largely chronological lines and Volume III includes the delightful secular cantata, No. 208, *Was mir behagt, ist nur die muntre Jagd*, which includes 'Sheep may safely graze'. All these works come from Bach's Weimar years. For the most part the singing here is of a high order of accomplishment – in particular Andreas Scholl and Elisabeth von Magnus, and the instrumental playing is certainly more finished than is often the case in the Teldec set, though here it is by no means always as fresh or secure as on the Japanese series now underway from BIS (see below). In No. 54, *Widerstehe doch der Sünde*, Suzuki surpasses Koopman in expressive power, and even when he doesn't, the string-playing yields in vigour and polish and sonority to the Japanese. Besides offering various appendices, in No. 63, *Christen, ätzet diesen Tag*, and in No. 162, *Ach! ich sehe, jetzt, da ich zur Hochzeit gehe*, Koopman gives alternative versions, giving him an undoubted advantage over the opposition.

Volume IV: *Cantatas Nos. 198; 201; 204; 209; 211; 214–15.*

**(*) Erato 0630 15562-2 (3); with Larsson, Bongers, Grimm, Stam, Von Magnus, De Groot, Agnew, Ovenden, Mertens, Bentvelsen.

The fourth volume is given over to secular cantatas of the Leipzig period (1726–34). Foremost among them is the 1727 cantata, BWV198, *Lass Fürstin, lass noch einen Strahl* or the 'Funeral Ode' cantata. The noble opening chorus is perhaps wanting in breadth (rhythms are often over-accentuated) and Koopman's soloists are uneven, particularly Lisa Larsson whose confidence and intonation are occasionally vulnerable (she is better in BWV 209, *Non sà che sia dolore*). Generally speaking, the men are stronger. Koopman is rather breathless in the opening sinfonia. All the same there are many felicities in the set and some expert and beautifully light wind-playing. The recording is absolutely first class.

Volume V: *Cantatas Nos. 202; 205–6; 207a; 212–13.*

**(*) Erato 0630 17578-2 (4); with Larsson, Rubens, Grimm, Bongers, Von Magnus, Prégardien, Mertens.

The fifth volume completes the survey of the Leipzig secular cantatas up to the so-called 'Peasant' Cantata, *Mer hahn en neue Oberkeet*, BWV 212. There is some distinguished singing from Klaus Mertens and Christian Prégardien and some highly accomplished and felicitous solo instrumental playing (there are some wonderfully poetic oboe obbligatos). Lisa Larsson seems far more at ease in BWV 202, *Weichet nur, betrübte Schatten*, than she was in the earlier volume, though elsewhere intonation occasionally troubles Elisabeth von Magnus. Generally speaking, this gives more consistent pleasure than earlier releases in the series, and the recordings are excellent.

Volume VI: *Cantatas Nos. 50; 59; 69; 69a; 75–6; 104; 179; 186; 190.*

**(*) Erato 3984 21629-2 (3); with Ziesak, Von Magnus, Agnew, Mertens.

With one exception the cantatas in the present set come from 1723–34. Admirers of Koopman's series will know what to expect from earlier issues: meticulously balanced but at times rather business-like tempi. However, the singing of Ruth Ziesak, Paul Agnew and Klaus Mertens is eminently satisfying and the occasional lapses in intonation which marred earlier cantatas are absent. The standard of instrumental performance remains high and the recordings are refreshingly clean and well detailed.

Volume VII: *Cantatas Nos. 24–5 ; 67; 95; 105; 136; 144; 147–8; 173; 181; 184.*

**(*) Erato 3984 23141-2 (3); with Larsson, Bartosz, Von Magnus, Türk, Mertens.

This volume continues where its predecessor left off, in exploring the first annual cycle of cantatas that Bach composed in Leipzig in 1723–4, including the well-known *Herz und Mund und Tat und Leben*. The character of Koopman's survey is by now well known, and admirers need not hesitate; even if there is inevitably some unevenness in the individual cantatas, few performances disappoint either in accomplishment or in the quality of sound the engineers produce.

Volume VIII: *Cantatas Nos. 40; 46; 60; 64–5; 77; 81; 83; 89; 89a; 90; 109; 167.*

*** Erato 3984 25488-2 (3); with Röschmann, Von Magnus, Bartosz, Dürmüller, Mertens.

The eighth volume brings 12 cantatas as well as the appendix to the *Cantata No. 89, Was soll ich aus dir machen, Ephraim?.* Like its two immediate predecessors, it is devoted to the first annual cycle of Leipzig cantatas from 1724–5. Koopman still sticks to solo voices in the chorus of *Ich glaube, lieber Herr, hilf meinem* (BWV 109) but, for the most part, the cantatas have the positive elements of earlier sets (light accents and well-ventilated textures) without too many of the negative ones (indifferent singing and all-too-brisk tempi). Of the soloists Dorothea Röschmann has a radiant and glorious quality that enhances the music's claims (try her in *Du sollst Gott, deinen Herren, lieben,* BWV 77). The recorded sound is of pleasing clarity.

Volume IX: *Cantatas Nos. 37; 48; 66; 70; 86; 138; 153; 154; 166; 173a (Durchlauchtster Leopold); 194.*

(N) *** Erato 3984 27315-2 (3). Rubens, Stam, Larsson, Landauer, Prégardien, Mertens, Amsterdam Bar. Ch. & O, Koopman.

The present volume continues the first cycle of cantatas that Bach composed in Leipzig in 1723–4, during a period of intense and concentrated creativity. (An exception is *Durchlauchtster Leopold* BWV 173a, a secular cantata written in Cöthen. It was re-worked as a sacred work as *Erhöhtes Fleisch und Blut* BWV 173, and as such it is included in Vol. VII of the Koopman series. No. 66, *Erfreut euch, ihr Herzen*, also originates from the composer's time in Cöthen.) The qualities of Ton Koopman's cycle are well known, and the project continues to go from strength (or near strength) to strength. The performances unfold effortlessly and with great naturalness; they were recorded in Amsterdam in 1998 and have exemplary clarity and warmth, which could be applied equally to the interpretations. The odd blemish – some suspect intonation from Sibylla Rubens and the occasionally less-than-beautiful tone from the counter-tenor Bernhard Landauer – does not detract from the overall artistic excellence and depth that Koopman achieves. His version of *Warum betrübst du dich,* BWV 138, is among the most eloquent and searching readings he has given us so far. This is an enjoyable and satisfying set, enhanced by excellent, authoritative notes from Christoph Wolff.

Complete Cantatas: BIS Masaaki Suzuki Series with Japan Bach Collegium

Cantatas Nos. 4; 150; 196.

*** BIS CD 751; with Kuriso, Tachikawa, Katano, Kooy.

The organist and harpsichordist Masaaki Suzuki went to the Sweelinck Conservatoire in Amsterdam where he became a pupil of Ton Koopman. Since 1990 he has directed the Bach Collegium Japan and teaches at the Tokyo National University of Fine Arts and Music, from which many of the soloists are drawn. The only European soloist in the first issues is Peter Kooy, also from the Sweelinck Conservatory. Like Koopman, Suzuki uses a higher pitch (A = 465) with its concomitant brighter sound, and he also favours female voices. This naturally places an additional hurdle before

the soprano, Yumiko Kuriso, which she surmounts with conspicuous distinction. In many ways, the results of the pupil outstrip those of the master, for these performances radiate more joy in music-making and give more consistent pleasure than many European ones. The strings are clean, and the sense of inhibition – of excessive awareness of the constraints of period performance that occasionally mar the Harnoncourt–Leonhardt set – is refreshingly absent here. Knowing the problems European languages pose for the Japanese, their German diction is more than acceptable. The continuing evidence below suggests that the remainder of the series (which is also including the other major choral works) is going to be as enjoyable as this first instalment – and as well recorded – and this is obviously going to occupy a key contribution in the Bach discography. Recommended with enthusiasm.

Cantatas Nos. 12; 54; 162; 182.

*** BIS CD 791; with Kuriso, Mera, Sakurada, Kooy.

Readers will recognize the opening of No. 12, *Weinen, Klagen, Sorgen, Zagen,* as a model for the *Crucifixus* of the *B minor Mass* and Suzuki gives it with feeling and gravitas, while his characterization elsewhere – both in No. 54, *Widerstehe doch der Sünde,* and in No. 162, *Ach! ich sehe, jetzt, da ich zur Hochzeit gehe* – inspires confidence. No grumbles about the quality of the singing, the instrumental response or the present and pleasing sound, which is in the best traditions of the house.

Cantatas Nos. 18; 152; 155; 161; 163.

*** BIS CD 841; with M. Suzuki, Schmithüsen, Mera, Sakurada, Kooy.

Cantatas Nos. 21 (with 3 alternative movements); 31.

*** BIS CD 851; with Frimmer, Türk, Kooy.

Cantatas Nos. 21; 147.

(N) *** BIS CD 1031. Nonoshita, Blaze, Türk, Kooij, Concerto Palatino (BWV 21), Bach Coll. Japan, Suzuki.

This is Vol. XII in Masaaki Suzuki's survey and the fifth devoted to the cantatas that Bach composed in 1723. There are several versions of *Ich hatte viel Bekümmernis* (BWV 21). The so-called Weimar version from 1716 which Bach transposed into D minor for Hamburg in 1720, appeared in Vol. VI of the Suzuki series with some alternative arias. This present version is the revision Bach made in 1723 for Leipzig in which the orchestral texture is enriched. Both cantatas receive performances of great vitality and spirit; the soloists are first rate and the recordings have great presence.

Cantatas Nos. 22–3; 75.

*** BIS CD 901; with M. Suzuki, Mera, Türk, Kooy.

Cantatas Nos. 24; 76; 167.

*** BIS CD 931; with M. Suzuki, Blaze, Türk, Urano.

Cantatas Nos. 25; 50; 64; 69a; 77.

(N) *** BIS CD 1041. Nonoshita, Blaze, Sollek-Avella, Türk, Sakurada, Kooij, Concerto Palatino (BWV 25 & 64), Bach Coll. Japan, Suzuki.

Volume XIII continues with the cantatas from Bach's first

year at Leipzig, 1723. The performances radiate freshness and enthusiasm, and their vitality is matched by a wonderfully present recorded sound. Masaaki Suzuki's series continues to be a viable first choice in this repertoire, and nothing here inclines us to doubt its dependable excellence.

Cantatas Nos. 46; 95; 136; 138.

*** BIS CD 991; with M. Suzuki, Wessel, Sakurada, Kooy.

Cantatas Nos. 61; 63; 132; 172.

*** BIS CD 881; with Schmithüsen, Mera, Sakurada, Kooy.

Turning to a Japanese group for the whole cantata cycle was a bold step which has been more than vindicated. As in the earlier issues the singers are uniformly excellent and can give many European soloists and choirs a lesson in diction; their German sounds immaculate. Yoshikazu Mera is a counter-tenor of the highest quality, and the remaining soloists have nothing to fear from comparison with those in the Leonhardt–Harnoncourt set or the Koopman survey on Erato – quite the contrary. Above all, the playing has sensitivity allied to vitality, and scholarship blended with imagination. The recordings are very well balanced and finely detailed, very much in the best traditions of BIS. If you find that any of the cantatas listed above fill gaps in your collection, there is no reason to hesitate – and if you are just starting out on a complete collection, this would be a viable first choice.

Cantatas Nos. 71; 106; 131.

*** BIS CD 781; with M. Suzuki, Yanagisawa, Mera, Türk, Kooy.

The present disc collects some of the earliest in the canon from Bach's time at Mühlhausen. Some may feel that Suzuki's slow tempo at the opening of No. 106, the *Actus tragicus* or *Gottes Zeit ist die allerbeste Zeit*, is a little too much of a good thing, but others (like us) may well be convinced by the breadth and space he brings to it. The singing is of a high standard throughout, and Midori Suzuki gives particular pleasure in No. 71, *Gott ist mein König*, with her freshness and expressiveness – as for that matter do Aki Yanagisawa and Gerd Türk. Freshness is what characterizes the chorus and instrumentalists too and what communicates a greater intensity of feeling than many rivals. The BIS sound is first class in terms of both clarity and ambience.

Cantatas Nos. 105; 179; 186.

*** BIS CD 951; with Persson, Blaze, Sakurada, Kooy.

Suzuki's survey of the Bach cantatas continues to go from strength to strength. Here it has the benefit of excellent soloists in Miah Persson, a Swedish soprano of real quality, and the tenor Makoto Sakurada. It seems invidious to single them out since both the counter-tenor, Robin Blaze, and Peter Kooy are hardly less impressive. *Herr, gehe nicht ins Gericht* (BWV 105) faces formidable competition, but it more than withstands any comparison you might care to make. The balance does not place the soloists too far forward and the sound is as vivid, warm and clear as you could want.

Cantatas Nos. (i) 163; (ii) 165; (iii) 185; (iv) 199.

*** BIS CD 801; with (i–ii) Yanagisawa; (i–iii) Tachikawa, Sakurada, Schreckenberger; (iii–iv) M. Suzuki.

Suzuki treats this incomparable music with an appropriate sense of awe and at no time does one feel any trace of routine. The musical and technical standard of this BIS series is maintained at the highest level.

Cantatas: Karl Richter DG Archiv Series with Munich Bach Choir & Orchestra

Cantatas Nos. (i) 4; (ii) 51; (i) 56; (i; iii) 140; (iv) 147; (ii) 202.

(B) *** DG Double (ADD) 453 094-2; with (i) Fischer-Dieskau; (ii) Stader; (iii) Mathis; Schreier; (iv) Buckel, Töpper, Van Kesteren, Engen, Ansbach Festival Soloists.

Richter's stereo Bach cantata series for DG, which spanned two decades beginning in the late 1950s, is shown at its finest in this well-chosen half-dozen which are all among Bach's finest works in this form. No. 4, *Christ lag in Todesbanden*, is early. Richter seems wholly in sympathy with the music and secures some splendid choral singing and dignified playing from the orchestra. Fischer-Dieskau is featured both here and in the solo cantata, *Ich will den Kreuzstab gerne tragen*. Some might feel that he is at times a little too expressive and over-sophisticated, but he pays characteristic attention to the text. Richter, too, is at times a trifle heavy-handed, but this remains a memorable account. No. 51, *Jauchzet Gott* demands an abnormally high tessitura from the solo soprano, and Maria Stader is in splendid voice here (a virtuoso performance which is also most moving) and also in the Wedding Cantata, *Weichet nur*, which is one of Bach's most immediately appealing works. Here the discipline of the choir is not always impeccable; but these performances truly belong to Stader, and her singing is firm and clear and shows no sense of strain. No. 140, *Wachet auf, ruft uns die Stimme* (which opens the programme), shows Richter's team at their most impressive throughout, with all the soloists on excellent form and the obbligato wind players, Manfred Clement (oboe) and Edgar Shann (cor anglais), making notable contributions, here as elsewhere. The gloriously heartwarming sound from the Munich orchestra is utterly different from what one would expect from a period-instrument performance today. *Herz und Mund und Tat und Leben* is another very successful performance, with both the soprano and contralto arias beautifully sung by Ursula Buckel and the rich-timbred contralto, Hertha Töpper, respectively. The tenor, John van Kesteren, is also impressive. This cantata contains the famous chorale, *Wohl mir, dass ich Jesum habe* (better known as 'Jesu, joy of man's desiring'), and this is presented spaciously and warmly. All in all, this set with its first-class CD transfers can be given the warmest welcome.

Cantatas (for the latter part of the Church year) Nos. 5; 26; 38; 55–6; 60; 70; 80; 96; 106 (Actus tragicus); 115–16; 130; 139–40; 180.

(B) **(*) DG (ADD) 439 394-2 (5); with Mathis, Buckel,

Schmidt, Töpper, Schreier, Haefliger, Fischer-Dieskau, Adam, Engen.

This Richter box collects cantatas that Bach composed for the last ten Sundays of Trinity, plus three others, a Reformation Festival piece (No. 80), a cantata for St Michael's Day (No. 130) and Bach's funeral cantata, *Gottes Zeit* – the so-called *Actus tragicus*; it is given a first-rate performance, with fine solo singing and committed direction. Most of these cantatas are chorale-based and nearly all emerge with the dignity and majesty one expects from these forces. They were all recorded in the Munich Herkulessaal, for the most part in 1978, and the sound is warm and spacious. Karl Richter's heavy tread seems over the years to have moderated into a more flexible and human gait, though a certain inflexibility and lack of imagination still surface occasionally.

Cantatas (for the middle Sundays after Trinity) Nos. 8–9; 17; 27; 33; 45; 51; 78; 100; 102; 105; 137; 148; 178–9; 187; 199.

(B) **(*) DG (ADD) 439 387-2 (6); with Buckel, Mathis, Stader, Hamari, Töpper, Schreier, Haefliger, Van Kesteren, Fischer-Dieskau, Engen.

This box offers the cantatas composed for the sixth Sunday after Trinity through to the seventeenth. Again the spacious venue is the Munich Herkulessaal. The chorus is probably larger than it should be, but the results are invariably musical, and Richter shows greater flexibility and imagination than often has been the case. Just occasionally his heavy touch is felt, but so much of this set is first rate that reservations can be all but overruled. The soloists are thoroughly dependable.

Cantatas (for Ascension Day; Whitsun; Trinity) Nos. 10–11; 21; 24; 30; 34; 39; 44; 68; 76; 93; 129; 135; 147; 175.

(B) **(*) DG (ADD) 439 380-2 (6); with Mathis, Buckel, Reynolds, Töpper, Schreier, Haefliger, Van Kesteren, Fischer-Dieskau, Moll, Engen.

The first performance offered here is the glorious Ascension Cantata, *Lobet Gott in seinen Reichen* (No. 11), which opens and closes joyfully with resplendent trumpets. All four soloists are first rate, and Anna Reynolds is especially memorable in her famous aria, *Ach, bleib doch, mein liebstes Leben*, warmly supported by the strings of the Munich ensemble. Richter's other performances have a breadth and sense of space that are really quite impressive. He makes heavy weather of *Ein ungefärbt Gemüte* (No. 24), but on the whole the dignity of these performances outweighs the occasional pedestrian moments. On the whole a successful box.

Cantatas: Gardiner DG Archiv Series

Cantatas for Easter Nos. 6; 66.

(N) *** DG 463 580-2. Soloists, Monteverdi Ch., E. Bar. Sol., Gardiner.

Cantatas for Ascension Day Nos. 11; 37; 43; 128.

(N) *** DG 463 583-2. Argenta, Blaze, Rolfe Johnson, Genz, Varcoe, Hagen, Monteverdi Ch., E. Bar. Sol., Gardiner.

Cantata for Feast of Circumcision: No.16; Cantatas for 21st & 23rd Sundays after Trinity Nos. 98; 139.

(N) *** DG 463 586-2. Fuge, Ragin, Podger, Schwarz, Monteverdi Ch., E. Bar. Sol., Gardiner.

Cantatas for Whitsun Nos. 34; 59; 74; 172.

(N) *** DG 463 584-2. Soloists, Monteverdi Ch., E. Bar. Sol., Gardiner.

Cantatas for Advent Nos. 36; 61; 62.

(N) *** DG 463 588-2. Argenta, Lang, Rolfe Johnson, Bär, Monteverdi Ch., E. Bar. Sol., Gardiner.

Cantatas for Christmas Nos. 63; 64; 121; 133.

(N) *** DG 463 589-2. Soloists, Monteverdi Ch., E. Bar. Sol., Gardiner.

Cantatas for the 3rd Sunday after Epiphany Nos. 72; 73; 111; 156.

(N) *** DG 463 582-2. Soloists, Monteverdi Ch., E. Bar. Sol., Gardiner.

Cantatas for the Feast of the Purification of Mary Nos. 82; 83; 125; 200.

(N) *** DG 463 585-2. Tyson, Agnew, Harvey, Monteverdi Ch., E. Bar. Sol., Gardiner.

Cantatas for 9th Sunday after Trinity Nos. 94; 105; 168.

(N) *** DG 463 590-2. Soloists, Monteverdi Ch., E. Bar. Sol., Gardiner.

Cantatas Nos. 106; 118; 198.

(N) *** DG 463 581-2. Argenta, Chance, Rolfe Johnson, Varcoe, Monteverdi Ch., E. Bar. Sol., Gardiner.

Cantatas for 11th Sunday after Trinity Nos. 113; 179; 199.

(N) *** DG 463 591-2. Soloists, Monteverdi Ch., E. Bar. Sol., Gardiner.

During the 250th anniversary of Bach's death in 2000 John Eliot Gardiner embarked on an ambitious project to perform all the cantatas on the appropriate days of the liturgical year in a variety of English and European venues. Deutsche Grammophon had planned to record the whole series, but the costs involved, the emergence of rival versions at budget prices, and the magnificent BIS series from Japan prompted them to reconsider the viability of the project.

The final outcome was the release of the CDs listed above. Some are live performances and two are re-issues: DG 463 581-2 (which includes a memorable account of *Gottes Zeit ist die allerbeste Zeit* from 1990) and the *Advent Cantatas* (DG 463 588-2, from 1992), though it must be noted that both are still offered at premium price, even though the playing time of the former is less than an hour. Come to that, the two newly recorded *Easter Cantatas* (DG 463 580-2) are 48:16 minutes and *Nos. 16, 98 & 139* (DG 463 586-2) even less: 45:30. To be perfectly fair the *Ascension Day Cantatas* (DG 463 583-2) are better value for money (78:30).

Gardiner's admirers are unlikely to be too concerned about this, as his feeling for style and sense of drive strike a responsive chord with many music-lovers. His choice of soloists is unerring, and the musicianship of the Monteverdi Choir and the English Baroque Soloists always imposing. Rhythmic articulation is light but well defined, and there is great technical finesse and unanimity of ensemble. Some may find him a little too crisp and clean and at times a shade too brisk, even in the poignant funeral cantata *Lass, Fürstin, lass noch einen Strahl* BWV 198.

Cantatas Nos. 140; 147.

(N) (M) *** DG Dig. 463 587-2. Holton, Chance, Rolfe Johnson, Varcoe, Monteverdi Ch., E. Bar. Sol., Gardiner.

These popular Bach cantatas are coupled in highly accomplished performances. The level of instrumental playing is polished, and Ruth Holton, Anthony Rolfe Johnson, Michael Chance and Stephen Varcoe make equally satisfying contributions. The recordings are immediate and well balanced. A strong recommendation, especially now that it is available at mid-price.

It goes without saying that in the course of these beautifully recorded performances there is much to refresh the spirit alongside much that has spirit rather than a sense of the spiritual. Gardiner is marvellously alive to the texture and dedicated and enthusiastic, but he can also be unyielding and lack breadth and majesty. Despite such reservations and the fact that Suzuki's series with the Bach Collegium of Japan is even more rewarding, Gardiner's performances are undoubtedly of a consistently high calibre. Both the documentation and presentation are of the usual fine Archiv standard.

Other cantata groupings

Cantatas Nos. (i) 4; (ii) 56; 82.

(M) (**(*)) DG (IMS) mono 449 756-2. (i–ii) Fischer-Dieskau; (i) Frankfurt Hochschule Ch., 1950 Bach Festival O, Lehman; (ii) Ristenpart CO, Ristenpart.

These recordings, reissued as one of DG's 'Originals', come from 1950–51. Fischer-Dieskau's artistry is heard to excellent effect and nowhere better than in *Ich habe genug*, which is sung exquisitely. The choral cantata, *Christ lag in Todesbanden*, receives a dignified and expressive reading. Though the sound is not as vivid or present as one might expect, it is eminently acceptable. A valuable issue, as a reminder both of an earlier Bach style and of Fischer-Dieskau's consummate artistry.

Cantatas Nos. 8; 51; 78; 80; 140; 147.

(B) **(*) O-L Double (ADD) 455 706-2 (2). Soloists, Bach Ens., Rifkin.

Joshua Rifkin's performances opt for the one-to-a-part principle not only in his instrumental ensemble but also as far as the choruses are concerned. He opts for female sopranos rather than boy trebles but uses adult male altos. Not all will find his solutions congenial, but there is some good singing in this series, and the playing is lively enough. One feels the need for greater weight and a more full-blooded approach at times, but this is outweighed by the sensitivity and intelligence that inform these excellently balanced recordings.

Cantatas for the Ascension, Advent, Christmas and Easter: (i) Ascension: 11 *(Ascension Oratorio)*; 43; 44; (ii) Advent: 36; 61; 62; (iii) Christmas: 57; 110; 122; (iv) Easter: 66 *(Easter Oratorio)*, BWV 249.

(M) ** HM HMX 2908070 (4). (i; iv) Schlick, Patriasz; (i–

ii) Prégardien; (i–iv) Kooy; (ii) Rubens; (ii–iii) Connolly; (iii) Jezovšek, Padmore; (iv) Wessel, Taylor; Ghent Coll. Voc., Herreweghe.

On the whole these are sympathetic and musical performances of well-chosen seasonal cantatas with good soloists, the only minor blot being the soprano and tenor duet in *Unser Mund sei voll Lachens*, where Vasiljka Jezovšek is insecure. The style of the music-making, although admirably refined, is generally a trifle wanting in the joy that this period of the Christian church calendar evokes. The account of the *Easter Oratorio* is a different matter, as is its apt Easter cantata coupling, where both singers and players are very spirited and vividly recorded. Fortunately this disc is available separately (HMC 901513).

Cantatas Nos. 28; 85; 90; 119; 140; 147.

(B) ** Erato Ultima (ADD) 3984 28166-2 (2). Friesenhausen, Lisken, Jelden, McDaniel, Scherler, Huber, Stämpfli, Wenk, Graf, Giebel, Hellman, Krebs, Heinrich Schütz Ch., Pforzheim CO, Werner.

The present performances were recorded between 1963 and 1970, and they serve as a reminder that the 1990s were not the sole arbiter of musical truth. Authenticity of feeling and humanity are every bit as important as period instruments. There are some distinguished solo contributions from Agnes Giebel and Helmut Krebs, particularly in BWV 147 (*Herz und Mund und Tat und Leben*), and Georg Jelden, and some fine obbligato playing too from Maurice André in *Es reisset euch ein schrecklich Ende* (BWV 90). The Heinrich Schütz Chorale is not always as finely focused or vital as one would like, but generally the set gives satisfaction. Werner is a stylist and this tells. The recordings are very good if not as wide-ranging or as transparent in detail as modern sets.

Cantatas Nos. 35; 53; 82.

(M) *** HM HMT 7901273. Jacobs, Ens. 415, Banchini.

Ich habe genug, best known in its form for baritone and obbligato oboe, is here, but sung by a male alto. The present performance finds the excellent René Jacobs in very good form. The playing of Ensemble 415 and Chiara Banchini is eminently spirited and stylish, and the opening concerto movement in *Geist und Seele wird verwirret* (BWV 35) has a refreshing vigour. The fine one-movement *Schlage doch, gewünschte Stunde* (BWV 53) – once attributed to Bach but now thought to be by Georg Melchior Hoffmann – is omitted from Rilling's survey on Hänssler. This enhances the claims of this excellently recorded mid-price issue. Some find Jacobs's tone a little chilly but there is great intensity here.

Cantatas Nos. 35: Sinfonias (only); (i) 56; 82; 158.

*** Decca 466 570-2. (i) Goerne; Salzburg Bach Ch. & Camerata Academica, Norrington.

All three cantatas for bass are on the theme of death and the liberation it brings, and they are interspersed on this disc with two spirited instrumental sinfonias. As you would expect from a pupil of Fischer-Dieskau and Schwarzkopf, Goerne's feeling for and projection of words are impeccable and he invests both *Ich habe genug* and *Ich will den Kreuzstab* with great expressive eloquence. Norrington is sometimes given to exaggeration, but for the most part he is supportive. The Decca balance places the voice rather close, perhaps to help the lower end of the register, but the sound is fresh and vivid. Impressive and satisfying accounts of these cantatas.

Cantatas Nos. 35; 169; 170.

**(*) Finlandia 3984 25325-2. Groop, Ostrobothnian CO, Kangas.

Monica Groop gives us three solo cantatas for alto, with the important organ obbligato parts played most expertly by Håkan Wikman. The orchestral playing is fresh and has a welcome liveliness, to which the recording engineer does justice. Groop is in good voice, though hers is commanding rather than moving singing.

Cantatas Nos. 39; 73; 93; 105; 107; 131.

(B) **(*) Virgin VBD5 61721 (4). Schlick, Mellon, Lesne, Brett, Kooy, Ghent Coll. Voc. Ch. & O, Herreweghe – *Masses (Missae breves)*. **(*)

These six cantatas are all among Bach's most rewarding works in this genre. With such a starry cast it is not surprising that the solo singing is of the very highest calibre, as is the instrumental playing (on period instruments), especially in the provision of obbligatos. The choral singing is stylishly sympathetic too, and these performances are all warmly enjoyable, with the single proviso that the resonant acoustic (as with the coupled *Missae breves*) takes the edge off the vocal projection and produces just a degree of blandness.

Cantatas for the 1st, 2nd and 3rd days of Christmas, Nos. 40; 57; 63–4; 91; 110; 121; 133; 151.

(M) **(*) Teldec (ADD) 0630 17366-2 (3). Soloists, Ghent Coll. Voc., Leonhardt Consort, Leonhardt; VCM, Harnoncourt.

A gathering of Bach's cantatas for the Christmas season. The ear has to accept moments of less than perfect intonation from the treble soloists of the Vienna Boys' (notably Detlef Bratsch in No. 91), although on the plus side Peter Jelosits makes a fine contribution to No. 53. Similarly among the original instruments, the horns are sometimes wildly astray in their upper harmonics (as in the introduction for the same cantata (*Gelobet seist du Jesu Christ*). The Ghent chorus are not always absolutely reliable either: they are not completely secure in No. 133; yet they are at their best in No. 151, a splendid cantata. But overall there is much to enjoy here.

Cantatas Nos. (i) 51: Jauchzet Gott in allen Landen (complete); (ii) 68: Also hat Gott die Welt geliebt: Aria: Mein gläubiges Herz (only); 199: Mein Herze schwimmt im Blut; (iii) 202: Weichet nur, betrübte Schatten (both complete); (ii) 208: Was mir behagt: Recitative and Aria: Schafe können sicher weiden (only); (iv) STOLZEL, attrib. BACH: Aria: Bist du bei mir.

(M) (***) EMI mono CDH5 67206-2. Schwarzkopf, (i) Philh. O, cond. Gellhorn; (ii) Dart; (iii) Concg. O, Klemperer; (iv) Moore.

EMI have gathered together a superb collection of Schwarzkopf's Bach recordings, made between 1946 (the aria known in English as 'Sheep may safely graze') and 1958 (*Cantata No. 199*). What is especially fascinating is the live recording which was taken from a performance of *Cantata No. 202* with Klemperer and the Concertgebouw, even more vehement and characterful at generally faster speeds than in the more controlled studio recording made later the same year, 1957, and now issued on Testament (see below). *Bist du bei mir*, long attributed to Bach, makes a delightful supplement, with Gerald Moore at the piano. Excellent transfers, though the Netherlands Radio recording with Klemperer is less full, if very atmospheric.

Cantatas Nos. 51; 82a; 84; 199; 202 (Wedding Cantata); 209.

(BB) *** Virgin 2 x 1 VBD5 61644-2 (2). Argenta, Ens. Sonnerie, Huggett.

Nancy Argenta recorded these cantatas in the early 1990s. Not only does she give us a radiantly brilliant account of *Jauchzet Gott in allen Landen*, one that belongs among the best, but also superb versions of both the *Wedding Cantata* and *Non sà che sia dolore*. As is well known, Bach was particularly happy with *Ich habe genug* and scored it for other voices including soprano, transcribing the oboe obbligato for flute. Argenta's performance is arguably the finest we have in this form and in all six cantatas included in this package, the Ensemble Sonnerie and Monica Huggett give exemplary support. In every way a distinguished issue and not least in the quality of the recorded sound.

Cantatas Nos. 51; 202; 209.

(M) *** Teldec (ADD) 3984 21711-2. Giebel, André, Leonhardt, Concerto Amsterdam, Schroeder, or Leonhardt Consort.

Agnes Giebel gives a dazzling account of *Jauchzet Gott* – and so for that matter does the trumpeter, Maurice André. In the so-called *Wedding Cantata* Giebel sings superlatively and Gustav Leonhardt's continuo support is beyond praise. *Non sà che sia dolore* is also sung excellently, and here Giebel is most stylishly accompanied by the Leonhardt Consort.

Cantatas Nos. 51; 202; 210.

*** DG 459 621-2. Schäfer, Mus. Ant. Cologne, Goebel.

Christine Schäfer, in this handsomely presented volume, couples two of Bach's wedding cantatas with the familiar *Jauchzet Gott in allen Landen*. Unusually, this is given in Wilhelm Friedemann Bach's arrangement, which adds a second trumpet and timpani to Bach's trumpet, strings and continuo. In all three she is in radiant voice and delights us with her beauty of tone and virtuosity. Reinhardt Goebel and his Musica Antiqua Cologne are spirited and vital, though there are times, particularly in the closing *Alleluia*, where the onward drive is somewhat unremitting. DG have provided one of their most expertly balanced recordings.

Cantatas Nos. 54; 169; 170.

*** Hyp. CDA 66326. Bowman, King's Consort, King.

James Bowman is on impressive form and his admirers need not hesitate here. The present disc is very desirable and the King's Consort under Robert King give excellent support. Good recorded sound.

Cantatas Nos. 55, BWV 189 (attrib. Georg Melchior Hoffmann); BWV 160 (by Telemann); Arias from Cantatas Nos. 5, 13, 26 & 102.

*** Ph. 442 786-2. Schreier, C. P. E. Bach CO.

Peter Schreier, who directs from the larynx as it were, includes two tenor cantatas once numbered in the Bach canon but now attributed to others. That leaves only one cantata (No. 55) for solo tenor as being *echt*-Bach. The opening of the Telemann piece is particularly delectable, and the whole work delights. Schreier sings and directs superbly, and the playing of the C. P. E. Bach orchestra will give solace to readers with an aversion to period-instrument ensembles. Exemplary recording-balance with plenty of warmth.

Cantatas Nos. 55; 82a; Sinfonias & Arias from Cantatas Nos. 4, 7, 18, 43, 139, 198, 212, & 249.

(N) *** Virgin VC5 45420-2. Bostridge, Europa Galante, Biondi.

Among Bach's copious output there is only one cantata for solo tenor, *Ich arme Mensch, ich Sündenknecht* BWV 55. Here Bostridge has attached a transcription of *Ich habe genug* in its soprano version (BWV 82a). He also performs tenor arias from a number of other cantatas, all of which reveal his fine musical intelligence and beauty of tone. Some may find his diction too carefully projected (he certainly dots his 'i's and crosses his 't's with enormous care), but others will find much to reward them here, not least the superb musicianship of Fabio Biondi and his Europa Galante, and the excellent Virgin Classics recording.

Cantatas Nos. 56; 82; 99; 106 (Actus tragicus); 131; 158.

(B) *** Double Decca Dig 458 087-2 (2). Soloists, Bach Ens., Rifkin.

Joshua Rifkin's series (where the soloists are one-to-a-part in the chorales) is somewhat uneven, but in the two solo cantatas (Nos. 56 and 82), Jan Opalach is magnificent and is excellently supported by Rifkin and his group. *Der Friede sei mit dir* (No. 158) is much more of a rarity but is hardly less rewarding. On the companion disc the performance of *Gottes Zeit* (the so-called *Actus tragicus*) has considerable merit. *Aus der Tiefen* (No. 131) is hardly less fine and the singers are all first class. As elsewhere in this series, one feels the need for greater weight but overall this is a worthwhile reissue.

(i) Cantatas Nos. 67; 130. Masses (Missae breves): (ii) BWV 233–4; (iii) BWV 235–6.

(B) **(*) Double Decca (ADD) 466 754-2 (2). (i) Ameling, Watts, Krenn, Krause, Lausanne Pro Arte Ch., OSR, Ansermet; (ii–iii) Hickox Singers & O, Hickox, with (ii) Jenkins; (ii–iii) Eathorne, Esswood, Roberts; (iii) Langridge.

In Ansermet's accounts of *Cantatas Nos. 67* and *130*, the orchestra may not be the finest in the world (though the flute playing of André Pepin is certainly in that bracket), and they are hardly 'authentic' (though they are not particularly *Romantic* either), but there is plenty of character here. They are very well recorded and they offer much good singing.

Hickox's mid-1970s performances bring more polished orchestral playing, fine singing and excellent recording. BWV 233 and 234 offer many beauties: the *A major Mass*, which draws on *Cantata No. 67* for its *Gloria*, is the more inspired, but it is hard to understand why all four of these works are relatively neglected. The two other *Masses*, BWV 235 and BWV 236, are equally well performed, with the contribution of the choir shining out.

Cantata No. 82: Ich habe genug.

☼ (M) (***) EMI CDH7 63198-2. Hotter, Philh. O, Bernard – BRAHMS: *Lieder.* (***) ☼

One of the greatest cantata performances ever. Glorious singing from Hans Hotter and wonderfully stylish accompanying from Anthony Bernard and the Philharmonia. This 1950 mono recording was never reissued on LP, and it sounds eminently present in this fine transfer.

Cantatas Nos. (i) 82; (ii) 159; (iii) 170.

☼ (M) *** Decca (ADD) 430 260-2. ASMF, Marriner, with (i) Lord; (i–ii) Shirley-Quirk; (ii–iii) Baker; (ii) Tear, St Anthony Singers.

John Shirley-Quirk's performance of *Ich habe genug* is much to be admired, not only for the sensitive solo singing but also for the lovely oboe obbligato of Roger Lord. But this reissue is to be prized even more for the other two cantatas. Both Dame Janet Baker and Shirley-Quirk are in marvellous voice, and *Vergnügte Ruh'* makes a worthy companion. This is among the half-dozen or so cantata records that ought to be in every collection.

(i) Cantatas Nos. 82: Ich habe genug; 169: Gott soll allein mein Herze haben; (ii) Aria: Bist du bei mir. Cantata arias: No. 6: Hochgelobter; No. 11: Ach bleibe doch; No. 34: Wohl euch ihr auserwählten Seelen; No. 129: Gelobet sei der Herr; No. 161: Komm, du süsse Todesstunde; No. 190: Lobe, Zion, deinen Gott. Christmas Oratorio: Bereite dich. Easter Oratorio: Saget, saget mir geschwinde. Magnificat: Et exultavit. St. John Passion: Es ist vollbracht.

(N) (B) **(*) EMI double forte (ADD) CZS 5 74282-2 (2). J. Baker, with (i) Bath Festival O, Menuhin; (ii) ASMF, Marriner – HANDEL: *Italian Cantatas.* ***

In the two complete cantatas, recorded in 1966, Janet Baker is expressive and intelligent, if not quite achieving the heights she does in the rest of the programme. The collection of arias that follow emanate from a 1975 LP, of which the sweet and contemplative ones dominate. These are beautiful, deeply felt performances, and an excellent case is made for including the alternative cantata version, *Ach bleibe doch*, of what became the *Agnus Dei* in the *B minor Mass*. The accompaniments are understanding (the gamba solo in *Es ist vollbracht* adding extra poignancy) and the recordings are excellent.

Cantatas Nos. (i) 82; 202 (Wedding); (ii) 208 (Hunt).

(N) (B) **(*) Hyp. Dyad CDD 22041 (2). Kirkby; (i) Thomas, Taverner Players, Parrott; (ii) J. Smith, S. Davies, George, Parley of Instruments, Goodman.

In the much recorded No. 82, *Ich habe genug*, David Thomas

gives a good but not inspired account of the solo part, and although the odd intonation blemish is of little importance, memories of Hotter, Souzay, Fischer-Dieskau and others are not banished. Kirkby is much more successful in the *Wedding Cantata* (*Weichet nur*) and as usual delights the listener, though some may feel that the excellent Taverner Players under Parrott could bring greater flair and lightness of touch to this felicitous score. The performance of the *Hunt Cantata*, however, is excellent in every way. The cantata is rich in melodic invention of the highest quality and is well served by excellent soloists (Kirkby again standing out) and first-class instrumental playing. As in the other works, the recording is natural and well balanced. The only snag is the short measure on the second disc (just over 43 minutes), but Kirkby's delightful singing more than compensates.

Cantatas Nos. 102 & 151.

(N)(M) *** Decca (ADD) 466 819-2. Harper, Baker, Veasey, Watts, Bowman, Pears, Fischer-Dieskau, Shirley-Quirk, Wandsworth School Ch., Aldeburgh Fest. S, Ambrosian Singers, ECO, Britten – PURCELL: *Celebrate This Festival*. ***

The cantata, *Herr, deine Augen* (No. 102), was recorded in Blythburgh Church as part of the 1965 Aldeburgh Festival. That was the year when Dietrich Fischer-Dieskau was persuaded to come to Aldeburgh to give the first performance of the cycle which Britten had just written for him, the *Songs and Proverbs of William Blake*. His superb contribution to this cantata came as a fine supplement, commanding and immaculate in both the expressive recitative and the lively arioso. The performance is equally memorable for the deeply felt singing of Dame Janet Baker in the aria, *Weh der Seele* ('Alas for the soul').

The other cantata, *Süsser Trost* (No. 151), was recorded at St Andrew's, Holborn, in December 1968, also with a formidable line-up of soloists, and with Britten inspiring his choir to sing with bright, clear tone and incisive attack. Heather Harper excels herself in the long opening aria, with Helen Watts strong and positive in her noble account of the other aria. Coupled with a lively account of the Purcell Ode taken from the opening concert of the Queen Elizabeth Hall, this makes a valuable addition to Decca's Britten at Aldeburgh series.

Cantatas Nos. 158; 203. Arias and Chorales from Cantatas Nos. 8; 13; 73; 123; 157; 159.

(M) *** EMI CDM5 67202-2. Fischer-Dieskau, St Hedwig's Cathedral Ch., Schwalbé, Nicolet, Rampal, Koch, Poppen, Picht-Axenfeld, Veyron-Lacroix, BPO, Forster.

An outstanding collection, mostly from 1958, which has been out of the catalogue ever since. For its reissue EMI have added the secular cantata, *Amore traditore*, which dates from 1960, and the excerpts from *Cantata No. 123*, recorded a decade later. Fischer-Dieskau, in splendid voice, sings here two complete cantatas plus six individual arias, usually with accompanying chorale. Their range of pitch is wide, of emotion still wider, yet the great baritone proves time and time again that he is absolutely at home in this field. The choir and orchestra under Karl Forster give him excellent

support, and the list of obbligato soloists is full of star names, including Aurèle Nicolet and Rampal. The early stereo lends a convincingly spacious realism to what was already a finely balanced ensemble and the CD transfer is admirable. Full texts and translations are included.

Cantatas Nos. (i) 197 (Wedding Cantata); (ii) 205: Der Zufriedengestellte Aeolus.

(M) *** Teldec ADD/Dig. 0630 12321. (i) Treble and alto soloists from V. Boys' Ch., Von Egmond, Ch. Viennensis; (ii) Kenny, Lipovšek, Equiluz, Holl, Arnold Schönberg Ch.; VCM, Harnoncourt.

The performance of *Gott ist unsre Zuversicht* does not come from the complete Teldec set, above, but was recorded independently in 1969. On a large scale it is finely performed, though the aria '*Schläfert aller Sorgen*' is a little sluggish. The use of boy treble and alto soloists may not be to all tastes, but they put up a good showing and the recording is excellent. No. 205 is a much later recording (from 1983) and is digital. The performance is very good indeed, and the recording has a decently spacious acoustic and no lack of detail. Recommended.

Cantatas Nos. 199; 202. Arias from Cantatas Nos. 68; 208.

*** Testament (ADD) SBT 1178. Schwarzkopf, Philh. O, Dart – MOZART: *Ch'io mi scordi di te?* (***)

Testament have here gathered together Schwarzkopf recordings made in 1955–8 that for various reasons were never published. What is clear is the superb quality of the singing here, with Sidney Sutcliffe, the principal oboe of the Philharmonia, matching Schwarzkopf's artistry in some of his obbligato solos. It is especially fascinating to compare the two versions (in German) of 'Sheep may safely graze', recorded a year apart in 1957 and 1958 – the second one far more dramatic in the recitative, and generally more freely expressive. The version here of *Cantata No. 199*, recorded only two days before the one included on the EMI Références issue (see above), is also more romantically expressive at a rather broader speed, a change in the opposite direction. The poised Schwarzkopf predominates, but the vehement Schwarzkopf also repeatedly comes through vividly, directly reflecting the singer's strong, positive character. Excellent transfers.

Cantatas Nos. 199; 202; 209.

(B) *** Naxos 8.550431. Wagner, Capella Istropolitana, Brembeck.

Mein Herze schwimmt im Blut (BWV 199) comes from Bach's Weimar years, and Friederike Wagner proves both sympathetic and lively; and both *Weichet nur, betrübte Schatten*, popularly known as the 'Wedding Cantata', and No. 209, *Non sa che sia dolore*, are given thoroughly enjoyable performances. Not for devotees of authentic-performance practice, but enjoyable for those who prefer a more traditional approach. Decent recording too.

Cantatas Nos. 202; 210 (Wedding Cantatas). Cantata No. 82 (excerpt): Ich habe genug. Arias (attrib.): Bist du

bei mir (*BWV 508*, probably by Gottfried Stölzel);
Gedenke doch, mein Geist (*BWV 509*, Anon.).

*** O-L 455 972-2. Kirkby, AAM, Hogwood.

This is among the most delightful of all the records of Bach's solo secular cantatas. Emma Kirkby, in her freshest voice, is ideally cast – as the lovely opening aria, *Weichet nur*, from the more famous of the two *Wedding Cantatas*, immediately shows. Her singing is no less ravishing in *Schlummert ein* from BWV 82, *Schweigt, ihr Flöten* ('Hush, you flutes' – Bach here isn't meaning to be taken seriously) from BWV 210, or the most famous 'Bach aria' which is not written by Bach, *Bist du bei mir*. The accompaniments from Hogwood and his Academy of Ancient Music could not have a lighter touch or more finesse, and the obbligato playing (of which there is a great deal) could not be more sensitive or more fluent. What a long way period-instrument playing has come in the last decade towards beguiling the ear! The recording is most natural and very well balanced indeed.

Cantata No. 208 (Hunt Cantata).

**(*) Hyp. CDA 66169. Smith, Kirkby, Davis, George, Parley of Instruments, Goodman.

This is a cantata rich in melodic invention of the highest quality. The performance has the benefit of excellent soloists and first-class instrumental playing. However, the measure is short compared with its competitors.

Cantatas Nos. (i) 208 (Hunt Cantata); 212 (Peasant Cantata).

(M) *** Teldec 4509 97501-2. Blasi, Holl; (i) with Kenny, Equiluz; Arnold Schönberg Ch., VCM, Harnoncourt.

Harnoncourt offers admirably ebullient accounts of a pair of Bach's secular cantatas, celebrating the name-days of two local dignitaries. The solo contributions in both works are splendid, and Blasi and the robust Robert Holl both enjoy themselves hugely in the boisterous *Peasant Cantata*. The musical interest of this remarkably inspired cantata (considering its ragbag of a text) is Bach's use of various old melodies familiar to his audience. The exuberance of the performance carries over to Harnoncourt's accompaniments – no scholarly rectitude here – and the recording is first rate.

Cantatas Nos. 211 (Coffee Cantata); 212 (Peasant Cantata).

*** O-L 417 621-2. Kirkby, Rogers, Covey-Crump, Thomas, AAM, Hogwood.

(N) ** Analekta Fleur de Lys FL 2 3136. LeBlanc, Polegato, Nils Brown, Tafelmusik, Lamon.

Emma Kirkby is particularly appealing in the *Coffee Cantata* and her father is admirably portrayed by David Thomas. Hogwood opts for single strings, and some may find they sound thin; however, there is a corresponding gain in lightness and intimacy. The recording is altogether first class.

Tafelmusik is one of the liveliest and most musical of period ensembles, whose work we have consistently admired. However, this coupling of two of the most popular Bach secular cantatas does not offer a serious challenge to its main competitors. Brett Polegato conveys some sense of

character, but Suzie LeBlanc is no match for Emma Kirkby, and the ensemble's playing is not as alert and sparkling as we have come to expect.

Major choral works

Christmas Oratorio, BWV 248.

*** DG 423 232-2 (2). Rolfe Johnson, Argenta, Von Otter, Blochwitz, Bär, Monteverdi Ch., E. Bar. Sol., Gardiner.

*** BIS CD 941/2. Frimmer, Mera, Türk, Kooy, Bach Collegium, Japan, Suzuki.

*** Decca 458 838-2 (2). Bott, Chance, Agnew, King, George, New L. Consort, Pickett.

*** Erato 0630 14775-2 (2). Larsson, Von Magnus, Prégardien, Mertens, Amsterdam Bar. Ch. & O, Koopman.

(B) *** EMI (ADD) double forte CZS5 69503-2 (2). Ameling, Baker, Tear, Fischer-Dieskau, King's College, Cambridge, Ch., ASMF, Ledger.

(N) (M) **(*) RRC Regis 2004 (2). Russell, Padmore, Wyn-Rogers, George, Sixteen, Christophers.

(i) Christmas Oratorio; (ii) Motets BWV 225-230.

(N) (M) **(*) H.M. HMX 2908113/115 (3 plus CD-Rom). (i) Roschmann, Scholl, Gura, Hager; (ii) Rubens, Kiehr, Fink, Turk, Kooy; Berlin RIAS Chamber Choir, Alte Musik Ac., Jacobs.

The freshness of the singing and playing in the DG set is a constant pleasure. Far more than usual, one registers the joyfulness of the work, from the trumpets and timpani at the start onwards. Anthony Rolfe Johnson makes a pointful and expressive Evangelist, and also outstanding is Anne Sofie von Otter with her natural gravity and exceptionally beautiful mezzo. Beauty of tone consistently marks the singing of Nancy Argenta, Hans-Peter Blochwitz and Olaf Bär. The sound is full and atmospheric.

As in his recordings of the Bach cantatas, Masaaki Suzuki directs an exceptionally fresh and alert reading of the *Christmas Oratorio*, bringing out the joy of Bach's inspiration, with outstandingly crisp singing from the chorus. Speeds are often fast, but in the beautiful cradle-song, *Schlafe mein Liebster*, relaxed pacing allows full expressiveness, here with Yoshikazu Mera as a characterful male alto soloist. Mera in florid writing does not always avoid the intrusive 'h', but that is one of the few blemishes in the solo singing, with Gerd Türk a fine Evangelist and Peter Kooy a firmly focused bass. Warm, atmospheric sound, though with the choir behind the instruments in the main choruses. This makes a fine alternative to the Gardiner version.

Philip Pickett takes an intimate, relatively small-scale view. Textures are transparent and refinement is the keynote, but this Bach performance also has plenty of vigour, with generally brisk speeds and sprung rhythms. The scale is reflected in the refined singing of Paul Agnew as the Evangelist, but the soprano Catherine Bott, and the counter-tenor Michael Chance are the soloists who stand out, not just from the rest but from most rivals in other versions. The tenor Andrew King is crisp and agile in his arias and, though Michael George is not as cleanly focused as he might be, his is a strong, sensitive contribution. Atmospheric recording which sets the limited forces in a helpful acoustic.

Koopman with his superb choir and orchestra directs a relaxed and genial account of the *Christmas Oratorio*. The Erato recording-balance favours instruments over voices, but most compellingly so, on a relatively intimate scale. The four soloists also sing the arias, and that includes the Evangelist, Christoph Prégardien, with his sweetly tuned tenor, who translates with no sense of strain from one role to the other. The others may not be as distinctive, but each voice is fresh and clear, well caught in the recording.

With generally brisk tempi (controversially so in Dame Janet's cradle-song, *Schlafe mein Liebster*, in Part II) Philip Ledger's 1976 King's performance is an intensely refreshing account which grows more winning the more one hears it, helped by four outstanding and stylish soloists. The King's acoustic gives a warm background to the nicely styled performance of choir and orchestra and, although in the CD transfer the choral focus is not absolutely clean, the sound overall is attractively balanced.

René Jacobs, with excellent soloists, offers a fresh, alert reading of the *Christmas Oratorio*, generally well-paced with one idiosyncrasy that for many will be crucial. Though in big choruses Jacobs tends to favour speeds faster than usual, light and crisp, he regularly adopts slow, even ponderous, speeds for the chorales, with pauses between lines, reminding one of the old tradition when big choirs were used for this work. He also favours speeds on the slow side for such key numbers as the great cradle-song of Part 2, *Schlafe mein Liebster*, movingly sung by the countertenor, Andreas Scholl. The extra time-length involved means that the break between the two CDs comes before the end of Part 3, leaving three numbers to be included on the second disc. In this bargain package the third disc contains Jacobs's excellent readings of Bach's six *Motets*, recorded in 1995, two years before the *Oratorio*. The beautifully matched team of soloists is nicely contrasted against the fresh RIAS Chamber Choir, light and resilient. The main booklet is generously supplemented with background information on the CD-Rom which comes as part of the package.

Harry Christophers conducts a crisp and sympathetic reading, very well played and sung, which at speeds generally a little slower than Gardiner's does not quite match that rival in exhilaration and intensity. But it remains an enjoyable performance. He has a first-rate quartet of soloists – where Gardiner has different soloists for the arias from those for the Christmas narrative – with the tenor, Mark Padmore, particularly impressive not just in the arias but as the Evangelist. Good, atmospheric recording, with trumpet and drums dramatically prominent. Now reissued by Regis at mid-price this is well worth considering.

With a characterful line-up of soloists, notably Howard Crook as the Evangelist and Michael Chance as male alto, Herreweghe offers a lively reading, well recorded, which yields to the finest rivals in the choral singing, not quite as crisply disciplined as it might be (Virgin VCD7 59530-2).

Christmas Oratorio: Arias and choruses.

(M) **(*) DG 463 003-2. Janowitz, Ludwig, Wunderlich, Crass, Munich Bach Ch. & O, Richter.

While Karl Richter's complete recording would hardly be a top choice, this selection is worth considering. He takes an unvarying view of the chorales, but there is good choral work and the fine solo singing includes glowingly beautiful contributions from Christa Ludwig and the late Fritz Wunderlich, even if Franz Crass, the bass, is coarse and unyielding.

Easter Oratorio, BWV 249; Cantata No. 66: Erfreut euch, ihr Herzen.

*** HM HMC 901513. Schlick, Wessel, Taylor, Kooy, Coll. Voc., Herreweghe.

Easter Oratorio, BWV 249; Magnificat in D, BWV 243.

(M) *** Decca (ADD) 466 420-2. Ameling, Watts, Krenn, Krause, V . Ac. Ch., Stuttgart CO, Münchinger.

(i) *Easter Oratorio;* (ii) *Magnificat in D, BWV 243.* Cantata Nos. (i) 4: *Christ lag in Totesbanden;* (ii) 11: *Lobet Gott in seinen Reichen (Ascension Cantata); Chorale: Nun ist das Heil und die Kraft* (from BWV 50).

(BB) ** Virgin 2 x 1 VBD5 61647-2 (2). (i–ii) Van Evera, Trevor, Daniels, Kooy, Thomas; (ii) Kirkby, Tubb, Cable, Crook, Jochens, Charlesworth, Grant; Taverner Consort & Players, Parrott.

Bach's *Easter Oratorio* derives from a secular cantata, more than once revised. It opens with a joyful *Sinfonia* and an *Adagio* with oboe solo (very well played in the Herreweghe account), followed by a lively chorus ('Come hasten, come running, ye swift feet') with trumpets, but then it depends very much on the soloists, who blend beautifully together in their introductory recitativo before taking their individual roles with distinction – as Mary Magdalen, Peter and John respectively. The chorus and trumpets then return to end the work joyfully. The apt coupling of the *Easter Cantata*, BWV 66, with its lovely closing *Alleluja* completes a disc which is fresh and vivid and will be hard to surpass.

The Decca coupling is one of Münchinger's very best records. The *Easter Oratorio* and *Magnificat* share the same group of soloists – and very impressive they are. Münchinger tends to stress the breadth and spaciousness of both works, and the contribution of the Stuttgart orchestra and the Vienna Academy Choir could hardly be finer, while the vintage Decca recordings have captured the detail with admirable clarity and naturalness.

Both sets of performances on Virgin are on a small scale, as Andrew Parrott favours one voice to a part in choruses. Without doubt the effect is refreshingly clear, for the singers are expert and the balance, even with Bach's exultant trumpets, is well managed. The solo singing is always good, often excellent, Caroline Trevor memorable in the alto solo, *Esurientes implevit bonis*, in the *Magnificat*. The instrumental support too is pleasingly fresh, with fine obbligato playing. But in the end the ear craves more weight.

Epiphany Mass (1740) (includes Cantatas BWV 65; BWV 180; Missa brevis in F, BWV 233).

*** DG 457 631-2 (2). Monoyios, Davidson, Daniels, Harvey, Gabrieli Cons. & Players, Congregational Choirs of Freiberg & Dresden, McCreesh).

Paul McCreesh has assembled here almost three hours of music to represent what might have been heard at Epiphany celebrations in the St Thomas church in Leipzig around 1740, when Bach was in charge. It transforms one's response to the *Missa brevis in F*, for example (in the Lutheran form of *Kyrie* and *Gloria* alone), to hear it like this instead of comparing it unfavourably with the great *B minor Mass*. So too with the cantatas, carols, chorales and organ pieces which make up the varied sequence, all performed superbly.

Magnificat in D, BWV 243.

*** BIS CD 1011. Persson, Nonoshita, Tachikawa, Türk, Urano, Bach Collegium, Japan, Suzuki – KUHNAU: *Magnificat in C*; ZELENKA: *Magnificats in C & D*. ***

*** Chan. 0518. Kirkby, Bonner, Chance, Ainsley, Varcoe, Coll. Mus. 90, Hickox – VIVALDI: *Gloria*. ***

*** EMI CDC7 54283-2. Hendricks, Murray, Rigby, Heilmann, Hynninen, ASMF Ch. & O, Marriner – VIVALDI: *Gloria*. ***

(B) *** Naxos 8.554056. Crookes, Whitaker, Trevor, Robinson, Gedge, Oxford Schola Cantorum, N. CO, Ward – VIVALDI: *Gloria*. ***

Magnificat in D, BWV 243; Cantata No. 21.

(N)(M) *** Virgin VM5 61833-2. De Reyghere, Jacobs, Prégardien, Lika, Netherlands Chamber Ch., Petite Band, Kuijken.

(i) Magnificat, BWV 243; (ii) Motets: Singet dem Herrn; Der Geist hilft unser Schwacheit auf; Jesu meine Freude, BWV 225–7.

(M) ** DG (ADD) 463 010-2. (i) Tomowa-Sintow, Baltsa, Schreier, Luxon, German Op. Ch., Berlin, BPO, Karajan; (ii) Regensburg Domspatzen, V. Capella Academica, Schneidt.

Magnificat in E flat, BWV 243a.

(B) *** Double Decca (ADD) 458 370-2 (2). Palmer, Watts, Tear, Roberts, King's College Ch., ASMF, Ledger – J. C. BACH: *Magnificat*; A. SCARLATTI: *St Cecilia Mass*. ***

Masaaki Suzuki's account of the better-known D major version of the *Magnificat* with his Japanese forces is quite exhilarating and is the most recommendable now available. He has good soloists, including the Swedish soprano Miah Persson and the German tenor Gerd Türk, as well as some impressive Japanese singers: the instrumental playing is of altogether outstanding quality. Ideal for those who don't now respond either to traditional modern-instrument performances or to authentic period orchestras, for Suzuki's players have the virtues of both: the warmth and vitality of the former and the clarity of the latter.

Both Richard Hickox and Neville Marriner couple the *Magnificat* with the popular D major *Gloria*, RV 589, of Vivaldi, and for collectors seeking this coupling the clear choice is between period and modern instruments. Those who like the former will gravitate towards Hickox, who directs a most musical account and has the benefit of such fine singers as Emma Kirkby, Michael Chance and Stephen Varcoe, and good Chandos recording. Marriner's performance with the Academy is well paced and executed with precision and fine musical intelligence. No quarrel with the

soloists either or with the splendidly warm and present recording. Both can be recommended with confidence.

Splendidly framed by the vigorous opening and closing choruses with their resplendent trumpets, Kuijken's reissued version of the *Magnificat* from 1988 performed by the excellent Netherlanders and La Petite Bande makes a strong mid-priced recommendation. There are some first-class contributions from Greta de Reyghere and Christoph Prégardien, with lovely singing from the soprano and a finely matched oboe obbligato in the aria *Quia respexit*; there are moments of vulnerable intonation from the oboe, but this is a small blemish. The recorder-decorated alto solo *Esurientes implevit* and the memorably rhythmic bass aria (with one of Bach's most catchy tunes) are equally impressive. In contrast the duet for alto and tenor *Et misericordia* is very touching. The choral singing is both warmly expressive (especially in *Suscepit Israel*) and as lightly articulated as you could wish. The coupling is one of Bach's most expansive and celebrated Weimar cantatas, *Ich hatte viel Bekümmernis*. The plangent opening *Sinfonia* creates the mood for this searchingly poignant work, which again gives the soprano and tenor plenty of opportunities for *espressivo*, individually and in a duo, after which the trumpets return for the intricate closing chorus of praise. Above all there is a sense of breadth and majesty fully worthy of Bach. A highly recommendable disc in every way.

The fresh and lively Naxos version of the *Magnificat* is also now attractively re-coupled with an outstanding version of Vivaldi's *Gloria*, also using modern instruments. None of the soloists from the choir, all of them stylish, is identified on the reissue; our listing of their names is retained from the original issue.

Philip Ledger's account of the E flat version, recorded by Argo in the late 1970s, is also most attractive, highly recommendable if boys' voices are preferred in the chorus, and is excellent value. The soloists are first class. This now comes as a Double Decca, with Alessandro Scarlatti's splendid *St Cecilia Mass* added, also performed with striking vigour and moving expressive feeling.

Karajan's reading of the D major *Magnificat* makes it an orchestral work with subsidiary chorus and, although the ingredients are polished and refined, the results are artificial, even though the soloists are excellent. However, the three best-known motets bring highly enjoyable performances which have a lusty freshness, enhanced by the brightness of the boy trebles of the Regensburger Domspatzen.

(i) Masses (Missae breves): in F, BWV 233; in G, BWV 236. Trio Sonata in C, Transposed to D, BWV 529.

*** Chan. 0653. (i) Argenta, Chance, Padmore, Harvey, instrumental soloists; Purcell Qt.

Masses (Missae breves): in A, BWV 234; in G min., BWV 235.

*** Chan. 0642. Gritton, Blaze, Padmore, Harvey, Purcell Qt.

Masses (Missae breves), BWV 233–6; Magnificat in D, BWV 243.

*** Ph. 438 873-2 (2). Bonney, Remmert, Trost, Bär, Berlin RIAS Chamber Ch., C. P. E. Bach CO, Schreier.

Masses (Missae breves): BWV 233–4; Kyrie eleison in F, BWV 233a.

*** Häns. CD 92.071. Brown, Schäfer, Danz, Taylor, Quasthoff, Schöne, Gächinger Kantorei, Budapest Franz Liszt CO, Bach Collegium, Stuttgart, Rilling.

Masses (Missae breves): BWV 235–6; Sancti in C; D; G; D, BWV 237–8, 240–41; Christe eleison in G min., BWV 242; Credo in unum Deum, BWV 1081.

*** Häns. CD 92.072. Oelze, Ziesak, Danz, Remmert, Prégardien, Quasthoff, Gächinger Kantorei, Bach Collegium, Stuttgart, Rilling.

Masses (Missae breves): BWV 233–6; Sanctus in D, BWV 238.

(M) **(*) Virgin VBD5 61721 (4). Mellon, Lesne, Crook, Prégardien, Kooy, Ghent Coll. Voc. Ch. & O, Herreweghe – *Cantata No. 39,* etc. **(*)

There have been various good modern-instrument performances of these so-called short or Lutheran Masses over the years, including the fine earlier set under Hickox, now available within a generous and inexpensive Double Decca (see above under *Cantata No. 67*). But the authentic period-instrument performances on Chandos must now take pride of place. Although the soloists provide the one-voice-to-a-part chorus, their voices blend so richly together that one is not conscious of any lack of body or contrast: indeed the effect is glorious, while in the F major work the vigorous trumpeting horns add to the joyfulness of the *Gloria* and *Cum Sancto Spiritu*. The solo singing is splendid, and the overall balance quite excellent. The first disc uses a *Trio Sonata* to act as a kind of extended opening sinfonia, and very effectively too. This is the CD to try first, and you will surely want the other one also.

The Schreier set can be warmly recommended too, for he also includes a fine, fresh account of the *Magnificat*. He has excellent soloists, notably Barbara Bonney and Olaf Bär, and the Philips digital sound is first class. Schreier uses a chamber chorus, and stylistically these modern-instrument performances show that he has absorbed much that is attractive from period-instrument practice, with his lively tempi and fresh orchestral textures. Moreover the ambience is particularly pleasing, bringing atmosphere without clouding detail.

The Masses on the first of the two Hänssler discs were recorded in the early 1990s and the *Kyrie in F*, BWV 233a, in 1999. Similarly, on the second, the recording of the *G minor*, BWV 235, was made in 1992 and the remaining recordings in 1999. These are eminently well-recorded (and recommendable) mid-priced accounts, with fine singing from Christine Oelze and Christoph Prégardien.

Herreweghe's recordings of these four *Missae breves* are now grouped rather arbitrarily with six cantatas (admirably sung), in a four-CD boxed set. The performances are authentic, quite spirited and certainly stylish. The snag – both here and in the coupled cantatas – is the very resonant ecclesiastical acoustic which, while it provides a smooth freedom from period-instrument abrasiveness, also takes some of the edge off the choruses and detracts from the presence of the soloists. Even so, the performances are warmly enjoyable.

Mass in B min., BWV 232.

*** DG 415 514-2. Argenta, Dawson, Fairfield, Knibbs, Kwella, Hall, Nichols, Chance, Collin, Stafford, Evans, Milner, Murgatroyd, Lloyd-Morgan, Varcoe, Monteverdi Ch., E. Bar. Sol., Gardiner.

(N) *** BBC (ADD) BBCL 4062-2 (2). Hill, J. Baker, Pears, Shirley-Quirk, New Philharmonia Ch. and O., Giulini.

(***) BBC mono BBCL 4008-7. Danco, Ferrier, Pears, Boyce, BBC Ch., Boyd Neel O, Enescu.

*** Hyp. CDA 67201/2 (2). Fritter, Mrasek, Schloderer, Fraas, Rolfe Johnson, George, Tölz Boys' Ch., King's Cons. Ch., King's Cons., King.

(B) *** EMI double forte CZS5 68640-2 (2). Donath, Fassbaender, Ahnsjö, Hermann, Holl, Bav. R. Ch. & O, Jochum.

(B) *** Arts 47525-2 (2). Invernizzi, Dawson, Banditelli, Prégardien, Mertens, Swiss R. Ch., Lugano, Sonatori de la Gioiosa Marca, Fasolis.

(M) *** Virgin VMD5 61337-2 (2). Kirkby, Van Evera, Iconomou, Immler, Kilian, Covey-Crump, D. Thomas, Soloists from Tölz Boys' Ch., Taverner Cons. & Players, Parrott.

(B) *** None. Ultima Double 7559 79563-2 (2). Nelson, Baird, Dooley, Minter, Hoffmeister, Brownlees, Opalach, Bach Ens., Rifkin.

(B) **(*) Naxos 8.550585/6. Wagner, Schäfer-Subrata, Koppelstetter, Schäfer, Elbert, Slovak Philharmonic Ch., Cappella Istropolitana, Bembreck.

(N)(M) **(*) Regis RRC 2002 (2). Dubose, Denley, Bowman, Ainsley, George, Sixteen & O, Christophers.

Mass in B min., BWV 232 (i) (complete); (ii) (excerpts).

(M) (***) EMI mono CHS5 67207-2 (2). (i) Schwarzkopf, Höffgen, Gedda, Rehfuss, V. Singverein, Philh. O, Karajan; (ii) Schwarzkopf, Ferrier, VSO, Karajan.

(i) *Mass in B min.; (ii) Cantata No. 80; Magnificat, BWV 243.*

(N) (M) **(*) H.H. HMX 2908110.2 (3). (i) Zomer, Gens, Scholl, Prégardien, Kooy, Müller-Brachman; (ii) Schlick, Mellon, Lesne, Crook; Coll. Voc. Ch. & O, Herreweghe. (with CD-Rom 'The Bach Companion').

John Eliot Gardiner gives a magnificent account of the *B minor Mass,* one which attempts to keep within an authentic scale but which also triumphantly encompasses the work's grandeur. Gardiner masterfully conveys the majesty (with bells and censer-swinging evoked) simultaneously with a crisply resilient rhythmic pulse. The choral tone is luminous and powerfully projected. The regular solo numbers are taken by choir members making a cohesive whole. The recording is warmly atmospheric but not cloudy.

In the echoing acoustic of St Paul's Cathedral – remarkably well-tamed by the BBC engineers – Giulini conducts a spacious, dedicated reading. This was a City of London Festival event in 1972, and from first to last one breathes in the atmosphere of a great occasion, thanks not only to the inspired conductor but to a superb quartet of soloists, notably Dame Janet Baker, whose contributions shine out with heartwarming fervour. Peter Pears, then 62, is in fine, clear voice, as is the bass, John Shirley-Quirk, with the soprano, Jenny Hill, fresh and bright. The chorus is not so clearly focused as the soloists, particularly in the meditative numbers, yet in vigorous sections and in the great censer-swinging rhythms of the *Sanctus* the weight and bite of the singing come over thrillingly.

Mindful no doubt of the cathedral's reverberant acoustic, Giulini adopts speeds on the broad side even for a traditional, large-scale performance, but soloists and chorus alike sustain them superbly, as do the orchestra, distinguished by such soloists as the horn-player Alan Civil, in the obbligato solo for the *Quoniam*. As an illuminating supplement an interview with Giulini by John Amis is included at the end.

In the BBC Legends series, the 1951 studio performance is indeed legendary. Suzanne Danco was in her prime, as were Kathleen Ferrier, Peter Pears and Bruce Boyce, Leslie Woodgate's BBC Chorus and, at the helm, the incomparable Georges Enescu. Menuhin pays tribute to his mentor in a moving note. The standards of the orchestral playing fall short of what one might expect in a modern commercial recording (the horn is somewhat tentative in the *Quoniam*) but the singing is glorious and the engineers have worked miracles on the sound which, though two-dimensional, is much better than you might expect. Even if you already have a modern stereo version of the *B minor Mass*, this is an essential supplement.

With the distinctive continental tone of the Tölzer Boys, very different from their English counterparts, Robert King's vigorous and alert reading has extra freshness, with 24 boys set brightly against 12 of the King's Consort tenors and basses. The individual finesse of the boy singers is impressively demonstrated in the solos. This is a reading which consistently brings out the joy of Bach's inspiration, not least in the great celestial outbursts of the *Sanctus* and the final *Dona nobis pacem*. Warm, atmospheric recording.

Jochum's memorable, dedicated (1980) performance, marked by resilient rhythms, remains among the most completely satisfying versions even today. The choral singing – by far the most important element in this work – is superb and, though the soloists are variably balanced, they make a fine, clear-voiced team to leave Bach's inspired music resonating in the listener's memory. The digital recording is admirably spacious and clear. Documentation is just about adequate, but with no text.

The Arts label offers a first-rate version at super-bargain price using period instruments. The five soloists are excellent, all with fresh young voices, and with Lynne Dawson radiant in *Laudamus te*. The Lugano Choir of Swiss Radio is outstanding too, with the elaborate counterpoint clean and transparent, thanks also to the recording. Fasano favours fast speeds in period style, giving a joyful lightness to *Et resurrexit*, and making the *Sanctus* happy rather than weighty.

Karajan's 1952 recording was a pioneering set, and the freshness and clarity of the mono sound are astonishing in this excellent EMI transfer. With Schwarzkopf at her most radiant, the quartet of soloists, then still young, stands comparison with any rival since and, though characteristically for the time Karajan adopts a broad speed for the great opening *Kyrie*, the performance is the more remarkable for its period in the briskness and clarity in choruses like the

Gloria, with the *Sanctus* exhilarating in its combination of freshness and weight, leading to a light, crisp *Osanna*. The five fragmentary excerpts that come as a supplement, recorded at a rehearsal in 1950, are equally valuable, and not only because of Kathleen Ferrier's contribution alongside Schwarzkopf. Karajan's speeds in that 1950 rehearsal are a degree faster than in the studio recording of two years later.

Parrott, hoping to re-create even more closely the conditions Bach would have expected in Leipzig, adds to the soloists a ripieno group of five singers from the Taverner Consort for the choruses. Speeds are generally fast, with rhythms sprung to reflect the inspiration of dance; however, the inner darkness of the *Crucifixus*, for example, is conveyed intensely in its hushed tones, while the *Et resurrexit* promptly erupts with a power to compensate for any lack of traditional weight. Soloists are excellent, with reduction of vibrato still allowing sweetness as well as purity, and the recording, made in St John's, Smith Square, is both realistic and atmospheric.

Following the pattern of his other Bach recordings, Herreweghe offers a period performance which thoughtfully avoids extremes, favouring moderate or even slow speeds by period-style standards. He is well served by his choir, though the recording has them placed behind the orchestra, not always cleanly focused on detail. The soloists are all first rate, with Véronique Gens and Andreas Scholl outstanding.

The reissue is at mid-price but now runs to three discs, which makes the set no more competitive, unless you also want the *Magnificat* and the cantata *Ein feste Burg* in its later arrangement by W. F. Bach, who added trumpets and timpani to the orchestra. The latter is very successful, with outstanding soloists, but the *Magnificat* is more uneven, especially in matters of pacing, although here Gerard Lesne distinguishes himself in the *Suscepit Israel*, and both sopranos sing their arias beautifully. The choral sound is vivid but not always too sharply focused.

A CD-Rom (which we have not explored) comes with the set giving, among other information, the geographical background to this music and the composer's genealogy.

Joshua Rifkin here presents Bach's masterpiece in the form of one voice to a part in the choruses; and the listener gets a totally new perspective when – at generally brisk speeds – the complex counterpoint is so crisp and clean, with original instruments in the orchestra adding to the freshness and intimacy. The soloists also sing with comparable brightness, freshness and precision, even if lack of choral weight means that dramatic contrasts are less sharp than usual. An exciting pioneering set, crisply and vividly recorded.

The Naxos set offers a chamber-scale performance on modern instruments. The orchestral playing is first rate and the soloists are a reliable team, with the contralto, Martina Koppelstetter, outstanding in her two big solos, *Qui tollis* and *Agnus Dei*, the latter taken broadly with fine concentration. In the big extrovert moments like the opening of the *Kyrie* and the *Sanctus*, the chorus are bold and confident; at times elsewhere there is less bite, though one doesn't want to make too much of this; Brembeck's pacing is well judged, and this set is still very recommendable in the budget range.

Harry Christophers, with the Sixteen expanded to 26 singers, gives a fresh, direct period performance, marked by well-chosen speeds and bright choral singing. It wears its period manners easily and the stylistic plainness, less detailed in matters in such matters as appoggiaturas, is certainly refreshing, but rarely allows the sharply distinctive characterization which marks such versions as Gardiner's on DG. The great Sanctus lacks a little in gravity and the slightly distanced recording takes some of the impact from bright, vigorous movements, where trumpets are less forward than usual. The soloists make an excellent team, though Catherine Dubosc's vibrato is obtrusive at times.

Unlike his earlier, EMI set, Karajan's 1974 DG performance is marked by his characteristic smoothness of Bach style – he conveys intensity, even religious fervour, but the sharp contours of Bach's majestic writing are often missing. But there is a strong sense of the work's architecture, and the highly polished surfaces do not obscure the depths of this music (DG Double 459 460-2).

When released in 1960, Shaw's RCA version was a pioneering set at the cutting edge of authentic performance: a complement of five soloists, a small chorus and orchestra. From a modern point of view, it seems a dated approach to the score, though not with any interpretative extremes, except in its slow tempi, which will seem laboured for most listeners. The most remarkable thing about this set is the recording: it is astonishingly full and vivid (RCA 09026 63529-2).

Despite excellent women soloists and bright choral sound, the Arte Nova version (74321 63632-2) cannot be recommended. From the ponderous account of the opening *Kyrie* onwards, Joshard Daus proves an uninspiring conductor, often choosing funereal speeds, with rhythms unsprung. In this price category the Arte Nova is far preferable for a period performance, the Naxos for one on modern instruments.

Richter's performance dates from the early 1970s and is obviously deeply felt. The choral work is well focused, firm and distinct; among the soloists Hertha Töpper is disappointing, but the others, Fischer-Dieskau in particular, are most impressive. But there are far finer versions in this price range (DG 463 004-2).

Motets: *Singet dem Herrn ein Neues Lied; Der Geist hilft unser Schwachheit auf; Jesu, meine Freude; Fürchte dich nicht, ich bin bei dir; Komm, Jesu, komm!; Lobet den Herrn alle Heiden, BWV 225–30.*

(M) *** Teldec 0630 17430-2. Stockholm Bach Ch., VCM, Harnoncourt.

**(*) Hyp. CDA 66369. The Sixteen, Christophers.

To Bach's motets, which include some of the greatest music he ever wrote for chorus, went the honour of being the first of his vocal music to be issued digitally in 1980. The Teldec recording is very successful indeed, beautifully fresh and clear, the acoustic attractively resonant without clouding detail, and the accompanying instrumental group giving discreet yet telling support. The vigour and joy of the singing come over splendidly. This is one of Harnoncourt's most impressive Bach records, while the Stockholm chorus show stamina as well as sympathy. At mid-price this must now be the prime recommendation for these six works.

Harry Christophers and The Sixteen give elegant readings,

beautifully tuned and balanced, of the six principal motets, not as strongly characterized as Harnoncourt's but consistently refreshing and satisfying.

St John Passion, BWV 245.

*** DG 419 324-2 (2). Rolfe Johnson, Varcoe, Hauptmann, Argenta & soloists, Monteverdi Ch., E. Bar. Sol., Gardiner.

*** BIS CD 921/22. Schmithüsen, Mera, Türk, Sakurada, Hida, Urano, Kooy, Bach Collegium, Japan, Suzuki.

*** Erato 4509-94675-2 (2). Schlick, Wessel, De Mey, Türk, Kooy, Mertens, Netherlands Bach Soc. Ch., Amsterdam Bar. O, Koopman.

*** (N) (M) Regis RRC 2003 290241 (2). Ainsley, Bott, Agnew, Chance, King's College, Cambridge, Ch., Brandenburg Cons., Cleobury.

*** Häns. CD 98.170. Banse, Danz, Schade, Taylor, Goerne, Schmidt, Rilling, Stuttgart Gächinger Kantorei & Bach-Collegium, Rilling.

(B) **(*) RCA Twofer 74321 49181-2 (2). Augér, Schreier, Ude, Adam, Lorenz, Reiss, Leipzig Thomanerchor & GO, Rotzsch.

(i) St John Passion, BWV 245; (ii) Cantata No. 10: Meine Seele erhebt den Herren.

(B) **(*) Double Decca 460 223-2 (2). (i) Watts, Krenn, Rintzler; (i–ii) Ameling; (i) V. Ac. Ch.; (ii) Ellenbeck, Berry, Hamari, Hollweg, Prey, Stuttgart Hymnus Ch.; Stuttgart CO, Münchinger.

Gardiner conducts an exhilarating performance. Speeds are regularly on the fast side but, characteristically, Gardiner consistently keeps a spring in the rhythm. Chorales are treated in contrasted ways, which may not please the more severe authenticists, but, as with so much of Gardiner's work, here is a performance using authentic scale and period instruments which speaks in the most vivid way to anyone prepared to listen, not just to the specialist. Soloists – regular contributors to Gardiner's team – are all first rate. Warm and atmospheric, yet clear and detailed recording.

Suzuki directs an urgently refreshing reading of the *St John Passion*, with fine singing from the chorus giving dramatic impact to the 'turba' choruses. The big choruses at beginning and end are beautifully sung too, though there the voices are set back behind the orchestra and are rather lightweight. Suzuki's feeling for the natural timing of numbers – generally on the fast side in the modern period manner – is impeccable, and the soloists make an excellent team, with Gerd Türk an outstanding Evangelist, light and clear.

The great glory of the Koopman version is the vividly dramatic singing of the choir. The soprano, Barbara Schlick, is pure and silvery, setting the pattern for clear, fresh voices. The other soloists complete a fine team, with Guy de Mey an expressive Evangelist, well contrasted with the solo tenor in the arias, Gerd Türk, and with the Jesus of Peter Kooy contrasted against Klaus Mertens in the arias and incidental roles, though not everyone will like the hooty counter-tenor of Kai Wessel.

Stephen Cleobury conducts a lively, well-paced reading using period instruments, with an excellent team of characterful soloists and with the fresh-toned choir of King's College Choir, including boy-trebles, adding dramatic bite.

What specially distinguishes this set is that the alternative numbers which Bach wrote for the revival in 1725 are given in an appendix. John Mark Ainsley is a warmly expressive tenor Evangelist, nicely contrasted with the lighter-toned Paul Agnew, who sings the tenor arias. Among the others, Catherine Bott is warmer and more tenderly expressive than almost any latterday rival, and the counter-tenor, Michael Chance, sounds in fuller, warmer voice here than in Gardiner's version, a question of recording balance, with the Cleobury performance setting the soloists close so as to counteract the reverberant acoustic of King's College Chapel. Most enjoyable.

The Rilling version on Hänssler uses rather larger forces than on most period versions and, paradoxically, modern instruments are used in period style, using today's higher pitch. Speeds in recitative tend to be broader in a relatively traditional way, but that allows the soloists, notably the superb Evangelist, Michael Schade, to bring out the meaning of the words most vividly, with an electrifying sense of drama, most important in this work. The other soloists are outstanding too, all of them young singers with firm, characterful voices, and they sound particularly well on record. The third disc comes as a (free) appendix, giving not just the five alternative numbers which Bach wrote for the 1725 revival but also detailed changes in various numbers, setting fragments from the original against the amended versions. These are explained in a spoken commentary between items, so that it is vital for English-speaking listeners to get the English-language version, instead of Hänssler's main German issue, which also has a single-language booklet of notes.

Rotzsch's version was recorded for Ariola in 1975–6 and, using modern instruments, presents a performance which in some ways anticipates period practice, with chorales and recitative generally brisk. The soloists make a strong and characterful team, with Peter Schreier as the Evangelist at his very peak, clear and true and more powerful than most, as well as deeply expressive. It is good too to hear Arleen Augér in the soprano arias. Full, warm sound. A good 'twofer' package.

Münchinger's reading matches his other recordings of Bach's choral works, with a superb line-up of soloists, all of them clear-toned and precise, and a fresh, young-sounding tenor as Evangelist, Dieter Ellenbeck. Though Münchinger does not equal a conductor like Britten in individuality of imagination, he points the musical balance of the score most satisfyingly, without idiosyncrasy. For sound scholarly reasons he uses organ continuo with no harpsichord. The Cantata is very well performed too, and the recordings are excellent. Good value.

The alternative Hänssler set under Eckhard Weyand offers a crisp and fresh reading using modern instruments, very well recorded. The manner is plain, the speeds are well chosen, and it is interesting to hear Christine Schäfer at the very beginning of her career, recorded in 1990. Otherwise, at full price hardly a first choice (CD 98.968).

Though the dramatic turba choruses are freshly done, recitatives are well paced and the women soloists are first rate, Joshard Daus as a Bach interpreter leans too far towards the ponderous old German tradition in chorales and big choruses. That is so even though the Europa choir and Akademie orchestra are modest in size. Helen Kwon is outstanding among the soloists, unfazed by the slow speed for her first aria, *Ich folge dir*. Lothar Odinius is a fresh-toned Evangelist, untroubled by high tessitura, though he is ungainly in the first tenor aria. It does not help that the chorus is rather backwardly balanced (Arte Nova 74321 67251-2).

St John Passion, BWV 245 (sung in English).

🌑 (B) *** Double Decca (ADD) 443 859-2 (2). Pears, Harper, Hodgson, Tear, Howell, Shirley-Quirk, Wandsworth School Boys' Ch., ECO, Britten.

Britten characteristically refuses to follow any set tradition, whether baroque, Victorian or whatever, and, with greater extremes of tempo than is common (often strikingly fast), the result makes one listen afresh. The soloists are all excellent, Heather Harper radiant, and the Wandsworth School Boys' Choir reinforces the freshness of the interpretation. A superb bargain.

St Mark Passion (reconstructed Andor Gomme, with recitatives and turbas by Reinhard Keiser).

**(*) ASV Dig CDGAX 237 (2). Ovenden, Mirfin, Gomme, Towers, Gilchrist, Thompson, Gonville & Caius College, Cambridge, Ch., Cambridge Bar. Camerata, Webber – KEISER: *Laudate pueri Domini.* **(*)

The *St Mark Passion* was performed in Leipzig in 1731 at a difficult time for the composer. Bach simply used existing material, and there is strong evidence that he used the various movements of the *Cantata No. 198* or *Trauer-Ode*, 'Ode of Mourning', to provide the opening and closing choruses and three of the six arias. Andor Gomme, editor of the edition used here, explains his decision to adapt the recitatives from the *St Mark Passion* of Reinhard Keiser, Bach's senior by a decade, to fill in the narrative sections. The result in no way rivals the two great Bach Passions we know, but it offers much fine music normally buried. This performance may not be ideal – with the period instruments of the Cambridge Baroque Camerata often rough – but the Caius Chorus is fresh and alert, as is the solo singing, with Jeremy Ovenden a clear-toned Evangelist, Ruth Gomme the bright, fresh soprano and the counter-tenor, William Towers, excellent in the alto arias and such roles as that of Judas. Keiser's ambitious setting of *Psalm 112* provides a welcome makeweight. Warmly atmospheric sound.

St Matthew Passion, BWV 244.

*** DG 427 648-2 (3). Rolfe Johnson, Schmidt, Bonney, Monoyios, Von Otter, Chance, Crook, Bär, Hauptmann, Monteverdi Ch., E. Bar. Sol., Gardiner.

*** BIS CD 1000/1002 (3). Türk, Kooy, Argenta, Blaze, Sakurada, Urano, Sollek-Avella, Hagiwara, Odagawa, Bach Collegium Japan Ch. & O, Suzuki.

(N) *** Teldec 8573-81036-2 (3). Fink, Magnus, Röschmann, Schäfer, Goerne, Henschel, Prégardien, Schade, M. Schäfer, Widmer, Schoenberg Ch., VCM, Harnoncourt.

*** Channel CCS 11397 (3). Türk, Smits, Zomer, Scholl, Mammel, Kooy, St Bavo Cathedral, Haarlem Boys' Ch.,

Netherlands Bach Society Bar. O and Ch., Van
Veldhoven.

(M) *** EMI (ADD) CMS5 67538-2 [567542] (3). Pears,
Fischer-Dieskau, Schwarzkopf, Ludwig, Gedda, Berry,
Hampstead Parish Church Ch., Philh. Ch. & O, Klemperer.

(B) *** Naxos 8.550832/4. Mukk, Gáti, Németh, Verebits,
Köves, Cser, Korpás, Kiss, Csenki, Hungarian R. Children's
Ch., Hungarian Festival Ch. & State SO, Oberfrank.

**(*) HM HMC 951676.68 (3). Bostridge, Selig, Rubens,
Scholl, Güra, Henschel, Schola Cantorum Cantate Domino,
Ghent Coll. Voc. Ch. & O, Herreweghe.

**(*) Ph. 454 434-2 (3). Der Meel, Sigmundsson, Kiehr,
Julsrud, Schubert, Brummelsroete, Bostridge, Spence, Kooy,
Van der Kamp, St Bavo Cathedral, Haarlem Boys' Ch.,
Netherlands Chamber Ch., O of 18th Century, Brüggen.

(N) (M) ** DG (ADD) 463 635-2 (3). Haefliger, Seefried,
Töpper, Fischer-Dieskau, Engen, Fahlberg, Munich Bach
Ch. & Boys' Ch., Richter.

Gardiner's version of the *St Matthew Passion*, the culminating issue in his Bach choral series for DG Archiv, brings
an intense, dramatic reading which now makes a clear first
choice, not just for period-performance devotees but for
anyone not firmly set against the new authenticity. The
result is an invigorating, intense telling of the story, with
Gardiner favouring high dynamic contrasts and generally
fast speeds, which are still geared to the weighty purpose of
the whole work. He and his performers were recorded in
what proved an ideal venue, The Maltings at Snape, where
the warm acoustic gives body and allows clarity to period
textures.

Masaaki Suzuki provides a fresh and beautifully sung
reading of the most challenging of all Bach choral works.
The light, crisp qualities which have shone from his previous
recordings are present here too, with the choir bright and
resilient, and with an outstanding team of soloists led by the
free-toned Gerd Türk as the Evangelist, and with Nancy
Argenta outstanding among the others. If the result is a little
short on devotional intensity in the culminating sections of
the work, that is partly the result of the rather close-up
recording, with solo voices and orchestra not always cleanly
separated. More seriously, the double choir in the great
double-choruses at the beginning and end is more backwardly balanced than elsewhere, set behind the orchestra,
so that the dramatic impact is lessened. Nevertheless, this
remains a powerful achievement.

When Harnoncourt made his pioneering recording of the
St Matthew Passion in 1970, he took the doctrinaire view that
it should be sung by all-male forces. The result was fresh, if
at times abrasive. This new version, recorded in 2000, takes
a less extreme view, and the result is lighter, generally faster,
yet with a gravity implied that, benefiting from an exceptionally strong and consistent team of soloists, has all necessary
weight and intensity. Christoph Prégardien is the mellifluous
Evangelist, crisply expressive in his narration, with Matthias
Goerne singing not just beautifully but movingly as Jesus.
The Arnold Schoenberg Choir has rightly established the
highest reputation among central European choirs, here
singing with power as well as freshness. Harnoncourt's
rhythmic control may not be as resilient as some, but his is

a consistently imaginative approach, giving concentration
and fine detail over the great span of this masterpiece,
making this a leading contender among the many rival
versions, recorded in clear, open sound.

The Channel Classics version with Jos van Veldhoven was
recorded live in 1997 in the same Utrecht venue as Brüggen's
(see below). You would never register that from the
recording, which is more spacious and balanced less close,
though van Veldhoven's manner is lighter and more flexible.
His team of soloists is also young and fresh, with Gerd Türk
a fine Evangelist – as he is for Suzuki in Japan – and
with Andreas Scholl singing the alto role beautifully, a real
highlight of the set.

While it certainly will not appeal to the authentic lobby,
Klemperer's 1962 Philharmonia recording of the *St Matthew
Passion* represents one of his greatest achievements on
record, an act of devotion of such intensity that points of
style and interpretation seem insignificant. The whole cast
clearly shared Klemperer's own intense feelings, and one can
only sit back and share them too, whatever one's preconceptions.

At bargain price the new version from Naxos uses modern,
not period, instruments but, following authentic trends, has
brisk speeds and well-sprung rhythms. Though the performance takes no less than 35 minutes less than, say, Richter's,
in its alertness it never seems rushed, with the Hungarian
State Symphony Orchestra and Festival Choir on excellent
form, conducted by Géza Oberfrank. A refreshingly lithe
and young-sounding Evangelist, József Mukk, leads a team
of Hungarian soloists with fresh, clear voices. The obbligato
wind-playing is also attractive (if closely balanced) and the
recording is spacious and full, and kind to voices.

Herreweghe made his first recording of the *St Matthew
Passion* in 1985, a fresh, eager performance with many fine
solo contributions. This later version offers more-polished
contributions from chorus and orchestra, a degree smaller
in scale than before, and again the line-up of mainly young
soloists is an impressive one. The set is well worth hearing
for the inspired singing of Ian Bostridge as the Evangelist,
headily beautiful and finely detailed. Andreas Scholl too is
superb in the alto numbers, singing with sensuously
beautiful tone, not least in *Erbarme dich*. Werner Güra
projects the tenor arias with clear, fresh tone, and the others
follow a similar pattern of youthful freshness. It is a fine
reading, beautifully paced, but some listeners may well feel
that here polish and perfection have not been matched by
spiritual intensity. The Harmonia Mundi set comes with an
extra CD-ROM disc which helpfully provides a survey of
the life of Bach and the background to the Passion, linking
it with musical excerpts.

Recorded live in Utrecht, a year earlier than van Veldhoven's set, in vivid, immediate sound, Frans Brüggen's
reading is typically fresh and alert, with speeds generally
fast but not invariably so, when Brüggen is consistently
thoughtful. With a very light-toned Evangelist (Nico van
der Meel) telling the story expressively, this is an intimate
reading, with the freshness intensified by the singing of the
soloists, mostly young.

Karl Richter's pioneering 1958 recording for DG Archiv
with Munich forces has some fine singing, both from the

chorus and from the soloists who include the young Fischer-Dieskau as baritone soloist. Though Richter represented the authentic cause at the time, using relatively small forces, his speeds are very slow indeed by the standards of period performance today. Though there is a glow and dedication in the music-making, with Ernst Haefliger a radiant Evangelist and Irmgaard Seefried producing ravishing sounds, the performance has come to sound stodgy – not just a question of speeds but of rhythmic squareness. Vocally the disappointment is the fruity contralto, Hertha Töpper, a key soloist in this work. This is now re-issued as one of DG's Originals, so costs more than its earlier bargain-priced incarnation, and it is a pity that DG did not choose instead Richter's later dedicated (1979) version, still rhythmically heavy, but with Dame Janet Baker's singing a crowning glory.

Ozawa's speeds are mostly fast, but the results sound less period-like than balletic, with modern instruments tending to smooth lines. Mark Ainsley as the Evangelist and Quasthoff as Jesus are splendid, but all the soloists are first rate, as is the choral singing. Excellent recording, but even so this is far from a first choice (Philips 462 515-2).

St. Matthew Passion, BWV 244 (in English).

(B) (**(*)) Dutton mono 2CDAX 2005 (3). Greene, Suddaby, Ferrier, Cummings, Bach Ch., Jacques O, Jacques –
PERGOLESI: Stabat Mater. (**)

In 1947/8 Decca recorded the St Matthew Passion, based on the annual performances conducted by Dr Reginald Jacques, and that is what Michael Dutton has here transferred immaculately to CD, with the bonus of the 1946 Decca recording of the Pergolesi Stabat Mater, also with Ferrier as soloist. The Bach is very much a performance of its time, with measured speeds and an expressively devotional manner, in the chorales and recitatives as well as in the big choruses. Only the 'turba' choruses commenting on the action are brisk in the way one would now expect. Eric Greene is the noble Evangelist and the sweet-toned Elsie Suddaby shines out in the soprano arias, but it is Ferrier who instantly on each entry conveys quite a different degree of intensity from the rest, immediately magnetic. Sadly Henry Cummings is too woolly-toned to give much pleasure, but the atmosphere of a performance at that time is vividly caught. Having an English text is well justified, when the words are so clear.

Schemelli's musicalisches Songbook: 57 sacred songs.

*** CPO 99407-2 (2). Schlick, Mertens, Van Asperen, Möller.

Bach was the principal contributor to the important collection of hymns published in Leipzig in 1736 when he was Kapellmeister there. Some are settings of traditional hymntunes, some with improvements by Bach, and some are original. This is the biggest selection yet recorded of Bach's work on the Songbook, and though this is not a set to play from end to end, it is good to have these dedicated performances from two stylish soloists, very well recorded.

Vocal collections

Arias: Bist du bei mir; Cantata 202: Weichet nur, betrübte Schatten. Cantata 209: Ricetti gramezza. St Matthew Passion: Blute nur; Ich will dir mein Herze schenken.

**(*) Delos D/CD 3026. Augér, Mostly Mozart O, Schwarz –
HANDEL: Arias. **(*)

Arleen Augér's pure, sweet soprano, effortlessly controlled, makes for bright performances of these Bach arias and songs, very recommendable for admirers of this delightful singer, well coupled with Handel arias.

Arias: Mass in B min.: Agnus Dei; Qui sedes. St John Passion: All is fulfilled. St Matthew Passion: Grief for sin.

(M) (***) Decca mono 433 474-2. Ferrier, LPO, Boult –
HANDEL: Arias. (***) ◉

On 7 and 8 October 1952, Kathleen Ferrier made her last and perhaps greatest record in London's Kingsway Hall, coupling four arias each by Bach and Handel. The combined skill of John Culshaw and Kenneth Wilkinson ensured a recording of the utmost fidelity by the standards of that time. Now it re-emerges with extraordinary naturalness and presence.

Orchestral transcriptions

Chaconne from solo Violin Partita No. 2, BWV 1004 (orch. Raff); Chorales: O Mensch, bewein' dein' Sünde gross, BWV 622 (orch. Reger); Wachet auf, BWV 645 (orch. Bantock); Fantasia & Fugue in C min., BWV 537 (orch. Elgar); Fugue à la gigue in G, BWV 377(orch. Holst); 'Giant Fugue' (Wir glauben all' an einen Gott), BWV 680 (orch. Vaughan Williams & Foster); Passacaglia & Fugue in C min., BWV 582 (orch. Respighi). Preludes & Fugues: in C, BWV 545 (orch. Honegger); in E flat (St Anne), BWV 552 (orch. Schoenberg).

(N) *** Chan. 9835. BBC PO, Slatkin.

Flying boldly in the face of period performance, these transcriptions by nine celebrated composers, including Respighi, Elgar, Holst, Vaughan Williams, Schoenberg and Raff, bring out the grandeur of Bach's vision in his organ music. That is greatly helped by the sumptuous Chandos sound and the magnificent playing of the BBC Philharmonic under Leonard Slatkin. The only nineteenth-century composer here, Raff, tackles not organ music but the great Chaconne from the solo Violin Partita in D minor, enhancing its epic scale in colourful orchestration. Respighi is weightily dramatic in the Passacaglia and Fugue in C minor, and so is Schoenberg in the St Anne Prelude and Fugue, while Honegger even uses a saxophone in the Prelude and Fugue in C. Most imaginative of all is the Fantasia and Fugue in G minor, with Elgar glorying in percussion and harp.

Piano transcriptions

Chaconne (from Partita No. 2 in D min., BWV 1004) (arr. Busoni).

(M) *** Nim. NI 8810. Busoni (piano) – CHOPIN:
Preludes **; LISZT: *Etudes d'exécution transcendante*,
etc. ***

This is the nearest we shall ever come to hearing Busoni play
and the impression (with a first-class modern recording
taken from a piano-roll) gives an uncanny feeling of the
artist's presence. His famous transcription of the Bach *Chaconne* is almost as much Busoni as it is Bach, but it is none
the less compelling for that. The recording dates from 1925,
but the reproduction makes it sound as if it were made
yesterday.

Transcriptions: arr. BUSONI: *Chaconne* (from *Violin
Partita No. 2*); *Chorales: Ich ruf' zu dir; Nun freut euch,
lieben Christen; Nun komm der Heiden Heiland; Wachet
auf; Toccata & Fugue in D min.* arr. LISZT: *Prelude &
Fugue in A min.* arr. LORD BERNERS: *In dulci jubilo.* arr.
MYRA HESS: *Jesu, joy of man's desiring.* arr. KEMPFF:
Siciliano. arr. LE FLEMING: *Sheep may safely graze.* arr.
RACHMANINOV: *Suite from Partita No. 3 in E.*

*** ASV CDDCA 759. Fergus-Thompson (piano).

A highly entertaining collection, played with much flair and,
in the case of the lyrical pieces at the centre of the recital
(notably Wilhelm Kempff's delightful *Siciliano* and Dame
Myra Hess's famous arrangement of *Jesu, joy of man's desiring*), stylish charm.

Partita in B min. (arr. from Unaccompanied Violin
Partita No. 1, BWV 1002).

(N) (BB) *** EMI Debut CDZ5 74017-2. Batiashvili (piano) –
BRAHMS: *Violin Sonata No. 1*; SCHUBERT: *Rondo in
B min., D895.* ***

Bach playing of great refinement and beauty of tone
by this gifted young player. The Georgian-born Elisabeth
Batiashvili studied with Mark Lubotsky and came to international attention when at the age of sixteen she won second
prize at the Sibelius Competition in Helsinki. Now
twenty-two she makes her EMI debut with this mixed programme. More a calling-card for the artist than a disc for
the collector who will probably want all the Bach *Partitas* or
the Brahms *Sonatas*. None the less, this is a most distinguished and satisfying recital that gives pleasure and is well
worth the modest outlay.

Arrangements: Bach–Reger

(i) *Orchestral Suite No. 2 in B min. for Flute & Strings*
(with continuo by Max Reger); *Bach–Reger Suite in
G min.* (selected and arr. Reger); *Aria: O Mensch, bewein
dein Sünde gross.*

*** MDG 321 0940-2. Stuttgart CO, Russell Davies; (i) with
Gérard.

A fascinating collection. Throughout there is a nineteenth-
century amplitude. The *Bach–Reger Suite in G minor*, which
is made up of movements from the keyboard *Partitas* and
English Suites, is scored very like a typical set of Reger
variations: the *Courante*, which features oboe, flute and
bassoon, may be anachronistic but is very felicitous. The

Stuttgart orchestra plays very sympathetically (as does the
excellent, nimble flautist) and Dennis Russell Davies seeks
a performing style which Reger would have recognized.
Excellent recording.

Arrangements: Bach–Stokowski

*Adagio in C, BWV 564; Chorales: Jesus Christus Gottes
Sohn* (from *Easter Cantata*); *Komm süsser Tod; Mein Jesu;
Sheep may safely graze; Wir glauben all' an einen Gott
(Giant Fugue), BWV 680. Fugue in G min. (Little), BWV
578; Passacaglia & Fugue in C min., BWV 582; Suite No. 3
in D, BWV 1068: Air. Toccata & Fugue in D min., BWV
565; Violin & Harpsichord Sonata No. 4, BWV 1017:
Siciliano; Well-Tempered Clavier, Book 1, Prelude No. 24.*

*** Chan. 9259. BBC PO, Bamert.

This sumptuously recorded Chandos CD brings together the
dozen published Stokowski Bach transcriptions. Bamert's
warmly sympathetic readings obviously follow his mentor's
way with this music, if without quite managing the naturally
spontaneous rubato which was one of Stokowski's special
gifts. Nor is the playing as vital and electrifying as the great
conductor's own record. But the result is very enjoyable, and
the Chandos stereo here is very much in the demonstration
bracket.

*Chorale Prelude: Wir glauben all' an einen Gott ('Giant
Fugue'), BWV 680; Easter Cantata, BWV 4: Chorale;
Geistliches Lied No. 51: Mein Jesu, BWV 487; Passacaglia &
Fugue in C min., BWV 582; Toccata & Fugue in D min.,
BWV 565; Well-Tempered Clavier, Book 1: Prelude No. 8 in
E flat min., BWV 853* (all orch. Stokowski).

(M) *** Decca (ADD) 448 946-2. Czech PO, Stokowski (with
Concert of miscellaneous orchestral transcriptions).

Stokowski's flamboyant arrangements of Bach organ works
are presented here with spectacular, closely balanced but
truthful Phase Four sound to match. Stokowski, over ninety
at the time, challenges his players in expansive tempi, but
the results are passionate in concentration. The famous *D
minor Toccata and Fugue* is a shade less vital here than in
Stokowski's earlier, mono version with the Philadelphia
Orchestra, but the stereo sumptuousness is ample compensation. Most remarkable of all is the mighty *Passacaglia and
Fugue in C minor*, highly romantic in its decorative detail
but moving steadily to an overwhelming climax.

Arrangements: Bach–Stokowski and Bach–Ormandy

arr. Stokowski: (i) *Brandenburg Concerto No. 5, BWV
1050; Chorale Preludes: Ich ruf' zu dir, Herr Jesu Christ,
BWV 177; Nun komm, der Heiden Heiland, BWV 62; Wir
glauben all' einen Gott, BWV 437.* arr. Ormandy:
(ii) *Chorale: Wachet auf, ruft uns die Stimme, BWV 140;
Passacaglia & Fugue in C min., BWV 582; Toccata, Adagio
& Fugue in C, BWV 564; Toccata & Fugue in D min.,
BWV 565.*

** Sony Heritage mono MH2K 62345 (2). Phd. O,
(i) Stokowski; (ii) Ormandy (with C. P. E. BACH: *Concerto
for Orchestra* (arr. Steinberg) **; J. C. BACH: *2 Sinfonias*

for Double Orchestra, Op. 18/1 & 3 *(*); W. F. BACH: Sinfonia in D min., F.65 **).

Stokowski's version of the *Fifth Brandenburg* is surprisingly restrained and detail comes through well. The three *Chorale Preludes* are warmly expressive without emotional hyperbole. On the other hand, although Ormandy's arrangement and performance of the famous *Toccata and Fugue in D minor* are not far removed from Stokowski's, his *Toccata, Adagio and Fugue* is so flamboyant and freely romanticized that not a great deal of Bach remains. The *Passacaglia and Fugue in C minor* is very weightily done indeed, but with refined woodwind playing to provide contrast. The outer-movement allegros of the paired J. C. Bach *Sinfonias* are also rather heavy-going; the slow movements are more successful, as is the work by Wilhelm Friedemann and Maximilian Steinberg's arrangement of C. P. E. Bach, which has a delicately played central *Andante*. The Stokowski sound is first class, the Ormandy recordings are full-blooded and beefier.

BACH, Wilhelm Friedemann (1710–84)

Harpsichord Concertos: in D, F.41; in F, F.44; in A min., F.45.

**(*) HM HMC 901558 Egarr, L. Bar., Medlam.

These three concertos always hold the listener's attention in these lively performances from Richard Egarr. The earliest work here, in A minor, has a sunny *Cantabile* slow movement. The *Molto adagio* of the F major work is more poignant in feeling and shows the composer at his most darkly expressive, while the *Presto* finale is quirky in its rhythmic high spirits. The London Baroque provide alert, polished accompaniments, but the sharp-edged timbre of leader Ingrid Seifert and her period style, with its swelling out on individual notes, may not appeal to all, although the ear does adjust to it.

Double Concerto for 2 Harpsichords in D, F46.

(N) (BB) **(*) Teldec 0630 12326-2 [id.]. Uittenbosch, Curtis, VCM, Harnoncourt – C. P. E. BACH: *Double Concerto for Harpsichord & Fortepiano* ***; J. C. BACH: *Sinfonia Concertante in F.* **(*)

The version of this attractive little four-handed work on Teldec is well played, though tuttis are a bit gruff and rather heavily accented.

Sinfonia in D, F.64.

(B) **(*) Naxos 8.553289. Salzburg CO, Lee – C. P. E. BACH: *Sinfonias.* **(*)

Sinfonia in D, F.64; Adagio & Fugue in D min., F.65.

*** Cap. 10 283. Concerto Köln – J. C. F. BACH: *Sinfonia;* C. P. E. BACH: *Harpsichord Concerto;* J. C. BACH: *Sinfonia.* ***

Wilhelm Friedemann's three-movement *Sinfonia in D major* was intended for use as an introduction to the Whitsun cantata, *Dies ist der Tag*. The better-known *Adagio and Fugue in D minor* may possibly have originally formed the last two

movements of a symphony. It is a very extraordinary and expressive piece. It is played by the Cologne period group with great expressive vitality and is well recorded.

The *Sinfonia* is also given a lively account in Salzburg; modern instruments are used, but textures are clean and fresh and the recording is faithful and well balanced.

6 Sonatas for flute duet, F.54–9.

*** MDG 311 984402. Hüteler, Schmidt-Casdorf.

These works must be fun to play, especially when the two instruments chirrup together, as in the first-movement *Allegro* of No. 2, dance along graciously, as in the final *Gigue* of the same work, or chase each other's tails, as in the *Presto* finale of No. 4. Slow movements are innocent, but yet have a thoughtful melancholy. Overall, the final work in F minor is the most individual of the six, but all are different and this simple polyphony stands up to repeated listenings. The performances here are technically immaculate, have a pleasing spontaneous simplicity, and are beautifully recorded.

Fantasias in C min., F.2; A min., F.23; 12 Polonaises, F.12.

(BB) ** CPO 999 501-2. Hoeren (fortepiano).

Fantasia in C min., F.2; 8 Fugues, F.31; March, F.30; Prelude, F.29; Sonatas: in G, F.7; F min., F.8; Suite in G min., F.24.

(B) ** HM HMA 1901305. Rousset (harpsichord).

Christophe Rousset (on the harpsichord) makes a good deal more of the *C minor Fantasia* than does Harald Hoeren, who is more impressive in the A minor work. That is perhaps the best thing on the disc except for the *E minor Polonaise* (No. 10), which is quite touchingly done. The E flat minor piece (No. 8) is also thoughtfully presented. Otherwise Hoeren dispatches these works directly and cleanly without trying to make too much of them. They are interesting in that apart from their metre they have virtually nothing about their character to suggest the Polish dance form. Good recording and a very reasonable price.

The extraordinary *Fantasia in C minor* has a darkly dramatic opening, then immediately evokes memories of Johann Sebastian's *Chromatic Fantasia* in its florid brilliance. The two sonatas are also impressive works. Christophe Rousset was nineteen when he recorded this recital and he plays with remarkable maturity and discernment throughout. He certainly brings out the diversity of the eight succinct miniature *Fugues* which readily demonstrate Wilhelm's contrapuntal mastery.

Polonaise in E flat, F.12/5.

(B) *** DHM (ADD) 05472 77440-2. Tilney – J. S. BACH: *Oboe Sonatas;* C. P. E. BACH: *Oboe Sonata.* **(*)

Wilhelm Friedmann's *Polonaise* is not a lively dance form in the modern sense, but a fairly placid piece with a constantly repeated refrain. Played here very simply, it is rather engaging.

BAERMANN, Heinrich (1784–1847)

Adagio for Clarinet & Orchestra.

*** ASV CDDCA 559. Johnson, ECO, Groves – CRUSELL: *Concerto No. 2* *** ✪; ROSSINI: *Introduction, Theme & Variations* ***; WEBER: *Concertino.* ***

Heinrich Baermann's rather beautiful *Adagio*, once attributed to Wagner, is offered by a young clarinettist who plays the work warmly and sympathetically.

BAGUER, Carlos (1768–1808)

Symphonies Nos. 12 in E flat; 13 in E flat; 16 in G; 18 in B flat.

*** Chan. 9456. LMP, Bamert.

The Catalan composer Carlos Baguer was born in Barcelona and spent his musical life there. The orchestra of the Barcelona Opera gave evening concerts, to which symphonies were introduced in the 1780s, and those of Haydn were to dominate the musical scene from 1782 onwards. Baguer soon adopted the four-movement Haydn pattern, and these symphonies date from a decade later. The craftsmanship is sound but conventional, as is the scoring, although there is some pleasingly assured invention. Although there is a certain warm graciousness to the writing, it is surprising that there is no local colour and no gypsy influences, not even in the finales. The performances here are nicely turned, and beautifully recorded in the best Chandos manner.

BAINES, William (1899–1922)

The Chimes; Coloured Leaves; Etude in F sharp min.; Idyll; The Naiad; Paradise Gardens; 7 Preludes; Silverpoints; Tides; Twilight Pieces.

*** Priory PRCD 550. Parkin.

William Baines spent his whole life in Yorkshire. It is his piano music for which he is renowned, and this collection explains why. He had a natural feeling for keyboard colouring and his music shows cross-influences from many sources, including Cyril Scott, Scriabin and the twentieth-century French school. However, his rhapsodic melodic style is undoubtedly individual and his use of irregular rhythms is so smoothly employed that they seem imperceptible. The greater number of these pieces are pictorial and the harmonic progressions are often quite strikingly effective; but Baines was at his finest when writing reflectively, and the three *Twilight Pieces* are delightful, while the brief *Etude in F sharp minor*, which ends the recital somewhat abruptly, is melodically quite haunting. Eric Parkin proves an ideal advocate of this rewarding music, and he is very naturally recorded.

BAINTON, Edgar (1880–1956)

Symphony No. 2 in D min.

*** Chan. 9757. BBC PO, Handley – CLIFFORD: *Symphony;* GOUGH: *Serenade.* ***

Edgar Bainton was born in London and was a pupil of Stanford. The *Symphony No. 2* is exactly contemporaneous with the Hubert Clifford work with which it is coupled. It is in one movement but falls into a dozen or so short sections, all played without a break. Its outlook is overtly romantic, but whereas Clifford's music has a stronger affinity with, say, Bliss or Walton, Bainton is closer to Arnold Bax. He certainly knows how to score and, although this symphony is uneven in quality of ideas, there is a lot of it that is both inventive and rewarding. A worthwhile and enterprising issue with first-rate playing from the BBC Philharmonic under Handley, and excellent recording.

Miniature Suite (for 2 pianos).

*** Olympia OCD 683. Goldstone and Clement (with BURY: *Prelude & Fugue in E flat* ***) – HOLST: *The Planets,* etc.; ELGAR: *Serenade in E min.* ***

Bainton's charming *Miniature Suite* is played and recorded most persuasively. Frank Bury's *Prelude and Fugue* is equally well crafted and makes an apt and enjoyable bonus. Bury's career was cut sadly short when as a commando he was killed during the Battle of Normandy in 1944.

BAIRD, Tadeusz (1928–81)

Colas Breugnon: Suite.

(M) *** EMI (ADD) CDMS5 65418-2. Polish CO, Maksymiuk – SZYMANOWSKI: *Violin concertos Nos. 1–2.* **(*)

Baird's delightful neo-classical suite (for flute and strings) has much in common with Warlock's *Capriol Suite*. It is beautifully played and recorded.

BAIRSTOW, Edward (1874–1946)

Organ Sonata in E flat.

*** Priory PRCD 401. Scott (St Paul's Cathedral organ) (with William HARRIS: *Sonata* ***) – ELGAR: *Sonata No. 1.* ***

Bairstow's *Organ Sonata* was written in 1937 and is Elgarian in feeling; the central Scherzo produces a blaze of orchestral sound unsurpassed by Elgar in either of his works for the instrument. The performance here is admirable and the St Paul's Cathedral organ is just right for it. The third work on the disc, a much more conventional sonata by William Harris (1883–1973), at least has a rather pleasing central *Adagio*.

Anthems and choral settings: *Blessed City, Heavenly Salem; Blessed Virgin's Cradle Song; Evening Canticles in D; If the Lord had not helped me; Jesu, grant me this I pray; Jesu, the very thought; Lamentation* (from *Jeremiah*);

Let all mortal flesh keep silence; Lord I call upon thee; Lord thou hast been our refuge; Save us, O Lord.

*** Priory PRDC 365. York Minster Ch., Moore; Scott Whiteley.

Bairstow is (rightly) best known for his moving and comparatively short anthem, *Let all mortal flesh keep silence*; but, as this collection shows, he wrote much else that gives full rein to his subtle understanding of choral blending and instinctive response to liturgical texts. The gloriously expansive *Blessed City, Heavenly Salem*, which opens the concert, makes the firmest of Christian statements, and the depth of the composer's religious feeling is expressed touchingly in the poignant *Jesu, the very thought of you*. The performances here are very well prepared and excitingly committed and spontaneous, while the excellent organ accompaniments could hardly be bettered.

BALADA, Leonardo (born 1933)

(i) *Piano Concerto No. 3;* (ii) *Concierto mágico for guitar & orchestra;* (iii) *Music for Flute & Orchestra.*

🏵 (N) (BB) *** Naxos 8.555039. (i)Torres-Pardo; (ii) Fisk; (iii) Martinez; Barcelona Symphony & Catalonia Mat. O, Serebrier.

Born in Barcelona, Balada subsequently moved across the Atlantic to study at Juilliard with Copland, and is now Professor of Composition at Pittsburgh. Spurning serialism, all his music is intensely communicative. Indeed, there is no better entry into his very Spanish sound world than with the *Third Piano Concerto*.

Audaciously popular in style, the rumbustious first movement is based on the infectious rhythm of a pasodoble, as used at a bull-fight, and the brilliant orchestration seeks to re-create the baudy atmosphere of that event partly by simulating an organillo (a metallic folk organ-grinder). The bizarre orchestral effects are dazzling, while the pianist responds with infectious roulades. The second movement is hardly less exotic in its mysterious evocation of a medieval Andalusian scenario, with piano creating an effect of dripping water, and the finale opens by continuing that primitive evocation, before the piano wittily interrupts with a *Jota*, with the orchestra soon joining in exuberantly, before the clamour evaporates and the movement ends gently. The *Concierto mágico* draws on Andalusian gypsy music and the influence of Rodrigo is apparent. The toccata-like first movement pulses with intense flamenco rhythms, while the nocturnal central *Luna* is rhapsodic and improvisatory in feeling and the *zapateado* finale in the form of a sparkling *moto perpetuo*.

The *Music for Flute and Orchestra* draws on Catalan folk melodies for each of its two movements, the first introduced ruminatively by the soloist, while the second becomes a launching pad for a lilting virtuoso display, against a background of flashing orchestral colours. All three works are superbly played and Serebrier's accompaniments combine atmosphere with infectious gusto. The Naxos recording is enormously vivid, and for sheer joyful exuberance this Naxos triptych is hard to beat.

Violin Concerto No. 1; Fantasías sonoras; Folk Dreams; Sardana.

(N) *** Naxos 8.554708. (i) Cárdenes; Barcelona SO, Aeschbacher.

Balada's *First Violin Concerto* is strongly influenced by Catalan folk idioms. Its textures and thematic style are highly individual, and the first movement ends with an engagingly simple minuet. This leads into an ecstatic and yet meditative *Adagio* (beautifully played by Andrés Cárdenes), and on to a deliciously folksy toccata-like finale, full of sparkling bravura from soloist and orchestra alike. It has a hesitant coda, slightly grotesque, almost like a Haydn joke seen through a glass darkly.

The intensely atmospheric three-movement *Fold Dreams* is Dali-influenced in its pictorial surrealism, the three movements drawing in turn on Latvian, Catalonian and (in the delectably jiggy finale) very recognizable Irish folk themes. *Sardana* is the national dance of Catalonia, and Balada's 'symphonic movement' is a brilliantly scored popular kaleidoscope of rhythm and colour, perhaps a trifle long, but always imaginative. *Fantasías sonoras* is minimalist, based on an ear-tickling variation of a simple melodic cell. All in all, a highly rewarding collection, splendidly played and recorded, and with excellent documentation. Ballada's music is well worth exploring, particularly at Naxos price.

BALAKIREV, Mily (1837–1910)

Piano Concertos Nos. 1 in F sharp min., Op. 1; 2 in E flat, Op. posth.

*** Hyp. CDA 66640. Binns, E. N. Philh. O, Lloyd-Jones – RIMSKY-KORSAKOV: *Concerto*. ***

The one-movement *First Piano Concerto* (*Youth*) is modelled on Balakirev's adored Chopin. It is well served by Malcolm Binns's intelligent and sensitive performance, which also has the advantage of fine orchestral support and recording. It also has the only available account of the more characteristic *Second Concerto*. This was left incomplete and was finished after his death by Lyapunov.

Symphony No. 1 in C.

🏵 (M) *** EMI mono CDM5 66595-2. Philh. O, Karajan – ROUSSEL: *Symphony No. 4*. (***) 🏵

Symphony No. 1 in C; In Bohemia (symphonic poem); *King Lear Overture.*

**(*) Chan. 9667. BBC PO, Sinaisky.

Symphonies Nos. 1–2: Overture on Russian Themes; Symphonic Poems: Russia; Tamara.

(B) **(*) Hyp. Dyad CDD 22030 (2). Philh. O, Svetlanov.

Karajan's pioneering version of No. 1, recorded in November 1949, remains unequalled as a performance, even by Beecham and Svetlanov. The *Symphony* is an endearing piece, finely wrought, melodious, brilliantly scored and memorable. The Scherzo sounds mercurial and effervescent in Karajan's hands, and the slow movement is done with great sensitivity. However, this CD has been deleted just as we go to press.

The most recent challenge to Karajan's pre-eminence has come from Chandos, and E. G.'s view is that not since that Philharmonia account has there been a version of this glorious Russian symphony quite so richly expressive, with outstanding playing from the BBC Philharmonic opulently recorded. I. M. and R. L. are less enthusiastic than E. G., but we are all agreed that the two Balakirev rarities make strong and characterful fill-ups.

Hyperion have now paired their Svetlanov accounts as a Duo. The performances bring more beautiful playing from the Philharmonia Orchestra: the soaring clarinet solo at the beginning of the slow movement of No. 1 is rapturously done and in the *Second Symphony* the effect is cultured, the sound pleasingly natural. However, there is some disagreement concerning Svetlanov's grip on the proceedings, and especially so in the first three movements of the *First*, although in the finale the emotional thrust is undeniable. The reading of the *Second* also has a spacious breadth; however, while agreeing that it is tauter than that of the *First*, E. G. suggests that it needs greater concentration. *Tamara* too – almost as extended as a one-movement symphony – needs to be stronger and more purposeful, although *Russia* is more successful.

Symphony No. 2 in D min.; (i) Piano concerto No. 1 in F sharp min.; Tamara.

*** Chan. 9727. (i) Shelley; BBC PO, Sinaisky.

Though the *Second Symphony* cannot compare with the *First* in scale or memorability, Vassily Sinaisky makes a most persuasive case for it in his warm and thrustful performance. He underlines the high dramatic contrasts, drawing playing from the BBC Philharmonic that is incisive and pointed in such a movement as the Cossack Dance of the *Scherzo* as well as sweetly refined in the lyrical slow movement. *Tamara* is played with similar panache, and Howard Shelley is a powerful soloist in the single movement of the *Piano Concerto*, relishing the bravura writing. Warm, full Chandos sound.

Islamey (oriental fantasy).

✪ *** Teldec 4509 96516-2. Berezovsky (with LIADOV: *Preludes;* MEDTNER: *Fairy Tales;* RACHMANINOV: *Etudes-tableaux* ***) – MUSSORGSKY: *Night on a Bare Mountain.* *** ✪

(M) *** EMI (ADD) CDM7 64329-2. Gavrilov – PROKOVIEV: *Concerto No. 1;* TCHAIKOVSKY: *Piano Concerto No. 1,* etc. ***

An amazing account of *Islamey* from Boris Berezovsky. Stunning, effortless virtuosity. Berezovsky makes an ideal Rachmaninov interpreter too, and it would be difficult to flaw these fine accounts of four of the Op. 39 set of *Etudes-tableaux*. Berezovsky is also a champion of Medtner and has an obvious affinity with his music. He has all the subtlety, poetic feeling and keyboard mastery that this music calls for. The Liadov *Preludes* too are played impeccably. This is in every respect an outstanding recital.

Gavrilov's dazzling account of Balakirev's fantasy is also outstandingly charismatic; it is well recorded, too. It comes in harness with an equally dazzling version of Prokoviev's

First Piano Concerto and a performance of the Tchaikovsky *B flat minor Concerto* which is rather less convincing.

Piano Sonata in B flat min.

**(*) Olympia (ADD) OCD 354. Amato – DUTILLEUX: *Sonata.* **(*)

**(*) Kingdom KCLCD 2001. Fergus-Thompson – SCRIABIN: *Sonata No. 3, etc.* **(*)

The Balakirev is arguably the greatest Russian piano sonata of the pre-1914 era. Donna Amato gives a musicianly account of it, well paced and authoritative. The recording is very lifelike, and this is a most desirable issue, even if the playing time at 47 minutes is not particularly generous.

Gordon Fergus-Thompson, too, is fully equal to the considerable demands of this remarkable *Sonata* and he offers excellent playing, though the recording is reverberant and the piano not always dead in tune. Fergus-Thompson also includes Balakirev's arrangement of Glinka's *The Lark* as an encore.

BANCHIERI, Adriano (1568–1634)

Barca di Venetia per Padova.

(B) *** HM HMC 90856.58 (3). Ens. Clément Jannequin, Visse – MARENZIO: *Madrigals* **(*); LASSUS; VECCHI: *Madrigal Comedies.* ***

Adriano Banchieri's *Barca di Venetia per Padova* ('Boat from Venice to Padua') is a diverting kaleidoscope of short madrigals, but linked – and at times dominated – by a robust (semi-parlando) tenor 'Argomento' which briefly but histrionically underlines the details of the voyage. With the passengers including lawyers, a student, a fisherman, a music-master and a bookseller, a drunken German and a pair of courtesans, the solos and ensembles are wildly contrasted and include a quintet in different dialects, a touching *madrigal affettuoso* ('provided' by the musician) and a no less charmingly lyrical *Madrigal cappriccioso*. The performance here has polish, vitality and style, and it is vividly recorded, too. It makes a highly stimulating and at times touching entertainment and, with its apt Marenzio coupling, comes as part of a Harmonia Mundi bargain CD trio of '*Comédies madrigalesques*' which is well worth exploring.

Festino nella sera del giovedi grasso avanti cena, Op. 18; Il Zabaione musicale.

(BB) *** Naxos 8.553785. R. Svizzara (Lugano) Ch., Sonatori de la Gioiosa Marca, Treviso, Fasolis.

Banchieri again here presents a pair of musical entertainments built on varied sequences of madrigals. *Il Zabaione musicale* consists of an introduction and three Acts, made up of 17 very brief madrigals. The *Festino* – an 'Entertainment for the Eve of Carnival Thursday before Dinner' – is a sequence of 21 very light-hearted madrigals, some of them involving animal and bird noises, as for example the memorable quartet for owl, cuckoo, cat and dog. Diego Fasolis draws superb singing from his Lugano choir, with incisively crisp ensemble, colourfully enhanced by brass and timpani.

Excellent recording, made in the studios of Radio Lugano. A splendid example of Naxos enterprise. Full texts and an English translation are provided.

BANTOCK, Granville (1868–1946)

Celtic Symphony; Hebridean Symphony; The Sea Reivers; The Witch of Atlas.

*** Hyp. CDA 66450. RPO, Handley.

Vernon Handley conducts warmly atmospheric performances of four of Bantock's Hebridean inspirations. Most ambitious is the *Hebridean Symphony* of 1913, with nature music echoing Wagner and Delius as well as Sibelius, whose music Bantock introduced into Britain. The two tone-poems are attractive too, but best of all is the *Celtic Symphony*, a late work (written in 1940) which uses strings and six harps. This is in the grand string tradition of Vaughan Williams's *Tallis Fantasia* and Elgar's *Introduction and Allegro*, a beautiful, colourful work that deserves to be far better known. With warm, atmospheric recording to match, Handley draws committed performances from the RPO.

Pagan Symphony; Fifine at the Fair; 2 Heroic Ballads.

*** Hyp. CDA 66630. RPO, Handley.

A fine successor to Handley's earlier pairing of the *Celtic* and *Hebridean Symphonies*. The *Pagan Symphony* dates from 1928, so it comes mid-way between the others, and the writing brings touches of Elgar as well as German influences. It is tuneful and well crafted. Perhaps it isn't as individual a work as *Fifine at the Fair*, with which Beecham understandably identified; but Handley is equally at home in this colourful tone-poem, and it is good to have it presented in stereo as vivid as this. The two *Ballads* are rather more conventional but still make a considerable impression.

The Pierrot of the Minute: Overture.

(M) *** Chan. 6566. Bournemouth Sinf., Del Mar – BRIDGE: *Summer* etc.; BUTTERWORTH: *Banks of Green Willow.* ***

Bantock's overture is concerned with Pierrot's dream in which he falls in love with a Moon Maiden, who tells him their love must die at dawn, but he will not listen. He wakes to realize that his dream of love lasted a mere minute. The writing is often delicate and at times Elgarian, and the piece is well worth investigating. The 1978 recording sounds remarkably fresh.

(i) *Sapphic Poem for Cello & Orchestra;* (ii) *Sappho.*

*** Hyp. CDA 66899. RPO, Handley, with (i) Lloyd Webber; (ii) Bickley.

The passion behind each of these nine songs, introduced by an extended orchestral Prelude, is vividly brought out by the RPO under Vernon Handley and sumptuously recorded. The mezzo, Susan Bickley, sings radiantly and with fresh clear tone, rapt and intense in the final song, *Music of the golden throne*. The concertante piece for cello and small orchestra, written in 1906, makes the perfect coupling – a

warmly expressive meditation on the same theme, with Julian Lloyd Webber a dedicated soloist.

Symphony No. 3 (The Cyprian Goddess); Dante and Beatrice; Helena (Variations on the Theme HFB).

*** Hyp. CDA 66810. RPO, Handley.

Vernon Handley again draws from the RPO ripely persuasive performances. *The Cyprian Goddess* echoes Strauss in its sumptuous orchestration and melodic writing, and in its refinement it has something of the elegiac tone of late Strauss. The *Helena Variations*, written in tribute to his wife, echo the freshness and variety of Elgar's newly completed *Enigma*, while *Dante and Beatrice* is a free-ranging programme work which in its warmth and dramatic contrasts echoes Tchaikovsky's *Romeo and Juliet*. Whatever the echoes, in each piece Bantock establishes his own distinctive voice, here more tautly controlled than in his expansive, middle-period works. First-rate sound.

BARBER, Samuel (1910–81)

Adagio for Strings, Op. 11.

*** Argo 417 818-2. ASMF, Marriner – COPLAND: *Quiet City;* COWELL: *Hymn;* CRESTON: *Rumor;* IVES: *Symphony No. 3.* ***

(B) *** DG 445 129-2. LAPO, Bernstein – BERNSTEIN: *Candide Overture;* COPLAND: *Appalachian Spring;* SCHUMAN: *American Festival Overture.* ***

(M) *** DG 427 806-2. LAPO, Bernstein – BERNSTEIN: *Candide: Overture,* etc. *** (with GERSHWIN: *Rhapsody in Blue* **(*)).

(M) *** DG 439 528-2. LAPO, Bernstein – COPLAND: *Appalachian Spring* ***; GERSHWIN: *Rhapsody in Blue.* **(*)

*** Koch Schwann 3-7243-2. New Zealand SO, Sedares – DELLO JOIO: *The Triumph of St Joan,* etc. ***

(M) **(*) Penguin/Decca 460 656-2. Baltimore SO, Zinman – BERNSTEIN: *Candide Overture,* etc. **(*); COPLAND: *Appalachian Spring,* etc. ***

Marriner's 1976 performance of Barber's justly famous *Adagio* is arguably the most satisfying version we have had since the war, although Bernstein's alternative has the advantage of digital recording. The quality of sound on the remastered Argo CD retains most of the richness and body of the analogue LP, but at the climax the brighter lighting brings a slightly sparer violin-texture than on the original LP.

Bernstein recorded the *Adagio* earlier for Sony, but the later DG recording (alternatively coupled), slow and intense, is just as deeply felt and has the advantage of modern digital sound.

The principal interest of this Koch CD is the coupled music by Norman Dello Joio, but the programme ends with a deeply felt account of Barber's *Adagio*.

Zinman's account of the Barber *Adagio* is beautifully played and richly and atmospherically recorded, but the level of tension is not very high and the effect is elegiac rather than passionate.

*Adagio for Strings; (i) Cello Concerto, Op. 22; Medea
(ballet suite) Op. 23.*

(N) (BB) *** Naxos 8.559088. (i) Warner; RSNO, Alsop.

Barber's *Cello Concerto* of 1945 is more elusive than the
Violin Concertos, but Wendy Warner concentrates on its
sometimes wry lyricism, and she articulates with brilliant
point in the gentle scherzando passage of the finale. Marin
Alsop is a persuasive partner, relishing the often plangent
orchestral backcloth and securing a splendidly committed
response from the Scottish players, both here and in the
often astringent score for *Medea*. The selection is generous
with the atmospheric central portrayal of Medea herself and
her dance of vengeance made the focal point of the score.
The famous *Adagio for Strings* then becomes essentially an
elegy, but reaches a passionate climax. Fine, vivid recording
though the massed upper strings could have more weight.

*(i) Adagio for Strings; (i–ii) Cello Concerto, Op. 22; (ii–
iii) Cello Sonata, Op. 6.*

*** Virgin VC7 59565-2. (i) SCO; Saraste; (ii) Kirshbaum;
(iii) Vignoles.

Kirshbaum's view of the Barber *Cello Concerto* is darker and
spikier than those of his direct rivals, and rather more urgent
in the outer movements, yet it is played just as beautifully. He is equally convincing in Barber's other, much rarer
cello work, the *Cello Sonata* of 1932. Roger Vignoles copes
well with the piano-writing. The celebrated *Adagio*, coolly
done, makes a worthwhile fill-up. Spacious, well-focused
recording.

*(i) Adagio for Strings; (ii) Piano Concerto, Op. 38;
(iii) Violin Concerto, Op. 14; (iv) 2nd Essay for Orchestra,
Op. 17; Overture: The School for Scandal, Op. 5.*

(M) **(*) Sony (ADD) SMK 60004. (i) Phd. O, Ormandy;
(ii) Browning, Cleveland O, Szell; (iii) Stern, NYPO,
Bernstein; (iv) NYPO, Schippers.

Barber's first popular success, the *School for Scandal* overture, has a Waltonesque orchestral brilliance and a most
touching secondary theme. The *Piano Concerto* never quite
adds up to the sum of its parts. However, the performance
here from its dedicatee is not helped by the forward balance
of the (originally CBS) recording or the shallowness of the
fortissimo piano-tone and the fierceness of the tuttis. The
Violin Concerto is a different matter and Stern's performance
with Bernstein is unsurpassed (see below). The famous *Adagio* is played with great eloquence by the Philadelphia
strings under Ormandy and the early (1957) stereo is impressively spacious. The *Second Essay*, like the light-hearted
Overture, is played superbly by the New York Philharmonic
Orchestra under Schippers. The recording is brightly lit but
acceptable.

*Adagio for Strings; (i) Piano Concerto, Op. 38. Medea's
Meditation and Dance of Vengeance, Op. 23a.*

*** ASV CDDCA 534. (i) Joselson; LSO, Schenck.

In Barber's *Concerto* Tedd Joselson is marvellously and dazzlingly brilliant, as well as being highly sensitive and poetic,
with an unforced and responsive orchestral contribution

from the LSO under Andrew Schenck. The LSO also give a
singularly fine account of the *Medea* excerpt (not to be
confused with the suite) and a restrained and noble one of
the celebrated *Adagio*.

*(i) Adagio for Strings; (i; ii) Violin Concerto; (i) Essays
Nos. 1–3; Medea: Medea's Dance of Vengeance, Op. 23a;
School for Scandal: Overture Op. 5; (iii; iv) Canzone for
Flute & Piano, Op. 38a; (iv; v) Cello Sonata, Op. 6; (iii; v)
Summer Music, Op. 31 (for wind quintet). (iv) (Piano)
Excursions, Op. 20; Nocturne (Homage to John Field),
Op. 33; Souvenirs, Op. 28.*

(N) (B) *** EMI double forte CZS 5 74287-2 (2). (i) St Louis
SO, Slatkin; (ii) Oliveira; (iii) Baxtresser; (iv) Margalit;
(v) Stepansky; Robinson, Drucker, Le Clair, Myers.

A splendid anthology of excellent modern recordings comprising some of Barber's most rewarding music. Slatkin's
accounts of the orchestral pieces are superbly played and
recorded, and he includes all three of the *Essays*, which is
quite rare, as well as the amusing *School for Scandal Overture*.
Elmar Oliveira's version of the *Violin Concerto* reacts to the
nostalgia of the *Andante* with a vein of bitter-sweet yearning
that is most affecting. It is a fine performance overall with a
brilliantly played finale. The chamber music is especially
valuable, with the performers producing that spontaneous
feeling that they have lived with the music before performing
it. The *Canzone for Flute and Piano* has an Elysian, soaring
melody (slightly French in atmosphere) which Jeanne Baxtresser plays very beautifully. The *Cello Sonata* has a powerful
impulse and is given the most eloquent advocacy here, while
the *Excursions* have wit and elegance. The shorter pieces are
all distinctive and well worth having and this whole bargain
Double cannot be too highly recommended.

*Adagio for Strings, Op. 11; Essays Nos. 1, Op. 12; 2, Op. 17;
Music for a Scene from Shelley, Op. 7; Overture, The
School for Scandal, Op. 5; Symphony No. 1, Op. 9.*

*** Argo 436 288. Baltimore SO, Zinman.

These performances are very alert and vital, particularly that
of the *First Symphony*,; the recording has superb presence
and detail. Apart from the first two *Essays* for orchestra,
Zinman's disc includes the more rarely heard *Music for
a Scene from Shelley*, sumptuously scored and gloriously
atmospheric. This adds greatly to the attractions of an
already desirable issue, and Zinman and his excellent
orchestra play the *Overture* to Sheridan's *The School for
Scandal*, with equal commitment. Strongly recommended.

*(i) Adagio for Strings; Essay No. 2 for Orchestra, Op. 17;
Medea's Meditation and Dance of Vengeance, Op. 23a; The
School for Scandal Overture; (ii) Vanessa: Intermezzo; (i;
iii) Andromache's Farewell, Op. 39.*

*** Sony (ADD) MHK 62837. (i) NYPO; (ii) Columbia SO;
Schippers; (iii) with Arroyo (with (ii) MENOTTI: *Overture:
Amelia al ballo*; BERG: *Wozzeck: Interlude*; D'INDY:
Fervaal: Introduction ***).

This appealingly packaged Heritage reissue celebrates the
work of the fine American conductor, Thomas Schippers,
and also makes an excellent Barber anthology, with the New

York Philharmonic recordings originally compiled for the composer's seventieth birthday. The original LP offered *Dover Beach*, but here instead we are offered *Andromache's Farewell*, with text taken from Euripides' *The Trojan Women*, a superb vehicle for Martina Arroyo at her finest. The new transfers greatly improve on the old LPs, the sound now full and atmospheric. Then, after Menotti's buoyantly vivacious *Amelia al ballo Overture*, the pungency of Berg's *Wozzeck Interlude* brings one up short, but balm follows with the beautiful closing *Fervaal Introduction* of Vincent d'Indy. Not surprisingly the documentation concentrates on Schippers's career, but the music itself is not neglected.

(i) Adagio for Strings; (ii) Essay No. 2 for Orchestra; Music for a Scene from Shelley; Serenade for Strings, Op. 1; (ii; iii) A Stopwatch and an Ordnance Map, Op. 15; (iv) Chorus: Let down the bars, O Death! (ii; v) A Hand of Bridge (chamber opera), Op. 35.

(M) *** Van. (ADD) 08.4016.71. (i) I Solisti di Zagreb, Janigro; (ii) Symphony of the Air, Golschmann; (iii) with Robert De Cormier Chorale; (v) with Neway, Alberts, Lewis, Maero; (iv) Washington Cathedral Ch., Callaway.

An admirable and highly rewarding anthology of works by a composer whose *Adagio for Strings* has wrongly overshadowed his achievement elsewhere. Excellent singing and playing throughout.

Adagio for Strings; Knoxville, Summer of 1915; Songs, Op. 13: Nocturne; Sure on the Shining Night.

*** EMI CDC5 55358-2. Hendricks, LSO, Tilson Thomas – COPLAND: *Quiet City*, etc. ***

Knoxville, to a poem by James Agee, is one of the most evocative pieces of its kind, and it is the more magical here for the authentically American inflexions that Hendricks gives it, together with glowing string-tone. The two songs which Barber orchestrated from his Opus 13 are most beautifully done too, while the celebrated *Adagio* is taken at a flowing tempo with no self-indulgence or sentimentality at all. A radiant disc.

Cave of the Heart (original version of *Medea*).

*** Koch 3-7019-2. Atlantic Sinf., Schenck – COPLAND: *Appalachian Spring.* ***

The original version of *Medea* was entitled *Cave of the Heart*; in this original form it sounds much darker in feeling and harder-edged, and it has stronger Stravinskian overtones. The effect in this full-blooded, vividly present recording is, if anything, brawnier than the more sumptuous revision. A most interesting and stimulating score.

Cello Concerto, Op. 22.

*** Chan. 8322. Wallfisch, ECO, Simon – SHOSTAKOVICH: *Cello Concerto No. 1.* ***

Wallfisch gives an impressive and eloquent reading, and the elegiac slow movement is especially fine. Wallfisch is forwardly balanced, but otherwise the recording is truthful; the orchestra is vividly detailed.

(i) Piano Concerto, Op. 38; (ii) Violin Concerto, Op. 14. Souvenirs, Op. 28.

*** Telarc CD 80441. (i) Parker; (ii) McDuffie; Atlanta SO, Levi.

Robert McDuffie is a powerful violinist with a formidable technique, if not as individual an artist as many rivals in this warmly romantic *Violin Concerto*. His reading makes an excellent coupling for Jon Kimura Parker's outstanding performance of the *Piano Concerto* and the suite, *Souvenirs*, in its orchestral form. The performance is rather tauter and more purposeful than the fine one which John Browning (the pianist for whom the work was written) recorded for RCA (see above). However, the latter offers a fine account of the *Symphony* and will suit collectors who already have the *Violin Concerto*.

Violin Concerto, Op. 14.

*** Decca 452 851-2. Bell, Baltimore SO, Zinman – BLOCH: *Baal Shem*; WALTON: *Violin Concerto.* ***

(M) *** Sony (ADD) SMK 64506. Stern, NYPO, Bernstein – MAXWELL DAVIES: *Violin Concerto.* ***

*** DG 439 886-2. Shaham, LSO, Previn – KORNGOLD: *Violin Concerto* etc. *** ●

*** Sony SK 89029. Hahn, St Paul CO, Wolff – MEYER: *Violin Concerto.* ***

*** EMI CDC5 55360-2. Perlman, Boston SO, Ozawa – BERNSTEIN: *Serenade;* FOSS: *3 American Pieces.* ***

(i) Violin Concerto. Adagio for Strings.

(M) *** Sony SMK 63088. (i) Stern; NYPO, Bernstein – SCHUMAN: *In Praise of Shahn*, etc. ***

Joshua Bell's passionate playing in the Barber, full of tender poetry, is well matched by the excellent orchestra, ripely and brilliantly recorded, with the soloist well forward but not aggressively so. This now takes pride of place, but Stern and Shaham have their own insights to offer.

Isaac Stern gave the Barber *Violin Concerto* its stereo première in 1964, and his performance, which is consistently inspired, is of superlative quality. It has warmth, freshness and humanity, and the slow movement is glorious. The CBS forward balance for the orchestra is less than ideal, but the recording is otherwise very good and has been impressively remastered. This comes alternatively coupled with Bernstein's 1971 account of the *Adagio*, measured and intense, and many will count the two fine William Schuman works a more apt coupling than the Maxwell Davies.

Gil Shaham's performance of the Barber also has great virtuosity and is a reading of strong profile, with every moment of dramatic intensity properly characterized. The effect is warm and ripe, with the sound close and immediate, bringing out above all the work's bolder side but not missing the withdrawn, tender lyricism of the heavenly *Andante*. This really *is* good – and worthy to rank alongside the Stern/Bernstein (Sony). Indeed, it is to be preferred to the richly extrovert Perlman account.

Hilary Hahn, still only nineteen when she made this recording, gives an outstanding performance of the Barber *Concerto*, at once romantic and thoughtful, bringing out heartfelt emotion without overplaying it. This is distinctive, both in using a chamber orchestra, making up in clarity for any loss of weight, and in offering the most unusual coupling, a warmly approachable work specially written for Hahn by the double-bass player and composer, Edgar Meyer. The close balance for the soloist does not allow a genuine pianissimo, but otherwise this stands among the finest of all versions.

For Perlman the kernel of the Barber *Concerto* lies in the central slow movement; he plays with a warmth and intensity that even he has rarely matched. Weight, power and virtuoso brilliance then come together in his dazzling account of the finale.

Essays Nos. 1, Op. 12; 2, Op. 17; 3, Op. 47.

*** Chan. 9053. Detroit SO, Järvi – IVES: *Symphony No. 1.* ***

In terms of both sonority and approach, Neeme Järvi's account of these appealing works differs from the American competitors. The strings have a lightness and subtlety and are highly responsive. The recording is very natural and present, and beautifully balanced.

Essay for Orchestra No. 3, Op. 47; Fadograph of a Yestern Scene, Op. 44; Medea: Suite, Op. 23.

*** Koch 3-7010-2. New Zealand SO, Schenck.

A welcome recording of two Barber rarities from the 1970s in sympathetic performances by the New Zealand orchestra under Andrew Schenck. The recording has outstanding clarity and definition, but the acoustic has the very slightly dry quality of a studio rather than the expansiveness of a concert hall.

Medea (ballet): Suite.

(M) *** Mercury (ADD) 432 016-2. Eastman-Rochester O, Hanson – GOULD: *Fall River Legend*, etc. ***

Howard Hanson's performance is both polished and dramatic, and the brilliant 1959 Mercury recording has astonishing clarity and vivid presence.

Souvenirs.

*** Koch 3-7005-2. New Zealand SO, Schenck – MENOTTI: *Amahl*, etc. ***

Souvenirs is an absolutely enchanting score which has bags of charm and, unlike the delightful Menotti with which it is coupled, every idea is so memorable that it instantly replaces the one that came before. It is very well played here by the New Zealand Symphony Orchestra under Andrew Schenck and is eminently well recorded too. Strongly recommended.

Symphonies Nos. 1, Op. 9; 2, Op. 19; Adagio for Strings; Overture, The School for Scandal.

*** Chan. 9684. Detroit SO, Järvi.

Symphonies Nos. 1, Op. 9; 2, Op. 19; Essay for Orchestra No. 1; Overture: The School for Scandal, Op. 5.

☯ (BB) *** Naxos 8.559024. RSNO, Alsop.

Marin Alsop is a shooting star in the firmament of international conductors. The two symphonies are played with passionate commitment and deep lyrical feeling by the Scottish orchestra. The account of the complete *Second Symphony* will surely confirm the reputation of a wartime work which the composer partly withdrew in despondency after its neglect. The *First Essay for Orchestra* also generates a powerful atmosphere when played with such depth of feeling. With spectacular recording, this exciting collection is very strongly recommended.

The *First Symphony* also comes off well in Neeme Järvi's hands, as does the wartime *Second*. The ubiquitous but none the less moving *Adagio* and the *Overture: The School for Scandal* complete a disc that could well serve as an admirable entry point into Barber's world. The Detroit orchestra turn in polished playing and the recording is rich and vivid, the sound fuller than in the Naxos alternative.

CHAMBER MUSIC

Canzone for Violin & Piano.

*** DG 453 470-2. Shaham, Previn – COPLAND: *Sonata*, etc.; GERSHWIN: *3 Preludes*; PREVIN: *Sonata*. ***

This brief, songful piece, with material from the slow movement of Barber's *Piano Concerto*, provides a valuable makeweight in Shaham and Previn's fine collection of American violin music.

(i) *Serenade for String Quartet, Op.1; String Quartet, Op. 11; (i; ii) Dover Beach, Op. 3; (ii; iii) 3 Songs (The daisies; With rue my heart is laden; Bessie Bobtail), Op. 2; 3 Songs (Rain has fallen; Sleep now; I hear an army), Op. 10; Sure on This Shining Night; Nocturne, Op. 13/3–4; Solitary Hotel; Despite and Still, Op. 41/4–5; 3 Songs (Now I have fed and eaten up; A green lowland of pianos; O boundless, boundless evening), Op. 45.*

*** Virgin VC5 45033-2.(i) Endellion Qt; (ii) Allen; (iii) Vignoles.

The *Serenade*, Op. 1, was written when Barber was only nineteen, with the first two of its three brief movements belying any idea of a lightweight work. The Endellion Quartet play with the hushed gravity and clear intensity that it deserves, and their reading of the Opus 11 *Quartet* has points of advantage over even the finest rivals, with more mystery and variety of expression. With Thomas Allen a superb soloist, this account of *Dover Beach* conveys mystery and builds to a thrilling climax on the poet's expression of love. In the solo songs Allen and Vignoles opt consistently for speeds on the fast side, so that the slow tango of the Joyce setting, *Solitary Hotel*, is more clearly established.

String Quartet, Op. 11.

**(*) DG 435 864-2. Emerson Qt – IVES: *Quartets Nos. 1–2.*

The Emerson Quartet play with brilliance and technical expertise. The tone is rich, their tonal blend immaculate and their ensemble impeccable; but their expressive eloquence sounds over-rehearsed. All the same, it is in its way stunningly played and eminently well captured by the DG engineers.

Summer Music.

*** Crystal (ADD) CD 750. Westwood Wind Quintet –

CARLSSON: *Nightwings;* LIGETI: *Bagatelles;* MATHIAS: *Quintet.* ***

(BB) **(*) Naxos 8.553851-2. Michael Thompson Wind Quintet − HINDEMITH: *Kleine Kammermusik* **(*); JANACEK: *Mládí* **(*); LARSSON: *Quattro tempi.* **

Samuel Barber's *Summer Music* is an evocative mood-picture of summer, a gloriously warm and lyrical piece. The Crystal CD offers superbly committed and sensitive playing and vivid, warm recording.

The Michael Thompson Wind Quintet offer the piece with an enterprising choice of coupling and give an expressive account. The playing is wonderfully accomplished and sensitive, but the close balance does rob it of atmosphere.

PIANO MUSIC

Ballade, Op. 46; 4 Excursions, Op. 20; Interlude, Op. posth.; Nocturne (Homage to John Field), Op. 33; Sonata, Op. 26; Souvenirs, Op. 28.

*** Virgin VC5 45270-2. McCawley.

This CD accommodates Barber's entire output for the piano. Leon McCawley plays excellently, even in the prodigiously difficult *Sonata*, written for Horowitz. McCawley's account is highly convincing, breathtakingly so in the dazzling *Scherzo* and the formidable closing *Fuga*. The *Souvenirs*, too, are brilliantly played; he makes a great deal of the *Pas de deux*. The posthumous *Interlude* is also well worth having; and this well-recorded survey displaces Angela Brownridge's Hyperion disc, which omits the latter piece as well as the *Souvenirs*.

VOCAL MUSIC

Agnus Dei.

*** Hyp. CDA 66219. Corydon Singers, Best − BERNSTEIN: *Chichester Psalms;* COPLAND: *In the Beginning,* etc. ***

Barber's *Agnus Dei* is none other than our old friend the *Adagio*, arranged for voices by the composer in 1967. Matthew Best's fine performance moves spaciously and expansively to an impressive climax.

(i) *Andromache's Farewell;* (ii) *Dover Beach;* (iii) *Hermit Songs;* (iv) *Knoxville: Summer of 1915.*

(M) (***) Sony (ADD) mono/stereo MPK 46727. (i) Arroyo, NYPO, Schippers; (ii) Fischer-Dieskau, Juilliard Qt; (iii) L. Price, composer; (iv) Steber, Dumbarton Oaks O, Strickland.

This collection of vintage recordings makes a splendid mid-priced Barber compendium, representing four of his finest vocal works, all in superb performances. Excellent CD transfers. No texts are provided, but words are exceptionally clear.

Despite and Still (song-cycle), *Op. 41; 10 Hermit Songs, Op. 29; Mélodies passagères, Op. 27; 3 Songs, Op. 2; 3 Songs, Op. 10; 4 Songs, Op. 13; 2 Songs, Op. 18; 3 Songs,*

Op. 45; Beggar's Song; Dover Beach; In the Dark Pinewood; Love at the Door; Love's Caution; Night Wanderers; Nuvoletta; Of That So Sweet Imprisonment; Serenades; A Slumber Song of the Madonna; Strings in the Earth and Air; There's Nae Lark.

*** DG 435 867-2 (2). Studer, Hampson, Browning; Emerson Qt.

Barber's style, easily lyrical, sensitively responding to the cadences of English verse, remained remarkably consistent. Cheryl Studer sings beautifully in the *Hermit Songs,* but it is Thomas Hampson who establishes the full flavour of the collection, which includes a sprinkling of vigorous, extrovert songs. He is particularly fine in Barber's best-known song, the extended *Dover Beach.* In that, Hampson is accompanied immaculately by the Emerson Quartet. Otherwise it is John Browning who sharpens the focus and heightens the fantasy in deeply sympathetic accompaniments. Excellent, natural recording, first-class documentation and full texts.

(i) *Hermit Songs, Op. 29;* (ii) *Knoxville: Summer of 1915* (cantata); (i) *Songs: The Daisies; Nocturne; Nuvoletta; Sleep now.* (ii) *Antony and Cleopatra* (opera): scenes: *Give me some music; Give me my robe.*

(M) (***) RCA (ADD) mono/stereo 09026 61983-2. L. Price, with (i) composer (piano); (ii) New Philh. O, Schippers.

Knoxville: Summer of 1915 has never been done more hauntingly than by Leontyne Price here, and it is well coupled with the heroine's arias from the opera *Antony and Cleopatra.* Far rarer is the private recording of the *Hermit Songs,* also specially written for her. Accompanied by the composer, Price is more rugged than Studer in the collected song edition, but just as intense. The mono sound is very limited but conveys the atmosphere of a historic occasion. Otherwise good stereo sound.

The Lovers, Op. 43; Prayers of Kierkegaard, Op. 30.

*** Koch 3-7125-2. Duesing, Reese, Chicago Ch. & SO, Schenck.

The Lovers is a substantial choral cantata setting nine erotic poems by the Chilean, Pablo Neruda. It makes a moving sequence, with the soloist, Dale Duesing, matching the responsiveness of the outstanding Chicago Symphony Chorus. *The Prayers of Kierkegaard* is a tougher, more uncompromising work, but approachable too, again with magnificent writing for chorus.

BARGIEL, Woldemar (1828–97)

Octet in C min. for Strings, Op. 15a.

(N) (B) *** Hyp. Helios CDH 55043. Divertimenti − MENDELSSOHN: *Octet.* ***

Woldemar Bargiel was Clara Schumann's step-brother and wrote this remarkable *Octet* while a student at the Leipzig Conservatoire. Of course it is not a masterpiece of the same order as the Mendelssohn, with which it is coupled here, but it has natural dignity and real substance. Bargiel has great facility: his invention is of quality and distinction, and his writing shows independence of mind. It would be worth duplicating the Mendelssohn recording for the sake of this compelling music. Divertimenti play it with total commitment and understandable enthusiasm.

BARRAUD, Henry (born 1900)

Offrande à une ombre.

(M) **(*) Mercury [434 389-2]. Detroit SO, Paray – CHAUSSON: *Symphony*; LALO: *Le roi d'Ys*, etc. **(*)

Barraud was a prolific composer whose style owes something to Dukas and Roussel. *Offrande à une ombre* is an effective ten-minute piece which is eminently well played by the Detroit orchestra and Paray. The recording was made in 1957 and appears in stereo for the first time.

BARRIOS, Agustin (1885–1944)

Las abejas; Aconquija; Aire de Zamba; La catedral; Choro de saudade; Cueca; Julia Florida; Una limosna por el amor de Dios; Maxixa; Mazurka appassionata; Medallon antiguo; Preludios: in C min.; in G min. Un sueño en la floresta; Valses Nos. 3–4; Vallancico de Navidad.

*** Sony SK 64396. Williams.

Aconquija; Aire de Zamba; La catedral; Cueca; Estudio; Una limosna por el amor de Dios; Madrigal (Gavota); Maxixa; Mazurka appassionata; Minuet; Preludio; Un sueño en la floresta; Valse No. 3; Vallancico de Navidad.

(M) *** Sony (ADD) SBK 47669. Williams – PONCE: *Folia de España.* ***

This full-price CD duplicates almost all the music on John Williams's first (bargain-priced) recital of music by this fine Paraguayan composer and has the advantage of the complete background silence of digital recording. The playing is of the highest calibre and has both concentration and charisma. However, the earlier disc offers about 10 minutes' more music by including the Ponce *Variations* and it remains very attractive in its own right.

Humoresque; Junto a tu corazion – Vals; Mabilita; Madrigal – Gavota; Maxixe; Pepita; Sarita (Mazurka); Suite Andina; Tu y Yo (Gavota romántica) U sueño en la floresta; Vals, Op. 8/4; Vidalita con variaciones; Villancido de Navidad.

(N) (BB) *** Naxos 8.554558. Gori.

As this collection is designated Volume I, presumable Naxos are planning a complete coverage of Barrios's guitar music. The first instalment from the international prize-winning Greek virtuoso Antigoni Gori plays in a rather more romantic style than John Williams. But Gori's ebb and flow of rubato is a natural response to the line of the music and her playing always sounds spontaneous. She is very well recorded, and the back-up documentation is first class. Incidentally, the attractive four-movement *Suite Andina*, which closes the recital, is an arbitrary grouping of four independent pieces (*Aconquija, Aire de Zamba, Córdoba* and *Cueca*).

BARTÓK, Béla (1881–1945)

Concerto for Orchestra.

(M) *** Decca 417 754-2. Chicago SO, Solti – MUSSORGSKY: *Pictures at an Exhibition.* ***

(N) *** Australian Decca Eloquence (ADD) 467 602-2. Israel PO, Mehta – JANACEK: *Taras Bulba*; KODALY: *Concerto for Orchestra.* ***

⊛ (M) (***) Dutton Lab. mono CDK 1206. Concg. O, Van Beinum – STRAVINSKY: *The Rite of Spring.* (***)

(N) (BB) (***) Naxos mono 8.110105. Boston SO, Koussevitzky – MUSSORGSKY: *Pictures at an Exhibition.* (**(*))

(B) **(*) EMI double forte (ADD) CZS5 72664-2 (2). Chicago SO, Ozawa – JANACEK: *Sinfonietta* ***; LUTOSLAWKI: *Concerto for Orchestra* **(*); STRAVINSKY: *Firebird ballet.* **(*)

(M) **(*) Telarc CD 82010. Los Angeles PO, Previn – JANACEK: *Sinfonietta.* **(*)

Concerto for Orchestra; Divertimento for Strings.

*** Conifer 75605 51324-2. RPO, Gatti.

Daniele Gatti's account of the *Concerto for Orchestra* belongs with the best. The orchestral playing is first class and Gatti gets phrasing of great imagination and subtlety of colouring. The central music has great atmosphere and sense of mystery, and the performance grips you from start to finish. No other version is better recorded than this beautifully realistic and finely balanced disc. The *Divertimento* is hardly less successful.

Solti gave Bartók's *Concerto for Orchestra* its CD début. The upper range is very brightly lit indeed, which brings an aggressive feeling to the upper strings. This undoubtedly suits the reading, fierce and biting on the one hand, exuberant on the other. Superlative playing from Solti's own Chicago orchestra, and given vivid sound.

It is curious that Mehta's splendid 1976 *Concerto for Orchestra* has had to wait so long for its CD release (though only on Australian Decca). Unlike most Israel Philharmonic recordings, this one was made in Kingsway Hall, London, and the sound is rich and full, and if Mehta's performance lacks the last degree of bite that you find with Solti, its combination of brilliance and warm expressiveness is very attractive. The finale has a measure of jollity in it (what Bartók called its ' life-assertion') at a tempo that allows the strings to articulate their rushing semi-quavers clearly. The recording was in the demonstration bracket in its day (the mid-1970s), with translucent woodwind, firmly focused brass, and plenty of sheen on the strings. It is reissued as part of an excellent triptych on the Australian Eloquence label, which, unlike the UK series, contains full sleeve notes.

Eduard van Beinum's recording dates from the early 1950s and it is astonishing how vivid is the work's impact. Bartók's vision springs to life in an extraordinarily fresh way. If you feel a little tired of this piece, listen to van Beinum, for he renews one's enthusiasm for this score as do few others. The sound is quite astonishing in detail and sonority.

The thrilling issue in the Naxos Historical series offers a radio recording of the first performance of the *Concerto for Orchestra* which Koussevitzky gave in Boston on December 30, 1944, four weeks after the New York première. It is a tribute to the virtuoso qualities of the Boston Orchestra that the playing is not merely brilliant but has a tension and authority missing from many latter-day performances. Though the sound is limited, with some odd balances and changes of volume, the glowing warmth of the Koussevitzky orchestra, as well as the brilliance, are vividly conveyed, making one easily forget that this is 1944 mono radio sound. The opening of the slow introduction may be more ponderous than we are used to, but that is very much the exception. The textual oddity is that the original five-bar pay-off in the finale is used, where latterly the 24-bar alternative has been universally adopted – far more effective.

Ozawa's EMI reissue produces dazzling playing from the Chicago orchestra. The performance is full of life and energy. There are more searching and more atmospheric accounts available, but this stands alongside the Solti version for brilliance. However, the CD transfer brings sound which, though most vivid, is rather two-dimensional.

Previn and the Los Angeles Philharmonic give a comfortable, relaxed reading of Bartók's *Concerto*. For Previn, it is above all a work of fun, although there is no lack of excitement in the finale. The Telarc recording captures the full bloom of the orchestra.

Concerto for Orchestra; Dance Suite; The Miraculous Mandarin: suite.

(N) (M) *** Decca (ADD) 467 686-2. LSO, Solti.

There will be many who prefer Solti's earlier (1965) LSO version of the *Concerto for Orchestra*, for this recording – outstanding in its day – shows its age only marginally in the brightly lit string tone; in all other respects it is of high quality. Kingsway Hall affords a pleasing warmth of colouring and the performance has all the fire and passion one could wish for, but with a touch more wit and idiosyncrasy than the later Chicago version (see above). There is more spontaneity too than in the later digital account, and one senses Solti's Hungarian upbringing more readily here, for he allows himself certain rubato effects not strictly marked in the score, absorbing the inflexions of Hungarian folksong, very much an influence of Bartók's last-period lyricism. The inclusion of two fill-ups is welcome. The title of *Dance Suite* (written in the early 1920s – generally his most dissonant period) may suggest something rather trivial, but Bartók's inspired composition gives us a work that can be enjoyed on many different levels, especially when the performance is so strong and fiery and the recording exemplary. The streak of ruthlessness in Solti's approach that sometimes mars performances of less earthy music is then given full rein in *The Miraculous Mandarin suite*, recorded with comparable vividness and colour two years earlier, and again benfiting from the Kingsway Hall ambience.

(i) *Concerto for Orchestra;* (ii) *Piano Concertos Nos. 1–3;* (i; iii) *Violin Concerto No. 2 in B min.*

(B) *** Ph. (ADD) Duo 438 812-2 (2). (i) Concg. O, Haitink;

(ii) Kovacevich, LSO or BBC SO (in *No. 2*), C. Davis;

(iii) Szeryng.

This is as enticing a bargain Bartók collection as you could find. Haitink's 1960 *Concerto for Orchestra* is more subtle, less tense than Solti's mid-priced version, although the element of dramatic contrast is not missing. Szeryng joins Haitink for the *B minor Violin Concerto* with equally satisfying artistic results. Kovacevich's direct, concentrated readings of the three *Piano Concertos* are hardly less persuasive. Sir Colin Davis accompanies sensitively and vigorously. No complaints about the bright, full recording in all four concertos.

(i) *Concerto for Orchestra;* (ii) *Dance Suite; 2 Portraits, Op. 5; Mikrokosmos* (orch. Serly): *Bourrée; From the Diary of a Fly.*

(M) *** Mercury (ADD) 432 017-2. (i) LSO; (ii) Philh. Hung., Dorati.

Dorati secures outstandingly brilliant and committed playing from the LSO. The recording, made in Wembley Town Hall, shows characteristic expertise of balance. The rest of the programme was recorded in 1958 in the Grosse Saal of the Vienna Konzerthaus, which affords Dorati's fine orchestra of Hungarian émigrés plenty of body without blurring outlines.

Concerto for Orchestra; (i) The Miraculous Mandarin (complete ballet).

(BB) **(*) Virgin Classics 2 x 1 VBD5 61754-2 (2). (i) Dumont Singers; Melbourne SO, Iwaki – STRAVINSKY: *Agon,* etc. **(*)

Concerto for Orchestra; The Miraculous Mandarin (ballet suite).

*** EMI CDC5 55094-2. CBSO, Rattle.

Rattle's superb Bartók coupling offers a brilliant studio recording of the violent *Miraculous Mandarin* ballet suite married to a live recording of the *Concerto for Orchestra*, both of which draw on an exceptionally wide emotional and expressive range. Rich, full and well-balanced recording, to match the brilliance of the performances. There are no finer readings of either work.

Iwaki and the Melbourne orchestra present the complete *Miraculous Mandarin* ballet, not just the suite, as coupling for the *Concerto for Orchestra*. The recording is excellent, spacious and full, and the playing is finely pointed but is often too well-mannered for Bartók, lacking something in fierceness and excitement.

Concerto for Orchestra; Music for Strings, Percussion & Celesta.

*** EMI CDC7 54070-2. Oslo PO, Jansons.

(M) **(*) DG (ADD) 457 890-2. BPO, Karajan.

**(*) Chant du Monde Praga (ADD) PR 254047. Czech PO, Lehel; or Leningrad PO, Mravinsky.

(M) ** Sony (ADD) SMK 60730. NYPO, Bernstein.

Concerto for Orchestra; Music for Strings, Percussion & Celesta; Hungarian Sketches.

(M) *** RCA (ADD) 09026 61504-2. Chicago SO, Reiner.

Concerto for Orchestra; 4 Orchestral Pieces, Op. 12.

**(*) DG 437 826-2. Chicago SO, Boulez.

Jansons and the Oslo Philharmonic give outstanding performances of both works, making this a fine recommendation in this now-favourite coupling. Unfortunately, as we go to press this set has been withdrawn.

Reiner's version of the *Concerto for Orchestra* was recorded in 1955, but in its latest CD format the sound approaches demonstration standard in its spacious warmth, clarity and impact. The performance is most satisfying, with plenty of cutting edge. The *Music for Strings, Percussion and Celesta*, recorded three years later, suffers from a forward balance which prevents a true pianissimo, yet the concentration of the playing all but overcomes this defect, and the set of five *Hungarian Sketches* is utterly seductive when played and recorded with such vividness of colour and a natural understanding of the music's rhythmic impetus.

Karajan is right in treating Bartók emotionally, but comparison with Solti points the contrast between Berlin romanticism and earthy Hungarian passion. Karajan's moulding of phrases is essentially of the German tradition. The *Music for Strings, Percussion and Celesta* has well-upholstered timbre, and here Karajan's essentially romantic view combines with the recording to produce a certain urbanity.

In the Mravinsky version of the *Music for Strings, Percussion and Celesta* the slow movement has tremendous mystery and intensity, and it makes one regret the rather less than opulent sound. The *Concerto for Orchestra*, conducted by György Lehel, has both a magisterial sweep and a sensitive ear for detail. The recording is warm and spacious and truthfully balanced – and infinitely superior to that accorded Mravinsky.

Boulez secures brilliant playing from the Chicago orchestra, but they are able to relax in the central movements, and the finale is very powerfully driven indeed. The *Four Orchestral Pieces* was the nearest Bartók came to writing a symphony, complete with Scherzo and melancholy slow movement.

Bernstein's coupling of Bartók's two most popular pieces brings gripping performances, typical of his work in New York at the end of the 1950s and beginning of the 1960s. Although the recording is fairly forward, the dynamic range is surprisingly wide, and because of the drama of the playing there is still plenty of contrast. However, the very brightly lit violins are thin above the stave. Yet for the animal energy which Bernstein finds in Bartók, this is still a record worth hearing.

Piano Concertos Nos. 1–3.

*** Teldec 0630 13158-2. Schiff, Budapest Festival O, Fischer.

*** Ph. 446 366-2. Kocsis, Budapest Festival O, Fischer.

*** EMI CDC7 54871-2. Donohoe, CBSO, Rattle.

(M) *** DG (ADD) 447 399-2. Anda, Berlin RSO, Fricsay.

(M) *** Decca Dig./ADD 448 125-2. Ashkenazy, LPO, Solti.

(B) **(*) Naxos 8.550771. Jandó, Budapest SO, Ligeti.

(i) *Piano Concertos Nos. 1–2;* (ii) *2 Portraits, Op. 5.*

(M) *** DG 457 909-2. (i) Pollini, Chicago SO; (ii) Minz, LSO; Abbado.

András Schiff's colourful, winning performances of Bartók's three piano concertos are totally idiomatic, brilliantly and warmly accompanied by the fine Budapest orchestra, bringing out point and sparkle. His depth of meditation in the slow movements matches that which he brings equally to Bach and Schubert.

The Kocsis performances, extracted from the Philips box listed below, remain a strong alternative choice, although Peter Donohoe and Sir Simon Rattle also give first-class accounts and they have the advantage of equally impressive sound.

The Géza Anda recordings with Ferenc Fricsay from the beginning of the 1960s are rather special. Both artists show a feeling for the music's inner world and its colouring, which is magnetic in the slow movements yet urgent, incisive and red-blooded too. The recording is remarkably atmospheric, yet still tangible in detail.

The partnership of Ashkenazy and Solti combines with vintage Decca sound. The *Second* and *Third Concertos* spark off the kind of energy and dash one would usually expect only at a live performance. The *First Concerto*, recorded digitally in 1981, is even tougher, urgent and biting, and the slow movements in all three works bring a hushed inner concentration, beautifully captured in warmly refined recording.

Jandó is on top form, playing with exciting bravura throughout. The energy of the motoric *First Concerto* is not brutalized, and in the slow movements the resonance of the recording ensures that there is plenty of atmosphere, even if in outer movements the violent brass interjections could be more cleanly focused. Apart from the excess of resonance, the recording is vivid and well balanced.

The DG concerto coupling celebrates an exuberant Italian partnership. Rhythms in fast movements are freely and infectiously sprung to bring out the bluff Bartókian high spirits. The vividly recorded Chicago orchestra is in superb form. The ear is then sweetened by Minz's warmth in the *Portraits*. This is an excellent recommendation in its own right, but most collectors will want all three piano concertos.

(i) *Piano Concertos Nos. 1–3. Allegro barbaro; 14 Bagatelles, Op. 6; 4 Dirges, Op. 9a; 2 Elegies, Op. 8b; First Term at the Piano; For Children, Books I–IV; 3 Hungarian Folksongs from Csík; 3 Hungarian Folk Tunes; Rumanian Christmas Carols; 6 Rumanian Folk Tunes; 2 Rumanian Dances, Op. 8a; 3 Rondos on Folk Tunes; Sonatina; 3 Studies, Op. 18; Suite, Op. 14.*

*** Ph. (IMS) 446 368-2 (4). Kocsis; (i) Budapest Festival O, Fischer.

The calibre of this Philips set cannot be denied, but it is relatively expensive: four full-price CDs for the price of three. Kocsis's recordings of the three concertos are as idiomatic as they are vibrant, and the *Third* is superbly done, among the finest on record. The Philips recording is admirably bold and full-bodied. But many may prefer to approach the solo piano music separately.

Piano Concerto No. 3.

(BB) *** Arte Nova 74321 52248-2. Sherman, SWF SO, Gielen

– BERG: *3 Pieces from the Lyric Suite;* CARTER: *Piano Concerto,* etc. ***

**(*) EMI CDC5 56654-2. Argerich, Montreal SO, Dutoit – PROKOVIEV: *Piano Concertos Nos. 1 & 3.* **(*)

Gielen directs an intense, crisply pointed account of the Bartók *Concerto,* matched by the sharply rhythmic, well-pointed playing of Russell Sherman. This makes a generous and unusual coupling of twentieth-century masterpieces, well recorded.

Elegant playing from Martha Argerich in the Bartók *Third Concerto* which is new to discography. There is a wonderful, improvisatory feel to much of it, though at times in the slow movement she caresses a phrase in a way that draws attention to her rather than to Bartók. Very distinguished playing, but not a first recommendation. Excellent support from the Montreal orchestra under Dutoit, and good recording.

(i) *Viola Concerto* (two versions; ed. Péter Bartók & ed. Serly); *Two Pictures, Op. 10.*

(B) *** Naxos 8.554183. Xiao, Budapest PO, Kovacs – SERLY: *Rhapsody for Viola & Orchestra.* ***

Viola Concerto (ed. Tibor Serly).

*** EMI CDC7 54101-2. Zimmermann, Bav. RSO, Shallon – HINDEMITH: *Der Schwanendreher.* ***

*** Sony SK 57961. Ma, Baltimore SO, Zinman – ALBERT: *Cello Concerto;* BLOCH: *Schelomo.* ***

Having a première recording of Bartók on Naxos makes an unmissable bargain. His *Viola Concerto* was the uncompleted work which, soon after his death, Tibor Serly put together from sketches. Now Bartók's son Péter, with the scholar Paul Neubauer, has re-edited those sketches. Though the differences are small, this first recording of the revised version, superbly played, proves fascinating, sounding closer to the *Concerto for Orchestra.* With the rich-toned Chinese viola-player, Xiao, as soloist, that version is here presented alongside Serly's. The warmly atmospheric *Two Pictures* and a viola work by Serly make a good coupling.

Tabea Zimmermann plays with great eloquence and taste, and the balance is flattering. The soloist is helped, but she is not so far forward as to mask orchestral detail, which is wonderfully present and beautifully placed.

Yo-Yo Ma plays it at the correct pitch on the alto violin, or vertical viola, in which the instrument is fitted with a long end-pin and played upright like a cello. His performance has characteristic finesse and eloquence, and it gains from the transparent sound which Zinman draws from the Baltimore orchestra.

(i) *Viola Concerto; Violin Concerto No. 1;* (ii) *Rhapsodies Nos. 1–2.*

(M) *** EMI CDM7 63985-2. Menuhin, (i) New Philh. O, Dorati; (ii) BBC SO, Boulez.

Menuhin with his strongly creative imagination plays these concertos with characteristic nobility of feeling, and he and Dorati make much of the Hungarian dance rhythms. There is a comparably earthy, peasant manner in Menuhin's playing of the two *Rhapsodies,* and it is matched by Boulez's approach, warm and passionate rather than clinical. The

soloist is rather close. However, the balance responds to the controls, and this remains one of Menuhin's most worthwhile reissues.

Violin Concertos Nos. (i) *1;* (ii) *2.*

(M) *** Sony (ADD) SMK 64502. Stern, (i) Phd. O, Ormandy; (ii) NYPO, Bernstein.

(M) *** Decca Dig./ADD 425 015-2. Chung, Chicago SO or LPO, Solti.

(BB) *** Naxos 8.554321. Pauk, Nat. Polish RSO (Katowice), Wit.

*** Nim. NI 5333. Hetzel, Hungarian State SO, Fischer.

Stern brings to the mature masterpiece an enviable combination of tautness and lyricism, steely strength and melting beauty of tone; Bernstein is evidently in complete sympathy with both the music and the soloist, and the overall impression is of an understanding between these two inspirational artists. The 1961 recording brings a balance which favours the soloist in a manner typical of CBS, but otherwise it sounds well in its successfully remastered format.

Though on Decca the soloist is again rather forwardly balanced, the hushed intensity of the writing, as well as bitingly Hungarian flavours, is caught superbly, thanks to the conductor as well as to the soloist, and there is no sentimental lingering.

György Pauk plays both concertos with exemplary musicianship and is given very good support by the Polish National Radio Orchestra at Katowice. No one investing in this coupling need feel disappointed, and the sound has great warmth and naturalness. Though not a first choice, this offers value for money and gives musical satisfaction.

Gerhart Hetzel plays both concertos with great feeling and understanding. These are performances of strong but unintrusive personality. Both concertos are very well recorded, with a natural, excellent balance which helps the soloist to just the right extent, and it must rank among the very best now available.

Violin Concerto No. 2 in B min.

(M) *** EMI (ADD) CDM5 66060-2. Perlman, LSO, Previn – CONUS: *Violin Concerto;* SINDING: *Suite.* ***

** Ph. 456 542-2. Mullova, LAPO, Salonen – STRAVINSKY: *Violin Concerto.* ***

Violin Concerto No. 2; 2 Rhapsodies for Violin & Orchestra.

*** DG 459 639-2. Shaham, Chicago SO, Boulez.

(i) *Violin Concerto No. 2; Second Suite for Orchestra* (revised, 1943 version).

(M) **(*) Mercury (IMS) (ADD) 434 350-2. (i) Menuhin; Minneapolis SO, Dorati.

Shaham's reading of the *Second Violin Concerto* is full of flair and imagination, taut and intense, while Boulez draws superb playing from the Chicago orchestra. The hushed intensity of Shaham's playing in the slow movement has rarely been matched. The two *Rhapsodies* make an ideal coupling. Full-bodied, well-detailed sound.

Perlman's is a superb performance, totally committed and full of youthful urgency and spontaneity. The 1973 recording is full and gains much from the Kingsway Hall acoustics, though Perlman is balanced characteristically forward. However, as we go to press the set has been withdrawn.

Menuhin's third version of the *Second Violin Concerto* (1957) is much better recorded than either of his earlier records and remains thoroughly worthwhile, with the solo playing demonstrating those special qualities of lyrical feeling and warmth for which he was justly famous. The rare coupling makes this Mercury reissue doubly attractive. The *Second Orchestral Suite* is a colourful, half-hour-long piece in four movements. Dorati is a persuasive advocate, and the characteristically graphic Mercury recording has no lack of primary colours.

Viktoria Mullova gives a brilliant enough account of Bartók's marvellous *Concerto*. But there is all too little of the warmth or humanity that others from Menuhin onwards have found in this powerful score.

Dance Suite; Divertimento; Hungarian Sketches; 2 Pictures.

**(*) DG (IMS) 445 825-2. Chicago SO, Boulez.

Pierre Boulez and the Chicago orchestra are here rather smoother and less sharply focused than usual. So the *Dance Suite* has its Hungarian flavours muted and in the *Divertimento* the contrasts between solos and tutti are underplayed, though the slow movement and the slower movements among the *Two Pictures* and the five *Hungarian Sketches* are done most poetically.

(i) Dance Suite; (ii) Music for Strings, Percussion & Celesta; (i) The Wooden Prince (complete), Op. 13.

(M) **(*) Sony (ADD) SM2K 64100 (2). (i) NYPO; (ii) BBC SO; Boulez – SCRIABIN: *Poème de l'exstase*. ***

In *The Wooden Prince* Boulez is the most compelling of advocates, maintaining his concentration throughout; the *Dance Suite* brings a performance just as warm, but a degree less precise. The 1975 analogue recording was originally among CBS's best. The *Music for Strings, Percussion and Celesta* suffers from the artificial balance sometimes favoured by CBS. However, for those who can overlook this, there are genuine rewards in this magnetic music-making, and the Scriabin coupling is quite superb.

Divertimento for Strings.

⚫ *** Chan. 9816. Norwegian CO, Brown – JANACEK: *Idyll*, etc. *** ⚫

*** MDG 321 0180-2. Polish CO, Maksymiuk – BRITTEN: *Variations on a Theme of Frank Bridge*. ***

(N) ** Ph. 462 594-2. Saito Kinen O, Ozawa – DVORAK: *Serenade for Strings* **; WOLF: *Italian Serenade*. ***

Iona Brown gives an arrestingly vibrant account of a piece that can sound dour but here is life-enhancing. The concentration is matched with playing of virtuosity and warmth, and demonstration-standard sound of great presence.

The Polish version under Jerzy Maksymiuk is also among the best. The playing is never less than distinguished and the recording very fine indeed.

With the allegro animated and well-pointed, the opening movement reveals the Saito Kinen Orchestra at their finest.

However, the slow movement, too square, lacks the hushed dedication required, though the jollity and vigour of the finale are infectious. The Wolf is superbly done, though sadly the Dvořák, sluggish in the first movement, lets the whole disc down. Good, undistracting sound.

(i) Divertimento for Strings; (ii) Music for Strings, Percussion & Celesta; (iii) Sonata for 2 Pianos & Percussion.

**(*) Oxford OOCD-CD2 (1/2) (2). (i–ii) Oxford O da Camera, Sacher; (ii–iii) Fry, Holland; (iii) Berman, Lemin.

In September 1995, within months of his own ninetieth birthday, the commissionee, Paul Sacher, recorded these live performances with the Oxford Orchestra da Camera, and he here introduces each with his own unique commentary in English. At speeds generally broader than usual, these unique performances may lack the vitality and bite of the finest rivals, but they have a compelling warmth and concentration. The two discs may be obtained from the orchestra direct (2 Axtell Close, Kidlington, Oxford).

Hungarian Pictures.

(N) (M) *** Chan. 6625 [id.]. Philh. O, Järvi – ENESCU: *Roumanian Rhapsodies 1–2*; WEINER: *Hungarian Folkdance Suite*. ***

The *Hungarian Pictures*, drawn from various folk-based pieces and originally written for piano, are lightweight Bartók and vividly entertaining. They are superbly played here and given spectacular sound. They are aptly coupled, not only with Enescu's pair of *Roumanian Rhapsodies* but also with an equally engaging suite by Leó Weiner.

Hungarian Sketches; Rumanian Folk Dances.

(M) *** Mercury (ADD) 432 005-2. Minneapolis SO, Dorati – KODALY: *Dances*, etc. ***

Dorati, himself a Hungarian, provided the pioneer stereo recording of these works, yet the 1956 sound is vivid and full and wears its years very lightly. The Minneapolis orchestra, on top form, provides plenty of ethnic feeling and colour.

The Miraculous Mandarin (complete ballet), Op. 19.

(*) Delos DE 3083. Seattle SO, Schwarz – KODALY: *Háry János*, etc. *

(i) The Miraculous Mandarin (complete ballet); Divertimento for String Orchestra; (ii) Sonata for 2 Pianos & Percussion.

(M) *** Mercury (ADD) 434 362-2. (i) BBC SO (with BBC chorus); (ii) Frid and Pons, LSO members; Dorati.

(i) The Miraculous Mandarin (complete); Hungarian Peasant Songs; Hungarian Sketches; Romanian Folk Dances; Transylvanian Dances.

*** Ph. 454 430-2. (i) Hung. R. Ch.; Budapest Festival O, Fischer.

(i) The Miraculous Mandarin (complete ballet); (ii) Hungarian Pictures; (i) Music for Strings, Percussion & Celesta; (iii) Rhapsody for Piano & Orchestra; (ii) Suite No. 1, Op. 3; 2 Pictures, Op. 10.

(B) **(*) Double Decca (ADD) 448 276-2 (2). (i) Detroit SO, Dorati; (ii) Israel PO, Mehta; (iii) Rogé, LSO, Weller.

The Miraculous Mandarin (complete); *Music for Strings, Percussion & Celesta.*

** DG 447 747-2. Chicago SO, Boulez.

(i) *The Miraculous Mandarin* (complete); (ii) *2 Portraits, Op. 5.*

(M) *** DG (IMS) 445 501-2. LSO, Abbado; (i) with Amb. S.; (ii) Minz – JANACEK: *Sinfonietta.* ***

(i) *The Miraculous Mandarin* (complete). *4 Orchestral Pieces, Op. 12;* (ii) *3 Village Scenes.*

(M) *** Sony (ADD) SMK 45837. (i) Schola Cantorum; (ii) Camerata Singers; NYPO, Boulez.

Iván Fischer's account of *The Miraculous Mandarin* is possibly the best ever committed to disc, and certainly the best recorded. The sound is in the demonstration category, with enormous range and depth. It has vivid presence and impact, and the balance is both truthful and refined. The performance has collected golden opinions almost everywhere (it was voted *Gramophone* magazine's 1998 orchestral award) for the performance has virtuosity, bite and real flair.

The Miraculous Mandarin was always one of Dorati's favourite concert pieces. The performance is as brilliant as anyone could want and the coupled *Divertimento*, apart from a perhaps too steady account of the finale, is interpreted with similar red-blooded Hungarian passion. The 1964 Mercury recording sounds marvellously full and vivid, not in the least dated. The coupled account of the *Sonata for Two Pianos and Percussion* is comparably red-blooded, and certainly spontaneous, if not as subtle in the central movement as some recordings; but the boisterous finale has wit as well as bravura.

Abbado directs a fiercely powerful performance of Bartók's barbarically furious ballet (including the wordless chorus in the finale) but one which, thanks to the refinement of the recording, makes the aggressiveness of the writing more acceptable while losing nothing in power. The Janáček coupling is highly appropriate and equally successful; before that, however, the ear is sweetened by Minz's warmth in the *Portraits.*

On Sony, Boulez also proves a strong and sympathetic advocate in all this music, and his approach is surprisingly warm. This is even more striking in *The Miraculous Mandarin.* The New York orchestra responds with deeply expressive playing and, with spacious recording, many will prefer it on that account.

The two major works on the Double Decca, the complete *Miraculous Mandarin* ballet and the *Music for Strings and Percussion*, are recorded digitally, and the range and brilliance of the sound are spectacular. This makes up for any lessening of tension in the actual performances compared with Dorati's previous recordings of both works for Mercury. Mehta gives a fine performance of the five *Hungarian Pictures.* They have great charm, and the glowing orchestral colours are well realized here. The Israel Philharmonic, recorded in Kingsway Hall, sounds far finer than when it faces the microphones on home ground. Pascal Rogé shows genuine feeling for the keyboard colour of Bartók's *Rhap-*

sody: in his hands the music is far from abrasive, with an atmospheric recording to match. The rest of the programme is in the hands of Antal Dorati. In the *Suite No. 1*, Dorati's approach is strong and vigorous to match the music's character, as it is in the much more advanced *Pictures* of 1910.

Gerard Schwarz directs the Seattle orchestra in a powerfully atmospheric account of Bartók's malignant ballet-score, not as idiomatically aggressive as some, but with plenty of grip and excitement at the climax. Aptly and generously coupled with Kodály, this too can be recommended strongly.

In his later, DG recording, Boulez takes a characteristically objective view of both works. The playing is brilliant and the recording full and detailed; but with Boulez it is a musical tapestry and not much more. His objectivity works better in the *Music for Strings, Percussion and Celesta*, which begins with the most refined pianissimo.

The Miraculous Mandarin (ballet suite).

(M) *** RCA 09026 63315-2 [id]. Chicago SO, Martinon – HINDEMITH: *Nobilissima visione*; VARESE: *Arcana.* ***

Martinon's *Miraculous Mandarin* suite is brilliantly played, with this conductor's natural elegance giving the quieter passages of the score a chilling beauty which is often quite haunting, and the recording, though it could be richer, certainly sounds better than it did on LP.

Music for Strings, Percussion & Celesta.

(N) (M) **(*) DG (ADD) 463 640-2. BPO, Karajan (with STRAVINSKY: *Agon* ***).

In DG's latest transfer Karajan's recording (also available coupled with the *Concerto for Orchestra* – see above) offers very beautiful sound, with playing to match. There may not be enough abrasiveness for Bartók, but detail is admirably clear and the overall effect is undoubtedly seductive, as is the equally marvellously played Stravinsky coupling.

Two Pictures, Op. 10.

*** Sony SK 58949. La Scala, Milan, PO, Muti – STRAVINSKY: *Le Baiser de la fée.* ***

A puzzling coupling, but Muti gets an orchestral response that stands up well to the competition from native Hungarians.

Rhapsodies for Violin & Orchestra: Nos. 1 in G min.; 2 in D min.

(B) *** [EMI Red Line CDR5 69806]. Chung, CBSO, Rattle – DVORAK: *Violin Concerto.* ***

(M) ** Sony (ADD) SMK 64503. Stern, NYPO, Bernstein – PROKOVIEV: *Violin Concertos.* **(*)

Kyung Wha Chung gives commanding, inspired performances, full of fire and imagination.

Stern and Bernstein seem less happy with the *Rhapsodies* than with the mature *Concerto.* The first is played well enough; however, neither Stern nor Bernstein seems comfortable in the second, and the constant rhythmic thrusting becomes monotonous.

The Wooden Prince, Op. 13 (complete ballet); *Hungarian Pictures.*

*** Chan. 8895. Philh. O, Järvi.

The Wooden Prince (complete); *Music for Strings, Percussion & Celesta.*

(M) **(*) Mercury (ADD). LSO, Dorati.

The Wooden Prince (complete); (i) *Cantata profana.*

*** DG 435 863-2. Chicago SO Ch. & SO, Boulez; (i) with Aler, Tomlinson.

Since he recorded *The Wooden Prince* earlier with the New York Philharmonic (for CBS/Sony), Boulez's view has grown noticeably more expansive and a degree warmer, though at times the DG recording puts an edge on the sound to the point of abrasiveness. The enigmatic *Cantata profana* of 1930 is superbly done, with the Chicago Symphony Chorus responding in total confidence to the challenge of the thorny choral writing, and with John Aler incisive in the taxing tenor role.

Järvi's red-blooded performance relates the work to romantic sources. The drama of the fairy story is told in glowing colours. The opulent playing of the Philharmonia is greatly enhanced by the full, vivid Chandos recording. The suite, *Hungarian Pictures*, provides a colourful if trivial makeweight.

Dorati's performances of both works are brilliantly authentic. *The Wooden Prince* is given a fresh, dynamic reading, vivid in its detail, with the reminders of Stravinsky and the Debussian textures brilliantly caught. The *Music for Strings, Percussion and Celesta* is comparably atmospheric, the playing full of tension, and Dorati brings out the Hungarian dance inflexions in the finale. The recordings, from 1964 and 1960 respectively, hardly sound their age.

CHAMBER AND INSTRUMENTAL MUSIC

Contrasts for Clarinet, Violin & Piano.

*** EMI CDC5 56816-2. Collins, Juillet, Argerich – LISZT: *Concerto pathétique;* PROKOVIEV: *Quintet.* ***

*** Delos D/CD 3043. Shifrin, Bae, Lash – MESSIAEN: *Quatuor.* ***

(i) *Contrasts. Mikrokosmos: excerpts.*

(M) (***) Sony mono MPK 47676. Composer, (i) with Szigeti, Goodman.

(i; ii) *Contrasts;* (ii) *2 Rhapsodies; Rumanian Folk Dances.* (Solo) *Violin Sonata.*

*** Hyp. CDA 66415. Osostowicz, with (i) Collins; (ii) Tomes.

(i) *Contrasts. Violin Sonatas Nos. 1–2.*

(B) *** Naxos 8.550749. Pauk, Jandó, (i) with Berkes.

Contrasts was commissioned by Benny Goodman. In 1940 Bartók added a further movement, and it was in this form that the three artists on Sony made their recording. That same year Bartók recorded 31 pieces from *Mikrokosmos*, and these performances are indicative of the wide range and delicacy of keyboard colour that Bartók commanded. The

sound is surprisingly good, given that it is over half a century old! An indispensable issue.

Like the companion pieces on the EMI CD, this performance of *Contrasts* comes from live concerts at the Saratoga Arts in 1998. There have been many good versions since Szigeti, Benny Goodman and Bartók himself committed it to disc, but this must be a first choice among them.

David Shifrin and his colleagues from Chamber Music Northwest admirably capture the diverse moods of Bartók's triptych, including the mordant wit and vitality of the outer sections and the dark colouring of the centrepiece. They are very well recorded in an agreeable acoustic.

Hyperion's coupling of the Bartók *Contrasts, Rhapsodies* and the *Sonata for Solo Violin* is a distinguished and well-recorded issue which finds all these artists on excellent form. Krysia Osostowicz is as good as almost any of her rivals in the *Sonata for Solo Violin*, and the remainder of the programme is hardly less impressive.

The Naxos collection is very highly recommendable too, particularly when these works are played by such experienced artists as György Pauk and his fellow Hungarian, Jenö Jandó. The refinement and subtlety of Pauk's playing here is very persuasive. In the superb account of *Contrasts*, in which Kálmán Berkes joins them, the balance is better than in the *Sonatas*. Outstanding value.

(i) *44 Duos. Solo Violin Sonata.*

(B) *** Naxos 8.550868. Pauk, (i) with Sawa.

György Pauk's impressive recording of the remarkable *Solo Sonata* of 1944 is commanding, and everywhere his pacing seems just right and his playing effortless. In the *44 Duos* Pauk, partnered by the Japanese violinist, Kazuki Sawa, offers expertly judged and splendidly characterful accounts of these pieces. The Naxos recording is very good indeed and enhances the attractions of this super-bargain issue.

Piano Quintet.

(B) **(*) ASV CDQS 6217. Bradbury, Silvestri String Qt – SCHUMANN: *Piano Quintet.* **(*)

(i–ii) *Piano Quintet;* (i; iii) *Andante* (for violin and piano); *Rhapsodies Nos. 1 & 2.*

(B) *** Naxos 8.550886-2. (i) Jandó; (ii) Kodály Qt; (iii) Pauk.

The *Piano Quintet* dates from 1903–4. A substantial work, it is wholly uncharacteristic. The *Andante* for violin and piano comes from 1902 and is slight but charming. The two *Rhapsodies* come from 1928 and are popular in style. Very good playing from György Pauk and alert playing from Jandó, whose humming is at times faintly audible. No quarrels with either recording or performances.

On ASV Quicksilva, the artists make a good case for this eclectic and predominantly romantic score. The performances and recording are both recommendable – though not perhaps in preference to the Naxos coupling.

Rhapsody No. 1; Rumanian Folk Dances.

**(*) Decca 455 488-2 (2). Haendel, Ashkenazy (with Recital: 'The Decca Years, 1940–1947' (***)) – ENESCU: *Violin Sonata No. 3;* SZYMANOWSKI: *Mythes.* **(*)

This is playing of the old, humane school, these artists neither afraid to phrase generously nor fearful of sounding old-fashioned. The coupled earlier performances are of much interest and include a rare partnership with Noel Mewton Wood in the Beethoven *G major Sonata*, plus some of the records Haendel made for Decca during and just after the war, expertly restored in these transfers.

Roumanian Folk Dances (arr. Székely).

(N) *** Erato 8573-85769-2. Repin, Berezovsky – STRAUSS: *Violin Sonata*; STRAVINSKY: *Divertimento*. ***

Repin and Berezovksy give an exemplary account of these Székely transcriptions as a makeweight in their outstanding Strauss–Stravinsky recital. There is nothing flashy about this impeccable and relaxed music-making.

Sonata for 2 Pianos & Percussion.

*** Sony MK 42625. Perahia, Solti, Corkhill, Glennie – BRAHMS: *Variations on a Theme by Haydn*. ***
*** Chan. 9398. Safri Duo & Slovak Piano Duo – LUTOSLAWKI: *Paganini Variations* ***; HELWEG: *American Fantasy*. **

On Sony an unexpected and highly creative partnership produces a vivid and strongly characterized performance. The recording is vivid to match, giving the players great presence.

The Slovak Piano Duo and the Safri Duo, two Danish percussion players, are all dazzlingly alive and vital. All the same, their CD labours under a handicap: it is not good value at full price, lasting about 50 minutes.

String Quartets Nos. 1–6.

*** Decca 455 297-2 (2). Takács Qt.
(N) *** DG 463 576-2 (2). Hagen Qt.
(B) *** Erato Ultima 3984 25594-2 (2). Keller Qt.
*** DG 423 657-2 (2). Emerson Qt.
(B) **(*) Ph. (ADD) Duo 442 284-2 (2). Novák Qt.
(M) **(*) Audivis V 4809 (3). Végh Qt.
**(*) EMI CDS7 47720-8 (3). Alban Berg Qt.
(**(*)) ASV CDDCS 301 (3). Lindsay Qt.

It is difficult to go far wrong among the available recordings of the Bartók *Quartets*. The Takács Quartet bring to these masterpieces the requisite virtuosity, tonal sophistication and command of idiom. These are full-blooded accounts of enormous conviction, with that open-air quality which suggests the fragrance of the forests and lakes of Hungary. The recording is excellent, and this Decca set now takes its place at the top of the list.

The Hagen Quartet have all the requisite fire and virtuosity for these marvellous scores. Apart from their immaculate technical address they bring individual interpretative insights to bear as well. One or two expressive emphases in the *Third Quartet* may disturb some listeners but on the whole theirs is a set with strong claims to commend it – among which is the vivid recording. Not necessarily a first recommendation but certainly among the finest in the catalogue.

The Keller Quartet are another Hungarian group who made their recordings in the Salle de Musique de la Chaux-de-Fonds, where the Végh recorded their second cycle. The performances are totally idiomatic, intense yet natural; at their new and highly competitive price they are among the best you can find.

The Emerson Quartet project very powerfully and, in terms of virtuosity, finesse and accuracy, outstrip most of their rivals. If at times their projection and expressive vehemence are a bit too much of a good thing, these are concentrated and brilliant performances that are very well recorded.

The Novák Quartet, a fine Czech group, bring plenty of grip to their performances and there is certainly no lack of fire and expressive intensity. If not as polished as the Tokyo versions, they have the advantage of being complete on a pair of Duo CDs. So there is no question of their bargain status, as the recording is firm and well balanced.

The analogue Végh recordings date from 1972, but the CD transfers are managed splendidly and there is bite without edginess on top. The Végh players sometimes respond with more expressive warmth than some would expect to be applied to Bartók, but which prevents the music from becoming too aggressive and, above all, they produce an effect of seeming spontaneity. But this mid-priced set involves three discs.

The Alban Berg Quartet's are very impressive performances indeed, technically almost in a class of their own. They are very well recorded too, but at times they appear to treat this music as a vehicle for their own supreme virtuosity.

The Lindsay performances, searching, powerful and expressive, are now reissued together. The digital recording, though first class, occupies three discs which, like the Alban Berg set, places it at a distinct disadvantage to the DG Emerson version.

The DG set by the Hungarian Quartet has considerable authority: the Hungarians were the first to record Nos. 5 and 6, and their leader gave the première of the *Violin Concerto*. But they do not quite convey the full intensity that distinguishes the best rival versions and this seems a curious choice for DG's Legendary 'Originals' (457 740-2).

String Quartet No. 4.

(N) **(*) ECM 465 776-2. Zehetmeir Qt – HARTMANN: *String Quartet No. 1*. **(*)

No quarrels with the Zehetmeir's performance of the *Fourth Quartet* (1928), although collectors will probably be more attracted by one of the complete Bartók cycles. The Hartmann coupling, which was written five years later, is an interesting piece and is otherwise not available. However, the disc runs to only 43 minutes which, at full price, is poor value for money. Three stars for artistic merit, none for economy.

Violin Sonata No. 1; Sonatina (trans. André Gertler); Rhapsody No. 2 for Violin & Piano; Hungarian Folksongs (trans. Tivadar Országh); Hungarian Folk-Tunes (trans. Jozsef Szigeti).

*** ASV CDDCA 883. Stanzeleit, Fenyö.

(Solo) Violin Sonata; Violin Sonata No. 2; Rhapsody No. 1; Rumanian Folk Dances.

*** ASV CDDCA 852. Stanzeleit, Fenyö.

Susanne Stanzeleit and her partner, Gusztáv Fenyö, are completely inside the idiom. The *Violin Sonata No. 1* and the *Rhapsody No. 2* are every bit as well played and recorded as the *Solo Sonata* and the *Second Sonata* for violin and piano (1922), and the performances are as good as any you can find in the current catalogue. The recording, too, is altogether first rate.

PIANO MUSIC

Allegro barbaro; 6 Dances in Bulgarian Rhythm; 3 Hungarian Folksongs; 15 Hungarian Peasant Songs; Mikrokosmos (excerpts); 3 Rondos on Slovak Folk Tunes; Sonatina.

(B) **(*) Naxos 8.550451-2. Szokolay.

Balázs Szokolay is a highly musical player. His performances are always vitally intelligent and perceptive, and he is acceptably recorded. This is a thoroughly recommendable recital and excellent value, though Szokolay is by no means as well recorded as Kocsis on Philips, nor does he quite have the latter's subtlety or distinction.

Allegro barbaro; 4 Dirges, Op. 9a; First Term at the Piano; 3 Hungarian Folksongs from Csík; Romanian Christmas Carols; 2 Romanian Dances, Op. 8a; 3 Rondos on Folk Tunes; 3 Studies, Op. 18; Suite, Op. 14.

*** Ph. 442 016-2. Kocsis.

14 Bagatelles, Op. 6; 2 Elegies, Op. 8b; 3 Hungarian Folk Tunes; 6 Rumanian Folk Tunes; Sonatina.

✿ *** Ph. 434 104-2. Kocsis.

3 Burlesques, Op. 8c; 7 Esquisses, Op. 9b; 10 Easy Pieces; 15 Hungarian Peasant Dances; Improvisations on Hungarian Peasant Songs, Op. 20.

✿ *** Ph. Dig./ADD 462 902-2. Kocsis.

Dance Suite; Kossuth: Marche Funèbre; 4 Pieces; Rhapsody, Op. 1 (long and short versions).

(N) *** Ph. 464 639–2 Kocsis.

For Children, Books 1–4.

*** Ph. 442 146-2. Kocsis.

Bartók playing doesn't come any better than this – nor does piano recording. Kocsis penetrates to the very centre or soul of this music more deeply than almost any other rival. He is scrupulously attentive to Bartók's own wishes as shown not only in autographs and revised editions of the published scores but as expressed on record. Kocsis can produce power and drama when required, but he also commands a wide-ranging palette and a marvellously controlled vitality. The sound is never beautified, but it is also never aggressive; indeed his playing calls to mind Bartók's own injunction that performances must be 'beautiful but true'. This is likely to be the classic set for a long time to come, and the recorded sound is altogether natural and realistic.

14 Bagatelles; 3 Hungarian Folk Songs; Out of Doors; 2 Romanian Dances, Op. 8a; Romanian Christmas Carols; Sonatina; Sonata.

(N)(M) *** Ph. 464 676-2. Kocsis.

This representative collection, chosen as one of Philips's '50 Great Recordings', comes from the Kocsis complete survey, and as it includes the *Sonata* and *Sonatina* and is superbly recorded, it can be highly recommended to those not willing or able to purchase the premium-priced set.

For Children (Books 1–4) complete; *Mikrokosmos (Books 1–6)* complete.

(M) *** Teldec (ADD) 9031 76139-2 (3). Ránki.

Dezsö Ránki here shows his musicianship and plays all 85 pieces with the utmost persuasion and with the art that conceals art, for the simplicity of some of these pieces is deceptive; darker currents lurk beneath their surface. He gives us the composer's original edition of 1908–9. Ránki also plays the *Mikrokosmos* with an effortless eloquence and a welcome straightforwardness. He is very clearly if forwardly recorded, and he is given a realistic presence.

Mikrokosmos (complete).

**(*) Ph. 462 381-2 (2). Kocsis (with Mocsári in Nos. 43–44, 55, 68, 74 & 95; Lukin in Nos. 65, 74, 95, 127).

(B) **(*) HM (ADD) HMA 190968/9. Helffer (with Austbö).

Bartók originally intended the piano pieces he began composing in 1926 as a pedagogic exercise with his young son, Péter, in mind and that is exactly the way Kocsis plays the first third of the 153 pieces. Most music-lovers will undoubtedly concentrate on the second half of the work, where the playing really begins to grip the ear, with greater colour and more flexibility of line to bring these brief pieces fully to life. Martá Lukin seems an admirable choice for the four vocal settings, and Karoly Mocsári takes the second part in the pieces for piano duo. The recording is excellent.

Claude Helffer also gives an intelligent account of all six books, but his approach at times goes to the other extreme, as he tends to invest detail with rather more expressive emphasis than this most simple of music can bear. However, Harmonia Mundi's cueing is ungenerous (there are only 12 bands to cover the whole series!). If you don't mind that, this is good value in the bargain range.

VOCAL MUSIC

Cantata profana.

*** Decca 458 929-2. Daróczy, Agache, Hungarian R. and TV Ch. and Children's Ch., Schola Cantorum Budapestiensis, Budapest Festival O, Solti — KODALY: *Psalmus Hungaricus*; WEINER: *Serenade.* ***

Solti's very last recording sessions in Budapest in June 1997 resulted in inspired performances. This reading of the *Cantata profana* is both warm and idiomatic, marred only by the unsteadiness of the tenor soloist. Solti came finally to regard the cantata as symbolic of his own life, with the allegory of the stag returning home reflecting his own return to Hungary after almost sixty years of exile.

OPERA

Bluebeard's Castle (sung in Hungarian).

*** EMI CDC5 65162-2. Tomlinson, Von Otter, Elès (nar.), BPO, Haitink.

*** DG 447 040-2. Norman, Polgár, Chicago SO, Boulez.

(M) *** Decca (ADD) 466 377-2. Berry, Ludwig, LSO, Kertész.

(M) *** Sony (ADD) SMK 64110. Nimsgern, Troyanos, BBC SO, Boulez.

(**(*)) Bluebell mono ABCD 075. Nilsson, Sönnerstedt, Swedish R. O, Fricsay – SCHIERBECK: *The Chinese Flute.* (**(*))

(i) *Duke Bluebeard's Castle;* (ii) *Cantata profana.*

(M) *** DG (ADD) stereo/mono 457 756-2. (i) Töpper; (i–ii) Fischer-Dieskau; (ii) Krebs, Berlin RIAS Ch., St Hedwig's Cathedral Ch.; (i–ii) Berlin RSO, Fricsay.

Never before has Bartók's darkly intense one-Acter been given such a beautiful performance on disc, intense and concentrated, as by Bernard Haitink in EMI's live recording of a concert performance with the Berlin Philharmonic. Anne-Sofie von Otter conveys new tenderness in Judith, with John Tomlinson magisterially Wagnerian as the implacable Bluebeard, both singing superbly, naturally balanced, not spotlit. Most impressive of all, Haitink builds the performance to a terrifying climax, when Judith is consigned to darkness with her predecessors.

Boulez, in his tautly intense DG version, opts for marginally faster speeds than he did in his earlier, Sony recording, with voices close to add to the involvement. László Polgár is superb as Bluebeard – firm, dark and incisive as well as idiomatic. Jessye Norman is a magisterial Judith. She may not be a believable victim, but this is still a glorious performance, matching the beauty of the Chicago orchestra's playing, weighty and rich on detail.

In 1965 Kertész set new standards with his version of *Bluebeard's Castle* with Christa Ludwig and Walter Berry. There is still a strong case for preferring the reading conducted by a Hungarian – especially as the Decca sound reaches demonstration standard in its remastering for Decca's Legends series – but on performance Haitink's later, EMI CD has the balance of advantage.

On Sony, Boulez revealed himself as an impressively warm Bartókian; the soloists are vibrantly committed and the recording is outstandingly vivid, presenting the singers in a slightly contrasted acoustic as though on a separate stage. At the time Boulez had rarely if ever made a finer Bartók record, but his newer DG version is even finer. A full libretto is provided.

Fricsay pioneered *Bluebeard's Castle* in stereo and his 1958 recording rightly won a *Grand Prix du Disque*. The snag is that the performance was tactfully cut so that it could fit on to a 12-inch LP. But it certainly stands the test of time. Fischer-Dieskau is a memorable Bluebeard, even if the tone-quality of the voice is perhaps too heroic, not quite sinister enough. Herta Töpper never made a better record than this: she is a superb Judith, even if not always perfectly steady. However, the vivid remastering emphasizes the close balance of the soloists, which is less than ideal. But despite this fault

and despite the cuts, this remains a fine achievement. For the reissue DG have coupled Fricsay's arresting, indeed inspired, account of the remarkably original *Cantata profana*, recorded seven years earlier, with passionate contributions from both Helmut Krebs and the splendidly incisive chorus. Both recordings were made in the Jesus-Christus Kirche. A worthy candidate for DG's series of Legendary Originals. Full translations are included.

Bluebell offer a CD taken from a Swedish Radio broadcast from 1953 with Nilsson and Bernhard Sönnerstedt, a wonderful baritone who never sought an international career. Fricsay casts a powerful spell and gets wonderfully eloquent results. There are some cuts which would rule it out of court were it not for the powerfully distilled and extraordinary atmosphere Fricsay evokes, and the superlative quality of both soloists.

BAX, Arnold (1883–1953)

Cathaleen-ni-Hoolihan; (i) *Concertante for 3 Wind Instruments & Orch.; London Pageant; Tamara Suite* (orch. Parlett).

(N) *** Chan. 9879. BBC PO, Brabbins; (i) Callow, Bradbury, Goodall.

According to the useful notes, the tone-poem *Cathaleen-ni-Hoolihan* began life in 1903 in Bax's student years as the slow movement of a quartet. The score of *Tamara* was inspired by Karsavina, Diaghilev's prima ballerina for whom Bax fell when the Ballet Russes came to London in 1911. He never finished the orchestration and the present 23-minute suite was compiled by the Bax scholar Graham Parlett. (Bax returned to one of its ideas for the incidental music he wrote nine years later for *The Truth about the Russian Dancers*.) *London Pageant* comes from the Coronation year 1937, which also brought the more successful *Crown Imperial* of Walton. The *Concertante for Cor Anglais, Clarinet, Bassoon and Orchestra* finds Bax at the very end of his creative life in being composed for the Henry Wood memorial concert in 1949. Not top-drawer Bax but the *Pastoral* is delightful and in any event second-best Bax is better than many other composers firing on all cylinders. The performances are first class, persuasive in every way, and so, too, is the richly sonorous recording.

(i) *Christmas Eve; Dance of Wild Irravel; Festival Overture; Nympholept; Paean;* (ii) *Tintagel.*

**(*) Chan. 9168. (i) LPO; (ii) Ulster O; Thomson.

These shorter works were originally used as fillers for the separate issues of the symphonies, and it might have been more generous of Chandos to reissue them at mid-price. Apart from *Tintagel, Nympholept* is probably the most interesting piece. The *Paean* and the *Dance of Wild Irravel* may strain the allegiance of some. Performances and recordings give absolutely no cause for complaint.

(i) *Concertante for Piano (Left Hand) & Orchestra. In memoriam;* (ii) *The Bard of the Dimbovitza.*

*** Chan. 9715. BBC PO, Handley with (i) Fingerhut; (ii) Rigby.

In memoriam is vintage Bax and its main theme was re-used in his score for David Lean's *Oliver Twist*. The *Concertante for Piano (Left Hand)* was written in 1949 for Harriet Cohen, who had injured her right hand the previous year, but after its première under Barbirolli and a Prom performance some weeks later, it languished unheard. Margaret Fingerhut is a most persuasive advocate, and that no doubt helps the positive impression it makes here. *The Bard of the Dimbovitza* offers settings of Romanian peasant songs. Exemplary performances from the BBC Philharmonic under Vernon Handley and state-of-the-art recording.

(i) *Cello Concerto. Cortège; Mediterranean; Northern Ballad No. 3; Overture to a Picaresque Comedy.*

*** Chan. 8494. (i) Wallfisch; LPO, Thomson.

The *Cello Concerto* is rhapsodic in feeling and Raphael Wallfisch plays it with marvellous sensitivity and finesse, given splendid support by the LPO under Bryden Thomson. The other pieces are of mixed quality: in the *Overture to a Picaresque Comedy* Bryden Thomson sets rather too measured a pace for it to sparkle as it should. The recording maintains the high standards of the Bax Chandos series.

(i) *Violin Concerto. Golden Eagle* (incidental music): *Suite; A Legend; Romantic Overture.*

*** Chan. 9003. (i) Mordkovitch; LPO, Thomson.

The *Violin Concerto* is full of good, easily remembered tunes, yet there is a plangent, bitter-sweet quality about many of its ideas and an easy-going Mediterranean-like warmth that is very appealing. Lydia Mordkovitch plays it with commitment and conviction. The *Romantic Overture* is for chamber orchestra and has a prominent role for the piano. All this music is new to the catalogue, and the concerto deserves to be popular.

(i) *Violin Concerto;* (ii) *Symphony No. 3.*

(N) (BB) (***) Dutton mono CDLX 7111. (i) Kersey, BBCSO, Boult; (ii) Hallé O, Barbirolli

Barbirolli's wartime recording of Bax's *Third Symphony*, made in the winter of 1943–4 when he was rebuilding the Hallé orchestra, has never been surpassed as an interpretation, the first ever recording of a Bax symphony and still one of the finest. EMI did an early CD transfer, but this Dutton version brings astonishingly full and vivid sound, heightening the power of the performance. It is good too to have another powerful performance in the *Violin Concerto*, a work very different in mood from that of the symphonies. Eda Kersey recorded this with Boult and the BBC Orchestra in Bedford in 1944, a recording made for the BBC Archive and not for general issue. The result again is astonishingly vivid, with Eda Kersey, sadly short-lived, demonstrating her virtuoso flair and depth of feeling in a reading faster and more urgent in all three movements than the fine modern version from Lydia Mordkovitch on Chandos.

The Garden of Fand; The Happy Forest; November Woods; Summer Music.

*** Chan. 8307. Ulster O, Thomson.

The Celtic twilight in Bax's music is ripely and sympatheti-

cally caught in the first three items, while *Summer Music*, dedicated to Sir Thomas Beecham and here given its first ever recording, brings an intriguing kinship with the music of Delius. The Chandos recording is superb.

The Garden of Fand (symphonic poem); *Mediterranean; Northern Ballad No. 1; November Woods; Tintagel* (symphonic poems).

*** Lyrita (ADD) SRCD 231. LPO, Boult.

Sir Adrian Boult's recording of *The Garden of Fand* is full of poetry and almost erases memories of Beecham's magical account. *Tintagel* is no less involving and beguiling and, though not as uninhibited as Barbirolli's, is equally valid. The *Northern Ballad No. 1*, though less memorable than either *Fand* or *Tintagel*, is well worth having, as is *November Woods*, a lush, romantic score. *Mediterranean*, a Spanish picture postcard and almost a waltz, has an endearing touch of vulgarity uncharacteristic of its composer. Excellent sound.

In the Faery Hills; Into the Twilight; Rosc-Catha; The Tale the Pine-Trees Knew.

*** Chan. 8367. Ulster O, Thomson.

The Tale the Pine-Trees Knew is here done with total sympathy. The other three tone-poems form an Irish trilogy. The performances and recording are well up to the high standard of this series.

Malta G.C. (film score: complete); *Oliver Twist: Suite* (film-scores).

(M) *** ASV CDWHL 2058. RPO, Alwyn – ARNOLD: *The Sound Barrier.* ***

Both these film-scores are in the form of a series of miniatures; on the whole, *Oliver Twist* stands up more effectively without the visual imagery. Kenneth Alwyn conducts the RPO with fine flair and commitment.

On the Sea-Shore.

*** Chan. 8473. Ulster O, Handley – BRIDGE: *The Sea;* BRITTEN: *Sea Interludes.* ***

Bax's Prelude, *On the Sea-Shore*, makes a colourful and atmospheric companion to the masterly Bridge and Britten pieces on the disc, played and recorded with similar warmth and brilliance.

Spring Fire; Northern Ballad No. 2; Symphonic Scherzo.

*** Chan. 8464. RPO, Handley.

Highly idiomatic playing from Vernon Handley and the RPO, and a thoroughly lifelike and characteristically well-detailed recording from Chandos.

Symphonic Variations for Piano & Orchestra; Morning Song (Maytime in Sussex).

*** Chan. 8516. Fingerhut, LPO, Thomson.

Margaret Fingerhut reveals the *Symphonic Variations* to be a work of considerable substance with some sinewy, powerful writing in the more combative variations, thoughtful and purposeful elsewhere. This CD is in the demonstration class.

Symphonies Nos. 1–7.

(M) *** Chan. 8906/10. LPO or Ulster O, Thomson.

Chandos have repackaged the cycle of seven symphonies, and it makes better sense for those primarily interested in these richly imaginative works to pay for five rather than seven CDs. The recordings continue to make a strong impression. For those who prefer to have the symphonies separately and with their original couplings, we list full details below.

Symphony No. 1 in E flat; Christmas Eve.

*** Chan. 8480. LPO, Thomson.

Symphonies Nos. (i) 1 in E flat; (ii) 7 in A flat.

*** Lyrita (ADD) SRCD 232. LPO, (i) Fredman; (ii) Leppard.

Symphony No. 2; Nympholept.

*** Chan. 8493. LPO, Thomson.

Symphony No. 3; Paean; The Dance of Wild Irravel.

*** Chan. 8454. LPO, Thomson.

Symphony No. 4; Tintagel.

*** Chan. 8312. Ulster O, Thomson.

Symphony No. 5; Russian Suite.

*** Chan. 8669. LPO, Thomson.

Symphony No. 6; Festival Overture.

*** Chan. 8586. LPO, Thomson.

Symphony No. 7 in A flat; (i) 4 Songs: Eternity; Glamour; Lyke-Wake; Slumber Song.

*** Chan. 8628. (i) Hill; LPO, Thomson.

Bax's symphonies remain controversial and some listeners find their quality of invention and argument less intensely sustained than the composer's shorter orchestral tone-poems. Nevertheless they have a breadth of imagination which the smaller structures do not always carry. The Lyrita coupling is particularly generous (78 minutes) and the performances by Myer Fredman and Raymond Leppard respectively are powerful and finely shaped and can well hold their own with the later, Chandos digital versions. The Lyrita 1970s analogue sound, too, is vivid and clear.

The Chandos couplings have their own interest. *Christmas Eve* is an early work, coming from the Edwardian era, and it displays a less developed idiom than the symphonies. The four songs offer great contrasts of manner and style, and Martyn Hill presents them very sensitively.

Symphony No. 1; The Garden of Fand; In the Faery Hills.

(BB) *** Naxos 8.553525. RSNO, Lloyd-Jones.

This first disc in what Naxos plan to be a Bax series offers warmly idiomatic readings of two early symphonic poems, as well as the *First Symphony*, in recording less weighty than in rival versions (such as that on Chandos at full price) but finely detailed. In the two symphonic poems, more specifically inspired by Irish themes, Lloyd-Jones draws equally warm and sympathetic performances from the Scottish orchestra, bringing inner clarity to the heaviest scoring. First-rate sound, though Bryden Thomson on Chandos has even richer recording.

Symphony No. 3; The Happy Forest (symphonic poem).

(BB) *** Naxos 8.553608. RSNO, Lloyd-Jones.

David Lloyd-Jones continues his admirable Bax series with a warmly idiomatic account of the *Third Symphony* of 1929, spacious in the long first movement and the meditative slow movement, defying any diffuseness of argument. The playing of the Royal Scottish Orchestra is clear and refined, helped by the transparency of the recording, clarifying often thick textures. From earlier in Bax's career *The Happy Forest*, described as a 'nature poem', provides a refreshing contrast in its youthful energy, tauter, less expansive.

Symphony No. 5; The Tale the Pine-Trees Knew.

(N) (BB) *** Naxos 8.554509. RSNO, Lloyd-Jones.

Dedicating his fine symphony of 1932 to Sibelius, Sir Arnold Bax openly echoes the example of that Finnish master, not least in nagging ostinato rhythms. There is also a northern chill in the writing, freshly caught and cleanly recorded in this fine performance from David Lloyd-Jones and the Royal Scottish National Orchestra. Where Bax elsewhere can seem diffuse, with passages rather like improvisations written down, there is a tautness here, again reflecting the example of Sibelius. The music remains very British in flavour, with the triumphant conclusion in a brazen major key affirming that. *The Tale the Pine-Trees Knew* of 1931, another northern inspiration, makes the ideal coupling. An excellent bargain. Another fine addition to the Naxos Bax series.

The Truth about the Russian Dancers (incidental music); From Dusk till Dawn (ballet).

*** Chan. 8863. LPO, Thomson.

The Truth about the Russian Dancers is vintage Bax, full of characteristic writing decked out in attractive orchestral colours. *From Dusk till Dawn* has many evocative ideas with some impressionistic orchestral touches. Not top-drawer Bax, but often delightful, and very well played by the London Philharmonic under Bryden Thomson, and splendidly recorded.

Winter Legends; Saga Fragment.

*** Chan. 8484. Fingerhut, LPO, Thomson.

The *Winter Legends*, for piano and orchestra, comes from much the same time as the *Third Symphony*, to which at times its world seems spiritually related. The soloist proves an impressive and totally convincing advocate for the score, and it would be difficult to imagine the balance between soloist and orchestra being more realistically judged. The companion piece is a transcription of his one-movement *Piano Quartet* of 1922. A quite outstanding disc.

CHAMBER AND INSTRUMENTAL MUSIC

Cello Sonata in E flat; Cello Sonatina in D; Legend Sonata in F sharp min.; Folk Tale.

** ASV CDDCA 896. Gregor-Smith, Wrigley.

The *Cello Sonata* has many characteristic touches and an

imaginative slow movement. Bernard Gregor-Smith and Yolande Wrigley are both highly sensitive and responsive players. In the *Sonata* the recording does not give quite enough back-to-front depth and there is a touch of glassiness about the sound. Things are a bit better in the *Folk Tale* (1920), but the recording is sufficiently wanting in bloom to inhibit a three-star recommendation.

Clarinet Sonata.

(*) Chan. 8683. Hilton, Swallow – BLISS: *Clarinet Quintet;* VAUGHAN WILLIAMS: *6 Studies.* *

(i) *Clarinet Sonata;* (ii) *Elegiac Trio* (for flute, viola & harp); (iii) *Harp Quintet;* (iv) *Nonet;* (v) *Oboe Quintet.*

*** Hyp. CDA 66807. (i; iv) Collins; (i) Brown (piano); (ii; iv) Davies; (ii–v) Chase; (ii–iv) Kanga; (iii–v) Crayford, Van Kampen; (iii; v) Juda; (iv) Wexler, McTier, Brown (cond.); (iv–v) Hulse.

Bax's *Clarinet Sonata* opens most beguilingly, and Janet Hilton's phrasing is quite melting. Moreover the Bliss coupling is indispensable.

The Hyperion performances are of exemplary quality. In the chamber-music field Bax wrote with a fantasy and sensibility that are no less captivating than in *The Garden of Fand* or *Tintagel*. The members of the Nash Ensemble, including Michael Collins in the *Clarinet Sonata* and Gareth Hulse in the *Oboe Quintet*, seem totally attuned to the idiom, and they play with their usual artistry and dedication. Excellent recording.

Concerto for Flute, Oboe, Harp & String Quartet; In memoriam, for Cor Anglais, Harp & String Quartet; Threnody & Scherzo for Bassoon, Harp & String Sextet; (i) Octet for Horn, Piano & String Sextet; String Quintet.

*** Chan. 9602. (i) Fingerhut; ASMF Ch. Ens.

In memoriam is the earliest piece here (it comes from 1917 and originally bore the subtitle, 'An Irish Elegy' – an obvious allusion to the Easter uprising). The *Octet* is arguably the most appealing work in this collection. However, most of this music is captivating; the performances are absolutley first class and the recording in the best traditions of the house.

Elegiac Trio; Fantasy Sonata for Harp & Viola; Harp Quintet; Sonata for Flute & Harp.

(N) (BB) *** Naxos 8.554507. Nichols, Ito, Honoré, Pillai, Storey, McGhee.

Ideal late-night listening for a balmy summer evening: a collection of Bax chamber music centred around the harp. We have the *Quintet for Harp and Strings* played by an accomplished group called Mobius, which also performs the seductive *Elegiac Trio* for flute, viola and harp, the imaginative *Fantasy Sonata* for viola and harp and the *Sonata for Flute and Harp*. This is all beguiling music (except perhaps for the folksy finale of the *Quintet*), the neglect of which is quite puzzling. There are distinguished alternatives but none are coupled together like this or priced so competitively.

(i) Harp Quintet; (ii) Piano Quartet. String Quartet No. 1.

*** Chan. 8391. (i) Kanga; (ii) McCabe; English Qt.

The *First String Quartet* is music with a strong and immediate appeal. The *Harp Quintet* is more fully characteristic and has some evocative writing to commend it, alongside the *Piano Quartet* with its winning lyricism. These may not be Bax's most important scores, but they are rewarding, and the performances are thoroughly idiomatic and eminently well recorded.

Oboe Quintet.

*** Chan. 8392. Francis, English Qt – HOLST: *Air & Variations*, etc.; MOERAN: *Fantasy Quartet*; JACOB: *Quartet.* ***

Bax's *Oboe Quintet* is a confident, inventive piece. Sarah Francis proves a most responsive soloist, though she is balanced too close; in all other respects the recording is up to Chandos's usual high standards, and the playing of the English Quartet is admirable.

(i) Piano Quintet in G min. String Quartet No. 2.

**(*) Chan. 8795. Mistry Qt; (i) with Owen Norris.

The *Piano Quintet* is symphonic in scale. The playing of the Mistry Quartet is dedicated and David Owen Norris is the excellent and sensitive pianist. The *Second Quartet* is tauter and more powerful. The performance has plenty of feeling and the recording is excellent.

Rhapsodic Ballad (for solo cello).

*** Chan. 8499. Wallfisch – BRIDGE: *Cello Sonata;* DELIUS: *Cello Sonata;* WALTON: *Passacaglia.* ***

The *Rhapsodic Ballad* for cello alone is a freely expressive piece, played with authority and dedication by Raphael Wallfisch. The recording has plenty of warmth and range.

Viola Sonata in G.

(***) Biddulph mono LAB 148. Primrose, Cohen – BLOCH: *Suite;* HINDEMITH: *Sonata.* (***)

The legendary William Primrose made this recording of the Bax *Viola Sonata* with Harriet Cohen in the late 1930s, and it serves as a reminder of his sumptuous tone and glorious musicianship.

Violin Sonatas Nos. 1 in E; 2 in D.

*** Chan. 8845. Gruenberg, McCabe.

The *Second* is the finer of these two sonatas and is thematically linked with *November Woods*. Rhapsodic and impassioned, this is music full of temperament. Erich Gruenberg is a selfless and musicianly advocate and John McCabe makes an expert partner.

Violin Sonata No. 2 in D min.

(N) *** Global Music Network GMN CO113. Little, Roscoe – ELGAR: *Violin Sonata.* ***

As in the Elgar *Sonata*, with which it is aptly coupled, Tasmin Little gives a powerful big-scale reading of the four-movement Bax *Sonata No. 2*, relishing the virtuosity of the writing, with Martin Roscoe similarly brilliant. This is a strong, extrovert reading rather than a meditative one, but it leaves you in no doubt of the strength of this relatively early work, with the second movement a sparkling, fantastic dance and the slow movement a warmly lyrical interlude. An excellent if unusual coupling for Tasmin Little's fine version of the Elgar, very well recorded.

Violin sonatas Nos. 2 in D; 3 (1927); Sonata in F.

(N) *** ASV CDDCA 1098. Gibbs, Mei-Loc Wu.

Strictly speaking there are four sonatas; the first comes from 1910 and was inspired by Bax's experiences in Russia but the two numbered sonatas recorded here come from the 1920s. The *Second* was written during the war but revised in 1921, while the two-movement *Third* comes from 1927. The *Sonata in F* comes from the following year and Baxians will recognise it as a kind of prototype of the magical *Nonet* (1930). No Baxian will want to be without it particularly in these fluent and committed performances.

PIANO MUSIC

Apple-Blossom Time; Burlesque; The Maiden with the Daffodil; Nereid; O Dame Get Up and Bake Your Pies (Variations on a North Country Christmas Carol); On a May Evening; The Princess's Rose-garden (Nocturne); Romance; 2 Russian Tone Pictures: Nocturne (May Night in the Ukraine; Gopak); Sleepy-Head.

**(*) Chan. 8732. Parkin.

The smaller pieces are not among Bax's most important works, but in Eric Parkin's hands they certainly sound pleasingly spontaneous.

Piano Sonatas Nos. 1 in E flat; 2 in G; Legend.

*** Continuum CCD 1045. McCabe.

Both Bax's *Piano Sonatas* are convincing in John McCabe's hands – in fact, more convincing than the *Legend*. A thoroughly enterprising issue, excellently recorded.

Piano Sonatas Nos. 1–2; Country Tune; Lullaby (Berceuse); Winter Waters.

**(*) Chan. 8496. Parkin.

Piano Sonatas Nos. 3 in G sharp min.; 4 in G; A Hill Tune; In a Vodka Shop; Water Music.

**(*) Chan. 8497. Parkin.

These *Sonatas* are grievously neglected in the concert hall. Eric Parkin proves a sympathetic guide in this repertoire. The recording is on the resonant side, but the playing is outstandingly responsive.

VOCAL MUSIC

I sing of a maiden; Mater ora filium; This world's joie.

(M) *** EMI CDM5 65595-2. King's College, Cambridge, Ch., Cleobury – FINZI: *Choral Music;* VAUGHAN WILLIAMS: *Mass.* ***

Bax's ambitious setting of a medieval carol, *Mater ora filium*,

is one of the most difficult *a cappella* pieces in the choral repertory. Here under Stephen Cleobury the King's College choir gives it a virtuoso performance, with trebles performing wonders in the taxingly high passages. It is particularly apt, too, when the original inspiration for the piece came from Bax hearing Byrd's *Mass in Five Voices*. The other two Bax pieces, also setting medieval texts, are done most beautifully too, with the unaccompanied voices vividly recorded against the spacious acoustic of King's Chapel. Besides the original Finzi coupling, the reissue includes a splendid analogue performance of Vaughan Williams's beautiful *Mass in G minor*.

BEACH, Amy (1867–1944)

(i) Piano Concerto in C sharp min., Op. 45; (ii) Piano Quintet in F sharp min., Op. 67.

**(*) Ara. Z 6738. Polk; (i) ECO, Goodwin; (ii) Lark Qt.

Amy Beach's *Piano Concerto* (1898–9) is an expansive, warmly romantic work written in a post-Lisztian style, with pleasingly lyrical melodies which recall other composers including Grieg and, in the dramatic first movement, Dvořák. In short, though its style is essentially eclectic, the composer's skill ensures that the concerto holds the listener's attention throughout, especially in a performance so lyrically sympathetic and sparkling as that by Joanne Polk, persuasively accompanied by Paul Goodwin and the ECO and very well recorded. It was a pity, though understandable, that the chosen coupling was the ubiquitous *Piano Quintet*. However, this is also presented passionately, with the lovely slow movement movingly done, though the balance here has the string quartet a shade too close and the acoustic lacks depth – those wanting the concerto will certainly not be disappointed at the quality of the performances of either work.

Symphony in E min. (Gaelic).

*** Chan. 8958. Detroit SO, Järvi (with BARBER: *Symphony No. 1* etc. ***).

Amy Beach was largely self-taught. Her *Symphony in E minor* operates at a high level of accomplishment and has a winning charm, particularly its delightful and inventive second movement. Once heard, this haunting movement is difficult to exorcize from one's memory. A very persuasive performance by the Detroit orchestra under Neeme Järvi, and good recorded sound.

CHAMBER MUSIC

Piano Quintet in F sharp min., Op. 67.

*** ASV CDDCA 932-2. Roscoe, Endellion Qt – CLARKE: *Piano Trio,* etc. ***

(i) Piano Quintet in F sharp min., Op. 67; Piano Trio in A min., Op. 50; (ii) Theme & Variations for Flute & String Quartet.

⚫ Chan. 9752. (i) Ambache; (ii) Keen; The Ambache.

Amy Beach's glorious 1908 *Piano Quintet* with its passionately lyrical first movement and hauntingly beautiful *Adagio* is already available in a fine performance on ASV, coupled with music by Rebecca Clarke. But the Chandos version from Diana Ambache and her group is even richer, more passionately involving, and the coupling with two other fine chamber works is more apt. The *Theme* for the *Flute Variations* (1916) has a touching nostalgia and, with exquisite flute-playing from Helen Keen, this music comes over as equally deeply felt. The *Piano Trio* is a late work (1939), the opening movement delicate in the manner of Fauré. The catchy finale might almost be a lively dance movement from Dvořák's American period, but the luxuriantly expansive centre-piece is all Beach's own. These are marvellous performances of three very highly rewarding works, superbly recorded.

With Martin Roscoe's characterful playing well matched by the masterly Endellion Quartet, the performance on ASV is magnetic and very well recorded.

PIANO MUSIC

By the Still Waters; Far Awa'; Gavotte fantastique; A Humming Bird; 3 Morceaux caractéristiques, Op. 28; Out of the Depths; Scherzino: A Peterboro Chipmunk; Scottish Legend; Variations on Balkan Themes, Op. 60; Young Birches.

*** Ara. Z 6693. Polk.

Ballad, Op. 6; A Cradle Song of the Lonely Mother; The Fair Hills of Eire, O!; A Hermit Thrush at Eve; A Hermit Thrush at Morn; Prelude & Fugue, Op. 81; Les Rêves de Columbine: suite française, Op. 65; Valse-caprice, Op. 4.

*** Ara. Z 6704. Polk.

Eskimos, 4 Characteristic Pieces, Op. 64; Fantasia fugata, Op. 87; From Grandmother's Garden, Op. 97; 5 Improvisations, Op. 148; Nocturne, Op. 107; 4 Sketches, Op. 15; Tyrolean Valse-fantaisie, Op. 116. Transcription: R. STRAUSS: *Serenade.*

*** Ara. Z 6721. Polk.

Arabesque are now exploring Amy Beach's piano music in depth and confirming the consistency of its quality. The *Variations on Balkan Themes* readily demonstrates her ability to sustain a major work. The imaginative pictorial evocations from nature are capped by the beautiful evocation of *Young Birches*, while the nocturnal *Cradle Song of the Lonely Mother* is quite haunting. Beach's ability to assimilate different styles in a single work is never better displayed than in the attractive *Four Sketches*, Op. 15, where at times Schumann, Beethoven, Mendelssohn and Liszt all look over her shoulder; while the disarming simplicity of characterization in *Eskimos* and *From Grandmother's Garden* is quite delightful. Joanne Polk is an understanding and persuasive advocate, capturing the music's special combination of sophistication and innocence with fine spontaneity. She is most truthfully recorded.

Ballad in D flat, Op. 6; Hermit Thrush at Eve; at Morn, Op. 91/1–2; Nocturne, Op. 107; Prelude & Fugue, Op. 81; 4

Sketches, Op. 15; (i) Suite for 2 Pianos on Irish Melodies, Op. 104.

*** Koch 3-7254-2. Erskin, (i) with Supove.

Amy Beach continues to surprise as we discover more of her music. Her invention is always pleasing, and sometimes an apparently trivial piece becomes more than that – witness the *Valse caprice*. The *Four Sketches* (*In Autumn, Phantoms, Dreaming* and *Fireflies*) are charmingly evocative, yet her imposing *Prelude and Fugue* is impressively worked out. Virginia Erskin is thoroughly sympathetic, never undervaluing a piece, and Kathleen Supove makes a fine partner in the demanding but by no means predictable *Suite for Two Pianos on Irish Melodies*.

BEAMISH, Sally (born 1956)

The Caledonian Road; The Day Dawn; (i) No, I'm Not Afraid; (ii) The Imagined Sound of Sun on Stone.

(N) *** BIS CD 1161. Swedish CO, Rudner; (i) Beamish; (ii) Harle.

Sally Beamish began her career as a violist in the London Sinfonietta before turning to full-time composition when she was in her 30s. Her musical speech is direct and often powerful, and she has a genuine feeling for nature. *The Imagined Sound of Sun on Stone*, a concerto for soprano saxophone and chamber orchestra, is most resourceful in its handling of the instrument and imaginative in its musical content, and it is played brilliantly here by John Harle and the Swedish Chamber Orchestra. All four pieces are inventive and well worth getting to know, and the BIS recording is state-of-the-art.

(i) Cello Concerto (River); (ii) Viola Concerto; (iii) Tam Lin (for oboe and orchestra).

*** BIS CD 971. (i) Cohen; (ii) Dukes; (iii) Hunt; Swedish CO, Rudner.

Tam Lin is a scena for oboe and small orchestra including harp and percussion but no violins. It is based on a Scottish ballad in which the elfin knight, Tam Lin, is saved from damnation by the love of a girl, Janet. The composer calls the *Viola Concerto* 'a personal response to the story of the Apostle Peter's denial of Christ' and casts the solo viola as Peter's voice, the horn being associated with Jesus. The three denials are punctuated by illustrations of Christ's trial in film-like contrasts. The *Cello Concerto* illustrates poems from Ted Hughes's 'River' collection, with orchestral colourings suggested by the words. The music is consistently imaginative, with clean, luminous textures. The writing is eventful and holds the listener in its spell. Robert Cohen and Philip Dukes, the dedicatees who commissioned the cello and viola works respectively, give committed performances, as does the oboist, Gordon Hunt, with distinctive plangent tone. Excellent support from the Swedish players, very well recorded.

BECK, Franz Ignaz (1734–1809)

Sinfonias: in B flat; D; G; in D, Op. 10/2; in E, Op. 13/1.

(BB) *** Naxos 8.553790. Northern CO, Ward.

Sinfonias in G min.; E flat; D min., Op. 13/3–5.

(BB) *** CPO 999 390-2. La Stagione, Frankfurt, Schneider.

Franz Ignaz Beck's three-movement *Sinfonias* are concise and sharply characterized, even if they are little more than Italian overtures. The *D major Sinfonia* is the exception, with a Haydnesque pattern of four movements. Ideas are fresh, scoring simple but felicitous. The graceful *Largo* of the *B flat major* work, with its string cantilena floating over a pizzicato bass, is worthy of Boccherini, and the *E major*, Op. 13/1, is a winning little work with a diverting finale. The performances on Naxos could hardly be more persuasive, warmly elegant and full of vitality. The recording, too, is first class.

The CPO disc offers mature later works (especially the *G minor*, with the themes interrelated) which are very much in the Haydn *Sturm und Drang* style. The *D minor Sinfonia* is for strings alone, but the *E flat major*, which has a remarkably searching *Adagio*, uses the horns most effectively as soloists in the *Minuet* and *Trio* and in the closing section of the finale. The period performances here are aggressively full of gusto and vitality, creating a sound-world very different from that on the Naxos collection.

BEECKE, Ignaz von (1733–1803)

String Quartets Nos. 9 in G; 11 in G; 16 in B flat, M.9, 11 & 16.

*** CPO 999 509-2. Arioso Qt.

Ignaz von Beecke is not to be confused with Franz Ignaz Beck, above (although he was an almost exact contemporary). He began his career in the military, but later taught himself the harpsichord and became a virtuoso on that instrument, admired by Haydn and playing in duet with Mozart (in Frankfurt in 1790). Later he became a travelling court musical director, performing his own symphonies as well as those by others. Beecke's string quartets were less well known in his own time than his symphonies. They are finely crafted, cultivated works which Haydn would surely not have been ashamed to own. The disarming warmth of the opening of the *G major*, M.11 (which is first on the disc), leads to a fine opening movement with two striking themes; the *Minuet* comes second and is equally personable, and after the elegant *Adagio* the finale is as spirited as you could wish. The *B flat Quartet* is in three movements and is hardly less pleasing, with a songful *Adagio* marked *sotto voce*. The companion *G major* work brings a striking minor-key slow movement, opening with a grave slow fugue; the *Minuet* lightens the mood and prepares for a most engaging finale. All three works are thoroughly diverting when played with such warmth, vitality and finesse, and this excellent quartet is very naturally recorded.

BEETHOVEN, Ludwig van
(1770–1827)

The DG Complete Beethoven Edition

(B) **(*) DG ADD/Dig. 453 700-2 (87) – MOZART: *Piano Concerto No. 20.*

DG's Complete Beethoven Edition was issued as a 20-volume, 87-CD set to celebrate the company's centenary, packaged in a substantial, suitcase-like cardboard box with an illustrated book. Most collectors would do better to concentrate on individual volumes, all available separately in the mid-price range.

Volume 1: *Symphonies Nos. 1–9.*

(M) *** DG (ADD) 453 701-2 (5). BPO, Karajan (with Janowitz, Rössel-Majdan, Kmentt, Berry, V. Singverein in *No. 9*).

Karajan's second Beethoven symphony cycle, recorded in 1961 and 1962, is generally the most successful of his four. The refinement of detail never undermines the dramatic urgency of the whole cycle. The *Pastoral* is the one real failure of the set, hard-driven and unyielding. The *Ninth Symphony* is strong and refined, with an urgency that carries the argument through from first to last. This set is also available in a separate bargain-price box – see below (DG 429 036-2).

Volume 2: *Complete Concertos: Piano Concertos Nos. (i; ii) 1–2; (i; iii) 3–5; (iv) in E flat, WoO 4; (v) in D, Op. 61 (arr. composer); Violin Concertos: (vi) in D, Op. 61; (vii) in C, WoO 5; (viii) Triple Concerto in C, Op. 56; (ix) Romances Nos. 1–2; (x) Romance cantabile for Piano, Flute & Bassoon in E min., H. 13; (xi) Rondo for Piano & Orchestra in B flat, WoO 6.*

(M) ** DG ADD/Dig. 453 707-2 (5). (i) Pollini, VPO; (ii) Jochum; (iii) Boehm; (iv) Ander, Berlin CO, Gülke; (v) ECO, Barenboim (piano & cond.); (vi; viii) Mutter, BPO, Karajan; (vii) Kremer, LSO, Tchakarov; (viii) with Zeltser, Ma; (ix) Shaham, Orpheus CO; (x) Patrick Gallois, Pascal Gallois, Philh. O, Myung-Whun Chung (piano and cond.); (xi) Richter, VSO, Sanderling.

The Concerto box, with the juvenilia and completed fragments included, is a mixed bag. The choice of Pollini's first piano concerto cycle is controversial, though the reserve in Pollini's playing is counterbalanced by the warmth of his accompanists. Anne-Sophie Mutter's early and beautiful recording of the *Violin Concerto* with Karajan makes an excellent choice, the result being entirely convincing. In the *Triple Concerto* Yo-Yo Ma and Mark Zeltser, as well as Mutter herself, are full of imagination but are not a well-matched team.

Gil Shaham in the two *Romances* is outstanding, but the problems of the compilers are displayed in the extra works. Like the other juvenilia, the *E flat Piano Concerto* of 1784 (completed, like the *Romance*, by the Swiss musicologist Willy Hess) and the first movement of a *C major Violin Concerto* (probably 1790–92) are attractive and fresh but not very individual. The arrangement of the *Violin Concerto* for piano and orchestra alters the character of the music entirely, substituting charm for spiritual depth, though Barenboim gives a dedicated performance.

Volume 3: *Orchestral Works & Music for the Stage:* (i–ii) *12 Contredanses, WoO 14;* (iii) *12 German Dances, WoO 8; Minuets: WoO 7;* (i; iv) *WoO 3; Ritterballett, WoO 1; Wellington's Victory, Op. 91;* (v–vi) Overtures: *Coriolan, Op. 62; Zur Namensfeier, Op. 115;* (vii) Overture and Ballet Music: *The Creatures of Prometheus, Op. 43;* Overtures and Incidental Music: (i; vi; viii; x–xii) *The Consecration of the House, H.118 (Opp. 113–14, 124, WoO 98);* (with ix) *The Ruins of Athens, Op. 113;* (i; vi; xiii) *Egmont, Op. 84;* (xiv) *King Stephen, Op. 117;* Miscellaneous Items: (xviii–xix; xxi) *Es ist vollbracht, WoO 97; Germania, WoO 94;* (i; vi; ix; xv) *Leonore Prohaska, WoO 96;* (xvi) *2 Arias for the Beautiful Shoemaker's Wife, WoO 91; Tarpeja, WoO 2:* (xvii) *Entr'acte;* (xxi) *Triumphal March;* (xix–xxi) *Vestas Feuer, H.115.*

(M) **(*) DG ADD/Dig. 453 713-2 (5). (i) BPO; (ii) Maazel; (iii) ASMF, Marriner; (iv) Karajan; (v) VPO; (vi) Abbado; (vii) Orpheus CO; (viii) Augér, Hirte, Crass; (ix) McNair; (x) RIAS Chamber Ch.; (xi) Berlin R. Ch.; (xii) Klee; (xiii) Studer, Ganz; (xiv) Fischer-Dieskau, Jackwerth, Rühl, Mende, Aljinovicz, Santa Cecilia Ch. & O, Myung-Whun Chung; (xv) Eichhorn; (xvi) Gedda, Rothenberger, Convivium Musicum München, Keller; (xvii) Gothenberg SO, Järvi; (xviii) BBC Singers; (xix) Finley; (xx) Kuebler, Leggate, Gritton; (xxi) BBC SO, A. Davis.

The Creatures of Prometheus is splendidly done by the Orpheus Chamber Orchestra. Abbado (who also directs the overtures) gives excellent accounts of the music for *The Consecration of the House* and *Egmont;* Klee is equally impressive in *The Ruins of Athens. King Stephen,* conducted by Myung-Whun Chung, was newly recorded (in Rome) and includes spoken melodrama (Fischer-Dieskau). Other more striking rarities include *Germania* and an operatic trio, *Vestas Feuer,* dramatically sung. Karajan's version of *Wellington's Victory* is very well played, but there is no sense of occasion; he is happier with the much lighter *Ritterballett,* presenting these dance vignettes affectionately. Marriner and his Academy are equally felicitous in the *German Dances* and *Minuets.* The recording is consistently excellent throughout.

Volume 4: (i) *Fidelio* (complete); (ii) *Leonore* (complete); Overtures: (iii) *Fidelio, Op. 72c; Leonora Nos.* (iv) *1, Op. 138;* (v) *2, Op. 72a;* (vi) *3, Op. 72b.*

(M) *** DG ADD/Dig. 453 719-2 (4). (i) Janowitz, Kollo, Jungwirth, Sotin, Popp, Dallapozza, Fischer-Dieskau, V. State Op. Ch.; (ii) Martinpelto, Begley, Hawlata, Best, Oelze, Schade, Miles, Bantzer, Monteverdi Ch.; (i; iii–iv) VPO; (i; iii) Bernstein; (iv) Abbado; (ii; v) ORR, Gardiner.

Gardiner presents this first version of the opera *Fidelio* as a masterpiece in its own right, confirming his passionate belief that *Leonore* is the more spontaneous and immediate work compared with the more considered *Fidelio* of ten years later. The performance is discussed in more detail below, under its separate issue.

Bernstein's reading of *Fidelio* is full of dramatic flair. The recording was made in conjunction with live performances by the same cast at the Vienna State Opera. Lucia Popp as Marzelline is particularly enchanting, and Gundula Janowitz sings most beautifully as Leonore. Kollo as Florestan is strong and intelligent, as are the rest of the cast.

Volume 5: *Piano Sonatas Nos. 1–32.*

(M) *** DG 453 724-2 (8). Kempff.

More than any other pianist, Kempff has the power to make one appreciate and understand Beethoven in a new way, thanks to his magnetism, his unfailing sense of spontaneity, his ability to clarify textures and and his lyrical flow, with extreme speeds avoided. Kempff may be erratic over observing exposition repeats, but the sense of live communication is what matters, not least in the late sonatas, with sharp, clean attack set against sublime lyricism.

Volume 6: *Piano Works:* (i) *Allegrettos in B min., WoO 61; in C min., WoO 53; H.69; Allegretto quasi andante in G min., WoO 61a; Allemande in A, WoO 81;* (ii) *Andante favori, WoO 57; Bagatelles: Opp. 33; 119;* (iii) *126;* (ii) *WoO 52; WoO 56;* (iii) *'Für Elise', WoO 59;* (i) *WoO 60;* (viii) *Canons à 2 in A flat, G, H.274/5; Ecossaises:* (vi) *WoO 83;* (i) *WoO 86; Fantasia in G min., Op. 77; Fugue in C, H.64; 12 German Dances, WoO 13; 7 Ländler in D, WoO 11; 'Lustig-traurig' in C min., WoO 54; 6 Minuets, WoO* (ii) *10;* (i) *82;* (ii) *Polonaise in C, Op. 89;* (i) *Prelude in F min., WoO 55;* (ii) *Rondos in A, WoO 49; in C, Op. 51/1; WoO 48; in G, Op. 51/2;* (i) *Rondo a capriccio in G ('Rage over the lost penny'), Op. 129;* (ix) *Sonatas, WoO 47, Nos. 1 in E flat; 2 in F min.; 3 in D;* (i) *in C, WoO 51; 2 Sonata Movements in F, WoO 50;* (ii) *6 Variations in F, Op. 34; Variations in C min., WoO 63; in F, WoO 64; in D, WoO 65; in C, WoO 68; in G, WoO 70;* (i) *in A, WoO 66; in C, WoO 72; in B flat, WoO 73; in F, WoO 75, 76; in G, WoO 77;* (iv) *15 Variations & Fugue on a Theme from Prometheus (Eroica Variations), Op. 35;* (vi) *32 Variations on an Original Theme in C min., WoO 80;* (vii) *33 Variations on a Waltz by Diabelli, Op. 120;* (v) *12 Variations on a Russian Dance, WoO 71; Variations on 'God save the King', WoO 78, and 'Rule, Britannia', WoO 79; 9 Variations on 'Quant'è più bello', WoO 69;* (i) *Waltzes, WoO 84–5. Works for Piano Duet:* (ix, x) *Grosse Fuge in B flat, Op. 134; 3 Marches, Op. 45; Sonata in D, Op. 6. Solo Pieces for Miscellaneous Instruments:* (xi) *Fugue in D, WoO 31. Grenadier March, H.107; 5 Pieces, WoO 33 (both works for mechanical clock). 2 Preludes through All 12 Major Keys, Op. 39.*

(M) ** DG ADD/Dig. 453 733-2 (8). (i) Cascioli; (ii) Pletnev; (iii) Ugorski; (iv) Gilels; (v) Mustonen; (vi) Kempff; (vii) Barenboim; (viii) Olbertz; (ix) Demus; (x) Shetler; (xi) Preston (organ).

Gilels's magisterial account of the *Eroica Variations* is well contrasted with Barenboim's intensely personal reading of the *Diabelli Variations,* giving the illusion of an improvisation, full of dramatic contrasts. Outstanding among the other recordings is Pletnev's *Bagatelles,* Opp. 33 and 119, but Ugorski is far less imaginative in Op. 126. Many of the lesser-known pieces are entrusted to Gianluca Cascioli, who does not disappoint. Olli Mustonen's stylish recordings of the four lesser sets of *Variations* come from Decca.

Volume 7: (i) *Violin Sonatas Nos. 1–10;* (ii) *6 German Dances, WoO 42;* (iii) *Rondo in G, WoO 41; 12 Variations on Mozart's 'Se vuol ballare' from Le nozze di Figaro, WoO 40.*

(M) *** DG ADD/Dig. 453 743-2 (4). (i) Kremer, Argerich; (ii) Garrett, Canino; (iii) Menuhin, Kempff.

Having two such volatile artists as Gidon Kremer and Martha Argerich in partnership for the Beethoven *Violin Sonatas* makes for exciting results, spontaneous and fresh in the last and most enigmatic of the sonatas, *No. 10 in G.* In that final work the contrasts of mood are caught vividly, with rapt mystery at the very start giving way to lightness. This set is also available separately – see below. The *German Dances, Rondo* and *Variations* are slight but are stylishly presented.

Volume 8: *Cello Sonatas: Nos. 1–5; 7 Variations on 'Bei Männern, welche Liebe fühlen', WoO 46; 12 Variations on 'Ein Mädchen oder Weibchen', Op. 66, both from Mozart's Die Zauberflöte. 12 Variations on 'See the conqu'ring hero comes' from Handel's Judas Maccabaeus, WoO 45.*

(M) *** DG 453 748-2 (2). Maisky, Argerich.

Mischa Maisky and Martha Argerich make a characterful partnership, giving exhilarating performances that yet at times are over-concerned on detail.

Volume 9: *Piano Trios:* (i) *Nos. 1–9; 10 (14 Variations on an Original Theme in E flat), Op. 44; 11 (10 Variations on 'Ich bin der Schneider Kakadu'), Op. 121a;* (ii) *Allegretto in E flat, H.48; Trio in E flat (arr. of Septet, Op. 20), Op. 38;* (iii) *Trio in D (arr. of Symphony No. 2), Op. 36.*

(M) **(*) DG ADD/Dig. 453 751-2 (5). (i) Kempff, Szeryng, Fournier; (ii) Beaux Arts Trio; (iii) Besch, Brandis, Boettcher.

The Kempff–Szeryng–Fournier set of trios is a distinguished one, most successful in the early trios, though the sound is dated. The other items are well done, if of limited interest.

Volume 10: *String Trios Nos. 1–4; Serenade in D, Op. 8.*

(M) **(*) DG 453 757-2 (2). Mutter, Giuranna, Rostropovich.

This starry trio of soloists certainly offers splendid playing, but the recording is rather forward and dry and is not intimate enough.

Volume 11: The Early Quartets: (i) *String Quartets Nos. 1–6, Op. 18/1–6;* (ii) *Fugue from Handel's 'Solomon' Overture, H.36; Minuet in A flat, H.33;* (iii) *Preludes & Fugues in F, H.30; in C, H.31; String Quartets in F,* (ii) *H.32 (Op. 18/1 first version);* (i) *H.34 (arr. of Piano Sonata, Op. 14/1).*

(M) **(*) DG ADD/Dig. 453 760-2 (3). (i) Amadeus Qt; (ii) Hagen Qt; (iii) Mendelssohn Qt.

The Op. 18 quartets inspire the Amadeus to their finest playing, the character of the playing at once polished and

intimate. The 1961 recording still sounds well. The other items are interesting rarities.

Volume 12: The Middle Quartets: *String Quartets Nos. 7 in F; 8 in E min., 9 in C (Rasumovsky), Op. 59/1–3; 10 in E flat (Harp), Op. 74; 11 in F min., Op. 95.*

(M) **(*) DG 453 764-2 (2). Emerson Qt.

We are at odds over the Emerson performances of the middle-period Beethoven quartets. E. G. finds them very compelling indeed, with pianissimos of breathtaking delicacy and vibrant attack of fortissimos. R. L. agrees that their playing is in a class of its own technically, but he feels that the thrust is inappropriate in music composed before the discovery of electricity.

Volume 13: The Late Quartets: *String Quartets Nos. 12 in E flat, Op. 127; 13 in B flat, Op. 130; 14 in C sharp min., Op. 131; 15 in A min., Op. 132; 16 in F, Op. 135; Grosse Fuge, Op. 133.*

(M) ** DG (ADD) 453 768-2 (3). LaSalle Qt.

Technically, the LaSalle Quartet are impressive, with their unanimity of ensemble and fine tonal blend, but there is no sense of mystery and little feeling of inwardness or depth. The recordings (made between 1972 and 1977) are of fine analogue quality.

Volume 14: *Chamber Works:* (i) *Canon in A, WoO 35;* (ii–iii) *Duets, in G for 2 Flutes, WoO 26;* (i) *in A for 2 Violins, WoO 34; in E flat for Viola & Cello, WoO 32;* (iv) *Fugue in D for String Quintet, Op. 137;* (v–vi) *Horn Sonata in F, Op. 17;* (i) *6 Ländler for 2 Violins & Bass, WoO 15; 6 Minuets for 2 Violins & Bass, WoO 9;* (vii) *Piano & Wind Quintet, Op. 16;* (viii; xii) *Piano Quartets Nos. 1–3;* (ix) *Pieces for Mandolin & Piano: Adagio, WoO 43b; Sonatinas in C, WoO 44a; in C min., WoO 43a; Variations in D, WoO 44b;* (i) *Prelude & Fugue in E min. for 2 Violins & Cello, H.29;* (x) *Serenade in D for Flute, Violin & Viola, Op. 25;* (iv) *Septet in E flat, Op. 20;* (xi) *Sextet in E flat, Op. 81b;* (xii–xiii) *String Quintet in C, Op. 29;* (ii; xiv) *Themes with Variations for Piano & Flute, Opp. 105 & 107;* (xv) *Trio in B flat for Piano, Clarinet & Cello, Op. 11;* (v; xvi) *Trio in G for Piano, Flute & Bassoon, WoO 37.*

(M) **(*) DG ADD/Dig. 453 772-2 (6). (i) Hagen Qt, Posch; (ii) Gallois; (iii) Rampal; (iv) VPO Ens.; (v) Barenboim; (vi) Bloom; (vii) Levine, Vienna–Berlin Ens.; (viii) Eschenbach; (ix) Fietz, Webersinke; (x) Zoeller, Brandis, Ueberschaer; (xi) Seifert, Klier, Drolc Qt; (xii) Amadeus Qt (members); (xiii) Aronowitz; (xiv) Licad; (xv) Kempff, Leister, Fournier; (xvi) Debost, Sennedat.

Best here are the early *Piano Quartets* of 1785, written in Bonn, not great works but most persuasive as played here. Outstanding too are the *C major String Quintet* with the Amadeus and Cecil Aronowitz (one of their finest recordings) and the *Septet.* Barenboim is an inspired pianist in both the *G major Trio*, for piano, flute and bassoon, with principals from the Orchestre de Paris, and the *Horn Sonata* with the brilliant Myron Bloom. The early *E flat Sextet*, Op. 81, was recorded for the 1970 Edition and sounds remarkably fresh. So does the 1970 Zoeller–Brandis–

Ueberschaer set of the *Serenade*, Op. 25. The Levine Vienna–Berlin Ensemble version of the Op. 16 *E flat Quintet* for piano and wind, which was made in 1986, is less satisfactory, but the Op. 11 *Trio* with Karl Leister, Pierre Fournier and Wilhelm Kempff is a delight.

Volume 15: *Wind Music:* (i–ii) *Ecossaise in D, WoO 22;* (iii) *3 Equale for 4 Trombones, WoO 30;* (i–ii) *Marches, WoO 18–20, WoO 24, WoO 29;* (i) *Octet in E flat, Op. 103;* (i–ii) *Polonaise in D, WoO 21;* (iv) *Rondino in E flat, WoO 25;* (i) *Sextet in E flat, Op. 71;* (v) *Trio in C, Op. 87; Variations on Mozart's 'Là ci darem la mano', both for 2 oboes and cor anglais.*

(M) *** DG (ADD) 453 779-2 (2). (i) BPO (members);
(ii) cond. Priem-Bergrath; (iii) Philip Jones Brass Ens.;
(iv) Netherlands Wind Ens.; (v) Holliger, Elhorst, Bourgue.

Belying its opus number, the *C major Trio*, Op. 87, for the unlikely combination of cor anglais and two oboes, is an early work, dating from 1794 and impressive in scale. The *'Là ci darem' Variations*, in a similar scoring, were not published until the twentieth century. The attractive *Rondino for Wind Octet* is given a crisp, clean performance by the Netherlands Wind Ensemble (also from Philips); the *Wind Sextet*, Op. 71, and *Octet in E flat*, Op. 103, are DG recordings from 1970, played by members of the Berlin Philharmonic Orchestra, equally alert and civilized, while Hans Priem-Bergrath directs the Berlin ensemble in lively accounts of the marches and dances.

Volume 16: *Lieder:* (i) *Abendlied unterm gestirnten Himmel;* (iv; ix) *Abschiedsgesang an Wiens Bürger;* (i) *Adelaide; Als die Geliebte sich trennen wollte; Andenken; An die ferne Geliebte, Op. 98;* (iii; ix) *An den fernen Geliebten, Op. 75/5; An die Geliebte* (ii; ix) *2nd version;* (i) *3rd version; An die Hoffnung, Op. 32* (1st version), *Op. 94* (2nd version); (iii; ix) *An einen Säugling;* (ii; ix) *An Laura; An Minna;* (i) *4 Ariettas & a Duet, Op. 82; Aus Goethes Faust, Op. 75/3; Der Bardengeist; Das Blümchen Wunderhold, Op. 52/8;* (vii; x) *Der edle Mensch;* (ii; ix) *Elegie auf den Tod eines Pudels; Erhebt das Glas mit froher Hand; Feuerfarb', Op. 52/2; Der freie Mann; Gedenke mein!;* (i) *Das Geheimnis; Gesang aus der Ferne* (vi; x) *1st version;* (i) *2nd version;* (iii; ix) *Der Gesang der Nachtigall; Gretels Warnung, Op. 75/4;* (i) *In questa tomba oscura; Der Jüngling in der Fremde;* (iii; ix) *Kennst du das Land, Op. 75/1;* (ii; ix) *Klage;* (v; x) *Der Knabe auf dem Berge;* (ii; ix) *Des Kriegers Abschied;* (iv; ix) *Kriegslied der Österreicher;* (i) *Der Kuss; Die laute Klage; Die Liebe, Op. 52/6;* (viii; x) *Das liebe Kätzchen;* (i) *Der Liebende; Das Liedchen von der Ruhe, Op. 52/3; 6 Lieder, Op. 48; 3 Lieder, Op. 83; 2 Lieder, WoO 118; Maigesang, Op. 52/4;* (iii; ix) *Man strebt, die Flamme zu verhehlen;* (iv; ix) *Der Mann von Wort;* (i) *Marmotte, Op. 52/7; Merkenstein* (vi; x) *WoO 144* (1st version), (ii–iii; ix) *Op. 100* (2nd version); (iii; ix) *Mollys Abschied, Op. 52/5; Neue Liebe, neues Leben* (vi; x) *WoO 127* (1st version), (i) *Op. 75/2* (2nd version); (ii; ix) *Oh care selve, o cara;* (i) *Opferlied; La partenza;* (ii; ix) *Plaisir d'aimer; Punschlied; Que le temps me dure* 1st version; (v; x) 2nd version; (i) *Resignation; Ruf vom Berge; Schilderung eines Mädchens; Sehnsucht, WoO 146;*

(iii; ix) *Sehnsucht, WoO 134* (4 versions); (ii; ix) *Ein Selbstgespräch; So oder so; La tiranna;* (i) *Urians Reise um die Welt, Op. 52/1; Vita felice; Der Wachtelschlag; Zärtliche Liebe; Der Zufriedene, Op. 75/6.*

(M) **(*) DG ADD/Dig. 453 782-2 (3). (i) Fischer-Dieskau,
Demus; (ii) Schreier; (iii) Stolte; (iv) Leib; (v) Helzel;
(vi) Maus; (vii) Person; (viii) Horn; (ix) Olbertz;
(x) Hilsdorf.

Fischer-Dieskau gives searching readings of the Beethoven songs, recorded in 1966, revealing their mastery, too little appreciated. Demus is a sensitive accompanist and the recording is good. For much of the rest DG draw on Telefunken recordings dating mainly from the 1970s, with Peter Schreier in excellent form. However, his colleagues are less reliable, including Adele Stolte in the duets.

Volume 17: *Folksong Arrangements: 7 British Songs, WoO 158b; 25 Irish Songs, WoO 152; 20 Irish Songs, WoO 153; 12 Irish Songs, WoO 154; 25 Scottish Songs, WoO 108; 12 Scottish Songs, WoO 156; 26 Welsh Songs, WoO 155; Songs of Various Nationalities, WoO 157, 158a & c.*

(M) *** DG 453 786-2 (7). Lott, Watson, Wyn-Davies,
Philogene, Walker, Murray, Ainsley, Robinson, Spence,
Allen, Maltman; Layton, Osostowicz, Blankestijn, Smith,
Martineau.

This is an enchanting kaleidoscopic collection of folksong arrangements, mainly British. So Beethoven's setting of *Auld lang syne* has a vigorous Scottish snap to it, and he treats *God save the King* canonically, while *Charlie is my darling* is in 2/4 time, and *The miller of Dee* is made the darker by a stylized accompaniment. Altogether 168 songs are included, ending with a disc of non-British settings just as fascinating, regularly bringing surprises in his accompaniments for piano trio. Malcolm Martineau as accompanist is the linchpin, regularly providing the sparkle needed, and almost all the singing is first rate. An outstanding set in every way.

Volume 18: *Secular Vocal Works:* (i) *Abschiedsgesang;* (ii) *Ah! perfido, Op. 65;* (iii) *Bundeslied, Op. 122; Elegischer Gesang, Op. 118;* (i; iv–vi) *Cantata campestre; Hochzeitslied; Lobkowitz-Kantate;* (vii) *Chor auf die verbündeten Fürsten;* (i) *Gesang der Mönche;* (viii; xi) *Mit Mädeln sich vertragen; Prüfung des Küssens;* (ix–xi) *Ne' giorni tuoi felici;* (ix; xi) *No, non turbati; Primo amore;* (iii; xii) *Opferlied, Op. 121b;* (viii–xi) *Tremate, empi, tremate, Op. 116;* (i; vi; xiii) *43 Canons & Musical Jokes;* (i) *18 Italian Partsongs.*

(M) ** DG ADD/Dig. 453 794-2 (2). (i) Berlin soloists;
(ii) Studer, BPO, Abbado; (iii) Amb. S., LSO, Tilson
Thomas; (iv) Jehser; (v) Olbertz; (vi) Knothe; (vii) BBC
Singers, BBC SO, A. Davis; (viii) Vogel; (ix) Kuhse;
(x) Büchner; (xi) Berlin Staatskapelle, Apelt; (xii) Haywood;
(xiii) Berlin Singakademie Ch.

This two-disc set contains much that will intrigue the dedicated Beethovenian – the *43 Canons and Musical Jokes*, for instance. For three of the more important inclusions DG have drawn on the Sony catalogue for outstanding performances from Michael Tilson Thomas of the *Bundeslied, Opferlied* (with Lorna Haywood an impressive soloist) and the remarkable *Elegischer Gesang* ('Elegiac song'). Cheryl Studer's dramatic account of *Ah! perfido* is new, as are most of the more trivial items.

Volume 19: *Large Choral Works: (i–iii) Cantatas on the Accession of Emperor Leopold II, WoO 88; (iii–iv) On the Death of Emperor Joseph II, WoO 87; (v) Choral Fantasia for Piano, Chorus & Orchestra in C min., Op. 80; (vi) Christus am Oelberge, Op. 85; (vii) Der glorreiche Augenblick, Op. 136; (i; viii–ix) Mass in C, Op. 86; (ix) Meeresstille und glückliche Fahrt, Op. 112; (x) Missa solemnis in D, Op. 123.*

(M) *** DG ADD/Dig. 453 798-2 (5). (i) Margiono; (ii) Shirnell; (iii) German Opera Ch. & O, Thielemann; (iv) Schäfer, Bieber, Von Halem; (v) Kissin, RIAS Ch., BPO, Abbado; (vi) Harwood, King, Crass, V. Singverein, VSO, Klee; (vii) Orgonasova, Vermillion, Robinson, Hawlata, Ch. di voci bianche dell'Arcum, St Cecilia Ac. Ch. & O, Myung-Whun Chung; (viii) Robbin, Kendall, Miles; (ix) Monteverdi Ch., ORR, Gardiner; (x) Studer, Norman, Domingo, Moll, Leipzig R. Ch., Swedish R. Ch., VPO, Levine.

Levine's account of the *Missa solemnis* is outstanding. Gardiner's period performance of the *Mass in C* is excellent too, revealing it as a masterpiece. Both are discussed below. In Beethoven's oratorio, *Christus am Oelberge*, James King underlines the operatic quality, and the radiance of Elizabeth Harwood's voice is powerfully caught, while Franz Crass is comparably intense. Bernhard Klee draws lively playing from the Vienna Symphoniker. The two youthful cantatas from Beethoven's Bonn period commemorating regal death and accession bring fine new recordings directed by Christian Thielemann, aptly combining vitality and gravitas. The Viennese celebration, *Der glorreiche Augenblick*, conducted by the ever-perceptive Myung-Whun Chung, is equally telling, with Luba Orgonasova an outstanding soloist. An essential purchase, particularly for those who want the two *Masses*.

Volume 20: Historic Recordings: *Piano Concertos Nos. (i) 3 in C min., Op 37; (ii–iii) 5 in E flat (Emperor), Op. 73; (iv) Violin Concerto in D, Op. 61. Symphonies Nos. (v) 3 in E flat (Eroica), Op. 55; (vi) 5 in C min., Op. 67; (vii) 7 in A, Op. 92; (viii) 9 in D min. (Choral), Op. 125. Overtures: (ix) Coriolan, Op. 62; (x) Egmont, Op. 84; Leonore No. 2, Op. 72; (ix) Leonore No. 3, Op. 72. Violin Sonatas Nos. (xii; ii) 5 in F, 'Spring', Op. 24; (xiii; ii) 9 in A, 'Kreutzer', Op 47; (ii) Rondo a capriccio in G, Op. 129. (xiv) An die ferne Geliebte (song-cycle), Op. 98. Lieder: Andenken, WoO 136; In questa tomba oscura, WoO 133; Der Wachtelschlag, WoO 129. Zärtliche Liebe, WoO 123 – (xv) MOZART: Piano Concerto No. 20 in D min., K.466 (with cadenzas by BEETHOVEN).*

(M) (***) DG (ADD) mono/stereo 453 804-2 (6). (i) Fischer, Bav. RSO, Fricsay; (ii) Kempff; (iii) BPO, Raabe; (iv) Wolfsthal, BPO, Gurlitt; (v–ix) BPO; cond. (v) Schuricht; (vi) Nikisch; (vii) Fricsay; (viii) Busch, with Lindberg-Torlind, Jena, Sjöberg, Byrding, Danish R. Ch. & O; (ix) Furtwängler; (x) Berlin Op. O, Klemperer;

(xii) Schneiderhan; (xiii) Kulenkampff; (xiv) Schlusnus, Peschko & Rupp; (xv) Richter, Warsaw PO, Wislocki.

Earliest here is the 1913 Nikisch account of the *Fifth Symphony*, the first complete recording of any symphony. The wartime (1941) set of the *Eroica* from Carl Schuricht and the Berlin Philharmonic brings a totally dedicated reading, vibrant and alive. Ferenc Fricsay's recording of the *Seventh Symphony* has a fire, a gravitas and an integrity that make a powerful impression. The *Ninth Symphony* was made in the autumn of 1950 under Fritz Busch, an undistracting, classical account. Among the concertos, Annie Fischer's 1957 account of the *Third*, with the Bavarian Radio orchestra under Fricsay, and Wilhelm Kempff's fine (1936) *Emperor Concerto* are most impressive. Josef Wolfsthal's 1929 account of the *Violin Concerto* offers breathtaking mastery, making one regret that this pupil of Carl Flesch died in his early thirties. The 1959 account by Sviatoslav Richter of Mozart's *D minor Concerto*, K.466, made in Warsaw, is included because of the Beethoven cadenzas the great Russian pianist used. The 1935 set of the *Kreutzer Sonata* with Georg Kulenkampff and Wilhelm Kempff is remarkable for its purity. Handsome presentation.

Other recordings

Piano Concertos Nos. 1–5.

*** Sony S3K 44575 (3). Perahia, Concg. O, Haitink.
*** Ph. 462 781-2 (3). Brendel, VPO, Rattle.

(i) Piano Concertos Nos. 1–5; (ii) Triple Concerto for Violin, Cello & Piano, Op. 56.

(M) *** Sony (ADD) SB3K 48397 (3). (i) Fleisher, Cleveland O, Szell; (ii) Stern, Rose, Istomin, Phd. O, Ormandy.

Piano Concertos Nos. 1–5; Rondos, Op. 51/1–2.

(M) (***) DG mono 435 744-2 (3). Kempff, BPO, Van Kempen.

Piano Concertos Nos. 1–5; Rondo in B flat, WoO 6; Piano Concerto No. 4, Op. 58 (for piano and string quintet; reconstructed Hans-Werner Küthen); (i) Choral Fantasia, Op. 80. Symphony No. 2 in D (arr. for piano, violin & cello).

*** DG 459 622-2 (4). Levin (fortepiano), ORR, Gardiner, (i) with Monteverdi Ch. and instrumental & vocal soloists.

(i) Piano Concertos Nos. 1–5; 6 Bagatelles, Op. 126; 'Für Elise'.

(B) **(*) Decca (ADD) 443 723-2 (3). Ashkenazy, (i) Chicago SO, Solti.

(i) Piano Concertos Nos. 1–5. Diabelli Variations, Op. 120.

(M) **(*) Decca (IMS) 433 891-2 (3). Backhaus; (i) VPO, Schmidt-Isserstedt.

(i) Piano Concertos Nos. 1–5. Piano Sonata No. 23 (Appassionata), Op. 57.

*** Teldec 3984 26801-2 (*Nos. 1–2*); 3984 26802-2 (*Nos. 3–4*); 3984 26900-2 (*No. 5 & Piano Sonata*). Schiff, Dresden State O, Haitink (available separately).

(i) Piano Concertos Nos. 1–5. 32 Variations in C min., WoO 80.

**(*) Ph. 464 142-2 (3). Uchida; (i) Bav. RSO or Concg. O, Sanderling.

Piano Concertos Nos. 1–5; (i) *Choral Fantasia, Op. 80.*

(M) *** EMI (ADD) CMS7 63360-2 (3). Barenboim, New Philh. O, Klemperer, (i) with John Alldis Ch.

(B) *** EMI CfP CD-CFP 6025 (*No. 1 & Choral Fantasia*); CD-CFP 6026 (*Nos. 2 & 4*); CD-CFP 6027 (*Nos. 3 & 5*). Lill, SNO, Gibson.

(M) ** Sup SU 3540-2. Panenka, Prague SO & (i) Ch., Smetáček.

Playing with exceptional clarity and incisiveness, András Schiff with ideal, equally transparent support from Haitink and the Dresden Staatskapelle offers one of the most refreshing, deeply satisfying Beethoven concerto cycles of recent years. While often choosing speeds on the fast side, Schiff never sounds rushed or breathless. The brightness of Schiff's tone may mean that in hushed passages, such as the solos in the central *Andante* of No. 4, he is reluctant to use a veiled tone, but the singing cantabile of his playing is equally persuasive. He crowns the cycle with a scintillating account of the *Emperor Concerto*, electrifying from first to last, aptly coupled with the most heroic sonata of Beethoven's middle period, the *Appassionata*. Clear, well-balanced sound to match. The discs are available separately.

Perahia, with Haitink a deeply sympathetic partner, gives masterly performances, as close to the heart of this music as any. The sound is full and well balanced. This set has now reverted to full price and is well worth it.

Alfred Brendel offers this new Philips set as his third and last recorded survey of the Beethoven concertos, made in Vienna with Sir Simon Rattle. With each concerto recorded immediately after live performances, the results have an extra spontaneity, usually at speeds marginally faster than in his previous recordings. The dynamic range is greater too, with hushed *pianissimos* more intense, and with Rattle encouraging lightness in his accompaniments. The ambience of the Musikverein casts a warm, natural glow over the proceedings and adds the necessary weight to the *Emperor*. A fine achievement.

Fleisher's 1961 cycle with Szell represents this unique musical partnership at its peak, in performances consistently fresh and intense. In the lively account of the *Triple Concerto*, recorded in Philadelphia, the soloists are placed unnaturally forward.

Robert Levin's cycle of the five Beethoven piano concertos plus the *Choral Fantasia* – on balance the finest yet using fortepiano, despite flaws in the *Emperor* – is here collected in a four-disc box with the valuable bonus of two chamber arrangements. The first is a deft arrangement for piano trio of his *Second Symphony* made by Beethoven himself. The other is more intriguing – an arrangement only recently reconstructed – of the *Fourth Piano Concerto* with the solo part modified by Beethoven and with the orchestral accompaniment neatly transcribed for string quintet. The result is all the more refreshing on period instruments.

The combination of Barenboim and Klemperer, recording together in 1967–8, brings endless illumination, with Klemperer's measured weight set against Barenboim's youthful spontaneity, specially compelling in slow movements. The

Choral Fantasia too is given an inspired performance. The remastered sound is clear and full.

Carefree delight runs through the earlier of Kempff's two cycles of the Beethoven *Piano Concertos*. Even more than in his stereo cycle, this one (recorded in mono in 1953) finds Kempff at his most individual, turning phrases and pointing ornamentation with rare sparkle and sense of fun. The CD transfer offers immediate, well-detailed sound.

John Lill has never been more impressive on record than in his set of the Beethoven concertos, recorded in 1974–5. In each work he conveys spontaneity and a vein of poetry that in the studio have too often eluded him. Gibson and the Scottish National Orchestra provide strong, direct support, helped by very good analogue recording using the spacious City Hall, Glasgow. Very competitive with other versions at whatever price.

The partnership of Ashkenazy and Solti is fascinating, with Solti's fiery intensity contrasted with Ashkenazy's introspective qualities. Ashkenazy brings a hushed, poetic quality to every slow movement, while Solti's urgency maintains a vivid forward impulse in outer movements. At times, as in the *C minor Concerto*, the music-making may seem too tautly intense, but freshness dominates. On CD the sound is fierce at times, while the piano tone is rather shallow.

Mitsuko Uchida is obviously at home in the earlier concertos but she finds ample power throughout, with weighty accompaniments from Sanderling and the two German orchestras involved. Some may find her spacious approach a little too relaxed, but this set is a fine memento of a deeply committed artist, warmly recommended to her many admirers. The early *C minor Variations*, incisively performed, make an apt if rather ungenerous fill-up for the *Emperor*.

Backhaus recorded the Beethoven concertos with Schmidt-Isserstedt in 1958–9 when he was in his mid-seventies (the *Diabelli Variations* date from 1955). Though his bold style is lacking in grace and wit, the authority is unassailable, and the early stereo recordings are remarkably fresh, even if the close balance prevents a real pianissimo.

The Supraphon set comes from 1964–71 and made relatively little impact at the time. Jan Panenka is a highly musical player and proves himself a thoughtful Beethoven interpreter. However, he does not have quite the dramatic fire and sense of scale of pianists like Kempff or Leon Fleischer, whose set with Szell and the Cleveland Orchestra also comes from this period, and which still inspires great admiration. Panenka still gives much pleasure all the same, even if others convey a grandeur and power that eludes this combination.

Piano Concertos Nos. 1, Op. 15; 3, Op. 37.

(N) (M) **(*) RCA (ADD) 09026 63057-2. Rubinstein, Boston SO, Leinsdorf.

Piano Concerto No. 2 in B flat, Op. 19.

(N) (M) **(*) RCA (ADD) 09026 63059-2. Rubinstein, Boston SO, Leinsdorf – BRAHMS: *Piano Concerto No. 1.* **(*)

Piano Concertos Nos. 4, Op. 58; 5 (Emperor).

(N) (M) **(*) RCA (ADD) 09026 63058-2. Rubinstein, Boston SO, Leinsdorf.

Rubinstein's Beethoven cycle with Leinsdorf, recorded in the 1960s, shows him in a much more favourable technical light than his later series with Barenboim. His account of the *First Concerto* is sparkling, totally spontaneous-sounding, and conveys the joy rather than the stress of early Beethoven. There are no half-tones, and no dynamic much below *mezzo forte* (partly a question of recording and close balance), but the sense of presence is vividly conveyed in bright yet not brittle piano timbre, bringing out the clarity of the articulation against the full-bodied but none too clear orchestral sound in the warm Boston acoustic.

The readings of Nos. 2 and 3 reflect Rubinstein's mastery as a Chopin interpreter. The rubato often is not very Beethovenian, although it is full of expressive feeling. Again the sparkle and spontaneity of the playing are vividly projected by the bright, forward recording of the piano against a resonant orchestral backcloth.

In the gentle opening solo of No. 4 Rubinstein's manner is easy and confidential, with no hush or sense of great arguments impending. The exchanges of the slow movement are cleanly and sharply contrasted, with little inner intensity but with keen persuasion. The finale is wonderfully volatile with rhythms neatly pointed.

In the *Emperor* passage work is a little sketchy, and the slow movement, taken at a fast speed, becomes a bright, untroubled interlude. Yet Rubinstein's fresh individuality is winning from first to last.

Piano Concertos Nos. 1–4.

(B) *** DG (ADD) Double 459 400-2 (2). Kempff, BPO, Leitner.

(B) *** EMI (ADD) double forte CZS5 69506-2 (2). Gilels, Cleveland O, Szell.

(i) *Piano Concertos Nos. 1–4; (ii) Romances for Violin & Orchestra Nos. 1–2, Opp. 40 & 50.*

(B) *** Ph. (ADD) Duo 442 577-2 (2). (i) Kovacevich, BBC SO, C. Davis; (ii) Grumiaux, Concg. O, Haitink.

Kempff's analogue stereo accounts from the early 1960s (also available in a three-disc bargain box, 427 237-2) still sound remarkably good for their age, with a warm ambience and natural piano timbre; the wisdom Kempff dispensed is as fresh as ever. Leitner's contribution is distinguished and there is memorable orchestral playing throughout, especially in slow movements. Here Kempff's profound sense of calm is remarkable, while finales sparkle joyously.

Gilels is an incomparable Beethoven player, unfailingly illuminating and poetic. Szell, tautly controlled, gives rhythms an exhilaraing lift and has tremendous grip, and the playing of the Cleveland Orchestra is beyond reproach, with a rhythmical point that has an exhilarating lift. The recordings, made in Severance Hall in 1968, are dry and clear but with ample atmosphere.

The first four concertos bring characteristically crisp and refreshing readings from Kovacevich and Davis. These are model performances, with Kovacevich conveying a depth and thoughtful intensity that have rarely been matched. The recording, from the early 1970s, is refined and well balanced and has been admirably transferred to CD. Grumiaux's

Romances date from a decade earlier, but the sound is full and the solo playing is peerless.

Piano Concerto No. 1 in C, Op. 15.

**(*) EMI CDC5 56974-2. Argerich, Concg. O, Wallberg – MOZART: *Piano Concerto No. 25.* **(*)

Argerich, recorded live, offers playing white-hot with the inspiration of the moment, full of sparkle, even if her approach to the slow movement is on the cool side. The radio sound is good, but the coughing of the audience is at times intrusive.

(i) *Piano Concerto No. 1 in C, Op. 15; Egmont Overture; String Quartet No. 16, Op. 135:* excerpts: *Lento; Vivace* (arr. **Toscanini**).

(BB) (**) Naxos mono 8.110826. (i) Dorfman; NBC SO, Toscanini.

Ania Dorfman was a pianist who – with her crisp, clean articulation and preference for fast speeds – matched Toscanini well, making the *First Concerto* an exuberant expression of youthful high spirits, rather than an anticipation of the middle period. No one was more dramatic than Toscanini in the *Egmont Overture*. The two arrangements from Op. 135 were Toscanini party-pieces. The sound is typically limited and dry but has a satisfying body in tuttis.

(i; iii) *Piano Concerto No. 1 in C, Op. 15;* (i; ii; iv) *Choral Fantasia, Op. 80;* (ii; iv) *Meeresstille und glückliche Fahrt, Op. 112.*

(N) (B) **(*) DG 469 549-2. VPO with (i) Pollini; (ii) V. State Op. Ch.; cond. (iii) Jochum or (iv) Abbado.

In the *C major Concerto* Pollini is sometimes wilful, but with refreshing clarity of articulation. Brisk rather than poetic, his performance vividly reflects the challenge of an unexpected partnership between pianist and conductor. The recording was taken from live performances, but betrays little sign of that. In the big opening solo of the *Choral Fantasia*, in effect a Beethovenian improvisation written down, Pollini is at his most magnetic, and indeed his performance is compelling throughout. The rare choral work, which acts as filler, also benefits from the spontaneous intensity of feeling conveyed here.

Piano Concertos Nos. 1–2.

*** Sony SK 42177. Perahia, Concg. O, Haitink.

(B) *** Ph. (ADD) 422 968-2. Kovacevich, BBC SO, C. Davis.

(B) *** Decca 448 982-2. De Larrocha, Berlin RSO, Chailly – SCHUBERT: *Moment musical No. 6.* ***

(M) *** DG 445 504-2. Argerich, Philh. O, Sinopoli.

(M) *** Virgin VER5 61296-2. Tan (fortepiano), LCP, Norrington.

*** DG 437 545-2. Zimerman, VPO.

Piano Concertos Nos. 1–2; Rondo in B flat, WoO 6.

(N) *** Simax PSC 1181. Berezovsky, Swedish CO, Dausgaard.

Piano Concertos Nos. 1–2; Piano Concerto No. 1 (2nd **performance, with cadenzas by Glenn Gould).**

*** EMI CDC5 56266-2. Vogt, CBSO, Rattle.

Murray Perahia's coupling of Nos. 1 and 2 brings strong and

thoughtful performances which draw a sharp distinction between the two works. No. 2, the earlier, brings a near-Mozartian manner in the first movement; but then, rightly, a deep and measured account of the slow movement takes Beethoven into another world, hushed and intense. The *First Concerto* finds Perahia taking a fully Beethovenian view from the start. Bernard Haitink proves a lively and sympathetic partner, with the Concertgebouw playing superbly. Warm recording.

Lars Vogt's EMI issue comes with a bonus disc containing a repeat performance of the *First Concerto* using Glenn Gould's weirdly atonal cadenzas instead of Beethoven's. That is more than a gimmick, for the young German pianist combines magnetism with keen imagination. His crisp, clean articulation and preference for transparent textures (matched by Rattle's work with the orchestra) remind one of Wilhelm Kempff, while his extreme speeds reflect the example of Artur Schnabel. Excellent, transparent sound.

Thomas Dausgaard and the Swedish Chamber Orchestra produced an impressively fresh Beethoven cycle based on Jonathan Del Mar's scholarly editions of the symphonies and have now turned their attention to the piano concertos with Boris Berezovsky as the soloist. Berezovsky was a distinguished Tchaikovsky prize winner, but he has been rather overshadowed by his countryman Pletnev. His Beethoven has real stature: it has sparkle and zest, and both concertos are paced beautifully and full of vitality. In terms of their pianism and interpretation they are to be recommended among the best. Very good sound, as one would expect from a record produced by Andrew Keener.

Philips have now restored to the catalogue Stephen Kovacevich's recordings of the Beethoven concertos separately on their Virtuoso label to make a clear first bargain choice for this coupling.

Alicia de Larrocha, in an uneven cycle with the Berlin Radio Symphony Orchestra under Chailly, gives delightful performances, lightly pointed, on a Mozartian scale, with beautifully poised accounts of both slow movements. Full, vivid recording.

The conjunction of Martha Argerich and Giuseppe Sinopoli in Beethoven produces performances which give off electric sparks, daring and volatile. Argerich is jaunty in allegros, and slow movements are songful, not solemn. Vivid sound in a reverberant acoustic.

Melvyn Tan's coupling of the first two concertos, using a fortepiano, brings performances of natural, unselfconscious expressiveness. Even when Tan's speeds for slow movements are very fast indeed, his ease of expression makes them very persuasive, while conveying necessary gravity.

Zimerman, completing the cycle he began with Bernstein, directs the Vienna Philharmonic in bright, elegant, often witty performances that bring home the point that these are early works. Bright recording.

Jos van Immerseel gives lively and stylish performances on Sony, but his fortepiano convinces less readily than the instrument played by Melvyn Tan, whose coupling of these two concertos has more sparkle.

Piano Concertos Nos. 1, 2 & 4; 6 Bagatelles, Op. 126.

(N) (B) **(*) Double Decca 468 558-2 (2). Ashkenazy, VPO Mehta.

Ashkenazy gives sparkling and relaxed readings of the first two concertos, with Mehta's tactful accompaniments adding to the joyful manner of the first movement of No. 1, where Ashkenazy opts not for Beethoven's biggest cadenza but for the much shorter first option of the three. Each slow movement is thoughtful in an unmannered way, and these are both readings which stay within the brief of early Beethoven. The relaxation and sense of spontaneity which mark this Vienna cycle then bring a performance of the *Fourth Concerto* that may lack something in heroic drive, but which in its relative lightness never loses concentration, and brings a captivating sparkle to the finale. Though this may not be as powerful as Ashkenazy's earlier Chicago reading with Solti, it is fresher and more natural. The six *Bagatelles* make an attractive if ungenerous bonus. Good, bright, well-detailed recording made in the highly suitable ambience of the Sofiensaal.

Piano Concertos Nos. (i) 2–3; (ii) 4–5 (Emperor).

✪ (BB) *** Royal DCL 705752 (2). (i) Arrau; (ii) Richter-Haaser; Philh. O; (i) Galliera; (ii) Kertész.

Arrau's 1959 interpretation of the *Second Concerto* strikes an ideal balance between the work's Mozartian characteristics and Beethovenian character, although it looks forward rather than backwards. Arrau's sensitive and imaginative playing of the beautiful *Adagio* and the crisp, saucy rhythms of the *Rondo* are an unalloyed delight for the listener. The recording too is most naturally balanced. The *C minor Concerto* has a spacious gravitas: there are no Mozartian echoes here, and again Arrau's reading is commanding from his very first entry. Both performances are enhanced by particularly fine playing from the Philharmonia under Galliera, and the early stereo could hardly be more natural.

Richter-Haaser's *G major Concerto* is comparably memorable and, although his reading has more of the grand manner than, say, Kempff's account, spontaneity breathes in every bar. Again first-rate recording (from the early 1960s). The *Emperor* brings less of the feeling of a live performance. The approach is the same but the achievement less memorable. The *Emperor* has some beautiful playing in the slow movement and is by no means to be dismissed; but three bull's-eyes out of four make this an indispensable bargain. The analogue recording is well up to standard.

Piano Concertos Nos. 2; 4.

(M) *** Sony (ADD) SBK 48165. Fleisher, Cleveland O, Szell.

Leon Fleisher, partnered by George Szell, is both powerful and intense in his spontaneous-sounding performance of No. 2, giving weight to early Beethoven. In No. 4 they are even more searching, with the soloist's refreshingly imaginative playing matched by glorious sounds from the Cleveland Orchestra. The bright, forward recordings have satisfying fullness and body.

Piano Concertos Nos. 2; 5 (Emperor).

(*(**)) BBC mono BBCL 4028-2. Hess, BBC SO, Sargent
(includes interview with John Amis).

Recorded in the Royal Albert Hall at Prom performances, this issue in the BBC Legends series gives the most vivid idea of the dynamism and depth of Myra Hess as a Beethoven interpreter. The *Emperor* is the more remarkable for the leonine quality of the performance, a vitally spontaneous reading which exploits the widest expressive range, at once heroic and poetic. The meditative intensity of the slow movement, rapt and refined, leads on to an exuberant account of the finale. No. 2, recorded three years later, also brings a remarkable performance: fresh, poetic and youthfully urgent in the first movement, dedicated in the slow movement, and sparkling and witty in the finale. However, it is important to stress the considerable difference here in recording quality between No. 5 (1957) and No. 2 (1960). It is quite possible that the latter comes from a private off-air tape rather than a BBC mastertape. The sound is more opaque, has *very* limited frequency range and suffers from distortion.

(i) *Piano Concerto No. 3. Coriolan Overture* (with rehearsal sequence).

(B) (***) Naxos mono 8.110804. (i) Hess; NBC SO, Toscanini
(with WAGNER: *Götterdämmerung: Siegfried's Rhine Journey* (***)).

On this live recording of a 1946 broadcast Dame Myra Hess gives a thrilling performance, one of her very finest on disc, with the outer movements crisply articulated and beautifully sprung at high speed and the slow movement warmly expressive, bringing out a rare warmth in Toscanini too. *Coriolan* is high-powered, dry and incisive, and the Wagner makes a welcome fill-up.

Piano Concerto No. 3; Rondo in B flat, WoO6.

(N) (M) *(*) DG (ADD) 463 649-2. S. Richter, VSO, Sanderling
– MOZART: *Piano Concerto No. 20.*

Richter's performance, now reissued as one of DG's 'Originals', is too chilly and detached to be wholly convincing. Like Schnabel, Richter takes the slow movement very slowly indeed, but unlike Schnabel he provides little warmth and the result is curiously square. The finale is very hard-driven.

The *Rondo* is a different matter. Richter's sparkling account is effortlessly brilliant, but not to the exclusion of all else: there is subtlety here and even a touch of humour, but above all complete spontaneity and a sense of enjoyment throughout. The recording has come up well with clean piano tone and a fresh overall balance.

Piano Concertos Nos. 3 in C min., Op. 37; 4 in G, Op. 58.

*** DG (IMS) 429 749-2. Zimerman, VPO, Bernstein.
*** Sony SK 39814. Perahia, Concg. O, Haitink.
(B) *** Ph. (ADD) 426 062-2. Kovacevich, BBC SO, C. Davis.
*** Ph. 446 082-2. Uchida, Concg. O, Sanderling.

Zimerman finds freshness and poetry in both Nos. 3 and 4, very sympathetically accompanied by Bernstein, who exactly matches his soloist in the thoughtful dialogue of the central

Andante of No. 4. Bright sound that yet does not allow a full pianissimo.

Perahia gives readings that are at once intensely poetic and individual but also strong, with pointing and shading of passage-work that consistently convey the magic of the moment caught on the wing, helped by fine, spacious and open recorded sound.

The Philips versions of Nos. 3 and 4 from the searching partnership of Kovacevich and Sir Colin Davis make an excellent bargain alternative to Perahia, with well-focused transfers.

Uchida proves a strong interpreter in Beethoven's *C minor Concerto*, understandingly supported by Sanderling. No. 4 is freely improvisational, both poetic and strongly held together. With superb Concertgebouw recording, this is refreshingly individual, with a feeling of live music-making and a fine sampler of her complete set (see above).

Piano Concertos Nos. 3, Op. 37; 4 in G, Op. 58.

(N) (M) ** RCA (ADD) 09026 63078-2. Rubinstein, LPO, Barenboim.

Piano Concerto No. 5 (Emperor); Piano Sonata No. 18, Op. 31/2.

(N) (M) **(*) RCA (ADD) 09026 63079-2. Rubinstein, LPO, Barenboim.

Rubinstein's cycle of Beethoven concertos with Barenboim was recorded in 1975 when the octogenarian pianist was in exuberant mood. The sessions saw each concerto completed quicker than expected, and much of the drive behind that comes over powerfully, although the slips of finger are too many and too noticeable to allow full enjoyment. It might have been different had Rubinstein not insisted on so close a balance for the piano, which is vividly caught. The accompaniments, beautifully played by the LPO, are at times masked behind the piano-tone, something this otherwise impressive remastering for reissue in the 'Rubinstein Edition' cannot alter, although the balance is more equal in the sparkling *Emperor Concerto*. The *E flat Sonata* makes a fine bonus, full of character, especially the *Scherzo* and the *Presto* finale; it was very well recorded (also in 1975).

Piano Concertos Nos. (i) 4 in G, Op. 58; (ii) 5 in E flat (Emperor).

(N) (M) *** SMK 8971. Perahia, Concg. O, Haitink.
(M) *** DG (ADD) 447 402-2. Kempff, BPO, Leitner.
(N) ☻ (M) *** Decca mono/stereo 467 126-2. Curzon, VPO, Knappertsbusch.
(B) *** DG (ADD) 439 483-2. Pollini, VPO, Boehm.
(N) (M) *** Ph. 464 681-2. Arrau, Dresden State O, Davis.

Perahia's accounts are strong, spacious and thoughtful with characteristic touches of poetry. Haitink is a responsive partner – each movement immediately takes wing.

The Kempff/Leitner performances bring another outstanding mid-priced recommendation. In the *Fourth Concerto* Kempff's delicacy of fingerwork and his shading of tone-colour are unsurpassed. Though his version of the *Emperor* is not on an epic scale, Kempff's exceptionally wide range of tone and dynamic gives it power in plenty.

Curzon's refinement and reflective poetry is wonderfully

refreshing in both concertos; moreover, he found a perfect partner in Hans Schmidt-Isserstedt. The *Fourth Concerto* is an Elysian performance, full of delicate lyrical feeling, the slow movement unsurpassed on record, not even by Kempff. Moreover, the 1954 mono recording, made in the Musikverein, is of outstanding quality, with warm, luminous piano tone and a clear, transparent orchestral image, not lacking bloom.

The *Emperor* is stereo, made in the Sofiensaal three years later. Again it is a refined and thoughtful reading. Curzon's playing in the slow movement is beautifully controlled and brings out the poetry gently and movingly. The first movement certainly does not lack compulsion, and the finale is the only movement where one feels his approach shifts the viewpoint back almost to Mozart; there is a restraint about the essentially rumbustious movement that some may feel to be almost too much of a good thing. Yet the keen intelligence of the playing and the inner concentration working throughout the reading keep it fully alive.

The Vienna Philharmonic plays strongly and authoritatively under Knappertsbusch, and the new transfer of the 1957 master has miraculously cleaned up the sound, the orchestral tuttis now full and not edgy and the piano quality very impressive indeed. This makes an ideal coupling for Decca's Legends series. But the Rosette is for the *Andante* of the *G major*, which recalls the notion that Beethoven had Orpheus's plea for the return of Euridice in mind. This Decca disc completely replaces Curzon's radio recordings with the Bavarian Radio Symphony Orchestra under Kubelik made two decades later (Audite 95.459), but his more robust 1971 BBC Festival Hall account of the *Emperor* with Boulez makes a fascinating alternative (see below).

The bargain Classikon coupling offers two of the most strikingly individual performances from Pollini's earlier cycle, excellently transferred. After the poised account of the *Fourth Concerto*, the distinction of Pollini's interpretation of the *Emperor* is never in doubt, with the slow movement elegant and the finale urgent and energetic.

Arrau's 1984 account of the *Emperor* has long been a primary recommendation, standing high among countless other versions. The wonder is that, in a recording made when he was over eighty, he sounds so uninhibited and carefree. There are technical flaws, and the digital recording made in Dresden's Lukas Kirche is rather resonant in the bass. But with Sir Colin Davis and the Dresden State Orchestra as electrifying partners, the voltage is even higher than in his earlier versions of the mid 1960s. The slow movement flows more freely, less hushed and poised than before, while the finale at a relaxed speed is joyful in its jaunty rhythms. Intensely individual, the very opposite of routine, this is from first to last a performance which reflects new searching by a deeply thoughtful musician. It is a thrillingly expansive *Emperor* which will give much satisfaction and is truly worthy to be included in the Philips collection of '50 Great Recordings'. The snag is that it is now coupled with No. 4, recorded at the same time, which is altogether less successful.

Here Arrau's weighty view brings speeds slower than usual, and for many, despite countless individual touches and excellent orchestral playing, the sluggishness will hamper enjoyment. The bass-heavy recording also adds to the impression of ponderousness. Even so this disc must be given the strongest recommendation for the superb account of the *Emperor* alone.

(i; ii; iii) *Piano Concerto No. 4;* **(i; iv)** *Symphony No. 5 ;* **(i; v)** *Overture: Leonore III;* **(vi)** *String Quartet No. 9 (Razumovsky), Op. 59/3);* **(i)** *Piano Sonatas Nos. 17 (Tempest); 21 in C, Waldstein).*

(N) (BB) **(*) DG Panorama (ADD/DDD) 469 112-2 (2).
  (i) VPO; (ii) Pollini; (iii) Boehm; (iv) Carlos Kleiber;
  (v) Abbado; (vi) Emerson Qt.

A seemingly random collection of Beethoven which offers Carlos Kleiber's famous account of the *Fifth Symphony* (more sensibly coupled with the *Seventh* on the Originals label) and Pollini's distinguished reading of the *Fourth Concerto*. Though he is not quite as convincing in the *Tempest* sonata and it only sporadically seems to draw us into its world, he is on top form in the *Waldstein*. Those who like high-powered Beethoven will enjoy the Emerson's *Third Razumovsky Quartet*. A not terribly well conceived programme on the bargain Panorama label.

Piano Concerto No. 5 in E flat (Emperor), Op. 73.

*** DG 429 748-2. Zimerman, VPO, Bernstein.
*** BBC Legends (ADD) BBCL 4020-2. Curzon, BBC SO, Boulez – MOZART: *Piano Concerto No. 26 (Coronation).* ***

(i) *Piano Concerto No. 5 (Emperor). Piano Sonata No. 7 in D, Op. 10/3.*

(M) (***) EMI mono CDH7 61005-2. Fischer, (i) with Philh. O, Furtwängler.

Piano Concerto No. 5 (Emperor); Piano Sonata No. 30 in E, Op. 109.

⚫**(B) ***** Ph. (ADD) 422 482-2. Kovacevich, (i) LSO, C. Davis.

(i) *Piano Concerto No. 5 (Emperor). Overtures: Coriolan, Op. 62; Creatures of Prometheus, Op. 43; Leonora No. 3.*

(N) (M) *** Chan. 6612. (i) Lill; CBSO, Weller.

Piano Concerto No. 5 (Emperor); Grosse Fuge in B flat, Op. 133.

(B) *** EMI CD-EMX 2184. Kovacevich, Australian CO.

Piano Concerto No. 5 (Emperor); **(i)** *Choral Fantasia, Op. 80.*

(M) **(*) EMI CDM5 67329-2. Barenboim, New Philh. O, Klemperer, (i) with John Alldis Ch.
(*) DG 447 771-2. Levin (fortepiano), ORR, Gardiner, (i) with Monteverdi Ch.

Kovacevich is unsurpassed as an interpreter of this most magnificent of concertos. His superb account for Philips, now on Virtuoso, has set a model for everyone and, with its late sonata coupling, remains the strongest recommendation, very well transferred. His version with the soloist directing from the keyboard is recognizably from the same inspired artist, though speeds are consistently faster and the manner is sharper and tauter. The piano sound on the digital recording is brighter, if not so well balanced. The *Grosse Fuge* on Eminence makes an unusual but apt coupling.

Zimerman reserves for the *Emperor* his most powerful playing and Bernstein sensitively encourages him into spontaneous-sounding expressiveness, turning phrases with consistent imagination.

The partnership of the introspective Clifford Curzon and the incisive Boulez may not seem a promising one, but in this live performance (recorded in 1971 at the Royal Festival Hall) the challenge between the two brings electrifying results. Curzon is at his most taut and incisive, while finding depths of poetry, and Boulez proves a surprisingly sympathetic interpreter of Beethoven, matching his soloist in subtle dynamic shading, while bringing home the work's dramatic power. Full, forward recording.

On Chandos, John Lill's bold, authoritative Beethoven style brings breadth and majesty to the opening movement, with the slow movement serene and the finale vigorously joyful. Walter Weller's performances of the three overtures are splendidly alive. The CBSO is on top form throughout, and the full, resonant sound is of the best Chandos vintage. An outstanding alternative mid-priced choice.

The Barenboim/Klemperer partnership in the *Emperor* produces a remarkable degree of concentration from pianist and conductor alike and provides an astonishingly fresh experience. The performance – with a number of unimportant 'fluffs' unedited – has a striking sense of spontaneity, as has the magnificent account of the *Choral Fantasia*. The new transfer of the 1967 Abbey Road recording brings out a hint of harshness on the massed strings, but the piano is caught admirably.

When Gardiner's orchestra is fuller-bodied than those on rival versions, the discrepancy with the solo fortepiano is underlined, and the 1812 instrument chosen is disconcertingly twangy at the top. Speeds are moderate, with the finale given an exhilarating performance. The performance of the *Choral Fantasia* too has fine panache. As a supplement, Levin offers on separate tracks two alternative improvisations of his own, easily interchangeable with the one Beethoven published years after the first performance.

Edwin Fischer's 1951 recording with Furtwängler and the Philharmonia Orchestra is one of the classics of the gramophone, an *Emperor* both imperious and imperial. The *D major Sonata*, recorded in 1954, is not to be missed either, made at Fischer's last recording session.

(i) *Piano Concerto No. 5 (Emperor)*. *32 Variations on an Original Theme in C min.*, WoO 80; *12 Variations on a Russian Dance from 'Das Waldmädchen' (Wranitzky)*, WoO 71; *6 Variations on a Turkish March from 'The Ruins of Athens'*, Op. 76.

(B) *** EMI double forte (ADD) CZS5 69509-2 (2). Gilels,
   (i) with Cleveland O, Szell – DVORAK: *Symphony No. 8*. **(*)

Of the many versions of the *Emperor Concerto* available, few are finer than Gilels's, with strength matched by poetry, and with Szell offering the strongest backing. The *C minor Variations* are superbly done, and the other two sets bring the strongest characterization too. Bright, full sound.

(i) *Piano Concerto No. 5 (Emperor)*; (ii) *Piano Concerto in E flat*, WoO 4 (arr. & orch. Willy Hess); (iii) *Violin Concerto in D*, Op. 61; (iv) *Triple Concerto for Violin, Cello & Piano in C*, Op. 56.

(B) **(*) Ph. (ADD) Duo 442 580-2 (2). (i) Kovacevich, LSO,
   C. Davis; (ii) Grychtolowna, Folkwang CO, Dressel;
   (iii) Krebbers, Concg. O, Haitink; (iv) Szeryng, Starker,
   Arrau, New Philh. O, Inbal.

Kovacevich's superb 1969 account of the *Emperor* is here part of an attractive Duo compilation which includes also the early *E flat Piano Concerto* (WoO 4) which the composer wrote when he was only fourteen, here offered in a spirited performance in a reconstruction by Willy Hess. Krebbers's 1974 recording of the *Violin Concerto* is outstanding. In his hands the slow movement has a tender simplicity which is irresistible. The companion account of the *Triple Concerto* with Arrau, Szeryng and Starker is less strongly projected, losing concentration at very unhurried tempi. Yet the set remains highly recommendable.

(i) *Piano Concerto No. 5 (Emperor)*; (ii) *Triple Concerto for Violin, Cello & Piano in C*, Op. 56.

(M) *** Sony (ADD) SBK 46549. (i) Fleisher, Cleveland O,
   Szell; (ii) Stern, Rose, Istomin, Phd. O, Ormandy.

Leon Fleisher, who worked with Szell with special understanding, gives a reading of the *Emperor* impressive for its dramatic vigour. Stern, Rose and Istomin make an inspired trio of soloists in the *Triple Concerto*, sadly marred by their close balance.

(i) *Piano Concertos Nos. 1–5*. (ii) *Violin Concerto*. *Symphonies Nos. 1–9*; *Overtures: Consecration of the House*; *Egmont*; *Leonora No. 3*.

(N) (B) **(*) Decca (ADD) 467 892-2 (8). (i) Backhaus;
   (ii) Szeryng with LSO; otherwise VPO, Schmidt-Isserstedt
   (with Sutherland, Horne, King, Talvela & V. Stata Op. Ch. in
   No. 9).

Backhaus's authoritative, overtly classical set of the *Piano Concertos* is also available separately (see below), but Schmidt-Isserstedt's vintage cycle of the symphonies, recorded in the Sofiensaal in the mid- to late 1960s, is new to CD. It presents a consistently musical view, not lacking strength, and without distracting idiosyncrasies. All the symphonies are beautifully played – the character of the VPO coming over strongly – and very well recorded. Apart from the *Pastoral*, clean and classically straightforward, but entirely lacking charm, there is no outright disappointment here, and the series culminates in a splendid account of the *Ninth*, one which does not quite scale the heights but which, particularly in the slow movement and the finale (with outstanding soloists), conveys visionary strength.

For some a reservation may be that the performances are not so strikingly indvidual as to compel repeated hearings, although the *Fourth* must be excepted from this general comment. It is a symphony well suited to Schmidt-Isserstedt's thoughtful poetic style. The *Fifth* – not a symphony that regularly gets successful performances on record – also stands out, with a first movement that has both bite and breathing space, a nicely measured *Andante* and a gloriously triumphant finale. Only the *Scherzo* invites controversy in its slow tempo; the *Seventh*, similarly, is compelling throughout. The first movement of the *Eighth* is slower than usual, and although the *Allegretto* is crisp and light, the *Minuet* is rather heavily pointed, with a Brahmsian touch in the *Trio*.

These are all performances that one can live with, but their mood is essentially serious: only rarely do they spark one off with fresh joy in Beethoven. The first two symphonies (again with generally slow tempi), although the playing is nicely detailed, are seriously lacking in charm. Szeryng's account of the *Violin Concerto* derives from the Philips catalogue and dates from 1965. His is a strongly lyrical performance, withdrawn in the *Larghetto*, yet creating a dreamy, hushed atmosphere where the gentle beauty of mood is the highlight of the reading, well supported by his partner.

Violin Concerto in D, Op. 61.

(M) *** EMI CDM5 66900-2 [566952]. Perlman, Philh. O, Giulini.

◉ (M) *** DG (ADD) 447 403-2. Schneiderhan, BPO, Jochum – MOZART: *Violin Concerto No. 5.* ***

(M) (***) EMI mono CDM5 66975-2 [566990]. Menuhin, Philh. O, Furtwängler – MENDELSSOHN: *Violin Concerto.* (***)

*** EMI CDC7 54072-2. Kyung-Wha Chung, Concg. O, Tennstedt – BRUCH: *Violin Concerto No. 1.* ***

(B) *** DG (ADD) Double 453 142-2 (2). Zukerman, Chicago SO, Barenboim – BRAHMS: *Concerto* **(*); MENDELSSOHN; TCHAIKOVSKY: *Concertos.* ***

(M) *** DG (ADD) 463 078-2. Zukerman, Chicago SO, Barenboim – HAYDN: *Sinfonia concertante in B flat.* ***

(M) *** RCA (ADD) 09026 61742-2. Heifetz, Boston SO, Munch – BRAHMS: *Concerto.* ***

(M) *** RCA (ADD) 09026 68980-2. Heifetz, Boston SO, Munch – MENDELSSOHN: *Violin Concerto.* ***

*** Sony SK 60584. Hahn, Baltimore SO, Zinman – BERNSTEIN: *Serenade.* ***

(***) BBC (ADD) BBCL 4019-2. Menuhin, Moscow PO, D. Oistrakh – MOZART: *Sinfonia concertante, K.364.* (***)

**(*) EMI CDC7 54574-2. Kennedy, N. German RSO, Tennstedt – BACH: (Unaccompanied) *Violin Sonatas and Partitas.*

(BB) *** Belart (ADD) 461 355-2. Campoli, LPO, Krips – MENDELSSOHN: *Violin Concerto.* ***

(BB) **(*) Virgin 2 x 1 VBD5 61504-2 (2). Seiler, City of L. Sinf., Hickox – HAYDN; MENDELSSOHN: *Concertos.* **(*)

(***) APR Signature mono APR 5506. Huberman, VPO, Szell – LALO: *Symphonie espagnole.* (**(*))

(**(*)) Testament mono SBT 1083. Haendel, Philh. O, Kubelik – BRUCH: *Violin Concerto No. 1.* (**(*))

(N) (BB) (***) Naxos mono 8.110936. Heifetz, NBC SO, Toscanini – BRAHMS: *Violin Concerto.* (***)

(i) Violin Concerto. Overtures: Consecration of the House; Leonora No. 3.

(M) **(*) Sony (ADD) SMK 63153. (i) Stern; NYPO, Bernstein.

(i) Violin Concerto; (ii) Romances Nos. 1 in G, Op. 40; 2 in F, Op. 50.

◉ *** Teldec 9031 74881-2. Kremer, COE, Harnoncourt.

*** EMI CDC7 49567-2. Perlman, BPO, Barenboim.

(***) Testament mono SBT 1109. Menuhin; (i) Lucerne Festival O; (ii) Philh. O, Furtwängler.

(B) *** Ph. (ADD) 420 348-2. Grumiaux; (i) Concg. O, C. Davis; (ii) New Philh. O, De Waart.

(B) *** Penguin/Ph. (ADD) 460 647-2. Grumiaux; (i) Concg. O, C. Davis; (ii) New Philh. O, De Waart.

(BB) *** Naxos 8.550149. Nishizaki, Slovak PO (Bratislava), Jean.

Gidon Kremer's Teldec account with Nikolaus Harnoncourt and the Chamber Orchestra of Europe offers one of his most commanding recordings, both polished and full of flair, with tone ravishingly pure. The controversial point is the cadenza in the first movement, for (like Schneiderhan) he uses a transcription of the big cadenza which Beethoven wrote for his piano arrangement of the work, but with added piano as well as timpani. He also plays violin versions of the other cadenzas and flourishes that punctuate Beethoven's piano version. One of the most refreshing versions of the concerto ever put on disc, backed up by crisp, unsentimental readings of the two *Romances*.

Perlman's outstanding first digital recording of Beethoven's *Violin Concerto* is rightly reissued as one of EMI's 'Great Recordings of the Century'. This is the finer of his two EMI versions. The element of slight understatement, the refusal to adopt too romantically expressive a style, makes for a compelling strength, perfectly matched by Giulini's thoughtful, direct accompaniment. The beautiful slow movement has a quality of gentle rapture, almost matching Schneiderhan's sense of stillness; and the finale, joyfully and exuberantly fast, is charged with the fullest excitement. The digital recording is satisfyingly full and spacious.

Wolfgang Schneiderhan's stereo version of the *Violin Concerto* is among the greatest recordings of this work: the serene spiritual beauty of the slow movement has never been surpassed on record. Schneiderhan uses cadenzas transcribed from Beethoven's piano version of the concerto. In DG's 'Legendary Recordings' series, the transfer of the well-balanced 1962 recording is fresh and realistic. The Mozart coupling is apt and generous.

Recorded only months before the conductor's death, Menuhin's version with Furtwängler is another classic which emerges with extraordinary freshness in the latest transfer. Here the bond between the conductor and his younger soloist brought an extra intensity to a natural musical alliance between two inspirational artists, both at their peak. Rarely has the Beethoven concerto been recorded with such sweetness and tenderness, yet with firm underlying strength. With its distinguished coupling, it is a compact disc which defies the years. One hardly registers that it is a mono recording.

Kyung-Wha Chung's EMI performance, recorded live in the Concertgebouw, is searching and intense. Next to Perlman on another live recording from EMI, Chung is lighter and more mercurial. The element of vulnerability adds to the emotional weight, above all in the wistfully tender slow movement, while the outer movements are full of flair. The recording is full and atmospheric.

Testament offers an alternative Menuhin recording that has been buried for 50 years. Recorded in August 1947, this was his first version of the Beethoven concerto and his first inspired collaboration with Furtwängler. The visionary spaciousness of the reading defied the fashion of the time for a brisk approach (largely promoted by Heifetz and Toscanini). Five years later, Menuhin and Furtwängler made their definitive LP recording, above; but here there is extra poetry and tenderness, particularly in the slow movement; and the CD transfer is first rate.

Grumiaux's beautiful account is both classical and deeply felt. Warmly recorded, this bargain disc stands high in the list of versions. The *Romances*, too, are most persuasive. The concerto, together with the *F major Romance*, is also available on a Duo issue, with the concertos of Brahms, Mendelssohn and Tchaikovsky (442 287-2), and also as a Penguin Classic, with an introductory essay by John Fortune.

Those looking for a super-bargain, digital version will find Nishizaki's spontaneous performance a match for many by more famous names. With excellent backing from the Slovak Philharmonic under Kenneth Jean, her playing is individual yet unselfconscious. The *Larghetto* is poised and serene, and the finale buoyant. The two *Romances* are also very well played. The digital recording is excellent, with resonant, spacious orchestral sound.

Zukerman's 1977 recording of the Beethoven *Violin Concerto* comes on a DG Double with three key recordings by Milstein. With Barenboim, Zukerman gives a spacious and concentratedly persuasive account of the first movement. The slow movement is rapt in its simplicity. For anyone wanting these four key concertos, this is an excellent recommendation. It also comes at mid-price, attractively recoupled with a fine performance of the Haydn *B flat Sinfonia concertante*.

Heifetz's unique performance is available coupled with either Brahms or Mendelssohn. RCA's digital transfer of a recording originally made in the very earliest days of stereo has a fine sense of realism and presence, and the extra immediacy of CD reinforces the supreme mastery of a performance which may adopt fast speeds but never sounds rushed.

With pure, refined tone, Hilary Hahn gives a dedicated performance, with the poetry of the work never underplayed, but without self-indulgence. The hushed beauty of the central *Larghetto* – taken on the slow side – leads on to a clean-cut, athletic account of the finale. Clear, well-balanced sound.

The reissue of Isaac Stern's performance on Sony shows the intense creative relationship established between this artist and Bernstein at an early peak in both their respective careers. Stern's reading has a tremendous onward flow with his personality strongly projected, yet (in spite of the forward balance of the soloist) Bernstein keeps the orchestra well in the picture and the energy of the music-making is compulsive. The caveat is that the close (1959) recording prevents any real *pianissimo*, but Sony has improved the original sound to an acceptable level by modern standards. The two overtures make a good bonus.

In 1963 the Moscow Philharmonic Orchestra visited London's Royal Albert Hall, and Menuhin joined them in the Beethoven *Violin Concerto* with no less a figure than David Oistrakh conducting. There is something rather special about this reading with Oistrakh (the slow movement is seraphic) and those who treasure memories of the occasion will welcome its reincarnation in this BBC recording, which is warm and truthful.

Nigel Kennedy's version was recorded live at a single performance in Lübeck, presented complete with encores (movements from the solo Bach *Sonatas* and *Partitas*). Like his interpretation of the Brahms, Kennedy's reading is wilfully slow but always persuasive, even when, after the big Kreisler cadenza in the first movement, he and Tennstedt threaten to come to a dead halt. The cadenza in the finale brings the most controversial point: Kennedy's improvisation which lapses into quarter-tones.

Campoli's early stereo Decca version has an appealing, freshly spontaneous lyricism, and the slow movement has depth and a simple poetry. Krips is in obvious sympathy with his soloist, and the orchestra displays a pleasingly light touch in the finale. This Belart reissue is even more notable for the captivating Mendelssohn coupling. A splendid bargain.

An impressive account from Mayumi Seiler which stands up well against distinguished bargain-priced competition. Hickox is slightly below his finest form and is a bit stiff in the opening of the first movement, but his soloist soars lyrically and is movingly serene in the slow movement, creating an ethereal thread of sound for the secondary theme; she then dances away in the finale. The sound is good, and the couplings include two concertos each by Haydn and Mendelssohn, all offered for the cost of a single medium-priced CD!

Huberman's 1934 performance is another classic version, raptly intense – as in the magical opening to the first-movement coda – but taken at speeds that flow easily, far faster overall than is now the rule. The APR transfer is first rate, with the violin immediate and full of presence.

The partnership of Heifetz and Toscanini in the Beethoven *Violin Concerto* makes for legendary results, uniquely powerful and purposeful, with the purity of the violinist's playing, notably above the stave, making up for any lack of tenderness. Heifetz's example leads Toscanini to a rare gentleness in the slow movement, while the finale is exhilarating in its rhythmic drive. The hard NBC recording is nicely mellowed in the Naxos transfer, if with some audible hiss. An ideal coupling with Heifetz's 1939 version of the Brahms.

Ida Haendel's 1951 recording is an exceptionally powerful one, commanding and concentrated even at spacious speeds. In a transfer of Testament's highest standard, it makes a welcome, if relatively expensive, reissue, in coupling with an outstanding account of the Bruch concerto.

Kyung Wha Chung's 1979 Decca performance is superseded by her later, full-priced, EMI version with Tennstedt, for the earlier account, measured and thoughtful, lacks compulsion thanks to the prosaic conducting of Kondrashin (460 014-2).

The Zehetmair/Brüggen partnership is for authenticists only. The *Romances* are placed first and are far from romantic, with the *G major* very brisk and unbeguiling. So is the opening of the concerto, with the timpani taps very dry, the orchestral exposition strongly accented and dramatically gruff. It is as if Brüggen is not persuaded that this work is the epitome of radiant Beethoven lyricism. Zehetmair uses the first-movement cadenza, with timpani, favoured by Schneiderhan, but plays it as if it were by Paganini, and the great reprise of the main theme is all but thrown away in the closing pages. Fortunately the *Larghetto* relaxes more, and Zehetmair's playing is often very beautiful, quite ethereal. Brüggen is merely supportive, and the bold gruffness returns to usher in the invigorating finale, again mirrored by the soloist in his cadenza (Ph. 462 123-2).

(i) *Violin Concerto;* (ii) *Triple Concerto in C, Op. 56.*

(M) ** Sony (ADD) SM2K 66941 (2). Stern, with (i) NYPO, Barenboim; (ii) Rose, Istomin, Phd. O, Ormandy – BRAHMS: *Concertos.* ***

Stern's recording of the *Violin Concerto* with Barenboim, dates from 1975 and is not as imaginative as his earlier one with Bernstein. Stern is less spontaneous-sounding than in his earlier version, though the sound is fuller. The *Triple Concerto*, recorded a decade earlier in 1964, brings a recording from three friends who reveal their personal joy in making music together, though the soloists are balanced too close.

Clarinet Concerto in D (arr. Pletnev from *Violin Concerto, Op. 61*).

*** DG 457 652-2. Collins, Russian Nat. O, Pletnev – MOZART: *Clarinet Concerto.* ***

Michael Collins offers a daring transcription for the clarinet of the Beethoven *Violin Concerto*. The warmth of Beethoven's lyricism is brought out more richly in the tone of the clarinet, not just in the slow movement – where Collins feels the advantages are greatest – but in the long first movement too. Apart from the obvious point that no double-stopping is possible on the clarinet, the main difference in the transcription involves a downward octave transposition of the solo line over many sections in all three movements. Pletnev has managed it so deftly that, with passage-work shifted to register comfortably for the clarinet, it consistently sounds natural. The wonder is that Collins makes light of all problems so that one can readily enjoy the music in a new way.

Triple Concerto for Violin, Cello & Piano in C, Op. 56.

(M) *** EMI (ADD) CDM5 66902-2 [566954]. D. Oistrakh, Rostropovich, S. Richter, BPO, Karajan – BRAHMS: *Double Concerto.* ***

*** RCA 09026 68964-2. Browning, Zukerman, Kirshbaum, LSO, Eschenbach – BRAHMS: *Double Concerto.* ***

(B) *** EMI double forte CZS5 69331-2 (2). D. Oistrakh, Oborin, Knushevitzky, Philh. O, Sargent – BRAHMS: *Double Concerto;* MOZART: *Violin Concerto No. 3;* PROKOFIEV: *Violin Concerto No. 2.* ***

(BB) *** CfP Double CDCFPSD 4775 (2). Zimmermann, Cohen, Manz, ECO, Saraste – DVORAK: *Cello Concerto;*

ELGAR: *Cello Concerto;* TCHAIKOVSKY: *Variations on a Rococo Theme.* ***

(i) *Triple Concerto. Piano Concerto in D* (arr. from *Violin Concerto*), *Op. 61a.*

(BB) *** Naxos 8.554288. Jandó; (i) with Kang, Kliegel; Nicolaus Esterházy O, Drahos.

(i) *Triple Concerto. Overtures: King Stephen, Op. 117; Leonora No. 3, Op. 72b; The Ruins of Athens, Op. 113.*

(M) **(*) DG (ADD) 447 907-2. (i) Mutter, Ma, Zeltser; BPO, Karajan.

(i; ii; iii) *Triple Concerto;* (ii) *2 Romances for Violin & Orchestra, Opp. 40 & 50;* (i; iv) *Romance cantabile for Piano, Flute & Bassoon with 2 Oboes & Strings in E min.*

**(*) DG 453 488-2. (i) Myung-Whun Chung, (ii) Kyung-Wha Chung, (iii) Myung-Wha Chung; (iv) Patrick Gallois, Pascal Gallois; Philh. O, Myung-Whun Chung.

(i) *Triple Concerto;* (ii) *Symphony No. 10: 1st movt* (realized & completed Cooper).

(M) *** Chan. 6501. (i) Kalichstein–Laredo–Robinson Trio, ECO, Gibson; (ii) CBSO, Weller.

(i) *Triple Concerto;* (ii) *Choral Fantasia.*

*** EMI CDC5 55516-2. Barenboim (piano & cond.) with (i) Perlman, Ma; (ii) German Op. Ch.; BPO.

*** Ph. 438 005-2. (i) Beaux Arts Trio; (ii) Pressler, Mid-German R. Ch.; Leipzig GO, Masur.

On the EMI recording, a breathtaking line-up, led by David Oistrakh. This is warm, expansive music-making that confirms even more clearly than before the strength of the piece. The new transfer is remarkably vivid and has firmed up the orchestral tuttis most satisfactorily. Now coupled in EMI's 'Great Recordings of the Century' with a similarly commanding account of the Brahms *Double Concerto*, this is an irresistible mid-priced bargain.

With such starry soloists as Perlman, Ma and Barenboim, it is not surprising that these too are strongly characterized, spontaneous-sounding performances. Here are great musicians who challenge and respond to one another, phrase by phrase, just as Oistrakh, Rostropovich and Richter did. Barenboim as conductor here keeps the tension taut, as soloist conveying in the opening cadenza of the *Choral Fantasia* the impression of a Beethovenian improvisation.

Not only does Menahem Pressler's playing in the later Beaux Arts recording of the *Triple Concerto* with Masur sparkle brightly, he is an inspired soloist in the *Choral Fantasia*. He sets a pattern of joyfulness, taking the work less seriously than usual, with witty pointing of the variations.

The partnership of Dong-Suk Kang, Maria Kliegel and Jenö Jandó may not be familiar, but it is none the less formidable. All three are accomplished soloists and are so good that it seems invidious to single any one of them out. Béla Drahos draws clean-cut, consistently alert playing from the orchestra, more crisply detailed than in most versions. Beethoven's piano version of the *Violin Concerto* makes an apt and exceptionally generous coupling. Jenö Jandó uses his artistry to minimize any ungainliness in the piano-writing, articulating as cleanly and crisply as he does in the *Triple Concerto*.

On RCA, three distinguished American artists (Browning, Zukerman and Kirshbaum) also form a winning team, particularly impressive in the central *Largo*, where Kirshbaum's opening cello solo is most subtly shaped from its hushed start. The finale is then light and sparkling.

The earlier EMI recording, now on double forte, also features distinguished Russian soloists and dates from the early days of stereo, yet the sound is excellent for its period, the balance one of the most successful this concerto has received even now. Sargent is authoritative, and his soloists make a good team.

On Classics for Pleasure, with first-rate, modern, digital recording and with Robert Cohen leading an excellent team of prize-winning young soloists (his solo in the slow movement is superb), this makes an outstanding bargain version, keenly competitive. Jukka-Pekka Saraste and the ECO provide a lively, understanding accompaniment, and the performance has splendid spontaneity throughout. However, this set has just been withdrawn.

The 1984 Chandos version of the *Triple Concerto* is exceptionally well recorded. Sharon Robinson, the cellist, takes the lead with pure tone and fine intonation, though both her partners are more forceful artists. A clean-cut, often refreshing view of the work, it is coupled with Weller's strong version of Barry Cooper's completion of the first movement of Beethoven's projected *Tenth Symphony*.

On DG, after Karajan's very positive opening tutti, the soloists seem rather small-scale, but each of these players makes a positive contribution. Yo-Yo Ma's playing is not immaculate but his natural expressiveness makes for an enjoyable version, well recorded. The overtures bring superlative playing from the Berlin Philharmonic.

The Chungs (also on DG) make a characterful trio and give a very fine account of the *Triple Concerto* which conveys a feeling of spontaneous chamber-playing, with the finale taken thrillingly fast, with sparkling results. However, the two *Romances*, beautifully played though they are, and the short, insignificant E minor fragment do not enhance the competitiveness of what is after all a premium-priced disc.

12 Contredanses, WoO 14; 12 German Dances, WoO 8; 12 Minuets, WoO 7; 11 Mödlinger Dances, WoO 17.

(BB) *** Naxos 8.550433. Capella Istropolitana, O. Dohnányi.

It is always a delight to catch Beethoven relaxing and showing how warmly he felt towards the Viennese background in which he lived. The excellent Capella Istropolitana group used for the recording is of exactly the right size, and they play the music with light, rhythmic feeling and with plenty of spirit.

The Creatures of Prometheus: Overture & Ballet Music, Op. 43 (complete).

*** Hyp. Dig CDA 66748. SCO, Mackerras.
(BB) *** Naxos 8.553404. Melbourne SO, Halász.

Here, in fresh, vigorous performances, Sir Charles Mackerras and the Scottish Chamber Orchestra bring out not only the drama of the piece but also the colourful qualities which made Beethoven a great composer of light music. The ballet ends with the number that gave him one of his most fruitful

themes, used for the finale of the *Eroica Symphony*. Highly recommended.

The Naxos issue provides an excellent bargain version. The playing is neat and fresh, with rhythms well pointed. Though the string sound is at times a little cloudy, dramatic passages such as the military trumpets and timpani of the *Allegro con brio* (No. 8) are very well caught, bringing out the panache of the playing. In the big *Adagio* (No. 5) the important cello solo confirms the quality of the Melbourne players.

OVERTURES

Overtures: The Consecration of the House; Coriolan; The Creatures of Prometheus; Egmont; Fidelio; King Stephen; Leonora Nos. 1–3; 72b; The Ruins of Athens; Zur Namensfeier.

(M) *** DG (ADD) (IMS) 427 256-2 (2). BPO, Karajan.

Karajan's set of overtures, recorded in the 1960s, brings impressive performances that have stood the test of time, with a command of structure and detail as well as the virtuosity one expects from the Berlin Philharmonic. The sound is fresh and bright.

(i) *Overtures: The Consecration of the House; Coriolan; The Creatures of Prometheus; Egmont; Fidelio; King Stephen; Leonora Nos. 1–3; The Ruins of Athens; Zur Namensfeier;* (ii) *12 Contredanses, WoO 14; 12 German Dances, WoO 8; 12 Minuets, WoO 7.*

(B) *** Ph. (ADD) Duo 438 706-2 (2). (i) Leipzig GO, Masur;
(ii) ASMF, Marriner.

Masur's performances of the *Overtures* are more direct than those of Karajan, satisfying in their lack of mannerism. The Philips recording from the early 1970s is of high quality, and the remastering has enhanced its vividness and impact. To complete the second CD, Marriner and the Academy offer a splendid foil with the dance music. Even as a composer of light music, Beethoven was a master.

Overtures: The Consecration of the House; King Stephen; (i) *Egmont (incidental music), Op. 84: excerpts.*

(M) *** EMI (ADD) CDM5 67335-2. (i) Nilsson; Philh. O or New Philh. O, Klemperer (with MENDELSSOHN: *Overture: The Hebrides (Fingal's Cave), Op. 26;* MOZART: *Overtures: Don Giovanni; Die Entführung aus dem Serail; Le nozze di Figaro ***).

It was a good idea of EMI to gather these overtures together as part of the Klemperer Legacy, for they are all outstanding performances. There is some really inspired playing in the Beethoven group. Even the trivial *King Stephen* is given strength, and *The Consecration of the House* has seldom sounded so magnificent on record. The *Egmont* items too have an added dimension, with Birgit Nilsson at her most eloquent in *Die Trommel Gerühret* and *Freudvoll und Leidvoll*. The music portraying Clärchen's death is given a touching nobility. *Fingal's Cave*, too, is a magnificent performance, spacious and powerful, and his *Don Giovanni* stands out among the Mozart overtures; *Le nozze di Figaro* is also played superbly.

Overtures: *Coriolan; Creatures of Prometheus; Egmont; Fidelio; Leonora Nos. 1–3; Ruins of Athens.*

(*) Virgin VCS5 45364-2. Bremen German Chamber Philh. O, Harding.

Daniel Harding gives strong, distinctive readings of eight Beethoven overtures. As the name of the Bremen orchestra suggests, these are performances on a chamber scale. With his chosen players Harding favours extreme speeds, with slow introductions very solemn and measured, leading to hectic allegros which press home the drama of Beethoven's writing. Though all four overtures for *Fidelio* are included, as well as four others, it is a pity that *The Consecration of the House* was not included, if necessary by omitting *The Ruins of Athens*.

Overtures: *Coriolan; Creatures of Prometheus; Egmont; Fidelio; Leonora Nos. 1 & 3; The Ruins of Athens.*

(BB) *** RCA Navigator 74321 21281-2. Bamberg SO, Jochum.

Jochum presents a superb collection of overtures, naturally spontaneous and full of warmth and drama. The finest performance is of *Leonora No. 3*, making a thrilling end to the programme. The Bamberg Symphony Orchestra are in excellent form and the recording has a full, spacious acoustic.

Overtures: *Coriolan; Leonore No. 2.*

(M) (***) EMI mono CHS5 65513-2 (3). BPO or VPO, Furtwängler – BRAHMS: *Symphonies Nos. 1–4, etc.* (**(*))

These studio recordings of Beethoven overtures, the one from Vienna in 1947, the other from Berlin in 1954, make a fine supplement to Furtwängler's Brahms cycle, with Vienna mellower-sounding than Berlin.

Overture: *Leonore No. 3, Op. 72a.*

(N) *** BBC (ADD) BBCL 4056-2. BBC SO, Kempe – DVORAK: *Symphony No. 9 (New World)* ⬤; PROKOFIEV: *The Love for Three Oranges: Suite.* ***

Like the other two works on Kempe's mixed disc of live Prom performances from August 1975, *Leonore No. 3* brings a performance of tingling intensity. Treated as an encapsulation of the whole opera, it could hardly be more dramatic, with each change of mood sharply defined. So the emergence of the main allegro theme in a glowing C major leads to violent conflict in the development section, with horns blazing, until the off-stage trumpet has just as powerful an impact as when heard in the opera house. With joy piled on joy the final coda seems to burst over in frenzy.

SYMPHONIES

Symphonies Nos. 1–9; 10 (realized Dr Barry Cooper): *1st movt.*

(M) *** Chan. 7042 (5). CBSO, Weller (with Barstow, Finnie, Rendall, Tomlinson, CBSO Ch. in *No. 9*).

Symphonies Nos. 1–9.

(BB) *** Arte Nova 74321 65410–2 (5). Zurich Tonhalle O, Zinman (with Ziesak, Remmert, Davislim, Roth, Swiss Chamber Ch. in *No. 9*).

(B) *** CfP CDBOXLVB 1 (5). RLPO, Mackerras (with Rodgers, D. Jones, Bronder, Terfel, RLPO Ch. in *No. 9*).

(N) *** DG 469 000-2 (5). BPO, Abbado; with Mattila, Urmana, Moser, Quasthoff & Swedish R. Ch. in No. 9.

*** DG 439 900-2 (5). ORR, Gardiner (with Orgonasova, Von Otter, Rolfe Johnson, Cachemaille, Monteverdi Ch. in *No. 9*).

(B) *** RCA 74321 20277-2 (5). N. German RSO, Wand (with Wiens, Hartwig, Lewis, Hermann, combined Ch. from Hamburg State Op. and N. German R. in *No. 9*).

*** Teldec 2292 46452-2 (5). COE, Harnoncourt (with Margiono, Remmert, Schasching, Holl, Arnold Schönberg Ch. in *No. 9*).

(B) *** DG (ADD) 463 088-2 (5). BPO, Karajan (with Janowitz, Rössel-Majdan, Kmentt, Berry, V. Singverein in *No. 9*).

(*) Ph. 446 067-2 (6). Dresden State O, C. Davis (with Sweet, Rappé, Frey, Grundheber, Dresden State Op. Ch. in *No. 9*).

(*) Everest (ADD) EVC 901014 (5). LSO, Krips (with Vyvyan, Verrett, Petrak, Bell, BBC Ch. in *No. 9*).

(N) (M) (**(*)) EMI mono CHS5 67496-2 (5). VPO or Stockholm PO, Furtwängler (with soloists & Ch. in *No. 9*).

(N) (M) *(*) Teldec 3984 27838-2 (6). Berlin State O, Barenboim (with Isokoski, Lang, Gambill, Pape & Berlin German State Op. Ch. in No. 9).

(i) *Symphonies Nos. 1–9; Overtures: Consecration of the House; Coriolan; Creatures of Prometheus; Egmont; Fidelio; King Stephen; Leonora No. 2; The Ruins of Athens;* (ii) *Missa solemnis.*

(BB) **(*) Nimbus NI 1760 (7). Hanover Band, (i) cond. Goodman or Huggett (with Harrhy, Bailey, Murgatroyd, George, Oslo Cathedral Ch. in *No. 9*); (ii) Hirsti, Watkinson, Murgatroyd, George, Oslo Cathedral Ch., cond. Kvam.

Symphonies Nos. 1–9; Overtures: *Coriolan; Egmont.*

(B) **(*) O-L 452 551-2 (5). AAM, Hogwood (with Augér, Robbin, Rolfe Johnson, Reinhardt, L. Symphony Ch. in *No. 9*).

Symphonies Nos. 1–9; Overtures: *Coriolan; Egmont; Fidelio; Leonora No. 3.*

** DG 439 200-2 (6). BPO, Karajan (with Perry, Baltsa, Cole, Van Dam, V. Singverein in *No. 9*).

Symphonies Nos 1–9; Overtures: *Coriolan; Egmont; Leonora No. 3.*

(B) **(*) Decca (ADD) 430 792-2 (6). Chicago SO, Solti (with Lorengar, Minton, Burrows, Talvela, Chicago Ch. in *No. 9*).

Symphonies Nos. 1–9; Overtures: *Creatures of Prometheus; Egmont; Fidelio.*

(BB) *** Royal HR 703732 (5). BPO, Cluytens (with Brouwenstijn, Meyer, Gedda, Guthrie, St Hedwig's Cathedral Ch. in *No. 9*).

Even more so than Sir Charles Mackerras on Eminence, David Zinman has learnt from the example of period performance and has consistently presented performances of all the symphonies, early and late, which have a transparency not usually achieved with modern instruments, helped by the clear, fresh acoustic of the Zurich hall. There is an important advantage too that this is the first modern-instrument cycle to use the new edition prepared by Jonathan Del Mar, with important modifications in the text. Zinman also allows a degree of ornamentation beyond convention. What matters above all is that not only are the performances electrifying, with the players responding to the challenge of fast speeds in observance of Beethoven's metronome markings, but there is also refinement and tenderness in slow movements, even in the face of fast-flowing tempi. The sound is vivid and beautifully balanced, making this a front-runner among recommendations for cycles using modern instruments.

Sir Charles Mackerras's Beethoven cycle is also among the most recommendable of all at any price, beautifully recorded and interpretatively refreshing, in a refined way steering a satisfying mid-course between traditional and period performance. So the brass have a satisfying braying roundness and the timpani echo period practice, not only in the sharp attack with hard sticks but also in their prominent balance, as in the finale of No. 5. Speeds are on the fast side, but it is a measure of Mackerras's mastery that rhythms are always beautifully sprung without any hint of breathlessness and with consistently refined detail.

Few conductors change their approach to Beethoven quite so radically as Claudio Abbado has done. It was in the late eighties with the Vienna Philharmonic that Abbado recorded his earlier set of the Beethoven symphonies for DG, with disappointing results. They were comfortable middle-of-the-road readings that lacked dramatic tension, despite being based on live performances. Signs of change came in 1996, when his live recording of the *Ninth Symphony* with the Berlin Philharmonic, made by Sony at the Salzburg Easter Festival, not only brought the biting intensity missing before but also involved markedly faster speeds.

In this latest set the transformation is complete. Abbado is still far from being an interventionist interpreter of Beethoven. Explaining his approach in a searching interview in the booklet, he pays tribute to the work of period-performance practitioners, which has influenced his thinking about both playing-technique and choice of speeds, and to the scholarly editions of all nine works prepared by Jonathan Del Mar, which offer authentic texts and valid alternatives.

The contrasts are astonishing, with overall timings of each work over five minutes shorter this time than before. Moreover, thanks to lighter playing-techniques and the use of smaller string forces textures are consistently clarified, helped by lighter recorded sound. There is then ample weight in the finale of the *Ninth*, where the chorus and soloists are far better balanced and more cleanly focused than before. Though there is no mention of it, these are live recordings, consistently conveying a dramatic intensity missing in the earlier cycle. Like the conductor, the Berlin players were responding to a challenge.

Other cycles such as Sir Charles Mackerras's on EMI Eminence and David Zinman's on Arte Nova may go even further towards learning from period performance, but Abbado now offers his finest Beethoven revelation yet.

Gardiner's cycle makes a clear first choice for those wanting period performances. These are exhilarating performances which have bite and imagination and a sense of spontaneity. Like others, Gardiner observes Beethoven's own fast metronome markings, but allowing himself expansion in the slow movements of the *Eroica* and the *Ninth*. With Jonathan Del Mar a scholarly helper, his amendment of the marking for the Turkish March in the finale of the *Ninth* is twice as brisk as Norrington's and leads logically into the fugue. The set comes in full, luminous sound, complete on only five discs, with a sixth containing an illustrated talk by Gardiner in three languages.

Wand's digital set with the North German Radio Orchestra, recorded between 1985 and 1988, makes another first-class bargain choice, offering performances without idiosyncrasy yet full of character. In the finale of the *Ninth* the combined choruses of North German Radio and Hamburg State Opera, well balanced, sing with fervour, and the closing pages bring a thrilling culmination. RCA have now made Wand's discs available separately at mid-price: *Nos. 1 & 6* (74321 20278-2); *Nos. 2 & 7* (74321 20279-2); *Nos. 3 & 8* (74321 20280-2); *Nos. 4–5* (74321 20281-2); *No. 9* (74321 20282-2).

Reflecting his work as a period-performance pioneer, Harnoncourt makes rhythms light and textures clean, with sparing string vibrato. Periodically, as in the first movement of the *Eroica*, he adopts a hectically fast tempo, but that is the exception. Regularly, his choice of speeds is geared to bringing out the refined expressiveness of this brilliant young orchestra. The *Ninth*, recorded almost a year after the rest, makes a fine culmination, though the dry manner in the great *Adagio*, taken at a flowing speed, underplays the emotional depth. Excellent sound.

Recorded between 1957 and 1960, the Cluytens set offers excellent traditional readings, very well played and in a very good full, open recording. Cluytens's reading of the *Pastoral* has always been highly regarded, but the other performances are comparably impressive: weighty, often at relatively broad speeds, but with resilient rhythms. At super-bargain price, another excellent recommendation.

Of Karajan's four recorded cycles, the 1961–2 set (DG 463 088-2) is the most compelling, combining high polish with a biting sense of urgency and spontaneity. There is one major disappointment, the over-taut reading of the *Pastoral*, which in addition omits a vital repeat in the Scherzo. Otherwise these are incandescent performances, superbly played. On CD the sound is still excellent. On five CDs at bargain price, this offers outstanding value.

Walter Weller's Beethoven cycle for Chandos is among his finest achievements on record. He draws from the City of Birmingham Symphony Orchestra a warm, refined, Viennese quality, to remind you that this conductor started his career as concertmaster of the Vienna Philharmonic. The Chandos sound is full and glowing to match. Now available at medium price, including Barry Cooper's realization of the *Tenth Symphony*.

The pioneering Hanover Band period-instrument performances are well worth considering, when the Nimbus package is so inexpensive. These are all readings which convey the fire and exuberance of live performance; setting them in a reverberant acoustic means that the woodwind sometimes appear disembodied. Monica Huggett directs Nos. 1–2 and 5; Roy Goodman Nos. 3–4 and 6–9. In the later recordings Goodman draws consistently fresh, individual readings from his team, with rhythms well sprung in exhilarating *allegros*. Consistently the feeling of spontaneity is most winning. The overtures (also shared by the two conductors) are just as characterful, and it is specially good to have the fresh and gripping account of the *Missa solemnis*, conducted by Terje Kvam, chorus-master of the Oslo Cathedral Choir.

Hogwood's set makes another period-instrument recommendation in the lower price-category. It is vividly recorded, with a keen sense of presence and ample weight in the *Ninth*, with the London Symphony Chorus full and vivid. Hogwood also has the finest quartet of soloists, though in the first movement he is too rigid. His pointing of rhythms is not always as alert or imaginative as that of his direct rivals but, with clean, well-disciplined playing, it is consistently satisfying.

Solti's first cycle with his own Chicago orchestra has a firm centrality to it, following the outstandingly successful version of the *Ninth*, with which he started the series. The performance of the *Eroica* has comparable qualities, with expansive, steady tempi and a dedicated, hushed account of the slow movement. The CD transfers bring an admirable consistency, with plenty of weight in the bass balancing the bright top register. At bargain price, Solti admirers should not miss this set, particularly as these performances are more satisfying than those in his later, digital series.

As a Beethoven interpreter Krips is in the central tradition, with speeds rather broader than has latterly become the rule. In the *Pastoral* or the *Eighth* one registers that here is a great Schubertian, for Krips makes the music sing, yet in the great opening movements of the *Eroica* and No. 9 weight and incisiveness go together. He is helped by the sharp focus of the 1960 sound, transferred with fine presence but with an acid edge on high violins. Only No. 5 is a degree disappointing, well shaped and pointed but lacking some of the tensions needed. Not a prime recommendation until the price is reduced.

In opulent sound Sir Colin Davis takes a spacious view of the Beethoven symphonies, drawing beautiful playing from the Dresden State Orchestra. At broad speeds he gives each symphony a concentrated strength, though the grinding dissonances at the heart of the development section in the first movement of the *Eroica* are warm rather than violent. Reflecting the mature responses of a conductor in his late sixties, this is comfortable Beethoven. Anyone wanting a mellow view will be well pleased.

In Karajan's last, digital set, the recording seems to have been affected by the need to make a version on video at the same sessions. The gain is that these performances have keener spontaneity, the loss that they often lack the brilliant, knife-edged precision of ensemble one has come to regard as normal with Karajan. The six discs are now remastered to Digital Gold standards – for comments see the individual issues below – and are offered at a slightly reduced price for the set: six CDs for the price of five.

By unearthing a live recording of No. 2, made in the Royal Albert Hall in 1948, and borrowing a radio recording of No. 8 made in Stockholm, EMI has put together a complete Furtwängler cycle – and very impressive it is interpretatively. The sound of those two *ad hoc* recordings may be rough, with heavy background noise, but the performances are electrifying. No. 9 comes in the dedicated performance given at Bayreuth in 1951, but the others are EMI's studio versions, not always as inspired as Furtwängler's live performances but still magnetic and, with well-balanced mono sound, well transferred. The five CDs are now also available separately: *Nos. 1 & 3* (CDH5 67490-2); *Nos. 2 & 4* (CDH5 67491-2); *Nos. 5 & 7* (CDH5 67492-2); *Nos. 6 & 8* (CDH5 67493-2). The *Choral* is reviewed separately below.

Barenboim, even more than most of today's conductors, has a lifelong devotion to the work of Furtwängler, a point which is regularly reflected in his readings of the Beethoven symphonies. Speeds tend to be broad in the Furtwängler manner, often very broad as in the first movements of the *Eroica* and *Ninth*, and he encourages a fair flexibility within movements. This is the orchestra with which he has been working regularly over his years at the Deutsche Oper in Berlin, and they are certainly responsive to his demands, but what undermines most of these performances is a curious lack of tension. In taking a broad, flexible view the big essential, as the finest Furtwängler performances demonstrate, is that the expressive freedom must seem to develop spontaneously. In that Barenboim, while still achieving creditable results, tends to fall short. The result is a series of run-throughs rather than genuine performances, not helped by a rounded recording that could with advantage be brighter.

Muti's Beethoven cycle, like Toscanini's, is beset by problems of recorded sound which are serious, if obviously of a less extreme kind. Even his version of the *Ninth*, the last of the symphonies to be recorded, has sound almost as opaque as the earliest. This is a very serious *Ninth*; but where one expects a Toscaninian spark from Muti to ignite the music, too much of the performance here is rhythmically square and stolid (EMI CZS5 72923-2).

Very well played and recorded, Michael Gielen's cycle with the South-West German Radio Orchestra offers fresh, direct and generally brisk readings, sounding matter-of-fact, missing the element of mystery and suspense in key passages. Excellent singing from choir and soloists in the culminating work. But when compared with the Arte Nova set this is a non-starter (EMI CMS5 60089-2).

Symphonies Nos. 1–9; Overture: Egmont; Missa solemnis, Op. 123.

(N) (M) (**(*)) RCA mono 74321 66656-2 (6 & 1). Soloists, Robert Shaw Ch., NBC SO, Toscanini.

Symphonies Nos. 1–4; Overture: Egmont.

(M) (**(*)) RCA mono 74321 55835-2 (2). NBC SO, Toscanini.

Symphonies Nos. 5–8.

(M) (**(*)) RCA mono 74321 55836-2 (2). NBC SO, Toscanini.

(i) *Symphony No. 9 (Choral)*; (ii) *Missa solemnis.*

(M) (**(*)) RCA mono 74321 55837-2 (2). Merriman, Robert

Shaw Ch., NBC SO, Toscanini, with (i) Farrell, Peerce, Scott; (ii) Marshall, Conley, Hines.

The harshness of sound on Toscanini's late recordings has till now defied even the cleverest transfer engineers. But here, in completely new transfers, you have sound with more body and atmosphere than before, letting one appreciate in relative comfort the unique intensity of Toscanini in Beethoven, even in No. 7, where some harshness remains. Speeds are often hectic, with tensions built up to breaking point, but the thrill of a Toscanini event is consistently caught, particularly in the *Eroica* and in the inspired coupling of the *Ninth Symphony* with the *Missa solemnis*.

As can be seen, these CDs come either in three double-disc boxes, available separately, or in a mid-priced box which also includes a seventh CD demonstrating the contrast in sound between past CD issues and the new 20-bit re-mastering.

Symphonies Nos. 1 in C, Op. 21; 2 in D, Op. 36; 3 in E flat (Eroica), Op. 55; 8 in F, Op. 93.

(B) *** EMI double forte CZS5 73323-2 (2). Concg. O, Sawallisch.

Symphonies Nos. 4 in B flat, Op. 60; 5 in C min., Op. 67; 6 in F (Pastoral), Op. 68; 7 in A, Op. 92.

(B) *** EMI double forte CZS5 73326-2 (2). Concg. O, Sawallisch.

Symphony No. 9 in D min. (Choral), Op. 125; (ii) Piano Concerto No. 5 (Emperor).

(B) **(*) EMI double forte CZS5 73329-2 (2). (i) Price, Lipovšek, Seiffert, Rootering, Düsseldorf Städtischer Musikverein, Concg. O; (ii) Egorov, Philh. O; Sawallisch – MOZART: *Piano Concerto No. 20.* **(*)

Much of Sawallisch's Concertgebouw set is greatly admired, but undoubtedly the first of these three double forte reissues is the one to go for. The orchestral playing is of a high standard throughout and Sawallisch has a fine sense of proportion. The *First Symphony* immediately sounds fresh and vibrant; the *Second* and the *Eighth* receive lovely, alert accounts that give much pleasure, and textures are clean and transparent. The *Eroica* receives a performance of some stature and has great breadth and dignity; the orchestral playing is a joy in itself. The mellow acoustic of the Concertgebouw Hall must, however, have encouraged Sawallisch into middle-aged spread for the *Fifth Symphony*, but blazing brass introduces an altogether more electrifying view of the finale. A relaxed view of the *Pastoral* is more sympathetic, but the sound is not ideally clear. Sawallisch's version of the *Choral Symphony* was recorded live, but its sense of occasion is surprisingly muted, with admirably chosen speeds but with playing too relaxed, lacking dramatic tension. Even the finale, with its impressive soloists, is disappointing when the chorus is placed backwardly and the singing lacks sharpness of focus. To fill up the set, Egorov gives a refreshingly direct but still individual account of the *Emperor*.

Symphonies Nos. 1–4.

(B) *** Ph. (ADD) Duo 454 032-2 (2). Leipzig GO, Masur.

Symphonies Nos. 5–8.

(B) ** Ph. (ADD) Duo 454 035-2 (2). Leipzig GO, Masur.

(i) *Symphony No. 9 (Choral);* (ii) *Overtures: Consecration of the House; Fidelio; Leonora Nos. 1–3;* (iii) *Choral Fantasia.*

(B) *(*) Ph. (ADD) Duo 454 038-2 (2). (i) Tomowa-Sintow, Burmeister, Schreier, Adam, Ch.; (i–ii) Leipzig GO, Masur; (iii) Brendel, LPO, Haitink.

Kurt Masur's earlier, analogue Beethoven cycle has much to recommend it in its natural, unforced expressiveness and finely disciplined playing. The *Eroica* is exceptionally fine, particularly its nobly paced slow movement, and in the *Fourth Symphony* Masur is marvellously alert. The *Ninth* is spacious and well proportioned, but not as strongly characterized as many, so that the third of the Duo sets is the least recommendable, despite the inclusion of Haitink's fine account of the *Choral Fantasia* with Brendel.

Symphonies Nos. 1–2.

*** DG 447 049-2. ORR, Gardiner.

(BB) *** Arte Nova 74321 63645-2. Zurich Tonhalle O, Zinman.

(N) *** RCA 74321 66458-2. NDR SO, Wand.

(B) *** Ph. (ADD) 432 274-2. ASMF, Marriner.

Symphonies Nos. 1–2; Overture: Coriolan.

(M) *** Sony (ADD) SMK 64460. Columbia SO, Walter.

Symphonies No. 1 in C, Op. 21; No. 2 in D, Op. 36; Ritterballet, WoO 1.

(N) *** Simax PSC 1179. Swedish CO, Dausgaard.

This Simax coupling is the first volume in what will be a complete survey of Beethoven's orchestral music. These are engagingly fresh performances, stylish and elegant, and plenty of spontaneous excitement in the outer movements. They combine the vigour of period performance with the richness of a modern orchestra, and if the following discs are as good as this, it will be a cycle of considerable importance. The early but delightful ballet music is a bonus, and the sound is superb.

Rather than treating the two early symphonies as Mozartian in the way most period performers do, John Eliot Gardiner uses his sonorous but clean-textured forces to bring out the power and revolutionary bite of the young Beethoven, opting for speeds on the fast side. Vivid, immediate sound in both the live recording of No. 1 and the studio one of No. 2.

Using the Bärenreiter scores newly edited by Jonathan Del Mar, David Zinman conducts electrifying performances of the first two symphonies, with a rather smaller band of strings than in later works. With textures transparent and rhythms crisply sprung at generally fast speeds, the results consistently reflect the influence of period performance. For the *Andantes* in both symphonies there is a hushed dedication.

As in his earlier outstanding Beethoven symphony cycle from the 1980s, recorded with the same orchestra, Gunter Wand conducts fresh, alert readings of the first two symphonies, recorded live respectively in 1997 and 1999. Interpretative differences are tiny, with speeds often just a fraction broader, but the tensions of a live occasion help to give an extra point to the new accounts. Textures also tend to be a shade lighter and more transparent than before, with extra detail. Only in the slow movement of No. 2 is the result more self-conscious, less easily lyrical.

Marriner presents the first two symphonies on modern instruments but on an authentic scale with a Mozart-sized orchestra, and the result is fresh and lithe, with plenty of character but with few, if any, quirks and mannerisms, most realistically captured in the fine (1970) analogue recording.

Bruno Walter's CBS recordings were made in 1958–9 in Hollywood in warm, well-balanced sound with the Columbia Symphony, a pick-up orchestra of outstanding musicians. The most controversial point about his interpretation of the *Second Symphony* is the slow movement, which is taken very slowly indeed, with much rubato.

Karajan's digital Beethoven series brings some surprisingly slack ensemble in the recording of the first two symphonies. The performances are relaxed in good ways too, with Karajan's flair and control of rhythm never leading to breathless speeds (DG 439 001-2).

Symphonies Nos. 1; 3 in E flat (Eroica).

(B) *** CfP CD-CFP 6067. RLPO, Mackerras.

*** Teldec 9031 75708-2. COE, Harnoncourt.

(M) **(*) Virgin VM5 61374-2. LCP, Norrington.

Symphonies Nos. 1; 3 (Eroica); Fidelio: Overture.

(B) (**(*)) Naxos mono 8.110802-3. NBC SO, Toscanini.

With Mackerras, the *First* is fresh and alert in a Haydnesque way, while the *Eroica* has ample power, with heightened dynamic contrasts and with the flowing speed for the Funeral March still conveying dedication. First-rate recording.

Harnoncourt's *Eroica* brings an extremely fast tempo in the first movement, and his austere view of the great Funeral March is chillingly intense. The result is as individual as it is powerful. No. 1, too, is splendidly alive.

Norrington's No. 1 lacks the lively energy of the best of the series, but the *Eroica* is one of the most successful performances, exceptionally fast and with rhythms well sprung, yet with natural gravity in the Funeral March.

Though the Naxos transfer is variable – with drying-noises in part of the *Eroica* slow movement and intrusive American radio announcers introducing the performances – Toscanini's 1939 account of the *Eroica* is one of the very greatest ever recorded, incandescent from first to last. The *First Symphony* too has a sparkle missing in later Toscanini.

Symphonies Nos. 1; 4; Egmont overture.

(M) *** DG (ADD) 419 048-2. BPO, Karajan.

Karajan's 1977 version of No. 1 is exciting, polished and elegant; in No. 4 the balance is closer, exposing every flicker of tremolando, helped by a recording with fine presence and body.

Symphonies Nos. 1; 6 (Pastoral).

(M) *** EMI (ADD) CDM5 66792-2. Philh. O, Klemperer.

(M) **(*) DG (ADD) 447 901-2. VPO, Bernstein.

(BB) **(*) Naxos 8.553474. Nicolaus Esterházy Sinfonia, Drahos.

Symphonies Nos. 1; 6 (Pastoral); Overture: Egmont.

(B) **(*) Sony (ADD) SBK 46532. Cleveland O, Szell.

Klemperer gives No. 1 a magnetic performance, and his account of the *Pastoral* is one of the very finest of all his recordings. The Scherzo may be eccentrically slow but, with superbly dancing rhythms, it could not be more bucolic, and it falls naturally into place within the reading as a whole. The exquisitely phrased slow movement and the final *Shepherd's Hymn* bring peaks of beauty, made the more intense by the fine, digital transfer.

Bernstein's cycle of the Beethoven symphonies for DG with the Vienna Philharmonic Orchestra offers live recordings, tactfully edited. In No. 1 the *Allegros* are fast but not hectic, the slow introductions and slow movements carefully moulded but not mannered. The reading of the *Pastoral* is most characterful, persuasively combining joy and serenity.

In his Beethoven series for Naxos, Drahos offers fresh, spontaneous-sounding performances, beautifully played by a chamber-sized group from Budapest, with recording outstandingly vivid. Plainer and less subtle than the finest versions, these lively, well-sprung performances still make excellent bargains.

Szell's dynamic performance of the *First Symphony* makes up for any absence of charm. In the *Pastoral*, Szell is subtle in his control of phrasing, for all the firmness of his style. However, it is a pity that the close-up sound robs the slow movement of much of its gentleness and delicacy of atmosphere.

Symphonies Nos. 1; 7.

(BB) **(*) ASV (ADD) CDQS 6066. N. Sinfonia of England, Hickox.

Hickox's view of both works is unaffected and direct, finely detailed yet substantial. The lack of idiosyncrasy makes for easy listening. The CD transfer is full, with a resonant bass.

Symphonies Nos. 2–4; 6 (Pastoral); 7–9 (Choral); Overture: Leonora No. 3.

(M) ** EMI Dig./ADD CDS5 56837-2 (8). Munich PO, Celibidache (with Donath, Soffel, Jerusalem, Lika, Philharmonic Ch. in *No.* 9) (with SCHUMANN: *Symphony No.* 2 **) – BRAHMS: *Symphonies 1–4; Haydn Variations; German Requiem.* **

Sergiu Celibidache is the latest cult figure, and his followers will eagerly snap up his records in much the same way as do Furtwängler's admirers. Even so, he is too idiosyncratic to gain more than a guarded recommendation.

Symphonies Nos. 2; 4; Overture: Leonora No. 3.

(B) (**) Naxos mono 8.110815/6 (2). NBC SO, Toscanini.

Though the sound is often rough and crumbly and the NBC radio announcements intrusive, it is good to have these CD versions, taken from Toscanini's legendary Beethoven cycle of 1939. They represent him at his peak, incandescent and tense – arguably too much so for these symphonies – but less brittle than in his later NBC recordings, issued by RCA.

Symphonies Nos. 2; 5.

*** Teldec 9031 75712-2. COE, Harnoncourt.

(M) **(*) EMI (ADD) CDM5 66794-2. Philh. O, Klemperer.

(B) **(*) Sony (ADD) SBK 47651. Cleveland O, Szell.

(BB) **(*) Naxos 8.553476. Nicolaus Esterházy Sinfonia, Drahos.

Harnoncourt's exuberance does not imply a lack of weight in the *Fifth*. The slow movement is particularly fine and the finale grows seamlessly out of the Scherzo. The playing has fine bite and lift, making this a clear first choice for this coupling in the premium price-range.

The new coupling in EMI's 'Klemperer Legacy' series underlines the consistency of his approach to Beethoven, with the *Second Symphony*, like the *First*, sounding the more powerful through weighty treatment. Only in the finale is the result too gruff. The *Fifth* is less electric than his earlier, mono version but, with exposition repeats observed in both outer movements, this retains its epic quality. Clean, natural CD transfers, with ample weight.

With marvellously clean articulation from the strings in the first movement, Szell's No. 2 has the adrenalin running free; yet here, as in the similarly brilliant account of No. 5, he understands the need to give full scope to the lyrical elements.

Béla Drahos on Naxos conducts clean-cut readings of both works, with the excellent, well-balanced recording capturing the chamber scale very effectively. No. 2 is less dramatic than some. In No. 5, the call of fate at the opening may seem lightweight, but on a chamber scale this is refreshing in its clarity, easily flowing in the middle movements, taut in the outer movements.

Symphonies Nos. 2; 7.

(M) *** DG (ADD) 419 050-2. BPO, Karajan.

(N) (B) *** DG (ADD) 469 545-2. VPO, Bernstein.

In Karajan's *Second*, the firm lines give the necessary strength. The *Seventh* is tense and exciting, with the conductor emphasizing the work's drama rather than its dance-like qualities.

The alternative disc offers two of Bernstein's finest performances from his 'live' 1979 Vienna cycle. In No. 2 the tension rises superbly at the end of the finale. He seems intent on emphasizing how much bigger a symphony this is than No. 1. If the tautness in *No. 7* is less marked than in his earlier New York recording, here that makes for extra spring and exhilaration in the lilting rhythms of the first movement, while the *Allegretto* is reposeful without falling into an ordinary *Andante*, and the last two movements have the adrenalin flowing with a sense of occasion. The recordings are full and bright.

Symphonies Nos. 2; 8.

(B) *** CfP CD-CFP 6068. RLPO, Mackerras.

(M) *** Virgin VM5 61375-2. LCP, Norrington.

(BB) **(*) ASV (ADD) CDQS 5067. N. Sinfonia, Hickox.

Mackerras rounded off his outstanding Beethoven cycle with performances of these two even-numbered works which bring out the dramatic bite in performances at once refined and full of sharp contrasts, with exhilarating results.

The coupling of Nos. 2 and 8 shows the London Classical Players to be an authentic group with a distinctive sound, sweeter and truer in the string section than most. In fol-lowing Beethoven's own metronome markings for both symphonies the results are exhilarating, never merely breathless.

Richard Hickox directs his chamber-scale orchestra in fresh, warm and relaxed readings. Playing is refined and rhythms resilient, with the focus sharper in No. 8 than in No. 2.

Symphony No. 3 (Eroica).

(M) **(*) DG (ADD) (IMS) 447 444-2. LAPO, Giulini (with SCHUMANN: *Manfred Overture ***).

(B) **(*) Ph. 410 044-2. ASMF, Marriner.

(M) **(*) Sony (ADD) SMK 60692. NYPO, Bernstein.

Symphony No. 3 (Eroica); Grosse Fuge.

✪ (M) *** EMI (ADD) CDM5 66793-2. Philh. O, Klemperer.

Symphony No. 3 (Eroica); Overture: Egmont.

**(*) DG 439 002-2. BPO, Karajan.

Symphony No. 3 (Eroica); Overture: Coriolan.

(N) (m) **(*) DG (ADD) 463 643-2. Berlin PO, Boehm.

Symphony No. 3 (Eroica); Overture: Leonora No. 3.

(M) **(*) DG (ADD) 419 049-2. BPO, Karajan.

The digital remastering of Klemperer's spacious 1961 version of the *Eroica* weightily reinforces its magnificence, keenly concentrated to sustain speeds slower than in his earlier, mono account. The *Grosse Fuge* has monolithic strength.

Marriner's version is outstanding, for the impression is of weight and strength, coupled with a rare transparency of texture and extraordinary resilience of rhythm, with sforzandos made clean and sharp. The Funeral March is most compelling, and the recorded sound is among the best ever in this symphony. But without a coupling, even at bargain price, its appeal is diminished.

Bernstein's very fast opening *Allegro* has a tautness that reminds one of a Toscanini performance. He takes the exposition repeat, and there is no slackening of tension whatever. The speed for the Funeral March is also on the fast side, but in that respect he anticipates modern practice. The Scherzo is slower than usual, almost a jolly country-dance, and the finale shows Bernstein at his most ebullient. The speed is again very fast, but the dash and bravura take the listener along magnificently. The 1964 Manhattan Center recording is a bit harsh, but that adds to the similarity with Toscanini's version. Bernstein's comments about the work make a fascinating bonus.

Karajan's 1977 account (419 049-2) brings fiery intensity, with the Funeral March more concentrated than in his earlier recordings. An exciting performance of *Leonora No. 3* makes a fair bonus. The sound is well defined and clean.

Karl Boehm's Berlin recording of the *Eroica* from the 1960s has been chosen for reissue as one of DG's 'Originals'. It has all the sanity and good sense that distinguished his Vienna recording made a decade later, but has the additional virtue of greater spontaneity. Unhurried, lyrical, less taut and powerful than Karajan, there is nevertheless a lot to admire here, even if there are other versions that have greater incandescence. The recording has been successfully remastered and sounds remarkably vivid. But the coupling, finely played as it is, is ungenerous.

The gain in Karajan's last, digital version of the *Eroica* (439 002-2) lies most of all in the Funeral March, very spacious and intense, with high dynamic contrasts. The playing lacks something of the knife-edged bite associated with him. The recording is clean and firm, but there is a degree of congestion in big tuttis. An epic reading.

Giulini's refined and individual reading, with its very measured view of the first movement, wins only a qualified recommendation, yet it remains a striking example of a conductor transforming an orchestra.

Symphonies Nos. 3 (Eroica); 4.

(BB) *** Arte Nova 74321 59214-2. Zurich Tonhalle O, Zinman.
*** DG 447 050-2. ORR, Gardiner.

David Zinman and the Tonhalle Orchestra give outstanding performances of both symphonies. The string and wind articulation in both symphonies is phenomenally crisp and clear so that there is no feeling of excessive haste. In the *Eroica*, even with the exposition repeat observed, the first movement lasts barely 15 minutes, and the Funeral March at a flowing speed still conveys darkly tragic intensity, not least at the close. First-rate recording, with ample bloom on the sound.

Gardiner's fast speeds mean that, like Zinman, he can fit Nos. 3 and 4 on the same disc. The *Eroica*'s first movement is presented purposefully, with full weight and biting intensity. The Funeral March has natural gravity, even at a flowing speed, with high dynamic contrasts. In No. 4, the sublime melody of the slow movement is sweeter than usual with period violins.

Symphonies Nos. 3 (Eroica); 5 in C min., Op. 67.

(N) (M) (***) Decca mono 467 125-2. Concg. O, Erich Kleiber.

The superbly remastered reissue in Decca's Legends series joins together two great performances from the early LP era, which have never before sounded so impressive on disc. Kleiber's 1950 *Eroica* is wonderfully intense and dramatic, and it includes the repeat of the exposition in the first movement to make the whole structure more staggeringly monumental. If anything, the *Fifth* is even finer. The cumulative excitement of the first movement is achieved without any sense of over-driving, and the slow movement brings a warmly lyrical feeling in the strings to offset the tension elsewhere. The preparation of the finale is unforgettable, and when the great tune sweeps in triumphantly, timpani pounding underneath, it combines dignity and power. Kleiber keeps up the concentration right through to the thrilling coda. The new transfers are wonderfully full and clear, the famous Concertgebouw acoustic faithfully captured, without edginess and stridency.

Symphonies Nos. 3 (Eroica); 5; 7.

(N) (M) **(*) Decca (ADD) 467 679-2. VPO, Solti.

Here is a fascinating encounter with the conducting of the young firebrand Georg Solti, making some of his first records with the VPO in the late 1950s. Produced by John Culshaw and superbly engineered by James Brown and Gordon Parry,

they were recorded in the Sofiensaal in 1958 (Nos. 5 and 7), and 1959 (No. 3). The VPO playing is marvellous and the detail and range of the sound does the orchestra full justice.

In the *Eroica* Solti immediately establishes his personality and authority with crisply percussive opening chords and (with the first movement exposition included) he maintains a high level of tension. The *Funeral March* is taken simply and slowly, the dynamics well controlled, giving a dedicated rather than an intense account. By contrast the *Scherzo* is thrillingly fast (with splendid Viennese horn playing) and the finale romps along to an exciting conclusion.

Alas, the reading of the *Fifth* is much less successful. Solti chooses a very fast tempo for the opening movement, and with such precise, efficient articulation the result cannot help but be physically exciting. But already the feeling is of the playing being too forced, and in the slow movement this comes out in full measure and the overall effect is of ponderousness. Solti exaggerates the climaxes, sometimes crudely, and the power of the finale is visceral rather than an expression of incandescent joy.

However the merits of Solti's *Seventh* are substantial: in many ways this is the finest of the three performances. The reading sounds spontaneous and the control of dynamic is particularly impressive throughout, with some fine pianissimos, delicate and precise. The climax of the *Allegretto* is splendidly graduated. Precision too gives the *Scherzo* a wit and point and the finale is crisp and exciting.

When these performances first appeared on LP we commented that 'there is something lacking at present in Solti that prevents him from giving a really great Beethoven performance'. But this set remains a fascinating example of his early work with the VPO and Decca can be justly proud of the recordings, which never sound their age and are a demonstration of how to balance a Beethovenian orchestra within an ideal ambience.

Symphonies Nos. 3 (Eroica); 8.

(M) **(*) Sony (ADD) SMK 64461. Columbia SO, Walter.
(B) **(*) Sony (ADD) SBK 46328. Cleveland O, Szell.
(BB) **(*) Naxos 8.553475. Nicolaus Esterházy Sinfonia, Drahos.

Walter's *Eroica* is not monumental, as Klemperer and Toscanini's were in different ways; but the ripeness harks back to the years of pre-war Vienna. The digitally remastered recording is aptly expansive, with rich horns and full-bodied strings. The *Eighth* has comparatively slow speeds, an interesting and sympathetic, rather than a compelling reading.

Szell's is a fine performance in the Toscanini tradition, hard-driven and dramatic. The digital remastering is very successful: the sound is firm, full and brilliant. The performance of the *Eighth* is also compelling. The first-movement repeat is taken and the performance is not overdriven.

Drahos's performances on Naxos benefit greatly from superb sound and have the same qualities of freshness and spontaneity that mark the other initial disc in the series, making a good bargain, even if there are more searching readings of the *Eroica*.

Symphony No. 4.

*** Orfeo (ADD) C 522 991 B. VPO, Boehm – MAHLER: *Lieder eines fahrenden Gesellen;* SCHUMANN: *Symphony No. 4.* ***

Symphonies Nos. 4–5; Egmont: Overture.

(M) **(*) Sony (ADD) SMK 63079. NYPO, Bernstein.

This Orfeo issue vividly portrays the mastery of Karl Boehm in varied repertoire, electrifying from first to last. His account of No. 4 is bitingly intense in the fast movements, with sharply rhythmic attack, and tender and sweet in the spacious slow movement.

Bernstein's earlier (1962) New York recording of the *Fourth Symphony* brings a powerful performance at urgent speeds, but the playing has both polish and concentration and the slow movement has an appealingly relaxed *espressivo*. The *Fifth* (from a year earlier) is also one of the finest of the Bernstein cycle, strong and dramatic, concentrated and vital.

Symphonies Nos. 4; 6 (Pastoral).

✿ (M) *** Sony (ADD) SMK 64462. Columbia SO, Walter.
(B) *** CfP CD-CFP 6069. RLPO, Mackerras.

Walter's reading of the *Fourth* is splendid, the finest achievement of his whole cycle. There is intensity and a feeling of natural vigour in every bar. Like his recording of the *Fourth*, the *Pastoral* represents the peak of his Indian summer in the American recording studios, an affectionate, finely integrated performance from a master, with beautifully balanced sound. This has also been reissued separately on a Super Audio CD (SS 6012) requiring special playback facilities.

Mackerras adopts consistently fast speeds in both symphonies, except in the slow introduction to No. 4. Crisp, light articulation allows for superb definition from the strings, and Mackerras's subtle rubato ensures that the opening of the *Pastoral* avoids any feeling of rigidity. With hard sticks used by the timpanist, the Storm has rarely sounded so thrilling, resolving on an ecstatic, glowing finale.

Symphonies Nos. 4; 7.

(M) *** EMI (ADD) CDM5 66795-2. Philh. O, Klemperer.
(M) *** Virgin VM5 61376-2. LCP, Norrington.
*** Teldec 9031 75714-2. COE, Harnoncourt.
(BB) *** Naxos 8.553477. Nicolaus Esterházy Sinfonia, Drahos.

Symphonies Nos. 4; 7; King Stephen Overture.

(B) *** Sony (ADD) SBK 48158. Cleveland O, Szell.

Klemperer's *Fourth* brings one of the most compelling performances of all, with its measured but consistently sprung pulse allowing for persuasive lyricism alongside power. The 1955 recording of the *Seventh* sounds all the more vivid in its stereo version. Speeds are consistently faster, the tension more electric, with phrasing moulded more subtly than in the later version. The sound is remarkably full, with good inner detail.

Szell is at his finest in both symphonies. Along with powerful outer movements, tense and spontaneous-sounding, go exceptional accounts of the slow movements in both symphonies, and in No. 7 Szell makes the second

movement a genuine *Allegretto*, with keen concentration taking it almost as fast as a period specialist.

The coupling of Nos. 4 and 7 also shows Norrington at his very best. In the *Seventh*, sforzandos are sharply accented and rhythms lightly sprung. He follows Beethoven's metronome markings – as in the brisk second-movement *Allegretto* – but finds time for detail and fine moulding of phrase.

Brilliant, vital readings from Harnoncourt, with high contrasts in the slow movement of No. 4, bringing soaring lyricism over nagging rhythmic figures below. In the outer movements of No. 7 – wonderfully spirited – the horns shine out, adding to the joyous release after an *Allegretto* full of under-the-surface tension.

The coupling of Nos. 4 and 7 is one of the most successful of the Drahos Naxos series. No. 4 has a joyful vitality, while in No. 7 Drahos keeps a spring in the rhythms without forcing the pace, lifting the finale with bouncing accents, leading to a thrilling coda. An excellent bargain.

Symphony No. 5.

(M) *** DG (IMS) 445 502-2. LAPO, Giulini – SCHUMANN: *Symphony No. 3 (Rhenish).* ***
(N) (M) **(*) Ph. (ADD) 464 682-2. Concg. O, Szell – SIBELIUS: *Symphony No. 2.* ***

Symphony No. 5; (i) Triple Concerto.

(B) (**(*)) Naxos mono 8.110801. NYPO, Toscanini, (i) with Piastro, Schuster, Dorfman.

Giulini's 1982 Los Angeles recording of Beethoven's *Fifth* brings an outstandingly fine performance, majestic and powerful. The slow movement is glorious; the horn entry in the Scherzo is thrilling and the finale overwhelming in its force and grandeur. Outstanding digital sound, clear, full and well balanced, and the Schumann coupling is hardly less distinguished.

Szell's 1966 Concertgebouw is not quite so intense as his Cleveland recording on Sony (coupled with *No. 2*), but is still recommendable with fine playing and full-bodied recording. However, one wonders how many collectors will want the new coupling with the Sibelius *Second*, good though that is.

The 1933 account of the *Fifth Symphony* brings a Toscanini performance to treasure, warmer and more refined than his later readings with the NBC Symphony Orchestra, showing a degree of flexibility that was missing later. The *Triple Concerto*, recorded in 1942, brings a tautly controlled performance, with three of Toscanini's favourite players as soloists. They are recorded clearly, but in both works the orchestral sound is very limited, not helped by often-heavy surface noise.

Symphony No. 5; (i) Egmont: Overture & Incidental Music, Op. 84 (complete).

✿ (BB) *** Warner Apex 8573 89078-2. NYPO, Masur; (i) with McNair, Quadflieg (narr.).

Masur's NYPO account of the *Fifth Symphony*, coupled with the complete *Egmont* incidental music, was recorded in the Avery Fisher Hall in 1992 and is one of his very finest achievements on record. The performance of the symphony, more rugged than Giulini's, is immensely powerful, compelling from the first bar to the last. The reading is given even greater weight by Masur's observing both the repeat of the *Scherzo* and of the finale's exposition, which is made doubly successful by the thrust and joyful momentum of the last movement.

As if that were not enough, he also provides the finest account of the complete *Egmont* incidental music in the catalogue, opening with a thrillingly positive account of the *Overture*. The central *Intermezzi* are most sensitively played, and Sylvia McNair is a highly responsive and rich-voiced soloist. Will Quadflieg speaks his melodrama with dignity (separately banded, in German, untranslated in the notes) before the trumpets anticipate the finale exultant paean of victory. The full-bodied sound is ideal for both works, with warm string tone as well as a vivid overall brilliance and projection.

Symphonies Nos. 5–6 (Pastoral).

(BB) **(*) Arte Nova 74321 49695-2. Zürich Tonhalle O, Zinman.

**(*) DG 447 062-2. ORR, Gardiner.

(B) **(*) DG (ADD) 439 403-2. BPO, Karajan.

**(*) DG 439 004-2. BPO, Karajan.

(M) **(*) Virgin VM5 61377-2. LCP, Norrington.

(M) (**(*)) Avid mono AMSC 583. (i) LPO, Weingartner; (ii) VPO, Walter.

Symphonies Nos. 5–6 (Pastoral); Coriolan: Overture.

(BB) (*(*)) Naxos mono 8.110823. NBC SO, Toscanini.

David Zinman conducts the Tonhalle Orchestra in unusually direct and incisive readings. The use of Jonathan Del Mar's Bärenreiter edition in No. 5 brings a full repeat of the Scherzo and Trio before the usual partial and lightweight reprise of the Scherzo, leading into the mysterious link to the finale. If in No. 5 Zinman's approach works extremely well, the *Pastoral* is more problematical. The opening allegro, at a brisk speed, has plenty of energy but not much warmth. The slow movement by contrast is spaciously done, and the Storm is biting rather than atmospheric, with the finale plain, strong and intense, rather than warmly persuasive. The sound is fresh and clean, perhaps a little lacking in weight, although it suits the performances.

Gardiner's fast speeds in No. 5, recorded live, bring allegros of manic energy and thrust, pushing the music to the limit. The *Pastoral*, at comparably fast speeds, is crisp and light, with fine shading of phrase and dynamic, not least in the slow movement, though the big violin melody in the finale inevitably lacks the full sweetness of modern strings. Vivid, forward sound, full of presence.

Karajan's 1962 *Fifth* (439 403-2) is thoroughly recommendable, if anything more intense than his 1977 version, more spacious in the *Andante* and with blazing horns in the finale. The *Pastoral* is a brisk, lightweight performance, very well played, marred only by the absence of the repeat in the Scherzo. The sound has freshness and body.

Karajan's digital versions of the *Fifth* and *Sixth* (439 004-2) present characteristically strong and incisive readings, so that the fast speed for the first movement of the *Pastoral* no longer sounds too tense.

No. 5 shows Norrington at his most exciting and inspired,

relishing his fast speeds, while the finale has an infectious swagger. No. 6 is disappointing, with the EMI sound not so refined or clear, with Norrington surprisingly fussy at times. The *Scene by the Brook*, for example, fails to flow when the phrasing is so short-winded.

Felix Weingartner's *Fifth Symphony*, recorded with the London Philharmonic in 1933, is Beethoven pure and true, straightforward and plain; there is no lack of character and fire. The recording sounds less dated than one might expect, though there is a curious touch of dryness, characteristic of these Avid transfers. Bruno Walter's 1936 account of the *Pastoral*, with the Vienna Philharmonic, is taut and brisk, yet feels expansive. This is a vintage performance, though the strings are not quite sweet enough above the stave.

The 1939 account of Beethoven's *Fifth Symphony* is a tough, urgent reading, typical of Toscanini, a degree more sympathetic than his later versions. The Naxos transfer is less full than those from RCA, and the same thin, often crumbly sound also mars both the *Coriolan Overture* (with the opening chords like bangs on a tin box) and his urgently dramatic version of the *Pastoral*.

Symphonies Nos. 5; 7.

⦿ (M) *** DG (ADD) 447 400-2. VPO, C. Kleiber.

(B) *** CfP CD-CFP 6070. RLPO, Mackerras.

*** DG 449 981-2. Philh. O, Thielemann.

(M) *** Penguin/Decca 466 211-2. Philh. O, Ashkenazy.

(M) **(*) Sony (ADD) SMK 64463. Columbia SO, Walter.

(N) (BB) (**) Naxos mono 8.110926. Berlin St. Op. O, Richard Strauss.

Symphonies Nos. 5; 7; Overtures: Coriolan; Fidelio.

(M) **(*) RCA (ADD) 09026 68976-2. Chicago SO, Reiner.

Symphonies Nos. 5; 8; Fidelio: Overture.

(M) *** DG (ADD) 419 051-2. BPO, Karajan.

If ever there was a legendary recording, it is Carlos Kleiber's version of the *Fifth* from the mid-1970s. In Kleiber's hands the first movement is electrifying but still has a hushed intensity. The slow movement is tender and delicate, with dynamic contrasts underlined but not exaggerated. In the Scherzo, the horns (like the rest of the VPO) are in superb form; the finale then emerges into pure daylight. In Kleiber's *Seventh*, symphonic argument never yields to the charm of the dance. Incisively dramatic, his approach relies on sharp dynamic contrasts and thrustful rhythms. A controversial point is that Kleiber, like his father, maintains the pizzicato for the strings on the final phrase of the *Allegretto*, a curious effect. The latest digital remastering has again greatly improved the sound.

Sir Charles Mackerras and the Royal Liverpool Philharmonic also give revelatory performances of both the *Fifth* and *Seventh*. Tempi are on the fast side in all four movements but, thanks to rhythmic control, they never sound hectic. The superb recording is both weighty and atmospheric.

Karajan's 1977 version of the *Fifth* (419 051-2) is magnificent in every way, tough and urgently incisive, with fast tempi bringing weight as well as excitement. The coupling is an electrically intense performance of the *Eighth*, plus the *Fidelio Overture*.

Christian Thielemann, opting for broad speeds and resonant textures, reminds one of the weighty Klemperer with this same orchestra – yet with speeds fluctuating in a manner far closer to Furtwängler. The results are magnetic; with outstanding playing from the Philharmonia and vivid digital recording, this is an excellent recommendation for anyone wanting a traditional view with modern sound.

On Penguin Classics, Ashkenazy's reading of the *Fifth*, urgent and vivid, is notable for its rich, Kingsway Hall recording. Well-adjusted speeds here, with joyful exuberance a fair substitute for grandeur. The reading of the *Seventh* is equally spontaneous. Highly recommended, especially for those for whom outstanding recording quality is a priority. The accompanying literary essay is by Arthur Miller.

Reiner's opening of the *Fifth* is measured, but then he spurts forward impulsively and excitingly. The slow movement is expansive, its principal melody flowing warmly to make a link with the *Pastoral Symphony*, and the finale, taken fast, caps a somewhat mannered interpretation exhilaratingly. The *Seventh* is particularly impressive in the first and third movements, where power is combined with fine rhythmic lift, while the fast tempo for the finale draws unscampering brilliance from the Chicago orchestra. Marginally less impressive are the symphony's slow introduction and the *Allegretto* second movement, where Reiner's manner at fastish speeds is cooler. Both the overtures are impressively played, *Coriolan* boldly dramatic.

In Bruno Walter's reading of the *Fifth*, the first movement is taken very fast but lacks a little in nervous tension. The middle two movements by contrast are slow, and the finale, taken at a spacious, natural pace, is joyful rather than dramatic. Walter's *Seventh* has a comparatively slow first-movement *Allegro*, and the *Allegretto* also seems heavier than usual (partly because of the rich, weighty recording), but this still gives the illusion of an actual performance. Note that Walter's version of the *Fifth* has also been issued on a Super Audio CD (SS 6506) coupled with Schubert's *Unfinished Symphony*.

Richard Strauss, long recognized as a great Mozart interpreter, here demonstrates his mastery in relation to Beethoven. Recorded in the 1920s for what was designed as a Beethoven centenary project, these are above all dynamic, bitingly energetic performances, not always well-disciplined but always magnetic. That is so despite the astonishingly fluid tempi, rarely staying quite the same for more than a few bars. In the *Fifth* the sound is limited, but the Naxos transfer is undistracting, never getting in the way of the performance.

The *Seventh*, recorded in 1926 just as electrical recording was introduced, comes in drier sound, but the boxiness is something you get used to. Though the second movement *Allegretto* is rather heavy, the rest is well sprung with a delightfully witty pay-off in the *Scherzo*. Sadly the finale brings an enormous cut, designed to fit the movement on to a single 78 side.

Symphony No. 6 (Pastoral).

(M) *** DG (ADD) 447 433-2. VPO, Boehm – SCHUBERT: *Symphony No. 5.* ***

(***) Cala mono CACD 0523. NY City SO, Stokowski – MOZART: *Sinfonia concertante, K.297b.* (***)
(N) ** CBC (ADD) PSCD 2021. Toronto SO, Ančerl – MARTINU: *Symphony No. 5.* **

Symphony No. 6 (Pastoral); Overtures: Coriolan; Creatures of Prometheus.

(BB) *** ASV (ADD) CDQS 6053. N. Sinfonia, Hickox.

Symphony No. 6 (Pastoral); Overtures: Egmont; Leonora No. 3.

(B) *** Decca 448 986-2. Philh. O, Ashkenazy.

Symphony No. 6 (Pastoral); Overture: Leonora No. 3.

(B) **(*) [EMI Red Line CDR5 72551]. Phd. O, Muti.
(N) * Ph. 462 595-2. Saito Kinen O, Ozawa.

Boehm's 1971 version of the *Pastoral* is as fine as any, a beautiful, unforced reading, one of the best played and (in its day) one of the best recorded. It still sounds fresh in its current reissue in DG's 'Originals' series with a Schubert coupling.

Ashkenazy's warm performance, thanks to spacious tempi, brings a feeling of lyrical ease and repose, with glowing playing from the Philharmonia and rich Kingsway Hall recording. The two overtures make a good bonus. An excellent bargain.

Hickox directs a persuasively paced reading, with a small orchestra used in order to give a performance of high contrasts, intimate in the lighter textures but expanding dramatically in the tuttis, while the finale, fresh and pure, brings a glowing climax. With warm analogue recording, this is one of the best of the Hickox Beethoven series. The two *Overtures* come in vigorously dramatic readings.

With the first two movements youthfully urgent, Muti's is an exhilarating performance, fresh and direct. The recording is warm and wide-ranging, though the high violins do not always live up to the 'Philadelphia sound'.

The Cala CD offers Stokowski's first commercial recording of the *Pastoral*, made in Carnegie Hall in 1945. As Edward Johnson points out in his excellent notes, there is 'no want of rustic jollity in the opening movement', but 'Stokowski's *Scene by the Brook* is certainly more *Adagio* than *Andante*'. However, he sustains this leisurely tempo with affectionate ease and gives a radiant account of the finale. The violins sing out freshly and radiantly, and the only real complaint about the sound is the restricted dynamic range. A memorable account just the same.

Karel Ančerl's concert performance of the *Pastoral Symphony* from 1972 was available briefly on Tahra Records in the mid-1990s. It is well shaped and unfolds naturally and musically, although it is not as compelling as the recent Testament reissue of a performance by the Berlin Philharmonic and André Cluytens in 1955. Good, but not special, with decent sound.

No one could fault the actual playing of the Saito Kinen Orchestra on Philips, but Ozawa's reading is curiously faceless and lacking in expressive vitality. In spite of fine recording, the result is uninspiring and anonymous.

Symphonies Nos. 6 (Pastoral); 8.

*** Teldec 9031 75709-2. COE, Harnoncourt.

(BB) *** Belart (ADD) 450 058-2. Concg. O, Jochum.

There is nothing over-tense about Harnoncourt's *Pastoral*, even though the brook flows freely; No. 8 has drama and bite and resilience too. A fine coupling.

Jochum's Concertgebouw coupling on Belart (originally Philips), dating from the end of the 1960s, still sounds extremely well, resonantly full-bodied, vivid and clear. Like his newer EMI recording, this is a leisurely reading, the countryside relaxing in sunshine. The *Eighth* too is given an outstanding performance, with plenty of energy. A fine alternative view of two of Beethoven's friendliest symphonies.

Symphony No. 7 (see also under *Missa solemnis*, below).

✿ (B) *** EMI double forte (ADD) CZS5 69364-2 (2). RPO, C. Davis – SCHUBERT: *Symphony No. 9* ***; ROSSINI: *Overtures.* **(*)

*(**) BBC (ADD) BBCL 4005-2. BBC SO, Stokowski – BRITTEN: *Young Person's Guide* **(*); FALLA: *El amor brujo.* *** ✿

**(*) DG 431 768-2. Boston SO, Bernstein – BRITTEN: *Peter Grimes: Sea Interludes.* **(*)

Symphony No. 7; Egmont Overture; Septet in E flat, Op. 20 (arr. Toscanini).

(BB) (*(*)) Naxos mono 8.110814. NBC SO, Toscanini.

Sir Colin Davis's early (1961) *Seventh* brings a great, electrifying performance. Originally issued as a bargain LP, it dominated the catalogue in the early stereo era. It sounds splendid in this digital remastering, with the horns coming through thrillingly in the codas of both outer movements.

Stokowski's reading sounds pretty breathtaking too and has great power and concentration. It is a performance of high contrasts, with the first movement pressed hard and the slow speed for the *Allegretto* made persuasive through subtle phrasing and rhythmic control. Stokowski then mutilates the Scherzo by eliminating the second reprise of the Trio and the third repeat of the Scherzo proper. Nevertheless, this is an exceptional performance. The couplings are outstanding (the Falla in particular is stunning) and the sound very good for its age.

Leonard Bernstein, recorded live with the Boston Symphony Orchestra, at the very last concert he ever conducted at Tanglewood on 19 August 1990, takes an expansive view, quite different from his previous recordings, consistently conveying the joy of Beethoven's inspiration while springing rhythms infectiously. First-rate sound, despite the problems of live recording at Tanglewood, and an unusual coupling.

It was a favourite party-piece of Toscanini to get his NBC orchestra to play the Beethoven *Septet*, with the strings agile in parts designed for solo instruments. The sound in that is fuller and firmer than on the rest of the disc, where the thin, crumbly recording which marks most of the Naxos transfers of Toscanini's 1939 Beethoven cycle spoils the impact of these searingly dramatic performances of both the *Egmont Overture* and the *Seventh Symphony*, an interpretation broadly in line with his classic New York Philharmonic reading of three years earlier.

Symphonies Nos. (i) 7; (ii) 8; (iii) 9 (Choral).

(B) ** DG Double (ADD) 459 463-2 (2). (i) VPO; (ii) Cleveland O; (iii) Donath, Berganza, Ochman, Stewart, Bav. RSO; Kubelik.

Kubelik's *Seventh Symphony*, with the VPO, is beautifully played and well recorded but lacks the drama of his earlier account with the Bavarian RSO. The *Eighth Symphony* receives a robustly enjoyable performance in Cleveland, with the choice of tempi always well judged. For the challenging *Ninth Symphony*, Kubelik used his own Bavarian orchestra. It is a warm and understanding performance, leading on consistently to the high spirits of the finale. But there is a missing dimension of conveyed power and greatness here. The performances are recorded well (in the mid-1970s).

Symphonies Nos. 7–8.

*** DG 423 364-2. VPO, Abbado.

*** DG 447 063-2. ORR, Gardiner.

(BB) **(*) Arte Nova 74321 56341-2. Zürich Tonhalle O, Zinman.

(B) **(*) [EMI Red Line CDR5 69785]. Phd. O, Muti.

The *Seventh* has always been a favourite symphony with Abbado, and the main allegro of the first movement is beautifully judged; as also is the *Eighth*, which is instantly established as more than a 'little' symphony. As in the *Seventh*, speeds are beautifully judged, giving the impression of live performance. A splendid coupling.

With Gardiner, the first movements of both No. 7 and No. 8 are very highly charged, with textures and rhythms lightened. Though there is comparable thrust in the finale of No. 7, the speed is not extreme. The *Allegretto* and Scherzo are fast and light too, as are the comparable movements of No. 8, leading to a hectic finale. Firm, forward sound.

Zinman's coupling has similar qualities to his earlier, less recommendable one of Nos. 5 and 6. That works very well in No. 7, with speeds on the brisk side, but still with rhythmic resilience, notably in the *Allegretto*. In No. 8, Zinman, like Toscanini, takes a rather fierce view of this most compact of the symphonies, with a clipped manner and a fast speed in the first movement and with little or no charm in the middle movements. With clean, crisp ensemble and vivid recording, the power of the piece is reinforced.

The vigour and drive of Muti's account of the *Seventh* are never in doubt – but, surprisingly, the ensemble of the Philadelphia Orchestra is not immaculate. There is spontaneity, but it is paid for by a lack of precision. The *Eighth* is also lively, and it brings greater polish.

Symphony No. 8; Overtures: Coriolan; Fidelio; Leonora No. 3.

**(*) DG 439 005-2. BPO, Karajan.

Symphony No. 8; Overtures: Coriolan; Leonora Nos. 1–3.

(M) ** EMI (ADD) CDM5 66796-2. Philh. O, Klemperer.

Karajan's more relaxed view of the *Eighth* (compared with his 1977 version) is almost always pure gain, a massive reading of Beethoven's 'little' symphony, with fierceness part of the mixture in the outer movements. The three overtures are made Olympian too, with *Coriolan* specially impressive.

Klemperer's approach to the *Eighth* is deliberate and heavy. His approach has its justification at the wonderful climax of the development in the first movement, leading over into the recapitulation, but the finale plods for much of its length. In the three *Leonora Overtures* he is strong rather than volatile but, with high tension, the result is neither dull nor heavy. Full-bodied transfers.

Symphony No. 9 (Choral).

(B) *** CfP CD-CFP 6071. Rodgers, D. Jones, Bronder, Terfel, RLPO Ch. & O., Mackerras.

(BB) *** Arte Nova 74321 65411-2. Ziesak, Remmert, Davislim, Roth, Swiss Chamber Ch., Zurich Tonhalle O, Zinman.

*** Sony SK 62634. Eaglen, Meier, Heppner, Terfel, Swedish R. Ch., Ericson Chamber Ch., BPO, Abbado.

*** Testament SBT 1177. Nordmo-Løvberg, Ludwig, Kmentt, Hotter, Philh. Ch. & O., Klemperer.

(M) *** DG (ADD) 415 832-2. Tomowa-Sintow, Baltsa, Schreier, Van Dam, V. Singverein, BPO, Karajan.

*** DG (ADD) (IMS) 429 861-2. Anderson, Walker, König, Rootering, various Chs., Bav. RSO, Dresden State O, etc., Bernstein.

*** DG 447 074-2. Orgonasova, Von Otter, Rolfe Johnson, Cachemaille, Monteverdi Ch., ORR, Gardiner.

(M) (***) EMI mono CDM5 66901-2 [566953]. Schwarzkopf, Höngen, Hopf, Edelmann, Bayreuth Festival Ch. & O., Furtwängler.

(M) *** DG 445 503-2. Norman, Fassbaender, Domingo, Berry, V. State Op. Ch., VPO, Boehm.

(B) *** DG (ADD) 439 495-2. G. Jones, Schwarz, Kollo, Moll, V. State Op. Ch., VPO, Bernstein.

*** DG 453 423-2. Kringelborn, Palmer, Moser, Titus, Dresden State Op. Ch., Dresden State O, Sinopoli.

*** Teldec 9031 75713-2. Margiono, Remmert, Schasching, Holl, Arnold Schönberg Ch., COE, Harnoncourt.

(BB) *** ASV CDQS 6069. Harper, Hodgson, Tear, Howell, Sinfonia Ch., L. Symphony Ch. (members), N. Sinfonia, Hickox.

(M) *** Penguin/Decca (ADD) 460 622-2. Lorengar, Minton, Burrows, Talvela, Chicago Ch. & SO, Solti.

(BB) *** Naxos 8.553478. Papian, Donose, Fink, Otelli, Nicolaus Esterházy Ch. & O, Drahos.

**(*) DG 439 006-2. Perry, Baltsa, Cole, Van Dam, V. Singverein, BPO, Karajan.

(M) **(*) Virgin VM5 61378-2. Kenny, Walker, Power, Salomaa, Schütz Ch., LCP, Norrington.

(N) ** (m) RCA (ADD) 09026 63682-2. Marsh, Veasey, Domingo, Milnes, Pro Musica Ch., New England Ch., Boston SO, Leinsdorf – SCHOENBERG: *Survivor from Warsaw.* **(*)

(N) (M) ** DG (ADD) 463 626-2. (i) Seefried, Forrester, Haefliger, Fischer-Dieskau, St Hedwig's Cathedral Ch., BPO, Fricsay.

(N) (m) (*) Orfeo Mono C533001B. Seefried, Wagner, Dermota, Greindl, Vienna State Op. Ch., VPO, Furtwängler.

(i) Symphony No. 9. Fidelio: Overture.

(B) **(*) Sony (ADD) SBK 46533. (i) Addison, Hobson, Lewis, Bell, Cleveland O Ch.; Cleveland O, Szell.

(M) **(*) Sony (ADD) SMK 63152. Arroyo, Sarfaty, De Virgilio, Scott, Juilliard Ch., NYPO, Bernstein.

Symphony No. 9; Overture: Coriolan.

(M) *** DG (ADD) 447 401-2. Janowitz, Rössel-Majdan, Kmentt, Berry, V. Singverein, BPO, Karajan.

Symphony No. 9; Overture: Creatures of Prometheus.

(M) ** EMI (ADD) CDM5 66797. Nordmo-Løvberg, Ludwig, Kmentt, Hotter, Philh. Ch. & O., Klemperer.

(i) Symphony No. 9; (ii) Choral Fantasia.

(BB) (**(*)) Naxos mono 8.110824. Westminster Ch., NBC SO, Toscanini, with (i) Novotna, Thorborg, Peerce, Moscona; (ii) Dorfman.

Mackerras conducts the Royal Liverpool Philharmonic in an inspired account of the *Ninth*, one which has learnt from the lessons of period performance, and, like period specialists, Sir Charles has taken careful note of Beethoven's controversial metronome markings. The recording is outstanding, warm yet transparent and with plenty of body; and the singing in the finale is fine, even if the tenor, Peter Bronder, is on the strenuous side.

David Zinman, too, crowns his Beethoven cycle with a magnificent account of the *Ninth*, using the new Bärenreiter Edition, opting for the fast speeds which have latterly come to be thought authentic, always giving the music the deeper qualities needed and with a sense of hushed dedication in the slow movement, even when taken at a flowing speed. The finale crowns his performance, with the chamber chorus not only fresh and dramatic but deeply dedicated too in the prayerful sections. The soloists are an excellent team of young-sounding singers, and the sound is full and well balanced. On a separate track the last half of the finale is given in an alternative version, with a pause included towards the end, representing Beethoven's first thoughts, later amended.

Claudio Abbado directs a recording made at the 1996 Salzburg Easter Festival. Throughout, it captures the electricity of a great occasion. The finale with a superb quartet of soloists and fine Swedish choirs brings the feeling of climax too often missing in recordings of the *Ninth*. Highly recommended.

The previously unpublished live recording of Klemperer conducting Beethoven's *Ninth* on Testament is magnetic from beginning to end. The occasion at the Royal Festival Hall in November 1957 was the very first concert of the newly founded Philharmonia Chorus – the culmination of Klemperer's first Beethoven symphony cycle in London. He followed that up immediately by recording the *Ninth* in the studio with exactly the same forces; but in all four movements this live performance has an extra bite and intensity at marginally faster speeds. In every way it is preferable to the published EMI studio recording, when even the sound is both warmer and kinder to the voices.

Of the three stereo recordings Karajan has made of the *Ninth*, his 1977 account (415 832-2) is the most inspired, above all in the *Adagio*, where he conveys spiritual intensity at a slower tempo than before. In the finale, the concluding eruption has an animal excitement rarely heard from this highly controlled conductor. The soloists make an excellent team. The sound has fine projection and drama.

Recorded live on the morning of Christmas Day 1989 after the fall of the Berlin Wall, Bernstein's Berlin version brings a historic performance that has something special to say, not only because Bernstein substitutes the word 'Freiheit', 'Freedom', for 'Freude', 'Joy', in the choral finale. The orchestra, drawn mainly from Germany, also included players of the Kirov Theatre Orchestra in Leningrad, the New York Philharmonic, the Orchestre de Paris and the LSO. The choirs similarly came from East and West Germany, while the soloists represented four countries: America (June Anderson), Britain (Sarah Walker), Germany (Klaus König) and Holland (Jan-Hendrik Rootering). For many, the uniqueness of this version and the emotions it conveys will make it a first choice, despite obvious flaws.

With Gardiner there is no mystery in the tremolos at the start of the Ninth, but the movement at its brisk speed builds up inexorably. The slow movement is far faster than usual but still conveys repose. The finale is urgent and dramatic, and the quartet of fresh-voiced soloists is exceptionally strong. An exuberant conclusion confirms this as a clear first choice among period versions.

It is thrilling to have such a splendid new transfer of Furtwängler's historic recording, made at the reopening of the Festspielhaus in Bayreuth in 1951. The chorus may not be ideally focused in the background, and the audience noises are the more apparent on CD, but the extra clarity and freshness impressively enhance a reading without parallel. The spacious, lovingly moulded account of the slow movement is among Furtwängler's finest achievements on record and, with an excellent quartet of soloists, the finale crowns a performance fully worthy of reissue among EMI's 'Great Recordings of the Century'.

Karl Boehm's reading is spacious and powerful. Overall there is a sense of a great occasion; the concentration is unfailing, reaching its peak in the glorious finale, rugged and strong. With a fine, characterful team of soloists and a freshly incisive chorus of singers from the Vienna State Opera. Strongly recommendable.

Karajan's 1962 version (447 401-2) is less hushed and serene in the slow movement than either of his later versions, but the finale blazes even more intensely, with Janowitz's contribution radiant in its purity. This reflected the electricity of the Berlin sessions, when it rounded off a cycle recorded over two weeks. The Coriolan coupling is an added bonus.

Bernstein's characterful VPO account (439 495-2) conveys immediate electricity at the very start, and the first movement is presented at white heat from first to last. In the finale Gwyneth Jones's hard-edged soprano will not please everyone. Otherwise this is a superb account, sung and played with dedication. The recording is bright, full and immediate.

Sinopoli's powerful version was recorded live in 1996 at the annual Palm Sunday performance of the Ninth in Dresden, giving a sense of occasion. He takes a rugged view, warmly sympathetic but largely without mannerism. The weight of the chorus is caught splendidly, with high dynamic contrasts and with the soloists an undistractingly well-matched team.

For some listeners the fast pace of the slow movement of Harnoncourt's Ninth will seem a drawback, but otherwise the performance caps the cycle splendidly, with a very compelling account of the finale.

Hickox's performance, beautifully paced, using an orchestra of the size Beethoven originally had, brings some of the advantages of period performance: clarity of articulation and texture; otherwise one might not realize that the string band is any smaller than one on a regular recording of the Ninth. This is the most successful issue in his Beethoven series for ASV. The performance culminates in a glowing account of the choral finale with four excellent soloists. At super-bargain price this is very competitive indeed.

If you regard the sublime slow movement as the key to this epic work, then Solti is clearly with you in his earlier, analogue version. Here is Innigkeit of a concentration rarely heard on record, even in the Ninth. In the first movement Solti is searing in his dynamic contrasts – maybe too brutally so – while the precision of the finale, with superb choral work and solo singing, confirms this as one of the finest Ninths on CD. The descriptive essay is written by Philip Ziegler.

As bitingly dramatic as Toscanini in the first movement and electrically intense throughout, Szell directs a magnetic account of the Ninth which demonstrates the glories of the Cleveland Orchestra. The chorus sings with similar knife-edged ensemble, set behind the orchestra. The performance of the Fidelio Overture is electrifying.

Béla Drahos with his outstanding chamber orchestra from Budapest gives a refreshingly direct performance of the Ninth, typically dramatic, with the Adagio following period practice in its flowing speed, sweet and beautifully moulded rather than hushed. With a superb chorus and well-matched soloists, the finale is urgently intense, working to a superb climax. Exceptionally vivid and full sound, well detailed.

Bernstein's Sony performance offers a finely shaped first movement which has genuine breadth and eloquence, a bitingly dramatic Scherzo that verges on the frenetic, a slow movement of considerable warmth, although with not quite enough inwardness and repose, and an intense and dramatic finale with some fine contributions from the soloists and chorus. The 1964 recording is better than it was on LP but lacks sophistication.

The high point of Karajan's digital version of the Ninth (439 006-2) is the sublime slow movement, here exceptionally sweet and true, with the lyricism all the more persuasive in a performance recorded in a complete take. The power and dynamism of the first two movements are also striking, but the choral finale is flawed above all by the singing of the soprano, Janet Perry, far too thin of tone and unreliable. The sound of the choir has plenty of body, and definition has been improved in this remastered version.

In December 1939 Toscanini rounded off his Beethoven symphony cycle in New York with these apocalyptic performances of the Ninth and the Choral Fantasia on Naxos, and the atmosphere of a great occasion comes over vividly. Quite apart from the searing thrust and drama of Toscanini's approach to both works, it is good to have in the slow movement a keener impression than usual of Toscanini's ability to mould phrases affectionately with hushed intensity. The soloists in the Ninth make a superb quartet, with the firm dark bass, Nicola Moscona, particularly impressive. Ania Dorfman's solo playing in the *Choral Fantasia* is marked by a bright tone and diamond-clear articulation. The Naxos transfers, though very limited, have more body than most in this Toscanini series of 1939.

Fricsay's account of the *Ninth* was the first to come out in stereo in the late 1950s. It is undoubtedly a significant performance, well-shaped and full of vitality, though tempi are fairly broad, save in the *Scherzo*. The *Adagio* is particularly beautiful, and only the finale seems lacking in weight. The recording is well balanced (the soloists forward, but the chorus well in the picture) and sounds remarkably good for its age, and though this is not as recommendable as Karajan or Boehm, it is finer than we had remembered it, and a fair choice for inclusion among DG's 'Originals'. The Overture is played as an introduction.

Klemperer's 1958 sound is amazingly good for its period, with the finale fresher and better balanced than in many recent recordings. However, his weighty vision is marred by a disappointing quartet of soloists; and the slow speeds for the first two movements come to sound ponderous. Yet the flowing account of the slow movement shows Klemperer at his finest. The new CD transfer offers extra refinement.

Among versions at super-bargain price, Rahbari's Brussels version, digitally recorded, makes a good recommendation, vigorous and spontaneous. The first movement is strong and purposeful, the Scherzo excitingly fast, with the slow movement sustaining measured speeds well; and the finale is helped by confident choral and solo singing. The recording is reverberant, but not so as to muddle an involving performance (Discover DICD 920151).

Peter Maag favours a traditional reading of the *Ninth*, tense and dramatic but often warm and relaxed, with a spacious account of the great *Adagio*, lovingly moulded. The playing is not always ideally polished, and in the finale the baritone soloist is wobbly in his opening solo, but this is a weighty performance, well recorded and well worth its super-bargain price (Arts 47248-2).

Weingartner's 1935 account of the *Ninth Symphony* was a mainstay of the 78-r.p.m. catalogue. It remains impressive, as in his whole cycle presenting Beethoven truthfully without any intervening filter or interpretative veneer. Weingartner's soloists are also good, particularly the magisterial Richard Mayr. Over 60 years old, it still ranks high among *Ninth*s. The transfer is fair but not outstanding (Avid AMSC 591).

Leinsdorf's Beethoven *Ninth* is brilliantly played and recorded, but misses the heights of the greatest performances. The fill-up is a rarity and surprisingly inappropriate.

Sharp, exhilarating intensity comes over in Norrington's reading of the *Ninth*, with many of Beethoven's fast metronome markings justified in the results, even the fast-slowing speed for the Adagio. A serious snag is the singing of the male soloists, with the baritone, Petteri Salomaa, tremulous, and the plaintive-sounding tenor, Patrick Power, cruelly exposed in the drum-and-fife march passage, taken slowly. Reverberant recording still allows the bite of timpani and valveless horns to cut through the texture.

Dedicated as Furtwängler's spacious reading is, the Austrian radio recording from the 1951 Salzburg festival on Orfeo is too seriously marred by intrusive audience noises and by sour woodwind to provide serious rivalry to Furtwängler's historic Bayreuth performance on EMI from the same summer, in which the soloists are even finer as well.

(i) *Symphony No. 9 (Choral)*; (ii) *Missa Solemnis*.

(N) (B) *** DG (ADD) Panorama 469 262-2 (2). (i) Jones, Schwarz, Kollo, Moll, V. Konzertvereinigung, VPO, Bernstein; (ii) Moser, Schwarz, Kollo, Moll, Hilversum R. Ch., Bernstein.

Both performances on the Panorama coupling are highly recommendable, each is discussed under its separate issue. Curiously the only slight reservation concerns the contribution of the soprano soloist (different in each case). There is a very slight saving in purchasing the two performances together.

Wellington's Victory (Battle Symphony), Op. 91.

🔘 **(M)** *** Mercury (ADD) 434 360-2. Cannon & musket fire directed by Gerard C. Stowe, LSO, Dorati (with separate descriptive commentary by Deems Taylor) – TCHAIKOVSKY: *1812*, etc. *** 🔘

This most famous of all Mercury records was one of the most successful classical LPs of all time, selling some two million copies in the analogue era. Remastered for CD, it sounds even more spectacular than it ever did in its vinyl format, vividly catching Beethoven's musical picture of armies clashing. The presentation, with handsome colour reproductions of appropriate paintings (and excellent documentation), is a model of its kind.

CHAMBER MUSIC

Cello Sonatas Nos. 1–5.

(N) (B) *** Ph. (ADD) 464 677-2 (2). Rostropovich, Richter.

(***) Testament mono SBT 2158 (2). Piatigorsky, Solomon – BRAHMS: *Sonata No. 1*; WEBER: *Sonata in A*. **(***)**

(i) Cello Sonatas Nos. 1–5; (ii) 7 Variations on 'Bei Männern', WoO 46; 12 Variations on 'Ein Mädchen', Op. 66 (both from Mozart's Die Zauberflöte); 12 Variations on 'See the conqu'ring hero comes', WoO 45 (from Handel's Judas Maccabaeus).

(B) *** Ph. (ADD) Duo 442 565-2 (2). (i) Rostropovich, Richter; (ii) Gendron, Françaix.

(M) *** EMI double forte (ADD) CZS5 7333-2 (2). Du Pré, Barenboim.

(B) *** DG Double (ADD) 453 013-2 (2). Fournier, Kempff.

(M) *** DG (IMS) (ADD) 437 352-2 (2). Fournier, Gulda.

(B) *** EMI (ADD) CZS5 69422-2 (2). P. Tortelier, Heidsieck.

(B) **(*)** Hyp. Dyad CDD 22004 (2). Pleeth, Tan (fortepiano).

Cello Sonatas Nos. 1–5; 7 Variations on 'Bei Männern'; 12 Variations on 'Ein Mädchen'; 12 Variations on 'See the conqu'ring hero comes'.

*** DG 431 801-2 and 437 514-2. Maisky, Argerich.

(i–ii) Cello Sonatas Nos 1–5; (ii–iii) Horn Sonata in F, Op. 17.

(B) *** Decca Double ADD/Dig. 466 733-2 (2). (i) Harrell; (ii) Ashkenazy; (iii) Tuckwell.

Made in the early 1960s, the classic Philips performances by Mstislav Rostropovich and Sviatoslav Richter, two of the instrumental giants of the day, have withstood the test of time astonishingly well and sound remarkably fresh in this transfer. The performances of the *Variations* by Maurice Gendron and Jean Françaix have an engagingly light touch and are beautifully recorded. At its new price this reissue is very tempting.

The Rostropovich/Richter set has been effectively remastered and has (rightly) been included in the Philips collection of '50 Great Recordings'. But the *Variations* are not included (the two discs together play for 109 minutes) so the Duo alternative is obviously preferable.

The Harrell/Ashkenazy mid-1980s performances are very fine too: they are unfailingly sensitive and alert, well thought out and yet seemingly spontaneous, with superb digital recording. The inclusion in this Double Decca issue of the *Horn Sonata*, equally recommendable (from 1974), makes this particularly attractive for those who regard sound-quality to be of importance.

The set of performances by Jacqueline du Pré with Daniel Barenboim was recorded live for the BBC during the Edinburgh Festival of 1970. The playing may not have the final polish of a studio-made version, but the concentration and intensity of the playing are wonderfully caught.

Fournier and Kempff also recorded their cycle of the sonatas at live festival performances. These fine artists were inspired by the occasion to produce unexaggeratedly expressive playing and to give performances which are marked by their light, clear textures and rippling scale-work, even in the slow introductions, taken relatively fast. In this remastering as a DG Double, the sound is beautifully clear.

Fournier's earlier accounts, made in the Brahms-Saal of the Vienna Musikverein in 1959, though not less spontaneous, have more gravitas. Gulda's contribution is strong: he is more than a passive partner. The recording of both instruments is close but full, natural and beautifully balanced.

Mischa Maisky and Martha Argerich make a strong, characterful partnership, offering strikingly detailed, exhilarating performances, vividly recorded. Also available in DG's Beethoven Edition.

The Tortelier set with Eric Heidsieck dates from the early 1970s. The performances are distinguished and make a useful alternative, with a bolder style than that of Fournier and Kempff on DG. The CD transfer is natural and clean.

The Piatigorsky–Solomon 1954 performances have an aristocratic poise and a patrician elegance that put them in the highest class. The recordings are in mono, and the transfers by Paul Bailey present them in the best possible light.

Though the cello is balanced rather forwardly in relation to the fortepiano, the Hyperion collection makes an attractive issue for anyone wanting period versions. Despite the balance, it is Tan who easily dominates the set and makes the allegros sparkle, notably in the *Variations*.

On ASV's bargain Quicksilva label, Richard Markson, very well partnered by Osorio, gives full-toned, direct readings.

Allegros are fresh and lively, though such a deep movement as the great *Adagio* from the last sonata, No. 5, misses the mystery implied. Warm and immediate recording, made in Wigmore Hall, London. Particularly with no fill-up on this two-disc set, it does not quite compete, even in this price category (CDQSS 235).

Cello Sonata No. 3 in A, Op. 69.

(M) (***) EMI mono CDM5 67008-2. Casals, Schulhof –
   BACH: (Unaccompanied) *Cello Suite No. 1*; BRAHMS:
   Cello Sonata No. 2. (***)

Cello Sonatas Nos. 3; 5.

(M) *** EMI CDM7 69179-2. Du Pré, Kovacevich.

The Du Pré/Bishop–Kovacevich recordings of Nos. 3 and 5 come from 1966, the year after Jacqueline had made her definitive record of the Elgar *Concerto*. They stand among her very finest recordings. Du Pré's tone ranges from full-blooded fortissimo to the mere whisper of a half-tone in performances using the most expressive rubato. With excellent recording, the CD transfer is crisp and fresh.

For the *A major Sonata*, way back in 1930, Casals chose Otto Schulhof. He is a thoughtful pianist and their playing is wonderfully natural, unforced and musical. The frail, dry sound soon ceases to worry the experienced ear.

Clarinet Trio in B flat, Op. 11.

(M) *** CRD (ADD) 3345. Nash Ens. (with ARCHDUKE
   RUDOLPH OF AUSTRIA: *Clarinet Trio in B flat ***).

The Nash Ensemble's account of Beethoven's *Clarinet Trio* has a royal rarity as a coupling. Archduke Rudolph was a son of the Austrian Emperor, but his claim to fame is as a pupil and friend of Beethoven. His *Clarinet Trio* is incomplete: of the closing rondo only a fragment survives, and this performance ends with the slow movement, a set of variations on a theme by yet another prince, Louis Ferdinand of Prussia. The playing is thoroughly persuasive, with some attractive pianism from the excellent Clifford Benson. Much the same goes for the performance of the Beethoven *Trio*, and this is well worth investigating for interest.

(i) Horn Sonata in F, Op. 1; (ii) Sextet for Horn & Strings, Op. 81b.

(B) *** EMI Debut CDZ5 72822-2. (i) Clark (Waldhorn),
   Govier (fortepiano); (ii) Ens. Galant, Montgomery (horn)
   – BRAHMS: *Horn Trio*; MOZART: *Horn Quintet*,
   etc. ***

Andrew Clark consistently relishes the ripe, fruity, often tangy tone of the Waldhorn, demonstrating that, although such a piece as the slow movement of the Beethoven sonata brings uncomfortable technical problems, the extra tensions involved can add to the intensity of a performance. There is a flamboyance in the playing which carries the day. Gerald Govier is a persuasive advocate of the fortepiano. On one of EMI's cheapest labels this makes a splendid and stimulating bargain, very well recorded.

Notturno, Op. 42.

*** EMI CDC5 55166-2. Caussé, Duchable – REINECKE:

Fantasiestücke ***; SCHUBERT: *Arpeggione Sonata.* **(*)

Beethoven's *Notturno* is an 1803 arrangement by Franz Xaver Kleinheinz of the *Serenade*, Op. 8, for string trio. It is a slight work, but Gérard Caussé and François-René Duchable give a nicely turned and musicianly account. Exemplary recording.

Piano Quartets Nos. 1–3.

(BB) **(*) Discover DICD 920254. Scheuerer Qt.

The enterprising Discover label does it again by giving Beethoven's three early *Piano Quartets* their CD début. Written in Bonn when the composer was fifteen, they are obviously Mozart-influenced, as the charming *Rondo* finales of Nos. 1 and 3 readily demonstrate, particularly the one in *D major* (otherwise less interesting), which is a lollipop. The central *Adagio* of No. 3 hints at the mature Beethoven, and the opening *Adagio assai* of No. 1 even more so – beginning like the slow movement for a piano concerto. The four sibling performers play throughout with pleasing freshness and vitality. The balance is good within a fairly resonant acoustic. This is well worth its modest cost.

Piano Trios Nos. 1–11.

(M) *** Ph. 438 948-2 (3). Beaux Arts Trio.

Piano Trios Nos. 1–3; 8; 10.

(M) *** Sony (ADD) SM2K 64510 (2). Stern, Rose, Istomin.

Piano Trios Nos. 4–7; 9; 11.

(M) *** Sony (ADD) SM2K 64513 (2). Stern, Rose, Istomin.

Piano Trios Nos. 1–9; 10 (Variations on an Original Theme in E flat), Op. 44; 11 (Variations on 'Ich bin der Schneider Kakadu'), Op. 121a; Allegretto in E flat, Hess 48.

*** EMI CDS7 47455-8 (4). Ashkenazy, Perlman, Harrell.

(M) **(*) EMI CMS7 63124-2 (3). Barenboim, Zukerman, Du Pré.

(BB) **(*) Naxos 8.550946 (*Nos. 1–2*); 8.550947 (*Nos. 3, 8, 10 & 12*); 8.550948 (*Nos. 5–6*); 8.550949 (*Nos. 7 & 11*). Stuttgart Piano Trio.

(M) **(*) Teldec 9031 73281-2 (3). Trio Fontenay.

Piano Trios Nos. 1–11; Trio in E flat (from Septet), Op. 38.

(BB) **(*) Arte Nova 74321 51621-2 (4). Seraphim Trio.

Piano Trios Nos. 1–11; Trios, Op. 38; in D (from Symphony No. 2); Trio movement in E flat.

(B) **(*) Ph. (IMS) ADD/Dig. 468 411-2 (5). Beaux Arts Trio.

Piano Trios Nos. 5 (Ghost); 6 in E flat, Op. 70/1–2; 7 (Archduke); 10 (Variations in E flat), Op. 44; 11 (Variations on Ich bin der Schneider Kakadu).

(N) (B) **(*) Teldec Ultima 8573 87821-2 (2) (from above). Trio Fontenay.

Piano Trios Nos. 7 (Archduke); 9.

*** EMI CDC7 47010-2. Ashkenazy, Perlman, Harrell.

Ashkenazy, Perlman and Harrell lead the field in this repertoire. The recordings, made over a period of five years and at various locations, offer sound that is consistently fresher, warmer and more richly detailed than with most other rivals. The playing is unfailingly perceptive and full of those musical insights which make one want to return to the set, but as we go to press it has been withdrawn, along with the separate coupling of the *Archduke* and *No. 9 in B flat.*

The Stern/Rose/Istomin recordings were made between 1968 and 1970, though the *Archduke* is earlier and was recorded in Switzerland in 1965. The performances are outstanding: strong, polished and alive. Istomin is always thoughtful and imaginative in slow movements, while Rose, although a less extrovert artist than Stern, holds his own by the warmth and finesse of his lyrical phrasing. One of the highlights of the set is the *Archduke*, commandingly bold and immediate, with a glorious slow movement; the *Ghost Trio* also shows these artists at their most communicative. These two performances are available separately (SBK 53514). The recording, improved on CD, is characteristically forward, in the CBS manner of the late 1960s.

The Barenboim/Zukerman/Du Pré set (by omitting Nos. 4 and 8) is fitted economically on to three mid-priced CDs. Even more than usual, the individual takes involved long spans of music, often complete movements, sometimes even a complete work. The result is music-making of rare concentration, spontaneity and warmth. The excellent recording has been freshened on CD.

In their analogue set from 1965 the Beaux Arts are let down by the ungenerous tone of their leader, Daniel Guilet; but this matters little, against the refreshing spontaneity of the playing as a whole. Tempi are admirably chosen (save in the *Ghost Trio*, which is very brisk, though the work's drama is projected brilliantly) and phrasing is marvellously alive. They convey a sense of music-making in the home rather than in the concert hall, with the naturally balanced recording attractively combining warmth and intimacy.

The Arte Nova set is as complete as most collectors will want, and it remains the least expensive way to collect this highly rewarding music. The Seraphim Trio have a splendid pianist in Gottfried Hefele, who dominates musically while conforming to an apt chamber scale. The playing is freshly spontaneous throughout – the group readily conveys joy and exhilaration, especially in the delightful early works on the second and third discs. The recording is well balanced and the acoustic pleasing, but the string timbre is somewhat dry. Though the *Archduke Trio* is given a rather lightweight reading, it does not lack repose in the slow movements, typically expressive. A first-rate bargain.

The Naxos performances have a good deal in common with those by the Seraphim Trio in the same price range but they have the additional advantage of being available separately. However, the Arte Nova set offers all eleven works on four CDs, whereas the Stuttgart series has already used that number of discs and is not yet complete. The early Op. 1 set is very successful, played with finesse and with a simplicity of style that is very appealing. The Stuttgart players are good at characterizing variations: Op. 44 is particularly successful and rhythmically most engaging. The first movement of the *Ghost Trio* is very brisk indeed, and the nervous intensity of the Stuttgart players permeates the performance, although the arrival of the 'Ghost' is eerily effective. The *E flat Trio* is rather more relaxed and the central movements are played appealingly. The performance of the *Archduke* is comparatively mellow – not without character, but not really distinctive. The *Kakadu Variations* come off well, and the *Allegretto in B flat*, WoO 39, is pleasingly done. Throughout the series the players are not helped by the close microphones in the Clara Wieck Auditorium, but this seems more noticeable in the later works. On the whole the Arte Nova set is the one to go for.

The Fontenay versions were recorded between 1990 and 1992 in the Teldec studios in Berlin. Alert and intelligent playing throughout, attentive phrasing and bright, well-lit recorded sound. The *Ghost* is rather closely balanced – the Op. 1 *Trios* are much better. Very good playing, without the last touch of humanity and depth, as found in the Beaux Arts performances – particularly in their earlier set from the 1960s.

There is also an attractive Ultima Double which includes the *Archduke*, one of the most impressive performances in the set, vibrant with an eloquent slow movement, and vividly recorded. The *Variations*, too, are attractively done; Op. 44 is particularly diverting.

Unlike their earlier set, the later Beaux Arts box offers everything Beethoven composed (or arranged) for this grouping, so that five well-filled CDs are involved; four of the recordings are digital. The transfers are well up to the usual high Philips standard and the performances are most accomplished and musical, if not quite matching the earlier Beaux Arts set in freshness and sparkle.

Piano Trios Nos. 1 in E flat; 2 in G, Op. 1/1–2.

(B) *** HM HMA 1901361. Cohen, Höbarth, Coin.
(N) *** MDG 303 1051-2. Trio Parnassus.
*** Hyp. CDA 66197. L. Fortepiano Trio.

Even more than in the recordings by the Fortepiano Trio, Patrick Cohen's group shows how fresh, alive and clear-textured these engaging works can be made to sound on period instruments, and how effective is the fortepiano, not only in the vivacious allegros but also in the slow movement of the *E flat major* and the *Largo con espressione* of the *G major*. The recording is first class, and this is a real bargain.

The Trio Parnassus use modern instruments, but their spiritedly vibrant style, with bold accents, is every bit a match for their period-instrument competitors. It is balanced by a warm legato from the excellent pianist (Chia Chou) in slow movements, and the finale of Op. 1/2 has exhilarating dynamism. The recording is vividly realistic.

The London Fortepiano Trio play with considerable virtuosity, particularly in the finales, which are taken at high speed and with fine attack. The use of a fortepiano serves to enhance clarity of texture in this particular repertoire.

Piano Trios Nos. 1, Op. 1/1; 4, Op. 11; Allegretto in B flat, WoO 39.

(N) *** Nimbus NI 5508. Vienna Piano Trio.

Piano Trios Nos. 2–3, Op. 1/2–3.

(N) *** Nimbus NI 5661. Vienna Piano Trio.

The Vienna Piano Trio on Nimbus is a first class ensemble which gives alert, vital readings that engage the listener's sympathy completely. As with the Dvořák trios from this source, they are well recorded, with a clean, well-focused sound. The performances give pleasure, although competition is stiff in this repertoire; however, in their own right these are superb artistically.

Piano Trios Nos. 4, Op. 11; 5 (Ghost); 7 (Archduke).

(N)(M) *** Ph. (ADD) 464 683-2. Beaux Arts Trio.

From the Beaux Arts Trio a generous triptych to represent their art among Philips's '50 Great Recordings'. These recordings date from 1965 but do not sound their age, and the *Archduke* is a particularly successful transfer, with an attractive bloom on the sound, yet detail is clear. This performance has more spontaneity than their later version and the overall feeling is of lightness and grace. The scherzo is a delight, and elsewhere there is an attractive pervading lyricism. Some might like a weightier approach, but this is highly rewarding in its own way. The Op. 11 *Trio* is usually heard in its clarinet version. The Beaux Arts players are again on excellent form here and they project the drama and intensity of the *Ghost Trio* to brilliant effect.

Piano Trio No. 7 in B flat (Archduke), Op. 97.

(B) *** EMI double forte (ADD) CZS5 69367-2 (2). D. Oistrakh, Knushevitzky, Oborin (with KODALY: *3 Hungarian Folksongs;* SUK: *Love Song;* WIENIAWSKI: *Légende;* YSAYE: *Extase* ***) – BRAHMS: *Violin Sonatas Nos. 1–2* **(*); SCHUBERT: *Piano Trio No. 1.* ***

On EMI double forte, a well-rounded, thoroughly alive performance by three eminent soloists experienced enough as chamber-music players to allow the necessary blend of personalities. They are rugged and assured in the first movement, brilliant in the last, and only a shade less compelling in the intervening movements. The 1958 recording is smooth and well balanced. The encores come from a concurrent recital disc. Oistrakh is placed rather near the microphones, but his tone is pure and exceptionally rich, with remarkable changes of tone-colour – listen to the little-known but seductive Ysaÿe work and the *Hungarian Folksongs* by Kodály.

Piano & Wind Quintet in E flat, Op. 16.

(M) *** Sony SMK 42099. Perahia, members of ECO – MOZART: *Quintet.* ***
(N) *** CBC MCVD 1137. Kuerti, Campbell, Mason, Sommerville, McKay – MOZART; WITT: *Quintets.* ***
✹ (***) Testament mono STB 1091. Gieseking, Philh. Wind Ens. – MOZART: *Quintet, etc.* (***) ✹
(N) *** Erato 4509 96359-2. Barenboim, Soloists of Chicago SO – MOZART: *Piano & Wind Quintet.* **(*)

First choice for Beethoven's *Piano and Wind Quintet* lies with Perahia's CBS version, recorded at The Maltings. The first movement is given more weight than usual, with a satisfying culmination. In the *Andante*, Perahia's playing is wonderfully poetic and serene, and the wind soloists are admirably responsive. With the recording balanced most realistically, this issue can be warmly recommended.

A totally winning performance, too, from this group of leading Canadian wind soloists, appropriately led by the Viennese-born pianist Anton Kuerti. They play together with total rapport and their performance has great freshness and all the spontaneity of live music-making. The finale is particularly infectious. The recording has great vividness and realism – indeed, it is in the demonstration bracket. This can be strongly recommended alongside the Sony disc, and has the considerable advantage of including additionally the attractive quintet by Friedrich Witt, who modelled his work closely on the quintets by Mozart and Beethoven.

Ideal chamber-music-making in the earlier version by Walter Gieseking and members of the Philharmonia Wind (Dennis Brain, Sidney Sutcliffe, Bernard Walton and Cecil James). Recorded in 1955, it has few rivals in tonal blend and perfection of balance and ensemble. The mono sound comes up wonderfully fresh in this Testament transfer.

Barenboim here puts down his baton to join players from his Chicago Orchestra (Hansjörg Schellenberger, oboe, Larry Combs, clarinet, Dale Clevenger, horn, and Daniele Damiano, bassoon), who distinguish themselves in the engaging interplay of the *Andante*. Barenboim too is in good form – the first movement proceeds jauntily, and the finale too is sprightly but nicely relaxed. This is very enjoyable and well recorded, if perhaps not a first choice.

Septet in E flat, Op. 20.

(B) *** Decca 448 232-2. V. Octet (members) – MOZART: *Clarinet Quintet*. ***

(N)(BB) *** Warner Apex 8573 89080-2. Berlin Soloists – MOZART: *Horn Quintet*. ***

**(*) Nim. NI 5461. BPO Octet – HINDEMITH: *Octet*. **(*)

Septet, Op. 20; Clarinet Trio, Op. 11.

(BB) *** Virgin 2 x 1 VBD5 64109-2 (2). Nash Ens. (with SCHUBERT: *Octet* **).

(i) *Septet, Op. 20;* (ii) *Wind Sextet in E flat, Op. 81b.*

*** Hyp. CDA 66513. Gaudier Ens.

(B) **(*) Ph. Virtuoso 426 091-2. BPO Octet (members), (i) with Klier.

The Vienna Octet have been justly famous for their recordings of Beethoven's *Septet* for Decca, and this newest version of 1991 is no disappointment. Brio and good humour mark the performance, with a warmly elegant account of the slow movement contrasted with the high spirits of the Minuet and the Scherzo. The finale is no less infectious.

The young members of the Gaudier Ensemble also give an exuberant performance, bringing the *Septet* home as one of the young Beethoven's most joyfully carefree inspirations. The rarer *Sextet* for two horns and string quartet makes a generous coupling. Excellent sound, with the wind well forward.

The Virgin issue brings uneven quality in the coupling. There is pure magic in these Beethoven performances, and so the *Clarinet Trio* finds each player, not just the fine clarinettist Michael Collins, but also the pianist Ian Brown and the cellist Christopher van Kampen. An apt sense of fun also infects the *Septet*, with allegros exhilaratingly fast. Good, atmospheric sound, but the coupled Schubert *Octet* is not so successful either technically or musically.

Of the three recordings from Berlin, that by the Soloists on Apex is a clear first choice. This is a most affectionate

account, beautifully played and warmly recorded in a pleasing acoustic. The players are given a nice presence without being on top of the listener. The Mozart coupling is attractive too, and this reissue is most competitively priced.

The Berlin Philharmonic Octet on Nimbus also give a delightful, characterful account of the *Septet* with playing polished and refined. The only snag is that the recording, made in the Teldec Studios, Berlin, is rather too closely balanced. Recommended none the less.

An amiably refined performance of the *Septet* from the excellent Berlin Philharmonic group on Philips, with plenty of life in the outer movements, but rather a solemn view taken of the slow movement. The analogue recording is excellent; many will like its warm ambience. The *Sextet*, for two horns and string quartet, is also very well played and recorded.

Serenade in D, Op. 8 (arr. Matiegka).

*** Mer. CDE 84199. Conway, Silverthorne, Garcia – KREUTZER; MOLINO: *Trios*. ***

*** Koch 3-7404-2. Still, Alemany, Falletta – KREUTZER: *Grand Trio;* SCHUBERT: *Quartet for Flute, Guitar, Viola & Cello*. ***

Beethoven's early *Serenade* for string trio was arranged for violin, viola and guitar by the Bohemian composer and guitarist, Wenceslaus Matiegka. On Meridian, Gerald Garcia has rearranged it for the present delightful combination, offering the violin part to the flute, and giving the guitar a more taxing contribution. As a companion piece for the rare Kreutzer and Molino items, it makes a charming oddity, very well played and warmly recorded.

On Koch, Matiegka is also associated with another piece included in this entertaining triptych, as it was his *Notturno* that Schubert transcribed to make his *Quartet* for a rather similar combination of instruments. Matiegka's Beethoven transcription is equally felicitous, and the result here, with fine playing and recording, consistently charms the ear.

String quartets

String Quartets Nos. 1–16; Grosse Fuge, Op. 133.

(M) *** ASV CDDDCS 305 (3) (*Nos. 1–6, 10–11*); CDDCS 207 (2) (*Nos. 7–9*); CDDCS 403 (4) (*Nos. 12–16; Grosse Fuge*). Lindsay Qt.

(M) *** Valois (ADD) V 4400 (8). Végh Qt.

*** Valois (ADD) V 4401 (*Nos. 1 & 5*); V 4402 (*Nos. 2–4*); V 4403 (*Nos. 6–7*); V 4404 (*Nos. 8–9*); V 4405 (*Nos. 10 & 12*); V 4406 (*Nos. 11 & 15*); V 4407 (*Nos. 13 & Grosse Fugue*); V 4408 (*Nos. 14 & 16*). Végh Qt.

(B) *** Ph. (ADD) 454 062-2 (10). Italian Qt.

(B) *** Cal. ADD CAL 3633.9 (7). Talich Qt.

(M) (***) EMI mono CZS7 67236-2 (7). Hungarian Qt.

*** EMI CDS7 54587-2 (4) (*Nos. 1, 3–4, 7, 10, 12–14*); CDS7 54592-2 (4) (*Nos. 2, 5–6, 8–9, 11, 15–16; Grosse Fuge; Cavatina from Op. 130*). Alban Berg Qt.

(B) *** EMI ADD/Dig. CZS5 77606-2 (7). Alban Berg Qt.

(B) *** Hyp. Helios CDH 55021/8 (8). New Budapest Qt.

(B) **(*) DG 463 143-2 (7). Amadeus Qt.

(BB) **(*) Arte Nova 74321 63637-2 (9). Alexander Qt (also available separately).

The great merit in the earlier Lindsay recordings of Beethoven lies in the natural expressiveness of their playing, most strikingly in slow movements, which brings a hushed inner quality too rarely caught on record. The sense of spontaneity necessarily brings the obverse quality: these performances are not as precise as those in the finest rival sets; but there are few Beethoven quartet recordings that so convincingly bring out the humanity of the writing, its power to communicate. They offer superb performances of Op. 59. Their insights are not often rivalled, let alone surpassed, in modern recordings. As to the sound, this set is comparable with most of its competitors and is superior to many; artistically, it can hold its own with the best. The Lindsays also get far closer to the essence of the late quartets than most of their rivals, with the benefit of very well-balanced recording. They regularly find tempi that feel completely right, conveying both the letter and the spirit of the music in rich, strong characterization. These are among the very finest versions to have been made in recent years and, at mid-price, are excellent value.

For long a first choice, the Végh performances, recorded in the mid-1970s, have rightly been acclaimed for their expressive depth. That intonation is not always immaculate matters little in relation to the wisdom and experience conveyed. There is no cultivation of surface polish, though there is both elegance and finesse. The CD transfers have a far cleaner image than the original LPs. The eight discs are now available together at mid-price.

The Italian performances, superbly stylish, are now offered in a bargain box of unbeatable value. The Végh versions, in some ways even finer, are at mid-price, but on eight discs instead of ten, so the difference in cost is relatively marginal. The latest Philips remastering is most impressive, with the sound much smoother than before and very naturally balanced. In the *Rasumovsky Quartets* in particular, their tempi are perfectly judged and every phrase is sensitively shaped, while the late quartets receive satisfyingly thoughtful and searching interpretations.

The Talich set now returns in a slipcase at bargain price. They have an impressive technical address, not less formidable than any of their rivals. Their performances have the merit of directness and simplicity of utterance; as music-making there is a refreshing naturalness about their approach, which especially suits Op. 18, even if they are sometimes inclined to be a little measured and wanting in urgency. First movement exposition repeats are observed, except in Nos. 1 and 6. In the middle-period works they win our confidence by the essentially private character of their performances. There is nothing jet-setting here: instead one feels like an eavesdropper on an intimate discourse, with real understanding of what this music is all about. In the late quartets their penetrating accounts can hold their own with the very finest, and the quality of the recorded sound, though not in any way spectacular, is eminently clean and firmly defined, the instruments well placed within a pleasing, not too resonant analogue ambience.

The Hungarian Quartet's first recorded cycle of the Beethoven quartets, with the mono sound firm and full, is superb, with tonal beauty never an end in itself. Polished ensemble goes with a sense of spontaneity in readings fresh and direct. The spacious, unhurried playing of the great slow movements here has rarely been matched. Those primarily concerned with the music as opposed to sound-quality will quickly adjust to the EMI mono recording.

The Alban Berg's second digital set, recorded at public concerts (CDS7 54587-2 and 54592-2), seeks to ensure the greater intensity and spontaneity generated in the presence of an audience. On balance, these performances are freer and more vital than those in the earlier set, but the differences are small. Though the very perfection of ensemble and sheer beauty of sound are not always helpful in this repertoire, these performances are not superficial or slick. Recommended to admirers of this ensemble who are prepared to pay premium price.

The Alban Berg Quartet's earlier performances are characterized by assured and alert playing, a finely blended tone and excellent attack; they generally favour brisk tempi in the first movements, which they dispatch with exemplary polish and accuracy of intonation. Occasionally a tendency to exaggerate dynamic extremes (Op. 59/3, for example) is evident and sounds self-conscious, but by any standards this is superb quartet playing. Other versions have displayed greater depth of feeling in this repertoire – including their own live performance cycle on the same label – but this well-packaged, beautifully recorded set (from 1978–83) at bargain price is well worth considering.

The New Budapest Quartet offer fine performances, always intelligent, with many considerable insights. Throughout the cycle their playing is distinguished by consistent (but not excessive) refinement of sonority, perfect intonation and excellent ensemble and tonal blend. With first-class Hyperion recording, they fully deserve three stars. If the very opening disc of Op. 18/1–2 lacks a little in vitality, this is not a problem elsewhere. They are less searching than the Végh or the Lindsays. At times one feels that they are somehow too clean and occasionally somewhat less than fully characterized. Yet this is always fully committed music-making with plenty of life, and as a super-bargain box (eight CDs for the price of five Helios discs, offered in a slipcase) they are certainly well worth considering: overall, the performances have more depth than those of their Amadeus competitors.

The Amadeus Quartet are at their very best in the Op. 18 *Quartets*, where their mastery and polish are heard to excellent advantage. The smooth and beautifully balanced DG recording from the early 1960s disguises its age. In the middle-period and late quartets, their richly blended tone and refinement of balance are always in evidence and are caught equally well by the DG engineers, but their playing does not always penetrate very far beneath the surface, particularly in the late quartets. There is some superb playing and immaculate ensemble in this cycle, which cannot help but give pleasure, but there are more searching accounts to be found. The set is now offered at bargain price in DG's Collector's Edition and is well documented.

No one investing in the Arte Nova accounts of the Op. 18 *Quartets* listed above will be disappointed. The San Francisco-based Alexander Quartet won the London International String Quartet Competition in 1985. Although these are super-bargain discs, they are top-drawer performances, with excellent if over-bright recordings of interpretations of fine musical intelligence. Generally speaking, the Alexander Quartet's approach is selfless and dedicated; the readings are well thought through and distinguished by considerable tonal finesse. In the E flat, Op. 127, tempi are intelligently chosen (the scherzando third movement could not be bettered), though there is a certain fierceness in tuttis. The close balance does not rob the slow movement of its sense of mystery, which is a tribute to the tonal finesse these players command. The great A minor Quartet, Op. 132 (74321 37312-2), is undeniably impressive. Lovely pianissimo playing, both in the opening and in the Heiliger Dankegesang, which has keen concentration. One of the best in the set. The B flat Quartet and the Grosse Fuge (74321 54455-2) come off well. They convey the sense of struggle and possess great lucidity of texture. The C sharp minor Quartet, Op. 131 (74321 63675-2), is less successful. In the fugal opening the sense of awe that you find in the greatest performances is missing. Their tempo, too, is just a bit too fast.

String Quartets Nos. 1–6, Op. 18/1–6; Op. 14/1 (arr. Beethoven); (i) String Quintet.

(N)*** ASV CDDCA 1111 (Nos. 1–3); CDDCA 1112 (Nos. 4–5 & Op. 14); CDDCA 1113 (No. 6 & *Quintet*). Lindsay Qt; (i) with L. Williams.

String Quartets Nos. 1–6, Op. 18/1–6.

(M) (***) Sony mono M2K 52531 (2). Budapest Qt.

(M) **(*) Ph. (ADD) 426 046-2 (3). Italian Qt.

(M) **(*) Cal. (ADD) CAL 9633 (*Nos. 1–3*); CAL 9634 (*Nos. 4–6*). Talich Qt.

The Lindsay Quartet are setting out on a new recorded cycle of the Beethoven string quartets after an interval of almost twenty years. With the Hungarian Quartet, noted Beethoven interpreters, among their early tutors in the 1960s, the Lindsays have from the start had Beethoven as a central pillar of their repertory, so that with fair justice they have to regard themselves as in the warm, intense tradition of the Busch and Vegh quartets, very different from the highly polished groups who have come to the fore. Already in the Opus 18 quartets the trends are clear, all encouraging.

Consistently throughout these performances, speeds are a fraction faster than before, in *Scherzos* often markedly so, with interpretations tauter and more positive, as well as more spontaneous sounding. If the two key *Adagios* which point forward to the visionary qualities of the late quartets – the D minor slow movement of No. 1 in F and in the deeply mysterious *Adagio, La Malinconia*, at the start of the finale of No. 6 – the speeds, as in the rest, are a fraction more flowing than before, but the hushed intensity is even greater, with no hint of heaviness inappropriate to these early works.

It is good to find Beethoven's own transcription for quartet of his little piano sonata, Opus 14, No. 1, taking its place so naturally among the regular masterpieces, with the finale wittily pointed. The *String Quintet* too is an apt

supplement, beautifully done with Louise Williams as the extra viola.

The celebrated set by the Budapest Quartet first appeared in the UK on the Philips label in 1956. Unlike their 1960s re-make, the sonority is perfectly focused and the readings have weight, animation and dedication, commanding the music's architecture and expressive detail, captured in sound of outstanding fidelity, given the period. The Sony engineers have produced transfers of excellent quality.

The Italian performances are superb. The only reservations concern No. 2 and No. 4: the latter is perhaps a little wanting in forward movement, while the conventional exchanges at the opening of No. 2 seem a shade too deliberate. The balance is truthful, but the digital remastering brings out a thinness in the treble.

The Talich have great directness and simplicity of utterance, even if their accounts are not as inspired as they were later on in the cycle. Most often they find the right tempo and in the first movement of the A major, Op. 18/5, have a wonderful freshness and spontaneity. Even if there are moments of prose, there is no lack of poetry elsewhere. Clean, present recording, even if it is a bit on the dry side. Recommended – but not in preference to, say, the Quartetto Italiano on Philips.

String Quartets Nos. 1; 4; 6; 9 (Rasumovsky); 11; (i) String Quintet in C, Op. 29.

✹ (M) (***) Sony mono MH2K 62870 (2). Budapest Qt, (i) with Milton Katims.

String Quartets Nos. 12; 14–16 (with Minuet from Quartet No. 5 in A, Op. 18/5).

✹ (M) (***) Sony mono MH2K 62873 (2). Budapest Qt.

These two-CD Sony sets collect the 78-r.p.m. cycle on which this group embarked during the war years between 1940 and 1945. The careful CD transfers are clean at the top and tonally full-bodied, belying their age. Such is the calibre of the playing that they even invite comparison with the legendary Busch set, with the fugal opening of the Budapest Op. 131 just as searching and technically more secure than the Busch. Elegant presentation reproduces facsimiles of the original 78-r.p.m. albums and their handsome labels. An outstanding, highly treasurable reissue at upper-mid-price.

(i) *String Quartets Nos. 1; 9; 11–12; 14–16; (ii) Violin Sonata No. 3 in E flat, Op. 12/3.*

✹ (M) *** EMI mono CHS5 65308-2 (4). (i) Busch Qt; (ii) Busch, Serkin – SCHUBERT: *String Quartet No. 8.* ***

Listening to the Busch Quartet's pre-war HMV accounts of the quartets, one feels that no group since has ever penetrated deeper into the heart of these scores. In addition to the Beethoven quartets there is a bonus in the form of the *Violin Sonata in E flat*, Op. 12, No. 3, from Busch and Serkin, playing of warmth and humanity, and a sparkling account of the early B flat Quartet, D.112, of Schubert. These are classics of the gramophone and not to be missed, excellently remastered and transferred.

String Quartets Nos. 1 in F; 4 in C min., Op. 18/1 & 4.

(N) *** MDG 307 0853-2. Leipzig Qt (with qt movements:

SCHUBERT: *in G min., D.173: Allegro con brio*;
ROMBERG: *in F, Op. 1/3: Andante*; MOZART: *No. 23 in F, K.590 – Allegro ***).

The Leipzig Quartet have made a strong impression in earlier recordings. So far MDG have issued two other Beethoven discs which comprise the *Rasumovsky* quartets together with *Opp. 74, 131 & 135*. The group is not glamorous or glitzy and so has attracted less attention than some of its high-powered colleagues. However, it has immaculate polish and tonal finesse and is immensely musical in its approach. This is humane, old-world music-making, civilized without any intrusive over-sophistication. Tempi in the *F major Quartet* are judged beautifully, and the performances are unhurried, although they never lack forward movement. The tonal blend and internal balance are impeccable. The *C minor* is perhaps a shade fast, with the exception of the finale, in which the speed is judged admirably. As the two quartets run to less than fifty minutes MDG fill out the remaining minutes with individual bits and pieces which the assiduous collector may have already acquired. In such a competitive field this will undoubtedly diminish the disc's appeal given its premium price. Artistically, however, the performances are a great success, and the recording is natural and well balanced.

String Quartets Nos. 1, Op. 18/1; 14, Op. 131.

*** Cap. 10510. Petersen Qt.

Both in Op. 131 and in the less successful *F major Quartet*, Op. 18, No. 1, the Petersen Quartet prove dedicated and characterful, and this is a satisfying alternative recommendation in digital sound.

String Quartets Nos. 3, Op. 18/3; 7, Op. 59/1.

*** Channel CCS 6094. Orpheus Qt.

The Orpheus Quartet's account of the *First Rasumovsky Quartet* is among the best in recent years. This is very natural playing, well attuned to the period, deeply felt without being over-intense. The recording has clarity and presence.

String Quartets Nos. 4–5, Op. 18/4–5; 13, Op. 130; Grosse Fuge.

(BB) **(*) Virgin Classics 2 x 1 VBD5 61748 (2). Borodin Qt.

For finesse and beauty of sound in Beethoven the Borodins are unmatched, even by the Alban Berg. In the early quartets the elegance and warmth of the playing are an undoubted pleasure; yet, eloquent as it is on the surface, the searching quality that Beethoven calls for is passed by. The *Grosse Fuge* demands and receives great attack and gusto, yet the players are even more in their element in the lighter, substituted finale. The sound is very realistic, so at its modest price this set still offers much to enjoy.

String Quartets Nos. 4, Op. 18/4; 10 (Harp), Op. 74; 14, Op. 131.

(M) (***) Biddulph mono LAB 056-7. Rosé Qt – BACH: *Double Concerto, etc.* (***)

These performances bring us as close as we can possibly get to the kind of strongly characterized playing Brahms and Mahler would have heard. The recordings were made in 1930 and 1932, the *C sharp minor* in 1927, and this accounts for the rather primitive sound.

String Quartets Nos. 4, Op. 18/4; 15, Op. 132.

*** Cap. 10722. Petersen Qt.

The *Heiliger Dankgesang* inspires the Petersen Quartet to playing of great depth, even though at other points they press ahead very slightly. An outstanding recommendation.

String Quartets Nos. 7–9 (Rasumovsky), Op. 59/1–3; 10 in E flat (Harp).

(N) (BB) *(*) Teldec Ultima 8573 80000-2 (2). Vermeer Qt.

String Quartets Nos. 7–9 (Rasumovsky), Op. 59/1–3; 10 (Harp), Op. 74; 11, Op. 95.

(M) *** Ph. (ADD) 420 797-2 (3). Italian Qt.

(N) (**(*)) Bridge mono 9099A. Budapest Qt.

The remastered Italian set still sounds well. Superb playing is marked by purity of intonation, perfectly blended tone and immaculate ensemble and attack. With tempi perfectly judged and every phrase sensitively shaped, these performances remain a strong recommendation at mid-price.

The Vermeer Quartet give us eminently well-proportioned and serious accounts, which are somewhat handicapped by the dryish, cramped acoustic which entails a certain loss of bloom. The playing is eminently well drilled and the choice of tempi sensible. Dynamic markings are at times a bit generalized (*mf* instead of *p*), though this may well be the fault of the close balance. These are readings to respect rather than warm to.

The Budapest Quartet recorded three complete cycles of the Beethoven quartets in the studio, one in the days of 78 r.p.m. discs, a second during the days of mono LPs and a third for stereo. In addition there are four complete cycles in the archives of the Library of Congress as well as a number of individual performances at the disposal of the planners of this set. In one instance, the account of *Op. 74* from 1941, a defective master, compelled the group to patch with about a minute-and-a-half of a performance from 1946, from the closing bars of the *Scherzo* to the second double bar-line of the variation finale. These performances were recorded at concerts given at the Library of Congress during and immediately after the Second World War; only in the *E minor*, *Op. 59, No. 2*, which was recorded in 1960, do we hear the ensemble in its last years. The personnel – Joseph Roisman, Alexander Schneider, Boris Kroyt and Mischa Schneider – is modified only once, in the *C major Rasumovsky* from 1946 when Edgar Ortenberg replaced Mischa Schneider. The *F major Rasumovsky* was the first the Budapest recorded, with its all Russian personnel in 1929. This version from 1941 has all the momentum, dramatic contrast and inevitability of growth you find in the later mono LP version. There is the tremendous grip of the LP version enlivened by the spontaneity of the concert hall. The slow movement of the *E minor*, recorded in 1960, also seems more searching and thoughtful than the 1950s set, even though its first movement is not as technically immaculate. The recordings from the 1940s are pleasingly full-bodied, and although the acoustic is rather dry, there is no lack of colour. Indeed in sonic terms they hold up well against the commercial LPs from the 1950s, and it is obvious that a great deal of care has gone into their refurbishment. The Budapest was always impressive in this repertoire (except perhaps for its last cycle in the 1960s), and the listener soon forgets any sonic limitations or the occasional blemish. A valuable document.

String Quartets Nos. 7 in F (Razumovky No. 1); 10 in E flat (Harp), Op. 74.

(BB) ** DG 469 028-2. Amadeus Qt.

Here is an inexpensive way to sample the Amadeus style. In the *Adagio* of the first *Razumovsky* the playing is undoubtedly concentrated, but one senses a missing dimension. In the slow movement of the *Harp Quartet* the essential simplicity of Beethoven's cantilena is well conveyed, and certainly the Scherzo has bold attack. Yet the closing *Allegretto*, with variations, seems calculated and lacking in genial humanity. The recording from the early 1960s has been transferred immaculately.

String Quartets Nos. 8, Op. 59/2; 10 (Harp), Op. 74.

(BB) *** Naxos 8.550562. Kodály Qt.

String Quartets Nos. 9, Op. 59/3; 12, Op. 127.

(BB) *** Naxos 8.550563. Kodály Qt.

String Quartet No. 13, Op. 130; Grosse Fuge.

(N) (BB) *** Naxos 8.556593. Kodály Qt.

String Quartets Nos. 14, Op. 131; 16, Op. 135.

(N) (BB) *** Naxos 8.556594. Kodály Qt.

String Quartets Nos. 15, Op. 132; in F (arr. of Piano sonata, Op. 14/1.

(N) (BB) *** Naxos 8.556592. Kodály Qt.

The Kodály have the benefit of very good recorded sound, with a particularly good balance, and the actual playing is very fine, with judiciously chosen tempi and expertly moulded phrasing. No one getting any of these discs is likely to be disappointed, although they are not a first choice in the bargain range.

String Quartet No. 10 (Harp), Op. 74.

(BB) **(*) Discover DICD 920171. Sharon Qt (with RAVEL: *Quartet* **(*)) – MOZART: *Quartet No. 1.* ***

The Sharon Quartet give a most enjoyable account of the *Harp Quartet*, very well matched, expressive and sensitive in the *Adagio* and perceptive in the closing *Allegretto con variazioni*. The sound is a shade reverberant, but the blend is attractively full.

String Quartets Nos. 10 (Harp), Op. 74; 11, Op. 95; 16, Op. 135.

**(*) Harmonia Mundi HMU 907254. Eroica Qt.

These are thought-provoking readings, but at the same time there is some ugly or vulnerable intonation here and there, most notably in the slow movement of the *F major*, Op. 135, and indeed at the very opening of the *Harp*. All the same, this is an interesting and rewarding disc.

String Quartet No. 11 in F min., Op. 95.

(*) DG 457 615-2. Hagen Qt – SCHUBERT: *String Quartet No. 15.* *

The Hagen Quartet brings plenty of dramatic intensity to the *F minor Quartet*, Op. 95: the first movement has great concentration, though all four movements are on the brisk side (and perhaps even a mite aggressive). But there is much expressive power in, and a powerful musical intelligence behind, everything they do. The DG recording has exemplary warmth and clarity.

String Quartets Nos. 12–16; Grosse Fuge, Op. 133.

(N) (M) *** Ph. (ADD). 464 684-2 (3). Italian Qt.
(**(*)) Testament mono SBT 3082 (3). Hollywood Qt.

String Quartets Nos. 12–13; 16; Grosse Fuge, Op. 133.

(B) *** Ph. (ADD) Duo 454 711-2 (2). Italian Qt.

String Quartets Nos. 12, Op. 127; 16, Op. 135.

(B) *** Ph. (ADD) 422 840-2. Italian Qt.
(B) **(*) [EMI Red Line CDR5 69791]. Alban Berg Qt.

String Quartet No. 13, Op. 130; Grosse Fuge, Op. 133.

(B) **(*) [EMI Red Line CDR5 69792]. Alban Berg Qt.

String Quartets Nos. 14–15.

(B) **(*) Ph. (ADD) Duo 454 712-2 (2). Italian Qt.
(B) **(*) [EMI Red Line CDR5 69793]. Alban Berg Qt.

The merits of the Italian Quartet's performances are very considerable and their separate reissue on a pair of Philips Duos is very competitive, even if the second of the two sets seems short measure at only 90 minutes. However, there is an alternative bargain coupling of Op. 127 and Op. 135 which some collectors may find useful. The remastered sound is very satisfying. But probably the best buy is the three-disc mid-priced set reissued as one of Philips's '50 Great Recordings'.

The renowned (1957) Hollywood set of the late Beethoven *Quartets* is one of the classic sets. Technically, the Hollywood players are superior and their virtuosity in the *Grosse Fuge* has to be heard to be believed. But there is no playing to the gallery at any time: this is Beethoven perfectly played without any thought of display. The recordings are mono but have plenty of presence.

Some listeners may find that the sheer polish of the Alban Berg Quartet gets in the way. The recordings do full justice to the magnificently burnished tone that they command and the perfection of blend they so consistently achieve.

String Quartet No. 13, Op. 130; Grosse Fuge, Op. 133.

(N) *** ASV CDDCA 1117. Lindsay Qt.
**(*) Nim. NI 5465. Brandis Qt.

This second installment of the Lindsays' new cycle of the Beethoven *Quartets* amply confirms in this late masterpiece the promise of the first issue of the Op. 18 quartets. What is striking in this performance compared with the Lindsays' version of 20 years earlier is the extra intensity, the hushed tension conveyed as in a live performance, making this a far more searching experience. As before, both Beethoven's original idea for a finale, the *Grosse Fuge*, and the far lighter replacement are included, each prefaced by a different performance of the *Cavatina*. Subtly modified, it is dark and weighty as prelude to the *Grosse Fuge* (which is then given a shattering performance, crisper and more urgent than before), easily lyrical before the regular finale, an ultimate demonstration of the players' responsiveness.

Like the Lindsays, the Brandis also offer both finales to this great quartet. Theirs is a good performance, humane in its musical approach, with tempi well judged and refreshingly selfless in approach. The Nimbus recording is undistracting.

String Quartets No. 14, Op. 131; 16, Op. 135 (versions for string orchestra).

*** DG 435 779-2. VPO, Bernstein.
(N) **(*) DG 463 579-2. VPO, Previn – VERDI: String
Quartet **(*)

Not long before he died, Bernstein nominated his string-orchestra version of Op. 131 as his personal favourite among his own recordings, and he draws dedicated playing from the Vienna Philharmonic, finding a concentration and an inner quality too often missing in recordings by four players alone. The CD version adds a similar string version of Op. 135, a work which Toscanini had presented in this form a generation earlier.

André Previn here follows the example of Leonard Bernstein in recording with the Vienna Philharmonic Mitropoulos's understanding arrangement for full strings of this most demanding of quartets. The result is to add weight, while softening the sharpness of inspiration. Unfortunately the reverberance of the recording softens the focus still further, so that the great set of slow variations of the fourth movement sounds almost Mahlerian in places. None the less, the extra power of the finale brings compensation. With an imaginative coupling in the comparable Verdi arrangement this certainly makes an illuminating disc.

String Trios Nos. 1 in E flat, Op. 3; 2 in G; 3 in D; 4 in C min., Op. 9/1–3; Serenade in D, Op. 8.

(B) *** Ph. (ADD) Duo 456 317-2 (2). Grumiaux Trio.
(B) *** DG Double (ADD) 459 466-2 (2). Italian String Trio.

String Trio No. 1; Serenade in D, Op. 8.

*** Hyp. CDA 67253. Leopold String Trio.

String Trios Nos. 2–4.

*** Hyp. CDA 67254. Leopold String Trio.

The young Beethoven, in preparation for writing string quartets, composed the three Op. 9 *String Trios* in 1798. They have a winning originality, each well contrasted with the others. The delightful seven-movement *Serenade* was published in 1797. The performances by the prize-winning Leopold Trio are particularly alive and fresh, and the Hyperion recording is remarkably real and vivid.

The return of the fine performances by the Grumiaux Trio on a Philips Duo is a cause for celebration. Their playing is supremely musical and marvellously effortless; these artists are content to let the music speak for itself. In addition, the recording is fresh and full-bodied in the best Philips chamber-music tradition. The *Serenade*, Op. 8,

though polished, is perhaps not quite as persuasive as the rest of the programme.

The Italian performances are immaculately played, full of vitality and vivid in sound. They stand alongside the equally fine accounts on Philips Duo, and choice is a matter of taste: the Philips set is rather more mellow in performance and recording, but both are equally valid interpretations.

VIOLIN SONATAS

Violin Sonatas Nos. 1–10.

*** DG 447 058-2 (3). Kremer, Argerich.
(M) *** Decca 421 453-2 (4); 436 892-2 (*Nos. 1–3*), 436 893-2 (*Nos. 4–5*), 436 894-2 (*Nos. 6–8*), 436 895-2 (*Nos. 9–10*). Perlman, Ashkenazy.
(N) (B) *** Ph. (ADD) 468 406-2 (4). Oistrakh, Oborin.
(M) (***) DG mono 463 605-2. Schneiderhan, Kempff.
(M) *** Sony Dig./ADD SM3K 64524 (3). Stern, Istomin.
(M) (***) Ph. mono 442 625-2 (5). Grumiaux, Haskil – MOZART: *Violin Sonatas*. (***)
(BB) **(*) EMI double forte (ADD) CZS5 73647-2 (2) (*Nos. 1–6*); CZS5 73650-2 (2) (*Nos. 7–10*). Zukerman, Barenboim – TCHAIKOVSKY: *Trio*. *(**)

(i) Violin Sonatas Nos. 1–10; (ii) Romances for Violin & Orchestra Nos. 1–2, Opp. 40 & 50.

(B) **(*) Ph. (ADD) Duo 446 521-2 (2) (*Nos. 1–5; Romances*); (ADD) Duo 446 524-2 (2) (*Nos. 6–10*). Szeryng; (i) Haebler; (ii) Concg. O, Haitink.

Having two such volatile artists as Kremer and Argerich in partnership for the Beethoven *Violin Sonatas* makes for exciting, heart-warming results. Perlman and Ashkenazy may be more centrally recommendable for being just as communicative and less idiosyncratic, but Kremer and Argerich have one magnetized from first to last by their individuality in performances that consistently sound spontaneous and fresh. Note that all ten sonatas are squeezed on to only three discs. Also available in DG's Beethoven Edition.

Perlman and Ashkenazy's performances offer a blend of classical purity and spontaneous vitality that is hard to resist; moreover, the realism and presence of the recording in its CD format are very striking. They are also now available (in the UK only) on four separate mid-priced CDs.

The 1962 versions by David Oistrakh and Lev Oborin are also performances to treasure. There is a relaxed joy in the music-making, an almost effortless lyricism and an infectious sparkle. Some might feel a lack of inner tension, and the recording is rather wider in separation than we favour nowadays, but it is a beautiful sound in every other respect.

Kempff's earlier, mono set of the *Violin Sonatas*, in which he is partnered by the estimable Schneiderhan, dates from 1953. The combination of Schneiderhan's refinement and classical sense of poise with Kempff's concentration and clarity makes these performances highly competitive, even compared with Kempff's later set with Menuhin. Schneiderhan's playing has greater finish and his lyrical line sings sweet and true. One has only to sample the *Spring* or

Kreutzer Sonatas to discover the calibre of this partnership, spontaneous, dramatic and full of insights, while Kempff's opening of the slow movement of the *C minor Sonata*, Op. 30/2, is unforgettable, and his partner joins him in comparable rapt concentration. The recording obviously does not separate violin and piano as clearly as in the stereo set, but the internal balance could hardly be bettered and the sound is natural, with a particularly attractive piano-image, fuller than Kempff sometimes received in later years. A worthy candidate for DG's 'Originals'.

The performances by Stern and Istomin have striking rhythmic strengths as well as lyrical appeal: how delightfully the lilting opening theme of *No. 2 in A major* dances along, and how superbly the great *Adagio* of the *C minor*, Op. 30/2, is sustained. This and the very first sonata are analogue and were recorded in 1969; the remainder are digital and date from 1982–3. The *Spring Sonata* is more intense than some versions; the *C minor*, Op. 30/2, has similar electricity, and the *Kreutzer* is splendid. The recording has fine presence, with the close balance suiting the highly projected style of music-making.

Arthur Grumiaux and Clara Haskil made their celebrated recordings in 1956–7, and they still sound remarkably well for their age. The performances are wonderfully civilized and aristocratic. All ten sonatas are fitted on three CDs at mid-price, as opposed to the four of Perlman and Ashkenazy, but they come in harness with two further CDs (equally desirable) of Mozart's mature *Violin Sonatas*, as part of the 'Clara Haskil Legacy'. The discs at present are not available separately.

Zukerman and Barenboim, friends and colleagues, are both strong and positive artists and they consistently strike imaginative sparks off each other, yet there is a hint too that they may have been conscious of earlier criticism that their collaborations were too idiosyncratic. So these are very much central performances which, although not the most imaginative we have had, are a safe recommendation. At bargain price, in good sound, with an exciting performance of the Tchaikovsky *Piano Trio* as a bonus, this is worth considering.

Szeryng's timbre is small and thin, much less ample than Perlman's, yet firmly focused, with the recording slightly more flattering in the later sonatas. There is always a poised line and a natural warmth in his phrasing of slow movements, and allegros often gain from this relative lack of opulence. With the two *Romances for Violin and Orchestra* included for good measure, this pair of Duos, taken together, make a good bargain, though there are preferable recommendations for these sonatas.

Anne-Sophie Mutter and Lambert Orkis were recorded at live performances, and there is no want of liveliness, expressive intelligence and tonal finesse. At the same time, there are too many impulsive touches, holding up the flow of the musical argument, and there are some agogic distortions too. Mutter's playing (and that of her distinguished partner) has much personality, is commanding, masterly and undeniably compelling. However, the idiosyncrasies are intrusive (DG 457 619-2).

Violin Sonatas Nos. 1–3, Op. 12/1–3.

(BB) *** Naxos 8.550284. Nishizaki, Jandó.

Violin Sonatas Nos. 4, Op. 23; 10, Op. 96; 12 Variations on Mozart's 'Se vuol ballare', WoO 40.

(BB) *** Naxos 8.550285. Nishizaki, Jandó.

Violin Sonatas Nos. 4; 5 in F, Op. 24 (Spring)

(N) (BB) **(*) EMI double forte (ADD) CZS5 74292-2 (2). Kagaan, S. Richter – MOZART: *Violin Sonatas.* **(*)

Naxos offer a winning combination here, in performances wonderfully fresh and alive. Takako Nishizaki's timbre, though not large, is admirably suited to Beethoven and she is in complete rapport with Jandó, who is in excellent form. The *Mozart Variations*, too, are winningly done. The recording is most naturally balanced and the acoustic is spacious without clouding the focus.

Kagaan and Richter offer performances which are very strong on personality and the results are both distinguished and compelling. There are touches of exaggeration here and there: staccato is very staccato, and the first movement of the *A minor* is fast and nervously intense, but there is no doubting the stature of these readings. The 1976 recording is excellent, and so too is the Mozart coupling.

Violin Sonatas Nos. 5 (Spring); 9 (Kreutzer).

(M) *** Decca (ADD) 458 618-2. Perlman, Ashkenazy.
(N) (BB) *** Warner Apex 8573 89079-2. Vengerov, (i) Golan; (ii) Markovich.
(BB) *** Naxos 8.550283. Nishizaki, Jandó.
(B) *** DG (ADD) 459 356-2. Menuhin, Kempff.
(B) **(*) [EMI Red Line CDR5 69789]. Yehudi & Jeremy Menuhin.

Couplings of the *Spring* and *Kreutzer Sonatas* are legion, and the combination of Perlman and Ashkenazy in Decca's Legends series must take pride of place.

Maxim Vengerov was just emerging on to the international stage when he made his recordings for Teldec, the *Kreutzer* first in 1991, the *Spring* a year later. Of his two partners, Alexander Markovich obviously proved the most stimulating, for in the impulsive account of *Spring Sonata* one feels that Itamar Golan adds comparatively little, although he leads on well enough. But in the *Kreutzer*, and especially the central variations, Vengerov and Markovich find an affinity. The finale is taken with great dash. Perlman and Ashkenazy have more poise and greater subtlety, but this is undoubtedly infectious when Vengerov's playing is so technically dazzling. Indeed, it would be churlish to award this inexpensive reissue fewer than three stars, for the vivid immediacy of the recording – which makes the forwardly placed violin sound larger than life – suits the impetuous manner of the music-making – alive in every bar.

If Takako Nishizaki does not produce a large sound, the balance with Jandó is expertly managed, and the result is very natural and real. The performances are delightful in their fresh spontaneity. An excellent bargain.

There is no doubt that Menuhin and Kempff give inspirational accounts of both works, and the current transfer of a recording dating from the beginning of the 1970s is well balanced and has good presence.

In 1986 Yehudi Menuhin re-recorded these works, this time with his son. Jeremy plays remarkably well, if not quite matching Hephzibah in the slow movement of the *Kreutzer*. Menuhin's timbre may be less rounded than formerly and his technique less refined, but the nobility of line is still apparent, and the spontaneity and family chemistry are as potent as ever. The *Kreutzer* finale is joyfully spirited. Excellent recording in a resonant acoustic.

Violin Sonatas Nos. 6–8, Op. 30/1–3.

(BB) *** Naxos 8.550286. Nishizaki, Jandó.

All three of the Op. 30 *Sonatas* on one CD represents very good value, particularly with playing of such quality.

Violin Sonatas Nos. 8, Op. 30/3; 9, Op. 47; 10, Op. 96.

(B) *** Cal. (ADD) CAL 6251. Messiereur, Bogunia.

Strong, direct accounts of Beethoven's last three sonatas, of striking spontaneity and recorded with great presence and vividness. This playing, if not always subtle, leaps out of the speakers. This disc is well worth its modest cost.

Violin Sonata No. 9 in A (Kreutzer), Op. 47.

*** EMI CDC5 56815-2. Perlman, Argerich – FRANCK: *Violin Sonata*. ***

Perlman and Argerich, both big musical personalities, strike sparks off each other in this vividly characterful reading of the *Kreutzer*, recorded live. Ensemble is not always immaculate, and audience noises intrude, but this playing could not be more vital, with the first movement fiery and dramatic, the slow movement warmly expressive, and the finale sparkily volatile. The recording, not as immediate as most of Perlman's studio recordings, gives a better idea than usual of his full range of dynamic and tone. Well coupled with a comparable reading of the Franck.

Wind music

Chamber Music for Wind (complete).

(M) **(*) CPO 999 658-2 (4). Consortium Classicum (as below).

Allegro & Minuet for 2 Flutes in G, WoO 26; Duo No. 1 in C for Clarinet & Bassoon, WoO 27/1; Septet in E flat, Op. 20.

**(*) CPO 999 162-2. Consortium Classicum.

Duo No. 2 in F for Clarinet & Bassoon, WoO 27/2; Fidelio: Harmoniemusik: Overture, Arias & Scenes (arr. SEDLAK); Variations on Mozart's 'Là ci darem la mano'.

** CPO 999 437-2. Consortium Classicum.

Wind Octet in E flat, Op. 103; Rondino in E flat, WoO 25; Trio for 2 Oboes & Cor Anglais in C, Op. 87.

**(*) CPO 999 438-2. Consortium Classicum.

Duo No. 3 in B flat for Clarinet & Bassoon, WoO 27/3; Grenadier March in B flat, WoO 29; Quintet in E flat for Oboe, 3 Horns & Bassoon; Wind Sextet in E flat, Op. 71.

**(*) CPO 999 439-2. Consortium Classicum.

The Consortium Classicum are a highly musical and eminently stylish group, and anyone wanting all Beethoven's important music for wind ensemble will find the CPO recordings well balanced and pleasing. The *Allegro and Minuet for Two Flutes* and the *Clarinet and Bassoon Duos* are played most winningly and have great charm, while the *Trio for Two Oboes and Cor Anglais*, a little-known but thoroughly rewarding work in the composer's wind output, is most persuasively presented. The *Grenadier March* is an engaging lollipop. However, few will want to repeat the 38-minute selection (*Harmoniemusik*) from *Fidelio* very often and, while Druschetsky's wind octet arrangement of the *Septet*, Op. 20, comes off spontaneously here, most collectors will prefer to have the original scoring. The four key works are available together on ASV in rather more characterful performances (see below): their superiority is most apparent in their more imaginative response to slow movements.

(Wind) Octet in E flat, Op. 103; Quintet in E flat for Oboe, 3 Horns & Bassoon; Rondino in E flat for Wind Octet, WoO 25; Sextet in E flat, Op. 71.

*** ASV CDCOE 807. Wind Soloists of COE.

The wind soloists of the Chamber Orchestra of Europe give strong and stylish performances of this collection of Beethoven's wind music, marked by some outstanding solo work, notably from the first oboe, Douglas Boyd. They are recorded in warm but clear sound, with good presence.

Octet in E flat, Op. 103; Rondino in E flat, WoO 25; Septet in E flat, Op. 20 (arr. for wind nonet by Jiří Druzěcky).

*** EMI CDC5 56817-2. Sabine Meyer Wind Ens.

The arrangement of the Op. 20 *Septet* was made by a leading composer of Harmoniemusik, who adds a double-bassoon to the usual octet. In this dazzling performance (with Sabine Meyer astonishingly agile in the rapid triplets of the finale) it is just as attractive as the original. An outstanding disc, beautifully recorded, representing early Beethoven at his most winning.

SOLO PIANO MUSIC

Piano Sonatas Nos. 1–32 (complete).

*** Nonesuch 7559 79328-2 (10). Goode.

⊕ (B) (***) DG mono 447 966-2 (8 + bonus disc). Kempff.

(BB) *** EMI (ADD) CZS5 72912-2 (10). Barenboim.

(BB) *** Nim. NI 1774 (11). Roberts.

(B) *** DG 463 127-2 (9). Barenboim.

(B) *** Decca (ADD) 443 706-2 (10) (with *Andanti favori*). Ashkenazy.

⊕ (M) (***) EMI mono CHS7 63765-2 (8). Schnabel.

(M) **(*) Decca Dig./ADD 433 882-2 (8). Backhaus.

Piano Sonatas Nos. 1–32; Diabelli Variations, Op. 120.

(BB) *** Arte Nova 74321 40740-2 (10): Vol. 1: *Nos. 1–3* (74321 27762-2); Vol. 2: *Nos. 4; 13–14 (Moonlight); 24* (74321 30459-2); Vol. 3: *Nos. 5–7; 26 (Les Adieux)* (74321 30460-2); Vol. 4: *Nos. 8 (Pathétique); 12 (Funeral March); 27–8* (74321 27764-2); Vol. 5: *Nos. 9–10; 29 (Hammerklavier)* (74321 37851-2); Vol. 6: *Nos. 11; 22–3 (Appassionata); 25* (74321 39101-2); Vol. 7: *Nos. 15 (Pastoral); 19–20; 21 (Waldstein)* (74321 34012-2); Vol. 8: *Nos. 16–17 (Tempest); 18* (74321 37311-2); Vol. 9: *Nos. 30–33* (74321 39102-2); Vol. 10:

Variations on a Waltz by Diabelli, Op. 120 (74321 27761-2).
Perl.

***Piano Sonatas Nos. 1–32; 6 Variations in F, Op. 43;
Variations & Fugue in E flat on a Theme from
'Prometheus' (Eroica), Op. 35; 32 Variations in C min.,
WoO 80.***

(M) *** Ph. (ADD) 432 301-2 (11). Arrau.

In America, Goode has often been likened to Schnabel or
Serkin, rugged Beethovenians, but that is misleading. It is
not just the power of Goode's playing that singles him out,
but the beauty, when he has such subtle control over a
formidably wide tonal and dynamic range. Even at its
weightiest, the sound is never clangorous. Particularly in the
early sonatas, Goode brings out the wit and parody, while
slow movements regularly draw sensuously velvety legato.
Helped by unusually full and clear recording, with no haze
of reverberation, the clarity of his articulation is breathtaking, as in the running semiquavers of the finale of the
Appassionata Sonata. Above all, Goode has a natural gravity
which compels attention. One has to go back to the pre-
digital era to find a Beethoven cycle of comparable command
and intensity. A clear first choice for those wanting a modern
digital cycle.

Those who have cherished Kempff's later, stereo cycle for
its magical spontaneity will find this quality conveyed even
more intensely in his mono set, recorded between 1951 and
1956. The interpretations are the more personal, the more
individual, at times the more wilful; but for any listener
who responds to Kempff's visionary concentration, this is a
magical series. No other set of the sonatas so clearly gives
the impression of new discovery. Amazingly, the sound has
more body and warmth than the stereo set. A ninth disc
comes free, celebrating Kempff's achievement in words and
music, on the organ in Bach, on the piano in Brahms,
Chopin and Beethoven (a masterly pre-war recording of the
Pathétique Sonata) and accompanying Fischer-Dieskau in
four of his own songs.

Barenboim's earlier set of the Beethoven *Sonatas*,
recorded for EMI when he was in his late twenties, remains
one of his very finest achievements on record. The readings
often involve extreme tempi, both fast and slow, but the
spontaneous style is unfailingly compelling. At times Barenboim's way is mercurial, with an element of fantasy. But
overall this is a keenly thoughtful musician living through
Beethoven's great piano cycle with an individuality that
puts him in the line of the master pianists. The admirably
balanced recordings were made at Abbey Road between 1967
and 1970, and the remastered quality brings a most believably
natural piano-image.

The young Chilean pianist Alfredo Perl responds superbly
to the challenge of a complete Beethoven sonata cycle, giving
searching accounts of works both early and late, always fresh
and spontaneous-sounding, consistently finding depths of
concentration in the most demanding of Beethoven's slow
movements. Particularly in the early sonatas, his manner is
impulsive, often with allegros fast in the Schnabel manner,
yet with technical problems solved masterfully and with no
fudging of detail. Slow movements by contrast are generally
spacious, but not so exaggeratedly so that the music loses

momentum or a sense of lyrical line. The cycle is splendidly
rounded off in accounts of the late sonatas that transcend
everything else, not least the *Hammerklavier*, where the slow
movement has a sublime purity. The performance of the
Diabelli Variations is equally commanding and imaginative.
Overall, Perl's readings are far more individual and characterful than those of his direct rival on super-bargain disc,
Jenö Jandó on Naxos, yet they are never wilful. Like the
Naxos set, this one offers the discs separately if required.
The sound is first rate, though inner textures are not always
ideally clear, and this stands alongside the finest surveys of
the Beethoven sonatas, irrespective of price.

Bernard Roberts's cycle – his second for Nimbus – can be
warmly recommended, the more so when it too comes
at super-bargain price. These are dedicated, undistracting
readings which consistently reflect Roberts's mastery as a
chamber-music pianist, intent on presenting the composer's
arguments as clearly as possible, not drawing attention to
himself. Always spontaneous-sounding, Roberts's approach
to Beethoven has an element of toughness, whether in the
early works or the late, a point that comes out the more
clearly when the individual discs mix works of different
periods. The mature sonatas are marked by rugged power,
with Roberts's virtuosity given full rein, as in the finale of
the *Appassionata*. The digital sound is full-bodied, with the
piano set in a helpful, quite intimate acoustic.

Spontaneity and electricity, extremes of expression in
dynamic, tempo and phrasing, as well as mood, mark Daniel
Barenboim's DG cycle, as they did his much earlier one for
EMI. Some of the more extreme readings have been modified
to fall short of provocation or eccentricity. This time spontaneity is even more evident, though that means he has a
tendency at times to rush his fences, particularly in the early
sonatas. All three movements of the *Waldstein* are more
lyrical this time, and that applies to the late sonatas too, not
just in slow movements but equally strikingly in the great
fugal movements, where inner parts are brought out more
clearly and warmly. The role of such a cycle as this is not to
set Barenboim's readings as though in amber, fixed for ever,
but to act more nearly as a living document of a performer
at a particular point in his career. The sound is full and
spacious, more consistent than before. The CD transfers, on
one disc less than Barenboim's EMI set, are of consistently
high quality.

In the early sonatas Ashkenazy's manner is strong, direct
and concentrated. His readings of the middle-period sonatas
are as masterly and penetrating as anything he has given us,
and he is impressive in the late sonatas too, with a rapt sense
of repose in the slow movement of Op. 109 (*No. 30 in E
major*), while the last two sonatas are played with a depth
and spontaneity which put these readings among the finest
available. The *Hammerklavier*, one of the last to be recorded,
is not quite on this level, hardly monumental. Generally the
sound is excellent, if not always quite as full and natural as
Barenboim's bargain-price EMI set.

Arrau's Beethoven cycle, recorded during the 1960s, is a
survey of great distinction. The Chilean master possessed a
quite distinctive keyboard sonority, richly aristocratic and
refined. The late sonatas show his artistry at its most consummate: outstanding (one of the very finest records he ever

made) is his *Hammerklavier*, which represents his art at its most fully realized. No apologies need be made for the recordings, which belie their age.

For many music-lovers and record collectors of an older generation, Schnabel was the voice of Beethoven; returning to this pioneering set again, one realizes that his insights were deeper than those of almost anyone who followed him, though his pianism has been surpassed. This is one of the towering classics of the gramophone and, whatever other individual Beethoven sonatas you may have, this is an indispensable reference point.

Backhaus recorded his survey over a decade, from 1958 to 1969 (with the exception of the *Hammerklavier*, which came much earlier, in 1953, and is mono). As it happens, the latter represents the peak of the cycle, offering playing of great power and concentration. Backhaus's direct, sometimes brusque manner does not derive from any lack of feeling but rather from a determination to present Beethoven's thoughts adorned with no idiosyncratic excrescences. At his best, as in the *Waldstein* and *Appassionata Sonatas*, the performances present a characteristic mixture of rugged spontaneity and wilfulness which can be remarkably compelling. His massive, rather gruff style naturally suits the later rather than the earlier sonatas, but even the powerful accounts of Op. 109 and Op. 111 do not always leave the music quite enough space to breathe. But overall the set is a formidable achievement, a reminder of a keyboard giant. The recording is remarkably faithful, but with a limited dynamic range.

Piano Sonatas Nos. 1, Op. 2/1 ; 3, Op. 2/3; 32, Op. 111.

(N) ✹ (***) Testament mono SBT 1188. Solomon.

Piano Sonatas Nos. 7, Op. 10/3; 8 (Pathétique), Op. 13; 13; 14 (Moonlight), Op. 27/1–2.

(N) ✹ (***) Testament mono SBT 1189. Solomon.

Piano Sonatas Nos. 17; 18, Op. 31/2–3; 21 (Waldstein), Op. 53; 22, Op. 54.

(N) ✹ (***) Testament mono SBT 1190. Solomon.

Piano Sonatas Nos. 23 (Appassionata), Op. 57; 28, Op. 101; 30 & 31, Opp. 109–110.

(N) ✹ (***) Testament mono SBT 1192. Solomon.

Piano Sonatas Nos. 26 (Les adieux); 27, Op. 90; 29 (Hammerklavier), Op. 106.

(N) ✹(***) Testament mono SBT 1191. Solomon.

This five-CD set provides a welcome reminder of Solomon's artistry and stature. Alas, it was never completed as his stroke in 1956 brought his career prematurely to an end. All these discs are available separately, and no one who cares about Beethoven and great piano playing should lose this opportunity of acquiring them. Solomon was the least assertive of musicians, yet the most deeply satisfying, and his interpretations never obscure Beethoven's intentions. His approach has a unique gravity, an Olympian serenity and an unforced naturalness; Bryce Morrison once spoke of the 'outer sobriety yet inner strength and radiance' of his playing. These performances are among the pinnacles of Beethoven playing,

and the transfers have never sounded better, surpassing in every respect the earlier EMI Référence issues.

Piano Sonatas Nos. 1 in F min.; 2 in A; 3 in C, Op. 2/1–3.

*** Sony SK 64397. Perahia.

*** Ph. 442 124-2. Brendel.

*** Chan. 9212. Lortie.

(BB) **(*) Naxos 8.550150. Jandó.

As his accounts of the concertos have shown, Murray Perahia is as authoritative and sensitive an interpreter of Beethoven as he is of Mozart. These are commanding accounts of the greatest elegance and freshness. The *C major Sonata* is arguably the best we have had since the days of Kempff.

Alfred Brendel's is distinguished, highly characterful playing, marked by superb control. Too controlled, some might say, for one sometimes feels the need, not so much for the unexpected, since Brendel is full of surprises, but for a more volatile, bad-tempered quality. Vividly alive recording.

Louis Lortie has the benefit of an immediate and truthful recording, greatly enhancing his playing. He brings his usual refined musical intelligence to all three of the Op. 2 *Sonatas*, giving ample evidence of his instinctive musicianship and artistry.

Jenö Jandó's complete recording of the Beethoven *Piano Sonatas* is also available in two flimsy slip-cases, each comprising five CDs (8.505002 and 8.505003). This first CD (actually Volume 3) establishes Jandó's credentials as a strong, unidiosyncratic Beethovenian. The piano sound is full and bold.

Piano Sonatas Nos. 3; 29 (Hammerklavier); 6 Bagatelles, Op. 126.

(N) *** BBC (ADD) BBCL 4052-2. Richter.

Sviatoslav Richter's Beethoven recital of the early *C major Sonata, No. 3, Op. 2,*, the *Hammerklavier* and the *6 Bagatelles* comes from the Aldeburgh Season of 1975 and was unannounced in the Festival brochure. In accordance with Richter's penchant for little-known venues, it was held in Blythburgh Church rather than one of the larger venues. The opening of the *Hammerklavier* explodes like some galactic force, and the intensity and fire of the performance carries all before it. There is a tremendous spontaneity as well as a magnificence about it. Unusually for Richter he does not repeat the exposition in the first movement of *Op. 2, No. 3*. Both this piece and the *Bagatelles* complete a memorable musical occasion which fortunately escaped oblivion in the BBC Archives. Very acceptable sound.

Piano Sonata No. 4 in E flat, Op. 7.

(M) * DG ADD/Dig. 457 762-2. Michelangeli – SCHUBERT: *Piano Sonata in A min.* **; BRAHMS: *4 Ballades.* ***

This is a curiously aloof and detached reading of the Op. 7 *Sonata* – as if the artist were viewing the sonata's progress without ever involving himself in its evolution. Coupled with some superb Brahms and controversial Schubert, this CD is a curate's egg.

Piano Sonatas Nos. 4; 13 in E flat, Op. 27/1; 19–20, Op. 49/ 1–2; 22 in F, Op. 54.

(BB) **(*) Naxos 8.550167. Jandó.

The performances of both the *E flat Sonata*, Op. 7, and the *Sonata quasi una fantasia*, Op. 27/1, in which Jandó is totally responsive to Beethoven's wide expressive range, show the excellence of this series, and the three shorter works are also freshly presented.

Piano Sonata Nos. 4; 15 (Pastoral); 20.

*** Ph. 446 624-2. Brendel.

Spacious and majestic are the words that spring to mind when the *E flat Sonata*, Op. 7, gets under way, and Brendel takes a magisterial view of the whole sonata. The *Pastoral* is now more inward-looking and has more gravitas, and some may find it less congenial. Few, however, will find it less than thought-provoking.

Piano Sonatas Nos. 4; 22; 23 (Appassionata); 25.

(N) **(*) EMI CDC5 56965-2. Kovacevich.

Stephen Kovacevich continues his magisterial survey with fine recordings of the *E flat Sonata*, Op. 7 and the glorious yet somewhat underrated *F major*, Op. 54 which Solomon plays so wonderfully (see above), the *Appassionata* and the little *G major*, Op. 79. As earlier in the cycle there is playing of characteristic mastery and subtlety. Op. 7 comes off best and the dramatic power of the *Appassionata* is well conveyed, although there is not so much a hectoring quality as a sense of overprojection. Those collecting the cycle will find much illumination, but it is not quite the equal of some of the earlier issues in this most distinguished survey.

Piano Sonatas Nos. 5–7; 15 (Pastoral).

*** EMI CDC5 56761-2. Kovacevich.

Stephen Kovacevich here offers one of his finest collections yet, with fresh and intense readings of four early sonatas, undisturbed by quirky mannerisms. Not that Kovacevich misses Beethoven's wit and humour, whether in all three Op. 10 works or in Op. 28, the *Pastoral*, among the most amiable of all. One is tempted to say that this cycle is to our time what the Schnabel and Kempff sets were to theirs (and no praise could be higher), and the EMI engineers have got the sound right.

Piano Sonatas Nos. 5–7, Op. 10/1–3; 25 in G, Op. 79.

(BB) *** Naxos 8.550161. Jandó.

The three splendid Op. 10 *Sonatas* show Jandó at his most perceptive and unselfconscious.

Piano Sonatas Nos. 5; 32 in C min., Op. 111; 32 Variations in C min.

*** EMI CDC5 65136-2. Vogt.

Lars Vogt here explores three of the many facets of Beethoven writing in the key of C minor. The most demanding of all, Op. 111, finds him at his most concentrated and penetrating. The EMI recording is first class. However, at the time of going to press this set has been withdrawn.

Piano Sonatas Nos. 7; 14 (Moonlight); 28, Op. 101.

(**(*)) Testament mono SBT 1070. Anda.

These recordings come from 1955–8, during the heyday of Géza Anda's years as a Columbia (EMI) artist. The outstanding performance is the other-worldly account of the *A major Sonata*, Op. 101. All three sonatas are played with a vibrant sense of line, and the recordings are fresh and clean.

Piano Sonatas Nos. 7; 23 (Appassionata).

(M) *** Sony SMK 39344. Perahia.
(M) **(*) RCA 09026 68977-2. Horowitz.

Intense, vibrant playing from Perahia in the *D major Sonata*, with great range of colour and depth of thought, and the *Appassionata* brings a performance of comparable stature.

In both sonatas, Horowitz's combination of drama, poetry and impulsive flair also conveys a considerable depth of intellectual power. Unfortunately the dry recording is not fully worthy of the playing.

Piano Sonatas Nos. 8 (Pathétique); 9–10; 11 in B flat, Op. 22.

*** EMI CDC5 56586-2. Kovacevich.

Readers jaded by a surfeit of Beethoven and who feel reluctance to invest in yet another sonata recital will be surprised at how compelling an experience this is. Playing of stature, and excellent EMI recording.

Piano Sonatas Nos. 8 (Pathétique); 14 (Moonlight); 15 (Pastoral); 17 (Tempest); 21 (Waldstein); 23 (Appassionata); 26 (Les Adieux).

(B) *** Ph. (ADD) Duo 438 730-2. Brendel.
(B) *** Double Decca (ADD) 452 952-2 (2). Ashkenazy.

All the performances here are taken from Brendel's analogue cycle for Philips; they are impressive and the recording is consistently excellent. The *Tempest*, Op. 31/2, is finely conceived and thoroughly compelling, and the central movements of the *Pastoral* resonate in the memory. Outstanding too is Brendel's account of the *Waldstein*.

The comparable Decca collection of named sonatas shows Ashkenazy consistently as a penetrating and individual Beethovenian. The *Moonlight* is poetic and unforced, and he brings concentration together with spontaneity of feeling to the *Tempest*, with an impressive command of keyboard colour. Taking a broadly lyrical view, the *Waldstein* is splendidly structured, and the *Appassionata* is superb. The very good analogue recordings are excellently transferred to CD.

Piano Sonatas Nos. 8 (Pathétique); 14 (Moonlight); 17 (Tempest); 23 (Appassionata).

(N)(BB) **(*) Warner Apex (ADD) 8575 89225-2. Pires.

Maria-João Pires's recordings date from 1977 and show her already emerging as an individual artist. Her performances are clear, and direct, the Appassionata strikingly authoritative, the *Tempest* more personalized and enjoyably so. Fine analogue recording, truthfully transferred. Good value at Apex price.

Piano Sonatas Nos. 8 (Pathétique); 14 (Moonlight); 21 (Waldstein); 23 (Appassionata).

(M) *** DG (ADD) 447 404-2. Kempff.

Everything Kempff does has his individual stamp; above all, he never fails to convey the deep intensity of a master in communication with Beethoven, as in the magic of his measured reading of the finale of the *Waldstein*. The *Appassionata* is characteristically clear and classically straight. The recording has gained in firmness with the clean sound of the digital remastering.

Piano Sonatas Nos. 8 (Pathétique); 14 (Moonlight); 23 (Appassionata).

(B) **(*) EMI (ADD) CDM5 66796-2 [566991]. Barenboim.
(BB) **(*) Naxos 8.550045. Jandó.

There is a rhapsodic feel to Barenboim's approach which is very convincing. The *Appassionata*, like the *Pathétique*, is rather wild and rhapsodic in the first movement, and the slow speed for the central variations brings a simple, natural intensity which contrasts well with the lightness and clarity of the finale. The sound is first class, with excellent sonority.

Jandó's clean, direct style and natural spontaneity are particularly admirable in the slow movements of the *Pathétique* and *Appassionata*, warmly lyrical in feeling, yet not a whit sentimental. Only in the coda of the finale of the *Appassionata* does one feel a loss of poise, when the closing *presto* becomes *prestissimo* and the exuberance of the music-making nearly gets out of control.

Piano Sonatas Nos. 8 (Pathétique); 14 (Moonlight); 23 (Appassionata); 26 (Les Adieux).

(N) ✪ (BB) *** RCA (ADD) 74321 68006-2. Rubinstein.
(N)(M) *** Ph. 464 680-2. Brendel.

Artur Rubinstein had never recorded the *Moonlight* previously, and he brings to it a combination of freshness and maturity to make it stand out even among many fine recorded versions, with an improvisatory feeling in the opening movement. The *Pathétique* has a youthful urgency in the outer movements, and the impulsive surge of feeling in the *Appassionata* is equally compelling. The recordings, made in the Manhattan Center, New York City, sound firmer and fuller than they did on LP. A superb bargain.

Gathered together to be included as one of Philips's '50 Great Recordings', Brendel's performances date from 1994, and are part of his third cycle of the Beethoven *Sonatas*. The gentle, beautifully controlled opening of the *Moonlight* sets the seal on these interpretations, considered and full of wisdom. But Brendel's playing certainly does not lack impulse and spontaneity, as is readily shown by the opening movement of the Appassionata. Slow movements are songful, yet have depth and character, and Brendel's instinctive feeling for the line of Beethoven's music is never shown more readily than in his wonderfully sympathetic account of Les Adieux. The recording, made in The Maltings, is totally real.

Piano Sonatas Nos. 8 (Pathétique); 21 (Waldstein); 23 (Appassionata).

✪ (B) *** DG ADD/Dig. 447 914-2. Gilels.
(M) **(*) Ph. (IMS) 454 686-2. Arrau.

Piano Sonatas Nos. 8 (Pathétique); 23 (Appassionata); 31, Op. 110.

(B) *** DG Dig./ADD 439 426-2. Gilels.

Gilels's account of the *Appassionata* is among the finest ever made, and so is that of the *Waldstein*. He is technically perfect as well as searching and profound. If the *Pathétique* does not quite equal that, such are the strengths of his playing that the reading still leaves a profound impression. In this sonata the 1980 digital recording is balanced too close, bringing a touch of hardness. The good analogue recordings of the other two sonatas are preferable.

The *Pathétique* and *Appassionata Sonatas* are also available on Classikon, in a coupling with Op. 110, and this makes a formidable bargain alternative, for the *A flat Sonata*, too, is given a searching performance. This was recorded (digitally) five years later than the *Pathétique* with the balance better judged.

Arrau's performances are magnificently recorded. This helps to make his *Appassionata* very commanding, with gloriously rich timbre in the central *Andante*, powerful and commanding in the same way as his *Emperor Concerto*. The *Waldstein* is impressive too, though the *Pathétique* (recorded in 1986 when Arrau was eighty-three) is a little lacking in colour and vitality.

Piano Sonatas Nos. 9–10, Op. 14/1–2; 24, Op. 78; 27, Op. 90; 28, Op. 101.

(BB) *** Naxos 8.550162. Jandó.

Opp. 90 and 101 show this artist at full stretch. These are demanding works and Jandó does not fall short, particularly in the eloquent slow movements. The piano sound is most believable.

Piano Sonatas Nos. 10, Op. 14/2; 19–20, Op. 49/1–2.

(M) *** Ph. (ADD) 464 710-2. S. Richter – LISZT: *Piano Concertos Nos. 1–2*. ***

These three sonatas (sonatinas in all but name) are among those works that most budding amatuer pianists have tried to play. Richter presents them with disarming ease and simplicity, and with the utmost eloquence. He is beautifully recorded (in 1963), but this was a curious coupling for his famous versions of the Liszt concertos with Kondrashin, dating from two years earlier, which also had a London venue.

Piano Sonatas Nos. 11–12; 19–20.

*** Chan. 9755. Lortie.

Performances of vital and unfailing intelligence, which make one think afresh about the music itself. What we have heard so far of Louis Lortie's Beethoven odyssey makes one feel that it is worth placing alongside Stephen Kovacevich's sonata cycle on EMI; it is certainly not inferior to it. The Chandos recording is state of the art and wonderfully natural. A most distinguished issue.

Piano Sonatas Nos. 11, Op. 22; 29 (Hammerklavier).

(BB) **(*) Naxos 8.550234. Jandó.

From its very opening bars, the *Hammerklavier* is commanding; there is rapt concentration in the slow movement, and the closing fugue runs its course with a powerful inevitability. Again, most realistic recording.

Piano Sonatas Nos. 12, Op. 26; 16 & 18, Op. 31/1 & 3.

(BB) **(*) Naxos 8.550166. Jandó.

Volume 7 with its trio of middle-period sonatas can be recommended with few reservations. No. 18 is a considerable success, and there is much to stimulate the listener's interest here. Excellent sound.

Piano Sonatas Nos. 12 in A flat, Op. 26; 13 in E flat, Op. 27/1; 14 in C sharp min. (Moonlight); 19 in G min., Op. 49/1; 20 in G, Op. 49/2.

(N) *** EMI CDC5 57131-2. Stephen Kovacevich.

Stephen Kovacevich's Beethoven always sounds freshly thought-out and the first movement of the *A flat Sonata, Op. 26* is no exception. However well you know it or how often you have heard it, Kovacevich remains an illuminating guide. Yet at no point in the sonata or its companion is there any point-making or attention-seeking. The same goes for his poetic and thoughtful account of the *Moonlight* and its beautiful E flat companion. Very few pianists command the natural sense of repose that Kovacevich produces in the first movement of the latter, at the point where the main E flat idea gives way to pianissimo C major chords. These performances were recorded on the Royal Festival Hall's Steinway in the studios at Lyndhurst Hall and the sound is absolutely first class. A most satisfying and distinguished issue.

Piano Sonatas Nos. 13 & 14 (Moonlight), Op. 27/1–2; 15 (Pastoral); 26 (Les Adieux).

(M) *** DG 445 593-2. Barenboim.

Spontaneity and electricity, extremes of expression in dynamic, tempo and phrasing, as well as mood, mark Barenboim's performances. The lyrical flow in the *Pastoral* is as evident as the spontaneity of the music-making.

Piano Sonatas Nos. 14 (Moonlight); 21 (Waldstein); 23 (Appassionata).

(N) (M) *** Virgin VM5 61834-2. Pletnev.
(B) *** Penguin/Decca (ADD) 466 210-2. Ashkenazy.

Some will find the Pletnev *Moonlight* rather mannered, but he has the capacity to make you listen intently and he finds the right depths in the slow movement and finale of the *Waldstein*. The account of the *Appassionata* is masterly. The engineering is immaculate. A fine mid-price reissue.

These three performances are included on Ashkenazy's Double Decca above, which is economically the better proposition. But anyone wanting just these three sonatas will not be disappointed with this disc on either musical or technical grounds. The *Moonlight Sonata* is among the finest in the catalogue.

Piano Sonatas Nos. 15–18; 30–32.

(M) (**) Sony mono SM3K 52642 (3). Gould.

'Wilful yet charismatic' is a phrase to which many have recourse whenever Glenn Gould's name is mentioned. There are no doubts as to his pianism or control or the quality of his musicianship; but his late Beethoven, for all its intelligence, is quirky and marred by his vocal contributions. It can be recommended only to his admirers.

Piano Sonatas: No. 15 (Pastoral); (Kurfürstensonaten) in E flat, F min., D, WoO 47/1–3; in C (incomplete), WoO 51; Sonatinas: in G, F, Anh. 5/1–2.

(BB) **(*) Naxos 8.550255. Jandó.

Jenö Jandó's playing is fresh, clean and intelligent and, if the two *Sonatinas* are not authentic, they make agreeable listening here. The *Pastoral Sonata* is admirably done.

Piano Sonatas Nos. 15 (Pastoral); 17 (Tempest); 18.

(M) *(**) DG 463 079-2. Gilels.

Gilels's performances of the Op. 31 sonatas have excited universal acclaim, and rightly so. It is a pity that the engineers placed the piano too far forward, bringing out the percussive qualities too much, but there is no doubting the impact of these readings. The snag with this CD is the very strange performance of the *Pastoral*, with little sense of flow and only occasional glimpses of the wisdom and humanity one associates with this great artist. But this CD is worth considering at mid-price for Op. 31/2–3.

Piano Sonatas Nos. 16–17 (Tempest); 18, Op. 31/1–3.

*** EMI CDC5 55226-2. Kovacevich.
(N) *** Chan. 9842. Lortie.

Kovacevich offers playing of insight and of unfailing artistry that illumines and delights the listener. It is in the same class as his Opp. 110 and 111.

Louis Lortie's ongoing Beethoven sonata cycle is second only to Stephen Kovacevich's magisterial cycle on EMI, and in some instances (thanks to the quality of the Snape recording) it is every bit as fine. Apart from its artistic merits – Lortie rarely puts a finger wrong – it benefits from outstanding natural recording quality. Lortie's playing is tremendously alive and vibrant, and the vivid nature of the sound makes for supremely satisfying listening.

Piano Sonata No. 17 (Tempest).

✿ (B) *** EMI (ADD) double forte CZS5 69340-2 (2). Sviatoslav Richter – HANDEL: *Suites Nos. 9–16.* *** ✿

Richter makes the most of possibilities of contrast. He plays the opening extremely slowly and then, when the allegro comes, he takes it unusually fast. Far from being odd, this effect is breathtaking. Excellent Abbey Road sound.

Piano Sonatas Nos. 17–18; 23 (Appassionata).

(N) (M) *** Sony SMK 89713. Perahia.

Wonderfully concentrated performances. All these readings have the blend of authority, finesse and poetry that distinguishes this great artist at his best.

Piano Sonatas Nos. 17 (Tempest); 21 (Waldstein); 26 (Les Adieux).

(BB) **(*) Naxos 8.550054. Jandó.

Jenö Jandó offers here three famous named sonatas, and very enjoyable they are in their direct manner.

Piano Sonatas Nos. 17 (Tempest); 29 (Hammerklavier).

(M) *** DG (ADD) (IMS) 419 857-2. Kempff.

Kempff's preference for measured allegros and fastish andantes gives a different weighting to movements from the usual, but the results are profoundly thoughtful.

Piano Sonatas Nos. 21 (Waldstein); 24, Op. 78; 31, Op. 110.

*** EMI CDC7 54896-2. Kovacevich.

Compared with Richard Goode – whose cycle has appeared complete – Kovacevich allows himself a degree more expressive freedom, giving foretastes of romantic music to come. The *Waldstein* as well as Op. 110 has a visionary quality. As with some others in the series, the piano is set at a distance in a reverberant acoustic, blurring the edges.

Piano Sonatas Nos. 24, Op. 78; 29 (Hammerklavier).

*** Sony (ADD) SMK 52645. Gould.

Gould's *Hammerklavier* must be the slowest version ever, and he takes every opportunity to linger over linking passages, coming virtually to a halt at the start of the development section. By personal magnetism the result is compelling, aptly rugged and muscular. The other movements too have their Gouldian eccentricities. Unhelpfully dry, if full and immediate, recorded CBS sound of 1970. In the little Op. 78 *Sonata*, Gould, consciously avoiding lightness and charm, is again magnetic.

Piano Sonatas Nos. 27, Op. 90; 28, Op. 101; 29 (Hammerklavier); 30, Op. 109; 31, Op. 110; 32, Op. 111.

✿ (B) *** DG Double (ADD) 453 010-2 (2). Kempff.
✿ (M) (***) EMI mono CHS7 64708-2 (2). Solomon.
(B) *** Ph. (ADD) Duo 438 374-2 (2). Brendel.

Kempff has never been more inspirationally revealing than in these performances of the last six Beethoven sonatas. These are all great performances, and the remastered recordings have been enhanced to an extraordinary degree, to give an uncannily realistic piano-image, helped by the immediacy of Kempff's communication.

Solomon's classic performances present Beethoven pure and unadulterated, with the *Hammerklavier Sonata* one of the greatest recordings of the work ever made. The sound emerges in startling freshness and fullness. Magisterial, thoughtful, lyrical performances that make many later versions sound shallow.

Brendel's set is among the most distinguished Beethoven playing of the analogue era. The recordings, made in the 1970s, are most realistic and satisfying in the CD transfers. The documentation too is first rate.

Piano Sonatas Nos. 27–8; 30–31.

(M) *** DG (ADD) 457 900-2. Gilels.

As a Beethoven interpreter Gilels is almost peerless and, though his reading of the *E minor Sonata*, Op. 90, has some idiosyncratic rubato in the glorious second movement, its sunny, almost Schubertian atmosphere is very appealing. In the other three works he is at his most inspired. The final two sonatas bring performances of enormous authority and power. These are digitally recorded; Nos. 27 and 28 come from the early 1970s and are transferred excellently.

Piano Sonatas Nos. 27–8; 32, Op. 111.

*** EMI CDC7 54599-2. Kovacevich.

Stephen Kovacevich's Op. 90 is among the finest in the catalogue; in the *A major*, Op. 101, the serene first movement has a subtlety of colour and tone that long resonates with the listener, while the short slow movement seems to commune with another world. The *C minor*, Op. 111, is similarly searching. The recording is excellent.

Piano Sonatas Nos. 28, Op. 101; 29 (Hammerklavier).

(N) (M) *** DG (ADD) 463 639-2. Gilels.

This reissue is an obvious candidate for DG's 'Originals' series. Gilels is at his most inspired in both sonatas, playing with the sort of rapt concentration that makes one forget that these are not live performances. His *Hammerklavier* is a reading of supreme integrity. Olympian, subtle, imperious, one of the finest ever recorded. However, allowances have to be made for the digital recording which is close and bright, and harder than ideal. The more elusive Op. 101 is also given a superb reading, with a deeply expressive first movement and *Adagio* before the contrapuntal finale. Here the analogue recording of a decade earlier is first-rate and very well transferred.

Piano Sonatas Nos. 28–9 (Hammerklavier); 30–32.

(B) *** Decca Double ADD/Dig. 452 176-2 (2). Ashkenazy.
(M) **(*) DG 449 740-2 (2). Pollini.

Distinguished performances from Ashkenazy, and an impressive sense of repose in the slow movement of Op. 109, while the account of No. 28 is searching and masterly. This was Ashkenazy's second recording of the *Hammerklavier* and the performance is fresher, more spontaneous than the earlier version, but less monumental. The last two sonatas are played with a depth and spontaneity which put them among the finest available. The analogue recordings date from between 1971 and 1980, and the remastering is very successful. The *Hammerklavier* is a digital recording and has a touch of hardness on top.

Pollini's recordings of the late sonatas, which won the 1977 *Gramophone* Critics' award for instrumental music, contain playing of the highest mastery. The remastering for reissue as a DG 'Original' has brought no marked improvement, but the two discs are now packaged like a DG Double and are offered at a special price.

Piano Sonatas Nos. 30–32.

*** Ph. (IMS) 446 701-2. Brendel.
*** MusicMasters 67098-2. Feltsman.
(M) *** Cal. Dig./ADD CAL 6648. Södergren.
(BB) *** Naxos 8.550151. Jandó.
(N) ** BIS CD 1120. Freddy Kempf.

Rounding off the latest Brendel Beethoven cycle, these performances are searching and concentrated. They draw one into Beethoven's world immediately, with an eloquence that is all the more potent for being selfless. The recordings, made at the Henry Wood Hall and at The Maltings, Snape, are excellent, real and full of presence.

Vladimir Feltsman demonstrates in the last three sonatas that age is not an essential prerequisite, even with the most searching of Beethoven's works. In the first movement of Op. 109 he is freely rhapsodic to the point of wildness, with the piano made to clatter. In Op. 110 Feltsman's fresh, simple account of the measured paragraphs of the final fugue happily tends to cancel out any disappointment over the bright forcefulness earlier. Op. 111 then comes as a culmination, for here his many qualities focus splendidly, not just in the drama of the compressed first movement but also in the spaciousness of the final *Arietta*.

Inger Södergren's analogue accounts of Opp. 110 and 111 are musically most impressive; she is obviously a pianist of keen musical insights. These performances are fit to keep exalted company, and the recordings are most naturally balanced. A first-class mid-priced recommendation.

The last three sonatas of Beethoven, offered in Naxos's Volume 4, are very imposing indeed in Jandó's hands. There is serenity and gravitas in these readings and a powerful control of structure.

Freddy Kempf plays very well and is gifted with good fingers and a good mind. However, the recording, which was made in the former Swedish Royal Academy of Music, tends to be a bit bottom- and middle-heavy, and there is more to this music than this artist uncovers.

Piano Sonatas Nos. 30–32; Variations on a Theme of Diabelli, Op. 120; 6 Bagatelles, Op. 126; 11 Bagatelles, Op. 119; Ecossaise, WoO 86; Klavierstücken, WoO 61 & 61a; Waltzes, WoO 80.

(M) **(*) Audivis NC 40001 (2). Heisser.

Heisser is a thoughtful pianist whose clear, precise articulation commands admiration and who radiates clarity of thought. There is a strong sense of musical purpose throughout and a refreshing absence of interpretative point-making. If he does not offer the insights of the very finest interpreters in this very demanding repertoire, his performances are still distinctive, and the sound of the recording is very much in the demonstration bracket.

Miscellaneous piano music

Allegretto in C min., WoO 53; Allegretto, WoO 61; Allegretto quasi andante, WoO 61; Bagatelles, WoO 52 & 56; in B flat, WoO 60; in C; 2 Bagatelles: 'Für Elise', WoO 59; 12 German Dances, WoO 8; 7 Ländler, WoO 11; 6 Ländler, WoO 15; Minuet in C; 6 Minuets WoO 10.

(BB) **(*) Naxos 8.553795. Jandó.

Allegretto in C min., H.69; Bagatelle in C (Lustig-Traurig), WoO 54; Fantasia, Op. 77; 12 German Dances, WoO 13; 7 Contredanses, WoO 14; 6 Ecossaises, WoO 83; Fugue in C, H.64; Minuet in E flat, WoO 82; Polonaise in C, Op. 89; 2 Preludes, Op. 39; Prelude in F min., WoO 55; (Concerto) Rondo in C, WoO 48; (Concerto) Finale in C, H.65.

(BB) **(*) Naxos 8.553798. Jandó.

It is always a joy to witness Beethoven relaxing. This collection of shorter piano pieces may offer no great music, but they have a freshness and vitality that is an endless delight. Jenö Jandó is at his finest in the two *C minor Allegrettos* and the *C major Rondo*. He opens the second disc with an appropriately impulsive and enjoyable account of the Op. 77 *Fantasia*. Elsewhere his clear, direct manner certainly evokes the spirit of Beethoven. The set of six *Ecossaises* (in essence, contredanses, and little to do with Scotland) are rhythmically very jolly and emerge as an exhilarating offering. The two *Preludes*, Op. 39, modulating through all the major keys in turn, have their fascination too, as has the solo arrangement of the final coda of the *Third Piano Concerto*, which completes the second disc buoyantly. With playing fresh and clear, this is for the most part a delightful supplement to Jandó's cycle of Beethoven sonatas for Naxos.

Andante favori, WoO 57; 2 German Dances, Hess 67; 12 Minuets, WoO 7; Rondo in A, WoO 49; 2 Rondos, Op. 51/1 & 2; Rondo a capriccio in G, Op. 129.

(N) (BB) *** Naxos 8.553799. Jandó.

With such lightweight items as the two *German Dances* and the *Twelve Minuets* Jandó's fresh, alert manner unobtrusively enhances their charms. That follows the pattern of his earlier Naxos discs of Beethoven's shorter piano pieces. This one also includes equally winning performances of the headlong *Rage over a Lost Penny* and the substantial set of variations, *Andante favori*, that Beethoven originally intended as a middle movement for the *Waldstein Sonata*. Also included are three *Rondos* from early in his career, respectively from 1796, 1798 and 1783, when the composer was only 12. Excellent sound.

Allegretto in C min., WoO 53; Andanti favori, WoO 57; 'Für Elise', WoO 59; 6 Variations on an Original Theme in F, Op. 34.

(M) *** Virgin VER5 61161-2. Tan (fortepiano) – SCHUBERT: Moments musicaux, etc. ***

Melvyn Tan is a spirited artist and a persuasive exponent of the fortepiano. The *F major Variations* come off splendidly; this is a thoroughly enjoyable recital and is recorded with great realism and presence in the Long Gallery of Doddington Hall in Lincolnshire.

Andante favori in F, WoO 57; Bagatelles, Opp. 33, 119: C min., WoO 52; C, WoO 56; 6 Minuets, WoO 10; Rondos: Nos. 1 in C, 2 in G, Op. 51; in C, WoO 48; in A, WoO 49; 6 Variations in F on an Original Theme, Op. 34; 9 Variations in C min. on a March by Dressler, WoO 63; Variations on a Swiss Song, WoO 64; 24 Variations in D on Righini's 'Venni Amore', WoO 65; 12 Variations in C on Haibel's 'Menuet à la Viganò'; 6 Variations in G on Paisiello's 'Nel cor più non mi sento', WoO 70.

(N) *** DG 457 493-2 (2). Pletnev.

These performances are extracted from the magisterial DG compilation issued in 1997 to mark that company's own centenary. They are articulated with characteristic mastery and clarity with no nuance of phrasing or dynamic left unobserved. Pletnev always makes an individual sound and brings his own special insights to bear on this repertoire. The sound is very clean and well focused.

7 Bagatelles, Op. 33; 11 Bagatelles, Op. 119; 6 Bagatelles, Op. 126.

(B) *** Ph. 426 976-2. Kovacevich.

(BB) **(*) Naxos 8.550474. Jenö Jandó.

Bagatelles, Opp. 33; 119; 126; WoO 52 & 56.

*** Chan. 9201. John Lill.

Beethoven's *Bagatelles*, particularly those from Opp. 119 and 126, have often been described as chips from the master's workbench; but rarely if ever has that description seemed more apt than in these searchingly simple and completely spontaneous readings by Kovacevich.

John Lill characteristically takes a serious view of these miniatures, bringing out their relationship to some of the full masterpieces.

Jandó plays with a crisply rhythmic style, almost at times as if he were thinking of a fortepiano. Then, in the later works, he finds more depth of tone and is thoughtful as well as flamboyant. He is given an excellent, modern, digital recording.

7 Bagatelles, Op. 33; 6 Bagatelles, Op. 126; 6 Variations in F, Op. 34; 15 Variations with Fugue in E flat (Eroica), Op. 35; 32 Variations on an Original Theme in C min., WoO 80.

(M) *(**) Sony (ADD) SM2K 52646 (2). Gould (piano).

6 Bagatelles, Op. 126; 6 Ecossaises, WoO 83; 'Für Elise', WoO 59; 15 Variations & Fugue on a Theme from 'Prometheus' (Eroica Variations), Op. 35.

*** Ph. 412 227-2. Brendel.

6 Bagatelles, Op. 126; Polonaise in C, Op. 89; Variations & Fugue on a Theme from 'Prometheus' (Eroica Variations), Op. 35.

*** Nim. NIM 5017. Roberts.

In bravura Alfred Brendel may not quite match his own early playing (on Vox) in this collection of shorter pieces, but his consistent thoughtfulness and imagination bring out the truly Beethovenian qualities of even the most trivial pieces.

Bernard Roberts gives a characteristically fresh and forthright reading of the *Eroica Variations*, recorded in exceptionally vivid sound. He may not have quite the flair of Brendel, but the crispness and clarity of his playing are most refreshing. The shorter pieces bring performances even more intense, with the *Bagatelles* – for all their brevity – given last-period intensity.

Glenn Gould's *Bagatelles* and *Variations* are better and less quirky than his Beethoven *Piano Sonatas*, which are not competitive. Gould fanatics can invest in them; others who are not converted can be assured that any eccentricity is positive and thought-provoking. Not a first choice but deserving of a place in the catalogue.

5 Variations in D on Arne's 'Rule, Britannia', WoO 79; 6 Variations in F on an Original Theme, Op. 34; 6 Variations in D on an Original Theme, Op. 76; 7

Variations in F on 'Winter's Kind, willst du ruhig schlafen?', WoO 75; 8 Variations in C on Grétry's 'Une fièvre brûlante', WoO 72; 8 Variations in F on Süssmayer's 'Tändeln und Scherzen', WoO 76; 10 Variations in B flat on Salieri's 'La stessa, la stessissima', WoO 73.

*** DG 457 613-2. Cascioli.

Gianluca Cascioli is an immensely alert and intelligent player with a keen wit and brilliant articulation; his refinement of colour and dynamics with delicacy of touch is everywhere in evidence. He makes the most of all these pieces, and no one investing in this disc is likely to be disappointed. Even if the recording is brightly lit, it has striking clarity and realism.

6 Variations in F, Op. 34; 6 Variations on 'Nel cor più non mi sento', WoO 70; 15 Variations & Fugue on a Theme from 'Prometheus' in E flat (Eroica Variations), Op. 35; 32 Variations in C min., WoO 80.

(BB) **(*) Naxos 8.550676. Jandó.

6 Variations in F, Op. 34; 15 Variations & Fugue on a Theme from 'Prometheus' in E flat (Eroica Variations), Op. 35; 2 Rondos, Op. 51; Bagatelle: 'Für Elise', WoO 59.

*** Chan. 8616. Lortie.

The Canadian pianist Louis Lortie is an artist of distinction; his readings have both grandeur and authority. This account of the *Eroica Variations* belongs in exalted company and can be recommended alongside such magisterial accounts as that of Gilels.

Jenö Jandó essays the same strong, direct style in his performances of the two major sets of variations as he does in the sonatas. Occasionally his forceful manner in Op. 35 and the *C minor Variations* reaches the point of brusqueness, but no one could deny the strength of this playing. His approach is appropriately lighter in Op. 34 and the very agreeable short set based on the duet by Paisiello. Excellent recording, clear and vivid, to match the other issues in his Naxos series.

33 Variations on a Waltz by Diabelli, Op. 120.

(N) *** Virgin VC5 454682. Anderszewski.

*** Hyp. CDA 66763. Kinderman.

*** Ph. (ADD) 426 232-2. Brendel.

(B) *** Ph. 422 969-2. Kovacevich.

(N) *** DG 459 645-2. Pollini.

33 Variations on a Waltz by Diabelli, Op. 120; 32 Variations in C min., WoO 80.

(BB) *** ASV CDQS 6155. Frith.

Piotr Anderszewski is the self-critical young Polish pianist who competed at Leeds in 1990 and broke off his performance of the Webern *Variations, Op. 27* in disappointment at his playing in the semi-finals and withdrew. His Wigmore performance of the *Diabelli* the following year excited rave reviews and this searching and finely recorded account is quite simply the most outstanding, most thoughtful and impressively played version of the *Diabelli Variations* to have appeared for many years.

William Kinderman's version on Hyperion is fresh and well thought out, sparkling with life and character, and it is almost worth buying the present disc for the sake of his illuminating liner-notes. He is very well recorded, too.

Now reissued in the lowest price-range and with an equally fine account of the *32 Variations on an Original Theme in C minor* thrown in for good measure, the ASV reissue is also very competitive. Benjamin Frith gives a fresh and clear reading; tense and dedicated, this conveys Beethoven's mastery without exaggeration or self-indulgence. Clear, realistic recording to match.

On Philips, Alfred Brendel, here working in the studio, captures the music's dynamism, the sense of an irresistible force building up this immense structure, section by section. It would be hard to imagine a more dramatic reading, sparked off by the cheeky wit of Brendel's treatment of the Diabelli theme itself. The whirlwind power of the whole performance is irresistible, and the piano sound is full and immediate.

Stephen Kovacevich also gives one of the most deeply satisfying performances ever recorded. He may at times seem austere, but his concentration is magnetic from first to last, with fearless dynamic contrasts enhanced in the excellent CD transfer. The reading culminates in the most dedicated account of the concluding variations, hushed in meditation and with no hint of self-indulgence. On the cheapest Philips label, it is a bargain that no Beethovenian should miss.

The *Diabelli* is the Everest of variations, along with the *Goldberg*, of course. Maurizio Pollini scales its heights with magisterial aplomb: he is a master pianist whose clarity of articulation and musical intelligence are second to none, and he makes impressive sense of the architecture of this extraordinary work. However, for all his insights and mastery he seems at times cool and aloof: there is a perfection which commands admiration rather than involvement from the listener. He rattles off variations 10 and 11, and although the sublime *Andante* (No. 20) is thoughtful Brendel and Stephen Kovacevich find infinitely greater depths and a wider range of characterization. The DG recording made in the Herkulesaal in Munich has impressive body and presence.

VOCAL MUSIC

Adelaide; Der Kuss; Resignation; Zärtliche Liebe.

(M) *** DG (ADD) 449 747-2. Wunderlich, Giesen –
SCHUBERT: *Lieder;* SCHUMANN: *Dichterliebe.* ***

Wunderlich was thirty-five when he recorded these songs, and the unique bloom of the lovely voice is beautifully caught. Though the accompanist is too metrical at times, the freshness of Wunderlich's singing makes one grieve again over his untimely death.

Abendlied unter gestirntem Himmel; Adelaide; An die ferne Geliebte, Op. 98; An die Hoffnung; Andenken; Aus Goethes Faust; Ich liebe dich; Der Kuss; Der Liebende; Lied aus der Ferne; Mailied; Mit einem gemalten Band; Neue Liebe, neues Leben; Resignation; Sehnsucht; Seufzer eines Ungeliebten und Gegenliebe; Der Wachtelschlag; Wonne der Wehmut.

(*) Decca (IMS) 444 817-2. Schreier, Schiff.

As in Schubert, the inspired partnership of Peter Schreier and András Schiff results in deeply felt, finely detailed readings of an excellent selection of Beethoven songs, notably in such songs as *An die Hoffnung*. Though the voice is at times gritty and no longer sounds youthful, the depth of feeling is never underplayed, with high dramatic contrasts, yet again heightening one's estimate of Beethoven as songwriter. Well-balanced sound.

Adelaide; An die ferne Geliebte, Op. 98; An die Geliebte; An die Hoffnung; Aus Goethes Faust; Klage; Der Liebende; Das Liedchen von der Ruhe; 6 Lieder aus Gellert; Mailied; Neue Liebe, neues Leben; Sehnsucht; Wonne der Wehmut.

*** Hyp. CDA 67055. Genz, Vignoles.

The German baritone Stephan Genz not only has a voice of warm, velvety beauty, but he already shows a rare depth of understanding. In the very first song here, *An die Hoffnung* ('To Hope') – Beethoven's response to suffering – he sings with rapt concentration, using the widest range of expression, while songs like *Adelaide* bring out his honeyed tone, allied to flawless legato. That contrasts with the youthful energy of the brisk songs and the biting irony of Goethe's *Song of the Flea*, taken very fast. A disc to have one reassessing Beethoven as songwriter, with the mould-breaking cycle, *An die ferne Geliebte*, as a fine climax.

(i–iv) Cantata on the Death of Emperor Joseph II, WoO 87; (ii–v) Cantata on the Accession of Emperor Leopold II, WoO 88. Meeresstille und glückliche Fahrt, Op. 112; (ii) Opferlied.

⊕ *** Hyp. CDA 66880 [id]. (i) Watson; (ii) Rigby; (iii) Mark Ainsley; (iv) Van Dam; (v) Howarth; Corydon Singers & O, Best.

Arguably Beethoven's first major masterpiece, WoO 87 was one of the few early, unpublished works of which he approved: when he came to write *Fidelio* he used the soaring theme from the first of the cantata's soprano arias for Leonore's sublime moment in the finale, *O Gott! Welch ein Augenblick*. The aria is sung radiantly here by Janice Watson. Relishing the tragic C minor power of the choruses, Matthew Best conducts a superb performance, incisive and deeply moving, with excellent soloists as well as a fine chorus. The second cantata, much shorter, written soon afterwards, brings anticipations of the *Fifth Symphony* and of the choral finale of the *Ninth*, while the two shorter pieces – with Jean Rigby as soloist in the *Opferlied* – make a generous fill-up, equally well performed. The atmospheric recording combines weight and transparency.

Che fa il mio bene? (2 versions); *Dimmi, ben mio; Ecco quel fiero istante!; In questa tomba oscura; T'intendo, si, mio cor.*

*** Decca 440 297-2. Bartoli, A. Schiff – HAYDN: *Arianna a Naxos;* MOZART: *Ridente la calma;* SCHUBERT: *Da quel sembiante appresi,* etc. ***

These rare Italian songs come as part of a recital which has an outstanding account of Haydn's *Arianna a Naxos* as its highlight. *La Partenza* has a winningly ingenuous simplicity

and the *Ariettas* (including two completely contrasting settings of *Che fa il mio bene?*) are also full of charm.

Christus am Olberge, Op. 85.

(M) **(*) Sony (ADD) MPK 45878. Raskin, Lewis, Beattie,
Temple University Chs., Phd. O, Ormandy.

**(*) HM (ADD) HMC 905181. Pick-Hieronimi, Anderson, Von
Halem, Ch. & O Nat. de Lyon, Baudo.

Ormandy is at his most purposeful and warmly understanding in Beethoven's oratorio (a stronger and more interesting work than has often been thought), and the soloists
are outstandingly fine, with the pure-toned Judith Raskin
very aptly cast as the Seraph and with Richard Lewis at
his freshest and most expressive as Jesus (a Florestan-like
figure).

Monica Pick-Hieronimi brings powerful Leonore-like
qualities to her role as the Seraph. Baudo directs an energetic
and lively account of it which, if lacking the utmost refinement of detail, generates urgency and breadth in the fine
closing section.

(i) Egmont: Overture & Incidental Music (complete), Op. 84 (see also under Symphony No. 5); (ii) Leonora Overture No. 3.

(BB) *** Discover DICD 920114. (i) Gauci, Schortemeier,
Belgian R. & TV O; (ii) LPO; Rahbari.

Egmont (incidental music), Op. 84: complete recording, with narration based on the text by Grillparzer, and melodrama from the play by Goethe.

(M) **(*) Decca (ADD) 448 593-2. Lorengar, Wussow (narr.),
VPO, Szell.

Alexander Rahbari offers all ten movements of Beethoven's
Egmont music, not just the selection made by Szell. Such
rarities as the third and fourth entr'actes and the melodrama,
Süsse Schlaf, with Schortemeier as the speaker, may not be
important, but they provide an attractive supplement to the
well-known items. Both in *Egmont* and in the *Leonora No. 3
Overture* (with the LPO) Rahbari conducts crisp, well-
sprung, often exciting performances, with Miriam Gauci
the warm-toned soprano. Atmospheric recording, pleasantly
reverberant.

Szell uses a text by the Austrian poet, Franz Grillparzer.
The music is interspersed at the appropriate points, including dramatic drum-rolls in Egmont's final peroration,
this last scene being from Goethe's original. The Decca
presentation, with Klaus-Jürgen Wussow the admirably
committed narrator, is most dramatic. Szell's conducting is
superb, the music marvellously characterized, and the songs
are movingly sung by Pilar Lorengar. A full translation is
included, but there are no separating bands for the spoken
narrative, so that it is impossible to programme the CD to
listen to just the music.

Mass in C, Op. 86.

(BB) *** Belart (ADD) 461 317-2. Palmer, Watts, Tear, Keyte,
St John's College, Cambridge, Ch., ASMF, Guest –
BRUCKNER: *Motets.* ***

(i) Mass in C, Op. 86; Meeresstille und glückliche Fahrt (Calm Sea and a Prosperous Voyage), Op. 112.

*** DG 435 391-2. Margiono, Robbin, Kendall, Miles,
Monteverdi Ch., ORR, Gardiner.

In this long-underrated masterpiece, Gardiner gives just
as refreshing a performance as his earlier, prize-winning
account of the *Missa solemnis*. Aptly clear-toned soloists
match the freshness of the Monteverdi Choir. As an imaginatively chosen coupling Gardiner offers the dramatic soprano
scena, *Ah! perfido*, with Charlotte Margiono as soloist, and
the brief choral cantata, *Meeresstille und glückliche Fahrt*.

George Guest's reading is intimate and, with boys' voices
in the choir and a smaller band of singers, less dramatic; yet,
with splendid recording, the scale works admirably and the
result is refreshing. Excellent value at super-bargain price.

(i) Mass in C, Op. 86; (ii) Missa solemnis, Op. 123.

(B) **(*) Ph. (ADD) Duo 438 362-2 (2). (i) Eda-Pierre, Moll;
(ii) Tomowa-Sintow, Lloyd; (i–ii) Payne, Tear, L. Symphony
Ch., LSO, C. Davis.

The freshness of the choral singing and the clarity of the
sound make Sir Colin Davis's an outstandingly dramatic
version of the *Mass in C*. The cry, 'Passus' ('suffered'), in the
Credo has rarely been presented so tellingly on record, and
the quartet of soloists is first rate. The *Missa solemnis* too
receives a fine performance, if not quite so intense. The 1977
recording, well focused, spacious and atmospheric, is given
a natural, concert-hall balance and the CD transfer is first
class. Good documentation.

Missa solemnis in D, Op. 123.

*** DG 435 770-2 (2). Studer, Norman, Domingo, Moll,
Leipzig R. Ch., Swedish R. Ch., VPO, Levine.

*** DG 429 779-2. Margiono, Robbin, Kendall, Miles,
Monteverdi Ch., E. Bar. Sol., Gardiner.

*** HM HMC 901557. Mannion, Remmert, Taylor,
Hauptmann, La Chapelle Royale Coll. Voc., O des Champs
Elysées, Herreweghe.

(N) *** Häns. 93006 (2). Halgrimson, Kallisch, Aler, Miles,
North German R. Ch., South West German R. Vocal Ens. &
SO, Norrington.

(B) *** DG (ADD) Double 453 016-2 (2). Janowitz, Ludwig,
Wunderlich, Berry, V. Singverein, BPO, Karajan – MOZART:
Coronation Mass. **(*)

(M) **(*) EMI (ADD) CDM5 67546-2 [567547]. Söderström,
Höffgen, Kmentt, Talvela, New Philh. Ch., Klemperer.

(B) *** Sony (ADD) SBK 53517. Arroyo, Forrester, Lewis, Siepi,
Singing City Chs., Phd. O, Ormandy.

(M) **(*) DG 445 543-2 (2). Cuberli, Schmidt, Cole, Van Dam,
V. Singverein, BPO, Karajan – MOZART: *Mass
No. 16.* **(*)

(M) **(*) Teldec 9031 74884-2 (2). Mei, Lipovšek, Rolfe
Johnson, Holl, Arnold Schönberg Ch., COE, Harnoncourt.

(i) Missa solemnis in D. Symphony No. 7 in A, Op. 92.

(**(*)) BBC mono BBCL 4016-2 (2). (i) Milanov, Thorborg,
Von Pataky, Moscona, BBC Choral Soc.; BBC SO, Toscanini
– CHERUBINI: *Anacréon Overture* ***; MOZART:
Symphony No. 35. (***)

(i) *Missa solemnis in D;* **(ii)** *Choral Fantasia in C, Op. 80.*

(M) **(*) Sony (ADD) SM2K 47522 (2). (i–ii) Westminster
Ch.; (i) Farrell, C. Smith, Lewis, Borg; NYPO, Bernstein,
(ii) with Rudolf Serkin – HAYDN: *Mass No. 12.* ***

The 1991 Salzburg Festival honoured its late music director,
Herbert von Karajan, in this performance of Beethoven's
Missa solemnis, conducted by James Levine. With a starry
quartet of soloists, the live recording has an incandescence
that conveys the atmosphere of a great occasion, and the
DG engineers have obtained rich, weighty sound. For such
an intense visionary experience, defying the conventional
view of Levine, this is a version not to be missed. Also
available in DG's Beethoven Edition.

Gardiner's inspired reading matches even the greatest of
traditional performances on record in dramatic weight and
spiritual depth, while bringing out the white heat of Beethoven's inspiration with new intensity. Though the performers are fewer in number than in traditional accounts,
the Monteverdi Choir sings with bright, luminous tone, and
the four soloists are excellent. The recording is vivid too.
Even those who normally resist period performance will find
this compelling.

Philippe Herreweghe's live recording of the *Missa solemnis*
(edited together from two performances) makes a good
alternative to Gardiner's prize-winning version on DG Archiv for a period-scale reading. Even at the start, with its
odd balance, there is no mistaking that we are on a visionary
journey, with an inner quality intensely conveyed. Though
the choir is balanced distantly, the sharpness of attack is
refreshing, amply justifying a performance on a relatively
intimate, period scale. The four young soloists make an
excellent team, headed by the sweet, firm, Canadian soprano,
Rosa Mannion, previously heard as Dorabella in the
Gardiner *Così.*

While the Hänssler version is not a period performance
such as one might expect from Norrington, his allegiances
are apparent, as in passages where the strings play with little
or no vibrato. His speeds, too, reflect a period performer's
preference for following Beethoven's own demanding
metronome markings. Yet what this version demonstrates
above all is not a doctrinaire view but a concern for bringing
out the thrilling originality of Beethoven's inspiration in this
visionary late masterpiece. The end of the *Gloria* brings
white-hot excitement, as wild syncopations and head-reeling
modulations emerge in urgent accelerando.

Although this radio recording, made in Stuttgart by the
South West German Radio engineers, was not of a live
performance, the thrill of it suggests that it was recorded in
a straight take. The chorus sing throughout with a winning
fervour. Their total confidence in tackling Beethoven's
taxing demands, as in cruelly exposed entries, brings incandescent results. The soloists are fresh and cleanly focused,
even if the tenor, John Aler, is a little strained under pressure.
Alastair Miles repeats his fine reading of the bass part,
as already heard in the Gardiner version, while Amanda
Halgrimson and Cornelia Kallisch both sing with gloriously
firm, full tone. The recording also helps to bring out the
highly dramatic contrasts of dynamic that regularly mark
this score, again emphasizing the originality of inspiration.

One can almost hear Beethoven speaking the words as he
revealed their meaning afresh.

On Karajan's earlier (1966) analogue recording, made in
the Jesus-Christus-Kirche, both the chorus and, even more
strikingly, the superbly matched quartet of soloists convey
the intensity and cohesion of Beethoven's deeply personal
response to the liturgy, best of all the ill-fated Fritz Wunderlich, singing radiantly. Now on a DG Double, it is attractively
coupled with Mozart's *Coronation Mass.*

On Sony, Bernstein is at his most intense in his fine,
dedicated account of Beethoven's supreme choral masterpiece. It is an inspirational performance, though it is a
drawback that it overlaps on to a second disc when, with an
overall playing time of about 77 minutes, it could have been
accommodated on a single CD. However, the couplings are
well worth having, especially the Haydn (digital) *Theresia
Mass.* Serkin's *Choral Fantasia* opens with a solo cadenza
almost to rival Brendel's.

The glory of Klemperer's set is the superb choral singing of
the New Philharmonia Chorus. The soloists are less happily
chosen: Waldemar Kmentt seems unpleasantly hard and
Elisabeth Söderström does not sound as firm as she can be.
This now comes on a single CD as one of EMI's 'Great
Recordings of the Century'.

Toscanini's legendary May 1939 account of Beethoven's
Missa solemnis with a formidable quartet of soloists is a
markedly broader, warmer performance than the one from
New York once available on RCA; the sound, though limited,
is satisfyingly full-bodied. The recordings of Beethoven's
Seventh and Mozart's *Haffner,* similarly warmer than his
New York performances, date from 1935. Though the sound
is crumbly at times, the thrill of Toscanini in full flight is
vividly conveyed.

On a single disc in Sony's Essential Classics series at
budget price, Ormandy's 1967 Philadelphia recording makes
an excellent bargain. Ormandy takes a bold and firm view
of this masterpiece. It may not plumb all the spiritual depths
of the work but, with four outstanding soloists and an
excellent, well-focused choir, he takes you magnetically
through the drama of the piece. The vintage recording gives
plenty of body to the sound, both of voices and of orchestra.

In his later version for DG, Karajan (445 543-2) conducts
a powerful reading marked by vivid and forward recording
for orchestra and soloists, less satisfactory in rather cloudy
choral sound. This was one of Karajan's recordings made in
conjunction with a video film, which brings both gains and
losses. The sense of spontaneity, of a massive structure
built dramatically with contrasts underlined, makes for extra
magnetism, but there are flaws of ensemble and flaws of
intonation in the singing of Lella Cuberli.

Like Levine's performance of a year earlier, Harnoncourt's
was recorded live at the Salzburg Festival, but it represents
the new, post-Karajan era at that grandest of music festivals.
Like Harnoncourt's Beethoven symphony cycle, this performance conveys the dramatic tensions of a live occasion,
with finely matched forces performing with freshness and
clarity. The rather distanced sound makes the results marginally less involving than either the Levine version or John
Eliot Gardiner's period performance.

The Ruins of Athens (incidental music; arr. Richard Strauss).

(N) *** Koch 3-6536-2. Arnesen, Windmuller, Selig, Bamberg Ch. & SO, Rickenbacher.

This radical arrangement of Beethoven's incidental music for Kotzebue's play was one of the rare failures among the projects which Strauss devised with Hugo von Hofmannsthal. It was Hofmannsthal's idea to flesh out the handful of incidental pieces that Beethoven wrote for the play, with suitable borrowings from Beethoven's early ballet, *Prometheus*, including the overture. Only a master as confident as Strauss would have dared to monkey with Beethoven's ideas as he does, cutting and reordering them to form an hour-long entertainment, with only two minutes of original Strauss – a brief interlude which quotes motifs from the *Eroica* and *Fifth* symphonies. The result is a colourful if curious amalgam, freshly enjoyable with Rickenbacher the dramatic conductor.

OPERA

Fidelio (complete).

(N) ✿ **(M)** *** EMI (ADD) CMS5 67364-2 (2) [567361]. Ludwig, Vickers, Frick, Berry, Crass, Philh. Ch. & O, Klemperer (with *Overture: Leonora No. 3*).

(BB) *** Naxos 8.660070/71. Nielsen, Winbergh, Moll, Titus, Lienbacher, Pecoraro, Hungarian R. Ch., Nicolaus Esterházy Sinf., Halász.

*** Ph. 426 308-2 (2). Norman, Goldberg, Moll, Wlaschiha, Coburn, Blochwitz, Dresden State Op. Ch. & O, Haitink.

*** Teldec 4509 94560-2 (2). Margiono, Seiffert, Bonney, Skovhus, Leiferkus, Polgár, Van der Walt, Arnold Schönberg Ch., COE, Harnoncourt.

(M) *** EMI (ADD) CMS7 69290-2 (2). Dernesch, Vickers, Kélémen, Ridderbusch, German Op. Ch., BPO, Karajan.

(B) *** DG (ADD) Double 453 106-2 (2) (includes *Overture: Leonora No. 3*). Leonie Rysanek, Haefliger, Fischer-Dieskau, Frick, Seefried, Lenz, Engen, Bav. State Op. Ch. & O, Fricsay.

(M) (***) EMI mono CHS7 64496-2 (2). Flagstad, Patzak, Schoeffler, Greindl, Schwarzkopf, Dermota, V. State Op. Ch., VPO, Furtwängler.

**(*) Telarc CD 80439 (2). Beňačková, Rolfe Johnson, Raimondi, Vogel, Kapellman, Mark Ainsley, Edinburgh Festival Ch., SCO, Mackerras.

Klemperer's great set of *Fidelio*, now rightly reissued as one of EMI's 'Great Recordings of the Century', has been freshly remastered by Allan Ramsay. For some reason, the Overture, though full-bodied, lacks absolute sharpness of focus; but, once the singers enter, the quality of the splendid 1962 Kingsway Hall recording is very apparent, with the voices beautifully caught in relation to the orchestra, all within a glowing ambience. The result is a triumph to match the unique incandescence and spiritual strength of the performance, superbly cast, which leads to a final scene in which, more than in any other recording, the parallel with the finale of the *Choral Symphony* is underlined. It remains first choice, and the drop in price is a move in the right direction. The

documentation, including a full translation, is in every way excellent. The *Overture: Leonora No. 3*) has been added as a postlude, an outstanding performance excellently transferred.

The new Naxos *Fidelio* from Budapest offers a first-rate modern cast incisively directed by Michael Halász, and very well recorded. Inga Nielsen is an outstanding Leonore, with every note sharply focused, using the widest tonal and dynamic range from bright fortissimo to velvety half-tone. Few singers on disc in recent years begin to rival her account of the *Abscheulicher*, ranging from venomous anger to radiant tenderness. Gösta Winbergh makes a formidable Florestan, with Alan Titus a firm, sinister Pizarro and Kurt Moll a splendid Rocco. Only the Don Fernando falls short, with a voice too woolly to focus cleanly. Even making no allowance for price, this version is among the very finest to have arrived in years, gaining in clarity and incisiveness from the relatively small scale.

The unsurpassed nobility of Jessye Norman's voice is perfectly matched to this noblest of operas. In detail of characterization she may not outshine Christa Ludwig, Klemperer's firm and incisive Leonore, but her reading is consistently rich and beautiful, bringing a new revelation. With excellent digital sound and with strong, forthright conducting from Haitink, this is the finest of modern versions, even if it does not replace Klemperer or Karajan.

As you would expect, Nikolaus Harnoncourt, tackling *Fidelio*, reflects the climate of period performance, even though modern instruments are used. The casting matches this approach, with the central role of Leonore given to a singer best known till now for singing Mozart and Bach, Charlotte Margiono. The voice here is warmer than we have known it, so that the *Abscheulicher* has a bite and clarity which make up for not pinning you back in your seat. Barbara Bonney is well contrasted with Margiono. Peter Seiffert sings with unforced clarity as Florestan, and Deon van der Walt is a fresh Jaquino, with Sergei Leiferkus an aptly sinister Pizarro, László Polgár a darkly resonant Rocco and Boje Skovhus a noble Don Pedro. Highlights (70 minutes) are available on Teldec 0630 13800-9.

Comparison between Karajan's strong and heroic reading and Klemperer's version is fascinating. Both have very similar merits, underlining the symphonic character of the work with their weight. Even so, Karajan uses bass and baritone soloists who are lighter than usual, for both the Rocco (Ridderbusch) and the Don Fernando (Van Dam) lack heft in their lower registers. Yet they sing dramatically and intelligently, while the Pizarro of Zoltan Kélémen is made to sound the more biting and powerful. Jon Vickers as Florestan is, if anything, even finer than he was for Klemperer, and Helga Dernesch as Leonore gives a glorious, thrilling performance. The orchestral playing is superb.

The Fricsay set dates from 1957, yet the result is astonishingly modern-sounding, lacking little or nothing in body. As for Fricsay's clear, fresh direction, it matches the excitement and keen tension of a Toscanini performance. Ernst Haefliger is a fine, clear-cut Florestan, lyric in timbre rather than fully heroic, and Frick and Fischer-Dieskau offer strong, intense characterizations, with Pizarro's aria chilling in its villainy. Rysanek's Leonore is also impressive, and her *Ab-*

scheulicher is both dramatic and beautifully shaded. Irmgard Seefried makes an enchanting Marzelline. In this bargain package no libretto translation is included, but there is a well-cued synopsis. The *Leonore No. 3 Overture* is included as a supplement after the opera.

Taken from performances at the Salzburg Festival in 1950, Wilhelm Furtwängler conducts an incomparably starry cast. This is an Austrian Radio recording, previously available only in pirated versions, but here treated to sound which captures the voices on stage with astonishing vividness. The epic scale of Kirsten Flagstad's voice as Leonore sometimes blasts the microphone, but it is a joy to hear such forthright power and security. Elisabeth Schwarzkopf is a delight as Marzelline, vivacious in the dialogue and masterfully sustaining Furtwängler's expansive speed for the Act I quartet. With dialogue included, this is even more compelling than Furtwängler's studio recording.

Like Harnoncourt, Mackerras with modern instruments takes period practice into account. Voices are closer than usual, making the storytelling both more intimate and more intense, most strikingly in the opening scenes. The sudden switch from genial domesticity to the world of the prison and Pizarro comes over with chilling force. That is typical of Mackerras's response to the drama, so that the confrontation quartet of Act II makes one sit up afresh, with Gabriela Beňačková as Leonore bitingly defiant in the face of Pizarro. Beňačková's voice has grown a degree edgier and less predictable at the top, but this is still a warmly expressive as well as a powerful performance. But Anthony Rolfe Johnson as Florestan, responsive though he is, too often brings out an unevenness in the voice, intensified by close-up recording. Siegfried Vogel is a clean-cut Rocco, less elderly than usual, and Ildikó Raimondi is a charming Marzelline, well contrasted with Beňačkova.

In Barenboim's version the links are provided in the booklet, and the recording simply omits dialogue, except in passages of accompanied melodrama. The other oddity is that Barenboim prefers the magnificent *Leonora No. 2 Overture* to the usual one for *Fidelio* and he reverses the order of the first two numbers, with Marzelline's little aria coming first. Barenboim is a dedicated Beethoven interpreter, but this is not one of his most inspired recordings. It is worth hearing for Plácido Domingo's heroic account of the role of Florestan, clean and incisive, if strained at times. Waltraud Meier becomes shrill under pressure, and Soile Isokoski with her marked vibrato is a matronly Marzelline. René Pape is an excellent, firm Rocco, but Falk Struckmann is wobbly and strained as Pizarro, and Kwangchul Youn is a lightweight Fernando (Teldec 3984 25249-2).

The second Naxos version offers a historic radio recording of a live performance, given in 1940 at the Metropolitan Opera in New York with Bruno Walter conducting and Kirsten Flagstad as Leonore. For many it will immediately be ruled out by the limited, often crumbly sound, even if the performance under Walter is urgently passionate at high voltage. Flagstad naturally dominates the performance vocally, even more vital than in her Salzburg reading under Furtwängler (EMI). Alexander Kipnis as Rocco and Herbert Janssen as Don Fernando stand out among the rest, with the others in the cast generally disappointing (Naxos mono 8.110054/55).

Fidelio: highlights.

(M) *** DG (ADD) 445 461-2 (from complete set, with Janowitz, Kollo, Sotin, Jungirth, Fischer-Dieskau, Popp; cond. Bernstein).

It is good to have a set of highlights from the Bernstein set, recorded in conjunction with live performances at the Vienna State Opera. Janowitz sings most beautifully as Leonore and, although Hans Sotin is not an especially villainous Pizarro, his vocal projection is impressive. Kollo is an intelligent and musicanly Florestan and Lucia Popp is at her delightful best as Marzelline. The selection is generous (71 minutes), including the *Overture* and the final scene, and contains a cued synopsis of the narrative.

Leonore (complete).

*** DG 453 461-2 (2). Martinpelto, Begley, Best, Miles, Oelze, Hawlata, Schade, Monteverdi Ch., ORR, Gardiner.
** MDG 337 0826-2 (2). Coburn, Baker, Lafont, Martin-Bonnet, Neidhardt-Barbaux, Von Halem, Kobel, Cologne R. Ch., O of Beethovenhalle, Bonn, Soustrot.

Gardiner's argument, brilliantly expressed in a note, is that *Leonore* in 1804 is the more spontaneous and immediate work, while *Fidelio* of ten years later is retrospective and considered in its response to tyranny and injustice. He goes on to claim that the portraits of both hero and heroine are more poignant in the earlier version, where later they are presented as more self-assured and certain, more universal. Admittedly one misses some dramatic moments, such as the cry of '*Abscheulicher*' at the start of the heroine's big aria. One also misses the great fortissimo outburst from the chorus at the start of the final scene, but the *Leonore* solution is even more evocative, with the chorus getting closer and closer in its signalling of freedom.

Hillevi Martinpelto in the title-role on DG conveys youthful ardour as well as power, well contrasted with the sweetly expressive Marzelline of Christiane Oelze. Kim Begley emerges in sharply focused, heroic strength as Florestan, with Michael Schade providing an ideal lyric contrast as Jaquino. Franz Hawlata as Rocco and Alastair Miles as Don Fernando are both first rate, and if Matthew Best as Pizarro comes too close to sing-speech, he is certainly evil-sounding.

Marc Soustrot here offers the première recording of Beethoven's first revision, made for performances in 1806, a year after the original. In practice, this 1806 text, enjoyable in its own right, lacks some of the freshness of 1805, while failing to match the final version of 1814. It does not help that Soustrot is far less dramatic than Gardiner. The performance, well recorded, is reliable rather than inspired, led by Pamela Coburn as a warm-toned Leonore, Mark Baker a lyrical Florestan, and Christine Neidhardt-Barbaux a sweetly charming Marzelline, but with Jean-Pierre Lafont a wobbly Pizarro.

BELLINI, Vincenzo (1801–35)

Oboe Concerto in E flat.

(B) *** Double Decca (ADD) 452 943-2 (2). Lord, ASMF, Marriner – HANDEL: *Oboe Concertos* etc.; VIVALDI: *Miscellaneous Concertos.* ***

Bellini's *Oboe Concerto* is brief but delectable. Its operatic lyricism is well understood by Roger Lord and Marriner, and their performance is not surpassed.

Sinfonias in C; D; E flat.

*** Koch 3-6733-2. Krakow State PO, Bader – DONIZETTI: *Sinfonias.* ***

Bellini's *Sinfonias* are elegant, rather more serious in mood and style than the Donizetti works with which they are coupled. Each has a long, gracious introduction. They have excellent ideas, well put together, and the secondary themes all have charm, as indeed has the principal theme of the *C major*. All three are very well played and recorded, and this collection is well worth exploring.

OPERA

(i) *Beatrice di tenda*; (ii) *Norma*; (iii) *I puritani*; (iv) *La sonnambula*.

(N) (B) **(*) Decca (ADD) 467 789-2 (10). Sutherland with (i) Pavarotti, Opthof; Veasey, Amb. Op. Ch.; (i; ii) LSO; (ii) Horne, Alexander, Cross; LSO Ch.; (iii) Duval, Capecchi, ROHCG Ch. & O; (iii; iv) Ch. & O of Maggio Musicale, Fiorentino; (iv) Monti, Corena, L. Op. Ch., Nat. PO; all cond. Bonynge.

As with Sir Colin Davis's Berlioz opera sets for Philips, Decca have now gathered Bonynge's four key Bellini recordings with Sutherland from the 1960s in a Collector's Edition at bargain price. This means that her earlier versions of *Norma*, *I puritani* and *La sonnambula* have been chosen, where in the latter two instances her later versions are preferable (see below). However, there is much beautiful singing here and these are vintage Decca recordings.

Beatrice di Tenda (complete); Arias: *Norma: Casta diva. I Puritani: Son vergin vezzosa; Oh rendetemi la speme. La sonnambula: Ah, non credea mirarti.*

(M) *** Decca (ADD) (IMS) 433 706-2 (3). Sutherland, Pavarotti, Opthof, Veasey, Ward, Amb. Op. Ch., LSO, Bonynge.

Beatrice di Tenda, with a story involving a string of unrequited loves, is a splendid vehicle for an exceptional prima donna with a big enough voice and brilliant enough coloratura. Dame Joan Sutherland had made it her own when this recording was made in 1966, a dazzling example of her art with Bonynge, a natural Bellini conductor. The supporting cast could hardly be better, with Pavarotti highly responsive. The recording, of Decca's best vintage, has been transferred to CD with vivid atmosphere and colour. Four famous arias are provided as a filler: one from Sutherland's 1964 *Norma*,

two from her 1963 *I Puritani* and one from the 1962 *La sonnambula*.

I Capuleti ed i Montecchi (complete).

*** RCA 09026 68899-2 (3). Kasarova, Mei, Vargas, Chiummo, Alberghini, Bav. R. Ch., Munich RO, R. Abbado.
*** Teldec 3984 21472-2 (2). Larmore, Hong, Groves, Aceto, Lloyd, Scottish CO, Runnicles.
(M) **(*) EMI CMS7 64846-2 (2). Baltsa, Gruberová, Raffanti, Howell, Tomlinson, ROHCG Ch. & O, Muti.

Taking three discs instead of the usual two, the RCA set offers an important bonus in an alternative version of the Tomb Scene by Nicolai Vaccai, dating from five years before Bellini's version. There are also a couple of alternative versions of arias ornamented by Rossini. Quite apart from that, Roberto Abbado conducts a beautifully sprung, warmly sympathetic reading, less hard-driven than the EMI live recording conducted by Muti. The sound too is warm, full and well balanced, preferable to the EMI. Vocally the principal glory of the set lies in Kasarova's characterful and stylish performance as Romeo, firmer and more consistent than Baltsa's on EMI. Eva Mei makes a sweet and girlish Giulietta, sensitive and true, if lacking some of the deeper insights of Gruberová on EMI. The rest of the cast is first rate, with Ramón Vargas outstanding in the tenor role of Tebaldo (Tybalt).

Donald Runnicles offers a fresh and sympathetic reading of Bellini's 'Romeo and Juliet' opera with an outstanding cast. The benefit of having the Scottish Chamber Orchestra instead of a full-blown symphony orchestra is that the woodwind and brass have a fairer balance against the strings. Jennifer Larmore is warm, fresh and firm as Romeo, youthfully ardent. Most remarkable of all is the Korean soprano Hei-Kyung Hong as Juliet, at once pure and warm of tone and passionate of expression, equally bringing out the youthfulness of the heroine. As Tebaldo, Paul Groves is clear and stylish, even though the tone is not Italianate, and Robert Lloyd is a commanding Lorenzo. Though the competition is strong, the Teldec set scores both in its casting and in its fullness of sound.

Muti's set was recorded live at Covent Garden in March 1984. With the Royal Opera House a difficult venue for recording, the sound is hard and close. Agnes Baltsa makes a passionately expressive Romeo and Edita Gruberová a Juliet who is not just brilliant in coloratura but also sweet and tender. Muti's conducting is masterly, especially striking at the end of Act I, when the five principals sing a hushed quintet. With excellent contributions from the refined tenor Dano Raffanti (as Tebaldo), Gwynne Howell and John Tomlinson, it is a performance to blow the cobwebs off this once-neglected opera.

Norma (complete).

(M) *** Decca (ADD) 425 488-2 (3). Sutherland, Horne, Alexander, Cross, Minton, Ward, L. Symphony Ch., LSO, Bonynge.
(***) EMI mono CDS5 56271-2 (3). Callas, Stignani, Filippeschi, Rossi-Lemeni, La Scala, Milan, Ch. and O, Serafin.

**(*) Decca 414 476-2 (3). Sutherland, Pavarotti, Caballé, Ramey, Welsh Nat. Op. Ch. & O, Bonynge.

(M) **(*) EMI (ADD) CMS5 66428-2 (3). Callas, Corelli, Ludwig, Zaccharia, Ch. & O of La Scala, Milan, Serafin.

Norma: highlights.

(M) *** Decca (ADD) 421 886-2 (from above complete recording with Sutherland, Horne; cond. Bonynge).

(M) **(*) EMI (ADD) CDM5 66662-2 (from above complete recording with Callas, Corelli; cond. Serafin).

In her first, mid-1960s recording of *Norma*, Sutherland was joined by an Adalgisa in Marilyn Horne whose control of florid singing is just as remarkable as Sutherland's own. The other soloists are very good indeed. A most compelling performance, helped by the conducting of Richard Bonynge; and the Walthamstow recording is vivid but also atmospheric in its CD format.

In Callas's earlier, mono set, the mono recording is opened out impressively in the new transfer, and the sense of presence gives wonderful intensity to one of the diva's most powerful performances, recorded at the very peak of her powers. Balance of soloists is close but Callas justifies everything, even the cuts. The veteran, Ebe Stignani, as Adalgisa is a characterful partner in the sisters' duets, but Filippeschi is disappointingly thin-toned and strained, and Rossi-Lemeni is gruff.

Though Dame Joan Sutherland was fifty-eight when her second *Norma* recording was made, her singing is still impressive, but Pavarotti is in some ways the set's greatest strength, easily expressive as Pollione. Caballé as Adalgisa seems determined to outdo Sutherland in cooing self-indulgently. Full, brilliant, well-balanced recording of the complete score.

By the time Callas came to record her 1960 stereo version, the tendency to hardness and unsteadiness in the voice above the stave, always apparent, had grown serious; but the interpretation was as sharply illuminating as ever, a unique assumption, helped by Christa Ludwig as Adalgisa, while Corelli sings heroically. Serafin as ever is the most persuasive of Bellini conductors.

Il Pirata (complete).

(M) *(**) EMI mono CMS5 66432-2 (2). Callas, Ego, Ferraro, Peterson, Watson, Sarfaty, American Op. Soc. Ch. & O, Rescigno.

(M) ** EMI (ADD) CMS5 67121-2 (2). Cappuccilli, Caballé, Martí, Raimondi, Rome R. & TV Ch. & O, Gavazzeni.

Recorded live at a concert performance in New York in January 1959, the Callas version is flawed, with harsh sound and intrusive audience noises. Though Callas herself shows signs of vocal deterioration, with top notes often raw and uneven, hers is a fire-eating performance, totally distinctive, instantly magnetic from the moment she utters her first word, 'Sorgete', in Act I. The rest of the cast is indifferent, with Constantine Ego strenuous in the tenor role of Ernesto. The second disc offers an alternative recording of the final scene, made in Amsterdam six months later, with Rescigno conducting the Concertgebouw Orchestra and with Callas in smoother vocal form, helped by less raw recording.

Gavazzeni's is the first complete recording. Caballé is well

suited to the role of the heroine, though by her highest standards there is some carelessness in her singing, with clumsy changes of register. Nor are the conducting and presentation sparkling enough to mask the comparative poverty of Bellini's invention. Caballé's husband, Bernabé Martí, battles valiantly with the difficult part of the pirate. The 1970 recording flatters the voices and has plenty of atmosphere.

I Puritani (complete).

*** Decca (ADD) 417 588-2 (3). Sutherland, Pavarotti, Ghiaurov, Luccardi, Caminada, Cappuccilli, ROHCG Ch. & O, Bonynge.

(***) EMI mono CDS5 56275-2 (2). Callas, Di Stefano, Panerai, Rossi-Lemeni, La Scala, Milan, Ch. & O, Serafin.

(M) **(*) Decca (ADD) 448 969-2 (2). Sutherland, Duval, Capecchi, Flagello, Elkins, De Palma, Maggio Musicale Fiorentino Ch. & O, Bonynge.

(M) **(*) EMI (ADD) CMS7 69663-2 (2). Caballé, Kraus, Manuguerra, Hamari, Ferrin, Amb. Op. Ch., Philh. O, Muti.

Whereas her earlier set was recorded when Sutherland had adopted a soft-grained style, with consonants largely eliminated, her singing brings fresh, bright singing, rich and agile. Pavarotti emerges as a Bellini stylist, with Ghiaurov and Cappuccilli making up an impressive cast, but with Anita Caminada disappointing as Enrichetta. Vivid, atmospheric recording.

In 1953, when she made this recording, Callas's voice was already hard on top and with some unsteadiness, but her portrayal is uniquely compelling. None of the other soloists is ideal, though most of the singing is acceptable. The mono sound is now opened up and the solo voices project well. Like other EMI/Callas recordings, this has been handsomely redocumented.

In her later set, Joan Sutherland slides about too freely in *portamento*, but the beauty and freshness of the sound, as well as the phenomenal agility, are what matter above all. The final *Ah, non giunge* is dazzling. In her earlier recording, Pierre Duval controls his ringing tenor well, powerful at the top, and Renato Capecchi is a strong Riccardo, if not always well focused. Though Bonynge conducts most sympathetically, controlling ensembles well, the text has cuts, confirming this as less recommendable than Sutherland's later set.

Riccardo Muti's attention to detail and pointing of rhythm make for refreshing results, and the warm, luminous recording is excellent. But both the principal soloists – here below form – indulge in distracting mannerisms, hardly allowing even a single bar to be presented straight in the big numbers, rarely sounding spontaneous. The big ensemble, *A te, o cara*, at slow speed loses the surge of exhilaration which Sutherland and Pavarotti show so strongly.

I Puritani: highlights.

(M) (***) EMI mono CDM5 66665-2 (from above recording, with Callas, Di Stefano, cond. Serafin).

The Callas highlights offer an hour of music – a dozen excerpts, and Elvira features in all but four of them – so this will be a useful disc for those not wanting to stretch to the full-priced complete set. The remastered sound is now surprisingly good.

La sonnambula (complete).

*** Decca 417 424-2 (2). Sutherland, Pavarotti, D. Jones, Ghiaurov, L. Op. Ch., Nat. PO, Bonynge.

(B) *** Naxos 8.660042/3. Orgonasova, D'Artegna, Papadjiakou, Giménez, Dilbèr, De Vries, Micu, Netherlands R. Ch. and CO, Zedda.

(***) EMI mono CDS5 56278-2 (2). Callas, Monti, Cossotto, Zaccaria, Ratti, La Scala, Milan, Ch. and O, Votto.

(M) **(*) Decca (ADD) 448 966-2 (2). Sutherland, Monti, Elkins, Stahlman, Corena, Maggio Musicale Fiorentino Ch. & O, Bonynge.

Sutherland's singing in her later version is even more affecting and more stylish than before, generally purer and more forthright, if with diction still clouded at times. The challenge of singing opposite Pavarotti adds to the bite of the performance, crisply and resiliently controlled by Bonynge.

The Naxos issue offers the finest version of the opera at any price since Joan Sutherland's. Luba Orgonasova is an expressive and characterful heroine, agile and pointed in her phrasing of coloratura, deeply affecting in the tender legato of *Ah non credea mirarti*, with tone delicately varied. Raul Giménez is equally stylish as Elvino, the rich landowner, using his light Rossinian tenor most sensitively, with Alberto Zedda, scholar as well as conductor, pointing the accompaniment lightly. The other principals are not quite on this level but they make an excellent team. As usual with Naxos opera issues, there is a libretto in Italian but only a detailed summary of the plot in English.

Substantially cut, the Callas version was recorded in mono in 1957, yet it gives a vivid picture of the diva at the peak of her powers. Nicola Monti makes a strong rather than a subtle contribution, but he blends well with Callas in the duets; and Fiorenza Cossotto is a good Teresa. Again, the remastered recording for the Callas Edition shows considerable improvement.

In Sutherland's earlier version, her use of *portamento* is often excessive, but the freshness of the voice is a delight, Bonynge's direction is outstanding, and the casting is first rate too, with Nicola Monti a Bellini tenor. Both Sylvia Stahlman as Lisa and Margareta Elkins as Teresa sing beautifully and with keen accuracy. Even Fernando Corena's rather coarse, *buffo*-style Rodolfo has an attractive vitality. The recording has come up vividly on CD.

COLLECTIONS

Scenes and arias from: *Bianca e Fernando; Norma* (including *Casta diva*); *Il Pirata.*

**(*) Sony SK 62032. Eaglen, OAE, Elder – WAGNER: Excerpts from: *Götterdämmerung*, etc. **(*)

It shows the versatility of Jane Eaglen, a singer who has both Brünnhilde and Norma in her stage repertoire, that she dares to couple Bellini and Wagner. With such a massive voice it is amazing in Bellini cabalettas that she can tackle coloratura divisions with such agility, even if the results can be ungainly, and the legato in Bellini's soaring melodies is not as seamless as it might be. The period instruments of the Orchestra of the Age of Enlightenment add attractive colour.

BENDA, Jiří Antonín (1722–95)

Sinfonias Nos. 1 in D; 2 in G; 3 in C; 4 in F; 5 in G; 6 in E flat.

(BB) **(*) Naxos 8.553408. Prague CO, Benda.

Sinfonias Nos. 7 in D; 8 in D; 9 in A; 10 in G; 11 in F; 12 in A.

(BB) **(*) Naxos 8.553409. Prague CO, Benda.

The Bohemian Benda family was something of a musical dynasty in Europe over a period of some 300 years. Jiří's twelve three-movement symphonies are conventional but are kept alive by the rhythmic vigour of the allegros and the graceful but uneventful *Andantes*. Occasionally he features a solo flute or (as in the *Larghetto* of No. 7) a pair of flutes, in No. 9 a songful oboe, or in No. 6, one of the finest of the series, a solo violin takes a concertante role; the scoring for woodwind and horns in the finale is very effective. But the orchestration is seldom a striking feature, and these sinfonias are best approached singly, rather than in a group. Christian Benda is a more recent member of the family clan, and he directs the excellent Prague Chamber Orchestra with vigour and spirit, shaping slow movements with affection. The Naxos recording is admirably fresh and truthful, and the ambience is most pleasing.

VOCAL MUSIC

(i) *Ariadne auf Naxos. Pygmalion.*

(BB) **(*) Naxos 8.553345. Quadlbauer, Uray; (i) Schell; Prague CO, Benda.

Ariadne auf Naxos and *Pygmalion* equally demonstrate Benda's ability to illuminate classical stories, making the central characters believable. *Pygmalion*, with libretto adapted from a French text of Jean-Jacques Rousseau, is the lighter piece, with a happy ending. Performances under Christian Benda are as impressive as that of *Medea* on the companion disc, but again texts and translations are separated, and no internal tracks are provided. First-rate sound and good acting, though as Pygmalion Peter Uray is not as clear in his delivery as the Ariadne, Brigitte Quadlbauer.

Medea (complete).

(BB) **(*) Naxos 8.553346. Schell & speaking cast, Prague CO, Benda (with J. J. BENDA: *Violin Concerto in G: Grave* ***).

Christian Benda here presents a most characterful and compelling version of what may be counted as Jiří Benda's masterpiece, the melodrama *Medea*. Not only is the playing of the Prague Chamber Orchestra tautly committed, the performance offers an impressive team of actors, led by

Hertha Schell. Irritatingly, the Naxos booklet gives the German text and English translation on different pages. The fill-up is a treasure. Christian Benda as solo cellist gives a most moving performance of a deeply expressive violin concerto slow movement, as arranged for cello. Excellent sound, with good balance between speaking voices and orchestra.

BENJAMIN, Arthur (1893–1960)

Concertino for Piano & Orchestra; Concerto quasi una fantasia for Piano & Orchestra.

** Everest (ADD) EVC 9029. Crowson, LSO, composer.

Benjamin's *Concertino* dates from 1929 and was inspired directly by Gershwin's *Rhapsody in Blue*. The jazz influence is mainly rhythmic and is felt at its strongest in the work's closing pages. The writing is fluent, the style eclectic, similar in many ways to the *Concerto quasi una fantasia* of 1949, particularly in the scherzando sections. Lamar Crowson gives spirited accounts of them here and is well, if not impeccably, accompanied by the LSO under the composer's direction. The 1959 recording is rather dry.

Symphony No. 1; Ballad for String Orchestra.

**(*) Marco 8.223764. Queensland SO, Lyndon-Gee.

The composer had served in each World War, and when his symphony was written, in 1944–5, he was surely reflecting his personal experience in both conflicts. The opening of the first movement with its violent drum-beats immediately creates a darkness of mood which is seldom to lift throughout the work. The *Ballad* is hardly less disconsolate in feeling, again expressing its melancholy through an on-going string cantilena. Here the Queensland strings are especially impressive, and Christopher Lyndon-Gee always responds convincingly to the emotional intensity which all this music carries. The recording is spacious if a little two-dimensional.

(i) *Cello Sonatina;* (ii) *Viola Sonata;* (iii) *Violin Sonata; 3 Pieces for Violin & Piano; Jamaican Rumba;* (iv) *Le Tombeau de Ravel* (for clarinet and piano).

(N) *** Tall Poppies TP 134. Tall Poppies Ensemble: Munro with (i) Pereira; (ii) Van Stralen; (iii) Harding; (iv) Jenkin.

Although opening with a lilting account of the *Jamaican Rumba* in the 1944 arrangement for violin and piano, dedicated to and played by Heifetz, the earliest music here is also for violin and piano, a set of *Three Pieces*. A lively *Humoresque* and *Carnavalesque* (with a curious tolling bell introduction) frame a ghostly *Arabesque*. The *Violin Sonatina* followed in 1924, with its opening movement, *Tranquilly flowing*, becoming increasingly passionate, followed by a perky *Scherzo* and a charming closing *Rondo*.

The *Cello Sonatina* of 1938 is perhaps the most warmly lyrical of Benjamin's string duos, easily melodic but with a highly rhythmic closing *March*. The *Viola Sonata*, written in 1942 for William Primrose, is a particularly fine work combining a haunting *Elegy* with a nostalgic *Waltz*, and ending with a boldly virtuosic *Toccata*.

But especially beguiling is the *Tombeau de Ravel* written for Gervase de Peyer, which exploited that artist's melting cantabile timbre and his virtuosity in six quixotic central waltz interludes, which are framed by an introduction and finale. All the performances here are of high quality and show a composer of great resource who always captures and holds the listener's ear. The recording is excellent.

Pastoral Fantasy (for string quartet); *5 Spirituals* (for cello & piano); *Viola Sonata; 3 Violin Pieces; A Tune & Variations for Little People; Violin Sonatina.*

(N)(M) *** Dutton Epoch CDLX 7110. Locrian Ens.

This excellent Dutton collection duplicates the *Viola Sonata*, and *Violin Sonata*, and the *Three Pieces* also offered on the Tall Poppies disc above, with the performances here if anything more persuasive, no less passionate, and often with appealing touches of fantasy. The *Three Violin Pieces* are more intimate in style and presented in a different order. These artists are completely inside all this music and have the advantage of the warm acoustic of The Maltings, Snape. The *Five Spirituals* are delightful vignettes which ought to be in the regular cello repertoire, while the *Pastoral Fantasy* is in the best tradition of English pastoralism. The composer avoids quoting actual folksongs, yet introduces a seductive pastiche *Musette* within the scherzo, which is marked *Andante molto languido*. The *Tune* on which he bases his *Variations for Little People* is also very beguiling. This disc has a price advantage over its equally admirable Tall Poppies competitor, but both collections are well worth investigating.

PIANO MUSIC

Brumas Tunes; Chinoiserie; Elegiac Mazurka; Fantasies I–II; Haunted House; Jamaican Rumba; Let's Go Hiking; 3 New Fantasies; Odds and Ends I–II; Pastorale, Arioso & Finale; Romance-impromptu; Saxophone Blues; Scherzino; Siciliana; Suite.

*** Tall Poppies TP 105. Munro.

Australian born, Arthur Benjamin's *Jamaican Rumba* was the result of a professional examination visit to England in 1938, and it soon became a worldwide hit. He did not repeat that success, yet his other genre pieces here are full of attractive ideas and comparably catchy rhythmic invention, at times cool in the jazz sense of the word (*Saxophone Blues*), at others (the *Odds and Ends* or the *Fantasies*, for instance) offering writing of charming but indelible simplicity. Benjamin's piano writing has the elegance and sophistication of the French School, and his 1926 *Suite* is distinctly Ravelian. The outer sections of the *Pastorale, Arioso and Finale* scintillate and they demand the utmost virtuosity. Ian Munro revels in the music's dashing bravura. Throughout he plays with great style and elegance and with obvious affection. This is a wholly delightful recital, with never a dull moment throughout its 78 minutes. The recording is admirably natural. (If you find it difficult to obtain this CD, you can order it direct from Tall Poppies, PO Box 373, Glebe, NSW 2037, Australia.)

BENJAMIN, George (born 1960)

(i) *Ringed by the Flat Horizon;* (ii) *At First Light. A Mind of Winter.*

*** Nim. NI 5075. (i) BBC SO, Elder; (ii) Walmsley-Clark, L. Sinf., composer.

Ringed by the Flat Horizon is a 20-minute orchestral piece, with the big climax masterfully built. *A Mind of Winter* is a 9-minute setting of *The Snowman* by Wallace Stevens, beautifully sung by the soprano Penelope Walmsley-Clark. Sound of great warmth and refinement to match the music makes this a collection well worth exploring.

Piano Sonata.

** Nim. Single NI 1415. Composer.

George Benjamin's *Piano Sonata* dates from 1978, when he was still a student at the Paris Conservatoire. The influences are predominantly Gallic, and in particular the music of Messiaen. Benjamin is also a very good pianist; but the recording, made in 1980, sounds rather synthetic. A 'single', this runs to 22 minutes 26 seconds.

BENNETT, Richard Rodney
(born 1936)

Guitar Concerto (for guitar and chamber ensemble).

(M) *** RCA (ADD) 09026 61598-2. Bream, Melos Ens., Atherton – ARNOLD: *Concerto;* RODRIGO: *Concierto de Aranjuez.* ***

Bennett's concerto, written in 1970, is dedicated to Julian Bream. It is imaginatively conceived, and its variety of texture, glittering and transparent, consistently intrigues the ear. If the work's idiom and language start out from the twelve-tone system, there is nothing difficult for the listener to assimilate. The performance, like its Arnold coupling, is definitive, and the 1972 recording is first class in every way.

(i) *Violin Concerto. Diversions; Symphony No. 3.*

*** Koch 3-7431-2. (i) Gluzman; Monte Carlo PO, DePreist.

The earliest of the three works here, the *Violin Concerto* of 1975 in two contemplative movements, was written when Bennett was bringing his idiom closer to that of his highly successful film music, embracing tonality more firmly. Vadim Gluzman plays superbly. Joseph DePreist is also most persuasive, drawing well-drilled, strongly committed playing from the Monte Carlo Philharmonic. The *Symphony*, dating from 1987, in three compact movements, is bleaker but the *Diversions* of 1990 bring an attractive set of variations on a theme like an Irish jig.

Film music: (i) *Enchanted April; Far from the Madding Crowd; Four Weddings and a Funeral: Love theme;* (ii) *Lady Caroline Lamb (Elegy for Viola & Orchestra); Murder on the Orient Express; Tender is the Night: Nicola's Theme.*

(N) *** Chan. 9867. (i) Miller; (ii) Dukes; BBC PO, Gamba.

Sir Richard Rodney Bennett ranks alongside Sir Malcolm Arnold as an outstanding English composer of film scores of quality that can stand up in their own right, away from the cinema screen. Bennett's music displays a ready flow of memorable melody, more lushly romantic, less whimsical than Arnold's, but equally ready to move across to sophisticated popular rhythms. His orchestral palette is equally rich, and *Murder on the Orient Express*, in which the train theme is in lilting waltz-time, is a splendid example of his musical diversity, also including a catchy tango. The lovely, evocative opening of *Far from the Madding Crowd*, with a solitary flute answered by a solo oboe, and then taken up by the strings, is romantic English pastoralism at its most elegiacally haunting. Later the score brings in folksy dance-rhythms, then the opening sequence returns more romantically, but with a closing passage that could well have been written by Vaughan Williams. *Lady Caroline Lamb* inspired a two-movement concertante work for viola (here Philip Dukes) and orchestra, and introduces one of the composer's most delectable melodies which is rapturously expanded at the climax.

Nicola's Theme is more modern in outline, but hardly less indelible, but the atmospheric writing for *Enchanted April*, with its solo ondes martenot, is (at 19 minutes) perhaps a little over-extended. The romantic theme from *Four Weddings and a Funeral* stood out from an otherwise pop-music backcloth. Rumon Gamba and the BBC Philharmonic are splendidly eloquent advocates of all this music, and they are sumptuously recorded.

Impromptu; (i) *Memento* (for flute & strings); *Sonatina;* (ii) *Summer Music; Winter Music.*

(N) *** Koch 3-7505-2. Still, (i) New Zealand CO, Sedares; (ii) De Witt Smith.

This collection makes an attractive introduction to Bennett's chamber music featuring the flute for which he seems to have an almost gallic affinity. *Summer Music* with its contrasting *Allegro tranquillo, Siesta* and *Games*, was written in 1982 for young performers, and is immediately accessible and attractive. The poetic solo *Impromptu* and two-movement *Sonatina* are both improvisatory in feeling. *Winter Music*, with its central *Spectrale* evocation, is very striking but Bennett's long breathed lyricism (sometimes a little wan) can be heard at its most individual in the work for flute and strings, *Memento*, where the memorable closing *Elegiac Blues* is far more searching than one might expect. The performances by Alexa Still are admirable and she is well partnered by Susan De Witt Smith and the responsive New Zealand Chamber Orchestra under James Sedares. The recording is most natural and very well balanced.

Sonata after Syrinx; 6 Tunes for the Instruction of Singing-Birds.

*** Koch 37355-2H1. Auréole Trio (members) – MAW: *Flute Quartet, etc.* ***

The *Sonata after Syrinx* takes Debussy's piece as the starting point for an appealing and civilized discourse for the same combination. The *Six Tunes for the Instruction of Singing-*

Birds are for solo flute and are brilliantly played by Laura Gilbert.

BENNETT, Robert Russell (1894–1981)

Abraham Lincoln (A Likeness in Symphonic Form); Sights and Sounds (An Orchestral Entertainment).

(BB) ** Naxos 8.5509004. Moscow SO, Stromberg.

Robert Russell Bennett, the orchestrator of many famous musicals, is best known on record for his Gershwin score, the *Symphonic Picture of Porgy and Bess*. The present works show his great orchestral skill, but the quality of the invention does not match the vividly imaginative orchestral sounds. There are *longueurs* in the four-movement *Lincoln Portrait*, and the various American *Sights and Sounds* are little more than clever orchestral effects. Only the evocation of a *Night Club*, with its saxophone riff, has anything approaching a memorable idea. The orchestral playing and the commitment of the conductor cannot be faulted, and nor can the recording. But the end result does not encourage repeated listenings.

BENOIT, Peter (1834–1901)

Hoogmis (High Mass).

(BB) *(**) Discover DICD 920178. George, Belgian R. & TV Philharmonic Ch., Koninklijk Vlaams Antwerp Music Conservatoire Ch. & Caecilia Chorale, Gemengd Ars Musica Merksem Ch., Zingende Wandelkring Saint Norbertus Ch., Belgian R. & TV PO, Rahbari.

The bargain Discover label offers a fascinating rarity, the *Hoogmis (High Mass)*, by the Belgian composer, Peter Benoit, a contemporary of Brahms. Alexander Rahbari's account with the BRTV Philharmonic Orchestra of Brussels and massed choirs, with the tenor, Donald George, taking the solos in the *Benedictus* and *Dona nobis pacem*, has all the thrust you need for an ambitious work lasting 55 minutes, with echoes of Beethoven. The live recording, though atmospheric and full of presence, brings washy sound.

BENTZON, Jørgen (1897–1951)

Divertimento for Violin, Viola & Cello, Op. 2; Intermezzo for Violin & Clarinet, Op. 24; Sonatina for Flute, Clarinet & Bassoon, Op. 7; Variazioni interrotti for Clarinet, Bassoon, Violin, Viola & Cello, Op. 12; (i) Mikrofoni No. 1, for Baritone, Flute, Violin, Cello & Piano, Op. 44.

**(*) dacapo 8.224129. Danish Chamber Players; (i) with Bertelsen.

Jørgen Bentzon's music has a clean, fresh, diatonic feel to it, though some of it sounds a bit manufactured. By far the best piece here is the *Mikrofoni*, Op. 44, though it is let down by the solo baritone, and by far the wittiest is the *Variazioni interrotti*.

BENTZON, Niels Viggo (born 1919)

(i) Piano Concerto No. 4, Op. 96. 5 Mobiles, Op. 125.

** dacapo 8.224110. (i) Blyme; Aarhus SO, Schmidt.

The veteran Danish composer Niels Viggo Bentzon was enormously prolific. There are at least 20 symphonies and as many piano sonatas, and 15 piano concertos! The *Five Mobiles* is an inventive score but the *Fourth Piano Concerto* is distinctly uneven in inspiration. Readers should try the symphonies listed below, which are full of fantasy and invention.

Feature on René Descartes, Op. 357.

(*) BIS (ADD) CD 79. Danish Nat. R. O, Schmidt (with JORGENSON: *To Love Music;* NORBY: *The Rainbow Snake* *).

Krönik om René Descartes ('Feature on René Descartes') comes from 1975. The first movement gives a 'musical version of the Cartesian vortex which refers to a medieval notion of rotating heavenly bodies moving at enormous speed', and the final movement addresses Descartes's celebrated proposition, *Cogito ergo sum*. A well-prepared performance and good recording, but this is not the composer at his best.

Symphonies Nos. 3, Op. 46 (1947); 4 (Metamorphoses), Op. 55 (1949).

*** dacapo DCCD 9102. Aarhus SO, Schmidt.

Both the symphonies recorded here are teeming with invention: the pastoral opening of the *Third* unleashes a rich flow of ideas, all of memorable quality. The *Fourth (Metamorphoses)* is a most imaginative work, visionary music: powerful, concentrated and inventive. Along with the *Sixth* and *Seventh Symphonies* of Holmboe, this is arguably the finest Nordic symphony after Nielsen, and Ole Schmidt and the Aarhus orchestra play it with conviction and passion. The recording is very good indeed, with plenty of detail and a good balance. Two remarkable works.

Symphonies Nos. 5 (Ellipser), Op. 61; 7 (De tre versioner), Op. 83.

⚫ *** dacapo 8.22411. Aarhus SO, Schmidt.

Bentzon's early symphonies offer real vision and their textures glow luminously. Both the *Seventh* and the *Fifth* have a sense of space and individuality (deriving from tonal composers Copland, Nielsen, Hindemith and Stravinsky). It is no exaggeration to call the *Seventh* a masterpiece, an impressive study in thematic metamorphosis. Fine performances and recording.

Piano Sonatas Nos. 3, Op. 44; 5, Op. 77; 9, Op. 104.

** dacapo 8.224103. Llambías.

Bentzon's *Sonata No. 3* is an exceptionally fine work, not dissimilar to the sonatas of Tippett or the sole sonata of Robert Simpson, and inferior to neither. Rodolfo Llambías's approach is highly discursive and he lays bare all of No. 3's many beauties rather too lovingly. All the same, in the absence of any alternatives, these remarkable sonatas demand a hearing. Unfortunately the acoustic is over-reverberant.

BERG, Alban (1885–1935)

Chamber Concerto for Piano, Violin & 13 Wind Instruments, Op. 6.

(M) *** DG (ADD) 447 405-2. Barenboim, Zukerman, Ens. InterContemporain, Boulez – STRAVINSKY: Concerto in E flat, etc. ***

(i) Chamber Concerto; (ii) 3 Pieces for Orchestra; (iii) Violin Concerto.

(M) ** Sony (ADD) SMK 68331. (i) Barenboim, Gavrilov; (i–ii) BBC SO; (iii) Zukerman, LSO; (i–iii) Boulez.

(i) Chamber Concerto; (ii) Violin Concerto.

(M) ** Sony (ADD) SMK 64504. Stern, with (i) P. Serkin, LSO members, Abbado; (ii) NYPO, Bernstein.

On DG, Boulez sets brisk tempi in the Chamber Concerto, seeking to give the work classical incisiveness; but the strong and expressive personalities of the pianist and violinist tend towards a more romantic view. The result is characterful and convincing, and not at all intimidating. Sadly, Boulez omits the extended repeat in the finale. The recording is attractively atmospheric.

Stern's Sony issue couples Berg's two concertante works with violin, made 26 years apart. The 1959 recording of the Violin Concerto underlines the coarser side of the performance, in which Stern takes a red-blooded, romantic view of the work. Though there is coarseness in the Chamber Concerto too, this is a virtuoso performance. The digital sound is very immediate indeed.

Boulez's personality again strongly dominates the sharply focused Sony performances of the Chamber Concerto and Op. 6 Orchestral Pieces from 1967. The Violin Concerto, with Zukerman as soloist very close indeed, was recorded two decades later, in 1984. His strong, urgent reading matches Boulez's toughness, a robust rather than a subtle or poetic reading, with the elegiac quality missing.

Violin Concerto.

(M) *** DG 447 445-2. Perlman, Boston SO, Ozawa (with RAVEL: Tzigane; STRAVINSKY: Concerto ***).

(M) *** Decca 460 005-2. Chung, Chicago SO, Solti (with BACH: Violin Partita No. 2 & Sonata No. 3 **).

*** DG 437 093-2. Mutter, Chicago SO, Levine – RIHM: Gesungene Zeit, etc. ***

(BB) *** RCA Navigator (ADD) 74321 29243-2. Hoelscher, Cologne RSO, Wakasugi – SCHOENBERG: Verklaerte Nacht; WEBERN: Passacaglia for Orchestra. ***

(M) *** Sup. (ADD) SU 1939-2 011. Suk, Czech PO, Ančerl (with BRUCH: Concerto **; MENDELSSOHN: Concerto **(*)).

(M) *** EMI (ADD) CDM7 63989-2. Menuhin, BBC SO, Boulez – BLOCH: Violin Concerto. ***

Perlman's performance is above all commanding. The Boston orchestra accompanies superbly and, though the balance favours the soloist, the recording is excellent. The current transfer shows the Boston acoustic at its most seductive.

No one excels Kyung Wha Chung in tenderness and poetry. The violin is placed well in front of the orchestra, but not aggressively so. The recording is brilliant in the Chicago manner, more spacious than some from this source, but not everyone will want the Bach coupling.

Anne-Sophie Mutter begins the Concerto with a pianissimo of much delicacy. She proceeds to give an intensely passionate reading, both freely expressive and intensely purposeful, with James Levine and the Chicago orchestra matching her in subtle shading. As an imaginative coupling, Mutter offers a concerto written for her by the forty-year-old German composer Wolfgang Rihm.

Ulf Hoelscher, well balanced in this fine (1977) Cologne recording, gives a passionately dedicated account of Berg's concerto, splendidly supported by Wakasugi and the excellent Cologne Radio Orchestra. This comes at the lowest possible price with two other key twentieth-century works, both very well played and recorded, although the documentation is totally inadequate.

Suk's sweet, unforced style movingly brings out the work's lyrical side without ever exaggerating the romanticism. A most beautiful performance, with the excellent (1965) recording transferred to CD very firmly and naturally.

Menuhin's is a warm and vibrant performance and, though technically this is not as dashing or immaculate a performance as several others on record, it is one that compels admiration for great artistry. Well coupled with the Bloch.

(i) Violin Concerto; (ii) Lyric Suite: 3 Pieces; 3 Pieces for Orchestra, Qp. 6.

(B) *** DG 439 435-2 (without 3 Orchestral Pieces). (i) Szeryng, Bav. RSO, Kubelik; (ii) BPO, Karajan.
(***) Testament mono SBT1004. (i) Krasner, BBC SO, Webern; (ii) Galimir Qt.

Henryk Szeryng gives a persuasive, perceptive and sympathetic account of the Berg Concerto, and he is very well accompanied by the Bavarian orchestra under Kubelik, with a first-rate CD transfer. As coupling in DG's Classikon series, you have two of Karajan's key recordings of Berg's orchestral music.

The Testament CD is of great interest in bringing back to life a broadcast of the Violin Concerto by Louis Krasner (who commissioned it and gave its first performance), laden with a unique intensity of feeling. The sound quality is poor (it comes from the soloist's own acetates) but the spirit is powerful and vibrant, and the BBC orchestra play superbly. It comes with another 1936 recording, the Galimir Quartet's pioneering Polydor 78s of the Lyric Suite – impeccably played but recorded in a horribly dry acoustic.

Lyric Suite: 3 Pieces.

(BB) *** Arte Nova 74321 52248-2. SWF SO, Gielen – BARTOK: Piano Concerto No. 3; CARTER: Piano Concerto, etc. ***

Michael Gielen's passionate devotion to this Berg work comes out in his warmly expressive, finely detailed reading, very well played and recorded. This may be an unexpected coupling, but it is a refreshing one.

Lyric Suite: 3 Pieces; 3 Pieces for Orchestra, Op. 6.

(M) *** DG (ADD) 457 760-2. BPO, Karajan – SCHOENBERG: *Variations;* WEBERN: *Passacaglia.* ***

(M) *** DG (ADD) 427 424-2 (3). BPO, Karajan – SCHOENBERG; WEBERN: *Orchestral Pieces.* ***

Karajan's purification process gives wonderful clarity to Berg's often complex scores, with expressive confidence bringing out the romantic overtones. For those who resist Berg's style, Karajan's way is most likely to convert, for these are magnificently played and recorded accounts, available either separately or in a set.

Lyric Suite: 3 Pieces; (i) 5 Altenberglieder, Op. 4.

(BB) *** Arte Nova 74321 27768-2. (i) Orsanic; SWFSO, Gielen – ZEMLINSKY: *Lyric Symphony.* ***

The three movements from his *Lyric Suite* make an ideal coupling for the Zemlinsky *Lyric Symphony*, the work which Berg quotes and which prompted his title. They are beautifully played and recorded here, as are the five settings of Altenberg poems, crisp and compact yet full of emotion, here sung superbly with fresh tone and clean attack by the soprano, Vlatka Orsanic. First-rate recording. A pity the documentation does not match the musical excellence.

3 Pieces for Orchestra, Op. 6; 5 Orchestral Songs, Op. 4; (i) Lulu: Symphonic Suite.

(M) *** DG (ADD) 449 714-2. (i) M. Price; LSO, Abbado.

Abbado makes it clear above all how beautiful Berg's writing is, not just in the *Lulu* excerpts but in the early Opus 4 *Songs* and the Opus 6 *Orchestral Pieces.*

Lyric Suite for String Quartet; String Quartet, Op. 3.

(M) *** Teldec (ADD) 3984 21967-2. Alban Berg Qt – URBANNER: *Quartet No. 3;* WEBERN: *6 Bagatelles,* etc. ***

The *Lyric Suite* is very accessible in its chamber-music format, while the Op. 3 *Quartet* is another of Berg's undoubted masterpieces. The performances are excellent, the recording bright but with plenty of ambience. This eponymous quartet's later (digital) EMI version of the *Lyric Suite* and *Third Quartet* (CDC5 55190-2) is arguably the best ever but now seems short measure at 47 minutes.

Piano Sonata, Op. 1.

(N) *** Ph. 468 033-2. Uchida – SCHOENBERG: *Piano concerto; Klavierstücke, Opp. 11 & 19;* WEBERN: *Variations, Op. 27.*

(BB) *** Naxos 8.553870. Hill – SCHOENBERG: *Piano Pieces,* etc.; WEBERN: *Variations.* ***

(B) **(*) Cal. Approche (ADD) CAL 6203. Södergren (with J. S. BACH: *Keyboard Collection* **(*)).

** DG 423 678-2. Pollini (with DEBUSSY: *Etudes* **).

In the Berg *Piano Sonata, Op. 1*, as in the remainder of her programme devoted to the Second Viennese school, Uchida is very persuasive indeed. The main work on the disc,

Schoenberg's *Piano Concerto*, receives one of its most successful readings on record.

Peter Hill's account of the Berg *Sonata* on Naxos has more than just its bargain price to commend it. He is a pianist of proven intelligence and sensitivity and is decently recorded. It comes with the Schoenberg piano music, played with no less expertise and authority.

Inger Södergren's performance has real character, but she softens its angst. Those attracted to her enjoyably relaxed Bach coupling may well be converted to enjoying her Berg too. The recording is pleasingly full.

Pollini gives an impressive account, as powerful as any on disc, but it is not helped by a clinical, closely balanced recording, and the Debussy *Etudes* with which it is coupled are seriously wanting in atmosphere and poetry.

7 Early Songs.

*** DG 437 515-2. Von Otter, Forsberg – KORNGOLD; STRAUSS: *Lieder.* ***

(N) *** Sony SK 61720. Eaglen, LSO, Runnicles – WAGNER: *Wesendonck Lieder;* STRAUSS: *Four Last Songs.* ***

*** Decca 466 720-2. Bonney, Concg. O, Chailly – MAHLER: *Symphony No. 4.* **(*)

In the seven early songs of Berg, Anne Sofie von Otter and Bengt Forsberg offer inspired playing and singing, drawing out the intensity of emotion to the full without exaggeration or sentimentality. Along with Strauss and Korngold songs, a fascinating programme, magnetically performed.

Though miniature in scale, these beautifully crafted early songs of Berg also inspire Jane Eaglen to produce sumptuous sounds, giving them almost Wagnerian scale to match her fine accounts of the *Wesendonck Lieder*. Runnicles draws ravishing sounds from the LSO to match. An excellent, imaginative coupling.

Barbara Bonney also sounds spontaneous and warm in the seven early Berg songs which come as a coupling for Mahler's *Fourth Symphony*, and Chailly and the orchestra too sound a degree more involved than in the Mahler.

Lulu (with orchestration of Act III completed by Friedrich Cerha).

(M) *** DG 463 617 (3). Stratas, Minton, Schwarz, Mazura, Blankenheim, Riegel, Tear, Paris Op. O, Boulez.

*** Chan. 9540 (3). Haupman, Jaffe, Straka, Juan, Danish Nat. RSO, Schirmer.

Boulez's pioneering recording of Berg's *Lulu* in its full three-act form brings an intensely involving performance, very well cast. Teresa Stratas's bright, clear soprano, well recorded, fits the ruthless heroine perfectly, and Yvonne Minton is most moving as Countess Geschwitz. Firm, clear recording, excellently remastered.

Recorded at a series of live performances, the Chandos version is strongly and purposefully conducted by Ulf Schirmer. Constance Haupman makes Lulu a girlish, vulnerable figure, as well as thrusting and selfish. Her singing is commendably precise, even if under pressure the tone grows shrill. As Dr Schön, Monte Jaffe relies too heavily on unpitched sing-speech, but his is a vividly characterful performance too; and among the others Peter Straka makes a fresh, clear Alwa and Julia Juan a touchingly mature Geschwitz. Boulez's studio version for DG may have a more immediate impact, but this provides an excellent alternative.

Maazel's performance was recorded live by Austrian Radio, allowing little bloom on the voices. Even under Maazel there is far too little tension in the orchestral playing, whether in interludes or accompanying the singers. Julia Migenes is characterful in the title-part, treating it in cabaret style, often using plain speech rather than sing-speech. A good cast is largely wasted (RCA 74321 57734-2).

Wozzeck (complete).

*** Decca 417 348-2 (2). Waechter, Silja, Winkler, Laubenthal, Jahn, Malta, Sramek, VPO, Dohnányi − SCHOENBERG: *Erwartung.* ***

(M) (***) Sony mono MH2K 62759 (2). Harrell, Farrell, Jagel, Mordino, Herbert, Music & Arts High School Ch., Schola Cantorum Ch., NYPO, Mitropoulos − KRENEK: *Symphonic Elegy* (***); SCHOENBERG: *Erwartung.* (**(*))

(M) *** EMI CDS5 56865-2 (2). Skovhus, Denoke, Olsen, Merritt, Blinkhof, Sacher, Hamburg State Op. Ch. & State PO, Metzmacher.

**(*) Teldec 0630 14108-2 (2). Grundheber, Meier, Baker, Wottrich, Clark, Von Kannen, German Opera, Berlin, Ch. & Children's Ch., Berlin State O, Barenboim.

**(*) DG (IMS) 423 587-2 (2). Grundheber, Behrens, Haugland, Langridge, Zednik, V. State Op. Ch., VPO, Abbado.

Dohnányi, with refined textures and superb playing from the Vienna Philharmonic, presents an account of *Wozzeck* that not only is more accurate than any other on record but is also more beautiful.

Dimitri Mitropoulos's electrifying recording of *Wozzeck* was recorded live at a concert performance in Carnegie Hall, New York, in April 1951 and, though the sound is only mono, the result in this transfer is extraordinarily vivid. In the title-role Mack Harrell not only characterizes well, but he brings out musical beauty in the writing. As for Eileen Farrell as Marie, the power and biting precision of her singing as well as the vividness of her characterization make the character central to the whole opera, not just an attendant figure. The Sony transfer is excellent, leaving room for generous fill-ups on the second disc. A full libretto with translations is provided in a separate booklet.

Ingo Metzmacher's live recording for EMI was made at the Hamburg State Opera, with Metzmacher drawing powerful, clean-textured playing from his orchestra, firmly establishing this as a high romantic work, whatever its modernist credentials. The casting is strong too, with Bo Skovhus singing with clean focus in the title-role, and with Marie superbly sung by Angela Denoke, sensuous on the one hand, tenderly affecting on the other. Otherwise, the production on a bare stage seems to have encouraged each character to overact, Skovhus included, even while the results are exceptionally vivid, with the sense of a live performance consistently adding to the dramatic impact.

Barenboim's Teldec version of *Wozzeck* was recorded live at the Deutsche Staatsoper in Berlin in 1994. With Grundheber even finer than under Abbado, Barenboim leads

a warmly expressive performance. The cast is an outstanding one, with such characterful singers as Graham Clark (Captain) in incidental roles. Less successful is Waltraud Meier as Marie, with an uneven, grainy quality in the voice.

The Abbado version, recorded live in the opera house, is very compelling in its presentation of the drama, given extra thrust through the tensions of live performance. The cast is first rate − but the drawback is you get not only intrusive stage noises, but the voices are set behind the orchestra, with the instrumental sound putting a gauze between listener and singers.

BERIO, Luciano (born 1925)

Différences; 2 Pieces; (i) Sequenza III; (ii) Sequenza VII; (i) Chamber Music.

(M) *** Ph. (IMS) (ADD) 426 662-2. (i) Berberian; (ii) Holliger; Juilliard Ens. (members), composer.

The biggest work here is *Différences* for five instruments and tape; but the two virtuoso solos − *Sequenza III* for voice and *Sequenza VII* for oboe − are if anything even more striking in their extensions of technique and expressive range. First-rate sound, well transferred.

Eindrücke; Sinfonia.

(N) (BB) *** Warner Apex 8573 89226-2. Pasquier, New Swingle Singers, O Nat. de France, Boulez.

In 1969 Berio's *Sinfonia*, written for the New York Philharmonic, made a far wider impact on the music world than is common with an avant-garde composer. Boulez records the complete work for the first time in this fine Erato version. *Eindrücke* is another powerful work, much more compressed, bare and uncompromising in its layering of strings and wind. An outstanding bargain.

(i) Recital I (for Cathy); (ii) Folk-song Suite; (iii) 3 Songs by Kurt Weill (arr. Berio).

(M) *** RCA (ADD) 09026 62540-2. Berberian, with (i) L. Sinf.; (ii−iii) Juilliard Ens.; all cond. composer.

Recital I is the most elaborate, colourful work that Berio ever wrote for Cathy Berberian. Against fragmentary accompaniment from the instrumental band, the soloist in this semi-dramatic piece thinks back through her repertoire as a concert-singer from Monteverdi to the present day, a brilliant collage of musical ideas. With Berberian at her most intense, the result is very compelling. Excellent recording. Also included is a sparkling collection of folksongs arranged for Berberian with twinkling ingenuity by Berio. The record concludes with three Kurt Weill songs, arranged by Berio, with Berberian relishing every word.

BERKELEY, Lennox (1903–89)

Divertimento in B flat, Op. 18; Partita for Chamber Orchestra, Op. 66; Serenade for Strings, Op. 12; (i) Sinfonia concertante for Oboe & Chamber Orchestra, Op. 84:

Canzonetta (only). *Symphony No. 3 in 1 Movement,
Op. 74; Mont Juic.*

*** Lyrita (ADD) SRCD 226. LPO, composer; (i) with Winfield
– with BRITTEN: *Op. 9.*

The *Divertimento* is enchanting, with its four stylish and
highly inventive movements, while the *String Serenade*, similarly in four sections, is hardly less attractive and brings a
beautiful *Lento* closing movement. In its rather weightier
tone of voice the *Partita* offers contrast, while the fourth
movement from the *Sinfonia concertante* makes a splendid
interlude before the closing *Symphony No. 3,* a concise,
one-movement work, slightly more austere in its lyricism.
The recording, too, from the early 1970s, is first class. The
programme opens with the charmingly spontaneous *Mont
Juic* suite which Berkeley wrote in collaboration with Benjamin Britten, two movements each.

*Concertino, Op. 49; Duo for Cello & Piano, Op. 81/1; Elegy
for Violin & Piano, Op. 35/2; Introduction & Allegro for
Solo Violin, Op. 24; Oboe Quartet, Op. 70; Petite suite for
Oboe & Piano; Sextet, Op. 47; Toccata for Violin & Piano,
Op. 33/3.*

(M) *** Dutton Lab. CDLX 7100. Endymion Ens.

Fine new recordings of Lennox Berkeley's elegantly
fashioned music. It is fastidiously crafted and musically
rewarding, unpretentious, urbane and charming. The Endymion Ensemble do it proud, and so does the natural and
well-balanced recording.

Horn Trio, Op. 44.

(N) *** Erato 8523 80217-2. Pyatt, Levon Chilingirian, Donohoe
– BRITTEN: *Canticle No. 3; Now sleeps the crimson petal;*
WOOD: *Horn Trio.* ***

This attractive collection of twentieth-century chamber
works centres on the seductive playing of David Pyatt,
winner of the BBC Young Musician of the Year competition
in 1988. Since then he has made a handful of exceptionally
fine recordings, challenging comparison with the finest
horn-players. The Lennox Berkeley *Horn Trio* was recorded
by EMI in the mid-1950s, soon after it was written, with
Colin Horsley (who commissioned the work) at the piano
and Dennis Brain on the horn, but that mono recording
disappeared all too quickly. This superb Erato version is
very welcome, for this is one of Berkeley's most appealing
chamber works, beautifully crafted and with a central slow
movement and a slow, lyrical variation in the long finale
which are among his most moving inspirations.

(i) *Music for Piano 4 Hands: Sonatina, Op. 39; Theme &
Variations, Op. 73; Palm Court Waltz, Op. 81/2. (Solo
piano music): 5 Short Pieces, Op. 4; 6 Preludes, Op. 23;
Sonata, Op. 20.*

*** British Music Society BMS 416CD. Terroni, (i) with Beedle.

A generous selection of the cultivated and tuneful piano
music of Lennox Berkeley: the fine *Sonata* with its sensuously
coloured *Adagio,* the often witty *Preludes* and the five
charming *Short Pieces,* which often have a whiff of Poulenc,
the *Sonatina* with another elegantly individual slow move-

ment, and the more complex *Theme and Variations.* Raphael
Terroni is an accomplished and sympathetic exponent, with
Norman Beedle an admirable partner in the *Music for Piano
Four Hands.* The piano recording is most natural. The CD
is available direct from the British Music Society, 7 Tudor
Gardens, Upminster, Essex.

*Improvisation on a Theme of Falla, Op. 55/2; Mazurka,
Op. 101/2; 3 Mazurkas (Hommage à Chopin), Op. 32;
Paysage; 3 Pieces; Polka, Op. 5a; 6 Preludes, Op. 23; 5 Short
Pieces, Op. 4; Sonata, Op. 20.*

**(*) Kingdom KCLCD 2012. Headington (piano).

With the exception of the *Sonata,* all these pieces are miniatures, some of considerable elegance. Christopher Headington was a sympathetic exponent, completely attuned
to the idiom. The recording is eminently serviceable and
truthful.

6 Preludes, Op. 23.

**(*) Paradisum PDS-CD2. Clegg – RAWSTHORNE: *Complete
Piano Music.* **(*)

John Clegg presents the whole of Rawsthorne's output for
the piano. Lennox Berkeley's charming and accomplished
miniatures complete a valuable disc: the only snag is the
rather claustrophobic acoustic.

BERKELEY, Michael (born 1948)

*(i–ii) Clarinet Concerto; (i) Flighting; (iii; ii) Père du doux
repos (Father of Sweet Sleep from Speaking Silence).*

*** ASV Single CDDCB 1101. (i) Johnson; (ii) N. Sinfonia,
Edwards; (iii) Herford.

The *Clarinet Concerto* was written for Emma Johnson. The
soloist's concentration leads one magnetically through a
thicket of virtuoso writing, often marked by stratospheric
shrieks, which she consistently makes compelling, thanks
also to the dedicated accompaniment under Sian Edwards.
As 'fitting pendants' come two shorter works, a setting of a
sonnet by the sixteenth-century French poet, Pontus de
Tyard, leading to a solo clarinet piece built on related material.

BERLIN, Irving (1888–1989)

Annie Get Your Gun (musical).

✪ *** EMI CDC7 54206-2. Criswell, Hampson, Graee, Luker,
Amb. Ch., L. Sinf., McGlinn.

John McGlinn follows up the pattern of his best-selling set
of Jerome Kern's *Show Boat* with another performance that
is at once scholarly and pulsing with life. Not only is the
singing strong, characterful and idiomatic, the whole performance – not least from the players of the London Sinfonietta – is full of fun. Kim Criswell as Annie, with her electric
personality and bitingly bright voice, is a natural successor
to Ethel Merman, the original Annie Oakley. Equally remarkably, Thomas Hampson makes an ideal hero, an opera-
singer with an exceptionally rich and firm baritone who gets

inside the idiom. However, this has been deleted as we go to press.

BERLIOZ, Hector (1803–69)

Complete orchestral works

(i) *Grande symphonie funèbre et triomphale, Op. 15;* (i–ii) *Harold in Italy, Op. 16;* (i; iii) *Lélio, Op. 14b; Overtures:* (i) *Béatrice et Bénédict;* (iv) *Benvenuto Cellini;* (i) *Le Carnaval romain, Op. 9; Le Corsaire, Op. 21; Les Francs-juges, Op. 3; Le Roi Lear, Op. 4; Waverley, Op. 1;* (v) *Rêverie et caprice* (for violin and orchestra), *Op. 8;* (vi–vii) *Symphonie fantastique, Op. 14;* (i; vii) *Tristia, Op. 18* (excerpt): *Marche funèbre pour la dernière scène d'Hamlet;* (i) *La Damnation de Faust, Op. 24* (excerpts): *Menuet des follets; Marche hongroise;* (i; viii) *Romeo and Juliet, Op. 17;* (i) *Les Troyens à Carthage, Part II, Prélude, Act III;* (ix) *Les Troyens, Act IV: Royal Hunt and Storm; Marche pour l'entrée de la reine; Ballet Music.*

(B) *** Ph. 456 143-2 (6). (i) LSO; (ii) with Imai; (iii) with Carreras, Allen, Constable (piano), Jowitt (clarinet), Scheffel-Stein (harp); (iv) BBC SO; (v) Grumiaux, New Philh. O, De Waart; (vi) Concg. O; (vii) with Alldis Ch.; (viii) with Kern, Shirley-Quirk, Tear, L. Symphony Ch.; (ix) ROHCG O; all (except *Op. 8*) cond. C. Davis.

(i) *Harold in Italy, Op. 16; Symphonie fantastique, Op. 14; La Damnation de Faust: Hungarian March. Roméo et Juliette, Op. 17:* orchestral excerpts: *Roméo seul . . . Grande fête chez Capulet; Scène d'amour; La Reine Mab (scherzo). Les Troyens:* (ii) *Royal Hunt and Storm.*

(B) **(*) Double Decca 455 361-2 (2). Montreal SO, Dutoit; (i) with Zukerman; (ii) with Montreal Ch.

Dutoit's version of *Harold in Italy*, with speeds on the broad side and Zukerman an individual, warmly expressive soloist, is very richly recorded. Again in the *Symphonie fantastique*, it is the spectacular, wide-ranging recorded sound that is the first point to note, and also the broad speeds. The four extended orchestral excerpts from *Roméo et Juliette* then follow, with Dutoit and his orchestra at their finest, playing warmly as well as brilliantly. The *Royal Hunt and Storm* comes from the complete set of *Les Troyens* and includes the chorus.

Harold in Italy.

(B) (**(*)) Dutton Lab. mono CDEA 5013. Primrose, Boston SO, Koussevitzky – R. STRAUSS: *Till Eulenspiegel* (***).

(i; ii) *Harold in Italy. Overtures:* (ii) *Le Corsaire;* (iii) *King Lear;* (ii) *Les Troyens: Trojan March.*

(N) (**(*)) BBC mono BBCL 4065-2. (i) Riddle; (ii) RPO; (iii) BBC SO; Beecham.

(i) *Harold in Italy, Op. 16;* (ii) *La Damnation de Faust, Op. 24: Hungarian March; Ballet des sylphes; Menuet des follets;* (iii) *Les Troyens: Trojan March;* (iv) *Royal Hunt and Storm.*

(B) **(*) Sony (ADD) SBK 53255. (i) De Pasquale; (i; iii) Phd.

O, Ormandy; (ii) Phd. O, Munch; (iv) O de Paris, Barenboim.

(i) *Harold in Italy, Op. 16;* (ii) *La Mort de Cléopâtre.*

(M) **(*) Sony (ADD) SMK 60696. (i) Lincer; (ii) Tourel; NYPO, Bernstein.

(i) *Harold in Italy;* (ii) *Tristia (Méditation religieuse; La Mort d'Ophélie; Marche funèbre pour la dernière scène de Hamlet), Op. 18.*

*** Ph. 446 676-2. (i) Caussé; (ii) Monteverdi Ch.; ORR, Gardiner.

(i) *Harold in Italy;* (ii) *Tristia, Op. 18. Les Troyens à Carthage: Prelude to Act II.*

(B) *** Ph. (ADD) 416 431-2. (i) Imai; (ii) Alldis Ch.; LSO, C. Davis.

Gardiner's pioneering account of *Harold in Italy* on period instruments is searingly dramatic, the more biting in its impact with textures transparent, yet with plenty of weight and high dynamic contrasts. Gérard Caussé here produces spare sounds, making the result quite eerie. The three separate movements of *Tristia* are equally refreshing and dramatic, with sharp dynamic contrasts. Excellent sound.

In addition to a noble account of *Harold* in which Nobuko Imai is on top form, the Philips analogue CD offers the *Tristia*, which includes the haunting *Funeral March for the Last Scene of Hamlet* given with chorus; this CD also offers the *Prelude* to Act II of *Les Troyens*. The sound is natural and realistic, with impressive transparency and detail. Reissued on the Philips Virtuoso bargain label, this is formidable value.

Ormandy's 1965 recording of *Harold in Italy* with the Philadelphia Orchestra is warmly recommendable, with Joseph de Pasquale a thoughtful and cultured soloist, even though the sound is not as transparent as with some rivals. For all that, this is an impressive *Harold*, superbly played. The three excerpts from *La Damnation de Faust* were recorded in 1963, when Munch was guest conductor in Philadelphia, and they have a Beecham-like elegance. Daniel Barenboim's recording of the *Royal Hunt and Storm* from *Les Troyens* with the Orchestre de Paris is less distinguished but has the benefit of better sound. Good value.

In his earlier CBS/Sony recording, Bernstein drives hard, but the dramatic excitement is justification and the result is undeniably thrilling, yet with plenty of warmth in the swinging *Pilgrims' March*. The reverberant recording is certainly atmospheric, but the top is fierce. Jennie Tourel sings with great eloquence in *La Mort de Cléopâtre*, and Bernstein gives her splendid dramatic support. This recording was also made in 1961, yet the sound is much fuller and more convincingly balanced than the main work.

The radio recordings of Beecham in full flight are most welcome, particularly when so many of his studio recordings of Berlioz for EMI have disappeared. The mono radio sound is beefy and immediate, if limited, with fine transfers by Paul Baily. All these items confirm how Beecham in live performances of Berlioz conveyed a red-blooded manic intensity, to match the composer's revolutionary wildness, making almost any rival seem cool. The *Corsaire Overture* has a fierceness and thrust entirely apt to the Byronic subject, culminating in a swaggering climax that verges on the frenetic. Beecham took a similar approach in his studio performances, but these are even more uninhibited in their excitement, including *King Lear* with the BBC Symphony Orchestra, not his own RPO.

Harold in Italy, recorded in 1956 with the dynamic range compressed so as to magnify pianissimos, is valuable for having as soloist Beecham's chosen leader of the RPO violas, Frederick Riddle, who in 1937 made the first ever recording of the Walton *Viola Concerto*, arguably still the finest interpretation ever. Here his expressive warmth and responsiveness to Beecham's volatile inspiration make up for intonation problems highlighted by the close, dry sound. The *Trojan March* makes a swaggering encore, an electrifying performance from the historic opening concert of the Colston Hall in Bristol in 1951.

Koussevitzky's 1944 recording of *Harold in Italy* was the first ever available commercially, an urgent, red-blooded version, and Primrose's reading reflects that – warmer and more colourful than his others on disc. Though the Dutton transfer has far more body than an earlier Biddulph issue, it still does not capture the full quality of the original 78s, with tuttis sounding rather opaque, damped down in comparison with the Strauss. Even so, the disc brings a wonderful demonstration of the mastery of a supreme conductor who has still not had his full due.

(i) *Harold in Italy, Op. 16;* (ii) *Symphonie fantastique, Op. 14;* (iii) Overtures: *Béatrice et Bénédict; Benvenuto Cellini; Le Carnaval romain; Le Corsaire; Les Francs-juges.*

(B) **(*) EMI double forte (ADD) CZS5 73338-2 (2).
(i) McInnes; (i–ii) O Nat. de France, Bernstein; (iii) LSO, Previn.

Bernstein gives a performance of *Harold in Italy* that is both exciting and introspective. With French players, his slightly more relaxed manner than with the NYPO (see below) is in some ways more authentic. Donald McInnes is a violist with a superbly rich and even tone. He responds at all times to the conductor, yet has plenty of individuality. The 1976 recording of this work has an opulent spread and plenty of warmth, but the CD transfer has brought a degree of shrillness to the upper range of the violins, although the solo viola timbre seems unaffected. Bernstein also directs a brilliant and understanding performance of the *Symphonie fantastique* which captures more than most the wild, volatile quality of Berlioz's inspiration. Again there is a disconcerting tendency to shrillness in the upper strings. The overtures provide a rich bonus and are otherwise very well recorded, but it is a pity about the unnatural treble response, which was certainly not on the analogue LPs. Under Previn, the swing-along melody of *Les Francs-juges* swaggers boldly.

Overtures: *Béatrice et Bénédict; Benvenuto Cellini; Le Carnaval romain; Le Corsaire; Les Francs-juges; Le Roi Lear; Waverley.*

● *** RCA 09026 68790. Dresden State O, C. Davis.

Mercurial, full of vitality and poetic feeling, wonderfully light in articulation, and superbly played and recorded. This completely supersedes Sir Colin's recordings on Philips in

every way. A glorious issue, outstanding in every way, and now the best Berlioz overtures disc in the catalogue.

Overtures: *Béatrice et Bénédict; Benvenuto Cellini; Le Carnaval romain; Le Corsaire; Les Francs-juges; Le Roi Lear; Les Troyens à Carthage (Prélude); Waverley.*

**(*) Decca 452 480-2. Montreal SO, Dutoit.

The performances on this compilation disc have all appeared in the late 1980s or early 1990s. The Montreal brass are especially commanding at the opening of *Les Francs-juges*, and later the famous swinging melody has a proper ebullience, while *Le Roi Lear* has plenty of weight. Brilliant recording and a fine ambient effect. But these performances do not capture the spirit of this composer to the same extent as the Davis disc.

Overtures: *Béatrice et Bénédict; Le Carnaval romain, Op. 9; Le Corsaire, Op. 21; Rob Roy; Le Roi Lear, Op. 4.*

(M) **(*) Chan. 8316. SNO, Gibson.

Rob Roy finds Gibson and the SNO at their most dashingly committed. *King Lear*, another rarity, also comes out most dramatically and, though *Béatrice et Bénédict* is not quite so polished, the playing is generally excellent. With first-rate digital recording, this can be recommended at mid-price.

Overtures: *Le Carnaval romain; Le Corsaire. La Damnation de Faust: Hungarian March.*

(M) **(*) Decca (IMS) (ADD) 448 571-2. Paris Conservatoire O, Martinon – BIZET: *Jeux d'enfants;* IBERT: *Divertissement;* SAINT-SAENS: *Danse macabre*, etc. ***

Martinon's Berlioz recordings have been added as a bonus for this reissue of his highly praised 1960 collection of French music; although the playing is both brilliant and exciting, it is not on the level of the later performances.

Rêverie et caprice, Op. 8.

(M) *** DG 445 549-2. Perlman, O de Paris, Barenboim – LALO: *Symphonie espagnole;* SAINT-SAENS: *Concerto No. 3.* ***

Perlman's ripely romantic approach to the *Rêverie* brings out the individuality of the melody and, with a sympathetic accompaniment from Barenboim, the work as a whole is given considerable substance. First-rate digital recording.

Symphonie fantastique, Op. 14.

(M) *** Ph. 464 692-2. Concg. O, C. Davis.
*** BBC (ADD) BBCL 4018-2. New Philh. O, Stokowski (with conversation with Deryck Cooke) – SCRIABIN: *Poème de l'extase.* ***
*** Ph. 434 402-2. ORR, Gardiner.
(B) (***) Dutton Lab. mono CDEA 5504. Hallé O, Barbirolli (with WAGNER: *Die Meistersinger: Suite* (***)) – FAURE: *Shylock: Nocturne.* (***)
(B) *** [EMI Red Line CDR5 72552]. Phd. O, Muti.
(M) (***) Dutton Lab. mono CDK 1208. Concg. O, Van Beinum (with BEETHOVEN: *Creatures of Prometheus: Overture* (LPO)) – SCHUBERT: *Symphony No. 5* (***).
(M) **(*) EMI (ADD) CDM5 67034-2. Philh. O, Klemperer

(with HUMPERDINCK: *Hänsel und Gretel: Overture & Dream Pantomime* (**(*))).

(M) **(*) Sony (ADD) SMK 60968. NYPO, Bernstein (with 'Berlioz takes a trip' – a talk on the *Symphonie fantastique* by Leonard Bernstein).

(M) **(*) Virgin VM5 61379-2. LCP, Norrington (with *Les Francs-juges*).

(M) **(*) Telarc CD 82014. Cleveland O, Maazel.

Symphonie fantastique; Overtures: Béatrice et Bénédict; Le Carnaval romain.

(N)(BB) ** Warner Apex 8573 89533-2. LPO, Mehta.

(i) *Symphonie fantastique;* (ii) *Overture: Benvenuto Cellini; Les Troyens: Royal Hunt and Storm.*

(M) **(*) Sony (ADD) SMK 60135. (i) LSO; (ii) NYPO; Boulez.

Symphonie fantastique; Overture: Le Carnaval romain.

(BB) **(*) Virgin 2 x 1 VBD5 61513-2. RPO, Menuhin – BIZET; CHAUSSON: *Symphonies.* **(*)

(B) ** Ph. 422 253-2. LSO, C. Davis.

(i) *Symphonie fantastique;* (ii) *Overtures: Le Carnaval romain; Le Corsaire.*

(BB) **(*) ASV (ADD) CDQS 6090. RPO, Bátiz.

Symphonie fantastique; Overtures: Le Carnaval romain; Le Corsaire. La Damnation de Faust: Marche hongroise. Les Troyens: Trojan March.

(M) **(*) Mercury (IMS) (ADD) 434 328-2. Detroit SO, Paray.

Symphonie fantastique; La Damnation de Faust: Ballet des sylphes; Menuet des feux follets.

(M) **(*) DG 463 080-2. BPO, Karajan.

Sir Colin Davis's 1974 Concertgebouw recording has dominated the catalogue for two decades. Now reissued at mid-price, it still remains a primary recommendation. The performance has superb life and colour, the slow movement memorably atmospheric and the final two movements very exciting. If the sound does not quite match recent rivals in brilliance and definition, the overall balance is very satisfying and believable.

A really high-voltage performance from Stokowski and the New Philharmonia Orchestra of the *Symphonie fantastique*, recorded in 1968. The great conductor was eighty-six and in astonishing form. Though this would not be a first choice, every bar is stamped with personality. There are characteristic expressive exaggerations, but everything rings true and has conviction. The sound is acceptable, though not all the strands in the texture are ideally balanced. This comes in tandem with an outstanding performance of *Le poème de l'extase* and a conversation between the great conductor and Deryck Cooke.

Gardiner with his Orchestre Révolutionnaire et Romantique uses the extra sharpness of focus to add to the dramatic bite. In his electrifying, warmly expressive performance, heightening Berlioz's wild syncopations, he is second to none in conveying the astonishing modernity of music written within three years of Beethoven's death.

The Dutton Barbirolli disc offers superb CD transfers of three recordings which he made for EMI in his early years. This version of the *Symphonie fantastique* was recorded in 1947, just when Barbirolli had built the Hallé into what was widely accounted to be the finest orchestra in the country. This is a spacious, beautifully moulded reading, taut and urgent in the last three movements. The Fauré *Nocturne* makes a fine if brief bonus.

The balance of fierceness against romantic warmth in Muti's own personality works well in this symphony so that he holds the thread of argument together firmly, without ever underplaying excitement. The sound is among the best that Muti has had in Philadelphia. A strong bargain recommendation.

Eduard van Beinum's *Symphonie fantastique* was the first post-war recording he made, in 1947, on six 78-r.p.m. shellac discs. *The Record Guide*, writing in 1951 and regretting its deletion, called it the 'best of all' at the time – understandably so. Superbly cultured playing from this great orchestra, and the recording is yet another tribute to Decca's post-war engineering.

From the first movement onwards (which is not without its impetuous feeling but is far more clearly symphonic than usual) Klemperer conveys a rugged strength which, in the massiveness of the *Witches' Sabbath* for example, brings you close to Satan himself. There is certainly no lack of adrenalin and the *March to the Scaffold*, its rhythms clipped, is also given commanding power; the close is made the more impressive by a recording that is outstanding for its period (the early 1960s), sounding superbly expansive in this new transfer. The music from *Hänsel und Gretel* is also on the whole successful within its expansive Klempererian mantle, with some superb horn-playing in the overture.

Paray's exciting, hard-pressed reading is passionate and mercurial. The first movement immediately spurts away, and it is only the conductor's firm grip that prevents the movement from getting out of hand. The other movements too are fast, with great verve in the last two. Brilliant recording, with a tendency to thinness in the violins. The encores are similarly exciting and vivid.

Boulez's New York account of the *Symphonie fantastique* is intensely individual, crisp and intense, with clarity the essential, as unatmospheric as could be. Boulez's accounts of the *Royal Hunt and Storm* and the *Benvenuto Cellini Overture* are also exciting but unevocative (Sony SMK 60135).

Menuhin's reading of the *Symphonie fantastique* is full of character and he brings his own humanistic insights, yet the bizarre power of the final two movements is relished. The RPO play very well for him, and the recording is first class, brilliant, but with a satisfyingly full and resonant bass. The overture is enjoyable in a similar way, not just treated as a vehicle for orchestral virtuosity.

Bernstein's NYPO performance is compelling, emerging all the more strongly on this, its CD début, with the 1963 recording sounding vivid and full. The virtuosity, especially in the last movement, is in no doubt; the only caveat is the rather unconvincing rubato in the first movement.

Karajan's 1975 performance of the *Symphonie fantastique* brings wonderful playing from the BPO. There is great intensity in the opening movement (without repeat), particularly in the hushed strings, with the orchestra bringing out many subtle nuances of detail. The two final movements are quite exciting, and the recording is very good. The fill-ups are attractive but not so well recorded. But this is not a top choice.

Sir Colin Davis's earlier, LSO recording does not match his Concertgebouw performance of a decade later. The final two movements are very exciting but the tension is not consistently maintained in the first movement, and the *Adagio* is a little detached.

Bátiz's ASV CD is fully competitive in the super-bargain range, with excellent digital recording, brilliant and well balanced. He brings the score vividly to life, consistently warm, intensely persuasive. One has the feeling of live music-making, and the two overtures are equally strong and spontaneous.

In his second digital recording, Bátiz really lets his hair down. He is clearly well in control and the Philharmonia respond with remarkable virtuosity; but not all will take to the frenetic neurosis of his opening movement, with its wild changes of tempi. The waltz too is supercharged, and after the idyllic calm of the *Scène aux champs* the *Marche au supplice* mordantly prepares the way for the grotesque satanic ritual of the finale, where the bells toll for a monstrous, doom-laden climax. Brian Culverhouse's vivid recording-balance certainly matches Bátiz's conception; but when one turns to the brilliant RPO performances of the pair of overtures (common to both CDs) one realizes that a little more poise is advantageous in Berlioz.

Norrington does his utmost to observe the composer's metronome markings; but where his Beethoven is consistently fast, some of these speeds are more relaxed than we are used to – as in the *March to the Scaffold* and the *Ronde du sabbat*. His lifting of rhythms prevents the music from dragging, with period instruments giving new transparency; *Les Francs-juges Overture* is disappointingly low-key.

Mehta's view of the *Symphonie fantastique* is strong and well sustained, with the LPO playing superbly; but it is not remarkable for poetry. The weighty recording quality reinforces that impression. As fill-up Mehta offers comparable direct and well-played readings of the two overtures, with the weight of the recording helping rather than hindering the mercurial qualities of *Béatrice et Bénédict*, thanks to crisp ensemble. But the performance of the *Symphonie* is not a front runner, even at Apex price.

Maazel's rather plain reading for Telarc compares with the finest rivals only in its spectacular recording of demonstration quality. With no fill-up, the disc has a playing time of only 49 minutes.

On DG, Boulez directs a powerful, sure-footed and beautifully played reading which is lacking emotional thrust. With rhythms crisp but unsprung, the result is unpersuasive, out of synch with the inspiration of an arch-romantic. The first two sections of *Tristia* are far warmer, but the weirdly atmospheric *Funeral March for the Last Scene of Hamlet* receives a disappointingly plain, detached reading (DG 453 432-2).

Symphonie fantastique; (i) Lélio (Le Retour à la vie), Op. 14b.

(B) *** EMI (ADD) Rouge et Noir CZS5 69550-2 (2). (i) Gedda, Burles, Van Gorp, Sendrez, Topart, Fr. R. Ch., ORTF Nat. O, Martinon.

Berlioz intended *Lélio* as a sequel to the *Symphonie fantastique*, and Martinon conveniently offers the works paired at bargain price. His account of the *Symphonie* is uniquely seductive, for though he is brilliant he never presses on too frenetically. The finale, with its tolling bells of doom, has a flamboyance and power to match any available, and the 1973 sound remains remarkably vivid. *Lélio* quotes the *idée fixe* from the *Symphonie*, which helps the listener to feel at home. Unfortunately, at the time of going to press this set has been withdrawn.

(i) Symphonie fantastique; (ii) Lélio (Le Retour à la vie); (iii) La Mort de Cléopâtre; (iv) Les Nuits d'été, Op. 7; (v) Béatrice et Bénédict: Overture & Entr'acte; Overtures: Benvenuto Cellini; Le Carnaval romain. Les Troyens: Royal Hunt and Storm.

(M) *** Sony SM3K 64103 (3). (i–ii) LSO, (ii) with Jean-Louis Barrault (narr.), Mitchinson, Shirley-Quirk, L. Symphony Ch.; (iii–iv) Minton, BBC SO, (iv) with Burrows; (v) NYPO; all cond. Boulez.

Coupled with a unique reading of the *Symphonie fantastique* (clear-headed and intense rather than atmospheric), *Lélio* shows Boulez at his most searchingly convincing. The dramatic scena, *La Mort de Cléopâtre*, an early work which yet gives many hints of the mature Berlioz, makes a particularly suitable companion, as it offers specific quotations of material later used in the *Symphonie fantastique* (the *idée fixe*) and the *Roman Carnival Overture* (the melody of the introduction). Yvonne Minton's account is dramatically incisive and strongly committed. *Les Nuits d'été* is shared by Minton and Stuart Burrows, both at their finest. The 1972 New York collection of overtures is warmer, less concerned with sharpness of detail than the earlier recordings, yet they still show toughness. Overall this is strongly recommended to Boulez admirers.

Symphonie fantastique; (i) Roméo et Juliette, Op. 17 (complete).

(B) *** RCA (ADD) Twofer 74321 34168-2. Boston SO, Munch, (i) with Elias, Valletti, Tozzi and Ch.

Symphonie fantastique; Roméo et Juliette: Love Scene (only).

(M) *** RCA (ADD) 09026 68979-2. Boston SO, Munch.

Roméo et Juliette offers a near-ideal performance, and Munch's approach is sharp and dramatic. The stabbing agony of the frenzied allegro following Juliet's death has a frightening impact, and the jollity of the Capulets' party is taut and brittle. Yet the romanticism of the love music shows the depth of Munch's sympathy. The virtuosity of singers and orchestra is matched by the brilliance of the early stereo. At their price, these performances should be snapped up, even if you have either of the Davis versions.

Collectors content with just the *Love Scene* from *Roméo et Juliette* will find the single disc equally recommendable and the transfers to CD just as impressive.

(i) Grande symphonie funèbre et triomphale; (ii) Overtures: Benvenuto Cellini; Le Carnaval romain; Le Corsaire; Les Francs-juges; (iii) Les Troyens: Royal Hunt

and Storm; Ballet Music; Trojan March; (iv) *La Mort de Cléopâtre.*

(B) *** Erato ADD/Dig. Ultima Double 3984 24229-2 (2).
    (i) Chorale Populaire de Paris, Musique des Gardiens de la Paix, Dondeyne; (ii) Strasbourg PO, Lombard; (iii–iv) New PO of R. France, Amy, (iv) with Denize.

Désiré Dondeyne's 1958 performance of the *Grande symphonie funèbre et triomphale*, spaciously recorded in Notre Dame, is exciting and convincing in a specially French way. The wind and brass group (with a convincing solo trombone) has an authentic tang, with the chorus at the end producing an exhilaratingly robust fervour. The sound has plenty of spectacle and bite. Nadine Denize is equally at home in *La Mort de Cléopâtre*, which combines dramatic flair with a moving closing section. The four key overtures, recorded digitally two decades later, are also very well played, and the programme ends with excerpts from *Les Troyens*, the *Royal Hunt and Storm* without chorus but still impressive. Excellent recording throughout, but the documentation is totally inadequate, with no texts.

VOCAL MUSIC

(i–ii) *La Damnation de Faust; L'Enfance du Christ, Op. 25; Herminie; Lélio; La Mort de Cléopatre; Les Nuits d'été; Roméo et Juliette; Requiem Mass; Te Deum.* (i) *Mélodies: La Belle Voyageuse; Le Captive; Le Chasseur danois; Le Jeune Pâtre breton; Zaïde.*

(B) *** Ph. (ADD) 462 252-2 (9). (i) Soloists; (ii) John Alldis Ch., LSO Ch., Amb. S., Wandsworth School Boys' Ch.; LSO, C. Davis.

This impressive bargain box of Sir Colin Davis's recordings of the major Berlioz vocal works can be recommended with enthusiasm. Many of them are still available separately and are discussed below. *Roméo et Juliette* has great vitality and atmosphere. *Lélio* is presented without the spoken dialogue, and is convincing within its structural limitations. The *Te Deum* conveys drama without unwanted excesses of emotion, and the expansive choral climaxes and Nicolas Kynaston's fine organ contribution are impressively contained. Dame Janet Baker sings with passionate intensity in the two dramatic scenes, *Herminie* and *La Mort de Cléopâtre*, but *Les Nuits d'été* is presented with different singers singing different songs, with Sheila Armstrong the finest of the group, especially in the final exhilarating *L'Île inconnue*. In the other songs Josephine Veasey's contribution is also an individual one; but Frank Patterson, the weakest of the soloists, lacks the necessary charm. Nevertheless this is a small blot on what is overall a splendid achievement.

La Damnation de Faust (complete).

(N) (BB) *** LSO Live LSO 008CD (2). Sabbatini, Shkosa, Pertusi, Wilson-Johnson, LSO and Ch., C. Davis.

*** Decca 444 812-2. Pollet, Leech, Cachemaille, Philippe, Montreal Ch. & SO, Dutoit.

*** Ph. (ADD) 416 395-2 (2). Veasey, Gedda, Bastin, Amb. S., Wandsworth School Boys' Ch., L. Symphony Ch., LSO, C. Davis.

*** Decca 414 680-2 (2). Riegel, Von Stade, Van Dam, King, Chicago Ch. & SO, Solti.

(B) **(*) DG (ADD) Double 453 019-2 (2). Mathis, Burrows, McIntyre, Paul, Tanglewood Festival Ch., Boston Boys' Ch. & SO, Ozawa.

(**) BBC mono BBCL 4006/7 (2). Crespin, Turp, Roux, Shirley-Quirk, L. Symphony Ch., LSO, Monteux.

(i) *La Damnation de Faust;* (ii) *La Mort de Cléopâtre.*

(B) **(*) EMI (ADD) double forte CZS5 68583-2 (2). Baker;
    (i) Gedda, Bacquier, Thau, Paris Opera Ch., O de Paris, Prêtre; (ii) LSO, Gibson.

Though in the LSO Live series, Sir Colin Davis's new version at super-bargain price offers a performance and sound which in every way match and even outshine any rival in a strongly competitive field. Recorded at the Barbican in October 2000, it is rivetingly dramatic. This strange mixture of opera and concert-work can so easily seem wayward in its treatment of Goethe with its episodic sequence of scenes, yet even more than in his classic 1973 recording for Philips Davis involves you in the painful quandary obsessing Faust, never letting tension slip for a moment. This time the playing of the LSO is even more refined, with rhythms even more lightly sprung, as in the witty treatment of Mephistopheles's *Flea song*, characterfully sung by Michele Pertusi, weighty yet agile.

As Faust, Gabriele Sabbatini is more overtly emotional than any rival, Italianate in his expressiveness with the occasional half-sob. Yet the involvement is what matters, helped by his radiant tonal range down to a perfectly controlled head-voice. The Albanian soprano Enkelejda Shkosa is a warm, vibrant Marguerite, with a flicker in the voice giving a hint of the heroine's vulnerability.

Not just the LSO but the London Symphony Chorus too are in searing form, and the recording brings out the detail of Berlioz's orchestration with ideal transparency, though the transfer is at rather a low level, needing fair amplification for full impact. Though, like other issues in the LSO Live series, this comes at super-budget price, making an astonishing bargain, the complete text is provided in the booklet, along with Davis Cairns's authoritative notes, if in microscopic print.

Dutoit follows up his epic recording of *Les Troyens* with an account of this unique work which fully brings out its operatic qualities. The choice of mainly French-speaking soloists intensifies the storytelling element, with singers balanced so as to allow words to be heard, and with the atmospheric warmth of the Montreal sound adding to the illusion of a stage picture. Richard Leech is not the most characterful Faust but, unlike many, he sings clearly and without strain. Françoise Pollet is a warm, expressive Marguerite, tenderly affecting in her two big solos, and Gilles Cachemaille, though not the most powerful Mephistopheles, is brilliant at pointing words and bringing out the wry humour.

Both Nicolai Gedda as Faust and Jules Bastin as Mephistopheles are impressive in Davis's fine 1974 Philips set. The response of the chorus and orchestra is highly intelligent and sensitive, and the recording perspective is outstandingly natural and realistic.

Solti's performance, searingly dramatic, is given stunning digital sound to make the *Ride to Hell* supremely exciting. But with Frederica Von Stade singing tenderly, this is a warmly expressive performance too; and the *Hungarian March* has rarely had such sparkle and swagger. The extra brightness matches the extrovert quality of the performance, less subtle than Davis's.

Most valuable in the EMI *Damnation de Faust* is Janet Baker's Marguerite, sung most beautifully. Prêtre is not always perceptive and, though there are many dramatic touches, the set does not outshine either Markevitch or Ozawa in this price-range. Berlioz's early scena on the death of a famous classical heroine, *La Mort de Cléopâtre*, is most movingly done.

Now offered, economically priced, on a DG Double (with translation and full documentation included), Ozawa's performance provides an alternative in a much more moulded style; but, with superb playing and generally fine singing, the results are seductively enjoyable.

The BBC recording is of a relay from the Royal Festival Hall on 8 March 1962, and it conveys a real sense of occasion. The Monteux performance is a distinguished one with a first-rate cast, and the sound wears its years very lightly.

L'Enfance du Christ, Op. 25.

*** Hyp. CDA 66991/2. Rigby, Miles, Finley, Aler, Howell, Corydon Singers & O, Best.

(B) *** Erato Ultima 3984 25595-2 (2). Von Otter, Rolfe Johnson, Van Dam, Cachemaille, Bastin, Monteverdi Ch., Lyon Op. O, Gardiner.

**(*) Ph. (ADD) 416 949-2 (2). Baker, Tappy, Langridge, Allen, Herincx, Rouleau, Bastin, Alldis Ch., LSO, C. Davis.

(BB) **(*) Naxos 8.553650/1. Lagrange, Piquemal, Bernardi, Ch. Regional Vittoria de l'Ile de France, Maîtrisse de R. France, Lille Nat. O, J.-C. Casadesus.

L'Enfance du Christ; La Belle Voyageuse, Op. 2/4; Chant sacré; Hélène, Op. 2/2; Quartetto e coro dei magi; Sara la baigneuse, Op. 11.

(N) *** Decca 458 915-2 (2). Graham, Le Roux, Ainsley, Cokorinos, Wentzel, Getz, Belleau, Montreal Ch. & SO, Dutoit.

(i) L'Enfance du Christ; (ii) Méditation religieuse; La Mort d'Ophélie; Sara la baigneuse; (iii) La Mort de Cléopâtre.

(B) *** Double Decca (ADD) 443 461-2 (2). (i) Pears, Morison, Cameron, Rouleau, Frost, Fleet, Goldsbrough O; (i–ii) St Anthony Singers; (ii–iii) ECO, (iii) with Pashley; all cond. C. Davis.

(i) L'Enfance du Christ; (ii) Roméo et Juliette (orchestral music only).

(B) *** EMI double forte (ADD) CZS5 88586-2 (2). (i) De Los Angeles, Gedda, Soyer, Blanc, Depraz, Cottret, René Duclos Ch., Paris Conservatoire O, Cluytens; (ii) Chicago SO, Giulini.

This atmospheric oratorio for Christmas, so different from almost any other Berlioz work, has been lucky on disc, but never has it been recorded with quite such glowing sound as in its latest Montreal Decca version, rich and full yet cleanly focused. As in his other major Berlioz recordings,

Dutoit is a warm, urgent interpreter, generally favouring speeds a degree faster than those of Sir Colin Davis. Susan Graham is superb as the Virgin, giving a fresh, heartfelt performance, with François Le Roux a clear, idiomatic Joseph and John Mark Ainsley a fluent Narrator. Excellent singing from the Montreal Choir, both in the main work and the rare and valuable fill-ups.

Vividly recorded in beautifully balanced digital sound, immediate yet warm, Matthew Best's version offers a keenly dramatic view. So Alastair Miles conveys pure evil in Herod's monologue at the start and, with words exceptionally clear, Joseph's pleas for shelter are movingly urgent. Jean Rigby is a fresh, young-sounding Mary, with Gerald Finley warm and expressive as Joseph. John Aler is a powerful Reciter and Gwynne Howell a strong, benevolent-sounding Father of the family. This makes an ideal choice for those who want an imaginative view and a superb modern recording.

Sir Colin Davis's 1961 recording of *L'Enfance du Christ* (originally made for L'Oiseau Lyre) is by no means inferior to his later, Philips set. At times the earlier performance was fresher and more urgent, and Peter Pears was a sweeter-toned, more characterful narrator. Elsie Morison and John Cameron are perfectly cast as Mary and Joseph, and Joseph Rouleau makes an impressive contribution as the Ishmaelite Father. This Double Decca reissue in atmospheric sound also offers an invaluable collection of off-beat vocal works, with fine choral singing and a splendid contribution from Anne Pashley.

John Eliot Gardiner in his vivid reading also has the advantage of fine modern recording, made in the Church of Sainte-Madeleine, Pérouges, very well balanced and atmospheric. Among the soloists, Anne Sofie von Otter's Mary is outstanding, singing with rapt simplicity. Gardiner often – though not always – adopts brisker tempi than Davis, and his vibrancy brings a new dimension to some of the music. Now it is very competitive, even if Davis's choice of pacing is even more apt.

In Davis's second version, for Philips, the beautifully balanced recording intensifies the colour and atmosphere of the writing, so that the *Nocturnal March* in the first part is wonderfully mysterious. There is a fine complement of soloists, and though Eric Tappy's tone as narrator is not always sweet, his sense of style is immaculate. Others are not always quite so idiomatic, but Janet Baker and Thomas Allen both sing beautifully.

Gedda may not be as sensitive as Pears on the first Davis version, but de Los Angeles is superlative and so is Ernest Blanc as Herod. The orchestra gives sensitive support to the fresh choral singing. The coupling is one of Giulini's best records from the same period (1969). The Chicago orchestra responds with fine discipline and beauty of tone, and also with great conviction in an incandescent performance. Good recording quality, though the focus is not always absolutely clean.

Casadesus and the Lille orchestra give a fresh and direct account of Berlioz's sacred trilogy. The tenor, Jean-Luc Viala, makes an excellent narrator and the mezzo, Michèle Lagrange, a touching Mary, and if the others are not so distinguished they form a satisfying team. Casadesus's approach can be well assessed from the flowing speed for the most celebrated number, the *Shepherds' Farewell*. The set includes in its excellent booklet full French text with English translation. Clear, pleasing sound.

'Chant d'amour': La Mort d'Ophélie; Zaïde.

*** Decca 452 667-2. Bartoli, Chung – BIZET; DELIBES; RAVEL: *Mélodies.* ***

Cecilia Bartoli's collection of French songs is one of the most ravishing of her records yet, and these Berlioz items are among the highlights. Myung-Whun Chung's contribution is both imaginative and supportive (see below under Recitals).

Irlande, Op. 2: excerpts; Mélodies: La Belle Voyageuse; Adieu, Bessy!; Le Coucher du soleil; Elégie; L'Origine de la harpe.

⚫ *** EMI CDC5 55047-2. Hampson, Parsons – LISZT; WAGNER: *Lieder.* *** ⚫

Thomas Hampson gives glowing performances of five of the nine songs, using translations from English texts by the poet Thomas Moore, which Berlioz wrote very early in his career. In their expressive warmth they make a perfect match for the fascinating selections of songs by Wagner and Liszt, with Geoffrey Parsons adding to the impact. Warm, helpful sound.

Mélodies: Aubade; La Belle Voyageuse; La Captive; Le Chasseur danois; Le Jeune Pâtre breton; La Mort d'Ophélie; Les Nuits d'été; Zaïde.

*** Erato 4509 99768-2. Montague, Robbin, Fournier, Crook, Cachemaille, Lyon Op. O, Gardiner.

Like Davis before him, John Eliot Gardiner here divides the six keenly atmospheric songs of *Les Nuits d'été* between four singers, in some ways an ideal solution when his choice of singers is inspired and the presiding genius of the conductor makes this a memorable Berlioz disc.

Mélodies: (i) La Belle Isabeau; La Belle Voyageuse; La Captive; Le Matin; La Mort d'Ophélie. (ii) Les Nuits d'été (song-cycle); (ii–iii) Roméo et Juliette: Prologue: Premiers transports (Strophes).

*** DG 445 823-2. Von Otter, with (i) Royal Stockholm Op. Ch.; Garben; (ii) BPO, Levine; (iii) Berlin RIAS Chamber Ch.

This is a most attractive compilation. The five solo songs here are among the most moving and individual of all, notably the longest, *La Mort d'Ophélie*. In *Les Nuits d'été* von Otter is fresh and radiant, bringing out the dramatic contrasts between the songs, and the poise and weight of *Strophes* from *Roméo* is magical.

Messe solennelle; Resurrexit (revised version).

(M) *** Ph. 464 688-2. D. Brown, Viala, Cachemaille, Monteverdi Ch., ORR, Gardiner.

This massive work, completed in 1824, is uneven, but the glow of inspiration shines out over any shortcomings. Gardiner conducts with characteristic flair and a sense of drama, bringing brilliant singing from the Monteverdi Choir, though the choral sound is backwardly balanced. A second,

modified and slightly expanded version of the violent *Resurrexit* is included as a supplement, a revised version that Berlioz himself acknowledged.

Les Nuits d'été (song-cycle).

(M) *** Decca (ADD) 460 973-2. Crespin, SRO, Ansermet – RAVEL: *Shéhérazade* *** ⚫ (with *Recital of French Songs* ***).

(N) (***) Testament mono SBT 3203 (3). Los Angeles, Boston SO, Munch – DEBUSSY: *La Demoiselle élue;* MASSENET: *Manon.* (***)

Les Nuits d'été (song-cycle); Mélodies: La Belle Voyageuse; La Captive; Zaïde.

(BB) *** Virgin 2 x 1 VBD5 61469-2 (2). Baker, City of L. Sinf., Hickox – BRAHMS: *Alto Rhapsody*, etc.; MENDELSSOHN: *Infelice*, etc.; RESPIGHI: *La sensitiva.* ***

(i) Les Nuits d'été; (ii) La Mort de Cléopâtre.

(M) *** DG 445 594-2. O de Paris, Barenboim, with (i) Te Kanawa; (ii) Norman.

With Régine Crespin's richness of tone, and with Ansermet at his finest accompanying brilliantly, this glowing performance is truly legendary – a *tour de force*. Moreover, the Ravel coupling is even more inspired, and the superb new transfers enhance the listener's pleasure further.

This Virgin two-for-one at mid-price is a treasure-chest of Janet Baker's later recordings, made in the early 1990s, including her later recording of *Les Nuits d'été* and other orchestral songs (see above). Her classic EMI reading with Barbirolli is now coupled on a double forte with *Roméo et Juliette* (see below).

The coupling of Jessye Norman in the scena and Kiri Te Kanawa in the song-cycle makes for a ravishing Berlioz record, with each singer at her very finest. Norman has natural nobility and command as the Egyptian queen in this dramatic scena, while Te Kanawa encompasses the challenge of different moods and register in *Les Nuits d'été* more completely and affectingly than any singer on record in recent years.

Victoria de Los Angeles's RCA recording of *Les Nuits d'été*, like Debussy's *La Demoiselle élue*, both dating from 1955, makes a splendid, generous bonus to the classic Monteux version of Massenet's *Manon*, recorded in Paris, also in 1955. Though there is more edge on the American recording than the EMI, making the voice a shade less golden, the charm of the lovely voice is still a delight.

Requiem Mass, Op. 5.

(***) BBC mono BBCL 4011-2. Lewis, RPO Ch., RPO, Beecham.

(BB) *(*) Naxos 8.554494/5. Schade, Toronto Mendelssohn Ch. & Youth Ch., Elora Festival O, Edison.

(i) Requiem Mass. Overtures: Benvenuto Cellini; Le Carnaval romain; Le Corsaire.

**(*) DG 429 724-2 (2). (i) Pavarotti, Ernst-Senff Ch.; BPO, Levine.

(i) Requiem Mass; (ii) Symphonie fantastique.

(B) *** EMI double forte Dig./ADD CZS5 69512-2 (2). (i) Tear, LPO Ch., LPO; (ii) LSO; Previn.

Requiem Mass; Messe solennelle: Resurrexit. Tantum ergo. Veni creator.

*** Decca 458 921-2 (2). Mark Ainsley, Montreal Ch. & SO, Dutoit (with BORTNYANSKY, arr. Berlioz: *Pater Noster; Adoremus*).

(i) *Requiem;* (ii) *Te Deum.*

(N)(M) **(*) Ph. (ADD) 464 689-2 (2). (i) Dowd;
(ii) Tagliavini; Wandsworth School Boys Ch., LSO Ch., LSO, Davis.

Previn's 1980 Walthamstow recording of Berlioz's great choral work offers spectacular digital sound, with the gradations of pianissimo breathtakingly caught, to make the great outbursts of the *Dies irae* and the *Tuba mirum* the more telling. There is a fine bloom on the voices, while the separation of sound gives a feeling of reality to the massed brass and multiple timpani. Previn's view is direct and incisive, not underlining expressiveness but concentrating on rhythmic qualities. If Previn misses animal excitement, the contrasts of the closing *Agnus Dei* are movingly captured. Robert Tear, balanced close, is a sensitive soloist. The *Symphonie fantastique* in Previn's dramatic, strongly structured reading makes a generous fill-up, also very well recorded.

Though Beecham's live recording, made at the Royal Albert Hall in December 1959, comes in mono only, the BBC sound is warm and full. The weight and intensity of the performance and the sense of a great occasion are caught vividly, not least in the great outburst of brass bands, widely separated, in the *Tuba mirum*. Although the professional choir takes a little time to settle down, the Beecham magic gets to work quickly, to make this one of the most compelling performances on disc. The tenor, Richard Lewis, is in superb form in the *Sanctus*, his voice given a halo of reverberation. A most cherishable historic issue.

As in *Les Troyens*, Dutoit favours speeds generally a degree or two more flowing than usual. The choral sound is beautifully integrated, with unrivalled weight in the climaxes, thanks to the recording. Where the singing of the Montreal choir does not quite match that of the finest rival versions is in attack. This is a performance a degree more relaxed, less bitingly dramatic, but one which is held strongly together in both structure and argument. Thanks to the ripe and resonant recording, the sounds of the last trump in the *Dies irae* are magnificent, with massed brass and timpani exceptionally well defined. The tenor soloist in the *Sanctus*, John Mark Ainsley, is sensitive rather than heroic, with the recording exaggerating the vibrato. The rare fill-ups are welcome, if not especially generous. The two pieces for women's choir – *Veni creator* unaccompanied, *Tantum ergo* with organ – reveal Berlioz at his simplest, touchingly so, as do the Bortnyansky arrangements. The *Resurrexit* is the most ambitious piece here with its vision of the last trump, later modified for the *Requiem*. Among rival versions of that main work, the Previn still has very strong claims, more biting than Dutoit; yet on recording grounds Dutoit is a first choice among digital versions.

For Sir Colin Davis's recording of the *Requiem* Philips

went to Westminster Cathedral, and though one can hear individual voices in the choir, thanks to the closeness of the microphones, the large-scale brass sound is formidably caught and the choral fortissimos are glorious, helped by the fresh cutting edge of the Wandsworth School Boys' Choir. The LSO provides finely incisive accompaniment. In the Te Deum Davis conveys the massiveness without pomposity, the drama without unwanted excesses of emotion, and his massed forces respond superbly. The only disappointment comes in the singing of Tagliavini, reasonably restrained by the standards of most Italian tenors, but not really in style with the others, or for that matter Berlioz. The recording is aptly brilliant and atmospheric.

Levine's account of the *Requiem*, one of his Berlioz series with the Berlin Philharmonic, cannot quite match the vintage Colin Davis, and the Ernst-Senff Choir falls short of its usual standards in some ragged entries. Pavarotti is a characterful, imaginatively expressive soloist, and three of Berlioz's most popular overtures come in excellent performances.

The chief merits of this disappointing Naxos account of the Berlioz *Grande messe des morts* – a difficult work to hold together – are the singing of the Toronto Mendelssohn Choir, atmospherically recorded, and of the sweet-toned tenor, Michael Schade, in the *Sanctus*. Otherwise this is an underpowered reading, lacking the biting intensity of rival versions, though the recording of the brass in the *Tuba mirum* section is rich and ripe.

Roméo et Juliette, Op. 17 (both original (1839) and standard (1846) versions of the score).

*** Ph. 454 454-2 (2). Robbin, Fouchécourt, Cachemaille, Monteverdi Ch., ORR, Gardiner.

Roméo et Juliette, Op. 17.

🏵 *** Ph. 442 134-2. Borodina, Moser, Miles, Bav. R. Ch., VPO, C. Davis.

(N) * Häns. CD 93.005 (2). Denize, Beczala, Lika, Baden-Baden & Freiburg SWR SO, Cambreling –
MESSIAEN: *L'Ascension.* *

(BB) *** LSO Live 0003CD (2). Barcellona, Tarver, Anastassov, LSO Ch., LSO, Sir Colin Davis.

In his newest Philips recording of *Roméo et Juliette* Sir Colin Davis's interpretative approach remains basically unchanged, yet he now offers greater depth, colour and body. Olga Borodina has the full measure of the Berlioz style, Thomas Moser is no less ardent and idiomatic, and Alastair Miles is a fine Friar Laurence. Apart from its all-round artistic excellence, this scores over all-comers in the sheer quality of the sound which reproduces the whole range of Berlioz's fantastic score in all its subtle colourings in remarkable detail and naturalness.

In the LSO Live series of super-budget discs this recording of Berlioz's great dramatic symphony builds in many important ways on what Sir Colin Davis has revealed to us in his two previous versions, both for Philips. This two-disc issue preserves what by any reckoning was an electrifying event at the Barbican in January 2000. Davis's view of the work has remained fundamentally unchanged, though his speeds at the Barbican are marginally broader until the concluding sections from Juliette's funeral onwards. The live Barbican recording may not match in opulence either the 1993 recording with the Vienna Philharmonic or the 1968 recording with the LSO, for the Barbican acoustic (as recorded) is drier. Yet the refinement of the sound, with orchestra and chorus set at a slight distance, brings pianissimos of breathtaking delicacy, focused in fine detail. The *Queen Mab Scherzo*, for example, gains in lightness and gracefulness.

The three young soloists are first-rate, characterizing strongly. The Italian, Daniela Barcellona, controls her vibrant mezzo well in the strophes, and the American tenor, Kenneth Tarver, sings his *Scherzetto* with fluency and sparkle, while the tangily Slavonic timbre of the Bulgarian bass, Orlin Anastassov, stands out well in the Friar Lawrence episodes.

Without usurping Davis's versions, the Gardiner set enables you to make your own choice from among the discarded material reproduced in the Appendices of the New Berlioz Edition. Gardiner has a good team of soloists and draws an expert response from his Orchestre Révolutionnaire et Romantique. He presses ahead at times with too unyielding a grip, and phrases do not always unfold naturally and breathe as freely as they would if a Beecham were on the podium. However, there is keen intelligence and imagination here, and the recording is absolutely first class, beautifully balanced and transparent in texture.

Sylvain Cambreling's version with the SWR Orchestra of Baden-Baden benefits from clean, refined sound, but lacks the tautness and weight which is needed to hold Berlioz's episodic structure together. The playing and singing are worthy, with the mezzo, Nadine Denize a characterful soloist, but too often the performance sounds cautious, lacking the flair necessary in Berlioz. The Messiaen piece makes a good supplement, but that too sounds unidiomatic, lacking in tension.

Roméo et Juliette (excerpts); *Les Troyens à Carthage: Prelude & Royal Hunt and Storm.*

(BB) **(*) Naxos 8.553195. San Diego Ch. and SO, Talmi.

Yoav Talmi and the San Diego orchestra offer a far more generous selection from Berlioz's great dramatic symphony than usual, lasting well over an hour. Talmi secures brilliant playing from his orchestra, with admirably crisp ensemble in such show-pieces as the *Queen Mab Scherzo*, and with satisfying warmth in the great Love Scene. It is good too on this very well-filled disc to have the *Prelude* to *Les Troyens* and the *Royal Hunt and Storm* (complete with offstage chorus) as makeweights. The recording is clean and detailed but lacks full weight.

Te Deum, Op. 22.

(N) *** Virgin VC5 45449-2. Alagna, O de Paris, Nelson; Alain.

*** DG 410 696-2. Araiza, L. Symphony Ch., LPO Ch., Woburn Singers, Boys' Ch., European Community Youth O, Abbado.

(i) *Te Deum*; (ii) *Les Nuits d'été* (song-cycle).

(B) ** Sony (ADD) SBK 63043. (i) Dupouy, Ch. d'Enfants de Paris, Maîtrisse de la Resurrection, Ch. & O de Paris, Barenboim; (ii) Minton, Burrows, BBC SO, Boulez.

When most of Berlioz's major works have been recorded many times over, it is surprising that the *Te Deum* has been relatively neglected. This latest version under a dedicated Berlioz interpreter, John Nelson, not only has a fuller, more brilliant sound than previous versions, with the complex textures well terraced, it offers two extra instrumental movements that Berlioz suggested should be included for performances celebrating victory, both with military overtones – a Prelude using one of the work's main themes in fugato and a rather corny 'March for the Presentation of the Colours'. It is good too to have Roberto Alagna as an imaginative soloist in the prayer, *Te ergo quaesummus*, and Marie-Claire Alain warmly idiomatic on the organ of the Madeleine, Paris.

The DG recording of the *Te Deum* from Abbado is very impressive. The sound is wide-ranging, with striking dynamic contrasts: Abbado brings great tonal refinement and dignity to this performance, and the spacious sound helps. Francisco Araiza is the fine soloist.

Barenboim's Paris version of the *Te Deum* brings a strong and characterful performance, occasionally exaggerated but with fine choral singing and a stylish tenor soloist, and fine playing from the organist, Jean Guillou. The recording is full and vivid. In *Les Nuits d'été* the six songs are shared between male and female voices. Yvonne Minton brings an almost operatic flair to *Le spectre de la rose*, *Sur les lagunes* and especially *L'Île inconnue*, and Stuart Burrows is hardly less ardent in his heady opening *Villanelle*, while both *Absence* and *Au cimetière* are touchingly done, although his wide vibrato is sometimes intrusive.

OPERA

Complete operas

(i) *Béatrice et Bénédict;* (ii) *Benvenuto Cellini;* (iii) *Les Troyens, Parts 1 & 2.*

(B) *** Ph. (ADD) 456 387-2 (9). (i) Baker, Tear, Watts, Van Allan, Alldis Ch., LSO; (i–ii) Eda-Pierre, Bastin, Lloyd; (ii) Gedda, Massard, Blackwell, Herincx, Cuénod, Berbié, BBC SO; (ii–iii) Soyer, ROHCG Ch.; (iii) Veasey, Vickers, Lindholm, Glossop, Begg, Partridge, Wandsworth School Boys' Ch., ROHCG O; all cond. C. Davis.

Sir Colin Davis's recordings of the three Berlioz operas (with *Benvenuto Cellini* made first in 1969, *Béatrice et Bénédict* following in 1972 and the series crowned with *Les Troyens* in 1977) makes another superb bargain package, with consistently fine CD transfers. The one blot on the set is the omission of libretto translations, although the synopses are adequately cued. If Janet Baker and Robert Tear understandably stand out in *Béatrice et Bénédict*, the rest of the cast is also first rate. Similarly, it is Nicolai Gedda in superb form who dominates *Benvenuto Cellini*, but his colleagues do not let him down. Even more than the other two operas, *Les Troyens* was an ambitious team-project, with singers, chorus and orchestra all inspired by Davis and with Josephine Veasey a superb Dido. The Philips engineers rise to the occasion in capturing the opera's spectacle with brilliance, atmosphere and refined detail.

Béatrice et Bénédict (complete).

*** Ph. (ADD) (IMS) 416 952-2 (2). Baker, Tear, Eda-Pierre, Allen, Lloyd, Van Allan, Watts, Alldis Ch., LSO, C. Davis.

*** Erato 2292 45773-2 (2). Graham, Viala, McNair, Robbin, Bacquier, Cachemaille, Le Texier, Lyon Opera Ch. & O, Nelson.

(i) *Béatrice et Bénédict* (complete); (ii) *Chant de la Fête de Pâcques; Irlande (9 Mélodies), Op. 2; La Mort d'Ophélie, Op. 18/2; Le Trébuchet, Op. 13.*

(B) *** Double Decca (ADD) 448 113-2 (2). (i) Veasey, Mitchinson, Cantelo, Cameron, Watts, Shirley-Quirk, Shilling, St Anthony Singers, LSO, C. Davis; (ii) Cantelo, Watts, Tear, Salter, Monteverdi Ch., Gardiner; Tunnard (piano).

Béatrice et Bénédict presents not just witty and brilliant music for the heroine and hero (on Philips, Janet Baker and Robert Tear at their most pointed) but sensuously beautiful passages too. First-rate solo and choral singing, brilliant playing and sound that is refined and clear in texture, bright and fresh, even if minimal hiss betrays an analogue source.

The Lyon Opera version conducted by John Nelson makes an excellent alternative to the vintage Colin Davis recording. In spacious, modern, digital sound it offers substantially more of the French dialogue, well spoken by actors but more dryly recorded than the musical numbers. Susan Graham is a characterful Béatrice, lighter in the big aria than Janet Baker for Davis but aptly younger-sounding. Jean-Luc Viala is a comparably light Bénédict, pointing the fun in his big aria, and Sylvia McNair and Catherine Robbin are superb as Héro and Ursule.

Above all, the early (1962) Oiseau-Lyre set is a triumph for Sir Colin Davis, who readily responds to Berlioz's quirkiness, bringing out the delicacy and the humour. The singing is equally fresh and vigorous, with April Cantelo coping splendidly with Héro's fearsome opening aria. Josephine Veasey as Béatrice presents an appropriately formidable figure, John Mitchinson is a distinctive Bénédict. To make the Double Decca reissue even more tempting, Decca have added the contents of a third LP of little-known vocal Berlioz, including the nine songs grouped together under the title *Irlande*. The performances are all of a high standard.

Les Troyens, Parts I & II (complete)

✿ (N) (BB) *** LSO Live 0010CD (4). Heppner, DeYoung, Land, Mingardo, Mattei, Milling, LSO & Ch., C. Davis.

*** Ph. (ADD) 416 432-2 (4). Veasey, Vickers, Lindholm, Glossop, Soyer, Partridge, Wandsworth School Boys' Ch., ROHCG Ch. & O, C. Davis.

*** Decca 443 693-2 (4). Lakes, Pollet, Voigt, Montreal Ch. & SO, Dutoit.

Recorded live at performances (and rehearsals) in the Barbican in London, Sir Colin Davis's second recording of this epic opera magnificently crowns his whole career as a Berlioz interpreter on record, generally outshining even his earlier pioneer version of 30 years earlier. The first wonder is that the sound of chorus and orchestra, so far from being cramped in that setting, is even fuller, more spacious and certainly brighter and clearer than on the earlier Philips

recording, or even the opulent digital recording given to Charles Dutoit in his Montreal set for Decca. Interpretatively, one difference between the new reading and the old is that, contrary to what happens with many conductors in their seventies, Davis is marginally faster in all five acts, a degree more thrustful with the excitement of a live occasion consistently adding extra intensity. No applause is included at the ends of acts, presumably by the use of rehearsal tapes.

The casting too is marginally even finer than before. Petra Lang, a last-minute substitute as Cassandra, is superb, firm, rich and intense, investing every phrase with emotional power, instantly establishing her dominance in the very first scene. Opposite her, Peter Mattei makes a powerful Chorebus. Both in *The Fall of Troy* and *The Trojans at Carthage* Ben Heppner excels himself, not just heroic with his unstrained *Heldentenor*, but finding a degree of refinement in the love duet of Act 3 that few rivals can match, let alone on disc. Michelle DeYoung may not be quite so rich and firm a Dido as Josephine Veasey on Davis's earlier set, but the vibrancy of her mezzo is warmly caught by the microphones, and her death monologue is the more moving for the vulnerability she conveys. The rest make an excellent team without any significant shortcoming. Though the set comes on four discs at super-budget price, full libretto and notes are provided, though printed in very small type.

Throughout his earlier Philips recording Davis compels the listener to concentrate, to achieve the epic logic of Berlioz's masterly setting. Only in the great love scene of *O nuit d'ivresse* would one have welcomed the more expansive hand of a Beecham. Veasey makes a splendid Dido, singing always with fine heroic strength, with Vickers a ringing Aeneas. The Covent Garden Chorus and Orchestra excel themselves in virtuoso singing and playing, and the sound quality is superbly vivid. However, fine though it is, this set is now superseded by Davis's new LSO Live digital recording.

Dutoit's Decca recording was linked to concert performances of each of the two parts of the opera, recorded in spectacular digital sound. Interpretatively the contrasts between Dutoit and Davis in his first Philips recording are quickly established. Dutoit is more volatile than Davis, consistently preferring faster speeds – reflecting the metronome markings – bringing not just thrilling allegros but lyrically flowing andantes. However, in his later LSO set Davis is much closer to Dutoit in his pacing.

On Decca Cassandra's first solo is most persuasively moulded at a flowing speed, with Deborah Voight far warmer than Berit Lindholm for Davis on Philips. However, both are upstaged by Petra Lang in the newest version. As Dido, the soprano on Decca, Françoise Pollet sings with rich, even tone, sensuously feminine, even if she lacks the weight of a mezzo, and though Gary Lakes as Dido is less heroic than Jon Vickers, he is more sensitive in the love duet. Duitoit includes the brief prelude that Berlioz wrote in 1863 for separate performances of the second part of the opera. The other textual addition comes in Act I. After the Andromache scene there is an extra scene, lasting six minutes, which the Berlioz scholar Hugh MacDonald, editor of the Barenreiter score, has orchestrated from the surviving piano score.

Les Troyens: Grand scenes.

(M) *** Decca 458 208-2 (from complete recording, with Lakes, Pollet, Voigt, Montreal Ch. & SO; cond. Dutoit).

The scenes here have been judiciously chosen and include the spectacular *Trojan March* at the end of Act I, so powerfully dominated by the foreboding of Deborah Voigt's Cassandra. In the final solo, Françoise Pollet portrays the distraught Dido, all purpose gone in the disjointed recitative, a closing sequence of great dramatic power that alone makes this Opera Gala CD worth considering. It is well packaged, with a full translation included.

BERNERS, Lord (1883–1950)

Luna Park; March; (i) *A Wedding Bouquet.*

** Marco 8.223716. (i) RTE Chamber Ch.; RTE Sinf., Alwyn.

Stravinsky spoke of Lord Berners as 'droll and delightful'. Apart from Constant Lambert, he was the only English composer taken up by Diaghilev. *Luna Park* (1930) was written for a C. B. Cochran revue, with choreography by Balanchine. *A Wedding Bouquet* was choreographed by Frederick Ashton and mounted at Sadler's Wells in 1937, with décor and costumes, as well as music, by Berners. This is good light music. Performances are decent, as are the recordings, but the acoustic does not permit tuttis to open out.

Les Sirènes (ballet; complete); *Caprice péruvien; Cupid and Psyche* (ballet suite).

** Marco 8.223780. Blennerhassett, RTE Sinf., Lloyd-Jones.

Les Sirènes was not a great success and the music, despite some bright moments, does not sustain a high level of invention. The *Caprice péruvien* was put together expertly by Constant Lambert with Berners's help. The ballet *Cupid and Psyche* was another Ashton work, mounted in 1939. Good performances, but not well polished. Again the recordings are wanting in bloom.

The Triumph of Neptune (ballet): extended suite; *Fantaisie espagnole; Fugue in C min.; 3 Morceaux; Nicholas Nickleby* (film music).

*** Olympia OCD 662. RLPO, Wordsworth.

Barry Wordsworth captures the character of this music remarkably well. Moreover, the *Trois morceaux* and the *Fantaisie espagnole* are new to the catalogue. They are Gallic in inspiration and are attractively imaginative. The recording is good without being in the demonstration class; detail is well defined and there is plenty of body. Originally issued on EMI, this rather surprisingly reappears on the Olympia label and is very welcome.

Piano music: Le Poisson d'or; Dispute entre le papillon et le crapaud; The Expulsion from Paradise; Fragments psychologiques; March; 3 Petites marches funèbres; Polka; Valse. (i) *Songs: A long time ago; Come on Algernon; The Rio Grande; Theodore or The Pirate King; 3 Chansons; 3 English Songs; Lieder Album* (3 *Songs in the German Manner); Red roses and red noses.*

(N) **(*) Marco 8.22159. (i) Partridge; Vorster.

Lord Berners was a diplomat as well as a musician and essentially self-taught, but he was the only English composer who was admired by both Diaghilev and Beecham. Both responded to Berners's witty eccentricity and hints of Gallic wit, within a musical style which often retained an underlying Englishness – demonstrated subtly here in the opening *Polka.* Berners was a painter and poet too; the miniscule, lovelorn *Le Poisson d'or* was based on his own poem and has a certain Debussian atmosphere, while the *Trois petites marches* and *Fragments psychologiques* are Satiesque, and not just in their titles. The longest of the piano pieces is the engagingly nostalgic *Valse.*

Berners's pastiche of German *Lieder* has the piano opening gruffly to contrast a lyrical vocal line romantically addressing a white pig. The French *chansons*, however, are not parodies, but readily idiomatic, with *La Fiancée du timbalier* engagingly spirited. Of the English songs, Tom Filuter's dialogue is brilliantly chimerical, and the 1920 set are most winning, especially the opening *Lullaby.*

The three later songs of 1921 are a charming rediscovery of the English folk idiom, while the sentimental *Red roses and red noses* has a flowing lyrical line. It is followed by the irrepressible *Come on Algernon,* about the insatiable Daisy, who always 'asked for more!' – a perfect music-hall number, written for the film *Champagne Charlie;* it makes a delightful pay-off to end the recital. Ian Partridge obviously relishes the many stylistic changes like a vocal chameleon, and his words are clear too. Len Vorster backs him up splendidly and is completely at home in the solo piano music. The recording is truthful and this makes a fine introduction to an underrated composer, who has a distinct voice of his own.

BERNSTEIN, Leonard (1918–90)

Candide: Overture.

(B) *** DG (ADD) Classikon 445 129-2. LAPO, composer – BARBER: *Adagio for Strings;* COPLAND: *Appalachian Spring;* SCHUMAN: *American Festival Overture.* ***

Candide: Overture; Facsimile (choreographic essay); *Fancy Free* (ballet); *On the Town* (3 dance episodes).

(B) *** [EMI Red Line CDR5 72091]. St Louis SO, Slatkin.

Candide: Overture; Fancy Free (ballet); *On the Waterfront:* symphonic suite; *West Side Story:* symphonic dances.

(M) *** Sony (ADD) SMK 63085. NYPO, composer.

(i) *Candide: Overture;* (ii) *On the Town* (3 dance episodes); (i) *West Side Story:* symphonic dances; (iii) *America.*

(M) *** DG 427 806-2. (i) LAPO; (ii) Israel PO; (iii) Troyanos with O; composer – BARBER: *Adagio* ***; GERSHWIN: *Rhapsody in Blue.* **(*)

(i) *Candide: Overture;* (ii) *On the Waterfront:* symphonic suite; (iii) *Prelude, Fugue & Riffs;* (i) *West Side Story:* symphonic dances.

(M) *** DG 447 952-2. (i) LAPO; (ii) Israel PO; (iii) Schmidl, VPO; composer.

Candide: Overture; West Side Story: **symphonic dances.**

(B) **(*) Penguin/Decca 460 656-2. Baltimore SO, Zinman – BARBER: *Adagio for Strings* **(*); COPLAND: *Appalachian Spring,* etc. ***

For many, this Sony compilation, issued under the 'Bernstein Century' logo, will be the ideal way of acquiring this orchestral theatre and film music. The fizzing account of the *Candide Overture* has never been surpassed and the sparkling *Fancy Free* ballet score is hardly less rhythmically seductive. The symphonic dances from *West Side Story* confirm Bernstein as a truly great tunesmith; apart from the music's life-enhancing vitality, the closing section is infinitely touching. The recordings, made between 1960 and 1963, have never sounded better: bright and free, with plenty of ambient space.

Bernstein's later, live, Los Angeles account of the sparkling *Candide Overture* has tremendous flair, his speed a fraction slower than in the earlier, New York studio recording for CBS/Sony. On Classikon it is part of an aptly chosen bargain collection of music by four key twentieth-century American composers.

Bernstein's Israeli recordings sound fuller than his earlier versions on Sony, and the *Prelude, Fugue and Riffs,* also recorded live, is vibrant and rhythmic, with Peter Schmidl a comparatively reticent soloist. The alternative collection offers the same performances but with alternative couplings, including a characteristically intense account of Barber's *Adagio.* The *Rhapsody in Blue* is, however, less successful than Bernstein's earlier, CBS/Sony account.

Though Slatkin cannot quite match Bernstein himself in the flair he brings to his jazzier inspirations, this EMI bargain collection is very attractive. Slatkin directs a beautiful, refined reading of the extended choreographic essay, *Facsimile.* As a gimmick, the song *Big stuff,* before *Fancy Free,* is recorded in simulation of a juke-box, complete with 78-r.p.m. surface-hiss and a blues singer with a very heavy vibrato. The sound otherwise is full rather than brilliant.

Zinman's *Candide Overture* is lively enough, but the orchestral playing lacks the sheer exuberance of Bernstein's own account, and the *West Side Story Dances,* although very well played, similarly have less rhythmic bite than the composer's own performance. The compensating factor is the richly expansive Baltimore recording, which approaches demonstration standard.

(i) *Candide Overture; On the Waterfront:* **symphonic suite.** (i; ii) *Serenade after Plato's 'Symposium'.* (i; iii) *Chichester Psalms.* **Highlights from:** (iv) *Candide;* (v) *On the Town;* (vi) *West Side Story.*

(N) (BB) *** DG Panorama ADD/Dig. 469 115-2 (2). (i) Israel PO; with (ii) Kremer; (iii) V Boys' Ch.; (iv) Soloists, LSO Ch., LSO; all cond. Composer; (v) Soloists, L. Voices, Tilson Thomas; (vi) Te Kanawa, Carreras & Soloists, Ch. & O, Bernstein.

This Panorama survey makes a really excellent sampler of Bernstein's special contribution to twentieth-century music, with the *Chichester Psalms* and the *Serenade* showing the

other side of a composer who was still perhaps at his most inspired in the world of the musical theatre. The *On the Town* highlights are taken from Tilson Thomas's excellent complete recording, but the rest are from Bernstein's superb accounts of his own music. The recordings are all first rate, and if no texts are provided this is still worthwhile and inexpensive.

(i) *Concerto for Orchestra (Jubilee Games);* (ii) *Dybbuk* (ballet): *Suites Nos. 1–2.*

(M) *** DG 447 956-2. (i) Chama, Israel PO; (ii) Sperry, Fifer, NYPO; composer.

The *Concerto for Orchestra* opens with the aleatory raucousness of *Free-Style Events,* featuring vociferous orchestral shouts. The final touching *Benediction* is eloquently sung here by José Eduardo Chama. The live recording brings music-making of striking intensity, not always immaculate.

The two suites taken from *Dybbuk* are no shorter than the original ballet, dividing the score broadly between passages involving vocal elements and those that are purely instrumental. Bernstein directs strong, colourful performances, cleanly and atmospherically recorded, with excellent vocal contributions from Paul Sperry and Bruce Fifer. The transfer to CD is first rate.

Divertimento for Orchestra; (i) *Facsimile* (choreographic essay); (ii) *Prelude, Fugue & Riffs. West Side Story:* symphonic dances (original version).

*** Virgin VC5 45295-2. CBSO, Järvi, with (i) Marshall; (ii) Meyer.

Järvi and the CBSO clearly enjoy themselves, especially in the elegantly polished and very spirited account of the *Divertimento.* There is some beautiful woodwind-playing in *Facsimile* and, not surprisingly, Wayne Marshall's contribution is glitteringly idiomatic. The same could be said for Sabine Meyer in the very jazzy account of the *Prelude, Fugue and Riffs,* while in the *West Side Story Dances* Järvi relishes the romantic melodies, which are exquisitely played, and finds plenty of rhythmic venom for the *Rumble.*

Divertimento; (i) *Halil;* (ii) *3 Meditations* (from *Mass*) for cello and orchestra; *A Musical Toast.*

(M) *** DG Dig./ADD 447 955-2. Israel PO, Bernstein; with (i) Rampal; (ii) Rostropovich.

The *Divertimento,* easily and cheekily moving from one idiom to another, is often jokey. *Halil,* for flute and strings, and the *Meditation* also beautifully reflect the individual poetry of the two artists for whom they were written and who perform in masterful fashion here. The other two party-pieces were recorded live in fizzing performances, *A Musical Toast* for André Kostelanetz, and *Slava* (a 'political overture, fast and flamboyant') to celebrate Rostropovich in Washington. Excellent recording throughout.

Dybbuk (ballet): **complete.**

(M) *** Sony (ADD) SMK 63090. Johnson, Ostendorf, NY City Ballet O, composer.

Bernstein wrote his ghoulish ballet on lost spirits for Jerome Robbins and the New York City Ballet in 1974, when this splendidly atmospheric recording was made. The score presents much the same happy and colourful amalgam of influences that you find in other Bernstein ballets. The vocal parts, although fairly substantial (and very well done), are merely incidental. The recording is brightly lit but spacious.

Facsimile (choreographic essay); (i) *Fancy Free* (ballet); *On the Town* (3 dance episodes).

(M) *** DG Dig./ADD 447 951-2. (i) Mense; Bernstein (vocals); Israel PO, composer.

The beach scenario of *Facsimile* recalls Poulenc's *Les Biches*. It is an attractively inventive and at times charming score. The companion ballet, *Fancy Free*, is another attractive example of Bernstein's freely eclectic style. The Israel Philharmonic does not match the New York Philharmonic Orchestra in virtuosity but it still plays with tremendous spirit and also enjoys excellent recording. What makes this version of *Fancy Free* special is Bernstein's own performance of the blues number, *Big stuff*, as the ballet's epilogue. Together with the colourful and vigorous dances from *On the Town* they are given vivid, if close-up, digital sound.

(i) *Fancy Free* (ballet) (ii) *On the Town* (3 dance episodes); (iii) *Prelude, Fugue & Riffs*; (iv) *Serenade after Plato's Symposium* (for solo violin, string orchestra, harp & percussion).

(M) (**(*)) CBS mono/stereo SMK 60559. (i) Columbia SO; (ii; iv) NYPO; (iii) Benny Goodman & Columbia Jazz Combo; (iv) Francescatti; all cond. composer.

Bernstein's pioneering 1956 mono recording of *Fancy Free* is here joined with his exhilarating early New York performance of the dance episodes from *On the Town*, together with the (stereo) *Prelude, Fugue and Riffs*, with its dedicatee as soloist, and the second recording of the *Serenade after Plato's Symposium*, where Zino Francescatti's response brings out the Hebrew flavour of the lyrical writing. But, like Stern before him, he is closely balanced, as is the orchestra, and Bernstein's passionate climaxes are given an aggressive fierceness.

3 Meditations for Cello & Orchestra (from *Mass*).

(B) *** DG (ADD) Double 437 952-2 (2). Rostropovich, Israel PO, composer – BOCCHERINI: *Cello concerto No. 2;* GLAZUNOV: *Chant du ménestrel;* SHOSTAKOVICH: *Cello Concerto No. 2;* TARTINI: *Cello Concerto;* TCHAIKOVSKY: *Andante cantabile* etc.; VIVALDI: *Cello Concertos.* ***

Bernstein's concertante piece, *Meditations for Cello and Orchestra*, is fully worthy of the subtlety of Rostropovich's art, and he plays it masterfully. This is part of a remarkably generous Double DG bargain anthology.

Serenade after Plato's Symposium (for solo violin, string orchestra, harp & percussion).

*** DG 445 186-2. Kremer, Israel PO, composer – GLASS; ROREM: *Violin Concerto.* ***
*** EMI CDC5 55360-2. Perlman, Boston SO, Ozawa – BARBER: *Violin Concerto;* FOSS: *Three American Pieces.* ***

*** Sony SK 60584. Hahn, Baltimore SO, Zinman – BEETHOVEN: *Violin Concerto.* ***
(M) *(**) Sony (ADD) SMK 64508. Stern, Symphony of the Air, composer – DUTILLEUX: *Violin Concerto.* ***

(i) *Serenade after Plato's Symposium;* (ii) *Songfest* (cycle of American poems).

(M) *** DG (ADD) 447 957-2. (i) Kremer, Israel PO; (ii) Dale, Elias, Williams, Rosenheim, Reardon, Gramm, Nat. SO of Washington; composer.

The *Serenade* ranks among Bernstein's most inspired creations, full of ideas, often thrilling and exciting and equally often moving. Gidon Kremer has all the nervous intensity and vibrant energy to do justice to this powerful and inventive score. *Songfest*, too, is one of the composer's most richly varied works. Characteristically, Bernstein often chooses controversial words to set and by his personal fervour welds a very disparate group of pieces together into a warmly satisfying whole. It was also an excellent idea for this fine benchmark recording to be recoupled with two other Kremer recordings of American concertos, if of different vintage. Both DG recordings are of excellent quality, atmospheric and clear.

In the *Serenade* Perlman may initially seem almost too confident, missing an element of fantasy in Bernstein's personalized meditation on Plato's *Symposium*, where the more reticent view of Gidon Kremer with the composer conducting seems to delve deeper. Yet Perlman brings home the more tellingly how each movement leads thematically out of the preceding one, until the final movement, much the longest, with its references back to the beginning. He also makes it seem a warmer piece, thanks to his range of rich tone-colours, set against the richness of the Boston string-sound.

As in the Beethoven coupling, Hilary Hahn gives an intense, deeply felt performance, crowned by a rapt account of the big *Adagio* fourth section, *Agathon*. Excellent sound.

Stern's temperament makes him an ideal soloist, and he plays very beautifully and with intense feeling. The snag is the balance of the early 1956 stereo, with the violin right out in front and climaxes unpleasantly coarse. There is no mistaking the adrenalin flow, but the lack of any kind of refinement in the orchestral tuttis is a severe drawback.

Symphonies Nos. 1 (Jeremiah); 2 (The Age of Anxiety); (i) *Chichester Psalms.*

(M) *** DG (ADD) 457 757-2. Israel PO, composer, (i) with soloists from the Vienna Boys' Choir.

Symphonies Nos. (i) *1;* (ii) *2;* (iii) *I hate music!; La bonne cuisine.*

(M) *** Sony SMK 60697. (i–ii) NYPO, composer, with (i) Tourel; (ii) Entremont; (iii) Tourel, composer.

Symphony No. 2 (The Age of Anxiety) (for piano & orchestra).

(N) *** Hyp. CDA 67170. Hamelin, Ulster O, Sitkovetsky – BOLCOM: *Piano Concerto 2.* ***

(i) *Symphony No. 2;* (ii) *Serenade after Plato's Symposium.*

(M) (**(*)) CBS mono/stereo SMK 60558. (i) Foss, NYPO; (ii) Stern, Symphony of the Air; composer.

The *Jeremiah Symphony* dates from Bernstein's early twenties and ends with a moving passage from *Lamentations* for the mezzo soloist (on DG, Christa Ludwig). As its title suggests, the *Second Symphony* was inspired by the poem of W. H. Auden, though no words are set to music in this purely orchestral work. The *Chichester Psalms* is one of the most attractive choral works written in the twentieth century: its jazzy passages are immediately appealing, as is the intrinsic beauty of the reflective sequences. These live performances with the Israel Philharmonic are not quite as polished or forceful as those Bernstein recorded earlier in New York, but the warmth of his writing is fully conveyed in these excellent recordings. With a playing time of just under 80 minutes, this DG Originals CD is exceptionally good value.

On Sony, with Jennie Tourel as soloist not as steady as Christa Ludwig on DG, there is a strong reminder of the lament Prokofiev included in his *Alexander Nevsky* music. In the Auden-inspired *Second Symphony*, with a piano obbligato impressively played by Philippe Entremont, there is no doubting Bernstein's own commitment, and that certainly comes over in these performances, which are even more concentrated and gripping than the later, DG versions; if the CBS/Sony Manhattan Center recording is not so well balanced, it is still exceptionally vivid. The reissue is made exceptionally valuable by the inclusion of the two engaging song-cycles, the first expressing the thoughts of a ten-year-old girl ('*I'm a person too, like you!*'), the second dwelling on culinary delights, from *Plum pudding* to how to prepare rabbit stew in a hurry. They are charmingly sung by Jennie Tourel, accompanied by Bernstein himself at the piano.

The alternative account of No. 2 is his very first (1950) mono version with Lukas Foss. The clear, forward mono sound reinforces the work's eclecticism, with the *Dirge* stridently dissonant, and the jazz interjections of the *Masque* contrasting boldly with the closing *Epilogue*. Foss is by turns evocative and dazzling, but he is too forwardly recorded. The 1956 performance of the *Serenade* has Stern even more naturally attuned to the score than Francescatti in the later stereo version (see above), but the recording again suffers from the unnaturally forward balance.

Any new version of a major Bernstein work has to stand comparison with Bernstein's own recordings, and even by that test this fine Hyperion account of *The Age of Anxiety* stands up well. As in Bernstein's recording with Lukas Foss, the piano soloist is presented as a concerto soloist, not only balanced forwardly, but encouraged to play characterfully, with expressive warmth. Marc-André Hamelin is outstanding in that role, subtler than Foss with a wider expressive and dynamic range, helped by refined recording and accompaniment. Under Sitkovetsky, the Ulster Orchestra plays brilliantly, giving cogency to the odd, programme-based structure.

(i) *Symphony No. 3 (Kaddish)*; (ii) *Chichester Psalms.*

(M) *** DG 447 954-2. (i) Caballé, Wager, V. Boys' Ch.; (ii) Soloist from V. Boys' Ch.; (i–ii) Wiener Jeunesse Ch., Israel PO, composer.

(M) *** CBS (ADD) SMK 60595. (i) Montealegre, Tourel, Columbus Boychoir; (ii) Bogart; (i–ii) Camerata Singers, NYPO, composer.

*** Erato 3984-21669-2. (i) Mattila, Menuhin; (ii) Mills; French R. Ch. & PO, Sado.

The *Third Symphony*, written in memory of John F. Kennedy, also coupled with the *Psalms*, is recorded on DG in its revised version (with a male speaker) which concentrates the original concept of a dialogue between man and God, a challenge from earth to heaven.

The Sony recordings were made in the Manhattan Center in the mid-1960s; the acoustic is agreeably spacious, and many may prefer them to the later, Israeli, DG versions. However, the spoken dialogue in the *Kaddish Symphony* is recited here with melodramatic fervour by Felicia Montealegre (Mrs Bernstein at the time) and this is a serious stumbling block. However, the performance of the *Chichester Psalms* is vividly projected by singers and players alike.

Menuhin, with his thoughtful, measured tones, is the opposite of most narrators in the *Kaddish Symphony* but the emotion is just as intensely conveyed. Karita Mattila is a radiant soprano soloist and the choir sings brilliantly, but at relatively measured speeds this does not have the dramatic bite of Bernstein's own recordings, though the sound here is fuller and clearer. In the *Chichester Psalms* the choir and orchestra seem more at home in Bernstein's jazzy syncopations, giving a dazzling performance, vividly recorded, with Joseph Mills from the New College, Oxford, choir a fine treble soloist.

VOCAL MUSIC

Arias & Barcarolles. On the Town: Some other time; Lonely town; Carried away; I can cook. Peter Pan: Dream with me. Songfest: Storyette, H. M.; To what you said. Wonderful Town: A little bit in love.

*** Koch 37000-2. Kaye, Sharp; Barrett, Blier.

Arias and Barcarolles for two soloists and piano duet is a family charade of a work. It is a charming piece, given here – with the composer himself approving the performance – in the original version with piano and excellent, characterful soloists. The bizarre title relates to a comment made by President Eisenhower, after he had heard Bernstein play a Mozart concerto: 'I like music with a theme, not all them arias and barcarolles.' It became a Bernstein family joke. That half-hour work, very well recorded, is coupled with an equivalent collection of eight of Bernstein's most haunting songs and duets.

Chichester Psalms (reduced score).

*** Hyp. CDA 66219. Martelli, Corydon Singers, Masters, Kettel, Trotter; Best – BARBER: *Agnus Dei*; COPLAND: *In the Beginning*, etc. ***

Martin Best uses the composer's reduced orchestration. The treble soloist's chaste contribution is persuasive and the choir scales down its pianissimos to accommodate him. Excellent, atmospheric sound, set in a church acoustic.

Mass (for the death of President Kennedy).

(M) **(*) Sony (ADD) SM2K 63089 (2). Titus (celebrant), Scribner Ch., Berkshire Boys' Ch., Rock Band & O, composer.

Outrageously eclectic in its borrowings from pop and the avant garde, Bernstein's *Mass* presents an extraordinary example of the composer's irresistible creative energy. The recording is vividly present but has a convincing ambience.

Songs: La bonne cuisine (French and English versions); I hate music (cycle); 2 Love Songs; Piccola serenata; Silhouette; So pretty; Mass: A simple song; I go on. Candide: It must be so; Candide's lament. 1600 Pennsylvania Ave: Take care of this house. Peter Pan: My house; Peter Pan; Who am I; Never-Never Land.

*** Etcetera KTC 1037. Alexander, Crone.

A delightful collection, consistently bearing witness to Bernstein's flair for a snappy idea as well as his tunefulness. Roberta Alexander's rich, warm voice and winning personality are well supported by Tan Crone at the piano. The recording is lifelike and undistracting.

A White House Cantata.

(N) *** DG 463 448-2. Hampson, Anderson, Hendricks, Tarver, Acquah, Watson, Jenkins, L. Voices, LSO, Nagano.

A White House Cantata is a slimmed-down concert version of *1600 Pennsylvania Avenue*, the Broadway musical with book and lyrics by Alan Jay Lerner which Bernstein wrote to celebrate the US Bicentennial in 1976. It was a terrible flop on Broadway, but following what the composer himself planned, the cantata picks out a sequence of superb Bernstein numbers, both hauntingly lyrical and catchily vigorous. Movingly interwoven in this wittily irreverent survey of American history is the deeper strand of black emancipation. Nagano draws electrifying performances from singers and orchestra alike, with Thomas Hampson and June Anderson strongly cast as successive Presidents and Presidents' wives, and Barbara Hendricks and Kenneth Tarver as the attendant black couple.

STAGE WORKS

Candide (musical: original Broadway production): Overture & Excerpts.

(M) *** Sony SK 48017. Adrian, Cook, Rounseville and original New York cast, Krachmalnick.

This exhilarating CBS record encapsulates the original 1956 Broadway production and has all the freshness of discovery inherent in a first recording, plus all the zing of the American musical theatre. The lyrics, by Richard Wilbur, give pleasure in themselves. Brilliantly lively sound.

Candide (final, revised version).

✿ *** DG 429 734-2 (2). Hadley, Anderson, Green, Ludwig,

Gedda, D. Jones, Ollmann, L. Symphony Ch., LSO, composer.

(i) Candide (final, revised version); (ii) West Side Story: complete recording.

✿ *** DG 447 958-2 (3). (i) Hadley, Anderson, Green, Ludwig, Gedda, D. Jones, Ollmann, L. Symphony Ch., LSO; (ii) Te Kanawa, Carreras, Troyanos, Horne, Ollmann, Ch. and O; composer.

The composer's complete recordings of *Candide* and *West Side Story* have been coupled together on three mid-priced discs to make an irresistible bargain for those who have not already acquired one or the other of these inspired scores. *Candide* is a triumph, both in the studio recording (which Bernstein made immediately after concert performances in London) and in the video recording of the actual concert at the Barbican, bringing out not just the vigour, the wit and the tunefulness of the piece more than ever before, but also an extra emotional intensity. There is no weak link in the cast. Jerry Hadley is touchingly characterful as Candide, and June Anderson as Cunegonde is not only brilliant in coloratura but also warmly dramatic. It was an inspired choice to have Christa Ludwig as the Old Woman, and equally original to choose Adolph Green for the dual role of Dr Pangloss and Martin. Nicolai Gedda also proves a winner in his series of cameo roles, and the full, incisive singing of the London Symphony Chorus adds to the weight of the performance without inflation.

What is missing in the CD set is the witty narration, prepared by John Wells and spoken by Adolph Green and Kurt Ollmann in the Barbican performance. As included on the video of the live concert (Laser disc DG 072 423-1; VHS DG 072 423-3), those links leaven the entertainment delightfully. Even those with the CDs should investigate the video version, which also includes Bernstein's own moving speeches of introduction before each Act.

Candide also remains available separately, costing approximately the same price.

Bernstein's recording of the complete score of *West Side Story* takes a frankly operatic approach in its casting, but the result is highly successful, for the great vocal melodies are worthy of voices of the highest calibre. Tatiana Troyanos, herself brought up on the West Side, spans the stylistic dichotomy to perfection in a superb portrayal of Anita. The clever production makes the best of both musical worlds, with Bernstein's son and daughter speaking the dialogue most affectingly. Bernstein conducts a superb instrumental group of musicians 'from on and off Broadway', and they are recorded with a bite and immediacy that is captivating. The power of the music is greatly enhanced by the spectacularly wide dynamic range of the recording.

A Quiet Place (complete).

(M) *** DG 447 962-2 (2). White, Ludgin, Morgan, Brandstetter, Kazaras, Vocal Ens., Austrian RSO, composer.

In flashbacks in Act II of *A Quiet Place*, Bernstein incorporates his 1951 score, *Trouble in Tahiti*, with its popular style set in relief against the more serious idiom adopted for the main body of the opera. Bernstein's score is full of thoughtful and warmly expressive music, but nothing quite matches the sharp, tongue-in-cheek, jazz-influenced invention of *Trouble in Tahiti*. The recording was made in Vienna, with an excellent cast of American singers and with the Austrian Radio orchestra responding splendidly on its first visit to the Vienna State Opera.

(i) *Trouble in Tahiti.* (ii) *Facsimile.*

(M) **(*) Sony (ADD) SMK 60969. (i) NYPO; (ii) Williams, Patrick, Butler, Clarke, Brown, Columbia Wind Ens.; composer.

Trouble in Tahiti (1952), for which Bernstein wrote both words and music, is a very successful precursor to *West Side Story*; its style lies between the musical and the opera house. There is no lack of good tunes and memorable rhythmic numbers, and the performance has great flair and theatrical adrenalin. The recording is remarkably vivid. The ballet score, *Facsimile*, is very well played but makes less than its fullest rhythmic effect here. The composer's later version for DG (see above) is clearly preferable.

West Side Story (complete recording).

*** DG 457 199-2. Te Kanawa, Carreras, Troyanos, Horne, Ollman, Ch. & O, composer.

The composer's own recording of *West Side Story* is now reissued complete on a single disc, but is also available on three mid-priced CDs, coupled with *Candide*, which is also indispensable (see above).

West Side Story (film soundtrack recording).

(M) **(*) Sony SK 48211. Nixon, Bryant, Tamblyn, Wand, Chakaris, Ch. & O, Green.

Few musicals have transferred to the screen with more success than *West Side Story*, and many will feel that, even though the principals' voices are ghosted, the soundtrack recording is preferable to Bernstein's own version using opera stars. The film was splendidly cast and the 'ghosts' were admirably chosen. In the romantic scenes, 'Tonight' and 'One hand, one heart', the changes from sung to spoken words are completely convincing and the tragic (mostly spoken) final scene – here included on record for the first time – is very moving. Russ Tamblyn, who sings his own songs, is first class and Marni Nixon and Jim Bryant as the pair of lovers sing touchingly and with youthful freshness. The performance is conducted vibrantly by Johnny Green, and it is a pity that the CD gives an edge both to voices and to the brilliant orchestral playing.

Wonderful Town.

*** EMI CDC5 56753-2. Criswell, McDonald, Hampson, Barrett, Gilfry, L. Voices, Birmingham Contemporary Music Group, Rattle.

Wonderful Town was one of Leonard Bernstein's earliest successes, but it has unfairly tended to be eclipsed by the later success of *West Side Story*. Here, in a fizzing performance, starrily cast, Rattle rights the balance in a performance at once vigorously idiomatic and also refined in the many lyrical moments. The two characterful sisters finding their feet in the big city are brilliantly played here by Kim Criswell and Audra McDonald, not just charismatic as actresses,

but singing superbly. Thomas Hampson as Robert just as commandingly bestrides the conflicting problem of Broadway and the classical tradition, and Brent Barrett in the secondary role of Wreck delightfully brings in the cabaret tradition. Such numbers as 'Ohio', 'A little bit in love', 'Conversation piece' and 'Wrong note rag', rounded off with the big tune of 'It's love', can be appreciated for their full musical quality, with Rattle and his talented Birmingham group relishing the jazzy idiom. Bright, forward sound to match, and a helpful booklet which gives the full text.

BERWALD, Franz (1796–1868)

(i–ii) *Piano Concerto in D*; (i; iii) *Duo in D for Violin & Piano*; (i) *Musical Journal: Tempo di marcia in E flat*; *Piano Piece No. 2: Presto feroce. Rondeau-bagatelle in B flat*; *Theme & Variations in G min.*

** Genesis (ADD) GCD 111. (i) Erikson; (ii) Swedish RSO, Westerberg; (iii) Grünfarb.

Greta Erikson's 1971 recording of the *Piano Concerto* is serviceable, very nimble and cleanly articulated, but somewhat wanting in poetry. Josef Grünfarb gives a finely turned account of the *D major Duo*, but this partnership is less persuasive than Marieke Blankestijn and Susan Tomes on Hyperion.

Violin Concerto in C sharp min., Op. 2.

(BB) **(*) Naxos 8.554287. Ringborg, Swedish CO, Willén – AULIN: *Violin Concerto No. 3*; STENHAMMAR: 2 *Sentimental Romances.* **(*)

The Berwald concerto is an early work; its ideas are pleasing and mellifluous, very much in the Spohr tradition. Tobias Ringborg plays well, though he is not as spirited as was Tellefsen (EMI). Good recorded sound. The two Stenhammar pieces are rarities and sound persuasive in his hands. Apart from Christian Bergqvist's record on Musica Sveciae, this newcomer is the only current version of Tor Aulin's well-crafted *C minor Concerto*. A decent performance and good, well-balanced recorded sound.

Symphony in A (1820; fragment); Symphonies Nos. 1–4; Overtures: Estrella de Soria; The Queen of Golconda.

*** Hyp. CDA 67081/2. Swedish RSO, Goodman.

Roy Goodman's set with the Swedish Radio Symphony Orchestra has the advantage of including the early fragment of the *Symphony in A major* which has been completed – and very well, too – by Duncan Druce, and makes its début on records. Goodman is always alert and intelligent, though he tends to favour brisk tempi. He starts the *Sinfonie singulière* far too quickly and is forced to pull back when the brass enter. There is a certain loss of breadth here, and again in the *Sinfonie sérieuse*. The *Overture* to *The Queen of Golconda* comes off very well. Berwald's orchestration tends to be top-heavy, and the cool acoustic of the Berwald Hall in Stockholm slightly accentuates that.

Symphonies Nos. 1 in G min. (Sérieuse); 2 in D (Capricieuse); 3 in C (Singulière); 4 in E flat.

(M) *** DG 445 581-2 (2). Gothenburg SO, Järvi.

Symphonies Nos. 1–4; Overture: Estrella de Soria; Play of the Elves (Elfenspiel); Racing; Reminiscences from the Norwegian Mountains.

(B) **(*) EMI double forte (ADD) CZS5 73335-2 (2). RPO, Björlin.

Symphonies Nos. 1–4; (i) Konzertstück for Bassoon & Orchestra.

*** BIS CD 795/6. (i) Davidsson; Malmö SO, Ehrling.

As his earlier recordings of Berwald demonstrate, Sixten Ehrling has a natural feeling for the classic Swedish symphonist. Tempi are all well judged and there is an admirable lightness of touch. There is plenty of breadth in the *Sinfonie sérieuse* and no want of sparkle in the *E flat Symphony*. The *Konzertstück*, composed in 1827 (the year before the *Septet*), is a charming piece, much in its manner. This could well be regarded as a first choice in this repertoire.

Neeme Järvi's set is still highly recommendable; this is music that is wholly in the life-stream of the Gothenburg orchestra. The only reservation one might make concerns the brisk opening movement to the *Sinfonie singulière*, but Roy Goodman is even faster. Järvi's account of the *E flat Symphony* has marginally greater sparkle and lightness of touch. The DG recording is excellent in every way, and the warmer acoustic of the Gothenburg Concert Hall may sway some readers in favour of this set, particularly in view of the much more modest outlay involved.

The orchestral playing under the late Ulf Björlin is a little deficient in vitality; the recordings were made during a heatwave. Others may be more vital and alert, and Björlin does not succeed in creating the same degree of tension in shaping melodic lines. The *Reminiscences from the Norwegian Mountains* is attractively atmospheric, while *Play of the Elves* is a delightful piece. The *Overture, Estrella de Soria* is full of resourceful and finely drawn ideas. There are no alternatives at this very reasonable cost, and the EMI engineers have provided excellent recording, clear and quite full-bodied.

Symphony No. 1; Overtures: Drottningen av Golconda; Estrella de Soria. Tone-poems: Festival of the Bayadères; Play of the Elves; Reminiscences from the Norwegian Mountains.

*** Bluebell (ADD) ABCD 047. Swedish RSO, Ehrling.

The *Sinfonie sérieuse* was recorded in 1970 and is arguably the finest account of the work ever recorded (including Ehrling's later BIS version). It is beautifully played and unerringly paced. The overtures and tone-poems were recorded in 1966. Excellent performances, more vital and imaginative than the RPO versions by the late Ulf Björlin. Very well recorded, too.

Symphonies Nos. 3–4.

(M) (***) DG mono 457 705-2. BPO, Markevitch –
   SCHUBERT: *Symphony No. 4.* (***)

In the mid-1950s Markevitch pioneered this pair of Berwald symphonies and he gave superlative performances, with the Berlin Philharmonic proving outstandingly responsive. The DG recordings, made in the Berlin Jesus-Christus-Kirche, also come from a vintage period. The remastering has been outstandingly successful, and these fine readings celebrate an underestimated conductor at the peak of his interpretative form. The Schubert coupling is also very fine indeed.

CHAMBER MUSIC

Duos: in B flat for Cello & Piano; in D for Violin & Piano; Duo Concertant in A min. for 2 Violins; Concertino in A min. for Violin & Piano: fragment; Fantasy on 2 Swedish Folk-Melodies.

(N) (BB) *** Naxos 8.554286. Rondin; Lundin; Ringborg, Bergström.

None of these pieces is top-drawer Berwald, and none come anywhere near the string quartets in quality. However, there is no other commercial recording of the *Duo concertant* or the other pieces here. The *Duo for Cello and Piano* (1857), played persuasively by Mats Rondin and Bengt-Ake Lundin, alludes to material from the *A minor Quartet*. (Incidentally the title page of the score states that it was written for cello or violin, although it is rarely played on the latter.) In both the *Duo* and the *Quartet* the piano is hyperactive, as it tends to be in the roughly contemporaneous *Piano Quintets*. Berwald wrote the *Duo concertant* around 1816–17 for himself and his young brother to play. It is quite inventive and well written, although it is nowhere as individual as the *G minor Quartet* (1818). The *Fantasy for Piano* does not survive in Berwald's hand but judging from its use of the keyboard, it could well be by him. The *Duos* fill out the picture as does the fragment of the *A minor Concertino* that he wrote for Cristina Nilsson. The playing throughout is accomplished, although Bengt-Ake Lundin dominates in the *Duos*, not because his playing is anything other than sensitive and intelligent, but because of the recording balance. The sleeve and cover state incorrectly that the *Duo in D major* is in D minor, but this issue is well worth exploring; in this work Susan Tomes plays with the great flair and finesse.

Grand Septet in B flat.

(M) *** CRD 3344. Nash Ens. – HUMMEL: *Septet.* ***

Berwald's only *Septet* is an imaginative work which deserves a secure place in the repertoire instead of on its periphery. It is very well played by the Nash Ensemble, and is finely recorded.

Grand Septet in B flat; Piano & Wind Quartet in E flat; Piano Trio in F min.

*** Hyp. CDA 66834. Gaudier Ens.

The *Quartet in E flat for Piano and Wind* of 1819 is good but not vintage Berwald, though it could not sound more persuasive in this performance. The *Grand Septet* (1828) is a captivating piece, and so is the inventive *F minor Piano Trio* of 1851. Delightful performances, on which it would be difficult to improve, and excellent recording too. This augurs well for this enterprise.

Piano Quintet No. 1 in C min.; Piano Trio No. 4 in C; Duo in D for Violin & Piano.

**(*) Hyp. CDA 66835. Tomes, Gaudier Ens.

The *Piano Quintet* (1853) comes off marvellously. Susan Tomes is both sensitive and expert, and the Gaudier Ensemble are hardly less distinguished. In the *Piano Trio No. 4* and in the less inventive *D major Duo* the balance makes her sound too dominant. True, the *Duo* is for piano and violin – not the other way round – but the violinist, Marieke Blankenstijn, an impeccable artist, sounds far too pale and reticent. The Naxos recordings of the three *Piano Quintets* by Bengt-Ake Ludin and the Uppsala Chamber Soloists are, alas, not recommendable.

Piano Trios Nos. 1 in E flat; 2 in F min.; 3 in D min.

(N) (BB) *** Naxos 8.555001. Prunyi, Kiss, Onczay.

These three mature piano trios echo the symphonies in their sharp originality, full of surprising twists and turns, often like a more quirky Mendelssohn. The second of the three is the most striking in a troubled F minor, starting with a broodingly intense first movement. Excellent performances from three Hungarian players, very well recorded.

Piano Trios No. 4 in C; in C (1845); in C & E flat (fragments).

(N) (BB) *** Naxos 8.555002. Dráfi, Modrian, Kertész.

In the second CD the other Hungarian team is first class. The recordings were made respectively in the Italian Institute in Budapest and the Festetič Castle at Keszthely and are bright and well detailed.

String Quartet No. 1 in G min.

(M) *** CRD (ADD) 3361. Chilingirian Qt – WIKMANSON: Quartet. ***

The *G minor Quartet* is a remarkably assured piece, and the first movement is full of audacious modulations, with themes both characterful and appealing. The Chilingirian players give a well-shaped and sensitive account of it. They are truthfully recorded, and the coupling – another Swedish quartet – enhances the attractions of this issue. Strongly recommended.

String Quartets Nos. 1; 2 in A min.; 3 in E flat.

*** BIS CD 759. Yggdrasil Qt.

First-rate performances by this young Swedish ensemble of their great compatriot's output in this medium. They are both original and rewarding. This gifted ensemble play them very well indeed and are splendidly recorded. Anyone who enjoys the Mendelssohn or Schumann *Quartets* should not delay in investigating this music.

BESOZZI, Alessandro (1702–93)

Sonatas for Oboe & Bassoon Nos. 1–6.

*** Tactus TC 700210. Baccini, Perfetti (with Celegbin).

Alessandro Besozzi was both a composer and an outstanding oboist from the age of twelve onwards; he lived in Turin with his brother, Girolami, a fine bassoonist. Their lives were so intertwined, both personally and musically, that they became a star act – even dressing alike, down to the smallest detail, according to Charles Burney. Mozart was another admirer. Alessandro's music has grace and charm and makes virtuoso demands on the oboe, while for the most part the bassoon trundles or scurries below. Yet at times he has much more than a continuo, playing with the oboe, or echoing a phrase. The performances here are admirable, catching the music's galant charm and its underlying geniality; the two instruments are nicely balanced.

BIBER, Heinrich (1644–1704)

Balletae a 4 Violettae Nos. 1–7; Battalia in D; Peasants' Churchgoing Sonata in B flat a 6; Sonatas Nos. 1–2 a 8 for 2 Clarini, 6 Violae; 3–4 a 5 Violae; Sonata a 7 for 6 Trumpets, Tramburin & Organ (168).

(N) (B) *** Teldec Ultima (ADD) 8573 87793-2 (2). VCM, Harnoncourt – *Requiem in F min.*, etc. ***

This is a good and varied introduction to Biber's music. The battle sequence itself has some hair-raising instrumental effects, including barbaric pizzicati representing the cannon. The picture of '*the dissolute company*' brings a half-minute of well-organized instrumental cacophony. In the *March* there is a bizarre fife-and-drum imitation by violin and double-bass. The piece closes with a *Lament of the Wounded Musketeers*. The *Sonatas* for strings and clarini (and notably the *Peasants' Churchgoing*) show lyrical pictorial effects as well as dramatic ones. The performances have great character – Nikolaus Harnoncourt was always good at explosive accents – and are very well recorded. This now comes as part of an Ultima Double coupled with vocal music (see below).

Ballettae à 4 Violettae; Battalia à 10; Sonata Sancti Polycarpi à 9. Sonatae tam Aris quam Aulis servientes: I à 8 & VII à 5. Sonata à 3 (for sackbut, violins & continuo); Sonata à 6 (for trumpet, violins, viols & continuo); Sonata à 6 (die Pauern Kirchfarth genandt); Sonata à 7 (for trumpets, timpani & continuo); Sonata pro tabula (for recorders, violins, viols & continuo). (i) Requiem in F min.; (ii) Serenada (der Nachtwächter).

(B) *** Double Decca (ADD) 458 081-2 (2) New L. Consort, Pickett; (i) with Bott, Bonner, Robson, Mark Ainsley, George; (ii) Grant – SCHMELZER: *Balletti & Sonate.* ***

This Double Decca derives from the Oiseau-Lyre label and currently offers just about the best Biber anthology in the catalogue. Philip Pickett's *Battle* sequence is less explosive than Harnoncourt's but many will admire its greater musicality. Pickett calls the *Serenade* (in which Simon Grant participates characterfully) and the *Peasants' Churchgoing Sonata* 'a programmatic tour de force' and the other instrumental sonatas are hardly less impressive. The *Sonata à sept* for trumpets and timpani is imposingly sonorous, while the *Sonata Sancti Polycarpi* uses the eight brass instruments in two antiphonal groups. The *Sonata pro tabula* alternates recorders, violins and viols with considerable charm, and the *Sonata No. 7* (*Tam Aris quam Aulis servientes*) offers a comparable interplay between trumpet duo, violi and viols. The *Sonata à trois* is most remarkable of all, featuring sackbut and solo violins with comparable ingenuity. The artists contributing are all experts, original instruments are used to pleasing effect, and the engineers have managed an almost perfect balance so that all the polyphonic lines are clear and well matched. In the *F minor Requiem* Pickett lays out his forces as they would have been positioned in Salzburg Cathedral in the 1690s, using three choral groups. The piece is powerful and makes a stronger effect here than in the 1968 Harnoncourt performance. Fine singing, remarkable music and excellent recording make this a very desirable Double indeed.

Battaglia; (Lute) Passacaglia in C min.; Partita VII for 2 Viole d'amore & Continuo; Violin Sonata (Solo representativa) with Continuo.

**(*) Teldec 3984 21464-2. Il giardino armonico (with
    ZELENKA: *Fanfare; anon: Tune for the Woodlark;*
    ONOFRI: *Ricercare for Viola da gamba & Lute)* – LOCKE:
    The Tempest. **(*)

The most impressive work here is the *Partita for Two Viole d'amore and Continuo*, a powerful piece concluding with a very fine *Arietta variata* which is in essence a chaconne. It is very well played indeed. So too is the *Solo Violin Sonata representativa*, a much lighter piece whose main interest is an ingenious series of bird and animal imitations: nightingale, cuckoo, cock and hen, and even a miaowing cat. If the lute *Passacaglia* is rather pale, the familiar *Battle* sequence is just the opposite and suits the generally rather aggressive period-instrument style, which also affects the coupled music by Matthew Locke. Rather bitty, anyway.

(12 Sonatae) Fidicinium sacro-profanum; Balletti lamentabili; (i) Passacaglia for Solo Violin; (ii–iii) Laetatus sum; (iii) Nisi Dominus; (ii) Serenada (der Nachtwächer).

*** Chan. 0605 (2). (i) Mackintosh; (ii) Harvey; (iii) Wistreich;
    Augmented Purcell Qt.

The *Fidicinium sacro-profanum* probably appeared in 1682 as part of the celebrations for the 1,100th anniversary of the founding of the Archdiocese of Salzburg. They are characteristically inventive works, varying between three and eight linked sections of considerable variety (rhythmic as well as melodic) and interest, very much the precursor of the concerto grosso. They are presented here with great freshness and give consistent pleasure. To add contrast, the Purcell Quartet intersperse them with other key works: the solo *Nisi Dominus* (Richard Wistreich in excellent form) and the dramatic duet setting of *Laetatus sum*, which is equally stimulating. Later, Peter Harvey returns as the Nightwatchman, singing against a winning pizzicato accompaniment. The famous *Battle* evocation is as impressive here as in any competing version. The second disc opens with the *Balletti lamentabili*, in which a haunting *Sonata* and a delicate closing *Lamenti* frame an *Allemande, Sarabande, Gavotte* and *Gigue*, all of which, for all their dance rhythms, maintain a mood of gentle melancholy. The programme ends with Biber's masterly *Passacaglia for Solo Violin*, which undoubtedly anticipates Bach's unaccompanied violin music. It is played superbly by Catherine Mackintosh. A splendid

set, among the Purcell Quartet's finest achievements. The recording is very real indeed.

Harmonia artificiosa-ariosa (7 Partitas), Nos. 1–3 & 5 for 2 Scordatura Violins & Continuo; 4 for Scordatura Violin, Viola di braccio & Continuo; 6 for 2 Violins & Continuo; 7 for 2 Violas d'amore & Continuo (complete).

*** Auvidis E 8572. The Rare Fruits Council.
(M) *** Chan. 0575/6. Purcell Quartet with Wallfisch.

These complete recordings of Biber's masterly *Harmonia artificiosa-ariosa* show us the amazing range of these seven partitas (or suites) which were published posthumously in 1712. Each work consists of a very free opening *Prelude* or a more structured *Sonata* (slow–fast–slow), usually improvisatory in feeling, and includes the usual dance-forms of *Allemande* and *Sarabande*, plus an *Aria* with divisions, and often closes with a lighthearted *Gigue*, although the *Third* ends with a remarkable *Canon in uniso*, liberally decorated with violin cascades. In many ways the three sets of performances are alike, and they certainly share the spontaneity and scholarship of the very best period-instrument performances. Tempi are usually similar, although the Purcell Consort tend to bring a slightly more spacious *espressivo* to slower movements. Their extra weight (with use of organ continuo) is especially telling in the passacaglias. The curiously named Rare Fruits Council also play with great energy and virtuosity and, again, effectively use an organ to add colour and weight to the texture. They are balanced rather forwardly, which reduces the dynamic range somewhat, but some of the solo passages have striking delicacy, and the chaconne-like variations of the closing *Seventh Partita* are very powerfully integrated. In short, you cannot go wrong with either of these recordings. We have listed the Rare Fruits Council first, as Auvidis manage to squeeze all seven partitas on to a single CD. Chandos have been forced to use a pair, playing for 43 minutes and 47 minutes respectively. But the cost has been reduced accordingly to upper-mid-price.

Harmonia artificiosa-ariosa: Partitas III & V. Rosenkranz Sonata No. 10; Passacaglia No. 16 for Solo Violin; Sonata No. VI; Sonata representativa (for violin & continuo).

*** BIS CD 608. Lindal, Ens. Saga.

Heinrich Biber is fast emerging as a major personality, and the melancholy *Passacaglia* for solo violin is totally memorable. But the hit of the programme is the *Sonata representativa* with its bird evocations – they are more than just imitations – including the nightingale, thrush, cuckoo (a most striking approach) and cockerel. Maria Lindal is a splendid soloist and the style of the playing here is vibrantly authentic: the ear quickly adjusts to the plangent (but in no way anaemic) timbres which suit this repertoire admirably.

12 Sonatae tam Aris, quam Aulis servientes.

*** Auvidis E 8630. Rare Fruits Council, Karemer.
*** Chan. 0591. Bennett, Laird, McGillivray, Cronin, Purcell Qt.
(B) ** Hyp. Helios CDH 55041. Parley of Instruments,
    Goodman, Holman.

Biber's *Sonatae tam Aris, quam Aulis servientes* are among

his most immediately attractive works, their direct appeal comparable with the Bach *Brandenburgs*. They combine appealing expressive elements and great rhythmic vitality. This robustly extrovert new recording from the Rare Fruits Council is full of character, vividly colourful and alive. In about half the sonatas (Nos. 1, 4, 7, 10 and 12) the authentic string group of seven players plus continuo are joined by one or two trumpets, and here the effect is quite spectacular. The works for strings alone, however, are splendidly full-bodied and colourful (helped by the liberal use of organ in the continuo). The energy and expressive vigour of the music-making here bubbles over. Highly recommended.

The Chandos complete set from the augmented Purcell Quartet is also excellent in every way, full of life and imaginative detail. The sound is first class, but the Rare Fruits Council remains first choice.

Indeed, by their side the much more intimate performances from the Parley of Instruments, sympathetically played though they are, sound rather pale. This Helios reissue is inexpensive, but the Auvidis Astrée disc is well worth the extra money.

8 Violin Sonatas (for violin & continuo) (1681); *Sonata pastorella; Sonata representativa in A* (for solo violin); *Passacaglia for Solo Violin; Passacaglia for Lute.*

*** HM HMU 907134/5 (2). Romanesca (Manze, North, Toll).

These phenomenally difficult *Sonatas*, with their high tessitura and bizarre effects, can be played only by a violinist of remarkable technical gifts. Such is Andrew Manze. He conveys to the full the tension that always springs from strong performances of technically demanding music, yet at the same time he retains an essentially expressive style, also featuring the improvisatory feeling in the writing, to say nothing of its sublimely volatile unpredictability. The recording has a fine, spacious acoustic, and only those who find the abrasiveness of authentic fiddling aurally difficult should stay away from this highly stimulating pair of discs.

Violin Sonatas Nos. 2, 3, 5, 7 (1681); *Passacaglia for Solo Violin;* (i) *Nisi Dominus for Violin, Bass Voice & Continuo.*

(N) *** ASV CDGAU 203. Huggett, Sonnerie; (i) with Guthrie.

Monica Huggett's period-instrument timbre and style of attack are no less gutsy and vibrant than those of Andrew Manze, with plenty of vibrant edge on the phrasing. But this is superbly alive playing and the unaccompanied solo flourishes of the *Second Sonata in D minor* surely anticipate Bach, as the unaccompanied *Passacaglia* reminds one initially of his famous *Chaconne*. But it comprises 65 repetitions of the ground – G, F, E flat, D – and some might feel that – for all Monica Huggett's skill – it outlasts its welcome; others may find it hypnotic. The Psalm setting, so resonantly, dramatically and touchingly sung by Thomas Guthrie, recalls Monteverdi. Here the violin figurations are clearly as important as the vocal line and the continuo, using organ as well as theorbo, gives fine support. Excellent, vividly forward recording.

VOCAL MUSIC

Missa Bruxellensis.

⬤ *** Alla Vox AV 9808. Soloists, La Capella Reial de Catalunya, Les Concerts des Nations, Savall.

This gloriously festive *Missa Bruxellensis* – a late (perhaps final) work, dating from 1700 – is scored for two eight-voice choirs, groups of wind, strings, trumpets, horns and trombones, and a bass continuo of organs and bassoons. The disposition of the soloists, choristers and instruments in the stalls, around the transept and in the cathedral choir was designed to add to the sense of spectacle, and the music is fully worthy of its ambitious layout. Its imaginative diversity, with continual contrasts between tutti and soli of great expressive power, shows the composer working at full stretch. The *Kyrie* opens in great splendour with the two antiphonal choirs and festive trumpets (*cornets à bouquin*). The closing *Agnus Dei* has the soloists singing radiantly but with piercing dissonance from Biber's extraordinary sustained suspensions, with the full forces then entering for the closing *Amen*. The performance here, superlatively recorded in the echoing – but never blurring – acoustics of Salzburg Cathedral, re-creates the work's première, and is truly inspired. This marvellous disc cannot be too highly recommended.

Missa Salisburgensis

*** DG 457 611-2. Gabrieli Cons. and Players, Mus. Ant., Cologne, McCreesh; Goebel.

**(*) Erato 3984 25506-2. Soloists, Amsterdam Bar. Ch. & O, Koopman.

Paul McCreesh in partnership with Reinhold Goebel turns to one of the grandest of all ecclesiastical events, when in Salzburg Cathedral in 1682 they celebrated the 1,100th anniversary of Salzburg as a centre of Christianity. Though the score survived, there is no specific mention of the composer – all was created for the glory of God alone – but shrewd detective work, described in the note, clearly points to Heinrich von Biber, who was soon to be appointed Kapellmeister to the archbishop. The blaze of sound on the disc is magnificent, with widely spaced antiphonal groups, choirs and instrumentalists, thrillingly capturing massive contrasts of sound.

Koopman's version of Biber's spectacular score has the obvious merit of being recorded in its original venue, Salzburg Cathedral. But the long reverberation period tends to blur the choral clarity, and it also affects the brilliance of the trumpets. Koopman's spacious approach must also have been dictated by the problems of resonance and, fine though his account is, it cannot match the superb DG version.

Requiem à 15 in A.

*** DHM 05472 77344-2. Almajano, Van der Sluis, Elwes, Padmore, Huijts, Van der Kamp, Netherlands Bach Festival Ch. & O, Leonhardt – STEFFANI: *Stabat Mater.* ***

Requiem à 15 in A; Vesperae à 32.

*** Erato 4509 91725-2. Bongers, Grimm, Wessel, De Groot,

Reyans, S. Davies, Steur, De Koning, Amsterdam Bar. Ch. &
O, Koopman.

As might be expected from the major key, Biber's A major
setting is more robust than its companion in F minor. It is
a gloriously exultant piece. Here death has very little sting,
with the promises of forgiveness and heaven to come. The
polyphonic and polychoral writing is spread across a wide
proscenium, with brass and voices echoing each other ambitiously in overlapping phrases. Although the *Vespers* is
hardly less complex and its writing is equally inventive, this
work depends more on continual contrast to makes its effect,
with the soloists consistently used in alternation with the
more massive choral and brass outbursts. Under Koopman
the performances here are inspired, with the solo team
matching voices and singing splendidly together.

Leonhardt's account is also very fine indeed. There is no
lack of spectacle, but the acoustic of Pieterskerk, Utrecht, is
ideally free from excessive resonance so that the results are
particularly fresh with remarkably clear detail, yet there is
the right warmth of ambience and a bloom on the excellent
soloists, choir and orchestra alike. The performance has
plenty of vitality and, for those interested in having a
beautiful setting of *Stabat Mater* by Biber's contemporary,
Agostino Steffani, this is an excellent alternative recommendation.

Requiem in F min.; Sonata St Polycarp à 9 (for 8 trumpets
and bass); *In festo trium regium muttetum Natale
(Epiphany cantata); Laetatus sum à 7 (cantata).*

(N) (B) *** Teldec Ultima (ADD) 8573 87793-2 (2). Soloists, V.
Boys' Ch., Ch. Viennensis, VCM, Harnoncourt – *Balletae;
Battalia, etc.* ***

The *F minor Requiem* has since been recorded with greater
success by Philip Pickett (see the Double Decca collection,
above). Alongside it, Harnoncourt's version tends to lack
consistency of musical purpose, despite fine moments. The
Polycarp Sonata, however, using eight trumpets, makes a
thrilling sound, and the two cantatas contain music that is
both beautiful and striking. The sound is excellent. This
disc now comes as part of an Ultima Double, paired with
orchestral and incidental music (see above).

BILLINGS, William (1746–1800)

Anthems and fuging tunes: *Africa; As the hart panteth;
Brookfield; Creation; David's Lamentation; Emmaus;
Euroclydon; Hear my Pray'r; I am the Rose of Sharon; Is
any afflicted?; Jordan; The Lord is ris'n indeed; O Praise
the Lord of Heaven; Rutland; Samuel the Priest (Funeral
Anthem); Shiloh.*

(N) ⊛ (BB) *** HM HMX 3957048. His Majesties's Clerkes,
Hillier.

William Billings was a Boston tanner and singing-master
who flourished in New England in the early period of the
emergence of the new American nation, and his anthems
and what he engagingly called 'fuging tunes' are wonderfully
fresh, and appealing. Although they are usually simply structured they are written in an idiom which has broken away

from the sober Lutheran tradition. The opening anthem
here *O Praise the Lord of Heaven* has a joyous spirited vigour
in its part-writing, and the repeated phrase, 'singing and
making melody' which enlivens *Is any afflicted* avoids any
possible hint of sanctimoniousness. Indeed the exuberant
sailors' anthem, *Euroclydon*, sounds for all the world like a
sea-shanty. Yet *Africa* has a simple touching melancholy,
which reminds one a little of the *Coventry Carol*.

Billings' funeral anthem *Samuel the Priest* is similarly
touching, but his very characteristic text 'merrily they sing'
restores the cheerfulness to *Shiloh*, while the Easter anthem
The Lord is ris'n indeed, with its joyful 'Alleluias', is wonderfully direct and exultant. Two of the 'hits' in his own time
were the plain one-stanza *Brookfield* and the magnetic,
hymn-like *Jordan*, but *Rutland*, often touchingly expressive,
brings an almost madrigalesque flavour to the linear interplay. The spirit of this music brings to mind the visually
striking white churches of New England, rather than the
devotional atmosphere of a cathedral. To quote the *Chicago
Tribune*, the music is sung with 'impeccable musicianship,
full-throated tone, warmth and security of blend and expressive intelligence', and, one might add, with great vitality
by His Majestie's Clerkes under Paul Hillier. It is beautifully
recorded in a not too reverberant acoustic; the words are
clear, but a website address is given from which full texts
can be obtained.

BINGE, Ronald (1910–79)

(i) *Elizabethan Serenade;* (ii; iii) *Saxophone Concerto;*
(iii) *Saturday Symphony;* (iv) *At the End of the Day;
Autumn Dream; Butterflies; Candles on the Table;
Farewell Waltz; Fugal Fun; Give Me a Ring; Homeward;
Inamorata; The Last of the Clan; I Like Your Smile; The
Look in Your Eyes; Man in a Hurry; Miss Melanie; The
Moon Looks Down; Morning Light; Perhaps I'm Young;
Sailing By; A Scottish Rhapsody; I Sent You Roses; The
Sound of Music is Everywhere; A Star is Born; Tango
Corto; There's a Light in Your Eyes; Under the Sun;
Waiting for Moonlight; The Watermill; What Do You
Know?; When You are Young.*

(N) (M) *** ASV (ADD) CDWLZ 245. (i) Nat PO, Gerhardt; O,
Walter Heller; (ii) Voss; (iii) S German RO, Composer;
(iv) Walter Heller & his Orchestra; Orchestra Raphael,
Hotter; or Dreamland Orchestra.

Ronald Binge's most famous pieces must be the *Elizabethan
Serenade* (which rightly opens disc 1), *Sailing By*, which has
been played at the closing of BBC Radio 4, accompanying the
Shipping Forecast, since 1973, or the delightful watercolour
portrait of *The Water Mill*. As this CD shows, his fund of
melody was unquenchable, and with his deftness of orchestration, it resulted in some first-class light classical music of
the type that blossomed in the 1950s and 1960s. The *Saxophone Concerto* and *Saturday Symphony* (conducted here by
the composer) are much longer than his usual short
character pieces, though are just as enjoyable. The recordings
(mainly from the 1960s) are taken from a variety of sources
but mostly feature Walter Heller & his Orchestra. Recom-

mended to all lovers of good tunes. The recordings range from very good to thoroughly acceptable, and it is fascinating to note that the performers of four of the pieces are unknown.

BIRTWISTLE, Harrison (born 1934)

Carmen Arcadiae mechanicae perpetuum; Secret Theatre; Silbury Air.

*** Etcetera KTC 1052. L. Sinf., Howarth.

Silbury Air is one of Birtwistle's 'musical landscapes', bringing ever-changing views and perspectives on the musical material and an increasing drawing-out of melody. With melody discarded, *Carmen Arcadiae mechanicae perpetuum* (*The Perpetual Song of Mechanical Arcady*) superimposes different musical mechanisms to bring a rhythmic kaleidoscope of textures and patterns. The title of *Secret Theatre* is taken from a poem by Robert Graves which refers to 'an unforeseen and fiery entertainment', and there is no doubting the distinctive originality of the writing, utterly typical of the composer. Howarth and the Sinfonietta could hardly be more convincing advocates, recorded in vivid, immediate sound.

(i) *Earth Dances;* (ii) *Endless Parade* (for trumpet, vibraphone and strings); (iii) *Five Distances for Five Instruments;* (iv) *Panic;* (iii) *Secret Theatre; Tragoedia;* (iii; vi) *3 Settings of Celan for Soprano & 5 Instruments.*

(N) (M) *** Decca 468 804-2 (2). (i) Cleveland O, Dohnányi; (ii) Hardenberger, BBC PO, Howarth; (iii) Ens. InterContemporain, Boulez; (iv) Harle, BBC SO, Andrew Davis; (vi) with Whittlesey.

There is no more individual or intractable voice in British music today than Harrison Birtwistle. Pierre Boulez, who directs the majority of the items here, has been his champion for many years, and he delivers performances sharply focused and powerfully intense. It was *Tragoedia* which in 1965 alerted us to a formidable new voice in British music, conveying deep, dark emotions behind a brutal façade. It is not a tragedy in the conventional sense but a ritual in eight compact, tensely argued sections. *Secret Theatre* over a span of nearly half an hour presents another ritual, contrasting timbres and moods, dance and song, with the brutality tempered by overt lyricism. The close of the piece is hauntingly poetic, one of Birtwistle's most telling moments.

The five players in *Five Distances* are widely separated (an instruction not well conveyed in the otherwise excellent originally DG recording) and this shorter piece is comparably intense. The Celan settings are a poignant and eloquent tribute to a Romanian-Jewish poet who suffered severely in the Second World War. The soloist, Christine Whittlesey, manages its angular vocal lines with richly beautiful tone throughout.

Earth Dances is yet another slow-moving ritual, brilliantly written for the orchestra, here superbly played in Cleveland, while the piece for trumpet and orchestra moves solo instrument through a kaleidoscopic processional of constantly changing aural images of great imaginative diversity. Its

language is yet again far from easily assimilable, but both performances and the Philips recording are outstandingly fine. The most famous item here is *Panic*, performed at the Last Night of the Proms in September 1995, its seemingly interminable progress causing near panic among the audience, many of whom found it chaotic and completely incomprehensible. So does I. M. Neither he nor R. L. finds Birtwistle's music particularly rewarding: the enthusiasm expressed above belongs to E. G.

(i; iii) *Melencolia I;* (ii; iii) *Meridian;* (iii) *Ritual Fragment.*

*** NMC CD 009. (i) Pay; (ii) King, Thompson, Van Kampen; L. Sinf. Voices; (iii) L. Sinf. (members); Knussen.

The NMC Birtwistle disc has the London Sinfonietta under Oliver Knussen in three works revealing the composer at his most uncompromising. *Ritual Fragment* was inspired by the death of Michael Vyner, the dynamic and influential artistic director of London Sinfonietta. Just as dark and even more obsessive are the two longer works on the disc, *Melencolia I* and *Meridian*, the latter the grimmest of love-songs.

Secret Theatre; Ritual Fragment; (i) *Nenia: The Death of Orpheus.*

(N) (B) *** CPO 9993602. (i) Hardy; Musikfabrik NRW, Kalitzke.

It is fascinating to compare this German reading of Birtwistle's impressive *Secret Theatre* with Boulez's on Decca. The playing of Musikfabrik may not seem so powerful, partly because of a less forward recording, but the concentration builds up with comparable intensity, and the final climax is, if anything, even more uninhibited. *Nenia: The Death of Orpheus*, the earliest work here, is an elegiac piece in which the soloist's vocalizing is punctuated by percussive sing-speech, an early example of the composer's obsession with the Orpheus legend which culminated in the large-scale opera, *The Mask of Orpheus*. *Ritual Fragment*, dating from 1990, is not just dark and intense but at times angry, demonstrating that, for all the brutality of expression, Birtwistle's emotions are fundamental.

OPERA

The Mask of Orpheus (complete).

(M) *** NMC D 050 (3). Garrison, Bronder, Rigby, Owens, Opie, Ebrahim, BBC Singers & O, A. Davis.

Birtwistle's *The Mask of Orpheus* is one of the most challenging operas ever written. The idiom may not be as abrasive as in some of Birtwistle's other works, often with lyrical vocal lines, but the telling and retelling of the Orpheus legend, with one version superimposed on another and with music reflecting that, makes it hard to take in for the listener who is unprepared. Even so, one cannot miss the magnetic intensity of Birtwistle's score. The words are fluid, so that the printed text gives only an outline of what is presented. Act I is broadly based on the death of Eurydice, poisoned by a snake; Act II follows Orpheus in his progress through the Underworld over 17 arches; and Act III, with its structure echoing the movement of the tide on a beach, rounds off the epic scheme, ending in Orpheus's death at the hands of the Dionysiac women, and the final fading of the myth.

With Andrew Davis controlling his massed forces masterfully, helped by Martyn Brabbins as assistant conductor, the intense originality of a score dotted with havens of sheer beauty, is never in doubt. Central to success is the thrilling performance of the American tenor, Jon Garrison, as Orpheus the man, well supported by Peter Bronder as Orpheus the myth. Jean Rigby and Anne-Marie Owens, less prominent in the story, similarly take on the divided and superimposed role of the heroine, Eurydice woman and myth. The recorded sound is superb, vivid in conveying the different musical layers, electronic as well as instrumental and vocal. The documentation is very full. It is good that NMC have issued this important set as 'three discs for the price of two'.

Punch and Judy (complete).

*** Etcetera KTC 2014 (2). Roberts, DeGaetani, Bryn-Julson, Langridge, Wilson-Johnson, Tomlinson, L. Sinf., Atherton.

Punch and Judy is a brutal, ritualistic piece. It may not make easy listening, but nor is it easy to forget for behind the aggressiveness Birtwistle's writing has a way of touching an emotional chord, just as Stravinsky's so often does. Stephen Roberts is outstanding as Punch, and among the others there is not a single weak link. David Atherton, conductor from the first performances, excels himself. The clear, vivid recording, originally made by Decca for their enterprising LP Headline series, has been licensed by Etcetera.

BIZET, Georges (1838–75)

L'Arlésienne (complete incidental music; ed. Riffauld).

*** EMI CDC7 47460-2. Orféon Donstiarra, Toulouse, Capitole O, Plasson.

The score of the complete incidental music that Michel Plasson and his excellent French forces have recorded is based on the 1872 autograph, and the singing of the Orféon Donstiarra is as excellent as the orchestral playing. The less familiar music is every bit as captivating as the suites, so that the performance has great charm, and the EMI recording is very good indeed. Strongly recommended.

L'Arlésienne: Suites Nos. 1–2; Jeux d'enfants.

*** Decca Australia Eloquence (ADD) 460 505-2. Cleveland O, Maazel – FRANCK: Symphony. **

(i) *L'Arlésienne: Suites Nos. 1–2;* (ii) *Symphony in C.*

(M) *** EMI (ADD) CDM5 67231-2 [567259]. (i) RPO; (ii) French Nat. R. O; Beecham.

(B) **(*) [EMI Red Line CDR5 69881]. ASMF, Marriner.

L'Arlésienne: Suites Nos. 1–2; Symphony in C; (i) *Carmen:* highlights.

(B) **(*) Erato Ultima 0630 18947-2 (2). Strasbourg PO, Lombard; (i) with Crespin, Ply, Pilou, Van Dam, Denize, Carminati, Ch. of Opéra du Rhin.

L'Arlésienne: Suites Nos. 1–2; Carmen: Suite No. 1.

(M) *** DG (ADD) (IMS) 423 472-2. LSO, Abbado.

L'Arlésienne: Suites Nos. 1–2; Carmen: Suites Nos. 1–2.

(M) *** Decca 466 421-2. Montreal SO, Dutoit.

(i) *L'Arlésienne: Suites Nos. 1–2; Carmen: Suites Nos. 1–2;* (ii) *Jeux d'enfants.*

(M) **(*) Ph. (ADD) 446 198-2. (i) ASMF, Marriner; (ii) Concg. O, Haitink.

With playing that is both elegant and vivid, and with superb, demonstration-worthy sound, Dutoit's polished yet affectionate coupling of the *L'Arlésienne* and *Carmen* suites makes a clear first choice.

Beecham's famous Bizet coupling now rightly reappears as one of EMI's 'Great Recordings of the Century'. His magical touch is especially illuminating in the two *L'Arlésienne* suites, and the early (1956) stereo gives the RPO woodwind striking luminosity yet plenty of body. The *Symphony* too sounds freshly minted. Although the playing here has slightly less finesse, its zest is in no doubt, especially in the finale, and the oboe soloist in the slow movement distinguishes himself.

Among other analogue couplings of the *L'Arlésienne* and *Carmen* suites, Abbado's 1981 DG recording also stands out. The orchestral playing is characteristically refined, the wind solos cultured and eloquent, especially in *L'Arlésienne*, where the pacing of the music is nicely judged.

Reissued on Australian Decca is one of Maazel's very best recordings: the music glitters and sparkles, and the sound (from the late 1970s) is altogether outstanding. Maazel chooses fast tempi in the *L'Arlésienne* suites, though not so fast that it sounds rushed, while the *Jeux d'enfants* is a delight, with some really delicate pianissimo playing from the Cleveland Orchestra. Unfortunately the coupling is not so outstanding (though still acceptable). Although Beecham and Dutoit are in a class of their own in *L'Arlésienne*, this Australian bargain CD will surely appeal to audiophiles.

Marriner's EMI account of Bizet's *Symphony*, which is generous with repeats in the outer movements, does not quite re-create the sparkling lightness of touch of his earlier Argo (Decca) version. In the first movement there is plenty of energy, but not the same sense of complete spontaneity. But it is still very enjoyable, and the two *L'Arlésienne* suites are beautifully played, the *Adagietto* given a gossamer delicacy. The Abbey Road recording is first class.

Marriner's Philips collection is generous, offering 11 items from *Carmen* and both *L'Arlésienne* suites, while Haitink's *Jeux d'enfants* is delectably played and superbly recorded in the Concertgebouw. The London recording, too, is attractively rich and naturally balanced. But the musical characterization – despite fine LSO playing, notably from the flautist, Peter Lloyd – is sometimes lacking in flair and the last degree of *brio*.

The Strasbourg performances under Alain Lombard date from the mid-1970s. The two *L'Arlésienne* suites are nicely turned, and the *Symphony* too is alive and well, with an elegant oboe solo in the *Adagio* and an infectiously spirited finale. The analogue sound is full and pleasing, rather than especially brilliant. What makes this Ultima Double especially tempting is the substantial set of highlights from a spontaneously vivid, complete recording of *Carmen*. Régine Crespin is in excellent voice, exuding a sexy sultriness, and she is well partnered by Gilbert Ply, a boldly romantic Don José. Van Dam's vigorous delivery of the 'Toreador's song' certainly carries the day. Lombard directs the proceedings with evident relish, helped by the enthusiasm of the Rhine Opera Chorus and warmly atmospheric recording with plenty of depth.

Carmen: Suites Nos. 1–2; Jeux d'enfants.

(B) **(*) [EMI Red Line CDR5 69861]. O Nat. de France, Ozawa – LALO: Symphonie espagnole; SARASATE: Zigeunerweisen. **(*)

Very good performances from the Orchestre National de France under Ozawa, and the recording is both vivid and atmospheric. If the couplings are suitable, this is worth considering, even if other accounts of this much-played repertoire have even more character.

Jeux d'enfants (Children's games), Op. 22.

(M) *** Decca (ADD) (IMS) 448 571-2. Paris Conservatoire O, Martinon – BERLIOZ: Overtures **(*); IBERT: Divertissement ***; SAINT-SAENS: Danse macabre, etc. ***

(N) **(*) BBC (ADD) BBCL 4039-2. PO, Boult – RAVEL: Daphnis et Chloé: Suite No. 2; SCHUBERT: Symphony No. 8 (Unfinished); SIBELIUS: Symphony No. 7 **(*).

Martinon's memorable account of Jeux d'enfants is reissued in the 'Classic Sound' series. The crisp trumpet fanfares in the opening piece set the seal on a performance notable for its vivid colour and delicacy of feeling. The sound is remarkably good.

Was Sir Adrian stepping in for Giulini on this occasion (a Prom from 1964?), for Jeux d'enfants, the Unfinished Symphony and Ravel's Daphnis was very much Giulini repertoire? In any event the Bizet is performed with the elegance, sparkle and tenderness one associates with the younger Italian maestro. Marvellous playing from the Philharmonia and a good BBC recording, which lacks only the last degree of range and sparkle.

Roma suite; Symphony in C.

(BB) **(*) ASV CDQS 6135. RPO, Enrique Bátiz.

Bátiz's performances are attractive, with very good playing from the RPO. Although he omits Patrie, Bátiz has a considerable price advantage and he receives excellent (1990) digital recording. In the Symphony the sound is full and weighty, adding to the impression that the performance is less lighthearted than usual in the first movement (repeat included), though there is no lack of vitality and, with its more serious manner, it is still both effective and enjoyable.

Symphony in C.

(M) *** Sony (ADD) SBK 48264. Nat. PO, Stokowski (with MENDELSSOHN: A Midsummer Night's Dream ***) – SMETANA: Vltava. ***

*** DG 423 624-2. Orpheus CO – BRITTEN: Simple Symphony; PROKOFIEV: Symphony No. 1. ***

(N) (M) *** Häns. CD 93013. Stuttgart SW RSO, Prêtre – RAVEL: Daphnis et Chloé: suite 2; La Valse. ***

(BB) **(*) Virgin 2 x 1 VBD5 61513-2 (2). SCO, Saraste –

BERLIOZ: Symphonie fantastique, etc.; CHAUSSON: Symphony. **(*)

(M) ** Sony (ADD) SMK 61830. NYPO, Bernstein – OFFENBACH: Gaîté parisienne, etc. **; SUPPE: Beautiful Galathea: overture. ***

Stokowski's exhilaratingly polished account of the Bizet Symphony was recorded at Abbey Road in May/June 1977, only three months before he died; it is a superb example of his last vintage recording period, as vital and alive as anything he recorded in his youth. David Theodore's oboe solo in the Adagio is very elegantly done and the moto perpetuo finale is wonderfully light and sparkling. A fine bargain coupling, ranking alongside Beecham. The couplings, too, show Szell at his finest.

The freshness of the seventeen-year-old Bizet's Symphony is also well caught by the Orpheus group, who present it with all the flair and polished ensemble for which they are famous. First-rate sound, most realistic in effect.

Saraste gives a distinctly purposeful account of the first movement, rhythmically strong and bold; the Adagio, with a rich-timbred oboe solo, blossoms romantically in the strings, and the Scherzo has striking impetus to lead to a high-spirited finale. The effect of the recording is fuller than that provided by the Orpheus group on DG, and the Scottish performance is enjoyable in its own way. Good value if you want all three works.

In a vivid live recording the Stuttgart Orchestra shows its paces impressively in Bizet's delightful symphony, particularly the strings. Prêtre's tempo for the opening movement (exposition repeat included) is just right, with a nice rhythmic lift, and the Adagio brings a memorable oboe solo. The unnamed principal has an almost vocal vibrato, and he phrases exquisitely. In the very brisk moto perpetuo finale the strings articulate with tremendous bustling precision, yet the second theme is able to relax and lilt seductively. The Liederhalle, Stuttgart, has a most attractive acoustic and the recording, although digital, has an almost analogue ambient warmth. If you want the couplings this disc is highly recommendable.

Bernstein's 1963 performance also brings much to enjoy. The finale, in particular, has tremendous brilliance which is most infectious, and the slow movement is affectionately done. On the downside, the first movement lacks the charm it ideally needs and the recording sounds a bit glassy, though it is better than it was on LP.

PIANO MUSIC

Jeux d'enfants, Op. 22.

*** Ph. 420 159-2. Katia & Marielle Labèque – FAURE: Dolly; RAVEL: Ma Mère l'Oye. ***

The Labèque sisters characterize Bizet's wonderfully inventive cycle of twelve pieces with vitality, great wit and delicacy of feeling and touch. Superb recording in the best Philips tradition.

VOCAL

'Chant d'amour': Mélodies: *Adieux de l'hôtesse arabe; Chant d'amour; La Coccinelle; Ouvre ton coeur; Tarantelle.*

*** Decca 452 667-2. Bartoli, Chung – BERLIOZ; DELIBES; RAVEL: *Mélodies.* ***

These delightful Bizet songs come as part of an outstanding recital of French repertoire, readily demonstrating the versatility of Cecilia Bartoli, who is so sympathetically accompanied by Myung-Whun Chung. Both voice and piano are recorded beautifully. The collection is considered more fully in our Recitals section, below.

OPERA

Carmen (complete).

*** DG 410 088-2 (3). Baltsa, Carreras, Van Dam, Ricciarelli, Barbaux, Paris Op. Ch., Schoenberg Boys' Ch., BPO, Karajan.

(N) (M) *** EMI CMS5 67357-2 [567353] (3). De los Angeles, Gedda, Micheau, Blanc, French R. Ch. & O, Beecham.

(B) *** DG 427 440-2 (3). Horne, McCracken, Krause, Maliponte, Manhattan Op. Ch., Met. Op. O, Bernstein.

(M) *** RCA 74321 39495-2 (3). L. Price, Corelli, Merrill, Freni, Linval, V. State Op. Ch., VPO, Karajan.

**(*) Decca 414 489-2 (2). Troyanos, Domingo, Van Dam, Te Kanawa, Alldis Ch., LPO, Solti.

** EMI CDS 56281-2 (3). Callas, Gedda, Guiot, Massard, Duclos Ch., Children's Ch., Paris Nat. Op. O, Prêtre.

** Teldec 0630 12672-2 (3). Larmore, Moser, Gheorghiu, Ramey, Bav. State Op. Ch. & O, Sinopoli.

Karajan's DG set of *Carmen* makes a first choice among modern versions. In Carreras he has a Don José who is lyrical and generally sweet-toned. José van Dam is incisive and virile, the public hero-figure; which leaves Agnes Baltsa as a vividly compelling Carmen, tough and vibrant, yet with tenderness under the surface.

Beecham's speeds are not always conventional but they always *sound* right. And, unlike so many strong-willed conductors in opera, Beecham allows his singers room to breathe and to expand their characterizations. De los Angeles's portrayal of Carmen is absolutely bewitching, and when in the Quintet scene she says *Je suis amoureuse* one believes her absolutely. Naturally the other singers are not nearly as dominant as this, but they make admirable foils; Nicolai Gedda is pleasantly light-voiced as ever, Janine Micheau is a sweet Micaëla, and Ernest Blanc makes an attractive Escamillo. The glowing stereo recording was made in the Salle Wagram, Paris, at widely separated sessions between 1958 and 1959, but in Allan Ramsay's excellent new transfer this hardly shows at all. The hall acoustic makes the chorus sound very resonant but gives an attractive theatrical atmosphere to the solo voices, caught naturally and without edginess, and well balanced in relation to the orchestra. At its new mid-price, this famous set reasserts its position near the top of the list of recom-

mendations and makes a worthy addition to EMI's 'Great Recordings of the Century'. Beecham adds his own special touch to the orchestral interludes. The documentation cannot be faulted, including session photographs and a full translation.

Bernstein's 1973 *Carmen* was recorded at the New York Metropolitan Opera. Some of his slow tempi are very controversial, but what really matters is the authentic tingle of dramatic tension which permeates the whole entertainment. Marilyn Horne – occasionally coarse in expression – gives a fully satisfying reading of the heroine's role, a vivid characterization. The rest of the cast similarly works to Bernstein's consistent overall plan. It is very well transferred and comes on three bargain CDs.

Karajan's RCA version, made in Vienna in 1964, owes much to Leontyne Price's seductive, smoky-toned Carmen. Corelli has moments of coarseness but his is still a heroic performance. Robert Merrill sings with gloriously firm tone, while Mirella Freni is enchanting as Micaëla. With recording full of atmosphere, and attractively repackaged at mid-price, this is a very strong contender.

Solti's Decca performance is remarkable for its new illumination of characters. Tatiana Troyanos is one of the subtlest Carmens on record. Escamillo too is more readily sympathetic, not just the flashy matador who steals the hero's girl, whereas Don José is revealed as weak rather than just a victim. Troyanos's singing is delicately seductive too, with no hint of vulgarity, while the others make up a consistent singing cast. Though the CD transfer brings out the generally excellent balances of the originally analogue recording, it exaggerates the bass, although the voices retain their fine realism and bloom.

Maria Callas was ideally suited to the role of Carmen, but her complete recording is disappointing. One principal trouble is that the performance, apart from her, lacks a taut dramatic rein, with slack ensemble from singers and orchestra alike. The moment the heroine enters, the tension rises; but by Callas's standards this is a performance roughhewn, strong and characterful but lacking the full imaginative detail of her finest work. The set has been remastered and a new booklet prepared for this latest reissue.

Sinopoli directs a thoughtful, clean-textured but generally unidiomatic reading of *Carmen*, matched by Jennifer Larmore in the title-role, singing with clear, firm tone, but never sounding sensuous or earthy in the way one requires of this red-blooded character. Thomas Moser as Don José sings cleanly, better served by the microphones than usual, and Samuel Ramey is a heroic Escamillo, though he is not helped in the 'Toreador's song' by Sinopoli's rather slow and detached manner. Most recommendable is the characterful Micaëla of Angela Gheorghiu, but this remains a curiosity of a set.

It would be hard to imagine a less French-sounding account of *Carmen* than the performance given live at the Met. in New York in March 1941, and offered here in a raucous radio recording, close and boxy. Gladys Swarthout is far too little represented on disc, and her magnificent contralto, firm and rich, is an instrument of wonder. The downside is that, though musically her singing is masterly, her characterization resembles Margaret Dumont in a Marx Brothers movie pretending to be a voluptuous young gypsy. Licia Albanese does not sound innocent enough for Micaëla, with the tone not pure enough. Leonard Warren may have been a heroic performer, but the voice with its juddery vibrato too easily comes to sound woolly, not incisive enough for the bullfighter. Only the American tenor Charles Kullman survives the test well, singing with sensitivity and refinement as Don José. The French Canadian Wilfred Pelletier directs a perfunctory account of the score, with the hard-pressed chorus almost comically unidiomatic. With so many excruciating French accents – and not a single French-speaking singer among the soloists – one wonders why they bothered to use the original language (Naxos mono 8.110001/2).

Carmen: highlights.

(M) *** Decca (ADD) 458 204-2 (from above complete set, with Troyanos; cond. Solti).

(M) *** DG (ADD) 457 901-2. (from above complete set, with Horne, McCracken, Krause; cond. Bernstein).

(B) **(*) DG (ADD) 439 496-2 (from complete set, with Berganza, Domingo, Cotrubas, Milnes, Amb. S., LSO, Abbado).

(M) ** EMI (ADD) CDM5 66663-2. (from above complete set, with Callas, Gedda; cond. Prêtre).

The reissued mid-price set of highlights from Solti's sharply characterful set is generous (75 minutes) and handsomely repackaged in a slipcase. A full translation is included, and the remastered recording sounds both brilliant, full-bodied and atmospheric, though still somewhat over-weighted in the bass. This is also available on Penguin Classics (460 652-2) – but with only 61 minutes included and no translation this is a non-starter.

The DG Galleria disc can also be recommended, offering 70 minutes of well-chosen excerpts from the Bernstein set recorded at the Met., the only snag being that the synopsis is not linked to the 14 different cues. However, luckily *Carmen* is not a difficult opera to follow!

The bargain highlights selection on DG Classikon offers a fairly generous sampler of the Berganza/Domingo/Abbado set, with some 69 minutes of well-chosen excerpts, including all the hits. The documentation relates the music to the narrative in a brief but succinct synopsis.

The Callas set of highlights returns to the original (1964) selection, offering 61 minutes of key items relevant to the narrative; so Callas sings in only about half the excerpts.

Les Pêcheurs de perles (complete).

(M) (***) EMI mono CMS5 652662 (2). Angelici, Legay, Dens, Noguera, Théâtre Nat. de l'Opéra-Comique Ch. & O, Cluytens.

Unavailable since the early days of LP, this superb EMI/Cluytens set of 1954 offers the finest, most warmly expressive performance on disc of this delectable opera. Ironically, its nearest rival is the Philips set of the previous year under Jean Fournet, also in mono (currently unavailable), both of them outshining later, stereo sets. Cluytens is an even more sensitive conductor than his Philips rival, less four-square, getting the music to flow flexibly; and his cast, idiomatically French, has no weak link. Martha Angelici as the heroine,

Leila, is both sweet and bright, with no Gallic shrillness, and Henry Legay has a degree of heroic timbre in the rounded, lyric quality of his tenor, while Michel Dens, as in other French opera recordings of the period, proves a firm, characterful baritone. With excellent choral and orchestral work, · one gets the impression of a stage experience translated to the studio. The mono transfer is a little dull on orchestral sound, but it captures voices vividly.

BLACHER, Boris (1903–75)

(i) *Alla marcia; Chiarina;* (ii) *Dance Scenes (La Vie).*

*** Largo 5142. (i) Berlin RSO; (ii) LPO; Shariff.

In addition to the early *Alla marcia* (1934), this CD couples two ballets: *Dance Scenes* and *Chiarina.* There is some Stravinsky in the former, and its sophistication, irony and syncopation (it embraces tango and rumba, as had Milhaud's *Saudades do Bresil*) would not have found favour with the Nazi notion of 'culture'. An inventive but uneven score. The post-war ballet is more wholly successful and elegantly mingles sambas and polkas with the cool, poised atmosphere of Stravinsky in *Baiser de la fée* mode. Very good performances under Noam Shariff, himself a Blacher pupil, and excellent recorded sound.

Concertante Musik; (i) *Concerto for Clarinet & Chamber Orchestra. Fürstin Tarakanowa: Suite, Op. 19a; 2 Inventionen, Op. 46; Music for Cleveland, Op. 53.*

(N) *** Ondine ODE-912-2. (i) Dimitri Ashkenazy; Deutsches SO, Berlin, Vladimir Ashkenazy.

The *Concertante Musik* of 1937 was the first Blacher work to find its way on to record. Incidentally, it was conducted by Carl Schuricht (not Johannes Schüler as the label said, as Schuricht was blacklisted) and its relaxed air and clever syncopations found no favour with the Nazi authorities. It is strongly diatonic and possesses a dry wit that is quite captivating. Its economy and lightness of touch are also to be found in the Suite from the opera *Fürstin Tarakanowa* and for that matter the *Zwei Inventionen* of 1954. Those who know Blacher's dazzling *Variations on a Theme of Paganini* will know what to expect: a resourceful and inventive musical mind and expert orchestration – in short, civilized musical discourse. The *Concerto for Clarinet and Chamber Orchestra,* written for the clarinettist of the Deutsches Symphonie-Orchester, Berlin, is highly entertaining and Dimitri Ashkenazy gives a good account of it. His father directs lithe and vital performances and is recorded with exemplary clarity. Strongly recommended.

Variations on a Theme of Paganini Op. 26.

*** Decca 452 853-2. VPO, Solti – ELGAR: *Enigma Variations;* KODALY: *Peacock Variations.* ***

Attractively coupled with comparable sets by Elgar and Kodály, the Blacher *Paganini Variations* make a delightful fill-up, a brilliant quarter-hour-long work not nearly as well known outside Germany as it should be. The performance is infectious in its pointing of rhythm, and jazzy syncopations are consistently interpreted with a sense of fun. The

Decca engineers have done wonders in splendidly capturing the unique acoustic of the Musikverein.

Der Grossinquisitor (oratorio; complete).

*** Berlin Classics 0093782 BC. Nimsgern, Leipzig R. Ch., Dresden PO, Kegel.

The Grand Inquisitor strikes a serious note; Blacher's oratorio draws for its inspiration on Dostoevsky's *The Brothers Kara-mazov*. The musical idiom remains strongly neo-classical, with Stravinsky and Hindemith closely in view. There is some powerful writing here, and the composer is well served by the distinguished soloist and the fine Dresden orchestra under Herbert Kegel. Very good, well-balanced recorded sound with fine definition and no lack of warmth.

BLAKE, Howard (born 1938)

Clarinet Concerto.

*** Hyp. CDA 66215. King, ECO, composer – LUTOSLAWSKI: *Dance Preludes;* SEIBER: *Concertino.* ***

Howard Blake provides a comparatively slight but endearing *Clarinet Concerto* which is played here with great sympathy by Thea King, who commissioned the work.

(i) Violin Concerto (Leeds). A Month in the Country (film incidental music): Suite; Sinfonietta for Brass.

*** ASV CDDCA 905. (i) Edlinger; E. N. Philh., Daniel.

It was the success of his music for *The Snowman* that gave Howard Blake the encouragement and the artistic breathing-space to write his beautiful and stimulating *Violin Concerto*. Christiane Edlinger is the soloist in what proves to be an inspired performance, caught 'on the wing'. The only snag is the excessively wide dynamic range of the recording. Blake's suite of string music written for the film *A Month in the Country* brings moments of comparable bitter-sweet, elegiac feeling. It is played most sensitively, as is the brass *Sinfonietta*, sonorous and jolly by turns. In terms of overall concert-hall realism, the recording is impressive and this record is strongly recommended.

BLISS, Arthur (1891–1975)

Adam Zero (ballet; complete); A Colour Symphony.

(BB) *** Naxos 8.553460. N. Philh. O, Lloyd-Jones.

Full of striking ideas and effects to illustrate four heraldic colours, the *Colour Symphony* here receives a refined and idiomatic reading, marked by superb wind-playing. More valuable still is the first complete recording of the ballet, *Adam Zero*, in which the process of creating a ballet is presented as an allegory for the ongoing life-cycle. Lloyd-Jones directs a dramatically paced performance, amply con-firming this as one of Bliss's most inventive, strongly co-ordinated scores, shamefully neglected. Full, well-balanced sound.

(i–ii) Adam Zero (ballet): Suite; Mêlée fantasque; Hymn to Apollo; (i–iii) Rout for Soprano & Orchestra; (i; iv–v) Serenade for Orchestra & Baritone; (i; vi–vii) The World is Charged with the Grandeur of God.

*** Lyrita (ADD) SRCS 225. (i) LSO; (ii) cond. composer; (iii) with Woodland; (iv) Shirley-Quirk; (v) cond. Priestman; (vi) with Amb. S.; (vii) cond. Ledger.

The *Mêlée fantasque* (well named) is even more striking than *Adam Zero*, with strong Stravinskian influences but with a characteristic elegiac section at its centre. After the *Hymn to Apollo*, although the rest of the programme is primarily vocal, it is in fact the orchestral writing that one remembers most vividly, for the *Serenade* has two purely orchestral movements out of three. The orchestra is almost more important than the voice in *Rout*. The solo vocal perform-ances throughout this CD are of high quality, with John Shirley-Quirk giving a swashbuckling account of the finale of the *Serenade*. In *The World is Charged with the Grandeur of God* it is again the orchestration that shows the composer's imagination at work. The recordings date from the early 1970s and are of high quality.

(i) Checkmate: Suite; Hymn to Apollo; (ii) Music for Strings; (iii) Clarinet Quintet; (ii, iv) Lie strewn the white flocks.

(B) *** Chan. 2-for-1 241-1 (2). (i) Ulster O, Handley; (ii) N. Sinfonia, Hickox; (iii) Hilton, Lindsay Qt; (iv) D. Jones, N. Sinfonia Ch.

The first of a new series of Chandos 2-for-1 Doubles makes an impressive Bliss survey. The *Music for Strings* is surely the key work here, and Hickox directs it spontaneously and with deeply expressive feeling. Vernon Handley conducts with complete authority and evident enthusiasm both the *Check-mate Suite* and the less familiar *Hymn to Apollo*. In the masterly *Clarinet Quintet* (see below) Janet Hilton and the Lindsays are totally persuasive, and the recording is most naturally balanced. The Pastoral, *Lie strewn the white flock*, is another of Bliss's most memorable works and is brought vividly to life by the passionate singing of the Northern Sin-fonia Chorus. Della Jones sings the *Pigeon song* touchingly, and the recording is demonstration class. On the whole, this is to be preferred to the Hyperion version (see below).

Checkmate (ballet): 5 Dances.

(M) *** Chan. 6576. West Australian SO, Schönzeler – RUBBRA: *Symphony No. 5* ***; TIPPETT: *Little Music.* **(*)

The five dances from *Checkmate* on the Chandos issue are well played under Hans-Hubert Schönzeler and, with its valuable Rubbra coupling, this is welcome back in the cata-logue at mid-price.

(i) Cello Concerto; A Colour Symphony; (ii) The Enchantress (scena for contralto and orchestra).

(M) *** Chan. 7073. (i) Wallfisch; (ii) Finnie; Ulster O, Handley.

Raphael Wallfisch is a powerful soloist in the *Cello Concerto*. This is a reading which brings out the red-blooded warmth of the writing, with the soloist strongly supported by the Ulster Orchestra under Handley. They are equally persuasive accompanying Linda Finnie in the extended scena which Bliss wrote for Kathleen Ferrier nearly 20 years earlier. There, Bliss was inspired by the individual artistry of a great musician – even though, as he himself said, he found it hard to reconcile the goodness of Ferrier with the character of Simaetha, the central figure in the passage of Theocritus which he chose to set. For this reissue Chandos have added Vernon Handley's authoritative and enthusiastic account of the *Colour Symphony* and throughout the recording is warm and atmospheric.

Piano Concerto.

(N) (M) **(*) Divine Art (ADD) 2–4206. Barnard, Philh. O, Sargent.

Bliss's *Piano Concerto* was commissioned by the British Council for the New York World Fair in 1939. It is a powerful work in the nineteenth-century Romantic tradition, and at the time it was hoped it could prove to be a British 'Emperor' concerto. It certainly displays a sense of design on a large scale, and Bliss manipulates his concertante forces and develops his themes with boldness and assurance. The snag is that those themes, although often lyrically attractive, are not strong or memorable enough in themselves. Even so, Trevor Barnard's excellent performance with Sargent and the Philharmonia is commanding, and there is much to enjoy. Barnard is obviously in complete sympathy with the music, and he gives a strong, passionate reading and displays considerable virtuosity. The original recording of the piano is excellent, but rather forward, while the orchestra is recessed and not ideally transparent, as is obvious in the opening tutti. Once the work gets underway the balance is effective enough, but the AAD CD transfer does not seem to improve the orchestral focus as much as it might. Nevertheless, a thoroughly worthwhile CD reissue.

Discourse for Orchestra; Miracle in the Gorbals (complete ballet); Things to Come (complete film score, reconstructed Christopher Palmer).

(BB) **(*) Naxos 8.553698. Queensland SO, Lyndon-Gee.

The Naxos issue is most valuable for offering not only a première recording of the *Discourse for Orchestra*, but the complete ballet score of *Miracle in the Gorbals*, colourful and vigorous in illustrating the sordid but moving tale of murder and salvation in the slums of Glasgow. The 18 brief sections are strongly contrasted in mood and atmosphere and are here given a warmly committed performance by the Queensland orchestra, as is the *Discourse*, even though the strings are challenged by the violin writing. The five movements from *Things to Come* are also welcome in Christopher Palmer's reconstruction of the original opulent scoring, though it is astonishing to find the famous *March* omitted. Good, warm sound.

Film music: Caesar and Cleopatra: Suite (ed. & arr. Easterbrook and Binney); Royal Palaces Suite; Things to Come: Concert Suite (reconstructed Lane); War in the Air: theme; March: Welcome the Queen.

(N) ❂ *** Chan. 9896. BBC PO, Gamba.

It seems extraordinary that Bliss's great pioneering film score for *Things to Come*, some 45 minutes of music, became lost in its original form. But in the formative years of the British cinema, as in Hollywood's early era of 'talkies', that was not an unusual occurrence.

Bliss had collaborated closely with H. G. Wells on the project, but in the final cut of the movie the recorded score no longer matched the action. Lionel Salter was called in at the last moment to edit Bliss's score and Muir Mathieson to record it. The premiere of the film put the music into the 'hit' category, and the public immediately wanted records of the truncated excerpts they had heard in the cinema.

Various records and arrangements were made but, fortunately for posterity, Sir Henry Wood had kept the test pressings of his 1935 78s of the original score, and eight of the ten sides were discovered in the late 1990s in the Archive Library of the Royal Academy of Music – fine recordings in mint condition – including unique copies of the uncut *Prologue* and *Epilogue*. The two 78 sides unaccounted for probably contained the *Rebuilding* sequence, and the records of the delightful *Ballet for Children*, the unforgettable *March*, and the highly imaginative *Pestilence* and *Attack* are reflected accurately by the published edition.

Now, thanks to Philip Lane, we can at last hear this inspired, wonderfully orchestrated score as Bliss conceived it, with the closing *Epilogue* so full of Elgarian nobilmente spirit. Bliss had been uniquely fired by his subject: his later music seldom approached its melodic memorability nor its vivid strength of characterisation. Moreover the performance here has tremendous flair and conviction and is fully worthy of the score, as is the state-of-the-art Chandos recording.

Caesar and Cleopatra had a chequered career as a film, with almost everything going wrong in production, and Bliss's score was never used. Fortunately it exists in a faded working manuscript, and again shows him in inspirational form. The various pieces and fragments have been skilfully put together here and the result is both atmospheric (the haunting evocation of the sea) and tangible, with attractive dance interludes for the Banquet scene, including a charming *Waltz*, followed by a delicate *Barcarolle*. The closing *Supply Sequence* shares the strong rhythmic flavour of *Things to Come*.

War in the Air, with its Waltonesque opening fanfare, was a splendid title and closing-credits piece of considerable panache, written for the BBC who produced this fifteen-episode documentary in 1954, as an answer to the famous American NBC series *Victory at Sea*.

The *Royal Palaces Suite* was written twelve years later for a BBC TV documentary broadcast on Christmas Day 1966, with a narration by Sir Kenneth Clark. It displays plenty of regality and also shows the composer at his most diverting and tuneful in the charming Waltz for *The Ballroom in Buckingham Palace*.

This admirable programme opens with Bliss's best march in the Elgarian tradition, written for a Pathé newsreel of the return of the young Queen Elizabeth from a Commonwealth tour in 1954, and altogether this splendid CD confirms Bliss as a composer of resource, who could write good tunes to order – at least in the early part of his career.

(i) *Introduction & Allegro;* (ii) *Theme & Cadenza for Violin & Orchestra.*

(BB) (***) Belart mono 461 353-2. (i) LSO, composer;
(ii) Campoli, LPO, Boult – ELGAR: *Violin Concerto.* (***)

The *Introduction and Allegro* (for full orchestra) sounds very impressive in this virile performance under the composer's direction. The *Theme and Variations* is shorter but no less striking. It was originally written for a radio play, written by the composer's wife. The performance, with Campoli a first-rate soloist, is authentic and vividly alive. The excellent mid-1950s Decca recording is well transferred, to make this a very desirable coupling.

(i) *Music for Strings;* (ii) *A Knot of Riddles;* (iii) *Pastoral.*

(M) (***) EMI (ADD) CDM5 67117-2. (i) LPO, Boult;
(ii) Shirley-Quirk, LCO (members), Morris; (iii) Michelow; Knight, Bruckner-Mahler Ch. of L., LCO, Morris.

Music for Strings represents one in the long series of successful works for strings by British composers, and here it receives a glowing performance under its most understanding interpreter. The LPO relish the beautifully judged virtuoso writing, and the recording is first rate. The remaining works here are two attractive song-cycles that show Bliss's art at its least demanding. He conceived the *Pastoral* (*Lie strewn the white flocks*) as a classical fantasy using mezzo-soprano, chorus, flute, timpani and strings. *A Knot of Riddles* is just as easy on the ear – arguably too easy – with English riddles translated from the Anglo-Saxon and provided with a solution by the soloist after each one. It is here sung with fine point by John Shirley-Quirk. Good recording.

CHAMBER MUSIC

Clarinet Quintet.

*** Redcliffe RR 010. Cox, Redcliffe Ens. – RAWTHORNE: *Clarinet Quartet;* ROUTH: *Clarinet Quintet.* ***
*** Chan. 8683. Hilton, Lindsay Qt – BAX: *Sonata;* VAUGHAN WILLIAMS: *Studies.* ***

The *Clarinet Quintet* is Bliss's masterpiece. The flowing lyricism of the opening movement is matched by the intense valedictory feeling of the *Adagietto*, in which the composer remembers his younger brother, Kennard, killed at the Somme in 1916. The work could not be better played than in this very beautiful performance by Nicholas Cox and members of the Redcliffe Ensemble. The recording, too, in the glowing acoustic of St George's, Brandon Hill, Bristol, is quite ideal.

Janet Hilton and the Lindsays also have the measure of the *Clarinet Quintet*'s autumnal melancholy; the recording is natural and well focused.

Conversations; Madam Noy; (i–ii) *Rhapsody;* (ii) *Rout. The Women of Yueh; Oboe Quintet.*

*** Hyp. CDA 66137. Nash Ens., with (i) Rolfe Johnson;
(ii) Gale.

The predominant influence in *Rout*, for soprano and chamber orchestra, and in the *Rhapsody*, with its two word-less vocal parts, is Ravel. The *Oboe Quintet* is a work of considerable quality. The music assembled here represents Bliss at his very best. A lovely disc which can be warmly recommended, and eminently well engineered, too.

String Quartets Nos. 1 in B flat; 2 in F min.

*** Hyp. CDA 66178. Delmé Qt.

These performances by the Delmé Quartet are not only thoroughly committed but enormously persuasive, and they can be recommended even to readers not normally sympathetic to this composer.

Piano Sonata.

** Divine Art 2-5011. Barnard – BUSONI: *24 Preludes.* **

Piano Sonata; Pieces: *Bliss (One-Step); Miniature Scherzo; Rout Trot; Study; Suite; Triptych.* arr. of BACH: *Das alte Jahr vergangen ist* ('The old year has ended').

*** Chan. 8979. Fowke.

The biggest work on the Chandos disc is the *Sonata*. Its neo-romantic rhetoric is less convincing than some of the earlier pieces Bliss composed, in particular the *Suite* (1925). There are some other lighter pieces, like the *The Rout Trot* and *Bliss (One-Step)*, written in the 1920s when his inspiration was at its freshest. Good performances and excellent recording, made in The Maltings, Snape.

Trevor Barnard played the *Sonata* to Bliss in the late 1950s and the composer made some annotations and corrections in the printed score that are incorporated here. But collectors should note that the Divine Art recording is distinctly monochrome and lacklustre. The Chandos disc is the one to go for.

VOCAL MUSIC

Lie strewn the white flocks.

(N) (B) *** Hyp. Helios CDH 55050. Minty, Pierce, Holst Singers & O, Davan Wetton – BRITTEN: *Gloriana: Choral Dances;* HOLST: *Choral Hymns from Rig Veda.* ***

Bliss's *Pastoral* is given a winning performance by the Holst Singers and Orchestra, with the choral sections (the greater part of the work) aptly modest in scale but powerful in impact. With glowing sound and very attractive works for coupling, this is an outstanding bargain issue.

BLOCH, Ernest (1880–1959)

(i) *America (Epic Rhapsody);* (ii) *Concerto Grosso No. 1 for Strings & Piano.*

(N) *** Delos DE 3135. Seattle SO, Schwarz; (i) with Seattle Ch.; Michaelian.

In 1927 the American magazine *Musical America* offered a $3000 prize for the best symphonic work on an American theme by an American composer. Bloch – who had emigrated to the USA only eleven years previously – felt eminently qualified, and submitted his epic rhapsody to a panel of judges which included Stokowski, Koussevitzky and

Stock. Not surprisingly, as it overflows with an endearingly naive and sentimental patriotism, it won hands down, with Stokowski declaring it to be a noble and masterly score.

Its three sections, lasting in total some 39 minutes, describe the struggles and hardships and the hours of joy and sorrow of the emergence of the American nation, leading to a finale which declares, in the words of Walt Whitman: 'As he sees the farthest he has the most faith.' Bloch throws a rugged view of ragtime and the mastery of man over machines into the melting pot and even a suggestion of the inevitable collapse. But fortunately it doesn't happen, and instead the work climaxes with a heartfelt anthem of praise, which the composer recounted came to him on the steamer on his arrival in New York Harbor in August 1916. It makes a superbly grandiloquent end to an endearingly contrived patchwork-quilt of ideas from both the Old and New worlds, ranging from *Half a pound of tuppeny rice* to *Swanee River*.

The performance could hardly be better, the playing (and singing) more enthusiastic or more spectacularly recorded, and the documentation includes not only the words and melody of the anthem (so that one can sing along) but a layout of the musical narrative, detailing the source of the melodies and quoting from Whitman's prose. The *Concerto Grosso* with its piano obbligato (one of the composer's finest shorter works) makes a refreshing postlude, again splendidly played and recorded.

Baal Shem.

*** Decca 452 051-2. Bell, Baltimore SO, Zinman – BARBER; WALTON: *Violin Concerto.* ***

(B) *** EMI Début CDZ5 73501-2. Shapira, ECO, Hazlewood – BRUCH: *Violin Concerto No. 1* **; BUNCH: *Fantasy* **; SARASATE: *Zigeunerweisen.* **(*)

Bloch's own (1939) orchestrations of his three popular Hasidic pieces for violin and piano, *Baal Shem*, offers a fine, unusual makeweight for Bell's prize-winning disc of the Barber and Walton concertos.

The EMI account of *Baal Shem* forms part of a début recital by the 24-year-old Israeli violinist, Ittai Shapira, designed to show off his artistry. A gifted player, who is perhaps more at home in this triptych than he is in the Bruch. A very fine performance, and very well recorded too.

Violin Concerto.

(M) *** EMI (ADD) CDM7 63989-2. Menuhin, Philh. O, Kletzki – BERG: *Violin Concerto.* ***

(i) Violin Concerto. Baal Shem.

*** ASV CDDCA 785. (i) Guttman; RPO, Serebrier (with SEREBRIER: *Momento; Poema* **).

(i) Violin Concerto; Hebrew Suite for Violin & Orchestra; (ii) Schelomo (Hebrew Rhapsody).

(M) ** Sup. SU 3169-2 011. (i) Bress, Prague SO, Rohan; (ii) Navarra, Czech PO, Ančerl.

Menuhin's deeply felt and finely recorded 1963 account is passionate and committed from the very first note, and any weaknesses in the score are quite lost when the playing is so compelling. Paul Kletzki accompanies with equal distinction. The Kingsway Hall recording sounds very well indeed.

The newcomer from Michael Guttman has both fire and colour, and no attempt is made to rein in the freely rhapsodic flow of the piece. It also has well-balanced, modern, digital recording.

Hyman Bress's recording is a thoughtful, ruminative account, well worth hearing and totally unforced. At the time of writing the *Hebrew Suite* is not otherwise available in its orchestral form. André Navarra's 1964 account of *Schelomo* is more high-voltage. Not a first choice, but those investing in these performances will find that there is musical satisfaction to be had here.

String Quartet No. 2 (1945); Night (1925).

(N)(BB) (***) Dutton mono CDBP 9713. Griller Qt – DVORAK: *Quartet No. 12 (American);* MOZART: *Adagio & Fugue.* ***

It is sad that the string quartets of Ernest Bloch have become so neglected. When this second of the five quartets appeared in 1945, Bloch's reputation was at its highest, and it was greeted (by Ernest Newman among others) as a successor to late Beethoven. This recording appeared two years later and consolidated such views, only to have its impact dissipated when Bloch went on to write three more quartets in the same vein which have far less cohesion. In No. 2 the material, strong and memorable, is worked into tautly constructed arguments, never more convincingly than with the Griller Quartet in their heyday just after the war. It was then the leading British quartet of the time, perfectly matched, and helped here by early Decca ffrr recording superbly transferred by Dutton. The Dvořák and Mozart items are equally recommendable.

(i) Israel Symphony; (ii) Schelomo.

(M) **(*) Van. 08 4047.71. (i) Christensen, Basinger, Fraenkel, Politis, Heder, Watts; (ii) Nelsova; Utah SO, Abravanel.

Bloch's *Israel Symphony* is a large-scale work, but the music has something in common with the soundtracks of Hollywood's biblical epics. The performance here has vigour and spontaneity, and the only snag is that the soloists, who are introduced at the end of the work, are wobbly and not especially distinguished. *Schelomo* is an appropriate coupling. The recordings were made in 1967 and are transferred to CD with great success.

Schelomo (Hebraic Rhapsody) for cello and orchestra.

(BB) *** Virgin 2 x 1 VBD5 61490-2. Isserlis, LSO, Hickox – ELGAR: *Cello Concerto;* KABALEVSKY: *Cello Concerto No. 2;* R. STRAUSS: *Don Quixote;* TCHAIKOVSKY: *Rococo Variations,* etc.

(M) *** DG 457 761-2. Fournier, BPO, Wallenstein – BRUCH: *Kol Nidrei;* LALO: *Cello Concerto;* SAINT-SAENS: *Cello Concerto No. 1.* ***

*** RCA RD 60757. Harnoy, LPO, Mackerras – BRUCH: *Adagio on Celtic Themes,* etc. ***

*** Sony 57961. Ma, Baltimore SO, Zinman – ALBERT: *Cello Concerto;* BARTOK: *Viola Concerto.* ***

(M) *** Sony (ADD) SBK 48278. Rose, Phd. O, Ormandy – FAURE: *Elégie* ***; LALO: *Concerto* **(*); TCHAIKOVSKY: *Rococo Variations.* ***

** MDG 0321 0215-2. Schmid, NW German PO, Roggen –
HONEGGER: *Cello Concerto.* **

The dark intensity of Isserlis's solo playing and the sharp, dramatic focus of Hickox in the big, climactic orchestral tuttis are magnetic, preventing Bloch's youthful outpouring on Solomon and the Song of Songs from sounding self-indulgent. Warm, refined recording. This now comes as part of a highly recommendable and very generous bargain Virgin Double which includes key cello works by five different composers, all in first-class performances.

Fournier is a bit too closely balanced in this fervent performance, but the sound is very beautiful and he is excellently supported by the Berlin Philharmonic under Wallenstein. Apart from the balancing of the cello, the 1967 recording is excellent.

Harnoy also catches the passionate, Hebraic feeling of the melodic line and in this is matched by Mackerras, whose central climax is riveting. Fine, well-balanced and expansive sound.

Yo-Yo Ma is more cultured and refined than many of his current rivals, but there are moments when Solomon drops his voice, as it were, and dispenses his wisdom in a whisper rather than with full-throated fervour. This comes with an interesting first recording of a rewarding *Cello Concerto* by the New York composer, Stephen Albert.

A darkly passionate, rhapsodical account from Leonard Rose, with an equally strong accompaniment from Ormandy. The recording-balance is close, which reduces the possible dynamic range, but the compelling power of the music-making triumphs – this very good 71-minute compilation is worthy of a fine (perhaps underrated) cellist.

Ulrich Schmid gives a thoroughly idiomatic and well-recorded performance. However, all its rivals offer more generous couplings: at only 42 minutes' playing time, this is not a viable recommendation.

Voice in the Wilderness.

**(*) Australian Decca Eloquence 466 907-2. Starker, Israel PO, Mehta – BERLIOZ: *Harold in Italy.* **(*)

Voice in the Wilderness is a rather diffuse piece which at times sounds for all the world like the soundtrack of a Hollywood biblical epic, while at others its textures are so vivid and imaginative that such thoughts are promptly banished. Starker's is a finely played account, vividly recorded. Mehta seems just a bit lacking in intensity, but there is little current competition on CD, so this is well worth considering if the coupling is attractive.

3 Nocturnes for Piano Trio.

*** Simax PSC 1147. Grieg Trio – MARTIN: *Piano Trio on Irish Folktunes;* SHOSTAKOVICH: *Piano Trios.* ***

The first *Nocturne* (*Andante*) finds Bloch in Hebraic–Debussy mode, while the second (*Andante quieto*) is more overtly romantic and less interesting, though the Grieg Trio play it with much feeling, as they do the final *Tempestuoso.* The couplings further enhance the value of this issue, arguably the best the Grieg Trio have given us.

Violin Sonatas Nos. 1; 2 (Poème mystique); Abodah (Yom Kippur Melody); Melody; Suite hébraïque.

(BB) *** Naxos 8.554460. Kremer, Over.

In Miriam Kremer and Simon Over the sonatas have sympathetic advocates: both artists play with exemplary taste and sensitivity, and Simon Over produces a wonderful range of colour. So for that matter does Kremer, who has great refinement of tone. Good recordings, with plenty of space round the aural image.

Suite in A min. for Viola & Piano.

(***) Biddulph mono LAB 148. Primrose, Kitzinger – BAX; HINDEMITH: *Sonatas.* (***)

Primrose and his excellent partner make the strongest case for this piece and, considering its provenance, the sound is amazingly good.

BLOMDAHL, Karl-Birger (1916–68)

Symphonies Nos. 1–2; 3 (Facetter).

*** BIS CD 611. Swedish RSO, Segerstam.

Karl-Birger Blomdahl's *First Symphony* is not particularly individual. At the same time, a strong symphonic impulse runs through it. The *Third* is a dark and powerful piece; though it is, as one critic put it, 'deficient in thematic vitality', there is a powerful atmosphere. Good performances by the Swedish Radio Orchestra under Segerstam, and excellent BIS recording.

BLOW, John (1649–1708)

Ode on the Death of Mr Henry Purcell; Amphion Anglicus (songs): Cloë found Amintas lying all in tears; Why weeps Asteria; Loving above himself (Poor Celadon); Shepherds, deck your crooks; Ah Heav'n! What is't I hear?; Epilogue: Sing, sing ye muses.

(B) *** Sony (ADD) SBK 60097. Jacobs, Bowman, soloists, Leonhardt Consort, Leonhardt.

(i) *Ode on the Death of Mr Henry Purcell. Fugue in G min.; Grounds: in C min.; in D min.; Sonata in A; Suite in G.*

**(*) Virgin VC5 45342-2. (i) Lesne, Dugardin; La Canzona – PURCELL: *Songs & Duets.* **(*)

Ode on the Death of Mr Henry Purcell: Mark how the lark and linnet sing. Ah, heav'n! What is't I hear?.

*** Hyp. CDA 66253. Bowman, Chance, King's Consort, King – PURCELL: *Collection.* ***

The *Ode on the Death of Mr Henry Purcell* is a most welcome addition to the catalogue, particularly as it is performed so superbly here under Gustav Leonhardt. There are some striking chromaticisms and dissonances and some inventive and noble music. James Bowman is the only native singer, but the others (notably René Jacobs) are no less intelligent and stylish. Both the performance and recording are fine for this short but rewarding disc.

Where Leonhardt on RCA is spacious in his concept and more detailed in his concern for word-meanings, so that the result is also more polished, Robert King's spontaneous style is infectious, with the orchestral comments engagingly animated. Both performances are highly rewarding, and in the last resort couplings will dictate choice. The Hyperion disc is more expensive but includes an extra quarter of an hour's music.

Gérard Lesne and his fellow counter-tenor give a stylish performance, reflecting that of the younger master, but it is good to identify the character of Blow himself more clearly in the instrumental pieces of his which punctuate the series of Purcell songs and duets. The recorder players of La Canzona are on the abrasive side, not helped by the close recordings, but this makes an attractive and illuminating disc.

Venus and Adonis.

(N) *** HM HMC 901684. Joshua, Finley, Blaze, Clare College Chapel Ch., OAE, Jacobs.

(B) *** HM HMA 190 1276. Argenta, Dawson, Varcoe, Covey-Crump, L. Bar. & Ch., Medlam.

René Jacobs conducts a lively performance of Venus and Adonis, bringing out the dramatic bite of a piece that inevitably suffers by comparison with Purcell's Dido and Aeneas. Speeds are on the brisk side, never rushed, and Rosemary Joshua makes a delightful Venus, bright and sweet, singing with ravishing tone in her big solo towards the end. Gerald Finley, clear and firm, makes a splendid Adonis, and it is good to have a counter-tenor, not a soprano, in the role of Cupid, the excellent Robin Blaze. Fresh, incisive singing from the Clare College Chapel Choir, and clear, atmospheric sound. This now completely replaces the L'Oiseau-Lyre version under Philip Pickett, which at consistently slower speeds sounds dull by comparison, despite the characterful Venus of Catherine Bott.

Charles Medlam with London Baroque gives a period performance and takes care that the early instruments are well blended rather than edgy and that the choral sound is full, bright and clean. The soloists too are all remarkable for sweetness and freshness of tone. This record is now offered at bargain price in the Musique d'Abord series so makes a genuine alternative to René Jacobs's version.

BOCCHERINI, Luigi (1743–1805)

Complete cello concertos

Cello Concertos Nos. 1 in E flat, G.474; 2 in A, G.475; 3 in D, G.476; 5 in D, G.478.

(BB) *** Naxos 8.553572. Hugh, Scottish CO, Halstead.

Cello Concertos Nos. 4 in C, G.477; 6 in D, G.479; 7 in G, G.480; 8 in C, G.481.

(BB) *** Naxos 8.553571. Hugh, Scottish CO, Halstead.

Cello Concertos Nos. 1–8.

(BB) **(*) Arte Nova 85094-2 (2). Klein, Hamburg Soloists.

Cello Concertos Nos. 3 in D, G.476; 7 in G, G.480; 9 in B flat, G.482. (i) Aria accademica in B flat, G.557.

**(*) Auvidis E 8517. Coin, Limoges Bar. Ens., Coin; (i) with Almajano.

Cello Concertos Nos. 4 in C, G.477; 6 in D, G.479; 7 in G, G.480; 8 in C, G.481.

(M) *** Teldec (ADD) 9031 77624-2. Bylsma, Concerto Amsterdam, Schröder.

Cello Concertos Nos. 5 in D, G.478; 7 in G, G.480.

** Sony SK 60680. Ma, Amsterdam Bar. O, Koopman – BACH: Chorales. **

Cello Concerto No. 6 in D, G.479.

(B) *** DG (ADD) Double 437 952-2 (2). Rostropovich, Zurich Coll. Mus., Sacher – BERNSTEIN: 3 Meditations; GLAZUNOV: Chant du ménestrel; SHOSTAKOVICH: Cello Concerto No. 2; TARTINI: Cello Concerto; TCHAIKOVSKY: Andante cantabile etc; VIVALDI: Cello Concertos. ***

(i) Cello Concertos Nos. 6 in D, G.479; 7 in G, G.480; (ii) 9 in B flat, G.482; 10 in D, G.483.

(B) *** Erato Ultima (ADD) 3984 201040-2 (2). Lodéon; (i) Lausanne CO, Jordan; (ii) Bournemouth Sinf., Guschlbauer.

Naxos has now begun an impressive new series covering Boccherini's twelve cello concertos. (Our listing uses the Gérard catalogue, so the collector must be careful to identify the contents of each CD by the Gérard numbers.) They are beautifully performed on modern instruments but with concern for period practice, and superbly recorded. There is dedicated playing not just from the soloist but also from the excellent Scottish Chamber Orchestra under Anthony Halstead. Tim Hugh offers substantial cadenzas not only in the first movements of each work but also in slow movements and finales too. The formula in all these works is similar, even though each has its individual delights, with strong, four-square first movements, slow movements that sound rather Handelian, and galloping finales. Throughout, Hugh and Halstead make a stimulating partnership and all these works spring appealingly to life.

The Romanian musician, Emil Klein, successfully manages the joint roles of solo cellist and conductor of the Hamburg Soloists. He proves to be an excellent player with a small, sweet, cleanly focused timbre, his intonation secure in the instrument's upper range. Sharply articulated bravura adds to the character of the performances, while slow movements are shaped with touching eloquence. The Hamburg Soloists are a somewhat larger chamber group than their name suggests, although their tonal spectrum is amplified by a rather too reverberant acoustic. The nicely alert playing from the orchestra adds to the listener's pleasure.

Rostropovich's No. 6 is so compelling that reservations are swept aside. He is given an alert accompaniment by Sacher, and the recording has fine body and presence. This is now part of a self-recommending DG Double bargain anthology.

Christophe Coin directs his excellent Limoges period-instrument group from the cello, and they accompany most stylishly. With his small-toned baroque cello, his playing is subtle and fastidiously elegant, its expressive feeling never worn on the sleeve. He is the exact opposite of Rostropovich, and those who enjoy intimacy in these works will find this much to their taste.

Anner Bylsma is a fine player, well suited to this repertoire, while Schröder's accompaniments are most stylish and full of vitality. The 1965 recording is first class and, like so many of Teldec's *Das alte Werk* series, the immaculate CD transfer makes the very most of the sound.

Yo-Yo Ma has now taken up a period cello, and this coupling of Bach chorales with Boccherini does not work out very well. Ton Koopman directs with rhythmic point and finds plenty of orchestral colour, but Ma's at times somewhat recessive solo contribution is stylistically insecure, the timbre rather dry, and the playing itself lacking in charm. Finales come off best, though Koopman's cadenzas are not a great asset.

Lodéon's playing is stylish and eloquent, and in the *G major Concerto*, G.480, he is wonderfully fresh and fervent; in his hands the better-known *D major Concerto*, G.479 (also recorded by Bylsma and Rostropovich), has tenderness and depth. He is well accompanied by both groups, but the two Lausanne performances (from 1981) have slightly superior sound. The snag to this pair of records is the playing time of only 85 minutes, whereas the competing Bylsma collection manages to get four concertos (including G.479 and G.480) on to a single mid-priced CD.

(i) *Cello Concerto No. 9 in B flat* (original version, revised Gendron); (ii–iii) *Flute Concerto in D, Op. 27* (attrib.; now thought to be by Franz Pokorny); (iv) *Symphonies Nos. 3 in C; 5 in B flat, Op. 12/3 & 5;* (v) *Guitar Quintets Nos. 4 in D (Fandango); 9 in C (La Ritirata di Madrid);* (vi) *String Quartet in D, Op. 6/1;* (iii) *String Quintet in E, Op. 13/5: Minuet* (only).

(B) *** Ph. Duo 438 377-2 (2). (i) Gendron, LOP, Casals;
(ii) Gazzelloni; (iii) I Musici; (iv) New Philh. O, Leppard;
(v) Pepe Romero, ASMF Chamber Ens.; (vi) Italian Qt.

This most attractive anthology is well documented, and the famous *Minuet* could hardly be presented more winningly, the one digital recording here. It is also good that Gendron's version of the *Cello Concerto* is included, for he pioneered the return of the original version (without Grützmacher's reworking), and he plays it admirably. The *Flute Concerto* is a *galant* piece, elegantly played by Gazzelloni, and one can see why it was mistakenly attributed. Both *Symphonies* are full of vitality in these excellent performances under Raymond Leppard and are very well recorded. The Italian Quartet's performance of the *D major Quartet* is notable for its freshness and refinement. The charming *Guitar Quintets* are unfailingly warm and sensitive, and they are well recorded too, although there is a touch of thinness on top.

Cello Concerto in B flat (arr. Grützmacher).

(M) *** EMI (ADD) CDM5 66896-2 [566948]. Du Pré, ECO,
Barenboim – HAYDN: *Concertos Nos. 1–2.* ***
*** Sony (ADD) MK 39964. Ma, St Paul CO, Zukerman – J. C.
BACH: *Sinfonia concertante, etc.* **(*)

(BB) *** Naxos 8.550059. Kanta, Capella Istropolitana, Breiner
– HAYDN: *Cello Concertos Nos. 1–2.* ***

Working for the first time in the recording studio with her husband, Daniel Barenboim, Jacqueline du Pré was inspired to some really heart-warming playing, broadly romantic in style – but then that is what Grützmacher plainly asks for. Du Pré's admirers will surely feel that this is an apt choice for reissue as one of EMI's 'Great Recordings of the Century', and the disc now offers two Haydn cello concertos instead of one.

Yo-Yo Ma also chooses the Grützmacher version. He plays it with taste and finesse, not wearing his heart on his sleeve as obviously as du Pré, but with his warm, if refined, timbre and style not missing the romanticism. The recording is first class.

Ludovít Kanta's playing is distinguished by imaginative and musicianly phrasing and a warm tone. The Slovak players under Peter Breiner give a good account of themselves, and this can hold its own against versions costing twice or three times as much.

Complete symphonies

28 Symphonies (complete).

(M) *** CPO 999 401-2 (8). Deutsche Kammerakademie,
Neuss, Goritzki.

In this first complete survey of the Boccherini symphonies, Johannes Goritzki's achievement is remarkable. Himself a cellist, he shows a natural feeling for Boccherini's special combination of *galant* and classical styles, revealing the music's strengths rather than its weaknesses, making the most of its colour and revelling in its fecundity of invention and easy tunefulness. The playing – on modern instruments – of the German Chamber Academy Orchestra of Neuss is alert, polished and warmhearted, besides showing a nice feeling for Boccherini's delicate *Andantinos*, which are never sentimentalized. The recording is excellently balanced and has plenty of life and bloom. All the discs are available separately at premium price, but the box comes at mid-price and is well worth considering.

Volume 1: *Sinfonia in D, G.490; Sinfonia concertante in C for 2 Violins & Cello, Op. 7, G.491; Sinfonia with Solo Guitar in C, Op. 10/3, G.523.*

*** CPO 999 084-2. Deutsche Kammerakademie, Neuss,
Goritzki.

The early *Sinfonia in D*, G.490, originated as an (Italian) overture to a cantata, *La confederazione del Sabini con Roma.* Dating from 1765, it has a most engaging, dancing finale, while the charming central *Andante grazioso* was also featured in the *Cello Concerto*, G.478. The *Sinfonia concertante*, G.491, first heard in Paris in 1768, is a wholly different matter – an ambitious work of considerable character and immediate appeal. The *Sinfonia* with obbligato solo guitar is an arrangement of G.491, made some years later for the Marquis de Benevent, an amateur guitarist. The role is not demanding and, agreeable though this arrangement is, the original work is far more impressive.

Volume 2: *Symphonies: in D; in E flat; in C, Op. 12/1–3, G.503–5.*

*** CPO 999 172-2. Deutsche Kammerakademie, Neuss, Goritzki.

Volume 3: *Symphonies: in D min.; in B flat; in A, Op. 12/ 4–6, G.506–8.*

*** CPO 999 173-2. Deutsche Kammerakademie, Neuss, Goritzki.

The Op. 12 *Symphonies* of 1771 mark Boccherini's full entry into his own *galant* symphonic world, even if at times he is still thinking in terms of concertante writing, especially in Op. 12/3. Allegros are full of vigour, yet that melancholy element which is part of his musical personality is always apparent, and it immediately appears in the plaintive *Andantino* of the D major work, while its *Minuet amoroso* opens with cellos to remind us that the cello was the composer's own instrument.

Volume 4: *Symphonies: in B flat; in E flat; in C; in D; in B flat, Op. 21/1–5, G.493–7.*

*** CPO 999 174-2. Deutsche Kammerakademie, Neuss, Goritzki.

Boccherini composed his Op. 21 set of 1775 during a congenial period in his life when he was living in Aranjuez, and this is reflected in their generally lighthearted manner. They are all three-movement works, elegant and tuneful, yet by no means lacking in strength; the flutes frequently colour the scoring appealingly, as in the opening movement of the first of the set. The slow movements are usually dainty *Andantinos*, and the composer favours *dolce* and *con grazia* flavourings. Finales are usually vigorous, with bouncing energy; alternatively, those of the second and third of the set are gracious Minuets.

Volume 5: *Symphonies: in A, Op. 21/6, G.498; in D; in E flat; in A, Op. 35/1–3, G.509–11.*

*** CPO 999 175-2. Deutsche Kammerakademie, Neuss, Goritzki.

Volume 6: *Symphonies: in F; in E flat; in B flat, Op. 35/4– 6, G.512–14; in C, Op. 37/1, G.515.*

*** CPO 999 176-2. Deutsche Kammerakademie, Neuss, Goritzki.

The last of the Op. 21 series is in A and is richly scored, with aurally striking use of the highly crooked horns. The charmingly delicate *Andantino grazioso* leads naturally into the elegant finale – a Minuet without a Trio.

The Opus 35 group of 1782 marks a further step forward in maturity. They are all still three-movement works, but the scoring is more expansive, yet the ideas in the allegros are as invigorating as ever.

The energetic first symphony of the Op. 37 set (one of the composer's most fertile works) is in four movements, setting the pattern for the rest of the series. Its first movement returns to Boccherini's concertante style, with pairs of oboes, bassoons, flutes and a solo violin, and the spirited monothematic finale brings a panoply of colour, with chirping trills adding to the gaiety.

Volume 7: *Symphonies: in D min.; in A, Op. 37/3–4, G.517–18; in C min., Op. 41, G.519.*

*** CPO 999 177-2. Deutsche Kammerakademie, Neuss, Goritzki.

By the time he wrote his Opus 37 symphonies in 1786–7 Boccherini was established as the director of the Duchess of Osuna's court orchestra in Madrid. These mature four-movement works are obviously Haydn-influenced, but the lively invention and rich scoring remain Boccherini's own. The last work in this set of three uses the woodwind throughout as freely as the string groups. The horns shine through in the *A major* finale which, with its single striking theme, is reminiscent of the finale of Haydn's *Symphony No. 88*. Moreover, the outer movements of the powerful C minor work, Op. 41 (1788), have much in common with Haydn's *Sturm und Drang*, with a lovely *Pastorale* to give peaceful contrast. This key work is one of the composer's most imaginative symphonies.

Volume 8: *Symphonies: in D, Op. 42, G.520; in D, Op. 45, G.522; in D, G.500.*

*** CPO 999 178-2. Deutsche Kammerakademie, Neuss, Goritzki.

Boccherini's last two symphonies, Opp. 42 and 45, were written in 1789 and 1792 respectively, while the composer was in the employ of the King of Prussia. They are both first-class works, clearly following the pattern Haydn had established; but, as ever with Boccherini, they remain highly individual in colour. After this, G.500 is unduly simplistic and unadventurous, and it is more likely to be spurious than an early work wrongly catalogued. However, Goritzki makes the very most of its brief *Presto* finale, avoiding a sense of anticlimax.

Other recordings

Symphonies, Op. 12/1–6.

(B) *** Ph. (ADD) Duo 456 067-2 (2). New Philh. O, Leppard.

The Philips set is well worth exploring, particularly as Leppard consistently secures playing from the highly alert New Philharmonia Orchestra that is polished, elegant and never superficial. The 1971 recording is excellent and so is the CD transfer, losing nothing of the bloom but firming up the overall focus admirably.

Symphonies: in D, G.490; in D min. (La casa del diavolo), Op. 12/4; in A; in F, Op. 35/3–4.

(B) **(*) HM HMA 1901291. Ensemble 415, Banchini.

The period-instrument performances by the excellent Ensemble 415, led by Chiara Banchini, are very enjoyable. The slight drawback is the resonance of the recording which tends to cloud the busier fortissimos.

Symphonies: in D; in E flat; in A; in F; in E flat; in B flat, Op. 35/1–6.

*** Hyp. CDA 66903. L. Festival O, Pople.

Symphonies: in C; in D min.; in A, Op. 37/1, 3 & 4, G.515, 517–18; in D, Op. 42, G.520.

*** Hyp. CDA 66904. L. Festival O, Pople.

In the mid-1990s, Hyperion embarked on a Boccherini series with Ross Pople directing lively, characterful and polished performances with his excellent chamber orchestra. As can be seen above, these are attractive and mature works. The Hyperion sound is pleasingly fresh and open, and this is a most enjoyable pair of discs, but not necessarily preferable to the CPO series.

CHAMBER MUSIC

Cello Quintet, Op. 37/7.

(N) *** Australian Decca Eloquence (ADD) 421 637-2. ASMF – MENDELSSOHN: Octet. ***

The Quintet is an inspired piece and makes this disc worth getting for its own sake, though the coupled performance of Mendelssohn's Octet is a particularly fine one. The 1968 recording remains rich and full, and this Australian Eloquence CD has full sleeve notes.

Cello Sonatas: in C min., G.2 (first version); in A, G.4 (first version); in G, G.5; in C, G.17; in F min.

(N) (BB) *** Naxos 8.554324. C. & S. Benda.

Boccherini could hardly be boring if he tried and these cello sonatas (of which he wrote thirty-four!) are full of attractive invention. The Naxos disc is described as Volume I, so no doubt more are to follow. They could hardly be more persuasively played. The A major Sonata which opens the disc is particularly enticing, warmly melodic and with fizzing display passages which Christian Benda handles with easy virtuosity against the simple fortepiano backing. The finale is marked Affetuoso which sums up this team's approach throughout. The jolly opening movement of the G major is an Allegro militaire, while the moto perpetuo finale of the C major is as busy as a bumble-bee. The F minor Sonata was only discovered as recently as 1987 and has a lovely Cantabile siciliano for its slow movement which is quite haunting in the hands of these players. In short this is a first-class disc, very naturally recorded.

Cello Sonatas: in D min., G.2b; in A, G.4; in G, G.5; in A, G.13; in G, G.15; in C min., G.18.

(N) **(*) Praga PRD 250 147. Kaňka, Tůma, Hejný.

These Prague recordings feature a full continuo, and the result is like a cello duet accompanied by a (dwarfed) backwardly balanced harpsichord. The playing is eloquent and spirited but the effect is muddled and much less enjoyable than the splendid Naxos versons.

Flute Quintets (for flute, violin, viola, 2 cellos), Op. 17/1–6, G.419–24).

(BB) *** Naxos 8.553719. Magnin, Janáček Qt.

The Op. 17 Quintets are comparatively familiar and certainly rewarding, and they are very well played and recorded here. This Naxos disc is excellent value.

Flute Quintets, Op. 55/1–6, G.431–6 (for flute & string quartet).

(N) (B) *** CPO 999 382-2. Faust, Auryn Qt.

These six Flute (or oboe) Quintets are late works, dating from 1797 and show the composer at his most felicitous and charming. Without the scoring for 2 cellos used in the earlier works, the flute dominates even more readily. All but one are two-movement works – usually with a Minuet following an Andantino or Allegretto. In the catchy opening work the first movement is marked con vivacità, and a second Allegretto follows. In No. 5, however, the perky Minuet is framed by two Andante movements; No. 6 is the only work in the minor key and ends delicately. Michael Faust is a first-rate flautist and his performances here are vivacious and elegant, and recorded with a vivid presence.

Guitar Quintets Nos. 1–7, G.445–51; 9 (La ritirata di Madrid), G.453.

(B) *** Ph. Duo (ADD) 438 769-2 (2). P. Romero, ASMF Chamber Ens. (members).

Boccherini wrote or arranged 12 guitar quintets, but only the present eight have survived, plus another version of No. 4 in D (Fandango), G.448. Although some of the music is bland, it is nearly all agreeably tuneful in an unostentatious way, and there are some highly imaginative touches, with attractive hints of melancholy and underlying passion. These performances by Pepe Romero (often willing to take a relatively minor role) and members of the ASMF Chamber Ensemble are wholly admirable, and Philips are especially good at balancing textures of this kind in the most natural way, the guitar able to be assertive when required without overbalancing the ensemble.

Guitar Quartets Nos. 4 in D (Fandango), G.448; 5 in D, G.449; 6 in G, G.450.

(N) (BB) *** HM 3957026. Savino, Artaria Qt.

It is good to have performances on period instruments which create such a natural balance between the strings and the guitar. Although textures are less ample, they can also be attractively delicate, and there is no lack of warmth in the lovely Pastorale which forms the second movement of the most famous work (No. 9), with its Fandango finale. Here there is a spirited contribution from Peter Mund with his castanets. The other D major Quartet, G.449 has a charming opening movement and a diverting closing Theme and Variations, based on the same theme. Performances are stylishly intimate with recording to match. Most recommendable.

Guitar Quintets Nos. (i) 4 in D (Fandango), G.448; 7 in E min., G.451; 9 in C (La ritirata di Madrid), G.453.

(N) (BB) *** ASV CDQS 6244. Carter, Bingham Qt; (i) with Parker (castanets).

(B) *** DG (ADD) 449 852-2. Yepes, Melos Qt; (i) with Tena.

The ASV group have the advantage of first-class modern digital recording and the effect is more robust and present than with Yepes and the Melos. Here the castenet player adds a real sparkle to the lively Fandango, and the famous Retreat from Madrid is first brought forward to make a remarkably vivid climax before receding into the distance. Excellent, spirited playing from all concerned makes a clear first choice.

In the DG bargain compilation from 1971 the playing is expert and, in the boisterous *Fandango* finale of No. 4, Lucero Tena also makes a glittering contribution with his castanets. *La ritirata di Madrid* is used as the finale of the C major work. This picturesque evocation is created with a set of 12 brief variations set in a long slow crescendo, followed by a similarly graduated decrescendo, a kind of Spanish patrol, with the 'night watch' disappearing into the distance at the end.

Quintet No. 9: La ritirata di Madrid ('Procession of the Night Watch in Madrid'): orchestral version.

(M) *** DG (ADD) 457 914-2. BPO, Karajan – ROSSINI: *String Sonatas.* **(*)

This colourful and original work, which sets out to evoke music heard in Madrid at night, responds wonderfully to the full Karajan treatment. The playing is glorious, with sound to match, but it is also available, with better couplings, on one of DG's 'Originals' (449 724-2) as a bonus for Respighi's *Pines* and *Fountains of Rome*.

Piano Quintets: in E min.; in F; in D, Op. 56/1–2 & 5, G.407–8 & G.411.

*** Auvidis E 8518. Cohen, Mosaïques Qt.

Piano Quintets: in B flat; in E min.; in C, Op. 57/2–3 & 6, G.414–15 & G.418.

*** Auvidis E 8721. Cohen, Mosaïques Qt.

There are 12 piano quintets, and Patrick Cohen and the Mosaïques Quartet are obviously embarking – so far with great success – on a complete set. There is drama and grace and warmth of feeling, balanced by elegance, in this music; and the playing here also emphasizes its vitality. Slow movements are particularly eloquent, and the use of period instruments in no way inhibits the expressive range of the music.

Piano Quintets: in E flat; in A min.; in E min.; in C, Op. 56/3 & 6, Op. 57/3 & 6, G.410, G.412, G.415, G.418.

(B) *** DHM (ADD) 05472 77448-2. Les Adieux.

This is a particularly attractive group of Boccherini works, and it is made the more so by its reissue on the bargain Baroque Esprit label. The lovely *E minor* and the *A minor* both have those hints of beguiling, almost sultry melancholy that makes this composer's musical language so distinctive. This accomplished period-instrument group turn in performances of great finesse and charm, though the recording-balance places the listener very much in the front row of the salon.

String Quartets, Op. 32/1–6.

(N) (BB) *** Teldec (ADD) 8573 85565-2 (1–3); 8573 85566-2 (4–6). (Available separately) Esterházy Qt.

This set dates from 1780, about the same period as Haydn's Op. 33. They may ultimately lack the depth and vision of Haydn and Mozart, but to listen to this pioneering recording is to be amazed that music of this quality has been so long neglected. Its originality, the quality of the inspiration, its freshness and grace can scarcely be exaggerated, and these performances on original-period instruments are both com-

mitted and authoritative, with no want of charm to boot. The Esterházy Quartet are led by Jaap Schröder and theirs is thoroughly rewarding music-making. The Quartet was beautifully recorded in Haarlem, Holland, in 1976 and the new CD transfer of these two Das alte Werk discs is outstandingly natural. The documentation is sparse, and the overall playing time of the pair of CDs is only 89 minutes, but all of them are enjoyable and the set now comes in the lowest price range.

String Quartets: in C; in G min.; in A, Op. 32/4–6.

(BB) *** CPO 999 202-2. Nomos Qt.

These are three most attractive works, of Boccherini's best quality. All three slow movements are expressively potent; the *Andantino lentarello* of the *A major* is particularly searching, and the following Minuet is hardly less striking. The Nomos is a first-class group, using modern instruments but in such a way as to provide textures which are fully blended and sweet while avoiding nineteenth-century opulence. The recording is excellent.

String Quartet in E flat, Op. 58/2.

(M) *** Cal. (ADD) CAL 6698. Talich Qt – HAYDN: *Quartet No. 74*; MENDELSSOHN: *Quartet No. 2*; MICA: *Quartet No. 6*. ***

The Talich are on top form and are recorded very naturally, so that this well-planned collection amounts to more than the sum of its parts.

String Quintets Op. 11/5; Op. 25/1, 4 & 6.

(N) *** Virgin VC5 45421-2. Europe Galante.

Boccherini's quintets are an unfailing delight and their sunny, gentle aspect at times masks a touching melancholy. The Europe Galante play with great sympathy and style and round things off with the famous Minuet. A most attractive issue.

String Quintet in E, Op. 13/5.

**(*) Sony SK 53983. Stern, Lin, Laredo, Ma, Robinson – SCHUBERT: *String Quintet in C.* **

This is the quintet with the famous 'Boccherini Minuet', and it is exquisitely played. An enjoyable if not distinctive account overall, and the recording balance seems less upfront than the coupling.

VOCAL MUSIC

(i) *Stabat Mater* (first version); (ii) *String Quintet in C min., Op. 31/4, G.328.*

(N) (M) **(*) HM HMX 2981378. (i) Mellon, Ens. 415, Banchini; (ii) Banchini, Gatti, Moreno, Dieltiens, Brugge.

(i) *Stabat Mater, G.532* (first version); *Concert Arias: Ah, no! son io che parlo; Care luci. Symphonies: in D min. (La casa del Diavolo), Op. 12/4 (G.506); in C, Op. 21/3 (G.523); in A, Op. 37/4 (G.518).*

(B) *** Erato Ultima 3984 24230-2 (2). (i) Gasdia; I Solisti Veneti, Scimone.

Stabat Mater (1800 version).

*** Hyp. CDA 67108. Gritton, Fox, Bickley, Agnew, Harvey,
King's Consort, King – D´ASTORGA: *Stabat Mater*. ***

Boccherini originally wrote his *Stabat Mater* in 1781 for solo
soprano and strings. But, stimulated by the ongoing success
of Pergolesi's famous 1736 setting of the same text, he revised
the work in 1800 for two sopranos and a tenor, increasing
its dramatic range and power.

On Erato, the first version is gloriously sung by Cecilia
Gasdia. The beautiful sequence of movements towards the
close contains some exquisite music, and in the despairing
closing *Quando corpus morietur* Gasdia is very moving indeed. The two concert arias which follow take Mozart as
their model. They are brilliantly sung: Claudio Scimone
provides highly sensitive support, then on the second disc
(with his I Solisti Veneti) he offers vital and expressive
accounts of three symphonies, including not only *La casa
del Diavolo* but also a most appealing concertante work in
C major which has prominent obbligato parts for oboe,
violin and guitar, which are most sympathetically played
here. The digital sound is bright and immediate, but there
is plenty of ambient warmth.

The pure-voiced Agnès Mellon also makes a gently
touching case for the earlier version and she is expressively
and authentically supported by the refined playing of Chiara
Banchini and her four colleagues of Ensemble 415, who also
give a sensitive account of the *String Quintet* which acts as
filler. If the effect of the vocal work with period-instrument
accompaniment is comparatively restrained, many will
enjoy the gently luminous sense of spirituality which pervades this Harmonia Mundi version, with the closing
Quando corpus morietur gravely reflective and tender. The
recording is very natural.

Boccherini's ambitious revision is masterly in increasing
the range and expressive power of the work. With first-class
soloists, Robert King's performance is as moving as it is
gripping in the more dramatic moments. Notable are the
lovely soprano duets, so beautifully sung by Susan Gritton
and Sarah Fox, contrasting with the dramatic trios with
tenor, and the closing *Quando corpus morietur* (another trio)
is exquisitely managed. The apt coupling, a fine setting of
the same text, written nearly a century earlier by an almost
unknown Spanish composer, increases the value of this disc.

BOECK, August de (1865–1937)

Symphony in G.

(B) *** Discover DICD 920126. Brussels BRT PO,
Rickenbacher – GILSON: *De Zee*. ***

The *Symphony in G* of August de Boeck is a ripely exotic
work, full of Russian echoes. You might describe it as the
Borodin symphony that Borodin didn't write, sharply
rhythmic in the fast movements and sensuous in the slow
movement, brilliantly orchestrated and full of tunes that are
only marginally less memorable than those of the Russian
master. Well played and recorded and, at Discover International's bargain price, an ideal disc for experimenting
with.

BOËLLMANN, Léon (1862–97)

*Cello Sonata in A min., Op. 40; 2 Pieces for Cello & Piano,
Op. 31.*

*** Hyp. CDA 66888. Lidström, Forsberg – GODARD: *Cello
Sonata in D min.*, etc. ***

Boëllmann is best known for his organ music and in particular the *Suite gothique*, whose final Toccata is a familiar
cheval de bataille. The *A minor Sonata* reveals him to be a
cultured and imaginative musician. Mats Lidström and
Bengt Forsberg play with such passion and conviction that
they almost persuade one that this piece is worthy to rank
alongside the Brahms *Sonatas*. The recording is very acceptable, if rather close. Strongly recommended.

BOIELDIEU, François (1775–1834)

Harp Concerto in 3 Tempi in C.

⬤ (M) *** Decca 425 723-2. Robles, ASMF, Brown –
DITTERSDORF; HANDEL: *Harp Concertos*, etc. *** ⬤

Boieldieu's *Harp Concerto* has been recorded before but
never more attractively. The (originally Argo) recording is
still in the demonstration class and very sweet on the
ear. To make the reissue even more attractive, three beguiling
sets of *Variations* have been added, including music by
Handel and Beethoven and a *Theme, Variations and Rondo
Pastorale* attributed to Mozart.

La Dame blanche (complete).

(M) *** EMI CMS5 56355-2 (2). Blake, Verzier, Naouri,
Fouchécourt, Deletré, Massis, Delunsch, Brunet, Dehont,
Vajou, Ch. de R. France, Paris Ens. O, Minkowski.

Completed in 1826, this lighthearted adaptation of Walter
Scott's novel sparkles from first to last, helped by the inspired
direction of Marc Minkowski with an excellent team of
soloists who all sing with a natural feeling for the idiom.
This is a piece which with its many lively ensembles points
directly forward to Donizetti's *Daughter of the Regiment*
and even to Offenbach's two gendarmes from *Geneviève de
Brabant*. Here the cast has no weak link, with the outstanding
Rossinian tenor Rockwell Blake matched by the others, not
least Annik Massis as Anna and Mireille Delunsch as Jenny.
For some non-French speakers there may be rather too
much dialogue, but that can easily be worked around on
CD. Warm, well-balanced sound.

BOISMORTIER, Joseph Bodin de
(1689–1755)

*Ballets de village: Nos. 1–4, Op. 52; Gentilesse No. 5, Op. 45;
Sérénade No. 1, Op. 39.*

(N) (BB) *** Naxos 8.554295. Le Concert Spirituel, Niquet.

Boismortier's four *Ballets de village* are colourful sets of
pastoral dances which make vivid use of rustic instruments
– the musette and hurdy-gurdy – with an underlying drone,

in concert with wind and string instruments, in continuous lively three-part writing. The three-movement *Gentillessse* is rather more refined. However the *Sérénade*, Op. 39, with its eighteen sections is much more ambitious. Here the texture is based on flutes violins, and oboes. There is an opening *Ouverture* and an extended closing *Chaconne*. In between come more dances, Gavottes, a Gigue, a Sarabande, a fast and piquantly vivacious *Villageoise* introduced by the the treble recorder, as well as an *Entrée rustique* an elegant *Air gracieux*, a charming *Air modéré* and even a *Choeur imaginaire*. Boismortier's invention is unflagging, the instrumental colouring ear-catching, and when played with such authenticity and sparkle this is very attractive, if not to be taken in a continuous sequence. The recording is excellent.

(i) Bassoon Concerto; (ii) Musette (Zampognae) Concerto; Fragments mélodiques (French dance suite); Sérénade or Symphonie française No. 2. Stage works: Daphnis et Chloé: Chaconne; Les Voyages de l'amour: Entrées des génies élémentaires.

(N) (BB) *** Naxos 8.554456. (i) Le Chenadec; (ii) Maillard; Le Concert Spirituel, Niquet.

Naxos at last are filling out a fuller picture of Joseph Bodin de Boismortier, tax collector (for the French Royal Tobacco Company) as well as musician. As this collection shows, he composed with easy facility so that a contemporary writer portrayed him in verse:

'Happy is he, Boismortier, whose fertile quill,

Each month, without pain, conceives a new air at will.'

The *Bassoon Concerto* shows this facility most agreeably, as does the equally engaging work for musette (Boismortier chose the Italian name to describe the instrument) with its underlying drone . His orchestral palette is shown even more colourfully in the two collections of dances, felicitously and lightly scored for flutes, oboes, hurdy-gurdy, musette and strings. One of his specialities was to write inventive chaconnes in duple instead of triple time. Both the *Fragments mélodiques* and *Sérénade* end with a typical example. But his finale for *Daphnis et Chloé* (which is used to open the concert) is even more individual and deserves to be better known. Most remarkable of all is the *Entrées des génies élémentaires*, a bubbling kaleidoscope of contrasting character dances. Hervé Niquet directs his excellent ensemble with animation and finesse, and both his soloists are in good form. A first-class disc in every way, well worth exploring.

6 Concertos for 5 Flutes, Op. 15/1–6.

(BB) ** Naxos 8.553639. Soloists of Concert Spirituel.

Although Boismortier's invention holds up well throughout, his predilection for block chords in slow movements means that the music has relatively little variety of colour. These excellent players blend and match their timbres expertly, often presenting a very homogeneous sound, the effect emphasized by the close balance. A disc to recommend primarily to amateur flautists.

6 Flute Sonatas, Op. 91.

*** Analekta FL2 3008. Guimond, Beauséjour.

Boismortier's Op. 91 is elegant and well crafted, and these sonatas nicely blend French and Italian influences. All except the first, which has an opening Sicilienne, are in the fast–slow–fast Italian tradition. They are played beautifully and stylishly by this excellent French-Canadian duo: Claire Guimond on the baroque flute and Luc Beauséjour. They play with an appealing delicacy to charm the ear, yet there is an underlying robustness which makes the music seem far from merely trivial. The recording (as one expects from this Canadian label) is expertly balanced and altogether natural.

(i) Suites for Solo Flute Nos. 3, 5 & 6; (ii) Harpsichord Suites Nos. 1–4 (1731).

(B) *** Cal. (ADD) CAL 6865. (i) Urbain; (ii) Lagacé.

Harpsichord Suite No. 1 .

(B) ** Cal. CAL 6838. Lagacé – RAMEAU: *6 Concerts en sextuor*. **

These four *Harpsichord Suites* were Boismortier's only works for harpsichord. They are very much in the style of the *Pièces de clavecin* of Rameau, and Boismortier follows his practice in giving each movement a colourful sobriquet. *La Cavernesque*, which begins the *First Suite*, is aptly titled. The invention is attractive, if perhaps not as individual as with Rameau, although the finale of the last suite shows Boismortier writing a very characterful set of variations. Mireille Lagacé is an excellent advocate and she uses a restored Hemsch, which is truthfully recorded and suits the repertoire admirably. Interleaved with the harpsichord works are three suites for unaccompanied flute. Again the playing is highly responsive, to make this a rewarding concert.

The first suite is also played expertly by Lagacé, and the recording is realistic, provided you turn down the volume.

(i) (i) Suites for Solo Flute No. 4; Nos 3 & 6 (with continuo); (ii) Harpsichord Suites Nos. 1–4.

(N) (BB) *** Naxos 8.554457. (i) Savignat, Plubeau; (iii) Martin.

The harpsichord which Béatrice Martin uses on the Naxos disc is not named, but if anything it is an even more attracive instrument that that used by Mireille Legacé, warmly resonant yet well focused. Anne Savignat plays the charming *Fourth Flute Suite* as a solo work, but in Nos. 3 and 6 she is partnered by Christine Plubeau who plays a simple bass line on the viola da gamba. Certainly these performances are every bit the equal of those on their Calliope competitor and again make one reflect that the works for harpsichord ought to be far better known.

BOITO, Arrigo (1842–1918)

Mefistofele (complete).

**(*) Decca (IMS) 410 175-2. Ghiaurov, Pavarotti, Freni, Caballé, L. Op. Ch., Trinity Boys' Ch., Nat. PO, Fabritiis.

(M) **(*) Decca (ADD) 440 054-2. Siepi, Del Monaco, Tebaldi, Cavalli, Santa Cecilia Academy, Rome, Ch. & O, Serafin.

The modern digital recording given to the Fabritiis set brings obvious benefits in the extra weight of brass and percussion – most importantly in the heavenly Prologue. With the principal soloists all at their best – Pavarotti most seductive, Freni finely imaginative on detail, Caballé consistently sweet and mellifluous as Elena – this is a highly recommendable set.

On the earlier (1958) Decca Rome set, Serafin, the most persuasive Italian conductor of his day, draws glorious sounds from his performers, even from Mario del Monaco, who is here almost sensitive. Tebaldi is a rich-toned Margherita – almost too rich-toned for so frail a heroine – and Siepi makes an excellent Mefistofele. The Decca engineers came up trumps: the stereo remains remarkably spacious, particularly in the Prologue, making a good mid-priced alternative to the later Decca version.

Mephistofele: scenes.

(M) **(*) Decca (ADD) 458 242-2. Siepi, Tebaldi, Di Stefano, St Cecilia, Rome, Ch. & O, Serafin.

This selection disc is a curiosity. At about the same time, Decca recorded the opera complete with the same forces except for the tenor (see above). This obviously represents the results of an unfinished project, and admirers of Giuseppe di Stefano – a subtler artist than Mario del Monaco, his Decca rival at that time – will be pleased to have this sample of his work in the late 1950s. His characterization is strong, and he gets good support from Siepi and Tebaldi. Excellent recording for its period.

BOLCOM, William (born 1938)

Piano Concerto.

(N) *** Hyp. CDA 67170. Hamelin, Ulster O, Sitkovetsky – BERNSTEIN: *Symphony No. 2 (The Age of Anxiety).* ***

William Bolcom is above all a communicator, never afraid of drawing on popular music of every kind, and translating his sources. So this colourful piano concerto, written in 1976 as an offbeat celebration of the US Bicentennial, ranges wide in its moods, with the first movement bringing a jewelled sequence of ideas, both bright and dark, and with the slow movement a gentle dialogue between piano and orchestra. The most striking and most provocative movement is the finale, in which Bolcom, Ives-like, hilariously offers a whirling pot-pourri of American popular themes, from *Yankee Doodle* by way of Sousa and others to ragtime and jazz, punctuated by a sort of last post on a cornet, using a hymn-tune. It is great fun, but intentionally with sinister overtones, and Hamelin and his accompanists respond superbly. An unusual and attractive fill-up for the Bernstein.

BONONCINI, Antonio (1677–1726)

La decollazione de S. Giovanni Battista (oratorio; complete).

*** Tactus TC 675201. Van Goethen, Barazzoni, D. Piccini, F. Piccini, Bianconi, Guastalla Bar. Op. O, Volta.

Antonio Bononcini's oratorio, *La decollazione de S. Giovanni*

Battista, dramatizes the story of St John the Baptist's fatal encounter with Herod and Salome – using an Angel to make narrative comments – in a series of brief recitatives and often very beautiful *da capo* arias. Herod's central aria, *Nulla si nieghi* (with cello obbligato), is finely projected by the excellent bass, Virgilio Bianconi. John the Baptist is a male alto role (Michael Van Goethen), and it is his soliloquy, *Bacio l'ombre e le catane*, movingly sung here, which is the emotional centre of the work. Bononcini's music protrays Salome herself as an almost ingenuous charmer, with Daniella Piccini here responding with ravishing tone and simplicity of line. It is the chorus (formed by the five soloists) which makes the touchingly tragic final comment on the outcome, *Morir il giusto*. The performance here is outstanding in every way, and Sandro Volta keeps this often lovely music flowing forward most appealingly. The recording is first class. Alas, the libretto is in Italian only, with no translation.

Stabat Mater.

(B) *** Decca Double (ADD) 443 868-2 (2). Palmer, Langridge, Esswood, Keyte, St John's College, Cambridge, Ch., Philomusica, Guest – PERGOLESI: *Magnificat in C,* etc. **(*); D. SCARLATTI: *Stabat Mater;* A. SCARLATTI: *Domine, refugium factus es nobis,* etc.; CALDARA: *Crucifixus;* LOTTI: *Crucifixus.* ***

Antonio Bononcini is not to be confused with Handel's rival, Giovanni, his older brother. Antonio's *Stabat Mater* is a work of genuine melodic distinction and affecting tenderness; there are some striking harmonies, even moments of drama, and in general a nobility and simple expressiveness that leave a strong impression. The St John's performance is wholly admirable and is very well recorded.

BONONCINI, Giovanni (1670–1755)

Cello Sonata in A min.; Trio Sonata for 2 Violins & Continuo in D min. (i) Cantatas: *Già la stagion d'amore; Lasciami un sol momento; Misero pastorello; Siedi, Amarilli mia.*

*** Virgin VC5 45000-2. Lesne, Il Seminario Musicale.

Giovanni Bononcini's cantatas were popular and were published in London in 1721. They reveal their composer to be far more than a mere historical figure. *Lasciami un sol momento* stands out as a particularly moving work, with its melancholy opening aria ('Leave me but for one moment, O bitter memory of my betrayed love') leading to a bravura finale, *Soffro in pace* ('I bear these chains in peace'). The instrumental works are also highly inventive and characterful: the *Lento* of the lively *Trio Sonata* is gently touching and its finale wonderfully spirited. All this music is worth knowing, and the advocacy of these fine artists brings it fully to life. The expressive eloquence of Gérard Lesne's singing could not be more winning, using the most felicitous ornamentation. The recording too is first class.

BORODIN, Alexander (1833–87)

'The World of Borodin': (i) In the Steppes of Central Asia; Prince Igor: (ii) Overture; (ii–iii) Polovtsian Dances; (iv) Symphony No. 2 in B min.; (v) String Quartet No. 2: Nocturne; (vi) Scherzo in A flat; (vii–viii) Far from the shores of your native land; (vii, ix) Prince Igor: Galitzky's Aria.

(M) *** Decca (ADD) 444 389-2. (i) SRO, Ansermet; (ii) LSO, Solti; (iii) with L. Symphony Ch.; (iv) LSO, Martinon; (v) Borodin Qt; (vi) Ashkenazy; (vii) N. Ghiaurov; (viii) Z. Ghiaurov; (ix) L. Symphony Ch., LSO, Downes.

'Essential Borodin': Symphonies Nos. (i) 1 in E flat; (ii) 2 in B min.; (iii) 3 in A min.; In the Steppes of Central Asia; (iv) String Quartet No. 2 in B min.; (v–vi) Song: From the shores of your far-off native land. Prince Igor: (vii) Overture; (vii–viii) Polovtsian Dances; (v; viii–ix) Galitzky's Aria; Konchak's Aria.

(B) *** Double Decca (ADD) 455 632-2 (2). (i) RPO, Ashkenazy; (ii) LSO, Martinon; (iii) SRO, Ansermet; (iv) Borodin Qt; (v) N. Ghiaurov; (vi) Z. Ghiaurov; (vii) LSO, Solti; (viii) L. Symphony Ch.; (ix) LSO, Downes.

The 'World of Borodin' is an extraordinarily successful disc. There can be few if any other collections of this kind that sum up a composer's achievement so succinctly or that make such a rewarding and enjoyable 76-minute concert. Solti's Prince Igor Overture is romantic, and very exciting too; there is no finer account in the current catalogue, and the same can be said for the Polovtsian Dances, with splendid choral singing. The Nocturne follows the Overture so effectively that one might have thought it the composer's own plan. Ansermet's In the Steppes of Central Asia is warm and atmospheric. After Nicolai Ghiaurov has reminded us of the melancholy side of the Russian spirit, we come finally to Martinon's unsurpassed 1960 LSO performance of the B minor Symphony, notable for its fast tempo for the famous opening theme. The strong rhythmic thrust suits the music admirably, the Scherzo has vibrant colouring and the slow movement, with a beautifully played horn solo, is most satisfying. The sound has remarkable presence and sparkle.

Decca have now happily expanded the programme to fit on to a Double, and in doing so they represent the composer even more comprehensively for very little extra outlay. Ashkenazy's reading of the First Symphony is less high-powered than Martinon's superb account of No. 2, but its many delights come over richly, thanks not only to the quality of the RPO playing but also to the warm (1992) digital recording. Ansermet's touch in the unfinished Third is attractively alive and spontaneous, with some delightful moments from the SRO woodwind. What makes this extended programme especially attractive is the inclusion of the whole of the Second String Quartet, rather than just the slow movement. The performance by the eponymous Borodin Quartet is masterly in every respect. In Prince Igor Ghiaurov now adds a second role by singing Konchak's aria from Act II in addition to Galitzky's aria from Act I.

In the Steppes of Central Asia; (i) Nocturne (from String Quartet No. 2) arr. for violin & orchestra by Rimsky-Korsakov; Petite suite (orch. Glazunov); (ii; iii) Requiem (orch. Stokowski, arr. Simon); Prince Igor: Overture; (iii) Chorus of Polovtsian Maidens; Dance of Polovtsian Maidens; Polovtsian March; Polovtsian Dances.

(M) **(*) Cala CACD 1029. Philh. O, Simon, with (i) Chase; (ii) Boughton; (iii) BBC SO Ch.

An interesting and valuable anthology. Borodin's 5-minute piano piece called Requiem is played in Stokowski's flamboyantly expansive orchestration, to which Geoffrey Simon has very effectively added solo tenor and male chorus. The piece is ingeniously based on 'Chopsticks' but has an exaggerated dynamic range. In the Steppes of Central Asia would have been more effective with greater dynamic contrast, a warmly languorous performance. In the March and the famous Polovtsian Dances, the singing of the BBC Chorus is of a high standard, though Geoffrey Simon's direction is lively rather than electrifying, both here and in the Overture. Rimsky-Korsakov's concertante arrangement of the famous Nocturne for violin and orchestra – in spite of Stephanie Chase's pleasing advocacy – gives the piece the character of a salon encore, charming but insouciant. The Petite suite, a set of six piano miniatures orchestrated by Glazunov, comes off very engagingly.

Prince Igor: Overture & Polovtsian Dances.

(BB) *** Virgin 2 x 1 VBD5 61751-2 (2). RLPO Ch. & O, Mackerras – MUSSORGSKY: Pictures, etc. **; RIMSKY-KORSAKOV: Scheherazade **(*); TCHAIKOVSKY: The Tempest. ***

A splendid account of the Prince Igor Overture from Mackerras. The Polovtsian Dances proceed with comparable brilliance and fervour, with the Royal Liverpool Philharmonic Choir producing an expansive lyrical tone and joining in the frenzy of the closing section with infectious zest. Excellent recording too, vivid and full; if only the Mussorgsky and Rimsky-Korsakov couplings had produced comparable electricity, this super-bargain double would have been a world-beater. As it is, it is good value.

Symphonies Nos. 1 in E flat; 2 in B min.; 3 in A min. (completed Glazunov); In the Steppes of Central Asia; Nocturne (orchestrated Nicolai Tcherepnin); Petite suite (arr. Glazunov); Prince Igor: Overture; (i) Polovtsian Dances.

*** DG (IMS) 435 757-2 (2). Gothenburg SO, Järvi; (i) with Gothenburg Ch.

For those wanting all three symphonies, the Järvi DG set remains recommendable. The alternative versions by Serebrier (ASV CDDCA 706) and Gunzenhauser (Naxos 8.550238) each have the advantage of being offered on a single CD but are undistinctive.

Järvi's First has plenty of individuality and colour; the slow movement is radiant, the Scherzo beautifully sprung and the finale made to anticipate the Prince Igor Overture in its bright, rhythmic pointing. The Second is a strong, spacious reading; however, alongside Martinon, the first movement is somewhat lacking in bite and thrust. The Third

Symphony (completed by Glazunov), comes off vividly, although it is not as strong a work as the other two. The other pieces are played equally well by the excellent Gothenburg orchestra, notably the *Petite suite*, although there are some reservations about Tcherepnin's very exotic orchestration of the famous *Nocturne* from the *D major String Quartet*, and perhaps Järvi doesn't pull out all the stops in his undoubtedly vivid account of the *Polovtsian Dances*. Yet the Swedish choral singing, if not uninhibited, is vital enough and even includes a brief solo interpolation representing the Khan. The digital recording throughout is from DG's top drawer.

Symphony No. 1 in E flat.

(BB) **(*) Finlandia 0927 40597-2. Norwegian R. O,
   Rasilainen – TCHAIKOVSKY: *Symphony No. 2*. ***

A very enjoyable and recommendable account of this delightful symphony from the Norwegian Radio Orchestra and their Finnish conductor is spirited, and is well enough played and recorded if you want the coupling. It certainly gives pleasure.

Symphony No. 2 in B min.

(***) Testament mono SBT 1048. Philh. O, Kletzki –
   TCHAIKOVSKY: *Manfred Symphony*. (***)

(N) (M) *(*) Ph. (ADD) 464 735-2. Concg. O, Kondrashin –
   RINSKY-KORSAKOV: *Scheherazade*. ***

(BB) *(*) Belair BAM 9724. New Russian O, Poltevsky –
   RIMSKY-KORSAKOV: *Tsar Saltan: Suite*. ***

Kletzki draws superb playing from the Philharmonia at a vintage period in the mid-1950s. The ravishing account of the slow movement has Dennis Brain at his peak in the big horn solo, backed by Bernard Walton on the clarinet and Sidney Sutcliffe on the oboe producing whispered pianissimos that caress the ear. The first movement is brisk and dramatic, while in the Scherzo the tonguing of the woodwind makes for phenomenal precision. As for the transfer, after a dull opening the bite and immediacy of the brass and woodwind are so vivid they give an illusion of stereo.

Kondrashin's rather brisk live account of the *Second Symphony* has the advantage of fine orchestral playing, though it is let down by some intrusive audience noise and a lapse of intonation in the slow movement. Kondrashin's outstanding *Scheherazade* is a different matter, but fortunately is also available alternatively coupled.

At super-bargain price on the Belair label comes Poltevsky's version with an excellent orchestra drawn from a range of Moscow orchestras. Impossibly heavy at the start, with fluctuation of tempo in the first movement, and the other three movements are taken broadly too. A disc worth hearing for an electrifying account of the *Tsar Saltan Suite*.

Sextet (2 movements).

** Mer. CDE 84211. Arienski Ens. – ARENSKY: *Quartet* ***;
   TCHAIKOVSKY: *Souvenir de Florence*. **

Borodin composed his *Sextet* on a visit to Heidelberg in 1860 but, unfortunately, only two of its movements survive. The Arienski Ensemble play with enthusiasm and conviction and are decently recorded.

String Quartets Nos. 1 in A; 2 in D.

(BB) *** Arte Nova 74321 51633-2. Russian Qt.

The popularity of Borodin's *Second Quartet* has tended to get in the way of appreciation of the equally delightful *First Quartet*, making this a very welcome coupling at bargain price. The Russian Quartet, a group of women players with exceptionally warm, fruity tone, make persuasive advocates of both works, with charm and tender lyricism brought out in the *First Quartet* and with sweetness and warmth in the *Second Quartet*. Warm, immediate sound to match.

String Quartet No. 2 in D.

*** Decca 452 239-2. Takács Qt – SMETANA: *String Quartet No. 1*. ***

(***) Testament mono SBT 1061. Hollywood Qt –
   GLAZUNOV: *5 Novelettes*; TCHAIKOVSKY: *String Quartet No. 1*. (***)

(BB) *** CfP Double (ADD) CDCFPSD 4772 (2). Gabrieli Qt –
   BRAHMS: *Clarinet Quintet* **(*); DVORAK: *String Quartet No. 12* ***; SCHUBERT: *String Quartet No. 14*. ***

(M) *** Classic fM 75605 57027-2. Chilingirian Qt – DVORAK:
   Quartet in F; SHOSTAKOVICH: *Quartet No. 8*. ***

(M) **(*) Cal. (ADD) CAL 6202. Talich Qt – TCHAIKOVSKY:
   Quartet No. 1. ***

(M) **(*) Decca (ADD) 425 541-2. Borodin Qt –
   SHOSTAKOVICH; TCHAIKOVSKY: *Quartets*. **(*)

An outstanding version of Borodin's *D major Quartet* comes from the Takács group, who play with fine ensemble and plenty of feeling, yet bring subtlety of colour and delicacy of texture, as well as warmth, to the famous *Notturno*. The recording has striking presence, and the Smetana coupling is hardly less impressive.

Although later recordings may match the Hollywood version, it is still a performance with persuasive freshness and ardour. The sound has been improved, and the addition of the Glazunov, which is new to the catalogue, enhances the disc's value. The playing time runs to one second short of 80 minutes.

As part of an outstanding Classics for Pleasure Silver Double compilation of Romantic string quartets, the Gabrielis offer a finely wrought, sensitive and thoroughly polished performance of the Borodin, warm in feeling. At less than half the price of its main competitor, this is excellent value, for the recording is first class and beautifully transferred to CD.

On the Classic fM label the Chilingirian Quartet offer powerful, incisive performances of an apt and generous coupling. With Levon Chilingirian an exceptionally alert leader, rhythms in the Borodin are consistently well sprung, with no sentimentality in a warmly expressive account of the celebrated slow movement.

The Talich performance is characteristically refined and beautifully played, although the performance lacks something in Slavonic voluptuousness. The digital recording is however first class, full and naturally balanced. Moreover, the Tchaikovsky coupling is outstanding in every way.

The Borodins' version of the *Second Quartet* on Decca is very fine, though the forward recording, rich-textured, approaches fierceness in the present CD transfer, and most will prefer a softer-grained effect.

Prince Igor (opera): complete.

*** Ph. 442 537-2 (3). Kit, Gorchakova, Ognovienko, Minjelkiev, Borodina, Grigorian, Kirov Ch. & O., St Petersburg, Gergiev.

*** Sony S3K 44878 (3). Martinovich, Evstatieva, Kaludov, Ghiuselev, Ghiaurov, Miltcheva, Sofia Nat. Op. Ch. & Festival O, Tchakarov.

(M) **(*) EMI (ADD) CMS5 66814-2 (2). Chekerliiski, Christoff, Todorov, Sofia Nat. Theatre Op. Ch. & O, Semkow.

Gergiev's electrifying account of Borodin's epic opera reflects not only his own magnetic qualities as a conductor but also the way he has welded his principal singers as well as the chorus and orchestra into a powerful team. Acts I and II are given in reverse order from the usual, with the substantial Prologue here followed by the first Polovtsian scene and its spectacular dances. Only then do you get the scene at Prince Galitsky's court, leading up to Yaroslavna's great lament, here sung superbly by Galina Gorchakova. Otherwise Gergiev generally follows that well-established edition, but he has included material omitted from Borodin's copious sketches, notably an extended monologue of lament for Igor himself as a prisoner of Khan Konchak in Act III: 'Why did I not fall on the field of battle?' That alone puts this ahead of the fine rival Sony recording from Tchakarov with Bulgarian forces, and Gergiev is even more sharply dramatic, generally adopting faster speeds. On the solo casting, honours are much more even. The two principal women here, not just Gorchakova but Olga Borodina too as Konchak's daughter, Konchakovna, are both magnificent, even finer than their Bulgarian rivals, but neither principal bass Vladimir Ognovienko as Galitsky nor Bulat Minjelkiev as Konchak can match the vocal richness or character of the Bulgarians, Ghiuselev and Ghiaurov, both older-sounding but still compelling. Gegam Grigorian in the tenor role of Igor's son gives a lusty performance, while Mikhail Kit as Igor himself, though often gritty and even fluttery of tone, sings thoughtfully and intelligently, making him a fair match for his Bulgarian rival.

On Sony, Boris Martinovich makes a firm, very virile Igor, and both the principal women have vibrantly Slavonic voices which still never distract in wobbling. The dramatic tension in this long work is held very well and its richness of invention over its very episodic span comes across vividly, notably in all its memorable melody and high colour.

In the colourful EMI recording, Act III is omitted entirely, on the grounds that it was almost completely the work of Rimsky-Korsakov and Glazunov. Boris Christoff as both Galitzky and Konchak easily outshines all rivals. Jerzy Semkow with his Sofia Opera forces is most sympathetic, but the other soloists are almost all disappointing, with the women sour-toned and the men often strained and

unsteady. The sound is limited but agreeably atmospheric.

Prince Igor: Overture & Polovtsian Dances.

(M)*** EMI CDM5 66983-2. Beecham Choral Soc., RPO, Beecham – RIMSKY-KORSAKOV: *Scheherazade.* ***

Prince Igor: Polovtsian Dances.

(M) **(*) Mercury (IMS) (ADD) 434 308-2. L. Symphony Ch., LSO, Dorati – RIMSKY-KORSAKOV: *Capriccio espagnol,* etc. ***

(N)(BB) (***) Dutton mono CDBP 9712. LPO, Fitelberg – RIMSKY-KORSAKOV: *Scheherazade; Skazka.* ***

Beecham's 1957 performance of the *Polovtsian Dances* – now reissued as one of EMI's 'Great Recordings of the Century' – sweeps the board, even though it omits the percussion-led opening *Dance of the Polovtsian Maidens.* Beecham draws an almost Russian fervour from his choristers. The recorded sound is little short of astonishing in its fullness, vividness and clarity.

Dorati's Mercury recording is not among the most refined from this source, but no one could say that the effect lacks vividness or boisterous vitality, and the climax is exhilarating.

The Polish conductor Gregor Fitelberg recorded the *Polovtsian Dances* for Decca in 1946, a fresh, colourful reading enhanced by early Decca ffrr recording at its most impressive, very well transferred by Dutton. It makes an attractive fill-up for the Rimsky-Korsakov items from Ansermet and Constant Lambert.

BØRRESEN, Hakon (1876–1954)

At Uranienborg or Tycho Brahe's Dream (ballet); (i) Romance for Cello & Orchestra. The Royal Guest: Prelude.

**(*) dacapo 8.224105. Aalborg SO, Hughes; (i) with Brendstrup.

The Royal Guest, a one-Act opera from 1919, was Børresen's greatest success, and its *Prelude* whets the appetite. The 12 numbers that constitute the ballet *At Uranienborg or Tycho Brahe's Dream* are given a committed performance, as is the *Romance,* played by Henrik Brendstrup and written in 1908 at the time of the *Second Symphony.* Owain Arwel Hughes and his Aalborg musicians sound as if they are enjoying themselves. But the acoustic of the Aalborg hall is not ideal: the sound is tubby in climaxes and lacks transparency.

Symphonies Nos. 2 in A (The Sea), Op. 7; 3 in C, Op. 21.

*** CPO 999 353-2. Frankfurt RSO, Schmidt.

Both symphonies have a lot going for them. The delightful Scherzo of No. 1 is as transparent in its orchestration as Mendelssohn, and the first movement has a Dvořákian sense of openness and space. Attractive works, not the last word in originality, but presented very persuasively by Ole Schmidt and the Frankfurt Radio Orchestra, and well recorded.

BORTKIEWICZ, Sergei (1877–1952)

Piano Concerto No. 1 in B flat min., Op. 16.

*** Hyp. CDA 66624. Coombs, BBC Scottish SO, Maksymiuk
– ARENSKY: *Piano Concerto.* ***

Sergei Bortkiewicz's concerto is conservative in idiom, a conventional, romantic, virtuoso offering without much individual flavour. Stephen Coombs takes its considerable difficulties in his stride and plays the work as if it was great music – and at times he almost persuades one that it is. He receives excellent support from the BBC Scottish Orchestra under Jerzy Maksymiuk, and good recording quality.

BORTNYANSKY, Dmitri (1751–1825)

Sacred Concertos No. 1–35.

*** Chan. 9729 *Nos. 1–9;* 9783 *Nos. 10–16;* (N) 9840 *Nos. 17–23;* (N) 9878 *Nos. 24–29.* Russian State Symphonic Capella, Polyansky.

Bortnyansky was born in the Ukraine but was soon recruited for the Court Cappella at St Petersburg. He studied with Galuppi in Italy. On his return to Russia in 1779 he became Kapellmeister of the Court Cappella, where he remained for the rest of his life; during the last years of Catherine the Great's reign the liturgy ended with these choral concertos, of which there are 35 in all. They are more indebted to the Italian motet than to Byzantine traditions of chant, but Bortnyansky wrote for voices with consummate expertise and no mean artistry. As Philip Taylor puts it in his notes, 'the music unfolds according to its own laws [and] it is the evolution of the melodic ideas and the way they are distributed among the different voice registers that give the concertos their entirely distinctive character'.

The performances by the Russian State Symphonic Capella under Valeri Polyansky have great eloquence, and though there is a long period of reverberation in the acoustic of both the Dormition Cathedral, Smolensk, and St Sophia's Cathedral, Polotsk (where the recordings were made in 1989–90), the sound is beautifully focused. They have taken some time to reach us, but their welcome is no less warm.

The third and fourth discs are new to the present volume and maintain the high standard of the previous two, with Bortnyansky's musical inspiration showing no sign of falling off.

Presumably there is one more issue to come to complete the set, although a further eight unpublished concertos have recently been discovered. Anyone who loves Russian choral music and that country's sonorous liturgical vocal tradition should explore this highly rewarding and superbly recorded series.

BÖRTZ, Daniel (born 1943)

Trumpet Concerto (Songs & Dances).

(N) *** BIS CD 1021. Hardenberger, Malmö SO, Varga –

RABE: *Sardine Sarcophagus;* SANDSTROM: *Trumpet Concerto No. 2.* ***

Börtz's *Trumpet Concerto* is highly imaginative and has a compelling quality thanks to his feeling for sound and colour, whether or not you respond to the idiom. It is subtitled *Songs and Dances* and is one of four concertos with related titles. Hardenberger is quite stunning, as is the BIS recording.

Sinfonias Nos. 1; 7; Parados; Strindberg Suite.

*** Chan. 9473. Stockholm PO, Rozhdestvensky.

Daniel Börtz is never boring, though his limited range of expressive devices makes it hard to listen to all these pieces straight off, despite the refined sense of orchestral colour. The music is too static, with extensive use of chord-clusters and strong dynamic contrasts, but both the *First* and *Seventh Symphonies* are powerfully atmospheric. The playing of the Stockholm orchestra is superb and the Chandos recording is of demonstration standard: marvellously present, well balanced and realistic.

BOTTESINI, Giovanni (1821–89)

(i) Double-Bass Concertino in C min.; (i–ii) Duo concertante on Themes from Bellini's 'I Puritani' for Cello, Double-Bass & Orchestra; (i) Elégie in D; (i; iii) Passioni amorose (for 2 double-basses); Ali Baba Overture; Il diavolo della notte; Ero e Leandro: Prelude.

*** ASV CDDCA 907. (i) Martin; (ii) Welsh; (iii) Petracchi; LSO, Petracchi, or (iii) Gibson.

A contemporary said of Bottesini's virtuoso playing, 'Under his bow the double-bass sighed, cooed, sang, quivered,' and it does all those things here on the flamboyant bow of Thomas Martin, himself a musician of the strongest personality. For the *Passioni amorose* the conductor, Francesco Petracchi, exchanges his baton for another bow to join his colleague, establishing a close, decisive partnership. Further contrast is provided in the *Duo concertante* on melodies of Bellini. The programme is interspersed with colourful orchestral miniatures. The *Sinfonia, Il diavolo della notte,* turns naturally from warm lyricism to galloping liveliness, and the brief *Ali Baba Overture* brings a spirited whiff of Rossini. The recording engineers have done marvels to balance everything so convincingly, and this programme is surprisingly rewarding and entertaining.

Gran duo concertante for Violin, Double-Bass & Orchestra; Gran concerto in F sharp min. for Double-Bass; Andante sostenuto for Strings; Duetto for Clarinet & Double-Bass.

**(*) ASV CDDCA 563. Garcia, Martin, Johnson, ECO, Litton.

The ASV recording combines the *Gran duo concertante* with another *Duetto for Clarinet and Double-Bass* which Emma Johnson ensures has plenty of personality, though none of this amiable music is very distinctive. The recording is excellent, well balanced and truthful.

Capriccio di bravura; Elegia in Re; Fantasia on 'Beatrice di Tenda'; Fantasia on 'Lucia di Lammermoor'; Grand allegro di concerto; Introduzione e bolero; Romanza drammatica; (i) *Romanza: Une bouche aimée.*

(*) ASV CDDCA 626. Martin, Halstead; (i) with J. Fugelle.

Thomas Martin is a superb virtuoso of the double-bass and he obviously relishes these display pieces, but some of the high tessitura is inevitably uncomfortable. The recording is most realistic.

BOUGHTON, Rutland (1878–1960)

(i) *Oboe Concerto No. 1 in C; Symphony No. 3 in B min.*

(B) *** Hyp. Helios CDH 55019. (i) Francis; RPO, Handley.

Rutland Boughton's *Third Symphony* is expertly fashioned, often imaginative and, save in the rumbustious Scherzo (where the closing pages are clumsily scored), hardly puts a foot wrong. The *Oboe Concerto* is hardly less rewarding. It opens a little floridly but its pastoralism soon asserts itself, blossoms in the *Adagio espressivo*, and colours the gaily dancing finale. The recording of the *Symphony* approaches the demonstration bracket and the performances are totally committed, even if the strings of the RPO are not quite on top form. A bargain well worth seeking out.

Pastoral.

(B) *** Hyp. Helios CDH 55008. Francis, Rasumovsky —
HARTY: *3 Pieces;* HOWELLS: *Sonata;* RUBBRA: *Sonata.* ***

Boughton's enchanting *Pastoral* for oboe and string quartet makes a delightful pendant to this fine collection of English music for oboe and piano. It has a disarmingly attractive, folksy pastoral melody, which haunts the memory. The performance could hardly be more persuasive.

Bethlehem (choral drama).

*** Hyp. CDA 66690. Field, Bryan, Bryson, R. Evans, Bowen, Peacock, Opie, MacDougall, Van Allan, Seaton, Campbell, I. Boughton, Matheson-Bruce, Holst Singers, New L. Children's Ch., City of L. Sinf., Melville.

Boughton's score, lyrical and undemanding, with carols punctuating the scenes as chorales punctuate the Bach Passions, is an aptly fresh and innocent setting of an edited version of the Coventry Nativity Play. The role of the villainous Herod unexpectedly is consigned to a tenor. Alan G. Melville conducts a warm, fluent performance that is generally well sung, though for the central role of the Virgin Mary it would have been better to have had a sweeter voice than Helen Field's. Alan Opie and the two other wise men are outstanding, and the three shepherds characterize well in their pastoral cavortings. The score has been discreetly cut to fit the two Acts on a single CD with little loss. First-rate, well-balanced sound.

The Immortal Hour (opera): complete.

(B) *** Hyp. Dyad CDD 22040 (2). Kennedy, Dawson, Wilson-Johnson, Davies, Mitchell Ch., ECO, Melville.

Analysed closely, much of *The Immortal Hour* may seem like Vaughan Williams and water; but this fine performance,

conducted by a lifelong Boughton devotee, brings out the hypnotic quality which had 1920s music-lovers attending performances many times over, entranced by its lyrical evocation of Celtic twilight. The simple tunefulness goes with a fine feeling for atmosphere. The excellent cast of young singers includes Anne Dawson as the heroine, Princess Etain, and Maldwyn Davies headily beautiful in the main tenor rendering of the *Faery song*. Warm, reverberant recording, enhanced in its CD format, and this delightful opera is not to be missed at its new Dyad price.

BOULANGER, Lili (1893–1918)

Faust et Hélène; Psaume 24; Psaume 130: Du fond de l'abîme; D'un matin de printemps; D'un soir triste.

*** Chan. 9745. Dawson, Murray, Bottone, MacKenzie, Howard, CBSO Ch., BBC PO, Y. P. Tortelier.

Faust et Hélène has astonishing beauty and a natural eloquence. Like *Psaume 26, Du fond de l'abîme* and the other music on the disc, it offers testimony to an altogether remarkable talent. There is a distinguished team of soloists (Lynne Dawson and Bonaventura Bottone in the cantata and Ann Murray in one of the Psalms) and first-rate contributions from the Birmingham Chorus and the BBC Philharmonic under Yan Pascal Tortelier.

Psaume 24; Psaume 130: Du fond de l'abîme; Pie Jesu.

⚙ **(*)** BBC (ADD) BBCL 4026-2. Price, Greevy, Partridge, Carol Case, BBC Ch., BBC SO, N. Boulanger — FAURÉ: *Requiem.* **(*)** ⚙

Lili Boulanger died in her mid-twenties, but not before committing some remarkable music to paper, including the *Pie Jesu*, dedicated to her sister Nadia. The latter certainly conveys her fervour and belief in these remarkable scores, and *Du fond de l'abîme* is a work of astonishing originality and imagination. Recorded at a live concert in the Fairfield Halls, Croydon, the BBC engineers provide more than acceptable sound and the balance is skilfully done. A rather special musical document.

BOULEZ, Pierre (born 1925)

Eclat-Multiples; Rituel: In memoriam Bruno Maderna.

(M) *** Sony (ADD) SK 45839. BBC SO, Ens. InterContemporain, composer.

Eclat-Multiples appeared first in 1964 simply as *Eclat*, a brilliant showpiece, an exuberant mosaic of sounds; but then, in 1970, it started developing from there in the pendant work, *Multiples. Rituel* is the most moving music that Boulez has ever written, inspired by the premature death of his friend and colleague, Bruno Maderna. This record, very well played and recorded, provides both a challenge and a reward.

(i) *Livre pour cordes;* (ii) *Pli selon pli.*

(M) *** Sony (ADD) SMK 68335. (i) New Philh. O strings; (ii) Lukomska, Bergman, Stingle, D'Alton, BBC SO; composer.

Pli selon pli (literally 'fold upon fold') comes from the poet Mallarmé, and Boulez's layers of invention are used to illuminate as centrepieces three Mallarmé sonnets. The luminous texture of Boulez's writing is endlessly fascinating and, for the listener with an open mind, this is a rewarding way of widening experience of the avant garde. *Livre pour cordes* is a less demanding piece, but one equally worth studying. Definitive performances and excellent (late-1960s) recording under the composer's sharp-eared and electrifying direction.

(i) *Dialogue;* **(ii)** *Répons.*

(*) DG 457 605-2. (i) Damiens; (ii) Soloists, Ens. InterContemporain, composer.

Boulez chose the title *Répons* in reflection of the interplay of solo and ensemble voices in Gregorian chant; but even an unprepared listener can appreciate the sensuous element in this work for six contrasted soloists, an instrumental ensemble of 24 players, and computerized sound developed from that of the soloists. Though a two-channel stereo recording cannot convey the full impact, this is a powerful performance that gives a fair impression of the live event. *Dialogue* applies similar techniques to a solitary clarinet, with more limited but tonally revealing results.

Domaines.

(N) (B) ** HM HMA 195930. Ens. Portal, Musique Vivante, Masson.

Domaines was first performed in 1968 as a work for solo clarinet, but two years later Boulez rewrote the score to include a responding concertante ensemble of 20 additional instrumentalists including percussion, divided into five groups arranged in a circle. The solo clarinet moves among them throughout the performance, yet remains a fulcrum. The music itself, which is extremely fragmented, is divided into six cahiers and in the first half of the work the soloist determines the order in which these shall be played and dominates the proceedings. In the second *Mirror* half, the conductor of the ensemble makes the choice and the soloists reflect the instrumental tuttis (often little more than bursts of notes and bizarre instrumental colour) which are now more elaborate. Clearly any performance has a strong visual element which an audio recording cannot capture, but the stereo here readily conveys the mobility of the soloist. Although all the music is in score, the effect of this obviously expert performance is almost aleatory, even improvisational, and few will find the composer's musical logic easily comprehensible. Although this is a bargain reissue, the playing time is only just over half an hour, which many will say is quite long enough!

Piano Sonatas Nos. 1–3.

(BB) *** Naxos 8.553353. Biret.

The Boulez sonatas are well served by the gramophone – particularly No. 2, which Pollini has recorded for DG (see 447 431-2). Those with an interest in this repertoire will be well rewarded by Idil Biret on Naxos; she is more than equal to their technical demands and is given good sound.

BOWEN, York (1884–1961)

PIANO MUSIC

Ballade No. 2, Op. 87; Berceuse, Op. 83; Moto perpetuo from Op. 39; Preludes, Op. 102, Nos. 1 in C; 2 in C min.; 6 in D min.; 7 in E flat; 8 in E flat min.; 10 in E min.; 15 in G; 16 in G min.; 18 in G sharp min.; 19 in A; 20 in A min.; 21 in B flat; 22 in B flat min.; Romances Nos. 1, Op. 35/1; 2, Op. 45; Sonata No. 5 in F min., Op. 72. Toccata, Op. 155.

⊛ *** Hyp. CDA 66838. Hough.

Few new discs of piano music are as magical as this: magnetic performances that come as a revelation, demonstrating that this long-neglected composer was a master of keyboard writing. Hough, always compelling on disc, not only technically brilliant but spontaneously expressive, consistently conveys his love for Bowen's music, starting with 13 of the 24 *Preludes*. He puts them in his own, very effective order, bringing out the contrasted qualities of jewelled miniatures, reflecting Rachmaninov on the one hand, Ireland and Bax on the other, but with a flavour of their own. The most powerful, most ambitious work is the *Sonata No. 5*, with two weighty, wide-ranging movements separated by an *Andante* interlude. Vivid piano-sound and illuminating notes by Francis Pott and Hough himself.

BOYCE, William (1710–79)

Overtures Nos. 1–9.

(M) *** Chan. 6531. Cantilena, Shepherd.

Overtures Nos. 10–12; Concerti grossi: in B flat; in B min.; in E min.

(M) *** Chan. 6541. Cantilena, Shepherd.

Though these works do not quite have the consistent originality which makes the Boyce *Symphonies* so refreshing, the energy of the writing – splendidly conveyed in these performances – is recognizably the same, with fugal passages that turn in unexpected directions. Cantilena's performances readily convey the freshness of Boyce's inspiration. The recording is oddly balanced but is both atmospheric and vivid and provides a refreshing musical experience.

Symphonies Nos. 1–8, Op. 2.

*** DG 419 631-2. E. Concert, Pinnock.

(N) (M) *** CRD 3356. Bournemouth Sinf., Thomas.

Pinnock's disc of the Boyce *Symphonies* wears its scholarship very easily and in so doing brings not only lively, resilient playing but fresh revelation in the treatment of the *vivace* movements. Nicely scaled recording, bright but atmospheric.

Thomas's tempi are often brisk, and are certainly swifter-paced than Pinnock's 'new look'. But even against such strong competition as this, the buoyant playing of the Bournemouth Sinfonietta still gives much pleasure by its sheer vitality. Bright, clear sound and a price advantage.

12 Trio Sonatas (1747).

**(*) Chan. 0648 (2). Coll. Mus. 90, Standage.

12 Trio Sonatas (1747); *Sonatas Nos. 13–15* (unpublished).

*** Hyp. CDA 67151/2. Parley of Instruments or Parley
  Baroque O, Holman.

Boyce gave the English trio sonata a new lease of life at a
time when the format was in danger of falling into neglect,
and they are consistently inventive and a good example of
baroque 'easy listening'. Not only that, but they seem to get
more and more attractive, and the second disc is more
enjoyable than the first. As an appendix, Peter Holman has
discovered three extra sonatas (here numbered 13–15) which
survive in a manuscript in the Cambridge Fitzwilliam Museum. There is evidence to suggest that these sonatas were
sometimes played in orchestral form, so the Hyperion
recording alternates orchestral and chamber performance,
with Nos. 1, 3, 5, 7–9, 11 and 13 heard on a full string group.
These period performances are vigorously alert and stylish,
with slow movements refined yet warmly relished, especially
those that remind the listener a little of Handel. Excellent
recording without edginess.

Simon Standage and Collegium Musicum 90 offer one
instrument to a part throughout. The performances are
fresh and alive, the recording clean and clear. However,
the competing set from Peter Holman, with the Parley
instrumental groups on Hyperion, is in almost every way
preferable.

Anthems: *By the waters of Babylon; I have surely built thee
an house; The Lord is King, be the people never so
impatient; O give thanks; O praise the Lord; O where shall
wisdom be found?; Turn thee unto me; Wherewithal shall a
young man; Organ Voluntaries Nos. 1, 4 & 7.*

(M) *** CRD 3483. New College, Oxford, Ch., Higginbottom;
  Cooper.

These five verse anthems and three others in a rather more
ambitious ternary format are all of high quality, broadly
following a Purcellian tradition. The beautiful *By the waters
of Babylon* is perhaps the finest of the latter, but the verse
anthem, *I have surely built thee an house*, is also very commanding, as is the opening *O where shall wisdom be found?*.
Three organ voluntaries are included to add variety and,
with such strong, well-integrated performances and excellent recording in a highly suitable acoustic, this can be truly
recommended.

Ode for St Cecilia's Day.

*** ASV CDGAU 200. Burrowes, Purefoy, Watts, Edgar-Wilson,
  George, New College, Oxford, Ch., Hanover Band, Lea-Cox.

Boyce's *Ode for St Cecilia's Day* uses a text by his friend
John Lockman, celebrating Apollo and the Muses as well as
St Cecilia, patron saint of music. It is only at the very end
that the saint herself appears in the last aria, sung in this
performance by a boy chorister, the fresh-voiced Patrick
Burrowes. This has similar vigour to *The Secular Masque*,
recorded earlier by Graham Lea-Cox with the same choir
and orchestra, with comparably lively results in the choruses,

if with less distinguished singing from the soloists. Good,
atmospheric sound.

The Secular Masque. Overtures: *Birthday Ode for George
III* (1768); *King's Ode for the New Year* (1772); *Ode for
St Cecilia's Day.*

*** ASV CDGAU 176. Howarth, Kuhlmann, Daniels, Robinson,
  Varcoe, Thomas, New College, Oxford, Ch., Hanover Band,
  Lea-Cox.

The Secular Masque represents Boyce at his freshest and most
unbuttoned. So 'Diana's song' – which Boyce published
separately – with elaborate horn parts, brims with rustic
jollity and is sung radiantly here by Judith Howarth. 'Mars's
song', *Sound the trumpet, beat the drum*, also has Boyce
responding with engaging directness, vigorous and
colourful. Each of the overtures here, including the one for
the *Secular Masque*, follow a similar form in two, three
or four brief movements. Graham Lea-Cox draws lively
performances from the Hanover Band, the choir and his
excellent team of soloists. Warm, full sound.

Solomon (*serenata*).

*** Hyp. CDA 66378. Mills, Crook, Parley of Instruments,
  Goodman.

William Boyce's *Solomon* is a totally secular piece, a dialogue
between She and He, with the verses freely based on the
Song of Solomon. As this stylish and alert period performance
using young, fresh-voiced soloists makes clear, it has some
delightful inspirations, less influenced by Italian models
than by popular English song. First-rate sound.

BRADE, William (1560–1630)

Hamburger Ratsmusik: excerpts.

(BB) ***DHM 05472 77476-2. Hespèrion XX, Savall.

This collection of dances is absolutely delightful, varied in
content and instrumental colour and expertly played and
recorded. Those content with a short selection, including
music from just the 1609 and 1615 collections, will find this
bargain disc most enjoyable.

BRÆIN, Edvard Fliflet (1924–76)

Anne Pedersdotter (opera): complete.

*** Simax PSC3121 (2). Ekeberg, Handssen, Carlsen, Sandve,
  Thorsen, Norwegian Nat. Op. Ch. & O, Andersson.

Edvard Fliflet Bræin was a highly talented Norwegian
composer who died in his early fifties. His opera, *Anne Pedersdotter* (1971), is based on the most famous witchcraft trial in
Norway: the burning of Anne Pedersdotter in Bergen in 1590.
Fliflet Bræin called it 'a symphonic opera' and, like Schoeck's
Venus, its invention unfolds in an effortlessly organic fashion;
in other words, his is the art that conceals art. It is effective
music-theatre and many of its ideas, as so often with Bræin,
are memorable. It gets a fine performance here, with good
singing from Kjersti Ekeberg as the eponymous heroine, Svein
Carlsen as her husband, Absolon Pedersøn-Beyer, and Kjell

Magnus Sandve as his son by his first marriage. The Norwegian Opera forces under the baton of Per Ake Andersson are excellent, and the recording, produced by Michael Woolcock, is very good indeed. Strongly recommended.

BRAHMS, Johannes (1833–97)

Piano Concertos Nos. 1 in D min., Op. 15; 2 in B flat, Op. 83.

(BB) *** Virgin 2 x 1 VBD5 61412-2. Hough, BBC SO, A. Davis.
** DG 457 837-2 (2). Pollini, BPO, Abbado.

(i) *Piano Concertos Nos. 1–2.* (ii) *Academic Festival Overture; Tragic Overture; Variations on a Theme of Haydn, Op. 56a.*

(B) *** EMI double forte (ADD) CZS5 72649-2 (2).
(i) Barenboim, Philh. O; (ii) VPO; Barbirolli.

(B) **(*) Ph. (ADD) Duo 438 320-2 (2). (i) Arrau; Concg. O, Haitink.

Piano Concertos Nos. 1–2; Tragic Overture, Op. 81; Variations on a Theme of Haydn, Op. 56a.

(B) **(*) DG (ADD) Double 453 067 (2). Pollini, VPO, Boehm (*No. 1*) or Abbado (*No. 2*).

(i) *Piano Concertos Nos. 1–2; Tragic Overture; Variations on a Theme of Haydn.*

(B) *(*) EMI (ADD) CZS5 72013-2 (2). Arrau, Philh. O, Giulini.

(i) *Piano Concertos Nos. 1–2. Variations & Fugue on a Theme of Handel, Op. 24; Waltzes, Op. 39.*

(M) *** Sony Heritage (ADD) MH2K 63225 (2). Fleisher;
(i) Cleveland O, Szell.

(i) *Piano Concertos Nos. 1–2. 4 Ballades, Op. 10; 8 Pieces, Op. 76; Scherzo in E flat, Op. 4.*

(B) *** Ph. (ADD) Duo 442 109-2 (2). Kovacevich; (i) LSO, C. Davis.

(i) *Piano Concertos Nos. 1–2. 4 Ballades, Op. 10; Theme & Variations in D min. (from String Sextet, Op. 18).*

(M) *** Ph. 446 925-2 (5). Brendel, (i) BPO, Abbado –
SCHUMANN: *Collection.* ***

(i) *Piano Concertos Nos. 1–2. Capriccio in B min., Op. 76/2; Intermezzi: in E, Op. 116/6; in E flat, Op. 117/1; in E min.; in C, Op. 119/2–3; Rhapsody in B min., Op. 79/1; 6 Pieces, Op. 118.*

(M) **(*) Decca (ADD) (IMS) 433 895-2 (2). Backhaus;
(i) VPO, Boehm.

(i) *Piano Concertos Nos. 1–2. Fantasias, Op. 116.*

(M) *** DG (ADD) 447 446-2 (2). Gilels; (i) BPO, Jochum.

The Gilels performances can still hold their own against virtually all the competition, but the two concertos are also available separately – see below. However, the present set is offered at a reduced price and the remastered recording is quite outstanding.

Barenboim's performance of the *First Piano Concerto* with Barbirolli is among the most inspired ever committed to disc. The playing is heroic and marvellously spacious. In the *Second Concerto* the first two movements remain grandly heroic and the slow movement has something of the awed

intensity you find in the middle movement of the *First*, while the finale erupts gracefully into rib-tickling humour. This is a performance to love in its glowing spontaneity. Of the fill-ups, the *Academic Festival Overture* could do with more sparkle, while the *Tragic Overture* and *Haydn Variations* show the conductor at his finest. The late-1960s recordings have transferred splendidly to CD.

Stephen Hough gives keenly distinctive and deeply thoughtful readings of both Brahms concertos, so that with refined recording the transparency of textures may be disconcerting to those who insist on a fat Brahms sound. He adopts the widest range of tone and dynamic, with the recording beautifully capturing the hushed pianissimos in both works, not least in both slow movements. Both recordings were made in 1989.

Leon Fleisher's two concerto recordings are both masterly examples of joint inspiration, bringing out the point that these are in many ways symphonies with piano, when Szell's direction is so powerful and incisive as well as warmly expressive. Not that Fleisher in any way lacks individuality, for the crisp confidence of his virtuosity has a sureness in its musical and emotional thrust that carries one magnetically on. The sound is among the best offered by CBS at that period, with the piano balanced forwardly but not aggressively so. Generously, this Heritage issue also includes solo recordings by Fleisher of the *Handel Variations* and *Waltzes*, similarly crisp and concentrated, though the 1956 mono sound here is rather clattery.

In the *D minor Concerto* Kovacevich plays with great tenderness and lyrical feeling. Similarly, No. 2 combines poetic feeling and intellectual strength and reflects an unforced naturalness that compels admiration. The accounts of the *Ballades* and the Op. 76 *Klavierstücke* have both fire and tenderness and are truthfully recorded.

Brendel's digital recordings of the two Brahms concertos with Claudio Abbado and the Berlin Philharmonic show him at his finest. His control of Brahmsian rubato is masterly, easily flexible but totally unexaggerated, and the basic tempi are set well and steadily. The balance is not too forward and the effect is warmly satisfying. The account of the Op. 10 *Ballades* is also a performance of distinction. The digital recording is first class.

Arrau's Philips readings undoubtedly have vision and power, and the *D minor Concerto* is majestic and eloquent. There is some characteristic agogic distortion that will not convince all listeners and, by the side of Gilels, Arrau seems idiosyncratic. In the *Second Concerto* his playing has a splendid combination of aristocratic finesse and warmth of feeling, and in both concertos Haitink and the Royal Concertgebouw Orchestra give excellent support.

Arrau's first stereo versions for EMI, made at the beginning of the 1960s, suffer from the feeling of a lack of affinity with the recording studio that has often afflicted him in the past. Nor is Giulini the ideal conductor for him, polished and weighty without being really inspired. Arrau provides some delicious moments in the more graceful passages of No. 1 but is never fiery in the way Curzon, for instance, is with Szell. The *Second Concerto* has a certain massive strength, helped by the full-bodied sound, but overall it hardly adds up to a very convincing performance.

Although Pollini and the Vienna Philharmonic under Karl Boehm are given finely detailed recording, in the *First Piano Concerto* other versions (notably Gilels) provide greater wisdom and humanity. Not that Pollini is wanting in keyboard command, but he is a little short on tenderness and poetry. All too often here he seems to have switched on the automatic pilot and, although the *B flat Concerto* under Abbado is much fresher and offers some masterly pianism, there are warmer and more spontaneous accounts to be had.

DG have also now paired together Pollini's two Brahms concertos, recorded live with Abbado in 1997–8. No. 1 is handicapped by a balance which places the piano very forward in relation to the orchestra. The *Second Concerto* is much more satisfactory in this respect: indeed the sound is very satisfactory. The performance too is of some distinction, but this set is poor value at premium price.

Backhaus recorded the *First Concerto* in 1953 and no apologies need be made for the mono recording, the performance has great impetus and authority. The *Second Concerto* was made in the Sofiensaal in 1967 when Backhaus was in his eighties, and the rugged strength of his conception is matched by playing of remarkable power. His is a broad, magisterial account. The recording wears its years remarkably lightly: it sounds fresh and full-bodied and is finely detailed. The solo pieces date from 1956 and Backhaus is again in excellent form.

Piano Concerto No. 1 in D min., Op. 15.

*** Ph. 420 071-2. Brendel, BPO, Abbado.

(M) *** Decca (ADD) 466 376-2. Curzon, LSO, Szell – FRANCK: *Symphonic Variations;* LITOLFF: *Scherzo.* ***

(N) (M) **(*) RCA (ADD) 09026 63059-2. Rubinstein, Boston SO, Leinsdorf – BEETHOVEN: *Piano Concerto No. 2 in B flat, Op. 19.* **(*)

(BB) **(*) ASV (ADD) CDQS 6083. Lill, Hallé O, Loughran.

(M) ** Chan. 6621 (2). Margalit, LSO, Thompson (with MENDELSSOHN: *Capriccio Brillant* **) – SCHUMANN: *Concerto;* SAINT-SAENS: *Concerto No. 2.* **

(N) (BB) *(*) Naxos 8.554088. Biret, Polish Nat. R. SO, Wit – SCHUMANN: *Introduction & Concert Allegro.* *(*)

(M) *(*) Sony (ADD) SMK 60675. Gould, NYPO, Bernstein.

(i) *Piano Concerto No. 1; Variations & Fugue on a Theme of Handel, Op. 24.*

(***) Testament mono SBT 1041. Solomon, (i) Philh. O, Kubelik.

(i) *Piano Concerto No. 1; 4 Ballades, Op. 10.*

(M) *** DG (ADD) 439 979-2. Gilels; (i) BPO, Jochum.

(N) ** Australian Decca (ADD) 466 724-2. (i) Rubinstein, Israel PO, Mehta; (ii) Katchen.

(i) *Piano Concerto No. 1; 4 Ballades, Op. 10; Scherzo in E flat min., Op. 4.*

(B) *** Ph. (ADD) 442 110-2. Kovacevich; (i) LSO, C. Davis.

(i) *Piano Concerto No. 1; (ii) 2 Songs, Op. 91.*

⬤ *** EMI CDC7 54578-2. (i) Kovacevich, LPO, Sawallisch; (ii) Murray, Imai.

Noble and dedicated, Stephen Kovacevich's EMI account of the Brahms *D minor Concerto* is a performance of stature

which belongs in the most exalted company; indeed, it must now take precedence. Moreover it is accorded fine digital sound which has all the warmth and spaciousness one could ask for, together with splendid presence and detail. There is a welcome fill-up in the form of the two Op. 91 *Songs* with viola, by Anne Murray and Nobuko Imai. However, as we go to press, this set has been withdrawn.

Gilels's reading of the *D minor Concerto* has magisterial strength blended with a warmth, humanity and depth that are altogether inspiring. The *Ballades* have never been played so marvellously on record, and the recording is very believable.

Brendel too produces a consistently beautiful sound and balances the combative and lyrical elements of the work with well-nigh perfect judgement.

Clifford Curzon's 1962 recording, produced by John Culshaw in Kingsway Hall, returns to the catalogue, superbly remastered. The fierceness of attack in the upper strings, especially in the powerful opening tutti, sounds naturally focused on CD, adding a leonine power to Szell's orchestral contribution, and the piano tone is admirably natural.

Kovacevich's earlier, Philips account of the *D minor Concerto* is also available on a Duo, which pairs it with the *Second Concerto* and also includes the solo piano music (see above). Those who want the *First Concerto* alone should be well satisfied with this separate issue on the Philips Virtuoso bargain label.

Serkin's 1968 account with Szell, his third on LP, brought tremendous command and grandeur. This is undoubtedly a memorable performance, and the support from Szell and the Cleveland Orchestra has great power. The CBS/Sony recording has been considerably improved, but the balance still lacks a natural perspective and the sound ideally needs more opulence and depth.

Solomon's magisterial account with Rafael Kubelik and the Philharmonia Orchestra has a majestic grandeur and blends the dramatic power of youth with the wisdom of old age. Of course the 1952 recording does not possess the range or bloom of subsequent versions, but the transfer succeeds in making it sound astonishingly present. Of his celebrated 1942 set of the Brahms *Handel Variations* one is tempted to say the same.

The partnership between Rubinstein and Leinsdorf in the D minor Concerto is quite different from his bonding with Ormandy in No. 2. Leinsdorf opens massively, with a degree of fierceness, but Rubinstein's entry is immediately more lyrical, with the orchestral strings then answering warmly. The slow movement is spaciously sustained, with lovely luminous pianism and rapt concentration shared between piano and orchestra. The closing section, gently glowing, contrasts with the burst of high spirits in the finale, where Rubinstein is engagingly fresh and the Boston players respond vigorously. Undoubtedly this reading is compulsive, and if the remastered 1964 recording – though much improved – shows signs of its age, there is plenty of orchestral body with the piano immediate and realistically caught.

John Lill has the measure of the work's fire and drama, yet his playing is fundamentally classical. He is given warm and spirited support from Loughran and the Hallé, even though woodwind intonation in one or two places is not wholly above reproach. At times there is a slightly reserved quality that inhibits unqualified recommendation.

Rubinstein admirers will be happy to learn that his 1975 Decca recording of Brahms's *First Concerto* has made it on to CD. With more than a sprinkling of wrong notes, this can never be a general recommendation, but the character and drive of the man in his late eighties emerge vividly. To hear such a performance in the concert hall one would readily pay far more, though here the piano is balanced too forwardly. Katchen's characterfully played and recorded *Ballades* make a useful coupling. This CD is nothing if not a collector's item.

Israela Margalit is a most musical exponent of this most leonine of concertos, and on the whole Bryden Thompson proves a sound partner. However, the sumptuous Chandos recording has the violins backwardly balanced at the very opening, blunting the orchestral attack. While this account, which has no lack of poetic feeling, is far more than just an also-ran and there is much to admire, the overall impression makes it less commanding than the finest available versions, and its new format is not particularly economical.

Idil Biret plays with genuine Brahmsian warmth, and her pianism is powerful and compelling. The Polish Orchestra is fully committed too. However, Wit's opening ritornello is romantically wayward, which prevents any sense of strong forward thrust that is so essential in the first movement of this concerto, and this approach is shared by the soloist. The slow movement does not lack expressive warmth, but it is only in the brilliant finale that the performance is totally convincing. The spacious recording gives no cause for complaint.

Glenn Gould's performance carries a prefatory disclaimer from Bernstein, something rarely encountered in the concert hall and unprecedented on disc. Recorded at a Carnegie Hall concert in New York in April 1962, the performance is new to the catalogue; it finds the Canadian pianist at his most wilful and self-conscious. Of course it offers moments of insight, but for the most part this is for Gould *aficionados* only. Others will be spectacularly underwhelmed.

Piano Concerto No. 2 in B flat, Op. 83.

*** Ph. 432 975-2. Brendel, BPO, Abbado.

(N) (M) *** RCA (ADD) 09026 63071-2. Rubinstein, Phd. O, Ormandy – SCHUMANN: *Fantasiestücke.* ***

(BB) **(*) ASV (ADD) CDQS 6088. Lill, Hallé O, Loughran.

(B) **(*) Sony (ADD) SBK 53262. Serkin, Cleveland O, Szell – R. STRAUSS: *Burleske.* *(**)

(**(*)) Testament mono SBT 1170. Fischer, BPO, Furtwängler – FURTWANGLER: *Symphonic Concerto: Adagio.* (**)

(N) (BB) ** Naxos 8.554089. Biret, Polish Nat. R. SO, Wit – SCHUMANN: *Introduction & Allegro appassionato.* *(*)

(i) *Piano Concerto No. 2; 4 Ballades, Op. 10.*

(M) *** DG (ADD) 439 466-2. Gilels; (i) BPO, Jochum.

(i) *Piano Concerto No. 2. Intermezzi: in B flat min., Op. 117/2; in C, Op. 119/3; Rhapsody in G min., Op. 79/2.*

(***) Testament mono SBT 1042. Solomon, (i) Philh. O, Dobrowen.

(i) *Piano Concerto No. 2; (ii) 5 Lieder, Op. 105.*

**(*) EMI CDC5 55218-2. Kovacevich; (i) LPO, Sawallisch; (ii) Murray.

(i) *Piano Concerto No. 2; Symphony No. 1 in C min., Op. 61; Serenade No. 1 in D: Allegro molto.*

(B) (**(*)) Naxos mono 8.110805/6. (i) Horowitz; NBC SO, Toscanini; (with broadcast commentary by Gene Hamilton).

(i) *Piano Concerto No. 2; (ii) Cello Sonata in D (arr. of Violin Sonata in G, Op. 78).*

**(*) Sony SK 63229. Ax; with (i) Boston SO, Haitink; (ii) Ma.

The partnership of Gilels and Jochum produces music-making of rare magic, and the digital remastering has improved definition: the sound is full in an appropriately Brahmsian way. Readers will note that this reissue is now recoupled with the *4 Ballades*, Op. 10 (instead of the *Fantasias*, Op. 116), which seems perverse when the Gilels version of the *First Concerto* has the same coupling.

Brendel is massive and concentrated and has greater depth than in his earlier account with Haitink. It is a worthy successor to their *D minor*, though in terms of humanity and wisdom it does not displace the celebrated Gilels–Jochum version.

When Rubinstein's second 1971 stereo recording of the *B flat Concerto* appeared on LP, the performance was welcomed by us as distinguished, but was dismissed for its less than ideal recorded sound. Since then his earlier 1958 account with Krips has held its place on CD among the top recommendations. That reading emphasized the bright and luminous aspects of the work, but RCA have chosen now to reissue the wholly different partnership with Ormandy in the 'Rubinstein Edition', with the remastered recording completely transformed. It was made in the Philadelphia Scottish Rites Cathedral whose warm acoustics are just right for Brahms.

The piano is forwardly placed, but the timbre, bright and glowing on top, has splendid body and a sonorous bass. The orchestra too is richly and spaciously caught; although the upper range lacks the last degree of refinement, the balance overall is most impressive. Ormandy – a splendid Brahmsian – and Rubinstein are at one, and their reading is much weightier and more powerful and exciting than the earlier version. Yet the luminosity remains, displayed in the orchestral playing as well as the pianism. The recapitulation of both the first movement and the lovely *Andante* bring moments of magical anticipation, and in the slow movement Samuel Mayes, the solo cellist, reprises his lovely theme gently and touchingly. There is contrasting lyricism too in the middle section of the passionate *Scherzo* while the skipping finale ripples along light-heartedly with Rubinstein's charismatic articulation balanced by a glowing orchestral response. This is an account to be reckoned with, strikingly spontaneous and greatly enjoyable, and it can be placed alongside those of Gilels, Barenboim, and Brendel. The Schumann coupling is comparably fine: the opening movement, *Des Abends*, comes as gentle balm after the bold closing pages of the concerto.

The commanding Solomon version of the *B flat Concerto* with Issay Dobrowen and the Philharmonia Orchestra comes from 1947. There is a leonine nobility about this performance and an immediacy, spontaneity and dramatic fire that sweep all before it. Like his recording of the *D minor Concerto*, this is a classic account which no admirer of this artist (or of Brahms, for that matter) should pass over. The piano is not always perfect (the C above the stave is out of tune in one passage) but the pianist is! The listener soon forgets the sonic limitations and is swept along by the performance.

The magisterial and autumnal *Second Piano Concerto in B flat* from Emanuel Ax and the Boston Symphony under Bernard Haitink on Sony has tremendous breadth. It strikes the right balance between the rhapsodic and the symphonic, the seemingly improvisatory solo writing and the sinewy orchestral texture. Ax is a perceptive and thoughtful artist whose beautiful pianism impresses, as does the eloquent orchestral playing. The fill-up, an arrangement by an unknown hand of the *G major Sonata* transposed to D major for cello, is played with refinement but is hardly an urgent addition to the catalogue.

After his noble and dedicated account of the *First Piano Concerto* with Wolfgang Sawallisch and the LPO, Stephen Kovacevich's version of its successor brings admiration tinged with disappointment. It does not match this partnership's *First* and does not take wing in quite the same way. However, the set has been withdrawn as we go to press.

John Lill's 1982 version with the Hallé Orchestra under James Loughran is in many ways a strong account, well thought out, finely paced and without the slightest trace of self-indulgence. It is the space and power of Brahms's conception that are given priority, rather than his poetry.

Serkin achieves an ideal balance between straightforwardness and expressiveness, while the slow movement has a genuine 'inner' intensity. He chooses a comparatively slow speed for the finale, but the flow and energy of the music are not impaired. Unfortunately the piano tone is not as full as one would ideally like, but the remastering produces a firm orchestral image, and the hall ambience contributes to a Brahmsian sonority.

The partnership of Edwin Fischer and Wilhelm Furtwängler produced inspired music-making, both in the 1943 wartime German radio recording of the Brahms concerto and in the slow movement from the conductor's own ambitious concerto, recorded in 1939. The sound in the Brahms is limited, but the piano is bright and clear, and the performance has such energy and warmth, rapt in the slow movement, that one readily forgives any flaws and intrusive audience noises.

Though, with announcements, the Naxos Horowitz/Toscanini version spreads to a second disc, and the 1940 sound is rough, this offers not only a glowing account of the *First Symphony* but a performance of the *Second Concerto* which makes it a symphony with piano. Even the mighty virtuoso, Horowitz, Toscanini's son-in-law, is outshone. The first movement of the *Serenade No. 1* acts as a light-hearted overture.

The spacious, boldly romantic approach of Idil Biret and Antoni Wit works much better in the *Second Concerto* than in the *First*, helped by the warmth of the full-bodied recording. There is no doubting the power and virtuosity of the solo playing or the committed response of the Polish Orchestra.

However, at times the forward momentum of the first movement is inclined to lapse, and Biret in her forcefulness becomes rhythmically heavy. The close of the leisurely *Andante* lacks the concentration necessary to sustain a high level of tension, but the lilting finale is a success.

Piano Concertos Nos. (i) 1; (ii) 2; (iii) Violin Concerto.

(B) **(*) Double Decca ADD/Dig. 452 335-2 (2). (i) Lupu, LPO, de Waart; (ii) Ashkenazy, LSO, Mehta; (iii) Belkin, LSO, Fischer.

Radu Lupu's approach to the *First Piano Concerto* is deeply reflective and intelligent, full of masterly touches and an affecting poetry which falls short of the thrusting combative power of a Serkin or Curzon. Decca produce a particularly truthful sound-picture. This could be recommended enthusiastically to those who want a second, alternative view. However, Ashkenazy's account of the *Second Piano Concerto* is less successful, its chief shortcoming being a lack of tension. On the other hand, Boris Belkin's performance of the *Violin Concerto* is direct and spontaneous, a spaciously warm reading that makes a strong impression. No complaints about the recorded sound.

Violin Concerto in D, Op. 77.

*** Decca 444 811-2. Bell, Cleveland O, Dohnányi – SCHUMANN: *Violin Concerto.* ***

(BB) *** Royal Long Players (ADD) DCL 705742 (2). Menuhin, BPO, Kempe – DVORAK; SIBELIUS; TCHAIKOVSKY: *Violin Concertos.* ***

(M) *** EMI CD-EMX 2203. Little, RLPO, Handley – SIBELIUS: *Violin Concerto.* ***

(M) *** RCA (ADD) 09026 61742-2. Heifetz, Chicago SO, Reiner – BEETHOVEN: *Violin Concerto.* ***

(M) *** DG 445 515-2. Mutter, BPO, Karajan – MENDELSSOHN: *Violin Concerto.* ***

*** EMI CDC7 54580-2. Perlman, BPO, Barenboim.

(N) (BB) (***) Naxos mono 8.110936. Heifetz, BSO, Koussevitzky – BEETHOVEN: *Violin Concerto.* (***)

*** ASV (ADD) CDDCA 748. Xue-Wei, LPO, Bolton – MENDELSSOHN: *Violin Concerto.* ***

*** Chan. 8974. Udagawa, LSO, Mackerras – BRUCH: *Concerto No. 1.* ***

(M) (***) EMI mono CDH7 61011-2. Neveu, Philh. O, Dobrowen – SIBELIUS: *Violin Concerto.* (***)

(***) Testament mono SBT 1037. Martzy, Philh. O, Kletzki – MENDELSSOHN: *Violin Concerto.* (***)

(***) Testament mono SBT 1038. Haendel, LSO, Celibidache – TCHAIKOVSKY: *Violin Concerto.* (***)

(M) (***) EMI (ADD) CDM5 66977-2 [566992]. Perlman, Chicago SO, Giulini.

**(*) EMI CDC7 54187-2. Kennedy, LPO, Tennstedt.

(N) (BB) **(*) EMI Encore (ADD) CDE5 74724-2. D. Oistrakh, Fr. Nat. RSO, Klemperer – MOZART: *Sinfonia concertante.* **

(B) **(*) DG (ADD) Double 453 142-2 (2). Milstein, VPO, Jochum – BEETHOVEN; MENDELSSOHN; TCHAIKOVSKY: *Violin Concertos.* ***

(*) DG 457 075-2. Mutter, NYPO, Masur (with SCHUMANN: *Fantasy, Op. 131* *).

(i) *Violin Concerto in D. Tragic Overture, Op. 81.*

(B) *** Ph. 422 972-2. (i) Krebbers; Concg. O, Haitink.

Joshua Bell's commanding performance of the Brahms *Violin Concerto* is full of flair, demonstrating not only his love of bravura display, but also his ready gift for turning a phrase individually in a way that catches the ear, always sounding spontaneous. Full, atmospheric recording and a no less outstanding coupling put this among the very finest versions.

The Royal super-bargain collection of 'Great Violin Concertos' includes four outstanding recordings and is alone worth its modest cost for Menuhin's performance of the Brahms with Kempe and the Berlin Philharmonic at the end of the 1950s – one of his supreme achievements in the recording studio. He was in superb form, producing tone of resplendent richness, and the reading is also notable for its warmth and nobility. Kempe and the Berlin Philharmonic were inspired to outstanding playing – the oboe solo in the slow movement is particularly beautiful. The sound is remarkably satisfying and well balanced and the present transfer is wholly admirable.

Tasmin Little gives a warmly satisfying account of the Brahms, at once brilliant and deeply felt. At mid-price the disc is even more recommendable, as it also contains an equally searching and exuberant account of the Sibelius *Violin Concerto*.

Like the Beethoven with which it is coupled, the CD transfer of Heifetz's dazzling performance makes vivid and fresh what on LP was originally a rather harsh Chicago recording, more aggressive than the Boston sound in the Beethoven. With the CD, the excellent qualities of RCA's Chicago balance for Reiner come out in full, giving a fine, three-dimensional focus.

Hermann Krebbers gives one of the most deeply satisfying readings of the Brahms *Violin Concerto* ever recorded: strong and urgent yet at the same time tenderly poetic, and always full of spontaneous imagination. But instead of offering another major concerto, the Philips bargain reissue gives us just the *Tragic Overture*.

In many ways the playing of Anne-Sophie Mutter combines the unforced lyrical feeling of Krebbers with the flair and individuality of Perlman. Needless to say, Karajan's accompaniment is strong in personality and the Berlin Philharmonic play beautifully; the performance represents a genuine musical partnership between youthful inspiration and eager experience. The coupling is hardly less attractive.

Perlman's newest digital account of the Brahms finds him at his most commanding, powerful and full of nonchalant flair. With Perlman the advantage of a live recording is that, as here, there is an extra warmth of commitment, with no sense that the performance has been achieved too easily. There is no fill-up, but few will complain with a reading that is so strong and compelling.

Recorded in 1939 with Koussevitzky and the Boston Orchestra as powerful partners, Heifetz's first recording of the Brahms concerto is typically strong and purposeful, with the structure firmly held together. Speeds in all three movements are faster than we are now used to, but never seem rushed or perfunctory. The patrician purity of Heifetz's playing brings concentration to the slow movement, while the finale is incisive and dramatic, with double-stopping crisply in time. The Naxos transfer is relatively mellow, masking the roughness in the mono sound. An ideal coupling with the Heifetz/Toscanini Beethoven.

Xue-Wei's version of the Brahms is fresh and well mannered. There is a degree of emotional reticence here compared with more flamboyant performers but, with Ivor Bolton drawing first-rate playing from the LPO, it is a performance to live with and it can be warmly recommended. The sound is first rate too.

Hideko Udagawa gives a powerful, persuasively spontaneous-sounding reading. Her biting attack on the most taxing passages is often thrilling, even if her violin-sound is not always the sweetest. Mackerras draws comparably powerful playing from the LSO. Warm, full and well-balanced recording.

Ginette Neveu's is a magnificent performance, urgently electric, remarkable not just for sweetness of tone and her pinpoint intonation but also for the precision and clarity of even the most formidable passages of double stopping. The EMI transfer from the original 78s brings satisfyingly full-bodied sound, surprisingly good on detail.

Johanna Martzy's is an exceptionally warm and persuasive account of the Brahms, marked by a very wide range of dynamic and tone. Few versions of whatever period can match the hushed tenderness of Martzy in the coda of the first movement, and so it is too in the slow movement, while the finale is played with Hungarian point and flair. Kletzki proves an ideal accompanist. The Testament reissue, superbly transferred, at last does justice to a long-underappreciated artist.

Ida Haendel, too, gives a powerful, full-toned reading of the Brahms. Recorded in mono in 1953, it comes up very freshly and intensely in this superb CD transfer from Testament, and the clarity and bite of the playing, as well as its strength and nobility, are splendidly caught, confirming the mastery of a great violinist too little heard on disc.

EMI have chosen Perlman's distinguished earlier account of 1976 for reissue in their 'Great Recordings of the Century' series. He is finely supported by Giulini and the Chicago Symphony Orchestra and gives a reading of a darker hue than is customary, with a thoughtful, searching slow movement, rather than the autumnal rhapsody which it so often becomes. The spacious recording is warm and full-bodied. It places the soloist rather too forward, but admirers of Perlman looking for an alternative performance need not hesitate.

Kennedy's version of the Brahms is by a fair margin the slowest ever put on disc, but his devotion to the work give an intensity to sustain all the eccentricities. Tennstedt draws concentrated playing from the LPO, the whole richly recorded.

The conjunction of two such positive artists as Oistrakh and Klemperer makes for a reading characterful to the point of idiosyncrasy, monumental and strong rather than sweetly lyrical. Oistrakh sounds superbly poised and confident; in the finale, if the tempo is a shade deliberate, the total effect is one of clear gain. The 1961 recording seems smoother than in its most recent incarnation.

For all the beauty and brilliance of the playing, this is not quite the flawless Milstein reading of the Brahms that he had previously put on record for other companies. Jochum secures playing of great warmth and distinction from the Vienna Philharmonic, and the hint of unease in the soloist is only relative. Those who want to hear Milstein in fine (1974) analogue sound can be safely directed here, for there are no such reservations about the other three performances on this DG Double.

In her New York recording, Anne-Sofie Mutter cannot quite match the mastery of her early version with Karajan. Her tone, as recorded, is less evenly beautiful, and live performance brings idiosyncrasies and the occasional flaw. It remains an enjoyable, warm-hearted version, recommendable for the unusual Schumann coupling.

Violin Concerto (with cadenzas by Busoni, Joachim, Singer, Hermann, Auer, Ysaÿe, Ondricek, Kneisel, Marteau, Kreisler, Tovey, Kubelik, Busch, Heifetz, Milstein, Ricci).

*** Biddulph LAW 002. Ricci, Sinf. of London, Del Mar.

The veteran Ruggiero Ricci not only gives a strong, assured performance of the concerto, he adds no fewer than 16 cadenzas as well, any of which can be programmed into the main performance on CD. Though Ricci is no longer as fiery or incisive as he once was, his is an attractive performance of the concerto, well recorded.

(i) *Violin Concerto in D, Op. 77;* (ii) *Double Concerto for Violin, Cello & Orchestra in A min., Op. 102.*

(B) **(*) Sony (ADD) SBK 46335. Stern, (ii) with Rose; Phd. O, Ormandy.

(M) **(*) Sony SM2K 66941 (2). Stern, with (i) NYPO, Mehta; (ii) Rose, Phd. O, Ormandy – BEETHOVEN: *Concertos.* **(*)

Stern's glorious (1959) account of the *Violin Concerto* with Ormandy is now given a coupling that is both generous and suitable, the mid-1960s' collaboration with Leonard Rose in the *Double Concerto*. The two soloists unfailingly match each other's playing, with Ormandy always an understanding accompanist. The only drawback is the characteristically forward balance of the soloists.

In the later (1978) version there are many thoughtful touches, but the orchestral playing under Mehta is not particularly distinguished; it is a little undercharacterized, and the recording is not in the first flight either. The mid-1960s recording of the *Double Concerto* is another matter. Here, each soloist has a creative ear in pointing a comment so that the response is made to sound like an unfolding conversation. The forward balance brings glorious tone, even if this means that there are no pianissimos. The CD transfer is well managed; the sound overall is full and clear.

(i; ii) *Violin Concerto;* (i) *Hungarian Dances Nos. 1 & 5; Symphony No. 3;* (iii) *Alto Rhapsody;* (iv) *Violin Sonata No. 1;* (v) *3 Intermezzi, Op. 117; 6 Pieces, Op. 118.*

(N) (B) ** DG Panorama [ADD/DDD] 469 124-2 (2). (i) BPO, Karajan; (ii) with Mutter; (iii) Ludwig, VPO, Boehm; (iv) Zukerman, Barenboim; (v) Kempff.

Karajan's digital recording of the *Third Symphony* is a disappointment: it is a relatively routine reading, not helped by the sound quality, which is not clear enough in the tuttis and inclines to shrillness. Mutter is splendid in the *Violin Concerto*, with Karajan providing a strong accompaniment to the soloist's youthful inspiration and eager experience. Although she is rather closely balanced and there is a touch of fierceness in the upper range in the tuttis, the sound is generally warm and vivid. Christa Ludwig's 1977 account of the *Alto Rhapsody* is strong and eloquent, and the chamber music items are all first class. A slightly random mixture of works, but acceptable enough at bargain Panorama price.

(i) *Violin Concerto;* (ii) *Violin Sonata No. 3 in D min., Op. 108.*

**(*) Teldec 0630 17144-2. Vengerov; (i) Chicago SO, Barenboim; (ii) Barenboim (piano).

For E. G., Maxim Vengerov here triumphantly tackles one of the most formidable war-horses among violin concertos, playing not just for display but with far deeper insights, the inspiration of the moment captured at white heat. Using the widest dynamic and tonal range, this is a performance of extremes, just as felicitous in bravura as in lyrical purity. Vengerov uses a formidable cadenza he has written himself. The account of the *Violin Sonata* is inspired too, with Vengerov bringing out the mystery of this minor-key work, and with Barenboim at the piano freely spontaneous too. Excellent sound, with no spotlighting of the violin. R. L., while not denying that Vengerov's technique is dazzling and spectacular, and admitting that he produces a wonderful sound, finds the performance of the concerto open to the charge of being a bit too gleaming and slick, a kind of 'Brahms on Madison Avenue', and no match for the classic accounts listed above.

(i) *Violin Concerto in D;* (ii) *Violin Sonata No. 3 in D min., Op. 108;* (iii) *Variations on a Theme of Paganini, Op. 35.*

(M) (***) EMI mono CDH5 66421-2. (i–ii) Szigeti; (i) Hallé O, Harty; (ii–iii) Petri.

EMI have restored to circulation Szigeti's 1928 recordings with the Hallé Orchestra and Sir Hamilton Harty. Szigeti somehow blends serenity with a nervous intensity that is quite distinctive, and the transfer engineers have managed to bring colour to the faded sound. The *D minor Sonata*, which he recorded with Egon Petri in 1937, is a reminder of their distinguished partnership, while Petri himself is represented by his celebrated account of both books of the *Paganini Variations*. Exemplary transfers by Andrew Walter and Simon Gibson.

Double Concerto for Violin, Cello & Orchestra in A min., Op. 102.

(M) *** EMI (ADD) CDM5 66902-2. D. Oistrakh, Rostropovich, Cleveland O, Szell – BEETHOVEN: *Triple Concerto.* ***

(B) *** EMI double forte CZS5 69331-2 (2). D. Oistrakh, Fournier, Philh. O, Galliera – BEETHOVEN: *Triple*

Concerto; MOZART: *Violin Concerto No. 3*; PROKOFIEV: *Violin Concerto No. 2*. ***
*** Teldec 0630-15870-2. Perlman, Ma, Chicago SO, Barenboim – MENDELSSOHN: *Violin Concerto*. ***
(N) (BB) (***) Naxos mono 8.110940. Heifetz, Feuermann, Philadelphia O, Ormandy – BRUCH: *Scottish Fantasy*; GLAZUNOV: *Violin Concerto*.
(M) *** RCA (ADD) 09026 63531-2. Heifetz, Piatigorsky, RCA Victor SO, Wallenstein – J. S. BACH: *Double Violin Concerto in D min.*; MOZART: *Sinfonia concertante*. ***
*** RCA 09026 68964-2. Zukerman, Kirshbaum, LSO, Eschenbach – BEETHOVEN: *Triple Concerto*. ***
(BB) *** Naxos 8.550938. Kaler, Kliegel, Nat. SO of Ireland, Constantine – SCHUMANN: *Cello Concerto*. ***
(N) (M) *(*) BBC (ADD) BBCL 4050-2. Menuhin, Rostropovich, LSO, Colin Davis – MENDELSSOHN: *Violin Concerto*. J. S. BACH: *Violin Concerto in E, BWV 1042*. *(*)

This 1969 EMI recording of the *Double Concerto* has claims to be regarded as one of the finest of all versions. If it places the soloists too far forward, few will grumble when the playing is so ripely, compellingly Brahmsian and the solo timbres so richly projected. The *Andante* is glorious. Szell's powerful tutti and warmly sympathetic backing keep the Cleveland Orchestra well in the picture. Coupled with an equally arresting version of Beethoven's *Triple Concerto*, this is fully worthy of its reissue as one of EMI's 'Great Recordings of the Century'.

David Oistrakh's first stereo account with Fournier dates from 1959, but the recording was balanced by Walter Legge and the sound is remarkably satisfying. The performance is distinguished, strong and lyrical – the slow movement particularly fine – and, with Galliera and the Philharmonia providing excellent support, this version, coupled with three other outstanding concerto recordings, makes an ideal choice for bargain-hunters.

Perlman, in collaboration with Yo-Yo Ma, is more volatile, more flexible than when his partners were Rostropovich and Haitink on EMI. Although in the outer movements the speeds are noticeably faster than before, Perlman and Ma are both freer, broadening more markedly in moments of repose, while the finale dances with extra lightness. A great performance, well recorded, and well coupled with Perlman's (1993) Chicago version of the Mendelssohn.

Recorded in December 1939 in very good sound for the period, the Philadelphia account of the Brahms *Double Concerto* finds Heifetz perfectly matched with Emanuel Feuermann, as near a cellist counterpart to the violin wizard as could ever be found. This is the most powerful performance ever put on disc, passionate as well as purposeful, if lacking a little in tenderness. The incisiveness of the playing in the most taxing bravura passages makes for exciting results. Generously coupled with Heifetz's pioneering account of the Glazunov concerto and his 1947 version of the *Scottish Fantasy*, the Naxos issue brings a first-rate transfer.

Although Wallenstein is not as fine an accompanist as Ormandy, he provides a sympathetic backcloth for the 1960 Heifetz–Piatigorsky partnership which, even if it does not quite match Heifetz's earlier version with Feuermann, is still

a strong, warm-hearted account with a strikingly brilliant finale. The 1960 recording, although a bit close, has been improved out of all recognition compared to the harsh quality of the LP, and there is certainly no lack of warmth here.

Zukerman and Kirshbaum are even more persuasive in their Brahms performance than they are in the Beethoven *Triple Concerto* with which it is coupled, helped by the warm, positive accompaniment from the LSO under Eschenbach. Speeds are on the broad side – arguably too much so in the central Andante – but this can safely be recommended to anyone wanting a recent recording of this generous coupling.

The Brahms and Schumann concertos make an excellent and apt coupling, here presented on the Naxos super-budget label in warmly spontaneous-sounding recordings, very well recorded. Ilya Kaler is as clean in attack and intonation as is Maria Kliegel, who earlier impressed with her Naxos coupling of the Dvořák and Elgar *Cello Concertos*.

Some imperious and masterly playing from Rostropovich on the BBC disc goes some way to redeem a vulnerable performance by Menuhin. The recording comes from a Prom in 1964 and sounds well for its period. However, this is no match for the best now in the catalogue.

Hungarian Dances Nos. 1–21 (complete).

🏵 (BB) *** Naxos 8.550110. Budapest SO, Bogár.
(B) *** Decca 448 240-2. RPO, Weller (with DVORAK: *Slavonic Dances, Op. 46/1–3 & 6–8*, cond. Dorati **(*)).
(M) **(*) Chan. 7072. LSO, Järvi.
**(*) Ph. 462 589-2. Budapest Festival O, I. Fischer.

The Budapest recording of the Brahms *Hungarian Dances* is sheer delight from beginning to end. The playing has warmth and sparkle, and the natural way in which the music unfolds brings a refreshing feeling of rhythmic freedom. Bogár's rubato is wholly spontaneous. The recording is warm and full yet transparent, with just the right brilliance on top. This is an outright winner among the available versions.

The RPO also play with wonderful spirit, as if they were enjoying every moment, and Walter Weller secures excellent playing from every department of the orchestra. The Kingsway Hall recording is lively and bright, eminently truthful in timbre and with good, natural perspective. Moreover the Decca Eclipse reissue offers six *Slavonic Dances* from Dvořák's Op. 46 as a considerable bonus. Dorati's performances have comparable *brio*.

The Chandos recording is characteristically sumptuous and Järvi is warmly affectionate, attractively coaxing the rubato of a dance like No. 7 in F major. There is plenty of spirit and flexibility elsewhere, and this set is certainly warmly enjoyable. Yet both Weller and (especially) Bogár are even more spontaneously Hungarian in spirit.

Ivan Fischer's performances are warmly enjoyable and obviously have an authentic Hungarian underlay, including players of the 'gypsy violin' and cimbalom. But it is the gentler numbers (Nos. 3 and 4, for instance), which come off best, and even here, for all the elegance of the playing, at times the rubato sounds just a trifle calculated. The recording is full and natural, but this does not alter our allegiance to the splendid Naxos set.

Hungarian Dances Nos. 1, 3, 5–6, 17–20.

(M) *** DG (ADD) 447 434-2. BPO, Karajan – DVORAK: *Scherzo capriccioso*, etc. **(*)

Karajan's performances have great panache and brilliance and the brightly lit (1959) recording is given added fullness in the current remastering, and the superlative orchestral playing is by turns warmly affectionate and dazzling.

Hungarian Dances Nos. 1, 5–7, 19, 21.

(N) (M) **(*) Decca (ADD) 467 122-2. VPO, Reiner – DVORAK: *Slavonic Dances;* STRAUSS: *Death and Transfiguration; Till Eulenspiegel.* **(*)

Reiner's coupling of Brahms and Dvořák dances was a favourite record of the late John Culshaw, and the 1960 Sofiensaal recording wears its years fairly lightly. Reiner indulges himself in rubato and effects of his own but the affection of the music making is obvious. This transfer on Decca's Legend label misses two of the dances on the original LP and on the previous Classic Sound CD incarnation which will be a bit frustrating for some collectors, but the CD plays for just under 79 minutes. Dazzling Strauss couplings.

Serenades Nos. 1 in D, Op. 11; 2 in A, Op. 16.

(M) *** Sony SMK 60134. LSO, Tilson Thomas.
(N) ✪ *** Australian Decca Eloquence (ADD) 466 672-2. LSO, Kertész.
(B) **(*) Ph. (ADD) 432 510-2. Concg. O, Haitink.
** Telarc CD 80522. SCO, Mackerras.

Serenades Nos. 1–2; Hungarian dances Nos. 1, 3 & 10.

(BB) *** ASV CDQS 6216. Philh. O, D'Avalos.

Michael Tilson Thomas's digital recordings of the two *Serenades* tends to sweep the board, irrespective of price. His account of the glorious D major work has a sunny geniality and a youthful radiance that are most persuasive, and the A major is equally fresh. He gets admirable results from the LSO, and these readings have both vitality and sensitivity. The Sony recordings are natural and well detailed.

It is a great pity that Kertész's classic performances are only available as an import, which means that although they are on a bargain label in Australia, they cost much more here. But these readings remain as fresh as ever. Recorded in the mid-sixties, they have an unforced spontaneity, as well as robust vigour when called for. The recording in its new transfer is full and vivid, and this remains very highly recommendable on all counts.

Francesco D'Avalos, too, gets some splendid playing from the Philharmonia. A fine, inexpensive alternative to the Sony coupling, which remains first choice.

Haitink's account of the *D major Serenade* is finely proportioned, relaxed yet vital. The Concertgebouw wind-playing is particularly distinguished. However, the resonant Concertgebouw acoustic does not afford the same degree of freshness and transparency to the sound-picture as on the competing Sony and ASV versions: the effect is more symphonic, less light-hearted. The *A major Serenade* has lighter scoring (Brahms's string section omits violins altogether) and, while the recording is warm, it is yet more lucid in detail. But this is not a first choice.

Mackerras's performances of the two *Serenades* are curiously disappointing. They are short of the conductor's usual vigorous enthusiasm and, although they have affectionate touches and are well played, they lack the kind of 'live' spontaneity and warm geniality that makes Tilson Thomas's performances on Sony so persuasive.

(i) *Serenades Nos. 1–2; Academic Festival Overture;* (ii) *Tragic Overture;* (i) *Variations on a Theme of Haydn;* (i, iii) *Alto Rhapsody, Op. 53.*

(B) **(*) EMI double forte (ADD) CZS5 68655-2 (2). (i) LPO; (ii) LSO; (iii) with J. Baker, Alldis Ch.; all cond. Boult.

Sir Adrian Boult's warmly lyrical approach to the two *Serenades* is less ebullient and sparkling than that of Tilson Thomas or D'Avalos, yet he gives pleasure in a different way. Boult's way with these delightful scores is engaging enough to blunt any criticism, when the late-1970s Abbey Road recording is suitably full. What makes this inexpensive double forte reissue even more attractive is the inclusion of Janet Baker's devoted account of the *Alto Rhapsody*, the performance essentially meditative. The *Academic Festival Overture* opens the programme in a rather more extrovert fashion, and the *Variations* are also vividly presented and strongly characterized, the sound here rather more lively. The eloquent *Tragic Overture* also shows Boult as a true Brahmsian. In playing time (just under two hours), however, this is rather less generous than some double fortes.

Serenade No. 1 in D, Op. 11.

*** Finlandia 3984-25327-2. Royal Stockholm PO, A. Davis – STENHAMMAR: *Serenade for orchestra.* *** ✪

Andrew Davis and the Stockholm orchestra give a spirited account of Brahms's early masterpiece. Davis's direction is as sympathetic as the players' response. The recording is very good, even if the texture could be more transparent. However, Stenhammar's glorious *Serenade* is a logical and useful coupling, and this performance is very special.

Tragic Overture, Op. 81.

(M) *** EMI (ADD) CMS5 66109-2 (2). BPO, Karajan – BRUCKNER: *Symphony No. 8;* HINDEMITH: *Mathis der Maler.* ***

A strong and impulsive yet highly sympathetic performance from Karajan, showing him at his most charismatic. It is very well played and excellently recorded in the Berlin Jesus-Christus-Kirche in 1970. However, the set has been withdrawn as we go to press.

SYMPHONIES

Symphonies Nos. 1–4.

(B) *** DG (ADD) Double 453 097-2 (2). BPO, Karajan.
(M) **(*) Mercury (ADD) (IMS) 434 380-2 (2). LSO or (in No. 2) Minneapolis SO, Dorati.
(M) **(*) DG 429 644-2 (3). BPO, Karajan.

(B) **(*) RCA 74321 20283-2 (2). N. German RSO, Wand.

(M) (**(*)) DG mono 449 715-2 (2). BPO, Jochum.

(B) (**(*)) RCA mono Twofer 74321 55838-2 (2). NBC SO, Toscanini.

** DG (ADD) 459 635-2(3). SW German R. O, Stuttgart, Celibidache.

Symphonies Nos. 1–4; Academic Festival Overture; Tragic Overture; Variations on a Theme of Haydn.

**(*) Erato 4509 94817-2 (4). Chicago SO, Barenboim.

Symphonies Nos. 1–4; Academic Festival Overture; Tragic Overture; Variations on a Theme of Haydn; (i) Hungarian Dances Nos. 17–21.

(M) **(*) Sony (ADD) SB3K 48398 (3). Cleveland O, Szell; (i) Phd. O, Ormandy.

Symphonies Nos. 1–4; Academic Festival Overture; Tragic Overture; Variations on a Theme of Haydn; (i) Alto Rhapsody; Fragment from Goethe's Harz Journey in Winter; (ii) Gesang der Parzen (Song of the Fates); Nänie; Schicksalslied.

*** DG 435 683-2 (4). BPO, Abbado; (i) with Lipovšek, Senff Ch.; (ii) Berlin R. Ch.

Symphonies Nos. 1–4, Hungarian Dances Nos. 1, 3 & 10; Variations on a Theme of Haydn.

(M) (**(*)) EMI mono CHS5 65513-2 (3). BPO or VPO, Furtwängler – BEETHOVEN: *Overtures*. (***)

Symphonies Nos. 1–4; Tragic Overture; Variations on a Theme by Haydn.

(***) Testament mono SBT 3167 (3). Philh. O, Toscanini.

(BB) *** RCA Navigator (ADD) 74321 30367-2 (3). Dresden State O, K. Sanderling.

*** Telarc CD-80450 (4). SCO, Mackerras.

(***) Testament mono/stereo SBT 3054 (3). BPO, Kempe.

**(*) DG (IMS) 427 602-2 (3). BPO, Karajan.

Symphonies Nos. 1–4; Variations on a Theme by Haydn; (i) German Requiem.

(M) ** EMI Dig./ADD CDS5 56837-2 (8). Munich PO, Celibidache; (i) with Augér, Philharmonic Ch. & Munich Bach Ch. (members) – BEETHOVEN: *Symphonies Nos. 2–4; 6 (Pastoral); 7–9 (Choral); Leonora Overture No. 3* ** (with SCHUMANN: *Symphony No. 2* **).

Symphonies Nos. 1–2; Academic Festival Overture; Variations on a Theme of Haydn; Tragic Overture.

(B) **(*) Double Decca (ADD) 452 329-2 (2). Chicago SO, Solti.

(i) *Symphonies Nos. 3–4;* (ii) *Hungarian Dances Nos. 1–21.*

(B) *** Double Decca ADD/Dig. 452 332-2 (2). (i) Chicago SO, Solti; (ii) RPO, Weller.

Abbado's remains the most successful of the modern, digital cycles and still makes a clear first choice, with playing at once polished and intense, glowingly recorded. The set gains from having a generous collection of imaginatively chosen couplings: the rare, brief, choral works, as well as the usual supplements in the overtures and variations.

The concerts on Testament preserve the two legendary occasions in the autumn of 1952 when, in a Brahms cycle at the Royal Festival Hall, Toscanini conducted the Philharmonia Orchestra on his one visit to London after the war. It is fascinating to compare these readings of the Brahms symphonies with those which Toscanini recorded in the same twelve months with the NBC Symphony Orchestra in New York. Where the New York performances, resonant and superbly drilled, have a hardness and rigidity, with dynamic contrasts ironed out, the Philharmonia ones consistently bring a moulding of phrase and subtlety of rubato which bear out the regular Toscanini instruction to 'Sing!'. And, in contrast with most Toscanini recordings, the hushed playing is magical. Though mono recordings made in the Royal Festival Hall are inevitably limited in range, the clarity and definition of the EMI recording quickly make one forget such limitations and the intrusive coughing. The glorious horn-playing of Dennis Brain has a rich bloom, and the timpani is thrillingly focused, arguably too prominent but very dramatic. Not only Brain's horn but the woodwind contributions of Gareth Morris on flute, Sidney Sutcliffe on oboe and Frederick Thurston on clarinet are markedly sweeter than their counterparts in Toscanini's own NBC orchestra. Even so, there are a couple of blips to note, which in context hardly matter. The chorale on trombones just after the great horn theme in the introduction to the finale of No. 1 brings a series of split notes, and the finale of No. 4 is disturbed by firecrackers let off by pranksters. Toscanini was completely unfazed, giving a magnificent reading, not just full of adrenalin in the drama of the movement but with a heart-stopping flute solo from Morris in the slow 3/2 variation. A set to restore Toscanini's unique reputation as a conductor without equal, when too many of his commercial discs give only a limited view of his mastery.

Anyone wanting Karajan's readings of the four Brahms symphonies should be well satisfied with the DG Double, which offers his recordings made in the late 1970s. The current remastering makes the most of the analogue sound. The playing of the Berlin Philharmonic remains uniquely cultivated: the ensemble is finely polished yet can produce tremendous bravura at times, and there is no lack of warmth. Karajan's interpretations, with lyrical and dramatic elements finely balanced, changed little over the years. A very real bargain, hard to beat.

Otherwise Kurt Sanderling's 1971–2 Dresden recordings make an excellent choice. They have a warmth and humanity that stand out from the general run of Brahms cycles, with the Dresden orchestra responding to Sanderling's direction with playing of an unaffected and natural eloquence, so that the performances can stand comparison with any in the catalogue at any price. Their return to circulation is cause for celebration.

Mackerras uses forces of the same size as Brahms would have had at his disposal in Meiningen. The smaller numbers remove some of the thick-textured, overweight quality that the strings can produce in Brahms, while retaining their warmth and richness. The strings are often thinned out to single part at times, and the effect is – strangely enough – enriching. The set includes the very first version of the slow movement of the *First Symphony* as it was originally performed at Karlsruhe and Cambridge. There are fascinating differences both in the order of the material and, at times, in the harmony. The playing is exemplary and has no lack of warmth, and the same must be said of the recording. Well worth getting.

Like Furtwängler, Kempe is freely expressive, but his freedom is very different, with far less extreme changes of tempo. Speeds and timings are often very similar, but results are strikingly different. First and foremost, Kempe has his finger on the natural flow and pulse of these symphonies in a way that calls to mind only the most exalted comparisons. The *Second* and the *Fourth* are both mono, and the sound is less transparent and fresh – but, ironically, they are at least as vivid and are rather better focused. The *Tragic Overture* is one of the best ever committed to disc. Excellent transfers.

Those who think of Solti as a conductor who always whips up excitement may be surprised at the sobriety of his approach here. These are important and thoughtful statements, lacking only a degree of the fantasy and idiosyncrasy which make fine performances great. However, it is the second of the two Doubles which offers the two finest performances: Solti's big-scale view of the *Third Symphony* is most compelling, and the *Fourth* shows him at his most vibrantly individual, with the *Andante moderato* second movement treated more like an Adagio, unfailingly pure and eloquent. This second box also includes Walter Weller's splendid, complete, digital set of the *Hungarian Dances*.

While not an obvious first choice, Dorati's Mercury set of the Brahms symphonies, made between 1957 and 1963, is also a competitive proposition at mid-price, always vital and interesting. The recording throughout is brightly lit in the Mercury manner, a bit fierce at times, but there is supporting body (Watford Town Hall was the venue). No listener could fail to be stimulated by this musicianly, strongly involved and involving music-making.

Günter Wand's Brahms set is highly recommendable for providing spontaneously compelling readings of all four works, very well played. The snag is that the early digital recording (1982/3) brings a degree of fierceness on violin tone in all but No. 2 and verges on shrillness in No. 3. Wand's is a consistently direct view of Brahms, yet the reading of each symphony has its own individuality. Wand's version of the *Second* is the pick of his Brahms series, a characteristically glowing but steady reading, recorded with a fullness and bloom that are missing in the companion issues. In the *Third Symphony* his wise way with Brahms, strong and easy and steadily paced, works beautifully. By contrast, the version of No. 4 initially seems understated. But it is quite a strong reading and provides a generally satisfying culmination to an inexpensive modern set of the four symphonies and is well worth considering.

Szell's powerful view of Brahms is consistently revealed in this masterful series of performances, recorded in the 1960s when he had made the Cleveland Orchestra America's finest. His approach is generally plain and direct, crisp and detached rather than smooth and moulded. Speeds are broad and, in the manner of the time, no exposition repeats are observed, not even in No. 3. Though the sound, as transferred, is not as full as on the original LPs, it is clear and bright, with superb detail.

With variably focused sound, Karajan's last cycle of the Brahms symphonies (on three CDs) is not his finest; but he remained a natural Brahmsian to the last, and this compilation, with Nos. 2 and 3 on the second disc, and No. 4 coupled with the *Variations*, makes a better investment than the original issues, for those who must have digital sound. However, this set is at full price.

Jochum's mono DG recordings of the Brahms symphonies are characteristically wayward and could hardly be regarded as a primary recommendation, even though the concentration of the playing generally holds the readings together. The Berlin Philharmonic playing is splendid throughout, and the mono recordings, made between 1951 and 1956, are amazingly good, full and clear, far more detailed and vivid than the original LPs.

Toscanini's NBC Brahms is high-powered but full of lyricism of an Italianate warmth. The *First Symphony* starts very fast and intensely, but often speeds are surprisingly broad, and the *Fourth Symphony*, Toscanini's favourite, brings a magnificent performance. Though RCA's new processing for this reissue has not transformed the original sound quite as well as it has in the Beethoven symphonies, harsh still on high violins, it now has ample body to let one enjoy these readings in rather more aural comfort.

Barenboim dons his Furtwänglerian mantle for his Erato accounts of the first two symphonies which, though very well played, suffer from his wilful flexibility and eccentric structural control. Barenboim's inspirational volatility works well in the *Third Symphony*, which does not lose its ongoing purpose and brings beautiful orchestral playing in the central movements. No. 4 is finest of all, a highly concentrated interpretation that moves forward powerfully; even though the tempo for the *Andante* is slow, it is presented ardently and is capped by a gripping performance of the closing *Passacaglia*.

Furtwängler's EMI compilation brings together the live recording of the *First Symphony* that he made with the Vienna Philharmonic in 1952 and live recordings of the remaining three symphonies made with the Berlin Philharmonic in 1948 and 1952, presumably taken from radio sources. The performance of the *First* is perhaps the best and it has the best sound, which otherwise is disappointingly thin, lacking in body and with some harshness; but the electricity of Furtwängler in Brahms is vividly captured.

Sergiu Celibidache's DG performances come from his appearances with the Stuttgart Radio (Südfunk) Orchestra in the 1970s. These certainly produce tone of the utmost refinement and subtlety. The sheer intentness of the playing and the tonal sheen produced by the Stuttgart group is nearly always in evidence but there is a certain want of real forward momentum and of sinew. Beauty rather than truth is dominant. The 1974–6 recordings come up well and there is a bonus rehearsal disc devoted to the first movement of the *Fourth Symphony*.

Celibidache's EMI set boxes all four Brahms symphonies, the *Requiem* and the *Haydn Variations*, and couples them with Schumann's *Second Symphony* and an incomplete Beethoven cycle on eight CDs not available separately. Celibidache dwells on beauty of sound and refinement of texture. He is happy to pull phrases completely out of shape. In the *Haydn Variations* he is lethargic and at times positively funereal.

Symphonies Nos. 1–3; Academic Festival Overture; Tragic Overture.

⚫ (B) *** EMI double forte CZS5 69515-2 (2). LPO, Jochum.

Jochum's EMI stereo versions of the Brahms symphonies were made in the Kingsway Hall in 1976; the analogue recordings, produced by Christopher Bishop, are outstandingly full and vivid. These remastered discs indeed sound better than almost any of their mid- or bargain-priced competitors. The LPO playing is excellent, the spontaneity of its performances carrying the listener along on a wave of inspiration, and this also applies to the exuberant *Academic Festival Overture* and the hardly less vibrant *Tragic Overture*. The high drama of the *First Symphony* immediately shows Jochum at his most persuasive. Equally, No. 2 is a warmly lyrical reading, expansive in the first movement, fast and exciting in the finale. The inner movements are beautifully played. The *Third Symphony* represents the peak of Jochum's cycle, and this is among the most rewarding versions of this work, irrespective of price. He conveys the full weight and warmth of the work with generally spacious speeds, finely moulded.

Symphony No. 1 in C min., Op. 68; (i) Alto Rhapsody, Op. 53.

(B) **(*) CfP 573 4332. (i) Greevy, Hallé Ch.; Hallé O, Loughran.

Symphony No. 2 in D, Op. 73; Academic Festival Overture.

(B) **(*) CfP 573 4342. Hallé O, Loughran.

Symphony No. 3 in F, Op. 90; Tragic Overture.

(B) **(*) CfP 573 4352. Hallé O, Loughran.

Symphony No. 4 in E min., Op. 98; Variations on a Theme of Haydn, Op. 56a.

(B) **(*) CfP 573 4362. Hallé O, Loughran.

This set of the Brahms symphonies, recorded at the end of the 1970s, crowned James Loughran's highly successful period as principal conductor of the Hallé Orchestra. These performances are justly renowned, for the whole orchestra shows a natural feeling for the Brahms style throughout all four symphonies. Loughran's readings of the first two are notable for their lyrical strength, the *First* with a refreshing, spring-like quality, the *Second* with a naturally warm flow carrying the listener on, even while the basic approach is direct and unfussy. By contrast, the *Third Symphony* is unexpectedly measured in tempo, yet on repetition this emerges as an unusually satisfying account. In the *Fourth* Loughran's approach is unobtrusively direct. Overall, the Hallé ensemble and string-tone are not always quite as polished as in the versions from metropolitan orchestras, but the sense of spontaneity is ample compensation. Bernadette Greevy gives a forthright, warmly enjoyable account of the *Alto Rhapsody*, and the two overtures and *Variations* also come off very well. Full, atmospheric recording, excellent for the period. Unfortunately this set has been deleted just as we go to press.

Symphony No. 1 in C min., Op. 68.

(M) *** DG (ADD) 447 408-2. BPO, Karajan – SCHUMANN: *Symphony No. 1.* ***
(BB) **(*) ASV CDQS 6101. RLPO, Janowski.
(N) *** Simax PSC 1206. Oslo PO, Jansons – JOACHIM: *Hamlet Overture.* ***
(N) (BB) (***) Dutton Lab. mono CDBP 9705. Hollywood Bowl SO, Stokowski – FALLA: *El amor brujo.* (**(*))
(M) ** DG (IMS) 445 505-2. VPO, Bernstein – BEETHOVEN: *Overtures: Coriolan; Egmont.* **

Symphony No. 1; Academic Festival Overture; Variations on a Theme of Haydn.

(M) **(*) Sony (ADD) SMK 64470. Columbia SO, Walter.

(i) *Symphony No. 1;* (ii) *Academic Festival Overture;* (iii) *Alto Rhapsody.*

(M) (***) Dutton Lab. mono CDK 1210. (i) Concg. O, Van Beinum; (ii) LSO; (iii) Ferrier, LPO Ch., LPO; (ii–iii) Kraus.

Symphony No. 1; Variations on a Theme of Haydn.

(BB) **(*) Naxos 8.550278. Belgian R. PO, Brussels, Rahbari.

(i) *Symphony No. 1; Variations on a Theme of Haydn;* (ii) *Hungarian Dances Nos. 17–21.*

(B) **(*) Sony (ADD) SBK 46534. (i) Cleveland O, Szell; (ii) Phd. O, Ormandy.

Symphony No. 1; Tragic Overture; (i) Alto Rhapsody.

⚫ (M) *** EMI (ADD) CDM5 67029-2. Philh. O, Klemperer, (i) with Ludwig, Philh. Ch.

Symphony No. 1; (i) Gesang der Parzen (Song of the Fates).

*** DG 431 790-2. BPO, Abbado, (i) with Berlin R. Ch.

Klemperer's 1956–7 Kingsway Hall recording remains among the greatest performances this symphony has ever received on disc. This is Klemperer at his very finest, and his reading remains unique for its authority and power, supported by consistently superb Philharmonia playing. The sound is both clear and full-bodied. The *Alto Rhapsody* also shows Klemperer at his most masterful and Ludwig on fine form: it is a beautifully expressive performance.

After a spacious introduction, Abbado launches into a warm, dramatic reading, rhythmically well sprung and finely shaded, with the full power of the great dramatic climaxes brought out in the finale, from the rapt pianissimo of the opening onwards. The *Gesang der Parzen* makes an unusual and warmly attractive coupling, very well sung. A clear first choice among modern recordings.

Karajan's 1964 recording of Brahms's *First Symphony* (the conductor's third version of five – DG 447 408-2) seems by general consensus to be regarded as his finest. The control of tension in the first movement is masterly, the orchestral playing is of superlative quality and the result is very powerful, with the finale a fitting culmination. The remastering has restored the original, full, well-balanced, analogue sound, with plenty of weight in the bass. The coupling with Schumann's *First Symphony* makes this a very desirable record indeed.

Following up his other Brahms symphony recordings for Simax, Jansons in a live recording directs a spacious reading of the *First*, which brings out its lyricism as well as its weight of argument. He is helped by a spacious acoustic in a venue, the Oslo Concert Hall, once counted difficult and dry. The refinement as well as the power and intensity of the playing cannot be faulted. Warmly recommended for those who have collected Jansons's earlier Brahms discs, as well as those curious about the rare and atmospheric Joachim overture.

Walter's first two movements of the *First Symphony* have a white-hot intensity that shows this conductor at his very finest. The third movement begins with a less-than-ravishing clarinet solo and, though the 6/8 section is lively enough, the playing is not as crisp as in the first two movements. In the finale the performance reasserts itself, although some might find the big string-tune too slow. The performance of the *Variations* is relaxed and smiling, and the genial account of the *Academic Festival Overture* gains from the extra brightness on top.

Szell's account of No. 1 is one of the most impressive of his set. His bold, direct thrust gives the outer movements plenty of power and impetus, and the inner movements bring relaxation and a fair degree of warmth.

All the van Beinum recordings on the Dutton disc were made in the autumn of 1947, only two years after the end of the Second World War. In all, he made three recordings of the *First Symphony*; this earliest recording has a great sense of spontaneity. Ferrier's classic record of the *Alto Rhapsody*, with the LPO and chorus with Clemens Kraus (newly rehabilitated after the war), and his exemplary *Academic Festival Overture* come up splendidly and in this fine transfer leave no doubt as to the quality of Decca's post-war engineering.

Opening powerfully with thundering timpani in the manner of Klemperer, though with generally more relaxed tempi, Alexander Rahbari on Naxos gives an account of Brahms's *First* that is certainly recommendable. It is a strong, direct reading, spacious yet with plenty of impetus. A good choice for those with limited budgets.

Janowski's plain yet sympathetic reading is greatly enhanced on a CD which is full-bodied, clearly detailed and well balanced. The added fullness is much more flattering to the orchestral timbres and makes a very satisfying sound overall.

Stokowski's characteristic ebb and flow of rubato is individual yet warmly felt, following the Brahmsian contours persuasively and giving the performance a constant expressive power. His rich lower strings combine with mellow wind and resonant brass, while the violins soar. The urgent, crisply articulated rhythms in the first movement give the reading a consistently strong momentum, and in the slow movement the violins play with extrovert lyrical passion. Similarly, in the finale, after the noble horn fanfare, the strings articulate their famous tune with gutsy bow contact. There is an involving sense of 'live' music-making here, and as usual the sophisticated Dutton transfer makes the very most of the original master.

The finale in Bernstein's version brings a highly idiosyncratic reading, with the great melody of the main theme presented at a speed very much slower than the main part of the movement. In the reprise it never comes back to the slow tempo, until the coda brings the most extreme slowing for the chorale motif. These two points are exaggerations of

accepted tradition and, though Bernstein's electricity makes the results compelling, this is hardly a version for constant repetition. The remastered sound is fully acceptable.

(i) *Symphonies Nos. 1–2; Academic Festival Overture;*
(ii) *Tragic Overture;* (i) *Variations on a Theme of Haydn; Variations & Fugue on a Theme by Handel* (arr. Rubbra).

(B) ** Sony SB2K (ADD) 63287 (2). (i) Phd. O, Ormandy;
   (ii) Nat. PO, Stokowski.

Ormandy's manner is direct and warmly purposeful, with speeds (on the broad side) which are generally kept steady, even in exciting codas. The glories of the Philadelphia sound are resonantly exploited with close but not aggressive focus in these 1960s recordings. A rarity is the arrangement of the *Handel Variations* by Edmund Rubbra, which – in a rather un-Brahmsian way – gives the principal soloists of the Philadelphia Orchestra marvellous opportunities to shine. The one item conducted by Stokowski brings a complete contrast, a 1977 recording which demonstrates what fire and energy the nonagenarian conductor had only six months before he died, with fast speeds and electric tension. This is very much a three-star performance and needs to be recoupled.

Symphony No. 2 in D, Op. 73.

(***) Testament mono SBT 1015. BBC SO, Toscanini –
   MENDELSSOHN: *Midsummer Night's Dream:* excerpt;
   ROSSINI: *Semiramide: Overture.* (***)

Symphony No. 2; Academic Festival Overture.

(M) ** DG 445 506-2. VPO, Bernstein.

Symphony No. 2; Academic Festival Overture; Tragic Overture.

(B) **(*) Penguin/Decca 460 623-2. Chicago SO, Solti.

Symphony No. 2; Variations on a Theme of Haydn.

*** DG 423 142-2. BPO, Karajan.

Symphony No. 2; (i) *Alto Rhapsody.*

*** DG 427 643-2. (i) Lipovšek, Senff Ch.; BPO, Abbado.

Among modern versions Abbado's now stands as an easy first choice, particularly when, with Marjana Lipovšek a radiant soloist, it also contains a gravely beautiful account of the *Alto Rhapsody.* Abbado's approach to Brahms is generally direct, but his control of rhythm and phrase makes the performance instantly compelling.

Karajan's digital version of the *Second Symphony* is a magnificent reading, even warmer and more glowing than his previous versions, with consistently fine playing from the Berlin Philharmonic, who approach with striking freshness a symphony that they must have played countless times. As in the *First Symphony*, Karajan omits the first-movement exposition repeat, but compensates with an appealing performance of the *Haydn Variations.*

Toscanini's account with the BBC Symphony Orchestra on Testament, recorded in 1938, will come as a revelation to those who view the legendary Italian as a hard-driving, demonic maestro. Tempi are relaxed, the first movement is unhurried and the mood is sunny and smiling. There is none of the hard-driven momentum and over-drilled intensity that marked his final, NBC version. The sound calls for tolerance, but the playing is worth it.

A powerful, weighty performance from Solti, its lyrical feeling passionately expressed in richly upholstered textures. The reading displays a broad nobility, but the charm and delicately gracious qualities are much less a part of Solti's view. Yet the lyric power of the playing is hard to resist, especially when the recording is so full-blooded and brilliant. Solti includes the first-movement exposition repeat and offers in addition a lively *Academic Festival Overture* and a splendidly committed *Tragic Overture*.

Bernstein in his live recording directs a warm and expansive account, notably less free and idiosyncratic than the *C minor Symphony*, yet comparably rhythmic and spontaneous-sounding. Considering the limitations of a live concert, the recording sounds well. But this is by no means a first choice, even at mid-price.

Symphonies Nos. 2–3.

*** Simax PSC 1204. Oslo PO, Jansons.
(M) *** Sony (ADD) SMK 64471. Columbia SO, Walter.
(M) *** EMI (ADD) CDM5 67030-2.. Philh. O, Klemperer.
(B) *** DG (ADD) 429 153-2. BPO, Karajan.
(B) *** Sony (ADD) SBK 47652. Cleveland O, Szell.

Jansons draws incandescent playing from his Oslo Philharmonic in outstanding versions of both symphonies. The refinement of the playing and the subtlety of Jansons's dynamic shading go with an approach which is at once direct and refreshing, with generally steady speeds yet warmly expressive on detail. Whereas in No. 3 Jansons observes the exposition repeat in the first movement, in No. 2 he omits it, a justifiable decision when it is very much a question of proportion. These now stand among the very finest versions of both symphonies; a formidable addition to the Simax catalogue, recorded in full, well-detailed sound.

The Bruno Walter coupling of the *Second* and *Third Symphonies* is very recommendable indeed. Walter's performance of the *Second* is wonderfully sympathetic, with an inevitability, a rightness which makes it hard to concentrate on the interpretation as such, so cogent is the musical argument. Walter's pacing of the *Third* is admirable, and the vigour and sense of joy which imbue the opening of the first movement (exposition repeat included) dominate throughout, with the second subject eased in with wonderful naturalness.

Klemperer's account of No. 2 is also a great performance, the product of a strong and vital intelligence. Alongside Walter, he may seem a trifle severe and uncompromising, but he was at his peak in his Brahms cycle and he underlines the power of the symphony without diminishing its eloquence in any way. Again in No. 3 there is a severity about his approach which may at first seem unappealing, but which comes to underline the strength of the architecture. The remastered recording, made concurrently and in the same venue as No. 1, is very impressive.

Karajan's 1964 reading of the *Second* is among the sunniest and most lyrical accounts, and its sound is competitive even now. The companion performance of the *Third* is marginally less compelling but is still very fine. He takes the opening

expansively and omits the exposition repeat. But clearly he sees the work as a whole: the third movement is also slow and perhaps slightly indulgent, but the closing pages of the finale have a memorable autumnal serenity. A bargain.

The Cleveland Severance recordings have been improved immeasurably. The orchestral virtuosity remains and at times Szell's care for detail does become predominant, but the underlying ardour and warmth are in no doubt, especially in the *Adagio*, while the *Allegretto grazioso* has an appealing simplicity. The *Third* is a magnificent performance. Overall, this is a reading to set alongside that of Bruno Walter, even if (as in the *Second Symphony*), the exposition repeat is omitted.

Symphony No. 3 in F, Op. 90.

(N) *** BBC (ADD) BBCL4058-2. BBC Northern SO, Monteux (with ROSSINI: *L'Italiana in Algeri Overture* **(*)) – SCHUMANN: *Symphony No. 4.* ***
(***) Testament mono SBT 1173. Philh. O, Cantelli – MENDELSSOHN: *Symphony No. 4.* (***)

Symphony No. 3; Tragic Overture; (i) Song of Destiny (Schicksalslied).

*** DG 429 765-2. BPO, Abbado; (i) with Senff Ch.

Symphony No. 3; Variations on a Theme of Haydn.

*** Erato 4509 95193-2. Chicago SO, Barenboim.
(BB) *** ASV CDQS 6103. RLPO, Janowski.

Abbado directs a glowing, affectionate performance of No. 3, adopting generally spacious speeds and finely moulded phrasing but never sounding self-conscious, thanks to the natural tension which gives the illusion of live, spontaneous music-making. The rich, well-balanced, clean-textured recording underlines the big dramatic contrasts. This now heads the list of modern digital recordings of this symphony.

Monteux's musical schooling was in Mozart, Beethoven and Brahms, and they were his first love. As a young man Monteux had played viola in the Geloso Quartet, performing among other things Grieg's quartet for the composer himself. The Geloso also played one of the Brahms quartets at a concert which the composer himself attended. Afterwards Brahms told them, 'It takes the French to play my music properly. The Germans all play it much too heavily.' This comment bears fruit in a performance that is beautifully played, admirably shaped and full of vigour.

Barenboim's volatile approach works well in the *Third Symphony* and, although there must be some minor reservations about his freely spacious treatment of both central movements, they are beautifully played and warmly lyrical. The first movement (exposition repeat very much part of the interpretation) has plenty of power and a glowing lyrical feeling. The finale has exciting thrust and the valedictory ending is managed most sensitively. The *Variations*, too, are full of imaginative touches.

Cantelli's 1955 version of Brahms's *Third*, justly famous in the mono LP era, is among the warmest, most glowing accounts ever put on disc, with Dennis Brain's glorious horn-playing, ripely recorded, crowning the whole incandescent performance. Sadly, in mono, it has been available only rarely in the years since 1955, making this superbly transferred reissue very welcome, particularly when the coupling is an equally unforgettable, previously unissued version of the Mendelssohn.

The *Third* is also the finest of Janowski's Brahms cycle, with surging outer movements (exposition repeat included) and the central *Andante* and *Poco allegretto* given an appealing, unforced, Brahmsian lyricism. An exciting and satisfying performance, given bright, full, digital sound, not absolutely refined on top. The *Variations* also have plenty of impetus and are strongly characterized. In its price-range this is very recommendable.

Symphonies Nos. 3–4.

(M) *** DG (ADD) 437 645-2. BPO, Karajan.

(M) **(*) Teldec 4509 92144-2. Cleveland O, Dohnányi.

In his 1978 recording Karajan gives superb grandeur to the opening of the *Third Symphony* but then characteristically refuses to observe the exposition repeat. Comparing this reading with Karajan's earlier (1964) version (coupled with No. 2), one finds him more direct and strikingly more dynamic and compelling. In the *Fourth Symphony* Karajan refuses to overstate the first movement, starting with deceptive reticence. His easy, lyrical style, less moulded in this 1978 reading than in his 1964 account, is fresh and unaffected and highly persuasive. The Scherzo, fierce and strong, leads to a clean, weighty account of the finale.

Those for whom quality of sound is of the highest consideration will certainly find Dohnányi's mid-priced Cleveland coupling tempting. The performances are clean and direct and superbly played, but the result finally lacks something in Brahmsian magic.

Symphony No. 4 in E min., Op. 98.

(M) *** DG 457 706-2. VPO, C. Kleiber.

(N) *** Simax PSC 1205. Oslo PO, Jansons – JOACHIM:
   Overture: *Heinrich IV*. ***

**(*) BBC (ADD) BBCL 4003-2. BBC SO, Kempe –
   SCHUBERT: *Symphony No. 5*. **(*)

Symphony No. 4; Academic Festival Overture.

*** Erato 4509 95194-2. Chicago SO, Barenboim.

(M) *** EMI (ADD) CDM5 67031-2. Philh. O, Klemperer (with
   SCHUMANN: *Overtures: Genoveva, Op. 81; Manfred,
   Op. 115* **).

(BB) **(*) ASV CDQS 6104. RLPO, Janowski.

Symphony No 4; Tragic Overture.

(M) *** DG (IMS) 445 508-2. VPO, Bernstein.

Symphony No. 4; Tragic Overture; (i) Song of Destiny (Schicksalslied).

(M) *** Sony SMK 64472. Columbia SO, Walter, (i) with
   Occidental College Concert Ch.

Symphony No. 4; Variations on a Theme by Haydn.

(BB) **(*) RCA Navigator (ADD) 74321 30367-2. Dresden State
   O, K. Sanderling.

Symphony No. 4; Variations on a Theme of Haydn; (i) Nänie.

*** DG 435 349-2. BPO, Abbado, (i) with Berlin R. Ch.

Symphony No. 4; (i) Fest-und Gedenksprüche, Op. 109; 3 Motets, Op. 110; Warum ist das Licht gegeben, Op. 74/1.

*** Decca 455 510-2. (i) MDR Ch., Leipzig; Leipzig GO,
   Blomstedt.

Of recent versions, Herbert Blomstedt's account with his new orchestra, the Leipzig Gewandhaus, is the finest and it is also among the most satisfying accounts on disc. It offers cultured playing, a reading that blends a highly developed sense of classical proportion with finely controlled feeling. It combines the classicism of the pre-war accounts by Boehm and Weingartner with the warmth and fire of Bruno Walter. First-class recording too. As a fill-up Blomstedt directs some fine *a cappella* pieces, which are sung with great eloquence and restraint. A distinguished record, well worth acquiring.

Abbado rounds off his outstanding series with an incandescent performance of the *Fourth*, marked by strong, dramatic contrasts and finely moulded phrasing. The coupling is exceptionally generous, not just the *Haydn Variations* but the rare choral piece to words by Schiller, *Nänie*.

Carlos Kleiber's famous version is a performance of real stature and much strength, with the attention to detail one would expect from this great conductor. A gripping and compelling performance, at the opposite end of the scale from Walter's coaxingly lyrical approach. DG have successfully remastered the 1981 sound, which now has more than sufficient weight in the bass and more bloom than before. The violins under pressure still sound somewhat shrill at fortissimo, but this adds to the edge of the performance, and there is room for the strings to expand in the *Andante*. The finale has tremendous thrust. Even without a coupling, this carries the strongest recommendation at mid-price.

Walter's opening is simple, even gentle, and the pervading lyricism is immediately apparent; yet power and authority are underlying. A beautifully moulded slow movement, intense at its central climax, is balanced by a vivacious, exhilarating Scherzo. The finale has an underlying impetus so that Walter is able to relax for the slow middle section. The new transfer is very successful: the recording has never sounded fresher or warmer and there is plenty of necessary weight in the bass. The *Tragic Overture* has characteristic breadth and vigour, while the *Song of Destiny*, both warm and dramatic, displays the capability of the chorus to good effect. The recording is excellent. This has also been issued as one of Sony's 'Super Audio' CDs which needs a special CD player (SS 6113).

Klemperer's granite strength and his feeling for Brahmsian lyricism make his version one of the most satisfying ever recorded. The finale may lack something in sheer excitement, but the gravity of Klemperer's tone of voice, natural and unforced in this movement as in the others, makes for compelling results. Among the fill-ups the *Academic Festival Overture* is made to sound grand rather than high-spirited, but the Schumann couplings are muscularly massive and Germanic, rather than incandescent. Excellent transfers.

Barenboim's Chicago reading is grippingly compulsive. He takes the *Andante* more slowly than marked but, with a richly ardent response from the Chicago strings, the result is eloquently convincing, with much refined orchestral detail.

After an excitingly ebullient Scherzo, the finale sets off with a powerful thrust that carries through to the final bar, though Barenboim's flexible style prevents any feeling of rigidity. The *Academic Festival Overture* is unusually expansive, bringing superb playing from the Chicago brass. Throughout, the sound is suitably full-bodied within the aptly resonant acoustics of Chicago's Orchestra Hall.

Jansons with the Oslo Philharmonic directs a performance which underlines the contrasts between the first two movements, predominantly lyrical and reflective, and the last two, with their sharper impact. As in the rest of Jansons's Brahms series the playing is polished and refined, the more magnetic for being recorded live. The recording beautifully captures the delicacy of the pianissimo playing of the strings, while offering ample warmth and power in the last two movements. The Joachim Overture *Heinrich IV*, finer than the earlier *Hamlet Overture*, makes an apt if not very generous bonus, when it was so admired by Brahms.

Bernstein's 1981 Vienna version of Brahms's *Fourth*, recorded live, is exhilaratingly dramatic in fast music, while the slow movement brings richly resonant playing from the Vienna strings, not least in the great cello melody at bar 41, which with its moulded rubato comes to sound surprisingly like Elgar. This is easily the finest of Bernstein's Vienna cycle and, with generally good sound, is well worth considering.

Kempe's account with the BBC Symphony Orchestra comes from 1974 and (according to the label information) the Festival Hall. Such is the warmth and openness of the acoustic that the Albert Hall would seem the more likely venue. It is a beautifully natural account, relaxed and yet held together well, and totally free from eccentricity. Kempe gets excellent playing from the BBC Symphony Orchestra, and the CD captures all the atmosphere of a live occasion.

Sanderling's super-bargain Dresden version has genuine fire and eloquence. It is finely recorded (in 1971), beautifully played and splendidly shaped. However, it has a sense of enjoyment that makes it a very rewarding performance indeed, and the *Variations* are also very successful. The warmth of the Dresden acoustic means that the quality remains pleasingly full, although the violins sound a little thin on top.

Following the success of the *Third*, Janowski gives a refreshingly direct reading of the *Fourth*. Speeds are unexceptionable, with the second-movement *Andante*, introduced very gently, slower than usual but certainly expressive. The recording sounds vivid and full on CD, and the weight of the final *Passacaglia* is well established. The coda of the symphony, like the overture which follows, brings real excitement.

(i) *Symphony No. 4;* (ii) *German Requiem, Op. 45;* (iii) *Schicksalslied, Op. 54.*

(B) **(*) EMI double forte ADD/Dig. CZS5 69518-2 (2).
  (i) LPO, Jochum; (ii) Norman, Hynninen; (ii–iii) BBC Symphony Ch., LPO Ch., LPO, Tennstedt.

In the *Fourth Symphony*, Jochum's very opening phrase establishes the reading as warmly affectionate, and he combines a high degree of expressive flexibility with a rapt concentration which holds the symphonic structure strongly

together. It demonstrates Jochum's passionate feeling for Brahms, with its spirit of soaring lyricism and – in the finale especially – a strong, even irresistible forward momentum. Although the performance has its idiosyncrasies of tempo, it is highly compelling in every bar, and it is a great pity that the appeal of this inexpensive reissue is somewhat diluted by the performance of the coupling, which may not be to all tastes.

In the *Requiem* Tennstedt brings speeds slower than on any rival version. His dedication generally sustains them well. What does sound monumental rather than moving is Jessye Norman's solo, *Ihr habt nun Traurigkeit*, though the golden tone is glorious. The *Schicksalslied* is also given a spacious, strong performance, with the London Philharmonic Choir singing dedicatedly, and the 1984–5 digital recording spacious to match.

Variations on a Theme of Haydn (St Anthony Chorale), Op. 56a.

(**) Sony mono MHK 63328. NYPO, Walter – MAHLER:
  Symphony No. 1. (**)

Walter's mono account comes from 1953 and appeared in the UK in 1955. It is naturally not as fresh or as open as his later stereo version, but it has the warmth and fine musicianship that characterize everything Walter did.

(i) Variations on a Theme of Haydn; (ii) Variations & Fugue on a Theme by Handel, Op. 24 (arr. Rubbra).

(N) *** Australian Decca Eloquence (ADD/DDD) 467 608-2.
  (i) VPO, Kertész; (ii) Cleveland O, Ashkenazy; – DVORAK:
  Symphonic Variations. ***

Rubbra's orchestration of the *Handel Variations* is hugely enjoyable, with a vivid orchestral palate, which becomes ever more imaginative as it goes along. Beginning in a very neo-baroque manner, with Clarke's *Trumpet Voluntary* springing to mind, all 25 variations are a delight. Ashkenazy's performance is superb and the recording (digital) excellent. The more familiar *Haydn Variations* is warmly recorded and receives a strongly affecting performance under István Kertész, perhaps more so with the knowledge that the conductor was tragically drowned just before the final sessions finished. The orchestra completed the recording without him, and it was released as a tribute to this much-admired musician.

CHAMBER MUSIC
Complete chamber music

(i–ii) *Cello Sonatas Nos. 1–2;* (iii–iv) *Clarinet Quintet in B min., Op. 115;* (v–vi) *Clarinet Sonatas Nos. 1–2;* (v; vii) *Clarinet Trio in A min., Op. 114;* (ii; viii–ix) *Horn Trio in E flat, Op. 40;* (x–xi) *Piano Quartets Nos. 1–3;* (iv; xii) *Piano Quintet in F min., Op. 34;* (x) *Piano Trios Nos. 1–4;* (xiii) *String Quartets Nos. 1–3;* (iv) *String Quintets Nos. 1–2; String Sextets Nos. 1–2;* (ii; ix) *Violin Sonatas Nos. 1–3.*

(B) *** Ph. (ADD) 454 073-2 (11). (i) Starker; (ii) Sebök;
  (iii) Stähr; (iv) BPO Octet (members); (v) Pieterson; (vi) H.
  Menuhin; (vii) Pressler, Greenhouse; (viii) Orval;

(ix) Grumiaux; (x) Beaux Arts Trio; (xi) Trampler (viola); (xii) Haas; (xiii) Italian Qt.

This Philips bargain box of Brahms's chamber music happily combines a series of warmly appealing recordings made in Germany with other distinguished contributions from the Beaux Arts Trio and the Quartetto Italiano. Grumiaux and Starker lead the instrumental duos with slightly less success, but Starker and Sebök compensate by their passionate and subtle response to the *Cello Sonatas* (this is a Mercury recording and is discussed separately below). The Berlin performance of the *Clarinet Quintet* (led by Herbert Stähr) is exceptionally beautiful, an outstanding version in every way. In the *Clarinet Trio* George Pieterson is the soloist, and this account with members of the Beaux Arts group offers a very well-integrated recording. The balance in the *Horn Trio* is managed even more adroitly. The Beaux Arts set of *Piano Trios* includes the *A major Trio*. The performances are splendid, with strongly paced, dramatic allegros, consistently alert, and with thoughtful, sensitive playing in slow movements. The sound is first class.

Cello Sonata No. 1 in E min., Op. 38.

(***) Testament mono SBT 2158. Piatigorsky, Rubinstein – BEETHOVEN: *Cello Sonatas;* WEBER: *Sonata in A.* (***)

Piatigorsky's patrician account of the *E minor Sonata* with Artur Rubinstein was recorded in Paris in the summer of 1936. It has been out of the catalogue for nearly half a century, and Testament has put matters right with this exemplary transfer.

Cello Sonatas Nos. 1 in E min., Op. 38; 2 in F, Op. 99.

*** DG 410 510-2. Rostropovich, Serkin.

(M) *** Mercury (ADD) 434 377-2. Starker, Sebök – MENDELSSOHN: *Cello Sonata No. 2.* ***

*** Channel Classics CCS 5483. Wispelwey, Komen.

*** Hyp. CDA 66159. Isserlis, Evans.

*(*) Ph. 456 402-2. Schiff, Oppitz.

Cello Sonatas Nos. 1–2; in D min., Op. 108 (arr. of *Violin Sonata in D min.*).

*** Sony SK 48191. Ma, Ax.

Cello Sonatas Nos. 1–2; Songs without Words: Feldeinsamkeit; Die Mainacht; Minnelied; Mondenschein; Nachtwandler; Sommerabend; Der Tod, das ist die kühle Nacht.

**(*) DG 459 677-2. Maisky, Gililov.

(i) *Cello Sonatas Nos. 1–2;* (ii) *Variations & Fugue on a Theme by Handel, Op. 24.*

*** EMI CDC5 56440-2. (i) Harrell; (i–ii) Kovacevich.

The partnership of the wild, inspirational Russian cellist and the veteran Brahmsian Serkin, pianist on DG, is a challenging one. It proves an outstanding success, with inspiration mutually enhanced, whether in the lyricism of Op. 38 or the heroic energy of Op. 99. Good if close recording.

The performances by Lynn Harrell and Steven Kovacevich are magnificent and commanding, and might well be a first choice for many, particularly in view of Kovacevich's finely

judged and eloquent Handel *Variations and Fugue*. However, as we go to press this set has been withdrawn.

Starker was on his finest form when he made his Mercury recordings, and he had a splendid and understanding partner in György Sebök. These highly spontaneous performances rank alongside those by Rostropovich and Serkin: they have ardour and subtlety and an impressive sense of line. The 1964 recording is very well balanced, the acoustic is warm, yet the focus is admirably clear.

The Dutch partnership, Pieter Wispelwey and Paul Komen, offers something rather different. The cellist plays a nineteenth-century Bohemian cello and the pianist a Viennese period-instrument: thus theirs is the only version of the sonatas to approximate to the sound Brahms himself might have heard. There is nothing anaemic or academic about their playing and no sense of scholarly inhibition. These are full-blooded performances, vivid in feeling and passionate, at no time wanting in eloquence.

Using gut strings, Isserlis produces an exceptionally warm tone, here nicely balanced in the recording against the strong and sensitive playing of his regular piano partner. In every way these perceptive and well-detailed readings stand in competition with the finest.

As always, Ma produces tone of great beauty and refinement, and Ax plays with great sensitivity, though there are times when he is in danger of overpowering his partner.

Mischa Maisky has exceptional refinement of tone at his disposal as well as much expressive eloquence, and the engineers do him and his partner justice. His phrasing is at times tinged with affectation, and some will find him a bit gushing and oversweet. He emotes a bit too heavily in the seven song transcriptions. Recommended to Maisky's following rather than to a wider constituency.

Heinrich Schiff is also well recorded and gives a noble account of the two sonatas, with natural and warm recorded sound on Philips, but the attractions of his recording are diminished by his somewhat pedestrian partner.

(i) *Cello Sonatas Nos. 1–2;* (ii) *Violin Sonatas Nos. 1–3; F.A.E. Sonata: Scherzo.*

(B) **(*) Virgin 2 x 1 Double VBD5 61415-2 (2). (i) Rose; (ii) Laredo; (i–ii) Pommier.

Rose achieves a fine partnership with Pommier, with whom he is ideally balanced, and though the recording is a trifle too close it is very truthful. Not surprisingly, these are strong, searching performances, especially the passionate *F major Sonata*. The *Violin Sonatas* used the same venue the previous year, but here Laredo is not flattered by the close microphones, and this makes his ardent Brahmsian response seem a bit fierce at times. Once that is said, these too are impressively committed performances.

Cello Sonata No. 2 in F, Op. 99.

(M) (***) EMI mono CDM5 67008-2. Casals, Horszowski – BACH: (Unaccompanied) *Cello suite No. 1 in G;* BEETHOVEN: *Cello Sonata No. 3.* (***)

(i) *Cello Sonata No. 2;* (ii) *Clarinet Quintet in B min., Op. 115;* (iii) *Horn Trio in E flat, Op. 40;* (iv) *Piano Trio*

No. 1 in B, Op. 8; (v) Violin Sonata No. 3 in D min., Op. 108.

(B) *** Double Decca (ADD) 452 341-2 (2). (i; iv) Starker; (i; iv–v) Katchen; (ii) Brymer, Allegri Qt; (iii) Tuckwell, Perlman, Ashkenazy; (iv–v) Suk.

The recordings of the *Piano Trio* and the *Cello Sonata* represent the results of Julius Katchen's last recording sessions before his untimely death. They were held at The Maltings, and the results have much warmth. The *Cello Sonata* is given a strong and characterful performance, while Jack Brymer gives a masterly and finely poised account of the *Clarinet Quintet* which in terms of polish and finesse can hold its own with the very best. The highlight of this set is the superbly passionate performance of Brahms's marvellous *Horn Trio* from Tuckwell, Perlman and Ashkenazy. By contrast, Josef Suk's personal blend of romanticism and the classical tradition in the *Violin Sonata* is warmly attractive but small in scale.

The celebrated (1936) Paris recording of the Brahms *F major Sonata*, Op. 99, with Casals and Horszowski has had numerous incarnations, most recently on EMI Références, but its splendours do not fade. It remains one of the most moving accounts of this leonine score on disc.

Clarinet Quintet in B min., Op. 115.

*** DG 459 641-2. Shifrin, Emerson Qt – MOZART: *Clarinet Quintet.* ***

(B) *** HM HMN 911 691. Carbonare, Hery, Binder, Bone, Pouzenc – MOZART: *Clarinet Quintet.* ***

(BB) **(*) CfP Double CDCFPSD 4772 (2). Puddy, Gabrieli Qt – BORODIN: *String Quartet No. 2*; DVORAK: *String Quartet No. 12*; SCHUBERT: *String Quartet No. 14.* ***

(i) *Clarinet Quintet; (ii) Clarinet Sonata No. 2.*

(M) *** Chan. 6522. Hilton, (i) Lindsay Qt; (ii) Frankl.

(i) *Clarinet Quintet; (ii) Clarinet Trio in A min.*

*** Hyp. CDA 66107. King, (i) Gabrieli Qt; (ii) Georgian, Benson (piano).

(BB) **(*) Naxos 8.550391. Balogh, (i) Danubius Qt; (ii) Jandó, Onczay.

(i) *Clarinet Quintet; String Quartet No. 1.*

(M) (**(*)) EMI mono CDH7 64932-2. (i) Kell; Busch Qt.

(i) *Clarinet Quintet; String Quartet No. 2.*

*** MDG 307 079-2. (i) Leister; Leipzig Qt.

(i) *Clarinet Quintet; (ii) String Quintet No. 2 in G, Op. 111.*

(N) (B) *** H.M. HMA 1951349. (i) Portal; (ii) Caussé, Melos Qt.

** EMI CDC5 56759-2. (i) Meyer; (ii) Schlichtig; Alban Berg Qt.

David Shifrin's newest recording of the Brahms *Quintet* is outstandingly fine. He establishes a natural partnership with the Emersons; the outer movements, while warmly lyrical, are much more characterful and positive than in his earlier version. Yet the *Adagio* achieves a gentle, ruminative, almost improvisational quality. The recording is admirably balanced and the equally recommendable Mozart coupling has an appealing simplicity.

The performance from the Leipzig Quartet, with Karl

Leister, is second to none. The quartet and its distinguished soloist produce impressive results in what is surely Brahms's most serene utterance, and the *A minor Quartet* also receives an authoritative and musical performance. For those wanting this particular coupling, this disc can certainly be recommended.

In Harmonia Mundi's bargain series, 'Les nouveaux interprètes', the talented young performers are led by Alessandro Carbonare. He produces exceptionally beautiful, liquid tone-colours over the widest dynamic range, with ear-catching *pianissimos* making the slow movement the high point, but with his entries in all four movements magically gentle. The string players provide consistently sympathetic support.

Janet Hilton's essentially mellow performance of the *Clarinet Quintet*, with the Lindsay Quartet playing with pleasing warmth and refinement, has a distinct individuality. Her lilting syncopations in the third movement are delightful. Hilton's partnership with Peter Frankl in the *E flat Clarinet Sonata* is rather less idiosyncratic and individual; nevertheless this performance offers considerable artistic rewards.

Thea King and the Gabrieli Quartet give a radiantly beautiful performance of the *Clarinet Quintet*, as fine as any put on record, expressive and spontaneous-sounding, with natural ebb and flow of tension as in a live performance. The recording of the strings is on the bright side, very vivid and real.

On Harmonia Mundi the warm resonance of the recording gives an almost orchestral richness of timbre to the Melos group, joined by Gérard Causé, yet they open the *Adagio* of Op. 111 (which comes first on the disc) with an exquisite delicacy of texture and feeling. The sound in the *Clarinet Quintet* is equally beguiling and Michael Portal matches the strings with his gently luscious tone in the *Clarinet Quintet*, with the beautiful slow movement dreamily ruminative, and the theme and variations finale hardly less delightful. This coupling is highly recommendable in all respects, much more rewarding than the alternative from EMI.

Keith Puddy's earlier, CfP account with the Gabrielis of this elusive work rises to fine, intense poetry in the slow movement and in the visionary closing pages of the finale. There is a spontaneity in the playing here which is a vital quality in this work, far more important than mechanical precision.

József Balogh is a highly sensitive player with a lovely tone. He is well supported by the Danubius Quartet, and their account of the *Clarinet Quintet* is a rewarding one, with warmth and atmosphere, rising to considerable heights of intensity in the *Adagio*. The *Clarinet Trio* is an enjoyably fresh account, though not quite so memorable, except in the *Andantino grazioso*, which is delightfully done; with excellent recording, this is still a worthwhile disc, and inexpensive to boot.

Reginald Kell's beauty of tone was legendary and his 1937 account of the *Clarinet Quintet* with the Busch Quartet is among the greatest recordings of the piece. Kell's vibrato was not to all tastes, but his playing here is at its most refined and the Busch produce a splendidly autumnal slow movement. The *Quartet*, from 1932, may not be as polished as in some more recent accounts (and certainly sounds its age), but the playing is full of imagination and vitality. However, as we go to press the set has been withdrawn.

Sabine Meyer joins the Alban Berg Quartet for a good rather than outstanding account of the *Clarinet Quintet*, and there are more moving accounts to be had and more memorable versions of the *G major Quintet*.

(i) *Clarinet Quintet;* (ii) *Clarinet Sonatas Nos. 1–2;* (iii) *String Quintet No. 2.*

(B) **(*) Delos Double DE 3706. (i–ii) Shifrin; (i; iii) Chamber Music Northwest; (ii) Rosenberger (with SCHUMANN: *Fantasiestücke, Op. 73* **(*)).

David Shifrin's earlier (1988) account of the *Clarinet Quintet* has a glowing delicacy of feeling and is played with lovely tone and much warmth from the supporting Northwest string group. However, the mellow atmosphere persists throughout and, although the performance is very easy to enjoy, there is too little difference of character between the four movements. One would have liked more bite and character from the strings, especially in the finale. This applies equally to the *G major Quintet*, where it is the lyrical warmth of the *Adagio* that remains in the memory. The two *Clarinet Sonatas* are songful and have great warmth, and again Shifrin's richly lyrical phrasing gives much pleasure. He has fine support from Carol Rosenberger. These performances, less volatile than those of Ralph Manno and Alfredo Perl on Arte Nova (see below), are very satisfying in a quite different way, for Shifrin's tone is consistently beautiful. So are the three Schumann *Fantasy Pieces*, especially the wistful opening number, which might well be another movement by Brahms.

(i) *Clarinet Quintet;* (ii) *Piano Quintet, Op. 34. String Quintets Nos. 1–2.*

(B) *** Ph. (ADD) Duo 446 172-2 (2). (i) Stähr; (ii) Haas; BPO Octet (members).

The Berlin performance of the *Clarinet Quintet* is both beautiful and faithful to Brahms's instructions. The delicacy with which the 'Hungarian' middle section of the great *Adagio* is interpreted gives some idea of the insight of these players. It is an autumnal reading, never forced, and is recorded with comparable refinement. The two *String Quintets* are also admirably served by these same players (with Dietrich Gerhard, viola, replacing the clarinettist, Herbert Stähr). The performances combine freshness and polish, warmth with well-integrated detail. For the *Piano Quintet* Werner Haas joins the group and they give a strongly motivated, spontaneous account of this splendid work that is in every way satisfying. The piano is balanced most convincingly. The recordings come from the early 1970s and the sound is remarkably full and warm, the richness of texture suiting the *String Quintets* especially well. This is among the finest bargains in the Philips Duo list.

Clarinet Sonatas Nos. 1 in F min.; 2 in E flat, Op. 120/1–2.

*** Chan. 8563. De Peyer, Prior.

(BB) *** Naxos 8.553121. Berkes, Jandó.

(BB) *** Arte Nova 74321 27767-2. Manno, Perl.

Superb performances from Gervase de Peyer and Gwenneth Prior, commanding, aristocratic, warm and full of subtleties of colour and detail. The recording too is outstandingly realistic.

No one buying the Naxos CD coupling the two late *Clarinet Sonatas* is likely to have any regrets. They are beautifully played and freshly recorded by this distinguished Hungarian duo, and they would be recommendable even in a higher price-bracket.

Ralph Manno establishes a strong partnership with Alfredo Perl and these volatile performances are full of imaginative light and shade. In the *F minor*, the slow movement is freely ruminative, the *E flat major* opens most persuasively and is equally strong on contrast. There is some most winning playing in the *Andante* and the brief finale is full of energy. The well-balanced recording is most realistic and vivid.

(i) *Clarinet Sonatas Nos. 1–2;* (ii) *String Quartets Nos. 1–3.*

(B) *** Ph. (ADD) Duo 456 320-2 (2). (i) Pieterson, H. Menuhin; (ii) Italian Qt.

The *Clarinet Sonatas* are very well played by George Pieterson and Hephzibah Menuhin. The autumnal twilight of the lovely *Andante un poco adagio* of the *F minor* is appealingly caught, and the following *Allegretto grazioso* flows engagingly. The *E flat Sonata* is more direct, less coaxing but strongly characterized, with plenty of light and shade. Vivid recording from 1980 adds to the feeling of boldness. The three *String Quartets* are marvellously played by the Quartetto Italiano. As always with the Philips remastering of analogue recordings (here from 1967, 1970 and 1971 respectively), the CD transfers are admirably truthful in timbre and balance.

Clarinet Trio in A min., Op. 114.

*** RCA 09026 63504-2. Collins, Isserlis, Hough – FRUHLING: *Clarinet Trio;* SCHUMANN: *Märchenerzählungen,* etc. ***
*** Sony Dig SK 57499. Stoltzman, Ax, Ma – BEETHOVEN: *Clarinet Trio* ***; MOZART: *Clarinet Trio (Kegelstatt).* **

(i) *Clarinet Trio; Clarinet Sonatas Nos. 1–2.*

*** Nim. NI 5600. Leister, Bognár; (i) with Boettcher.

It would be hard to imagine a finer performance of the Brahms *Clarinet Trio* than on the RCA disc. All three of these fine young musicians are natural recording artists, never failing to sound spontaneously expressive, always conveying the feeling of live music-making, so that their interchanges are magnetic. It makes an imaginative coupling having the Brahms masterpiece alongside the long-buried but delightful Frühling *Trio* and the arrangements of Schumann items for the same forces.

With Stolzman, Ax and Ma, the *Clarinet Trio* comes off well and finds this team in excellent form. This is also one of the most recommendable of current versions, with Stoltzman playing with great sensitivity.

The Nimbus recording gives the artists rather less space round the aural image than we would like. All the same,

Karl Leister and his two distinguished colleagues play with expressive eloquence and artistry. These performances have warmth and spontaneity.

(i) *Clarinet Trio;* (ii) *Horn Trio in E flat; Piano Trios Nos. 1–3.*

*** Hyp. CDA 67251/2. Florestan Trio, with (i) Hosford;
   (ii) Stirling.

(i) *Clarinet Trio;* (ii) *Horn Trio;* (iii) *Piano Trios Nos. 1–4.*

(B) *** Ph. (ADD) Duo 438 365-2 (2). (i) Pieterson; (ii) Orval,
   Grumiaux, Sebök; (i; iii) Beaux Arts Trio.

The Florestan set of the *Piano Trios* is the finest since the Beaux Arts comparable grouping, in terms of both performance and recording. There is a freshness and spontaneity that rekindles one's own enthusiasm for this music, and such is its dedication that one is left marvelling at the richness and quality of Brahms's inventive resource. The same must be said of the *Horn Trio* and the late *A minor Clarinet Trio*. The recorded sound is very natural and lifelike and brings the players into your living room.

George Pieterson is a first-rate artist and his account of the *Clarinet Trio* with members of the Beaux Arts group offers masterly playing from all three participants. The balance in the *Horn Trio* is perhaps the most successful on record. The fine horn player, Francis Orval, achieves this without any loss of personality in his playing. As for the *Piano Trios*, the performances are splendid, with strongly paced, dramatic allegros, consistently alert and thoughtful, and with sensitive playing in slow movements. The sound is first class and the resonance of Bernard Greenhouse's cello is warmly caught without any clouding of focus. The CD transfer has brightened the top a little, but not excessively.

***Horn Trio in E flat, Op. 40* (see also above).**

(B) *** EMI Debut CDZ5 72822-2. Clark (Waldhorn), Martin,
   Govier – BEETHOVEN: *Horn Sonata, etc; MOZART: Horn
   Quintet, etc.* ***

(M) **(*) Decca (ADD) 452 887-2. Tuckwell, Perlman,
   Ashkenazy – FRANCK: *Violin Sonata.* ***

Andrew Clark's performance using a period Waldhorn, as Brahms wanted, is most stimulating. There is a flamboyance in the playing which makes such a movement as the finale of the Brahms *Trio* thrilling, and Clark's virtuosity is well matched by his partners, also using period instruments. On one of EMI's cheapest labels it makes a splendid bargain. Warm, full sound.

A superb performance of Brahms's marvellous *Horn Trio* from Tuckwell, Perlman and Ashkenazy. They realize to the full the music's passionate impulse. The 1968 recording has been remastered for reissue in Decca's Classic Sound series, but the attempt to provide a more sharply defined sound-picture has brought a curious loss of focus at times, verging on distortion at climaxes.

(i) *Horn Trio in E flat, Op. 40;* (ii) *Piano Quintet in F min., Op. 34.*

(N) (M) *** CRD 3489. Nash Ens. (members); (i) Lloyd;
   (ii) Brown.

The CRD re-issue of the *F minor Piano Quintet* and the *Horn Trio* played by the Nash Ensemble is very competitive. The playing is refreshingly unforced, with the *Quintet* underpinned firmly by the incisive playing of the pianist Ian Brown. In the *Horn Trio* Frank Lloyd produces an exceptionally rich tone and helps the group to give a raptly beautiful account of the *Adagio*; the galloping finale is then performed with joyful panache. Tempos are well chosen, and there is great naturalness of phrasing. These players convey the sense of music-making in the home rather than concert hall, and they have lively, faithfully recorded sound in their favour.

(i) *Horn Trio in E flat;* (ii) *String Sextet No. 2.*

✪ (B) *** Sony SBK 63209. (i) Bloom, Tree, Serkin;
   (ii) Carmirelli, Toth, Naegele, C. Levine, Arico,
   Reichenberger.

The performance of the *Horn Trio*, recorded at the Marlboro Festival in 1960, is unforgettable. Myron Bloom's horn playing is superb, and Michael Tree matches his lyrical feeling, while Rudolf Serkin holds the performance together so that the listener is carried along by the exhilaration of the moment. Recorded in 1967, the *G major String Sextet* has been remastered very effectively and the players given striking presence. There is a degree of thinness on the violin timbre but no lack of body, and the performance is both warm and refined: it seems to gather tension as it proceeds. The finale is particularly successful.

Hungarian Dances Nos. 1–2, 4 & 7.

*** EMI CDC7 54753-2. Chang, Feldman – TCHAIKOVSKY:
   Violin Concerto. ***

It may be an ungenerous coupling for the Tchaikovsky *Concerto*, but Chang's performances of four of the Brahms *Hungarian Dances* – recorded with Jonathan Feldman in New York – are delectable.

Piano Quartets Nos. 1 in G min., Op. 25; 2 in A, Op. 26; 3 in C min., Op. 60.

*** Sony S2K 45846 (2). Laredo, Stern, Ma, Ax.

(i) *Piano Quartets Nos. 1–3; Piano Trio in A, Op. posth.*

(B) *** Ph. (ADD) Duo 454 017-2 (2). Beaux Arts Trio, (i) with
   Trampler.

(i) *Piano Quartets Nos. 1–3;* (ii) *Piano Trios Nos. 1–3.*

(M) *** Sony Dig./ADD SM3K 64520 (3). Stern, with
   (i) Laredo, Ma, Ax; (ii) Rose, Istomin.

The Beaux Arts set of *Piano Quartets* is self-recommending at Duo price, with the *A major Piano Trio* thrown in as a bonus. Thoughtful, sensitive playing in slow movements, lively tempi in allegros, characteristic musicianship plus spontaneity combine to make these recordings highly recommendable throughout, alongside the Stern Sony set, which is in a higher price-bracket.

The Stern–Laredo–Ma–Ax partnership produces some pretty high-voltage playing and a real sense of give-and-take; there is genuine musical rapport. The listener is placed rather closer to the artists than some readers might like. All the same, no one investing in the Sony set is likely to be in the least disappointed.

This Sony set of the *Piano Quartets* is still available separately on two premium-priced CDs, but the three-disc set is the one to go for. This includes equally fine versions of the *Piano Trios*, recorded in New York two decades earlier, in 1964 and 1966. Here Stern joins with Rose and Istomin to give committed, romantic performances of comparable magnetism. The remastering has improved the original recording out of all recognition, especially in relation to the piano sonority.

(i) Piano Quartets Nos. 1–3; Piano Quintet; String Quartet No. 2.

(***) Testament mono SBT 3063 (3). (i) Aller; Hollywood Qt – SCHUMANN: *Piano Quintet*. (***)

The Hollywood Quartet's versions of the Brahms *Piano Quartets* have hardly been surpassed, and the *A minor Quartet* has tremendous grip and an ardent lyricism. They seem to be more or less ideal performances. Due to the microphone placement there is a strident quality in the upper register in the *A minor Quartet*, but it can easily be tamed. There was nothing in the least strident about their tone in the flesh. Performances of this integrity do not come often.

(i) Piano Quartet No. 1; 4 Ballades, Op. 10.

(M) **(*) DG (ADD) 447 407-2. Gilels, (i) with Amadeus Qt.

Gilels is in impressive form, and most listeners will respond to the withdrawn delicacy of the Scherzo and the gypsy fire of the finale. The slow movement is perhaps somewhat wanting in ardour, and the Amadeus do not sound as committed or as fresh as their keyboard partner. The DG recording is well balanced and sounds very natural in its new transfer. Moreover, in the *Ballades* Gilels offers artistry of an order that silences criticism.

Piano Quartet No. 1 in G min. (orch. Schoenberg); Variations & Fugue on a Theme by Handel, Op. 24 (orch. Rubbra).

*** Chan. 8825. LSO, Järvi.

The current craze for Schoenberg's transcription of the Brahms *Piano Quartet in G minor* is puzzling. However, Neeme Järvi's new version with the LSO is as good as any. It is performed with some enthusiasm and is well recorded.

Piano Quartet No. 2 in A.

(BB) *** ASV CDQS 6199. Schubert Ens. of London – MENDELSSOHN: *Piano Quartet No. 1*. ***

Musicianly and well-recorded performances that will give satisfaction at this (or any other) price level. Sensible tempi and very well-articulated phrasing.

Piano Quartet No. 3 in C min., Op. 60.

(BB) *** ASV CDQS 6198. Schubert Ens. of London – MENDELSSOHN: *Piano Quartet No. 3*. ***

The Schubert Ensemble of London, which includes the pianist William Howard, give a commendable account. They do not perhaps penetrate all its depths, but readers attracted

by the coupling can be assured that the ASV version is well worth the modest outlay required.

Piano Quintet in F min., Op. 34.

*** BBC (ADD) BBCL 4009-2 (2). Curzon, Amadeus Qt – SCHUBERT: *Trout Quintet*. ***

(BB) *** Naxos 8.550406. Jandó, Kodály Qt – SCHUMANN: *Piano Quintet*. ***

*** Ph. 446 710-2. P. Serkin, Guarneri Qt – HENZE: *Piano Quintet*. ***

(i) Piano Quintet; String Quartets Nos. 1–3.

(N) (B) *** Teldec Ultima 8573 87802-2 (2). (i) Virzaladze; Borodin Qt.

(i) Piano Quintet; String Sextet No. 1 in B flat, Op. 18.

(B) **(*) DG (ADD) 439 490-2. (i) Eschenbach, Amadeus Qt (augmented).

Clifford Curzon is captured at his most spontaneously expressive in his live performance with the Amadeus Quartet, recorded at the Royal Festival Hall in 1974. Similarly the Amadeus Quartet are at their most compelling. Ensemble may not be quite as polished as in a studio performance, but the warmth and power are ample compensation, and the bonus disc of Schubert's *Trout Quintet* makes a very attractive package.

The fine Naxos account has a great deal going for it, even though it does not include the first-movement exposition repeat. The playing is boldly spontaneous and has plenty of fire and expressive feeling. The opening of the finale also has mystery and overall, with full-bodied recording and plenty of presence, this makes a strong impression. It is certainly a bargain.

Recorded in 1995, Peter Serkin and the Guarneri Quartet's account of the Brahms *Quintet* must rank among the most thoughtful and penetrating of recent recordings. Naturally it is technically impeccable but there is no want of spontaneity and poetic feeling. Those who have found the Guarneris rather chromium-plated and streamlined in the past will find a lot to surprise them in this challenging and powerfully conceived reading. The Philips recording is first class. However, no doubt the coupling will be a prime influence here.

The Teldec performances of the *Quintet* and *Second Quartet* were recorded in 1990 at The Maltings, Snape, and benefit from its warm and vibrant acoustic. The *Piano Quintet* receives a commanding yet sensitive treatment with Elizo Virzaladze making a positive contribution to the proceedings. In the *A minor Quartet* the Borodins have an agreeably unforced sense of forward movement, and in tonal blend and ensemble they are impeccable. Nos. 1 and 3 were recorded two years later at the Teldec Berlin Studios, and here the digital recording is still firm and truthful, but a shade close and bright.

The first movement of No. 1 sets off with considerable impetus, but the thoughtfulness of the performance establishes itself within a few bars. The inner movements of this quartet have much grace and delicacy of feeling, while in No. 3 the subtle treatment of the variations which make up the last movement is a high point of the reading. These latter performances offer much to admire and enjoy, but the playing lacks the kind of spontaneity that really grips the listener and which these players displayed more readily at Snape.

Christoph Eschenbach gives a powerful – sometimes over-projected – account of his part in the *Quintet*, yet this is undoubtedly a moving performance with plenty of vitality, and the Amadeus players remain well in the picture. The performance of the *Sextet* lacks something in purity of style, but the obvious tonal warmth and the undoubted merits of the ensemble, coupled with very good late-1960s recording, make this a pretty good recommendation for those with limited budgets.

Piano Trios Nos. 1 in B, Op. 8 (original, 1854 version); 1 in B, Op. 8 (1889 version); 2 in C, Op. 87; 3 in C min., Op. 101 (see also above).

(BB) *** Arte Nova 74321 51641-2 (2). Trio Opus 8.

Piano Trios Nos. 1 in B, Op. 8; 2 in C, Op. 87; 3 in C min., Op. 101; 4 in A, Op. posth.

(N) (B) *** Teldec Ultima 8573 87792-2 (2). Trio Fontenay.

Piano Trios Nos. 1–2.

(M) *** Decca (IMS) 421 152-2. Katchen, Suk, Starker.
*** DG 447 055-2. Pires, Dumay, Wang.

(i) Piano Trios Nos. 1–3; (ii) Cello Sonata No. 2 in F; (iii) F.A.E. Sonata: Scherzo.

(B) *** Double Decca (ADD) 448 092-2 (2). Katchen, with (i–ii) Starker; (i; iii) Suk.

Powerful, spontaneous playing with a real Brahmsian spirit, given excellent, modern recording, puts these admirable performances by the Trio Fontenay at the top of the list.

The Katchen/Suk/Starker performances of the first two *Piano Trios* are warm, strong and characterful, while the tough *C minor Trio* and the epic, thrustful *Cello Sonata* bring a comparably spontaneous response. If the sound of the CD transfers is a little limited in the upper range, the ear is grateful that no artificial brightening has been applied, for it provides a real Brahmsian amplitude which is very satisfying. Highly recommended in either format.

The prize-winning Trio Opus 8 have recorded not only Brahms's final, revised version of 1889 but also the twenty-year-old composer's original (1854) score, his first major chamber work for strings. They make a very good case for it. Throughout all three works speeds are on the broad side, but that helps to give even the most compressed of these *Trios*, Op. 101 *in C minor*, heroic power in the outer movements. All three trios are played with great verve and commitment and excellently crisp ensemble, while slow movements have fine concentration and lyrical warmth. The account of the *C major Trio*, Op. 87, is particularly fine. The pianist, Michael Hauber, leads the ensemble vibrantly. The cellist, Mario de Secondi, is a strikingly songful player, and his warm tone helps to offset the digital brightness on the violin timbre. This may need taming on some reproducers, but the recording is otherwise vivid and full, and the ambience pleasing.

Augustin Dumay and Maria João Pires are joined by the young Chinese cellist, Jian Wang. His contribution is certainly eloquent here and the performances overall have authority and finesse. Though the recording is not absolutely ideal in every respect, it does have a pleasing warmth and amplitude. The performance has personality and earns three stars.

String Quartets Nos. 1 in C min.; 2 in A min., Op. 51/1–2; 3 in B flat, Op. 67 (see also under Clarinet Sonatas).

(B) *** Teldec (ADD) 4509 95503-2 (2). Alban Berg Qt (with DVORAK: *String Quartet No. 13****).
*** EMI CDS7 54829-2 (2). Alban Berg Qt.
**(*) Claves 50-9404/5 (2). Quartet Sine Nomine.

String Quartets Nos. 1–3; (i) Clarinet Quintet.

(M) (***) EMI Rouge et Noir mono CHS5 66422-2 (2). Léner Qt, (i) with Draper.

String Quartets Nos. 1–3; (i) Piano Quintet in F min., Op. 34.

(M) *** Hyp. Dyad CDD 22018 (2). (i) Lane; New Budapest Qt.

String Quartets Nos. 1–2.

*** Chan. 8562. Gabrieli Qt.
(N) (BB) *** Naxos 8.554271 Ludwig Qt.
(**(*)) Biddulph mono LAB. Busch Qt – SCHUMANN: *Violin Sonata No. 2* (***) (with REGER: *Violin Sonata No. 5, Op. 84: Allegretto* (***)).
**(*) Simax PSC1156. Vertavo Qt.

The analogue Teldec Alban Berg performances were made in the mid-1970s when the quartet was on peak form, highly polished yet completely fresh in their musical responses. This set is strongly recommended and can stand alongside the best in the catalogue, even if the Dvořák coupling is not quite as fine as the Brahms.

The New Budapest Quartet bring warmth and spontaneity to all three scores, responding to their dramatic fervour and lyrical flow in equal measure. Their intonation is altogether impeccable and they are scrupulously attentive to Brahms's dynamic markings, with pleasing results in terms of clarity and transparency. They also offer an excellently shaped and musicianly account of the *F minor Piano Quintet*, with responsive playing from Piers Lane, and they are among the best and most naturally recorded to have appeared in recent years.

On EMI, the performances have all the finesse and attack one expects from the Alban Berg Quartet, along with impeccable technical address. The *A minor* has just the right kind of dramatic intensity and the range of colour and dynamics they produce in all three works is impressive. The EMI engineers produced well-detailed, truthful sound. These are all performances of quality and can be recommended even to those who find this ensemble at times a little too glossy.

The Sine Nomine Quartet are splendidly recorded in a helpful acoustic and the effect here is just like a series of live performances. The playing, though well integrated, responsive and with plenty of Brahmsian spirit, has not the degree of sophistication and finesse the Alban Berg Quartet displays, but it does have consistent vitality and spontaneity; the *Third, B flat major Quartet* is particularly alive: it leaps out of the speakers towards the listener, and again the closing variations are a highlight of the performance.

Richly recorded in an agreeably expansive ambience, the Gabrielis give warm, eloquent performances of both the Op. 51 *Quartets*, deeply felt and full-textured without being heavy; the *Romanze* of Op. 51, No. 1, is delightfully songful. There are both tenderness and subtlety here, and the sound is first class.

The Naxos issue is an eminently satisfactory bargain. Indeed it provides more musical pleasure than one might find from more celebrated ensembles and the recording has good presence and is well balanced.

The Busch recorded the *C minor Quartet*, Op. 51/1, for HMV in 1932, but the post-war *A minor*, Op. 51/2 (made in 1947 on four Columbia LXs when the ensemble were past their prime), came as a disappointment. There is no lack of insight but the playing is less polished. Busch and his colleagues were profound musicians and there is always something to learn from them, despite the frail sound. Excellent transfers and interesting couplings.

The Vertavo are a young Norwegian quartet. There is evident feeling in these well-prepared performances, though a trace of self-consciousness can be discerned in the wide dynamic range they cultivate. When they play softly, they certainly let you know it. All the same, these are thoroughly recommendable accounts even if they do not displace first recommendations.

The Léner ensemble offer music-making from another age: civilized, free from expressive exaggeration and with nothing overprojected or forced. The quartets unfold in a totally natural way – well, not quite wholly natural, for Léner's portamenti, very much of its period, tend to date them. Portamenti apart, there is much to savour here. Connoisseurs of the clarinet will find Charles Draper's account of the *B minor Quintet* of particular interest, and his slow tempo at the very opening had Brahms's own imprimatur. The transfers and annotations are excellent.

String Quartet No. 2 in A min., Op. 51/2.

(BB) **(*) ASV CDQS 6173. Lindsay Qt – MENDELSSOHN: *String Quartet No. 6*. *(*)

The Lindsays are in fine fettle here and, besides generating spontaneous excitement, the playing has much imagination and subtlety. This was a live recording and the microphones are too close, but the ear adjusts to the fierceness given to the players' attack when the performance has such spontaneous thrust.

String Quintets Nos. 1 in F, Op. 88; 2 in G, Op. 111.

*** Hyp. CDA 66804. Raphael Ens.
*** DG 453 420-2. Hagen Qt, Caussée.

With the *First Quintet* opening seductively, these are fine, vital performances of both works from the Raphael Ensemble. Indeed, these performances are on the same level of distinction as their accounts of the *String Sextets* and, like that companion Hyperion disc, the recording is very present indeed, which to some ears may seem a minor drawback.

The Hagen Quartet and Gérard Caussée give highly enjoyable accounts of the two *Quintets*, and the DG engineers

give them good recorded sound. No need to say more than that it can rank alongside the Raphael Ensemble on Hyperion.

String Quintet No. 2 in G, Op. 111.

*** Naim CD 010. Augmented Allegri Qt – BRUCH: *String Quintet*. ***
*** Nim. NI 5488. Brandis Qt, with Dean – BRUCKNER: *String Quintet*. ***

The second of the two string quintets makes the ideal coupling for the long-buried Bruch *Quintet*, which was also the product of old age. Very well played and recorded by the Allegri.

The Brandis version of the *G major Quintet* offers good value in being coupled with Bruckner's *F major Quintet*. The Brandis are a fine quartet and they give a warm and sympathetic account of this lovely work; the Nimbus recording is natural and lifelike.

String Sextet No. 1 in B flat, Op. 18.

(***) Biddulph mono LAB 093. Pro Arte Qt, with Hobday, Pini – SCHUBERT: *String Quintet in C*. (***)

String Sextets Nos. 1 in B flat, Op. 18; 2 in G, Op. 36.

*** Hyp. CDA 66276. Raphael Ens.
*** Chan. 9151. ASMF Chamber Ens.
*** Sony S2K 45820 (2). Stern, Lin, Ma, Robinson, Laredo, Tree.
*** Signum SIGCD 013. Hausmusik, London.

The *Sextets* are among Brahms's most immediately appealing chamber works. The Raphael Ensemble are fully responsive to all their subtleties as well as to their vitality and warmth. In short, these are superb performances; the recording is very vivid and immediate, although some ears might find it a shade too present.

The Chandos alternative is also highly recommendable, with both *Sextets* again accommodated on one CD without sacrificing the exposition repeats, so that at almost 78 minutes the Academy of St Martin-in-the-Fields offer excellent value for money. Moreover, these well-prepared and musical performances are perceptive and intelligent, and they receive finely detailed and present recording.

On Sony the rapport and interplay so vital in chamber-music playing is in ample evidence. There is a keen awareness of the warmth and generosity of feeling, as well as of the strength and architecture, of these masterpieces, and the engineering is impressive. This can be recommended alongside the Raphael Ensemble, which are accommodated on one CD, so many may feel that this remains the 'best buy'.

Hausmusik are dedicated to the performance of nineteenth-century music on the instruments of the time. The instrumental timbre is lighter and more transparent, but there is no lack of warmth. The sonority is less well upholstered and rich than in modern versions, but tempi are well chosen and the playing is unfailingly sensitive and musical. It is a more than welcome addition to the catalogue, but for most collectors it will be a supplement rather than an alternative to the existing recommendations.

The impeccable technical address of the Pro Arte Quartet shows on the Pro Arte reissue here, and their warmth and finesse make their Brahms as satisfying as any account recorded since. Needless to say, some allowance has to be made for the 1935 recording, eminently well transferred though it is.

Violin Sonata No. 1 in G., Op. 78.

(N) (M) *** EMI Debut CDZ5 74017-2. Batiashvili, Chernyavska – BACH: *Partita No. 1*; SCHUBERT: *Rondo in B min., D895*. ***

The Georgian-born Elisabeth Batiashvili studied with Mark Lubotsky and came to international attention when at the age of sixteen she won second prize at the Sibelius Competition in Helsinki. Now twenty-two she makes her EMI debut with a mixed programme. The disc is a calling-card for the artist rather than the collector who will probably want all three Brahms Sonatas. Taken purely on its merits, however, this is a lovely performance, suitably relaxed and lyrical. Ms Batiashvili is sensitively partnered by Milana Chernyavska and the balance on the recording expertly judged.

Viola Sonatas Nos. 1; 2 in E flat, Op. 120/1–2.

⚫ *** Virgin VC7 59309-2. Tomter, Andsnes – SCHUMANN: *Märchenbilder*. ***

Viola Sonatas Nos. 1–2; F.A.E. Sonata: Scherzo.

**(*) Chan. 8550. Imai, Vignoles – SCHUMANN: *Märchenbilder*. **(*)

Viola Sonatas Nos. 1–2; (i) 2 Songs with Viola, Op. 91.

*** RCA 09026 63293-2. Bashmet, Muntian.

Lars Anders Tomter and Leif Ove Andsnes bring a wide range of colour to this music and they phrase with an unforced naturalness that is very persuasive. Very well balanced, though there is a slight bias in favour of the piano.

The *Viola Sonatas* are also played superbly by Yuri Bashmet, whose sumptuous tone and refined musicianship, along with the expert support of Mikhail Muntian, are persuasive. Finely poised and well-proportioned accounts, among the finest around, although Tomter and Andsnes are rather special.

Nobuko Imai is an almost peerless violist and it is difficult to flaw her accounts of the two Op. 120 *Sonatas* with Roger Vignoles. The reverberant acoustic does not show the piano to good advantage but, apart from that, this is an impressive issue.

Viola Sonatas Nos. 1–2; Violin Sonatas Nos. 1–3; F.A.E; Sonata: Scherzo.

(B) *** DG Double (ADD) 453 121-2 (2). Zukerman, Barenboim.

The Zukerman–Barenboim performances of the *Viola Sonatas* may be a little sweet for some tastes, but they are easy to enjoy, spontaneous-sounding, with the expressiveness never sounding contrived, always buoyant. In the *Violin Sonatas*, they produce songful, spontaneous-sounding performances that catch the inspiration of the moment. The sound itself is very natural, with good presence. The lively *Scherzo in C minor* from the *F.A.E. Sonata* is thrown in for good measure.

Violin Sonatas Nos. 1–2.

(B) **(*) EMI (ADD) double forte CZS5 69367-2 (2). I. Oistrakh, Ginzburg – BEETHOVEN: *Archduke Trio*; SCHUBERT: *Piano Trio No. 1*. ***

Violin Sonatas Nos. 1 in G, Op. 78; 2 in A, Op. 100; 3 in D min., Op. 108.

*** Sony SK 45819. Perlman, Barenboim.

(M) *** EMI CDM5 66893-2 [566945]. Perlman, Ashkenazy.

(N) (M) *** RCA (ADD) 09026 63041-2. Szeryng, Rubinstein.

*** DG 435 800-2. Dumay, Pires.

(N)(M) *** Decca (ADD) 466 393-2. Suk, Katchen.

(***) Testament mono SBT 1024. De Vito, Fischer; Aprea (in No. 2).

(M) **(*) Ph. (ADD) (IMS) 446 570-2. Grumiaux, Sebök.

(N) (BB) * EMI Encore CDE5 7725-2. Mutter, Weissenberg.

Violin Sonatas Nos. 1–3; Scherzo from F.A.E. Sonata.

(N) (M) **(*) DG (ADD) 463 653-2 (2). Schneiderhan, Seeman.

Violin Sonata No. 2 in A.

*** Orfeo (ADD) C489981B. D. Oistrakh, S. Richter – PROKOFIEV: *Sonata No. 1*. ***

The Sony recording, made at a live recital in Chicago, finds Perlman in far more volatile form, more urgently persuasive with naturally flowing speeds and more spontaneous rubato than he adopts in his spacious readings with Ashkenazy on EMI. Barenboim too is less aggressive and more fanciful than he was with Zukerman on DG.

Perlman and Ashkenazy bring out the trouble-free happiness of these lyrical inspirations, fully involved yet avoiding underlying tensions. In their sureness and flawless confidence at generally spacious speeds, these are performances which carry you along, cocooned in rich sound. But not all will agree that this is a suitable candidate for EMI's 'Great Recordings of the Century'.

Szeryng – whose timbre and control of vibrato are immediately recognizable – and Rubinstein are at their finest in this triptych of Brahms sonatas. This artistic partnership makes the best of both worlds, for both players show themselves as fine virtuosi and willing partners, and are equally imbued with the Brahmsian spirit. The performances are sophisticated yet committed, strongly felt yet careful in matters of detail and balance. Excellent transfers.

Augustin Dumay and Maria João Pires on DG are certainly among the most interesting of the other CD couplings. They bring temperament and finesse to all three sonatas and, though there are one or two interpretative touches that may not enjoy universal appeal, these are unlikely to inhibit pleasure. These are artists of strong personality: certainly those with a special admiration for this partnership need not hesitate.

The Suk/Katchen partnership was recorded in the Kingsway Hall in 1967. Suk's personal blend of romanticism and the classical tradition is warmly attractive but small in scale. These are intimate performances, but none the worse for that, and they are refreshingly enjoyable, particularly as the sound and balance are excellent.

Gioconda De Vito's accounts of the *G major* and *D minor Sonatas* with Edwin Fischer from 1954 show warmth and finesse in equal measure, and her playing conveys a sense of expressive freedom. Fischer's playing is characteristically magisterial; and the *A major Sonata*, which she recorded with her usual partner, Tito Aprea, is hardly less beautiful. This is all rather special playing, and few allowances need be made for the excellent mono recording.

While other versions of these works may be more volatile and passionate, Grumiaux, expertly partnered by Sebök, is very persuasive, never short of warmth and character. The recording too is beautifully balanced and natural.

Schneiderhan and Seeman, for all their classical expertise, give the impression in the first and third sonatas of an unromantic, almost cool approach, which hardly agrees with Brahms in his pastoral *G major* mood, or his fiery *D minor* mood. However No. 2 shows the team in a much more favourable light. The *A major*, a sunny and radiant work, here benefits from a warm approach, stressed by the violinist's rounded tone and the pianist's glowing left-hand playing, especially of the arpeggio passages. They are also in good form for the delightful and less often heard *Scherzo* from a sonata based on the motto 'F.A.E.' (frei aber einsam – free but lonely), whose other movements were written by Schumann and Dietrich.

Igor Oistrakh finds a rich tone and a fine lyrical line for two essentially lyrical works, and he is accompanied sympathetically by Anton Ginzburg. The recording of both instruments is beautiful, but the piano is backwardly balanced in a resonant acoustic and the violin is well forward. This is not disastrous, but it may irritate those who rightly consider that these are works for violin *and* piano.

The Orfeo disc is rather special. It records the Oistrakh–Richter partnership at the very top of its form in a live concert at the 1972 Salzburg Festival. The playing silences criticism and the recording from ORF (Austrian Radio) is perfectly serviceable.

This was one of Anne-Sophie Mutter's earliest recordings for EMI, and this gifted young violinist scores over some rivals by the vividness of the recorded sound. But the attractions of this reissue end there. Her playing is accomplished enough and not wanting in ardour or imagination, but Alexis Weissenberg proves insensitive and lacking in feeling. He conveys little pleasure – and there are few performances in the concert hall or on record that have less magic. Not recommended even at super-budget price.

Violin Sonata (arr. from Clarinet/Viola Sonata, Op. 120/ 2); Hungarian Dances Nos. 2, 5, 8 & 9 (arr. Joachim).

*** Ph. 462 621-2. Suwana, Berezovsky – DVORAK: *4 Romantic pieces*, etc.; JANACEK: *Violin Sonata.* ***

Brahms's own transcription of the *Sonata*, Op. 120/2 – originally written for clarinet or viola – brings eminently civilized music-making; but the arrangement, though understandable when clarinet or viola recitals were rare, is hardly necessary when the gramophone has rendered the originals so readily available. However, this is distinguished playing, wholly natural and unforced. The recording is superb in every way.

PIANO MUSIC
Piano music, four hands

Hungarian dances Nos. 1–21; 18 Liebeslieder Waltzes, Op. 52a.

(BB) *** Naxos 8.553140. Matthies, Köhn.

The Naxos edition of Brahms piano duets brings lively and winning performances. It makes a generous and very attractive coupling to have all 21 *Hungarian Dances* in their original form, coupled with the piano-duet version of the first and more popular set of *Liebeslieder Waltzes*. Crisp, clean ensemble, matched by well-focused sound.

German Requiem, Op. 45 (arr. for piano, 4 hands).

(BB) ** Naxos 8.554115. Mattheis, Köhn.

Brahms's piano-duet arrangement of his great choral work succeeds better than might be expected. Though the whole project may seem odd, what does come out of this warmly expressive performance is the spring-like lyricism of Brahms's writing. On the other hand, having piano tone alone does emphasize the fact that the work is predominantly slow. A curiosity, well recorded.

Serenades Nos. 1 in D, Op. 11; 2 in A, Op. 16.

(BB) *** Naxos 8.553726. Matthies, Köhn.

Brahms's two *Serenades*, among his earliest orchestral works – the *Second* without violins – have an open innocence which translates well to the plainer medium of piano duet in Brahms's own arrangements. The duo of Matthies and Köhn, very well recorded, bring out an extra freshness and clarity. An attractive addition to their Naxos series.

Sonata for 2 Pianos in F min., Op. 34b; Variations on a Theme of Haydn, Op. 56b.

(BB) *** Naxos 8.553654. Matthies, Köhn.

This third volume in Naxos's series brings fresh and alert performances of two of the most important works, each of them better known in alternative forms. What the German duo demonstrate is that the two-piano format brings formidable advantages in bite and attack, as well as some disadvantages. Speeds are sensibly chosen for the sonata, as they are in Brahms's own piano-duet version of the *Variations on a Theme of Haydn*, again clarified. Bright, clear sound to match.

Variations on a Theme by Haydn, Op. 56a.

*** Sony MK 42625. Perahia, Solti – BARTOK: *Sonata for 2 Pianos & Percussion.* ***

Murray Perahia and Solti bring out the fullest possible colouring in their performance, so that one hardly misses the orchestra.

Solo piano music

4 Ballades, Op. 10; 7 Fantasias, Op. 116; Hungarian Dances Nos. 1–10; (i) Nos. 11–21; 3 Intermezzi, Op. 117; 8 Piano Pieces, Op. 76; 6 Piano Pieces, Op. 118; 4 Piano Pieces,

Op. 119; Piano Sonatas Nos. 1 in C, Op. 1; 2 in F sharp min., Op. 2; 3 in F min., Op. 5; 2 Rhapsodies, Op. 79; Variations on a Hungarian Song, Op. 21/2; Variations on a Theme by Paganini, Op. 35; Variations & Fugue on a Theme by Handel, Op. 24; Variations on a Theme by Schumann, Op. 9; Variations on an Original Theme, Op. 21/1; Waltzes, Op. 39.

(B) *** Decca (ADD) stereo/mono 455 247-2 (6). Katchen, (i) with J.-P. Marty.

Katchen's magisterial survey of Brahms's keyboard music was made for Decca between 1962 and 1965, save for the last three *Ballades*, which come from the 1950s and are in mono. Although we would rank the Gilels *Ballades* and some of the Kempff recordings of the later pieces as special (not to mention Solomon's mono account of the *F minor Sonata* (Testament) and, indeed, some of the other recordings of this work listed separately below), those wanting a comprehensive survey need look no further. Katchen is an eminently faithful and sound interpreter who brings refined musicianship and a natural authority to this repertoire; he is given the benefit of Decca recording which was excellent for its period, and remains so. The six CDs are offered at a very low price and, although they are not available separately, they still make a tremendous bargain. In addition to the three *Ballades*, the following are mono recordings: the *Schumann Variations*, Nos. 1, 5 and 7 of the *Fantasias* and Nos. 11–21 of the *Hungarian Dances*.

4 Ballades, Op. 10.

(M) *** DG ADD/Dig. 457 762-2. Michelangeli – SCHUBERT: *Piano Sonata in A min.* **; BEETHOVEN: *Piano Sonata No. 4.* *

Michelangeli produces a wonderfully blended tone and fine, mellow sonority. The *Ballades* are given a performance of the greatest distinction, without the slightly aloof quality that sometimes disturbs his readings; and the 1981 digital recording is excellent. The couplings, alas, are not in the same league.

4 Ballades, Op. 10; Intermezzo, Op. 117/2; 6 Piano Pieces, Op. 118; Piano Sonata No. 3, Op. 5; 2 Rhapsodies, Op. 79; Variations & Fugue on a Theme by Handel, Op. 24; Variations on a Theme by Paganini, Op. 35.

(B) **(*) Double Decca (ADD) 452 338-2 (2). Katchen.

Julius Katchen's style in Brahms is distinctive. In general the bigger, tougher pieces come off better than, for example, the gentle *Intermezzo*. But such pieces as the two *Rhapsodies* are splendidly done, and so are the *Ballades*. The *Sonata* receives a commanding performance.

4 Ballades, Op. 10; Scherzo in E flat, Op. 4; Piano Sonatas Nos. 2 in F sharp min., Op. 2; 3 in F min., Op. 5; Variations & Fugue on a Theme by Handel, Op. 24; Variations on a Theme by Paganini, Op. 35.

(M) **(*) Ph. (ADD) 432 302-2 (3). Arrau.

The 1970s sound does justice to the wonderful sonority this great pianist produced, although he is at times characteristically 'personal', notably so in the *F minor Sonata*, where he

does indulge in some generous rubato. Yet his playing is always stamped by a kind of wisdom that holds the listener, and there is no want of virtuosity in the *Handel* and *Paganini Variations*.

4 Ballades, Op. 10; Piano Sonata No. 3 in F min., Op. 5.

(BB) **(*) Naxos 8.550352. Biret.

As a pupil of Kempff, Idil Biret has a fine understanding of this repertoire, although her approach is more muscular than Kempff's. Thus the first of the four *Ballades* opens with enticing lyrical feeling but has the most powerfully dramatic climax, to match the feeling of the Scottish ballad, *Edward*, on which it is based. The fourth *Ballade* is gravely beautiful and shows her at her finest. The *Sonata* opens commandingly and its lyrical side is well balanced. These performances are full of character. Good recording, made in the Heidelberg studio.

4 Ballades, Op. 10; Variations & Fugue on a Theme by Handel, Op. 24; Variations & Fugue on a Theme by Schumann, Op. 9.

(BB) *** ASV CDQS 6161. Osorio.

Jorge Federico Osorio's account of the *Variations and Fugue on a Theme by Handel* is tremendously impressive. He possesses an unfailing sense of the Brahms style, giving us playing that is selfless and with no hint of the idiosyncratic. The four *Ballades* are also played with fine sensitivity and character. On top of all this, ASV provide excellent, well-focused sound, with plenty of depth, and this now comes in the super-bargain category.

7 Fantasias, Op. 116.

*** Ottavio OTRC 39027. Cooper – SCHUMANN: *Abegg variations*, etc. ***

(M) **(*) DG 445 562-2. Kissin – LISZT: *Concert Paraphrases of Schubert Lieder*, etc. ***; SCHUBERT: *Wanderer Fantasia.* **(*)

Imogen Cooper's stirring account of the *Capriccio* which opens the set captures the listener immediately, and the variety of colour and mood gives enormous pleasure throughout. The gentle *Intermezzi* are most beautiful, for the recording does this memorable playing full justice. The listening experience here is as if one was present at a live recital.

The Kissin recording comes from 1991 and finds the young virtuoso in masterful form. There is perhaps more to these extraordinary pieces than he uncovers but his pianism is glorious, and he is beautifully recorded too.

7 Fantasias, Op. 116; 3 Intermezzi, Op. 117; 8 Pieces, Op. 76; 6 Pieces, Op. 118; 4 Pieces, Op. 119.

(B) *** EMI double forte (ADD) CZS5 69521-2 (2). Alexeev – SCHUMANN: *Etudes symphoniques.* ***

Fantasias, Op. 116; 3 Intermezzi, Op. 117; 6 Pieces, Op. 118; 4 Pieces, Op. 119.

(M) **(*) DG (ADD) 437 249-2. Kempff.

Dmitri Alexeev's playing has authority and he produces an ideally weighted sonority, with the correct blend of colour.

He brings the right kind of tenderness and insight to the quieter pieces. His mastery of rubato is consummate and these performances generally hold their own against any now before the public. With its excellent Schumann coupling this is very highly recommendable.

Kempff's style in Brahms is characteristically individual: poetry emphasized rather than brilliance, subtle timbres rather than virtuosity. It follows that Kempff shines in the gentle fancies of Brahms's last period, with his magic utterly beguiling in the *Intermezzi in A minor, E major* and *E minor* from Op. 116, and especially in the lovely *E flat major Andante* of Op. 117.

(i) *Fantasias, Op. 116; Intermezzi, Op. 117;* (ii) *Pieces, Op. 76;* (i) *Pieces, Opp. 118/119;* (ii) *Rhapsodies Nos. 1 in B min.; 2 in G min., Op. 79/1–2;* (i) *Variations & Fugue on a Theme by Handel, Op. 24;* (iii) *Variations on a Theme by Paganini, Op. 35.*

(B) *(**) Ph. Duo ADD/Dig. 442 589-2 (2). (i) Kovacevich; (ii) Varsi; (iii) Harasiewicz.

The performances by Stephen Kovacevich can receive the strongest recommendation. He finds the fullest range of emotional contrast in the Op. 116 *Fantasias* but is at his finest in the Op. 117 *Intermezzi* and the four *Klavierstücke*, Op. 119, and it seems perverse that Philips then turned to recordings by Dinorah Varsi of the two *Rhapsodies* and eight *Klavierstücke*, Op. 76, when Kovacevich has also recorded them. However, these are already available, coupled with the two piano concertos, on another Duo. Varsi's playing is at times very impulsive. Adam Harasiewicz, however, plays the *Paganini Variations* with some flair and towards the end produces some exciting bravura. Generally the recordings are very good; Kovacevich's Op. 116 and Op. 118 are digital.

7 Fantasias, Op. 116; 8 Pieces, Op. 76; 2 Rhapsodies, Op. 79.

(BB) **(*) Naxos 8.550353. Biret.

Idil Biret readily captures the graceful intimacy of the *A flat* and *B flat Intermezzi*. Of the two *Rhapsodies*, the second is particularly fine, boldly spontaneous, its dark colouring caught well. The *Fantasias*, Op. 116, bring some beautifully reflective playing, notably in the three *Intermezzi* grouped together (in E major and E minor), while the framing *G minor* and *D minor Capriccios* are passionately felt, the latter ending the recital strongly. This is all impressively characterized Brahms playing, and the recording does not lack sonority.

3 Intermezzi, Op. 117; 6 Pieces, Op. 118; 4 Pieces, Op. 119; 2 Rhapsodies, Op. 79.

*** Decca (ADD) 417 599-2. Lupu.
(B) **(*) Cal. (ADD) 6679. Södergren.

Radu Lupu's late Brahms is quite outstanding in every way. There is great intensity and inwardness, when these qualities are required, and a keyboard mastery that is second to none. This is undoubtedly one of the most rewarding Brahms recitals currently before the public.

Inger Södergren's Brahms is imaginative and poetic: her performances of the three *Intermezzi* are enticingly intimate, while there is a commanding volatility and passion in the

Rhapsodies. She brings out all the colour of the Op. 118 *Pieces* and captures their variety of mood and atmosphere.

Piano Sonatas Nos. 1 in C, Op. 1; 2 in F sharp min., Op. 2.

*** Decca 436 457-2. Richter.

Recorded in Mantua in February 1987, these performances show Sviatoslav Richter at his most commanding. He makes the most heavily chordal piano writing sound totally pianistic and there is exquisite shading of tone and flawless legato. Both slow movements are coloured most subtly and the opening of the finale of the *F sharp minor Sonata* has a wonderful improvisational feeling. The playing throughout has the spontaneity of live music-making and the Decca engineers have secured most realistic sound.

Piano Sonata No. 3 in F min., Op. 5; 4 Ballades, Op. 10.

(N) *** Hyp. CDA 67237. Hough.
*** Teldec 0630-14338-2. Barenboim.
(N) ** EMI CDC5 57125-2. Vogt.

Piano Sonata No. 3; 4 Ballades; Intermezzo in E, Op. 116/6; Romance in F, Op. 118/5.

(N) (M) **(*) RCA 09026 63068. Rubinstein.

Piano Sonata No. 3; Intermezzi: in E flat, Op. 117/1; in C, Op. 119/3.

(M) *** Decca (ADD) 448 578-2. Curzon – SCHUBERT: *Piano Sonata No. 21.* ***

Piano Sonata No. 3; 6 Pieces, Op. 118.

(N) (BB) **(*) ASV CDQS 6193. Vakarelis.

Piano Sonata No. 3; Theme & Variations in D min. (from String Sextet, Op. 18).

(M) *** Decca (ADD) 448 129-2. Lupu – SCHUBERT: *Sonata No. 5, etc.* ***

The *F minor Sonata* and the *Ballades, Op. 10*, are virtually contemporary, separated by less than a year. They are a young man's music – the composer only just having entered his twenties. Stephen Hough gives us a finely conceived, naturally paced and beautifully controlled account of both pieces. The intellect and emotions, the 'classical' Brahms and youthful romanticism are well balanced. The recorded sound is very good and lifelike.

Curzon's account of the *F minor Sonata* is special. His approach is both perceptive and humane, and his playing has great intensity and freshness and, above all, is spontaneous-sounding, both in the *Sonata* and in the two *Intermezzi* which act as encores. The 1962 recording was among the finest of its day.

Noble, dignified and spacious are the adjectives that spring to mind when listening to Lupu's Op. 5. His view is inward, ruminative and always beautifully rounded. The arrangement of the slow-movement theme and variations from the *B flat major String Sextet* in his hands seems tailor-made for the piano. The 1981 digital recording is most realistic, the piano set slightly back, the timbre fully coloured and the focus natural.

Barenboim's *Sonata* and *Ballades* are distinguished by an effortless technical command and excellent musical characterization and insight. Although he is not necessarily a first choice, this generally well-recorded account is certainly most impressive.

Rubinstein's impulsive way with Brahms, not only in the *Sonata* but also in the *Ballades* (recorded a decade later), brings a mercurial quality which is undoubtedly spontaneous, even if in the later pieces one misses the extremes of tension and repose. The splendid remastering of the 1959 recording of the *Sonata* has brought a greater fullness of colour and timbre; indeed, the piano image is commendably real and present. The *Intermezzo* and *Romance* are beautifully played, and this reissue is most welcome.

Janis Vakarelis treats the *Sonata* as a volatile expression of youthful genius, yet finds a touching simplicity in the *Andante*. He has the full poetic measure of the *Intermezzo*, then rounds off his reading in a passionate, powerfully structured account of the finale. The Op. 18 *Pieces* are given the strength and poise of maturity, with the two final items particularly characterful. Vakarelis is most realistically recorded, and if not a first choice for the *Sonata*, this disc is well worth its modest cost.

Lars Vogt, who has made so strong an impression in recent years, is less concerned in allowing Brahms to speak for himself. He commands a wide range of keyboard colour and a refined imagination. But ultimately his is a performance of extremes in terms of dynamics (the loud passages are very powerful even allowing for the rather close balance) and exaggerations in rubato, pulling the flow of the line out of place to make an expressive point. This is something one can take in one's stride in the concert hall but is less satisfying on CD.

Variations on a Theme by Paganini, Op. 35.

(BB) *** Koch Discovery DICD 920423. Brancart – LISZT: *Paganini Etudes.* ***

Evelyne Brancart has superb technique, fine musicianship and sensitivity; the recording is rather bright and forward but yields pleasing results. An enjoyable recital – though, even at super-bargain price, rather short measure at 47' 40".

ORGAN MUSIC

11 Chorale Preludes, Op. 122; Chorale Prelude & Fugue on 'O Traurigkeit, O Herzeleid'; Fugue in A flat min. (original and published versions); *Preludes & Fugues: in A min.; G min.*

*** Nim. NI 5262. Bowyer (organ of Odense Cathedral).

11 Chorale Preludes, Op. 122; Chorale Prelude & Fugue on 'O Traurigkeit, O Herzeleid'; Fugue in A flat min.; Preludes & Fugues: in A min.; G min.

(M) *** CRD 3404. Danby (organ).
(N) (M) ** Simax PSC 1137. Kordstoga (organ of Oslo Cathedral).

Kevin Bowyer has the advantage of the splendid Danish organ in Odense Cathedral, which combines a full tone and a warmly coloured palette with a clear profile. Like Nicholas Danby, Bowyer is obviously at home both in the early *Preludes and Fugues*, in which he produces considerable bravura (helped by the fresh, bright sound of the organ),

and in the very late set of *Chorale Preludes*. He then closes the recital with Brahms's original manuscript forms of the two earliest pieces (which we have already heard in their published formats), the *Chorale Prelude and Fugue on 'O Traurigkeit'* and the unpolished *A flat minor Fugue*. The disc is very well documented.

Nicholas Danby, playing the organ of the Church of the Immaculate Conception in London, gives restrained, clean-cut readings which yet have a strong profile. Choice between these two discs might well depend on preference for the type of organ used. The effect on CRD is rather more incisive but has firmness and weight of tone and certainly does not lack amplitude.

As Kåre Nordstoga demonstrates in his flamboyant account of the opening *Prelude in G minor*, the organ at Oslo Cathedral is a magnificent instrument. It is ideal for this repertoire, colourfully resonant yet allowing detail to register clearly, which is especially telling in the *Chorale Preludes*. But, alas, after that brilliant opening, Norstoga becomes more didactic and favours very steady tempi, especially in the *Fugues*.

VOCAL MUSIC

Vocal ensembles: *Ballads & Romances, Op. 75; 14 Children's Folksongs; 49 Deutsche Volkslieder; Duets, Opp. 20; 28; 61; 66; Liebeslieder, Op. 52; Neue Liebeslieder, Op. 65; Quartets, Opp. 31; 64; 92; 112; Zigeunerlieder, Op. 103.*

(M) *** DG Dig./ADD 449 641-2 (4). Mathis, Fassbaender, Schreier, Fischer-Dieskau; Engel, Sawallisch, Kahl; N. German R. Ch., Jena.

This box from DG's Brahms Edition includes all his vocal ensembles for solo voices with piano, and they receive fresh, brightly affectionate performances from an almost ideally chosen quartet of distinguished singers, accompanied by excellent, imaginative pianists. There is much treasure to be found throughout these four discs, recorded with a nice balance between intimacy and immediacy.

Choral works: Female chorus: *Ave Maria, Op. 12; 13 Canons, Op. 113; Psalm 13, Op. 27; 3 Geistliche Chöre, Op. 37; 4 Songs, Op. 17; 12 Songs & Romances, Op. 44.* **Male chorus:** *7 Canons; Little Wedding Cantata; Songs, Op. 41; 23 German Folksongs.* **Mixed chorus:** *Begräbnisgesang, Op.13; 3 Fest- und Gedenksprüche, Op. 109; Marienlieder, Op. 22; Motets, Opp. 29; 74; 110; Geistliches Lied, Op. 30; Songs, Opp. 42; 62; 104; Songs & Romances, Op. 93a; Tafellied Dank der Damen, Op. 93b.*

(M) *** DG 449 646-2 (4). Mathis, Murray, Hahn, Dickel, Kahl, Rohde, Schroeder, Winkler; N. German R. Ch., Jena.

This four-disc collection, also from the DG Brahms Edition, of his unaccompanied choral music ranges wide, representing all periods of his career in intimate, warmly characterful writing, whether in motets, part-songs, canons or folksong settings. It contains much buried treasure, not least the fine *Motets for Double Chorus*, Opp. 109 and 110. The Hamburg choir gives radiant performances, beautifully recorded with no hint of routine: the sound is both clear and pleasingly atmospheric. Highly recommended.

Choral works with orchestra: (i) *Alto Rhapsody, Op. 53;* (ii) *German requiem, Op. 45; Nänie, Op. 82;* (iii) *Rinaldo, Op. 50;* (iv) *Song of destiny (Schicksalslied), Op. 54; Song of the Fates, Op. 89;* (v) *Song of Triumph, Op. 55.*

(M) **(*) DG 449 651-2 (3). (i) Fassbaender; (ii) Bonney, Schmidt, V. Op. Ch., VPO, Giulini; (iii) Kollo; (v) W. Brendel; (i; iii–v) Prague Philharmonic Ch., Czech PO, Sinopoli.

Giulini's performance of the *German Requiem* is deeply dedicated but one which at spacious speeds lacks rhythmic bite. Meditation is a necessary part of Brahms's scheme, but here, with phrasing smoothed over and the choral sound rather opaque, there is too little contrast. Fassbaender makes a strong, noble soloist in the *Alto Rhapsody*, but it is the other works which command first attention in such a collection, not least the *Triumphlied* of 1870, to which Sinopoli, helped by incandescent singing from the Czech choir, brings Handelian exhilaration. There is freshness and excitement too in the other rare works, with Sinopoli lightening the rhythms and textures. In *Rinaldo*, for example – the nearest that Brahms came to writing an opera – Sinopoli moulds the sequence of numbers very dramatically. René Kollo is the near-operatic soloist. The recordings, made in Prague, bring sound which is warm and sympathetic, with the orchestra incisively close and the chorus atmospherically behind, if sometimes a little confusingly so.

LIEDER

Lieder: *Ach, wende diesen Blick; Die Mainacht; Heimweh; Mädchenlied; Meine Liebe ist grün; O kühler Wald; Ständchen; Unbewegte laue Luft; Von ewiger Liebe; Wie rafft' ich mich auf; Wiegenlied;* (i) *2 Songs with Viola (Gestilte Sehnsucht & Geistliches Wiegenlied), Op. 91; 3 Volkslieder: Dort in den Weiden; Sonntag; Vergebliches Ständchen. 8 Zigeunerlieder, Op. 103/1–7 & 11.*

*** DG (IMS) 429 727-2. Von Otter, Forsberg, (i) with Sparf.

Anne Sofie von Otter gives these Brahms Lieder the natural freshness of folksong which so often they resemble. She phrases unerringly, holding and changing tension and mood as in a live recital, and her accompanist is strongly supportive. In the Op. 91 settings they are joined by Nils-Erik Sparf, who plays with admirable taste.

Lieder: *Agnes; Alte Liebe; Dein blaues Auge hält so still; Dort in den Weiden; 2 Songs, Op. 91; Gold überwiegt die Liebe; Immer leiser wird mein Schlummer; Der Jäger; Klage I–II; Die Liebende schreibt; Liebesklage des Mädchens; Liebestreu; Des Liebsten Schwur; Das Mädchen, Op. 85/3; Mädchenfluch, Op. 95/1; Mädchenlied. Op. 107/5; Das Mädchen spricht; 5 Ophelia Lieder; Regenlied; 6 Romanzen und Lieder, Op. 84; Salome; Sapphische Ode; Spanisches Lied; Der Schmied; Therese; Todessehnen; Die Trauernde; Vom Strande; Von waldbekränzter Höhe; Vorschneller Schwur; Wie melodien zieht; 8 Zigeunerlieder, Op. 103.*

(B) *** DG (ADD) Double 459 469-2 (2). Norman, Barenboim.

This double CD concentrates on Brahms's 'women's songs'. Jessye Norman's tone is full and golden. Her imagination even matches that of Fischer-Dieskau, and no praise could be higher. Her voice is ideally suited to many of these songs, and if occasionally there is a hint of an over-studied quality this is of little consequence, considering the overall achievement. Barenboim's accompaniments are superb, contributing much to the success of this recital. The recording is excellent and this is a real bargain.

Lieder: *An die Nachtigall; Bottschaft; Dein blaues Auge hält so still; Feldeinsamkeit; Der Gang zum Liebchen; Geheimnis; Im Waldeseinsamkeit; Komm bald; Die Kränze; Die Mainacht; Meine Liebe ist grün; Minnelied; Nachtigall; O wüsst ich doch den Weg zurück; Sah dem edlen Bildnis; Salamander; Die Schale der Vergessenheit; Serenade; Sonntag; Ständchen; Von ewiger Liebe; Von waldbekränzter Höhe; Wie bist du, Meine Königin; Wiegenlied; Wir Wandelten.*

(BB) *** Virgin 2 x 1 VBD5 61418-2 (2). Allen, Parsons – WOLF: *Lieder.* ***

Thomas Allen gives fresh, virile performances of a particularly attractive collection of Brahms songs. There is less underlining of words than Fischer-Dieskau or Bär give us but still a keen and detailed feeling for meaning as well as mood. There are many such felicities here, with Geoffrey Parsons an ever-sympathetic accompanist and with sound more cleanly focused than in earlier Lieder issues from this source. Now coupled with an equally desirable recital of Wolf songs, with the two CDs offered for the cost of one mid-priced disc, this is a set not to be missed by any lover of German Lied, even though no translations are provided.

Lieder: *An eine Aolsharfe; Auf dem See; Dein blaues Auge; Botschaft; Brauner bursche führt zum Tanze; Dämmrung senkte sich von oben; Feldeinsamkeit; Frühlingstrost; Immer leiser wird mein Schlummer; Juchhe; Kommt dir manchmal in den Sinn; Lerchengesang; Liebestreu; Mädchenlied; Das Mädchen spricht; Die Mainacht; Meine Liebe ist grün; Mein wundes Herz verlangt; O wüss ich doch den Weg zurück; Ständchen; Vergebliches Ständchen; Von Strande; Wiegenlied; Wie Melodien zieht es mir.*

(BB) **(*) Arte Nova 74321 59216-2. Rao, Gelius.

Lan Rao has a fresh, pretty soprano which she uses most sensitively, if within a rather limited tonal range. The items which stand out are those, like *Wiegenlied* or *Immer Leiser,* which involve poised legato and the gentlest dynamics. Response to word-meaning is good, even if such a witty number as *Vergebliches Ständchen* is rather undercharacterized. Nevertheless, with well-balanced recording, the disc makes an attractive bargain on the Arte Nova label.

Alto Rhapsody; 4 Songs, Op. 17.

(BB) *** Virgin 2 x 1 VBD5 61469-2 (2). J. Baker, London Symphony Ch., City of L. Sinf., Hickox – BERLIOZ: *Les Nuits d'été,* etc.; MENDELSSOHN: *Infelice,* etc.; RESPIGHI: *La Sensitiva.* ***

Though the Virgin recording of the *Alto Rhapsody* was made

after Janet Baker's retirement from the concert platform, the voice is in glorious condition, superbly controlled. This is a more openly expressive and spacious reading than her earlier, EMI one with Boult, matching her performances in the two Mendelssohn items. The four early Brahms songs, Opus 17, for women's chorus with two horns and harp accompaniment, are delightfully done.

(i–ii) *Alto Rhapsody*; (ii) *Begrabnisgesang, Op. 13; Gesang der Parzen, Op. 89*; (iii) *Geistlicheslied, Op. 30*; (iv) *2 Motets, Op. 29*; (iii) *2 Motets, Op. 74; 3 Motets, Op. 110*; (ii) *Nänie, Op. 82*; (v) *Rinaldo, Op. 50*; (ii) *Song of Destiny (Schicksalslied), Op. 54.*

(B) *** Double Decca Dig./ADD 452 582-2 (2). (i) Van Nes; (ii) San Francisco Ch. and SO, Blomstedt; (iii) New English Singers, Preston; (iv) King's College, Cambridge, Ch., Cleobury; (v) King, Ambrosian Ch., New Philh. O, Abbado.

The recordings of the five key choral works here, the *Alto Rhapsody*, *Begrabnisgesang* (Funeral hymn), *Gesang der Parzen* (*Song of the Fates*), *Nänie* and the *Song of Destiny* (*Schicksalslied*), come from an outstanding 1989 collection using the Davis Symphony Hall, San Francisco, where the Decca team have made many outstanding records. This is no exception, with inspired singing from the splendid San Francisco Choir. Jard van Nes's moving account of the *Alto Rhapsody* can stand alongside the famous versions from Dame Janet Baker and Kathleen Ferrier, although it differs from both; again the choral contribution is splendid. The King's College Choir under Cleobury then follows on with the two lovely *a cappella* five-part motets of Op. 29. Both these earlier (1860) Brahms settings pay tribute to the Bach tradition, whereas the later motets of Op. 74 (1877) and especially the three of Op. 110 (1889) look forward as well as backwards in style. The final item on the second disc is the most substantial and the least satisfactory. James King's rather coarse Heldentenor approach to the 40-minute cantata *Rinaldo* is less than ideal for music that is much more easily lyrical than Wagner. However, Abbado ensures that the performance overall is fairly convincing. In any case the rest of the content of this set is more than worth its asking price.

(i) *Alto Rhapsody; Deutsche Volkslieder:* (ii) *Ach, englische Schäferin; All mein' Gedanken; Da unten im Tale; Dort in den Weiden;* (iii) *Es war einmal ein Zimmergesell;* (ii) *Es wohnet ein Fiedler; In stiller Nacht; Maria ging aus wandern; Mein Mädel hat einen Rosenmund; Schwesterlein; Die Sonne scheint nicht mehr;* (iii) *Verstohlen geht der Mond auf.* (ii) *Wach auf, mein' Herzensschöne.* (iv) *Lieder: Am Sonntagmorgen; Botschaft; Heimweh II; Junge Lieder I; Die Mainacht; Minnelied; O liebche Wangen; Regenlied; Sonntag; Uber die Heide; Von ewiger Liebe.*

(B) *** DG 439 441-2. (i) Ludwig, V. Singverein, VPO, Boehm; (ii) Mathis or Schreier, Engel; (iii) N. German R. Ch., Jena; Kahl; (iv) Fischer-Dieskau, Barenboim.

Christa Ludwig's strong and eloquent account of the *Alto Rhapsody* and the Lieder recital from Fischer-Dieskau and Barenboim are capped by a well-chosen selection from

Brahms's folksong arrangements: simple, glowing settings, the product of a lifetime's love affair with the music. Edith Mathis and Peter Schreier capture their innocent spirit delightfully, never overplaying their hands. Karl Engel accompanies sympathetically and the Chorus of North German Radio (digitally recorded) provides two of the attractive choral settings.

(i) *Alto Rhapsody*; (ii) *German Requiem, Op. 45*; (iii) *Song of Destiny (Schicksalslied), Op. 54*; (iv) *Geistliches Lied, Op. 30*; (v) *Vier ernste Gesänge (4 Serious Songs), Op. 121*; (vi) *2 Songs with Viola, Op. 91.*

(B) **(*) Double Decca ADD/Dig. 452 344-2 (2). (i; vi) Watts; (i) SRO, Ansermet; (ii) Te Kanawa, Weikl, Chicago Ch. & SO, Solti; (iii) Amb. Ch., New Philh. O, Abbado; (iv) King's College, Cambridge, Ch., Cleobury; (v) Holl, A. Schiff; (vi) Parsons, Aronowitz.

Solti favours very expansive tempi, smooth lines and refined textures in the *Requiem*. There is much that is beautiful, even if the result overall is not as involving as it might be. Kiri Te Kanawa sings radiantly, but Bernd Weikl with his rather gritty baritone is not ideal. Fine recording, glowing and clear. Helen Watts gives a sensitive account of the *Alto Rhapsody*, while the *Song of Destiny* brings a refined contribution from the Ambrosian Chorus with Abbado directing strongly. Helen Watts, too, is in good form in her sensitive performances of the two songs with viola as well as piano accompaniment. Cecil Aronowitz plays his obbligato with great finesse, and the combination of voice, viola and piano is particularly effective in *Gestillte Sehnsucht*. The contributions of Robert Holl, accompanied by András Schiff, are slightly marred by the slow tempi chosen but are well sung, with due note taken of the texts.

49 Deutsche Volkslieder; 14 Folksongs for Children.

(M) *** DG (ADD) (IMS) 449 087-2 (2). Mathis, Schreier, Engel; N. German R. Ch., Jena.

The writing here represents Brahms at his most engagingly domestic in these lovely folksong settings and the *Volks-Kinderlieder*, originally designed for the family of Robert and Clara Schumann. There is much to treasure here and the performances are fresh and brightly affectionate. The sound is first class and the documentation includes full translations. Recommended.

German Requiem, Op. 45.

⊛ *** Ph. 432 140-2. Margiono, Gilfry, Monteverdi Ch., ORR, Gardiner.

(N) (BB) *** Warner Apex 8573 89081-2. Price, Ramey, Ambrosian Singers, RPO, Previn.

(N)(BB) *** HM LSO Live LSO 0005CD. Blackwell, Wilson-Johnson, LSO Ch., LSO, Previn.

(M) *** EMI CDM5 66903-2 [566955]. Schwarzkopf, Fischer-Dieskau, Philh. Ch. & O, Klemperer.

(B) *** DG 459 355-2. Popp, W. Brendel, Prague Philharmonic Ch., Czech PO, Sinopoli.

(M) (***) EMI mono CDH7 64705-2. Grümmer, Fischer-Dieskau, St Hedwig's Cathedral Ch., BPO, Kempe.

(B) **(*) EMI CZS7 67819-2 (2). Norman, Hynninen, LPO Ch.,
   LPO, Tennstedt – SCHUMANN: *Requiems.* ***

(N) (B) **(*) Sony [ADD] SBK 89308. Contrubas; Prey; New
   Phil. Ch. & O, Maazel.

(i) *German Requiem;* (ii) *Alto Rhapsody; Song of Destiny
(Schicksalslied), Op. 54; Academic Festival Overture; Tragic
Overture; Variations on a Theme by Haydn.*

(B) **(*) Ph. (ADD) (IMS) Duo 438 760-2 (2). (i) Lipp, Crass;
   (ii) Heynis; V. Singverein; VSO, Sawallisch.

(i) *German Requiem; Burial Song, Op. 13.*

(M) *** Virgin VM5 61605-2. (i) L. Dawson, Bär; L. Schütz Ch.,
   LCP, Norrington.

Gardiner's 'revolutionary' account of the *German Requiem*
brings a range of choral sound even more thrilling than in
the concert hall. With period instruments and following
Viennese practice of the time, speeds tend to be faster than
usual, though the speed for the big fugue is surprisingly
relaxed. Charlotte Margiono makes an ethereal soprano
soloist, while Rodney Gilfry, despite a rapid vibrato, is aptly
fresh and young-sounding. One could not ask for a more
complete renovation of a masterpiece that is often made to
sound stodgy and square.

It is the seeming simplicity of Previn's dedicated approach
in his earlier Teldec recording, with radiant singing from the
chorus and measured speeds held steadily, that so movingly
conveys an innocence in the often square writing, both in
the powerful opening choruses and in the simple, songful
Wie lieblich. The great fugatos are then powerfully presented.
Both soloists are outstanding, Margaret Price golden-toned,
Samuel Ramey incisively dark. The recording, of high
quality, is warmly set against a helpful church acoustic with
the chorus slightly distanced.

Following up the live recordings made by Sir Colin Davis
for the LSO's own label, comes this second recording from
André Previn, Conductor Laureate, in a work he is specially
close to. With incandescent singing from the London Symphony Chorus, finely shaded over the widest dynamic range,
this is a powerful, dedicated reading which emphasizes the
drama of the piece in high contrasts. The impact of the
chorus is all the greater, when the recording gives the impression of a relatively compact group – more a question of the
Barbican acoustic rather than actual size. In its freshness it
defies any idea of this as a turgid piece, as once condemned
by Bernard Shaw. Though speeds are on the fast side – with
the overall timing some ten minutes shorter than in most
rival versions – the flow makes the music all the more
magnetic, removing any hint of sentimentality. Good clear
soloists and first-rate sound.

Norrington, using period forces, comes into direct rivalry
with Gardiner in his Philips version, recorded 18 months
earlier. At speeds even faster and taking a plainer view, but
drawing equally fine singing from his choir, Norrington
lacks some of Gardiner's dramatic flair, but Lynne Dawson
sings with ravishing sweetness in her central solo and Olaf
Bär brings a lieder-like intensity to the baritone solos, even
if he lacks a degree of darkness. Unlike Gardiner and most
other rivals, Norrington offers a brief coupling, the dark
Burial Song with wind accompaniment.

Klemperer's reading has been effectively remastered for
reissue as one of EMI's 'Great Recordings of the Century'.
Measured and monumental, the performance defies precon-
ceived doubts. The speeds are consistently slow – too slow
in the *vivace* of the sixth movement, where Death has little
sting – but, with dynamic contrasts underlined, the result
is uniquely powerful. The solo singing is superb and the
Philharmonia Chorus were at the peak of their form. The
new CD transfer is excellent.

Sinopoli's DG version brings a performance of extremes
– generally measured but consistently positive and often
dramatically thrilling – helped by the wide-ranging
recording, excellent soloists and an incisive contribution
from the Prague Philharmonic Chorus. The 1983 digital
recording is full, clear and realistically balanced.

Rudolf Kempe's mono recording of 1955 is incandescent,
glowing with warmth, a characteristic example of his dedicated intensity, and, though the mono recording is limited
on orchestral sound, the voices are caught vividly and atmospherically, with the choir the more involving for being
forwardly balanced. There is vintage singing too from
Fischer-Dieskau and Elisabeth Grümmer sounds sweetly
radiant, superbly sustaining Kempe's exceptionally slow
speed for *Ihr habt nun Traurigkeit.*

Tennstedt's is an unusually spacious view of the *Requiem,*
with a reverential manner always alert, never becoming
merely monumental. Jorma Hynninen proves an excellent
soloist. On CD, generally fine, spacious recording which
matches the spaciousness of the interpretation.

Maazel directs a strong unaffected performance, most
impressive in the great choral climaxes, notably so in *Denn
alles Fleisch.* There is a fair sense of spontaneous music-
making here, and the warm 1976 recording is apt for the
music. The soloists are both in good voice, though Contrubas's beautiful tone has a hint of unsteadiness, no doubt
exaggerated by the recording. Fair value as Sony provide
texts and translations.

In the *German Requiem* Sawallisch may not penetrate the
spiritual depths as deeply as a conductor like Kempe, but
the music flows naturally. It is a deeply satisfying version,
with an account of the final movements both dramatic and
ethereal. Franz Crass's dark bass colouring make his solos
tonally distinctive, but the singing of Wilma Lipp in *Ihr habt
nun Traurigkeit* is a blot, wobbly and plaintive-sounding.
However, what makes this inexpensive set worth considering, even against the competition, is Aafje Heynis's
lovely singing in the *Alto Rhapsody.* It is even more dedicated
and 'inner' than Kathleen Ferrier's, and the tonal shading is
most beautiful. The emotionally more turbulent *Song of
Destiny* is also a considerable success. Not all collectors will
need the overtures, but they are well enough played and
recorded, although the early date (1959) of the *Variations*
shows in the violin timbre.

German Requiem, Op. 45 (sung in English).

*** Telarc CD 80501. Chandler, Gunn, Mormon Tabernacle
   Ch., Utah SO, Jessop.

(N) (BB) (**) Naxos mono 8.110839. Chiesa, Janssen,
   Westminster Ch., NBC SO, Toscanini.

Craig Jessop directs a dedicated reading of a new translation by Robert Shaw which for English-speaking listeners will communicate warmly, not least thanks to the extra immediacy of the words. The choir, which too often has been recorded mushily, here emerges far fresher than before, and the two soloists are both first rate. Janice Chandler has a warm, creamy soprano, and Nathan Gunn has a youthfully clear baritone which he uses with finesse and passion. Full, warm sound, not always ideally transparent; but this remains a fully worthy tribute to Shaw.

In January 1943, at the height of the Second World War, Toscanini conducted his performance of the Brahms *Requiem* in New York, understandably choosing an English text rather than German. As one would expect it is high-powered, starting with a refreshing, urgent account of the opening Beatitude setting, *Blessed are they*. After that the next movement, *Behold, all flesh is grass*, is very broad indeed, prevented from sounding sluggish only by Toscanini's high-voltage intensity, which equally sustains the other movements. Herbert Janssen as the baritone soloist dramatic and clean-cut, provides Lieder-like detail. Viviane della Chiesa is the fresh, creamy-toned soprano in the fourth movement, and the Westminster Choir adds to the drama, even though backwardly balanced. Limited mono sound, less harsh than many commercial NBC recordings of the period.

3 Gesänge, Op. 42; (i) 4 Gesänge, Op. 17; 5 Gesänge, Op. 104; (ii) 6 Quartette, Op. 112; Zigeunerlieder, Op. 109.

(N)⬤ *** Chan. 9805. Danish Nat. R Ch., Parkman; with
(i) Yeats, McClelland, Lind; (ii) Forsberg.

Brahms's shorter choral works are still too little known by many collectors who are almost over-familiar with his orchestral and chamber music, so we have given this Chandos disc a Rosette, not only in response to the splendid performances it contains, but also in the hope of enticing readers to explore. The Danish National Radio Choir have already brought us a fine collection of motets, including the *Marienlieder* (see below). Here they turn their attention to some of the lovely unaccompanied *Gesänge*, and include also as a highlight of the concert the luscious settings of Op. 17, which have delectable harp accompaniments and obbligatos for one or two horns. *Sehnsucht*, the first of the six piano-accompanied *Quartets* which follow, has one of the composer's most seductive melodies, and the robust set of *Zigeunerlieder* which close the recital, sung with great vigour, show the composer at his most infectiously boisterous.

Liebeslieder Waltzes, Op. 52.

*** BBC (ADD) BBCB 8001-2. Harper, J. Baker, Pears, Hemsley, Britten & Arrau (piano duet) – ROSSINI: *Soirées musicales;* TCHAIKOVSKY: *4 Duets.* ***

Britten was allergic to the music of Brahms, but you would never know that from this magical performance of the *Liebeslieder Waltzes*. As an inspired accompanist he is joined by Claudio Arrau in a perfect partnership. The soloists make an outstanding and characterful team, whooping away throughout, with Janet Baker striking a deeper note in the poignant seventh waltz. Full, clear, radio sound.

Liebeslieder Waltzes, Op. 52; New Liebeslieder Waltzes, Op. 65/15.

(M) (***) Decca mono 425 995-2. Seefried, Ferrier, Patzak, Günter, Curzon, Gá – MAHLER: *Kindertotenlieder.* (**)

Liebeslieder Waltzes, Op. 52; New Liebeslieder Waltzes, Op. 65; 3 Quartets, Op. 64.

*** DG 423 133-2. Mathis, Fassbaender, Schreier, Fischer-Dieskau; Engel & Sawallisch (pianos).

On DG one of the most successful recordings yet of the two seductive but surprisingly difficult sets of *Liebeslieder Waltzes*. The CD has fine realism and presence.

Recorded at the Edinburgh Festival in September 1952, the Decca historic performance brings a dazzling team together. Though it is not the most relaxed account, there are countless touches of imagination, not least from the very distinctive tenor, Julius Patzak, and the ever-responsive Clifford Curzon taking the upper piano part. Limited but clear sound.

(i–ii) Liebeslieder Waltzes, Op. 52 (2 performances); (iii) Waltzes, Op. 39; Waltzes for Piano Duet, Op. 39, (iv) Nos. 2, 6 & 15; (v) Nos. 1, 2, 5, 6, 10, 14 & 15.

(M) (***) EMI mono CDH5 66425-2. (i) Seefried, Höngen, Meyer-Welfing, Hotter; (i, iv) Wührer; Von Nordberg; (ii) De Polignac, Kedroff, Cuénod, Conrad; (ii, v) Lipatti, Boulanger; (iii) Backhaus.

This historic tribute to Brahms in waltz-time makes a fascinating study, with two early recordings of the first *Liebeslieder Waltzes* – one very Viennese, one very French – set in contrast and the Opus 39 *Waltzes* offered in a variety of performances, with the popular *Waltz in A flat*, as well as two others, appearing in no fewer than three versions each, from Backhaus solo, from Wührer and Von Nordberg in Vienna and from Lipatti and Boulanger in Paris, all very different and equally winning. The vocal teams in the *Liebeslieder Waltzes* are strikingly different too, with the Viennese much slower and more inclined to linger, with voices beautifully blended, where the Parisian performances are brisk and incisive, with voices (not least Hugues Cuénod's high tenor) clearly separated, despite the limited mono recording of 1937. Good, smooth transfers.

Motets

Sacred motets: *Ach, arme Welt, du trügest mich, Op. 110; Es ist das Heil uns kommen her, Op. 29; O Heiland reiss die Himmel auf, Op. 74.*

**(*) Paraclete Press GDCG 107. Dei Cantores, Patterson – MENDELSSOHN: *Motets.* **(*)

Brahms's *Es ist das Heil* owes a debt to Bach in its four-part chorale followed by a five-part fugue, where the part-writing could be more sharply delineated. But the other two works have a simple eloquence which is well caught by these persuasively committed performances, beautifully recorded.

Ave Maria, Op. 12; 3 Fest- und Gedenksprüche, Op. 109; Geistliches Lied, Op. 30; 2 Motets, Op. 29; 2 Motets, Op. 74; 3 Motets, Op. 110; Psalm 13, Op. 27.

(BB) *** Naxos 8.553877. St Bride's Ch., R. Jones; Morley (organ).

Throughout his composing career, from his Hamburg days onwards, Brahms was devoted to writing choral music, both religious and secular, superbly crafted. In their first recording, Robert Jones and the choir of St Bride's, Fleet Street, give fresh, clear performances. They are beautifully scaled to give the illusion of church performance, helped by warm, atmospheric recording.

3 Fest- und Gedenksprüche, Op. 109; Marienlieder, Op. 22; 2 Motets, Op. 29; 2 Motets, Op. 74; 3 Motets, Op. 110.

*** Chan. 9671. Danish Nat. R. Ch., Parkman.

The programme from the Danish Radio Choir is made especially attractive by the inclusion of the seven *Marien-lieder*, which include some of Brahms's simplest and most beautiful lyrical inspirations. They are gloriously sung by this justly famous Danish choir, who are on splendid form throughout the disc and are beautifully recorded.

3 Fest- und Gedenksprüche, Op. 109; Missa canonica, Op. posth.; 2 Motets, Op. 29; 2 Motets, Op. 74; 3 Motets, Op. 110.

*** HM HMC 901951. Berlin RIAS Chamber Ch., Creed.

This collection of Brahms's *a cappella* choral music includes the rare fragments (*Sanctus, Benedictus* and *Agnus Dei*, all set in German, from the *Missa canonica*. There is a distinctive advantage in having German-born singers in this repertoire, and the performances by the RIAS Chamber Choir directed by Marcus Creed could hardly be more eloquent, especially the four beautiful *Festal & Commemorative Sentences*, Op. 109. The recording is first class.

(i) *Rinaldo, Op. 50; Begräbnisgesang, Op. 13; Gesang der Parzen, Op. 89;* (ii) Arr. of Schubert *Ellens Gesang II.*

(N) *** EMI CDC5 56983-2. Ernst-Senff Ch., Berlin, Dresden PO & Ch., Michel Plasson; (i) Davislim; (ii) Gens.

Rinaldo is a rarity these days: this newcomer from Dresden with the Ernst Senff Choir of Berlin and the Dresden Chorus and Philharmonic under Michel Plasson is the first for almost 20 years. Its opening pays homage to Beethoven and the writing for voices is masterly – hardly surprising since Brahms spent much time conducting choirs. Indeed the piece began life as an entry for a male-chorus competition, and as Malcolm Macdonald writes in his authoritative study *Master Musicians* it is both absorbing and deeply felt. The *Gesang der Parzen (Song of the Fates)* has a classical power and dignity that come over well in this fine recording. Steve Davislim rises heroically to the demands of the solo tenor role and sings with great intelligence. Highly recommended.

Die schöne Magelone (song-cycle).

**(*) Orfeo C490 981B. Fischer-Dieskau, S. Richter.

Dietrich Fischer-Dieskau has done more than any other singer to bring this once-neglected song-cycle back into the repertory, a love-story from the age of chivalry. This Orfeo version offers a live Salzburg Festival recording, made in July 1970, and though audience noises occasionally intrude,

the thrust and impulse of the reading are irresistible. As a bonus come his three encores of other Brahms songs. No texts are given or even translations of titles.

(i) *Vier ernste Gesänge, Op. 121; An die Nachtigall;* (ii) *Dein blaues Auge;* (i) *Erinnerung;* (ii) *Der Gang zum Liebchen; Geheimnis;* (i) *Die Mainacht;* (ii) *Meine Liebe ist grün; O kühler Wald;* (i) *O wüsst' ich doch den Weg zurück;* (ii) *Ruhe, Süssliebchen;* (i) *Sonntag; Ständchen; Vergebliches Ständchen; Verrat; Von ewige Liebe;* (ii) *Vor dem Fenster; Ein Wanderer; Wiegenlied; Wie Melodien zieht es mir; Wir wandelten.*

(M) (***) EMI mono CDH5 66426-2. Kipnis, with (i) Moore; (ii) Wolff.

The performances here are a revelation, with Kipnis using his firm, dark bass with its very Russian timbre to bring out word-meaning and dramatic point with an intensity rarely matched. So the *Four Serious Songs* are both incisively powerful and movingly poetic, with legato perfectly controlled, as it is in such a taxing song as *Von ewige Liebe*. It is fascinating to find Kipnis, very much a virile singer, tackling songs normally sung by women, such as *Vergebliches Ständchen, Wiegenlied* or *Sonntag*, with a point and charm rarely matched, so that at times with his head voice he sounds like a bass version of Richard Tauber. The transfers, focusing on the voice, retain some surface noise but not enough to be intrusive.

Vier ernste Gesänge, Op. 121; Lieder: Auf dem Kirchhofe; Botschaft; Feldeinsamkeit; Im Waldeseinsamkeit; Minnelied III; Mondenschein; O wüsst' ich doch den Weg zurück; Sapphische Ode; Sommerabend; Ständchen.

❀ (M) (***) EMI (SIS) CDH7 63198-2. Hotter, Moore – BACH: *Cantata No. 82: Ich habe genug.* (***) ❀

Glorious singing from Hans Hotter, wonderfully accompanied by Gerald Moore. An excellent transfer.

BRAUNFELS, Walter (1882–1954)

Die Vögel (complete).

*** Decca 448 679-2 (2). Kwon, Wottrich, Kraus, Holzmair, Görne, Berlin R. Ch., German SO, Berlin, Zagrosek.

This charming opera, based on Aristophanes' *The Birds*, brings warm, uncomplicated music, yet the innocence of the writing and the clarity of the composer's own libretto avoid any feeling of sentimentality. The very opening magically introduces the Nightingale, a coloratura role sung at the first performance by Maria Ivogun. Another ravishing sequence is the long duet which opens Act II, between the Nightingale and Good Hope, a tenor role beautifully sung by Endrik Wottrich. Helen Kwon as the Nightingale sings not just brilliantly but with sensuous beauty and a formidable range of tone. The rest of the cast could hardly be bettered, with such outstanding singers as Wolfgang Holzmair and Matthias Görne in smaller roles. Zagrosek conducts a glowing performance, superbly played and recorded.

BRETÓN, Tomàs (1850–1923)

La Dolores (complete).

*** Decca 466 060-2 (2). Matos, Domingo, Lanza, Beltrán, Pierotti, Liceu Grand Theatre Ch., Badalona Conservatoire Children's Ch., Barcelona SO, Ros Marbà.

Bretón may not be the most original of composers, a contemporary of Puccini who writes fluently in an undemandingly melodic style, but *La Dolores* still makes enjoyable listening. With the melodramatic story confidently handled – including crowd choruses, such colourful genre pieces as a lively *Jota*, and echoes of popular repertory operas such as an offstage bullfight at the end of Act II – the result is rather like Mascagni in a plainer idiom. Ros Marbà conducts a lively performance, with Domingo in splendid voice. As the heroine of the title, Elisabete Matos is on the shrill side but sings warmly and idiomatically, and Tito Beltrán is an impressive second tenor. Full-blooded sound to match.

BRIAN, Havergal (1876–1972)

Symphony No. 1 (Gothic).

*** Marco Polo 8.223280/1. Jenisová, Pecková, Dolezal, Mikulás, Slovak Philharmonic Ch., Slovak Nat. Theatre Op. Ch., Slovak Folk Ens. Ch., Lucnica Ch., Bratislava Chamber Ch. & Children's Ch., Youth Echo Ch., Czech RSO (Bratislava), Slovak PO, Lenárd.

The first of the symphonies here receives a passionately committed performance from Slovak forces. Despite a few incidental flaws, it conveys surging excitement from first to last, helped by a rich recording which gives a thrilling impression of massed forces. The final *Te Deum*, alone lasting 72 minutes, brings fervent choral writing of formidable complexity, with the challenge taken up superbly by the Czech musicians.

Symphony No. 3 in C sharp min.

(B) **(*) Hyp. Helios CDH 55029. Ball, Jacobson, BBC SO, Friend.

The *Third Symphony* began life as a concerto for piano; this perhaps explains the prominent role given to two pianos in the score. The work is full of extraordinarily imaginative and original touches, but the overall lack of rhythmic variety is a handicap. The playing of the BBC Symphony Orchestra under Lionel Friend is well prepared and dedicated, but the recording does not open out sufficiently in climaxes. Even so, this is well worth considering at Helios price.

BRICCIALDI, Giulio (1818–81)

Wind Quintet in D, Op. 124.

(BB) *** Naxos 8.553410. Avalon Wind Quintet – CAMBINI: *Wind Quintets Nos. 1–3.* ***

Giulio Briccialdi was an Italian flautist of considerable fame during his lifetime. His *Wind Quintet in D major* is carefree, empty, lightweight – and utterly charming. It is played

expertly by these young German musicians, and the recording is as delightfully natural as the playing. Well worth its three stars.

BRIDGE, Frank (1879–1941)

Berceuse; Canzonetta; Suite for Strings; There is a willow grows aslant a brook; Serenade; The Two Hunchbacks; Threads.

*** Conifer 75605 51327-2. Britten Sinfonia, Cleobury.

This delightful collection has much in common with similar compilations of the lighter miniatures of Elgar. The beautiful *Suite for Strings* and the inspired, Butterworth-like *There is a willow grows aslant a brook* are masterpieces, but the vignettes are charming, notably the *Intermezzi* from incidental music for a children's play, *The Two Hunchbacks* and the gentle *Andante* and winning little *Waltz* from another play called *Threads*. The playing is warmly sympathetic and polished, and beautifully recorded.

Cherry ripe; Enter Spring (rhapsody); *Lament; The Sea* (suite); *Summer* (tone-poem).

(M) *** EMI (ADD) CDM5 66855-2. RLPO, Groves.

Writing in the early years of the last century, the composer confidently produced a magnificent seascape in the wake of Debussy, *The Sea*, but *Summer* was free of conventional pastoral moods, while in the last and greatest of Bridge's tone-poems, *Enter Spring*, he was responding to still wider musical horizons. Groves's warm advocacy adds to the impressiveness. First-rate recording, most successfully remastered.

Cherry ripe; Sir Roger de Coverley; Suite for Strings; There is a willow grows aslant a brook.

**(*) Koch 3-7139-2. New Zealand CO, Braithwaite – DELIUS: *Sonata for Strings.* **(*)

A nicely played, pastel-shaded performance of Bridge's *Suite for String Orchestra*, with the delicacy of feeling in the lovely, ethereal *Nocturne* making amends for any lack of robustness elsewhere. The folksong arrangements are also attractively done and, if Britten's old ECO recording of *Sir Roger de Coverley* was even wittier, the poignant 'impression' (the composer's own term), *There is a willow grows aslant a brook*, is beautifully played. The modern, digital recording is both fresh and transparent.

(i) *Enter Spring;* (ii) *The Sea.*

(N) (M) *** BBC mono/stereo BBCB 8007-2. (i) New Phil. O; (ii) ECO, Britten – HOLST: *Fugal Concerto, etc.*; BRITTEN: *The Building of the House Overture.* ***

Benjamin Britten as Frank Bridge's devoted pupil conveys a warmth and depth of understanding which transforms two of Bridge's finest, most ambitious orchestral works, both evocative and intensely imaginative, giving them a focus that other interpreters do not always find. The radio recordings have been very well transferred.

The Sea (suite).

*** Chan. 8473. Ulster O, Handley – BAX: *On the Sea-Shore*; BRITTEN: *Sea Interludes*. ***

The Sea receives a brilliant and deeply sympathetic performance from Handley and the Ulster Orchestra, recorded with a fullness and vividness to make this a demonstration disc.

Suite for Strings.

*** Chan. 8390. ECO, Garforth – IRELAND: *Downland Suite*, etc. ***

*** Nim. NI 5068. E. String O, Boughton – BUTTERWORTH: *Banks of Green Willow*, etc.; PARRY: *Lady Radnor's Suite*. ***

Suite for String Orchestra; Summer; There is a willow grows aslant a brook.

(M) *** Chan. 6566. Bournemouth Sinf., Del Mar – BANTOCK: *Pierrot of the Minute*; BUTTERWORTH: *Banks of Green Willow*. ***

Summer is beautifully played by the Bournemouth Sinfonietta under Norman Del Mar. The same images of nature permeate the miniature tone-poem, *There is a willow grows aslant a brook*, an inspired piece, very sensitively managed. The *Suite for Strings* is equally individual. Its third movement, a *Nocturne*, is lovely. The CD transfer is excellent and one can relish its fine definition and presence.

The ECO also play well for David Garforth in the *Suite for Strings*. This performance is extremely committed; it is certainly recorded excellently, with great clarity and presence.

The Nimbus collection is more generous and is certainly well chosen. Here Bridge's *Suite* again receives a lively and responsive performance, from William Boughton and his excellent Birmingham-based orchestra, treated to ample, sumptuously atmospheric recording, more resonant than its competitors.

CHAMBER MUSIC

Cello Sonata.

(M) *** Decca (ADD) 443 575-2. Rostropovich, Britten – SCHUBERT: *Arpeggione Sonata*. **(*)

*** Chan. 8499. Raphael & Peter Wallfisch – BAX: *Rhapsodic Ballad*; DELIUS: *Sonata*; WALTON: *Passacaglia*. ***

Cello Sonata; 2 Pieces: Meditation; Spring Song.

**(*) ASV CDDCA 796. Gregor-Smith, Wrigley – DEBUSSY; DOHNANYI: *Sonatas*. **(*)

Bridge wrote his *Cello Sonata* during the First World War. The playing on Decca is of an altogether rare order, even by the exalted standards of Rostropovich and Britten, and the recording, made at The Maltings in 1968, has immediacy, warmth and great response.

It is a distinctive world that Bridge evokes in the *Cello Sonata* and one to which Raphael Wallfisch and his father, Peter, are completely attuned, and they are beautifully recorded.

The ASV account by Bernard Gregor-Smith and Yolande Wrigley is also played with intensity and sensitivity. The recording is a bit close, but those wanting the coupling (and the Dohnányi is an excellent piece) need not hesitate.

3 Idylls for String Quartet.

*** Hyp. CDA 66718. Coull Qt – ELGAR: *Quartet* **(*); WALTON: *Quartet*. ***

As this superb, purposeful performance by the Coull Quartet shows, the *Three Idylls*, each marked by sharp changes of mood as a phantasie-form, make up a satisfying whole, a quartet in all but name. They provide a superb bonus to a fine performance of the Elgar and an outstanding performance of the Walton *Quartet*. Excellent sound.

Phantasie Quartet.

(N) (M) *** Decca [ADD] 466 823-2. Brainin, Schidlof, Lovett, Britten – JANACEK: *Poháðka*; SHOSTAKOVICH: *7 Blok Romances; Cello Sonata*. ***

With Britten joined by members of the Amadeus Quartet, the BBC recording of the *Phantasie Quartet* receives a performance of high contrasts, a perfect example of the way Britten's example inspired those around him in performances at the Aldeburgh Festival. So far from seeming wayward, the distinctive layout prescribed for the Cobbett Prize seems tautly logical.

(i) *Phantasie Quartet in F sharp min. Phantasie Trio in C min.; Piano Trio No. 2.*

(N) (B) *** Hyp. Helios CDH 55063. Dartington Trio, (i) with Patrick Ireland.

The playing of the *Phantasie Trio* by the Dartington Trio is of exceptional eloquence and sensitivity. They are no less persuasive in the *Phantasie Quartet*. Their account of the visionary post-war *Piano Trio No. 2* of 1929 is completely inside this score. The Hyperion recording is altogether superb, in the demonstration bracket, perfectly natural and beautifully proportioned, and this is even more attractive on the bargain Helios label.

String Quartets Nos. 1 in E min.; 4 (1937).

** Mer. CDE 84369. Bridge Qt.

The eponymous Bridge Quartet give committed and dedicated accounts of the *First Quartet* of 1906 and the much darker, searching *Quartet* Bridge completed four years before his death. The overall sound is lustreless and uninviting, and to be frank the playing could have a little more finish. However, we are not spoilt for choice in this interesting repertoire.

String Quartets Nos. 2 in G min.; 3.

*** Mer. CDE 843111. Bridge Qt.

Bridge's *Second Quartet*, written in 1915, immediately captures the listener's attention and brings together a sequence of movements thematically linked, each of which has a wide range of moods and tempi, phantasy-style. The *Third Quartet*, written a decade later, shows affinities with the Second Viennese School, yet, after the intensity of the argument and a haunting central *Andante*, the work has a valedictory close. The two quartets are superbly played by this eponymous group, who are right inside the music. The recording is first class.

String Sextet.

*** Chan. 9472. ASMF Chamber Ens. – GOOSENS: *Concertino*, etc. ***

Frank Bridge's *Sextet* is a substantial piece that fills in the picture of the development of the composer before the First World War. The Academy of St Martin-in-the-Fields Chamber Ensemble plays with great eloquence.

PIANO MUSIC

Arabesque; Capriccios Nos. 1–2; Dedication; Fairy Tale Suite; Gargoyle; Hidden Fires; In Autumn; 3 Miniatures; Pastorals, Sets 1–2; Sea Idyll; 3 Improvisations for the Left Hand; Winter Pastoral.

*** Continuum CCD 1016. Jacobs.

Berceuse; Canzonetta; 4 Characteristic Pieces; Dramatic Fantasia; Etude Rhapsodic; Lament; Pensées fugitives; 3 Pieces; 4 Pieces; 3 Poems; Scherzettino.

*** Continuum CCD 1018. Jacobs.

Piano Sonata; Graziella; The Hour-glass; 3 Lyrics; Miniature Pastorals, Set 3; Miniature Suite (ed. Hindmarsh); *3 Sketches.* arr. of BACH: *Chorale: Komm, süsser Tod, BWV 478.*

*** Continuum CCD 1019. Jacobs.

Peter Jacobs provides a complete survey of the piano music of Frank Bridge, and it proves an invaluable enterprise. The recorded sound is very good indeed: clean, well defined and present, and the acoustic lively. Calum MacDonald's excellent notes tracking Bridge's development over these years are worth a mention too.

VOCAL MUSIC

Songs: Disc 1: *Adoration; Blow, blow, thou winter wind; Come to me in my dreams; Cradle Song; Dawn and evening; A dead violet; The Devon maid; A dirge; E'en as a lovely flower; Fair daffodils; Far, far from each other; Go not, happy day; If I could choose; Lean close thy cheek; Music, when soft voices die; My pent-up tears oppress my brain; Night lies on the silent highways; The primrose; So perverse; Tears, idle tears; The violets blue; When most I wink; Where'er my bitter tear drops fall; Where is it that our soul doth go?.*

Disc 2: *All things that we clasp; Day after day; Dear, when I look into thine eyes; Dweller in my deathless dreams; Goldenhair; Into her keeping; Isobel; Journey's end; The last invocation; Love is a rose; Love went a-riding; Mantle of the blue; O that it were so!; Speak to me my love; So early in the morning, O; Strew no more red roses; Thy hand in mine; 'Tis but a week; What shall I your true love tell?; When you are old and gray; Where she lies asleep.*

*** Hyp. CDA 67181/2(2). Watson, Winter, MacDougall, Finley, Chase; Vignoles.

Bridge's song output was extensive and of quality. The first disc covers the songs from 1901 through to 1908, ending with the *Three Songs with Viola* with Louise Winter and Roger Chase; and the second carries them through to the Tagore settings and Humbert Wolfe *Journey's End* of 1925. By this time Bridge's musical language had undergone a complete change. Not that the early songs are ever mere Edwardian ballads, but one would be hard put to guess that they were by the same composer as *Dweller in my deathless dreams*. All four singers give thoroughly committed performances, and it would be invidious to single any one of them out for special praise. Roger Vignoles is superb throughout and Hyperion's recording is expertly balanced. Special mention, too, for the informative and judicious presentation.

BRITTEN, Benjamin (1913–76)

An American Overture; Ballad of Heroes; The Building of the House; Canadian Carnival; (i) Diversions for Piano (left-hand) & Orchestra; Occasional Overture; Praise we great men; Scottish Ballad; Sinfonia da Requiem; Suite on English Folk Tunes: A time there was . . .; Young Apollo; (ii) 4 Chansons françaises.

(B) *** EMI CZS5 73983-2 (2). (i) Donohoe; (ii) Gomez; CBSO Ch., CBSO, Rattle.

A valuable compilation from the various recordings of Britten's music, most of it rare, which Rattle has made over the years. It is good to have the *Diversions for Piano (left-hand) & Orchestra*, with Peter Donohoe as soloist – amazingly this was the first version in stereo – and the most cherishable item of all is the radiant performance given by Jill Gomez of the four *Chansons françaises*, the remarkable and tenderly affecting settings of Hugo and Verlaine composed by the 15-year-old Britten. This fine collection is now all the more desirable at its new bargain price.

An American Overture; (i) King Arthur Suite (arr. Hindmarsh); (i–ii) *The World of the Spirit* (cantata).

*** Chan. 9487. BBC PO, Hickox, with (i) Britten Singers; (ii) Gordon, Rigby, Mitchell, Reed.

The two main works here both derive from music written for radio productions, an epic dramatization of the *King Arthur* story by D. G. Bridson in 1937 and the religious cantata, *The World of the Spirit*, in 1938, using a sequence of texts prepared by R. Ellis Roberts. Though the mature Britten style is identifiable only occasionally, the invention and imagination are characteristic from first to last. The fanfares which open the *King Arthur* music have the flavour of the film music of the period, but with a clear, Britten-like slant. The religious cantata, *The World of the Spirit*, follows the pattern of *The Company of Heaven* of the previous year, but the wide range of texts prompts Britten to use an astonishing range of techniques. The result is a fascinating mosaic of contrasting elements, culminating at the end of the second of the three parts in an open imitation of Walton's *Belshazzar's Feast*. Full texts are given. *An American Overture* makes a good companion-piece to the radio-inspired works. First-rate singing from soloists and choir alike in the cantata, helped by full and rich recording.

An American Overture; Sinfonia da Requiem, Op. 20; Peter Grimes: 4 Sea Interludes & Passacaglia, Op. 33.

(BB) **(*) Naxos 8.553107. New Zealand SO, Fredman.

Myer Fredman conducts warm and purposeful performances of this group of orchestral works from early in Britten's career. Dramatic and atmospheric points are well made with the help of a warm hall acoustic and full-ranging recording. Recommendable at super-budget price.

A Time There Was (suite on English folk tunes), Op. 90; Johnson over Jordan (suite, arr. P. Hindmarsh); Young Person's Guide to the Orchestra, Op. 34; Peter Grimes: 4 Sea Interludes.

*** Chan. 9221. Bournemouth SO, Hickox.

A time there was is the suite which Britten wrote at the very end of his life, characteristically original and with a new, elusive vein. The Johnson over Jordan Suite is drawn from the incidental music which Britten wrote in 1939 for an experimental play of J. B. Priestley, in which music and mime played an integral part. If the style is uncharacteristic of the later Britten, the colour and vitality are most winning, played here with verve.

A Time There Was . . . (suite on English folk tunes), Op. 90; Lachrymae: Reflections on a Song of Dowland (arr. for orchestra); Prelude & Fugue for 18-part String Orchestra, Op. 29; Simple Symphony, Op. 4; Variations on a Theme of Frank Bridge; Young Person's Guide to the Orchestra, Op. 34. (i) Song-cycles: Les Illuminations, Op. 18; Nocturne, Op. 60; (i; ii) Serenade for Tenor, Horn & Strings, Op. 31. Gloriana: Courtly Dances. Peter Grimes: 4 Sea Interludes.

(B) **(*) Nim. NI 1751 (3). E. String O or ESO, Boughton; with (i) Hadley; (ii) Halstead.

This inexpensive bargain box will seem to many collectors an admirable way of collecting Britten's key orchestral works plus the three major song-cycles. In the latter, Jerry Hadley is a dramatic and involving soloist; his is not far short of an operatic approach, with the crystal-clear projection of words and histrionic power of his singing compensating for some lack of subtlety in word-colouring. Les Illuminations (in easily colloquial French) is strikingly fresh and spontaneous, and in the Nocturne, which opens magnetically and evocatively, the orchestral playing is full of tension. Anthony Halstead's horn contribution in the Serenade is hardly less impressive. William Boughton shows himself a fine Britten advocate throughout, and the works both for strings and for full orchestra are most sympathetically played and certainly do not lack vitality. The recording (for the most part made in the Great Hall of Birmingham University) is outstandingly rich and resonant in a characteristic Nimbus way, while the powerful evocation of the Peter Grimes Sea Interludes is enhanced by the acoustic of Birmingham's Symphony Hall – one of the first recordings to be made there. Excellent value.

The Building of the House: Overture, Op. 79.

(N) (M) *** BBC mono/stereo BBCB 8007-2. ECO, Composer – BRIDGE: The Sea, etc.; HOLST: Fugal Concerto, etc. ***

Written for the opening of the Maltings Concert Hall in June 1967, The Building of the House Overture comes in a performance Britten conducted only two days after the premiere. The excitement of the occasion is carried over, even though the choral entry is initially off-pitch. A historic supplement to Britten's revealing interpretations of Bridge and Holst, well transferred from a radio recording.

Piano Concerto in D, Op. 13.

*** EMI CDC5 56760-2. Andsnes, CBSO, Järvi – ENESCU: Legend for Trumpet & Piano; SHOSTAKOVICH: Piano Concerto No. 1. ***

(M) **(*) Chan. (ADD) 6580. Lin, Melbourne SO, Hopkins – COPLAND: Concerto. **(*)

(M) **(*) Hyp. CDA 66293. Servadei, LPO, Giunta – KHACHATURIAN: Piano Concerto. **(*)

(i) Piano Concerto, Op. 13; (ii) Violin Concerto, Op. 15.

(M) *** Decca (ADD) 417 308-2. (i) Richter; (ii) Lubotsky; ECO, composer.

Leif Ove Andsnes and Järvi fils were recorded at a live concert in Symphony Hall. Their account of this rewarding and brilliant concerto ranks along with the very best in the catalogue. Andsnes has all the virtuosity the score calls for, plus the thoughtfulness and inner feeling required in the slow movement. First-rate sound.

Richter is almost incomparable in interpreting the Piano Concerto, not only the thoughtful, introspective moments but also the Liszt-like bravura passages. With its highly original sonorities the Violin Concerto makes a splendid vehicle for another Soviet artist of the time, Mark Lubotsky. Recorded in The Maltings, the playing of the ECO under the composer's direction matches the inspiration of the soloists.

Gillian Lin cannot match Richter in detailed imagination but, from her sharp attack on the opening motif onwards, she gives a strong and satisfying reading, well accompanied by Hopkins and the Melbourne orchestra.

With good, well-balanced, digital recording, Annette Servadei gives a strong, dedicated, muscular performance. She is particularly impressive in the hushed and sustained passacaglia, entitled Impromptu, which provided Walton with the theme of his Variations on an Impromptu of Britten.

Violin Concerto in D min., Op. 15.

(N) *** Chan. 9910. Mordkovitch, BBCSO, Hickox – VEALE: Violin Concerto. ***

(M) *** EMI (ADD) CDM7 64202-2. Haendel, Bournemouth SO, Berglund – WALTON: Violin Concerto. ***

*** Classico CLASSCD 233. Azizjan, Copenhagen PO, Vänskä – WALTON: Violin Concerto. **(*)

(i) Violin Concerto, Op. 15; (ii) Serenade for Tenor, Horn & Strings, Op. 31.

(BB) *** CfP Double CDCFPSD 4754 (2). (i) Friend; (ii) Partridge, Busch; LPO, Pritchard – TIPPETT: Concerto for Double String Orchestra ***; VAUGHAN WILLIAMS:

Tallis Fantasia, etc. ***; WALTON: *Belshazzar's Feast*. **(*)

(i) *Violin Concerto, Op. 15;* (ii) *Symphony for Cello & Orchestra, Op. 68.*

(N) (BB) *** Naxos 8.553882. (i) Hirsch; (ii) Hugh; BBC Scottish SO, Yuasa.

Lydia Mordkovitch follows up her distinguished series of recordings of British violin concertos with an outstandingly thoughtful and intense reading of the Britten, fascinatingly coupled with an unjustly neglected work by John Veale. The hushed opening, which can seem just sweet and easy, here conveys mystery and expectation thanks to Mordkovitch, and the tautness and purposefulness of her bravura playing then keeps the wayward structure together, helped by warmly responsive playing from the BBC Symphony under Hickox. The central *Scherzo* is full of flair with Mordkovitch finding a Russian echo in the lyrical episode, while the big test of the *Passacaglia* finale finds both soloist and orchestra at their most concentrated, leading a touchingly poignant account of the coda. The opulent Chandos recording, finely detailed, bringing out the richness of Mordkovitch's tone and the high dramatic contrasts of the orchestra, adds greatly to the impact.

Like the Naxos coupling of Walton's *Violin* and *Cello Concertos*, this Britten pairing is an outstanding disc in every way, not just a fine bargain. As in the Walton, Tim Hugh gives a superb reading of Britten's *Cello Symphony*, strong and purposeful, making light of the formidable technical demands, and the gritty double-stopping, with lyrical moments standing out. Rebecca Hirsch gives a spacious reading of the *Violin Concerto*, her tone clear and fresh rather than warmly romantic. The scherzando writing of the middle movement is full of fun, and the elegiac close of the finale is made poignant by understatement. Full, clear recording, with timpani specially vivid.

Rodney Friend proves a masterful soloist, magnificently incisive and expansive. As for Ian Partridge – one of the most consistently stylish of recording tenors – he gives a reading often strikingly new in its illumination, more tenderly beautiful and purer than Peter Pears's classic reading, culminating in a heavenly performance of the final Keats sonnet setting. With vivid recording, this is part of a highly desirable Silver Double aptly entitled 'The Best of England', with only James Loughran's account of Walton's *Belshazzar's Feast* below the high standard of the rest.

Ida Haendel's ravishing playing places the work firmly in the European tradition. She brings panache and brilliance to the music, as well as great expressive warmth. This is a reading very much in the grand manner, and it finds Paavo Berglund in excellent form. The recording is full and realistic.

Sergej Azizjan in the Britten adopts a manner at once lighter in the quicksilver bravura passages and more intimate and poetic in lyrical writing, ending with a deeply felt account of the closing pages, one of Britten's deepest inspirations up to that time. Though some will still prefer the bigger-boned approach of Ida Haendel, such a fine and illuminating performance as Azizjan's is equally welcome, as is the coupling.

Violin Concerto, Op. 15 (original version).

(M) **(*) EMI mono CDM5 66053-2. Olof, Hallé O, Barbirolli – HEMING: *Threnody*; RUBBRA: *Symphony No. 5*, etc. (***)

Allowances have to be made for the quality of this première recording, made by Theo Olof and the Hallé Orchestra under Barbirolli in 1948. At work on a revised version of the score, Britten never sanctioned its release, though he can hardly have entertained any doubts as to the virtuosity and dedication of the soloist or of Sir John, who had championed the piece in his New York days. Well worth hearing. The limited sound is a handicap.

(i) *Double Concerto in B min. for Violin, Viola & Orchestra. 2 Portraits for Strings; Sinfonietta* (version for small orchestra); (ii) *Young Apollo* (for piano, string quartet and strings), *Op. 16.*

*** Erato 3984 25502-2. (i) Kremer, Bashmet; (ii) Lugansky; Hallé O, Nagano.

Of the many works which Britten left in his bottom drawer to be discovered only after his death, none is more rewarding than this striking three-movement *Double Concerto for Violin and Viola*. What he left was the short score with indications of orchestration, which Colin Matthews had little difficulty in completing. Though the chromatic writing in the *Double Concerto* betrays something of the same influence, it is stylistically less radical than the *Sinfonietta*, warmer and more recognizably the work of Britten, with its distinctive melodies and orchestration both spare and striking. It receives a magnetic reading here from the two high-powered Russian soloists, with Kent Nagano and the Hallé Orchestra. The *Sinfonietta* comes in a version that Britten made in America, for small orchestra rather than solo instruments, and the *Two Portraits*, written when Britten was 16, a vigorous, purposeful picture of a friend, and a reflective, melancholy one of himself, with the viola solo beautifully played by Bashmet. A revelatory disc.

(i) *Diversions for Piano (left hand) & Orchestra, Op. 21;* (ii) *Sinfonia da Requiem, Op. 20;* (iii) *Young Person's Guide to the Orchestra, Op. 34.*

(M) **(*) Sony Dig./ADD SBK 62746. (i) Fleisher, Boston SO, Ozawa; (ii) St Louis SO, Previn; (iii) LSO, A. Davis.

The *Diversions* is a wartime work, highly inventive and resourceful, whose neglect over the years is puzzling. Fleisher gives a sensitive and intelligent account with great sympathy and skill. His playing has strong character and he receives fine support from Ozawa and the Boston orchestra, and fine recording. The St Louis orchestra plays with great spirit in the *Sinfonia da Requiem* and Previn's performance is deeply felt, if not quite a match for the composer's own. The 1963 recording is well detailed. Andrew Davis also directs an account of the *Young Person's Guide* that is bright and workmanlike, enjoyable enough, and the (1975) Abbey Road recording sounds well on CD.

(i) *Lachrymae, Op. 48a. Movement for Wind Sextet;* (ii) *Night Mail* (end sequence). *Sinfonietta; The Sword in*

the Stone (concert suite for wind and percussion);
(iii) *Phaedra, Op. 93.*

*** Hyp. CDA 66845. (i) Chase; (ii) Hawthorne; (iii) Rigby;
Nash Ens, Friend.

Lachrymae, for viola with string accompaniment, is played
here with the beauty intensified, thanks to the firm, true
playing of Roger Chase. Both the *Sinfonietta* and the *Wind
Sextet* movement of 1930 are astonishingly accomplished for
a teenage composer, reflecting the mature Britten style only
occasionally. The concert suite for wind and percussion was
drawn from music for a radio production of T. H. White's
ironic Arthurian piece, *The Sword in the Stone*, and brings
some delightful Wagner parodies. It is also good to have
the final sequence from Britten's music for the GPO film
documentary, *Night Mail*, with Auden's rattling verse
spoken by Nigel Hawthorne. In the dramatic scena, *Phaedra*,
Jean Rigby sings beautifully but lacks the biting intensity of
Janet Baker. Excellent playing from the Nash Ensemble, and
first-rate recording.

(i; ii) *Lachrymae (Reflections on a Song by Dowland)
Op. 48a; (i) Prelude & Fugue, Op. 29; Simple Symphony,
Op. 4; Variations on a Theme of Frank Bridge, Op. 10;
(ii) Elegy for Solo Viola.*

⚫ *** Virgin VC5 45121-2. (i) Norwegian CO, Brown;
(ii) Tomter.

Iona Brown gives performances of the *Simple Symphony* and
the *Frank Bridge Variations* to match the composer's own.
The *Simple Symphony* fizzes with youthful energy, yet Brown
brings an unusually wide and expressive range to the poignant *Sentimental Sarabande*, which elevates Britten's writing
far beyond any suggestion of juvenilia. The *Frank Bridge
Variations* have never sounded more emotionally powerful
on record and in the *Lachrymae* Lars Anders Tomter is an
outstanding soloist, not least in the touching full presentation of Dowland's tune in the haunting coda. He follows
the *Lachrymae* with an ardent account of the solo *Elegy*. The
recording is of demonstration quality.

(i; ii) *Lachrymae, Op. 48a; (ii) Simple Symphony, Op. 4;
Variations on a Theme of Frank Bridge, Op. 10; Young
Apollo, Op. 16. (iii) Death in Venice: Suite (arr. Bedford);
(iv) Peter Grimes: 4 Sea Interludes & Passacaglia.*

(B) *** Chan. 2-for-1 241-2 (2). (i) Montreal I Musici, Turovsky;
(ii) Golani; (iii) ECO, Bedford; (iv) Ulster O, Handley.

Young Apollo is particularly successful here, with vivid
recording capturing the unusual textures with piano and
string quartet as well as strings. Rivka Golani is a resonant
soloist in *Lachrymae*, and the *Variations* and *Simple Symphony* have similar heft, helped by the rich, upfront
recording. Representing Britten's operas, Steuart Bedford's
Death in Venice Suite is well worth having, and Handley's
Peter Grimes excerpts are second only to Previn's splendid
EMI recording, helped by richly atmospheric digital sound
of demonstration quality. This is one of the most recommendable of Chandos's new two-for-one Doubles.

(i) *Matinées musicales; Soirées musicales; (ii; iv) Young
Person's Guide to the Orchestra; (iii; iv) Peter Grimes: 4
Sea Interludes & Passacaglia.*

(M) *** Decca (ADD) 425 659-2. (i) Nat. PO, Bonynge;
(ii) LSO; (iii) ROHCG O; (iv) composer.

Bonynge's sparkling versions of the *Matinées* and *Soirées
musicales* are here reissued, coupled with Britten's accounts
of the *Young Person's Guide to the Orchestra* and the *Sea
Interludes & Passacaglia.*

*Prelude & Fugue for 18-part String Orchestra, Op. 29;
Simple Symphony, Op. 4; Variations on a Theme of Frank
Bridge.*

(BB) *** ASV CDQS 6215. N. Sinfonia, Hickox.

This triptych of string works on ASV's super-bargain Quicksilva label is notable for an outstandingly fine account of the
Frank Bridge Variations which stands up well alongside not
only the composer's own version but also Karajan's superb
mono, Philharmonia account. Hickox's reading encompasses the widest range of emotion and style. The rich
string sonorities resonate powerfully in the glowing ambience of All Saints' Quayside Church, Newcastle, and in the
Simple Symphony the reverberation recalls Britten's own
famous account, made in The Maltings. Hickox's approach
is less light-hearted than Britten's, but it remains a very
compelling performance. The *Prelude and Fugue* is comparably eloquent, although here the playing is marginally less
assured. The recording is first class, with the bright upper
range well supported by the firm bass.

The Prince of the Pagodas (complete).

⚫ *** Virgin VCD7 59578-2 (2). L. Sinf., Knussen.

The multicoloured instrumentation – much influenced by
Britten's visit to Bali – is caught with glorious richness in
Oliver Knussen's really complete version. Most importantly,
he opens out more than 40 cuts, most of them small, which
Britten sanctioned to fit his own Decca recording on to four
LP sides. The performance is outstanding and so is the
sound.

Simple Symphony (for strings), Op. 4.

*** DG 423 624-2. Orpheus CO – BIZET: *Symphony;*
PROKOFIEV: *Symphony No. 1.* ***

(i) *Simple Symphony, Op. 4; (ii) The Young Person's Guide
to the Orchestra (Variations & Fugue on a Theme of
Purcell), Op. 34; Peter Grimes: 4 Sea Interludes.*

(B) *** [EMI Red Line CDR5 72564]. (i) ASMF; (ii) Minnesota
O; Marriner.

(i) *Simple Symphony, Op. 4; (ii; iii) Les Illuminations,
Op. 18; (ii; iv) Serenade for Tenor, Horn & Strings, Op. 31.*

(B) *** DG Dig./ADD 459 358-2. (i) Orpheus CO; (ii) Tear;
(iii) Philh. O; (iv) Clevenger, Cleveland O; Giulini.

(i) *Simple Symphony, Op. 4; (ii) Variations on a Theme of
Frank Bridge, Op. 10; (iii) Young Person's Guide to the
Orchestra. Peter Grimes: 4 Sea Interludes.*

(N) **(*) Australian Decca Eloquence mono/stereo 467 237-2.

(i) ECO, Composer; (ii) ASMF, Marriner; (iii) Concg. O, van Beinum.

Rarely have the *Four Sea Interludes* been recorded with such bite and dramatic flair as here under van Beinum. Though the *Young Person's Guide* has some wildness in the playing, the excitement of the performance makes it memorable, and the mono sound is basically full and warm. The stereo recordings are quite superb, with the composer's incomparable performance of the *Simple Symphony*, and Marriner's vivid account of the *Frank Bridge Variations*, both classic versions.

The engaging *Simple Symphony*, spick and span and sparkling in its Orpheus performance, also makes a stimulating introduction to an excellent bargain programme. In 1979 Robert Tear recorded the two favourite Britten cycles for DG with Giulini, who presents both cycles as full-scale orchestral works; though some detail may be lost, the strength of Britten's writing amply justifies it. Tear is at his finest in both cycles, more open than in his earlier recording of the *Serenade*. As we know from other records, Dale Clevenger is a superb horn-player, and it is good to have a fresh view in such music. Soloists are balanced rather close in an otherwise excellent, vivid recording.

The *Simple Symphony* goes well alongside the Bizet and Prokofiev works, especially when played as freshly and characterfully as here by the Orpheus group. Britten himself found more fun in the *Playful Pizzicato*, but the reading is all-of-a-piece and enjoyably spontaneous. Excellent, realistic sound.

Marriner's Minnesota accounts of the *Young Person's Guide* and the *Peter Grimes Interludes* are very well played and, if his direct approach is a little stiff, the digital sound is first rate, clean and clear, yet warmly atmospheric. The youthful *Simple Symphony* is delightfully spirited and fresh. This is available only in the USA.

Sinfonia da Requiem, Op. 20.

(M) *** EMI CDM7 64870-2. CBSO, Rattle – SHOSTAKOVICH: *Symphony No. 10.* **

Rattle's view of the *Sinfonia da Requiem* is unashamedly extrovert yet well detailed. The EMI recording is admirably vivid and clear, but the Shostakovich coupling is less convincing.

(i) Sinfonia da Requiem, Op. 20; (ii) Symphony for Cello & Orchestra, Op. 68; (iii) Cantata misericordium, Op. 69.

(M) *** Decca (ADD) 425 100-2. (i) New Philh. O; (ii) Rostropovich, ECO; (iii) Pears, Fischer-Dieskau, London Symphony Ch., LSO; composer.

All the performances on the Decca CD are definitive, and Rostropovich's account of the *Cello Symphony* in particular is commanding. The CD transfers are managed admirably.

Sinfonia da Requiem, Op. 20; The Young Person's Guide to the Orchestra, Op. 34; Peter Grimes: 4 Sea Interludes & Passacaglia, Op. 33.

(M) **(*) Virgin VM5 61835-2. RLPO, Pešek.

Though Libor Pešek fails to convey the full ominous weight of the first movement of the *Sinfonia da Requiem*, he then directs a dazzling account of the central *Dies Irae Scherzo*, taken breathtakingly fast, and finds an intense repose in the calm of the final *Requiem aeternam*. The *Sea Interludes* sound relatively unatmospheric, but the *Young Person's Guide* is very well detailed. The recording is comfortably reverberant.

Sinfonia da Requiem, Op. 20; Peter Grimes: 4 Sea Interludes & Passacaglia.

❂ (B) *** EMI double forte (ADD) CZS5 72658-2 (2). LSO, Previn – SHOSTAKOVICH: *Symphonies Nos. 4 & 5.* **(*)

Previn gives a passionately intense reading of the *Sinfonia da Requiem*, the most ambitious of Britten's early orchestral works, written after the death of his parents. It is warmer than the composer's own, less sharply incisive but presenting a valid alternative. So too in the *Four Sea Interludes*, with Previn springing the bouncing rhythms of the second interlude – the picture of *Sunday Morning in the Borough* – even more infectiously than the composer himself. These superb performances are presented in expansive 1970s recordings of demonstration quality. It is a pity that the Shostakovich coupling is only partly recommendable: the *Fourth Symphony* is very successful but the *Fifth* fails to take off. Nevertheless a good double forte.

Sinfonietta, Op. 1.

*** BIS CD 540. Tapiola Sinf., Vänskä – *Nocturne*, etc. ***

The *Sinfonietta* is busier in its textures than mature Britten; it is here presented with rare strength and warmth to make it totally convincing. It is very well recorded and comes with an attractive collection of vocal music.

Symphony for Cello & Orchestra, Op. 68.

*** Virgin/EMI VC5 45356-2. Truls Mørk, CBSO, Rattle – ELGAR: *Cello Concerto.* ***

*** Ph. 454 442-2. Lloyd Webber, ASMF, Marriner – WALTON: *Cello Concerto.* ***

(*) Russian Disc RDCD 11108. Rostropovich, Moscow PO, composer – SAUGUET: *Mélodie concertante.* *

(i) Symphony for Cello & Orchestra, Op. 68. Death in Venice: suite, Op. 88 (arr. Bedford).

*** Chan. 8363. (i) Wallfisch; ECO, Bedford.

This is the second recording Truls Mørk has made of the *Cello Symphony*. He is completely attuned to the Britten sensibility, playing with ardour and vision. Rattle gets a superb response from the Birmingham players and the sound is state-of-the-art, with particularly impressive depth and naturalness of perspective. The best account of the piece to have appeared for some years, and highly recommended.

Julian Lloyd Webber, too, in passionately committed readings brings out the power of each work and also the beauty, remarkably so in the grittily taxing Britten piece. Helped by sumptuous Philips sound, he and Sir Neville Marriner also demonstrate the extraordinary originality of Britten's scoring in a way beyond almost any rival, but they find an extra expressive warmth.

Sounding less improvisatory than Rostropovich, Wallfisch and Bedford are more purposeful, and the weight and range of the brilliant and full Chandos recording quality add to the impact, with Bedford's direction even more spacious than the composer's. Steuart Bedford's encapsulation of Britten's last opera into this rich and colourful suite makes a splendid coupling.

The special interest of the Russian Disc issue is that it includes a recording of the very first performance of the *Cello Symphony* on 12 March 1964, given by its dedicatee and 'onlie begetter', with Britten himself conducting. It is not as well recorded as the version Rostropovich and Britten made for Decca not long afterwards, but there is great intensity and concentration here.

Variations on a Theme of Frank Bridge, Op. 10.

⚫ (M) (***) EMI mono CDM5 66601-2. Philh. O, Karajan –
VAUGHAN WILLIAMS: *Tallis Fantasia* (***) ⚫;
STRAVINSKY: *Jeu de cartes.* (**)
*** MDG 321 0180-2. Polish CO, Maksymiuk – BARTOK:
Divertimento. ***

If all digital CDs of the 1990s sounded like this Karajan mono recording of the early 1950s, there would be no need for a *Penguin Guide*. The sound is astonishingly fresh and vivid, and the playing of the Philharmonia strings is of the highest distinction. They produce beautifully blended tone, rich and full-bodied, yet marvellously delicate at the *pianissimo* end of the dynamic spectrum. Karajan's reading is unaffected yet impassioned, electrifying in the *Funeral Music*. Alas, this splendid CD has been withdrawn just as we go to press.

Among recent accounts of Britten's youthful masterpiece, this Polish version under Jerzy Maksymiuk is among the best. Each variation is expertly shaped and well characterized, and the piece is held together very well by Maksymiuk. Rather short measure at 52 minutes, but nevertheless an issue of quality.

Variations on a Theme by Frank Bridge; Young Person's Guide to the Orchestra; Peter Grimes: 4 Sea Interludes & Passacaglia.

(N) (BB) *** Warner Apex 8573 89082-2. BBC SO, A. Davis.

In his admirable British music series for Teldec, Andrew Davis gives full weight as well as brilliance to these masterpieces from early in Britten's career, making a particularly attractive triptych. The *Frank Bridge Variations*, set here against the more popular Purcell set, gain particularly from large-scale treatment, with each variation strongly characterized. Excellent recording. This is one of the outstanding bargains among the Warner Classics super-bargain Apex series.

Young Person's Guide to the Orchestra (Variations & Fugue on a Theme of Purcell), Op. 34.

**(*) BBC (ADD) BBCL 4005-2. BBC SO, Stokowski –
BEETHOVEN: *Symphony No. 7* *(**); FALLA: *El amor brujo.* *** ⚫
(M) **(*) Virgin VM5 61782-2. RLPO, Pešek – PROKOFIEV:
Peter and the Wolf; SAINT-SAENS: *Carnival of the Animals.* ***

Stokowski's 1962 Prom performance with the BBC Sym-

phony Orchestra is quite spectacular. The whole occasion was highly charged and the quality of the orchestral response pretty breathtaking. Even if the opening is very relaxed, almost lethargic, this is a reading of outstanding personality and intensity, the sound very good for its age.

Libor Pešek and the Royal Liverpool Philharmonic Orchestra give a detailed and brilliantly played account of Britten's *Young Person's Guide to the Orchestra*. Tension is comparatively relaxed, but the closing fugue is lively and boldly etched.

Young Person's Guide to the Orchestra (with narration).

(BB) *** Naxos 8.554170. Everage, Melbourne SO, Lanchbery –
POULENC: *The Story of Babar* *** ⚫; PROKOFIEV: *Peter and the Wolf.* ***
(M) **(*) Decca Phase Four 444 104-2. Connery, RPO, Dorati
– PROKOFIEV: *Peter and the Wolf,* etc. **(*)

Using her own enthusiastically expanded version of the original commentary, Dame Edna Everage is sure to draw any young possum into the world of the orchestra. Her exuberance offsets any twee moments, and the Melbourne orchestra illustrate vivid instrumental descriptions with splendidly alive and colourful playing. The Naxos recording is excellent and, with its highly enjoyable couplings, this inexpensive triptych is warmly recommendable.

Sean Connery's voice is very familiar and his easy style is attractive. His narration should go down well with young people, even if some of the points are made heavily. The orchestral playing is first rate and the vivid, forwardly balanced recording – with a Decca Phase Four source – is effective enough. The performance has plenty of colour and vitality.

CHAMBER MUSIC

(i) *Cello Sonata in C, Op. 65;* (Unaccompanied) *Cello Suites Nos. 1, Op. 72; 2, Op. 80.*

(M) *** Decca (ADD) 421 859-2. Rostropovich; (i) with composer.

The *Cello Sonata* was written specially for Rostropovich. The idiom itself is unexpected, sometimes recalling Soviet models, as in the spiky *March*, perhaps out of tribute to the dedicatee. Although technically it demands fantastic feats from the cellist, it is hardly a display piece. It is an excellent work to wrestle with on a record, particularly when the performance is never likely to be outshone. The recording is superb in every way. It is here aptly coupled with two of the *Suites for Unaccompanied Cello.*

(i) *Cello Sonata, Op. 65;* (ii) *Elegy for Solo Viola;* (iii) *6 Metamorphoses after Ovid, for Solo Oboe, Op. 49;* (iv) *Suite for Violin & Piano, Op. 6.*

(B) *** EMI CZS5 73989-2 (2). (i) Welsh, Lenehan;
(ii) Silverthorne; (iii) Carter; (iv) Barantschick, Alley –
WALTON: *Piano Quartet,* etc. ***

In the *Cello Sonata*, Moray Welsh and John Lenehan make no attempt to ape the famous Rostropovich account but instead choose their own approach, which is thoughtful, ardent and strong and highly spontaneous. Paul Silverthorne gives a touchingly valedictory account of the *Elegy* and Roy Carter is rhapsodically free in the six piquant oboe miniatures, capturing their wistful innocence to perfection. But perhaps the most remarkable of all is the compellingly alive account of the early *Suite for Violin and Piano*. As if anticipating the *Cello Sonata*, the five movements are beautifully contrasted. Throughout, the recordings, made in the Conway Hall, have a pleasing degree of resonance; the effect is present in the most natural way. At its new bargain price, and with a superb coupling, this is strongly recommended.

Cello Suites (Suites for Unaccompanied Cello) Nos. 1, Op. 72; 2, Op. 80; 3, Op. 87.

(N) *** Virgin VC5 45399-2. Mørk.
*** BIS CD 446. Torleif Thedéen.

The Norwegian cellist Truls Mørk gives richly eloquent accounts of all three suites. He produces a magnificent sound and has a flawless technique. There is an impressive sense of space, a refusal to impress us or be rushed, and a depth of insight that is quite special. Even if you have the pioneering Rostropovich set or one of its successors you will find something new here.

Torleif Thedéen has magnificent tonal warmth and eloquence, and he too proves a masterly advocate of these *Suites*, which sound thoroughly convincing in his hands, if not quite so powerful as Rostropovich in the concertos and sonatas.

Cello Suite No. 3.

(N) (M) *** Virgin VM5 61849-2. Isserlis – TAVENER: *The Protecting Veil.* ***

Steven Isserlis brings out the spiritual element in a work which draws on traditional Russian themes, including Orthodox Church music, and such a performance relates well to the Tavener work with which it is coupled.

(i) *Gemini Variations* (for violin, flute and piano duet), Op. 72; (ii) *2 Insect Pieces* (for oboe and piano); (iii) *Russian Festival* (for brass); (iv; v) *Birthday Hansel,* Op. 92; (iv; vi–viii) *Cantata academica,* Op. 62; (iv; vii; ix; x) *Cantata misericordium,* Op. 69; (iv; xi; xii) *Canticle II (Abraham and Isaac);* (xiii; x) *Children's Crusade,* Op. 82; (iv; xii) *6 Hölderlin Fragments,* Op. 61; (xiv) *The Poet's Echo.*

(N)(M) *** Decca ADD 468 811-2 (2). (i) Gábor and Zoltán Jeney; (ii) Holliger, Schiff; (iii) Philip Jones Brass, Iveson; (iv) Pears, (v) Ellis; (vi) Vyvyan, Watts, Brannigan, (vii) LSO Ch., LSO, (viii) Malcolm; (ix) Fischer-Dieskau; (x) cond. Burgess; (xi) Proctor; (xii) composer (piano); (xiii) Soloists, Wandsworth School Boys' Ch.; (xiv) Vishnevskaya, Rostropovich.

This collection is called 'Rarities' and ranges from the *Insect Pieces* for oboe and piano of 1935 and the sonorous *Russian Funeral* of 1936 to *A Birthday Hansel* (a Burns setting celebrating the seventy-fifth birthday of the Queen Mother), completed the year before the composer's death. The 1957 recording of *Abraham and Isaac*, with an eloquent contribution from Norma Procter, is new to the catalogue. The

Gemini Variations were commissioned by the Hungarian Jeney twins, who perform the piece here. Britten's ingenuity in switching the two young performers between one instrument and another (violin, flute and piano) is never interrupted and the final cadence brings a real coup, when all four instruments are somehow sounded together.

More than anything the *Cantata academica*, written for Basle University, is an expression of joy and optimism, while in the *Cantata misericordium* (telling the story of the Good Samaritan) the composer's theme is the resolution of stress in a peace and tranquillity which come from within. At its close the beautiful *Dormi nunc* ('Sleep now') in a gentle 9/8 rhythm makes a blissful resolution.

(i; ii) *Lachrymae, Op. 48;* (ii; iii; iv) *Canticle No. 3: Still falls the rain, Op. 55;* (iii; v) *Our Hunting Fathers, Op. 8;* (ii; iii) *Who are these children?, Op. 84.*

(M) (**(*)) BBC mono/stereo BBCB 8014-2. (i) Major; (ii) composer (piano); (iii) Pears; (iv) Brain; (v) LSO, composer.

This valuable issue in the BBC's 'Britten the Performer' series fills in two gaps in the list of his own works which he recorded – the early cantata, *Our Hunting Fathers* and the extended, enigmatic viola piece, *Lachrymae. Our Hunting Fathers* created something of a scandal when it was first performed, at the Norwich Festival in 1936, thanks to its anti-blood-sports theme, prompted by W. H. Auden. The composer in his interpretation here, biting and urgent to the point of violence in climaxes, reflects what he must have felt in writing the work. Pears is in superb voice too, focused sharply in this rather dry mono BBC studio recording of 1961. In *Lachrymae*, the playing of Britten at the piano magnetizes the ear almost as in an improvisation, with the viola player Margaret Major characteristically warm in a beautifully sustained reading.

With its clutch of brief nursery-rhyme settings in the Scots dialect, *Who are these children?* may initially seem a relatively lightweight piece, but they only serve to intensify, by contrast, the darkness of the four more substantial war-inspired songs, with both Britten and Pears at their finest. It is good, too, to have this 1956 Aldeburgh Festival account of the *Canticle No. 3* with Dennis Brain as horn soloist, warm even in face of a dry acoustic. The big snag is the absence of texts – particularly serious in the case of the little-known Soutar poems.

The *Children's Crusade*, written for the fiftieth anniversary of the Save the Children Fund, is darker, a setting of a Brecht poem which in the most direct way, with vivid percussion effects, tells of children lost in Poland in 1939. *The Poet's Echo*, Britten's setting of Pushkin in the original Russian, was written for Vishnevskaya. Her voice, with its Slavonic unevenness, is not the most suited in controlling the subtle line of such delicate songs, but with the help of her husband the performance is warm and highly atmospheric. The six *Hölderlin Fragments*, with Peter Pears responding eloquently, reflect a highly individual response to the German language and the sensitive word-painting of Hölderlin. (Surprisingly for Decca, no translations are included for either of these cycles.)

6 Metamorphoses after Ovid, Op. 49; Phantasy Quartet, Op. 2; 2 Insect Pieces; Temporal Variations.

**(*) MDG MDG 3010925-2. Schmalfuss, with Mannheim Qt (members) or Watanabe.

(i) *6 Metamorphoses after Ovid; (i–ii) Phantasy Quartet, Op. 2; (i; iii) 2 Insect Pieces; Temporal Variations; (iii) Holiday Diary, Op. 5; Night Piece; 5 Waltzes.*

*** Hyp. CDA 66776. (i) Francis; (ii) Delmé Qt (members); (iii) Dussek.

(i) *6 Metamorphoses after Ovid; 2 Insect Pieces; (ii) Suite for Harp, Op. 83.*

*** Mer. (ADD) CDE 84119. (i) Watkins; Ledger; (ii) Ellis – *Tit for Tat*, etc. ***

Sarah Francis gives strong and distinctive characterizations not only to the *Ovid* pieces but also to the early *Phantasy Quartet* and to the pieces for oboe and piano as well. Michael Dussek proves a magnetic interpreter of the solo piano music, bringing out the sparkle of the boyhood waltzes (or 'Walztes' as the boy Britten called them) and the *Holiday Diary*. He then finds intense poetry and magic in the *Night Piece*.

Sarah Watkins gives biting and intense performances of the unaccompanied *Metamorphoses*, as well as the two early *Insect Pieces* with Philip Ledger. The sound is full and immediate, set convincingly in a small but helpful hall. It was for Osian Ellis that Britten wrote the *Harp Suite*, and Ellis remains the ideal performer.

Gernot Schmalfuss plays expertly and is excellently supported by the pianist Mamiko Watanabe and members of the Mannheim Quartet. Excellent recording, too, though it is not very realistically marketed – 46' 47'' playing time is rather short measure for a premium-price disc.

String Quartets: in F (1928); in D (1931); 2, Op. 36.

*** Chan. 9664. Sorrel Qt.

String Quartets Nos. 1 in D, Op. 25; 2 in C, Op. 36; 3 Divertimenti.

(BB) *** Naxos 8.553883. Maggini Qt.

String Quartet No. 3, Op. 94; Quartettino (1930); Alla marcia (1933); Simple Symphony.

(BB) *** Naxos 8.554360. Maggini Qt.

String Quartet No. 1 in D, Op. 25a.

(M) *** CRD 3351. Alberni Qt – SHOSTAKOVICH: *Piano Quintet.* **(*)

String Quartets Nos. 2 in C, Op. 36; 3, Op. 94.

(M) *** CRD 3395. Alberni Qt.

String Quartet No. 3, Op. 94.

❁ *** Koch 3-6436-2. Medici Qt – JANACEK: *Quartet No. 1;* RAVEL: *Quartet;* SHOSTAKOVICH: *Quartet No. 8;* SMETANA: *Quartet No. 1.* *** ❁

*** ASV CDDCA 608. Lindsay Qt – TIPPETT: *Quartet No. 4.* ***

It is a revelation to find Britten at 14 strongly influenced by Beethoven. This première recording by the Sorrel Quartet of the *F major* work of 1928, his first written under the

tutelage of Frank Bridge, is strong and confident, with hints of later Britten. The *D major Quartet* of 1931 was revised by the composer himself not long before he died, tonally equivocal, with hints of Bergian influence. Warmly performed, they make a fine coupling for the magnificent *Second Quartet*, here made to start waywardly, leading to a passionate, concentrated reading, helped by wide-ranging sound.

The Maggini give clean, direct performances of the first two numbered quartets, not as intense as some but fresh and thoughtful, well coupled with the three colourful *Divertimenti* of 1936. Clean, slightly distanced sound. This makes a formidable bargain as its competitors all involve more than one disc.

The Maggini's second CD is even finer than their first. They give a strongly characterized reading of Op. 94. The *Poco adagio* of the *Quartettino* is particularly searching, while the account of the *Simple Symphony* (which opens the programme) is as sprightly and sparkling as you could wish. First-class recording. The almost Mahlerian *Alla marcia* is the musical source of the penultimate movement of the song-cycle, *Les Illuminations*, written six years later. This pair of Naxos discs all but trumps the opposition.

The Alberni Quartet have good ensemble and intonation, and they play with great feeling; moreover, the CDs are available separately. The recording is vivid and clear. But the Naxos discs are more generous.

The Medici Quartet, in inspired form, are totally involved in Britten's valedictory *Third Quartet*, with its rarefied atmosphere and ethereal slow movement. The *Burlesque* is splendidly robust and the long final *Passacaglia* is sustained with complete concentration. The recording, like the playing, gives the impression of live music-making.

The Lindsay performance also brings one of the most expansive and deeply expressive readings on record. The ASV recording is vivid, with fine presence; but extraneous sounds are intrusive at times: heavy breathing, snapping of strings on finger-board, etc.

Suite for Violin & Piano, Op. 6.

(B) *** EMI Début CZS5 72825-2. Zambrzycki-Payne, Presland – GRIEG: *Violin Sonata No. 3;* SZYMANOWSKI: *Violin Sonata, Op. 9.* ***

Unlike some Début releases, which concentrate on pieces that serve more purpose as a visiting card for the artist than as a useful addition to the catalogue, this makes good sense on both scores. The Britten is a rarity, and though there is a rival account this has tremendous personality and life. What an imaginative and characterful piece it is! Rafal Zambrzycki-Payne's partner, Carole Presland, is a superb player too. The Abbey Road recording is expertly balanced and sounds very natural. A most desirable disc.

VOCAL MUSIC

Advance Democracy; (i) A Boy Was Born, Op. 3; 5 Flower Songs, Op. 47; Sacred and Profane, Op. 91.

*** Chan. 9701. Finzi Singers; (i) Lichfield Cathedral
  Choristers, Spicer.

Advance Democracy, with its adventurous choral writing,
sets the seal on a wide-ranging group of works representing
Britten: both early (the nativity cantata, *A Boy Was Born*,
written at the age of 19) and late (*Sacred and Profane*, dating
from 1975, the year before Britten died, which poignantly
sets death-obsessed medieval lyrics). The five *Flower Songs*,
written in 1949, demonstrate Britten's gift for writing occasional music, pointful and elegant. Under Paul Spicer the
Finzi Singers give virtuoso performances, vividly caught in
the warm and atmospheric Chandos recording.

*A.M.D.G.; Chorale after an Old French Carol; 5 Flower
Songs; Hymn to the Virgin; Sacred and Profane, Op. 91;
Gloriana: Choral Dances.*

(N) *** Hyp. CDA 67140. Polyphony, Layton.

Under Stephen Layton the brilliant group, Polyphony, give
superb performances of a wide range of Britten's unaccompanied choral music, from the *Hymn to the Virgin*, written
in 1930 when the teenage composer was confined to the
school sickbay, to *Sacred and Profane*, one of his last works,
settings of medieval texts both religious and secular. Originally written for solo voices, they present a formidable challenge for a choir, taken up masterfully by Polyphony. They
equally combine refinement and strength in the other,
widely varied works, from the delicate *Flower Songs* to the
often lusty dances from the Elizabethan opera, *Gloriana*,
incisively done. *A.M.D.G.* is a work never performed until
long after Britten's death, sensitive settings of poems by
Gerard Manley Hopkins, written in 1939 when Britten was
in the United States, and remaining unperformed, when
Britten and Pears stayed on in America for three years.
Finely balanced sound to match the refined beauty of the
performances.

*Antiphon; Festival Te Deum; Hymn to St Cecilia; A Hymn
of St Columba; Hymn to St Peter; Hymn to the Virgin;
Jubilate Deo; Missa brevis; Rejoice in the Lamb; Te Deum
in C. (Organ) Prelude & Fugue on a Theme of Vittoria.*

(BB) *** Naxos 8.554791. St John's College Ch., Robinson.

This collection of 11 choral works may omit the much-
recorded *Ceremony of Carols* but as a result it gives a wider
view of Britten's achievement in this area, with Barry Holden's
excellent notes relating each work to the composer's career
and personal associations. The biting attack of these young
singers is enhanced by refined recording which thrillingly
brings out the wide dynamic contrasts. The *Prelude and Fugue*
for organ with its elaborate counterpoint is also brilliantly
done. The booklet includes full texts.

Cabaret songs (to words of W. H. Auden): *As it is, plenty;
Calypso; Funeral blues; O tell me the truth about love;
Johnny; When you're feeling like expressing your affection.*
*Blues: Blues; Boogie-Woogie; The Clock on the Wall; The
Spider and the Fly.*

*** Unicorn DKPCD 9138. Gomez, Jones, Instrumental Ens. –
  PORTER: *Songs.* **(*)

These are all fun-pieces, and as a bonus Jill Gomez includes

the jazzy song, *As it is, plenty*, from the cycle, *On This Island*.
The accompanist, Martin Jones, is more deadpan in five
classic Cole Porter songs which Jill Gomez also sings. To fill
the disc, an instrumental ensemble plays Daryl Runswick's
inventive arrangements of four blues numbers by Britten,
drawn from the operetta *Paul Bunyan*, as well as his early
incidental music for plays.

*A Boy was Born, Op. 3; A Ceremony of Carols, Op. 28;
Rejoice in the Lamb, Op. 30.*

(N) **(*) Australian Decca Eloquence 467 612-2. Masters,
  Barley, King's College, Cambridge, Ch., Cleobury.

Stephen Cleobury's refined, beautifully controlled readings
from 1990, originally on Argo, now reappear on Australian
Decca's Eloquence label. This was always an excellent
grouping of these three early Britten works, all with the
sound of boy trebles as a source of inspiration. These performances, set against a reverberant acoustic, may lack the
bite and earthiness of the readings Britten himself is known
to have preferred, but they still have plenty of energy and
can still be recommended as they have a character of their
own.

*A Boy Was Born; Christ's Nativity; Hymn to the Virgin;
Jubilate in C; Shepherd's Carol; Te Deum in C.*

*** Hyp. CDA 66285. Gritton, Wyn-Rogers, Holst Singers,
  St Paul's Cathedral Choristers, Layton; Goode (organ).

Here is a disc to illustrate Britten's special fascination with
the Christmas story, including *Christ's Nativity*. The writing
has many bold and original touches typical of the mature
composer, not least in the opening cries of *Awake!*. Steven
Layton conducts a finely controlled performance, full of
sharp dynamic and rhythmic contrasts. Despite speeds
slower than usual, the performance of the cantata, *A Boy
Was Born*, of 1934 has similar merits, with the *Jubilate* and
Te Deum made the more vigorous by the organ accompaniment of David Goode. Atmospheric, spacious choral sound.

*A Boy Was Born, Op. 3; Festival Te Deum, Op. 32; Rejoice
in the Lamb, Op. 30; A Wedding Anthem, Op. 46.*

*** Hyp. CDA 66126. Corydon Singers, Westminster Cathedral
  Ch., Best; Trotter (organ).

All the works included here are sharply inspired. The refinement and tonal range of the choirs could hardly be more
impressive, and the recording is refined and atmospheric to
match.

5 Canticles.

*** Hyp. CDA 66498. Rolfe Johnson, Chance, Opie, Vignoles,
  Williams, Thompson – PURCELL, arr. BRITTEN: *An
  Evening Hymn*, etc. ***

*Canticles Nos. 1, My beloved is mine, Op. 40; 2, Abraham
and Isaac, Op. 51; 3, Still falls the rain, Op. 55; 4, Journey of
the Magi, Op. 86; 5, Death of St Narcissus, Op. 89. A
Birthday Hansel.* arr. of PURCELL: *Sweeter than roses.*

(M) *** Decca (ADD) 425 716-2. Pears, Hahessy, Bowman,
  Shirley-Quirk, Tuckwell, Ellis, composer.

This Decca CD brings together on a single record all five

of the miniature cantatas to which Britten gave the title 'Canticle', plus the *Birthday Hansel*, written in honour of the seventy-fifth birthday of Queen Elizabeth the Queen Mother, and a Purcell song-arrangement. A beautiful collection as well as a historical document, with recording that still sounds well.

The newer Hyperion versions make an excellent alternative. Rolfe Johnson's tenor is sweeter even than Pears's, most of all in the fifth of the *Canticles, The Death of St Narcissus*, written with harp accompaniment at the very end of Britten's life. Like the fourth, *The Journey of the Magi*, it sets a T. S. Eliot poem. The three Purcell realizations are shared among the soloists, one apiece, all representing Purcell at his most beautiful and intense.

Canticle No. 1; Folksong arrangements: Down by the Salley Gardens; Little Sir William; The trees they grow so high; O Waly Waly; 7 Sonnets of Michelangelo, Op. 22; Winter Words, Op. 52.

(N) (B) *** Hyp. CDH 55067. Rolfe-Johnson, Graham Johnson.

In this 1985 recording, now reissued at bargain-price on Hyperion's Helios label, Anthony Rolfe-Johnson is at his most mellifluous. It is his strength as an interpreter of Britten's songs that without imitating Peter Pears he can convey similar intensity, bringing out dramatic points very much as the composer's inspirer did. The *Michelangelo Sonnets* have a freshness and exuberance apt for that earliest of the song-cycles with piano, and the folksongs are deliciously pointed, notably *Little Sir William*. Even more valuable are the first and most neglected of the *Canticles*, setting an equivocal poem by the Jacobean Francis Quarles, as well as the Hardy song-cycle, *Winter Words*, surprisingly neglected on disc when it contains some of the most striking and atmospheric of all Britten's songs, exactly evoking the world of Hardy. As in so many song issues Graham Johnson – who earlier worked at Aldeburgh with Britten – proves an ideal accompanist. Refined, well-balanced sound.

(i) *Canticles Nos. 1–3. Folksong arrangements: The ash grove; La belle est au jardin d'amour; The bonny Earl o'Moray; The brisk young widow; Ca' the yowes; Come you not from Newcastle?; The foggy foggy dew; The Lincolnshire Poacher; Little Sir William; The minstrel boy; O can ye sew cushions?; Oliver Cromwell; O waly waly; The plough boy; Quand j'étais chez mon père; Le roi s'en va-t'en chasse; The Sally Gardens; Sweet Polly Oliver; The trees they grow so high. Song-cycles: On this Island, Op. 11; 7 Sonnets of Michelangelo, Op. 22; Winter words, Op. 52.*

(N) (M) *** EMI (ADD) CZS 573995-2 (2). Tear, Ledger;
(i) with Bowman; Tuckwell.

Abraham and Isaac, much the longest of the three canticles, draws its text, as *Noyes Fludde* does, from the Chester Miracle Plays. Britten conveys the drama of the situation with extraordinary economy. Naturally, much depends on the concentration of the tenor soloist as well as the pianist for both have passages that sound almost like extemporization. Much more concentrated is the third canticle, *Still falls the rain*, to words by Edith Sitwell. It was written in memory of the

pianist, Noel Mewton Wood. Here the horn obbligato as played by Alan Civil is ripely effective.

Tear, trained in the Aldeburgh tradition, gives renderings that are both individual and authentic, but his performances cannot quite match those on Decca. However, they are still very sensitive, and the mid-1970s stereo is even more atmospheric than on the earlier disc. The use of a countertenor (Bowman) for the second voice in *Abraham and Isaac* allows the eerie setting of God's words (the two soloists in octaves) to be more smoothly matched to produce an aptly disembodied effect.

Tear is at his freshest and most communicative in the three cycles and the folksong arrangements. It was a generous idea to include not only the intensely atmospheric Hardy settings of *Winter words* and the deeply expressive Michelangelo settings but also the rarer settings of Auden (*On this island*), which date from the beginning of Britten's career. These last may be less felicitous than the later songs, but they are still strikingly individual. In the folksongs, close as Tear's interpretations are to those of Peter Pears, he has a sparkle of his own, helped by the resilient accompaniment of Sir Philip Ledger. In any case, some of these songs are unavailable in Pears versions, and the EMI collection is a delight on its own account. *Oliver Cromwell* (which ends the first of the two discs) is among the most delectable of pay-off songs ever written. Excellent recording throughout.

Canticle No. 3; Now sleeps the crimson petal.

(N) *** Erato 8523 80217-2. Rolfe Johnson, Pyatt, Donohoe –
BERKELEY: *Horn Trio, Op. 44*; WOOD: *Horn Trio.* ***

The two Britten vocal items make an attractive supplement to the two fine horn trios that constitute the main works on this mixed disc celebrating the seductive playing of David Pyatt. Britten's Tennyson setting was originally designed for the *Serenade for Tenor, Horn and Strings*, but was discarded for not fitting in with the final scheme. Anthony Rolfe Johnson is at his most mellifluous, as he is in the *Canticle No. 3*, where he intones Edith Sitwell's elegiac words with hypnotic intensity, well matched by Pyatt and Donohoe.

A Ceremony of Carols. Deus in adjutorium meum; Hymn of St Columba; Hymn to the Virgin; Jubilate Deo in E flat; Missa brevis, Op. 63.

*** Hyp. CDA 66220. Westminster Cathedral Ch., Hill; (i) with
S. Williams; J. O'Donnell (organ).

Particularly impressive here is the boys' singing in the *Ceremony of Carols*, where the ensemble is superb, the solo work amazingly mature and the range of tonal colouring a delight. Along with the other, rarer pieces, this is an outstanding collection, beautifully and atmospherically recorded.

(i; ii) *A Ceremony of Carols, Op. 28*; (i; iii) *Friday Afternoons, Op. 7; Francie; King Herod and the cock; The oxen*; (i) *Sweet was the song*; (iv) *Song: The birds*; (iv; v; iii) *3 2-part Settings of Walter de la Mare: The Ride-by-nights; The Rainbow; The Ship of Rio. A Wealden Trio.*

(B) *** Naxos 8.553183. (i) New L. Children's Ch., Corp;
(ii) Kanga; (iii) Wells; (iv) Hopper; (v) Attree; Kenyon.

Ronald Corp directs bright, refreshing performances of a

delightful collection of Britten choral pieces written for children's voices. The New London Children's Choir is relatively large and is recorded against a lively hall acoustic, but there is no lack of impact, and the tenderness of expression as well as the liveliness is consistently refreshing. Though the *Processional* is recorded statically, losing in atmosphere, the *Ceremony of Carols* brings ensemble remarkably crisp for a biggish choir, and these performances justify the decision to have full ensemble treatment for all of the *Friday Afternoons* sequence. A splendid bargain.

(i) *A Ceremony of Carols, Op. 28; Hymn to St Cecilia, Op. 27;* (ii) *Jubilate Deo;* (i) *Missa brevis in D, Op. 63;* (ii) *Rejoice in the Lamb* (Festival cantata), *Op. 30; Te Deum in C.*

(M) *** EMI (ADD) CDM7 64653-2. King's College, Cambridge, Ch.; (i) Ellis, Willcocks; (ii) Bowman, Ledger.

The King's trebles may have less edge in the *Ceremony of Carols* than their Cambridge rivals at St John's College, and the *Missa brevis* can certainly benefit from a throatier sound, but the results here are dramatic as well as beautiful. Philip Ledger's 1974 version of the cantata, *Rejoice in the Lamb*, have timpani and percussion added to the original organ part. Here the biting climaxes are sung with passionate incisiveness, while James Bowman is in his element in the delightful passage which tells you that 'the mouse is a creature of great personal valour'. The *Te Deum* setting and *Jubilate* make an additional bonus and are no less well sung and recorded.

(i) *A Ceremony of Carols;* (ii) *Shepherd's Carol; A Boy Was Born; Jesus, as Thou art our Saviour.*

(M) *** ASV CDWHL 2097. Christ Church Cathedral Ch., Grier; with (i) Kelly; (ii) Bicket (with Collection: 'Carols from Christ Church' ***).

A first-class account of Britten's *Ceremony of Carols*, attractively vigorous, full of rhythmic energy. There is an earthy quality which reflects the composer's own rejection of over-refined choirboy tone, yet the two treble solos are both delicate and radiantly assured. The dialogue *Shepherd's Carol* is also sung most effectively. The reissue is combined with a dozen other carols by various composers, mostly English, making for an enticing Christmas CD.

4 *Chansons françaises; Les Illuminations; Serenade for Tenor, Horn & Strings.*

(M) **(*) Chan. 7112. Lott, Rolfe Johnson, Thompson, SNO, Thomson.

Felicity Lott gives a strong and sensitive performance of the four *French songs*, as she does of the other early French cycle on the disc, *Les Illuminations*, bringing out the tough and biting element rather than the sensuousness. Anthony Rolfe Johnson, soloist in the *Serenade*, gives a finely controlled performance, but Michael Thompson is not as evocative in the horn solo as his most distinguished predecessors. Bryden Thomson draws crisp, responsive playing from the SNO.

Curlew River (1st parable for church performance).

*** Koch-Schwann 3-1397-2. Milhofer, Hargreaves, Hughes-Jones, M. Evans, Guildhall Chamber Ens., Angus.

(M) *** Decca (ADD) 421 858-2. Pears, Shirley-Quirk, Blackburn, soloists, Instrumental Ens., composer and Tunnard.

**(*) Ph. 454 469-2. Langridge, Allen, Keenlyside, Saks, Richardson, L. Voices, ASMF (members), Marriner.

Recorded at a single performance in St Giles', Cripplegate, with students of the Guildhall School of Music, this superb Koch version of *Curlew River* is in many ways even more involving than the original recording of almost 30 years earlier, with a live performance, often at broader speeds, conveying dramatic tension hypnotically. In particular, the predicament of the madwoman searching for her child becomes more touching when the voice is as young and clear as Mark Milhofer's. The words are commendably clear, and the bite of the chorus and of the instrumental ensemble (notably horn and percussion) makes this a moving experience, with stage and audience noises at a minimum.

In Britten's own version, which has its own special character, Harold Blackburn plays the Abbot of the monastery who introduces the drama, while John Shirley-Quirk plays the ferryman who takes people over the Curlew River and Peter Pears sings the part of the madwoman who, distracted, searches fruitlessly for her abducted child. The recording is outstanding even by Decca standards.

Marriner conducts a fresh, clean-cut reading, Philip Langridge gives a sensitive account of the central role of the Madwoman, but neither he nor the others can quite match the example of Britten's own original recording in mystery or warmth, while Pears is unique in conveying the tender vulnerability of the Madwoman.

Folksong Arrangements: *The ashgrove; At the mid hour of night; Avenging and bright; La Belle est au jardin d'amour; Bird scarer's song; Bonny at morn* (2 versions)*; The Bonny Earl o'Moray; The brisk young widow; Ca'the yowes; Come you not from Newcastle?; David of the white rock; Dear harp of my country!; Early one morning; Eho! Eho!; The False knight along the road; Fileuse; The foggy, foggy dew; How sweet the answer; Il est quelqu'un sur terre; I was lonely and forlorn; I will give my love an apple; The last rose of summer; Lemady; The Lincolnshire poacher; Little Sir William; Lord! I married me a wife; Master Kilby; The miller of Dee; The minstrel boy; La Noël Passée; O can ye sew cushions?; O the sight entrancing; Oft in the stilly night; Oliver Cromwell; O Waly, Waly; The plough boy; Quand j'étais chez mon père; Rich and rare; Le Roi s'en va-t'en chasse; Sail on, sail on; Sailor-boy; The sally gardens; Sally in our alley; She's like the swallow; The shooting of his dear; The soldier and the sailor; Sweet Polly Oliver; There's none to soothe; The trees they grow so high; Voici printemps.*

(N)(B) *** Hyp. Dyadd CDD 22042 (2). Anderson, Nathan, MacDougall; Martineau, Lewis, Ogden.

Now reissued as a Dyadd Double, this is a delightfully varied set, conveniently bringing together the seven volumes of folksong settings, five with piano accompaniment, and one each with guitar and harp. Jamie MacDougall, youthfully fresh and clear, has the majority of the songs, and though he may not be as characterful as Peter Pears, for whom they were written, his directness and clear diction are just as winning, undaunted as he is by singing not just in French but in Welsh for two of the songs in the volume with harp. Lorna Anderson, also fresh and clear, provides contrast in six of the seven volumes, with the second soprano, Regina Nathan, warmer in tone, singing all nine of the Irish songs in the final volume. Much of the success of the collection, certainly its variety, is owed to Malcolm Martineau, who relishes the sharp originality of Britten's piano writing, making one regret that he wrote so few solo piano pieces. Bryn Lewis on the harp and Craig Ogden on the guitar are equally idiomatic. First-rate sound. Full texts are given in the notes.

Folksong arrangements: *The ash grove; Avenging and bright; La belle est au jardin d'amour; The bonny Earl o' Moray; The brisk young widow; Ca' the yowes; Come you not from Newcastle?; Early one morning; The foggy, foggy dew; How sweet the answer; The last rose of summer; The Lincolnshire poacher; The miller of Dee; The minstrel boy; Oft in the stilly night; O waly, waly; The plough boy; Le roi s'en va-t'en chasse; Sally in our alley; Sweet Polly Oliver; Tom Bowling.*

(M) *** Decca (ADD) 430 063-2. Pears, Britten.

It is good to have the definitive Pears/Britten collaboration in the folksong arrangements. Excellent, faithful recording, well transferred to CD.

(i) *The Golden Vanity;* (ii) *Noye's Fludde.*

(M) *** Decca (ADD) 436 397-2. (i) Wandsworth School Boys' Ch., Burgess, composer (piano); (ii) Brannigan, Rex, Anthony, East Suffolk Children's Ch. & O, E. Op. Group O, Del Mar.

The Wandsworth boys are completely at home in *The Golden Vanity* and sing with pleasing freshness. The coupling was recorded during the 1961 Aldeburgh Festival, and not only the professional choristers but the children too have the time of their lives to the greater glory of God. All the effects have been captured miraculously here, most strikingly the entry into the Ark, while a bugle band blares out fanfares, with the stereo readily catching the sense of occasion and particularly the sound of *Eternal Father* rising above the storm at the climax of *Noye's Fludde.*

The Holy Sonnets of John Donne, Op. 35; Harmonia sacra (realizations of Pelham HUMFREY): *Hymn to God the Father; Lord I have sinned* (realization of William CROFT): *A Hymn on Divine Musick. The Way to the Tomb* (incidental music for Ronald Duncan's masque): *Evening; Morning; Night.* W. H. Auden settings: *Fish in the unruffled lakes; Night covers up the rigid land; To lie flat on the back with the knees flexed.* Songs: *Birthday song for Erwin; Cradle song for Eleanor; If thou wilt ease thine heart; Not even summer yet; The red cockatoo; Um Mitternacht; When you're feeling like expressing your affection; Wild with passion.*

⚙ *** Hyp. CDA 66823. Bostridge, Johnson.

In the Donne *Sonnet* cycle, written when the composer returned in deep shock after playing at the death camp of Belsen at the end of the war, Bostridge makes one concentrate afresh on Britten's powerful response to Donne's grittily uncompromising poems. His voice may be lighter than that of Pears, but in its lyrical beauty it can encompass a wider range of tone and dynamic. So in the opening sonnet one registers the anger of the words even more bitingly than with Pears, thanks also to the inspired accompaniment of Graham Johnson. The disc also offers inspired performances of 18 of the Britten songs which earlier fell by the wayside: the four Auden settings, which include a provocatively sexual one, a dreamily atmospheric setting of *Fish in the unruffled lakes* and a jolly cabaret song. The evocative title given to this CD collection, 'The Red Cockatoo', refers to the shortest song of all, a striking setting of Arthur Waley.

(i) *Les Illuminations* (song-cycle), *Op. 18;* (ii) *Nocturne;* (iii) *Serenade for Tenor, Horn & Strings, Op. 31.*

(M) *** Decca (ADD) 436 395-2. (i–iii) Pears; (i) ECO; (ii) wind soloists; (ii–iii) LSO strings, composer; (iii) with Tuckwell.
(BB) ** Naxos 8.553834. A. Thompson, M. Thompson, Bournemouth Sinf., Lloyd-Jones.

With dedicated accompaniments under the composer's direction, these classic Pears versions of *Les Illuminations* and the *Serenade* (with its horn obbligato superbly played by Barry Tuckwell) make a perfect coupling, with the *Nocturne* from 1960 making an ideal addition on CD. Pears, as always, is the ideal interpreter, the composer a most efficient conductor, and the fiendishly difficult obbligato parts are played superbly. The recording is brilliant and clear, with just the right degree of atmosphere although the transfer of *Les Illuminations* is brighter than the other two works.

This same coupling is welcome at super-bargain price, and David Lloyd-Jones draws vivid and responsive playing from the Bournemouth Sinfonietta, with Michael Thompson an outstanding horn soloist. Adrian Thompson is a sensitive and characterful singer who understands the idiom, unafraid of high tessitura, but the microphone brings out the heavy vibrato in the voice, often as a disagreeable wobble.

Nocturne, Op. 60.

(M) **(*) BBC (ADD) BBCB 8013-2. Pears, ECO, Britten – SHOSTAKOVICH: *Symphony No. 14.* **(*)

Nocturne, Op. 60; Now sleeps the crimson petal; Serenade, Op. 31 (both for tenor, horn & strings).

*** BIS CD 540. Prégardien, Lanzky-Otto, Tapiola Sinf., Vänskä – *Sinfonietta.* ***

This vivid live broadcast performance contrasts well with Britten and Pears's studio recording for Decca (see above). Peter Pears here sounds warmer and sweeter, balanced a little backwardly and so set against a helpful ambience. The obbligato instrumentalists in each song, by contrast, are more closely balanced than in the Decca recording, adding to the impact of such a song as the Wordsworth with its terrifying timpani solo, superbly played by James Blades. Not just Blades but all the soloists here from the ECO are even more attuned to Britten's idiom than their LSO counterparts on Decca. Sadly, no texts are included.

Osmo Vänskä brings together not only the two best-loved orchestral song-cycles but also the supplementary Tennyson setting intended for the *Serenade* and the elusive work, the *Sinfonietta*, which Britten honoured as his Opus 1. Christophe Prégardien has an ideally light and sweet tenor which, even in the high tessitura of the *Lyke-Wake Dirge* from the *Serenade*, shows no strain whatever. Though one detects that he is not English, that is a tribute to his articulation, and he is totally in tune with the idiom. Excellent, spacious sound, if with the tenor soloist slightly backward.

(i) *Noye's Fludde, Op. 59. A Ceremony of Carols, Op. 28.*

*** Somm SOMMCD 212. (i) Wyn-Rogers, Luxon, Wilson-Johnson; Finchley Children's Music Group, Wilks.

Noye's Fludde is here delightfully fresh and energetic, capturing the atmosphere of a live performance very well, with its processions of birds and animals and the off-stage Voice of God. With Benjamin Luxon providing a sonorous Voice of God, David Wilson-Johnson a characterful Noye and Catherine Wyn-Rogers a fruity Mrs Noye, all the other roles are performed sharply and incisively by members of the group. *A Ceremony of Carols*, given with comparable freshness and confidence, makes an ideal coupling, also well recorded.

On This Island; Folk-song arrangement: *The Salley Gardens.*

(M) *** BBC (ADD) BBCB 8015-2. Pears, composer – SCHUBERT: *7 songs;* WOLF: *7 Mörike Lieder* *** (with ARNE: *Come away death; Under the greenwood tree;* QUILTER: *O mistress mine;* TIPPETT: *Come unto these yellow sands;* WARLOCK: *Take, O take those lips away* ***).

Britten's early song-cycle, set to poems by his friend W. H. Auden, is especially valuable, as he did not otherwise record it, and typically it brings a bitingly dramatic reading. Inspired performances of the Lieder by Schubert and Wolf, as well as the sharply contrasted Shakespeare settings by a wide range of British composers.

(i) *Our Hunting Fathers, Op. 8;* (ii) *Serenade for Tenor, Horn & Strings, Op. 31;* (i) *Folksong arrangements: Oliver Cromwell; O waly, waly.*

**(*) EMI CDC5 56871-2. Bostridge; with (i) Britten Sinf., Harding; (ii) Neunecker, Bamberg SO, Metzmacher.

Ian Bostridge's radiantly lyrical tenor is ideally suited to the works which Britten wrote for Peter Pears, providing new insights in the *Serenade*, and the early song-cycle on an anti-blood-sports theme, *Our Hunting Fathers*, makes a welcome alternative. Bostridge gives a most illuminating account of the solos, bringing out the bite of the texts prepared by W. H. Auden, and Daniel Harding's direction is beautifully textured at spacious speeds – but next to the venom of Britten's own urgent performance it seems a degree too relaxed.

The Prodigal Son (3rd parable), *Op. 81.*

(M) *** Decca (ADD) 425 713-2. Pears, Tear, Shirley-Quirk, Drake, E. Op. Group Ch. & O, composer and Tunnard.

The last of the parables is the sunniest and most heart-warming. Britten cleverly avoids the charge of oversweetness by introducing the Abbot, even before the play starts, in the role of Tempter, confessing he represents evil and aims to destroy contentment in the family he describes: 'See how I break it up' – a marvellous line for Peter Pears. An ideal performance is given here with a characteristically real and atmospheric Decca recording.

Purcell realizations: *Orpheus Britannicus: The knotting song; 7 Songs* (1947); *6 Songs* (1948); *O Solitude; 5 Songs* (1960); *Celemene; 6 Duets* (1961). *Harmonia sacra: The Blessed Virgin's expostulation; The Queen's Epicedium; Saul and the Witch of Endor; 3 Divine Hymns* (1947); *2 Divine Hymns & Alleluia* (1960). *Miscellaneous songs* (1971): *Dulcibella; When Myra sings.*

*** Hyp. CDA 67061/2. Lott, Gritton, S. Walker, Bowman, Ainsley, Bostridge, Rolfe Johnson, Jackson, Keenlyside; Johnson.

As a result of giving recitals with Peter Pears during and after the war, Britten was encouraged to make a series of realizations using the figured basses Purcell provided in his big collections, *Orpheus Britannicus* and *Harmonia sacra*. The accompaniments for piano may defy latter-day ideas of authenticity, but Britten imaginatively follows the harmonic indications given, to produce entirely distinctive results, introducing a lyricism rare in keyboard continuo. With an outstanding team of soloists and with Graham Johnson as the inspired pianist, this collection stands as a monument to the devotion of one English master to another. The first disc, drawn from the *Orpheus Britannicus* collection, includes songs like *Fairest isle*, better known in the context of *King Arthur* or other entertainments. The second, from *Harmonia sacra*, has darker, weightier and more extended items, notably the magnificent scena, *Saul and the Witch of Endor*, involving three singers and with side-slipping chromatics as daring as any Purcell ever imagined. The tenor Ian Bostridge displays high mastery and Simon Keenlyside sings magnificently in the dark, bass items like *Job's curse* and the late *Let the dreadful engines*. Excellent, well-balanced sound.

St Nicholas; Hymn to St Cecilia.

*** Hyp. CDA 66333. Rolfe Johnson, Corydon Singers, St George's Chapel, Windsor, Ch., Girls of Warwick University Chamber Ch., Ch. of Christ Church, Southgate, Sevenoaks School, Tonbridge School, Penshurst Ch. Soc., Occasional Ch., Edwards, Alley, Scott, ECO, Best.

(i) *St Nicholas, Op. 42;* (ii) *Rejoice in the Lamb, Op. 30.*

(M) (***) Decca mono 425 714-2. (i) Hemmings, Pears, St John Leman School, Beccles, Girls' Ch., Ipswich School Boys' Ch., Aldeburgh Festival Ch. & O; R. Downes; (ii) Hartnett, Steele, Todd, Francke, Purcell Singers, G. Malcolm; composer.

For the first time in a recording, the congregational hymns

are included in Matthew Best's fresh and atmospheric account of *St Nicholas*, adding greatly to the emotional impact of the whole cantata. Though the chorus is distanced slightly, the contrasts of timbre are caught well, with the waltz-setting of *The birth of Nicholas* and its bath-tub sequence delightfully sung by boy-trebles alone. The *Hymn to St Cecilia* is also beautifully sung, with gentle pointing of the jazzy syncopations in crisp, agile ensemble and with sweet matching among the voices.

However, Britten's first recordings of his own works have a freshness and vigour unsurpassed since. Britten's performances capture the element of vulnerability, not least in the touching setting of words by the deranged poet, Christopher Smart, *Rejoice in the Lamb*.

Serenade for Tenor, Horn & Strings.

(B) *** DG (ADD) 439 464-2. Tear, Clevenger, Chicago SO, Giulini – DELIUS: *On hearing the first cuckoo*, etc; VAUGHAN WILLIAMS: *Greensleeves*, etc. ***

(i) *Serenade for Tenor, Horn & Strings, Op. 31;* (ii) Arr. of folksongs: *Avenging and bright; The bonny Earl O'Moray; The last rose of summer; Sally in our alley.*

(N)(M) (**(*)) Decca mono 468 801-2. Pears with (i) Brain, Boyd Neel String O, composer; (ii) Composer (piano) – WALTON: *Façade*. ***

(i) *Serenade for Tenor, Horn & Strings, Op. 31;* (ii) *7 Sonnets of Michelangelo, Op. 22; Winter Words, Op. 52.*

(M) (***) Decca mono 425 996-2. Pears, (i) Brain, Boyd Neel String O, composer; (ii) composer (piano).

This early 1944 account of the *Serenade*, with Pears in freshest voice and Dennis Brain's superb horn playing, has never been surpassed. The transfer from 78s is admirably faithful, complete with surface rustle, and one soon forgets the dry acoustic and early provenance of the recording. Yet surely the clicks could have been removed! Four folk songs recorded in stereo have been added for this reissue.

The alternative Decca compilation brings together some of Britten's historic early recordings. This first recording of the *Serenade*, though not helped by unatmospheric sound, is wonderfully intense. The first recording of the Hardy song-cycle, *Winter Words*, has never been matched by more recent recordings, an evocative performance with Britten drawing magical sounds from the piano in support of Pears. This version of the *Michelangelo Sonnets* is not quite as fresh-toned as the even earlier EMI one, but it still offers a searching performance. Limited but clear mono sound.

Robert Tear's 1977 interpretation of the *Serenade* is very much in the Aldeburgh tradition set by Pears, and Giulini has long been a persuasive advocate of Britten's music. He presents the cycle as a full-scale orchestral work and Tear is at his finest, more open than in his earlier, EMI recording. Dale Clevenger is a superb horn-player. It is good to have a fresh view of the music, especially when inexpensively coupled with fine performances of music by Delius and Vaughan Williams.

Songs & Proverbs of William Blake, Op. 74; Tit for Tat; 3 Early Songs: *Beware that I'd ne'er been married; Epitaph; The clerk;* Folksong arrangements: *Bonny at morn; I was

lonely; Lemady; Lord! I married me a wife!; O waly, waly; The Salley Gardens; She's like the swallow; Sweet Polly Oliver.*

**(*) Chan. 8514. Luxon, Williamson.

Benjamin Luxon's lusty baritone gives an abrasive edge, whether to early songs, folksong settings or the Blake cycle. Only rarely does he become too emphatic. Excellent, sensitive accompaniment and first-rate recording.

(i) *Spring Symphony, Op. 44;* (ii) *Cantata academica;* (iii) *Hymn to St Cecilia.*

(M) *** Decca (ADD) 436 396-2. (i–ii) Vyvyan, Pears; (i) Procter, Emanuel School, Wandsworth, Boys' Ch., ROHCG O, composer; (ii) Watts, Brannigan; (ii–iii) L. Symphony Ch.; (ii) LSO; (ii–iii) Malcolm.

(i–ii) *Spring Symphony, Op. 44;* (ii) *5 Flower Songs (for mixed chorus), Op. 47;* (ii–iii) *Hymn to St Cecilia, Op. 27.*

*** DG 453 433-2. (i) Hagley, Robbin, Mark Ainsley, Choristers of Salisbury Cathedral, Philh. O; (ii) Monteverdi Ch.; (iii) with Preston-Dunlop, Ross, Vickers, Mitchell, Savage; Philh. O, Gardiner.

(i) *Spring Symphony, Op. 44; Peter Grimes: 4 Sea Interludes.*

(M) *** EMI (ADD) CDM7 64736-2. (i) Armstrong, J. Baker, Tear, St Clement Dane's School Boys' Ch., L. Symphony Ch.; LSO, Previn.

(i) *Spring Symphony, Op. 44;* (ii) *Welcome Ode, Op. 95;* (iii) *Psalm 150, Op. 67.*

**(*) Chan. 8855. (i) Gale, Hodgson, Hill, Southend Boys' Ch., LSO; (ii) City of London Schools' Ch., LSO; (iii) City of London Schools' Ch. and O; Hickox.

Jennifer Vyvyan and Peter Pears are both outstanding, and Britten shows that no conductor is more vital in his music than he himself. The Decca reissue couples the work to the *Cantata academica*, with its deft use of a 12-note row, written for Basel, and the *Hymn to St Cecilia*. The setting exactly matches the imaginative, capricious words of Auden. Performances are first class and so is the CD transfer.

Like Britten, Previn makes this above all a work of exultation, a genuine celebration of spring; but here, more than in Britten's recording, the kernel of what the work has to say comes out in the longest of the solo settings, using Auden's poem, *Out on the lawn I lie in bed*. With Janet Baker as soloist it rises above the lazily atmospheric mood of the opening to evoke the threat of war and darkness. The *Four Sea Interludes*, which make a generous bonus, are presented in their concert form, with tailored endings.

John Eliot Gardiner provides a striking contrast with Britten himself, a performance that clarifies the complex textures at speeds generally flowing more briskly than usual. Gardiner draws equally refined playing from the Philharmonia; though the result is less wild and rustic-sounding in the bluff final chorus, the sharpness of focus makes it intensely refreshing, while the two fill-ups also demonstrate the Monteverdi Choir's astonishing virtuosity, with the syncopated rhythms of the *Hymn to St Cecilia* superbly sprung and the rare *Flower Songs* just as fresh.

With more variable soloists – the tenor Martyn Hill outstandingly fine, the soprano Elizabeth Gale often too edgy – Hickox's version of the *Spring Symphony* does not quite match the composer's own in gutsy urgency. But this CD brings the advantage of a first recording of Britten's last completed work, the *Welcome Ode*. The third work, equally apt, is the boisterous setting of *Psalm 150*.

(i) *Tit for Tat;* (ii) Folksong arrangements: *Bird scarer's song; Bonny at morn; David of the White Rock; Lemady; Lord! I married me a wife!; She's like the swallow.*

*** Mer. CDE 84119. Shirley-Quirk; (i) Ledger; (ii) Ellis – 6 *Metamorphoses* etc. ***

John Shirley-Quirk is unrivalled in the sharp yet subtle way he brings out the irony in these boyhood settings of De la Mare poems. It is also good to have him singing the six late folk-settings with harp accompaniment, here played by Osian Ellis, for whom they were originally written.

War Requiem, Op. 66.

*** Decca (ADD) 414 383-2. Vishnevskaya, Pears, Fischer-Dieskau, Bach Ch., London Symphony Ch., Highgate School Ch., Melos Ens., LSO, composer.

(N) ☼ *** BBC (ADD) BBCL 4046-2. Woytowicz, Pears, Wilbrink, Wandsworth School Boys' Ch., Melos Ens., New Philh. Ch., New PO, Giulini.

*** EMI CDS7 47034-8. Söderström, Tear, Allen, Trebles of Christ Church Cathedral Ch., Oxford, CBSO Ch., CBSO, Rattle.

**(*) DG 437 801-2 (2). Orgonasova, Rolfe Johnson, Skovhus, Monteverdi Ch., Tölz Boys' Ch., N. German R. Ch. & SO, Gardiner.

(BB) ** Naxos 8.553558/9. Russell, Randle, Volle, Scottish Festival Ch., St Mary's Episcopal Cathedral, Edinburgh, Ch., BBC Scottish SO, Brabbins (with Boddice).

(i) *War Requiem;* (ii) *Ballad of Heroes, Op. 14; Sinfonia da Requiem, Op. 20.*

*** Chan. 8983/4. (i) Harper, Langridge, Shirley-Quirk; (ii) Hill; St Paul's Cathedral Choristers, London Symphony Ch., LSO & CO, Hickox.

Richard Hickox's Chandos version rivals even the composer's own definitive account in its passion and perception. Hickox thrusts home the big dramatic moments with unrivalled force, helped by the weight of the Chandos sound. The boys' chorus from St Paul's Cathedral is exceptionally fresh. Heather Harper is as golden-toned as she was at the very first Coventry performance, fearless in attack. Philip Langridge has never sung more sensitively on disc, and both he and John Shirley-Quirk bring many subtleties to their interpretations. Adding to the attractions of the set come two substantial choral works, also in outstanding performances. Britten's own 1963 recording of the *War Requiem* comes near to the ideal. Though Vishnevskaya is abrasive in the soprano solos, she sings with incomparable emotional intensity. The 1963 recording has now been carefully and lovingly remastered and it now also includes a rehearsal sequence. The vivid realism of the sound-balance now comes over the more strikingly, with uncannily precise placing and balancing of the many different voices and instruments,

and John Culshaw's contribution as producer is the more apparent. A remarkable achievement.

Recorded live by the BBC in 1969, this thrilling account of the *War Requiem* finds Giulini as the principal conductor bringing the sort of biting, even wild intensity and deep dedication to Britten's score that marked his readings of the Verdi *Requiem*. The spacious Albert Hall acoustic enhances the electric atmosphere, while Britten himself conducts the Melos Ensemble just as dramatically in the Wilfred Owen settings. Peter Pears as tenor soloist is matched by the fresh, clear Dutch baritone, Hans Wilbrink, while Stefania Woytowicz is the bright, incisive soprano, alongside the New Philharmonia Chorus at its most brilliant. A bargain squeezed onto a single disc at rather more than mid-price.

With Elisabeth Söderström a more warmly expressive soloist than the oracular Vishnevskaya, the human emotions behind the Latin text come out strongly. If Tear does not always match the subtlety of Pears on the original recording, Allen sounds more idiomatic than Fischer-Dieskau. Rattle's approach is warm, dedicated and dramatic, with fine choral singing (not least from the Christ Church Cathedral trebles). The various layers of sound are well managed on the digital recording, if not quite with the definition of the finest rivals.

Recorded live in Lübeck by the North German Radio Orchestra and Choir under their chief conductor, John Eliot Gardiner, this is a thoughtful rather than a dramatic reading. It is intense and compelling, but it is seriously undermined by dim, inconsistent recording, with soloists and chorus often ill-focused. Richard Hickox's Chandos version is warmer and more powerful as an interpretation, as well as far better recorded.

What works far better than Gardiner's CD is the video version of the same performance (LaserDisc 072 198-1; VHS 072 198-3), set in the beautiful Marienkirche in Lübeck. With the singers in close-up, the ear tends to ignore bad balances. Another advantage is that on a single VHS cassette there is no break in the middle.

The glory of the Naxos version, on two bargain discs, is the sound, with spatial contrasts caught thrillingly and atmospherically, and the boys' choir in particular beautifully caught, clear but at a distance. The choral singing generally is excellent, vivid and immediate in the big climaxes of such sections as *Dies irae*. Under Martyn Brabbins for the full orchestral sections, and under Nigel Boddice for the chamber orchestra settings of the Wilfred Owen poems, the BBC Scottish Symphony Orchestra plays with fine point and precision, underlining the drama of the piece. The weakness is the solo singing, with Thomas Randle sounding strained and Michael Volle unidiomatic, and with Lynda Russell's fruity soprano too often edgy and uneven.

It is always revealing to have non-British performances of British music, and Kurt Masur directs a thoughtful, dedicated reading of the *War Requiem* with three first-rate American soloists. The virtuoso chamber group accompanying the Owen poems is made up of excellent players from the New York Philharmonic, and the choirs cannot be faulted, with the off-stage boys precisely placed. That said, this does not have the dramatic intensity of the finest versions, and the soloists are not helped by a relatively dry acoustic. With no fill-up it makes an expensive buy (Teldec 0630 17115-2).

Winter Words (song-cycle), Op. 52.

(BB) *** ASV CDQS 6172. I. Partridge, J. Partridge –
PURCELL: 'Sweeter than Roses' (songs). ***

Ian Partridge with his heady, fresh tenor gives keenly sensitive performances of atmospheric Hardy settings. He is admirably supported by his sister, Jennifer, who makes the very most of the imaginative piano-writing, whether in simulating railway noises in Midnight on the Great Western, or the creaks of The little old table. Excellent late-1970s recording. A worthy coupling for a warmly sympathetic collection of favourite Purcell songs.

OPERA

Albert Herring (complete).

**(*) Decca (ADD) 421 849-2 (2). Pears, Fisher, Noble,
Brannigan, Cantelo, ECO, Ward, composer.

Britten's own 1964 recording of the comic opera, Albert Herring, remains a delight. Peter Pears's portrait of the innocent Albert was caught only just before he grew too old for the role, but it is full of unique touches. Sylvia Fisher is a magnificent Lady Billows, and it is good to have so wide a range of British singers of the 1960s presented so characterfully. The recording, made in Jubilee Hall, remains astonishingly vivid.

Billy Budd (original four-act version; complete).

*** Erato 3984 21631-2 (2). Hampson, Rolfe Johnson,
Halfvarson, Manchester Boys' Ch., Hallé Ch. & O, Nagano.
(**) VAIA mono 1034-3 (3). Pears, Uppman, Dalberg, Alan,
G. Evans, Langdon, ROHCG Ch. & O, composer.

Billy Budd (revised version; complete).

*** Chan. 9826 (3 for 2). Keenlyside, Langridge, Tomlinson,
Opie, Bayley, Best, LSO Ch., LSO, Hickox.
*** Decca (ADD) 417 428-2 (3). Glossop, Pears, Langdon,
Shirley-Quirk, Wandsworth School Boys' Ch., Amb. Op. Ch.,
LSO, composer (with Holy Sonnets of John Donne; Songs &
Proverbs of William Blake ***).

Hickox's brilliant Chandos version of Billy Budd, with the finest cast of principals yet assembled, uses the revised two-Act score. Not only does he demonstrate the extra tautness of the revision, he also finds an extra emotional thrust. In Philip Langridge the role of Vere has found its most thoughtful interpreter yet, so that from the start his self-searching is the key element in the whole work. Far from the final monologue of Vere as an old man seeming to be a tailing-off, here it provides the most powerful conclusion, a cathartic resolution on the words: 'He has saved me and blessed me'. Comparably magnetic is John Tomlinson's Claggart, the personification of evil, chillingly malevolent in every inflexion, oily in the face of authority. Equally, Simon Keenlyside as Billy gains over all rivals in the fresh, youthful incisiveness of the voice, movingly shaded down to a rapt half-tone for the lyrical monologue sung by Billy about

to die. Helped by sound of spectacular quality, Hickox at marginally broader speeds conveys more mystery in reflective moments than even Britten himself did. His expansiveness means that the set spills over on to a third disc but, with three discs for the price of two, that brings no disadvantage.

On Erato we have a complete recording of Britten's original four-Act version of his opera, Billy Budd, above all urgent and intense, more dramatic, less reflective than Britten's own recording for Decca of the revised two-Act version. Not only that, Thomas Hampson brings to the title-role an extra beauty alongside heroic power. It includes the important assembly scene on the deck of HMS Indomitable – removed in the revision – when the crew greet Captain Starry Vere, establishing his character. It also provides a thrilling fortissimo close to the original Act I, superbly achieved in Kent Nagano's powerful performance with the Hallé Orchestra and Choir. Set against the velvet-toned Hampson, Anthony Rolfe Johnson as Vere has some grit in his voice, creating a believable character at once rugged and introspective. Eric Halfvarson as the evil Claggart is not as sinister as some of his predecessors but, apart from some roughness in the upper register, it is a forceful, incisive performance, matching the urgency of Nagano's approach. Among the others, Gidon Saks is superb as the Sailing Master, Mr Flint; Martyn Hill is most characterful as the whining Red Whiskers, and the veteran, Richard Van Allan, is ideally cast as old Dansker, with Andrew Burden clear-toned as the victimized Novice. Coming on two discs instead of three, this has a clear advantage over existing sets.

On Decca, Britten himself has an outstanding cast, with Glossop a bluff, heroic Billy and Langdon a sharply dark-toned Claggart, making these symbol-figures believable. Magnificent sound, and the many richly imaginative strokes – atmospheric as well as dramatic – are superbly managed. The extravagant layout on three CDs begins with the John Donne Holy Sonnets (sung by Pears) and the Songs & Proverbs of William Blake (sung by Fischer-Dieskau), with the Prologue and Act I of the opera beginning thereafter. They are equally ideal performances.

Though the sound is very scrubby, disconcertingly so at the very start, the historic recording of the very first performance of the opera in December 1951 is valuable for the fresh, youthful-sounding performance of Theodor Uppman in the title-role, as well as Peter Pears as Captain Vere, clearer and more flexible than in his studio recording of 16 years later. There is no libretto. It is interesting that, though the orchestra sounds dim and limp at the start, Britten as conductor whips up searing tension through the opera.

Death in Venice (complete).

*** Decca (ADD) 425 669-2 (2). Pears, Shirley-Quirk,
Bowman, Bowen, Leeming, E. Op. Group Ch., ECO,
Bedford.

Thomas Mann's novella, which was made into an expansively atmospheric film, far removed from the world of Mann, here makes a surprisingly successful opera. Pears's searching performance in the central role of Aschenbach is set against the darkly sardonic singing of John Shirley-Quirk in a sequence of roles as the Dionysiac figure who draws Aschenbach to his destruction and, though Steuart Bedford's assured conducting lacks some of the punch that Britten would have brought, the whole presentation makes this a set to establish the work outside the opera house.

Gloriana (complete).

*** Decca 440 213-2 (2). Barstow, Langridge, D. Jones, Summers, WNO Ch. & O., Mackerras.

Without effacing memories of earlier interpreters, Josephine Barstow gives a splendid performance as the Virgin Queen, tough and incisive, with the slight unevenness in the voice adding to the abrasiveness. Only in the final scene when, after the execution of Essex, the queen muses to herself in fragments of spoken monologue does her reading lack weight, but, just before that, the final confrontation between Elizabeth and Essex brings a thrilling climax, when Elizabeth attacks her lover not for infidelity but for treason. Philip Langridge's portrait of Essex is just as striking, consistently bringing out the character's arrogant bravado. The rest of the cast is equally starry, with Alan Opie as the queen's principal adviser, Sir Robert Cecil, balefully dark rather than sinister, with the warm-toned Della Jones as Essex's wife and the abrasive Yvonne Kenny as his sister, Lady Penelope Rich, equally well cast. Sir Charles Mackerras directs his Welsh National Opera forces in a performance that brings out the full splendour of this rich score. The Decca recording is comparably splendid.

Gloriana: Choral Dances.

(N) (B) *** Hyp. Helios CDH55050. Hill, Owen, Holst Singers & O., Davan Wetton – BLISS: *Lie strewn the white flocks*; HOLST: *Choral Hymns from the Rig Veda*. ***

The composer's own choral suite, made up of unaccompanied choral dances linked by passages for solo tenor and harp, makes an excellent coupling for the equally attractive Bliss and Holst items. Excellent, atmospheric recording.

A Midsummer Night's Dream (complete).

*** Decca (ADD) 425 663-2 (2). Deller, Harwood, Harper, Veasey, Watts, Shirley-Quirk, Brannigan, Downside and Emanuel School Ch., LSO, Britten.

** Ph. 454 122-2 (2). McNair, Asawa, Lloyd, Bostridge, Watson, Mark Ainsley, LSO, C. Davis.

Britten again proves himself an ideal interpreter of his own music and draws virtuoso playing from the LSO. Peter Pears has shifted to the straight role of Lysander. The mechanicals are admirably led by Owen Brannigan as Bottom; and among the lovers Josephine Veasey (Hermia) is outstanding. Deller, with his magical male alto singing, is the eerily effective Oberon.

Sir Colin Davis's cast is a strong one, with the lovers aptly taken by generally younger, if less characterful, singers than in rival sets. The LSO play brilliantly but, thanks to a rather dry acoustic, there is little of the atmospheric magic which makes the composer's own original so compelling. Davis is also a more metrical, more literal, less freely expressive interpreter. Sylvia McNair as Tytania has pure, silvery tone,

and Ian Bostridge is masterly in the tenor role of Flute. As Bottom, the dark-toned Robert Lloyd responds strongly, with fine feeling for words, but a serious snag is the choice of the counter-tenor Brian Asawa as Oberon, with a marked vibrato which makes him sound too womanly.

(i) Owen Wingrave (complete); (ii) 6 Hölderlin Fragments, Op. 61; (iii) The Poet's Echo, Op. 76.

*** Decca (ADD) 433 200-2 (2). (i) Pears, Fisher, Harper, Vyvyan, J. Baker, Luxon, Shirley-Quirk, ECO, composer; (ii) Pears, composer; (iii) Vishnevskaya, Rostropovich.

Britten's television opera marked a return after the *Church Parables* to the mainstream pattern of his operatic style, with a central character isolated from society. Each of the seven characters is strongly conceived, with the composer writing specially for the individual singers in the cast. The performance is definitive and the recording very atmospheric. The set is filled out with the *Six Hölderlin Fragments* and *The Poet's Echo*, Russian settings of Pushkin, written for Vishnevskaya, who performs them with her husband at the piano.

Paul Bunyan (complete).

*** Chan. 9781 (2). Gritton, Streit, Robinson, Egerton, Broadbent, White, Coleman-Wright, Graham, Royal Opera Ch. & O., Hickox.

*** Virgin VCD7 59249-2 (2). Lawless, Dressen, Comeaux Nelson, soloists, Ch. & O of Plymouth Music Series, Minnesota, Brunelle.

The much-admired Covent Garden production of *Paul Bunyan* was recorded live at the Sadler's Wells Theatre in 1999. Though there are intrusive stage noises, the Chandos sound vividly captures the dramatic atmosphere of this ballad opera with its witty libretto by W. H. Auden, so full is it of colourful, distinctive invention. Hickox directs a warmly idiomatic reading which gains over the only previous version in featuring such fine singers as Susan Gritton as Tiny and Kurt Streit as Johnny Inkslinger. The Chandos sound is more open and atmospheric than the studio recording for Virgin, which yet in many ways gains from the closeness of the voices.

Aptly, that first recording of Britten's choral operetta comes from the state, Minnesota, where the story is set. When the principal character is a giant who can appear only as a disembodied voice, the piece works rather better on record or radio than on stage. Musically, Britten's conscious assumption of popular American mannerisms does not prevent his invention from showing characteristic originality. Recorded in clean, vivid sound, with Philip Brunelle a vigorous conductor, it is an excellent first recording.

Peter Grimes (complete).

*** Chan. 9447/8 (2). Langridge, Watson, Opie, Connell, Harrison, Opera London, L. Symphony Ch., City of L. Sinf., Hickox.

(N) ⚫ (M) *** Decca (ADD) 467 682-2 (2). Pears, C. Watson, Pease, J. Watson, Nilsson, Brannigan, Evans, Ch. and O of ROHCG, composer.

*** EMI CDC7 54832-2 (2). Rolfe Johnson, Lott, Allen, Ch. & O of ROHCG, Haitink.

(B) *** Ph. (ADD) Duo 462 847-2 (2). Vickers, Harper, Summers, Bainbridge, Cahill, Robinson, Allen, ROHCG Ch. & O., C. Davis.

The rhythmic spring which Hickox gives this colourful score harks back to the composer's classic set, and Chandos backs him up with an exceptionally rich recording, with bloom on the voices and full, immediate orchestral sound. The casting of Philip Langridge in the title-role is central to the set's success. As on stage, he is unrivalled at conveying the character's mounting hysteria, and the result is chilling. Janice Watson makes a most touching Ellen Orford, younger and less maternal than her rivals, but all the more tender, with the golden tones of the voice well caught. The others make a superb team, with Alan Opie an outstanding Balstrode and John Connell commanding as lawyer Swallow at the start.

The Decca recording of *Peter Grimes* was one of the first great achievements of the stereo era. Few opera recordings can claim to be so definitive, with Peter Pears, for whom it was written, in the name-part, Owen Brannigan (another member of the original team) and a first-rate cast. Britten conducts superbly and secures splendidly incisive playing, with the whole orchestra on its toes throughout. The recording, superbly atmospheric, has so many felicities that it would be hard to enumerate them, and the Decca engineers have done wonders in making up aurally for the lack of visual effects. Reissued on the 'Legends' series at mid-price, this costs far less than it did but lacks text or libretto.

On EMI, Anthony Rolfe Johnson brings out the inward intensity of Grimes, singing most beautifully, hardly troubled by the high tessitura. Felicity Lott makes a tenderly sympathetic Ellen Orford, and Sarah Walker is unforgettable as Mrs Sedley, the laudanum-taking gossip. Thomas Allen is a wise and powerful Balstrode, making the Act III duet with Ellen an emotional resolution. The Covent Garden Chorus and Orchestra benefit from the extra range and vividness of EMI's digital recording adding to the impact.

Sir Colin Davis takes a fundamentally darker, tougher view of *Peter Grimes* than the composer himself. Jon Vickers's powerful, heroic interpretation sheds keen new illumination on what arguably remains the greatest of Britten's operas. Heather Harper as Ellen Orford is most moving, and there are fine contributions from Jonathan Summers as Captain Balstrode and Thomas Allen as Ned Keene. The recording is full and vivid, with fine balancing. Now reissued as a Duo, this is a genuine bargain.

(i) *Peter Grimes* (scenes); (ii) *The Rape of Lucretia* (abridged); (iii) French Folksong Arrangements: *La belle est au jardin d'amour; La fileuse; Quand j'étais chez mon père; Le roi s'en va-t'en chasse; Voici le printemps;* (iv) English Folksongs: *The Ash grove; The Bonny Earl o' Moray; Come you not from Newcastle?; The foggy, foggy dew; Heigh ho, heigh hi!; The King is gone a-hunting; Little Sir William; O, waly, waly; Oliver Cromwell; The plough boy; The Salley Gardens; Sweet Polly Oliver; There's none to soothe.*

(M) (***) EMI mono CMS7 64727-2 (2). (i–ii) Cross, Pears;

(i) Evans, E. Op. Group Chamber O; (ii) BBC Theatre Ch., ROHCG O; (i–ii) Goodall; (iii) Wyss; (iv) Pears; (iii–iv) composer.

Both of these abridged recordings of Britten's earliest operas, made in the 1940s, have a freshness and energy that reflect the excitement they aroused at their first appearance. They illustrate both the resilient energy of Peter Pears at this early stage, lighter and fresher of voice than later, and the urgent intensity of Reginald Goodall. Though the recordings, transferred from 78s, are boxy in sound, the closeness adds to the bite and impact, demonstrating the character and point of Joan Cross as Ellen Orford. It was a role written for her, as was the Female Chorus part in *Lucretia*. In the latter opera it is good to have Nancy Evans in the title-role, tenderly affecting, with the contrasts between the heroine's tragic grief and the beauty of the serving maids' Flower Duet superbly brought out. The recordings of folksong settings are delightful, made not just by Peter Pears for both Decca and EMI, but by Sophie Wyss (for whom *Les Illuminations* was written). The wit and point of such songs as *The foggy, foggy dew* and *Little Sir William* come out even more charmingly than in later recordings, with Britten as accompanist at his most inspired.

Peter Grimes: 4 Sea Interludes & Passacaglia.

*** Chan. 8473. Ulster O, Handley – BAX: *On the Sea-shore;* BRIDGE: *The Sea.* ***

Handley draws brilliant, responsive playing from the Ulster Orchestra in readings that fully capture the atmospheric beauty of the writing, helped by vivid recording of demonstration quality.

The Rape of Lucretia (complete).

*** Chan. 9254/5. Rigby, Robson, Pierard, Maxwell, Miles, Rozario, Gunson, City of L. Sinf., Hickox.

(i) *The Rape of Lucretia* (complete); (ii) *Phaedra, Op. 93.*

*** Decca (ADD) 425 666-2 (2). (i) Pears, Harper, Shirley-Quirk, J. Baker, Luxon, ECO, composer; (ii) J. Baker, ECO, Bedford.

In combining on CD *The Rape of Lucretia* with *Phaedra,* Decca celebrates two outstanding performances by Dame Janet Baker, recorded at the peak of her career. Among other distinguished vocal contributions to the opera Peter Pears and Heather Harper stand out, while Benjamin Luxon makes the selfish Tarquinius into a living character. The seductive beauty of the writing – Britten then at his early peak – is caught splendidly, the melodies and tone-colours as ravishing as any he ever conceived.

Though the soloists in the Britten recording – notably Janet Baker in the title-role – are more sharply characterful and well contrasted, the alternative views presented on Chandos are comparably convincing. Jean Rigby as Lucretia may lack the warmth and weight of Baker, but she gains from having a younger-sounding voice. Equally, the timbre of Nigel Robson as the Male Chorus, rather darker than Peter Pears's, adds to the dramatic bite of his characterization, virile in attack. Catherine Pierard as the Female Chorus has a more sensuous voice, making it a more involved commentary. Quite apart from its unique authority, Britten's Decca set (also at full price) comes with a valuable fill-up in *Phaedra*, the work he wrote for Janet Baker; but the Chandos rival gives an equally strong, in some ways more dramatic view of a masterly opera.

The Turn of the Screw.

(M) (***) Decca mono 425 672-2 (2). Pears, Vyvyan, Hemmings, Dyer, Cross, Mandikian, E. Op. Group O, composer.

**(*) Ph. (IMS) (ADD) 446 325-2 (2). Donath, Tear, Harper, June, Watson, Ginn, ROHCG O (members), C. Davis.

Though the recording is in mono only, the very dryness and the sharpness of focus give an extra intensity to the composer's own incomparable reading of his most compressed opera. Peter Pears as Peter Quint is matched superbly by Jennifer Vyvyan as the Governess and by Joan Cross as the housekeeper, Mrs Grose. It is also fascinating to hear David Hemmings as a boy treble, already a confident actor. Excellent CD transfer.

Sir Colin Davis's 1981 Covent Garden recording has the benefit of spacious and atmospheric sound, and his ability to relax, to vary the expression, brings many dividends. There is no weak link in the singing cast, with Robert Tear underlining the devilish side of Peter Quint's character, more forcefully sinister than was Peter Pears, but at times too melodramatic. Helen Donath sings feelingly as the Governess, making her a neurotic character; but she hardly erases memories of Jennifer Vyvyan. The treble, Michael Ginn, as Miles, is excellent, and Heather Harper as Miss Jessel is a warmly persuasive ghost. The playing of the Covent Garden orchestra is superb, to bring out the formidable compassion of the piece, and the transfer to CD is first class.

Collection

'The world of Britten': (i–ii) *Simple Symphony*; (iii; ii) *Young Person's Guide to the Orchestra*; (iv–v) *Folksong arrangements: Early one morning; The plough boy*; (vi) *Hymn to the Virgin*; (iv; vii; iii; ii) *Serenade for Tenor, Horn & Strings: Nocturne*. Excerpts from: *Ceremony of Carols; Noye's Fludde; Spring Symphony; Billy Budd; Peter Grimes*.

(M) *** (ADD) Decca 436 990-2. (i) ECO; (ii) cond. composer; (iii) LSO; (iv) Pears; (v) composer (piano); (vi) St John's College Ch., Guest; (vii) Tuckwell; & various artists.

The Britten sampler is well worth having for the composer's own vibrant account of the *Variations on a Theme of Purcell* and the *Simple Symphony*, where the *Playful Pizzicato* emerges with wonderful rhythmic spring and resonance (in the warm Maltings acoustics). The Pears contributions are very enjoyable too, notably the haunting *Nocturne* from the *Serenade*, with Barry Tuckwell in splendid form. Excellent sound throughout, although the tuttis in the *Young Person's Guide to the Orchestra* could with advantage have had a more expansive sonority.

BROSSARD, Sébastien de (1655–1730)

Elevations et motets (for 1, 2, or 3 voices): Festis laeta sonent; O Domine quia refugium; Oratorio seu Dialogus poenitentis animae cum Deo; Psallite superi; Qui non diliget te; Salve Rex Christe; Templa nunc fumet.

(B) **(*) Opus 111 OPS 10-002. Rime, Fouchécourt, Honeyman, Delétré, Parlement de Musique, Gester.

Sébastien de Brossard came from Normandy to take a position as Chapel Master at Strasbourg Cathedral. These motets are mostly dialogue cantatas. *O Domine quia refugium* is a fine example, although the expressive and touching *Qui non diliget te* (for which the composer wrote the text) is a solo work, and very beautifully sung by Noémi Rime. *The dialogue of the repentant soul with God* is shared by soprano and tenor: it is not especially dramatic, but the pace quickens as forgiveness is given. The final work, *Festis laeta sonent cantibus organa* (*May the organ ring out with solemn songs*), is very well sung by the tenor, Jean-Paul Fouchécourt; but Brossard's weakness lies in the lack of a more robust spirit to many of these interchanges – surprising from a musician who was an advocate of the introduction of Italian styles into French music. Excellent recording and full texts.

BRUCH, Max (1838–1920)

Adagio on Celtic Themes, Op. 56; Ave Maria, Op. 61; Canzone, Op. 55; Kol Nidrei, Op. 55.

*** RCA RD 60757. Harnoy, LPO, Mackerras – BLOCH: *Schelomo, etc.* ***

Ofra Harnoy has the full measure of Bruch's sombre, Hebraic lyricism in the best-known piece here, *Kol Nidrei*, and she receives warm support from Mackerras. The rest of the programme creates a lighter mood, with the engaging *Adagio on Celtic Themes* recalling the *Scottish Fantasia*. An excellent recording, made in Watford Town Hall.

Double Concerto in E min., for Clarinet, Viola & Orchestra, Op. 88.

(B) *** Hyp. Dyad CDD 22017 (2). King, Imai, LSO, Francis (with Concert – see below ***).

Bruch's *Double Concerto* is a delightful work, with genuinely memorable inspiration in its first two lyrical movements and with a roistering finale making a fine contrast. Clarinet and viola are blended beautifully, with melting phrasing from Thea King. The recording is excellent. This is part of an excellent two-disc set, including other attractive concertante works by Mendelssohn, Crusell, Spohr and other less familiar names.

(i) *Double Concerto in E min. for Clarinet, Viola & Orchestra; Romance for Violin & Orchestra*; (ii) *8 Pieces for Clarinet, Viola & Piano.*

(N) (BB) *** Warner Apex 8593 89229-2. Meyer, Caussé; (i) Lyon Op. O, Nagano; (ii) Duchable.

The performance of the *Double Concerto* from Paul Meyer and Gérard Caussé is affectionately mellow, yet not missing the lilt of the lively finale. Caussé's timbre is so warm and full that here the balance between wind and stringed soloists is more equal than on Hyperion. Caussé then goes on to give a richly romantic account of the *Romance*, another work with an endearing melodic flow. The *Eight Pieces* are much rarer, another late work (from 1910). They are full of charm, their romanticism pastel-shaded, but they are by no means insubstantial (*No. 3* extends to nearly eight minutes). These highly sympathetic performances are beautifully recorded, and this Apex reissue makes a fine bargain.

Double Piano Concerto in A flat min., Op. 88a.

*** Chan. 9711. Güher and Süther Pekinel, Philh. O, Marriner – MENDELSSOHN: *Double Piano Concerto in E;* MOZART: *Double Piano Concerto in E flat, K.365.* ***

**(*) Ph. 432 095-2. Katia & Marielle Labèque, Philh. O, Bychkov – MENDELSSOHN: *Double Concerto.* **(*)

The Max Bruch *Double Concerto* is well worth hearing in a performance as strong, sympathetic and well recorded as the one on Chandos. With some attractive themes it makes a welcome rarity, whatever its limitations.

Bychkov is heavy-handed at the start, but the contrapuntal writing for the pianos that follows is agreeable in a Reger-like way. The Labèques play with bravura and panache and are given good solid support. The recording is full and resonant but lacks transparency, and the effect is surely heavier than need be.

Violin Concertos Nos. 1 in G min.; 2 in D min., Op. 44; 3 in D min., Op. 58; Serenade for Violin & Orchestra, Op 75; Scottish Fantasy, Op. 46.

(B) *** Ph. (ADD) Duo 462 167-2 (2). Accardo, Leipzig GO, Masur.

This Philips Duo gathers together Bruch's three *Violin Concertos*, plus two other major concertante works. Although no other piece quite matches the famous *G minor Concerto* in inventive concentration, the delightful *Scottish Fantasia*, with its profusion of good tunes, comes near to doing so, and the first movement of the *Second Concerto* has two soaringly lyrical themes. The *Third Concerto* brings another striking lyrical idea in the first movement and has an endearing *Adagio* and a jolly finale. The engagingly insubstantial *Serenade* was originally intended to be a fourth violin concerto. Throughout the set Accardo's playing is so persuasive in its restrained passion that even the less inspired moments bring pleasure. With Accardo balanced rather close, the orchestral recording is full and spacious.

Violin Concerto No. 1 in G min., Op. 26.

(N) (M) *** Sony SMK 89715. Lin, Chicago SO, Slatkin – MENDELSSOHN: *Concerto;* VIEUXTEMPS: *Concerto No. 5.* ***

*** EMI CDC7 54072-2. Chung, LPO, Tennstedt – BEETHOVEN: *Concerto.* ***

*** ASV CDDCA 680. Wei, Philh. O, Bakels – SAINT-SAENS: *Concerto No. 3.* ***

(M) *** EMI (ADD) CDM5 66906-2 [566958]. Menuhin, Philh. O, Susskind – MENDELSSOHN: *Concerto.* ***

(B) *** [EMI Red Line CDR5 69863]. Perlman, LSO, Previn – MENDELSSOHN: *Violin Concerto.* ***

(M) *** DG 449 091-2. Mintz, Chicago SO, Abbado – DVORAK: *Concerto.* ***

(N) (M) *** DG 463 641-2. Mutter, BPO, Karajan – MENDELSSOHN: *Violin Concerto.* ***

(**(*)) Testament mono SBT 1083. Haendel, Philh. O, Kubelik – BEETHOVEN: *Violin Concerto.* (**(*))

*** Chan. 8974. Udagawa, LSO, Mackerras – BRAHMS: *Concerto.* ***

(BB) *** EMI CES5 68524-2 (2). Menuhin, LSO, Boult – MENDELSSOHN: *Violin Concerto, etc.* ***

*** EMI CDC7 49663-2. Kennedy, ECO, Tate – MENDELSSOHN: *Concerto;* SCHUBERT: *Rondo.* ***

(M) **(*) Sony SMK 66830. Stern, Phd. O, Ormandy – TCHAIKOVSKY: *Méditation, etc.* ***; WIENIAWSKI: *Violin Concerto No. 2.* **(*)

(M) **(*) Sony SBK 48274. Zukerman, LAPO, Mehta – LALO: *Symphonie espagnole;* VIEUXTEMPS: *Concerto No. 5.* **(*)

(N) **(*) EMI CDC5 56906-2. Znaider, LPO, Lawrence Foster – NIELSEN: *Violin Concerto, Op. 33.* **(*)

(N) **(*) Australian Decca Eloquence [ADD] 461 369-2. Ricci, LSO, Gamba – MENDELSSOHN: *Violin Concerto* **(*). SAINT-SAENS: *Havanaise etc.* ***

(N) (M) **(*) DG (ADD) 463 651-2. Morini, Berlin RO, Fricsay – DVORAK: *Violin Concerto* ***; GLAZUNOV: *Violin Concerto* **.

(B) ** EMI Début CDZ5 73501-2. Shapira, ECO, Hazlewood – BLOCH: *Baal Shem* ***; BUNCH: *Fantasy* **; SARASATE: *Zigeunerweisen.* **(*)

(N) (BB) (**) Naxos mono 8.110902. Menuhin, LSO, Landon Ronald – ELGAR: *Violin Concerto.* (***)

Cho-Liang Lin is accompanied most sensitively by Slatkin and the Chicago orchestra, and this reading is totally compelling in its combination of passion and purity, strength and dark, hushed intensity. The recording is excellent.

Compared with her earlier Decca recording, Kyung Wha Chung's expressive rubato in her EMI version is more marked, with her freedom vividly conveying magic such as you find in her live performances, and the finale is again impulsive in its bravura. An exceptionally attractive version.

Xue Wei's approach to the concerto is at once passionately committed and refined in its delicacy of detail. He is accompanied superbly by Kees Bakels, while Wei can equally seduce the listener with a most magical *pianissimo*. The slow movement is ravishing in its poetic flair, and the finale is full of fire.

Menuhin's performance with Susskind, now reissued as one of EMI's 'Great Recordings of the Century', has long held an honoured place in the catalogue. The performance has a fine spontaneity, the work's improvisatory quality very much part of the interpretation, and there is no doubting the poetry Menuhin finds in the slow movement or the sparkle in the finale. The bright, forward sound of the 1960 recording has transferred vividly and naturally to CD.

Perlman gives a glowing, powerful account that is almost too sure of itself. With Previn and the LSO backing him up richly, this is a strong, confident interpretation, forthrightly masculine. The opulent, full recording suits the performance. This is available only in the USA.

Shlomo Mintz's compelling playing makes the listener hang on to every phrase. The vibrato is wide, but his approach is so distinctive and interesting that few listeners will resist. The Chicago Symphony Orchestra plays with great brilliance and enthusiasm, and Abbado's direction is most sympathetic. The vivid recording has transferred splendidly to CD.

In Anne-Sophie Mutter's hands the concerto has an air of chaste sweetness, shedding much of its ripe, sensuous quality, but retaining its romantic feeling. There is a delicacy and tenderness here which is very appealing and, although the tuttis have plenty of fire, Karajan sensuously scales down his accompaniment in the lyrical passages to match his soloist. The digital recording provides a natural balance and a vivid orchestral texture.

Ida Haendel's magnificent (1948) reading of the Bruch, rather like her accounts of the Brahms and Tchaikovsky, reissued earlier by Testament, combines power and great warmth, with the first movement strong and purposeful, the second passionate in its lyricism, and the third brilliant and sparkling. An excellent transfer, but it is a pity this is offered at full price.

Full of temperament, Hideko Udagawa gives a persuasively passionate performance of the Bruch, very well recorded, and, with strong, colourful playing from the orchestra, the hushed opening of the slow movement is caught beautifully.

Menuhin's second stereo recording of the Bruch *Concerto* was made in the early 1970s, and the lovely slow movement is given a performance of great warmth and humanity. Boult accompanies admirably, and the recording is fuller and more modern than the earlier version with Susskind, even if the solo playing is technically less immaculate.

Kennedy's totally unsentimental view may not have quite the individual poetry of the very finest versions, but it is coupled with an outstanding account of the Mendelssohn and the rare Schubert *Rondo*.

Stern's vintage account from 1966 with Ormandy is one of the classic recordings of the work, warm-hearted and passionate, with a very involving account of the slow movement. The finale, too, has wonderful fire and spirit. Ormandy's accompaniment is first class and triumphs over the unrealistic balance, with the violin far too far in front.

Zukerman's reissued Sony triptych shows him at his finest, and it is a pity that the close-up balance brings inevitable reservations. His Bruch is a passionately extrovert performance, tempered by genuine tenderness in the slow movement. The brilliantly lit recording with its larger-than-life effect is overwhelming.

Ricci has an outstanding technique and has a very characteristic tone which, alongside Perlman's rich sound, for example, sounds more febrile. But the performance here has fine intensity and there is a natural warmth which brings out the music's temperament without indulging it. The 1958 recording only hints its age in the tuttis, but is amazingly full and vivid, and this performance – especially with Gamba's full-blooded conducting, remains individual and enjoyable.

Nikolaj Znaider comes from Denmark but is of Russian parentage and made a very strong impression at the 1999 Ysaÿe (or rather Queen of the Belgians) Competition in Brussels, taking the first prize in a very strong field. His Bruch *Concerto No. 1 in G minor* is very fine indeed, well thought out and fervent. He has very good support from Lawrence Foster and the LPO but there is a slight self-awareness that prevents it going to the top of the list.

Erica Morini's account with Fricsay dates from the late 1950s, but still sounds remarkably fresh, and the tender performance of the famous slow movement is quite memorable. However, on LP this version last appeared on DG's bargain label, which is where it belongs. The current reissue is most notable for Martzy's coupled account of the Dvořák *Concerto*.

Wonderfully talented though Ittai Shapira is, this account of the *G minor Concerto* does not sweep all before it. He needs a little more sense of abandon, though Charles Hazlewood's rather steady, almost sedate tempi do not help.

The young Yehudi Menuhin's first recording dates from 1931 (the year before the coupled Elgar concerto). The transfer, made by Mark Obert-Thorn from pre-war RCA Victor pressings, is not very flattering to Menuhin's tone in the outer movements, which is thin and edgy, and the orchestra sounds very rough in the main tutti of the first movement. However, the slow movement shows Menuhin's true eloquence both in his richness of timbre and in his beauty of line.

Violin Concerto No. 1 in G min., Op. 26; Scottish Fantasy, Op. 46.

(M) *** Decca (ADD) 460 976-2. Chung, RPO, Kempe – MENDELSSOHN *Concerto*. ***

(B) *** Decca/Penguin (ADD) 460 620-2. Chung, RPO, Kempe.

(M) *** RCA (ADD) 09026 61745-2. Heifetz, New SO of L., Sargent – VIEUXTEMPS: *Concerto No. 5*. ***

The magic of Kyung Wha Chung, always a spontaneously inspired violinist, comes over beguilingly. However, Decca have upstaged the Penguin Classics issue by reissuing the recordings on their Legends label, with the Mendelssohn *Concerto*. Chung goes straight to the heart of the famous *G minor Concerto*, finding mystery and fantasy as well as more extrovert qualities. Just as strikingly in the *Scottish Fantasia* she transcends the episodic nature of the writing to give the music a genuine depth and concentration, above all in the lovely slow movement. Kempe and the RPO accompany sympathetically, well caught in a glowing recording.

Heifetz plays with supreme assurance, and the slow movement shows this fine artist in masterly form. Heifetz's panache and the subtlety of his bowing and colour bring a wonderful freshness to Bruch's charming Scottish whimsy. Sargent accompanies sympathetically, and though the soloist is balanced much too closely, there is never any doubt that Heifetz can produce a true *pianissimo*.

Violin Concertos Nos. 1; 3 in D min., Op.58.

(N) ** CBC SMCD 5207. Ehnes, Montreal SO, Dutoit.

It is surprising that this generous coupling of the first and third concertos of Bruch is so rare, with no rival currently available. Far more ambitious than the popular *G minor Concerto*, *No. 3* vies in scale with the concertos of Beethoven and Brahms. James Ehnes, brilliant young Canadian virtuoso from Manitoba, is an impressive soloist with an exceptionally pure, sweet tone above the stave – important when so much of the solo writing lies up there. In both works he is both deeply reflective and brilliant, with double-stopping exceptionally clean and incisive. Where the issue falls down, most surprisingly, is in the contribution of Dutoit and the Montreal Symphony Orchestra, dull in sound and square in performance, rather lacking forward momentum, not helped by backward balance,

Violin Concerto No. 2 in D min., Op. 44.

*** Delos DE 3156. Hu, Seattle SO, Schwarz – GOLDMARK: *Violin Concerto.* ***

Violin Concerto No. 2; Scottish Fantasy, Op. 46.

**(*) EMI CDC7 49071-2. Perlman, Israel PO, Mehta.

(i) *Violin Concerto No. 2. Symphony No. 3 in E, Op. 51.*

*** Chan. 9738. (i) Mordkovitch; LSO, Hickox.

It was Bruch's fate never quite to match the exuberant lyricism of his ever-popular *First Violin Concerto*, and it would be idle to pretend that the themes here are as instantly memorable. Yet in such warmly expressive, spaciously conceived readings as these, the coupling of symphony and concerto on Chandos offers a welcome alternative to the general run of Bruch issues that concentrate on one genre or the other. In the *Third Symphony* Hickox takes an affectionate view of the work. Speeds are broad in the first three movements, markedly so in the *Adagio*, with the chorale theme spacious and dedicated, and the surging theme which opens the finale has a hint of English folksong. In the *Second Violin Concerto*, Lydia Mordkovitch gives a raptly intense reading, making the long, slow first movement (in sonata form) into a deeply reflective meditation, punctuated by virtuoso flurries, readily justifying her spacious speeds, and with ripe Chandos recording bringing out the warmth and bite of her bravura playing, often in thorny double-stopping.

Nai-Yan Hu is ideally balanced and well accompanied by Schwarz and the Seattle orchestra. Hu's soaring lyrical lines underline the music's warmth and consistent melodic inspiration. Though Perlman strikes a high profile in his EMI version, the sympathetic warmth of this Hu/Schwarz partnership and the concert-hall fullness of the Delos recording are preferable.

Perlman may be less intimately reflective in both works than he was when he recorded this coupling before with the New Philharmonia, but in the fast movements there are ample compensations in the sharp concentration from first to last.

(i) *Violin Concerto No. 3 in D min., Op. 58. Symphony No. 1 in E flat, Op. 28.*

*** Chan. 9784. (i) Mordkovitch; LSO, Hickox.

The *Third Violin Concerto* is twice as long as either of the first two concertos, laid out spaciously on the lines of Beethoven or Brahms; yet Bruch characteristically allows himself plenty of lyrical lingering, which inspires Lydia

Mordkovitch to playing of rapt intensity down to magical *pianissimos*. The slow movement is the most typical of Bruch, again with Mordkovitch responding warmly to this hushed meditation, before the vigorous *moto perpetuo* finale. The *Symphony No. 1*, written soon after the popular *Violin Concerto in G minor*, is also based on striking material, with the four movements including a Mendelssohnian *Presto* (prompting dazzling playing from the LSO) and a ripely lyrical slow movement. As in the earlier disc, Hickox is a warmly expressive but never self-indulgent interpreter, and the Chandos recording is full and atmospheric.

(i) *Double Concerto for Violin & Viola, Op. 88; Kol Nidrei, Op. 47; Romance for Viola & Orchestra, Op. 85.*

*** RCA 09026 63292-2. Bashmet, LSO, Järvi; (i) with Tretyakov – WALTON: *Viola Concerto.* ***

Bruch's fund of melodic invention, usually a youthful gift, stayed with him well into his seventies, as the *Double Concerto* and the *Romance* winningly demonstrate. The latter work for viola and orchestra of 1912 harks straight back to the slow movement of the *G minor Violin Concerto*. It is a radiant piece and draws a heartfelt performance from Bashmet, as does the well-known *Kol Nidrei*, made the more poignant with viola taking the place of cello. The *Double Concerto* brings extra sensuousness, thanks also to the puretoned playing of Viktor Tretyakov, a perfect foil for the resonant Bashmet.

Kol Nidrei, Op. 47.

*** EMI CDC5 56126-2. Chang, LSO, Rostropovich – FAURE: *Elégie* ***; SAINT-SAENS: *Cello Concerto No. 1* ***; TCHAIKOVSKY: *Rococo Variations.* *** ●

*** DG 427 323-2. Haimovitz, Chicago SO, Levine (with LALO: *Concerto*; SAINT-SAENS: *Concerto No. 1* ***).

(M) *** RCA (ADD) 74321 84112-2 (2). Lloyd Webber, Nat. PO, Gerhardt – DELIUS: *Concerto; Serenade*; HOLST: *Invocation*; LALO: *Concerto*; RODRIGO: *Concierto como un divertimento*; VAUGHAN WILLIAMS: *Fantasia on Sussex Folk Tunes* *** (with recital *Celebration*: FAURE: *Elégiê*; VILLA-LOBOS: *Bachianas brasileiras No. 5*; POPPER: *Gavotte*; SAINT-SAENS: *Samson et Dalila: Softly awakes my heart*; FALLA: *El amor brujo: Ritual Fire Dance*; BACH: *Arioso*; BRIDGE: *Scherzetto*; CANTELOUBE: *Baïlèro* ***).

(M) *** DG (ADD) 457 761-2. Fournier, LOP, Martinon – BLOCH: *Schelomo*; LALO: *Cello Concerto*; SAINT-SAENS: *Cello Concerto No. 1.* ***

The phenomenally gifted 13-year-old Korean-born cellist, Han-Na Chang, catches the intense atmosphere of Bruch's Hebrew melody with a natural sensitivity, spontaneous in her dynamic contrasts; and indeed the extraordinary poise and assurance of this playing, matched by her ability to touch the listener, reminds one of the young Yehudi Menuhin. Her mentor accompanies her with great sympathy and the Abbey Road recording is beautifully balanced.

Matt Haimovitz, born in Israel, has a natural feeling for the piece, and his performance, balancing restraint with expressive intensity, is serenely moving. The Lalo concerto is equally distinguished.

The RCA Double celebrates Julian Lloyd Webber's fiftieth birthday. His performance of *Kol Nidrei* has both ardour and an underlying delicacy. Gerhardt accompanies persuasively and both artists capture the Hebrew feeling of the melodic line. The recording is warmly resonant but acceptably so, although it is a bit over-lush for some of the encores. The highlights are the Popper, Villa-Lobos and the Bridge *Scherzetto*, and the Falla *Ritual Fire Dance* is a surprise success, played with plenty of bite.

If Fournier's performance lacks the last degree of romantic urgency, it makes up for it in the beauty and style of the solo playing, and he is well supported by Martinon's Lamoureux Orchestra.

Scottish Fantasy (for violin & orchestra), *Op. 46*.

(B) *** EMI CD-EMX 2277. Little, Royal SNO, Handley –
   LALO: *Symphonie espagnole.* ***
(N) (BB) (***) Naxos mono 8.110940. Heifetz, LPO, Barbirolli
   – BRAHMS: *Double Concerto;* GLAZUNOV: *Violin Concerto.*

It is an excellent idea to couple Bruch's evocation of Scotland with Lalo's of Spain, both works in unconventional, five-movement, concertante form. Tasmin Little takes a ripe, robust and passionate view of both works, projecting them strongly, as she would in the concert hall. In this she is greatly helped by the fine, polished playing of the Scottish orchestra under Vernon Handley, a most sympathetic partner. The recording is superb, with brass in particular vividly caught. Unlike Meyers on RCA, Little plays the Guerriero finale absolutely complete. An outstanding bargain on the Eminence label.

Bruch's *Scottish Fantasy* was always a favourite work with Heifetz, and although his pioneering 1947 version cannot quite match his stereo remake with Sargent and the LSO in thoughtful intensity, the passion and brilliance of the playing are most compelling, with the songful *Adagio* section even more moving in its simpler, more flowing manner, hushed and dedicated. Generously coupled with the powerful Brahms performance and the exuberant account of the Glazunov, another first recording. Good Naxos transfers if with audible surface hiss and not quite as sophisticated as the EMI remastering.

Symphonies Nos. 1–3; (i) Adagio appassionato, *Op. 57; Konzertstück, Op. 84; In memoriam, Op. 65; Romanze, Op. 42 (all for violin and orchestra).*

(B) *** Ph. (ADD) Duo 462 164-2 (2). (i) Accardo; Leipzig GO,
   Kurt Masur.

This collected edition contains much attractive music, beautifully played and recorded, guaranteed to delight anyone wanting undemanding symphonies as alternatives to those of Brahms and Schumann. Masur's performances with the Leipzig Gewandhaus Orchestra are characteristically warm and refined, with smooth recording to match, but sparkle is largely missing. Room has also been found for Accardo's *Konzertstück*, one of Bruch's last works. *In memoriam* is finer still, and the *Adagio appassionato* and *Romanze* are strongly characterized pieces. Accardo's advocacy is very persuasive here.

Symphonies Nos. 1 in E flat, *Op. 28; 2 in F min., Op. 36; 3 in E, Op. 51.*

**(*) EMI CDS5 550 046-2 (3). Gürzenich O or Cologne PO,
   James Conlon.

In James Conlon's convincing performances, both orchestras (it is not clear which plays which work) emphasize the music's Brahmsian and Schumannesque derivations. A good case is made for the *Third Symphony* here, with the romantic opening richly done, the slow-movement variations warmly effective, and the Scherzo (which the composer regarded as the finest movement in each of these works) is made to sound original in its scoring. Only the finale lets the piece down. The orchestral playing is committed throughout, even if at times greater drive is needed from the conductor. There is no fill-up, and the second CD plays for only 36 minutes.

String Quintet in A min., *Op. posth.*

*** Naim CD 010. Augmented Allegri Qt – BRAHMS: *String Quintet No. 2.* ***

Bruch's *A minor Quintet* was one of two he wrote for sheer joy at the age of 80. It is an unashamed throwback in idiom to Beethoven and Brahms, but the freshness of ideas and argument is most winning. Like the Brahms *G major Quintet*, with which it is ideally coupled, it is very well performed and vividly recorded.

VOCAL MUSIC

Moses (oratorio; complete).

*** Orfeo C 438 982 H. Volle, Gambill, Whitehouse, Bamberg
   Ch. & SO, Flor.

Bruch's oratorio celebrating the story of Moses – as the composer said, from where Handel's *Israel in Egypt* leaves off – regularly recalls Mendelssohn's *Elijah*. The fresh, bright opening chorus leads on to a series of strong and colourful choruses. The story is then filled in with solos from the three characters – Moses a baritone, Aaron a tenor and The Angel of the Lord a soprano. The result may not be as vividly dramatic as *Elijah*, but in a warm and purposeful performance under a conductor with strong Mendelssohnian sympathies it makes its mark, thanks also to striking melodic material. Bright, clear, well-balanced sound.

Odysseus (Scenes from the Odyssey), *Op. 41.*

**(*) Koch Schwann 3-6557-2 (2). Kneebone, Maultsby,
   Nylund, Lange, Mann, Gärtner, Holzer, NDR R. Ch.,
   Hanover R. PO, Botstein.

Written in 1872, when the composer was in his mid-30s, *Odysseus* is far less adventurous than the concertos that have remained in the repertory. It is all easy on the ear but there is a blandness not only in the musical invention but also in the treatment of the text, which is static and undramatic. Even the joyful concluding chorus seems to imitate *Elijah*. Nevertheless, with a cast led by two American singers, Jeffrey Kneebone and Nancy Maultsby, it is an amiable piece, well presented and freshly recorded.

BRUCKNER, Anton (1824–96)

Symphonies Nos. 00; 0; 1–9. Overture in G min.; String Quintet: Adagio.

(N) (BB) *** Arte Nova 74321 85290-2 (12). Saarbrücken RSO, Skrowaczewski.

Symphonies Nos. 0; 1–9.

(B) **(*) Ph. (ADD) 442 040-2 (9). Concg. O, Haitink.
(B) **(*) Decca Dig./ADD 448 910-2 (10). Chicago SO, Solti.

Symphonies Nos. 1–9.

(M) *** DG (ADD) 429 648-2 (9). BPO, Karajan.
(N) (b) *** EMI (ADD) CZS5 73905-2 (9). Dresden State O, Jochum.
(B) *** DG (ADD) 429 079-2 (9). BPO or Bav. RSO, Jochum.

Recorded between 1991 and 2001, Skrowaczewski's cycle of all eleven symphonies offers dedicated, intense readings which bring out the ruggedness of Bruckner as well as the beauty. Warmly expressive and refined as the playing is, the approach is direct, with steady but not inflexible speeds the rule. The recording is open and well balanced, allowing even heavy textures to be clarified. Exceptionally, the set includes the two early, unnumbered symphonies, both fine, attractive works, as well as the *Overture* and *Adagio*. Where Tintner in his rival bargain cycle for Naxos offers Bruckner's first thoughts on each symphony, Skrowaczewski prefers the regular Haas edition, as revised.

The reappearance of Karajan's magnificent cycle, long a yardstick for others – and at mid-price – is warmly welcomed. We have sung the praises of these recordings loud and long, and in their new format they are outstanding value.

Jochum's DG cycle was recorded between 1958 and 1967. No apology need be made for the performances or the quality of the recorded sound, which wears its years lightly. Jochum brought a unique sense of mystery and atmosphere to Bruckner that more than compensates for the occasional freedom he permitted himself. He communicates a lofty inspiration to his players, and many of these readings can more than hold their own with later rivals.

Eugen Jochum's second Bruckner cycle was recorded in Dresden with the magnificent Staatskapelle between 1975 and 1980 in the last days of analogue. His approach here differs little from his earlier DG set: he always favoured the Nowak editions, but the Dresden set has the richer, more opulent sound. Jochum had wisdom and nobility as well as a sense of vision, and his lifelong feeling for Bruckner's music and grasp of its architecture shine through in every bar.

Haitink's grasp of the architecture is strong and his feeling for beauty of detail refined, though he only hints at the spiritual dimension in these works. Preferring the Haas editions, he secures consistently fine playing from the Concertgebouw Orchestra. The CD transfers bring much more vivid sound than on LP, yet the overall balance is always convincing.

Solti recorded the whole cycle between 1979 (No. 6) and 1995 (No. 5). The two early symphonies are very impressive, but the *Third* is the one failure, relatively crude and coarse.

Otherwise, the series culminates in an inspired account of the *Eighth* and the *Ninth*, similarly spacious, with the music given full time to breathe. Other performances may be more deeply meditative, but the power of Solti and the brilliance of the playing and the digital recording are formidable.

Symphony No. 00 in F min. (Study Symphony); String Quintet: Adagio (arr. for strings).

*** Ondine ODE 920-2. German SO, Berlin, Ashkenazy.

Symphony No. 00 in F min. (Study Symphony); Symphony No. 4: Volkfest Finale (1878).

(BB) *** Naxos 8.554432. RSNO, Tintner.

It is good that Tintner in his superb Bruckner cycle for Naxos here fills in what might easily have been two gaps. The composer was 39 when he completed this *F minor Symphony*, but the progressions and effects point forward to what we now recognize as fully Brucknerian, with sharp contrasts and sudden changes of direction in the argument. With excellent playing and recording – as in the rest of the series – Tintner could not be more persuasive; as a welcome bonus he adds the very rare second version of the finale of the *Fourth Symphony*, which Bruckner entitled *Volkfest*, 'Festival of the People'. Strikingly different, particularly at the start, from the 1880 version of that movement generally performed, it is well worth hearing in a fine performance like this, even if it hardly displaces the usual version.

Ashkenazy conducts his Berlin orchestra in a strong and purposeful reading. His speeds are consistently fast, his manner direct but still expressive, bringing out the inner intensity of the fine slow movement. The lovely *Adagio* of the *String Quintet* in string orchestra format brings just as dedicated a performance, an excellent bonus. Full, warm sound. However, the Naxos set has a considerable price advantage.

Symphonies Nos. 0 in D min. (Die Nullte); 8 in C min. (1887 Nowak edition).

(BB) *** Naxos 8.554215/6. Nat. SO of Ireland, Tintner.

There are few Bruckner interpreters more persuasive than Georg Tintner. In a moving note he passionately argues the case for Bruckner's original (1887) version of No. 8, fresh and spontaneous. Most conductors opt for the 1889–90 revision, edited by either Haas or Nowak. The differences are major and there is much that will take you completely by surprise. The result is an intense, keenly concentrated reading, with total dedication in the playing, which rises to supreme heights in the long *Adagio* slow movement, where the refined *pianissimo* playing of the Irish orchestra is magically caught by the Naxos engineers. Even for those with rival versions, this makes a very necessary recommendation, particularly when the two-disc package brings so generous and revealing a coupling as the *D minor Symphony (Die Nullte)* in a very good performance. Tintner powerfully brings out the Brucknerian qualities in embryo, and again he is served very well by the Irish orchestra, even if the weight of big tuttis is less than in some others of this series.

Symphony No. 1 in C min.

(BB) *** Arte Nova 74321 59226-2. Saarbrücken RSO, Skrowaczewski.

Symphony No. 1 in C min.; (i) Helgoland.

*(*) Teldec 0630 16646-2. BPO, Barenboim, (i) with male
voices of Berlin R. Ch. and Ernst-Senff Ch.

Skrowaczewski draws dedicated, tautly sprung playing from
the Saarbrucken orchestra in what remains a problematic
work. At speeds on the fast side, this is a fresh and urgent
reading which yet brings out the hushed intensity of the
spacious second-movement *Adagio*. Beautifully recorded in
a helpful acoustic, it is a match for almost any version at
whatever price.

Barenboim's Teldec version has a welcome fill-up in the
symphonic chorus, *Helgoland*, but that is one of its few advan-
tanges. This is a warm, weighty reading, at times heavy-
handed, which does not reveal the Berlin Philharmonic at its
polished best. The recording is rather cloudy in tuttis.

*Symphonies Nos. 1 in C min. (1866 version, revised
Carragan); 3 in D min.: Adagio (1876).*

(BB) *** Naxos 8.554430. RSNO, Tintner.

As with other symphonies in his mould-breaking Bruckner
series for Naxos, Georg Tintner opts for the earliest version
of the *Symphony No. 1*. The principal differences here are in
the finale, which brings angular writing and orchestration
more radical than in the revisions. Tintner in his dedicated
performance, with refined playing from the Scottish
orchestra, amply justifies his choice, powerfully bringing out
the bald originality of the writing. The generous makeweight
also offers a rare text, a version of the slow movement of the
Symphony No. 3 unearthed by the Bruckner editor, Leopold
Nowak, which was composed in 1876, between the original
one of 1873 and the shortened one of 1877. Again the intensity
and refinement of the performance sustain the expansiveness compellingly. Clear, atmospheric sound, at once
transparent and weighty in climaxes.

Symphony No. 2 in C min. (original, 1872 score).

(BB) *** Naxos 8.554006. Nat. SO of Ireland, Tintner.

In his Bruckner series for Naxos, Georg Tintner here firmly
favours the composer's first thoughts, arguing that later
revisions are not improvements. He therefore opts for the
edition of the original (1872) score, presenting the work at
its most expansive and with the middle two movements in
reverse order from usual. The Scherzo has an extra repeat,
but more important is the expansion of both the slow
movement and the finale, here presented in concentrated
performances that feel not a moment too long. The coda of
the *Andante* brings a horn solo at the very end (substituted
by Herbeck in 1876), challenging to the player, which is
more strikingly beautiful than the clarinet solo with which
Bruckner replaced it. Excellent, refined playing from the
Irish orchestra and full, rich sound, with the brass gloriously
caught.

Symphony No. 2 in C min.

*** Decca (IMS) 436 154-2. Concg. O, Chailly.
*(*) Teldec 3984-21485-2. BPO, Barenboim.

Chailly uses the complete, Haas edition. It is a beautifully
simple reading, with the slow-movement climax nobly

graduated, a strong Scherzo without repeats (the Trio has a
tuneful charm) and a finale that is not pressed forward
ruthlessly but generates a positive and exciting closing section. The Decca recording is spacious and luminous.

Barenboim's latest version of the *Second*, recorded at concerts in the Philharmonie in 1997, comes as something of a
disappointment. He opts for the Nowak version of Bruckner's
score and the playing is curiously routine and uninspired. The
recording, too, is nothing to write home about.

Symphony No. 3 in D min. (original, 1873 version).

(BB) *** Naxos 8.553454. RSNO, Tintner.

Symphony No. 3 in D min. (1877 version).

*** Ph. 422 411-2. VPO, Haitink.

Symphony No. 3 in D min. (1877 version with 1876 Adagio).

*** Hyp. CDA 67200. BBC Scottish SO, Vänskä.

Symphony No. 3 in D min. (1889 version).

(BB) *** Arte Nova 74321 651412-2. Saarbrücken RSO,
Skrowaczewski.

With characteristic boldness, Georg Tintner opts here to
record the very rare first version, far more expansive than
the final revised version normally heard. The score was lost
for almost a century and was finally published only in 1977.
Tintner masterfully holds the vast structure together, even
though his speeds in the three expanded movements are
daringly slow. The first movement alone lasts over half
an hour, yet the concentration of the performance, with
dynamic contrasts heightened, never falters for a moment,
with playing from the Scottish orchestra both powerful and
refined. The slow movement too is rapt and dedicated, with
pianissimos of breathtaking delicacy. The Scherzo is then fast
and fierce, before the spacious account of the finale. Tintner
in every way justifies his daring and revelatory choice of text.

Even among Bruckner's symphonies the text of the *Symphony No. 3* remains bafflingly problematic, with a wider
range of different versions than any. The key point about
Vänskä's version, given a brilliant and refined performance
by the BBC Scottish Symphony, is that he uses a long-buried
text for the *Adagio* slow movement. It was only discovered
when the orchestral parts for the 1877 performance of the
revision completed that year were found to have extensive
corrections and pastings-over. Once these were removed,
another complete version of the *Adagio* was revealed, more
expansive, with more quotations from Wagner included.
The notes clarify these points, making an excellent case
for preferring this text. Vänskä effectively heightens the
Wagnerian qualities of the score, while drawing a ripe Brucknerian sound from his players, helped by full, atmospheric
recording.

Haitink gives us the 1877 version, favoured by many
Bruckner scholars. Questions of edition apart, this is a performance of great breadth and majesty, and Philips give it a
recording to match. The playing of the Vienna Philharmonic
is glorious throughout, and even collectors who have
alternative versions should acquire this magnificent issue.

Skrowaczewski offers a super-budget version of the *Third*
which in both performance and recording rivals more expensive versions. Unlike Tintner he opts for the usual text,

following Bruckner's final reworking in his third version of the work. As in Skrowaczewski's other Bruckner recordings for Arte Nova, the playing of the Saarbrücken orchestra is strong and intense, with opulent sound to match. So the slow movement is sweet and warm in its lyrical flow, and the finale glows with resplendent brass.

Symphonies Nos. 3–4 (Romantic) (original versions: 1873/4).

(N) (B) **(*) Teldec/Ultima 8573 87801-2 (2). Frankfurt RSO, Inbal.

There are three versions of both the *Third* and *Fourth* symphonies. The 1873 version of No. 3 is by far the longest (the first movement alone lasts 24 minutes). Now that Tintner has chosen it for his Naxos cycle, this pioneering version by Inbal is less important. But the Ultima reissue includes also the *Fourth*, and no one has recorded the 1874 original before. The Scherzo here is a completely different and very fiery movement, and the opening of the finale is also totally different. Inbal's performances are good, paying scrupulous attention to dynamic refinements, while the playing of the Frankfurt Radio Orchestra shows a keen feeling for atmosphere. The recording is fully acceptable, though the climaxes in No. 4 almost (but not quite) reach congestion. A fascinating reissue, the more attractive with the two discs offered for the price of one.

Symphonies Nos. 3 in D min.; 4 in E flat (Romantic) (Nowak editions).

(B) *** Double Decca (ADD) 448 098-2 (2). VPO, Boehm.

There are many who admire Boehm's Bruckner, and he certainly controls the lyrical flow of these two symphonies convincingly, helped by first-rate playing from the VPO. Both recordings offer vintage Decca sound from 1970 and 1973 respectively; each has the advantage of the spacious acoustics of the Sofiensaal, and the balance provides splendid detail and a firm sonority. Boehm's sobriety was also his strength; in every bar he gives the impression that he knows exactly where he is going and, choosing the Nowak edition, he shapes each structure compellingly.

Symphonies Nos. 3–4 (ed. Nowak); 5 (ed. Haas).

(N) *(**) 459 663-2 (4) (with rehearsal sequence). Stuttgart SW RSO, Celibidache (with MOZART: *Symphony No. 35 (Haffner)* ***).

There is no question that these live recordings show the grip and control which Celibidache exerts over his orchestra; moreover, the level of tension is high. The orchestral playing too is superb in its tonal warmth and body, and refinement of detail, but the conductor's constant lingering continually distorts the music's flow and structure. Even the *Scherzi* bring exaggerated contrasts when the *Trios* arrive. Nevertheless, the finale of the *Third Symphony* generates considerable excitement. The *Fourth* opens with characteristically moulded phrasing from the horn and strings, where absolute simplicity is paramount. The timings of the outer movements are 19 and 24 minutes respectively; indeed, for all the beauty of the playing the finale seems endless. The overall playing time for *No. 5* is 83 minutes against Sinopolis's 77,

but it seems longer. What is so surprising is that the coupled Mozart performance cannot be faulted – it is stylish, beautifully played and attractively paced. The recordings are of high quality, but these (expensive) records can only be given a very guarded recommendation to those interested in the art of a remarkable if extraordinarily self-aware conductor.

Symphonies Nos. 3–9; (i) Mass No. 3 in F min.; (ii) Te Deum.

** EMI CDC5 56688-2. (i) M. Price, Soffel, Straka, Hölle; (i–ii) Munich Philharmonic Ch.; (ii) Price, Borchers; Ahnsjö, Helm, Munich Bach Ch.; Munich PO, Celibidache.

Some good judges have been persuaded by Celibidache's sense of texture and his obvious dedication, but for others the eccentricities place an insurmountable obstacle between the composer and the listener. He manages to linger for more than 100 minutes over the *Eighth Symphony* as opposed to Jochum's or Karajan's 83, and he takes 20 minutes longer than Furtwängler. Likewise his *Ninth* lasts 68 minutes, whereas most interpreters take under the hour. These performances are difficult to grade: for Celibidache devotees they will rate three stars no doubt, since both the orchestral response and the recorded sound are not to be faulted; others, exasperated by his funereal tempi, may not wish to accord them any at all!

Symphonies Nos. 3 in D min.; 7 in E.

(B) *** EMI double forte (ADD) CZS5 68652-2 (2). Dresden State O, Jochum.

Eugen Jochum gives these massive structures an easy, warm, unforced concentration which brings out their lyricism as well as their architectural grandeur. He uses the Nowak edition; with his understanding of Bruckner developing towards a more direct and monumental approach, the authority is never in doubt, and this is matched by splendid playing from the Dresden orchestra.

Symphony No. 4 in E flat (Romantic).

*** RCA 09026 68839-2. Berlin PO, Wand.
(M) *** DG 449 718-2. BPO, Jochum (with SIBELIUS: *Night Ride and Sunrise, Op. 55* with Bav. RSO (***)).
(M) *** DG (ADD) 439 522-2. BPO, Karajan.
(BB) *** Naxos 8.554128. RSNO, Tintner.
(B) *** Ph. (ADD) 442 044-2. Concg. O, Haitink.
(M) *** Decca (ADD) Legends 466 374-2. VPO, Boehm.
(BB) *** Arte Nova 74321 72101-2. Saarbrücken RSO, Skrowaczewski.
(M) **(*) Sony (ADD) SMK 64481. Columbia SO, Walter.
(B) **(*) [EMI Red Line CDR5 69795]. BPO, Muti.
(M) **(*) EMI CDM5 66094-2. BPO, Karajan.
** Teldec 0630 17126-2. Concg. O, Harnoncourt.
(N) (M) (**) Sup. mono SU 3467–2 001. Czech PO, Konwitschny.

Symphony No. 4 in E flat; Overture in G min.

(***) Testament mono/stereo SBT 1050. Philh. O, Von Matačič.

Günther Wand's Berlin version of the *Fourth Symphony* crowns his achievement as one of our greatest Bruckner conductors. The recording derives from a concert at the Philharmonie in Berlin and conveys a sense of occasion so often missing in the studio. Wand knows what this music is about and has the command of its architecture and space. One feels immediately comfortable in his hands, dedicated and purposeful, with consistently warm textures from the Berlin Philharmonic. Speeds are perfectly judged; rubato is more extreme than in most studio readings, but the massive structure is lucidly held together in total concentration. Keenly dramatic, capped by towering climaxes, it offers full, rich sound, if with *pianissimos* not quite as hushed as they might be. This is much more successful than Wand's earlier recordings with the NDR Cologne Orchestra and must rank alongside the finest now in the catalogue; for collectors wanting a premium-priced version, this will probably be first choice.

Jochum's way with Bruckner is unique. So gentle is his hand that the opening of each movement or even the beginning of each theme emerges into the consciousness rather than starting normally. The purist may object that, in order to do this, the conductor reduces the speed far below what is marked, but Jochum is for the listener who wants above all to love Bruckner. The recording has been enhanced in this reissue in DG's 'Originals' series, and a fascinating mono recording of Sibelius's *Night Ride and Sunrise* has been added. Jochum was not thought of as a Sibelian, but this performance is most impressive.

Karajan's opening (on his DG version) has more beauty and a greater feeling of mystery than almost anyone else on CD. As in his earlier, EMI record, Karajan brings a keen sense of forward movement to this music as well as showing a firm grip on its architecture. His slow movement is magnificent. The current remastering of the 1975 analogue recording, made in the Philharmonie, is very impressive. The sound may lack the transparency and detail of the very finest of his records, but it is full and firmly focused.

There are not many versions as fine as Georg Tintner's on Naxos, at whatever price. With extreme *pianissimos* magically caught, full of mystery, this is an exceptionally spacious reading, deeply reflective and poetic, which brings out the Schubertian qualities in Bruckner, sweet and songful as well as dramatic. The playing of the Scottish National Orchestra is as refined as the recording, with subtly terraced dynamics beautifully clear.

Haitink's performance is noble and unmannered; the opening horn solo is arresting and the orchestral playing is eloquent. The new CD transfer is excellent, and this is good value and a primary bargain choice, although Jochum on DG is worth the extra cost.

Boehm's fine 1973 version with the VPO, here reissued on Decca's Legends label is discussed above in its coupling with No. 3.

Skrowaczewski's reading of Bruckner's most popular symphony is characteristically strong and refined, with extreme dynamic contrasts heightened by the excellent recording, so that the crescendo at the start of the finale is exceptionally powerful. Only in the third-movement Scherzo does he adopt a tempo at all out of the ordinary, challenging the horns in daringly fast hunting calls, which yet are finely disciplined.

Although not quite as impressive as his Bruckner *Ninth*, Bruno Walter's 1960 recording is transformed by its CD remastering, with textures clearer, strings full and brass sonorous. The superbly played 'hunting horn' Scherzo is wonderfully vivid. Walter makes his recording orchestra sound remarkably European in style and timbre. The reading is characteristically spacious. Walter's special feeling for Bruckner means that he can relax over long musical paragraphs and retain his control of the structure, while the playing has fine atmosphere and no want of mystery.

With warm, slightly distanced sound, the sensuous beauty of the Berlin Philharmonic string section has rarely been caught so beautifully. Muti as a Brucknerian has a fine feeling for climax, building over the longest span, and his flexible phrase-shaping of Brucknerian melody, very different from traditional rugged treatment, reflects a vocal style of expressiveness. With that extra warmth and high dramatic contrasts, Muti takes Bruckner further south than usual.

Karajan's 1970 recording for EMI, made in the Berlin Jesus-Christus-Kirche and now reissued in the Karajan Edition, at high voltage combines simplicity and strength. The playing of the Berlin Philharmonic is very fine. The resonance means that there is a touch of harshness on the considerable fortissimos, while *pianissimos* are relatively diffuse. However, at the time of going to press this issue has become unavailable.

Lovro von Matačič's Philharmonia account of the *Fourth Symphony* dates from 1954 and used the Franz Schalk–Karl Loewe edition of 1889, with cuts in the Scherzo and finale. This fine Testament transfer pays tribute to the acute ears of the Walter Legge/Douglas Larter recording team, with the sound beautifully blended. When it was issued in the USA, the *Overture in G minor* was added two years later, and this was also recorded in stereo. The performance has both lucidity and majesty, with Dennis Brain's horn-playing outstanding.

Harnoncourt's is a relatively objective view of Bruckner, rugged and purposeful, less emotional than most. Dynamic shading is precisely caught and the Concertgebouw Orchestra plays with typical refinement, with refined recording to match. But there are many more compelling versions than this.

Konwitschny's reading (using the 1886 score) is above all warmly lyrical, even in the Scherzo (which rather lacks bite and effervescence). The kernel of his reading is the *Andante quasi allegretto*, which is more like an *Andante molto*. But the mono sound is full, and the concentration of the very fine orchestral playing holds the listener, even if the dynamic range is restricted and the brass tuttis are congested.

From Salonen on Sony, beautiful orchestral sound, and the unaffected opening paragraphs give promise of a fine performance, but there is soon an abrupt lurch forward which is convincing at no level. The playing of the Los Angeles Philharmonic and the Sony recording are of the highest order, and one only wishes that they were at the service of a selfless interpreter. Recommended to this conductor's admirers rather than Bruckner's (Sony SK 63301).

Symphonies Nos. 4; 9 in D min.

(N) (B) *** DG Panorama (ADD) 469 265-2 (2). BPO, Karajan.

For this Panorama reissue DG have chosen Karajan's mid-1970s recordings. In the case of No. 9 this later version, fine as it is, was not preferable to the 1966 account, which is available on Galleria (see below). In the later reading Karajan clearly wanted to convey a tougher, more majestic impression, and the interpretation concentrates on strength and impact. As before, however, the playing of the Berlin Philharmonic is both technically immaculate and dedicated. The recording balance is closer than before, but the current transfers of both symphonies are truthful and not without analogue atmosphere.

Symphony No. 5 in B flat.

⊛ *** DG 460 527-2. Dresden State O, Sinopoli.
*** Decca 433 819-2. Concg. O, Chailly.
*** RCA 09026 68503-2. BPO, Wand.
*** BBC (ADD) BBCL 4033-2. BBCSO, Horenstein.
*** EMI CDC5 551255. LPO, Welser-Möst.
(M) (***) EMI mono CDH5 56750-2. VPO, Furtwängler.
(N) (M) ** Ph. 464 693-2. Concg. O, Jochum.

Sinopoli's disc appeared in the very month of his untimely death, a wonderful memorial, characterful and strong in a positive, even wilful way distinctively his. The Dresden Staatskapelle responds with playing of incandescent intensity, totally allied with the conductor in silencing any stylistic reservations. This is a reading of high dramatic contrasts, with the towering climaxes of the outer movements both rugged and refined, purposeful and warm, with the variegated structure of the finale tautly held together. This is a live recording, and the inspiration of the moment comes over at full force. The energy of the *Scherzo* and the passion of the slow movement complete the picture of an exceptionally high-powered reading, recorded in glowing sound.

Chailly gave us an outstanding Bruckner *Seventh* with the Berlin Radio Symphony Orchestra in the early days of CD which still ranks high among all the competition (see below), and this version of the *Fifth* is, if anything, even finer. The Royal Concertgebouw Orchestra play with sumptuous magnificence, and Chailly's overall control of a work that is notable for its diversive episodes is unerring, moving towards an overwhelming final apotheosis. The *Adagio* is very beautiful and never sounds hurried. The Decca recording is superb, with the brass attacking brilliantly. An easy first choice.

In his later version Günter Wand forsakes the Cologne and Hamburg orchestras (with which he made his earlier recordings) in favour of the Berlin Philharmonic. The present disc was put together from three concert performances given in January 1996. Wand, an experienced and selfless interpreter, gives a noble reading, magnificently played.

Horenstein's magisterial account of the *Fifth Symphony* with the BBC Symphony Orchestra has the advantage of relatively rich and vivid sound and comes from a 1971 Prom. It is an eloquent and compelling performance of a symphony which Horenstein (to the best of our knowledge) never recorded commercially.

The London Philharmonic play eloquently for Franz

Welser-Möst in their live recording, made in the Konzerthaus, Vienna, in late May–early June 1993 before an attentive and silent audience. There are some potentially disruptive agogic touches, but Welser-Möst succeeds in persuading you that they have logical motivation. The wide-ranging dynamics are well captured by the engineers.

Furtwängler's account of the *Fifth Symphony* comes from the invaluable Salzburg Archives and was recorded at the 1951 Salzburg Festival. (The remainder of the concert included Mendelssohn's *Fingal's Cave* and Mahler's *Lieder eines fahrenden Gesellen* with the 26-year-old Fischer-Dieskau.) Considering its age, the sound is remarkably good; and the performance has that blend of warmth, majesty and radiance which distinguishes the best Furtwängler. However, as we go to press this set has been withdrawn.

Jochum's 1964 Concertgebouw account last appeared on Polygram's super-bargain Belart label. Now it is reissued at mid-price as a very doubtful candidate for inclusion among Philips's '50 Great Recordings'. Jochum's performance undoubtedly has the electricity of live music-making, but the acoustic of the recording is rather confined, with two-dimensional brass sonorities. It was made at a concert in Ottobeuren Abbey Germany in 1964 yet the string timbre is curiously dry for an ecclesiastical ambience, and most listeners will want a more expansive sound in this work.

Symphonies Nos. 5 in B flat (1878 edition); *Symphony No. 6 in A* (original version).

(B) **(*) EMI double forte CZS5 72661-2 (2). Dresden State O, Jochum.

Jochum's DG account of the *Fifth Symphony* (with the Bavarian Radio Orchestra) was one of the earliest and one of the finest of his first cycle, and DG should consider issuing it as one of their 'Originals'. However, the Dresden version also has a very impressive slow movement, and the *Sixth* is similarly compelling. The CD transfers are admirably spacious, and the Dresden strings have plenty of depth. But the brass is rather too brightly lit, and, especially in the climaxes of the *Sixth Symphony*, the effect is brash.

Symphony No. 6 in A.

*** Decca 458 189-2. Concg. O, Chailly – WOLF: *4 Goethe Lieder*. ***
(M) *** EMI (ADD) CDM5 67037-2. New Philh. O, Klemperer – WAGNER: *Wesendonk Lieder*. **
(M) **(*) DG (ADD) 477 525-2. BPO, Karajan.
(BB) **(*) Arte Nova 74321 54456-2. Saarbrücken RSO, Skrowaczewski.

Chailly's reading of the *Sixth Symphony* is at once refined and powerful at spacious speeds, a performance which is warmly emotional at every turn without a trace of sentimentality. In the slow movement as in the first, the extreme *pianissimos* have a breathtaking beauty. The pointing of rhythms in the Scherzo has a Mendelssohnian lightness, and in the finale too fantasy is set against Brucknerian power. The recording is of demonstration quality. The Wolf songs, superbly sung with the composer's own orchestrations, make a valuable and generous fill-up.

Klemperer directs a characteristically strong and direct

reading. It is disarmingly simple rather than overly expressive in the slow movement (faster than usual), but is always concentrated and strong, and the finale is held together particularly well. Splendid playing from the orchestra, with the mid-1960s recording clear and bright, yet full-bodied in this remastering for 'The Klemperer Legacy'.

Karajan is not as commanding here as in his other Bruckner recordings, yet this is still a compelling performance, tonally very beautiful and with a glowing account of the slow movement that keeps it in proportion. The 1979 analogue recording might ideally have been more expansive.

Skrowaczewski guides his forces with unerring purpose and nobility. Tempi are well judged throughout and phrases shaped with refinement. The string-tone needs perhaps to be weightier, but this is a very good performance.

Symphony No. 7 in E.

*** Teldec 3984 24488-2. VPO, Harnoncourt.

(BB) *** Naxos 8.554269. RSNO, Tintner.

(M) *** Ph. (ADD) 446 580-2. Concg. O, Haitink.

(M) *** EMI (ADD) CDM5 66095-2. BPO, Karajan.

(N) *** RCA 74321 68716-2. BPO, Günter Wand.

(M) (***) Dutton Lab. mono CDK 1205. Concg. O, Van Beinum (with TCHAIKOVSKY: *Waltz* from *Serenade for Strings*(***)).

(M) **(*) DG 445 553-2. VPO, Giulini.

**(*) Decca 466 574-2. Berlin RSO, Chailly.

(N) **(*) Hans. CD 93.027. SW RSO, Stuttgart, Sanderling.

(M) **(*) EMI (ADD) CDM5 67330-2. Philh. O, Klemperer (with RAMEAU: *Gavotte with Variations* **).

(M) ** Sony SMK 64481. Columbia SO, Walter.

** EMI CMS5 56425-2. CBSO, Rattle.

Harnoncourt's outstanding performance of the *Seventh* was recorded live in the Sofiensaal and is one of his very finest records. The sound is magnificent, the Viennese strings have a radiant sheen and the brass is gloriously sonorous. The performance could hardly be more compelling. In the slow movement the cymbal crash at the climax is omitted, but even this does not spoil its impact, and in the beautiful coda Harnoncourt draws out the resemblance in the valedictory overlapping horn parts to Wagner's *Das Rheingold*. The Scherzo is extremely vivid, yet what is so striking about the reading overall is its appealing lyrical feeling, with its moments of gentle restraint. This has to compete with Tintner, Karajan and Haitink, but it is very highly recommendable in its own right. Harnoncourt admirers need not hesitate.

Like his other Bruckner recordings for Naxos, Tintner's account of No. 7 brings a performance both subtle and refined, concentrated from first to last, often at spacious speeds. The glow of Brucknerian sound is caught beautifully, with the full nobility of the slow movement brought out. The Scherzo is not as rugged as it can be but, with sprung rhythms, the dance element is infectious. An outstanding bargain to rival any version.

Haitink's 1978 version offers a fine alternative at mid-price. The recording is wide in range and refined in detail, yet it retains the ambient warmth of the Concertgebouw. Haitink's reading is more searching than his earlier version,

made in the 1960s. The Concertgebouw Orchestra play with their accustomed breadth of tone and marvellously blended ensemble.

Karajan's outstanding EMI version also shows a superb feeling for the work's architecture, and the playing of the Berlin Philharmonic is gorgeous. The recording has striking resonance and amplitude. This EMI reading, generally preferable to his later, digital recording for DG, has a special sense of mystery.

This RCA disc offers Günter Wand's third recording of the *Seventh Symphony*; the earlier performances were with the Cologne Radio or NDR Orchestra. It has the benefit of the Berlin Philharmonic and excellent recorded sound. As always with Wand everything is phrased beautifully, and there is a fine balance between beauty of incident and the grandeur of the whole. Taken on its own, it is thoroughly recommendable, but it would not be a first choice.

Eduard van Beinum's reading, one of the finest ever put on record, brings a wonderfully persuasive response from the Concertgebouw Orchestra, not only rich in sonority but refined and often surprisingly transparent in texture, so that the effect of Bruckner's scoring is lighter than usual, especially in the lilting Scherzo. The great *Adagio* has superb concentration. Given another of Dutton's miraculous transfers, the 1947 Decca recording sounds both spacious and full-bodied. The Tchaikovsky *Waltz* which acts as encore is sheer delight.

Giulini shapes each paragraph lovingly – indeed, at times some might think too lovingly: the Vienna strings are occasionally prone to a little too much sweetness. All the same, here are some wonderful things and music-making of affecting eloquence, even though there is a lack of consistent forward movement. The DG recording has splendid warmth.

We thought highly of Chailly's Bruckner *Seventh* when it first appeared in 1984, and we ranked it among the finest of its period. There are so many superb *Sevenths* now in the catalogue that, fine though it is, it perhaps no longer enjoys its old pre-eminence. It seems scarcely credible that Decca have chosen to reissue it at full price – small wonder the industry is in such dire straits!

Sanderling's is a spacious, powerfully expressive reading and he gets fine playing and rich string tone from the Stuttgart Orchestra. The advantage of a live performance is that, with the musicians fully committed, he feels able to relax instead of pressing on, and this brings moments where the tension ebbs somewhat, while in the slow movement the climax falls short of being overwhelming. The recording is good but not nearly as fine as Harnoncourt's.

Klemperer's first movement is slow and, although both here and in the second movement the tension is far from low, some listeners may find it difficult to concentrate to the end. The Scherzo goes well, and in the finale Klemperer makes the lovely chorale melody glow most beautifully, but as an overall reading this can be strongly recommended only to keen Klemperer admirers. The Rameau *Gavotte*, recorded eight years later, makes a piquant bonus, the manner far from authentic but most winning when played with such elegance and finish.

Walter's reading concentrates on detail at the expense of structure. The outer movements bring many illuminating touches and the final climax of the first is built imposingly, but overall the tension is held loosely, and in the *Adagio*, which is kept moving fairly convincingly, the climax is disappointing. The 1963 recording sounds fuller and more spacious than the original LPs.

Rattle's reading of No. 7 brings opulent sound from the Birmingham orchestra, with exceptionally spacious speeds well sustained and with subtle terracing of dynamics. Even so, this is not the most tensely dramatic of Rattle's recorded performances. Recommended to those who value Bruckner for his heavenly length.

Symphonies Nos. 7 (ed. Haas); 8–9 (ed. Nowak).

*(**) DG (ADD) 445 471-2 (4). Stuttgart SW RSO, Celibidache
– SCHUBERT: *Symphony No. 5.* **(*)

Symphony No. 8 in C min. (ed. Nowak).

(M) *(*) EMI ZDCB5 56696-2 (2). Munich PO, Celibidache.

Celibidache's Bruckner is for the dedicated initiate rather than the true Brucknerian; for the former, the DG set, extremely well recorded at live performances, will be self-recommending and probably preferable to the Munich version of No. 8 on EMI, where, while he dwells lovingly on the admittedly many beauties, he does not really hold the structure together.

Celibidache's Stuttgart *Seventh* is nearly seven minutes longer than Harnoncourt's version, and it must be said that in the 24-minute slow movement one has to be very patient while waiting for the climax to arrive! Scherzi are lively enough and, although on the whole the account of the *Eighth* is the most convincing of the three, Celibidache conveys a sense of apotheosis at the end of each work. The orchestral response is very impressive, and one can imagine how in the concert hall the audience came under the conductor's spell. The set includes rehearsal sequences from *Symphonies Nos. 7* and *8*, and the coupled performance of Schubert's *Fifth Symphony* also shows Celibidache in a favourable light.

Symphony No. 8 in C min.

(N) *** DG 459 678-2. VPO, Boulez.

✿ *** DG 427 611-2 (2). VPO, Karajan.

*** Ph. (IMS) 446 659-2. VPO, Haitink.

(M) *** EMI (ADD) CMS5 66109-2 (2). BPO, Karajan –
BRAHMS: *Tragic Overture;* HINDEMITH: *Mathis der Maler.* ***

(B) *** DG (ADD) 463 263-2. BPO, Jochum.

(M) *** EMI (ADD) CDM7 64849-2. LPO, Tennstedt.

*** RCA 09026 68047 (2). N. German RSO, Wand.

(N) (M) **(*) Chan. 7080 (2). LPO, Järvi – REGER: *Variations & Fugue on a Theme of Beethoven.* ***

(N) **(*) BBC (ADD) BBCL 4067-2. Hallé O, Barbirolli.

(N) ** Teldec 8573 81037-2. BPO, Harnoncourt.

With taut control Pierre Boulez directs a tough, intense reading of this most expansive of the Bruckner symphonies, one which is also warmly expressive in the great Bruckner melodies, helped by glowing playing from the Vienna Philharmonic in this live recording, made at the International Bruckner Festival at St Florian in 1996. The terracing of the textures, as well as their clarification, typical of Boulez, is beautifully caught by the fine DG recording. After the weighty first movement, the *Scherzo* is light and resilient with refined textures, and the great slow movement proceeds magnetically, in Boulez's hands a powerful symphonic structure rather than a visionary statement. The finale – using the more expansive text of the Haas Edition – is then rugged and bitingly dramatic, with Boulez's use of rubato warmly idiomatic. A fine, distinctive reading, the more attractive in being fitted on a single disc.

Karajan's last version of the *Eighth Symphony* is with the Vienna Philharmonic Orchestra and is the most impressive of them all. The sheer beauty of sound and opulence of texture is awe-inspiring but never draws attention to itself: this is a performance in which beauty and truth go hand in hand. The recording is superior to either of its predecessors in terms of naturalness of detail and depth of perspective.

Bernard Haitink and the Vienna Philharmonic make a formidable combination; add to them the doyen of Philips engineers, Volker Strauss, and the results are outstanding. The performance is magnificent in its breadth and nobility; not only does it possess great dramatic sweep, its slow movement has a greater depth than his earlier reading. The Vienna Philharmonic play with great fervour and warmth, and the recorded sound is sumptuous.

The newest transfer of Karajan's 1958 Berlin Philharmonic recording is remarkably successful. The EMI sound is spacious and, if the sonorities are not quite as sumptuous as we would expect today, the strings do not lack body and the brass make a thrilling impact. Like Karajan's later versions for DG, this has compelling power, with the slow movement concentratedly conveying dark and tragic feelings. However, this set has just been withdrawn as we go to press.

Jochum's earlier (1964) DG account of the *Eighth*, like the later EMI Dresden version, uses the Nowak Edition, which involves cuts in the slow movement and finale. In addition, here he more often presses the music on impulsively in both the outer movements and especially in his account of the *Adagio*, where the climax has great passion and thrust. The DG recording is rather less full-blooded, but is cleaner in detail and very well balanced, and this bargain Classikon disc is worth any Brucknerian's money.

The plainness and honesty of Tennstedt in Bruckner is heard at its finest in his impressive account of the *Eighth*. The inwardness and hushed beauty of the great *Adagio* in particular are superbly projected in unforced concentration. Here he is in favour of Nowak without the additional material in the recapitulation. Fine, well-balanced recording, with the CD clarity filled out by the fullness of ambience. Like the Karajan issue above, this is now unavailable.

Günter Wand is as far removed from the jet-set maestro as it is possible to get, and his later recording of the *Eighth Symphony* has patrician eloquence. It is the product of three live concerts from December 1993 and is a straightforward, selfless reading of integrity and vision. This comes on two CDs, packaged as one and costing as much. Given its artistic claims and the very truthful sound, it is certainly worth considering.

Neeme Järvi's reading with the LPO is warmly spontaneous from first to last, helped by opulent Chandos sound in this 1986 recording. The thrust of argument is persuasively conveyed throughout, as in a live performance, thanks to

Järvi's easy control of rubato, with weighty brass set against silky string tone. The *Scherzo* is warm with no hint of menace, and the slow movement cocoons one in a sensuous bath of sound, before the weighty finale, even if the result is not always quite as detailed as in the finest versions. At mid-price with the rare Reger fill-up it is still a good recommendation.

Barbirolli's Hallé version comes from a live Royal Festival Hall broadcast of 1970. The recording is well balanced, but limited in range and dynamic and the brass tuttis could ideally be more expansive. But its Festival Hall brightness is fully acceptable when the performance is so concentrated. Barbirolli's reading of the slow movement is deeply felt and warmly passionate in his characteristic manner, and the Hallé players respond eloquently both here and in the beautifully shaped and thrilling finale. The applause at the close is well deserved.

Detailed and thoughtful, Harnoncourt's Berlin version, recorded live in the Philharmonie, yet fails to hang together. The detail often comes to sound fussy and self-conscious, with rubato that does not always sound spontaneous or even warm, and with rhythms too often evenly stressed, failing to lift. That said, there is much to admire in the refined playing of the Berlin Philharmonic, yet, using the more questionable Nowak Edition, a two-disc version without fill-up is not a good recommendation.

Symphony No. 8 in C min. (*Scherzo; Adagio; Finale* only).

(***) Koch Schwann mono/stereo 314482. Prussian State O, Karajan.

Karajan's 1944 recording was among those which were spirited off to the then Soviet Union after the collapse of Nazi Germany. Technically the sound is quite astonishing – and the finale, an early example of stereo, is little short of incredible. Not only is it extraordinary in terms of sound, it is also of exceptional artistic interest. The finale has a breadth and spaciousness, a grandeur and, above all, a sense of repose, that Karajan did not surpass in his later recordings.

Symphonies Nos. (i) 8 in C min.; (ii) 9 in D min.

*** BBC (ADD) BBCL 4017-2 (2). (i) LSO; (ii) BBC SO; Horenstein.

(B) *** EMI double forte (ADD) CZS5 73827-2 (2). Dresden State O, Jochum.

(M) (***) DG mono 449 758-2 (2). (i) Hamburg PO; (ii) Bav. RSO; Jochum.

These BBC recordings of performances at the Royal Albert Hall in 1970 reveal the genius of Jascha Horenstein more tellingly than almost any of his studio recordings. Though he draws out the warm expressiveness in Bruckner's lyrical writing, moulding phrases, he takes a rugged view of the overall structure, not least in his rapt account of the great *Adagio* in *Symphony No. 8*. Fine as the LSO is in that symphony with its brighter string-tone, the performance of the *Ninth* with the BBC Symphony brings even finer playing, strong and purposeful. Warm, atmospheric, radio sound.

With the benefit of wide-ranging, full-blooded recording, Jochum's Dresden version of the *Eighth* is a performance of incandescent warmth. His flexible, spontaneous-sounding

style in Bruckner is here consistently persuasive from the mysterious opening of the first movement onwards. As in his earlier vesion for DG, Jochum opts for the Nowak edition. The quality is vivid for much of the time, but the climaxes are not without a touch of harshness and a hint of congestion. The Dresden account of the *Ninth* is another splendid example of Jochum's art, with the strings made to sound weighty and sonorous by the Dresden acoustic. Jochum is again at his most convincing here, giving an impression of spontaneity such as you would expect in the concert hall.

Jochum's mono recordings of the *Eighth* and *Ninth Symphonies* date from 1949 and 1954. The DG sound is technically of astonishingly fine quality, particularly in the gloriously played *Adagio* of the *Eighth*, which has a remarkably wide dynamic range. Jochum gives a feeling of total spontaneity as the music ebbs and flows foward. The conductor's sense of vision and his unique understanding of Bruckner's spiritual base come over as strongly here as in his later, stereo versions, if not more so.

Symphony No. 9 in D min.

🏵 (M) *** Sony SMK 64483. Columbia SO, Walter.

(M) *** DG 429 904-2. BPO, Karajan.

(BB) *** Naxos 8.554268. RSNO, Tintner.

*** RCA 74321 63244-2. BPO, Wand.

*** Teldec 9031 72140-2. BPO, Barenboim.

*** DG 427 345-2. VPO, Giulini.

(B) **(*) DG Classikon 445 126. BPO, Jochum.

(*) Decca 455 506-2. Concg. O, Chailly (with BACH, orch. WEBERN: *Musical Offering: Fuga ricercata a 6* *).

(**) BBC Legends mono BBCL 4034-2 (2). Hallé O, Barbirolli – MAHLER: *Symphony No. 7.* (**)

(N) (BB) ** Arte Nova 74321 80781-2. Saarbrucken SO, Skrowaczewski.

(N) (M) *(*) Orfeo mono C548001B. Bavarian Radio SO, Schuricht.

Symphony No. 9 in D min.; Adagio for String Orchestra (3rd movt of *String Quintet*, arr. Stadlmair).

*** Decca 458 964-2. Leipzig GO, Blomstedt.

Bruno Walter's 1959 account of Bruckner's *Ninth Symphony* represents the peak of his achievement during his Indian summer in the CBS recording studios just before he died. His mellow, persuasive reading leads one on through the leisurely paragraphs so that the logic and coherence seem obvious where other performances can sound aimless. Some may not find the Scherzo vigorous enough to provide the fullest contrast, but the final slow movement has a nobility which suggests that after this, anything would have been an anticlimax.

The DG Galleria reissue of Karajan's 1966 recording offers a glorious performance of Bruckner's last and uncompleted symphony, characteristically moulded and displaying a simple, direct nobility that is sometimes missing in this work. Even in a competitive field, this disc stands out at mid-price, to rank alongside Bruno Walter's noble 1959 version.

Like others in his Bruckner series, Georg Tintner's Naxos recording of the *Ninth Symphony* is a match in every way for the finest rival versions, whatever the price. The refinement of *pianissimos* brings out the full mystery of the massive outer movements, while the delicate fantasy of the Scherzo is brilliantly touched in at high speed, with a touch of wildness. The final *Adagio* builds up in exultation: this may not have been planned as the finale, but here it becomes the most deeply satisfying conclusion. The playing of the Royal Scottish National Orchestra is superb, with recording at once transparent and refined, as well as weighty.

Blomstedt lays out the terrain with great clarity, the vistas with which we are presented have an awesome grandeur and, as always with this conductor, there is nobility. He stands high on the current list of recommendations, and his issue offers a useful fill-up in the shape of a transcription by Hans Stadlmair of the slow movement of the *String Quintet* for full strings.

Günter Wand, using what he describes as the 'original version', now directs an incandescent performance which gains from being recorded not only live but with the Berlin Philharmonic. The concentration is unremitting, with tension maintained through the stillest *pianissimos*, and the opulence of the Berlin players, most strikingly with the strings and brass, gives one a satisfying cushion of sound throughout, with climaxes of shattering weight. Tiny things may go wrong (some ugly wind intonation at 10 minutes 45 seconds into the slow movemement) but they are few and unlikely to worry most listeners. Wand brings the same sense of authority and wisdom to this extraordinary score, and he is certainly superbly recorded.

Daniel Barenboim's Berlin account has depth and strength, with the advantage of superb orchestral playing, and the recorded sound has splendid body and transparency. One of the strongest of newer recommendations.

Giulini's *Ninth* is also a great performance, the product of deep thought. There is the keenest feeling for texture and beauty of contour, and he distils a powerful sense of mystery from the first and third movements. The DG recording is spacious and transparent.

Jochum's reading has greater mystery than any other, and the orchestral playing reaches a degree of eloquence that disarms criticism. If at times he tends to phrase too affectionately, he is still magnetic in everything he does. The 1966 recording sounds remarkably fine. An excellent bargain version.

Chailly conducts a soberly dedicated reading of the *Ninth*, with the Concertgebouw playing superbly. If in his spacious view of the finale he lacks the concentration of the finest versions, this is still worth considering by those who prefer an objective reading. Excellent sound, rather less full-bodied than some from this source. The Webern arrangement of Bach makes an imaginative fill-up.

Barbirolli's account of the *Ninth* with the Hallé Orchestra comes from a 1966 Promenade Concert and has much finer recorded sound than his valuable reading of the Mahler *Seventh*. Sir John does not exactly linger and his first movement is at times quite rushed. Though there is that individual Barbirolli intensity, this does not show him at his best.

Skrowaczewski with his Saarbrucken Orchestra conducts a clean-cut, strongly structured reading, which yet fails to convey the sort of biting intensity which has marked his

finest Bruckner readings with this orchestra. One gets too little feeling of dedication in this unfinished work dedicated to the Love of God. Speeds are unexceptionable, and the playing generally refined, but even in the super-bargain category Tintner's Naxos version is far preferable.

Schuricht's Orfeo disc offers a live broadcast reading (in mono only) recorded in the Herkulessaal in Munich in 1963, yet there is too little of the tension one would expect of a live event, even if there are moments of frenetic *accelerando* which suggest the inspiration of the moment. Schuricht is better remembered by his studio recordings.

CHAMBER MUSIC

String Quintet in F.

*** Nim. NI 5488 Brandis Qt, with Dean – BRAHMS: *String Quintet No. 2.* ***

String Quintet in F; Intermezzo for String Quintet.

(*) Hyp. CDA 66704. Raphael Ens. – R. STRAUSS: *Capriccio: Sextet.* *

(M) **(*) CRD 3456. Alberni Qt.

The Brandis version of the *Quintet* offers a splendid coupling in Brahms's *G major Quintet*, Op. 111, and their playing stands up well alongside the current competition. They are well recorded and have a natural feeling for the space and pacing of this piece. For those attracted by the coupling, this could well be a first choice.

The Raphael Ensemble, coupling their performance with the *Intermezzo in D minor* and the opening *Sextet* from Strauss's *Capriccio*, are ardently full-blooded in an eloquent account and have the benefit of rich recorded sound.

The Alberni version comes from the early 1980s without any additional fill-up. It is well played without affectation and, taken in isolation, is most satisfying. Hardly a first choice.

VOCAL MUSIC

Masses Nos. (i) 1 in D min. (for soloists, chorus and orchestra); 2 in E min. (for 8-part chorus and wind ensemble); (ii) 3 in F min. (for soloists, chorus and orchestra).

⊕ (M) *** DG (ADD) 447 409-2 (2). (i) Mathis, Schiml, Ochman, Ridderbusch; (ii) Stader, Hellman, Haefliger, Borg; Bav. R. Ch. & O, Jochum.

Masses Nos. 1–3; Aequalis Nos. 1 & 2; Motets: Afferentur regi virgines; Ave Maria; Christus factus est; Ecce sacardos magnus; Inveni David; Locus iste; Os justi; Pange lingua; Tota pulchra es, Maria; Vexilla regis; Virga Jesse; Libera me; Psalm 150; Te Deum.

*** Hyp. CDS 4407 (3). Soloists, Corydon Singers and O; ECO Wind Ens., Best; T. Trotter (organ).

Bruckner composed his three *Masses* between 1864 and 1868, although all three works were revised two decades later. Each contains magnificent music; Eugen Jochum is surely an ideal interpreter, finding their mystery as well as their eloquence, breadth and humanity. The *Kyrie* of the *E minor* swelling out gloriously from its gentle opening is breath-taking, while the fervour of the passionate *F minor* work is extraordinarily compelling, with the intensity and drive of an inspirational live performance. Throughout all three works the scale and drama of Bruckner's inspiration are fully conveyed. In these outstanding new transfers, the warmly atmospheric analogue recordings from the early 1970s are given remarkable vividness and presence. A splendid choice for DG's 'Original' series of Legendary Recordings.

It makes good sense to assemble all of the Bruckner choral music that the Corydon Singers and Matthew Best have done during the last few years in one three-CD set. They are very fine indeed and make a splendid modern alternative to Jochum; when eloquent and natural, Best's direction is imaginative and he achieves a wide tonal range.

Mass No. 1 in D min.; Motets: Ave Maria; Christus factus est; Locus iste; Os justi; Tota pulchra.

(N) *** DG 459 674-2. Orgonasova, Fink, Prégardien, Schulte, Monteverdi Ch., Vienna PO, Gardiner

Gardiner in his live recording, made in 1996, gives a warm and powerful reading of this strongly characterized setting of the *Mass*, with the helpful acoustic of the Vienna Musikverein adding atmosphere without the washiness of a church acoustic. The soprano, mezzo and tenor soloists are first-rate, though the curious timbre of the bass is less attractive. In both the Vienna performance and the separate recording of the five *Motets*, made in 1998 in a church in Norfolk, the Monteverdi Choir are in incandescent form, at once immaculate yet warmly dedicated, responding to Gardiner's characterful direction.

Mass No. 2 in E min.; Mass in C.

(N) *** Chan. 9863. Kuznetzova, Golub, Russian State Symphonic Cappella, Russian State SO, Polyansky.

There is something seraphic about the *E minor Mass*. It may not have the grandeur and majesty of the later symphonies, but there is a simplicity of invention and an elevation of feeling that are affecting, particularly when it is recorded so beautifully and performed with the eloquence of Polyansky and his Russian forces on Chandos. The early *C major Mass* is a most welcome coupling.

Missa solemnis in B flat min.; Psalms 112, 150.

(BB) *** Virgin 2 x 1 VBD5 61501-2 (2). Oelze, Schubert, Dürmüller, Hagen, Bamberg Ch. & SO, Rickenbacher – MOZART: *Requiem*. ***

Bruckner's *Missa solemnis* is a comparatively early work (1854), written a decade before the *D major Mass*. It is given a strong, fresh performance here, with a good solo team, although the soprano, Christiane Oelze, sounds a bit hard at times. The two Psalm settings are 30 years apart, with *Psalm 150* (1892) obviously the more mature: both are sung eloquently. The chorus, as in the Mozart coupling, are set back in a spacious acoustic. Altogether this makes a thoroughly worthwhile bargain Double, unexpectedly pairing early Bruckner with late Mozart.

Motets: Afferentur regi; Ave Maria; Christus factus est; Ecce sacerdos; Iam lucis orto sidere; Inveni David; Libera me; Locus iste; Os justi; Pange lingua; Salvum fac populum tuum; Tantum ergo; Tota pulchra es; Vexilla regis; Virga Jesse.

(BB) *** Naxos 8.550956. St Bride's Church Ch., Jones.

(i) Motets: Afferentur regi; Ave Maria; Christus factus est; Ecce sacerdos; Locus iste; Os justi; Pange lingua; Tota pulchra es; Vexilla regis; Virga Jesse. (ii) Psalm 150; Te Deum.

(M) *** DG (ADD) 457 743-2 (2). (i) Bav. R. Ch.; (ii) Stader, Wagner, Haefliger, Lagger, German Op. Ch., Berlin, BPO; Jochum.

Motets: Afferentur regi; Ecce sacerdos; Inveni David; Os justi; Pange lingua.

(BB) *** Belart (ADD) 461 317-2. St John's College, Cambridge, Ch., ASMF, Guest – BEETHOVEN: *Mass in C*. ***

This Naxos disc is the first commercial recording of the St Bride's Church Choir, and very impressive it is, for with crisp, clear ensemble and fresh tone from boyish-sounding sopranos they give warmly sympathetic performances of these fine Bruckner motets, an excellent selection covering most of the best known. The recording is full and vivid, set against a helpful church acoustic which does not obscure detail.

On DG, the ten motets are sung superbly and are among Jochum's most distinguished recordings. With excellent soloists, the performances of the two larger-scale works here have fine eloquence and admirable breadth and humanity and no lack of drama and, with some fine singing from Maria Stader and Ernst Haefliger, as well as superbly loving orchestral support from the Berliners, this has a special eloquence. The original recordings tended to be distanced; in making the sound more present and clear the remastering is undoubtedly fresher and brighter.

The St John's performances are of the highest quality and the recording is marvellously spacious. They come in the lowest price range, coupled with a fine account of Beethoven's *C major Mass*.

Requiem in D min.; Psalms 112 & 114.

(*) Hyp. CDA 66245. Rodgers, Denley, M. Davies, George, Corydon Singers, ECO, Best; T. Trotter (organ).

Matthew Best here tackles the very early setting of the *Requiem* which Bruckner wrote at the age of 25. The quality of the writing in the Psalm settings also varies; but with fine, strong performances from singers and players alike, including an excellent team of soloists, this is well worth investigating by Brucknerians. First-rate recording.

Te Deum.

(N) (B) *** Warner Apex 8573 89128-2. Spreckelsen, Ankerson, Adalbert Kraus, Moll, Bielefeld Musikvereins Ch., Philh. Hungarica, Stephani – BRUCKNER: *Te Deum*. ***

(B) **(*) DG Double (ADD) 453 091-2 (2). Tomowa-Sintow, Baltsa, Schreier, Van Dam, V. Singverein, VPO, Karajan – VERDI: *Requiem Mass*. **(*)

An outstanding account of Bruckner's 1884 setting of the *Te*

Deum from Martin Stephani, vibrantly direct and gripping, with an excellent team of soloists and very fine choral singing over a wide range of dynamic. Stephani is fully sympathetic to the composer's deeply felt religious feeling. The well-balanced recording provides a warm acoustic while giving chorus bite and amplitude. Text and translation are included. A bargain.

Karajan's analogue account of the *Te Deum* is spacious and strong, bringing out the score's breadth and drama. This is very satisfying and, if the Verdi coupling is acceptable, is self-recommending.

BRUHNS, Nicolaus (1665–97)

2 Preludes in E min.; Preludes: in G ; G min.; (i) Fantasia on 'Nun komm der Heiden Heiland'.

*** Chan. 0539. Kee (organ of Roskilde Cathedral, Denmark), (i) with Rehling – BUXTEHUDE: *Chorale Preludes.* ***

Just five Bruhns organ works survive (all included in this recital). Though he uses the term '*Praeludium*', each consists of an introduction and one or two fugues, written with an eager flair that recalls the early organ works of the young Bach, who certainly knew of this music. The *Fantasia on 'Nun komm der Heiden Heiland'* has its *cantus firmus* introduced by a soprano voice, and she returns to repeat the chorale (undecorated) at a central point, after three variants. Piet Kee presents all this music with splendid life and colour, and his Danish organ, recently restored, brings vivid registration which is a pleasure to the ear. The recording is in the demonstration bracket.

BRÜLL, Ignaz (1846–1907)

Piano Concertos Nos. 1 in F, Op. 10; 2 in C, Op. 24; Andante & allegro, Op. 88.

*** Hyp. CDA 67069. Roscoe, BBC Scottish SO, Brabbins.

Like so many issues in Hyperion's admirable romantic piano concerto series, this brings real revelation about a composer who till now has seemed a shadowy figure, one of a Viennese group associated with Brahms. Both the concertos are early works, the *Second* built on rather more distinguished material than the *First*, and their innocent flamboyance is superbly caught in these brilliant performances, with Martin Roscoe excelling himself in his dazzling virtuosity. The *Andante & allegro*, a much later work, provides a warmly expressive makeweight. Full, well-balanced sound of best Hyperion quality.

BRUMEL, Antoine (c. 1460– c. 1520)

Missa: Et ecce terrae motus; Lamentations. Magnificat secundi toni.

*** GIMCD 454 926. Tallis Scholars, Phillips.

It is not just the contrapuntal ingenuity of Brumel's music that impresses but the sheer beauty of sound with which we are presented. Brumel was not only one of the first to write a polyphonic *Requiem* but the very first to make a polyphonic setting of the sequence, *Dies irae, dies illa*. This is a more severe work than the glorious 12-part Mass which occupies the bulk of this CD, and it is written in a more medieval tonal language. The Tallis Scholars are very impressive. They opt for a unique solution to the *Agnus Dei*, which is incomplete in the Munich manuscript. The texture in their performance has great transparency and clarity, and this disc can be highly recommended.

BUNCH, Kenji (born 1973)

Fantasy for Violin & Orchestra.

(B) ** EMI Début CDZ5 73501-2. Shapira, ECO, Hazlewood – BLOCH: *Baal Shem ***; BRUCH: *Violin Concerto No. 1 in G min., Op. 26 **; SARASATE: *Zigeunerweisen. **(*)

This piece forms part of a début recital. It was written for this gifted player, who is described by the composer as playing a Joachim-like role in its gestation. It would be unkind to press the parallel with Brahms further, for this is a very thin, amorphous piece – quite sub-Bloch.

BURGON, Geoffrey (born 1941)

Acquainted with Night; Cançiones del Alma; Lunar Beauty; Nunc dimittis; This ean Night; Worldës Blissë.

(M) *** EMI CDM5 66527-2. Bowman, Brett, City of L. Sinf., Hickox.

This collection of Geoffrey Burgon's music for counter-tenor has at the centre his most celebrated piece, the setting of the *Nunc dimittis* used as theme-music in the television adaptation of John Le Carré's *Tinker, Tailor, Soldier, Spy*, originally for treble but well within counter-tenor range. In the three settings of St John of the Cross, *Cançiones del Alma*, Burgon was consciously seeking to get away from Anglican church-choir associations of the counter-tenor voice, and some of the bell-like effects are most beautiful. *Worldës Blissë* was prompted by a dream of a counter-tenor and oboe in duet; while in *This ean Night* he dared to set the same text as Britten and Stravinsky in the *Lyke-Wake Dirge*, producing distinctive results in the tangy duetting of counter-tenors. The performances are strongly committed, with James Bowman taking the lion's share of solos. The recording gives an aptly ecclesiastical glow to the sound while keeping essential clarity.

At the round earth's imagined corners; But have been found again; Laudate Dominum; Magnificat; Nunc dimittis; A prayer to the Trinity; Short Mass; This World; 2 Hymns to Mary.

**(*) Hyp. CDA 66113. Chichester Cathedral Ch., Thurlow.

Burgon's famous *Nunc dimittis* is well matched here with the *Magnificat* which he later wrote to complement it and a series of his shorter choral pieces, all of them revealing his flair for immediate, direct communication, and well performed. First-rate recording.

(i) *The Calm; Merciless Beauty;* **(ii)** *A Vision.*

*** ASV CDDCA 1059. (i) Bowman; (ii) Jenkins, (i) City of London Sinf., (ii) ASMF, (i; ii) composer.

In *Merciless Beauty* the alto voice blends so closely with the orchestra that James Bowman seems an integral part of the texture, within semi-voluptuous scoring. All these seven songs are about love, but the most striking is the title-number (a setting of Chaucer) while the closing *Campionesque for Anna* matches the opening *Western wind* in its languorously exotic line. The tenor cycle, *A Vision*, offers settings of John Clare (1793–1864) and pictures the countryside as seen through the eyes of a sensitive farmworker-poet. These songs are generally more restrained and reflectively touching. An interlude, *Voices from the Calm* (originally a ballet score), offers instrumental writing, with the counter-tenor voice again laminated in, and is no less evocative in feeling. The closing *Voices from the Calm*, a dream couplet by Walt Whitman (which also inspired the ballet), returns to voices – overlapping vocal lines. All the performances are warmly sensitive and beautifully recorded in an ideally warm ambience.

BUSH, Geoffrey (born 1920)

Symphonies Nos. **(i)** *1;* **(ii)** *2 (Guildford);* **(iii)** *Music for Orchestra;* **(iv)** *Overture Yorick.*

*** Lyrita ADD/Dig. SRCD 252. (i) LSO, Braithwaite; (ii) RPO, Wordsworth; (iii) LPO; (iv) Philh. O; (iii–iv) Handley.

Geoffrey Bush's music is consistently warm and appealing. This very well-filled disc brings together fine Lyrita recordings made between 1972 and 1982, and adds a superb, completely new recording of the *Symphony No. 2*. The vigorous *Yorick Overture* has all the exuberance of a Walton overture, with wit and warm lyricism nicely balanced. The first of the two symphonies is a positive, three-movement structure centring on an elegiac slow movement with blues overtones, written in memory of Constant Lambert, quoting from *The Rio Grande*. The *Second Symphony* is outgoing, too, no formal exercise but a warm statement of personal feeling, built on a strong and complex structure in four linked sections, the first and last suitably genial and festive. *Music for Orchestra* is 'a miniature symphony', with the string parts carefully written so that they are not beyond the reach of inexperienced players. All the performances and recordings are outstandingly good, notably that of the *Symphony No. 2*, conducted by Barry Wordsworth.

Farewell, Earth's Bliss; 4 Hesperides Songs; A Menagerie; **(i)** *A Summer Serenade.*

*** Chan. 8864. Varcoe, Thompson, Westminster Singers, City of L. Sinfonia, Hickox, (i) with Parkin.

The delightful *Summer Serenade* of seven song-settings has long been Bush's most frequently performed work, and this first recording glowingly brings out the sharp contrasts of mood within and between the songs, with instrumentation just as felicitous as the choral writing. It is well coupled with a solo song-cycle of comparable length, *Farewell, Earth's Bliss*, with Stephen Varcoe the baritone soloist; four songs

from Herrick's *Hesperides*, also for baritone and strings; and three for unaccompanied voices, including an insistently menacing setting of Blake's *Tyger*. The tenor Adrian Thompson, not ideally pure-toned, contributes to only two of the *Serenade* songs; otherwise these are near-ideal performances in warm, open sound.

BUSONI, Ferruccio (1866–1924)

Piano Concerto.

*** Hyp. CDA 67143. Hamelin, CBSO, Elder.

Busoni's *Piano Concerto* is arguably the most formidable in his repertory, but in such an inspired reading as Hamelin's it emerges as a genuine Everest of a work. The challenge it presents has already sparked off an impressive list of recordings, but Hamelin's is the finest yet. Even before the piano enters, the opening tutti, four minutes long, establishes the rapt, glowing intensity of the performance, thanks to Mark Elder's dedicated conducting of the Birmingham orchestra, with radiant recording to match. Above all, Hamelin and Elder bring out the warmer, more colourful qualities behind the five massive movements, the dedication of the long *Pezzo serioso* beautifully sustained.

Violin Sonatas Nos. 1 in E min., Op. 29; 2 in E min., Op. 36a.

*** Chan. 8868. Mordkovitch, Postnikova.

Busoni's two *Violin Sonatas* are rarities in the concert hall. There is no current alternative to the *First*, and Lydia Mordkovitch and Victoria Postnikova are impressive advocates of this somewhat uneven piece. The *Second* is a one-movement work, dating from 1898, with a *langsam* opening, a Presto and a most beautiful *Andante* section leading to a set of variations. Mordkovitch and her partner give a sympathetic reading and, with excellent recording, this disc should be sought out by admirers of this composer.

SOLO PIANO MUSIC

Indianisches Tagebuch (4 Studies); Sonatinas Nos. 1–6; Toccata.

(N) *** CPO 999 702-2. Pontinen.

Busoni composed his six *Sonatinas* over a decade between 1910 and 1920. His choice of title is deceptive, for they are by no means simply structured works and their textures are characteristically prolix. (One often feels with this composer that there are too many notes!) The most famous is No. 6 (*Super Carmen*), which is rather like a Lisztian concert paraphrase, only more sophisticated in its seductive interweaving of themes from Bizet's opera. Pontinen plays with matching subtlety and he is equally sensitive to the essentially serene atmosphere of No. 4, subtitled *In diem navitatis Christi MCMXVII*. No. 5 is a free reworking of the *Fantasy and Fugue in D minor*, once attributed to Bach, but since discovered unauthentic.

The four studies which make up the *Indian Diary* are based on Native American Indian folk themes. All this music is very demanding technically, and the closing Toccata prodigiously so, but Roland Pontinen not only responds warmly to Busoni's lyrical writing, but meets all the many challenges with easy virtuosity and flair. He is excellently recorded.

An die Jugend: Giga bolero e variazione. Elegies: All'Italia; Berceuse; Turandots Frauengemach. Exeunt omnes; Fantasia nach J. S. Bach; Indianisches Tagebuch (Red Indian Diary), Book I; Sonatinas Nos. 2; 6 (Kammerfantasie on 'Carmen'); Toccata. Transcription of Bach: Prelude & Fugue in D, BWV 532.

*** Chan. 9394. Tozer.

Elegies Nos. 1 (Nach der Wendung); 7 (Elegy); Fantasia in modo antico, Op. 33b/4; Macchiette medioevali; Sonatinas Nos. 4 (In diem navitatis Christi MCMXVII); 6 (Kammerfantasie on Bizet's 'Carmen'); Suite campestre. arr. of BACH: *Choral preludes: Ich ruf' zu dir, Herr Jesu Christ; Nun komm, der Heiden Heiland.*

*** Olympia OCD 461. Stephenson.

Both these collections are thoroughly worthwhile and they overlap very little. William Stephenson is possibly the more natural Busoni interpreter and his programme is very stimulating. Yet the Chandos disc assembles nearly 80 minutes of Busoni's piano music and makes an admirable and well-chosen introduction to it. Most pieces come off very well indeed, and often brilliantly, from the *Exeunt omnes* and the *Elegien* to the *Indianisches Tagebuch* and the attractive *Turandots Frauengemach*. This is an excellent CD, very well recorded and thoroughly recommendable, but not in preference to the Olympia selection, if one has to make an outright choice between them.

4 Elegies; Sonatina seconda; Toccata. arr. of Bach: Toccata & Fugue in D min., BWV 565; Chorales: Ich ruf zu dir, Herr; Wachet auf.

*** MDG 312 0436-2. Tanski.

Claudius Tanski proves a most persuasive Busoni interpreter, having the questing mind and sensitivity this repertoire calls for, not to mention the abundant technical prowess. He plays four of the *Elegies*, Nos. 3–6. Both in Busoni's visionary pieces and in the transcriptions of the Bach, he is more than equal to the technical and imaginative challenges this music presents. Artistically this is three-star playing and, though the recording is not in the demonstration bracket, it is superior to Trevor Barnard (see below).

Fantasia contrappuntistica; Fantasia after J. S. Bach; Toccata.

**(*) Altarus (ADD) AIR-2-9074. Ogdon.

Ronald Stevenson calls Busoni's remarkable *Fantasia contrappuntistica* a masterpiece and, listening to John Ogdon's performance, one is tempted to agree. The *Fantasia after J. S. Bach* was written a year earlier and is among Busoni's most concentrated and powerful piano works. The balance places Ogdon rather far back and, as the acoustic is somewhat reverberant, the piano sounds a little clangy.

24 Preludes, Op. 37.

** Divine Art 2-5011. Barnard – BLISS: *Piano Sonata.* **

Trevor Barnard offers an intelligently planned disc, since neither the Bliss *Piano Sonata* nor the Busoni *Preludes* are otherwise available. However, the recording is a bit monochrome and shallow; the playing itself, though serviceable and conscientious, falls short of distinction.

OPERA

(i) *Arlecchino* (complete); (ii) *Turandot* (complete).

*** Virgin VCD7 59313-2 (2). (i) Richter, Mohr, Holzmair, Huttenlocher, Dahlberg, Mentzer; (ii) Gessendorf, Selig, Dahlberg, Schäfer, Kraus, Holzmair, Struckmann, Sima, Rodde; Lyon Op. Ch. & O, Nagano.

Arlecchino ('Harlequin') is a sparkling comedy that builds on *commedia dell'arte* conventions with a point rarely matched in opera, though for the non-German-speaking listener a snag of the piece is that the title-role is a speaking part, a deterrent to frequent repetition. Even so, it would be hard to imagine a finer performance than this, with the conductor's finesse matched by a brilliant German cast with no weak link.

Busoni's *Turandot* evokes a fantasy fairy-tale atmosphere in a piece that is light in texture, with motivation aptly quirky rather than realistic. The surreal atmosphere is enhanced when the improbable theme for the evocative interlude before Act II is not Chinese but English – *Greensleeves*. Again Nagano's conducting gives a thrusting intensity to a piece that might seem wayward, and the casting is comparably brilliant, with Mechthild Gessendorf masterly as Turandot and Stefan Dahlberg heady-toned as Kalaf. The recording is vividly atmospheric, with plenty of presence.

Doktor Faust (opera) complete.

**(*) Erato 3984 25501-2 (3). Henschel, Begley, Hollop, Jenis, Kerl, Fischer-Dieskau, Lyon Opera Ch. & O, Nagano.

(M) **(*) DG (ADD) 427 413-2 (3). Fischer-Dieskau, Kohn, Cochran, Hillebrecht, Bav. Op. Ch. & R. O, Leitner.

Kent Nagano and his Lyon Opera forces fill an important gap in the catalogue with this first really complete recording of Busoni's masterpiece, using the score as completed after Busoni's death by his pupil, Philipp Jarnach. The set seeks to get the best of both worlds by also offering the extended realization of the closing scenes prepared by Anthony Beaumont with the help of newly discovered extra sketches. Fischer-Dieskau here recites the opening and closing superscriptions, normally omitted in stage productions. Dietrich Henschel may not be as searching or weighty an interpreter as Fischer-Dieskau, but the clarity and incisiveness of his singing are most impressive, leading to a noble account of the death scene, one of the passages expanded in the Beaumont version. He is well contrasted with the powerful Mephistopheles of Kim Begley, a tenor role that is Wagnerian in its demands. The rest of the cast is first rate, with voices well forward; but the impact of the performance is slightly blunted by the backward balance of the orchestra, distanced in a more spacious acoustic.

Unfortunately, the DG recording is full of small cuts; however, with superb, fierily intense conducting from Leitner, it fully conveys the work's wayward mastery, the magnetic quality which establishes it as Busoni's supreme masterpiece, even though it was finished by another hand. The cast is dominated by Fischer-Dieskau, here in 1969 at his very finest; and the only weak link among the others is Hildegard Hillebrecht as the Duchess of Parma.

BUTTERWORTH, Arthur

(born 1923)

Symphony No. 1, Op. 15.

*** Classico CLASSCD 274. Munich SO, Bostock – GIPPS: *Symphony No. 2.* ***

How is it possible for a symphony of this quality to be so neglected by the British musical establishment? It is powerful, imaginative and atmospheric. Arthur Butterworth comes from Manchester and played in the Hallé and Scottish National Orchestras. His *First Symphony* is a large-scale, 40-minute work which Sir John Barbirolli premièred in 1957. Sibelian in outlook (but none the worse for that) and with an innate feeling for the landscape of northern England and Scotland, it is powerfully argued and arresting – the product of a resourceful musical mind. It resonates in the memory, and Douglas Bostock and the Munich orchestra capture both its sombre mood and its stormy climaxes; the composer had the desolate Cape Wrath in mind in the last movement, where the music's whirlwind energy is splendidly conveyed. The recording is excellent, spacious and full-bodied.

BUTTERWORTH, George

(1885–1916)

(i) *The Banks of Green Willow; 2 English Idylls; A Shropshire Lad* (rhapsody); (ii) *A Shropshire Lad* (cycle of 6 songs); *Bredon Hill* and other songs: *O fair enough are sky and plain; When the lad for longing sighs; On the idle side of summer; With rue my heart is laden.*

(N) (M) *** Decca (ADD) 468 802-2. (i) ASMF, Marriner; (ii) Luxon, Willinson.

In his orchestral pieces and songs (almost all of which are included here) George Butterworth's music created an idealized picture of a rural England before the First World War, in which the composer was killed by a sniper's bullet. The orchestral rhapsody, *A Shropshire Lad*, with its yearning lyricism, represents the English folksong school at its most captivatingly atmospheric, and the other three works are in a similar appealing pastoral vein, and again have moments of passionate feeling. Marriner's performances with the Academy have stood the test of time. They are very beautiful and utterly evocative. The recording, vivid and wide-ranging, dates from 1976 and the CD remastering shows just how good it is.

Benjamin Luxon's performances of the songs, in partnership with David Willinson, are equally persuasive. Unlike the orchestral works they do not draw on actual folk-tunes.

Benjamin Luxon's approach, dramatic as well as sympathetic, reveals these settings as not quite the unassuming miniatures they may sometimes seem. But while he can project his tone and words with great power, his delicate half-tones are equally impressive, and he underlines the aptness of music to words often set by British composers, but never more understandingly than here. Again well-balanced, vivid recording from the mid-1970s.

The Banks of Green Willow.

(M) *** Chan. (ADD) 6566. Bournemouth Sinf., Del Mar – BANTOCK: *The Pierrot of the Minute: overture;* BRIDGE: *Summer*, etc. ***

The Banks of Green Willow; 2 English Idylls; A Shropshire Lad (rhapsody).

*** Nim. NI 5068. E. String O, Boughton – BRIDGE: *Suite;* PARRY: *Lady Radnor's Suite.* ***

Boughton secures from his Birmingham-based orchestra warm and refined playing in well-paced readings. In an ample acoustic, woodwind is placed rather behind the strings.

On Chandos, Del Mar gives a glowingly persuasive performance of *The Banks of Green Willow*, which comes as part of another highly interesting programme of English music devoted also to Butterworth's somewhat older contemporaries, Bantock and Frank Bridge. The digital transfer of a 1979 analogue recording has the benefit of even greater clarity without loss of atmosphere.

A Shropshire Lad (rhapsody).

(N) (M) (**) Cala mono CACD 0528. NBC SO, Stokowski – ANTHEIL: *Symphony No. 4;* VAUGHAN WILLIAMS: *Symphony No. 4.* (***)

Stokowski in this evocative Butterworth tone poem draws ravishing, sensuous sounds from the NBC Orchestra, notably the strings, unrecognizable as Toscanini's players. Sadly, the 1944 radio recording, cleanly focused and well transferred, is marred by some 'wow' on the tape.

Love Blows as the Wind (3 songs).

(M) *** EMI (ADD) CDM7 64731-2. Tear, CBSO, Handley – ELGAR; VAUGHAN WILLIAMS: *Songs.* ***

These three charming songs (*In the year that's come and gone, Life in her creaking shoes, Coming up from Richmond*), to words by W. E. Henley, provide an excellent makeweight for a mixed bag of orchestral songs based on the first recording of Vaughan Williams's *On Wenlock Edge* in its orchestral form. The sound is clear, yet enjoyably warm and atmospheric.

BUXTEHUDE, Diderik (c. 1637–1707)

CHAMBER MUSIC

6 String sonatas (without Opus numbers): *in C min. D, BuxWV 266–7; in F, BuxWV 269; in G; in A min.; in B flat, BuxWV 271–3.*

*** da capo 8.224005. Holloway, Weiss, Ter Linden, Rasmussen, Mortensen.

*** da capo 8.224121 (as above, in a box with complete da capo catalogue).

These unpublished works come from an (undated) collection held in Uppsala, Sweden. They are scored for a more varied ensemble than the Op. 1 and Op. 2 sonatas and their other principal difference is that they contain considerably more solos than in the published collections. They are certainly no less inventive. Both the *G major*, BuxWV 271 (which opens the disc), and the *B flat major*, BuxWV 273 (which is a considerably expanded version of Op. 1/4), are particularly attractive; the former, with a series of violin solos and a sprightly closing fugato, shows the composer at his most varied and light-hearted. BuxWV 266 (which closes the disc) is the most concentrated and complex of all. The same thematic material is re-used and varied throughout the work. There is a central, freely ruminative ('fantastic') violin solo, and the sonata culminates with a brief, sustained slow finale. The writer of the excellent accompanying notes, Nils Jensen, suggests that this (appropriately) C major work deserves the epithet of Buxtehude's *'Jupiter Sonata'*. Performances throughout are excellent in every way and the recording well up to standard. As can be seen above, this CD comes either in a normal jewel-case or also (subject to availability) in a box with a complete da capo catalogue.

7 Trio Sonatas, Op. 1, BuxWV 252–8.

*** da capo 8.224003. Holloway, Mortensen, Ter Linden.

7 Trio Sonatas, Op. 2, BuxWV 259–65.

*** da capo 8.224004. Holloway, Mortensen, Ter Linden.

Trio Sonatas: in G; B flat & D min., Op. 1/2, 4 & 6 (BuxWV 253, 255 & 257); in D & G min., Op. 2/2–3, (BuxWV 260–1).

*** ASV (ADD) CDGAU 110. Trio Sonnerie.

Trio Sonatas for Violin, Viola da gamba & Harpsichord: in A min., Op. 1/3; in B flat, Op. 1/4; in G min., Op. 2/3; in E, Op. 2/6 (BuxWV 254–5, 261; 264).

(B) *** HM (ADD) HMA 901089. Boston Museum Trio.

Buxtehude was nearly sixty when he published his *Sonatas*, Op. 1 and Op. 2. Each contains seven works and together they ambitiously explore all the major and minor keys, beginning with F major and omitting only F minor and B flat minor. What is immediately striking about both Op. 1 and Op. 2 is not just the variety of invention, but the way Buxtehude heightens the contrasting vitality of his allegros by introducing them with *Lentos* or *Adagios* of considerable expressive intensity. On the whole, the sonatas of Opus 2 are less quirky and seem more mature than those of Op. 1. The very first, the *Sonata in B flat*, in five movements, brings an eloquent central *Grave* (a dialogue between violin and cello) plus much to divert the listener throughout. No. 5, in A major, opens with a bouncing but brief *Allegro*; then comes a violin solo, marked *Concitato*, followed by a similarly improvisatory viola da gamba contribution. Nos. 6 and 7, both with noble opening slow sections, and very well balanced in their expressive and vigorous content, make a satisfying conclusion to a fine series. With John Holloway a

very stylish leader, the performances here are expert, fresh and alive, using period instruments brightly without edginess or unattractive linear squeezing. The group is very well balanced and the recording immediate and real.

In their well-chosen selection, the Trio Sonnerie show enthusiasm and expertise, and their virtuosity is agreeably effortless and unostentatious.

The Boston Museum Trio are a highly accomplished group who display an exemplary feeling for style. The music here is unfailingly inventive and, despite the obvious Italianate elements, distinctive. Not only are the playing, recording and presentation of high quality, but the cost is modest.

KEYBOARD MUSIC
Complete harpsichord music

Volume 1: *Aria in A min., BuxWV 249; Canzona in C, BuxWV 166; Canzonetta in A min., BuxWV 225; Chorale Variations: Wie schöne leuchtet der Morgernstern, BuxWV 223; Fugue in B flat, BuxWV 176; Partita: Auf meinen lieben Gott, BuxWV 179; Suites: in C, BuxWV 226; in D, BuxWV 233; Toccata in G, BuxWV 165.*

*** da capo 8.224116. Mortensen.

Volume 2: *Aria: More Palatino in C, BuxWV 247; 2 Canzonettas in G, BuxWV 171–2; Chorale: Nun lob, meine Seele, den Herren, BuxWV 215; Courante zimble in A min., BuxWV 245; Fugue in C, BuxWV 174; Suites: in E min., BuxWV 235; in G min., BuxWV 242.*

*** da capo 8.224117. Mortensen.

Volume 3: *Aria: La Capricciosa in G, BuxWV 250; Canzonetta in D min., BuxWV 168; Prelude in G, BuxWV 162; Suites: in F, BuxWV 238; in A, BuxWV 243.*

*** da capo 8.224118. Mortensen.

Buxtehude's keyboard and organ music is not clearly defined: much of it could be played on organ, harpsichord or clavichord, although the works requiring the pedal were obviously intended primarily for the organ. The modestly conceived but very agreeable *Suites* (each a group of four dance movements: *Allemande, Courante, Sarabande* and *Gigue*) were obviously intended for the domestic keyboard. In his excellent survey Lars Ulrik Mortensen has carefully chosen the works most suitable for the harpsichord, including chorales and other sets of variations (notably the *Arias*) which were Buxtehude's strongest suit and in which he displays consistent ingenuity and musical skill, always holding the listener's interest. The selected fugues are all jauntily appealing. Mortensen uses a copy of a Ruckers harpsichord made by Thomas Mandrop-Poulsen, an excellent instrument on which he produces a remarkable range of colour (it includes also a muted effect). His performances are of the highest order, spontaneous and flexible, and exciting in their sheer dexterity.

Volume 3 brings what is undoubtedly Buxtehude's keyboard masterpiece, *La Capricciosa*, a virtuoso showpiece nearly 30 minutes in length, consisting of 32 variations on an *Aria in G minor*, a bergamasca which is later transformed variously into a gigue, sarabande and minuet. The composer's kaleidoscopic invention knows no bounds, and this work clearly anticipates Bach's *Goldberg Variations*. It is less profound, but is continually diverting and it requires both imagination and brilliance from its performer. Superbly played here, it makes this third collection the obvious point for the collector to enter Buxtehude's very rewarding keyboard world.

ORGAN MUSIC

Canzonetta in G, BuxWV 171; Ciaconas: in C min., BuxWV 159; in E min., BuxWV 160; Chorales: Ach, Herr, mich armen Sünder, BuxWV 178; Der Tag der ist so freudenreich, BuxWV 182; Durch Adams Fall ist ganz verderbt, BuxWV 183; In dulci jubilo, BuxWV 197; Komm, heiliger Geist, Herr Gott, BuxWV 199; Nimm von uns, BuxWV 207; Nun komm der Heiden Heiland, BuxWV 211; Wie schön leuchtet der Morgenstern, BuxWV 223. Fugue in C, BuxWV 174; Magnificat primi toni, BuxWV 203; Passacaglia in D min., BuxWV 161; Preludes: in A min., BuxWv 153; in C, BuxWV 137; in D, BuxWV 139; in D min., BuxWV 140; in E min., BuxWV 142; in F, BuxWV 145; in F sharp min., BuxWV 146; in G min., BuxWV 149. Te Deum laudamus, BuxWV 218; Toccatas: in D min., BuxWV 155; in F, BuxWV 156.

(M) *** Erato 0630 12979-2 (2). Alain (Schnitger-Ahrend organ, Groningen).

Marie-Claire Alain's admirable, mid-priced two-disc set on Erato currently seems just about the best buy for those wanting a comprehensive survey of Buxtehude's splendid organ music. The magnificent opening *Prelude in C* shows not only how ideally the Groningen organ suits this repertoire (weighty yet never clouding sonorities) but also the full calibre of Buxtehude's music. Beginning floridly and thrillingly over massive pedals, Alain presents it powerfully and spontaneously, and she is equally impressive in registering the chorales, using a wide palette of colour: they are gently paced but never drag. The second disc opens with the ebullient *Fugue in C* which is so like the *Fugue à la gigue* attributed to Bach (BWV 577). Then, after the impressive chaconnes, the *Canzonetta in G* is piped deliciously. The complex *Magnificat primi toni* and the large-scale chorale fantasia on the *Te Deum* (in which Buxtehude and Alain always ensure that the *cantus firmus* emerges clearly) make one understand why Bach so admired this music. The arresting *Toccata in D minor*, with its dramatic pauses, undoubtedly influenced Bach's most famous organ work in the same key. Superb playing throughout, and demonstration-standard recording.

Canzona in D min., BuxWV 168; Choral fantasia on Gelobet seist du, Jesu Christ, BuxWV 188; Ciacona in E min., BuxWV 160; Fugue in C, BuxWV 174; Magnificat primi toni, BuxWV 203; Passacaglia in D min., BuxWV 161; Prelude in D min., BuxWV 140; Prelude in F sharp min. (transposed into G min.), BuxWV 146; Toccatas: in D min., BuxWV 155; in F, BuxWV 157.

(BB) *** Arte Nova 74321 63633-2. Oster (Arp-Schnitger organ, St Jacobi, Hamburg).

Although the mid-priced two-disc collection from Marie-Claire Alain still remains the most comprehensive and desirable introduction to Buxtehude's organ music for the general collector, this super-bargain sampler by Rainer Oster is very attractive in its own right. Oster presents all this music spontaneously in vivid colours, delightfully registered. He closes with the compelling *Toccata in D minor*, which shows so well the influence Buxtehude exerted over the young Bach, who walked so far to hear him play. The recording is first class.

Canzona in E min., BuxWV 169; Canzonetta in G, BuxWV 171; Ciacona in E min., BuxWV 160; Chorales: Ach Herr, mich armen Sünder, BuxWV 178; In dulci jubilo, BuxWV 197; Komm, Heiliger Geist, Herre Gott, BuxWV 199; Vater unser im Himmelreich, BuxWV 219; Magnificat primi toni, BuxWV 203; Preludes: in C, BuxWV 137; in D, BuxWV 139.

(*) Chan. 0514. Kee (organ of St Laurent Church, Alkmaar) – SWEELINCK: *Collection*. *

Piet Kee's performance of the opening *Magnificat primi toni* is magnificent. The closing *Ciacona in E minor* is impressive too, while the *Canzonetta in G* is deliciously registered, with piping flute colouring. One's reservations concern the presentation of the chorales, which, Kee suggests, 'require poetic expression'. Perhaps they do, but they also need to be moved on rather faster. The Chandos recording is superb.

Chorales: Auf meinen lieben Gott, BuxWV 179; Gott der Vater wohn uns bei, BuxWV 190; Nimm von uns, Herr du treuer Gott, BuxVW 207; Nun komm der Heiden Heiland, BuxWV 211; Puer natus in Bethlehem, BuxWV 217; Von Gott will ich nicht lassen (2 settings), BuxWV 220/221.

*** Chan. 0539. Kee (organ of Roskilde Cathedral, Denmark) – BRUHNS: *Preludes*. ***

The restored baroque organ at Roskilde Cathedral has a palette to tempt the most jaded listener and, although Piet Kee still persists in playing these chorales and their variants rather slowly, his piquant registration is very effective, so that they serve as attractively serene interludes between the remarkably flamboyant *Preludes* by Buxtehude's precociously inspired pupil, Nicolaus Bruhns, whose genius was sadly cut short when he died before his mentor, at the early age of 32. The recording is of demonstration quality.

Chorales: Christ unser Herr zum Jordan kam; Durch Adams Fall ist ganz verderbt; Ein feste Burg ist unser Gott; Erhalt uns, Herr, bei deinem Wort; Es ist das Heil uns kommen her; Es spricht der unweisen Mund wohl; Gelobet seist du, Jesu Christ; Gott der Vater, wohn uns bei; Magnificat primi toni; 2 Preludes & Fugues in A min.; Preludes & Fugues: in C; F sharp min.

(B) *** HM (ADD) HMA 190942. Saorgin (Schnitger organ of the Church of St Michel de Zwolle, Holland).

The Schnitger organ is sensitively and colourfully registered by René Saorgin; he is particularly impressive in the serene, reflective chorales, *Durch Adams Fall* and *Es spricht der unweisen Mund wohl*, while the elaborations of the

Magnificat are finely made. Excellent recording, vividly transferred.

Ciaconas: in C min.; E min., BuxWV 159–60; Passacaglia in D min., BuxWV 161; Preludes & Fugues: in D; D min.; E; E min., BuxWV 139–42; in F; F sharp min., BuxWV 145–6; in G min., BuxWV 149.

(M) *** DG (IMS) (ADD) 427 133-2. Walcha (organ of Church of SS Peter and Paul, Cappel, Germany).

Helmut Walcha has the full measure of this repertoire, and these performances on the highly suitable Arp Schnitger organ in Cappel, Lower Saxony, are authoritative and spontaneous. The 1978 recording is excellent and the disc comprises generous measure, 73 minutes.

(i) *Preludes & Fugues: in G min.; F. Chorales: Herr Christ, der einig Gottes Sohn; In dulci jubilo; Lobt Gott, ihr Christen allzugleich; Chorale Fantasy: Gelobet seist du, Jesu Christ. Cantatas: (ii) In dulci jubilo; Jubilate Domino.*

(B) *** HM (ADD) HMA 190700. (i) Saorgin (organ of St Laurent Church, Alkmaar); (ii) Alfred Deller, Deller Cons., Perulli, Chapuis.

A good, inexpensive sampler of Buxtehude, dating from 1971. The opening *Prelude and Fugue in G minor* is fully worthy of the young J. S. Bach and, like its companion, is played splendidly by René Saorgin. The chorales are more static and less interesting than Bach's treatment of the same ideas. Of the cantatas, *In dulci jubilo* is a florid piece for four voices with instrumental accompaniment, while *Jubilate Domino* is a solo cantata accompanied by viola da gamba and organ continuo. Deller is in good form throughout.

VOCAL MUSIC

Cantatas: An Filius non est Dei, BuxWV 6; Cantate Domino, BuxWV 12; Frohlocket mit Händen, BuxWV 29; Gott fähret auf mit Jauchzen, BuxWV 33; Herr, wenn ich nur Dich habe, BuxWV 39; Heut triumphieret Gottes Sohn, BuxWV 43; Ich bin die Auferstehung, BuxWV 44; Ich habe Lust absuzcheiden, BuxWV 46; Ihr lieben Christen, BuxWV 51; In dulci Jubilo, BuxWV 52; Jesus dulcis memoria, BuxWV 56; Jesu meines Lebens Leben, BuxWV 62; Jubilate Deo, BuxWV 64; Mein Gemüt erfreuet sich, BuxWV 72; Nichts soll uns scheiden, BuxWV 77; Nun danket alle Gott, BuxWV 79; Wie wird erneuet, wie ird erfreuet, BuxWV 110 (0630 17759-2 (3)). Membra Jesu nostri, BuxWV 75 (0630 17760-2).

(M) *** Erato 0630 17758-2 (4). Schlick, Frimmer, Chance, Jacobs, Prégardien, Kooy, Hanover Boys' Ch., Amsterdam Bar. O, Koopman.

All the works in the main three-disc collection are of a pietist religious character, although the music readily expands into joyously extrovert expressions of praise. The usual pre-Bach layout is observed: a short instrumental sonata followed by a short vocal concerto, an aria with interspersed instrumental interpolations and a final ensemble. Some are more ambitious, including chorus, trumpets and cornetts, and even trombones, and drums too. The brass-writing is inevitably primitive but highly effective in its stylized way. The solo singing is excellent, accompaniments are alive, textures transparent, and the recording balance is altogether excellent. The collection is capped by the inclusion of a moving and beautifully sung version of *Membra Jesu nostri*. Sufficient to say that the performances are of the highest quality, beautifully sung by the same group of soloists, and choir. The recording is both spacious and clear, and the style is expressively reverential, while conveying the music's humanity.

Cantatas: Befiehl dem Engel, BuxWV 10; Fürwahr, er trug unsere Krankhelt, BuxWV 31; Gott hilf mir, BuxWV 34; Herzlich lieb hab ich Dich, O Herr, BuxWV 41; Ich suchte des Nachts, BuxWV 50; Nun danket alle Gott, BuxWV 79.

*** HM HMC 901629. Cantus Köln, Junghänel.

This eminent German group give extremely stylish and cultured accounts of these lovely pieces, and no one wanting a representative anthology of Buxtehude cantatas is likely to be unpersuaded by this splendid recording.

Membra Jesu nostri, BuxWV 75.

(M) *** DG (IMS) 447 298-2. Monteverdi Ch., E. Bar. Sol., Gardiner – SCHUTZ: *O bone Jesu.* ***
*** BIS CD 871. Hida, Midori Suzuki, Yanagisawa, Anazawa, Mera, Sakurada, Ogasawara, Bach Collegium, Japan, Maasaaki Suzuki.
(BB) *** Naxos 8.553787. Trogu, Invernizzi, Balconi, Cecchetti, Carnovich, R. Svizzera (Lugano) Ch., Sonatori de la Gioiosa Marca, Treviso, Accademia Strumentale Italiana, Verona, Fasolis (with ROSENMULLER: *Sinfonia XI* ***).

Membra Jesu nostri; Heut triumphieret Gottes Sohn, BuxWV 43.

**(*) HM HMC 901333. Concerto Vocale & Instrumental Ens., Jacobs.

The *Membra Jesu nostri* is a cycle of seven cantatas, each addressed to different parts of the body of the crucified Christ, all of a simple, dignified, expressive power that make a strong impression. John Eliot Gardiner's is the most searching and devotional; the Concerto Vocale, though beautifully sung, is less atmospheric both as a performance and as a recording. The Harmonia Mundi is more forwardly balanced; the Gardiner has more space and the sense of one of Buxtehude's own *Abendmusik*. Compare the sixth of the cantatas, *Ad cor*, and the more reverential approach and feeling of the Gardiner version tells. But both issues can be recommended; the impressive *Heut triumphieret Gottes Sohn* comes with the Harmonia Mundi disc and a Schütz *Geistliches Konzert*, *O bone Jesu*, related in spirit, comes on the Archiv recording, which is now offered at mid-price.

On BIS, Suzuki's Japanese ensemble bring a remarkably authentic feeling for period to this lovely work (Maasaaki Susuki worked with Ton Koopman for many years) and, although the recording is made in a rather reverberant acoustic environment, this does not seriously diminish the pleasure this set gives. However, unlike both its competitors, it is without a coupling.

The performance from the Swiss-Italian Radio and ensembles from Verona and Treviso under Diego Fasolis is marginally less polished and accomplished vocally, but it has feeling and depth. They are most expertly balanced and the sound is excellent in every way. Those wanting a bargain need not hesitate.

BYRD, William (1543–1623)

The Byrd Complete Edition, Volume I: (i) *Alma redemptoris mater a 4; Audivi vocem de caelo a 5; Christe qui lux es a 5; Christe redemptor omnium a 4; De lamentorum Jerimiae prophetae a 5; Domine quis habitat a 9; Ne perduas cum impiis a 5; Omni tempore benedic Deum a 5; Peccavi super numerum a 5; Vide Dominum quoniam tribulor a 5. Propers for the Lady Mass in Advent a 5: (Rorate caeli; Tollite portas/Ave Maria; Ecce virgo).* Consort pieces: (i) *Christe qui es lux a 4; Miserere a 4; Sanctus a 3; Sermone blando a 4.*

*** ASV CDGAU 170. Cardinall's Musick, Carwood;
   (ii) Friedeswide Consort.

Cardinall's Musick are putting us in their debt by preparing (in new editions by David Skinner) a complete recorded survey of one of the greatest Elizabethan English composers, William Byrd. Although not all of it is of equal quality, the overall standard is very high, and most of it was published during the composer's lifetime, though not the superb *Peccavi super numerum*, which close the recital. Volume I commences the series with a programme of the early manuscript works, which are used to frame the three Gradualia for the Lady Mass in Advent. At a centre point in each group of motets, a recorder consort provides two contrasting instrumental pieces. Most of this music is virtually unknown: it is all sung with great conviction, richly blended and convincingly paced. The recording was made in the Fitzalan Chapel at Arundel Castle, which provides an ideal acoustic, resonant yet never blurring detail.

The Byrd Complete Edition, Volume II: *Ad Dominum, cum triblarer a 8 Alleluya – Confitemi Domino a 3; Alleluya – Laudate pueri Dominum a 3; Ave regina caelorum a 5; Decantabat populus a 5; Deus in adjutorium a 6; Hodie Christus natus est a 4/6; O admirable commertium a 4/7; O magnum mysterium a 4/8–9; O salutaris hostia a 6. 5 Propers for the Nativity a 4 (1607).* BYRD/SHEPPARD/MUNDY: *In exitu Israel a 4.*

*** ASV CDGAU 178. Cardinall's Musick, Carwood.

Volume 2 is, if anything, even more stimulating than Volume 1, including as it does *O salutaris hostia* with its extraordinarily plangent harmonic clashes – the most musically daring work in the composer's whole output. Also harmonically striking is the extended psalm-setting, *In exitu Israel*, which was a composite work shared by Byrd with William Mundy and John Sheppard, who wrote the lion's share, setting seven of the fourteen verses. The Propers for Christmas and the three associated Gradualia provide the central core of the recital. But the exultant *Decantabat populus* and the two closing motets – the noble and melancholy *Deus in adjutorium* (here reconstructed) and the heartfelt and passionate *Ad Dominum cum tribularer* – are among

the composer's finest, most individual and most passionate works. Both reflect the frustrations of the Catholic-faithful living in Protestant England. The eloquent performances truly reflect this anguish, and again this splendid group are superbly recorded.

The Byrd Complete Edition, Volume III: Early Latin church music: *Benigne fac Domine; Christus qui lux est; Circumspice Jerusalem; Domine ante te omne desiderium; Domine Deus omnipotens; Petrus beatus; Reges Tharsis et insulae; Sacris solemnis; Super flumina Babylonia; Te lucis; 4 Propers for Epiphany.*

*** ASV CDGAU 179. Cardinall's Musick, Carwood (with Philippe DE MONTE: *Quomodo cantabimus* ***).

In Volume 3, Cardinall's Musick turn to rare music, mostly pieces which Byrd left unpublished. Many of these motets have had to be reconstructed, their inner parts restored with scholarly care. The four *Propers for Epiphany* come from an incomplete set of Gradualia, published in 1607, yet this music shows Byrd at his most imaginative. Most moving of all is the culminating item, an eight-part setting of four verses from Psalm 136, reflecting the trials of a recusant Catholic in Elizabeth I's England, with the poignant message (in Latin), 'How shall we sing the Lord's song in a strange land?' Also included is a fine setting of Psalm 136 by the Flemish Philippe de Monte which prompted Byrd to write his response. Performances throughout are beautifully shaped, yet with great underlying intensity.

The Byrd Complete Edition, Volume IV: *Cantiones sacrae*, Book I (1575): complete.

*** ASV CDGAU 197. Cardinall's Musick, Carwood.

Byrd published the first of his three books of *Cantiones sacrae* in conjunction with his teacher and mentor, Thomas Tallis, contributing 17 motets to this initial collection. *Tribue Domine . . ., Te deprecor . . ., Gloria Patri* (here sung together as the penultimate number before *Libera me, Domine*) were given separate numbers to reach this total. Although these ASV performances encounter considerable competition in the present catalogue, this is, at present, the only recommendable CD (74 minutes) offering the entire contents of Book I, and the performances are beautifully blended, while Andrew Carwood's tempi move the music on at what seems a natural pacing. The recording is well up to the fine standard of this series.

The Byrd Complete Edition, Volume V: (i) *Masses for 3, 4 & 5 Voices;* (ii) *Organ Fantasia in C & D min.; Voluntary a 3.*

✿ (N) *** ASV CDGAU 206. (i) Cardinal's Music, Carwood; (ii) Russill.

Byrd's three great Masses were written for recusant private performance in English country houses. They were celebrated in secret against a background of oppression and fear, for penalties were severe, especially for celebrant priests. Yet if anything, the associated dangers tended to enhance the degree of devotion, and certainly Byrd's music celebrates the Eucharist with a very special combination of serenity and intensity. Perhaps the most beautiful is the *Mass for 3*

Voices, which comes second here and is performed with great eloquence, but in all three the performers sing the *Credo* with a growing depth of feeling, while the following *Sanctus* makes a gently rapturous contrast. The closing *Agnus Dei* of the *Mass for 5 voices* is ravishingly seraphic. The performances are admirably paced and authentically chamber-scaled with two voices to a part, yet the ambience of Fitzalan Chapel, Arundel Castle, brings the richest blend of sound. Carwood has chosen to perform the *Mass for 4 voices* with the combination of alto, tenor, baritone and bass voices (instead of SATB), and this gives a mellower sonority than usual, but works well. The three organ voluntaries that act as introductions and interludes are taken from *My Lady Nevells Booke* and are admirably played on an appropriate (modern) chest organ by Patrick Russill. The opening *Fantasia in D minor* demands genuine bravura but is also notable for quoting from the *Salve Regina* chant, a significant indication of the faith of its listeners. It is difficult to conceive of finer or more moving performances or more natural sound, and the clarity of detail is remarkable.

The Byrd Complete Edition, Volume VI: Music for Holy Week and Easter (1605 & 1607): (i) *Adoramus te; Angelus Domini; Christus resurgens; Haec dies; Holy Saturday Vespers; Mane vobiscum; Mass Propers for Easter Day; Passion Domini nostri Jesu Christi secundum Johannem; Plorans plorabit; Post dies octo.*

(N) *** ASV CDGAU 214. Cardinall's Musick, Carwood,
(i) with Russill (organ)

Shortly after publishing his three Masses Byrd began his comprehensive anthology of Graduela (Mass Propers for the Church Year). The First Book was published in 1605, a difficult time for Catholics in England, because of the Gunpowder Plot which took place in that same year. Undeterred, Byrd followed with the Second Book in 1607 and all the music in this collection comes from these two books. The penetential opening lament, *Plorans plorabit* ('My eyes shall weep sore') is one of his finest, and very moving in its expressive polyphony.

Yet a warning has to be given that roughly half the disc consists, not of polyphony, but of chanting by solo voices. The *St John Passion*, 35 minutes long, with – inexplicably – no dividing tracks, is almost entirely of chant in Latin. The greatest part of the setting is monodic plainsong using three voices – Chronista (the narrator), Christus (singing the words of Jesus in a lower voice) and Synagoga (the choir who sing the words of Pilate and Peter) – and also those of the crowd with the briefest of commentary in turba choruses. With complete text and translation it becomes hypnotic, but hardly an experience to be repeated often.

The rest of the programme however is richly appealing, especially the *Holy Saturday Vespers* which in their *Alleluias* anticipate the joyous and imaginative *Mass Propers for Easter Day* (the word *Alleluia* is not spoken in Lent). The remaining group of Easter motets are all brief, but tellingly expressive until the final four-part *Christus resurgens* which makes its effect with a direct emotional simplicity. This is one of Byrd's earliest known works, and fascinating in prompting diverse opinions, being regarded as crude by some, as a masterpiece

by others. The performances and recordings are well up to the high standard of this ever-rewarding series offering beautiful atmospheric sound.

OTHER RECORDINGS

Complete consort music: *Christe qui lux a 4, Nos. 1–3; Christe redemptor a 4; Fantasia a 3, Nos. 1–3; Fantasia a 4, No. 1; Fantasia a 5 (Two in One); Fantasia a 6, Nos. 2–3; In nomine a 4, Nos. 1–2; In nomine a 4, Nos. 1–5; Miserere a 4; Pavan & Galliard a 5; Pavan & Galliard a 6; Prelude & Ground a 5; Sermon blande blando a 3; Sermon blando a 4, No. 1; Te lucis a 4, No. 2, verse 2.*

*** Virgin VC5 45031-2. Fretwork, with Wilson (lute).

Fretwork have completed their survey of Byrd's consort music, which is now fitted on to a single CD. The grave feeling of much of this music is apparent in the opening *Prelude and Ground a 5*; then the mood quickly lightens as the texture is woven in more swiftly moving configurations to make a typically satisfying whole. *Browning* has the alternative title of *The leaves be green* and consists of divisions on a popular song, while the *Fantasia a 6*, which closes the concert, is a masterly compression of ideas into a fluid structure as powerful as Purcell's famous *Chaconne*. Performances have consistent authority and freshness and, although the recording seems rather close, it is vivid and realistic.

Music for Consorts and Virginals: *Browning; The Carman's whistle; A fancie; Fantasia a 6; French Corantos; The Irish March; My Lord of Oxenford's Maske; Pavan; Pavan a 5; Pavan: Belle qui tiens ma vie; Pavan: Mille Regretz; 2 Pavans & Galliards; Pavan & Galliard a 6; Pavan & Galliard: Kinbourough Good; Praeludium & Ground; The Queen's Alman.*

*** Auvidis E 8611. Capriccio Stravagante, Sempé.

Skip Sempé and his colleagues play every note with that authenticity of feeling which is so often missing from period performance. Sempé has poetic feeling, an astonishing keyboard flair and rare artistry. The sound of his Skowroneck harpsichord is vividly reproduced. One of the best CDs of its kind to have appeared in the last few years, and a splendid introduction to the composer.

Music for viols: *Browning; 2 Fantasias a 3 in C; Fantasias a 4 in D & G; Prelude & Voluntary;* (i) *Prelude (Pavana, Gagliarda Ph. Tregian); Ut re mi fa sol la* (for harpsichord); (ii–iii) *Delight is dead;* (ii) *Farewell false love;* (iii) *My mistress had a little dog; Rejoice unto the Lord;* (ii–iii) *Who made thee, Hob, forsake the plough?* (ii) *Ye sacred muses.*

*** Lyrichord LEMS 8015. (i) Bagger; (ii) Crout; (iii) Lipnik; NY Cons. of Viols.

The New York Consort of Viols play with an attractive blend of timbre, and everything they play is thoroughly alive. The harpsichordist, Louis Bagger, plays with great bravura when *Ut re mi fa sol* becomes more and more florid as it proceeds. The two vocal soloists work well together, especially in the rustic dialogue song, *Who made thee, Hob, forsake the plough?*. Tamara Crout sings with great charm in her solo numbers: with the lightest touch in the charming song about the 'murdered' pet dog, and very expressively in *Rejoice unto the Lord* and the touching *Ye sacred muses*. In every way this is a most rewarding programme, excellently balanced and recorded.

Consort, keyboard music, anthems and songs: *Fantasia for 4 viols; Fantasia No. 2 for 6 viols; Fantasia No. 3 for 6 viols; Galliard; Have mercy upon me, O God; In nomine No. 2 for 4 viols; In Nomine No. 5 for 5 viols; Pavane;* (i) (Keyboard) *John, come kiss me now; Pavan in A min.; Qui passe (for my Lady Nevell);* (Vocal) (ii) *Christ rising again; Fair Britain isle; In angel's weed; Rejoice unto the Lord; Susanna fair; Triumph with pleasant melody.*

(BB) *** Naxos 8.550604. Rose Consort, Red Byrd; (i) Roberts (harpsichord or virginals); (ii) Bonner.

Here is a useful and inexpensive cross-section of Byrd's secular output that gives a good idea not only of its artistic riches but of its sheer variety. Both the ensembles recorded here, the Rose Consort of viols and Red Byrd, are in good form, and Timothy Roberts and Tessa Bonner are sensitive and expert exponents of this repertoire. The recorded sound is eminently clean and well balanced, and there is plenty of space round the aural image, which greatly enhances the undoubted attractions of an attractive anthology.

Complete keyboard music.

(M)*** Hyp. CDA 665551/7. Moroney (harpsichords, muselar virginal, organ, chamber organ, clavichord).

Davitt Moroney's impressively comprehensive *Gramophone* award-winning undertaking includes also the organ music played on the highly suitable Ahrend organ of L'Eglise-Musée des Augustins, Toulouse, which Moroney often registers with ear-tickling skill, as in the *Gloria tibi trinitas* or in the first version of the *Fancie for my Ladye Nevell*. To add maximum variety, he also uses a number of keyboard instruments based on north European seventeenth-century models, including a clavichord by the estimable Thomas Goff, a chamber organ by Martin Goetz and Domenic Gwynn, and harpsichords by Hubert Bédard and Reinhard von Nagel. The most fascinating of these instruments is the so-called muselar virginal (by John Philips of Berkeley after a 1650 Couchet), which has a remarkably rich timbre and also a beautiful painting on the lid (a colour photograph is printed on the back of the liner-notes). Moroney tells us that, for all its fullness of sound, the instrument fell out of favour because of a drawback, its very characteristic 'amplified' mechanical clicks, especially in rapid left-hand scales. However, this instrument is heard at its finest and most spectacular (on Disc 7) in Byrd's description of *The Battel*, with its introductory *Marche* and a *Galliard for the Victorie*. Quite as fascinating aurally are the five items with which Moroney closes his programme. Four different versions of the *Praeludium to the Fancie* from Book 12 are given, each heard on a different instrument, and he concludes with the *Fantasia* from Book 13, one of the composer's most complex and original pieces, presented with considerable

flair. Throughout, the playing is committed, authoritative and nicely embellished, if at times a shade didactic. The recording is most realistic, though it is important not to set the volume level too high. The accompanying notes are as thorough as they are scholarly and comprehensive. The set is offered at a special price: seven discs for the cost of five.

Keyboard music (from above): *The Battell: The Trumpets; The Bells; The Carman's Whistle; Christ qui lux; Fantasia; Galliard; Galliard for the Victorie; Galliard to Johnson's Delighte; Go from my window; A Grounde; Miserere I & II; Have with yow to Walsingham; My Ladye Nevell's Grownde; O quam gloriosum est regnum; 7th Pavaian; A Pavion; Praeludium to the Fancie; Ut, re, mi, fa, sol, la.*

(N) *** Hyp. CDA 66558. Moroney (harpsichords, muselar virginal, organ, chamber organ, clavichord).

A well-chosen 78-minute programme from Davitt Moroney's distinguished survey, including favourite items like the hypnotic portrayal of *The Bells*, the jolly *Carman's Whistle* (on chamber organ), *The Trumpets* from *The Battell* to demonstrate the extaordinary sound of the muselar virginal (here sounding something like a highly amplified jew's harp!), but given a less bizarre image in the following *Galliard for the Victorie*. In complete contrast the pair of delicate *Misereres* are played on a small clavichord, so you will have to be careful with the volume control. As with the complete set the documentation is first class.

VOCAL MUSIC

Anthems: *Praise our Lord, all ye Gentiles; Sing joyfully; Turn our captivity.* **Motets:** *Attolite portas; Ave verum corpus; Christus resurgens; Emendemus in melius; Gaudeamus omnes; Justorum animae; Laudibus in sanctis Dominum; Non vos relinquam; O magnum mysterium; O quam suavis; Plorans plorabit; Siderum rector; Solve iubente Deo; Veni, Sancte Spiritus; Visita quaesumus Domine.*

*** Coll. COLCD 110. Cambridge Singers, Rutter.

John Rutter brings a composer's understanding to these readings, which have a simple, direct eloquence, the music's serene spirituality movingly caught; and the atmospheric recording is very faithful, even if detail could be sharper. The programme is divided into four groups: Anthems; then Motets: of penitence and prayer; of praise and rejoicing; and for the Church year.

Motets in paired settings: *Ave verum corpus* (with PHILIPS: *Ave verum corpus*); *Haec dies* (with PALESTRINA: *Haec Dies*); *Iustorum animae* (with LASSUS: *Iustorum animae*); *Miserere mei* (with G. GABRIELLI: *Miserere mei*); *O quam gloriosum* (with VICTORIA: *O quam gloriosum*); *Tu es Petrus* (with PALESTRINA: *Tu es Petrus*).

(B) *** CfP CD-CFP 4481. King's College, Cambridge, Ch., Willcocks.

This is an imaginatively devised programme of motets in which settings of Latin texts by Byrd are directly contrasted with settings of the same words by some of his greatest contemporaries. As was the intention, quite apart from adding variety to the programme the juxtaposition makes one listen to the individual qualities of these polyphonic masters the more keenly and register their individuality. The recording emerges with remarkable freshness on CD, and the singing is most beautiful.

Cantiones sacrae, Book I (1575): *Laudate pueri; O lux beata trinitas; Tribue Domine.* Book II (1589): *In resurrectione tua; Laetentur coeli; Ne irascaris; O quam gloriosum; Tribulationes civitatum.* Book III (1591): *Cantate Domino; Esurge Domine; Haec dies; Recordare Domine; Salve Regina.*

(BB) *** ASV CDQS 6211. Sarum Consort, Mackay.

Cantiones sacrae, Book 1: *Aspice Domine; Domine secundum multitudinem; Domine tu iurasti; In resurrectione tua; Ne irascaris Domine; O quam gloriosum; Tristitia et anxiestas; Vide Domine afflictionem; Virgilate.*

(N) (M) **(*) CRD 3420. New College, Oxford, Ch., Higginbottom.

Cantiones sacrae, Book 2: *Circumdederunt me; Cunctis diebus; Domine, non sum dignus; Domine, salva nos; Fac sum servo tuo; Exsurge, Domine; Haec dicit Dominus; Haec dies; Laudibus in sanctis Dominum; Miserere mei, Deus; Tribulatio proxima est.*

(N) (M) **(*) CRD 3439. New College, Oxford, Ch., Higginbottom.

Although all three Books of *Cantiones sacrae* were written to be sung in Latin, some of the more successful were translated and sung in English. Their musical range is wide. The Sarum Consort is a finely balanced and blended group, admirably directed by Andrew Mackay, whose pacing and control of light and shade cannot be faulted. The recording, made in the ideal acoustic of Milton Abbey, is clear, yet rich in choral ambience. Excellent documentation, with full texts and translations, makes this a first-rate bargain.

Though the New College Choir under its choirmaster, Edward Higginbottom, does not sing with the variety of expression or dynamic which marks its finest Oxbridge rivals, it is impossible not to respond to the freshness of its music-making. The robust, throaty style suggests a Latin feeling in its forthright vigour, and the directness of approach in these magnificent *Cantiones sacrae* is most attractive, helped by recording which is vividly projected, yet at once richly atmospheric.

The Great Service (with anthems).

*** Gimell CDGIM 911. Tallis Scholars, Phillips.

Peter Phillips and the Tallis Scholars give a lucid and sensitively shaped account of Byrd's *Great Service.* Theirs is a more intimate performance than one might expect to encounter in one of the great English cathedrals; they are fewer in number and thus achieve greater clarity of texture. The recording is quite excellent: it is made in a church acoustic (the Church of St John, Hackney) and captures detail perfectly. It includes three other anthems, two of which (*O Lord make thy servant*

Elizabeth and *Sing joyfully unto God our strength*) are included on the rival EMI disc.

Mass for 3 voices; Mass for 4 voices; Mass for 5 voices.

⊛ (M) *** Decca (ADD) 433 675-2. King's College, Cambridge, Ch., Willcocks.
(B) **(*) HM (ADD) HMA 90211[id.]. Deller Cons.

Masses for 3, 4 & 5 voices; Ave verum corpus.

*** Gimell CDGIM 945. Tallis Scholars, Phillips.

Masses for 3, 4 & 5 voices; Ave verum corpus; Magnificat; Nunc dimittis.

(B) *** Double Decca 452 170-2 (2). King's College, Cambridge, Ch., Willcocks – TAVERNER: *Western Wynde Mass.* ***

Although later versions of the *Mass for 5 voices* have produced singing that is more dramatic and more ardent, the King's Choir versions of the *Masses for 3 and 4 voices,* dating from 1963, remain classics. Under Willcocks there is an inevitability of phrasing and effortless control of sonority and dynamic that completely capture the music's spiritual and emotional feeling. On Double Decca the 1959 recordings of the *Ave verum, Magnificat* and *Nunc dimittis* have been added, representing a more reticent, less forceful style than some might expect. But the singing is still affectingly beautiful and the sound comparably spacious, and the coupled Taverner programme shows the choir on top form.

Peter Phillips is a master of this repertoire; undoubtedly these performances have more variety and great eloquence so that, when the drama is varied with a gentler mood, the contrast is the more striking. The sound made by the Scholars in Merton College Chapel is most beautiful, both warm and fresh.

Whether or not it is historically correct for Byrd's Masses to be sung by solo voices, the great merit of the French Harmonia Mundi performances is their clarity, exposing the miracle of Byrd's polyphony, even though the tonal matching is not always flawless. The 1968 recording is clean and truthful, although it lacks something in ecclesiastical atmosphere.

Mass for 4 voices; Mass for 5 voices; Infelix ego.

(BB) *** Naxos 8.550574. Oxford Camerata, Summerly.

This coupling from the Oxford Camerata represents one of Naxos's most enticing bargains. The full-throated singing has spontaneous ardour but no lack of repose in the music's more serene moments. Summerly offers the motet, *Infelix ego,* as a bonus. These readings are distinctive in a different way from those by the Tallis Scholars. The recording is outstandingly vivid.

Masses a 5: In assumptione beauae mariae virginis; In tempore Paschali (Propers). Antiphons: *Ave Regina coelorum; Salve Regina.* Motet: *Regina coeli.*

(M) *** HM HMT 7905182. Chanticleer.

After three beautiful Masses, Byrd wrote more music that could be used for private Mass celebration by Roman Catholics living in Protestant England. Besides a great many motets, he left sequences of Mass Propers which could be used for certain key feast-days of the church year. They can be grouped quite effectively and sung independently, and that is what the dozen singers of Chanticleer do here. They have chosen two main sequences, the first connected with Easter (the Mass *In tempore Paschali*) and the second for the *Assumption of the Blessed Virgin Mary*. Intonation is not always absolutely immaculate, but the singing always has expressive conviction; one finds oneself carried along by the very spontaneous flow, with very little pause between movements. A well-documented collection, including translated texts.

Byrd Song: *Fantasia a 4; In nomine Nos. 1–2 a 4; Fair Britain Isle; In fields abroad; Lullaby; My Mistress had a little dog; O Lord how vain; Rejoice unto the Lord; Susanna fair; Though Amaryllis dance in green; Though I be Brown; La Verginella; Ye sacred muses.*

(N) *** Simax PSC 1191. McGreevy, Partridge, Phantasm.

Geraldine McGreevy dominates this attractive recital, opening with the lovely *La Verginella*, and very touching in the surprisingly melancholy *Fair Britain Isle* and the poignant *Lullaby*, though perking up for *Susanna fair* and *Though Amaryllis dance in green*. Ian Partridge is in good voice too, although his contribution is perhaps less striking. These are all songs in which the vocal line is part of the polyphonic texture of the viol accompaniment which Phantasm handle admirably, as they do their three solo consort pieces. Excellent recording with no edginess on the string timbres.

BYSTRÖM, Oscar (1821–1909)

Symphony in D min.; Andantino; Concert Waltzes Nos. 1 & 3; Overture in D; Overture to Herman Vimpel.

** Sterling CDS 1025-2. Gävle SO, Spierer.

Oscar Byström is an interesting figure. He was an accomplished pianist and conductor who, like his fellow Swede Berwald, pursued a career outside music alongside his work as a composer. His *Symphony in D minor* is clearly influenced by Berwald. The second group of the first movement is delightful and the work as a whole has much to commend it. The overtures all come from much the same period and are pleasing, though no one would make great claims for them. They are well served on this CD.

CABEZÓN, Antonio de (1510–66)

'Music for the Spanish Kings': *Keyboard Tablatures* (excerpts, arr. Savall) inc. Cabezón's arrangements of music by CRECQUILLON and WILLAERT.

(N) (BB) *** Virgin 2 x 1 VBD5 61875 (2). Hespèrion XX, Savall (with fifteenth- and sixteenth-century music from the Spanish Courts of Alphonso I, Ferdinand I and Charles V ***).

Cabezón was Philip II of Spain's favourite court musician and he accompanied his king on journeys to Italy, Germany and the Netherlands – and to London, where his virtuoso playing may well have served to inspire the flowering of English virginal music. He was one of the greatest contrapuntalists of his age, and his output is preserved in the form of keyboard tablatures, intended for keyboard, harp or vihuela. Jordi Savall's group of vihuela players produce some glorious sounds here, as do the highly accomplished brass players.

The eighteen pieces recorded on the first of these two discs are transcribed mainly for groups of vihuela de arco and brass, as well as two vihuela de mano. Their polyphonic inventiveness is heard to clear advantage in this form. In addition to the music of Cabézon himself there are his arrangements of music by Crecquillon and Willaert.

Early Spanish music benefited from the intermingling of Arab and Christian cultures and the companion CD includes earlier music from the Spanish court, offered in conjectural instrumentation, using brass and simple percussion liberally, although Hayne van Ghizeghem's melancholy piece for viols, *De tous biens plaine*, makes a striking contrast. Throughout the disc Montserrat Figuerras makes a major contribution in the various cancións and dance songs. Highlights include the villanesca, *O Dio se vede chiaro*, with its alternating moods, and *Amor, che t'o fat hio*, an engaging love song with a distinct flamenco flavour. Most affecting of all is Antonio Valente's villancico, *Ay luna que reluzes*, beautifully sung, and haunting in quite a modern way. Also included on the second disc is an extra instrumental piece by Cabézon, the memorable and winningly scored *Diferencias sobre el cano del caballero*. The closing *Galliarda Napolitana* of Antonio Valente and the villanesca all napolitana, *Vecchie letrose*, by Adrian Willaert, both have potential hit status. Again excellent recording.

CAGE, John (born 1912)

Concerto for Prepared Piano & Chamber Orchestra (1950/51); *The Seasons* (ballet); *Seventy-Four* (for orchestra), *Versions I & II; Suites for Toy Piano* (original and orchestral version, scored by Lou Harrison).

*** ECM; 465 140-2. (i) Tang (prepared piano; toy piano); American Composers' Orchestra, Russell Davies.

Seventy-Four, hypnotic in atmosphere, is nevertheless remarkably static. *The Seasons* is in the composer's own words 'an attempt to express the traditional Indian view as quiescence (winter), creation (spring), preservation (summer), and destruction (fall)'. It is not easy to follow, but certainly has plenty of movement, and its textures are exotic. The simplistic *Suite for Toy Piano* has also been ingeniously scored by Lou Harrison and most listeners will respond to the vividly contrasting sonorities of this instrumental version, which has instant appeal. The performances here are dedicated and of the highest calibre, and the recording excellent.

Piano music (1933–50): *Ad Lib; Crete and Dad; 3 Easy Pieces; Jazz Study; 5 Metamorphoses; Ophelia; 2 Pieces (1935); 2 Pieces (1946); A Room; Quest (2nd movement); The Seasons; Soliloquy; Triple-Paced (first version).*

(N) *** MDG 613 0793-2. Schlweiermacher.

MDG are undertaking a complete survey of John Cage's piano music, and the present collection represents the composer's first compositional period. All the music here is readily accessible; indeed, the *Three Easy Pieces* have charm as well as simplicity. The *Jazz Study* and *Ad Lib* are rhythmically catchy without being predictable. The haunting picture of *A Room* is matched by the evocative nature of much of the writing in *The Seasons*. The *Metamorphosis* suite is rather more formidable, but distinctly rewarding. In short, if you want to explore Cage's piano repertoire this is the place to start: the performances are first class and so is the recording.

Piano music (1960–92): *ASLP; The Beatles (1962–70); Etudes boreales* (for a percussionist using a piano); *One* (4 versions for 1–4 pianos).

(N) *** MDG 613 0791-2. Schlweiermacher.

The key work here is *One*, written in four versions between 1987 and 1990, in which a series of notes or simple chords are played widely separated, with the four pianos placed in different positions. The silence between the notes and note groups, and the implications of time and space, are all important. In the second version of 1989, the Brahms *Lullaby* appears and reappears, apparently played on a musical-box, and no reason for this is given in the analytical notes. The other works are similarly fragmented. But the exception, which will fascinate the non-specialist listener, is the bizarre mélange of Beatles tunes, at times only barely recognizable, and with the music finally ending in mid-air. The performances are obviously authoritative and the recording is first class, both in the reproduction of the pianos and the dimensional layout.

CALDARA, Antonio (c. 1670–1736)

Sonata da camera in E min., Op. 1/5; Trio Sonata in D, Op. 2/3; (i) Cantatas: *D'improvviso amore felice; Medea in Corinto; Soffri mio caro Alcino; Vicino a un rivoletto.*

(B) **(*) Virgin 2 x 1 VBD5 61588-2 (2). (i) Lesne, Il Seminario Musicale – STRADELLA: *Motets.* **(*)

Gérard Lesne is in his element in these fine cantatas. The most immediately striking is *Medea in Corinto*, based on the legend of the betrayal of Medea by Jason of Golden Fleece fame. But the finest and most extended is the memorable *Vicino a un rivoletto*, where the voice shares a long, echoing interchange with a solo violin (splendidly played here) followed by a gravely noble arioso with cello obbligato. The two *Sonatas* are used as interludes, but they are fine works in their own right – the melancholy *Adagio* of the four-movement *Trio Sonata*, Op. 1/5 is particularly affecting. These performances could hardly be more authentic or more communicative and they are naturally balanced and recorded. The one great snag is the absence of either translations or adequate notes about the music.

Christmas Cantata (Vaticini di Pace); Sinfonias Nos. 5 & 6.

(B) *** Naxos 8.553772. Enid Haines, Dayiantis-Straub, Lane, Arnot, Aradia Baroque Ens., Mallon.

Caldara, an Italian contemporary of Bach and Handel, wrote this rare and delightful cantata for the Christmas celebrations in Rome in 1712. Preceded by an overture, it is a free-running sequence of 14 arias for the allegorical characters of Peace, Human Heart and Divine Love, with Justice initially representing Old Testament values. Peace, in the longest and most beautiful of the arias, a siciliano, then woos Justice to mercy through a vision of the Infant Christ. This Canadian performance is fresh and lively, with four excellent soloists (notably Mary Enid Haines as Peace) and a good period-instrument ensemble. A rarity made doubly enticing at Naxos super-bargain price.

Crucifixus.

(B) *** Double Decca (ADD) 443 868-2 (2). Palmer, Langridge, Esswood, Keyte, St John's College, Cambridge, Ch., Philomusica, Guest – BONONCINI: *Stabat Mater ***; PERGOLESI: *Magnificat in C; Stabat Mater **(*); D. SCARLATTI: *Stabat Mater; A. SCARLATTI: *Domine, refugium factus es nobis; O magnum mysterium; LOTTI: Crucifixus.* ***

The *Crucifixus* is an elaborate sixteen-part setting of great eloquence, texturally rich and concentrated into a few seconds short of five minutes. It follows on naturally after Bononcini's beautiful *Stabat Mater*.

Maddalena ai piedi di Cristo (oratorio; complete).

*** HM HMC 905221/22 (2). Kiehr, Dominguez, Fink, Scholl, Messthaler, Türk, Schola Cantorum Basiliensis O, Jacobs.

This oratorio about Mary Magdalene at the feet of Christ, an early work dating from around 1700, inspired Caldara to an astonishing sequence of *da capo* arias most of them brief, but with several longer ones given to Maddalena herself, notably the heartfelt *Pompo inutile*, inspiring Maria Cristina Kiehr to warm, golden tone, or the agonized *In lagrime stemprato*, depicting falling tears. In contrasting characterization, her sister Marta has such jolly numbers as *Vattene, corri, vola*, with Rosa Dominguez bright and agile. The role of Christ is given to a tenor, but neither of his two arias is reflective, and the biggest proportion of arias go to the counterpart characters of Earthly Love (a mezzo, Bernarda Fink) and Heavenly Love (a counter-tenor, Andreas Scholl), both of them singing superbly, subtly contrasted in tone. René Jacobs draws fresh and alert playing from the Schola Basiliensis Orchestra, with the instruments, including varied continuo, set in a warm acoustic slightly behind the singers.

Missa Sanctorum Cosmae et Damiani; Gradual: *Benedicta et venerabilis es;* Motet: *Caro meo vere es cibus.*

*** Virgin VC5 45387-2. Frimmer, Popken, Jochens, Mertens, Westfalia Kantorei, Capella Agostino Steffani, Lajos, Rovatkay (with Franz TUMA: *Sonata a 4 in E min.; Sonata a 5 in E min.* ***).

Caldara's *Missa Sanctorum Cosmae et Damiani* is a joyfully extrovert work, both lyrical and high spirited and fully scored with trumpets gleaming. The subdivisions of the *Gloria*, the heart of the work, with soloists and chorus alternating, are enhanced by instrumental obbligati: the alto's *Dominus Deus* features a trombone, the soprano's contribution to *Domine fili* is ornamented by a bravura trumpet. Two short, but attractive *String Sonatas* by Caldara's Bohemian contemporary, Tuma are used as interludes between the Mass, the very touching motet, *Caro meo* (a soprano–alto duet), and the closing, more ambitious Marian gradual, *Benedicta et venerabilis es*. Very well sung and excellently recorded, this collection will give much pleasure.

CAMBINI, Giuseppe Maria
(1746–1825)

Wind Quintets Nos. 1 in B; 2 in D min.; 3 in F.

(B) *** Naxos 8.553410. Avalon Wind Quintet – BRICCIALDI: *Wind Quintet in D.* ***

These *Wind Quintets* are doubtless inconsequential but they are charming, particularly when played so superbly and elegantly by these fine young German musicians. The recording is expertly balanced and very natural. Slight music, but so well served that it will give much pleasure.

CAMPION, Thomas (1567–1620)

Lute Songs: *Are you not what your fair looks express?; Author of light; Awake thou spring of speaking grace; Beauty is but a painted hell; Beauty, since you so much desire; Come you pretty false-eyed wanton; The Cypress curtain of the night; Fair, if you expect admiring; Fire, fire; I care not for these ladies; It fell upon a summer's day; Kind are her answers; Love me or not; Never love unless you can; Never weather-beaten sail; O never to be moved; Pined I am, and like to die; See where she flies; Shall I come, sweet love to thee?; So tired are all my thoughts; Sweet exclude me not; Your fair looks.*

(N) (B) **(*) HM HCX 3957023. Minter, O'Dette.

Thomas Campion was an almost exact contemporary of Dowland but his lute songs are much less well known – undeservedly so, for although his settings were rather less individually distinctive, their lyrical melancholy is often comparably affecting, as *Love me or not* and *The Cypress curtain of the night, Never weather-beaten sail* and the lovely *Author of light* readily demonstrate. Most touching of all is the plaintive *Shall I come, sweet love to thee?*, while the livelier and lighter-hearted *I care not for these ladies* is quite catchy. Drew Minter has an appealing alto voice and forms a sensitive vocal line, and (not surprisingly) Paul O'Dette's accompaniments are highly supportive. The balance is excellent and this disc is very good value, but the recital would have been even more attractive if several different singers had been employed, affording greater variety of timbre.

Lute songs: *Author of light; Beauty, since you so much desire; Come let us sound with melody; Come you pretty fals-ey'd wanton; Faire, if you expect admiring; Fire, fire, fire, fire!; Her rosie cheeks; I care not for these ladies; It fell on a sommers daie; Jacke and Jone they think no ill; Most sweet and pleasing are thy ways; Never weather-beaten saile; Shall I come, sweet love to thee?; Sweet exclude mee not; The Sypres curtain of the night; There is a garden in her face; There is none, O none but you; Though you are yoong and I am olde; Thou joy'st, fond boy; To musicke bent; Tune thy musicke to thy hart; Turn all thy thoughts to eyes; What is it that all men possess?; When to her lut Corrina sings; Vaile, love mine eyes (with ROSSETER: My sweetest Lesbia; When then is love but mourning?; ANON.: Miserere my maker).*

(B) **(*) Naxos 8.553380. Rickards, Linell.

Thomas Campion's song output was second only to Dowland's and he shared that composer's ability to touch the listener with melancholy. *Author of light, The Sypres curtain of the night* and *Though you are yoong and I am olde* are outstanding examples, but there are many others here. Of course, there are lighter settings too. *I care not for these ladies* could hardly have naughtier implications in its repeated pay-off line: 'She never will say no'. Steven Rickards, a young American counter-tenor, has a pleasing voice and delivery. At times one listens in vain for more variety of colour, but his presentation is appealingly simple, as are the lute accompaniments of Dorothy Linell, who attempts no elaborations or embellishments. They are well recorded in a pleasing acoustic and, with full texts included, this is yet another enterprising Naxos disc well worth its modest cost.

CAMPRA, André (1660–1744)

Cantatas: *Arion; La Dispute de l'Amour et de l'Hymen; Enée et Didon; Les Femmes.*

(B) *** HM HMA 1901238. Feldman, Visse, Gardeil, Les Arts Florissants, William Christie.

Jill Feldman is at her most spirited and eloquent in the dramatic narrative of *Arion* and Dominique Visse's tangy alto is equally telling in the altercation of the conflicting interests of Marriage and Love which need to be resolved harmoniously. *Les Femmes* is sung with both feeling and sparkle by Jean-François Gardeil. The most ambitious of the four works is a brilliant duet celebrating the nuptials of Aeneas and Dido. With sensitive and strongly paced accompaniments from Christie and Les Arts Florissants, it is difficult to imagine that these works could be re-created more tellingly, helped by the presence and atmosphere of the excellent recording.

Requiem Mass.

**(*) HM (ADD) HMC 901251. Baudry, Zanetti, Benet, Elwes, Varcoe, Chapelle Royale Ch. & O, Herreweghe.

This *Requiem* is a lovely work, with luminous textures and often beguiling harmonies, and its neglect is difficult to understand. Herreweghe's performance, with refined solo and choral singing, is pleasing and sympathetic if comparatively cool. The recording is refined, to match the performance.

OPERA

Idoménée (tragédie-lyrique): complete.

(B) *** HM (ADD) HMX 2901396.98 (3). Deletré, Piau,
Zanetti, Fouchécourt, Boyer, Les Arts Florissants, William
Christie.

In this first complete recording of any opera by Campra,
Christie opts for the later revision of the piece which the
composer made for the revival in 1731. Christie with his
talented Les Arts Florissants team presents the whole work
with a taut feeling for its dramatic qualities, though there is
nothing here to compare with the big moments in Mozart's
opera. The matching of voices to character is closer here
than we would conventionally expect in Mozart, and in the
breadth of its span and its frequent hints as to what Purcell
might have achieved had he tackled a full-length opera, this
is a fascinating work, vividly recorded. It is all the more
attractive reissued in Harmonia Mundi's bargain opera
series. An excellent booklet with full translation is included.

CANNABICH, Johann Christian

(1731–98)

*Symphonies Nos. 47 in G; 48 in B flat; 49 in F; 50 in
D min.; 51 in D; 52 in E, Op. 10/1–6.*

(N) (B) *** Naxos 8.554340. Nicolaus Esterházy Sinf., Grodd.

*Symphonies Nos. 59 in D; 63 in D; 64 in F; 67 in G; 68 in
B flat.*

(N) (B) *** Naxos 8.553960. Lukas Consort, Lukas.

Christian Cannabich was born and made his career in
Mannheim, where in 1774 he became conductor of what at
that time was the most celebrated orchestra in Europe.
Cannabich was to be described by Mozart as the finest
conductor he had ever encountered, but was also a prolific
and accomplished, if not always individual, symphonist. His
six works published in 1772 as Op. 10 are each in three
movements and effectively scored for flutes (or oboes),
and horns. Opening movements are conventional, but the
expressively gracious slow movements and lively finales
more than compensate, and very soon we encounter the
famous Mannheim 'crescendo' (the opening movement of
No. 51 provides a very striking example). There are even
hints of Mozart. The performances are lively, stylish and
well recorded.

The second group of symphonies (though still in three
movements) mark a considerable step forward. The scoring
of No. 59 uses the oboes more freely as soloists, and its
Andante is strikingly gracious. But when we reach the dramatic opening of No. 63 the scoring is much more ambitious,
using trumpets and timpani, as well as full woodwind, including clarinets. All the celebrated Mannheim effects are
here with an emphatic unison in the introduction, plus the
carefully regulated, almost Rossinian crescendos. The lilting
oboe melody of the slow movement contrasts with the
strong, Mozartean finale.

No. 64 brings more crescendo sequences, and the *Andante*

is again very fetching, to be followed by another bold finale,
featuring the horns, which are again used most effectively
in Nos. 67 and 68. No. 68 begins amiably but energetically,
and the solo horns are given the full limelight with the
principal theme of the *Andante*. The light-hearted second
subject of the finale again demonstrates the variety of
Cannabich's invention and the whole movement displays
his deft use of orchestral colour. Viktor Lukas and his Consort give admirable performances, full of life and with the
necessary light and shade. They are again very well recorded
and this pair of inexpensive discs provides a most stimulating
introduction to a composer/conductor justly renowned in
his own time.

Flute Quintets, Op. 7/3–6.

*** CPO CPO 999 544-2. Camerata Köln.

Cannabich's *Flute Quintets* are for one (or usually two)
flutes, violin, viola and cello, and sometimes have optional
keyboard parts. The music is elegant, well crafted and
charming, if very lightweight, with the 'concertante' flute
parts always dominant. Excellent performances here and
natural recording within a pleasing ambience.

CANNING, Thomas (born 1911)

Fantasy on a Hymn Tune by Justin Morgan (for double
string quartet and string orchestra).

*** Everest (ADD) EVC 9004. Houston SO, Stokowski –
R. STRAUSS: *Don Juan* etc. ***

The Pennsylvanian composer, Thomas Canning, has clearly
modelled his *Fantasy* on the Vaughan Williams *Tallis fantasia*. Although the contrast with the secondary string group
is less ethereal, in Stokowski's hands the work reaches a
thrilling climax, and this fine if derivative piece is well worth
having on disc when the recording is so rich and well
focused. This CD is offered at slightly under premium price.

CANTELOUBE, Marie-Joseph

(1879–1957)

Songs of the Auvergne: Series 1–5 (complete).

(B) *** Double Decca 444 995-2 (2). Te Kanawa, ECO, Jeffrey
Tate – VILLA-LOBOS: *Bachianas brasileiras No. 5*. ***

(i) *Chants d'Auvergne: Series 1–5* (complete);
(ii) Appendix: *Chants d'Auvergne et Quercy: La Mère
Antoine; Lorsque le meunier; Oh! Madelon, je dois partir;
Reveillez-vous, belle endormie. Chants paysans Béarn:
Rossignolet qui chants. Chants du Languedoc: La fille d'un
paysan; Moi j'ai un homme; Mon père m'a plasée; O up!;
Quand Marion va au moulin. Chants des Pays Basques:
Allons, beau rossignol; Comment donc Savoir; Dans le
tombeau; J'ai une douce amie; Le premier de tous les
oiseaux.*

🏵 (M) *** Van. (ADD) 08.8002.72 Davrath, O, (i) la Roche;
(ii) Kingsley.

It was Netania Davrath who in 1963 and 1966 – a decade

before the De los Angeles selection – pioneered a complete recording of Canteloube's delightful song-settings from the Auvergne region of France, plus an important appendix of 15 more, collected by Canteloube and admirably scored by Gershon Kingsley, very much in the seductive manner of the others. While her voice has a lovely, sweet purity and freedom in the upper range, she also brings a special kind of colour and life to these infinitely varied settings. The accompaniments are freshly idiomatic, warm but not over-upholstered, and the CD transfers retain all the sparkle and atmosphere of the original recordings.

In Dame Kiri Te Kanawa's recital the warmly atmospheric Decca recording brings an often languorous opulence to the music-making. In such an atmosphere the quick songs lose a little in bite, and *Baïlèro*, the most famous, is taken extremely slowly. With the sound so sumptuous, this hardly registers and the result remains compelling, thanks in large measure to sympathetic accompaniment from the ECO under Jeffrey Tate. At Double Decca price, this now makes a formidable bargain.

Chants d'Auvergne: L'Antouèno; Baïlèro; 3 Bourrées; Lou Boussu; Brezairola; Lou coucut; Chut, chut; La Délaïssádo; Lo Fiolairé; Jou l'pount d'o Mirabel; Malurous qu'o uno fenno; Passo pel prat; Pastourelle; Postouro, sé tu m'aymo; Tè, l'co, tè.

☸ (B) *** EMI CD-EMX 9500. Gomez, RLPO, Handley.

Jill Gomez's selection of these increasingly popular songs, attractively presented on a mid-price label, makes for a memorably characterful record which, as well as bringing out the sensuous beauty of Canteloube's arrangements, keeps reminding us, in the echoes of rustic band music, of the genuine folk base. An ideal purchase for the collector who wants just a selection.

Chants d'Auvergne: Baïlèro; 3 Bourrées; Brezairola; Lou Boussu; Lou coucut; Chut, chut; La Délaïssádo; Lo Fiolairé; Jou l'pount d'o Mirabel; Malurous qu'o uno fenno; Oï ayaï; Pastourelle; La pastrouletta; Postouro, sé tu m'aymo; Tè, l'co, tè; Uno jionto postouro.

(B) *** Virgin Classics 2 x 1 VBD5 61742-2. Augér, ECO, Tortelier – RAVEL: *Alborada; Shéhérazade*, etc. **(*)

Arleen Augér's lovely soprano is ravishing in the haunting, lyrical songs like the ever-popular *Baïlèro*. In the playful items she conveys plenty of fun, and in the more boisterous numbers the recording has vivid presence. Augér returns to sing Ravel's exotic song cycle *Shéhérazade* as part of a new coupling, which includes four of that composer's key orchestral works.

CAPLET, André (1878–1925)

La Masque de la mort rouge (Conte fantastique); Divertissements for Harp; (i) Les Prières, for soprano, harp & string quartet; (ii) 2 Sonnets, for soprano & harp; (i–iii) Septet à cordes vocales et instrumentales.

(B) *** HM (ADD) HMA 1901417. Cabel, Ens. Musique Oblique; with (i) Coste; (ii) Piau; (iii) Deguy.

This bargain-priced Harmonia Mundi reissue is highly recommendable, offering the more intimate, chamber version of the *Conte fantastique* for harp and strings, based on Edgar Allen Poe's *Masque of the Red Death*. In the other three major works, female voices are richly integrated with the string quartet, and the composer makes a great success of this combination of voices and strings, especially in the *Septet*, using a trio of two sopranos and a mezzo. Beautiful singing, sensitive playing and warmly atmospheric sound add to the listener's aural pleasure. Two solo *Divertissements* for harp make an agreeable central interlude.

Epiphany (Fresco for Cello & Orchestra after an Ethiopian Legend).

(B) *** EMI Début CZS5 73727-2. Phillips, Bav. Chamber PO, Plasson – FAURE: *Elégie*; LALO: *Cello Concerto*. ***

'Fresco' is a perfect description of this impressionistically etched evocation, which depicts the arrival in Bethlehem of Caspar, the black member of the three kings, the bringer of gold to 'honour the King of the World'. Caplet creates a fascinating opening texture of woodwind colour, which the cello first embroiders, then rhapsodically dominates. There is a long central cadenza placed against a steady drumbeat, then the work ends with an exotic dance when the King's young black retainers join in the celebration. Caplet's sound imagery is oriental and yet French (just as Ravel's can be), but the work demands, and receives here, enormous bravura from the cello soloist. The clear recording and the skill of the conductor ensure that, without loss of allure, every detail is in focus.

CARDOSO, Frei Manuel (c. 1566–1650)

Lamentatio; Magnificat secundi toni.

(B) *** Naxos 8.553310. Ars Nova, Bo Holten – LOBO: *Motets*; MAGALHAES: *Missa O Soberana luz* etc. *** (with Concert of Portuguese polyphony ***).

Cardoso's serene, flowing polyphony with its forward-looking use of augmented chords is heard at its most striking in the *Magnificat*, while his *Lamentatio* for six voices is touchingly beautiful. Remarkably eloquent singing from this fine Danish choir and good recording in a suitably ecclesiastical acoustic. The rest of the programme is hardly less stimulating.

Missa Miserere mihi Domine; Magnificat secundi toni.

*** HM HMC 901543. European Vocal Ens., Herreweghe.

Once again in the *Missa Miserere mihi Domine* we are aware of the extraordinary individuality of Cardoso's polyphony and its powerful and sumptuous expressive content. The composer's forward-looking use of harmonic relationships is also a striking feature of the *Magnificat*, a shorter but no less impressive work. The performers here really sound as if they believe both in the music and in the words they are singing, and the recording, made in L'Abbaye aux Dames de Saintes, is fully worthy of their richly sonorous blend of tone.

Requiem (*Missa pro defunctis*).

(B) *** Naxos 8.550682. Oxford Schola Cantorum, Summerly
– LOBO: *Missa pro defunctis.* ***

*Requiem: Magnificat; Motets, Mulier quae erat; Non
mortui; Nos autem gloriari; Sitivit anima mea.*

❀ *** Gimell (ADD) CD GIM 921. Tallis Scholars, Phillips.

Cardoso's *Requiem* opens in striking and original fashion.
The polyphony unfolds in long-breathed phrases of unusual
length and eloquence, and both the motets, *Mulier quae erat*
('A woman, a sinner in that city') and the short *Nos autem
gloriari* ('Yet should we glory'), are rich in texture and
have great expressive resplendence. Cardoso's use of the
augmented chord at the opening of the *Requiem* gives his
music some of its distinctive stamp. The Tallis Scholars sing
with characteristic purity of tone and intonation, and they
are splendidly recorded. A glorious issue.

In Summerly's Naxos account, Cardoso's *Missa pro defunctis* is not as dramatic in its contrasts as the coupled
setting of Duarte Lôbo. As with the Lôbo coupling, a solo
treble makes a brief but effective introduction for each
movement, a device which works very touchingly. The performance by Oxford Schola Cantorun is beautifully paced
and the calibre of the singing itself is very impressive indeed,
as is the Naxos recording.

CARISSIMI, Giacomo (1605–74)

*Abraham et Isaac; Ezecha (Hezekiah); Jephte (oratorios);
Missa septimi toni (for unaccompanied double choir);
Motets: O quam pulchra es; O vulnera doloris; Salve, salve
puellule; Tolle sponsa.*

(B) **(*) Erato Ultima (ADD) 3984 24231 (2). Smith, Serafim,
Huttenlocher, Rosat, Elwes, Silva, Rossier, Dufour, Lisbon
Gulbenkian Foundation Ch. & O, Corboz.

This Ultima Double makes a fine introduction to this gifted
composer. The soloists are excellent throughout, with Philip
Huttenlocher standing out, particularly as Jephte. The three-
movement choral *Mass* (*Kyrie–Gloria–Credo*) is also well
sung, although here the recording aims at sonority, rather
than aiming to separate the two choral groups. The other
snag is the lack of full documentation and texts. But the four
solo cantatas (given in turn to soprano, bass, tenor, and in
the case of *Tolle sponsa*, soprano, bass and chorus) are so
freshly sung and offer such enjoyable music that criticism is
all but disarmed. No complaints about the vivid projection
of the sound here.

Duos & cantatas: *A piè d'un verde alloro; Bel tempo per
me; Così volete, così sarà; Deh, memoria è che più chiedi;
Hor che si Sirio; Il mio cor è un mar; Lungi homai deh
spiega; Peregrin d'ignote sponde; Rimati in pace homai;
Scrivete, occhi dolente (Lettera amorosa); Tu m'hai preso à
consumare; Vaghi rai, pupille ardenti.*

(B) *** HM HMA 1901262. Concerto Vocale, Jacobs.

Carissimi's achievement as a sacred composer has long overshadowed his secular music, whose riches are generously
displayed here and whose inspiration and mastery are im-

mediately evident. These are performances of great style and
are beautifully recorded. A bargain.

(i) *Jephte;* (ii) *Jonas;* (iii) *Judicium Salomonis (The
Judgement of Solomon)* (oratorios).

*** Mer. CDE 84132. Coxwell, Hemington Jones, Harvey,
Ainsley, Gabrieli Cons. 8 Players, McCreesh.

No opening sinfonia survives for *Jephte*, and Paul McCreech
chooses to preface this oratorio with a Frescobaldi *Toccata*,
which works well. *Jepthe* is affectingly presented, and the
McCreech performance brings overt expressive feeling, despite some vocal insecurities at the very top. Overall these
are well-prepared and intelligent accounts. The continuo
part is imaginatively realized with some pleasing sonorities
(organ, double harp, chitarrone, etc.) and, despite some
undoubted minor shortcomings, these are most convincing
accounts of all three works, if on a fairly intimate scale
However, the back-up documentation is inadequate.

CARLSSON, Mark (born 1952)

Nightwings.

*** Crystal CD 750. Westwood Wind Quintet – BARBER:
Summer Music; LIGETI: *Bagatelles;* MATHIAS:
Quintet. ***

In *Nightwings* the flute assumes the persona of a dreamer,
the taped music may be perceived as a dream-world, and
the other four instruments appear as characters in a dream.
On this evidence, however, the conception is in some respects more interesting than the piece itself. Excellent
playing and recording.

CARMINA BURANA (*c.* 1300)

Carmina Burana – Songs from the Original Manuscript.

**(*) HM (ADD) HMC 90335. Clemencic Cons., René
Clemencic.

This was the collection on which Carl Orff drew for his
popular cantata. The original manuscript comprises more
than 200 pieces from many countries, dating from the late
eleventh to the thirteenth century, organized according to
subject-matter: love songs, moralizing and satirical songs,
eating, drinking, gambling and religious texts. René Clemencic's performances, recorded in 1977, have immense spirit
and liveliness, and there is much character. The presentation
suffers slightly from over-reverberant sound, though this at
times brings a gain in atmosphere.

The Great Mystery of the Passion (Passion play realized
Marcel Pérès).

(N) (B) *** HMA 1901323.24 (2). Soloists, Ens. Organum,
Marcel Pérès.

The Carmina Burana manuscript, found in the monastery
of Benediktheuren, is most famous for its secular texts, but
it includes valuable liturgical and sacred material too, and
its centrepiece is the framework of a narrative Passion drama,
written in both Latin and an ancient Southern German

dialect. Any modern re-creation is inevitably conjectural in the widest sense. The music itself is written in neumes (without a clef for definitive pitch indication) so that the melodic line is at best approximate.

In addition the unwieldy nature of the text itself induced Pérès both considerably to condense the original and also to expand it, using extraneous musical material and adding a narrator to link the sequences.

Authentic or not, the result works surprisingly well if you enjoy the basic idiom of monody and rich choral organum. There is a great deal of chant, but the resonant opening Palm Sunday processional with interchanging male and female voices is arresting, and the Pérès reconstruction then introduces the key characters.

Mary Magdalene (sinuously and darkly portrayed by Cyrille Gerstenhaber) is heard celebrating the world's pleasures and buying cosmetics 'that I may entice young men', followed by Domenique Visse's commanding Angel announcing the coming of Jesus, leading to his meeting with Mary and her renunciation and forgiveness.

Judas (Bruno Boterf) is boldly rather than weakly characterized, and Jesus himself (Françoise Fauché) is given a strong rich-voiced presence. The resurrection of Lazurus is followed by Judas's betrayal, Jesus on the Mount of Olives, his arrest and Peter's denial. The work's dramatic climactic sequence is very powerful – the Trial and the Flagellation, with its melancholy female chorus contrasting with the shouts of the Jews for Jesus's Crucifixion, and finally Mary's poignant lament (Astrid Maugard), with the closing choral Deposition both grieving and nobly exultant.

The performance under Pérès is splendidly sung, by principals and chorus alike, and (with the help of the excellent translation) the narrative is brought vibrantly to life, within a cathedral-like atmosphere.

CARPENTER, John Alden (1876–1951)

Adventures in a Perambulator; Symphonies Nos. 1–2.

(N) (B) *** Naxos 8.558065. Nat. SO of Ukraine, McLaughlin Williams.

John Alden Carpenter came from a wealthy Illinois family, and in spite of receiving every encouragement to develop his musical talent (which showed itself when he was still quite young), he put the family business first, eventually becoming Vice-President. His musical training included study under Elgar and this shows in his confident handling of the orchestra. *Adventures in a Perambulator* (which includes encounters with *Dogs*, *Dreams*, *The Lake*, *The Hurdy-Gurdy* and *The Policeman*) is charmingly scored and pleasantly tuneful. The *First Symphony*, a well-planned single-movement work, divided into five linked sections, is hardly more ambitious. But again its invention is warmly attractive and its nostalgic atmosphere holds the listener in its undemanding spell.

The *Second* opens more dramatically but similarly does not probe any depths, seeking mainly to divert, especially the jolly, boisterous finale. The Ukraine Orchestra obviously enjoy this music and play it very well indeed. The Naxos

recording is first class and the documentation includes the composer's own notes for *Adventures in a Perambulator*.

CARTELLIERI, Casimir Anton (1772–1807)

Clarinet Concertos Nos. 1 in B flat; 2 – Adagio pastorale; 3 in E flat.

*** MDG 301 0527-2. Klöcker, Prague CO.

Hardly a household name, Casimir Anton Cartellieri was born in Danzig and eventually found his way to Vienna. His three *Clarinet Concertos* (only the slow movement of the second survives) are expertly laid out for the instrument. While they are not searching or profound, they are astonishingly inventive and full of both charm and wit. Dieter Klöcker and the Prague Chamber Orchestra give thoroughly committed accounts of these delightful pieces, and the MDG recording is immaculate.

Double Concerto for 2 Clarinets in B flat; (i) Flute Concerto in G; Movement for Clarinet & Orchestra in B flat.

*** MDG MDG 301 0960-2. Klöcker, Arnold; (i) Brandkamp; Prague CO.

The *Concerto for Two Clarinets* reaffirms the strong impression made by its companions above. It bubbles over with high spirits and has a strikingly original opening. Klöcker and his pupil, Sandra Arnold, give a masterly account of the piece, and Kornelia Brandkamp is hardly less expert in the diverting and delightful *Flute Concerto*. As always with the Dabringhaus und Grimm label, the recordings are beautifully balanced and very natural. Not great music, perhaps, but very rewarding all the same.

CARTER, Elliott (born 1908)

(i; ii) Oboe Concerto; (iii) Esprit rude; (ii) Penthode (for 5 groups of instruments); (iv; ii) A Mirror on Which to Dwell.

(N) (B) *** Warner Apex. 8573 89227-2. (i) Holliger; (ii) Ens. Intercontemporain; (iii) Cherrier, Troutet; (iv) Bryl-Julson, Boulez.

A recording of a concert given for the composer in Paris to celebrate his eightieth birthday, for which he expresses gratitude and admiration in the notes, besides giving a full analysis of his music. The *Oboe Concerto* was written for Heinz Holliger, who gives a superb performance of a work which is underlyingly lyrical and appealing, even though the soloist is confronted with 'widely varying mercurial moods, sometimes bursting out dramatically'. *Esprit rude* ('rough breathing') is an even less predictable duet for flute and clarinet, and the atmospheric *Penthode* ('concerned with the experiences of connectedness and isolation') written for five groups of four players, is no more easy to unravel.

In the song cycle, setting poems of Elizabeth Bishop, one cannot but admire the expertise of Phyllis Bryn-Julson, accurately leaping from note to note against often bizarre accompaniments, and producing a remarkably expressive line of real tonal beauty in the fourth song, *Insomnia*, and the deeply expressive if enigmatic closing setting, *O Breath*. The recording is admirable, clear and well balanced. A classic and indispensable reissue.

(i) *Piano Concerto; Variations for Orchestra.*

*** New World (ADD) NW 347. (i) Ursula Oppens; Cincinnati SO, Gielen.

The *Concerto* is a densely argued piece, complex in its structure, with a concertino of seven instruments, surrounding the piano, who act as 'a well-meaning but impotent intermediary'. The *Variations* is an inventive and fascinating work, splendidly played by these Cincinnati forces. The recording was made at concert performances and is excellent.

Piano Concerto; Concerto for Orchestra; 3 Occasions for Orchestra.

(B) *** Arte Nova 74321 27773-2. Oppens, SWF SO, Gielen.

Piano Concerto; 3 Occasions for Orchestra.

(B) *** Arte Nova 74321 52248-2. Oppens, SWF SO, Gielen – BARTOK: *Piano Concerto No. 3;* BERG: *3 Pieces from the Lyric Suite.* ***

Michael Gielen directs strong, purposeful readings, very well played, of this taxing music, clarifying the thornily complex arguments with the help of vivid, sharply focused sound. Even with Ursula Oppens a powerful soloist, the *Piano Concerto*, dating from 1964–5, is the most formidable piece for the unprepared listener. That leads naturally on to the *Concerto for Orchestra* of 1969. More approachable than either is the third work, a collection of three pieces, written between 1986 and 1989, which display to the full the astonishing vitality and questing originality of a composer of rising eighty. In performances like these, recorded live, the tension is magnetic and this makes an inexpensive introduction to one of the most intractable of twentieth-century composers.

The alternative disc brings together two of Gielen's outstanding Carter performances but offering the generous alternative coupling of Bartók and Berg works.

Concerto for Orchestra.

(M) *** Sony (ADD) SMK 60203. NYPO, Bernstein – IVES: *Central Park in the Dark* etc. ***

It is apt that on the Bernstein CD, Elliott Carter's key avant-garde orchestral work from 1969 should follow on after Ives, for its writing seems naturally to derive from that earlier master in its complexity. However, the argument here is much more thorny, the texture densely interwoven and prismatic; its energy is unquestioned, but its linear fragmentation is daunting. Certainly it could hardly be played with more expertise or display more conviction; and the close (1970) recording-balance ensures that every detail is well defined.

CARULLI, Ferdinando (1770–1841)

Guitar Concerto in A.

(M) **(*) DG (IMS) (ADD) 439 984-2. Behrend, I Musici – GIULIANI: *Concerto in A* ***; VIVALDI: *Guitar Concertos* **(*).

The Italian virtuoso Ferdinando Carulli made his reputation in Paris, where this innocent post-Mozartian one-movement piece was written. It is elegantly played by Behrend and I Musici and immaculately recorded. A touch more vitality would have been welcome, but this is enjoyable enough.

CARVALHO, João De Sousa (1745–98)

Te Deum.

(M) *** DG (ADD) 453 182-2. Bosabalian, Saque, Gonzales, Mitchinson, Malta, Gulbenkian Chamber Ch. & O, Salzmann – ALMEIDA: *Beatus vir* etc.; SEIXAS: *Adebat Vincentius* etc.; TEIXEIRA: *Gaudate, astra.* ***

The Portuguese composer João De Sousa Carvalho was a contemporary of Mozart. During the course of this splendid and powerfully expressive work there is much thrilling writing for double chorus, and the florid arias – like Mozart's – are often semi-operatic in style, making great demands on the soloists, who generally rise to the occasion here, especially the fine mezzo, Carmen Gonzales, and the tenor, John Mitchinson. The performance here is eloquently moving and spaciously recorded (in 1970). Even if the double chorus at times could be more sharply defined, the overall focus and balance are very good. The reissue is made the more attractive by the substantial couplings from three major Portuguese baroque composers, all little known.

CARVER, Robert (c. 1484–c. 1568)

Mass: Cantate Domino for 6 Voices.

*** ASV CDGAU 136. (i) Lovett; Hamilton, Capella Nova, Tavener – ANGUS: *All my Belief;* (i) *The Song of Simeon.* ANON.: *Descendi in hortum meum.* BLACK: *Ane lesson upone the feiftie psalme; Lytill Blak.* PEEBLES: *Psalms 107; 124; Si quis diligit me.* ***

Most of the pieces, by David Peebles (who flourished 1530–76), John Black (c. 1520–87) and John Angus (fl. 1562–90), come from *Musica Britannica* Vol. XV ('Music of Scotland, 1500–1700') and appear on record for the first time. Though the authorship of the *Mass: Cantate Domino* is not definitely established, it is related to the five-part *Fera pessima* by Robert Carver and is almost certainly a re-working, possibly by Carver himself, of the earlier, five-part piece for six voices. In any event, this is a record of much interest, well sung and recorded.

Mass Dum sacrum mysterium in 10 parts; Motets: *Gaude flore Virginali; O bone Jesu.*

*** ASV CDGAU 124. Cappella Nova, Tavener.

The motet *O bone Jesu*, is in 19 parts and is of exceptional luminosity and richness. The 10-part *Mass, Dum sacrum mysterium*, is undoubtedly the grandest in scope, the most extended in development and the richest in detail. The motet, *Gaude flore Virginali* for five voices, though less sumptuous, has some adventurous modulations. The Cappella Nova under Alan Tavener give a thoroughly dedicated account of all three pieces, though the pitch drops very slightly in the *Gaude flore Virginali*. The recording is very good indeed.

Masses: Fera pessima for 5 voices; Pater creator omnium for 4 voices.

*** ASV CDGAU 127. Cappella Nova, Tavener.

Missa: L'Homme armé for 4 Voices; Mass for 6 Voices.

*** ASV CDGAU 126. Cappella Nova, Tavener.

These two CDs, together with his ten-part *Missa Dum sacrum mysterium* (and probably the *Cantata Domino* listed above), represent the complete sacred music of the early-sixteenth-century Scottish composer, Robert Carver. The six-part *Mass* of 1515 is cyclic (each Mass section opens with similar music), and the presence of other common material suggests that it is a parody Mass, possibly based, it is thought, on an earlier Carver motet.

Like the *L'Homme armé*, the *Fera pessima* is another *cantus firmus* Mass and dates from 1525; its companion, the four-part *Pater creator omnium*, comes from 1546 and reflects the changing style of the period. It survives only in incomplete form; the two missing parts in the *Kyrie* and *Gloria* have been added by Kenneth Elliott. Committed singing from the Cappella Nova and Alan Tavener, and very well recorded too.

CARWITHEN, Doreen (born 1922)

(i) Concerto for Piano & Strings. Overtures: ODTAA ('One damn thing after another'); Bishop Rock; Suffolk Suite.

*** Chan. 9524. (i) Shelley; LSO, Hickox.

Doreen Carwithen here emerges as a warmly communicative composer in her own right, owing rather more to Walton's style than that of her husband (William Alwyn). The two overtures in their vigour and atmospheric colour relate readily to her film music, the one inspired by John Masefield's novel, *ODTAA*, the other inspired by the rock in the Atlantic that marks the last contact with the British Isles, stormy in places, gently sinister in others. The charming *Suffolk Suite* uses melodies originally written for a film on East Anglia. Much the most ambitious work is the *Concerto for Piano and Strings*, with powerful virtuoso writing for the piano set against rich-textured strings. A deeply melancholy slow movement – in which the piano is joined by solo violin – leads to a strong finale which in places echoes the Ireland *Piano Concerto*. Howard Shelley is the persuasive soloist, with Richard Hickox and the LSO equally convincing in their advocacy of all four works. Warm, atmospheric sound.

(i) Violin Sonata; (ii) String Quartets Nos. 1 & 2.

*** Chan. 9596. (i) Mordkovitch, Milford; (ii) Sorrel Quartet.

The *First Quartet*, written in 1948 when she was still a student, firmly establishes Doreen Carwithen's personal idiom, tautly constructed in three movements. The result, identifiably English, yet points forward, though it is only in the *Second Quartet* of 1952, in two extended movements, that one detects a hint that she may have been studying the quartets of Bartók; with warmly expressive performances from the well-matched Sorrel Quartet. The *Violin Sonata*, written later, brings high dramatic contrasts, most strikingly in the central *Vivace*, a moto perpetuo in 9/8 rhythm. Lydia Mordkovitch, as ever, proves a passionate advocate, finding a depth and poignancy in the lyrical writing that may reflect her Russian roots. Julian Milford makes an ideal partner, though the piano is rather backwardly balanced. Otherwise the recording is first-rate.

CASELLA, Alfredo (1883–1947)

La Giara (Symphonic Suite), Op. 41 bis; Paganiniana (Divertimento for Orchestra), Op. 65; Serenata for Chamber Orchestra, Op. 46 bis.

(B) Naxos 8.553706. Italian Swiss RSO, Benda.

The performance of *Paganiniana* and the performance here by the Italian Swiss Radio under Christian Benda is as bright-eyed, polished and sympathetic as its competitor, below. Both the *Serenata*, which is precociously good humoured (it opens with a drole bassoon solo) and touchingly nostalgic by turns, and the ballet *La Giara*, are unashamedly eclectic. But Casella has a ready fund of good tunes and they are delectably scored. The ballet also includes a melancholy vocal interlude, *The Story of the Girl Seized by Pirates*, sensitively sung by Marco Beasley, affecting, but not in the least sentimental. The recording is first class, vividly atmospheric. This collection is well worth having, but don't play all three works at once.

Paganiniana, Op. 65.

(***) Testament mono SBT 1017. St Cecilia, Rome, O, Cantelli – DUKAS: *L'Apprenti sorcier*; FALLA: *Three-Cornered Hat*; RAVEL: *Daphnis et Chloé: Suite No. 2.* (***)

Paganiniana is a delightful effervescent score. Cantelli's pioneering record dates from 1949 and comes up sounding very well in a marvellously transferred Testament issue which also offers his 1955–6 Philharmonia recording of the *Daphnis* suite and his 1954 *Three-Cornered Hat*. Elegant playing.

CASTELNUOVO-TEDESCO, Mario (1895–1968)

Guitar Concerto No. 1 in D, Op. 99.

(M) *** Sony (ADD) SMK 60022. Williams, ECO, Groves – RODRIGO: *Concierto de Aranjuez*; VILLA-LOBOS: *Guitar Concerto.* ***

(B) *** Naxos 8.550729. Kraft, N. CO, Ward – RODRIGO; VILLA-LOBOS: *Concertos.* ***

(M) **(*) DG (IMS) (ADD) 449 098-2. Yepes, LSO, Navarro –
HALFFTER: *Concerto; RODRIGO: Fantasía.* **

On Naxos another first-class version of this slight but attractive Concerto, which is well suited by the relatively intimate scale of the performance. The recording is well balanced and vivid, and the soloist, Norbert Kraft, has plenty of personality and the accompaniment is fresh and polished. Typically excellent Naxos value.

Narciso Yepes plays this Concerto admirably, receiving attentive support from Navarro and the LSO and fresh, vivid recording from DG; for the two coupled works, however, his partner was Odón Alonso and the results are less impressive, with a dry studio acoustic not flattering the music-making. The Naxos CD is a far more attractive proposition.

*Cello Sonata, Op. 50; Notturna sull'acqua, Op. 82a
;Scherzino, Op. 82b; I Nottambu i (Variazione fantastiche),
Op. 47; Paraphrase on Rossini's Largo al factotum;
Toccata, Op. 83; Valse on the Name of Gregor Piatigorsky.*

*** Biddulph LAW 024. Green, Moyer.

Castelnuovo-Tedesco's *Cello Sonata* is a splendid work, opening with a striking main theme (marked *Arioso e sereno*) followed by a highly inventive *Aria with Variations* to act as slow movement and finale combined. The fairy-light *Scherzino* which follows, although written seven years later, might have been an additional movement. The two nocturnal pieces are full of Mediterranean atmosphere. Serenity and passion are interchanged and whirling Spanish dance rhythms follow, but the perfumes of the night return to end the work gently. The two witty encores sparkle, with Tchaikovsky's *Sleeping Beauty Waltz* making a surprise entry in the Piatigorsky tribute. Nancy Green is in full sympathy with this repertoire and she plays very persuasively indeed, with excellent support from her partner, Frederick Moyer. An excellent digital sound balance is afforded to these artists. Recommended to all lovers of the cello.

SOLO GUITAR MUSIC

*Aranci in fiore, Op. 87a; Capriccio, Op. 195/18;
Escarramán, Op. 177/1–5; La guarda cuydadosa, Op. 177/6;
3 preludi mediterranei, Op. 176; Variations à travers les
siècles, Op. 71; Variations plaisantes sur un petit air
populaire, Op. 95; Tarantella, Op. 87b.*

(N) (B) **(*) Naxos 8.554831. Micheli.

This is the début CD of the young Italian, Lorenzo Micheli, who won first prize in the 1999 Guitar Foundation of America Competition. To his credit he refrains from duplicating the familiar Villa Lobos or Sor repertoire and concentrates on rarities by his countryman Castelnuovo-Tedesco. The music is slender in substance but far from unappealing. Artistically this is first-rate, as Lorenzo Micheli plays with assurance and elegance, but he is balanced very closely.

CATALANI, Alfredo (1854–93)

A Sera; Serenatella; String Quartet in A.

*** ASV CDDCA 909. Puccini Qt – PUCCINI: *Crisantemi;
Fugues; Quartet etc.* ***

The elegant *Serenatella* and the romantically melancholy *A Sera*, were arranged by the composer from piano originals, and Catalani understandably thought well enough of the latter to use it for the prelude to Act III of his most famous opera, *La Wally*. The *String Quartet in A* is less consistent, but its scale is impressive, with the extended slow movement providing a moving expressive climax, confidently handled. A delightful disc, warmly played and atmospherically recorded.

La Wally (opera): complete.

(B) *** Double Decca (ADD) 460 744-2 (2). Tebaldi, Del
Monaco, Diaz, Cappuccilli, Marimpietri, Turin Lyric Ch.,
Monte Carlo Op. O, Fausto Cleva.

The title-role of *La Wally* prompts Renata Tebaldi to give one of her most tenderly affecting performances on record, a glorious example of her singing late in her career. Mario del Monaco begins coarsely, but the heroic power and intensity of his singing are formidable, and it is good to have the young Cappuccilli in the baritone role of Gellner. The sound in this late-1960s recording is superbly focused and vividly real. Reissued as a Double this is now one of Decca's prime operatic bargain sets. The new-style synopsis should prove attractive to newcomers to the opera.

CATOIRE, Georgy (1861–1926)

Piano music: *Caprice, Op. 3; Chants de crépuscule (4
Morceaux), Op. 24; Intermezzo, Op. 6/5; 3 Morceaux,
Op. 2; 5 Morceaux, Op. 10; 4 Morceaux, Op. 12; Poème,
Op. 34/2; Prélude, Op. 6/2; 4 Préludes, Op. 17; Prélude,
Op. 34/3; Scherzo, Op. 6/3; Valse, Op. 36; Vision (Etude),
Op. 8.*

*** Hyp. CDA 67090. Hamelin.

Georgy Catoire was born in Moscow to parents of French extraction. His music has been all but forgotten, which makes this dazzling collection of his piano music especially welcome, prompting Hamelin to astonishing feats of virtuosity combined with poetry. Catoire left a big collection of piano miniatures, of which this collection of twenty-eight is an attractive sample. They are played in order of opus number, giving an idea of Catoire's development from echoing Chopin, Liszt and Tchaikovsky to adventuring more towards the world of Wagner and of the French Impressionists. If there is a Russian he echoes, it is Scriabin, and it is the fluency of his writing for the keyboard rather than memorability of material which strikes home, with Hamelin an ideal interpreter. Yet for all these influences, in many ways he is his own man, and his music, particularly the *Morceaux*, is often very seductive. Marc-André Hamelin also shows how he can tickle the ear with a scherzando lightness as in the two engaging pieces from Op. 6. This is not a recital to play continuously, but drawn on it will give much refreshment and pleasure. Hamelin is given an outstandingly natural recording, bright, yet with full sonority and colouring.

CAVALLI, Francesco (1602–76)

La Calisto (complete).

**(*) HM HMC 901515/17 (3). Bayo, Lippi, Keenlyside, Pushee, Mantovani, Concerto Vocale, Jacobs.

La Calisto (complete version – freely arranged by Leppard).

(M) *** Decca (ADD) 436 216-2 (2). Cotrubas, Trama, J. Baker, Bowman, Gottlieb, Cuénod, Hughes, Glyndebourne Festival Op. Ch., LPO, Leppard.

Leppard's freely adapted version of an opera written for Venice in the 1650s is the more delectable because of the brilliant part given to the goddess, Diana, taken by Dame Janet Baker. In this version she has the dual task of portraying first the chaste goddess herself, then in the same costume switching immediately to the randy Jupiter disguised as Diana, quite a different character. The opera is splendidly cast. Parts for such singers as James Bowman draw out their finest qualities, and the result is magic. Linfea, a bad-tempered, lecherous, ageing nymph, is portrayed hilariously by Hugues Cuénod. The recording, made at Glyndebourne, is gloriously rich and atmospheric. A full libretto is provided.

Jacobs directs a lively account, recorded in vivid, immediate sound, helped by some characterful, generally well-sung solo performances. In the title-role Maria Bayo is sweet and fresh, and Alessandra Mantovani as Diana sings warmly, though with some unsteadiness. The disappointment is that when Jove is disguised as Diana, the part is sung by the weighty baritone, Marcello Lippi, taking the role of Jove, in a piping falsetto. Graham Pushee, a reliable but hooty counter-tenor, takes the role of Endimione and the comic role of the nymph, Linfea, is taken by a male singer, Gilles Ragon, capable but nowhere near as characterful as Hugues Cuénod at Glyndebourne. However inauthentic the Leppard version is, it conveys more intense enjoyment than this and, though the vigour and variety of Cavalli's inspiration are brought out well by Jacobs and his team, the Decca mid-priced reissue is the one to go for.

La Didone (ed. Hengelbrock & Bratschke).

**(*) DHM/BMG 05472 77354-2 (2). Kenny, Howarth, Dale, Balthasar Neumann Ens., Thomas Hengelbrock.

La Didone, one of Cavalli's earliest operas, tells the story of Dido and Aeneas, starting apocalytically with the fall of Troy. In this recording, taken from live performances at the Schwetzingen Festival, the conductor, Thomas Hengelbrock, has edited and cut the original score, with Detlef Bratschke filling out the spare treble and bass lines. The result has nothing like the lusciousness of Leppard's arrangements of Cavalli, but with lavish continuo avoids the bleakness of some realizations. Yvonne Kenny as Dido and Laurence Dale as Aeneas are both excellent in strongly characterized performances, standing out from most of the others, though

Judith Howarth sings powerfully as Aeneas's doomed wife, Creusa. Not a magnetic performance but a valuable one. Atmospheric sound disturbed by stage noises.

CERHA, Friedrich (born 1926)

String Quartets Nos. 1–3; (i) *8 Movements after Hölderlin Fragments for String Sextet.*

*** CPO CPO 999 646-2. Arditti Qt; with (i) Kakuska, Erben.

Friedrich Cerha is best known as a champion of the second Viennese school and as the scholar-composer who completed the third Act of Alban Berg's *Lulu*. The three quartets recorded here come from the period 1989–92: the *First Quartet* is subtitled *Maqam*, inspired by Arab music. It makes liberal use of microtones, as does, though to a lesser extent, the minimalist *Second* inspired by his contact with the Papuan peoples at Sepik in New Guinea. The *Hölderlin Fragments* (1995) are settings for string sextet without voice, though the poems which inspired them are reproduced in the excellent and detailed booklet. The Arditti Quartet play with great expertise and attention to detail, and are vividly recorded. Recommended for those with a special interest in contemporary Austrian music.

CERTON, Pierre (died 1572)

Chansons: *Amour a tort; Ce n'est a vous; C'est grand pityé; De tout le mal; En espérant; Entre vous gentilz hommes; Heilas ne fringuerons nous; Je l'ay aymé; Je neveulx poinct; Martin s'en alla; Plus nu suys; Que n'est auprès de moy; Si ta beaulté; Ung jour que Madame dormait.* Mass: *Sur le pont d'Avignon.*

(B) *** HM (ADD) HMA 190 1034. Boston Camerata, Cohen.

The Mass, *Sur le pont d'Avignon*, has genuine appeal, and the chansons also exercise a real charm over the listener. The Mass is performed *a cappella*, and the chansons enjoy instrumental support. In both sacred and secular works the Boston Camerata bring freshness, musical accomplishment and stylistic understanding to bear; the recording, made in a spacious acoustic, creates the most beautiful sounds.

CESTI, Antonio (1623–69)

Cantatas: *Amanti, io vi disfido; Pria ch'adori.*

(B) **(*) HM (ADD) HMA 1901011. Concerto Vocale – D´INDIA: *Duets, Laments & Madrigals.* **(*)

Cesti's 17-minute cantata, *Pria ch'adori*, is a serenata for two voices, after the Monteverdi style, including even a *Lamento d'Arianna* in duet form. *Amanti, io vi disfido* is a much shorter, bravura piece. The performances by Judith Nelson and René Jacobs are certainly pleasingly fresh, and the distinguished instrumental group includes William Christie providing the continuo.

CHABRIER, Emmanuel (1841–94)

Bourrée fantasque; España (rhapsody); Joyeuse marche; Menuet pompeux; Prélude pastorale; Suite pastorale; Le Roi malgré lui: Danse slave; Fête polonaise.

*** EMI CDC7 49652-2. Capitole Toulouse O, Plasson.

Bourrée fantasque; España (rhapsody); Joyeuse marche; Suite pastorale; Gwendoline: Overture. Le Roi malgré lui: Danse slave; Fête polonaise.

(M) *** Mercury (ADD) 434 303-2. Detroit SO, Paray – ROUSSEL: *Suite.* **(*)

Chabrier is Beecham territory and he calls for playing of elegance and charm. Michel Plasson and his excellent Toulouse forces bring just the right note of exuberance and *joie de vivre* to this delightful music. The recording is eminently satisfactory, though it is a shade resonant and, as a result, lacks the last ounce of transparency. Even so, the effect suits the music, and the elegant performance of the delightful *Suite pastorale* ensures a strong recommendation for this EMI CD, but it has been deleted just as we go to press.

The finely played and idiomatically conducted Mercury collection of Chabrier's best orchestral pieces does not disappoint. Paray's whimsically relaxed and sparkling account of *España* gives great pleasure and his rubato in the *Fête polonaise* is equally winning. The *Suite pastorale* is a wholly delightful account, given playing that is at once warm and polished, neat and perfectly in scale, with the orchestra beautifully balanced. The *Marche joyeuse* was recorded in Detroit's Old Orchestral Hall a year before the rest of the programme.

España (rhapsody).

⭘ (B) *** Dutton Lab. mono CDEA 5017. LPO, Sir Thomas Beecham (with Concert: 'Beecham Favourites' *** ⭘).

España (rhapsody); Habanera; Joyeuse marche; Lamento; Prélude pastorale; Suite pastorale; Le Roi malgré lui: Danse slave; Fête polonaise.

(B) **(*) Naxos 8.554248. Monte-Carlo PO, Niquet.

España; Fête polonaise; Gwendoline overture; Habanera; (i) Larghetto for Horn & Orchestra. Marche joyeuse; Prélude pastorale; Suite pastorale.

*(**) DG 447 751-2. (i) Janezic; VPO, Gardiner.

España (rhapsody); Suite pastorale.

*** Chan. 8852. Ulster O, Y. P. Tortelier – DUKAS: *L'Apprenti sorcier; La Péri.* **(*)

Beecham's fizzing 1939 recording has never been surpassed and is unsurpassable. The superb Dutton transfer restores all the warmth and bloom of the original 78-r.p.m. disc, made in the Kingsway Hall, where the glowing ambience adds to the lustre of a sparkling recording often used for demonstration in its day. The rest of this concert is hardly less enticing for Beecham aficionados.

A very well-recorded programme on Naxos, played with considerable idiomatic flair if without always the very last degree of finesse (*Sous-bois*, for instance, could be more delicate in the bass). But the rumbustious pieces have plenty of sparkle and *España* does not lack gusto. Enjoyable and good value for money.

Gardiner's DG collection is disappointing. The fortissimos bring coarseness into the music-making and readily become tiring to listen to. Easily the most attractive and refined playing comes in the charming *Suite pastorale*, with the rustling leaves in *Sous-bois* delicately caught. The performances certainly do not lack vigour but are hardly subtle in rhythmic feeling. Clearly the VPO are not at home in this repertoire and, for all the brilliance of Gardiner's approach, *España* becomes heavy-going, with its over-enthusiastic bass drum, while the orchestra is not very seductive either in nudging the rhythms of the *Habanera*.

Yan Pascal Tortelier and the excellent Ulster Orchestra give an altogether first-rate account of Chabrier's delightful *Suite pastorale*, distinguished by an appealing charm and lightness of touch. There is a spirited account of *España*, too.

PIANO MUSIC

Aubade; Ballabile; Caprice; Feuillet d'album; Impromptu; Pièces pittoresques; Ronde champêtre; (i) 3 Valses romantiques.

*** Unicorn (ADD) DKPCD 9158. Stott, (i) with Burley.

For those wanting a representative single-CD selection, Kathryn Stott provides the ideal answer. She plays this long-neglected but rewarding repertoire with intelligence, wit and elegance. Perhaps the very last ounce of charm is missing, but there is enough of it to provide delight. She is moreover recorded with great presence and fidelity; the piano-sound is very alive, natural and fresh.

Bourrée fantasque; 5 Pièces posthumes; 10 Pièces pittoresques; Suite de valses.

(B) **(*) ASV CDQS 6166. Schiller.

Alan Schiller, if not quite as sympathetic as Kathleen Stott on Unicorn-Kanchana, can play tenderly (as in the *Feuillet d'album* from the *Pièces posthumes*) as well as brilliantly, and he is only occasionally percussive. He lifts rhythms nicely in the *Bourrée fantasque* and characterizes strongly. On the whole tempi are well chosen and his rubato is convincing. Good, clear piano recording.

OPERA

Briseis (complete).

⭘ *** Hyp. CDA 66803. Rodgers, Padmore, Keenlyside, Harries, George, BBC Scottish SO, Jean-Yves Ossonce.

Starting with a ripely seductive sailors' chorus, few operas are as sensuous as *Briseis*. On disc it matters little that this is a torso. The writing is not just sensuous but urgent, a warm bath of sound that is also exhilarating. Casting is near ideal, with Joan Rodgers in the title-role rich and distinctive, and with Mark Padmore as the sailor, Hylas, equally warm, producing heady, clear tenor tone. Symbolizing the forces of Christian good, Simon Keenlyside as the Catechist and

Kathryn Harries as the mother of Briseis, cured through faith, both sing with character and apt resonance. Full, atmospheric sound.

Gwendoline (complete).

*(**) HM ED 13059 (2). Kohutková, Henry, Garino, Brno Philharmonic Ch., Slovak PO, Penin.

Like the unfinished *Briseis*, recorded by Hyperion, *Gwendoline* is a high romantic opera written in the shadow of Wagner with many sensuous sequences, not just the love-duets but such evocative choral passages as the *Epithalamium*. The final love-death brings more echoes of the final trio of Gounod's *Faust* than it does of Wagner, with the idiom identifiably French throughout. This live recording offers a performance flawed vocally but with Jean-Paul Penin drawing playing that is both sensitive and passionate from the Slovak Philharmonic. In the title-role Adriana Kohutková sings sympathetically but with bright tone that leads to shrillness on top. Didier Henry's grainy baritone grows rough under pressure, hardly heroic-sounding, and Gérard Garino's fine, clear tenor sounds far too youthful for the aged Armel. Nevertheless, a very enjoyable first recording, with first-rate sound.

L'Etoile (complete).

✪ *** EMI CDS7 47889-8 (2) [Pathé id.]. Alliot-Lugaz, Gautier, Bacquier, Raphanel, Damonte, Le Roux, David, Lyon Opéra Ch. and O, Gardiner.

This fizzing operetta is a winner: the subtlety and refinement of Chabrier's score go well beyond the usual realm of operetta, and Gardiner directs a performance that from first to last makes the piece sparkle bewitchingly. Colette Alliot-Lugaz and Gabriel Bacquier are first rate and numbers such as the drunken duet between King and Astrologer are hilarious. Outstandingly good recording, with excellent access.

CHADWICK, George (1854–1931)

Overtures: Melpomene; Rip van Winkle. Tam O'Shanter (symphonic ballad).

*** Chan. 9439. Detroit SO, Järvi – RANDALL THOMPSON: *Symphony No. 2.* **

The *Rip van Winkle* overture, new to the catalogue, is an early work well laid out for the orchestra, as for that matter are the other two pieces. *Melpomene* derives its title from the muse of tragedy and has been compared by some commentators to the symphonic poems of Franck or Dukas. *Tam O'Shanter* (1915) is brilliantly scored and enormously vital and rumbustious. Good playing from the Detroit Orchestra under Neeme Järvi and natural, lifelike recording.

Serenade for Strings.

*** Albany TROY 033-2. V. American Music Ens., Earle – GILBERT: *Suite.* ***

This very well-crafted piece by the so-called 'Boston classicist' gives much pleasure. It is quite beautifully played by this excellent Viennese group, drawn from younger members of the Vienna Symphony Orchestra. The sound too is first rate,

a successful example of a 'live recording' bringing no loss in realism and a gain in spontaneity.

Symphonic Sketches.

(M) **(*) Mercury (ADD) [434 337-2]. Eastman-Rochester O, Hanson – MACDOWELL: *Suite* **(*); PETER: *Sinfonia.* **

The first two movements, *Jubilee* and *Noel*, come from 1895 and, written in the wake of Dvořák's American visit, rather endearingly recall that composer's music. The third and fourth movements were written later: indeed the charming third movement, *Hobgoblin*, did not see the light of day until 1904. The suite is very well played and brilliantly and glowingly recorded. Not great music perhaps, but amiably melodic and colourfully orchestrated.

Symphonies Nos. 2 in B flat; 3 in F.

*** Chan. 9685. Detroit SO, Järvi.

Chadwick's *Second Symphony* dates from the early 1880s, though its delightful *Scherzo* was premièred two years ahead of the rest of the work. When this was first heard it had to be encored, which is hardly surprising. It has an engaging, cheeky quality (one contemporary review in the Boston *Transcript* wrote that 'it positively winks at you') and Järvi makes the very most of it. The *Third Symphony* is hardly less fresh and appealing. It breathes much the same air as Brahms, Dvořák and Svendsen; it is very compelling in so persuasive a performance as given here by Järvi and his Detroit Orchestra. The *Largo* is beautifully shaped and the *Scherzo* delightfully light and piquant. Absolutely first-class recording too.

CHAMINADE, Cécile (1857–1944)

Piano trios Nos. 1 in G min., Op. 11; 2 in A min., Op. 34; Pastorale enfantine, Op. 12; Ritournelle; Serenade, Op. 29 (all 3 arr. Marcus); Serenade espagnole (arr. Kreisler).

*** ASV CDDCA 965. Tzigane Piano Trio.

In these two *Piano Trios* Chaminade confidently controls larger forms, building on a fund of melody. The two central movements of the *Piano Trio No. 1* are charming, a passionately lyrical *Andante* and a sparkling, Mendelssohnian Scherzo. The *Piano Trio No. 2*, in three movements, without a Scherzo, is weightier, almost Brahmsian, with themes rather more positive. Three of the four miniatures which come as fill-ups have been arranged for trio by the Tzigane's pianist, Elizabeth Marcus.

PIANO MUSIC

Air à danser, Op. 164; Air de ballet, Op. 30; Automne; Autrefois; Contes bleus No. 2, Op. 122; Danse créole, Op. 94; Guitare, Op. 32; La Lisonjera, Op. 50; Lolita, Op. 54; Minuetto, Op. 23; Pas des écharpes, Op. 37; Pas des sylphes: Intermezzo; Pierette, Op. 41; 3 Romances sans paroles, Op. 76/1, 3 & 6; Sérénade, Op. 29; Sous la masque, Op. 116; Toccata, Op. 39; Valse arabesque.

*** Chan. 8888. Parkin.

Album des enfants, Op. 123/4, 5, 9 & 10; Op. 126/1, 2, 9 & 10; Arabesque, Op. 61; Cortège, Op. 143; Inquiétude, Op. 87/3; Le Passé; Prelude in D min., Op. 84/3; Rigaudon, Op. 55/6; Sérénade espagnole; Sonata in C min., Op. 21; Les Sylvains, Op. 60; Valse-ballet, Op. 112; Valse brillante No. 3, Op. 80; Valse No. 4, Op. 91.

*** Hyp. CDA 66846. Jacobs.

Arlequine, Op. 53; Au pays dévasté, Op. 155; Chanson brétonne; Divertissement, Op. 105; Etudes de concert, Op. 35: Impromptu; Tarantella. Etude symphonique, Op. 28; Feuillets d'album, Op. 98: Elégie. Gigue in D, Op. 43; Libellules, Op. 24; Pastorale, Op. 114; Pièces humoristiques Op. 87: Sous bois; Consolation. Nocturne, Op. 165; Passacaille in E, Op. 130; Poème romantique, Op. 7; Tristesse, Op. 104; Valse tendre, Op. 119; Scherzo-valse, Op. 148.

*** Hyp. CDA 66706. Jacobs.

Autrefois; Callirhoë; Elévation in E; Etude mélodique in G flat; Etude pathétique in B min.; Etude scholastique; La Lisonjera; L'Ondine; Pêcheurs de nuit; Romance; Scherzo in C; Sérénade in D; Solitude; Souvenance; Thème varié in A; Valse romantique; Waltz No. 2.

*** Hyp. CDA 66584. Jacobs.

Artistically these pieces are rather stronger than one had suspected and, although they are by no means the equal of Grieg or early Fauré, they can hold their own with Saint-Saëns and are more inventive than the *Brises d'orient* of Félicien David. There is a quality of gentility that has lent a certain pallor to Chaminade's charms, but both pianists here make out a stronger case for her than most people would imagine possible. Both are well recorded and in this respect there is little to choose between the two. Nor is there much to choose as far as the performances are concerned; both are persuasive, though Parkin has a slight edge over his colleague in terms of elegance and finesse. If you want a single disc collection you might choose the Chandos disc. If you seek a complete survey stay with Jacobs.

CHARPENTIER, Gustave

(1860–1956)

Louise (complete).

(N)(B) (***) Naxos mono 8.110102/4. Moore, Jobin, Pinza, Doe, Met. Op. Ch. & O, Beecham.

This completely gives the lie to any idea that Grace Moore was primarily a film star rather than a genuine prima donna. Helped by Sir Thomas Beecham at his most warmly understanding, obviously enjoying his wartime stint at the Met in New York (1943), she gives an enchanting performance as Charpentier's heroine. The voice is not just brilliant and flexible, with trills and ornaments flawlessly executed, but warm too, bringing out the tenderness of the writing. Her French is totally idiomatic, with the Canadian, Raoul Jobin, a stylish hero and Ezio Pinza gloriously resonant as the heroine's father. Clearer, fuller, if limited mono sound than in most radio recordings from this source.

Louise (gramophone version conceived and realized by the composer).

(M) (***) Nim mono NI 7829. Vallin, Thill, Pernet, Lecouvreur, Gaudel, Ch. Raugel & O, Eugène Bigot.

These substantial excerpts from *Louise* were recorded in 1935 under the 75-year-old composer's supervision; they feature two ideally cast French singers as the two principals, Ninon Vallin enchanting in the title-role and the tenor, Georges Thill, heady-toned as the hero, Julien. The original eight 78-r.p.m. records are fitted neatly on to a single CD, and – in the selection of items, made by the composer himself – just the delights and none of the *longueurs* of this nostalgically atmospheric opera are included. The voices are caught superbly in the Nimbus transfers, but with an early electrical recording like this the orchestral sound becomes muddled. Yet even Nimbus has rarely presented voices as vividly as here.

CHARPENTIER, Marc-Antoine

(1643–1704)

Ballet music: *La Descente d'Orphée aux Enfers; Médée; Les Plaisirs de Versailles.*

*** Erato 3984 26129-2. Les Arts Florissants, Christie – RAMEAU: *Les Fêtes d'Hébe; Hippolyte et Aricie* ***.

This recording celebrated the twenty-fifth anniversary of William Christie and Les Arts Florissants by combining colourful, lightweight ballet sequences from major dramatic works by Charpentier with more extended ballets of Rameau. These shorter selections are characteristically colourful and played with great vivacity and colour.

Concert à 4 (for viols), H.545; Musique de théâtre pour Circé et Andromède; Sonata à 8 (for 2 flutes & strings), H.548.

**(*) HM HMA 1901244. London Baroque, Medlam.

These pieces are most expertly played here by the members of London Baroque (though the string sound still does not entirely escape the faint suspicion that it has been marinaded in vinegar) and will reward investigation. The sound is excellent.

9 Noëls; Christmas motets: *Canticum in nativitatem Domini, H.393; In nativitatem Domini canticum, H.314; In nativitatem Domini canticum: Chanson, H.416; In nativitatem Domini Nostri Jesus Christi, H.414.*

(B) *** Naxos 8.554514. Arcadia Ensemble, Mallon.

In this Christmas disc with a difference, the talented Canadian group, the Arcadia Ensemble, warmly recorded, present the nine charming sets of simple variations Charpentier wrote on French Christmas carols, or Noëls. Standing out from the rest is the minor-key *Or nous dites Marie*, with chromatic writing like Purcell's. Those instrumental pieces are set alongside a sequence of lively vocal motets on a Christmas theme, culminating in a miniature Nativity oratorio.

Motets: *Alma redemptoris; Amicus meus; Ave regina; Dialogus inter Magdalenam et Jesum; Egredimini filiae Sion; Elevations; O pretiosum; O vere, o bone; Magdalena lugens; Motet du saint sacrement; O vos omnes; Pour le Passion de notre Seigneur* (2 settings); *Salve regina; Solva vivebat in antris Magdalena lugens.*

*** HM (ADD) HMA 1901149. Concerto Vocale.

Half of the motets on this record are for solo voice and the others are duets. Among the best and most moving things here are *O vos omnes* and *Amicus meus*, which are beautifully done. Another motet to note is *Magdalena lugens*, in which Mary Magdalene laments Christ's death at the foot of the Cross. Expressive singing from Judith Nelson and René Jacobs, and excellent continuo support. Worth a strong recommendation.

Ave Maris stella, H.63; Domine salvum sine organo in C, H. 290; Messe pour le Port-Royal, H.5; Motet: Flores o Gallia, H.342; Magnificat pour le Port-Royale, H.81; O salutaris hostia, H.261; Psaume Laudate Dominum, H. 182; Veni creator pour un dessus sel au catechisme, H. 69.

*** Auvidis/Astrée E 8598. Les Demoiselles de Saint-Cyr, Mandrin.

In the mid 1680s, Charpentier composed several works 'for Port Royale'. There were two convents: one in the Chevreuse valley, south of Versailles, which was situated on a low-lying, marshy site; and the second, to which many of the nuns repaired, in the Faubourg Saint-Jacques in Paris, for which most of this repertoire was written. The music is scored for female voices only and is generally austere in style. The main work, after which the record is titled, is the *Messe pour le Port-Royale* for three soloists, chorus and organ. This is supplemented by various other pieces, psalm settings and the fine *Magnificat* also written for the convent. This is reposeful music, predominantly meditative in character, and very persuasively performed by Les Demoiselles de Saint-Cyr under Emmanuel Mandrin with Michel Chapuis providing the solo organ interludes. A rewarding issue.

(i) *Caecilia, virgo et martyr, H.397; De profundis, H.189;* (ii) *Elévation; In obitum augustissimae nec son piissimae gallorum Reginae lamentum; Luctus de morte augustissimae Mariae Theresiae Galliae.*

(B) *** Erato 3984 24232-2 (2). (i) Degelin, Reyghere, Mols, James, Meens, Van Croonenborgh, Ghent Madrigal Ch. & Cantabile; (ii) Degelin, Verdoodt, Smolders, Crook, Vandersteene, Widmer, Namur Chamber Ch.; (i; ii) Musica Polyphonica, Devos.

Charpentier's present setting of the *De profundis* is lavishly scored (soloists, double-chorus, two orchestras with flutes and continuo) and was composed in 1683 for the funeral of Louis XIV's first Queen, Marie Thérèse. It is an impressive and moving piece, and this somewhat restrained performance catches its gravitas, even if some of the grandeur and power eludes Devos, although he uses considerable forces. *Caecilia virgo et martyr* fares much better, although collectors will find some textual differences from William Christie's earlier recording (see below). All three works on the second disc further lament the death of the Queen. Clearly the event

moved Charpentier deeply, and each reflects the paradox of the Christian faith in contrasting grief with joy and hope in the life hereafter. Here Devos's performances could hardly be bettered, bringing out all the music's drama, joy, and depth of feeling. The recordings, both made in spacious acoustics are also first class and this Erato Ultima Double is highly recommended. Such a collection can only further enhance the growing recognition of Charpentier's stature.

Caecilia, virgo et martyr; Filius prodigus (oratorios); *Magnificat.*

(B) *** HM HMA 190066. Grenat, Benet, Laplenie, Reinhard, Studer, Les Arts Florissants, Christie.

The music's stature and nobility are fully conveyed here. The *Magnificat* is a short piece for three voices and has an almost Purcellian flavour. One thing that will immediately strike the listener is the delicacy and finesse of the scoring. All this music is beautifully recorded; the present issues can be recommended with enthusiasm, especially at Musique d'abord price.

In nativitatem Domini nostri Jesus Christi (canticum), H.414; Pastorale sur la naissance de notre Seigneur Jésus Christ, H.483.

*** HM (ADD) HMC 901082. Les Arts Florissants Vocal & Instrumental Ens., Christie.

This *Canticum* has much of the character of an oratorio. The invention has great appeal and variety. The *Pastorale* is a most rewarding piece, and the grace and charm of the writing continue to win one over to this eminently resourceful composer. This collection by William Christie is self-recommending, so high are the standards of performance and recording, and so fertile is Charpentier's imagination.

In nativitatem Domini nostri Jesus Christi, H.416; Pastorale sur la naissance de notre Seigneur Jésus Christ H.482.

*** HM (ADD) HMC 905130. Les Arts Florissants Vocal & Instrumental Ens., Christie.

The cantata is one of Charpentier's grandest, a finely balanced edifice in two complementary halves, separated by an instrumental section, an eloquent evocation of the night. The little pastorale was written in the tradition of the ballet de cour or divertissement. This is enchanting music, elegantly played and excellently recorded.

Leçons de ténèbres for Maundy Thursday.

*** HM (ADD) HMC 901005. Jacobs, Nelson, Verkinderen Kuijken, Christie, Junghänel, Concerto vocale, Jacobs.

These *Leçons de ténèbres* are eloquent and moving pieces, worthy of comparison with Purcell. René Jacobs's performance, like that of his colleagues, is so authentic in every respect that it is difficult to imagine it being surpassed. The recording is as distinguished as the performances.

The first of the *Leçons ténèbres* sung on Maundy Thursday (or rather the previous evening) concerns the *Lamentations of Jeremiah*, and Charpentier's melismatic setting is sung with great eloquence by René Jacobs. Yet one must remember that this music was written for nuns (the names of the sisters who sang them are known) and Charpentier observed that the leading soprano should possess a '*voix touchante*' rather than a '*voix brillante*'. So it is here, in the second and third lessons, with Judith Nelson's *dolce* leading the small female group, accompanied as the composer suggested by a continuo of bass viol, organ and theorbo.

Leçons de ténèbres for Wednesday in Holy Week.

*** Virgin VC5 45107-2. Greuillet, Pelon, Lesne, Purves, Il Seminario Musicale.

Leçons de ténèbres for Maundy Thursday.

*** Virgin VC5 45075-2. Piau, Lesne, Honeyman, Harvey, Il Seminario Musicale.

Leçons de ténèbres for Good Friday.

*** Virgin VC7 59295-2. Lesne, Mellon, Honeyman, Bona, Il Seminario Musicale.

Leçons de ténèbres for Wednesday in Holy Week, Maundy Thursday & Good Friday.

(M) *** Virgin Veritas EMI VMT5 61483-2 (3). Gérard Lesne & soloists, Il Seminario Musicale, Lesne.

This complete series of Charpentier's *Leçons de ténèbres* from Il Seminario Musicale offers music of great variety and beauty, featuring soloists who are naturally attuned to this repertoire. The accompaniment is provided by a varied instrumental group, and their use is consistently imaginative and refreshing to the ear. The Psalms are sung by a small choral group. The effect is warm yet refined and the lyrical melancholy of much of this music is quite haunting, and the acoustic of L'Abbaye Royale de Fontevraud is ideal for the music. The documentation is first class. Although these three CDs are individually in the premium price-range (and well worth every penny), they are now issued as a medium-price set in a slipcase, and any collector attracted to this remarkable and inspired composer should consider them.

Litanies de la Vierge; Missa Assumpta est Maria; Te Deum.

(N) (M) *** HM HMX 2981 1298. Soloists, Les Arts Florissants, William Christie.

Marc-Antoine Charpentier's best-known choral work, the *Te Deum*, which is introduced not only by the famous fanfare 'Prélude' but before that by Philidor's *Marche des timbales*. The performance of the *Te Deum* is almost certainly the finest in the catalogue, and the CD includes also the much less familiar but no less beautiful *Missa Assumpta est Maria* and the more restrained *Litanies de la Vierge*. Framed by a *Kyrie* and closing *Agnus Dei*, the seven movements each radiantly describe one of the Virgin's mystical attributes, followed by an intercessionary prayer. This is a deeply devotional work for eight singers, two viols and continuo, and the composer himself participated in its first performance. An outstanding disc in every way, beautifully recorded.

Magnificat, H.74; Te Deum, H.146.

**(*) EMI CDC7 54284-2. Upshaw, Murray, Robinson, Aler, Moll, Ch. & ASMF, Marriner.

These spirited accounts come from the early 1990s and are what one might call mainstream performances, very expert and accomplished in every way, and very well recorded. A useful coupling, although Christie's account of the *Te Deum* is even finer.

Méditations pour le Carême; Le Reniement de St Pierre.

(B) *** HM HMA 1905151. Les Arts Florissants, William Christie.

The *Méditations pour le Carême* are a sequence of three-voice motets for Lent with continuo accompaniment (organ, theorbo and bass viol) that may not have quite the same imaginative or expressive resource as the coupling, but which are full of nobility and interest. *Le Reniement de Saint Pierre* is one of Charpentier's most inspired and expressive works and its text draws on the account in all four Gospels of St Peter's denial of Christ. The performances maintain the high standards of this ensemble, and the same compliment can be paid to the recording.

(i) Messe de minuit pour Noël (Midnight Mass for Christmas Eve); (ii) Te Deum.

(N) (B) *** EMI Encore CDE5 74726-2 (ADD). (i) Cantelo, Gelmar, Partridge, Bowman, Keyte, King's College Ch., ECO, Willcocks; (ii) Lott, Harrhy, Brett, Partridge, Roberts, King's College Ch., ASMF, Ledger.

There is a kinship between Charpentier's lovely *Christmas Mass* and Czech settings of the Mass that incorporate folk material, even the *Kyrie* having a jolly quality about it. The King's performance is warm and musical, but there isn't much Gallic flavour. The recording comes from the late 1960s and certainly now has more bite than it did; but reservations remain about the basic style of the singing. The coupling is the best known of the *Te Deum* settings, and this time the King's performance has a vitality and boldness to match the music and catches also its douceur and freshness. A splendid bargain on EMI's new super-bargain label.

(i) Missa Assumpta est Maria; (ii) Te Deum.

(N) (B) *** Teldec 0630 12465-2. Bonner, Pendlebury, Davidson, Del Pozo, Robertson, (i) Brough; (ii) Davies; Clarkson, Grant, St James's Singers & Bar. Players, Bolton.

Ivor Bolton's account of the *Te Deum* is vigorous and eloquent by turns. He has a fine team of soloists (Teresa Bonner, serenely pure of tone in *Te ergo quaesumus*) and there is also a spiritedly robust contribution from the period trumpets, essential for the famous opening *Prélude*. The *Missa Assumpta est Maria* is presented with two examples of the organ *in alternim*: the organist, John Toll, offers a verse improvisation at the centre of the *Kyrie*, while in the *Sanctus/Benedictus* sequence he interpolates a *Fugue et caprice* (No. 9) by François Roberday. Again the vocal soloists (who make a major contribution to the setting) blend well, both together and with the excellent choir, and the performance is full of life. The instrumental group is also expressively responsive, especially in the three *Symphonies* (one at the opening, the other two framing the *Agnus Dei*). This fine bargain coupling can be recommended alongside William Christie's disc (see above), although the Harmonia Mundi issue also includes the beautiful *Litanies de la Vierge*.

Miserere, H.219; Motets: *Pour la seconde fois que le Saint Sacrament vient au même reposoir, H.372; pour le Saint Sacrement au reposoir, H.346. Motet pour une longue offrande, H.434.*

*** HM HMC 901185. Mellon, Poulenard, Ledroit, Kendall, Kooy, Chapelle Royale, Herreweghe.

Charpentier's *Motet pour une longue offrande* is one of his most splendid and eloquent works. The *Miserere* was written for the Jesuit Church on Rue Saint-Antoine, whose ceremonies were particularly sumptuous. All four works on the disc are powerfully expressive and beautifully performed. The recording, made in collaboration with Radio France, is most expertly balanced.

Les Quatre Saisons (Quatuor anni tempestates). Psalms of David Nos. 41: Quemadmodum desiderat cervus; 75: Notus in Judaea Deus; 126: Nisi Dominus.

(B) **(*) Op. OPS 10-004. Rimi, Delétré, Parlement de Musique, in Gester.

Charpentier's *Four Seasons* is a group of four motets for two voices, drawing its inspiration from the 'Song of Songs', but it is a comparably routine inspiration. In the celebration of *Spring*, the two soprano voices here (the second unnamed) are not ideally matched and their vibratos clash. But in *Summer* and *Autumn*, their dialogue interchanges are much more pleasing and in *Winter*, the bravura scales (suggesting the gales, perhaps) come off quite effectively. With the Psalm settings, the vocal writing is of an altogether different order and the three singers respond to Charpentier's stimulating variety of colour and mood. *Nisi Dominus* brings some lovely solo work from Noémi Rimi and the vocal blending is often impressive. After a charming 'piping' instrumental introduction, the bass opens Psalm 75 rather gruffly, but the agreeable vigour of this opening makes way for a very touching centrepiece, before the buoyant close. The style of Le Parlement de Musique is robust rather than refined, and while the recording is vivid, the focus is not always quite clean. But this inexpensive disc is still worth trying. Full texts and translations are provided.

Le Reniement de Saint Pierre – histoire sacrée.

(M) **(*) Erato 4509 97409-2. Robin, Chamonin, Maurant, Richez, Lesueur, Veyron-Lacroix, Ch. Caillard – COUPERIN: *Audite omnes et expanescite* etc. **

Charpentier's *Le Reniement de Saint Pierre* is a deeply expressive work and the performance, which presumably comes from the early 1960s, is also deeply felt. Both the singing and playing give pleasure, and the poignant dissonances of the final chorus make a strong impression. In some ways Christie's Harmonia Mundi performance (see above) is even finer, but it is not more moving. There are minor reservations about the Erato coupling, but on the whole this is a valuable reissue.

OPERA AND THEATRE MUSIC

Actéon (complete).

(B) *** HM HMA 1951095. Visse, Mellon, Laurens, Feldman, Paut, Les Arts Florissants Vocal & Instrumental Ens., Christie.

Actéon is particularly well portrayed by Dominique Visse; his transformation in the fourth tableau and his feelings of horror are almost as effective as anything in nineteenth-century opera! The other singers are first rate, in particular the Diane of Agnès Mellon. Alert playing and an altogether natural recording, as well as excellent presentation, make this a most desirable issue and a real bargain.

(i) *Amor vince ogni cosa* (pastoraletta); (ii) *Les Plaisirs de Versailles;* (iii) *3 Airs on Stanzas from Le Cid.*

*** Erato/Warner 0630 14774-2. (i) Petibon, Lallouette; (i; ii) Daneman, Piolino, (ii) Károlyi, Duardin, Gardeil; (i; iii) Agnew, Les Arts Florissants, Christie.

Les Plaisirs de Versailles is a 'mini-opera' in which the characters are Music, Conversation, Le Jeu, Comus and Un Plaisir. They engage in a vociforous dialogue which is in turns lyrical, dramatic, and bizarrely humorous, arguing at length about which is the most essential of the King's pleasures, with Comus mediating and suggesting fine wines, pastries, and sweetmeats. Finally the protagonists are reconciled and the piece ends with a happy chorus.

Amore vince ogni cosa is a charming pastoral conversation piece (with shepherds' chorus) about unrequited love. The three ardent airs from Corneille's *Le Cid* make a passionate central interlude. Throughout the solo singing is delightful and full of lively and charming characterization, while the Charpentier's orchestration is equally diverting. With William Christie and his Arts Florissants providing elegant, sparkling accompaniments, this splendidly recorded collection is treasure trove indeed.

Les Arts Florissants (opéra et idyle en musique).

(B) *** HM (ADD) HMA 1901083. Les Arts Florissants Vocal & Instrumental Ens., William Christie.

Les Arts Florissants is a short entertainment in five scenes; the libretto tells of a conflict between the Arts, who flourish under the rule of Peace, and the forces of War, personified by Discord and the Furies. This and the little Interlude that completes the music include some invigorating and fresh invention, performed very pleasingly indeed by this eponymous group under the expert direction of William Christie. Period instruments are used, but intonation is always good and the sounds often charm the ear. The recording is excellent. A bargain.

David et Jonathas (complete).

(B) **(*) HM (ADD) HMA 190 1289/90. Lesne, Zanetti, Gardeil, Visse, Les Arts Florissants, Christie.

Christie's version of *David et Jonathas* may not always be especially dramatic, but it has a notably sure sense of authentic Baroque style and scale, as well as fine choral singing. However, only one of Christie's soloists is really outstanding:

the characterfully distinctive counter-tenor, Dominique Visse, who gives a vivid, highly theatrical performance. Those who relish authenticity above all else will clearly take to this version, very well recorded.

La Descente d'Orphée aux Enfers (chamber opera; complete).

*** Erato 0630 11913-2. Agnew, Daneman, Zanetti, Petibon, Károlyi, Gardeil, Les Arts Florissants, William Christie.

Charpentier's compact setting of this famous story starts with lightweight, sparkling movements in dance rhythms, but then dramatically changes tone with the death of Euridice, a moment superbly interpreted by Sophie Daneman. The following lament of Orphée is just the first of his moving and expressive solos, each of them brief but intense and beautifully sung by Paul Agnew. They culminate in a sequence when he seeks to charm Pluton in the Underworld, finally succeeding. The piece ends with the lamenting of Pluton's subjects at losing Orphée and his musical magic. With Christie drawing superb playing and singing from his well-chosen team, it is good to have such a delightful rarity revived, probably given once at the time and no more.

Le Malade imaginaire (incidental music).

*** HM HMC 901336. Zanetti, Rime, Brua, Visse, Crook, Gardeil, Les Arts Florissants, Christie.

This sequence of extended prologue and three *intermèdes* tingles with energy, and is superbly realized on this first recording of the complete incidental music, much of which was lost for three centuries. With well balanced, warmly refined sound, Christie – though he uses percussion dramatically – is light in his textures and rhythms, often opting for fast speeds. The format is cumbersome, with a single disc contained in a double jewel-case, but the libretto is very readable.

Médée (complete).

✿ *** Erato 4509 96558-2 (3). Hunt, Padmore, Delétré, Zanetti, Salzmann, Les Arts Florissants, Christie.

Médée (tragédie-lyrique): complete.

(M) **(*) HM (ADD) HMX 2901139.41 (3). Feldman, Ragon, Mellon, Boulin, Bona, Cantor, Les Arts Florissants, Christie.

In his second recording of this rare opera, again with his group, Les Arts Florissants, Christie was glad to be able to open out the small cuts that were made before so as to fit the LP format. The success of his new interpretation is readily borne out in the finished performance, which easily surpasses the previous one in its extra brightness and vigour, with consistently crisper and more alert ensembles, often at brisker speeds, with the drama more clearly established. The casting is first rate, with Lorraine Hunt outstanding in the tragic title-role. Her soprano has satisfying weight and richness, as well as the purity and precision needed in such classical opera; and Mark Padmore's clear, high tenor copes superbly with the role of Jason, with no strain and with cleanly enunciated diction and sharp concern for word-meaning. The others follow Christie's pattern of choosing cleanly focused voices, even if the tone is occasionally gritty.

Christie's highly communicative first recording of *Médée* in 1985 has excellent soloists and the performance has a vitality and sense of involvement which bring out the keen originality of Charpentier's writing, his implied emotional glosses on a formal subject. Les Arts Florissants in the stylishness of its playing on period instruments matches any group in the world and the recording is excellent. This reissue is admirably documented and includes a full libretto with translation and makes an excellent bargain. However, the new Erato interpretation easily surpasses the earlier one in extra brightness and vigour with the drama even more clearly established.

CHAUSSON, Ernest (1855–99)

Poème for Violin & Orchestra.

*** EMI (ADD) CDC7 47725-2. Perlman, O de Paris, Martinon
 – RAVEL: *Tzigane;* SAINT-SAENS: *Havanaise* etc. ***

(M) *** Decca (ADD) 460 006-2. Chung, RPO, Dutoit –
 DEBUSSY; FRANCK: *Violin Sonatas.* *** ✿

(M) **(*) RCA (ADD) 09026 61753-2. Heifetz, RCA Victor SO, Solomon – LALO: *Symphonie espagnole* (**(*));
 SAINT-SAENS: *Havanaise* etc.; SARASATE:
 Zigeunerweisen. (***)

Perlman's 1975 recording, with the Orchestre de Paris under Jean Martinon, of Chausson's beautiful *Poème* is a classic account by which newcomers are measured. The digital transfer exchanges some of the opulence of the original for a gain in presence, but Perlman's glorious tone is undiminished, even if now the ear perceives a slightly sharper outline to the timbre.

Chung's performance is deeply emotional, if not as opulent as Perlman's; but, with committed accompaniment from the RPO and excellent (1977) recording, this makes an apt bonus for superb performances of the Debussy and Franck *Violin Sonatas.*

Heifetz is recorded very closely, as if in the glare of a spotlight, and the performance is robbed of much of its subtlety. Even so, the playing itself is quite remarkable.

(i) Poème for Violin & Orchestra; (ii) Poème de l'amour et de la mer.

*** Chan. 8952. (i) Tortelier; (ii) Linda Finnie; Ulster O, Tortelier – FAURE: *Pavane* etc. ***

No quarrels with Yan Pascal Tortelier's playing in the *Poème,* which he directs from the bow. There is consistent beauty of timbre and, what is more important, refinement of feeling. In the *Poème de l'amour et de la mer* Linda Finnie can hold her own with the very best; her feeling for the idiom is completely natural and her voice is beautifully coloured; among newer recordings this has very strong claims. Indeed in rapport between singer and orchestra none is better.

Symphony in B flat, Op. 20.

(B) **(*) Virgin VBD5 61513-2 (2). French RPO, Janowski –
 BERLIOZ: *Symphonie fantastique; Le Carnaval romain;*
 BIZET: *Symphony.* ***

(M) **(*) Mercury (ADD) [434 389-2]. Detroit SO, Paray –

BARRAUD: *Offrande à une ombre*; LALO: *Le roi d'Ys*; *Namouna*. **(*)

Symphony in B flat; (i) *Poème*.

(B) *** RCA 2-CD (ADD) 74321 84591 (2). (i) D. Oistrath; Boston SO, Munch – DEBUSSY: *La Mer* etc. ***

Symphony in B flat, Op. 20; *Soir de fête*, Op. 32; *La Tempête*, Op. 18; *Viviane*, Op. 5.

*** Chan. 9650. BBC PO, Y. P. Tortelier.

Symphony in B flat; *Soir de fête*, Op. 32; *La Tempête*, Op. 18: 2 *Scenes*.

**(*) Chan. 8369. Radio-Télévision Belge SO, Serebrier.

Yan Pascal Tortelier and the BBC Philharmonic give thoroughly idiomatic and well-played accounts of all these Chausson pieces. They more than hold their own against any of the competitors, given the excellence of the sound.

However, Munch's 1962 Boston account is very compelling indeed and he clearly has great sympathy for the style. This was one of his very best records and David Oistrath's *Poème* is peerless.

Serebrier's account is more logically coupled with other Chausson pieces, *Soir de fête* plus two scenes from the incidental music for *The Tempest*. Serebrier's account of the *Symphony* has real conviction and receives good recording, but on balance Torvelier is preferable.

Janowski's highly idiomatic reading of the Chausson *Symphony* is the finest of the three performances on this inexpensive Virgin Double. It is very well played, and the performance has a strong impetus, particularly in the passionate finale, with the Franckian undertones well brought out throughout. The recording is very good.

Paul Paray's 1956 performance of the Chausson *Symphony* is first class and the recording is much better than we remembered from its mono version.

CHAMBER MUSIC

Andante & Allegro (for clarinet and piano); *Piano Trio in G min.*, Op. 3; *Pièce for Cello & Piano*, Op. 39; *Poème* Op. 25 (arr. for violin, string quartet & piano).

*** Hyp. CDA 67028. Neidlich, Devoyon, Hoffman, Graffin; Chiligirian Qt.

The *Poème* appears here in a newly discovered arrangement by the composer. There is a complete naturalness and conviction about this performance in which Graffin is a wonderfully persuasive soloist. The remaining pieces including the early *Piano Trio* come off well and can hold their own against any rival. The rich acoustic environment enhances the appeal of these dedicated performances.

Concerto in D for Violin, Piano & String Quartet, Op. 21.

*** Essex CDS 6044. Accardo, Canino, Levin, Batjer, Hoffman, Wiley – SAINT-SAENS: *Violin Sonata No. 1*. ***

Salvatore Accardo and Bruno Canino and their four colleagues convey a sense of effortless music-making and of pleasure in making music in domestic surroundings. Accardo is particularly songful in the third movement, light

and delicate elsewhere. It is a thoroughly enjoyable account, recorded in a warm acoustic.

Piano Quartet in A, Op. 30; *Piano Trio in G min.*, Op. 3.

(B) **(*) HM HMA 1901115. Les Musiciens.

The Op. 30 *Piano Quartet* of 1896 is one of Chausson's finest works. Les Musiciens are recorded rather closely, and their performance is lacking some of the subtlety and colour one knows this ensemble can command. The effect both here and in the early *G minor Trio*, Op. 3, is somewhat monochrome. However, the playing is both warm and spontaneous, and the ambience of the acoustic is pleasing.

Piano Trio in G min., Op. 3.

*** Ph. 411 141-2. Beaux Arts Trio – RAVEL: *Trio in A min.* ***

The early *G minor Trio* will come as a pleasant surprise to most collectors, for its beauties far outweigh any weaknesses. The playing of the Beaux Arts Trio is superbly eloquent and the recording is very impressive on CD.

String Quartet in C min., Op. 35 (completed Vincent d'Indy).

(N) *** Hyp. CDA 67097. Chilingirian Qt. – D´INDY: *String Quartet No. 1*. ***

(B) *** Naxos 8.553645. Quatuor Ludwig – FRANCK: *Piano Quintet*. ***

Prompted by César Franck in 1889, French composers produced a series of fine string quartets, of which only Debussy's and Ravel's remain in the regular repertory. This superb disc from the Chilingirians, sensitively played and beautifully recorded, is a revelation. Chausson's work, completed by Vincent d'Indy after the composer's tragic death, has echoes of his teacher, Franck, touched in with point and elegance.

The Quatuor Ludwig also play it with conviction and aplomb. The recording is excellent, and this is also highly recommendable if you want the coupling.

VOCAL MUSIC

3 *Chansons de Shakespeare*; 3 *Lieder de Camille Mauclair*; 2 *Poèmes de Verlaine*; *Mélodies*: *L'albatross*; *L'âme de bois*; *Amour d'antan*; *Apaisement*; *L'aveu*; *Cantique à l'épouse*; *La caravanne*; *Chanson*; *Chanson perpétuelle*; *Le charme*; *La cigale*; *Le colibri*; *Dans la forêt*; *La dernière feuille*; *Hébé*; *Marins dévots à la vierge Marie*; *Les morts*; *Nanny*; *Nocturne*; *Nos souvenirs*; *Nous, nous aimerons*; *La nuit*; *Les papillons*; *La pluie*; *Printemps triste*; *Le rideau de ma voisine*; *Le reveil*; *Sérénade*; *Sérénade italienne*; *Serres chaudes*; *Le temps des lilas*.

(N) *** Hyp. CDA 67321/2. Lott, Murray, Trakas, Greevy, Johnson; Chiligirian Qt.

Graham Johnson, as much a devotee of French *mélodie* as of German *Lieder*, here turns his searchlight attention to an area seriously neglected. These two superb, revelatory discs contain all the regularly published songs of Chausson, plus five songs drawn from manuscript sources. Beautifully performed, they come with the same kind of scholarly notes that Johnson provides for his Schubert and Schumann series. As he says, Chausson may not be one of the four or five really great composers of French *mélodie*, but the beauty and sensitivity of his settings of a wide range of poets – all vividly portrayed in Johnson's notes – make the whole set a delight, plotting the composer's development from his student years to his untimely death in a cycle accident.

What consistently comes out far more than in Chausson's instrumental music is his gift of tunefulness, fresh and memorable. It may be that paradoxically these songs are underprized simply because their melodies are so easy on the ear, as though true *mélodie* should be more difficult for the listener. Not that they lack refinement in any way, and the piano accompaniments. particularly in the early songs, from the sparkling first item, *Les papillons*, are models of refinement and imagination, consistently inspiring Johnson as accompanist.

The singers too are all fine artists. Ann Murray is charming throughout in the great majority of the songs for female voice, with Dame Felicity Lott confined to five intense Maeterlinck settings, written in 1896 four years before his death, when he and Debussy were encouraging each other's enthusiasm for that poet. The third principal singer, the American, Chris Pedro Trakas, is a great discovery, with his heady light tenor and unfailingly sensitive response to the French words. The last songs, setting Verlaine and Shakespeare, lead finally to a delicate setting of Albert Jounet and as an apt conclusion a ravishing song with string quartet accompaniment to words by Charles Cros, a poet, also credited in France with inventing the gramophone. Vignettes of each poet as well as the commentary add to the delights of the set.

Mélodies: *Le colibri; Hébé. Nocturne; (i) La nuit. Printemps triste; (i) Réveil. Le temps des lilas.*

*(*) DG 459 682-2. Schäfer, Gage; (i) with Doufexis – DEBUSSY: *Mélodies* *(*).

Christine Schäfer's recital would be more welcome were she more completely at ease in the style, and her French more idiomatic. Hers is a lovely voice, but even so this collection disappoints. Very good recorded sound.

(i) *La Légende de Sainte Cécile, Op. 22; (ii) La Tempête, Op. 18.*

(M) *** EMI CDM5 55323-2 (2). (i) Verner, Choeur de Femmes de Radio France; (ii) Dale, Farman, Todorovitch, Le Roux, Lafont, Ens. O de Paris, Kantorow.

La Tempête comprises a dozen or so settings and is scored for unusual forces: three strings, flute, harp and celeste. In *La Légende de Sainte Cécile*, the shades of Wagner and Franck are never far away but, as always with this composer, the invention is fluent, the music often imaginative and always rewarding. The performances are expert and persuasive and the recording very natural. This is something of a find. However, as we go to press this set has been deleted.

CHÁVEZ, Carlos (1899–1978)

Symphonies Nos. (i) *1;* (ii) *2;* (i) *4;* (iii) *Baile (Symphonic Painting); The Daughter of Colchis (Symphonic Suite).*

** ASV CDCA 1058. (i) RPO; (ii) Mexico PO; (iii) Mexico State SO; Bátiz.

Sinfonia de Antigona (Symphony No. 1); Sinfonia India (Symphony No. 2); Sinfonia Romantica (Symphony No. 4).

**(*) Everest (ADD) EVC 9041. New York Stadium SO, composer.

These Everest performances carry the authority of the composer's direction and include the best known, *Sinfonia India*, which is based on true Indian melodies. It has a savage, primitive character which is very attractive. The 1958 recording is detailed and bright, if not absolutely sharp in focus because of the resonance, and is somewhat wanting in real depth and weight. Nevertheless this is a valuable reissue, and it is a pity that it is not offered in a lower price range.

Enrique Bátiz produces good results from his various orchestras and the sound is more than acceptable. But the Everest remains a first choice.

CHERUBINI, Luigi (1760–1842)

Anacréon Overture.

(***) BBC BBCL mono 4016-2 (2) BBC SO, Toscanini – BEETHOVEN: *Missa solemnis; Symphony No. 7 (**(*));* MOZART: *Symphony No. 35 (Haffner). (***)*

Cherubini's fine *Anacréon Overture* enjoyed considerably more exposure in the 1930s and 1940s. (At the time of writing there is no modern recording at all!) Toscanini's account comes from 1935 and finds the BBC Symphony Orchestra at its most responsive and alert. For a 1930s broadcast the sound, though not the highest of fi, is really very good indeed.

String Quartets Nos. 1 in E flat; 6 in A min.

*** CPO 999 463-2. Hausmusik.

String Quartets Nos. 2 in C; 5 in F.

(N) *** CPO 999 464-2. Hausmusik.

String Quartets Nos. 3 in D min.; 4 in E.

(N) *** CPO 999 465-2. Hausmusik.

String Quartets Nos.1 in E flat; 2 in C.

*** BIS CD 1003. David Qt.

String Quartets Nos. 3 in D min.; 4 in E.

*** BIS CD 1004. David Qt.

Cherubini's quartets are of very high quality and it is good to have outstanding new recordings of them. Listening to them makes one realize the justice of Beethoven's admiration for the composer, for Cherubini's art is informed by lofty ideals and often noble invention. His melodic inspiration is often distinguished and instinctive, there is always a fine musical intelligence at work and polished craftsmanship is always in evidence.

The *First Quartet* (1814) apparently uses ideas borrowed from the operas of Méhul, but one would hardly guess that they were not the composer's own, with all four movements springing readily from the same basic material. The *Third* and *Fourth* quartets are if anything even finer. All four works bring an exhilarating response from this excellent BIS group, who are superb individual players yet tonally perfectly integrated. They are thoroughly at home in Cherubini's sound world. In short these modern-instrument performances could hardly be bettered, and the recording, as one expects from this label, is in every way first class.

The performances by Hausmusik on period instruments are also of the very highest quality. Although textures are less ample, inner detail is wonderfully clear, there is no lack of warmth and the playing itself is highly eloquent. Their account of the *Larghetto* of No. 1 is both searching and dramatic, and as it so happens the *Fifth Quartet in F*, which they alone offer, is one of their finest performances, with the beautiful *Adagio* wonderfully hushed and serene, and the *Scherzo*'s *Trio*, with its recurring dainty rising scale, is also deliciously played.

The group's perfect tonal blending in the *Larghetto sostenuto* of No. 3 is equally satisfying, and this is again apparent at the opening *Allegro maestoso* of No. 4, while the *Scherzo* is again played with dainty rhythmic point. The opening of No. 6 is similarly perceptive and, throughout, finales are full of zest and energy. In short, except for those allergic to period instruments, this set leads the field, and the recording is strikingly vivid and present.

Requiem in C min.

(B) *** EMI doubleforte CZS5 68613-2 (2). Ambrosian Ch., Philh. O, Muti – VERDI: *Requiem*. ***

The *C minor Requiem*, the best known, was called by Berlioz 'the greatest of the greatest of his [Cherubini's] works'. Muti directs a tough, incisive reading, underlining the drama. The digital recording is excellent.

Requiem Mass No. 2 in D min.

(M) *** DG (ADD) 457 744-2. Czech PO & Ch., Markevitch – MOZART: *Coronation Mass*. ***

Beethoven revered Cherubini and listening to the *D minor Requiem* one can see why. Cherubini's inspiration is always dignified and fluent, and there is a nobility about his music that is imposing. One tends to think of Cherubini as one of those 'historical personages', but this original and often exciting work shows that in his old age (he was 76 when he wrote it) he was looking to the future and not the past. The performance is an outstandingly alive one and the recording has a wide dynamic range, making a remarkable impact in the climaxes. It becomes less immediate in the quieter passages and is notably withdrawn at the very beginning. But DG's current remastering has improved this considerably.

OPERA

Medea (complete).

(M) ** EMI (ADD) CMS5 66435-2 (2). Callas, Scotto, Pirazzini, Picchi, La Scala Ch. & O, Serafin (with BEETHOVEN: *Ah! perfido* **).

The 1957 studio recording of *Medea* is a magnificent example of the fire-eating Callas. She completely outshines any rival. A cut text is used and Italian instead of the original French, with Serafin less imaginative than he usually was; but, with a cast more than competent – including the young Renata Scotto – it is an enjoyable set. Callas's recording of the Beethoven scena, *Ah! perfido*, makes a powerful fill-up, even though in this late recording (1963/4) vocal flaws emerge the more.

CHOPIN, Frédéric (1810–49)

Complete Chopin Editions

DG Complete Chopin Edition.

(B) **(*) DG Dig./ADD 463 047-2 (17).

To commemorate the 150th anniversary of Chopin's death, DG assembled, for the first time, the complete works of Chopin – even making several new recordings to fill in the gaps. Where this edition falls down in places is in the choice of performance. There are many outstanding Chopin recordings here – notably from Argerich, Pollini and Zimerman – but there are several where DG might have made a better choice, the *Waltzes* and *Mazurkas* for example. At a bargain price and with a lavishly illustrated booklet, it is still good value and one can always supplement this set with other recordings. The merits of each volume, which are available separately, are discussed below.

Volume 1: Works for piano and orchestra: (i; ii) *Piano Concerto Nos. 1 in E min., Op. 11;* (i; iii) *2 in F min., Op. 21;* (i; iii) *Andante spianato et Grande polonaise brillante, Op. 22;* (iv) *Grande fantasia on Polish airs, Op. 13;* (v) *Krakowiak concert rondo, Op. 14;* (iv) *Variations on 'Là ci darem la mano' from Mozart's Don Giovanni, Op. 2.*

(M) *** DG (ADD) 463 048-2 (2). (i) Zimerman; (ii) Concg. O, Kondrashin; (iii) LAPO, Giulini; (iv) Arrau, LPO, Inbal; (v) Askenase, Hague Residente O, Otterloo.

Krystian Zimerman's Chopin Concerto recordings are fresh, poetic and individual accounts, always sparkling and beautifully characterized. DG have chosen for the *E minor Concerto* to use his 'live' 1979 performance at the Concertgebouw (recorded by Hilversum Radio), rather than the studio one with Giulini, perhaps as there is a touch more spontaneity in the former. If the piano is marginally too close in both Concertos, the sound is acceptable, with surprisingly little difference between the studio and concert sources. Claudio Arrau's contributions (originally Philips) are very fine too: the playing is immaculately aristocratic; but his use of rubato will not suit everyone. Askenase's *Krakowiak concert rondo* – dating from 1959, but still sounding good – is most enjoyable and the programme ends with a sparkling account of the *Andante spianato et Grande polonaise brillante* from Zimerman.

Volume 2: (i) *Ballades Nos. 1–4;* (ii) *Barcarolle, Op. 60; Berceuse, Op. 57; Etudes, Op. 10, 1–12; Op. 25, 1–12;* (iii) *3 Ecossaises, Op. 72/3; 3 Nouvelles études;* (i) *Fantasy in F min., Op. 49;* (iii) *Funeral March, Op. 72/2.*

(M) *** DG Dig./ADD 463 051-2 (2). (i) Zimerman; (ii) Pollini; (iii) Ugorski.

Krystian Zimerman's impressive set of the *Ballades* and the *Fantasy* are touched by distinction throughout and have spontaneity as well as tremendous concentration to commend them and the 1987 recordings are of high DG quality. Maurizio Pollini's electrifying account of the *Etudes*, from 1972, remains as satisfying as ever with the remastering sounding fresh and full. The *Barcarolle* and *Berceuse* (1990) are hardly less impressive. This disc is completed by a series of mainly trifles recorded in 1999 (excepting the *Funeral March*, Op. 72/2) and well played by Anatol Ugorski. This is an outstanding set.

Volume 3: (i) *Mazurkas 1–49.* Mazurkas without Opus numbers: (ii) *2 Mazurkas in A min.: (ami Emile Gaillard); (notre temps); Mazurka in A flat; 2 Mazurkas in B flat; Mazurkas in C; D; & G.*

(M) *(*) DG 463 054-2 (2). (i) Luisada; (ii) Zilberstein.

The gifted Tunisian-born pianist Jean-Marc Luisada brings considerable elegance and finesse to the *Mazurkas* but alas, has difficulty in finding real simplicity of expression and Chopin's line is so often the victim of wilful rubato. There are some good things during the course of this survey, but they are too few and far between to permit anything other than the most qualified recommendation. For the *Mazurkas* without Opus numbers, DG have made new recordings with Lilya Zilberstein, which although they are better played and have novelty value, do not compensate for the poor set of the famous ones. Good recordings, but this is the least attractive set in the DG's Chopin Edition.

Volume 4: Nocturnes Nos. 1–21.

(M) *** DG 463 057-2 (2). Barenboim.

Barenboim's playing is of considerable eloquence, the phrasing beautifully moulded, yet with undoubted spontaneous feeling. If compared with Rubinstein these performances lack a mercurial dimension, they have their own character, with moments of impetuosity preventing any suggestion of blandness. The 1981 recording is first class.

Volume 5: Polonaises and minor works: (i) *Andante spianato et Grande polonaise brillante, Op. 22;* (ii) *Polonaises Nos. 1–7;* (iii) *3 Polonaises, Op. 71; Polonaises (without Opus numbers): in A flat; B flat; B flat min.; G min.; G flat & G sharp min.; Album Leaf in E; 2 Bourrées; Cantabile in B flat; Fugue in A min.; Galop marquis in A flat; Largo in E flat.*

(M) *** DG Dig./ADD 463 060-2 (2). (i) Argerich; (ii) Pollini; (iii) Ugorski.

Pollini offers magisterial playing, in some ways more commanding than Rubinstein (and better recorded) though not more memorable. Argerich's *Andante spianato* (1974) is everything it should be: wonderfully relaxed to start with

and extrovertly sparkling in the *Grande polonaise.* Ugorski fills in the gaps with some of Chopin's early works: interesting to hear, sometimes entertaining, but containing only glimpses of the greatness that was to emerge. Excellent value.

Volume 6: Impromptus, Preludes, Rondos and Scherzos: (i) *Impromptus Nos. 1–3; 4 (Fantaisie-impromptu);* (ii) *24 Preludes, Op. 28; Prelude in C sharp min., Op. 45; Prelude in A flat, Op. posth.;* (iii) *Rondo in C min., Op. 1; Rondo (La mazur) in F, Op. 5;* (iv) *Rondo in E flat, Op. 16;* (v) *Rondo for 2 Pianos in C, Op. posth. 73;* (vi) *4 Scherzos.*

(M) **(*) DG Dig./ADD 463 063-2 (2). (i) Bunin; (ii) Argerich; (iii) Zilberstein; (iv) Pletnev; (v) Bauer and Bung; (vi) Pollini.

The *Preludes* show Martha Argerich at her finest, spontaneous and inspirational, though her moments of impetuosity may not appeal to all tastes. But her instinct is sure, with many poetic and individual touches. Stanislav Bunin follows on with the *Impromptus* and here the result is not so impressive: he is technically brilliant, but can be self-aware and idiosyncratic at times. There is no want of intellectual power or command of keyboard colour in Pollini's accounts of the *Scherzi.* This is eminently magisterial playing. Zilberstein's account of two of the *Rondos* is enjoyable enough, but not as imposing as the Pletnev *Rondo in E flat* which follows, nor as beautifully recorded. This set concludes with Bauer and Bung in the *Rondo for Two Pianos*: here the recording, dating from 1958, is rather thin in sound with noticeable tape hiss, but the performance is acceptable.

Volume 7: Piano Sonatas and Variations: (i) *Piano Sonatas Nos. 1 in C min., Op. 4;* (ii) *2 in B flat min., Op. 35; 3 in B min., Op. 58;* (iii) *Introduction & Variations on a German National Air, Op. posth.;* (iv) *Introduction & Variations on a Theme of Moore for Piano (Four Hands), Op. posth.;* (i) *Variations in A major (Souvenir de Paganini);* (iii) *Variations brillantes in B flat major, Op. 12;* (v) *Variation No. 6 from the Cycle 'Hexameron'.* Miscellaneous pieces: *Allegro de concert, Op. 46;* (vi) *Bolero, Op. 19; Tarantella, Op. 43.*

(M) **(*) DG 463 066-2 (2). (i) Zilberstein; (ii) Pollini; (iii) Vásáry; (iv) Vl. and Vo. Ashkenazy; (v) Vl. Ashkenazy; (vi) Ugorski.

This set opens with a newly recorded version of the *First Sonata*, well played by Lilya Zilberstein. Of course, having the two most famous *Sonatas* in equally famous performances following, puts it rather in the shade. Pollini's readings of the *Second* and *Third* are enormously commanding. Both works are played with great distinction, but the balance is just a shade close. The second CD is of lighter fare taken from a variety of sources: Vásáry opens with an enjoyable set of the Op. 12 *Variations*, recorded in 1965 and sounding just a little thin. The Ashkenazys are borrowed from Decca and are in excellent form. Zilberstein's and Ugorski's contributions have been newly made and are (like the sound) good without being exceptional. On the whole a worthwhile set.

Volume 8: Chamber Music and Waltzes: (i) *Cello Sonata in G min., Op. 65;* (ii) *Grand duo concertant for Cello & Piano in E;* (i) *Introduction & polonaise brillante for Cello & Piano in C, Op. 3;* (iii) *Piano Trio in G min. Op. 8;* (iv) *Waltzes 1–17;* (v) *Waltzes in E flat (Sostenuto); in A min., Op. posth.*

(M) **(*) DG Dig./ADD 463 069-2 (2). (i) Rostropovich and Argerich; (ii) Bylsma and Orkis; (iii) Beaux Arts Trio; (iv) Luisada; (v) Zilberstein.

It seems a curious idea to combine the chamber music with the *Waltzes*, particularly as the recordings DG chose for the bulk of the latter are not inspired. Compared to the best available, these accounts seem pale, even though the recorded sound (1990) is good. The chamber music on the second CD is far stronger: the *Piano Trio*, an early work, is not wholly characteristic of Chopin, but is certainly of interest. The Beaux Arts' performance could hardly be improved upon and the 1970 recording (originally Philips) is excellent. With such characterful artists as Rostropovich and Argerich challenging each other, a memorable account of the *Cello Sonata*. The contrasts of character between expressive cello and brilliant piano are also richly caught in the *Introduction and polonaise* and the recording is warm and vivid. In between these two works is the *Grand duo concertant*, played by Anner Bylsma and Lambert Orkis. But the performance does not have the excellence of the Rostropovich/Argerich ones which flank it, nor as flattering a recording.

Volume 9: *17 Songs, Op. posth. 74; Czary, Op. posth.; Dumka, Op. posth.*

(M) **(*) DG 463 072-2. Szmytka, Martineau.

The Polish soprano Elzbieta Szmytka (newly recorded in 1999) has the full measure of these songs and is well supported by Malcolm Martineau. If these performances don't quite erase memories of the Söderström and Ashkenazy CD (a Decca issue that is currently withdrawn), they are well recorded and are much more than a stopgap. One is surprised how few recordings there have been of these songs, generally a neglected area of Chopin's output, for they are often surprisingly emotional and no lover of this composer or of song in general should be without them. The CD plays for under 47 minutes – Chopin disappointingly not having written enough songs to really fill up a CD!

Idil Biret Complete Chopin Edition

Piano Concerto No. 1, Op. 11; Andante spianato et Grande Polonaise brillante, Op. 22; Fantasia on Polish Airs, Op. 13.

(B) **(*) Naxos 8.550368 (with Slovak State PO, Stankovsky).

Piano Concerto No. 2, Op. 21; Krakowiak, Op. 14; Variations on Mozart's 'Là ci darem la mano', Op. 2.

(B) ** Naxos 8.550369 (with Slovak State PO, Stankovsky).

Ballades Nos. 1–4; Berceuse, Op. 57; Cantabile; Fantaisie, Op. 49; Galop marquis; Largo; Marche funèbre; 3 Nouvelles études.

(B)** Naxos 8.550508.

Mazurkas, Op. posth: in D; A flat; B flat; G; C; B flat;

Rondos, Op. 1, Op. 16 & Op. 73; Rondo à la Mazurka, Op. 5; Souvenir de Paganini; Variations brillantes; (i) *Variations for 4 Hands; Variations on a German Theme; Variations on Themes from 'I Puritani' of Bellini.*

(B) *** Naxos 8.550367 ((i) with Martin Sauer).

Nocturnes Nos. 1–21.

(B) *** Naxos 8.550356/7 (available separately).

Polonaises Nos. 1–6; 7 (Polonaise fantaisie).

(B) **(*) Naxos 8.550360.

Polonaises Nos. 8–10, Op. 71; in G min.; B flat; A flat; G sharp min.; B flat min. (Adieu); G flat, all Op. posth.; Andante spianato et Grande Polonaise in E flat, Op. 22 (solo piano version).

(B) **(*) Naxos 8.550361.

Piano Sonatas Nos. 1, Op. 4; 2 (Funeral March); 3, Op. 58.

(B) *** Naxos 8.550363.

Waltzes Nos. 1–19; Contredanse in G flat; 3 Ecossaises, Op. 72; Tarantelle, Op. 43.

(B) ** Naxos 8.550365.

The Turkish pianist, Idil Biret, has all the credentials for recording Chopin. Among others, she studied with both Cortot and Wilhelm Kempff. She has a prodigious technique and the recordings we have heard so far suggest that overall her Chopin survey is an impressive achievement.

Her impetuous style and chimerical handling of phrasing and rubato are immediately obvious in the *First Concerto*, and she makes a commanding entry in the *F minor Concerto*; in the *Larghetto*, too, the solo playing brings a gently improvisational manner, and the finale really gathers pace only at the entry of the orchestra (which is recorded rather resonantly throughout). Of the other short concertante pieces, the opening of the *Andante spianato* is very delicate and there is some scintillating playing in the following *Grande Polonaise* and *Fantasia on Polish Airs* – and a touch of heaviness, too, in the former. The introductory *Largo* of the *Mozart variations* is a bit too dreamy and diffuse but, once the famous tune arrives, the performance springs to life. Similarly, the introduction to the charming *Krakowiak Rondo* hangs fire, but again the *Rondo* sparkles, with the rhythmic rubato nicely handled, though the orchestral tuttis could ideally be firmer.

The *Ballades* bring impetuously romantic interpretations where the rubato at times seems mannered; the *Berceuse* is tender and tractable, the *Fantaisie in F minor* begins rather deliberately but opens up excitingly later; though the playing is rather Schumannesque, it is also imaginative; the three *Nouvelles études*, too, are attractively individual.

The disc called *Rondos and Variations* (8.550367) is worth anyone's money, showing Biret's technique at its most prodigious and glittering.. Much of the music here is little known and none of it second rate. The *Nocturnes* are a great success in a quite different way, the rubato simple, the playing free and often thoughtful, sometimes dark in timbre, but always spontaneous. The recording is pleasingly full in timbre. The *Polonaises* demonstrate Biret's sinewy strength: the famous *A major* is a little measured, but the *A flat* is fresh and exciting and the whole set commanding, while the

Polonaise fantaisie shows imaginative preparation yet comes off spontaneously like the others. The recital ends with a fine account of the solo piano version of the *Andante spianato* (quite lovely) and *Grande Polonaise*, which is more appealing than the concertante version.

The three *Sonatas* are fitted comfortably on to one CD and, irrespective of cost, this represents one of the finest achievements in Biret's series so far. The *Waltzes* brought charismatic playing, giving opportunities for exciting bravura, but too many of these pieces are pressed on without respite. The *Ecossaises* and *Tarantelle* are also thrown off at almost breakneck speed.

Opus Chopin edition

Piano Concerto No. 2 in F minor, Op. 21; Fantasy on Polish Airs, Op. 13.

*** Opus 111 OPS 2008. Olejniczak, Das Neue Orchester, Spering (with ELSNER: *Overture, Lezek Bialy;* KURPINSKI: *Overture, Zamek na Czorsztynie;* PAER: *La Biondina in gondoletta* (with Olga Pasiechnyk)).

Etudes, Op. 25; 24 Preludes, Op. 28; Piano Sonata No. 2.

*** Opus 111 OPS 2009. Sokolov.

'Chopin's Last Concert in Paris' (with music by Bellini, Donizetti, Mozart and Meyerbeer).

*** Opus 111 OPS 2012. Olejniczak, Pasiechnyk, etc.

The 150th anniversary of Chopin's death brought a flurry of activity from various companies, none more original or imaginative than that of the Paris-based Opus 111 label. There are ten volumes in all (OPS 2006–15) handsomely produced and intelligently planned, two of which we list above. The first, *Racines* (*Roots*) (OPS 2006), produces the traditional folk music and dances that Chopin would have heard in his youth and that played such a formative role in his musical development. Not only do we get so much fascinating folk material – mazurkas, polkas and obereks – but we also hear instruments of the period including the suka, an eighteenth-century string instrument. This affords a most useful insight into the world that the boy Chopin must have encountered. A second two-CD set brings 9 *Polonaises* and 23 *Mazurkas* played by Janusz Olejniczak (OPS 2007). But it is the third set (detailed above) which should make the most convenient entry point into this series. It reproduces on period instruments the programme on which Chopin made his Warsaw début after his triumph in Vienna, with the *F minor Concerto* and the *Fantasy on Polish Airs*. The programme also included overtures by his teacher, Jozef Elsner, and by Karol Kurpinski and soprano variations by Ferdinando Paër. Janusz Olejniczak strikes us as wonderfully idiomatic and is far more convincing than any other account we have heard on period instruments. He has fine poetic feeling and a refined sensitivity, and Das Neue Orchester under Christoph Spering give splendid support as well as spirited accounts of the overtures.

Grigory Sokolov's two-CD set of the *Etudes*, Op. 25, the *Preludes*, Op. 28 and the *Second Piano Sonata* is also something of a must, certainly well worth shortlisting, for he is an artist of real insight and vision. When one proceeds to

his recital entitled *Chopin privé* (*Chopin at Home*) (OPS 2010), he proves a most imaginative player. Another disc, *Chopin intime* (OPS 2011), offers readings of his correspondence with Georges Sand together with appropriate music illustrations. The letters are beautifully read by Sonia Rykiel and Andrzej Seweryn of the Comédie-Française, and English and German translations are given in the accompanying booklet for those whose French is a little fractured.

One of the most absorbing issues (listed above) is a reconstruction of Chopin's last concert in Paris in February 1848. Janusz Olejniczak shines in the Chopin pieces, and the Bellini, Donizetti, Meyerbeer and Mozart items are equally well served by the team that Opus 111 have assembled. Few records so successfully convey the atmosphere of this poignant occasion – and a sense of what concerts were like at that period. The remaining discs – jazz improvisations by the Andrzej Jagodzinski Trio (OPS 2013), and 'Chopin tomorrow' (OPUS 2014), are not mandatory purchases, though they have their rewards, as does the last CD, which presents some of the writings about Chopin by such diverse thinkers and writers as Nietzsche, Heine, Proust, Gide, Hermann Hesse and Tolstoy. An enterprising and thought-provoking set which is well worth exploring, but two of the listed discs (OPS 2008 and 2012) are outstanding.

OTHER CHOPIN RECORDINGS
Concertos and concertante music

(i) *Piano Concertos Nos. 1–2; Ballades Nos. 1–4; Barcarolle; Fantasia in F min.; Impromptus Nos. 1–4 (Fantaisie-impromptu); Nocturnes Nos. 1–21; Preludes Nos. 1–28; Scherzos Nos. 1–4; Waltzes Nos. 1–19.*

(N) (B) **(*) Ph. (ADD) 468 391-2. (7) Arrau; (i) with LPO, Inbal.

Arrau's survey was recorded over a decade in the 1970s. The two piano concertos came first and set the seal on his approach, immaculately aristocratic, but with personal touches of rubato which will not convince everybody. His expressive hesitations do not always grow naturally out of what has gone before. The LPO under Inbal give loyal support, but the piano is forwardly balanced to dominate the proceedings.

The *Préludes* followed in 1974, with each and every one bearing the imprint of a strong personality, to which not all listeners respond. Yet these performances appear to spring from a strong inner conviction. The *Ballades*, too, are particularly impressive and, as always with the Philips recordings of this artist, there is unfailing beauty of tone. Among the *Impromptus* the *Fantaisie-impromptu*, with its nobly contoured central melody, is a highlight: the piano timbre is richly coloured and full in the bass. Some of the rubato Arrau adopts in the *Nocturnes* may again strike some listeners as a shade too personal, but his artistry is unique and he is eminently well served by the engineers.

(i) *Piano Concertos Nos. 1–2. Nocturnes Nos. 1–19; Waltz, Op. 64/2.*

(M) (***) EMI mono CHS7 64491-2 (2). Rubinstein, (i) with
LSO, Barbirolli.

(i) *Piano Concertos Nos. 1 in E min., Op. 11; 2 in F min.,
Op. 21. Andante spianato et Grande Polonaise brillante,
Op. 22; Barcarolle, Op. 60; Berceuse, Op. 57; Mazurkas
Nos. 1–51; Nocturnes Nos. 1–19; Polonaises Nos. 1–7;
Scherzi Nos. 1–4: Waltz in C sharp min., Op. 64/2.*

(M) (***) EMI mono CHS7 64933-2 (5). Rubinstein, (i) with
LSO, Barbirolli.

*Andante spianato et Grande Polonaise brillante, Op. 22;
Barcarolle, Op. 60; Berceuse, Op. 57; Mazurkas Nos. 1–51;
Polonaises Nos. 1–7; Scherzi Nos. 1–4; Waltz in C sharp
min., Op. 64/1.*

(M) (***) EMI mono CHS7 64697-2 (3). Rubinstein.

The five-CD set listed above falls into two parts, the first
consisting of the two piano Concertos, recorded with Barbirolli and the LSO in 1937 (*E minor*) and 1931 (*F minor*), the *C
sharp minor Waltz*, recorded in 1930, and the celebrated set
of the *Nocturnes* from 1936–7. This is additionally available
on a two-CD Références set. The second set of three CDs
comprises the *Mazurkas* (recorded in 1938), some of the
most totally idiomatic Chopin playing ever committed to
record, the 1932 *Scherzi* and the *Polonaises* (1934) and various
other pieces. Rubinstein was at the height of his powers
when he made these recordings and he rarely equalled and
never surpassed them in the post-war, LP era. The *Mazurkas*
and *Nocturnes* have a poetic spontaneity and aristocratic
finesse that are totally convincing. But those sets have been
deleted as we go to press.

*Piano Concertos Nos. (i) 1 in E min., Op. 11; (ii) 2 in
F min., Op. 21.*

*** DG (ADD) 415 970-2. Zimerman, LAPO, Giulini.
**(*) Sony SK44922. Perahia, Israel PO, Mehta.
*** EMI CDC5 56798-2. Argerich, Montreal SO, Dutoit.
(M) *** Mercury (ADD) [434 374-2]. Bachauer, LSO, Dorati.
(B) *** RCA Navigator (ADD) 74321 17892-2. Ax, Phd. O,
Ormandy.
(B) *** Naxos 8.550123. Székely, Budapest SO, Németh.
(B) *** DG 429 515-2. Vásáry, BPO, (i) Semkow; (ii) Kulka.
(M) **(*) EMI ADD CDM5 67232-2 [567261]. François,
Monte-Carlo Op. O, Frémaux.
(B) ** Ph. (ADD) 434 145-2. Arrau, LPO, Inbal.
** DG 459 684-2. Zimerman, Polish Festival Orchestra.
** Hyp. CDA 66647. Demidenko, Philh. O, Schiff.

The CD coupling of Zimerman's performances of the two
Chopin Concertos with Giulini is hard to beat. Elegant,
aristocratic, sparkling, it has youthful spontaneity and at the
same time a magisterial authority, combining sensibility
with effortless pianism. Both recordings are cleanly detailed.

Perahia's effortless brilliance and refinement of touch
recall artists like Hofmann and Lipatti. Mehta provides a
highly sensitive accompaniment once the soloist enters but
is curiously offhand and matter-of-fact (indeed almost
brutal) in the orchestral ritornelli. The sound is dryish and
far from ideal. The three stars are for Perahia's playing, not
the sound!

In Martha Argerich's newest EMI coupling her pianism

remains as mercurial and her virtuosity as incandescent
as ever; indeed she has rarely sounded as captivating or
characterful. Charles Dutoit gets good playing from the
Montreal Orchestra. Admirers of Argerich (and we might
add Chopin) need not hesitate.

Gina Bachauer obviously sees these as full-bloodedly romantic Concertos and Dorati gives her every support and
the orchestral playing is first class. Passage-work scintillates
and her phrasing and rubato have fine sensitivity. Both slow
movements bring appealing delicacy, and finales have a
lilting panache. With Mercury's spaciously realistic Watford
Town Hall recording of orchestra and piano alike, and an
excellent balance, this is very enjoyable indeed but no longer
available in the UK.

Emanuel Ax offers genuinely poetic playing and the finale
of the *F minor*, with its light, chimerical touch is particularly
pleasing. The digital recording is not quite top-drawer in
the matter of transparency. Yet it provides a full sound
for the Philadelphia Orchestra, and Ormandy is a highly
sensitive accompanist in both works.

Evgeny Kissin's programme was recorded at the Moscow
Conservatory in 1984 when he was a boy of twelve, though
he sounds like a seasoned master. There is no lack of depth
and poetic feeling, and this still remains a pretty extraordinary feat. Kissin follows the Concertos with three encores,
again proclaiming his mastery of this repertoire, with the
closing waltz thrown away with captivating insouciance. The
applause is well justified and the recording is excellent.

István Székely is particularly impressive in the *E minor
Concerto*, but in both works he finds atmosphere and poetry
in slow movements and an engaging dance spirit for the
finales, with rhythms given plenty of character. Németh
accompanies sympathetically; the orchestral contribution
here is quite refined. The recording is resonantly full, not
absolutely clear on detail; but the piano image is bold and
realistic. A splendid bargain in every sense of the word.

Vásáry's approach is much more self-effacing: his gentle
poetry is in clear contrast with the opulent orchestral sound.
Yet soloist and orchestra match their styles perfectly in both
slow movements, which are played most beautifully, and the
finales have no lack of character and sparkle and, with
recording that retains its depth and bloom, this makes a fine
bargain coupling.

If François's rather grand first entry in the *E minor* is
slightly mannered, there is much fine playing here, and the
solo contribution in the finales of both the Concertos often
scintillates. Frémaux's accompaniments of outer movements are strong in vitality, and certainly supportive in the
beautiful *Larghettos*, where again much of the solo playing
is persuasive. The remastering of the late 1960s recordings
gives both the forwardly placed soloist and the orchestra a
vivid presence.

Arrau's performances with Inbal are marred by rubato,
which at times seems mannered. The early 1970s recording
is average (with the piano too forward) and has a surprising
amount of tape hiss.

DG marked the 150th anniversary of the composer's death
with a newly recorded pairing of the two Concertos from
Krystian Zimerman. Alas, any sense of momentum or naturalness is submerged by uncharacteristically disruptive ru-

bato. Both Concertos are the same – full of intrusive touches and pulled out of shape. Far better to have his earlier set with Giulini and the Los Angeles Orchestra, elegant, aristocratic and sparkling.

Nikolai Demidenko produces consistent beauty of sound but his rubati can be disruptive, influenced by moments of disturbing self-consciousness. Probably the best things are in the middle movements, though even these are not always allowed to speak for themselves. Heinrich Schiff gets an excellent response from the Philharmonia Orchestra. For the dedicated admirer of the pianist rather than of the composer.

Piano Concerto No. 1 in E min., Op. 11.

(M) *** DG (ADD) 449 719-2 Argerich, LSO, Abbado – LISZT: *Piano Concerto No. 1.* ***

(B) **(*) Naxos 8.550292. Székely, Budapest SO, Németh – LISZT: *Concerto No. 1.* **(*)

** Decca 460 019-2. Ashkenazy, Deutsches SO, Berlin – GLAZUNOV: *Chopiniana.* **

(i) *Piano Concerto No. 1. Barcarolle in F sharp, Op. 60; Preludes, Op. 28/1, 3, 6, 10, 15–17, 20–21 & 24; Scherzo No. 3, Op. 39.*

(B) **(*) DG (ADD) 439 459-2. Argerich; (i) LSO, Abbado.

(i) *Piano Concerto No. 1. Berceuse in D flat, Op. 57; Fantaisie in F min., Op. 49; Fantasie-impromptu in C sharp min., Op. 66.*

*** DG 457 585-2. Pires; (i) COE, Krivine.

(i) *Piano Concerto No. 1. Etudes: in E, Op. 10/3; A flat, Op. 25/1; Fantaisie-impromptu in C sharp min., Op. 66; Impromptu No. 3 in G flat, Op. 51; Mazurkas: in A min., Op. 68/2; B flat, Op. 7/1; Nocturne No. 2 in E flat, Op. 9; Waltz No. 12 in F min., Op. 70/2.*

(B) **(*) Belart (ADD) 461 149-2. Vásáry; (i) BPO, Semkow.

(i) *Piano Concerto No. 1. Ballade No. 1, Op. 23; Nocturnes Nos. 4 & 5, Op. 15/1–2; 7, Op. 27/1; Polonaise No. 6, Op. 53.*

(M) *** EMI (ADD) CDM5 67548-2 [567549]. Pollini, (i) Philh. O, Kletzki.

Piano Concerto No. 1 in E min., Op. 11; Variations on 'La ci darem', Op.2; Waltz in A min., Op.34/2.

*** Sony (ADD) SK 60771. Ax, (for piano) OAE, Mackerras.

Pollini's classic recording still remains among the best available of the *E minor Concerto*. This is playing of such total spontaneity, poetic feeling and refined judgement that criticism is silenced. The digital remastering has been generally successful. The additional items come from Pollini's first EMI solo recital, and the playing is equally distinguished, the recording truthful.

Maria João Pires's concerns centre on the more inward-looking side of Chopin rather than its incandescence or brilliance, but this is a performance of substance and she is given eminently responsive support from the Chamber Orchestra of Europe and Emmanuel Krivine. The solo pieces are thoughtful, sensitive accounts and there are no quarrels with the DG recording.

As with the companion version of No. 2 this Sony disc from Emanuel Ax offers period performances unlikely to be

outshone for their imagination and poetry. Using a full-toned Erard piano of 1851, Ax produces warm, full tone which yet allows extra agility, thanks to the light action. The transparency of textures is a delight, with the writing for left hand brilliantly articulated. Mackerras enhances the drama of these readings by drawing out a wide range of dynamics from the OAE. The Opus 2 variations are relatively trivial, but Ax gives them both wit and poetry, and solo piano encore again finds Ax tenderly poetic. Excellent sound.

With persuasive support from Abbado, Martha Argerich provides some lovely playing, especially in the slow movement. Perhaps in the passage-work she is rather too intense, but this is far preferable to the rambling style we are sometimes offered. This version is now reissued in two different formats. The first comes as one of DG's 'Originals' in a coupling with an equally individual and charismatic account of Liszt's *First Concerto*; for the bargain Classikon alternative a miscellaneous programme of encores has been added, showing well the impulsive qualities of her solo playing.

Vásáry's fine mid-1960s Belart (originally DG) recording of the *E minor Concerto* gives great pleasure. He is beautifully recorded with a good balance and fine piano-tone. The recital which follows is rather more uneven. The pianist's self-effacing style is at its most effective in the *E major Etude* and the justly famous *E flat Nocturne*. However, he finds plenty of brilliance for the closing *Fantaisie-impromptu*. Again good recording.

István Székely's account is also available with the *F minor Concerto* (see above), but those preferring a Liszt coupling should find this alternative coupling equally satisfactory.

Ashkenazy's recording of the *E minor Concerto* is strangely enough his first. While his pianism is elegant, there is little real magic here. Excellent Decca sound.

(i) *Piano Concerto No. 1;* (ii) *Romanze only. Berceuse in D flat, Op. 67; Chant polonaise (arr. Liszt); Etudes: in E, Op. 10/1; in G flat, Op 10/5 (2 versions); Mazurkas: in B flat min., Op. 24/4; in C sharp min., Op. 63/3 (3 versions); in G, Op. 67/1; Waltzes: in C sharp min., Op. 64/ 1; in E min., Op. posth.*

(***) Biddulph mono LHW 040. Rosenthal; with (i) Berlin State Op. O, Weissmann; (ii) NBC SO, Black.

Listening to this painstaking transfer by Ward Marston, it is easy to understand why Moriz Rosenthal was held in such veneration. His poetic feeling and extraordinary delicacy of touch come across in the smaller pieces. In the *E minor Concerto* his playing is of enormous elegance and refinement of tone, which can be discerned even in this primitive 1930 recording. The recordings all date from 1929–31 when this artist was in his late sixties to early seventies, save for the slow movement of the Concerto, which survives in a live broadcast marking the pianist's seventy-fifth birthday. Some allowances must be made for the frail sound but the playing has unfailing beauty and finesse.

Piano Concerto No. 2 in F min., Op. 21.

(B) *** Decca Penguin (ADD) 460 653-2. Ashkenazy, LSO, Maazel – TCHAIKOVSKY: *Piano Concerto No. 1.* ***

(M) *** Decca (ADD) 448 598-2. Ashkenazy, LSO, Zinman –

BACH: *Clavier Concerto No. 1;* MOZART: *Piano Concerto No. 6.* **(*)

(N) (B) (***) Naxos mono 8.110612. Cortot, O., Barbirolli – SCHUMANN:*Piano Concerto in A min., Op. 56.* (***)

(N) *(*) Decca 467 093-2. Thibaudet, Rotterdam PO, Gergiev – GRIEG: *Piano Concerto in A min., Op. 16.* *(*)

(i) *Piano Concerto No. 2 in F min., Op. 21. 24 Preludes, Op. 24.*

(B) **(*) Belart 461 055-2 (ADD) De Larrocha; (i) SRO, Comissiona.

Ashkenazy's 1965 recording is a distinguished performance: his subtlety of phrasing and rubato are a constant source of pleasure. The recitativo section in the *Larghetto* is shaped with mastery, and there is a delectable lightness of touch in the finale. David Zinman and the LSO are obviously in full rapport with their soloist and the vintage recording has been remastered most satisfactorily.

This performance is available in Decca's 'Classic Sound' series (less ideally coupled with Bach and Mozart), but the (cheaper) Penguin Classics disc, with its excellent Tchaikovsky coupling, is the better deal. The author's note is by Angela Huth.

Alicia de Larrocha is an artist of personality and temperament, and her performance of the Concerto is highly poetic. It is supported by a strongly characterful accompaniment from Comissiona. Her *rubati* carry total conviction, whereas in the *Preludes* they sometimes seem more idiosyncratic. Fine Decca engineering from the 1970s.

Cortot, who recorded so much Chopin between the wars and for so many embodied the spirit of Chopin at that period, never committed the *E minor Concerto* to disc. The *Second*, recorded in 1935 at the Abbey Road Studios, sounds wonderfully fresh and is as individual as one would expect from this great artist. Mark Obert-Thorn gets a very good sound from the shellac originals.

Of course there are good things in Thibaudet's well-recorded account (among them Gergiev's accompaniment in the slow movement) but they do not add up enough to make a serious challenge to the existing competition. This much-admired (and rightly so) artist does not produce the wonderful range of colour that he has in his pianistic armoury and the overall impression left is surprisingly anonymous.

Piano Concerto No. 2; Andante spianato et Grande polonaise brillante, Op. 22; Grand fantasia on Polish Airs for Piano & Orchestra in A, Op. 13.

*** Sony SK 63371. Ax (fortepiano), OAE, Mackerras.

Emanuel Ax plays on an 1851 Erard piano helped by Mackerras. The sound is full and firm, and Ax uses the extra clarity of an early instrument – with none of the twang associated with fortepianos – to intensify the poetry of the writing. The two other, more trivial concertante works are equally made the more winning by the freshness of approach from both soloist and conductor, with witty pointing and moments of pure magic. Well worth exploring.

(i) *Piano Concerto No. 2. Ballades Nos. 1–4; Barcarolle, Op. 60; Berceuse, Op. 57* (2 versions); *Chants polonais,*

Op. 74 (trans. Liszt); *Etudes, Op. 10/1–12* (2 versions); *Op. 25/1–12* (2 versions); *Nouvelles études; Impromptus, Opp. 29, 36; Nocturnes Opp. 9/2; 15/1–2; 27/1; 55/1–2; 24 Preludes, Op. 28; Prelude in C sharp min., Op. 45; Piano Sonatas Nos. 2, Op. 35; 3, Op. 58; Waltzes Nos. 1–14.*

(M) (***) EMI mono CZS7 67359-2 (6). Cortot, (i) with O, Barbirolli.

Cortot's spontaneity, poetic feeling and keyboard refinement are heard to prodigal effect on these six CDs. Several alternative versions (for example, both sets of the Opp. 10 and 25 *Etudes* from 1934 and 1942 are included) offer food for thought. But in any event this is playing of a quite special quality: aristocratic yet full of fire and spontaneity. The transfers are strikingly good and bring Cortot very much before one's eyes.

(i) *Piano Concerto No.2. Ballade No. 1 in G min., Op. 23; Barcarolle in F sharp min., Op. 60; Berceuse in D flat, Op. 57; Fantaisie-impromptu in C sharp min., Op. 66; Mazurkas: in B flat, Op. 7/1; in D, Op. 33/2; in A min., Op. 68/2; Nocturnes: in E flat, Op. 9/2; in G min., Op. 37/1; Polonaises Nos. 3 in A (Military), Op. 40/1; 6 in A flat, Op. 53; Scherzo No. 2 in B flat min., Op. 31; Sonata No. 2 in B flat min. (Funeral March), Op. 35* (complete). *Waltzes: in A flat, Op. 34/1; in D flat (Minute), Op. 64/1; in E min., Op. posth.*

(B) *** RCA (ADD) Twofer 74321 34175-2 (2) [(M) Rubinstein, (i) Symphony of the Air, Wallenstein.

Including as it does complete performances of the *F minor Piano Concerto* and an unsurpassed *Funeral March Sonata*, this RCA Twofer must be counted a top choice among all the bargain collections of Chopin's piano music. Rubinstein's playing was in a class of its own. The orchestral tuttis in the *Concerto* are dry and studio-ish, but the piano timbre and colouring are unimpaired, especially in the delicate filigree of the slow movement. Otherwise the sound is always good, and often very good.

(i) *Piano Concerto No. 2. Mazurkas Nos. 5 & 7, Op. 7/1 & 3; 15 & 17, Op. 24/2 & 4; 20–21, Op. 30/3–4; 22–23 & 25, Op. 33/1–2 & 4; 27, Op. 41/2; 32, Op. 50/3; 41, Op. 63/3; 45, Op. 67/4; 47 & 49, Op. 68/2 & 4; Piano Sonata No. 3, Op. 58; Waltzes Nos. 1–14.*

(B) **(*) EMI (ADD) CZS5 68226-2 (2). Malcuzynski; (i) with LSO, Susskind.

Malcuzynski's recordings were made between 1959 and 1961. They project their musical personality with great intensity. This is especially apparent in his brilliant and highly individual collection of the fourteen *Waltzes*, where the crisp, assured playing is very attractive in the more extrovert numbers, thrown off with splendid panache. But his collection of *Mazurkas*, is brilliantly successful in every way. The playing is again immensely polished, yet finds an infinite range of mood and expression in a very well-chosen programme. The performance of the *B minor Sonata* is undoubtedly commanding, mannered perhaps, yet certainly not insensitive. But there is a dimension missing compared with Rubinstein. The Concerto is a disappointment. Again Malcuzynski offers confident, extrovert playing which inevitably provides much excitement, but this is altogether too glittering to be an ideal account of Chopin's delicate inspiration. The LSO under Susskind provide good support and the recording is bold, rather loud and rather over-projected. But there is nothing pallid or routine about this Chopin playing, and this inexpensive 'Profile' is a thoroughly worthwhile reissue.

Les Sylphides (ballet; orch. Douglas).

⚫ (B) *** DG (ADD) 429 163-2. BPO, Karajan – DELIBES: *Coppélia*: suite; OFFENBACH: *Gaîté parisienne*: excerpts. ***

(B) *** Sony (ADD) SBK 46550. Phd. O, Ormandy – DELIBES: *Coppélia; Sylvia: Suites ***; TCHAIKOVSKY: *Nutcracker Suite.* **(*)

(B) **(*) Ph. (ADD) Duo 438 763-2 (2). Rotterdam PO, Zinman – DELIBES: *Coppélia;* GOUNOD: *Faust: Ballet Music.* **(*)

(B) **(*) Decca 448 984-2. Nat. PO, Bonynge – MASSENET: *Thaïs: Méditation* with Kennedy; ROSSINI/RESPIGHI: *La Boutique fantasque.* **(*)

Karajan conjures consistently beautiful playing from the Berlin Philharmonic Orchestra, and he evokes a delicacy of texture which delights the ear throughout. The sound is full and atmospheric, and this is one of Karajan's very finest recordings. At bargain price it is unbeatable, coupled on CD not only with *Coppélia* (although the suite is not complete) but also with Offenbach's *Gaîté parisienne*.

The Philadelphia strings are perfectly cast in this score and, although the CBS sound is less svelte than the DG quality for Karajan, it is still very good. Ormandy begins gently and persuasively. Later the lively sections are played with irrepressible brilliance.

David Zinman's approach is less suavely characterful than Karajan's, but he secures smoothly beautiful playing from his Rotterdam orchestra and there is no lack of vitality. Most enjoyable, when the 1980 recording is so natural and resonantly full (obviously more modern than the DG).

Bonynge's performance shows a strong feeling for the dance rhythms of the ballet, and the orchestral playing is polished and lively. Bonynge also has the advantage of excellent (1982) digital recording, made in the Kingsway Hall. Nigel Kennedy plays very appealingly in the Massenet lollipop which acts as an encore. Even so, Karajan remains unsurpassed in this beautiful score.

Les Sylphides (orchestrations by Leroy Anderson and Peter Bodge).

(M) ** RCA ADD 09026 63532-2. Boston Pops O, Fiedler – LISZT: *Les Préludes; Mazeppa* *; PROKOFIEV: *The Love for Three Oranges: Suite.* **(*)

Apart from a few distracting tempi, *Les Sylphides* receives a generally good performance by Fiedler, dating from 1960, and in lively 'Living Stereo' sound. The souped-up orchestration has some nice moments, but the familiar Roy Douglas version is by far the more successful.

CHAMBER MUSIC

Cello Sonata in G min., Op. 65; Grand duo concertante in E on Themes from Meyerbeer's 'Robert le Diable'; Nocturne in C sharp min., Op. posth. (arr. Piatigorsky); *Etudes: in E min., Op. 25/7; D min., Op. 10/6* (arr. Glazunov; ed. Feuermann); *Waltz in A min., Op. 34/3* (arr. Ginsburg).

(B) *** Naxos 8.553159. Kliegel, Glemser.

Fresh and ardent performances of the *Sonata* and the re-maining two pieces that comprise Chopin's complete output for cello and piano. The Naxos collection also throws in some cello arrangements for good measure. These gifted and accomplished young artists are also very well recorded indeed and, at the price, this is a bargain.

Cello Sonata in G min., Op. 65.

(N) (B) *** EMI CZS5 74333-2 (2). Tortelier, Ciccolini – FAURE; MENDELSSOHN; RACHMANINOV: *Cello Sonatas.* ***

Tortelier's recordings of the Chopin and Rachmaninov son-atas, which were made in the 1960s in the Salle Wagram, come up sounding fresh. They occupied a commanding position in the catalogue during the early 1970s and rightly so! The same goes for the Fauré, which Tortelier recorded with Eric Heidsieck as a fine partner. Although he is accom-panied less well in the two Mendelssohn sonatas (recorded in 1978), this reissue is still highly competitive at the price.

Waltzes, arranged for cello & piano, Vol. I: Etude in E min., Op. 25/7; Grande valse brillante in D, Op. 18; Mazurkas in G min., Op. 67/2; in C, Op. 67/3; in A min., Op. 67/4 & Op. 68/2; in B flat (op. posth.); *Nocturne in C sharp min.* (op. posth.); *Polonaise brillante in C, Op. 3; Preludes No. 2 in A min., Op. 28; No. 3 in G; No. 4 in E min., Op. 28; 6 in B min., Op. 28; No. 7 in A, Op. 28; Scherzo* (from *Cello & Piano Sonata, Op. 65); Valse Brillante in A, Op. 34/1 & A min., Op. 34/2; Valse in A, Op. 42.*

(N) **(*) Channel Classics CCS 16298. Wispelwey, Lazic.

This is an oddity. Pieter Wispelwey has followed up the example of the nineteenth-century Russian cellist and composer, Carl Davidov, in transcribing Chopin piano pieces for cello and piano. The opening one, the popular *D major Waltz*, Opus 18, arranged by Davidov, is unpromising, with the cello not bright enough to sustain the melody well. Wispelwey's own transcriptions in partnership with his pianist, Dejan Lazic, of *Mazurkas, Preludes* and other Chopin pieces, are much more effective, and find both players in sparkling form, though the closeness of the sound is un-helpful. Other transcriptions by Glazunov and Piatigorsky are also included, as well as the *Scherzo* from Chopin's *Cello Sonata* and an early *Polonaise in C*, which Chopin himself wrote for cello and piano. Recommended above all for cellists.

SOLO PIANO MUSIC
Vladimir Ashkenazy Chopin Edition

Albumblatt in E; Allegro de concert in A, Op. 46; Barcarolle in F sharp, Op. 60; Berceuse in D flat, Op. 57; Boléro in A min., Op. 19; 2 Bourrées; Cantabile in B flat; Fugue in A min.; Galop marquis; Hexameron: Variation in E min.; Largo in E flat; 3 Nouvelles études; Rondo in E flat, Op. 16; Souvenir de Paganini (Variations in A); Tarantelle in A flat, Op. 43; Variations brillantes in B flat, Op. 12; Wiosna (Spring) from Op. 74/2. Ballades Nos. 1–4; Scherzi Nos. 1–4. 12 Etudes, Op. 10; 12 Etudes, Op. 25. Impromptus Nos. 1–3; 4 (Fantaisie-impromptu). 24 Preludes, Op. 28; Preludes: in C sharp min., Op. 45; in A flat. Mazurkas Nos. 1–29; Nos. 30–68 (including 2 versions of Op. 68/4). Nocturnes Nos. 1–12. Nos. 13–21. Polonaises Nos. 1–6; No. 7, Polonaise-fantaisie; Nos. 8–16. Sonata No. 1; Contredanse in G flat; 3 Ecossaises; Marche funèbre in C min., Op. 72/2; Rondo in C min., Op. 1; Rondo à la Mazur in F, Op. 5; Rondo in C, Op. 73; Variations on a German National Air; (i) Variations in D (for piano duet – with Vovka Ashkenazy) (443 750-2). Sonatas Nos. 2–3; Fantaisie in F min., Op. 49 (443 749-2). Waltzes Nos. 1–19 (443 746-2).

(B) *** Decca ADD/Dig. 443 738-2 (13).

Ashkenazy made his Chopin recordings for Decca over a decade from 1974 to 1984, using seven different locations, yet the recorded sound is remarkably consistent, always natural in colour and balance and with a good presence, whether from an analogue or a digital source. Consistently persuasive, these readings combine poetry with flair and (as in the *Ballades*) often bring a highly communicated warmth. The bravura brings genuine panache, whether in the large-scale, virtuoso pieces like the *Scherzi* or in the chimerical approach to a miniature like the *Souvenir de Paganini*. At bargain price this set makes an unbeatable investment.

Andante spianato et Grande polonaise, Op. 22.

(***) BBC mono 4031-2. Richter, LSO, Kondrashin – LISZT: *Piano Concertos Nos. 1–2; Hungarian Fantasia.* (***)

Both in the *Andante* and the *Polonaise*, Richter is at his most magical, not just brilliant but intensely poetic too, the more moving in a live performance. The playing has great delicacy and bravura. The BBC's mono recording balances him much closer than the orchestra and at times his pedalling is audible.

Ballades Nos. 1–4; Allegro de concert, Op. 45; Introduction & Variations on 'Je vends des scapulaires', Op. 12.

(M)*** CRD (ADD) CRD 3360. Milne.

Ballades Nos. 1-4; Barcarolle, Op. 60; Berceuse, Op. 57; Scherzo No. 4 in E, Op. 54.

**(*) RCA 09026 63259. Kissin.

Ballades Nos. 1–4; Barcarolle, Op. 60; Fantaisie in F min., Op. 49.

*** DG 423 090-2. Zimerman.

Ballades Nos. 1–4; Etudes; Waltzes (complete).

(N) (B) ** EMI double forte (ADD) CZS 5 74290-2 (2). Anievas.

Ballades Nos. 1–4; Etudes: in E; C sharp min., Op. 10/3–4; Mazurkas: in F min., Op. 7/4; in A min., Op. 17/4; in D, Op. 33/2; Nocturne in F, Op. 15/1; Waltzes: in E flat (Grande valse brillante), Op. 18; in A flat, Op. 42.

⚫ *** Sony SK 64399. Perahia.

Ballades Nos. 1–4; Fantasia in F min., Op. 49; Prelude in C sharp min., Op. 45.

**(*) DG 459 683-2. Pollini.

Ballades Nos. 1–4; Nocturnes Nos. 1–21 (complete).

(B) *** Double Decca (ADD) 452 579-2 (2). Ashkenazy.

Ballades Nos. 1–4; Scherzi Nos. 1–4; Prelude in C sharp min., Op. 45.

(M) *** Decca (ADD) 466 499-2. Ashkenazy.

Ballades Nos. 1–4; Scherzi Nos. 1–4; Tarantelle, Op. 43.

(M)*** RCA (ADD) 9026 63045–2. Rubinstein.

One has to go back to Hofmann, recorded in 1937, to find a more searching or poetic account of the *G minor Ballade* than Murray Perahia's. His *Waltzes* prompt thoughts to turn to the classic post-war Lipatti set, but comparison does not find Perahia less poetic. Moreover the Sony engineers do him justice. In every respect a masterly recital which readers should not miss.

Krystian Zimerman's impressive set of the *Ballades* and the other two works on this disc are also touched by distinction throughout and have spontaneity as well as tremendous concentration to commend them, and the modern digital recording is of fine DG quality.

However, Rubinstein's readings are unique and the digital remastering has been highly successful. The performances of the *Ballades* are a miracle of creative imagination, with Rubinstein at his most inspired. The *Scherzi*, which gain most all from the improved sound (they were originally very dry), are both powerful and charismatic. The *Tarantelle* may seem musically less interesting, but in Rubinstein's hands it is a glorious piece, full of bravura.

Ashkenazy's readings of the *Ballades* are thoughtful and essentially unflashy; the rubato arises naturally from his personal approach to the music. The intimacy of the recording allows him to share this with the listener. The recording is admirably natural and satisfying. The *Nocturnes* were recorded over a decade, from 1975 to 1984. The playing is splendidly imaginative and atmospheric. As always, Ashkenazy is completely attuned to Chopin's unique sound-world, and the CD transfers are impeccable.

Those wanting the alternative coupling with *Scherzi* will find the reissue in Decca's Legends series equally attractive. In the *Scherzi* the playing is chimerically dazzling, and the isolated Op. 45 *C sharp minor Prelude*, a pianistic tone poem in its own right, makes an ideal interlude before the *B minor Scherzo* bursts in on the listener. Very good recording, particularly impressive in the *Scherzi*, which have a fine depth of sonority.

Hamish Milne gives thoughtful and individual perform-ances of the *Ballades*. They may initially sound understated, but in their freshness and concentration they prove poetic and compelling. Similarly he plays the two rarities with total conviction, suggesting that the *Allegro de concert* at least (originally a sketch for a third piano Concerto) is most unjustly neglected. The recorded sound is first rate.

Kissin's *Four Ballades* were recorded in the Sudwestfunk studios in Freiburg and although the sound is natural enough, climaxes tend to be muddy in the reverberant acoustic. The *G minor Ballade* is curiously wayward and wanting in momentum. Of course, there are many beautiful things – particularly the *Barcarolle* – but at other times Kissin is intrusive and not content to leave Chopin to speak for himself.

Pollini's CD is so modestly filled that however impressive the playing, it strikes us as poor value. Only 48 minutes of music at full price is a lot to ask – even if it is Pollini. The performances are commanding, masterly and well recorded.

Agustin Anievas is at his best in the 1966 recording of the *Etudes*, which remains fresh, with charm and bravura used to bring out a wide range of expression. The *Waltzes* (which include the five posthumous ones) don't have quite the same flair, though there is still much to enjoy, especially in the reflective passages, and the same can be said of the *Ballades* (1975). The recordings are pretty ordinary next to the best ones, but this set is a fair bargain.

Barcarolle, Op. 60; Berceuse, Op. 57; Cantabile in B flat; Contredanse in G flat; Fantaisie in F min., Op. 49; Feuille d'album in E; Fugue in A min.; Funeral March in C min., Op. 72/2; Largo in E flat; 3 Nouvelles-études, Op. posth.; Polonaise-fantaisie, Op. 61; Souvenir de Paganini in A (Variations).

(B) *** Sony ADD/Dig. SBK 53515. Fou Ts'ong.

Fou Ts'ong's programme is enterprising – how many readers, we wonder, have heard Chopin's succinct little *Fugue in A minor*? The smaller pieces are played with a distinction and dedication that completely win one over, and the closing *Paganini variations* are disarmingly attractive. The recording, partly analogue, partly digital, is good but not quite top-drawer: in general the analogue items sound best. But this 66-minute bargain recital is well worth exploring.

Barcarolle, Op. 60; Berceuse, Op. 57; Fantaisie in F min., Op. 49; Impromptus Nos. 1–3, Opp. 29, 36 & 51

*** Sony MK 39708. Perahia.

Perahia is a Chopin interpreter of the highest order. There is an impressive range of colour and an imposing sense of order. This is highly poetic playing and an indispensable acquisition for any Chopin collection. The CBS recording does him justice.

Barcarolle, Op. 60; Berceuse, Op. 57; Scherzi Nos. 1–4.

**(*) DG 431 623-2. Pollini.

Berceuse, Op. 57; Fantaisie in F min., Op. 49; Scherzi Nos. 1–4.

*** Chan. 9018. Shelley.

Howard Shelley offers much the same programme as Maurizio Pollini on DG. He has the advantage of a more sympathetic recording. But there is a greater freshness and tenderness about his approach and though he is obviously totally inside this music, he manages to convey the feeling that he is discovering it for the first time.

There is no want of intellectual power or command of keyboard colour in Maurizio Pollini's accounts of the Chopin *Scherzi*. This is eminently magisterial playing with powerfully etched contours and hard surfaces that inspires more admiration than pleasure.

Etudes, Op. 10/1–12; Op. 25/1–12; 3 Nouvelles études.

*** Chan. 8482. Lortie.
(N) ✹ *** Erato 8573-80228-2. Lugansky.
(B) *** Warner Apex 8573 89083-2. Berezovsky.

Etudes, Op. 10/1–12; Op. 25/1–12.

*** DG (ADD) 413 794-2. Pollini.

Etudes, Op. 10/1–12; Op. 25/1–12; Ballades Nos. 1 & 3.

(B) *** [EMI Red Line CDR5 69799]. Gavrilov.

Etudes, Op. 10/1–12; Op. 25/1–12; Fantaisie in F min., Op. 49; Piano Sonatas Nos. 1–3.

(B) *** Double Decca (ADD) 466 250-2 (2). Ashkenazy.

Ashkenazy recorded his Chopin survey as far as possible in chronological order. The sets of *Etudes* from 1975 offer playing of total mastery and can be recommended alongside Pollini and more recently Louis Lortie on Chandos (offering the finest recorded sound of all). The *C minor Sonata* (No. 1) is an early work (1827) and not deeply characteristic. Ashkenazy's account (1976) enjoys classic status alongside the more recent version of Andsnes. His 1980 performance of the *Funeral March Sonata* (No. 2) is no less dazzling than his earlier live recording of 1972 and in some respects surpasses it. It has wonderful panache. The *B minor Sonata*, recorded a year later, is also memorable and involving an authoritative account of the *F minor Fantasy* provides an excellent makeweight in very realistic sound.

Nikolai Lugansky is a year or so younger than Yevgeni Kissin or Leif Ove Andsnes but by no means as well known. In the 1980s Melodiya released an outstanding LP of a recital made when Lugansky was thirteen, in which he played Bach, Scriabin and Rachmaninov. It is evident that he has survived the pressures of childhood exposure and developed into a perceptive and refined musician whose playing radiates virtuosity yet eschews ostentation. He produces a beautiful sound at every dynamic and is unconcerned with showmanship or high-voltage display. Small wonder that he was a protégé of Tatiana Nikolayeva or a winner of the Tchaikovsky Competition. He is a real artist with consummate delicacy of fingerwork and fluidity of phrasing. We much admired his Vanguard recording of the Rachmaninov *Fourth Concerto*, and this set of the Chopin *Etudes* is every bit as fine. It is a musician's Chopin and for the serious music lover rather than the piano fancier. A most distinguished and valuable recording.

Marvellous playing, too, from the 23-year-old Boris Berezovsky in 1991. He had been placed fourth at Leeds in 1987 and first at Moscow in 1990, and this was his first major recording for Teldec. Just try the dazzling Op. 10/2 or the gentle poetry of the famous *E major Etude* which follows, while the three final *Studies* of Op. 25 show his wide range of dynamic, natural sensitivity, and compelling power. Then the closing *Nouvelles études* are coaxed disarmingly. In short this is a thrilling disc, and would be highly recommendable if it cost far more. The recording brings a touch of hardness at fortissimo level, but is certainly truthful in all respects and readily reflects Berezovsky's warm colouring of the lyrical writing.

Louis Lortie's set of the 24 *Etudes* can also hold its own with the best. His playing has a strong poetic feeling and an effortless virtuosity. He is beautifully recorded at The Maltings, Snape (whose acoustic occasionally clouds the texture).

Pollini's record also comes from 1975 and sounds splendidly fresh in its digitally remastered form. These are vividly characterized accounts, masterly and with the sound eminently present, although not as full in sonority as the more recent versions.

Andrei Gavrilov's performances of the *Etudes* bring an exuberant virtuosity that is impossible to resist. Even if some of the tempi are breathtakingly fast, the sustained legato and his poetic feeling are indisputable. The impulsive bravura is often engulfing, so that one feels the need to take a breath on the soloist's behalf after the furious account of the *Revolutionary Study*; but this is prodigious playing, given a bold, forward recording to match. The *Ballades* are also impulsive but full of romantic feeling too.

Etudes, Op. 25/1–12; Sonata No. 2 in B flat min., Op. 35 (Funeral March).

(N) *** Opus 111 OPS 30-289. Sokolov.

These performances are extracted from a ten-volume set produced for the Chopin celebrations in 1999 (and discussed above). Grigory Sokolov's electrifying playing of the *Études, Op. 25* and the *Second Piano Sonata* is something of a must: he is a virtuoso whose technique is matched by real insight. When Olejnicsak 'sits down in front of an 1831 Pleyel piano', the sleeve tells us, 'Chopin's strength, tenderness, and virtuosity re-emerge as never before.'

Mazurkas Nos. 1–59, Op. 6/1–4; Op. 7/1–5; Op. 17/1–4; Op. 24/1–4; Op. 30/1–4; Op. 33/1–4; Op. 41/1–4; Op. 50/1–3; Op.56/1–3; Op. 59/1–3; Op. 63/1–3; Op. 67/1–4; Op. 68/1–4; & Op. 68/4 (revised version); Nos. 60–68, Op. posth.

(B) *** Double Decca Dig./ADD 448 086-2 (2). Ashkenazy.

Mazurkas Nos. 1–51.

(M) *** RCA (ADD) 09026 63050–2 (2). Rubinstein.

As can be seen, Ashkenazy's survey of Chopin's *Mazurkas* is the most comprehensive available. Ashkenazy's are finely articulated, aristocratic accounts and he includes all the posthumously published *Mazurkas*. The Decca recordings (often digital) are more modern and more natural than that afforded to Rubinstein.

Rubinstein could never play in a dull way to save his life, and in his hands these fifty-one pieces are endlessly fascinating, though on occasion in such unpretentious music one would welcome a completely straight approach. As with the *Ballades* and *Scherzi*, the digital remastering has brought a much more pleasing piano timbre.

Nocturnes Nos. 1–19 (see also under Ballades).

(M) *** RCA (ADD) 09026 63049–2(2) Rubinstein.

Nocturnes Nos. 1–21.

*** DG 447 096-2 (2). Pires.

(BB) *** Arte Nova 74321 82185-2 (2); or 74321 30494-2 (1–10); 74321 54451-2 (11–21) (available separately). Castro.

(B) *** DG 453 022-2 (2). Barenboim.

(B) **(*) Sony SB2K 53249 (2). Fou Ts'ong.

**(*) Hyp. CDA 66341/2. Rév.

Nocturnes Nos. 1–21; Barcarolle; Fantaisie-impromptu.

**(*) Regis RRC 2034 (2). Stott.

Nocturnes Nos. 1–21; Barcarolle, Op. 60; Fantaisie in F min., Op. 49.

(N) (M) *** Ph. (ADD) 464 694-2 (2). Arrau.

Nocturnes Nos. 1–21; Impromptus Nos. 1–4 (Fantaisie-impromptu).

(B) **(*) Ph. (ADD) Duo 456 336-2. Arrau.

Nocturnes Nos. 1–21; Mazurkas Nos. 13 in A min., Op. 17/4; 32 in C sharp min., Op. 50/3; 35 in C min., Op. 56/3; Waltzes Nos. 3 in A min.; 8 in A flat, Op. 64/3; 9 in A flat; 10 in B min., Op. 69/1-2; 13 in D flat, Op. 70/3.

(B) **(*) EMI Double fforte (ADD) CZS5 73830-2 (2). Weissenberg.

Rubinstein in Chopin is a magician in matters of colour; his unerring sense of nuance and the seeming inevitability of his rubato demonstrate a very special musical imagination in this repertoire. The recordings were the best he received in his Chopin series for RCA, and this mid-priced reissue is most handsomely repackaged.

However, Pires gives performances of great character, her playing often bold as well as meltingly romantic and brings the right poetic feel to this music. Hers is the art that conceals art, and that serves the composer to perfection. She uses the widest dynamic range and is recorded with a brilliant presence as well as a basically warm sonority. .

To have an outstanding set of the *Nocturnes*, digitally recorded and in the lowest possible price-range, seems almost too good to be true, but the Brazilian pianist, Ricardo Castro, offers a series of performances to compete with almost any in the catalogue. The degree of concentration, and thoughtful simplicity of approach is consistent throughout both discs, his nuancing and rubato managed with convincing spontaneity. The recording, made in two quite different venues, is of high quality, clear and natural.

Barenboim recorded the *Nocturnes* in 1981 and he was very beautifully recorded. Phrasing is beautifully moulded, seemingly spontaneous, thoughtful and poetic, and becoming really impetuous only in the music's more passionate moments.

Arrau's approach creates tonal warmth coupled with inner tensions of the kind one expects in Beethoven and this is a very compelling cycle, full of poetry, the rubato showing an individual but very communicable sensibility. Although Arrau's Chopin is seldom mercurial, it is never inflexible, and it has its own special insights. The *Fantaisie-impromptu* with its finely contoured central melody is a highlight. As always, the Philips piano recording is of the highest standard

Arrau's set also comes as one of Philips's '50 Great Recordings' coupled with the *Barcarolle* and *Fantaisie in F minor*, which are among his finest Chopin recordings.

As is immediately apparent in the *Fantaisie-impromptu* which acts an introduction to her survey, Kathryn Stott's Chopin is very romantic, seldom understated and uses the widest dynamic range. Yet at times she touches the listener by her very calmness. Rubato is convincingly managed and overall her playing has a stronger profile than that of Lívia Rév. She is most realistically recorded.

Fou Ts'ong sometimes reminds one of Solomon – and there can surely be no higher tribute. He is at his very best in the gentle, poetic pieces; in the more robust *Nocturnes* his rubato is less subtle, the style not so relaxed. But this is undoubtedly distinguished and, with good transfers of well-balanced recording from the late 1970s, this is competitive at budget price.

Lívia Rév is an artist of refined musicianship and impeccable taste, selfless and unconcerned with display or self-projection. Indeed there are times when she comes too close to understatement. But still these are lovely performances and the recording has great warmth.

Alexis Weissenberg is a thoughtful, serious artist and a natural Chopin player with highly poetic feeling for rubato. But at times he gets impulsively carried away, and occasionally some of the elusive nocturnal quality is lost. The *Mazurkas* too are very volatile, but here the strong rhythmic pointing is more appropriate, and the *Waltzes* sparkle more delicately. Overall one would not want to make too much of Weissenberg's passionate outbursts, for much of his playing is memorably gentle and affecting, helped by a natural piano sound, which has fine colour and sonority.

Nocturnes Nos. 1–19; Scherzi Nos. 1–4.

(N) (B) (*(**)) Naxos mono 8.110659/60. Rubinstein.

The Naxos transfers are of Rubinstein's London recordings made at Abbey Road in 1932 (the *Scherzi*) and 1937 (the *Nocturnes*). They are transferred from 78 originals (in excellent condition) by Stuart Rosenthal, with some backgound noise still present at times. One also feels that in the *Nocturnes* a little more space could have been allowed between each piece. But although the sound is less impressive, not as wide-ranging as EMI's own transfers, this is fair value at the Naxos price.

Nocturnes Nos. 1–19; Waltzes Nos. 1–14.

(N) (BB) Dutton (ADD) 2CDBP 9715 (2). Lympany.

Recorded respectively in 1960 and 1959, these readings of the Chopin *Nocturnes* and *Waltzes* from Moura Lympany are classics that should never have been allowed to languish in the deletions cupboard. It is good to be reminded just how tenderly poetic her Chopin-playing was, warm and deeply felt but fresh and unexaggerated. These are finer readings than many that have been regularly available over the years, with excellent early stereo beautifully refurbished by Dutton in refined and full-bodied sound.

Polonaises Nos. 1–16, Op. 26/1–2; Op. 40/1–2; Op. 44; Op. 53; Polonaise-fantaisie, Op. 61; Op. 71/1–3; Op. posth./

1–6. Albumblatt in E; Allegro de concert, Op. 46; Barcarolle in F sharp, Op. 60; Berceuse in D flat, Op. 57; 2 Bourrées; 3 Nouvelles études; Fugue in A min.; Galop marquis; Tarantelle in A flat, Op. 43; Wiosna (arr. from Op. 74/2).

(B) *** Double Decca ADD/Dig. 452 167-2 (2). Ashkenazy.

Polonaises Nos. 1–7; Andante spianato et Grande polonaise brillante.

(M) *** RCA (ADD) 09026 63048–2. Rubinstein.
(M) *** DG (ADD) 457 711-2. Pollini.

Polonaises Nos. 1–6; 7 (Polonaise-fantaisie); Andante spianato & Grande polonaise brillante; Nocturnes Nos. 1, 2, 4, 5, 8, 9, 11, 13–19.

(B) ** Royal (ADD) DCL 705712 (2) Ohlsson.

Ashkenazy's performances of the *Polonaises* are of the highest calibre and the recording is of Decca's best. The second CD contains some items that are quite short (the piano transcription of Chopin's song *Wiosna* lasts for barely a minute, but it is very fetching). But there are substantial works too: the *Barcarolle* and *Berceuse*, the latter meltingly done, and the *Allegro de concert* and *Nouvelles études* also show Ashkenazy at his finest. At Double Decca price this pair of CDs is self-recommending.

Master pianist that he was, Rubinstein seems actually to be rethinking and re-creating each piece, even the hackneyed *Military* and *A flat* works, at the very moment of performance in this recording, made in Carnegie Hall. His easy majesty and natural sense of spontaneous phrasing give this collection a special place in the catalogue, and the *Andante spinato* and *Grande polonaise* obviously inspire him.

Pollini's set offers playing of outstanding mastery as well as subtle poetry, and the DG engineers have made a satisfactory job of the new transfer, although the hardness on top remains something to which the ear must adjust. Nevertheless this is magisterial playing, in some ways more commanding than Rubinstein (and rather more tangibly recorded), though not more memorable.

In the *Polonaises*, Ohlsson demonstrates a weighty style and technique very much of the American school, but with it all he is thoughtful. When he uses a flexible beat it is only rarely that the result sounds wilful. The EMI recording is very good, but while this inexpensive reissue makes an excellent visiting card, it seems a pity that neither of his surveys was offered complete.

24 Preludes, Op. 28; Prelude in C sharp min., Op. 45. Andante spianato et Grande polonaise in E flat, Op. 22; Polonaise-fantaisie in A flat, Op. 61.

*** Chan. 9597. Lortie.

24 Preludes, Op. 28; Preludes Nos. 25–26; Scherzi Nos. 1–4; Waltzes Nos. 1–19.

(B) *** Double Decca (ADD) 460 991-2 (2). Ashkenazy.

24 Preludes, Op. 28; Preludes Nos. 25–26; Barcarolle, Op. 60; Polonaise No. 6 in A flat, Op. 53; Scherzo No. 2 in B flat min., Op. 31.

(M) **(*) DG (ADD) 415 836-2. Argerich.

24 Preludes, Op. 28; Preludes Nos. 25–26; Berceuse, Op. 57; Fantasy in F min., Op. 4.

*** Hyp. CDA 66324. Rév.

24 Preludes, Op. 28; Scherzos Nos. 1 in B min., Op. 20; 2 in B flat min., Op. 31; 4 in E, Op. 54.

*** Naim NAIMCD 028. Gimse.

24 Preludes, Op. 28; Etudes, Op. 10/4–6; Op. 25/1–2; 6 & 12.

**(*) Erato 0630 11726-2. Lympany.

24 Preludes, Op. 28; Piano Sonata No. 2 in B flat minor, Op. 35; Polonaise in A flat, Op. 53.

** RCA 09026 63535-2. Kissin.

Louis Lortie's expertly recorded account of the *Preludes* is among the best we have had in recent years. He has poetic feeling, character and finesse in equal measure. Not all his interpretative decisions will convince everyone, but on the whole this is enjoyable and distinguished Chopin playing.

Ashkenazy's 1979 set of the *Preludes* combines drama and power with finesse and much poetic delicacy when called for. The *Waltzes* were recorded over the best part of a decade. There is an impressive feeling for line throughout, an ability to make each waltz seem spontaneous and yet as carefully wrought as a tone-poem. The *Scherzi* have characteristic panache, the playing imbued with imaginative insights and spontaneity. Again excellent recording.

The *Preludes* show Martha Argerich at her finest, spontaneous and inspirational, though her moments of impetuosity may not appeal to all tastes. But her instinct is sure, with many poetic, individual touches. The other pieces are splendidly played.

Lívia Rév's playing has an unforced naturalness that is most persuasive. She is an artist to her fingertips and, though she may not have the outsize musical personality of some great pianists, she does not have the outsize ego either. She includes not only the extra *Preludes*, but two other substantial pieces as well.

Håvard Gimse is a cultured player, whose talent is primarily lyrical. He is at his best in the self-communing, poetic side of these wonderful pieces but there is no want of fire, though perhaps more could be made of the dramatic and dynamic contrasts in the *B minor Scherzo*. The Sofienberg Church in Oslo offers an excellent acoustic and the recording is pleasingly natural.

Dame Moura Lympany plays the whole set as an ongoing sequence and then adds a baker's half-dozen hand-selected *Etudes* for good measure in which her pedalling covers the not always quite precise articulation (in Op. 25/12, for instance). The piano recording is truthful, warm rather than brilliant.

Kissin's new recital offers some masterly, indeed dazzling pianism, but we miss the fresh, spontaneous quality that has distinguished most of his earlier recitals. He makes pretty heavy weather of the *E minor Prelude* (No. 9) though the close RCA balance probably makes him sound heavier than he is.

Preludes, Op. 28, Nos. 1–11; 14–16; 20 & 23.

(M) ** Nimbus NI 8810. Busoni (piano) – BACH: *Chaconne;* LISZT: *Etudes d'exécution transcendante* etc. ***

Busoni's Duo-Art piano-roll recordings (from 1923) project his Chopin manner truthfully, and he proves no stylist in this music. Indeed much of his playing, if strong in character, is heavy going. *No. 20 in C minor* opens very stolidly indeed, but the closing *F major* (No. 23), recorded four years after the rest of the sequence, brings a much lighter touch. Excellent sound.

Scherzos Nos. 1–4; Introduction & Variations on a German Air; Variations on 'Là ci darem la mano', Op. 2.

**(*) Hyp. CDA 66514. Demidenko.

Scherzos Nos. 1–4; Polonaise-fantaisie, Op. 61.

(M) *** Ph. 442 407-2. Arrau.

Arrau's last recording of the four *Scherzi* was made in Munich, just after the artist's eightieth birthday. However, these accounts are full of wise and thoughtful perceptions and remarkable pianism, recorded with great presence and clarity. The Philips engineers seem to produce piano quality of exceptional realism.

Nikolai Demidenko plays with magisterial keyboard authority and command of colour. There are narcissistic and idiosyncratic touches to which not all listeners will respond; all the same, there is still much that will (and does) give pleasure.

Piano Sonatas Nos. 1 in C min., Op. 4; 2 in B flat min. (Funeral March), Op. 35; 3 in B min., Op. 58.

(M) *** Decca (ADD) 448 123-2. Ashkenazy.

Piano Sonatas Nos. 1–3; Etudes, Op. 10/6; Op. 25/3, 4, 10 & 11; Mazurkas, Op. 17/1–4.

(B) *** Virgin 2 x 1 Double VBD 5 45187-2 (2). Andsnes.

Leif Ove Andsnes has the advantage of state-of-the-art piano-sound and his recital comes in a slim, two-for-the-price-of-one CD pack. Andsnes proves as idiomatic an interpreter of Chopin as he has done of Grieg. He also makes out a very good case for the early *C minor Sonata*, Op. 4, which is less well represented on disc and which he plays with real conviction and flair. The other pieces generally come off well and collectors can invest in this set with complete confidence.

Ashkenazy's accounts enjoy classic status, and certainly well recorded, with very vivid sound. They are also available as part of a Decca Double combined with the *Etudes* and *Fantasy in F minor* – see above.

Piano Sonata No. 2 in B flat min., Op. 35.

(***) Testament mono STB 1089. Gilels – MOZART: *Sonata No. 17;* SHOSTAKOVICH: *Preludes & Fugues Nos. 1, 5 & 24. (***)*

The *B flat minor Sonata* was recorded in New York and first appeared in 1984. The passage of time has not dimmed its classic status or its poetic intensity and, although some allowances have to be made for the recorded sound, they are few.

Piano Sonata No. 2 in B flat min., Op. 35; Barcarolle in F sharp, Op. 60; Nocturnes Nos. 5 in F sharp, Op. 15/2; 13 in C min., Op. 48/1; 15 in E, Op. 62/2; 20 in C sharp min., Op. posth.; Scherzo No. 2 in B flat min., Op. 31.

(N) (M) **(*) Virgin VM5 61836–2. Pletnev.

Pletnev is a master pianist: in his hands the finale of the *Sonata* has a wizardry comparable only with Horowitz and Rachmaninov. However, this is not a self-effacing performance and the expressive posturing will disappoint his growing circle of admirers. Of course, there are marvellous things here too – the *C minor Nocturne* is one – but on the whole this is masterly pianism first and Chopin second.

Piano Sonatas Nos. 2 in B flat min. (Funeral March), Op. 35; 3 in B min., Op. 58.

*** DG (ADD) 415 346-2. Pollini.

*** Sony (ADD) MK 76242. Perahia.

Piano Sonatas Nos. 2 (Funeral March); 3 in B min., Op. 58; Barcarolle, Op. 60; Berceuse Op. 59; Fantaisie in F min., Op. 49..

(M)*** RCA (ADD) 09026 63046-2. Rubinstein.

Rubinstein's readings of the two finest *Sonatas* are unsurpassed, with a poetic impulse that springs directly from the music and a control of rubato to bring many moments of magic. The sound is improved, too, and the addition of the *Barcarolle* and *Berceuse* make this mid-priced reissue all the more desirable.

Murray Perahia's technique is remarkable, but it is so natural to the player that he never uses it for mere display; always there is an underlying sense of structural purpose. The dry, unrushed account of the finale of the *B flat Sonata* is typical of Perahia's freshness, and the only pity is that the recording of the piano is rather clattery and close.

Pollini's performances are commanding; his mastery of mood and structure gives these much-played *Sonatas* added stature. The slow movement of Op. 35 has both drama and atmosphere, so that the contrast of the magical central section is all the more telling. Both works are played with distinction, but the balance is just a shade close.

Piano Sonata No. 3 in B min., Op. 58; Mazurkas, in A min., Op. 17/4; in B flat min., Op. 24/4; in D flat, Op. 30/3; in D, Op. 33/2; in G; in C sharp min., Op. 50/ 1 & 3; in C, Op. 56/2; in F sharp min., Op. 59/3; in B; in F min.; in C sharp min., Op. 63/1–3; in F min., Op. 68/4.

*** RCA 09026 62542-2. Kissin.

Piano Sonata No. 3 in B min., Op. 58; Barcarolle, Op. 60; Fantaisie-impromptu, Op. 66; Impromptus Nos. 1–3, Opp. 29, 36 & 51.

*** Chan. 9175. Shelley.

Piano Sonata No. 3 in B minor, Op. 58; Polonaise No. 6 in A flat, Op. 53.

(B) **(*) EMI Début CDZ5 73500-2. Slobodyanik – SCHUMANN: *Kinderszenen, Op. 15; Papillons, Op. 2.* **

Piano Sonata No. 3 in B min., Op. 58.

(B) ** EMI doubleforte (ADD) CZS5 69527-2 (2). Anievas – LISZT: *Sonata* ***; RACHMANINOV: *24 Preludes* etc. **(*)

Evgeny Kissin plays not only with an effortless mastery but with a naturalness and freshness that silence criticism. His sense of poetry and his idiomatic rubato are combined with impressive technical address and impeccable taste.

An outstanding Chopin recital from Howard Shelley whose interpretative powers continue to grow in stature. His playing has poetic feeling and ardent but well-controlled temperament. Very good sound.

Alex Slobodyanik is now in his mid-twenties and on the brink of a promising career. His account of the *B minor Sonata* is sensitive and intelligent and, along with the Schumann couplings, serves as an admirable visiting card for this young artist. At the same time, it does not have quite the strong personality of some of his CD rivals.

Agustin Anievas gives a strong if not absolutely distinctive performance of the lesser-known *B minor Sonata*. However, the slow movement has the same thoughtfulness and sensitivity that distinguish his performance of the Liszt *Sonata*, and the bravura of the finale is striking. Good recording. If the couplings are suitable, this is worth considering.

Waltzes Nos. 1–14; Impromptus Nos. 1–4 (Fantaisie impromptu); Bolero, Op. 19.

(N) (M)***RCA (ADD) 09026 63047–2. Rubinstein.

Waltzes Nos. 1–14; Barcarolle, Op. 60; Mazurka in C sharp min., Op. 50/3; Nocturne in D flat, Op. 27/2.

✪ (M) (***) EMI mono CDM5 66904-2 [66956]. Dinu Lipatti.

Waltzes Nos. 1–17; Polonaises: in G min.; in B flat, Op. posth.

(B) *** ASV CDQS 6149. Schiller.

Rubinstein's performances of the waltzes have a chiselled perfection, suggesting finely cut and polished diamonds, and his clear and relaxed accounts of the *Impromptus* make most other interpretations sound forced by comparison. The digital remastering has softened the edges of the sound-image, and there is an illusion of added warmth.

Lipatti's classic performances were recorded by Walter Legge in the rather dry acoustic of a Swiss Radio studio at Geneva in the last year of Lipatti's short life, and with each LP reincarnation they seem to have grown in wisdom and subtlety. The reputation of these meticulous performances is fully deserved, and they are rightly reissued as part of EMI's 'Great Recordings of the Century' series.

Allan Schiller's playing of the *Waltzes* is always musical and often very sensitive, though there are one or two in which he could have allowed his imagination freer rein. Very good recording quality. Well worth its modest asking price.

RECITAL COLLECTIONS

'Favourite piano works': Ballades Nos. 1 in G min., Op. 23; 3 in A flat, Op. 47; Barcarolle, Op. 60; Etudes: in E; in G flat (Black Keys); in C min. (Revolutionary), Op. 10/3, 5 & 12; in A min. (Winter Wind), Op. 25/11; Fantaisie-impromptu, Op. 66; Mazurkas: in B flat, Op. 7/1; in D, Op. 33/1; Nocturnes: in E flat, Op. 9/2; in F sharp min., Op. 15/2; in B, Op. 32/1; in F min., Op. 55/1; Polonaises: in A (Military), Op. 40/1; in A flat, Op. 53; Preludes: in D flat (Raindrop), Op. 28/15; in C sharp min., Op. 45; Scherzos Nos. 1 in B flat min., Op. 31; 3 in C sharp min., Op. 39; Waltzes: in E flat (Grande valse brillante), Op. 18; in A min., Op. 34/2; in D flat (Minute); in C sharp min.,

Op. 64/1-2; in A flat, Op. 69/1; in B min., Op. 69/2; in G flat, Op. 70/1.

(B) *** Double Decca Dig/(ADD) 444 830-2 (2). Ashkenazy.

Most music-lovers would count themselves lucky to attend a recital offering the above programme with a total playing time of 130 minutes. The first CD, which is all-digital, opens commandingly with the *Grande valse brillante* and closes with the *Polonaise in A flat*; the second (an analogue collection, but of excellent technical quality) begins with the *A flat Ballade* and ends with the *Scherzo in C sharp minor*. Overall the recordings date from between 1972 and 1984.

Ballade No. 1 in G min.; Berceuse in D flat; Etudes, Op. 10/ 1, 5, 6, & 12 (Revolutionary); Impromptu No. 1 in A flat, Op. 29; Mazurkas: in B flat, Op. 7/1; in C, Op. 67/3; in A min., Op. 68/2; in A flat, Op. posth.; Polonaise No. 6 in A flat, Op. 53; Scherzos No. 3 in C sharp min.; 4 in E, Op. 54; Waltzes Nos. 3 in A min., Op. 34/2; 14 in E min., Op. posth.

(B) **(*) DG (ADD) 439 406-2. Vásáry.

An excellent bargain recital,. The layout is attractive, opening poetically with the *G minor Ballade* and *Berceuse*, ranging through the *Waltzes, Etudes, Scherzos* (very well done) and *Mazurkas*, and ending with the *A flat Polonaise*. The sound is a fraction dry but firm and believable. The documentation is impressive.

'Favourites': Ballade No. 1 in G min.; Fantaisie-impromptu, Op. 66; Mazurkas: in B flat, Op. 7/1; in D, Op. 33/2; Nocturnes: in E flat, Op. 9/2; in F sharp, Op. 15/2; in B, Op. 32/1; Polonaise in A flat, Op. 53; Scherzo in B flat min., Op. 31; Waltzes: in E flat (Grande valse brillante), Op. 18; in A min., Op. 34/2; in A flat; B min., Op. 69/1–2; in G flat, Op. 70/1.

(B) *** Penguin Decca 460 614-2. Ashkenazy.

On Penguin Classics, another attractive recital, with many favourites, played with Ashkenazy's customary poetic flair and easy brilliance. The digital recordings were made at various times during the early 1980s but match surprisingly well: the sound has striking realism and presence. The special note is by Kazuo Ishiguro, author of *The Remains of the Day*. But the Double Decca above is even more enticing.

Ballade No. 1 in G min.; Mazurkas Nos. 19 in B min., 20 in D flat, Op. 30/2–3; 22 in G sharp min., 25 in B min., Op. 33/1 & 4; 34 in C, Op. 56/2; 43 in G min., 45 in A min., Op. 67/2 & 4; 46 in C; 47 in A min., 49 in F min., Op. 68/ 1–2 & 4; Prelude No. 25 in C sharp min., Op. 45; Scherzo No. 2 in B flat min., Op. 31.

**(*) DG (ADD) (IMS) 413 449-2. Michelangeli.

Although this recital somehow does not quite add up as a whole, the performances are highly distinguished. Michelangeli's individuality comes out especially in the *Ballade* and is again felt in the *Mazurkas*, which show a wide range of mood and dynamic. The *Scherzo* is extremely brilliant, yet without any suggestion of superficiality. The piano tone is real and lifelike.

Ballade No. 4 in F min., Op. 52; Berceuse, Op. 57; Etudes, Opp. 10/3, 8 & 9; 25/1–3; Fantaisie in F min., Op. 49; Mazurka in A min., Op. 68/2; Nocturnes in E flat, Op. 9/2; D flat, Op. 27/2; Polonaise in A, Op. 40/1; A flat, Op. 53; Waltzes in A flat, Op. 42; E min., Op. posth.

(**(*)) Testament mono SBT 1030. Solomon.

This anthology affords ample proof of Solomon's power to distil magic in pretty well whatever composer he touched. Most of these 78 recordings were made between 1942 and 1946; the F minor *Fantaisie* is pre-war (1932), a wonderfully searching account, and the sheer delicacy and poetry of the playing shine through the often frail recorded sound. Good transfers.

Ballade No. 4 in F min., Op. 52; Fantaisie in F min., Op. 49; Mazurkas: in G; in A flat; in C sharp min., Op. 50/ 1–3; Nocturnes: in D flat, Op. 27/2; in E, Op. 62/2; Polonaise in A flat, Op. 53; Scherzo No. 4 in E, Op. 54; Waltz in C sharp min., Op. 64/2.

(M) *** Van. 99122. Lugansky.

Nikolai Lugansky's playing is selfless, full of character and unfailingly musical throughout this recital. There is nothing ostentatious or in the least sensational about him; he is a refined and natural artist whose playing gives much pleasure and at its best is touched by distinction.

Barcarolle in F sharp min., Op. 60; Berceuse in D flat, Op. 57; Mazurkas Nos. 13 in A min., Op. 17/4; 23 in D, Op. 33/2; 33 in B, Op. 56/1; Nocturnes Nos. 1 in B flat min., Op. 9/1; 8 in D flat, Op. 27/2; 10 in A flat, Op. 32/2; 12 in G, Op. 37/2; 17 in B, Op. 62/1; Polonaises Nos. 3 in A, Op. 40/1; No. 6 in A flat (Héroïque); Scherzo No. 2 in B flat min., Op. 31 Waltzes: in C sharp min., Op. 64/2.

(M) (**(*)) EMI mono CDM5 67007-2. Rubinstein.

The present selection, carefully arranged to make a satisfactory ongoing recital, dates from between 1928 (the charismatic account of the *Barcarolle*, which sounds unbelievably good) and 1939 (the *B flat Mazurka*, Op. 56/1). Certainly the younger Rubinstein (he was in his forties) has a wonderfully chimerical touch, especially in some of the *Nocturnes* and indeed the *Berceuse*, which he paces fairly briskly. In the *Mazurkas* his rubato is as uniquely personal as it is convincing. The transfers are a shade dry, and at times a little lacking in sonority, but pretty faithful otherwise.

Etudes: in G flat, Op. 10/5; in G sharp min.; in C sharp min., Op. 25/6–7; 3 Ecossaises, Op. posth. 72/3; Fantasy in F min., Op. 49; Impromptu in A flat, Op. 29; Sonata No. 3 in B min., Op. 58; Waltzes: in A flat; A min., Op. 34/1–2; in E min., Op. posth.

*** DG 453 456-2. Pletnev.

Opening with the great *F minor Fantasy* and closing with the *B Minor Sonata*, both superbly done, Pletnev's well-planned recital has all the hallmarks of a live recital, plus the technical advantage of studio recording. Such is his command of tonal colour elsewhere that one is scarcely aware of the piano's hammers even in fortissimo passages. But interpretatively things are less straightforward and he is often wilful. His rubato in the *B minor Sonata* is at times intrusive. The *G flat* and *G sharp minor Etudes* are dazzling, as is the famous *E minor Waltz* (written when the composer was twenty) and the *Ecossaises*, which are even earlier, are deliciously frothy. Yet the *C sharp minor Etude* takes the listener into a wholly different world and is very touching, as is the slow movement of the *Sonata*. For all one's reservations about the personal element, this is very distinguished playing indeed.

Fantaisie in F min., Op. 49; Nocturnes in C sharp min., Op. 27/1; in D flat, Op. 27/2; in A flat, Op. 32/2 ; Polonaise in F sharp min., Op. 44; Scherzo No. 2 in B flat min., Op. 31; Waltzes: in A flat, Op. 34/1; in A min., Op. 34/2; in A flat, Op. 42.

❀ *** RCA 09026 60445-2. Kissin.

Evgeny Kissin's Chopin anthology comes from a Carnegie Hall recital given early in 1993 when he was still only twenty-one. His virtuosity and brilliance are always harnessed to musical ends and there is total dedication to Chopin and no indulgence. Chopin playing of real quality and well recorded, though the sound is a bit thick in the bass.

Fugue in A min., Op. posth.; Lento con gran espressione in C sharp min., Op. posth.; Nocturnes: in E flat, Op. 9/2; in C min., Op. posth.; Polonaise in B flat min., Op. posth.; Waltzes in A min., Op. 34/2; in A min. Op. posth.; in E min.; in F sharp min., Op. posth.

(*) Etcetera KTC 1231. Antoni – FIELD: *Largo; Nocturnes,* etc. *

The primary purpose of this CD is to make a direct comparison with similar works, written even earlier, by John Field, who invented the *Nocturne* in the year Chopin was born. Some of the similarities between the two young composers have already been documented (notably Field's *E flat major Romance* and Chopin's famous *Nocturne* in the same key from Opus 9). But other musical links are equally fascinating. Helge Antoni plays simply and poetically and this serves to point up his comparisons. He is naturally recorded in a pleasing acoustic.

Mazurkas in A min., A flat, F sharp min., Op. 59/1–3; Nocturne in F, Op. 15/1; Polonaise in A flat, Op. 53; Scherzo No. 3 in C sharp min., Op. 39; Sonata No. 3 in B min. Op. 58.

** EMI (ADD) CDC5 56805-2. Argerich.

Argerich's recital is called *The Legendary 1965 Recording*. It was made at the Abbey Road Studios in June of that year. Hence EMI were never able to issue it for contractual reasons. There are numerous felicities in the *Mazurkas* and the *Nocturne* but Argerich went on to make a finer account of the *B minor Sonata* for DG. The sound is surprisingly shallow and hard.

VOCAL MUSIC

Songs: *The bridegroom; Drinking song; Faded and vanished; Reverie (Dumka); Handsome lad; Hymn from the tomb; Lithuanian song; The maiden's wish; Melodia*

(Elegy; Lamento); The messenger; My darling; Out of my sight; The ring; Sad river; Spring; There where she loves; The two corpses; The warrior; Witchcraft. Songs arr. Pauline Viardot from Chopin Mazurkas: *Berceuse* (from Op. 33/3); *Faible coeur* (from Op. 7/3); *La Danse* (from Op. 50/1); *La Fête* (from Op. 6/4); *Plainte d'amour* (from Op. 6/1).

*** Hyp. CDA 67125. Kryger, Spencer.

Chopin wrote these songs for relaxation, just to please himself, never publishing them, and that may explain why the Polish flavour is so strong. He was reflecting his own early background, and the results are charming. Mazurka rhythms abound, as in the haunting *Handsome lad*, with the collection rounded off in the one song which goes deeper, *Melodia*, the heartfelt lament of an exile. The five arrangements of Chopin Mazurkas made for her own use by the leading singer, Pauline Viardot, are comparably charming, making the ideal fill-up. Urszula Kryger, with her vibrant Slavonic tone well controlled, makes the most sympathetic interpreter, sensitively accompanied by Charles Spencer.

Songs: *Hulanka; Melodya; Moja Piesczotka (My sweetheart); Narzeczony (The bridegroom); Niema czego Trzeba (There is no need); Spiew Grobowy (Hymn from the tomb); Wiosna (Spring).*

(B) ** Belart (ADD) 461 626-2. Tear, Ledger – *Songs.* **

Robert Tear and Philip Ledger couple songs by two composers. Both are Slavic, Chopin the simpler of the two as a songwriter is directly reflecting the folk music of Poland. Robert Tear commendably sings in Polish, but his style is often not direct enough to capture the full freshness. The snag is the absence of adequate documentation with texts and translations. But this disc is very inexpensive and collectors may well be tempted by its modest cost.

CILEA, Francesco (1866–1950)

Adriana Lecouvreur (complete).

*** Decca 425 815-2 (2). Sutherland, Bergonzi, Nucci, d'Artegna, Ciurca, Welsh Nat. Op. Ch. & O, Bonynge.

(M) **(*) Decca (ADD) (IMS) 430 256-2 (2). Tebaldi, Simionato, Del Monaco, Fioravanti, St Cecilia, Rome, Ac. Ch. & O, Capuana.

Sutherland's performance in the role of a great tragic actress could not have been warmer-hearted. She impresses with her richness and opulence in the biggest test, the aria *Io son l'umile ancella*, an actress's credo, and her formidable performance is warmly backed up by the other principals, and equally by Richard Bonynge's conducting, not just warmly expressive amid the wealth of rich tunes, but light and sparkling where needed, easily idiomatic.

Tebaldi's consistently rich singing misses some of the flamboyance of Adriana's personality but in her characterization both *Io son l'umile ancella* and *Poveri fiori* are lyrically very beautiful. One wishes that Del Monaco had been as reliable as Tebaldi but, alas, there are some coarse moments among the fine, plangent top notes. Simionato is a little more variable than usual but a tower of strength nevertheless. The recording is outstanding for its time (early 1960s), brilliant and atmospheric.

L'Arlesiana (complete).

(M) ** EMI (ADD) CMS5 66762-3 (2). Zilio, Kelen, Spacagna, Barry Anderson, Hungarian State Ch. & O, Rosekrans.

As an opera story the oddity of *L'Arlesiana* is that the girl from Arles herself is never seen or heard. The principal female role is for Federico's mother, Rosa, warmly sung in this performance by Elena Zilio, and Barry Anderson is equally strong and firm in the role of Baldassare, the old shepherd who acts as the understanding adviser to all the others. The role of the hero, Federico, originally created by the young Caruso, is taken by Péter Kelen, a tenor inclined to overdo the histrionics, often using his tenor with restraint, as in the most celebrated aria, *E la solita storia*, but then indulging in excessively emotional outbursts. The conductor, Charles Rosekrans, brings out the warmth of the lyricism, but the dramatic thrust is not always strong enough. A useful stop-gap at mid-price.

CIMAROSA, Domenico (1749–1801)

Double Flute Concerto in G.

(N) **(*) RCA 09026 63701-2. James & Jean Galway, LMP – DEVIENNE: *Flute Concertos*. ***

Although not momentous music, Cimarosa's concerto for a pair of flutes has undeniable charm, and its gay final *Rondo* is quite memorable. The only drawback is the composer's emphasis on florid writing, with the two solo instruments playing consistently in thirds and sixths. Here although Galway is well up to form the playing of his partner, Jean, while technically accomplished, is paler in timbre and personality. Even so, with good accompaniment and excellent sound this is agreeable enough.

Piano Sonatas, Volumes I–III, Nos. 1–62 (complete).

(N) *** Arcobaleno AAOC 93672 (2). Crudelli.

Marcella Crudelli is not only a pianist of distinction, she is also an eminent teacher (at the Rome Santa Cecilia Academy) and musicologist, and it is to her we owe this new, revised edition of the complete three volumes of Cimarosa's sonatas. They are simple single-movement works, ranging in length from half a minute to just over four minutes. They have a good deal in common with Scarlatti's sonatas, offering considerable variety of mood and style, although they are not as searching. In her notes the pianist speaks of 'their balance and contrast in feeling, rhythm, and melody' to provide 'a sequence of well-proportioned and articulated musical episodes intended to solicit the listener's attention'. This they certainly do and continue to hold it.

Crudelli uses a modern piano and plays stylishly with crisp clear timbre and articulation. But there is charm as well as scholarship in her advocacy. She begins with Volume III (where Nos. 2 *in D minor* and the brilliantly familiar 3 *in D major* immediately catch the attention) and works her way back to Volume I. But the quality of the music is consistent and the earliest sonatas are hardly less ear-

catching. The recording gives the piano a clean clear image (there is never any suggestion of over-pedalling) so that these performances are both authentic and spontaneous. This is a most enjoyable set, and it is a pity that the documentation is so limited.

Requiem (rev. Negri).

(B) *** Ph. (ADD) 422 489-2. Ameling, Finnila, Van Vrooman, Widmer, Montreux Fest. Ch., Lausanne CO, Negri.

The choral writing in Cimarosa's *Requiem* is most assured, and the Montreux Festival Chorus conveys a feeling of spacious eloquence. It is a pity that the recording is too reverberant to produce an incisive edge to the choral sound; its warm atmosphere, however, adds to the feeling of weight and serenity. The soloists are very good, notably Elly Ameling and Kurt Widmer. Vittorio Negri secures excellent playing from the Lausanne orchestra and the CD transfer enhances the 1969 recording, which does not seem too dated. A recommendable bargain reissue.

Il maestro di cappella (complete).

(M) *** Decca (ADD) 433 036-2 (2). Corena, ROHCG O, Quadri – DONIZETTI: *Don Pasquale*. ***

Corena's classic assumption of the role of incompetent Kapellmeister has been out of the catalogue for too long. Corena shows complete mastery of the buffo bass style, and he is so little troubled by the florid passages that he can relax in the good humour. The vintage 1960 recording is clear and atmospheric, with the directional effects naturally conveyed.

CIURLIONIS, Mikalojus Konstantinas (1875–1911)

Concord, VL255; Folksong transcriptions : *Did the winds blow, VL274; Oh, my mother, VL277; A willow on the hill, VL289; Fugue in B flat minor, VL345; Impromptu, VL181; Nocturne, VL178; Pater Noster, VL260; Preludes: VL169; VL182a; VL184; VL186; VL187; VL188; VL239; VL325; VL335; VL338; VL331; VL337a; VL310; 4 Variations on 'Run, you fields', VL279; 5 Variations on 'You, my forest', VL276; 6 Variations on 'Sefaa Esec', VL258.*

(M) **(*) EMI CDM5 66791-2. Landsbergis.

Ciurlionis was something of a polymath, for in addition to his achievements as the leading Lithuanian composer of his day, he was also a painter (and is exhibited in Kaunas). The piano pieces here are mostly miniatures, often poetic and lyrical; some are quite slight but others come near to the language of Szymanowski. Professor Landsbergis is a sensitive player but the instrument on which he plays is a bit hard and not in ideal condition and nor is the recording acoustic ideal. An interesting issue all the same.

CLARKE, Rebecca (1886–1979)

(i) *Piano Trio;* (ii) *Viola Sonata.*

⊕ *** ASV CDDCA 932. Roscoe, with (i) Watkinson, Waterman; (ii) Jackson – BEACH: *Piano Quintet.* ***

Born and educated in Britain, Rebecca Clarke was a frequent visitor to the United States and lived there permanently from the Second World War onwards. She played the viola herself, and the bitingly romantic *Sonata*, superbly written for the instrument, is here given a warm and purposeful performance. The *Piano Trio* of two years later (1921) is, if anything, even more striking, with clean-cut, thrusting themes bringing echoes of Bartók and Bloch which never submerge Clarke's individual voice. The performances by Roscoe with members of the Endellion Quartet are masterly, with full-bodied, well-balanced recording.

CLEMENS NON PAPA, Jacob

(*c.* 1510/15–*c.* 1555/6)

Missa Pastores quidnam vidistis; Motets: *Pastores quidnam vidistis; Ego flos campi; Pater peccavi; Tribulationes civitatum.*

⊕ *** Gimell CDGIM 013. Tallis Scholars, Phillips.

This admirable disc serves as an introduction to the music of Jacob Clement or Clemens non Papa (who was jokingly known as Clemens-not-the-Pope, so as to distinguish him from either Pope Clement VII or the Flemish poet, Jacobus Papa). The beauty of line and richness of texture in the masterly *Missa Pastores quidnam vidistis* are unforgettable in this superb performance by the Tallis Scholars. The programme opens with the parody motet associated with the Mass, which has a glorious eloquence. Of the other motets, *Pater peccavi*, solemnly rich-textured, is especially memorable; but the whole programme is designed to reveal to twentieth-century ears another name hitherto known only to scholars. The recording is uncannily real and superbly balanced. It was made in the ideal acoustics of the Church of St Peter and St Paul, Salle, Norfolk.

CLEMENTI, Muzio (1752–1832)

(i) *Piano Concerto in C. Symphonies: in B flat & D, Op. 18; Nos. 1 in C; 2 in D; 3 (Great National) in G; 4 in D; Minuetto pastorale; Overtures in C & D.*

(M) ** ASV CDDCS 322 (3). (i) Spada; Philh. O, D'Avalos.

Symphonies: in B flat & D, Op. 18/1–2; Symphonies Nos. 1–4; Overtures in C & D; Minuetto pastorale.

(M) ** ASV CDDCS 247 (2). Philh. O, D'Avalos.

Symphonies: No. 1; in B flat & D, Op. 18/1–2 .

*** Chan. 9234. LMP, Bamert.

Symphonies Nos. 1–4.

(B) *** Erato Ultima (ADD) 3984 21039-2 (2). Philh. O, Scimone.

Six of Clementi's 20 symphonies survive. The four numbered works are all scored for much larger forces than the Op. 18 set and even include trombones. Their musical content explains Clementi's high reputation in his lifetime as a composer for the orchestra, not just the piano. If the *Great National Symphony* is the most immediately striking, with *God save the King* ingeniously worked into the third movement, the other works are all boldly individual. The *Fourth* is a remarkably powerful symphonic statement which brings some striking modulations, and there is some unexpected chromatic writing. Moreover Clementi's use of the orchestra is often very imaginative, though his indebtedness to the Haydn of the *London Symphonies* is very striking.

Bamert's performances are on a chamber scale and are refreshingly alive and polished. They are given top-class Chandos sound. If you want just one CD of Clementi symphonies, this is the one to have, and indeed the music here is rather engaging.

The performances by Claudio Scimone and the Philharmonia Orchestra are strong and sympathetic, and the recording (made in London's Henry Wood Hall in 1978) is full, resonant and natural, bringing weight as well as freshness. Now that Erato have accommodated these so economically both in price and in space on the shelf, they deserve a warm recommendation.

D'Avalos gets spirited playing from the Philharmonia, though he is not as strong on subtleties of phrasing as Scimone. The ASV performances are now available either in a three-disc set including the *Piano Concerto* (an arrangement of a piano sonata, where Piero Spada appears as the secure and accomplished soloist) or even more economically on a pair of CDs without the concerto. The bonus items are common to both.

PIANO MUSIC

Capriccio in B flat, Op. 17; Fantasia on 'Au clair de la lune'; Preludio alla Haydn, Preludio alla Mozart (both from Op.19); Sonatas: in F min., Op. 13/6; in F, Op. 33/2; in G min., Op. 34/2.

(N) *** Teldec 3984 26731-2. Staier (fortepiano).

These are superb performances. Andreas Staier uses an 1802 Broadwood from his own personal collection, which is in perfect condition. The ear immediately adjusts to its special timbre when the playing is so full-blooded, commanding and exciting, producing great bravura. Staier underlines Clementi's forward-looking style, which so often (and especially in the Op. 34 *G minor Sonata*) anticipates Beethoven. The lighter *Capriccio* with its wide range of mood and colour is very persuasively presented indeed, as are the delightfully innocent variations on *Au clair de la lune*, and this is a collection to convert the most doubtful listener to the cause of the fortepiano for music of this period.

Piano Sonatas in G min., Op. 7/3; in F min., Op. 13/6; in B flat, Op. 24/2; in F sharp min.; in D; Op. 25/5–6.

**(*) D & J Athene ATH CD 4. Katin.

Peter Katin plays a square piano, which has subsequently

been restored. So the sounds he creates are as authentic as one could find. The work which comes off best in his recital is the *G minor Sonata*, Op. 7/3, which sounds so effective on the fortepiano. The slow movement of the *F sharp minor*, Op. 25/5, sounds very direct, seeking no romantic overtones; generally, Peter Katin's approach is plainspun to suit the somewhat dry sonority of his instrument. He is very realistically recorded.

Piano Sonatas: in F min., Op. 13/6; in F sharp min., Op. 25/5; in G, Op. 34/2.

(N) ** Hänssler 98.114. Sager (piano).

Piano Sonatas: in F min., Op. 13/6; in B flat, Op. 24/2; in F sharp min., Op. 25/5; in G, Op. 37/1.

*** Accent ACC 67911D. Van Immerseel (fortepiano).

Very fleet and brilliant performances from Jos van Immerseel. The slow movements of these Sonatas have some considerable expressive depth, and the outer ones are full of a brilliance that is well served by this eminently skilful and excellent artist.

Christopher Sager is less concerned than others to draw the parallel between Clementi and Beethoven. Playing with appealing gentleness, he is at his best in slow movements – the *Lento e patetico* of Op. 25/5 and the *Adagio* of the *F minor Sonata*, where he is less commanding in the *agitato* of the opening movement and the finale. The outer movements of the *G minor Sonata*, too, although presented very musically, are less than stormy. He is very well recorded, but this CD only extends to 47'40".

Piano Sonatas: in B flat, Op. 24/2; in G; in F sharp min., Op. 25/2 & 5; in D, Op. 37/2; 6 Progressive Sonatinas, Op. 36.

(B) *** Naxos 8.550452. Szokolay.

Balázs Szokolay made a strong impression at the Leeds Piano Competition some years back and we have much admired his Naxos records of some of the Grieg *Lyric Pieces* (see below). This Clementi anthology is hardly less successful and his playing inspires enthusiasm. Decent recording; excellent value.

Piano sonatas: in D, Op. 25/6; in A, Op. 33/1; in A, Op. 50/1; in G min. (Didone abbandonata), Op. 50/3.

(N) (M) *** CRD 3500. Roscoe.

This is one of the very finest available collections of Clementi's keyboard sonatas, and Martin Roscoe makes a very persuasive case for playing them on a modern instrument. He is particularly searching in the *Adagio sostenuto* of the late *A major Sonata*, Op. 50/1, and how impressively he pedals in the dolorous *Introduzione (Largo patetico e sostenuto)* of the *G minor Sonata (Didone abbandonata)*, then presenting the *Adagio dolente* most touchingly, and finding plenty of drama in the agitated finale. Yet the gallant early D major work is joyfully spirited and full of charm. The recording is very natural, well up to the high standard we expect from this label.

Piano Sonatas in G; B min.; D, Op. 40/1–3.

(B) *** Naxos 8.553500. De Maria.

After their earlier success with the Hungarian pianist Balázs Szokolay, Naxos have elected to continue with Pietro De Maria – and he, too, is hardly less captivating. His account of the three *Sonatas* of Op. 40 is impeccable not only in terms of virtuosity but in musicianship and artistry. His playing is meticulous, beautifully articulated, his command of dynamics and naturalness of phrasing admirable. He is accorded first-class sound, fresh and present, as one might expect from the acoustic of St George's, Brandon Hill, Bristol. Very good value for money.

CLÉRAMBAULT, Louis-Nicolas
(1676–1749)

Sonata No. 1 (Anonima) in G; Simphonie à 5 in G min.; (i) Harpsichord Suite No. 2 in C min.; (ii) Cantatas: Orphée; Léandre et Héro.

(N) (B) **(*) Naxos 8.553744. Les Solistes du Concert Spirituel. (i) Rannou; (ii) with Piau.

Nicolas Clérambault – son of a violinist who played in the 'Vingt-quatre violins du Roi' – made his name first as an organist, in 1715 establishing himself in the organ-loft of Saint-Sulpice. From the 1720s onwards he also held private concerts in his house in the rue du Four and it was here that his instrumental music was introduced. His *Sonatas* followed the Corellian model, but the invention of No. 1 is indeed very anonymous. and does not show him at his best. The three-minute *Simphonie*, however, turns out to be an engaging single-movement *Chaconne*.

The *Harpsichord Suite* follows the French style of Couperin, but Blandine Rannou fails to make the most of it by choosing consistently slow tempi, until the closing *Gigue*, which sparkles. However, as can be seen below, it was his cantatas which made Clérambault's reputation, and two of the finest are included here, beautifully sung by Sandrine Piau.

Both include 'strong and tender airs', which are exquisite duets with a solo flute, and the example in *Orfée* – a supplication to Pluto – is quite ravishing here. This cantata ends happily with a 'Cheerful air', as the power of love is celebrated (before Orpheus tragically looks back). The accompaniments by Les Solistes du Concert Spirituel are admirably alive and stylish and this Naxos disc is well worth getting for the cantatas alone.

Cantatas: Apollon et Doris; L'Isle de Délos; Léandre et Héro; Pirame et Tisbé.

(M) *** Opus 111 10-006. Poulenard, Ragon, Ens. Amalia.

Between 1710 and 1742 Clérambault produced some twenty-six cantatas for varying instrumental combinations. Both *Léandre et Héro* and *Pirame et Tisbé* come from 1713 and are redolent of tragedy, and exhibit a sensibility of great refinement. *L'Isle de Délos* comes from 1716 and evokes the pleasures of the island, while *Apollon et Doris* (1720) serves to reaffirm the feeling that as a master of the secular chamber cantata he was second to none. Affecting performances from Isabelle Poulenard and Gilles Ragon, well supported throughout by the Ensemble Amalia. The recording is first-rate.

Cantatas: *La Muse de l'opéra ou les Caractères lyrques; La Mort d'Hercule; Orphée; Pyrame et Tisbé.*

(N) (B) *** HM HMA 1901329. Rime, Fouchécourt, Rivenq, Les Arts Florissants, Christie.

Here is a further diverting programme of Clérambault's more distinctive cantatas, all but *Orphée* written between 1713 and 1716, very popular in their day and admired by the King. Jean-Paul Fouchécourt's light-voiced tenor style could not be more French in his characterization of *Pyrame et Tisbé*, tender and dramatic by turns, and Nicolas Rivenq is resonantly eloquent in *La Mort d'Hercule*. Noèle Rime's approach is comparably histrionic in the remaining two works – the *Tempeste* in *La Muse de l'opéra* suits her admirably; but she can charm lyrically too in her duets with the flute. She opens *Orphée* with grace, but this is a splendidly operatic performance full of temperament and character, if not quite as tonally ravishing as with Sandra Piau on Naxos. Here as throughout, Christie's accompanying group gives lively, stylish backing and the recording is excellent. Texts and translations are provided, but curiously the libretto of *Orphée* ends before the closing three numbers, as if the translator could not come to terms with the upbeat ending.

Motets: *Domine à 3 with 2 Violins; Domine salvum; Domine salvum, prière pour le Roy; Exultet omnium; Magnificat à 3 parties; O delicis affluens; O piissima, o sanctissima; Panis angelicus; Salve regina antienne.*

(N) *** Virgin VC5 45415-2. Lesne, Padmore, Ramon i Monzó, Il Seminario Musicale.

This splendid Virgin collection shows that Clérambault's sacred music, written during his early tenure of Saint-Sulpice, could be every bit as inspired as his cantatas, the scoring equally delightful. Here the opening *Panis angelicus* is full of expressive intensity, without a hint of sentimental underlay, while the spirited *Exultet omnium*, dedicated to Saint-Sulpice himself, is full of ardour, especially the exultant *Venite, accurite*, and the closing *Grex tuus gaudeat*. The Marian solo motet *O deliciis affluens* beautifully sung, is charmingly lighthearted, and the *Salve Regina antienne*, also dedicated to the Virgin, has much expressive delicacy. Both this work and the *Magnificat* bring splendid writing for the vocal trio in concert, but the vocal interchanges are no less memorable, as in the dialogue of the *Domine à troix voix*. The two brief but noble settings of *Domine salvum* were used as prayers for the King at the conclusion of services, and again the ear is struck by the simplicity and colour of the accompaniments. Throughout this recital, with the inestimable Gerald Lesne leading a superb solo team, one is struck by celebratory joy of the writing, so good-humoured and full of faith in life itself. The recording is first class. Highly recommended.

Le Triomphe d'Iris (pastorale).

(B) *** Naxos 8.554455. Méchaly, Geoffroy-Dechaume,

Goubioud, Bona, Duthoit, Novelli, Lombard, Le Concert Spirituel, Niquet.

Clérambault also produced lively court entertainments like this delightful Pastorale. Parallel to the *Grand opéra*, France had developed a less-imposing genre called the *Petit opéra* which comes close to the Masque in England. In a manner typical of that style and period the present work presents a story of two pairs of shepherd and shepherdess lovers, Daphnis and Sylvie, and Tircis and Philis, brought together at the end by the goddess, Iris, representing Love. What matters most is the vitality of Clérambault's writing in a sequence of brief arias, choruses and dances, underlined in the rhythmic bite of this performance from the period instruments of Le Concert Spirituel. The refined, very French team of singers is well drilled and agile, untroubled by brisk speeds. Clear, refined recording to match.

CLIFFORD, Hubert (1904–59)

Symphony.

*** Chan. 9757. BBC PO, Handley – BAINTON: *Symphony No. 2*; GOUGH: *Serenade.* ***

Australian born, Hubert Clifford came to England to study at the Royal College of Music in London with Vaughan Williams. He never returned to Australia and after a spell of teaching joined the BBC as head of Light Music Programmes. He subsequently became director of music for Alexander Korda. His four-movement *Symphony* is an ambitious score which runs to forty-three minutes. It is compelling, expertly fashioned and vividly scored, even if no distinctive voice emerges. Its idiom at times comes close to the English film music of the 1940s and 1950s. It is well argued and it would be difficult to imagine a more persuasive and convincing account than it receives from the BBC Philharmonic and Vernon Handley or better-recorded sound. An enterprising release.

COATES, Eric (1886–1958)

Ballad; By the sleepy lagoon; London Suite; The Three Bears (phantasy); *The Three Elizabeths* (suite).

(M) *** ASV CDWHL 2053. East of England O, Nabarro.

Nabarro has the full measure of Coates's leaping allegros and he plays the famous marches with crisp buoyancy. *The Three Bears* sparkles humorously, as it should; only in *By the sleepy lagoon* does one really miss a richer, more languorous string-texture. Excellent, bright recording, and the price is right.

Calling All Workers March; Dambusters March; The Jester at the Wedding; London Suite; The Merrymakers Overture; The Three Elizabeths Suite. (i) Songs: *The Green hills o' Somerset; Stonecracker John.*

(N) (M) ** BBCM 5011–2. BBC Concert O, Boult; (i) with Wallace.

An exceptionally generous collection (76 minutes) of Eric Coates favourites, including the three best-known marches:

Dambusters, Knightsbridge (once used as the introduction to the BBC's vintage radio show, 'In Town Tonight') and *Calling All Workers*, specifically written as the signature-tune for later wartime broadcasts of 'Music while you work'. Most importantly, the programme includes Coates's finest orchestral work, *The Three Elizabeths* (1944), in which the Queen Mother (*Elizabeth of Glamis*) got the best tune – scored for the oboe, and with a delightful, Scottish snap (although as played here it does not beguile the ear as much as it can). Queen Elizabeth II (then a princess) was celebrated with yet another swinging march. The charming and little-known ballet suite, *The Jester at the Wedding*, is played quite delightfully and Boult sees that the marches have plenty of rhythmic swing. The fine bass-baritone, Ian Wallace, is also on hand to give resonant accounts of two of Coates's most successful ballads. The orchestral playing is lively enough, if not immaculate; but the recording, although quite satisfactorily balanced in the Hippodrome Studio, Golders Green, does not flatter the violins and suggests that there were not too many of them. Good value, nevertheless.

The Four Centuries: Suite; The Jester at the Wedding: Ballet Suite; The Seven Dwarfs.

(M) **(*) ASV CDWHL 2075. East of England O, Malcolm Nabarro.

Nabarro offers a particularly delectable account of *The Jester at the Wedding Ballet Suite*. *The Four Centuries* is a masterly and engaging pastiche of styles from four different periods, and again it receives a performance of some subtlety, although at times one wishes for a more opulent sound from the violins, and the closing jazzy evocation of the 1930s and 1940s could be more uninhibitedly rumbustious. *The Seven Dwarfs* is an early work (1930), a ballet written for a short-lived London revue.

The Three Elizabeths (suite).

(M) **(*) Mercury (ADD) [434 330-2]. London Pops O, Fennell – GRAINGER: *Country gardens* etc. **

Fennell's performance is notable for its spirit and polish: the closing march, *The Youth of Britain*, sounds particularly fresh and alert, while the slow movement is nicely expressive. But the 1965 Mercury recording, made in Watford Town Hall, though fuller and with a more attractive ambience than the coupled Grainger items, still lacks something in expansiveness, though not clarity of detail. A pity this is no longer available in the UK.

VOCAL MUSIC

Songs: *Always as I close my eyes; At sunset; Bird songs at eventide; Brown eyes I love; Dinder courtship; Doubt; Dreams of London; Green hills o'Somerset; Homeward to you; I heard you singing; I'm lonely; I pitch my lonely caravan; Little lady of the moon; Reuben Ranzo; Song of summer; A song remembered; Stonecracker John; Through all the ages; Today is ours.*

(M) *** ASV CDWHL 2081. Cook, Terroni.

Eric Coates, as well as writing skilful orchestral music, also produced fine Edwardian ballads which in many instances transcended the limitations of the genre, with melodies of genuine refinement and imagination. Brian Rayner Cook, with his rich baritone beautifully controlled, is a superb advocate and makes a persuasive case for every one of the 19 songs included in this recital. His immaculate diction is infectiously demonstrated in the opening *Reuben Ranzo* (a would-be sailor/tailor), in which he breezily recalls the spirited projection of another famous singer of this kind of repertoire in the early days of the gramophone, Peter Dawson. The recording is admirably clear.

COLERIDGE-TAYLOR, Samuel (1875–1912)

4 Characteristic Waltzes, Op. 22; Gipsy Suite, Op. 20; Hiawatha Overture, Op. 30; Othello Suite, Op. 79; Petite suite de concert, Op. 77; Romance of the Prairie Lilies, Op. 39.

*** Marco 8.223516. Dublin RTE Concert O, Leaper.

Coleridge-Taylor wrote much delightful orchestral music, the most famous being the charming *Petite suite de concert*. It opens robustly, before turning into a graceful waltz; the two central movements are reflectively pastoral, and the suite ends in a lively Tarantella.

The composer's feeling for the genre is also apparent in the *4 Characteristic Waltzes*. Each is nicely coloured: there is a nostalgic *Valse bohémienne*, a countrified *Valse rustique* (the oboe so easily conjuring up the countryside), a stately *Valse de la reine*, and a lively *Valse mauresque*.

The *Gipsy Suite* is a piquantly coloured four-movement work of considerable appeal, whilst the *Othello Suite*, beginning with a lively dance, has an engaging *Willow song* and ends with a stirring *Military March*. Performances and recording are excellent, and this is altogether a winning if essentially lightweight collection, perhaps more for aficionados than the general collector.

Scenes from The Song of Hiawatha (complete).

(M) *** Decca 458 591-2 (2). Field, Davies, Terfel, WNO Ch. & O, Alwyn.

Part One of Coleridge-Taylor's choral trilogy based on Longfellow's epic poem is still regularly performed by choral societies in the north of England. The reasons for the neglect of Parts Two and Three, *The Death of Minnehaha* and *Hiawatha's Departure*, are made only too clear by this complete recording: there is a distinct falling-off in the composer's inspiration, so fresh and spontaneously tuneful in Part One. Indeed, when the main theme of *Hiawatha's Wedding Feast* returns in Part Three with the words 'From his place rose Hiawatha', one realizes how memorable it is, compared with what surrounds it. Of course the choral writing is always pleasingly lyrical and makes enjoyable listening. Part Two has plenty of drama, and towards the end Helen Field has a memorably beautiful solo passage, which she sings radiantly, echoed by the chorus, 'Wahonomin! Wahonomin! Would that I had perished for you.' There is also an almost Wagnerian apotheosis at the actual moment of the Farewell, which is sung and played here with compelling grandiloquence. Kenneth Alwyn directs a freshly spontaneous account and has the advantage of excellent soloists (including an early appearance on CD by Bryn Terfel as Hiawatha, now featured prominently on the front of the reissue), though the Welsh Opera Choir do not seem at home in the idiom. The recording while vivid, lacks the glowing ambient effect of the Royal Albert Hall, which would have been a much better venue.

CONFREY, Edward (1895–1971)

African suite; Amazonia; Blue Tornado; Coaxing the Piano; Dizzy Fingers; Fourth Dimension; Jay Walk; Kitten on the Keys; Meandering; Moods of a New Yorker (suite); Rhythm Venture; Sparkling Waters; Stumbling Paraphrase; Three Little Oddities; Wisecracker Suite.

*** Marco 8.223826. Andjaparidze.

Older collectors will surely remember *Kitten on the Keys* and perhaps *Dizzy Fingers* and *Coaxing the Piano* (all dazzlingly played here). Confrey established his international fame as a precocious virtuoso pianist/composer in the early 1920s. His music has a witty charm and is clearly influenced by French impressionism as well as Gershwin and the Scott Joplin rags. The Georgian pianist Eteri Andjaparidze gives engagingly sparkling performances of the bravura pieces including the ingenious closing *Fourth Dimension*, with its amazingly virtuosic cross-hand accents, and is equally at home in the more relaxed ragtime of *Jay Walk*, *Stumbling* and the sauntering gait of *Meandering*. But she also relishes the atmosphere and charm of the gentler pieces among the *Oddities* and the suites (two of the *Moods of a New Yorker* recall the tranquil simplicity of MacDowell's *To a wild rose*). A most entertaining collection given excellent piano recording.

CONSTANTINESCU, Paul
(1909–63)

The Nativity (Byzantine Christmas Oratorio).

**(*) Olympia (ADD) OCD 402 (2). Petrescu, Kessler, Teodorian, Bömches, Bucharest Enescu Ch. & PO, Basarab.

Paul Constantinescu's *Byzantine Christmas Oratorio* is an extended work of some quality in three parts: *Annunciation*, *Nativity* and *The Three Magi*. This impressive performance comes from the late 1970s. Constantinescu writes effectively both for the chorus and for solo voices, and his orchestration too is expert. The soloists are excellent (and in different circumstances might well have made names for themselves outside their native country) and the analogue recording is very good indeed. Readers with an interest in the exotic and a touch of enterprise are recommended to investigate this set.

CONUS, (Konius, or Konyus), Julius (1869–1942)

Violin Concerto in E min.

(M) *** EMI (ADD) CDM5 66060-2. Perlman, Pittsburgh O, Previn – BARTOK: *Violin Concerto No. 2;* SINDING: *Suite.* ***

**(*) Chan. 9622. L. Edwin Csüry, I Musici de Montréal, Turovsky – DAVIDOV: *Cello Concerto No. 2 in A min., Op. 14;* GLAZUNOV: *Piano Concerto No. 2.* **(*)

Julius Conus's *Violin Concerto* is a ripely romantic piece in one continuous movement with only a few memorable ideas but with luscious violin writing. Here the opening is very commanding and Perlman's first entry quite magical; he shows his supreme mastery in giving the piece new intensity, helped by fine playing from Previn and the Pittsburgh orchestra. The 1979 recording is vivid and, if the violin is very close, Perlman's tone is honeyed. However, as we go to press this has been deleted.

Csüry is a most musical player and he plays this *Concerto* very sympathetically, even if he is no match for Perlman. Turovsky's Montreal band give him admirable support.

COOKE, Arnold (born 1906)

Clarinet Concerto.

*** Hyp. (ADD) CDA 66031. King, NW CO of Seattle, Francis – JACOB: *Mini-Concerto;* RAWSTHORNE: *Concerto.* ***

Arnold Cooke's music contains an element of Hindemithian formalism, carefully crafted, but the slow movement of this Concerto soars well beyond. Thea King makes a passionate advocate, brilliantly accompanied by the Seattle Orchestra in excellent 1982 analogue sound, faithfully transferred.

COPLAND, Aaron (1900–90)

Appalachian Spring (complete recording of full score); Billy the Kid (ballet suite); Rodeo: 4 Dance Episodes.

(N) ❁ *** RCA 09026 63511-2. San Francisco SO, Tilson Thomas.

It was Eugene Ormandy who in 1954 persuaded Copland to score the complete *Appalachian Spring* – hitherto only available in its original chamber version – for full orchestra. It is still not in print, existing only in manuscript, but Michael Tilson Thomas's superb recording confirms Ormandy's view that the work would expand magnificently.

In the normal concert suite the variations on *Simple Gifts* which form the climax are presented in an uninterrupted sequence, but in the ballet the sequence is broken by an additional episode in which a revivalist appears and warns the central couple in the story of what Copland called ' the strange and terrible aspects of human fate'. The complete ballet here runs to 36 minutes, and in this magnificently played and very moving performance is revealed as a twentieth-century masterpiece to rank (with its two more lightweight companions) alongside the three key Stravinsky ballets, including *The Rite of Spring*.

The opening is wonderfully serene, and Tilson Thomas finds infinite detail and colour throughout, while creating a richly evocative tapestry of great beauty, helped by a recording of extraordinary range and breadth.

The other performances of the two cowboy ballets are similarly imaginative and compelling, giving the impression of coming to the music for the first time. Rhythms are crisply lifted, the lyrical music is tender and touching, and the feeling of infinite open spaces ever-present. This is the finest single CD in the Copland discography and not to be missed, even if you already have other versions of this vivid music.

Appalachian Spring (ballet; complete original version)

*** Koch 3-7019-2. Atlantic Sinf., Schenck – BARBER: *Cave of the heart.* ***

Appalachian spring (complete: original chamber score); *Billy the Kid*: excerpts: *Waltz; Prairie Night; Celebration Dance. Down a Country Lane; 3 Latin American Dances; Music for the Theatre; Quiet City;* (i) *Old American Songs* (sets 1–2); (ii) *8 Poems of Emily Dickinson.*

(B) *** Teldec 3984 28169-2 (2). Saint Paul Chamber Orchestra, Wolff; with (i) Hampson; (ii) Upshaw.

Appalachian Spring (ballet suite: original chamber version); *Billy the Kid* (ballet suite); *Fanfare for the Common Man; Music for the Theatre.*

(M) **(*) Classic fm 76505 570362. Eos O, Sheffer.

This Koch International issue offers a welcome chance to hear a modern digital recording of *Appalachian Spring* in its original form for thirteen instruments and the bright, upfront recording presents the chamber version in the best possible light. This is a most interesting and stimulating issue.

Hugh Wolff and his fine Saint Paul Orchestra are completely at home here and it is good to have the original version of *Appalachian Spring* played (and recorded) so beautifully. The composer's markings of the last two sections – 'like a prayer' and 'very calm' – are also perfectly evoked. *Quiet City* brings some impressive solo playing from cor anglais (Thomas Tempel) and trumpet (Gary Bordner), but here the textural balance is less delicately atmospheric and less well integrated than in the famous Marriner version. It is good to have the composer's own scoring of his engaging *Down a Country Lane* (originally a piano piece). However, the other highlights are the two superbly sung song cycles. In the *Old American Songs*, Thomas Hampson is in a special class. His noble delivery of *At the river* followed by the deliciously lighthearted *Ching-a-ring* is unforgettable. So is Dawn Upshaw's eloquent set of the *Emily Dickinson Poems*, now easily the finest on record (*Going to heaven* is marvellously sung), yet like Hampson she can both ravish and tickle the ear by turns. The closing song, *The chariot*, has a touching simplicity. It is a pity that only three excerpts were included from *Billy the Kid* (there was plenty of room on the disc for the whole ballet!), but they make an enjoyable postlude. Very highly recommended.

The Eos is a chamber-sized orchestra, made up of first-class players, resident in New York. Here they are custom-built for the original score (but only include the suite) of *Appalachian Spring*, which, truthfully recorded, is more striking for its rhythmic zest and vivid woodwind detail than the richer sweep of string tone which comes with a full orchestral version like Hickox's below. The same approach gives the sharpest focus to the popular rhythmic elements of *Music for the Theatre* and the *Billy the Kid* ballet suite, where the gentle nostalgia of *Prairie Night* and *Billy's Death* are more gently caught by the small string group. The *Celebration Sequence* is very wittily pointed, while the final view of *The Open Prairie* certainly does not lack evocative power; but again some might prefer a more lavish patina of orchestral tone.

'Celebration' Vol. 1: (i) *Appalachian Spring* (ballet: complete original chamber version; with rehearsal sequence); (ii) *Billy the Kid* (ballet): *Suite; Danzón Cubano; Down a Country Lane;* (iii) *El salón Mexico;* (ii) *Fanfare for the Common Man; Quiet City; Rodeo* (4 dance episodes). (iv) *Nonet for Strings.*

(N) (M) *** Sony (ADD) SM2K 89323 (2). (i) Columbia Chamber Ens.; (ii) LSO; (iii) New Philh. O; (iv) Columbia String Ens; all cond. composer.

This is the first of three mid-priced Doubles celebrating the centenary of Copland's birth with key recordings from the Sony catalogue. The sound has been effectively remastered, but many of these famous performances are still available in alternative compilations. The exception is the *Nonet for Strings* (recorded in 1962), which has not appeared on CD before. It is a powerful triptych with two 'Slow and solemn' sections framing a rhythmic centrepiece. The recording is good if a bit close. The other novelty, *Down a Country Lane*, began life as film music and then became a piano piece, before being scored as it is heard here. The original version of *Appalachian Spring* brings an alert, refreshing account, and although only 13 instruments are used (because of the slender resources of the Martha Graham Ballet Company) the effect certainly does not lack fullness of atmosphere. A rehearsal sequence is included, with the composer's directions to his players as pertinent as they are clear.

Appalachian Spring (ballet) *Suite.*

*** Everest (ADD) EVC 9003. LSO, Walter Susskind – GOULD: *Spirituals* ***; GERSHWIN: *American in Paris.* **(*)
(B) *** DG Classikon 445 129-2 [(M).import]. LAPO, Bernstein – BARBER: *Adagio for Strings;* BERNSTEIN: *Candide Overture;* SCHUMAN: *American Festival Overture.* ***
(M) *** DG 439 528-2. LAPO, Bernstein – BARBER: *Adagio for Strings* ***; GERSHWIN: *Rhapsody in Blue.* **(*)

Susskind's dramatic and sympathetic reading of what is perhaps Copland's finest orchestral score is most spaciously and vividly recorded. Although it is an English performance, it compares very favourably indeed with the composer's own – see below – and the American-style engineering with wide dynamics adds plenty of drama, but not at the expense of amplitude. With its apt Gould coupling – no less well done – this is an outstanding reissue. It is a pity that it is

---

offered at only slightly less than full price, but it is worth its cost.

Bernstein's DG version of *Appalachian Spring* was recorded at a live performance, and the conductor communicates his love for the score in a strong yet richly lyrical reading, and the compulsion of the music-making is obvious. The recording is close but not lacking in atmosphere, and it sounds extremely vivid. It is offered in alternative couplings, a recommendable bargain Classikon compilation of four key twentieth-century American works, or at mid-price, with Bernstein at the piano in his rather less recommendable second recording of Gershwin's *Rhapsody in Blue*.

(i) *Appalachian Spring; Billy the Kid* (complete ballet); (ii) *Dance Symphony;* (iii) *Danzón Cubano; El salón México;* (ii) *Fanfare for the Common Man; The Red Pony* (suite); (i) *Rodeo* (complete ballet).

(B) *** EMI Double Fforte CZS5 73653-2 (2). (i) St Louis SO, Slatkin; (ii) Mexico City PO, Bátiz; (iii) Dallas SO, Mata.

A first-class collection. Slatkin's was the first complete recording of *Billy the Kid*, which includes about ten minutes of extra music omitted from the usual suite – including two delightful waltzes. The complete ballet *Rodeo* consists essentially of the usual four colourful movements, though here a piano interlude is included (an old upright piano of 'doubtful' lineage was used for this recording, according to the original booklet). Both are given terrific performances under Slatkin, and the sound is superb. Bátiz's orchestra doesn't have the technical excellence of Slatkin's, but he is a lively and persuasive interpreter of Copland. The *Dance Symphony* is well done, though the ensemble is not as precise as it could be. *The Red Pony* suite – a colourful and nostalgic score for Lewis Milestone's film – is among the most endearing lighter scores Copland wrote and is very enjoyable. Mata's Dallas performances of *Danzón Cubano* and *El salón México* are as good as any – brilliant performances in demonstration sound. In every sense this set is a splendid bargain.

(i) *Appalachian Spring* (ballet) *Suite; Billy the Kid: Ballet Suite;* (ii) *Clarinet Concerto;* (i) *Danzón Cubano; Fanfare for the Common Man; John Henry; Letter from Home;* (i; iv) *Lincoln Portrait;* (iii) *Music for Movies;* (i) *Our Town; An Outdoor Overture; Quiet City; Rodeo (4 Dance Episodes);* (iii) *El salón México;* (i) *Symphony No. 3;* (v) *Las agachadas.*

(M) *** Sony (ADD) SM3K 46559 (3). (i) LSO; (ii) Goodman, Columbia Symphony Strings; (iii) New Philh. O; (iv) with H. Fonda; (v) New England Conservatory Ch.; composer.

Sony here offer a comprehensive anthology of the major orchestral works, ballet suites and film scores dating from Copland's vintage period, 1936–48. The composer directs with unrivalled insight throughout. The remastering for CD is done most skilfully, retaining the ambience of the originals, while achieving more refined detail.

(i) *Appalachian Spring* (ballet) *Suite; Billy the Kid* (ballet) complete; (ii) *Danzón Cubano; El salón México.*

(M) *** Mercury (ADD) [434 301-2]. (i) LSO; (ii) Minneapolis SO, Antal Dorati.

(i) *Appalachian Spring; Billy the Kid* (suite); (ii) *El salón México;* (i) *Rodeo: 4 Dance Episodes.*

(M) *** RCA (ADD) 09026 63467-2. (i) Phd. O, Ormandy; (ii) Dallas SO, Mata.

Appalachian Spring (ballet): *Suite; Billy the Kid* (ballet) *Suite; Fanfare for the Common Man; Rodeo (4 Dance Episodes).*

(B) **(*) Naxos 8.550282. Slovak RSO (Bratislava), Gunzenhauser.

(i) *Appalachian Spring;* (ii) *Billy the Kid* (suite); *Rodeo* (suite).

(B) *** RCA Navigator (ADD) 74321 21297-2. (i) Boston SO, composer; (ii) Morton Gould and his Orchestra.

Dorati pioneered the first stereo recording of the complete *Billy the Kid* ballet, and the 1961 Mercury LP caused a sensation on its first appearance for its precision of detail and brilliance of colour, while the generous acoustics of Watford Town Hall added ambient warmth. The gunshots (track 13) were and remain electrifying, with their clean percussive transients, while the LSO playing combines tremendous vitality and rhythmic power with genuine atmospheric tension. For the CD, earlier (1957) Minneapolis versions of the *Danzón Cubano* and *El salón México* have been added. The recording is crisp and clean to suit his approach. This CD has been withdrawn in the UK.

Under Ormandy the playing of the Philadelphia Orchestra is wonderfully rich and refined and of course totally idiomatic in this repertoire, even if his *Appalachian Spring* does not surpass the composer's own on the same label. The 1969 recording lacks the impact of rival versions, but is fully acceptable. Mata's performances date from 1978 and there's nothing to grumble about sonically at all. Nor is there about the performances: they are lively and enjoyable and show just how good the Dallas Orchestra was at that time.

The Bratislava Orchestra play with such spontaneous enjoyment in *Rodeo* and *Billy the Kid* that one cannot help but respond. Gunzenhauser, a fine conductor of Czech music, is equally at home in Copland's folksy, cowboy idiom and all this music has plenty of colour and atmosphere. If some of the detail in *Appalachian Spring* is less sharply etched than with Bernstein, the closing pages are tenderly responsive. The recording is admirably colourful and vivid with a fine hall ambience, and the spectacle of the *Fanfare for the Common Man* is worth anybody's money. A bargain.

Copland's first recording of *Appalachian Spring*, recorded in Boston in 1959, has an appealing breadth and warmth of humanity, helped by the Symphony Hall resonance: the Shaker climax is wonderfully expansive. Morton Gould conducts the other two ballets with enormous zest and vitality, and 'his' orchestra play as if their very lives depended on it. The early (1957) stereo is a little dated but remains arrestingly spectacular and the quieter, evocative writing is haunting, distilling a special combination of tender warmth and underlying tension. The *Corral Nocturne* and wistful *Saturday Night Waltz* in *Rodeo* are especially fine, and here Gould also includes the *Honky-Tonky Interlude* on an appropriate piano. The closing *Hoe-Down* is refreshingly folksy and has great rhythmic energy.

(i) *Appalachian Spring* (ballet) *Suite;* (ii) *Ceremonial Fanfare;* (iii) *Dance Symphony; El salón México;* (i) *Fanfare for the Common Man;* (i; iv) *Lincoln Portrait;* (v) *Music for Movies;* (vi) *Quiet City;* (iii) *Rodeo: 4 Dance Episodes;* (vii) *Old American Songs* (excerpts): *Simple gifts; Ching-a-ring-chaw; Long time ago; I bought me a cat; At the river.*

(B) *** Double Decca ADD/Dig. 448 261-2 (2). (i) LAPO, Mehta; (ii) Philip Jones Brass Ens.; (iii) Detroit SO, Dorati; (iv) Peck; (v) L. Sinf., Howarth; (vi) ASMF, Marriner; (vii) Horne, ECO, Davis.

Mehta's performance of *Appalachian Spring* is one of the most distinguished of several fine recordings he made for Decca in the late 1970s, which also included the spectacular *Fanfare for the Common Man* and the *Lincoln Portrait,* with Gregory Peck a comparatively laid-back narrator who speaks Lincoln's prose with dignity and restraint. Dorati's perform-ances of the *Dance Symphony, El salón México* and *Rodeo* were digitally recorded in 1981. They are notable for their bright, extrovert brilliance, having evidently been chosen for their immediate, cheerful qualities, and the only reservation is that, somewhat surprisingly, Dorati's treatment of jazzy syncopations is rather literal. But as sound this is very impressive, and the performances have much vitality. The evocative opening picture of the *New England Countryside* occupies the same musical world as *Appalachian Spring.* Again fine playing from the London Sinfonietta under Elgar Howarth and vivid recording. Marriner's account of *Quiet City* is second to none, but the highlight of the second CD is Marilyn Horne's delightful performances of five *Old American Songs:* the rhythmic sparkle of *Ching-a-ring-raw* and the charm of *I bought me a cat* contrasting with the moving simplicity of the closing *At the river.* Excellent value.

Appalachian Spring (ballet suite); Fanfare for the Common Man.

(B) *** Penguin Decca 460 656-2. Detroit SO, Dorati – BARBER: *Adagio for Strings;* BERNSTEIN: *Candide Overture; West Side Story Dances.* **(*)

Dorati's Decca *Appalachian Spring* (the suite, not the com-plete score) is among the finest and most brilliant versions on record, and the *Fanfare* makes a superb impact, both helped by the expansive Detroit ambience. However, the Baltimore performances which act as couplings are at a lower level of tension.

(i) Appalachian Spring (ballet): Suite; Fanfare for the Common Man; An Outdoor Overture; (ii) 3 Latin-American Sketches; (i) Rodeo (4 Dance Episodes); (ii) El salón México.

(M) *** Sony (ADD) SMK 60133. (i) LSO; (ii) New Philh. O; composer.

This generously filled (79 minutes) CD is drawn from the composer's more comprehensive anthology above. It is emi-nently recommendable. Copland's own account of *Appa-*

lachian Spring is particularly evocative and beautifully recorded.

(i) Appalachian Spring (ballet suite); (ii) Fanfare for the Common Man; (i; iii) Quiet City; (iv) Piano Sonata.

(M) **(*) Virgin VM5 61702-2. (i) City of L. Sinf, Hickox; (ii) LPO, Davis; (iii) with Steele-Perkins, McQueen; (iv) Lawson.

It is easy to enjoy Richard Hickox's warmly atmospheric account of Copland's greatest ballet score. The full orchestral version is made seductively opulent by the spacious recording, and the same comment applies to the rich textures of *Quiet City,* embroidered by first-class trumpet and cor anglais soloists who are perhaps a shade too forwardly bal-anced. Yet the principal attraction in this 'centenary tribute' is the inclusion of the rarely recorded *Piano Sonata.* Peter Lawson's highly concentrated, yet essentially cool reading is rhythmically strong but emotionally spare until the solilo-quizing closing sequence which is touchingly sustained.

Appalachian Spring (ballet) Suite; (i) Piano Concerto. Symphonic Ode.

**(*) Delos DE 3154. (i) Hollander; Seattle SO, Schwarz.

The glowing acoustics of the Seattle Opera House smooth some of the abrasiveness away from Lorin Hollander's im-pressive account of Copland's *Piano Concerto* and also filter out some of the glitter from the jazzy piano-writing. Simi-larly, *Appalachian Spring* loses some of the bite in the dance rhythms, although the glowing woodwind detail and the richly expansive closing variations on *A Gift to be Simple* are more than compensation. The exultantly monumental close of the pungently flamboyant *Symphonic Ode* is given similar weight and breadth. The Seattle orchestra plays splendidly throughout and Schwarz is a master of all this repertoire.

Appalachian Spring (ballet) Suite; Short Symphony.

*** Pro Arte CDD 140. St Paul CO, Russell Davies – IVES: *Symphony No. 3.* ***

On Pro Arte, using a smaller ensemble than is usual, Russell Davies conducts fresh and immediate performances of both the *Short Symphony* and the well-known suite from *Appa-lachian Spring,* which was originally conceived for chamber orchestra. The recording is bright and forward to match the performances. An excellent and recommendable anthology.

Ceremonial Fanfare; John Henry (A Railroad Ballad); Jubilee Variations; (i) Lincoln Portrait; (ii) Old American Songs, Set 1; An Outdoor Overture; The Tender Land: The Promise of Living.

*** Telarc CD 80117. Cincinnati Pops O, Kunzel; (i) with Hepburn (nar.); (ii) Milnes.

Katharine Hepburn's remarkable delivery of Abraham Lin-coln's words quite transcends any limitations in Copland's *Lincoln Portrait* and makes it an undeniably moving experi-ence, and Kunzel, clearly inspired by the authority of her reading, punctuates the text with orchestral comments of singular power. The shorter pieces are also given splendid life. Sherrill Milnes's highly infectious performance of the first set of *Old American Songs* shows a spirited boisterousness that recalls Howard Keel in *Seven Brides for Seven Brothers*. Altogether a collection that is more than the sum of its parts, given superlative Telarc recording, highly spectacular and realistic, yet with natural balance.

Clarinet Concerto.

*** ASV CDDCA 568. MacDonald, N. Sinfonia, Bedford – FINZI: *Concerto*; MOURANT: *Pied Piper*. ***

*** Chan. 8618. Hilton, SNO, Bamert – NIELSEN: *Concerto*; LUTOSLAWSKI: *Dance Preludes*. ***

(i) Clarinet Concerto. Music for the Theatre; Music for Movies; (ii) Quiet City.

**(*) Music Masters 7005-2. (i) Blount; O of St Luke's, Russell Davies; (ii) with Gekker, Taylor.

Copland's splendid *Clarinet Concerto* is at last coming into its own, on record at least. George MacDonald gives a virtuoso performance, not quite as dramatic and full of flair as that of the dedicatee, Benny Goodman, but in many ways subtler in expression and particularly impressive in the long lyrical paragraphs of the first of the two movements.

Janet Hilton's performance is soft-grained and has a light touch, yet she finds plenty of sparkle for the finale and her rhythmic felicity is infectious. She is at her very finest, however, in the gloriously serene opening, where her tender poetic lilt is ravishing.

William Blount is a rich-toned soloist, with spacious, long-drawn phrasing in the opening movement, which some might find too languid, contrasting with the brilliant central cadenza and roisterously jazzy finale. The vibrant *Music for the Theatre* with its brash *Prologue* and *Dance* and ironic *Burlesque* nicely offsets the mellower New England evocations of *Music for Movies*, although here *Sunday Traffic* makes another lively contrast and the *Threshing Machines* are very busy too. *Quiet City* is beautifully evoked. This is a reissue of a 1988 CD, but the vivid projection and warmth of the sound suggest more modern provenance.

(i; ii) Piano Concerto; (iii) Dance Symphony; (ii) Music for the Theatre; (iii) 2 Pieces for String Orchestra; Short Symphony (Symphony No. 2); Statements; Symphonic Ode; (iv; ii) Symphony for Organ & Orchestra.

(M) *** Sony (ADD) SM2K 47232 (2). (i) Composer (piano); (ii) NYPO, Bernstein; (iii) LSO, composer; (iv) with E. Power Biggs.

This second Sony Copland collection covers early orchestral and concertante music written between 1922 and 1935 and is, if anything, more valuable than the first box. The 1923 *Rondino*, the second of his *Two Pieces for String Orchestra*, is the earliest work here. The *Lento* is a totally memorable piece. The *Symphony for Organ and Orchestra* is a powerful and strikingly innovative work, dating from 1924. It is given an extremely idiomatic and responsive performance by Power Biggs, and Bernstein balances the overall sounds with great skill. The pungently flamboyant *Symphonic Ode*, commissioned by the Boston Symphony, helped the orchestra to celebrate its fiftieth anniversary. All these performances have a definitive authority combined with total spontaneity of response from the participants which makes them compelling listening, and the recordings – dating from

between 1964 and 1967 – are very well engineered, extremely vivid in the excellent CD transfers.

Piano Concerto.

(M) *** Van. (ADD) 08.4029.71. Wild, Symphony of the Air, composer – MENOTTI: *Piano Concerto*. **(*)

(M) **(*) Chan. 6580. Lin, Melbourne SO, John Hopkins – BRITTEN: *Piano Concerto*. **(*)

This Vanguard record, with Earl Wild, a supreme piano virtuoso, providing a glittering account of the piano part, is very recommendable. The 1961 recording is first rate.

Gillian Lin, too, is undoubtedly successful in the Copland *Concerto*, bringing out the jazz element in this syncopated music. The 1978 stereo recording is well balanced and realistically transferred to CD.

(i–ii) Piano Concerto; Connotations for Orchestra; (iii) El salón México; (ii) Music for the Theatre (suite).

(M) *** Sony (ADD) SMK 60177. (i) Composer (piano); (ii) NYPO; (iii) (mono) Columbia SO; Bernstein.

El salón México, which was Bernstein's earlier mono recording, was made with the Columbia Symphony in 1951. It has great vitality and bite: no one coaxes that sleazy dance-hall rhythm quite like Bernstein. The programme opens with the suite of *Music for the Theatre*, with its spaciously atmospheric *Prologue*, unmistakably and uniquely by Copland (few composers have such indelible harmonic fingerprints); the poignant *Interlude*, shared by cor anglais and trumpet, is very reminiscent of *Quiet City*. If you already have Bernstein's disc of the ballet scores, this would be a splendid way to continue an exploration of Copland's music: the opening of the *Piano Concerto* is utterly haunting. *Connotations* (which also includes the piano within the orchestra) is less obviously popular in appeal but is undoubtedly magnetic. The present transfers are first class.

(i) Connotations; (ii) Dance Panels; Down a Country Lane; (i) Inscape; (ii) 3 Latin-American Sketches; Music for a Great City; Orchestral Variations; Preamble for a Solemn Occasion; The Red Pony (film score).

(M) *(**) Sony (ADD) SM2K 47236 (2). (i) NYPO, Bernstein; (ii) LSO or New Philh. O, composer.

This third Copland box from Sony is something of a disappointment – not the music, which is even rarer than before and of great interest. *The Red Pony* is vintage Copland, and the *Orchestral Variations*, though strictly an orchestral version of the *Piano Variations* of 1930, make a unique and impressive contribution to Copland's oeuvre. *Connotations* and to a lesser extent *Inscape*, the major work of the composer's final period, are serially orientated. *Dance Panels* is an abstract ballet without a narrative line, and *Music for a Great City*, with its jazz influences and nocturnal scene, derives from another film-score (*Something Wild*). The performances are all extremely successful, but the CD transfers are over-bright and, for all their vividness of detail, tiring to the ear, particularly the thin violins and the more pungent climaxes of the later works.

Film music: *The City; From Sorcery to Science; The Cummington Story* (suite, arr. Sheffer); *The North Star* (suite).

(N) *** Telarc CD 80583. Eos O, Sheffer.

Superb performances and brilliantly recorded premiere recordings of some colourful Copland film scores. From *Sorcery to Science* gave Copland a chance to write some amusing character pieces, including portrayals of a *Chinese Medicine Man, The Witch's Cauldron, The Alchemist* and *African Voodoo*, ending with *The Modern Pharmacy* and *March of the Americans*. It is all great fun and makes an entertaining ten-minute suite. With *The City*, Copland again demonstrates his usual knack for producing a totally American sound-world, while *The North Star*, a war-time film, has striking passages too. Not all the music here is first-rate Copland, but it is worth hearing, especially in such committed performances. The sleeve notes are helpful and informative.

Film music: *The Heiress* (suite, reconstructed Arnold Freed); *Music for Movies; Our Town; Prairie Journey (Music for Radio); The Red Pony* (suite).

*** RCA 09026 61699-2. Saint Louis SO, Slatkin.

Copland's film score for *The Red Pony* is one of his most delightful works, with its series of charming folksy vignettes, all warmly characterized, following the film narrative. The music for *The Heiress* dates from the same year (1948) and is more emotionally plangent, distinctly Hollywoodian in its sweeps of string tone, but Copland also slips into the score a hint of Martini's *Plaisir d'amour* to represent the amorous suitor. *Music for Movies* (which draws primarily on the films *The City* and *Of Mice and Men*) is a series of pastoral evocations, some quite lively, set in the New England countryside, while the shorter piece derived from *Our Town* has a similar warm nostalgic feeling. The closing *Prairie Journey* (1936), commissioned as 'Music for Radio' by CBS, is cast in a single vibrant movement built from nagging ostinatos, but with nostalgic interludes. In its balletic way it anticipates the scores of *Rodeo* and *Billy the Kid*. All this music is played with great affection and the most vivid colouring by the excellent Saint Louis Orchestra under the ever persuasive Leonard Slatkin, with the glowing ambience of Powell Symphony Hall adding much to the listener's pleasure.

Quiet City.

*** Argo (ADD) 417 818-2. ASMF, Marriner – BARBER: *Adagio;* COWELL: *Hymn;* CRESTON: *Rumor;* IVES: *Symphony No. 3.* ***

Marriner's 1976 version is both poetic and evocative, and the playing of the trumpet and cor anglais soloists is of the highest order. The digital remastering has brought added clarity without loss of atmosphere.

Quiet City; (i) *8 Poems of Emily Dickinson.*

*** EMI CDC5 55358-2. (i) Hendricks; LSO, Thomas – BARBER: *Adagio for Strings* etc. ***

This is an intensely beautiful disc, especially *Quiet City*, with solo trumpet and cor anglais (superbly played by Maurice Murphy and Christine Pendrill) creating great atmospheric intensity. The freshness and sharp imagination of the accompaniments are enhanced in support of vocal lines lovingly matched to Dickinson's distinctive poetic style. Radiant singing from Hendricks, and equally sensuous sounds from the orchestra. However, this has just been deleted.

Statements for Orchestra.

*** Everest (ADD) EVC 9039. LSO, Goossens – ANTHEIL: *Symphony No. 4.* **(*)

Statements for Orchestra (1934–5), as the bald title suggests, is one of Copland's less expansive works, but its six vignettes, *Militant, Cryptic* (hauntingly scored for brass and flute alone), *Dogmatic* (but disconsolate), *Subjective* (an elegiac soliloquy for strings), the witty *Jingo* and the thoughtfully *Prophetic* conclusion, reveal a compression of material and sharpness of ideas that are most stimulating. Goossens's performance is first rate in every way; so is the LSO playing, and the atmospheric (1959) recording sounds hardly dated at all.

Symphony No. 3; Billy the Kid (ballet): *Suite.*

** Everest (ADD) EVC 9040. LSO, Copland.

Symphony No. 3; Quiet City.

*** DG 419 170-2. NYPO, Bernstein.

Symphony No. 3; (i) *Symphony for Organ & Orchestra.*

(M) **(*) Sony (ADD) SMK 63155. (i) E. Power Biggs; NYPO, Bernstein.

Dating from 1959, the composer's first recordings of *Billy the Kid* and his *Third Symphony* (made at Walthamstow) are presented in stereo of sharp clarity with inner detail remarkably clear; the violins, however, are distinctly thin, which makes fortissimos sharp-edged, in spite of the basically warm ambience. The LSO are obviously coming fresh to *Billy the Kid*, playing with plenty of rhythmic bite. They give a far less virtuoso performance of the *Symphony*, which is convincing as an expression of emotion in the opening movement and the *Andantino*, but less than perfect in the playing of the brilliant Scherzo.

With Bernstein conducting Copland's *Third Symphony*, you appreciate more than with rival interpreters that this is one of the great symphonic statements of American music. The electricity of the DG performance is irresistible. The recording is full-bodied and bright, but its brashness is apt for the performance. The hushed tranquillity of *Quiet City*, another of Copland's finest scores, is superbly caught by Bernstein in the valuable fill-up.

In his earlier CBS/Sony recording Bernstein built the music up in a manner that the material will not quite stand and the result does not always avoid a feeling of inflation. The account of the work for organ and orchestra is discussed above. The Avery Fisher Hall recordings, from 1966 and 1967 respectively, sound suitably spacious in these fine new transfers, although the organ balance is close, and in this latter work tuttis have an element of harshness.

'Celebration' Vol. 2: (i; ii) *Duo for Flute & Piano;* (i; iii) *Piano Quartet;* (i; iii; iv) *Sextet for Clarinet, Piano & String Quartet;* (i; v) *Vitebsk (Study on a Jewish Theme for Piano Trio;* (vi) *Billy the Kid* (excerpts, arr. for piano, Lukas Foss). (Vocal) (vii; i) *Old American Songs, Sets I–II* (viii; i) *12 Poems of Emily Dickinson;* (with (ix) *Lincoln Portrait*).

(M) **(*) SM2K 89326 (ADD) stereo/mono (2). (i) Composer;
 (ii) Shaffer; (iii) Juilliard Qt. (members); (iv) Wright;
 (v) Carlyss, Adam; (vi) Levant; (vii) Warfield; (viii) Lipton;
 (ix) Sandburg, NYPO, Kostelanetz.

Copland wrote very little chamber music, obviously preferring to express himself on a fuller orchestral canvas. But the few works he left us ought to be more often heard (and recorded): it is extraordinary that Sony have not been able to include the *Violin Sonata* here.

The early *Vitebsk* (1928) opens with a spiky two-note rhythmic violin figure, but the music's underlying lyricism soon comes to the fore on the cello, and its harmonic character, rhythmic freedom and syncopated touches are already hinting at the later style of the ballet music. The performance has both intensity and impetus, but one could wish that the microphones were not so very close to Earl Carlyss's violin, which is made to sound thin and fierce.

The *Sextet* is the composer's 1936 arrangement of the *Short Symphony* of three years earlier, its concentration and terse argument the more sharply etched by the sparse instrumentation. The performance could not be more spontaneously committed (Harold Wright opening the central *Lento* very evocatively) and the close balance, if far from ideal, is not destructive.

In the masterly and challenging *Piano Quartet* (1950) Copland so thoroughly absorbed twelve-note technique into his own harmonic and rhythmic vocabulary that, from the haunting opening *Adagio serio* onwards, one could hardly guess this is a serial work. It is a comparatively austere triptych and was designed to show that he sought to achieve 'an idiom that might be accessible only to cultivated listeners'. Yet Copland could not help being immediate in communication, and the closing *Non troppo lento* is powerfully expressive.

The *Duo for Flute & Piano* (1971) is very listener-friendly, melting and poetic on Elaine Shaffer's lips and in the finale witty and gallically diverting, and Oscar Levant's performance of the piano arrangements of *The Open Prairie, Street in a Frontier Town* and *Celebration Day* from *Billy the Kid* are attractively fresh and idiomatic.

It is good that Sony decided to include Martha Lipton's pioneering mono LP of the *Emily Dickinson Poems*. With the composer at the piano the performance has an appealing directness, and feeling for the the words. The voice is very well caught by the microphones. Similarly William Warfield sings the *Old American Songs* with great freshness, and his mono set with the composer is vividly projected. It was André Kostelanetz who commissioned the *Lincoln Portrait*, which explains the inclusion of his 1958 recording. He conducts it dramatically and committedly. Carl Sandburg was Lincoln's biographer and his narration is attractively unpontifical and warmly casual. The orchestral recording is brilliant but lacks a really rich amplitude.

Violin Sonata; Nocturne for Violin & Piano.

*** DG 453 470-2. Shaham, Previn – BARBER: *Canzone for Violin & Piano;* GERSHWIN: *3 Preludes;* PREVIN: *Sonata.* ***

The *Violin Sonata* of 1944 represents the Copland of 'wide-open spaces', with broad intervals and open harmonies as in the ballets *Rodeo* and *Billy the Kid*. Shaham with his wide and beautiful contrasts of tone is an ideal interpreter, with Previn the thoughtful partner. The *Nocturne* dates from Copland's Paris period, charming in 1920s style.

PIANO MUSIC

Piano Sonata; 4 Piano Blues; Scherzo humoristique: The Cat and the Mouse.

*** Nim. NI 5585. Anderson – GERSHWIN: *3 Preludes; Arrangements of Songs; An American in Paris.* ***

Mark Anderson gives an outstanding account of the *Piano Sonata*, making it seem emotionally warmer and less texturally and harmonically spare than usual. His reading will surely make new friends for the work, it is 'freely expressive' (as the first movement is marked by the composer), and with the restless rhythmic mood of the central *Vivace* spontaneously caught, with even a brief jazz inflection. The closing *Andante sostenuto* is movingly tapered down and leaves the listener aware that this is a remarkably individual and original work. The *Four Piano Blues* are in Copland's easily accessible style and are also very well characterized, while the witty portrait of *Le Chat et la souris* makes a brilliant encore for what is a live recital in Nimbus's own concert hall.

VOCAL MUSIC

(i) *In the Beginning. Help us, O Lord; Have mercy on us, O my Lord; Sing ye praises to our King.*

*** Hyp. CDA 66219. (i) Denley; Corydon Singers, Best –
 BARBER: *Agnus Dei;* BERNSTEIN: *Chichester Psalms.* ***

In the Beginning is a large-scale, fifteen-minute motet for unaccompanied chorus and soprano solo, written in 1947, and the long span of the work is well structured with the help of the soprano soloist, here the fresh-toned Catherine Denley. The chorus is just as clear and alert in its singing, not only in the big motet but also in the three delightful little pieces which come as an appendix. Vivid recording, full of presence.

'Celebration' Vol. 3: (i; ii) *In the Beginning;* (ii; iii) *Lark;* (iv) *Old American Songs, Sets I–II;* (v) *12 Poems of Emily Dickinson;* (vi) *The Tender Land* (opera: abridged version).

(M) **(*) Sony (ADD) SM2K 89329 (2). (i) Miller, (ii) New
 England Conservatory Ch., Composer; (iii) with Hale;
 (iv) Warfield, Columbia SO, Composer; (v) Addison,

Composer (piano); (vi) Clements, Turner, Treigle, Cassily, Fredericks, Choral Arts Soc., NYPO, Composer.

By the time he came to re-record the orchestral settings of the *Old American Songs* in 1962 William Warfield had made them completely his own and he sings them with great warmth and affection, bringing genuine American style to support a richly vigorous voice and a real talent for this repertoire. Needless to say Copland's direction of the orchestra is a delight from start to finish. In the settings of Emily Dickinson, he accompanies at the piano with even more relish than he did previously for Martha Lipton, and Adele Addison's creamy voice adds to the listener's pleasure, especially in the lyrical songs like *Heart we will forget him* and *Sleep is supposed to be*. She readily brings out the American folk associations and this performance is more seductive than the earlier version, if perhaps characterized less strongly.

The two choral works, *In the Beginning* more ambitious in scale than *Lark*, both have strong soloists, but in neither case is the singing of the New England Conservatory Chorus ideally vibrant and biting, although with the composer directing the performances are still compelling, and they are well enough recorded.

The abridged recording of *The Tender Land* is another matter, for Copland proves a first-class opera conductor. The excerpts are atmospherically and vividly recorded and there is no weak link in the cast. Joy Clements sings appealingly as the heroine, Laura, matched by Richard Cassily, her ardent lover, Martin, while Norman Treigle is a resonant Grandpa. And the great quintet, *The promise of living*, which closes Act I, is thrillingly sung. The opening of Act II, marked 'lively and rough', has all the vigour one could want in an opera which is closely attuned to the style of a musical, as has the later barn dance sequence, and the Act II love duet is movingly passionate, leading to an idyllic close.

Old American Songs: Sets 1 & 2 (original versions).

** Chan. 8960. Willard White, McNaught (with collection: *American Spirituals; Folk-songs from Barbados and Jamaica* ***).

Characteristically White's opulent bass comes with a pronounced vibrato which on disc tends to get exaggerated. Yet with its helpful acoustic the Chandos recording captures the richness of his voice most attractively, very characterfully black in its evocations.

OPERA

The Tender Land (arr. Sidlin; complete).

**(*) Koch 3-7480-2 (2). Hanson, Vargas, MacNeil, Webster, Zeller, Hansen, Third Angle New Music Ens., Murry Sidlin.

When the conductor Murry Sidlin approached Aaron Copland suggesting that he should arrange this opera for an ensemble of thirteen instruments, 'achieving a Copland sound similar to *Appalachian Spring*', he received an immediate reply – 'What a good idea!' That is the version recorded here, which in default of a current recording of the original is welcome for offering a fresh, sensitive reading of a

work which matches the simple plot with music in Copland's most open-air American mood. Sidlin has modified the score in other ways too – with the composer's approval – adapting the Introduction to the original Act III as a prelude to the whole work, and inserting arrangements of two of Copland's Old American folk-songs – *Zion's Walls* and *Long time ago* – in the party scene of Act II.

Though it would be better still to have the original restored to the catalogue, this is an enjoyable, unpretentious reading of the revised score, with a cast of fresh young singers, well supported by the ensemble. This is a gentle rather than fiery opera, which is well suited to listening on disc. The intimate, relatively dry acoustic is apt for the work as arranged.

CORELLI, Arcangelo (1653–1713)

Concerti grossi, Op. 6/1–12.

(B) *** Hyp. Dyad CDD 22011 (2). Brandenburg Consort, Goodman.

*** HM HMC90 1406/7. Ensemble 415, Banchini.

*** DG 423 626-2 (2). E. Concert, Pinnock.

(B) *** Naxos 8.550402/3. Capella Istropolitana, Krechek.

(B) **(*) Ph. (ADD) Duo 456 326-2 (2) [(M) id. import]. I Musici.

(B) **(*) Double Decca (ADD) 443 862-2. ASMF, Marriner.

Concerti grossi, Op. 6/1–6.

*** HM Opus OPS 30-147. Europa Galante, Biondi.

Concerti grossi, Op. 6/7–12.

*** HM Opus OPS 30-155. Europa Galante, Biondi.

In its usual string version, Corelli's glorious set of *Concerti grossi*, Op. 6, is now very well represented in the catalogue in all price-ranges. For those who prefer period performances there is plenty of choice. However, although a clear-cut recommendation is difficult, the balance of advantage in authenticity seems to lie between Goodman and Banchini. One can invest in either with confidence. Roy Goodman and the Brandenburg Consort use the smaller forces (17 string players) plus harpsichord continuo, archlute and organ; Harmonia Mundi's Ensemble 415, with Chiara Banchini and Jesper Christensen, number 32 strings and a comparably larger continuo section with several archlutes, chitarrone, harpsichords and organ. The richer bass and altogether fuller sonority may cause some readers to prefer it. However, there is a sense of style and a freshness of approach in the Goodman version that is very persuasive. In both instances the recorded sound is first class.

The newest set, from the appropriately named Europa Galante, is as fine as any. The chamber-sized ripieno of period instruments (2,2,2,1,1) offers crisp detail yet no feeling of any lack of sonority, and the elegant playing is alert and vital yet smiles pleasingly: these musicians are obviously enjoying the music and so do we. The soloists are excellent, as is the recording.

The DG performances bring not only an enthusiasm for this music but a sense of its spacious grandeur. The English Concert are entirely inside its sensibility, and the playing of the concertino group (Simon Standage, Micaela Comberti and Jaap Ter Linden) is wonderfully fresh-eyed and alert, yet full of colour.

At super-bargain price, the Naxos set by the Capella Istropolitana under Jaroslav Krechek represents very good value indeed. The players are drawn from the Slovak Philharmonic and have great vitality and, when necessary, virtuosity to commend them. The digital recording is clean and well lit, but not over-bright, and makes their version strongly competitive.

I Musici bring a full sonority and expert musicianship to these *Concertos*. They are especially good in slow movements, where the playing has an agreeable lightness of touch and often creates delicately radiant textures. In allegros, rhythms are less bouncy than with Goodman, and the effect is less exhilarating. Yet there is an appealing warmth here, and certainly the Philips recording provides beautifully rich string-sound. Good value as a Duo, but not a first choice.

The reissued ASMF version uses a performing edition by Christopher Hogwood and has been prepared with evident thought and care. Yet compared to the issues mentioned above, there is at times a hint of blandness

Concerti grossi, Op. 6/1–6.

(N) (B) **(*) HM HCX 3957014. Philh. Bar. O, McGegan.

We are only offered Volume I of McGegan's 1990 complete set of Corelli's *Concerti grossi*, and we must hope that Volume II is to follow, for this makes a good recommendation for those wanting a bargain set of the concertos on period instruments. The performances, intimately small-scaled as they are, combine a spirited vivacity with expressive feeling, and although slow movements are moved on more briskly than with Pinnock (who still leads the authentic field) the balance of tempi is generally convincing. One might like rather more textural warmth, but the transparency is appealing and the continuo comes through as it should and overall the balance is very good.

Concerti grossi, Op. 6/1, 3, 7, 8 (Christmas), 11 & 12.

(M) *** DG 447 289-2. E. Concert, Pinnock.

At mid-price, with the *Christmas Concerto* included, this will admirably suit those collectors who want an original-instrument version and who are content with a single-disc selection.

Concerti grossi, Op. 6/1–12 (complete; with wind and brass, arr. Sardelli).

✿ *** Tactus TC 650307 (No.s 1–6); TC 650308 (Nos. 7–12). Modo Antiquo, Sardelli.

Of all the discoveries made so far by the enterprising Tactus label, this is the most fascinating. Modern scholarship has revealed that it was not unusual in Corelli's time to have fully scored performances of baroque concerti grossi, doubling the strings with wind and brass as available, and that is what happening in these thoroughly stimulating period performances by Modo Antiquo. Their conductor, Federico Sardelli, has obviously given much thought to his choice of instrumentation. For instance, trumpets are only used in

Nos. 1, 4 and 7 (all in D major) and then only where appropriate. Oboes are featured with equal discernment in Nos. 3, 7 and 10; recorders are used most sparingly, but always to felicitous effect. For the most part the wind are only added to the ripieno, but just occasionally they play phrases drawn from the concertino, and there is a splendid baroque interplay of colours.

At times the listener is reminded of Vivaldi, but as Corelli's original string textures (and style) predominate, the listener need not worry that the music's essential character is lost. Phrasing is both warm and refined, allegros are alert and vivacious and the excellent recording ensures that this music is given an entirely fresh lease of life.

Oboe Concerto (arr. Barbirolli).

*** Dutton Lab./Barbirolli Soc. CDSJB 1016. Rothwell, Hallé O, Barbirolli – HAYDN; MARCELLO: *Oboe Concertos* *** (with Recital: C. P. E. BACH; LOEILLET; TELEMANN: *Sonatas* etc. **

Barbirolli's *Concerto* is cunningly arranged from a trio Sonata and in its present form it makes one of the most enchanting works in the oboe repertoire. The performance here is treasurable and the clear, natural recording projects the music admirably.

CHAMBER MUSIC

Sonate da chiesa, Op. 1/1–12; Op. 3/1–12.

(N) (B) *** HM HMA 1951344/5. L. Baroque, Medlam.

Corelli's two dozen *Church Sonatas* Op. 1 (1681) and Op. 3 (1689) are brim-full of attractive invention, with Op. 3 more adventurous, both in the part-writing in the lively fugues and the harmonic implications throughout. They are different from the chamber sonatas in that the continuo is for organ (most winningly presented here), while the structure opens with a slow *Grave* or *Largo*, followed by three more movements, usually (but not invariably) fast–slow–fast. The sparkling final sonata of Op. 12, after the opening *Grave*, has four fast movements in a row. Throughout these works each movement is brief, but the contrapuntal writing is ever-felicitous and the music brims over with appealing invention. These period-performances from Charles Medlam and his excellent London Baroque group could not be fresher or more appealing and they are beautifully recorded. If so far you have only heard Corelli's *Concerti grossi*, try this pair of inexpensive CDs (handsomely presented) and you will discover why Corelli was so admired in his own time, and his influence so far-reaching.

Sonate da camera (Trio Sonatas), Op. 2/1–11.

** Tactus TC 650306. Il Ruggiero.

Sonate da camera (Trio Sonatas), Op. 2/1–12; Op. 4/1–12.

(B) *** HM HMA 1901342/3. L. Baroque, Medlam.

Corelli's *Sonate da camera*, Opp. 2 and 4 are more light-hearted than the *Sonate da chiesa*, Op. 1 and Op. 3, and yet it is not possible to draw clear distinctions between the different formats. Corelli was incapable of writing trivially, and of the earlier chamber Sonatas of Op. 2, the *Second* and *Sixth* both have extended slow opening *Allemandes* while the remarkable No. 4 *in E minor* has a very touching central *Adagio* in addition its solemn opening *Prelude*. The final work of Op. 2 (omitted on the Tactus disc) is a single-movement *Ciacona* which deserves to be better known. London Baroque under Charles Medlam catch the varying moods of these rewarding works to perfection, and they are beautifully recorded.

Il Ruggiero, the alternative period-instrument group on Tactus, play rather soberly for Italians. Although dance movements are deft and vigorous, the overall texture is close-grained so that although the opening *Preludes* and slow movements have a sombre dignity, the serious mood predominates and there is an absence of elegant, lighthearted contrast.

Trio Sonatas, Op. 1/9, 10 & 12 (Ciacona); Op. 2/4; Op. 3/5; Op. 4/1; Violin Sonata, Op. 5/3; Concerto grosso in B flat, Op. 6/5.

(M) *** Virgin VER5 61210-2. L. Baroque, Medlam.

Trio Sonatas, Op. 1/9; Op. 2/4 & 12 (Ciacona); Op. 3/12; Op. 4/3; Op. 5/3, 11 & 12 (La Folia).

*** Hyp. CDA 66226. Purcell Qt.

The quality of invention in these pieces underlines the injustice of their neglect. The players from the English Concert dispatch them with a virtuosity and panache that are inspiriting, and their evident enthusiasm for this music is infectious. This is a most impressive and rewarding issue – and excellently recorded into the bargain.

The Hyperion disc is one of six designed to illustrate the widespread use in the eighteenth century of the famous *La Folia* theme. It includes a varied collection of sonate da chiesa and sonate da camera. Excellent performances from all concerned, and recording to match.

12 Violin Sonatas, Op. 5; Sonata in A, Op.5/9 (elaborated Geminiani).

*** Hyp. CDA 66381/2. Locatelli Trio.
(B) **(*) Ph. Duo 462 306-2 (2). Grumiaux, Castogne (harpsichord).

Corelli's Opus 5 was published in 1700 as *Twelve Sonate a violino e violone o cimbalo*. Though not now as familiar as his concerti grossi, they were enormously popular and influential in their day and were even used by his contemporaries as vehicles for improvised or written elaboration and ornamentation. The Hyperion set includes Geminiani's elaborated version of No. 9, using a manuscript in the latter's own handwriting. Needless to say, the originals stand up perfectly well without such accretions. They are in essence suites of usually five (sometimes four) movements and the later works incorporate dance forms – Corrente, Sarabanda, Giga etc. No. 12 is a set of variations on the famous *La Folia*. These period performances by the Locatelli Trio are eminently alive and stylish. Allegros sparkle, decoration seems entirely apt and Adagios have a sympathetic expressive line and there is imaginative use of dynamic contrast. The recording balance cannot be faulted. These versions make an obvious first choice, yet it has to be admitted that Elizabeth

Wallfisch's period violin does not produce such a beautiful timbre as Arthur Grumiaux's.

Grumiaux has a glorious tone, and on his bow Corelli's beautiful slow movements are phrased simply and with an appealingly warm lyricism. At times he gives the impression of echoing a phrase to striking effect. Moreover, he and Riccardo Castagnone are eminently well recorded – although the violin balance is close. But Grumiaux has no cello continuo; at times he plays in a more nineteenth-century fashion than we are accustomed to nowadays, and his vibrato is distinctly apparent. While it is difficult to resist playing of such tonal beauty and warmth, there just a hint of blandness which slightly diminishes the appeal of this reissue. The transfer of the mid 1970s recording is immaculate.

Trio Sonatas, Op. 5/1–6.

(B) *** HM HMX 290853.55 (3) [(M) id.]. Banchieri, Christensen, Contini, Gohl – TARTINI: *Concerti grossi*; VIVALDI: *Chamber Sonatas*. ***

Chiara Banchieri and her colleagues present the first six sonatas with them with vitality, warmth and finesse. Their period-instrument manners are not excessive, and the acoustic resonance adds to the body of the sound without impairing clarity. In this Harmonia Mundi bargain-priced Trio presentation, Corelli's music is aptly linked with Sonatas of Vivaldi and – rather less obviously – with Concertos of Tartini.

Trio Sonatas, Op. 5/1, 3, 6, 11 & 12 (La Folia).

*** Accent ACC 48433D. S. & W. Kuijken, Kohnen.

When authenticity of spirit goes hand in hand with fine musical feeling and accomplishment, the results can be impressive, as they undoubtedy are here, drawing one into the sensibility of the period. This is a thoroughly recommendable selection which deserves to reach a wider audience than early-music specialists; the recording is natural and the musicianship refined and totally at the service of Corelli.

CORNELIUS, Peter (1824–74)

Der alte Soldat, Op. 12/1; 3 Chorgesänge, Op. 11; Die Könige, Op. 8/3; Leibe: Ein Zyklus von 3 Chorliedern, Op. 18; 3 Psalmlieder, Op. 13; So weich und warm; Requiem; Trauerchöre, Op. 9; Trost in Tränen, Op. 14; Die Vätergruft, Op. 19.

(N) *** Hyp. CDA 67206. Polyphony, Layton.

Building on the German tradition of amateur choral societies, Peter Cornelius developed the genre of unaccompanied choral pieces like these, starting with the one which became by far the most famous, *Die Könige* ('The Three Kings'). Cornelius, a lifelong devotee of German verse, responded to the words with keen sensitivity, heightening the poems he set to make the genre an equivalent to Lieder, spanning a wide range of moods and atmosphere with beautifully crafted choral effects. Stephen Layton's brilliant group, Polyphony, prove ideal as interpreters, refined on detail, polished in ensemble while giving thrust and intensity to each item. Beautifully balanced and atmospheric recording to match.

6 Weihnachtslieder, Op. 8: Christbaum; Die Hirten; Die Könige; Simeon; Christus der Kinderfreud; Christkind.

⚫ *** EMI CDC5 56204-2. Bär, Deutsch (with Recital: *Christmas Lieder* *** ⚫).

Peter Cornelius was born on Christmas Eve, so perhaps it is not surprising that his set of *Weihnachtslieder* so readily captures the seasonal mood. Cornelius's settings have a winningly tender simplicity, and the final *Christkind* turns the mood into light-hearted happiness. Olaf Bär sings with a natural beauty of line and phrase and much affection, and his accompanist, Helmut Deutsch, is wonderfully supportive. However, as we go to press this has been deleted.

CORNYSH, William (c. 1468–1523)

Adieu, adieu my heartes lust; Adieu, courage; Ah Robin; Ave Maria, mater Dei; Gaude, virgo, mater Christi; Magnificat; Salve regina; Stabat Mater; Woefully arrayed.

⚫ *** Gimell CDGIM 914. Tallis Scholars, Phillips.

Cornysh's music is quite unlike much other polyphony of the time and is florid, wild, complex and, at times, grave. The Tallis Scholars give a magnificent, totally committed account of these glorious pieces – as usual their attack, ensemble and true intonation and blend are remarkable. Excellent recording.

Ave Maria mater Dei; Gaudi virgo mater Christi (motets); Magnificat; Salve Regina.

*** ASV CDGAU 164. Cardinall's Musick, Carwood – TURGES: *Magnificat*; PRENTES: *Magnificat*. ***

In his survey of early Tudor polyphony, Andrew Carwood, with his keenly responsive group, Cardinall's Musick, here presents all four of Cornysh's surviving liturgical works, including a fine *Magnificat* and a radiant *Salve Regina*, alongside even more elaborate *Magnificats* by two composers far less well-known but just as inspired. Complex and beautiful, the *Magnificat* of Turges is the most expansive of all, while Prentes's *Magnificat*, closely following Cornysh's, even outshines that model both in scale and sublimity.

CORRETTE, Michel (1709–95)

6 Organ Concertos, Op. 26.

(B) *** HM (ADD) HMA 190 5148. Saorgin (organ of L'Eglise de l'Escarène, Nice), Bar. Ens., Bezzina.

These lively and amiable Concertos are here given admirably spirited and buoyant performances, splendidly recorded using period instruments. The orchestral detail is well observed and René Saorgin plays vividly on an attractive organ. Michel Corrette's invention has genuine spontaneity and this makes an enjoyable collection to dip into, though not to play all at one go.

Sonatas: for Bassoon & Continuo: in F & G (Les Délices de la solitude), Op. 20/1 & 5; for Flute & Continuo: in E min.; D min., Op. 13/2 & 4; for Harpsichord & Flute in E min., Op. 15/4; for Oboe & Continuo in D min. (L'Ecole d'Orphée). Suite for Recorder & Continuo in C min. (from Les Pièces, Op. 5). (Harpsichord): Les Amusements du Parnasse: La Furstemberg & Variations; Le Sabotier hollandois & Variations; Premier livre de pièces de clavecin: Suite in D (complete); Suite No. 3 (Les Etoiles): Rondeau, Op. 12 (both from Op. 12).

*** Mer. CDE 84325. Carroll, Rowland, Civil.

The rather agreeable *Oboe Sonata* comes from *L'Ecole d'Orphée*, a violin tutor, and the Op. 5 *Pièces*, from which the *Suite for Recorder and Continuo* is taken, were primarily designated for the musette (an aristocratic set of bagpipes). However, the composer suggested a whole range of alternatives. The versatile and expert Paul Carroll has mastered all the baroque instruments featured in these works and plays each of them with spirit and character. But it is perhaps his harpsichord music for which Corrette is best remembered – and justly so. The *D major Suite* is strikingly inventive. David Rowland plays them on excellent modern copies of two different period instruments, and he is beautifully recorded. The instrumental works, too, are naturally balanced. An entertaining 73 minutes – but not necessarily to be taken all at once.

COUPERIN, Armand-Louis
(1725–1789)

Pièces de clavecin excerpts: L'Affligée; Allemande; L'Arlequine ou la Adam; La Blanchet; La de Boisgelou; La du Breüil; La Chéron; Courante la de Croissy; L'Enjouée; La Foucquet; Gavottes 1 & 2; La Grégoire; L'Intrépide; Menuets 1 & 2; La Turpin; La Seimillante ou la Joly; Les Tendres Sentimens; La Victoire.

**(*) CPO 999 312-2. Hoeren (harpsichord).

Armand-Louis Couperin was distantly related to both François and Louis. His *Pièces de clavecin* were published in 1751 in two books, and here we are offered a good selection of 19 pieces and some, such as the *Allemande* and *La Grégoire* show a debt to Rameau but others such as *L'Affligée* and *La Chéron* are more forward-looking. Harald Hoeren, a pupil of Kenneth Gilbert and Gustav Leonhart, plays an instrument by Klaus Ahrend based on Flemish models of the 1750s. He is a persuasive artist, though he is not helped by the rather close recording balance. Satisfactory results can be obtained by a low-level setting of the volume control.

Pièces de clavecin: L'Affligée; La du Breüil; Les Tendres Sentimens.

**(*) BIS CD 982. Hirosawa (harpsichord) – FRANCOIS COUPERIN; LOUIS COUPERIN: *Pièces de clavecin.* **(*)

Another thunderous harpsichord so closely balanced that immediate action is called for to reduce the level setting. No quarrels however with Ms Hirosawa's playing, which has great expressive feeling. Her account of *L'Affligée* has greater poignancy than Harald Hoeren's and if the volume is turned down a satisfactory result can be secured.

COUPERIN, François (1668–1733)

Les Apothéoses: L'Apothéose composé à la mémoire immortelle de l'incomparable M. de Lully; La Parnasse ou l'Apothéose de Corelli.

(N) (M) *** Astrée ES 9947. Hespèrion XX, Savall.

Couperin's two great linked instrumental works, both called *apothéoses*, between them ardently espouse the virtues of the conflicting French and Italian influences on early eighteenth-century music. The composers Lully and Corelli are thus united in the Elysian fields, with the French and Italian muses playing each other's music. It is a delightful conception. Each work has a sequence of stylized classical vignettes. *L'Apothèose de Lully* is programmatic and evokes Apollo and Mercury; *L'Apothéose de Corelli* is an eloquent Trio sonata, but also with titled movements, grave, expressive and lively by turns. The performances by Savall and Hespèrion XX have splendid life, grace and refinement of feeling. The gossamer delicacy of *Plaint des mêmes* in the former is matched by the exquisite playing in the fourth section, *Corelli . . . s'endorf . . .* in the latter. Each movement is introduced briefly in French by Bernard Hervé (who never outstays his welcome), and the documentation includes translations. This rewarding music could hardly be more attractively presented, and the recording is excellent.

Concerts royaux Nos. 1 in G; 2 in D; 3 in A; 4 in E min.

(B) *** Sony (ADD) SBK 60370. Kuijken Ens.
*** ASV CDGAU 101. Trio Sonnerie.

The *Concerts royaux* can be performed in a variety of forms. Kuijken and his distinguished colleagues (Franz Brüggen, flute, Jürg Schaeftlein, oboe, Milan Turkovic, bassoon, with continuo) feature a variety of wind-colouring to pleasing effect, and the 1971 recording is well balanced if forward. This reissue also has the advantage of economy.

On the alternative ASV Gaudeamus disc the Trio Sonnerie give them in the most economical fashion (violin, viola da gamba and harpsichord) and the contribution of all three musicians is unfailingly imaginative. Excellent recording.

Les Goûts réunis: Nouveaux concerts Nos. 5–7; 9; 10–11; 12; 14.

(B) **(*) Sony (ADD) SB2K 60714 (2). Kuijken Ens.

Les Goûts réunis: Nouveaux concerts: Nos. 5–14. .

(B) **(*) DG Double (ADD) 459 484-2 (2). Brandis, Aurèle Nicolet, Sax, Holliger, Ulsamer, Strehl, Jaccottet.

Couperin followed his four initial *Concerts royaux* of 1722 with eight more, published two years later. He acknowledged that the music combined the French and Italian styles with his title *Les Goûts réunis*. The Kuijken Ensemble use period instruments and one only has to sample the opening *Prélude* (*gracieusement*) of the Fifth concert, the central *Sarabande* (*grave*), or the closing *Musette* (*dans le goût de Carillon*) to find how attractive is their sound world. The *Ninth Concert*

has a linking programme and its eight dance movements contrast the many facets of love. *Concert* No.12 is effectively scored for a pair of viols, but in general Couperin left the instrumentation up to the performers, and Kuijken has researched and followed Couperin's own practice. The playing too is idiomatic and pleasing and the balance is excellent. This is most rewarding but why were Nos. 8 and 13 omitted – there is plenty of room on the second disc, which only plays for 50 minutes.

The DG set, using modern instruments, has lively musicality to commend it and the recording is clearly focused and natural; indeed, it sounds highly realistic in its latest bargain format. If there are some reservations, it is because these artists do not seek to find the music's peculiarly French flavour. *Notes inégales* are not always observed and there are inconsistencies in matters of ornamentation. But the non-specialist listener will find that there is much to delight the ear, for the playing itself is sensitive and alert.

KEYBOARD MUSIC

L'Art de toucher le clavecin, Harpsichord Suites, Book 2, Ordre 8; Book 3, Ordre 14; Book 4: Ordre 21.

(N) (B) *** Double Decca (ADD) 468 555-2 (2). Malcolm (harpsichord) – RAMEAU: *Pièces de clavecin.* **(*)

With the complete Harmonia Mundi sets by Rousset and Kenneth Gilbert currently withdrawn, Malcolm's excellent anthology from 1969 is left to serve as a satisfactory introduction to Couperin's art. Malcolm is at his very finest and plays with great elegance and flair. The balance is somewhat close, but the harpsichord image is clear and vivid. However, he is rather less stylistically secure in the coupled music of Rameau.

Harpsichord Suites, Book 1, Ordre 1; Concerts royaux Nos. 1–2.

(B) *** Naxos 8.550961. Cummings (harpsichord).

Harpsichord Suites, Book 3: Ordre 13.

**(*) BIS CD 982. Hirosawa (harpsichord) – ARMAND-LOUIS COUPERIN; LOUIS COUPERIN: *Pièces de clavecin.* **(*)

Laurence Cummings has already won golden opinions from us for his admirable and idiomatic earlier recital of Louis Couperin (see below), and his account of the *Premier ordre* of François is hardly less fine. Cummings plays a modern instrument by Michael Johnson modelled on a Taskin, and he produces pleasing and musical results. Both artistically and in terms of recorded sound, this is a valuable addition to the catalogue.

Asami Hirosawa couples the marvellous *Treizième ordre* with two of Louis Couperin's *Suites* and three pieces by Armand-Louis. She is thoroughly inside the French style and shows a natural feeling for its rhythmic flexibility. A very close microphone balance produces pretty deafening results but a drastic reduction of volume makes for more satisfactory listening.

(i) *Messe à l'usage ordinaire des paroisses* (with plainsong chosen by Emmanuel Mandrin); (ii) *Messe propre pour les couvents de religieux et religieuses* (with *Ordinaire de la messe du 6 ton* de Henry D'Mont (1610–84).

(N) *** Erato (i) 0630 17581-2; (ii) 3984 25507-2 (available separately). Alain (Cliqiot organ of Saint-Pierre de Poitiers Cathedral); (i) Chanteurs de la Chapelle de Versailles, Mandrin; (ii) Compagnie Musicale, Catalane, Cabré.

Messe à l'usage ordinaire des paroisses; Messe propre pour les couvents de religieux et religieuses (reconstructed by Jean Saint-Arromen to include Plainchant and Motets: *Domine salvum fac Regem* (2 versions); *Quid retribuam tibi dominum*).

(M) *** Virgin Veritas/EMI VED5 61298-2 (2). Brosse (organ of Saint-Bertrand, Saint-Bertrand de Comminges), with Poulenard, Des Longchamps, Le Roux, Val-de-Grâce Gregorian Ch.

(i) *Messe à l'usage ordinaire des paroisses;* (ii) *Messe propre pour les couvents de religieuses* (reconstructed by Edward Higginbottom to include plainchant, taken from Nivers's *Graduale romanaomonasticum* of 1658).

(B) *** Double Decca (ADD) 455 026-2. Hurford (organ of St-Pierre, Toulouse), with (i) Gentlemen of Ch. of New College, Oxford; (ii) Ladies of Oxford Chamber Ch.; Higginbottom.

Marie-Claire Alain is here at her very finest, playing the magnificently characterful historic organ at Poitiers Cathedral. Indeed at times the plangent mixtures verge on the bizarre. In contrast the chosen plainsong is unelaborate, and sung with simple eloquence, echoing back into the cathedral. Men's voices are used in the *Mass for the Parishes*, women's voices for the *Mass for the Convents*. But the success of these recordings is Alain's triumph, combined with superb engineering.

Whether in the *Dialogue sur les Trompettes et le Chromhorne* (for the *Kyrie eleison*) and the *Dialogue sur les grands les grands jeux* (of the *Gloria*) in the *Mass for the Parishes*, or the *Fugue sur le trompette* (in the *Christe eleison*) or the *Plain-jeu* (of the *Gloria*) of the *Mass for the Convents*, the Poitiers organ produces a wonderful panoply of sound and the gentler registration is hardly less colourful. Yet the underlying intensity of Alain's playing ensures that the celebratory meaning of this remarkable music communicates equally compellingly.

Jean-Patrice Brosse also has the full measure of this music and the Saint-Bertrand organ brings the necessary plangent French timbre. In the *Mass for Parishes* the plainsong interpolations are mostly brief and always simple, although the *Credo* is an obvious exception. Brosse faithfully follows the composer's indicated registrations, and there are many piquant sounds throughout both works, using solo stops or combinations. In reconstructing his conjectural performances, Jean Saint-Arromen has added short motets within the Elévation for the *Benedictus* and *Agnus Dei*, and these are sung effectively enough by Jacques des Longchamps (alto) and François Le Roux (baritone); which emphasizes the dedicated spiritual nature of Couperin's overall conception. These beautifully recorded performances give a splendid illusion of being in the cathedral.

Peter Hurford plays the two organ Masses on the restored organ, designed by Robert Delaunay in 1683, of Saint-Pierre des Chartreux. The Decca engineers have made an excellent job of marrying the acoustic with that of the Chapel of New College, Oxford, and they capture the atmosphere of both to splendid effect. Edward Higginbottom's reconstruction is less elaborate that that of Jean Saint-Arromen, using plainchant economically to follow on simply after the organ dialogues. Male voices of the New College, Oxford, Choir are used in the *Messe des paroisses*, while in the *Messe des couvents* women's voices are an obvious choice. They sing very beautifully and the effect is memorable, particularly when Hurford is such an obvious master of Couperin's organ writing, which is again superbly recorded. It cannot be denied that the French voices used in the Erato and Virgin alternative recordings do bring an added feeling of vocal authenticity. But both versions have their own merits.

VOCAL MUSIC

Leçons de ténèbres pour Mercredi Saint.

(B) *** HM (ADD) HMA 195 1210. Deller, Todd, Perulli, Chapuis.
*(*) HM HMC 901133. Jacobs, Darras, Concerto Vovâle, Jacobs – PURCELL: *Divine hymn; Evening hymn.* CLARKE: *Blest be those sweet regions.* **(*)

Leçons de ténèbres pour le Mercredi Saint Nos.1–3; Quatre versets du motet.

*** Erato/Warner 0630 17067-2. Sophie Daneman, Patricia Petibon, Les Arts Florissants, William Christie.

Leçons de ténèbres pour le Mercredi Saint; Magnificat; Motets: Laetentur coeli; Victoria! Christo resurgenti.

** O-L 466 776-2. Les Talens Lyriques, Rousset.

Couperin's first two *Leçons de ténèbres pour le Mercredi Saint* were written for solo soprano, the third for two voices. One would have thought that the Oiseau-Lyre performances would have been ideal, with two excellent soloists and the accompaniments directed by Christophe Rousset. Sandrine Piau and Véronique Gens take turns in the first two *Leçons* and match their voices convincingly in the third, and later in the *Magnificat* and motets. Yet the result is disappointingly cool and chaste and curiously unmoving. The most effective piece here is the fervent closing Easter motet, *Victoria! Christo resurgenti*, where the *Alléluias* have real emotional resonance.

However, this newcomer with Sophie Daneman, Patricia Petibon and Les Arts Florissants must probably rank as the best. They are among the most intense and inward-looking of Couperin's works and are heard to striking effect in these intimate and poignant performances. The first two *Leçons* are divided between the two sopranos, who join together for the last. As the *Trois leçons de ténèbres* take less than forty minutes, the *Quatre versets du motet* (eight minutes) make an ungenerous fill-up. However, these are exquisite performances and are beautifully recorded.

Neither Jacobs's nor Deller's versions are authentic, since this music, written for a convent, did not envisage performances by male voices. In every other respect, however,

Deller's account has a wonderful authenticity of feeling, and a blend of scholarship and artistry that gives it a special claim on the attention of collectors.

On the other hand René Jacobs's singing seems emotionally overloaded and over-dramatized. Although his phrasing and intonation cannot be faulted, the result is curiously unmoving. He is joined in the *Third Lesson* by Vincent Darras. The other pieces on the disc are much more successful. Purcell's *Divine* and *Evening* hymns (the latter doubtfully attributed) are quite eloquently sung, and a remarkably fine *Hymn* from Jeremiah Clarke (of *Trumpet voluntary* fame) is most successful of all.

Messe propre pour les couvents.

(B) *** Arte Nova 74321 65413-2. Ens. Canticum, Erkens; Deutsch (Koenig organ, St Avold, France) – MARD: *Te Deum.* ***

Couperin's two organ masses, one for the parishes and the other for the monastery chapels, are both interspersed with chant. Helmut Deutsch uses the Koenig organ at the former St Nabor Abbey in St Avold, France, modelled on a 1776 instrument by Mercadier de Belesta. Very impressive and vivid recorded sound, and fine playing. Arte Nova give details of the registration of the organ but are not wholly scrupulous elsewhere. But this remains a genuine bargain!

Motets: *Audite omnes et expanescite; Pour le jour de Pâques. 3 Leçons de ténèbres.*

(M) ** Erato (ADD) 4509 97409-2. Sautereau, Collard, Ens., Laurence Boulay – CHARPENTIER: *Le Reniement de Saint Pierre.* **(*)

Both Nadine Sautereau and Janine Collard show themselves to be thoroughly at home in this idiom, and the instrumental ensemble under Laurence Boulay is admirably discreet. In the first of the *Leçons de ténèbres* Mme Sautereau sings occasionally on the flat side of the note, but for the most part both the singing and playing give pleasure.

Motets: *Domine salvum fac regem; Jacunda vox ecclesiae; Laetentur coeli; Lauda Sion salvatorem; Magnificat; O misterium ineffabile; Regina coeli; Tantum ergo sacramentum; Venite exultemus Domine; Victoria! Christo resurgenti.*

(B) *** HM (ADD) HMA 1901150. Feldman, Poulenard, Reinhart, Linden, Moroney.

The motets on this record cover a wider spectrum of feeling and range of expressive devices than might at first be imagined. The performances are eminently acceptable, with some particularly good singing from Jill Feldman; the recording is made in a spacious and warm acoustic.

COUPERIN, Louis (c. 1626–61)

Harpsichord suites: in A min.; in C; in D; in F (including Le Tombeau de M. de Blancrocher).

(B) *** Naxos 8.550922. Cummings (harpsichord).

Pièces de clavecin: Suites in A min. & C.

**(*) BIS CD 982. Hirosawa (harpsichord) – ARMAND-LOUIS COUPERIN; FRANCOIS COUPERIN: *Pièces de clavecin.* **(*)

Laurence Cummings plays a modern copy of a Ruckers, which is very well recorded by Naxos. His selection is generous and he arranges his own groupings. His decoration is convincing and he plays with much spontaneity and flair. The CD offers some 75 minutes of music and is one of Naxos's best bargains.

Asami Hirosawa couples two of Louis Couperin's suites with pieces by Armand-Louis and Couperin-le-grand. She is an impressive advocate, admirably flexible in such pieces as the *Prélude à l'imitation de Mr. Froberger*. We occasionally felt the need for greater variety of colour, though she is not helped by a very close microphone balance.

COUPERIN, Marc Roger Normand (1663–1734)

Livre de tablature de clavecin (c. 1695): complete.

*** Hyp. CDA 67164. Moroney (harpsichord).

Marc Roger Normand's book contains fifty-seven pieces – many attributed to other composers including Chambonnières, Le Bègue and Lully. His choice is unerringly perceptive. Virtually all these miniatures are very personable, especially those by Paul de la Pierre and members of his family. Normand was a first cousin of François Couperin and was clearly a first-rate. Apart from his own works he includes an extended set of variants (twenty-seven couplets) on the famous *Folies d'Espagnes*. Moroney is a persuasive advocate. He plays with style and spontaneity and consistently entertains the listener. He uses a splendid Italian virginal dating from the seventeenth century, which is beautifully recorded and this collection can be very highly recommended.

COWARD, Noël (1899–1973)

After the Ball: *I knew that you would be my love. Bitter Sweet: I'll see you again; Zigeuner. Conversation Piece: I'll follow my secret heart; Never more; Melanie's aria* (sung in French); *Charming. Operette: Dearest love; Where are the songs we sung? Countess Mitzi. Pacific 1860: Bright was the day; This is a changing world.*

(B) *** Belart (ADD) 450 014-2. Sutherland, Coward, soloists, Ch. & O, Bonynge.

Sutherland does not always get right inside the characters Coward created (she tries very hard with Countess Mitzi). But all this is swept aside in the sheer pleasure of hearing such a wonderful voice sing such delightful music. Sutherland's tonal lustre and sense of line in *I'll see you again* are incomparable, as are her display of fireworks in *Zigeuner*, and her gentle delicacy in *I knew that you would be my love*, with its ravishing final cadence. Noël Coward's own vocal contributions are quite small but they magically create atmosphere, and Richard Bonynge's affectionate and stylish conducting is a model.

COWELL, Henry (1897–1965)

Hymn & Fuguing Tune No. 10 for Oboe & Strings.

*** Argo (ADD) 417 818-2. Nicklin, ASMF, Marriner –
   BARBER: *Adagio;* COPLAND: *Quiet City;* CRESTON:
   Rumor; IVES: *Symphony No. 3.* ***

This likeable *Hymn and Fuguing Tune,* by a composer otherwise little known, is well worth having and is expertly played
and recorded here. The digital remastering has slightly clarified an already excellent recording.

COWEN, Frederick (1852–1935)

*Symphony No. 3 in C min. (Scandinavian); The Butterfly's
Ball: Concert Overture; Indian Rhapsody.*

** Marco 8.220308. Slovak State PO (Kosice), Leaper.

The *Symphony No. 3* (1880) shows (to borrow Hanslick's
judgement) 'good schooling, a lively sense of tone painting
and much skill in orchestration, if not striking originality'.
But what Cowen lacks in individuality he makes up for in
natural musicianship and charm. His best-known work is
the *Concert Overture, The Butterfly's Ball* (1901), which is
scored with Mendelssohnian delicacy and skill. The *Indian
Rhapsody* (1903) with its naïve orientalisms carries a good
deal less conviction. The performances are eminently lively.
The recording is pleasingly reverberant but somewhat
lacking in body.

CRESTON, Paul (born 1906)

A Rumor.

*** Argo (ADD) 417 818-2. ASMF, Marriner – BARBER:
   Adagio; COPLAND: *Quiet City;* COWELL: *Hymn;* IVES:
   Symphony No. 3. ***

A Rumor is a witty and engaging piece and is played here
with plenty of character by the Academy under Sir Neville
Marriner. It completes a thoroughly rewarding and approachable disc of twentieth-century American music that
deserves the widest currency. The sound is first class.

*Symphonies Nos. 1, Op. 20; 2, Op. 35; 3 (Three Mysteries),
Op. 48.*

(B) *** Naxos 8.559034. Ukraine National SO, Kuchar.

Paul Creston was among the most approachable of American
symphonists. The *First,* is exuberantly colourful and strongly
rhythmic with clean-cut themes. The titles of the four compact movements – *With Majesty, With Humour, With Serenity* and *With Gaiety* – reflect the openness of the emotions.
No. 2 is much darker, with each of its two substantial
movements, moving from darkness towards a lightened
mood. No. 3 outlines the life of Christ with a peaceful
opening, almost pastoral, representing the Nativity and
leading to a joyful allegro. The second movement, representing the Crucifixion, is a heartfelt lament, avoiding
bitterness and anger, before the Resurrection finale, where
Creston is at his most specifically American, almost Cop-

land-like, with jagged syncopations leading on to a triumphant close. The Ukraine Orchestra, very well rehearsed,
plays with warmth and an idiomatic flair surprising from a
non-American band, and is very well recorded.

Symphony No. 2, Op. 35.

*** Chan. 9390. Detroit SO, Järvi – IVES: *Symphony
   No. 2.* ***

*Symphony No. 2, Op. 35; Corinthians XIII, Op. 82; Walt
Whitman, Op. 53.*

*** Koch 37036-2 or KI 7036. Krakow PO, Amos.

Järvi's well-recorded and excellently performed Chandos
version of No. 2 makes a viable alternative choice and can
be if the Ives coupling is preferred.

   The *Second Symphony* is also played with real enthusiasm
and affection by these Polish forces and is very well recorded,
even though the sound could do with greater transparency
in the upper range. The coupling too is of great interest.

*Symphony No. 3 (Three Mysteries), Op. 48; Invocation &
Dance; Out of the Cradle; Partita for Flute, Violin &
Strings.*

*** Delos DEL 3114. Seattle SO, Schwarz.

Gerard Schwarz gives a fervent and committed account of
No. 3, drawing excellent playing from his Seattle orchestra.
The exhilarating *Invocation and Dance,* the *Partita,* which is
somewhat more austere, and the less successful *Out of the
Cradle,* benefit not only from Schwarz's committed advocacy
but also from superb engineering. The sound is in the
demonstration class.

String Quartet, Op. 8.

(***) Testament mono SBT 1053. Hollywood Qt – DEBUSSY:
   Danse sacrée etc. RAVEL: *Introduction & Allegro;*
   TURINA: *La oración del torero;* VILLA-LOBOS: *Quartet
   No. 6.* (***)

The *String Quartet,* Op. 8, is a pleasing, well-fashioned piece,
slightly Gallic in feeling. The *Adagio* unfolds with eloquence.
It could not be better served than it is by the Hollywood
Quartet, recorded in 1953: the playing is stunning, and the
recording, too, is very good for its period, even if the acoustic
is on the dry side.

CRUSELL, Bernhard (1775–1838)

*Clarinet Concertos Nos. 1 in E flat, Op. 1; 2 in F min.,
Op. 5; 3 in E flat, Op. 11.*

⊕ *** ASV CDDCA 784. Johnson, RPO/ECO, Herbig; Groves;
   or Schwarz.

(N) *** Ondine ODE 965-2. Kriiku, Finnish RSO, Oramo.

(B) *** Virgin VBD5 61585-2 (2). Pay, OAE – WEBER: *Clarinet
   Concertos.* ***

*** Hyp. CDA 66708. King, LSO, Francis.

Crusell, born in Finland but working in Stockholm most of
his career, was himself a clarinettist and these delightful
Concertos demonstrate his complete understanding of the
instrument. There are echoes of Mozart, Weber and Rossini

in the music, with a hint of Beethoven. No one brings out the fun in the writing quite as infectiously as Emma Johnson, and this generous recoupling (74 minutes) bringing all three Concertos together is a delight. With well-structured first movements, sensuous slow movements and exuberant finales, Johnson establishes her disc as a first choice above all others.

With full, bright, immediate sound, the Finnish clarinettist, Kari Kriiku, gives dazzling performances of these three delightful clarinet concertos. He is even more daring than his rivals on disc, regularly choosing speeds that stretch virtuosity to the limit, particularly in the finales. By choosing exceptionally fast speeds in Nos. 1 and 2 Kriiku brings out an extra scherzando quality, sharp and spiky, with crisply dotted rhythms. Partly as a result of the immediacy of the recording Kriiku's pianissimos are not as extreme as they might be, yet in flair and panache he is second to none, superbly supported by the purposeful playing of the Finnish National Radio Orchestra under Sakari Oramo.

Pay uses a reproduction of a nine-key clarinet as made around 1810 by Heinrich Grenser; Crusell himself is known to have used a ten-key Grenser clarinet. The slight edginess of the sound goes well with Pay's preference for fastish – often very fast – speeds which yet never get in the way of his imaginative rhythmic pointing. The results in outer movements are exhilarating. They sparkle with wit, while slow movements have a flowing songfulness that is comparably persuasive. The Virgin recording, made at Abbey Road studio, is clear, well balanced and atmospheric.

Thea King with her beautiful, liquid tone also makes an outstanding soloist. Her approach is often more serious, especially in the *Second Concerto*, where she brings out the Beethovenian character of the first movement, while the *Andante pastorale* slow movement is played with the widest range of tone-colour. Throughout, she is well accompanied by Alun Francis; and the resonant Hyperion recording, with the soloist balanced forward, emphasizes the feeling of added gravitas.

Clarinet Concerto No. 1 in E flat, Op. 1.

*** ASV CDDCA 763. Johnson, RPO, Herbig – KOZELUCH; KROMMER: *Concertos.* ***

Even though many collectors may prefer the CD containing all three of the Crusell Concertos, Emma Johnson's version of the *First Clarinet Concerto* makes a highly attractive compilation with lesser-known but enticing works by Kozeluch and Krommer.

Clarinet Concerto No. 2 in F min., Op. 5.

*** ASV CDDCA 559. Johnson, ECO, Groves – BAERMANN: *Adagio;* ROSSINI: *Introduction, Theme & Variations;* WEBER: *Concertino.* ***

Crusell's *Second Clarinet Concerto* made Emma Johnson a star, and in return she put Crusell's engagingly lightweight piece firmly on the map. Her delectably spontaneous performance is now caught on the wing and this recording sounds very like a live occasion.

Concertino for Bassoon & Orchestra in B flat; Introduction et air suédois for Clarinet & Orchestra, Op. 12; Sinfonia concertante for Clarinet, Horn, Bassoon & Orchestra, Op. 3.

*** BIS BIS CD 495. Hara, Korsimaa-Hursti, Lanski-Otto, Tapiola Sinf., Vänskä.

The most substantial piece here is the *Sinfonia concertante for Clarinet, Horn, Bassoon and Orchestra*. The finale is a set of variations on a chorus from Cherubini's opera, *Les Deux Journées*. The much later *Concertino for Bassoon and Orchestra* is an altogether delightful piece, which quotes at one point from Boïeldieu. It is played with appropriate freshness and virtuosity by László Hara. The *Introduction et air suédois for Clarinet and Orchestra* is nicely done by Anna-Maija Korsimaa-Hursti. The Tapiola Sinfonietta, the orchestra of Esspoo, play with enthusiasm and spirit for Osmo Vänskä, and the BIS recording has lightness, presence and body.

Clarinet Quartets Nos. 1 in E flat, Op. 2; 2 in C min., Op. 4; 3 in D, Op. 7.

(B) *** Hyp. Helios CDH 55031. King, Allegri Qt (members).

These are captivatingly sunny works, given superb performances, vivacious and warmly sympathetic, Thea King's tone is positively luscious and the sound is generally excellent. The CD transfer is highly successful and its migration to the bargain-price Helios label makes it even more attractive.

Divertimento in C, Op. 9.

(B) **(*) Hyp. Helios CDH 55015. Sarah Francis, Allegri Qt – KREUTZER: *Grand Quintet;* REICHA: *Quintet.* **(*)

Crusell's *Divertimento* has charm and grace, and the performance here is nicely played and recorded; it is now offered at bargain-price.

Introduction & Variations on a Swedish Air (for clarinet and orchestra), Op. 12.

(B) *** Hyp. Dyad CDD 22017 (2). King, LSO, Francis (with Concert ***).

The Weberian Crusell *Variations* show Thea King's bravura at its most sparkling. It is far from being an empty piece; its twists and turns are consistently inventive. This is part of an excellent two-disc set including other attractive concertante works by Max Bruch, Mendelssohn, Spohr and other less familiar names.

CUI, César (1835–1918)

(i) Suite concertante (for violin & orchestra), Op. 25. Suite miniature No. 1, Op. 20; Suite No. 3 (In modo populari), Op. 43.

**(*) Marco 8.220308. (i) Nishizaki; Hong Kong PO, Schermerhorn.

These pieces have a faded period charm that is very appealing (try the *Petite marche* and the equally likeable *Impromptu à la Schumann* from the *Suite miniature*) and are very well played by the Hong Kong Philharmonic. Takako Nishizaki is the expert soloist in the *Suite concertante*. An interesting issue that fills a gap in the repertoire, and very decently recorded too.

CURZON, Frederick (1899–1973)

The Boulevardier; Bravada (Paso doble); Capricante (Spanish Caprice); Cascade (Waltz); Dance of an Ostracised Imp; Galavant; In Malaga (Spanish Suite); Punchinello: Miniature Overture; Pasquinade; La Peineta; Robin Hood Suite; (i) Saltarello for Piano & Orchestra; Simionetta (Serenade).

*** Marco 8.223425. (i) Cápová; Slovak RSO (Bratislava), Leaper.

The best-known piece here is *Dance of an Ostracised Imp*, a droll little scherzando. But the *Galavant* is hardly less piquant and charming, the delicious *Punchinello* sparkles with miniature vitality, and the *Simonetta* serenade is sleekly beguiling. Curzon liked to write mock Spanishry, and several pieces here have such a Mediterranean influence. Yet their slight elegance and economical scoring come from cooler climes farther north. Both *In Malaga* and the jolly *Robin Hood Suite* are more frequently heard on the (military) bandstand, but their delicate central movements gain much from the more subtle orchestral scoring. The performances throughout are played with the finesse and light touch we expect from this fine Slovak series, so ably and sympathetically conducted by Adrian Leaper. The recording is admirable.

DA CREMA, Giovanni Maria
(died *c.* 1550)

Con lagrime e sospiri (Philippe Verdelot); De vous servir (Claudin de Sermisy); Lasciar il velo (Jacques Arcadelt); O felici occhi mieie (Arcadelt); Pass'e mezo ala bolognesa; Ricercars quinto, sexto, decimoquarto, decimoquinto, duodecimo, tredecimo; Saltarello ditto Bel fior; Saltarello ditto El Giorgio; Saltarello ditto El Maton.

(BB) *** Naxos 8.550778. Wilson (lute) – DALL´AQUILA: *Lute Pieces.* ***

The pieces here are taken from a *First Lute Book* which Da Crema published in 1546. The inclusion of the dance movements alongside reflective pieces like *Con lagrime e sospiri* gives variety to an attractive programme, and the *Pass'e mezo ala bolognesa* is rather catchy. The performances are of the highest order, and Christopher Wilson is recorded most naturally. Well worth exploring, especially at such a modest cost.

DALL'ABACO, Evaristo Felice
(1675–1742)

Concerti a quattro de chiesa, Op. 2/1, 4, 5 & 7; Concerti a più instrumenti, Op. 5/3, 5 & 6; Op. 6/5 & 11.

*** Teldec 3984 22166-2. Concerto Köln.

Dall'Abaco's foreign travels exposed him to both French and Italian influences and he draws on them just as it suits him. We also find him astutely keeping up with public taste and subtly modifying his style over the years. Of the four *Concerti a quattro da chiesa*, taken from his Opus 2 (1712), *No. 5 in G minor* is a particularly fine work, worthy of Corelli. The Op. 5 set of *Concerti a più instruments* (*c.* 1719) brings predominantly French influences, and very appealing they are. Opus 6 (*c.* 1734) is more forward-looking, *galant* in style, with amiable allegros and nicely expressive cantabiles. All in all, this is a most stimulating collection. The Concerto Köln's virtuosity brings a sparkling response, with the group's somewhat abrasive string-timbres infectiously bending to the composer's force of personality. They are splendidly recorded. A real find.

DALLAPICCOLA, Luigi (1904–75)

Tartiniana for Violin & Orchestra.

(M) (***) Sony mono SMK 60725. Posselt, Columbia SO, Bernstein – LOPATNIKOFF: *Concertino;* SHAPERO: *Symphony.* (***)

Dallapiccola's *Tartiniana* was composed at Tanglewood and reworks themes from Tartini's sonatas in a refreshing neo-classical style; the language is neo-classic and diatonic. Good playing from Ruth Posselt and Bernstein's orchestra, and the 1953 mono recording comes up well in this well-transferred and intelligently planned compilation.

VOCAL MUSIC

(i) Canti di Prigionia; (i; ii) 2 Cori di Michelangelo Buonarroti il Giovane; (iii) 5 Fragmenti di Saffi; 2 Liriche di Ancreonte; 6 Carmina Alcani; (ii) Tempus destruendi – Tempus aedificandi.

(N) (BB) *** Warner Apex 8593 89230-2. (i) New L. Chamber Ch., (ii) Jansen, Gwynn; (iii) Moffat; Ens. InterContemporain, Zender.

This excellently sung and atmospherically recorded collection offers a fine survey of Dallapiccola's highly individual vocal writing, from the comparatively direct madrigal style of the early *Michelangelo Cori* (1933), to the unpredictable choral lines and sustained dissonances – gentle and passionate – of *Tempus destruedi – Tempus aedificandi* written nearly forty years latter. The evocatively ear-tweaking *Preghiera* of the *Canti di Prigionia* (1938–41) for chorus, with pianos, harps and percussion, moves inexorably towards its first and subsequent climaxes while the second movement (*Invocazione di Boezio*) surprises by introducing the *Dies irae*, no doubt influenced by the composer's reaction at the time of composition to Mussolini's announcement of Italy's adoption of Fascism.

But it is in the three central song cycles of the early 1940s, with their colourful and often dextrous accompaniments, in which Dallapiccola shows himself as both an original and an expressive communicator. Even if the melodic lines twist about impulsively, and not always logically, the effect is aurally magnetic when they are so confidently and sympathetically sung and accompanied. The one snag is that while texts are provided, there are no translations.

DALL'AQUILA, Marco (c. 1480–1538)

Amy souffrez (Pierre Moulu); La cara cosa; Priambolo; Ricercars Nos. 15, 16, 18, 19, 22, 24, 28, 33, 70 & 101; 3 Ricercar/Fantasias; La Traditora.

(BB) *** Naxos 8.550778. Wilson (lute) – DA CREMA: *Lute Pieces.* ***

Marco dall'Aquila was a much-admired Venetian composer/lutenist in his day. These are relatively simple pieces, rhythmically active but often dolorous; *Amy souffrez* and *La cara cosa* are among the more striking, but the *Ricercars* can be haunting too. They are beautifully played by Christopher Wilson, and the recording is admirably balanced.

DAMASE, Jean-Michel (born 1928)

Quintet for Flute, Harp, Violin, Viola & Cello; Sonata for Flute & Harp; Trio for Flute, Harp & Cello; Variations 'Early Music' for Flute & Harp.

*** ASV CDDCA 898. Noakes, Tingay, Friedman, Atkins, Szucs.

Jean-Michel Damase was a pupil of Alfred Cortot and Henri Büsser, and his chamber music (and in particular the *Trio for Flute, Harp and Cello* and the *Quintet*) has a fluent, cool charm. It is beautifully fashioned, and those coming to it for the first time will find it very attractive, with touches of Poulenc without his harmonic subtlety. It is nicely played and very well recorded.

DANZI, Franz (1763–1826)

Bassoon Concertos Nos. 1–2 in F; 3 in C; 4 in G min.

(N) (BB) *** Naxos 8.554273. Holder, New Brandenburg Philharmonie, Pasquet.

Danzi was himself a cellist and wrote a fine concerto for his own instrument, but he also, perhaps not surprisingly, had a natural affinity for the bassoon, and all four of these tuneful concertos readily exploit the instrument's potential for gentle melancholy and humour. The former is well displayed in the first two movements of the *G minor Concerto*, while the *Polonaise* finale could hardly be more jaunty. The first of the two *F major* works opens amiably (like that of Hummel), has a winning slow movement, but is most famous for the finale with its variations on the Austrian folk song *A Schüsserl und a Reinderl*. The *Second F major Concerto* is perhaps the most familiar, with its delightfully lyrical opening movement and doleful centrepiece which is followed by another infectious *Polonaise*. The *C major Concerto* is somewhat more sober until its finale which brings another felicitous set of variations. Albrecht Holder (who prepared the *C major* work for publication) is a splendidly stylish soloist with a most appealing timbre, and his cadenzas are

nicely judged. He is most sympathetically accompanied by Nicolás Pasquet and his excellent Brandenburg chamber orchestra. The Naxos recording balances the soloist forwardly, but the orchestra is well in the picture and the warm resonance is flattering. A first class CD in every way which will be hard to surpass.

(i; ii) Concertante for Flute & Clarinet in B; Op. 41; (i) Flute Concerto No. 2 in D min., Op. 31; (ii) Fantasia on Mozart's 'La ci darem la mano' for Clarinet & Orchestra.

*** RCA 09026 61976-2. (i) Galway; (ii) Meyer, Württemberg CO, Faerber.

Danzi wrote four flute concertos which suggest a style midway between eighteenth-century classicism and the more romantic manner of Weber. The dramatic minor-key opening of No 2, included here, is remarkably like Mozart's *D minor Piano Concerto*, but James Galway's entry immediately lightens the mood; he also plays the charming *Larghetto* very persuasively, and the finale trips along delightfully. His partnership with Sabine Meyer affords equal felicity in the *Concertante*, with the two soloists carolling together most engagingly. They have plenty of good tunes to share, and in Danzi's *Fantasia* Meyer clearly enjoys all the bravura roulades with which Mozart's famous theme is decorated, after its delectably gentle entry. The accompaniments by Faerber with his Württemberg Chamber Orchestra are stylishly supportive and the recording is both full and well balanced.

Horn Concerto in E.

(BB) *** Teldec 0630 12324-2 [id.]. Baumann, Concerto Amsterdam, Schröder – HAYDN, ROSETTI: *Horn Concertos.* ***

Danzi's *Horn Concerto* is a straightforward affair. Baumann plays the piece sympathetically and is well accompanied. This CD is more attractive now it is in the budget range.

Bassoon Quartets Nos. 1 in C; 2 in D min.; 3 in B flat.

(M) *** CRD 3503. Thompson, Coull Qt.

These three charming *Quartets* have a *galant* innocence and a gentle, lyrical feeling. Danzi seeks primarily to capture the bassoon's doleful, lyrical character; its lighter side is not dismissed but he never becomes too jocular. In short, these are slight but appealing works, and they are presented here with affectionate warmth and spirit, and they are beautifully recorded.

(i) Piano Quintet in F, Op. 53. Wind Quintets, Op. 67/1–3.

*** BIS CD 539. (i) Derwinger; BPO Wind Qt.

Danzi was one of the first composers to cultivate the wind quintet; these diverting pieces, played with much distinction and recorded with great clarity and presence, offer unexpected pleasure. The *Piano Quintet* is insubstantial, but rather delightful all the same.

Wind Quintets, Op. 56/1–3; Wind Sextet in E flat.

(N) (BB) *** Naxos 8.553576. (i) Michael Thompson Wind Quintet.

(i) *Wind Quintets, Op. 67/1–3;* (ii) *Horn Sonata No. 1 in E flat, Op. 28.*

(N) (BB) *** Naxos 8.553570. (i) Michael Thompson Wind Quintet; (ii) Thompson; Fowke.

(i) *Wind Quintets, Op. 68/1–4;* (ii) *Horn Sonata No. 2 in E min., Op. 44.*

(N) (BB) *** Naxos 8.554694. (i) Michael Thompson Wind Quintet; (ii) Thompson; Fowke.

Danzi's three sets of ever-engaging *Wind Quintets* were published in 1821 and 1823–4 respectively). For these elegant recordings the horn soloist, Michael Thompson, has gathered around him a superbly balanced group of London's leading wind players, including Jonathan Snowden (flute), Derek Wickens (oboe), Robert Hill (clarinet) and John Price, a bassoonist with a particularly appealing musical presence. They combine to give polished and beautifully blended performances of this charmingly conversational music, for which Danzi had such a ready penchant. Their melodic invention is innocent, but is as appealing as it is seemingly inexhaustible.

The interflow of the part-writing and the blending of the wind colours has a smiling Bohemian graciousness; yet the jaunty allegros often demand sudden bursts of virtuosity (sometimes hair-raising) from individual players – notably bassoon and horn – which are met here with astonishing aplomb. In short this delightful music could not be more attractively or expertly presented, while the recording is beautifully balanced and natural.

The first disc also includes Danzi's *First Horn Sonata* of 1804, probably modelled on Beethoven's similar work of three years earlier, although the style is more romantic in its writing for the horn. Thompson and Philipe Fowke are admirable partners, the latter making a particularly appealing contribution to the easy-going opening movement, while Thompson has bravura in reserve for the finale. The *Second Horn Sonata* of 1813 is even more lyrically gallant (the piano part especially so), especially in the theme and variations finale.

The *Wind Sextet*, which is the bonus on the second CD, is in the tradition of wind *Harmoniemusik*, which reached its zenith with Mozart's later serenades. Danzi's work is not quite on that level, but is fluently appealing, with a spirited finale which has much in common with Mozart's *Gran partita* for thirteen wind instruments. Again, excellent sound.

Wind Quintets, Op. 56/1–2; Op. 68/1–2.

(N) (M) *** Sup. 11 1264-2. Academia Wind Quintet.

Czech players have a special feeling for the Bohemian light-heartedness of Danzi's writing for wind instruments, and the matched colouring of their instruments plus the characterful horn timbre bring a distinct individuality. The Academia Wind Quintet from the Prague Conservatory is no exception. They offer here two pairs of hand-picked quintets from Opp. 56 and 68 and play them with a rippling facility and endearing insouciance. They are beautifully recorded.

DA PONTE, Lorenzo (1749–1838)

L'ape musicale.

**(*) Nuova Era 6845/6 (2). Scarabelli, Matteuzzi, Dara, Comencini, Teatro la Fenice Ch. & O, Parisi.

This greatest of librettists was no composer, but he was musical enough to devise a pasticcio like *L'ape musicale* ('The musical bee') from the works of others, notably Rossini and Mozart. The first Act – full of Rossinian passages one keeps recognizing – leads up to a complete performance of Tamino's aria, *Dies Bildnis*, sung in German at the end of the Act. Similarly, Act II culminates in an adapted version of the final cabaletta from Rossini's *Cenerentola*. The sound is dry, with the voices slightly distanced. The stage and audience noises hardly detract from the fun of the performance.

D'ASTORGA, Emanuele (c. 1680–1757)

Stabat Mater.

*** Hyp. CDA 67108. Gritton, Bickley, Agnew, Harvey, King's Consort Ch., King's Consort, King – BOCCHERINI: *Stabat Mater.* ***

Emanuele d'Astorga's *Stabat Mater* predates Boccherini's – with which it is coupled – by nearly a century and, unlike that work (and the Pergolesi setting on which it is based), is written like a miniature oratorio with soloists and chorus. The chorus opens and closes the work – the opening with touching melancholy, but the closing *Christe quam sit hinc exire* much more upbeat. In between, the various solos and duets are expressively quite intense, and overall this is a remarkably accomplished and rewarding piece, especially when sung as eloquently as it is here with excellent soloists and a fine choral contribution, all very well recorded.

(c)Dauvergne, Antoine (1713–97)

Concerts de simphonies: Premier Concert in B flat, Op. 3/1; Deuxième Concert in F, Op. 3/2; Quatrième Concert in A, Op. 4/2.

(M) *** Virgin VM5 61542-2. Concerto Köln.

Dauvergne's *Concerts de simphonies*, Opp. 3 and 4, are a real find, full of attractive ideas and catchy rhythms. Each begins with an Overture and ends with a Chaconne. One has only to sample the skipping *Andantino* of Op. 3/2, the engaging *Minuetto grazioso* or the penultimate *Presto* (with its fizzing groups of double triplets and double quadruplets) to confirm that Dauvergne is a composer of individuality. The performances here have both grace and much vigour: the period-instrument playing is polished and aurally pleasing, and often has real bravura. The recording too is first class. Well worth seeking out.

(i) *Les Troqueurs (opéra-bouffon et ballet; complete). Concerts de simphonies in F, Op. 3/2.*

(B) *** HM HMA 1901454. (i) Saint-Palais, Marin-Degor, Rivenq, Salzmann; Cappella Coloniensis.

Clearly influenced by Pergolesi's *La Serva padrona, Les*

Troqueurs ('The Barterers') is a splendid little work in its own right. Two pairs of engaged lovers decide to exchange partners until the temperamental explosions of one of the ladies (Margot) makes her substitute paramour quickly change his mind; all is resolved when the original relationships are resumed. The two pairs of singers are not individually outstanding (indeed their voices are very alike), but their repartee is ever vivacious, and Christie deftly keeps the pot boiling with his excellent and stylish Cappella Coloniensis. At the close of the opéra-comique the orchestra then entertains us with a *Concert of Symphonies*, in essence an elegant little suite, altogether very winning. The recording is excellent and, with full translation included, this is a bargain not to be missed.

DAVYDOV, Karl (1838–89)

Cello Concerto No. 2 in A min., Op. 14.

**(*) Chan. 9622. Ziumbrovsky, I Musici de Montréal, Turovsky – CONUS: *Violin Concerto*; GLAZUNOV: *Piano Concerto No. 2.* **(*)

Davydov (or Davïdov) was one of the greatest cellists of his day – Tchaikovsky described him as 'the king of cellists'. His *A minor Concerto* is rather bland, almost Mendelssohnian, but it is an excellent visiting card for the soloist, Alexander Ziumbrovsky, who plays with a fine and natural musicianship.

DAWSON, William (1899–1990)

Negro Folk Symphony.

*** Chan. 9909. Detroit SO, Järvi –ELLINGTON: *Harlem, The River; Solitude.* ***

William Dawson began life the son of a poor Alabama labourer, yet he worked his way up to become Director of Music at the Tuskegee Institute. His *Negro Folk Symphony* is designed to combine European influences and Negro folk themes. All three movements are chimerical. The music is rhapsodic and has plenty of energy and ideas, but they are inclined to run away with their composer. Järvi, however, is persuasive and has the advantage of excellent orchestral playing and first-class Chandos sound.

DEBUSSY, Claude (1862–1918)

Complete Orchestral Music (as below).

(M) **(*) Chan. 7019 (4). Soloists, Ulster O, Y. P. Tortelier.

La Boîte à joujoux; Children's Corner (orch. Caplet); *Danse (Tarantelle styrienne*, orch. Ravel); *Marche écossaise sur un thème populaire; Petite suite* (orch. Büsser). (Chan. 7017)

(i) *Fantaisie for Piano & Orchestra*; (ii) *Danse sacrée et danse profane for Harp & Strings; L'Isle joyeuse* (orch. Molinari); (iii) *La plus que lente*; (iv) *Première rapsodie for Clarinet & Orchestra*; (v) *Rapsodie for Alto Saxophone*

& Orchestra (orch. Roger-Ducasse); *Sarabande* (orch. Ravel); *Suite bergamasque: Clair de lune* (orch. Caplet). (Chan. 7018; with (i) Queffélec; (ii) Masters; (iii) Bell (cimbalom); (iv) King; (v) McChrystal)

Images; Jeux; Khamma. (Chan. 7016)

La Mer; Nocturnes; Printemps; Prélude à l'après-midi d'un faune. (Chan. 7015)
As can be seen, Chandos have now assembled Debussy's orchestral music (previously coupled with Ravel) in an upper-mid-priced box in recordings which generally represent the state of the art. There are excellent soloists in the concertante works. The subtlety and atmosphere of *La Boîte à joujoux* are captured splendidly, and the concertante works are equally sensitive. Not all the performances are a first choice, but the shorter works come off particularly well. CHAN 7017 and 7018, now available separately, are very desirable indeed.

2 Arabesques (orch. Mouton); (i) *La Cathédrale engloutie* (orch. Stokowski); *La Mer; Petite suite* (orch. Henri Büsser); *Pagodes* (orch. Grainger). *Première rapsodie for Clarinet & Orchestra; Suite bergamasque: Clair de lune* (orch. Caplet).

(M) *** Cala CACD 1001. (i) Campbell; Philh. O, Simon.

Geoffrey Simon's warm, urgent reading of *La Mer*, very well recorded, comes in coupling with six items originally involving piano. Debussy did his own arrangement of the *Clarinet Rhapsody* and admired André Caplet's arrangement of *Clair de lune* as well as Henri Büsser's of the *Petite suite*. Stokowski's freely imagined orchestral version of *La Cathédrale engloutie* is effectively opulent, and the most fascinating instrumentation of all comes in Percy Grainger's transcription of *Pagodes*, with an elaborate percussion section simulating a Balinese gamelan.

(i) *Berceuse héroïque*; (ii; iii) *Danses sacrées et profanes* (for harp and strings); (ii) *Images; Jeux; Marche écossaise; La Mer*; (ii; iv) *Nocturnes*; (ii) *Prélude à l'après-midi d'un faune*; (ii; v) *Première rapsodie for Clarinet & Orchestra.*

❀ (B) *** Ph. Duo (ADD) 438 742-2 (2). Concg. O, (i) Van Beinum; (ii) Haitink; with (iii) Badings; (iv) Women's Ch. of Coll. Mus.; (v) Pieterson.

This Duo must now rank as the finest Debussy collection in the CD catalogue. Although the programme as a whole is directed by Haitink, it is good that his distinguished predecessor, Eduard van Beinum, is remembered by the opening *Berceuse héroïque*, played with great delicacy and a real sense of mystery, with the early (1957) stereo highly effective. For the *Danses sacrées et profanes* Haitink takes over, with elegant playing from the harpist, Vera Badings, who is excellently balanced. Haitink's reading of *Images* is second to none and is beautifully played by the wonderful Dutch orchestra; this applies equally to *Jeux*, while in the *Nocturnes* the choral balance is judged perfectly, and few versions are quite as beguiling and seductive as Haitink's. His *La Mer* is comparable with Karajan's 1964 recording. The hazily sensuous *Prélude à l'après-midi d'un faune* and the undervalued *Clarinet Rhapsody* are also played atmospherically, although the former is more overtly languorous in Karajan's hands. Again, the Philips recording is truthful and natural, with beautiful perspectives and realistic colour, a marvellously refined sound.

Berceuse héroïque; Images; Jeux; Marche écossaise; La Mer; Musiques pour le Roi Lear; Nocturnes; Prélude à l'après-midi d'un faune; Printemps.

(B) *** EMI double forte (ADD) CZS5 72667-2 (2). Fr. R. & TV Ch. & O, Martinon.

Martinon's is a very good *Images*, beautifully played, with the orchestral detail vivid and glowing. *Jeux* is also very fine, with the sound attractively spacious. *La Mer* enjoys the idiomatic advantage of fine French orchestral playing, even if it does not quite match Karajan or Haitink. The *Musiques pour le Roi Lear* is a real rarity; the colourful *Fanfare* remains impressive, and *Le Sommeil de Lear* is highly evocative. The *Nocturnes* are beautifully played, as indeed is *Printemps*, with Martinon penetrating its charm. At bargain price these are competitive recommendations, and the current transfers are warmly atmospheric; even if the upper end of the range is rather brightly lit, there is plenty of depth in the sound.

La Boîte à joujoux; Children's Corner (orch. Caplet); *Danse* (orch. Ravel); (i) *Danses sacrées et profanes.* (ii) *Fantaisie for Piano & Orchestra; La plus que lente; Khamma; Petite suite* (orch. Büsser); (iii) *Première rapsodie for Clarinet & Orchestra.* (iv) *Rapsodie for Saxophone.*

(B) *** EMI double forte (ADD) CZS5 72673-2 (2). Fr. R. & TV O, Martinon; with (i) Jamet; (ii) Ciccolini; (iii) Dangain; (iv) Londe.

Children's Corner and *La Boîte à joujoux* contain much to enchant the ear, as does the tuneful *Petite suite*. The rarity here is *Khamma*. This and the two *Rapsodies* are underrated and, although there are alternative versions of all these pieces, none is more economically priced. The performances are sympathetic and authoritative, and the recordings have been remastered successfully. The sound is full and spacious with an attractive ambient glow.

Children's Corner; Danse (Tarantelle styrienne) (arr. Ravel); *Estampes: La Soirée dans Grenade* (arr. Stokowski). *L'Isle joyeuse; Nocturnes; Préludes: Bruyères; La Fille aux cheveux de lin.*

(M) *** Cala CACD 1002. Philh. O, Simon.

Geoffrey Simon's version of the three *Nocturnes* is colourful and atmospheric, with nothing vague in *Fêtes*. The orchestrations of piano music include Stokowski's vivid realization of *La Soirée dans Grenade*, as well as Ravel's magical re-interpretation of *Danse* and André Caplet's sensitive orchestration of *Children's Corner*. Full, vivid recorded sound.

Danse; Images: Ibéria, Marche écossaise; La Mer; Nocturnes: Nuages; Fêtes (only); (i) *La Demoiselle élue.*

(B) (***) Naxos mono 8.110811-2. NBC SO, Toscanini, (i) with Novotna, Glaz, Schola Cantorum Women's Ch.

These are incandescent, sharply focused performances, quite unlike any others and offering the longest of the irascible

rehearsals which are a fascinating feature of the series. It is specially valuable to have the three rare works – the *Marche écossaise* of 1908; the *Danse*, an early piano piece orchestrated by Ravel; and the early lyric poem, *La Demoiselle élue* – with clean-cut soloists.

Danse sacrée et danse profane (for harp and string orchestra).

(***) Testament mono SBT 1053. Mason Stockton, Concert Arts Strings, Slatkin – CRESTON: *Quartet;* RAVEL: *Introduction & Allegro;* TURINA: *La oración del torero;* VILLA-LOBOS: *Quartet No. 6.* (***)

Felix Slatkin and his Hollywood colleagues give as atmospheric an account of the *Danse sacrée et danse profane* as any on record, and Anne Mason Stockton is the excellent harpist. The mono recording dates from 1951 but is uncommonly good. This comes as part of a remarkably fine anthology of Hollywood Quartet recordings.

(i) *Danses sacrées et profanes; Images. Jeux; La Mer;* (ii) *Nocturnes; Printemps;* (iii) *Première rapsodie for Clarinet & Orchestra.*

(M) **(*) Sony (ADD) SM2K 68327 (2). New Philh. O or (i) Cleveland O; Boulez; with (i) Chalifoux; (ii) Alldis Ch.; (iii) De Peyer.

Jeux, a work of seminal importance in Boulez's development, is here given very persuasively. The *Images* are carefully shaped and balanced and, like the coolly distinctive *Danses sacrées et profanes*, were recorded in Cleveland and gain from the ambience of Severance Hall, even if the balance is close. *La Mer* and the *Prélude à l'après-midi d'un faune* (which certainly does not lack passionate feeling) are a good deal better than some accounts, but *La Mer* cannot compare with the Karajan version from the same era. Needless to say, Gervase de Peyer gives a distinguished account of the lovely *Clarinet Rhapsody*, and the contribution of the John Alldis Choir to *Sirènes*, the third of the *Nocturnes*, is poised, even if the effect overall is cool rather than ethereal. But those who respond to Boulez's clarity of vision in this repertoire will find that the Sony engineers have made a marvellous job of these transfers to CD, maximizing the ambient effect and retaining the sharply defined detail.

Danses sacrées et profanes; Images; Jeux; Prélude à l'après-midi d'un faune.

(N) (M) *** Sup. (ADD) SU 3478-2 011. Czech PO, Baudo (with Patras).

Recorded in the attractive acoustics of the Dvořák Hall of the Rudolfinum, Prague, these were among the finest recordings Supraphon made during the analogue LP era. The *Prélude* and *Jeux* date from 1977. Perhaps in the latter the rhythmic impetus lacks the final degree of bite, and the reverberation prevents any real *pianissimos*, but the acoustic is so well judged that one cannot complain. This elusive work is clothed in richly glowing colours, with ravishingly seductive string textures, while Baudo displays a subtle feeling for the music's ebb and flow. He also lets the famous *Prélude* unfold with a natural progress. The flautist has a wide vibrato, but his phrasing is most beautiful and the rest of the orchestra catch the opening mood and let the central climax of the piece flower quite spontaneously. At the very opening of *Images* the piquant oboe solo is ear-catching. *Les Parfums de la nuit* waft languorously in the evening breeze, and the opening of *Le Matin d'un jour de fête* is hauntingly evocative before the orchestra blazes into life. This, like the *Danse sacrée*, was recorded a decade later with comparable success.

6 Epigraphs antiques (orch. Ansermet); *Estampes: Pagodes* (orch. André Caplet); *Printemps* (suite symphonique; original (1887) choral version, reconstructed Emil de Cou); *Prélude: La puerta del vino* (orch. Henri Büsser); *Suite bergamasque* (orch. Gustave Cloez & André Caplet).

**(*) Ara. Z 6734. San Francisco Ballet O, De Cou; (i) with soloists and Ch.

A fascinating disc, and most fascinating of all is the original choral version of *Printemps*, which sounds positively voluptuous in this superbly rich recording. Emil de Cou has gone back to the full original manuscript and provided his own highly convincing re-scoring. The result will intrigue all Debussians and its seductive impact will surely thrill all listeners. The orchestrated piano pieces are also very successful. In the *Suite bergamasque*, *Clair de lune* sounds lovely on strings, and both the *Minuet* and *Passepied* are effective in orchestral dress. Ansermet himself recorded his fastidiously scored *Epigraphs antiques* (originally written for piano duet) and one would have liked rather more of the sharply etched detail for which his version was famous. But de Cou goes for atmospheric evocation and certainly No. 2 (*Pour le tombeau sans nom*), with its instant reminder of *Images*, is very beguiling; and the whole set is made to sound lustrous in its impressionistic colouring. The San Francisco Ballet Orchestra plays very well indeed, and the spacious acoustic provides an impressively full and naturally balanced sound-picture.

Fantaisie for Piano & Orchestra.

*** Ph. (IMS) 446 713-2. Kocsis, Budapest Festival O, Fischer – RAVEL: *Concertos.* **

(N) (BB) *** Warner Apex (ADD). 8573 89232-2. Quéffelec, Monte Carlo Op. O, Jordan – RAVEL: *Piano Concertos.* ***

Zoltán Kocsis's credentials as a Debussy interpreter scarcely need asserting. His account of the *Fantaisie* is both lucid and delicate and can be recommended with confidence. This would be a clear first choice, but the two Ravel concertos with which it is coupled are not.

The Warner Apex disc offers an inexpensive coupling of the major works for piano and orchestra by both Debussy and Ravel, and in Anne Quéfelec's hands the *Fantaisie* makes a very pleasing impression indeed and is very well recorded.

(i) *Fantaisie for Piano & Orchestra. Préludes, Books I–II.*

(N) (B) **(*) Decca Double (ADD) 468 552-2 (2). Kars; (i) with LSO, Gibson (with MESSIAEN: *Catalogue d'oiseaux: Le Merle bleu. Vingt regards sur l'Enfant-Jésus: Regard de l'esprit de joie; Regard du silence.* **(*))

The *Fantaisie* remains a Debussy rarity. Written between

1889 and 1890 it was withdrawn by the composer just as its first performance under Vincent d'Indy was about to take place. If it does not find Debussy's language fully formed it is still well worth hearing, and this was its first successful appearance on LP (in 1970). Jean-Rodolphe Kars plays it with great sympathy, and is well accompanied and very well recorded. His set of *Préludes* again show him naturally suited to Debussy and a pianist of undoubted sensibility and impeccable keyboard control. However, his playing here is a little disappointing, somewhat wanting in colour and atmospheric tension. There is much beautiful pianism and he is again truthfully recorded, but keener characterization is called for in this inspired music.

Images.

(M) **(*) DG (ADD) 463 615-2. Boston SO, Tilson Thomas – TCHAIKOVSKY: *Symphony No. 1.* **(*)

Images; Jeux; Le Roi Lear (incidental music).

*** [EMI Red Line CDR5 72095]. CBSO, Rattle.

Images; La Mer; (i) Nocturnes.

(N) (***) Australian P. Eloquence mono/stereo 464 636-2. Concg. O, Beinum, with (i) Women's voices of the Coll. Mus.

Images: Ibéria. La Mer (with rehearsal); (i) *Nocturnes.*

(**) DG (ADD) 453 194-2 (3 + 1). Stuttgart SWR RO, Celibidache; (i) with SWR Female Ch. – RAVEL: *Alborada*, etc. **

Images; Nocturnes; (i) Le Martyre de Saint-Sébastien: (symphonic fragments); *La Mer; Prélude à l'après-midi d'un faune; Printemps* (orch. Büsser).

(B) *** Double Decca 460 217-2 (2). Montreal SO, Dutoit, (i) with chorus.

In *Images* Rattle is memorably atmospheric, while in *Jeux* he is just a touch more expansive than most rivals, and also more evocative, though he does not depart from the basic metronome markings. Haitink probably remains a first choice in this score, for he has atmosphere and a tauter grip on the music's flow. The *King Lear* excerpts sound splendid. First-rate recording, very vivid but beautifully balanced.

In *Images* and the *Nocturnes* Dutoit is freer than some with rubato, as well as in his warm, expressive moulding of phrase. His sharp pointing of rhythm, as in the Spanish dances of *Ibéria* or the processional march in *Fêtes*, is also highly characteristic of his approach to French music. By contrast, the remaining works are strong rather than evocative, although few versions of *L'après-midi* match this one in the seductive beauty of Timothy Hutchins's flute-playing. For those who like these impressionistic masterpieces to be presented in full colour, with a vivid feeling for atmosphere, this is an ideal choice.

Michael Tilson Thomas's set of the *Images* dates from the early 1970s. The approach is youthfully impulsive and enjoyable and conveys the atmosphere of *Gigues* and the languor of the middle movement of *Ibéria* better than many eminent rivals. It is not a top choice but is still thoroughly recommendable.

Beinum's performances here have genuine atmosphere

and beauty, nothing overstated, yet much nuance and detail captured. The *Images* are mono recordings from the 1950s, but sound remarkably full and sophisticated, while the rest of the stereo recordings, from the late 1950s, sound only just a bit dated under pressure, though always remain warm. Well worth investigating at its bargain price.

As so often with Celibidache, attention focuses primarily on the conductor and the refinement of sonority he can command. And he does produce a beautiful sound from the Stuttgart orchestra, who give a slow-motion account of the three *Nocturnes*, taking well over half an hour. His *Ibéria* is almost as ruinous, and *Les Parfums de la nuit* at almost 13 minutes is intolerable. However, it is not only a matter of the static tempi; the affected phrasing is even more unpleasing. It is only fair to add that Celibidache's admirers, who include many respected musicians and critics, respond positively. The recordings come from the 1970s and are not always as successfully balanced as is usual from Südwestfunk.

Images: Ibéria (only).

(M) *** RCA GD 60179. Chicago SO, Reiner – RAVEL: *Alborada* etc. *** 🌑

Images: Ibéria. La Mer; (i) *Nocturnes; Prélude à l'après-midi d'un faune.*

🌑 (M) *** Ph. (ADD) 464 697-2. Concg. O, Haitink; (i) with female ch.

Images: Ibéria. La Mer; Prélude à l'après-midi d'un faune.

(M) *** Mercury (IMS) 434 343-2. Detroit SO, Paray – RAVEL: *Ma Mère l'Oye.* ***

Haitink's magical performances and recordings (from the mid- to late 1970s), extracted from Haitink's Duo above, have stood the test of time and remain unsurpassed. Indeed, the allure of the orchestral sound as remastered here is quite unforgettable. An admirable choice for Philips's set of '50 Great Recordings'.

Fritz Reiner and the Chicago orchestra give a reading that is immaculate in execution and magical in atmosphere. This marvellously evocative performance, and the Ravel with which it is coupled, should not be overlooked, for the recorded sound with its natural concert-hall balance is greatly improved in terms of body and definition.

Paray, in 1955, gave us the first stereo recording of *La Mer*, which is very exciting, balancing powerful evocation and firm overall control. The balance is slightly recessed, which provides plenty of atmosphere and a hazy, warm luminosity to the glowingly voluptuous account of *L'Après-midi* with its ardently beautiful string climax. *Images* is equally fine. The recording is without sharply delineated detail; yet for body, natural concert-hall balance and richness of orchestral colour there are few stereo recordings made in the mid- to late-1950s to match this.

Jeux; La Mer; Nocturnes: Nuages, Fêtes (only).

(***) Testament mono SBT 1108. St Cecilia Ac., Rome, O, De Sabata – RESPIGHI: *Fountains of Rome.* (***)

Jeux; La Mer; (i) *Nocturnes.*

** RCA 74321 64616-2. VPO, Maazel; (i) with Schoenberg Ch.

Jeux; La Mer; Nocturnes; Prélude à l'après-midi d'un faune.

(M) ** Sony (ADD) SMK 60972. NYPO, Bernstein.

Victor de Sabata's 1947 account with his Rome orchestra of *Jeux* brings great character and atmosphere to this wonderful score. Although the two purely orchestral *Nocturnes* first appeared on record in 1948, de Sabata's account of *La Mer* did not; it makes its first appearance now, but it is still music-making of quality that deserves a place in any Debussy collection.

The VPO play magnificently for Lorin Maazel, although the readings are not so memorable as to displace Haitink in *Jeux* and the *Nocturnes*, or Karajan in *La Mer*, not forgetting the likes of Reiner and Paray. Nor, strangely enough, is the recording particularly outstanding, though it is very good.

There is plenty to admire in the orchestral playing under Bernstein, which is of considerable virtuosity, but these performances, notably of *La Mer* and the *Prélude*, are very personal readings indeed. Bernstein has undoubted feeling for atmosphere, but the resulting performance has an air of self-indulgence, magnetic as it is. The phrasing in *Prélude à l'après-midi d'un faune* is very self-conscious in places, and *Jeux* too lacks a consistent forward pulse.

Le Martyre de Saint Sébastien (symphonic fragments).

(N) ** RCA 74321 72788-2. NDR SO, Wand – MUSSORGSKY: *Pictures at an Exhibition.* **

Günter Wand's account of the four fragments from *Le Martyre de Saint-Sébastien* comes from a concert performance in 1982, and the disc is obviously addressed to Wand fans. The conductor had great feeling for this work, and his is an idiomatic and sympathetic account. However, it is not superior to Tilson Thomas, who offers the complete score, and it comes with yet another *Pictures at an Exhibition*. At 54 minutes and full price, this is unlikely to make the pulse quicken.

La Mer.

(M) *** DG (ADD) 447 426-2. BPO, Karajan – MUSSORGSKY: *Pictures;* RAVEL: *Boléro.* ***

(M) *** RCA (ADD) 0926 68079-2. Chicago SO, Reiner – RESPIGHI: *Fountains & Pines of Rome.* *** 🌑

(M) **(*) RCA (ADD) 09026 61500-2. Boston SO, Munch – IBERT: *Escales* ***; SAINT-SAENS: *Symphony No. 3.* *** 🌑

(**) Orfeo (ADD) C 488 981 B. BPO, Mitropoulos – MENDELSSOHN: *Symphony No. 3;* SCHOENBERG: *Variations.* (**)

(N) (M) ** Chan. 6615. Detroit SO, Järvi – MILHAUD: *Suite provençale;* RAVEL: *Boléro; La Valse.* **

La Mer; Images: Iberia. Nocturnes: Nuages; Fêtes (only). *Prélude à l'après-midi d'un faune; Printemps.*

(B) *** [RCA 2-CD (ADD) 74321 84591-2(2)]. Munch/Boston SO, Munch – CHAUSSON: *Symphony* etc. ***

La Mer; (i) *Nocturnes; Prélude à l'après-midi d'un faune.*

(B) *** Penguin/DG 460 636-2. O de Paris, Barenboim, (i) with Ch.

La Mer; (i) *Nocturnes; Prélude à l'après-midi d'un faune; Printemps.*

(N) (BB) **(*) EMI Encore CDE5 74727-2. Capital Toulouse O, Plasson; (i) with female ch.

La Mer; Nocturnes: Nuages; Fêtes (only). *Prélude à l'après-midi d'un faune; Printemps* (symphonic suite).

(BB) *** RCA Navigator (ADD) 74321 21293-2. Boston SO, Munch.

La Mer; Nocturnes: Nuages; Fêtes (only); *Le Martyre de Saint-Sébastien* (symphonic fragments); *Prélude à l'après-midi d'un faune.*

(***) Testament mono SBT 1011. Philh. O, Cantelli.

La Mer; Prélude à l'après-midi d'un faune.

(M) *** DG (ADD) 427 250-2. BPO, Karajan – RAVEL: *Boléro*, etc. ***

After more than three decades Karajan's 1964 account of *La Mer* is still very much in a class of its own. It enshrines the spirit of the work as effectively as it observes the letter, and the superb playing of the Berlin orchestra, for all its virtuosity and sound, is totally self-effacing. It is now available, coupled with Karajan's outstanding (1966) record of Mussorgsky's *Pictures at an Exhibition* and a gripping account of Ravel's *Boléro*, but we prefer the original coupling of the *Prélude à l'après-midi d'un faune* and Ravel's *Daphnis et Chloé*, which are equally unforgettable.

Reiner's 1960 recording, coupled with Respighi's *Fountains* and *Pines of Rome*, has great warmth and atmosphere, while the pianissimo opening has enormous evocative feeling and the *Jeux des vagues* has a haunting sense of colour. Of course the marvellous acoustics of the Chicago Hall contribute to the appeal of this superbly played account: the effect is richer and fuller than in Karajan's remastered DG version, and Reiner's record gives no less pleasure.

The new CD transfers have completely transformed the Munch recordings, the Boston acoustic now casting a wonderfully warm aura over the orchestra, and the sound is gloriously expansive and translucent. There is marvellous Boston playing here, especially from the violins. Munch's inclination to go over the top may not appeal to all listeners, but the results are very compelling when the orchestral bravura is so thrilling. The *Prélude* makes a ravishing interlude, expanding to a rapturous climax. The permutation of music is more generous on the 2-disc reissue.

Barenboim's 1978 coupling of *La Mer* and *Nocturnes*, reissued on DG's Classikon bargain label, offers not only first-class analogue recording but performances which, although highly individual in their control of tempo, have great electricity and ardour. The *Prélude à l'après-midi d'un faune* has comparable languor to *Sirènes*, the last of the *Nocturnes*, if not quite the same refinement of feeling. Excellent sound for its period.

Michael Plasson and the Orchestre Capitole de Toulouse offer value for money on EMI's super-budget label Encore, in that the traditional coupling of *La Mer*, *Nocturnes* and the *Prélude* is supplemented by a lovely performance of *Printemps*, very refined and beautifully recorded. The very well characterized and equally finely played *La Mer* can hold its own with the best. The two orchestral *Nocturnes* have plenty of atmosphere, but *Sirènes* is let down by uncertain intonation and poor tone from the female voices of the Choeur de Toulouse Midi-Pyrénées. The reverberance of Halle-aux-Grains poses some problems, but they are more completely overcome here than in many earlier recordings.

Karajan's 1978 analogue re-recording of *La Mer* for EMI may not have quite the supreme refinement of his earlier, DG version – partly a question of the warmer, vaguer recording – but it has a comparable concentration, with the structure built persuasively and inevitably. The *Prélude* has an appropriate languor, and there is a commanding warmth about this performance, beautifully moulded; but again the earlier version distilled greater atmosphere and magic.

Cantelli's account of the four symphonic fragments from *Le Martyre de Saint-Sébastien* is one of the most beautiful performances he ever committed to vinyl; the textures are impeccably balanced and phrases flawlessly shaped. Its atmosphere is as concentrated as that of the legendary first recording under Coppola. *La Mer* and the *Prélude à l'après-midi d'un faune* are hardly less perfect, and the transfers are excellent.

Neeme Järvi's version of *La Mer* has a fair amount going for it; it has a subtle sense of flow and a good feeling for texture. There are some oddities, including a slowing down in the second part of *De l'aube à midi sur la mer* some way before the passage Satie referred to as 'the bit he liked at about quarter to eleven'. Given the sheer quantity and quality of the competition, however, this is not really a front-runner.

The Orfeo *La Mer* was recorded at the Salzburg Festival in 1960 and is a magical and atmospheric performance. Mitropoulos casts a strong spell, but the frequency range is narrow and the sound of the strings above the stave is shrill and strident.

Nocturnes: Nuages; Fêtes; (i) Sirènes.

(B)*** Decca/Penguin 460 649-2. Montreal SO, Dutoit; (i) with female ch. – RAVEL: *Le Tombeau de Couperin; La Valse;* SATIE: *3 Gymnopédies.* ***

Dutoit's *Nocturnes* have a persuasive ebb and flow of languorous rubato, while the glittering processional in *Fêtes* is sharply rhythmic. The atmospheric recording is well up to the expected high Montreal standard, and the couplings are equally fine.

Petite suite (orch. Büsser).

(B) *** Sony (ADD) SBK 63056. Cleveland O, Lane – RAVEL: *Introduction & Allegro* etc.; SATIE: *Gymnopédies Nos. 1 & 3.* ***

It is good to have a first-class performance of Debussy's *Petite suite* in Büsser's charming orchestration on a bargain label. The warmly atmospheric recording dates from the late 1960s when Louis Lane was a colleague of George Szell at Cleveland and the orchestra was still at the peak of its form.

Prélude à l'après-midi d'un faune; La Cathédrale engloutie (orch. Stokowski).

(M) (**(*)) Cala mono CACD 0526. NBC SO, Stokowski – GOULD: *2 Marches for Orchestra;* HOLST: *The Planets.* (***)

The *Prélude à l'après-midi d'un faune* derives from a NBC

broadcast dating from March 1943. Apart from a couple of blemishes (the opening has a fair amount of swish), the sound is acceptable, but the performance is more than that: it is individual and compelling, with the faun's reverie celebrated with some particularly lush string-playing. The same comments apply to Stokowski's superb account of his transcription of *La Cathédrale engloutie*, dating from a February 1944 broadcast but sounding rather shrill. There are some technical faults: a sudden brief drop in level quite early on, some pitch fluctuation, etc., but the magnetism of the performance is never in doubt. Two attractive fill-ups for an individual account of *The Planets*.

Première rapsodie (for clarinet and orchestra).

*** EMI CDC5 56832-2. Meyer, Berlin PO, Abbado – MOZART: *Clarinet Concerto;* TAKEMITSU: *Fantasma/Cantos.* ***

This evocative Debussy work reveals to the utmost Sabine Meyer's special gift for using the clarinet seductively. Not only is this a beautiful performance, it is a dramatic one too, with high contrasts underlined, helped by immaculate playing from the Berlin Philharmonic under Abbado. An unusual but magical coupling for the Mozart masterpiece.

COLLECTIONS

2 Arabesques (arr. MOUTON); Bruyères (arr. GRAINGER); La Cathédrale engloutie (arr. STOKOWSKI) ; Children's Corner (arr. CAPLET) ; Danse – Tarantelle Styrienne (arr. RAVEL); L'Isle Joyeuse (arr. MOLINARI); La Mer.

(N) (M) **(*) Cala CACD 1024. PO, Simon.

Geoffrey Simon's warm, urgent reading of *La Mer* is coupled here to various orchestrations of Debussy's piano music. Debussy himself approved of Caplet's sensitive orchestration of *Children's Corner* ('so gorgeously apparelled', he said), with its reference to *Tristan* in the final *Golliwog's Cakewalk* underlined by the orchestration. The recording is good, if a bit cavernous, and doesn't capture the bass drum in the delectable *Tarantelle Styrienne* in the way that Ansermet's old Decca recording did. But it is all enjoyable.

Clair de lune (arr. CAPLET); The Girl with the Flaxen Hair (arr. GLEICHMANN); Night in Granada (arr. STOKOWSKI); Nocturnes; Pagodas (arr. GRAINGER); Petite suite (arr. BUSSER); Première rapsodie.

(N) (M) **(*) Cala CACD 1025. Philh. O, Simon.

The second Geoffrey Simon Debussy CD, like the first, includes several rarities, plus an excellent account of the *Nocturnes*. Grainger's arrangement of *Pagodas* is especially charming, with its elaborate percussion section simulating Balinese gamelan, and Büsser's famous arrangement of the *Petite suite* is always a delight. As with the companion CD, the sound is a bit cavernous, clouding some of the textures at times. These two new Cala compilations are replacements for earlier collections discussed above.

CHAMBER MUSIC

Cello Sonata in D min.

(M) *** Decca (ADD) 460 974-2. Rostropovich, Britten – SCHUBERT: *Arpeggione Sonata* **(*); SCHUMANN: *5 Stücke in Volkston.* ***

**(*) ASV CDDCA 796. Gregor-Smith, Wrigley – BRIDGE; DOHNANYI: *Sonatas.* **(*)

(i) Cello Sonata; (ii) Violin Sonata.

(*) Chan. 8458. (i) Turovsky; (ii) Dubinsky; Edlina – RAVEL: *Piano Trio.* *

Cello Sonata; Petite pièce for Clarinet & Piano; Première rapsodie for Clarinet & Piano; Sonata for Flute, Viola & Harp; Violin Sonata; Syrinx for Solo Flute.

*** Chan. 8385. Athena Ens.

Like Debussy's other late chamber works, the *Cello Sonata* is a concentrated piece, quirkily original. The classic version by Rostropovich and Britten has a clarity and point which suit the music perfectly. The recording is first class and, if the couplings are suitable, this holds its place as first choice. It is fully worthy of reissue in Decca's latest Legends series.

The most ethereal of the pieces on Chandos is the *Sonata for Flute, Viola & Harp*, whose other-worldly quality is beautifully conveyed here. In the case of the other sonatas, there are strong competitors but, as a collection, this is certainly recommendable.

Bernard Gregor-Smith and Yolande Wrigley play with great refinement and authority, as well as much sensitivity. They are perhaps too closely balanced but this does not prevent their record being a highly desirable one.

Yuli Turovsky gives a well-delineated, powerful account with Luba Edlina. In the *Violin Sonata*, Rostislav Dubinsky and Edlina (his wife) are in excellent form, though this is red-blooded Slavonic Debussy rather than the more ethereal, subtle playing of a Grumiaux.

(i) Danses sacrées et profanes; (ii) Cello Sonata; (iii) Sonata for Flute, Viola & Harp; (iv) String Quartet; (v) Syrinx; (vi) Violin Sonata.

(M) **(*) Cal. Dig./ADD CAL 3822.4 (3). (i; iii) Pierre; (i) La Follia Ens.; (ii) Pernoo; (ii; vi) Rigollet; (iii) Xuereb; (iii; v) Beaumadier; (iv; vi) Roussin – RAVEL: *Chamber Music,* etc. **

The *String Quartet in G minor* was recorded in 1972 – and very good it is, too. The three sonatas are digital and recent and, like the *Danses sacrées et profanes* and *Syrinx*, come from 1997. They are very well played, though none would necessarily be a first choice. A more than serviceable recommendation all the same.

Le Petit Nègre; Petite pièce; Première rapsodie; Rapsodie for Cor Anglais; Rapsodie for Saxophone; Sonata for Flute, Viola & Harp; (i) Syrinx.

(B) *** Cala CACD 1017 (2). Bennett, Daniel, Campbell, Gough; (i) Haram & Ens. – SAINT-SAENS: *Chamber Music.* ***

The *Rapsodie for Cor Anglais*, with which this Cala Duo

opens, is more familiar in its form for alto saxophone; it was originally to have been called *Rapsodie mauresque*. Nicholas Daniel plays it with great sensitivity. It is also heard in its alternative form, splendidly played by Simon Haram. The performance of the *Sonata for Flute, Viola & Harp* is highly sensitive.

Piano Trio in G (1880).

*** Hyp. CDA 67114. Florestan Trio – FAURE; RAVEL: *Piano Trios*. ***

(*) Ara. Z 6643. Kaplan Carr Trio – FAURE: *Piano Trio* *; SAINT-SAENS: *Piano Trio*. **(*)

(BB) **(*) Naxos 8.550934. Joachim Trio – RAVEL: *Piano Trio*; SCHMITT: *Piano Trio: Très lent*. **(*)

Debussy's *Piano Trio*, a product of his teenage years, may reveal few signs of his mature style but it makes a very apt and delightful coupling for the Ravel and Fauré works, representing different periods of each composer's career. With personnel drawn from the piano quartet group, Domus, led by the pianist Susan Tomes, the Florestans follow up the success of their prize-winning Schumann disc for Hyperion in a strong and urgent reading, at once highly polished and flexibly expressive. Vivid sound.

The Golub–Kaplan–Carr Trio also give a very good account of this slender piece, and they are decently recorded.

The Joachim Trio play with consistent sensitivity and finesse. This is a thoroughly musical account and beautifully recorded; but it would not necessarily be a first choice, though the attractive price-tag (and the agreeable Schmitt bonus) makes it competitive.

Sonata for Flute, Viola & Harp.

*** Koch 3-7016-2. Atlantic Sinf. – JOLIVET: *Chant de Linos*; JONGEN: *Concert*. ***

The three members of the Atlantic Sinfonietta are well balanced and achieve a feeling of repose and mystery. This is the best of the recent recordings of this enormously civilized and ethereal music, but the Melos version remains special, and we await its return to the catalogue.

String Quartet in G min., Op. 10.

⚫ (M) *** DG 463 082-2. Melos Qt – RAVEL: *String Quartet*. *** ⚫

*** DG (IMS) 437 836-2. Hagen Qt – RAVEL; WEBERN: *Quartets*. ***

*** Sony SK 52554. Juilliard Qt – DUTILLEUX; RAVEL: *Quartets*. ***

(M) *** Ph. 464 699-2. Italian Qt – RAVEL: *Quartet*. ***

(N) (B) *** DG (ADD) 469 591-2. LaSalle Qt. – RAVEL: *Quartet*. ***

(B) *** CfP CD-CFP 4652. Chilingirian Qt – RAVEL: *Quartet*. ***

(N) (B) *** EMI Début CDZ5 74020-2. Belcea Qt – DUTILLEUX: *Ainsi la nuit*. RAVEL: *String Quartet*. ***

(BB) **(*) Naxos 8.550249. Kodály Qt – RAVEL: *Quartet* etc. ***

**(*) ASV CDDCA 930. Lindsay Qt – RAVEL: *String Quartet* **(*); STRAVINSKY: *3 Pieces*. **(*)

(N) (M) **(*) EMI CDM5 67550-2 [567551]. Alban Berg Qt. –

RAVEL: *String Quartet* **(*); STRAVINSKY: *Concertino; Double Canon; 3 Pieces*. ***

(N) (BB) ** Warner Apex 8573 89231-2. Keller Qt – RAVEL: *Quartet*. **

The outstanding Melos recording was made in 1979 and is in every way a great performance. The playing of the Melos Quartet is distinguished by perfect intonation and ensemble, scrupulous accuracy in the observance of dynamic markings, a natural sense of flow and great tonal beauty. It would be difficult to imagine a finer account of the Debussy than this, and the sound in its latest Galleria format remains very impressive.

The Hagen Quartet on DG produce the greatest refinement of sound without beautifying the score; they also enjoy the benefit of superb engineering. Indeed, if pressed, this might well be a first choice, at least among recent issues.

The Juilliard performance is impressive, in spite of the wide vibrato these players employ; but one barely notices this except when making a direct comparison. Their first movement is not as fresh and ardent as some others, but overall this is very satisfying and they are well recorded.

It need hardly be said that the playing of the Quartetto Italiano is outstanding. Perfectly judged ensemble, weight and tone still make this a most satisfying choice and, even if it is rather short measure, the Philips recording engineers have produced a vivid and truthful sound-picture. However, it has now been promoted from bargain to mid-price.

The LaSalle Quartet are also on top form and their reading takes place of honour alongside the Quartetto Italiano. The 1971 recording was of high quality and the CD transfer in no way degrades its natural sound balance. This reissue now has a price advantage, now that the Philips competitor has been reissued at mid-price.

At bargain price, the Chilingirian coupling is in every way competitive. They give a thoroughly committed account with well-judged tempi and very musical phrasing. The Scherzo is vital and spirited, and there is no want of poetry in the slow movement. The recording has plenty of body and presence and has the benefit of a warm acoustic: the sound is fuller than on the version by the Italian Quartet.

The Belcea Quartet was formed in 1994 and won first prize at the Osaka International Competition in 1999 and at Bordeaux, in what was formerly the Evian Competition. These young players pay scrupulous attention to dynamics and make fine judgements regarding tempos and can hold their own with the best. They have enviable tonal finesse, and their phrasing is sensitive and internal balance excellent. A brightly lit recording, although there is a touch of glare.

As we know from their Haydn recordings, the Kodály Quartet are an excellent ensemble, and they too give a thoroughly enjoyable account. There are moments here (in the slow movement, for example) when the Kodály are touched by distinction. This music-making has the feel of a live performance: these players also have the benefit of a generous fill-up and very good recorded sound. Excellent value.

The Lindsays play with their usual aplomb and panache. There are splendid things here, notably the youthful fire of the opening movement and the finely etched finale. They do not always match the *douceur* and *tendresse* which the Quartetto Italiano and the Hagen find, but they are always stimulating. Fine recording.

Technically the Alban Berg are in a class of their own, yet, strangely enough one finishes listening to this with greater admiration than involvement. Not that they are in any way outside Debussy's world; rather the performance beautifies the work and has comparatively little spontaneous feeling. It is superbly recorded, but is not a first choice, unless the outstanding Stravinsky coupling is wanted.

The Keller Quartet is a Hungarian group, formed when the players were still studying at Budapest. They came to wider attention when they won a number of international prizes in 1990. They offer the Debussy and Ravel *Quartets* alone, but their CD is in the lowest price-range. However, they rush and over-dramatize the first movement of the Debussy – in fact the whole work is rather hurried along, and there is just too much paprika here to make this a three-star recommendation.

Syrinx; Bilitis (arr. Lenski). (i) *La plus que lente.*

*** EMI CDC5 56982-2. Pahud; (i) Kovacevich – PROKOFIEV: *Flute Sonata;* RAVEL: *Chansons madécasses.* ***

Syrinx has rarely sounded more erotic or other-worldly. The *Bilitis* is a transcription by Karl Lenski of the *Six épigraphes antiques* for piano duet (1914). Emmanuel Pahud, first flute of the Berlin Philharmonic, is sensitive both to every nuance and dynamic subtlety and to the spirit of this highly effective transcription. Stephen Kovacevich gives a beautifully characterized account of Debussy's satire of a salon waltz, *La plus que lente*, as good as any and better than most.

Violin Sonata.

✪ (M) *** Decca (ADD) 460 006-2. Chung, Lupu – FRANCK: *Violin Sonata* *** ✪; CHAUSSON: *Poème.* ***

*** DG (IMS) 445 880-2. Dumay, Pires – FRANCK: *Violin Sonata;* RAVEL: *Berceuse,* etc. ***

*** Virgin VC5 45122-2. Tetzlaff, Andsnes – JANACEK: *Sonata;* RAVEL: *Sonata;* NIELSEN: *Sonata No. 2.* ***

(B) *** CfP 573115-2. Little, Lane – POULENC: *Violin Sonata;* RAVEL: *Violin Sonata,* etc. ***

(BB) *** Arte Nova 74321 59233-2. Contner, Rogatchev – FRANCK; SAINT-SAENS: *Violin Sonatas.* ***

Kyung Wha Chung plays with marvellous character and penetration, and her partnership with Radu Lupu could hardly be more fruitful. Nothing is pushed to extremes and everything is in perfect perspective. The recording sounds admirably real.

Augustin Dumay and Maria João Pires give as idiomatic and sensitive an account of the Debussy *Sonata* as one could wish for, and those wanting their particular coupling with Franck and Ravel need not really hesitate.

However, Christian Tetzlaff and Leif Ove Andsnes provide as expert and imaginative a partnership as any of their rivals. The sheer interest of their couplings, not least the Nielsen *G minor Sonata*, and the quality of the performances make this also one of the strongest contenders in the current catalogue.

Tasmin Little and Piers Lane also give a highly dedicated performance which tautly holds together the often fragmen-tary argument, making the result sound spontaneous in its total concentration. Excellent sound and a first-rate coupling.

Mirijam Contner is a superb young violinist with plenty of fire and temperament, one who plays the elusive Debussy *Sonata* from the heart, as though improvising the music, helped by the understanding pianist. Full tone and immaculate technique. Well-balanced sound ensures a warm welcome for this excellent CD in the lowest price-range.

PIANO MUSIC
Piano duet

Danses sacrées et profanes; En blanc et noir; Lindaraja; Nocturnes (trans. RAVEL); *Prélude à l'après-midi d'un faune.*

(B) *** Hyp. Helios CDH 55014. Coombs, Scott.

Stephen Coombs and Christopher Scott made an outstanding début with this fine recording, which leads the field in this repertoire. Very highly recommended.

En blanc et noir.

(N) (M) *** Decca (ADD) 466 821-2. Richter, Britten – MOZART: Piano Sonata in C, K.521, etc. SCHUBERT: *Andante varié,* D.823. ***

As in the Mozart and Schubert duets Britten and Richter are inspired partners in music of a composer specially close to them. The elusiveness of late Debussy brings a performance of dream-like fantasy, as though the notes are being spontaneously re-created, catching the magic of live performance on the wind.

En blanc et noir; 6 Epigraphes antiques; Lindaraja; Petite suite; Nocturnes: Nuages, Fêtes (arr Ravel).

*** Ph. 454 471-2. K. and M. Labèque.

The Labèque sisters focus on brilliance and sparkle, and their performances will stimulate and astonish. Martha Argerich and Stephen Kovacevich found more repose in their classic version of *En blanc et noir* but the Labèques' virtuosity is not in question, nor is the excellence and presence of the Philips recording.

(i) En blanc et noir; Lindaraja. (Piano): Estampes; Images I & II; L'Isle joyeuse; Masques.

(B) *** EMI (ADD) CES5 72376-2 (3). Collard, (i) with Béroff – RAVEL: *Piano Music.* ***

Distinguished playing from Jean-Philippe Collard in the *Estampes* and the two sets of *Images*, and his collaboration with Michel Béroff in *En blanc et noir* is hardly less successful. The recording, made in the early 1970s at the Salle Wagram, is less satisfactory but good enough to warrant a full three-star recommendation on artistic grounds.

(i) En blanc et noir; 6 Epigraphes antiques; Lindaraja; Marche écossaise; Petite suite. (Solo piano): Ballade slave; Berceuse héroïque; Danse (Tarantelle styrienne); Danse bohémienne; D'un cahier d'esquisses; 12 Etudes; Hommage

à Haydn; Masques; Nocturne; Le Petit Nègre; La plus que lente; Rêverie; Suite bergamasque; Valse romantique.

(B) *** Ph. Duo (ADD) 438 721-2 (2). Haas, (i) with Lee.

2 Arabesques; Children's Corner; Estampes; Images, Books 1–2; L'Isle joyeuse; Mazurka; Pour le piano; Préludes, Books 1–2.

(B) **(*) Ph. Duo (ADD) 438 718-2 (2). Haas.

The playing of Werner Haas is rarely routine. Book 2 of the *Préludes* and many of the pieces from Book 1 are very well worth having; the *Images* are pretty good too, and many of the shorter pieces in the second listed volume are neatly and sensitively characterized. What makes its companion pair of CDs indispensable is the splendid collection of Debussy's music for piano duet (four hands or two pianos), recorded a decade later, in which Haas is joined by Noël Lee. The *Petite suite* is delightfully fresh, and *En blanc et noir* and the *Six épigraphes antiques* are very distinguished indeed. The (early 1960s) piano recording throughout is well up to Philips's high standard.

Solo piano music

2 Arabesques; Ballade; Berceuse héroïque; Children's Corner; Danse; Danse bohémienne; D'un cahier d'esquisses; Estampes; 12 Etudes; Hommage à Haydn; Images 1–2; L'Isle joyeuse; Masques; Mazurka; Nocturne; Le Petit Nègre; La plus que lente; Pour le piano; Préludes, Books 1–2; Rêverie; Suite bergamasque; Valse romantique.
(i) *Fantaisie for piano & orchestra.*

(M) (***) EMI mono CHS5 65855-2 (4). Gieseking; (i) with Hessischen R. O, Schröder.

Gieseking's Debussy enjoyed legendary status in the 1930s and 1940s, and EMI are to be congratulated for not only restoring to circulation the famous recordings he then made but also even adding to them. The two sets of *Préludes* date from 1953 and 1954, as indeed do most of the recordings collected here. The earliest is *Children's Corner* from 1951, which is also the date of the Frankfurt recording of the *Fantaisie*. The latter calls for some (albeit not great) tolerance, but the remaining performances sound better than ever. Gieseking's artistry is too well known to need further exegesis or advocacy. A marvellous set which all pianists should investigate.

2 Arabesques; Danse bohémienne; D'un cahier d'esquisses; Estampes; Images oubliées; L'Isle joyeuse; Morceau de concours; Nocturne; Pour le piano; Préludes, Books 1–2 (complete); Masques; Rêverie.

*** Decca 452 022-2 (2). Thibaudet.

Beautifully recorded, Jean-Yves Thibaudet's wide range of tone and dynamic is used with great imagination, and his playing often suggests an improvisatory quality. The music's subtlety of colour, with half-lights as well as sudden blazes of light (as in the stunning *Feux d'artifice*), is fully understood by this fine artist, and there is no question as to the spontaneity of his playing. The *Préludes* are among the finest on record.

Ballade; Berceuse héroïque; Children's Corner; Danse (Tarantelle styrienne); Elégie; Etudes, Books I & II; Etude retrouvée (reconstructed Roy Howatt); Hommage à Haydn; Images I & II; Mazurka; Page d'album; Le Petit Nègre; La plus que lente; Suite bergamasque; Valse romantique.

*** Decca 460 247-2 (2). Thibaudet.

This completes Jean-Yves Thibaudet's survey of Debussy's solo piano music, and Debussy-playing doesn't come any better than this. As before, these performances are full of evocative atmosphere (especially the *Images*), and ever imaginative in their infinite variety of colour and dynamic. Even the early pieces, especially the gentle *Ballade*, have an added poetic dimension, and the more familiar works, *Children's Corner* and *Suite bergamasque*, sound wonderfully fresh. The quirky vignettes like *Le Petit Nègre*, *Hommage à Haydn* and the charmingly brief *Page d'album* are delightfully done, and the sombre *Berceuse héroïque* is darkly memorable. But most impressive are the *Etudes*, unsurpassed on record in their strong characterization, flair and virtuosity – not even by Mitsuko Uchida's famous Philips set – and, with Decca's recording so real and immediate, they project with vivid spontaneity as at a live recital. These four CDs make a clear first choice among modern digital recordings of this totally absorbing repertoire.

2 Arabesques; Ballade slave; Berceuse héroïque; Children's Corner; Danse (Tarantelle styrienne); Danse bohémienne; D'un cahier d'esquisses; Elégie; Estampes; Etudes, Books I–II; Hommage à Haydn; Images, Books I–II; Images oubliées; L'Isle joyeuse; Masques; Mazurka; Morceau de concours; Nocturne; Page d'album; Le Petit Nègre; La plus que lente; Pour le piano; Préludes, Books 1–2; Suite bergamasque; Valse romantique.

(BB) *** ASV CDQS 432 (4). Fergus-Thompson.
(N) (BB) ** EMI CZS5 73813-2 (5) (also includes *La Boîte à joujoux; Epigraphes antiques; Etude retrouvée*). Ciccolini.

This ASV set represents an extraordinary bargain in offering distinguished performances of Debussy's complete solo piano music, admirably recorded, for a lot less than the cost of two premium-priced CDs. Gordon Fergus-Thompson's survey maintains a consistently high standard of artistry. His set of the elusive *Etudes* is altogether excellent, and so is *Pour le piano*. He finds the full charm and character of *Children's Corner*, while the shorter pieces, the *Arabesques*, the quirky *Le Petit Nègre* and *Rêverie* for instance, are beguilingly presented. The evocation of this unique repertoire is perceptively caught throughout, not least in the *Images*. If one places his sets of *Préludes* alongside those of Gieseking or Arrau, they are less individually distinctive, yet the characterization remains telling. Throughout, this playing shows a genuine feeling for the Debussy palette and, with fine, modern, digital recording, the piano-image mellow and true, these records will give great satisfaction.

The Italian pianist Aldo Ciccolini has made his career in France and taught for some years at the Paris Conservatoire. He is perhaps best known to collectors for his LP recordings of Satie and Poulenc, although his repertoire and range is more extensive. His complete Debussy survey is not of uniform excellence, and at times he can appear inattentive to dynamic shadings and tonal finesse, although the recording itself is a shade restricted in range. Nevertheless he brings considerable atmosphere to *Et la lune descend sur le temple qui fut* and other pieces.

2 Arabesques; Berceuse héroïque; D'un cahier d'esquisses; Hommage à Haydn; Images, Books 1–2; L'Isle joyeuse; Page d'album; Rêverie.

*** Ph. 422 404-2. Kocsis.

Artistically, this new recital is if anything even more distinguished in terms of pianistic finesse, sensitivity and tonal refinement than Kocsis's earlier (1983) Debussy collection (Ph. 412 118-2) – see below.

2 Arabesques; Children's Corner; Etudes, Books I & II; Estampes; Images, Books I & II; Le Petit Nègre; La plus que lente; Pour le piano; Préludes, Books I & II.

(N) (BB) *(**) EMI CZS5 74122-2 (3). Béroff.

On the original LPs Michel Béroff's accounts of the *Préludes* and *Estampes* had a compelling sense of atmosphere and a wonderful sensitivity and tonal finesse. However, these transfers have brought the aural image forward and succeed in robbing the performances of much of their magic. Some tinkering with the controls will help, and there is still pleasure to be derived from Béroff's artistry, but justice has not been done to the sonority that this fine Debussian produces.

2 Arabesques; Children's Corner; Estampes; Images, Books I–II; L'Isle joyeuse; Pour le piano; Préludes, Book 1; Rêverie; Suite bergamasque.

(B) *** Double Decca (ADD) 443 021-2 (2). Rogé.

Pascal Rogé's playing is distinguished by a keen musical intelligence and sympathy, as well as by a subtle command of keyboard colour, and this Double Decca set must receive the warmest welcome. *Children's Corner* is played with neat elegance and the characterization has both charm and perception, while the *Suite bergamasque* and *Pour le piano* and the *Images* are no less distinguished. In *Estampes* there are occasional moments when the listener senses the need for more dramatic projection, but Rogé brings genuine poetic feeling to the first book of the *Préludes*. The CD transfers are clear and firm.

2 Arabesques; Children's Corner; Estampes; Images, Books I–II; Masques; Préludes, Books 1–2.

(M) (***) Sony mono SM2K 60795 (2). Casadesus.

Robert Casadesus's accounts of the *Préludes* are (like Gieseking's before him) legendary. They were made in 1953–4 and the other works followed (except for the appealing account of *Children's Corner* which came first in 1950, yet sounds extremely good, if closely balanced). The new transfers are impressive, and there is now very little difference in quality between the two Books of *Préludes*. There is some marvellous playing in *Estampes* and in both Books of *Images* (notably *Mouvement*, *Cloches à travers les feuilles* and *Poissons d'or*), while the performances of *Book 2* of the *Préludes* show the pianist at his finest: *Brouillards* and *Feuilles mortes*, for instance, are superbly atmospheric, and *Feux d'artifice*

repeats the ready virtuosity we have already encountered in *Images*, glittering with fiery brilliance. The reissue is handsomely packaged and offered at mid-price, rather than in Sony's more expensive Heritage series.

2 Arabesques; Children's Corner; Estampes; L'Isle joyeuse; Le Petit Nègre; La plus que lente; Rêverie; Suite bergamasque: Clair de lune.

(N) *** Chan. 9912. Tabe.

Among newer recordings of Debussy piano music Kyoko Tabe's recital is eminently successful. She has a good feeling for atmosphere and a keen musical intelligence. The playing time runs to 65 minutes so there would have been room for the whole of the *Suite bergamasque*. All the same, this is a fine issue on every count.

(i) 2 Arabesques; Danse; L'Isle joyeuse; Masque; La plus que lente; Pour le piano; (ii) Préludes, Books 1–2 (complete); (i) Suite bergamasque.

(B) *** DG Double (ADD) 453 070-2 (2). (i) Vásáry; (ii) Ciani.

Vásáry is at his finest in the *Suite bergamasque*, and *Clair de lune* is beautifully played, as are the *Arabesques*. Ciani has a fine technique (witness *Feux d'artifice*) and plays both Books of *Préludes* with intelligence and taste. Both artists are very well recorded indeed. There is a good deal of Debussy's best-known piano music here, offered inexpensively, and this is a very satisfying pair of discs in its own right.

Ballade; Children's Corner; Elégie; Le Petit Nègre; La plus que lente; Mazurka; Morceau de concours; Nocturne; Préludes: Books 1–2; Valse romantique.

* Ph. 456 568-2 (2). Kocsis.

This set proves a major disappointment. Dynamic markings, always scrupulously observed in his previous Debussy CDs, are disregarded in the most cavalier fashion. There are explosive whirlwinds, capricious sforzati and little sense that he really cares about this music. Of course there are good things, but they are too few to redeem this set.

Children's Corner Suite.

(N) (BB) **(*) Naxos 8.550885. Biret – SCHUMANN: *Kinderszenen;* TCHAIKOVSKY: *Album for the Young.* ***

Idil Biret takes the opening movement very briskly and impetuously, but the performance then settles down and is sensitive and well characterized, especially the closing *Golliwog's Cakewalk*. Good recording and recommendable couplings too.

Children's Corner; Images, Books I–II; Préludes, Books 1–2.

**(*) DG (ADD) 449 438-2 (2). Michelangeli.

'Immaculate' is one of the words that spring to mind when one hears Michelangeli's Debussy. There is no doubt that his performances of *Children's Corner* and the two sets of *Images* are very distinguished. The *Préludes* undoubtedly bring piano playing which is pretty flawless. At the same time, it is very cool and detached and, although Book 2 excited enormous enthusiasm in some quarters, both Books here will strike many as somewhat glacial and curiously unatmospheric. Moreover the set is uncompeti-tively priced.

Estampes; Images, Books I–II; Préludes, Books 1–2.

(M) *** Ph. (IMS) (ADD) 432 304-2 (2). Arrau.

Claudio Arrau's versions of these solo piano works by De-bussy are very distinguished. The piano timbre in these 1978–9 analogue recordings has a consistent body and re-alism typical of this company's finest work.

Estampes; Images oubliées; Pour le piano; Suite bergamasque.

*** Ph. 412 118-2. Kocsis.

An exceptionally atmospheric and intelligently planned re-cital from Zoltán Kocsis. The playing is enormously refined and imaginative, and every nuance is subtly graded. The Philips engineers have captured the piano with exceptional realism and fidelity.

Estampes; Préludes, Books 1–2 (complete); Images: Reflets dans l'eau.

(BB) *** CfP Double CDCFPSD 4805 (2). Egorov.

The Classics for Pleasure Double has the advantage of con-siderable economy. Youri Egorov is a very fine player indeed; he gives performances of commanding keyboard technique, exquisite refinement and atmosphere. The recording is very good, a shade too reverberant perhaps, but this must rank high in current CD sets of the complete Préludes.

Etudes, Books I–II.

✹ (M) *** Ph. 464 698-2. Uchida.

Mitsuko Uchida's remarkable account of the Etudes on Philips is not only one of the best Debussy piano records in the catalogue and arguably her finest recording, but also one of the best ever recordings of the instrument. It is even more attractive at mid-price and is certainly worthy of inclusion among Philips's selection of '50 Great Recordings'.

Préludes, Books 1–2 (complete).

✹ (M) *** EMI mono CDM5 67233-2 [567262]. Gieseking.
*** DG 435 773-2 (2). Zimerman.
(B) **(*) RCA Twofer 74321 49185-2 (2). Collard.
(B) **(*) Nonesuch Ultima 7559 79474-2 (2). Jacobs.

Gieseking's classic set of both Books of the Debussy Préludes takes its rightful place as one of EMI's 'Great Recordings of the Century' and now has proper documentation. The current remastering again confirms the natural realism of the 1953–4 Abbey Road recording, with Book 1 produced by Geraint Jones and Book 2 by Walter Legge, although there is a touch of hardness on forte passages.

There is no want of atmosphere or poetic feeling in Krystian Zimerman's account of the Préludes. This is a very distinguished performance indeed, though some may find the level of intensity too much to live with. Yet his playing is imaginative and concentrated. The DG recording is sensi-tively balanced, but there is more than a hint of hardness in climaxes.

Catherine Collard's RCA set brings the problem that the reflective qualities of her playing mean that her total timing is 85 minutes – too long for a single CD. But this is a very distinguished set, and her playing has superb technical command and flair, matched by her evocative imagination. She brings a penetrating understanding to this many-faceted music. The recording is first class, cleanly focused and fully coloured, the ambience virtually ideal.

As with Collard on RCA, Paul Jacobs's choice of occasion-ally slower tempi means that his complete set of Préludes stretches over a pair of CDs, although offered as an Ultima Double. Jacobs's playing is highly evocative, and he can be quirky too, as in the engagingly lighthearted account of La Danse de Puck. There is much to appeal here, but in the last resort this Nonesuch set cannot be a top recommendation.

Préludes, Book 1; Images oubliées (1894).

(M) **(*) Channel CCS 4892. Van Immerseel.

The special interest of Jos van Immerseel's recording of the first Book of Préludes lies in his instrument, an Erard of 1897, of the kind which Debussy would have known and played. The sonority is gentle and veiled and curiously seductive except in forte passages; the timbre, particularly in the upper register of the instrument, is monochrome and dry, and this tells in a piece such as La Sérénade interrompue. There is a real turn-of-the-century feel to the shadowy sound-world of Des pas sur la neige and the first of the Images oubliées. An interesting appendix for a Debussy discography, but essentially this is an issue for specialist collections.

Préludes, Book 1; L'Isle joyeuse.

*(*) DG 445 187-2. Pollini.

Maurizio Pollini may be Maurizio Pollini, but only 43 minutes is on the stingy side for a full-price disc. Ce qu'a vu le vent d'ouest sounds as if he is attacking Rachmaninov or Prokofiev. There are good things too, and the pianism and control are masterly (as in Des pas sur la neige), but generally speaking one remains outside Debussy's world. The recording was made in Munich's Herkulessaal and has abun-dant clarity and presence.

VOCAL MUSIC

3 Ballades de François Villon; 3 Chansons de France; Fêtes galantes (2nd series); Noël des enfants qui n'ont plus de maison; 3 Poèmes de Stéphane Mallarmé; Le Promenoir des deux amants.

(M) **(*) Auvidis V 4803. Kruysen, Lee.

Bernard Kruysen was perhaps the most distinguished Dutch baritone of his day. The present recital comprises the con-tents of one 1971 LP which, at just under 40 minutes, is distinctly poor value even at mid-price. Artistically these are strong performances, aristocratic in demeanour and well characterized. Kruysen is sensitively and perceptively accompanied by Noël Lee, and well recorded too.

3 Chansons de Charles d'Orléans.

*** Ph. 438 149-2. Monteverdi Ch., ORR, Gardiner – FAURE: Requiem; RAVEL; SAINT-SAENS: Choral Works. ***

With Gardiner and his period forces bringing out the medi-eval flavour of these charming choral settings, this adds to a generous and unusual coupling for Gardiner's expressive reading of the Fauré *Requiem*.

La Demoiselle élue.

(N) (***) Testament mono SBT 3203 (3). Los Angeles, Boston SO, Munch – BERLIOZ; *Les Nuits d'été;* MASSENET: *Manon.* ***

The combination of Munch's purposeful understanding of this wayward work, together with the charm of Victoria de los Angeles, make this an exceptional performance, even though in limited 1955 mono sound. As in the Berlioz song-cycle, the RCA recording may not capture the full golden beauty of the singer's voice, but these two works make a valuable bonus for the classic Monteux version of Massenet's *Manon*.

Le Martyre de Saint-Sébastien (incidental music): complete.

*** Sony SK 48240. Caron; McNair, Murray, L. Symphony Ch., LSO, Tilson Thomas.

Michael Tilson Thomas here records the complete incidental music in a form that the composer approved, using a nar-rator, Leslie Caron, to provide the spoken links between sections. What it shows is how much richer and more varied the complete score is than the usual symphonic fragments. This is as near an ideal performance as could be imagined, with Sylvia McNair singing radiantly in the principal so-prano roles, with brilliant playing from the LSO and glorious recording which brings out the full atmospheric beauty of the choral singing, often off-stage.

Mélodies: La Belle au bois dormant; Beau soir; 3 Chansons de Bilitis; Fêtes galantes I; Fleur des blés; Noël des enfants qui n'ont plus de maison; Nuit d'étoiles.

*** Virgin VC5 45360-2. Gens, Vignoles – FAURE; POULENC: *Mélodies.* ***

Véronique Gens gives an impressive and imaginative ac-count of these songs, allowing Debussy's subtle art to register without any expressive exaggeration. She certainly makes a beautiful sound and has the benefit of Roger Vignoles' intelligent support, and excellent and natural recording.

Mélodies: Dans la forêt du charme et de l'enchantement, Op. 36/2; Fêtes galantes I; Nuits blanches; Proses lyriques; 4 Mélodies, Op. 13.

*(*) DG 459 682-2. Schäfer, Irwin – CHAUSSON: *Mélodies.* *(*)

Christine Schäfer is not really any more successful with Debussy than she is with Chausson. Non-French speakers may be less worried by some imperfect pronunciation, and her voice is one of striking beauty, but this is not the best recording this wonderful singer has given us, nor is it among the best recitals.

OPERA

Pelléas et Mélisande (complete).

*** DG 435 344-2 (2). Ewing, Le Roux, Van Dam, Courtis, Ludwig, Pace, Mazzola, Vienna Konzertvereingung, VPO, Abbado.

*** Decca (IMS) 430 502-2 (2). Alliot-Lugaz, Henry, Cachemaille, Thau, Carlson, Golfier, Montreal Ch. & SO, Dutoit.

(B) *** Naxos 8.660047-9 (3). Delusch, Theruel, Arapian, Bacquier, Jessoud, Ch. Regional Nord/Pas de Calais, O Nat. de Lille, J.-C. Casadesus.

*** EMI CMS5 67057-2 [567168] (3). Stilwell, Von Stade, Van Dam, Raimondi, Ch. of German Op., Berlin, BPO, Karajan.

(M) **(*) Sony (ADD) SM3K 47265 (3). Shirley, Söderström, McIntyre, Ward, Minton, ROHCG Ch. & O, Boulez.

(***) EMI mono CHS7 61038-2 (3). Joachim, Jansen, Etcheverry, Paris CO, Désormière (with *Mélodies*).

(***) Testament mono SBT 3051 (3). Jansen, De los Angeles, Souzay, Froumenty, Collard, French Nat. R. O, Cluytens.

Claudio Abbado's outstanding version broadly resolves the problem of a first recommendation in this opera, which has always been lucky on record. If among modern versions the choice has been hard to make between Karajan's sumptu-ously romantic account, almost Wagnerian, and Dutoit's clean-cut, direct one, Abbado satisfyingly presents a per-formance more sharply focused than the one and more freely flexible than the other, altogether more urgently dra-matic. The casting is excellent, with no weak link.

Charles Dutoit brings out the magic of Debussy's score with an involving richness typical of that venue which has played so important a part in the emergence of the Montreal orchestra into the world of international recording. This is not the dreamy reading that some Debussians might prefer, but one that sets the characters very specifically before us as creatures of flesh and blood, not mistily at one remove.

Though the spaciousness of Casadesus's sensitive and poetic reading means that the Naxos set stretches to three discs rather than two, the result is most compelling, with fresh, young voices helping to make the drama more in-volving. Mireille Delusch is a bright and girlish Mélisande, well matched against the high baritone of Gérard Theruel as a boyish Pelléas. The others are first rate too, including the veteran, Gabriel Bacquier, aptly sounding old as Arkel. The voices are to the fore in the recording, with every word made clear, and the orchestra, with a modest band of strings, adds to the chamber-scale intimacy. The libretto comes in French only, but with good notes and a synopsis in English.

EMI have restored the rich and passionate Karajan set to the catalogue, as one of their 'Great Recordings of the Century'. It is a performance that sets Debussy's masterpiece as a natural successor to Wagner's *Tristan*, with the orches-tral tapestry at the centre and the singers providing a verbal obbligato; but Karajan's concentration carries one in total involvement through a story that can seem inconsequential. Frederica von Stade is a tenderly affecting heroine and Richard Stilwell a youthful and upstanding hero, set against the dark, incisive Golaud of Van Dam. The playing of the

Berlin Philharmonic is both polished and deeply committed.

Boulez's sharply dramatic view of Debussy's atmospheric score is a performance which will probably not please the dedicated Francophile – for one thing there is not a single French-born singer in the cast – but it rescues Debussy from the languid half-tone approach which for too long has been accepted as authentic. He is supported by a strong cast; the singing is not always very idiomatic but it has the musical and dramatic momentum that stems from sustained experience on the stage. In almost every way this has the tension of a live performance.

In Roger Désormière's wartime recording, Etcheverry is arguably the most strongly characterized Golaud committed to disc, and neither Joachim's Mélisande nor Jansen's Pelléas has been readily surpassed. A *Pelléas* without atmosphere is no *Pelléas*, and this classic reading puts you under its spell immediately. A further inducement for collectors is a generous selection of Debussy songs from Maggie Teyte and the celebrated recording of *Mes longs cheveux* by the original Mélisande, Mary Garden, accompanied on the piano by Debussy himself in 1904. A very special set.

It is good to see the Cluytens (1956) recording return to currency. Victoria de los Angeles as Mélisande is often affecting and always sings the role exquisitely, and readers will obviously want the set for her. Souzay's Golaud is also magnificent vocally. André Cluytens gets superior playing from the Orchestre National de la Radiodiffusion Française and casts a strong spell, even if he does not always distil as powerful an atmosphere. The transfer is altogether exemplary, a model of its kind, and the well-focused mono sound gives unalloyed pleasure.

Rodrigue et Chimène (opera; completed Langham Smith; orch. Denisov).

*** Erato 4509 98508-2 (2). Brown, Dale, Jossoud, Van Dam, Bastin, Le Texier, Lyon Op. Ch. & O, Nagano.

In the years immediately before he started work on his masterpiece, *Pelléas et Mélisande*, Debussy all but completed this opera to a much more conventional libretto, telling the story of El Cid. Richard Langham Smith reconstructed the rest, and Edison Denisov did the inspired orchestration, adding music from other sections to fill in a few gaps. The best comes first, with radiant singing from Laurence Dale, ideal as Rodrigue, and the fresh and expressive soprano, Donna Brown, as Chimène. Atmospheric off-stage choruses are distinctive too, but little of Act III gives much clue as to the identity of the composer, enjoyable though it is. Kent Nagano's superb recording brings vividly atmospheric sound. José van Dam sings strongly and clearly as the heroine's father, Don Diègue, with the veteran, Jules Bastin, in splendid voice as Don Gomez.

DE LA BARRE, Michel (c. 1675–1745)

Flute Suites Nos. 2 in C min.; 4 in G min.; 6 in C; 8 in D; Sonata No. 1 in B flat.

**(*) ASV CDGAU 181. Hadden, Walker, Carolan, Headley, Sayce.

Michel de la Barre played the transverse flute at the Court of Louis XIV with the status of Flûte de la Chambre. His suites are among the earliest pieces written for the remodelled instrument, and they have a certain pale charm, balancing a pervading melancholy with brighter, more lively airs, gigues and chaconnes. The charming *Sonata* is for a pair of unaccompanied flutes, the *Suites* for solo flute with continuo, here harpsichord, viola da gamba and theorbo. These expert period-instrument performances are stylishly refined and delicate, and certainly pleasing if taken a work at a time.

DELAGE, Maurice (1879–1961)

4 Poèmes hindous.

*** Testament mono SBT 1135. Micheau, O de la Radiodiffusion Française, Cluytens – STRAVINSKY: *Le Rossignol.* *** ⬤

The *Quatre poèmes hindous* make an ideal coupling for *Le Rossignol*. These four songs are very much in the received post-Debussian tradition and are exquisitely sung by Janine Micheau. While the mono sound is less transparent than is ideal, the recording is expertly transferred and gives great pleasure.

DELALANDE, Michel-Richard (1657–1726)

Symphonies pour les soupers du roy (complete).

*** HM HMC 901337/40 (4). Ensemble La Simphonie du Marais, Reyne.

In the last years of his life, Louis XIV could choose from among a dozen suites to accompany his meal. This is the first time all have been committed to disc. Each of these four CDs contains between 36 and 45 individual movements, much of it as charming and inventive as the familiar excerpts. The young members of the Ensemble La Simphonie du Marais, led by Hugo Reyne, give thoroughly fresh and stylish accounts of them.

Cantate Domino; De profundis; Regina coeli.

*** ASV CDGAU 141. Ex Cathedra Chamber Ch. & Bar. O, Skidmore.

Jeffrey Skidmore with his fine, Birmingham-based choir and orchestra presents vividly characterized performances of three of Delalande's 'grands motets', written to be performed simultaneously with the daily celebration of Mass at Louis XIV's court. *De profundis* is a magnificent piece, as are the two lighter, joyful motets. As the title indicates, *Regina coeli* has a Marian text, while *Cantate Domino* represents the peak of Delalande's long career. With their sequences of brief, sharply contrasted movements, these motets, in performances as lively and sensitive as these, can be warmly recommended to many more than baroque specialists. Warm, full sound.

Confitebor tibi Domine; Super flumina Babilonis; Te Deum.

(B) *** HM HMA 1951351. Gens, Piau, Steyer, Fouchécourt, Piolino, Corréas, Les Arts Florissants, Christie.

Confitebor tibi Domine (1699) and *Super flumina Babilonis* (1687) have much expressive writing, and the performances under William Christie are light and airy but not wanting in expressive feeling. The more familiar *Te Deum* is given as good a performance as any that has appeared in recent years. The sound is airy and spacious, and the performances combine lightness and breadth.

3 Leçons de ténèbres.

(M) *** Erato 4509 98528-2. Etcheverry, Charbonnier, Boulay.

Delalande brings a distinctive personal stamp to these settings and is no less a master of the ariosa style than his contemporaries; indeed, in melodic richness some of this is even finer than the Couperin version. And the continuo realization (viola da gamba, harpsichord, chamber organ) was spontaneous and not prepared in every detail beforehand; it sounds fresh and immediate. Micaëla Etcheverry is an excellent soloist; she sings with considerable lyrical beauty, and the artists are eminently well balanced and recorded. A welcome reissue.

DE LA RUE, Pierre (c. 1460–1518)

Missa de feria; Missa Sancta Dei gentrix; Motet: Pater de celis Deus; (i) Motets arr. for lute: *O Domine, Jesu Christe; Regina coeli; Salve Regina.*

*** Hyp. CDA 67010. (i) Gothic Voices, Page; (i) Wilson and Rumsey (lutes).

Pierre de la Rue is still an unfamiliar name, yet he was prolific. His music seems solemn, partly because he is fond of lower vocal ranges, but his ready use of intervals of the third and sixth gives it a harmonic lift and a special individuality. The *Missa de feria* is in five parts and is vocally richer than the more austerely concise *Missa Sancta Dei gentrix* in four; but they are distantly related by sharing an identical musical idea on the words 'Crucifixus' and 'et resurrexit'. The canonic imitation which is at the heart of Pierre's polyphony is heard even more strikingly in the superbly organized six-part motet *Pater de celis Deus*. To provide interludes Christopher Wilson and his partner play three of his lute-duet intabulations, and their closing *Salve Regina* makes a quietly serene postlude. Christopher Page and his Gothic Voices are thoroughly immersed in this repertoire and period, and these stimulating performances could hardly be more authentic. The recording too is well up to standard.

DELDEN, Lex van (1919–88)

(i) *Concerto for Double String Orchestra, Op. 71; Piccolo Concerto, Op. 67;* (ii) *Musica sinfonica, Op. 93;* (iii) *Symphony No. 3 (Facets), Op. 45.*

*(**) Etcetera stereo/mono KTC 1156. Concg. O; (i) Jochum; (ii) Haitink; (iii) Szell.

The idiom of the Dutch composer, Lex van Delden, is predominantly tonal. The strongest of the works here are the *Third Symphony* and the brilliant *Piccolo Concerto* for twelve wind instruments, timpani, percussion and piano. Van Delden is inventive and intelligent, and these four pieces leave you wanting to hear more. The recordings were made at various times and are of varying quality, all in the Concertgebouw Hall and taken from various broadcast tapes, the two concertos conducted by Jochum in 1968 and 1964 respectively (the latter is mono), the *Musica sinfonica* with Haitink in 1969, and the *Third Symphony* with Szell, again mono, in 1957.

DELIBES, Léo (1836–91)

Complete ballets: (i) *Coppélia;* (ii) *Sylvia;* (iii) *La Source.*

(B) *** Decca ADD/Dig. 460 418-2 (4). (i) Nat. PO; (ii) New Phil. O; (iii) ROHCGO; Bonynge.

Complete ballets: (i) *Coppélia;* (ii) *Sylvia.*

(M) *** Mercury (IMS) (ADD) 434 313-2 (3). (i) Minneapolis SO, Dorati; (ii) LSO, Fistoulari.

Delibes's *Coppélia* (1870), which was greatly admired by Tchaikovsky, marked a turning point in the history of ballet music and is his masterpiece. Bonynge's digital recording sparkles from start to finish. There is tremendous energy in the many vigorous numbers and the contribution of the woodwind is a continual delight. Not as consistently inspired as *Coppélia*, *Sylvia* is more serious and symphonic in approach. But there are many exciting set-pieces, much piquant colouring and a haunting *leitmotif* which runs throughout. The New Philharmonia play with tremendous energy and style, and the 1972 recording is as brilliant as you could wish. *La Source* is the composer's first ballet, though he wrote only Acts II and III. Its elegantly lightweight style was a success and alerted the world to his talent for writing for the dance theatre, with his felicitous use of the orchestral palette readily discernible – clearly showing this as a forerunner for *Coppélia* and *Sylvia*. The complete ballet is given here, with Acts I and IV written by Minkus whose contribution is rather more melancholy than Delibes's but is well written and enjoyable. The ROHCG Orchestra plays with great style and the digital recording is warm and detailed – well up to the house standard. At bargain price, this set is exceptional value.

Both Mercury recordings are very early stereo (*Coppélia* 1957, *Sylvia* 1958), but neither sounds its age and *Sylvia*, using the expansive acoustics of Watford Town Hall, approaches the demonstration bracket. Fistoulari was among the very greatest of ballet interpreters, and this shows him at his most inspired. The LSO play superbly for him, the woodwind ensemble is outstanding and the solo playing most beautiful. Dorati's recording of *Coppélia* makes a lively contrast. This Minneapolis recording is rather more confined at the bottom end, but the conductor's vivid combination of energy and grace is appealing in a score that teems with bright melodies and piquant orchestral effects.

Coppélia (ballet): complete.

(B) *** Erato Ultima 8573 84250-2 (2). Lyon Opéra O, Nagano.
*** Decca (IMS) 414 502-2 (2). Nat. PO, Bonynge.

(B) *** Double Decca (ADD) 444 836-2. SRO, Bonynge –
MASSENET: *Le Carillon.* ***

(B) **(*) Ph. Duo (ADD) 438 763-2. Rotterdam PO, Zinman –
CHOPIN: *Les Sylphides;* GOUNOD: *Faust: Ballet
Music.* **(*)

Delibes's delightful score for *Coppélia* is available in a number of different formats, but Kent Nagano's complete set rises fairly easily to the top of the current list of recommendations. The performance has many felicities and the Orchestre de L'Opéra de Lyon bring a sure sense of style to this elegantly crafted and engagingly tuneful music. Their playing is polished yet warm and graceful and, under the lively yet nicely detailed direction of Kent Nagano, the spontaneity of the music-making seems to grow as the ballet proceeds. The recording has a nicely judged acoustic, warm yet clear.

The only slight drawback to Bonynge's digital recording is the relatively modest number of violins which the clarity of the digital recording makes apparent. In all other respects the recording is praiseworthy, not only for its vividness of colour but for the balance within a concert-hall acoustic (Walthamstow Assembly Hall).

On the Double Decca reissue of his earlier (1969) analogue set, Bonynge secures a high degree of polish from the Suisse Romande Orchestra, with sparkling string and wind textures, and with sonority and bite from the brass. The Decca recording sounds freshly minted and, with its generous Massenet bonus, little-known music of great charm, this set remains very competitive.

David Zinman's performance of *Coppélia* is beautifully played and most naturally recorded. The warm acoustic of the Rotterdam concert hall certainly suits Delibes's colourful scoring, and the gracefully delicate string-playing is nicely flattered. The performance has no want of vigour or refinement and, if it is without the sheer character of Nagano's or Bonynge's performances, it is still very enjoyable in its own right.

Coppélia (ballet; complete); *La Source: Suites Nos. 2 & 3;
Intermezzo: Pas de fleurs.*

(BB) *** Naxos 8.553356/7. Slovak RSO (Bratislava), Mogrelia.

The Bratislava orchestra plays with characteristic finesse and grace and with glowing lyrical feeling. There is both drama and vitality. The recording is warm and spacious, with the orchestra set slightly back. Other versions may have more surface brilliance, but most lovers of ballet music will enjoy the naturalness of perspective and the attractively smooth string-quality. *La Source* somes off equally well. The *Pas de fleurs Grande valse* is a real lollipop and in the two suites the music (selected rather arbitrarily) has plenty of colour and rhythmic life.

Coppélia: extended excerpts; *Sylvia:* extended excerpts.

(B) *** EMI (ADD) CZS5 69659-2 (2). Paris Op. O, Mari.

Jean-Baptiste Mari uses ballet tempi throughout, yet there is never any loss of momentum, and the long-breathed string-phrasing and the felicitous wind solos are a continual source of delight. Mari's natural sympathy and warmth make the very most of the less memorable parts of the score for *Sylvia* (and they are only slightly less memorable). Seventy-five minutes are offered from each ballet. The sound is fresh.

Coppélia (ballet): suite (excerpts).

(B) *** DG (ADD) 429 163-2. BPO, Karajan – CHOPIN: *Les
Sylphides* *** 🅞; OFFENBACH: *Gaîté parisienne:*
excerpts. ***

Karajan secures some wonderfully elegant playing from the Berlin Philharmonic Orchestra and his lightness of touch is generally sure. The *Csárdás*, however, is played very slowly and heavily, and its curiously studied tempo may spoil the performance for some. The recording is very impressive; but it is a pity that in assembling the CD the suite had to be truncated (with only 71 minutes' playing time, at least one more number could have been included). As it is, the *Scène et valse de la poupée*, *Ballade de l'épi* and the *Thème slav varié*, all present on the original analogue LP, are omitted here.

(i) *Coppélia* (ballet) suite; (ii) *Sylvia* (ballet) suite.

(B) *** Sony (ADD) SBK 46550. Phd. O, Ormandy – CHOPIN:
Les Sylphides ***; TCHAIKOVSKY: *Nutcracker
Suite.* **(*)

Ormandy and the Philadelphia Orchestra are on top form here. The playing sparkles and has a fine sense of style. Both suites are done in a continuous presentation but are, unfortunately, not banded. The recording is notably full and brilliant in the CBS manner.

Coppélia: suite; *Kassya: Trepak; Le Roi s'amuse:* suite; *La
Source:* suite; *Sylvia:* suite.

(BB) **(*) Naxos 8.550080. Slovak RSO (Bratislava), Lenárd.

An attractive hour of Delibes, with five key items from *Coppélia*, including the *Music for the Automatons* and *Waltz*, four from *Sylvia*, not forgetting the *Pizzicato*, and four from *La Source*. Perhaps most enjoyable of all are the six pastiche ancient 'airs de danse', provided for a ballroom scene in Victor Hugo's play, *Le Roi s'amuse*. They are played most gracefully, and the excerpts from the major ballets are spirited and nicely turned. Vivid sound.

Sylvia (ballet): complete.

(B) *** Double Decca (ADD) 448 095-2 (2). New Philh. O,
Bonynge – MASSENET: *Le Cid.* ***

(BB) *** Naxos 8.553338/9. Razumovsky Sinfonia, Mogrelia –
SAINT-SAENS: *Henry VIII Ballet Music.* ***

Sylvia is played by Richard Bonynge with wonderful polish and affection, and the recording is full, brilliant and sparkling in Decca's best manner. The CDs offer a splendid Massenet bonus, another recording out of Decca's top drawer.

Mogrelia's performance of *Sylvia* above all is spacious, bringing out the music's pastel-shaded lyricism yet finding plenty of weight for the more vigorous music depicting the hunters. The *Divertissement* of Act III (which includes some of the best numbers, including the famous *Pizzicato*) is vividly done. However, in the performance as a whole, glowing sentience takes precedence over vitality, and some might find the atmosphere a little sleepy at times. Excellent, naturally balanced recording.

VOCAL MUSIC

Les Filles de Cadiz.

*** Decca 452 667-2. Bartoli, Myung-Whun Chung (with VIARDOT: *Les Filles de Cadiz; Hai Luli!; Havanaise* ***) − BIZET; BERLIOZ; RAVEL: *Mélodies.* ***

Cecilia Bartoli could hardly be more seductive or more Carmen-like than she is here in Delibes's most famous song, *Les Filles de Cadiz*; here, within a delectable recital of French songs, it is placed alongside the setting of the same poem made by the great prima donna, Pauline Viardot, giving a refreshingly different view. The other Viardot items too are highly engaging in this memorable collection of French mélodies.

OPERA

Lakmé (complete).

*** EMI CDC5 56569-2 (2). Dessay, Kunde, Van Dam, Haldan, Toulouse Capitole Ch. & O, Plasson.
(B) *** Double Decca 460 741-2 (2). Sutherland, Berbié, Vanzo, Bacquier, Monte Carlo Op. Ch. & O, Bonynge.

Lakmé is a strange work, not at all the piece one would expect knowing simply the famous *Bell Song*. The glory of the EMI set is the fresh, girlish portrayal of the heroine by Natalie Dessay, starrily seductive with her silvery, girlish tone, first heard ravishingly from afar. Technically, she is superb too, and the *Bell Song* becomes a narrative, not just a coloratura display piece. As Gerald, Gregory Kunde has an appealingly light and heady tenor, sounding totally idiomatic. José van Dam as the vengeful Nilakantha is not as menacing as some, but he sings with satisfying firmness. Delphine Haldan's fruity mezzo contrasts rather than blends with Dessay's soprano in the popular *Flower duet* but with Plasson warmly expressive, generally taking an expansive view, the sensuousness of the score is well brought out, helped by atmospheric Toulouse recording, though not as sharply focused as the vintage Decca recording, with Bonynge more bitingly dramatic.

The performance on Decca seizes its opportunities with both hands. Sutherland swallows her consonants, but the beauty of her singing, with its ravishing ease and purity up to the highest register, is what matters; and she has opposite her one of the most pleasing and intelligent of French tenors, Alain Vanzo. Excellent contributions from the others too, spirited conducting and brilliant, atmospheric recording. The reissue as a Double Decca makes a splendid bargain and the new-style synopsis will prove especially helpful for newcomers to this opera.

DELIUS, Frederick (1862–1934)

The Delius Collection

With many of the performances directed by the composer's devoted amanuensis and dedicated interpreter, Eric Fenby, the Unicorn Delius Collection can be given the strongest recommendation. Quite apart from the consistent quality of the music-making, the warm and spacious digital sound seems ideally suited to music which depends on atmosphere and evocation to make its fullest effect.

Volume 1: (i–ii) *Dance Rhapsody No. 1* (ed. Beecham); (i; iii) *Dance Rhapsody No. 2; Fantastic Dance;* (iv) (Piano) *Preludes Nos. 1–3; Zum Carneval* (polka); (v; i; iii) *Song of the High Hills.*

✪ *** Unicorn UKCD 2071. (i) RPO; (ii) Del Mar; (iii) Fenby; (iv) Parkin; (v) Amb. S.

Norman Del Mar and Eric Fenby, both natural Delians, give spontaneously volatile performances of the *Dance Rhapsodies*, and the spacious recording with its wide dynamic range captures well the music's sudden mood-changes. The *Fantastic Dance* is an agreeable late miniature. Eric Parkin also breathes Delian air naturally. The *Preludes* for piano are typical miniatures, the *Polka* an oddity. The piano is naturally caught. But the highlight of this well-planned programme is the *Song of the High Hills*, written in 1911. Fenby draws a richly atmospheric performance, here finely balanced within an evocative sound-picture.

Volume 2: (i–ii) *Piano Concerto;* (iii–iv) *Violin Concerto;* (v) *Irmelin: Prelude; A Late Lark; A Song of Summer.*

*** Unicorn UKCD 2072. RPO; (i) Fowke; (ii) Del Mar; (iii) Holmes; (iv) Handley; (v) Fenby.

Philip Fowke, in partnership with Del Mar, rides confidently over the orchestra in this impassioned account of the one-movement *Piano Concerto*; Ralph Holmes and Vernon Handley form a comparable symbiosis in their strong and beautiful account of the *Violin Concerto*. A Late Lark was the last composition which Delius was able to finish, except for a few bars, before the arrival of Eric Fenby; while *A Song of Summer* is the finest of the works which Fenby subsequently took down from the composer's dictation; the performance is loving and dedicated. The programme opens with a ravishingly atmospheric account of the *Irmelin Prelude*.

Volume 3: (i) *Koanga: La Calinda;* (i–iii) *Idyll;* (i–iv) *Songs of Sunset;* (v) *A Village Romeo and Juliet: Walk to the Paradise Garden.*

*** Unicorn UKCD 2073. RPO; (i) Fenby; with (ii) Lott, (iii) Allen; (iv) Walker, Amb. S.; (v) Del Mar.

The love-scene entitled *Idyll* was rescued from an abortive opera project (*Margot la rouge*). It becomes a beautiful, extended duet in this impressive performance by Felicity Lott and Thomas Allen. Allen is no less persuasive in the *Songs of Sunset*, where he is joined by Sarah Walker, and this fine recording brings ravishing sounds from the Ambrosians, with both soloists deeply expressive. The concert opens with Norman Del Mar's languorously brooding yet passionate account of the *Walk to the Paradise Garden* and ends with Fenby's expansive performance of *La Calinda*, which begins with deceptive delicacy. First-class digital sound throughout.

Volume 4: (i) *Cello Sonata;* (ii) *Violin Sonatas Nos. 1–3.*

*** Unicorn Dig./ADD UKCD 2074. (i) Lloyd Webber;
  (ii) Holmes; Fenby.

Julian Lloyd Webber is a warmly persuasive advocate of the *Cello Sonata* and Fenby partners him admirably. The three *Violin Sonatas*, particularly the last, are also among the finest of Delius's chamber works. Though Fenby as pianist may not be a virtuoso, the natural affinity of his playing and that of Ralph Holmes makes this one of the most treasurable and moving of Delius recordings. The *Cello Sonata* was recorded digitally in 1981 and is set in a natural and pleasing acoustic. The *Violin Sonatas*, dating from a decade earlier, are also atmospheric in ambience, but the violin timbre has just a hint of thinness on top.

Volume 5: Orchestral songs: (i) *The bird's story;* (ii) *I-Brasil;* (i) *Le ciel est par-dessus le toit;* (ii) *La lune blanche;* (i) *Let springtime come;* (ii) *Il pleure dans mon coeur;* (iii) *To daffodils; Twilight fancies; Wine roses.* Songs with piano: (iii) *Autumn;* (i) *Avant que tu ne t'en ailles;* (iii) *Chanson d'automne;* (i) *Le ciel est par-dessus le toit;* (ii) *I-Brasil;* (i) *In the garden of the Seraglio; Irmelin Rose;* (iii) *Let springtime come;* (ii) *La lune blanche; Il pleure dans mon coeur; Silken shoes; So white, so soft, so sweet is she;* (i) *Sweet Venevil;* (iii) *To daffodils; Twilight fancies;* (i) *The violet.*

*** Unicorn UKCD 2075. (i) Lott; (ii) Rolfe Johnson;
  (iii) Walker; RPO, Fenby, or Fenby (piano).

All the orchestral songs here are sung in the original language, whereas in the larger collection of English, French and Scandinavian songs – in which Eric Fenby accompanies on Delius's own piano – except for three in German, the Scandinavian settings are sung in English. Apart from the early *Twilight fancies* they are little known, but they consistently reflect the composer's feeling for words. The duplications in both versions are particularly welcome. All three soloists sing most understandingly and characterfully. Excellent recording.

Volume 6: (i) *Fennimore and Gerda: Intermezzo;* (ii) *Paris (The Song of a Great City;* ed. Beecham); (iii–iv) *Suite for Violin & Orchestra;* (i; v) *An Arabesque.*

*** Unicorn UKCD 2076. RPO, cond. (i) Fenby; (ii) Del Mar;
  (iii) Handley; with (iv) Holmes; (v) Allen, Amb. S.

Paris is spaciously conceived by Norman Del Mar, and the splendidly atmospheric Unicorn sound-picture suits this evocatively leisurely reading. In Fenby's hands, *An Arabesque* emerges as a masterpiece. The emotional thrust of the opening sequence, superbly sung by Thomas Allen and with passionate singing from the chorus too, subsides into characteristic Delius reflectiveness. The early *Suite for Violin and Orchestra* is played with much understanding; and Fenby closes the programme with a warmly evocative account of the best-known piece here, the lovely *Intermezzo* from *Fennimore and Gerda.*

Volume 7: (i) *2 Aquarelles;* (i; iv) *Caprice & Elegy;* (ii; v) *Légende;* (iii) *Life's Dance;* (i; vi) *Cynara;* (i; vii) *Songs of Farewell.*

*** Unicorn UKCD 2077. RPO, cond. (i) Fenby; (ii) Handley;
  (iii) Del Mar; with (iv) Lloyd Webber; (v) Holmes; (vi) Allen;
  (vii) Amb. S.

Once again Eric Fenby draws loving and dedicated performances from the RPO and the Ambrosian Singers: the *Songs of Farewell* are most beautiful; and Thomas Allen is very impressive in *Cynara. Life's Dance,* certainly does not lack ebullience in Norman Del Mar's hands, and Ralph Holmes and Handley again find an admirable partnership in the *Légende.* The two gentle *Aquarelles* for strings, together with the *Caprice and Elegy* (dedicated to Fenby) for cello and small orchestra, make an attractive central interlude in the programme. Julian Lloyd Webber is very persuasive as soloist in the latter piece. As throughout this series, the recording is warmly atmospheric and beautifully balanced.

Other orchestral recordings

Air & Dance; Fennimore and Gerda: Intermezzo. Hassan: Intermezzo & Serenade; Koanga: La Calinda. On Hearing the First Cuckoo in Spring; A Song Before Sunrise; Summer Night on the River; A Village Romeo and Juliet: The Walk to the Paradise Garden. (i) *Sea Drift.*

(M) *** Decca (ADD) 440 323-2. ASMF, Marriner;
  (i) Shirley-Quirk, L. Symphony Ch., RPO, Hickox.

These are lovely performances, warm, tender and eloquent. They are played superbly and recorded (in 1977) in a flattering acoustic though, with a relatively small band of strings, the sound inevitably has less body than with a full orchestral group. *Sea Drift* was recorded three years later, in 1980, and is a total success. Rather than lingering, Richard Hickox is urgent in his expressiveness, but there is plenty of evocative atmosphere. John Shirley-Quirk sings with characteristic sensitivity, and the chorus – trained by Hickox – is outstanding. The effect of the CD transfer is most real and tangible, the chorus set back within a warm ambience.

Air & Dance; Florida Suite; North Country Sketches; On Hearing the First Cuckoo in Spring.

(N) (M) *** Chan. 6628. LPO or Ulster O, Handley.

Vernon Handley's splendid Ulster coupling of the comparatively rare *Florida Suite* (written in America) and the *North Country Sketches* (which evokes the seasons on the Yorkshire moors) has always been a staple of the CD catalogue. In the latter work a Debussian influence is revealed and Handley's refined (yet warm) approach to the early (1887) *Florida Suite* clearly links it with later masterpieces, with the famous *La Calinda* delightfully presented. The recording is superbly balanced within the very suitable acoustics of the Ulster Hall, and it is hardly less impressive in the two bonuses from the LPO, which are equally beautifully played. The *Air and Dance* dates from 1915 and was dedicated to the National Institute for the Blind. A highly recommendable reissue.

American Rhapsody (Appalachia); Norwegian Suite (Folkeraadet: The Council of the People); Paa Vidderne (On the Heights); Spring Morning.

** Marco Polo 8.220452. Slovak PO, Bratislava, Hopkins.

Paa Vidderne, the most substantial piece here, is rather melodramatic but has a distinct melodic interest. *Spring Morning* is shorter and similarly picaresque, but the *Folkeraadet Suite* displays a sure orchestral touch and is most attractive in its diversity of invention. The *American Rhapsody* is a concise version of *Appalachia* without the chorus, given here in its original (1896) format. John Hopkins brings a strong sympathy and understanding to this repertoire and secures a committed and flexible response from his Czech players in music which must have been wholly unknown to them.

(i) Appalachia; Sea Drift; (ii) A Song before Sunrise; Koanga: La Calinda.

(N) *** Australian Decca Eloquence (ADD)467 60-2.
(i) Shirley-Quirk, LSO Ch., RPO, Hickox; (ii) ASMF, Marriner.

Hickox's 1977 LP of *Appalachia* and *Sea Drift* is an early example of this conductor's natural affinity with Delius. These are fresh and dedicated performances, urgent in their expressiveness rather than lingering. John Shirley-Quirk sings with characteristic sensitivity, and the chorus is outstanding. The trusty Marriner items are always good to hear, and the sound throughout this generous CD is superb. Texts are included in this Australian Eloquence release, as are excellent notes by Christopher Palmer.

(i; ii) Appalachia; (iii) Brigg Fair; (i; ii) Hassan: Closing Scene; Irmelin Prelude; Koanga: La Calinda (arr. by Fenby).

(N) (BB) Naxos mono 8.110906. (i) LPO; (ii) BBC Ch.;
(iii) Beecham SO; all cond. by Beecham.

(i) Eventyr (Once upon a Time); Hassan: Incidental Music; (i; ii) Koanga: Closing Scene; (iii) On Hearing the First Cuckoo in Spring; (i) Paris; (iii) Summer Night on the River.

(N) (BB) Naxos mono 8.110904. (i) LPO; (ii) London Select Ch.; (iii) RPO; all cond. by Beecham.

These recordings are mostly pioneering accounts of Delius made by his finest interpreter, Sir Thomas Beecham, between 1927 and 1934, and in artistic terms they are without peer. However, it is sad that the transfers are so wanting in timbre and colour that it is impossible to recommend them. No one who has the originals or has heard the LP transfers by A. C. Griffith would recognize them. Let us hope that Dutton Laboratories or Ward Marston will restore them.

2 Aquarelles (arr. Fenby); Brigg Fair; Dance Rhapsodies Nos. 1–2 (ed. Beecham); Florida Suite; In a Summer Garden; North Country Sketches. On Hearing the First Cuckoo in Spring; Summer Night on the River (both ed. Beecham); The Walk to the Paradise Garden.

(B) **(*) Double Decca 460 290-2 (2). WNO O, Mackerras.

Mackerras is just as warmly sympathetic in these Delius orchestral pieces as in his complete opera recording, *A Village Romeo and Juliet*. The contrast between the two performances of the interlude, *The Walk to the Paradise Garden*, reflects the contrast between the orchestras, the Welsh more direct and passionate. The *Dance Rhapsodies*, music which is far from rhapsodic, here receive fresh, taut performances. In the shorter works Mackerras is warmly sympathetic, with the woodwind playing in particular excellent. But the recording, made in the Brangwyn Hall, Swansea, is less spacious, less sensuous than the Austrian-made one of the opera, lacking Delian mystery. The massed strings in particular have too much brightness; one requires more lambent textures in this music.

2 Aquarelles (arr. FENBY); Fennimore and Gerda: Intermezzo. Hassan: Intermezzo & Serenade (all arr. BEECHAM); Irmelin: Prelude. Late Swallows (arr. FENBY); On Hearing the First Cuckoo in Spring; A Song Before Sunrise; Summer Night on the River.

(M) *** Chan. 6502. Bournemouth Sinf., Del Mar.

The 49-minute concert creates a mood of serene, atmospheric evocation – into which Eric Fenby's arrangement of *Late Swallows* from the *String Quartet* fits admirably – and the beauty of the 1977 analogue recording has been transferred very well to CD, with all its warmth and bloom retained.

2 Aquarelles; Fennimore and Gerda: Intermezzo. On Hearing the First Cuckoo in Spring; Summer Night on the River.

(M) *** DG (ADD) 439 529-2. ECO, Barenboim – VAUGHAN WILLIAMS: *Lark Ascending*, etc.; WALTON: *Henry V*. ***

Barenboim's luxuriant performances have voluptuous sensuousness, and their warm, sleepy atmosphere should seduce many normally resistant to Delius's pastoralism. The couplings are no less enticing.

Brigg Fair; Dance Rhapsody No. 2; Fennimore and Gerda: Intermezzo (arr. FENBY); Florida Suite: Daybreak – Dance (La calinda) (revised & edited Beecham); Irmelin: Prelude; On Hearing the First Cuckoo in Spring; Sleigh Ride; Song before Sunrise; Summer Evening (arr. BEECHAM) Summer Night on the River.

(N) ✿ (M) *** EMI CDM5 67552 [567553]. RPO, Beecham.

The further remastering of Beecham's stereo Delius recordings, made at Abbey Road at the end of the 1950s, continues to demonstrate a technological miracle. No doubt Sir Thomas's meticulous ear for subtlety of balance contributed much to this, but the EMI producer and engineer, Lawrence Collingwood and Christopher Palmer respectively, must share the credit. The result brings these unsurpassed performances into our own time with an uncanny sense of realism and presence. The delicacy of the gentler wind and string textures is something to marvel at, as is the orchestral playing itself. Beecham's fine-spun magic, his ability to lift a phrase is apparent from the very opening of *Brigg Fair*, which shows Delius at his most inspired and Beecham's orchestra at their most incandescent. The shorter pieces (especially the ravishing *Intermezzo* from *Fennimore and*

Gerda) bring superb wind solos, while Beecham often conjures a lazy sentient warmth from the strings - as in *On Hearing the First Cuckoo in Spring*, but more especially in *Summer Night on the River*, which no other conductor has matched since. The *Sleigh Ride* shows Beecham twinkling and sparkling, and he is no less persuasive in the excerpt from the *Florida Suite*. But why is this not complete? The admirable documentation is by Lyndon Jenkins. Sheer magic, and fully worthy to be included in EMI's 'Great Recordings of the Century'.

Brigg Fair; Dance Rhapsody No. 2; On Hearing the First Cuckoo in Spring; In a Summer Garden.

(B) *** Sony (ADD) SBK 62645. Phd. O, Ormandy –
VAUGHAN WILLIAMS: *Fantasias*, etc. ***

Ormandy and his great orchestra, on peak form in the early 1960s, give warm, stirring and highly romantic performances of these four masterpieces. Ormandy and his engineers do not seek the fragility, the evanescence of Delius's visions; for that one can turn to Beecham. But this music responds well to a riper approach and there is no danger here of Delius sounding faded. The sound is remarkably full and expansive, far more convincing than the original LP. With its equally involving coupling, this is a true bargain.

(i) *Brigg Fair; La Calinda* (arr. Fenby); *In a Summer Garden; Fennimore and Gerda: Intermezzo. Hassan: Intermezzo* and (iii) *Serenade* (arr. Beecham); (ii) *Irmelin: Prelude;* (i) *Late Swallows* (arr. Fenby); *On Hearing the First Cuckoo in Spring; A Song before Sunrise;* (ii) *A Song of Summer;* (i) *Summer Night on the River;* (ii) *A Village Romeo and Juliet: Walk to the Paradise Garden* (arr. Beecham); (i; iv) *Appalachia* (with brief rehearsal sequence).

(M) *** EMI (ADD) CMS5 65119-2. (i) Hallé O; (ii) LSO; Barbirolli; (iii) with Tear; (iv) Jenkins, Amb. S.

Sir John shows an admirable feeling for the sense of light Delius conjures up and for the luxuriance of texture his music possesses. The gentle evocation of *La Calinda* contrasts with the surge of passionate Italianate romanticism at the climax of *The Walk to the Paradise Garden*. Barbirolli's style is evanescent in repose and more romantic than the Beecham versions but, with lovely playing from both the Hallé and the LSO, the first-rate analogue sound from the mid- to late 1960s adds to the listener's pleasure. *Appalachia* is given an admirably atmospheric reading that conveys the work's exotic and vivid colouring.

Brigg Fair; In a Summer Garden; On Hearing the First Cuckoo in Spring; Paris (The Song of a Great City); Summer Night on the River; A Village Romeo and Juliet: Walk to the Paradise Garden.

(N) (BB) *** Warner Apex 8573 89084-2. BBC SO, A. Davis.

A superb disc. Beecham may be very special in these lovely scores but it is good to have state-of-the-art modern recordings, admirably spacious and atmospheric and with an excitingly wide dynamic range. The closing section of *Brigg Fair*, with Davis's slow sustained march tempo leading to an impulsive accelerando and a great surge of passion, is thrilling, and shows, like the similarly volatile account of *Paris*, how deeply Andrew Davis responds to this music. But he can be languorous too (a legacy from Barbirolli perhaps), as at the beginning of the *Walk to the Paradise Garden;* later the BBC strings sing out with full-blooded fervour at the climax, superbly caught by the engineers, and Davis tapers down the coda very beautifully indeed. *On Hearing the First Cuckoo in Spring* and the *Summer Night on the River* both bring a feeling a hazy rapture with lovely woodwind detail. In short this is post-Beecham Delius with a new approach from a conductor who feels this music in his very being.

Caprice & Elegy (for cello and chamber orchestra).

*** RCA 09026 61695-2. Starker, Philh. O, Slatkin – ELGAR: *Cello Concerto;* WALTON: *Cello Concerto.* **(*)

As a bonus to the Elgar and Walton concertos, Janos Starker offers these two tender and evocative Delius miniatures, originally dictated to Eric Fenby, with chamber orchestra accompaniment. The reserve which marks his view of the major works here evaporates in warm, sweet playing.

(i) *Caprice & Elegy;* (ii–iii) *Piano Concerto;* (iv–v) *Violin Concerto;* (vi; iii) *Hassan: Intermezzo & Serenade; Koanga: La Calinda;* (v) *On Hearing the First Cuckoo in Spring;* (vii) *Legend for Violin & Piano.*

(***) Testament mono SBT 1014. (i) Harrison, CO, Fenby; (ii) Moiseiwitsch, Philh. O; (iii) Lambert; (iv) Sammons; (v) Liverpool PO, Sargent; (vi) Hallé O; (vii) Holst, Moore.

The greatest treasure here is the first ever recording of the *Violin Concerto*, made in 1944 and featuring the original soloist, Albert Sammons, arguably the most eloquent and moving account of the work ever committed to disc. Moiseiwitsch's recording of the *Piano Concerto*, also the first ever, is hardly less powerful, making a very good case for this warm but less cogent piece. The other items range from the 1930 recording of the *Caprice and Elegy* by Beatrice Harrison, the dedicatee, with suspect intonation and plentiful portamento, to Sargent's 1947 recording of the *First Cuckoo*, very warm and free in its rubato. Constant Lambert is also a first-rate interpreter of Delius, as the *Hassan* and *Koanga* excerpts show. This transfer has higher surface-hiss than later issues on this label, but the disc must be strongly recommended.

Cello Concerto.

*** EMI CDC5 55529-2. Du Pré, RPO, Sargent (with Recital. ***)

The EMI disc offers what was du Pré's first concerto recording, and this recital is a transfer of the material mainly from her very first EMI sessions in 1962 which gave such clear promise of glories to come. Most recommendable, although readers will note that it remains at full price.

(i) *Cello Concerto;* (ii) *Hassan: Serenade* (arr. for cello and orchestra).

(N) (M) *** RCA (ADD) 74321 84112-2 (2). Lloyd Webber, (i) Philh. O, Handley; (ii) Nat.PO, Gerhardt – BRUCH: *Kol Nidrei;* HOLST: *Invocation;* LALO: *Concerto;* RODRIGO: *Concierto como un divertimento;* VAUGHAN WILLIAMS:

Fantasia on Sussex Folk Tunes. *** (with Recital
'Celebration' ***)

Lloyd Webber is inside the idiom and plays the concerto
(the composer's own favourite among his four concertos)
with total conviction. Its lyricism is beguiling, but the work
proceeds in wayward fashion and the soloist must play every
note as if he believes in it ardently – and this Lloyd Webber
and his partners do. The RCA balance is ideal and conveys
an almost chamber-like quality at times with great warmth
and clarity. The *Hassan Serenade* makes a seductive encore,
with sound even more balmy.

Violin Concerto.

(M) **(*) EMI (ADD) CDM7 64725-2. Menuhin, RPO, Davies
– ELGAR: *Violin Concerto.* ***

Menuhin's account, well accompanied and recorded in 1976,
does not show the polish of his playing in earlier years, and
the timbre is not always ideally sweet; but he gives a heartfelt
performance, and the semi-improvisational freedom and
radiant beauty of the writing above the stave are caught
superbly. The Abbey Road recording is truthful, warmly
atmospheric and well balanced.

Dance Rhapsodies Nos. 1–2; In a Summer Garden; North Country Sketches; A Village Romeo and Juliet: Walk to the Paradise Garden.

**(*) Chan. 9355. Bournemouth SO, Hickox.

Hickox is a sensitive and flexible Delian and the Bournemouth orchestra play passionately for him, especially in the
Walk to the Paradise Garden. The *Dance Rhapsodies* are not
held together quite so persuasively as by Eric Fenby, who
also has the advantage of smoother and more natural string
recording. *In a Summer Garden* is both ardent and luxuriant
in its shimmering summer heat-haze, while the wintry landscape of the *North Country Sketches* brings almost crystalline
iciness from the violins. But the recording, made in the
Winter Gardens, Bournemouth, although basically full and
spacious, brings a somewhat two-dimensional effect in
catching the fervent sweep of violin-tone, as if the microphones were a little too close.

Fennimore and Gerda: Intermezzo. Irmelin: Prelude. Koanga: La Calinda (arr. Fenby). On Hearing the First Cuckoo in Spring; Sleigh Ride; A Song before Sunrise; Summer Night on the River; A Village Romeo and Juliet: The Walk to the Paradise Garden.

(B) *** CfP (ADD) CD-CFP 4304. LPO, Handley.

Those looking for a bargain collection of Delius should find
this very good value; Handley's approach to *The Walk to the
Paradise Garden* is strongly emotional, closer to Barbirolli
than to Beecham.

Florida Suite; Idylle de printemps; Over the Hills and Far Away; La Quadroone; Scherzo; (i) Koanga: Closing Scene.

(BB) *** Naxos 8.553535. E. N. Philh. O, Lloyd-Jones; (i) with
Glanville, Lees, Evans, Francis, Peerce, Thomas.

Several of the works here are new to disc, including the *Idylle
de printemps*, fresh and charming, leading to an ecstatic

climax. *La Quadroone* and *Scherzo* were originally planned
as movements in a suite. Lloyd-Jones has clearly learnt from
Beecham's example in his glowing and intense readings of
the other three works, with the orchestra's woodwind soloists excelling themselves in delicate pointing, not least in the
haunting *La Calinda*, included in the *Florida Suite. Over the
Hills and Far Away*, raptly done, is richly evocative too, and
the epilogue to the opera, *Koanga*, rounds off a generously
filled disc with music both sensuous and passionate, featuring six female vocal soloists from Opera North, three
sopranos and three mezzos.

On Hearing the First Cuckoo in Spring; Summer Night on the River.

(B) *** DG (ADD) 439 464-2. ECO, Barenboim (with
BRITTEN: *Serenade*) – VAUGHAN WILLIAMS:
Greensleeves, etc. ***

Hazily sensuous in the summer sunshine, Barenboim's performances are warmly and enticingly recorded, and here
offered as part of a fine bargain collection of English music.

On the Mountains (symphonic poem); (i) Paa vidderne (melodrama). (ii) 7 Songs from the Norwegian.

(N) *** Classico CLASSCD 364. RLPO, Bostock; (i) Hall;
(ii) Lund (with GRIEG: *Norwegian Bridal Procession*, orch.
Delius ***).

'Vidde' is unique to Norwegian and means the desolate
heather and rock of the high mountains rather than just
plain mountain. So both Delius's *Paa vidderne* and the
slightly earlier tone poem are best translated as *On the
Heights.* The latter was first performed in 1891 and was
recorded by Beecham in 1946. The 40-minute *Paa vidderne*
(1888) was never performed in Delius's lifetime, and its
première was given in 1981 on Norwegian television; this is
the first recording in this format of this great rarity. It
was originally intended for tenor and orchestra but finally
emerged as a melodrama, with Ibsen's poem being declaimed. Delius had first met Grieg in 1887, not long after
the composition of Grieg's own melodrama *Bergliot*, but
although he spoke good Norwegian by this time, Delius set
Ibsen's text in German; in this case Douglas Bostock uses
Lionel Carley's fine English translation from the Ibsen original. There is a lot of Grieg here, but much that only Delius
could have written, often highly imaginative and rather
haunting. However, the medium is not really satisfactory
(Grieg had warned Delius as to the impracticality of the
genre), and Peter Hall has to assert himself over the full
orchestra, and in climaxes the result is not pleasing. All the
same the piece is always interesting and often moving. The
Songs from the Norwegian are also given in English. Bostock
is a first-rate conductor and gets vitally fresh and responsive
playing from the Royal Liverpool Philharmonic. There is
plenty of air around the aural image, and the recording
balance is judged most musically.

Over the Hills and Far Away; Paris (The Song of a Great City); (i) Sea Drift.

(N) (M) ((***)) Sony mono SMK 89430. RPO, Beecham;
(i) with Boyce & BBC Ch.

Beecham's interpretations of Delius are uniquely compelling: the early tone-poem *Over the Hills and Far Away* comes over with great atmosphere and both *Paris* and *Sea Drift*, with Bruce Boyce as soloist, are special, so it is sad that Sony's standards of transfer have deteriorated since these mono recordings of the early 1950s first appeared on CD. An extra top-emphasis goes with more muddled inner textures, so that even in *Paris* – the most successful of the transfers here – the percussion sounds shallow and unnatural. When Beecham never managed to record *Sea Drift* in stereo sound, it is specially sad that the chorus sounds ill-focused and rather crumbly in a work that cries out for evocative atmosphere. With all the reservations over transfers the performances remain irreplaceable.

(i) *2 Pieces for Strings;* (ii) *7 Danish Songs; Irmelin Suite*.

** Dinemic DCCD 019. (i) Philh. O; (ii) Farley, Rhein PO; Serebrier.

Delians will welcome this issue, which brings rare repertoire: the Danish songs have not been recorded before. However, the value of these performances is diminished by the recording, which is far too reverberant and by no means well focused.

Sonata for Strings (arr. from *String Quartet* by Eric Fenby).

(*) Koch 3-7139. New Zealand CO, Braithwaite – BRIDGE: *Suite*, etc. *

It was Sir John Barbirolli who in 1963 commissioned Delius's amanuensis, Eric Fenby, to score the 'Late swallows' slow movement of the *String Quartet* for full orchestral strings, and in 1977 he completed the arrangement of the whole work. It is arguable whether the other movements transcribe as effectively as the third (marked by the composer 'Slow and wistfully'), but the performance here is persuasive and the warm yet transparently natural sound seems right for the music.

CHAMBER MUSIC

Cello Sonata.

*** Chan. 8499. R. and P. Wallfisch – BAX: *Rhapsodic Ballad;* BRIDGE: *Cello Sonata;* WALTON: *Passacaglia*. ***

Cello Sonata (in one movement); *2 Pieces for Cello & Piano; Romance; Hassan: Serenade*.

*** Ph. 454 458-2. Lloyd Webber, Forsberg – GRIEG: *Cello Sonata*. ***

Julian Lloyd Webber offers a most attractive coupling of the complete cello-and-piano music of both Delius and Grieg, composers closely linked both in musical style and as personal friends. Since he last recorded the Delius *Cello Sonata* (for Unicorn in 1981) Lloyd Webber has refined and deepened his reading, making it tauter than before. He is just as warmly sympathetic in the shorter pieces.

In the alternative version of the *Cello Sonata* the Chandos performers give as strong and sympathetic an account as is to be found. They are also excellently recorded.

(i) *Cello Sonata. Violin Sonatas Nos.* (ii) *1–2;* (iii) *3*.

(B) *** EMI CZS5 73992-2 (2). (i) Welsh; (ii) Graham; (iii) Barantschick; (i–iii) Margalit – ELGAR: *Piano Quintet*, etc. **(*)

Those looking for modern, digital recordings of these four works will find that these performances by members of the LSO are in every way satisfying. Moray Welsh provides warm tone and much depth of feeling in the *Cello Sonata* and Janice Graham's passionate advocacy in the earlier *Violin Sonatas* matches that of Alexander Barantschick in the *Third*. Israela Margalit's pianism in all four works is full of personality, and the recording is resonant and forwardly balanced, and satisfyingly full. However, the Elgar couplings are rather less memorable.

String Quartet.

*** ASV CDDCA 526. Brodsky Qt – ELGAR: *Quartet*. ***

In this music, the ebb and flow of tension and a natural feeling for persuasive but unexaggerated rubato is vital; with fine ensemble but seeming spontaneity, the Brodsky players consistently produce that. First-rate recording.

String Quartet; *2 Movements* (1888).

(N) ** Meridian CDE 84401. Bridge Qt – GRIEG: *String Quartet in G min., Op. 27;* (with: GRAINGER: *Molly on the Shore*). **

Three composers linked by friendship share this Meridian CD, which features not only Delius's *Quartet*, but two movements of a string quartet from 1888, the year in which Delius and Grieg met in Leipzig. Its existence was known for a long time, as Delius had sent the entire score to Sinding in the hope that it would interest the Brodsky Quartet (who had played the Grieg work earlier that year), but nothing came of it. Two or three years ago Michael Schonfield, the violist of the Bridge Quartet, discovered a manuscript of two movements (the third and fourth) and a fragment of another, and consequently they make their début on record here. The first, the *Adagio*, is the more individual of the two, with many Griegian touches that serve as a reminder that this is the period of the *Florida Suite*. The musicians are totally inside the idiom and responsive to the ebb and flow of the musical ideas, but the performance is a little wanting in tonal finesse and the intonation is occasionally wry. The recording is a shade reverberant. The Grieg is played with genuine ardour and imagination, although there are finer, more authoritative accounts before the public. But Delians will obviously want this disc.

Violin Sonatas Nos. *1–3; in B, Op. posth*.

● *** Conifer 75605 51315-2. Little, Lane.

This is the first disc to bring together all four of Delius's *Violin Sonatas*, here performed magnetically, with Tasmin Little's deeply felt playing superbly matched by Piers Lane; these are works that find Delius at his most meltingly lyrical. The rarity is the earliest and longest, written in 1892 but not published until 1977, less distinctive than the three numbered works, but already very characteristic. The others are tauter and more compact than one expects of Delius, culminating in the haunting masterpiece that, when blind and paralysed, he dictated to his amanuensis, Eric Fenby.

VOCAL MUSIC

(i) *Appalachia: Chorus* (arr. B. SUCHOFF) Songs: *An den Sonnenschein; Ave Maria; Durch den Wald; Frühlingsabruch; Her ute skai gildet saa; Little birdie; On Craig Ddu. Two Songs to be Sung of a Summer Night on the Water:* No. 1, without words; No. 2, with tenor solo; *Sonnenscheinlied; The splendour falls on castle walls; The streamlet's slumber song. Hassan,* Act I: *Chorus;* Act II: *Chorus of beggars and dancing girls; Irmelin,* Act I (arr. E. LUBIN): (i) *Chorus. A Village Romeo and Juliet: Wanderer's Song* (male voices); *Wedding music.*

*** Somm SOMMCD 210. Douse, Ball, Elysian Singers of London, Greenhall with (i) Nolan.

Though you would hardly recognize the early part-songs of 1887 as the work of Delius, their Englishness is attractive, making a delightful prelude to an evocative sequence freshly performed. In chronological order, it follows the composer's development through his early operas, with appropriate sequences turned into separate numbers – those from *A Village Romeo and Juliet* and *Appalachia* involving accompaniments for organ and piano respectively. The climax comes with the two haunting *Songs to be Sung of a Summer Night on the Water.* The *Hassan* items too are vintage Delius, before the final Tennyson setting rather pales in face of Britten's far more vivid setting in the *Serenade.* Warm, atmospheric sound.

(i) *An Arabesk. A Mass of Life: Prelude.* (ii) *Songs of Sunset,* Parts 1–7; (iii) Part 8. Songs: (iv) *I-Brasil; Le ciel est pardessus le toit; Cradle song; Irmelin Rose; Klein Venevil; The nightingale; Twilight fancies; The violet; Whither.*

(N) (***) Somm mono BEECHAM 8. (i, ii) Roy Henderson, L. select Ch.; (ii) Haley; (iii) Nancy Evans, Llewellyn, BBC Ch. (iv) Labbette; LPO or RPO, Beecham (or (iv) Beecham, piano).

Drawn from discs in Beecham's own private collection, mostly unissued till now, this collection includes several treasures, notably the live recording of the *Songs of Sunset,* made at the 1934 Leeds Festival. Far more than any rival, Beecham conveys a virile thrust and energy in the writing, partly by opting for faster speeds. Both in this, with its seven linked sections, and in the single span of *An Arabesk,* a setting of Jens Peter Jacobsen in Philip Heseltine's translation, the line of the argument is clarified. Roy Henderson is the clean-cut, sensitive baritone soloist in both, sounding very English, with Olga Haley a fresh, bright mezzo soloist in the *Songs of Sunset.* The test pressings sadly lack the final section, but a substitute is provided for that section, taken from a 1946 recording with Nancy Evans and Redvers Llewellyn, which Beecham initially rejected. The ends of 78 sides tend to have a noisy surface, but there is ample body in the sound.

Dora Labbette is the enchanting soprano soloist in all the separate songs, bright and silvery, attacking even the most

exposed high notes with astonishing purity and with magical *pianissimos.* Four of the ten come in the beautiful orchestral versions, with the rest accompanied at the piano by Beecham himself. He may have been only a good amateur pianist, but his natural magnetism still shines out.

An Arabesk; 2 Danish Songs; 5 Danish Songs (orch. Bo Holten); *7 Danish Songs* (1897); *Fennimore and Gerda: Intermezzo. Lebenstanz; Sakuntala.*

(N) *** Danacord DACOCD 536. Bonde-Hansen, Reuter, Danish Nat. Op. Ch., Aarhus Chamber Ch. and SO, Holten.

This collection of Danish inspirations, beautifully performed and recorded, reveals Delius at his most characteristic, drawing on his deep sympathy for Scandinavia and its culture. Tending to favour speeds a shade faster than usual, Bo Holten brings out the emotional thrust of such a piece as *An Arabesk,* rather as Beecham used to. The longest of the vocal pieces here, *An Arabesk,* dates from 1911, but the others were written much earlier, music reflecting the younger Delius, active and virile. The *Seven Danish Songs* of 1897 come in Delius's own sensuous orchestrations, with the self-quotations in the ballad-like *Irmelin Rose* the more telling in orchestral form, while *Summer nights* is magically transformed in its atmospheric evocation of a sunset.

Delius also orchestrated two separate Danish songs, *The violet* and *Summer landscape,* as well as *Sakuntala,* which has prompted Holten to orchestrate five other Danish songs, so as to form another orchestral cycle. These, too, are more beautiful than with piano. Singing in the original Danish, the two soloists both have fresh young voices, clear and precise. The choral singing in *En Arabesk* is also excellent.

The *Intermezzo* from *Fennimore and Gerda* – drawn from two of the opera's interludes – is relatively well known, but *Life's Dance,* inspired by a play of Helge Rode, is a rarity, originally conceived in 1899, with the depiction of death at the end peaceful, not at all tragic. The Aarhus orchestra responds warmly to Holten's idiomatic direction, with refined playing closely balanced in a helpful acoustic.

(i) *A Mass of Life* (sung in German); (ii) *Requiem.*

*** Chan. 9515 (2). (i) Rodgers, Rigby, Robson; (ii) Evans; (i–ii) Coleman-Wright; Waynflete Singers, Bournemouth Ch. & SO, Hickox.

(N) (*(**)) Sony mono SM2K 89432 (2). Raisbeck, Sinclair, Craig, Boyce, LPO Ch., RPO, Beecham (with introductory talk by Beecham).

Hickox gives a glowing account of this ambitious setting of a German text drawn from Nietzsche's *Also sprach Zarathustra.* He is helped by excellent singing and playing from his Bournemouth forces, and by fine solo singing, notably from the soprano, Joan Rodgers. The full and atmospheric Chandos recording confirms the primacy of this version even over the excellent previous recordings. The *Requiem,* half an hour long, makes the ideal coupling, emerging as a fine example of Delius's later work, not as distinctive in its material as the *Mass,* but with an element of bleakness tempering the lushness of the choral writing. Here too – with Rebecca Evans this time as soprano soloist – Hickox conducts a most persuasive performance, ripely recorded.

Among Beecham's mono recordings of Delius this incandescent reading of the most ambitious of his concert works has been seriously neglected in the age of CD. The music's pantheism and sense of ecstasy are eloquently conveyed and, whatever its odd weakness, the performance has tremendous conviction and authority. It brings out afresh how excellent the four soloists are – with Bruce Boyce taking on much the biggest role – but above all the thrust and concentration of the chorus, notably in the opening sections of both halves, which are among the most vigorous of all Delius's inspirations. The transfer is generally clear and full-blooded, if with a rather glassy top-emphasis that makes percussion sound shallow and tinny. The first disc, offering rather short measure, includes a spoken introduction from Beecham himself, at his most endearingly pompous in trumpeting the claims of Delius as a composer unlike any other. The booklet includes the full German text and rather stilted English translation. Though Richard Hickox's excellent Chandos version, superbly recorded, brings out even more the richness of this most ambitious of Delius's non-operatic scores, with a performance hardly less incandescent, the persuasiveness of Beecham in Delius remains irresistible.

4 Old English Lyrics. Songs: *I-Brasil; Indian love song; Love's philosophy; The nightingale; The nightingale has a lyre of gold; Secret love; Sweet Venevil; Twilight fancies.*

**(*) Chan. 8539. Luxon, Willison – ELGAR: *Songs.* **(*)

This group of Delius songs draws most persuasive performances from Luxon and Willison, sadly marred by the rough tone which has latterly afflicted this fine baritone. Excellent, well-balanced recording.

Sea Drift.

(M) ** EMI (ADD) CDM5 65113-2. Noble, RLPO Ch. & O, Groves – STANFORD: *Songs of the Fleet*, etc. **(*)

(i) *Sea Drift; Songs of Farewell; (i; ii) Songs of Sunset.*

*** Chan. 9214. (i) Terfel; (ii) Burgess; Bournemouth Symphony Ch., Waynflete Singers, Southern Voices, Bournemouth SO, Hickox.

In this second recording of Delius's masterpiece Hickox finds even more magic, again taking a spacious view – which keeps the flow of the music going magnetically. Bryn Terfel adds to the glory of the performance, the finest since Beecham, as he does in the *Songs of Sunset*, with Sally Burgess the other characterful soloist. The *Songs of Farewell*, helped by incandescent choral singing, complete an ideal triptych, presented in full and rich Chandos sound.

Sir Charles Groves could be a persuasive Delian, but his 1973 recording of *Sea Drift* is rather too matter-of-fact, failing to convey the surge of inspiration that so exactly matches the evocative colours of Walt Whitman's poem about the seagull, a solitary guest from Alabama. The recording is very good.

OPERA

Fennimore and Gerda (complete).

*** Chan. 9589. Stene, Howarth, Tucker, Coleman-Wright, Danish Nat. R. Ch. & SO, Hickox.

Fennimore and Gerda, the sixth and last of Delius's operas, may suffer from a lopsided libretto but it has some of his most inspired vocal music. Fennimore, the first heroine, dominates the first nine of the eleven scenes, with Gerda, the second heroine, introduced only at the end to provide an idyllic conclusion. Using the original German, Hickox's reading is aptly sensuous – far warmer than the only previous recording on EMI, conducted by Meredith Davis (CDM5 66314-2) – with fresh-voiced principals headed by Randi Stene as Fennimore, Judith Howarth as Gerda and Peter Coleman-Wright and Mark Tucker as rivals in this very Scandinavian love-tangle.

DELLO JOIO, Norman (born 1913)

The Triumph of St Joan (Symphony); Variations, Chaconne & Finale.

*** Koch Schwann 3-7243-2. New Zealand SO, Sedares – BARBER: *Adagio for Strings.* ***

Norman Dello Joio's *Triumph of St Joan Symphony* makes a welcome CD début here and has worn well. The music is spacious, dignified and imaginative. The *Variations, Chaconne and Finale* is a little earlier and a good deal less convincing. However, the disc is well worth investigating for the sake of the symphony (and there are good things in the companion work).

DENISOV, Edison (born 1929)

Film music: *An Ideal Husband; Turtle Tortilla; Une étoile sans nom (A Nameless Star)* (suites arr. YOURI KASPAROV).

(N) ** Chant du Monde RUS 288172. Russian Cinema O, Jrupka.

Edison Denisov was born in Siberia and turned to music after initially studying mathematics. His work was frowned upon in the USSR during the 1960s, but one of his avant-garde pieces was taken up by Pierre Boulez, and he subsequently settled in France. Although his music for the cinema is less important than his more serious works, he wrote prolifically for the medium, composing for over 60 films in a variety of idioms. The suites from three of his films have been arranged by his pupil Youri Kasparov and are fashioned expertly and orchestrated with some flair. Well played and recorded, but ultimately unmemorable.

DERING, Richard (c. 1580–1630)

Motets: *Ardens est cor meum; Ave Maria gratia plena; Ave verum corpus; Factum est silentium; Gaudent in coelis; O crux ave spes unica; O bone Jesu; O quam suavis; Quem vidistis, pastores?.*

(M) **(*) EMI CDM5 66788-2. King's College, Cambridge, Ch., Cleobury – PHILIPS: *Motets.* **(*)

Richard Dering and his older contemporary, Peter Philips, were Catholic expatriates who lived in the Spanish-dominated southern Netherlands. This CD contrasts and compares the two composers' settings of the same texts, drawing on Dering's *Cantiones sacrae* of 1617 and the *Cantica sacra* of 1618 and the posthumously published set of 1662. The performances are faithful, though sometimes a bit stiff; the actual sound, though good, is not ideal in focus or blend – partly perhaps (but not solely) due to the recording. However, this has been deleted as we go to press.

DETT, R. Nathaniel (1882–1943)

8 Bible Vignettes; In the Bottoms; Magnolia Suite.

**(*) New World NW 367. Oldham.

Robert Nathaniel Dett was the first African American to gain a Bachelor of Music degree. His writing is at times colourful and, though limited in its range of expressive devices, attractive, particularly so in the suite, *In the Bottoms*, which evokes the moods and atmosphere of life in the 'river bottoms' of the Deep South. However, this is not a disc to be taken all at once. Denver Oldham is a persuasive enough player, and he is decently recorded.

DEVIENNE, François (1769–1803)

Flute Concertos Nos. 7 in E min.; 8 in G.

(N) *** RCA 09026 63701-2. Galway, LMP – CIMAROSA: *Double Flute Concerto.* **(*)

Galway's dedication of this CD as his 'Homage à Rampal' is evidence of his regard and admiration for the great French flautist. Certainly Galway's own playing is worthy of his early mentor, celebrated with these two elegant, well-crafted works of Devienne. Their bold opening tuttis have a classical impetus, but Galway is going a little far in his notes to suggest an association (in the first movement of the *G major* work) with Beethoven. However, its finely contoured *Largo* is played very beautifully, and the infectious hopping and skipping *Polonaise* finale is delightful. The companion work is very similar, although here the slow movement is more formal. With performances of this calibre both concertos are worth returning to, for Galway's tone and phrasing are very persuasive. Excellent recording.

DEVREESE, Godfried (1893–1972)

(i) *Cello Concertino;* (ii) *Violin Concerto No. 1. Tombelène* (choreographic suite).

*** Marco 8.223680. (i) Spanoghe, (ii) De Neve. Belgian R. & TV PO (Brussels), Devreese.

Godfried Devreese, a Belgian composer, is imaginative as well as a gifted and colourful orchestrator, and this suite from *Tombelène* gives pleasure. His *Violin Concerto No. 1* also sounds balletic in inspiration, and if you respond to the Bloch and Delius concertos, you would find much here to engage your sympathies. The *Cello Concertino* (1930)

originally appeared scored for 15 wind instruments, celesta, harp, six double-basses and variously tuned side-drums. The present version is re-scored by his son, Frédéric, for more practical forces; it, too, is imaginative without possessing a strong individual voice. Very good performances and vivid, well-detailed recording.

DIAMOND, David (born 1915)

(i) *Concert Piece for Flute & Harp. Concert Piece for Orchestra.* (i) *Elegy in Memory of Ravel. Rounds for String Orchestra; Symphony No. 11: Adagio.*

*** Delos DE 3189. Seattle SO, Schwarz, (i) with Glorian Duo.

The *Rounds for String Orchestra* (1944) is a masterpiece and ought to be part of the international repertoire. It conjures up the vastness of the American continent but suggests also the presence of humanity, while the vigorous closing movement encapsulates barn-dance energy. The *Concert Piece for Orchestra* is also snappily rhythmic, more jagged, with a cool, elegiac counterpart and a sudden resolution. The *Elegy for Ravel* is unexpectedly troubled and dissonant, but the delicately evoked *Concert Piece for Flute and Harp* is far closer to Ravel's world. The eloquent *Adagio* from the *Eleventh Symphony* has been described as Brucknerian. All this music is played superbly by the fine Seattle orchestra, and the disc is worth considering for the *Rounds* alone.

(i) *Concerto for Small Orchestra;* (ii) *Symphonies Nos 2; 4.*

*** Delos D/CD 3093. (i) NY CO; (ii) Seattle SO; Schwarz.

The *Second Symphony* is a large-scale work, and it has great sweep and power. The music unfolds with a sense of inevitability and purpose. The *Concerto for Small Orchestra* is original in form; there are two parts which open and conclude with a fanfare, with two preludes and fugues in between. The Mediterranean-like *Fourth Symphony* with its glowing, luminous textures sounds even more relaxed and lyrical in this performance than in Bernstein's account from the 1960s. Dedicated and expert performances from the Seattle orchestra under Gerard Schwarz. The acoustic is spacious and the balance very well judged.

(i) *Violin Concerto No. 2. The Enormous Room; Symphony No. 1.*

*** Delos DE 3119. (i) Talvi; Seattle SO, Schwarz.

The *First Symphony* is an urbane and intelligently wrought piece which has a strong sense of both purpose and direction. The *Second Violin Concerto* is a bit Stravinskian with a dash of Walton and keeps the excellent soloist fully stretched. *The Enormous Room* shows the composer at his most imaginative. It derives its title from e. e. cummings's 'high and clear adventure'. It is rhapsodic in feeling, with orchestral textures of great luxuriance. Excellent performances from Gerard Schwarz and the Seattle orchestra, and outstanding recording.

(i) *Kaddish for Cello & Orchestra. Psalm; Romeo and Juliet; Symphony No. 3.*

*** Delos DE 3103. (i) Starker; Seattle SO, Schwarz.

The *Third Symphony* is a four-movement work of no mean power. The *Romeo and Juliet* music is an inventive score, full of character and atmosphere, which shows Diamond as a real man of the orchestra; and the Seattle orchestra proves an eloquent advocate. *Kaddish* is a more recent piece and is played here by its dedicatee, János Starker.

Symphony No. 4.

(M) **(*) Sony (ADD) SMK 60594. NYPO, Bernstein –
    HARRIS: *Symphony No. 3* **(*); THOMPSON: *Symphony No. 2.* **(*)

Bernstein recorded David Diamond's *Fourth Symphony* way back in 1958. He obviously has great feeling for this euphonious and beautifully shaped work, and in his hands every note means something. Wonderfully eloquent and, even though the recorded sound cannot match the recent account from Gerard Schwarz on Delos, it is a rather special record.

Symphony No. 8; Suite No. 1 from the Ballet, Tom; (i) *This Sacred Ground.*

*** Delos DE 3141. (i) Parce, Seattle Ch., Seattle Girls' Ch.,
    NorthWest Boys' Ch.; Seattle SO, Schwarz.

The *First Suite from the Ballet, Tom* inhabits much the same musical world as Aaron Copland. The *Eighth Symphony* makes use of serial technique but will still present few problems to those familiar with Diamond's earlier music, for it remains lyrical and thought-provoking. It culminates in a double fugue of considerable ingenuity. *This Sacred Ground* is a short setting for soloist, choirs and orchestra of the Gettysburg Address, and it may not travel so well. Committed performances and excellent, natural, recorded sound.

DIBDIN, Charles (1745–1814)

(i) *The Brickdust Man* (musical dialogue); (ii) *The Ephesian Matron* (comic serenata); (iii) *The Grenadier* (musical dialogue).

*** Hyp. CDA 66608. (i) Barclay, West; (ii) Mills, Streeton,
    Padmore, Knight; (iii) Bisatt, West, Mayor; Opera Restor'd,
    Parley of Instruments, Holman.

Dibdin, best known as the composer of *Tom Bowling*, the song heard every year at the Last Night of the Proms, here provides three delightful pocket operas, the shorter ones officially described as musical dialogues and *The Ephesian Matron* as a comic serenata. *The Grenadier* (dating from 1773) lasts well under a quarter of an hour, using a text that is possibly by David Garrick. The brief numbers – duets and solos – are linked by equally brief recitatives, then rounded off with a final trio. The other two pieces are just as delightful in these performances by a group that specializes in presenting just such dramatic works of this period in public. Excellent Hyperion sound.

DIEPENBROCK, Alphons
(1862–1921)

Elektra Suite; (i) *Hymn for Violin & Orchestra. Marsyas Suite; Overture: The Birds.*

*** Chan. 8821. (i) Verhey; Hague Residentie O, Vonk.

The *Birds Overture*, written for a student production of Aristophanes, is rather delightful if very Straussian, with some vaguely Impressionistic touches. The *Marsyas Music* (1910) is expertly and delicately scored with touches of Strauss, Reger and Debussy. Good performances from the Residentie Orchestra under Hans Vonk, and eminently truthful recording quality. Recommended.

(i) *Hymne an die Nacht;* (ii) *Hymne;* (i) *Die Nacht;* (iii) *Im grossen Schweigen.*

*** Chan. 8878. (i) Finnie; (ii) Homberger; (iii) Holl; Hague
    Residentie O, Vonk.

This second volume brings four symphonic songs, all of great beauty and with an almost Straussian melancholy. There are touches of Reger and Debussy as well as Strauss, and all four pieces are expertly and delicately scored. Good performances from all three soloists and the Residentie Orchestra under Hans Vonk, and very good recording indeed.

DITTERSDORF, Carl Ditters von
(1739–99)

Double-Bass Concertos Nos. 1 in D; 2 in D (Krebs 171/2).

(N) *** Hyp. CDA 67179. Nwanoku, Swedish CO, Goodwin –
    VANHAL: Double-Bass Concerto in D. ***

The double-bass can make a cumbersome concerto soloist, but Chi-Chi Nwanoku, regular member of distinguished ensembles ever since her student days, makes light of any problems in these concertos. She is amazingly agile and incisive in allegros, well-tuned and expressive in lyrical slow movements. Jan Vaňhal and Carl Ditters von Dittersdorf, exact contemporaries, were both inspired to write these works by the playing of the eighteenth-century virtuoso, Johann Matthias Sperger, himself the composer of seventeen double-bass concertos. The Vaňhal is charming enough, but the two Dittersdorf works are more distinctive, making up an ideal coupling very well recorded.

(i) *Double-Bass Concerto in E;* (ii) *Flute Concerto in E min.;* (iii) *Symphonies in C & D.*

** Olympia (ADD) OCD 405. (i) Thomas, Arad PO, Boboc;
    (ii) Costea, Cluj-Napoca PO, Cristescu; (iii) Oradea
    Philharmonic CO, Ratiu.

The *C major* is an agreeably conventional three-movement symphony, but the *D major* is more elaborate, with an infectious opening movement, an engaging *Chanson populaire d'Elsass* for its *Andante*, a minuet with two trios and a set of variations for its modestly paced finale. Both the concertos are attractive and require considerable bravura from their soloists. The recorded sound varies somewhat but is always fully acceptable and quite well balanced.

Harp Concerto in A (arr. Pilley).

✿ (M) *** Decca (ADD) 425 723-2. Robles, ASMF, Brown —
BOIELDIEU; HANDEL: *Harp Concertos*, etc. *** ✿

Dittersdorf's *Harp Concerto* is a transcription of an unfinished keyboard concerto with additional wind parts. It is an elegant piece, thematically not quite as memorable as the Boieldieu coupling, but captivating when played with such style.

6 Symphonies after Ovid's Metamorphoses.

**(*) Chan. 8564/5 (2). Cantilena, Shepherd.

All the *Ovid Symphonies* have a programmatic inspiration and relate episodes from the *Metamorphoses* of Ovid, such as *The Fall of Phaeton*, which are vividly portrayed. *The Rescue of Andromeda by Perseus* is a particularly effective work (it has an inspired *Adagio*) and the slow movement of the *D major*, *The Petrification of Phineus and his Friends*, is a delight. *The Transformation of the Lycian Peasants into Frogs* could hardly be more graphic and is full of wit. This is inventive and charming music that will give much pleasure, and it is generally well served by Cantilena under Adrian Shepherd. There is also a set on Naxos (8.553368/9) acceptably performed by the Failoni Symphoy Orchestra under Hanspeter Gmür, but the Chandos versions have much more character and are worth the extra cost.

Symphonies in A min. (Il delirio delli compositori, ossia Il gusto d'oggidi) (Grave a2); in A (Sinfonia nazionale nel gusto di cinque nazioni) (Grave A10); in D (Il Combattimento delle passioni umani) (Grav D16).

(N) (BB) *** Naxos 8.553975. Failoni O, Grodd.

Of these three symphonies, descriptive of human moods rather than programmatic, the *A minor*, concerned with the delirium of the composer, is obviously not meant to be taken too seriously. Written in the mid 1770s, it opens a little nervily and very much in the minor mode, but its main ideas are engagingly contrasted and in the more extrovert *Andantino* the rhythmic feeling is lively but firmly controlled. The canonic Minuet leads to a flowing Trio which reminds us of the work's sobriquet with a witty, sudden displaced accent; but the energetic finale, if not predictable, dispels any doubts about the composer's peace of mind.

The D major *Battle of the Human Passions* of 1771, with its seven movements, is more of a suite than a symphony. Opening with a portentous 'Halleluija' *maestoso* ('Pride'), it includes a *'Mad'* (but not very mad) *Minuet* for strings alone, and depicts a tender humility, contentment, a very positive constancy, and a touching melancholia. The finale is the epitome of vivacity, yet with mercurial mood changes.

The *Sinfonia of Five Nations* – Germany, Italy (unflatteringly crude), France, England, and (surprisingly) Turkey – dates from around 1766 and is really another suite, given its variety by rhythm as much as melody. Easily the best movement is the finale, boisterous and elegant by turns. Excellent performances throughout – Uwe Grodd is a persuasive exponent – and good recording; but, apart from

the ingenious *A minor Symphony*, musically this is far less rewarding than the companion triptych of untitled symphonies below.

Symphonies: in D min. (Grave d1); F (Grave F7); G min. (Grave g1).

(N) (BB) *** Naxos 8.553974. Failoni O, Grodd.

The three works collected here – far more than the later and more famous programmatic symphonies based on Ovid – show Dittersdorf at his most inventive, learning and absorbing influences from both Haydn and Mozart. The *F major Symphony* is the earliest here, probably dating from the early 1760s, and a very personable little work it is, opening with a pertly succinct theme which soon expands in a characteristic Mannheim crescendo; the brief *Andante* has comparable charm, and after an elegant Minuet featuring the horns, they return exuberantly to lead the finale.

The *G minor Symphony*, which comes from the close of the same decade, is altogether more turbulent. It must have been highly regarded in its day, for the manuscript survives in a number of copies and is listed in three major publisher's catalogues of the time. The symphony is contemporary with the beginning of Haydn's *Sturm und Drang* period, with which it has much in common. The use of the violins and (again) the horns in the first movement is individual and striking; the fine, flowing *Andante* might easily be mistaken for Haydn, and there is a first class Minuet with the flute leading the Trio. But it is the remarkable finale which sets the seal on the work's originality by cyclically returning to the bold opening theme of the first movement with even greater thrust, with a graceful answering passage from the violins. Yet another surprise is in store when, just before the coda, the key suddenly changes to a sunny G major, and the mood lightens before a final satisfyingly bold statement of the opening theme.

The *D minor Symphony* dates from the mid to late 1770s and its warmly lyrical opening *Adagio* immediately coaxes the ear with just a hint of Beethoven's *Pastoral Symphony*, although its mood is darker. The following *Allegro* is more positively classical, its character Mozartian, but the witty Minuet with its chirruping rhythms is closer to Haydn, whose spirit also dominates the genial finale. The performances here are first class in every way, the playing polished, responsive and vigorous, and the recording is excellent. This is an easy first choice among the available discs of Dittersdorf symphonies.

DOCKER, Robert (1918–92)

(i) *3 Contrasts for Oboe & Strings*; (ii) *Legend*; *Pastiche Variations* (both for piano and orchestra); *Air*; *Blue Ribbons*; *Fairy Dance Reel*; *Scènes de ballet*; *Scène du bal*; *The Spirit of Cambria*; *Tabarinage*.

*** Marco 8.223837 Dublin RTE Concert O, Knight; with (i) Presley; (ii) Davies.

Robert Docker is probably best known as a composer of film music (including a contribution to *Chariots of Fire*). His *Legend*, which opens this collection, is a tuneful example of a miniature 'film-concerto'. The closing *Pastiche Variations*, opening with a horn solo, is more expansive and romantic, but witty too. Based on *Frère Jacques*, it has something in common with Dohnányi's *Nursery-Theme Variations*. William Davies proves a most persuasive soloist. In between comes an attractive lightweight suite of *Scènes de ballet*, three engaging *Contrasts for Oboe and Strings* (lovely playing from David Presley), and a series of engaging short pieces. Perhaps the best known is the catchy *Tabarinage*. The delicate *Scène du bal* is a very English waltz despite its French title. There are also some spirited folksong arrangements. *The Spirit of Cambria* (although the composer is a Londoner) was written for St David's Day in 1972 and effectively uses four different traditional Welsh melodies. All this music is played with polish and warmth by the Dublin Radio Orchestra under Barry Knight, and is pleasingly recorded.

DODGSON, Stephen (born 1924)

(i) *Flute Concerto* (for flute and strings); (ii) *Duo Concertant for Violin, Guitar & Strings*; (iii) *Last of the Leaves* (cantata for bass, clarinet and strings).

*** Biddulph LAW 015. (i) Stallman; (ii) Kantorow, Gifford; (iii) George, Bradbury; N. Sinfonia, Zollman.

Dodgson wrote his *Flute Concerto* for the American flautist, Robert Stallman, who is the fine soloist on this disc. The *Duo Concertant* also receives a persuasive performance. With its hints of an English Stravinsky, this is another work that is at once thoughtful and charming. *Last of the Leaves* is a cantata for bass soloist accompanied by clarinet and strings, more consistently autumnal and elegiac. Framing the work are settings of poems by Austin Dobson and Harold Monro, with the necessary contrast provided by the best-known poem, G. K. Chesterton's *The Donkey*. Though Michael George's noble bass voice is not caught as sweetly as it might be, it is a tenderly moving performance, with John Bradbury equally expressive, and with the Belgian conductor, Ronald Zollman, as in the other works, a sympathetic accompanist.

(i) *Guitar Concerto* (for guitar and chamber orchestra). *Partita No. 1 for Solo Guitar*.

(B) **(*) Sony (ADD) SBK 61716. Williams; (i) with ECO, Groves – RODRIGO: *Concierto de Aranjuez*, etc. **(*)

John Williams proves an eloquent and authoritative exponent, and the *Concerto* could hardly hope for a more persuasive performance. Much the same goes for the *Partita*, and these make original and worthwhile couplings for the ubiquitous Rodrigo works. The recording is good but not exceptional.

Piano Sonatas Nos 1; 3 (*Variations on a Rhythm*); 6.

Claudio CC 4941-2. Roberts.

Piano Sonatas Nos 2; 4; 5.

Claudio CC 4431-2. Roberts.

Those who know Stephen Dodgson's guitar music may initially be disconcerted that the style here is grittier, more demanding and quirky at times, as in the multiple move-

ments of the *Sonata No. 4*. In that work the note-writer, Professor Wilfrid Mellers, highlights an 'Alice in Wonderland' quality – apt from a composer distantly related to the Dodgson who was author of that fantasy, Lewis Carroll.

That comes on CC 4431-2, but the companion CD, CC 4941-2, gives a wider insight into the composer's development, from the *Sonata No. 1* of 1959, in which English echoes can still be detected, to the more freely expansive writing of the *Sonata No. 6* of 1994, inspired by Bernard Roberts's performances on the first disc. Most ingenious in its complex organization is the *Sonata No. 3* of 1983, subtitled *Variations on a Rhythm*, with Dodgson at his most original. Excellent, well-balanced sound.

DOHNÁNYI, Ernst von (1877–1960)

Piano Concertos Nos. 1 in E min., Op. 5; 2 in B min., Op. 42.

*** Hyp. CDA 66684. Roscoe, BBC Scottish SO, Glushchenko.

These concertos are well wrought, with a melodic warmth that fails to be indelible, but they provide bravura for the soloist and contrast for the orchestra. The present performances are surely unlikely to be surpassed for their commitment, and the playing is finished as well as ardent; the recording, too, is excellent.

Konzertstück for Cello & Orchestra, Op. 12.

*** Chan. 8662. Wallfisch, LSO, Mackerras – DVORAK: *Cello Concerto*. ***

Dohnányi's *Konzertstück* has many rich, warm ideas, not least a theme in the slow movement all too close to *Pale hands I loved beside the Shalimar*, and none the worse for that. Wallfisch's performance, as in the Dvořák, is strong, warm and committed, and the Chandos sound is first rate.

(i) *Konzertstücke for Cello & Orchestra, Op. 12*; (ii) *Cello Sonata in B flat min., Op. 8*; *Ruralia Hungarica, Op. 32d; Adagio ma non troppo*.

(BB) *(*) Naxos 8.554468. Kliegel; with (i) Esterházy O, Halász; (ii) Jandó.

In the *Konzertstücke* Maria Kliegel proves a persuasive soloist, though the Nicolaus Esterházy Orchestra is distinctly subfusc. She is no less successful in the *Cello Sonata*, where she is well supported by the ubiquitous Jenö Jandó. The recording, particularly in the cello version of the so-called *Gypsy Andante* from the *Ruralia Hungarica*, is poor. Recommendable only for the *Cello Sonata*.

Symphony No. 1 in D min., Op. 9.

*** Telarc CD 80511. LPO, Botstein.

Symphony No. 1; American Rhapsody, Op. 47.

*** Chan. 9647. BBC PO, Bamert.

Dohnányi's *First Symphony* is something of a find. It is not just accomplished; the scoring shows real flair. A large-scale piece, some 55 minutes in duration, it reveals a strong sense of form. Telarc's account with the LPO under Leon Botstein has grip and fervour, and it benefits from first-rate recorded sound.

Mathias Bamert has the advantage of the BBC Philharmonic and excellent engineering from the BBC/Chandos team. There is surprisingly little to choose between the two performances: the Telarc sound is brighter, the Chandos richer, and both have plenty of body and presence. Whichever you opt for, you will find this most rewarding music.

Symphony No. 2, Op. 40; Symphonic Minutes, Op. 36.

*** Chan. 9455. BBC PO, Bamert.

Dohnányi's *Symphonic Minutes* are richly inventive and have enormous charm. The *Second Symphony* is a generally well-argued and finely crafted piece and is well worth getting to know, even if (at nearly 50 minutes) it rather outstays its welcome. The playing of the BBC Philharmonic under Mathias Bamert is vital and sensitive, and the Chandos recording is in the best traditions of the house.

Variations on a Nursery Tune, Op. 25.

(B) *** Double Decca (ADD) 458 361-2 (2). Katchen, LPO, Boult – LISZT: *Piano Concertos 1–2, etc.* ***

(M) *** Decca (ADD) 448 604-2. Katchen, LPO, Boult – RACHMANINOV: *Piano Concerto No. 2, etc.* ***

Variations on a Nursery Tune, Op. 25; Suite in F sharp min., Op. 19; The Veil of Pierrette: Suite, Op. 18.

*** Chan. 9733. Shelley, BBC PO, Bamert.

(i) *Variations on a Nursery Tune, Op. 25. Capriccio in F min., Op. 28.*

*** Chesky CD-13. Wild; (i) New Philh. O, C. von Dohnányi – TCHAIKOVSKY: *Piano Concerto No. 1.* ***

For all their popularity, Dohnányi's variations on 'Twinkle, twinkle, little star', with their witty parodies, have been meanly treated on disc. The brilliant version with Howard Shelley the sparkling soloist is especially welcome when it offers two other examples of Dohnányi the charmer. The *Wedding Waltz* from the mimed entertainment, *The Veil of Pierrette*, was once well known, dashingly Viennese, as are the other three movements, previously unrecorded, including a *Merry Funeral March* which parodies Mahler. The *Suite* too is engagingly colourful. Brilliant performances, sumptuously recorded.

Katchen's 1959 set of the *Nursery Variations* has the advantage of Decca's finest vintage stereo. The performance is both perceptive and spontaneous, as full of wit as it is of lilt and flair, and the recording is very beautifully balanced – indeed, in the demonstration bracket for its period. There are alternative couplings.

A scintillating account of the piano part from Earl Wild is matched by a witty accompaniment directed by the composer's grandson, who doesn't miss a thing. Splendid vintage analogue recording from the early 1960s. The *Capriccio*, brilliantly played, acts as an encore (before the Tchaikovsky coupling), but the recording is rather recessed.

Cello Sonata in B flat min., Op. 8.

**(*) ASV CDDCA 796. Gregor-Smith, Wrigley – BRIDGE; DEBUSSY: *Sonatas.* **(*)

On ASV the *Cello Sonata* is played with great expertise and fine musicianship by this excellent duo partnership. The recording is just a bit too bright and forward to be ideal but, with that proviso, the disc can be cordially recommended.

(i) *Piano Quintet No. 1 in C min., Op. 1. String Quartet No. 2 in D flat, Op. 15.*

**(*) Chan. 8718. (i) Manz; Gabrieli Qt.

Piano Quintets Nos. 1 in C min., Op. 1; 2 in E flat min., Op. 26; Serenade in C, Op. 10.

*** Hyp. CDA 66786. Schubert Ens. of London.

(i–ii) *Piano Quintets Nos. 1–2; (i) Suite in the Old Style, Op. 24.*

*** ASV CDDCA 915. (i) Roscoe; (ii) Vanbrugh Qt.

Dohnányi wrote the first of his two *Piano Quintets* when still in his teens; it is ripely Brahmsian, built strongly on memorable themes. The *Second Quintet*, dating from 20 years later, just after the *Nursery Variations*, is sharper and more compact, with Hungarian flavours more pronounced, if never Bartókian. The *Suite in the Old Style*, for piano alone, is an amiable example of pre-Stravinsky neo-classicism, again beautifully written for the instrument. The Vanbrugh Quartet is well matched by Martin Roscoe in keen, alert performances, warmly recorded.

The Schubert Ensemble also give us the *Serenade for String Trio*. A clear three-star recommendation for the Hyperion disc and their excellent pianist, William Howard.

Wolfgang Manz's performance of Dohnányi's *First Piano Quintet* lacks something in fantasy and lightness of touch. But the bigger-boned, somewhat Brahmsian effect of this performance is certainly compelling, if less strong on charm. The *Second String Quartet* is a strong piece, splendidly played by the Gabrielis, and beautifully recorded.

Serenade for String Trio.

(N) (B) *** Virgin 2 x 1 VBD5 61904-2 (2). Domus – MARTINU: *Piano Quartet No. 1 etc.* DVORAK: *Bagatelles.* KODALY: *Intermezzo.* SUK: *Piano Quartet.* ***

The Dohnányi *Serenade for String Trio* comes from 1902 and was first recorded in an unforgettable performance by Heifetz, Primrose and Feuerman. The three players from the Domus team meet its demands with admirably alert and sensitive playing and can more than hold their own with recent rival accounts. This performance comes as part of a rewarding and inexpensive programme from Domus which has an eminently natural recorded sound.

Sextet in C for Piano, Clarinet, Horn, Violin, Viola & Cello, Op. 37.

*** ASV CDDCA 943. Endymion Ens. – FIBICH: *Piano Quintet.* ***

The Endymions play with great feeling and panache; they are splendidly recorded and can be strongly recommended.

String Quartets Nos. 1 in A, Op. 7; 2 in D flat, Op. 15.

(M) *** Koch (ADD) 316352. Artis Qt, Vienna.

The *First Quartet* comes from Dohnányi's mid-twenties and, though not the equal of the *Second* in the quality of its ideas, is still well worth investigation. The idiom is still heavily indebted to Brahms and Strauss, but none the worse for that. The playing of the Artis Quartet of Vienna is persuasive and the recordings, which come from the 1980s, are very present.

String Quartets Nos. 2 in D flat, Op. 15; 3 in A min., Op. 33.

*** ASV CDDCA 985. Lyric Qt – KODALY: *Intermezzo for String Trio.* ***

These two quartets are separated by two decades. Dohnányi's emerging personality is already much in evidence. The *Third Quartet* is a finely crafted and richly inventive score, conservative in idiom. The Lyric Quartet play with commitment and conviction that more than outweighs the odd moment of inelegance.

Violin Sonata in C sharp min., Op. 21; Andante rubato (Ruralia Hungarica).

**(*) Biddulph LAW 015. Shumsky, Lipkin – WEINER: *Violin Sonatas Nos. 1 & 2.* **(*)

Oscar Shumsky and Seymour Lipkin were recorded in New York in 1993 and they make out an excellent case for this neglected but fine sonata. Shumsky's playing is not quite as polished or masterly as it was in the early 1980s, but it is still supremely musical. This is a worthwhile addition to the catalogue.

PIANO MUSIC

6 Concert Etudes, Op. 28; Pastorale; Ruralia Hungarica, Op. 32a; Variations on a Hungarian Folk Song, Op. 29.

⚫ (BB) *** Naxos 8.553332. Pawlik.

The *Six Concert Etudes*, Op. 28, of 1916 are among the most technically demanding pieces in the repertoire. Markus Pawlik was still in his twenties when he recorded these pieces, and his playing is remarkable for its dazzling virtuosity, sensitivity, finesse and good taste. His dexterity and wonderful clarity of articulation in the *D flat Etude* are remarkable. His is a formidable talent, and we hope to hear much more of him. Decent recorded sound. Recommended with all enthusiasm.

DONIZETTI, Gaetano (1797–1848)

Ballet music from: L'assedio di Calais; Dom Sébastien; La favorita; Les martyres.

(B) *** Ph. (ADD) (IMS) Duo 442 553-2 (2). Philh. O, De Almeida – ROSSINI: *Ballet Music.* **(*)

The ballet music from four of Donizetti's operas, which were presented in Paris, provides sparkling, refreshing dances of no great originality, but they are delivered here with great zest and resilience and fine solo playing, and are excellently recorded.

Il Barcaiolo; Cor Anglais Concerto in G; Oboe Sonata in F; (Piano) Waltz in C.

*** Mer. (ADD) CDE 84147. Polmear, Ambache O, Ambache (with PASCULLI: *Concerto on Themes from 'La Favorita'; Fantasia on 'Poliuto'*; LISZT: *Réminscences de Lucia di Lammermoor*).

The *Sonata in F* is an agreeable piece with a fluent *Andante* and a catchy finale; and the vignette, *Il barcaiolo*, is even more engaging. The *Cor Anglais Concerto* centres on a set of variations that are not unlike the fantasias on themes from his operas by Pasculli. However, these demand the utmost bravura from the soloist. Diana Ambache proves a sympathetic partner and gives a suitably flamboyant account of Liszt's famous *Lucia* paraphrase.

(i) Clarinet Concertino in B flat. Study No. 1 for Solo Clarinet.

(BB) *** ASV CDQS 6242. Farrall; (i) with Britten Sinfonia, Daniel – MERCADANTE: *Clarinet Concertos;* ROSSINI: *Variations in B flat & C.* ***

Donizetti's *Clarinet Concertino* is also available in a recommendable anthology (see below) but Joy Farrall's performance is hardly less winning, and she is most stylishly accompanied and beautifully recorded. She gets a chance to show her mettle first in the bravura of the solo *Study*. This generous collection is one of the highlights of the ASV Quicksilva bargain catalogue.

(i) Clarinet Concertino in B flat; (ii) Cor Anglais Concertino in G; (iii) Flute Concertino in C min.; (iv) Oboe Concertino in F; (v) Double Concertino in D min. for Violin & Cello; (vi) Sinfonia a soli instrumenti di fiato in G min. Sinfonia in D min. per la Morte di Capuzzi.

⚫ *** Marco 8.223701. (i) B. Kovács; (ii) Girgás; (iii) I. Kovács; (iv) J. Kiss; (v) A. Kiss, J. Kiss Domonkos; (vi) Soloists, Budapest Camerata, L. Kovács.

We already know the *Concertino for Cor Anglais*, which is played here with a delectable timbre and a nice feeling for light and shade. The *Clarinet Concertino* brings a touch of melancholy to its opening cantilena, yet the finale chortles. The *Flute Concertino* also opens with an eloquent aria, but the closing rondo is irrepressibly light-hearted, with an infectiously carefree, Rossinian wit. The *Oboe Concerino* has a vigorous hunting finale, played here with bouncing zest. The *Double Concertino*, in three movements, is the most ambitious work. In short, all these concertos are most winning, as elegant as they are inventive, and all the expert soloists (several of whom seem to be interrelated) smilingly convey the music's Italian sunshine. The concertos are framed by two contrasting *Sinfonias*. Both are played very persuasively, and throughout the collection László Kovács and his Budapest chamber orchestra provide supportive and stylish accompaniments. The recording could hardly be bettered, and the result is a collection which will give great and repeated pleasure.

Sinfonias in A; D min. (both arr. Benedek); D (arr. Angerer).

**(*) Marco 8.223577. Failoni CO, Oberfrank.

Sinfonias in C; D; D min.

*** Koch 3-6733-2. Krakau State PO, Bader – BELLINI: *Sinfonias.* ***

The *D major Sinfonia* is a delightfully spontaneous piece with a graciously beautiful *Larghetto*. The D minor work opens darkly, but the sun soon comes out and at times we are reminded of Rossini. The *Larghetto* is pensive. The *A major* has a fine, siciliano-like *Larghetto cantabile*. Fine, stylish performances on Koch, very well recorded, and the *C major Symphony* is also very infectious. On Marco Polo too the works are well played and flatteringly recorded; a touch more wit and sparkle would not have come amiss, but the music is well worth having.

String Quartet in D (arr. for string orchestra).

(B) *** Double Decca (ADD) 443 838-2 (2). ASMF, Marriner – ROSSINI: *String Sonatas Nos. 1–6* (with CHERUBINI: *Etude No. 2 for French Horn & Strings* (with Tuckwell); BELLINI: *Oboe Concerto in E flat* (with Lord) ***).

This delightful 'prentice work has a sunny lyricism and a melodic freshness that speak of youthful genius. The composer's craftsmanship is obvious and the writing is such that (unlike Verdi's *String Quartet*) it lends itself readily to performance by a string orchestra, especially when the playing is so warm-hearted and polished and the recording transferred so immaculately to CD. A fine bonus for the irresistible Rossini *String Sonatas*.

CHAMBER MUSIC

Introduzione for Strings; String Quartets Nos. 10 in G min.; 11 & 12 in C.

(BB) *** CPO 999 279-2. Revolutionary Drawing Room.

This excellent CPO series reveals Donizetti to be a considerable contributor to the string quartet medium, offering works that in their craftsmanship and quality of invention can stand comparison with all but the very finest of Haydn. These three and the following four, Nos. 13–16, all date from around 1821, when the composer was in his early twenties. They are very much Haydn-influenced (in the best sense), especially the witty downward scale which forms the diverting Minuet finale of No. 10 and the winning outer movements of No. 11. These players are completely at home on their period instruments: their execution is fresh, vital and expressive, without any linear eccentricities. The simple eloquence of the melancholy *Introduzione*, which opens the disc and which reflects the composer's grief (in 1829) over his stillborn child, is most affecting, while the Theme and Variations which forms the *Andante* of No. 12 is beautifully shaped.

String Quartet No. 13 in A.

(M) *** CRD 3366. Alberni Qt – PUCCINI: *Crisantemi*; VERDI: *Quartet.* ***

This is an endearing work with a Scherzo echoing that in Beethoven's *Eroica* and with many twists of argument that are attractively unpredictable. It is given a strong, committed performance and is well recorded.

String Quartets Nos. 13 in A; 14 in D; 15 in F.

(BB) **(*) CPO 999 280. Revolutionary Drawing Room.

No. 14 in D is programmatic, and we hear the storm gathering immediately at the opening: its full force is soon sweeping through the music. The hushed *Adagio* sadly contemplates the havoc left behind, but the genial Minuet suggests that life goes on, with repairs carried out in the Trio, while the hammering workmen sing to themselves. The *F major* opens thoughtfully, but the genial spirit of the first movement again recalls Haydn, and that master's humanity is also reflected in the *Andante*. All these quartets are played with spirit, warmth and finesse, and the recording is vivid, though this disc is not quite as smooth as CPO 999 279, revealing a degree of edge on the timbre of the lead violin.

String Quartets Nos. 16 in B min.; 17 in D; 18 in E min.

(BB) *** CPO 999 282-2. Revolutionary Drawing Room.

No. 16 is the last of the 1821 quartets; the jolly, energetic triplets of its first movement are clearly forward-looking, almost Schubertian. The *Largo* is thoughtfully serene, even sombre. No. 17 was written four years later and is noticeably more warmly romantic. Finest of the whole series is the mature *E minor Quartet* of a decade later, splendidly assured in its light-hearted first movement, which the composer used as a basis for his *Linda di Chamonix Overture*. The tranquil yet searching *Adagio* is very touching, and the gypsy rondo of the *alla polacca* finale confirms this as Donizetti's masterpiece in the form; and it ought to be much better known. It is splendidly played; indeed, the performances throughout this CD are among the finest in the series, and the recording is first class, too – that edge on the leader's tone (noticed above) has disappeared, and the balance is excellent.

Requiem.

(M) ** Decca (ADD) (IMS) 425 043-2. Cortez, Pavarotti, Bruson, Washington, Arena di Verona Lyric Ch. & O, Fackler.

There are many passages in Donizetti's *Requiem* which may well have influenced Verdi when he came to write his masterpiece. Donizetti's setting lasts for 65 minutes but its inspiration is short-winded, and it is not helped here by limited performance and recording, deriving from the Cime label. The singing and playing are generally indifferent. Pavarotti, recorded in 1979, is the obvious star, singing flamboyantly in his big solo, *Ingemisco*. Of curiosity value only.

OPERA

Anna Bolena (complete).

*** Decca 421 096-2 (3). Sutherland, Ramey, Hadley, Mentzer, Welsh Nat. Op. Ch. & O, Bonynge.

(M) (**(*)) EMI mono CMS5 66471-2 (2). Callas, Simionato, Rossi-Lemeni, G. Raimondi, Carturan, La Scala, Milan, Ch. & O, Gavazzeni.

In the 1987 recording of *Anna Bolena*, Joan Sutherland crowns her long recording career with a commanding performance. Dazzling as ever in coloratura, above all exuberant in the defiant final cabaletta, she poignantly conveys the tragedy of the wronged queen's fate with rare weight and gravity. Samuel Ramey as the king is outstanding in a fine, consistent cast. Excellent recording.

The Callas recording was made live at La Scala in 1957, with the great diva at her most searingly magnetic. This is a performance which, despite the occasional sour note, has one marvelling at the imaginative phrasing and subtlety of dynamic shading, with top notes firm and clear, if characteristically edgy. Gavazzeni proves a most sympathetic conductor and, though the rest of the cast is no match for Callas, there is characterful if rather inflexible singing from Simionato as Giovanna and a fresh, clear contribution from Gianni Raimondi in the relatively small tenor role of Percy, here made the smaller by cuts. Nicola Rossi-Lemeni as Henry VIII is positive but gritty of tone in a less than convincing characterization. The radio sound is dry and limited and with occasional interference, but for Callas fans this is well worth hearing.

L'assedio di Calais (complete).

*** Opera Rara (ADD) OR 9 (2). Du Plessis, Jones, Focile, Serbo, Nilon, Platt, Glanville, Smythe, Treleaven, Harrhy, Bailey, Mitchell Ch., Philh. O, Parry.

The Opera Rara set is one of the most invigorating of all the complete opera recordings made over the years by that enterprising organization. With Della Jones and Christian du Plessis in the cast, as well as a newcomer, Nuccia Focile, as Queen Eleanor, David Parry conducts the Philharmonia in a fresh, well-sprung performance which gives a satisfying thrust to the big ensembles. The one which ends Act II, including a magnificent sextet and a patriotic prayer for the chorus, brings the opera's emotional high point. When, in Act III, Edward III's big aria turns into a sort of jolly waltz song, the music seems less apt.

Don Pasquale (complete).

*** RCA 09026 61924-2 (2). Bruson, Mei, Allen, Lopardo, Bav. R. Ch., Munich R. O, R. Abbado.

*** EMI CDS7 47068-2 (2). Bruscantini, Freni, Nucci, Winbergh, Amb. Op. Ch., Philh. O, Muti.

(M) *** Decca (ADD) 433 036-2 (2). Corena, Sciutti, Oncina, Krause, V. State Op. Ch. & O, Kertész – CIMAROSA: *Il maestro di cappella.* ***

Roberto Abbado's Munich set for RCA is on balance the finest modern version of Donizetti's sparkling comedy. Not only does Abbado spring rhythms cleanly and lightly, they are made the more infectious by the clarity of focus. The cast has no weak link. Renato Bruson may accentuate Pasquale's comic lines with little explosions of underlining but that helps to distinguish him sharply as a *buffo* character from his opposite number, Malatesta, here sung with rare style and beauty by Thomas Allen, as well as with a nicely timed feeling for the comedy. Frank Lopardo as Ernesto shades his clear tenor most sensitively, singing his *Serenade* with far more refinement than most latter-day rivals. Eva Mei sings the role of Norina with an apt brightness and precision

(including an excellent trill), even if others have presented a more characterful heroine.

Muti's is a delectably idiomatic-sounding reading, one which consistently captures the fun of the piece. Freni is a natural in the role of Norina, both sweet and bright-eyed in characterization, excellent in coloratura. The *buffo* baritones, the veteran Bruscantini as Pasquale and the darker-toned Leo Nucci as Dr Malatesta, steer a nice course between vocal comedy and purely musical values. Muti is helped by the beautifully poised and shaded singing of Gösta Winbergh, honey-toned and stylish as Ernesto. Responsive and polished playing from the Philharmonia, and excellent studio sound.

Under Kertész, Corena is an attractive *buffo*, even if his voice is not always focused well enough to sing semiquavers accurately. Juan Oncina, as often on record, sounds rather strained, but the tenor part is very small; and Krause makes an incisive Malatesta. Graziella Sciutti is charming from beginning to end, bright-toned and vivacious, and remarkably agile in the most difficult passages. The 1964 Decca recording is excellent, with plenty of atmosphere as well as sparkle.

Don Pasquale (complete; in English).

(M) *** Chan. 3011 (2). Shore, Dawson, Banks, Howard, Mitchell Ch., LPO, Parry.

There are obvious benefits from having a comic opera in English rather than the original language, and David Parry and a lively team of soloists, using Parry's own translation, deliver a well-paced, jolly and amiable performance. The interplay of characters is caught well and but the celebrated patter duet between Don Pasquale and Dr Malatesta, wonderfully articulated, brings none of the traditional comic wheezing at the end – on the whole an advantage. Andrew Shore and Jason Howard are good *buffo* singers, characterful if a little gruff, with Howard's Malatesta rather younger-sounding than usual, a believable brother of Norina. Lynne Dawson is fresh, sweet and agile as the heroine, and Barry Banks is a clear and unstrained Ernesto. Full sound, atmospheric enough to give warmth to the voices without obscuring words. If your preference is for opera in English, you can't go wrong with this.

L'elisir d'amore (complete).

*** Decca 455 691-2 (2). Gheorghiu, Alagna, Scaltriti, Alaimo, Lyon Opera Ch. & O, Pidò.

(M) *** Erato 4509 98483-2 (2). Devia, Alagna, Spagnoli, Praticò, Tallis Chamber Ch., ECO, Viotti.

*** Decca (ADD) 414 461-2 (2). Sutherland, Pavarotti, Cossa, Malas, Amb. S., ECO, Bonynge.

(M) *** Sony M2K 79210 (2). Cotrubas, Domingo, Evans, Wixell, ROHCG Ch. & O, Pritchard.

(B) **(*) Double Decca (ADD) 443 542-2 (2). Gueden, Di Stefano, Corena, Capecchi, Mandelli, Maggio Musicale Fiorentino Ch. & O, Molinari-Pradelli.

(N) (BB) (***) Naxos mono (ADD) 8.110125/26 (2). Sayao, Tagliavini, Valdengo, Baccaloni, Lenchner, Met. Op. Ch. & O, Antonicelli (with excerpts from LEONCAVALLO: *Pagliacci;* PUCCINI: *La Bohème* (**)).

(M) **(*) RCA 74321 25280-2 (2). Popp, Dvorsky, Weikl, Nesterenko, Munich R. Ch. & O, Wallberg.

(M) **(*) EMI (ADD) CMS5 65658-2 (2). Carteri, Alva, Panerai, Taddei, La Scala, Milan, Ch. & O, Serafin.

Angela Gheorghiu and Roberto Alagna help to make the new Decca version of Donizetti's sparkling comedy a winner. Alagna's voice is weightier and is recorded closer than in his earlier, Erato version, a portrait of the innocent Nemorino on the hefty side, with a newly unearthed variant of the great aria, *Una furtive lagrima*, which proves no advantage, neither tender nor subtle. Otherwise the set is excellent all round, with Gheorghiu an enchanting Adina, tenderly poignant in her final solo. Roberto Scaltriti as Belcore and Simone Alaimo as Dulcamara are both firm and characterful.

The mid-priced Erato set is a light, generally brisk account of the score, and it provides an ideal modern alternative to Richard Bonynge's version. Mariella Devia cannot match Sutherland for beauty of tone in the warmly lyrical solos but she sparkles more, bringing out what a minx of a heroine this is. Roberto Alagna's tenor timbre was then lighter, if not quite so firm, and, like Devia, he brings out the lightness of the writing delectably. His performance culminates in a winningly hushed and inner account of the soaring aria, *Una furtiva lagrima*. Rounding off an excellent cast, Pietro Spagnoli is a fresh, virile Belcore, and Bruno Praticò a clear, characterful Dr Dulcamara, an excellent *buffo* baritone, making the very most of a voice on the light side. The sound is first rate.

Joan Sutherland makes Adina a more substantial figure than usual, full-throatedly serious at times, at others jolly like the rumbustious Marie; in the key role of Nemorino, Luciano Pavarotti proves ideal, vividly portraying the wounded innocent. Spiro Malas is a superb Dulcamara, while Dominic Cossa is a younger-sounding Belcore, more of a genuine lover than usual. Bonynge points the skipping rhythms delectably and the recording is sparkling to match, with striking presence.

On the Sony reissue, delight centres very much on the delectable Adina of Ileana Cotrubas. Plácido Domingo by contrast is a more conventional hero and less the world's fool than Nemorino should be. Sir Geraint Evans gives a vivid characterization of Dr Dulcamara, though the microphone sometimes brings out roughness of tone, and Ingvar Wixell is an upstanding Belcore. The stereo staging is effective and the remastered recording bright and immediate.

With Hilde Gueden at her most seductive, the very early (1955) Decca stereo recording offers a delightful, spontaneous-sounding performance. Not just Gueden but the other soloists too are strikingly characterful, with Giuseppe di Stefano at his most headily sweet-toned, singing with youthful ardour, Fernando Corena a strong and vehement Dulcamara and Renato Capecchi well contrasted as Sergeant Belcore, though not quite so firm of tone, but both splendidly comic. Even without a libretto it makes a good bargain, with two CDs offered for the price of one.

One great benefit from the Naxos Historical series has been to expand our knowledge of the Brazilian soprano Bidu Sayao, who for many years was such a favourite at the Met in New York, but who was hardly known in Europe, making far too few commercial recordings. As a total charmer among lyric sopranos she is perfectly cast here as Adina, giving a sparkling portrayal opposite the young, golden-toned Tagliavini as Nemorino. Like all Italian tenors of his generation, he has his unstylish habits, but echoing Gigli he gives a winningly delicate account of *Una furtiva lagrima*, as well as entering into the fun of the piece. Giuseppe Valdengo could hardly be stronger as a firm, powerful Belcore, and the veteran, Salvatore Baccaloni, in traditional buffo bass style milks every comic point as the quack, Dulcamara, with Antonicelli timing the comedy to a nicety. Clear, if limited, mono sound. As a supplement come two delightful live recordings of Sayao – Nedda's communing with the birds in *Pagliacci* and the *Bohème* duet, *O soave fanciulla*, with Giuseppe di Stefano.

Wallberg's recording is marked by a charming performance of the role of Adina from Lucia Popp, bright-eyed and with delicious detail, both verbal and musical. Nesterenko makes a splendidly resonant Dr Dulcamara with more comic sparkle than you would expect from a great Russian bass. Dvorsky' and Weikl, both sensitive artists, sound much less idiomatic, with Dvorsky''s tight tenor growing harsh under pressure, not at all Italianate, and Weikl failing similarly to give necessary roundness to the role of Belcore.

The La Scala set had a fine cast in its day (1959). Alva is a pleasantly light-voiced and engaging Nemorino. Carteri's Adina ideally should be more of a minx than this, but the part is nicely sung all the same. Panerai as Belcore once again shows what a fine and musical artist he is, and Taddei is magnificent, stealing the show as any Dulcamara can and should. The drawback is Serafin's direction. The La Scala chorus is lively enough, and it is not that the orchestral playing is slipshod, but they provide less sparkle than they should.

L'elisir d'amore: highlights.

*** Decca 466 064-2 (from above complete recording, with Gheorghiu, Alagna, Scaltriti; cond. Pidò).

(N) (BB) ** Naxos 8. 554704. (from complete recording with La Scola, Ruffini, Alaimo, Frontali, Hungarian State Op.Ch. & O, Pier).

Decca's set of highlights includes a full translation; the playing time is 76 minutes.

Naxos's complete recording of this sparkling opera (8.66045/6) is very well played and warmly recorded, but is sadly flawed by the choice of tenor to sing Nemorino. Vincenzo La Scola is far too strenuous in his delivery. The great legato test-piece included here, *Una furtiva lagrima*, finds him less coarse, but this is a knowing not an innocent characterization. The others are better chosen, with Alessandra Ruffini bright-toned and vivacious as Adina, Simone Alaimo an excellent Dulcamara, and Roberto Frontali agile and characterful as Belcore. But this set is best approached through this generous and well-chosen selection of highlights (77 minutes).

The Elixir of Love (complete; in English).

(M) **(*) Chan. 3027 (2). Banks, Plazas, Holland, Shore, Williams, Mitchell Ch., Philh. O, Parry.

This lively account in English under David Parry brings out the high spirits of the piece, even if inevitably there are resulting echoes of Gilbert and Sullivan. Central to the performance's success is the vivacious Adina of Mary Plazas, sparkling and sweet-toned, guaranteed to ensnare any man around. Barry Banks gives a forthright performance as the innocent hero, Nemorino, even if the tone is not really Italianate enough for this music, whatever the language. Ashley Holland as Sergeant Belcore and Andrew Shore as Dr Dulcamara are lively and characterful, agile in rapid patter, even if their voices could be more sharply focused.

Emelia di Liverpool (complete). L'eremitaggio di Liwerpool (complete).

*** Opera Rara (ADD) OR 8 (3). Kenny, Bruscantini, Merritt, Dolton, Mitchell Ch., Philh. O, Parry.

The very name, Emelia di Liverpool, makes it hard to take this early opera of Donizetti seriously. In this set, sponsored by the Peter Moores Foundation, we have not only the original version of 1824 but also the complete reworking of four years later, which was given the revised title noted above. Such a veteran as Sesto Bruscantini makes an enormous difference in the buffo role of Don Romualdo in Emelia, a character who speaks in Neapolitan dialect. His fizzing duet with Federico (the principal tenor role, sung superbly by Chris Merritt) sets the pattern for much vigorous invention. With fresh, direct conducting from David Parry, this is a highly enjoyable set for all who respond to this composer.

La favorita (complete).

(M) **(*) Decca (ADD) (IMS) 430 038-2 (3). Cossotto, Pavarotti, Bacquier, Ghiaurov, Cotrubas, Teatro Comunale Bologna Ch. & O, Bonynge.

La Favorita may not have as many memorable tunes as the finest Donizetti operas, but red-blooded drama provides ample compensation. Fernando is strongly and imaginatively sung here by Pavarotti. The mezzo role of the heroine is taken by Fiorenza Cossotto, formidably powerful if not quite at her finest, while Ileana Cotrubas is comparably imaginative as her confidante, Ines, but not quite at her peak. Bacquier and Ghiaurov make up a team which should have been even better but which will still give much satisfaction. Bright recording.

La Favorite (complete opera; sung in French).

(N) *** RCA 74321 66229-2 (2). Kasarova, Vargas, Michaels-Moore, Colombara, Bav. R. O, Munich R. O, Viotti.

With a fine cast, strongly led by the Russian mezzo, Vesselina Kasarova, in the title role, this is an excellent set. It also fills an important gap, as up to now the more melodramatic Italian version has generally been preferred on disc over this original version, written by Donizetti for Paris. It may seem an odd choice to have non-French principals for this opera in French, but both Kasarova and the tenor Ramon Vargas are fine, characterful artists who brilliantly exploit the piece's drama. The text has been slightly tailored to fit the complete opera onto two discs, with the ballet severely cut. For many

the three-disc Decca set in Italian, with Richard Bonynge, Fiorenza Cossotto and the young Pavarotti, will be even more recommendable, with a very complete text that seeks to bring together the merits of both the French and the Italian versions, and the Decca sound more brilliant than on this RCA recording.

La Fille du régiment (complete).

*** Decca (ADD) 414 520-2 (2). Sutherland, Pavarotti, Sinclair, Malas, Coates, ROHCG Ch. & O, Bonynge.

It was with this cast that La Fille du régiment was revived at Covent Garden, and Sutherland immediately showed how naturally she takes to the role of Marie, a vivandière in the army of Napoleon. She is in turn brilliantly comic and pathetically affecting, and Pavarotti makes an engaging hero. Monica Sinclair is a formidable Countess in a fizzing performance of a delightful Donizetti romp that can confidently be recommended both for comedy and for fine singing. Recorded in Kingsway Hall, the CD sound has wonderful presence and clarity of focus.

(i) Gabriella di Vergy (1838 version); (ii) Scenes from 1826 version.

**(*) Opera Rara ORC 3 (2). (i) Andrew, Du Plessis, Arthur, Tomlinson, J. Davies, Winfield; (ii) Harrhy, Jones; RPO, Francis.

Dating from 1979 and transferred well to CD, this Opera Rara set of Gabriella di Vergy (not to be confused with Gemma di Vergy) presents the rediscovered score, written in the composer's hand, of a piece which Donizetti himself never heard. It was unearthed by Don White and Patric Schmid and makes one wonder how this inventive score with its many sparkling cabalettas and superb Act II finale could have been neglected for so long. The cast is a capable one, with Alun Francis, as ever, a sympathetic conductor; it is interesting to hear John Tomlinson early in his career, slightly miscast. It is fascinating to have as appendix three excerpts from the original, 1826 score, with Della Jones taking the role of the hero, Raoul, later rewritten for tenor.

Lucia di Lammermoor (complete).

*** Decca (ADD) 410 193-2 (2). Sutherland, Pavarotti, Milnes, Ghiaurov, Davies, Tourangeau, ROHCG Ch. & O, Bonynge.

(B) *** Double Decca (ADD) 460 747-2 (2). Sutherland, Cioni, Merrill, Siepi, St Cecilia Ac., Rome, Ch. & O, Pritchard.

(M) *** DG 459 491-2 (2). Studer, Domingo, Pons, Ramey, Amb. Op. Ch., LSO, Marin.

(M) (***) EMI mono CMS5 66441-2 (2). Callas, Di Stefano, Gobbi, Arie, Ch. & O of Maggio Musicale Fiorentino, Serafin.

(B) **(*) Ph. (ADD) Duo 446 551-2 (2). Caballé, Carreras, Sardinero, Ramey, Murray, Ahnsjö, Amb. S., New Philh. O, López-Cobos.

**(*) EMI CDS5 56284-2 (2). Callas, Tagliavini, Cappuccilli, Ladysz, Philh. Ch. & O, Serafin.

*(*) Sony S2K 63174 (2). Rost, Ford, Michaels-Moore, Miles, L. Voices, Hanover Band, Mackerras.

Though some of the girlish freshness of voice which marked

the 1961 recording had disappeared by the 1971 set, Sutherland's detailed understanding was intensified. Power is there as well as delicacy, and the rest of the cast is first rate. Pavarotti, through much of the opera not as sensitive as he can be, proves magnificent in his final scene. The sound-quality is superb on CD. In this set, unlike the earlier one, the text is absolutely complete.

The 1961 Sutherland version of *Lucia* now reappears as a splendid bargain in Double Decca format. Though consonants were being smoothed over, the voice is obviously that of a young singer, and dramatically the performance was close to Sutherland's famous stage appearances of that time, full of fresh innocence. Her coloratura virtuosity remains breathtaking, and the cast is a strong one, with Pritchard a most understanding conductor. The reissue has Decca's new-style synopsis, with a 'listening guide' for newcomers to the opera.

On DG, Cheryl Studer makes an affecting heroine, singing both brilliantly and richly, and Plácido Domingo rebuts any idea that his tenor is too cumbersome for Donizetti. This is the finest version yet in digital sound, with the young Romanian, Ion Marin, drawing fresh, urgent playing from the LSO. The rest of the cast is outstandingly strong too, with Juan Pons as Lucia's brother, Enrico, and Samuel Ramey as the teacher and confidant, Raimondo, Bide-the-Bent.

Callas's earlier, mono set dates from 1953. The diva is vocally better controlled than in her later, stereo set (indeed some of the coloratura is excitingly brilliant in its own right), and there are memorable if not always perfectly stylish contributions from Di Stefano and Gobbi. As in the later set, the text has the usual stage cuts, but the remastered sound is impresssive.

The idea behind the set with Caballé is an opera for a dramatic soprano, not a light coloratura. Compared with the text we know, paradoxically transpositions are for the most part upwards. López-Cobos's direction hardly compensates for the lack of brilliance and, José Carreras apart, the singing, even that of Caballé, is not very persuasive. Although only a synopsis of the plot is included, it is generously cued.

The Callas stereo version was recorded in Kingsway Hall in 1959, with her edgy top notes cleanly caught. Her flashing-eyed interpretation of the role of Lucia remains unique, though the voice has its unsteady moments. One instance is at the end of the Act I duet with Edgardo, where Callas on the final phrase moves sharpwards and Tagliavini – here past his best – flatwards. Serafin's conducting is ideal, though the score, as in Callas's other recordings, still has the cuts which used to be conventional in the theatre.

The Sony set under Mackerras benefits textually from the conductor's new edition of the score, absolutely complete with illicit transpositions removed. Unlike his rivals, Mackerras uses a period orchestra, but the benefits of that are very limited, when the players seem out of tune with the idiom, too often sounding square and failing to lift rhythms. Anthony Michaels-Moore is excellent as Enrico, and Alistair Miles makes a strong Raimondo. Bruce Ford is a fluent and stylish Edgardo, but the tone as recorded is often gritty, while Andrea Rost, bright and flexible in coloratura, yet

sings with too sour a tone to give much pleasure, the final blot on a disappointing set.

Lucia di Lammermoor: highlights.

(M) *** Decca (ADD) 421 885-2 (from above complete recording, with Sutherland, Pavarotti; cond. Bonynge).

(M) **(*) EMI (ADD) CDM5 66664-2 (from above complete recording, with Callas, Tagliavini, cond. Serafin).

For those who have chosen either Callas or Sutherland's earlier, complete set, the 63-minute selection from the latter's 1971 version should be ideal.

A satisfactory hour-long selection from Callas's 1959 Kingsway Hall stereo recording, with the diva not as completely in vocal control as she was in her earlier, mono sets.

Lucrezia Borgia (complete).

(M) *** Decca (ADD) (IMS) 421 497-2 (2). Sutherland, Aragall, Horne, Wixell, London Op. Voices, Nat. PO, Bonynge.

Sutherland is in her element here. Aragall sings stylishly too, and although Wixell's timbre is hardly Italianate he is a commanding Alfonso. Marilyn Horne in the breeches role of Orsini is impressive in the brilliant *Brindisi* of the last Act, but earlier she has moments of unsteadiness. The recording is characteristically full and brilliant.

Maria Padilla (complete).

**(*) Opera Rara (ADD) ORC 6 (3). McDonall, Jones, Clark, Du Plessis, Earle, Caley, Kennedy, Davies, Mitchell Ch., LSO, Francis.

Maria Padilla even matches *Lucia di Lammermoor* in places, with the heroine ill-used by the prince she loves, Pedro the Cruel. When the obligatory mad scene is given not to the heroine but to her father, even a tenor such as Graham Clark – future star in Bayreuth – can hardly compensate, however red-blooded the writing and strong the singing. In the title-role Lois McDonall is brightly agile, if at times a little raw. Alun Francis directs the LSO in a fresh, well-disciplined performance and, as ever with Opera Rara sets, the notes and commentary contained in the libretto are both readable and scholarly.

Maria Stuarda (complete).

(M) *** Decca (ADD) 425 410-2 (2). Sutherland, Tourangeau, Pavarotti, Ch. & O of Teatro Comunale, Bologna, Bonynge.

In Donizetti's tellingly dramatic opera on the conflict of Elizabeth I and Mary Queen of Scots, the contrast between the full soprano Maria and the dark mezzo Elisabetta is underlined by some transpositions, with Tourangeau emerging as a powerful villainess in this slanted version of the story. Pavarotti turns Leicester into a passionate Italian lover, not at all an Elizabethan gentleman. As for Sutherland, she is at her most fully dramatic too, and the great moment when she flings the insult *Vil bastarda!* at her cousin brings a superb snarl; Richard Bonynge directs an urgent account of an unfailingly enjoyable opera. Unusually for Decca, the score is slightly cut. The recording is characteristically bright and full.

Mary Stuart (complete; in English).

(M) **(*) Chan. 3017 (2). Baker, Plowright, Rendall, Opie, Tomlinson, E. Nat. Op. Ch. & O, Mackerras.

Mary Stuart was the opera chosen at the ENO just before Janet Baker decided to retire from the opera stage in 1982, and this comes from a series of performances at the Coliseum. Though far from ideal, the result is strong and memorable, with Dame Janet herself rising nobly to the demands of the role, snorting fire superbly in her condemnation of Elizabeth as a royal bastard and, above all, making the closing scenes before Mary's execution deeply moving. Her performance is splendidly matched by that of Rosalind Plowright, though the closeness of the recording of the singers makes the voices sound rather hard. The singing of the rest of the cast is less distinguished, with chorus ensemble often disappointingly ragged, a point shown up by the recording balance.

Poliuto (complete).

(M) (***) EMI mono CMS5 65448-2 (2). Callas, Corelli, Bastianini, Zaccaria, La Scala Ch. and O, Votto.

In 1960 Maria Callas returned to La Scala, having missed the two previous seasons, and had a triumph. This live recording, made at the time, demonstrates the scale of that triumph, with Callas's musical imagination and intensity of communication at their very peak. Corelli gives a heroic performance, noticeably subtler and more sensitive in scenes opposite Callas than when he is on his own. Callas herself consistently shows why this role inspired her, both in her natural gravity and poised intensity in slow music and in her biting brilliance in coloratura, marred slightly by the characteristic edge on the voice. Bastianini and Zaccaria complete the top Scala team of principals and, though the chorus is often rough, Votto heightens the dramatic impact in his conducting. Variable and limited mono sound, now effectively remastered.

Rosmonda d'Inghilterra: highlights.

(N) *** Opera Rara ORR 214. Fleming, Ford, Miricioiu, Miles, Montague, Philh. O, Parry.

It was in 1994, just before her spectacular rise to international superstar status, that Renée Fleming contributed to Opera Rara's splendid recording of this long-neglected Rossini opera. Shrewdly that company here offers 76 minutes from the opera, covering substantially all the vocal highspots involving the heroine. The result is a formidable demonstration of Fleming's art, with her sumptuous voice then at its freshest. With starry casting for the other characters too, the quality of her contribution, far from being dimmed, is enhanced still further, with Nelly Miricioiu and Diana Montague nicely contrasted, and with Bruce Ford and Alastair Miles ideally cast. Strong purposeful direction from David Parry and full, vivid sound. Unlike most Opera Rara issues, this one does not provide texts, only a summary of plot for each item.

Ugo, conte di Parigi (complete).

*** Opera Rara (ADD) (3). D. Jones, Harrhy, J. Price, Kenny, Arthur, Du Plessis, Mitchell Ch., New Philh. O, Francis.

The 1977 recording of *Ugo, conte di Parigi* was the result of formidable detective work, revealing in this early opera of 1832 a strong plot and some fine numbers, including excellent duets. Matching such singers as Janet Price and Yvonne Kenny, Maurice Arthur sings stylishly in the title-role with a clear-cut tenor that records well. Della Jones and Christian du Plessis, regular stalwarts of Opera Rara sets, complete a stylish cast. Reissued on CD, thanks to the Peter Moores Foundation, it offers a fresh and intelligent performance under Alun Francis, and the scholarly, readable notes and commentary, as well as libretto and translation, are models of their kind.

Collection: 'Donizetti Divas': excerpts from: (i) *Alfredo il Grande;* (ii) *L'assedio di Calais;* (iii) *Chiara e Serafina;* (iv) *Dom Sébastien de Portugal;* (v) *Emilia di Liverpool;* (vi) *Gabriella di Vergy;* (vii) *Maria De Rudenz;* (viii) *Maria Padilla;* (ix) *Rosmonda d'Inghilterra;* (x) *Ugo Conte di Parigi;* (xi) *Zoraisa di Granata.*

(N) *** Opera Rara (ADD) ORR 213. (i; iii) D. Jones; (ii) Focile, Di Plessus; (iii; v) Kenny; (iii) Davies; (iv) Elkins; (vi) Andrew; (vii; ix) Miricioiu; (vii) MacFarland, Ford; (viii) McDonall; (ix) Fleming; (x) Price; Harrhy; (xi) Cullagh; Montague with var. orchestras & conductors.

Recorded with various singers and orchestras between 1977 and 1990, this collection of Donizetti rarities brilliantly exploits the sparkling style of Della Jones as exponent of Donizetti. The various items have been compiled from earlier recordings from Opera Rara, complete operas as well as the earlier volumes of the '100 Years of Italian Opera' series, yet in sound and above all in vocal quality the results are splendidly consistent. Anyone looking to explore the neglected side of Donizetti's vast output without venturing into complete operas will find this most illuminating.

Arias: *Don Pasquale: Com'è gentil. Don Sebastiano: Deserto in terra. Il Duca d'Alba: Inosservato, penetrava . . . Angelo casto e bel. La Fille du régiment: Ah! mes amis . . . Pour mon âme; Pour me rapprocher de Marie. L'elisir d'amore: Quanto è bella; Una furtiva lagrima. La Favorita: Una vergine, un' angelo di Dio; Si, che un solo accento; Favorita del re! . . . Spirto gentil. Lucia di Lammermoor: Tombe degli avi miei; Tu che a Dio spigasti l'ali. Maria Stuarda: Ah! rimiro il bel sembiante.*

(M) *** Decca (ADD) 458 203-2. Pavarotti, with various orchestras & conductors.

A cleverly chosen compilation of Pavarotti recordings of Donizetti from various sources – not just complete sets but previous recital discs. It is good to have one or two rarities along with the favourite numbers, including Tonio's celebrated 'High-C's' solo from the Act I finale of *La Fille du régiment*. Sound from different sources is well co-ordinated. In all, 13 items are included, and this makes an attractive reissue in Decca's Opera Gala series, rather handsomely presented with an additional outer slip-case. Full translations are included.

Arias: *L'elisir d'amore: Prendi, prendi per me sei libero. La figlia del reggimento: Convien partir. Lucrezia Borgia: Tranquillo ei posa! . . . Come'è bello!.*

(M) ** EMI (ADD) CDM5 66464-2. Callas, Paris Conservatoire O, Rescigno – ROSSINI: *Arias.* **(*)

Reissued as part of EMI's Callas Edition, and very well recorded in 1963–4, this is a good example of the latter-day Callas, not always sweet-toned, and at times demonstrating less than the usual fire. If the singing rarely shows her at her most imaginative, and if there are fewer phrases that stick in the memory by their sheer individuality, that is not Donizetti's fault. Yet there is still much to admire, and the remastering flatters the voice by providing a warmly atmospheric orchestral backing. Excellent documentation: full translations are provided.

DOPPER, Cornelis (1870–1939)

Symphony No. 2; Pään I in D min. ; Pään II in F min. (symphonic studies).

(N) *** Chan. 9884. Hague Residentie O, Bamert.

Older readers may dimly recall an early recording of Dopper's *Ciaconna gotica*, but apart from that his music has remained unrepresented in the catalogue. Of humble origins, Dopper rose to eminence in Dutch musical life as Mengelberg's assistant at the Concertgebouw, where he conducted the first Dutch performances of Debussy's *La Mer*, Ravel's *Rapsodie espagnole* and Sibelius's *Second Symphony* – as well as much else besides. During his lifetime, Dopper's music was championed by Richard Strauss, Monteux and Mengelberg among others. He composed seven symphonies, the *Second* dating from 1903. The writing is cultured in the spirit of Brahms and Dvořák although the symphony is conservative in idiom, inclined to be diffuse and does not exhibit strong individuality. Nor for that matter do the two *Pääns* composed during the First World War. Very good performances by the fine Hague Residentie Orchestra under Matthias Bamert. Excellent recording, too, but this is not repertoire that we suspect will invite frequent repetition.

DOWLAND, John (1563–1626)

The Collected Works (complete).

(B) *** O-L (ADD) 452 563-2 (12). Kirkby, Simpson, York Skinner, Hill, D. Thomas, Consort of Musicke, Rooley.

Volume 1: *First Booke of Songs 1597.*

Volume 2: *Second Booke of Songs 1600.*

Volume 3: *Third Booke of Songs 1603.*

Volume 4: *A Pilgrimes Solace 1612 (beginning) (Fourth Booke of Songs).*

Volume 5: *A Pilgrimes Solace 1612 (conclusion) (Fourth Booke of Songs).* Keyboard transcriptions of Dowland's music: ANON.: *Can she excuse* (2 versions); *Dowland's almayne; Frogs' galliard; Pavion solus cum sola;* BYRD: *Pavana lachrymae.* FARNABY: *Lachrimae pavan.* MORLEY: *Pavana and Galiarda.* PEERSON and BULL: *Piper's Paven and Galliard.* SCHILDT: *Paduana lachrymae.* SIEFERT: *Paduana (la mia Barbara).* WILBYE: *The Frogge* (Tilney (harpsichord)).

Volume 6: *Mr Henry Noell Lamentations 1597; Lachrimae 1604.*

Volume 7: Sacred songs: *An heart that's broken and contrite; I shame at mine unworthiness; Sorrow, come!.* Psalms: *All people that on earth do dwell* (2 versions); *Behold and have regard; Lord to thee I make my moan; My soul praise the Lord; Put me not to rebuke O Lord. A Prayer for the Queen's most excellent Majesty.* Instrumental music (mainly anon. arrangements): *Comagain (Comagain sweet love); Pavan lachrymae* (both arr. VAN EYCK); *Earl of Essex galliard; Galliard; If my complaints; Lachrimae; Lachrimae; Lachrimae Doolande; Lady Rich galliard; Lord Willoughbie's welcome home; My Lord Chamberlaine his galliard; Pipers Pavan; Solus cum sola pavan; Sorrow stay.*

Volume 8: Lute music: (i) *Almain; Almain; Can she excuse; Coranto; Dr Case's Pavan; A Dream; Fantasia; Fantasia; Lachrimae; Loth to depart; Melancholy galliard; Mr Dowland's midnight; Mrs Vaux galliard; Preludium; The Queen's galliard; Resolution; Sir John Smith, his almain;* (ii) *Aloe; Come away; Fancy (Fantasia); Galliard; John Dowland's galliard; Mr Giles Hobie's galliard; Pavan; The Earl of Essex, his galliard; The Lady Clifton's spirit (Galliard); The Most Sacred Queen Elizabeth, her galliard; What if a day.* (i) Bailes; (ii) Lindberg.

Volume 9: Lute music: (i) *Complaint; A Fancy (Fantasia); The Frog galliard; Galliard on 'Walsingham'; Galliard to Lachrimae; Jig; Lachrimae; Mignarda; Semper Dowland semper dolens;* (ii) *Captain Dogorie Piper's galliard; Dowland's first galliard; Dowland's galliard; 2 Fancies (Fantasias); 2 Galliards; Go from my window; Lady Hunsdon's puffe; Lady Laiton's almain; Lord Willoughbie's welcome home; Mr Langton's galliard; Mrs Clifton's almain; Pavan; Piper's pavan; Sir Henry Guilforde, his almain; Tarleton's jig; Walsingham.* (i) Lindberg; (ii) North.

Volume 10: Lute music: (i) *Pavana Johan Douland;* (ii) *Can she excuse; Farewell Fancy; Farewell (on the 'In nomine' theme); The Frog galliard; 2 Galliards; The King of Denmark's galliard; Lachrimae; La mia Barbara; Lord Strang's march; Mrs Brigide Fleetwood's pavan; Mrs Nichol's almain; Mrs Norrish's delight; Mrs Vaux's jig; Mrs White's nothing; Mrs White's thing; Mrs Winter's jump; The Shoemaker's wife, a toy; Sir Henry Umpton's funeral;* (iii) *Forlorn hope fancy; Galliard; Orlando sleepeth; Robin; Solus cum sola; The Lord Viscount Lisle, his galliard.* (i) North; (ii) Rooley; (iii) Wilson.

Volume 11: Lute music: *A Coy toy; Almain; Earl of Derby, his galliard; Fancy (Fantasia); Fortune my foe; Mr Knight's* galliard; Sir John Langton's pavan; Sir John Souch his galliard; Tarletone's riserrectione; The Lady Rich, her galliard; The Lady Russell's pavan. Consort music (arrangements): Almain a 2; Can she excuse galliard; Captain Piper's pavan and galliard; Dowland's first galliard; Fortune my foe; The Frog galliard; Katherine Darcie's galliard; Lachrimae antiquae novae pavan and galliard; Lachrimae pavan; La mia Barbara pavan and galliard; Mistress Nichols alman a 2; a 5; Mr John Langton pavan and galliard; Round Battell galliard; Susanna fair; Tarleton's jigge.

Volume 12: Consort music: Lady if you so spite me; Mistress Nichols alman; Pavan a 4; Volta a 4; Were every thought an eye. A Musicall Banquet 1610: works collected by Robert Dowland.

This set, recorded over half a decade in the late 1970s, is a remarkable achievement. The discs originally appeared separately, but are now available only in a bargain box, well documented and with full texts provided. The contents of the First Booke of Songes of 1597 were recorded in the order in which they are published, varying the accompaniment between viols, lute with bass viol, voices and viols, and even voices alone.

The Second Booke contains many of Dowland's best-known songs, such as Fine knacks for ladies, I saw my lady weep and Flow my tears. Incidentally, the last two are performed on lute and two voices, the bass line being sung by David Thomas; this is quite authentic, though many listeners will retain an affection for its solo treatment. The solo songs are given with great restraint and good musical judgement, while the consort pieces receive expressive treatment. Emma Kirkby is at her freshest and most appealing in Come, ye heavy states of night and Clear or cloudy.

In the Third Booke David Thomas gives an excellent account of himself in What poor astronomers they are, and Emma Kirkby's voice is again a delight. Apart from a certain reluctance to characterize, this disc also commands admiration.

A Pilgrimes Solace (1612), Dowland's Fourth Booke of Songs, appeared when he was fifty, and here it spreads over more than a single CD. In a collection pervaded by melancholy, variety has been achieved here by using contrasts of texture: some of the songs are performed in consort, others are given to different singers. The second of the two CDs also includes some interesting 'transcriptions', but they are less 'transcriptions for the keyboard of Dowland', rather pieces composed 'after' Dowland.

Volumes 6 and 7 offer a superb collection of motets and sacred songs, an invaluable counterpart to the better-known secular works, instrumental and vocal. The recording is first rate. The Lachrimae are most beautiful pieces and are played with splendid taste. The instrumental music which closes Volume 7 is an anthology of arrangements of Dowland's music, presented not as second-best (as we today think of arrangements) but as a genuine illumination, a heightening of the original inspiration. Particularly attractive are the items for two or more lutes.

Volumes 8, 9, 10 and 11 concentrate on Dowland's huge output of lute music. Though Dowland is best known for his melancholy – semper dolens etc. – he has far greater range than the popular imagination would give him credit for. Of particular note are some of the Fantasias from Jakob Lindberg (who uses a bandora as well as a lute); their chromatic boldness and fantasy place them among the greatest music for this instrument. Both Christopher Wilson and Anthony Bailes play very freely and expressively.

The second half of Volume 11 and the first part of Volume 12 concentrate on the consort music. Three of the Pavans and Galliards come from Thomas Simpson's Opusculum (1610) and two of the Pavans are direct recompositions of Dowland's Lachrimae. Marvellous playing comes in the pieces from Simpson's Taffel-consort (1621).

The final Volume concludes with 'A Musicall Banquet' (1610) which Robert Dowland, the great lutenist's son, compiled and published but which he did not compose. The composers range from his celebrated father to lesser-known masters such as Holborne and Tessier, or more familiar ones such as Caccini. Not all the performances are equally satisfying, but overall this box cannot be recommended too highly, though essentially it is meant to be dipped into rather than taken a whole CD at a time. The CD transfers are of the very highest quality.

CONSORT MUSIC

Consort music: Captain Digorie Piper, his pavan and galliard; Fortune my foe; Lachrimae; Lady Hunsdon's almain; Lord Souche's galliard; Mistress Winter's jump; The shoemaker's wife (a toy); Sir George Whitehead's almain; Sir Henry Guildford's almain; Sir Henry Umpton's funeral; Sir John Smith's almain; Sir Thomas Collier's galliard; Suzanna.

*** Hyp. CDA 66010. Extempore String Ens.

The Extempore Ensemble's technique of improvising and elaborating in Elizabethan consort music is aptly exploited here in an attractively varied selection of pieces by Dowland; on record, as in concert, the result sounds the more spontaneous. Excellent recording.

Consort music, lute solos and songs: Captain Digorie Piper his galliard; The King of Denmark's galliard; M. Buctons galliard; The Earle of Essex galliard; M. George Whitehead his galliard; M. Giles Hobies galliard; M. Henry Noel his galliard; M. Nicholas Gryffith his galliard; Mistress Nichols almand; Mr John Langton's pavan; M. Thomas Collier his galliard; Semper Dowland semper dolens; Sir Henry Umpton's funerall; Sir John Such his galliard. Lute: A Fancy; Farewell (In nomine). Lute and bass viol: Dowlands adieu for Master Oliver Cromwell. Songs: All ye who love or fortune; Burst forth my tears; Can she excuse my wrongs; Lasso vita mia; A shepherd in a shade; Stay sweet awhile.

(BB) *** Naxos 8.553326. Rose Consort of Viols, with Heringman and King.

Catherine King's fresh voice and simplicity of line are all her own and she is very touching in the melancholy songs. The Rose Consort, lively enough in the galliards, also show their sensitivity to Dowland's doleful moods, notably in the famous *Semper Dowland semper dolens*, but also in the lament for Oliver Cromwell, played sombrely on bass viol and lute. The two lute solos, very well played by Jacob Heringman, offer further contrast, and the whole programme is recorded most naturally.

Lachrimae, or Seaven Teares.

*** BIS CD 315. Dowland Consort, Lindberg.

Jakob Lindberg and his consort of viols give a highly persuasive account of Dowland's masterpiece. The texture is always clean and the lute clearly present.

Lachrimae: 7 Passionate pavans. Consort settings: *Captain Piper his galiard; The Earl of Essex galiard; The King of Denmarks galiard; M. Bucton his galiard; M. George Whitehead his almand. M. Giles Hoby his galiard; M. Henry Noell his galiard; M. John Langtons pavane; M. Nicholas Gryffith his galiard; M. Thomas Collier his galliard with two trebles; Mrs Nichols Almand; Semper Dowland, semper dolens; Sir Henry Umptons funerall; Sir John Souch his galiard.*

*** Virgin VC5 45005-2. Fretwork, with Wilson.

This is a reissue of Fretwork's 1989 recording of excerpts from the *Lachrimae*, for which the 'passionate' pavans serve as introduction. Structurally they form a variation sequence, linked by a falling fourth at the opening of the first *Lachrimae antiquae* and by other common motifs of melodic line and harmony, an innovative procedure at the time. They are distinguished also by their pervading melancholy but are followed by a newly recorded collection of Dowland's own galliards, so one can choose to move over to more cheerful music at any time. All the performances are of undoubted merit and are well recorded.

COMPLETE LUTE MUSIC

Complete lute works: Volumes 1–5.

(M) *** HM HMX 2907160.64 (5).

Complete lute works, Volume 1: *Almain, P 49; Dr Cases Pauen; A Dream (Lady Leighton's paven); A Fancy, P 5; Farwell; Frogg galliard; Galliards, P 27; P 30; P 35; P 104; Go from my windowe; The Lady Laitons Almone; Mellancoly galliard; M. Giles Hobies galliard; Mistris Whittes thinge; Mr Knights galliard; Mrs whites nothing; Mrs Winters jumpp; My Ladie Riches galyerd; My lord willobies wellcome home; Orlando sleepeth; Pavan P 18; Pavana (Mylius 1622); Piece without a title, P 51; What if a day.*

*** HM HMU 907160. O'Dette (lute and orpharion).

Dowland wrote about 100 lute solos, using every musical form familiar at the time. Where either divisions (variations) or ornaments are obviously missing, Paul O'Dette has supplied his own – and very convincing they are. The music on this first disc is particularly rich in ideas. *Orlando sleepeth* is a hauntingly delicate miniature and it is played, like *Mrs Winters Jumpp* and *Go from my window*, on the orpharion,

a wire-strung instrument very like the lute but with a softer focus in sound because 'the fingers must be easily drawn over the strings, and not sharply gripped or stroken, as the lute is'. O'Dette is an acknowledged master of this repertoire: his playing, which can be robust or with the most subtle nuance, is by a natural and unexaggerated expressive feeling.

Complete lute works, Volume 2: *Aloe; As I went to Walsingham; Can she excuse; Captain Candishe his galyard; Captain Digorie Piper his galliard; A coye joye; Dowlands first galliard; Dowland's galliard; Farwell (An 'In nomine'); Fantasia; Lachrimae; Mayster Pypers pavyn; Mignarda; Mounsieur's almaine; Mrs Brigide fleetwoods paven alias Solus sine sola; Mrs vauxes galliarde; Mrs vauxes gigge; My lady hunnsdons puffe; Sir Henry Guilforde his almaine; Sir John Smith his almain; Sir John Souche his galliard; Solus cum sola; Suzanna galliard; Sweet Robyne.*

*** HM HMU 907161. O'Dette (lute).

Dowland's use of other composers' music is very prevalent in this programme, and several of the works are not certainly his but are of such a quality that the attribution is just. Once again Paul O'Dette constantly beguiles the ear with his feeling for the special mood and colour of Dowland's writing, and the recording is impeccable.

Complete lute works, Volume 3: *Dowlands adew for Master Oliver Cromwell; A Fancy, P 7; Forlorne hope fancye; Fortune my foe; Lord Strangs march; Mistresse Nichols almand; The most high and mightie Christianus, the fourth King of Denmark, his galliard; The most Sacred Queene Elizabeth, her galliard; Mr Dowlands midnight; Mr Langtons galliard; Mrs Cliftons allmaine; A Pavan, P 16; The Queenes galliard; The Right Honourable Ferdinando Earle of Darby, his galliard; The Right Honourable the Lady Cliftons spirit; Semper Dowland semper dolens; Sir John Langton, his pavin; Tarletones riserrectione; Tarletons Willy; Wallsingham & A galliard on Wallsingham.*

*** HM HMU 907162. O'Dette.

Dowland was never satisfied with his music; he was always revising and rethinking earlier works. The exotic *King of Denmark's galliard*, the opening item here, was originally called the 'Battle galliard' because of its bugle-calls, so engagingly portrayed on the lute. *Queen Elizabeth's* not dissimilar *galliard* was originally written for someone else. Generally the third volume of this excellent series has more extrovert music, but there are still interludes of melancholy. The closing *Semper Dowland semper dolens* (extended to seven minutes) speaks for itself.

Complete lute works, Volume 4: *Almand, P 96; Awake sweet love – Galliard; Come away; Coranto, P 100; Fancy, P 6; Fantasia, P 71; Frog Galliard; Galliard, P 82; Galliard on a galliard by Daniel Bachelar; Galliard to Lachrimae; Lachrimae, P 15; The Lady Russells pavane; La mia Barbara; Loth to depart; My Lord Wilobies welcome home; Pavana; Preludium; The Right Honourable the Lord*

Viscount Lisle, his galliard; The Right Honourable Robert, Earl of Essex, his galliard; The shoemaker's wife – A Toy.

(*) HM HMU 907163. O'Dette.

For his fourth volume, Paul O'Dette uses two different lutes as appropriate, an 8-course and a 10-course, both after Hans Frei. For the most part this is a low-key programme, very much in the '*semper dolens*' mood. Of course there are highlights, like the famous *Fantasia*, P 71, and the mood perks up for the galliard written for the Earl of Essex, while the galliard after Daniel Bachelar is also very striking and the penultimate piece, *La mia Barbara*, is very charmingly presented. But overall this is not one of the more memorable of the O'Dette collections.

Complete lute works, Volume 5: *Almande; Captain Pipers Galliard; Doulands Rounde Battell Galyarde; Earl of Darbies Galliard; Earl of Essex Galliard; 2 Fancies; A Fantasie; Gagliarda; Galliard; Hasellwoods Galliard; A Jig; Mistris Norrishis Delight; Pavana Dowland Angli; Pavana lachrimae; Pavin; Sir Henry Umpton's Funerall; Sir Thomas Monson his Pavin and Galliard; Squires Galliard; Une jeune fillette.*

*** HM HMU 907164. O'Dette.

Volume 5 includes a fascinating mixture of genuine Dowland and music written by other composers very much in the Dowland manner. *Une jeune fillette* (with its extended divisions) is probably by Bachelar. The sombrely memorable *Sir Henry Umpton's Funerall* is certainly by Dowland but was originally conceived as a consort piece, as was *Haselwood's Galliard*. Three items are probably by Dowland's son, Robert, including the rather fine *Pavin and Gaillard for Sir Thomas Monson* and the very characterful *Almande*, which appears to be derived from a piece by Robert Johnson. Dowland's own splendid closing *Fantasie* comes from a late manuscript, but in a profusely ornamented version, which suggests that it is not completely authentic. Dowland was known not to favour excess ornamentation, which he called 'blind divisions'. Yet it makes a lively ending to a fine concert, which is full of good things.

Music for lute or (i) orpharion: (i) *Can she excuse me; A Dream. Fancies, P 6 & P 73; Fantasie, P 1a; Farwell; Frog galliard; Lachrimae, P 15; Lady Hunsdon's puffe; Melancholy galliard; Mignarda; The most high and mightie Christianus, the fourth King of Denmark, his galliard; Mr Knights galliard; Mrs Brigide Fleetwood's pavan alias Solus sine sola; Mrs Vaux Jig;* (i) *Mrs Winters jump; My Lord Willoughby's welcome home;* (i) *Orlando sleepeth; Resolution; The Right Honourable The Lord Viscount Lisle, his galliard; Semper Dowland semper dolens; The Shoemaker's wife; Sir John Smith his almain; Tarleton's riserrection; Walsingham.*

*** BIS Dig CD 824. Lindberg (lute or (i) orpharion).

Those not collecting Paul O'Dette's complete series will find this BIS CD offers a cross-section of many of the finest of Dowland's lute pieces. The programme is generous (75 minutes) and Jacob Lindberg is no less at home in this repertoire than his colleague on Harmonia Mundi. He is particularly successful in the lively (battle) galliard written

for the King of Denmark, which is full of personality, as is the gentle piece called *Resolution*. The orpharion is used to atmospheric effect in the four works for which it was intended. *Semper Dowland, semper dolens* is presented most eloquently, as is the remarkable *Farwell*; and the divisions on *Walsingham* are played with a nice flow and an unexaggerated bravura. The recording is first class.

VOCAL MUSIC

A Musicall Banquet (Collection, 1610).

(N) *** Decca 466 917-2. Scholl, Karamazov, Märkl, Coin.

As can be seen above, *A Musicall Banquet* (although compiled by his son) is included in the final volume of the collected works of John Dowland, and while several of the finest songs are attributed to him, most of them are by others, including two engaging chansons by Pierre Guédron, and Caccini's very beautiful *Amarilli mia bella* (ravishingly presented by Andreas Scholl) and the equally touching *Dovro dunque morire?* Batchelar's *To plead my faith* is hardly less memorable and another highlight is Guillaume Tessier's delicate *In a grove most rich of shade*, while the anonymous *Sta notte mi sognana* brings some delectably nimble decoration. Indeed this repertoire is perfectly designed for Scholl's lovely voice and subtle musicianship, and the continuo accompaniment is never intrusive. The recording is most naturally balanced, but with the pervading melancholy atmosphere it might have been a good idea to have used more than one voice to add variety of timbre.

Ayres and Lute-lessons: *All ye whom love; Away with these self-loving lads; Come again sweet love; Come heavy sleep; Go Christal teares; If my complaints; My thoughts are winged; Rest awhile;* (Lute): *Semper Dowland, semper dolens. A shepherd in a shade; Stay sweet awhile; Tell me, true love; What if I never speede; When Phoebus first did Daphne love; Wilt thou unkind.* (Lute)*Prelude & Galliard.*

(B) **(*) HM (ADD) HMA 901076. Deller Consort, M. Deller; Spencer.

Dowland's 'ayres' were designed for a consort of singers as well as for solo singer and lute, and it is good to hear them in this form. Two of the Lute Lessons are excellently played by Robert Spencer. The performances for the most part give consistent pleasure. The sound is excellent.

Can she excuse my wrongs?; Come again! Sweet love doth now invite; Come, heavy sleep; Fine knacks for ladies; Flow my tears; His golden locks; If my complaints could passions move; In darkness let me dwell; I saw my lady weep; Lady, if you so spite me; Me, me and none but me; Now, O now I needs must part; Say love if ever thou did'st find; Sorrow stay; Stay awhile thy flying; Think'st thou then by feigning?; Time stands still; When Phoebus first did Daphne love; Wilt thou unkind thus reave me?. Lute solos: Fortune my foe; Melancholy galliard. (With *Galliards* by Mary, Queen of Scots. Attrib. FRANCIS CUTTING: *Greensleeves (Divisions).* ANON.: *Bonny Sweet Robin; Callino; Kemp's Jig.*)

(BB) *** Naxos 8.553381. Rickards, Linell (lute).

Steven Rickards has a light, precise counter-tenor voice which he uses very imaginatively in this sequence of 19 madrigals, including many of Dowland's finest. So a lively number like *Fine knacks for ladies* has a crispness and spring to bring out its lightness; even more impressively Rickards, with tone rock-steady and little or no hooting, superbly sustains the long legato lines of such great madrigals as *Flow my tears, I saw my lady weep* and *Come, heavy sleep*. There are also well-chosen lute solos from Dorothy Linell, supplementing her excellent accompaniments. The recording, made in New York, is clear and well balanced. Full texts and good notes are provided.

Can she excuse my wrongs?; Come again! Sweet love doth now invite; Far from triumphing court; Flow so fast, ye fountain; In darkness let me dwell; I saw my lady weep; Lady, if you so spite me; Thou almighty God; Shall I sue?; Weep you no more, sad fountains. Lute solos: Lachrimae antiquae pavane; Semper Dowland, sempre dolens.

*** Lyrichord (ADD) LEMS 8011. Oberlin, Iadone (lute).

One can hardly believe that this recital was recorded in 1958, so fresh and vivid is the sound. Russell Oberlin's very special counter-tenor timbre is beautifully caught. *I saw my lady weep* is most moving, while *Flow my tears* soars; but most touching of all is the closing *In darkness let me dwell*. Joseph Iadone contributes two of Dowland's most famous instrumental pieces. The only drawback to this disc is the comparatively short playing-time of 48 minutes.

Ayres: Can she excuse my wrongs?; Come again, sweet love; Come heavy sleep; Flow not so fast, ye fountains; From silent night; Go nightly cares; In darkness let me dwell; I saw my lady weep; Shall I sue?. Consort pieces: Captain Digory Piper's pavane and galliard; The First galliard. Lute lessons: Melancholy galliard; Mistess White's nothing; Mistress Winter's jump; My Lady Hunsdon's puff. Lute duets: My Lord Chamberlain's galliard; My Lord Willoughby's welcome home. Lute lessons: Orlando sleepeth; Sir John Smith's almain; Tarlton's resurrection.

(M) *** HM (ADD) HMT 90245. Deller, Consort of Six, Spencer.

Alfred Deller's collection is admirably planned and beautifully recorded. He is in excellent voice, while variety is provided by interweaving his solos with lute pieces and music for Elizabethan consort of six instruments (two viols, flute, lute, cittern and bandora). The recording is naturally balanced and nothing in the recital outstays its welcome.

'Earth, water, air and fire': Lute songs: Come again, sweet love doth now invite; Shall I strive; Sleep, wayward thoughts; Woeful heart; Would my conceits. Pilgrims Solace: Toss not my soul; From silent night; Go nightly cares; Sorrow stay; In darkness let me dwell; Though mighty God.

*** ASV CDGAU 187. Consort of Musicke, Rooley (with LOCKE: *Break, distracted heart.* MORLEY: *Deep lamenting; Leave now mine eyes.* TOMKINS: *O let me live*

for true love; Weep no more; WEELKES: *Cease sorrows now;* DE SERMISY: *Las, je m'y plains ***).*

The note accompanying this stimulating concert suggests that the four elements were 'everywhere in English lyrics' during Dowland's time, 'celebrating England as a veritable Arcadia'. Fresh response to word-meaning is the keynote, not just in Dowland but in items by his friends, Tomkins, Morley and Weelkes, and, notably, Matthew Locke's melodramatic *Break, distracted heart*, sung by 'Two despairing men and two despairing women', ending with a spoken dialogue between the two principal characters, before they do away with themselves! The closing sequence, in complete contrast, brings the most intense illumination of all, Dowland's five devotional songs, *The Pilgrimes Solace*, crowned by an extended motet, *Thou Mighty God*, visionary and uplifting.

Lute songs, Book I (1597): Awake sweet love; All ye whom love or fortune hath betraid; Can she excuse my wrongs with vertues cloak?; Come again: sweet love doth now invite; Deare, if you change, ile never chuse again; Goe crystal teares; If my complaints could passions move; Sleep wayward thoughts. Book II (1600): Come ye heavie states of night; Fine knacks for ladies; Flow my teares fall from your springs; If fluds of teares could cleanse my follies past; I saw my lady weepe; Shall I sue, shall I seek for grace?; Stay sorow stay; Tymes eldest sonne, old age the heire of ease . . . Then sit thee down and say thy 'Nunc dimittis' . . . When others sings 'Venite exultemus'.

*** Metronome METCD 1010. Agnew, Wilson.

Lute songs, Book III (1603): Behold a wonder here; Flow not so fast ye fountaines; I must complaine, yet do enjoy; Lend your eares to my sorrow good people; Say love if ever thou didst finde; Time stands still; Weepe you no more sad fountaines; What if I never speed; When Phoebus first did Daphne love. A Musicall Banquet (1610): In darkness let me dwell; Lady if you so spight me. A Pilgrim's Solace (1612): If that a sinners sighes be angels foode; Love those beames that breede Shall I strive with wordes to move; Stay time while thy flying; Thou mightie God . . . When Davids life by Saul . . . When the poore criple.

*** Metronome METCD 1011. Agnew, Wilson.

Paul Agnew's tenor voice has a certain darkness of colouring in the middle range that seems just right for the dolour of such songs as *Come ye heavie states of night* and *Flow not so fast ye fountaines*, or the despondent *If that a sinners sighes be angels foode* (a lovely performance), yet he can lighten it attractively for lively numbers like *What if I never speede* or *Fine knacks for ladies*. On the first disc, *Come again: sweet love doth now invite* has a passionate forward flow that is almost operatic. In the tripartite *Tymes eldest sonne* Dowland separates the three stanzas with excerpts from the actual liturgy, while *Thou mightie God* maintains its lamenting mood consistently throughout its three semi-narrative sections. Christopher Wilson's intimate accompaniments could not be more gently supportive, and the recording balance is admirable within a pleasingly atmospheric acoustic. Each disc is handsomely presented with a beautifully printed booklet containing full texts and illustrations, all within a slipcase.

Four-part lute songs, Book I: *Awake with these self-loving lads; If my complaints could passions move; Now! oh now I needs must part; Think'st thou then by thy feigning.* **Book II:** *Fine knacks for ladies.* **Book III:** *Me, me and none but me; Say love, if ever thou didst find; What if I never speed?; When Phoebus first did Daphné love.* **Book IV:** *In this trembling shadow; Stay, sweet awhile; Tell me true love; Wherever sin sore wounding.* **Solo:** *Tell me true love.*

(*) Lyrichord LEMS 8031. Saltire Singers, Dupré.

The Saltire Singers are a superb vocal group from the early 1960s. Patricia Clark and Edgar Fleet were both performers with Deller's Consort, and Desmond Dupré was Deller's lutenist. The vocal blend here is ravishing. Seldom have individual singers matched their voices more richly in this repertoire, with Patricia Clark leading with a sweet, soaring soprano, her gentle touch of vibrato ideal for Dowland's melodic lines. The choice of songs too is admirable, offering some of Dowland's very finest inspirations. The extended *Tell me true love* brings opportunities for lovely solo contributions from each member of the team; but most touching of all is the melancholy *Wherever sin sore wounding*, which shows Dowland at his most profound. The recording of the voices could hardly be bettered, except that at times they tend to overwhelm the lute. The only other small caveat is the relatively short measure (44 minutes), but the quality of the singing more than compensates. Full texts are provided.

DRAESEKE, Felix (1835–1913)

(i) *Piano Concerto in E flat, Op. 36. Symphony No. 1 in G, Op. 12.*

** MDG 335 0929-2. (i) Tanski; Wuppertal SO, Hanson.

Felix Draeseke was best known as a critic and he is scantily represented on CD. The *First Symphony*, composed in 1873, has touches of *Lohengrin* and there are even reminders of Berlioz as well as Schumann and Brahms. The *Piano Concerto* (1885–6) is inevitably Lisztian, though much more conventional. Claudius Tanski makes out a good case for it, and the American George Hanson pilots us through these raffish backwaters with some skill. Decent sound, but not a disc that excites enthusiasm.

DREYSCHOCK, Alexander (1818–69)

Piano Concerto in D min., Op. 137.

*** Hyp. CDA 67086. Lane, BBC Scottish SO, Willén –
KULLAK: *Piano Concerto in C min.* ***

This is one of the very finest of Hyperion's 'Romantic Piano Concerto' series. Piers Lane rises to the occasion with glittering dexterity and fine romantic flair, while the orchestra provides enthusiastic support, introducing the endearing main theme of the *Andante* with affectionate warmth. As in the coupled Kullak concerto, there are echoes of Liszt and Chopin in the passage-work, and the strong finale combines Weberian brilliance with Mendelssohnian sentiment in the charming secondary theme. The splendidly balanced recording presents the polished dialogue between solo piano and the often flamboyant orchestra in an ideal perspective.

DU FAY, Guillaume (c. 1400–1474)

Secular Music (complete).

(B) *** O-L 452 557-2 (5). Penrose, Covey-Crump, Elwes, Elliott, Hillier, George, Medieval Ens. of L., P. and T. Davies.

Volume 1: *Belle, que vous ay ie mesfait; Ce jour de l'an voudray joye mener; Entre vous, gentils amoureux; Helas, et quant vous veray?; Invidia nimica; J'ay mis mon cueur et ma pensée; Je donne a tous les amoureux; Je requier a tous amoureux; Je veuil chanter de cuer joyeux; L'alta belleza tua, virtute, valore; Ma belle dame, je vous pri; Mon chier amy, qu'aves vous empensé; Mon cuer me fait tous dis penser; Navré je sui d'un dart penetratif; Par droit je puis bien complaindre et gemir; Passato è il tempo omaj di quei pensieri; Pour ce que veoir je ne puis; Resvellies vous et faites chiere lye; Resvelons nous, resvelons, amoureux; Se madame je puis veir.*

Volume 2: *Adieu ces bon vins de Lannoys; Belle plaissant et gracieuse; Belle, veullies moy retenir; Belle, vueillies vostre mercy donner; Bien veignes vous, amoureuse liesse; Bon jour, bon mois, bon an et bonne estraine; Ce moys de may soyons lies et joyeux; Dona i aredenti ray; Estrines moy, je vous estrineray; He, compaignons, resvelons nous; Helas, ma dame, par amours; J'atendray tant qu'il vous playra; J'ay grant (dolour); Je me complains piteusement; Je ne puis plus ce que y'ai peu; Je ne suy plus tel que souloye; La belle se siet au piet de la tour; La dolce uista; Ma belle dame souveraine; Portugaler; Pour l'amour de ma doulce amye (2 versions); Quel fronte signorille in paradiso; Vergene bella, che di sol vestita.*

Volume 3: *Bien doy servir de volente entiere; Ce jour le doibt, aussi fait la saison; C'est bien raison de devoir essaucier; Craindre vous vueil, doulce dame de pris; Dona gentile, bella come l'oro; Donnes l'assault a la fortresse; Entre les plus plaines danoy; Hic iocundus sumit mundus; Je prens congie de vous, amours; Las, que feray? Ne que je devenray?; Mille bonjours je vous presente; Mon bien, m'amour et ma maistresse; Pouray je avoir vostre mercy?; Qu'est devenue leaulte?; Seigneur Leon, vous soyes bienvenus; Se la face ay pale.*

Volume 4: *Adieu m'amour, adieu ma joye; Adieu, quitte le demeurant de ma vie; Belle, vueilles moy vangier; J'ayme bien celui qui s'en va; Je languis en piteux martire; Je n'ai doubté fors que des envieux; Juvenis qui puellam; Lamentatio sanctae matris ecclesiae constantinopolitanae; Ne je ne dors ne je ne veille; Or pleust a dieu qu'a son plaisir; Par le regart de vos beaux yeux; Puisque celle qui me tient en prison; Puisque vous estez campieur; Se la face ay pale (2 versions); S'il est plaisir que je vous puisse faire; Trop lonc temps ai esté en desplaisir; Va t'en, mon cuer, jour et nuitie; Vo regard et doulce maniere.*

Volume 5: *De ma haulte et bonne aventure; Departes vous, male bouche et envie; Dieu gard la bone sans reprise; Du tout m'estoie abandonné; En triumphant de Cruel Dueil; Franc cuer gentil, sur toutes gracieuse; Helas mon dueil, a ce cop sui ie mort; Je ne vis onques la pareille; Je vous pri, mon tres doulx ami; Les douleurs, dont me sens tel somme; Le serviteur hault guerdonné; Malheureulx cueur, que vieulx tu faire?; Ma plus mignonne de mon cueur; Mon seul plaisir, ma doulce joye; O flos florum virginum; Resistera . . .; Vostre bruit et vostre grant fame.*

What will surprise those who dip into these discs is the range, beauty and accessibility of this music. There is nothing really specialized about this art beyond the conventions within which the sensibility works. The documentation is thorough and the performances have great commitment and sympathy to commend them. The actual sound-quality is of the first order, and readers who investigate the contents of this box will be rewarded with much delight. The discs are not available separately, but we are glad to see that the box is available on both sides of the Atlantic.

Chansons: *Adieu ces bons vins de Lannoys; Belle, que vous ay je mesfait; Bon jour, bon mois; Ce jour de l'an; Donnes l'assault à la fortress; Helas mon dueil; J'ay mis mon cuer; Mon chier amy; Par droit je puis bien complaindre; Pas le regard de vos beaux yeux; Pour l'amour de ma doulce amye; Puisque vous estez campieur; Quel fronte signorille La doce vita; Resvelliés vous et faites chiere lye; Resvelons nous; Se la face ay pale; Vergene Bella.*

(BB) ** Naxos 8.553458. Landauer, Unicorn Ens., Posch.

This Naxos anthology offers some 17 items, which are freely interpreted, taking the text as a guideline rather than a rigid musical framework, and they are given with some panache. There is an improvisatory freedom that would doubtless delight in the concert hall but is perhaps less satisfying on repetition. Well recorded, but ultimately not as rewarding as the performances in the more authoritative Oiseau-Lyre set.

Missa L'homme armé; Motet: *Supremum est mortalibus bonum.*

(BB) *** Naxos 8.553087. Oxford Camerata, Summerly.

Jeremy Summerly and his Oxford Camerata give a powerfully expressive and wholly convincing account of Du Fay's masterly cyclic Mass using a Burgundian chanson as its basis. We hear this sung first in its original format as an introduction, and its message, 'The armed man should be feared', makes a dramatically appropriate contrast with the motet, *Supremum est mortalibus*, which is a peace song. The latter was written some 30 years earlier, yet it shows just as readily the remarkable inventiveness and eloquence of this fifteenth-century French composer. The Mass movements are interspersed with plainchant in the same Dorian mode. With vivid yet atmospheric recording this can be given the strongest recommendation.

Missa Santi Anthoni de Padua. Hymnus: *Veni creator spiritus.*

*** DG 447 772-2. Pomerium, Blachly.

Missa Santi Anthoni de Padua. Motet: *O proles Hispaniae / O sidus Hispaniae.*

*** Hyp. CDA 66854. Binchois Cons., Kirkman.

We have a choice of style of performance for this beautiful music. The Binchois Consort is a small, intimate, all-male group, while Alexander Blachly's Pomerium is a much larger choir, although the whole ensemble is used only in the Ordinary movements. This makes for greater dynamic contrast; moreover, the two recording acoustics are different, the DG Archiv recording being made in the richly resonant Grotto Church of Notre Dame in New York, whereas the Hyperion ambience is drier and the inner detail emerges with much greater clarity. Pomerium offer as a bonus Du Fay's setting of the hymn, *Veni creator spiritus*, while the Binchois Consort performs a motet with two texts also associated with St Anthony. Both recordings are first class.

Motets: *Apostolo glorioso; Balsamis et munda cera; Ecclesie militantis; Fulgens iubar ecclesiae Dei; Magnanime gentes laudes; Moribus et genere; Nuper rosarum flores; O gemma lux; O Sancte Sebastiane; Rite majorem Jacobus; Salve flos Tusce gentis; Supremum est mortalibus; Vasilissa ergo gaude.*

(N) *** HM HMC 901700. Huelhas Ens., Van Nevel.

Du Fay was especially renowned in his time for his rhythmic motets, all thirteen of which are included here. The polyphonic character of these works is dependent on a constantly repeated rhythmic formula or period (of no determined length). But, as always with this composer, the expressive character of the music still predominates, and its underlying structural complexity is seldom obvious to the listener – nor should it be.

The music soars and there is no better example than the celestial polyphony of *Eccesie militantis* with its complex final pages, or the more sombre motet which gives the disc its title, *O gemma lux*. The exultant *Rite majorem Jacobus* ends with a bold stroke of dissonance in its final cadence, but the flowing *Virgo, virga virens* which closes the concert creates a lovely expressive serenity. The voices are underpinned by instruments, usually sonorous sackbuts, which support the implied harmony without weighing down the polyphony. The performances here are most eloquent, very well paced, and beautifully recorded in a very suitable abbey acoustic.

DUKAS, Paul (1865–1935)

L'Apprenti sorcier (The Sorcerer's Apprentice).

*** DG 419 617-2. BPO, Levine – SAINT-SAENS: Symphony No. 3. ***

(M) **(*) Chan. 6503. SNO, Gibson – ROSSINI (arr. RESPIGHI): La Boutique fantasque; SAINT-SAENS: Danse macabre. **(*)

(***) Testament mono SBT1017. Philh O, Cantelli – CASELLA: Paganiniana; FALLA: Three-Cornered Hat; RAVEL: Daphnis et Chloé: Suite No. 2. (***)

Levine chooses a fast basic tempo, though not as fast as Toscanini (who managed with only two 78 sides), but achieves a deft, light and rhythmic touch to make this a real orchestral Scherzo. Yet the climax is thrilling, helped by superb playing from the Berlin Philharmonic Orchestra. The CD has an amplitude and sparkle which are especially telling.

Gibson secures excellent playing from the SNO, if without the sheer panache of some of his competitors. The recording (made in City Hall, Glasgow, in 1972) is less overtly brilliant than Levine's but has plenty of atmosphere. The Chandos disc, however, is ungenerous with a playing time of only 37 minutes.

Cantelli's 1954 mono account still remains one of the very best performances ever recorded, and it is splendidly transferred.

L'Apprenti sorcier (The Sorcerer's Apprentice) (with spoken introduction).

(BB) **(*) Naxos 8.554463. Morris (nar.), Slovak RSO, Jean – RAVEL: *Ma Mère l'Oye ***. SAINT-SAENS: *Carnival of the Animals. **(*)

In this Naxos triptych clearly aimed at young children, Johnny Morris provides a concise and effective narrative introduction. The performance is alive and well paced; it takes a while to generate the fullest tension, but any child should respond to this imagery. The recording is excellent, spacious and vivid.

L'Apprenti sorcier; La Péri.

(*) Chan. 8852. Ulster O, Y. P. Tortelier – CHABRIER: *España*, etc. *

L'Apprenti sorcier; La Péri: Poème dansé (with Fanfare); Symphony in C.

*** RCA 09026 68802-2. O. Nat de France, Slatkin.

**(*) Telarc CD 80515. Cincinnati SO, López-Cobos.

(i) L'Apprenti sorcier; (ii) La Péri; (iii) Symphony in C; (ii) Ariane et Barbe-bleue: Act III Prelude.

(M) **(*) EMI (ADD) CDM7 63160-2. (i) (mono) Philh. O, Markevitch; (ii) (stereo) Paris Op. O, Dervaux; (iii) (stereo) ORTF, Martinon.

L'Apprenti sorcier; La Péri (with Fanfare); Polyeucte: Overture.

🏵 (M) *** Ph. (ADD) 454 127-2. Rotterdam PO, Zinman – D'INDY: *Symphonie sur un chant montagnard. **

(N) (M) *** Sup. (ADD) SU 3479–2 011. Czech PO, Almeida.

(i) L'Apprenti sorcier; (ii) La Péri (with Fanfare); Symphony in C; (iii) Piano Sonata in E flat min.; La Plainte; Prélude, élégiaque; Variations, Interlude & Finale.

(N) (BB) ** Erato Ultima Dig./ADD. 8573 88051-2 (i) Nouvel P O; (ii) SRO, Jordan; (ii) Hubeau.

Symphony in C; Polyeucte: Overture.

*** Chan. 9225. BBC PO, Y. P. Tortelier.

Dukas's *La Péri* was written for Diaghilev in 1912. David Zinman's 1978 recording is arguably the finest account of Dukas's colourful score ever to have been put on record. Only in the introductory *Fanfare* could some ears crave more sonic brilliance from the well-balanced recording, and that comment might also be applied to *L'Apprenti sorcier*.

The *Polyeucte Overture* is not dissimilar in style to *La Péri* but has less interesting material; it is presented equally effectively.

Yan Pascal Tortelier gives a very good performance indeed of *La Péri*, with plenty of atmosphere and feeling, and *L'Apprenti sorcier* is equally successful as a performance.

Very fine playing from the Orchestre National under Leonard Slatkin and a very well-shaped account of Dukas's fine *Symphony* plus a highly persuasive and atmospheric account of *La Péri*. Extremely well recorded too. This can be warmly recommended alongside Yan Pascal Tortelier on Chandos; the different choice of couplings will no doubt be a decisive factor, but there is not a great deal to choose between them if it is just the *Symphony* you are after.

The same sound engineer, Mikloslav Kulhan, who balanced Baudo's outstanding Debussy record above was also at the controls for Almeida's Dukas collection, made in the same venue in 1973 and hardly less successful, although he rightly sought to give the strings added brilliance for the passionate climax of *La Péri*. Almeida's performance is sensuous and gripping, and the orchestral playing has both intensity and allure if perhaps not quite the subtlety and feeling for detail shown by Zinman in Rotterdam. *Polyeucte*, an early work with Wagnerian echoes, is also extremely successful, especially the closing Andante tranquillo. But what makes this Supraphon disc very competitive is the sparkling *L'Apprenti sorcier*, the main theme winningly jaunty and ideally paced, and reaching a brilliant climax, with superb roistering horns and the whole orchestra on its toes.

Martinon brings real vigour and feeling to the *Symphony in C* and the 1974 recording comes up well. *La Péri* was recorded in 1957 and wears its years well, though the orchestral playing is not first class. Markevitch's 1953 Philharmonia account of *L'Apprenti sorcier* (mono, of course) is brilliantly played, but there is an ugly edit (cut-off reverberation) halfway through. Still, this is worth having.

After the richly resonant *Fanfare*, the diaphanous opening of *La Péri* is beautifully played in Cincinnati, and the climax has proper sensuous passion. The orchestra is equally committed in the *Symphony*, but Jesús López-Cobos does not manage to retain the same degree of grip on the structure of the first movement as Leonard Slatkin or Yan Pascal Tortelier. The slow movement, however, is very successful on Telarc and the finale very spirited. *L'Apprenti sorcier* is lively too, but without quite the wit and rhythmic buoyancy of the very finest accounts. The Telarc recording is impressively full-bodied and well balanced, but the hall resonance does not provide quite enough transparency to reveal the fullest detail in the more complex climaxes.

Armin Jordan's account of *L'Apprenti sorcier* is not without impetus but is rhythmically rather heavy. However, his reading of the *Symphony* has conviction and the Suisse Romande Orchestra play well for him. He is equally sensitive to atmosphere in *La Péri* and the Erato recording is eminently satisfactory.

The second disc is less distinctive, for Jean Hubeau's performances of the piano music are acceptable rather than distinguished. The finale of the *Sonata* (its longest movement) has a rather good tune, but one feels more could have been made of it, and the *Variations* too are given uneven advocacy. However, the *Prélude élégiaque* (on the name of Haydn) is more appealingly presented.

Ariane et Barbe-bleue (opera): complete.

(M) *** Erato 2292 45663-2 (2). Ciesinski, Bacquier, Paunova, Schauer, Blanzat, Chamonin, Command, Fr. R. Ch. & O, Jordan.

Ariane et Barbe-bleue is, like Debussy's *Pelléas*, set to a Maeterlinck text, but there is none of the half-lights and the dream-like atmosphere of the latter. The performance derives from a French Radio production and is, with one exception, well cast; its direction under the baton of Armin Jordan is sensitive and often powerful. The recording is eminently acceptable. The complete libretto is included, and this most enterprising and valuable reissue is strongly recommended.

DU MONT, Henry (1610–1684)

Allemande à 3; Pavane à 3; Saraband à 3; Symphonie à 3 (for 2 violins & continuo); *Allemande en tablature; Allemande grave; Allemande sur les anches* (all for organ); *Pavane pour clavecin.* Dialogue motets: *Dialogus angelis et peccatoris; Dialogus de Anima; In lectulo meo; In te Domine; Litanies à la Vierge.*

(N)(M) *** Virgin VM5 61531-2. Les Talens Lyriques, Rousset.

Symphonies: in D; G. Motets: *Benedic anima mea; Domine quid multiplicati sunt; Magnificat; Nisi Dominus; O panis angelorum; Pulsate tympane.*

(N) (M) *** Virgin VM5 61675-2. Les Pages et Chantres de la Chapelle, Musica Aeterna Ens., Schneebeli.

Henry de Thier was born near Liège and probably adopted the title Du Mont, the French translation of his Walloon name, to help his advancement when he settled in Paris just before 1640. It was a shrewd move, for he was to become Master of Music in the King's Chapel, a shared post, but one in which he prospered.

Between them this pair of Virgin CDs give us a satisfactory survey of his output, with the first disc rather upstaged by the second, for Du Mont's *grands motets* are vocally and instrumentally quite spectacular.

However, Rousset, in his more diverse collection with Les Talens Lyriques, introduces some of the chamber and instrumental music, in which a noble expressive gravity predominates, although there are engaging dance-like interludes. He has chosen (quite authentically) to use mean-tone temperament, a tuning system based on thirds, which lends a distinctive colour to the organ music. And, in the interests of an ideal balance, his singers and instrumentalists are sited in the organ loft!

The harpsichord *Pavane* with which Rousset closes the concert himself is one of its highlights, and the other is the echo motet, *In lectulo meo*, in which Sandrine Piau shines radiantly in a duet with herself. The five-voice *Litanies à la Vierge* (with continuo) is another serenely beautiful work. But the most important and striking of these dialogue motets is the ambitious *Dialogus de Anima* – almost an oratorio –

for five singers, in which God, a sinner and an angel converse, with the piece ending with a splendid five-part chorus. This is most vividly performed, and recorded, and with full texts and translations this disc, while perhaps of specialist appeal, can be recommended highly.

However, the collection of Du Mont's *grands motets*, composed for the Chapel Royal, shows the composer at his most inspired. They are in an exultant post-Renaissance style, using soloists, solo ensembles, small chorus, and large five-part chorus in combination. Grandest of all is the superb *Magnificat* featuring a double choir (large and small) and solo group to make a kind of three-dimensional intercourse. The sense of spectacle here reminds the listener of Gabrieli, even if Du Mont's instrumental scoring is much more modest.

The performances rise to the occasion, and if there is a momentary slight lapse of intonation among the soloists, it is not of great moment when overall these singers and instrumentalists are fully worthy of this exuberant music. The recording is first class and the only snag is that texts and translations are omitted.

DUNCAN, Trevor (born 1924)

Children in the Park; Enchanted April; The Girl from Corsica; High Heels; Little Debbie; Little Suite; Meadow Mist; Maestro Variations; Sixpenny Ride; St Boniface Down; La Torrida; Twentieth-Century Express; Valse mignonette; The Visionaries: Grand March; Wine Festival.

*** Marco 8.223517. Slovak RSO (Bratislava), Penny.

Trevor Duncan is perhaps best known for the signature-tune to the TV series, 'Dr Finlay's Casebook', the *March* from the *Little Suite*, which is offered here along with the other two numbers which make up that suite. But more of his popular pieces are included: the *Twentieth-Century Express*, with its spirited 'going on holiday' feel, the exotic *Girl from Corsica*, and the tunefully laid-back *Enchanted April*, which was also used in a television programme. All the music here is nostalgically tuneful, with enough invention of melody and colour to sustain interest. Andrew Penny and the Bratislavan orchestra sound as though they have played it all for years, and recording is excellent. Full and helpful sleeve-notes complete this attractive collection of good-quality light music.

DUNSTABLE, John (d. 1453)

Missa Rex seculorum. Motets: *Albanus roseo rutilat – Quoque ferundus eras – Albanus domini Laudus; Ave maris stella; Descendi in ortum meum; Gloria in canon; Preco preheminence – Precursor premittur – textless – Inter natos mulierum; Salve regina mater mire; Specialis Virgo; Speciosa facta es; Sub tuam protectionem; Veni sancte spiritus – Veni creator spiritus.*

*** Metronome METCD 1009. Orlando Cons.

The Orlando Consort present their generous, 74-minute survey with an impressive combination of direct, impassioned feeling and style. If the splendid *Missa Rex seculorum* is of doubtful attribution, every piece here, motets and antiphons alike, is clearly by a major composer with a highly individual voice. The recording is excellent in every way and this CD, which won the *Gramophone*'s Early Music Award in 1996, offers the collector an admirable and highly rewarding entry into this composer's sound-world.

Motets: *Agnus Dei; Alma redemptoris Mater; Credo super; Da gaudiorum premia; Gaude virgo salutata; Preco preheminenciae; Quam pulcra es; Salve regina misericordiae; Salve sceme sanctitatis; Veni creator; Veni sancte spiritus.*

*** Virgin VER5 61342-2. Hilliard Ens., Hillier.

These motets give a very good idea of Dunstable's range, and they are sung with impeccable style. The Hilliard Ensemble has perfectly blended tone and impeccable intonation, and their musicianship is of the highest order. Some collectors may find the unrelieved absence of vibrato a little tiring on the ear when taken in large doses; but most readers will find this a small price to pay for music-making of such excellence, so well recorded.

DUPARC, Henri (1848–1933)

Mélodies (complete): *Au pays où se fait la guerre; Chanson triste; Elégie; Extase; La fuite (duet); Le galop; L'invitation au voyage; Lamento; Le Manoir de Rosamonde; Phidylé; Romance de Mignon; Sérénade; Sérénade florentine; Soupir; Testament; La vague et la cloche; La vie antérieure.*

*** Hyp. CDA 66323. Walker, Allen, Vignoles.

The Hyperion issue is as near an ideal Duparc record as could be. Here are not only the 13 recognized songs but also four early works – three songs and a duet – which have been rescued from the composer's own unwarranted suppression. Roger Vignoles is the ever-sensitive accompanist, and the recording captures voices and piano beautifully, bringing out the tang and occasional rasp of Walker's mezzo and the glorious tonal range of Allen's baritone.

DUPHLY, Jacques (1715–89)

Pièces pour clavecin: *La Bouchon; Courante; La Félix; La Forqueray; Les Graces; La d'Héricourt; Légèrement; Menuets; Rondo in D; Rondeau in D min.; La Vanlo; La Victoire; La de Villeneuve.*

*** ASV CDGAU 108. Meyerson (harpsichord).

These performances come from the mid-1980s (still analogue, and none the worse for that) and are very spirited and characterful. Though none of this music can lay a claim to greatness, it has undoubted charm and grace. Mitzi Meyerson plays a Goble harpsichord and uses no fewer than four tunings during the course of the recital. There are excellent notes by Nicholas Anderson. Recommended.

DUPRÉ, Marcel (1886–1971)

Symphony in G minor for Organ & Orchestra, Op. 25.

*** Telarc CD 80136. Murray, RPO, Ling – RHEINBERGER: *Organ Concerto No. 1.* ***

If you enjoy Saint-Saëns's *Organ Symphony*, you'll probably enjoy this. The organ's contribution is greater, although it is not a concerto. It is a genial, extrovert piece, consistently inventive if not as memorably tuneful as its predecessor. The performance has warmth, spontaneity and plenty of flair, and the recording has all the spectacle one associates with Telarc in this kind of repertoire.

ORGAN MUSIC

Chorale & Fugue, Op. 57; 3 Esquisses, Op. 41; Preludes & Fugues: in B; G min., Op. 7/1 & 3; Le Tombeau de Titelouse: Te lucis ante terminum; Placare Christe servulis, Op. 38/6 & 16; Variations sur un vieux Noël, Op. 20.

*** Hyp. CDA 66205. Scott (St Paul's Cathedral organ).

An outstandingly successful recital, more spontaneous and convincing than many of the composer's own recordings in the past. Dupré's music is revealed as reliably inventive and with an atmosphere and palette all its own. John Scott is a splendid advocate and the St Paul's Cathedral organ is unexpectedly successful in this repertoire.

6 Chorales, Op. 28; 2 Chorales, Op. 59; 24 Inventions, Op. 50; 4 Modal Fugues, Op. 63.

(BB) *** Naxos 8.553862. Biery.

The 24 *Inventions*, Op. 50, which are divided to begin and end this CD, are, like Bach's *Well-Tempered Clavier*, composed in all the major and minor keys. They are distinguished by fastidious craftsmanship and considerable imagination, as are the 79 *Chorales*, Op. 28 (1930). The *Chorales*, Op. 59, and the *Four Modal Fugues* come from the 1960s. James Biery is an excellent advocate and the recording, made on the Casavant organ of the Cathedral of Saints Peter and Paul, in Providence, Rhode Island, is splendidly lifelike and has great clarity and definition. A rewarding issue.

DURUFLÉ, Maurice (1902–86)

Fugue sur le thème du carillon des heures de la Cathédrale de Soissons; Prélude, adagio et choral varié sur le thème du Veni Creator; Prélude sur l'Introit de l'Epiphanie; Prélude et fugue sur le nom d'Alain, Op. 7; Scherzo, Op. 2; Suite, Op. 5.

**(*) Delos D/CD 3047. Wilson (Schudi organ of St Thomas Aquinas, Dallas, Texas).

The producer of this record, which contains all Duruflé's organ music, consulted the composer before choosing the present organ, and the performances of Duruflé's often powerful and always engagingly inventive music are of the highest quality. The account of the closing *Toccata* of the *Suite*, Op. 5, has breathtaking bravura, and if here (as elsewhere) detail is not sharply registered, the spontaneity and power of the playing are compulsive.

Requiem, Op. 9.

*** Teldec 4509 90879-2. Larmore, Hampson, Amb. S., Philh. O, Legrand – FAURE: *Requiem*. ***

(B) *** Sony (ADD) SBK 67182. Te Kanawa, Nimsgern, Amb. S., Desborough School Ch., New Philh. O, A. Davis – FAURE: *Requiem*. ***

(B) *** Decca Eclipse 448 711-2. Palmer, Shirley-Quirk, Boys of Westminster Cathedral Ch., L. Symphony Ch., LSO, Hickox – FAURE: *Pavane*; POULENC: *Gloria*. ***

(M) *** Decca 466 418-2. King, Keyte, St John's College, Cambridge, Ch., Cleobury (organ), Guest – FAURE: *Requiem*. ***

Requiem, Op. 9; Messe Cum jubilo, Op. 11; 4 Motets sur les thèmes grégoriens, Op. 10; Notre père, Op. 14 (both for a cappella choir).

*** EMI CDC5 56878-2. (i) Von Otter, Hampson, Alain; Orfeon Donostiarra, O de Capitole Toulouse, Plasson.

*** Nim. NI 5599. (i) Turpin, Clements, Morton (treble); Farrington, St John's College Cambridge Ch., Robinson.

Requiem, Op. 9 (3rd version); 4 Motets, Op. 10.

*** Hyp. CDA 66191. Murray, Allen, Corydon Singers, ECO, Best; Trotter (organ).

(i–iii) Requiem. Op. 9; (ii) 4 Motets, Op. 10; (iii) (Organ) Prélude et fugue sur le nom d'Alain.

(B) *** Double Decca (ADD) 436 486-2. (i) King, Keyte; (ii) St John's College, Cambridge, Ch.; (iii) Cleobury (organ); Guest – FAURE: *Requiem*, etc.; POULENC: *Messe*, etc. ***

*(*) DG 459 365-2. Bartoli, Terfel, Santa Cecilia Nat. Ac. Ch. & O, Chung – FAURE: *Requiem*. *(*)

Duruflé wrote his *Requiem* in 1947, overtly basing its layout and even the cut of its themes on the Fauré masterpiece. Michel Legrand uses the full orchestral version and makes the most of the passionate orchestral eruptions in the *Sanctus* and *Libera me*. He strikes a perfect balance between these sudden outbursts of agitation and the work's mysticism and warmth. The Ambrosian Choir sing ardently yet find a treble-like purity for the *Agnus Dei* and *In Paradisum*, while Jennifer Larmore gives the *Pie Jesu* more plangent feeling than its counterpart in the Fauré *Requiem*. The recording, made in Watford Town Hall, is spacious and most realistically balanced. A clear first choice in the premium price-range.

However, Andrew Davis directs a warm and atmospheric reading of Duruflé's beautiful setting with the Desborough School Choir, and this makes an excellent bargain alternative. He too uses the full orchestral version with its richer colourings. Kiri Te Kanawa sings radiantly in the *Pie Jesu*, and the darkness of Siegmund Nimsgern's voice is well caught. In such a performance Duruflé establishes his claims for individuality, even in the face of Fauré's setting. The recording is nicely atmospheric.

Hickox tempers the richness of the orchestral version by using boys' voices in the choir. He relishes the extra drama of orchestral accompaniment with biting brass at the few

moments of high climax. Felicity Palmer and John Shirley-Quirk sing with deep feeling and fine imagination, if not always with ideally pure tone. The recording has a pleasantly ecclesiastical ambience, which adds to the ethereal purity of the trebles, and the stereo spread is wide.

Using the chamber-accompanied version, with strings, harp and trumpet – a halfway house between the full orchestral score and plain organ accompaniment – Best conducts a deeply expressive and sensitive performance of Duruflé's lovely setting of the *Requiem*. With two superb soloists and an outstandingly refined chorus, it makes an excellent recommendation, well coupled with the motets, done with similar freshness, clarity and feeling for tonal contrast. The recording is attractively atmospheric yet quite clearly focused.

The (originally Argo) St John's version also uses boy trebles instead of women singers, even in the solo of the *Pie Jesu* – exactly parallel to Fauré's setting of those words, which was indeed first sung by a treble. The alternative organ accompaniment is used here, not as warmly colourful as the orchestral version, but very beautiful nevertheless. The 1974 recording is vividly atmospheric. To this have been added the *Four Motets*, on plainsong themes, which are also finely sung. The organ piece, another sensitive example of Duruflé's withdrawn genius, makes a further bonus, especially when one realizes that this generous pair of mid-price CDs includes also the *Mass* and *Salve Regina* of Poulenc.

The later St John's performance under Christopher Robinson also uses the highly effective organ-accompanied score. With a superb contribution from Ian Farrington, this works admirably, especially in the *Libera me*, but it has to be admitted that an orchestra makes a spectacular contribution to the *Gloria* (and elsewhere) and again later adds much colour to the lovely *Messe cum Jubilo*.

Plasson's performance was recorded in the spaciously resonant acoustic of Toulouse's Notre Dame La Daurade and, as is immediately obvious in the opening *Kyrie*, the chorus is backwardly placed, floating in a misty atmosphere; although at climaxes the vocal sound expands thrillingly, at other times Plasson's comparatively relaxed pacing mean that the music-making has less tension. The warmer voice of Thomas Hampson has a special appeal; on the other hand, while Anne Sophie von Otter sings beautifully and eloquently, her vibrato brings a hint of the opera-house at the climax of the *Pie Jesu*.

The characterful contributions of Cecilia Bartoli and Bryn Terfel add to the point of the newest DG coupling with Fauré. Memorably, Terfel gives the *Dies irae* section of the *Libera me* an apt violence. Sadly, the chorus is so dim and distant, with the dynamic range of the recording uncomfortably extreme, that the disc cannot be recommended.

(i–ii) Requiem, Op. 9; (ii–iv) Mass Cum jubilo, Op. 11; (ii) 4 Motets on Gregorian Themes, Op. 10; (iv) 3 Dances for Orchestra, Op. 10; (Organ) (v) Prélude, adagio & choral varié sur Veni Creator, Op. 4; (vi) Prélude et fugue sur le nom d'Alain, Op. 7; Scherzo, Op. 2; (v) Suite, Op. 5: Prelude in E flat min.; Sicilienne.

⬤ (B) *** Erato Ultima 3984 24235-2 (2). (i) Bouvier, Depraz, Philippe Caillard Ch., LAP; (ii) Stéphane Caillat Ch.;

(iii) Soyer; (iv) French R. O; all cond. composer;
(v) composer or (vi) Marie-Madeleine Duruflé-Chevalier (organ).

This is a particularly valuable set as it gathers together two-thirds of Duruflé's entire output. It centres on the now familiar *Requiem*, given a spontaneously dedicated performance which blossoms into great ardour at emotional peaks. The less familiar but no less beautiful *Mass Cum jubilo* receives a comparably inspirational account, its gentler passages sustained with rapt concentration, with beautiful playing from the French Radio Orchestra. The soloists in both works rise to the occasion, and the choral singing combines passionate feeling with subtle colouring: the Chorale Stéphane Caillat are at their finest in the four brief *a cappella* motets which are no less memorable. The three orchestral *Dances* are impressionistic in feeling, and the French Radio Orchestra play with appealing delicacy in the central *Danse lente* and with ecstatic vigour in the closing *Tambourin*, which recalls the Dukas of *L'Apprenti sorcier*. The colourful organ works are shared between the composer and his daughter, using organs at Soissons Cathedral and L'Eglise Saint Etienne-du-Mont, Paris. The excellent recordings, spaciously atmospheric, date from between 1959 and 1963. Not to be missed.

DUTILLEUX, Henri (born 1916)

Cello Concerto (Tout un monde lointain).

*** EMI (ADD) CDC7 49304-2. Rostropovich, O de Paris, Baudo – LUTOSLAWSKI: *Cello Concerto*. ***

(i) *Cello Concerto (Tout un monde lointain)*; (ii) *Violin Concerto (L'Arbre des songes)*.

*** Decca 444 398-2. (i) Harrell; (ii) Amoyal; Fr. Nat. O, Dutoit.

(i) *Cello Concerto (Tout un monde lointain)*; *Métaboles*; *Mystères de l'instant*.

*** Chan. 9565.(i) Pergamenschikov; BBC PO, Y. P. Tortelier.

Dutilleux's *Cello Concerto* is a most imaginative and colourful score which exerts an immediate appeal and sustains it over many hearings. Rostropovich plays it with enormous virtuosity and feeling; the Orchestre de Paris under Serge Baudo gives splendid support, while the 1975 recording is immensely vivid, with Rostropovich looming larger than life but given great presence.

Boris Pergamenschikov rises to the challenge and, although Rostropovich's remains an almost mandatory recommendation, thanks to the composer's authority, the excellence of the orchestral playing under Yan Pascal Tortelier and the Chandos recording earn it a three-star grading. The *Métaboles* and the *Mystères de l'instant* are played expertly and persuasively.

Both Pierre Amoyal and Lynn Harrell are first class and withstand the exalted comparisons they confront. The Decca recording is finer than that of rivals, clean, well detailed and with great presence and refinement.

Violin Concerto (L'Arbre des songes).

(M) *** Sony (ADD) SMK 64508. Stern, O Nat. de France, Maazel – BERNSTEIN: *Serenade*. *(**)

(i) *Violin Concerto (L'Arbre des songes)*; *Timbres, espaces, mouvement*; (ii) *2 Sonnets de Jean Cassou*.

*** Chan. 9504. (i) Charlier; (ii) Hill, N. Davies; BBC PO, Y. P. Tortelier – ALAIN: *Prière*. ***

Dutilleux's *Violin Concerto*, written for Isaac Stern, is a beautiful work, and the underlying romantic fervour finds Stern playing with warm commitment, strongly accompanied by Maazel and the Orchestre National. First-rate recording.

In terms of artistry and musicianship Charlier yields nothing to his rivals, and Yan Pascal Tortelier gives us the *Timbres, espaces, mouvement* (*La Nuit étoilée*) from 1979 as a makeweight. The *Deux sonnets de Jean Cassou* come in Dutilleux's own orchestral transcription, in which Martyn Hill and Neal Davies are effective soloists.

Le Loup (ballet): Symphonic Fragments.

(M) *** EMI (ADD) CDM7 63945-2. Paris Conservatoire O, Prêtre – MILHAUD: *Création du monde*; POULENC: *Les Biches*. ***

Dutilleux's score for *Le Loup*, with its 'Beauty and the Beast' storyline bringing a tragic ending, is dominated by a haunting, bitter-sweet waltz theme of the kind that, once heard, refuses to budge from the memory. But the invention throughout has plenty of colour and variety, and Dutilleux's orchestral palette is used individually to great effect. Prêtre makes a persuasive case for the suite and this vivid recording is part of a highly attractive triptych of French ballet scores.

(i) *Symphonies Nos. 1–2 (Le Double)*; (ii) *Métaboles*; (iii) *Mystère de l'instant* (for 24 strings, cymbalum & percussion); (ii) *Timbres, espace, mouvement (La Nuit étoilée)*; (iv) *Ainsi la nuit* (string quartet); (v) *Les Citations* (diptych for oboe, harpsichord, double-bass & percussion); (vi) *3 Strophes sur le nom de Sacher* (for unaccompanied cello); (vii–viii) *Figures de résonances* (for 2 pianos); (vii) *Piano Sonata; 3 Préludes Nos. 1–3*; (ix; viii) *2 Sonnets de Jean Cassou*.

(M) *** Erato Dig./ADD 0630 14068-2 (3). (i) O de Paris, Barenboim; (ii) O Nat. de France, Rostropovich; (iii) Zurich Coll. Mus., Sacher; (iv) Sine Nomine Qt; (v) Bourgue, Dreyfus, Cazauran, Balet; (vi) Geringas; (vii) Joy; (viii) composer; (ix) Cachemaille.

These three Erato CDs afford an excellent survey of Dutilleux's orchestral, chamber and instrumental music. The symphonies are well played and the recording of both is eminently serviceable. *Métaboles* is otherwise the best-known orchestral work here, alongside *Timbres, espace, mouvement*, and it is good to have both under the baton of Rostropovich. *Mystère de l'instant* is a set of ten miniatures, splendid played by the Collegium Musicum under Paul Sacher and digitally recorded. The chamber and instrumental music is equally successful. The recordings are very fine and the documentation is excellent, illustrated with photographs of the composer and major participants.

Symphonies Nos. 1–2.

⬤ *** Chan. 9194. BBC PO, Y. P. Tortelier.

Marvellously resourceful and inventive scores, which are given vivid and persuasive performances by Yan Pascal Tortelier and the BBC Philharmonic Orchestra. The engineers give us a splendidly detailed and refined portrayal of these complex textures – the sound is really state-of-the-art. This issue supersedes Serge Baudo's version with the Orchestre National de Lyon of the *First Symphony*, coupled with *Timbres, espace, mouvement*.

Symphony No. 1; Timbres, espace, mouvement.

(M) *** HM HMT 7905159. O. Nat. de Lyon, Baudo.

In Dutilleux's *First Symphony* there is a sense of forward movement: you feel that the music is taking you somewhere. *Timbres, espace, mouvement* is a more recent work, dating from 1978. Serge Baudo is an authoritative interpreter of this composer, and the Lyon orchestra also serve him well. The engineering is superb and the balance is thoroughly realistic.

Symphony No. 2; Métaboles; Timbres, espace, mouvement.

(N) **(*) Finlandia 3984 25324-2. Toronto SO, Saraste.

Jukka-Pekka Saraste and the Toronto Symphony Orchestra offer exactly the same repertoire as Semyon Bychkov and the Orchestre de Paris on Philips, and those who were fortunate to invest in that need read no further. Not that these performances are in any way inadequate; far from it, they are eminently serviceable and having been made in the presence of Dutilleux himself, must, we assume, carry his imprimatur. But the string sonority is not as rich and the recording does not have quite the transparency or body of the Philips, which is currently withdrawn.

Ainsi la nuit (String Quartet).

*** Sony SK 52554. Juilliard Qt – DEBUSSY; RAVEL: *Quartets*. ***

(N) (B) *** EMI Début CDZ5 74020-2. Belcea Qt – DEBUSSY, RAVEL: *String Quartets*. ***

This impressive account from the Juilliard Quartet is the finest yet, offering superb playing and recording. The music conjures up the moods and impressions surrounding the idea of 'night' – not night itself so much as its aura.

The Belcea accounts of the Debussy and Ravel quartets are pretty impeccable, and their Dutilleux is hardly less sensitive. One's first impression of *Ainsi la nuit* is of fragmentation and delicate wisps of texture, but gradually its power and logic emerge. The Belcea players are extraordinarily sensitive to its dynamic range and produce a performance of great finesse. At a budget price and with good sound, this enjoys a strong competitive advantage.

(i) Ainsi la nuit; (ii) Les Citations (diptych for oboe, harpishord, double-bass & percussion); (iii) 3 Strophes sur le nom de Sacher (for unaccompanied cello); (iv; v) Figures de résonances (for 2 pianos); (iv) Piano Sonata; 3 Préludes; (v; vi) 2 Sonnets de Jean Cassou.

(N) (B) **(*) Erato Ultima (ADD) 8573 88047-2 (2). (i) Sine Nomine Qt; (ii) Bourgue, Dreyfus, Cazauran, Balet; (iii) Geringas; (iv) Joy; (v) Composer; (vi) Cachemaille.

These chamber and instrumental pieces are drawn from the boxed set above, originally issued to celebrate the composer's eightieth birthday. They include the *Piano Sonata* of 1947 in the hands of the pianist most closely associated with it over the years, Geneviève Joy – and played with great zest and panache too! Joy is no less effective in the *Préludes*.

Dutilleux is a composer of keen imaginative awareness and consistent inventive quality, who always holds the listener. *Les Citations* is a case in point. *Ainsi la nuit* is very well played here, and the composer himself participates in the *Figures de résonances* for two pianos, and accompanies the excellent Gilles Cachemaille in the only vocal item, the remarkable *Deux sonnets de Jean Cassou*, composed during the occupation of France, the one violent, the other, in the words of the composer, 'a lyrical outpouring of infinite tenderness'. Dutilleux is the author of the brief notes for this reissue. The recording is excellent, but no texts and translations are provided for the *Sonnets*, and as the present pair of CDs has a total playing time of only 88 minutes, the boxed set above, which is handsomely documented and illustrated, is a far better investment, as long as it remains available.

Piano Sonata.

**(*) Olympia OCD 354; Archduke MARC 2. Amato – BALAKIREV: *Sonata*. **(*)

Donna Amato gives a totally committed and persuasive account of this brilliant sonata, and the recording is very truthful.

DVOŘÁK, Antonín (1841–1904)

(i) *American Suite, Op. 98b;* (ii) *Czech Suite, Op. 39; Nocturne for Strings in B, Op. 40; Polka for Prague Students in B flat, Op. 53a; Polonaise in E flat; Prague Waltzes;* (i) *Slavonic Dances Nos. 1–16, Op. 46/1–8, Op. 72/1–8;* (ii) *Slavonic Rhapsody No. 3, Op. 45.*

(B) *** Double Decca Dig./ADD 460 293-2 (2). (i) RPO; (ii) Detroit SO; Dorati.

(i) *American Suite in A, Op. 98b;* (ii) *Serenade for Strings in E, Op. 22; Serenade for Wind in D min., Op. 44.*

(B) *** Decca 448 981-2. (i) RPO, Dorati; (ii) LPO, Hogwood.

Dvořák's *American Suite* has clear influences from the New World. It is slight but charming music. Dorati has its measure and the RPO are very responsive. The Kingsway Hall recording balance suits the scoring rather well, but the *Slavonic Dances*, recorded at the same time (1983), are not so sweet here in the upper range of the strings, although otherwise the sound is full and pleasing. Dorati's performances have characteristic brio, the RPO response is warmly lyrical when necessary and the woodwind playing gives much pleasure. The *Czech Suite* can sometimes outstay its welcome, but certainly not here. The other items too have the brightness and freshness that mark out the *Slavonic Dances*, especially the *Polka* and *Polonaise* with their attractive rhythmic spring. The most charming piece of all is the set of *Waltzes*, written for balls in Prague – Viennese music with a Czech accent – while the lovely *Nocturne* with its subtle drone bass makes a winning interlude. The *Slavonic Rhapsody*, with its opening suggesting a troubadour and his harp, makes a vivacious end to what the documentation rightly describes as 'two-and-a-half hours of Dvořák's most tuneful orchestral music'.

The two *Serenades* also receive fresh, bright, spring-like accounts from Hogwood and the LPO in clean, slightly recessed sound. Textually, this version of the *String Serenade* is unique on record in that it uses the original score, newly published, in which two sections (one of 34 bars in the Scherzo and the other of 79 bars in the finale), missing in the normal printed edition, are now included.

Cello Concerto in B min., Op. 104.

☀ (M) *** DG (ADD) 447 413-2. Rostropovich, BPO, Karajan – TCHAIKOVSKY: *Rococo Variations*. *** ☀

(N) *** Teldec 8573-85340-2. Du Pré, Swedish RSO, Celibidache – SAINT-SAENS: *Cello Concerto No. 1*. ***

*** Sony SK 67173. Ma, NYPO, Masur – HERBERT: *Cello Concerto No. 2*. ***

*** Chan. 8662. Wallfisch, LSO, Mackerras – DOHNANYI: *Konzertstück*. ***

(BB) *** CfP (ADD) 574 8792. Cohen, LPO, Macal – ELGAR: *Cello Concerto*. ***

(M) (***) EMI mono CDH7 63498-2. Casals, Czech PO, Szell – ELGAR: *Concerto* (**(*)); BRUCH: *Kol Nidrei*. (***)

(*) EMI (ADD) CDC5 55527-2. Du Pré, Chicago SO, Barenboim – ELGAR: *Concerto*. *

(N) **(*) Virgin VM5 61838–2. Mørk, Oslo PO, Jansons – TCHAIKOVSKY: *Variations on a Rococo Theme*. **(*)

**(*) Finlandia 4509 98886-2. Noras, Finnish RSO, Oramo (with SCHUMANN: *Cello Concerto **).

(i) *Cello Concerto. Scherzo capriccioso* (with rehearsal).

(BB) (**) Naxos mono 8.110819. (i) Kurtz; NBC SO, Toscanini.

The intensity of lyrical feeling and the spontaneity of the partnership between Karajan and Rostropovich ensures the position of their DG disc at the top of the list of recommendations for this peer among nineteenth-century cello concertos. The orchestral playing is glorious. Moreover, the analogue recording, made in the Jesus-Christus-Kirche in September 1969, is as near perfect as any made in that vintage analogue era, and the CD transfer has freshened the original.

It comes as a welcome surprise to have two radio recordings of Jacqueline du Pré to supplement her much-loved studio versions of these same works. The Dvořák, recorded in Sweden in 1967, is even more valuable than the Saint-Saëns, while the Swedish Radio recording brings excellent sound, even better than on her EMI studio recording made in Chicago two years later. Her reading here is even more warmly spontaneous than the later one. Evidently, du Pré did not just tolerate the typical exaggerations of a Celibidache reading, but responded positively to them.

Yo-Yo Ma's partnership with Masur brings an extra weight of expression and a firmer control, making for a performance that is both more commanding and more spontaneous-sounding than his earlier version with Maazel (see below). Ma's expressiveness is simpler and nobler in such great lyrical passages as the second-subject melody, and the result is one of the finest versions available, ideal if one wants for coupling the Victor Herbert concerto, which sparked off Dvořák's inspiration.

Rafael Wallfisch's is also an outstanding version, strong and warmly sympathetic, masterfully played. The excitement as well as the warmth of the piece comes over as in a live performance, and Wallfisch's tone remains rich and firm in even the most taxing passages. The orchestral playing, the quality of sound and the delightful, generous and unusual coupling all make it a recommendation which must be given the strongest advocacy.

Robert Cohen is strong and forthright, technically very secure, with poetry never impaired by his preference for keeping steady speeds. The result is most satisfying, helped by a comparably incisive and understanding accompaniment from the Czech conductor, Zdenek Macal. With first-class recording, orchestrally full-bodied and with a truthful balance, this is now reissued coupled with the Elgar concerto.

Casals plays with astonishing fire and the performance seems to spring to life in a way that eludes many modern artists; the rather dry acoustic of the Deutsches Haus, Prague, and the limitations of the 1937 recording are of little consequence. This disc is one of the classics of the gramophone.

Jacqueline du Pré's version is newly transferred for a so-called 'dream coupling' with her unique Elgar performance. The original harshness of the Chicago Dvořák recording has been tamed and, though the exaggeratedly forward balance of the cello is still very noticeable, the sound has filled out nicely and is clearly detailed; the inspirational result is very rewarding.

A fine lyrical performance from an impressive young Norwegian soloist. Truls Mørk has not the largest instrumental personality, but Jansons provides a refined orchestral introduction to set the scene for the arrival of his young soloist, who phrases both with ardour and with gently hushed tenderness when playing on a half-tone. The elegiac episode recalling earlier ideas just before the close of the finale is touchingly done. An enjoyable performance, given vivid, modern sound, but one which pales beside the glorious romanticism of the Rostropovich–Karajan partnership.

The excellent Finnish cellist, Arto Noras – well remembered for making the first recording of the Bliss *Cello Concerto* – gives a sensitive reading of the Dvořák, not helped by the backward balance of the soloist. Most impressive are the tender moments, not least the epilogue, raptly done.

Edmund Kurtz is a strong enough soloist to persuade Toscanini to relax more than he often did, so that the big melodies are allowed a degree of expansion. So it is that though the slow movement opens in a matter-of-fact way, Kurtz quickly warms the atmosphere, bringing the conductor with him, and the meditation of the epilogue finds them both similarly relaxed. The *Scherzo capriccioso* also finds Toscanini at his warmest, relishing the lilting rhythms, even finding charm. Sadly, the rehearsal sequence, with Toscanini muttering in the distance, brings little or no illumination.

(i) *Cello Concerto;* (ii) *Rondo in G min., Op. 94;* (iii) *Silent Woods, Op. 68/5.*

(M) *** Sony SMK 66788. Ma, BPO, Maazel.

**(*) Channel CCS 8695. Wispelwey; (i) Netherlands PO, Renes; (ii–iii) Giacometti (piano or harmonium) (with ARENSKY: *Chant triste;* DAVIDOV: *Am Springbrunnen, Op. 20/2;* TCHAIKOVSKY: *Andante cantabile, from Op. 11* **(*)).

Ma's rapt concentration and refined control of colour bring an elegiac dimension to this reading. Maazel, having provided a spaciously powerful orchestral introduction (with superb BPO playing), accompanies with understanding and great sensitivity, fining down the orchestral textures so that he never masks his often gentle soloist, yet providing exuberant contrasts in orchestral fortissimos. The twilight evocation of *Silent Woods* is equally well caught. However, we are inclined to prefer Ma's later recording, with Masur, in many ways more commanding, more spontaneous-sounding.

The Dutch cellist, Pieter Wispelwey, equally at home in period or modern style, here gives a more intimate reading than most on disc, with rather more *portamento* than usual, bringing out autumnal tone-colours, as he does in the shorter pieces which come as fill-up. The performance may be less bitingly dramatic than most, but the concentration and expressive warmth make it extremely compelling. Three of the shorter pieces – in all of which Wispelwey uses gut strings – have harmonium accompaniment. That is most effective in the Tchaikovsky and the Arensky (which sounds as though it is about to turn into Tchaikovsky's song, *None but the lonely heart*), but then sounds muddled in Dvořák's *Silent Woods*. Happily the *Rondo* comes with piano accompaniment, as does the Davidov. Excellent sound.

(i) *Cello Concerto;* (ii) *Symphony No. 8 in G, Op. 88.*

(B) *** DG (ADD) 439 484-2. (i) Fournier; (i–ii) BPO; (i) Szell; (ii) Kubelik.

Pierre Fournier's reading of the *Cello Concerto* has a sweep of conception and a richness of tone and phrasing that carry the melodic lines along with exactly the mixture of nobility and tension the work demands. DG's recording, dating from 1962, is forward and vivid, with a broad, warm tone for the soloist. Kubelik's *Eighth* is appealingly direct and the polished, responsive playing of the Berlin Philharmonic adds to the joy and refinement of the performance, making for a highly recommendable bargain coupling.

(i) *Cello Concerto;* (ii) *Symphony No. 9 (From the New World).*

(M) *** Ph. (ADD) 442 401-2. (i) H. Schiff; Concg. O; (i) C. Davis; (ii) Dorati.

(BB) (***) Naxos 8.110901. (i) Feuermann; Berlin State Op. O, cond. (i) Taube, (ii) E. Kleiber.

Schiff's earlier reading of the *Concerto* (from the beginning of the 1980s) brings an unexaggerated vein of poetry akin to the approach of Yo-Yo Ma's first recording: its range of emotion is on a relatively small scale, though satisfying in its intimacy. This performance sounds extremely well in its CD transfer. Dorati's *New World* is characteristically vibrant

and extrovert; indeed, the level of tension is high in the outer movements, and the finale ends with a thrilling surge of adrenalin.

Emanuel Feuermann's pioneering account of the *Cello Concerto* was made in 1928–9. Feuermann, a passionate soloist, at times seems intent on showing just how fast he can play, with phenomenally clean articulation but with the occasional flaw of intonation. Well transferred by Mark Obert-Thorn from pre-EMI Parlophone pressings, the sound is limited but clear. Erich Kleiber's 1929 recording of the *New World Symphony* equally brings an electrifying performance, fast and furious in allegros and tenderly expressive in the slow movement. The surface noise is sometimes obtrusive but hardly detracts from the impact of an at times inspirational reading.

Piano Concerto in G min., Op. 33.

(M) *** EMI (ADD) CDM5 66895-2 [566947]. Richter, Bav. State O, C. Kleiber – SCHUBERT: *Wanderer Fantasia.* ***

(i) *Piano Concerto, Op. 33; The Water Goblin (symphonic poem), Op. 107.*

(BB) *** Naxos 8.550896. (i) Jandó; Polish Nat. RSO, Wit.

Richter plays the solo part in its original form (and not the more pianistically 'effective' revision by Wilém Kurz which is published in the Complete Edition), and his judgement is triumphantly vindicated. This is the most persuasive and masterly account of the work ever committed to disc; its ideas emerge with an engaging freshness and warmth, while the greater simplicity of Dvořák's own keyboard writing proves in Richter's hands to be more telling and profound. Carlos Kleiber secures excellent results from the Bavarian orchestra, and the 1977 recording has clarity and good definition to recommend it.

An infectiously fresh and warmly lyrical account from Jandó and the highly supportive Polish National Radio Orchestra under Antoni Wit. Jandó conveys his own pleasure, and Wit's accompaniment glows with colour; he then offers a splendidly vibrant and colourful portrayal of *The Water Goblin*, one of the composer's most vividly melodramatic symphonic poems. The recording is spacious and realistically balanced. The violins are a shade overbright but otherwise the sound is excellent. Very enjoyable and well worth its modest cost.

Violin Concerto in A min., Op. 53.

(N) *** Teldec 4509 96300-2 . Vengerov, MYPO, Masur – ELGAR: *Violin Sonata.* ***

(B) *** CfP CD-CFP 4566. Little, RLPO, Handley – BRUCH: *Concerto No. 1.* ***

*** EMI CDC7 54872-2. Zimmermann, LPO, Welser-Möst – GLAZUNOV: *Concerto.* ***

(N) (M) *** Virgin VM5 61910-2. Tetzlaff, Czech PO, Pešek – LALO: *Symphonie espagnole.* ***

(M) *** DG 449 091-2. Mintz, BPO, Levine – BRUCH: *Concerto No. 1.* ***

(M) *** Ph. (ADD) 420 895-2. Accardo, Concg. O, C. Davis – SIBELIUS: *Violin Concerto.* ***

(N) (M) *** DG mono 463 651-2. Martzy, Berlin R SO, Fricsay

— BRUCH: *Violin Concerto No. 1;* GLAZUNOV: *Violin Concerto **.*

(BB) *** Royal Long Players DCL 705742 (2). Krebbers, Amsterdam PO, Kersjes — BRAHMS; SIBELIUS; TCHAIKOVSKY: *Violin Concertos.* ***

(M) (***) Dutton Lab. mono CDK 1204. Haendel, Nat. SO, Rankl — SAINT-SAENS: *Introduction & Rondo capriccioso;* TCHAIKOVSKY: *Violin Concerto.* (***) ✿

Violin Concerto; Masurek.

(N)*** Ph. 464 531-2. Suwanai, Budapest Fest. O, Ivan Fischer — SARASATE: *Carmen Fantasy; Zigeunerweisen.* ***

Violin Concerto; Romance in F min., Op. 11.

(B) *** [EMI Red Line CDR5 69806]. Chung, Phd. O, Muti — BARTOK: *Rhapsodies.* ***

**(*) EMI (ADD) CDC7 47168-2. Perlman, LPO, Barenboim.

(BB) *** Naxos 8.550758. Kaler, Polish Nat. RSO (Katowice), Kolchinsky — GLAZUNOV: *Concerto.* ***

(M) *** Sup. (ADD) SU 1928-2 011. Suk, Czech PO, Ančerl — SUK: *Fantasy.* ***

** Decca 460 316-2. Frank, Czech PO, Mackerras — SUK: *Fantasy in G min.* ***

Maxim Vengerov pairs the Dvořák concerto with the Elgar *Sonata.* There seems to be no particular reason for the coupling, although Elgar once played under Dvořák's baton in the *D major Symphony* and was a great admirer. Vengerov performs not only with the effortless brilliance and dazzling technical command that one expects but with poetic feeling, freshness and spontaneity. Here virtuosity is at the service of artistry. He receives splendid support from Kurt Masur and the New York Philharmonic (they are recorded at a concert performance) and the balance between the soloist and orchestra is judged expertly. Unfortunately the Elgar is less satisfying.

Tasmin Little brings to this concerto an open freshness and sweetness, very apt for this composer, that are extremely winning. The firm richness of her sound, totally secure on intonation up to the topmost register, goes with an unflustered ease of manner, and the recording brings little or no spotlighting of the soloist; she establishes her place firmly with full-ranging, well-balanced sound that co-ordinates the soloist along with the orchestra.

In 1990 Akiko Suwanai was the youngest-ever winner of the Tchaikovsky Competition, and though she has made relatively few recordings since then, her virtuoso flair leaps out from every note both in the Dvořák and in the Sarasate pieces which come as brilliant prelude. In the concerto Suwanai is daring, urgent and volatile, adopting the widest range of dynamic and tone down to whispered *pianissimos* that convey a mood of deep meditation, as in the opening of the slow movement. The finale, taken faster than usual, is above all exciting, if with rhythms rather less sprung than in more relaxed readings. Though none of these performers is strictly Slavonic, the Slavonic flavours have rarely been brought out so vividly in this boldly rhapsodic concerto. The colourful *Masurek* (or mazurka) makes an apt link between the Sarasate showpieces and the concerto. Full, brilliant sound, with the violin marginally spot-lit.

Frank Peter Zimmermann's account of the Dvořák con-certo is full of spirit. His rhythms are lightly sprung and he conveys great delight in this genial yet underrated score. This performance too is highly recommendable. Certainly the LPO under Franz Welser-Möst are supportive, and the EMI recording is first class.

There is dazzling playing from Shlomo Mintz, whose virtuosity is effortless and his intonation astonishingly true. There is good rapport between soloist and conductor, and the performance has the sense of joy and relaxation that this radiant score needs. The digital sound is warm and natural in its upper range.

Adding to the list of excellent recordings of the Dvořák *Violin Concerto,* Tetzlaff's version brings not only a unique and generous coupling in the Lalo *Symphonie espagnole* but an obvious advantage in having the composer's compatriots accompanying, with crisp ensemble and rhythms deliciously sprung. Tetzlaff's performance, distinguished by quicksilver lightness in the passage-work, is both full of fantasy and marked by keen concentration and a sense of spontaneity. With the violin balanced naturally, not spot-lit, the slow movement has a hushed intensity at the opening, which gives extra poignancy to Tetzlaff's tender, totally unsentimental phrasing. In romantic freedom of expression Tetzlaff comes somewhere between Chung on the one hand and the re-strained Zimmermann on the other. Characteristically, Pešek makes orchestral textures clear, bringing out extra detail even in the heaviest tuttis, despite reverberant recording. Very recommendable.

In his Philips recording, Accardo is beautifully natural and unforced, with eloquent playing from both soloist and orchestra. The engineering is altogether excellent, and in a competitive field this must also rank high.

Kyung Wha Chung gives a heartfelt reading of a work that can sound wayward. The partnership with Muti and the Philadelphia Orchestra is a happy one, with the sound warmer and more open than it has usually been in the orchestra's recording venue. She finds similar concentration in the *Romance.* This CD is available only in the USA.

Perlman and Barenboim still sound pretty marvellous and show all the warmth and virtuosity one could desire. This CD also has the eloquent and touching *F minor Romance.* Perlman is absolutely superb in both pieces: the digital remastering undoubtedly clarifies and cleans the texture, though there is a less glowing aura about the sound above the stave. However, this EMI record remains at premium price and offers no other music.

Martzy's full-blooded performance dates from the late 1950s but remains one of the finest in the catalogue, fully worthy of place among DG's 'Originals'. Martzy possesses a virtuoso technique dominated by the mind of a fine mu-sician, so that the listener feels an agreeable sense of security and pleasure even in the most fiery passages. The several luscious and lyrical tunes emerge with the bloom of youthful innocence upon them, and their kinship with folk-song adds constantly to their all-pervading charm. Fricsay's accom-paniment is masterly, and if he is not ideally served by the recording acoustic, his insistence on clarity of texture compensates for this small disadvantage.

Krebbers offers a characteristically fresh and incisive reading, bringing out the Czech overtones in the first movement and giving a simple and reposeful account of the slow movement and an infectiously lilting one of the finale. He receives good support from the Amsterdam orchestra and the recording is extremely vivid, perhaps a bit too brightly lit but not lacking support in the lower range. The CD transfer is excellent, and this is part of an extraordinarily attractive super-bargain package which is consistently enjoyable throughout.

The performance of the Russian violinist, Ilya Kaler, has great romantic warmth and natural Slavonic feeling, and he is given excellent support by Kolchinsky and the Polish orchestra. The very resonant acoustics of the recording, made in the Concert Hall of Polish Radio, give the soloist a somewhat larger-than-life image against a widely resonant orchestral backcloth. But the effect is easy to enjoy when the playing is so ardent; moreover these artists offer (besides the Glazunov) the *Romance in F minor*, and that is also beautifully played.

Suk's earlier performance is back in the catalogue at mid-price, effectively remastered, recoupled with the Suk *Fantasy*. Its lyrical eloquence is endearing, the work is played in the simplest possible way, and Ančerl accompanies glowingly. Readers will note that, since its last appearance, the *Romance* has been restored, an equally delightful performance. This is one of Suk's very finest records.

The Dutton Lab. transfer offers the last recording Ida Haendel made for Decca in July 1947 before she moved to EMI. It is a memorable and endearing performance, with some really lovely playing in the *Adagio* and an engagingly spirited finale. The expert transfer brings sound which is full and atmospheric, the violin timbre sweet and natural, and one soon adjusts to the mono sound-picture, even if tuttis are not ideally clear.

Pamela Frank plays the *Concerto* with virtuoso assurance, but she is a degree more reticent than her finest rivals on disc. Where she scores is in the light, lilting account of the *Furiant* finale. The *Romance* is persuasively done at a flowing speed, but neither Dvořák work is helped by the backward balance of the orchestra. By far the most compelling performance on the disc is of the Suk fill-up.

Czech Suite, Op. 39; A Hero's Song, Op. 111; Festival March, Op. 54; Hussite Overture, Op. 67.

(BB) **(*) Naxos 8.553005. Polish Nat. RSO (Katowice), Wit.

Antoni Wit is most impressive in *A Hero's Song*. There is an outburst of patriotic hyperbole towards the close (with thundering trombones), but Wit generates excitement without letting things get out of hand. The performance of the *Czech Suite* is warm and relaxed, nicely rustic in feeling, but again is affected by the resonance.

Czech Suite in D, Op. 39; Notturno for Strings, Op. 40; Serenade for Strings, Op. 22.

*** Ara. Z 6697. Padova CO, Golub.

David Golub takes a more relaxed view than usual of the opening movement of the adorable *Czech Suite* (no harm in that), and he presents the quicker movements with an unforced charm that is captivating. The Padua Chamber Orchestra respond to his sensitive direction with evident

sympathy in the *Serenade*, though he tries to make a little too much of the contrasting idea of the first movement. Generally very well-judged tempi. Enjoyable and musical playing, enhanced by a natural recording.

Overtures: Carnival, Op. 92; Hussite, Op. 67; In Nature's Realm, Op. 91; My Home, Op. 62; Othello, Op. 93; Scherzo capriccioso, Op. 66. Symphonic Poems: The Golden Spinning Wheel, Op. 109; The Noonday Witch, Op. 108; The Water Goblin, Op. 107; Symphonic Variations, Op. 78.

(B) *** Double Decca (ADD) 452 946-2 (2). LSO, Kertész.

Overtures: Carnival; In Nature's Realm; Othello; Scherzo capriccioso.

**(*) Chan. 8453. Ulster O, Handley.

Overtures: Carnival; In Nature's Realm; Othello; Scherzo capriccioso; Symphonic Variations.

**(*) ASV CDDCA 794. RPO, Farrer.

Overture: My Home. Symphonic Poems: The Golden Spinning Wheel; The Hero's Song, Op. 111; The Noonday Witch; The Water Goblin; The Wood Dove, Op. 110.

(B) Chan. 2-for-1 241-3 (2). RSNO, Järvi.

Kertész's vintage Decca sound from the 1960s and 1970s stands up well, and Kertész was very much at home in this repertoire. He makes the very most of the brilliant *Carnival Overture* and also offers an outstanding version of the *Scherzo capriccioso*. *Carnival* forms a triptych with *Othello* and *In Nature's Realm*, linked by a recurring main theme. These pieces, like the melodramatic symphonic poems, are also handled very evocatively: all have the most vivid colouring. So has the *Hussite Overture*, where the drama is comparably red-blooded. *My Home*, a more spontaneously inspired work, is even more successful, while the Brahmsian derivations of the *Symphonic Variations* are all but submerged when the playing has such spirit and freshness.

Many will be attracted to Neeme Järvi's collection for the modern digital sound, warmly atmospheric in typical Chandos style, not always clean on detail but firmly focused. These recordings were all fill-ups for Järvi's integral set of the symphonies. The real rarity here is *The Hero's Song*, Dvořák's very last orchestral work. Järvi's strongly committed, red-blooded performance minimizes any weaknesses. *My Home* is given an exuberant performance, bringing out the lilt of the dance rhythms, and Järvi is a dramatic advocate of *The Water Goblin*. He also brings out the storytelling vividly in *The Noonday Witch*, while the most memorable of all the symphonic poems, *The Golden Spinning Wheel*, has plenty of drama and atmosphere, helped by the fine bloom of the recording. The only snag here is the relative short measure.

Handley's excellent performances put the three works in perspective. Superbly recorded, this now seems short measure at premium price.

John Farrer scores over Handley by including also the *Symphonic Variations*, here given a performance of great freshness. The three linked overtures have comparable warmth and delicacy of colouring. There is plenty of drama too, and the only slight disappointment is that *Carnival*, while vigorous enough and with a richly hued central section, could have been even more exuberant. The *Scherzo capriccioso* is brightly vivacious.

Symphonic poems: *The Golden Spinning Wheel, Op. 109; The Noonday Witch, Op. 108; The Wood Dove, Op. 110.*

(BB) *** Naxos 8.550598. Polish Nat. RSO (Katowice), Gunzenhauser.

The Polish orchestra seem thoroughly at home in Dvořák's sound-world and Gunzenhauser gives warm, vivid performances and is especially evocative in the masterly *Golden Spinning Wheel*. There is shapely string phrasing and a fine, sonorous contribution from the brass. The concert hall of Polish Radio in Katowice has expansive acoustics – just right for the composer's colourful effects.

Legends, Op. 59; Miniatures, Op. 75a; Notturno in B, Op. 40; Prague Waltzes.

(N) 🏵 *** Ph. 464 647-2. Budapest Festival O, Fischer.

The *Legends* come from 1881, the year of the *Sixth Symphony*, and are endearing, captivating, gloriously inventive pieces, the charm and character of which are conveyed wonderfully by Iván Fischer and the Budapest Festival Orchestra and recorded as sumptuously as their outstanding Bartók discs. All of these pieces, including the poignant *Notturno* and the delightful *Prague Waltzes*, are performed with great feeling and style and convey Fischer's affection for them. The *Legends* have been well served in the past by Raymond Leppard, Charles Mackerras, and such Czech conductors as Kubelik and Karel Sejna, and Fischer's version is every bit as idiomatic and better recorded, so that this recording now serves as a first recommendation.

Scherzo capriccioso, Op. 66; Slavonic Dances, Opp. 46/1, 3 & 7; 72/2 & 8.

(M) **(*) DG (ADD) 447 434-2. BPO, Karajan – BRAHMS: *8 Hungarian Dances.* ***

Virtuoso performances from Karajan which remain stylish because of the superbly polished ensemble. The *Scherzo capriccioso* is exhilarating, but the lilt of the lyrical secondary tune does seem a trifle calculated. However, coupled with eight of the Brahms *Hungarian Dances*, this reissue certainly shows the Karajan/BPO combination in dazzling form.

Serenade for Strings in E, Op. 22.

(M) *** EMI (ADD) CDM5 66760-2. RPO, Stokowski – VAUGHAN WILLIAMS: *Tallis Fantasia;* PURCELL: *Dido and Aeneas: Dido's Lament.* ***

(BB) *** Virgin Classics 2 x 1 VBD5 61763-2 (2). LCO, Warren-Green – ELGAR: *Introduction & Allegro*, etc.; SUK: *Serenade;* TCHAIKOVSKY: *Serenade;* VAUGHAN WILLIAMS: *Greensleeves*, etc. ***

(BB) **(*) Naxos 8.550419. Capella Istropolitana, Krček – SUK: *Serenade.* ***

(N) *(*) Ph. 462 594-2. Saito Kinen O, Ozawa – BARTOK: *Divertimento for Strings* **(*); WOLF: *Italian Serenade.* ***

Serenade for Strings; Serenade for Wind in D min., Op. 44.

*** ASV CDCOE 801. COE, Schneider.

*** Ph. (IMS) (ADD) 400 020-2. ASMF, Marriner.

Serenade for Strings; Serenade for Wind; Miniatures, Op. 74a.

(BB) *** Discover DICD 920135. Virtuosi di Praga, Vlček.

The Stokowskian magic is very apparent in his 1975 EMI recording of the *String Serenade*, not only in the ripeness of the string playing but also in the masterly control of tension. Thus the opening is slow and affectionate, but there is concentration in every bar and the lyrical flow is highly engaging. In the second movement Stokowski's delicacy at a quick tempo is exhilarating, and the lilting Scherzo is matched by the warmth of the *Larghetto*. The RPO strings are kept on their toes throughout, and the wide-ranging Abbey Road recording offers the most beautiful string-sound.

The young players of the Chamber Orchestra of Europe give winningly warm and fresh performances of Dvořák's *Serenades*, vividly caught in the ASV recording.

Christopher Warren-Green and the excellent London Chamber Orchestra bring their characteristically fresh, spontaneous approach to the Dvořák *Serenade*, and the amazingly generous couplings make this one of Virgin's most desirable 2 x 1 super-bargain collections.

Marriner's Philips performances are direct without loss of warmth, with speeds ideally chosen, refined yet spontaneous-sounding; in the *Wind Serenade* the Academy produce beautifully sprung rhythms, and the recording has a fine sense of immediacy.

The wind players of the Virtuosi di Praga give a bright, idiomatic performance of Opus 44, using characteristically reedy tones. The *String Serenade* is done with equal understanding, though the recording catches an edge on high violins. The rare *Miniatures* for string trio provides an attractive makeweight. An excellent bargain in full, bright sound.

Fine playing from the Capella Istropolitana on Naxos, and flexible direction from Jaroslav Krček. His pacing is not quite as sure as in the delightful Suk coupling, and the *Adagio* could flow with a stronger current, but this is still an enjoyable and well-recorded performance.

The magical opening of Dvořák's *String Serenade* has rarely seemed so stodgy or sluggish as with Ozawa, creating the most unpromising impression at the start of this variable disc. The other four movements of that delightful work bring a gradual improvement, until the *Allegro vivace* finale, biting and delicate, at last finds these talented players back in form, but the initial impact remains. Apart from the slow movement of the Bartók, the rest is brilliantly done, particularly the Wolf. Good sound, warm rather than brilliant.

Serenade in D min. for Wind, Op. 44.

(M) *** CRD 3410. Nash Ens. (with KROMMER: *Octet-partita* ***).

(N) (BB) *** Naxos 8.554173. Oslo PO Wind Soloists – ENESCU: *Dixtuor;* JANACEK: *Mládi.* ***

(**(*)) Testament mono SBT 1180. L. Bar. Ens., Haas – MOZART: *Serenades Nos. 11 & 12.* (**(*))

**(*) EMI CDC5 55512-2. Sabine Meyer Wind Ens. – MYSLIVICEK: *Octets Nos. 1–3.* **(*)

The Nash Ensemble can hold their own with the competition

in the *D minor Serenade*, and their special claim tends to be the coupling, a Krommer rarity that is well worth hearing. The CRD version of the Dvořák is very well recorded and the playing is very fine indeed, robust yet sensitive to colour, and admirably spirited.

The Oslo wind soloists on Naxos give us a genuine bargain. Here is a performance of real quality that can stand alongside the finest on offer. Crisp rhythms predominate, and a good sense of line and tonal finesse. These artists recorded this repertoire on the Victoria label in the early 1990s under a conductor. These are different and better accounts in every way. No need to hesitate.

Karl Haas's preference for fast speeds and metrical rhythms is well illustrated in this reading of Dvořák's *Wind Serenade*, in which the opening march has more of a military flavour than usual. As a generous supplement to Mozart's two great serenades for wind octet, this makes an ideal coupling of three of the greatest of all wind works, performed by an ensemble that included some of the finest British players of the post-war period, including Dennis Brain, Frederick Thurston and Terence Macdonagh. Vivid, immediate sound, well transferred.

The Sabine Meyer Ensemble have elegance but are perhaps a little laid back by comparison with some current rivals. Yet they give undoubted pleasure, and the EMI recording is excellent.

Slavonic Dances Nos. 1–16, Op. 46/1–8; Op. 72/1–8.

*** Decca (IMS) 430 171-2. Cleveland O, Dohnányi.

(M) *** DG (ADD) 457 712-2. Bav. RSO, Kubelik.

✿ (M) *** Sony SBK 48161. Cleveland O, Szell.

*** Telarc 80497. Atlanta SO, Levi.

(M) *(**) Mercury (IMS) (ADD) 434 384-2. Minneapolis (Minnesota) SO, Dorati.

**(*) DG 447 056-2. Russian Nat. O, Pletnev.

Dohnányi's rhythmic flexibility and the ebb and flow of his rubato are a constant delight. The recording is superb, very much in the demonstration bracket, with the warm acoustics of the Cleveland Hall ideal in providing rich textures and brilliance without edge. A delightful disc.

Kubelik's set, now issued as one of DG's 'Originals', offers polished, sparkling orchestral playing. The sound has greater refinement and a rather wider range of dynamic than the competing Sony disc and for that reason many will choose it in preference to Szell, for Kubelik has a very special feeling for Dvořák and the playing of the Bavarian orchestra brings a thrilling virtuosity and a special panache of its own.

In Szell's exuberant, elegant and marvellously played set of the *Slavonic Dances* the balance is close (which means pianissimos fail to register) but the charisma of the playing is unforgettable and, for all the racy exuberance, one senses a predominant feeling of affection and elegance. The warm acoustics of Severance Hall ensure the consistency of the orchestral sound. This is also available on one of Sony's new Super Audio CDs which require a special CD player (SS 7208).

The Atlanta Symphony Orchestra enter a hotly competitive field and emerge with flying colours. The playing has exhilaration, warmth and flexibility, helped by the pleasing ambience of Symphony Hall and Levi's easy-going rubato. The strings have plenty of bloom – indeed the sound is richly blended rather than sharply detailed. Perhaps the cymbals (as in the very first dance) could emerge with more transient bite, but better this than artificial brightness: the brilliance comes from the orchestra's response, with the conductor at his affectionate best in the second set (Opus 72).

Dorati's performances have splendid brio and Slavonic flair. They are also very well played, and the gentler, lyrical sections are often quite delightful. The snag is the curiously confined recording, full-bodied but somehow unable to expand properly.

Refinement and crispness of ensemble are the keynotes of Mikhail Pletnev's distinctive reading. The approach is at times almost Mozartian in its elegance, with little of the earthier, Slavonic qualities and with even the wildest furiants kept under control and the extrovert joy of the music rather underplayed. Yet consistently Pletnev and his Russian players make one marvel at the beauty of the instrumentation, and this is a disc to give a fresh view of well-loved music. However, the acoustic of the Concert Hall of Moscow Conservatory is not particularly flattering, and competition is strong.

Slavonic Dances Nos. 1, 3, 8–10.

(N) (M) **(*) Decca (ADD) 467 122-2. VPO, Reiner – BRAHMS: *Hungarian Dances.* STRAUSS: *Death and Transfiguration; Till Eulenspiegel.* **(*)

Reiner's way with Dvořák is indulgent but has plenty of sparkle, and the VPO are clearly enjoying themselves; any reservations about the conductor's idiosyncrasies are minor when the playing is so vivacious. Good 1960 recording and splendid Strauss couplings makes this disc worth considering.

(i) 3 Slavonic Rhapsodies, Op. 45; (ii) Rhapsody in A min., Op. 14.

(BB) *** Naxos 8.550610. Slovak PO, (i) Košler; (ii) Pešek.

Dvořák's three *Slavonic Rhapsodies* of 1878 are surprisingly rarely heard either on record or in the concert hall. Although they are spirited in the way of the *Slavonic Dances*, they are much more like symphonic poems without a programme and, while overflowing with characteristic ideas and colourful scoring, they are also loosely constructed and melodramatic. But it is the earlier *Rhapsody in A minor* that is the most ambitious work here. It is very nationalistic in feeling, and has plenty of attractive Slavonic themes, some quite lilting. Libor Pešek's performance is splendid, with a vigorous response from the orchestra, who even bring off the bombastic, patriotic coda. This is every bit as enjoyable as the Op. 45 *Rhapsodies*, although it is not as sophisticated as No. 3. This Naxos collection would be recommendable even if it cost far more.

Suite in A, Op. 98b.

(M) (***) Supraphon mono SU 1924-2 001. Czech PO, Sejna – MARTINU: *Concerto for Double String Orchestra,* etc. (***)

A lovely performance of the beautiful *A major Suite,*

recorded in mono in 1956; but the real attraction on this disc are the Martinů pieces – especially the *Third Symphony* – which are very special.

Symphonic Variations.

(N) *** Australian Decca Eloquence (ADD) 467 608-2. LSO, Kertész. BRAHMS – *Haydn Variations.* ***

Kertész's account of the underrated *Symphonic Variations* is outstanding, with the conductor bringing out all the Brahmsian overtones as well as the Czech composer's freshness of spirit. The 1970s recording remains vivid and full, and with two excellent couplings this is certainly a desirable CD.

SYMPHONIES

Symphonies Nos. 1–9.

(M) *** Chan. 9008/13. SNO, Järvi.

Symphonies Nos. 1–9; American Suite; Carnaval Overture; Czech Suite; Overtures: My Home; Othello; In Nature's Realm; Scherzo capriccioso; The Wild Dove.

(N) (BB) **(*) Virgin VB5 61853-2 (8). RLPO, or Czech PO, Pešek.

Symphonies Nos. 1–9; Overtures: Carnival; In Nature's Realm; My Home. Scherzo capriccioso.

✿ **(B)** *** Decca (ADD) 430 046-2 (6). LSO, Kertész.

Symphonies Nos. 1–9; Overture: Carnival. Scherzo capriccioso; The Wood Dove.

(B) **(*) DG 463 158-2 (6). BPO, Kubelik.

Neeme Järvi has the advantage of outstanding, modern, digital recording, full and naturally balanced. The set is offered at upper mid-price, six CDs for the price of four. Only the *Fourth Symphony* is split centrally between discs; all the others can be heard uninterrupted. But there are no fillers, as with Kertész on Decca.

For those not wanting to go to the expense of the digital Chandos/Järvi set, István Kertész's bargain box is an easy first choice among the remaining collections of Dvořák symphonies. The CD transfers are of Decca's best quality, full-bodied and vivid, with a fine ambient effect. It was Kertész who first revealed the full potential of the early symphonies, and his readings gave us fresh insights into these often inspired works. To fit the symphonies and orchestral works on to six CDs, some mid-work breaks have proved unavoidable; but the set remains a magnificent memorial to a conductor who died sadly young.

Pešek's recording of the *First Symphony* is new to the catalogue. He obviously identifies readily with its anticipations of the mature Dvořák, coaxing the lyrical secondary theme of the first movement, yet not missing the drama. The focal point of his reading is the warmly spacious account of the *Adagio*, with affectionate detail throughout, and the tension well sustained in spite of the comparatively leisurely tempo.

The *Scherzo/Allegretto* too has its full share of folksy charm and the intractable finale certainly has plenty of energy. The playing of the Liverpool orchestra is most responsive and it

is the recordings made in in that orchestra's city which tend to stand out in Pešek's cycle. Indeed the *Second Symphony* sparkles less consistently than it might, even if the Czech Philharmonic playing is always idiomatically persuasive.

The *Third* (once more recorded in Liverpool) is undoubtedly a highlight of the series. Here the rhythmic freshness of the writing is well brought out and Pešek gives a radiant account of the lovely second subject and is masterly in controlling the long development section. He shows similar concentration in sustaining a very slow speed for the central *Adagio* to make a fine contrast with the urgency of the finale.

For No. 4 Pešek returns to the Czech Orchestra and they are at their lilting best in the *Scherzo*, where the main theme is given an infectious lolloping gait, and again in the finale, which is as racy and vigorous as anyone could want. But Pešek's reading fails to develop sufficient thrust in the first movement, nor does he attempt to disguise the Wagnerian influences which sometimes weigh heavily on the slow movement.

No. 5 is characteristically fresh and direct, but markedly cooler than most other accounts. Here the Czech recording, rather distant but refined, adds to the coolness, although with native Czechs performing, there is plenty of power as well as authenticity.

No. 6 brings a slow and relaxed view of the first movement, with its clear echoes of Brahms's *Second*, also in D major. Unfortunately, with less body to the sound than the music needs – a question of the Czech recording, rather edgy and bright and not full enough – the result lacks dramatic tension. Moreover, in observance of an indication that the composer put on the autograph after an early performance, the exposition repeat in the first movement is omitted.

For Nos. 7 and 8 Pešek returned to Liverpool, and these performances are among the most stimulating of the whole cycle. The opening of the *D minor* (No. 7) may lack the ominous and mysterious atmosphere of some performances, but the slow movement is warm and relaxed, and the *Scherzo* becomes a happy, folk-like dance, despite the minor key, while Pešek's speed in the finale also allows him to give a lift to the stamping dance-rhythms. No. 8 receives a similarly refreshing performance, persuasive in a light and relaxed way, with the folk element again brought out, particularly in the middle movements, and finishing with a lilting *Scherzo*. Both performances benefit from the full, clear sound.

The *New World* (No. 9) is enjoyable too, very well played and impressively recorded. It is at its best in the *Scherzo*, which has striking character, and the nicely relaxed Trio. But elsewhere Pešek's mellowness produces a reading that could use more adrenalin and overall this account is just a little lacking in spontaneity and grip.

Among the extra items, which are all well and idiomatically presented, the Czech Orchestra are at their most seductive in the *Othello Overture*, while in Liverpool the *Scherzo capriccioso*, in which the central repeat is observed, is particularly sympathetic, and the *American Suite* is presented with a beguilingly affectionate touch. Although uneven, this set, with its advantage of (for the most part) excellent modern digital recording, remains a pretty formidable bargain.

Kubelik's set from the late 1960s and early 1970s has much

to recommend it, first and foremost being the glorious playing of the Berlin Philharmonic and the natural idiomatic warmth Kubelik brings to his music-making. He seems less convinced by the earlier symphonies, and in No. 3 there is an element of routine, something which does not happen with Kertész on Decca. In spite of some idiosyncratic touches, however, Kubelik achieves glowing performances of Nos. 6–9, and especially No. 7; in No. 8 he is also more compelling than his Decca competitor. The remastered DG sound is impressively wide-ranging and is especially fine in the last (and greatest) three symphonies. Many will also be glad to have his memorable account of *The Wood Dove*.

Symphony No. 1 in C min. (The Bells of Zionice), Op. 3; Overture Carnaval; The Wood Dove.

(N) (B) **(*) DG 469 550-2. Bav. RSO, Kubelik.

Symphony No. 1; A Hero's Song, Op. 111.

*** Chan. 8597. SNO, Järvi.

Symphony No. 1; Legends, Op. 59/1–5.

(BB) *** Naxos 8.550266. Slovak PO or Czecho-Slovak RSO, Gunzenhauser.

The first of Dvořák's nine symphonies is on the long-winded side. Yet whatever its structural weaknesses, it is full of colourful and memorable ideas, often characteristic of the mature composer. Järvi directs a warm, often impetuous performance, with rhythms invigoratingly sprung in the fast movements and with the slow movement more persuasive than in previous recordings. The recording is warmly atmospheric in typical Chandos style.

Though on a super-bargain label, the competing Bratislava version rivals Järvi's Chandos disc both as a performance and in sound. The ensemble of the Slovak Philharmonic is rather crisper, and the recording, full and atmospheric, has detail less obscured by reverberation. The first five of Dvořák's ten *Legends* make a generous coupling: colourful miniatures, colourfully played.

This is the first time Kubelik's recording of the *First Symphony* (taken from his boxed set) has been issued separately and we can understand why from the conductor's comments – here abbreviated – included with the disc: 'It is regrettable that the composer's own honourable decision to discard this work was not respected. Nevertheless I have consented to the recording of this work, partly because this symphony contains the germ of the many stylistic feaures of his later works. These are present in embryo. They give a hint of his eventual mastery, but at the same time this early symphonic essay shows us how far Antonín Dvořák had to travel along the road which was to lead to his mature achievements as a symphonist.'

That said, Kubelik gives a bright and direct reading of the work; freshly incisive in the first movement and in the *Adagio* both refined and intense. Indeed it is pressed forward so strongly that the time-span is more than three minutes shorter than with Pešek's more recent version, discussed above. The *Allegretto/Scherzo* has a folksy rhythmic feeling, and only the repetitive finale remains elusive. A dashing *Carnaval* and a finely played, atmospheric account of *The Wood Dove* completes an interesting reissue.

Symphonies Nos. 1–3.

(B) *** Double Decca 466 739-2 (2). LSO, Kertész .

Kertész 's vibrant accounts of the first three Dvořák symphonies sound as fresh today – in sound and in performance – as they did around 30 years ago. These early symphonies are by no means among his greatest works but it is fascinating to hear the development of the young composer. If there are some long-winded passages, there are equally some delightful ones, and by the *Third Symphony* the full exuberance of Dvořák's genius is clearly felt. This Double Decca is listed as Volume I: presumably the rest of the cycle will follow. However, the complete set is already available in a bargain box.

Symphony No. 2 in B flat, Op. 4; Legends, Op. 59/6–10.

(BB) *** Naxos 8.550267. Slovak PO or Czecho-Slovak RSO, Gunzenhauser.

Symphony No. 2; Slavonic Rhapsody No. 3 in A flat, Op. 45.

**(*) Chan. 8589. SNO, Järvi.

With speeds more expansive than those of Neeme Järvi, his Chandos rival, Gunzenhauser gives a taut, beautifully textured account, very well played and recorded, clearly preferable in every way, even making no allowance for price. The completion of the set of *Legends* makes a very generous coupling (73 minutes).

Järvi's performance, characteristically warm and urgent, is let down by the reverberant Chandos sound, here missing the necessary sharpness of focus, so that the tangy Czech flavour of the music loses some of its bite. The *Slavonic Rhapsody* is done with delicious point and humour, with the sound back to Chandos's normally high standard.

Symphony No. 3 in E flat, Op. 10; Carnival Overture, Op. 92; Symphonic Variations, Op. 78.

*** Chan. 8575. SNO, Järvi.

Järvi's is a highly persuasive reading, not ideally sharp of rhythm in the first movement but totally sympathetic. The recording is well up to the standards of the house, and the fill-ups are particularly generous.

Symphonies Nos. 3; 6 in D, Op. 60.

(BB) *** Naxos 8.550268. Slovak PO, Gunzenhauser.

These exhilarating performances of the *Third* and *Sixth Symphonies* are well up to the standard of earlier records in this splendid Naxos series. Gunzenhauser's pacing is admirably judged through both works, and rhythms are always lifted. Excellent, vivid recording in the warm acoustics of the Bratislava Concert Hall.

Symphonies Nos. 3; 7 in D min., Op. 70.

*** DG 449 207-2. VPO, Chung.

Myung-Whun Chung has the full measure of both the *E flat* and, especially, the *D minor Symphony*. The playing in both symphonies is impressive and they deserve – but do not receive – state-of-the-art recorded sound. There needs to be a better-ventilated, more spacious orchestral texture, such as Chandos provide for Bělohlávek (in No. 7). All the same, the stature of the performances is such as to warrant a full three-star recommendation.

Symphony No. 4 in D min., Op. 13; (i) Biblical Songs, Op. 99.

*** Chan. 8608. SNO, Järvi, (i) with Rayner Cook.

Järvi's affectionate reading of this early work brings out the Czech flavours in Dvořák's inspiration and makes light of the continuing Wagner influences, notably the echoes of *Tannhäuser* in the slow movement. This is a performance to win converts to an often underrated work. The recording is well up to the Chandos standard.

Symphonies Nos. 4; 8 in G, Op. 33.

(BB) **(*) Naxos 8.550269. Slovak PO, Gunzenhauser.

Gunzenhauser's *Fourth* is very convincing. In his hands the fine lyrical theme of the first movement certainly blossoms, and the relative lack of weight in the orchestral textures brings distinct benefit in the Scherzo. The slow movement, too, is lyrical without too much Wagnerian emphasis. The naturally sympathetic orchestral playing helps to make the *Eighth* a refreshing experience, even though the first two movements are rather relaxed and without the impetus of the finest versions. The digital sound is excellent, vivid and full, with a natural concert-hall ambience.

(i) Symphony No. 5 in F, Op. 76; (ii) Carnival Overture, Op. 92; (iii) The American Flag (cantata), Op. 102.

(B) **(*) Sony Dig./ADD SBK 60297. (i) Philh. O, A. Davis; (ii) NYPO, Mehta; (iii) Evans, McDaniel, St Hedwig's Cathedral Ch., Berlin RIAS Chamber Ch., Berlin RSO, Tilson Thomas.

Andrew Davis's account of the *Fifth Symphony*, freshly played but somewhat undercharacterized, is rather more successful than his *Sixth*, but there is nothing special about Mehta's *Carnival Overture*. What makes this bargain CD well worth considering is *The American Flag*. It was was commissioned for the composer's visit to the New World in 1892, and Dvořák's setting has real flair. The opening sections addressing the American Eagle are spirited enough, but when the tenor (as the Foot Soldier) presents the *First Address to the Flag*, Dvořák produces an infectiously jigging tune, which is then taken up enthusiastically by the chorus; the work continues in this vein until its effective closing apotheosis. The singing of both soloists is first rate and the combined choruses are magnificent. The analogue recording could not be bettered, and this surely needs to be re-coupled more aptly with Tilson Thomas's account of the *American Suite* (see below).

Symphony No. 5; Othello Overture, Op. 93; Scherzo capriccioso, Op. 66.

✪ *** EMI CDC7 49995-2. Oslo PO, Jansons.

Symphony No. 5; The Water Goblin, Op. 107.

*** Chan. 8552. SNO, Järvi.

Jansons directs a radiant account of this delectable symphony, and the EMI engineers put a fine bloom on the Oslo sound. With its splendid encores, equally exuberant in

performance, this was one of the finest Dvořák records in the catalogue, but it has just been deleted!

Järvi is also most effective in moulding the structure, subtly varying tempo between sections to smooth over the often abrupt links. His persuasiveness in the slow movement, relaxed but never sentimental, brings radiant playing from the SNO, and Czech dance-rhythms are sprung most infectiously, leading to an exhilarating close to the whole work, simulating the excitement of a live performance.

Symphonies Nos. 5; 7 in D min., Op. 70.

(BB) *** Naxos 8.550270. Slovak PO, Gunzenhauser.

Gunzenhauser's coupling is recommendable even without the price advantage. The beguiling opening of the *Fifth*, with its engaging Slovak wind solos, has plenty of atmosphere, and the reading generates a natural lyrical impulse. The *Seventh*, spontaneous throughout, brings an eloquent *Poco adagio*, a lilting Scherzo and a finale that combines an expansive secondary theme with plenty of excitement and impetus.

Symphony No. 6 in D, Op. 60; The Wood Dove, Op. 110.

*** Chan. 9170. Czech PO, Bělohlávek.

Bělohlávek conducts a glowing performance of No. 6, rich in Brahmsian and Czech pastoral overtones, helped by satisfyingly full and immediate Chandos sound. This easily takes precedence over the Järvi version (CHAN 8350). His reading of the late symphonic poem is comparably warm and idiomatic in a relaxed way.

Symphonies Nos. 6; 8.

✪ (N) *** DG 469 046-2. VPO, Chung.

The first movement of No. 6 surpasses in breadth and power (and in the natural way in which it unfolds) almost anything between the *C major (Great)* of Schubert and the *Second* of Brahms, the shadows of both of which are clearly visible. It is luminous and innocent, as is the *Eighth*, another glowing and life-enhancing score generously coupled here. Both symphonies are served supremely well by Chung and the Vienna Orchestra and the DG engineers. It is certainly the best we have had since the famous Decca set from Kertesz (with the Bruegel covers!).

Symphony No. 7 in D min., Op. 70; Nocturne for Strings, Op. 40; The Water Goblin, Op. 107.

*** Chan. 9391. Czech PO, Bělohlávek.

Bělohlávek knows better than his direct rivals how to draw out idiomatic warmth from the Czech Philharmonic, and he is helped by satisfyingly full and glowing Chandos sound. Fresh, well paced and intelligently shaped, this is a thoroughly recommendable reading, paired with an excellent account of *The Water Goblin* and the eloquent, poignant *Nocturne for Strings*. In this spacious reading of the *Nocturne* the Czech strings produce ravishing sounds, and *The Water Goblin* is similarly relaxed and warm rather than sharply dramatic.

Symphonies Nos. 7; 8 in G, Op. 88.

*** EMI CDC7 54663-2. Oslo PO, Jansons.

(M) *** Mercury (IMS) (ADD) 434 312-2. LSO, Dorati.

(M) *** DG (ADD) 457 902-2. BPO, Kubelik.

(B) **(*) Sony (ADD) SBK 67174. Philh. O, A. Davis.

Mariss Jansons's readings of both works are outstandingly fine, with the dramatic tensions of the *D minor* work bitingly conveyed, yet with detail treated affectionately, and with rhythms sprung exhilaratingly. No. 8 is given a performance of high contrasts too, with the slow movement warmly expansive and the whole crowned by a winningly spontaneous-sounding account of the finale, rarely matched in its exuberance. Excellent sound. This makes a new first choice for this coupling, although at mid-price there are strongly recommendable alternatives, notably Dorati on Mercury.

Dorati's coupling brings an extraordinary successful account of No. 7 with the spontaneous feel of a live performance enhanced by the vividly realistic concert-hall balance of the (1963) Mercury recording – one of their very finest. The interpretation is free, the *Poco adagio* is impulsive and the Scherzo lifts off with a sparkle. The finale has enormous energy and bite, and an exuberant thrust, leading on to a thrilling coda. The *Eighth Symphony* was recorded four years earlier, with the acoustic of Watford Town Hall again providing a highly convincing ambience. Dorati's reading proves comparably vibrant.

Kubelik's splendid performances are also available on a DG Double, including also the *New World Symphony* and *The Wood Dove* (see below), which is better value; those wanting just Nos. 7 and 8 will find the present Galleria disc eminently satisfactory.

Andrew Davis's coupling with the Philharmonia was recorded at EMI's Abbey Road studios. Yet, with the violins given a bright sheen, the sound is more like a CBS recording than a mellower, EMI offering. Davis's comparatively lightweight account of the *Seventh* has an attractive lyrical freshness; the *Eighth* is much more compulsive and dramatically spontaneous, making the most of the music's dynamic contrasts, with high drama in the climaxes of the *Adagio*, which also has plenty of expressive feeling, and a sense of vibrant energy throughout the outer movements. The finale is thrilling (although there is some raucous tone from the brass) and there is no doubt about the individuality of the reading as a whole.

Symphonies Nos. (i) 7; (ii) 8; 9 (New World); Overture: Carnival, Op. 92; Scherzo capriccioso, Op. 66.

(B) **(*) EMI double forte (ADD) CZS5 68628-2 (2). (i) LPO; (ii) Philh. O; Giulini.

Symphonies Nos. 7–9 (New World); Scherzo capriccioso.

(B) *** Double Decca 452 182-2 (2). Cleveland O, Dohnányi.

(i) Symphonies Nos. 7–8; (ii) 9 (New World); (i) Symphonic Variations, Op. 78.

(B) *** Ph. (ADD) Duo 438 347-2 (2). (i) LSO; (ii) Concg. O; C. Davis.

Dohnányi's Cleveland performances make an admirable Double Decca triptych. However, Dohnányi's *New World*, superbly played and recorded, like the equally outstanding recordings of Nos. 7 and 8, also fails to observe the first-movement exposition repeat. That said, there is much to praise in this grippingly spontaneous performance, generally direct and unmannered but glowing with warmth. The great cor anglais melody in the *Largo* and the big clarinet solo in the finale are both richly done, with the ripe and very well-balanced Decca recording adding to their opulence. The sound is spectacularly full and rich. In the *Scherzo capriccioso* Dohnányi brings out the Slavonic dance sparkle and moulds the lyrical secondary theme with comparable affectionate flair.

Giulini is at his finest in both the *Seventh* and the *New World*. In the *D minor Symphony* he and the LPO players really make the music sing, and the Dvořákian sunshine keeps breaking out. The glowing (1976) recording encourages rounded textures and rounded phrases. No. 8 (like the *New World*), recorded with the Philharmonia 14 years earlier, brings a similar mellow approach, but the result is comparatively disappointing. Giulini's speeds are on the slow side, especially in the *Adagio* and rather bland *Allegretto*, while the finale opens in a somewhat subdued fashion. Frankly this does not altogether come off. The *New World* is a different matter, refreshingly direct. The remastering gives the sound plenty of warmth and projection.

Sir Colin Davis's performances of Nos. 7 and 8, with their bracing rhythmic flow and natural feeling for Dvořákian lyricism, are appealingly direct yet have plenty of life and urgency. In the *New World*, however, the very directness has its drawbacks. The cor anglais solo in the slow movement brings an appealing simplicity. The reading is completely free from egotistical eccentricity and, with beautiful orchestral playing throughout, this is enjoyable in its way. The set is made the more attractive by the inclusion of the *Symphonic Variations* – one of Dvořák's finest works, much underrated by the public – and here Davis's performance has striking freshness. The remastering of all the recordings is very successful.

Symphonies Nos. 7–9 (New World); Legends, Op. 59/4, 6 & 7; Scherzo capriccioso; Serenade in D min., Op. 44.

(BB) *** Royal Classics (ADD) HR 703992 (3). Hallé O, Barbirolli (with BRAHMS: *Double Concerto* with Campoli and Navarra **).

Barbirolli's red-blooded performances of Dvořák's last three symphonies are offered here with other works on three CDs, in separate jewel cases within a slip case, at the lowest possible price. They make a very remarkable bargain. The *Seventh* and *Eighth* symphonies sustain characteristically high adrenalin levels and splendidly warm lyrical feeling. The *Eighth* (engineered by the Mercury team) is especially fine, sounding like a live performance, rather than a studio account: it received a Rosette from us on its individual issue. The *New World* is comparably spontaneous and exciting, with a ravishingly warm slow movement (beautiful wind and string playing) and a thrilling finale. The other works come off well too, the *Legends* affectionately lyrical, while the *Scherzo capriccioso* bounces buoyantly. The *Wind Serenade* is an unexpected bonus, an intimate performance of persuasive charm. The playing is good too, and the recording limited but satisfactory.

Symphonies Nos. 7; 9 (New World).

(B) *** EMI CD-EMX 2202. LPO, Mackerras.

At mid-price, Mackerras's coupling offers performances of both works which are among the finest ever. With Mackerras, tragedy is not uppermost in the *D minor Symphony* but rather Dvořákian openness. After a hushed, mysterious opening it is the lilting joy of the inspiration that makes the performance so winning. In the *New World* he takes a warmly expansive view, remarkable for a hushed and intense account of the slow movement and superb playing from the LPO. However, this coupling is currently withdrawn.

Symphony No. 8 in G; The Golden Spinning Wheel, Op. 109.

**(*) Chan. 9048. Czech PO, Bělohlávek.

(i) *Symphony No. 8; Nocturne for strings, Op. 40;*
(ii) *Overtures: Carnival, Op. 92; In Nature's Realm, Op. 91.*

(M) *** Chan. 7123. (i) LPO; (ii) Ulster O; Handley.

Symphony No. 8; Slavonic Dances Nos. 3, Op. 46/3; 10, Op. 72/2.

(B) **(*) EMI double forte (ADD) CZS5 69509-2 (2). Cleveland O, Szell – BEETHOVEN: *Piano Concerto No. 5,* etc. ***

Symphony No. 8; The Wood Dove, Op. 110.

*** Chan. 8666. SNO, Järvi.

Järvi's highly sympathetic account of the *Eighth* underlines the expressive lyricism of the piece, the rhapsodic freedom of invention rather than any symphonic tautness, with the SNO players reacting to his free rubato and affectionate moulding of phrase with collective spontaneity. The warm Chandos sound has plenty of bloom, with detail kept clear, and is very well balanced.

Handley's admirable (1983) recording is direct, with the opening relatively straight, not eased in. But that is the very virtue of the reading: it has an ongoing freshness, and its affectionate touches – as in the way Handley lilts the glorious string melody at the centre of the Scherzo – are subtle, not egocentric. Indeed, with first-class playing from the LPO, the life and spontaneity of the performance are most winning. The *Nocturne* makes a most agreeable encore and is also beautifully played. The Ulster Orchestra takes over in the two overtures, linked by a recurring leitmotif, both most attractively done, with *In Nature's Realm* glowing with evocative colour. The recording contributes, of course: it is of Chandos's usual high standard.

Szell's reading of the *Eighth Symphony* is strong and committed, consistent from first to last, and marvellously played. With full-bodied (1970) sound, it remains both distinctive and very enjoyable. The pair of *Slavonic Dances* are mellower than the earlier, complete set on Sony but are still a fine example of Cleveland orchestral bravura. The transfers are first class – this is a richer sound than on many records from this source.

Bělohlávek directs the Czech Philharmonic in a warmly idiomatic reading of No. 8. He is helped by a satisfyingly beefy recording with plenty of bloom that yet focuses the players more sharply than most recordings with this orchestra. Though basic speeds are on the fast side, Bě-lohlávek is never reticent over giving full expansiveness to linking passages, so adding to the warmth. The longest and richest of Dvořák's late symphonic poems is given similarly idiomatic treatment – but in a version with cuts, a considerable drawback.

Symphonies Nos. 8 in G; 9 (New World).

(N) *** Ph. 464 640-2. Budapest Fest. O, Iván Fischer.
(M) *** DG (ADD) 447 412-2. BPO, Kubelik.
(M) *** Sony (ADD) SMK 64484. Columbia SO, Walter.

A superb new coupling of Dvořák's two greatest symphonies goes straight to the top of the list. Needless to say Fischer includes the exposition repeat of the *New World*, and both performances are uncommonly imaginative and marvellously played. Fischer's readings combine freshness with refinement, and thoughtfulness with passion, and he has a splendid ear for detail. One notes in particular the magical *pianissimo* at the reprise of the main theme of the finale of the *G major Symphony* on the strings, with the following passage touchingly nostalgic, to match a similar delicacy of feeling at the gentle close of the *Largo* of the *New World*. This is ravishingly played, with a meltingly simple cor anglais solo. Yet the brass can blaze brilliantly when required and the Budapest trombones have a splendidly exuberant rasp. The recording is of Philips's very finest. Not to be missed.

Rafael Kubelik's performances of the last Dvořák symphonies are among the finest ever recorded. They are superbly played, and the recordings sound admirably fresh, full yet well detailed, the ambience attractive. Kubelik's account of the *Eighth* is without personal idiosyncrasy, except for a minor indulgence for the phrasing of the glowingly lyrical string-theme in the trio of the Scherzo. The orchestral balance in the *G major Symphony* is particularly well judged. Kubelik's marvellously fresh *New World*, recorded in the Jesus-Christus-Kirche, also remains among the top recommendations, providing one does not mind the omission of the first movement's exposition repeat. There is a choice of formats. The *Eighth* and *Ninth* symphonies are reissued as 'Legendary Recordings' in DG's 'Originals' series at midprice, and the *New World* is additionally available on a DG Classikon bargain CD (439 436-2), coupled with five sparkling *Slavonic Dances* (see below).

Walter's account of Dvořák's *Eighth* was one of the last recordings he made (in 1962) but the overall lyricism never takes the place of virility, and Walter's mellowness is most effective in the *Adagio*. His pacing is uncontroversial until the finale, which is steadier than usual, more symphonic, though never heavy. The *New World* was recorded two years earlier. Once more this is not a conventional reading, but it is one to fall in love with. Its recognizably Viennese roots lead to a more relaxed view of the outer movements than usual. Nevertheless, as so often with Walter, there is an underlying tension to knit the structure together and the result is more involving and satisfying than some other rivals which have greater surface excitement. The new transfers are admirable.

Symphony No. 9 in E min. (From the New World), Op. 95.

⊕(N) *** BBC (ADD) BBCL 4056-2. BBC SO, Kempe –

BEETHOVEN: *Overture: Leonore No. 3.* PROKOFIEV: *The Love for Three Oranges; Suite.* ***

(N) (M) *** DG 463 650-2. BPO, Fricsay — LISZT: *Les Préludes;* SMETANA: *Má Vlast: Vltava.* ***

(M) *** Mercury (ADD) 434 317-2. Detroit SO, Paray — SIBELIUS: *Symphony No. 2.* **

(M) (***) Mercury (IMS) mono 434 387-2. Chicago SO, Kubelik — MOZART: *Symphony No. 38.* (**)

**(*) DG 439 009-2. VPO, Karajan — SMETANA: *Vltava.* **(*)

(M) ** EMI (ADD) CDM5 67033-2. Philh. O, Klemperer — HAYDN: *Symphony No. 101.*

(N) (M ** Virgin VM5 61837–2. Houston SO, Eschenbach — TCHAIKOVSKY: *Francesca da Rimini.* **

Symphony No. 9 in E minor, Op. 95 (From the New World); American Suite, Op. 98.

(N) *** Classic fM 75605 57043-2. Prague SO, Pešek (with SMETANA: *Má Vlast: Vltava* ***).

Symphony No. 9 (New World); Overtures: Carnival; Othello.

(B) *** Penguin/Decca (ADD) 466 212-2. LSO, Kertész.

Symphony No. 9 (New World); Overture: Othello.

**(*) DG 457 651-2. BPO, Abbado.

Symphony No. 9 (New World); (ii) Czech Suite; Prague Waltzes.

(B) *** Decca 448 245-2. (i) VPO, Kondrashin; (ii) Detroit SO, Dorati.

Symphony No. 9 (New World); Overture: My Home, Op. 62.

*** Chan. 8510. SNO, Järvi.

(i) Symphony No. 9 (New World); (ii) Serenade for Strings.

(M) **(*) Sony SBK 46331. (i) LSO, Ormandy; (ii) Munich PO, Kempe.

(i) Symphony No. 9 (New World); (ii) Slavonic Dances Nos. 1, 2, 7 & 8, Op. 46/1, 2, 7 & 8; 16, Op. 72/8.

(B) *** DG (ADD) 439 436-2. (i) BPO; (ii) Bav. RSO; Kubelik.

Symphony No. 9 (New World); Slavonic Dances Nos. 1, 3 & 7, Op. 46/1, 3 & 7; 10 & 15, Op. 72/2 & 7.

(M) *** DG (ADD) 435 590-2. BPO, Karajan.

Symphony No. 9 (New World); Slavonic Dances Nos. 6, 8, & 10, Op. 46/ 6 & 8, 72/2.

(N) (BB) **(*) Warner Apex 8573 89085-2. NYPO, Masur.

Symphony No. 9 (New World); Symphonic Variations, Op. 78.

(B) *** CfP 574 9432. LPO, Macal.

Symphony No. 9 (New World); The Water Goblin, Op. 107.

*** Teldec 3984 25254-2. Cong. O, Harnoncourt.

Kondrashin's Vienna performance of the *New World Symphony* was one of Decca's first demonstration CDs. Recorded in the Sofiensaal, every detail of Dvořák's orchestration is revealed within a highly convincing perspective. Other performances may exhibit a higher level of tension but there is a natural spontaneity here. The cor anglais solo in the *Largo* is easy and songful, and the finale is especially satisfying, with the wide dynamic range adding drama and the refinement

and transparency of the texture noticeably effective as the composer recalls ideas from earlier movements. The budget-priced Eclipse CD is enhanced by Dorati's bright, fresh Detroit versions of the *Czech Suite* and the even rarer *Prague Waltzes* (Viennese music with a Czech accent).

Recorded live, Harnoncourt's first movement, with its bold, clipped rhythms and a nice relaxation for the lyrical second group, generates plenty of excitement, with exposition repeat made part of the structure. The *Largo* by contrast is gentle, with the cor anglais solo very delicate, almost like an oboe, and with some superb pianissimo string-playing to follow. The Scherzo lilts as it should, and the finale is well thought out so that it moves forward strongly, yet it can look back to the composer's reprise of earlier themes with touching nostalgia. This CD is made the more attractive by the superbly atmospheric and magnetic account of *The Water Goblin* , one of Dvořák's most colourful symphonic poems.

Among earlier analogue accounts, Kertész's LSO version (now on Penguin Classics) stands out. It remains one of the finest performances ever committed to record, with a most exciting first movement (exposition repeat included) in which the introduction of the second subject group is eased in with considerable subtlety; the *Largo* brings playing of hushed intensity to make one hear the music with new ears. Tempi in the last two movements are perfectly judged. Reissued, very successfully remastered, with equally fine accounts of *Othello* and the *Carnival Overture*, this remains very competitive, but for most collectors the Kondrashin version is even more attractive. In the UK the special note is by Paul Bailey, in the USA by Wendy Wasserstein.

Kempe's *New World Symphony* brings a memorable performance, dedicated, with *pianissimos* of breathtaking delicacy. In a rapt account of the slow movement, taken at a flowing speed the opening cor anglais solo has a folk-like innocence, which poignantly reflects the emotions of Dvořák in American exile. The other three movements have a similar Slavonic flavour, each involving dramatic extremes of dynamic, vividly caught by the BBC engineers and superbly transferred. This is a quite exceptional account, the most illuminating and compelling to have appeared for some years. And while they make a curious mixture for a single disc, each of the three contrasted works on this CD have a rare intensity, coming from the two Prom concerts that Kempe conducted in August 1975 on the eve of his taking over as Chief Conductor of the BBC Symphony Orchestra in succession to Pierre Boulez. Plainly the players were responding with joy to the new man.

Fricsay's reading is unashamedly romantic, and a favourite of I.M.'s. He makes a considerable and affectionate *ritardando* at the entry of the first movement's secondary theme, but with superb playing from the Berlin Philharmonic his unashamed use of *rubato* and *accelerando* is managed so spontaneously that it becomes part of the structure. The great *Largo* opens gently and luminously, and is imbued throughout with tender warmth. The sparkling dance rhythms of the *Scherzo* are full of verve, and the finale is similarly exhilarating, with its central nostalgic interlude hardly less telling. The first movement exposition repeat is omitted, as it usually was at the beginning of the 1960s, but this remains a splendid example of Fricsay's vibrantly personal style. The recording has been vividly remastered and with its equally fine couplings this was an obvious candidate for DG's 'Originals'.

Another highly recommendable mid-priced account of the *New World* comes from the Prague Symphony Orchestra under Libor Pešek on the Classic fM label. It is coupled with another much-recorded piece, Smetana's evocation of the *Vltava* from *Má Vlast* and a relative rarity, Dvořák's *American Suite, Op. 98*, which was composed as a piano work a year after the symphony and orchestrated in 1895. Even in an over-crowded field this is a competitive issue at this price; these perennially fresh masterpieces are all well characterised and spirited and recorded vividly. The documentation presents the repertoire with enthusiasm and puts the music in the context of its period.

Macal as a Czech takes a fresh and unsentimental view of the *New World Symphony*. His inclusion of the repeat balances the structure convincingly. With idiomatic insights there is no feeling of rigidity, with the beauty of the slow movement purified, the Scherzo crisp and energetic, set against pastoral freshness in the episodes, and the finale again strong and direct, bringing a ravishing clarinet solo. The *Symphonic Variations*, which acts as coupling, is less distinctive but is well characterized. A fine bargain recommendation.

Karajan's 1964 DG analogue recording is preferable to his digital version. It has a powerful lyrical feeling and an exciting build-up of power in the outer movements. The *Largo* is played most beautifully, and Karajan lets the orchestra speak for itself, which it does, gloriously. The rustic qualities of the Scherzo are brought out affectionately, and altogether this is very rewarding. The recording is full, bright and open. This is now reissued, sounding as good as ever, coupled with five favourite *Slavonic Dances*, given virtuoso performances.

Kubelík's DG *New World* (see above) remains among the top recommendations. It is brightly transferred in this Classikon reissue, where it is recoupled with five sparkling *Slavonic Dances*.

Järvi's opening introduction establishes the spaciousness of his view, with lyrical, persuasive phrasing and a very slow speed, leading into an allegro which starts relaxedly but then develops in big, dramatic contrasts. The expansiveness is underlined when the exposition repeat is observed. The *Largo* too is exceptionally spacious, with the cor anglais player taxed to the limit but effectively supported over ravishingly beautiful string-playing. The Scherzo is lilting rather than fierce, and the finale is bold and swaggering.

Paray's 1960 *New World* is uncommonly fresh. In the first-movement allegro he is airy and graceful; the exposition repeat is not observed. The *Largo*, with its poised cor anglais melody, makes a gentle contrast, and the Scherzo is admirably vivacious. The finale goes furiously, and its spontaneity leaves the listener with the rare feeling that the music really has been made while he or she was listening. The recording, made in Detroit's Cass Technical High School auditorium, is well balanced in a typically natural, Mercury way and adds to the freshness of effect.

Abbado's opening *Othello Overture* is superbly done and combines warmly observed detail with an ongoing concentration that is more elusive in the symphony – the more surprisingly so, as these are live performances. In the *New World*, the Berlin Philharmonic often play gloriously, but excitement is more sporadic – welling up at the end of the first movement, and emerging throughout a sparkling account of the Scherzo. But, although beautifully played, the *Largo* is very relaxed, and the forward sweep one needs in the finale is elusive, so this cannot be counted among the finest versions of this much-recorded work. The sound is first class, fully and glowing, but 58 minutes is short measure for a premium-priced CD.

Kurt Masur's recording was taken from a live concert given in the Avery Fisher Hall in October 1991, and the Teldec engineers have made light of the hall's notoriously unhelpful acoustic. Though the sound is on the dry side, it not only has a fair bloom but conveys an extremely wide dynamic range. The slow movement is particularly fine, with *pianissimos* that have you catching your breath, and with Masur's very straight, simple phrasing conveying a tender intensity. Moreover, there is a precision of ensemble to rival that of a studio performance.

Masur's very direct manner in the fast movements brings strong, dramatic results, but with very forward sound, and the percussion standing out (the timpani almost deafening at times), the results are on the aggressive side. This is not among the warmer readings of this much-recorded work, yet with an attractive coupling of three *Slavonic Dances*, winningly done, it makes a worthwhile addition to the catalogue at its very modest cost.

Kubelík's Mercury recording of the *New World Symphony* was almost as celebrated in its day (1951) as his *Pictures from an Exhibition*. The Chicago players are kept constantly on their toes. There is no first-movement exposition repeat but the *Largo* is played most beautifully, with the one proviso that the cor anglais soloist is not ripe-toned and has what comes across as a rather nervous vibrato. The sparkling Scherzo, crisply rhythmic and full of idiomatic character, then leads to a thrilling finale, where the tension is held at the highest level until the very last bar. Here the sound, hitherto remarkably good, tends to become a bit shrill.

Under Ormandy, the playing of the LSO has life and spontaneity, and the rhythmic freshness of the Scherzo (achieved by unforced precision) is matched by the lyrical beauty of the *Largo* and the breadth and vigour of the finale. Perhaps the reading has not the individuality of the finest versions, but the sound is full and firm in the bass to support the upper range's brilliance. For coupling, we are offered an essentially mellow account of the *String Serenade*, directed by Kempe with affectionate warmth.

Karajan's digital recording of the *New World Symphony* is enjoyably alive and does not lack spontaneity, although the VPO playing is less refined than on either of Karajan's analogue versions with the BPO, especially in the *Largo*. However, those wanting a Karajan performance in modern, digital sound could be well satisfied with this.

Eschenbach's reading with the Houston orchestra is strong and often thoughtful, played and recorded with refinement, but it often sounds self-conscious and over-prepared, not at all idiomatic with a very slow tempo indeed for the Largo. That brings out the refined beauty of the Houston string tone, and generally ensemble is excellent. It would have been much better to have this under-appreciated orchestra in music less frequently recorded than the New World. Hardly a first choice, but perhaps recommendable to those who want the unusual coupling.

Klemperer is given good recording for its date (1963) and fine playing from the Philharmonia Orchestra. The *Largo* is very beautiful but, although the conductor's deliberation in the first movement brings a well-detailed account of the score, the Scherzo and finale are too solid to be totally convincing. Admirers of this conductor's style will probably not be disappointed.

CHAMBER AND INSTRUMENTAL MUSIC

Bagatelles, Op. 47 (for string trio & harmonium).

(N) **(B)** *** Virgin 2 x 1 VBD5 61904-2 (2). Domus –
  MARTINU: *Piano Quartet No. 1*, etc. DOHNANYI:
  Serenade. KODALY: *Intermezzo.* SUK: *Piano Quartet.* ***

Dvořák's endearing *Bagatelles* for string trio and harmonium never fail to captivate and charm. They are a welcome ingredient in this well-priced compilation of predominantly Czech chamber music. The sympathetic Domus performances (from 1989–90) are recorded expertly and well balanced.

Piano Quartets Nos. 1 in D, Op. 23; 2 in E flat, Op. 87.

⚙ *** Hyp. CDA 66287. Domus.

The Dvořák *Piano Quartets* are glorious pieces, and the playing of Domus is little short of inspired. This is real chamber-music playing: intimate, unforced and distinguished by both vitality and sensitivity. Domus are recorded in an ideal acoustic and in perfect perspective; they sound wonderfully alive and warm.

Piano Quartet No. 2 in E flat, Op. 87; Piano Quintet in A, Op. 81.

(BB) *** ASV CDQS 6200. Clementi Ens.

A very enjoyable account of the *A major Piano Quintet* given by an accomplished and musical group new to records. The quintet is refreshingly unmannered and pleasingly musical, and this modestly priced and well-engineered ASV disc will give a lot of pleasure in both works and it can be especially recommended to those wanting modern, digital sound.

(i) Piano Quartet No. 2; (ii) Romantic Pieces, Op. 78; Violin Sonatina in G, Op. 100.

(N) *** Sony SK 62597. (i) Ax, Laredo, Stern, Ma; (ii) Stern, McDonald.

A starry line-up here for the *E flat Piano Quartet* with Emanuel Ax, Jaime Laredo, Yo-Yo Ma and Isaac Stern, who also plays the *G major Sonatina* and the *Romantic Pieces* with the pianist Robert McDonald. The *E flat Piano Quartet* was sketched immediately after the famous *A major Piano Quintet*, and though not quite its equal, it is full of character and appealing melodic inspiration. The *Violin Sonatina* and

the *Romantic Pieces* are rather light in comparison, though such is their charm that few will complain.

(i) Piano Quintet in A, Op. 81. String Quartets Nos. 5, Op. 9: Romance; 10 in E flat, Op. 51; 12 in F, (American), Op. 96; 13 in G, Op. 106; 14 in A flat, Op. 105; String Quintet in E flat, Op. 97; 5 Bagatelles for 2 Violins, Cello & Harmonium, Op. 47; Cypresses; 2 Waltzes (for string quartet); Terzetto (for 2 violins & viola in C), Op. 74.

(N) **(M)** *** ASV CDDCS 446 (4). The Lindsays with (i) P. Frankl.

A splendid compilation, gathering together many of Dvořák's key chamber works and including not only the *American Quartet* but also the lovely *Quintet*, which has similar transatlantic connections. Incidentally and importantly, they include the repeat in the first movement of this work, with its lead-back. The less well-known *E flat major Quartet* has a slow movement marked *Dumka (Elegia)*: its mood is at first wistful then more energetic, but there is a nostalgic *Romanza* to follow before the dancing finale. The twelve *Cypresses* are arrangements of songs but are so winningly melodic that the words are not missed. The two *Waltzes* are also charmingly folksy, characterful and strongly contrasted. The *Bagatelles* feature a by no means backward harmonium, the effect engagingly piquant. None of this music is uninspired and most of it shows the composer at his finest. The performances are characteristically warm and vital, and the recording is first class, clearly focused but with a pervading bloom.

Piano Quintet in A, Op. 81.

*** ASV CDDCA 889. Frankl, Lindsay Qt – MARTINU: *Piano Quintet No. 2.* ***
(M) *** Decca (ADD) 448 602-2. Curzon, VPO Qt – SCHUBERT: *Trout Quintet.* ***

Piano Quintet in A; Piano Quartet No. 2 in E flat, Op. 87.

**(*) DG 439 868-2. Pressler, Emerson Qt (augmented).

Piano Quintet in A; Piano Trio No. 4 in E min. (Dumky), Op. 90.

(BB) *** Virgin 2 x 1 Double VBD5 61516-2 (2). Nash Ens. – SAINT-SAENS: *Carnival of the Animals*, etc. ***

(i) Piano Quintet in A. String Quartet No. 10 in E flat, Op. 51.

*** Decca 466 197-2. (i) Haefliger; Takács Qt.

(i) Piano Quintet in A; String Quartet No. 12 in F (American), Op. 96.

*** Testament (ADD) SBT 1074. (i) Stepán; Smetana Qt – JANACEK: *String Quartet No. 1.* ***

(i) Piano Quintet in A. String Quintet in G, Op. 77.

*** Hyp. CDA 66796. Gaudier Ens., (i) with Tomes.

This ASV account of Dvořák's glorious *Piano Quintet* by the Lindsays with Peter Frankl is the finest of modern versions and can readily stand comparison with the famous early Decca account with Clifford Curzon. Apart from Peter Frankl's fine contribution, one especially responds to Bernard Gregor-Smith's rich cello-line. Because of the resonance, the recording is full and warm, and if there is just a hint of thinness on the violin timbre the balance with the piano is particularly well managed.

Andreas Haefliger and the Takács Quartet can hold their own with the best. Haefliger is, as always, a deeply musical player and his approach, like that of the Takács, is sober and dedicated without any oversweetness. Some may find the tempo of the first movement a little too measured. Both here and in the *E flat Quartet*, Op. 51, the Takács acquit themselves in exemplary fashion and the recorded sound is, in the best traditions of the house, bright and present.

With Susan Tomes (also of Domus) the inspired pianist, the Gaudier Ensemble give a sparkling performance of the *Piano Quintet*, full of mercurial contrasts that seem entirely apt and with rhythms superbly sprung. The *G major String Quintet* is lighter than most rival versions, with speeds on the brisk side and with Marieke Blankestijn's violin pure rather than rich in tone. Very well recorded, this makes an excellent recommendation if you fancy the coupling. In neither work are the exposition repeats observed.

It is surprising that the coupling of the *A major Piano Quintet* and the *Dumky Trio* has not been chosen more often. The Nash Ensemble offer warmly enjoyable performances of both, with genuine intimacy of feeling and no lack of vitality. They are eminently well recorded and give considerable satisfaction. The Saint-Saëns couplings are delightful, and this inexpensive Virgin Double is splendid value for money.

The wonderfully warm and lyrical (1962) performance of Dvořák's *Piano Quintet* by Clifford Curzon is a classic record, one by which all later versions have come to be judged, and the CD transfer retains the richness and ambient glow of the original analogue master, while improving definition and presence. The piano timbre remains full and real. This performance is available coupled with Schubert's *Trout Quintet* in Decca's 'Classic Sound' series.

In terms of tonal finesse and bloom the Smetana Quartet had few peers, and their ensemble is perfect. Moreover the quality of the mid-1960s recorded sound is as good as many being produced today. The *Piano Quintet*, in which they are joined by Pavel Stepán, is glorious even if the acoustic is slightly drier than is ideal. No quarrels with the *F major Quartet* either. The sound is analogue and has great warmth.

Menahem Pressler joins the Emerson Quartet in powerful, intense accounts of these two magnificent works. The *Lento* of the *Second Piano Quartet* is given with a rapt, hushed concentration to put it among the very finest of Dvořák's inspirations. The performance of the *Quintet* is comparably positive in its characterization, but the DG New York recording gives an unpleasant edge to high violins, making the full ensemble abrasive.

(i) *Piano Quintet in A, Op. 81. String Quintets Nos. 1–3, Opp. 1, 77 & 97; String Sextet in A, Op. 46.*

(B) *** Ph. (ADD) Duo 462 284-2 (2). (i) Kovacevich; BPO Octet (members).

This is the first time all these works have been gathered together on CD, and they make up a very enticing Duo. The Opus 1 *String Quintet in A minor* was written in 1861 when the composer was twenty; the *G major String Quintet* is also an early work, and there is plenty to be found in its beautiful

Poco andante and the vital finale. The masterly and endearingly characteristic Opus 97 *Quintet* (1893) dates from the composer's American years. The Berlin Philharmonic soloists play most eloquently; these performances are both musical and polished. They are splendidly matched in the *Piano Quintet* by Stephen Kovacevich, who at times is perhaps a little over-reticent but whose clarity of articulation is a marvel. The recordings, from 1968 and 1972, occasionally show their age just a little in the upper range of the string timbre in fortissimos. But there is a pleasing ambient fullness and the sound is generally well balanced.

Piano Trios Nos. 1 in B flat, Op. 21; 2 in G min., Op. 26; 3 in F min., Op. 65; 4 in E min. (Dumky), Op. 90.

*** Ara. Z 6726-2 (2). Golub, Kaplan, Carr.

(N) 🌑 (M) **(*) Sup. (ADD) SU 3545-2 (2). Suk Trio (Panenka, Suk, Chuchro).

(N) (B) *** Teldec Ultima 8573 87789-2 (2). Trio Fontenay.

(B) **(*) Ph. (ADD) Duo 454 259-2 (2). Beaux Arts Trio.

David Golub, Mark Kaplan and Colin Carr make an ideally balanced group; Golub produces a wide range of keyboard colour and combines subtlety with a vital yet flexible rhythmic grip. Kaplan plays with great artistry, and we can't remember hearing cello-playing of greater eloquence in these trios than we get from Colin Carr. Splendidly characterized playing and totally idiomatic in style. Throughout there is feeling and freshness, yet nothing is overstated. The recording places one fairly near the artists, but there is room for the music to expand in climaxes and the overall effect has plenty of presence. An altogether delightful set which gives great pleasure.

The finest Czech musicians have a very special feeling for Dvořák's chamber music, a naturalness of impulse which is totally disarming. One has only to listen to these glorious Dvořák performances from the Suk Trio to find their complete rapport with the composer and their warmth for the music surfacing again and again, notably in the often inspired pianism of Jan Panenka, and Josef Suk's delicate lyricism; but the cellist, Josef Churchro, is also a most responsive player, witness his solo at the opening of the *Adagio* of the *First Trio*, which Suk takes up so exquisitely.

Throughout the set their readings have the benefit of great concentration and intellectual grip. They hold the architecture of each movement together most impressively, yet can relax in an instant, as in the delectable *Allegretto grazioso* of No.3 with its rhythmic sparkle and sense of light and shade.

They are perhaps finest of all in the *Dumky*, with its constant changes of mood, and ebb and flow of tempi. They play with enormous commitment and find more to captivate the listener here than even the Beaux Arts manage, with Panenka's contribution especially magical.

The original recordings, dating from 1977/8, were of high quality, but while the analogue warmth and ambient glow are fully retained in the CD transfer, and the piano sounds especially fresh, the recording shows its age in the violin timbre, which is a little thin in the higher register, and this may trouble some ears. But these performances remain unsurpassed.

First-class playing and expertly balanced modern recording combine to make the version by the Trio Fontenay very attractive indeed, especially at Ultima price. Wolf Harden, the pianist, dominates – but only marginally so: his colleagues match him in lyrical ardour, and they are as sympathetic to Dvořák's warm lyricism as to the Czech dance characteristics of the livelier allegros.

The Beaux Arts versions of the *Piano Trios* come from the end of the 1960s. The *F minor* is played with great eloquence and vitality. And what sparkling virtuosity there is in the *Scherzo* of the *G minor*, Op. 26. The splendours of the *Dumky* are well realized in an account of great spontaneity and freshness. The recording is naturally balanced and splendidly vivid; only a degree of thinness on the violin timbre gives any grounds for reservation. At Duo price this is excellent value.

Piano Trios Nos. 1–2.

*** Chan. 9172. Borodin Trio.

(N) (BB) *** Naxos 8.55439. Joachim Trio

Piano Trios Nos. 1; 4 (Dumky).

*** Nim. NI 5472. Vienna Piano Trio.

The Vienna Piano Trio show admirable musicianship and sensitivity in the *B flat Trio* and in the famous *Dumky Trio*, and they are very well recorded too.

We liked the Borodins' earlier recording of the *F minor Piano Trio* (see below) and find much to admire in the present disc: these are spontaneous yet finely shaped performances, very well recorded.

Fresh, vital playing from this excellent Naxos group. Very good recording too, and though not to be preferred to the Beaux Arts, this is eminently recommendable and worth the money.

Piano Trio No. 3 in F min., Op. 65.

**(*) Chan. 8320. Borodin Trio.

Piano Trios No. 3–4 (Dumky).

*** Sony MK 44527. Ax, Kim, Ma.

*** Hyp. CDA 66895. Florestan Trio.

(B) *** HM HMA 901404. Trio de Barcelona.

(M) **(*) Ph. (ADD) 426 095-2. Beaux Arts Trio.

Piano Trio No. 4 in E min. (Dumky), Op. 90.

*** Chan. 8445. Borodin Trio – SMETANA: *Piano Trio.* ***

The performances by the Ax/Kim/Ma trio have warmth and freshness. The *F minor Trio* is given a powerful yet sensitive reading and the recording is faithful and natural. A marginal first choice for this coupling.

However, the Hyperion disc offers an eminently satisfying alternative. These are musicianly and refined performances that will give much pleasure, and the recording, too, is excellent.

The accounts of both *Trios* from the Trio de Barcelona are also first rate and hold up well against the competition, including the Beaux Arts Trio – which is no mean compliment. They really have the measure of this music and portray its changing moods, dramatic fire and lyrical repose, bringing both poetic feeling and refined musicianship to

both pieces. Warm, well-defined, excellent sound. A fine bargain.

The Beaux Arts' 1969 performances of Op. 65 and the *Dumky* still sound fresh and sparkling, though the recording on CD is a little dry in the violin timbre; the *F minor*, arguably the finer and certainly the more concentrated of the two, is played with great eloquence and vitality.

The playing of the Borodin Trio in the *F minor Trio* has characteristic ardour and fire; such imperfections as there are arise from the natural spontaneity of a live performance. But in the *Dumky Trio* it is the spontaneous flexibility of approach to the constant mood-changes that makes the splendid Borodin performance so involving. The recording here is naturally balanced and the illusion of a live occasion is striking.

4 Romantic Pieces, Op. 75; Slavonic Dances, Op. 46/2; Op. 72/2 & 8 (arr. Kreisler).

*** Ph. 462 621-2. Suwana, Berezovsky – BRAHMS: *Sonata*, etc.; JANACEK: *Violin Sonata.* ***

Akiko Suwana and Boris Berezovsky make out the strongest case for these charming pieces: their playing is wonderfully natural and unforced. The recording is quite remarkably alive and brings the artists into your living room. A recital of distinction.

String Quartets Nos. 1–14; Cypresses, B.152; Fragment in F, B.120; 2 Waltzes, Op. 54, B.105.

(B) *** DG (ADD) 463 165-2 (9). Prague Qt.

Dvořák's *Quartets* span the whole of his creative life. The glories of the mature *Quartets* are well known, though it is only the so-called *American* which has achieved real popularity. The beauty of the present set, made in 1973–7, is that it offers more *Quartets* (not otherwise available) plus two *Quartet Movements*, in *A minor* (1873) and *F major* (1881), plus two *Waltzes* and *Cypresses* for good measure, all in eminently respectable performances and decent recordings. The present transfers are managed most satisfactorily, with a nice balance between warmth and presence. At bargain price, neatly packaged and with good documentation, this is self-recommending.

String Quartets Nos. 5 in F min., Op. 9; 7 in A min., Op. 16.

(BB) *** Naxos 8.553377. Vlach Qt.

String Quartets Nos. 8 in E., Op. 80; 11 in C, Op. 61.

(BB) *** Naxos 8.553372. Vlach Qt.

String Quartet No. 9 in D min., Op. 34; Terzetto in C (for 2 violins and viola), Op. 74.

(BB) *** Naxos 8.553373. Vlach Qt.

String Quartets Nos. 10 in E flat, Op. 51; 14 in A flat, Op. 105.

(BB) *** Naxos 8.553374. Vlach Qt.

Although there is stiffer competition now that DG have reissued the Prague Quartet set of the Dvořák canon at bargain price, the Vlach is as good a way of exploring this repertoire as any. Their tonal matching seals their claims to be an outstanding international group, and there is nothing 'bargain basement' about the performances except their price. The playing is cultured and has warmth and vitality, and there can be no grumbles so far as the quality of the recorded sound is concerned; it is natural, well focused and warm. The dark intensity on a whispered pianissimo which marks the hushed opening of Op. 105, one of Dvořák's masterpieces, leads on to performances of exceptional strength and refinement, and throughout the series the vigorous movements bring exhilaratingly sprung rhythms and slow movements that are deeply expressive. So far this has been one of Naxos's success stories, and we are inclined to think the series strongly competitive even alongside most of the full-priced alternatives.

String Quartet No. 7 in A min., Op. 16; Cypresses.

**(*) Chan. 8826. Chilingirian Qt.

String Quartets Nos. 8 in E, Op. 80; 9 in D min., Op. 34.

**(*) Chan. 8755. Chilingirian Qt.

String Quartets Nos. 10 in E flat; 11 in C, Op. 61.

**(*) Chan. 8837. Chilingirian Qt.

Chandos provide very fine recorded sound for the Chilingirians, who play with sensitivity in all five *Quartets*. These are straightforward, well-paced readings that are eminently serviceable. Some collectors may perhaps feel that they fall short of the very highest distinction, but they are unfailingly musicianly and vital.

String Quartets Nos. 10 in E flat, Op. 51; 14 in A flat, Op. 105.

(N) ** EMI CDC5 57013-2. Alban Berg Qt.

The strengths of the Alban Berg Quartet are well known: impeccable ensemble, refined in tonal blend and superb polish. These recordings are of concert performances given in the Mozartsaal of the Vienna Konserthaus in 1999. Surprisingly, given its provenance, the *E flat Quartet* is a little bland and uninvolved, while the great *A flat Quartet, Op. 105* has more fire than charm. The sound is a bit close and wanting in transparency and bloom.

String Quartet No. 12 in F (American), Op. 96.

(BB) *** CfP (ADD) Double CDCFPSD 4772 (2). Gabrieli String Qt – BORODIN: *String Quartet No. 2* ***; BRAHMS: *Clarinet Quintet* **(*); SCHUBERT: *String Quartet No. 14.* ***

*** EMI CDC7 54215-2. Alban Berg Qt – SMETANA: *Quartet.* ***

(M) *** Classic fM 75605 57027-2. Chilingirian Qt – BORODIN: *Quartet No. 2;* SHOSTAKOVICH: *Quartet No. 8.* ***

(N) (BB) (***) Dutton mono CDBP 9713. Griller Qt. BLOCH: *Quartet No. 2; Night;* MOZART: *Adagio & Fugue.* (***)

(***) Testament mono SBT 1072. Hollywood Qt – KODALY; SMETANA: *Quartets.* (***)

(M) **(*) DG (IMS) (ADD) 437 251-2. Amadeus Qt – SMETANA: *String Quartet No. 1.* **(*)

String Quartet No. 12 (American); Cypresses.

*** DG 419 601-2. Hagen Qt – KODALY: *Quartet No. 2.* ***

The Hagen Quartet make an uncommonly beautiful sound, and their account of this masterly score is very persuasive indeed. Their playing is superbly polished, musical and satisfying, and they play the enchanting *Cypresses*, which Dvořák transcribed from the eponymous song-cycle, with great tenderness. The recording is altogether superb, very present and full-bodied.

Another thoroughly satisfying account of the *American Quartet* comes from the Gabrielis, notable for its warmth, vitality and polish, and a touching account of the slow movement. As part of a Classics for Pleasure Silver Double it makes an outstanding reissue, given first-class (1973) sound, smoothly yet vividly transferred to CD.

The Alban Berg have their finger on the vital current that carries its musical argument forward. Phrasing is shaped dextrously and the polish and elegance of their playing are never in danger of diminishing the spontaneous-seeming character of this music.

On Classic fM, the Chilingirian Quartet give powerful, incisive performances, though they are recorded a bit too forward. Levon Chilingirian's violin-tone is given a slight edge by the full, immediate recording. In the Dvořák the big contrasts of mood and atmosphere are brought out, with the slow movement yearningly beautiful and the fast movements given an infectious spring.

When this brilliant version of Dvořák's *American Quartet* was recorded in 1948, the Grillers were at their peak, unassailably the leading such group in Britain. Perfectly matched, they bring out the exhilaration of the fast music, notably in a dazzling account of the finale, and the yearning beauty of the slow movement. This was a fine early example of Decca's prowess in using its ffrr process, and Dutton in the CD transfer secures astonishingly vivid results. Well coupled with the masterly but neglected Bloch *Quartet* and the Mozart masterpiece.

The Hollywood Quartet is pretty well self-recommending, and their account of the *F major Quartet* is everything one would expect: impeccable in terms of execution, ensemble and taste. This was a quartet which brought real artistry to everything they played.

Admirers of the Amadeus will certainly want their 1977 coupling of Dvořák and Smetana, recorded in Finland. This is a strongly conceived performance, full of ardour. The Scherzo and exhilarating finale show their brilliance of ensemble at its most appealing and infectious. The sound is vivid, full and immediate.

String Quartets Nos. 12 (American); 13 in G, Op. 106.

*** ASV CDDCA 797. Lindsay Qt.

In the *American Quartet* the Lindsays' account is certainly among the very best in terms of both performance and recording. The *G major* is also played very well, with much the same dedication and sensitivity. An outstanding issue.

String Quartets Nos. 12 (American); 14 in A flat, Op. 105.

**(*) Chan. 8919. Chilingirian Qt.

These Chilingirian performances are well up the standard of their fine series, even if their version of the *American Quartet* would not be a first choice. The recording is first class, and those needing this coupling will not be disappointed.

String Quartet No. 12 (American); (i) String Quintet in E flat, Op. 97.

*** Erato 4509 96968-2. Keller Qt; (i) with Deeva.

Dvořák wrote the second of his string quintets, the one with extra viola, at the same period as the popular *American Quartet*, similarly using thematic material with American inflexions, so that the two works make an apt and attractive coupling. The Keller Quartet give outstanding readings of both works, crisp and fanciful, with light, clear textures and with speeds generally on the fast side. The tenderness of the lyricism is beautifully caught in consistently imaginative phrasing, and the Erato recording is beautifully balanced.

String Quartet No. 13 in G, Op. 106; Quartet Movement in F, B.120; 2 Waltzes, Op. 54.

**(*) Chan. 8874. Chilingirian Qt.

The playing of the Chilingirians has momentum and vitality and, though there are moments when they could make more of dynamic nuance, these are sympathetic and well-recorded performances. They include the *Quartet Movement in F major* that Dvořák had originally intended for the piece, as well as two of the *Waltzes* he arranged from the Op. 54 piano pieces.

String Quartet No. 14 in A flat, Op. 105.

(N) *** DG 469 066-2. Hagen Qt – KURTAG: *Hommage à Mihály Abdrás;* SCHULHOFF: *5 Pieces.* ***

String Quartet No. 14 in A flat, Op. 105; Terzetto in C, Op. 74.

*** Testament SBT 1075. Smetana Qt – JANACEK: *String Quartet No. 2.* ***

The Smetanas observe the traditional cut in the finale of Op. 105, from 11 bars before fig. 11 until 4 bars after fig. 12. This is a wonderful performance. Moreover it comes with the *Terzetto in C* for two violins and viola, a rarity in the concert hall, played freshly and elegantly, and their outstanding account of Janáček's *Intimate Letters*, which is new to the British catalogues.

The Hagen Quartet give us a hybrid offering with what seems a somewhat arbitrary coupling. Their performance is in many ways competitive, with spritely rhythms and imaginative phrasing, though it falls short of being a first recommendation. Putting aside differences of price, the Vlach on Naxos remains the more satisfying choice.

String Quintets: (i) in G, Op. 77; (ii) in E flat, Op. 97.

*** Bayer BR 100 184CD. Stamitz Qt, with (i) Hudec; (ii) Talich.

String Quintets: in G, Op. 77; in E flat, Op. 97. Intermezzo in B, Op. 40.

*** Chan. 9046. Chilingirian Qt with D. McTier.

Artistically, honours are pretty evenly divided between the Stamitz Quartet and the Chilingirians in the quintets. The Stamitz Quartet is perhaps balanced more forwardly but is recorded pleasantly, and the Chilingirian set on Chandos

has more air round the sound but without any loss of focus. Both performances have the warmth and humanity that Dvořák exudes, but the Chilingirians undoubtedly score in including the beautiful *B major Intermezzo* that the composer had originally intended for the *G major Quintet* and which he subsequently expanded into an independent work for full strings, the *Nocturne*, Op. 40. This tips the balance in its favour.

String Quintet in E flat, Op. 97; String Sextet in A, Op. 48.

*** Hyp. CDA 66308. Raphael Ens.

The *E flat major Quintet*, Op. 97, is one of the masterpieces of Dvořák's American years, and it is most persuasively given by the Raphael Ensemble, as is the coupled *Sextet*. It is also very well recorded, though we are placed fairly forward in the aural picture.

Violin Sonatina in G, Op. 100.

(N) *** Praga PRD 250 153. Remés, Kayahara – JANACEK; MARTINU; SMETANA: *Violin Sonatas.* ***

Considering its disarmingly melodic freshness, it is astonishing that Dvořák's *Violin Sonatina* is so rarely heard and recorded. Although it is full of charm, its four movements are by no means diminutive in character, and the composer probably chose the title to emphasize its unpretentiousness. This splendidly sensitive account from Václav Remes, admirably partnered by Sachiko Kayahara, is a sheer delight, and has an authentic Czech lilt and is full of character. The recording is very good indeed and so are the couplings.

Piano duet

Slavonic Dances Nos. 1–16, Op. 46/1–8; Op. 72/1–8.

(BB) *** Naxos 8.553138. Matthies, Köhn.

The brilliant piano duo of Silke-Thora Matthies and Christian Köhn are most persuasive performers, radiating their own enjoyment, bringing out inner parts, giving transparency to even the thickest textures, subtly shading their tone and, above all, consistently springing rhythms infectiously, with an idiomatic feeling for Czech dance music. The forwardly balanced recording brings out the brightness of the piano while letting warmth of tone come forward in such gentler dances as No. 3 in D. An excellent bargain.

7 Organ Preludes & Fugues.

(N) **(*) BIS CD 1101. Ericsson – GLAZUNOV: *Preludes & Fugues,* etc. SIBELIUS: *Intrada,* etc. ***

These pieces – five preludes, a fughetta and two fugues – are graduation exercises that Dvořák wrote on leaving the Prague Organ School. They are played very well here and show the fluency and technical proficiency you would expect from any gifted student, but no sign of individuality.

VOCAL AND CHORAL MUSIC

Biblical Songs, Op. 99; Gipsy Melodies, Op. 55; In Folk Tone, Op. 73; Love Songs, Op. 83.

(N) *** Sup. SU 3437-2. Peckova, Gage.

Though each of these four song-cycles has been treated to a series of recordings in the past, it is good to have a complete disc of Dvořák songs, and certainly one as fine as this. It makes a generous coupling too, with Dagmar Peckova an inspired interpreter, sensitively supported by Irwin Gage. Hers is an ideal voice for this repertory, unmistakably Slavonic in timbre, yet firm and pure as well as rich. She retains a freshness specially apt for the songs inviting a girlish manner, including the most famous of this composer's songs, the fourth of the seven *Gipsy Songs, Songs My Mother Taught Me*, sounding fresh and new.

The four cycles are also most welcome for representing the full span of Dvořák's career. Earliest in inspiration are the eight *Love Songs*, charming pieces which already reveal an unquenchable lyrical gift. Next chronologically are the *Gipsy Songs* of 1880, bold and colourful, which are here nicely contrasted by Peckova and Gage with the four simpler, less exotic songs, *In Folk Tone*, of six years later.

The brisker songs are the ones when Dvořák most directly echoes his *Slavonic Dances*. Last and longest is the cycle of ten *Biblical Songs*, setting texts from the Psalms, written – again at high speed – in 1894, when Dvořák in the United States was feeling homesick. More often they are sung by male singers, gaining from weight and gravity, but here with the mezzo, Peckova, they prove just as moving and intense. Full texts are given, but translations in German and French as well as English come on separate pages, making it far more difficult to follow songs line by line. Clear, well-balanced sound.

(i) *Requiem, Op. 89;* (ii) *6 Biblical Songs from Op. 99.*

🏵 (B) *** DG (ADD) Double 453 073-2 (2). (i) Stader, Wagner, Haefliger, Borg, Czech PO & Ch., Ančerl; (ii) Fischer-Dieskau, Demus.

This superb DG set from 1959 brings an inspired performance of Dvořák's *Requiem* which here emerges with fiery intensity, helped by a recording made in an appropriately spacious acoustic that gives an illusion of an electrifying live performance, without flaw. The passionate singing of the chorus is unforgettable and the German soloists not only make fine individual contributions but blend together superbly in ensembles. DG have added Fischer-Dieskau's 1960 recordings of six excerpts from Op. 99. He is at his superb best in these lovely songs. (The numbers included are: *Rings an den Herrn; Gott, erhöre meine inniges Flahen; Gott ist mein Hirte; An den Wassern zu Babylon; Wende dich zu mir;* and *Singet ein neues Lied.*) Joerg Demus accompanies sensitively, and the recording balance is most convincing.

(i) *Requiem, Op. 89;* (ii) *Mass in D, Op. 86.*

(B) *** Double Decca (ADD) 448 089-2 (2). (i) Lorengar, Komlóssy, Isofalvy, Krause, Amb. S., LSO, Kertész; (ii) Ritchie, Giles, Byers, Morton, Christ Church Cathedral Ch., Oxford, Cleobury (organ), Preston.

Kertész conducts with a total commitment to the score and he secures from singers and orchestra an alert and sensitive response. The recording, which has the advantage of the Kingsway Hall ambience, has a lifelike balance, and for this Double Decca reissue the work has been sensibly recoupled with Simon Preston's beautifully shaped Christ Church account of the *Mass in D*, recorded six years later. In both works the CD remastering shows how good were the original recordings.

Saint Ludmila (oratorio), *Op. 74.*

*** Orfeo C 513992H (2). Aghová, Breedt, Beczala, Vele, Prague Chamber Ch., WDR Cologne Ch. & SO, Albrecht.

Saint Ludmila was written for the 1886 Leeds Festival, but overall the result, like the choral ballad *The Spectre's Bride*, is a winningly vigorous, dramatic work, reflecting the composer we know from the symphonies in its rhythmic strength and lyrical warmth. It is a piece full of white-hot inspiration, punctuated with lively choruses and arias, often feeling operatic. The oratorio tells how Ludmila, the daughter of a Serb prince, married the Prince of Bohemia and, by her conversion in 874, turned the whole nation to Christianity. As is to be expected, since it comes from the same period as the *Seventh Symphony*, there are many glorious pages. The final section leads to a triumphant choral finale which in places echoes that of Beethoven's *Ninth*.

This Orfeo issue offers a strong, colourful performance which points the drama well, using four first-rate Czech-speaking soloists and with the Cologne choir augmented by the Prague Chamber Choir. The result is both polished and idiomatic, helped by warm, full sound, even though the chorus is set behind the orchestra.

Stabat Mater, Op. 58.

*** Telarc 2CD 80506 (2). Goerke, Simpson, Olsen, Berg, Atlanta SO & Ch., Shaw.

(N) *** DG 471 022-2 (2). Zvetkova, Donose, Botha, Scandiuzzi, Saxon St Op. Ch., Dresden State O, Sinopoli.

(i) *Stabat Mater;* (ii) *Legends Nos. 1–10, Op. 59.*

(B) *** DG (ADD) Double 453 025-2 (2). (i) Mathis, Reynolds, Ochman, Shirley-Quirk, Bav. R. Ch. & SO; (ii) ECO; Kubelik.

The *Stabat Mater* blazed the trail for Dvořák's cause during his lifetime and inspires the late Robert Shaw to considerable heights. He brings great dedication and obvious feeling to this score and gets a fine response from the Atlanta Symphony Orchestra and Chorus and an admirable line-up of soloists. Its lyrical breadth and gentleness come over well in this new Telarc recording, and the only possible grumble might be the lack of real front-to-back depth of perspective in the balance.

Recorded only months before his untimely death in April 2001, this vividly dramatic account of Dvořák's *Stabat Mater* makes a fine memorial to Giuseppe Sinopoli, a conductor who, controversial or not, rarely lacked inspiration. Here the performance, recorded live, so far from reflecting the Victorian good manners of traditional readings emerges at white heat.

Sinopoli's is an operatic approach to a work which, thanks to the obsessively mournful text, can lack variety. The opposite is true with Sinopoli, with the weightiest tuttis gloriously caught in the rich DG recording, set in total contrast with hushed, intense *pianissimos*. The quartet of soloists, all idiomatic, is consistently fine, and the chorus sings incandescently throughout. On two discs without coupling, the extravagant layout is a drawback, but so special a performance is ample compensation.

Kubelik is consistently responsive and this is a work which benefits from his imaginative approach. The recording, made in the Munich Herkulessaal, is of very good quality. The ten *Legends* are beautifully played by the ECO. This music ought to be better known, with its colourful scoring and folksy inspiration of a high order. Again very good recording.

OPERA

Dimitrij (complete).

**(*) Sup. 11 1259-2 (3). Vodička, Drobková, Hajossyová, Aghová, Mikulas, Prague R. Ch., Czech PO Ch. and O, Albrecht.

Dimitrij, Dvořák's attempt to write a really grand opera, contrasts large-scale ensemble scenes with intimate ones full of lyrical ideas as ripely inspired as he ever conceived for an opera. The title-role is taken by the tenor, Leon Marian Vodička, whose Slavonic timbre is very apt for the music, even if he is strained at times. Drahomira Drobková as Marfa and Magdalena Hajossyová as Marina sing strongly, but it is Livia Aghová as Xenia who with sweet, pure tone brings out the beauty of Dvořák's melodies more than anyone. Gerd Albrecht draws brilliant playing from the Czech Philharmonic, though the choral singing is less well disciplined. This recording follows a reconstruction of Dvořák's original score of 1882 and contains sections of the score never previously heard this century.

The Jacobin.

*** Sup. (ADD) 11 2190-2 (2). Zítek, Sounová, Přibyl, Machotková, Blachut, Prusa, Tuček, Berman, Katilena Children's Ch., Kuhn Ch., Brno State PO, Pinkas.

The background to *The Jacobin* is one of revolt and political turmoil, but Dvořák was more interested in individuals, so this is more a village comedy than a tract for the times. The sequence of exuberant, tuneful numbers (dances and choruses, as well as arias) is more than enough to make the piece a delight on disc. Jiři Pinkas draws lively and idiomatic performances from a first-rate cast, including such stalwarts as Vilem Přibyl as the hero (a little old-sounding but stylish) and the veteran tenor Beno Blachut giving a charming portrait of the heroine's father. Václav Zítek sings the heroic part of the Jacobin himself with incisive strength and Daniela Sounová is bright and clear as the heroine. The analogue sound is clear and firmly focused. A full libretto/translation is included.

The Jacobin: highlights.

(M) **(*) Sup. (ADD) 11 2250-2 (from above complete recording, cond. Pinkas).

The highlights disc is at medium price and, with 62 minutes' playing time, makes a good sampler. However, there is no libretto included, not even a synopsis, which is unhelpful in an unfamiliar work of this kind.

Kate and the Devil (complete).

**(*) Sup. (ADD) 11 1800-2 (2). Barová, Ježil, Novák, Sulcová, Suryová, Horáček, Brno Janáček Op. Ch. & O, Pinkas.

This is a charming comic fantasy about the girl who literally makes life hell for the devil who abducts her. It inspired a score that might almost be counted an operatic equivalent of his *Slavonic Dances*, full of sharply rhythmic ideas, colourfully orchestrated. The role of Kate is very well taken by Anna Barová, firm and full-toned, with Jirka sung attractively by Miloš Ježil, though his Slavonic tones are strained on top. The snag is the ill-focused singing of Richard Novák as the Devil, characterful enough but wobbly. Jiři Pinkas persuasively brings out the fun and colour of the score, drawing excellent singing from the chorus; and the 1979 recording has plenty of space, agreeably warm and atmospheric. The libretto is well produced and clear, but it assumes that the set is on three CDs instead of two, with Acts II and III together on the second.

Rusalka (complete).

*** Decca 460 568-2 (3). Fleming, Heppner, Hawlata, Zajick, Urbanová, Kusnjer, Kloubová, Kühn Mixed Ch., Czech PO, Mackerras.

*** Sup. 10 3641-2 (3). Beňačková-Cápová, Novák, Soukupová, Ochman, Drobková, Prague Ch. & Czech PO, Neumann.

Dvořák's late masterpiece, *Rusalka*, is rapidly overtaking Smetana's *Bartered Bride* as the world's favourite Czech opera, and rightly so. Here Decca offers not only ripely atmospheric sound but what in almost every way is the ideal cast, with the Czech Philharmonic incandescent under Sir Charles Mackerras. Renée Fleming gives a heartfelt performance, having performed the role on stage many times. That experience is reflected in the intensity of her sharply detailed performance, with the voice consistently beautiful over the widest range. Ben Heppner too, with his powerful tenor at once lyrical and heroic, is ideally cast, also a singer with long stage experience of his role as the Prince. Franz Hawlata as the Watergnome, Rusalka's father, and Dolora Zajick as the witch, Ježibaba, are both outstanding too, with even the smaller roles cast from strength, using leading singers from the Prague Opera. In his inspired conducting Mackerras does not resist the obvious Wagnerian overtones, yet Czech flavours are never underplayed in the many colourful dance rhythms.

Dvořák's fairy-tale opera is also given a magical performance by Neumann and his Czech forces, helped by full, brilliant and atmospheric recording. The title-role is superbly taken by Gabriela Beňačková-Cápová, and the famous *Invocation to the moon* is enchanting. Vera Soukupová as the Witch is just as characterfully Slavonic in a lower register, though not so even; while Wieslaw Ochman sings with fine, clean, heroic tone as the Prince, with timbre made distinctive by tight vibrato. Richard Novák brings out some of the Alberich-like overtones as the Watersprite, though the voice is not always steady. The banding could be more generous, but a full translation is included. However, the Decca set makes a clear first choice.

Rusalka: highlights.

*** Decca 466 356-2 (from above complete recording, with Fleming, Heppner; cond. Mackerras).

(M) ****(*)** Sup. 11 2252-2 (from above complete recording; cond. Neumann).

The splendid Decca recording of *Rusalka* runs to three CDs and there will be those collectors who will be satisfied with just highlights; and here the heroine's famous *Invocation to the moon* opens a well-chosen 74-minute selection. Texts and translations are included.

The Supraphon disc offers an hour of music. But the current mid-priced reissue has neither libretto nor synopsis, merely a list of the excerpts.

Wanda (complete).

(N) ****(*)** Orfeo C149003F (3). Romanko, Tchistjakova, Straka, Daniluk, Kusnjer, Breedt, Prague Chamber Ch., WDR Ch., & SO Cologne, Albrecht.

In five acts, *Wanda* was Dvořák's idea of a grand opera after the manner of Meyerbeer. Happily, he of all composers was incapable of being pompous, and his glowing lyricism, with its winning Czech inflections, is what stands out in the varied sequence of attractive ensembles. The opera dates from 1876, the year after he composed his eternally fresh *Fifth Symphony*, and much of that freshness is carried over to the opera, with orchestration light and transparent.

Sadly, Dvořák was not a natural opera-composer, and for all the delights of the music, this Polish subject involving Princess (later Queen) Wanda and two rivals for her love, the Cracow knight Slavoj and the German Prince Roderick, is hardly gripping dramatically.

Yet on disc it is well worth investigating, and Gerd Albrecht, using a revised and expanded edition of a score thought to be lost in the Second World War, conducts a strong, purposeful performance, with fine teamwork in the ensembles. The principal male soloists, Peter Straka as Slavoj and Ivan Kasnjer as Roderick, are both first rate, but the warm, idiomatic singing of the principal women, Olga Romanko in the title role and Irina Tchistjakova as her sister, Božena, is marred by the unevenness of their very Slavonic voices. Excellent singing from the joint Czech and German choirs, and full, well-balanced radio recording.

DYSON, George (1883–1964)

(i) *Violin Concerto. Children's Suite* (after Walter De La Mare).

🌑 ******* Chan. 9369. (i) Mordkovitch; City of L. Sinfonia, Hickox.

Dyson's *Violin Concerto* is a richly inspired, warmly lyrical work, and the third-movement *Andante* for violin and muted strings, divided into variations, brings a rare hushed beauty, superbly achieved in this dedicated performance. Lydia Mordkovitch gives a reading both passionate and deeply expressive. The *Children's Suite* reflects qualities similar to those in the concerto, not least a tendency to switch into waltz-time and a masterly ability to create rich and transparent orchestral textures, beautifully caught in the opulent Chandos recording. Two rarities to treasure.

(i) *Concierto leggiero* (for piano & strings); *Concerto da camera; Concerto da chiesa* (both for string orchestra).

*** Chan. 9076. (i) Parkin; City of L. Sinfonia, Hickox.

This splendid Chandos CD brings not only an engagingly light-textured concertante item for piano but also two powerful and eloquent works in the great tradition of English string music. The writing shows both a strongly burning creative flame as well as new influences from outside. The performances here are wonderfully fresh and committed and the string recording has plenty of bite and full sonority, while the balance with the piano is quite admirable. Highly recommended.

Symphony in D.

**(*) Chan. 9200. City of L. Sinfonia, Hickox.

Dyson's *Symphony* was composed in 1937. Its best movement by far is the third, an attractive and diverse theme and variations. The finale is confident in its use of ideas from *The Canterbury Pilgrims* with majestic scoring for the brass, but the charming second-movement *Andante* is rather slight and the first movement, marked *Energico*, flags. An enjoyable piece, nevertheless, very well played and resonantly and realistically recorded, in the way of Chandos.

CHAMBER MUSIC

3 Rhapsodies (for string quartet).

(N) (B) ******* Hyp. Helios CDH 55045. Divertimenti – HOWELLS: *In Gloucestershire (String Quartet No. 3).* *******

Although its spirit is lighter, more capricious, the first of Dyson's *Rhapsodies* follows on quite naturally after the gentle close of Howells's haunting portrayal of the Gloucestershire countryside. The second, a dark elegy, makes a haunting contrast, but the third is again essentially light-hearted in its lyrical grace. Surprisingly, the work was inspired by Dante and written after a Mediterranean holiday. Its changing moods are most sensitively caught by this excellent group, and the Hyperion recording is of high quality.

(Organ) *Fantasia & Ground Bass. 3 Choral Hymns; Hierusalem; Psalm 150; 3 Songs of Praise.*

(N) (B) ******* Hyp. Helios CDH55046. Hill, St Michael's Singers, Trotter, RPO, Rennert.

Where the organ piece unashamedly builds on an academic model, *Hierusalem* reveals the inner man more surprisingly, a richly sensuous setting of a medieval poem inspired by the thought of the Holy City, building to a jubilant climax. It is a splendid work and is backed here by the six hymns and the Psalm setting, all of them heartwarming products of the Anglican tradition. Performances are outstanding, with Jonathan Rennert drawing radiant singing and playing from his team, richly and atmospherically recorded.

(i–ii) *The Canterbury Pilgrims. Overture at the Tabard Inn;* (i) *In Honour of the City.*

*** Chan. 9531 (2). (i) Kenny, Tear, Roberts; (ii) London
Symphony Ch.; LSO, Hickox.

Chandos provide us with the long-awaited recording of
Dyson's best-known work, preceded by the Overture based
on its themes. Here the soloists all have major contributions
to make, for Dyson's characterization of the individual pilgrims is strong; but the glory of the piece is the choruses,
which are splendidly sung here. *In honour of the city*, Dyson's
setting of William Dunbar, appeared in 1928, nine years
before Walton's version of the same text; Dyson, however,
unlike Walton, uses a modern version of the text, as he
does in *The Canterbury Tales*, and to fine direct effect. The
splendid Chandos recording is fully worthy of the vibrant
music-making here.

EBEN, Petr (born 1929)

Job; Laudes; Hommage à Buxtehude.

(N) *** Hyp. CDA 67194. Halgeir Schiager (organ of Hedvig
Eleonora Kykran, Stockholm).

In his homeland this Czech composer of choral and organ
music is a famous improviser/recitalist on both organ and
piano. Eben is another of the East European musicians who
survived Buchenwald concentration camp and emerged with
his spirit unbroken. His is undoubtedly a major new voice
in the field of organ music – the most exciting since Messiaen. His music is tonal, but wholly original, both in its
complexities and in its mixed sonorities. Those British
music-lovers who think of *Job* as synonymous with only
Vaughan Williams must think again. Eben regards the theme
of Job as 'the wager between Satan and God on the fate of a
human being', and the eight titled movements cover what
befalls Job and his personal response, ending with a set of
variations on a Bohemian chorale to designate God's
blessing, 'for Christ is truly the personification of the innocent sufferer to the very end'. It is an extraordinary work
and sonically riveting, as indeed is the four-part *Laudes*, all
based on a Gregorian melody, which reflects 'our deep
ingratitude to our fellow men and to the world, and above
all to its Creator'. The *Hommage à Buxtehude* alternates
toccata and fugue, and although based on two quotations
from that composer's music has a quirky rhythmic individuality that would have astonished its dedicatee. This is astonishing music, superbly played and recorded. Just try the very
opening of *Job* with its sombrely menacing pedal motif and
you will surely want to hear the whole work (some 43
minutes long).

EBERLIN, Johann (1702–62)

*Christus factus est; Cum sancto spiritu; Dextera Domini;
Mass in C; Pater si non potest; Tenebrae facta sunt; Tonus
octavus; Tonus secundus.*

(N) *** ASV CDGAU 205. Rodolfus Ch., Allwood; Whitton
(organ).

A generation younger than Bach, Johann Eberlin was the
predecessor of Mozart's father, Leopold, as Kapellmeister to
the Archbishop of Salzburg, so inevitably influencing the
boy Mozart. Eberlin was above all a master of counterpoint,
as the liturgical music here consistently demonstrates – two
crisply compact settings of the Mass and three fine motets.
In lively performances like these from the Rodolfus Choir,
using editions prepared by the conductor, Ralph Allwood,
far from sounding academic, they emerge bright and refreshing, full of adventurous harmony, looking forward as
well as back. The same is true of the sets of organ pieces,
brief exercises in counterpoint that Bach himself would have
approved. Warm, clear sound.

ECKHARD, Johann Gottfried
(1735–1809)

*Keyboard Sonatas, Op. 1/1–3; Op. 2/1–2; in G; Menuet
d'Exaudet with Variations.*

(BB) *** Discovery DICD 920392. Haudebourg (fortepiano).

Johann Gottfried Eckhard's published keyboard sonatas included on this disc are forward-looking and they embody
expressive and dynamic markings characteristic of the piano.
His music is played persuasively by Brigitte Haudebourg
and is recorded decently.

EDWARDS, Ross (born 1943)

Piano Concerto.

(N) **(*) Australian ABC Eloquence 426 483-2. Henning,
Queensland SO, Fredman – WILLIAMSON: *Double Piano
Concerto* **(*); SCULTHORPE: *Piano Concerto.* **(*)

An enterprising disc of Australian piano concertos. Ross
Edwards's example is no masterpiece, but it has a certain
enjoyable vitality. The slow movement, using pentatonic
scales, gives it a Japanese flavour, and the finale is tuneful
and fun. The performance is good, though the recording is
only average.

EGK, Werner (1901–83)

The Temptation of St Anthony (cantata).

(M) *** DG (IMS) (ADD) 449 097-2. J. Baker, Koeckert Qt,
Bav. RSO (strings), composer – ORFF: *Catulli
Carmina.* ***

Egk's *Temptation of St Anthony* shows him at his best: it is
in effect a song-cycle, and Janet Baker, who was in particularly good voice at this period of her career (the mid-1960s),
sings it with great beauty. The recording, too, is good, and
this can be recommended as a sampler for those who want
to investigate Egk's music for themselves.

EISLER, Hanns (1898–1962)

Deutsche Sinfonie, Op. 50.

*** Decca (IMS) 448 389-2. Wangemann, Markert, Görne,
Lika, Gütschow, Schwarz, Senff Ch. Leipzig GO, Zagrosek.

The *Deutsche Sinfonie* consists of 11 disparate movements mostly composed during Eisler's period of exile after the Nazis came to power. Seven of the movements are Brecht settings. Despite its unusual provenance, the work seems to hang together and, for all the reminders of Shostakovich, Hindemith and Mahler, it makes a strong impression. Eisler's is not a strongly individual voice but this piece is worth getting to know. The various soloists and the two speaking roles are as impressive as the orchestral playing, which is scrupulously prepared. The recording is state-of-the-art.

Prelude and Fugue on B-A-C-H for String Trio, Op. 46; String Quartet, Op. 75.

(N) (BB) *** CPO 999 341-2. Leipzig Qt – ADORNO: *String Quartet*, etc. ***

Hanns Eisler wrote relatively little chamber music. The *Prelude and Fugue on B-A-C-H* comes from 1934, the year after he left Berlin for the United States, and the *String Quartet* was written four years later. Rather anonymous music, composed at the time he was renewing his faith in his teacher, Schoenberg.

'The Hollywood Songbook': Anakreontische Fragmente; An den kleinen Radioapparat; Auf der Flucht; Automne californian; 5 Elegien; Epitaph auf einen in der Flandernschlacht Gefallenen; Erinnerung an Eichendorff und Schumann; Die Flucht; Frühling; Gedenktafel für 4000 Soldaten; Die Heimkehr; Hollywood-Elégie No. 7; Hölderlin-Fragmente; Hotelzimmer 1942; In den Weiden; Der Kirschdieb; Die Landschaft des Exils; Die letzte Elégie; 2 Lieder nach Wofrten von Pascal; Die Maske des Bösen; Der Mensch; Nightmare; Ostersonntag; Panzerschlacht; Der Schatzgräber; Der Sohn; Speisekammer 1942; Spruch; Unber den Selbstmond; Vom Sprengen des Gartens; Winterspruch.

*** Decca 460 582-2. Goerne, Schneider.

Hanns Eisler went to Los Angeles but, unlike many, reacted violently against the culture of Hollywood. So it is that the 'Hollywood Songbook', far from being a celebration, is a collection of Lieder reflecting bitterness, cynicism and disillusion. This disc offers a mixed group of 46 brief songs, mainly to words by Bertolt Brecht, which reflect both Eisler's studies with Schoenberg and a desire to communicate directly, standing very much in the central tradition of the German Lied, which Eisler felt was in direct conflict with everything that Hollywood represented. Matthias Goerne is an ideal interpreter with his incisive baritone and feeling for words, very well accompanied by Eric Schneider.

Lieder: An den kleinen Radioapparat; An den Schlaf; An die Hoffnung; An die Uberlebenden; Andenken; Auf der Flucht; Despite these miseries; Diese Stadt hat mich belehrt; Elegie (2 settings); Errinerung an Eichendorff und Schumann; Frühling; Gedenkktafel für 4000 Soldaten; Hotelzimmer; In den Hügeln wird Gold gefunden; In den Weiden; In der Frühe; In der Stadt; Jeden Morgen; Die Landschaft des Exils; Die letzte Elegie; Die Maske des Bösen; Monolog des Horatio; The only thing; Die Stadt ist nach den Engeln gennant; Spruch (2 versions); Uber den

Selbstmord; Uber die Dauer des Exils; Unter den grünen Pfefferbäumen; Verfehite Liebe; Zufluchtsstätte.

(N) (BB) *** Warner Apex 8573 89086-2. Fischer-Dieskau, Reimann.

Many of this collection of Eisler *Lieder* are also included on Matthias Goerne's Decca recital. Eisler did more than set the words to music: he modified nearly all the texts to fit his music, and Brecht, though none too pleased, in the end accepted the alterations with good grace. With the Hölderlin settings Eisler described his versions as 'Hölderlin fragments'. But the succinct, pithy result, with most of the songs between only one and two minutes in length, increases their strength of character. Eisler's musical style is far from 'popular' but always invigorating, and it is good to have a darker-voiced Fischer-Dieskau (recorded in 1987) illuminating them with his special feeling for word-meanings, which were so important to the composer. Aribert Reimann accompanies supportively and the recording is most vivid. The translations provided refer to Brecht's original texts and do not take into account Eisler's revisions.

ELGAR, Edward (1857–1934)

(i–ii) Adieu; Beau Brummel: Minuet; (i; iii) 3 Bavarian Dances, Op. 27; Caractacus, Op. 35: Woodland Interlude. Chanson de matin; Chanson de nuit, Op. 15/1–2; Contrasts, Op. 10/3; Dream Children, Op. 43; (iv) Enigma Variations, Op. 36; (i; iii) Falstaff, Op. 68: 2 Interludes. (iv) Pomp and Circumstance Marches Nos. 1–5, Op. 39; (i; iii) Salut d'amour; Sérénade lyrique; (i; iii; v) Soliloquy for Oboe (orch. Gordon Jacob); (i–ii) Sospiri, Op. 70; The Spanish Lady: Burlesco. The Starlight Express: Waltz. Sursum corda, Op. 11.

(B) *** Chan. 2-for-1 241-4 (2). (i) Bournemouth Sinf.; (ii) Hurst; (iii) Del Mar; (iv) RSNO, Gibson; (v) with Goossens.

Sir Alexander Gibson's reading of *Enigma* has stood the test of time and remains very satisfying, warm and spontaneous in feeling, with a memorable climax in *Nimrod*. The 1978 recording, made in Glasgow's City Hall, remains outstanding. The *Pomp and Circumstance Marches*, too, have fine *nobilmente* and swagger. The rest of the programme is a collection of miniatures directed by either George Hurst or Norman Del Mar – both understanding Elgarians. Elgar wrote the *Soliloquy* for Leon Goossens, who plays it with his long-recognizable tone-colour and feeling for phrase. Most of the other pieces in Norman Del Mar's programme are well known, but they come up with new warmth and commitment here, and the 1976 recording, made in the Guildhall, Southampton, has an appealing ambient warmth and naturalness. George Hurst recorded his Elgar rarities a year earlier in Christchurch Priory, and again the recording has plenty of body, but there is more thinness in the sound of the violins in these items than with Del Mar.

'A Portrait of Elgar': 3 Bavarian Dances, Op. 27; Carissima; Chanson de matin; Chanson de nuit, Op. 15/1–2; Cockaigne Overture, Op. 40; Dream Children, Op. 43;

Enigma Variations, Op. 36; Froissart Overture, Op. 19; Gavotte (Contrasts), Op. 10/3; Introduction & Allegro for Strings, Op. 47; May Song; Mazurka, Op. 10/1; Nursery Suite; Pomp and Circumstance Marches Nos. 1–5, Op. 39; Rosemary, 'That's for remembrance'); Sérénade lyrique; Serenade for Strings, Op. 20; Salut d'amour, Op. 12; Spanish Lady (suite); The Wand of Youth Suite No. 2, Op. 1b.

(B) **(*) Nim. NI 1769 (4). E. SO or E. String O, Boughton.

This very inexpensive four-disc set is made up of four separate Elgar collections, and Disc 3 duplicates the *Chanson de matin* and *Chanson de nuit*, already included on Disc 2. However, the latter collection (including the *Nursery Suite* plus the *Dream Children* and most of the miniatures) is particularly attractive, for William Boughton's performances are graceful and sympathetic and have plenty of character. The *Introduction and Allegro* has a ripely overwhelming climax, but the fugal argument is not lost. The *Enigma Variations* have many pleasingly delicate touches of colour, with the brass and organ making a fine effect in the finale. There is an easy swagger about the *Pomp and Circumstance Marches*. The warmly reverberant acoustic of the Great Hall of Birmingham University gives the performances of these larger-scale works a spacious scale that is entirely apt. What is more questionable is the scale conveyed by the recording (in the same acoustic) for the other, lighter and more intimate pieces. The manner is sparkling, the playing refined and well detailed, with rhythms nicely sprung, but the large scale implied tends to inflate the music, particularly in the *Wand of Youth* excerpts.

'The Lighter Elgar': (i) *Beau Brummel: Minuet;* (ii) *Carissima;* (i) *Chanson de matin, Op. 15/2;* (ii) 3 *Characteristic Pieces, Op. 10: Mazurka; Sérénade mauresque; Contrasts: The Gavottes AD 1700 & 1900;* (i) *Dream Children, Op. 43/1–2;* (ii) *May Song; Mina; Minuet, Op. 21; Rosemary (That's for remembrance); (ii–iii) Romance for Bassoon & Orchestra, Op. 62;* (i) *Salut d'amour, Op. 12;* (ii) *Sevillana, Op. 7; Sérénade lyrique;* (iv) *The Starlight Express, Op. 78: Organ grinder's songs: My old tunes; To the children.* (i) *The Wand of Youth Suite No. 1: excerpt: Sun Dance.*

❁ (M) *** EMI (ADD) CDM5 65593-2. (i) RPO, Collingwood; (ii) N. Sinfonia, Marriner; with (iii) Chapman; (iv) Harvey.

This beautifully recorded CD combines almost all the contents of two LPs. In the first Frederick Harvey joins the orchestra for two organ grinder's songs from the incidental music for *The Starlight Express*, and they have seldom been sung more winningly on record. It is these items one remembers most, but the second collection under Sir Neville Marriner is hardly less successful. All the music is pleasingly delightful in its tender moods and restrained scoring, favouring flute, bassoon and the clarinet in middle or lower register. Very much worth having is the rhapsodic *Romance for Bassoon and Orchestra* with Michael Chapman the elegant soloist. The Northern Sinfonia play with style and affection. Throughout, EMI have provided that warm, glowing sound that is their special province in recording Elgar's music.

(i–ii) *Chanson de matin; Chanson de nuit, Op. 15/1–2;* (iii–iv) *Enigma Variations;* (iii; ii) *In the South (Alassio), Op. 50;* (iii–iv) *Pomp and Circumstance March No. 5;* (iii) *The Starlight Express, Op. 78;* (iii; v) Songs: *My old tunes; To the children.*

(M) *** Dutton Lab. mono CDK 1203. (i) Boyd Neel String O; (ii) Neel; (iii) National SO; (iv) Sargent; (v) with Cummings, cond. Groves.

Boyd Neel's account of *In the South* has a fine thrusting impetus, and in that respect is surpassed (if it is) only by Silvestri's famous Bournemouth version. It sounds totally spontaneous, as does Sargent's *Enigma*, full of Elgarian character, warmth and colour – his finest performance on disc. The playing of the National Symphony Orchestra is most responsive and the powerful climax of *Nimrod* is superbly controlled. The finale makes a thrilling culmination, and it is followed by the ripest, most *nobilmente* account of the underrated *Fifth Pomp and Circumstance March* on record (which was the fill-up, side 8 of the 78-r.p.m. set). The *Chansons* are played with affectionate finesse, and the disc ends with the two charming (and inspired) organ grinder's songs from *The Starlight Express*, sung with great character (and splendid diction) by Henry Cummings in a style of received pronunciation that belongs to a bygone era. As always, the Dutton transfers are marvellously full and vivid. Sargent was recorded in the Kingsway Hall, Boyd Neel's *In the South* a month later at Wembley Town Hall, where the balance brings less body to the strings and less weight in the bass. But the sound is still pretty impressive. The *Chansons* and songs were recorded in the drier acoustic of Broadhurst Gardens but still sound fresh and clear.

Civic Fanfare; (i) *Piano Concerto: Slow movement. Crown of India: March; Hail Immemorial Ind.; Empire March; Polonia; The Spanish Lady: suite; Une voix dans le désert; The wind at dawn.*

(N) *** Classico CLASSCD 334. (i) Fingerhut; Ostergard, Hall, Munich SO, Bostock.

Douglas Bostock and the Munich Symphony Orchestra follow up their series of British rarities with this Elgar collection of occasional pieces and other rarities, including several first recordings. The two items here from the *Crown of India* – an 'Imperial masque' performed in London in 1912 at the time of George V's crowning at the Delhi Durbar – are the only two to have survived beyond the regular suite. The *March* is not as characterful as the well-known *March of the Mogul Emperors* and the extended song, *Hail Immemorial Ind.*, is no better than the corny opening words suggest, but this music is typically Elgarian, and so is the *Empire March* of 1924, written for the Wembley Exhibition.

The song, *The Wind at dawn*, like the *Crown of India* items a first recording, is the earliest music here, setting a poem by Elgar's future wife, similar in mood to *Sea Pictures*, with the mezzo-soprano, Mette Christina Ostergard, a clear, girlish soloist. The words (by the Belgian poet, Emil Cammaerts) are an embarrassment in the wartime piece, *A Voice in the Desert*, which, starting with melodramatic funeral drumbeats, involves both a speaker and a mezzo soloist in uneasy harness. *Polonia*, involving orchestra alone, has its moments of banality too, but works far better, even though the performance could be stronger.

The Spanish Lady Suite here is listed as a first recording, with the five brief movements newly recorded – *March, Morning Minuet, Fitzdottel, Fantastico* and *Bolero* – rather more striking than those in the well-known suite edited by Percy Young. The slow movement of the *Piano Concerto* was also edited by Dr Young, but even with a sympathetic performance from Margaret Fingerhut, that is a disappointing trifle, more of a salon piece than a genuine concerto movement. Yet for the dedicated Elgarian, even Elgar trivialities are a source of delight. The strings of the Munich Symphony are not always as well nourished as they might be, but Douglas Bostock is always persuasive with his Elgarian rubato. Lewis Foreman's scholarly notes greatly add to enjoyment.

(i) *Cockaigne Overture;* (ii) *Cello Concerto in E min.;* (iii) *Violin Concerto;* (i) *Enigma Variations, Op. 36;* (iv) *Pomp and Circumstance Marches Nos. 1–5, Op. 39.*

(B) *** Sony (ADD) SB2K 63247 (2). (i) Phd. O, Ormandy; (ii) Du Pré, Phd. O, Barenboim; (iii) Zukerman, LPO, Barenboim; (iv) Philh. O, A. Davis.

Jacqueline du Pré's outstanding second recording of the Elgar *Cello Concerto* is discussed below, as is Zukerman's ardent account of the *Violin Concerto*, recorded six years later – also with Barenboim. Andrew Davis brings plenty of imaginative flair to the five *Pomp and Circumstance Marches* and is sumptuously recorded. Ormandy's view of *Enigma* is characteristically forthright, lacking some Elgarian nuance – although *Nimrod* is finely shaped – but, with the help of glorious Philadelphia string-playing, urgently convincing just the same. Ormandy paints his picture of Edwardian London with even broader strokes of the brush in vivid primary colours and the Philadelphia players rise to his exultant direction. Again the expansively resonant sound adds to the sense of spectacle.

(i) *Cockaigne Overture;* (ii–iii) *Cello Concerto;* (iii) *Falstaff: Interludes;* (iv) *Froissart Overture;* (v) *In the South Overture.*

(M) (***) EMI mono CDM5 67298-2. (i) Royal Albert Hall O; (ii) Harrison; (iii) New SO; (iv) LPO; (v) LSO; all cond. composer.

Symphony No. 1 in A flat, Op. 55; Falstaff.

(M) (***) EMI mono CDM5 67296-2. LSO, composer.

Symphony No. 2 in E flat, Op. 63 **(including two rehearsal sequences).**

(M) (***) EMI mono CDM5 67297-2. LSO, composer.

The above three CDs are taken from EMI's Elgar Edition, currently withdrawn. It is thrilling to find that the recordings, made between 1927 and 1932, have a body and immediacy that give the most astonishing sense of presence. Consistently these are tough performances, with rhythms pressed sharply home and with speeds generally faster than has become normal today. In addition, Elgar's sense of line, his ability to mould rhythms with natural flexibility, regularly brings an extra emotional thrust and an extra

intensity and poignancy. Most thrilling of all is the *First Symphony*, where Elgar modifies some of the markings in the score on speed-changes; and this reading of *Falstaff*, too, has never been surpassed. *Symphony No. 2* comes with fascinating supplements, including a rehearsal of the Scherzo and an alternative take of the first part of the movement.

Cockaigne Overture, Op. 40; Enigma Variations, Op. 36; Introduction & Allegro for Strings; Serenade for Strings, Op. 20.

⊛ *** Teldec 9031 73279-2. BBC SO, A. Davis.

Andrew Davis's collection of favourite Elgar works is electrifying. The very opening of *Cockaigne* has rarely been so light and sprightly, and it leads on to the most powerful characterization of each contrasted section. The two string works are richly and sensitively done. Similarly the big tonal contrasts in *Enigma* are brought out dramatically, notably in Davis's rapt and spacious reading of *Nimrod*, helped by the spectacular Teldec recording. This is surely a worthy successor to Barbirolli in this repertoire and is an outstanding disc in every way.

Cockaigne Overture, Op. 40; Enigma Variations; Serenade for Strings, Op. 20.

(N) (**) Sony mono SMK 89405 RPO, Beecham.

Although Beecham and Elgar are not names one normally links together, Sir Thomas did in fact programme him far more often than you might think. In fact his repertoire included not only the above but *Falstaff*, the violin and cello concertos, *The Dream of Gerontius* and both the symphonies. (The notes tell us that he conducted an Elgar work on no fewer than 160 occasions!) His classic recordings of the *Cockaigne Overture*, the *Serenade for Strings* and the *Enigma Variations* were made in 1954 and have been out of currency for quite some time. His *Enigma* is wonderfully characterized, and among the most thoughtful accounts in its extensive representation on disc. Everything breathes naturally and is unerringly paced. Yet the transfers are disappointingly poor, with a top emphasis that makes high violins sound thin and steely. Though there has been an attempt to make the sound more immediate than on the original LPs, the results are generally shallow, with odd balances, so that in the finale of *Enigma* the organ is barely audible. Recommended for the interpretations only.

(i) *Cockaigne Overture;* (ii) *Froissart Overture, Op. 19; Pomp and Circumstance Marches, Op. 39, Nos* (i) *1 in D;* (ii) *2 in A min.; 3 in C min.;* (i) *4 in G;* (ii) *5 in C.*

(M) *** EMI (ADD) CDM5 66323-2. (i) Philh. O; (ii) New Philh. O; Barbirolli.

It is good to have *Cockaigne*, Barbirolli's ripe yet wonderfully vital portrait of Edwardian London, back in the catalogue – one of the finest of all his Elgar records. *Froissart* is very compelling too (though the CD transfer is slightly less flattering here), and Barbirolli makes a fine suite of the five *Pomp and Circumstance Marches*. The lesser-known Nos. 2 and 5 are particularly gripping, with plenty of contrast in No. 4 to offset the swagger elsewhere. Here the sound is as expansive as you could wish.

Cockaigne Overture; Introduction & Allegro for Strings,
Op. 47; Serenade for Strings, Op. 20.

(M) (***) EMI mono CMS5 66543-2 (2). Hallé O, Barbirolli –
VAUGHAN WILLIAMS: *Oboe Concerto*, etc. (***)

Barbirolli later recorded all three of these works in stereo,
but these mono versions from the early post-war period
have an immediacy and positive strength rarely matched.
Transfers are vivid and clear, with fine detail, only rarely
thin or edgy. With the important Vaughan Williams recordings, an outstanding double-disc issue.

Cockaigne Overture; Pomp and Circumstance Marches,
Op. 39/1–5; (i) Sea Pictures, Op. 37.

(B) *** CfP 574 0032. LPO, Handley, (i) with Greevy.

Bernadette Greevy, in glorious voice, gives the performance
of her recording career. The singer's magical illumination
of the words is a source of constant delight and her tenderness both in the *Sea slumber song* and the delightfully idyllic
In haven contrasts with the splendour of the big central and
final songs, where Handley revels in the music's surging
momentum. Here he uses a telling *ad lib.* organ part to
underline the climaxes of each final stanza. The recording
balance is ideal, the voice rich and clear against an orchestral
background shimmering with atmospheric detail. The
coupled *Marches* are exhilaratingly brilliant, and if Nos. 2
and (especially) 3 strike some ears as too vigorously paced,
comparison with the composer's own tempi reveals an authentic precedent. Certainly the popular *First* and *Fourth* have
an attractive, gutsy grandiloquence. *Cockaigne* is given a
performance that is expansive but never hangs fire. The
recording is excellent.

Cello Concerto in E min., Op. 85.

⚫ *** EMI (ADD) CDC5 56219-2. Du Pré, LSO, Barbirolli –
Sea Pictures. *** ⚫

*** EMI (ADD) CDC5 55527-2. Du Pré, LSO, Barbirolli –
DVORAK: *Cello Concerto.* **(*)

(M) Ph. 464 700-2. Lloyd Webber, RPO, Menuhin – WALTON:
Concerto. ***

*** Virgin VC5 45356-2. Mørk, CBSO, Rattle – BRITTEN: *Cello*
Symphony. ***

(M) (***) Revelation mono RV 10100. Rostropovich, Moscow
PO, Rakhlin – BRITTEN: *Cello Symphony.* (***)

(BB) *** CfP (ADD) 574 8792. Cohen, LPO, Del Mar –
DVORAK: *Cello Concerto.* ***

*** BIS CD 486. Thedéen, Malmö SO, Markiz – SCHUMANN:
Concerto. ***

*** Finlandia 4509 95768-2. Noras, Finnish RSO, Saraste –
LALO: *Cello Concerto.* ***

**(*) RCA (ADD) 09026 61695-2. Starker, Philharmonia Orch,
Slatkin – DELIUS: *Caprice & Elegy* ***; WALTON: *Cello*
Concerto. **(*)

(BB) *** Virgin 2 x 1 VBD5 61490-2 (2). Isserliss, LSO, Hickox
– BLOCH: *Schelomo;* KABALEVSKY: *Cello Concerto No. 2;*
R. STRAUSS: *Don Quixote;* TCHAIKOVSKY: *Rococo*
Variations, etc. ***

(M) (**(*)) EMI mono CDH7 63498-2. Casals, BBC SO, Boult
– DVORAK: *Concerto* (***) (with BRUCH: *Kol*
Nidrei (***)).

(i) *Cello Concerto; Enigma Variations.*

*** Ph. 416 354-2. (i) Lloyd Webber; RPO, Menuhin.

*** Australian Decca 450 021-2. (i) Harrell, Cleveland O,
Maazel; (ii) LAPO, Mehta.

(i–ii) *Cello Concerto; (iii) Enigma Variations; Pomp and*
Circumstance Marches Nos. 1 & 4.

*** Sony (ADD) SK 60789. (i) Du Pré; (ii) Phd. O; (iii) LPO;
Barenboim.

(i) *Cello Concerto; Enigma Variations; Serenade for*
Strings.

(B) *** Penguin/DG 460 624-2. (i) Maisky; Philh. O, Sinopoli.

Jacqueline du Pré was essentially a spontaneous artist. Her
style is freely rhapsodic, but the result produced a very
special kind of meditative feeling; in the very beautiful slow
movement, brief and concentrated, her inner intensity conveys a depth of espressivo rarely achieved by any cellist on
record. Brilliant virtuoso playing too in the Scherzo and
finale. CD brings a subtle extra definition to heighten the
excellent qualities of the 1965 recording, with the solo instrument firmly placed. Alongside the original pairing with Janet
Baker's *Sea Pictures,* EMI have now given an alternative
coupling with the Dvořák *Concerto,* and this much-loved
recording is given extra warmth and clarity in the new
transfer. However, we retain our allegiance to the original
pairing, which was earlier revamped when it won a platinum
disc award.

The Philips coupling of the *Cello Concerto* and the *Enigma*
Variations, featuring two artists inseparably associated with
Elgar's music, made the disc an immediate bestseller, and
rightly so. These are both warmly expressive and unusually
faithful readings, the more satisfying for fidelity to the score,
and Julian Lloyd Webber in his playing has never sounded
warmer or more relaxed on record, well focused in the
stereo spectrum. This performance also comes alternatively
coupled with the Walton *Concerto* at mid-price.

Jacqueline du Pré's second recording of the Elgar *Cello*
Concerto was taken from live performances in Philadelphia
in November 1970, and this is a superb picture of an artist
in full flight, setting her sights on the moment in the Epilogue
when the slow-movement theme returns, the work's innermost sanctuary of repose. Barenboim's most distinctive
point in *Enigma* is in giving the delicate variations sparkle
and emotional point, while the big variations have full
weight, and the finale brings extra fierceness at a fast tempo.
The recording has now been effectively remastered (the
sound in the concerto is particularly impressive in its clarity
of profile) and handsomely repackaged to include not only
a fine colour portrait of Du Pré but also a reproduction of
the familiar old LP sleeve. The programme now opens with
Barenboim's rumbustious accounts of the two favourite
Pomp and Circumstance Marches.

Truls Mørk has the requisite blend of fervour and dignity,
yet there is a freshness and directness here which is affecting.
Rattle and the Birmingham orchestra give excellent support,
and the recording has excellent internal balance and naturalness of perspective.

With eloquent support from Maazel and his fine orchestra
(the woodwind play with appealing delicacy), Lynn Harrell's

deeply felt reading balances a gentle nostalgia with extrovert brilliance. The slow movement is tenderly spacious, the Scherzo bursts with exuberance and, after a passionate opening, the finale is memorable for the poignantly expressive reprise of the melody from the slow movement – one of Elgar's greatest inspirations. The recording of the orchestra is brightly lit, but attractively so, and the cello image is rich and full, a little larger than life perhaps, but convincingly focused. In the *Enigma Variations*, Mehta proves a strong and sensitive Elgarian, and this is a highly enjoyable performance which has long been admired. The vintage Decca recording, with the organ entering spectacularly in the finale, is outstanding in its CD transfer – a real demonstration disc, and this is one of Mehta's very finest records.

The mid-priced mono Revelation disc offers an early account from Rostropovich. In the main arguments of each movement he uses the widest dynamic range, conveying a raptly reflective intensity, full of poignancy, to match even du Pré. Rakhlin proves a most sensitive Elgarian and has great feeling for the reticence and longing that this music conveys. The cello is far too forwardly balanced, making the orchestra sound dim by comparison, but the warmth of the reading is powerfully conveyed.

Mischa Maisky is highly persuasive in the *Cello Concerto* and, with Sinopoli a willing partner, gives a warmly nostalgic performance, essentially valedictory in feeling. The slow movement is deeply felt, but not in an extrovert way, and the soloist's dedication is mirrored in the finale. The mood of the *Concerto* is carried over into the other works here. The lyrical variations of *Enigma* are expressively relaxed and *Nimrod* has a simple, direct nobility. Though Sinopoli avoids the usual speeding-up at the end of the finale, the thrust of that and of the other vigorous climaxes is pressed home passionately. The *Serenade* is similarly expansive, and some may feel that the *Larghetto*, for all its sympathetic feeling, is too measured. The rich recording adds to the character of the readings, with the Philharmonia strings in particular playing superbly. The descriptive essay is written by Rosamund Pilcher.

Robert Cohen's performance is strong and intense, with steady tempi, the colouring more positive and less autumnal than usual. The ethereal half-tones at the close of the first movement are matched by the gently elegiac poignancy of the *Adagio*. Del Mar's accompaniment is wholly sympathetic, underlining the soloist's approach and his songful line. The 1978 Walthamstow recording is wide-ranging and brilliant but shows Cohen's tone as bright and well focused rather than especially resonant in the bass.

Two Nordic views of the Elgar *Cello Concerto* come from BIS and Finlandia. The former offers the young Swedish virtuoso, Torleif Thedéen, splendidly recorded with the Malmö orchestra, and the latter brings his Finnish colleague, Arto Noras, with Finnish Radio forces; both artists seem completely attuned to the Elgar sensibility. Thedéen has a nobility and reticence that are strongly appealing, and Noras is hardly less impressive. Neither will disappoint; both enrich and do justice to the Elgar discography.

János Starker in his seventies here turns to English repertory not previously associated with him, offering performances which reflect both the understanding and the intellectual strength that has always marked his playing. In the Elgar his tough, slightly wiry tone goes with a relatively objective approach, with flowing speeds generally kept steady; and Slatkin, as in his other Elgar recordings, shows his natural feeling for the idiom. Well-balanced sound.

The most distinctive point about Steven Isserlis's version of Elgar's *Cello Concerto* on Virgin is his treatment of the slow movement, not so much elegiac as songful. Using a mere thread of tone, with vibrato unstressed, the simplicity of line and the unforced beauty are brought out. The very placing of the solo instrument goes with that, rather more distant than is usual, with the refinement of Elgar's orchestration beautifully caught by both conductor and engineers. Now reissued as part of a Virgin Double covering concertate cello works by five different composers, this is an almost irresistible bargain.

Casals recorded the Elgar *Cello Concerto* in London in 1946, and the fervour of his playing caused some raised eyebrows. A powerful account, not least for Sir Adrian's contribution, even though its eloquence would have been even more telling were the emotion recollected in greater tranquillity. A landmark of the gramophone all the same, and the strongly characterized Max Bruch *Kol Nidrei* makes a fine encore.

(i) *Cello Concerto in E min., Op. 85*; (ii) *Violin Concerto in B min., Op. 61*.

(B) (***) Avid mono AMSC 587. (i) Casals, BBC SO, Boult; (ii) Sammons, New Queen's Hall O, Wood.

(i–ii) *Cello Concerto*; (iii) *Violin Concerto*; (ii) *Dream Children, Op. 43*.

(M) (**) Pearl mono GEM 0050. (i). Squire; (ii) Hallé O, Harty; (iii) Sammons, New Queens Hall O, Wood.

In some ways Albert Sammons's 1929 recording of the *Violin Concerto* has never been surpassed, although of course Menuhin's with the composer himself is also very special. The first Avid CD transfer of these recordings was singularly unsuccessful. But the second, current version is infinitely superior. The sound in both works is now excellent, the *Cello Concerto* full and with the soloist firmly focused, the *Violin Concerto* even more remarkable in its warmth and natural clarity, with the solo violin caught vividly and cleanly. Sammons's high level of concentration and the atmospheric magnetism generated in the unsurpassed account of the finale come over very directly to complete a remarkably compelling listening experience.

The Pearl transfer, boomy in the bass, cannot match the Avid. Noticeable surface hiss also exposes some 78-r.p.m. side-joins, but with little harm done. The W. H. Squire version of the *Cello Concerto* is far rarer, a noble reading which in the first three movements can match almost any in its concentration, but which then in the finale finds Squire's intonation less precise in what emerges as a rougher performance. The cello is vividly caught and, though the orchestra is relatively dim, one quickly adjusts to the sound. The miniature, *Dream Children*, also with Harty and the Hallé, is a charming makeweight.

(i) *Cello Concerto*; (ii) *Symphony No. 2*; (iii)*Enigma Variations; Pomp and Circumstance March No. 1 in D*; (iv) *Introduction & Allegro for Strings*; (v) *La Capricieuse; Salut d'amor.*

(N) (BB) *(*) DG Panorama (ADD/DDD) 469 136-2 (2).
(i) Fournier, BPO, Wallenstein; (ii) PO, Sinopoli; (iii) BBC SO, Bernstein; (iv) Orpheus CO; (v) Shaham, Silva.

Fournier's mid-1960s account of the *Cello Concerto* has fervour and conviction, but suffers a bit from a close microphone balance which obscures some of the orchestral detail. Sinopoli's account of the *Second Symphony* is some twenty minutes longer than Elgar's own, which gives you some idea of his approach. Although he is not unspontaneous, and the sound is consistently beautiful, one misses the leaping exhilaration which Elgar valued and which always characterizes great performances of this work. Bernstein's *Enigma* has the distinction of being one of the most perverse readings of this work committed to disc. Few will respond to its outrageous self-indulgence, not least in *Nimrod*, which is dragged out to almost unimaginable lengths. The Orpheus CO are disappointing in the *Introduction and Allegro*, which suggests that, at the time of recording, they were not yet inside this marvellous music.

Violin Concerto in B min., Op. 61.

*** EMI CDC5 56413-2 Kennedy, CBSO, Rattle – VAUGHAN WILLIAMS: *The Lark Ascending*. ***

(M) *** EMI (ADD) CDM7 64725-2. Menuhin, New Philh. O, Boult – DELIUS: *Violin Concerto*. **(*)

(M) *** Decca (ADD) 460 015-2. Chung, LPO, Solti – MENDELSSOHN: *Violin Concerto*. ***

(N) (***) (BB) Naxos mono 8.110939. Heifetz, LSO, Sargent – WALTON: *Violin Concerto*. (***)

(N) (BB) (***) Naxos mono 8.110902. Menuhin, LSO, Composer – BRUCH: *Concerto No. 1*. (**)

(***) Beulah mono 1PD 10. Campoli, LPO, Boult – MENDELSSOHN: *Violin Concerto*. (***)

(BB) (***) Belart mono 461 353-2. Campoli, LPO, Boult – BLISS: *Introduction & Allegro*, etc. (***)

(i) *Violin Concerto in B min. Cockaigne Overture, Op. 40.*

(BB) *** Naxos 8.550489. (i) Kang; Polish Nat. RSO (Katowice), Leaper.

(i) *Violin Concerto; In the South (Alassio)* (concert overture).

(B) *** Sony (ADD) SBK 62745. (i) Zukerman; LPO, Barenboim.

With this impressive remake of the Elgar *Violin Concerto*, Kennedy launched masterfully into his new career, refreshed after years of self-imposed exile from the regular concert platform. He made this new recording in Birmingham immediately after giving his first live concerto performance in years, and the reading has extra thrust and passion compared with his earlier recording of this epic work. The outer movements are faster and more freely expressive than before, the slow movement more expansive, with pianissimos of magical intensity, qualities equally impressive in the evocative Vaughan Williams piece.

Menuhin's second stereo recording, in partnership with Sir Adrian Boult, is hardly less moving and inspirational than his first. There is an added maturity in Menuhin's contribution to compensate for any slight loss of poise or sweetness of tone, and the finale – the most difficult movement to keep together – is stronger and more confident than it was. The 1966 Kingsway Hall recording is characteristically warm and atmospheric, yet vividly focused by the CD transfer. A record indispensable for its documentary value as well as for its musical insights.

Kyung Wha Chung's deeply felt performance is also available, coupled with Lynn Harrell's similarly moving account of the *Cello Concerto* (see above), altogether a more apt coupling. However, those collectors for whom the Mendelssohn *Violin Concerto* is more suitable will find Chung again on her finest form.

Zukerman was inspired to give a reading that gloriously combined the virtuoso swagger of a Heifetz with the tender, heartfelt warmth of the young Menuhin, plus much individual responsiveness, and culminating in a deeply felt rendering of the long accompanied cadenza. Barenboim is a splendid partner and, with full but clearly defined recording, naturally balanced, at EMI's Abbey Road studios, this is a version which all Elgarians should seek out. The coupling is an exciting and virile account of *In the South*, not quite as remarkable as the *Concerto* but a worthwhile bonus.

Dong-Suk Kang, immaculate in his intonation, plays the Elgar with fire and urgency. This is very different from most latter-day performances, with markedly faster speeds; yet those speeds relate more closely than usual to the metronome markings in the score, and they never get in the way of Kang's ability to feel Elgarian rubato naturally, guided by the warmly understanding conducting of Adrian Leaper. Irrespective of price, this is a keenly competitive version, with excellent, wide-ranging, digital sound, if with rather too forward a balance for the soloist.

Jascha Heifetz's unique readings of the Elgar and Walton violin concertos make an ideal coupling, well transferred on Naxos in mellower sound than on previous RCA transfers. The ease of his virtuosity leads in the Elgar to dazzling bravura at speeds faster than usual, bringing a rare volatile quality in music that can easily seem a struggle. Yet that ease goes with a passionate warmth in Elgar's great lyrical moments, with wide vibrato perfectly controlled, and with high harmonics ethereally pure. The great second subject melody is the more tenderly poignant for flowing easily. Heifetz treats the slow movement as a lyrical interlude, before the brilliant display of the finale leads to a deeply reflective account of the unaccompanied cadenza. Any idea of Heifetz as a chilly interpreter is firmly rebutted. Good 1949 mono sound.

Mark Obert-Thorn's transfer of the classic Menuhin account is taken from what he describes as pre-war RCA Victor 'Z' shellac pressings and the result is surprisingly successful, the soloist truthfully caught with a minimum of background noise, and the orchestral strings given plenty of body. The coupled Max Bruch, recorded the previous year, is less successful.

Campoli gives a deeply felt but highly individual account of Elgar's great concerto. One can judge one's reaction to this performance by the control of vibrato on the opening phrase of his first entry. This is an essentially romantic approach, full of warmth, but Campoli applies himself here with dedication to a work he obviously loves, and the result – with Boult securely and compellingly at the helm – is most rewarding. The 1954 Kingsway Hall recording has been impeccably transferred from the *ffrr* master tape by Tony Hawkins at the Decca studios. With its outstanding Mendelssohn coupling this is a fully worthy memento of a strikingly fine soloist.

With its alternative – and equally valuable – Bliss coupling, this is one of the most valuable mono reissues in Belart's 'Boult Historic Collection', although the Bliss couplings are not conducted by Boult but by the composer.

(i) *Violin Concerto in B min., Op. 64;* (ii) *Enigma Variations, Op. 36.*

(M) (***) EMI mono CDM5 66979-2 [CD5 66994].
   (i) Menuhin, LSO; (ii) Royal Albert Hall O, composer.

The 1932 Menuhin/Elgar recording of the *Violin Concerto* emerges on this newly remastered EMI CD with a fine sense of presence and plenty of body to the sound. As for the performance, its classic status is amply confirmed; in many ways no one has ever matched – let alone surpassed – the sixteen-year-old Menuhin in this work, even if the first part of the finale lacks something in fire. Elgar's own 1926 recording of *Enigma* is too well known for much further comment. But his accelerando surge just before he broadens the climax of *Nimrod* and the hustle and bustle of *G.R.S.* emphasize the spontaneous individuality of the reading. Although allowances have to be made for the sound, which is somewhat recessed at lower dynamic levels, the engineers have done wonders with the current remastering, and this coupling is surely worthy to take its place among EMI's 'Great Recordings of the Century'.

Coronation March, Op. 65; Froissart: Concert Overture, Op. 19; In the South (Alassio) (concert overture), *Op. 50; The Light of life: Meditation, Op. 29.*

*** ASV CDDCA 619. RPO, Butt.

Yondani Butt draws warm and opulent performances from the RPO. Both overtures have splendid panache. Rich, atmospheric recording, yet with plenty of brilliance – an excellent Elgar sound, in fact.

Crown of India: Suite, Op. 66; Enigma Variations, Op. 36; Pomp and Circumstance Marches Nos. 1–5.

(M) **(*) Sony (ADD) SBK 48265. LPO, Barenboim.

Barenboim's view of *Enigma* is full of fantasy. Its most distinctive point is its concern for the miniature element, while the big variations have full weight, and the finale brings the fierceness of added adrenalin at a fast tempo. Tempi are surprisingly fast in the *Pomp and Circumstance Marches* (though Elgar's also tended to be fast) and not all Elgarians will approve of the updating of Elgarian majesty. The rumbustious approach to the *Crown of India Suite* brings this patriotic celebration of the Raj vividly to life, though here the lack of opulence in the recording is a drawback. The marches, too, could do with a more expansive middle range, though *Enigma* is fully acceptable.

Dream Children, Op. 43; Elegy, Op. 58; In Moonlight; Nursery Suite; (i) *Romance for Bassoon and Orchestra, Op. 62; Serenade for Strings, Op. 20; Sospiri, Op. 70.*

(N) **(*) HM HMU 907258. ECO, Goodwin; (i) with Price.

A warmly nostalgic collection, beautifully played and recorded, if not quite so idiomatic in feeling as the performances by Boult and Handley . The *Serenade* and the boisterous items in the *Nursery Suite* bring contrast to what is all essentially gentle music. An attractive programme for a later summer evening.

Elegy for Strings, Op. 58; Sospiri, Op. 70; Serenade for Strings in E min., Op. 58.

(M) *** EMI CDM5 66541-2. City of L. Sinfonia, Hickox –
   PARRY: *English Suite,* etc. ***

Hickox draws beautifully refined string-playing from his City of London Sinfonia, notably in the three elegiac movements, the slow movement of the *Serenade* as well as the two separate pieces. An excellent coupling for the rare Parry items, excellently recorded.

Enigma Variations (Variations on an Original Theme), Op. 36.

*** Decca 452 853-2. VPO, Solti – BLACHER: *Paganini Variations;* KODALY: *Peacock Variations.* ***

(M) *** Decca (ADD) 452 303-2. LSO, Monteux – HOLST: *Planets.* ***

(BB) *** DG (ADD) 439 446-2. LSO, Jochum – HOLST: *Planets.* ***

(N) **(*) Cala (ADD) CACD 0524. LSO, Stokowski (with BRAHMS: *Symphony No. 1 in C min., Op. 68* **(*)).

(N) (M) **(*) BBC (ADD) BBCM 5002-2. BBC SO, Sargent – HOLST: *The Planets.* **(*)

(M) *** EMI (ADD) CDM7 64748-2. LSO, Boult – HOLST: *Planets.* ***

In contrast to Solti's brittle Chicago version of 1974, this warmly spontaneous-sounding 1997 account of the *Enigma Variations* reflects not just the special qualities of the great Viennese orchestra but the way in which Solti mellowed over the last two decades of his life. This is a heartfelt, incandescent performance, delicate and subtle on detail; and it is the more moving when Solti refuses to over-emote, for example in the great climax of *Nimrod,* taking it at a flowing speed. The Decca engineers place the orchestra vividly within the unique acoustics of the Musikverein, with close balance avoided, and a fine sense of spaciousness.

Monteux's *Enigma* remains among the freshest versions ever put on disc, and the music is obviously deeply felt. The reading is famous for the real *pianissimo* which Monteux secures at the beginning of *Nimrod,* the tension electric, and the superb climax is more effective in consequence. Differences from traditional tempi elsewhere are marginal and add to one's enjoyment. The vintage Kingsway Hall stereo was outstanding in its day and it is almost impossible to believe that this dates from 1958; with its stunning Holst coupling, this is one of the very finest (and most generous – 78 minutes) reissues in Decca's 'Classic Sound' series.

Like others – including Elgar himself – Jochum sets a very slow *Adagio* at the start of *Nimrod,* slower than the metronome marking in the score; unlike others, he maintains that measured tempo and, with the subtlest gradations, builds an even bigger, nobler climax than you find in *accelerando* readings. It is like a Bruckner slow movement in microcosm around which the other variations revolve, all of them delicately detailed, with a natural feeling for Elgarian rubato. The playing of the LSO matches the strength and refinement of the performance.

Stokowski adroitly guides the players of the Czech Philharmonic through Elgar's masterpiece, illuminating every bar with his special affection, and the result is gloriously rich in spontaneous feeling, casting an entirely new slant on a work that one felt one knew very well indeed. Stokowski's insights are special to himself. The coupling is a splendid version of Brahms's *First Symphony*, recorded live with the LSO at the Royal Festival Hall in 1972.

With the BBC engineers capturing the atmospheric thrill of a Prom performance in the Royal Albert Hall, Sir Malcolm Sargent's 1966 account of Elgar's *Enigma Variations* gives a better idea of why he was such a Proms favourite, with the result more spontaneous than almost any of his studio recordings. The live performance may be a degree less polished, but its thrust and urgency are irresistible, building up superbly to the final variations in which the BBC brass and the obbligato organ convey an extra frisson, even if the sound is pretty opaque and there are too many extraneous noises. But this is not an expensive disc and, with an equally warm and expressive account of *The Planets* as the generous coupling, in many ways this makes a more persuasive case for the conductor than the older EMI pairing of Sargent's studio recordings of the same works.

Boult's *Enigma* comes from the beginning of the 1970s, but the recording has lost some of its amplitude in its transfer to CD: the effect is fresh, but the violins sound thinner. The reading shows this conductor's long experience of the work, with each variation growing naturally and seamlessly out of the music that has gone before. Yet the livelier variations bring exciting orchestral bravura and there is an underlying intensity of feeling that carries the performance forward.

Enigma Variations; Coronation March, Op. 65; In the South (Alassio), Op. 50.

(BB) *** Naxos 8.553564. Bournemouth SO, Hurst.

George Hurst with the Bournemouth orchestra inspires richly expressive playing, full of subtle rubato which consistently sounds natural and idiomatic, never self-conscious. Like Elgar himself, he tends to press ahead rather than linger, as in the great climactic variation in *Enigma, Nimrod*, as well as in the finale and in the overture, *In the South*. The *Coronation March* also inspires an opulent, red-blooded performance, and the recording throughout is rich and sumptuous.

Enigma Variations; Elegy for Strings (2 versions); Introduction & Allegro for Strings (2 versions); Symphony No. 1 in A flat, Op. 55.

(B) (***) Dutton Double mono/stereo CDSJB 1017 (2). Hallé O, Barbirolli.

Barbirolli recorded both the *Enigma Variations* and the

beautiful *Elegy* (for which he had a special affection) three times, and the *Introduction and Allegro* six times! Here we are offered the third (1947 – mono) and fifth (1956 – stereo) versions of the latter. The interpretations are broadly the same, but they are both distinctly individual performances, the later one obviously gaining from the greater richness of stereo. Yet in the earlier, mono account the recapitulation of the big striding theme in the middle strings already has superb thrust and warmth. The *Enigma* recording is the first (in mono), also from 1947, and it sounds very well in the present transfer, though the later and very exciting Pye stereo version, and the 1962 HMV version (see below) are finer on both performance and sonic grounds. Which is not to say that this strikingly fresh earlier version is not worth having. But what makes the present collection special is the inclusion of the first (1956), originally Pye, stereo account of the *First Symphony*. While the later (1962) HMV version has the advantage of more modern recording and the Philharmonia playing is more polished than the Hallé's, the tempo of the first movement, after the march introduction, is much slower. The Hallé plays at a good sparkling allegro, and the music surges along. In the slow movement too there is greater warmth, with really affectionate playing in the three glorious main themes – the last one reserved for the very end of the movement. The remaining movements have comparable intensity, and in this new Dutton transfer the sound, though not as ripe as the later, EMI version, is much more than acceptable.

(i) Enigma Variations; (ii) Falstaff, Op. 68.

(M) *** EMI (ADD) CDM5 66322-2. (i) Philh. O; (ii) Hallé O; Barbirolli.

(B) **(*) [EMI (ADD) Red Line CDR5 72553]. LPO, Mackerras.

Ripe and expansive, Barbirolli's view of *Falstaff* is colourful and convincing; it also has fine, atmospheric feeling and the interludes are more magical here than in the Boult version. *Enigma*, too, was a work that Barbirolli, himself a cellist, made especially his own, with wonderfully expansive string-playing and much imaginative detail; the recording was made when he was at the very peak of his interpretative powers. The massed strings have lost some of their amplitude, but detail is clearer and the overall balance is convincing, with the Kingsway Hall ambience ensuring a pleasing bloom.

With recorded sound far more reverberant than is common in EMI recordings of Elgar, Mackerras's powerful readings of the composer's own favourite among his orchestral works, together with the most popular, are given a comfortable glow, while losing some inner clarity. The reading of *Falstaff* is superb, among the most electrically compelling put on disc; but *Enigma* is marred by mannered and self-conscious phrasing in the opening statement of the theme and the first variation, as well as in *Nimrod*. *Falstaff* is indexed very generously.

Enigma Variations; Falstaff; Grania and Diarmid: Funeral March.

*** EMI CDC5 55001-2. CBSO, Rattle.

In *Enigma*, Rattle and the CBSO are both powerful and

refined, overwhelming at the close, and they offer a generous and ideal coupling. *Falstaff* is given new transparency in a spacious reading, deeply moving in the hush of the final death scene, with the *Grania and Diarmid* excerpts as a valuable makeweight.

(i) *Enigma Variations;* (ii) *Pomp and Circumstance Marches Nos. 1–5, Op. 39.*

(M) *** (ADD) DG 429 713-2. RPO, Del Mar.

(M) *** EMI (ADD) CDM7 64015-2. (i) LSO; (ii) LPO, Boult.

In the *Enigma Variations* Del Mar comes closer than any other conductor to the responsive rubato style of Elgar himself, using fluctuations to point the emotional message of the work with wonderful power and spontaneity. The RPO plays superbly, both here and in the *Pomp and Circumstance Marches*, given Proms-style flair and urgency – although some might feel that the fast speeds miss some of the *nobilmente*. The reverberant sound here adds something of an aggressive edge to the music-making.

Boult's *Enigma* (also available coupled with Holst's *Planets* – see above) is self-recommending. Boult's approach to the *Pomp and Circumstance Marches* is brisk and direct, with an almost no-nonsense manner in places. There is not a hint of vulgarity and the freshness is most attractive, though it is a pity he omits the repeats in the Dvořák-like No. 2. The brightened sound brings a degree of abrasiveness to the brass.

(i) *Enigma Variations;* (ii) *Pomp and Circumstance Marches Nos. 1–5;* (iii) *Serenade for Strings.*

(B) *** Decca (ADD) 433 629-2. (i) LAPO, Mehta; (ii) LSO, Bliss; (iii) ASMF, Marriner.

If there are no special revelations from Mehta, the transition from the nobly conceived and spacious climax of *Nimrod* to a delightfully graceful *Dorabella* is particularly felicitous, and this is one of his very finest records. Marriner's elegantly played yet highly sensitive account of the *String Serenade* makes a fine bonus, and Sir Arthur Bliss's rumbustiously vigorous accounts of the *Pomp and Circumstance Marches* are worth anyone's money.

(i) *Enigma Variations; Pomp and Circumstance Marches Nos. 1 & 4; Salut d'amour, Op. 12;* (ii) *Serenade for Strings in E min., Op. 20.*

(BB) *** Naxos 8.554161. (i) Czecho-Slovak RSO; (ii) Capella Istropolitana; Leaper.

Though Leaper's slow account of the 'Enigma' theme makes an unpromising start, his reading of the *Variations* is most beautiful, with ripely resonant string-playing and with warmly expressive rubato in *Nimrod* suggesting that the Slovak players had been won over to Elgar by Leaper's advocacy. Most refined of all is the Capella Istropolitana's account of the *Serenade*, with the slow movement specially beautiful, finely shaded. An excellent compilation of Elgar's most popular orchestral pieces, brilliantly recorded.

Falstaff, Op. 68; Elegy, Op. 58; The Sanguine Fan (ballet), Op. 81.

(BB) *** Naxos 8553879. Northern Philh., Lloyd-Jones.

Rich, full Naxos sound with high dynamic contrasts adds satisfying weight to David Lloyd-Jones's taut and dramatic account of Elgar's elaborate Shakespearean portrait. Speeds are often on the fast side, but idiomatically so, with a natural feeling for Elgarian rubato and sprung rhythms. Both in *Falstaff* and in *The Sanguine Fan*, Lloyd-Jones draws fragmented structures warmly and persuasively together so that the late ballet-score emerges strongly, not just a trivial, occasional piece. The beautiful *Elegy* is most tenderly done, modest in length but no miniature. An outstanding bargain, competing with all premium-price rivals.

Falstaff, Op. 68; Imperial March, Op. 32; (i) *Sea Pictures, Op. 37.*

(B) *** Sony (ADD) SBK 63020. LPO, Barenboim; (i) with Minton.

Barenboim's habit of moulding the music of Elgar in flexible tempi, of underlining romantic expressiveness, has never been as convincing on record as here in *Falstaff*. Yvonne Minton uses her rich tone sensitively in Elgar's orchestral song-cycle, and she responds to this music richly and ardently. Barenboim is a persuasive Elgarian, and this makes a most welcome bargain reissue, with his ripe account of the *Imperial March* thrown in for good measure. The CD transfers are excellent, with the warmly atmospheric sound in the *Sea Pictures* particularly appealing.

Introduction & Allegro for Strings.

*** Ara. Z 6723. San Francisco Ballet O, Lark Qt., Jean-Louis Le Roux – HANDEL: *Concerto grosso in B flat, Op. 6/7;* SCHOENBERG: *Concerto for String Quartet & Orchestra after Handel's Concerto grosso, Op. 6/7;* SPOHR: *Concerto for String Quartet & Orchestra.* ***

(M) **(*) EMI CDM5 66761-2. City of L. Sinfonia, Hickox – VAUGHAN WILLIAMS: *Tallis Fantasia* **(*); WALTON: *Sonata for Strings.* ***

A passionately committed performance from the excellent San Francisco string-players, with a warmly tender contribution from the solo group. They are not entirely idiomatic – they do not quite let rip in the striding unison string-tune in the way that British players would – but their slower tempo remains convincing when the underlying fervour is in no doubt. The final climax is superb. Splendidly vivid recording.

Hickox's account of the *Introduction and Allegro* is slightly disappointing. The athleticism is exhilarating but lacks ripeness, especially in the great surging tune on unison strings, where the playing conveys forceful brilliance rather than ripeness of feeling (like Barbirolli). The recording, made in St Augustine's Church, Kilburn, is brightly lit by the close microphone placing but does not lack weight.

Introduction & Allegro for Strings, Op. 47; Serenade for Strings in E min., Op. 20.

(BB) *** Virgin Classics 2 x 1 VBD5 61763-2 (2). LCO, Warren-Green – DVORAK: *Serenade for Strings;* SUK: *Serenade;* TCHAIKOVSKY: *Serenade;* VAUGHAN WILLIAMS: *Greensleeves Fantasia, etc.* ***

(i–ii) *Introduction & Allegro for Strings;* (i) *Serenade for Strings;* (iii) *Elegy, Op. 58; Sospiri, Op. 70.*

⚫ (M) *** EMI CDM5 67240-2 [567264]. (i) Sinfonia of L.; (ii) Allegri Qt; (iii) New Philh. O; Barbirolli – VAUGHAN WILLIAMS: *Greensleeves & Tallis Fantasias.* *** ⚫

Barbirolli's famous record of English string music (the *Elegy* and *Sospiri* were added later) might be considered the finest of all his records and it remained in the catalogue at full price for over three-and-a-half decades. Now not only does it cost less, it rightly takes its place as one of EMI's 'Great Recordings of the Century', with the current remastering of an originally magnificent recording losing nothing, combining bite and excellent inner definition with the fullest sonority.

Christopher Warren-Green, leading his London Chamber Orchestra, directs the *Introduction and Allegro* with tremendous ardour. The whole work moves forward in a single sweep and the sense of a live performance, tingling with electricity and immediacy, is thrillingly tangible. It is very difficult to believe that the group contains only 17 players (6–5–2–3–1), with the resonant but never clouding acoustics of All Saints' Church, Petersham, helping to create an engulfingly rich body of tone. Appropriately, the *Serenade* is a more relaxed reading, yet it has plenty of affectionate warmth, with the beauty of the *Larghetto* expressively rich but not overstated. This now comes as part of one of the most desirable of Virgin's super-bargain doubles.

King Arthur: Suite; (i) *The Starlight Express* (suite), *Op. 78.*

(M) **(*) Chan. 6582. (i) Glover, Lawrenson; Bournemouth Sinf., Hurst.

The *King Arthur Suite* is full of surging, enjoyable ideas and makes an interesting novelty on record. *The Starlight Express Suite* is taken from music Elgar wrote for a children's play, with a song or two included. Though the singers here are not ideal interpreters, the enthusiasm of Hurst and the Sinfonietta is conveyed well, particularly in the *King Arthur Suite.* The recording is atmospheric if rather over-reverberant, but the added firmness of the CD and its refinement of detail almost make this an extra asset in providing a most agreeable ambience for Elgar's music.

Nursery Suite; Wand of Youth Suites Nos. 1 and 2, Op. 1a & b.

*** Chan. 8318. Ulster O, Thomson.

The playing in Ulster is attractively spirited; in the gentle pieces (the *Sun Dance, Fairy Pipers* and *Slumber Dance*), which show the composer at his most magically evocative, the music-making engagingly combines refinement and warmth. The *Nursery Suite* is strikingly well characterized, and with first-class digital sound this is highly recommendable.

Romance for Cello & Orchestra, Op. 62.

(M) *** EMI CDM7 64726-2. Lloyd Webber, LSO, Mackerras – SULLIVAN: *Cello Concerto,* etc. ***

Julian Lloyd Webber has rescued the composer's own ver-sion of the *Romance* for cello (originally for bassoon) and it provides a delightful makeweight for the Sullivan reissue, beautifully played and warmly recorded.

Symphonies Nos. 1–2; In the South (Alassio), Op. 50; Pomp and Circumstance Marches, Op. 39, Nos. 1 in D; 3 in C min.; 4 in G.

(B) **(*) Teldec Ultima 0630 18951-2 (2). BBC SO, A. Davis.

Symphonies Nos. 1–2; Overtures: Cockaigne; In the South.

(B) *** Double Decca (ADD) 443 856-2 (2). LPO, Solti.

Symphonies Nos. 1–2; Cockaigne Overture; Pomp and Circumstance Marches Nos. 1–5.

(B) **(*) Ph. Duo 454 250-2 (2). RPO or LSO, Previn.

Symphonies Nos. 1–2; Pomp and Circumstance March No. 5.

(B) **(*) EMI (ADD) double forte CZS5 69761-2 (2). Philh. O, Haitink.

In the *First Symphony* Solti's thrusting manner will give the traditional Elgarian the occasional jolt, but his clearing away of the cobwebs stems from the composer's own 78-r.p.m. recording, here with very much the same rich, committed qualities that mark out the Elgar performance. Again modelled closely on the composer's own surprisingly clipped and urgent reading, the *Second Symphony* benefits from virtuoso playing from the LPO and full, well-balanced sound. Fast tempi bring searing concentration, yet the *nobilmente* element is not missed and the account of the finale presents a true climax. The effect is magnificent. The CD transfers bring out the fullness satisfyingly as well as the brilliance of the excellent (1970s) sound, and this applies also to the sharply dramatic account of *Cockaigne. In the South,* recorded in 1979, is less successful, over-tense if still exciting. Here Solti is not helped by Decca recording in which the brilliance is not quite matched by weight or body (an essential in Elgar).

Previn's view of the opening movement of the *First Symphony* is spacious, with moulding of phrase and lifting of rhythm beautifully judged, to bring natural flexibility within a strongly controlled structure, steadier than usual in basic tempo. The syncopations of the Scherzo/march theme have an almost jazzy swagger, and the reading is crowned by a flowing account of the finale. There Previn confirms his ability to point Elgarian climaxes with the necessary heart-tug. The opening movement of the *Second* has a similar Elgarian ebb and flow, but here one senses an absence of thrust, and he does not display as tight a grip on the structure as Solti, although the *Larghetto* is deeply felt and is played eloquently by the LSO. *Cockaigne* is in a similar mould, though attractively affectionate and spirited. The five *Pomp and Circumstance Marches* are not quite as flamboyant as some versions but are beautifully sprung. The recordings were made at Abbey Road and the Philips sound certainly does not lack opulence.

With consistently slow tempi, Haitink's is a spacious reading of No. 1. The result is hardly idiomatic but, with superb playing from the Philharmonia under Haitink's concentrated direction, it is profound and moving, elegaically glowing with genuine Elgarian warmth. The *Second Sym-*

phony is more controversial, and here the CD transfer remains just a little disappointing, with the sound of the strings not as expansively opulent as expected. The opening movement in particular is very volatile, and throughout there are many wayward touches that fail to convince entirely on repeated hearing. Elgarians will miss some of the usual spring in the 12/8 compound time of the first movement. But for many the performance will be a revelation in its strength and depth of feeling.

With sound of demonstration quality, Andrew Davis conducts a broad, rather plain reading of the *First Symphony* which is yet highly idiomatic and is beautifully played. Sadly, the performance falls short at the very end, where the brassy coda fails to blaze as it should. However, Davis provides a strong and passionate account of the *Second*. It is an impetuous performance, but convincingly so, and the slow movement has great eloquence. The finale has splendid impetus, and one can only lament that Davis did not insist on the organ reinforcement at the climax. But he offers an exuberant *In the South* as a bonus. The recording is first class, with fine range and amplitude.

Symphony No. 1 in A flat; Chanson de matin; Chanson de nuit; Serenade for Strings, Op. 20.

(M) *** EMI (ADD) CDM7 64013-2. LPO, Boult.

(i) *Symphony No. 1 in A flat;* (ii) *Cockaigne Overture.*

(M) **(*) EMI (ADD) CDM7 64511-2. Philh. O, Barbirolli.
(B) *** Ph. (ADD) 416 612-2. RPO or LSO, Previn.

Symphony No. 1 in A flat; Imperial March, Op. 32.

(BB) *** Naxos 8.550634. BBC PO, Hurst.

On the bargain Naxos label comes a warmly sympathetic version of the *Symphony No. 1* from the BBC Philharmonic under George Hurst. Masterly with Elgarian rubato, he refreshingly chooses speeds faster than have become the norm, closer to those of Elgar himself. No one will be disappointed with Hurst's powerful reading, well coupled with the *Imperial March*.

Boult clearly presents the *First Symphony* as a counterpart to the *Second*, with hints of reflective nostalgia amid the triumph. His EMI disc contains a radiantly beautiful performance, with no extreme tempi, richly spaced in the first movement, invigorating in the syncopated march rhythms of the Scherzo, and similarly bouncing in the Brahmsian rhythms of the finale.

Previn's account is also available coupled to No. 2 on a Duo (see above) but as that is a marginally successful reading, many collectors may prefer to have the *A flat Symphony* with this bargain *Cockaigne* coupling.

In Barbirolli's later (1962) Philharmonia account on EMI there is a hint of heaviness where, after the march introduction, the music should surge along. The slow movement, too, is very slow: it is done more affectionately in the earlier, Pye version, which we hope will reappear in due course. The present transfer of a Kingsway Hall recording has lost some of the fullness in the violins; otherwise, it sounds very well. The *Cockaigne Overture* is one of Barbirolli's most notable Elgar recordings.

Symphony No. 2 in E flat, Op. 63.

(B) *** CfP (ADD) CD-CFP 4544. LPO, Handley.
(BB) *** Naxos 8.550635. BBC PO, Downes.

Symphony No. 2; Cockaigne Overture, Op. 40.

(M) *** EMI (ADD) CDM7 64014-2. LPO, Boult.

Symphony No. 2; The Crown of India (suite), *Op. 66.*

(M) *** Chan. (ADD) 6523. RSNO, Gibson.

(i) *Symphony No. 2;* (ii) *Elegy, Op. 58; Sospiri, Op. 70.*

(M) **(*) EMI (ADD) CDM7 64724-2. (i) Hallé O; (ii) New Philh. O; Barbirolli.

Handley's remains the most satisfying modern version of a work which has latterly been much recorded. What Handley conveys superbly is the sense of Elgarian ebb and flow, building climaxes like a master and drawing excellent, spontaneous-sounding playing from an orchestra which, more than any other, has specialized in performing this symphony. The sound is warmly atmospheric and vividly conveys the added organ part in the bass, just at the climax of the finale, which Elgar himself suggested 'if available': a tummy-wobbling effect. However, this has been withdrawn just as we go to press.

For his fifth recording of the *Second Symphony* Sir Adrian Boult, incomparable Elgarian, drew from the LPO the most richly satisfying performance of all. Over the years Sir Adrian's view of the glorious nobility of the first movement had mellowed a degree, but the pointing of climaxes is unrivalled. With Boult more than anyone else the architecture is clearly and strongly established, with tempo changes less exaggerated than usual. This is a version to convert new listeners to a love of Elgar although, even more than in the *First Symphony*, the ear notices a loss of opulence compared with the original LP. This is also very striking in *Cockaigne*, which opens the disc.

Downes uses an expansive speed in the first movement to give the writing its full emotional thrust, and the hushed tension of the slow movements leads up to towering climaxes, well controlled. The Scherzo is brilliant, delicate and witty, and the finale with its sequential writing is perfectly paced. The valedictory feeling at the close is very moving. Indeed, the only reservation is that the sound, though warm and refined, is a degree too distanced, so that the noble opening of the work does not have its full impact.

Gibson's recording shows his partnership with the RSNO at its peak, and this performance captures all the opulent nostalgia of Elgar's masterly score. The reading of the first movement is more relaxed in its grip than Handley's, but its spaciousness is appealing and, both here and in the beautifully sustained *Larghetto*, the richly resonant acoustics of Glasgow City Hall bring out the full panoply of Elgarian sound. The finale has splendid *nobilmente*. In the *Crown of India* suite Gibson is consistently imaginative in his attention to detail, and the playing of the Scottish orchestra is again warmly responsive.

Barbirolli's 1964 Kingsway Hall recording shows its age a little in the massed violins (especially by comparison with the richer tapestry for the two short string-pieces, beautifully played, which were recorded two years later). Barbirolli's ardour is never in doubt – witness the exuberant horn-playing in the first movement and the passion of the finale – but his interpretation is a very personal one, deeply felt but with the pace of the music often excessively varied, sometimes coarsening effects which Elgar's score specifies very precisely and weakening the structure.

Symphony No. 3 (from the composer's sketches, realized by Anthony Payne).

(BB) *** Naxos 8.554719. Bournemouth SO, Daniel.

Symphony No. 3: sketches and commentary by Payne.

(B) *** NMC NMCD 052. Gibbs, Norris, BBC SO, A. Davis.

Symphony No. 3 (completed from sketches, elaborated by Payne).

*** NMC NMCD 053. BBC SO, A. Davis.

As the original NMC recording of Anthony Payne's realization of Elgar's fragmentary sketches became a bestseller, it is not surprising that Naxos should want to issue a rival version at super-budget price. In every way this performance by the Bournemouth orchestra under Paul Daniel matches the earlier one from Andrew Davis. If on NMC the BBC Symphony sounds richer and more sumptuous, relating the work to earlier Elgar, the leaner sound of the Bournemouth orchestra brings out the originality even more, with textures clear and transparent. The passages such as the opening exposition section, which Elgar completed himself, again make it clear that he was pointing forward, developing his style. Daniel is particularly successful too in drawing the threads together in the finale, the movement which was the most problematic for Payne. The slow epilogue is even more moving here than in the earlier performance, ending in mystery on a question mark. First-rate sound.

Andrew Davis also gives an inspired performance and the playing of the BBC Symphony Orchestra is thoroughly committed. The symphony is very well recorded.

Anthony Payne's illustrated talk on the sketches gives precise details of his thinking and procedures. He discusses the exact state in which Elgar left the sketches, many of which were in full score, and what problems any conjectural completion would encounter, confirming that, whatever extra inspiration Elgar himself would have added to a finished score, this remains a wonderful bonus to our knowledge of the composer. The majority of the sketches were written out for violin and keyboard, and (on NMCD 052) Robert Gibbs plays the very instrument on which Elgar himself ran through the fragments with Reed. This bargain-price CD makes a splendid supplement to the recording of the complete work.

CHAMBER AND INSTRUMENTAL MUSIC

Piano Quintet in A min., Op. 84; Harmony Music No. 4: The Farmyard. Sospiri, Op. 70.

(B) **(*) EMI CZS5 73992-2 (2). Margalit, LSO (members) – DELIUS: *Violin Sonatas, etc.* ***

Piano Quintet in A min., Op. 84; String Quartet in E min., Op. 83.

(N) *** Chan. 9894. Sorrel Qt, with (i) Brown.
(BB) *** Naxos 8.553737. Maggini Qt, (i) with Donohoe.
(BB) *** Discover DICD 920485. Aura Ens., (i) with Fink.

Piano Quintet; Violin Sonata in E min., Op. 82.

*** Hyp. CDA 66645. Nash Ens. (members).

The Sorrel Quartet, perfectly matched by Ian Brown in the *Piano Quintet*, give exceptionally searching readings of these two late chamber works of Elgar. These are dedicated performances which understandingly bring out the contrast between the expansive *Quintet*, bold in its rhetoric, and the more intimate *Quartet*, with its terse, economical structure. The breadth of expression, using the widest dynamic range down to the most delicate *pianissimos*, intensifies the impact of each performance, magnetic and concentrated as if recorded live.

It is a big-boned reading of the *Quintet*, presenting the rhetoric with panache but without inflation, setting passionate climaxes against the most intimate expression in rapt concentration. The tenderness as well as the richness of the central *Adagio* are gloriously brought out, and so is the exuberant energy of the finale. In the *Quartet* the Sorrels find mystery and tenderness both in the crisply compact first movement and the haunting central *Piacevole*, leading on to a thrusting, sharply accented account of the finale.

The Naxos and Discover versions appeared simultaneously, both at super-bargain price, both very recommendable. The Naxos issue with the young British Maggini Quartet, joined by Peter Donohoe, promptly won an important record prize in France with stylish, nicely pointed, slightly understated readings. Yet it is the Aura Ensemble of Switzerland which, perhaps surprisingly, offers even more red-blooded, urgently expressive readings, helped by rich, forward sound. One hopes it is a sign that rare Elgar is at last communicating outside Britain.

With the violinist, Marcia Crayford, and the pianist, Ian Brown, both as the duo in the *Sonata* and as the key players in the *Quintet*, these performances on Hyperion are more volatile than usual; but it is the slow movements above all that mark these performances as exceptional. The central *Adagio* of the *Quintet*, far slower than usual, then brings the most dedicated playing of all, making this not just a lyrical outpouring but an inner meditation. Warm, immediate recording.

The EMI reissue is another instance in which the apparently logical pairing of two different sets of performances into a two-disc set brings uneven results. Both the pianist, Israela Margalit, and the cellist, Moray Welsh, are involved in the Delius couplings, and the latter makes an eloquent contribution here to the *Piano Quintet*'s slow movement. But overall, the performance, while musically sensitive, lacks the panache and sense of vigorous involvement generated by the competing version from Ian Brown and the Nash Ensemble, or indeed the Naxos and Discover super-bargain alternatives. Both the touching *Sospiri* and the excerpt from Elgar's *Harmony Music* for wind come off very successfully.

String Quartet in E min., Op. 83.

(N) *** Regis RRC 1015. Britten Qt – WALTON: *Quartet.* ***
*** ASV CDDCA 526. Brodsky Qt – DELIUS: *Quartet.* ***

**(*) Hyp. CDA 66718. Coull Qt – BRIDGE: *3 Idylls*;
  WALTON: *Quartet*. ***

There is a poignancy in this late work which the beautifully
matched members of the Britten Quartet capture to perfection. Not only do they bring out the emotional intensity,
they play with a refinement and sharpness of focus that
give superb point to the outer movements. With more
portamento than one would normally expect today, the result
is totally in style. Warmly expressive as the Gabrieli Quartet
are in the Chandos coupling of the same works, the Brittens
are even more searching.

The young players of the Brodsky Quartet take a weightier
view than usual of the central, interlude-like slow movement, but they amply justify it. The power of the outer
movements, too, gives the lie to the idea of this as a lesser
piece than Elgar's other chamber works. First-rate recording.

Though in the Elgar the Coulls sound almost too comfortable, less successful at conveying the volatile mood-changes,
their relaxed warmth is still very persuasive; and the Walton
performance, with the melancholy of the slow movement
intensified, is very fine. Excellent sound.

Violin Sonata in E min., Op. 82.

(N) *** Globe Musical Network GMN CO113. Little, Roscoe –
  BAX: *Violin Sonata No. 2*. ***
(N) *** Nim. NI 5666. Hope, Mulligan – FINZI: *Elegy*;
  WALTON: *Violin Sonata*. ***
(N) *** Teldec 4509 96300-2. Vengerov, Chachamov –
  DVORAK: *Violin Concerto*. ***
(BB) *** ASV (ADD) CDQS 6191. McAslan, Blakely –
  WALTON: *Violin Sonata*. ***
(M) **(*) EMI (ADD) CDM5 66122-2. Y. and H. Menuhin –
  VAUGHAN WILLIAMS: *Sonata* **(*); WALTON:
  ***Sonata*. (**)**

Violin Sonata; Canto popolare; La Capricieuse, Op. 17;
Chanson de matin, Op. 15/2; Chanson de nuit, Op. 15/1;
Mot d'amour, Op. 13/1; Offertoire, Op. 11 (arr. Schneider);
Salut d'amour, Op. 12; Sospiri, Op. 70; Sursum corda,
Op. 11.

⚙ ***** Chan. 9624. Mordkovitch, Milford.**

Violin Sonata; Canto popolare; Chanson de matin;
Chanson de nuit; Mot d'amour; Salut d'amour; Sospiri; 6
Easy pieces in the first position.

*** Chan. 8380. Kennedy, Pettinger.

Lydia Mordkovitch here transforms the elusive Elgar *Violin
Sonata*. In rapt and concentrated playing she gives it new
mystery, with the subtlest pointing and shading down to
whispered pianissimos. The shorter works include not only
popular pieces like *Salut d'amour*, *Chanson de matin* and
Sospiri, but rarities like a version of *Sursum corda* never
previously recorded and a little salon piece of 1893 which
Elgar inexplicably published under the pseudonym, Gustav
Francke. The young Nigel Kennedy has covered most of the
same works, but less subtly than Mordkovitch.

Tasmin Little gives a warmly romantic, freely expressive
reading of the Elgar *Violin Sonata*, presenting it as a big-scale
virtuoso work, where so often it has been underplayed. She
allows herself fair freedom over tempo, so that the second

subject is exceptionally broad, yet convincingly so, when as
ever she conveys spontaneity in every phrase. Equally, the
fantasy of the slow movement is brought out, even while she
prefers a rich rather than an intimate tonal palette. Her
volatility in the finale leads up to a magnificent conclusion.
Very well recorded, with the Bax *Sonata No. 2* an excellent
coupling, dating as it does from exactly the same period as
the Elgar.

The coupling of the Elgar and Walton *Violin Sonatas* on
Nimbus is an apt one, well supplemented by the Finzi.
The Elgar brings a performance of high contrasts both in
dynamic range – with Hope using daringly extreme pianissimos – and in flexibility of tempo. So in the first movement
the opening at an urgent speed gives way to a very broad
reading of the second subject, hushed and introspective.
Hope then treats the enigmatic slow movement as more
than an interlude, bringing out gravity through his dark
violin tone. In the finale, too, Hope conveys an improvisational quality, again using the widest dynamic range, finely
matched by Simon Mulligan – like Hope, a Menuhin protégé. Warm, atmospheric recording, less reverberant than
many from this source.

The Elgar *Violin Sonata* provides an unusual but inspired
coupling for the Dvořák concerto, with the charismatic
Vengerov giving a performance at once passionate and on a
big scale. He also brings out the thoughtful poetry of the
piece, with a vein of fantasy in the elusive slow movement.
It is good to find a leading Russian virtuoso so understanding
in an English work long under-appreciated. One can hardly
wait to hear Vengerov in the Elgar *Violin Concerto*. Excellent
sound.

At the start of the *Sonata*, Kennedy establishes a concerto-
like scale, which he then reinforces in a fiery, volatile reading
of the first movement, rich and biting in its bravura. The
elusive slow movement, *Romance*, is sharply rhythmic in its
weird Spanishry, while in the finale Kennedy colours the
tone seductively. As a coupling, Kennedy too has a delightful
collection of shorter pieces, not just *Salut d'amour* and
Chanson de matin but other rare chips from the master's
bench. Kennedy is matched beautifully throughout the recital by his understanding piano partner, Peter Pettinger,
and the recording is excellent.

Though Lorraine McAslan's performance cannot quite
match the virtuoso command and body of tone of Kennedy
on Chandos, hers is an impressive and warm-hearted version, full of natural imagination and bringing some rapt
pianissimo playing in the outer movements. She is helped
by the sympathetic partnership of John Blakely, who is
attractively incisive. The digital recording is faithful but
rather forward, which gives the violin-tone less bloom than
it might have. But this coupling with Walton is more than
worth its modest cost.

The Menuhins present a large-scale view of this sonata.
Unfortunately, though slow speeds bring their moments of
insight and revelation at the hands of a Menuhin, the result
overall is too heavy, and it is also marred by imperfect
intonation. The recording is first rate.

Music for wind

Adagio cantabile (Mrs Winslow's Soothing Syrup); Andante con variazione (Evesham Andante); 5 Intermezzos; Harmony Music No. 1.

(M) *** Chan. (ADD) 6553. Athena Ens.

4 Dances; Harmony Music Nos. 2–4; 6 Promenades.

(M) *** Chan. (ADD) 6554. Athena Ens.

As a budding musician, playing not only the violin but also the bassoon, Elgar wrote a quantity of brief, lightweight pieces in a traditional style for himself and four other wind-players to perform. He called it 'Shed Music'; though there are few real signs of the Elgar style to come, the energy and inventiveness are very winning, particularly when (as here) the pieces – often with comic names – are treated to bright and lively performances. Excellent recording, with the CD transfers sounding as fresh as new paint.

PIANO MUSIC
Piano duet

Serenade in E min. (composer's version for 2 pianos).

*** Olympia OCD 683. Goldstone and Clement (with BURY: *Prelude and Fugue in E flat* ***) – HOLST: *The Planets* (original version), etc.; BAINTON: *Miniature Suite.* ***

As with Holst's *Planets*, it is a surprise to find just how well this sounds on two pianos (especially the *Larghetto*) except that it is played so sensitively by this excellent duo, who are most faithfully recorded.

Solo piano music

Adieu; Concert Allegro, Op. 46; Dream Children, Op. 43; Enigma Variations, Op. 36 (arr. Elgar); Griffinesque; In Smyrna; Presto; Salut d'amour; Serenade; Skizze; Sonatina.

*** ASV CDDCA 1065. Garzón.

Adieu; Carissima; Chantant; Concert Allegro; Dream Children; Griffinesque; In Smyrna; May Song; Minuet; Pastorale; Presto; Rosemary; Serenade; Skizze; Sonatina.

**(*) Chan. 8438. Pettinger.

The main work on ASV is Elgar's own transcription of the *Enigma Variations*, which preceded the orchestral version by three months. It is marvellously played here but was, of course, made before the days when one could get to know the piece through the gramophone. However, if you are going to have this in its keyboard form, it could hardly be better played. The Spanish pianist María Garzón has sensitivity and fervour, and she plays it and the other Elgar pieces, such as the *Concert Allegro*, the *Sonatina* and *In Smyrna* (which Elgar composed after a Mediterranean cruise as a guest of the Royal Navy), as if she had been born and bred in Worcester rather than Madrid.

The Chandos record includes nearly all of Elgar's piano music. This has not established itself in the piano repertoire but, as Peter Pettinger shows, there are interesting things in

this byway of English music (such as the *Skizze* and *In Smyrna*). We get both the 1889 version of the *Sonatina* and its much later revision. Committed playing from this accomplished artist, and a pleasing recording too, with fine presence on CD.

ORGAN MUSIC

Organ Sonata No. 1 in G, Op. 28.

*** Priory PRDC 401. Scott (organ of St Paul's Cathedral) (with HARRIS: *Sonata* ***) – BAIRSTOW: *Organ Sonata.* ***

(BB) **(*) ASV (ADD) CDQS 6160. Bate (Royal Albert Hall organ) – with Recital: 'British Organ Music'. **(*)

.(i) *Organ Sonata No. 1 in G;* (ii) *Vesper Voluntaries, Op. 14: Introduction; Andante.*

(M) *** EMI CDM5 65594-2. (i) Sumsion (organ of Gloucester Cathedral); (ii) Robinson (organ of Worcester Cathedral) – *Choral music.* **(*)

Elgar's *Organ Sonata* is a ripely expansive piece, a richly inspired work, more of a symphony than a sonata. John Scott gives an excitingly spontaneous performance and the St Paul's Cathedral organ seems an ideal choice, although some of the *pianissimo* passages become rather recessed. The recording has plenty of spectacle and the widest dynamic range.

Herbert Sumsion's recording of the *Organ Sonata* on the organ at Gloucester makes a splendidly expansive sound, but the gentler pages, glowingly registered, are not as recessed as in some other versions. Sumsion opens grandly and rises to the work's closing climax. His performance is sympathetically idiomatic, though it could perhaps be more flamboyantly extrovert. He is very well recorded, as is Christopher Robinson in the relatively slight *Voluntaries*, used to make an interlude within the concert of choral music to which the *Sonata* acts as a pendant.

Jennifer Bate plays with all the necessary flair, with her rubato only occasionally sounding unidiomatic, bringing out the dramatic contrasts of dynamic encouraged by the vast Royal Albert Hall organ in its massive setting – emphasized by its facility for causing the sound-image to recede in quieter passages. The analogue recording brings good detail, even if the very wide dynamic range means that Bate's *piano* registers as *pianissimo* because of the distancing.

VOCAL AND CHORAL MUSIC

Choral music: *Angelus, Op. 56/1; Ave Maria, Op. 2/2; Ave maris stella, Op. 2/3; Ave verum, Op. 2/1; Give unto the Lord, Op. 74; O hearken thou, Op. 64; Te Deum and Benedictus, Op. 34.*

(M) **(*) EMI (ADD) CDM5 65594-2. Worcester Cathedral Ch., Robinson; Bramma – *Organ Sonata No. 1*, etc. ***

Elgar was one of a handful of Roman Catholics among our major English composers (Byrd was another). Like Byrd, he wrote much of his early sacred music within a Protestant tradition. *O hearken thou* is a coronation anthem, written in the composer's official capacity for the coronation of George

V. The genuinely Catholic works were written during Elgar's apprenticeship at St George's Church, Worcester. Both the *Ave verum* and the *Ave Maria* have a gentle, romantic colouring; but most memorable is the *Angelus*, with its repeated figure like an echoing bell. There is much in this programme to show an emerging musical individuality. Performances are sympathetic and alive, and the cathedral ambience is highly suitable for the music. The 1969 recording has been transferred admirably to CD. The coupled organ music increases the interest of this generously full reissue (76 minutes).

Angelus, Op. 56/1; Ave Maria; Ave maris stella; Ave verum corpus, Op. 2; Ecce sacerdos magnus; Fear not, O land; Give unto the Lord, Op. 74; Great is the Lord, Op. 67; I sing the birth; Lo! Christ the Lord is born; O hearken thou, Op. 64; O salutaris hostia Nos. 1–3.

*** Hyp. CDA 66313. Worcester Cathedral Ch., Hunt; Partington.

Though one misses the impact of a big choir in the *Coronation Anthem, O hearken thou*, and in the grand setting of Psalm 48, *Great is the Lord*, the refinement of Donald Hunt's singers, their freshness and bloom as recorded against a helpful acoustic, are ample compensation, particularly when the feeling for Elgarian phrasing and rubato is unerring. Vividly atmospheric recording, which still allows full detail to emerge.

Songs: *After; Arabian Serenade; Is she not passing fair; Like to the damask rose; Oh, soft was the song; Pleading; Poet's life; Queen Mary's song; Rondel; Shepherd's song; Song of autumn; Song of flight; Through the long days; Twilight; Was it some golden star?.*

**(*) Chan. 8539. Luxon, Willison – DELIUS: *Songs.* **(*)

Benjamin Luxon seemingly cannot avoid the roughness of production that has marred some of his later recordings, but he gives charming freshness to this delightful selection. Brilliant and sensitive accompaniment, and a very fine recording-balance.

The Apostles, Op. 49.

*** Chan. 8875/6. Hargan, Hodgson, Rendall, Roberts, Terfel, Lloyd, L. Symphony Ch., LSO, Hickox.

(M) *** EMI (ADD) CMS7 64206-2 (2). Armstrong, Watts, Tear, Luxon, Grant, Carol Case, Downe House School Ch., LPO Ch., LPO, Boult.

Where Boult's reading has four-square nobility, Hickox is far more flexible in his expressiveness, drawing singing from his chorus that far outshines that on the earlier reading. Most of his soloists are preferable too, for example Stephen Roberts as a light-toned Jesus and Robert Lloyd characterful as Judas. Only the tenor, David Rendall, falls short, with vibrato exaggerated by the microphone. The recording, made in St Jude's, Hampstead, is among Chandos's finest, both warm and incandescent, with plenty of detail.

Boult's performance gives the closing scene great power and a wonderful sense of apotheosis, with the spacious sound-balance rising to the occasion. Generally fine singing – notably from Sheila Armstrong and Helen Watts – and a

1973/4 Kingsway Hall recording as rich and faithful as anyone could wish for. The powerfully lyrical *Meditation* from *The Light of Life* makes a suitable postlude without producing an anticlimax, again showing Boult at his most inspirational.

The Banner of St George, Op. 33; (i) Great is the Lord (Psalm 48), Op. 67; Te Deum and Benedictus, Op. 34.

(M) *** EMI CDM5 65108-2. L. Symphony Ch., N. Sinfonia, Hickox; (i) with Roberts.

In telling the story of St George slaying the dragon and saving the Lady Sylene, Elgar is at his most colourful, with the battle sequence leading to beautifully tender farewell music (bringing one of Elgar's most yearningly memorable melodies) and a final rousing chorus. The three motets, written at the same period, bring 'Pomp and Circumstance' into church and, like the cantata, stir the blood in Hickox's strong, unapologetic performances, richly recorded.

(i) *The Black Knight* (symphony for chorus and orchestra); Part-songs: *Fly singing bird; The snow; Spanish serenade.* (ii) *Scenes from the Saga of King Olaf, Op. 30.*

(M) *** EMI CMS5 65104-2 (2). (i) RLPO Ch. & O, Groves; (ii) Cahill, Langridge, Rayner Cook, LPO Ch., LPO, Handley.

The Black Knight, Op. 3; Scenes from the Bavarian Highlands, Op. 27.

✪ *** Chan. 9436. L. Symphony Ch., LSO, Hickox.

The cantata *The Black Knight* is based on a similar story to that of Mahler's early cantata, *Das klagende Lied*, but Elgar's inspiration is more open and less tortured, with the orchestration already showing the mastery which was to bloom in *Enigma*. Hickox, helped by exceptionally rich and full recording, with vivid presence, consistently brings out the dramatic tensions of the piece as well as the refinement and beauty of the poetic sequences, to make the previous recording under Sir Charles Groves sound too easy-going, enjoyable though it is. The part-songs inspired by the composer's visit to Bavaria then add even more exhilaration, with the vigour and joy of the outer movements – better known in Elgar's orchestral versions – brought out winningly, and with the London Symphony Chorus at its freshest and most incisive. A disc to win new admirers for two seriously neglected works.

Charles Groves conducts a strong, fresh performance of *The Black Knight*, and the happiness and confidence of the writing are what come over with winning freshness, even though Elgarians must inevitably miss the deeper, darker and more melancholy overtones. The emotional thrust in Handley's reading confirms *King Olaf* as the very finest of the big works Elgar wrote before the *Enigma Variations* in 1899. In its big choruses its style keeps anticipating the later masterpieces, equally reflecting the influence of Wagner's *Parsifal*, but it grows even richer towards the end, with the exciting, dramatic chorus, *The Death of Olaf*, followed by an epilogue that transcends everything, building to a heart-tugging climax on the return of the 'Heroic Beauty' theme. Though strained at times by the high writing, Philip Langridge makes a fine, intelligent Olaf, Teresa Cahill sings with ravishing silver purity and Brian Rayner Cook brings out words with fine clarity; but it is the incandescent singing of the London Philharmonic Chorus that sets the seal on this superb set, ripely recorded, one of the finest in EMI's long Elgar history.

(i) *Caractacus, Op. 35. Severn Suite* (full orchestral version).

*** Chan. 9156/7. (i) Howarth, Wilson-Johnson, Davies, Roberts, Miles, L. Symphony Ch.; LSO, Hickox.

Elgar's *Caractacus* draws from Hickox and his splendid LSO forces a fresh, sympathetic reading, generally very well sung, with David Wilson-Johnson in the title-role, recorded in opulent Chandos sound. Much the most memorable item is the well-known *Imperial March*, introducing the final scene in Rome, made the more exciting with chorus. One even forgives the embarrassment of the concluding chorus which predicts that 'The nations all shall stand, and hymn the praise of Britain hand in hand.' The only reservation is that the earlier, EMI recording conducted by Sir Charles Groves was crisper in ensemble and even better sung, with even more seductive pointing of rhythm. For coupling, Hickox has the full orchestral arrangement of Elgar's very last work, originally for brass band, the *Severn Suite*.

(i) *Coronation Ode, Op. 44. The Spirit of England, Op. 80.*

(M) *** Chan. 6574. Cahill, SNO Ch. and O, Gibson; (i) with Collins, Rolfe Johnson, Howell.

Gibson's performances combine fire and panache, and the recorded sound has an ideal Elgarian expansiveness, the choral tone rich and well focused, the orchestral brass given plenty of weight, and the overall perspective highly convincing. He is helped by excellent soloists, with Anne Collins movingly eloquent in her dignified restraint when she introduces the famous words of *Land of hope and glory* in the finale; and the choral entry which follows is truly glorious in its power and amplitude. *The Spirit of England*, a wartime cantata to words of Laurence Binyon, is in some ways even finer, with the final setting of *For the fallen* rising well above the level of his occasional music.

The Dream of Gerontius, Op. 38.

*** Chan. 8641/2. Palmer, A. Davies, Howell, L. Symphony Ch. & LSO, Hickox – PARRY: *Anthems.* ***

(B)*** EMI (ADD) CZS5 73579-2 (2). Baker, Lewis, Borg, Hallé & Sheffield Philharmonic Ch., Amb. S. Hallé O, Barbirolli.

(i) *The Dream of Gerontius;* (ii) *Cello Concerto.*

(***) Testament mono SBT 2025 (2). (i) Nash, Ripley, Noble, Walker, Huddersfield Ch. Soc., Liverpool PO; (ii) P. Tortelier, BBC SO; Sargent.

(i) *The Dream of Gerontius;* (ii) *The Music Makers, Op. 69.*

✪ (M) *** EMI (ADD) CMS5 66540-2 (2). (i) Gedda, Watts, Lloyd, Alldis Ch., LPO Ch., New Philh. O; (ii) Baker, LPO Ch., LPO; Boult.

Boult's total dedication is matched by his powerful sense of drama. Indeed, it is difficult to conceive of a more powerful conclusion to Part I when Robert Lloyd (a magnificent Priest and Angel of Agony) and the chorus send Gerontius's soul on its way. The spiritual feeling is intense throughout, but the human qualities of the narrative are also fully realized. Boult's controversial choice of Nicolai Gedda in the role of Gerontius brings a new dimension to this characterization, and he brings the sort of echoes of Italian opera that Elgar himself – perhaps surprisingly – asked for. He is perfectly matched by Helen Watts as the Angel. It is a fascinating vocal partnership and is matched by the commanding manner which Robert Lloyd finds for both his roles. The orchestral playing is always responsive, and often, like the choral singing, very beautiful, while the dramatic passages bring splendid incisiveness and bold assurance from the singers. The 1976 Kingsway Hall recording (produced by Christopher Bishop) is extremely well balanced by Christopher Parker and has been remastered quite stunningly – especially at the bass end of the spectrum: the sound has great presence as well as ideal ambient warmth and atmosphere. It is technically, as well as musically, a truly great recording. The performance and recording of *The Music Makers*, made at Abbey Road a decade earlier, are also very successful. If only the whole piece lived up to the uninhibited choral setting of the *Nimrod* variation from *Enigma*, it would be another Elgar masterpiece. Nevertheless, Boult's dedication, matched by Janet Baker's masterly eloquence, holds the listener throughout, and the current transfer has brought a new vividness to the choral contribution.

Sir Malcolm Sargent, never finer on disc, in 1945 paced the score perfectly, drawing incandescent singing from the Huddersfield Choral Society. The soloists too, superbly led by Heddle Nash as Gerontius, have a freshness and clarity rarely matched, with Nash's ringing tenor consistently clean in attack. Though Gladys Ripley's fine contralto is caught with a hint of rapid flutter, she matches the others in forthright clarity, with Dennis Noble as the Priest and Norman Walker as the Angel of the Agony both strong and direct. The mono recording captures detail excellently; even if inevitably the dynamic range is limited and the chorus lacks something in body, such a climax as *Praise to the Holiest* has thrilling bite. The first and finest of Paul Tortelier's three recordings of the Elgar *Cello Concerto* makes an ideal coupling, emotionally intense within a disciplined frame. The 1953 recording is transferred very clearly and vividly. Like all the Testament transfers of EMI material, it comes with excellent background notes.

Barbirolli's red-blooded reading of *Gerontius* is the most heart-warmingly dramatic ever recorded; here it is offered, in a first-rate CD transfer, in coupling with one of the greatest Elgar recordings ever made: Janet Baker's rapt and heartfelt account of *Sea Pictures*. No one on record can match her in this version of *Gerontius* for the fervent intensity and glorious tonal range of her singing as the Angel, one of her supreme recorded performances; and the clarity of CD intensifies the experience. In terms of pure dedication the emotional thrust of Barbirolli's reading conveys the deepest spiritual intensity, making most other versions (though not Boult's) seem cool by comparison. The recording may have its hints of distortion, but the sound is overwhelming. Richard Lewis gives one of his finest recorded performances, searching and intense, and, though Kim Borg is unidiomatic in the bass role, his bass tones are rich in timbre, even if his projection lacks the dramatic edge of Robert Lloyd on the reissued Boult set.

Hickox's version outshines almost all rivals in the range and quality of its sound. Quite apart from the fullness and fidelity of the recording, Hickox's performance is deeply understanding, not always ideally powerful in the big climaxes but paced most sympathetically, with a natural understanding of Elgarian rubato. The soloists make a characterful team. Arthur Davies is a strong and fresh-toned Gerontius; Gwynne Howell in the bass roles is powerful if not always ideally steady; and Felicity Palmer, though untraditionally bright of tone with her characterful vibrato, is strong and illuminating. Though on balance Boult's soloists are even finer, Hickox's reading in its expressive warmth conveys much love for this score, and the last pages with their finely sustained closing *Amen* are genuinely moving.

(i) *The Kingdom, Op. 51*; (ii) *Coronation Ode, Op. 34.*

(M) *** EMI (ADD) CMS7 64209-2. (i) M. Price, Minton, Young, Shirley-Quirk, LPO Ch., LPO, Boult; (ii) Lott, Hodgson, Morton, Cambridge University Music Soc., King's College, Cambridge, Ch., New Philh. O, Band of Royal Military School of Music, Kneller Hall, Ledger.

The Kingdom; Sursum corda; Sospiri.

*** Chan. 8788/9. Marshall, Palmer, A. Davies, Wilson-Johnson, L. Symphony Ch., LSO, Hickox.

Boult was devoted to *The Kingdom*, identifying with its comparative reticence, and his dedication emerges clearly throughout a glorious performance. The melody which Elgar wrote to represent the Holy Spirit is one of the noblest that even he created, and the soprano aria, *The sun goeth down* (beautifully sung by Margaret Price), leads to a deeply affecting climax. The other soloists also sing splendidly, and the only reservation concerns the chorus, which is not quite as disciplined as it might be and sounds a little too backward for some of the massive effects which cap the power of the work. The coupling of the *Coronation Ode* is handy and certainly welcome, rather than particularly appropriate. It is far more than a jingoistic occasional piece, though it was indeed the work which first featured *Land of hope and glory*. All told, the work contains much Elgarian treasure, and Ledger is superb in capturing the necessary swagger and panache, disdaining all thought of potential bad taste. With recording of outstanding quality – among the finest made in King's College Chapel during the analogue era – and with extra brass bands, it presents a glorious experience. Excellent singing and playing, too, although the male soloists do not quite match their female colleagues. Both works are generously cued.

Hickox proves a warmly understanding Elgarian and his manner is more ripely idiomatic. His soloists make a characterful quartet. Margaret Marshall is the sweet, tender soprano, rising superbly to a passionate climax in her big solo, *The sun goeth down*, and Felicity Palmer is a strong and positive – if not ideally warm-toned – Mary Magdalene. David Wilson-Johnson points the words of St Peter most dramatically, and Arthur Davies is the radiant tenor. The fill-ups are not generous: the intense little string adagio, *Sospiri*, and the early *Sursum corda*.

The Light of Life (Lux Christi), Op. 29.

*** Chan. 9208. Howarth, Finnie, A. Davies, Shirley-Quirk, L. Symphony Ch., LSO, Hickox.

(M) **(*) EMI (ADD) CDM7 64732-2. Marshall, Watts, Leggate, Shirley-Quirk, RLPO Ch. & O, Groves.

Notably more than Sir Charles Groves in the earlier, EMI recording, Hickox conveys the warmth of inspiration of *The Light of Life* in glowing sound, with the chorus incandescent. The solo singing is richly characterful, even if the microphone catches an unevenness in the singing of the mezzo, Linda Finnie, and of John Shirley-Quirk; nevertheless he sings nobly as Jesus in the climactic 'Good Shepherd' solo. Arthur Davies as the blind man and the soprano, Judith Howarth, are both excellent, singing with clear, fresh tone.

Sir Charles Groves's understanding performance features four first-rate soloists and strongly involving, if not always flawless, playing and singing from the Liverpool orchestra and choir. The recording is vivid and full in EMI's recognizable Elgar manner and has been admirably transferred, with cleaner focus and no appreciable loss of amplitude.

(i) *The Music Makers, Op. 69. Chanson de matin; Chanson de nuit, Op. 15/1–2; Dream Children, Op. 43; Elegy, Op. 58; Salut d'amour, Op. 12; Sospiri, Op. 70; Sursum corda, Op. 11.*

**(*) Teldec 4509 92374-2. (i) Rigby, BBC Symphony Ch.; BBC SO, A. Davis.

The Music Makers; Sea Pictures, Op. 37.

*** Chan. 9022. Finnie, LPO Ch., LPO, Thomson.

(M) **(*) EMI CDM5 65126-2. Palmer, L. Symphony Ch., LSO, Hickox.

On Chandos the song-cycle and the cantata make a good coupling, with a contralto soloist as the key figure in each work. Bryden Thomson directs warmly expressive, spontaneous-sounding performances of both works, easily flexible in an idiomatic way, and this now makes a first choice among modern recordings.

Hickox's coupling of *Sea Pictures* and the big cantata, *The Music Makers*, brings strong, powerful performances, very individual in the song-cycle thanks to the urgent, tough and indeed characterful singing of Felicity Palmer. Hickox gives a convincing, red-blooded reading of the cantata, atmospherically recorded and with the voices well caught, but with reverberation masking some of the orchestral detail.

Andrew Davis conducts a dedicated, refined reading of *The Music Makers*, giving a rare intensity to the quotations from earlier works. Jean Rigby sings with clear, firm focus. The rather backward balance of the chorus prevents the performance from having the full impact it deserves; but the sound, both refined and atmospheric, consistently brings out the beauty of Elgar's orchestration, both in the cantata and in the very generous and imaginative selection of shorter pieces which come as coupling. Among the encores, the early *Sursum corda*, Op. 11, for brass, organ and strings, stands well between the two masterly elegiac pieces of his high maturity, *Elegy* and *Sospiri*.

3 Partsongs, Op. 18; 4 Partsongs, Op. 53; 2 Partsongs, Op. 71; 2 Partsongs, Op. 73; 5 Partsongs from the Greek

anthology, Op. 45; Death on the hills; Evening scene; Go song of mine; How calmly the evening; The Prince of Sleep; Weary wind of the West.

*** Chan. 9269. Finzi Singers, Spicer.

Elgar's part-songs span virtually the whole of his creative career, and the 22 examples on the Finzi Singers' disc range from one of the most famous, *My love dwelt in a northern land*, of 1889 to settings of Russian poems (in English translation) written during the First World War. The Finzi Singers under Paul Spicer give finely tuned, crisp and intense readings of all the pieces. The Hyperion two-disc collection also includes Elgar's ecclesiastical motets, but for the secular part-songs the Chandos performances are even finer.

4 Partsongs, Op. 53; 5 Partsongs from the Greek anthology, Op. 45. Choral songs: *Christmas greeting; Death on the hills; Evening scene; The fountain; Fly, singing bird; Goodmorrow; Go, song of mine; The herald; How calmly the evening; Love's tempest; My love dwelt; Prince of sleep; Rapid stream; Reveille; Serenade; The shower; Snow; Spanish serenade; They are at rest; The wanderer; Weary wind of the West; When swallows fly; Woodland stream; Zut! zut! zut!*

*** Hyp. CDA 66271/2. Worcester Cathedral Ch.; Donald Hunt Singers, Hunt; Swallow, Ballard; Thurlby.

The finest item on the Hyperion CD is the last, in which both choirs join, the eight-part setting of *Cavalcanti* in translation by Rossetti, *Go, song of mine*. It is also fascinating to find Elgar in 1922, with all his major works completed, writing three charming songs for boys' voices to words by Charles Mackay, as refreshing as anything in the whole collection. Atmospherically recorded – the secular singers rather more cleanly than the cathedral choir – it is a delightful collection for anyone fascinated by Elgar outside the big works.

Songs: *Pleading; 3 Songs (Was it some golden star?); Oh, soft was the song; Twilight), Op. 59; 2 Songs (The torch; The river), Op. 60.*

*** (M) EMI (ADD) CDM7 64731-2. Tear, CBSO, Handley – BUTTERWORTH: *Songs;* VAUGHAN WILLIAMS: *On Wenlock Edge,* etc. ***

At his most creative period in the early years of the century, Elgar planned another song-cycle to follow *Sea Pictures*, but he completed only three of the songs, his Op. 59. The other three songs here are even more individual, a fine coupling for Vaughan Williams and Butterworth. Incisive and characterful, yet expressively sympathetic performances from Robert Tear. The recording, well focused, is appropriately warm and atmospheric.

Scenes from the Bavarian Highlands, Op. 27 (orchestral version).

(M) *** EMI (ADD) CDM5 65129-2. Bournemouth Ch. & SO, Del Mar – STANFORD: *Symphony No. 3.* ***

The EMI recording uses the orchestral version of the score; although the choral recording is agreeably full, balances are not always ideal, with the choral descant in the *Lullaby*

outweighing the attractive orchestral detail. However, the performances are infectiously spirited, conveying warmth as well as vigour – Del Mar is a natural Elgarian. Moreover, the EMI coupling of the Stanford *Third Symphony* was a happy and generous choice.

Scenes from the Bavarian Highlands, Op. 27; Ecce sacerdos magnus; O salutaris Hostia (3 settings); *Tantum ergo; The Light of Life: Doubt not thy Father's care; Light of the World.*

(M) **(*) Chan. 6601. Worcester Cathedral Ch., Robinson; Wibaut; Bramma.

It is good to have a fine, mid-priced performance of the original piano-accompanied version of the charmingly tuneful *Bavarian Scenes*. Even without the orchestra, the music lifts up with remarkable freshness when the singing in Worcester is appropriately committed and spontaneous. The three versions of *O salutaris Hostia* are also worth having, and the strong performances of *Tantum ergo* and *Ecce sacerdos magnus* add to the interest of this reissue.

Sea Pictures (song-cycle), *Op. 37.*

⊛ *** EMI (ADD) CDC7 47329-2. Baker, LSO, Barbirolli – *Cello Concerto.* *** ⊛

(N) **(*) ABC Classics (ADD) 461 922-2. Elkins, Queensland SO, Albert – SHIELD: *Rosina;* WILLIAMSON: *The Growing Castle.* ***

Like du Pré, Janet Baker is an artist who has the power to convey on record the vividness of a live performance. With the help of Barbirolli she makes the cycle far more convincing than it usually seems, with often trite words clothed in music that seems to transform them. On CD, the voice is caught with extra bloom, and the beauty of Elgar's orchestration is enhanced by the subtle added definition.

This warm-hearted, atmospheric and beautiful account of the *Sea Pictures* makes an unexpected fill-up to Shield's sparkling rustic opera, *Rosina*. Margreta Elkins's voice is well captured in the 1983 recording. Though the orchestra lacks richness, it is perfectly acceptable. Texts are included along with very full documentation.

(i) *Sea Pictures, Op. 37;* (ii–iii) *The Starlight Express: Songs: O children, open your arms to me; There's a fairy that hides; I'm everywhere; Wake up, you little night winds; O stars, shine brightly; We shall meet the morning spiders; My old tunes are rather broken; O think beauty; Dustman, Laughter, Tramp and busy Sweep;* (iii) *Dream Children, Op. 43.*

(M) **(*) Decca 452 324-2. (i) D. Jones, RPO; (ii) Hagley, Terfel; (iii) Welsh Nat. Op. O; all cond. Mackerras – LAMBERT: *The Rio Grande.* **(*)

Under Mackerras the opening of the *Sea slumber-song* is simple and touching but he creates a big climax for *Sabbath morning at sea,* and Della Jones brings even more histrionic feeling to the final climax of *The swimmer.* She sings richly throughout; however, although *Where corals lie* is obviously deeply felt, one feels that not all the secrets of this music are fully revealed. The vocal numbers from *The Starlight Express* are well sung by Alison Hagley and Bryn Terfel, and Mackerras is as warmly affectionate in the delicately scored *Dream Children* as he is dramatic in the *Sea Pictures*.

The Spirit of England, Op. 80; O give unto the Lord (Psalm 29); Land of hope and glory; O hearken Thou (Offertory); *The Snow.*

(M) *** EMI CDM5 65586-2. Lott, L. Symphony Ch., N. Sinfonia, Hickox.

In his series of lesser Elgar choral works for EMI, Hickox conducts a rousing performance of *The Spirit of England*, adding three short choral pieces, including a setting of Psalm 29, and ending with *Land of hope and glory* in all its splendour. The London Symphony Chorus is in radiant form and Felicity Lott is a strong soloist in the main work. First-rate EMI digital sound, made at Abbey Road in 1987.

ELLER, Heino (1887–1970)

Dawn (tone poem); (i) *Elegia for Harp & Strings; 5 Pieces for Strings.*

*** Chan. 8525. (i) Pierce; SNO, Järvi – RAID: *Symphony No. 1.* ***

Dawn is frankly romantic – with touches of Grieg and early Sibelius as well as the Russian nationalists – and the *Five Pieces for Strings* have a wistful, Grieg-like charm. The *Elegia for Harp and Strings* of 1931 strikes a deeper vein of feeling and has nobility and eloquence, tempered by quiet restraint; there is a beautiful dialogue involving solo viola and harp which is quite haunting. Excellent performances and recording. Strongly recommended.

ELLINGTON, Edward Kennedy 'Duke' (1899–1974)

Harlem; The River: suite (orch. Collier); *Solitude* (trans. Morton Gould).

(N) *** Chan. 9909. Detroit SO, Järvi – DAWSON: *Negro Folk Symphony.* ***

Harlem is a wildly exuberant but essentially optimistic picture of Harlem as it used to be before the drug age. Ellington pictures a parade and a funeral, and ends with riotous exuberance. This is true, written-down, orchestral jazz, more authentic than Gershwin and marvellously played by musicians who know all about the Afro-American musical tradition. The trumpets are terrific.

The *River* was composed in 1970, intended as music for a ballet with choreography by Alvin Ailey, but this project proved abortive, and Ellington also saw the score as a river journey. The ideas are characteristically varied and imaginative, yet as orchestrated by Ron Collier the seven movements sound like an extended ballet sequence in an MGM film with big band interludes.

Solitude, which dates from Ellington's Cotton Club days, is much more subtly scored by Morton Gould, and in its orchestral format has a haunting almost Copland-esque

flavour, although it retains Ellington's own musical fingerprints. Splendid recording.

EMMANUEL, Maurice (1862–1938)

Sonatine bourguignonne; Sonatine pastorale; Sonatines Nos. 3–4; Sonatine No. 5 (alla francese); Sonatine No. 6.

⊕ *** Continuum (ADD) CCD 1048. Jacobs.

Maurice Emmanuel was born in Burgundy and celebrated his native province in the *Sonatine bourguignonne* (1893), drawing on folk tunes as well as featuring the carillon and chimes of the cathedral at Beaune, where he was a boy chorister. Later in his career he was to number Messiaen among his pupils, and his *Sonatine pastorale* (1897) is inspired by the birdsong which fascinated his more famous contemporary. The later works are impressionistic. The *Sonatine Hindous* contrasts with the elegant pastiche of the masterly *Sonatine alla francese* (1926), a 'French Suite' not so far removed from Ravel's *Tombeau de Couperin*. All this music is superbly played by Peter Jacobs. Not to be missed.

ENESCU, Georges (1881–1955)

Poème roumain (symphonic suite), *Op. 1;* (i) *Vox maris* (symphonic poem), *Op. 31. Voix de la nature (Nuages de l'automne sur le forêt).*

(BB) **(*) Arte Nova 74321 65425-2. Georges Enescu Ens., Bucharest PO & Ch., Mandeal; (i) with Diaconescu.

An inexpensive introduction to the Romanian composer for those who know him only through the *Roumanian Rhapsody No. 1* couples his very first opus, the *Poème roumain* (a two-movement symphonic suite for voices and orchestra), with one of his most eloquent works – the symphonic poem, *Vox maris*. There is a quasi-mystical feel to much of it, though it is a little overheated and amorphous. His *Voix de la nature* remained unfinished, but a fragment survives – its first movement, entitled *Nuages de l'automne sur le forêt*. It is scored for a small orchestra with an unusual group of solo strings: two each of violas and cellos and one double-bass. The recordings are a little coarse in climaxes and wanting in transparency and refinement.

Roumanian Rhapsody No. 1.

(M) *** Mercury (ADD) 432 015-2. LSO, Dorati – LISZT: *Hungarian Rhapsodies Nos. 1–6.* **(*)

Dorati finds both flair and exhilaration in this enticing piece, especially in the closing pages, and the Mercury sound from the early 1960s is of a vintage standard. The coupling with the Liszt *Hungarian Rhapsodies* is entirely appropriate.

Roumanian Rhapsodies 1–2, Op. 11/1–2.

(N) (M) *** Chan. 6625. RSNO, Järvi – BARTOK: *Hungarian Pictures.* WEINER: *Hungarian Folkdance Suite.* ***

Roumanian Rhapsodies Nos. 1–2; (i) *Symphonie concertante for Cello and Orchestra, Op.8; Suites for Orchestra Nos. 1 in C, Op. 9; 2 in C, Op. 20; 3 (Villageoise), Op. 27;* (ii) *Poème roumain, Op. 1.*

(B) **(*) Erato Ultima 3984 24247-2 (2). Monte Carlo PO,
   Foster; with (i) Maggio-Ormezowski; (ii) Male Ch. of
   Colonne O, & Ens. Audita Nova de Paris.

Järvi has a warmly idiomatic feeling for these amiable,
peasant-inspired rhapsodies, moulding phrases and linking
passages with spontaneity, drawing committed playing, with
plenty of subtle touches from the Royal Scottish National
Orchestra, ripely recorded. Although the first of the two
rhapsodies is much the more popular, and justly so, the
second is also lively and colourful. They are now aptly
coupled with comparably entertaining and colourful folk-
inspired music by Bartók and Weiner.

The *First Roumanian Rhapsody* combines a string of
glowing, folk-derived melodies with glittering scoring; the
Second, though still attractive, is not so indelible in its
melodies as the *First*. The *Poème roumain* has lyrical appeal
and uses an evocative, wordless male chorus with bells at the
opening, and later a solo violin; it features the Roumanian
national anthem as its finale. The *Symphonie concertante* is
an attractively written piece, again using national dances.
The cello soloist is excellent. The first two of the three *Suites*
are well crafted without being in the very first rank; they are
expertly laid out for the orchestra and have a charm and
appeal that ought to ensure them a wider following. The
Third (Village) Suite brings a series of pastoral scenes, followed by an evocation of the river in the moonlight and
more national dances to conclude. All this is well enough
served by the Monte Carlo orchestra under Lawrence Foster
and given the benefit of natural, spacious recording.

(i) *Symphony No. 3; Roumanian Rhapsody No. 1, Op. 11.*

** Chan. 9633. (i) Leeds Festival Ch.; BBC PO,
   Rozhdestvensky.

The *Third Symphony* dates from the middle of the First
World War and is a long, loosely constructed piece, scored
for large forces including six horns, organ, piano, two harps
and wordless chorus. Rozhdestvensky conducts with much
sympathy, though he could perhaps have adopted a brisker
tempo for the first movement. The performance lacks the
last ounce of urgency, and the same goes for the popular
Roumanian Rhapsody No. 1. Good Chandos sound.

Cello Sonatas Nos. 1 in F min.; 2 in C, Op. 26/1–2.

(BB) *** Arte Nova 74321 54461-2. Zank, Sulzen.

The *F minor Sonata* is very much in the received tradition,
inventive and well constructed, muscular in character and
Brahmsian in feeling. Though it is still conservative in approach, the *Second Sonata* of 1935 is far more individual and
searching in its musical language. Gerhard Zank is a masterly
and eloquent cellist, and he is well partnered by the Kansas-
born Donald Sulzen. Very clean, bright (perhaps overbright)
recording with plenty of presence. A rewarding disc and well
worth the modest asking price.

Dixtuor, Op. 14.

(N) (BB) *** Naxos 8.554173. Oslo PO Wind soloists –
   DVORAK: *Wind Serenade;* JANACEK: *Mládí.* ***

The *Dixtuor* or *Decet* is one of Enescu's most glorious scores.
It dates from 1906, six years after the celebrated *Octet*, and

is richly inventive: its sophisticated counterpoint and idyllic
charm are most appealing. The plaintive slow movement is
haunting. The Oslo wind soloists are artists of quality whose
reading challenges the finest at any price. Crisp rhythms, a
good sense of line and tonal finesse. These artists recorded
this piece on the Victoria label in the early 1990s but these
are different and better accounts in every way.

Légende for Trumpet and Piano.

*** EMI CDC5 56760-2. Hardenberger, Andsnes – BRITTEN:
   Piano Concerto; SHOSTAKOVICH: *Piano Concerto
   No. 1.* ***

A fine makeweight to the Shostakovich concerto which
provides an admirable opportunity for Håkon Hardenberger
to display his incredible legato phrasing.

Octuor in C, Op. 7.

*** Chan. 9131. ASMF Chamber Ens. – SHOSTAKOVICH: 2
   Pieces for String Octet; R. STRAUSS: *Capriccio: Sextet.*

(i) *Octuor;* (ii) *Dixtuor in D for winds, Op. 14.*

(BB) *** Arte Nova 74321 63634-2. Georges Enescu Ens. (from
   Bucharest PO), with Mandeal.
** Marco 8.223147. (i) Voces and Euterpe Qts; (ii) Winds of
   Iasi Moldova PO, Baciu.

Enescu's *C major Octuor* for strings (1900) is an amazingly
accomplished piece for a nineteen-year-old. It is a masterly
and inventive score whose inspiration flows with wonderful
naturalness. From the Academy of St Martin-in-the-Fields
Chamber Ensemble comes a very good performance and
recording.

On both Marco Polo and the Arte Nova super-bargain
label it is paired with a most valuable coupling, the *Dixtuor*
(or *Decet*) for wind instruments of 1906, one of Enescu's best
pieces. Both are impressively presented by the eponymous
Bucharest group.

No quarrels with the response of the Romanian strings,
and the *Dixtuor* is very well played by the winds of the Iasi
Moldova Philharmonic under Ion Baciu. But the Marco
Polo recording is far less impressive than the Chandos, or
the excellent quality offered by the Arte Nova bargain label.
That is the one to go for, on both artistic and price grounds.

String Quartets Nos. 1 in E flat; 2 in G, Op. 22/1–2.

(N) (BB) *** Naxos 8.554721. Ad Libitum Qt.

The Enescu quartets share the same opus number but are
separated by over three decades; the *First* comes from the
end of the First World War and the *Second* from the 1950s,
towards the end of the composer's life. Few works by this
extraordinary musician are without their rewards, and although neither quartet rises to the same imaginative heights
as *Oedipe* or the *Dixtuor* they are full of good things. They
are well played by this fine Romanian team and priced at
the right level. The adventurous collector will not baulk at a
fiver for repertoire that he or she does not know and will
find the outlay worthwhile.

Oedipe (opera): complete.

*** EMI CDS7 54011-2 (2). Van Dam, Hendricks, Fassbaender,

Lipovšek, Bacquier, Gedda, Hauptmann, Quilico, Aler, Vanaud, Albert, Taillon, Orfeon Donostiarra, Monte Carlo PO, Foster.

This is an almost ideal recording of a rare, long-neglected masterpiece, with a breathtaking cast of stars backing up a supremely fine performance by José van Dam in the central role of Oedipus. The idiom is tough and adventurous, as well as warmly exotic, with vivid choral effects, a revelation to anyone who knows Enescu only from his *Roumanian Rhapsody*. The only reservation is that the pace tends to be on the slow side, but the incandescence of the playing of the Monte Carlo Philharmonic under Lawrence Foster and the richness of the singing and recorded sound amply compensate for that, making this a musical feast.

ENGLUND, Einar (born 1916)

Symphonies Nos. 1 (War) (1946); 2 ('Blackbird') (1948).

**(*) Ondine ODE 751-2. Estonian SO, Lilje.

Einar Englund's *First Symphony* is, in his own words, 'an expression of euphoric joy'. He has a spontaneous and natural gift, and his musical language is closer to Shostakovich than to anyone else. The *Second Symphony* presumably acquired its nickname from the apparent evocation of birdsong at the very opening. Good performances and very acceptable (though not outstanding) recorded sound.

Symphonies Nos. 2 (Blackbird); 4 (Nostalgic); (i) Piano Concerto No. 1.

(BB) *** Naxos 8.553758 [id.]. Turku PO, Panula, (i) with Sivelöv.

The *Second Symphony* (1948) is full of imaginative things, though, like the *Fourth*, its debt to Shostakovich is heavy. In the *First Piano Concerto* (1955), with its touches of Prokofiev and strongly Gallic overtones, Niklas Sivelöv proves a most musical and accomplished soloist. Rather good performances and recording make this an admirable introduction to this gifted composer.

Symphonies Nos. 4 (Nostalgic); 5 (Fennica); The Great Wall of China (suite).

(N) *** Ondine ODE 9612. Tampere PO, Eri Klas.

The *Great Wall of China*, the first work of Englund to be put on record in the days of mono LP, is the incidental music for the play by Max Frisch. It sounds fresh and there is no lack of parody and pastiche, with touches of jazz (Englund himself was an accomplished jazz pianist). The *Fourth Symphony* was composed following the death of Shostakovich, to whom it is heavily indebted and from whose works it quotes. The *Fifth Symphony* recalls Englund's service in the Second World War with the spirit of tranquil recollection, unlike the *First*, which was written in the immediate wake of those terrible years. There are powerful things here, although the debt to Shostakovich undoubtedly hangs too heavily.

(i) *Symphony No. 6 (Aphorisms); (ii) Cello Concerto.*

*** Ondine ODE 951-2 [id.]. Tampere PO, Klas; with (i) Gustafsson, (ii) Tampere Philh. Ch.

The *Cello Concerto* (1954) precedes the *First Piano Concerto* and is highly imaginative. Shostakovich is still a presence in Englund's musical make-up, but his music is nevertheless quite haunting and his writing both inventive and resourceful; there is always something happening and the music unfolds naturally. The *Sixth Symphony* (1986) is a choral setting of Heraclitus, again inventive and direct in utterance. Jan-Erik Gustafsson is the eloquent soloist in the *Cello Concerto* and the orchestral support under Eri Klas is first class. The recording has much greater body and richness of detail than the Naxos disc listed above.

EYCK, Jakob van (1590–1657)

Der Fluyten Lust-hof (excerpts).

*** Auvidis E 8588. Feldman, Marq, Lislevand.

Jakob van Eyck was blind but, as his tombstone stated, 'What God took from his eyes he gave back in his ear.' He played the recorder 'like a bird' in the local park, to the delight of the weekend promenaders. *Der Fluyten Lust-hof*, published in two volumes, dates from the middle of the seventeenth century. Van Eyck wrote divisions and improvisations on famous tunes of the time, most of which came from France and England – half a dozen of Dowland's most famous numbers are featured. Jill Feldman sings with engaging purity of line and tone, and she has a knack for simple embellishment. The intimacy of the performances is nicely reflected in the recording.

FALLA, Manuel de (1876–1946)

(i) *Harpsichord Concerto;* (ii; iii) *El amor brujo;* (ii; iv; v); *Nights in the Gardens of Spain;* (vi) *The Three-Cornered Hat: Miller's Dance; Final Dance.* (vii) *La vida breve: Interlude & Dance No. 1.*

(N) **(*) Australian Ph. (ADD) 468 313-2. (i) Puyana, Mackerras; (ii) Markevitch; (iii) Spanish RTV SO; (iv) Lamoureux O; (v) Haskil; (vi) Paris Nat. Op. O, Benzi; (vii) Minneapolis SO, Dorati.

Markevitch provides real atmosphere at the beginning of *El amor brujo* and the orchestra is lively and committed. Clara Haskil admirers will be glad to have her dazzling and sultry account of the *Nights in the Gardens of Spain*, and Mackerras's direction of the *Harpsichord Concerto* is idiomatic and Puyana is a fine soloist – the rather dry acoustic suiting the music admirably. Benzi's excerpts from *The Three-Cornered Hat* with the Paris Opéra Orchestra have a typically French twang in the brass department, and Dorati's *La vida breve* excerpt is vividly played and recorded in the Mercury manner. The 1960s sound throughout is generally good, if not as rich and vivid as the rival Decca recordings of the same period.

El amor brujo (Love, the Magician; ballet) (original
version, complete with dialogue); (i) (Piano) *Serenata;
Serenata andaluza; 7 Canciones populares españolas.*

*** Nuova Era 6809. Senn, Carme Ens., Izquierdo; (i) Bodini.

By including the dialogue, spoken over music, the Nuova
Era issue provides the complete original conception of *El
amor brujo*, rather like a one-act zarzuela, with chamber
scoring. Martha Senn is perfectly cast in the role of the gypsy
heroine. She sings flamboyantly and often ravishingly, both
here and in the delectable *Canciones populares* and the other
two songs offered as coupling, and she is accompanied
very sympathetically. Luis Izquierdo directs the main work
atmospherically and finds plenty of gusto for the piece we
know as the *Ritual Fire Dance*; and the recording is suitably
atmospheric and vivid.

El amor brujo: complete.

🏵 *** BBC (ADD) BBCL 4005-2. Lane, BBC SO, Stokowski –
BEETHOVEN: *Symphony No. 7* *(**); BRITTEN: *Young
Person's Guide to the Orchestra.* **(*)

(M) *** Decca (ADD) 448 601-2. Mistral, New Philh. O,
Frühbeck de Burgos – ALBENIZ: *Suite española.* ***

(N) (B) (**(*)) Dutton Lab. mono CDBP 9705. Merriman,
Hollywood Bowl SO, Stokowski – BRAHMS: *Symphony
No. 1.* (***)

(M) **(*) BBC (ADD) BBCB 8012-2. Reynolds, ECO, Britten –
TCHAIKOVSKY: *Francesca da Rimini; Romeo and
Juliet.* **

(i) *El amor brujo* (complete); (ii) *Nights in the Gardens of
Spain.*

(M) *** Decca 430 703-2. (i) Tourangeau, Montreal SO,
Dutoit; (ii) De Larrocha, LPO, Frühbeck de Burgos –
RODRIGO: *Concierto.* *** 🏵

(B) **(*) DG (ADD) 439 458-2. (i) Berganza, LSO, Navarro;
(ii) Weber, Bav. RSO, Kubelik – RODRIGO: *Concierto de
Aranjuez.* **

Stokowski's account of Falla's *El amor brujo* was given at a
Prom in 1964 and has all the electricity of a live occasion.
This is an outstanding and thrilling performance. In almost
every movement Stokowski opts for fast speeds, with the
players of the BBC Symphony Orchestra challenged to the
limit, as in the *Ritual Fire Dance*, which is electrifying.
Consistently Stokowski finds colour and atmosphere, and
his soloist, Gloria Lane, with her fruity mezzo tone-colours,
sounds comparably idiomatic. In short, this is the most
gripping and hypnotic performance on or off record, and
the recording quality is very good indeed.

With recording in the demonstration class, Dutoit's performance has characteristic flexibility over phrasing and
rhythm and is hauntingly atmospheric. The sound in the
coupled *Nights in the Gardens of Spain* is equally superb,
rich and lustrous and with vivid detail. Miss de Larrocha's
lambent feeling for the work's poetic evocation is matched
by her brilliance in the nocturnal dance-rhythms.

The score's evocative atmosphere is hauntingly captured
by Raphael Frühbeck de Burgos, and, to make the most
striking contrast, the famous *Ritual Fire Dance* blazes brilliantly. Nati Mistral has the vibrant open-throated projection

of the real flamenco artist, and the whole performance
is idiomatically authentic and compelling. Brilliant Decca
sound to match.

Navarro conducts a vibrantly atmospheric account of *El
amor brujo* and Teresa Berganza is a strong, dark-throated
soloist. The LSO are on top form. The performance of *Nights
in the Gardens of Spain* is similarly compelling. With Margrit
Weber giving a brilliant account of the solo part, particularly
in the latter movements, the effect is both sparkling and
exhilarating.

Stokowski's magnetism is just as apparent in his 1956
recording of *El amor brujo* with the Hollywood Bowl
Orchestra. In this Dutton transfer the mono recording is
amazingly sharp and vivid: and the vibrant soloist, Nan Merriman, is very much with us. The Spanish rhythms and colours
are seductively caught, with plenty of bite in the famous *Ritual
Fire Dance*. But in this instance Stokowski upstages himself,
for the later BBC recording is even more electrifying.

Britten conducts a warmly evocative reading of the Falla
ballet. Not only does he bring out the atmospheric beauty
of the writing, he characteristically points rhythms in a
seductively idiomatic way, as in his treatment of the haunting
Pantomime. Anna Reynolds may not sound very Spanish,
but she too is warmly responsive and characterful. However,
the Tchaikovsky coupling ultimately lacks the kind of strong
adrenalin flow so essential in this repertoire.

(i; ii) *El amor brujo* (complete); (ii) *The Three-Cornered
Hat* (ballet): suite; (iii) *7 Spanish Popular Songs;*
(iv) *Psyché; Soneto a Córdoba.*

(M) **(*) EMI (ADD) CMS5 67587-2 (2). (i) De los Angeles;
(ii) Philh. O, Giulini; (iii) Soriano; (iv) Challan & String Trio
– *La vida breve.* ***

(i) *El amor brujo* (complete); (ii) *Nights in the Gardens of
Spain; The Three-Cornered Hat: Dance of the Neighbours;
Dance of the Miller; Finale (Jota).*

(N) (B) *** Sony (ADD) SBK 89291. (i) Philadelphia O,
(ii) Stokowski; (iii) Ormandy; (iv) Entremont.

(BB) **(*) RCA Navigator (ADD) 74321 24215-2. (i) Mistral;
(ii) Achucarro; LSO, Mata.

(i) *El amor brujo* (complete); (ii) *Nights in the Gardens of
Spain; La vida breve: Interlude and Dance.*

*** Chan. 8457. (i) Walker; (ii) Fingerhut, LSO, Simon.

Giulini's performances come from the early 1960s, and the
disc also includes Soriano's excellent account of *Nights in
the Gardens of Spain*. The Philharmonia playing is polished
and responsive and Giulini produces civilized, colourful
performances. The recording, too, is brightly coloured and,
although noticeably resonant in *The Three-Cornered Hat*,
the present transfers offer vivid and full-bodied sound. *El
amor brujo* is not as red-blooded here as it is in the hands of
Dutoit, but Victoria de los Angeles's contribution is an
undoubted point in its favour, as are the vocal bonuses.

The late Eduardo Mata's account of *El amor brujo* is much
more exciting than Giulini's. Mata, too, has an uninhibited
vocal soloist in Nancy Mistral and her singing is, if anything,
more earthy than Los Angeles's. *Nights in the Gardens of
Spain* brings a highly sympathetic contribution from Joa-

quin Achucarro, and the performance is both evocative and exciting, if not as delicately refined as the Soriano/Giulini account. The dances from *The Three-Cornered Hat* are more rhythmically subtle than usual, although here the LSO violin timbre sounds thinner. A good super-bargain triptych, nevertheless.

The brightly lit Chandos recording emphasizes the vigour of Geoffrey Simon's very vital account of *El amor brujo*, and Sarah Walker's powerful vocal contribution is another asset, her vibrantly earthy singing highly involving. The Simon/Fingerhut version of *Nights in the Gardens of Spain* also makes a strongly contrasted alternative to Alicia de Larrocha's much-praised reading and the effect is more dramatic, with the soloist responding chimerically to the changes of mood. The *Interlude and Dance* from *La vida breve* make a very attractive encore.

Stokowski's charismatic stereo Philadelphia recording of *El amor brujo* is fierce and sumptuous by turns. It was he who introduced the ballet to America, and its drama is vividly presented. The orchestra play with passionate conviction, and Shirley Verrett ranges between rich vibrato and raucous flamenco-like tone. The *Nights in the Gardens of Spain* receives a flamboyantly expressive performance from Entremont and Ormandy – both artists forming a true partnership, with a well-judged balance between glitter and a delicate blending of textures; real electricity is generated. The dances from the *Three-Cornered Hat* are strongly characterized too, though the violins sound a bit glassy here. The recordings date from the 1960s and are not outstanding, but do not detract from the vivid music-making.

(i) *El amor brujo (Love, the Magician)*; (ii) *The Three-Cornered Hat* (ballets; both complete).

(B) *** DG (ADD) 457 878-2. Berganza, (i) LSO, Navarro; (ii) Boston SO, Ozawa.

(i) *El amor brujo (Love, the Magician)*; (ii) *The Three-Cornered Hat* (ballet); *La vida breve: Interlude and Dance.*

(M) *** Decca (ADD) 466 991-2. SRO, Ansermet, with (i) de Gabarain; (ii) Berganza.

Listening to Ansermet's early 1960s version of *The Three-Cornered Hat*, you understand why his recordings are cherished by audiophiles: the sound is glitteringly brilliant and full. The performance has lots of character and shows the conductor and his orchestra on top form. *El amor brujo* is not quite so brilliant as a recording, or as a performance, but it is still very good, with plenty of nice touches here and there. It is always a pleasure to hear the *Interlude and Dance* from *La vida breve*: the *Dance* of which – a most catchy tune – is especially vivid here. A very colourful and worthy addition to Decca's Legends label.

Teresa Berganza links the comparable DG pairing. Both the recordings date from the late 1970s, and at that time Ozawa's Boston sound is vividly alive, even more so on CD, and has a wide dynamic range yet an admirable presence without distorting perspectives. *El amor brujo*, recorded in London's Henry Wood Hall, brings a slightly more recessed effect and the score's magical moments of evocation are beautifully done, while Berganza's contribution is vibrantly

idiomatic, and the responsive LSO playing (wind and strings alike) is comparably seductive in the *Pantomime* sequence.

'*Música española*': (i; ii) *El amor brujo* (ballet; complete); (iii; iv) *Harpsichord Concerto* (for harpsichord, flute, oboe, clarinet, violin & cello); (v) *Nights in the Gardens of Spain*; (vi; ii) *The Three-Cornered Hat* (ballet; complete); (ii) *La vida breve: Interlude and Dance*; (vii; iv) *Psyché*; (vii; viii; iv) *El retablo de Maese Pedro (Master Peter's Puppet Show).*

(M) *** Double Decca (ADD) 433 908-2 (2). (i) De Gabarain; (ii) SRO, Ansermet; (iii) Constable; (iv) L. Sinfonia, Rattle; (v) De Larrocha, LPO, Frühbeck de Burgos; (vi) Berganza; (vii) Smith; (viii) with Oliver, Knapp.

Ansermet's vivaciously spirited complete *The Three-Cornered Hat* is also available separately (see above). John Constable proves an admirable interpreter of the *Concierto* and there is no doubting the truth and subtlety of the balance or the excellence of the performance. *Psyché* is a setting of words by Jean Aubry for voice and a small instrumental grouping of the size used in the *Harpsichord Concerto*. Jennifer Smith is an excellent soloist and the orchestral response in both works is thoroughly alive and characterful. *Master Peter's Puppet Show* is not really an opera but a play within a play, both audience and performers being puppets. The singers are excellent. Simon Rattle shows himself completely at home in the Spanish sunshine, and the orchestral playing and recording are matchingly vivid.

Nights in the Gardens of Spain.

(M) (***) Ph. (IMS) mono 442 751-2 (2). Del Pueyo, LAP, Martinon – GRANADOS: *Danzas españolas* etc. ***

(N) (BB) *** Warner Apex 8573 89223-2. Heisser, Lausanne CO, López-Cobos – ALBENIZ: *Concierto fantástico; Rapsodia española;* TURINA: *Rapsodia sinfónica.* ***

(M) *** DG 463 085-2. Weber, Bav. RSO, Kubelik – MARTINU: *Fantasia concertante* ***; TCHEREPNIN: *10 Bagatelles* ***; WEBER: *Konzertstück.* **(*)

(i) *Nights in the Gardens of Spain. El amor brujo: Ritual Fire Dance.*

(M) **(*) RCA (ADD) 09026 63070-2. Rubinstein; (i) Phd. O, Ormandy – FRANCK: *Symphonic Variations* ***; SAINT-SAENS: *Concerto No. 2.* **(*)

Dating from 1955, Del Pueyo's *Nights in the Gardens of Spain* has never been surpassed. Martinon's magically evocative orchestral opening is matched by the delicacy of the solo entry, and the continuing dialogue between piano and the Paris orchestra brings incandescent subtlety of colour. The slightly diffuse orchestral tapestry presented by the warmly atmospheric recording, which sounds for all the world like stereo, suits the music admirably. Unforgettable.

The performance by Jean-François Heisser (with López-Cobos a highly idiomatic partner) is also first class in every way, combining warm evocation, brilliant colouring and excitement. The playing could hardly be more grippingly spontaneous, and the modern (1996) digital sound is vividly real. The couplings are equally attractive and this comes in the lowest price range.

Kubelik brings out all the excitement of Falla's vivid score, well supported by Margrit Weber (see above). Imaginative new couplings, too.

Rubinstein's 1969 Philadelphia version is an aristocratic reading, treating the work as a brilliantly coloured and mercurial concert-piece rather than a misty evocation, with flamenco rhythms glittering in the finale. The two encores which follow are even more arresting. This is now part of the Rubinstein Edition and has been impressively remastered.

(i) *Nights in the Gardens of Spain*; (ii) *The Three-Cornered Hat* (ballet; complete).

*** Teldec 0630 17415. Chicago SO, with (i) Barenboim
(piano), cond. Domingo; (ii) Larmore, cond. Barenboim.

The catalogue is well served by luminous recordings of Manuel da Falla's *Nights*, in fragrantly evocative Spanish gardens. But a first-class new version is very welcome indeed, and Barenboim and Domingo make a outstanding partnership, catching the perfumes of the Spanish night and the shimmering background of flamenco dance rhythms. The gentle entry into the jasmin-scented *Generalife* in Granada is subtly managed by Domingo, and the great climax at the end brings a thrilling burst of passion. From the glittering central 'Danza lejana' we are lead into the final sequence with sparkling pianism, and the closing pages bring a richly languorous apotheosis.

Barenboim moves from keyboard to rostrum for *The Three-Cornered Hat* and opens briskly and vigorously. Jennifer Larmore is the vibrant if not especially individual mezzo soloist. Again the superb Chicago Orchestra revels not only in the vivid colouring and bold rhythms, but also in the gentler moments. The Miller's *Farruca* brings a stoically gutsy pulse and the boisterous final *Jota* is vigorous and uninhibited. The live recording if not in the demonstration bracket is full-blooded and yet has plenty of transparency.

The Three-Cornered Hat (ballet; complete).

*** Chan. 8904. Gomez, Philh. O, Tortelier – ALBENIZ:
Iberia. ***

Yan Pascal Tortelier is hardly less seductive than Dutoit in handling Falla's beguiling dance-rhythms, bringing out the score's humour as well as its colour. The fine Chandos recording is full and vivid, if rather reverberant, and Jill Gomez's contribution floats within the resonance; but the acoustic warmth adds to the woodwind bloom and the strings are beguilingly rich. The closing *Jota* is joyfully vigorous.

The Three-Cornered Hat (ballet): *3 Dances*.

(B) *** Decca Penguin (ADD) 460 638-2. Montreal SO, Dutoit
– RODRIGO: *Concierto de Aranjuez; Fantasia para un
gentilhombre*. *** ⬤
(***) Testament mono SBT1017. Philh O, Cantelli – CASELLA:
Paganiniana; DUKAS: *L'Apprenti sorcier*; RAVEL:
Daphnis et Chloé: Suite No. 2. (***)

These three dances, taken from Dutoit's excellent 1981 complete ballet, make a colourful interlude between two outstanding performances of Rodrigo. The personal essay is by Victoria Glendinning.

It is good that Cantelli's excellent (1954) performances of these vivid dances are back in such fine transfers. Elegant, polished accounts, given very good mono sound.

GUITAR MUSIC

7 Spanish Popular Songs (*Suite populaire españolas*; arr. for guitar).

(B) *** [EMI Red Line CDR5 69850]. Barrueco – GRANADOS:
Danzas españolas. ***

Barrueco is a magician among the new school of guitarists, and his delicate nuances of colouring in these song transcriptions are matched by his seemingly spontaneous rhythmic freedom. Excellent recording too.

PIANO MUSIC

Fantasía bética.

(BB) **(*) ASV (ADD) CDQS 6079. Petchersky – ALBENIZ:
Suite española. **(*)

Falla's masterly *Fantasía bética* calls for more dramatic fire and projection than Alma Petchersky commands. But she is a musical and neat player, the recording is very acceptable and this recital (which also includes Granados's *Allegro de concierto*) is competitively priced.

Fantasia bética; 4 Piezas españolas.

(B) *** Double Decca (ADD) 433 926-2 (2). De Larrocha –
ALBENIZ: *Iberia; Navarra* etc.

These welcome and attractive couplings for Albéniz's *Iberia* are given exemplary performances and most realistic recording.

OPERA

La vida breve (complete).

(M) *** EMI (ADD) CMS5 67587-2 (2). De los Angeles,
Higueras, Rivadeneyra, Cossutta, Moreno, Orfeon
Donostiarra Ch., Nat. O of Spain, Frühbeck de Burgos – *El
amor brujo* etc. ***

La vida breve is a kind of Spanish *Cavalleria rusticana* without the melodrama, and the final scene is weakened by a fundamental lack of drama in the plot. Victoria de Los Angeles deepened her interpretation over the years and her imaginative colouring of the words gives a unique authority and evocation to her performance. The flamenco singer in Act II (Gabriel Moreno) also matches the realism of the idiom with an authentic 'folk' style. The other members of the cast are good without being memorable; but when this is primarily a solo vehicle for de los Angeles, and the orchestral interludes are managed so colloquially, this is readily recommendable. The recording remains atmospheric, as well as having increased vividness and presence.

FARNON, Robert (born 1917)

A la claire fontaine; Colditz March; Derby Day; Gateway to the West; How Beautiful is Night; 3 Impressions for Orchestra: 2, In a Calm; 3, Manhattan Playboy. Jumping Bean; Lake in the Woods; Little Miss Molly; Melody Fair; Peanut Polka; Pictures in the Fire; Portrait of a Flirt; A Star is Born; State Occasion; Westminster Waltz.

*** Marco 8.223401. Slovak RSO (Bratislava), Leaper.

Farnon's quirky rhythmic numbers, *Portrait of a Flirt, Peanut Polka* and *Jumping Bean*, have much in common with Leroy Anderson in their instant memorability; their counterpart is a series of gentler orchestral watercolours, usually featuring a wistful flute solo amid gentle washes of violins. *A la claire fontaine* is the most familiar. Then there are the film music, of which the *Colditz March* is rightly famous, and the very British genre pieces, written in the 1950s. All this is played by this excellent Slovak orchestra with warmth, polish and a remarkable naturalness of idiomatic feeling. The recording is splendid, vivid with the orchestra set back convincingly in a concert hall acoustic.

FASCH, Johann (1688–1758)

Chalumeau Concerto in B flat, FWV L:B1; Concerto in C min. for Bassoon & 2 Oboes, FWV L:C2; Concerto in D for 2 Horns, 2 Oboes & 2 Bassoons, FWV L:D14; Trumpet Concerto in D, FWV L:D1.

*** DG (IMS) 449 210-2. Soloists, E. Concert, Pinnock.

Fasch's *Suite in G minor* is attractively inventive and colourful, very much in the manner of Telemann. The *Trumpet Concerto* is a short, unambitious work, but Mark Bennett makes a fairly good case for it. The *Concerto for Chalumeau*, an early clarinet, is altogether more individual. Colin Lawson is completely in command of his period instrument, his tone is succulent, his performance winning. This work is a real find. The *Concerto*, which features a pair of horns makes considerable demands on the players in the jolly allegros which frame a *Largo*, where the sustained upper tessitura brings trills and other ornamentation. The *C minor Concerto for Bassoon and Two Oboes* is more of a concerto grosso and agreeable rather than distinctive. However, the excellence of the performances here and the fine recording make this a collection well worth exploring.

Quadros: in B flat, FWV N:B2; in D min., FWV N:d2; in F, FWV N:F2; in G min., FWV N:g1; Trio Sonatas: in D min., FWV N:d1; in G min., FWV N:g2; in F, FWV N:F6.

(N) ** HM HMC 905251. Arfken, Brüggemann, Agrell & continuo.

Fasch, a contemporary of J. S. Bach, wrote in a gallant manner without the lively polyphonic interest of his most famous contemporary. These are agreeable works, but the oboes generally play together in simple harmony, while the part-writing and imitation is comparatively ingenuous. The music is pleasing but no more. The recording closely inte-

grates the instruments – a degree more separation would have been welcome.

FAURÉ, Gabriel (1845–1924)

(i; ii) *Après un rêve;* Elégie (both for cello and orchestra); (iii) *Masques et bergamasques;* (ii; iv) *Pavane;* (ii; v) *Pelléas et Mélisande: Suite;* Harp: (vi) *Une châtelaine en sa tour;* Piano: (vii) *Dolly;* (viii) *Barcarolle No. 2; Nocturne No. 4;* (ix) *Cantique de Jean Racine;* Mélodies: (x) *Les berceaux; Le secret; Soir; L'horizon chimérique* (cycle). (xi) *Requiem.*

(N) (B) **(*) DG Panorama (ADD) 469 268-2 (2). (i) Erskin; (ii) Boston SO, Ozawa; (iii) Orpheus CO; (iv) Tanglewood Fest. Ch.; (v) Hunt; (vi) Zabaleta; (vii) Alfons & Aloys Kontarsky; (viii) Rogé; (ix) King's College Ch., Cambridge, Cleobury; (x) Souzay, Baldwin; (xi) Battle, Schmidt, Philh. Ch. & O, Giulini.

Although some of the performances here are inclined to excessive reticence, overall this well-planned collection makes a good introduction to Fauré's special sensibility. In the orchestral items Ozawa's understatement goes a shade too far at times, but *Pelléas et Mélisande* includes the rarely heard *Chanson de Mélisande* sung simply and sweetly by Lorraine Hunt. However, neither she nor the eminently musical cello soloist (Jules Erskine) in the two concertante pieces displays a strong individuality. The *Pavane* is almost certainly sung in French, though the words are inaudible, partly because of the Boston resonance; the choral embroidery, however, adds an agreeable touch of vitality to a rather solemn performance.

Masques et bergamasques springs to life in the hands of the Orpheus Chamber Orchestra and is played vigorously and warmly. Similarly, the Kontarskys give a vividly sympathetic account of *Dolly,* and Pascal Rogé plays the two piano pieces beautifully. Nicanor Zabaleta too is very beguiling in his own arrangement of *Une châtelaine en sa tour,* and Souzay is in his element in the *Mélodies.* However, though the King's performance of the *Cantique* cannot be faulted, Giulini returns to a comparatively withdrawn mood for the *Requiem.*

Using large-scale Philharmonia forces, he adopts consistently slow speeds and a very reverential manner. Such an approach usually makes the work too sentimental, but Giulini's care for detail in textures and his unexaggerated expressive style keep the result hushed and prayerful rather than sugary. Kathleen Battle sings glowingly in the *Pié Jesu,* sounding sumptuous but not really in style. Throughout the programme the warmly atmospheric recording is a considerable plus point, and this is certainly value for money, even if no texts are included.

Ballade for Piano & Orchestra, Op. 19.

☢ (N) (BB) (***) Dutton mono CDBP 9714. K. Long, Nat. SO, Boyd Neel; LEIGH: *Concertino;* MOZART: *Piano Concertos No. 15 & 24.* (***)

*** Chan. 8773. Louis Lortie, LSO, Frühbeck de Burgos – RAVEL: *Piano Concertos.* **(*)

(BB) **(*) Naxos 8.550754. Thiollier, Nat. SO of Ireland, De Almeida – FRANCK: *Symphonic Variations;* D´INDY: *Symphonie sur un air montagnard français.* **(*)

Recorded in 1944, Kathleen Long's classic recording of Fauré's *Ballade for Piano and Orchestra* remains among the most inspired ever, at once subtle and immediate in its communication, a perfect demonstration of Long's refined artistry. A fine supplement to the equally subtle readings of Mozart *Concertos* and the hauntingly effective Leigh *Concertino*. A magical (and very generous) CD, very well recorded and transferred.

Louis Lortie is a thoughtful artist and his playing has both sensitivity and strength. This is as penetrating and well recorded an account of Fauré's lovely piece as any now available; however, the coupling is not one of the preferred versions of the Ravel concertos.

Naxos offer an intelligently planned triptych. François-Joël Thiollier shows some imagination and sensitivity in Fauré's lovely *Ballade*, which is not represented as generously on CD as it should be. The orchestral playing is perfectly acceptable, without being in any way out of the ordinary; likewise the recording. All the same, it is worth the money.

(i) *Ballade for Piano & Orchestra, Op. 19. Dolly Suite;* (ii) *Elégie for Cello & Orchestra;* (iii) *Fantaisie for Flute & Orchestra* (orch. I. Aubert). *Masques et bergamasques, pavane* (orch. H. Rabaud); *Pénélope: Prelude.*

*** Chan. 9416. (i) Stott; (ii) Dixon; (iii) Davis; BBC PO, Tortelier.

Beautifully played and richly recorded, with Yan Pascal Tortelier a most understanding interpreter, this neatly brings together the most popular orchestral pieces of Fauré, miniatures which often convey surprising weight of feeling as well as charm, as for example the celebrated *Elégie*, here tenderly played by Peter Dixon. Kathryn Stott, brings out not only the poetry in the *Ballade for Piano and Orchestra*, but the scherzando sparkle of the virtuoso passages. Just as convincing are the *Fantaisie* for flute (soloist Richard Davis) and the ever-popular *Dolly Suite*, both arranged by other hands. The four brief movements of *Masques et bergamasques* are charmingly done and Tortelier's account of the *Overture* to *Masques et bergamasques* is second to none. Indeed, he has the measure of all the music on this disc, be it the poignancy of the *Pénélope Prelude* or the delicacy of the *Dolly Suite.*

(i) *Ballade for Piano & Orchestra;* (ii) *Requiem; Cantique de Jean Racine.*

(N) (BB) **(*) EMI Encore CDE5 74728-2. (i) Ogdon (ii) Burrowes, Rayner-Cook, CBSO, Ch., CBSO, Frémaux.

The elusive and delicate essence of Fauré's *Ballade* is not easy to capture, but John Ogdon's warmly affectionate approach is enjoyable and is notably sensitive in the central and closing sections of the work. Frémaux has a moulded style in the *Requiem* which does not spill over into too much expressiveness, and there is a natural warmth about this performance that is persuasive. Norma Burrowes sings beautifully; her innocent style is most engaging. The origin-ally reverberant recording has been refocused somewhat and does not lose too much of its ambient glow.

(i) *Berceuse, Op. 116; Dolly* (suite), *Op. 56; Masques et bergamasques, Op. 112; Pelléas et Mélisande* (suite), *Op. 80;* (ii) *Shylock* (suite), *Op. 57.*

(BB) *** Naxos 8.553360. Dublin RTE Sinf., Giorgiadis; with (i) Healy; (ii) Russell.

John Georgiadis with his rhythmic flair not only brings out the colour and vigour of the fast movements but, as a fine violinist himself, persuades his Irish players to draw out the expressive warmth of such numbers as *Tendresse* in the *Dolly Suite*. *Masques et bergamasques*, the *Dolly Suite* and the incidental music to *Pelléas et Mélisande* are all among Faurés best-loved works, and it is good too to have the rarer music for the Shakespeare-based play, *Shylock*, complete with two vocal movements sweetly sung by Lynda Russell. Michael Healy is the expressive violin soloist in the lovely *Berceuse*. Warm, atmospheric recording, transferred at rather a low level.

(i) *Elégie in C min.* (for cello and orchestra), *Op. 24.*

*** EMI CDC5 56126-2. Chang, LSO, Rostropovich – BRUCH: *Kol Nidrei* ***; SAINT-SAENS: *Cello Concerto No. 1* ***; TCHAIKOVSKY: *Rococo Variations.* *** ●
(B) *** EMI Début CZS5 73727-2. Phillips, Bavarian Chamber PO, Plasson – CAPLET: *Epiphany;* LALO: *Cello Concerto.* ***
(M) *** Sony (ADD) SBK 48278. Rose, Phd. O, Ormandy – BLOCH: *Schelomo* ***; LALO: *Concerto* **(*); TCHAIKOVSKY: *Rococo Variations.* ***
(B) *** DG (ADD) 431 166-2. Schiff, New Philh. O, Mackerras – LALO: *Cello Concerto;* SAINT-SAENS: *Cello Concerto No. 1.* ***

Han-Na Chang is a naturally inspirational artist, and on her sensitive bow the lovely and sometimes elusive *Elégie* is made to sound like a vocal aria, the shaping and use of light and shade unerring, with a dedicated accompaniment from her mentor, Rostropovich. The recorded sound is very beautiful.

From the impressive Xavier Phillips, a poetically songful and only marginally recessive performance, with orchestra and soloist at one in their response to Fauré's emotional and dynamic contrasts.

An ardent yet not over-pressed account from Leonard Rose of Fauré's lovely *Elégie* which admirably captures its idiom and its feeling of burgeoning yet restrained ecstasy. The recording is close, but the cello image is natural and firm. The rest of this collection is also highly recommendable.

Heinrich Schiff also gives an eloquent account of the *Elégie*, and he is finely accompanied and superbly recorded.

Pavane, Op. 60.

(B) *** Decca 448 711-2. ASMF, Marriner – DURUFLE: *Requiem;* POULENC: *Gloria.* ***

Marriner's warmly elegant account of the famous *Pavane* is used effectively on this Decca disc as an interlude between Duruflé's *Requiem* and Poulenc's *Gloria*, both fine performances.

(i) *Pelléas et Mélisande (incidental music), Op. 80;*
(ii) *Pavane, Op. 50.*

(B) *** Ph. Duo 462 309-2. Rotterdam PO, Zinman, with
Gomez; (ii) Fournet – SCHOENBERG: *Pelleas and
Melisande; Verklaerte Nacht.* SIBELIUS: *Pelléas et
Mélisande; Swan of Tuonela.* **(*)

Fauré's incidental music is beautifully played and to make
the selection complete, Jill Gomez gives a delightful account
of the song *The three blind daughters*, not previously
recorded. David's Zinman's refined approach suits Fauré
admirably and there is a pervasive tenderness and delicacy
(the *Sicilienne* is memorable). The 1979 analogue recording
too is naturally balanced and of high quality. Fournet's
account of the famous *Pavane* is also very sensitive.

Pelléas et Mélisande (suite), Op. 80; (i) *Pavane, Op. 50.*

*** Chan. 8952. (i) Renaissance Singers; Ulster O, Tortelier –
CHAUSSON: *Poème* etc. ***

These finely finished and atmospheric performances come
in harness with a fine account from the soloist-conductor
of Chausson's *Poème* and a perceptive and idiomatic performance of the *Poème de la mer et de l'amour.* Very good
orchestral playing and exemplary recording.

CHAMBER MUSIC

(i) *Allegretto Moderato for 2 Cellos;* (ii) *Andante. Elégie,
Op. 24; Papillon, Op. 77; Romance, Op. 69; Sérénade,
Op. 98; Sicilienne, Op. 78; Sonatas Nos. 1 in D min.
Op. 109; 2 in G min., Op. 117.*

**(*) RCA 09026 68049-2. Isserlis, Devoyon; with
(i) Waterman; (ii) Greer.

Steven Isserlis understands the essential reticence and refinement of Fauré's art. Perhaps he is at times a shade too
reticent in the music and could allow himself to produce a
more ardent and songful tone. The balance, which slightly
favours his partner, contributes to this impression. Pascal
Devoyon is a no less perceptive and sensitive artist. A welcome, then, for the artistry of these performances, but tinged
with slight disappointment at the less than ideal balance.

*Cello Sonatas Nos. 1 in D min., Op. 109; 2 in G min.,
Op.117.*

(N) (B) *** EMI (ADD) CZS5 74333-2 (2). Tortelier, Heidsieck
– CHOPIN; MENDELSSOHN; RACHMANINOV: *Cello
Sonatas.* ***

Cello Sonatas Nos. 1, Op. 109; 2, Op. 117; Après un rêve
(trans. Casals); *Elégie, Op. 24; Papillon, Op. 77; Romance,
Op. 69; Sicilienne, Op. 78; Sérénade, Op. 98.*

*** Opus 111 OPS 30-242. Bruns, Ishay.

*Cello Sonatas Nos. 1 in D min., Op. 109; 2 in G min.,
Op. 117; Elégie, Op. 24; Sicilienne, Op. 78.*

(M) *** CRD (ADD) CRD 3316. Igloi, Benson.

Noble performances from the late Thomas Igloi and Clifford
Benson that do full justice to these elusive and rewarding

Fauré sonatas, and the recording is clear, if not one of CRD's
finest in terms of ambient effect.

Noble performances too from both Tortelier and Heidsieck, who play with fervour and eloquence within the restrained expressive limits of the music. The fine EMI
recording brings both instruments into the living room most
vividly.

Peter Bruns plays the Tonino cello that Casals once owned
and Roglit Ishay plays an Erard. This has a more brittle
timbre than the modern piano but Fauré himself much
liked its lighter action. Those who want the sonatas in the
sonorities the composer himself might have heard should
investigate this, which in any case is probably a first choice
for this repertoire. These two artists both play with appropriate eloquence and the miniatures come off well.

(i) *Cello Sonatas Nos. 1 in D min., Op. 109; 2 in G min.,
Op. 117;* (ii) *Andante in B flat, Op. 75; Berceuse, Op. 16;
Elégie, Op. 24;* (iii) *Fantaisie, Op. 79; Morceau de concours;*
(ii) *Morceau de lecture;* (i) *Papillon, Op. 77;* (i–ii) *Piano
Trio in D min., Op. 120.* (ii) *Romance, Op. 28;* (i) *Serenade
in B min., Op. 98; Sicilienne, Op. 78;* (ii) *Violin Sonatas
Nos. 1 in A, Op. 15; 2 in E min., Op. 108;*

(B) *** EMI (ADD) CZS5 69261-2 (2). Collard; (i) Lodéon;
(ii) Dumay; (iii) Debost.

Piano Quartets Nos. (i; ii) *1 in C min., Op. 15;* (i; iii) *2 in
G min., Op. 45; Piano Quintets Nos. 1 in C min., Op. 89; 2
in D min., Op. 115;* (iii) *String Quartet in E min., Op. 121.*

(B) **(*) EMI (ADD) CZS5 69264-2 (2). (i) Collard;
(ii) Dumay, Pasquier, Lodéon; (iii) Parrenin Qt.

Dumay and Collard bring different and equally valuable
insights, and the performances of the *Piano Quartets* are
masterly. In addition, there are authoritative and idiomatic
readings of the two *Piano Quintets*, the enigmatic and other-
worldly *Quartet*, and on the first set above, the *Piano Trio*,
the two *Cello Sonatas*, (what a fine player Lodéon is!), plus
all the smaller pieces. True there are excellent accounts of
the *Violin Sonatas* elsewhere, from Grumiaux/Crossley and
Amoyal/Rogé, and the *Cellos Sonatas* are well served by both
Ingloi and Isserliss (see below); but many of the smaller
pieces are more elusive, and they are presented here with a
generally admirable standard of performance and recording.
This is enormously civilized music whose rewards grow with
each hearing; however, one has to accept that, because the
Paris Salle Wagram was employed for the recordings (made
between 1975 and 1978), close microphones have been used
to counteract the hall's resonance. The remastering has both
increased the sense of presence and brought a certain dryness
to the ambient effect, although the string timbres are fresh.

*Piano Quartet No. 1 in C min., Op. 15; Piano Quintet No. 1
in D min., Op. 89.*

*** Decca 455 149-2. Rogé, Ysaÿe Qt.

It goes without saying that Pascal Rogé and the Ysaÿe Quartet
give performances of great finesse and sensitivity. They are
perhaps more successful in the quintet than in the earlier
piece, where they must yield to Domus (Hyperion) who find
greater delight and high spirits in the scherzo. The recording
is very good though there is the occasional moment when

the reverberant acoustic affects the focus. This is scarcely worth mentioning and there is no cause to withhold a full three-star rating.

Piano Quartets Nos. 1 in C min., Op. 15; 2 in G min., Op. 45.

⚫ *** Hyp. CDA 66166. Domus.

*** Sony SK 48066. Ax, Stern, Laredo, Ma.

(BB) **(*) ASV Quicksilva CDQS6237. Schubert Ens. of London.

Domus have the requisite lightness of touch and subtlety, and just the right sense of scale and grasp of tempi. Their nimble and sensitive pianist, Susan Tomes, can hold her own in the most exalted company. The recording is excellent, too, though the balance is a little close, but the sound is not airless.

Sony's starry version of the two *Piano Quartets* with Emanuel Ax, Isaac Stern, Jaime Laredo and Yo-Yo Ma offers a serious challenge to the Domus account on Hyperion. The performances are of high quality and anyone could rest happy with them.

A very serviceable coupling on ASV, which offers very good value. Very musical playing, attentive to the letter and the spirit of these scores without, perhaps, the last ounce of distinction that the Domus team brought to them on Hyperion. Very well recorded indeed. Well worth the modest asking price – and more!

Piano Quartet No. 2 in G min., Op. 45; Piano Quintet No. 2 in C min., Op. 115.

*** Decca 455 150-2. Rogé, Ysaÿe Qt.

The playing of all concerned is excellent, alive and subtle with expert and sensitive contributions from the distinguished pianist. As in its predecessor the aural image is not in ideal focus, with Pascal Rogé very slightly too much to the fore and the quartet not as well defined. But such is the quality of the playing that it would be curmudgeonly to withhold a third star.

Piano Quintets Nos. 1 in D min., Op. 89; 2 in C min., Op. 115.

⚫ *** Hyp. CDA 66766. Domus, with Marwood.

*** Claves CD 50-8603. Quintetto Fauré di Roma.

The playing of Domus in these two masterpieces is as light, delicate and full of insight as one would expect. They make one fall for this music all over again. The second is among the masterpieces of Fauré's Indian summer as he approached his eighties. As this concentrated performance suggests, its autumnal lyricism brings likenesses to late Elgar, with the pianist, Susan Tomes, at her most sparkling in the mercurial Scherzo. Excellent sound.

The Quintetto Fauré di Roma also have the measure of Fauré's subtle phrasing and his wonderfully plastic melodic lines, and their performances are hard to fault. The recording, made in a Swiss church, is warm and splendidly realistic. This music, once you get inside it, has a hypnotic effect and puts you completely under its spell.

(i) Piano Quintet No. 2 in C min., Op. 115 (ii) Violin Sonata No. 1 in A, Op. 13; (iii) Dolly Suite (for piano duet), Op. 56.

(N) (M) **(*) CRD 3505. (i) Nash Ens; (ii) Crayford, Brown; (iii) Brown; Tomes.

A very fine account from Marcia Crayford and Ian Brown of the *A major Violin Sonata*, sensitive yet vital. Some may feel that they are brought too close to the artists, but the balance between the two instruments is musically judged. The *Dolly Suite* is beautifully done, and Ian Brown and Susan Tomes convey its charm and innocence in exemplary fashion. The balance in the *Second Piano Quintet* is less than ideal, the piano being rather too dominant, and in this respect the Domus version on Hyperion is to be preferred. Overall the sound on this disc is a bit too bright, but the playing is full of conviction and artistically this must carry a strong recommendation.

Piano Trio in D min., Op. 120.

*** Ara. Z 6643. Golub Kaplan Carr Trio – DEBUSSY: *Piano Trio* ***; SAINT-SAENS: *Piano Trio*. **(*)

*** Hyp. CDA 67114. Florestan Trio – DEBUSSY; RAVEL: *Piano Trios*. ***

Piano Trio in D min., Op. 120; (i) La Bonne Chanson, Op. 61.

(M) *** CRD (ADD) CRD 3389. Nash Ens., (i) with Walker.

David Golub, Mark Kaplan and Colin Carr give as understanding and idiomatic a performance of the sublime Fauré *Trio* as is to be found. They convey its understatement and subtlety of nuance to perfection, and the interplay among them is a model of the finest chamber-music-making. The recording is very good indeed, with plenty of warmth.

The Florestans offer a very apt coupling of three sharply contrasted French works. Fauré is represented in mellow old age, Debussy as a teenager and Ravel in high maturity. With personnel drawn from the piano quartet group Domus, led by the pianist Susan Tomes, they give an exceptionally strong, unapologetic reading, at once highly polished and flexibly expressive, revealing what power Fauré retained to the end of his life. Vivid sound.

The members of the Nash Ensemble also give a dedicated performance of the late, rarefied *Piano Trio*, capturing both the elegance and the restrained concentration. They are hardly less persuasive in the song cycle where the characterful warmth and vibrancy of Sarah Walker's voice, not to mention her positive artistry, come out strongly in this beautiful reading of Fauré's early settings of Verlaine, music both tender and ardent. The atmospheric recording is well up to CRD's high standard in chamber music.

String Quartet in E min., Op. 121.

*** Conifer 75605 51291-2. Miami Qt – SAINT-SAENS: *String Quartets Nos. 1 & 2*. ***

Fauré's only *Quartet* is among his most elusive scores and is very difficult to bring off. The Miami Quartet is equipped both with great understanding and refined musicianship, but are richly endowed with technical finesse and musical insight. Theirs is the finest account of the *Quartet* to have appeared for many years. The claims of their set are further enhanced by the interest of the coupling, the two *String Quartets* of Saint-Saëns.

Violin Sonatas Nos. 1 in A, Op. 13; 2 in E min., Op. 108.

(B) *** Hyp. Helios CDH 55030. Osostowicz, Tomes.

(M) *** Ph. 426 384-2. Grumiaux, Crossley – FRANCK: *Sonata.* **(*)

Violin Sonatas Nos. 1–2; Andante, Op. 75; Berceuse, Op. 16.

(BB) **(*) ASV CDQS 6170. Fujikawa, Osorio.

Violin Sonatas Nos. 1 in A, Op. 13; 2 in E min., Op. 108; Andante in B flat, Op. 75; Berceuse, Op. 16; Romance in B flat, Op. 28.

⚫ *** Decca 436 866-2. Amoyal, Rogé.

(BB) *** Naxos 8.550906. Kang, Devoyon.

Pierre Amoyal and Pascal Rogé are totally inside the idiom and convey its subtlety and refinement with freshness and mastery. There are admirable alternatives, but Amoyal and Rogé more than hold their own against them and throw new light on the three slight miniatures that they offer as a bonus. Impeccable recording, too. A lovely disc.

Dong-Suk Kang, splendidly partnered by another French pianist, Pascal Devoyon give us performances which are hardly less fine and which cost only a third as much as the Decca CD. Without disturbing our allegiance to other earlier issues, this is a welcome newcomer – and very good value for money.

Krysia Osostowicz and Susan Tomes bring an appealingly natural, unforced quality to their playing and they are completely persuasive, particularly in the elusive *Second Sonata*. The acoustic is a shade resonant but, such is the eloquence of these artists, the ear quickly adjusts. At Helios price, this is highly recommendable.

These *Sonatas* are also beautifully played and recorded on the Philips reissue. Moreover the two artists sound as if they are in the living-room; the acoustic is warm, lively and well balanced. An excellent mid-priced recommendation.

Mayumi Fujikawa and Jorge Federico Osorio produce playing of the highest accomplishment and finesse. There is genuine passion here and real commitment. They are recorded in a resonant hall, and the fairly close microphones are not always flattering to the violin's upper range under stress, although not too much need be made of this: Fujikawa often makes a beautiful sound, and particularly so in the lovely *Berceuse.*

PIANO MUSIC
Piano duet

Dolly, Op. 56.

*** Ph. (IMS) 420 159-2. K. and M. Labèque – BIZET: *Jeux d'enfants;* RAVEL: *Ma Mère l'Oye.* ***

The Labèque sisters give a beautiful account of Fauré's touching suite, their playing distinguished by great sensitivity and delicacy. The recording is altogether first class.

Solo piano

Ballade in F sharp, Op. 19; Barcarolles Nos. 1–13; (i) Dolly, Op. 56. Impromptus Nos. 1–5; Impromptu, Op. 86; Mazurka in B flat, Op. 32; 13 Nocturnes; Pièces brèves Nos. 1–8, Op. 84; 9 Préludes, Op. 103; Romances sans paroles Nos. 1–3; (i) Souvenirs de Bayreuth. Theme & Variations in C sharp min., Op. 73; Valses-caprices Nos. 1–4.

⚫ *** Hyp. CDA 66911/4 (4). Stott, (i) with Roscoe.

Both the *Thirteen Barcarolles*, written between 1880 and 1921, and the *Thirteen Nocturnes*, from an even wider period between 1875 and 1921, give a most illuminating view of Fauré's career, gentle and unsensational like the music itself, but with the subtlest of developments towards a sparer, more rarefied style. That comes out all the more tellingly when, as here, they are given in succession and are played with such poetry and spontaneous-sounding freshness. Stott earlier recorded for Conifer a generous selection of Fauré piano music, but, quite apart from the warmer, clearer and more immediate sound on the Hyperion issue, allowing for velvet tone-colours, the later performances are more winningly relaxed, ranging wider in expression. Each of the four discs contains well over 70 minutes of music, logically presented, with the *Nocturnes* spread between the third and fourth discs, framing the lighter pieces, including such duets as the witty Wagner quadrille, *Souvenirs de Bayreuth*, and the ever-fresh *Dolly Suite*, both with Stott ideally partnered by Martin Roscoe. A masterly set.

Ballade in F sharp, Op. 19; Mazurka in B flat, Op. 32; 3 Songs Without Words, Op. 17; Valses-caprices Nos. 1–4.

(M) *** CRD 3426. Crossley.

Crossley is especially good in the quirky *Valses-caprices*, fully equal to their many subtleties and chimerical changes of mood. He is extremely well recorded too.

Ballade in F sharp, Op. 19; Nocturnes Nos. 1–13 (complete); 9 Préludes, Op. 103; Theme & Variations in C sharp min., Op. 73.

(B) *** EMI (ADD) CZS5 69437-2 (2). Collard.

This is glorious music which ranges from the gently reflective to the profoundly searching. The *Nocturnes* offer a glimpse of Fauré's art at its most inward and subtle. The *Préludes* are comparably intimate, and this is all music to which Jean-Philippe Collard is wholly attuned. His account of the *Theme and Variations* is no less masterly, combining the utmost tonal refinement and sensitivity with striking keyboard authority. The recording is good, though it has not the bloom and body of the very finest piano records.

Barcarolles Nos. 1–13 (complete).

(M) *** CRD (ADD) CRD 3422. Crossley.

Paul Crossley has a highly sensitive response to the subtleties of this repertoire and is fully equal to its shifting moods. The CRD version was made in the somewhat reverberant acoustic of Rosslyn Hill Chapel, and is more vivid than the 1971 EMI recording of Jean-Philippe Collard.

Barcarolles Nos. 1–13; (i) Dolly; Impromptus Nos. 1–5; Mazurka, Op. 32; Pièces brèves Nos. 1–8, Op. 84; Romances sans paroles Nos. 1–3; (i) Souvenir de Bayreuth. Valses-caprices Nos. 1–4.

(B) **(*) EMI (ADD) CZS5 69431-2 (2). Jean-Philippe Collard, (i) with Rigutto.

Jean-Philippe Collard has the qualities of reticence yet ardour, subtlety and poetic feeling to penetrate Fauré's intimate world but, while Collard has exceptional beauty and refinement of tone at all dynamic levels, the only regret is that full justice is not done to it by the French engineers.

Barcarolles Nos. 1, 2, 4, Opp. 26, 41, 44; Impromptus Nos. 2 & 3, Opp. 31, 34; Nocturnes Nos. 4 & 5, Opp. 36–7; 3 Romances sans paroles, Op. 17; Valse-caprice, Op. 30.

*** Decca (IMS) 425 606-2. Rogé.

This CD makes an ideal single-CD introduction to Fauré's piano music. Rogé brings warmth and charm as well as all his pianistic finesse to this anthology, and his artistry is well served by the Decca engineers.

Barcarolles Nos. 1, Op. 26; 6, Op. 70; Impromptus Nos. 2, Op. 31; 3, Op. 34; Nocturnes Nos. 1, 3, Op. 33/1 & 3; 4, Op. 36; 6, Op. 63; 13, Op. 13; 8 Pièces brèves, Op. 84; Romance sans paroles No. 3, Op. 17/3.

*** Hyp. CDA 67074. Stott.

An admirably chosen collection, arranged in the form of a recital taken from Kathryn Stott's complete survey. The opening *Romance Without Words* is inviting and *A minor Barcarolle* and *E flat major* and *minor Nocturnes* are particularly winning, as are the charming eight miniatures of Op. 84. A pity the *C sharp minor Theme and Variations* was not included, but what is (69 minutes) is well worth having when played and recorded so persuasively.

Impromptus Nos. 1–5; 9 Préludes, Op. 103; Theme & Variations in C sharp min., Op. 73.

(M) *** CRD (ADD) CRD 3423. Crossley.

The *Theme and Variations in C sharp minor* is one of Fauré's most immediately attractive works; Paul Crossley plays it with splendid sensitivity and panache, so this might be a good place to start for a collector wanting to explore Fauré's special pianistic world. The recorded sound, too, is extremely well judged.

Nocturnes (complete); Pièces brèves, Op. 84.

(M) **(*) CRD (ADD) CRD 3406/7. Crossley.

Here the recording is rather closely balanced, albeit in an ample acoustic, but the result tends to emphasize a percussive element that one does not normally encounter in this artist's playing. There is much understanding and finesse, however, and the *Pièces brèves* are a valuable fill-up.

VOCAL MUSIC

Mélodies: Après un rêve; Au bord de l'eau; Aurore; Clair de lune; Dans les ruines d'une abbaye; En sourdine; Fleur; Green; Ici-bas; Mai; Mandoline; Nell; Nocturne; Notre amour; Le Papillon et la fleur; Le Pays des rêves; Les Présents; Prison; Les Roses d'Ispahan; Le Secret; Soir.

(BB) *** Virgin 2 x 1 Double VBS5 61433-2. Yakar, Lavoix (with BIZET: *Pastorale; Rose d'amour; Sonnet;* CHABRIER: *Chanson pour Jeanne; L'Île heureuse; Lied ***) –* HAHN: *Mélodies.* ***

Rachel Yakar with her warm, very French-sounding timbre is an ideal interpreter of French mélodie, bringing out the subtleties of word-meaning, though it is a pity that in this super-bargain double-disc issue no texts are provided, only a cursory survey of the genre. The selection of twenty-two songs could hardly be more attractive, with settings of individual poets grouped together, so that early and late settings of Verlaine can be compared and contrasted. Excellent (1991) recording from Radio France. Coupled with an equally imaginative collection of Hahn songs, plus extra cherishable items from Bizet and Chabrier, it is a delightful issue.

Mélodies: Après un rêve; Au bord de l'eau; Les Berceaux; Clair de lune; Lydia; Mandoline; Le Papillon et la fleur; Sylvie.

*** Virgin VC5 45360-2. Gens, Vignoles – DEBUSSY; POULENC: *Mélodies.* ***

Véronique Gens is a highly accomplished artist and certainly makes a beautiful sound. She allows Fauré's art to speak for itself, although there are times when you feel stronger characterization would not come amiss. She is sensitively accompanied by Roger Vignoles and recorded with great naturalness.

La Chanson d'Eve, Op. 95; Mélodies: Après un rêve; Aubade; Barcarolle; Les Berceaux; Chanson du pêcheur; En prière; En sourdine; Green; Hymne; Des jardins de la nuit; Mandoline; Le Papillon et la fleur; Les Présents; Rêve d'amour; Les Roses d'Ispahan; Le Secret; Spleen; Toujours!.

❂ *** Hyp. CDA 66320. Baker, Parsons.

Dame Janet Baker gives magical performances of a generous collection of 28 songs, representing the composer throughout his long composing career, including many of his most winning songs. Geoffrey Parsons is at his most compellingly sympathetic, matching every mood. Many will be surprised at Fauré's variety of expression over this extended span of songs.

3 Mélodies, Op. 23 (Les Berceaux; Notre amour; Le Secret); 5 Mélodies de Venise, Op. 58 (Mandoline; En sourdine; Green; A Clymene; C'est l'extase); Mélodies, Op. 39: 2, Fleur jetée; 4, Les Roses d'Ispahan.

(BB) *** Belart (ADD) 461 624-2. Palmer, Constable – RAVEL: *Chansons; Mélodies; Poèmes.* **(*)

Felicity Palmer has the measure of Fauré's subtle and elevated art, which she shows most impressively in the *Cinq mélodies de Venise*, while the closing *Fleur jetée* is sung with great passion. She has the advantage, moreover, of John Constable's imaginative accompanying and altogether first-class analogue recording from the mid-1970s, and although no texts or translations are included, it is still a bargain.

Requiem, Op. 48.

*** Teldec 4509 90879-2. Bonney, Hampson, Amb. S., Philh. O, Legrand – DURUFLE: *Requiem.* ***

(B) *** Sony (ADD) SBK 67182. Popp, Nimsgern, Amb. S., New Philh. O, Davis – DURUFLE: *Requiem.* ***

(M) *** EMI (ADD) CDM5 66894-2. De los Angeles, Fischer-Dieskau, Brasseur Ch., Paris Conservatoire O, Cluytens.

✿ **(*) BBC (ADD) BBCL 4026-2. Price, Carol Case, BBC Ch., BBC SO, Boulanger – BOULANGER: *Psaumes 24 & 130; Pie Jesu.* **(*) ✿

(M) *** Decca (ADD) 466 418-2. Bond, Luxon, St John's College, Cambridge, Ch., ASMF, Cleobury (organ), Guest – DURUFLE: *Requiem.* ***

(B) **(*) EMI (ADD) CZS5 69647-2 (2). Cook, Burrowes, CBSO Ch., CBSO, Frémaux – BERLIOZ: *Requiem.* **

(N) ** René Gailly CD 87 162. Coppé, Van der Crabben, Capella Brugensis, Collegium Brugense, Peire – POULENC: *Organ Concerto.* **

*(*) DG 459 365-2. Bartoli, Terfel, Santa Cecilia Nat. Ac. Ch. & O, Chung – DURUFLE: *Requiem.*

Requiem; Pavane, Op. 50.

(M) *** EMI (ADD) CDM7 64634-2. Armstrong, Fischer-Dieskau, Edinburgh Festival Ch., O de Paris, Barenboim – BACH: *Magnificat.* **

*** Ph. 446 084-2. (i) McNair, Allen; ASMF Ch. & O, Marriner (with KOECHLIN: *Choral sur le nom de Fauré;* SCHMITT: *In memoriam No. 2: Scherzo sur le nom de Gabriel Fauré;* RAVEL: *Pavane pour une infante défunte* ***).

(B) **(*) [EMI (ADD) Red Line CDR5 69858]. Chilcott, Carol Case, King's College, Cambridge, Ch., New Philh. O, Willcocks – PALESTRINA: *Missa Papae Marcelli.* **

(i; ii) *Requiem, Op. 48;* (i) *Pavane; Pelléas et Mélisande: Suite, Op. 80.*

*** Decca 421 440-2. (i) Te Kanawa, Milnes; (ii) Montreal Philharmonic Ch.; Montreal SO, Dutoit.

(N) (M) **(*) Ph. (ADD) 464 701-2. Rotterdam PO; (i) Ameling, Kruysen, Cherzempa, Netherlands R. Ch., Fournet; (ii) Zinman; with Gomez.

(i) *Requiem, Op. 48;* (ii) *Messe basse.*

(B) **(*) CfP CDCFP 6072. (i) Augér, Luxon; (ii) Smy; King's College, Cambridge. Ch., Ledger.

Requiem, Op. 48 (1893 version). Ave Maria, Op. 67/2; Ave verum corpus, Op. 65/1; Cantique de Jean Racine, Op. 11; Maria, Mater gratiae, Op. 47/2; Messe basse; Tantum ergo, Op. 65/2.

*** Collegium (ADD) COLCD 109. Ashton, Varcoe, Cambridge Singers, L. Sinfonia (members), Rutter.

Requiem, Op. 48 (1893 version); Ave verum corpus, Op. 65/1; Cantique de Jean Racine, Op. 11; Messe basse; Tantum ergo, Op. 65/2.

*** Hyp. CDA 66292. Seers, Poulenard, George, Corydon Singers, ECO, Best.

(i) *Requiem, Op. 48;* (ii) *Cantique de Jean Racine, Op. 11;* (ii; iii) *Messe basse.*

(BB) *** Naxos 8.550765. Beckley, Gedge, Schola Cantorum of Oxford, Oxford Camerata, Summerly (with DE SEVERAC: *Tantum ergo;* VIERNE: *Andantino;* with Carey, organ ***).

(B) *** Double Decca (ADD) 436 486-2 (2). (i) Bond, Luxon; (ii) Cleobury; (iii) Brunt; (i–iii) St John's College, Cambridge, Ch., Guest (i) with ASMF – FAURE: *Requiem;* POULENC: *Mass* etc. ***

(i; ii; iv) *Requiem, Op. 48;* (ii; iii) *Les Djinns, Op. 12;* (ii) *Madrigal, Op. 35.*

*** Ph. 438 149-2. (i) Bott, Cachemaille; (ii) Monteverdi Ch., Salisbury Cathedral Boy Choristers; (iii) Vatin; (iv) ORR, Gardiner – DEBUSSY: *3 Chansons de Charles d'Orléans;* RAVEL: *3 Chansons;* SAINT-SAENS: *3 songs.* ***

Requiem, Op. 48 (1894 version); Messe des pêcheurs de Villerville.

(M) (M) *** HM HMX 2981292. Mellon, Kooy, Audoli, Petits Chanteurs de Saint-Louis, Paris Chapelle Royale Ch., Musique Oblique Ens., Herreweghe.

John Rutter's inspired reconstruction of Fauré's original 1893 score, using only lower strings and no woodwind, opened our ears to the extra freshness of the composer's first thoughts. Rutter's fine, bright recording includes the *Messe basse* and four motets, of which the *Ave Maria* setting and *Ave verum corpus* are particularly memorable. The recording is first rate but places the choir and instruments relatively close.

The directness and clarity of Andrew Davis's reading go with a concentrated, dedicated manner, the fresh vigour of the choral singing achieves an admirable balance between ecstasy and restraint in this most elusive of Requiem settings, culminating in a wonderfully measured and intense account of the final *In paradisum.* Lucia Popp is both rich and pure, and Siegmund Nimsgern (if less memorable) is refined in tone and detailed in his pointing. The recording, made in a church, matches the intimate manner and, with its equally fine Duruflé coupling, this is a very highly recommendable bargain version .

John Eliot Gardiner with period forces also chooses the version of the *Requiem* with the original instrumentation. The darkness matches Gardiner's view of the work which he makes more dramatic than it often is. The mellow recording takes away some of the bite but, with excellent soloists – Catherine Bott radiantly beautiful in the *Pie Jesu,* Gilles Cachemaille vividly bringing out word-meaning – it makes an excellent choice. *Les Djinns* is specially welcome, with piano accompaniment on a gentle-toned Erard of 1874; and all the other pieces, including Fauré's enchanting *Madrigal,* are in various ways inspired by early French part-songs, with the medieval overtones brought out in the Debussy and with the humour of the Ravel nicely underlined.

Michel Legrand uses the full orchestral version of 1900 in the most dramatic way possible, yet the delicacy of the *In paradisum* reflects an equally sympathetic response to the gentler, mystical side of the music. Barbara Bonney's *Pié Jesu* with its simplicity and innocence is very touching. Thomas Hampson makes an eloquent contribution to the *Libera me,* and after the climax the flowing choral line shows the subtle range of colour and dynamic commanded by the

Ambrosian Singers (as well as the orchestra). With superb, spacious recording this performance is very compelling indeed, and it is coupled with an equally fine account of the Duruflé work which was inspired by Fauré's masterpiece.

Matthew Best's performance with the Corydon Singers uses the Rutter edition but presents a choral and orchestral sound that is more refined, set against a helpful church acoustic. *In paradisum* is ethereally beautiful. Best's soloists are even finer than Rutter's, and he too provides a generous fill-up in the *Messe basse* and other motets, though two fewer than Rutter.

Barenboim's 1975 recording has been splendidly remastered. The sound is firmer and better focused without loss of atmosphere. The Edinburgh Festival Chorus is freshly responsive so that, although their tone is beefier than in some versions, the effect is never heavy and the performance is given a strong dimension of drama. Sheila Armstrong's *Pie Jesu* is even more successful here than with de los Angeles. Fischer-Dieskau is not quite as mellifluous as in his earlier account with Cluytens, but he brings a greater sense of drama. A first-rate version, including a sensitive account of the *Pavane*.

The Los Angeles/Fischer-Dieskau version, made under the late André Cluytens in the early 1960s, has great expresssive eloquence and the choir, if not as fine as Rutter's or Gardiner's (to name but two) has a certain idiomatic advantage. It has always been a highly recommendable version with dedicated contributions from both soloists and the full, warmly atmospheric recording sounds very beautiful. However it has no coupling.

The Naxos version makes an excellent bargain choice for the *Requiem* in its original orchestration. The fresh, forward choral tone goes with a direct, unmannered interpretation from Jeremy Summerly, with soloists comparably fresh-toned and English-sounding. The recording brings out the colourings of the orchestra in sharp detail, with the organ and brass vividly caught. The performance of the *Messe basse* is comparably direct, made to sound a little square at times, but the *Cantique de Jean Racine* is most winningly done. The little meditative organ piece by Vierne and the unaccompanied motet by de Severac are pleasing makeweights.

Philippe Herreweghe, unlike Rutter and Best, tends to adopt speeds that are a degree slower than those marked. His soloists are more sophisticated than their British rivals, tonally very beautiful but not quite so fresh in expression. The recording has chorus and orchestra relatively close, but there is a pleasant ambience round the sound.

Not surprisingly, the acoustics of St Eustache, Montreal, are highly suitable for recording the regular full orchestral score of Fauré's *Requiem*, and the Decca sound is superb. Dutoit's is an essentially weighty reading, matched by the style of his fine soloists, yet the performance has both freshness and warmth and does not lack transparency. There are attractive bonuses.

The St John's account has a magic that works from the opening bars onwards. Jonathon Bond and Benjamin Luxon are highly sympathetic soloists and the 1975 (originally Argo) recording is every bit as impressive as its digital competitors, while the smaller scale of the conception is probably nearer to Fauré's original conception. The Double Decca reissue

offers exceptionally generous couplings, not only the Duruflé *Requiem* but other fine music by both Duruflé and Poulenc.

Marriner in his 1993 recording for Philips returns to the fuller re-orchestration. But where many larger forces encourage expansive speeds, Marriner's pacing is ideal, and the clean choral attack is matched by superb singing from Sylvia McNair and Thomas Allen. Though other versions convey even more magic, Marriner can be warmly recommended, particularly for those who fancy the instrumental pieces offered as coupling, including charming rarities by Koechlin and Schmitt.

Nadia Boulanger's account, recorded at Croydon's Fairfield Hall with the BBC Chorus and Symphony Orchestra, has dignity and gravity. Tempi throughout are on the slow side but seem absolutely right. The Introitus has what John Warrack's excellent notes call 'an almost tragic severity'. There may be better sung and played accounts of the *Requiem* but this has a keenly devotional feeling throughout and a special radiance that is moving. A rather special musical document.

Fournet's account of the *Requiem* is very dramatic, and while the singing of the Netherlands Radio Chorus rises to climaxes powerfully, in some other respects the performance is rather cool. The recording tends to make both soloists (who sing well enough) sound rather too close, and it does not flatter Kruysen. However the major coupling, David Zinman's highly refined and beautifully played account of the *Pelléas et Mélisande* suite, is a different matter. This is in every way outstanding. There is a pervasive tenderness and delicacy (the *Sicilienne* is memorable), and to make the selection complete, Jill Gomez gives a ravishing account of Mélisande's song, *The King's Three Blind Daughters*. The (1979) recording is in the demonstration bracket here, and for that matter the 1975 recording of the *Requiem* has come up pretty well in this remastering too. Full texts and translations are included, but this is hardly, as Philips suggest, a 'Great Recording'.

Frémaux has a moulded style which does not spill over into too much expressiveness, and there is a natural warmth about this performance that is highly persuasive. Norma Burrowes sings beautifully, her innocent style most engaging. However, this is coupled with a much less recommendable set of the Berlioz *Requiem*.

On the earlier (1967) King's version under Willcocks, the solo soprano role is taken appealingly by a boy treble, Robert Chilcott. The recording is very fine and splendidly remastered. The performance is eloquent and warmly moving, although some may feel its Anglican accents unidiomatic. The modest coupling is a melting version of the famous *Pavane*, with Gareth Morris playing the flute solo, given lovely, rich sound.

In the later (1982) digital King's College recording, Ledger presents the *Requiem* on a small scale, with considerable restraint. The singing is refreshingly direct, but anyone who warms to the touch of sensuousness in the work, its Gallic quality, may well find a degree of disappointment, though the *Sanctus* conveys drama. This is less beautiful a performance than the earlier one, now also reissued, which was made with the same choir by Sir David Willcocks. On the Classics for Pleasure reissue the comparatively brief *Messe basse*, also sweetly melodic, makes a rather more apt but still not generous alternative coupling.

On the latest DG coupling with Duruflé Myung-Whun Chung's speeds are often excessively slow, challenging even Bartoli's control in the *Pie Jesu*. The characterful singing of both soloists has to be balanced against dim and distant choral sound and an excessively wide dynamic range in the recording. Not recommended.

The Bruges performance uses the version from 1893 with chamber forces and is free from the glamour of star soloists or instrumentalists. It has the affecting simplicity you would expect to find in any university city performance. Hilde Coppé's *Pie Jesu* has great purity. Overall this is not accomplished enough to be a first recommendation, but the absence of star quality is not in itself a handicap. Decent recording.

FAYRFAX, Robert (1464–1521)

Albanus Domini laudans; Ave lumen gratie; Missa Albanus;
Antiphons: *Eterne laudis lilium; O Maria Deo grata.*

*** ASV CDGAU 160. Cardinall's Musick, Carwood.

The magnificent *Missa Albanus*, written for St Alban's Abbey (where Fayrfax was finally buried) is aptly coupled with two extended antiphons, just as elaborate in their polyphonic complexity. *O Maria Deo grata* is directly associated with this particular Mass, having also been written for St Alban's. *Eterne laudis lilium*, again written for St Alban's, won for Fayrfax the sum of 20 shillings from the much-loved Queen Elizabeth of York, wife of Henry VII, and is a dedicated tribute to St Elizabeth, mother of John the Baptist. Fresh and intense performances, beautifully balanced.

Antiphona Regali ex progenie; Magnificat Regali; Missa Regali ex progenie; Alas for the lak of her presens; Lauda vivi alpha et O; That was my woo.

*** ASV CDGAU 155. Cardinall's Musick, Carwood.

This collection is centred around the *Mass* and *Magnificat Regali ex progenie*, but opens with the extended votive antiphon *Lauda vivi Alpha et O*. The collection also includes two rare songs, including the plangent duet, *That was my woo*. The performances are very fine and if the Mass itself is not among the composer's most ambitious works, its textures are as strongly individual as ever. Splendid recording.

Antiphon: Tecum principium (plainsong); Missa tecum principium; Motet: Maria plena virtute; Music for recorders: Mese tenor; O lux beata trinitas; Parames tenor.

*** ASV CDGAU 145. Cardinall's Musick, Carwood; Frideswide Cons.

Though the *Missa tecum principium* is less complex than the brilliant Mass *O quam glorifica*, the argument is not just more direct but even more extended, with the four big sections lasting almost 50 minutes. The final sublime *Agnus Dei* is followed by three tiny instrumental pieces played on recorders by the Frideswide Consort. An extended votive antiphon, *Maria plena virtute*, then rounds off the disc with

the most moving music of all, a narrative on the Virgin Mary at the Cross, full of deeply personal responses immediately to involve the modern listener.

Ave Dei patris filia; Missa O quam glorifica; O quam glorifica (hymnus); Orbis factor (Kyrie). 3 secular songs: *Sumwat musyng; That was joy; To complayne me, alas.*

⊕ *** ASV CDGAU 142. Cardinall's Musick, Carwood.

The Mass, *O quam glorifica*, is the most complex that Fayrfax ever wrote. The rhythmic complexities too, sound wonderfully fresh to the modern ear, with conflicting speeds often involving bold cross-rhythms, parading the composer's closely controlled freedom, before bar-lines applied their tyranny. Above all this is music immediately to involve one in its radiant beauty. The separate antiphon or motet, *Ave Dei patris filia*, is comparably adventurous and beautiful, and is well supplemented by three secular part-songs for male voices. They even anticipate the Elizabethan madrigal, notably the third and most poignant, *To complayne me, alas*. Carwood draws inspired performances from his singers, crisp, dramatic and beautifully blended, and atmospherically recorded in the Fitzalan Chapel at Arundel Castle.

FERGUSON, Howard (born 1908)

(i) *Concerto for Piano & String Orchestra*; (ii) *Amore langueo, Op. 18.*

(M) *** EMI CDM7 64738-2. (i) Shelley; (ii) Hill, L. Symphony Ch.; City of L. Sinfonia, Hickox – FINZI: *Eclogue.* ***

Ferguson's concerto has something in common with the lyrical feeling of John Ireland's comparable work, and as with Ireland, the finale is gay and melodically carefree. Howard Shelley's performance is admirable and Hickox secures highly sympathetic response from the City of London Sinfonia string section. *Amore langueo* is an extended cantata, lasting just over half an hour. The setting, for tenor solo and semi-chorus, with a strong contribution from Martyn Hill, brings a powerful response in the present performance, and Ferguson's music moves with remarkable ease from the depiction of Christ's suffering on the Cross to the sometimes even playful atmosphere of lovers in the bedchamber. An unusual and rewarding piece, recorded with great vividness on CD.

Overture for an Occasion, Op. 16; Partita, Op. 5a; (i) 2 Ballads, Op. 1; (ii) The Dream of the Rood, Op. 19.

*** Chan. 9082. (i) Rayner Cook; (ii) Dawson, LSO Ch.; LSO, Hickox.

This collection includes a striking setting of the *Lyke-Wake dirge*, written in 1928 long before Britten. The *Partita* of 1935–6 is surprisingly dark until the last movement, with a weirdly enigmatic second movement and a lamenting slow movement. The *Overture for an Occasion*, written for the Queen's coronation, has the warmth and colour of comparable Walton works, and further echoes of Walton flavour the *Dream of the Rood*, a setting of an Anglo-Saxon poem with a radiant soprano solo introducing a sequence of richly atmospheric choruses. Hickox proves an ideal advocate, drawing incandescent singing and playing from his performers, with rich and clear Chandos sound to match.

(i) *Octet;* (ii; iii) *Violin Sonata No. 2, Op. 10;* (iii) *5 Bagatelles.*

*** Hyp. CDA 66192. (i) Nash Ens.; (ii) Chilingirian; (iii) Benson – FINZI: *Elegy.* ***

Ferguson's *Octet* is written for the same instruments as Schubert's masterpiece, a delightful counterpart. Those seeking a first-class modern version will find that the Nash Ensemble fill the bill admirably. The other works on the Hyperion disc display the same gift of easy, warm communication, including the darker *Violin Sonata* and Finzi's haunting *Elegy for Violin and Piano.*

(i) *Violin Sonatas Nos. 1, Op. 2; 2, Op. 10;* (ii) *4 Short Pieces;* (iii) *3 Sketches, Op. 14;* (iv) *Discovery* (song-cycle), *Op. 13;* (v) *5 Irish Folksongs, Op. 17;* (vi) *Love and reason;* (iv) *3 Mediaeval Carols, Op. 3.*

*** Chan. 9316-2. (i) Mordkovitch; (ii) Hilton; (iii) Butt; (iv) Mark Ainsley; (v) Burgess; (vi) Schneider-Waterberg; all with Benson.

This generous collection of Ferguson's chamber music, beautifully performed, provides a fine counterpart to Hickox's orchestral and choral disc. It is framed by the two *Violin Sonatas* (1931 and 1946), both powerful works, with Lydia Mordkovitch a rich and persuasive interpreter. Clifford Benson is the lynchpin among the performers, contributing to all the works here. The *Four Short Pieces* for clarinet and the *Three Sketches* for flute are delightful miniatures, as is the counter-tenor song, *Love and reason,* and the *Carols* and the *Discovery* cycle for tenor. Best of all is the colourful cycle of Irish folksongs for mezzo, vividly performed by Sally Burgess. Excellent, well-balanced sound.

(i) *Partita for 2 Pianos, Op. 56. Piano Sonata in F min., Op. 8.*

*** Hyp. CDA 66130. Shelley, (i) Macnamara.

The *Sonata* is a dark, formidable piece in three substantial movements, here given a powerful, intense performance, and for all its echoes of Rachmaninov is quite individual. The *Partita* is also a large-scale work, full of good ideas. Howard Shelley is joined for this two-piano version by his wife, Hilary Macnamara. Excellent, committed performances and first-rate recording, vividly transferred to CD.

FERNSTRÖM, John (1897–1961)

Wind Quintet, Op. 59.

(N) *** Phono Suecia PSCD 708. Amadé Wind Quintet – KALLSTENIUS: *Clarinet Quintet, Op. 17;* Sigurd von KOCH: *Piano Quintet.*

Although John Fernström was a prolific composer, much of his energy and time was consumed by work with orchestras and choirs in Southern Sweden. However, the *Wind Quintet* is well fashioned and civilized. The playing of the Amadé Quintet has plenty of finesse and elegance.

FERRANTI, Marco Aurelio Zani de (1801–78)

Exercice, Op. 50/14; Fantaisie variée sur le romance d'Otello (Assisa a piè), Op. 7; 4 Mélodies nocturnes originales, Op. 41a/1–4; Nocturne sur la dernière pensée de Weber, Op. 40; Ronde des fées, Op. 2.

*** Chan. 8512. Wynberg (guitar) – FERRER: *Collection.* ***

Simon Wynberg's playing fully enters the innocently compelling sound-world of this Bolognese composer; it is wholly spontaneous and has the most subtle control of light and shade. Ferranti's invention is most appealing, and this makes ideal music for late-evening reverie; moreover the guitar is most realistically recorded.

FERRER, José (1835–1916)

Belle (Gavotte); La Danse de naïades; L'Étudiant de Salamanque (Tango); Vals.

*** Chan. 8512. Wynberg (guitar) – FERRANTI: *Collection.* ***

José Ferrer is a less substantial figure than Ferranti, but these four vignettes are almost as winning as that composer's music. The recording has striking realism and presence.

FERROUD, Pierre-Octave (1900–36)

Symphony in A; Sérénade; Chirurgie (opera): Suite.

(N) ** Marco 8.225029. Württemberg PO, Davin.

This is the kind of repertoire off the beaten track that makes CD collecting these days so rewarding. Pierre-Octave Ferroud was a native of Lyons and is probably best-known to collectors for the *March* he contributed to the composite ballet *L'Eventail de Jeanne* in 1927. He was a pupil of Ropartz and Florent Schmitt and a composer of sufficient merit to warrant the attention of a conductor of stature: Pierre Monteux conducted the premières of the *Symphony in A* and the one-act comic opera *Chirurgie,* both composed in 1930. The *Sérénade* (1927) has charm and there is a hint of Roussel in the symphony. However, these performances are serviceable but no more.

FESCH, Willem de (1687–1761)

Concerti Grossi, Op. 2/6; Op. 3/3–4; Op. 5/2; Op. 10/4–5; (i) Violin Concertos, Op. 2/2 & 5; Op. 3/6; Op. 5/5.

*** Olympia OCD 450. (i) Nikolitch; O d'Auvergne, Arie van Beek.

De Fesch was born in Alkmaar, but his writing reflects influences absorbed from Italy and France, and also from Handel, of whom he was an almost exact contemporary. He must have been a pretty impressive fiddler himself, judging from the bravura demanded of the soloist in his violin concertos. The *Concerti grossi* are first rate. Op. 3/4 is very like a sinfonia concertante in the way de Fesch uses his solo group of two oboes plus genial bassoon. The five-movement *G minor* work, Op. 5/2, features a pair of flutes with equal felicity, its undoubted charm coming from delicate scoring and a melancholy atmosphere. The Orchestre d'Auvergne are an excellent chamber group and Gordon Nikolitch an estimable soloist. Although modern instruments are used, the light textures and resilient rhythms suggest a thorough knowledge of authentic practices. Excellent recording too. A strong recommendation for this pioneering CD.

FETLER, Paul (born 1920)

Contrasts for Orchestra.

(M) *** Mercury (ADD) [434 335-2]. Minneapolis SO, Dorati –
AURIC: *Overture;* FRANCAIX: *Piano Concertino;*
MILHAUD: *Le Boeuf sur le toit;* SATIE: *Parade.* ***

Paul Fetler's four-movement sinfonietta, *Contrasts*, is based on four notes (B flat, F, C, A flat), yet it is as impressive for its fine use of brass sonorities in the slow movement as for the neo-classical athleticism of the opening *Allegro* and the pervading energy of the finale where everything comes together. It is an eclectic work yet has distinct character. The performance is first rate, and so is the Mercury recording.

FIBICH, Zdeněk (1850–1900)

Symphonies Nos. 1 in F, Op. 17; 2 in E flat, Op. 38; 3 in E min., Op. 53.

(B) *** Chan. Double 9682 (2). Detroit SO, Järvi.

Anyone who has ever responded to Dvořák should hear the symphonies of his contemporary, Fibich – similarly echoing the cadences of Czech folk music, but with touches of Mendelssohn, no doubt developed by the composer's studies in Leipzig. There is a strong Bohemian feel to these works, and if, like so much of Fibich's music the *First Symphony*, which opens so invitingly is a little square, such is the excellence of Neeme Järvi's performance that it does not feel so. It is the best account so far on record. The performances of the *Second* and *Third* come into competition with a Supraphon issue from the Brno Orchestra under Jiři Walddans and Bělohlávek (11 0657-2) respectively. But on Chandos, opulent sound adds to the rustic charm of much of the writing, as well as heightening the warmth and drama of the playing. Moreover the Chandos recording scores in terms of fidelity and space, and the Detroit Orchestra respond with enthusiam to these scores. Overall this set is well worth exploring.

Symphonies Nos 1 in F, Op. 17; 2 in E flat, Op. 38.

(BB) ** Naxos 8.553699. Razumovsky SO, Mogrelia.

The Naxos issue of the first two symphonies offers fresh, clean-cut performances with transparent textures, making an attractive bargain issue, though they are pale beside Järvi's Chandos performances.

Piano Quartet in E min., Op. 11; Quintet for Violin, Clarinet, Horn, Cello & Piano, Op. 42.

*** MDG 304 0775-2. Villa Musica Ens.

The *E minor Piano Quartet* is an early piece, which enjoyed the approval of Hanslick, while its companion comes from 1893. The ideas though pleasing are a little square; they do not have the fresh, outdoor quality of Fibich's great compatriots. This is well-wrought music and beautifully played by these accomplished artists and excellently recorded.

Piano Quintet, Op. 42.

*** ASV CDDCA 943. Endymion Ens. – DOHNANYI:
Sextet. ***

Fibich's *Piano Quintet* is a relatively late piece; it comes from the last decade of his life and has much lively invention and no mean charm. The Endymions give a first-rate account of it and are excellently recorded.

Moods, Impressions & Reminiscences, Opp. 41, 44, 47 & 57.

*** Chan. 9381-2. Howard.

A generally preferable alternative to Rudoslav Kvapil's thoughtful and perceptive recital on Unicorn-Kanchana (DKPCD 9149). William Howard is equally sensitive to the varying moods of these pieces, and he is much more convincingly recorded.

Sarka (complete)

(N) *** Orfeo C 541 002H (2). Urbanová, Lotric, Kirilova, Jenis, Vienna Concert Ch., Vienna RSO, Cambreling.
(N) **(*) Sup. (ADD) SU 0036-2 612 (2). Depoltavá, Pribyl, Randová, Zítek, BRNO Janack Opera Ch., Brno State PO, Jan Stych.

Completed in 1897 only three years before the composer's death, Fibich's *Sarka*, based on the Czech legend of the predatory Sarka and her fellow Amazons, yet established itself as a central work in the Czech repertory, effectively preventing Janáček's compressed treatment of the same subject – written earlier but not produced until 1925 – from ever being appreciated. Fibich was aiming directly at writing a Wagnerian opera, especially in his echoes of *Tristan und Isolde* in the love duet for Sarka and Ctirad, the knight with whom she falls in love against her will. It is music of big, bold gestures, with any Czech flavours tending to echo Smetana rather than Dvořák.

As in so many grand romantic operas the weakness lies in melodic material that only fitfully sticks in the memory. Yet on disc this is a piece well worth hearing. On Orfeo Sylvain Cambreling conducts a strong and purposeful performance in a good, well-balanced radio recording. Both the principals, Eva Urbanová as Sarka and Janez Lotric as Ctirad, are outstanding, with their characterful Slavonic voices that yet focus beautifully, and the others make a strong team.

The Supraphon version dates from 1978 with warmly atmospheric analogue sound. Its great strength is the idiomatic conducting of Jan Stych, even though Eva Depoltavá in the title role is less characterful than Urbanová on Orfeo. Vilem Pribyl is a first-rate Ctirad, but the most outstanding singing comes from Eva Randová as the leader of the Amazons, Vlasta, rich and distinctive.

FIELD, John (1782–1837)

Piano Concertos Nos. 1 in E flat; 2 in A flat.

*** Chan. 9368. O'Rourke, LMP, Bamert.

Míceál O'Rourke embarks on a complete cycle of the Field concertos. The music of the present pair of concertos is uneven, but the Scottish slow movement of No. 1 features the folk tune *Within a mile of Edinburgh town* rather winningly. No. 2 brings a characteristic Field rondo with an engaging principal theme which becomes catchier as it is given more rhythmic treatment. The soloist is very persuasive, and he receives admirable support from Bamert and the London Mozart Players. First-class, naturally balanced recording.

Piano Concertos Nos. 1 in E flat; 3 in E flat.

(BB) *** Naxos 8.553770. Frith, Northern Sinfonia, Haslam.

Piano Concerto Nos. 2 in A flat; 4 in E flat.

(BB) *** Naxos 8.553771. Frith, Northern Sinfonia, Haslam.

Benjamin Frith has the bargain field to himself. His playing is characteristically sensitive and fresh, and he is well supported by the Northern Sinfonia and David Haslam. Very good, warm recording, in a decent acoustic. The second disc is particularly attractive.

Piano Concertos Nos. 2 in A flat; 3 in E flat.

*** Telarc CD 80370. O'Conor, SCO, Mackerras.

**(*) Teldec 3984 21475-2. Staier, Concerto Kölne, Stern.

These Telarc versions are beautifully recorded and the warm, naturally balanced sound gives the music the elegance it needs. The *Andantino* of No. 3 (not a part of the original concerto) brings a nicely rhapsodical feeling and uses one of the composer's daintiest *Nocturnes*, orchestrated to have a gentle string accompaniment. It is played with much grace and delicacy and is then followed by a Rondo, with a catchy, hopping main theme which is also one of Field's very best finales. John O'Conor plays throughout with great distinction and always displays the lightest touch and Mackerras accompanies with warmth and character.

The performances on Teldec are certainly authentic, with Staier's nimble, twinkling (some would say tinkly) roulades contrasting with the robust orchestral tuttis. But, as with the music of Chopin, it is difficult to prefer the sound here to that of the modern piano, except perhaps in the innocent *Rondo* which closes No. 2, which is delightfully pointed by Staier's crisp keyboard articulation.

Piano Concertos Nos. 3; 5 (L'incendie par l'orage).

*** Chan. 9495. O'Rourke, LMP, Bamert.

Míceál O'Rourke is well up to form in the *Third Concerto*. The coupling (No. 5) is notable mainly for its histrionic storm effects in the middle of the first movement, which climax with a bold stroke on the tam-tam. After this, the weather breaks and we are ready for the songful *Andante*,

before the comparatively robust and spirited finale which brings delicacy as well as brilliance from the soloist.

Piano Concertos Nos. 4 in E flat; 6 in C.

*** Chan. 9442. O'Rourke, LMP, Bamert.

O'Rourke continues his Chandos series with highly persuasive accounts of Nos. 4 and 6, with both works providing delightful slow movements. The *C major Concerto* is the more interesting of the two, giving the soloist some scintillating passage-work in the first movement and a lolloping Rondo finale. Excellent, sympathetic accompaniments and first-rate recording.

(i) Piano Concerto No. 7 in C; Divertissements Nos. l–2; Nocturne No. 16 in F; Rondeau in A flat. (ii) Quintetto.

*** Chan. 9534. O'Rourke, (i) LMP, Bamert (ii) Juritz, Godson, Bradley, Desbruslais.

Although the finale of Field's *Seventh Piano Concerto* is characteristically chirpy, some of the passage-work is a shade garrulous (not the fault of the soloist, who is well on form). However, the opening movement has a beautiful central *Lento* section which the composer later extracted and published as one of the nocturnes. What makes this disc treasurable is the series of lollipops which follow – the two *Divertissements*, *Rondeau* and *Nocturne*, every one of which has a really good tune. The serene single-movement *Piano Quintet* is also delicately charming. Performances and recordings are well up to the high standard of this excellent Chandos series.

Air du bon roi Henri IV; 2 Album Leaves in C min.; Andante inédit in E flat; Fantaisie sur un air russe, 'In the Garden'; Fantaisie sur l'air de Martini; Irish Dance: Go to the Devil; Marche triomphale; Nocturne in B flat; Nouvelle fantaisie in G; Polonaise en rondeau; Rondeau d'écossais; Rondo in A flat; Sehnsuchtswalzer; Variations in D min. on a Russian Song, 'My dear bosom friend'; Variations in B flat on a Russian Air, Kamarinskaya.

*** Chan. 9315. O'Rourke.

Míceál O'Rourke presents this (nearly 80-minute) recital with intelligence and taste. Most of this repertory is not otherwise available, and much of it has the quiet charm one expects from this delightful composer. Míceál O'Rourke proves a dedicated interpreter of real artistry. Recorded at The Maltings, Snape, he is admirably served by the Chandos team.

Nocturnes Nos. 1–16.

**(*) Athene ATH CD 1. Leach (fortepiano).

Joanna Leach uses three 'square' fortepianos, by Stodart and Broadwood (both from the 1820s) and a D'Almain from a decade later. The latter instrument most closely approaches the quality of a modern piano, though the Broadwood is not far behind. Joanna Leach coaxes poetic sounds from these comparatively recalcitrant instruments and plays this repertoire very sensitively. However, it cannot be denied that for most ears this music (with its remarkable anticipations of Chopin) sounds even better on a modern concert grand.

Nocturnes Nos.1–6; 9–10; 12–13; 17.

(N) (M) *** EMI (ADD) CDM5 67431-2. Adni – HARTY: *John Field Suite;* IRELAND: *The Holy Boy;* LEIGH: *Harpsichord concertino.* ***

Daniel Adni's fresh and sensitive playing, though not always quite free enough in its rubato, has one responding to the charm of this well-chosen selection. For samples try No. 4 in A major, or the Russian-tinged No. 10. The piano tone is full and firm. It was a happy idea to couple this recital with Harty's attractively arranged and orchestrated *John Field Suite.*

Nocturnes Nos. 1–9; Piano Sonatas Nos. 1 in E flat; 2 in A, Op. 1/1–2.

(BB) *** Naxos 8.550761. Frith.

Benjamin Frith's playing is delectably coaxing, and he makes these *Nocturnes* so often seem exquisitely like Chopin, yet still catches their naïve innocence, especially in the *A flat major* work. He hops, skips and jumps delightfully in the Irish Rondo finale of the *First Sonata* and is hardly less beguiling in the rather more imposing opening movement of the *Second.* The Naxos recording is first class, and made in a very pleasing acoustic.

Nocturnes Nos. 10–17; 18 (Midi); Piano Sonata No. 3 in C min., Op. 1/3.

(N) (BB) *** Naxos 8.550762. Frith.

Benjamin Frith continues his Naxos series with a second delectable instalment of the *Nocturnes,* including the famous No. 18 whose original title was *Midi* (or 'Twelve O'clock Rondo'). The *Third Sonata* occupies the mid-way point in the recital. Its first movement is just a little hectoring (Beethovenian con fuoco was not Field's natural element) but the closing *Rondo* simulates another popular air for its basis. As before, the recording is very natural.

Nocturnes 1, 2, 4–6, 8–16, 18.

*** Telarc CD-80199. O'Conor.

It would be difficult to better John O'Conor's sensitive and beautifully recorded accounts of his countryman's pioneering essays in the *Nocturnes.* He captures their character to perfection, and his tonal finesse is remarkable but never self-regarding. Strongly recommended.

Largo in C min.; Nocturnes in B flat; C min.; E min.; Prelude in C min.; Romance in E flat; Waltzes in A; E (Sehnsucht).

*** Etcetera KTC 1231. Antoni – CHOPIN: Recital. **(*)

Under the title 'Crossfire' this fascinatingly devised recital readily demonstrates links and influences between the music of John Field (who invented the Nocturne) and Chopin, his young Polish successor. Helge Antoni is a notably sensitive advocate of Field's music, and his simple style readily draws parallels with alternated pieces by Chopin. Field's *Nocturne in C minor* of 1812 is presented alongside Chopin's work in the same key, written twenty-five years later, and there are similar influences to be found in the *Waltzes.* A recital that is both stimulating and musically enjoyable too, as it is naturally recorded.

Piano Sonatas: Nos. 1 in E flat; 2 in A; 3 in C min., Op. 1/1–3; 4 in B.

**(*) Chan. 8787. O'Rourke.

Míceál O'Rourke plays these two-movement *Sonatas* written by his countryman with some flair. He is particularly good in the famous *Rondo* finale of the *First Sonata,* which he plays with real Irish whimsy and sparkling touch. The *Allegretto scherzando* of No. 3 also has hit potential.

FINZI, Gerald (1901–56)

Cello Concerto in A min., Op. 40.

*** Chan. 8471. Wallfisch, RLPO, Handley – K. LEIGHTON: *Veris gratia.* ***

Finzi's *Cello Concerto* is perhaps the most searching of all his works. Wallfisch finds all the dark eloquence of the central movement, and the performance overall has splendid impetus, with Handley providing the most sympathetic backing. The Chandos recording has an attractively natural balance.

Clarinet Concerto, Op. 31.

(N) (B) *** Hyp. Helios CDH 55101. King, Philh. O, Francis – STANFORD: *Clarinet Concerto.* ***

*** ASV CDDCA 568. MacDonald, N. Sinfonia, Bedford – COPLAND: *Concerto;* MOURANT: *Pied Piper.* ***

(i) *Clarinet Concerto, Op. 31;* (ii) *5 Bagatelles for Clarinet & Piano.*

*** ASV CDDCA 787. Johnson; (i) RPO, Groves; (ii) Martineau – STANFORD: *Clarinet Concerto etc.* ***

(i) *Clarinet Concerto, Op. 31; 5 Bagatelles for Clarinet & Strings (arr. Ashmore), Op. 23a; Love's Labour Lost: 3 Soliloquies, Op. 28.* (ii) *Introit in F for Solo Violin & Small Orchestra, Op. 6; Romance in E flat for String Orchestra, Op. 11; A Severn Rhapsody, Op. 3.*

(BB) *** Naxos 8.553566. (i) Plane; (ii) Hatfield; Northern Sinf., Griffiths.

(i) *Clarinet Concerto;* (ii) *Introit for Violin & Orchestra.*

(M) *** BBC (ADD) BBCM 5015-2. (i) Hilton, BBC Northern SO, Thomson; (ii) Jarvis, LPO, Boult – LEIGH: *Harpsichord Concertino* *** (with Concert: 'English Music' ***).

(i) *Clarinet Concerto. New Year Music: Nocturne; Romance for String Orchestra.* (ii) *Dies natalis.*

*** Ph. 454 438-2. (i) A. Marriner; (ii) Bostridge. ASMF, N. Marriner.

Emma Johnson is even more warmly expressive in the concerto than Thea King on her Hyperion disc, and with Sir Charles Groves and the RPO ideally sympathetic accompanists. Finzi's sinuous melodies for the solo instrument are made to sound as though the soloist is improvising them, and with extreme daring she uses the widest possible dynamic, ranging down to a whispered pianissimo that might be inaudible in a concert-hall.

Andrew Marriner gives a particularly sensitive account of the *Clarinet Concerto* in which simplicity is the keynote. Marriner is an admirable partner and secures some ravishingly gentle playing from the ASMF in the *Adagio*. The finale lilts engagingly. But it is the coupling with *Die natalis*, perhaps the composer's best-known work, that makes this Philips disc so enticing. Ian Bostridge's superb account of an inspired song-cycle that occupies a midway point between the vocal music of Elgar and Britten, but yet has the stamp of the composer's personality set firmly on every bar, is unsurpassed. Marriner accompanies with comparable warmth and subtlety of line and the atmospheric sound adds to the magic, when the orchestral playing is of such high quality.

On Helios Thea King also gives a definitive performance, strong and clean-cut. Her characterful timbre, using little or no vibrato, is highly telling against a resonant orchestral backcloth. Alun Francis is a most sympathetic accompanist. With Stanford's even rarer concerto this makes a most attractive bargain reissue, and the sound is excellent.

Finzi's *Clarinet Concerto* is also played most nimbly by Janet Hilton, admirably supported by Bryden Thomson, especially in the lovely *Adagio*, which is memorably intense. The present transfer is strikingly fresh and natural. The virtually unknown *Introit for Violin and Orchestra*, which brings another memorable theme, is a meditative, thoughtful piece, very well played by Gerald Jarvis and the LPO under Sir Adrian Boult in 1969 and again the current transfer gives a very pleasing sound picture, warm and natural. This is part of a 77-minute concert of English music including the delicious *Harpsichord Concertino* of Walter Leigh.

Robert Plane's highly responsive performance of the concerto also uses a wide range of dynamic, and movingly brings out the work's sense of improvisatory lyricism. Not to be outdone, the Naxos collection offers the *Three Soliloquies*, plus an orchestration of the five lovely *Bagatelles*, which is even more evocative than the original version with piano. The *Introit* for violin and orchestra is most sensitively played by Lesley Hatfield. The *Romance* is hardly less engaging, while *Severn Rhapsody* shows its composer spinning his pastoral evocation in the manner of Butterworth. All this music is most persuasively presented by the Northern Sinfonia under Howard Griffiths and the Naxos recording has plenty of warmth and atmosphere.

The coupling of Finzi and Copland makes an unexpected but attractive mix, with the Canadian clarinettist, George MacDonald, giving a brilliant and thoughtful performance, particularly impressive in the spacious, melismatic writing of the slow movement. Refined recording, with the instruments set slightly at a distance.

(i) *Clarinet Concerto*. (ii) *Eclogue for Piano & Strings; Love's Labour's Lost: Suite; Prelude for String Orchestra; Romance for Strings*.

(M) *** Nim. NI 5665. (i) Hacker; (ii) Jones; E. String O, Boughton.

Alan Hacker's reading of the *Concerto* is improvisatory in style and freely flexible in tempi, with the slow movement at once introspective and rhapsodic. The concert suite of incidental music for Shakespeare's *Love's Labour's Lost* is amiably atmospheric and pleasing in invention and in the colour of its scoring. The two string pieces are by no means slight and are played most expressively; the *Romance* is particularly eloquent in William Boughton's hands. For the reissue a sensitive account of the *Eclogue* has been added.

(i) *Clarinet Concerto; Romance for Strings, Op. 11*. (ii) *Dies natalis, Op. 8*; (iii) *Let us garlands bring, Op. 18*.

(N) **(*) CBC SMCD 5204. (i) Campbell; (ii) V. Anderson; (iii) Braun; Manitoba CO, Streatfeild.

The warmly expressive playing of the strings of the Manitoba Orchestra under Simon Streatfeild immediately strikes the ear at the opening of this generous Finzi collection from Canada, and they play the lovely *Romance* very beautifully. It was enterprising to offer a version of *Dies natalis* (written for 'high voice') with a soprano soloist, but although Valdine Anderson sings freshly and sensitively, her close vibrato will not seduce all ears, and she is no match for Ian Bostridge. However, Russell Braun is much more persuasive in the baritone cycle of Shakespearean songs, *Let us garlands bring*, and James Campbell is equally impressive in the *Clarinet Concerto*, playing very gently in the ravishing *Adagio* and with appealing whimsy in the catchy finale. Excellent recording too.

(i) *Concerto for Violin & Small Orchestra; Prelude, Op. 25; Romance, Op. 11* (both for strings); (ii) *In Years Defaced* (song-cycle, orchestrated by Finzi, Alexander, Roberts, Matthews, Payne and Weir).

(N) *** Chan. 9888. (i) Little; (ii) Mark Ainsley; City of L. Sinf., Hickox.

This is one of the most attractive CDs of the Finzi discography. Taking their cue from Finzi's own setting of *When I set out for Lyonesse*, the five other composers involved, all Finzi admirers, offer sensitive settings of a sequence of poems (four by Hardy) which together form a satisfying cycle, designed to celebrate the composer's centenary in 2001. All very much in style, they heighten the emotional thrust of each of these beautiful songs, all among Finzi's finest, and are sympathetically sung by John Mark Ainsley.

Apart from Finzi's brief march-like setting of the second poem, the first and last are the most striking. Colin Matthews brings out the mystery of Flecker's evocative poem *To a Poet a Thousand Years Hence*, while Anthony Payne (the understanding 'realizer' of Elgar's *Third Symphony*) provides a brilliant conclusion, more radical than the rest, with the compound-time setting of Hardy's *Proud Songsters*, quite different from Britten's setting of the same poem in *Winter Words*.

The *Concerto for Violin and Small Orchestra* was the first orchestral work of Finzi's to be performed, but was then neglected for over 70 years, until these same outstanding performers took it up for this recording. Drawing on Finzi's distinctive brand of pastoral writing, the outer movements are strong and vigorous, the central slow movement ethereally reflective. The warmly expressive *Prelude for Strings* was salvaged from a *Chamber Symphony* that was never completed, while the *Romance* is the most ravishing piece of all, with rich string writing echoing both Elgar and Vaughan Williams in its emotional surge. Ideal performances, richly recorded.

Eclogue for Piano & String Orchestra.

(M) *** EMI CDM7 64738-2. Shelley, City of L. Sinfonia, Hickox – FERGUSON: *Piano Concerto No. 2* etc. ***

(M) *** EMI CD-EMX 2239. Lane, RLPO, Handley – DELIUS: *Piano Concerto;* VAUGHAN WILLIAMS: *Piano Concerto.* ***

This is the central movement of an uncompleted piano concerto which the composer decided could stand on its own. It was Howard Ferguson who edited the final manuscript and set the title, and it is appropriate that this essentially valedictory piece should be coupled with his own concerto. The mood is tranquil yet haunting, and Shelley's performance brings out all its serene lyricism. The recording is admirably realistic.

This haunting work makes a valuable makeweight for the Eminence coupling of the Delius and Vaughan Williams *Piano Concertos.* Piers Lane gives it a tenderly sympathetic reading, even if this does not quite match in magic the Howard Shelley version on EMI.

Grand Fantasia & Toccata (for piano and orchestra), Op. 38; (ii) Intimations of Immortality, Op. 29.

(M) *** EMI CDM7 64720-2. (i) Fowke; (ii) Langridge, RLPO Ch.; RLPO, Hickox.

Finzi's setting of Wordsworth, with its rich, lyrical cantilena, brings constant reminders of the Elgar of *Gerontius,* while the writing remains essentially within the pastoral tradition of English song-setting. The performance here is wholly committed, with the fervour of the chorus echoing the dedication of the soloist. The choral recording is both spacious and brilliant. The coupling, a Bachian *Grand Fantasia,* is followed by a genial *Toccata,* fugal in style. The piece is played compellingly by Philip Fowke, and Hickox is a fine partner. Again vividly realistic sound. Highly recommended.

(i) Romance for Strings, Op. 11; (ii) Dies natalis, Op. 8; (iii) Earth and Air and Rain, Op. 16; (ii) For St Cecilia; (iv) Lo, the Full, Final Sacrifice, Op. 26: Amen (only); (v) Magnificat, Op. 36; (vi) In terra pax, Op. 39; (vii) Let us garlands bring, Op. 18.

(N) (M) *** Decca (ADD) 468 807-2 (2). (i) ASMF, Marriner; (ii) Langridge, LSO Ch., LSO, Hickox; (iii) Luxon, Willinson; (iv) New College, Oxford Ch., Higginbottom; (v) Hickox Singers, City of L. Sinf., Hickox (vi) Sweeney, Winchester Cathedral Ch., Bournemouth SO, Hill; (vii) Terfel, Martineau.

Marriner's account of the eloquent if brief *Romance for Strings* is second to none, and Hickox's performance of *Dies natalis* brings a notably sensitive and passionate soloist in Philip Langridge, who also contributes impressively to the cantata commissioned for the St Cecilia's Day celebration in 1947 (with a text by Edmund Blunden). Its opening is full of pageantry in the Elgarian tradition, although the mood softens in the second section.

In terra pax is another Christmas work, opening atmospherically with the baritone's musing evocation of the pastoral nativity scene. It is admirably sung by David Hill. Then comes a burst of choral splendour at the appearance of the Angel of the Lord, and after her gentle declaration of the birth of Christ comes an even more resplendent depiction of the 'multitude of the heavenly host', magnificently sung and recorded, and the music returns to the thoughtful, recessed mood of the opening.

The boldly set *Magnificat* of 1951 was an American commission and all three of these performances are strongly convincing. But why only include the brief *Amen* from *Lo, the Full, Final Sacrifice*?

In *Earth and Air and Rain,* Finzi's distinctive settings of Hardy, there is sometimes a flavour of Vaughan Williams, and in *When I set out for Lyonnesse* a distinct reminder of Stanford's *Songs of the Sea.* But in the touching *Waiting* both and the dramatic *Clock of the years* Luxon demonstrates the versatility of Finzi's word settings. Excellent accompaniments from David Willinson – his gentle postlude for the finale song, *Proud songsters,* ends the cycle movingly.

The five Shakespearean settings, *Let Us Garlands Bring,* are just as memorable in their contrasted ways, and are beautifully sung by Bryn Terfel. All in all this is a thoroughly worthwhile compilation, given excellent recording throughout.

Elegy for Violin & Piano.

(N) *** Nim. NI 5666. Hope, Mulligan – ELGAR: *Violin Sonata;* WALTON: *Violin Sonata.* ***

*** Hyp. CDA 66192. Chilingirian, Benson – FERGUSON: *Octet* etc. ***

The Finzi *Elegy* is a very apt makeweight for the Elgar and Walton sonatas, the only surviving movement from a projected violin sonata written in a hectic period for Finzi at the beginning of the Second World War. No other recording is currently listed, making this freely lyrical piece in Finzi's warmest pastoral vein especially welcome.

Finzi's moving little *Elegy for Violin and Piano* also makes an apt fill-up for the record of chamber music by his friend, Howard Ferguson.

Dies natalis.

(M) *** EMI CDM5 65588-2. Brown, ECO, Finzi – HOLST: *Choral Fantasia; Psalm 86;* VAUGHAN WILLIAMS: *5 Mystical Songs* etc. ***

Dies natalis is one of Finzi's most sensitive and deeply felt works, using meditative texts by the seventeenth-century writer, Thomas Traherne, on the theme of Christ's nativity. Finzi's setting is very well sung here by Wilfred Brown. The remastered recording sounds wonderfully fresh and is naturally balanced within a glowing acoustic.

Dies natalis; Intimations of immortality.

**(*) Hyp. CDA 66876. Mark Ainsley, Corydon Singers & O, Best.

Matthew Best, with John Mark Ainsley as soloist in both works, offers the ideal Finzi coupling. Using a relatively small orchestra, this is a more intimate reading of the latter work than on the earlier, EMI recording from Richard Hickox, yet it conveys an almost comparable concentration. Ainsley has a sweet if small voice, very apt for both works, even if under pressure there is some unevenness. The chorus sings with feeling, though the recording is not as vividly immediate as the analogue EMI recording which features the Royal Liverpool Philharmonic Choir and Orchestra.

God is Gone Up; Lo, the Full, Final Sacrifice; Magnificat.

(M) *** EMI CDM5 65595-2. King's College, Cambridge, Ch., Cleobury; Farnes – BAX: *Choral Music;* VAUGHAN WILLIAMS: *Mass.* ***

Both the extended anthem, *Lo, the Full, Final Sacrifice*, setting Richard Crashaw's version of an Aquinas hymn, and the *Magnificat* were commissioned works, the one for St Matthew's, Northampton, the other for Massachusetts; in their rich climaxes they bring out a dramatic side in Finzi along with his gentle beauty, splendidly conveyed by the King's choir. The recording, made in the Chapel, is so nicely balanced that part-writing is clear even against the ample acoustic.

FIORILLO, Federigo (1755– after 1823)

Violin Concerto No. 1 in F.

(B) *** Hyp. Helios CDH 55062. Oprean, European Community CO, Faerber – VIOTTI: *Violin Concerto No. 13.* ***

Fiorillo's *Concerto* is charmingly romantic. Adelina Oprean's playing can only be described as quicksilver: her lightness of bow and firm, clean focus of timbre are most appealing. She is given a warm, polished accompaniment and the recording is eminently truthful and well balanced.

FISCHER, Johann Caspar Ferdinand (c. 1670–1746)

Musical Parnassus, Volume 1: Suites Nos. 1–6 (Clio; Calliope; Melpomène; Thalia; Erato; Euterpe).

(BB) *** Naxos 8.554218. Beauséjour (harpsichord).

J. C. F. Fischer is remembered for his *Ariadne musica* (1715), a series of twenty preludes and fugues, each in a different key, thus anticipating Bach's *Wohltempierte Klavier*. His role in music history was to fuse the style of the Lullian suite with the classical core of dance suite movements favoured by Froberger. He published his *Musicalischer Parnassus* in 1738, which comprises nine suites named after the Muses. The first six are included on this disc and are often fresh and inventive, rarely routine. The Canadian Luc Beauséjour plays them with some flair and is very vividly recorded.

FLOTOW, Friedrich (1812–83)

Martha (opera; complete).

(M) *** RCA 74321 32231-2 (2). Popp, Soffel, Jerusalem, Nimsgern, Ridderbusch, Bav. R. Ch. and O, Wallberg.

Martha is a charming opera, and the cast of this 1978 recording (originating with Eurodisc) is as near perfect as could be imagined. Lucia Popp is a splendid Lady Harriet, the voice rich and full yet riding the ensembles with jewelled accuracy. Doris Soffel is no less characterful as Nancy, and Siegfried Jerusalem is in his element as the hero, Lionel, singing ardently throughout. Siegmund Nimsgern is an excellent Lord Tristan, and Karl Ridderbusch matches his genial gusto. Wallberg's direction is marvellously spirited and the opera gathers pace as it proceeds. The Bavarian Radio Chorus sings with joyous precision and the orchestral playing sparkles. The first-class recording has been vividly tranferred, though there is a touch of edge on the voices of Lady Harriet and Nancy. The libretto promised on the back of the box is in German only, but the story of this opera is very easy to follow.

FLOYD, Carlisle (born 1926)

Susannah (opera; complete).

*** Virgin VCD5 45039-2 (2). Studer, Ramey, Hadley, Lyon Op. Ch. & O, Nagano.

This is an updating of the story of Susanna and the Elders in the Apocrypha, which readily adapts to the background of a traditional community in the Appalachian mountains. The idiom is tuneful and unashamedly tonal, influenced by American folk-music. Most effective are the two big solos for the heroine, one in each of the compact Acts, both gloriously sung by Cheryl Studer, who as a native American sounds easily in character, taking to the idiom naturally. Samuel Ramey is similarly at home in this music, singing strongly with his richest tone, even if one can hardly believe in him as a vile hypocrite. With Jerry Hadley ideally cast as the tenor hero, Sam, Susannah's brother, who finally murders the predatory Blitch, the rest of the cast is first rate. The chorus and orchestra of the Lyon Opera are also inspired by their American conductor to give heartfelt, idiomatic performances. Excellent sound, as in previous Lyon Opera recordings with Nagano.

FOERSTER, Josef Bohuslav (1859–1951)

Symphony No. 4 in C min. (Easter), Op. 54; Springtime and Desire, Op. 93.

*** Sup. ADD/Dig. 111 822-2. Prague SO, Smetáček.

This beautiful if overlong symphony is both dignified and noble; its Scherzo is infectiously memorable and could be as popular as any of the *Slavonic Dances* if only it were known, and there is a sweep to the first movement that is most impressive. The finale is the least successful of the four movements, and here attention flags. All the same, the symphony wears well. To this analogue recording Supraphon add a 1985 account, digitally recorded, of his *Springtime and Desire*, a symphonic poem with a strong emphasis on the symphonic, and this, like the symphony, is a most welcome addition to the catalogue. Good performances, decent recording.

FORQUERAY, Antoine (1671–1745)

Harpsichord Suites Nos. 1 in D min.; 3 in D; 5 in C min.

(BB) *** Naxos 8.553407. Beauséjour (harpsichord).

These suites are transcriptions of music for the viol of uncertain provenance, and they were long thought to be by Forqueray's son, Jean-Baptiste. Whatever the case may be, the music itself is of quality and originality, and it is well served by the Canadian harpsichordist, Luc Beauséjour, as recorded at the Church of St Alphonse-de-Rodriguez in Quebec. He plays with great flair and zest, and the sound is first class.

Harpsichord Suites Nos. 3 in D; 5 in C min.

(N) (BB) *** Virgin 2 x 1 VBD5 61872-2 (2). Meyerson (harpsichord) – RAMEAU: *Pièces de clavecin en concerts.* ***

Mitzi Meyerson duplicates the *D major Suite* offered on Naxos, and includes also the equally ambitious *C minor* work, which like its companion has titled movements, with the majestic introduction dedicated to Rameau (whose *Pièces de clavecin en concerts* act as an attractive coupling for this inexpensive Double CD set). She plays a 1974 Rubio after a 1769 Taskin, its rich sonority well conveyed in the warm acoustic of Forde Abbey, Chard, Somerset, especially in the dramatically forceful closing portrait of *Jupiter*.

Pieces for 3 Viols in D min.; Suite for 3 Viols in D.

*** Virgin VC5 45358-2. Hantaï, Uemura, Verzier, Hantaï – MARAIS: *Pièces à violes.* ***

It is not absolutely sure that these works are by Forqueray, a contemporary of Marais, but they share the austere style we recognize in that composer's writing for viol consort. Whoever composed this six-movement *Suite*, it is music of considerable expressive depth, especially the eloquent *Sarabandes* and ends with a lively extended *Chaconne*. The performances here are sympathetically expert and very well recorded.

FÖRSTER, Christoph (1693–1745)

Horn Concerto in E flat.

(N) *** Arabesque Z 6750. Rose, St Luke's Chamber Ens. – HAYDN; Leopold MOZART; TELEMANN: *Horn Concertos.* ***

Christoph Förster was a contemporary of Bach and this, the earliest of the four concertos in this outstanding collection, is no less demanding of the soloist's virtuosity. The first movement centres on a catchy rhythmic figure in the strings,

which the horn then proceeds to decorate lavishly. The eloquent minor key theme of the *Adagio* is genuinely touching, and its distinctly baroque cantilena is well understood by soloist and orchestra alike. The dancing finale has an almost Vivaldian tinge and again demands great virtuosity, which is readily forthcoming here. Stewart Rose is a splendid player, secure in technique, his style buoyant and expressive by turns, and the orchestra of which he is principal provides him with warmly stylish accompaniments. The recording is first class.

FOSS, Lucas (born 1922)

3 American Pieces.

*** EMI CDC5 55360-2. Perlman, Boston SO, Ozawa – BARBER: *Violin Concerto;* BERNSTEIN: *Serenade.* ***

As the title suggests, Foss's *Three American Pieces* have a strong element of Copland-like folksiness, married to sweet, easy lyricism and with some Stravinskian echoes. Skilfully orchestrated for a small orchestra with prominent piano, all three of the pieces, not just the final allegro, *Composer's Holiday*, but the first two, *Early Song* and *Dedication*, have a way of gravitating into hoe-down rhythms, often with a surprising suddenness.

FOULDS, John (1880–1939)

Dynamic Triptych for Piano & Orchestra.

*** Lyrita (ADD) SRCD 211. Shelley, RPO, Handley – VAUGHAN WILLIAMS: *Piano Concerto.* ***

John Foulds's ambitious concerto brings a profusion of memorable ideas, not always well disciplined; but it makes for an attractive piece, particularly so in the last of the three movements, *Dynamic Rhythm*, with its extrovert references to Latin-American rhythms and the American musical. Played with dedication and beautifully recorded, it makes an interesting coupling for the masterly and underestimated Vaughan Williams *Piano Concerto*. Howard Shelley and the RPO under Handley give a highly persuasive account of the *Triptych*, and the 1984 recording is well up to the usual high Lyrita standard.

String Quartets Nos. 9 (Quartetto intimo), Op. 89; 10 (Quartetto geniale), Op. 97. Aquarelles, Op. 32.

✪ *** Pearl SHECD 9564. Endellion Qt.

The *Quartetto intimo*, written in 1931, is a powerful five-movement work in a distinctive idiom more advanced than that of Foulds' British contemporaries, with echoes of Scriabin and Bartók. Also on the disc is the one surviving movement of his tenth and last quartet, a dedicated hymn-like piece, as well as three slighter pieces which are earlier. Passionate performances and excellent recording, which is enhanced by the CD transfer. A uniquely valuable issue.

PIANO MUSIC

April, England; Egoistic; English Tune with Burden, Op. 89;
Essays in the Modes, Op. 78; Music-Pictures Groups VI
(Gaelic Melodies), Op. 81; VII (Landscapes), Op. 13;
Variations & Improvisations on an Original Theme, Op. 4.

*** BIS CD 933. Stott.

Kathryn Stott proves brilliant and persuasive in this repertoire. She also has the advantage of quite exceptionally
truthful and vivid recording quality. The *Essays in the Modes*
(1928), which opens the disc, is interesting stuff; one is
reminded of *Petrushka* in the first and of Busoni elsewhere.
Ms Stott characterizes these pieces and everything here with
strong personality. Try *Prismic*, the last of the *Essays*, and
the intelligence and wit of her playing will make a striking
impression. Foulds wrote for the piano throughout his life,
and if his music from the 1920s is obviously the more
rewarding, even the youthful *Variations and Improvisations
on an Original Theme* shows a pleasing fluency. Not great
music but, played like this, one is almost persuaded that it
is.

FRANÇAIX, Jean (born 1912)

Piano Concertino.

*** Decca (IMS) 452 448-2. Thibaudet, Montreal SO, Dutoit –
HONEGGER: *Concertino*; RAVEL: *Concertos.* **
(M) *** Mercury (ADD) [434 335-2]. Françaix, LSO, Dorati –
AURIC: *Overture*; FETLER: *Contrasts*; MILHAUD: *Le
Boeuf sur le toit*; SATIE: *Parade.* ***

Claude Françaix, the composer's daughter, made the first
recommendable stereo recording of this delectable, miniature, four-movement *Concertino* in 1965. The conductor's
touch is deliciously light in the outer movements and the
pianist's touch is neat and accomplished. Alas, it has been
withdrawn in the UK.

Jean Françaix's delightful *Concertino* also comes off well
in Thibaudet's hands. However, the two Ravel concertos,
the main works, while very well played and recorded, do not
present a strong challenge to existing recommendations.

*À huit (Octet); Clarinet Quintet; Divertissement for
Bassoon & String Quintet; (i) L'Heure du berger.*

*** Hyp. CDA 67036. Gaudier Ens. (i) Tomes.

*À huit (Octet); Clarinet Quintet; Divertissement for
Bassoon & String Quintet.*

**(*) MDG MDGL 3300. Ens.

Jean Françaix's music is always elegant and high-spirited,
never more so than in the four works collected here. *À huit*,
written for the Vienna Octet in 1972 and dedicated to the
memory of Schubert, is a delight. The *Clarinet Quintet* is a
relatively late work (1977) but full of the beguiling charm
that distinguishes so much of Françaix's invention. Despite
its wartime provenance, the *Divertissement for Bassoon and
String Quintet* manages to smile, while *L'Heure du berger*,
background music for a brasserie, comes off equally well.

Highly polished and characterful playing from all concerned
and excellent recording.

Highly accomplished playing from the Charis Ensemble
and eminently acceptable recording. But the Gaudier Ensemble offer the same repertoire as well as an elegant performance of *L'Heure du berger*. Though the Charis are very
good, the Gaudier have the competitive edge over them.

Wind Quintets Nos. 1 & 2; (i) L'Heure du berger.

*** MDG 603 0557-2. Kammervereinigung Berlin; (i) Zichner.

These Berliners put over Françaix's delightful *Wind Quintets*
with great charm and delicacy. These are performances that
radiate freshness and fun and, apart from the virtuosity of
the performances, the naturalness of the recording and the
balance are a continuing source of delight. *L'Heure du berger*
is a piano and wind sextet, but this is as good in its different
way. Delicious playing and enchantingly light-hearted
music.

FRANCK, César (1822–90)

Symphonic Variations for Piano & Orchestra.

🏵 (B) *** Decca (ADD) 433 628-2. Curzon, LPO, Boult –
    GRIEG: *Concerto* ***; SCHUMANN: *Concerto.* **(*)
(M) *** Decca (ADD) 466 376-2. Curzon, LPO, Boult –
    BRAHMS: *Piano Concerto No. 1*; LITOLFF:
    Scherzo. ***
(M) *** RCA (ADD) 09026 63070-2. Rubinstein; Symphony of
    the Air, Wallenstein (with PROKOFIEV: *Love for Three
    Oranges: March* ***) – FALLA: *Nights in the Gardens of
    Spain* etc. SAINT-SAENS: *Concerto No. 2.* **(*)
(M) (**(*)) EMI mono CDM5 66597-2. Gieseking, Philh. O,
    Karajan – GRIEG: *Piano Concerto*; SCHUMANN: *Piano
    Concerto.* (**(*))
(BB) **(*) ASV CDQS 6092 [(M) id.]. Osorio, RPO, Bátiz –
    RAVEL: *Left-Hand Concerto* ***; SAINT-SAENS:
    Wedding-Cake ***; SCHUMANN: *Concerto.* **(*)
(BB) **(*) Naxos 8.550754. Thiollier, Nat. SO of Ireland,
    Antonio de Almeida – FAURE: *Ballade*; D´INDY:
    Symphonie sur un chant montagnard français. **(*)

Clifford Curzon's 1959 recording of the Franck *Variations*
has stood the test of time; even after five decades there is no
finer version. It is an engagingly fresh reading, as notable
for its impulse and rhythmic felicity as for its poetry. The
vintage Decca recording is naturally balanced and has been
transferred to CD without loss of bloom. The Grieg *Concerto*
coupling is hardly less desirable, and there is also an alternative coupling with Brahms and Litolff, reissued in Decca's
Legends series.

Rubinstein's recording of the *Symphonic Variations* was
the first to appear in stereo. There is refinement and charm,
yet his bravura tautens the structure while his warmth and
freedom prevent it from seeming hard or in any way
aggressive. The 1958 recording was made in the Manhattan
Center, New York City, and has a warm atmosphere. The
two solo encores are marvellously done, particularly the
Prokofiev *March*.

Gieseking's performance dates from 1951. Artistically it

belongs among the very finest accounts of the work that were made in the 1950s, given its many beauties and the wonderful orchestral support from Karajan.

The ASV super-bargain disc offers fine performances of four concertante works including a really outstanding version of the Ravel *Left-Hand Concerto* and it adds up to more than the sum of its parts. It can receive a strong recommendation, for reservations about the Franck performance are minor. It has both poetry and impulse and lacks only a little in sparkle at the very end. It is very well recorded.

François-Joël Thiollier shows imagination, and the orchestral playing is perfectly acceptable without being in any way distinguished. All the same, many will find it tempting at this price.

(i) *Symphonic Variations for Piano & Orchestra;*
(ii) *Symphony in D min.; Les Eolides;* (iii) *Violin Sonata in A;* (iv) (Piano) *Prélude, choral et fugue;* (v) (Organ) *Cantabile in B; Choral No. 2; Pièce héroïque in B min.;*
(vi) *Panis angelicus.*

(B) **(*) Ph. (ADD) Duo 442 296-2 (2). (i) Bucquet, Monte Carlo Op. O, Capolongo; (ii) Concg. O, Otterloo; (iii) Grumiaux, Hajdu; (iv) Del Pueyo; (v) Cocherau (organ of Notre-Dame de Paris); (vi) Carreras.

Although the performances are variable, this Philips Duo set is certainly worth its asking price. Its highlights are Otterloo's splendid (1964) account of the *Symphony* (plus *Les Eolides*) and the Grumiaux/Hajdu performance of the *Violin Sonata* (see below). Otterloo's reading of the *Symphony* has tremendous thrust and its romantic urgency is impossible to resist when the orchestral playing is so assured. *Les Eolides* is a welcome bonus. Marie-Françoise Bucquet gives a perfectly satisfactory account of the *Symphonic Variations*, and Carreras sings his heart out in *Panis angelicus*. But del Pueyo's piano contribution is a routine one and Cocherau's organ pieces are also unmemorable, not helped by wheezily unflattering sound.

Symphony in D min.

⚙ (M) *** RCA (ADD) 09026 63303-2. Chicago SO, Monteux − STRAVINSKY: *Petrushka.* ***

(M) *** DG (ADD) 449 720-2. Berlin RSO, Maazel − MENDELSSOHN: *Symphony No. 5.* ***

(M) **(*) DG (ADD) (IMS) 445 512-2. O Nat. de France, Bernstein − ROUSSEL: *Symphony No. 3.* **(*)

**(*) Teldec 4509 98416-2. BPO, Mehta − SAINT-SAENS: *Symphony No. 3.* **(*)

** Australian Decca Eloquence (ADD) 460 505-2. Cleveland O, Maazel − BIZET: *L'Arlèsienne: Suites Nos. 1−2; Jeux d'enfants ***.*

(B) *(*) DG (ADD) 439 494-2 [(M) id. import]. Chicago SO, Barenboim − SAINT-SAENS: *Symphony No. 3.* **(*)

(i) *Symphony in D min.;* (ii) *Le Chasseur maudit;*
(iii) *Symphonic Variations for Piano & Orchestra.*

(BB) **(*) RCA Navigator (ADD) 74321 29256-2. (i−ii) Boston SO, Munch; (iii) Pennario, Boston Pops O, Fiedler.

(M) **(*) EMI (ADD) CDM7 64747-2. (i; iii) BPO, Karajan; (iii) with Weissenberg; (ii) Phd. O, Muti.

Symphony in D min.; Les Eolides; (i) *Symphonic Variations for Piano and Orchestra.*

(N) *** Chan. 9875 (i) Lortie, BBC PO, Tortelier.

Monteux exerts a unique grip on this highly charged Romantic symphony, and his control of the continuous ebb and flow of tempo and tension is masterly, so that any weaknesses of structure in the outer movements are disguised. The splendid playing of the Chicago orchestra is ever responsive to the changes of mood, and the most recent remastering by John Pfeifer for the Monteux Edition brings a further improvement; indeed, now the quality reflects the acoustics of Chicago's Orchestra Hall in the same way as the Reiner recordings, with textures full-bodied and glowing without loss of detail. The newest coupling is Monteux's uniquely authoritative 1962 Boston recording of *Petrushka*.

With brilliantly full Chandos recording enhancing Tortelier's warm, urgent reading of the *Symphony*, this new Chandos CD makes an outstanding recommendation for Franck's two most popular orchestral works, an ideal coupling, not as common as one might expect. The evocative tone-poem, *Les Eolides*, inspired by a poem of Leconte de Lisle, light and fanciful in its luminously scored evocation of the breezes of heaven, makes an attractive bonus. In the *Symphony*, with speeds far faster than usual, making the overall timing over five minutes less than with such rivals as Chailly and Karajan, Tortelier totally avoids the heaviness and sentimentality that can afflict this work. In the central *Allegretto*, after his urgent account of the first movement, Tortelier adopts a conventional tempo, with fine gradations of dynamic and a slightly raw-sounding cor anglais adding to the freshness. In the finale Tortelier is more distinctive than anywhere, with his fast speed for the *Allegro non troppo* challenging the players of the BBC Philharmonic to produce exciting rather than genial results. Louis Lortie is the excellent soloist in the *Symphonic Variations*, spontaneously poetic in the slow sections, sparkling and light in the scherzando finale.

Maazel's DG account is beautifully shaped, both in its overall structure and in incidental details. He adopts a fairly brisk tempo in the slow movement, which, surprisingly enough, greatly enhances its poetry and dignity; his finale is also splendidly vital . The work gains enormously from strong control and deliberate understatement, as well as from the refinement of tone and phrasing which mark this reading, for there is no lack of excitement. The recording, admirably well blended and balanced, is enhanced in this new CD transfer for DG's 'Originals'.

Bernstein conducts a powerful, warmly expressive performance which, thanks in part to a live recording, carries conviction in its flexible spontaneity. It has its moments of vulgarity, but that is part of the work; the reservations are of less importance next to the glowing, positive qualities of the performance. The recording is vivid and opulent, but with the brass apt to sound strident.

Munch's 1957 performance of the *Symphony in D minor* was always among the finest ever recorded, a performance of great élan, but it suffered − as it still does − from the internal balance of the orchestra, which lets the trumpets (with a nasal edge to their tone) coarsen the texture of the loud moments. Otherwise the warm Boston acoustics are heard to good effect. *Le Chasseur maudit* (recorded five years later) also sounds spectacular: Franck's horn-calls come over arrestingly. The *Symphonic Variations* are brilliantly played by Leonard Pennario. Altogether this Navigator compilation is well worth its modest cost.

Karajan's tempi are all on the slow side, but his control of rhythm prevents any feeling of sluggishness or heaviness. There is always energy underlying the performance, and by facing the obvious problems squarely Karajan avoids the perils. Weissenberg's account of the *Symphonic Variations* has less distinction, but the poetry of the lyrical sections is not missed and Karajan ensures that the orchestral contribution is a strong one. However, as we go to press this issue has been withdrawn.

Muti's is a strongly committed but unsentimental reading. The cor anglais solo in the *Allegretto* is most beautiful and the finale is particularly refreshing in its directness. *Le Chasseur maudit* is strongly presented, and the 1983 recording, robust and vivid, is certainly improved in its CD format, generally well integrated and among EMI's better Philadelphia records made in the 1980s, but there is a degree of glare on the otherwise brilliant digital recording.

Maazel's Decca account is exciting and brilliantly played and recorded, but a lack of lyrical tenderness robs the work of some of its more appealing qualities. The rich melody of the second subject finds Maazel introducing tenutos, which in so clipped and precise a performance seem obtrusive. Maazel's earlier account with the Berlin Radio Orchestra on DG is in almost every way preferable.

Mehta's live performance brings an individual and powerful reading with highly responsive playing from the BPO, whose playing style has a strong influence over the interpretation. Resolutely controlled, the outer movements have consistent thrust and generate plenty of adrenalin. The *Allegretto*, taken slowly, is gentle. In the finale Mehta maintains his grip firmly, so that the closing peroration is the more forceful. A compelling version, given full-bodied if not always refined sound, which is worth considering if the coupling is suitable.

Barenboim adopts a surprisingly plodding tempo in the first movement, the first subject lacking bite. There are also places where the reading is self-indulgent (Barenboim putting on his Furtwänglerian mantle) and, in an otherwise fine account of the slow movement, the cor anglais solo is disappointingly wooden. The 1976 sound, however, is firmer than the original and very acceptable.

(i) *Symphony in D min.;* (i; ii) *Symphonic Variations for Piano & Orchestra;* (iii; v) *Piano Quintet in F min.;* (iii; iv) *Violin Sonata;* (vi) *Prelude, choral et fugue.*

(B) **(*) Erato Ultima (ADD)/Dig. 3984 24234-2 (2). (i) O. Nat. de l'O.R.T.F., Martinon; (ii) with Entremont; (iii) Hubeau, (iv) Charlier; (v) Viotti Qt; (vi) Devoyon.

Not surprisingly, Jean Martinon's volatile account of the *D minor Symphony* is exciting, idiomatic and well held together, and Philippe Entremont makes a warm and sensitive contribution to the *Symphonic Variations*. The late 1960s stereo is full-bodied and is otherwise well balanced, with warmly coloured piano timbre. It is amazing how rarely the *Piano Quintet* has been recorded in recent years and Jean Hubeau's performance with the Viotti Quartet is faithful and committed, as is the ardent and sensitive account of the *Violin Sonata*, where he is joined by Olivier Charlier. These are digital recordings and in the *Quintet* the string timbre could be more sweetly focused, although there is no lack of ambience. No complaints about Pascal Devoyan's admirably sensitive response to the *Prélude, choral et fugue*, and here the sound is very good. At its modest cost this package is worth considering, even if the documentation is inadequate.

CHAMBER MUSIC

Cello Sonata in A (trans. of *Violin Sonata*).

(M) **(*) CRD (ADD) CRD 3391. Cohen, Vignoles (with DVORAK: *Rondo*) – GRIEG: *Cello Sonata*. **(*)

Robert Cohen gives a firm and strong rendering of the Franck *Sonata* in its cello version, splendidly incisive and dashing in the second-movement *Allegro*, but the recording is more limited than one expects from CRD, a little shallow. The addition of the Dvořák *G minor Rondo*, Op. 94, makes a pleasing bonus.

Flute Sonata in A (trans. of *Violin Sonata*).

(M) *** RCA (ADD) 09026 61615-2. Galway, Argerich – PROKOFIEV; REINECKE: *Flute Sonatas*. ***

Although the prospect of hearing the Franck *Violin Sonata* arranged for flute may strike you as unappealing, it is surprising how well this music responds to James Galway's transcription and his sweet-toned virtuosity. Argerich is in absolutely superb form here, and the recording, if just a trifle close is truthful, pleasingly fresh and well defined. An outstanding reissue.

Piano Quintet in F min.

(BB) *** Naxos 8.553645. Levinas, Quatuor Ludwig – CHAUSSON: *Quartet in C min*. ***

(***) Testament mono SBT 1077 Aller, Hollywood Qt – SHOSTAKOVICH: *Piano Quintet*. (***)

Michaël Levinas and the Quatuor Ludwig give a very impressive account of 'the king of piano quintets' (the phrase is Tournemire's). This is a very competitive account which is well worth its modest asking price. Michaël Levinas is a sensitive player, and those who are attracted by the enterprising Chausson coupling should consider the present disc. The standard of playing and recorded sound is high.

Edward Sackville-West and Desmond Shawe-Taylor, the authors of *The Record Guide*, spoke of the Aller/Hollywood version four decades ago as a 'clean-limbed performance ... the players' attack is extraordinarily vivid and the instrumental balance beautifully maintained'. Even if there is no mistaking the (1953) mono sound as being of its time, the performance has such eloquence and power that the music leaps out of the speakers with a vibrant intensity.

Piano Trios Nos. 2 in B flat (Trio de salon), Op. 1/2; 3 in B min., Op. 1/3; 4 in B min., Op. 2.

** Chan. 9742. Bekova Sisters.

These early trios come from Franck's student years and are in no way representative of his mature personality. They emanate from the world of Weber and Mendelssohn and offer little of real substance, even the fugal Op. 2, which he dedicated to Liszt. Eleonora Bekova, the pianist, proves the dominant personality in the trio and some will find her just a bit too assertive. Neither the music nor the playing is really three star but the recording is realistic in the best tradition of the house.

Viola Sonata in A (transcription of Violin Sonata).

*** Chan 8873. Imai, Vignoles – VIEUXTEMPS: *Viola Sonata* etc. ***

*** Simax PSC 1126. Tomter, Gimse – VIEUXTEMPS: *Viola Sonata* etc. ***

An all-Belgian coupling from these two violists, Imai and Tomter. The Franck loses a certain amount of its flamboyance and passion, and gains in a kind of measured dignity. Both performances listed above are exemplary if you want it in this form. There is absolutely nothing to choose between them; both are commanding performances and have an impressive eloquence.

Violin Sonata in A.

⬤ (M) *** Decca (ADD) 460 006-2. Chung, Lupu – DEBUSSY: *Violin Sonata* *** ⬤; CHAUSSON: *Poème.* ***

*** EMI CDC5 56815-2. Perlman, Argerich – BEETHOVEN: *Violin Sonata No. 9 in A (Kreutzer).* ***

(M) *** Decca 452 887-2. Perlman, Ashkenazy – BRAHMS: *Horn Trio.* **(*)

*** DG (IMS) .445 880-2. Dumay, Pires – DEBUSSY: *Violin Sonata in G min.*; RAVEL: *Berceuse* etc. ***

(M) *** DG (IMS) (ADD) 431 469-2. Danczowska, Zimerman – SZYMANOWSKI: *Mythes* etc. *** ⬤

(BB) *** Arte Nova 74321 59233-2. Contner, Rogatchev – DEBUSSY; SAINT-SAENS: *Violin Sonatas.* ***

(M) **(*) Ph. (ADD) 426 384-2. Grumiaux, Sebok – FAURE: *Sonatas.* ***

Kyung-Wha Chung and Radu Lupu give a glorious account, full of natural and not over-projected eloquence, and most beautifully recorded. The slow movement has marvellous repose and the other movements have a natural exuberance and sense of line that carry the listener with them. The 1977 recording is enhanced on CD and, with an apt Chausson coupling, this reissue remains very desirable indeed.

As in the Beethoven *Kreutzer Sonata*, Perlman and Argerich challenge each other to thrilling effect in this live EMI recording, made in Saratoga in 1999. Here, in a less formally structured sonata, their spontaneous interplay makes for an apt feeling of rhapsodic improvisation. The very opening finds Argerich deeply reflective before Perlman launches into the allegro at a far faster tempo. Some may resist the expressive freedom, whether in phrasing, rubato or in fluctuations of speed, but the magnetism will for most be irresistible, even when the playing is not immaculate, as in the second movement allegro. As in the Beethoven coupling, audience noises are intrusive at times.

How beautifully and simply Perlman and Ashkenazy on Decca open the first movement and how poetically Ashkenazy responds to the melody on Perlman's bow. Yet the second movement catches the listener by the ears with the thrust of its forward impulse and the intensity of its lyrical flow. There is no lack of flexibility, and the sheer ardour of the interpretation makes it a genuine alternative to the Chung/Lupu account.

The distinguished partnership of Augustin Dumay and Maria João Pires offers as assured and powerful an interpretation of Franck's indestructible *Sonata* as any now in the catalogue. They have a firm grip on line and combine both intellectual conviction and tenderness of feeling. The DG recording is more than acceptable, and readers wanting this particular coupling need not hold back.

Kaja Danczowska's account of the Franck is distinguished by a natural sense of line and great sweetness of tone, and she is partnered superbly by Krystian Zimerman. Indeed, in terms of dramatic fire and strength of line, this version can hold its own alongside the finest, and it is perhaps marginally better balanced than the Kyung-Wha Chung and Radu Lupu recording.

The brilliant young German violinist, Mirijam Contner, naturally responding to the French idiom, gives a passionate, warmly intense performance of the Franck sonata, not just in the extrovert passages but also as compellingly in the hushed musing at the very start, or the improvisatory sequence of the third movement. Very well accompanied, this makes up an outstanding disc of French violin sonatas, with excellent sound – an outstanding bargain.

Grumiaux's account, if less fresh than Chung's, has nobility and warmth to commend it. He is slightly let down by his partner, who is not as imaginative as Lupu in the more poetic moments, including the hushed opening bars.

ORGAN MUSIC

Andantino in E (arr. Vierne); *Cantabile; Chorals Nos. 2–3; Pièce héroïque; Prélude, fugue et variation, Op. 18.*

*** Chan. 8891. Kee (Cavaillé-Coll organ of Basilica de Santa Maria del Coro, San Sebastian).

The Dutch composer-organist Piet Kee omits the *Choral No. 1*, for which room could surely have been found, as the playing-time is only 61 minutes 43 seconds, but, apart from this, there can be few grumbles about his record. His interpretations strike an excellent balance between expressive freedom and scholarly rectitude.

3 Chorals (in E; B min.; A min.); 3 Pièces: (Fantaisie in A; Cantabile; Pièce héroïque); 6 Pièces: (Fantaisie No. 1 in C, Op. 16; Grande pièce symphonique, Op. 17; Prélude, fugue et variation, Op. 18; Pastorale, Op. 19; Pière, Op. 20; Final, Op. 21.

⬤ *** Erato 0630 12706-2 (2). Alain (Cavaillé-Coll organ of Saint-Etienne, Caen).

These two CDs include all of Franck's most important works for organ: the *Six pièces*, written between 1860 and 1862, the *Trois pièces* of 1878 and the *Trois chorals* of 1890, the last year of the composer's life. Marie Claire Alain recorded all these works on LP for Erato on a Cavaillé-Col organ at Lyons. Now she has returned to them, using an even finer instrument at Caen. The Cavaillé-Coll organs are as closely related to Franck's music as say, Peter Pears voice was to Britten's. These new performances are even finer than the earlier ones, full of spontaneous feeling and the registration brings some glorious sounds, notably in the Op. 16 *Fantaisie*, the *Third Choral*, where the detail is quite remarkably clear, and the exultant closing *Final*. The sympathy which this player brings to this music and the authority of the results gives this survey a special claim on the allegiance of collectors, and the digital recording is superb, very much in the demonstration bracket.

Choral No. 2.

*** Chan. 9785. Tracey (organ of Liverpool Cathedral), BBC PO, Tortelier – GUILMANT: *Symphony No. 2 for Organ & Orchestra, Op. 91*; WIDOR: *Symphony No. 3 for Organ & Orchestra*. ***

Franck's *Second Choral* is an expansive *Passacaglia*, which reaches a great climax and then gently fades away in the valedictory closing bars. Although the Liverpool organ is not entirely right for it (one needs better definition), Ian Tracey's performance can hardly be faulted, and the result is nothing if not spectacular, enough to make a suitable encore for the two concertante works.

Fantaisie in A; Pastorale.

*** Telarc CD 80096. Murray (organ of Symphony Hall, San Francisco) – JONGEN: *Symphonie Concertante*. ***

Michael Murray plays these pieces very well, although the San Francisco organ is not tailor-made for them. The Telarc recording is well up to standard.

PIANO MUSIC

Choral No. 3; Danse lente; Grand caprice; Les Plaintes d'une poupée; Prélude, aria et final; Prélude, choral et fugue.

*** Hyp. CDA 66918. Hough.

Stephen Hough's impressive *Prélude, choral et fugue* is worthy to rank alongside Murray Perahia's account (currently withdrawn), and no praise could be higher. In addition to the piano music, Hough gives us his own transcription of the *Third* of the Organ *Chorals*, which in his hands sounds as if it had been written for the piano, so splendidly is it played. A most distinguished record in every way.

Eglogue (Hirtengedicht), Op. 3; Les Plaintes d'une poupée; Prélude, aria et final; Prélude, choral et fugue; Premier grand caprice, Op. 5.

(BB) *** Naxos 8.554484. Wass.

Ashley Wass hails from Lincolnshire and came to international attention as first-prize winner of the 1997 World Piano Competition. Both the *Eglogue*, meditative with a massive central climax, and the *Grande caprice*, a flamboyant showpiece, were written when Franck was in his early twen-

ties. What Wass brings out in those and the major items is the technical brilliance of the keyboard writing. He uses a ravishing range of tone, lightening the *Prélude, aria et final* with a flowing speed in the *Prélude* and a mysterious opening for the *Final*. The two lyrical miniatures are charming, but most impressive is the finest of Franck's piano works, the *Prélude* and *Choral*, leading to a powerful, clean-cut account of the *Fugue*, which makes one want to hear Wass in Bach. Heavy fortissimos tend to clang – partly the eager pianist's fault – but otherwise the sound is full and vivid.

VOCAL MUSIC

Les Béatitudes.

(B) **(*) Erato Ultima 3984 24233-2 (2). Lebrun, Berbié, Stutzmann, Rendall, Vanaud, Loup, Ottevaere, French R. Ch. & Nouvel PO, Jordan.

Les Béatitudes has never really established itself. There is much writing of quality as one would expect, but also much that is pedestrian by the standards of the *Symphony*, the *Sonata* or *Psyché*. The recording was made at a live performance in Paris in 1985 and is sensitively shaped under the baton of Armin Jordan. The solo singers are more than adequate, the choral and orchestral contributions are also admirable, and the sound-picture is very natural.

Psyché (symphonic fragments).

(***) Testament mono SBT1128. René Duclos Ch., Paris Conservatoire O, Cluytens – RAVEL: *Daphnis et Chloë*. ***

It is logical that André Cluytens' sensitive account of *Daphnis* should be coupled with Franck's most sumptuous and imaginative score. Both are inspired by classical mythology. The 1954 recording is mono but the transfer is of high quality and no collector will fail to respond.

FRANKEL, Benjamin (1916–71)

(i) The Aftermath, Op. 17. Concertante lirico, Op. 27; 3 Sketches for Strings, Op. 2; Solemn Speech and Discussion, Op. 11; Youth Music, Op. 12.

(BB) *** CPO 999 221-2. (i) Dan; Northwest CO, Seattle, Francis.

All the works recorded here are for string orchestra. While the *Concertante lirico* is very attractive, one of the strongest pieces is *The Aftermath*, a song-cycle for tenor, strings and off-stage trumpet and timpani, to words of Robert Nichols. It is an evocative and imaginative piece. This issue, like others in this series, is recommended to all with an interest in contemporary music that has real individuality and eschews trendiness like the plague. The notes are exceptionally helpful and informative.

(i) Viola Concerto, Op. 45; (ii) Violin Concerto (In Memory of the Six Million), Op. 24; (iii) Serenade Concertante for Piano Trio & Orchestra, Op. 37.

*** CPO CPO 999 422-2. (i) Dean; (ii) Hoelscher; (iii) Smith, Lale, Emmerson; Queensland SO, Albert.

The *Violin Concerto* comes from 1951 when the holocaust was still a vivid and horrific memory. Its emotional core is the expressive and eloquent slow movement. Yet apart from its elegiac centre, the overwhelming impression the work leaves is powerful and positive, a testament to the strength of the human spirit. The *Viola Concerto* is much later and is hardly less memorable. Frankel's lyricism and his musical ingenuity are always in evidence. The composer describes the *Serenata concertante*, which is for piano trio and orchestra, as 'a street scene' in which passing traffic, a distant jazz band, lovers dancing and much else besides can be heard. It wears its serial organization lightly. Both Ulf Hoelscher and Brett Dean are impressive soloists in the two concertos and the Queensland Orchestra respond with supportive playing. The recording engineers serve these fine players faithfully and produce an impressive and wide-ranging sound. Strongly recommended.

Symphonies Nos. 1, Op. 33; 5, Op. 46; May Day Overture, Op. 22.

*** CPO 999 240-2. Queensland SO, Albert.

Benjamin Frankel was a master of the orchestra, and the *First Symphony* (1959) leaves no doubt that he was also a master symphonist. The music develops organically; Frankel has something of the strength of Sibelius combined with a Mahlerian anguish, and his serialism, like that of Frank Martin, never undermines tonal principles. The *Fifth Symphony*, too, is a well-argued and impressive score. The Queensland orchestra play with dedication, and the performances of both symphonies and the inventive *May Day Overture* are very well recorded too.

Symphonies Nos. 2, Op. 38 (1962); 3, Op. 40 (1964).

⚫ *** CPO 999 241-2. Queensland SO, Albert.

Like the *First*, his *Second Symphony* is a powerfully concentrated and finely argued piece which has a constant feeling of onward movement. While the *Second* springs from painful emotions, the *Third Symphony* with its almost Stravinskian opening is a compact one-movement work, predominantly positive in expression and compelling in its sense of purpose. Each symphony is prefaced by a paragraph or so of spoken introduction that the composer recorded at the time he conducted the first performance of these symphonies on the Third Programme. Once more the playing of the Queensland Orchestra is excellent, and so, too, is the recording.

Symphonies Nos. 4, Op. 44; 6, Op. 49; Mephistopheles' Serenade and Dance, Op. 25.

*** CPO 999 242-2. Queensland SO, Albert.

The *Fourth Symphony* is arguably one of the very finest of Frankel's works. It has a more restrained palette than its predecessors, yet its invention is both powerful and distinctive. The Scherzo has a memorable delicacy and the elegiac finale has great eloquence. The *Sixth* is dark and powerfully argued and gets very persuasive advocacy from the Queensland orchestra under Werner Andreas Albert, and very fine recording. Readers might well start either with this latest issue or with the coupling of Nos. 2 and 3.

Symphonies No. 7, Op. 50; 8. Op. 53; A Shakespearean Overture, Op. 29; Overture to a Ceremony, Op. 51.

(N) *** CPO 999 243-2. Queensland SO, Albert.

This issue all but completes the cycle of Benjamin Frankel's symphonies, with No. 6 still to come. The *Seventh* was commissioned by the Peter Stuyvesant Foundation for the LSO, who gave its première under André Previn in 1970. A thoughtful and searching piece, it was underrated at the time and we now have the opportunity of getting to know it for ourselves. The opening of the *Eighth* (1971) is vintage Frankel and the work as a whole has a sense of logic and purpose that marks his best music. All the same, those starting to investigate the cycle should not begin here; the *First* and *Fourth* are better entry points into Frankel's world. The resourceful and imaginative *Shakespearean Overture* was first given at the Edinburgh Festival by the National Youth Orchestra of Great Britain under Walter Süsskind, and is a welcome addition to the Frankel discography. There are ample and excellent notes, which also include eight music-type illustrations.

Bagatelles for 11 Instruments (Cinque pezzi notturni), Op. 35; Clarinet Quintet, Op. 28; Clarinet Trio, Op. 10; Pezzi pianissimi, Op. 41 (for clarinet, cello & piano); Early Morning Music.

(BB) *** CPO 999 384-2. Dean, Australian String Qt (members); Queensland Symphony Chamber Players.

The *Clarinet Quintet* is beautifully crafted and is expertly played by these Australian artists. The *Clarinet Trio* was composed in 1940, but Frankel's musical language and fluent invention are already in place. The short but disturbing *Pezzi pianissimi* are thoughtful, gentle pieces which resonate in the memory afterwards, as do the *Bagatelles for Eleven Instruments* of 1959. This work is serial but not 'atonal' – much in the same way as Frank Martin is. Excellent playing and recording make this another most desirable introduction to a much-neglected and underrated composer whose work is at last gaining ground.

FRASER-SIMPSON, Harold
(1872–1944)

The Maid of the Mountains (with James W. Tate).

(N) *** Hyp. CDA 67190. Kelly, Maltman, George, Suart, Burgess, Maxwell, Gamble, New London Light Op. Ch. & O, Corp.

The history of successful musicals is always fascinating and *The Maid of the Mountains* is no exception. Although it has a famous score accredited to Fraser-Simpson, including such a key number as the splendid *Love Will Find a Way*, when it was on its out-of-town try-out at the Prince's Theatre, Manchester, in 1916, its female lead, José Collins, decided that the score did not have enough popular hits. So her stepfather, James W. Tate, came to the rescue and wrote three of the show's most catchy numbers, *A Paradise for Two*, *A Bachelor Gay* and the duet, *When You're in Love*. The result was a resounding success and the show played for

1,352 performances, its run ending only when its leading lady decided that enough was enough! It is a winningly, lighthearted, cosy piece and still holds up well in the amateur theatre. But it is good to have such a lively professional account as this, from principals and excellent chorus alike, conducted by Ronald Corp, with a consistently vivacious spirit and clear words. The one slight snag is that the heroine, Teresa, sung by Janis Kelly, has a rather close, soubrettish vibrato. However, Richard Suart shines in the relatively small part of Tonio, with his Gilbertian solo *I Understood*, and the charming duet with Vittoria (Sally Burgess) *Over Here and Over There*, which also has a G. & S. flavour. Excellent recording and a full libretto.

FRESCOBALDI, Girolamo

(1583–1643)

Il primo libro de' madrigale a 5 (1608).

*** Opus 111 OPS 30-133. Concerto Italiano, Alessandrini.

Frescobaldi, born in Ferrara, was 25 when his first book of madrigals was published in 1608. They are songs about lovers, longing, admiring, often not daring to speak directly, about parting and loss, and always about passions unrequited. They produced a glorious stream of lyrical invention and a skill in construction remarkable in a composer at the outset of his career. Rinaldo Alessandrini and the Concerto Italiano have been winning golden opinions in this repertoire, and these delightful performances bear out their reputation for fine tuning and blending, and a richly expressive line. They not only give pleasure but should at last put this composer's name firmly in front of the public.

KEYBOARD MUSIC

Primo libro di toccate (1616): excerpts. *Il Secondo libro di toccata, canzoni, Versi d'hinni; Magnificat; Gagliarde, corrente*: excerpts. *Partite sopra l'aria della romanesca* (1624); *Aria di balletto* (1637).

(BB) *** Virgin 2 x 1 VBD5 61869-2 (2). Ross (harpsichord) – BACH: *Goldberg Variations.* **(*)

Scott Ross here surveys the keyboard music of a composer whose music demands a free, improvisatory style of performance, of which he is obviously a master. Indeed he presents this repertoire in a most appealing way, opening with four (very free) *Toccatas* from Book I. The excerpts from the Second Book are framed by two highly inventive sets of variations. The second is a rather engaging *Aria di balletto*, not unlike Handel's variations known as *The Harmonious Blacksmith*. Ross's easy bravura is particularly attractive here, and his Jean-Louis Val harpsichord is very vividly recorded. This no comes inexpensively coupled to Scott Ross's lively set of Bach's *Goldberg Variations*.

Primo libro di capricci (1624/6): *Capriccio sopra la bassa fiamenga. Primo libro di toccate du cimbalo et organa* (1637): *Partite 10 sopra passacaglia; Partite 14 sopra l'aria della romanesca; Toccata 9. Secondo libro di toccate,*

canzone (1627): *Canzona 3; Toccata 9. Quarto libro canzoni alla francese* (1645): *Canzon 3 della La Crivelli.*

(N) (BB) *** Teldec (ADD) 2292 43544-2. Van Asperen (harpsichord).

Like Scott Ross, this excellent Dutch harpsichordist splendidly conveys in these fine performances a feeling of the improvisatory style that the composer himself must have commanded. They concentrate on four keyboard genres: the canzone, the capriccio, the toccata and the partita. Bob van Asperen uses a harpsichord made by Martin Skowronek and modelled on an Italian instrument of the seventeenth century. The music is full of interesting chromatic touches. The 1970 recording is faithful but closely balanced: it needs to be reproduced at a comparatively low listening level.

FROBERGER, Johann (1616–67)

Capriccio in C, FbWV 632; Lamentation sur la mort de Ferdinand III in F, FbWV 633; Partitas: in C, FbWV 612; C min., FbWV 619; D, FbWV 611a; E flat, FbWV 631; in G (auff Die Maÿerin), FbWV 606; Toccatas: in A min., FbWV 101; D, FbWV 121; G, FbWV 103; Tombeau sur la mort de M. Blancheroche in C min., FbWV 632.

*** Virgin VC5 45259-2. Rampe (various harpsichords and virginals).

Siegbert Rampe brings this rewarding repertoire vividly to life on four different period instruments, each admirably chosen; bearing in mind that slight pitch changes are involved as well as the changing character of the instrument, Rampe is immediately commanding in the opening *Tombeau sur la mort de M. Blancheroche* and the similarly meditative *Lamentation for the Death of Ferdinand III*. Both these extended valedictions and the intervening *C minor Partita* are played on a double-manual 1628 Ruckers harpsichord, rebuilt a century later in Paris, which produces a satisfying body of tone. The first two *Partitas* are played on a Miklis Czech harpsichord, made in Prague in 1671, which gives an appropriately more lightweight effect; its pitch, too, is slightly higher. The three bold *Toccatas* are heard on a tangy Spanish instrument made in 1629, which is in splendid condition. In between comes the reflective and touching *Capriccio in C*, which seems ideally suited to the chosen (1587) virginal, made in Venice by Giovanni Celestini. The performances here are outstanding in every way and the recording is very real and believable.

FROHLICH, Johannes (1806–60)

Symphony in E flat, Op. 33.

*** Chan. 9609. Danish Nat. RSO, Hogwood – GADE: *Symphony No. 4.* ***

This delightful disc resurrects a long-buried work which proves far more than just a curiosity. Johannes Frederik Frohlich, born in 1806, was one of the fathers of Danish music. He wrote his *Symphony* in 1833, but it was so poorly played it sank without trace, and was never given again. Yet this is a totally refreshing, beautifully written work, not unlike the symphonies of another Scandinavian, Berwald; it also owes much to Weber. The writing is inventive and full of character, and the Danish Radio Orchestra under Christopher Hogwood play it with both spirit and conviction. It is well coupled here in splendid performances with the best-known symphony by another Dane, Niels Gade, devoted follower of Mendelssohn. Good recording too, if not Chandos's very finest.

FROST, Stephen (born 1959)

(i; ii) *Bassoon Concerto;* (iii) *Oboe Concerto;* (ii; iv) *The Lesson.*

**(*) Chan. 9763. (i) Birkeland; (ii) Bournemouth SO; (iii) Elmes, Ens. 2000; (iv) Bergset; cond. Harrison.

The work for oboe is undoubtedly the finer of these two concertos, succinctly inventive. The *Bassoon Concerto* is perhaps somewhat over-extended when its genial opening toccata gives way to a long central soliloquy, decorated with percussion but also featuring a solo piano, which is to provide a link into the energetic finale.

Both soloists are excellent players, and the performances overall are of high quality. *The Lesson* is a floating vocal melisma using the poem by W. H. Auden. The speaker is placed within the orchestra and no attempt is made to focus the words sharply (and no text is included) so one assumes they are merely a starting point for a piece which is above all evocative. Excellent recording.

FRÜHLING, Carl (1868–1937)

Clarinet Trio, Op. 114.

*** RCA 09026 63504-2. Collins, Isserlis, Hough – BRAHMS: *Clarinet Trio;* SCHUMANN: *Märchenerzählungen; Träumerei.* ***

It was the cellist Steven Isserlis who unearthed this warmly seductive trio for clarinet, cello and piano. Frühling was a composer writing against fashion in a frankly Brahmsian idiom, which yet has strong purpose and individuality, built on memorable themes. The Schumann suite is a fine makeweight, with Isserlis tackling the viola part on the cello. Michael Collins and Stephen Hough, equally magnetic as recording artists, are ideal partners.

FRYE, Walter (died 1475)

Missa Flos Regalis; Song: *Alas, alas.*

*** Signum SIGCD 015. Clerk's Group – Wickham (with ANON.: *Kyrie: Deus creator from Sarum Chant Prynncesse of Youthe.* BEDYNGHAM: *Myn hertis lust; Fortune alas; Mi very joy; So ys emprentid* ***) – PLUMMER: *Missa Sine nomine.* ***

This enterprising and very rewarding Signum collection is entitled 'Brussels 5557', as all the music is taken from a manuscript catalogued under that number, held in the Brussels Bibliothèque Royale. The presence of English music in an anthology which includes works by Du Fay confirms its importance, and indeed the *Missa Flos Regalis* is a remarkably individual setting. Frye's melismatic style is all his own, with the serene *Sanctus* followed by an even more beautiful *Agnus Dei.* We are then offered a group of memorable secular songs, including three by another virtually unknown composer, John Bedyngham, which are equally individual, especially the delightful *So ys emprentid,* although Frye's *Alas, alas* is perhaps finest of all. The performances, as one anticipates from this splendid group, are dedicated and impressively secure. The recording too could hardly be bettered, nicely set back in a warm ambience.

FUCHS, Robert (1847–1927)

Cello Sonatas Nos. 1 in D min., Op. 29; 2 in E flat min., Op. 83; Phantasiestücke, Op. 78.

*** Marco 8.223423. Drobinsky, Blumenthal.
*** Biddulph LAW005. Green, Palmer.

The *Cello Sonatas,* like the more Schumannesque *Phantasiestücke,* offer well-fashioned, cultured and civilized music (no mean virtues) which may not have a strongly original profile but is well worth investigating for all that. After long neglect these works are available in two different versions. To be frank, there is not much to choose between them; both offer very good performances; both are very well recorded and deserve their three stars, so no agonies of choice are required: you can safely invest in one or the other.

Clarinet Quintet, Op. 102.

*** Marco 8.223282. Rodenhäuser, Ens. Villa Musica – LACHNER: *Septet.* ***

This is beautifully crafted and speaks with the accents of Schubert and Brahms rather than with any strong individuality. It is nicely played by the Mainz-based Ensemble Villa Musica whose excellent clarinettist, Ulf Rodenhäuser, is worth a mention. A curiosity rather than a revelation then, but eminently well recorded.

String Quartets: in E, Op. 58; in A min., Op. 62.

(N) **(*) MDG 6031001-2. Minguet Qt.

Op. 62 was composed in the late 1890s and reveals how strong Brahms' gravitational pull was on Fuchs; its Minuet bears a more than passing resemblance to Brahms' quartet in the same key, Op. 51/2. The music is fashioned expertly (although the slow movement of Op. 58 is wanting in concentration), but a distinctive voice does not emerge. Good playing and an acceptable recorded sound.

String Trio in A, Op. 94.

*** MDG 634 0841-2. Belcanto Strings – REINECKE: *Trio in C min., Op. 249.* ***

In his day Robert Fuchs was a much admired teacher whose pupils included Mahler, Sibelius, Wolf, Franz Schmidt, Schreker and Zemlinsky! He was also a prolific composer, even if none of his works to reach the catalogues reveals evidence of a strong or original voice. Finely crafted and cultured music, very conservative for its date of composition (1910), but superbly played and recorded.

Piano Sonatas Nos. 1, Op. 19; 2, Op. 88.

*** Marco 8.223377. Blumenthal.

The early *F minor Sonata*, Op. 19, (1877) is again heavily indebted to Brahms. All the same it has a certain breadth and lyrical fertility that impress. The *Second Sonata*, Op. 88, is mature Fuchs. Its invention is more chromatic and there are hints of Reger and even of Debussy and Fauré. Although Fuchs may lack a strong individual voice, his musical thinking has the merit of breadth and span and these are both rewarding works, given such masterly and persuasive advocacy as they receive at the hands of Daniel Blumenthal.

FURTWÄNGLER, Wilhelm

(1886–1954)

Symphonic Concerto: Adagio.

(**) Testament Mono SBT 1170. Fischer, Berlin PO, Furtwängler – BRAHMS: *Piano Concerto No. 2.* (**(*))

It makes a valuable bonus to the radio recording of the Brahms concerto to have a further, very personal example of these two great artists' rapport in working together, in a movement from one of the conductor's most ambitious works. This may not be great music, but with its echoes of Bruckner leading to passionate climaxes it makes agreeable listening in this studio recording of 1939, even with limited sound.

Symphony No. 2 in E min.

(M) (***) DG mono 457 722-2 (2). BPO, Furtwängler – SCHUMANN: *Symphony No. 4.* (***) ✪

Furtwängler spoke of his *Second Symphony* as his spiritual testament. It is Brucknerian in its dimensions and sense of space. The first movement, lasting 24 minutes, is accommodated on the first CD, and the remaining three on the second. Furtwängler himself thought the present studio recording, made in the Jesus-Christus-Kirche, Berlin, in 1950 'stilted', but it sounds amazingly clear and warm in this transfer and readers should not be put off acquiring it. The Schumann coupling – one of Furtwängler's very finest mono records – makes a superb coupling.

FUX, Johann Joseph (1650–1741)

Il Concentus musico instrumentalis: Overtures (Suites) Nos. 2 in B flat; 4 in G min. Overtures (Suites) in B flat; D min.

(M) *** Van. 99705. Il Fondamento, Dombrecht.

Fux wrote a great many overtures or suites which combine the French and Italian styles, of which the present four are lively and quite colourful examples. They have a good deal in common with similar works of Telemann, even if not nearly so skilfully scored. Il Fondamento, a period-instrument group under Paul Dombrecht bring these works

to life quite vividly. They are agreeably recorded; though the sound could ideally be more transparent. But the thickness of texture is partly caused by the doubling up in the scoring, with the wind playing in tutti with the strings.

GABRIELI, Andrea (1520–86)

Aria della battaglia.

(B) ** Decca 448 993-2. Philip Jones Brass Ens., Jones – Giovanni GABRIELI: *Collection.* **(*)

The *Aria della battaglia* is a rambling piece lasting over ten minutes, rather too long to retain the listener's interest – at least in the present performance. It is very well played, without any dramatic dynamic contrasts, and tends to jog along rather than create any great degree of tension. The recording is clear and nicely resonant.

(i) *Ricercar a 4 del primo tuono; Ricercar a 4 del sesto tuono; Ricercar a 4 del duodecimo tuono; Ricercar per sonar a 8.* (ii) (Organ) *Canzon alla Francese: Petit Jacquet; Intonazione del sesto tuono; Madrigal: Ancor che co'l partire; Ricercar del settimo tuono.* (i; ii; iii) *Missa Pater peccavi;* Motets: (i; iii) *De profondis clamavi;* (i; iv) *O sacrum convivium.*

(N) *** Hyp. CDA 67167. (i) His Majestys Sackbutts & Cornets; Roberts (organ); (iii) His Majestys Consort of Voices, Roberts, (iv) with Pickard.

It is good to have first-class performances of some of Andrea Gabrieli's *Ricercari* on record, even if they are less spectacular, and indeed less varied than those of his nephew, Giovanni. The Mass setting (based on Andrea's own motet *Pater peccavi in caelum*) settles for very simple counterpoint – probably bearing the dictum of the Council of Trent in mind – but springs to life in the *Sanctus*.

Among the brass pieces the lively *Ricercar del settimo tuono* stands out, while the solo motet *O sacrum convivium* is simply and beautifully sung by Anna Sarah Pickard, whose vocal line is integrated within the 'accompaniment' by four sackbuts. The organ interludes are played by the group's director, Timothy Roberts, and the concert closes with the eight-part *Ricercar per sonar*, which is rather impressive. Excellent recording in a well-judged acoustic.

Madrigali e canzoni: *Angel del terzo ciel; Cantiam di Dio, Cantiamo; Canzona a 4; Come havrò pace in terra; Caro dolce ben mio; A le guacie i rose; Gratie che'l mio Signor; I'vo piangendo i miei passati tempi; Mentre la greggia errando; Mentr'io vi miro; Quanti, sepolti giù nel foco eterno; Hor che nel suo bel seno; O Dea; Piangi pur, Musa; Ricercare Va 4; Rimanti, Amor; O soave al mio cor dolce catena; Sento, sent' un rumor; Tirsi, che fai così dolente a l'ombra; Tirsi morir volea; Vaghi augeletti; La verginella è simile alla rosa; Vostro fui e sarò mentre ch'io viva.*

**(*) CPO 999 642-2. Weser-Renaissance Bremen, Cordes.

Andrea Gabrieli composed prolifically in most genres and this collection of madrigals, performed here by singers and instrumentalists of the Weser-Renaissance, brings together pieces from several different publications. Where the singers and instrumentalists are together, there is a tendency for nuances of word-colouring and dynamics to be ironed out. Although there are moments of dubious intonation, performances are generally dedicated, and the recording clean and well focused. A useful addition to the catalogue.

GABRIELI, Giovanni (1557–1612)

Music for Brass, Vol. 1: *Canzon a 12 in double eco; Canzon septimi toni a 8 No. 2; Canzon septimi e octavi toni a 12; Canzon noni toni a 8; Canzon noni toni a 12; Canzoni duodecimi toni a 10, Nos. 1 & 3; Canzoni VII; VIII; IX; XI; XIII; XIV; XVII; XXVIII; Sonata pian' e forte alla quarta bassa a 8.*

(BB) *** Naxos 8.553609. LSO Brass, Crees.

Starting with the *Canzon XVII* of 1615 in 12 parts, involving three choirs of instruments, Eric Crees and his brilliant players from the brass section of the LSO demonstrate at once what variety of tone they can produce, with the finest shading of timbre and texture. In the great *Sonata pian' e forte* of 1597 in eight parts and the even more striking *Double Echo Canzon in 12 Parts*, the playing is remarkable as much for its restraint and point as for its dramatic impact. Beautiful sound, both clear and atmospheric, not aggressive.

(i) *Canzon a 6; Canzon primi toni a 8; Canzon, La Spiritata, a 4; Canzon vigesimasettima a 8; Sonata a 3.* (i; ii) *Canzon per sonar a 4; Canzoni Nos. 4 a 6; 12 a 8; In ecclesiis; Jubilate Deo; O Jesu mi dulcissime; O magnum mysterium; Quem vidistis pastores?; Timor et tremor.*

(B) **(*) Decca 448 993-2. (i) Philip Jones Brass Ens., Jones; (ii) Soloists, King's College, Cambridge, Ch., Cleobury – Andrea GABRIELI: *Aria della battaglia.* **

The first group of *Canzoni* here is played immaculately on modern brass instruments. The *Sonata 3* comes off best; otherwise there seems to be a lack of tension and not the widest range of dynamic. In the rest of the programme, recorded four years later in 1986, the widely resonant acoustics of King's College Chapel make an admirable alternative to St Mark's for this repertoire. In the festive motet, *In ecclesiis*, with its three choirs plus organ and instrumental accompaniment, the complex layout is thrilling, and the Christmas motet, *Quem vidistis pastores?*, with its solo voices from the choir representing the shepherds, is very well managed. The canzoni for brass alone, which act as interludes, are undoubtedly enhanced by the King's ambience, and climaxes have real impact.

Sonata pian e forte.

(N) *** BBC BBCL mono 4059-2. LSO, Stokowski – LISZT: *Mephisto Waltz No. 1.* NIELSEN: *Symphony No. 6.* TIPPETT: *Concerto for Double String Orchestra.*

The *Sonata pian e forte* was a repertory piece in the 1940s and 50s, before the period-instrument movement got under way, and Stokowski evokes a rich individual sonority from his fine players.

Angelus ad pastores ait; Buccante in neomenia tuba; Canzon septimi toni a 8; Hodie Christus natus est; Hodie completi sunt; O Domine Jesu Christe; O magnum mysterium; Omnes gentes, plaudite manibus.

(B) **(*) EMI Double forte (ADD) CZS5 68631-2 (2). Cambridge University Musical Soc., Bach Ch., King's College Ch., Wilbraham Brass Soloists, Willcocks (with SCHEIDT: *In dulci jubilo* ***) – SCHUTZ: *Psalm 150* **(*); MONTEVERDI: *Vespers.* *(*)

Originally recorded in King's College Chapel, using quadraphonic sound, the CD transfer brings stereo which is notable for the opulent richness of brass and choral textures rather than inner clarity, yet is resonantly resplendent. There is an impressively wide dynamic range, as is shown by the serene motet, *O Domine Jesu Christe*. Added to the Gabrieli works is Scheidt's setting in eight parts of the famous *In dulci jubilo*, which is particularly successful. It is a pity that the principal Monteverdi coupling is not more recommendable.

GADE, Niels (1817–90)

Andante & Allegro (arr. Rachlevsky); *Novelettes, Opp. 53 & 58.*

*** Claves CD 50-9607. Kremlin CO, Rachlevsky.

This is eminently civilized writing, inventive and intelligent, full of charm, and the performances by the Kremlin Chamber Orchestra under Misha Rachlevsky are beyond praise. It is a joy to hear such natural and beautifully shaped phrasing and the recording is pleasingly natural and warm.

Novellettes in F, Op. 53; in E, Op. 58.

*** CPO CPO 999 516-2. German Chamber Academy Neuss, Goritzki – HAMERIK: *Symphony No. 6.* ***

These miniatures for strings, like most of Gade's music, are full of charm, and are excellently played by the Deutsche Kammerakademie with their splendid cellist-conductor Johannes Goritski. They have great lightness of touch and vital rhythmic articulation. First-rate sound.

Symphony No. 1 in C min. (On Sjølund's Fair Plains), Op. 5; Overture, Echoes from Ossian, Op. 1; Hamlet Overture, Op. 37.

*** Chan. 9422. Danish Nat. RSO, Kitaenko.

This performance of the engaging, folksong-inspired *First Symphony* has an unaffected quality and an unforced eloquence that give much delight. The two shorter works, *Hamlet* and the *Echoes from Ossian Overture*, are also very well played. The recording, made in the fine concert hall of Danish Radio, is absolutely first rate, natural in perspective, with plenty of presence and detail.

Symphonies Nos. 1 in C min. (On Sjøland's Fair Plains), Op. 5; 8 in B min., Op. 47.

*** BIS CD 339. Stockholm Sinf., Järvi.

Thirty years separate the *First Symphony* from his *Eighth* and last symphony, like the *First* much indebted to Mendelssohn. Despite this debt, there is still a sense of real mastery and a command of pace. The Stockholm Sinfonietta and Neeme Järvi give very fresh and lively performances, and the recording is natural and truthful.

Symphonies Nos. 2 in E, Op. 10; 7 in F, Op. 45.

*** BIS CD 355. Stockholm Sinf., Järvi.

Schumann thought No. 2 'reminiscent of Denmark's beautiful beechwoods'. The debt to Mendelssohn is still enormous here, but it is very likeable, more spontaneous than the *Seventh*, though this work has a delightful Scherzo. Splendid playing from the Stockholm Sinfonietta under Järvi, and good recording too.

Symphonies Nos. 2 in E, Op. 10; 8 in B min., Op. 47. Allegretto, un poco lento; Overture: In the Highlands, Op. 7.

(N) *** Chan. 8962. Danish Nat. RSO, Hogwood.

Hogwood's Chandos disc is announced as the first of a complete cycle. The *Second Symphony* was composed in 1843, hardly before the ink was dry on its predecessor, which Mendelssohn had championed in Leipzig. Schumann admired it, pronouncing it 'softer and less brisk than the *First*, and reminiscent of Denmark's beautiful beechwoods'; however, it is not as fresh as No. 1 or as fluent or well-proportioned as No. 3. The *Eighth Symphony* (1871) is very civilized, although the fact remains that Gade never really succeeded in making his escape from the orbit of Mendelssohn. Hogwood also gives us the *Allegretto, un poco lento*, the original slow movement of the *Eighth Symphony* (which Gade subsequently discarded), and an early overture, *In the Highlands*, with which Gade followed up the success of his *Ossian Overture*. Well shaped, solid performances and recommendable, although Neeme Järvi and the Stockholm Sinfonietta have the lighter touch and have greater transparency of sound.

Symphonies Nos. 3 in A min., Op. 15; 4 in B flat, Op. 20.

*** BIS CD 338. Stockholm Sinf., Järvi.

Gade's *Third* has great freshness and a seemingly effortless flow of ideas and pace, and a fine sense of musical proportion. No. 4 was more generally admired in Gade's lifetime, but its companion here is the more winning. It is beautifully played and recorded.

Symphonies Nos. 3 in A min., Op. 15; (i) 5 in D min., Op. 25.

**(*) dacapo DCCD 9004. (i) Malling; Coll. Mus., Copenhagen, Schønwandt.

Michael Schønwandt's performances of these two Gade symphonies are most musical, and distinguished by sensitive phrasing and a fine feeling for line. In the *Fifth Symphony*, the piano is less closely observed than it is in the BIS recording. Amalie Malling is the more reticent player, too, and plays with taste and grace. However, the 1988 recording though perfectly acceptable is not as good or as fresh sounding as its BIS rival which is on balance to be preferred.

Symphony No. 4 in B flat, Op. 20.

*** Chan. 9609. Danish Nat. RSO, Hogwood – FROLICH: *Symphony.* ***

In this best known of his eight symphonies, as in most of his works, Gade charmingly echoes Mendelssohn. Very well played and recorded, it makes an excellent coupling for the delightful, long-buried Frohlich symphony. The performance does not supplant Neeme Järvi, coupled with the *Third*, which has more transparent, better balanced recorded sound. All the same, a very recommendable disc, for the coupling is delightful.

Symphonies Nos.. (i) 5 in D min., Op. 25; 6 in G min., Op. 32.

*** BIS CD 356. Stockholm Sinf., Järvi; (i) with Pöntinen.

The *Fifth Symphony* is a delightfully sunny piece which lifts one's spirits; its melodies are instantly memorable, and there is a lively concertante part for the piano, splendidly played by the young Roland Pöntinen. The *Sixth Symphony* is rather more thickly scored and more academic. The recording is very good and, given the charm of the *Fifth Symphony* and the persuasiveness of the performance, this coupling must be warmly recommended.

CHAMBER MUSIC

Allegro in A min., for String Quartet; (i) Andante & Allegro molto in F min., for String Quintet. String Quartet in F (Wilkommen und Abschied); (ii) Octet in F, Op. 17.

**(*) BIS CD 545. Kontra Qt, with (i–ii) Nygaard; (ii) Egendal, Madsen, Ranmo.

All this music is youthful, and has charm and freshness of invention. Gade's work has a spontaneity – particularly the *F minor Quintet* – which is quite captivating. This is a useful supplement to the Kontra's recording of the three later *Quartets* discussed below, and in many ways it is to be preferred. The excellent performances are well recorded, but there is a slightly strident edge in tutti passages which inhibits a full three-star recommendation.

String Quartets Nos. 1 in F min., 2 in E min., 3 in D, Op. 63.

*** BIS CD 516. Kontra Qt.

These are pleasing works of great facility and are worth hearing, particularly in such good performances and recordings as we are given here. If they show too strong a gravitational pull of Mendelssohn, in terms of invention and craftsmanship they give a certain pleasure.

VOCAL MUSIC

(i) Efterklange af Ossian (Echoes from Ossian), Op. 1; (ii) Elverskud (The Elf-King's Daughter), Op. 30; (iii) 5 Partsongs, Op. 13.

*** Chan. 9075. (ii) Johansson, Gjevang, Elming, Danish Nat. R. Ch.; (iii) Danish Nat. R. Chamber Ch., Parkman; (i; ii) Danish Nat. RSO, Kitaienko.

(i) Elverskud Op. 30; (ii) Forårs-fantasi (Spring Fantasy), Op. 23.

*** dacapo 8.224051. (i) Elmark, Paëvatalu; (i; ii) Dolberg;

(ii) Dahl, Henning-Jensen, Byriel, Westenholz; (i) Tivoli Concert Ch.; Tivoli SO, Schønwandt.

Gade's *Elverskud*, variously translated as *The Elf-King's Daughter*, *The Erl-King's Daughter*, *The Fairy Spell* or *The Elf-Shot*, is a work of great appeal and the opening of the second half – an evocation of the moonlit world of the fairy hill – is little short of inspired. Michael Schønwandt's account has a good deal to recommend it. In some ways this Marco Polo disc scores over its Chandos rival: the solo singers are generally more satisfying and the conductor keeps a firmer grip on proceedings without any loss of poetic feeling or atmosphere. It also has the advantage of the more adventurous coupling, the *Forårs-fantasi* (*Spring Fantasy*), another of Gade's most delightful inspirations, radiant in its happiness and full of sun.

On Chandos *Elverskud* comes with Gade's very first opus, the delightful *Ossian Overture*. A further bonus is the set of *Five Partsongs*, Op. 13, beautifully sung by the Danish Radio Chamber Choir; the fourth, *Autumn song*, is particularly memorable and haunting. Gade never escapes the embrace of Mendelssohn for long; if his world is urbane, well ordered and free from any hint of tragedy, *Elverskud* again gives unfailing pleasure, particularly in such a persuasive performance and excellent recording.

Korsfarerne (The Crusaders), Op. 50.

**(*) BIS CD 465. Rorholm, Westi, Cold, Canzone Ch., Da Camera, Kor 72, Music Students' Chamber Ch., Aarhus SO, Rasmussen.

Gade's *Korsfarerne* is in three sections, *In the Desert*, *Armida* and *Towards Jerusalem*, and lasts the best part of an hour. The Danish forces assembled here do it proud, as do the BIS recording team, but the debt to Mendelssohn, say in the *Chorus of the Spirits of Darkness* which opens the second section, overwhelms any feeling of originality.

GALBRAITH, Nancy (born 1951)

Piano Concerto No. 1.

*** Ocean OR101. Zitterbart, Cincinnati CO, Lockhart –
ALONSO-CRESPO: *Overtures & Dances from Operas.* ***

The first movement of Nancy Galbraith's attractively colourful concerto uses what she calls 'sensuous rhythmic pulses' in the orchestra, minimalist style, from which the piano regularly surfaces in a concertante manner. In the atmospherically lyrical slow movement the piano achieves an essentially reflective solo role, before the orchestra re-asserts its dominance in a driving, energetic toccata-like finale, which has quite haunting lyrical interludes. This is writing that communicates directly to the listener. The performance here is persuasively full of life and colour and the recording excellent.

GALUPPI, Baldassare (1706–85)

Motets: *Arripe alpestri ad vallem*; (i) *Confitebor tibi, Domine.*

⊛ *** Virgin VC5 45030-2. Lesne, (i) with Gens, Harvey; Il Seminario Musicale.

These two very beautiful motets show Galuppi at his most inspired, and they are performed superbly by Gérard Lesne, who is joined by Véronique Gens and Peter Harvey in *Confitebor tibi* (praising God for His munificence), which brings a skill in its overlapping part-writing worthy of Mozart. The accompaniments from Il Seminario Musicale are refreshingly sensitive, alive and polished, while the recording has a natural presence.

GARDINER, Henry Balfour (1877–1950)

Humoresque; The Joyful Homecoming; Michaelchurch; Noel; 5 Pieces; Prelude; Salamanca; Shenandoah & Other Pieces (suite).

*** Continuum (ADD) CCD 1049. Jacobs.

Balfour Gardiner was at his finest in miniatures, and his writing has an attractive simplicity and innocence. Most of this music is slight, but its appeal is undeniable when it is presented with such authority and sympathy. It is very well recorded indeed.

GARDNER, John (born 1917)

Flute Concerto, Op. 220. Half-Holiday Overture, Op. 52; Irish Suite, Op. 231; Prelude for Strings, Op. 148a; Sinfonia Piccola for Strings, Op. 47; Symphony No. 3 in E min., Op. 189.

(M) *** ASV CDWHL 2125. Royal Ballet O, Sutherland; (i) with Stinton.

John Gardner was born in Manchester. After service in the RAF he joined the staff at St Paul's Girls' School at Hammersmith (following in famous footsteps). His first symphony was premièred at the Cheltenham Festival in 1951, and the opera *The Moon and Sixpence* at Sadler's Wells in 1957.

The catchy *Half-Holiday Overture* doesn't go on a moment too long. The *Flute Concerto*, written for Jennifer Stinton in 1995, has a relaxed conversational opening movement followed by a poignant *Nocturne*, and the rondo finale gives the flute plenty of opportunities for sparkling virtuosity.

The *Third Symphony* suggests influences from Shostakovich, which persist in the solemn threnodic *Adagio*. The finale restores the mood of genial humanity. The elegiac *Prelude for Strings* derives from a string quartet.

Most successful of all is the *Sinfonia Piccola*. The *Andante* proves to be a searching passacaglia, always a source of stimulation in the hands of a fine composer. The finale has a touch of Britten's *Simple Symphony* about it. The *Irish*

Suite genially celebrated the composer's eightieth birthday. Fine performances and an excellent recording serve to recommend this collection well, and congratulations to ASV for issuing it at mid-price.

GATES, Philip (born 1963)

Airs & Graces; Clarinet Sonata; Flute Sonata; Danzas del Sud; Mood Music; Rio Bound.

**(*) Shellwood Productions SWCD 15. Way, Kelly, Clarke, Willox, Composer.

Philip Gates obviously has a special feeling for the flute and is clearly influenced by twentieth-century French writing for this instrument, including the jazzy inflections. The engagingly cool nostalgia of the central movement of his *Sonata* has a few unpredictable interruptions from the piano, for which Gates also writes very naturally. The finale's rhythmic influences are Latin-American. The six *Airs and Graces* are lightweight vignettes, the most striking being *At Loch Leven* (with its Scottish snap in the melody) and the neatly syncopated *Rag-a-muffin*. The *Clarinet Sonata* flows amiably, with a bluesy central *Cantabile*. But it is the snappy finale that stands out. *Rio Bound* makes a good final encore. The *Mood Music* pieces for alto-saxophone are less striking. The *March Hare* gambols robustly, but *Sax-Blue* and *Soft-Shoe* are too predictable. The performances are excellent and so is the recording.

GAUBERT, Philippe (1879–1941)

Music for Flute and Piano: *Sonatas Nos. 1–3; Sonatine. Ballade; Berceuse; 2 Esquisses; Fantaisie; Nocturne et allegro scherzando; Romance; Sicilienne; Suite; Sur l'eau.*

*** Chan. 8981/2. Milan, Brown.

Gaubert had a genuine lyrical gift and his music has an elegance and allure that will captivate. He is eminently well served by Susan Milan and Ian Brown, and they are all well balanced by the Chandos engineers. Truthful sound; civilized and refreshing music, not to be taken all at one draught but full of delight.

Flute Sonatas 1–3; Madrigal; Orientale; 3 Aquarelles for Flute, Cello & Piano; Pièce romantique for Flute, Cello & Piano.

(N) **(*) Deux-Elles DXL 923. Thomas, Shaw, Scott.

Philippe Gaubert was a virtuoso flautist and composed extensively for the instrument. This anthology shows his refinement of craftsmanship and freshness of inspiration. Not great music but full of Gallic charm, which is well conveyed in these accomplished performances by Katryn Thomas and Richard Shaw, who are joined in the 3 *Aquarelles* and the *Pièce romantique* by the cellist Phoebe Scott. Decently recorded even if the acoustic is over-reverberant.

GAY, John (1685–1732)

The Beggar's Opera (arr. Pepusch and Austin).

⚜ (BB) *** CfP Silver Double (ADD) CDCFPSD 4778 (2). Morison, Cameron, M. Sinclair, Wallace, Brannigan, Pro Arte Ch. & O, Sargent.

The Beggar's Opera was the eighteenth-century equivalent of the modern American musical. It was first produced in 1728 and caused a sensation with audiences used to the stylized Italian opera favoured by Handel. This performance under Sargent is in every way first class and the soloists here could hardly be bettered, with Elsie Morison as Polly and Owen Brannigan a splendid Peachum. The linking dialogue is spoken by actors to make the result most dramatic, with every word crystal clear. The chorus is no less effective, and the recording has a most appealing ambience. Its sense of presence and atmosphere is remarkable, but alas, it has just been deleted as we go to press.

GEMINIANI, Francesco (1687–1762)

Concerti grossi, Op. 2/1–6; Op. 3/1–4.

(BB) *** Naxos 8.553019. Capella Istropolitana, Krĕcek.

This is part of an ongoing Naxos project to record all Geminiani's *Concerti grossi* using modern instruments but in a style which clearly reflects the freshness and vitality of period-instrument practice. The Capella Istropolitana offer excellent accounts of the whole of Op. 2 and the first four concertos of Op. 3 (with the remainder to follow), all invigoratingly enjoyable and very well recorded.

Concerti grossi, Op. 2/1–6; Concerti grossi after Corelli, Op. 5/3 & 5.

*** Sony SK 48043. Tafelmusik, Lamon.

Although these works are essentially concerti grossi, the frequent dominance of the solo violin in the concertino points the way to the solo concertos of Vivaldi. Jeanne Lamon takes this solo role and directs the performances with plenty of vitality, and the recording produces clean, full, yet transparent textures. The recording is bright and immediately balanced within the warm acoustic of Notre Dame Convent in Waterdown, Ontario, Canada.

Concerti grossi, Op. 3/5–6; Op. 7/1–6.

(BB) *** Naxos 8.553020. Capella Istropolitana, Krĕcek.

This CD continues the Naxos series of Geminiani's *Concerti grossi*, concluding Op. 3 and including the whole of Op. 7. However, the extra parts (in Nos. 3, 4 and 5 for flutes, and 6 for bassoon) are not used here as they are in Iona Brown's outstanding set with the ASMF, which remains a primary recommendation for Op. 7. Nevertheless the performances by the Capella Istropolitana match those on their first disc in freshness and vitality, and they are very well recorded. Bargain hunters need not hesitate.

12 Concerti grossi, Op. 5 (after Corelli).

(B) *** Ph. (IMS) (ADD) Duo 438 766-2 (2). Michelucci, Gallozzi, Bennici, Centurione, I Musici.

The music on which Geminiani based his Op. 5 is drawn from the splendid *Sonatas for Violin and Continuo* of Corelli with the same opus number. Their skilful adaptation to *concerto grosso* form features a viola in the solo group as well as violins and cello. The performances by I Musici – at their very finest – are admirable in all respects, spirited and responsive, polished yet never bland. The recording is first class too, wide-ranging, full and clearly detailed. Highly recommended.

(i) *12 Concerti grossi, Op. 5 (after Corelli)*; (ii; iii) *Cello Sonata in D min, Op. 5/2*; *Ornamented arrangement of Corelli's Sonata in A for Violin & Cello.*

(N) *** HM 907261.2 (2). (i) AAM, Manze; (ii) Watkin; (iii) McGillivray.

Fine as is I Musici's set of Corelli's Op. 5, it is surpassed by the new period instrument performance by the players of the Academy of Ancient Music, led from the bow by Andrew Manze. He is a superb soloist, but so are his colleagues and the transparency of the sound and refinement of textures in no way preclude warmth. Allegros are full of vigour (and bravura) while the exquisite delicacy of the solo contribution to slow movements makes the strongest possible case for authenticity in this music. If you want to sample the vigour and dynamic contrasts of this music-making, try the final work of the set with its winning variations on *La Folia*. As a bonus two further arrangements are offered, equally persuasive in performance. The recording is excellent and this make a clear first choice for Op. 5, unless you are unable to enjoy period performance manners – which here are totally without eccentricity.

Concerti grossi, Op. 7/1–6.

*** ASV CDDCA 724. ASMF, Brown.

The striking textural richness of Geminiani's Op. 7 is achieved by the composer's inclusion of *two* violas, one in the concertino and one in the ripieno, and to increase the colour range he adds a pair of flutes in Nos. 3, 4, and 5 and a solo bassoon in No.6 (which comes first on this CD). The music itself is equally rich, imaginative and vital and nobly expressive, aligning these works with the achievement of Handel and Corelli. There is a sense of scale and breadth too in these splendid ASMF performances under Iona Brown, who gave us a superb set of Handel's Op. 6. The leonine string sound has body and transparency, and the concertino is well focused and naturally separated from the main group. A splendid disc.

Concerti grossi: in D min. (La folia, from CORELLI: *Sonata in D min., Op. 5/12); in G min., Op. 7/2; Trio Sonatas Nos. 3 in F (from Op. 1/9); 5 in A min. (from Op. 1/11); 6 in D min. (from Op. 1/12); Violin Sonatas: in E min., Op. 1/3; in A, Op. 4/12.*

*** Hyp. CDA 66264. Purcell Band & Qt.

This record comes from Hyperion's 'La folia' series, though

the only piece using that celebrated theme is the arrangement Geminiani made of Corelli's *D minor Sonata*. Apart from the *G minor Concerto*, Op. 7, No. 2, the remainder of the disc is given over to chamber works. The Purcell Quartet play with dedication and spirit and convey their own enthusiasm for this admirably inventive music to the listener.

GERBER, Steven (born 1948)

(i) *Cello Concerto*; (ii) *Violin Concerto; Serenade for String Orchestra.*

(N) ✿ *** Koch 3-7501-2. (i) Brey; (ii) Nikkanen; Washington Nat. CO, Gajewski.

Steven Gerber is another outstanding composer of the new American school who has now turned his back on the atonality of his early compositions and, in the mid-1990s, returned to a lyrical tonal idiom. The beautiful *Violin Concerto* is a superb example. In the first movement he uses hauntingly memorable material from his college years and writes unashamedly tonally, and in sonata form. The elegiac central movement opens exquisitely but has a more extrovert middle section; then an improvisatory but written cadenza leads to a quirkily rhythmic finale in 5/4 time. It is announced by a solo trumpet, with the violin then continuing over an irregular timpani rhythm.

The *Cello Concerto* opens equally atmospherically and the soloist ruminates evocatively. The scoring is economical and very telling. Again the first movement uses modified sonata form (one of the themes on the bassoons brings a whiff of Sibelius) and the concerto, in the composer's words, 'is frequently pentatonic'. The brief central movement is an inventive *Scherzo* but alternating with a solemn chorale-like idea, and the finale, a *Passacaglia*, is based on the material of the opening movement. There is a central cadenza but, as with all fine passacaglias, the music finds a satisfying resolution – recreating the mood of the opening, but ending very postively. These are splendid works and both soloists are fully worthy of them, and completely inside this consistently memorable music. The *String Serenade* (an earlier work from 1989–90) is hardly less memorable and individual, opening with a yearning, expressive cantilena, but soon becoming rhythmically more spiky. The second movement is a splendidly inventive theme and variations, deftly using the techniques of minimalism (about which the composer expresses his doubts) as accompanimental figuration. This is real music, splendidly played and recorded, and this Koch CD cannot be too highly recommended to those who, like us, welcome the end of the twentieth-century's disastrous experiment with 'twelve-tone' writing.

GERHARD, Roberto (1896–1970)

(i) *Harpsichord Concerto. Symphony (Homenaje a Pedrell).*

*** Chan. 9693. (i) Tozer; BBC SO, Bamert.

Gerhard's unnumbered *Symphony* of 1941, written in homage to his teacher, Felipe Pedrell, is a far more approachable, less radical piece than his later works. Based on themes from an opera by Pedrell, it is openly tonal, with a Dvořák-like first movement, a warmly elegiac central slow movement and a jolly finale, with Spanish flavours increasingly emerging. The *Harpsichord Concerto*, written for Thurston Dart, is altogether grittier, revealing Gerhard's increasing confidence in handling serial argument. Excellent performances and full-ranging sound.

Concerto for Orchestra; Symphony No. 2 (original version).

*** Chan. 9694. BBC SO, Bamert.

Gerhard's *Concerto for Orchestra* provides an excellent introduction to this fascinating composer. Like the *Fourth Symphony*, it reflects a mood of controlled wildness, with the composer's exuberant enjoyment of exotic sound exploited to the full. It receives a warm, incisive performance from Bamert and the BBC Orchestra, who are comparably persuasive in the grittier arguments of the *Second Symphony*. This is the first recording, which goes back to his original score of 1959. It is a powerful work, in two long movements, each subdivided in two, with the pent-up energy of the first giving way to the stillness and concentration of the second. Oustanding rich and full recording.

(i) Piano Concerto; Epithalamion; Symphony No. 3 (Collages).

*** Chan. 9556. BBC SO, Bamert with (i) Tozer.

The key work here is the *Third Symphony* of 1960, which brings out Gerhard's fascination with electronic sounds, set in contrast with a large orchestra, hence the subtitle, *Collages*. The visual inspiration here was seeing a sunrise from a high-flying aircraft, with the physical element vital in Gerhard's ever-inventive, thornily complex writing. That is vividly captured in Bamert's powerful performance, which easily outshines those on earlier recordings. The *Piano Concerto* of 1951 is complex too in its thought, but readily approachable, and the *Epithalamion*, written for the wedding of friends, using a very large orchestra, represents the composer at his wildest. Full, rich sound.

(i) Violin Concerto; Symphony No. 1.

*** Chan. 9599. BBC SO, Bamert (i) with Charlier.

It was the belated first performance in 1955 of the *Symphony No. 1* that sparked off the surge of creativity which marked Gerhard's last years. The work's athematicism makes it initially less approachable than the coupled *Violin Concerto*, but it is a brilliant and rewarding piece. It is a work which richly repays repeated listening, and here under Bamert receives a powerful performance. The *Violin Concerto* is more immediately inviting, a neo-Romantic and haunting score with a strong sense of atmosphere: its slow movement has a sultry langour that recalls the Mediterranean. It is also a bravura work and the piece includes Spanish references, very like those in the opera *The Duenna*, written soon afterwards. Olivier Charlier is a brilliant advocate, not least in the dazzling finale. Rich, full-bodied sound. A fascinating and highly recommendable issue.

Symphony No. 4 (New York); Pandora Suite.

*** Chan. 9651. BBC SO, Bamert.

Roberto Gerhard's *Fourth Symphony* can be seen as the culminating achievement of his extraordinary last period. Throwing caution aside, he here indulges in his exuberant love of wild and exotic orchestral sounds. This half-hour, single-movement span is at once uninhibited yet tautly conceived, with complex and highly original textures that emerge with pin-point clarity in this superb recording conducted by Matthias Bamert. The *Pandora Suite* from 1942, written for the Kurt Jooss ballet in colourful tonal writing, reveals Gerhard at his most approachable.

Concert for 8; Gemini; Leo; Libra. (i) 3 Impromptus.

*** Largo LARGO 5134. Nieuw Ens., Spanjaard. (i) Snijders.

'I have a certain weakness for astrology in general and for horoscopes in particular,' wrote Gerhard in 1968, having just completed the third of his three astrological pieces for chamber ensemble. It is specially valuable to have all three on a single disc. With contrasted instrumental groups in each, this is Gerhard at his most personal: taut and abrasive, thornily inventive. The strongest and boldest of the three, as well as the longest, is *Leo*, his last completed work, a celebration of the star sign of his wife, Poldi. That association makes the close, written in the face of serious illness, specially poignant. The *Concerto for 8* – with an accordion among the instruments – is an apt extra, as are the three little piano *Impromptus*. Clean-cut performances and recording.

The Duenna (opera; complete).

*** Chan. 9520 (2). Van Allan, Clark, Glanville, Powell, Archer, Taylor, Roberts, Wade, Opera North Ch., E. N. Philh. O, Ros Marbá.

Sheridan's play, *The Duenna*, was originally presented with music by Thomas Linley. But Gerhard resolved to turn it into an opera, being attracted not just by the wit of the dialogue but with its setting in Seville. The work which resulted was the culmination of a period during the 1940s when the Spanish influence was strongest in his music and here the characteristic hints of atonality simply add extra spice to the Spanish flavours, with sensuously colourful instrumentation and lively dance rhythms to produce a superbly crafted, consistently inspired work, even if there is rather too much reliance on speech over music to fill gaps in the story. As the heroine, Donna Luisa, Susannah Glanville sings charmingly, rising to the challenge of her big monologue in Act II, one of the most tenderly lyrical passages in the whole opera, where Gerhard touches deeper emotions than one expects in an eighteenth-century comedy. Richard Van Allan makes an aptly gruff and characterful Don Jerome, the heavy father, and Neill Archer is an ardent hero. In the title-role of the Duenna, Claire Powell is firm and fruity, delightful in her duet with Don Isaac, the rich Jew who is tricked into marrying her. The recording, made in the Royal Concert Hall, Nottingham, is vivid and immediate, with fine presence, letting words be heard with commendable clarity even over the richest orchestral background.

GERMAN, Edward (1862–1936)

Berceuse; The Conqueror; Gipsy Suite; Henry VIII: 3 Dances; Merrie England: Suite; Nell Gwyn: Suite; Romeo and Juliet: Suite; Tom Jones: Waltz.

*** Marco 8.223419. Czecho-Slovak RSO (Bratislava), Leaper.

Richard III Overture; The Seasons; Theme & 6 Diversions.

** Marco 8.223695. RTE Concert O, Penny.

Symphony No. 2 in A min. (Norwich); Valse gracieuse; Welsh Rhapsody.

*(*) Marco 8.223726. Nat. SO of Ireland, Penny.

Of the three Edward German CDs listed above, the first is definitely the one to go for. These suites essentially consist of a string of piquant, rustic-type dances of considerable charm. Most of the composer's most famous numbers are here: the items from *Merrie England* and *Henry VIII*, the pseudo-exotic *Gipsy Suite*, the memorable *Waltz* from *Tom Jones*, plus a few rarities. All of it is effectively presented by the ever-reliable Adrian Leaper, and his Bratislava orchestra play as though they were from the home counties. Definitely an enticing collection in Marco Polo's valuable British Light Music series, most of which shows this composer at his best.

German's 'symphonic suite' *The Seasons* is appealingly tuneful, colourfully orchestrated and enjoyable. The darker colours in *Autumn* provide a certain gravitas, while *Winter* has plenty of scurrying strings and woodwind to paint the scene. If the *Richard III Overture* is no towering masterpiece, it is not dull either, and has enough ideas and a certain Romantic sweep to keep it going. A robust theme in D minor on the brass opens the *Theme and Six Diversions*, and the ensuing variations are enjoyable and nicely varied. The caveat is that although the music is well conducted and played with enthusiasm, the orchestra is a bit scrawny in the string department. Nor is the recording first class – it lacks richness and bloom. But the music's character does come through.

The *Second Symphony* was commissioned by the Norwich Festival (hence its title 'Norwich') in 1893. It has a certain charm – the spirits of Mendelssohn and Dvořák vaguely hover around in the background, but in the last resort, the writing fails to be memorable. The charming *Valse gracieuse* and the deservedly well-known *Welsh Rhapsody* show the composer on better form. The performances are committed, but the sound is only average.

Welsh Rhapsody.

(B) *** CfP (ADD) CD-CFP 4635. RSNO, Gibson – HARTY: *With the Wild Geese*; MACCUNN: *Land of Mountain and Flood*; SMYTH: *Wreckers Overture.* ***

Edward German is content not to interfere with the traditional melodies he uses in his rhapsody, relying on his orchestral skill to retain the listener's interest, and in this he is very successful. The closing pages, based on *Men of Harlech*, are prepared in a Tchaikovskian manner to provide a rousing conclusion. The CD transfer is very well managed, though the ear perceives a slight limitation in the upper range.

Piano music

Concert Study in A flat; Elegy in C min.; First Impromptu in E min.; Graceful Dance in F; Humoresque in E; Intermezzo in A min.; Mazurka in E; Melody in D flat; Melody in E flat; Polish Dance in E; Rêverie in A min.; Tarantella in A min.; Valse-caprice in A; Valse fantastique; Valsette in E min.

(N) ** Marco 8.223370. Cuckston.

These piano miniatures show Edward German at his best. This is unpretentious music of much charm and piquancy. The minor-keyed works are nostalgically disarming, sometimes quite serious, such as the seven-minute *Elegy in C*, sometimes carefree, like the *Tarantella*; but nothing outstays its welcome. Alan Cuckston's performances are good, but not outstanding, and the piano tone is a little harsh, perhaps due to the dry acoustic. Enjoyable and recommendable, never the less.

Merrie England (complete; without dialogue).

(BB) (**) CfP Double CDCFPSD 4796 (2). McAlpine, Bronhill, Glossop, Glynne, Sinclair, Kern, Rita Williams Singers, Collins O, Collins.

Although this recording dates from 1960, it cannot compare in stereo sophistication with EMI's *Beggar's Opera* of five years earlier. All the solo voices are close-miked, usually in a most unflattering way, and too often they sound edgy, while the chorus is made artificially bright; the orchestra is lively enough, but the violins are thin. However, it must be said that Michael Collins directs the proceedings in an attractively spirited fashion. Among the soloists, Howell Glynne is splendid as King Neptune, and Monica Sinclair sings with her usual richness and makes *O peaceful England* more moving than usual. Patricia Kern's mezzo is firm and forward, while McAlpine as Sir Walter Raleigh sings with fine, ringing voice. The Rita Williams Singers are thoroughly professional even if just occasionally their style is suspect. However, this has just been deleted as we go to press.

GERNSHEIM, Friedrich (1839–1916)

Symphonies Nos. 1 in G min., Op. 32; 2 in E flat, Op. 46; 3 in C min. (Miriam), Op. 54; 4 in B flat, Op. 62.

(BB) *** Arte Nova 74321 636352. Rheinland-Pfalz State PO, Köhler.

While revivals of long-forgotten composers can too often prove disappointing, this is a set that triumphantly demonstrates the joys of such an exercise in four richly inventive symphonies in Brahmsian mould, beautifully orchestrated and here presented in strong, sympathetic performances very well recorded. Yet though the cut of his melodies may echo that master, the results are still distinctive and always strongly and individually argued. The *First Symphony* comes from 1875, just before Brahms's *First*, and the *Fourth* from 1895. The ripe, warm melody of the second subject in that first symphony establishes the pattern, and from then on the musical material in each movement and its treatment consistently establish the confident mastery of a composer who may not plumb any depths of feeling, but who in his open optimism leaves you satisfyingly comforted, rather as Mendelssohn or Dvořák do in their symphonies. What Gernsheim offers, which so many minor composers do not, are memorable ideas persuasively presented, as in the *Tarantella* movement of the *Second Symphony* (or any of the Scherzos), the first movement of No. 3 (subtitled 'Miriam', having been inspired by a performance of Handel's *Israel in Egypt*), or the bold outer movements of No. 4. The performances by the Staatsphilharmonie Rheinland-Pfalz under Siegfried Köhler are dedicated. A happy discovery, the more welcome for being offered at super-budget price.

GERSHWIN, George (1898–1937)

An American in Paris.

**(*) Everest (ADD) EVC 9003. Pittsburgh SO, Steinberg –
COPLAND: *Appalachian Spring;* GOULD: *Spirituals.* ***

The recorded sound is rather dry and unexpansive, but otherwise vivid. Steinberg's performance is lively, idiomatic and convincing. The central blues tune is pleasingly sultry. Incidentally, the sleeve-note points out that the Parisian taxi horns that Steinberg adopts now date the piece irretrievably, as horn-tooting is now forbidden in Paris by law.

An American in Paris; Catfish Row (suite from *Porgy and Bess); Cuban Overture; Lullaby.*

(B) *** [EMI Red Line CDR5 72554]. St Louis SO, Slatkin.

Slatkin is clearly at home in *Catfish Row*, and he relishes the sophistication of Gershwin's own suite from *Porgy and Bess*. In the brash *Cuban Overture* some of the gutsy feeling of the piece is lost; while for *American in Paris*, although he often disguises the seams, he could at times be more extrovert. It is partly the gloriously ample acoustics of the Lovell Hall, St Louis, that makes everything seem opulent, especially the *Lullaby* (which derives from *Blue Monday*), in which the St Louis strings sound richly seductive.

(i) *An American in Paris; Cuban Overture;* (ii) *Funny Face: Overture* (orch. Don Rose); *Girl Crazy: Suite* (orch. Leroy Anderson); *Oh, Kay!: Overture* (orch. Rose); (i; iii) *Rhapsody in Blue;* (iv) *Porgy and Bess: Suite* (arr. Roland Shaw).

(B) *** Penguin Decca (ADD) 460 612-2. (i) Cleveland O, Maazel; (ii) Boston Pops O, Fiedler; (iii) with Davis; (iv) Frank Chacksfield and his Orchestra.

Ivan Davis is both a brilliant and a sophisticated soloist in the *Rhapsody*; the boisterous account of *Cuban Overture* is immensely spirited, and *An American in Paris* is given an upbeat reading, well held together. There are more sumptuous versions but with superb Cleveland playing, these performances are easy to enjoy. The original CD has been nicely expanded with characteristically lively Boston Pops performances of the series of marvellous show tunes which make up the theatre overtures, and Leroy Anderson's similarly brief pot-pourri from *Girl Crazy*. Frank Chacksfield's

account of Roland Shaw's brilliantly scored selection from *Porgy and Bess* lacks nothing in panache, and the luscious Decca sound here is outstanding of its kind. An exhilarating compilation. The author's note is by Humphrey Carpenter.

(i) *An American in Paris; Cuban Overture;* (ii) *Porgy and Bess: Symphonic Portrait;* (i; iii) *Rhapsody in Blue.*

(N) **(*) Decca Eloquence (ADD/DDD) 467 410-2.
(i) Cleveland O, Maazel; (ii) Detroit SO, Dorati; (iii) Ivan Davis.

Maazel's mid-1970s performances are brilliantly played and recorded – and certainly enjoyable – but one occasionally feels that the kernel of the two main works is missing: the great blues melody at the centre of *An American in Paris* sounds undernourished, and the *Cuban Overture* sounds an emptier piece than usual. However, Dorati's digital recording of Robert Russell Bennett's famous *Porgy and Bess* arrangement is quite superb, both as a recording and as a performance. The opening is evocatively nostalgic, and each one of these wonderful tunes is phrased with a warmly affectionate feeling for its character, yet never vulgarized. A good bargain, though as usual in the UK Eloquence series notes are not provided.

(i) *An American in Paris;* (ii) *Piano Concerto in F;* (iii) *Rhapsody in Blue.*

(M) *** EMI CDM5 66891-2 [566943]. Previn with LSO.

An American in Paris; (i) *Piano Concerto in F; Rhapsody in Blue; Variations on 'I got rhythm'.*

(BB) *** RCA 74321 68019-2. (i) Wild; Boston Pops O, Fiedler.

The digital remastering of Previn's EMI set, made at the beginning of the 1970s, has brought a striking enhancement of the recording itself. There is now much more sparkle. The performance of the *Concerto* was always a fine one by any standards, but now in the *Rhapsody* one senses many affinities with the famous Bernstein account. *An American in Paris* is exuberantly volatile, and the entry of the great blues tune on the trumpet has a memorable rhythmic lift.

The reissued CD on RCA brings essentially jazzy performances: Earl Wild's playing is full of energy and brio, and he inspires Arthur Fiedler to a similarly infectious response. The outer movements of the *Concerto* are comparably volatile and the blues feeling of the slow movement is strong. At the end of *An American in Paris* Fiedler (like Steinberg and Slatkin) adds to the exuberance by bringing in a bevy of motor horns. A splendid bargain.

An American in Paris; (i) *Rhapsody in Blue.*

⦿ (M) *** Sony (ADD) SMK 63086. NYPO, Bernstein, (i) Bernstein (piano) – GROFE: *Grand Canyon Suite.* ***

Bernstein's 1958–9 CBS (now Sony) coupling set the standard by which all subsequent pairings of *An American in Paris* and *Rhapsody in Blue* came to be judged. It still sounds astonishingly well as a recording. Bernstein's approach is inspirational, exceptionally flexible but completely spontaneous. The performance of *An American in Paris* is vividly characterized, brash and episodic; an unashamedly American view, with the great blues tune marvellously timed and phrased as only a great American orchestra can do it. This coupling is also available on one of Sony's Super Audio CDs – which needs special playback equipment (SS 89033).

Broadway and Film Music: *A Damsel in Distress:* suite, arr. McGlinn. *Stiff Upper Lip: Funhouse Sequence.* **Overtures:** *Girl Crazy; Of Thee I Sing; Oh, Kay!; Primrose; Tip-Toes.*

(B) **(*) EMI Double forte CZS5 68589-2 (2). New Princess Theatre O, McGlinn – KERN: *Overtures* **; PORTER: *Overtures & Film Music.* ***

This inexpensive two-disc Double forte set makes a pretty good collection for those who enjoy authentic re-creations of Broadway music composed by three of its greatest names. John McGlinn has recorded his selections using the original scores. The extended dance-sequence, *Stiff Upper Lip*, comes from a 1937 movie and has some good tunes. So has *Oh Kay!* (half a dozen) while *Girl Crazy* offers the irresistible *I got rhythm.* Elsewhere the famous melodies are more thinly spread, but the marvellous playing of the New York pick-up orchestra (gorgeous saxes and brass) has splendid pep. The lively, close-miked sound gives an authentic theatre-pit brashness, with very bright violins, although the background ambience is warm enough.

Catfish Row (suite from *Porgy and Bess*).

*** Telarc CD 80086. Tritt, Cincinnati Pops O, Kunzel – GROFE: *Grand Canyon Suite.* ***

Catfish Row was arranged by the composer after the initial failure of his opera. It includes a brief piano solo, played with fine style by William Tritt in the highly sympathetic Telarc performance which is very well recorded.

Piano Concerto in F; 'I got rhythm' – Variations for Piano & Orchestra; Rhapsody in Blue; Second Rhapsody.

✪ (M) *** Virgin VM5 61478-2. Marshall, Aalborg Symphony.

(M) *** Classic fM 76505 57012-2. Boriskin, Eos O, Sheffer.

With this dazzling Gershwin programme Wayne Marshall both acts as soloist and directs the orchestra. The performance of the *Rhapsody in Blue* outshines even Bernstein's famous New York account in its glittering brilliance and excitement. Marshall manages spontaneously to coalesce both the symphonic and jazz character of the piece, with a hell-for-leather 'bezaz' in the fast brass tuttis (the tuba comes through splendidly) contrasting with a rapturous account of the big tune, with saxophone timbre shining through the strings as it must. The disc opens with a scintillating account of the '*I got rhythm*' *Variations*, played with comparable bravura and panache, full of affectionate and witty touches. He opens the *Concerto* much faster than usual and this too is a peppy transatlantic reading, but one that can relax wonderfully for the heart-touching trumpet blues theme of the slow movement, superbly played here.

The *Second Rhapsody* is almost as dazzling as the first, with the closing pages winningly brought off. The recording is superb: the violins have just the right degree of brightness and edge to add bite where necessary.

Michael Boriskin is a native New Yorker, and he and Jonathan Sheffer immediately establish a partnership which brings an idiomatic and freshly individual approach to these two concertante masterpieces, which uniquely span the jazz world and the ethos of the concert hall. The keenly sophisticated and inventive '*I got rhythm*' *Variations* are no less glittering and are wonderfully infectious. The orchestral detail throughout is a joy (especially illuminating in the less inspired *Second Rhapsody*), while in the concerto the big climaxes open out to engulf the listener expansively and ardently. Boriskin's brilliant pianism is wittily skittish in the most infectious way, both in the *Rhapsody* and in the delectably played central section of the concerto's slow movement, which Neil Balm has opened so languorously with his trumpet. The finale brings dazzling yet totally unforced bravura. The recording is first rate.

Rhapsody in Blue (see also above, under *An American in Paris*).

(M) **(*) DG 439 528-2. Bernstein with LAPO – BARBER: *Adagio for Strings;* COPLAND: *Appalachian Spring.* ***

(M) **(*) Decca 430 726-2. K and M Labèque, Cleveland O, Chailly – ADDINSELL: *Warsaw Concerto;* GOTTSCHALK: *Grand Fantasia;* LISZT: *Hungarian Fantasia;* LITOLFF: *Scherzo.* ***

In his last recording of this work for DG, Bernstein rather goes over the top with his jazzing of the solos in Gershwin. Such rhythmic freedom was clearly the result of a live rather than a studio performance. This does not match Bernstein's inspired 1959 analogue coupling for CBS.

Although the Labèque duo play charismatically their account is made somewhat controversial by the addition of an improvisatory element (more decorative than structural). However, the playing does not lack sparkle and the recording is first class.

(i) *Rhapsody in Blue* (orchestral version); (ii) *Rhapsody in Blue* (piano solo version); *Preludes for Piano.* Songs: *Do it again; I'll build a stairway to paradise; I got rhythm; Liza; The man I love; Nobody but you; Oh, lady be good; Somebody loves me; Swanee; Sweet and low down; 'S' wonderful; That certain feeling; Who cares?.*

(N) (B) ** Sony (ADD) SBK 89369. (i) Entremont; Philadelphia O, Ormandy; (ii) Watts.

Entremont's account of the *Rhapsody in Blue* with Ormandy is bright and attractive, marred only by the recording, which sounds over-bright and brittle in the upper register. Only the keenest Gershwin collector is likely to want the solo piano version, even though André Watts's performance is thoughtful as well as brilliant. However, the songs are ever attractive, even without the vocals, and these assured if sometimes wilful performances have plenty of life. The recording (for which no dates are given) is a little hard, but acceptable.

Song arrangements for orchestra: *Bidin' my time; But not for me; Embraceable you; Fascinating rhythm; I got rhythm; Liza; Love is sweeping the country; Love walked in;*

The man I love; Oh, Lady be good; Someone to watch over me; 'S' wonderful (all arr. Ray Wright).

(M) **(*) Mercury (ADD) 434 327-2. O, Fennell – PORTER: *Song Arrangements.* **(*)

This is reputed to be Frederick Fennell's favourite record, and he directs every one of these famous tunes with affectionate style and a sparkling rhythmic lift. Unusually for this label, the smooth (1961) Mercury sound is multi-miked, yet it has plenty of ambience as well as both a silky lustre and a natural clarity. The orchestral playing is fully worthy of the sophistication of the scoring, and Gershwin's songs with their ripe tunefulness respond more easily than Cole Porter's to presentation without the lyrics.

3 Preludes (transcribed Heifetz for violin & piano).

*** DG 453 470-2. Shaham, Previn – BARBER: *Canzone for Violin & Piano;* COPLAND *Violin Sonata; Nocturne;* PREVIN: *Violin Sonata.* ***

Heifetz's evocative transcriptions of the three little Gershwin *Preludes,* brilliantly done, make a pointful addition to Shaham and Previn's fine recital.

PIANO MUSIC

Impromptu in 2 keys; 3 Preludes; Three-quarter Blues; Ballet (from *Primrose*); *Jazzbo Brown* (from *Porgy and Bess*); *Merry Andrew* (from *Rosalie*); *Overtures: Girl Crazy; Lady be Good. Promenade* (from *Shall we Dance*); *2 Waltzes in C* (from *Pardon my English*). Song arrangements: *Clap yo' hands; Do do do; Do it again; Fascinating rhythm; I got rhythm; I'll build a stairway to paradise; Liza; The man I love; My one and only; Nobody but you; Oh, Lady be good; Somebody loves me; Strike up the band; Swanee; Sweet and low down; 'S' wonderful; That certain feeling; Who cares?*

(N) (B) *** Hyp. CDH 55006. Brownridge.

Angela Brownridge offers Gershwin's meagre output of solo concert pieces for piano, opening with a Joplinesque early rag, *Rialto Ripples,* Gershwin's first instrumental number from 1916. She plays the *Three Preludes* very well indeed, and also includes piano interludes from various shows, like the pair of *Waltzes in C* which the composer and Kay Swift played as a piano duet in *Pardon my English.*

There are also two pot-pourri Overtures which are very spirited indeed, and then – by offering just chorus and verse – she finds room for eighteen of Gershwin's finest song arrangements, her playing scintillating and romantic by turns, yet always stylish. The recording is excellent. A bargain.

3 Preludes; An American in Paris (arr. Daly); *Songs* (arr. Gershwin): *Fascinating rhythm; I got rhythm; I'll build a stairway to paradise; The man I love; Oh Lady be good; Liza; Somebody loves me; Sweet and low down; 'S' wonderful; Who cares?*

(*) Nim. NI 5585. Anderson – COPLAND: *Piano Sonata,* etc. *

Recorded at a live recital in Nimbus's own concert hall, this is an enjoyable enough collection of Gershwin favourites. Mark Anderson plays very well, if without those subtle rhythmic inflections that mark most American performances and especially Gershwin's own piano-roll recordings. But why transcribe *An American in Paris?* It sounds so much better in its full orchestral costume.

Piano rolls

'The Piano Rolls' Vol. 1: (i) *An American in Paris;* (ii) *Idle dreams; Kicking the clouds away; Novelette in fourths; On my mind the whole night long; Rhapsody in Blue; Scandal walk; So am I; Swanee; Sweet and lowdown; That certain feeling; When you want 'em you can't get 'em, when you've got 'em you don't want 'em.*

*** None. 7559 79287-2. (i) Milne and Leith; (ii) composer.

This series, recorded by the composer between 1916 and 1926 using the Welte-Mignon and Duo-Art piano-roll systems, was reproduced through a 1911 pianola (operated by Artis Wodehouse) and then recorded in digital stereo – with the utmost realism. The result is as if Gershwin himself was playing in the studio. The four-handed arrangement of *An American in Paris* is a marvellous 'orchestral' performance and matches the composer in its flamboyance and breadth of style. *Rhapsody in Blue* is the composer's special arrangement. The sound is first class and admirably present.

'The Piano Rolls' Vol. 2: FREY: *Havanola.* CONRAD/ ROBINSON: *Singin' the blues.* GERSHWIN: *From now on.* AKST: *Jaz-o-mine.* SILVERS: *Just snap your fingers at care.* KERN: *Whip-poor-will.* GERSHWIN/DONALDSON: *Rialto ripples.* PINKARD: *Waitin' for me.* WENDLING/WILLS: *Buzzin' the bee.* C. SCHONBERG: *Darling.* BERLIN: *For your country and my country.* MORRIS: *Kangaroo hop.* MATTHEWS: *Pastime rag No. 3.* GARDNER: *Chinese blues.* SCHONBERGER: *Whispering.* GRANT: *Arrah go on I'm gonna go back to Oregon.*

** None. 7559 79370-2. Gershwin.

As can be seen, Volume 2 includes music by others, and few of these numbers even approach the quality of Gershwin's own output. But it is all played in good, lively style, although one senses that Gershwin was doing a professional job rather than acting as an enthusiastic advocate, and some pieces come off more appealingly than others. Frankly, much of this is cocktail bar music, although Chris Schonberg's *Darling* is a rather effective exception. Again the recording cannot be faulted.

'The Authentic George Gershwin' (piano arrangements of songs)

Volume 1 (1918–25): *Come to the moon; Drifting along with the tide; Fascinatin' rhythm; The half of it, Dearie, blues; Hang on to me; I'd rather Charleston; I was so young; Kicking the clouds away; Limehouse nights; The man I love; Nobody but you; Oh Lady be good; So am I; Swanee; Tee-oodle-um-bum-bo. Piano Concerto in F: slow movt. Rhapsody in Blue.*

(M) **(*) ASV CDWHL 2074. Gibbons.

Volume 2 (1925–30): *Clap yo' hands; Do, do, do; Embraceable you; He loves and she loves; I got rhythm (2 versions); Liza; Looking for a boy; Maybe; Meadow Serenade; My one and only; Someone to watch over me; Sweet and low-down (2 versions); 'S' Wonderful; Funny face; That certain feeling; When do we dance? An American in Paris (overture); Strike Up the Band (overture); Irish Waltz (Three-Quarter Blues); 3 Piano Preludes.*

(M) **(*) ASV CDWHL 2077. Gibbons.

Volume 3 (1931–37): *For you, for me, for evermore; Isn't it a pity; Jilted; Let's call the whole thing off; Our love is here to stay; They can't take that away from me. Cuban Overture; Second Rhapsody; Porgy and Bess: Suite. Good morning, Brother: excerpts. Variations on 'I got rhythm'.*

(M) **(*) ASV CDWHL 2082. Gibbons.

Volumes 1–3 (complete).

(M) **(*) ASV CDWLS 328 (3).

Jack Gibbons has transcribed Gershwin's own piano transcriptions from the records and piano rolls made by the composer himself, and in certain cases from recorded radio programmes and film sound-tracks. His playing is brightly idiomatic, fresh and spontaneous, and has received much praise for its closeness to the composer's own keyboard style. The modern digital recording adds to the appeal of this set. But the arrangements of the orchestral works and the solo piano versions of the *Rhapsody in Blue*, the *Second Rhapsody* and the *'I got rhythm' Variations* (drawn from the composer's four-handed versions) often sound rather prolix and are much less effective and enjoyable than the songs, although played with the same sense of style. There are also more impressive versions on disc of the three *Piano Preludes*.

Volume 4: *'The Hollywood Years': A Damsel in Distress: I can't be bothered now; The jolly tar and the milkmaid (2 versions); Put me to the test; Stiff upper lip; A foggy day in London town; Nice work if you can get it; Things are looking up. Goldwyn Follies: I was doing all right; Love walked in. Girl Crazy: Overture. Shall we Dance: French Ballet Class; Dance of the Waves; Slap that bass; Walking the dog; I've got beginner's luck; They all laughed; They can't take that away from me; Shall we dance. The Show is on; By Strauss.*

(N) (M) **(*) ASV CDWHL 2110. Gibbons.

In many ways Volume 4 is the most attractive of the Jack Gibbons anthologies so far. Opening with the original version of the *Girl Crazy Overture* he concentrates on numbers from two shows, *A Damsel in Distress* (which includes a pair of fascinatingly different versions of *The jolly tar and the milkmaid*), and *Shall we Dance*. Both are full of striking numbers, and he ends with the ever engaging *Love walked in* from *The Goldwyn Follies*. His easy undemanding style is as idiomatically engaging as ever, and the recording is well up to standard.

Piano arrangements of songs: Bidin' my time; But not for me; Clap yo' hands; Do, do, do; Embraceable you; Fascinating rhythm; A foggy day; Funny face; He loves and she loves; How long has this been going on; I got rhythm; I'll build a stairway to paradise; I've got a crush on you; Let's call the whole thing off; Liza; Love is here to stay; Love is sweeping the country; Love walked in; The man I love; Maybe; Mine; Of thee I sing; Oh, Lady be good; Somebody loves me; Someone to watch over me; Soon; Strike up the band; Swanee!; 'S' Wonderful; That certain feeling; They can't take that away from me; Who cares; Excerpts from: An American in Paris. Themes from Concerto in F; Piano Prelude No. 2. Rhapsody in Blue: excerpts.

(M) *** Van. 08.6002.71. Feyer (with Lucas, Mell, Salzberg, Caccavate).

The American Hungarian émigré pianist, George Feyer, is unsurpassed in this repertory, playing all these tunes with a rhythmic lift and naturally lilting inflexions that make one almost forget that most of them also had lyrics! The rhythmic backing is first class and the 1974 recording very real. Offering some 64 minutes of marvellous melody, this CD is in a class of its own. An ideal disc to titillate the ear and senses on a late summer evening.

VOCAL MUSIC

'Kiri Sings Gershwin': Boy wanted; But not for me; By Strauss; Embraceable you; I got rhythm; Love is here to stay; Love walked in; Meadow serenade; The man I love; Nice work if you can get it; Somebody loves me; Someone to watch over me; Soon; Things are looking up. Porgy and Bess: Summertime.

**(*) EMI CDC7 47454-2. Te Kanawa, New Theatre O, McGlinn (with Chorus).

In Dame Kiri's gorgeously sung *Summertime* from *Porgy and Bess*, the distanced heavenly chorus creates the purest kitsch. But most of the numbers are done in an upbeat style. Dame Kiri is at her most relaxed and ideally there should be more variety of pacing: *The man I love* is thrown away at the chosen tempo. But for the most part the ear is seduced; however, the pop microphone techniques bring excessive sibilants on CD.

OPERA AND MUSICALS

Girl Crazy (musical).

(M) *** Elektra None. 7559-79437-9. Blazer, Luft, Carroll, Korbich, O, Mauceri.

Girl Crazy, despite its hit numbers – *Embraceable you, I got rhythm* and *Bidin' my time* – has always been counted a failure; but this lively recording, with an ensemble of distinguished New York musicians conducted by John Mauceri, gives the lie to that. The story of love and misunderstanding is largely irrelevant, but the score has point and imagination from beginning to end, all the brighter here for having had the sugar-coating which Hollywood introduced in the much-mangled film version of 1943 removed. The casting is excellent. Judy Blazer takes the Ginger Rogers role of Kate, the post-girl, while Judy Garland's less well-known daughter, Lorna Luft, is delightful in the Ethel Merman part of the gambler's wife hired to sing in the saloon. David Carroll is the New Yorker hero, and Frank Gorshin takes the comic role of the cab driver, Gieber Goldfarb. The only serious reservation is that the recording is dry and brassy, aggressively so – but that could be counted typical of the period too. Undoubtedly a bargain at its new mid-price.

Lady Be Good (musical).

*** Elektra None. 7559 79308-2. Teeter, Morrison, Alexander, Pizzarelli, Blier, Musto, Ch. & O, Stern.

This charming score, dating from 1924 (just after *Rhapsody in Blue*), emerges as one of the composer's freshest. Such numbers as the title-song, as well as *Fascinatin' rhythm* and the witty *Half of it, dearie, blues*, are set against such duets as *Hang on to me* and *So am I*, directly reflecting the 1920s world that Sandy Wilson parodied so affectionately in *The Boy Friend*. *Lady Be Good* was the piece originally written for the brother-and-sister team of Fred and Adele Astaire, and the casting of the principals on the disc is first rate. These are not concert-singers but ones whose clearly projected voices are ideally suited to the repertory, including Lara Teeter and Ann Morrison in the Astaires' roles and Michael Maguire as the young millionaire whom the heroine finally marries. The score has been restored by Tommy Krasker, and an orchestra of first-rate sessions musicians is conducted by Eric Stern.

Oh Kay!

*** Elektra None 7559 79361-2. Upshaw, Ollman, Arkin, Cassidy, Westenberg, Larsen, Ch. & O of St Luke's, Stern.

The last in this splendid Nonesuch series of Gershwin musicals is in many ways the finest of all. With the music (including hits like *Someone to watch over me*, *Clap yo' hands*, *Do, do do* and the very catchy *Fidgety feet*) fitting neatly on to one CD, this is a fizzing entertainment. Dawn Upshaw is a highly enticing Kay, and she gets vivid support from Kurt Ollman as Jimmy, Adam Arkin as Shorty McGee and Patrick Cassidy as Larry. The cast could hardly be more naturally at home in Gershwin's sparkling score. Eric Stern directs with great flair and the recording is admirably vivid. Not to be missed.

Porgy and Bess (complete).

✪ *** EMI CDS7 49568-2 (3). White, Haymon, Blackwell, Clarey, Evans, Glyndebourne Ch., LPO, Rattle.

Simon Rattle here conducts the same cast and orchestra as in the opera house, and the EMI engineers have done wonders in establishing more clearly than ever the status of *Porgy* as grand opera. By comparison, Lorin Maazel's Decca version sounds a degree too literal, and John DeMain's RCA set is less subtle. More than their rivals, Rattle and the LPO capture Gershwin's rhythmic exuberance with the degree of freedom essential if jazz-based inspirations are to sound idiomatic. The chorus is the finest and most responsive of any on the three sets, and the bass line-up is the strongest. Willard White is superbly matched by the magnificent Jake of Bruce Hubbard and by the dark and resonant Crown of Gregg Baker. As Sportin' Life, Damon Evans gets nearer than any of his rivals to the original scat-song inspiration without ever short-changing on musical values. Cynthia Haymon as Bess is movingly convincing in conveying equivocal emotions, Harolyn Blackwell as Clara sensuously relishes Rattle's slow speed for *Summertime*, and Cynthia Clarey is an intense and characterful Serena. EMI's digital sound is exceptionally full and spacious.

Porgy and Bess: highlights.

*** EMI CDC7 54325-2; (from above recording, with White, Haymon; cond. Rattle).

Rattle's highlights disc is most generous (74 minutes) and most comprehensive. However, not all the tailoring is clean: *Summertime* ends rather abruptly and there is at least one fade.

Strike Up the Band (musical).

**(*) None. 7559 79273-2. Barrett, Luker, Chastain, Graae, Fowler, Goff, Lambert, Lyons, Sandish, Rocco, Ch. & O, Mauceri.

Strike Up the Band was the nearest that George and Ira Gershwin ever came to imitating Gilbert and Sullivan, although its two hit numbers, *The man I love* and *Strike Up the band*, are entirely characteristic. For all its vigour, the performance lacks something of the exuberance which marks the recordings of musicals conducted by John McGlinn for EMI. It may be correct to observe the dotted rhythms of *The man I love* as precisely as this performance does, but something is lost in the flow of the music, and to latterday ears the result is less haunting than the customary reading. The singers are first rate, but they would have been helped by having at least one of their number with a more charismatic personality. The second disc includes an appendix containing seven numbers used in the abortive 1930 revival.

GESUALDO, Carlo (c. 1561–1613)

Ave, dulcissima Maria; Ave, regina coelorum; Maria mater gratiae; Precibus et meritus beatae Mariae (motets). *Tenebrae responsories for Holy Saturday.*

*** Gimell CDGIM 915. Tallis Scholars, Phillips.

The astonishing dissonances and chromaticisms may not be as extreme here as in some of Gesualdo's secular music but, as elaborate as madrigals, they still have a sharp, refreshing impact on the modern ear which recognizes music leaping the centuries. The Tallis Scholars give superb performances, finely finished and beautifully blended, with women's voices made to sound boyish, singing with freshness and bite to bring home the total originality of the writing with its awkward leaps and intervals. Beautifully recorded, this is another of the Tallis Scholars' ear-catching discs, powerful as well as polished.

Leçons de ténèbres: Responsories for Maundy Thursday.

(B) *** HM (ADD) HMA 190220. Deller Cons., Deller.

The Responses for Holy Week of 1611 are as remarkable and passionately expressive as any of Gesualdo's madrigals, and in depth of feeling they should be compared only with the finest music of the age. The Deller Consort bring to this music much the same approach that distinguishes their handling of the madrigal literature. The colouring of the words is a high priority, yet it never oversteps the bounds of good taste. The consort blends remarkably well and intonation is excellent. This is temptingly inexpensive.

GETTY, Gordon (20th century)

The White Election (song-cycle).

*** Delos D/CD 3057. Erickson, Guzelimian.

The simple, even primitive, yet deeply allusive poetry of Emily Dickinson is sensitively matched in the music of Gordon Getty. Here he tackles a sequence of thirty-two songs, building them into an extended cycle in four linked parts 'to tell Emily's story in her own words'. If at times the tinkly tunes seem to be an inadequate response to profound emotions, the total honesty of the writing disarms criticism, particularly in a performance as dedicated and sensitive as this, with Kaaren Erickson a highly expressive artist with a naturally beautiful voice. The pianist too is very responsive.

GIBBONS, Orlando (1583–1625)

Fantasia in 2 Parts; 4 Fantasias in 3 Parts; 3 Fantasias in 6 Parts; Go from my window in 6 Parts. Galliard in 3 Parts; 2 Fantasias in 3 Parts; Fantasia in 4 Parts (all 4 'for the Great Dooble Bass'); In nomine in 4 Parts; In nomine in 5 Parts; Fantasia, Prelude & Ground (for organ). (i) The Cries of London: Parts I & II.

(M) **(*) Virgin VC5 45144-2. Fretwork, with Nicholson (organ); (i) with Red Byrd.

Easily the most interesting items here are the *Fantasias* (and *Galliard*), which feature – not too ostentatiously – 'the Great Dooble Bass' (in fact an oversized viol – pictured on the back of the excellent accompanying booklet). Its inclusion seemed to have inspired Gibbons to produce a sequence of his more attractive ideas. *Go from my window in 6 parts* is a set of divisions on a popular ballad which tends to outstay its welcome because of the lack of dynamic range in the music-making – a criticism which applies also to the simpler *Fantasias*. Paul Nicholson provides variety with his organ solos, but the most memorably expressive pieces are the pair of *In nomine* settings. In between come the two charming brief selections from the *Cries of London*, sung by the members of Red Byrd with a nice feeling for their popular declamatory style, yet with musical sophistication and good tuning.

Consort music: (i) Fantazia No. 1 for 2 Treble Viols; Fantazias Nos. 3 & 5 a 6; Fantazia No. 1 for Great Double Bass (for Organ & 3 Viols); Galliard a 3; Galliard a 6; Go not from my window a 6; In nomine a 4; Pavane a 6. Keyboard pieces: (ii) Almain in F; The fairest nymph (mask); Lincoln's Inn mask; The Lord of Salisbury his pavane and galliard. Organ Preludium in G. Vocal: (i; iii) Behold thou hast made my days; Glorious and powerful God (both for 5 voices & 5 viols). Solo voice & viols: (i; iv) Dainty fine bird; Fair is the rose; I feign not friendship where I hate; I see ambition never pleased; I tremble not at noise of war; I weigh not fortune's frown; The silver swan.

(BB) *** Naxos 8.550603. (i) Rose Consort of Viols; (ii) Roberts; with (iii) Red Byrd; (iv) Bonner.

This makes the perfect supplement to the excellent Naxos issue of Gibbons's church music, with twenty-two items that cover a wide range of songs as well as instrumental music. The players of the Rose Consort, with agreeably tangy string tone, contribute most of the instrumental pieces, culminating in two magnificent *Fantazias* in six parts: No. 3 with ear-catching harmonic clashes, No. 5 with side-slipping chromatic writing, pointing forward to later centuries.

Timothy Roberts is the soloist in keyboard music on harpsichord, virginals and organ, while the soprano, Tessa Bonner, is the bright-toned soloist in a sequence of songs with consort accompaniment. Standing out too are two fine anthems, one written for the funeral of a Dean of Windsor, with Red Byrd accompanied by the consort, five voices and five instruments.

Madrigals and motets (1612): Ah dear heart; Dainty fine bird; Fair is the rose; Fair ladies that to love; Farewell all joys; How art thou thralled; I feign not friendship; I see ambition never pleased; I tremble not at the noise of war; I weigh not fortune's frown; Lais now old; 'Mongst thousands good; Nay let me weep; Ne'er let the sun; Now each flowery bank of May; O that the learned poets; The silver swan; Trust not too much fair youth; What is our life?; Yet if that age.

(B) *** Double Decca (ADD) 458 093-2 (2) Consort of Musicke, Rooley – MORLEY; WILBYE: *Madrigals.* ***

Gibbons left only one book of madrigalian pieces, and the Consort of Musicke here present it complete. The vocal group includes well-known names and is led by the young Emma Kirkby, who opens the 1975 programme with a delightfully fresh, young-voiced solo performance of *The silver swan* (which is used as the title of the collection). She is accompanied by a quartet of viols, and half the pieces here are sung *and* played with viols, and sensitive attention is paid to phrasing and colour. Performances are eminently thoughtful; diction is not always first class, but it would be curmudgeonly to dwell on minor criticisms in so enjoyable an enterprise, for the set is expertly recorded and beautifully produced. It is not only a welcome addition to Gibbons's representation on record, but is equally valuable for the coupled repertoire by Morley and Wilbye. Full texts are included.

Anthems: Almighty and everlasting God; Blessed are all they; Glorious and powerful God; Lord, grant grace; O

Lord, how do my woes increase; Sing unto the Lord; This is the record of John; We praise Thee, O Father.

(B) *** Cal. Approche (ADD) CAL 6621. Clerkes of Oxenford, Wulstan – SHEPPARD: *Mass 'Cantate'; Respond: 'Spiritus Sanctus'.* ***

This collection of eight verse-anthems of Orlando Gibbons makes an admirable coupling for some lesser-known music of John Sheppard. They are written for solo groups as well as for the full choir, and often with instrumental accompaniments, and their style obviously recalls similar music by Purcell. By comparison they are not found wanting. They are splendidly sung and recorded, and this is a genuine bargain.

Anthems and verse anthems: Almighty and everlasting God; Hosanna to the Son of David; Lift up your heads; O Thou the central orb; See, see the word is incarnate; This is the record of John. Canticles: *Short service: Magnificat & Nunc dimittis. 2nd Service: Magnificat & Nunc dimittis.* Hymnes & Songs of the church: *Come kiss me with those lips of thine; Now shall the praises of the Lord be sung; A song of joy unto the Lord.* Organ Fantasia: *Fantasia for Double Organ; Voluntary.*

*** ASV CDGAU 123. King's College Ch., L. Early Music Group, Ledger; Butt.

This invaluable anthology was the first serious survey of Gibbons's music to appear on CD. It contains many of his greatest pieces. Not only are the performances touched with distinction, the recording too is in the highest flight and the analogue sound has been transferred to CD with complete naturalness. Strongly recommended.

Anthems: Almighty and everlasting God; Hosanna to the son of David; O clap your hands; O God, the King of glory; O Lord, in thy wrath; O Lord of Lords; Lift up your heads; Out of the deep; See, see, the word is incarnate; Second Service: Magnificat; Nunc dimittis. Short Service: Nunc dimittis. (Organ) Fantazia of 4 parts; Preludes in D min.; G.

(BB) *** Naxos 8.553130. Oxford Camerata, Summerly; Cummings.

Using his small professional choir, twelve singers at most, and often fewer, Jeremy Summerly directs fresh, finely focused readings of an outstanding collection of Gibbons's anthems. This may not have so much of the ecclesiastical aura of a traditional cathedral performance with boys' voices, but it amply makes up in clarity and incisiveness for any lack of weight and warmth. That is particularly so in the six magnificent unaccompanied full anthems which are included, where the astonishing harmonic clashes and progressions in the counterpoint come out with wonderful impact, generally with just a single voice per part.

In addition there are three fine verse anthems, drawing on the full complement of singers with organ accompaniment, plus Gibbons's two evening services, the short one much simpler than the second one. Three organ pieces are also included, though Laurence Cummings' account of the extended *Fantazia* in four parts is not as varied as it might be. Fine, clear, atmospheric sound.

Anthems and verse anthems: Behold, thou hast made my days; Blessed are they that fear the Lord; Glorious and powerful God; Great King of Gods; Hosanna to the son of David; If ye be risen again with Christ; O clap your hands; O God, the King of glory; O Lord in thy wrath rebuke me not; Sing unto the Lord; This is the record of John; Thou God of wisdom; Second Evening Service: Magnificat; Nunc dimittis. Organ Fantasia in A min (MB XX/12).

*** Hyp. CDA 67116. Blaze, Varcoe, Winchester Cathedral Ch., Hill; Farr or Baldock.

Orlando Gibbons's *Hosanna to the son of David* is among the very finest anthems of the period, a glory of English music, and aptly that is the opening item for this excellent collection of Gibbons's church music, very well performed and recorded. Robin Blaze is an outstandingly sweet-toned countertenor soloist, well matched by Stephen Varcoe in the verse anthems. The only pity is that the collection concentrates on verse anthems, nine of them plus the *Second Evening Service*, as against only three full anthems with their excitingly elaborate counterpoint. The *Fantasia in A minor* for organ makes an apt supplement.

GILBERT, Henry (1868–1928)

Suite for Chamber Orchestra.

*** Albany TROY 033-2. V. American Music Ens., Earle – CHADWICK: *Serenade for Strings.* ***

Henry Gilbert belonged to a time when almost all musical influences came from Europe and the American public did not value the output of its indigenous composers. This *Suite*, which harmonically is innocuous but which has an agreeable nostalgic languor, has something in common with Delius's *Florida Suite*, although Gilbert's invention is less indelible. An excellent performance here from members of the Vienna American Ensemble, who sound as if they are completely at home in the music, as well they might be. The recording is excellent.

GILLES, Jean (1668–1705)

Messe des morts (Requiem Mass).

(M) *** DG (ADD) 437 087-2. Rodde, Nirouët, Hill, U. Studer, Kooy, Ghent Coll. Voc., Col. Mus. Ant., Herreweghe (with CORRETTE: *Carillon des morts* ***).

Gilles's rhythmic and harmonic vigour (with plentiful false relations to add tang) is well caught in this performance on original instruments, and the singers find the music's expressive style admirably. The *Carillon* was included by Michel Corrette in his own edition of the Gilles *Requiem*, printed in 1764, and is appropriately included here as a postlude.

GILSON, Paul (1865–1942)

De Zee (suite).

(B) *** Discover DICD 920126. Brussels BRT PO,
   Rickenbacher – DE BOECK: *Symphony in G.* ***

Like August de Boeck, also represented on this disc, Paul
Gilson was a Belgian composer, born in 1865. His suite, *De
Zee*, like de Boeck's *Symphony* is full of Russian echoes. It is
a series of four seascapes halfway between Wagner's *Flying
Dutchman* and Debussy's *La Mer*, with Rimsky-Korsakov's
Scheherazade mixed in. Well played and recorded and, at
this bargain price, an ideal disc for experimenting with.

GINASTERA, Alberto (1916–83)

Harp Concerto, Op. 25.

*** Chan. 9094. Masters, City of L. Sinfonia, Hickox –
   GLIERE: *Concertos.* ***

Ginastera's 1956 *Harp Concerto*, full of vivid colours and
snappy, incisive rhythms, also has a highly atmospheric slow
movement. All its kaleidoscopic moods are keenly projected
by Rachel Masters in this refreshing and invigorating performance. Alert playing, too, from the City of London Sinfonia under Richard Hickox. Strongly recommended, as are
the two Glière concertos with which it is coupled.

(i) *Harp Concerto, Op. 25;* (ii) *Piano Concerto No. 1.
Estancia* (ballet suite), *Op. 89.*

*** ASV CDDCA 654. (i) Allen; (ii) Tarrago; Mexico City PO,
   Bátiz.

The *Harp Concerto* is brought fully to life here by Nancy
Allen and the Mexican orchestra. *Estancia* is a comparably
vivid piece of Coplandesque machismo, its character also
very successfully realized. The *First Piano Concerto* is mildly
serial but far from unattractive – and very brilliantly (and
sensitively) played by Oscar Tarrago. An excellent introduction to this composer.

Estancia (ballet suite); *Panambi* (choreographic legend).

*** Everest (ADD) EVC 9007. LSO, Goossens – ANTILL:
   Corroboree; VILLA-LOBOS: *Little Train of the
   Caipira.* **(*)

Both these brightly hued scores bring a high standard of
invention. *Panambi* is the earlier – written when the
composer was only twenty. It opens with a haunting picture
of *Moonlight on the Panama* and the *Lament of the Maidens*
is gently touching, while the *Invocations of the Powerful
Spirits* and *Dance of the Warriors* are powerfully primitive.
Estancia dates from a slightly later period. Again the scoring
is exotic and impressive, and the lively dances are full of
primeval energy, notably the closing *Malambo*, while the
lovely *Wheat Dance* brings another nostalgic interlude. The
performances are in every way first class and the atmospheric
recording brilliantly captures the composer's imaginatively
varied sound-world.

(i) *Cello Sonata, Op. 49. Danzas argentinas, Op. 2;
Estancia, Op. 8;* (i) *Pampeana No. 2, Op. 21* (rhapsody for
cello and piano). *Pequeña danza; Piano Sonata No. 1,
Op. 22; 5 Canciones populares argentinas:* (i) *Triste.* (arr.
Fournier)

*** ASV CDDCA 865. Portugheis, (i) with Natola-Ginastera.

The four-movement *Cello Sonata*, ardently rhapsodic, chimerical and full of atmosphere, is dedicated to Ginastera's
wife, who is the soloist here, while *Pampeana* is a rhapsody
which has an Argentinian flavour without using folk melodies. The *Piano Sonata No. 1* (1952) is a powerful, integrated
piece with a desolate *Adagio* and a brilliant, rhythmically
chimerical folk-dance finale. Alberto Portugheis is
thoroughly at home in this repertoire and plays compellingly
throughout. He is well recorded.

Piano music

*Canciones, Op. 3: Milonga. Malambo, Op. 7; 3 Piezas,
Op. 6; Piezas infantiles; Rondo sobre temas infantiles
argentinos, Op. 19; Sonatas Nos. 1, Op. 53; 3, Op. 58;
Toccata.*

*** ASV CDDCA 880. Portugheis.

The pieces for children are most welcoming and are delightfully varied and intimate: the *Milonga* is seductive in a
Latin-American way, as are the *Three Pieces*, Op. 6. The
Sonatas are harder nuts to crack: the first has a formidable
opening movement and a ferocious closing toccata, and the
Toccata, written for the organ and played with great bravura
here, is also a piece to make one sit up. Alberto Portugheis
is a first-rate artist, and his natural sympathies for the music's
idiom are apparent throughout. He is very well recorded.

GIORDANO, Umberto (1867–1948)

Andrea Chénier (complete).

(M) *** RCA (ADD) 74321 39499-2 (2). Domingo, Scotto,
   Milnes, Alldis Ch., Nat. PO, Levine.

**(*) Decca 410 117-2 (2). Pavarotti, Caballé, Nucci,
   Kuhlmann, Welsh Nat. Op. Ch., Nat. PO, Chailly.

(M) **(*) EMI (ADD) CMS5 65287-2 (2). Corelli, Stella, Sereni,
   Rome Op. Ch. & O, Santini.

Andrea Chénier with its defiant poet hero provides a splendid
role for Domingo at his most heroic and the former servant,
later revolutionary leader, Gérard, is a character well appreciated by Milnes. Scotto gives one of her most eloquent
and beautiful performances, and Levine has rarely displayed
his powers as an urgent and dramatic opera conductor more
potently on record, with the bright recording intensifying
the dramatic thrust of playing and singing.

Pavarotti may motor through the role of the poet-hero,
singing with his usual fine diction; nevertheless, the red-
blooded melodrama of the piece comes over powerfully,
thanks to Chailly's sympathetic conducting, incisive but
never exaggerated. Caballé, like Pavarotti, is not strong on
characterization but produces beautiful sounds, while Leo
Nucci makes a superbly dark-toned Gérard. Though this

cannot replace the Levine set, it is a colourful substitute with its demonstration sound.

The glory of the 1964 EMI version is the Chénier of Franco Corelli, one of his most satisfying performances on record with heroic tone gloriously exploited. The other singing is less distinguished. Though Antonietta Stella was never sweeter of voice than here, she hardly matches such rivals as Scotto or Caballé. The 1960s recording is vivid, with plenty of atmosphere, and has been transferred to CD most naturally, but the RCA set in the same price range, with Domingo and Scotto, remains a clear first choice.

Fedora (complete).

(M) **(*) Decca (ADD) 433 033-2 (2). Olivero, Del Monaco, Gobbi, Monte Carlo Nat. Op. Ch. & O, Gardelli – ZANDONAI: Francesca da Rimini. **(*)

Fedora will always be remembered for one brief aria, the hero's Amor ti vieta; but, as this highly enjoyable recording confirms, there is much that is memorable in the score, even if nothing else quite approaches it. Meaty stuff, which brings some splendid singing from Magda Olivero and (more intermittently) from Del Monaco, with Gobbi in a light comedy part. Fine, vintage (1969), atmospheric recording.

GIPPS, Ruth (born 1921)

Symphony No. 2, Op. 30.

*** Classico CLASSCD 274. Munich SO, Bostock – BUTTERWORTH: Symphony No. 1. ***

Ms Gipps studied with Vaughan Williams and during the war years played the oboe in the City of Birmingham Symphony Orchestra. She became a tireless champion of neglected repertoire and an excellent teacher. Her Second Symphony comes from 1945, the immediate post-war years, and though indebted to Vaughan Williams, is well argued and inventive. It is decently played and recorded.

GIULIANI, Mauro (1781–1828)

(i; ii) Guitar Concertos Nos. 1 in A, Op. 30; 2 in A, Op. 36; 3 in F, Op. 70; Introduction, Theme with Variations & Polonaise (for Guitar & Orchestra), Op. 65. (i) Grande ouverture, Op. 61; Gran sonata eroica in A; La Melanchonia; Variations on Ich bin a Kohlbauern Bub', Op. 49; Variations on a Theme by Handel, Op. 107; (i; iii) Variazioni concertanti, Op. 130.

(B) *** Ph. Duo (ADD) 454 262-2 (2). (i) Pepe Romero, (ii) with ASMF, Marriner; (iii) with Celedonio Romero.

Pepe Romero is a first-rate player, and his relaxed music-making and easy bravura bring an attractive, smiling quality. But what makes these concertos so distinctive are the splendid accompaniments provided by the Academy of St Martin-in-the-Fields under Marriner, and throughout there are many delightful touches from the orchestra. The F major Concerto begins with an engaging little march theme whose dotted contour reminds one of Hummel, and the amiable Siciliano that forms the slow movement is matched by an unforceful closing Polonaise. Hummel again comes rhythmically to mind in the first movement of the Second Concerto, which is for strings alone. The Introduction, Theme with Variations and Polonaise is like a mini-concerto and is given a performance of vitality and charm. The Op. 49 Variations are agreeable but slight, but the Sonata eroica hardly merits its grand sobriquet. The Variations concertanti for two guitars, in which Pepe is joined by Celedonio, is played with affection and ready virtuosity. The mid-1960s recording throughout is warm and refined, very easy on the ear.

Guitar Concerto in A, Op. 30.

(M) *** DG (IMS) (ADD) 439 984-2. Behrend, I Musici – CARULLI: Concerto in A ***; VIVALDI: Guitar Concertos. **(*)

(B) **(*) Decca (ADD) 448 709-2. Fernández, ECO, Malcolm – PAGANINI: Sonata; VIVALDI: Concertos. **(*)

Giuliani's A major Concerto is presented by Siegfried Behrend with much elegance and finesse and is immaculately recorded. Its catchy main theme is endearing; though the music overall is slight, it is nicely crafted.

A rather low-key, essentially chamber performance from the highly musical Eduardo Fernández, who refuses to show off. He is accompanied elegantly by Malcolm and the ECO and is most naturally recorded.

Duo concertante for Violin & Guitar, Op. 25.

(N) (BB) *** HM HCX 3957116. Huggett, Savino – PAGANINI: Grand Sonata; Sonata concertata. ***

Monica Huggett adopts her most silky timbre and plays most winningly in Giulini's ingenuous but extended Duo (37 minutes). Richard Savino has less to do but does it expertly. The Theme and Varations second movement also has considerable charm. The recording is ideally balanced and most realistic.

Variations on a Theme by Handel, Op. 107.

(B) *** Sony (ADD) SBK 62425. Williams (guitar) – PAGANINI: Caprice 24; Grand Sonata; D. SCARLATTI: Sonatas; VILLA-LOBOS: 5 Preludes. ***

The Variations are on Handel's famous Harmonious Blacksmith theme. Their construction is guileless but agreeable, and they are expertly played and well recorded. This is only a small part of a well-planned and exceptionally generous collection devoted mainly to Paganini and Domenico Scarlatti.

GLASS, Philip (born 1937)

(i; ii) Concerto for Saxophone Quartet & Orchestra; (ii) Symphony No. 2; (ii) Orphée, Act II, Scene 3: Interlude.

(N) *** None. 7559 79496-2. (i) Rascher Saxophone Qt.; (ii) Stuttgart CO; (iii) V. RSO; composer.

Philip Glass's Symphony No. 2, in three substantial movements, represents his music at its most mellifluous, his second-generation brand of minimalism. Written in 1993, it uses polytonality as a basic element, to a degree taking the place of contrasts traditional in symphonic form. The first movement, longest of the three, is lush and lyrical with melodies turning back on themselves, while the central slow movement jogs along similarly with minimalist 'till-ready' rhythms. The finale is bolder and brassier, with a piano bringing echoes of *Petrushka*. The *Interlude* from *Orphée* is vintage Glass, while the more compact *Saxophone Quartet Concerto* brings the liveliest music, with jazzy syncopations in the second movement and Spanish-American flavours in the finale varying Glass's persistent moderato writing. Excellent performances and well-balanced recording.

Violin Concerto.

*** Telarc CD 80494. McDuffie, Houston SO, Eschenbach – ADAMS: *Violin Concerto.* ***

*** DG 445 186-2. Kremer, VPO, Dohnányi – BERNSTEIN: *Serenade after Plato's Symposium;* ROREM: *Violin Concerto.* ***

Violin Concerto; Company; Akhnaten: Prelude & Dance.

(BB) **(*) Naxos 8.554568. Anthony, Ulster O., Yuasa.

Glass's *Violin Concerto*, with its hypnotic minimalist exploration of simple basic material, is one of his best and most approachable works. The repeated four-note downward scale on which the soloist weaves his serene soliloquy in the slow movement is particularly haunting, the effect very like a chaconne, which links it readily to the coupled Adams concerto.

Gidon Kremer's disc brings together recordings of three different vintages. His version of the Glass concerto dates from 1992 and proves a warmly expressive reading, characterizing strongly, helped by vivid recording made in the Musikverein in Vienna with the soloist closely balanced. However, Kremer's approach is in some ways less idiomatic than Robert McDuffie's reading, which is notable for the way that he gives a persuasively jazzy lift to the ostinato rhythms with their implied syncopations. His tone may not be as beautiful as Kremer's, but it is a warmly felt performance, which sustains its slower tempo for the long third movement convincingly. Very well recorded and more aptly coupled with the Adams concerto of 1993, this Telarc disc is in every way recommendable.

Adele Anthony is a talented violinist from Tasmania, who here gives a sweetly expressive reading of the Glass *Violin Concerto*, despite a rather plodding account of the very opening. In the central movement she finds a rare tenderness, as well as on the high harmonics at the end of the whole work. The concerto makes an excellent centrepiece for a complete disc of Glass's music, with Yuasa and the Ulster Orchestra equally persuasive in the four brief movements of *Company* and in the two orchestral passages from the opera, *Akhnaten*.

Company; Façades.

(N)) (M) *** Virgin VM5 61851-2. LCO, Warren-Green – ADAMS: *Shaker Loops* *** ⚫; REICH: *8 Lines* ***; HEATH: *Frontier.* ***

Company consists of four brief but sharply contrasted movements for strings; *Façades* offers a haunting cantilena for soprano saxophone, suspended over atmospherically undulating strings. The performances are full of intensity and are expertly played, and the recording is excellent.

Dance Pieces: Glasspieces; In the Upper Room: Dances Nos. 1, 2, 5, 8 & 9.

*** CBS MK 39539. Ens., dir. Riesman.

These two ballet scores bring typical and easily attractive examples of Glass's minimalist technique. Heard away from the stage, the music seems to have a subliminally hypnotic effect, perhaps because rhythmic patterns often repeat themselves almost endlessly.

String Quartets Nos. 2 (Company); 3 (Mishima); 4 (Buczak); 5.

*** Elektra-None 7559 79356-2. Kronos Quartet.

Happily, the quartets here are presented in reverse order, for the last of the four, No. 5, dating from 1991, presents Glass at his most warmly expressive and intense. Textures are luminous, shimmering in their repetitions rather than thrusting them home relentlessly. The Kronos Quartet, for whom the work was written, give a heartfelt performance, as they do of the *Quartet No. 4* (1990), written in memory of Brian Buczak, who died of AIDS. The valedictory mood is intensified by a lyrical and poignantly beautiful middle movement, leading to a noble finale. The *Quartet No. 2* (1983) consists of four brief movements originally written to accompany the staged soliloquy of a dying man, entitled *Company*. Again it is valedictory in tone but is far less tender. The *Quartet No. 3* (1985) is repetitive in the characteristic Glass manner, this time with six brief movements. Though Nos. 4 and 5 most clearly reveal the hand of a master, the earlier works also represent Glass at his most approachable, the more so when they are treated to magnetic performances by the Kronos Quartet, superbly recorded.

ORGAN MUSIC

(i) Dances 2 & 4; (ii) Duets & Canons (suite); (iii) Satyagraha (opera), Act III: Finale.

(N) *** Nimbus NI 5664. (i) Broadbent; (ii) Bower
(Marcusson organ in St Augustin's Chapel, Tonbridge School, Kent).

Sometimes one wonders with the music of Philip Glass whether the composer always means to be taken seriously, or if he is sometimes pulling our musical legs. The two *Dance* movements were written in the early 1970s. *Dance 2* represents the most basic form of minimalism, offering a hypnotically relentless ostinato for nearly twenty-five minutes, with very minor changes of the harmonic implications in the pedals.

Dance 4 is more musically eventful. Below the toccata-like sequence there is a galumphing figure in the bass and frequent if repetitious harmonic movement. A good deal more happens during this piece, although one feels that the composer, rather than creating forward movement, is going round in circles. The shorter (seven-minute) *Satyagraha* finale is sandwiched in between the two *Dances*, more lyrical in feeling, but hardly more motivated. All three pieces are played with devoted determination by Christopher Bowers Broadbent who never puts a foot or finger wrong.

Kevin Bowyer takes over for the *Duets and Canons* (1996)

creating a thoughtful, improvisatory feeling. All ten are brief and have liturgical titles, which the composer tells us are based on the plainsong of the Third Mass of the Nativity. They are rhythmically free (often quirkily so) and the changes in mood are provided primarily by the changes in registration (and modest variations in tempo). The *Sanctus*, for instance, is surprisingly dark and sombre, *Viderent omnes celestial*, but the closing *Agnus Dei and Bendictus* finally leave the listener in mid-air. The recording of the fine Marcusson organ at Tonbridge cannot be faulted.

OPERA

Akhnaten (complete).

*** Sony (ADD) M2K 42457 (2). Esswood, Vargas, Liebermann, Hannula, Holzapfel, Hauptmann, Stuttgart State Op. Ch. & O, Davies.

Akhnaten, Glass's powerful third opera, is set in the time of Ancient Egypt. Paul Esswood in the title-role is reserved, strong and statuesque; this is an opera of historical ghosts, and its life-flow lies in the hypnotic background provided by the orchestra; indeed the work's haunting closing scene with its wordless melismas is like nothing else in music. It offers a theatrical experience appealing to a far wider public than usual in the opera house; and here the Stuttgart chorus and orchestra give the piece impressively committed advocacy.

La Belle et la Bête (opera based on the film of Jean Cocteau; complete).

*** None-Elektra 7559 794347. Felty, Purnhagen, Kuether, Martinez, Neill, Zhou, Philip Glass Ens., Riesman.

What Glass has done here is to provide a new musical accompaniment to a showing of Cocteau's 90-minute film, *La Belle et la Bête*, dispensing with Auric's original film-music and synchronizing the singing-parts with the speech of the actors in the film. In the opening scenes the music is far lighter and more conventionally beautiful than most Glass, but then the poignancy of the story is more and more reflected in the score, both tender and mellifluous. The hypnotic quality of Glass's repetitions helps to enhance the magical atmosphere, while the use of the original French film-script prompts Glass to be more warmly melodic than usual. Glass's justification lies in the intensity of the score overall, with Janice Felty and Gregory Purnhagen both clearly focused in the central roles, though Purnhagen's baritone suggests from the start a heroic, not a bestial, figure. Vividly atmospheric sound.

Einstein on the Beach (complete).

*** Teldec 7559 79323-2 (3). Soloists, Philip Glass Ens., Riesman.

Glass himself explains the need for a new recording of this bizarre and relentless opera – as the surreal title implies, more dream than drama. Where the earlier recording had an abrasive edge, this new one is more refined, melding the different elements, electronic alongside acoustic, more subtly and persuasively than before. Even so, the first train

episode, over 20 minutes long, remains mind-blowing in its relentlessness. The impact is heightened by the vividness of the recording, with spoken voices in particular given such presence that they startle you as if someone had burst into your room. The vision remains an odd one, but with a formidable group of vocalists and instrumentalists brilliantly directed, often from the keyboard, by Michael Riesman, the new recording certainly justifies itself.

Satyagraha (complete).

*** Sony M3K 39672 (3). Perry, NY City Op. Ch. & O, Keene.

The subject here is the early life of Mahatma Gandhi and the text is a selection of verses from the *Bhagavadgita*, sung in the original Sanskrit and used as another strand in the complex repetitive web of sound. The result is undeniably powerful. Where much minimalist music in its shimmering repetitiveness becomes static, a good deal of this conveys energy as well as power. The writing for chorus is often thrilling, and individual characters emerge in only a shadowy way. The recording, using the device of overdubbing, is spectacular.

GLAZUNOV, Alexander (1865–1936)

A la mémoire de Gogol, Op. 86; A la mémoire d'un héros, Op. 8; (i) Chant du ménestrel for Cello & Orchestra, Op. 71; Concerto ballata for Cello & Orchestra, Op. 108; 2 Pieces for Cello & Orchestra, Op. 20.

(BB) *** Naxos 8.553932. Moscow SO, Golovschin (i) with Rudin.

The *Concerto ballata* is a late work, written for Casals and dating from 1931. The *Chant du ménestrel* is much earlier and comes from between 1900, the *Sixth* and *Seventh Symphonies*. It has an easy charm that delights the ear. *A la mémoire de Gogol* is a dignified, well-shaped piece, which belies (as does the *Concerto ballata*) Glazunov's reputation for scoring too thickly. We admired Alexander Rudin's recording of the Kabalevsky cello concertos, and his playing here is no less eloquent. The Moscow Orchestra plays well for Igor Golovschin and the sound has pleasing warmth and clarity.

Carnaval Overture, Op. 45.

(M) *** RCA High Performance 09026 63308-2. Boston Pops O, Fiedler – SHCHEDRIN: *Carmen* (ballet); SHOSTAKOVICH: *Hamlet*: incidental music. ***

Glazunov's vivacious, spring-like overture is most attractive, with a lilting main theme; the surprise is the gentle organ interlude at the centre. Fiedler's performance could hardly be more persuasive and the Boston playing is superbly spirited. Excellent recording too, splendidly remastered.

Carnaval Overture, Op. 45; Concert Waltzes Nos. 1–2, Opp. 47 & 51; Spring, Op. 34; Salomé (incidental music), Op. 90: Introduction; Dance.

(BB) **(*) Naxos 8.553838. Moscow SO, Golovschin.

This collection of shorter pieces by Glazunov makes up a delightful disc, bringing out the composer's amiable side.

There are some attractive ideas in *Spring* (*Vesna*), a charming work and refined and transparent in its orchestration, playing on birdsong and building to a sensuous climax. The more familiar *Concert Waltzes* contain some of Glazunov's most winning tunes, the one Tchaikovskian in flavour, the other Viennese. The novelty most likely to excite curiosity here is Glazunov's music for Oscar Wilde's *Salomé*, with Salome's dance leading to a Polovtsian climax. It is surprisingly conventional and tame, and Salome sheds her veils in a most unerotic fashion. But this cannot be blamed on the conductor, and generally these are warm, idiomatic performances, richly recorded.

Le Chant du destin, Op. 84; 2 Préludes, Op. 85; Suite caractéristique in D, Op. 9.

(BB) **(*) Naxos 8.553857. Moscow SO, Golovschin.

Le Chant du destin, written in 1907, is dominated by a sombre two-phrase theme which curiously reminds one of Gershwin's song, 'S' *wonderful*, only the mood and colouring are utterly different. The music, which is eloquently presented, still has its longueurs. The eight-movement *Suite caractéristique*, from two decades earlier, is vintage Glazunov, an orchestral transcription of piano pieces. The two *Preludes* date from 1906 and 1908 respectively. One remembers, in a sombre valedictory mood, Vladimir Stassov (famous for naming Balakirev and his contemporary group of Russian composers 'the mighty handful'); the second (much more extended) opens surprisingly like Tchaikovsky's *Francesca da Rimini* and this curious leitmotif dominates the early part of the piece. It is well played, as indeed is the *Suite*. The recording is very good too. At Naxos price this is worth considering.

Chant du ménestrel (for Cello & Orchestra), Op. 71.

(B) *** DG Double (ADD) 437 952-2 (2). Rostropovich, Boston SO, Ozawa – BERNSTEIN: *3 Meditations*; BOCCHERINI: *Cello Concerto No. 2*; SHOSTAKOVICH: *Cello Concerto No. 2*; TARTINI: *Cello Concerto*; TCHAIKOVSKY: *Andante cantabile* etc.; VIVALDI: *Cello Concertos*. ***
*** Chan. 8579. Wallfisch, LPO, Thomson – KABALEVSKY; KHACHATURIAN: *Cello Concertos*. ***

Glazunov's *Chant du ménestrel* shows the nostalgic appeal of 'things long ago and far away'. It is a short but appealing piece and is splendidly played by Rostropovich within a highly recommendable Double DG anthology. Alternatively, it becomes a welcome makeweight on the Chandos CD.

Chopiniana, Op. 46.

** Decca 460 019-2. Deutsches SO, Berlin, Ashkenazy – CHOPIN: *Piano Concerto No. 1*. **

Glazunov's scoring of various piano pieces, made in 1893, is at times rather thick but it makes a satisfactory fill-up to Ashkenazy's less than special account of the Chopin *E minor Concerto*.

(i) Concerto ballata for Cello & Orchestra, Op. 108; (ii) Piano Concerto No. 1, Op. 92.

*** Chan. 9528. (i) Dyachkov; (ii) Pirzadeh; I Musici de Montréal, Turovsky – ARENSKY: *Violin Concerto*. ***

The highly romantic *First Piano Concerto* is already well served by Stephen Coombs (see below). The *Concerto ballata* is also available on Naxos, but Yegor Dyachkov is a fine soloist, and the young Iranian-born Canadian pianist, Maneli Pirzadeh, proves a most poetic and brilliant exponent of the *Piano Concerto*. All in all this makes a highly recommendable coupling.

Piano Concertos Nos. 1 in F min., Op. 92; 2 in B flat, Op. 100.

**(*) Hyp. CDA 66877. Coombs, BBC Scottish SO, Brabbins – GOEDICKE: *Concertstück*. **(*)
(N) (BB) ** Naxos 8.553928. Yablonskaya, Moscow SO, Yablonvsky.

These two piano concertos are ripely lyrical, like a mixture of Brahms and Rachmaninov, but the inspiration is anything but tired or faded. In the *First Concerto*, an extended first movement – with echoes of Rachmaninov's *Second Symphony* – is followed by a long and elaborate set of variations, while the Liszt-like structure of the *Second Concerto* includes the most beautiful slow movement. As in his survey of Glazunov's piano music for the same label, Stephen Coombs is a persuasive advocate, and he always leaves one with the feeling that this music means more than it does. The BBC Scottish Symphony Orchestra under Martyn Brabbins give sympathetic support, and the only serious reservation one might make concerns the over-resonant recording acoustic.

Very good performances of both these genial pieces by this partnership but they do not by any means supplant the Hyperion alternative with Stephen Coombs, who is the more subtle pianist. We would continue to recommend his recording in spite of the price advantage of this newcomer.

Piano Concerto No. 2 in B, Op. 100.

**(*) Chan. 9622. Herskowitz, I Musici de Montréal, Turovsky – DAVIDOV: *Cello Concerto No. 2 in A min., Op. 14*. **(*) CONUS: *Violin Concerto*. **(*)

Matthew Herskowitz is not quite as persuasive an artist as, say, Stephen Coombs on Hyperion. However, the merit of this record is to explore Russian concertos of the second rank which deserve a place in your library.

Violin Concerto in A min., Op. 82.

*** Teldec 4509-90881-2. Vengerov, BPO, Abbado – TCHAIKOVSKY: *Violin Concerto*. ***
*** DG 457 064-2. Shaham, Russian Nat. O, Pletnev – KABALEVSKY: *Concerto*; TCHAIKOVSKY: *Souvenir d'un lieu cher* etc. ***
*** Erato 0630 17722-2. Mutter, Nat. SO, Rostropovich – PROKOFIEV: *Violin Concerto No. 1*; SHCHEDRIN: *Stihira*. ***
*** EMI CDC7 54872-2. Zimmermann, LPO, Welser-Möst – DVORAK: *Violin Concerto*. ***
⬤ (M) (***) EMI mono CDH7 64030-2. Heifetz, LPO, Barbirolli – SIBELIUS: *Violin Concerto* (**); TCHAIKOVSKY: *Violin Concerto*. (***)
(M) *** RCA (ADD) 09026 61744-2. Heifetz, RCA Victor SO, Hendl – PROKOFIEV: *Violin Concerto No. 2*; SIBELIUS: *Concerto*. ***

*** EMI CDC7 49814-2. Perlman, Israel PO, Mehta –
SHOSTAKOVICH: *Violin Concerto No. 1*. ***

(BB) *** Naxos 8.550758. Kaler, Polish Nat. RSO (Katowice),
Kolchinsky – DVORAK: *Concerto* etc. ***

(N) (B) (***) Naxos mono 8.110940. Heifetz, LPO, Barbirolli –
BRAHMS: *Double Concerto*; BRUCH: *Scottish
Fantasy*. (***)

(N) (M) ** DG (ADD) 463 651-2. Morini, Berlin RO, Fricsay –
BRUCH: *Violin Concerto No. 1* **; DVORAK: *Violin
Concerto* ***.

Outstanding as Vengerov's Tchaikovsky performance is, his
Glazunov is even more exceptional, for he gives a familiar
concerto extra dimensions, turning it from a display piece
into a work of far wider-ranging emotions, when he contrasts and shades the tone-colours so magically, keeping his
richest tone in reserve for the third theme. Predictably, the
dashing final section is breathtaking in its brilliance.

Gil Shaham gives a pretty dazzling account of the concerto
with Mikhail Pletnev and the Russian National Orchestra,
which can well hold its own with the current opposition. It
reminds us what a superb (and often touching) piece it is.
The coupling is unusual and readers attracted by it need not
hesitate. Good, ample sound.

Anne-Sophie Mutter is here more volatile and more freely
expressive than she has usually been on disc, sounding
totally spontaneous, and that is particularly impressive in
the Glazunov. The recording, made in the Kennedy Center,
Washington, is more airy and spacious than many from this
venue.

The Glazunov also comes up sounding delightfully fresh
in Frank Peter Zimmermann's hands. Among recent versions this can hold its head high: Zimmermann plays with
effortless virtuosity, great polish and great beauty of tone.
Franz Welser-Möst provides excellent support, and the
recording is outstandingly natural and realistic.

In the winter of 1934 Heifetz came to London to record
concertos for the very first time, and after his stylish account
of the Mozart *A major Concerto* he turned to the Glazunov, a
work previously unrecorded. The exuberance of his playing,
well matched by Barbirolli's sympathetic accompaniment,
makes it a uniquely compelling version, freely improvisational with a dedicated account of the *Andante sostenuto*
and an exuberant one of the swaggering finale. The Naxos
transfer is well balanced, if not quite so sophisticated as the
previous EMI remastering, with surface hiss occasionally
intrusive. A generous coupling just the same and splendid
value.

The command and panache of Perlman are irresistible
in this showpiece concerto, and the whole performance,
recorded live, erupts into a glorious account of the galloping
final section, in playing to match that even of the supreme
master in this work, Heifetz.

The Russian violinist Ilya Kaler gives a rapturously lyrical
performance, and Camilla Kolchinsky's accompaniment is
equally warm and supportive. The resonant acoustic of the
Concert Hall of Polish Radio gives a big, spacious orchestral
sound, but Ilya Kaler's tone is full to match, and the violin
playing can certainly accommodate the scrutiny of the fairly
close microphones.

Erica Morini's sweetly lyrical account is eminently acceptable, even if it is no challenge to the finest versions. Whether
it is worthy of a place among DG's 'Originals' is another
matter (although Johanna Martzy's account of the coupled
Dvořák most certainly is). However, Morini's is in every
respect a pleasing and well-recorded performance (it was
made in the late 1950s). There was an audible edit with a
drop in pitch at one point on the original LP, which we
assume DG have now corrected (at the time of going to
press we were unable to sample the reissue).

(i) *Violin Concerto. The Seasons* (ballet), *Op. 67*.

*** Chan. 8596. (i) Shumsky; SNO, Järvi.

Neeme Järvi obtains good results from the Scottish National
Orchestra in *The Seasons*, though tempi tend to be brisk. The
Chandos acoustic is reverberant and the balance recessed. In
the *Violin Concerto*, Oscar Shumsky is perhaps wanting the
purity and effortless virtuosity of Heifetz, but the disc as a
whole still carries a three-star recommendation.

From the Middle Ages, Op. 79; Scènes de ballet, Op. 52.

*** Chan. 8804. SNO, Järvi (with LIADOV: *A Musical
Snuffbox* ***).

***From the Middle Ages* (suite), *Op. 79; The Sea, Op. 28;
Spring, Op. 34; Stenka Razin, Op. 13.***

(M) *** Chan. 7049. SNO, Järvi.

Järvi makes out an excellent case for these charming Glazunov suites. Although this music is obviously inferior to
Tchaikovsky, Järvi has the knack of making you think it is
better than it is and the Chandos recording is up to the best
standards of the house. The first disc also includes a fine
account of Liadov's delightful *A Musical Snuffbox*.

The tone-poem *Spring* was written two years after *The
Sea* and is infinitely more imaginative; in fact it is as fresh
and delightful as its companion is cliché-ridden. At one
point Glazunov even looks forward to *The Seasons*. *Stenka
Razin* has its moments of vulgarity – how otherwise with
the *Song of the Volga Boatmen* a recurrent theme? – but it
makes a colourful enough opening item for this alternative
collection.

***Raymonda* (complete ballet).**

(BB) **(*) Naxos 8.553503/4. Moscow SO, Anissimov.

This Naxos version is played elegantly and affectionately,
and the Moscow upper strings are full and warm as recorded.
It does not lack life. But in seeking atmosphere, the playing
creates a less than vibrant effect, although this is partly
caused by Alexander Anissimov's tendency to luxuriant
tempi.

***Raymonda* (ballet), *Op. 57*: extended excerpts from Acts I
& II.**

**(*) Chan. 8447. SNO, Järvi.

Järvi chooses some 56 minutes of music from the first two
Acts, omitting entirely the Slavic/Hungarian Wedding *Divertissement* of the closing Act, and this contributes to the
slight feeling of lassitude. But with rich Chandos recording
this is a record for any balletomane to wallow in.

Les Ruses d'amore (ballet), Op. 61; Scènes de ballet (suite), Op. 52; Suite caractèristique, Op. 9; Triumphal March, Op. 40. Chopiniana (suite arr. from Chopin's works), Op. 46.

(B) *** BMG/Melodiya Twofer 74321 59055-2 (2). USSR SO, Svetlanov.

Les Ruses d'amore offers 55 minutes of music, not unlike *Raymonda*, though not perhaps quite as fine as *The Seasons*. The eight-movement *Suite caractèristique* has linking thematic material, but still sounds very like a ballet score. All this music is warmly and elegantly played, and directed with affectionate understanding by Svetlanov. *Chopiniana* consists of transcriptions of four major Chopin piano pieces, opening with the famous *Polonaise in A major* and closing with a lively *Tarantella* in the same key. It is agreeable enough, but not in the same class as the Roy Douglas score for *Les Sylphides*. The *Triumphal March* seems at first suprisingly lyrical, but it ends with a rumbustious climax, introducing and repeating ad lib the *Battle Hymn of the Republic*. The 1989–90 digital recording is excellent in every respect, full, vivid, and with plenty of ambient warmth.

The Seasons (ballet; complete), Op. 67.

*** Decca 433 000-2 (2). RPO, Ashkenazy – TCHAIKOVSKY: *Nutcracker.* ***

(B)*** Double Decca 455 349-2 (2). RPO, Ashkenazy – PROKOFIEV: *Cinderella.* ***

(M) *** EMI (ADD) CDM5 65911-2. Concert Arts O, Irving – SCARLATTI/TOMMASINI: *Good Humoured Ladies;* WALTON: *Wise Virgins.* ***

(M) **(*) Decca 460 315-2. SRO, Ansermet – KHACHATURIAN: *Gayaneh; Spartacus:* excerpts. ***

(BB) **(*) Naxos 8.550079. Czech RSO (Bratislava), Lenárd – TCHAIKOVSKY: *Sleeping Beauty Suite.* **

The Seasons (ballet), Op. 67; Concert Waltzes Nos. 1 in D, Op. 47; 2 in F, Op. 51.

(B) *** EMI Double forte (ADD) CZS5 69361-2 (2). Philh. O, Svetlanov – ARENSKY: *Variations on a Theme of Tchaikovsky ***; RIMSKY-KORSAKOV: *Scheherazade.* **

The Seasons (ballet) complete; Scènes de ballet, Op. 52.

*** Telarc CD CD 80347. Minnesota O, De Waart.

Ashkenazy's account of Glazunov's delightful ballet is the finest it has ever received. The RPO playing is dainty and elegant, refined and sumptuous, yet the strings respond vigorously to the thrusting vitality of the Autumnal *Bacchanale*. The Decca engineers, working in Watford Town Hall, provide digital sound of great allure and warmth, very much in the demonstration bracket. As can be seen this recording is also available less expensively on a Double Decca coupled with Prokofiev's *Cinderella* ballet.

But if you want *The Seasons* separately on a single CD, you will be hard put to better the Minnesota performance, elegant, polished, warm and alive, and given Telarc's top-drawer sound. The famous thrusting tune of *Autumn* is only marginally less athletic than with Ashkenazy. The *Scènes de ballet* make an ideal coupling, not quite as melodically distinctive but still very enjoyable and cosily tuneful, al-though the second-movement *Marionnettes* matches Delibes at his most piquant.

Robert Irving's 1960 recording still sounds astonishingly fresh, while the resonant ambience prevents the quality from being too dated. The Concert Arts Orchestra play with wit, warmth and precision. Irving shapes and points the melodies with consummate balletic feeling and his reading is delightfully evocative. The stirring tune of *Autumn* is taken very fast and has strikingly more vitality than with Svetlanov. However, as we go to press this set has been deleted.

Svetlanov's account is played most beautifully. His approach is engagingly affectionate; he caresses the lyrical melodies persuasively so that, if the big tune of the *Bacchanale* has slightly less thrust than usual, it fits readily into the overall conception. The glowing Abbey Road recording is excellent and vividly remastered. It comes in harness with a very Russian *Scheherazade*, which he recorded with the LSO but about which we have some reservations (see below), and Barbirolli's highly persuasive version of the endearing Arensky *Variations* for strings.

Ansermet's recording dates from 1966 and is of vintage Decca quality. The performance takes a little while to warm up, but perhaps that is not inappropriate in the opening *Winter* sequence, where the conductor's meticulous ear for detail is a plus point, for the wind playing throughout is engagingly pointed. At the opening of *Summer* one might wish for a richer, more sumptuous sound from the Suisse Romande violins, but the zestful opening of *Autumn* is firm to the point of fierceness.

Ondrej Lenárd gives a pleasing bargain account of Glazunov's delightful score, finding plenty of delicacy, while the entry of Glazunov's most famous tune at the opening of the *Autumn Bacchanale* is very virile indeed. The sound is atmospheric, yet with plenty of fullness.

Stenka Razin (symphonic poem), Op. 13.

*** Chan. 8479. SNO, Järvi.

Stenka Razin has its moments of vulgarity – how otherwise with the *Song of the Volga Boatmen* a recurrent theme? – but it makes a generous and colourful makeweight for Järvi's fine version of *Scheherazade*. The recording is splendid.

Symphonies Nos. 1 in E (Slavyanskaya), Op. 5; 4 in E flat, Op. 48.

(BB) **(*) Naxos 8.553561. Moscow SO, Anissimov.

Symphony No. 1 in E (Slavyanskaya), Op. 5; (i) Violin Concerto, Op. 82.

*** Chan. 9751. Russian State SO, Polyansky; (i) with Krasko.

What a remarkable and delightful work the Glazunov *First Symphony* is – not only on account of the composer's youth (he was a mere sixteen at the time) but also the quality and fertility of its invention and its expert craftsmanship!

Polyansky's pacing keeps the music alive throughout, and the finale, delightfully scored and in effect a set of variations on a simple theme, is one of the most successful closing movements for any of the composer's symphonies. Polyansky manages the tempi changes in an engagingly spontaneous way and the Chandos sound, full and with glowing wind colouring, is flattering. Julia Krasko plays the *Violin*

Concerto warm-heartedly and with confidence and ready bravura, and she receives fine support from the Russian Orchestra. The Chandos sound is well up to standard.

Both in the *First* and in the *Fourth*, Alexander Anissimov gets eminently sympathetic performances from the Moscow orchestra, though one can imagine livelier and lighter playing.

Symphony No. 2 in F sharp min., Op. 16. (i) *Coronation Cantata, Op. 56.*

*** Chan. 9709. Russian State SO, Polyansky (i) with Lutiv-Ternovskaya, Kuznetsova, Grivnov, Stepanovich, Russian State Symphonic Capella.

Symphonies Nos. 2 in F sharp min., Op. 16; 7 in F (Pastoral), Op. 77.

(BB) ** Naxos 8.553769. Moscow SO, Anissimov.

Glazunov's *Symphony No. 2* is full of very Russian themes that echo Borodin's *Prince Igor*, which Glazunov himself helped to complete after the composer's death. Though Polyansky's performance loses some concentration in the finale, it is warmly expressive and colourful, helped by rich, full recording. What makes the disc especially attractive is the substantial fill-up, the première recording of the *Coronation Cantata* which Glazunov wrote to celebrate the coronation of the last Tsar, Nicolas II. Framed by forthright choruses, the opening one in a swinging triple time, the middle five movements feature the four soloists in turn, culminating in an exhilarating movement, *Heaven and earth*, enriched with sensuously beautiful orchestration. A winning rarity, very well performed, with a strong team of soloists, all attractively Slavonic in timbre, even if the soprano grows edgy under pressure.

In Glazunov's *Second Symphony* Anissimov and the Moscow Symphony Orchestra respond to the music's Slavonic feeling, but overall without quite the degree of passion and drama the work demands, and the violins, as recorded, lack allure. However, the 'Pastoral' *Seventh* of 1902 (which makes a distinct melodic reference to Beethoven's work in the same key) is rather more successful. The recording is well balanced and full, if not top-drawer. With any reservations noted, this is fair value.

(i) *Symphony No. 3;* (ii) *Serenades Nos. 1 in A, Op. 7; 2 in F, Op. 11;* (i) *Stenka Razin, Op. 13.*

**(*) ASV CDDCA 903. (i) LSO; (ii) RPO; Butt.

Symphonies Nos. 3 in D, Op. 33; 9 in D min. (unfinished, orch. Gavril Yudin).

(BB) ** Naxos 8.554253. Moscow SO, Anissimov.

Yondani Butt's performance of the symphony is a good one and very well played. One would have liked a greater sense of soaring (over the throbbing wind chords) at the opening, but the response of the LSO catches the colour and melancholy of the slow movement, and the Scherzo (easily the best movement) has sparkle. But it is the two charming early *Serenades* that catch the ear, seductively played by the RPO.

Alexander Anissimov opens lightly and initially creates a Mendelssohnian atmosphere over the throbbing woodwind. His is a lyrical reading, with plenty of warmth, but as the

movement procedes, in spite of fine playing and some vigorous brass passages, the underlying pulse is that bit too relaxed to carry the music consistently forward; the same problem recurs in the finale. The main interest of this Naxos CD is the inclusion of the single movement of the composer's incomplete final symphony which he left sketched out in short score. The main themes are drawn from the slow introduction, but they are not memorable and although here Anissimov and his orchestra play the piece with passionate commitment they are unable to convince us that it is worth resurrecting.

Symphonies Nos. 4 in E flat, Op. 48; 5 in B flat, Op. 55.

*** Chan. 9739. Russian State SO, Polyansky.
*** ASV CDDCA 1051. Philh. O, Butt.

The *Fourth Symphony* dates from the year of Tchaikovsky's death (1893) and is a charming and well-composed work, held together structurally by a theme which Glazunov uses in all three movements. The *Fifth* written two years later is more imposing, but not so very different really, although the first movement is more vigorous. Throughout both works the Philharmonia playing under Butt is persuasively warm and sympathetic, helped by the spacious, well-balanced recording.

However, the Chandos competitor has the advantage of a fine Russian orchestra, which immediately establish a richly Slavic atmosphere of melancholy for the languorous opening theme of No. 4; and Polyansky is able to relax and re-create this mood at the very end of the first movement without losing concentration. The Chandos recording is glowingly warm in capturing string and woodwind timbres alike, yet the Scherzos of both symphonies sparkle translucently. The resonance means that the finales have less bite than with the ASV recording, and while they are played with robust Russian-dance vigour, Butt is exceptionally spirited in the finale of No. 5. It is a case of swings and roundabouts, for the ASV recording is clearer, if not more lustrous.

Symphonies Nos. 5; 8 in E flat, Op. 83.

(N) (BB) *** Naxos 8.553660. Moscow SO, Anissimov.

These are both delightful symphonies, even if the *Eighth* is rather thickly scored. However, Alexander Anissimov does his best to make the textures as clear and well ventilated as possible, and pays great attention to details of dynamics and balance. Try the scherzo of the *Fifth Symphony* and you will find much lightness of touch and a greater transparency than is often encountered in records of these works. His is a far more persuasive account of the *Eighth* than Svetlanov's LP version from the 1980s. Strongly recommended, especially at such a modest cost.

(i) *Symphony No. 6; Raymonda* (ballet), *Op. 57a: Suite;* (ii) *Triumphal March, Op. 40.*

*** ASV CDDCA 904. (i) LSO; (ii) RPO; Butt.

Symphony No. 6 in C min., Op. 58; The Forest (tone poem), *Op. 19.*

(BB) **(*) Naxos 8. 554293. Moscow SO, Anissimov.

Taken overall, Yondani Butt's is the preferred choice for

Glazunov's *Sixth*, helped by the open sound of the ASV recording, and the fine wind and brass contributions from the LSO; the brass chorale at the end of the *Variations* is effectively sonorous. The selection from *Raymonda* concentrates on the first two Acts and offers only a brief *Entr'acte* from Act III; most of the music in fact comes from Act I, some 21 minutes out of a selection lasting just over half an hour. The playing is both graceful and lively, and the recording has plenty of amplitude and warmth.

Anissimov also handles the symphony admirably and with the Moscow players responding persuasively, the performance is a great success. However, *The Forest* is an over-extended pantheistic tone poem, with an ingenuous programme. The performance is sympathetic, the recording very good, but Anissimov fails to persuade us that this piece is not too long for its material. Yet the work is rarely if ever performed, and the fine account of the symphony is worth its modest Naxos price.

CHAMBER MUSIC

5 Novelettes, Op. 15.

(***) Testament mono SBT1061. Hollywood Qt – BORODIN: *String Quartet No. 2;* TCHAIKOVSKY: *String Quartet No. 1.* (***)

The Hollywood Quartet bring a freshness and ardour to these charming compositions that is most persuasive.

String Quartets Nos. 3 in G (Slavonic), Op. 26; 5 in D min., Op. 70; The Fridays, Book 2: Kuranta; Prelude & Fugue in D min.

**(*) Olympia OCD 525. Shostakovich Qt.

The appeal of the *Third Quartet* is immediate and the thematic inspiration folk-like and of the highest level. The *Fifth Quartet* (1898) opens with a noble and expressive fugue, and on hearing it one is tempted to agree with Calvocoressi that this is the finest of the seven. Very good performances, though they are not the last word in polish; but they are rather too closely balanced for complete comfort.

String Quartets Nos. 6 in B flat, Op. 106; 7 in C, Op. 107.

** Olympia OCD 526. Shostakovich Qt.

The *Sixth* and *Seventh Quartets* have all the sad charm of old Russia. The Shostakovich Quartet generally play with conviction, though their performances are by no means as polished as those of Nos. 3 and 5. The recording is rather up-front and has some roughness on climaxes, but there is no alternative version of either work.

String Quintet in A, Op. 39.

*** Chan. 9878. ASMF Chamber Ens. – TCHAIKOVSKY: *Souvenir de Florence.* ***

Glazunov's *String Quintet* (with second cello) is a work of characteristic warmth and lyricism. The performance is thoroughly committed and persuasive, and very well recorded too. There is no alternative version in the catalogue – but, even if there were, this would be hard to beat.

Complete piano music

Piano Sonata No. 1 in B flat min., Op. 74; Grande valse de concert, Op. 41; 3 Miniatures, Op. 42; Petite valse, Op. 36; Suite on the Name 'Sacha'; Valse de salon, Op. 43; Waltzes on the Theme 'Sabela', Op. 23.

*** Hyp. CDA 66833. Coombs.

Easy Sonata; 3 Etudes, Op. 31; Miniature in C; 3 Morceaux, Op. 49; Nocturne, Op. 37; 2 Pieces, Op. 22; 2 Poèmes-improvisations; Sonatina; Theme & Variations, Op. 72.

*** Hyp. CDA 66844. Coombs.

Marking the start of a new Russian series, each of these two discs contains a major work, the *Piano Sonata No. 1* on the first and the *Theme and Variations*, Op. 72, on the second. For the rest, you have a dazzling series of salon and genre pieces, full of the easy charm and winning tunefulness that mark Glazunov's ballet, *The Seasons.* Stephen Coombs proves a most persuasive advocate, consistently conveying sheer joy in keyboard virtuosity to a degree rare in British pianists. Coombs plays with a natural warmth and a spontaneous feeling for line which give magic to pieces which otherwise might seem trivial. As well as the engaging *Variations*, Op. 72, simple in outline but elaborate and colourful in texture, the second disc offers what might be counted Glazunov's most assured piano work, the set of three *Etudes*, Op. 31.

Piano Sonata No. 2 in E min., Op. 75; Barcarolle sur les touches noires; Idyll, Op. 103; 2 Impromptus, Op. 54; In modo religioso, Op. 38; Prelude & 2 Mazurkas, Op. 25; Song of the Volga Boatmen, Op. 97 (arr. Siloti); (i) Triumphal March, Op. 40.

*** Hyp. CDA 66866. (i) Coombs; (i) Holst Singers, Layton.

The most substantial work here is the *Second Sonata* of 1901, which is better played than by any of its rivals we have heard. The most unusual piece is the transcription of a Wagnerian *Triumphal March*, written for the Chicago Exposition, which eventually introduces *Hail Columbus*, sung in Russian! Not all the music on this generously filled CD is of equal merit but most of it is rewarding, and the recording serves the music well.

4 Preludes & Fugues, Op. 101; Prelude & Fugue in D min., Op. 62; in E min. (1926).

*** Hyp. CDA 66855. Coombs.

The *D minor Prelude and Fugue* is not just a powerful essay in Bachian counterpoint, but a dramatic and compelling piece. The set of four, Op. 101, are not only intellectually rewarding but they are also artistically most satisfying and inventive pieces. The *E minor* from 1926 opens dramatically and is another impressive piece. The recording is eminently satisfactory, without any excessive reverberance.

Piano Sonatas Nos. 1 in B flat min., Op. 74; 2 in E min., Op. 75; Grande valse de concert in E flat, Op. 41.

**(*) Pearl (ADD) SHECD 9538. Howard.

As we have observed above, the Glazunov *Sonatas* are well

worth investigating, and the Pearl disc has the advantage of grouping them together in performances which are both committed and as well recorded. Admirers of Glazunov's art not following the Hyperion series should investigate this issue, which sounds extremely impressive.

ORGAN MUSIC

Fantasy, Op. 110; Preludes & Fugues: in D, Op. 93; in D min., Op. 98.

(N) *** BIS CD 1101. Ericsson – DVORAK: *Preludes & Fugues* **(*). SIBELIUS: *Intrada* etc. ***

These pieces leave no doubt as to Glazunov's contrapuntal mastery. The *Prelude and Fugue in D* was composed in the immediate wake of the *Eighth Symphony*, and the *D minor* (which also exists in a version for piano), with its powerfully wrought fugue, will surprise those who think of Glazunov as a dyed-in-the-wool conservative. The *Fantasy* was written for Marcel Dupré in 1934–5 towards the end of Glazunov's career and is well worth getting to know. Hans Ola Ericsson produces some splendid effects from the powerful new Gerald Woehl organ at St. Petrus Canisius, Friedrichshafen. The recording is in the demonstration class and has tremendous presence and range.

VOCAL MUSIC

Tsar Iudesyskiy (King of the Jews).

*** Chan. 9467. Russian State Symphony Ch. & SO, Rozhdestvensky.
(N) *** Chan. 9824. (i) Russian State Symphonic Capella; Russian State SO, Polyansky.

Glazunov's incidental music to Konstantin Romanov's *Tsar Iedesyskiy* (*King of the Jews*) offers considerable artistic rewards. There is an unaffected simplicity that is quite touching, and the naturalness of the musical inspiration outweighs any of its longueurs or miscalculations. Rozhdestvensky shapes each phrase with feeling and imagination, and he gets good results from his chorus and orchestra. Moreover, the quality of the recorded sound is first rate in every respect, with well-balanced choral and orchestral forces and a lifelike perspective. There are informative and helpful notes by David Nice.

Astonishingly Chandos have followed up Rozdestvensky's CD with another, using similar forces conducted by Valéry Polyansky. His version is hardly less compelling, although perhaps Rozhdestvensky is that bit more dramatic at the opening, and in portraying the Levite's trumpets (actually horns). But Polyansky's account is richly atmospheric and his singers are splendid. There is little in it, although some may be swayed by the more recent CD's inclusion of the music that Glazunov wrote in 1908 for a production of Oscar Wilde's *Salome*. It is agreeably sinuous and sumptuous, but the music for the famous *Dance* (for which Fokine provided choreography) is anything but erotic.

GLIÈRE, Reinhold (1875–1956)

The Bronze Horseman: Suite; (i) Horn Concerto, Op. 91.

** Chan. 9379. (i) Watkins; BBC PO, Downes.

The Bronze Horseman is not great music – nor, for that matter, is the *Horn Concerto*. Richard Watkins is a fine soloist in the latter; Downes gets good rather than really distinguished playing from the BBC Philharmonic, though the recording is excellent.

(i) Concerto for Coloratura Soprano, Op. 82; (ii) Harp Concerto, Op. 74.

*** Chan. 9094. (i) Hulse; (ii) Masters; City of L. Sinfonia, Hickox – GINASTERA: *Harp Concerto*. ***

This digital recording of Glière's lush concertos is highly competitive in both works. The recording is suitably rich and opulent, yet every detail is audibly in place. Eileen Hulse is an impressive soloist with excellent control, well-focused tone and a good sense of line, and she is excellently supported by the City of London Sinfonia and Richard Hickox. Nor need Rachel Masters fear comparison with her predecessor, Osian Ellis; so, given such excellent sound, this is all highly self-indulgent and sybaritic.

Symphony No. 2 in C min., Op. 25; Zaporozhy Cossacks, Op. 64.

**(*) Chan. 9071. BBC PO, Downes.

Not even the advocacy of Sir Edward Downes with his magnificent Manchester orchestra can conceal the banality of some of the writing in this early Glière symphony – it cannot compare with Glière's later and grander *Symphony No. 3. Zaporozhy Cossacks* is less ambitious but also contains banalities. Excellent performances and outstanding recording.

Symphony No. 3 in B min. (Ilya Murometz), Op. 42.

*** Chan. 9041. BBC PO, Downes.

Downes and the BBC Philharmonic in magnificent form give an urgently passionate performance of this colourful programme piece, more convincing than any rival in what can easily seem too cumbersome a work. Downes, taut and intense, relates the writing very much to the world of Glière's close contemporary, Rachmaninov. The recording, made in the concert hall of New Broadcasting House, Manchester, is one of Chandos's finest, combining clarity and sumptuousness.

GLINKA, Mikhail (1805–57)

(i) Andante Cantabile & Rondo in D min.; Jota aragonesa (Spanish Overture No. 1); Polka No. 1 (orch. Balakirev); Prince Kholmsky (incidental music): Overture & Entr'actes to Acts II–V. Recollections of a Summer Night in Madrid (Spanish Overture No. 2); Symphony on Two Russian Themes (orch. Shebalin); Waltz Fantasia; A Life for the Tsar (Ivan Susanin): Overture & Dances. (ii) Ruslan and Ludmilla: Overture; Dances; Tchernomor's March.

(B) *** BMG/Melodiya Twofer (ADD) 74321 53461-2 (2).
    (i) USSR SO; (ii) Bolshoi Theatre O; Svetlanov.

An eminently recommendable survey of Glinka's orchestral output. The performances embrace a considerable time-span (1963–90), though the majority are from the 1970s and 1980s. The playing of the USSR Symphony Orchestra is nothing if not expert and idiomatic; and the recordings, though variable in quality, are generally very good indeed.

Capriccio brillante on the Jota aragonesa (Spanish Overture No. 1); Kamarinskaya; Souvenir of a Summer Night in Madrid (Spanish Overture No. 2); Valse-fantaisie; A Life for the Tsar: Overture & Suite (Polonaise; Krakowiak; Waltz; Mazurka; Epilogue).

*** ASV CDDCA 1075. Armenian PO, Tjeknavorian.

The key work here is *Kamarinskaya*, a kaleidoscopic fantasy on two Russian folk songs. Tchaikovsky said it contained 'the whole of Russian music, just as the acorn holds within itself the oak tree'. The two Spanish overtures created another genre, the orchestral 'picture postcard', which Russian composers brought home from their travels abroad. Glinka's two pieces have a glitter and atmospheric appeal all of their own, especially the *Capriccio brillante*, featuring a 'jota aragonesa' also used by Liszt. But the seductive scoring of *Summer Night in Madrid* was in some ways even more influential. The *Valse-fantaisie* is a charmer, but the overture and suite from *A Life for the Tsar* are more conventional. The whole programme is played here with a natural vitality, great charm and a delightful feeling for its Russianness by a first-class orchestra under a conductor who is a composer himself. The bright recording, full-bodied and glowing, is one of the finest we have received from ASV.

Capriccio brillante on the Jota aragonesa (Spanish Overture No. 1); Kamarinskaya; Overture in D; Ruslan and Ludmilla: Overture & Suite; Souvenir of a Summer Night in Madrid (Spanish Overture No. 2); Symphony on Two Russian Themes; Valse-Fantaisie.

(N) *** Chan. 9861. BBC PO, Sinaisky.

Sinaisky duplicates the main items in Tjeknavorian's programme, but includes also the seductive *Symphony on Two Russian Themes*; not great music, but alluring in its orchestral palette and its anticipations of Borodin. Many will also prefer the fizzingly brilliant *Overture*, *March* and *Dances* (effectively a charming ballet suite) from *Ruslan and Ludmilla* to the excepts from *A Life for the Tsar*. Moreover, not only is the playing of the BBC Philharmonic under Sinaisky both warmly responsive and sparkling, but the state-of-the-art Chandos recording (brass, woodwind and strings alike) is even finer than the ASV alternative. Highly recommended.

Grand Sextet in E flat.

*** Hyp. CDA 66163. Capricorn – RIMSKY-KORSAKOV: *Quintet.* ***

Glinka's *Sextet* is rather engaging, particularly when played with such aplomb as it is here. The contribution of the pianist, Julian Jacobson, is brilliantly nimble and felicitous.

Trio pathétique in D min.

*** Chan. 8477. Borodin Trio – ARENSKY: *Piano Trio.* ***
(N) (BB) *** ASV CDQS 6187. Classic Trio – BRAHMS; GLINKA: *Clarinet Trios.* ***

Glinka's *Trio* is prefaced by a superscription; '*Je n'ai connu l'amour que par les peines qu'il cause*' ('I have known love only through the misery it causes'). It is no masterpiece – but the Borodins almost persuade one that it is. The Chandos recording is vivid and has excellent presence.

Glinka's *Trio pathétique* was originally scored for clarinet, piano and bassoon, with two optional changes in instrumentation. On ASV it works particularly well on clarinet, cello and bassoon, especially when played and recorded as persuasively as here.

PIANO MUSIC

Andalusian Dance, Las Mollares; Bolero; Contredanse, La couventine; Contredanse in G; Cotillon in B flat; A Farewell Waltz; French Quadrille; Galop; Grande valse in G; 6 Mazurkas; Polka; Polonaise in E; The Skylark (trans. Balakirev); Tarantella; Valse-favorite; Valse mélodique; Variations on a Theme by Mozart; Variations on the Terzetto from the Opera 'A Life for the Tsar' (trans. Alexandr Gourilyov).

** BIS CD 981. Ryabchikov.

Victor Ryabchikov's second survey of Glinka's piano music includes a supplement of three alternative versions of the *Variations on a Theme by Mozart*, plus Balakirev's transcription of *The Skylark*, made a few years after Glinka's death, and the *Variations on the Terzetto from the Opera 'A Life for the Tsar'* transcribed by Alexandr Gourilyov. No masterpieces are uncovered among these salon pieces, though there are some attractive numbers such as the *Bolero* and *A Farewell Waltz*. These are the kind of dances that you might have heard at any ball in Russia, and Ryabchikov plays them in the order you might have conceivably heard them in at such a function. Three-star playing and clear, rather forward recording made in the Melodiya Studios in Moscow but distinctly one-star music.

Variations on an Original Theme in F; Variations on the Romance 'Benedetta sia la madre'; Variations on Two Themes from the Ballet, Chao-Kang; Variations on The Nightingale (by Alabyev) Variations on a Theme from Anna Bolena (by Donizetti); Variations & Rondino brillante on a Theme from the Opera, I Capuleti e i Montecchi (by Bellini); Variations on a Theme from Faniska (by Cherubini); Variations on the Russian Folk-song 'In the shallow valley'.

** BIS CD 980. Ryabchikov.

All these variations were written when the composer was in his twenties. Ryabchikov suggests, in his thorough and authoritative notes, that 'the music is full of tenderness and expression, elegant simplicity and nobility'. Although he plays with evident feeling, he is handicapped by a rather forward recording. When he is playing above *forte* there is a touch of glare. The recording was made in Moscow, not by the familiar BIS team, and produced by the pianist himself.

Ruslan and Ludmilla (complete).

*** Ph. 446 746-2 (3). Ognovienko, Netrebko, Diadkova, Bezzubenkov, Gorchakova, Kirov Op. Ch. & O, Gergiev.

(M) **(*) BMG/Melodiya (ADD) 74321 29348 (3). Nesterenko, Rudenko, Yaroslavtsev, Sinyavskaya, Morozov, Fomina, Bolshoi Theatre, Moscow, Ch. & O, Simonov.

Gergiev in his Kirov recording, done live on stage, launches into this classic Russian opera with a hair-raisingly fast and brilliant account of the overture, and then characteristically brings out the subtlety of much of the writing, as well as the colour. The voices come over well, with Vladimir Ognovienko characterful as Ruslan, bringing out word-meaning, most impressively in his big Act II aria. Anna Netrebko is fresh and bright as Ludmilla, as well as agile, not as shrill as many Russian sopranos; but it is Galina Gorchakova as Gorislava who takes first honours, rich and firm, as is Larissa Diadkova in the travesti role of Ratmir, especially impressive in the delightful duet with Finn (Konstantin Pluzhnikov). A video recording is also available.

The Bolshoi recording on BMG/Melodiya at mid-price brings a warm and convincing account, typical of Bolshoi standards in the late 1970s, with Yevgeni Nesterenko magnificent as Ruslan, rich, firm and heroic. Another outstanding performance comes from Boris Morozov as the braggart, Farlaf, with his comic patter Rondo in Act II, not just brilliantly agile but resonant too and full of fun, reminding one of Chaliapin's famous recording. Alexei Maslennikov is most affecting in Finn's Ballad, and Nina Fomina is a rich, firm Gorislava. One snag is that Bela Rudenko as Ludmilla is shrill under pressure, and a few cuts are made in Act V; but it is still an enjoyable if uneven set.

GLUCK, Christophe (1714–87)

Alceste (Vienna version 1767; complete).

(B) *** Naxos 8.660066/68 (3). Ringholz, Lavender, Degerfeldt, Treichl, Martinsson, Drottningholm Theatre Ch. & O., Ostman.

This is the first recording of the Vienna version of Alceste, rather simpler and more direct in manner than the far better known French version of 1776. Here, Alceste's powerful aria Divinités du Styx becomes Ombre, larve, less imposing, and the intimate scale of the Drottningholm presentation reflects that, with a cast of young singers remarkable for their freshness rather than for their power.

Where the self-sacrificing heroine usually emerges as a formidable figure, here she is more girlish, more vulnerable, as portrayed by the American Teresa Ringholz, who is consistently pure and sweet, clear and true in every register, if a little lacking in variety. Her sweetness and purity are matched by the young Swedish soprano Miriam Treichl, in the role of Ismene, Alceste's confidante – a most promising singer, even if it is at times confusing to have such similar singers juxtaposed. The clear-toned British tenor Justin Lavender sings stylishly in the relatively small role of Admeto,

husband of Alceste, with Jonas Degerfeldt, aptly lighter and more youthful, as his confidant, Evandro.

After a dull start the chorus warms up well in Act II, with the period orchestra a little edgy but always alert under Ostman's direction. At Naxos price one can hardly complain that the opera is rather extravagantly laid out on three discs, when in any case that brings the advantage of one disc per act. Well-balanced sound, with voices well to the fore. Full libretto, synopsis and translation are provided.

Armide (complete).

*** DG 459 6716-2. Delunsch, Workman, Podles, Naouri, Ch. & Musiciens du Louvre, Minkowski.

Armide, the fifth of Gluck's 'reform' operas, written for Paris in 1777, is both passionate and dramatic in telling the story of the sorceress, Armide, and her unwilling love for the knight Renaud. It leads to a sensuous love duet in Act V before Renaud finally rejects her love. Using a libretto set by Lully almost a century earlier, Gluck develops a compellingly flexible structure, with arias, duets and recitatives merging in quick succession. Minkowski's treatment could not be more dramatic, persuasively leading one on at speeds on the brisk side. The cast is strong, powerfully led by Mireille Delunsch in the title role, singing with rich, firm tone, and with Charles Workman fresh and clean cut as the tenor hero, Renaud. In the brief but important role of La Haine, Ewa Podles sings with commanding intensity, and the minor roles are also well taken. The live recording gives weight and bite to the substantial instrumental band.

Der betrogene Kadi (complete).

(M) *** CPO/EMI CPO 999 552-2. Rothenberger, Donath, Gedda, Berry, Hirte, Marheineke, Bav. State Op. Ch. & O, Suitner.

Gluck wrote this light-hearted Singspiel, Die betrogene Kadi ('The Cheated Cadi'), in the year before he completed his first version of Orfeo, providing an astonishing contrast with that masterpiece. Unlike Mozart in Entführung, Gluck generally avoids the exotic, preferring a gentler style. Even so, he gives the Kadi a vigorous aria which may have given Mozart the idea for some of Osmin's music. The cast is a strong one, with Helen Donath providing a sweet contrast to the ever-bright Anneliese Rothenberger, and with Walter Berry as the Kadi and Nicolai Gedda as the hero, Nuradin, characterizing well. The 1978 EMI recording still sounds full and vivid.

Don Juan (ballet): complete.

(N)(M) *** Warner Apex 8573 89233-2-2. E. Bar. Soloists, Gardiner.

Reissued as part of the Gardiner Collection, this has much to recommend it especially at Apex price. The 1981 recording is full and modern. The performance too has a clean and dramatic profile.

Iphigénie en Aulide (complete).

(M) *** Erato 2292 45003-2 (2). Van Dam, Von Otter, Dawson, Aler, Monteverdi Ch., Lyon Op. O, Gardiner.

Gardiner here reconstructs the score as presented in the first revival of 1775; the recording conveys the tensions of a live performance without the distractions of intrusive stage noise. The darkness of the piece is established at the very start, with men's voices eliminated, and a moving portrait built up of Agamemnon, here sung superbly by José van Dam. In the title-role Lynne Dawson builds up a touching portrait of the heroine. Her sweet, pure singing is well contrasted with the positive strength of Anne Sofie von Otter as Clytemnestra, and John Aler brings clear, heroic attack to the tenor role of Achille. The performance is crowned by the superb ensemble-singing of the Monteverdi Choir in the many choruses.

Iphigénie en Aulide (complete in German; arr. Wagner).

(M) **(*) RCA (ADD) 74321 32236-2 (2). Moffo, Fischer-Dieskau, Schmidt, Spiess, Stewart, Augér, Bav. R Ch., Munich R. O, Eichhorn.

Wagner's arrangement used here, is, by the standards of modern purism, a total travesty and the use of German instead of French only reinforces the stylistic conflict. But with an urgently dramatic performance, with a formidable list of soloists, excellent choral singing and fine playing, this is enjoyable entertainment in its own right, with its enriched orchestration and harmony, its cuts and additions and its amended plot. Wagnerians at least need not hesitate. Good stage atmosphere in the recording. The German libretto comes without a translation.

Iphigénie en Tauride (complete).

✪ *** Ph. 416 148-2 (2). Montague, Aler, Thomas Allen, Argenta, Massis, Monteverdi Ch., Lyon Op. O, Gardiner.

(N) DG 471 133-2 (2). Delunsch, Keenlyside, Beuron, Naoure, Cousin, Louvre Ch. & O, Minkowski.

(N) Telarc CD 80546 (2). Goerke, Gilfry, Cole, Salters, Baker, West, Boston Baroque, Pearlman.

Gardiner's electrifying reading of *Iphigénie en Tauride* is a revelation. Though his Lyon orchestra does not use period instruments, its clarity and resilience and, where necessary, grace and delicacy are admirable. Diana Montague in the name-part sings with admirable bite and freshness, Thomas Allen is an outstanding Oreste, characterizing strongly but singing with classical precision. John Aler is a similarly strong and stylish singer, taking the tenor role of Pylade. The recording is bright and full.

Marc Minkowski launches into his characterful, highly distinctive reading in a performance of the overture with characterstically extreme speeds in both directions. Where Pearlman's Telarc version consistently takes a safe course, Minkowski's regularly offers a more personal, more challenging view, giving new insights into the music. It also sounds more idiomatic thanks to having a cast almost entirely made up of French speakers, who enunciate their words clearly to heighten the meaning.

That is specially true of Mireille Delunsch in the title-role, golden-toned and deeply affecting in her great aria, *O malheureuse Iphigénie!*. Simon Keenlyside as Oreste is hardly less idiomatic and characterful, with his sharply focused baritone. Yann Peuron as Pylade and Laurent Maouri as Thoas complete an outstanding team. Balance of merits between Minkowski and Pearlman could not be closer, and there is also the outstanding Gardiner version, which despite using modern instruments combines many of the merits of both.

With an excellent cast, led by Christine Goerke radiantly pure-toned in the title-role, Martin Pearlman directs his Boston forces in a fresh, direct reading of the last of Gluck's Reform operas, which unaffectedly brings out the dramatic bite as well as the beauty. Pearlman's choice of speeds is never extreme, always natural, and, besides Goerke, Rodney Gilfry as Oreste and Vinson Cole as Pylade with clean, heady tenor tone are both excellent. An excellent, safe choice for anyone wanting this masterpiece in a period performance.

Orfeo ed Euridice (complete).

*** Ph. 434 093-2 (2). Ragin, McNair, Sieden, Monteverdi Ch., E. Bar. Soloists, Gardiner.

(M)*** EMI CDC5 56885-2 (2). Hendricks, Von Otter, Fournier, Monteverdi Ch., Lyon Opera O, Gardiner.

(M) *** Erato 2292 45864-2 (2). J. Baker, Speiser, Gale, Glyndebourne Ch., LPO, Leppard.

*** Teldec 4509 98418-2 (2). Larmore, Upshaw, Hagley, San Francisco Op. Ch. & O, Runnicles.

(M) **(*) RCA 74321 32238-2 (2). Lipovšek, Popp, Kaufmann, Bav. R. Ch., Munich R. O, Hager.

Gardiner's newest set for Philips could not be more sharply contrasted with the earlier recording he made for EMI in 1989. Then he was persuaded at the Lyon Opéra to record the Berlioz edition, in French. But all along Gardiner has much preferred the tautness of the original, Vienna version in Italian, which here on Philips he presents with a bite and sense of drama both totally in period and deeply expressive. The element of sensuousness, not least in the beautiful singing of the counter-tenor, Derek Lee Ragin, in the title-role, complements the Elysian beauty Gardiner finds in such passages as the introduction to *Che puro ciel*. Sylvia McNair as Euridice and Cyndia Sieden as Amor complete Gardiner's outstanding solo team. One's only regret is that the set does not provide as a supplement such numbers written for Paris as *The Dance of the Blessed Spirits*.

EMI have reissued Gardiner's earlier, 1989 recording of the Berlioz edition of Gluck's opera sung in French. It is now at mid-price and many will be glad to have this set, which aimed at combining the best of both the Vienna and Paris versions, although he omits the celebratory ballet at the end of the opera. Anne Sophie von Otter is a superb Orphée, dramatically most convincing. The masculine forthrightness of her singing matches the urgency of Gardiner's direction; and both Barbara Hendricks as Euridice and Brigitte Fournier as Amour are also excellent. The chorus is Gardiner's own Monteverdi Choir, superbly clean and stylish, and the recording is full and well-balanced. However, his newest set, for Philips, is even finer (even though once again he does not include the ballet sequence).

The Erato version of *Orfeo ed Euridice*, directly based on the Glyndebourne production in which Dame Janet Baker made her very last stage appearance in opera, was recorded in 1982. Leppard presents the score with freshness and power, indeed with toughness. Nowhere is that clearer than in the great scene leading up to the aria, *Che farò*, where Dame Janet commandingly conveys the genuine bitterness and anger of Orpheus at Eurydice's death. Elisabeth Speiser as Eurydice and Elizabeth Gale as Amor are both disappointing but, as in the theatre, the result is a complete and moving experience centring round a great performance from Dame Janet. The complete ballet-postlude is included, delightful celebration music. The recording has been enhanced in the CD transfer, bright and vivid without edginess. At mid-price this makes a clear first choice.

Donald Runnicles also conducts a performance based on the 1869 Berlioz edition, generally adopting speeds a degree broader than those preferred by Gardiner in his EMI set, and with a smoother style. Jennifer Larmore makes a strong and positive Orphée, brilliant in the aria which in this edition ends Act I, rich and warm in rather broad treatment of the big aria, *J'ai perdu mon Eurydice*. Next to von Otter for Gardiner she sounds very feminine, and not quite as flexible. Dawn Upshaw is a charming Eurydice, and Alison Hagley a sweet-toned L'Amour, though she is balanced very backwardly, as is the chorus at times in what is otherwise a good recording. Unlike Gardiner, but like Leppard on Erato, Runnicles includes ballet music at the end.

Hager's Munich version brings a good, enjoyable, middle-of-the-road performance. Marjana Lipovšek has a beautiful, rich mezzo inclined to fruitiness, which yet in this breeches role is well able to characterize Orfeo strongly and positively. So *Che farò* is warm and direct in its expressiveness. Lucia Popp makes a delightful Euridice and Julie Kaufmann, though less distinctive, is fresh and bright as Amor. The chorus, on the heavyweight side, adds to the power of the performance, which uses the 1762 Vienna version of the score, though with instrumental numbers added from the Paris version. The libretto has the full Italian text without translation.

Orfeo ed Euridice (abridged version).

(B) (***) Dutton Lab. mono CDEA 5015. Ferrier, Ayars, Vlachopoulos, Glyndebourne Festival Ch., Southern PO, Stiedry.

Recorded in 1947 after the early post-war staging of the opera at Glyndebourne, this hour-long collection of excerpts concentrates on the contribution of Kathleen Ferrier in the title-role, giving a very vivid idea of her darkly intense reading. Stiedry keeps a taut rein on the performance while letting Ferrier emerge in full expressiveness. So the climactic aria, *Che farò*, is much faster than in Ferrier's later recording in English, but no less moving in context. In their brief contributions, Ann Ayars as Euridice and Zoë Vlachopoulos as Amor sing with clean precision. No text is provided; otherwise, this is an outstanding disc. The Dutton transfers are superb, offering astonishingly vivid and immediate sound.

Arias from: Iphigénie en Tauride; Orphée et Eurydice; Paride e Elena.

(N) *** Erato 8573 85768-2 . Graham, OAE, Bickett – MOZART: Arias from: *La clemenza di Tito; Idomeneo; Lucio Silla; Le nozze di Figaro.* ***

Masterly as is Susan Graham's singing of Mozart, in a wide range of arias, her Gluck performances are if anything even more revelatory, making one of the outstanding recital discs of recent years. These are all characters that she has portrayed on stage, and the characterization and ease with French words could not be more compelling, particularly in the three contrasted *Iphigénie Arias*. The voice is creamily beautiful, and though the best known of these items, Orpheus's *J'ai perdu mon Eurydice*, is on the slow side, Graham sustains her line flawlessly. Polished playing and well-balanced sound.

Arias: Orfeo ed Euridice: Che farò; Che puro ciel. Telemàco: Se per entro.

*** Virgin VC5 45365-2. Daniels, OAE, Bicket – MOZART; HANDEL: *Arias.* ***

Even in a generation that has produced an extraordinary crop of fine counter-tenors, the American David Daniels stands out for the clear beauty and imagination of his singing. The best-known items here – the two principal solos from Gluck's *Orfeo* – are done with a tender expressiveness that matches any performance by a mezzo, with Daniels's natural timbre, at once pure and warm, completely avoiding counter-tenor hoot. Not only that, his placing of the voice is flawless, with the florid singing equally impressive in its brilliance and precision.

GODARD, Benjamin (1849–95)

Cello Sonata in D min., Op. 104; 2 Pieces for Cello & Piano, Op. 61.

*** Hyp. CDA 66888. Lidström, Forsberg – BOELLMANN: *Cello Sonata in A min.* etc. ***

An interesting and compellingly played disc of off-beat repertoire. Benjamin Godard was a pupil of Vieuxtemps and his *D minor Sonata* is very much in the Schumann–Brahms tradition and is beautifully crafted and powerfully shaped, as are the *Aubade and Scherzo*. Mats Lidström and Bengt Forsberg play with such passion and conviction that they almost persuade you that this piece is worthy to rank alongside the Brahms sonatas. The recording is just a trifle on the close side, but it produces eminently satisfactory results. Strongly recommended.

GODOWSKY, Leopold (1870–1938)

53 Studies, Based on the Etudes of Chopin, Op. 10 & Op. 25 (complete).

✪ *** Hyp. CDA 67411/2. Hamelin.

Ian Hobson offers a selection of these legendary pieces on the Arabesque label and Carlo Grante has done them all in masterly fashion on Altarus, but Marc-André Hamelin supersedes them both. Godowsky's celebrated studies are of unbelievable difficulty, and arouse both excitement and admiration and, in some places, horror that some of their contortions should have been attempted at all. Godowsky's *tour de force* is realized with supreme virtuosity and – more to the point – artistry by Marc-André Hamelin. It is quite stunning, an extraordinary achievement even by Hamelin's own standards. No one with an interest in the piano should pass this by.

GOEDICKE, Alexander (1877–1957)

Concertstück in D (for piano and orchestra), Op. 11.

**(*) Hyp. CDA 66877. Coombs, BBC Scottish SO, Brabbins – GLAZUNOV: *Piano Concertos Nos. 1 & 2.* **(*)

Alexander Goedicke's *Concertstück* is far from negligible, both in its melodic invention and in its musical structure. Stephen Coombs is a brilliant and sympathetic interpreter of this music and the BBC Scottish Symphony Orchestra under Martyn Brabbins give every support. The recording is too reverberant – and this perhaps inhibits a full three-star recommendation.

GOEHR, Alexander (born 1932)

Metamorphosis/Dance, Op. 36; (i) Romanza for Cello & Orchestra, Op. 24.

(M) *** Uni UKCD 2039. (i) Welsh; RLPO, Atherton.

Moray Welsh plays the *Romanza* warmly and stylishly. *Metamorphosis/Dance*, inspired by the Circe episode in the *Odyssey*, is a sequence of elaborate variations, full of strong rhythmic interest. The performance is excellent.

GOETZ, Hermann (1840–76)

Francesca da Rimini: Overture; Spring Overture, Op. 15; (i) Nenie, Op. 10; (i–ii) Psalm 137, Op. 14.

(B) ** CPO 999 316-2. (i) N. German R. Ch.; (ii) Stiller; N. German R. PO, Hanover, Albert.

Hermann Goetz was born in the same year as Tchaikovsky. The best piece here is *Nenie*, which has a strong sense of purpose and a genuine lyrical flow. The *Francesca da Rimini Overture* comes from an opera its composer left unfinished. The musical language is very much in the tradition of Mendelssohn and Spohr, but the invention is of some quality, even if a little bland. Good performances from all concerned and decently balanced, well-rounded sound.

GOLIGHTLY, David (born 1947)

Symphony No. 1; 3 Seascapes.

(N) *** ASC CDCS 38. Prague PO, Sutherland.

It may seem extraordinary, but David Golightly's *Symphony No. 1*, written over a period of four years, was commissioned and dedicated to Middlesbrough Football Team and its Chairman, Steve Gibson. Essentially programmatic, it is effectively wrought with a first movement founded on a rhythmic ostinato (*Resoluto marcato*) 'for those who strive, knock hard on the door of fate', the scherzo reflecting the

lively optimism of visits to Wembley, the eloquent and imaginatively scored slow movement reflecting the pain of defeat in an idiom that reminded the writer a little of the spacious string writing of Howard Hanson.

The finale is a jaunty populist march, exotically scored, with the two-part structure reflecting the two halves of the game. The orchestral fanfares depict the team scoring. It is a happy extrovert inspiration and receives a fine performance under Gavin Sutherland in Prague and a full-blooded recording. The three *Seascapes* further demonstrate Golightly's vivid orchestral skill, using well-known folk-themes, like *Shenandoah*. The disc is available from ABC Records in Macclesfield, Cheshire (Phone 01625 423605; Fax 423802).

GOLDMARK, Karl (1830–1915)

Violin Concerto in A min., Op. 28.

✪ *** Delos DE 3156. Nai-Yuan Hu, Seattle SO, Schwarz – BRUCH: *Violin Concerto No. 2.* ***
*** EMI CDC7 47846-2. Perlman, Pittsburgh SO, Previn – KORNGOLD: *Violin Concerto.* ***
(BB) *** Naxos 8.553579. Tsu, Razumovsky Sinfonia, Yu Long – KORNGOLD: *Violin Concerto.* ***

(i) Violin Concerto in A minor, Op. 28. Overture, Prometheus Bound, Op. 38.

(N) *** EMI CDC5 56955-2. Sarah Chang, Cologne Gürzenich PO, Conlon.

Sarah Chang, the latest to take up the Goldmark *Violin Concerto*, gives a sensitive and virtuoso account. James Conlon is supportive and also provides a rarity, the overture *Prometheus Bound* as a fill-up. Excellent recording quality, but this is not a first choice.

The Taiwanese soloist Nai-Yuan Hu (pronounced Nigh-Yen Who) makes an outstanding début on CD with a coupling of two underrated concertos which on his responsively lyrical bow are made to sound like undiscovered masterpieces. The Goldmark is a tuneful and warm-hearted concerto that needs just this kind of songful, inspirational approach: Hu shapes the melodies so that they ravishingly take wing and soar. Moreover, Schwarz and the Seattle orchestra share a real partnership with their soloist, and provide a full, detailed backcloth in a natural concert-hall framework.

Not surprisingly, the concerto is also beautifully played by Perlman, whose effortless virtuosity and strong profile in the bravura passage-work are combined with striking lyrical poise. In the first-movement cadenza he is unsurpassed. However, the EMI balance places the violin in a forward spotlight so that orchestral detail does not always register as it should: in this respect the Delos alternative is in almost every way preferable.

Vera Tsu is another outstanding soloist. Her tone is rich, bringing out to the full the ripe romanticism of the Goldmark *Concerto*. Her attack is fearless in the many bravura passages, so that the dance rhythms of the dance-finale have a rare sparkle, and her hushed playing in the central slow movement at a very broad speed movingly demonstrates her inner concentration, helped by the equally beautiful, finely varied playing of the Razumovsky Sinfonia of Bratislava. Rich, full, open sound.

Rustic Wedding Symphony, Op. 26.

(M) *** Van. (ADD) 08 6151 71 [OVC 5002]. Utah SO, Abavanel – ENESCU: *Romanian Rhapsodies Nos. 1–2.* **

Rustic Wedding Symphony, Op. 26; Overtures: In Italy, Op. 49; In the Spring, Op. 36.

(BB) **(*) Naxos 8.550745. Nat. SO of Ireland, Gunzenhauser.

Rustic Wedding Symphony, Op. 26; Sakuntala Overture, Op. 13.

*** ASV CDDCA 791. RPO, Butt.

Goldmark's *Rustic Wedding Symphony* opens with a distinctly rustic theme on the lower strings, which when taken up by the horns (with woodwind birdsong overhead) is as magical as any passage in the romantic symphonic repertory. The hazily romantic evocation of a summer garden which forms the slow movement leads to a boisterous dance finale, with genial injections of fugato. Yondani Butt and the RPO clearly enjoy themselves. The recording has brightly lit violins, but plenty of bloom on the woodwind, and the only miscalculation of balance concerns the trombone entry in the first movement, which is too blatant and too loud. Otherwise this is in every way enjoyable. The *Overture Sakuntala* opens impressively but does not quite sustain its 18 minutes. Butt presents it with persuasive vigour and lyrical feeling, and does not shirk the melodrama.

The Utah acoustic is expansive and the music certainly blossoms here, for the playing has a pleasing freshness and spontaneity. Abravanel's approach is direct. There is plenty of warmth and the woodwind bring a Beechamesque charm to the inner movements. *In the Garden* is as deeply felt as anyone could want, and altogether, with its attractive Enescu coupling (recorded not quite so glowingly), this stands high in the list of recommendations, irrespective of price.

Gunzenhauser gives a fresh, bright-eyed account. He takes both the opening movement and the Andante (*In the Garden*) appreciably faster than does Butt, and he loses something in poise and spacious eloquence in consequence. But the overall performance is spontaneous and enjoyable. It is well recorded and, although the violins sound thin, that is almost certainly not the fault of the engineers. Of the two jaunty overtures, *In Italy* is especially vivacious and sparkling.

Symphony No. 2 in E, Op. 35; In Italy Overture, Op. 49; Prometheus Bound, Op. 38.

*** ASV CDDCA 934. Philh. O, Butt

Goldmark's *Second Symphony* is a highly confident piece with a strong opening movement, an ambivalent but appealing Andante, a vivaciously delicate Scherzo, which is Mendelssohn undiluted, and a characteristically folksy, dance-like finale. Yondani Butt has the work's full measure. The Lisztian *Promtheus Bound* on the other hand is overlong and melodramatic, and the main allegro is routine in its working out. Yet it has some winning lyrical ideas and Butt does his very best for it. The *Italian Overture* is genuinely

vivacious, though not especially Italianate: it has a rather beautiful nocturnal sequence as a central episode. The ASV recording is in every way excellent.

String Quartet in B flat, Op. 8. (i) String Quintet in A min., Op. 9.

**(*) ASV CDDCA 1071. Fourth Dimension String Qt; (i) with Smith.

Goldmark's *String Quartet in B flat* is a fluent, beautifully fashioned piece, very much in the Schumann and Mendelssohn tradition, though one is in no doubt that the musical argument is guided by a sense of purpose. The *String Quintet* is an even stronger piece, sure in its feeling for musical movement and with some good ideas. The Fourth Dimension String Quartet makes its début, with David Smith as the second cello in the quintet. Decent performances, though the tonal blend leaves something to be desired, and one would welcome greater richness of timbre.

GOLDSCHMIDT, Berthold
(1903–96)

(i) *String Quartets Nos. 2–3;* (ii) *Letzte Kapitel; Belsatzar.*

*** Largo LC 5115. (i) Mandelring Qt; (ii) Marks; Ars-Nova Ens., Berlin, Schwarz.

Berthold Goldschmidt was hounded from Nazi Germany in 1935 and settled in London. This disc collects his *Letzte Kapitel* for speaker and an instrumental ensemble, very much in the style of Kurt Weill, and the *Second Quartet*, which has something of the fluency of Hindemith. It is an excellently fashioned piece with a rather powerful slow movement, an elegy subtitled *Folia*. The CD is completed by *Belsatzar*, an *a cappella* setting of Heine, and the *Third Quartet*, a remarkable achievement for an 86-year-old, the product of a cultured and thoughtful musical mind. The performances are dedicated, the recordings satisfactory.

OPERA

(i) *Beatrice Cenci* (opera; complete). (ii) Songs: *Clouds; Nebelweben; Ein Rosenzweig.*

*** Sony S2K 66836 (2). Estes, Jones, Alexander, Kimm, Rose, Wottrich, Berlin R. Ch., German SO, Berlin, Zagrosek; (ii) Vermillion, composer.

Commissioned to write an opera for the Festival of Britain in 1951, Berthold Goldschmidt responded with this richly imaginative rendering of a melodramatic play of Shelley, in which Beatrice is portrayed not as a murderess but as the victim of an evil father. Much of the most moving music involves the relationship of Beatrice and her mother, Lucia, with Della Jones strongly cast against Roberta Alexander in the title-role, singing radiantly. Her big final aria brings the most moving moment of all. Simon Estes sings well, but is not evil-sounding enough to convey the full villainy of the father. Vividly recorded and powerfully conducted by Lothar Zagrosek, the set makes generous amends for the work's long neglect. The songs, with Iris Vermillion accompanied by the nonagenarian composer, make a delightful bonus.

GOOSSENS, Eugene (1893–1962)

Concertino for Double String Orchestra, Op. 47; Fantasy for 9 Wind Instruments, Op. 36; Symphony No. 2, Op. 62.

*** ABC 8.770013. Sydney SO, Handley.

The *Second Symphony* is an important work – and something of a discovery: its material is strong and the imaginative landscape it inhabits quite individual. There is a dark, Nordic feeling about the opening and a fertility of invention in the Scherzo that recalls Prokofiev. The *Concertino* is more effective for full strings than in its chamber form (see below), and the *Fantasy for Wind Instruments* (1924) has a touch of Stravinsky and Les Six. Expert playing from the ABC Sydney Orchestra of which Goossens was conductor in the 1950s, and well-prepared and meticulously shaped readings from Vernon Handley. Recommended with enthusiasm.

Concertino for String Octet, Op. 47; Phantasy Sextet, Op. 37.

*** Chan. 9472. ASMF Chamber Ens. – BRIDGE: *String Sextet.* ***

The *Concertino for String Octet, Op. 47* was subsequently scored for double string orchestra (see above). It has brightness and vitality, and is expertly laid out for the instruments, as is the 1923 *Phantasy Sextet, Op. 37*, commissioned by Elisabeth Sprague Coolidge. This is intelligent and inventive music, well played by the Academy of St Martin-in-the-Field and eminently well recorded by the ever-enterprising Chandos.

GÓRECKI, Henryk (born 1933)

(i) *Harpsichord Concerto;* (ii) *Little Requiem for a Polka (Kleines Requiem für eine Polka);* (iii) *Good Night (In Memoriam Michael Vyner)* for soprano, alto flute, 3 tam-tams and piano.

*** None. 7559 79362-2. L. Sinf.; (i) Zinman; (ii) Chojnacka, cond. Stenz; (iii) Upshaw, Bell, Constable, Hockings.

The *Little Requiem* (1993) opens with a single quiet bell-stroke; a piano (John Constable) then engages in a tranquil dialogue with the violins, to be rudely interrupted by a burst of bell-ringing; the energetic, marcato *Allegro impetutoso* follows. The piece ends with a raptly sustained elegiac *Adagio*, still dominated by the quietly assertive tolling bells.The two-movement *Harpsichord Concerto*, written a decade earlier, combines soloist and strings in a vibrant, jangly ménage. *Good Night* is nocturnally serene. The soprano voice enters only in the third movement, with a cantilena to Shakespeare's words from *Hamlet*: 'Good night ... and flights of angels sing thee to thy rest!'. Both here and in the *Little Requiem* the very atmospheric recording brings an added dimension to the communication from performers who are obviously totally committed to the composer's cause.

Symphony No. 3 (Symphony of Sorrowful Songs), Op. 36.

*** Elektra None. 7559 79282-2. Upshaw, London Sinf., Zinman.

Symphony No. 3 (Symphony of Sorrowful Songs), Op. 36; 3 Pieces in the Olden Style.

(BB) *** Naxos 8.550822. Kilanowicz, Polish Nat. RSO, Wit.
**(*) Koch Schwann 311041. Woytowicz, Berlin RSO, Kamirski; or Warsaw CO, Teutsch;

Scored for strings and piano with soprano solo in each of the three movements, all predominantly slow, Górecki's *Symphony No. 3* sets three laments taking the theme of motherhood. The first movement, nearly half an hour long, resolves on the central setting of a fifteenth-century text from a monastic collection. The second movement incongruously brings a switch to a sensuously beautiful idiom, with the soprano solo soaring radiantly. The third movement is the setting of a folksong with a two-chord ostinato as accompaniment, concluding in a passage of total peace. The Sinfonietta's fine performance, beautifully recorded, is crowned by the radiant singing of Dawn Upshaw.

Zofia Kilanowicz on Naxos has also obviously become immersed in the word-settings. In the work's closing section, with its hint of a gentle but remorseless tolling bell, Wit achieves a mood of simple serenity, even forgiveness. The *Three Pieces in Olden Style* make a fine postlude, the second with its dance figurations, the third with its fierce tremolando violins, like shafts of bright light, suddenly resolving to a very positive ending. All in all, this seems in many ways a 'best buy'.

The Koch performance is also most eloquent, with Woytowicz again completely at home in her solo role, but it is no more moving than either of the other versions and the analogue recording is not appreciably finer than that offered on Naxos.

Genesis I (Elementi per tre archi); Sonata for 2 Violins, Op. 10; String Quartets Nos. 1 (Already it is Dusk), Op. 62; 2 (Quasi una fantasia), Op. 64.

*** Olympia (ADD) OCD 375. Silesian Qt.

This record (74 minutes) contains all Górecki's chamber music written so far. The opening of the *Double Violin Sonata* is harsh and spiky and, although calm soon descends, it is an uneasy calm and the restlessness soon reasserts itself. *Genesis* is full of extraordinary effects: if this is the beginning of life, the bubblings and glissandi suggest a volatile primeval melting pot. The *First Quartet* opens with an emphatic chord which diminuendos; then mysticism takes over, with emphatic chordal interruptions; later there is a nagging ostinato which produces a climax of considerable power. The *Second Quartet* begins in an atmosphere of utter desolation; the effect is of a desperate plodding journey to nowhere. The *Arioso* slow movement begins in a mood of piercing despair. The finale moves on with a remorseless, toccata-like insistence, then the slow plodding of the work's opening reappears and, gradually becoming less insistent, returns the music to infinity. The playing throughout this collection combines power and intensity. The recording is of very high quality. The composer was present and there is something special about these performances.

VOCAL MUSIC

(i) *Miserere, Op. 44; Amen, Op. 35; Euntes ibant et flebant, Op. 32;* (ii) *Wuslo moja (My Vistula, Grey Vistula), Op. 46; Szeroka woda (Broad Waters): Choral Suite of Folksongs, Op. 39 (Oh, our River Narew; Oh, when in Powistle; Oh, Johnny, Johnny; She picked wild roses; Broad waters).*

*** None. 7559 79348-2. (i) Chicago Symphony Ch. & Lyric Op. Ch., Nelson; (ii) Lyra Chamber Ch., Ding.

Górecki's powerful *Miserere* was prompted by the political upheaval in Poland in 1981. Górecki set a text of only five words: *Domine Deus noster, Miserere nobis*; although the work's span is ambitious, it is sustained by profound intensity of feeling. The combined Chicago choirs maintain the sombrely atmospheric opening pianissimo with impressive concentration, and the dynamic climax of the piece, when the combined choirs sing in ten parts, is very compelling. The following *Euntes ibant et flebant* (for unaccompanied chorus) is simpler, more serene. The five folksong settings are also essentially expressive (even *Oh, Johnny, Johnny* is marked *Molto lento – dolce cantabile*) and all are harmonically rich. They are beautifully sung by the smaller group. The recording, made in the Church of St Mary of the Angels in Chicago, is admirable.

GOSSEC, François-Joseph (1734–1829)

Symphonies: in E flat; in D (Pastorella), Op. 5/2–3; in E flat; in F, Op. 12/5–6; in D (1776).

(N) *** Chan. 9661. L. Mozart Players, Bamert.

François-Joseph Gossec, composer of a remarkably forward-looking *Requiem*, also wrote some three dozen symphonies, the first dating from the 1750s and his last from 1809. His style is often close to Haydn – witness the delightful chirping second subject of the first movement of the *F major*, Op. 12/6 (published in 1769), the tenderly lyrical slow movement using muted strings and the jovial finale. The two symphonies from Op. 5 date from seven years earlier and here the scoring, which includes clarinets, brings a Mozartian elegance, besides a gallant charm in the *Romanza* second movement. The stately *Adagio* of the so-called *Pastorella*, however, looks backwards in its classical poise. In some ways most striking of all is the later three-movement D major work, with its striding opening theme, boldly Haydnesque, gentle central lament and cheerful finale. Its full scoring, which includes trumpets, shows a fine feeling for orchestral colour. But these are all highly enjoyable and rewarding works, especially when played with such spirit and finesse and so beautifully recorded.

Requiem (Missa pro defunctis).

(N) (BB) *** Warner Apex 8573 89234-2. Degelin, De Reyghere, Crook, Widmer, Maastrich Conservatory Ch. Ch., Musica Polyphonica, Devos.

Requiem (Missa pro defuntis); (i) *Symphony à 17.*

(N) (BB) *** Naxos 8.554750-51 (2). Invernizzi, Arruabarrena, Crook, Darbellay, Gruppo Vocale Cantemus, Svizzera Rad. Ch., Svizzera Italiana O, Hauschild, or (i) Fasolis.

The Belgium composer François-Joseph Gossec was a bold innovator, some of his writing even foreshadowing Berlioz. The opening of this 80-minute *Requiem* of 1760, with its ominous timpani and string-writing, is quite commanding, and the ensuing movements have a period mixture of baroque and classical writing, some interesting harmonic progressions and certainly some beautiful writing. It is in passages such as the *Mors stupebit et natura*, with its tremolo strings punctuated by the timpani, that one realizes how forward-looking this composer was. The performance, using modern instruments, is enjoyable, and generally well sung and played, though it's possible to imagine that Minkowski, for example, would make it more exciting. The sound is good – the San Lorenzo Cathedral doesn't produce an acoustic that is too wallowy. The 27-minute *Symphony* makes an enjoyable bonus, and this set is well worth investigating at the price, with full texts and translations included, along with informative sleeve-notes.

The alternative version from Devos uses period instruments and has the advantage of being on a single CD. It is also very enjoyable and has plenty of commitment and gusto. The soloists (with Howard Crook common to both versions) are good without being outstanding, but the chorus is impressive, with fine authentic-sounding brass support at the *Mors stupebit*. The recording too is excellent, so if you are not worried about the symphony and don't mind the absence of text and translation, this could be a better buy.

GOTTSCHALK, Louis (1829–69)

Grand Fantasia Triumfal for Piano & Orchestra.

(M) *** Decca 430 726-2. Ortiz, RPO, Atzmon – ADDINSELL: *Warsaw Concerto* ***; GERSHWIN: *Rhapsody* **(*); LISZT: *Hungarian Fantasia* ***; LITOLFF: *Scherzo.* ***

Gottschalk's *Grand Fantasia* has naïvety, and a touch of vulgarity too, but the performers here give it an account which nicely combines flair and a certain elegance, and the result is a distinct success.

(i; ii) *Grande Tarantelle for Piano & Orchestra;* (ii) *Symphony No. 1 (A Night in the Tropics);* (iii) *Music for one piano, four hands: L'étincelle; La gallina; La jota aragonesa; Marche de nuit; Orfa; Printemps d'amour; Radieuse; Réponds-moi; Ses yeux; Souvenirs d'Andalousie; Tremolo.* (2 pianos): *The Union (concert paraphrase on national airs).*

(M) *** Van. (ADD) 08.4051 71. (i) Nibley; (ii) Utah SO, Abravanel; (iii) List with Lewis or Werner.

With nearly 77 minutes of music this well-recorded Vanguard reissue makes an ideal introduction to Gottschalk's music. The *Grande Tarantelle* has a very catchy main theme; the two-movement *Night in the Tropics* uses its title of 'symphony' very loosely. The second movement is a kind of samba, rhythmically very winning. The music for piano, four hands, is played with flair and scintillating upper tessitura. The opening arrangement of *La jota aragonesa* heads an ear-tickling programme, with a touch of wit in the piece called *Tremolo*. When the participants move to two pianos for *The Union* concert paraphrase, the acoustic expands and the effect is properly grand. The orchestral recordings date from 1962, the piano pieces from 1976, and the sound is excellent throughout.

PIANO MUSIC

Complete solo piano music: 'An American Composer, bon Dieu!'

Volume 1: *Le Bananier (Chanson nègre), Op. 5; Le Banjo; Chanson de Gitano; Columbia (Caprice américain), Op. 34; Danza, Op. 33; Le Mancenillier, Op. 11; Mazurka; Minuit à Seville, Op. 30; Romanze; Souvenir de la Havana (Grand caprice de concert), Op. 39; Souvenir de Porto Rico, marche des Gibaros, Op. 31; Les Yeux créoles (Danse cubaine), Op. 37; Union (Paraphrase de concert), Op. 48.*

*** Hyp. CDA 66459. Martin.

Gottschalk invented the conception of the composer/recitalist in America, just as Liszt had in Europe. As a touring virtuoso he had great audience appeal, and if his music is lightweight it is well crafted and tuneful, paying homage to both Liszt and Chopin. Its exotic folk-influences are drawn colloquially and naturally from the Deep South, with syncopated rhythms the strongest feature.

Philip Martin's continuing complete survey on Hyperion is in every way distinguished. He is naturally sympathetic to the transatlantic idioms, yet he treats the music as part of the romantic mainstream, bringing out its various derivations. He plays with elegance, brilliance, style and above all spontaneity. He is very well recorded in an ideal acoustic. In Volume 1 he closes with the celebrated and grandiose *Union (Paraphrase de concert)*, which Gottschalk, a dedicated abolitionist, played for President Lincoln and his First Lady in 1864.

Volume 2: *Ballade; Berceuse, Op. 47; Caprice polka; Grand scherzo, Op. 57; La jota aragonesa (Caprice espagnol), Op. 14; Manchega (Etude de concert), Op. 38; Marche de nuit, Op. 17; Miserere du Trovatore (paraphrase de concert), Op. 52; Pasquinade (caprice), Op. 59; Polkas in A flat; in B flat; La Savane (Ballade créole), Op. 3; Scherzo romantique; Souvenirs d'Andalousie (Caprice de concert), Op. 22; Souvenir de Lima (Mazurka), Op. 74; Suis-moi! (Caprice), Op. 45; Ynés.*

*** Hyp. CDA 66697. Martin.

The *Paraphrase of Verdi's Miserere* all but upstages Liszt. One can imagine how the composer's contemporary audiences would have loved its melodrama, while both the *Jota aragonesa* and the similar *Souvenirs d'Andalousie* are a *tour de force* of extrovert dexterity. The *Caprice polka* is polished and sparkling, while the *Souvenir de Lima* returns to

an engagingly Chopinesque idiom. Again, a very good recording.

Volume 3: *Bamboula (Danse des nègres), Op. 2; La Chute des feulles (Nocturne), Op. 42; The Dying Poet (Meditation); Hercule (Grande étude de concert); Murmurs éoliens; O ma charmante, épargnes-moi (Caprice); Gottschalk's Melody; Grand fantaisie triomphale sur l'hymne national Brésilien; The Last Hope; Symphony No. 1 (La Nuit des tropiques)*: 1st movement: *Andante* (arr. Napoleão); *Tournament galop.*

*** Hyp. CDA 66915. Martin.

The Dying Poet and *The Last Hope* (which the composer described tongue in cheek as a '*succès de larmes*' (tears)) are treated with a nice discretion. *Hercule* (given a striking march theme with simple decorative variants) is built to a fine rhetorical climax, as is the slow movement of the *Symphony No. 1* (in this not entirely advantageous transcription). The closing, very orchestral *Tournament galop* is superbly thrown off. It has a Rossinian vivacity, but its roulades are very much Gottschalk's own.

Volume 4: *Apothéose (Grande marche solennelle), Op. 29; La Colombe (petite polka), Op. 49; Fantôme de bonheur (Illusions perdues), Op. 36; Forest Glade Polka (Les Follets), Op. 25; La Gitana (Caprice caractéristique), Op. 35; La Moissonneuse (Mazurka caractéristique), Op. 8; Morte!! (Lamentation), Op. 55; Ossian (2 Ballades), Op. 4/ 1–2; Pensée poétique; Polonia, Op. 35; Reflets du passé, Op. 28; La Scintilla (L'Etincelle: Mazurka sentimentale), Op. 20; Ricordati (Nocturne, méditation, romance), Op. 26; Le Songe d'une nuit d'été (Caprice élégant), Op. 9; Souvenir de Cuba (Mazurka), Op. 75.*

*** Hyp. CDA 67118. Martin.

If you decide to explore this enjoyable Hyperion survey, Volume 4 is a good place to start, for much of its content is little known and every piece is enjoyable. The Lisztian *Le Songe d'une nuit d'été*, the thoughtful *Pensée poétique*, *La Scintilla* (with its iridescence) all have great charm. *Morte!!* brings an elegaic contrast and has a distinctly sentimental ambience. *Polonia* is a jolly peasant dance, while the *Forest Glade polka* curiously anticipates the music of Billy Mayerl, and there is a flamboyant closing *Apothéose*, which takes a fair time to reach its zenith, but proceeds to do so with panache.

Bamboula; Le Bananier; Le Banjo; The Dying Poet; The Last Hope; The Maiden's Blush; Ojos criollos; Pasquinade; La Savane; Souvenir de Porto Rico; Suis-moi!; Tournament galop.

(M) *** Van. (ADD) 08.4050.71 [OVC 4050]. List.

Eugene List made this repertoire very much his own in the USA in the late 1950s and early 1960s, and his performances are second to none. The glittering roulades in *Le Bananier* and *Ojos criollos* are brought off with unaffected brilliance, and the plucking imitations at the close of *The Banjo* are equally successful. The pieces with sentimental titles are more appealing than their names might suggest, and the *Tournament galop* closes the recital at an infectious canter.

The recording dates from 1956 but doesn't sound its age at all: it is very well balanced and realistic.

Piano music for 4 hands: (i) *Le Bananier (Chanson nègre)*, *Op. 5; La Gallina (Danse cubaine), Op. 53; Grande tarantelle, Op. 67; La jota aragonesa (Caprice espagnol), Op. 14; Marche de nuit, Op. 17; Ojos criollos (Danse cubaine – Caprice brillante), Op. 37; Orfa (Grande polka), Op. 71; Printemps d'amour (Mazurka-caprice de concert), Op. 40; Réponds-moi (Danse cubaine), Op. 50; Radieuse (Grand valse de concert), Op. 72; La Scintilla (L'Etincelle – Mazurka sentimentale), Op. 21; Ses yeux (Célèbre polka de concert), Op. 66.* Solo piano music: *Le Banjo; Berceuse* (cradle song); *The Dying Poet* (meditation); *Grand scherzo; The Last Hope* (religious meditation); *Mazurka; Le Mancenillier* (West Indian serenade); *Pasquinade caprice; Scherzo romantique; Souvenirs d'Andalousie; Tournament galop; The Union: Concert Paraphrase on National Airs (The Star Spangled Banner; Yankee Doodle; Hail Columbia).*

(B) ** Nim. NI 7045/6 (2). Marks; (i) with Barrett.

Much of Gottschalk's music exists in alternative two- and four-handed arrangements and Alan Marks and Nerine Barrett make an effervescent Gottschalk partnership in the latter, playing the more dashing pieces to the manner born. The drawback is that this very personable piano duo are recorded – realistically enough – in an empty, resonant hall, and although one adjusts the effect is not advantageous.

The solo recital is still resonant, but not exaggeratedly so, and Alan Marks plays with considerable flair: the *Souvenirs d'Andalousie* glitters with bravura, his felicity of touch and crisp articulation bring much sparkle to the *Grand scherzo* and *Scherzo romantique*, while he sounds like a full orchestra in the *Tournament galop*. Most importantly, there is not a hint of sentimentality in *The Dying Poet* or *The Last Hope*, the composer's most famous piece. For those wanting an inexpensive survey of Gottschalk this Nimbus Double will serve well enough, but the Hyperion series is artistically and sonically preferable.

GOUGH, John (1903–51)

Serenade for Small Orchestra.

*** Chan. 9757. BBC PO, Handley – BAINTON: *Symphony No. 2 in D min.*; CLIFFORD: *Symphony*. ***

John Gough worked for a time as a studio manager or balance engineer in the BBC and was later Pacific Service Music Organizer during the war years. After the war he became a features producer during the period when that BBC department was at the height of its fame. The short but charming *Serenade for Small Orchestra* reveals a genuine creative talent and was written in 1931 for Hubert Clifford's wedding. Exemplary playing and first-rate recorded sound.

GOULD, Morton (1913–96)

Fall River Legend (ballet; complete).

*** Albany TROY 035. Peters, National PO, Rosenstock (with recorded conversation between Agnes de Mille and Morton Gould).

This complete recording of *Fall River Legend* opens dramatically with the Speaker for the Jury reading out the Indictment at the trial, and then the ballet tells the story of Lizzie Borden in flashback. Gould's music has a good deal in common with the folksy writing in Copland's *Appalachian Spring*, and it is given a splendidly atmospheric performance and recording by the New York orchestra under Rosenstock. There is also a 26-minute discussion on the creation of the ballet between Agnes de Mille and the composer.

Fall River Legend: Suite; Spirituals for String Choir & Orchestra.

(M) *** Mercury (ADD) [432 016-2]. Eastman-Rochester SO, Hanson – BARBER: *Medea: Suite*. ***

The composer's orchestral suite from the ballet is brightly played by the Eastman-Rochester Orchestra under the highly sympathetic Howard Hanson, who also gives an outstandingly vibrant account of the *Spirituals*. The 1959/60 Mercury recording has astonishing clarity, range and presence.

2 Marches for Orchestra.

(M) (***) Cala mono CACD 0526. NBC SO, Stokowski – DEBUSSY: *Prélude à l'après-midi d'un faune; La Cathédrale engloutie* (**(*)); HOLST: *The Planets*. (***)

These two stirring wartime marches were 'written in tribute to two of our gallant allies': the first is Chinese in character (complete with marching effects), the second colourfully employs two Red Army songs. An enjoyable end to a fascinating Stokowski disc and the sound, emanating from an NBC broadcast from March 1943, is fully acceptable.

Spirituals for String Choir & Orchestra.

*** Everest (ADD) EVC 9003. LSO, Susskind – COPLAND: *Appalachian Spring* ***; GERSHWIN: *American in Paris*. **(*)

It is unexpected to find an English performance of this essentially American piece, the more so as it has never been bettered, not even by the composer himself. The slow movement is really moving and *A Little Bit of Sin* is wittily pungent, while the wide-ranging recording (brightly lit in a transatlantic way) looks after the dramatic needs of *Protest* and the ambivalent exuberance of *Jubilee*. The couplings are hardly less welcome.

GOUNOD, Charles (1818–93)

Faust: Ballet Music & Waltz.

(B) **(*) Ph. Duo (ADD) 438 763-2. Rotterdam PO, Zinman – DELIBES: *Coppélia*; CHOPIN: *Les Sylphides*. **(*)

If without quite the panache of a Beecham, David Zinman's account of the *Faust Ballet Music* springs readily to life: it has polish and elegance. Very good (1980) recording in a warm acoustic ensures the listener's aural pleasure, making this collection a genuine bargain.

Symphonies Nos. 1 in D; 2 in E flat.

*** ASV CDDCA 981. O of St John's, Smith Square, Lubbock.

Symphonies Nos. 1 in D; 2 in E flat; Faust (Ballet Music): Suite.

*** Ph. 462 125-2. ASMF, Marriner.

Gounod's two symphonies – delightful, lyrical works full of sparkling invention – were written in quick succession when he was in his mid-thirties, his only extended orchestral works. They make an outstanding coupling in these splendid performances from Sir Neville Marriner and the Academy of St Martin-in-the-Fields, which – as the Philips disc also aptly includes the *Faust* ballet music – is now a clear leader in the field. The ASMF playing has sparkle, elegance and style, the recordings have clarity and presence.

Until now we have recommended the beautifully sprung and subtly phrased performances from John Lubbock and the Orchestra of St John's. In their lightness and transparency they too bring out the charm of the writing; Lubbock's care for detail and the refreshingly polished playing is matched by a pervading warmth. We hope, in view of the latest competition, ASV will decide to reissue the Gounod pairing on the Quicksilva label, when it would again be fully competitive.

Michel Plasson's mid-price coupling with the Orchestre du Capitole de Toulouse (on EMI CDM7 63949-2) remains eminently satisfactory. But the best is the enemy of the good, and in terms of both artistry and sound quality, it is no match for the Marriner and Lubbock discs.

Petite symphonie in B flat (for 9 wind instruments).

(M) *** Chan. (ADD) 6543. Athena Ens. – IBERT: *3 Pièces brèves;* POULENC: *Sextet.* ***

An astonishingly fresh and youthful work, the *Petite symphonie* in fact has impeccable craftsmanship and is witty and civilized. It makes ideal listening at the end of the day, and its charm is irresistible in a performance as full of *joie de vivre* as that provided by the Athena group, who are particularly light-hearted in the finale.

(i) Petite symphonie in B flat for Wind; (ii) Messe solennelle de Sainte-Cécile.

(N) (BB) ** EMI Encore CDE5 74730-2. (i) Hallé O (members), Barbirolli; (ii) Lorengar, Hoppe, Crass, Duclos Ch., Paris Conservatoire O, Hartemann.

Barbirolli's account (from the 1960s) of Gounod's witty and charming *Petite symphonie* still sounds well. The performance has plenty of character, yet a suitably light touch, and Barbirolli's affection is obvious. The Hallé players are in good form.

One also welcomes back to the catalogue Jean-Claude Hartemann's performance of this highly attractive Victorian mass. The *Credo* is the part to sample first – a rollicking

setting with more than a hint of a Beatles tune, and Gounod, having invented such a good tune, has no inhibitions about using it. Whatever the rhythms of the words he brings it back whenever he wants, ending with a very secular-sounding augmentation, almost in Hollywood style. If that is the most vulgar movement, it is also the most enjoyable. The rest is agreeable without being terribly memorable. This Paris performance is capable without being very distinguished and the recording is only fair, but at super-budget price this disc is worth exploring.

String Quartet Nos. 1 in D (Le Petit Quatuor); 2 in A; 3 in F.

*** Audivis V 4798. Daniel Qt.

In his last years, having finally abandoned opera, Gounod turned to these string quartets. They are really quite a find, and provide (though in a very different way) almost as much delight as the early symphonies. There are Mendelssohnian echoes in all three works, not least in the Scherzos, but this is more than just charming music, with Beethoven among the composer's models. The slow movement of the *A major* is quite captivating but then so are most of the movements. Outstanding performances from the Daniel Quartet and truthful recording.

Mélodies and songs: L'absent; The arrow and the song; Au rossignol; Ave Maria; Boléro; Ma belle amie est morte; La Biondina (song-cycle); Ce que je suis sans toi; Chanson de printemps; Clos ta paupière; Envoi de fleurs; The fountain mingles with the river; If thou art sleeping, maiden; Ilala; A lay of the early spring; Loin du pays; Maid of Athens; Mignon; My true love hath my heart; Oh happy home! o blessed flower!; Où voulez-vous aller?; La Pâquerette; Prière; Rêverie; Sérénade; Le Soir; Le Temps des roses; Trust her not!; Venise; The worker.

*** Hyp. CDA 66801/2. Lott, Murray, Rolfe-Johnson, Johnson.

Graham Johnson here devises an enchanting programme of 41 songs presenting the full span of Gounod's achievement not just in French *mélodie* (on the first of the two discs) but also in songs Gounod wrote during his extended stay in England. The soloists here are at their very finest. So on the first disc, after charming performances of the opening items from Felicity Lott, Ann Murray enters magically, totally transforming the hackneyed lines of *Ave Maria*, before tackling the most joyous of Gounod songs, the barcarolle-like *Sérénade*. Anthony Rolfe Johnson is comparably perceptive in *Biondina*, bringing out the Neapolitan-song overtones, as well as in six of the English settings. As in the Schubert series, Johnson's notes are a model of scholarship, both informed and fascinating.

Messe Chorale.

(N) (BB) *** Warner Apex. 8573 89235-2. Lausanne Vocal Ens., Corboz; Fuchs (organ) – SAINT-SAENS: *Mass.* **(*)

Gounod's *Messe Chorale*, an early work, could not be more different from his *Messe solennelle de Saint Cécile*. Drawing on the eighteenth-century tradition of French organ mass it intersperses choral sections with organ interludes, all based on the chosen Gregorian theme which acts like a leitmotif, reaching an expressive peak in the *Hosanna in excelsis* of the *Sanctus*. The *Benedictus* then leads via a brief fugue and a grand organ coda into the richly harmonized and finally serene *Agnus Dei*. Gounod's setting has an endearing simplicity, and it is beautifully sung and recorded here under Michel Cobos, with Marie-Claire Alain making a splendid foil for the choir on the magnificent organ of Lausanne Cathedral.

Messe solennelle de Saint Cécile.

*** EMI CDC7 47094-2. Hendricks, Dale, Lafont, Ch. and Nouvel O Philharmonique of R. France, Prêtre.

Gounod's *Messe solennelle*, with its blatant march setting of the *Credo* and sugar-sweet choral writing, may not be for sensitive souls, but Prêtre here directs an almost ideal performance, vividly recorded, with glowing singing from the choir as well as the three soloists.

Faust (complete).

◉ *** Teldec 4509 90872-2 (3). Hadley, Gasdia, Ramey, Mentzer, Agache, Fassbaender, Welsh Nat. Op. Ch. & O, Rizzi.

*** EMI CDS7 54228-2 (3). Leech, Studer, Van Dam, Hampson, Ch. & O of Capitole de Toulouse, Plasson.

(M) **(*) EMI (ADD) CMS7 69983-2 (3). De los Angeles, Gedda, Blanc, Christoff, Paris Nat. Op. Ch. and O, Cluytens.

Rizzi, with an outstanding cast and vividly clear recording, makes the whole score seem totally fresh and new. Jerry Hadley as Faust has lyrical freshness rather than heroic power, brought out in his headily beautiful performance of *Salut! demeure* and, like Rizzi's conducting, his singing has more light and shade in it than that of rivals. The tenderness as well as the bright agility of Cecilia Gasdia's singing as Marguerite brings comparable variety of expression, with the *Roi de Thulé* song deliberately drained of colour to contrast with the brilliance of the *Jewel song* which follows. Her performance culminates in an angelic contribution to the final duet, with Rizzi's slow speed encouraging refinement, leading up to a shattering moment of judgement and a fine apotheosis. Alexander Agache as Valentin may be less characterful than Hampson on the EMI set, but his voice is caught more richly; but it is the commandingly demonic performance of Samuel Ramey as Mephistopheles that sets the seal on the whole set, far more sinister than José van Dam on EMI. Like the EMI set, the Teldec offers a valuable appendix, not just the full ballet music but numbers cut from the definitive score – a drinking song for Faust and a charming aria for Siebel. EMI's supplementary items, four, all different, are more generous, but musically less interesting.

On EMI, Plasson comes near to providing another recommendable *Faust*, even if José van Dam's gloriously dark, finely focused bass-baritone does not have the heft of a full-blooded bass voice such as is associated with the role of Mephistopheles. Cheryl Studer conveys the girlishness of Marguerite, using the widest range of dynamic and colour. If Richard Leech's voice might in principle seem too light-

weight for the role of Faust, the lyrical flow and absence of strain make his singing consistently enjoyable. As Valentin, Thomas Hampson is strongly cast, with his firm, heroic baritone. The sound has a good sense of presence, set in a pleasantly reverberant acoustic which does not obscure necessary detail. In addition to supplementary numbers, the appendix offers the complete ballet music.

In the reissued Cluytens set, the seductiveness of De los Angeles's singing is a dream and it is a pity that the recording hardens the natural timbre slightly. Christoff is magnificently Mephistophelian. Gedda, though showing some signs of strain, sings intelligently, and among the other soloists Ernest Blanc has a pleasing, firm voice, which he uses to make Valentin into a sympathetic character. Cluytens's approach is competent but somewhat workaday. The set has been attractively repackaged and the libretto has strikingly clear print, to make a good mid-priced choice for this popular opera.

Faust (complete in English).

(M) *** Chan. 3014 (3). Clarke, Plazas, Miles, Magee, Montague, Walker, Geoffrey Mitchell Ch., Philh. O, Parry.

Faust, in a good English translation by Christopher Cowell, works brilliantly. The dramatic intensity is consistently heightened by David Parry's lively conducting, with the music paced to bring out the full impact of the big climaxes, and with freshness and sparkle given to such familiar numbers as the *Soldiers' Chorus*. The chorus is electrifying, and the cast of principals is first-rate. Paul Charles Clarke sings strongly in the title role (if not always sweetly), well-experienced from appearing in the Welsh National Opera production. Alastair Miles also sang with WNO, outstanding in every way as Mephistopheles, dark, firm and incisive, if not always sinister. Mary Plazas brings out the girlish innocence in Marguerite, sweet and pure, making light of the vocal challenges, above all giving joy to the *Jewel Song*. With singers as characterful as Diana Montague and Sarah Walker in smaller roles, this is the finest issue yet in the excellent Opera in English series promoted by the Peter Moores Foundation. The third disc includes the complete ballet music as a supplement.

Faust (abridged version).

(M) (**(*)) Naxos mono 8.110016/7. Jepson, Crooks, Pinza, Warren, Olheim, NY Met. Op. Ch. & O, Pelletier.

Naxos offers a performance broadcast from the Boston Opera House in April 1940. Richard Crooks's ringing tenor sounds more Italianate than French, but he makes an ardent Faust, and Ezio Pinza gives a vividly dynamic and characterful portrait of Mephistopheles, singing superbly and offering what must be the fastest account of the *Calf of Gold* aria on disc. Leonard Warren even in 1940 did not sound youthful enough for Valentin, with vibrato already obtrusive, and though Helen Jepson as Marguerite is a little shrill at times under pressure, it is a winning performance. Wilfred Pelletier proves an inspired conductor. Pacing the music very well, he draws excellent ensemble from the whole company, even if the radio recording has the orchestra presented rather dimly, well behind the singers. Applause and stage noises tend to be obtrusive, with the performance preceded and punctuated by an announcer summarizing the plot.

Faust (abridged version sung in English with ballet music; introduced by Sir Thomas Beecham).

(M) *** Dutton mono 2CDAX 2001 (2) Nash, Licette, Easton, Williams, Vane, Brunskill, Carr, BBC Ch. & SO, LPO, Beecham.

Beecham's 1929 recording, superbly transferred on the Dutton label, gives a vivid and refreshing idea of British opera performance in the 1920s. The old Chorley translation is used, stilted and creaking but memorable – 'What rubbishy wine!' says Mephistopheles. Voices are firm and cleanly projected, with the bright-toned Miriam Licette as Marguerite delivering a splendid trill at the start of the *Jewel Song*. Heddle Nash sings with heady tone as Faust, Harold Williams is a youthfully fresh Valentine and the distinctive flicker in Robert Easton's bass never gets in the way of clean focus in the role of Mephistopheles. Beecham himself is inspired, pointing rhythms and phrases infectiously, though, curiously, four of the 32 sides of the original 78s were conducted by Clarence Raybould. A supplement on the second CD includes a brief spoken introduction by Beecham, as well as the *Nubian Dance* and *Adagio* from the ballet music – otherwise omitted, like the *Walpurgisnacht* scene.

Faust: highlights.

(M) *** EMI (ADD) CD-EMX 2215 (from above complete set, with De los Angeles, Gedda; cond. Cluytens).

In the EMI (75-minute) set of excerpts the singing gives much pleasure, particularly that of de los Angeles and Christoff, and the choral contribution is spirited. Excellent value and an ideal way of sampling a performance which has many virtues.

Roméo et Juliette (complete).

*** EMI CDS5 56123-2 (3). Alagna, Gheorghiu, Vallejo, Van Dam, Keenlyside, Capitole de Toulouse Ch. & O, Plasson.
**(*) RCA 09026 68440-2 (2). Domingo, Swenson, Clarke, Ollmann, Miles, Bav. R. Ch., Munich R. O, Slatkin.
(B) (**(*)) Double Decca (IMS) mono 443 539-2 (2). Jobin, Micheau, Mollet, Rialland, Rehfuss, Opéra Nat. Ch. & O, Erede.

With Gheorghiu and Alagna inspired as the lovers, the EMI Toulouse set offers the finest performance on disc yet, in almost every way. Gheorghiu does not just sing sweetly without strain, the subtlety of her expression and her ability to rise to the demands of tragedy set her apart, and Alagna – who made such an impact in this role at Covent Garden early in his career – is youthfully ardent and unstrained. The rest of the cast is generally excellent too, with José van Dam as Frère Laurent and Simon Keenlyside as Mercutio both outstanding, though Marie-Ange Todorovitch, bright and agile as Stephano, is rather shrill. Given absolutely complete with the Act IV ballet music – not a dramatic gain – the set

takes three discs instead of two, but is well worth it. Warm, atmospheric sound.

Leonard Slatkin directs a strong account of Gounod's Shakespearean opera, lacking a little in Gallic point but generally well cast. Domingo may seem rather old for the role of Roméo, but he brings to it all of his characteristic finesse. Ruth Ann Swenson sings with warm, full tone as Juliette, but the waltz song lacks sparkle, and elsewhere too she sounds too mature. Alastair Miles is a very good Frère Laurent, and Susan Graham is charming as Stephano, but otherwise the cast does not match that in the EMI set, its one advantage being that it is offered on a pair of CDs. Full, well-focused recording.

It is an interesting comment that in 1953 Paris could offer a far finer team of singers than latterly, with the tenor Pierre Mollet, for example, light and airy as Mercutio, not least in the *Queen Mab Aria*, and Charles Cambon a fine Capulet. The only non-French singer, Heinz Rehfuss, projects with the clearest focus as Frère Laurent, while the roles of the two lovers are both warmly characterful. Janine Micheau is tenderly charming as a vulnerably girlish Juliette and, as Roméo, Raoul Jobin sings stylishly and with little of the pinched tone that too often has afflicted French tenors. The transfer is more than full-bodied enough to compensate for the slightly edgy top.

GRAF, Friedrich (1727–95)

6 Flute Quartets.

(N) *** MDG 311 0520-2. Hünteler, Festetics Qt (members).

Friedrich Hartmann Graf began his musical career as a timpanist in the band of a Dutch regiment, but after being both wounded in battle and taken prisoner decided to turn to the more peaceful flute. He developed into a virtuoso, becoming a colleague of Telemann in Hamburg in 1759. In his six quartets for flute, violin, viola and cello (dating from around 1775) the flute dominates, but the ensemble is elegantly integrated. They are gently melodious and full of charm, and taken one at a time make very pleasing listening. The performances here are beautifully turned and perfectly balanced in a warm acoustic. Undoubtedly lightweight, but beguiling.

GRAINGER, Percy (1882–1961)

Blithe Bells; Colonial Song; English Dance; Duke of Marlborough's Fanfare; Fisher's Boarding House; Green Bushes; Harvest Hymn; In a Nutshell (Suite); Shepherd's Hey; There were Three Friends; Walking Tune (symphonic wind band version); *We Were Dreamers.*

*** Chan. 9493. BBC PO, Hickox.

Hickox is masterly here, with rhythms always resilient, both in bringing out the freshness of well-known numbers like *Shepherd's Hey* and in presenting the originality and charm of such little-known numbers as *Walking Tune*. The BBC Philharmonic is in superb form, warmly and atmospherically recorded. By far the longest item is the suite, *In a*

Nutshell, which includes pieces like the *Arrival Platform Humlet*, well known on their own, and which has as its core a powerful and elaborate piece, *Pastoral*, which with its disturbing undertow belies its title.

Blithe Bells (Free Ramble on a Theme by Bach: Sheep may safely graze): Country Gardens; Green Bushes (Passacaglia); Handel in the Strand; Mock Morris; Molly on the Shore; My Robin is to the Greenwood Gone; Shepherd's Hey; Spoon River; Walking Tune; Youthful Rapture.

(M) *** Chan. 6542. Bournemouth Sinf., Montgomery.

For those wanting only a single Grainger orchestral collection, this could be first choice. Among the expressive pieces, the arrangement of *My Robin is to the Greenwood Gone* is highly attractive, but the cello solo in *Youthful Rapture* is perhaps less effective. Favourites such as *Country Gardens*, *Shepherd's Hey*, *Molly on the Shore* and *Handel in the Strand* all sound as fresh as new paint. The 1978 recording, made in Christchurch Priory, has retained all its ambient character in its CD transfer.

Children's March; Colonial Song; Country Gardens; Handel in the Strand; The Immovable 'Do'; Irish Tune from County Derry; Mock Morris; Molly on the Shore; My Robin is to the Greenwood Gone; Shepherd's Hey; Spoon River.

(M) ** Mercury (ADD) [434 330-2]. Eastman-Rochester Pops O, Fennell – COATES: *Three Elizabeths Suite.* **(*)

Lively and sympathetic performances from Fennell, and good playing. But the 1959 Mercury sound here is more dated than most CDs from this source: the acoustics of the Eastman Theatre in Rochester are too dry for Grainger's more expansive string writing in the *Colonial Song* and the *Irish Tune from County Derry*. The pithily rhythmic pieces like *Mock Morris* come off best as the sound is always clear and clean.

Country Gardens; In a Nutshell (Suite); Lincolnshire Posy; Train Music (ed. Rathburn); The Warriors.

*** EMI CDC5 56412-2. CBSO, Rattle – DEBUSSY (orch. Grainger): *Pagodes*; RAVEL (orch. Grainger): *La Vallée des cloches.*

'Grainger in a Nutshell' is the title of this EMI issue, a collection that in Rattle's dazzling, exhilaratingly wild performances aptly sums up this idiosyncratic composer's genius, echoing the title of the four-movement suite with which the disc opens. That charming piece starts with the *Arrival Platform Humlet* and ends with the equally characterful *Gum-Suckers' March*. The *Lincolnshire Posy* is a similar compilation of folk-based pieces brilliantly scored, and the disc ends with Grainger's most ambitious work, his thrillingly varied 'Music to an imaginary ballet', *The Warriors*, for huge orchestra. There are also idiosyncratic arrangements of Debussy and Ravel piano pieces and a spectacular version of his own *Country Gardens* specially written for Stokowski. Brilliant sound to match.

Irish Tune from County Derry; Lincolnshire Posy (suite); *Molly on the Shore; Shepherd's Hey.*

(M) *** ASV (ADD) CDWHL 2067. L. Wind O, Wick – MILHAUD; POULENC: *Suite française.* ***

First-class playing and vivid recording, with the additional attraction of delightful couplings, make this very highly recommendable.

The Warriors (music for an imaginary ballet).

*** DG 445 860-2. Philh. O, Gardiner – HOLST: *The Planets.* ***

Colourful and vigorous, *The Warriors* throbs with energy, at one point – in a gentler interlude – involving an offstage orchestra in Ivesian superimpositions. The result is hugely enjoyable in such a fine performance as Gardiner's. It makes an unexpected and valuable coupling for his brilliant account of the favourite Holst work. Dazzling sound.

(i) *Ye Banks and Braes o' Bonnie Doon.* (ii) *Colonial Song; Country Gardens.* (i) *The Gum-Suckers' March; Faeroe Island Dance; Hill Song No. 2.* (ii) *Irish Tune from County Derry.* (i) *The Lads of Wamphray March.* (ii) *Lincolnshire Posy.* (i) *The Merry King; Molly on the Shore.* (ii) *Shepherd's Hey.*

*** Chan. 9549. Royal Northern College of Music Wind O, with (i) Rundell, (ii) Reynish.

Even more than most issues in the Chandos Grainger series, this is a fun disc, with the brilliant young players of the Royal Northern College relishing the jaunty rhythms. Many of the pieces are well-known in Grainger's alternative arrangements, but this version of Grainger's most popular piece, *Country Gardens*, is not just an arrangement of the piano version, but as he explained himself a new piece in every way'. The *Faeroe Island Dance* in this late band version of 1954 has a pivoting ostinato for horns that echoes the opening of Vaughan Williams's *Fifth Symphony*, before launching into the dance proper with echoes of *The Rite of Spring*.

PIANO MUSIC

Colonial Song; Country Gardens; Handel in the Strand; Harvest Hymn; The Hunter in his Career; In a Nutshell (Suite): Gum-suckers' March. In Dahomey (Cakewalk Smasher); Irish Tune from County Derry; Jutish Medley; A March-Jig; The Merry King; Mock Morris; Molly on the Shore; Ramble on the Last Love-Duet from Richard's Strauss's Der Rosenkavalier; A Reel; Scotch Strathspey & Reel; Shepherd's Hey; Spoon River; Walking Tune.

**(*) Hyp. CDA 66884. Hamelin.

Marc-André Hamelin's articulation is phenomenally crisp, and the recording is excellent, but he misses the charm of some of these pieces, when he is often too metrical, pushing ahead a shade too fast in such pieces as *Country Gardens* or *Shepherd's Hey*, so that rhythms fail to spring infectiously as they should. Yet the choice of items is generous and apt.

Country Gardens; In a Nutshell (suite): *Gay but Wistful; The Gum-Suckers' March. Jutish Medley; March-Jog (Maguire's Kick); Molly on the Shore; One More Day my John; Ramble on the Last Love-Duet in Strauss's 'Der Rosenkavalier'; Sheep and Goat Walkin' to the Pasture; Shepherd's Hey; Spoon River; Sussex Mummers' Christmas Carol; Turkey in the Straw; The Warriors.* STANFORD: *Irish Dances* arr. GRAINGER: *Leprechaun's Dance; A Reel.*

*** Nim. NI 8809. Grainger (from Duo-Art piano rolls).

We have always been admirers of the Duo-Art player-piano recording system, and here Grainger's personality leaps out from between the speakers, yet the original rolls were cut between 1915 and 1929! It is good to have such a winningly vigorous *Country Gardens* and such a characterful *Shepherd's Hey*, while *Sheep and Goat Walkin' to the Pasture* has rhythmical character of the kind that makes one smile. *Gay But Wistful* is neither – nonchalant, rather – but endearing. The lyrical numbers like the touching *Sussex Mummers' Christmas Carol, One More Day My John* and the lilting *Zanzibar boat-song* have a winningly relaxed flair, and Grainger makes his arrangement of the Richard Strauss love-duet from *Der Rosenkavalier* sound intimately luscious and deliciously idiomatic. The recording is first class.

Complete: 'Dished up for Piano', Volumes 1–5.

(B) *** Nim. NI 1767 (5). Jones.

'Dished up for Piano', Volume 1: Andante con moto; Bridal Lullaby; Children's March; Colonial Song; English Waltz; Handel in the Strand; Harvest Hymn; The Immovable 'Do'; In a Nutshell (Suite) (Arrival Platform Humlet; Gay But Wistful; The Gum-Suckers' March; Pastoral); In Dahomey; Mock Morris; Peace; Sailor's Song; Saxon Twi-Play; To a Nordic Princess; Walking Tune.

'Dished up for Piano', Volume 2: Arrangements: BACH: *Blithe Bells; Fugue in A min.* BRAHMS: *Cradle Song.* Chinese TRAD.: *Beautiful Fresh Flower.* DOWLAND: *Now, O Now, I Needs Must Part.* ELGAR: *Enigma Variations: Nimrod.* Stephen FOSTER: *Lullaby; The Rag-Time Girl.* GERSHWIN: *Love Walked In; The Man I Love.* RACHMANINOV: *Piano Concerto No. 2: Finale* (abridged). R. STRAUSS: *Der Rosenkavalier: Ramble on the Last Love-Duet.* TCHAIKOVSKY: *Piano Concerto No. 1* (opening); *Paraphrase on the Flower Waltz.*

'Dished up for Piano', Volume 3: Folksong arrangements: *The Brisk Young Sailor; Bristol Town; Country Gardens; Died for Love; Hard-Hearted Barb'ra Helen; The Hunter in his Career; Irish Tune from County Derry; Jutish Medley; Knight and Shepherd's Daughter; Lisbon (Dublin Bay); The Merry King; Mo Ninghean Dhu; Molly on the Shore; My Robin is to the Greenwood Gone; One More Day My John* (2 versions, easy and complex); *Near Woodstock Town; The Nightingale and the Two Sisters; O Gin I were Where Gowrie Rins; Rimmer and Goldcastle; The Rival Brothers; Scotch Strathspey; Shepherd's Hey; Spoon River; Stalt Vesselil; Sussex Mummers' Christmas Carol; The Widow's Party; Will Ye Gang to the Hielands, Lizzie Lindsay?.*

Volume 4: Arrangements: ANON.: *Angelus ad Virginem.* BACH: *Toccata & Fugue in D min.* DELIUS: *Air & Dance.* FAURE: *Après un rêve; Nell.* Stephen FOSTER: *Lullaby* (Easy: Grainger). GRIEG: *Piano Concerto* (first movement). HANDEL: *Water Music: Hornpipe.* SCHUMANN: *Piano Concerto* (first movement). STANFORD: *4 Irish Dances.* GRAINGER: *At Twilight; The Bigelow March; Eastern Intermezzo; Tiger-Tiger; Klavierstücke in A min., B flat, D & E.*

Volume 5: Original works for up to six hands: BRAHMS: *Paganini Variation No. 12.* BYRD: *The Carman's Whistle.* (i) *Children's March;* DELIUS: *A Dance Rhapsody.* (i–ii) *English Dance.* (i) GERSHWIN: *Girl Crazy: Embraceable You.* (i–ii) *Green Bushes; Spoon River; Train Music; Up-Country Song;* (i–ii) *The Warriors* (music to an imaginary ballet); *Ye Banks and Braes o' Bonnie Doon; Zanzibar Boat-song.*

(with (i) McMahon; (ii) Martin).

Martin Jones's splendid Nimbus survey of Grainger's piano music is not now available on separate CDs, but they now come together in a slip-case at bargain price. The playing is refreshingly alive and spontaneous. Volume 1 is particularly attractive, and that is the place to start, for there is not a dull item here. There is plenty of dash in the folksong arrangements, and charm too, and they display a much greater range than one might have expected. The transcriptions are fascinating. The fourth and fifth volumes are the most enjoyable of all. Grainger's arrangements in Volume 4 are often very free, but Jones plays them with such spontaneity that they are freshly enjoyable in their own right. The opening *Four Irish Dances* of Stanford are attractively spiced. His 'concert version' of Bach's most famous *Toccata and Fugue* in based on the arrangements by Tausig and (mainly) Busoni: Jones excitingly gives it the full bravura treatment. But there are gentle, original pieces too, and the *Eastern Intermezzo* features peals of bells. *Tiger-Tiger* is simplicity itself, as is *At Twilight*, but this piece then ends with a bluesy 'added sixth' chord.

Volume 5 offers the original works for up to six hands, and the opening *Children's March*, in which Jones is joined on one piano by Richard McMahon, could not be more rumbustiously attactive. In *Ye Banks and Braes* (prolix but effective) and the lilting *Zanzibar Boat-Song* three players share a single piano. But in the intricate *Passacagalia on Green Bushes* (a *tour de force*, which steadily increases in pace and excitement), Philip Martin joins the other two to make up the six hands, on three pianos, and this is the complex scoring of both the 'rambling' *English Dance*, which is very diverting, and the closing *Warriors* ballet (which is complete). All the playing here is splendidly secure technically, and the performances not only have panache but also readily convey the enjoyment of the participants. The pianos are recorded reverberantly in the Nimbus manner – but it rather suits this repertoire, and the image is absolutely truthful.

VOCAL MUSIC

Anchor song (setting of Rudyard Kipling); *Thou gracious power* (setting of Oliver Wendell Holmes); Arrangements of folk songs: *Afterword; Air from County Derry; Brigg Fair; Early one morning; Handel in the Strand; I'm seventeen come Sunday; The lonely desert-man sees the tents of the Happy Tribes; Marching tune; Molly on the shore; 2 Sea chanties; Shallow Brown; Six dukes went a-fishing; There was a pig went out to dig; Ye banks and braes o' bonnie Doon.*

*** Chan. 9499. Padmore, Varcoe, Joyful Company of Singers, City of L. Sinf., Hickox; Thwaites.

In the darkly intense *Shallow Brown* Hickox has less prominent janglings than Gardiner (see below) in the accompaniment, but he has a clear advantage in opting for an excellent baritone soloist (Stephen Varcoe) instead of a rather uncertain soprano, with an equally fine choral ensemble. Hickox's version of the *County Derry* (the 'Londonderry air') is quite different from Gardiner's, for he has chosen a more extended, much more elaborate setting. *Ye banks and braes* is another item given in a version previously unrecorded, with a whistled descant. Among the pieces completely new to disc are the *Marching tune* and *Early one morning*. Also most striking is the brief, keenly original choral piece, *The lonely desert-man sees the tents of the Happy Tribes*, here given a dedicated performance, with the tenor intoning a theme from Grainger's orchestral piece, *The Warriors*, and the distant chorus chattering a chant borrowed from his *Tribute to Foster.*

(i) *Bell Piece. Blithe Bells;* (ii) *Children's March; Hill Songs I & II; The Immovable Do. Irish Tune from County Derry; Marching Song of Democracy; The Power of Rome and the Christian Heart.*

*** Chan. 9630. Royal Northern College of Music Wind O., Reynish or Rundell; with (i) Gilchrist; (ii) vocal group from band.

Where in their first collection (above) the splendid players of the Royal Northern College of Music Wind Orchestra clearly so enjoy Grainger's rhythmic buoyancy, here they equally relish his feeling for wind colour, as in the engaging *Hill Songs*, and rich sonorities, as in the powerful and remarkable *The Power of Rome and the Christian Heart*, and equally so in this characteristically imaginative arrangement of the *Londonderry Air* for band and pipe organ. *Bell Piece* (a 'ramble' on Dowland's melancholy air, *Now, O Now I Needs Must Part*), begins with a tenor solo with piano, before the wind players gently steal in. In the *Children's March* members of the band are invited twice to sing a vocalise when they are not playing. Altogether a fascinating and greatly enjoyable programme, strikingly well directed by Timothy Reynish and Clark Rundell.

The Crew of the Long Serpent; Danish Folk Song Suite; Kleine Variationen-Form; Stalt Vesselil (Proud Vesselil); To a Nordic Princess; (i) (Vocal) *Dalvisa; Father and Daughter (Fadit og Dóttir); The merry wedding; The rival brothers; Song of Värmland; Under un Bro (Bridge).*

*** Chan. 8721. Danish Nat. RSO, Hickox; (i) with Stephen, Reuter, Danish Nat. R. Ch.

From his earliest years Grainger was drawn to Scandinavian and Icelandic literature. This stimulating and rewarding collection centres on music directly influenced by his immersion in those cultures, all little known, except perhaps the *Danish Folk Song Suite*, with its highly exotic orchestration, winningly presented here. Among the other orchestral items the rollicking *Crew of the Long Serpent*, the colourful *Variations*, and the much more extended and lusciously scored *Tribute to a Nordic Princess* stand out. In the complex opening choral piece, *Father and Daughter*, a traditional Danish folk dance is mixed up with a theme of Grainger's own. The jolly, concerted *Merry wedding* is sung in English: it draws on a folk poem for its text, but is musically original. *Dalvisa* is a delightful vocalise, using the same melody Alfvén featured as the centrepiece in his *Midsummer Rhapsody*. Splendid performances and top-class Chandos sound.

Duke of Marlborough Fanfare; Green Bushes (Passacaglia); Irish Tune from County Derry; Lisbon; Molly on the shore; My Robin is to Greenwood Gone; Shepherd's Hey; Piano Duet; Let's Dance Gay in Green Meadow. Vocal and Choral: *Bold William Taylor; Brigg Fair; I'm Seventeen Come Sunday; Lord Maxwell's goodnight; The Lost Lady Found; The Pretty Maid Milkin' Her Cow; Scotch Strathspey and Reel; Shallow Brown; Shenandoah; The Sprig of Thyme; There Was a Pig Went Out to Dig; Willow Willow.*

(N) *** Australian Decca Eloquence (ADD) 467 234-2. Pears, Shirley-Quirk, Amb. S. or Linden Singers, Wansworth Boys' Ch., Britten or Bedford.

This collection is one of the best single disc anthologies of Grainger's music. The bulk of the collection derives from Britten's 1969 LP, and the sound in this transfer is extraordinarily full and vivid: indeed, the clarity of *There Was a Pig Went Out to Dig* has uncanny presence. It is altogether a delightful anthology, beautifully played and sung throughout. If Grainger's talent was smaller than his more fervent advocates would have us believe, his imagination in the art of arranging folk-song was prodigious. The *Willow Song* is a touching and indeed haunting piece and shows the quality of Grainger's harmonic resource. The *Duke of Marlborough Fanfare* is strikingly original, and so is *Shallow Brown*. Vocal and instrumental items are felicitously interwoven, and Decca's Australian team are to be congratulated in making this CD available.

Bold William Taylor; Colonial song; The Bridegroom Grat; Died for love; Free music; Harvest hymn; Hubby and Wifey; The Land O' the Leal; Lisbon; Lord Maxwell's goodnight; Lord Peter's Stable-Boy; Molly on the shore; The Nightingale; The old woman at the christening; The only son; The power of love; The shoemaker from Jerusalem; The two corbies; The two sisters; Walking tune; Willow willow; Ye Banks and Braes O'Bonnie Doon.

(N) **(*) Chan. 9819. D. Jones, Hill, Varcoe, ASMF Chamber Ens.

The present volume of the Chandos Grainger series is devoted to pieces (with or without vocal contributions) accompanied by various chamber ensembles. The opening instrumental version of *Lord Peter's Stable Boy* (scored for violin, cello, piano and harmonium) is characteristically fresh. Grainger's scoring is as vividly captivating as ever, and never more so than in his arrangements of *Lisbon* and *Walking tune* (both for wind quintet), or in accompanying the delightful melody of *The shoemaker of Jerusalem* (with flute, trumpet, strings and piano (four hands)). This was originally collected in Jutland and the infectiously quarrelsome *Hubby and Wifey* (Della Jones and Stephen Varcoe) comes from the same source.

In the solo songs some might feel Della Jones is a bit precocious in her sharp word enunciation (as in *The old woman at the christening*), but her gusto is endearing. Stephen Varcoe adopts a much simpler style most effectively in *Bold William Taylor*, and Martyn Hill spins the line of *Lord Maxwell's goodnight* and *The two corbies* very touchingly, accompanied by a rich string patina.

All three singers make a passionately sentimental contribution to the *Colonial song*, which some might feel goes a little over the top, but clearly it was what Grainger wanted. It opens with a warm cello solo (here beautifully played by Stephen Orton), and the cello features seductively in many other arrangements, notably *The Nightingale* and *The two sisters*, both using harmonium backing.

Free music is set for a normal string quartet and opens with eerie glissandi, but the quartet returns, cello-led, to end the recital with a rapturous account of *Molly on the shore*. Excellent recording, as usual from this source.

Folksong arrangements: *The bride's tragedy* (for chorus & orchestra); *Brigg Fair* (for tenor & chorus); *Danny Deever* (for baritone, chorus & orchestra); *Father and daughter* (*A Faeroe Island dancing ballad;* for 5 solo narrators, double chorus, & 3 instrumental groups); *I'm seventeen come Sunday* (for chorus, brass & percussion); *Irish tune from County Derry* (*Londonderry air;* for wordless chorus); *The lost lady found; Love verses from The Song of Solomon* (for tenor & chamber orchestra); *The merry wedding* (*Bridal dances;* for 9 soloists, chorus, brass, percussion, strings & organ); *My dark-haired maiden* (*Mi nighean dhu;* for mixed voices); *Scotch strathspey & reel – inlaid with several Irish & Scotch tunes & a sea shanty* (orchestral version); *Shallow Brown* (for solo voice or unison chorus, with an orchestra of 13 or more instruments); *The three ravens* (for baritone solo, mixed chorus & 5 clarinets); *Tribute to Foster* (for vocal quintet, male chorus & instrumental ensemble).

⚫ *** Ph. 446 657-2. Soloists, Monteverdi Ch., English Country Gardiner O, Gardiner.

Gardiner singles out the hypnotically measured sea-shanty, *Shallow Brown,* as the most 'searingly original' of Grainger's works and the most haunting. The performance here backs that up, with furious tremolandos from guitars and banjos, which Grainger called 'wogglings'. The richest, most exotic piece is the setting of *Love verses* from The Song of Solomon, while the longest and most elaborate items bring astonishingly original effects for both voices and orchestra, the richly evocative *Tribute to Stephen Foster* and the setting of a mock Scottish ballad by Swinburne, *The bride's tragedy*. The bitter element in some of the numbers provides a clue to the inspiration which fired Grainger, as in the grim setting of Kipling's *Danny Deever*, with its refrain, 'Oh they're hanging Danny Deever in the morning'. Superb sound, though (because of the complexity of textures) words are often inaudible. Full text and really outstanding notes.

Folksong arrangements: *Songs of the North (4 Scottish settings); 6 settings of Rudyard Kipling; The secret of the sea; Sailor's chanty.* Traditional folksong settings: *Bold William Taylor; British waterside; Creepin' Jane; Hard hearted Barb'ra; The lost lady found; The pretty maid milking her cow; Shallow Brown; Six dukes went afishin'; Willow willow.*

**(*) Chan. 9503. Varcoe, Thwaites.

Stephen Varcoe is obviously at home in these folksongs. Most of them are set fairly simply, as in the lovely opening of *Willow willow,* or the bold, jiggy narrative of *The lost lady found,* while *The pretty maid milking her cow* is very touching. These are essentially concert performances. However, Varcoe's vernacular account of Kipling's *Soldier soldier come from the wars* is especially successful, and *Hard hearted Barb'ra* is delightfully done, as is Grainger's own setting of Longfellow's *The secret of the sea. Shallow Brown,* which ends the programme, is very dramatic indeed, although some might feel that Varcoe goes over the top here, helped by Penelope Thwaites's strong accompaniment; indeed, she makes an admirable contribution throughout this well-recorded recital.

GRANADOS, Enrique (1867–1916)

(i) *Dante* (symphonic poem); *Goyescas: Intermezzo;* (i) *La maja y el ruiseñor. 5 Piezas sobre cantos populares españolas* (arr. Ferrer).

(N) *** ASV CDDCA 1110. Gran Canaria PO, Leaper; with
  (i) Herrera; (ii) Lucey.

Granados wrote little orchestral music. His *Dante* is a two-part symphonic poem which slowly gestated between 1895 and 1910. It is unexpectedly confident in its use of the orchestral palette. The first section opens in sombre despair to evoke Dante's journey with Virgil into the 'black malignant air' of the Inferno, while in the second we meet Paolo and Francesca, their love already anticipated in a sadly yearning theme in part one. Granados evokes his narrative using luscious post-Wagnerian chromaticism and even introduces voluptuous hints of Scriabin and early Schoenberg. *Francesca's Story* is a straightforward setting of Canto V of Dante's poem and here there are even hints of Puccini's *Madame Butterfly*. The vocal line is affectingly sung by Nancy Herrera, her fully coloured mezzo darkening the lower notes entreatingly. Adrian Leaper and the excellent Gran Canaria Orchestra play this remarkable score with languourous intensity. The enchanting highlight of *Goyescas*, *La maja y el ruiseñor* is simply and beautifully sung by Frances Lucey, and the opera's *Intermezzo* follows vibrantly. Anselm Ferrer's orchestration of five of the *Piezas sobre cantos populares* skilfully re-creates the music orchestrally – sultry and sparkling by turns. They are most winningly and flexibly presented, to make an entertaining centrepiece in a first-class collection that is atmospherically and vividly recorded.

(i) *Piano Quintet in G min. Piano music: A la Cubana, Op. 36; Aparición; Cartas de amor – Valses intimos, Op. 44; Danza caracteristica; Escenas poéticas* (2nd series).

(M) *** CRD (ADD) 3335. Rajna; (i) with Alberni Qt.

The *Piano Quintet* is a compact work, neat and unpretentious, in three attractive movements, including a charming lyrical Allegretto and a vigorous finale where the piano is most prominent. Among the solo items, the evocative pieces in the *Escenas poéticas II* are the most valuable, but even the more conventional colour-pieces that make up the rest of the disc are worth hearing in such perceptive readings. The CRD analogue recording is very good indeed and so are the CD transfers.

12 Danzas españolas; Escenas poeticas, Book II (arr. for guitar and orchestra).

(BB) *** Naxos 8.855037. Kraft, Razumovsky Sinf., Breiner.

These are attractive transcriptions for guitar and orchestra of Granados's piano pieces. The Canadian guitarist Norbert Kraft is a brilliant and effective player. If you want to try Granados in this orchestral garb rather than in its original keyboard form, you can invest in this with confidence.

GUITAR MUSIC

Cuentos para la juventud, Op. 1: Dedicatoria. Danzas españolas Nos. 4 & 5, Op. 37/4–5; Tonadillas al estilo antiguo: La maja de Goya. Valses poéticos.

❀ (BB) *** RCA Navigator 74321 17903-2. Bream (guitar) – ALBENIZ: *Collection;* RODRIGO: *3 Piezas españolas.* *** ❀

Like the Albéniz items with which these Granados pieces are coupled, these performances show Julian Bream at his most inspirational. The illusion of the guitar being in the room is especially electrifying in the middle section of the famous *Spanish Dance No. 5*, when Bream achieves the most subtle pianissimo. Heard against the background silence, the effect is quite magical. But all the playing here is wonderfully spontaneous. This is one of the most impressive guitar recitals ever recorded, and for this super-bargain reissue RCA have generously added the *Tres piezas españolas* of Rodrigo, recorded a year later and no less distinguished.

12 Danzas españolas (trans. for guitar).

(B) *** [EMI Red Line CDR5 69850]. Barrueco – FALLA: *Spanish Popular Songs.* ***

As in the Falla coupling, this is masterly playing, warmly coloured, subtly nuanced, and naturally idiomatic in its

rhythms, so that one might think that these piano pieces had been orginally intended for the guitar.

PIANO MUSIC

A la cubana; Allegro de concierto; Barcorola; Bocetos; Cantas de amor; Carezza (vals); Capricho español; Cuentos de la juventud; Danza caracteristica; 2 Danzas españolas; 12 Danzas españolas; Elisenda; Escenas poéticas I–II; Estudio; 6 Estudios espresivos en forma de piezas fáciles; 2 Gavotos; Goyescas, Books I–II; Goyescas: Intermezzo. 2 Impromptus; Libro de horas; Marche militaire; Moresque y canción arabe; Oriental, canción, variada, intermedio y final; Palsaje; Paises soñados; 6 Piezas sobre cantos populares españolas; Rapsodia aragonesa; Valse de concert; Valses intimos. Reverie (Improvisation; transcribed from a Duo Art piano roll).

(N) (BB) *** Nimbus NI 1734 (6). M. Jones.

The Nimbus six-disc set is described as 'the complete published works for the piano', but you will look in vain in the contents list for the *Goyescas* as they are listed (on the second CD) as *Los majos enamorados*, Parts I and II. The *Libro de horas* come between the two Books (which works well enough), with *El pelele* played quite separately. No reason is given for this in the sparse notes, the one drawback to the set, which is otherwise highly recommendable at its modest price. As can be seen, there is an equally recommendable shorter collection (which includes the *Goyescas* and also The Duo Art piano roll transcription of the composer playing an improvisation).

Allegro de concierto; Escenas románticas; Goyescas (complete); Goyescas: Intermezzo. Goyesca (El pele); Oriental, canción, variada, intermedio y final rapsodia aragonesa; Valse de concert; Reverie (Improvisation; transcribed from a Duo Art piano roll).

(BB) *** Nim. NI 5595/8 (4). Jones – ALBENIZ: *Iberia* etc. ***

As in the coupled collection of the major piano works of Albéniz, Martin Jones's instinctive sympathy with the Spanish idiom brings a remarkable freshness of approach to music which until now seems to have been the sole province on record of Alicia de Larrocha. His imaginative spontaneity throughout shows very personal insights; the playing, with its wide range of colour and dynamic, sparkles and glimmers and is full of poetry. The familiar *Goyescas* are vividly and warmly characterized, and the most famous number *Quejas, o la maja y el ruiseñor* is just as memorable here as in the hands of de Larrocha. The Nimbus recording is pleasingly real and natural and this set is highly recommendable.

A la pradera; Barcarola, Op. 45; Bocetos; Cuentos de la juventud, Op. 1; Mazurka, Op. 2; Mosque y Arabe; Sardana; Los soldados de cartón.

(M) *** CRD (ADD) 3336. Rajna.

Allegro de concierto; Capricho español, Op. 39; Carezza vals, Op. 38; 2 Impromptus; Oriental; Rapsodia aragonesa; Valses poéticos.

(M) *** CRD (ADD) 3323. Rajna.

Danzas españolas, Op. 37.

(M) *** CRD (ADD) 3321. Rajna.

Escenas románticas; 6 Piezas sobre cantos populares españoles; Danza lenta.

(M) *** CRD (ADD) 3322. Rajna.

6 Estudios expresivos; Estudio, Op. posth.; Impromptu, Op. 39; 3 Marches militaires; Paisaje, Op. 35; Pequeña suite (In the garden of Elisenda).

(M) *** CRD (ADD) 3337. Rajna.

Goyescas; Escenas poéticas (1st series); *Libro de horas.*

(M) *** CRD (ADD) 3301. Rajna.

Not all of Granados's piano works are as inventive as the *Goyescas*, but although this music is of uneven quality, Thomas Rajna plays it with great sympathy and flair. Apart from the *Danzas españolas*, some of the finest music is to be found in the *Escenas románticas* and in the other pieces on CRD 3322 and 3323. The later volumes, however, excellently played and recorded, should nonetheless be acquired, and not merely for the sake of completeness. The eight pieces on CRD 3336, opening with the beguiling innocent *Moresqe y Arabe*, are delightful, pleasingly contrasted in style and played with great character and spontaneity. The *Six Estudios* serve to point the formative influences in Granados's style – Schumann and, to a lesser extent, Fauré – while the other pieces, including the *Marches militaires* (in which Rajna superimposes the second piano part) are unfailingly pleasing. His account of *Goyescas* must yield to Alicia de Larrocha, but his interpretations are clear and persuasive and the music's greatness doe not elude him. The fill-ups, more immediately charming, less ambitious, are valuable, too. A distinguished set, welcome to the CD catalogue at mid-price.

Allegro de concierto; 12 Danzas españolas; El pelele.

(B) *** Double Decca ADD/Dig. 433 923-2 (2). De Larrocha – ALBENIZ: *Cantos de España; Suite española.* ***

Escenas románticas; Goyescas; 6 Piezas sobre cantos populares españoles.

(B) *** Double Decca ADD/Dig. 433 920-2 (2). De Larrocha – M. ALBENIZ: *Sonata;* SOLER: *Sonatas.* ***

These two Double Deccas are reissued as part of Decca's 'Música española' series. Alicia de Larrocha has an aristocratic poise to which it is difficult not to respond, and she plays with great flair and temperament in the *Danzas españolas*. *El pelele* is an appendix to the Goyescas collection and is brilliantly played, as is the *Allegro de concierto* (which is digitally recorded). The subtle, expressively ambitious *Escenas románticas* again show the amazingly wide range of Granados's piano music. They were recorded digitally, as were the *six Piezas sobre cantos populares*. However, many collectors may opt for the alternative coupling of *Goyescas* with Albéniz's *Iberia* (see below).

Allegro de concierto; El pelele; Goyescas: El fandango del Candil; Quejas a La Maja y el Ruiseñor.

(M) ** DG 459 430-2 (2). Pinzolas – ALBENIZ: *Iberia* (complete). **(*)

José María Pinzolas is rather less impressive here than in the coupled music of Albéniz. The dashing *Allegro de concierto* certainly has glittering bravura, and *El pelele* is characterful enough, but the two excerpts from *Goyescas* (and especially the lovely *Quejas o la maja y el ruiseñor*) are much more magnetic in the hands of Alicia de Larrocha.

12 Danzas españolas; 6 Escenas románticas; Goyescas.

(N) (B) **(*) Erato Ultima 8573 88046-2. Heisser.

Heisser's approach to this repertoire is engagingly chimerical. The *Danzas españolas* scintillate and the more intimate *Escenas románticas* are full of charm, played with an almost improvisatory flair. His approach to the *Goyescas* may seem a little lightweight compared with De Larrocha, but this is a highly individual approach, his digital dexterity sparkles, and he finds a captivatingly gentle touch for *La maja y el ruiseñor*. Very good recording.

12 Danzas españolas; Goyescas.

(M) *** Ph. (IMS) mono 442 751-2 (2). Del Pueyo – FALLA: *Nights in the Gardens of Spain.* ***

Eduardo del Pueyo's playing of the colourful *Spanish Dances* has much flair and poetic delicacy – sample *No. 2 in C minor*, so beautifully articulated – and the magical pianissimo at the centre of No. 5 makes one wonder if Julian Bream listened to Del Pueyo before making his equally memorable account of this famous piece. But it is in the *Goyescas* that Del Pueyo's evocation so immediately captures the Spanish atmosphere and especially in the haunting *Quejas o la maja y el ruiseñor*. The Falla coupling is perhaps even more remarkable.

12 Danzas españolas; Valses poéticos.

*** RCA 09026 68184-2. De Larrocha.

Alicia de Larrocha has already recorded the *Danzas españolas* definitively for Decca. Yet her newest version is every bit as perceptive, and her Spanish temperament remains naturally attuned to this repertoire. The spontaneity of feeling is there too, and the *Valses poéticos* are a delightful bonus. The RCA recording is very natural, fully coloured and with fine sonority. However, the Decca set offers a great deal more music for the same outlay.

Goyescas (complete).

⦿ (B) *** Double Decca 448 191-2 (2). De Larrocha – ALBENIZ: *Iberia* etc. ***

Goyescas (complete); *Escenas románticas; 6 Piezas sobre cantos populares españoles; Valses poéticos.*

(M) *** EMI CMS7 64524-2 (2) [CDMB 64524]. De Larrocha.

Alicia de Larrocha brings special insights and sympathy to the *Goyescas* (given top-drawer Decca sound in 1977); her playing has the crisp articulation and rhythmic vitality that these pieces call for, while she is hauntingly evocative in *Quejas o la maja y el ruiseñor*. The overall impression could hardly be more idiomatic in flavour nor more realistic as a recording. This Double Decca coupling with Albéniz's *Iberia* is very distinguished.

Alicia de Larrocha's EMI set of *Goyescas* derives from the Spanish Hispavox catalogue and was made in 1963, a decade before her first Decca set. The performance is more impulsive, at times more intensely expressive, if less subtle in feeling than the later version, and the recording, if not as fine as the Decca, is eminently realistic. The closing *Zapateado* of the *Cantos populares españoles* has a fire and sparkle characteristic of her playing at this stage of her career.

Goyescas (complete); *El pelele.*

**(*) Chan. 9412. Parkin.

Eric Parkin is obviously comfortable in the balmy Spanish climate and his performance of *Quejas ó la maja y el Ruiseñor* is as seductive as any. His approach to the gentler music is thoughtfully intimate, yet the brilliantly played *El pelele* brings plenty of extrovert sparkle. However, in the two more extended pieces of *Goyescas*, *Los requiebros* ('Flatteries') and especially *El amore y la muerte*, Alicia de Larrocha's combination of impulsiveness with ruminative evocation is that bit more temperamentally spontaneous. The Chandos recording cannot be faulted, but this is not a first choice.

GRAUN, Karl Heinrich (1704–59)

Cleopatra e Cesare (opera): 'Great arias'.

(M) *** HM HMT 7901602. Williams, Vermillion, Dawson, Gambill, RIAS Chamber Ch., Concerto Köln, Jacobs.

Taken from a complete three-disc set, recorded in Berlin in 1995, this generous, 77-minute collection of overture and ten arias plus two ensembles is consistently refreshing. In this selection, fast arias predominate – no doubt a wise choice – with all the principals singing most stylishly, with clean, agile attack, not least Janet Williams and Iris Vermillion in the twin title-roles, as well as Lynne Dawson, singing most beautifully as Cornelia, widow of Pompey. Janet Williams is sweetly affecting in her big Act III aria, and Iris Vermillion with her firm, strong mezzo makes a most characterful Caesar. Under René Jacobs, a sensitive director, there is no weak link in the rest of the cast either, and recorded sound is nicely balanced to convey an apt scale for this music.

GRAY, Steve (born 1947)

Guitar Concerto (for guitar & small orchestra).

✪ *** Sony SK 68337. Williams, LSO, Daniel – HARVEY: *Concerto antico.* *** ✪

The kernel of Steve Gray's *Guitar Concerto* (1987), written for its performer here, John Williams, is the long, expressively atmospheric slow movement, which reaches a bold expansive climax. The effect is haunting, but the jocular finale also brings loudly vociferous, even vulgar, orchestral outbursts – reflecting the composer's jazz-orientated background – and these probably come off better at a concert than on disc. However, the work ends with music of the

utmost delicacy. The performance here is surely definitive and the recording first class.

GRECHANINOV, Alexander (1864–1956)

(i) *Cello Concerto, Op. 8. Symphony No. 4, Op. 102.* (ii) *Missa festiva, Op. 154.*

*** Chan. 9559. Russian State SO, Polyansky with (i) Ivashkin. (ii) Russian State Symphonic Cappella, with Golub (organ).

The *Cello Concerto* is an early work, rather pale and conventional, but the *Fourth Symphony* is intensely Russian and its idiom more reminiscent of the 1880s than the 1920s. It is no masterpiece but if you feel at home in the world of Glière and Glazunov, it is worth investigating. Decent performances.

Symphony No. 1 in B min., Op. 6; (i) *Snowflakes, Op. 47; Missa Sancti Spiritus, Op. 169.*

*** Chan. 9397 (i) Russian State Symphony Cappella; Russian State SO, Polyansky.

The *First Symphony* is well-schooled music and, like so much Russian music of the period, its craftsmanship is not in question. *Snowflakes* is a middle-period work, written before Grechaninov moved to America after the Revolution; and it has charm. The *Missa Sancti Spiritus* comes from the other end of Grechaninov's long career, when he was living in America. Good performances and excellent recording.

Symphony No. 3, Op. 100; (i) *Cantata, Kvalite Boga (Praise the Lord), Op. 65.*

*** Chan. 9698. (i) Kuznetsova, Russian State Symphonic Cappella: Russian State SO, Polyanski.

The *Third Symphony* is said to be the composer's own favourite among his five essays in the genre. It has some of the pastoral charm of Glazunov's *Seventh*. While the ideas fall short of melodic distinction, they are sunny and genial, and the theme and variations that comprise the third movement have a delightful fairy-tale atmosphere. The cantata *Kvalite Boga* ('Praise the Lord') is earlier (1915), and if the ideas in themselves are not strong, the overall effect of the piece is. It is endearing and quite touching. The performances are very good, as is the recording. A very enjoyable disc.

All-Night Vigil (Vespers), Op. 59; Nunc dimittis (Lord now lettest Thou Thy servant), Op. 34/1; The Seven Days of the Passion; (i) *In Thy Kingdom, Op. 58/3. Now the Powers of Heaven, Op. 58/6.*

*** Hyp. CDA 67080. (i) Bowman; Holst Singers, Layton.

Grechaninov's *All-Night Vigil* was composed in 1912, three years before Rachmaninov's celebrated setting. It is a work of great beauty; radiance might be a better word, particularly as presented here by Stephen Layton and the Holst Singers. Marina Rakhmanova speaks of its grand ('essentially epic') scale, and its handling of choral texture is masterly. The singing is strikingly idiomatic and the Temple Church, London, provides an ideal acoustic. There is an ideal balance, too, between choir and the chant intoned by James Bowman in *In Thy Kingdom*. Really something of a triumph.

GREGORIAN CHANT

'Gregorian chant': Responsories; Hymns; Antiphons; Gospel tone: Vos estis sal terrae; Laudes seu Acclamationes; Gradual: Flores apparuerunt; Alleluia: Justus germinabit; Communions; Antiphon: Montes Gilboe; Ave verum corpus; Antiphonal Psalmody; Marian antiphons.

⚫ (M) *** Decca Penguin 460 641-2. L. Carmelite Priory Ch., McCarthy.

Mass Propers for Good Friday & Easter.

(M) *** DG (IMS) (ADD) 447 299-2. Abteikirche Münsterschwarzach, Joppich.

(BB) **(*) Naxos 8.550951. Nova Schola Gregoriana, Turco.

Mass Propers for the Church Year.

(BB) *** Naxos 8.550711. Nova Schola Gregoriana, Turco.

The liturgy of the Catholic Church has the Mass as its central focus. The Ordinary of the Mass – those elements that are unchanging through the Church year – has been set by countless composers and include the *Kyrie* ('Lord have mercy'), the *Gloria, Credo* and *Sanctus* ('Holy, holy, holy') and the *Agnus Dei* ('Lamb of God, who takes away the sins of the world, have mercy on us and grant us peace'). The Mass Propers are chants which change with the seasons of the year or the occasion of the celebration; they consist of Introit, Gradual, Alleluia, Tract, Offertory and Communion. These are amplified by Sequences (accretions to the liturgy) and Tropes (additions which amplify and heighten the meaning of the biblical text in prose or poetry). The changes brought about by the reforming Council of Trent in the sixteenth century removed many of these additions, but they are at the heart of medieval Church music.

To evaluate Gregorian Chant in a volume of this kind is hazardous and essentially subjective. However, for the general collector, there is one collection that stands out from all the others. Planned by the late Alec Robertson, who also provided the fascinating detailed notes describing the music's ecclesiastical and spiritual background, the beautifully sung and excellently recorded anthology now reissued by Decca as 'The World of Gregorian Chant' is the finest possible introduction to plainsong. Extra variety of tone is provided by the use of female voices as well as male. Edgar Fleet acts as cantor and John McCarthy directs the singing with dedication and authority, using a wide dynamic range and sometimes crescendos and diminuendos to simulate a processional effect. The recording, made in Brompton Little Oratory, London, in January 1961 is absolutely natural. The accompanying essay is by Richard Mabey.

DG's Archiv label offers a number of seasonal discs, such as the Gregorian chant for Good Friday and Easter from the Abteikirche Münsterschwarzach, led by Pater Godehard Joppich and recorded in 1981–2, while an inexpensive Naxos disc (with full texts provided, though no translations) by the Nova Schola Gregoriana, directed by the Italian scholar, Alberto Turco, covers this same area very effectively, and

this choir is recorded in the Parish Church of Quatrelle, Mantua, which provides a suitably atmospheric setting.

However, this fine choral group are heard to even better effect in an excellently chosen 75-minute compilation of chants taken from different Sundays in the Church year. The singing has a firm profile and is well recorded, not seeking to create a purely atmospheric effect. It is a pity that texts and translations are not provided, but the back-up notes are very helpful.

'Liturgia defuntorum': Gregorian chant for the dead (from the Order of Burial and for All Souls' Day).

(BB) **(*) Naxos 8.553192. Aurora Surgit, Randon.

To use a group of female voices in this repertoire (but with a male cantor) may not be completely authentic but the soaring monody gains a special character from the use of female trebles, and the added element of contrast in the responsories is also attractive. By no means all this music is solemn or dark in feeling: the closing group of chants, the *Libera me*, and especially the soaring *In paradisum – Chorus angelorum,* followed by the *Ego sum resurrectio,* are intended to give the Christian soul an eloquent send-off. Fine singing and atmospheric yet clear recording.

GRÉTRY, André-Ernest-Modeste (1741–1813)

Céphale et Procris (suite; ed. Mottl). Lucile (suite). Overtures: L'Ami de la maison; L'Amitié à l'épreuve; L'Epreuve villageoise; Guillaume Tell; Le Huron; Le Jugement de Midas; Le Magnifique; Silvain; Le Tableau parlant. Zémire et Azor (suite).

(N) **(*) CDDCA 1095. O de Bretagne, Stefan Sanderling.

This is Beecham territory. He rightly loved the graceful and delectably scored music of *Céphale et Procris* and *Zémire et Azor,* and he played it with exquisite elegance. He would also have known how to handle these overtures, especially *Le Jugement de Midas* with its thunderous storm sequence (here not really very spectacular), the attractive *L'Ami de la maison* and *L'Amitié à l'épreuve,* the very winning *Le Magnifique,* with its offstage drum beats, and the unexpected *Guillaume Tell,* with its woodwind piping and bustling allegro. Here it is all well played, but that special Beechamesque touch is absent. One has only to compare the famous *Air (Pantomime)* from *Zémire et Azor:* under Beecham it is quite magical, whereas Stefan Sanderling brings to it a simple, innocent charm. The ASV recording is pleasing, too, especially in relation to the strings, but it has a rather dead, boomy bass and a lack of real sparkle. Given that the disc was engineered by Brian Culverhouse, the acoustic of the Rennes Opera House must have proved intractable. Worthwhile for much music that is otherwise unavailable.

Zémire et Azor: Air de ballet.

⚫ (B) *** Dutton Lab. mono CDEA 5017. LPO, Beecham (with Concert: 'Beecham Favourites' *** ⚫).

The orchestral suite that Beecham fashioned from music

from Grétry's opera produced this famous lollipop, which *The Record Guide* (of Edward Sackville West and Desmond Shaw-Taylor) described as 'one of the most captivating morsels in the gramophone repertory'. It is exquisitely played here, especially the immensely delicate closing pianissimo reprise, where the Dutton transfer is wonderfully refined. This Beecham anthology, which includes also his justly renowned account of Chabrier's *España*, is an essential purchase, for every conceivable reason.

GRIEG, Edvard (1843–1907)

Complete music with orchestra

(i) *Bergliot* (melodrama for orchestra), *Op. 42*; (ii) *Piano Concerto in A Min.*; *2 Elegiac Melodies, Op. 34*; *Funeral March in Memory of Richard Nordraak*; *Holberg Suite, Op. 40*; *In Autumn, Op. 11*; *2 Lyric Pieces, Op. 68*; *Lyric Suite, Op. 54*; *Norwegian Dances, Op. 35*; *2 Norwegian Folk Melodies, Op. 53*; *2 Nordic Melodies, Op. 63*; *Old Norwegian Melody with Variations, Op. 51*; *4 Symphonic Dances, Op. 64*; *Symphony in C min.*; (iii) *Before a Southern Convent Op. 30*; (iv; v) *Orchestral Songs: The First Meeting; From Monte Pincio; Henryk Wergeland; Spring; A Swan*. (v; vi) *Landkjenning, Op. 31*; (v) *The Mountain Thrall, Op. 32*; (v; vii) *Olav Trygvason (Scenes), Op. 50*; (viii) *Peer Gynt* (complete incidental music); (ix) *Sigurd Jorsalfar* (incidental music).

(N) (B) *** DG 471 300-2 (6). Gothenburg SO (& Ch.), Järvi; with (i) Tellefsen (nar.); (ii) Zilberstein; (iii) Bonney, Stene, Women's Ch.; (iv) Bonney, (v) Hagegard; (vi) with Men's Ch.; (vii) Stene, Gjevang & Ch.; (viii) Bonney & Soloists.

This comprehensive coverage of Grieg's 'music with orchestra', with many of the performances unsurpassed, would make an ideal basis for any Grieg collection. Most are discussed below, although not Zilberstein's account of the *Piano Concerto*, one of the few disappointments. It is a good narrative performance and could never be called routine, but her reading is comparatively conventional, with few fresh insights. The documentation is excellent but the surprise is the omission of texts and translations for the vocal music, with only synopses deemed necessary. But the standard of recording is consistently high, and this six-disc bargain box is still remarkable value.

At the Cradle, Op. 68/5; Country Dance; 2 Elegiac Melodies, Op. 34; Holberg Suite, Op. 40; 2 Melodies, Op. 53.

*** Virgin VC5 45224-2. Norwegian CO, Brown – NIELSEN: *At the Bier of a Young Artist etc.* ***

The Norwegian Chamber Orchestra collect all of Grieg's music for strings. Very alert and responsive playing in a programme that offers such lovely music-making of great feeling and sensitivity. The recording, made in the glorious acoustic of Eidsvoll Church in Norway, is in the demonstration bracket.

Piano Concerto in A min. (original 1868/72 version); *Larviks-polka* (1858); *23 Small Pieces* (1859).

*** BIS CD 619. Derwinger, Norrköping SO, Hirokami.

This CD offers us a fascinating glimpse of how the concerto must have sounded to its contemporaries. Love Derwinger is the intelligent and accomplished soloist with the Norrköping orchestra, and he proves a sensitive guide in the collection of juvenilia that completes the disc. The *Larvikspolka*, written when Grieg was fifteen, is probably the very earliest of his piano pieces to survive, and the *Nine Children's Pieces* are all very slight in substance, but they fill out the picture of the young composer and the world in which he grew up. The concerto is well balanced and Love Derwinger's solo pieces are well recorded too.

Piano Concerto in A min., Op. 16.

(N) (M) *** Ph. (ADD) 464 702-2. Kovacevich, BBC SO, C. Davis – SCHUMANN: *Concerto.* ***

*** Sony SK 44899. Perahia, Bav. RSO, Davis – SCHUMANN: *Concerto.* ***

(B) *** Decca 433 628-2. Curzon, LSO, Fjeldstad – FRANCK: *Symphonic Variations* *** ✪; SCHUMANN: *Concerto.* ** (*)

*** EMI CDC7 54746-2. Vogt, CBSO, Rattle – SCHUMANN: *Concerto.* ***

(M) *** Decca (ADD) 466 383-2. Lupu, LSO, Previn – SCHUMANN: *Piano Concerto.* ***

(B) **(*) [EMI Red Line CDR5 69859]. Ousset, LSO, Marriner – SCHUMANN: *Piano Concerto.* **(*)

(***) EMI mono CDH7 63497-2. Lipatti, Philh. O, Galliera – CHOPIN: *Piano Concerto No. 1.* (**)

(M) (**(*)) EMI mono CDM5 66597-2. Gieseking, Philh. O, Karajan – FRANCK: *Symphonic Variations;* SCHUMANN: *Piano Concerto.* (**(*))

(N) *(*) Decca 467 093-2. Thibaudet, Rotterdam PO, Gergiev – CHOPIN: *Piano Concerto No. 2 in F min., Op. 21.* *(*)

(i) *Piano Concerto in A min.*; (ii) *Peer Gynt Suites Nos. 1–2*.

(B) **(*) DG 439 427-2. (i) Anda, BPO, Kubelik; (ii) BPO, Karajan.

(i) *Piano Concerto in A min.*; (ii) *Peer Gynt: Suites Nos. 1 & 2; Prelude; Dance of the Mountain King's Daughter*.

(M) *** Decca (ADD) 448 599-2. (i) Curzon, LPO; (ii) LSO; Fjeldstad.

(i) *Piano Concerto in A min., Op. 16. Solo piano music: Agitato* (1865); *Album Leaves, Op. 28/1 & 4; Lyric Pieces, Opp. 43, 54 & 65; Piano Sonata in E min., Op. 7; Poetic Tone Pictures, Op. 3/4–6*.

✪ (BB) *** Virgin 2 x 1 VBD5 61745-2 (2). Andsnes; (i) with Bergen PO, Kitaienko.

Whether in the clarity of virtuoso fingerwork or the shading of half-tone, Kovacevich is among the most illuminating of the many great pianists who have recorded the Grieg *Concerto*. He plays with bravura and refinement, the spontaneity of the music-making bringing a sparkle throughout, to balance the underlying poetry. The 1972 recording has been freshened most successfully and this now reappears as one of Philips's '50 Great Recordings'.

Perahia revels in the bravura as well as bringing out the lyrical beauty in radiantly poetic playing. He is commanding and authoritative when required, with the blend of spontaneity, poetic feeling and virtuoso display this music calls for. He is given sympathetic support by Sir Colin Davis and the fine Bavarian Radio Symphony Orchestra, and there is no finer version of the Grieg recorded in the digital age than this.

Curzon's approach to Grieg is wonderfully poetic and this is a performance with strength and power as well as lyrical tenderness. This reading is second to none in distilling the music's special atmosphere and is available coupled either with Franck and Schumann at bargain price or with more music by Grieg at mid-price in the 'Classic Sound' series. In its original format Fjeldstad's *Peer Gynt* was counted to be one of the really outstanding early Decca stereo LPs. The LSO is very sensitive, and the tender string-playing in *Solveig's Song* is quite lovely. Fjeldstad's persuasive direction is comparable with that of Beecham, making the listener feel he or she is experiencing this familiar music in a new way. The conductor builds up a blaze of excitement during *In the Hall of the Mountain King*. The early (1958) Kingsway Hall recording retains its glowing lustre, and only when the violins are under pressure above the stave is there some loss of sweetness.

Virgin Classics have now put together Andsnes's distinctive account of the *Piano Concerto* with his later piano recital, to which we gave a ◐. As a 2 x 1 Double it makes a remarkable bargain. In the concerto Andsnes wears his brilliance lightly. There is no lack of bravura and display, but no ostentation either. Indeed, he has great poetic feeling and delicacy of colour, and Grieg's familiar warhorse comes up with great freshness. He is excellently balanced in relation to the orchestra. His solo recital rightly won golden opinions. Besides the *Sonata* and various other short pieces, he offers three sets of the *Lyric Pieces*, including Op. 43, which opens with the famous *Butterfly*. Book VIII (Op. 65) is now included, with its touching *Melancholy* and lively *Wedding Day at Troldhaugen*, which Grieg later orchestrated, as he did Op. 54. Andsnes's virtuosity is always at the service of the composer and he plays with real imagination and lightness of touch.

Decca's remastering of Radu Lupu's fine 1973 Kingsway Hall recording, one of Decca's very best of the period, suits the style of the performance, which is boldly compelling in the outer movements, but has warmth and poetry too, especially striking in the slow movement, where Previn's hushed opening is particularly telling. Indeed, the orchestral contribution is a strong one throughout, while Lupu's playing has moments of touching delicacy, and this Decca performance must stand high on the list of mid- and bargain-priced recommendations.

Lars Vogt never allows his personality to obtrude; he colours the familiar phrases with great subtlety yet without the slightest trace of narcissism. He is very well supported by Rattle and the CBSO, and excellently recorded. An unusually sensitive player, his version, with the inevitable Schumann coupling, is eminently satisfying. Curzon, Kovacevich and

O'Hora are top recommendations, but among newcomers this has strong claims to be put among them.

Géza Anda's account of the *Piano Concerto* is more wayward than some but is strong in personality and has plenty of life. Kubelik's accompaniment is good too, and the 1963 recording sounds well. However, Karajan's analogue *Peer Gynt Suites* are in a class of their own. They were also recorded – a decade later – in the Berlin Jesus-Christus-Kirche but, for some reason, the CD transfer seems very brightly lit, although the fullness and analogue ambience are retained.

Ousset's is a strong, dramatic reading, not lacking in warmth and poetry but, paradoxically, bringing out what we would generally think of as the masculine qualities of power and drive. Marriner gives persuasive support, the sound is full, firm and clear, and this reading gives a refreshingly individual slant on a much-played work.

The famous 1947 Lipatti performance remains eternally fresh, and its return to the catalogue is a cause for rejoicing, although the ear now notices a slightly drier quality and a marginal loss of bloom.

Gieseking's 1951 recording with Karajan and the Philharmonia was overshadowed at the time by Lipatti and Curzon, understandably so. It was compared unfavourably with his pre-war account; but nevertheless, although some of the passage-work is open to the charge of being cursory, there is a great deal that gives delight – not least Gieseking's beautiful and poetic tone.

Thibaudet's very routine performance disappoints. There are good things, notably Gergiev's contribution in the slow movement, but for the most part Thibaudet's playing is curiously monochrome and overall this never fully springs to life.

2 *Elegiac Melodies*, Op. 34; *Erotik*; 2 *Melodies*, Op. 53; 2 *Norwegian Airs*, Op. 63.

(BB) **(*) Naxos 8.550330. Capella Istropolitana, Leaper – SIBELIUS: *Andante festivo* etc. ***

Adrian Leaper secures responsive and sensitive playing from the Capella Istropolitana in this Grieg collection, and the recording is very good indeed and the balance natural.

2 *Elegiac Melodies*; *Holberg Suite*, Op. 40.

(BB) **(*) ASV CDQS 6094 Swiss CO – SUK; TCHAIKOVSKY: *String Serenades*. ****

The Swiss Chamber Orchestra take the first movement of the *Holberg Suite* very briskly, but it is an enjoyably spick-and-span account, with good lyrical contrast; although the *Elegiac Melodies* lack opulence, these brightly recorded performances make a good bonus for outstanding versions of the Suk and Tchaikovsky *Serenades*.

2 *Elegiac Melodies* (*Heart's Wounds; The Last Spring*), Op. 34; *Holberg Suite*, Op. 40; 2 *Lyric Pieces* (*Evening in the Mountains; At the Cradle*); 2 *Melodies* (*Norwegian; The First Meeting*), Op. 53; 2 *Nordic Melodies* (*In Folk Style; Cow-Call*), Op. 63.

*** DG 437 520-2. Gothenburg SO, Järvi.

A most attractive and well-designed anthology. The *Holberg*

Suite is presented with much character, and the other folk melodies bring some beautiful playing from the Gothenburg strings. The two lovely *Elegiac Melodies* sound freshly minted and the innocent appeal of the much less familiar *Nordic Melodies* is fully captured. In the *Evening in the Mountains* the effect of oboe solo – backwardly placed as the composer intended – is piquantly and engagingly managed. The following *Cradle Song* is very touching. Excellent, bright, modern recording with a good ambient effect.

(i) 2 *Elegiac Melodies*, Op. 34; (ii) *Holberg Suite*, Op. 40; (iii) *Lyric Suite*, Op. 54; *Peer Gynt Suites Nos. 1*, Op. 46; 2, Op. 55; (iv) *String Quartet in G min.*, Op. 27; (v) *Violin Sonata No. 3*, Op. 45; (vi) *Lyric Pieces: Wedding-Day at Troldhaugen*.

(B) **(*) Finlandia Ultima 8573 81964-2 (2). (i) Ostrobothnian Chamber O, Kangas; (ii) Helsinki Strings; (iii) Norwegian Radio O, Rasilainen; (iv) New Helsinki Qt; (v) Söderblom, Tateno; (vi) Lagerspetz.

A generally recommendable set – the highlight being the New Helsinki Quartet's account of the *String Quartet*: a dramatic, well-shaped and vital performance, yet full of sensitivity and well recorded. In the *Peer Gynt* suites, the Norwegian Radio Orchestra, under their Finnish conductor, Ari Rasilainen, are certainly enjoyable, while the recording is good, but not outstanding. Similar comments apply to the lovely *Lyric Suite* (with the same forces) that follows. The *Holberg Suite* with the Helsinki strings comes off very well – lots of life in the vital outer movements matched by tenderness in the haunting *Andante religioso*. The *Sonata for Violin and Piano* receives a strong performance and is well recorded (the finale is especially captivating), and with two other attractive short fillers, this double Ultima CD is good value at bargain price, although there is virtually no information about the music in the documentation, only a short biography of the composer.

(i) 2 *Elegiac Melodies*, Op. 34; *Lyric Suite*, Op. 54: *Norwegian March & Nocturne*. *Norwegian Dance*, Op. 35/2; (i) *Peer Gynt Suites Nos. 1–2* (including *Solveig's lullaby*); (i) *Sigurd Jorsalfar: Homage March*, Op. 56/3.

(B) *** Sony SBK 53257. (i) Phd. O, Ormandy; (ii) Söderström, New Philh. O, Davis.

Andrew Davis offers freshly thought performances of the two *Peer Gynt Suites*, beautifully played and warmly recorded at Abbey Road in 1976. A special attraction is the singing of Elisabeth Söderström, not only in *Solveig's song* but also in *Solveig's lullaby*, which has been added to the second suite. The Ormandy recordings date from a decade earlier but they make up a most attractive anthology. The orchestral playing is very good indeed and Ormandy's warmth is obvious. The transfers are well managed.

Holberg Suite, Op. 40.

(B) *** Carlton IMP 30367 02242. Serenata of London – ELGAR: *Serenade*; MOZART: *Eine kleine Nachtmusik* etc. ***

The performance by the Serenata of London is first class in every way, spontaneous, naturally paced, and played with considerable eloquence. However, as we go to press this issue has been deleted.

Holberg Suite, Op. 40; Lyric Suite, Op. 54; 4 Norwegian Dances, Op. 35; Old Norwegian Romance with Variations, Op. 51; Peer Gynt (incidental music): Suites Nos. 1, Op. 46; 2, Op. 55; Sigurd Jorsalfar (suite), Op. 56; Symphonic Dances, Op. 64.

(B) ** Ph. Duo (ADD) 462 290-2 (2) ECO, or Philh. O, Leppard.

Leppard's performances included in the alternative Philips Duo above (the so-called '*Best of Grieg*' which offers also the *Piano Concerto*) are here extended to include instead more orchestral music. Leppard is at his very best in the *Old Norwegian Romance with Variations*. But the performances from Barbirolli – see below – have far more character.

Holberg Suite, Op. 40; Peer Gynt Suites Nos. 1 & 2.

*** DG 439 010-2. BPO, Karajan – SIBELIUS: *Finlandia; Valse triste; Swan of Tuonela*. ***

Karajan's performance of the *Holberg Suite* is the finest currently available. The playing has wonderful lightness and delicacy, with cultured phrasing not robbing the music of its immediacy, while in *Peer Gynt* many subtleties of colour and texture are revealed by the vividly present recording, clear and full and with a firm bass-line, especially in the thrillingly gutsy *In the Hall of the Mountain King*. Grieg's perennially fresh score is marvellously played. *Anitra* dances with elegance, and the *Death of Aase* is movingly eloquent. The digital recording now proves to be one of the best to have emerged from the Philharmonie in the early 1980s.

In Autumn Overture, Op. 11; Lyric Piece: Erotik, Op. 43/5; Norwegian Dances, Op. 35; Old Norwegian Romance with Variations, Op. 51.

*** Chan. 9028. Iceland SO, Sakari (with SVENDSEN: 2 *Icelandic Melodies* for strings ***).

The Iceland orchestra play very responsively for their Finnish conductor, Petri Sakari, who gives very natural and straightforward accounts of this endearing music. Highly musical performances, with no lack of personality, truthfully recorded. Very recommendable.

In Autumn, Op. 11; Peer Gynt Suites Nos. 1 & 2; Symphonic Dances, Op. 64.

(N) *** Erato 8573 82917-2. CBSO, Oramo.

This is one of the best Grieg discs of the last few years. The overture *In Autumn* is a revision of an early work Grieg made for the Birmingham Festival, and so it is an appropriate work for Sakari Oramo to include in his début recording with the Birmingham orchestra. In his hands the *Peer Gynt* suites sound as fresh as they must have been in the 1890s. Oramo and his players also convey the charm, sparkle and innocence of the *Symphonic Dances*, and the recorded sound is altogether first class. Highly recommended.

Lyric Suite, Op. 54; Norwegian Dances, Op. 35/1–4; Symphonic Dances, Op. 64. Sigurd Jorsalfor (incidental music): Homage March, Op. 56/3.

*** Barbirolli Society/ Dutton Lab. (ADD) CDSJB 1012. Hallé
O, Barbirolli.

The set of four *Symphonic Dances* is the earliest recording
here, dating from 1957. With Harold Lawrence leading a
team of Mercury engineers, the sound is if anything even
cleaner and brighter than the first-rate EMI quality for the
rest, recorded in 1969–70. Sir John brings out all their drama
and colour, and the orchestral wind soloists make an often
memorable contribution. There are characteristic touches
too in the rest of the programme, notably in the expressive
warmth of the *Nocturne* in the *Lyric Suite*, and in the *Homage
March* from *Sigurd Jorsalfar*. The *Norwegian Dances*, too, are
affectionately done and very positively presented. As ever,
Mike Dutton gives the sound plenty of body and weight,
not least in the *Symphonic Dances* and finally in the *Homage
March*, which rounds the selection off.

*Lyric Suite, Op. 54; Sigurd Jorsalfar (Suite), Op. 56;
Symphonic Dances, Op. 64.*

**(*) ASV CDDCA 722. RPO, Butt.

The *Symphonic Dances* are particularly successful here. They
are not easy to bring off, yet Butt and the RPO capture their
charm and energy without succumbing to melodrama in
No. 4. The *Lyric Suite*, too, is fresh and the trolls in the finale
have an earthy pungency. However, the outer movements
of *Sigurd Jorsalfar* bring an element of ponderousness. Excellent, vivid recording.

4 Symphonic Dances; Peer Gynt Suites Nos. 1–2.

(N) (BB) **(*) EMI Encore Dig./ADD CDE5 74731-2.
Bournemouth SO, Berglund (with ALFVEN: *Swedish
Rhapsody No. 1*; JARNEFELT: *Praeludium*. ***)

Berglund's attractive performances of the *Symphonic Dances*
are available on this inexpensive EMI Encore reissue coupled
with strongly characterized performances of the two *Peer
Gynt* suites. Here *Ingrid's Lament* is notably sombre, and
very well played. But elsewhere there is some lack of charm,
and the recording has the artificial brilliance that one used
to associate with EMI's hi-fi-conscious Studio Two techniques, so that the upper string sound is clear and vivid
rather than rich-textured. However, the inclusion of two
favourite encore pieces by Alfvén and Järnefelt – both based
on catchy melodies – makes this disc quite enticing.

Symphony in C min.; Symphonic Dances, Op. 64.

(N) *** Finlandia 8573 8777-2. Norwegian RO, Rasilainen.
(BB) ** Virgin Classics 2 x 1 VBD5 61621-2 (2). Bergen PO,
Kitaienko – Vocal music: *Bergliot; Olav Trygvason; Funeral
March*. ***

Grieg's *Symphony in C minor* is an early student work. It is
not particularly characteristic, although Grieg may have
been unduly self-critical in condemning it to total oblivion.
First choice now lies with the Norwegian Radio Orchestra
under Ari Rasilainen, whose performance is a strong one,
with plenty of impetus and a notably eloquent *Adagio*, its
coda particularly beautiful. Moreover, the *Symphonic Dances*
are outstandingly successful, the *First* and *Fourth* strongly
rhythmic, and the inner movements full of colour and
sparkle, with some lovely wind playing. As in the *Symphony*,

the recording is full-bloodedly resonant, adding to the
music's weight and substance.

Kitaienko and the Bergen Philharmonic offer a well-
prepared account of the *Symphony* and it is well recorded.
But the performance is by no means as persuasive as the
reading by Ari Rasilainen. Nor does Kitaienko's account of
the *Symphonic Dances* displace Rasilainen's account. The
principal appeal of this Virgin 2 x 1 Double is its economy
and the coupled vocal music, which is altogether more
successful.

CHAMBER MUSIC

Cello Sonata in A min., Op. 36.

**(*) CRD 3391. Cohen, Vignoles – FRANCK: *Cello
Sonata*. **(*)

Cello Sonata in A min., Op. 36; Intermezzo.

*** Ph. (IMS) 454 458-2. Lloyd Webber, Forsberg – DELIUS:
Cello Sonata; 2 Pieces; Romance; Hassan: Serenade. ***

*Cello Sonata in A min.; Intermezzo in A min.; Piano
Sonata, Op. 7.*

(BB) *** Naxos 8.550878. Birkeland, Gimse.

In their apt coupling of the complete cello and piano music
of both Delius and Grieg, Julian Lloyd Webber and Bengt
Forsberg give a magnetic performance of the Grieg sonata,
among the most inspired and intense of his longer works.
With plenty of light and shade, the pianissimos from both
cellist and pianist are daringly extreme, magically so in the
central slow movement with its haunting quotation from
Grieg's *Homage March*.

Oystein Birkeland and Håvard Gimse also give the sonata
an alive and sensitive account, coupled with the early and
unrepresentative *Intermezzo in A minor*. They are both
imaginative players and are decently recorded. Given the
modest outlay involved, this competes very strongly with its
rivals, but even if it were at mid- or full-price it would be
highly recommendable. Håvard Gimse's performance of the
early *Piano Sonata*, Op. 7, is also very good indeed.
Altogether a first-rate bargain.

In the folk element Cohen might have adopted a more
persuasive style, bringing out the charm of the music more,
but certainly he sustains the sonata structures well. The
recording presents the cello very convincingly. It has been
most naturally transferred to CD.

String Quartet No. 1 in G min., Op. 27.

(BB) *** Finlandia 0927 40601-2. New Helsinki Qt –
SIBELIUS: *Quartet in D min. Op. 56*. ***
(M) (***) Biddulph mono LAB 098. Budapest Qt – SIBELIUS:
Quartet; WOLF: *Italian Serenade*. (***)
(N) ** Meridian CDE 84401. Bridge Qt – DELIUS: *String
Quartet* (with GRAINGER: *Molly on the Shore* **).

*String Quartets Nos. 1 in G min., Op. 27; 2 in F
(unfinished).*

(BB) *** Naxos 8.550879. Oslo String Qt – JOHANSEN: *String
Quartet*. ***

String Quartets Nos. 1 in G minor, Op. 27; 2 in F (unfinished).

*** Hyp. CDA 67117. Chilingirian Qt.

String Quartets Nos. 1–2; (i) Andante con moto for Piano Trio. Fugue in F min.

*** Olympia OCD 432. Raphael Qt, (i) with Röling.

String Quartets Nos. 1–2; Fugue (1861).

*** Victoria VCD 19048. Norwegian Qt.
**(*) BIS CD 543. Kontra Qt.

The Naxos account of the quartets from the Oslo String Quartet, a relatively new group, proves the best of the lot – indeed it is the best version we have had since the Budapest. They would easily sweep the board even at full price, on account of their sensitivity, tonal finesse and blend, and the keenness of their artistic responses. They play only the first two movements of the *F major Quartet*, leaving room for a fine quartet by Grieg's biographer, David Monrad Johansen. The recording balance, made in the Norwegian Radio studios, is excellent, neither too forward nor too recessed.

The Chilingirians leave off where Grieg did, just as the Oslo Quartet do on Naxos. They have lavished much care on it. and their disc is expertly engineered by Arne Kaselborg and Andrew Keener. Recommended alongside the Naxos (which is also excellent in every way).

The version of the *First Quartet* from the New Helsinki Quartet couples it with the Sibelius *Quartet*. It is dramatic, well shaped and vital, yet full of sensitivity and can be strongly recommended among modern recordings, assuming price is no consideration. Apart from the excellence of the playing, the recording is also very present and well detailed. But the Naxos coupling makes a more obvious primary recommendation.

The Budapest Quartet's recording dates from 1936, but its attractions in terms of coupling here are strong. The Sibelius *Voces intimae* and the Hugo Wolf *Italian Serenade* are both superb performances and still remain unsurpassed. The Biddulph transfer is excellent.

The Raphael Quartet do not give quite as spirited an account of the *F major Quartet* as the Oslo Quartet, but their CD enjoys two points of special interest: they give us Julius Röntgen's conjectural realization of the sketches to the remaining two movements Grieg had planned for the *F major Quartet*; and they also include another rarity in the shape of the *Andante con moto* for piano trio.

The Norwegian Quartet may not be immaculate in terms of tonal blend or ensemble but the performances are decent and have plenty of spirit, and the recorded sound is excellent.

The Kontras play with much dramatic power and invest the music with great feeling; one would hesitate to speak of unforced eloquence. In this respect the Norwegians score, for their playing is somehow truer in scale. The BIS recording is excellent and, though not a first choice artistically, the disc is perfectly recommendable.

This Meridian issue of No. 1 celebrates the friendship between these three composers. The Bridge Quartet play with great feeling and no mean imagination, but there are better finished and more finely tuned accounts available.

Violin Sonatas Nos. 1 in F, Op. 8; 2 in G, Op. 13; 3 in C min., Op. 45.

*** DG 437 525-2. Dumay, Pires.
(N) *** Simax PSC 1162. Tonnesen, Smebye.
*** Chan. 9184. L. and E. Mordkovitch.

Like the *Piano Concerto*, the *Violin Sonatas* works possess extraordinary resilience and survive countless repetition. The French violinist, Augustin Dumay, and his distinguished partner, Maria João Pires, give poised, animated accounts of all three sonatas. Their performances are exemplary in every way, and the recorded sound is also excellent in terms of both balance and realism.

In each sonata Terje Tonnesen plays with much sweetness of tone and tenderness of feeling. His virtuosity is disarmingly effortless and there is a lyric and expressive grace that his captivating. His partner, Einar Henning Smebye, is sensitive and responsive, and the balance is excellent. For many this will be a first choice, although Dumay and Pires are in some ways more individual.

The same goes for Lydia and Elena Mordkovitch (*mère et fille*) on an admirably recorded Chandos CD. They, too, give splendidly fresh and well-shaped accounts of all three sonatas which give much pleasure in music-making. Affectionate yet virile performances – thoroughly recommendable.

Violin Sonata No. 3 in C min., Op. 45.

(B) *** EMI Début CZS5 72825-2. Zambrzycki-Payne, Presland
  – BRITTEN: *Suite for Violin & Piano, Op. 6;*
  SZYMANOWSKI: *Violin Sonata, Op. 9.* ***

Rafal Zambrzycki-Payne is the young Polish-born player who was the 1996 'BBC Young Musician of the Year'. In the *C minor Sonata*, he has a youthful ardour that carries the listener with him. There is a strong musical personality here and his partner Carole Presland is hardly less impressive. The Abbey Road recording is expertly balanced and sounds very natural.

PIANO MUSIC

Einar Steen-Nøkleberg Complete Naxos Series

Einar Steen-Nøkleberg has recorded every note of music Grieg composed for the piano. He has impressive musical credentials and is, among other things, the author of a book on Grieg's piano music and its interpretation. His survey displaces earlier sets in quality: he is responsive to mood and is searchingly imaginative in his approach.

Volume 1: *Funeral March in Memory of Rikard Nordraak; Humoresques, Op. 6; I love You (Jeg elsker dig), Op. 41/3; Melodies of Norway: The Sirens' Enticement. Moods (Stimmungen), Op. 73; 4 Piano Pieces, Op. 1; Sonata in E min., Op. 7.*

(BB) *** Naxos 8.550881. Steen-Nøkleberg.

Steen-Nøkleberg does not proceed chronologically: the first disc couples early and late Grieg – the very earliest of his published pieces, written while he was still studying at Leipzig, the *Humoresques*, Op. 6, and the *E minor Piano*

Sonata, Op. 7, alongside the *Stimmungen* ('Moods'), Op. 73, composed in the early years of the present century (1901–5). Whether the music is early or late, Steen-Nøkleberg plays with total sympathy and dedication, and he is beautifully recorded throughout in the Lindeman Hall of the Norwegian State Academy of Music. Only in the *Sonata* does he suffer a trace of self-consciousness.

Volume 2: *The First Meeting, Op. 52/2; Improvisations on 2 Norwegian Folksongs, Op. 29; Melodies of Norway: Ballad to St Olaf. 25 Norwegian Folksongs & Dances, Op. 17; 19 Norwegian Folksongs, Op. 66.*

(BB) *** Naxos 8.550882. Steen-Nøkleberg.

The second disc includes the remarkable *Nineteen Norwegian Folksongs*, Op. 66, which are contemporaneous with what many would see as Grieg's masterpiece, the song-cycle *Haugtussa*, which the composer himself spoke of as full of 'hair-raising' chromatic harmonies. (One of the folksongs appears in Delius's *On Hearing the First Cuckoo in Spring*.) But the earlier set, Op. 17, written not long after the first version of the *Piano Concerto*, is also full of delights.

Volume 3: *4 Album Leaves, Op. 28; Ballade, Op. 24; Melodies of Norway: Iceland. Pictures from Everyday Life (Humoresques), Op. 19; Poetic Tone-pictures, Op. 3; Sigurd Jorsalfar: Prayer, Op. 56/1.*

(BB) *** Naxos 8.550883. Steen-Nøkleberg.

Volume 4: *Holberg Suite, Op. 40; Melodies of Norway: I Went to Bed so Late. 6 Norwegian Mountain Melodies; Peer Gynt Suite No. 1, Op. 46/1: Morning. Norwegian Peasant Dances (Slåtter) Op. 72.*

(BB) *** Naxos 8.550884. Steen-Nøkleberg.

The third CD includes the poignant *Ballade in G min.*, Op. 24, composed by Grieg on the death of his parents, Steen-Nøkleberg is highly imaginative and, even if some may find his rubato a little extreme, the keyboard colouring is subtle and rich. He conveys a splendidly rhapsodic spontaneity and there is much feeling. This and the companion disc, with the *Seventeen Norwegian Peasant Dances* (*Slåtter*), Op. 72, deserve a particularly strong recommendation. These extraordinary pieces with their quasi-Bartókian clashes are most characterful in Steen-Nøkleberg's hands.

Volume 5: *Norway's Melodies Nos. 1–63.*

(BB) **(*) Naxos 8.553391. Steen-Nøkleberg.

Volume 6: *Norway's Melodies Nos. 64–117.*

(BB) **(*) Naxos 8.553392. Steen-Nøkleberg.

Volume 7: *Norway's Melodies Nos. 118–52 (EG 108).*

(BB) **(*) Naxos 8.553393. Steen-Nøkleberg.

The next three discs are devoted to *Norges Melodier* ('Norway's Melody'), an anthology Grieg made in the mid-1870s for a Danish publisher, of 'easy to play' arrangements of tunes, some of them charming, others less so Steen-Nøkleberg plays some on the house-organ or harmonium, some on the clavichord, some on a Graf piano to match those sonorities which would have been familiar in Norwegian homes in the 1870s, and some on a Steinway.

Volume 8: *Lyric Pieces: Book I, Op. 12; Book II, Op. 38; Book III, Op. 43; Book IV, Op. 47.*

(BB) *** Naxos 8.553394. Steen-Nøkleberg.

Volume 9: *Lyric Pieces: Book V, Op. 54; Book VI, Op. 57; Book VII, Op. 62.*

(BB) *** Naxos 8.553395. Steen-Nøkleberg.

Volume 10: *Lyric Pieces: Book VIII, Op. 65; Book IX, Op. 68; Book X, Op. 71.*

(BB) *** Naxos 8.553396. Steen-Nøkleberg.

Volumes 8–10 survey the delightful *Lyric Pieces*. They are admirably fresh and are presented with the utmost simplicity, yet are obviously felt. These performances come into direct competition with Daniel Adni's not quite complete but otherwise excellent set on an EMI forte double CD. Many will like to have the coverage absolutely complete, and the three Naxos discs cost about the same. The EMI piano-sound is perhaps very slightly warmer and fuller, but the Naxos recording is wholly natural and believable. Einar Steen-Nøkleberg is totally idiomatic and authoritative, and readers wanting a complete set need not hesitate.

Volume 11: *Bergliot, Op. 42; Peer Gynt Suites Nos. 1, Op. 46; 2, Op. 55; Sigurd Jorsalfar (Suite), Op. 22; (i) Olav Trygvason, Op. 50: 2 Pieces.*

(BB) *** Naxos 8.553397. Steen-Nøkleberg; (i) Norwegian State Institute of Music Chamber Ch., Schiøll.

Volume 12: *Agitato, EG 106; Albumblad, EG 109; Norwegian Dances, Op. 35; (i) Peer Gynt: excerpts, Op. 23 including Dance of the Mountain King's Daughter, Op. 55/5 (Op. 23/9); 3 Piano transcriptions from Sigurd Jorsalfar. Waltz Caprices, Op. 37. arr. of* HALVORSEN: *Entry of the Boyards.*

(BB) *** Naxos 8.553398. Steen-Nøkleberg; (i) Norwegian State Instute of Music Chamber Ch., Schiøll.

With the remaining four volumes we enter the realm of Grieg's transcriptions of his orchestral works and his juvenilia, as well as sketches for works that did not materialize. Most valuable are the *Waltz Caprices*, Op. 37, and the early *Agitato*, EG 106, and *Albumblad*, EG 109. Both these issues are recommendable but dispensable.

Volume 13: *2 Elegaic Melodies, Op. 34; 2 Melodies, Op. 53; 2 Nordic Melodies, Op. 63; Norwegian Melodies Nos. 6 & 22; 3 Piano Pieces, EG 105; 3 Piano Pieces, EG 110/112; Piano transcriptions of Songs, Op. 41.*

(BB) *** Naxos 8.553399. Steen-Nøkleberg.

Volume 14: *At the Halfdan Kjerulf Statue, EG 167; Canon a 4 voci for Organ, EG 179; Piano Concerto in B min. (fragments), EG 120; Larsvikspola, EG 101; Mountain Song, Norwegian Melodies Nos. 87 & 146, EG 108; 23 Small Pieces for Piano, EG 104; Piano Sonata Op. 7 (1st version: mvts 2 and 4); Piano transcriptions of Songs, Op. 52.*

(BB) *** Naxos 8.553400. Steen-Nøkleberg.

The last two volumes are another matter. Volume 13 brings rarities in the shape of the *Three Piano Pieces*, EG 105, and a further three, EG 110–112, all of which are otherwise available only on Love Dervinger's full-priced BIS record of the 1874 version of the *Piano Concerto*. The last volume is of particular interest in that it brings – in addition to various juvenilia – the sketches for a *Second Piano Concerto* – very Lisztian – and the first versions of the slow movement and finale of the Op. 7 *Sonata*.

Ballade, Op. 24; 4 Lyric Pieces: March of the Dwarfs; Notturno, Op. 54/3–4; Wedding Day at Troldhaugen, Op. 65/6; Peace of the Woods, Op. 71/4. Sonata in E min., Op. 7; arr. of songs: Cradle Song; I Love Thee; The Princess; You Cannot Grasp the Wave's Eternal Course. Peer Gynt: Solveig's Song.

**(*) Olympia (ADD) OCD 197. Katin.

The *Sonata* is not one of Grieg's finest works, but it has a touching *Andante* and is agreeably inventive, if perhaps conventionally so. Peter Katin gives it a clean, direct performance, and he is impressive in the rather dolorous set of variations which forms the *Ballade*. The song arrangements, too, come off well, and the four *Lyric Pieces* are presented very appealingly.

Carnival Scene, Op. 19/3; 7 Fugues, EG.184a–g. Lyric Pieces: Berceuse, Op. 38/1; Butterfly; To Spring, Op. 43/1 & 6; Melody, Op. 47/3; March of the Trolls; Scherzo; Bell-ringing, Op. 54/3, 5 & 6; Brooklet, Op. 62/4; In Ballad Vein; Wedding Day at Troldhaugen, Op. 65/5 & 6; Grandmother's Minuet, Op. 68/2. Piano Sonata in E minor, Op. 7.

⬤ *** DG 459 671-2. Pletnev.

There are fewer *Lyric Pieces* here than on Gilels's classic DG recording, which has held sway for more than a quarter of a century. But Pletnev finds room for the *E minor Sonata*, the *Carnival Scene*, and seven early *Fugues*. He brings great delicacy, control of keyboard colour, and freshness to Grieg's youthful *Sonata*, which can be recommended alongside Andsnes (Virgin – see above). The *Fugues* are student exercises from Grieg's Leipzig years, but Pletnev succeeds in making them sound like music. This CD is likely to be to the next quarter of a century what Gilels was to the last.

Lyric Pieces: Book I, Op. 12; Book II, Op. 38; Book III, Op. 43; Book IV, Op. 47; Book V, Op. 54; Book VI, Op. 57; Book VII, Op. 62; Book VIII, Op. 65; Book IX, Op. 68; Book X, Op. 71.

(BB) **(*) Arte Nova 74321 63647-2. Henschel.

Florian Henschel is both sensitive and intelligent and his survey is accorded very well-balanced recorded sound. The accompanying notes are short – just as well, perhaps, as they are the most ignorant we have seen

Lyric Pieces: Op. 12/3, 5, 7 & 8; Op. 38/1, 3 & 6; Opp. 43, 47 & 54; Op. 57; Opp. 62, 65, 68 & 71.

(B) *** EMI Double forte (ADD) CZS5 68634-2 (2). Adni.

Daniel Adni has also made a complete recording but, in order to fit the majority of the works on to two CDs (with a total playing time of 155 minutes), some of the earlier pieces from Books I and II have been omitted. Adni plays with genuine feeling for their character and a strong sense of atmosphere, and the 1973 EMI recording is very good indeed.

Lyric Pieces: Opp. 12/2, 7; 38/1, 3; 43/1-6 (1, 2, 4, 6 two versions); 47/2, 3, 4; 54/1, 3, 4, 6; 57/6; 62/3, 5, 6; 65/1, 2, 6 (6 two versions); 68/2, 3, 5; 71/2, 3, 4, 7; Norwegian Bridal Procession, Op. 19/2.

(BB) **(*) EMI mono CHS5 66775-2 (2).(BB)Gieseking –
MENDELSSOHN: *Songs Without Words.* **(*)

Gieseking was a distinguished interpreter of the *Lyric Pieces* as his pre-war 78s testify. However these recordings made towards the end of his life are not really his most inspired. Of course, some are touched by his special poetry but others sound a little as if he is on automatic pilot. The recorded sound too, is a little studio-bound.

Lyric Pieces: Op. 12/1; Op. 38/1; Op. 43/1–2; Op. 47/2–4; Op. 54/4–5; Op. 57/6; Op. 62/4 & 6; Op. 68/2, 3 & 5; Op. 71/ 1, 3 & 6–7.

⬤ (M) *** DG (ADD) 449 721-2. Gilels.

With Gilels we are in the presence of a great keyboard master whose characterization and control of colour and articulation are wholly remarkable. An altogether outstanding record in every way. This recording has been admirably remastered for reissue in DG's 'Originals' series and now sounds better than ever.

Lyric Pieces, Op. 12/1, 4 & 5; Op. 38/1–2, 5 & 7; Op. 43/1, 4 & 6; Op. 47, 1–4; Op. 54/1–4; Op. 57/6; Op. 62/3, 4 & 6; Op. 65/5–6; Op. 68/9; Op. 71/3 & 7.

(BB) *** Naxos 8.554051. Steen-Nøkleberg.

A compilation disc for those who do not want to invest in all three of this artist's discs of the *Lyric Pieces*. Very distinguished playing, though not to be preferred to Gilels's anthology in the DG 'Originals' series.

Lyric Pieces: Op. 12/1, 6; Op. 38/5; Op. 54/1, 4 & 5; Op. 57/4, 6; Op. 62/3, 4 & 6; Op. 65/1–4; Op. 68/2, 4 & 5; Op. 71/1.

**(*) Naxos 8.550650. Szokolay.

Lyric Pieces: Op. 12/3, 8; Op. 38/1; Op. 43/1, 3 & 6; Op. 47/ 3–7; Op. 54/3, 5–6; Op. 57/1–3; Op. 62/1–2, 5; Op. 65/6; Op. 71/7.

**(*) Naxos 8.550557. Szokolay.

Naxos are not always lucky with their piano recordings, but the two CDs that Balázs Szokolay has recorded are very good. Szokolay's playing is not as consistently subtle in colouring or as poetic in feeling as that of Leif Ove Andsnes, but it is pretty idiomatic. However, at super-bargain price it is without doubt very good value indeed, and although the balance is very slightly close, it is not oppressively so. Both CDs give pleasure.

'The long, long winter night': Norwegian Folksongs & Slåtter, Opp. 66 & 73.

*** EMI CDC5 56541-2. Andsnes (with recital Monrad
JOHANSEN: *Portraits, Op. 5*; SAEVERUD: *Slåtter og stev fra Siljastøl*; Geirr TVEITT: Hardanger folk tunes,
Op. 150; VALEN: *Variations, Op. 23*).

Here is a second unforgettable recital by Grieg's countryman, Leif Ove Andsnes, made the more attractive by the rarity of the repertoire included. His playing, ever sensitive and full of special insights, is a joy, and he is given EMI best quality piano sound.

VOCAL MUSIC

A capella choral music: (i) *At the Halvdan Kjerulf monument; Ave maris stella; Dona nobis pacem;* (ii) *4 Psalms, Op. 74; Holberg Cantata; Male-voice choruses: Election song; Impromptu; Inga Litamor; The late rose; Westerly wind.*

*** Simax PSC 1187. (i) Sandve; (ii) Vollestad; Oslo Ph. Ch., Skiöld.

Grieg's *a cappella* output is among the least known. This disc by the Oslo Philharmonic Choir offers a generous helping of it and presents it persuasively. His last work, the *Four Psalms, Op. 74,* dates from 1906 and is based on traditional tunes of popular Norwegian origin. The Oslo Philharmonic Choir produce a beautiful and well-blended sound. Good recording.

Orchestral songs: *Album lines, Departed; En svane (The swan); Eros* (orch. Reger) *Fra Monte pincio* (orch. Grieg); *Spillemnd (Fiddlers); The mountain thrall, Op. 26; The princess; 4 songs, Op. 60; 6 Songs, Op. 48; To the motherland. A vision* (orch Byl) *With a water-lily. Peer Gynt: Solveig's cradle song.*

*** Dinemec DCCD022. Farley, LPO or Philh. O, Serebrier.

This anthology collects 23 Grieg songs, three in the composer's own orchestrations but the vast majority in transcriptions by the conductor, José Serebrier. Some of them, like *Princessan (The Princess)* do not gain in the process, but the vast majority do, and Serebrier's orchestrations are both expert and idiomatic. Carole Farley does not use the white-toned, vibrato-free style favoured by some of the younger generation of Norwegian singers, but her disc is none the worse for that. Only occasionally is her vibrato obtrusive. For the most part she commands a wide expressive range and exhibits considerable feeling for the character of each of the songs. Moreover the orchestral support is sensitive and the recording well balanced.

Songs in historic performances (1888–1924): *Den første møte (First meeting); Dulgte kjaerlighed (Hidden love); En fuglevis (A bird-song); Eros; Fra Monte Pincio; Den gamle vise (The old song); God Morgen; Jag elsker Dig (I love thee); Jag reiste en deilig sommerkvaeld (I walked one balmy summer evening); Killingdans (Kids' dance); Kongekvadet (The king's song); Margretas Vuggesang (Margreta's cradle song); Mens jeg venter (On the water); Moderen synger (The mother's lament); Norønnafolket (The Northland folk); Og jeg vil ha mig en Hjertenskaer (Midsummer eve); Ragnhild; Solveig's song; Solveigs vuggevise (Solveig's lullaby); Stambogsrim (Album lines); En Svane (A swan); Takk for dit råd (Say what you will); Eine Traume (A dream); Trudom (Faith); Våren (Spring); Vaer hilset I Damer (Greetings, fair ladies).*

(*(**)) SIMAX mono PSC 1810 (3). Ackté, Anselmi, Barrientos, Bryhn-Landgaard, Bronnum, Burg, Burzio, Bye, Chaliapin,

Clément, Cornelius, Destinn, Eide, Elwes, Elizza, Farrar, Flagstad, Forsell, Galli-Curci, Gates, Gerhardt, Graarud, Gulbranson, Grieg, Hedemark, Heim, Hempel, Herold, Hultgren, Jadlower, Kernic, Kline, Kruszelnicka, Lehmann, Lütken, Lykseth-Schjerven, Monrad, Ohman, Olitzka, Rethberg, Schumann-Heink, Scheidemantel, Slezak, Stückgold, Schwarz, Tauber, Tetrazzini (various pianists).

As the cast-list shows, this is a veritable treasure-house of singing at the turn of the century, not only in northern Europe but elsewhere. Naturally in the early years of the gramophone singers tended to gravitate towards a handful of songs so that familiar numbers such as *Jag elsker Dig* and *En Svane* turn up in several versions, the former eleven times and the latter seven. There are no fewer than sixteen different versions of *Solveig's song,* including a few bars sung without accompaniment by Nina Grieg in 1889 when she would have been forty-four, and, although she is barely audible through the deluge of background noise, the voice is obviously of great purity. The roll-call of performers is pretty dazzling, ranging as it does from big names such as Aino Ackté (for whom Sibelius composed *Luonnotar*), to Chaliapin and Emmy Destinn (the copy of her *Mens jeg venter* is unfortunately pretty rough) and there are forty-seven singers in all, but the less familiar names also offer valuable insights into performance practice. There are nearly eighty performances altogether, and the quality of the recordings which have been subjected to the NoNoise system of reduction calls for more tolerance than many listeners will feel able to extend. This is a set for libraries, specialist collectors and students of song, and it is an invaluable resource into which to dip.

4 Songs, Op. 14; 6 Songs, Op. 49; Songs from Peer Gynt, Op. 55.

**(*) Victoria VCD 19038. Hirsti, Sandve, Skram, Jansen.

Marianne Hirsti possesses a voice of great purity; her intonation is spot-on, and the overall sound radiates a childlike innocence. She is heard at her best in, say, *Margaret's cradle song,* one of the four songs of Op. 15 and Grieg's very first setting of Ibsen. Characterization, on the other hand, is not always her strong suit; all the same, it's a beautiful voice. Knut Skram has lost some of the bloom his voice once possessed – though none of his artistry or musical intelligence. Good recordings throughout.

Songs: *At Rodane; A bird song; The first primrose; From Monte Pincio; Hope; I love but thee; I walked one balmy summer evening; Last spring; Margaret's cradle song; On the water; The princess; Spring showers; A swan; To her II; Two brown eyes; Upon a grassy hillside. 4 Poems from Bjørnstjerne Bjørnson's Fishermaiden, Op. 21; 6 Songs, Op. 48; Peer Gynt: Solveig's song; Solveig's cradle song.*

(BB) **(*) Naxos 8.553781. Arnesen, Eriksen.

An inexpensive and, at 70 minutes, well-filled CD, beautifully recorded and pleasingly sung. Bodil Arnesen has a voice of great purity and radiance. She sings marvellously in tune, though some may find that in this repertoire she has something of a 'little-girl', innocent quality that does not give the whole picture. This perhaps is troubling when you are listening to all the songs straight off. Taken a group at a time, she will touch most hearts, particularly in the setting of Bjørnson's *Prinsessen* and *Det første møte*. Erling Eriksen is an excellent pianist.

(i) *Bergliot, Op. 42;* (ii) *Den Bergtekne (The mountain thrall), Op. 32;* (iii & iv) *Foran sydens kloster (Before a Southern Convent);* (ii & iii) *7 Songs with Orchestra: Den første møde; Solveigs sang; Solveigs vuggesang; Fra Monte Pincio; En svane; Våren; Henrik Wegeland.*

(B) *** DG 469 026-2. (i) Tellefsen, (ii) Hagegård; (iii & iv) Bonney; (iii) Stene; Gothenburg SO, Järvi.

Before a Southern Convent is based on a Bjørnson poem which tells how Ingigerd, the daughter of a chieftain, has seen her father murdered by the villainous brigand, Arnljot. He was on the verge of raping her but relented and let her go; she seeks expiation by entering a foreign convent, and the piece ends with a chorus of nuns who admit her to their number. It's not great Grieg but it's well worth investigating, and is very naturally balanced. Generally speaking, the quality on all these DG recordings is excellent. *Bergliot* is an orchestral melodrama with narration, and one is aurally gripped, even while not understanding a word! For the whole collection is reissued without either texts or translations. It is sad that a company like DG could do this. Surely better to charge mid-price, and offer proper documentation.

(i) *Bergliot, Op. 42;* (ii) *Olav Trygvason, Op. 50; Funeral March for Rikard Nordraak.*

(BB) *** Virgin Classics 2 x 1 VBD5 61621-2 (2). (i) Fjeldstad; (ii) Kringelborn, Stene, Vollestad, Trondheim Ch.; Trondheim SO, Rudd – Orchestral music: *Symphony; Symphonic Dances.* **

The three scenes from *Olav Trygvason* are all that survives of Grieg's only operatic project. They show no great dramatic sense; indeed, they are more like a cantata than scenes from an opera. These Norwegian performances have great freshness and spirit, though the DG accounts have the greater polish and finesse. All the same, no one investing in these performances (offered most inexpensively) will have occasion to feel disappointed, even though the coupled orchestral works are less distinctive – see above.

Haugtussa (song-cycle), Op. 67; 6 Songs, Op. 48. Songs: Beside the stream; Farmyard song; From Monte Pincio; Hope; I love but thee; Spring; Spring showers; A swan; Two brown eyes; While I wait; With a waterlily (sung in Norwegian).

⚜ *** DG 437 521-2. Von Otter, Forsberg.

This recital of Grieg's songs by Anne Sofie von Otter and Bengt Forsberg is rather special. Von Otter commands an exceptionally wide range of colour and quality and in Bengt Forsberg has a highly responsive partner. Altogether a captivating recital, and beautifully recorded too.

(i) *Landkjenning (Land-sighting), Op. 31;* (i & ii) *Olav Trygvason, Op. 50; Peer Gynt Suites Nos. 1 & 2.*

*** DG 437 523-2. (i) Gjevang; (ii) Stene; (i; ii) Hagegård; Gothenburg SO, Järvi.

The three scenes that survive from the opera, *Olav Trygvason* and *Landkjenning* ('Land-sighting') are coupled together on DG with the two *Peer Gynt* suites. In the second tableau, the role of the priestess is sung by Anne Gjevang, the Erda in the Haitink *Ring* on EMI. Some may find her vibrato a bit excessive. The other soloists, Randi Stene and Håkan Hagegård, acquit themselves well, as does the Gothenburg Orchestra and Chorus under Neeme Järvi. The *Peer Gynt* suites are not new, though two of the numbers have been re-recorded. Recommended.

6 songs, Op. 25: Spillemnd (Fiddlers), En svane (A swan), Stambogsrim (Album lines), Med en vadnlilje (With a waterlily, Borte (Departed), En fuglevis (A birdsong).

*** Virgin VC5 45273-2. Kringelborn, Martineau – NIELSEN, RANGSTROM, SIBELIUS: *Songs.* ***

Solveig Kringelborn's anthology is called *Black Roses* after the famous Sibelius song she includes. The Op. 25 songs of Grieg including the famous *A swan*, are beautifully sung: she sets great store by a smooth legato and purity of tone, which she commands in abundance. Her characterization could perhaps be stronger; the overall effect when one listens to her record straight off is just a shade uniform. But she is possessed of a lovely voice and her pianist is quite superb. Excellent recording.

Peer Gynt (incidental music), Op. 23 (complete).

(M) *** Unicorn (ADD) UKCD 2003/4. Carlson, Hanssen, Bjørkøy, Hansli, Oslo PO Ch., LSO, Dreier.

Per Dreier achieves very spirited results from his soloists, the Oslo Philharmonic Chorus and our own LSO, with some especially beautiful playing from the woodwind; the recording is generally first class, with a natural perspective between soloists, chorus and orchestra. The Unicorn set includes 32 numbers in all, including Robert Henrique's scoring of the *Three Norwegian Dances*, following the revised version of the score Grieg prepared for the 1886 production in Copenhagen. This music, whether familiar or unfamiliar, continues to astonish by its freshness and inexhaustibility.

Peer Gynt (incidental music), Op. 23 (complete); Sigurd Jorsalfar (incidental music), Op. 56 (complete).

*** DG (IMS) 423 079-2 (2). Bonney, Eklöf, Sandve, Malmberg, Holmgren; Foss, Maurstad, Stokke (speakers); Gösta Ohlin's Vocal Ens., Pro Musica Chamber Ch., Gothenburg SO, Järvi.

Neeme Järvi's recording differs from its predecessor by Per Dreier in offering the Grieg Gesamtausgabe *Peer Gynt*, which bases itself primarily on the 26 pieces he included in the 1875 production rather than the final published score, prepared after Grieg's death by Halvorsen. This well-documented set comes closer to the original by including spoken dialogue, as one would have expected in the theatre. The CDs also offer the complete *Sigurd Jorsalfar* score, which includes some splendid music. The performances by actors, singers (solo and choral) and orchestra alike are exceptionally vivid, with the warm Gothenburg ambience used to creative effect; the vibrant histrionics of the spoken words undoubtedly add to the drama.

Peer Gynt: extended excerpts.

*** DG (IMS) 427 325-2. Bonney, Eklöf, Malmberg, Maurstad, Foss, Gothenburg Ch. & SO, Järvi.

*** Decca (IMS) 425 448-2. Malmberg, Haeggander, San Francisco Ch. & SO, Blomstedt.

(BB) *** Belart (ADD) 450 018-2. VPO, Karajan – SIBELIUS: En Saga etc. ***

Neeme Järvi's disc offers more than two-thirds of the 1875 score, and the performance has special claims on the collector who wants one CD rather than two (half the second CD of the set is taken up by *Sigurd Jorsalfar*).

Decca's set of excerpts makes a useful alternative to the Järvi disc. All but about 15 minutes of the complete score is here and the spoken text is included too, all admirably performed. Perhaps the Gothenburg acoustic is to be preferred to the Davies Hall, San Francisco. However, the Decca recording approaches the demonstration class.

Karajan's shorter set of excerpts (from 1962) makes a first-class super-bargain alternative on Belart, with a particularly fresh response from the VPO. It includes a beautiful account of *Solveig's song*, and the sound is warm and atmospheric. The Sibelius couplings are equally recommendable.

(i) Peer Gynt: excerpts. In Autumn (overture), Op. 11; An Old Norwegian song with Variations, Op. 51; Symphonic Dance No. 2.

❀ (M) *** EMI CDM5 66914-2 [566966]. (i) Hollweg, Beecham Ch. Soc.; RPO, Beecham.

Beecham showed a very special feeling for this score and to hear *Morning*, the gently textured *Anitra's Dance* or the eloquent portrayal of the *Death of Aase* under his baton is a uniquely rewarding experience. Ilse Hollweg makes an excellent soloist. The recording dates from 1957 and, like most earlier Beecham reissues, has been enhanced by the remastering process. The most delectable of the *Symphonic Dances*, very beautifully played, makes an ideal encore after *Solveig's Lullaby*, affectingly sung by Ilse Hollweg. The *In Autumn* overture, not one of Grieg's finest works, is most enjoyable when Sir Thomas is so persuasive, not shirking the melodramatic moments. Finally for the present reissue, we are offered *An Old Norwegian Folksong with Variations* (not previously released in its stereo format). It is a piece of much colour and charm, which is fully realized here.

Peer Gynt (incidental music): Overture; Suites 1–2. Lyric Pieces: Evening in the Mountain; Cradle Song, Op. 68/5; Sigurd Jorsalfar: Suite, Op. 56; Wedding Day at Troldhaugen, Op. 65/6.

(BB) **(*) Naxos 8.550140. CSSR State PO, Košice, Gunzenhauser.

A generous Grieg anthology on Naxos (70 minutes, all but 3 seconds) and the performances by the Slovak State Philharmonic Orchestra in Košice (in eastern Slovakia) are very fresh and lively and thoroughly enjoyable. There is wide dynamic range both in the playing and in the recording, and sensitivity in matters of phrasing.

Peer Gynt Suites Nos. 1 & 2, Opp. 46 & 55.

*** Finlandia/Warner 0630 17675-2. Norwegian Radio O, Ari Rasilainen. – SAEVERUD: Peer Gynt Suites. ***

The thinking behind this disc is to contrast the two sets of incidental music for Ibsen's *Peer Gynt*; Grieg's romantic setting of 1874 on which he later based his two orchestral suites, and Harald Sverud's anti-romantic incidental music of 1947. The idea is so obvious that it is surprising no one has done it before, though it has been done more than once in London concert halls, and on the radio. The Norwegian Radio Orchestra under their Finnish conductor, Ari Rasilainen give fresh, well-characterized accounts of the familiar suites and are very well recorded. They may not enjoy the same ranking as the Oslo Philharmonic (their strings do not possess the same tonal opulence or weight) but they are a good orchestra in their own right and these performances give pleasure.

(i) Peer Gynt: Suites Nos. 1–2. Lyric Suite, Op. 54; Sigurd Jorsalfar: Suite.

(M) *** DG 427 807-2. (i) Soloists, Ch.; Gothenburg SO, Järvi.

Järvi's excerpts from *Peer Gynt* and *Sigurd Jorsalfar* are extracted from his complete sets, so the editing inevitably produces a less tidy effect than normal recordings of the *Suites*. However, the performances are first class and so is the recording, and this comment applies also to the *Lyric Suite*, taken from an earlier, digital orchestral collection.

Peer Gynt Suites Nos. 1, Op. 46; 2, Op. 55; Lyric Suite: March of the Trolls, Op. 54/3. Norwegian Dance, Op. 35/2.

(M) ** Sony (ADD) SMK 63156. NYPO, Bernstein – SIBELIUS: Finlandia; The Swan of Tuonela; Valse triste. **

The slightly mannered performance of *Anitra's Dance* and the touch of melodrama in the *Second Suite* add individuality to Bernstein's performance of the *Peer Gynt* incidental music, of which the performances in general are good, though the 1967 recording is not especially distinguished. The two other Grieg pieces are attractive, but there are much better versions available of *Peer Gynt*.

GRIGNY, Nicolas de (1672–1703)

Organ Mass.

(M) *** Cal. CAL 6911. Isoir (Cliquot organ at the Cathedral of Saint-Pierre de Poitiers).

Nicolas de Grigny's fame as a composer rests upon one book, including 49 pieces of music, and the present Couperin-influenced *Organ Mass* which was very influential in its own right. The variety of the writing is remarkable, and certainly André Isoir's performance on the Cliquot organ at Poitiers Cathedral readily demonstrates the music's imaginative range. As a double encore we are offered an *Elévation en sol* and a *Symphonie* by Nicolas LeBegue, both strong pieces. The analogue recording is of fine quality.

GROFÉ, Ferde (1892–1972)

Grand Canyon Suite.

*** Telarc CD 80086 (with additional cloudburst, including real thunder). Cincinnati Pops O, Kunzel – GERSHWIN: *Catfish Row.* ***

(M) *** Sony SMK 63086. NYPO, Bernstein – GERSHWIN: *An American in Paris* etc. *** ●

The Cincinnati performance is played with great commitment and fine pictorial splendour. What gives the Telarc CD its special edge is the inclusion of a second performance of *Cloudburst* as an appendix with a genuine thunderstorm laminated on to the orchestral recording. The result is overwhelmingly thrilling, except that in the final thunderclap God quite upstages the orchestra, who are left trying frenziedly to match its amplitude in their closing peroration.

Bernstein treats the music as if it was a masterpiece of orchestral impressionism, while the famous *On the Trail* (John Corigliano the solo fiddler) has never sounded more infectiously witty. The closing storm has real spectacle, powerfully generated by the orchestral playing itself. The recording has never sounded half as good is it does here.

Grand Canyon Suite; Mississipi Suite.

(M) **(*) Mercury (ADD) 434 355-2. Eastman-Rochester O, Hanson – HERBERT: *Cello Concerto No. 2.* **

It is impossible not to respond to the pictorial vividness and gusto of Hanson's performances and, even if the studio-ish acoustic of the Eastman Theater is not ideally expansive, the 1958 Mercury stereo is brilliantly detailed in the *Grand Canyon Suite.* The *Mississippi Suite*, a much lesser piece, is also persuasively presented, especially the exuberant portrait of *Huckleberry Finn.* But the canyon storms rage much more spectacularly on the rival versions.

GRØNDAHL, Agathe Backer

(1847–1907)

6 Etudes de concert, Op. 11; 3 Etudes, Op. 22; 3 Morceaux, Op. 15; 4 Sketches, Op. 19; Suite, Op. 20.

(N) *** BIS CD 1106. Braaten.

Four years younger than Grieg, Agathe Grøndahl died only a few weeks before him. The annotator does her cause no service by placing her music on a level with Grieg and Kjerulf, for although she was much respected as a concert pianist in her day well beyond Scandinavia, her music has never escaped the shadows of Mendelssohn and Schumann. The folk-influenced Norwegian accents that inspired Nordraak, Grieg and Svendsen held little attraction for Grøndahl. Bernard Shaw hailed her as a great pianist and found some individuality in the songs but little in the piano pieces. On this disc they range from the *Concert Studies, Op. 11* of 1881, her first published composition, through to the *Trois études, Op. 22* of 1888; they are written capably but wanting in

originality. Geir Henning Braaten plays splendidly and is given an excellent BIS recording.

GRUENBERG, Louis (1884–1964)

Violin Concerto, Op. 47.

(N) (BB) (**) Naxos mono 8.110942. Heifetz, San Francisco SO, Monteux – PROKOFIEV: *Violin Concerto No. 2 in G min.* (***)

Commissioned by Heifetz, Louis Gruenberg, best known for his opera, *The Emperor Jones*, wrote his *Violin Concerto* in 1943. A massive 40 minute work, it has some warmly attractive material in a slightly jazzy idiom, and formidably exploits violin technique to stretch even Heifetz. But it seriously outlasts its welcome with much empty doodling. A comfortable transfer of the limited 1945 sound.

GUBAIDULINA, Sofia (born 1931)

(i) *Bassoon Concerto* (for bassoon and low strings); (ii) *Detto II* (for cello and chamber orchestra); (iii) *Misterioso* (for 7 percussion); (iv) *Rubaiyat* (cantata).

(M) *** BMG/Melodiya ADD/Dig. 74321 49957-2. (i) Popov, Chamber Ens., Meshchaninov; (ii) Monighetti, Chamber Ens., Nikolaevsky; (iii) Bolshoi Theatre O percussion, Grishkin; (iv) Yakovenko, Chambe Ens., Rozhdestvensky.

Sofia Gubaidulina belongs to the same generation as Alfred Schnittke and Edison Denisov. The *Rubaiyat*, a cantata for baritone and chamber orchestra, and the *Detto II* for cello and chamber forces were both recorded in the 1970s, as was the *Concerto for Bassoon and Low Strings. Misterioso* for seven percussion instruments is later (from 1990). Her music is unlikely to enjoy wide popular appeal – no harm in that – and readers who have become interested in this composer need not hesitate.

In Croce for Bayan & Cello; Seven Last Words for Cello, Bayan & Strings; Silenzio for Bayan, Violin & Cello.

(BB) *** Naxos 8.553557. Moser, Kliegel, Rabus, Camerata Transsylvanica, Selmeczi.

In Croce is an arrangement of a work for cello and organ, composed in 1979 and arranged for bayan or push-button accordion in 1993. The *Seven Last Words*, composed in 1982 for cello, accordion and strings, is probably the best entry-point into Gubaidulina's strange world, mesmerizing for some, boring for others. Maria Kliegel is an intense and powerful cellist, and Elsbeth Moser is a dedicated player long associated with this repertoire. Good recorded sound.

GUERRERO, Francisco (1528–99)

Missa de la batalla escoutez; Conditor alme siderum; Duo Seraphim clamabant (motet); In exitus Israel; Magnificat octavi toni; Pange lingua gloriosi; Regina caeli laetari, Alleluia (instrumental version).

*** Hyp. CDA 67075. Westminster Cathedral Ch., His Majestys Sackbutts and Cornetts, O'Donell.

The celebration of the quatrocentenary of Guerrero's death is at last bringing another important, but hitherto little-known Spanish composer before the public. The performances here (even in the *Mass*) use brass instruments as well as voices, following the *alternatim* style, which was a particular feature of Guerrero's music, where plainchant regularly alternates with polyphony. The Trinity motet, *Duo seraphim* opening descriptively with two solo trebles, uses twelve voices in three choirs to create wide contrasts of dynamic and texture. The *Missa de la batalla*, for five voices, uses a chanson of Jannequin, *La guerra*, as its basis, indicated by including the French word '*escoutez*' in its title. *Pange lingua gloriosi* uses a popular melody, a gently swinging Iberian song, ornamented with counterpoint, and moving from voice to voice, in many ways like a primitive theme and variations. Throughout the discs, the eloquent singing, and very well-balanced, never overwhelming brass choir makes this a varied and highly enjoyable introduction to a remarkable composer, of whom we shall surely discover much more.

Missa Sancta et immaculata; Hei mihi, Domine; Lauda mater ecclesia; Magnificat septimi toni; O lux beata Trinitas; Trahe me post te, Virgo Maria; Vexilla Regis.

*** Hyp. CDA 66910. Westminster Cathedral Ch., O'Donnell.

Guerrero's *Missa Sancta et immaculata* is based on the celebrated four-part motet of that name by his one-time master Christóbal de Morales. It comes from his *Liber primus missarum* which was published in Paris in 1566. The two serene motets *Hei mihi, Domine* and *Trahe me post te, Virgo Maria* come from the second book of masses (1582) and the three hymns, *Vexilla Regis*, composed for Passion Sunday, *O lux beata Trinitas* and the spirited *Lauda mater ecclesia* are of striking quality and character. The Westminster Cathedral Choir and James O'Donnell give performances of quite outstanding eloquence and purity. The recording is first-class and there are exemplary notes by Bruno Turner.

GUILMANT, Félix Alexandre
(1837–1911)

Symphony No. 1 for Organ & Orchestra, Op. 42.

*** Chan. 9271. Tracey (organ of Liverpool Cathedral), BBC PO, Tortelier – WIDOR: *Symphony No. 5* ***; POULENC: *Organ Concerto.* **(*)

This Guilmant *Symphony* (the composer's own arrangement of his *First Organ Sonata*) is a real find, with all the genial vigour of the famous work of Saint-Saëns. The first movement has a galumphing main theme and an equally pleasing secondary idea. It is followed by a tunefully idyllic *Pastorale* (with some delicious registration from Ian Tracey) and a rumbustiously grandiloquent finale. All great fun, and well suited to the larger-than-life resonance of Liverpool Cathedral with its long reverberation period.

Symphony No. 2 for Organ & Orchestra, Op. 91.

*** Chan. 9785. Tracey (organ of Liverpool Cathedral), BBC PO, Tortelier – FRANCK: *Choral No. 2;* WIDOR: *Symphony No. 3 for Organ & Orchestra.* ***

Guilmant's *Second Symphony* is a hugely effective transcription of his *Eighth Organ Sonata*. It opens gently with an anticipatory fanfare-like figure on the violins, then after the grandiose organ entry with tutti, the allegro sets off with infectious vigour. The *Adagio con affetto* is romantic, but still reminds us we are in a cathedral, as does the shorter *Andante sostenuto*, which follows the rumbustious Scherzo. The finale opens evocatively and then becomes instantly animated, working towards a splendidly grandiloquent ending. The performance has great gusto and if the wide resonance of Liverpool Cathedral prevents any chance of internal clarity, it certainly gives the music a superb impact. Full marks to the Chandos engineers.

GURNEY, Ivor (1890–1937)

Songs: All night under the moon; An epitaph; Bread and cherries; By a bierside; The cloths of heaven; Cradle song; Desire in spring; Down by the salley garden; Epitaph in old mode; 5 Elizabethan Songs; Even such is time; The fields are full; The folly of being comforted; Hanacker mill; In Flanders; I will go with my father a-ploughing; Most holy night; Nine of the clock; Severn Meadows; The singer; You are my sky.

(N) *** Hyp. CDA 67243. Agnew, Drake.

Ivor Gurney was born in Gloucester and became a chorister at the cathedral, later studying composition under Stanford and (after his wartime service) Vaughan Williams. Soldiering in the trenches in the First World War ruined his physical health, and probably led to a later mental deterioration and eventually complete mental collapse. But during his comparatively short creative life he composed over three hundred songs, the best of which are among the finest settings in the English language, their pervasive dolorous mood often drawing parallels with Dowland.

The *Five Elizabethan Songs* of 1913/14 are already establishing the melancholy quality of his melodic lines (even *Under the greenwood tree* is nostalgic in feeling). The wartime songs also include an intensely emotional Masefield setting, *By the bierside*, while *In Flanders* is full of longing for the Severn Hills.

The rich lyricism of *The fields are full of summer* and *The cloths of Heaven* and the gentle evocation of *Down by the salley gardens* are touching in a very direct way, the music's aura consistent in its pastoral evocation. Paul Agnew moulds the melodic lines with great sensitivity, his use of vocal colour illuminating the words, and Julius Drake accompanies with natural understanding. The recording is excellent, and this is another fine addition to the Hyperion treasure-house of vocal recordings.

GYROWETZ, Adalbert (1763–1850)

Symphonies: in E flat; F, Op. 6/2–3; in D, Op. 12/1.

*** Chan. 9791. LMP, Bamert.

The Bohemian composer Adalbert Gyrowetz, a talented contemporary of Haydn and Mozart, outlived both of them. The Gyrowetz symphonies are delightful, full of characterfully individual invention, with Gyrowetz adding *galant* touches of his own. The engaging bravura horn solo in the Trio of the Minuet of Op. 6/2 is truly Bohemian, as is the genial opening movement of Op. 6/3, while the *Andante* soon produces a winning arioso for the oboe followed by a bouncing half Scherzo, half Ländler and a Haydnesque finale. There are catchy ideas too in the *Andante* of the later *D major Symphony* and again in the nicely scored finale. In short these are most enjoyable works and they are played (on modern instruments) with great elegance and sparkle and are beautifully recorded. Well worth seeking out.

HAAS, Joseph (1879–1960)

Krippenlieder (6 Songs of the Crib), Op. 49.

⚫ *** EMI CDC5 56204-2. Bär, Deutsch (with Recital: *Christmas Lieder* *** ⚫).

These delightful strophic songs help to make Olaf Bär's collection of German Christmas Lieder most treasurable. Their romantic melodic style also features a strong folk element. In the lovely opening *Weihnachtslegende* the 'Hosianna! Alleluja!' is very winning indeed, while the somewhat graver closing *Die Heiligen drei König* brings a charming repeated 'Eia Christkindelein, eia'. Marvellously warm and subtle performances from Bär and Deutsch alike, and splendidly natural recording.

HADLEY, Patrick (1899–1973)

(i) Lenten Cantata. The cup of blessing; I sing of a maiden; My beloved spake; A Song for Easter.

*** ASV CDDCA 881. (i) Ainsley, Sweeney; Ch. of Gonville & Caius College, Cambridge, Webber; Hill or Phillips (organ) – RUBBRA: *Choral Music.* ***

The most substantial piece here is the *Lenten Cantata* or *Lenten Meditations* for two soloists, choir and orchestra (here given in an organ transcription), composed in 1963. Not a strongly individual voice, Hadley is nevertheless a refined craftsman whose feeling for line and texture is highly developed. The performances are of high quality, and so is the recording.

HAHN, Reynaldo (1875–1947)

Le Bal de Béatrice d'Este (ballet suite).

*** Hyp. CDA 66347. New London O, Corp – POULENC: *Aubade; Sinfonietta.* ***

Le Bal de Béatrice d'Este is a charming pastiche, dating from the early years of the century and scored for the unusual combination of wind instruments, two harps, piano and timpani. Ronald Corp and the New London Orchestra play it with real panache and sensitivity.

Piano Concerto in E.

*** Hyp. CDA 66897. Coombs, BBC Scottish SO, Ossonce – MASSENET: *Piano Concerto.* ***

Entitled *Improvisation*, the opening movement of this charming work starts with a theme which surprisingly has an English flavour, easily lyrical, leading on to variations full of sharp, sparkling contrasts. A brief, light-hearted Scherzo leads to a combined slow movement (*Reverie*) and finale (*Toccata*). What Stephen Coombs's inspired performance demonstrates, most sympathetically supported by Jean-Yves Ossonce with the BBC Scottish Symphony, is that, though no deep emotions are touched, this is a delightful piece, well worth reviving, here perfectly coupled with another concerto also uncharacteristic of its composer and written late in his career.

(i) Piano Quintet in F min. String Quartets Nos. 1 in A min.; 2 in F.

**(*) Audivis V 4848. (i) Tharaud; Quatuor Parisii.

Reynaldo Hahn is today remembered for his songs, but he also wrote a modest number of fine chamber works of which the *Piano Quintet* of 1921, with its Franckian undertones, was understandably the most popular during the composer's lifetime. It is a thoroughly rewarding piece, which deserves to return to the repertoire. It is persuasively played here, particularly by the pianist, Alexandre Tharaud, who is well inside its sensibility, and it is a pity that the recording of the strings does not produce riper textures. The *Second Quartet*, ambitiously modelled on the Franck quartet, was never published, but has a memorably atmospheric slow movement, the strings muted throughout. The *First Quartet* is a thoughtful, delicate evocation of considerable Gallic charm, with a yearning *Andantino* and a light-hearted finale. It is played most appealingly and here the recording is better balanced and more naturally integrated.

Mélodies: L'Air; A Chloris; L'Automne; 7 Chansons grises; La Chère Blessure; D'une prison; L'Enamourée; Les Etoiles; Fêtes galantes; Les Fontaines; L'Incrédule; Infidélité; Offrande; Quand je fus pris au pavillon; Si mes vers avaient des ailes; Tyndaris.

(B) *** Hyp. Helios CDH 55040. Hill, Johnson.

If Hahn never quite matched the supreme inspiration of his most famous song, *Si mes vers avaient des ailes*, the delights here are many, the charm great. Martyn Hill, ideally accompanied by Graham Johnson, gives delicate and stylish performances, well recorded. The reissue on the Helios bargain label should tempt collectors to sample this attractive repertoire, particularly when full translations are included.

Mélodies: L'Air; Chansons grises; D'une prison; L'Enamourée; Les Fontaines; L'Incrédule; Je me metz en vostre mercy; La Nuit; Quand je fus pris au pavillon; Le

Rossignol des lilas; Seule; Si mes vers avient des ailes; Le Souvenir d'avoir chanté.

(BB) *** Virgin 2 x 1 Double VBD5 61433-2. Yakar, Lavoix – FAURE: *Mélodies.* ***

Rachel Yakar with her warm, very French-sounding timbre is an ideal interpreter of the songs of Hahn, Bizet and Chabrier on this second disc of this well-conceived bargain-priced Double. It is a pity that in this reissue no texts are given, but Yakar's way of bringing out the subtleties of word-meaning goes with beautifully clear diction. Though Hahn cannot match the other composers in depth or imagination, his facile genius in 19 songs, including the seven *Chansons grises*, setting Verlaine, and the most popular of all, a teenage inspiration, *Si mes vers avaient des ailes*, brings many delights. Excellent (1988) recording from Radio France.

Mélodies: A Chloris; Au rossignol; Les Cygnes; D'une prison; Fêtes galantes L'Heure exquise; Infidelité; Je me souviens; Mai; Ma jeunesse; Nocturne; La Nymphe de la Source; Offrande; Paysage; Le Plus Beau Présent; Puisque j'ai mis ma lèvre; Quand la nuit n'est pas étoilée; Rêverie; Le Rossignol des lilas; Séraphine; Seule; Si mes vers avaient des ailes; Sur l'eau; Trois jours de vendange. Ciboulette: C'est sa banlieue (Y a des arbres); Non avons fait un beau voyage. O mon bel inconnu: C'est très vilain d'être infidèle. 10 Etudes Latines; 12 Rondels. Mozart (musical comedy): Air de la lettre. Une Revue: La Dernière (valse).

*** Hyp. CDA 67141/2. Lott, Bickley, Bostridge, Varcoe, L. Schubert Chorale, Layton, Johnson.

This is the most comprehensive collection of Hahn songs ever recorded, including a number of items never available before and even items from stage works. As in his Schubert edition for Hyperion, Graham Johnson masterminds the project to give endless new insights, whether in his ideal choice of soloists, his inspired playing or his illuminating notes. Specially valauable are the ten *Etudes latines*, both pure and sensuous in their classical evocation. Fine, atmospheric sound.

'La Belle Epoque': Mélodies: A Chloris; L'Automne; D'une prison; L'Enamorée; Dans la nuit; Fêtes galantes; Les Fontaines; Fumée; L'Heure exquise; Infidelité; Je me souviens; Mai; Nocturne; Offrande; Paysage; Le Printemps; Quand je fus pris au pavillon; Quand la nuit n'est pas étoilée; Le Rossignol des lilas; Si mes vers avaient des ailes; Trois jours de vendage. Etudes Latines: Lydé; Phyllis; Tyndaris.

*** Sony SK 60168. Graham, Vignoles.

The solemnity of Susan Graham's first song, *A Chloris*, with its Bachian pastiche may surprise those who think of Hahn as merely a dilettante tunesmith, and Graham finds the fullest range of expression in this charming collection. Hahn may fail to bring out the poignancy behind the Verlaine poem, *D'une prison*, but within his limited range he is a master. A good single-disc choice, made the more attractive by the glowing beauty of Graham's voice, sensuous in the most famous song, *Si vers avait des ailes*. Fine, sensitive accompaniment from Roger Vignoles.

HALÉVY, Jacques Fromental
(1799–1862)

La Juive (opera): complete.

*** Ph. (ADD) 420 190-2 (3). Varady, Anderson, Carreras, Gonzalez, Furlanetto, Amb. Op. Ch., Philh. O, Almeida.

La Juive ('The Jewess') was the piece that, along with the vast works of Meyerbeer, set the pattern for the epic French opera, so popular last century. Eléazar was the last role that the great tenor, Enrico Caruso, tackled. José Carreras sings well, but the role of the old Jewish father really needs a weightier, darker voice, such as Caruso had in his last years. Julia Varady as Rachel makes that role both the emotional and the musical centre of the opera, responding both tenderly and positively. In the other soprano role, that of the Princess Eudoxia, June Anderson is not so full or sweet in tone, but she is impressive in the dramatic coloratura passages. Ferruccio Furlanetto makes a splendidly resonant Cardinal in his two big solos, and the Ambrosian Opera Chorus brings comparable bite to the powerful ensembles. Antonio de Almeida proves a dedicated advocate.

HALFFTER, Ernesto (1905–89)

Automne malade; Dos canciones; Rapsodia Portugesa; Sonatina (ballet, complete).

*** ASV CDDCA 1099. Orquesta Filarmónica de Gran Canaria, Leaper.

Ernesto Halffter was a pupil of Manuel de Falla. Judging from this well-played and excellently recorded issue, his music is resourceful and full of bright colours. Halffter is a good craftsman and the quality of his melodic invention is high.

HALVORSEN, Johan (1864–1935)

Air norvégien, Op. 7; Danses norvégiennes.

(BB) *** Naxos 8.550329. Kang, Slovak (Bratislava) RSO, Leaper – SIBELIUS: *Violin Concerto;* SINDING: *Légende;* SVENDSEN: *Romance.* ***

Dong-Suk Kang plays the attractive *Danses norvégiennes* with great panache, character and effortless virtuosity, and delivers an equally impeccable performance of the earlier *Air norvégien.*

Askeladden: Suite; Gurre (Dramatic Suite), Op. 17; The Merchant of Venice: Suite.

*** Simax PSC 1198. Latvian Nat. SO, Mikkelsen.

Festival March; Kongen (The King): Suite; Tordenskjold (Suite); Vasantasena: Suite.

*** Simax PSC 1199. Latvian Nat. SO, Mikkelsen.

Halvorsen's main activity lay in the field of theatre music, and he composed extensively for the stage. The suite from *The Merchant of Venice* on the first CD is second-rate salon stuff, but that is the only disappointment. The music to

Holger Drachmann's play *Gurre* is not only expertly laid out for the orchestra but delightfully fresh. The idiom is indebted to Grieg but he obviously knew his Berlioz and Svendsen. *Sommernatsbryllup* ('Summer night's wedding') has much charm and brilliance and so has the opening *Aftenlandskap* ('Evening scene'), an atmospheric and appealing piece. *Aske-ladden* is a play for children, and the suite recorded here has abundant charm. The second disc brings music for Bjørnstjerne Bjørnson's play, *Kongen* ('The King'), whose delightful second movement, *Hyrdepigernes Dans* ('Dance of the Shepherdesses') is quite irresistible. It is difficult to get it out of your head. *Vasantasena* aspires to an oriental exoticism, which is quite endearing and charming. The Latvian National Orchestra play splendidly for Terje Mikkelsen, and the recording is state of the art, with beautifully transparent strings and with plenty of space round the sound.

HAMERIK, Asger (1843–1923)

Symphony No. 6 in G minor (Symphonie spirituelle), Op. 38.

*** CPO CPO 999 516-2. German Chamber Academy, Neuss, Goritski – GADE: *Novelletter, Opp. 53 & 58.* ***

Asger Hamerik belongs to the generation of Danish symphonists between Gade and Nielsen. His *Sixth Symphony (Symphonie spirituelle)* for strings comes from 1897 and is in the Gade–Schumann tradition. There is a *Seventh* and choral *Symphony*, composed the following year after which he gave up America and composing altogether, returning to retire in Copenhagen. No. 6 is quite an appealing work, and this is its first modern recording. First-class playing and recording.

HANDEL, George Frideric (1685–1759)

The Alchymist: Suite; Concerti a due cori Nos. 1–3; 2 Arias for Wind Band; Royal Fireworks Music; Water Music: Suites Nos. 1–3 (complete).

(B) **(*) O-L Double ADD/Dig. 455 709-2 (2). AAM, Hogwood.

A useful and attractive two-CD collection, bringing together rarities as well as the complete Fireworks and Water music. *The Alchymist* suite is jolly music but, presented here spiritedly, is much more conventional than the consistently inspired invention for the two great royal occasions. It was the *Water Music* with which Hogwood's Academy of Ancient Music made its début at the Proms in 1978, and the joy of that occasion is matched by this performance. While it may still seem disconcerting to hear the well-known *Air* taken so fast – like a minuet – the sparkle and airiness of the invention have rarely been caught on record so endearingly. Hogwood's account of the *Fireworks Music*, recorded two years later, can also be counted among the best available. The *Concerti a due cori*, sharing musical material taken from familiar works (including *Messiah*), are scored for two groups of wind instruments with an accompanying string

orchestra plus continuo. Horns are strongly featured in the *F major Concertos* (Nos. 1 and 3). The present (1983) performances are lively enough, but the recording is thinner. The two *Arias for Wind Band* include an arrangement of an actual operatic aria (from *Teseo*) and again are rather spoilt by the inaccurate tuning of the period horns.

Ballet music: Alcina: Overture; Acts I & III: Suites. Il pastor fido: Suite. Terpsichore: Suite.

(M) *** Erato 4509 99720-2. E. Bar. Sol., Gardiner.

John Eliot Gardiner is just the man for such a programme. He is not afraid to charm the ear, yet allegros are vigorous and rhythmically infectious. The bright and clean recorded sound adds to the sparkle, and the quality is first class. A delightful collection, and very tuneful too.

Concerti a due cori Nos. 1 in B flat; 2 in F; 3 in F; Overture in D; Solomon: Arrival of the Queen of Sheba; Concerto grosso in C (Alexander's Feast).

(M) *** Ph. (ADD) 454 131-2. ASMF, Marriner.

The *Concerti a due cori* were almost certainly written for performance with the three patriotic oratorios (No. 1 with *Joshua*, No. 2 with *Alexander Babus* and No. 3 with *Judas Maccabaeus*). They are full of good tunes. The performances here are rich-timbred and stylish, full of warmth, with modern instruments convey the grandeur of Handel's inspiration. This applies equally to the *Overture in D* and the better known *Concerto grosso* associated with *Alexander's Feast*. Only in the *Arrival of the Queen of Sheba* would a lighter touch have been beneficial.

Concerti a due cori Nos. 1 in B flat; 2–3 in F, HWV 332–4; Music for the Royal Fireworks.

*** Sony SK 63073. Tafelmusik, Lamon.

The Tafelmusik *Fireworks Music* is both boldly expansive and crisply rhythmic, with fine clean drums underpinning the brassily full textures of the outer sections, and plenty of character elsewhere. The *Concerti a due cori* are better played and much better tuned than Hogwood's set, and there are some fascinating sonorities here (familiar tunes emerge in new instrumental costume). The playing of the baroque horns is spectacular. This stands alongside Marriner's fine modern-instrument recording coupled with the *Alexander's Feast Concerto grosso* (see above).

(i) *Concerti a due cori Nos. 1–3; Concerti grossi, Op. 3/1–6; Op. 6/1–12; (ii) in C (Alexander's Feast). (iii); (i; iv) Oboe Concertos Nos. 1–3; (i; v) Organ Concertos Nos 1–6, Op. 4/1–6; 7–12, Op. 7/1–6; 13–16.*(i) *Music for the Royal Fireworks; Sonata: Il trionfo del tempo e del disinganno; Solomon: Arrival of the Queen of Sheba. Water Music: Suites 1–3 (complete).*

(B) *** Decca ADD/Dig. 458 333–2 (8). (i) ASMF, Marriner; (ii) L. Philomusica O, Jones; (iii) AAM, Hogwood; (iv) Lord; (v) Malcolm.

An outstanding collection. The great majority of the performances are from Marriner and his Academy on peak form. The *Concerti grossi*, Opp. 3 and 6, the *Fireworks* and *Water Music* remain among the finest performances ever committed to disc. Hogwood steps in for the *Concerti a due cori* and makes a less than ideal case for period instruments when directly contrasted with the greater sophistication (and incomparably precise intonation) which one takes for granted with the ASMF. Never mind, the effect is still stimulating and with first-class Decca (originally Argo) sound throughout, this box is worth any collector's consideration. Incidentally the Sonata: *Il trionfo del tempo e del disinganno* is short and sweet: it lasts for just under three minutes.

2 Concerti a due cori, Nos. 2–3, HWV 333–4; Concerti grossi, Op. 3/1–6; Op. 6/1–12; Concerto grosso in C (Alexander's Feast); Music for the Royal Fireworks; Water Music (both complete).

(B) **(*) DG 463 094–2 (6). E. Concert, Pinnock.

A generous bargain set of some of Handel's most famous orchestral music, which Pinnock's admirers will not want to miss. His accounts of the *Fireworks* and *Water Music* have tremendous zest and are among the best of the available period-instrument performances. The six Op. 3 concertos with their sequences of brief jewels of movements also find Pinnock and his English Concert at their freshest and liveliest, with plenty of sparkle and little of the abrasiveness associated with the earlier examples of authentic music-making. The twelve Op. 6 concertos however are not quite so recommendable: there is comparatively little sense of grandeur and few hints of tonally expansive beauty. But Pinnock's English Concert are never unresponsive and they offer much fine solo playing helped by an attractively atmospheric acoustic, and in spite of the above reservation, there is much to enjoy. The *Alexander's Feast Concerto grosso* also has vitality and imagination to recommend it, as have the *Concerti a due cori*, and all are well recorded.

Concerti grossi, Op. 3/1–6; Op. 6/1–12.

⊛ (M) *** Decca (ADD) 444 532-2 (3). ASMF, Marriner.

Concerti grossi, Op. 3/1–6 (including No. 4b); Concerti grossi, Op. 6/1–12.

(M) **(*) Teldec ADD/Dig. 4509 95500-2 (4). VCM, Harnoncourt.

This integral recording of the Handel *Concerti grossi* makes a permanent memorial of the partnership formed by the inspired scholarship of Thurston Dart and the interpretative skill and musicianship of Marriner and his superb ensemble, at their peak in the late 1960s. Dart planned a double continuo of both organ and harpsichord, used judiciously to vary textural colour and weight. Flutes and oboes are employed (with delightful effect) where Handel suggested in Op. 3, and in Op. 6 the optional oboe parts are used in concertos 1, 2, 5 and 6. The final concerto of Op. 3 features the organ as a solo instrument, a choice questioned by Christopher Hogwood in his researches. The three records come at a special lower-mid-price. But, alas, the superb CD transfer brings no separate cues for individual movements, only one band for each work.

The Teldec set is the most endearing of Harnoncourt's earlier authentic performances of baroque music. In Op. 3, tempi tend to be relaxed, but the performances are very enjoyable in their easy-going way, the ripe, fresh colouring

of the baroque oboes, played expressively, is most attractive to the ear, and the string-sound is unaggressive. Tuttis are curiously dry, suggesting that the microphones were close to the violins; otherwise the sound is very good and the whole effect quite distinctive. So it is in Op. 6, where the recording is much more ample. Unfortunately, Op. 3 (with its extra concerto) plays for 71 minutes at Harnoncourt's chosen tempi and Teldec have spread Op. 6 uneconomically over three more CDs, an expensive way of obtaining this music, even at mid-price.

Concerti grossi, Op. 3/1–6 including 4b, HWV 312–7.

(N) (B) *** Hyp. Helios CDH 55075 (with Concerto No. 4b). Brandenburg Consort, Goodman.

Roy Goodman's set achieves the best of both worlds by (like Harnoncourt before him) including the spurious (but very engaging) No. 4b and, like Hogwood (currently deleted), using an authentic version of No. 6, yet featuring the concertante organ concertante at its close as a bonus. The playing is rhythmically spirited and enjoyably light and airy: this is period instrument music-making at its most seductive, helped by some delightfully sensitive flute and oboe contributions from Rachel Brown and Katharina Arfken respectively. First-class recording, natural and transparent with a pleasing ambience. A fine bargain.

Concerti grossi, Op. 3/1–6.

*** Sony SK 52553. Tafelmusik, Lamon.
(N) (BB) *** Naxos 8.553457. Northern Sinf., Creswick.
*** DG (ADD) 413 727-2. E. Concert, Pinnock.
(M) **(*) Erato 2292 45998-2. E. Bar. Sol., Gardiner.

Those looking for a fine, digital recording of Op. 3, with its woodwind complement added to the strings and a concertante organ in No. 6, will find the Tafelmusik disc very satisfactory. The playing is fresh and unfussy – plainer than with Gardiner. It is alert, elegant and with plenty of warmth, and tempi are admirably judged. Original instruments are used but not flaunted too abrasively and the sound is first class, clear as well as full.

Barry Creswick and his excellent Northern Sinfonia provide a most enjoyably modern instrument version of Op. 3. They do not include 4b, nor give us the revised version of No. 6, but neither do most of their competitors, and with excellent playing throughout, freshly paced and most truthfully recorded, this is excellent value.

The six Op. 3 concertos with their sequences of brief jewels of movements also find Pinnock and the English Concert at their freshest and liveliest, with plenty of sparkle and little of the abrasiveness associated with 'authentic' performance.

Gardiner's analogue set from 1980 has transferred well to CD. Recorded in the Henry Wood Hall, textures are slightly more ample but still clear and admirably balanced. The starry cast-list includes Simon Standage and Roy Goodman among the violins, and the playing is both lively and stylish. There is a slight lack of finish in one or two places and some poor intonation in *No. 2 in B flat* – yet one also notes the imaginative treatment of the *Largo e staccato* of Op. 3/3 and its following *Adagio*, with Lisa Beznosiuk the engaging flute soloist.

Concerti grossi, Op. 3/1–6; Concerto grosso in C (Alexander's Feast); (i) *Music for the Royal Fireworks; Water Music* (complete).

(BB) *(*) Virgin 2 x 1 VBD5 61656-2 (2). Linde Consort; (i) with Cappella Coloniensis.

These are good, quite well-characterized performances, nicely recorded, but not much more than that. This repertoire is richly covered by excellent authentic and modern instrument versions, so we must relegate this Virgin Double – despite its bargain price – to the second division.

(i) *Concerti grossi, Op. 3/1–6;* (ii) *Organ Concertos Nos. 1–6, Op. 4/1–6.*

(B) **(*) Ph. (ADD) Duo (IMS) 442 263-2 (2) (i) ECO, Leppard; (ii) Chorzempa, Concerto Amsterdam, Schröder.

Among versions of Handel's Op. 3, Leppard's set also stands high. The playing is lively and fresh, and the remastered recording sounds very good. Leppard includes oboes and bassoons and secures excellent playing all round. In this Duo pairing we are also offered Daniel Chorzempa's set of Handel's Op. 4 *Organ Concertos*, and here we move over to period instruments. Chorzempa uses an appropriate Dutch organ and the balance is admirable. Regarding ornamentation, Chorzempa's approach is fairly elaborate and he interpolates a sonata movement from Op. 1 after the *Adagio* of the *Third Concerto*. The recording is again excellent, and those for whom the coupling is suitable will find this is good value.

(i) *Concerti grossi, Op. 3/1–6;* (ii) *Water Music: Suites 1–3.* (complete).

(B) ** Erato Ultima 3984 24243-2 (2). Les Musiciens du Louvre, Minowski; (ii) Amsterdam Bar. O, Koopman.

In Minowski's set of the *Concerti grossi* the original wind instruments at times steal so much of the limelight from the strings that one has the impression that these are solo concertos for oboe or, in the case of No. 3, recorder and flute. In No. 6 the organ dominates. String textures are bright and transparent, with the lightest possible sonority, and the continuo comes through intimately. With brisk allegros that are always alert and vivacious, the effect here is of hearing a completely new series of concertos.

Koopman's approach to the *Water Music*, again using period instruments, also brings an individual approach. In the first, *F major Suite*, it is not until the third movement *Allegro*, with the entry of the horns, that the music becomes robust. The second suite places elegance of style first and foremost, and the effect, engaging as it is in its way, seems more like eighteenth-century French court music. The opening of the third *D major Suite* has a ceremonial feeling, but overall this has the character of a chamber performance.

Concerti grossi, Op. 6/1–12.

*** Chan. 9004/6. I Musici de Montréal, Turovsky.

(BB) *** Belart (ADD) 461 329-2 (*Nos. 1–4*); 461 330-2 (*Nos.*

5–8); 461 331-2 (*Nos. 9–12*) (available separately). ECO, Leppard.

**(*) DG 410 897-2 (*1–4*); 410 898-2 (*5–8*); 410 899-2 (*9–12*). E. Concert, Pinnock.

12 Concerti grossi, Op. 6/1–12; Concerto grosso in C (Alexander's Feast).

**(*) Chan. 0600 (*Nos. 1–5*); 0616 (*Nos. 6–9*); 0622 (*Nos. 10–12; Alexander's Feast*) (available separately). Coll. Musicum 90, Standage.

I Musici de Montreal offer a refreshing and stimulating set of Handel's Opus 6. The group uses modern instruments and Yuli Turovsky's aims to seek a compromise between modern and authentic practice, by paring down vibrato in some of the expressive music. The concertino, Eleonora and Natalya Turovsky and Alain Aubut, play impressively, while the main group (6.3.1.1) produces full, well-balanced tone and Handel's joyous fugues are particularly fresh and buoyant. Turovsky paces convincingly, not missing Handel's breadth of sonority and moments of expressive grandeur. This could now be first choice for this wonderful music.

Simon Standage's Chandos set with Collegium Musicum 90 has been much admired and indeed, for its combination of delicately crisp rhythmic vitality and airy grace, it has much to offer. Yet anyone looking for weight of Handelian sonority in the ripieno will not find it here. Even though the main orchestral group is not small in numbers (5, 5, 3, 3, 1) and includes Handel's optional oboes and bassoon, the tutti is very much that of a small chamber group. Clearly, robustness is not part of Standage's conception: fresh, refined transparency is his hallmark and this means no bold, full contrasts with the concertino. The playing is of high calibre, though there is a complete absence of geniality, notably in the fugal writing, where Handel is so different from Bach. The Chandos recording is first class.

Leppard's 1967 Philips set is now offered on Polygram's Belart label for little more than the cost of just one of the Chandos CDs. Moreover it sounds splendid in its newly remastered format, not in the least dated. The main group is comparatively full-bodied, which means that Leppard's soloists stand out in greater relief, graceful and elegant. These performances, too, have plenty of spirit and lively rhythmic feeling, while the richer orchestral texture brings added breadth in slow movements. How beautiful is the famous melody from the very last concerto, marked *Larghetto e piano*, when played so smoothly and lyrically on modern instruments.

For all its 'authenticity', Pinnock's is never unresponsive music-making, with fine solo playing set against an attractively atmospheric acoustic. Ornamentation is often elaborate – but never at the expense of line. These are performances to admire and to sample, but not everyone will warm to them. If listened through, the sharp-edged sound eventually tends to tire the ear. The recording itself is first class.

Concerti grossi, Op. 6/1–10.

(B) **(*) EMI double fforte (ADD) CZS5 73344-2 (2). Bath Festival CO, Menuhin.

(i) *Concerti grossi, Op. 6/11–12; Water Music* (Suites 1–3; complete); (ii) *Violin Sonatas, Op. 1/3, 10, 12–15.*

(B) **(*) EMI double fforte (ADD) CZS5 73347-2 (2). (i) Bath Festival CO, Menuhin (ii) Menuhin, Malcolm, Gauntlet.

Menuhin gave us the first complete stereo set of Op. 6 in the early 1960s, recording the later concertos first and working backwards. He used a modest body of strings, and during the sessions it was suggested to the artists that a double continuo might be used, as was Handel's practice. But this does not appear to happen until what was originally the third LP, containing Nos. 1, 2, 4, and 5 (in this reissue the works are presented in a straightforward numerical sequence). In consequence, the performances of the first two concertos – the last to be recorded – are the finest of the set, both buoyant and rich in expressive feeling; the harpsichord contribution comes through splendidly. In the later concertos the harpsichord continuo is too backwardly balanced. But they are still very enjoyable. For the *Water Music* Menuhin used a new edition especially prepared by Neville Boyling, and his genial approach again demonstrates the humanity and freshness which always informed his music-making, with excellent playing and lively spontaniety throughout. Both recordings have been admirably transferred to CD. The Opus 1 *Violin Sonatas* were pioneering authentic versions, vital and stylish, using a well-balanced continuo (Ambrose Gauntlet, viola da gamba and George Malcolm, harpsichord). But here the CD transfer makes Menuhin's violin timbre sound slightly edgy. The 1963 Abbey Road recording is warm, fresh and clear in its new CD transfer.

Concerti grossi, Op. 6/1–4; Concerto grosso in C (Alexander's Feast).

*** Virgin.VC5 45348-2. OAE, McGegan.

Nicholas McGegan's Virgin Veritas disc was the first instalment of a most enjoyable new period instrument set. However, so far, the rest of the concertos have not materialized. Above all, the playing appealingly combines rhythmic vitality with a graceful warmth in slow movements, while Handel's fugal passages are spirited and joyous. The concertino (Elizabeth Wallfisch, Catherine Mackintosh, Alison Bury and Susan Sheppard) play most beautifully, without a suspicion of edginess. In the infectious account of the *Alexander's Feast Concerto*, the ripieno is further augmented, but textures remain fresh. The Abbey Road recording has just the right degree of resonance.

Concerto grosso in B flat, Op. 6/7.

*** Ara. Z 6723. San Francisco Ballet O, Lark Qt., Le Roux – SCHOENBERG: *Concerto for String Quartet & Orchestra after Handel's Op. 6/7;* ELGAR: *Introduction & Allegro for Strings;* SPOHR: *Concerto for String Quartet & Orchestra.* ***

What a pleasure to hear a Handel *concerto grosso* played for once on a full body of modern strings, emphasizing its warmth of sonority. But this is included as part of an imaginative concert of string music so that the listener can compare the original with Schoenberg's bizarre but aurally fascinating recomposed pastiche.

(i) *Flute Concerto in D* (attrib.); (ii) *Double Cello Concerto in G min.;* (iii) *Harp Concerto in B flat, Op. 4/6;* (iv) *Oboe Concertos Nos. 1–3.*

(BB) **(*) Arte Nova 74321 51634-2. (i) Beckett; (ii) Szucs; (iii) Wakeford; (iv) Messiter; L. Festival O, Pople.

An enjoyable collection of Handelian concertos, not all of them authentic. The *Harp Concerto* sounds as delectable as ever, and Malcolm Messiter is a neatly stylish soloist in the three works for oboe, although Ross Pople's accompaniments have not quite the degree of finesse which Marriner finds for Roger Lord. The agreeable *Flute Concerto* is almost certainly not by Handel, but it is well-played. The other novelty is the amiable work for a pair of cellos (although only one player is credited), arranged most effectively from a *Sonata in G minor* (HWV 393). The recording is truthful and pleasingly balanced.

(i) *Harp Concerto, Op. 4/6. Variations for Harp.*

⬤ (M) *** Decca (ADD) 425 723-2. Marisa Robles, (i) ASMF, Iona Brown – BOIELDIEU; DITTERSDORF: *Harp Concertos* etc. *** ⬤

Handel's Op. 4/6 is well known in both organ and harp versions. Marisa Robles and Iona Brown make an unforgettable case for the latter by creating the most delightful textures, while never letting the work sound insubstantial. The ASMF accompaniment, so stylish and beautifully balanced, is a treat in itself, and the recording is well-nigh perfect.

Harp Concertos from Organ Concertos in F (Op. 4/5); in B flat (Op. 4/6); in D min. (Op. 7/4).

(N) (B) **(*) DG (ADD) 469 544-2. Zabaleta, Kuentz CO, Kuentz – BACH: *Harp Concertos.* **

Handel himself offered an alternative version of his *Organ Concerto,* Op. 4/6 for harp, so there is a precedent for Zabaleta's transcriptions here of two other concertos, Op. 7/4, (which includes a neat improvised cadenza), and Op. 4/5. Zabeleta's playing is refined and full of light and shade, while Paul Kuentz provides warm, polished accompaniments. The result, pleasingly recorded, is certainly enticing, but utterly unlike today's period-authenticity.

(i) *Harpsichord Concerto, Op. 4/6. Suite No. 15: Air & Variations.*

(**(*)) Biddulph mono LHW 032. Landowska; with O, Bigot – BACH: *Concerto No. 1 in D min., BWV 1052* (**); HAYDN: *Concerto in D; Sonata No. 36 in C sharp min.: Minuet; German Dance No. 5.* (***)

We more usually hear this concerto on the organ or harp, but Wanda Landowska makes a fairly good case for the harpsichord, although her predilection towards grandeur means that her presentation is on the heavy side. The *Air and Variations* is played with much character and is made to be every bit as memorable as *The Harmonious Blacksmith.* The recording is vivid throughout and very well transferred.

Oboe Concertos Nos. 1–3; Air & Rondo (ed. Camden); (i) *Suite in G min.* (ed. Camden); Otho: *Overture.*

(BB) *** Naxos 8.553430. Camden, (i) Girdwood; City of London Sinfonia, Ward.

Oboe Concertos Nos. 1–3; Concerto grosso, Op. 3/3; Hornpipe in D, HWV 356; Overture in D, HWV 337/8; Sonata à 5 in B flat, HWV 288.

(B) **(*) Ph. (ADD) 426 082-2. Holliger, ECO, Leppard.

Oboe Concertos Nos. 1 in B flat, HWV 301; 2 in B flat, HWV 302a; 3 in G min., HWV 287; Largo in F, HWV 302b. Solomon: Arrival of the Queen of Sheba.

(B) *** Double Decca (ADD) 452 943-2 (2). Lord, ASMF, Marriner – BELLINI: *Oboe Concerto in E flat;* VIVALDI: *Miscellaneous Concertos.* ***

Handel's three *Oboe Concertos* have an immediate appeal, their style predominantly lyrical, and they are given sensitive, polished performances by Roger Lord and the Academy. Incidentally, the *Largo in F* uses the same musical material as the first movement of the *Second Concerto*, but with quite spectacular horn parts added to the accompaniment. With Bellini's brief but delightful concerto added for good measure, this makes a fine coupling for the Academy's generous programme of miscellaneous Vivaldi concertos, which are in every way recommendable. The vintage (originally Argo) sound is first class.

Anthony Camden, for years principal oboe of the LSO, here makes a very welcome solo appearance on disc, playing with typical point and style, using his attractively reedy tone. The regular oboe concertos are well supplemented by the *Suite in G minor* as edited by Camden, where he is joined by the prize-winning Julia Girdwood on the second oboe. The *Otho Overture* too features prominent roles for oboes in duet. Ward and the City of London Sinfonia are sympathetic accompanists using modern instruments. First-rate sound from All Saints, East Finchley. A fine alternative to Roger Lord with the ASMF.

Holliger, a masterly interpreter, does not hesitate to embellish repeats; his ornamentation may overstep the boundaries some listeners are prepared to accept. His playing and that of the other artists in this collection is exquisite, and the recording is naturally balanced.

Oboe Concertos Nos. 1 in B flat, HWV 301; 2, HWV 302a; 3, HWV 287; Sonatas for Oboe & Continuo in B flat, HWV 357; in F, HWV 363a; in G min., Op. 1/6, HWV 364a; in C min., Op. 1/8, HWV 366; Sonata in G min. for Oboe, Violins & Continuo, HWV 404.

*** Unicorn DKPCD 9153. Francis, L. Harpsichord Ens.

Sarah Francis is a superb baroque oboeist, at the same time directing the members of the London Baroque Ensemble with spirit and finesse. These performances are not only delightful, but a model of style. In the sonatas Handel's ever-engaging contrapuntal interplay is beautifully clear (the harpsichord comes through in perfect balance with the continuo), so that for sheer pleasure, these performances almost upstage the more familiar concertos. A collection that leads the field, not least for its excellent sound.

Organ Concertos: Op. 4/1–6; Op. 7/1–6.

⬤ (M) Erato 0630 17871-2 (2). Koopman, Amsterdam Bar. O.

(B) **(*) Teldec Ultima (ADD) 8573 87790-2 (2). Tachezi, VCM, Harnoncourt.

Organ Concertos Nos. 1–6, Op. 4/1–6.

*** Virgin VC5 45174-2. Van Aspenen, OAE.

Organ Concertos Nos. 7–12, Op. 7/7–6; 13 in F (The Cuckoo and the Nightingale), HWV 295; 14 in A, HWV 296; 15 in D min., BWV 304; 16 in D, BWV 305a.

*** Virgin VCD5 45236-2 (2). Van Asperen, OAE.

Organ Concertos, Op. 4/1–6; Op. 7/1–6; in F (The Cuckoo and the Nightingale), HVW 295; in A, HWV 296; in D min., HWV 304.

(M) *** DG 435 037-2 (3). Preston, E. Concert, Pinnock.

Ton Koopman's combined sets of Opp. 4 and 7 lead the field, complete on a pair of mid-priced CDs taken from the Koopman Handel Edition. They take precedence over all the competition, both as performances and as recordings. The playing has wonderful life and warmth, tempi are always aptly judged and, although original instruments are used, this is authenticity with a kindly presence, for the warm acoustic ambience of St Bartholomew's Church, Beek-Ubbergen, Holland, gives the orchestra a glowingly vivid coloration and the string timbre is particularly attractive. So is the organ itself, which is just right for the music. Ton Koopman plays imaginatively throughout and he is obviously enjoying himself: no single movement sounds tired and the orchestral fugues emerge with genial clarity. Koopman directs the accompanying group from the keyboard, as Handel would have done, and the interplay between soloist and ripieno is a delight. The sound is first class and the balance could hardly be better.

Bob van Asperen's survey is absolutely complete and its combination of musicianship and scholarship gives this Virgin set a special feeling of authenticity. Although the accompanying group is comparatively modest there is no feeling that the scale of the music is minimized. The recording could hardly be bettered. In Opus 4, van Asperen chooses an organ built by Goetz and Gwynne in 1985 using seventeenth-century models, and he directs the Orchestra of the Age of Enlightenment from the keyboard, as Handel would have done. The results are refreshingly alert and buoyant. From the orchestra there is expressive warmth as well as vitality, and no lack of weight when called for. For Op. 7 he turns to an equally appealing four-stop continuo organ by N. P. Mander Ltd. Also included here are the pair of concertos known as the 'Second set' (one is the famous *The Cuckoo and the Nightingale*) and the two final works, as published by Arnold in 1797. Throughout, in the places where Handel would have improvised, extra Handelian movements are interpolated (mainly from the keyboard suites and solo sonatas, and all listed in the synopsis), but van Asperen improvises shorter linking passages himself. A considerable achievement.

Simon Preston's set of the Handel *Organ Concertos* now comes on three discs. On the first, containing the six Op. 4 works, plus the *A major*, though the balance of the solo instrument is not perfect, the playing of both Preston and the English Concert is admirably fresh and lively. Ursula Holliger is outstanding on a baroque harp (taking the place of the organ) in Op. 4, No. 6, and she creates some delicious sounds. The second and third discs, containing the six Op. 7 works, plus the *The Cuckoo and the Nightingale* and the *D minor*, were recorded on the organ at St John's, Armitage, in Staffordshire, and are even more attractive for the warmth and assurance of the playing, which comes near the ideal for a period performance. The *A major* that completes the set was recorded earlier with Op. 4. For those wanting a complete set of the *Organ Concertos* this is also strongly recommended.

Herbert Tachezi also concentrates on the twelve concertos which make up Opp. 4 and 7. The ornamentation provided by the soloist was achieved spontaneously at the actual recording sessions, but Harnoncourt's accompaniments at times seem unadventurous and rhythmically too positive. But Tachezi's registration and flourishes give constant pleasure, and the chest organ (made by Jürgen Ahrend) is very well chosen for this repertoire. Although Handel's more robust and grander qualities are rather played down, the recording is fresh, full, transparent and cleanly transferred, and there is much to enjoy here. Good value at Ultima price.

Organ Concertos Op. 4/1–3; (i) Op. 4/4; (ii) Op. 4/6. Op. 7/1–6.

** Hyp. CDA 67291/2. Nicholson, Brandenburg Consort, Goodman; (i) with Clare College Ch., Cambridge; (ii) Kelly (harp).

Besides using Handel's own organ (still in excellent condition) in St Lawrence, Whitchurch, at Canons, near Edgware, north of London, the Nicholson/Goodman set offers a novelty in including Op. 4/4 in a 1737 version where Handel concluded the finale with an *Alleluia* chorus from *Athalia*, an eccentric idea which in the event is effective enough. Op. 4/6 is heard in the arrangement for harp, and the performance lacks charm. In any case the performances here are at times curiously didactic. The crisp rhythms with which these works abound, and which should sound amiably jaunty, are often here just that bit too rigid. Both playing and recording are otherwise fresh, but the competition is fierce and this is far from a first choice.

Organ Concertos, Op. 4/1–6.

(BB) *** Naxos 8.553835. Lindley, N. Sinf., Creswick.

A most enjoyable and inexpensive modern instrument performance of Op. 4, rhythmically jaunty and warmly expressive by turns. Simon Lindley is an excellent soloist and the piping reeds of the organ at Holy Cross Church, Fenham, seem very apt for the music. Op. 4/6 is played and registered with appealing delicacy to remind us of the alternative version for harp. The recording balance is admirable. Not a first choice overall but an undoubted bargain.

Organ Concertos, Op. 4/1, 2 & 4; Op. 7/1 & 4.

*** Erato 3984 25486-2. Alain, Freiburg Baroque O, Von Der Goltz.

This is perhaps a first instalment of a new digital recording of Handel's Op. 4 and Op. 7, but even if it were not, the disc includes five of Handel's most attractive concertos, and they are splendidly played on a Cavaillé-Coll organ with a superb baroque personality at Saint-Pierre des Chartreux, Toulouse. Although the Freiburg Baroque Orchestra uses period instruments, the effect is more robust than with Bob van Asperen's recordings, partly because of the larger personality of the organ. But Marie-Claire Alain's performances, too, are more extrovert and vivid. Goltz's orchestral support is stylish and refined, without ever being meagre (sample the fullness of the opening Adagio of Op. 7/4 with bassoons), and allegros have exhilarting buoyancy. The documentation includes a detailed plan of the registrations used. Most enjoyable.

Organ Concertos, Op. 4/2; Op. 7/3–5; in F (The Cuckoo and the Nightingale).

(M) *** DG 447 300-2. Preston, E. Concert, Pinnock.

This is more generous than the previous (full-price) sampler from Preston's series with Pinnock. Both performances and sound are admirably fresh.

(i) Piano Concerto in A (arr. Beecham). The Gods Go A-Begging (ballet, arr. BEECHAM): excerpts. The Origin of Design (suite de ballet, arr. BEECHAM).

(N) (***) Somm mono BEECHAM 7. (i) Betty Humby Beecham; LPO or RPO, Beecham.

This disc of Beecham's arrangements of Handel, like the companion issue of Delius recordings, draws on private discs in Beecham's own collection. Always elegant and warmly expressive, full of fun, Beecham flagrantly defies latter-day taste in baroque performance, yet is totally winning. The ten movements from the ballet *The Origin of Design* come from the very first recording sessions of Beecham's newly founded London Philharmonic in December 1932. They were never issued, when the following month he recorded some of the movements again. The performances are brilliant, with the players on their toes, not least the oboist, Leon Goossens. Seven of the movements from the later ballet *The Gods Go A-Begging*, made between 1933 and 1938, did get published, but all the rest, including the six movements from the same ballet recorded with the RPO in 1949, have never appeared in any format, inexplicably so.

The oddity is the four-movement *Piano Concerto* which Beecham cobbled together from various Handel movements (unidentified here) for his then wife, the pianist Betty Humby. It makes a curious confection, starting with a nine-minute *Chaconne* in which grandly spacious sections punctuate energetic variations. The result is exuberant, sounding less like Handel than twentieth-century pastiche. As in the Delius disc, transfers bring satisfyingly full-bodied sound, if with obvious limitations.

Music for the Royal Fireworks (original wind scoring).

*** Telarc CD 80038. Cleveland Symphonic Winds, Fennell – HOLST: *Military Band Suites.* *** ✹

Music for the Royal Fireworks; Concerto grosso in C (Alexander's Feast); Overtures: Alceste; Belshazzar; Samson; Saul. Solomon: Arrival of the Queen of Sheba.

(M) *** DG 447 279-2. E. Concert, Pinnock.

Music for the Royal Fireworks (original version);
(i) *Coronation Anthems* (see also below).

*** Hyp. CDA 66350. (i) New College, Oxford, Ch.; augmented King's Consort, King.

King provides the first ever period performance of Handel's *Royal Fireworks Music* to use the full complement of instruments Handel demanded, assembling no fewer than 24 baroque oboists and 12 baroque bassoonists, 9 trumpeters, 9 exponents of the hand horn and 4 timpanists. It all makes for a glorious noise. King's Handel style has plenty of rhythmic bounce, and the recording in its warmly atmospheric way gives ample scale. The coupled performances of the four *Coronation Anthems* are not as incisively dramatic as some but still convey the joy of the inspiration.

In 1978, in Severance Hall, Cleveland, Ohio, Frederick Fennell gathered together the wind and brass from the Cleveland Symphony Orchestra and recorded a performance to demonstrate spectacularly what fine playing and digital sound could do for Handel's open-air score. The overall sound-balance tends to favour the brass (and the drums), but few will grumble when the result is as overwhelming as it is on the CD, with the sharpness of focus matched by the presence and amplitude of the sound-image.

Pinnock's performance of the *Fireworks Music* has tremendous zest; this is still a top recommendation for those wanting a period-instrument version. The account of the *Alexander's Feast Concerto* has both vitality and imagination and is no less recommendable. The vigorous and exhilarating performances of five overtures, most of them hardly known at all but full of original ideas. All are freshly and cleanly recorded.

Music for the Royal Fireworks, HWV 351 (original wind scoring); *Concertos in D* (arr. from *Fireworks Music, HWV 335a; in F* (arr. from *Water Music*), HWV 331/316; *Occasional Suite in D* (arr. PINNOCK); *Passacaille, gigue et menuet* (arr. from *Trio Sonata, Op. 5/4*).

*** DG 453 451-2. E. Concert, Pinnock.

Pinnock's newest 1996 recording of the *Royal Fireworks Music* adds grandeur to vitality. It is superbly played, although fascinatingly the period horns do not quite produce the exciting edge that made Mackerras's early stereo Pye recording so memorable. The rest of the programme is agreeable occasional music, played with warmth and the new elegance which original-instrument performances have discovered recently, and the *Passacaglia, Gigue and Minuet* has the warmth of timbre one would expect from modern instruments. The two concertos have interpolated slow movements from other sources; the *Occasional Suite* (a pastiche in the manner of Beecham) draws on the *Overture* from the *Occasional Oratorio* (with a particularly beautiful oboe solo) plus excerpts from *Ariodante, Joshua* and *Alessandro Severo*. All most enjoyable in a most unexpected way: almost old-fashioned in its colour and popular appeal.

Music for the Royal Fireworks; Water Music (complete).

⊕ *** DG 435 390-2. Orpheus CO.

*** Virgin VC5 45265-2. L. Classical Players, Norrington.

(N) (M) *** Ph. 464 706-2. E. Bar. Sol., Gardiner.

(M) *** Classic fM 75605 570442. Scottish CO, McGegan.

(BB) *** Naxos 8.550109. Capella Istropolitana, Warchal.

The conductorless Orpheus Chamber Orchestra are little short of superlative in polished and alive performances that sweep the board. Although modern instruments are used, such is the Orpheus sense of baroque style, so crisp and buoyant are the rhythms, that the effect has much in common with a period performance without any of the snags. How warmly and elegantly they play the colourful and more intimate dances in the central *G major Suite* of the *Water Music*, and they begin with a riveting account of the *Royal Fireworks Music*, catching its sense of spectacle. Strings are used as Handel wished, but the wind and brass dominate. The recording is in the demonstration bracket, and these performances are so fresh that it is like listening to this marvellous music for the very first time.

Norrington uses a full orchestra but highlights the bright trumpets and braying horns to give both works a vividly robust open-air flavour. The dance movements have grace, but a lively grace, and it is the consistent vitality that makes these performances so stimulating. The overtures of both works bring the crispest double-dotting, while the outer movements of the *Fireworks Music* are as strong and rugged as you could want, without loss of polish or tuning.

Gardiner's *Fireworks* and *Water Music* were recorded eight years apart and have only now been combined on one CD. The *Royal Fireworks Music* brings an excellent reponse from the English Baroque Soloists, rhythms are alive and well articulated, and phrasing musical. Tempi are a bit on the fast side, and rather more grandeur might have been welcome in the closing sections. But the result remains fresh, if comparatively lightweight. The *Water Music*, however (with the *F major Suite* played first), is brighter, more resilient, full of vitality and colour, although the famous *Air* trips along in sprightly fashion, more like a dance movement. But this is period-instrument playing at its most stimulating and the sound picture is vivid and clear.

Nicholas McGegan and his excellent Scottish players, very well recorded in the Caird Hall, Dundee, use modern instruments but seek a style deriving from period-instrument experience, with brisk tempi and lifted rhythms, though somewhat more easygoing than Norrington. The Overture and finale of the *Royal Fireworks Music* are boldly expansive and in the *Water Music* textures are attractively light, phrasing neat and stylish. At mid-price this Classic fM pairing is very competitive.

Bohdan Warchal directs the Capella Istropolitana in bright and lively performances of the complete *Water Music* as well as the *Fireworks Music*, well paced and well scaled, with woodwind and brass aptly abrasive, and with such points as double-dotting faithfully observed. Textures are clean, with an attractive bloom on the full and immediate sound, to provide a strong bargain recommendation.

Music for the Royal Fireworks; Water Music (complete);
(i) *Oboe Concerto No. 2 in B flat.*

(B) **(*) Decca (ADD) 448 227-2. Stuttgart CO, Münchinger,
(i) with Koch.

Münchinger's style is a compromise between authenticity
and the German tradition. In the complete *Water Music* he
uses recorders most effectively; the balance, helped by
Decca's very transparent sound, is often attractively lightweight. If occasionally tempi seem a shade on the slow side,
there is much to enjoy both here and in the *Fireworks Music*.
First-class digital recording, vivid and well focused, and with
an oboe concerto (well played by Lothar Koch) thrown in
for good measure.

Music for the Royal Fireworks; Water Music Suite (arr.
Harty).

(M) **(*) Mercury (ADD) 434 398-2. LSO, Dorati – MOZART:
Serenade: Eine kleine Nachtmusik; Dances; Marches. **

Music for the Royal Fireworks: Suite; Water Music: Suite
(arr. Harty and Szell); *The Faithful Shepherd: Minuet* (ed.
Beecham); *Xerxes: Largo* (arr. Reinhardt).

(BB) *** Belart (ADD) 450 001-2. LSO, Szell.

Many readers will, like us, have a nostalgic feeling for the
Handel–Harty suites from which earlier generations got to
know these two marvellous scores. George Szell and the LSO
offer a highly recommendable coupling of them on a Belart
super-bargain issue, with Handel's *Largo* and the *Minuet*
from Beecham's *Faithful Shepherd Suite* thrown in for good
measure. The orchestral playing from the early 1970s is
outstanding, and the strings are wonderfully expressive in
the slower pieces. The horns excel, and the crisp new transfer
seems to add to the sheer zest of the music-making. A
splendid bargain.

Dorati also takes us back to the pioneering Harty suites,
vividly adapted for modern orchestra, and very good they
sound too in the glowing resonance of Watford Town Hall.
The 1957 recording hardly sounds at all dated. They could
hardly be better played, mixing elegance and warmth, although the leisured tempi in the *Fireworks Music* (particularly the *Alla siciliana*), now seem out of style.

Overtures:(i) *Agrippina; Alcina; Belshazzar; Deidamia;
Jephtha; Messiah; Radamisto; Rinaldo; Rodelinda;
Susanna;* (ii) *Samson.*

(M) **(*) DG (ADD) 457 903-2. (i) LPO, (ii) Munich Bach O;
Richter.

While today's ears are used to much lighter Handelian
textures, and Richter (recorded in 1969) is weighty, his
broadness of style is tempered by brilliantly alert playing
from the LPO, with allegros taken exhilaratingly fast. Those
who enjoy the German tradition in Handel will find this
partnership with a British orchestra fruitful and rewarding.
The *Messiah Sinfonia* is particularly fine. Richter's own
Munich Bach Orchestra is used for *Samson*, the closing item,
which has been added for the present reissue. They play
most impressively, with a strikingly fine contribution from
the horns.

Water Music: Suites Nos. 1–3 (complete).

(BB) *** ASV CDQS 6152. ECO, Malcolm.
(M) *** Vanguard 99713. Il Fondamento, Dombrecht –
TELEMANN: *Water Music.* ***
*** Hyp. CDA 66967. King's Cons., King – TELEMANN:
Water Music. ***
(B) *** [EMI Red Line CDR5 69809]. BPO, Muti.
*** DG 410 525-2. E. Concert, Pinnock.

This super-bargain set of the complete *Water Music* on the
ASV Quicksilva label from George Malcolm and the English
Chamber Orchestra makes an outstanding recommendation, except for those insisting on period instruments. This
is a most stylish realization of Handel's intentions, with the
closing dances of the *Third Suite in G* particularly elegant,
while the digital recording approaches demonstration standard. The playing is first class, articulation is deft and detail
admirable.

Il Fondamento is an excellent Belgian period-instrument
group; under the lively direction of Paul Dombrecht they
present Handel's *Water Music* with a nice mixture of verve
and elegance. The throaty reeds and robust brass ensure a
vigorous response, but the more graceful numbers in the
centre of the work have pleasing colour and much character.
This ranks high among the 'authentic' versions and is made
doubly attractive by being coupled at mid-price with Telemann's *Wassermusik*, not as inspired as Handel's but engagingly inventive and entertaining.

Robert King's is above all a performance of contrasts –
between the elegant lighter dance movement, the playing
warmly refined, and the set-piece allegros where the baroque
horns and trumpets burst forth exuberantly. They always
play with joyful vigour, with as much weight and more
brightness and bite than with modern instruments. The
strings are never edgy and often quite mellow as in the
famous *Air*. The coupling with Telemann's *Water Music*
works well.

The playing of the Berlin Philharmonic under Muti is
polished and elegant. In the *Overture* of the first suite, a
small instrumental group is featured as a neat counterpoint
to the main ripieno: throughout there is a strong emphasis
on contrast, with instrumental solos often treated in a concertante manner. The playing is very responsive and the
strings generally display a light touch, but the horns are
almost aggressive in their spirited vigour in the famous
fanfare tune. With a full, vivid, yet clear sound-picture, this
is very easy to enjoy. This is only available in the USA.

To offer the *Water Music* without the *Fireworks Music* at
full price now seems ungenerous, but Pinnock's first version
on DG Archiv remains very enticing. Speeds are consistently
well chosen and are generally uncontroversial. One test is
the famous *Air*, which here remains an engagingly gentle
piece. The recording is beautifully balanced and clear.

CHAMBER MUSIC
Complete chamber music

Volume 1: *Flute Sonatas: in E min., Op. 1a/b; in G, Op. 1/5; in B min., Op. 1/9; in D (HWV 378); Halle Sonatas Nos. 1–3.*

(M) *** CRD (ADD) CRD 3373. L'Ecole d'Orphée (Preston, Sheppard, Toll, Carolan).

Volume 2: *Oboe Sonatas Nos. 1 in B flat (HWV 357); in F (HWV 363a); in C min., Op. 1/8 (HWV 366); Violin Sonatas: in D min. (original version of Op. 1/1), HWV 359a; in A, Op. 1/3, HWV 361; in G min., Op. 1/6 (HWV 364a); in D, Op. 1/13 (HWV 371); Allegros for Violin & Continuo: in A min. (HWV 408); in C min., HWV 412.*

(M) **(*) CRD (ADD) CRD 3374; CRDC 4074. L'Ecole d'Orphée (Reichenberg, Holloway, Sheppard, Carolan).

The first pair of CDs in CRD's complete survey are very well recorded. Volume 1 contains the seven sonatas for flute (three are the so-called 'Halle' Trio Sonatas, published in 1730 and thought to be the product of Handel's youth) as well as a sonata recently discovered in Brussels, for flute and continuo in D major (HWV 378). The playing is always spirited and intelligent, and if Stephen Preston's eighteenth-century flute timbre sounds a little watery, his phrasing is often beguiling. David Reichenberg's Hailperin oboe is full of ripe colour, and the playing of both artists is immaculate.

Volume 3: *Trio Sonatas, Op. 2: Nos. 1 for Flute, Violin & Continuo in B min.; 2 in G min.; 3 in B flat for 2 Violins & Continuo; 4 in F for Recorder, Violin & Continuo; 5 in G min.; 6 in G min. for 2 Violins & Continuo.*

(M) **(*) CRD (ADD) CRD 3375. L'Ecole d'Orphée (Holloway, Comberti, Preston, Pickett, Sheppard, Wooley, Toll).

Volume 4: *Trio Sonatas, Op. 5 for 2 Violins & Continuo: Nos. 1 in A; 2 in D; 3 in E min.; 4 in G; 5 in G min.; 6 in F; 7 in B flat.*

(M) **(*) CRD 3376. L'Ecole d'Orphée (Holloway, Comberti, Sheppard, Carolan).

Volume 5: *Sinfonia in B flat (HWV 338); Trio Sonatas: in C min., Op. 2/1a; in F (HWV 392); in G min.(HWV 393); in E (HWV 394); in C (HWV 403).*

(M) **(*) CRD 3377. L'Ecole d'Orphée (Holloway, Comberti, Sheppard, Carolan).

The *Trio Sonatas* recorded by L'Ecole d'Orphée include the complete Op. 2 set, an alternative version of another sonata of Op. 2, the seven sonatas of Op. 5, and the three so-called 'Dresden' *Sonatas* (HWV 392–4). Only one of them (in F) is totally authentic, though whoever composed the remaining two was no mean figure. In addition there is a very attractive *Sinfonia in B flat* (HWV 338), which is written in trio sonata form. There are many musical riches here and no want of accomplishment in the performances. The two violins in use by John Holloway and Micaela Comberti have markedly different tone-quality.

Volume 4 of the CRD set includes Op. 5. Here Handel frequently borrows from himself, and much of this material

is also found in the overtures for the *Chandos Anthems* or in the dance music for his operas. No. 6 is familiar, as Handel himself re-used the material of the first and fourth movements for the *Cuckoo and the Nightingale Organ Concerto*. But one of the most exasperating features of these CD transfers, and one which makes them less easy to use than the original LPs, is that individual movements are uncued, only each complete work.

Volume 6: *Recorder Sonatas, Op. 1: Nos. 2 in G min. (HWV 360); 4 in A min. (HWV 362); 7 in C (HWV 365); 11 in F (HWV 369); in G (HWV 358); in B flat (HWV 377); in D min. (HWV 367a); Trio Sonata in F (HWV 405).*

(M) *** CRD (ADD) CRD 3378. L'Ecole d'Orphée (Pickett, Beckett, Sheppard, Carolan).

These much-praised CRD performances bring elegant and finished playing from the two recorder players and, besides the Op. 1 *Sonatas*, the programme includes a *G major Sonata*, first published in 1974, and the original D minor version of the *Flute Sonata, Op. 9/1*, which has an engaging second movement based on a minor-key variant of a famous allegro in the *Water Music*. Excellent, intimate recording, but again with the irritating drawback that individual movements are not cued, and the *D minor Sonata* has seven of them.

Sonatas, Op. 1: Nos. 1 in D min. (HWV 359a) (for violin & continuo); 1a in E min. (HWV 379); 1b in E min. (HWV 359b) (both for flute & continuo); 2 in G min. (HWV 360) (for recorder & continuo); 3 in A (HWV 361) (for violin & continuo); 4 in A min. (HWV 362) (for recorder & continuo); 5 in G (HWV 363b) (for flute & continuo); 6 in G min. (HWV 364a) (for violin & continuo); 7 in C (HWV 365) (for recorder & continuo); 8 in C min. (HWV 366) (for oboe & continuo); 9a in D min. (HWV 367a) (for recorder & continuo); 9b in B min. (HWV 367b) (for flute & continuo); 11 in F (HWV 369) (for recorder & continuo); 13 in D (HWV 371) (for violin & continuo); Halle Sonatas Nos. 1–3 (for flute & continuo), (HWV 374–6); Sonata for Oboe & Continuo in B flat (HWV 357); Sonata for Recorder & Continuo in B flat (HWV 377); Sonata for Violin & Continuo in G (HWV 358).

*** Hyp. CDA 66921/3. Wallfisch, Beznosiuk, Beckett, Tunnicliffe, Nicholson.

The Hyperion set concentrates on Op. 1, although illogically four of the violin sonatas, previously counted as being part of Handel's opus, have been omitted as spurious (HWV 368, 370 and 372–3). The fine *Halle Sonatas* have been included, plus some other miscellaneous works now considered to be authentic. The performances use period instruments and have the advantage of current practice, so both flute and oboe timbres have a strong baroque flavour but the violins are less raw-timbred than the quality offered by L'Ecole d'Orphée; on the other hand the playing itself is mellower and perhaps at times slightly less vital than on the more comprehensive CRD set.

Flute Sonatas (for flute and continuo): in E min., Op. 1/1a; in D, HWV 378; Halle Sonatas (for flute and continuo) Nos. 1–3; Oboe Sonatas (for oboe and continuo): Nos. 1 in

B flat (HWV 357); in F (HWV 363a), Op. 1/5; in C min. (HWV 366), Op. 1/8; Recorder Sonatas (for recorder and continuo): in G min. (HWV 360); in A min. (HWV 362); in C (HWV 365); in F (HWV 369), Op. 1/2, 4, 7 & 11; in B flat (HWV 377); in D min. (HWV 367a); Sinfonia in B flat for 2 Violins & Continuo, HWV 338; Trio Sonatas: in E min. for 2 Flutes & Continuo, HWV 395; in F for 2 Recorders & Continuo, HWV 405.

(B) *** Ph. Duo (ADD) 446 563-2 (2). ASMF Chamber Ens.

This superb Philips set assembles virtually all the important wind sonatas, plus a single Trio Sonata for two violins and continuo, on a pair of discs offered for the price of one. William Bennett uses a modern flute very persuasively in the Flute Sonatas and includes, besides the work from Op. 1 and the three Halle Sonatas, a more recent discovery from a Brussels manuscript. Nicholas Kraemer and Denis Vigay provide admirable support, and the recording is most realistic and present. In the Recorder Sonatas Michala Petri plays with her customary virtuosity and flair, and Neil Black is marvellously accomplished in the Oboe Sonatas. Both artists share an excellent rapport with their continuo players, who include George Malcolm (harpsichord), Denis Vigay (cello) and Graham Sheen (bassoon), and again the sound is exemplary, natural and spacious. Only those seeking original instruments need look elsewhere.

Flute Sonatas (for flute and continuo): in E min., HWV 359b; in G, HWV 363b; in B min., HWV 367b (6th movt); in A min., HWV 374; in E min., HWV 375 (4th movt); in B min., HWV 376; Oboe Sonatas (for oboe and continuo): in C min., HWV 366; in B flat, HWV 357, in F, HWV 363a (2nd movt); Recorder Sonatas (for recorder and continuo): in G min., HWV 360; in A min., HWV 362; in C, HWV 365; in D min., HWV 367a (movts 1-5, 7); in F, HWV 369; in B flat, HWV 377; Andante in D min., HWV 409.

(B) *** Sony (ADD) Double SBK 60100 (2). Brüggen, Haynes, Lange, Bylsma, Van Asperen (harpsichord and organ).

These performances, on period instruments, are most accomplished: Brüggen plays with characteristic mastery and so do his companions. There are some mannerisms: he swells all too predictably on sustained notes and is generous with stress accents. However, Handelians will want to consider the set for its scholarship and expertise, even though the flute is balanced rather close. This makes a clear alternative to Marriner's set, although it is not so complete, including only key movements from some works; and the documentation, by leaving out the opus numbers, is less clear.

Flute or Alto Recorder Sonatas: Op. 1/2, 4, 7, 9 & 11; in B flat.

*** HM HMU 907151. Verbruggen, Koopman, Linden.

Marion Verbruggen uses modern copies of two alto recorders from the early eighteenth century and a similar voice flute in D; the sounds here are appealingly mellow, with the continuo featuring cello, harpsichord and chest organ. The effect is intimate, expressive and lively by turns, but with no attempt at self-conscious bravura. The recording is beautifully balanced.

Recorder Sonatas, Op. 1/2, 4, 7, 11; in D min (Fitzwilliam), HWV 367a; Trio Sonata in F, HWV 405; Favourite Air (Lelio's Aria from Scipio); Gavotte, HWV 604; Gigue, HWV 599; Minuet, HWV 603.

(BB) *** Naxos 8.550700. Czidra, Harsányi, Pertis, Keleman.

A particularly attractive and generous anthology. These Hungarian musicians are first-class players and their accounts of the sonatas from Op. 1 and the Trio Sonata (for two recorders and continuo) are second to none. The encores (for various combinations) are most engaging, especially the Gavotte and Gigue. The recording is excellent.

(i) Trio Sonatas, Opp. 2/5; 5/4 & 7 for 2 Violins & Continuo; Italian cantatas: (i; ii) Notte placida e cheta; (i; ii; iii) Tra la fiamme.

*** Chan. 0620. (i) Purcell Qt (members); (ii) Bott; (iii) with Kershaw, Downer, Amherst, Manson.

An entirely delightful recital. The Trio Sonatas are full of attractive invention, notably an impressive passacaglia in Op. 5/4, and they are used to frame and act as an interlude between the two Italian cantatas, ravishingly sung by Catherine Bott. It is difficult to decide which of the two – Tra la fiamme (about Daedalus and Icarus) with its descriptive aria Among the flames, or Notte placida e cheta ('Calm and quiet night') – is the more enchanting. The recording is ideally balanced.

KEYBOARD MUSIC

Capriccio in F; Chaconne in G, HWV 435; Fantaisie in C; Prelude in D min.; Prelude & Allegro in G min.; Sonata in C; Suites Nos. 1 in A, HWV 426; 4 in D min., HMW 429; 7 in G min., HWV 432.

*** Erato 0630 14886-2. Baumont (harpsichord).

Olivier Baumont uses three different harpsichords for his well-devised programme: a 1707 Dumont for the Chaconne and G minor Suite, a 1652 Couchet for the other two Suites, and an anonymous Italian instrument from 1677 for the shorter works (the one-movement Sonata, the Capriccio, the contrasting G minor Prelude and Allegro and Fantaisie), all particularly appealing pieces from the composer's 'early youth'. Baumont plays the more extended final version of the Chaconne and his own version of the Suite No. 4, omitting the Prelude, 'as it represents a preliminary sketch for the opening movement of the Third Suite', and including instead a very beautiful Sarabande with variations (which you might recognize) taken from an autograph manuscript in the Fitzwilliam Museum at Cambridge. All in all this is a very stimulating and enjoyable collection, played with great vitality and splendidly recorded.

Suites Nos. (i) 1 in A; (ii) 2 in F; 3 in D min.; (i) 4 in E min.; (ii) 5 in E; (i) 6 in F sharp min.; 7 in G min.; (ii) 8 in F min.

⚫ (B) *** EMI double forte (ADD) CZS5 69337-2 (2). (i) Gavrilov; (ii) Richter.

Suites (i) Nos. 9 in G min.; (ii) 10 in D min.; 11 in D min.;

(i) *12 in E min.;* (ii) *13 in B flat;* (i) *14 in G;* (ii) *15 in D min.;* (i) *16 in G min.*

⚫ (B) *** EMI double forte (ADD) CZS5 69340-2 (2).
  (i) Richter; (ii) Gavrilov – BEETHOVEN: *Piano Sonata No. 17.* *** ⚫

These superb recordings of the Handel *Keyboard Suites* were recorded by Sviatoslav Richter and Andrei Gavrilov at the Château de Marcilly-sur-Maulne during the 1979 Tours Festival, and first appeared in 1983 in a handsome five-LP box, but never reissued as single- or double-pack LPs in the UK. They have been slow to reach CD, but EMI have made amends by issuing the set in first-class transfers, and in an economical format – two twin-CDs packaged as one, available separately, and competitively priced – and with Richter's famous 1961 account of Beethoven's *D minor Sonata*, Op. 31, No. 2, thrown in for good measure. The serenity and tranquillity of the slow movements and the radiance of the faster movements have never before been so fully realized. Not to be missed.

Harpsichord Suites Nos. 1–8, HWV 426/433; 6 Fugues or Voluntarys for Organ or Harpsichord, HWV 605/10; Fugues: in F; E, HWV 611/12.

*** Hyp. CDA 66931/2. Nicholson (harpsichord).

Harpsichord Suites Nos. 1–8.

(B) *** HM Musique d'Abord HMA 190447/48. Gilbert (harpsichord).

Paul Nicholson's playing is admirable, full of life yet with a degree of intimacy that is very appealing. He has an ideal (unnamed) harpsichord, which is perfect for this repertoire and which is superbly recorded. Nicholson's crisp and stylish ornamentation is never fussy, and he is generous with repeats. The most famous of the eight is, of course, No. 5 which has the variations known as *The Harmonious Blacksmith* as its finale, here ending in a blaze of bravura. Highly recommended, and unlikely to be surpassed in the near future.

Gilbert is a scholar as well as a distinguished player, and his version of the suites, recorded on a copy of a Taskin harpsichord by Bédard, makes a fine bargain alternative to Paul Nicholson's more comprehensive (and more expensive) set. Gilbert observes most first-half repeats but not those of the second, and he is as imaginative in the handling of decoration and ornamentation as one would expect. The recording is natural and very well balanced.

Harpsichord Suites Nos. 1 in B flat min.; 2 in G; 3 in D min.; 4 in D min.; 5 in E min.; 6 in G min.

*** Chan. 0644. Yates.

Vivacious and intelligent performances, competitively priced and very well recorded.

Harpsichord Suites Nos. 3 in D min.; 8 in F min.; 11 in D min.; 13 in B flat; 14 in G; 15 in D min.

(M) *** Lyrichord LEMS 8034 (2). Wolfe (harpsichord).

The Texan harpsichordist Paul Wolfe was a pupil and protégé of Wanda Landowska. He made these recordings in 1958/9, but the quality is extremely vivid, both real and

present, and the chosen acoustic excellent. While the performances are of high calibre, there is as much interest here in the instrument itself as the music-making. Wolfe had a harpsichord specially built for him by Frank Rutkowski of Stoney Creek, Connecticut. It is a magnificent creature, dubbed by its maker 'the *Queen Mary*' because of its length – nine feet! It has two manuals with a range of just over five octaves, and seven pedals to alter and mute the timbre and includes a buff (or lute) stop which creates a dry, pizzicato sound. The range of colour is aurally fascinating and Wolfe makes the very most of the tonal and dynamic contrasts possible in Handel's music, especially in the variations.

The playing itself is infectiously full of life; one's only comment is that Wolfe usually chose to pace the *Allemandes* very slowly and grandly, even the *Sarabande variée* in the 11th Suite, which is based on *La folia*. The deep bass stop (also favoured by Landowska) can be heard to its fullest effect in the *Prelude* of the *F minor Suite* (No. 8), which provides a lively end to the second disc. The two-CD set, which has 85 minutes of music, is offered at a special price.

VOCAL MUSIC

(i) *Aci, Galatea e Polifemo;* (ii) *Recorder Sonatas in F; C & G (transposed to F).*

(B) *** HM HMA 901253/4. (i) Kirkby, Watkinson, Thomas, L. Bar., Medlam; (ii) Piquet, Toll.

Aci, Galatea e Polifemo proves to be quite a different work from the always popular English masque, *Acis and Galatea*, with only one item even partially borrowed. Charles Medlam directs London Baroque in a beautifully sprung performance with three excellent soloists, the brightly characterful Emma Kirkby as Aci, Carolyn Watkinson in the lower-pitched role of Galatea, and David Thomas coping manfully with the impossibly wide range of Polifemo's part. The three recorder sonatas are comparably delightful, a welcome makeweight. Excellent sound, full of presence. Particularly enticing at bargain price.

Acis and Galatea (complete).

*** Erato 3984-25505-2 (2). Daneman, Petibon, Agnew, Cornwell, Ewing, Sinclair, Piolino, Le Monnier, Les Arts Florissants, Christie.

*** DG 423 406-2 (2). Burrowes, Rolfe Johnson, Hill, White, E. Bar. Sol., Gardiner.

(BB) ** Naxos 8.553188. Kym Amps, Robin Doveton, Angus Davidson, Van Asch, Scholars Bar. Ens., Van Asch.

Acis and Galatea; Il pastor fido: Hunting Scene.

(B) *** Double Decca 452 973-2 (2). Tear, Gomez, Langridge, Luxon, Ch. & ASMF, Marriner – Tear: *'Baroque Recital'.* ***

(i) *Acis and Galatea;* (ii) *Cantata: Look Down, Harmonious Saint.*

*** Hyp. CDA 66361/2; KA 66361/2. (i; ii) Ainsley; (i) McFadden, Covey-Crump, George, Harre-Jones; King's Cons., King.

Gardiner and Marriner are strong contenders in this field, but William Christie's new account on Erato is if anything even better and probably now a first recommendation alongside Robert King's Hyperion version. Christie gives us a chamber performance with forces similar to those Handel used for the Cannons performances. Tempi are inclined to be brisk and rhythms crisp but he has marshalled expert singers; Alan Ewing's Polyphemus is particularly good, well characterized and spirited. Indeed, the whole performance is full of life and personality, and William Christie holds everything together with finesse and grace. The sound, too, is well balanced and natural.

Robert King directs a bluff, beautifully sprung reading of *Acis and Galatea* that brings out its domestic jollity. Using the original version for five solo singers and no chorus, this may be less delicate in its treatment than John Eliot Gardiner's reading but it is, if anything, even more winning. The soloists are first rate, with John Mark Ainsley among the most stylish of the younger generation of Handel tenors, and the bass, Michael George, characterizing strongly. Claron McFadden's vibrant soprano is girlishly distinctive. This Hyperion issue provides a valuable makeweight in the florid solo cantata, thought to be originally conceived as part of *Alexander's Feast*, nimbly sung by Ainsley.

The refinement and rhythmic lift of the Academy's playing under Marriner make for a lively, engaging performance, marked by characterful solo singing from a strong team. The choruses are sung by a quartet drawn from a distinguished vocal sextet (Jennifer Smith, Margaret Cable, Paul Esswood, Wynford Evans, Neil Jenkins and Richard Jackson) and, with warmly atmospheric recording, the result is a sparkling entertainment. Robert Tear's tone is not always ideally mellifluous (for instance in *Love in her eyes sits playing*) but, like the others, he has a good feeling for Handelian style; the sweetness of Jill Gomez's contribution is a delight. The 1977 (originally Argo) recording is of vintage quality and this Double Decca reissue is made the more attractive by the inclusion of a further solo recital from Robert Tear of rare English baroque repertoire – music by Arne, Boyce and Hook, as well as Handel. Before this, as an interlude, comes a sprightly (orchestral) *Hunting Scene* from *Il pastor fido* consisting of a *March* and a pair of *Airs pour les chasseurs*.

Some of John Eliot Gardiner's tempi are idiosyncratic (some too fast, some too slow), but the scale of the performance, using period instruments, is beautifully judged, with the vocal soloists banding together for the choruses. Willard White is a fine Polyphemus. The authentic sounds of the English Baroque Soloists are finely controlled and the vibrato-less string timbre is clear and clean without being abrasive.

On a single disc at super-bargain price, the Naxos version is well worth hearing. David van Asch, leading the Scholars Baroque Ensemble, directs a brisk and light reading with Kym Amps as Galatea, sweeter and purer than she has sometimes been on disc, and Robin Doveton a light-toned Acis, stylish if not always firm in his legato singing. The counter-tenor, Angus Davidson, is rather unsteady as Damon, and though David van Asch as Polyphemus copes well with the with the wide range required, he is unresonant as the giant. Clear, well-balanced sound.

Agrippina condotta a morire; Armeda abbandonata; Lucrezia (Italian cantatas).

**(*) Virgin VC5 45283-2. Gens, Les Basses Réunies.

The only really well-known piece here is *Lucrezia*, which Dame Janet Baker has also recorded with distinction and whom Véronique Gens does not quite match. Nevertheless, she is convincingly and powerfully indignant at her violation, and in her closing suicidal aria, although at first touchingly vulnerable, she becomes really vehement as she determines vengeance '*nell'inferno*'. The abandoned Armida, against a bare accompaniment, laments her fate (*Ah crudele!*) to a particularly lovely melisma, and at the close she reveals her deep distress in a simple siciliana, movingly sung here. Agrippina, at her son Nero's mercy, contemplates her coming execution with all the volatile anger of her tempestuous character. Véronique Gens is here in her element, revelling in the dramatic mood changes and in the vocal bravura, where she is always in control. Her decoration is apt and she is persuasively accompanied.

Marian arias and cantatas: *Ah! Che troppo inequale; Donna, che in ciel; Haec est Regina;* G. B. FERRANDINI (attrib. HANDEL): *Il pianto di Maria*.

*** DG 439 866-2. Von Otter, Col. Mus. Ant., Goebel.

Dating from his years in Italy, these Handel works, directly linked to the worship of the Virgin Mary, inspire von Otter to give radiant performances. Ironically, the longest work, *Il pianto di Maria*, long attributed to Handel, has been found to be by G. B. Ferrandini; but it has many beauties, not least in a measured cavatina, *Se d'un Dio*. Both *Haec est Regina* and *Ah! che inequale* are strong, imaginative arias, and *Donna, che in ciel* is a superb, full-scale cantata with a fine overture and four splendid arias. Reinhard Goebel and his team give sympathetic support, though the period string-playing is on the abrasive side. Warm, immediate recording, which captures von Otter's firm mezzo superbly.

Ah! crudel, nel pianto mio; Armida abbandonata (cantatas).

(N) (B) * EMI Double forte (ADD) CZS 5 74284-2 (2). J. Baker, ECO, Leppard – BACH: *Cantatas*. ***

Dame Janet Baker delivers a strongly impassioned style for music which, though formal in layout, expresses far from normal emotions. Her singing is magnificent; even though the tessitura is a little high for a mezzo it brings a striking display of virtuosity as well as of incomparable tone-colour. Leppard's accompaniments are spirited and the recording is fresh, and this makes an admirable coupling for some of her equally beautiful Bach recordings.

Alexander's Feast; Concerto grosso in C (Alexander's Feast).

**(*) Ph. 422 053-2 (2). Watkinson, Robson, Brown, Stafford, Varcoe, Monteverdi Ch., E. Bar. Sol., Gardiner.

**(N) (M) ** Teldec (ADD) 3984 26796-2 (2). Palmer, Rolfe Johnson, Roberts, Stockholm Ch., VCM, Harnoncourt.

Alexander's Feast was the first and greatest of the odes by Dryden which Handel set to celebrate St Cecilia's Day. The invention is consistently on the highest level, without a single poor number.

The Philips version was recorded live at performances given at the Göttingen Festival, with sound that takes away some of the bloom on voices and instruments. What matters is the vigour and concentration of Gardiner's performance. Stephen Varcoe may lack the dark resonance of a traditional bass, but he projects his voice well. Nigel Robson's tenor suffers more than do the others from the dryness of the acoustic. The soprano, Donna Brown, sings with boyish freshness, and the alto numbers are divided very effectively between Carolyn Watkinson and the soft-grained counter-tenor, Ashley Stafford. The *Concerto grosso in C* was given with the oratorio at its first performance.

Harnoncourt's 1978 recording of *Alexander's Feast* is variably successful. The team of soloists is first rate, with Felicity Palmer, Anthony Rolfe-Johnson and Stephen Roberts all stylish, although Palmer's line is not always even and Roberts is too light of voice for the magnificent *Revenge, Timotheus cries*. The Stockholm Choir is consistently lively, a splendid ensemble, and the Concertus Musicus play with excellent precision, but the edginess that comes with authentic performance of this vintage (the horns sound awkward) is often disconcerting, albeit generally well served by the recording. It also seems perverse to include the *Concerto grosso* from Op. 3 as a fill-up, rather than the obvious choice of the concerto which carries the name of the vocal work.

L'allegro, il penseroso, il moderato.

(M) *** Erato (ADD) 2292 45377-2. Kwella, McLaughlin, Smith, Ginn, Davies, Hill, Varcoe, Monteverdi Ch., E. Bar. Sol., Gardiner.

(i) L'allegro ed il penseroso; (ii) Ode for St Cecilia's Day.

(B) *(*) Double Decca (ADD) 460 287-2 (2). (i) Morison, Delman, Harwood, Watts, Pears, Alan, St Anthony Singers, Philomusica of L.; (ii) Cantelo, Partridge, King's Coll., Cambridge, Ch., ASMF; Willcocks.

Taking Milton as his starting point, Handel illustrated in music the contrasts of mood and character between the cheerful and the thoughtful. Then, prompted by his librettist, Charles Jennens, he added compromise in *Il moderato*, the moderate man. The sequence of brief numbers is a delight, particularly in a performance as exhilarating as Gardiner's, with excellent soloists, choir and orchestra. The recording is first rate.

Somehow the Willcocks performance does not quite come to life, perhaps because it tries too hard. Pears sings intelligently as ever, but the other soloists are uneven in quality and seem unable to offer sufficient variety of tone colour and phrasing. The performance of the *Ode* is also disappointing. April Cantelo phrases sensitively and accurately, if with rather a white tone, but her singing seldom beguiles, and it is the tenor who brings the performance fully to life with *The trumpet's loud clangour*. The sound is excellent, but this set is altogether a non-starter.

Alpestre monte; Mi palpita il cor; Tra le fiamme; Tu fedel? Tu costante? (Italian cantatas).

*** O-L (IMS) 414 473-2. Kirkby, AAM, Hogwood.

The four cantatas here, all for solo voice with modest instrumental forces, are nicely contrasted, offer a spirited sequence of little arias rejecting a lover. Even 'A heart full of cares' in *Mi palpita il cor* inspires Handel to a charming, pastoral aria, with a delectable oboe obbligato, and even those limited cares quickly disperse. Light-hearted and sparkling performances to match.

Aminta e Fillide (cantata).

(B)*** Hyp. Helios CDH 55077. Fisher, Kwella, L. Handel O, Darlow.

In writing for two voices and strings, Handel presents a simple encounter in the pastoral tradition over a span of ten brief arias which, together with recitatives and final duet, last almost an hour. The music is as charming and undemanding for the listener as it is taxing for the soloists. This lively performance, beautifully recorded with two nicely contrasted singers, delightfully blows the cobwebs off a Handel work till now totally neglected. It is even more attractive on the bargain Helios label.

(i) Apollo e Daphne (cantata); (ii) Oboe Concerto in G min.

(B) *** HM (ADD) HMA 1905157. (i) Nelson, Thomas; (ii) Haynes; Philh. Bar. O; McGegan.

(N) (BB) *** Teldec 4509 98645-2. (i) Alexander, (ii) Hampson; VCM, Harnoncourt.

Apollo e Daphne, one of Handel's most delightful cantatas, tells how the determinedly chaste heroine, after an unwelcome and persistent pursuit by her godly suitor, finally escapes a fate worse than death by being transformed into a laurel bush. It has two strikingly memorable numbers, a lovely siciliano for Dafne with oboe obbligato and an aria for Apollo, *Come rosa in su la spina*, with unison violins and a solo cello. Both soloists are first rate, and Nicholas McGegan is a lively Handelian, though the playing of the orchestra could be more polished. The sound is over-resonant but has plenty of atmosphere. For the bargain-priced reissue (retaining the full documentation plus translation) a neat account of Handel's *G minor Oboe Concerto* has been added.

Harnoncourt's soloists, Roberta Alexander and the rich-voiced Thomas Hampson are hardly less impressive. They sing with great character, and there is some lovely wind playing from the Vienna Concentus Musicus. Harnoncourt keeps the action fizzing along with brisk tempi, and the delightful duet, *Una guerra ho dentro il seno* sparkles like Rossini. As a bonus we are offered Alexander's brilliant performances of Cleopatra's key arias from *Giulio Cesare*. This comes from a CD of highlights where she took to the coloratura with aplomb. Excellent recording, clear and atmospheric.

Athalia (oratorio; complete).

*** O-L 417 126-2 (2). Sutherland, Kirkby, Bowman, Jones, Rolfe Johnson, Thomas, New College, Oxford, Ch., AAM, Hogwood.

(BB) *** Naxos 8.554364/5. Scholl, Schlick, Holzhausen,

Reinhold, Brutscher, MacLeod, Junge Kantorei, Frankfurt
Bar. O, Martini.

As Queen Athalia, Dame Joan Sutherland sings boldly with
a richness and vibrancy to contrast superbly with the pure
silver of Emma Kirkby, not to mention the celestial treble
of Aled Jones, in the role of the boy-king, Joas. That The
casting is perfectly designed to set the Queen aptly apart
from the good Israelite characters led by the Priest, Joad
(James Bowman in a castrato role), and Josabeth (Kirkby).
Christopher Hogwood with the Academy brings out the
speed and variety of the score that has been described as
Handel's first great English oratorio. The recording is bright
and clean, giving sharp focus to voices and instruments
alike.

Very well cast and stylishly performed, using period instruments, the Naxos set makes an excellent bargain. Even
if the playing is not quite so crisp or purposeful as on the rival
(full-priced) set from Hogwood, the result is compellingly
dramatic. Outstanding among the singers is Barbara Schlick
as Josabeth, pure, sweet and expressive, and though Elisabeth
Scholl in the title role provides rather too little contrast
with her rather boyish tone not really apt for this'Jewish
Clytemnestra', her attack is clean and fresh. The castrato
role of Joad is taken by Annette Reinhold, who sounds
uncannily like a low counter-tenor, firm and secure, with
little vibrato. Good, undistracting recording.

Belshazzar (complete).

(M) **(*) Teldec 0630 10275-2 (3). Palmer, Lehane, Tear,
Esswood, Van der Bilt, Stockholm Chamber Ch., VCM,
Harnoncourt.

With authentic style and instruments set against a relatively
intimate acoustic, Harnoncourt's opening of the fine overture to Belshazzar on this Teldec recording may initially
seem gruff. The drama is the more pointed when the soloists,
led by Felicity Palmer and Robert Tear, keep the story-line
clearly in mind with their expressive enunciation of the
words. The other soloists, too, are excellent, notably Paul
Esswood with his fresh counter-tenor tone, and the bass,
Peter van der Bilt. Most enjoyable of all is the singing of the
fine Stockholm Chamber Choir, delectably light and pointed
in some of the end-of-scene choruses. Nikolaus Harnoncourt is at his best when given the chance to point a brisk
number with lifted rhythms, but he is less effective in warmer
music.

Carco sempre di gloria; La Lucrezia; Mi palpita il cor; Splenda l'alba in oriente (Italian cantatas). Trio sonata in G, Op. 5/4.

(N) (b **(*) Virgin x 2 VBD5 61803 (2). Gérard Lesne, Il
Seminario Musicale – SCARLATTI: Cantatas. **(*)

Gérard Lesne's collection of Handel cantatas makes an admirable coupling for those of Scarlatti, even if the finest, La
Lucrezia (a masterpiece), was intended for soprano voice.
Mi palpita il cor is also very theatrical and operatic in feeling,
while Caro sempre and Splenda l'alba pay homage to
St Cecilia. All these works combine bravura florid passages
(which bring no problems for this fine artist) with expressive
passages, which Lesne sings with much feeling. Il Seminario

Musicale provides admirable backing and offers a Trio sonata
as a central interlude. The only considerable snag about
this inexpensive reissue is the absence of vital texts and
translations.

Carco sempre di gloria; Splenda l'alba in oriente; Tu fedel? Tu constante? (Italian cantatas).

(N) **(*) Australian Decca Eloquence [ADD] 461 596-2. Watts,
ECO, Leppard – SCARLATTI: Cantatas. **(*)

These are sympathetic performances dating from the early
1960s. Helen Watts is direct in manner, rather than being
especially subtle in her use of vocal colouring, but the results
are free from indulgence. Leppard's direction stylish and
alive, and the recording is warm and vivid.

Carmelite Vespers.

(BB) *** Virgin 2 x 1 VBD5 61579-2 (2). Feldman, Kirkby, Van
Evera, Cable, Nichols, Cornwell, Thomas, Taverner Ch. &
Players, Parrott.

What Andrew Parrott has recorded here is a reconstruction
by Graham Dixon of what might have been heard in July
1707 at the church of the Carmelite Order in Rome for the
Festival of Our Lady of Mount Carmel. Dixon has put the
motets and Psalm settings in an order appropriate for the
service of Second Vespers, noting that it is not the only
possible reconstruction. So Dixit Dominus is introduced by
plainchant and a chanted antiphon, with similar liturgical
links between the other Handel settings – in turn Laudete
pueri, Te decus Virgineum, Nisi Dominus, Haec est Regina
Virginum, Saeviat Tellus and Salve Regina. Of these, the only
unfamiliar Handel piece is Te decus Virgineum – which
makes this not quite the new experience promised but a
nevertheless enjoyable way of hearing a magnificent collection of Handel's choral music. In a liturgical setting in 1707,
women's voices would not have been used, but the sopranos
and altos of the Taverner Choir produce an aptly fresh
sound, as does the fine group of soloists, headed by an
outstanding trio of sopranos: Emma Kirkby, Jill Feldman
and Emily Van Evera. The recording, made in St Augustine's,
Kilburn, London, has a pleasant and apt ambience, which
however does not obscure detail. At its modest price this
reissue is well worth having.

Chandos Anthems Nos. 1–11 (complete).

*** Chan. 0554/7. Dawson, Kwella, Partridge, Bowman,
George, Sixteen Ch. & O, Christophers.

Chandos Anthems Nos. 1: O be joyful in the Lord; 2: In the Lord put I my trust; 3: Have mercy on me, HWV 246/8.

*** Chan. 0503. Soloists, Sixteen Ch. & O, Christophers.

Chandos Anthems Nos. 4: O sing unto the Lord a new song; 5: I will magnify thee; 6: As pants the hart for cooling streams.

*** Chan. 0504. Soloists, Sixteen Ch. & O, Christophers.

Chandos Anthems Nos. 7: My song shall be alway; 8: O come let us sing unto the Lord; 9: O praise the Lord.

*** Chan. 0505. Soloists, Sixteeen Ch. & O, Christophers.

Chandos Anthems Nos. 10: The Lord is my light; 11: Let God arise.

*** Chan. 0509. Soloists, Sixteen Ch. & O, Christophers.

It is appropriate that a record label named Chandos should record a complete set of Handel's *Chandos Anthems*. This is now available on four CDs in a box (still at full price) and marks one of the most successful and worthwhile achievements of The Sixteen on CD. From the first of these fine works, which Handel based on his *Utrecht Te Deum*, to the last with its exuberant closing *Alleluja* the music is consistently inspired; it has great variety of invention and resourceful vocal scoring. The recordings are well up to the house standard.

Chandos Anthems: (i) As pants the hart; (ii; iii) I will magnify thee, O God; (iii) In the Lord put I my trust; (iv) Let God arise; (i) The Lord is my light; (iv, v) O praise the Lord with one consent.

(B) *** Decca (ADD) 458 389-2 (2). King's College, Cambridge, Ch., ASMF, Willcocks; with (i) Cantelo, Partridge; (ii) Friend; (iii) Langridge; (iv) Vaughan, Young; (v) Robinson.

Dating from 1965–73, this (originally Argo) series was never completed. Yet it has stood the test of time and only extreme authenticists will fail to respond to the warmth and beauty of the playing and singing, as well as its robust vigour. The recordings are bright and full, and if the CD transfer sometimes gives the sound a bit of an edge, many will find that appropriate in our 'authentic' age. A bargain, especially as texts are included.

(i) Coronation Anthems (complete); (ii) Concerti a due cori Nos. 2–3, HWV 333/4.

(M) *** DG 447 280-2. (i) Westminster Abbey Ch., Preston; (i–ii) E. Concert; (ii) Pinnock.

Coronation Anthems (complete); Judas Maccabaeus; See the conqu'ring hero comes; March; Sing unto God.

*** Ph. 412 733-2. ASMF Ch., ASMF, Marriner.

(i) 4 Coronation Anthems (complete); (ii) Ode for the Birthday of Queen Anne.

*** Australian Decca Eloquence (ADD) 466 676-2. (i) King's College Ch., ECO, Willcocks; (ii) Kirkby, Nelson, Minty, Bowman, Hill, Thomas, Christ Church Cathedral Ch., Oxford, AAM, Preston.

The extra weight of the Academy of St Martin-in-the-Fields Chorus compared with the Pinnock version seems appropriate for the splendour of music intended for the pomp of royal ceremonial occasions, and the commanding choral entry in *Zadok the Priest* is gloriously rich in amplitude, without in any way lacking incisiveness. The excerpts from *Solomon* are delightful.

Those who like sparer, period textures will favour Preston in the *Coronation Anthems* where, although the result is less grand, the element of contrast is even more telling. To have the choir enter with such bite and impact underlines the freshness and immediacy, with characterful period playing. An exhilarating version. The new coupling of the two *Con-*

certi a due cori is welcome, with the performances full of rhythmic vitality.

Willcocks's famous 1961 recording of these four anthems sound much better on CD than they ever did on LP, and are greatly enjoyable. They are coupled with a fine performance of the *Ode for the Birthday of Queen Anne*, recorded in the late 1970s, and sound very good indeed. An excellent bargain CD.

Coronation Anthem: Zadok the Priest.

(M) *** Decca (ADD) 458 623-2. King's College, Cambridge, Ch., ASMF, Marriner – HAYDN: *Nelson Mass;* VIVALDI: *Gloria, RV 589.* ***

Many collectors will be glad to have a separate recording of this fine King's performance of *Zadok the Priest* coupled with Vivaldi's most famous *Gloria* to say nothing of the favourite among Haydn's late masses. Moreover the current transfer has added to the impact of the choir, so that it soars out well over the orchestra.

Dettingen Te Deum; Dettingen Anthem.

*** DG 410 647-2. Westminster Abbey Ch., E. Concert, Preston.

The *Dettingen Te Deum* is a splendid work, continually reminding one of *Messiah*, written the previous year. Preston's Archiv performance with the English Concert makes an ideal recommendation, with its splendid singing, crisp but strong, excellent recording and a generous, apt coupling. This setting of *The King shall rejoice* should not be confused with the *Coronation Anthem* of that name. It is less inspired, but has a magnificent double fugue for finale. The recording is first class.

Dixit Dominus; Coronation Anthem: Zadok the Priest.

(M) *** Erato (ADD) 2292 45136-2. Palmer, Marshall, Brett, Messana, Morton, Thomson, Wilson-Johnson, Monteverdi Ch. & O, Gardiner.

Dixit Dominus; Nisi Dominus; Salve Regina.

*** DG 423 594-2. Augér, Dawson, Montague, Nixon, Birchall, Westminster Abbey Ch. & O, Preston.

Dixit dominus; Nisi dominus; Silete venti.

*** Chan. 0517. Dawson, Russell, Brett, Partridge, George, Sixteen Choir & O, Christophers.

Handel's *Dixit Dominus* divides into eight sections, and the setting, while showing signs of Handel's mature style in embryo, reflects also the Baroque tradition of contrasts between small and large groups. The writing is extremely florid and requires bravura from soloists and chorus alike. John Eliot Gardiner catches all its brilliance and directs an exhilarating performance, marked by strongly accented, sharply incisive singing from the choir and outstanding solo contributions. In high contrast with the dramatic choruses, the duet for two sopranos, *De torrente*, here beautifully sung by Felicity Palmer and Margaret Marshall, is languorously expressive, but stylishly so. Other soloists match that, and the analogue recording is first rate, proving ideal for CD remastering.

On DG Archiv *Dixit Dominus* is very aptly coupled with

fine performances of another – less ambitious – Psalm setting, *Nisi Dominus*, and a votive antiphon, *Salve Regina*, which Handel composed between the two. Preston here draws ideally luminous and resilient singing from the Westminster Abbey Choir, with a fine team of soloists in which Arleen Augér and Diana Montague are outstanding. The playing of the period orchestra, led by Roy Goodman, in every way matches the fine qualities of the singing.

Christophers' speeds tend to be more extreme, slow as well as fast, and the recorded sound, though full and well detailed, is less immediate. On balance Gardiner with his rather more bouncy rhythms remains the first choice, but the Chandos issue gains significantly from a much more generous third item. *Silete venti* allows the silver-toned Lynne Dawson to shine even more than in the other items, ending with a brilliant *Alleluia* in galloping compound time.

Esther (1718 version).

*** Regis 2025 (2). Russell, Randle, Padmore, Argenta, Chance, George, Sixteen Ch. & O, Christophers.

**(*) O-L 414 423-2 (2). Kwella, Rolfe Johnson, Partridge, Thomas, Kirkby, Elliott, Westminster Cathedral Boys' Ch., Ch. and AAM, Hogwood.

Esther was the first of Handel's oratorios with a substantial role for the chorus, and this period performance opts for the 1718 version of the oratorio. It may be odd structurally compared with later revisions – with Esther appearing only after the halfway point – but the six compact scenes in a single Act are crisper, so suiting modern taste. Christophers with a small choir of 18 singers offers an aptly intimate view, light and fresh, helped by bright, immediate recording. Lynda Russell and Nancy Argenta exceptionally sweet and pure in the soprano roles, with the two tenors sharply contrasted – Thomas Randle more heroic, Mark Padmore purer and more refined. Michael George gives fine Handelian thrust to the bass solos.

Like Christophers, Hogwood has opted for the original, 1718 score, and his rather abrasive brand of authenticity goes well with the bright, full recorded sound which unfortunately exaggerates the choir's sibilants. The elaborate passage-work is far too heavily aspirated, at times almost as though the singers are laughing. The vigour of the performance is unaffected and the team of soloists is strong and consistent, with the sweet-toned Patrizia Kwella sounding purposeful in the name-part, and Anthony Rolfe Johnson and Ian Partridge both outstanding in the tenor roles.

Funeral Anthem for Queen Caroline: The Ways of Zion do Mourn.

(M) **(*) Erato (ADD) 4509 96954-2. Burrowes, Brett, Hill, Varcoe, Monteverdi Ch. & O, Gardiner.

Queen Caroline was the most cultivated of the royal family of the Georges, and when she died in 1737 Handel was inspired to write a superb cantata in an overture and eleven numbers, including the splendid chorus, *How are the mighty fall'n*. He later used the material for the first Act of *Israel in Egypt*. Gardiner directs a stirring performance which brings out the high contrasts implicit in the music, making the piece energetic rather than elegiac. Excellent work from soloists, chorus and orchestra alike, all very well recorded. The only snag is the playing time of 44 minutes.

(i) Gloria; (ii) Dixit Dominus.

(N) *** BIS CD 1235. (i) Kirkby, R. Ac. of Music Bar. O, Cummings; (ii) Martinpelto, Von Otter, Stockholm Bach Ch., Drottingholm Bar. Ens., Ohrwall.

The existence of the *Gloria* has been known for some time, and there is a full score plus two sets of parts in London's Royal Academy of Music library. But only in September 2000 was it positively identified as a work by Handel, and an inspired one too. It was appropriate that Emma Kirkby, the reigning queen of baroque, was given the privilege of making the first recording, accompanied by an excellent modern instrument chamber group. She sings the florid opening exultantly and is even more impressive in the heady bravura of the closing *Cum sancto spirito*. Yet it is the beauty of her lyrical singing which stands out even more, and indeed her stylish control of ornamentation. The recording is vividly forward.

The performance of *Dixit Dominus* also has very fine soloists, although none quite to match Kirkby in easy flowing lines. But the chorus is equally important here and the singing of the Stockholm Choir has splendid vigour and bite. The recording is set further back here than in the *Gloria*, and effectively so, for the period-instrumental accompaniment is without edginess.

Israel in Egypt (oratorio).

(M) **(*) (IMS) (ADD) DG 429 530-2 (2). Harper, Clark, Esswood, Young, Rippon, Keyte, Leeds Festival Ch., ECO, Mackerras.

Israel in Egypt (oratorio; with The Lamentations of the Israelites for the Death of Joseph).

(M) **(*) Virgin VMD5 61350-2 (2). Argenta, Van Evera, Wilson, Rolfe Johnson, Thomas, White, Taverner Ch. & Players, Parrott.

(i) Israel in Egypt; (ii) Organ Concerto in F (The Cuckoo and the Nightingale), HWV 295.

*(**) Regis 2012 (2). (i) Jenkin, Dunkley, Trevor, MacKenzie, Evans, Birchall, The Sixteen; (ii) Nicholson; O of The Sixteen; Christophers.

(i) Israel in Egypt; (ii) Chandos Anthem No. 10: The Lord is my Light. Organ Concerto in F (The Cuckoo and the Nightingale).

(B) *** Double Decca (ADD) 443 470-2 (2). (i) Gale, Watson, Bowman, Partridge, McDonnell, Watts, Christ Church Cathedral, Oxford, Ch., ECO, Preston; (ii) Cantelo, Partridge, King's College, Cambridge, Ch., ASMF, Willcocks.

(i) Israel in Egypt. Coronation Anthems: Zadok the Priest; The King shall Rejoice.

(M) *** Ph. 432 110-2 (2). (i) Holton, Priday, Deam, Stafford, Chance, Collin, Kenny, Robertson, Salmon, Tindall, Tusa, Clarkson, Purves; Monteverdi Ch., E. Bar. Sol., Gardiner.

(i) Israel in Egypt: Lamentations of the Israelites for the Death of Joseph; (ii) The Ways of Zion do Mourn (funeral anthem).

(M) *** Erato (ADD) 2292 45399-2 (2). (i) Knibbs, Troth, Greene, Priday, Royall, Stafford, Gordon, Clarkson, Elliott, Kendall, Varcoe, Stewart; (ii) Burrowes, Brett, Hill, Varcoe; Monteverdi Ch. & O, Gardiner.

Israel in Egypt (complete 1739 version 1, including the original Part I: *The Ways of Zion do mourn*).

(N) **(*) Decca 452 295-2 (2). Gritton, Crabtree, Chance, Ogden, Bostridge, Varcoe, Herford, King's College Cambridge Ch., Brandenburg Consort, Cleobury.

In his Philips digital version of *Israel in Egypt* Gardiner secures subtler playing from his period instruments, not just more stylish and generally more lightly sprung than in the earlier, Erato version, but conveying more clearly the emotional and dramatic thrust. So the start is more mysterious, and such illustrative numbers as the hopping of the frogs during the plague choruses is even more delightfully pointed than before. As before, first-rate soloists have been chosen from the chorus, and the digital recording is full and well balanced. The *Coronation Anthems* are also winningly performed.

Using modern instruments, Gardiner made his Erato recording in 1978. His style here, crisply rhythmic, superbly sprung, with dozens of detailed insights in bringing out word-meaning, is very much what has since become his forte in period performances of Handel and others. The singing both of the chorus and of the twelve soloists chosen from its members is excellent, though, like all other modern recordings, this one slightly falls down in resonance on the most famous number, the duet for basses, *The Lord is a Man of War*. In almost every way Gardiner gains by presenting the *Lamentations* not as an introduction to the main oratorio, but as a supplement, with the same music given in its original form, with text unamended: the funeral cantata for Queen Caroline. Excellent, full-bodied, analogue sound.

Simon Preston, using a small choir with boy trebles and an authentically sized orchestra, directs a performance that is beautifully in scale. He starts with *The Cuckoo and the Nightingale Organ Concerto* – a procedure sanctioned by Handel himself at the first performance. Though Elizabeth Gale is not as firm a soprano as Heather Harper on Mackerras's alternative mid-priced Archiv set, the band of soloists is an impressive one and the ECO is in splendid form. The 1975 recording (originally Argo), vividly transferred, is warmly atmospheric. This Double Decca set generously includes the tenth Chandos anthem, *The Lord is my light*, remarkable for magnificent fugal writing, freshly performed by King's Choir under Sir David Willcocks.

It is the great merit of Stephen Cleobury's version of *Israel in Egypt*, with his King's College Choir that, on scholarly authority, he has reconstructed the first version of this ever-popular oratorio. What Handel originally did was to adapt the fine cantata he wrote on the death of Queen Anne as *The Lamentations of the Israelites for the death of Joseph*, and use that as the first part of what became *Israel in Egypt*. Unfortunately, after various permutations of the score, the version published after Handel's death was limited to the two later parts only, but this tripartite version solves the regular problem of finding an introduction, when usually an organ concerto is borrowed as an overture.

Recorded in 1995, but not issued for five years, the set is not as brilliant as one would expect from this source, with the King's Choir set back, not as bright-toned as usual. The earlier analogue Decca version under Simon Preston has a far sharper focus, and the performance too has more bite. With the period instruments of the Brandenburg Consort speeds are fast and textures light, but even in a period performance it would help to have more weight, with the Plague choruses evocative but rather lacking in impact. The soloists are first rate, notably the tenor, Ian Bostridge, characterful in linking recitative, with Susan Gritton the sweet-toned soprano. But all would benefit from a sharper projection from the recording.

Parrott directs a clean-cut, well-paced reading which wears its period manners easily. This may lack the distinctive insights of Gardiner's more sharply rhythmic versions, but with excellent choral and solo singing the performance is unlikely to offend anyone. Good, warm sound. Parrott follows the precedent of Handel's very first performance in using as the first part of the oratorio the cantata written on the death of Queen Caroline, *The Lamentations of the Israelites for the Death of Joseph*, with text duly adapted.

Mackerras's performance represents a dichotomy of styles, using the English Chamber Orchestra sounding crisp, stylish and lightweight and a fairly large amateur choir, impressively weighty rather than incisive. Thus the work makes its effect by breadth and grandiloquence rather than athletic vigour. The solo singing is distinguished, but its style is refined rather than earthy.

Christophers uses the *Lamentations* as a first part to the oratorio, and also – another nod towards Handelian performance-practice – adds the best-known of Handel's organ concertos, the *Cuckoo and the Nightingale*, between Parts One and Two. The playing and singing are bright, but sadly the Collins recording is so reverberant that there is a serious loss of inner detail.

Jephtha.

*** Ph. 422 351-2 (3). Robson, Dawson, Von Otter, Chance, Varcoe, Holton, Monteverdi Ch., E. Bar. Sol., Gardiner.

(M) *** Van. (ADD) 08 5091 73 (3). Young, Forrester, Grist, Watts, Lawrenson, Amor Artis Chorale, ECO, Somary.

John Eliot Gardiner's recording was made live at the Göttingen Festival in 1988 and, though the sound does not have quite the bloom of his finest studio recordings of Handel, the exhilaration and intensity of the performance come over vividly, with superb singing from both chorus and an almost ideal line-up of soloists. Nigel Robson's tenor may be on the light side for the title-role, but the sensitivity of expression is very satisfying. Lynne Dawson, with her bell-like soprano, sings radiantly as Iphis; and the counter-tenor, Michael Chance, as her beloved, Hamor, is also outstanding. Anne Sofie von Otter is powerful as Storge, and Stephen Varcoe with his clear baritone, again on the light side, is a stylish Zebul. As for the Monteverdi Choir, their clarity, incisiveness and beauty are a constant delight.

The Vanguard set was the first ever recording of *Jephtha*, made in 1969. It stands up surprisingly well against period performances so that anyone preferring modern instruments need not hesitate. The analogue sound, full, forward and bright, is well transferred, and the freshness and liveliness of Somary's direction, with brisk speeds lightly sprung, are worlds away from the old oratorio tradition. The singers make a formidably starry team with no weak link. Alexander Young, a superb Handel singer, recorded far too little; here he sings most beautifully as Jephtha, not least in *Waft her, angels*. The Canadian mezzo Maureen Forrester is caught richly and firmly as Hamor, and the others are first rate too. The small professional chorus is equally assured, producing bright, fresh tone, firmly and forwardly focused.

Joshua (complete).

⚫ *** Hyp. CDA 66461/2. Kirkby, Bowman, Ainsley, George, Oliver, New College, Oxford, Ch., King's Consort, King.

Emma Kirkby is here ideally sparkling and light in the role of Achsa, daughter of the patriarchal leader, Caleb (taken here by the bass, Michael George). Her love for Othniel, superbly sung by James Bowman, provides the romantic interest in what is otherwise a grandly military oratorio, based on the Book of Joshua. The brisk sequence of generally brief arias is punctuated by splendid choruses, with solo numbers often inspiring choral comment. The singing is consistently strong and stylish, with the clear, precise tenor John Mark Ainsley in the title-role. Robert King and his Consort crown their achievement in other Hyperion issues, notably their Purcell series, with polished, resilient playing, and the choir of New College, Oxford, sings with ideal freshness. Warm, full sound.

Judas Maccabaeus (complete).

(M) *** DG (ADD) 447 692-2 (3). Palmer, Baker, Esswood, Davies, Shirley-Quirk, Keyte, Wandsworth School Ch., ECO, Mackerras.

**(*) Hyp. CDA 66641/2 (2). Kirkby, Denley, Bowman, MacDougall, George, Birchall, Ch. of New College, Oxford, King's Consort, King.

(M) **(*) Van. (ADD) 08 4072 72 (2). Harper, Watts, Young, Shirley-Quirk, Amor Artis Ch., Wandsworth School Boys' Ch., ECO, Somary.

** HM HMU 907077/8 (with appendix). De Mey, Saffer, Spence, Thomas, UCLA, Berkeley, Chamber Ch., Philh. Bar. O, McGegan.

Judas Maccabaeus may have a lopsided story, with a high proportion of the finest music given to the anonymous soprano and contralto roles, Israelitish Woman and Israelitish Man; but the sequence of Handelian gems is irresistible, the more so in a performance as sparkling as DG's reissued 1976 recording under Sir Charles Mackerras. Though not everyone will approve of the use of boys' voices in the choir (inevitably the tone and intonation are not flawless), it gives an extra bite of character. Hearing even so hackneyed a number as *See, the conqu'ring hero* in its true scale is a delightful surprise. The orchestral group and continuo sound splendidly crisp. Ryland Davies and John Shirley-Quirk are most stylish, while both Felicity Palmer and Dame Janet crown the whole set with glorious singing, not least in a delectable sequence, towards the end of Act I,

on the subject of liberty. The recording quality is outstanding in its CD format, fresh, vivid and clear.

With some superb solo singing and refined instrumental textures, Robert King's performance can be recommended warmly, even though it is not as lively as some of his Purcell recordings. It is partly that the chorus is not as forward or as bright-toned as one wants in Handel; but there is much to enjoy, with Jamie MacDougall clean and bright if not always ideally firm in the title-role, and with the pure-toned Emma Kirkby well contrasted with the much warmer mezzo of Catherine Denley. Michael George gives splendid weight to the bass arias so central to Handel oratorio.

On Vanguard the solo singing is excellent, with Alexander Young a ringing tenor, and Helen Watts singing the opening aria in Act III exquisitely. Very good recording – the choruses could ideally have a crisper focus, but the effect is wholly natural – and a sense of commitment throughout from all departments.

Like Robert King's Hyperion version, McGegan's rival period performance lacks something of the grandeur which, like other late Handel choral works, this oratorio seems to require. This two-disc set generously offers an appendix, including two arias which Handel added after the first performance in 1747. In a first-rate line-up of soloists Lisa Saffer is outstanding in the key role of the Israelite Woman and, though Guy de Mey in the title-role is hardly idiomatic, his singing is clean and stylish. McGegan is rather more dramatic and incisive than King, but that advantage is offset by the dryness of the recording, typical of the venue in Berkeley, California.

Sacred cantatas: *Laudate pueri (Psalm 112); Cœlestis dum spirat aura; O qualis de cœlo sonus; Salve Regina. Trio Sonata in G min., HWV 27.*

⚫ (N) *** BIS CD 1065. Kirkby; L. Baroque, Medlam.

Emma Kirkby is in glorious voice throughout this splendid recital, floating the opening line of *Salve Regina* most beautifully, and then dashing away to a sparkling accompaniment in *Eja ergo*. Her closing *Alleluja!* in *O qualis de cœlo sonus* is wonderfully nimble, as is the flowing *Felix dies* ('Happy day') of *Cœlestis dum spirat aura*. Finest of all is the setting of *Psalm 112*, where she soars up to the heavens on a characteristic repeated phrase and sings flowingly and ravishingly against a particularly attractive accompaniment – in which the continuo with organ is delightfully conceived – capped by the spirited runs of the *Gloria Patri*. This is one of Kirkby's very finest Handel records. Her voice is caught with a lovely bloom, and the balance with the accompaniment is just about perfect. Not to be missed.

Lucrezia (cantata). Arias: *Ariodante: Oh, felice mio core . . . Con l'ali do constanza; E vivo ancore? . . . Scherza infida in grembo al drudo; Dopo notte. Atalanta: Care selve. Hercules: Where shall I fly? Joshua: O had I Jubal's lyre. Rodelinda: Pompe vane di morte! . . . Dove sei, amato bene? Serse: Frondi tenere e belle . . . Ombra mai fù (Largo).*

(M) *** Ph. (ADD) 426 450-2. Baker, ECO, Leppard.

Even among Dame Janet's most impressive records this

Handel recital stands out, ranging as it does from the pure gravity of *Ombra mai fù* to the passionate virtuosity in *Dopo notte* from *Ariodante*. Leppard gives sparkling support, and the whole is recorded with natural and refined balance. An outstanding disc, with admirable documentation.

Messiah (complete).

*** DG 423 630-2 (2). Augér, Von Otter, Chance, Crook, Tomlinson, E. Concert Ch., E. Concert, Pinnock.

⚙ *** BIS CD 891/892 (2). Midori Suzuki, Mera, Elwes, Thomas, Bach Collegium Japan, Masaaki Suzuki.

(M) *** Hyp. Dyad CDD 22019 (2). Dawson, Denley, Davies, George, Sixteen Ch. & O, Christophers.

*** HM HMC 901498.99-2 (2). Schlick, Piau, Scholl, Padmore, Berg, Les Arts Florissants, Christie.

*** DG 453 464-2 (2). Röschmann, Gritton, Fink, Daniels, Davies, Gabrieli Consort & Players, McCreesh.

*** Ph. 434 297-2 (2). Marshall, Robbin, Rolfe Johnson, Brett, Hale, Shirley-Quirk, Monteverdi Ch., E. Bar. Sol., Gardiner.

*** Decca 414 396-2 (2). Te Kanawa, Gjevang, Lewis, Howell, Chicago Ch. & SO, Solti.

(M) *** Ph. Duo (ADD) 464 703-2 (2). Harper, Watts, Wakefield, Shirley-Quirk, L. Symphony Ch., LSO, Davis.

(B) *** EMI (ADD) CZS7 62748-2 (2) [Ang. CDMB 62748]. Harwood, Baker, Esswood, Tear, Herincx, Amb. S., ECO, Mackerras.

(B) **(*) CfP (ADD) CD-CFPD 4718 (2). Morison, Thomas, Lewis, Milligan, Huddersfield Ch. Soc., RLPO, Sargent.

(M) **(*) EMI (ADD) CMS7 63784-2 (2) Trebles from King's, Bowman, Tear, Luxon, King's College, Cambridge, Ch., ASMF, Willcocks.

(BB) **(*) Naxos 8.550667/8. Amps, Davidson, Doveton, Van Asch, Scholars Bar. Ens.

(M) **(*) Van. (ADD) 08.4019 72 (2). Price, Minton, Young, Diaz, Amor Artis Chorale, ECO, Somary.

(M) *(*) Sony (ADD) SM2K 60205 (2). Addison, Oberlin, Lloyd, Warfield, Westminster Ch., NYPO, Bernstein.

Pinnock presents a performance using authentically scaled forces which, without inflation, rise to grandeur and magnificence, qualities Handel himself would have relished. The fast contrapuntal choruses, such as *For unto us a Child is born*, are done lightly and resiliently in the modern manner, but there is no hint of breathlessness, and Pinnock (more than his main rivals) balances his period instruments too to give a satisfying body to the sound. There is weight too in the singing of the bass soloist, John Tomlinson, firm, dark and powerful, yet marvellously agile in divisions. Arleen Augér's range of tone and dynamic is daringly wide, with radiant purity in *I know that my Redeemer liveth*. Anne Sofie von Otter sustains *He was despised* superbly with her firm, steady voice. Some alto arias are taken just as beautifully by the outstanding counter-tenor, Michael Chance. The tenor, Howard Crook, is less distinctive but still sings freshly and attractively.

With his excellent Japanese singers and players, Masaaki Suzuki has produced a series of intensely refreshing readings of baroque choral works, and here he excels himself. His crisp, sharp manner goes with transparent textures and sprung rhythms, and though modest forces are used the result has natural dramatic weight. The consistent alertness of the chorus is a delight but the fast speeds he tends to prefer never sound breathless, and he is never afraid to choose a spacious tempo, if the mood of the music demands it – as in the aria, *He was despised*, sung with seamless beauty by the male alto, Yoshikazu Mera. The soprano Midori Suzuki sings with radiant purity, notably in *I know that my Redeemer liveth*, and the two British soloists are excellent too, with John Elwes bright and eager and David Thomas caught at his warmest. This can readily be recommended alongside Pinnock, Christophers and Christie, and is a special favourite of I. M.'s

Christophers consistently adopts speeds more relaxed than those we have grown used to in modern performances, and the effect is fresh, clear and resilient. Alto lines in the chorus are taken by male singers; a counter-tenor, David James, is also used for the *Refiner's fire*, but *He was despised* is rightly given to the contralto, Catherine Denley, warm and grave at a very measured tempo. The team of five soloists is as fine as that on any rival set, with the soprano, Lynne Dawson, singing with silvery purity. The band of 13 strings sounds as clean and fresh as the choir. Even the *Hallelujah chorus* – always a big test in a small-scale performance – works well, with Christophers in his chosen scale, through dramatic timpani and trumpets conveying necessary weight. The sound has all the bloom one associates with St John's recordings. Now offered as a two-for-one Dyad, this is a real bargain.

More than most period performances William Christie gives the impression of a live performance caught on the wing, even though it was recorded in the studio. His preference for fast, resilient speeds and light textures, not least in choruses, never prevents him from giving due emotional weight to such key numbers as *He was despised*. That is superbly sung, with touching simplicity, firm tone and flawless intonation, by the counter-tenor, Andreas Scholl. The other singers too sound fresh and young, with the two sopranos, Barbara Schlick and Sandrine Piau, delectably counterpointed, both pure and true, making light of the elaborate divisions in such a number as *Rejoice greatly*. The treble, Tommy Williams, also sings with beautiful, firm clarity in the Angel's narration, *There were shepherds abiding in the fields*. The tenor, Mark Padmore, and the bass, Nathan Berg, complete the pattern, light by old-fashioned standards but fresh and cleanly focused. Christie in his text opts for Handel's later versions of numbers. Excellent sound, though the chorus is placed a little backwardly.

Using the Foundling Hospital version of the score, Paul McCreesh, in recreating the sort of performance Handel supervised there in 1754, seeks to present a 'thoroughly modern performance – A Messiah for the Millennium' as he puts it. If he has not quite achieved that, this is still a bright and individual reading, bringing out the drama of the music, with extreme speeds in both directions. The chorus copes well with some tempi that run the risk of breathlessness, and the soloists make an excellent team with their fresh, young voices. Good, warm sound.

Gardiner chooses bright-toned sopranos instead of boys for the chorus and he uses, very affectingly, a solo treble to sing *There were shepherds abiding*. Speeds are fast and light, and the rhythmic buoyancy in the choruses is very striking, though idiosyncratically Gardiner begins *Hallelujah!* on a pianissimo. *Why do the nations* and *The trumpet shall sound* (both sung with great authority) come over dramatically, and the soloists are all first class, with the soprano Margaret Marshall finest of all, especially in *I know that my Redeemer liveth*. Other highlights include Margaret Marshall's angelic version of *Rejoice greatly*, skipping along in compound time.

Sir Georg Solti inspires a vital, exciting reading. The Chicago Symphony Orchestra and Chorus respond to some challengingly fast but never breathless speeds, showing what lessons can be learnt from authentic performance in clarity and crispness. Yet the joyful power of *Hallelujah* and the *Amen chorus* is overwhelming. Dame Kiri Te Kanawa matches anyone on record in beauty of tone and detailed expressiveness, while the other soloists are first rate too, though Anne Gjevang has rather too fruity a timbre. Brilliant, full sound.

The LSO recording conducted by Sir Colin Davis, in the 1960s the first of a new generation of *Messiah* recordings, fresh and urgent, has not lost its impact, remastered in bright sound. Textures are beautifully clear and, thanks to Davis, the rhythmic bounce of such choruses as *For unto us* is really infectious. Even *Hallelujah* loses little and gains much from being performed by a chorus of this size. Excellent singing from all four soloists, particularly Helen Watts who, following early precedent, is given *For He is like a refiner's fire* to sing, instead of the bass, and produces a glorious chest register.

With Mackerras the chorus is not so fresh as Davis's LSO Choir but has a compensating breadth and body. More than Davis, Mackerras adopts Handel's alternative versions, so the soprano aria *Rejoice greatly* is given in its optional 12/8 version. A male alto is also included, Paul Esswood, and he is given some of the bass arias as well as some of the regular alto passages. Among the soloists, Dame Janet Baker is outstanding. Her intense, slow account of *He was despised* – with decorations on the reprise – is sung with profound feeling. The recording is warm and full in ambience and, with the added brightness of CD, sounds extremely vivid.

It is good to have Sir Malcolm Sargent's 1959 recording now restored to the catalogue in full for, apart from the pleasure given by a performance that brings out the breadth of Handel's inspiration, it provides an important corrective to misconceptions about pre-authentic practice. Sargent unashamedly fills out the orchestration, and though by the side of Davis, his tempi are very measured, but his pacing is natural, and, with a hundred-strong Huddersfield group, he gives weight and vigour to the choruses. There is some splendid singing from all four soloists, and Marjorie Thomas's *He was despised* is memorable in its moving simplicity. Remarkably clear CD transfer.

Often though *Messiah* may have been recorded, there is always room for alternative versions, particularly those which show a new and illuminating view of the work. Willcocks's recording, made in the Chapel at King's in 1971/ 2, has been described as the 'all-male *Messiah*', since a counter-tenor takes over the contralto solos, and the full complement of the trebles of King's College Choir sings the soprano solos, even the florid ones like *Rejoice greatly*; the

result is enchanting, often light and airy. The bigger choruses do not lack robust qualities. The sound is vivid and atmospheric. A gimmicky version, perhaps, but one that many will find refreshing and involving.

On the bargain Naxos label the Scholars Baroque Ensemble presents the oratorio on the smallest possible scale, with individual singers from the small chorus coming forward to sing the arias. In keeping with this approach, the performance is directed by one of the basses, David van Asch, and characteristically the booklet seeks as far as possible not to highlight individual contributions but to emphasize teamwork. At brisk speeds, with rhythms well sprung, this will please those who fancy such an approach, though the period instrumental sound is abrasive, and none of the singers has a voice of star quality. By their own definition, these are good choristers rather than great soloists.

Somary directs a crisp, small-scale performance that features sparkling orchestral playing (on modern instruments) and first-rate singing from soloists and chorus alike. His direction is not always consistent but it is never dull, and the recording is first class, warm yet bright and natural. This is an excellent choice for those wanting a relatively traditional approach and who have a special fondness for all or any of the soloists. The chorus is excellent, its size nicely judged.

Handel's masterpiece cannot fail to make an impact when conducted with such conviction and vigour (even if Bernstein indulges himself expressively in the *Pastoral Symphony*, and the *Hallelujah chorus* now sounds too slow and solid). He has the advantage of two outstanding soloists: Adele Addison's soprano arias, especially *I know that my Redeemer liveth*, are sung with ravishing purity of line, and Russell Oberlin's contribution is very distinguished indeed. His is a unique voice, and the plangent bite of the middle section of *He was despised* is unforgettable. The tenor and baritone have strong voices but are more conventional; the real snag is the chorus. They sing with conviction (especially in the lively *For unto us a child is born*) but the quavery soprano line is uningratiating and today we are used to crisper accuracy in the running passages.

Messiah (reorchestrated Sir Eugene Goossens).

⊛ (M) *** RCA (ADD) 09026 61266-2 (3). Vyvyan, Sinclair, Vickers, Tozzi, RPO Ch. & O, Beecham.

This is a performance flamboyantly reorchestrated, both dramatic and moving, which at every point radiates the natural flair of the conductor. The use of the cymbals to cap the choruses *For unto us a child is born* and *Glory to God* is unforgettable. Many of Beecham's tempi are slower than we expect today, but not the *Hallelujah chorus*, which is fast and resilient. Jennifer Vyvyan and Monica Sinclair both sing freshly. Jon Vickers brings to his tenor arias a heroic quality that is often welcome and effective. Giorgio Tozzi's English is sound and his management of the tricky bass arias (especially *Why do the nations*) compels admiration. The 1959 recording of the chorus and orchestra is full and expansive in its CD transfer and the soloists have remarkable presence and immediacy. The third disc with its 17-minute appendix of eight items – normally cut at the time this recording was made – comes as a bonus, as the set is priced as for two mid-range CDs.

(i) *Messiah* (complete).(ii) *Israel in Egypt* 3 Choruses: *But for His people; Moses and the children of Israel; The Lord is a man of war. Amaryllis Suite* (arr. Beecham): *Gavotte; Scherzo.*

(***) Biddulph mono WHL 059/61(3). (i) Suddaby, Thomas, Nash, Antony, Luton Choral Society; (ii) Leeds Festival Ch.; RPO, Beecham – BACH: *Christmas Oratorio: Sinfonia.* (***)

Issued only in the United States, never in Britain, this recording of 1947 is one of Beecham's rarest, an oddity but a fascinating one. Unlike his later RCA version of *Messiah* this one has no percussion trimmings in the orchestra, but as he explains in a spoken introduction, he uses choirs of different sizes for different numbers. Speeds are often extreme, commendably so in brisk numbers, while his expansive slow speeds bring persuasive Beechamesque moulding. A fine quartet of soloists includes the great tenor Heddle Nash. The *Israel in Egypt* excerpts date from 1934, celebrating Beecham's work at the Leeds Festival, the instrumental pieces from 1947.

Beecham rarely conducted Bach, and in this brief bonus he makes the *Sinfonia* sound like one of his arrangements of Handel.

Messiah (slightly abridged).

⚙ (B) (***) Dutton Lab. mono 2CDEA 5010 (2). Baillie, Ripley, Johnson, Walker, Huddersfield Ch. Soc., Liverpool PO, Sargent.

Sargent's first recording of Handel's *Messiah* is not complete. Following his usual performance practice, three numbers are cut from Part II and four from Part III. The recording venue was Huddersfield Town Hall in 1946, when that great Choral Society was still at its peak, and Handel's masterpiece is here brought vividly to life in a brilliant Dutton transfer from the 78s. What is so involving is the way this remarkably realistic and present recording (in many ways more vivid than the later stereo set), made in a series of four-minute takes, comes over with the tension of a live performance. There may be strictures about the style, not least the slow tempi (especially in Part II) and the orchestration (Prout's edition, plus additions from Mozart's version) and of course its weight and scale. But the chorus sings throughout with enormous conviction and the four fine soloists obviously live their parts, with their enunciation making every word clear. The star of the performance is Isobel Baillie. Her first entry in *There were shepherds* is a moment of the utmost magic, and what follows is utterly ravishing, while her gloriously beautiful *I know that my Redeemer liveth* has never been surpassed on record. Gladys Ripley sings *He was despised* with moving simplicity and restraint, and she warmly introduces *He shall feed his flock*, sharing it with Baillie, who re-enters exquisitely. At bargain price this is an essential investment for anyone who loves the English amateur choral tradition.

Der Messias (sung in German, arr. Mozart): complete.

(M) **(*) DG (ADD) (IMS) 427 173-2 (2). Mathis, Finnilä, Schreier, Adam, Austrian R. Ch. & O, Vienna, Mackerras.

Mozart's arrangement of *Messiah* is fascinating. It is not simply a question of trombones being added but of elaborate woodwind parts too – most engaging in a number such as *All we like sheep*, which even has a touch of humour. *The trumpet shall sound* is considerably modified and shortened. To avoid the use of a baroque instrument, Mozart shares the obbligato between trumpet and horn. Mackerras leads his fine team through a performance that is vital, not academic in the heavy sense. The remastered recording is excellent and a translation is provided.

Messiah (sung in English): highlights.

(N) (M) *** Ph. (IMS) 462 055-2 (from above set, cond. Gardiner).
(M) *** Penguin Decca 466 215-2 (from above set, cond. Solti).
(M) **(*) Classic FM 75605 57057-2. Kwella, Denley, Ainsley, Terfel, London Musici & Chamber Ch., Stephenson.
(M) *** [EMI Red Line (ADD) CDR5 72431] (from above set, cond. Mackerras).
(B) **(*) CfP (ADD) CD-CFP 9007 (from above stereo set, cond. Sargent).
(BB) **(*) ASV CDQS 6001. Kwella, Cable, Kendal, Drew, Jackson, Winchester Cathedral Ch., L. Handel O, Neary.
(BB) **(*) Belart (ADD) 450 045-2 (from above Philips Duo set, cond. Davis).
(M) **(*) Ph. 462 055-2. Marshall, Robbins, Brett, Hale, Monteverdi Ch., E. Bar. Sol., Gardiner.

Here Gardiner's collection reigns supreme, with the single caveat that *The trumpet shall sound* is missing.

Solti's selection on Penguin Classics is undoubtedly generous, including all the key numbers and much else besides. The sound is thrillingly vivid and full. The note is provided by Garrison Keillor.

Recorded for Conifer in 1989, Mark Stephenson's disc of favourite numbers offers fresh, bright performances vividly recorded in full, atmospheric sound. In style this follows the example of Colin Davis's vintage recording, using modern instruments but with choruses challengingly fast and with bright, crisp choral singing. It was recorded before Bryn Terfel became an international star, and his voice is gloriously dark and firm in his two solo passages. Sadly, *The trumpet shall sound* is not included. The others are impressive too, notably Patricia Kwella at her most golden. A pity this is not the complete oratorio.

Otherwise Mackerras is first choice (although available in the USA only), while the great and pleasant surprise among the bargain selections is the Classics for Pleasure CD of highlights from Sir Malcolm Sargent's 1959 recording; no one will be disappointed with *Hallelujah*, while the closing *Amen* brings a powerful apotheosis.

Brightly if reverberantly recorded in Winchester Cathedral, Martin Neary's collection of excerpts gives a pleasant reminder of the work of one of our finest cathedral choirs. In its authentic manner Neary's style is rather too clipped to convey deep involvement, but the freshness is attractive, with some very good solo singing.

Although it is not generous, the Belart set of highlights from Sir Colin Davis's mid-1960s recording is the least expensive high-quality selection currently available. It offers a dozen key items, including most of the favourites, but not *He was despised*.

The second mid-priced selection from Gardiner's set centres on the choruses (which feature bright-toned sopranos). Some arias are included, notably *The trumpet shall sound*, sung with great authority by Robin Hale; but too much is missing here: any selection from *Messiah* that omits *I know that my Redeemer liveth* can receive only a limited recommendation, even though the selection runs to 76 minutes. The presentation in Philips's 'Choral Collection' is handsome, but the notes are sparse and no texts are included.

The Occasional Oratorio.

**(*) Hyp. CDA 66961/2. Gritton, Milne, Bowman, Ainsley, George, New College, Oxford, Ch., King's Consort Ch. & Ens., King.

Handel's *Occasional Oratorio* offers a wonderful showcase of Handel at his most inspired and vigorous. The vigorous choruses in particular, some only a few seconds long, regularly punctuate the work to heighten the effect of the arias. The piece culminates in an adaptation of Handel's great coronation anthem, *Zadok the Priest*, with loyal cries of *God save the King* ringing out at the end. The whole performance is fresh and electrifying, with excellent singing from all the soloists. Susan Gritton and Lisa Milne, the clear-toned sopranos, are set against the increasingly dark counter-tenor tones of James Bowman, with John Mark Ainsley and Michael George both clear and fresh Handelian stylists. The chorus fares rather less well in a generally excellent recording for, though the ensemble is first rate, the backward balance takes some of the edge off the more dramatic choruses.

Ode for the Birthday of Queen Anne (Eternal source of light divine); Sing unto God (Wedding Anthem); Te Deum in D (for Queen Caroline).

*** Hyp. CDA 66315. Fisher, Bowman, Ainsley, George, New College, Oxford, Ch., King's Consort, King.

Handel's *Birthday Ode for Queen Anne* combines Purcellian influences with Italianate writing to make a rich mixture. King's performance is richly enjoyable, with warm, well-tuned playing from the King's Consort and with James Bowman in radiant form in the opening movement. The other two items are far rarer. Warmly atmospheric recording, not ideally clear on detail.

Ode for St Cecilia's Day.

*** DG (IMS) 419 220-2. Lott, Rolfe Johnson, Ch. & E. Concert, Pinnock.

*** ASV CDDCA 512. Gomez, Tear, King's College Ch., ECO, Ledger.

(M) *** Teldec (ADD) 0630 12319-2. Palmer, Rolfe Johnson, Stockholm Bach Ch., VCM, Harnoncourt.

Trevor Pinnock's account of Handel's magnificent setting of Dryden's *Ode* comes near the ideal for a performance using period instruments. Not only is it crisp and lively, it has deep tenderness too, as in the lovely soprano aria, *The complaining flute*, with Lisa Beznosiuk playing the flute obbligato most delicately in support of Felicity Lott's clear singing. Anthony Rolfe Johnson gives a robust yet stylish account of *The trumpet's loud clangour*, and the choir is excellent, very crisp of ensemble. Full, clear recording with voices vivid and immediate.

Those seeking a version with modern instruments will find Ledger's ASV version a splendid alternative. With superb soloists – Jill Gomez radiantly beautiful and Robert Tear dramatically riveting in his call to arms – this delightful music emerges with an admirable combination of freshness and weight. Ledger uses an all-male chorus; the style of the performance is totally convincing without being self-consciously authentic. The recording is first rate, rich, vivid and clear.

Harnoncourt's Teldec version of the *Ode*, recorded in 1979, comes up well in its digital transfer to CD. It is only slightly less recommendable than Trevor Pinnock's Archiv version, though the non-British choir, for all its fluency, sounds less comfortable than its rival and sings less crisply. Anthony Rolfe Johnson is excellent on both versions, while Felicity Palmer as soprano sings most characterfully. One special point in favour of Harnoncourt is his own striking cello playing in the beautiful setting of Dryden's second stanza, *What Passion cannot Musick raise and quell!* Now reissued in Teldec's Das Alte Werk mid-priced series.

La Resurrezione.

*** O-L (IMS) 421 132-2 (2). Kirkby, Kwella, Watkinson, Partridge, Thomas, AAM, Hogwood.

(B) *** HM HMA 1907027/8. Saffer, George, Nelson, Spence, Thomas, Phil. Bar. O, McGegan.

*** DG (IMS) 447 767-2 (2). Massis, Smith, Maguire, Ainsley, Naouri, Les Musiciens du Louvre, Minkowski.

In 1708, halfway through his four-year stay in Italy, the young Handel wrote this refreshingly dramatic oratorio. With opera as such prohibited in Rome, it served as a substitute, not solemn at all, but with dramatic and moving exchanges between the central characters. There is no chorus until the close, but Handel makes up for this with a wonderful palette of orchestra colour in his accompaniments, liberally featuring trumpets, recorders and oboes.

Hogwood directs a clean-cut, vigorous performance with an excellent cast. Emma Kirkby is at her most brilliant in the coloratura for the Angel, Patrizia Kwella sings movingly as Mary Magdalene and Carolyn Watkinson as Cleophas adopts an almost counter-tenor-like tone. Ian Partridge's tenor has a heady lightness as St John, and though David Thomas's Lucifer could have more weight he too sings stylishly. Excellent recording.

Nicholas McGegan's performance is as lively as one could wish and is excellently cast. Lisa Saffer is an appealing Angel, nimble (in breathtakingly florid coloratura) and touching, especially good in her dialogues with the boldly resonant Lucifer (Michael George). But Judith Nelson is equally affecting as Mary Magdelene, whereas Patricia Spence's dark contralto (as Cleophas) and Jeffrey Thomas's fresh tenor

St John bring plenty of dramatic contrast. The sounds from the period instruments of the Philharmonia Baroque Orchestra are ear-tickling, and the soloists join together for the life-assertive closing chorus. Excellent recording, both atmospheric and vivid, makes for a fine bargain alternative to Hogwood.

Marc Minkowski brings out the dramatic bite of this early Handel oratorio, often opting for extreme speeds, particularly fast ones, challenging his excellent soprano Annick Massis to the limit in the Angel's brilliant first aria. He may rarely relax in the way that Ton Koopman did on his earlier Erato version (currently withdrawn), but in this episodic piece there is much to be said for such a taut approach, with fine, clean-textured playing from Les Musiciens du Louvre. However Hogwood remains first choice and the enjoyable alternative from McGegan is in the bargain price-range.

Samson (complete).

*** Teldec 9031 74871-2 (2). Rolfe Johnson, Alexander, Kowalski, Scharinger, Venuti, Blasi, Arnold Schoenberg Ch., VCM, Harnoncourt.

Harnoncourt here conducts a Handel performance where Handelian grandeur shines out from the opening overture with its braying horns and genially strutting dotted rhythms. He is altogether warmer than before, and a fine team of singers, led by Anthony Rolfe Johnson in the title-role, is allowed full expressiveness, with speeds in slow numbers broader than one might expect. So the blind Samson's first aria, *Total eclipse*, is very measured, with Rolfe Johnson using the widest tonal and dynamic range. Though the recording catches some flutter in Roberta Alexander's voice as Dalila, she gives a characterful performance, well contrasted with Angela Maria Blasi, her attendant, who sings the lovely aria, *With plaintive note*, most beautifully. Maria Venuti in the climactic *Let the bright seraphim* at the end is not ideally pure-toned, but she sings strongly and flexibly. Other fine singers include Alastair Miles, magnificent in the bass role of the giant, Harapha, not least in *Honour and arms*, as well as the rich-toned counter-tenor, Jochen Kowalski as Micah and Christoph Prégardien in the tenor role of the Philistine. With the Schoenberg choir singing incisively, Harnoncourt presents the work not only with period instruments but on an authentic scale.

Saul (complete).

*** Ph. 426 265-2 (3). Miles, Dawson, Ragin, Ainslie, Mackie, Monteverdi Ch., E. Bar. Sol., Gardiner.

(M) *** DG (ADD) 447 696-2. Armstrong, Price, Bowman, Davies, English, Dean, McIntyre, Winfield, Leeds Festival Ch., ECO, Mackerras.

(BB) **(*) Naxos 8.554361/63 (3). MacLeod, Cordier, Schuch, Schlick, McFadden, Beekman, Junge Kantorei, Frankfurt Baroque O., Martini.

Gardiner's performance is typically vigorous in what represents Handel's full emergence as a great oratorio composer, with the widest range of emotions conveyed. The alternation of mourning and joy in the final sequence of numbers is startlingly effective. With Derek Lee Ragin in the

counter-tenor role of David, with Alastair Miles as Saul, Lynne Dawson as Michal and John Mark Ainslie as Jonathan, it is not likely to be surpassed on disc for a long time.

With an excellent combination of soloists Mackerras steers an exhilarating course in a work that naturally needs to be presented with authenticity but equally needs to have dramatic edge, and the result is powerful on one hand, moving on another. The contrast of timbre between Armstrong and Price is beautifully exploited, and Donald McIntyre as Saul, Ryland Davies as Jonathan and James Bowman as a counter-tenor David are all outstanding, while the chorus willingly contributes to the drama. An outstanding set, beautifully recorded (at the Leeds Triennial Music Festival in 1972) and vividly transferred to CD.

Joachim Carlos Martini on Naxos offers a clear, fresh, lively reading using period instruments, very well recorded, making an excellent bargain version. Outstanding among the soloists is the creamy-toned Barbara Schlick, who sings the role of Michal, Saul's daughter and David's wife. Singers with fresh, young voices fill the other roles effectively, if not always very characterfully. Stephan McLeod as Saul is a clear, firm baritone, rather than the dark bass the role ideally requires, and David Cordier as David is a very English-sounding counter-tenor, clean and cultivated. Claron McFadden in the dual role of Merab and the Witch of Endor is rather edgy, better suited to the second of those roles. The chorus sing well, but are not ideally focused. Otherwise the sound is fresh and clear.

Solomon (complete).

✪ *** Ph. 412 612-2 (2). Watkinson, Argenta, Hendricks, Rolfe Johnson, Monteverdi Ch., E. Bar. Sol., Gardiner.

*** DG 459 688-2 (3). Scholl, Dam-Jensen, Hagley, Bickley, Gritton, Agnew, Gabrieli Cons. & Players, McCreesh.

(M) **(*) Van. 08 5086 72 (2). Diaz, Armstrong, Tear, Rippon, Palmer, Amore Artis Chorale, ECO, Somary.

This is among the very finest of all Handel oratorio recordings. With panache, Gardiner shows how authentic-sized forces can convey Handelian grandeur even with clean-focused textures and fast speeds. The choruses and even more magnificent double choruses stand as cornerstones of a structure which may have less of a story-line than some other Handel oratorios – the Judgement apart – but which Gardiner shows has consistent human warmth. The Act III scenes between Solomon and the Queen of Sheba are given extra warmth by having in the latter role a singer who is sensuous in tone, Barbara Hendricks. Carolyn Watkinson's pure mezzo is very apt for Solomon himself, while Nancy Argenta is clear and sweet as his Queen, but the overriding glory of the set is the radiant singing of Gardiner's Monteverdi Choir. Its clean, crisp articulation matches the brilliant playing of the English Baroque Soloists, regularly challenged by Gardiner's fast speeds, as in *The Arrival of the Queen of Sheba*; and the sound is superb, coping thrillingly with the problems of the double choruses.

The great merit of Paul McCreesh's version of Solomon is that he includes every item that Handel wrote for the 1749 premiere, where even John Eliot Gardiner in his Philips version, one of his very finest recordings, omits five arias.

McCreesh and his team, taking a more relaxed view than Gardiner, though equally dramatic, are lighter in texture, though the recording, made in all Saints, Tooting, is a degree more reverberant. A controversial point is that where Handel originally wrote the title role for a woman singer, not a castrato, McCreesh opts for a counter-tenor, arguing that had Handel heard such an outstanding falsettist as Andreas Scholl, he would have been amply convinced. Scholl sings magnificently, and the rest of the team is strong too, with no weak link. The extra items, involving almost half an hour of music, mean that the work spreads on to three discs instead of two.

With a crisp professional chorus and a formidable line-up of soloists, Somary offers an enjoyable, infectiously sprung performance, marred by the choice of voice for the title-role. Handel himself opted for a mezzo rather than a castrato or a tenor, but here Somary, following now-discredited tradition, has a bass, singing an octave lower than written. Admittedly Justino Diaz sings with satisfyingly dark, firm tone to make the result dramatically very convincing, and the other soloists, drawn from among the finest British singers of the time, are all excellent.

Susanna.

**(*) HM HMU 907030/2. Hunt, Minter, Feldman, Parker, Jeffrey Thomas, David Thomas, U. C. Berkeley Chamber Ch., Philh. Bar. O, McGegan.

The wealth of arias and the refreshing treatment of the Apocrypha story of Susanna and the Elders make it ideal for records. McGegan's performance does not quite match those of his earlier Handel recordings, made in Budapest. This one was done live with a talented period group from Los Angeles. The main snag is that the dry acoustic brings an abrasive edge to the instrumental sound and takes away bloom from the voices. Yet with fine soloists including Lorraine Hunt (Susanna), Drew Minter (Joacim) and Jill Feldman (Daniel), this is far more than a mere stop-gap.

Susanna: highlights.

(M) **(*) HM HMT 7907168 (from above set, cond. McGegan).

Many collectors who might not want to stretch to the complete work on three full-priced CDs will welcome this 72-minute selection of highlights, particularly as it comes with full text and good documentation.

Theodora (complete).

(N) *** DG 469 061-2 (3). Gritton, Bickley, Blaze, Agnew, Davies, Gabrieli Cons. & Players, McCreesh.

*** HM HMU 907060/62 (3). David Thomas, Minter, Jeffrey Thomas, Hunt, Lane, Rogers, University of California (Berkeley) Chamber Ch., Philh. Baroque O, McGegan.

(N) (M) *** MDG 332 1019-2 (3). Zomer, Buwalda, Rasker, Schoch, Sol, Schweiser, Cologne Chamber Ch., Collegium Cartusianum, Neumann.

(M) **(*) Van. (ADD) 08.4075.72 (2). Harper, Forrester, Lehane, Young, Lawrenson, Amor Artis Ch., ECO, Somary.

**(*) Teldec 2292 46447-2 (2). Alexander, Blochwitz, Kowalski, Van Nes, Scharinger, Schönberg Ch., VCM, Harnoncourt.

Handel's penultimate oratorio, *Theodora*, initially a failure but one of his own favourites, has been fortunate in the age of CD, yet Paul McCreesh's version sweeps the board. Beautifully recorded in a sympathetic acoustic – less dry than on Nicholas McGegan's Harmonia Mundi version – it offers an outstandingly sensitive, well-paced reading ideally cast, using a text which gives alternative versions of numbers which Handel revised. Using a relatively large string section (26 players), McCreesh brings out the dramatic contrasts vividly in a work which in its telling of the story of Theodora, the early Christian martyr, has its elements of grandeur.

In the title role Susan Gritton sings radiantly, unaffectedly compassing the widest range of expression, a moving central focus to the drama, with the even-toned countertenor, Robin Blaze, equally impressive as Didymus, the Roman officer who becomes her fellow martyr. The mezzo, Susan Bickley, sings with simple dedication as Irene, with Paul Agnew elegant in the role of Septimius and Neal Davies an authoritative Valens, President of Antioch.

McGegan's spirited, exuberant performance gives the text absolutely complete and offers alternative numbers not included in the regular Handel edition. The fine team of soloists is impressively headed by Lorraine Hunt, who also shone in McGegan's earlier, prize-winning recording of *Susanna*, with the counter-tenor, Drew Minter, the tenor, Jeffrey Thomas, and the bass, David Thomas, again singing stylishly. They are not helped by the dry acoustic, but the sound is less aggressive than in the earlier set, and it means that words are crystal clear.

Peter Neumann's version on MDG, well played and sympathetically paced, would be very welcome but for the formidable competition from both McCreesh on DG Archiv and McGegan on Harmonia Mundi. The German cast is first-rate, admirably coping with an English text, led by the warm-toned Johanette Somer as Theodora and the excellent counter-tenor, Sytse Buwalda, as Didymus. The three discs come for the price of two.

The reissued Vanguard account is traditional in style and is directed by an understanding and intelligent Handelian, Johannes Somary. With fresh and sympathetic singing from soloists who are stylistically at home in Handel, the result is most enjoyable. Maureen Forrester in particular sings superbly, but all the singing is at least reliable, and the recording has transferred warmly and vividly to CD.

There is much to enjoy in the lively Teldec account, with fresh, clean textures typical of the Concentus Musicus, and with Harnoncourt thrusting in manner, occasionally to the point of being heavy-handed. The solo casting is strong, though this team of international singers does not always sound at home, either stylistically or in singing English. Roberta Alexander is the finest of the soloists, with the counter-tenor Jochen Kowalski exceptionally warm of tone but hardly sounding Handelian in the role of Didymus. Jard van Nes is warm and fruity as Irene and Hans Peter Blochwitz is light and fresh as Septimius. Bright, full recording.

The Triumph of Time and Truth.

*** Hyp. CDA 66071/2. Fisher, Kirkby, Brett, Partridge, Varcoe, L. Handel Ch. and O, Darlow.

Darlow's performance of Handel's very last oratorio is broad and strong and very enjoyable. The soloists have all been chosen for the clarity of their pitching – Emma Kirkby, Gillian Fisher, Charles Brett and Stephen Varcoe, with the honey-toned Ian Partridge singing even more beautifully than the others, but with a timbre too pure quite to characterize 'Pleasure'. Good atmospheric recording.

Utrecht Te Deum & Jubilate in D – see below, under *Alceste.*

OPERA

Admeto, re di Tessaglia (complete).

(M) *** Virgin (ADD) VMT5 61369-2 (3). Jacobs, Yakar, Gomez, Bowman, Cold, Dams, Van Egmont, Il Complesso Barocco, Curtis.

Admeto is among the very greatest of Handel's operas, and this recording, made in 1977 in Holland, was one of the first complete recordings of a Handel opera to attempt an authentic approach, and the most successful up to that time. Though recitatives are on the slow side, it stands the test of time, a fine performance, very well cast, played with refinement on period instruments and excellently recorded. Handel wrote *Admeto* with the three greatest singers of the time in mind, the castrato, Senesino, in the title-role, and the rival prima donnas, Cuzzoni and Bordoni, as Antigona and Alceste. Here the counter-tenor René Jacobs gives an understanding and characterful performance in the title-role, but it is Jill Gomez as Antigona who steals first honours, with magnificent singing, sweet, pure and strong of tone, with ornamentation beautifully crisp. Rachel Yakar is not so sweetly caught by the microphones, but hers is a stylish performance too, and the rest of the cast has no weak link, with James Bowman outstanding as Admeto's brother, Trasimede.

Agrippina (complete).

*** Ph. 438 009-2 (3). Jones, Miles, Ragin, Brown, Chance, Von Otter, Mosley, E. Bar. Sol., Gardiner.

*** HM HMU 907063/65 (3). Bradshaw, Saffer, Minter, Hill, Isherwood, Popken, Dean, Banditelli, Szilági, Capella Savaria, McGegan.

Agrippina was the second and last of the operas that Handel wrote during his stay in Italy between 1706 and 1710. His libretto was specially written for him by Cardinal Vincenzo Grimani, using historical characters from the time of the Emperor Claudius, in which the immoral goings-on in the court are treated with a lightness and vein of irony that marked operas in the previous century by Monteverdi and Cavalli.

This Gardiner recording comes into direct rivalry with the fine Harmonia Mundi version of 1991 under Nicholas McGegan, fresh and immediate with a generally youthful cast. Not just Della Jones, but most of the other principals

are a degree more characterful than their opposite numbers – Derek Lee Ragin as Nero (a counter-tenor clearly preferable to McGegan's soprano), Alastair Miles as the Emperor and Michael Chance as Ottone among them. The Philips sound is warmer and more spacious, with the period instruments sounding sweeter and less abrasive. Gardiner also has an extra ballet movement at the very end after the goddess Juno's epilogue aria, superbly sung here by Anne Sofie von Otter. Highlights are available on 456025-2.

McGegan's version is delightfully light-hearted, magnetic in its fanciful telling of the intrigues between the Emperor Claudius, his wife Agrippina, Nero her son and Poppea, as well as Otho (Ottone) and Pallas (Pallante). Nicholas McGegan is markedly sympathetic, and, with a fine bloom on voices and instruments, notably the brass, the performance is exhilaratingly fresh and alert. The cast is first rate, led by the silvery Sally Bradshaw as Agrippina, the bright Nero of Wendy Hill and the seductive Poppea of Lisa Saffer, all well contrasted in their equally stylish ways.

(i) *Alceste: Overture & Incidental Music;* (ii) *Anthem for the Foundling Hospital; Ode for the Birthday of Queen Anne;* (iii) *Utrecht Te Deum & Jubilate in D.*

(B) *** Double Decca 458 072-2 (2). (i; ii; iii) Kirkby, Nelson, Thomas, AAM (i) Cable, Thomas, Elliott, Ch., Hogwood (ii) Minty, Bowman, Hill, (ii; iii) Christ Church Cathedral Ch., Preston; (iii) with Brett, Covey-Crump, Elliott.

Handel left us much to enjoy in the impressively dramatic *Alceste Overture* in D minor and the *Grand entrée* for Admetus, Alceste and their wedding guests, which get the proceedings off to a fine start. There follows a series not just of solo items but also some simple tuneful choruses in which a small secondary vocal group participates. There is nearly an hour of freshly enjoyable music and Hogwood draws lively, sympathetic performances from his team. The *Ode* has its Italianate attractions and opens with a splendid counter-tenor aria from James Bowman, with an elaborate trumpet obbligato, superbly played here. But it is the much later *Founding Hospital Anthem* that is the more memorable, not just because it concludes with an alternative version of the *Hallelujah Chorus,* but also because the other borrowed numbers are also superb. The Utrecht pieces were written just before Handel came to London and were intended as a sample of his work. Preston directs performances which are characteristically alert and vigorous, particularly impressive in the superb closing *Glory be to the Father* with its massive eight-part chords. Throughout the team of soloists regularly associated with the Academy give of their best, and the recordings, made in 1977 and 1979 are splendidly transferred, clean and clear yet not losing their analogue atmosphere.

Alcina (complete).

*** EMI CDS7 49771-2 (3). Augér, Jones, Kuhlmann, Harrhy, Kwella, Davies, Tomlinson, Opera Stage Ch., City of L. Bar. Sinfonia, Hickox.

*** Erato 8573 80233-2 (3). Fleming, Graham, Dessay, Kuhlmann, Lascarro, Robinson, Naouri, Les Arts Florissants, Christie.

(i) *Alcina* **(complete); (ii)** *Giulio Cesare (Julius Caesar):* **highlights.**

(M) **(*) Decca 433 723-2 (3). Sutherland, Sinclair,
(i) Berganza, Alva, Sciutti, Freni, Flagello, LSO; (ii) Elkins,
Horne, Conrad, New SO; Bonynge.

It would be hard to devise a septet of Handelian singers more stylish than the soloists in Hickox's version. Though the American, Arleen Augér, may not have the weight of Joan Sutherland, she is just as brilliant and pure-toned, singing warmly in the great expansive arias. Even next to her, Della Jones stands out in the breeches role of Ruggiero, with an extraordinary range of memorable arias, bold as well as tender. Eiddwen Harrhy as Morgana is just as brilliant in the aria, *Tornami a vagheggiar,* usually 'borrowed' by Alcina, while Kathleen Kuhlmann, Patrizia Kwella, Maldwyn Davies and John Tomlinson all sing with a clarity and beauty to make the music sparkle. Hickox underlines the contrasts of mood and speed, conveying the full range of emotion, with warm, spacious sound, recorded at EMI's Abbey Road studio.

The fine Erato set was recorded live at a series of five performances at the Paris Opéra, with a cast of principals that would be hard to match. Though the auditorium of the Palais Garnier is dangerously large for such a Handel opera, the recording minimizes that problem, with arias well balanced, allowing the solo voices ample bloom without excessive reverberation. Only in recitatives do stage noises ever intrude, and the tensions of a live reading help to minimize the drawback of an opera containing only one ensemble number (the Act III terzetto) in addition to the traditional brief choral finale. Christie too is masterly at avoiding any monotony in the long sequence of da capo arias, with recitative superbly timed and reprises beautifully decorated. It is striking that the star singers here, each with an exclusive contract for another company – Fleming for Decca, Graham for Sony, and Dessay for EMI – are not just brilliant in tackling elaborate passage work and ornamentation, but are stylishly scrupulous in avoiding unwanted aspirates. Fleming is in glorious voice as Alcina, with Susan Graham characterizing well in the trouser-role of Ruggiero. Natalie Dessay as Alcina's sister, Morgana, relishes the challenge of the brilliant *Tornami a vagheggiar* (appropriated by Joan Sutherland in the unauthentic Decca set), helped by Christie's relatively relaxed tempo. He also sets relaxed speeds in some of the great slow arias such as *Verdi prati,* encouraging an expressive approach which yet remains within the bounds of period style. If the live EMI recording conveys dramatic tension more clearly, the contrast between voices is more marked in the earlier set, with the male singers exceptionally strong.

Although the 1962 Decca *Alcina* is less complete than the newer EMI set, it has the advantage of including some 50 minutes of highlights from *Giulio Cesare,* made a year later, which Sutherland did not undertake in a complete version. *Alcina,* however, represents the extreme point of what can be described as Sutherland's dreamy, droopy period. The fast arias are stupendous. But anything slow and reflective, whether in recitative or aria, has Sutherland mooning about the notes, with no consonants audible. Of the others, Teresa Berganza is completely charming in the castrato part of Ruggiero, even if she does not manage trills very well. Monica Sinclair shows everyone up with the strength and forthrightness of her singing. Both Graziella Sciutti and Mirella Freni are delicate and clear in their two smaller parts. Richard Bonynge draws crisp, vigorous playing from the LSO. The 30-year-old Walthamstow recording is vintage Decca, and the CD transfer hints at its age only in the orchestral string sound.

Not surprisingly, the *Giulio Cesare* highlights are used as a vehicle for Sutherland, and her florid elaborations of melodies turn *da capo* recitatives into things of delight and wonder. There is some marvellous singing from Marilyn Horne and Monica Sinclair too, and Bonynge conducts with a splendid sense of style. As a sample, try *V'adoro pupile* – Cleopatra's seduction aria. Full translations are provided in both works.

Almira **(complete).**

(BB) **(*) CPO 999 275-2 (3). Monoyios, Rozario, Gerrard,
Thomas, Nasrawi, MacDougall, Elsner, Fiori Musicale,
Lawrence-King.

Almira was Handel's first opera, written in Hamburg in 1704 and first given just before his twentieth birthday. Setting a libretto partly in German, partly in Italian and with a plot involving the loves of Almira, Queen of Castile, it is a long piece lasting almost four hours. The arias are generally more compact than in the mature Handel, with argument more constrained, less developed. Even so, one regularly detects a genuine Handelian flavour in the themes, and he himself borrowed a fair measure of the material here in later works. This recording, with three discs offered for the price of two, was made after a staging presented in both Halle and Bremen in 1994. Andrew Lawrence-King secures a fresh and well-paced – if rather plain – performance, with deft playing from the German period orchestra. Ann Monoyios is a light, bright Almira, with Patricia Rozario, taxed a little by the high tessitura. equally stylish as Edilia. The two principal tenor roles are very well taken by Jamie MacDougall and Douglas Nasrawi, with the third tenor, Christian Elsner, taking the comic servant role. David Thomas sings with clean attack in the bass role of the Prince of Segovia. Good, undistracting and well scaled in an intimate acoustic.

Amadigi di Gaula **(complete).**

*** Erato 2292 45490-2 (2). Stutzmann, Smith, Harrhy, Fink,
Musiciens du Louvre, Minkowski.

Minkowski's electrifying performance is one of his sharpest, dominated vocally by the magnificent young French contralto (no mere mezzo) of Nathalie Stutzmann in the title-role. She sings Amadigi's gentle arias most affectingly, notably the lovely *Sussurrate, onde vezzose,* and the two women characters, Amadigi's lover Melissa and Princess Oriana, are well taken by Eiddwen Harrhy and Jennifer Smith, with the brilliant arias for Prince Dardano of Thrace superbly sung by Bernarda Fink. It is a performance on an intimate scale, and the more involving for that.

Ariodante (complete).

*** HM HMU 907146/48 (3). Hunt, Gondek, Saffer, Lane, Cavallier, Muller, Wilhelmshaven Vocal Ens., Freiburger Bar. O, McGegan.

*** DG 457 271-2 (3). Von Otter, Dawson, Podles, Croft, Musiciens du Louvre, Minkowski.

(M) *** Ph. 442 096-2 (3). Baker, Mathis, Burrowes, Bowman, Rendall, Ramey, L. Voices, ECO, Leppard.

Ariodante is among the most richly inspired of Handel's operas. McGegan's performance on Harmonia Mundi, recorded in Göttingen in 1995 immediately after festival performances on stage, brings clear advantages. Not only is there an exceptionally strong and consistent cast, the text is far fuller and the period-instrument orchestra is full-bodied and sweetly tuned, with the experience of live performing adding to the dramatic bite. McGegan springs rhythms infectiously, making speeds that are faster than Leppard's seem natural, never breathless, letting the music relax where necessary, again influenced by live experience. In the castrato title-role Lorraine Hunt may not have the emotional weight of Dame Janet Baker, but hers is a fresh, clear and firm mezzo, which she uses most characterfully and imaginatively. Her big Act II aria, *Scherza infida*, in its positive strength even brings unexpected echoes of Kathleen Ferrier. The others too, mainly American singers, all have fresh, clean delivery and free flexibility, notably Juliana Gondek as the heroine, Ginevra, Lisa Saffer as Dalinda and Jennifer Lane as Polinesso. Nicolas Cavallier as the King may not have the richness of Samuel Ramey in Leppard's set, but his attack too is clean, and Rufus Muller in the tenor role of Lucanio, clear and firm, like the women sings elaborate divisions with ideal precision. Excellent recording with bloom on the voices, aptly intimate and full of presence.

On DG Archiv, with an outstanding starry team of soloists, Marc Minkowski conducts a high-powered reading of *Ariodante*, urgently dramatic and a compelling set in every way. Though Ann Sophie von Otter in the title role is not quite at her freshest, and Lorraine Hunt and Dame Janet Baker on rival sets give even more moving performances, her characterization is as strong as ever. Among the others Lynne Dawson and Ewa Podles are outstandingly fine, though by a very narrow margin the Harmonia Mundi set with Hunt remains first choice.

In the colourful, urgent performance under Raymond Leppard the castrato role of Ariodante is a challenge for Dame Janet Baker, who responds with singing of enormous expressive range, from the dark, agonized moments of the C minor aria early in Act III to the brilliance of the most spectacular of the three display arias later in the Act. Dame Janet's duets with Edith Mathis as Princess Ginevra, destined to marry Prince Ariodante, are enchanting too, and there is not a single weak member of the cast, though James Bowman as Duke Polinesso is not as precise as usual, with words often unclear. Consistently resilient playing from the English Chamber Orchestra and refined, beautifully balanced (1978) analogue recording, vividly transferred to CD.

Arminio (complete opera).

(N) *** Virgin VCD5 45461-2 (2). Genaux, McGreevy, Labelle, Custer, Petroni, Buwalda, Ristori, Il Complesso Barocco, Curtis.

Written at high speed in 1736 towards the end of Handel's career as opera-composer, *Arminio* is the most neglected of the ten of his operas with titles beginning with A. As this lively performance directed by Alan Curtis demonstrates from first to last, the complete neglect over 250 years is totally unjustified, even though the libretto by Antonio Salvi telescopes the story, based on Tacitus's account of Varo and the defeat of the Roman legions by the Germans. The piece starts in defiance of early-18th-century convention with a duet for hero and heroine immediately after the overture, and the sequence of brief arias rings changes of mood and voice with one delightful number after another. Recitatives are reduced to modest proportions in obedience to London taste, so that the overall span over the three acts fits neatly on to the two discs.

Standing out in the cast is Geraldine Mcgreevy, winner of the 1996 Kathleen Ferrier Award, who takes the key role of the heroine, Tusnelda, daughter of the German prince, Segeste. Tusnelda has far more arias than anyone, many of them vigorous, but including such deeply reflective numbers as the ravishing *Rendimi il dolce sposo*, which ends Act 2. In Act 3 she has in addition to another reflective aria two charming duets with voices in chains of thirds. Vivica Genaux as Arminio is not quite so well caught by the microphone, but the whole cast, including Dominique Labelle, an excellent second soprano as Sigismondo, are commendably agile in the florid writing, with the fresh-toned period band Il Complesso Barocco ever-responsive. Clear, well-balanced sound.

Flavio (complete).

*** HM HMC 901312/13 (2). Gall, Ragin, Lootens, Fink, *et al.*, Ens. 415, Jacobs.

Based on a staging of this unjustly neglected Handel opera at the 1989 Innsbruck Festival, René Jacobs' recording vividly captures the consistent vigour of Handel's inspiration. Handel's score was brilliantly written for some of the most celebrated singers of the time, including the castrato, Senesino. His four arias are among the highspots of the opera, all sung superbly here by the warm-toned and characterful counter-tenor, Derek Lee Ragin; almost every other aria is open and vigorous, with the whole sequence rounded off in a rousing ensemble. René Jacobs' team of eight soloists is a strong one, with only the strenuous tenor of Gianpaolo Fagotto occasionally falling short of the general stylishness. Full, clear sound.

Giulio Cesare (complete).

*** HM HMC 901385/7. Larmore, Schlick, Fink, Rorholm, Ragin, Zanasi, Visse, Concerto Köln, Jacobs.

*** Astree E 8558 (3). Bowman, Dawson, Laurens, James, Visse, La Grande Ecurie et la Chambre du Roy, Malgoire.

The counter-tenor René Jacobs, conducting the German group, Concerto Köln, is a warmly expressive rather than a severe period performer. The casting of the pure, goldentoned Barbara Schlick as Cleopatra proves outstandingly successful. Jennifer Larmore too, a fine, firm mezzo, with a touch of masculine toughness in the tone, makes a splendid Caesar. Together they crown the whole performance with the most seductive account of their final duet. Derek Lee Ragin is excellent in the sinister role of Tolomeo (Ptolemy); so are Bernarda Fink as Cornelia and Marianne Rorholm as Sesto, with the bass, Furio Zanasi, as Achille. Jacobs' expansive speeds mean that the whole opera will not fit on three CDs, but the fourth disc, at 18 minutes merely supplementary, comes free as part of the package, and includes an extra aria for the servant, Nireno, delightfully sung by the French counter-tenor, Dominique Visse. Firm, well-balanced sound. An excellent bargain-priced set of highlights is also available with texts and translations included for some 78 minutes of excerpts (HMA 1951458).

Jean-Claude Malgoire directs his outstanding cast in a fresh, free-running performance of Handel's most frequently performed opera. The counter-tenor James Bowman in the Malgoire set is strongly contrasted against the firm and purposeful mezzo, Jennifer Larmore. Bowman cannot quite match Larmore in the brilliance of his florid singing, but the timbre is firm and rich at less demanding speeds, and the portrait of a hero is conveyed convincingly. The contrast between Lynne Dawson as Cleopatra and Barbara Schlick is a key one too, for Dawson, following Malgoire's general approach, concentrates on beauty and classical poise, whereas Schlick brings out greater depth of expression. The contrast is similar over Giullemette Laurens as Cornelia as against Bernarda Fink, the one poised, the other more deeply expressive, often at broader speeds. By contrast the counter-tenor, Dominique Visse, is the more actively characterful as the villainous Tolomeo, where Derek Lee Ragin for Jacobs combines sharp characterization with cleaner vocalization. Malgoire's text is not quite as complete as Jacobs', with cuts in recitative.

Julius Caesar (complete in English).

(M) *** Chan. 3019 (3). Baker, Masterson, Walker, Jones, Bowman, Tomlinson, E. Nat. Op. Ch. & O, Mackerras.

Dame Janet Baker is in glorious voice and draws on the widest range of expressive tone-colours, and Valerie Masterson makes a charming and seductive Cleopatra, fresh and girlish, though the voice is caught a little too brightly for caressing such radiant melodies as those for V'adoro pupille ('Lamenting, complaining') and Piangero ('Flow my tears'). Sarah Walker sings with powerful intensity as Pompey's widow; James Bowman is a characterful counter-tenor Ptolemy, and John Tomlinson a firm, resonant Achillas, the other nasty character. The ravishing accompaniments to the two big Cleopatra arias amply justify the use by the excellent ENO Orchestra of modern, not period instruments. The full, vivid studio sound makes this one of the very finest of the invaluable series of ENO opera recordings in English, now being made available again by Chandos, sponsored by the Peter Moores Foundation.

Giustino (complete).

*** HM HMU 907130/32. Chance, Röschmann, Kotoski, Gondek, Lane, Padmore, Minter, Cantamus Halle Chamber Ch., Freiburg Baroque O, McGegan.

First heard in 1737 and never revived until 1967, the opera, Giustino, has been consistently underestimated. This splendid, lively set should do much to bring a full reassessment, for McGegan, with his fast, crisp manner and fondness for extra decoration in da capo repeats, brings out the element of sparkle and irony implied in the improbable story, treated refreshingly in dozens of brief arias. Michael Chance is outstanding in the title-role originally written for a castrato, and Dorothea Röschmann sings most movingly in the key role of Arianna. Drew Minter, stylish and intelligent as he is, fails to give enough bite to the villainous role of Amanzio; but there are few other disappointments, and the tenor, Mark Padmore, sings with virtuoso flair in the military role of Vitaliano. The German string-players are more abrasive than one expects nowadays, but this is a set to delight all Handelians, filling in an important gap.

Hercules (complete).

(M) *** DG 447 689-2 (2). Tomlinson, Walker, Rolfe Johnson, Smith, Denley, Savidge, Monteverdi Ch., E. Bar. Sol., Gardiner.

Gardiner's brisk performance of Hercules using authentic forces may at times lack Handelian grandeur in the big choruses, but it conveys superbly the vigour of the writing, its natural drama; and the fire of this performance is typified by the outstanding singing of Sarah Walker as Dejanira. John Tomlinson makes an excellent, dark-toned Hercules. Fresh voices consistently help in the clarity of the attack – Jennifer Smith as Iole, Catherine Denley as Lichas, Anthony Rolfe Johnson as Hyllus and Peter Savidge as the Priest of Jupiter. Refined playing and outstanding recording quality make this most welcome at mid-price.

Orlando (complete).

*** O-L 430 845-2 (3). Bowman, Augér, Robbin, Kirkby, D. Thomas, AAM, Hogwood.

*** Erato 0630 14636-2 (3). Bardon, Mannion, Summers, Joshua, Van der Kamp, Les Arts Florissants, Christie.

Handel's Orlando was radically modified to provide suitable material for individual singers, notably in the magnificent mad scene, which ends Act II on the aria, Vaghe pupille. That number, superbly done here by James Bowman, with appropriate sound effects, is only one of the virtuoso vehicles for the counter-tenor. For the jewelled sequences of arias and duets, Hogwood has assembled a near-ideal cast, with Arleen Augér at her most radiant as the queen, Angelica, and Emma Kirkby characteristically bright and fresh in the lighter, semi-comic role of the shepherdess, Dorinda. Catherine Robbin assumes the role of Prince Medoro strongly and David Thomas sings stylishly as Zoroastro. This is one of Hogwood's finest achievements on record, taut, dramatic and rhythmically resilient. Vivid, open sound.

William Christie's Erato recording of Orlando makes a valuable alternative. The most obvious difference is that where Hogwood has a male alto singing the title-role, Christie here opts for a fine mezzo, Patricia Bardon. Her approach is more overtly dramatic than James Bowman's for Hogwood, with moods and passions more positively characterized. The celebrated Mad scene ending Act II illustrates the point perfectly, with Christie and Bardon more violent, using bigger contrasts, ending in a scurrying *accelerando*, whereas the Bowman/Hogwood approach keeps some classical restraint to the end, pointing the drama of the moment in thunder effects. The Erato recording is warm and full, but is not as transparent or well separated as the earlier one, with Christie often opting for marginally broader speeds. His other soloists are all excellent, readily matching their rivals, not least the contralto, Hilary Summers, as Prince Medoro.

Ottone, re di Germania (complete).

*** Hyp. CDA 66751/3. Bowman, McFadden, Smith, Denley, Visse, George, King's Consort, King.

**(*) HM HMU 907073/5. Minter, Saffer, Gondek, Spence, Popken, Dean, Freiburg Bar. O, McGegan.

Previously unrecorded, *Ottone* simultaneously prompted these two versions, both of which have their points of advantage. Nicholas McGegan continues his impressive Handel series for Harmonia Mundi in a recording with the Freiburg Baroque Orchestra and with Drew Minter taking the title-role, while Robert King and his King's Consort offer a version on Hyperion with James Bowman as Ottone. When the women principals in McGegan's version have purer, firmer voices than their rivals, there is a strong case for preferring his set. As the heroine, Teofane, Lisa Saffer for McGegan is markedly sweeter and clearer than Claron McFadden for King. When it comes to the key castrato roles taken by counter-tenors, it is quite different. For McGegan, Drew Minter, a stylish singer, no longer has the power to give the many bravura arias the thrust they need, whereas for King, Bowman with his far richer tone continues to sing with enormous panache and virtuoso agility. Dominique Visse as the duplicitous Adalberto on King's set tends to overcharacterize, but the singing makes the rival version seem colourless. Add to that the extra richness and bloom on the instrumental sound in the Hyperion version, and the balance clearly goes in its favour.

Partenope (complete).

(M) *** DHM/BMG (ADD) GD 77109 (3). Laki, Jacobs, York, Skinner, Varcoe, Müller-Molinari, Hill, La Petite Bande, Kuijken.

With the exception of René Jacobs, rather too mannered for Handel, the roster of soloists here is outstanding, with Krisztina Laki and Helga Müller-Molinari welcome additions to the team. Though ornamentation is sparse, the direction of Sigiswald Kuijken is consistently invigorating, as is immediately apparent in the *Overture*; the 1979 recording sounds splendid in its CD format.

Radamisto (complete).

**(*) HM HMU 907111/13. Popken, Gondek, Saffer, Hanchard, Dean, Cavallier, Freiburger Bar. O, McGegan.

Radamisto is a magnificent work. The best-known aria, the plaintive *Ombra cara*, sung by Radamisto, leads on to a whole sequence of magnificent minor-key numbers in Act II, with some of the arias given to Zenobia, Radamisto's wife, marked by strange, sudden switches of mood. This first complete recording is very welcome in revealing much superb material, even if the period-performance manners are less sympathetic, with the strings of the Freiburg orchestra very abrasive, while recitative is on the heavy side. Yet there is some first-rate singing, with the title-role strongly taken by the firm-toned counter-tenor, Ralf Popken, even if he is occasionally hooty. It is not his fault that *Ombra cara* sounds rather stodgy, for he shades his tone most beautifully for the reprise. Juliana Gondek sings with full, warm tone as Zenobia, producing crisp trills and ornaments, though most of the others are not quite so successful. The recording, made in Göttingen after a festival production, is on the dry side but has plenty of presence.

Riccardo Primo (Richard the Lionheart).

*** O-L 452 601-2 (3). Mingardo, Piau, Lallouette, Scaltriti, Brua, Bertin, Les Talens Lyriques, Rousset.

Christophe Rousset conducts a lively, well-characterized performance of one of the rarest and one of the most elaborately scored of Handel's operas, even using a sopranino recorder for a delightful bird aria in Act III, for the princess of Navarre, Costanza, Richard's betrothed, Cuzzoni's role. It is a long opera, and you have to wait until Act III for many of the jewels in the score, which then round the piece off with great flair.

Vocally, the principal glory of this recorded performance is the singing of Sara Mingardo in the title-role, gloriously firm and true, so that such a showpiece as Richard's Act III aria, *All'orror delle procelle*, has one readily registering what must have been the impact of Senesino in the first performances. In quite a different mood, the duet between Richard and Costanza which ends Act II is enchantingly poetic, later adapted for Handel's last oratorio, *Jephtha*. Sandrine Piau as Costanza is tenderly expressive, even though (as recorded) the voice, sweet in tone, is not perfectly even, and Claire Brua in the Bordoni role of Pulcheria tends to be too gusty to enunciate elaborate divisions clearly, but the contrast between the rival ladies is well established. The counter-tenor, Pascal Bertin, is excellent as Oronte, and the two baritone roles are well taken by Roberto Scaltriti (aptly villainous-sounding) and Olivier Lallouette. First-rate, well-balanced sound.

Rinaldo (complete).

(N) *** Decca 467 087-2 (3). Daniels, Bartoli, Fink, Finley, Orgonasova, Taylor, AAM, Hogwood.

(M) *** Sony (ADD) SM3K 34592 (3). Watkinson, Cotrubas, Scovotti, Esswood, Brett, Cold, La Grande Ecurie et la Chambre du Roy, Malgoire.

It would be hard to devise a cast for this colourful and vigorous opera which would begin to match that on Hogwood's new Decca set. It was Handel's first opera for London and the first Italian opera specifically composed for the London stage, and it is surprising that such a strong and memorable piece has not been recorded more often. This Decca issue easily surpasses all competition.

The inspired and characterful counter-tenor, David Daniels, makes an ideal choice for the castrato role of Rinaldo, strong and imaginative in martial music, tenderly expressive in such a poignant aria as *Cara sposa*. Though the vibrant Cecilia Bartoli was considered for that role, she rightly preferred to tackle the gentler role of Rinaldo's wife, Almirena, and makes *Lascia ch'io pianga* one of the high points of the performance.

Luba Orgonasova is wonderfully contrasted in the fire-eating role of the sorceress, Armida, with Bernardo Fink bringing character to the recessive role of Goffredo, the Christian captain-general, and Gerald Finley firm and positive as Argante, King of Jerusalem.

Above all, Christopher Hogwood brings out not only the colour but the vigour of Handel's inspiration, with speeds on the fast side but never rushed, always sounding fresh. By contrast he allows full expansion on the big slow numbers, encouraging the expressiveness of his starry team, with brilliant, incisive playing from the Academy of Ancient Music.

The vigour of Malgoire's direction of an opera which plainly for him is very much alive, makes this a very attractive set, with the one caveat that it has been reissued without a translation (the full libretto is in Italian only). The elaborate decorations on *da capo* arias are imaginatively done, but most effectively the famous *Cara sposa* is left without ornamentation, beautifully sung by the contralto Rinaldo, Carolyn Watkinson. The finest singing comes from Ileana Cotrubas, but the whole team is convincing. The bright but spacious recording adds to the projection, and the magic sounds associated with the sorceress, Armida, such as the arrival of her airborne chariot, are well conveyed, and throughout Handel's invention is a delight.

Rodelinda, Regina de Langobardi (complete).

*** Virgin VCT5 45277-2(3). Daneman, Taylor, Thompson, Robbin, Blaze, Purves, Raglan Bar. Players, Kraemer.

Rodelinda, dating from 1725, has a plot typically involving disguises and forced coincidences, which may be hard for the modern listener to accept. Yet the variety of Handel's invention triumphs over all complication in clearly defining each character, not least the two villains, tenor and bass respectively. Nicholas Kraemer, drawing refined playing from the Raglan Baroque Players, has a winningly light touch. The singers in this live recording work very effectively as a team, characterizing sharply. Sophie Daneman as Rodelinda, with vibrato stilled, produces sound of bell-like purity and crisp ornamentation. Daniel Taylor, as the hero, Bertarido, uses his refined counter-tenor with subtlety and point, not least in the most famous aria, *Dove sei*, while the mezzo, Catherine Robbin, is superb as his disappointed sister, Eduige.

Rodrigo (complete).

*** Virgin VCD5 45897-2 (2). Banditelli, Piau, Fedi, Müller, Invernizzi, Calvi, Il Complesso Barocco, Curtis.

Rodrigo was Handel's very first Italian opera, written for the Medici court in Florence in 1707. It was not heard again until 1984, when Alan Curtis (the conductor here) directed a performance using a score he himself had prepared, with newly rediscovered material restored. This spirited performance has been neatly tailored to fit on two generously filled CDs, with cuts mainly of the *secco* recitatives. The freshness of the performance matches the freshness of Handel's youthful inspiration, with numbers generally more compact than in later Handel operas. Gloria Banditelli sings richly and firmly in the castrato role of Rodrigo, King of Spain, with Sandrine Piau sweet and bright as his wife Esilena, who is given many of the most memorable arias. Elena Cecchi Fedi sings edgily as Florinda but is well in character, and Rufus Müller is a strong Giuliano. A valuable first recording, with bright, fresh sound.

Semele (complete).

*** DG 435 782-2 (3). Battle, Horne, Ramey, Aler, McNair, Chance, Mackie, Amb. Op. Ch., ECO, Nelson.

(M) *** Van. (ADD) 08.5082 72 (2). Armstrong, Watts, Palmer, Tear, Diaz, Deller, Fleet, Amor Artis Chorale, ECO, Somary.

(M) **(*) Erato 2292 45982-2 (2). Burrowes, Jones, Lloyd, Thomas, Rolfe Johnson, Kwella, Penrose, Davies, Monteverdi Ch., E. Bar. Sol., Gardiner.

With its English words, *Semele* stands equivocally between the genres of opera and oratorio. DG's digital recording turns away from current fashion in using modern rather than period instruments, but the balance of advantage lies very much in its favour, compared with the Erato set of Gardiner; even period fanatics may well find it the better choice. Surprisingly, the Nelson performance is generally crisper and faster than Gardiner's, with rhythms sprung just as infectiously. Most importantly, he opens out the serious cuts made by Gardiner, following the old, bad tradition. If *Semele* – dating from 1744, three years after *Messiah* – is known as a rule only by its most celebrated aria, *Where'er you walk*, it contains many other superb numbers.

Though at times he favours slow, oratorio-like tempi, Somary still keeps in mind an operatic flavour, and the Amor Artis Chorale (a pseudonym for a well-known professional recording choir) sings splendidly, often with great vigour, and even attempts some attractive if inauthentic corporate ornamentation. Overall the performance has much charm and spirit with superb soloists. Like the rest of this Vanguard series from the 1970s, the fine recording allows excellent detail, yet is full and expansive.

Gardiner's 1981 version of *Semele* offers a period performance with the English Baroque Soloists using an excellent cast of British singers. Very well recorded, it has the very practical advantage of coming on only two mid-priced discs. The extensive cuts which make that possible are the traditional ones, some of them sanctioned by Handel himself. Gardiner's ability to use period performance with warmth and imagination makes it consistently compelling. Norma Burrowes is a sweet, pure Semele, and Anthony Rolfe Johnson is outstanding as Jupiter, singing *Where'er you walk* with a fine sense of line and excellent pacing.

Serse (Xerxes; complete).

*** Conifer 75605 51312-2 (3). Malafronte, Smith, Milne, Bickley, Asawa, Thomas, Ely, Ch. & Hanover Band, McGegan.

(M) **(*) Sony (ADD) SM3K 36941 (3). Watkinson, Esswood, Wenkel, Hendricks, Rodde, Cold, Bridier Vocal Ens., La Grand Ecurie et la Chambre du Roy, Malgoire.

Following Venetian fashion, Handel here wrote a piece built

on dozens of short numbers, which has humour and irony as part of the mixture. Even the most celebrated number, Xerxes' aria, *Ombra mai fù*, addressed to a plane tree, is hardly serious, rather illustrating the central character's quirky tastes. McGegan with light textures and generally brisk speeds, gives necessary momentum, while allowing his principals full expressiveness in such deeper numbers as the hero's Act II aria, *Il core spera e teme*, warmly sung by Judith Malafronte, as is *Ombra mai fù*. The counter-tenor Brian Asawa, in the role of Xerxes' brother, Arsamene, is equally expressive with rich even tone and fine agility, and Jennifer Smith as the heroine, Romilda, is particularly effective in her dramatic arias. Lisa Milne as her sister, Atalanta, nicely catches an ironic tone, with Susan Bickley fresh and agile as Amastre. Characterful baritone contributions from David Thomas (as a comic servant) and Dean Ely, with the chorus's brief interjections adding brightness and sparkle. Full, open sound.

On Sony Carolyn Watkinson may not be the most characterful of singers in the high castrato role of Xerxes himself, but it is good to have the elaborate roulades so accurately sung. The celebrated *Ombra mai fù* is most beautiful. Paul Esswood is similarly reliable in the role of Arsamene (originally taken by a woman) and the counter-tenor tone is pure and true. Barbara Hendricks and Anne-Marie Rodde are both outstanding in smaller roles, and the comic episodes (most unexpected in Handel) are excellently done. There are detailed stylistic points one might criticize in his rendering (for instance the squeeze effects on sustained string notes) but the vitality is never in doubt, and the close recording is vivid too. As in the rest of this series of Sony reissues, the snag is the absence of an English translation.

Silla (complete).

(N) *** Somm SOMMCD 227-8 (2). Bowman, Lunn, Marsh, Baker, Nicholls, Cragg, Dixon, London Handel O, Darlow.

Handel's early opera, *Silla*, is a curiosity. It is not known precisely when it was written, probably in 1713, and it is not even certain that it was ever performed in Handel's lifetime. The story about the predatory Roman dictator, Sulla (spelt Silla in the eighteenth century), is bizarre, with a forced happy ending, but over its compact span – three acts in under two hours – it has one delightful number after another, all relatively brief with no longueurs anywhere. Silla's slumber aria, *Dolce nume*, is ravishing, as is the touching aria for Silla's estranged wife, Metella, *Io noin chiedo più*, while Silla's aria, *La vendetta*, and that of his enemy, Claudio, *Con tromba guerriera*, with trumpets blazing, are fine examples of the martial Handel.

Denys Darlow conducts a fresh, stylish performance with his London Handel Festival forces, recorded live at the Royal College of Music. Textures are clean and rhythms light and resilient, with James Bowman in the title role leading a consistently reliable team. Rachel Nichollas as Metella is not as steady as the rest, but everyone copes very well with florid vocal writing, with a live occasion, well caught, adding to the magnetism.

The Sorceress (pasticcio).

**(*) Ph. (IMS) 434 992-2. Te Kanawa, AAM, Hogwood.

This pasticcio, with items drawn from a whole range of Handel operas, was devised for a Dutch television programme. The CD – like the video version, complete with ballet interludes – is taken from the soundtrack, providing in effect a sequence of seven arias, sung with characteristic poise and sumptuous tone by Dame Kiri, spiced with instrumental pieces, mostly brief. Though the plot is broadly based on the situation in *Alcina*, only one aria is taken from that opera, *Ombre pallide*, which, preceded by an accompanied recitative, makes up by far the longest item. It seems even longer thanks to Dame Kiri's somewhat languid performance. Otherwise, even with speeds on the slow side, Dame Kiri sings gloriously, with four of Cleopatra's arias from *Giulio Cesare* – including the seduction aria, *V'adoro pupille* – providing the cornerstones. Hogwood draws fresh sounds from the Academy of Ancient Music but he might have sounded even sharper at faster speeds. The sound is clear and well-balanced.

Tamerlano (complete).

(M) *** Erato 2292 45408-2. Ragin, Robson, Argenta, Chance, Findlay, Schirrer, E. Bar. Sol., Gardiner.

(M) **(*) Sony SM3K 37893-2 (3). Ledroit, Elwes, Van der Sluis, Jacobs, Poulenard, Reinhart, La Grande Ecurie et la Chambre du Roy, Malgoire.

John Eliot Gardiner's live concert performance of *Tamerlano* presents a strikingly dramatic and immediate experience. Leading the cast are two outstanding counter-tenors, whose encounters provide some of the most exciting moments: Michael Chance as Andronicus, firm and clear, Derek Lee Ragin in the name-part equally agile and more distinctive of timbre, with a rich, warm tone that avoids womanliness. Nigel Robson in the tenor role of Bajazet conveys the necessary gravity, not least in the difficult, highly original G minor aria before the character's suicide; and Nancy Argenta sings with starry purity as Asteria. The only snag is the dryness of the sound, which makes voices and instruments sound somewhat aggressive on CD.

Malgoire's performance style here is less abrasive than it has been on some other opera sets, but one looks in vain for an element of elegance or charm, despite consistently excellent contributions from a good band of soloists. The two counter-tenors are well contrasted – René Jacobs as ever a tower of strength – and Mieke van der Sluis is outstanding among the women. Some arias have been cut, but one has been added in Act I (*Nel mondo e nell'abisso*), and is well sung by the bass, Gregory Reinhardt. Good, clear, but not too dry sound gives a comparatively intimate effect, and the CD transfer is first class. The snag is that, as with the other reissues in this series, no translation is included with the full Italian libretto.

Teseo (opera; complete).

*** Erato 2292 45806-2 (2). James, Jones, Gooding, Ragin, Napoli, Gall, Les Musiciens du Louvre, Minkowski.

Using an Italian translation of a French libretto originally written for Lully 40 years earlier, Handel uniquely produced a hybrid between an Italian *opera seria* and a French tragédie lyrique, with the classical story of Theseus and Medea told in a brisk sequence of short arias. The score may not contain great Handel melodies, but it is characteristically fresh and imaginative. Marc Minkowski, among the liveliest of period performance specialists, brings out the inventiveness, helped by an excellent cast, dominated by British and American singers. These include Della Jones as Medea, Eirian James in the castrato role of Teseo, Julia Gooding as Agilea and characterful counter-tenors, Derek Lee Ragin and Jeffrey Gall, as Egeo and Arcane.

COLLECTIONS

Occasional songs: *7 Airs français, HWV 155; 4 Songs in Different Languages, HWV deest. 3 Theatre Songs, HWV 218 & 228; An answer to Collin's complaint; The beauteous Cloe; Di godere ha sperenza il mio core; The dream; From scourging rebellion; Hunting song; Je ne sçai quoi (Yes, I'm in love); Molly Mog; The poor shepherd; Stephon's complaint of love; The unhappy lovers. 4 Minuets; March in G.*

(N) **(*) Somm SOMMCD 226. Kirkby, Daniels, Instrumental Ens., & Ch., Nicolson.

Over two thousand songs are attributed to Handel and these so-called 'occasional' examples come from many sources. If not quite all of them are authentic, most of them have charm. Notably so the French songs, shared very colloquially by Emma Kirkby and Charles Daniels. Written in Rome in 1707, there are actually four songs and three recitatives. The most interesting is *Nos plaisirs serant peu durables*, a chaconne with ground bass, later used in *Alexander's Feast*, while the German Lied in the following group has a nimble cello obbligato, and the Spanish item has a rather lovely tune which Handel was also to re-use later.

Many of the English items are in a simple pastoral style. *The Dream (beneath a shady willow)* draws on the opening chorus of *Acis and Galatea* and *The beauteous Cloe* transforms a melancholy aria from *Ottone* into a lighthearted swain's praise of his beloved. The theatrical songs would fit readily into a piece like *The Beggar's Opera*, and that especially applies to the strophic songs, notably the patriotic numbers with chorus *Stand round my brave boys* and the lively closing *From scouring rebellion*. Both Emma Kirkby, who sings as sweetly as ever, and the fresh-voiced Charles Daniels have just the right, easy style for this undemanding repertoire and the performances are pleasingly spontaneous. The instrumental items are slight, but used as intermezzi they are effective enough. The accompaniments are ever-spirited and the recording excellent. Not an essential anthology perhaps, but one which shows another facet of Handel's vocal style. Full texts are included.

Arias: (i) *Cantanta à 3: La Rodinella. Admeto: Cangio d'aspetto. Alexander Balus: Convey me to some peaceful shore. Ottone: La Speranzaè giunta;Vieni, o figlio. Partenope: Voglio dire. Rinaldo: Lascia ch'io pianga. Rodelinda: Dove sei.* (ii) *Alcina: Pensa a chi geme. Alexander's Feast: Revenge, Timotheus cries. Ezio: Se un*

bell'ardier. *Hercules: The God of Battle. Samson: Honour and arms. Semele: Leave me, loathsome light. Susanna: Peace crowned with roses. Theodora: Wide spread his name.*

(N) ** Australian Decca Eloquence [ADD] 461 593-2. ASMF with (i) Greevy, cond. Leppard; (ii) with Robinson, cond. Ledger.

This CD pairs two LPs from the mid-1960s. Bernadette Greevy's fine, rich, if sometimes unwieldy contralto voice is well caught here. She is at her best in the expansive phrases where one is treated to a glorious stream of sound, though interpretations could be more imaginative, and it is a pity that she was reluctant to decorate the da capo arias. Leppard provides excellent accompaniments, Forbes Robinson had built up a formidable reputation at Covent Garden when these recordings were made, and he shows versatility in these often taxing arias. Though he fails to give them the variety one would ideally like, they are not dull, and all the items are firm favourites. This CD represents a good old-fashioned approach to Handel singing.

Airs, 'scènes célèbres', sinfonias and instrumental music from: *Alcina; Admeto; Giulio Cesare; Radamisto; Rodelinda; Serse. Concerto grosso (Alexander's Feast).*

❀ *** HM HMC 901685. Scholl, Berlin Akademie für Alte Musik.

Handel's most celebrated aria, *Ombra mai fù*, is radiantly sung here, with firm golden tone, alongside the equally lovely *Chiudetevi, miei lumi* from *Admeto*, and the glorious *Dove sei* from *Rodelinda*, with the programme capped by an unforgettably beautiful *Verdi prati* from *Alcina*. There are lively moments too, notably the genial *Va tacito*, which has a jolly horn obbligato. The splendid period-instrument accompaniments by the Berlin Akademie für Alte Musik make the 76-minute programme doubly diverting by playing sinfonias and dance movements (including an engaging suite from *Radamisto*) in between the arias. The Akademie end the programme with a superb account of the *Alexander's Feast Concerto grosso*, light and airy. None the less, it is Andreas Scholl's wonderfully stylish and moving singing that makes this record indispensable. The recording is full and immediate.

Opera arias: *Agrippina: Bel piacere. Orlando: Fammi combattere. Partenope: Furibondo spira il vento. Rinaldo: Or la tromba; Cara sposa; Venti turbini; Cor ingrato; Lascia ch'io pianga mia cruda sorta. Serse: Frondi tenere; Ombra mai fù.*

(M) *** Erato 0630 14069-2. Horne, I Solisti Veneti, Scimone – VIVALDI: *Orlando:* Arias. ***

Marilyn Horne (recorded at her peak in 1978) gives here virtuoso performances of a wide-ranging collection of Handel arias. The flexibility of her voice in scales and trills and ornaments of every kind remains formidable, and the power is extraordinary down to the tangy chest register. The voice is spot-lit against a reverberant acoustic. Purists may question some of the ornamentation, but most collectors will revel in the sheer confidence of this singing, and the reissue is made the more attractive by the apt inclusion of three key arias from Vivaldi's setting of one of the same operas, *Orlando*.

Arias: (i) *Agrippina: Pur ritorno a rimimiravi. Alexander's Feast: Revenge, Timotheus cries. Belshazzar: Oh, memory still bitter to my soul . . . Oppress'd with never-ceasing grief. Berenice: Si, tra i ceppi.* (ii) *Giulio Cesare: Va tacito e nascosto; Dall'ondoso periglio; Aure, deh per pietà.* (i) *Ottone: Con gelosi sospetti? . . . Dopo l'orrore. Samson: Honour and arms. Saul: To him ten thousands! . . . With rage I shall burst. Serse: Frondi tenere e belle? . . . Ombra mai fù. Solomon: Prais'd be the Lord . . . When the sun o'er yonder hills. Susanna: Down my old cheeks . . . Peace, crown'd with roses.*

(M) **(*) DG (IMS) (ADD) 449 551-2. Fischer-Dieskau; Munich Bach O; (i) Stadlmair; (ii) Richter.

Opening with an arresting performance of *Revenge, Timotheus cries* from *Alexander's Feast*, this 1977 collection then goes on to emphasize Handel's lyricism rather than the drama. Fischer-Dieskau is at his finest in *Ombra mai fu* from *Serse* (Handel's '*Largo*') with its beautifully controlled opening single-note crescendo. The voice is forwardly balanced and naturally caught; the orchestra is set in a resonant acoustic with modern-instrument textures are full rather than detailed, especially the two *Giulio Cesare* items now added, which were recorded much earlier (in 1969).

'*The Glories of Handel Opera*': *Alcina: Dream Music;* (i) *Sta nell'ircana pietrosa tana.* (ii) *Tornami a vagheggiar.* (iii) *Atalanta: Care selve.* (iv) *Berenice: Si, trai ceppi.* (v) *Ezio: Se un bell'ardire. Giulio Cesare:* (vi) *Da tempesta il legno infranto;* (i) *Piangero la sorte mia.* (vii) *Orlando: Ah stigie larve; Gia latra cerbero; Vaghe pupille, non piangente, no.* (viii) *Riccardo Primo: Atterrato il muro cada.* (ix) *Rinaldo: Laschia ch'io pianga. Rodelinda:* (x) *Dove sei;* (vi) *Io t'abbraccio.* (x) *Semele: Iris, hence away.* (xi) *Xerxes: Ombra mai fù.*

(M) *** Decca ADD/Dig. 458 249-2. (i) Berganza; (ii) Kirkby; (iii) Pavarotti; (iv) Evans; (v) Robinson; (vi) Sutherland (vii) Bowman; (viii) Mingardo; (ix) Greevy; (x) Horne; (xi) Tebaldi.

An ingenious anthology of Handel show-stoppers, drawing on a wide range of artists and recordings. With such a various programme, it makes stimulating listening, as much for the rarities as for the glittering showpieces. There recordings are nearly all bright and vivid, and full texts and translations are included as always in Decca's well-conceived Opera Gala series. Highly diverting.

Arias: *Alexander's Feast: The Prince, unable to conceal his pain; Softly sweet in Lydian measures. Atalanta: Care selve. Giulio Cesare: Piangerò. Messiah: Rejoice greatly; He shall feed his flock. Rinaldo: Lascia ch'io pianga. Samson: Let the bright Seraphim.*

**(*) Delos D/CD 3026. Augér, Mostly Mozart O, Schwarz – BACH: *Arias.* **(*)

Arleen Augér's bright, clean, flexible soprano is even more naturally suited to these Handel arias than to the Bach items

with which they are coupled. The delicacy with which she tackles the most elaborate divisions and points the words is a delight.

Arias from: *Giulio Cesare; Rinaldo; Rodelinda; Serse; Tamerlano.*

*** Virgin VC5 45326-2. Daniels, OAE, Norrington

Even in a generation that has produced a fine crop of counter-tenors, David Daniels stands out for the evenness and beauty of his voice, with an exceptionally rich lower register. Though the orchestra is not always as alert as it might be, his singing in this challenging group of arias, starting with *Ombra mai fù* from *Serse*, is warmly expressive in slow numbers and brilliantly dramatic in fast ones like *Al lampo dell'armi* from *Giulio Cesare*. Well-balanced sound.

Arias: *Judas Maccabaeus: Father of heaven. Messiah: O Thou that tellest; He was despised. Samson: Return O God of Hosts.*

⊛ (M) (***) Decca mono 433 474-2. Ferrier, LPO, Boult – BACH: Arias. (***)

Kathleen Ferrier had a unique feeling for Handel; these performances are unforgettable for their communicative intensity and nobility of timbre and line. She receives highly sympathetic accompaniments from Boult, another natural Handelian.

Arias: *Partenope: Sento amor; Ch'io parta?; Furibondo spira il vento. Tolomeo: Stille amare.*

*** Virgin VC5 45365-2. Daniels, OAE, Bicket – GLUCK, MOZART: *Arias.* ***

One of the *Partenope* arias provides the title for this exceptional disc of counter-tenor arias, ranging wide in its expressiveness, with David Daniels using his extraordinarily beautiful voice, clear and pure with none of the usual counter-tenor hoot, with the keenest artistry. Whether in deeply expressive lyrical numbers or in brilliant florid passages, his technique is immaculate, with the voice perfectly placed.

Overtures and Arias (1704–1726) from *Almira; Amadigi di Gaula; Giulio Cesare in Egitto; Rinaldo; Rodelinda; Rodrigo; Scipione* (with *March*); *Silla; Tamerlano.*

*** Hyp. CDA 66860. Kirkby, Brandenburg Consort, Goodman.

Overtures and Arias (1729–1741) from: *Alcina; Ariana in Creta; Atalanta; Berenice, regina d'Egitto; Deidamia; Ezio; Lotario; Partenope; Sosarme, re di Media.*

*** Hyp. CDA 67128. Kirkby, Brandenburg Consort, Goodman.

It might be thought that a collection interspersing Handel arias and overtures would not be particularly stimulating, but Emma Kirkby (in glorious voice) and Roy Goodman directing invigorating playing by the Brandenburg Consort prove just how enjoyable such a concert, or pair of concerts, can be. The first disc covers the first half of Handel's operatic career. After opening with Handel's second overture to *Almira*, Kirkby clears her throat with the sprightly roulades of *Vedrai s'a tuo dispetto*, and then enchants us with the melancholy line of *Perché viva il caro sposo* from *Rodrigo*. *Desterò dall'ampia Dite*, from *Amadigi di Gaula*, then brings a superb trumpet (Robert Farley) and oboe (Katharina Arfken) obbligato duet, and the oboe is again prominent in the introduction to the famous *V'adoro pupille* (from *Giulio Cesare*) while the lovely *Ombre piante* brings an echoing flute. Both are ravishingly sung and the trumpet returns for the lively closing regal number from *Scipione*.

Volume 2 deals with Handel's later operas and opens with the virtually unknown overture to *Lotario* (1729). Queen Adelaide's feisty aria which follows, shows Emma Kirkby at her nimblest, although she is hardly less dazzling in *Dite pace* from *Sosarme*. Other highlights include the lovely *Caro padre* from *Ezio* and the anguished recitative *Ah! Ruggiero* from *Alcina*, with its dramatic pauses, and a lovely flowing aria, *Ombre pallide*, both of which show Kirkby at her very finest. Perhaps the most delightful item here is *Chi t'intende?* from *Berenice*, where Kirkby clearly enjoys her continuing duet with the solo oboe. The closing number, *M'hai resa infelice*, comes from *Deidamia*. It opens with a touching lament and then its heroine curses Ulysses spectacularly for taking her lover Achilles away from her to the war against Troy.

Overtures and excerpts from *Jephtha; Joseph and His Brethren; Joshua; Solomon*. *Belshazzar: Let festival joy reign!*

**(*) Ara. Z 6720. Elwes, St Lukes CO.

There are lots of good tunes here and each selection includes a key aria strongly and dramatically sung by John Elwes. His manner is direct and forward, and he sings Handel's runs with gusto, using his vibrato with individuality. He tends to over-phrase in the lyrical music, yet can produce lovely tone in a number like *Waft her angels* (from *Jephtha*) which he does not attempt to decorate. Excellent recording, lively but with a nice degree of resonance.

HANSON, Howard (1896–1981)

(i) *Piano Concerto, Op. 36*. *For the First Time* (Suite); *Merry Mount Suite; Mosaics* (with composer's spoken analyses of all three orchestral works, concerning orchestral colour, pitch spectrum, musical form and 'tone relationships').

(M) *** Mercury (ADD) [434 370-2] (2). Eastman-Rochester O or Philh. O, composer (cond. & narrator); (i) with Mouledous.

Mercury not only pioneered many of Hanson's major works on record but also invited him to talk about his music. The three orchestral works here seem ideal for the purpose and his 'guide to the instruments of the orchestra' (directly related to the scoring of the *Merry Mount Suite*) is particularly instructive, the more so as the microphones have been set up to project solo instruments and groupings of woodwind, brass and strings with extraordinary realism and presence. The four-movement *Piano Concerto* is brilliantly played by Alfred Mouledous, especially in the Scherzo, marked *Allegro molto ritmico* (though they are not jazzy

rhythms) and the *giocoso* finale, while the slow movement is eloquently expressive. The recordings here are characteristically vivid, though occasionally very bright on top.

Symphonies Nos. 1–7; (i) *Piano Concerto in G. Elegy in Memory of Koussevitzky;* (i) *Fantasy Variations on a Theme of Youth, Op. 40. Mosaics; Merry Mount Suite, Op. 31; Pastorale for Oboe, Harp & Strings, Op. 38; Serenade for Flute, Harp & Strings, Op. 38; (ii) Lament for Beowulf, Op. 25; Song of Democracy.*

(M) *** Delos DE 3150 (4). Seattle SO, Schwarz; with (i) Rosenberger; (ii) Ch.

Gerard Schwarz has proved himself a master of Hanson's Nordic idiom and a consistently convincing interpreter of his symphonies, in which he secures high commitment and playing of the highest quality from the excellent Seattle orchestra. Carol Rosenberger is an excellent soloist in the two concertante piano works; the other soloists are drawn from the orchestra, and all make admirable contributions. This is all music which is easy to enjoy, and these artists are afforded full, brilliant recording from the Delos engineers within an expansive acoustic.

Symphonies Nos. 1 in E min. (Nordic), Op. 21; 2 (Romantic), Op. 30; (i) *Song of Democracy.*

(M) *** Mercury (ADD) [432 008-2]. Eastman-Rochester O, composer; (i) with Eastman School of Music Ch.

Hanson's own pioneering stereo recordings of his two best-known symphonies have a unique thrust and ardour. The *Song of Democracy* has plenty of dramatic impact and is also very well recorded.

Symphonies Nos. 1 in E min. (Nordic); 3; 5 (Sinfonia Sacra), Op. 43; (i) *Piano Concerto in G, Op. 36;* (ii) *Lament for Beowulf, Op. 25; Merry Mount: Suite, Op. 31.*

(B) *** Delos Double DE 3709 (2). Seattle SO, Schwarz; (i) with Rosenberger; (ii) with Symphony Ch.

Hanson is of Swedish descent and his music has a strong individuality of idiom and colour. The *First Symphony* is very like the more famous *Second* – warmly appealing, held together with indelible ideas which appear in all three movements. After getting to know these two works (which are also available coupled together on D/CD 3073) the musical terrain of the *Third* will seem familiar: the string threnodies surge purposely foward, there are similar rhythmic patterns and confident rhetorical gestures. The single movement *Sinfonia Sacra* – inspired by Christ's Passion – is also very succinct, again showing the composer's Nordic inheritance. The four-movement *Piano Concerto* (1948) is also compressed. Carol Rosenberger is a brilliant and responsive soloist. The *Lament for Beowolf* is an eloquent, elegiac piece with chorus which does not outstay its welcome. These Seattle performances have plenty of breadth and ardour. The recording, made in Seattle Opera House is gloriously expansive and the balance convincingly natural.

Symphonies Nos. 2 (Romantic), Op. 30; 4 (Requiem), Op. 34. Elegy (to the Memory of my Friend, Serge Koussevitsky), Op. 44.

(BB) **(*) Arte Nova 74321 43306-2. Jena PO, Montgomery.

David Montgomery has the full measure of the haunting, nostaglic feeling which permeates Hanson's symphonies, especially No. 2. The Jena Philharmonic cannot quite produce the body of tone that Schwarz has at his disposal with the superb Seattle orchestra on Delos, but there is no lack of vigour and spontaneity, with excellent brass playing, and in No. 4 Montgomery does not miss the Sibelian influences, especially in the sombre *Requiescat*. The touching tribute to Koussevitzky, who originally helped to put Hanson's music in front of the American public, is eloquently played. The Arte Nova recording is spacious and well balanced.

Symphonies Nos. (i) 2 (Romantic); 4 (Requiem); 6; (i–ii) 7 (Sea Symphony after Walt Whitman); (i) Elegy in Memory of Serge Koussevitzky; (i; iii) Fantasy Variations on a Theme of Youth (for piano and orchestra); (i) Mosaics; (iv) Serenade for Flute, Harp & Strings.

(B) *** Delos Double DE 3705 (2). (i) Seattle SO; (ii) Seattle Chorale; (iii) Rosenberger; (iv) Meredith, Jollies, NY Chamber Ens.; all cond. Schwarz.

A warm welcome for this introduction to the highly rewarding music of Howard Hanson, which includes his *Second Symphony*, melodically so memorable. Like this symphony, the *Fourth* has strong Nordic influences, and the *Sea Symphony* brings stirring choral writing to words of Walt Whitman. All three are superbly played in Seattle and Schwarz's powerful direction is thoroughly idiomatic and committed. The *Fantasy Variations* have a fine piano soloist in Carol Rosenberger. *Mosaics* is another set of variations, written in 1957 for Szell and the Cleveland Orchestra. The even briefer and delicately scored *Serenade* makes a delightful contrast, finely crafted. All this music is well worth getting to know, and much of it is very rewarding indeed. The recordings are in the demonstration bracket.

Symphony No. 3.

(***) Biddulph mono WHL 044. Boston SO, Koussevitzky (with MUSSORGSKY: *Khovanshchina: Prelude*. LIADOV: *The Enchanted Lake*. RIMSKY-KORSAKOV: *Legend of the Invisible City of Kitezh: Entr'acte. Dubinushka*. FAURE: *Pelléas et Mélisande: Prélude; La Fileuse; Mort de Mélisande* (**(*)).

With passionate playing from the Boston Orchestra, Koussevitzky's reading is powerfully committed, immediately establishing the northern atmosphere of Hanson's sound-world and building the finale steadily to its final climax with gripping concentration. The Biddulph transfer is very good, with sonic inadequacies easily forgotten. The other pieces, which come before the symphony, are all played superbly, but the sound is more variable. Highlights include the Mussorgsky *Khovanshchina Prelude*, sombrely paced, and the Liadov *Enchanted Lake*, both highly evocative and the latter remarkably full and atmospheric. The excerpts from Fauré's *Pelléas et Mélisande* are delicately done, although here climaxes are less refined.

Symphony No. 3; Elegy in Memory of my Friend Serge Koussevitzky, Op. 44; (i) Lament for Beowulf.

(M) *** Mercury (ADD) 434 302-2. Eastman-Rochester O, composer, (i) with Eastman School of Music Ch.

In the *Third Symphony* the string threnodies surge purposefully forward; there are similar rhythmic patterns and confident rhetorical gestures. This is highly accessible music. This applies also to the *Elegy*, while the cantata also makes an immediate impression and is very well sung. Here as in the orchestral works the 1958 Mercury sound is first rate. This disc is available only in the USA.

HARBISON, John (born 1938)

(i) Concerto for Double Brass Choir & Orchestra; (ii) The Flight into Egypt; (iii) The Natural World.

*** New World NW 80395-2. (i) LAPO, Previn; (ii) Anderson, Sylvan, Cantata Singers & Ens., Hoose; (iii) Felty, Los Angeles Philharmonic New Music Group, Harbison.

These three fine works provide an illuminating survey of the recent work of one of the most communicative of American composers today. The most striking and vigorous is the concerto he wrote as resident composer for Previn and the Los Angeles Philharmonic, and for the orchestra's brass section in particular. The other two works reveal the more thoughtful Harbison, the one a collection of three songs to nature poems by Wallace Stevens, Robert Bly and James Wright. *The Flight into Egypt* is a measured and easily lyrical setting of the story of the Holy Family fleeing from King Herod. Sanford Sylvan and the choir sing the main text, with Roberta Anderson interjecting as the Angel. Excellent performances and recording.

HARRIS, Roy (1898–1979)

(i) Violin Concerto; Symphonies Nos. 1; 5.

** Albany (ADD) AR012. (i) Fulkerston; Louisville O, Smith; Mester or Whitney.

The *First Symphony* is strong stuff, hardly less impressive than No. 3, but neither No. 5 nor the *Violin Concerto* adds greatly to our picture of its composer. Gregory Fulkerston gives a persuasive account of the solo part, but the strings of the enterprising Louisville Orchestra are wanting in body and lustre. The recordings are serviceable rather than distinguished.

Symphony No. 3.

(BB) **(*) Sony SMK 60594. NYPO, Bernstein – DIAMOND: *Symphony No. 4*; THOMPSON: *Symphony No. 2*. **(*)

This Sony account comes from 1961 and is quite simply the best LP/CD version artistically; only his mentor Koussevitzky's pioneering 78s have greater concentration and fire, and Bernstein runs him pretty close, even if the forwardly balanced recording is less than ideal. It comes with another classic of the American discography, the Diamond *Fourth Symphony*.

HARTMANN, Johan Peter Emilius

(1805–1900)

The Valkyrie, Op. 62.

** CPO 999 620-2 (2). Frankfurt RSO, Jurowski.

Written for Bournonville, Hartmann's ballet has a pretty lurid scenario, with plenty of blood and thunder. However, *The Valkyrie* remains curiously bland and tame, and its melodic ideas are obstinately unmemorable. Good playing and recording, and Bournonville fans will surely want it, but the music itself does not represent Hartmann at his best and we would hesitate to press its claims on non-specialists.

HARTMANN, Karl Amadeus

(1905–63)

(i) Chamber Concerto for Clarinet, String Quartet & Strings; (ii) Concerto funèbre for Violin & Strings; Symphony No. 4 for Strings.

(N) *** ECM 465 779-2. Munich CO, Christoph Poppen;
(i) Paul Meyer, Peterson Qt; (ii) Isabelle Faust.

The *Concerto funèbre*, the lament for the betrayal of Czecho-slovakia, is the best known work here, and Isabelle Faust holds her own alongside her rivals in previous recordings. The *Chamber Concerto* for the unusual combination of clarinet, string quartet and string orchestra (from 1935) is a rarity in which there are occasional touches of Bartók and at one point even Kodály. The performance of the *Fourth Symphony* comes off well. The playing here has eloquence, and the recording is absolutely first class. A well-filled disc which makes a more than serviceable calling-card for Hart-mann's music.

Symphonies Nos. 1–8.

(N) *** EMI CDS5 56911-2 (3). Bamberg SO, Metzmacher.

Ingo Metzmacher and his Bamberg Orchestra have been exploring the Karl Amadeus Hartmann symphonies over the last half-dozen years, and EMI have now collected them on these three CDs. All eight have been issued before on Wergo in performances by Kubelik and Zdeněk Macal, but these are currently out of circulation, and in any event this set is more economical. All the Hartmann symphonies up to the Sixth (1951–3) have their origins in earlier work. The *Third* (1949) is a conflation of movements from two different pieces written during the Second World War – the *Sinfonia tragica* (1940, revised 1943) and the *Klagegesang* (1944–5, revised 1946–7). The *Fourth* (1947), which is for string orchestra, was completed two years before the *Third*; it is sinewy and Bartókian but without the strong personality and memorability of the latter. The *Fifth*, subtitled *Symphonie concertante*, has its origins in a trumpet concerto from 1933. The *Sixth* is the most performed of all and was the first to be recorded, in the days of mono LP, but despite numerous recordings it has never gained more than a toe-hold on the repertory. Some find the post-expressionist language of Hartmann hard going, but he is a composer of both integrity

and substance and is well worth the effort. This expertly recorded set is now a strong recommendation.

Symphonies Nos. (i) 1 (Versuch eines Requiem); 6; Miserae.

*** Telarc CD 80528. LPO, Botstein; (i) with Van Nes.

Leon Botstein gives very committed accounts of the two symphonies recorded here. Jard van Nes is a distinct asset in the *First Symphony*. Those who want to investigate this challenging and respected composer (and who do not want to embark on the Metzmacher cycle) should find this a satisfying buy.

String Quartet No. 1 (Carillon).

(N) **(*) ECM 465 776-2. Zehetmeir Qt – BARTOK: *Quartet No. 4.* **(*)

The Hartmann *First Quartet* comes from 1933, and its sub-title, Carillon, alludes to the prize Hartmann's quartet won at a competition in Geneva in 1936. The Zehetmeir gives an intense and dedicated account of this work and readers with an interest in this composer need not entertain any serious artistic doubts. Bartók's *Fourth Quartet* (1928), whatever its merits, makes for short measure. The disc only runs to 43 minutes.

HARTY, Hamilton (1879–1941)

A Comedy Overture; (i) Piano Concerto; (ii) Violin Concerto; (iii) In Ireland (Fantasy). An Irish Symphony; (ii) Variations on a Dublin Air. With the Wild Geese. (iv) The Children of Lir; Ode to a Nightingale. Arrangement: Londonderry Air.

(M) *** Chan. 7035 (3). (i) Binns; (ii) Holmes; (iii) Fleming, Kelly; (iv) Harper; Ulster O, Thomson.

Bryden Thomson's box gathers together Harty's major orchestral and concertante works with great success, and each disc is also available separately – see below.

(i) Piano Concerto in B min.; (ii) Violin Concerto in D.

(M) *** Chan. 7032. (i) Binns, (ii) Holmes; Ulster O, Thomson.

Harty's *Piano Concerto*, written in 1922, has strong Rach-maninovian influences, but the melodic freshness remains individual in this highly sympathetic performance. Though the *Violin Concerto* has no strongly individual idiom, the invention is often touched with genuine poetry. Ralph Holmes gives a thoroughly committed account of the solo part and is well supported by an augmented Ulster Orchestra under Bryden Thomson.

An Irish Symphony; A Comedy Overture; (i) In Ireland (fantasy for flute, harp and orchestra). With the Wild Geese.

(M) *** Chan. 7034. Ulster O, Thomson, (i) with Fleming, Kelly.

An Irish Symphony; In Ireland; With the Wild Geese.

(N)(BB) *** Naxos 8.554732. Nat. SO of Ireland, O Duinn.

The *Irish Symphony* built on traditional themes, has won

great acclaim for its brilliant scoring and craftsmanship, with the Scherzo particularly engaging. It is extremely well played by the Ulster Orchestra under Bryden Thomson, while the *In Ireland Fantasy* is full of delightful Irish melodic whimsy. Melodrama enters the scene in the symphonic poem, *With the Wild Geese*, but its Irishry asserts itself immediately in the opening theme. Again a splendid performance and a high standard of digital sound.

The brief, dancing scherzo entitled *The Fair Day*, which may here be less genial on Naxos than it can be, but is the more exciting for being taken at breathtaking speed. The players of the National Symphony Orchestra of Ireland take up the challenge brilliantly, and bring all the necessary warmth to the other evocative movements, which like the two tone-poems, a generous fill-up, are atmospheric programme pieces inspired by Irish legends and places. Full, clear sound.

A John Field Suite.

(N) (M) *** EMI (ADD) CDM5 67431-2. Dilkes, E. Sinf. – FIELD: *Nocturnes;* IRELAND: *The Holy Boy;* LEIGH: *Harpsichord concertino.* ***

Harty's *John Field Suite* is lightweight charming music, mixing wit and Irish whimsy with nicely judged orchestral colouring. Dilkes's performance is sprightly and vividly recorded.

With the Wild Geese (symphonic poem).

(B) *** CfP (ADD) CD-CFP 4635. RSNO, Gibson – GERMAN: *Welsh Rhapsody;* MACCUNN: *Land of Mountain and Flood;* SMYTH: *Wreckers Overture.* ***

With the Wild Geese is a melodramatic piece about the Irish soldiers fighting on the French side in the Battle of Fontenoy. The ingredients – a jolly Irish theme and a call to arms among them – are effectively deployed; although the music does not reveal a strong individual personality, it is carried by a romantic sweep which is well exploited here. The 1968 recording still sounds most vivid, and this anthology makes a first-rate bargain.

Music for cello and piano: Butterflies; Romance & Scherzo, Op. 8; Wood-stillness.

(M) *** Dutton Epoch CDLX 7102. Fuller, Dussek – HURLSTONE: *Cello Sonata in D;* PARRY: *Cello Sonata in A.* ***

Slight but quite pleasing pieces that are fill-ups for the two cello sonatas by Hurlstone and Parry. Effective and accomplished playing from Andrew Fuller and Michael Dussek – and very well recorded too.

3 Pieces for Oboe & Piano.

(B) *** Hyp. Helios CDH 55008. Francis, Rasumovsky Qt. – BOUGHTON: *Pastorale;* HOWELLS: *Sonata;* RUBBRA: *Sonata.* ***

Harty's three oboe *Pieces*, played here with piano, were written for Henry Wood's 1911 Proms with an orchestral accompaniment. They are utterly charming in this more intimate version, and both artists respond to their disarming melodiousness, especially in the very Irish tune of the closing

A la campagne. The balance is too forward but the playing has delicacy of feeling and, if you turn the volume down, the effect is very pleasing.

VOCAL MUSIC

(i) *The Children of Lir; Ode to a Nightingale.*
(ii) *Variations on a Dublin Air.* Arrangement: *Londonderry Air.*

(M) *** Chan. 7033. Ulster O, Thomson, with (i) Harper; (ii) Holmes.

Harty's setting of Keats's *Ode to a Nightingale* is richly convincing, a piece written for his future wife, the soprano, Agnes Nicholls. The other work, directly Irish in its inspiration, evocative in an almost Sibelian way, uses the soprano in wordless melisma, here beautifully sung by Heather Harper. The performances are excellent, warmly committed and superbly recorded. The *Variations on a Dublin Air*, for violin and orchestra, and Harty's arrangement of the *Londonderry Air* have been added for the reissue.

HARVEY, Richard (born 1953)

Concerto antico (for guitar and small orchestra).

✪ *** Sony SK 68337. Williams, LSO, Daniel – GRAY: *Concerto.* *** ✪

Richard Harvey's highly atmospheric *Concerto antico* is easily the best concerto for the guitar since the work by Malcolm Arnold of several decades earlier, admirably written for the soloist and most imaginatively scored in the orchestra. As much a five-movement suite as a concerto, the piece uses old song- and dance-forms, but the composer's ideas are his own – and very tuneful they are, with an element of pastiche in their settings, yet nicely spiced with modern harmonic touches. In every way this is a masterly work, and it is played superbly by its commissioner and dedicatee, John Williams, splendidly accompanied by the LSO under Paul Daniel. The recording, ideally balanced, is of demonstration quality.

HASSE, Johann (1699–1783)

Sinfonias: in D, Op. 3/3; in F, Op. 3/5; Fugue in G min.
(i) *Motette: Chori angelici laetantes; Salve Regina in A;*
(ii) *Salve Regina in E flat.*

*** DG (IMS) 453 435-2. Musica Antiqua Köln, Goebel with (i) Fink. (ii) Bonney, Fink.

Given the commanding position he occupied in his lifetime, it is surprising that Hasse enjoys relatively little exposure on record. He was a truly international figure. Burney visited him in 1772 when he was living in Vienna, and it was for him that Hasse's daughters sang the *Salve Regina in E flat.* Bernarda Fink and Barbara Bonney share it with obvious delight. It is a lovely piece and the level of inspiration of its companions is high. The *Sinfonia in D* is the overture to *Cleofide,* the opera that put him on the map in Dresden in 1731. Quite apart from his work directing these performances, Reinhard Goebel has written richly informative notes: he calls the three vocal pieces here 'sublime in anyone's language' – and he is absolutely right. First-rate sound, very clean and well balanced.

(i; ii) Aria 'Ah Dio, ritornate' from La conversione di San'Agostino for viola da gamba and harpsichord; (iii; i–ii) Flute Sonata in B min., Op. 2/6; (ii) Harpsichord Sonata in C min. Op. 7/6; (iv; i–iii) Cantatas: Fille, dolce mio bene; Quel vago seno, O Fille; Venetian ballads: Cos e' sta Cossa?; Grazie agli inganni tuoi; No ste' a condanare; Si' la gondola avere', non crie'.

(M) *** CRD 3488. (i) Headley; (ii) Proud; (iii) Hadden; (iv) Baird.

The cantatas here are written in a pastoral style, with important flute obbligatos (a legacy from Frederick). They show much charm and distinct expressive feeling, and Julianne Baird has exactly the right voice for them, with a freshness of tone and purity of line matched by the right degree of ardour. The Harpsichord Sonata, alternating fast and slow movements, is inventive and good-humoured and the Aria for viola da gamba readily shows the composer's operatic style, while the Venetian ballads which close this elegantly performed and very well-recorded concert are also full of character, cultivated rather than folksy in their more popular idiom.

HAUG, Halvor (born 1952)

(i) Symphony No. 3 (The Inscrutable Life); Furuenes sang (Song of the Pines). (ii) Silence for Strings; Insignia: Symphonic Vision.

*** Simax PSC 1113. (i) Norrköping SO; (ii) ECO; Ruud.

The Norwegian composer Halvor Haug is a composer of substance. His sensibility is strongly Nordic and at one with the sounds and the landscape of those latitudes. The Third Symphony (1991–3) is a large-scale piece in two parts, lasting some 36 minutes. Its subtitle incidentally alludes to the famous Inextinguishable of Nielsen. This is meditative, concentrated in atmosphere and static. The ending uses a nightingale as does Respighi in The Pines of Rome but the effect will not convince all his admirers. Stillhet or 'Silence' (1977) is an evocation of tranquillity (a better translation might have been 'stillness'); and Song of the Pines (1987), a threnody on the desecration of the natural world, has real eloquence. Insignia (1993) is a response to the other-worldly landscape of the Lofoten islands. Ole Kristian Ruud gets good results from the Norrköping Orchestra and the sound is excellent.

HAYDN, Josef (1732–1809)

Cello Concertos in C & D, Hob XVIIb/1–2.

*** Ph. (IMS) 420 923-2. Schiff, ASMF, Marriner.

(M) *** EMI (ADD) CDM5 66896-2 [5 66948]. Du Pré, ECO, Barenboim OR LSO, Barbirolli – BOCCHERINI: Cello Concerto in B flat (arr. GRUTZMACHER).

(BB) *** Naxos 8.550059. Kanta, Capella Istropolitana, Breiner – BOCCHERINI: Cello Concerto. ***

**(*) Virgin VC5 45014-2. Mørk, Norwegian CO, Brown.

Cello Concertos Nos. 1 in C; 2 in D, Hob VIIb/1–2.

**(*) DG 463 180-2. Wang, Gulbenkian O, Tang.

(M) **(*) EMI CDM5 67234-2 [567263]. Rostropovich, ASMF.

(N) (BB) **(*) EMI Encore CDE5 74734-2. Harrell, ASMF, Marriner – VIVALDI: Concertos. **

(i) Cello Concertos in C; D, Hob VIIb/1–2. Overture in G (Lo speziale).

**(*) EMI CDC5 56535-2. (i) Chang; Dresden State O, Sinopoli.

(i) Cello Concertos in C; D, Hob VIIb/1–2. Sinfonia Concertante in B flat for Violin, Cello, Oboe, Bassoon & Orchestra, Hob I/105.

*** DHM/BMG 05472 77506-2. (i) Suzuki; La Petite Bande, Kuijken.

(i) Cello Concertos in C & D, Hob VIIb/1–2; (ii) Sinfonia Concertante in B flat. Symphony No. 13: Adagio cantabile in G.

*** RCA 09026 68578-2 (i) Isserlis; (ii) Blakenstijn, Boyd, Wilkie, COE, Norrington.

Cello Concertos in C & D, Hob VIIb/1–2; Symphony No.104. (arr. Salomon).

*** Channel Classics CCS 7395. Wispelwey, Florilegium.

Steven Isserlis is a commanding soloist in both cello concertos, and unlike many rivals he does not linger in slow movements, preferring flowing speeds. Nor does he race breathlessly in finales. Particularly with such a generous coupling, this makes a first choice among modern versions, if the Sinfonia Concertante is wanted also. Here the other soloists are distinguished principals from the COE, playing just as pointedly as Isserlis. Vivid and immediate sound.

Hidemi Suzuki is second only to Isserlis as a soloist in these two concertos, playing with fine tone, sensibility and refinement, and producing electrifying bravura in the finales – especially the C major which Kuijken takes exhilaratingly briskly. La Petite Bande provides the stylish soloists for the engaging Sinfonia concertante, and the balance is again just right.

Pieter Wispelwey is also an inspired soloist in the period performance with Florilegium, at times abrasive but always transparent in texture with the soloist's clean articulation allowing fast speeds in outer movements with no feeling of rush. The central Adagios by contrast are surprisingly slow, not as elegant as some, but deeply felt. Salomon's arrangement of Haydn's last symphony for flute, string quartet and piano makes an unusual if lightweight coupling.

Heinrich Schiff produces a beautiful sound, as indeed do the Academy under Marriner. These are impressively fresh-sounding modern instrument performances with lyrical and affectionate playing from all concerned. The recording has the realistic timbre, balance and bloom one associates with Philips.

Jacqueline du Pré's recording of the C major Concerto in April 1967 was the first she made with her husband, Daniel Barenboim, and she gives a performance of characteristic warmth and intensity. Equally, with Barbirolli scaling his accompaniment to match the inspirational approach of his young soloist, the performance of the better known *D major Concerto* is just as warm and expressive, and the romantic feeling is matched by an attractively full, well-balanced sound-picture.

Ludovít Kanta is a fine soloist. The excellent Naxos recording is made in a bright, resonant acoustic in which every detail is clearly registered, though the players are perhaps forwardly placed. The accompaniments are alert and fresh. Kanta plays contemporary cadenzas. An excellent bargain.

Truls Mørk gives characterful readings of both concertos, full of individual touches. The outer movements of the *C major* are daringly fast, though the opening movement of the *D major* brings a surprisingly relaxed approach. Both the slow movements are romantically spacious. Well recorded, though at premium price, with no extra work included, it is hardly a first recommendation.

Jian Wang gives authoritative, warm, finely conceived and detailed readings of both concertos; in the slow movements he adopts very spacious speeds, sustaining them well with rapt intensity, very much in the modern tradition, with no concern for period practice. Speeds otherwise are generally well chosen, even if the finale of the *C major* is hectically fast, challenging Wang (like Rostropovich) to wonderfully clean articulation. Warm, full sound. Excellent recording, but again no couplings.

Rostropovich's virtuosity is astonishing. True, there are moments of breathless phrasing, and Rostropovich's style has acquired a degree of self-indulgence in the warmth of expressiveness and this is reflected in the accompaniment from the ASMF, which he also directed. Just the same, the solo playing is very compelling for all its romantic emphasis and slow movements are certainly beautiful.

The attractions of Lynn Harrell's super-bargain coupling are enhanced by the inclusion of two Vivaldi concertos interspersed with Haydn (although the recorded sound is strikingly different). Harrell, rather after the manner of Rostropovich, seeks to turn these elegant concertos into big, virtuoso pieces, helped by Marriner's beautifully played accompaniments. Although touches of romantic expressiveness tend to intrude, the result is enjoyable, even if cadenzas are distractingly long.

The young Korean cellist Han-Na Chang gives warm but essentially refined readings of both concertos and in the beautiful slow movement of the *D major*, she draws out the melodic line exquisitely on a half-tone, and she conveys pleasure in what she does. Sinopoli affectionately fines down the orchestral accompaniment to match his soloist's delicacy, but some may prefer a more robust, more mature approach in eighteenth-century concertos. The Italian *overture* (in effect a miniature sinfonia) is most deftly played and makes an engaging interlude between the two works.

(i) *Cello Concerto No.1 in C, Hob VIIb/1;* (ii; iv) *Horn Concertos Nos. 1–2;* (iii; iv) *Trumpet Concerto in D.*

(M) *** Decca (ADD) 430 633-2. (i) Rostropovich, ECO, Britten; (ii) Tuckwell; (iii) Stringer; (iv) ASMF, Marriner.

Rostropovich's earlier (1964) stereo recording of the *C major*

Cello Concerto for Decca is warmly romantic, and some may feel he takes too many liberties in the slow movement, but with Britten accompaying it is magnetic throughout. A first-rate coupling in excellent 1966 versions of both the *Horn Concertos* by Barry Tuckwell in peak form and Alan Stringer's 1967 account of the *Trumpet Concerto*.

Cello Concerto No. 2 in D, Hob VIIb/2.

(M) **(*) BMG/Melodiya (ADD) 74321 40724. Shafran, USSR SO, Järvi – TCHAIKOVSKY: *Andante cantabile* etc. **(*)

Daniil Shafran enjoys cult status among cellists – understandably so, you may think, on hearing this 1962 account of the Haydn *D major Concerto*, made when Järvi was twenty-five. Shafran had a wonderfully rich, singing tone and an intensity that is always held within the right limits. He obviously inspired both the USSR Symphony Orchestra and Neeme Järvi. By the side of the finest recordings of the period, the sound is two-dimensional but it is more than adequate, and playing like this is very special.

(i) *Cello Concertos: in C, Hob VIIb/1; in D, Hob VIIb/2;* (ii) *Violin Concertos: in C; in A; in G, Hob VIIa/1, 3 & 4;* (ii; iii) *Double Concerto for Violin & Harpsichord in F, Hob XVIII/6.*

(B) *** Ph. Duo (ADD) 438 797-2 (2). ECO with (i) Walevska, De Waart; (ii) Accardo; (iii) Canino.

The three *Violin Concertos* are all early; the *C major*, written for Tomasini, is probably the best. The other two have come into the limelight fairly recently. Accardo plays with great elegance and charm. It would be idle to pretend that either they or the *Double Concerto for Violin and Harpsichord* is great music. in that the soloists are rather forward, but the the 1980 recording has been well transferred. The two cello concertos are much better known; Christine Walevska presents them freshly, well partnered by Edo de Waart and the ECO. She is balanced almost within the orchestra, to give an agreeable chamber-like quality to the music-making.

(i) *Cello Concertos in C, 406 VIIb/1; in D, VIIb/2;* (ii) *Trumpet Concerto;* (iii) *Symphonies Nos. 94 (Surprise); 100 (Military); 104 (London);* (iv) *Andante with Variations in F min., Hob XVII/6.*

(N) (B) ** DG Panorama (ADD/DDD) 469 148-2 (2).
(i) Fournier, Lucerne Fest. Strings, Baumgartner;
(ii) Herseth, Chicago SO, Abbado; (iii) BPO, Karajan;
(iv) Brendel.

Fournier plays with real style in his late 1960s recordings of the *Cello Concertos*, and if the accompaniments are not quite so distinguished, they are enjoyable, though the recording is a mite thin. Plush describes Karajan's well-known trio of Haydn symphonies: they are impressively played, with much power and dignity, if without the sparkle that Jochum and Colin Davis brought to them. Herseth's digital account of the *Trumpet Concerto* is well played and recorded, but lacks brio. The *Andante with Variations* (also digital) finds Brendel on top form, and even non-Brendel fans will admire his jewelled precision as well as his musical intelligence.

(i) *Harpsichord Concertos: in F, Hob XVIII/3; in G, Hob XVIII/4; in D, Hob XVIII/11; (i; ii) Double Concerto in F for Harpsichord & Violin, Hob XVIII/6; (iii) Concertini: in C, Hob XIV/3; in C, Hob XIV/11; in C, Hob XIV/12; Concertino (Divertimento) in G, Hob XIV/13; Concertino in F, Hob XIV/F2; Divertimenti in C, Hob XIV/4; in C, Hob XIV/7; in C, Hob XIV/8; in F, Hob XIV/9; in C, Hob XIV/C2.*

(B) *** Ph. Duo (ADD) 446 542-2 (2). Koopman;
- (i) Amsterdam Musica Antiqua or Amsterdam Bar. O;
- (ii) with Huggett; (iii) Goebel, Stuurop, Medlam.

Ton Koopman's admirable Philips Duo set covers the 14 concertante Haydn keyboard works listed in the Hoboken catalogue now thought to be authentic. The present coverage includes the ten small concertos from the 1760s called either *Divertimenti* or *Concertini*, which are of little real substance but which still make attractive, undemanding listening. Here the accompanying group is made up of Reinhard Goebel and Alda Stuurop (violins) and Charles Medlam (cello), all playing on period instruments. The four longer concertos, including the rightly famous *D major* (scored for oboes and horns) and the *Double Concerto for Violin, Keyboard and Strings*, Hob XVIII/6, use a larger accompanying group, which Koopman directs from the keyboard. As sound, these recordings could hardly be bettered: the balance is finely judged and the acoustic warm, with detail registered perfectly. The performances are alive and highly accomplished. Though occasionally Koopman might have allowed the music to unfold at a more leisurely pace, this invites the strongest recommendation.

(i) *Harpsichord Concerto in D, Hob XVIII/11. Sonata No. 36 in C sharp min.; Minuet; German Dance No. 5 (Ballo tedesco).*

(***) Biddulph mono LHW 032. Landowska; (i) with O, Bigot
- BACH: *Harpsichord Concerto No. 1 in D min., BWV 1052 (**). HANDEL: Concerto, Op. 4/6; Suite No. 15: Air & Variations. (**(*))*

With neatly scaled playing from Landowska, and a crisp clean accompaniment from Bigot, the Haydn concerto is much more attractive than its heavyweight Bach coupling and the encores too are very pleasing, especially the sharply rhythmic *German Dance*. The recording is surprisingly good (a bit thin on violin timbre, but not unpleasantly so) and this is a most refreshing view of Haydn, dating back to 1937.

Horn Concerto No. 1 in D, Hob VII/d3.

(N) *** Arabesque Z 6750. Rose, St Luke's Chamber Ens. – FORSTER; Leopold MOZART; TELEMANN: *Horn Concertos. ****

(BB) *** Teldec (ADD) 0630 12324-2. Baumann, Concerto Amsterdam, Schröder – DANZI: *Horn Concerto in E*; ROSETTI: *Horn Concerto in D min. ****

(N) (*(**) BBC mono BBCL 4066-2. Brain, BBC Midland O, Wurmser (with instrumental recital (***)).

Stewart Rose plays the outer movements ebulliently and, like Dennis Brain, phrases the eloquent slow movement richly, yet sonorously relishing the passages where the melodic line dips down into the horn's lower register. He has the big, broad tone typical of a modern wide bore instrument. The St Lukes Chamber Orchestra provide a lively, supportive accompaniment and the recording is excellent, as are the couplings. A first rate disc in every way.

Baumann's 1969 account has bold, classical lines, emphasized by the spacious sound of the remastered recording, which gives a full, open horn-timbre and expansive string-timbre. The *Adagio* is rather sombre here (it has some splendidly resonating low notes from the soloist), but the finale is spirited enough, and this is very attractive at its new budget price.

Dennis Brain's performance brings his characteristic combination of finesse and bonhomie but alas the BBC recording, already rough in the first movement, produces severe harmonic distortion in the *Adagio* which does not improve in the finale.

Oboe Concerto in C, Hob VIIg/C1.

*** Dutton Lab./Barbirolli Soc. (ADD) CDSJB 1016. Rothwell, Hallé O, Barbirolli – CORELLI; MARCELLO: *Oboe Concertos *** (with Instrumental Recital: C. P. E. BACH; LOEILLET; TELEMANN: Sonatas etc. **).*

Haydn's *Oboe Concerto* is of doubtful authenticity, but in this account played by Evelyn Rothwell, deftly accompanied by her husband, Haydn surely would have welcomed the attribution. The orchestra is given a very positive classicism by Barbirolli's firmness, and in the opening movement his wife's delicacy makes a delightful foil for the masculine orchestral presentation. The slow movement is well brought off and the delicacy of articulation returns in the finale. The 1958 recording is resonant and the skilful Dutton transfer almost entirely disguises its age.

Piano Concertos: in F, Hob XVIII/3; in G, Hob XVIII/4; in C, Hob XVIII/5; in F, Hob XVIII/7; in G, Hob XVIII/9; in C, Hob XVIII/10; in D, Hob XVIII/11; in C, Hob XIV/12; in G, Hob XIV/13; in F, Hob XVIII/F2; Divertimenti in C (for piano and strings), Hob XIV/C2 & XIV/4.

(N) (B) ** Teldec Ultima 8573-85192-2 (2). Entremont, V. CO.

More than half the concertos here are almost certainly spurious, and the music is pretty thin. Among the authentic concertos, the famous *D major*, Hob XVIII/11, readily stands out and is given a lively, robust account by Entremont and the Vienna Chamber Orchestra. He makes no attempt to emulate period manners, but the playing is bold and unsentimental and the articulation crisp. The recording is good, if rather forward, but it is now available inexpensively on the Ultima series.

Piano Concertos in F; in G; in D, Hob XVIII 3, 4 & 11.

*** EMI CDC5 56950-2. Andsnes, Norwegian CO.

Piano Concertos: in F, Hob XVIII/3; in G, Hob XVIII/4; in D, Hob XVIII/11.

*** Sony SK 48383. Ax, Franz Liszt CO.

(BB) *** Arte Nova 74321 51635-2. Smirnova, Sinfonia Varsovia, Schmidt-Gertenbach.

Piano Concertos: in F, Hob XVIII/3; in D, Hob XVIII/11.

(N) (M) ** Guild GMCD 7206. Thew, Zürich Camerata, Tschupp – KUHN: *Concierto de Tenerife.* **

Leif Ove Andsnes gives inspired performances of the three Haydn piano concertos that are fully authenticated, not just the early *F major* and *G major*, here made to sparkle brightly, but the best known and finest of the series, *No. 11 in D.* Andsnes justifies his generally brisk speeds for outer movements in subtle pointing of rhythm and phrase, articulating crisply – always individual without being self-conscious. His preference is for speeds on the slow side in middle movements, more measured than eighteenth-century manners might allow, but rapt and naturally expressive; in his hands and those of the Norwegian Chamber Orchestra, which he directs from the keyboard, these concertos blossom. These are fresh, poetic and brilliant performances, recorded with exemplary clarity.

Emanuel Ax also gives these concertos on the modern grand piano, and he does so with great elegance and finesse. He evidently enjoys a good rapport with the Franz Liszt Chamber Orchestra, who respond warmly to his direction, and throughout all three concertos the music sounds fresh and sparkling. The quality of the recording is outstanding; the piano sounds real and lifelike, and the balance is well struck. But Andsnes is a clear first choice.

These works are also played with freshness and point by Lisa Smirnova and admirably accompanied with a sure sense of style and a nice feeling for light and shade by Volker Schmidt-Gertenbach and the excellent Sinfonia Varsovia. The recording is beautifully balanced.

The Guild issue is a memorial to the American pianist Warren Thew, who lived in Zürich from 1956 until his untimely death in 1984. He was a composer and the author of around two hundred poems in the Rumanche language, which were published posthumously in 2000 to much acclaim. In the two Haydn concertos he is unfailingly musical and sensitive, though the Camerata Zürich is no match for the Norwegian Chamber Orchestra (and for Leif Ove Andsnes). The recording from 1972 is acceptable and well balanced, but wanting in range and freshness.

Piano Concertos in G, Hob XVIII/4; F, Hob XVIII/7; D, Hob XVIII/11.

(BB) *** Virgin 2 x 1 VBD5 61881-2 (2). Pletnev, Deutsche Kammerphilharmonie – *Piano Sonatas Nos. 33, 60 & 62 etc.* ***

The keyboard concertos are by general consent not the greatest Haydn and, of the records reviewed here, one is of doubtful authenticity: the *F major* (XVIII/7 in the Hoboken catalogue) is probably by Wagenseil; and not very much is known about the *G major*, which is very early. In both pieces, as well as in the well-known *D major Concerto*, Mikhail Pletnev offers playing of great character and personality. He obviously enjoys a splendid rapport with the Deutsche Kammerphilharmonie, and the colour and feeling Pletnev discovers in these pieces is a source of wonder, both distinctive and distinguished. This now comes inexpensively coupled on a Virgin Double with Pletnev's accounts of three key piano sonatas – a superb bargain.

(i) *Piano Concerto in D, Hob XVIII/11;* (ii) *Violin Concertos: in C; in G; Hob VIIa/1 & 4;* (ii–iii) *Double Concerto for Violin & Harpsichord in F, Hob XVIII/6.*

*** Sup. SU 3265-2. (i) Davidovich; (ii) Sitkovetsky; (iii) Hudeček; Prague CO, Sitkovetsky.

Here is the most winning of Haydn's solo keyboard concertos together with two of the violin concertos, including the *C major* with its engaging, serenade-like, cantabile slow movement. They are impeccably played, with just the right degree of expressive feeling. The piano used by Bella Davidovich has a crisp, clean timbre, rather like a fortepiano, only with more colour. What clinches the appeal of this attractive collection is the delightful account of the *Double Concerto*. Here the interplay of piano and violin is perfectly balanced. This disc makes a splendid case for the use of modern instruments in this repertoire when Sitkovetsky directs the accompanying group so stylishly, with the overall effect pleasingly intimate.

Trumpet Concerto in E flat.

*** Ph. 420 203-2. Hardenberger, ASMF, Marriner – HERTEL ***; HUMMEL ***; STAMITZ: *Concertos.* ***

(N) (M) *** Sony (ADD) SMK 37846. Marsalis, Nat. PO, Leppard – HUMMEL: *Concerto* *** (with L. MOZART: *Concerto* ***).

(B) *** CfP 573 4392. Balmain, RLPO, Kovacevich – MOZART: *Horn Concertos.* ***

*** EMI CDC5 55231-2. André, Franz Liszt O, Budapest, Rolla – HERTEL; HUMMEL: *Trumpet Concertos* ***; MARCELLO: *Concerto in D min.* **(*)

Hardenberger's playing of the noble line of the *Andante* is no less telling than his fireworks in the finale and, with Marriner providing warm, elegant and polished accompaniments throughout, this is probably the finest single collection of trumpet concertos in the catalogue. However, these performances are also available on a Philips Duo (464 028-2), containing the finest collection of concertante music for trumpet in the catalogue.

Marsalis is splendid too, his bravura no less spectacular, with the finale a tour de force, yet never aggressive in its brilliance. His way with Haydn is eminently stylish, as is Leppard's lively and polished accompaniment.

With Stephen Kovacevich as conductor, Ian Balmain favours extreme speeds for Haydn's delectable *Trumpet Concerto*, playing brilliantly. It makes an apt and attractive coupling for Claire Briggs's fine recordings of all four Mozart *Horn Concertos*, very well recorded.

Maurice André has recorded this work a number of times over the years, and his touch is as sure as ever, his phrasing if anything even more elegant. The Hertel and Hummel concertos are equally enjoyable, but the Marcello concerto was written for the oboe, and although André manages the high tessitura of the Adagio with skill and taste, such a transcription seems superfluous.

Violin Concertos Nos. 1 in C; 4 in G, HobVIIa/1 & 4; (i) *Double Concerto for Violin & Piano, HobVIII/6.*

(B) *** Hyp. Helios CDH 55007. Adelina Oprean, European CO; (i) with Justin Oprean.

Violin Concertos Nos. 1 in C; 4 in G, Hob VIIa/1 & 4;
(i) Sinfonia Concertante in B flat for Violin, Cello, Oboe,
Bassoon & Orchestra, Hob I/105.

(N) (B) *** Virgin x 2 VBD5 61800-2 (2). Wallfisch, OAE; (i) with
Watkin, Robson, Warnock – *Symphonies Nos. 26; 52; 53.* ***

Haydn's *Violin Concertos* are early works; the *C major* with
its winding, serenade-like melody is probably the finer, but
the *G major* too has an eloquent *Adagio* and a bustling finale.
Wallfisch leads the Orchestra of the Age of Enlightenment
from her bow and proves a highly sensitive soloist – these
performances are if anything even more impressive than
those of the Mozart concertos by the same soloist. Her
serenely reflective account of the *Adagio molto* of the *C
major* is memorable. In the *Sinfonia Concertante* the smiling
interplay of the various wind and string soloists has never
been bettered on record and the use of period instruments
brings a pleasing intimacy and plenty of spirit. The recording
is truthfully balanced and vivid. These performances now
come on a Virgin Double, coupled with three symphonies
admirably played by Kuijken's Petite Bande.

The Helios disc makes a good modern-instrument
alternative for those interested in the well-crafted (and very
well-played) *Double Concerto for Violin and Piano*, which
has a particularly striking dialogue between the two soloists
in the central *Largo*. In the two solo concertos, Adelina
Oprean proves a persuasive soloist with a dulcet but not
over-opulent timbre. The central cantilena of the *G major
Concerto*, with its pizzicato accompaniment, is delightful,
and she directs the orchestra in outer movements with
vigour and point. The sound is good too.

Violin Concertos Nos. 3 in A; 4 in G, HobVIIa/3–4.

(BB) **(*) Virgin 2 x 1 VBD5 61504-2 (2). Seiler, City of L. Sinf.
– BEETHOVEN; MENDELSSOHN: *Concertos.* **(*)

Unlike the coupled Beethoven and Mendelssohn concertos
on this generous Virgin bargain Double, the soloist Mayumi
Seiler also directs the orchestra. The effect is very much of
chamber performances – warm, polished and comparatively
intimate. The result is musically enjoyable, if not distinctive,
but this inexpensive two-disc set offers five concertos, all
very well played and recorded, for the cost of a single
medium-priced CD.

The Seven Last Words of Our Saviour on the Cross
(orchestral version).

(N)(M) **(*) EMI (ADD) CDM5 67423-2. VPO, Muti.

Of the different versions that Haydn made of his unique
devotional sequence of adagio movements, the purely
orchestral one presents most difficulties, lacking the intimacy of the string quartet version and the full gravity of the
choral one. This recording made by Austrian Radio at the
Salzburg Festival in August 1982 brings marginally slower
speeds than Muti's later Berlin version for Philips, but it gains
greatly in the extra tension conveyed in a live event. The scale
is more appropriate, too, more intimate thanks to a drier
acoustic. The spiritual dimension is not conveyed as it would
be with a quartet or a chorus (Muti is not the interpreter for
that), but it makes a moving experience nonetheless, with the
Vienna Philharmonic on excellent form.

*Sinfonia Concertante in B flat for Violin, Cello, Oboe,
Bassoon & Orchestra.*

(M) *** DG 463 078-2. Zukerman, Leonhard, Winters,
Breidenthal, LAPO, Barenboim – BEETHOVEN: *Violin
Concerto in D, Op. 61.* ***

*Sinfonia Concertante in B flat for Violin, Cello, Oboe,
Bassoon & Orchestra, Hob I/105.*

(BB) **(*) ASV CDQS 6140. Frieman, Pople, Anderson,
Gambold, L. Festival O, Pople – STAMITZ: *Sinfonias
Concertantes.* **(*)

Directing the players from the solo cello, Ross Pople draws
a strong and alert rather than an elegant performance from
his London Festival Orchestra, well recorded in bright,
firmly focused sound. Though the solo playing is not always
ideally refined, there is a winning sense of musicians acting
out a drama, at speeds that are comfortable, never exaggerated. The coupling of *Sinfonias Concertantes* by Stamitz is
very apt and attractive.

In Barenboim's enjoyably spontaneous performance the
four soloists work splendidly together as a team and the
Andante is particularly successful. The recording is well
balanced and well transferred.

SYMPHONIES

*Symphonies: A in B flat; B in B flat; Nos. 1 in D; 2 in C; 3
in G; 4 in D; 5 in A; 6 in D (Le Matin); 7 in C (Le Midi); 8
in G (Le Soir); 9 in C; 10 in D: 11 in E flat; 12 in E; 13 in D;
14 in A; 15 in D; 16 in B flat; 17 in F; 18 in G; 19 in D; 20 in
C; 21 in A; 22 in E flat (Philosopher); 23 in G; 24 in D; 25 in
C; 26 in D min. (Lamentatione); 27 in G; 28 in A; 29 in E;
30 in C (Alleluja); 31 in D (Hornsignal); 32 in A; 33 in C; 34
in D min.; 35 in B flat; 36 in E flat; 37 in C; 38 in C (Echo);
39 in G min.; 40 in F; 41 in C; 42 in D; 43 in F (Mercury);
44 in E min. (Trauer-symphonie); 45 in F sharp min.
(Farewell); 46 in B; 47 in G; 48 in C (Maria Theresa); 49 in
F min. (La Passione); 50 in C; 51 in B flat; 52 in C min.; 53
in D; 54 in G; 55 in E flat (School-Master); 56 in C; 57 in D;
58 in F; 59 in A (Fire); 60 in C (Il distratto); 61 in D; 62 in
D; 63 in C (La Roxelane); 64 in A; 65 in A; 66 in B flat; 67
in F; 68 in B flat; 69 in C (Laudon); 70 in D; 71 in B flat; 72
in D; 73 in D (La Chasse); 74 in E flat; 75 in D; 76 in in
E flat; 77 in B flat; 78 in C min.; 79 in F; 80 in D min.; 81 in
G; (82-87 'Paris Symphonies') 82 in C (The Bear); 83 in
G min. (La Poule); 84 in E flat; 85 in B flat (La Reine); 86
in D; 87 in A; 88 in G; 89 in F; 90 in C; 91 in E flat; 92 in G
(Oxford); (93-104 'London Symphonies') 93 in D; 94 in G
(Surprise); 95 in C min.; 96 in D (Miracle); 97 in C; 98 in
B flat; 99 in E flat; 100 in G (Military); 101 in D (Clock);
102 in B flat; 103 in E flat; No. 104 in D (London).*

*Symphonies Nos. 1–104; Symphonies A; B. Alternative
versions: Symphony Nos. 22 (Philosopher), 2nd version.
Symphony No. 63 (La Roxelane), 1st version. Symphony
No. 53 (L'Impériale): 3 alternative Finales: (i) A
(Capriccio); (ii) C (Paris version, attrib. Haydn); D:
Overture in D (Milanese version). Symphony No. 103:*

Finale (alternative ending). (i) *Sinfonia Concertante in B flat for Oboe, Bassoon, Violin & Cello.*

⚫ (B) *** Decca (ADD) 448 531-2 (33). Philh. Hungarica, Dorati; (i) with Engl, Baranyai, Ozim, Rácz.

Dorati was ahead of his time as a Haydn interpreter when, in the early 1970s, he made this pioneering integral recording of the symphonies. Superbly transferred to CD in full, bright and immediate sound, the performances are a consistent delight, with brisk allegros and fast-flowing *Andantes*, with textures remarkably clean. The slow, rustic-sounding accounts of Minuets are more controversial, but the rhythmic bounce makes them attractive too. The set remains as yet the only complete survey. It includes not only the *Symphonies A and B* (Hoboken Nos. 106 and 108) but also the *Sinfonia Concertante in B flat*, a splendidly imaginative piece with wonderful unexpected touches. Dorati's account – not surprisingly – presents the work as a symphony with unusual scoring, rather than as a concerto. As H. C. Robbins Landon tells us in the accompanying notes, the *Symphonies A and B* were omitted from the list of 104 authentic symphonies by error, as the first was considered to be a quartet – wind parts were discovered later – and the second a divertimento.

Dorati also includes as an appendix completely different versions of *Symphony No. 22* (*The Philosopher*), where Haydn altered the orchestration (a pair of flutes substituted for the cor anglais), entirely removed the first movement and introduced a new *Andante grazioso;* plus an earlier version of No. 63, to some extent conjectural in its orchestration, for the original score is lost. Of the three alternative finales for *L'Impériale* (No. 53), the first (A) contains a melody which Robbins Landon suggests 'sounds extraordinarily like Schubert'; the second (C) seems unlikely to be authentic; but the third (D) uses an overture which was first published in Vienna. 'In some respects,' Robbins Landon suggests, 'this is the most successful of the three concluding movements'. He feels the same about the more extended finale of the *Drum Roll Symphony*, which originally included 'a modulation to C flat, preceded by two whole bars of rests. But Haydn thought that this made the movement too long and crossed out the whole section. Robbins Landon continues: 'Perhaps Haydn was for once in his life too ruthless here.'

Symphonies Nos. 1; 2; 4; 5; 10; 11; 18; 27; 32; 37; Symphony A (Partita) in B flat.

**(*) O-L (ADD) 436 428-2 (3). AAM, Hogwood.

Symphonies Nos. 3; 14; 15; 17; 19; 20; 25; 33; 36; 108 (Partita).

**(*) O-L (ADD) 436 592-2 (3). AAM, Hogwood.

Symphonies Nos. 6 (Le Matin); 7 (Le Midi); 8 (Le Soir); 9; 12; 13; 16; 40; 72.

**(*) O-L (ADD) 433 661-2. AAM, Hogwood.

Symphonies Nos. 21; 22 (Philosopher); 23; 24; 28; 29; 30 (Alleluja); 31; 34.

**(*) O-L (ADD) 430 082-2 (3). AAM, Hogwood.

Symphonies Nos. 26; 42; 43 (Mercury); 44 (Trauer); 48 (Maria Theresia); 49.

**(*) O-L (ADD) 440 222-2 (3). AAM, Hogwood.

Symphonies Nos. 35; 38; 39; 41; 58; 59 (Fire); 65.

**(*) O-L (ADD) 433 012-2 (3). AAM, Hogwood.

Symphonies Nos. 45; 46; 47; 51; 52; 64.

*** O-L (ADD) 443 777-2 (3). AAM, Hogwood.

In his Haydn series Hogwood has mellowed in period-performance manners, compared with his pioneering set of the Mozart symphonies. The playing, too, is now more polished. He uses a small group of strings (about half the size of that chosen by Tafelmusik, who have the benefit of H. C. Robbins Landon's advice in this matter). In particular he avoids abrasiveness in slow movements which, though much leaner than with modern instruments, are sympathetically phrased though sometimes a little stiff. In general his direct, crisply rhythmic approach to these works tends not to convey the charm of Haydn. He offers all repeats, but for scholarly reasons no harpsichord continuo is employed. The finely detailed, firmly focused recording perfectly brings out the transparency of textures, while giving body to the sound. If you are a Hogwood aficionado, these boxes can be acquired with confidence, particularly the collection appropriately subtitled 'Climax of the *Sturm und Drang*'.

Symphonies Nos. 50; 54 (1st version); 55 (Schoolmaster); 56; 57; 60.

*** O-L (ADD) 443 781-2 (3). AAM, Hogwood.

In this group of symphonies from 1773–4, following the *Sturm und Drang* sequence, Hogwood's speeds are generally brisk, with typically crisp, transparent textures, but he occasionally allows himself to luxuriate in broader tempi, generally effectively. With second-half repeats regularly observed, these period performances come in pairs, only two per disc. As with the earlier issues in this Haydn series, the style of the AAM has mellowed a degree more than in their pioneering set of the Mozart symphonies on the same label, with a warmer approach to slow movements. A scholarly note explains Hogwood's continuing avoidance of harpsichord continuo. Clean, undistracting sound.

Symphonies Nos. 53 (L'Impériale); 54 (second version); (i) 61; 66; 67; 68; 69 (Laudon).

*** O-L (ADD) 460 776-2. AAM, Hogwood.

The ninth volume of Christopher Hogwood's series vividly demonstrates the merits of presenting these symphonies in chronological order, rather than in the old (sometimes misleading) numerical sequence. These works, all presumed to date from 1775–6, are here dubbed as 'theatrical and popular symphonies', simpler and less demanding than the *Sturm und Drang* masterpieces that preceded them. What these refreshing, clean-cut performances demonstrate is that Haydn was here turning his increasing technical command towards entertainment. Speeds for fast movements are characteristically brisk, but slow movements – exceptionally long with all repeats observed – are again taken broadly. With recording that heightens the transparency of texture, all the usual qualities of the Hogwood series are here, with braying natural horns, sharply percussive timpani and no harpsichord continuo.

Symphonies Nos. 1–5.

*** Hyp. CDA 66524. Hanover Band, Goodman.

Symphonies Nos. 6 (Le Matin); 7 (Le Midi); 8 (Le Soir).

*** Hyp. CDA 66523. Hanover Band, Goodman.

Symphonies Nos. 13–16.

*** Hyp. CDA 66534. Hanover Band, Goodman.

Symphonies Nos. 42; 43 (Mercury); 44 (Trauer).

**(*) Hyp. CDA 66530. Hanover Band, Goodman.

Symphonies Nos. 45 (Farewell); 46; 47.

**(*) Hyp. CDA 66522. Hanover Band, Goodman.

Symphonies Nos. 48 (Maria Theresia); 49 (La Passione); 50.

**(*) Hyp. CDA 66531. Hanover Band, Goodman.

Symphonies Nos. 70–72.

*** Hyp. CDA 66526. Hanover Band, Goodman.

Symphonies Nos. 76–78.

*** Hyp. CDA 66525. Hanover Band, Goodman.

Symphonies Nos. 82 (The Bear); 83 (The Hen); 84.

*** Hyp. CDA 66527; KA 66527. Hanover Band, Goodman.

Symphonies Nos. 90; 91; 92 (Oxford).

*** Hyp. CDA 66521; KA 66521. Hanover Band, Goodman.

Symphonies Nos. 93; 94 (Surprise); 95.

*** Hyp. CDA 66532. Hanover Band, Goodman.

Symphonies Nos. 101 (Clock); 102; Overture: Windsor Castle.

*** Hyp. CDA 66528. Hanover Band, Goodman.

From the very outset of his Hyperion project, Goodman, who began at the beginning with the low-numbered symphonies, established a winning manner in early Haydn and, as the series progressed, he showed that his dramatic approach (tougher than Kuijken, for instance, in his COE recordings for Virgin) was being fruitful in the middle-period and later works. The performances offer consistently alert and well-sprung readings, which generally favour fast Allegros and relatively spacious slow movements which more than in most period performances, give expressive warmth to Haydn's melodies, without overstepping the mark into romanticism. That Goodman is very much the positive director of the group is brought out by the generally close balance given to the harpsichord continuo, which is far more audible than in most versions. The recording is resonant, giving bloom to the strings, yet oboes and horns (and other wind and brass, when used) come through vividly. This Hyperion series is achieving a balance of style somewhere between the Hogwood approach and the fuller scale of Dorati, using modern instruments.

Symphonies Nos. 1–20.

(M) **(*) Nim. NI 5426/30. Austro-Hungarian Haydn O, Fischer.

The Nimbus project of recording all the Haydn symphonies on modern instruments in the Haydnsaal of the Esterházy Palace brings playing which is fresh yet warm, with the considerable reverberation adding to the weight and scale of the earlier symphonies, in a manner that some ears will relish but others may find too opulent. In the accompanying notes the conductor, Adám Fischer, comments that the chosen orchestra, which is made up of players from Vienna and Budapest, carries forward the tradition of Austro-Hungarian music-making. The playing itself is warm and elegant, and again and again in these early symphonies the ear enjoys the finesse of this music-making and its ripeness of texture, with the rich-toned Viennese horns soaring out over the strings when given an opportunity to do so. The woodwind are sprightly and offer plenty of colour, and in Nos. 6–8 the various orchestral solos are taken with distinction. The conductor's speeds are moderate. Slow movements are gracious and phrasing is cultivated; minuets are courtly and finales lively and resilient, without being rushed. The sound itself is rich in ambience and easy to enjoy, for it does not cloud.

Symphonies Nos. 40–54.

(M) *** Nim. NI 5530/4. Austro-Hungarian Haydn O, Fischer.

In Volume 3 of his ongoing series, Adám Fischer homes in on the *Sturm und Drang* works, but he is working in numerical order, so includes one or two other symphonies, though none that is not full of stimulating ideas (the theme and variations which forms the *Andante* of *L'Imperiale* is sheer delight). The orchestral playing is consistently warm and committed and of course there is none of the astringency of texture one expects with Hogwood, or squeezed violin phrasing that Brüggen and others insist is authentic. The result is richly enjoyable and slow movements in particular consistently gain from such a dedicated orchestral response. The *Adagio* opening of *La Passione* is gentle yet is intensely concentrated in feeling and the following *Allegro di molto* is crisp, fast and biting. Minuets are faster and racier than with Dorati, with plenty of dynamic contrasts – and finales, if helter-skelter, still retain an elegant poise. The unnamed *C major Symphony* (No. 50) and the following *B flat major* work are among the finest performances here, splendidly characterful – and in the *Adagio* of the latter there is a glorious horn solo, followed by the graceful *Allegretto* finale. The Viennese elegance of phasing, and polish combined with sparkle, oftens reminds one of Beecham in its friendly listener-appeal. The recording is first class, full and warm with a natural concert-hall ambience.

Symphonies Nos. 43; 44; 49; 52 in C min.; 59; 64 (Tempora mutantur).

(N) (B) *** Nimbus NI 7072/3. Austo-Hungarian CO, Fischer.

This Nimbus Double, centring on the *Sturm und Drang* era, makes a splendid sampler for Adam Fischer's Haydn cycle, played on modern instruments. Fischer is often at his most imaginatively persuasive in these works, and both orchestral playing and recording are first class. The slow movements of the *Mercury* and *Trauer* symphonies are both very beautiful, while the *Adagio* opening of *La Passione* is gentle yet intensely concentrated in feeling, and the following *Allegro di molto* is crisp, fast and biting. In the notes we are told by David Threasher that the nickname of No. 64 (*Tempora mutantur*) is based on a couplet by the Welsh epigrammist John Owen, which was used as an inscription on clocks and sundials.

Symphonies Nos. 55-69.

(M) *** Nim. NI 5590/4 (5). Austro-Hungarian Haydn O, Fischer.

With Adám Fischer a dedicated advocate, inspiring fresh, persuasive playing from his hand-picked orchestra, there is no slackening of standards in this fourth volume of Nimbus's projected Haydn cycle. This group of works follows up the *Sturm und Drang* sequence with symphonies regularly related to Haydn's theatre music, at times with eccentric effects, as in the six-movement *Il distratto*, No.60, or No. 67 with its col legno and hurdy-gurdy effects. In the helpful acoustic of the Haydnsaal of the Esterhazy Palace at Eisenstadt, the sound is at once warmly atmospheric and intimate, with high contrasts of dynamic and texture. Continuing to use modern, not period instruments, but with limited string vibrato, and Viennese oboes and horns standing out distinctively, these are recordings to challenge the long-time supremacy of Dorati's pioneering Decca set. In important ways, not just in the extra fullness of the digital sound, the new performances improve on the old, notably in the brisker speeds for Minuets. Fischer generally, tends to prefer speeds in slow movements a fraction more flowing than those of Dorati, while outer movements are regularly a degree more relaxed. Thanks to Fischer's springing of rhythm, speeds never drag, even if those dedicated to period practice might well prefer the more hectic Prestos and Prestissimos of the earlier set. These are performances which register Haydn's humour more clearly, even in the *Sturm und Drang* symphonies here, Nos. 58 and 59 (*The Fire*).

Symphonies Nos. 70-81.

(N) *** Nimbus NI 5652/5. Austo-Hungarian CO, Fischer.

With the exception of No. 72, which probably dates from the 1760s, Volume 5 of Adam Fischer's ever more attractive survey contains works written more or less consecutively over a compact period of just over four years (1778-82). Robbins Landon has emphasised that generally these are much more courtly works than their *Sturm und Drang* predecessors, and No. 79 is a characteristically elegant example.

No. 70 is not. It opens very dramatically and bursts with energy, then changes mood completely, before its minor-key slow movement which is a set of double variations. The brilliantly contrapuntal finale, based on a repeated note motif, also opens in the minor key and develops into a remarkable triple fugue. No. 71 brings another striking opening movement which may have been written earlier than the other three, and also has a very beautiful *Adagio*.

Symphony No. 72 immediately recalls the *Hornsignal Symphony* and the scoring for for horns is certainly virtuosic, with bravura upward scales and roulades in the first movement which even today remain fiendishly difficult. The *Andante* is a concertante movement featuring solo violin and flute and the finale, another *Andante*, offers more solo playing (including a double-bass contribution) within an enchanting set of variations. No. 73 is the best known. Its

slow movement offers more variations, this time on a song, *Gegenliebe*. The finale with its main hunting theme on horns and trumpet gives the symphony its title (*La chasse*). But what will continually strike the non-specialist listener when listening through these ever-diverting works is their wide range of mood, particularly in the two minor key symphonies (Nos. 78 and 80).

Development sections give a flashing reminder of Haydn's most concentrated manner. Kaleidoscopic sequences of keys whirl the argument in unexpected directions (especially in No. 80), while slow movements are winningly diverse. The *Adagio cantabile* of No. 74, the *Poco Adagio (Andante con variazioni)* of No. 75, the *Adagio* of No. 76 and the memorable flowing melody of No. 77 are all highly rewarding examples.

Haydn was incapable of being boring, and some of these works are in every way remarkable in their forward-looking progressions, often anticipating Mozart's most visionary works. The modern-instrument performances here combine vitality, intensity and warmth in ideal proportions and the recording reveals the full detail of Haydn's very felicitous scoring, besides having an attractive overall bloom.

Symphonies Nos. 82-87.

(M) **(*) Nim. NI 5419/20. Austro-Hungarian Haydn O, Fischer.

The expansive sound of the Austro-Hungarian Orchestra suits the *Paris Symphonies*. *La Poule* and *La Reine* (with its rhythmically powerful opening movement) both show Fischer and his players at their best, and finest of all is one of the least known, *Symphony No. 84 in E flat* with another remarkably original first movement. Slow movements are warm and poised: the *Largo* of No. 86 is particularly successful, as is the light-hearted trio of its Minuet, with a vigorous finale, lightly articulated, to round the work off. The sound is always satisfyingly full-bodied, with the violins resonantly rich. The weighty bass is not always absolutely clean, but generally the effect is very believable.

Symphonies Nos. 88-92; Sinfonia Concertante in B flat for Violin, Cello, Oboe, Bassoon & Orchestra.

(M) ** Nim. NI 5417/8. Austro-Hungarian Haydn O, Fischer.

As with the other issues in this Nimbus series the recording is full and pleasing, but here the warm resonance prevents sharpness of detail and also has the effect of blunting the string articulation. Too often one feels the need for more bite in allegros. Tempi are almost always relaxed, so that the famous slow movement of No. 88 in G, warmly expressive as it is, very nearly drags, although Fischer brings off the *Adagio* of the *Oxford Symphony* beautifully. Throughout Minuets are very stately indeed but finales dance gracefully and opening Adagios are warmly expressive; yet in the end there is an absence of conveyed exhilaration. The *Sinfonia Concertante* included on the second disc is a particularly pleasing performance, with most sympathetic solo playing.

Symphonies Nos. 93-104 (London Symphonies).

(M) **(*) Nim. NI 5200/4. Austro-Hungarian Haydn O, Fischer.

With three symphonies apiece on the first two discs of the five-disc Nimbus set, Fischer's cycle of all twelve *London Symphonies* makes a neat and attractive package, with consistently fresh, resilient and refined performances. Though these works were first given in the intimate surroundings of the Hanover Square Rooms in London, they were very quickly heard in this much grander setting, and the performances reflect the fact, with broad speeds and weighty tuttis made weightier by the reverberant Nimbus recording. Such a movement as the lovely *Adagio* of No. 102 with its soaring melody is given added beauty by the ambience and slow speed. The set can be warmly recommended to most who resist period performance when, even at broad speeds, rhythms are light and resilient. Never sounding breathless, Fischer's Haydn consistently brings out the happiness of the inspiration. These are very much performances to relax with.

Other miscellaneous symphonies

Symphonies Nos. 1–12.

(N) (M) *(*) Chan. 6618 (3). Cantilena, Adrian Sheppard.

Sheppard's set of Haydn's earliest symphonies is potentially attractive, but the playing in the first five is not well-enough rehearsed, and while the named works (Nos. 6–8) have more spirit and polish they are no match for Pinnock and Marriner. Nos. 9–11, although vigorous (except for the flaccid Minuets), still lack finesse. Pleasing sound, but although these discs do not have to compete in a crowded market even at mid-price they are too expensive to do so.

Symphonies Nos. 6 (Le Matin); 7 (Le Midi); 8 (Le Soir).

(B) *** DG 459 357-2. E. Concert, Pinnock.

(BB) *** Naxos 8.550722. N. CO, Ward.

(M) **(*) Teldec 2292 46018-2. VCM, Harnoncourt.

(N) (B) ** DG (ADD) 469 551-2. Prague CO, Klee.

These were almost certainly the first works that Haydn composed on taking up his appointment as Kapellmeister to the Esterházys. Pinnock's performances are polished and refined, yet highly spirited, with infectious allegros and quite generous *espressivo*. There is certainly weight here, yet essentially this is a bracing musical experience, with the genius of these early works fully displayed.

The Northern Chamber Orchestra under Nicholas Ward has wind players who relish their solos, so that the flute chirps merrily and the bassoon immediately has a chance to shine in the Trio of the Minuet of No. 6. In the *Andante* of *Le Soir* the strings create a chamber-music atmosphere, and it is the intimate scale of these performances that is so attractive. Modern instruments are used, but textures are fresh and the ambience of the Concert Hall of New Broadcasting House, Manchester, adds the right degree of warmth.

Harnoncourt is nothing if not dramatic. He opens No. 6 with an impressively controlled crescendo, beginning from an almost inaudible pianissimo, while the opening of the main allegro is characteristically gruff. But this music-making bursts with vitality, and a soothing flute solo soon appears to calm the listener. The very opening of Harnoncourt's slow movement (of No. 6) is austere but the atmosphere lightens, and it is again a flute which gaily introduces

the lively finale. So it is throughout, with tuttis edgily bold and with plenty of accents, yet with balancing passages of delicacy. The recording is as vivid as the playing; if Harnoncourt's eccentricities prevent an unreserved period-instrument recommendation, this will be welcomed by his admirers.

In the mid-1970s Bernhard Klee's performance of Haydn's three early Esterhazy symphonies was one of the recommended pioneering LPs of this triptych. In his day Klee scored over nearly all his competitors in both sensitivity and vitality, and the wind soloists from the Prague Chamber Orchestra showed the expertise and individuality one expects from Czech players. The string playing too is polished and alert, although now the upper range of the violin timbre sounds rather dated. However the addition of a good performance of the *Philosopher Symphony*, with some impressive horn playing, certainly makes the reissue value for money.

(i) *Symphonies Nos. 6 (Le Matin); 7 (Le Midi); 8; 22 (Philosopher); (ii) 26 (Lamentatione); (i) 31 (Horn Signal); 43 (Mercury); 44 (Trauer); 45 (Farewell); (ii) 47 (Palindrome); (i) 48 (Maria Theresia); 49 (La Passione); 53 (L'Impériale); 55 (Schoolmaster); 59 (Fire); 60 (Il distratto); 63 (La Roxelane); 69 (Laudon); 73 (La Chasse); 82 (L'Ours); 83 (La Poule); 85 (La Reine); 92 (Oxford); 94 (Surprise); 96 (Miracle); 100 (Military); 101 (Clock); 103 (Drum Roll); 104 (London).*

(B) **(*) Ph. (ADD)/Dig. 454 335-2 (10). (i) ASMF, Marriner; (ii) ECO, Leppard (directed from harpsichord).

This fine collection, recorded between 1968 and 1981, is beautifully transferred to CD and offers Philips's most natural sound-quality. Marriner and Leppard between them offer consistently elegant performances of 29 'named' symphonies, not all of them well known. Marriner has the lion's share; Leppard, conducting from the harpsichord, is in excellent form in the *Lamentatione* and the so-called *Palindrome*, with its set of slow-movement variations on a pair of invertible themes. Under Marriner the Academy playing is more polished and urbane than in the rival accounts under Dorati. Although ultimately there is an earthier quality in the music than Marriner perceives, these are most enjoyable performances, and they often have a compensating charm which Dorati misses (the *Schoolmaster*, for instance). Nos. 44 and 49 are among the highlights, and here Marriner follows Leppard by featuring a discreet harpsichord continuo. There is some excellent horn playing in both works. On the other hand the *Horn Signal* seems curiously undercharacterized. *Il Distratto* and *La Roxelane* both have theatrical connections, and in the former Dorati's account has the greater sense of theatre, while the Academy orchestral playing is more finished. The 'named' *Paris Symphonies* are distinguished by excellent ensemble and keen articulation; they have a winning charm, yet are lively and musical, again offering a distinct alternative to Dorati. No. 94 has a particularly fine performance of the variations which form the slow movement (the 'surprise' itself most effective) and there is most delightful woodwind detail in No. 96 – the oboe solo in the trio of the Minuet is a joy. The playing in the *Clock* is very spruce and clean, and the atmosphere at the opening of the *Drum Roll* is wonderfully caught. At bargain price the set offers excellent value, and if at times there is just a hint of blandness Marriner has set himself high standards and there is much to admire in each of these performances, which always rise above the routine.

Symphonies Nos. 6 (Le Matin); 45 (Farewell); 48 (Maria Theresia); 82 (The Bear); 92 (Oxford); 94 (Surprise).

(B) *** Nim. NI 7041/2. Austro-Hungarian Haydn O, Fischer.

Nimbus could hardly have made a better selection to demonstrate the excellence of their warmly stylish modern-instrument series of Haydn symphonies. The two *Sturm und Drang* works are particularly fine, with Fischer bringing out the originality of the *Adagio* of the *Farewell* and making the famous finale memorable by securing most elegant playing from the instrumentalists before they depart. The slow movement of the *Oxford* is also memorable, and the *Bear* is sheer delight. Perhaps it was a pity that No. 94 was included, as most collectors will already have it, but no one could fault the 'surprise' itself. The recording is of high quality, full bodied and resonant, but not blurred.

Symphonies Nos. 22 (Philosopher); 86; 102.

*** EMI CDC5 55509-2. CBSO, Rattle.

It is refreshing to have a coupling of symphonies from different periods of Haydn's career. One of the most striking of the early works, the *Philosopher*, with its trudging chorale on two cor anglais, comes with one of the *Paris Symphonies*, No. 86, and one of the final *London* set. If only No. 102 had a nickname, it would be even more widely appreciated as a supreme masterpiece with its exhilarating outer movements and the most beautiful of all Haydn slow movements. Rattle's speeds are on the fast side but not extreme. Only in the final *Presto* of No. 86 does Rattle opt for a hectic speed, making one marvel at the agility of the Birmingham horns in repeated triplets.

Symphonies Nos. 23; 24; 61.

(BB) *** Naxos 8.550723. N. CO, Ward.

The fresh, stylish approach of the Northern Chamber Orchestra is entirely suited to these three symphonies, and here Nicholas Ward makes a persuasive case for the use of modern instruments. No. 24 includes a leading semi-concertante flute part (nicely managed) and the *G major* has a wistful *Andante* for strings alone, and a vital *Presto* finale, well sprinkled with strongly accented quadruplets. The opening movement of No. 61 is obviously more mature and is presented with both character and charm. Excellent recording.

Symphonies Nos. 26 (Lamentatione); 35 38–39; 41–44; 45 (Farewell); 46–52; 58–59; 65.

**(*) Ph. 462 177-2 (5). OAE, Brüggen.

With four of the five discs containing four symphonies each instead of the usual two or three, Brüggen offers an attractive package of all the *Sturm und Drang* works, presented in what is deduced as chronological order. It makes an impressive series, with a relatively small group of OAE players crisply

responsive, even though Brüggen's preference for minimal vibrato brings much edgy and squeezed violin tone, the more obtrusive with so few instruments. Speeds are impeccably chosen, rarely if ever sounding rushed, with dynamic contrasts dramatically brought out. Aptly the sequence ends with the *Farewell Symphony*. The recordings, made in the Blackheath Concert Halls over a period of nearly three years are both warm and intimate.

Symphonies Nos. 26; 35; 38; 39; 41; 42; 43 (Mercury); 44 (Trauer); 45 (Farewell); 46; 47; 48 (Maria Theresia); 49 (La Passione); 50; 51; 52; 58; 59 (Fire), 65 (Sturm und Drang symphonies).

(B) *** DG 463 731-2 (6). E. Concert, Pinnock.

Pinnock's forces are modest (with 6.5.2.2.1 strings), but the panache of the playing conveys any necessary grandeur. It is a new experience to have Haydn symphonies of this period recorded in relatively dry and close sound, with inner detail crystal clear (harpsichord never obscured) and made the more dramatic by the intimate sense of presence, yet with a fine bloom on the instruments. Some may find a certain lack of charm at times, and others may quarrel with the very brisk one-in-a-bar minuets and even find finales a little rushed. However, at bargain price, it is certainly value for money.

Symphonies Nos. 26 (Lamentatione); 35; 49 (La Passione).

(BB) **(*) Naxos 8.550721. N. CO, Ward.

Although enjoyable, this disc from Nicholas Ward and his Northern Chamber Orchestra is not quite as fresh-sounding as his first. The playing remains elegant and the horns (in B flat alto) are splendid in the Minuet of No. 35. But the opening *Allegro assai con spirito* of the *Lamentatione* could do with a shade more bite, and in the *Adagio* the warm resonance makes the finely played oboe solo almost a cor anglais and the melodic line like a Handel aria. The opening slow movement of No. 49 is not as intense as it might be, though the *Allegro di molto* which follows has plenty of energy. The resonance of the BBC's Studio 7 in Manchester brings a pleasingly mellow sound-picture, but the string detail is not sharply defined.

Symphonies Nos. 26 (Lamentatione); 52; 53 (L'Impériale).

(N) (B) *** Virgin x 2 VBD5 61800-2 (2). La Petite Bande, Kuijken – *Violin Concertos 1 & 4; Sinfonia Concertante.* ***

These are fresh, vital, cleanly articulated performances which wear their authenticity lightly and even indulge in speeds for slow movements that are more expansive and affectionate than many purists would allow. These three symphonies now come coupled on a Virgin Double, coupled with two key violin concertos and the *Sinfonia Concertante in B flat* – see above.

Symphonies Nos. 30 (Alleluja); 55 (Schoolmaster); 63 (La Roxelane).

(BB) *** Naxos 8.550757. N. CO, Ward.

An entirely winning triptych of named Haydn symphonies, spanning a highly creative period from the three-movement *Alleluja* (1765), with its delightful woodwind contribution in the *Andante*, to *La Roxelane* (1780), where the *Allegretto* paints an engaging portrait of a flirtatious character in a play and the finale fizzes with energy. In between comes *The Schoolmaster*, whose Adagio brings a theme and variations of disarming simplicity. Alert and vivacious playing from all concerned; admirable pacing and first-class sound ensure a welcome for a disc that would be just as recommendable if it cost far more.

Symphonies Nos. 31 (Horn Signal); 59 (Fire); 73 (La Chasse).

*** Teldec 4509 90843-2. VCM, Harnoncourt.

This is one of Harnoncourt's very best records. All three symphonies are notable for their spectacular horn parts. The playing here – using natural horns – is superb, with throatily exuberant braying at the opening of the *Horn signal*, an equally striking contribution throughout the *Fire Symphony* (where the horns are crooked in A), and more cheerful hunting-calls in the spirited finale of *La Chasse*. The playing is not only extremely vital and polished but even has an element of charm (not something one can always count on from this source). The orchestra communicate their involvement throughout.

Symphonies Nos. 39; 70; 73 (La Chasse); 75.

⚫ (M) *** Van. (ADD) 08 6152 71. Esterházy O, Blum.

David Blum pioneered authentic chamber-orchestra performances of the mid-period Haydn symphonies (using modern instruments) in the early 1960s, so this fine Vanguard reissue makes a splendid reminder of his achievement. His alert stylishness is matched by the warmth of the slow movements, which are beautifully played and are made the expressive centrepiece of each symphony. Throughout all four symphonies Blum takes the Minuets at a spirited tempo, in that way anticipating modern practice. Outstanding among Haydn symphony issues.

Symphonies Nos. 42; 45 (Farewell); 46.

(M) *** DG (IMS) 447 281-2. E. Concert, Pinnock.

Haydn's famous *Farewell Symphony*, given a vibrant and characterful performance with a very beautiful slow movement, is here coupled with two apparently straightforward but still forward-looking works, No. 42 with its memorably solemn *Andantino e cantabile* and *No. 46 in B major*. Here the ethereal 6/8 *Poco Adagio* contrasts with an invigorating scherzando finale where the high horns (crooked in B alto) produce repeated bursts of hair-raising virtuosity. And Haydn has a characteristic trick up his sleeve for, just before the end, the Minuet returns, only to be swept away by a final rally from the horns.

Symphonies Nos. 43 (Mercury); 46–47.

(N) *** Naxos 8.554767. Cologne CO, Mühler-Brühl.

Helmut Mühler-Brühl and the Cologne Chamber Orchestra carry on the Naxos Haydn series with this excellent bargain version of three fascinating symphonies from his middle period, vividly recorded. For over ten years this orchestra played on period instruments, so many of the lessons of period performance have been taken on board. Mühler-

Brühl's choice of speeds cannot be faulted, with allegros crisp and alert and slow movements kept flowing. These three works date from the early 1770s, when Haydn was well established at Esterháza.

The nickname 'Mercury' for No. 43 probably relates to a stage work with a fine A flat slow movement opening on muted strings. No. 47 brings striking military horn-calls at the start, beautifully caught in this recording, but the most memorable of the three is No. 46, with its lilting B minor slow movement. Its extraordinary finale is then punctuated by sudden silences, with sharp modulations and an unexpected quotation from the preceding *Minuet*. Such quirkiness is what makes Haydn endlessly fascinating, from whichever period.

Symphonies Nos. 44 (Trauer); 88; 104 (London).

(BB) *** Naxos 8.550287. Capella Istropolitana, Wordsworth.

Symphonies Nos. 45 (Farewell); 48 (Maria Theresia); 102.

(BB) *** Naxos 8.550382. Capella Istropolitana, Wordsworth.

Symphonies Nos. 82 (The Bear); 96 (Miracle); 100 (Military).

(BB) *** Naxos 8.550139. Capella Istropolitana, Wordsworth.

Symphonies Nos. 83 (The Hen); 94 (Surprise); 101 (The Clock).

(BB) *** Naxos 8.550114. Capella Istropolitana, Wordsworth.

Symphonies Nos. 85 (La Reine); 92 (Oxford); 103 (Drum Roll).

(BB) *** Naxos 8.550387. Capella Istropolitana, Wordsworth.

Like Barry Wordsworth's recordings of Mozart symphonies, with the Capella Istropolitana on the Naxos label, this Haydn collection provides a series of outstanding bargains at the lowest budget price. The sound is not quite as clean and immediate as in the Mozart series – it is a little boomy at times in fact – and Wordsworth's preference for relatively relaxed speeds is a little more marked here than in his Mozart series, but the varied choice of works on each disc is most attractive. At their modest cost, these are well worth collecting.

Symphonies Nos. 45 (Farewell); 55 (Schoolmaster).

(M) (**(*)) Decca mono 458 869-2. Aldeburgh Fest. O, Britten – MOZART: *Piano Concerto No. 12 in A, K.414* (**(*)).

These two mid-period Haydn symphonies were recorded live at the 1956 Aldeburgh Festival; the sound is limited but close and immediate.

In the *Farewell* Britten brings out the *Sturm und Drang* drama of the piece, with dynamic contrasts underlined. His speeds in the last two movements are fresh and brisk – remarkably so for the period – relaxing for the *Adagio* epilogue. That is so beautifully timed over the departure of one player after another that the very end inspires laughter. The *Schoolmaster* is strongly characterized too. The offbeat, mid-air ending of the finale is also delectably timed, and – as in the *Farewell* – the amusement of the audience is clearly audible.

Symphonies Nos. (i) *45 (Farewell);* (ii) *88;* (iii) *104 (London).*

(B) *** DG (ADD) 439 428-2. (i) ECO, Barenboim; (ii) VPO, Boehm; (iii) LPO, Jochum.

A stimulating triptych of Haydn performances by three different conductors, all of whom have something positive to say about this repertoire. Barenboim's *Farewell Symphony* has much vitality and there is sensitive playing in the remarkable *Adagio*, one of Haydn's finest. Boehm and the VPO are at their very best in No. 88, with the slow movement gravely expansive. The playing has great polish and refinement, and Boehm's touch instantly charms in the spirited finale. Jochum's is among the most musically satisfying accounts of No. 104 in the catalogue; and all three recordings (from the 1970s) sound first class in their remastered form. A genuine bargain, playing for 77 minutes.

Symphonies Nos. 54; 56; 57.

(BB) *** Naxos 8.554108. Cologne CO, Müller-Brühl.

In vivid, full-ranging recordings made by German Radio, Müller-Brühl conducts lively performances with his excellent chamber orchestra of three symphonies from around 1774. Müller-Brühl, using modern instruments, yet reflects period practice in asking for very limited vibrato and light articulation from the strings.

Symphonies Nos. 69 (Laudon); 89; 91.

(M) **(*) Naxos 8.550769. Budapest Nicolaus Esterházy Sinfonia, Drahos.

The resonance of the Reformed Church, Budapest, prevents the sharpest definition here. The orchestra is set back and the internal balance is natural: the strings have bloom without edginess. This is alert, thoroughly musical playing with apt tempi. The *Andante con moto* of No. 89 is elegantly done, and the variations of the *Andante* of No. 91 are neatly handled (with an elegant bassoon solo). All in all this gives pleasure, but more brightness on top would have been welcome.

Symphonies Nos. 72; 93; 95.

(BB) *** Naxos 8.550797. Nicolaus Esterházy Sinfonia, Drahos.

These performances are polished, warm and spirited and, if the Naxos recording is on the reverberant side, it does not cloud textures. Four horns are featured prominently in No. 72 and provide many bravura flourishes and virtuoso scales in the opening movement; the playing here is first class. The orchestral response is equally impressive in the fine slow movements of these later works, and throughout Béla Drahos's pacing is matched by the overall sense of spontaneity and style.

Symphonies Nos. 74–76.

(BB) *** Naxos 8.554109. Cologne CO, Müller-Brühl.

The three symphonies, dating from the early 1780s, make an attractive group, characteristically lively in outer movements but each with slow movements involving the use of mysterious muted strings. Müller-Brühl, as in his other Haydn

recordings, favours broad adagios and Minuets that retain the idea of a stately dance. Yet the freshness and rhythmic resilience never fail to bring the performances to life. Like its companions, an excellent recommendation.

Symphonies Nos. 77–79.

(BB) *** Naxos 8.553363. N. CO, Ward.

For these three little-known but most engaging symphonies, written in 1782–3, Nicholas Ward could hardly be more persuasive. The colourful charm of Haydn's scoring in the *B flat Symphony* is most sensitively caught, the *Vivace* opening of *No. 78 in C minor* is highly dramatic, while both slow movements are eminently graceful. The *Minuets*, though not rushed, are suitably spirited and finales are deft and lively, especially the winning monothematic *Presto* of the *C minor* work, which includes some of the composer's genial pauses.

Symphonies Nos. 80; 81; 99.

(BB) *** Naxos 8.554110. Cologne CO, Müller-Brühl.

Müller-Brühl here couples two symphonies of 1783–4 with the first of the masterpieces which Haydn wrote for Salomon for the second of his two visits to London. No. 80 is remarkable for the dark intensity of the minor-key opening with its dramatic use of tremolo. Chromatic touches break in later too. In these later symphonies, unlike the earlier ones, Müller-Brühl does allow Minuets to acquire a hint of the Scherzo at brisker speeds. No. 99 is remarkable for Haydn's inclusion for the first time in a symphony of a pair of clarinets.

Symphonies Nos. 80; 87; 89.

(BB) *** ASV CDQS 6156. LMP, Glover.

No. 87 is the least known of the *Paris Symphonies*; but all three of these works show Haydn at his most inventive. *No. 80 in D minor* begins as though it were a throwback to the *Sturm und Drang* period, but then at the end of the exposition Haydn gives a winning smile. No. 89 ends with a dance movement which contains delectable *strascinando* (dragging) passages. Though textures are not as transparent as we are beginning to demand in an age of period performance – largely a question of the ambient recorded sound – these modern-instrument performances are both winning and lively.

Symphonies Nos. 82 (The Bear); 83 (The Hen); 84; 85 (La Reine); 86; 87 (Paris).

✿ (BB) *** Virgin Classics 2 x 1 Double VBD5 61659 (2) OAE, Kuijken.
*** Philips 462 111-2 (2). O. of the 18th Century, Brüggen.
(B) *** Double Decca (ADD) 448 194-2 (2). Philh. Hungarica, Dorati.
(B) *** Ph. Duo ADD/Dig 438 727-2 (2). ASMF, Marriner.

Sigiswald Kuijken's set of the *Paris Symphonies* – warmly and vividly recorded – is among the most enjoyable period-performance recordings of Haydn ever. Kuijken and his players wear their authenticity lightly and the slow movements are allowed to relax beautifully, while the one-in-a-bar treatment of the minuets produces a delightful Ländler-like swing. With dynamic contrasts underlined, the grandeur of Haydn's inspiration is fully brought out, along with the rigour; yet Kuijken gives all the necessary sharpness to the reminiscence of *Sturm und Drang* in the near-quotation of the *Farewell* in the first movement of No. 85, *La Reine*. The magnificence of that movement is underlined by the observance of the second-half repeat. Above all, he and his players convey the full joy of Haydn's inspiration in every movement and the reissue at bargain price is surely irresistible.

Frans Brüggen, continuing his excellent Haydn series with his talented Dutch period orchestra is here, as ever, an outstandingly characterful interpreter of Haydn, with rhythms beautifully sprung. These are strong, positive performances of the *Paris Symphonies*, helped by immediate sound giving a vivid sense of presence. There is no discrepancy in the quality for No. 86, recorded earlier than the rest. However, good as these performances are, they are upstaged by Kuijken, and not only just on price (the Philips set costs about three times as much as the Virgin Double!).

Dorati's set of *Paris Symphonies* makes a fine Double Decca bargain. These performances are well up to the high standard of his integral Haydn series, freshly stylish performances with plenty of vigour. The sinewy strength of the G minor opening of No. 83 for a moment brings a hint of *Sturm und Drang*, then yields its surprise as it gives way to the clucking of its titular *Hen*, while the variations which form its slow movement are matched in charm by those based on the French folksong (*La gentille et jeune Lisette*) which make up the *Romance: Allegretto* of No. 85. No. 84 has a first movement of the most delicate fantasy, while No. 87, after its sublime *Adagio*, ends in a mood of lithe high spirits. The only point of controversy here is Dorati's consistently slow tempi for the minuets, nicely pointed as they are.

From Marriner, spirited and well-played accounts of the *Paris Symphonies*, distinguished by excellent ensemble and keen articulation. Nos. 86 and 87 (and perhaps 84) are digital recordings, the remainder being analogue, though this is not indicated in the documentation. The playing has that touch of charm which is so essential in Haydn. It is possible to imagine performances of greater character and personality than these (in the slow movements there is a tendency to blandness) but they are lively and musical and a good alternative to the Dorati recordings, economically priced.

Symphony No. 83 in G min. (La Poule).

(N) *** BBC (ADD) BBCL 4038. Hallé O, Barbirolli – LEHAR: *Gold and Silver;* JOHANN STRAUSS SNR: *Emperor Waltz* etc.; R. STRAUSS: *Der Rosenkavalier Suite.* ***

This is one of Barbirolli's most cherishable records. The account of *Symphony No. 83* is delightful, with the 'Hen' clucking to the manner born. There is grace and simplicity in the *Andante* and exuberance in the finale, and the couplings are unmissable.

Symphonies Nos. 83 (The Hen); 84; 88.

(BB) *** ASV CDQS 6167. LMP, Glover.

A very winning companion for Jane Glover's earlier Haydn

triptych – see above. Once again there is a lesser known symphony, No. 84, (with its shapely Theme and Variations slow movement (elegantly played here) alongside two favourites. Jane Glover neatly enunciates the 'clucking second subject' which gives No. 83 its nickname, and finds a warm serenity for the noble slow movement of No. 88. Outer movements are as lively as you could wish and the recording is excellent. A genuine bargain.

Symphonies Nos. 83 (La Poule); 88; 96 (Miracle).

(M) (***) Dutton mono CDSJB 1003. Hallé O, Barbirolli.

Barbirolli's recording of No. 83 (*The Hen*), made in 1949, was the very first in the catalogue. Characteristically, he gives it an energetic reading full of fun and high dramatic contrasts. So the clucking of the second subject has rarely been pointed with more wit. No. 96, with which *The Hen* was originally coupled on LP, has freer, more open sound. The playing is a degree more polished and elegant, with no diminution of energy or wit, and again the flute and oboe emerge as stars in the Hallé team. No. 88 was recorded in 1953 but was never issued, maybe for lack of a coupling. He sustains the great melody of the *Largo* at a slow speed with elegance as well as warmth, and the fun of the finale is delightfully caught.

Symphony No. 88.

⚫ (M) (***) DG mono 447 439-2. BPO, Furtwängler –
SCHUBERT: *Symphony No. 9.* (***)

Even those who usually find Furtwängler's interpretations too idiosyncratic will be drawn to this glowing performance. The beauty of his shaping of the main theme of the slow movement is totally disarming, and the detail of the finale, lightly sprung and vivacious, is a constant pleasure. The Berlin Philharmonic plays marvellously well for him, and the 1951 recording in its remastered form it sounds admirably fresh, yet has plenty of body. Here it is coupled with Schubert's *Ninth Symphony*, an ideal candidate for reissue in DG's 'Originals'.

Symphonies Nos. 88 in G; 89 in F; 90 in C.

*** Sony SK 66253. Tafelmusik, Weil.

The Tafelmusik series from Sony was produced with the estimable H. C. Robins Landon as musicological and artistic consultant, who has expressed pleasure at the performances, which set new standards in this repertoire. The previous issues included symphonies nos. 41–43 (SK 48370); 44, 51–52 (SK 48371); 45–47 (SK 53986); 50, 64–65 (SK 53985); and the six *Paris Symphonies*, 82–87 (SK 66295/6). The size of the orchestra seems just about ideal, with twenty strings (7, 6, 3, 2, 2) against which woodwind, horns and sometimes trumpets are vividly balanced. Bruno Weil's tempi are apt, and his players are sensitive to details of phrasing and dynamics and obviously love Haydn. The performances are brimful of character and have irrepressible spirit. The sound is full yet admirably transparent. The first movement of No. 88 is not rushed and the noble tune of the slow movement is unerringly paced. No. 89 is particularly winning and the joke false ending of No. 90 is neatly done. Alas, as we go to press the whole series (including the present disc) has been deleted. Sony tell us they have no plans to reissue them at present, which is lamentable.

Symphonies Nos. 88–92 (Oxford).

(BB) ** Virgin 2 x 1 Double VBD5 61567-2 (2). La Petite Bande, Kuijken.

Kuijken's performances of this nicely balanced group of key Haydn symphonies have many of the qualities that made his set of the *Paris Symphonies* also on Virgin (see above) so winning. Yet with a gap of two years, and a change of orchestra to La Petite Bande, come differences which weigh significantly against this reissue. For these rather later symphonies, Kuijken has abandoned the use of harpsichord continuo, and his preference for very measured speeds in slow movements leads him to at least one serious miscalculation. At a funereal pace he makes the heavenly *Largo* of No. 88 far too heavy, seriously holding up the flow of the great melody with over-emphasis and exaggerated pauses. The sound is warm and well balanced, though violins could be better defined in tuttis; but overall this is something of a disappointment when compared with Kuijken's earlier achievement.

Symphonies Nos. 88; 92 (Oxford); 94 (Surprise).

(M) **(*) DG (IMS) 445 554-2. VPO, Bernstein.

All three G major symphonies emanate from concerts at the Musikvereinsaal in the mid-1980s, using the full strings of the Vienna Philharmonic and given a richly upholstered recording. For all his idiosyncrasies, Bernstein is never more winning than in Haydn, with a romantic, beautiful account of the *Largo*. The slow movement of the *Surprise* is also taken relaxedly, and the speed of the finale is challengingly fast. Good sound.

Symphonies Nos. 88; 104 (London).

(M) *** CRD (ADD) CRD 3370. Bournemouth Sinf., Thomas.

With an orchestra on a chamber scale, the playing has great freshness and vitality; indeed it is the urgency of musical feeling that Ronald Thomas conveys which makes up for the last ounce of finesse.

Symphony No. 92 (Oxford).

(M) (***) Dutton Lab mono CDEA 5003. Paris Conservatoire O, Walter – SCHUBERT: *Symphony No. 9.* (***)

These magnetic performances have one marvelling at the whirlwind energy and resilience of allegros in both the Schubert and the Haydn symphonies. Even Walter's broad tempos and expressive phrasing in slow movements are firmly controlled. The classic account of the *Great C major Symphony* of Schubert was made in London later the same year. However, this issue has now been deleted.

Symphonies Nos. 92 (Oxford); 104 (London).

(M) (***) DG mono 457 720-2. BPO, Rosbaud – MOZART: *Violin Concerto No. 4.* (***)

Hans Rosbaud is heard at his finest here, particularly in the beautifully played *Andante* of the *London Symphony*. Throughout, the playing of the Berlin Philharmonic

Orchestra has remarkable finesse and polish, and they are again at their most winning in both the Minuet of the *Oxford Symphony* and its sparkling finale. Rosbaud's tempi never languish, and the recording, clear and fresh, is impressively remastered.

Symphonies Nos. 93; 94 (Surprise); 97; 99; 100 (Military); 101 (Clock) (London Symphonies).

✪ (B) *** Ph. Duo (ADD)/Dig. 442 614-2 (2). Concg. O, Davis.

Symphonies Nos. 95; 96 (Miracle); 98; 102; 103 (Drum Roll); 104 (London) (London Symphonies).

✪ (B) *** Ph. Duo (ADD)/Dig. 442 611-2 (2). Concg. O, Davis.

Symphonies Nos. 93; 94 (Surprise); 97; 100 (Military); 103 (Drum Roll); 104 (London).

(B) *** Double Decca (ADD) 452 256-2 (2). Philharmonia Hungarica, Dorati.

Symphonies Nos. 94 (Surprise); 100 (Military); 104 (London).

(B) *** Penguin Decca (ADD) 460 628-2. Philharmonia Hungarica, Dorati.

Symphonies Nos. 95; 96 (Miracle); 98; 99; 101 (Clock); 102.

(B) *** Double Decca (ADD) 452 259-2 (2). Philharmonia Hungarica, Dorati.

Symphonies Nos. 93–104 (London Symphonies).

(BB) **(*) Arte Nova 74321 72109-2 (4). L. Fest. O, Pople.

Sir Colin Davis's Haydn series (recorded between 1975 and 1981) is one of the most distinguished sets he has given us over his long recording career, and its blend of brilliance and sensitivity, wit and humanity gives these two-for-the-price-of-one Duo reissues a special claim on the collector. There is no trace of routine in this music-making and no failure of imagination. The excellence of the playing is matched by Philips's best recording quality, whether analogue or digital. The Concertgebouw sound is resonant and at times weighty but has good definition. The *Allegretto* of the *Military Symphony* is properly grand and expansive, balanced by vital, sparkling outer movements. Excellent notes from Robin Golding. A bargain in every sense of the word.

Dorati and the Philharmonia Hungarica perform these final masterpieces with a glowing sense of commitment, and Dorati generally chooses rather relaxed tempi for the first movements – as in No. 93, which is deliciously lilting. In slow movements his tempi are on the fast side, but only in No. 94, the *Surprise*, is the result controversial. Though an extra desk of strings has been added to each section, the results are authentically in scale, and with intimacy comes extra dramatic force in sforzandos. A magnificent conclusion to a magnificent project and all the more desirable, now that this series is being economically reissued in Decca Double format.

The Penguin Classics disc joins the *Surprise* with its briskly paced slow movement, with two of the most popular named

London Symphonies, which are equally finely played and recorded. The personal comments about the music are from Bamber Gascoigne.

Jochum secures fine, stylish playing from the LPO, challenging them with often very fast tempi in outer movements. Those fast tempi sometimes prevent the music from having quite the lilt it has with Beecham or the gravitas of Sir Colin Davis; but the athletic exuberance of Jochum in Haydn, his ability to mould slow movements with tenderness that never spills over into unstylish mannerism (and to handle the sets of themes and variations to bring great diversity of atmosphere and mood), makes these wonderfully satisfying readings of Haydn's greatest symphonies. In the finale of No. 98 Jochum adds a harpsichord to the texture so that Haydn's charming little joke at the end can make its point all the better. The recording is naturally balanced and clear, with its warm reverberation presenting these works on a somewhat bigger scale, yet with rather less weight than Davis brings.

Ross Pople conducts his London Festival Orchestra in lively accounts of the twelve *London Symphonies*. They are neatly fitted, in numerical order, onto only four CDs thanks to the omission of the exposition repeat in No. 104. These are amiable rather than high-powered or highly polished readings, but with rhythms well lifted they are consistently enjoyable. Well paced, they bring brisk Ländler-like Minuets, and fresh, alert outer movements. Excellent value and well worth considering at their modest cost. But they do not upstage the superb Colin Davis set on a pair of Philips Duos.

Symphonies Nos. 93; 94 (Surprise); 97; 99; 102; 103 (Drum Roll).

(N) (B) ** Ph. Duo 468 546-2 (2). O of 18th Century, Brüggen.

Franz Brüggen's approach to the last symphonies of Haydn (of which his Philips Duo is the first instalment) brings remarkable contradictions of style. He is not helped by the resonant acoustic, which creates weighty textures and a focus that is not always quite clean in fortissimos. Openings and first movement allegros are generally portentous and large-scale, generating almost a Beethoven atmosphere, and, while slow movements bring the restrained 'authentic' string style, the expansive movements again often seem too inflated. Finales are usually snappy and the orchestral playing is of high quality with fine wind solos, but the end result fails to convince.

Symphonies Nos. 93; 95; 97.

(B) *** Sony (ADD) SBK 67175. Cleveland O, Szell.

With superb polish in the playing and precise phrasing it would be easy for performances such as these to sound superficial, but Haydn's music obviously struck a deep chord in Szell's sensibility and there is humanity underlying the technical perfection. Indeed there are many little musical touches from Szell to show that his perfectionist approach is a dedicated and affectionate one. There is also the most delectable pointing and a fine judgement of the inner balance. The recordings have been splendidly remastered and the sound is fuller and firmer than it ever was on LP. A highly recommendable reissue.

Symphonies Nos. 94 (Surprise); 96 (Miracle); 104 (London).

(M) **(*) DG 463 083-2. BPO, Karajan.

Karajan's *London Symphony* has impressive power and dignity with altogether splendid string playing from the Berlin Philharmonic, with none of the interpretative self-indulgence which sometimes marred this conductor's later performances. Similar comments also apply to the *Surprise* and *Miracle* symphonies: these are beautifully played works, weighty by modern standards, but not ponderous. With a playing time of 76 minutes, this is an excellent way to sample Karajan's plush approach to Haydn. Good recording.

Symphonies Nos. 96 (Miracle); 97; 98; 99.

(B) **(*)Teldec Ultima 3484 21337-2 (2). Concg. O, Harnoncourt.

Harnoncourt is nothing if not wide-ranging in his Haydn interpretations; the vigorous and polished Concertgebouw playing, with hard-driven allegros and contrasting moments of great delicacy, is certainly never dull. If one accepts the gruffness of manner, the fierce accenting and the weight of the orchestral tuttis, the *Miracle* is an impressive reading, with the secondary theme of the opening movement elegant enough, and No. 97 is similarly compelling. The recording is first class throughout.

Symphonies Nos. 96 (Miracle); 100 (Military); 103 (Drum Roll).

(B) *** [EMI Red Line CDR5 69810]. ECO, Tate.

Consistently Tate chooses speeds that allow the wit and sparkle of Haydn's writing to come out naturally, as in the second subject of the *Military* or in the joyful lilt of the 6/8 rhythms of the first-movement allegro in the *Drum Roll*. Tate's speeds bring out Haydn's humour far more than anything faster and fiercer would do. And always, with his slow speeds, crisp articulation ensures that the music sounds light and springy, never too heavy. Warm, well-balanced sound. A most attractive triptych.

Symphony No. 98.

(M) ** EMI (ADD) CDM5 67032-2. Philh. O, Klemperer – TCHAIKOVSKY: *Symphony No. 5*.

Symphony No. 101 (Clock).

(M) ** EMI (ADD) CDM5 67033-2. Philh. O, Klemperer – DVORAK: *Symphony No. 9*. **

Klemperer is not the first conductor one thinks of in relation to Haydn, and his approach is characteristically broad and measured. Although he shows his mastery in structuring and rhythmic pointing, these readings (for all their integrity) could not be further removed from modern rethinking about the way this music should be performed.

Symphonies Nos. 101 (Clock); 102; 103 (Drum Roll); 104 (London).

(B) *(**) Teldec Ultima 0630 18953-2 (2). Concg. O, Harnoncourt.

Harnoncourt's performances with the Concertebouw Orchestra, recorded in 1987–8, bring a curious stylistic mixture and bizarre eccentricities. In period-performance manner, first movements are fierce and emphatic and slow movements are clipped and short-winded (disastrously so in the glorious *Adagio* of No. 102). But there are occasional lapses into a smooth, modern manner. This is powerfully persuasive music-making, very well played and impressively recorded.

Symphonies Nos. 103 (Drum Roll); 104 (London).

*** DHM/BMG 05472 77362-2. La Petite Bande, Kuijken.

La Petite Bande are fully back on form in this highly stimulating coupling of Haydn's last two *London Symphonies*. After an arresting opening, the *Drum Roll* has a delightfully frisky opening *Allegro*, with delectably nimble oboe-playing at the second subject yet in no way lacking rhythmic weight. The *Andante* brings an appealing gravity, and after a dynamic *Minuet* the even more vigorous finale is played with winning dynamic subtlety. No. 104, too, opens very dramatically. The song-like slow movement brings a touching, ethereal delicacy from the strings, echoed later by the woodwind. After the jolly, swinging *Minuet*, the finale, for all its geniality, makes a brilliantly compelling conclusion. The orchestral sound is full, yet clean and fresh, with the powerful impact of the timpani never made over-resonant.

CHAMBER MUSIC

Divertimenti Nos. 1–12, Hob III/1–4; Hob II/6; Hob III/6–12.

(BB) *** Arte Nova 74321 31682-2 (4). Hamburg Soloists, Klein.

These string *Divertimenti* (given that name by Haydn himself) are in fact his earliest string quartets (including Op. 1 and Op. 2). The present works are all symmetrically structured in five movements. Each is framed by two outer *Prestos* within which there is an inner frame of two Minuets and at the centre an *Adagio*, the musical heart of each work, almost always containing the finest music. The other movements are well crafted but relatively conventional, although every so often there is something to catch the ear, for instance the hunting style of the opening movement of the very first work (which recurs in No. 6). Inexpensive, with excellent recording.

Divertimenti (Cassationa): in G, Hob II/1; in G, Hob II/G1; in C (Birthday), Hob II/11; in F, Hob II/20.

(M) **(*) Virgin VER5 61163-2. Linde Consort, Linde.

Two of the *Divertimenti* offered here are fairly ambitious (Hob II, Nos. G1 and 20), scored for a nonet (including a pair each of oboes and horns); the remaining two, written around 1765, are scored for a sextet (including flute and oboe), often used with charm and effectively demonstrating the special timbres of the early instruments played here. Overall the performances have plenty of character. The recording, made in a fairly reverberant acoustic, has a quite large-scale effect.

Divertimenti for Wind (Feld-Parthie) (for 2 oboes, 2, horns & 2 bassoons), Hob II/ 3, 7, 14–15, & 23; in D & G, Hob deest.

(N) ** Campanella C 130069. Berlin Haydn Ens.

Haydn's *Wind Divertimenti* or *Feld-Parthie* (which title indicates open-air performance) date from the early 1760s and are part of the Bohemian styled *Harmoniemusik*, of which Mozart was the supreme master. Haydn's contribution here is a series of five-movement suites, each including a pair of Minuets, often the most striking sections. They are jolly enough, with some lively writing for the horns (notably the hunting finale of *No. 3 in G major*, the Trio of the Minuet of the *D major*, Hob deest and its companion in G, where the principal horn rushes up the scale to a hair-raising G in alt). But at this early stage in his career, Haydn showed no great identification with the medium. Maybe a Viennese performance could find more charm in the music, but the present group, formed mainly of musicians from the Berlin Philharmonic, plays vigorously and robustly, but rather stiffly. They are faithfully but forwardly recorded, which gives striking presence, but prevents the widest range of dynamic.

(i) Flute Trios for 2 Flutes & Cello Nos. 1–4 (London), Hob IV/1–4; (ii) Flute Quartets, Op. 5, Nos. 1 in D, Hob II/D9; 2 in G, Hob II/G4; 3 in D, Hob II/D10; 4 in G, Hob II/1; 5 in D, Hob II/D11; 6 in C, Hob II/11.

*** Accent ACC 9283/4 (2). (i) Bernard Kuijken, Mark Hantaï, Wieland Kuijken; (ii) Bernard, Siegfried & Wieland Kuijken, François Fernandez.

The *London Trios* date from 1794 during Haydn's visit to England and the first two include variations on the song, *Trust not too much*. They are delightful works and receive felicitous performances from this authentic group on Accent who make the most winning sounds. The *Flute Quartets*, Op. 5, in the view of H. C. Robbins Landon may not all be by Haydn. It seems fairly certain, however, that the first two, also known as *Divertimenti*, are authentic, very early works from the 1750s. All the music is engaging when played with such finesse and warmth, although this is a set to be dipped into rather than taken in large doses. The recording is admirably fresh and realistic.

8 Notturni for the King of Naples, Hob II/25–32 (originally for lira organizzata, woodwind, horn and strings, arranged by Haydn for instrumental ensemble).

*** Sony SK 62878. Mozzafiato & L'Archibudello.

(B) *(*) Double Decca 458 075-2 (2). Music Party, Hacker.

These eight divertimenti, in three or four movements (although No. 6 has only two), were commissioned by King Ferdinand IV of Naples and written for the lira organizzata. Or rather a pair of them, for the King played in duet with his friend Norbert Hadrava, an Austrian diplomat. The lira comprised a keyboard and a revolving wheel and was really a modified hurdy-gurdy. It seems a pity that someone could not have managed a reconstruction of this seemingly fascinating instrument. Haydn's original scoring was for two lire, two horns, two clarinets (or later, violins), two violas, and cello (later with double-bass added). He thought sufficiently well of the works and brought them to London with him to play at the Salomon Concerts in 1791, with the lira parts given to flutes, or flute and oboe, and the clarinet parts for practical reasons allotted to violins, which also have independent solo roles in Nos. 7 and 8. This is the nearest Haydn came to writing wind divertimenti of the calibre of those by Mozart, and although this music is slight, it has much charm with particularly sprightly finales, including a jolly fugue for No. 5. (The last movement of No. 6 is lost, although the engaging *Andante* makes up for it.) No. 8 with a slow introduction before the first movement *Allegro* is like a miniature symphony without a minuet, and H. C. Robbins Landon has declared the touching *Adagio* as being the greatest single movement of the whole set. It is eloquently played here and these fresh, dedicated performances by the combined period-instrument groups, Mozzafiato (woodwind, horns and double-bass) and L'Archibudelli are very winning, with the clarinet parts restored. They are beautifully recorded.

The competing performances by Alan Hacker's Music Party stretch to a pair of discs (though costing approximately the same) but fail to take off in the same way; they are not helped by a resonant acoustic which slightly deadens the focus. Only the finales are really vivacious.

8 Notturni for the King of Naples, Hob II/25–32 (Nos. 1–6 only, Hob II/25–6; 29–32)

(N) (B) ** CPO 999 741-2Consortium Classicum, Klöcker.

Dieter Klöcker on CPO gets round the textural problem by using a pair of chamber organs placed to the left and right of his wind and string ensemble (two violas and a double bass), to give an antiphonal effect. The result is piquantly appealing at first, but the continuing use of the upper range of the organs loses its novelty after a time, although the music-making itself is elegant and pleasing. In any case this CPO set is incomplete.

Piano Trios Nos. 1–46, Hob XV:1–41; Hob XIV:C1 in C; Hob XV:C1 in C; Hob XIV6/XVI6 in G; Hob XV:f1 in F min.; Hob deest in D (complete).

✪ (B) *** Ph. 454 098-2 (9). Beaux Arts Trio.

It is not often possible to hail one set of records as a 'classic' in quite the way that Schnabel's Beethoven sonatas can be so described. Yet this set can be described in those terms, for the playing of the Beaux Arts Trio is of the very highest musical distinction. The contribution of the pianist, Menahem Pressler, is inspired, and the recorded sound on CD is astonishingly lifelike. The CD transfer has enhanced detail without losing the warmth of ambience or sense of intimacy. Now offered in a bargain box of nine CDs, this is a set no Haydn lover should miss: it is desert island music.

Piano Trios, Hob XV, Nos. 6–10.

(N) **(*) CPO 999 466-2. Trio 1790.

Piano Trios, Hob XV, Nos 11–14.

(N) **(*) CPO 999 467-2. Trio 1790.

The Beaux Arts Trio have long reigned supreme in this repertoire but those who are attracted by the idea of original

instruments might well consider this expert group Trio 1790, which is based in Cologne and was recorded there in the WDR studios. Mathias Fischer, its violinist, plays an instrument by Leopold Widhalm of Nuremberg, Philip Bosbach a copy of a cello made in 1640 in Southern Germany and Harald Hoeren a copy by Derek Adlam of a fortepiano from 1790 after Matthäus Heilmann. They are intelligent players, and their discs are priced economically. All the same this will remain an adjunct rather than a replacement for the Beaux Arts and the sublime Menaham Pressler.

Piano Trios, Hob XV, Nos. 18 in A, 19 in G min.; (i) Andante with Variations in F min., Hob XVII; (ii) Cantata: The Battle of the Nile, Hob XXV1b4; 2 Italian Duets, Hob XXVa1–2; The Spirit's Song, Hob XXV1a41

(N) *** ASV CDGAU 219 Four Nations Ens. (i) Appel; (ii) Monoyios, Nils Brown.

The Four Nations Ensemble is an acclaimed New York early-music ensemble which presents a handful of Haydn pieces from 1793 to 1800. *The Battle of the Nile*, from which the CD takes its title, was occasioned by Nelson and Lady Hamilton's visit to Esterháza. The Princess Esterhazy arranged for Haydn and some musicians to entertain his guests and Haydn was persuaded to compose this cantata to words by Cornelia Knight, who accompanied them on the visit, celebrating Nelson's victory. Although it is by no manner of means a masterpiece, it pays tribute to Haydn's enormous social versatility. This expert group play the two 1794 *Trios* with exemplary taste and vitality and Andrew Appel gives us a sensitive account of the *Andante with Variations in F minor* on a fine copy of an instrument by Anton Walter. The *The Battle of the Nile* is a rarity and is currently available in only one alternative. An enjoyable, well-played and beautifully recorded disc.

Piano Trios, Hob XV, Nos. 24–27.

(M) *** Ph. 422 831-2. Beaux Arts Trio.

These are all splendid works. No. 25 with its *Gypsy rondos* is the most famous, but each has a character of its own, showing the mature Haydn working at full stretch. The playing here is peerless and the recording truthful and refined.

Piano Trios in A, Hob XV 18; in C, Hob XV 21; Nos. 39 in G (Gypsy), Hob XV 25; in E flat, Hob XV 29.

*** Teldec 0630 15857-2. Trio Fontenay.

Piano Trios in A, Hob XV18; Nos. 38 in D; 39 in G (Gypsy), Hob XV24–25; in E flat, Hob XV29.

*** Nim. NI 5535. Vienna Piano Trio.

There is little to choose here between the Nimbus and Teldec performances: both are polished, warm and spirited, and both are beautifully recorded. Each collection is delightful, and both discs include the best-known *Gypsy Trio* with its sparkling closing rondo. It has to be said, too, that a modern piano adds much colour to these works, which are for the most part light-hearted, and even more in gentle expressive moments like the finale of the *D major Trio*, which is marked *Allegro, ma dolce*, to which Stefan Mendl, the fine pianist in the Vienna Trio, makes an appropriate response. Yet his colleague in the Fontenay group, Wolf Harden is an equally fine ensemble player.

Piano Trios No. 38 in D; 39 in G (Gypsy); 40 in F sharp min., Hob XV 24–26.

**(*) HM HMC 901514. Patrick Cohen, Erich Höbarth, Coin.

The Cohen Trio are in good form here and for those wanting period instrument performances their playing is pleasingly musical and the recording well balanced. However they, only provide three works, which is short measure (47 minutes).

Piano Trios Nos. 42 in E flat, Hob XV/30; 43 in C, Hob XV/27; 44 in E, Hob XV/28; 45 in E flat, Hob XV/29.

⬤ *** Sony SK 53120. Vera Beths, Anner Bylsma, Levin.

Piano Trios Nos. 43–45.

(B) **(*) HM HMC 901572. Patrick Cohen, Erich Höbarth, Christophe Coin.

This Sony group plays with immense flair and spirit and conveys the exhilaration of the finale of the *C major Trio* (No. 43, Hob XV/27) superbly well and the depth and poetry of the middle movements. Infectious in its high spirits and delight in music-making, and very well recorded! It is good to have modern digital alternatives to the justly famous Beaux Arts versions. Strongly recommended.

The Cohen Trio are not quite so successful in Haydn as they were in early Beethoven but their playing is still refreshing. In the *C major Trio* there are a few over-strong accents and an occasional touch of abrasiveness, brought by the close microphones. The players capture the *innocentement* of the *Andantino* and are at their finest in the robust vigour of the rustic dance which ends the piece boisterously. However the competing Sony disc offers an extra work and makes an obvious first choice.

String quartets (with list of keys and opus nos.)

String Quartets Nos. *1 in B flat; 2 in E flat; 3 in D; 4 in G; 5 in E flat; 6 in C (Op. 1/1–6); No 7 in A; No 8 in E (Op. 2/1–2); 9 in F; 10 in B flat (Op. 2/4 & 6); 19 in C; 20 in E flat; 21 in G; 22 in D min.; 23 in B flat; 24 in A (Op. 9/1–6); 25 in E; 26 in F; 27 in E flat; 28 in C min.; 29 in G; 30 in D (Op. 17/1–6); 31 in E flat; 32 in C; 33 in D min.; 34 in D; 35 in F min.; 36 in A (Op. 20/1–6); 37 in B min.; 38 in E flat; 39 in C; 40 in B flat; 41 in G; 42 in D (Op. 33/1–6); 43 in D min. (Op. 42); 44 in B flat; 45 in C; 46 in E flat; 47 in F sharp min.; 48 in F; 49 in D (Op. 50/1–6); 50–56 (The Seven Last Words of Our Saviour on the Cross, Op. 51); 57 in G; 58 in C; 59 in E (Op. 54/1–3); 60 in A; 61 in F min.; 62 in B flat (Op. 55/1–3); 63 in C; 64 in B min.; 65 in B flat; 66 in G; 67 in D; 68 in E flat (Op. 64/1–6); 69 in B flat; 70 in D; 71 in E flat (Op. 71/1–3); 72 in C; 73 in F; 74 in G min. (Op. 74/1–3); 75 in G; 76 in D min.; 77 in C; 78 in B flat; 79 in D; 80 in E flat (Op. 76/1–6); 81 in G; 82 in F (Op. 77/1–2); 83 in D min. (Op. 103).*

String Quartets Nos. 1–12; 19–83; String Quartet Fragments in D min. (Andante grazioso & minuet), Op. 103 (includes The Seven Last Words of Christ on the Cross, Op. 51/1–7, with readings selected by Reginald Barrett-Ayres).

(B) **(*) Decca 455 261-2 (22). Aeolian Qt.

The first complete recording of the Haydn *String Quartets* in stereo was Decca's project parallel to Dorati's integral recording of the symphonies. The performances were recorded over a period of four years between December 1972 and December 1976, using the critical edition by Reginald Barrett-Ayres and H. C. Robbins Landon. The recordings were made in two London churches, beginning with Opp. 71 and 74, followed by Op. 2. Though the performances of these late works are vigorously enjoyable, the engineers let the ecclesiastical acoustic provide the four players with a degree of 'helpful' reverberation which in Opp. 71 and 74 made them sound a little like a string orchestra, although the microphone placing ensures clarity of part-writing as well as warmth. By the time Decca came to record Op. 2, the problem was solved, and for the remaining sessions the recording team moved to St John's, Smith Square, where an excellent and realistic presence was consistently achieved, the profile of the leader (Emanuel Hurwitz) bright without being edgy.

It is not always an advantage in the early quartets of Opp. 1 and 2 that the Aeolian players are wedded to repeats. Nevertheless, on their own unpretentious level these are charming works, and Hurwitz readily takes his chances in such a *Quartet* as Op. 2/1, which includes stylish cadenzas. The Op. 3 *Quartets* are now claimed to be by Romanus Hofstetter, not by Haydn, and they have understandably been omitted from the present box.

Though few of the quartets of Opp. 9 and 17 are consistently inspired from beginning to end (the *G major*, No. 29, is a marvellous exception), they all contain their moments of magic, and by now the Aeolian group, having settled into their task, play with consistent freshness. The fine Op. 20 set is also given here in well-prepared and musical accounts, as are the six Op. 33 *Quartets*. Tovey describes them as 'the lightest of all Haydn's mature comedies', for by the time he wrote them, in 1781, many years after the Op. 20 group, Haydn was learning from the young Mozart. Mozart returned the compliment in the six masterpieces he dedicated to Haydn; in his turn, Haydn responded with his Op. 50 group, cogent in their monothematic form. The Aeolians came to these marvellous works fairly late on in their complete cycle, but the players' perception and energy are, if anything, keener than ever. Not all their tempi are beyond question, but the wonder is how consistently enjoyable their playing is.

The set is crowned by their admirable performances of the consistently inspired last *Quartets*, Opp. 77 and 76. The straight, unmannered approach disguises consistent imaginative thoughtfulness, and the music's characteristic touches of humour (as in the genial bouncing opening Allegro of Op. 77/1) are not missed. *The Seven Last Words of Jesus Christ* (Nos. 50–56, Op. 51) are treated as an appendix. Haydn confessed that it was 'no easy task to compose seven adagios, lasting approximately ten minutes each, and to succeed one another without fatiguing the listener'. But the result is profound, and the performances here avoid any risk of monotony by inserting poetry readings between movements. The texts (from John Donne, George Herbert, Robert Herrick and Edith Sitwell, among others) are aptly chosen and beautifully read by Sir Peter Pears. All told, this is a fine achievement. The documentation consists of an excellent essay by Lindsay Kemp. However, this set is now upstaged by the new Philips survey by the Angeles Quartet.

String Quartets Nos. 1–10; 19–83 (complete).

(N) (B) *** Ph. 464 650-2 (21). Angeles Qt.

(N) (BB) **(*) Naxos 8.502301 (23). Kodály Qt.

This complete survey by the Angeles Quartet comes on twenty-one CDs and was made over a period of five years (1994–9). Both the playing and the sound quality are of a consistently high standard: generally speaking the set is beautifully balanced without excessive reverberation and with great clarity; the players have warmth, intelligence and a refined tonal blend and their readings are full of character and wit. They leave you in no doubt that they have thought deeply about this music, but at the same time they never leave the impression that they are too studied or wanting in spontaneity.

The internal balance is very good indeed, even if one might occasionally welcome greater projection from the cellist. Tempos are finely judged, and there is a keen awareness of Haydn's developing stature throughout. One never gets the feeling that one is hearing the earlier quartets through the eyes and ears of the later quartets. The group's sense of characterization is pretty unerring, and it leaves you marvelling anew at the quality of Haydn's musical invention.

It is difficult to generalize about so vast an output or so ambitious a recording enterprise, but the Angeles Quartet brings greater elegance and polish to this music than the Aeolian set on 22 CDs, which comes from the early 1970s, and greater transparency of texture than the Kodály on Naxos and arguably greater finish. The Kodály does not lack warmth or a sense of style, and the consistently friendly warmth of these players' approach to Haydn's music is always endearing. Apparently they turned up at the Naxos recording venue at regular intervals ready to record a set or group of the quartets after they had lived with the music and reached the point that they felt fully prepared. The result almost always sounds spontaneous and usually carries the feeling of 'live' music-making.

The Kodály's playing was flattered by the warm acoustics of the Budapest Unitarian Church, which suited its mellow, civilised approach, although at times the engineers slightly miscalculated the microphone balance and captured a little too much resonance, bringing a degree of textural inflation. But the sound is always natural, the performances do not miss Haydn's subtleties or his jokes, and the group always communicates readily.

Those wanting to collect an inexpensive survey in instalments might prefer the Kodály set rather than the larger initial outlay of the Angeles Philips box. However, without forgetting or naming all the many excellent individual sets and collections by the Mosaïques (on period instruments), Tokyo (Op. 50), the Lindsays (especially in Op. 76) and

others, the Philips set ranks alongside the very best. Its claims are enhanced by an impressive essay by Richard Wigmore.

The Naxos discs (which come in a big slip-case in their original jewel-cases with excellent documentation) are all available separately, and as such are discussed below.

String Quartets: Nos. 1 (La Chasse), Op. 1/1; 32, Op. 20/2; 35, Op. 20/5; 46, Op. 50/3; 57; 58; 59, Op. 54/1–3; 65; 66, Op. 64/3–4; 74 (Rider), Op. 74/3; 77 (Emperor), Op. 76/3; 78 (Sunrise), Op. 77/2.

(**(*)) Testament mono SBT 3055 (3). Pro Arte Qt.

String Quartets: Nos. 6, Op. 1/6; 16; 17 (Serenade), Op. 3/4–5 (Hoffstetter); 31; 34, Op. 20/1 & 4; 38 (Joke); 39 (Bird); 42 (How do you do?), Op. 33/2, 3 & 6 (Le Matin); 49 (Frog), Op. 50/6; 60; 62, Op. 55/1 & 3; 68, Op. 64/6; 69, Op. 71/1; 72; 73, Op. 74/1–2; 81, Op. 77/1.

(**(*)) Testament mono SBT 4056 (4). Pro Arte Qt.

While LP and CD reissues have kept the name of the Busch Quartet alive, the Pro Arte is a less familiar one to modern collectors. In their hands the Haydn *Quartets* bring us a world of delight, wisdom and sanity, and few groups are better guides. They have great purity of style and an immaculate intonation and technique, while they seem always to hit on exactly the right tempo, which in turn enables phrasing to speak naturally. However, the actual sound of these recordings calls for a little tolerance. The violin, particularly above the stave, is wanting in bloom, and one would welcome more space between movements. Less than perfect sound, perhaps, as might be expected from their recording dates (1931–8), but impeccable Haydn playing.

String Quartets: Op. 1/0; Nos. 43, Op. 42; 83, Op. 103.

**(*) Mer. (ADD) ECD 88117. English Qt.

These fine players rise to all the challenges posed by this music, and the recorded sound is eminently truthful. There would have been room for another quartet on this disc, which offers rather short measure at 43 minutes.

String Quartets Nos. 1–4, Op. 1/1–4.

(BB) **(*) Naxos 8.550398. Kodály Qt.

String Quartets Nos. 5–6, Op. 1/5–6; 7–8, Op. 2/1–2.

(BB) **(*) Naxos 8.550399. Kodály Qt.

The Op. 1 and Op. 2 quartets are in essence five-movement divertimenti scored for four string players. These earliest works have not quite the unquenchable flow of original ideas that the early symphonies have but, in such fresh performances as these, they make easy and enjoyable listening even if, with the performances generous in observing repeats, some movements outstay their welcome. The resonant ambience of the Unitarian Church in Budapest seems not unsuitable for works which lie midway between divertimenti and quartets, and the focus seems brighter and sharper on the second CD, recorded in June 1991, two months after the first.

String Quartets Nos. 1, Op. 1/1; 67 (Lark), Op. 64/5; 74, Op. 74/3 (Rider).

*** DG 423 622-2. Hagen Qt.

The Hagen are supple, cultured and at times perhaps a little overcivilized, but in these three Haydn quartets they play flawlessly and are wonderfully alert and intelligent.

String Quartets Nos. 9–10, Op. 2/4 & 6 (Le Matin); 35, Op. 42.

(BB) **(*) Naxos 8.550732. Kodály Qt.

The Unitarian Church, Budapest, continues to provide a warm, flattering tonal blend but a texture that is a little too ample for early Haydn, while the fairly close microphones reduce the dynamic range. However, the Kodály's friendly style and elegant finish suit early Haydn. These performers find exactly the right degree of expressiveness for the *Adagio* of Op. 2/4 and are equally at home in the engaging *Andante ed innocentemente* which opens the first movement of Op. 42, a splendid work, written a quarter of a century later.

String Quartets Nos. 17 (Serenade), Op. 3/5; 38 (Joke), Op. 33/2; 76 (Fifths), Op. 76/2.

(B) **(*) Discover DIDCD 920172. Sharon Qt.

The Sharon Quartet are an excellent group and they give warm and spirited accounts of these three favourite quartets. They are recorded in the resonant acoustics of St John's Church in Cologne and, like some of the recordings made for Naxos by the Kodály Quartet, the resonance expands the texture, although not seriously enough to prevent enjoyment, for they make a bright, clean sound. They find charm in Hofstetter's famous *Serenade* of Op. 3 and are equally good in the *Variations* which form the slow movement of the *Fifths*; at the same time, they find the right approach to the *Joke* in the finale of Op. 33/2.

String Quartets Nos. 17 (Serenade), Op. 3/5; 63 (Lark), Op. 64/5; 76 (Fifths), Op. 76/2.

(B) *** Ph. (ADD) 426 097-2. Italian Qt.

First-class playing here; although the first movement of the *Lark* is a bit measured in feeling, the inauthentic*Serenade Quartet* is made to sound inspired, its famous slow movement played with exquisite gentleness. The *D minor Quartet* is admirably poised and classical in feeling. A real bargain.

String Quartets Nos. 19; 21–22, Op. 9/1, 3 & 4.

(BB) *** Naxos 8.550786. Kodály Qt.

String Quartets Nos. 20; 23; 24, Op. 9/2, 5 & 6.

(BB) *** Naxos 8.550787. Kodály Qt.

The Kodály Quartet are in excellent form throughout Opus 9. Their simple eloquence in all three slow movements on the first disc serves Haydn well: the *Largo* of Op. 9/3 is ideally paced and beautifully poised. The players then go on to give a captivating account of the finale. Indeed, all the finales here are superb, showing Haydn at full stretch. The last of the set in A major opens with a very attractive *Presto* in 6/8, which is delightfully buoyant here. Fortunately, the Naxos recording team (in December 1992 and January 1993) have mastered the acoustics of the Unitarian Church in Budapest. The microphones are in the right place, the sound is not inflated.

String Quartets Nos. 25–26; 28, Op. 17/1, 2 & 4.

(BB) *** Naxos 8.550853. Kodály Qt.

The Kodály Quartet seem very much at home in this music, which they approach with affection, yet with an appealing directness which leads to playing which is perfectly integrated, yet fresh. The recording could hardly be bettered: the balance is most natural.

String Quartets Nos. 27; 29; 30, Op. 17/3, 5 & 6.

(BB) *** Naxos 8.550854-2. Kodály Qt.

While the other works here are also played with pleasing warmth and finesse, the highlight of the second Naxos disc of Op.17 is the *D major Quartet* which has a searching, aria-like slow movement, dominated by the principal violin, which is played most eloquently here. This is the last of the set, and appropriately the last to be recorded in this highly distinguished Naxos series. The recording balance is quite admirable.

String Quartets Nos. 31–36, Op. 20/1–6.

❀ *** Astrée E 8784 (2). Mosaïques Qt.

String Quartets Nos. 31–33, Op. 20/1–3.

(BB) ** Naxos 8.550701. Kodály Qt.

String Quartets Nos. 34–36, Op. 20/4–6.

(BB) ** Naxos 8.550702. Kodály Qt.

Using period instruments, the four players of the Mosaïques Quartet create individual timbres which are pleasing to the ear and which have body and transparency, are perfectly matched and never edgy. There is no squeezed phrasing, and the use of vibrato is as subtle as the control of colour and dynamic. Intonation and ensemble are remarkably exact. Such is the calibre of this music-making and the strength of insight of these players that the character of these fine, relatively early works is communicated with seemingly total spontaneity. This is playing of rare distinction which is immensely revealing and rewarding, helped by state-of-the-art recording of complete realism and presence within an acoustic that provides the necessary intimacy of ambience.

The Naxos Kodály series brings polished, sympathetic playing of considerable warmth. Allegros are lively, but the acoustics of the Unitarian Church, Budapest, though providing beautifully rich string-textures, here make the effect almost orchestral and bring an element of blandness to the fine *Adagio* slow movements; throughout, the dynamic range of the playing is reduced by the microphone positioning. The theme and variations of the *Poco adagio e affettuoso* of the *D major Quartet*, Op. 20/4, are attractively characterized but badly need a wider dynamic contrast. This is even more striking in the *Fuga a quattro soggetti* which forms the finale of Op. 20/2.

String Quartets Nos. 31; 33; 34 (Sun), Op. 20/1, 3, & 4.

**(*) ASV CDDCA 1027. Lindsay Qt.

The Lindsays are at their finest in *No. 34 in D major* and make much of its theme and variations slow movement, brief Gypsy Minuet and scherzando finale. These recordings were apparently made under studio conditions and the playing in the slow movements of the other two quartets has slightly less concentration than one has come to expect from their 'live' recordings. The sound is first class, and the extra finish of the ensemble brings its own rewards.

String Quartets Nos. 32; 34, 35, Op. 20/2, 5 & 6.

*** ASV CDDCA 1057. Lindsay Qt.

These are three of Haydn's very greatest mid-period quartets, and the Lindsays have their full measure, with the feeling of 'live' music-making persisting throughout. The rich-textured opening of *No. 32 in C major* is immediately inviting, and the *Capriccio* second movement is most sensitively done, as is the lovely, rocking siciliano *Adagio* of *No. 34 in F minor*. The *Allegro di molto e scherzando* character of the first movement of the *A major* is perfectly caught. All three finales are fugal, and the lightness and keeness of articulation here is a joy. Excellent truthful recording. Very highly recommended.

String Quartets Nos. 32, Op. 20/2; 44, Op. 50/1; 76 (Fifths), Op. 76/2.

(BB) *** ASV CDQS 6144. Lindsay Qt.

Since these are public performances, one has to accept music-making reflecting the heat of the occasion, the odd sense of roughness (the finale of Op. 76, No. 2), for these artists take risks – and this is perhaps a shade faster than it would be in a studio. There is splendid character in these performances and plenty of musical imagination. These readings have a spontaneity which is refreshing in these days of retakes! The recordings are eminently truthful and audience noise is minimal. An excellent bargain.

String Quartets Nos. 34 (Sun), Op. 20/4; 38 (Joke), Op. 33/2; 39 (Bird), Op. 33/3; 61 (Razor), Op. 55/2; 67 (Lark), Op. 64/5; 77 (Emperor), Op. 76/3.

(M) *** ASV CDDCS 236 (2). Lindsay Qt.

All these performances show the Lindsays on top form; indeed the *Sun Quartet* is the finest performance on the full-priced CD from which it comes. Anyone wanting a grouping of these named quartets (all masterpieces) cannot go wrong here as the recordings are all vividly real: the *Emperor*, for instance, which was recorded live, is very present indeed. The only snag is that a compilation like this cuts across other collections which group together works of a single Opus number.

String Quartets Nos. 34, Op. 20/4; 47, Op. 50/4; 77 (Emperor), Op. 76/3.

*** ASV CDDCA 731. Lindsay Qt.

The Lindsay performances were again recorded at public performances, on this occasion in London's Wigmore Hall. The advantages this brings are twofold: higher spontaneity and a greater propensity to take risks. In all three performances the gains outweigh any loss, though the balance tends to cause some coarse-sounding tone in fortissimo passages.

String Quartets Nos. 35, Op. 20/5; 40, Op. 33/4; 70, Op. 71/2.

(BB) *** ASV CDQS 6146. Lindsay Qt.

The immediacy of the Lindsays' playing here is just as striking as before, yet at the rather serious opening of the *F minor*, Op. 20/5, the approach is appropriately sober and considered as well as spontaneous. This quartet also has a tender *Siciliano* slow movement which is played with affecting simplicity and grace. The account of the *B flat Quartet*, Op. 33/4, brings a burst of applause at the end, as well it might, with its deeply thoughtful *Largo* and engaging finale. Three marvellous works, recorded with striking presence.

String Quartets Nos. 37; 38 (Joke); 39 (Bird), Op. 33/1–3.

*** Kingdom KCLCD 2014. Bingham Qt.

String Quartets Nos. 37; 38 (Joke); 40, Op. 33/1–2 & 4.

**(*) ASV CDDCA 937. Lindsay Qt.

String Quartets Nos. 37–42, Op. 33/1–6.

*** Astrée E 8801 (2). Mosaïques Qt.

String Quartets Nos. 37–38 & 41, Op. 33/1–2 & 5.

(BB) **(*) Naxos 8.550788. Kodály Qt.

String Quartets Nos. 39–40 & 42, Op. 33/3–4 & 6.

(BB) **(*) Naxos 8.550789. Kodály Qt.

String Quartets Nos. 39 (Bird); 41 in G; 42, Op. 33/3, 5 & 6.

*** ASV CDDCA 938. Lindsay Qt.

String Quartets Nos. 40; 41; 42 (How do you do?), Op. 33/4–6.

*** Kingdom KCLCD 2015. Bingham Qt.

Although Haydn had written some fine quartets before these were published in 1782, this Op. 33 set proved a watermark. Here he finally established himself as complete master of a new medium.

Those wanting Op. 33 on period instruments can be recommended without reservation to the Mosaïques Quartet, whose performances are more penetrating than any of their competitors. Indeed the intensity of the playing is remarkable, with concentration held throughout the widest range of dynamic, and constantly uncovering hidden depths in these works, even in the *Joke Quartet*. There are touches of darkness, as well as serenity, in adagios; and finales dance with fairy lightness, while the crisply pointed *Allegretto* which ends Op. 33/6 has a Beechamesque rhythmic panache. Marvellous playing throughout, with every detail revealed in sound which is both transparent, yet never in the least textually meagre. The superb recording is perfectly balanced.

The tonal matching and ensemble of the Bingham Quartet are most impressive, with the leader, Stephen Bingham, a remarkably stylish player who really understands how to shape a Haydn phrase. Above all the Binghams convey their pleasure in the music, and every performance here sounds fresh. The recording was made at the Conway Hall, London, in 1990. The balance is a shade close, but the instruments are naturally focused, individually and as a group. Even if the range of dynamic is a little affected, the playing itself is full of light and shade so that if the volume level is carefully set one soon forgets this reservation in the sheer pleasure this music affords.

The Kodály Quartet play Op. 33 with an easy relaxed warmth. Their style is low-key so that the 'Joke' finale of Op. 33/2 is rather gentle and muted; on the other hand, the reason for the sobriquet of the *Bird Quartet* is affectionately conveyed and the finale is delightfully light-hearted. Slow movements are serene and quietly musical. Minuets are generally full of character, with the trios nicely realized, and this applies especially to the charming middle section of the Scherzo in the *Joke Quartet*. In short these are performances which convey the players' affection for this wonderful music with no possible desire to put their own personalities between composer and listener. The Naxos recording is wholly natural with the acoustics of the Budapest Unitarian Church beautifully caught without any textural inflation.

If the Kodály Quartet are exceptionally relaxed in Op. 33, the Lindsays are at the opposite end of the scale: vividly alert and with the playing full of tension, emphasized by the recording, where the microphones are close, giving striking presence and emphasizing the bite on the timbre of the leader, Peter Cropper. Fortunately, the superb ensemble stands up to such scrutiny. No one could say that the Lindsays miss the wit inherent in the finale of the *Joke*; yet, in spite of the gentle ending, the smile is weakened by the vibrant purposefulness. The performances here use the Henle Urtext edition, which differs quite substantially in phrasing and, in places, even in notes from the more familiar Peters Edition, especially at the opening of Op. 33/1. The second disc includes a Rosette-worthy account of Op. 33/3 with Haydn's birdsong exquisitely simulated.

String Quartet No. 39 in C (Bird), Op. 33/3.

✿ (N) (BB) *** Dutton mono CDBP 9702. Griller Qt – MOZART: *String Quartets Nos. 14–15 in D min., K.421 (Haydn Quartets).* *** ✿

This simply one of the finest Haydn Quartet recordings ever put on disc, and the Dutton transfer from the 1946 Decca ffrr 78s miraculously provides a sound quality superior to many modern digital stereo recordings. The Griller were in their absolute prime at the time. You need only sample the grace and finesse of the first movement, with its engaging chirping, the serene blending of timbre in the *Adagio* and the elegance of the closing *Rondo* to realize that this playing is very special indeed, as is the recording.

String Quartets Nos. 43, Op. 42; 67 (Lark), Op. 64/5; 79, Op. 76/5.

(BB) *** ASV CDQS 6145. Lindsay Qt.

The Lindsays are given a striking presence here and the spontaneity of their playing is gripping. The presto finales (particularly the moto perpetuo of *The Lark*, which overall is most strikingly done) offer fizzing bravura and the beautiful slow movement of Op. 76/5 is rapt in its quiet intensity. There are remarkably few moments of roughness of ensemble arising from the impetuosity of the playing.

String Quartets Nos. 44–49, Op. 50/1–6.

(BB) *** Naxos 8.553983 (Nos. 44–46); 8.553984 (Nos. 47–49) (available separately). Kodály Qt.

The Kodály Quartet are back to their finest form in Op. 50

and they are most naturally recorded. These are mellow performances, warm and polished, with perfect blending of timbre, yet refined detail. Slow movements are beautifully shaped, with the leader Attila Falway frequently distinguishing himself with the graceful finish of his phrasing. Allegros are spirited but unforced, Minuets have an affectionate modicum of wit, and finales are never rushed.

String Quartets Nos. 46 in E flat; 48 in F, Op. 50/3 & 5; 76 in D min.(Fifths), Op. 76/2; 83 in B flat, Op. 103.

(N) (B) ** Cal (ADD) CAL 6267. Suk Qt.

Fine peformances from the Suk Quartet, warm and polished. They have obviously lived with this music and play it with a natural impetus. The analogue recording, however, is rather recessed and though the sound is pleasing most listeners will seek better defined detail.

String Quartets Nos. 50–56 (The Seven Last Words of Our Saviour on the Cross), Op. 51.

✿ *** ASV CDDCA 853. Lindsay Quartet.
(N) *** Astrée E 8803. Mosaïques Qt.

String Quartets Nos. 50–56 (The Seven Last Words of Our Saviour on the Cross), Op. 51; 83, Op. 103.

(BB) *** Naxos 8.550346. Kodály Qt.

No work for string quartet, not even late Beethoven, presents more taxing interpretative problems than Haydn's *Seven Last Words of Our Saviour on the Cross*. The recording by the Lindsay Quartet, while offering all the devotional gravity that Haydn demands, brings not just an illuminating variety but also a sense of drama, and the performance makes no compromise for, unlike some others, the Lindsays observe the first-half repeats in each movement, extending the work to a full 70 minutes, instead of under an hour. After the long sequence of slow movements, the Lindsays' account of the final, brief Presto, *Il terremoto*, then conveys the full, elemental force of the earthquake. It is thrilling with so elusive a work to have so complete an answer in a single recording, with sound both well defined and glowingly beautiful, set against an apt church acoustic.

The slightly austere style of the Mosaïques Quartet is perfectly suited to the sometimes withdrawn expressive intensity of Haydn's collection of seven Adagios. The Introduction is immediately commanding, and throughout the playing combines strength with subtlety, with the fifth and sixth movements gaining from the lean timbre, delicacy of feeling and great concentration, and the seventh (which Haydn marks 'Pater in tuas manus commendo spiritum meum') finding a natural resolution. The final 'earthquake' could hardly be more forcefully telling. Excellent, vivid recording within a well-judged ambience.

The Kodály Quartet give a memorable performance, strongly characterized and beautifully played, with subtle contrasts of expressive tension between the seven inner slow movements. They also offer an appropriate bonus in Haydn's last, unfinished, two-movement *Quartet*. The recording is first rate, vividly present yet naturally balanced, like the other issues in this attractive Naxos series.

String Quartets Nos. 57–59, Op. 54/1–3.

*** ASV CDDCA 582. Lindsay Qt.
(BB) *** Naxos 8.550395. Kodály Qt.
*** Hyp. CDA 66971. Salomon Qt.

The present works show Haydn at his most inventive and resourceful. The playing of the Lindsay Quartet is splendidly poised and vital, and the recording is very fine indeed.

The Kodály players enter animatedly into the spirit of the music; the leader, Attila Falvay, shows himself fully equal to Haydn's bravura embellishments in the demanding first violin writing. The Naxos sound is fresh and truthful.

The Salomon Quartet, led by Simon Standage, play on period instruments, but there is nothing anaemic or edgy about the body of tone they command, and the pervading feeling here is of freshness, with finales spirited without being rushed off their feet. This is one of the very best records from these excellent players and the recording is first class.

String Quartets Nos. 57–59, Op. 54/1–3; 71; 73; 74, Op. 74/1–3.

(BB) *** Virgin 2 x 1 VBD5 61436-2 (2). Endellion Qt.

The Endellion Quartet were recorded in The Maltings, Snape (in 1988 and 1990 respectively), which provides an ideal acoustic environment. The playing is bright-eyed, fresh and vital, and in both sets they prove a sound guide to this repertoire. The sound is strikingly immediate but is beautifully integrated, and there are many moments of musical insight. With the two discs offered for the cost of a single mid-priced CD, this set is very competitive.

String Quartets Nos. 60; 61 (Razor); 62, Op. 55/1–3 (Tost Quartets).

*** ASV CDDCA 906. Lindsay Qt.
(BB) **(*) Naxos 8.550397. Kodály Qt.
**(*) Hyp. CDA 66972. Salomon Qt.

Here the Lindsays are heard under studio conditions, but in Holy Trinity Church, Wentworth, and the results, on the second set of *Tost Quartets*, are marginally less chimerical than in their live recordings, but not less dedicated or less vital. There is of course greater polish, as the fizzing finale of Op. 55/3 readily demonstrates. The recording is lifelike and vivid without excessive resonance.

Opus 55 brings playing from the Kodály Quartet which is undoubtedly spirited and generally polished, but the music-making at times seems plainer than usual in the Naxos series. The recording is bright and clear, with a realistic presence.

Generally fine playing from the Salomon Quartet in Op. 55, although this record is not quite as memorable as was Op. 54. The *Razor*, the second of the set, comes off very well indeed; but the slow movements in the two works on either side of it sound a shade too precise. The recording is truthful but rather close.

String Quartets Nos. 63–65, Op. 64/1–3.

*** Hyp. CDA 67011. Salomon Qt.
(BB) *** Naxos 8.550673. Kodály Qt.

String Quartets Nos. 66; 67 (Lark); 68, Op. 64/4–6.

*** Hyp. CDA 67012. Salomon Qt.
(BB) *** Naxos 8.550674. Kodály Qt.

Like Opp. 54 and 55, Haydn's Op. 64 set was dedicated to the violinist and businessman Johann Tost, who had led the second violins in the Eszterházy orchestra, and they show Haydn at his most inspired. The Salomon performances are well up to the standard of their versions of those earlier works. Their timbre is leaner than that of the estimable Kodály Quartet on Naxos (8.550673/4) but they blend beautifully and have their own insights to offer: their precise ensemble in no way inhibits commitment and feeling. The second of the two discs is particularly rewarding, with the famous opening movement of the *Lark* readily taking flight and the *Adagio* poised and intense. The Hyperion recording is admirably truthful.

These Kodály performances are all enjoyable, but the set seems to get better and better as it progresses. Op. 64/1–3 were recorded on 25–29 April 1992; the last to be done, the *B flat major*, is remarkably successful, with a vigorous opening *Vivace assai* and a rapt *Adagio*. The other three works were taped on 1–3 May, and clearly the group had found its top form. The *Adagio – cantabile e sostenuto* of No. 4 finds them at their most concentrated: the *Lark* has never soared aloft more spontaneously and the Minuet and finale of No. 6 close the set in a winningly spirited fashion. The warm acoustics of the Budapest Unitarian Church provide a mellow and expansive sound-image, but not an orchestral one, and detail remains clear. A most enjoyable set.

String Quartets Nos. 67 (Lark), Op. 64/5; 74 (Rider), Op. 74/3; 77 (Emperor), Op. 76/3.

(B) *** DG (ADD) 439 479-2. Amadeus Qt.

Here is a worthwhile triptych of named quartets for those seeking to sample the Amadeus Quartet in Haydn. Their superb ensemble is immediately noticeable at the opening of the *Lark Quartet*, as is Norbert Brainin's vibrato, giving the Amadeus sound its special stamp. The finale brings spiccato precision that dazzles the ear. The *Largo* of the *Rider Quartet* sounds just a little deliberate but its intensity is in no doubt, and the gutsy vibrancy of the playing in the finale is equally remarkable. These date from the 1970s; the *Emperor* was made a decade earlier and the recording is a trifle thinner. The performance shows these fine musicians in the best possible light.

String Quartets Nos. 69–71 (Apponyi Quartets), Op. 71/1–3; 72–74 (Rider), Op. 74/1–3.

(BB) *** Naxos 8.550394 (Nos. 69–71); 8.550396 (Nos. 72–74). Kodály Qt.
(M) *** Arcana A 918 (2). Festetics Qt.
**(*) Chan. 9416. Chilingirian Qt.

The *Apponyi Quartets* are among the composer's finest. The Naxos recordings by the Kodály Quartet are outstanding in every way and would be highly recommendable even without their considerable price advantage. The digital recording has vivid presence and just the right amount of ambience: the effect is entirely natural.

The Festetics Quartet continue their period-instrument Haydn series with beautifully judged performances of Opp. 71 and 74. The playing has the customary animation and finish, with detail perceptively observed, and well-blended yet beautifully transparent textures. As before, there is nothing vinegary here, and phrasing and line are impeccably musical. Minuets are pleasing, without heaviness (sample the Trio of Op. 71/3 for delectable articulation) and finales sparkle. These are three-star performances without a doubt, and the recording could hardly be better judged. One's only reservation concerns slow movements, sometimes a little solemn.

The Chilingirians' opening of the first of the *Apponyi Quartets* is very positive. This is spick-and-span playing, highly musical and full of character. Slow movements are well shaped and expressive and there are moments of wit, notably in the Minuet and Trio of No. 3. The recording is truthful. Yet this playing, although by no means plain, lacks something of the sunny quality the Kodály Quartet brings to this music.

String Quartets Nos. 71, Op. 71/3; 72 in C, Op. 74/1.

**(*) Hyp. CDA 66098. Salomon Qt.

String Quartets Nos. 73; 74, Op. 74/2–3.

**(*) Hyp. CDA 66124. Salomon Qt.

The Salomon Quartet use period instruments, vibrato-less but vibrant; the sonorities, far from being nasal and unpleasing, are clean and transparent. There is imagination and vitality here, and the Hyperion recording is splendidly truthful. However, each disc offers short measure.

String Quartet No. 74 (Rider), Op. 74/3.

(M) *** Cal. CAL 6698. Talich Qt – BOCCHERINI: *Quartet, Op. 58/2;* MENDELSSOHN: *Quartet No. 2;* MICA: *Quartet No. 6.* ***

The *Quartet in G minor*, Opus 74, No. 3, is one of Haydn's greatest quartets. It brings a very beautiful, serenely introspective *Largo assai* in which, in this searching Talich performance, one has the feeling of eavesdropping on private music-making. After the blithe Minuet, the finale is engagingly light and spirited. Superb playing and most natural recording, and the rest of the performances on this generously filled mid-priced CD (76 minutes) are equally distinguished.

String Quartets Nos. 74 (Rider), Op. 74/3; 77 (Emperor), Op. 76/3.

(B) *** Teldec 3984 21849-2. Alban Berg Qt.

Back in the early 1970s the Alban Berg Quartet displayed admirable polish, but the end-result was without that hint of glossy perfection which poses a problem with some of their more recent, digital recordings. The playing here has wonderful resilience and sparkle. The famous slow movement of the *Emperor Quartet* has seldom been put on record with such warmth and eloquence, and the slow movement of No. 74 is even more beautiful. Indeed the performance of this *Quartet* is masterly, with the rhythmic figure in the first movement which gives the work its title admirably managed.

The recording too is first class, full and clear, and this is one of the most rewarding of all Haydn quartet couplings. The playing time is only 45 minutes, but every one of them is treasurable and this disc is inexpensive.

String Quartets Nos. 75; 76 (Fifths); 77 (Emperor); 78 (Sunrise); 79; 80, Op. 76/1–6 (Erdödy Quartets).

(N) ❁ *** ASV CDDCA 1076 (*Nos.75–77*); CDDCA 1077 (*Nos. 78–80*). Lindsay Qt.

(N) *** Astrée E 8665 (2). Mosaïques Qt.

(BB) *** Naxos 8.550314 (*Nos. 75–77*); 8.550315; 4550315 (*Nos. 78–80*). Kodály Qt.

(B) **(*) Sony SB2K 53522 (2). Tokyo Qt.

String Quartets Nos. 75; 79; 80, Op. 76/1, 5 & 6.

*** EMI CDC5 56826-2. Alban Berg Qt.

String Quartets Nos. 76 (Fifths); 77 (Emperor); 78 t, Op. 76/2-4.

*** EMI CDC5 56166-2. Alban Berg Qt.

String Quartets Nos. 76 (Fifths); 77 (Emperor); 78 (Sunrise), Op. 76/2-4.

(BB) *** Naxos 8.550129. Kodály Qt.

The Lindsays crown their series of Haydn recordings with this superb set of the supreme masterpieces from Opus 76, marvellously played and truthfully recorded. In their hands these quartets are made to sound among the greatest ever written, which of course they are. The Lindsays have covered three of these works before, in live recordings, but this time not only is the sound more refined, the performances are too, while keeping the strength and warmth which characterizes all the Lindsays' playing. The first of the three may be less frequently performed than the others but after an exhilarating account of the chirpy first movement, where the delicacy of articulation and refinement of ensemble are most striking, the hushed, nobly restrained *Andante sostenuto* has in their hands a transcending Beethovenian depth and profundity. The purposeful first movement of the *Fifths* is taken briskly, but every detail tells, and here the lighter mood of the *Andante o più allegretto* is enchantingly caught. The famous slow movement of the *Emperor*, also, has unusual refinement as well as warmth, and this too is a performance as vital as it is polished. Very highly recommended.

The Kodály Quartet too are fully worthy of the composer's inexhaustible invention and make a splendid bargain recommendation. Their playing brings a joyful pleasure in Haydn's inspiration and there is not the slightest suspicion of over-rehearsal or of routine: every bar of the music springs to life spontaneously, and these musicians' insights bring an ideal combination of authority and warmth, emotional balance and structural awareness.

The leonine style and comparatively spare textures that are the essential feature of the playing of the Mosaïques Quartet are immediately apparent at the opening of first of the *Erdödy* set and undoubtedly cast a new and different light on Haydn's supreme masterpieces in this genre. The following *Adagio* is restrained and refined in texture, as indeed is the slow movement of the *Emperor*, yet there is an underlying warmth, and the following *Presto* Minuet (of

Op. 76/1) is articulated with great rhythmic zest and leads to a very winning Trio.

The clean articulation in the first movement of the *Fifths Quartet* is a joy in itself. A brisk tempo contrasts with the affectionate account of the *Andante*, and the finale, too, is agreeably light-textured. The delicacy of the opening of the *Sunrise Quartet*, and the almost vibratoless chording in the *Adagio* again creates a uniquely rarefied atmosphere. The laconic opening *Allegretto* of 76/5 is winningly played, preparing for the great *mesto cantabile* slow movement, which sustains a gentle nobility, with the rustic Minuet following warm-heartedly. The Hungarian finale then dances with the wind, cleanly articulated and exhilarating.

Every detail of the polyphonic interplay of the monothematic first movement of the last of the six in E flat major emerges clearly, but with no sense of didacticism and the withdrawn style of the playing underlines the mysterious, forward-looking *Fantasia* slow movement. Its Scherzo then leaps away nimbly, and the players make the most of the genial scalic Trio. The spirited closing movement with its offbeat rhythms completes a splendid performance, which shows this group at their very finest. The recording could hardly be bettered, transparent and beautifully focused within a pleasing ambience. If you already have a modern instrument recording of these marvellous works, this is surely an essential supplement.

The Alban Berg Quartet's set of Op. 76 offers peerless playing, with poised slow movements, simply and beautifully played, yet with every note perfectly in place. At times one might venture a suspicion that everything is too perfectly calculated, but such a judgment would be unfair, for Haydn's spirit hovers over this music-making. The balance between vigour and precision in the Minuet/Scherzo of Op. 76/1 is matched by the elegance of the *Allegretto* opening of Op. 76/5, and the finale of the same work is wonderfully crisp and vital. The first movement of the *Fifths Quartet* is presented with great energy and vigour. Perhaps they could smile a little more here. Nevertheless this is playing of distinction, bringing impeccable blending and ensemble. They are more relaxed for the opening movement of the *Emperor* and beguilingly pensive at the beginning of the *Sunrise*, although they can be vehemently dramatic too, as in the *Emperor*'s finale. But the three slow movements are played very beautifully, with much delicacy of feeling and sophistication of light and shade, and the rapt pianissimo for the *Adagio* of Op. 70/4 is affectingly intimate. Although the recording is brightly lit and the effect a shade too up-front, it is realistic and admirably balanced.

The Tokyo Quartet offer superb playing and an immaculate tonal blend, and they are unfailingly intelligent. Yet it is a pity that they do not relax a little more and allow the music to unfold at greater leisure, as do the Kodály players, for they do not convey the humanity and charm that distinguish the Naxos set. The recording is faithful, but they are not as well served by the engineers as they were by DG for their prize-winning Bartók cycle.

String Quartet No. 76, Op. 76/2.

(*) Testament mono SBT 1085. Hollywood Qt – HUMMEL: *Quartet in G *(*)*; MOZART: *Quartet No. 17.* ***(*)**

The Hollywood Quartet were recorded at a memorable concert in London's Royal Festival Hall in September 1957, which also included the Mozart coupling and, in the second half of the programme, the Schubert *C major Quintet*. These recordings have never been available before. The playing can only be described as impeccable, not surprisingly so, given the tonal beauty and musical sophistication these artists commanded; and the sound is astonishingly good for the period. There are a couple of minutes of balance test and a brief exchange among the players.

String Quartets Nos. 81; 82, Op. 77/1–2; 83, Op. 103.

*** Astrée E 8799. Mosaïques Qt.

(N) *** Praga 250 157. Kocian Qt.

*** Hyp. CDA 66348. Salomon Qt.

String Quartets Nos. 81; 82, Op. 77/1–2.

(BB) ** Naxos 8.553146. Kodály Qt.

Using period instruments to totally convincing effect, the Mosaïques Quartet give outstanding performances of Haydn's last three quartets. They play with much subtlety of colour and dynamic and bring total concentration to every bar of the music. The *D minor Quartet*, Haydn's last, is beautifully judged. The recording is absolutely real: the sound is transparent as well as immediate. This is among the finest of all Haydn quartet records.

Those preferring modern-instrument performances could hardly do better than invest in the Kocian Quartet. Allegros sparkle, ensemble is clean and true, and slow movements are beautifully played, notably the eloquent variations of Op. 77/2, but also the *Andante grazioso* of Haydn's last quartet, where the hint of melancholy is nicely understated. The recording is very real, the players not too close in an attractive acoustic.

The Salomon, recorded in a less ample acoustic, produce an altogether leaner sound but one that is thoroughly responsive to every shift in Haydn's thought. They seem to have great inner vitality and feeling.

The Kodály Quartet give comparatively robust performances of both works, made to seem even more robust by the close balance which reduces the dynamic range – not that the playing is notable for pianissimo contrast. This is warm, friendly music-making and in that respect (and in that respect only) preferable to the Festetics; but the latter's playing has considerably more subtlety, and they offer an extra work.

KEYBOARD MUSIC

Piano sonatas (with list of keys and Hoboken nos.)

1 in G (Hob XVI/8); 2 in C (Hob XVI/7); 3 in F (Hob XVI/9); 4 in G (Hob XVI/G1); 5 in G (Hob XVI/11); 6 in C (Hob XVI/10); 7 in D (Hob XVII/D1); 8 in A (Hob XVI/5); 9 in D (Hob XVI/4); 10 in C (Hob XVI/1); 11 in B flat (Hob XVI/2); 12 in A (Hob XVI/12); 13 in G (Hob XVI/6); 14 in C (Hob XVI/3); 15 in E (Hob XVI/13); 16 in D (Hob XVI/14); 17 in E flat (Hob deest); 18 in E flat (Hob deest); 19 in E min. (Hob deest); 20 in B flat (Hob XVI/18); 28 in D (Hob.XIV/5); 29 in E flat (Hob. XVI/45); 30 in D (Hob XVI/19); 31 in A flat

(Hob XVI/45); 32 in G min. (Hob XVI/44); 33 in C min. (Hob XVI/20); 34 in D (Hob XVI/33); 35 in A flat (Hob XVI/43); 36 in C (Hob XVI/21); 37 in E (Hob XVI/22); 38 in F (Hob XVI/23); 39 in D (Hob XVI/24); 40 in E flat (Hob XVI/25); 41 in A (Hob XVI/26); 42 in G (Hob XVI/27); 43 in E flat (Hob XVI/28); 44 in F (Hob XVI/29); 45 in A (Hob XVI/30); 46 in E (Hob XVI/31); 47 in B min. (Hob XVI/32); 48 in C (Hob XVI/35); 49 in C sharp min. (Hob XVI/36); 50 in D (Hob XVI/37); 51 in E flat (Hob XVI/38); 52 in G (Hob XVI/39); 53 in E min. (Hob XVI/34); 54 in G (Hob XVI/40); 55 in B flat (Hob XVI/41); 56 in D (Hob XVI/42); 57 in F (Hob XVI/47); 58 in C (Hob XVI/48); 59 in E flat (Hob XVI/49); 60 in C (Hob XVI/50); 61 in D (Hob XVI/51); 62 in E flat (Hob XVI/52).

Piano Sonatas Nos. 1–16; 17–19 (Hob Deest) 20; 28, Hob XIV/5; 29–62, Hob XVI/1–52 & G1; XVII/D1; The Seven Last Words on the Cross; Adagio in F; Capriccio in G on the song 'Acht Sauschneider müssen sein'; Fantasia in C; 7 Minuets from 'Kleine Tänz für die Jugend'; Variations in F min.; 5 Variations in D; 6 Variations in C; 12 Variations in E flat; 20 Variations in A.

(B) *** Decca (ADD) 443 785-2 (12). McCabe.

John McCabe made the first successful complete survey of the Haydn *Sonatas* for Argo between 1974 and 1977, including also *The Seven Last Words on the Cross*, an arrangement not made by the composer but approved by him. It is remarkably successful here. Indeed two things shine through John Mc-Cabe's performances: their complete musicianship and their fine imagination. In presenting them as he does on a modern piano, McCabe makes the most of the colour and subtlety of the music, and in that respect his style is more expressive, less overtly classical than Jandó's (see below) while the recording is made to sound somewhat softer-grained by the acoustic of All Saints' Church, Petersham. Given phrasing so clearly articulated and alertly phrased, and such varied, intelligently thought-out and wholly responsive presentation, this set can be recommended very enthusiastically. The recordings are of the very highest quality, truthful in timbre and firmly refined in detail, and they must be numbered among the most successful of this repertoire ever to be put on disc, for the piano is notoriously difficult to balance in eighteenth-century music. The set is most reasonably priced and the pianist provides his own extensive and illuminating notes. To sample the calibre of this enterprise, begin with *The Seven Last Words* – playing of unexaggerated expressive feeling that almost makes one believe this was a work conceived in pianistic terms.

*Adagios: in F, Hob XVII/9; in G, Hob XV/22 (II);
Allegrettos: in G after Hob III/41 (IV); in G, Hob XVII/10;
Arietta with 12 Variations in A, Hob XVII/2; Fantasia in C (Capriccio), Hob XVII/4 Piano Sonatas Nos. 17, Hob deest; 19, Hob XVI/47bis; 28, Hob XVI/5a (incomplete).*

(BB) *** Naxos 8.553826. Jandó.

Jandó is at his best in the simple *Adagios* and *Allegrettos* (that in G, Hob III/41, is an arrangement of the engaging variations from the *'How do you do?' Quartet, Op. 33/5*). He gives a strongly impulsive and exciting account of the

Fantasia in C, which ends the recital boldly. The two complete sonatas are a shade on the literal side, but still fresh, however he does not make much of the unfinished fragment of the first movement of *No. 28 in D*, where he tends to rush his fences. Though the good things here outweigh reservations, there is much to enjoy, and the recording is up to standard.

Andante with Variations in F min., Hob XVII/6; Piano Sonatas Nos. 59, Hob XVI/49; 60, Hob XVI/50; 62, Hob XVI/52.

*** Ph. Dig./ADD 446 921-2 (S). Brendel – MOZART: *Piano Concertos & Sonatas.* **(*)

This acts as a mere sampler of Brendel's outstanding Haydn recordings. In Hob XVI/49 (analogue), the first to be recorded, he observes all the repeats and the sound is first class. The rest of the programme is digital. His playing throughout is most distinguished, aristocratic without being aloof, concentrated without being too intense. Everything is cleanly articulated and finely characterized. Vivid, lifelike recording.

Piano Sonatas Nos. 1, Hob XVI/8; 2, Hob XVI/7; 3, Hob XVI/9; 4, XVI/G1; 5, XVI/11; 6, Hob XVI/10; 7, Hob XVII/D1; 8, Hob XVI/5; 9, XVI/4; 10, Hob XVI/1.

(N)(BB) *** Naxos 8.553824. Jandó.

There are no autograph manuscripts of Haydn's earliest sonatas, which were all written before 1766. The authenticity of No. 1 (Hob XVI/8) is certain and many of the others of these three-movement works bear the same musical fingerprint and a characteristic simplicity of style. Doubts have been expressed about No. 8 (Hob XVI/5), but it is attractively enough presented here. Indeed Jenö Jandó seems in his element throughout: his freshness of approach and stylistic confidence is consistently striking. The recording too is excellent, and overall this Naxos series can be recommended with confidence.

Piano Sonatas Nos. 3, Hob XVI/9; 13, Hob XVI/65; 14, Hob XVI/3; 22, Hob XVI/24; 29, Hob XVI/45; 45, Hob XVI/30.

(BB) **(*) Arte Nova 74321 59211-2. Piazzini.

Carmen Piazzini is an Argentine pianist of some quality who studied with such keyboard luminaries as Wilhelm Kempff and Hans Leygraf. This bargain-price disc offers six sonatas, played with fine musicianship and taste even if at times she is a little monochrome. She is very well recorded and, like John McCabe (Decca) and Jenö Jandó (Naxos), a sound guide for this repertoire in this price range. She is not the equal (nor are they) of Schiff or Andsnes.

Piano Sonatas Nos. 11, Hob XVI/2; 12, Hob XVI/12; 13, Hob XVI/6; 14, Hob XVI/3; 15, Hob XVI/13; 16, Hob XVI/14; 18, Hob XVI deest.

(BB) *** Naxos 8.553825. Jandó.

These early sonatas are all played freshly in Jandó's pleasingly direct style. All but one are simple three-movement works; the exception is *No. 13 in G*, which has an appealing additional *Adagio* which Jandö treats simply but appealingly.

The recording is truthful and this issue, Volume 8 in the series, cannot be faulted.

Piano Sonatas Nos. 11, Hob XVI/2; 31, Hob XVI/46; 39, Hob XVI/24; 47, Hob XVI/32.

*** Decca (IMS) 436 455-2. S. Richter.

Richter's crisp, classical style, with sparing use of the pedal and strong rhythmic feeling is immediately noticeable at the opening of the *B minor* work, bringing a feeling almost of a *moto perpetuo*, although the variations of colour and dynamic prevent any hint of monotony. The *Andante* is cool and gentle and the finale brings toccata-like brilliance of execution. So it is with the others here, though the *Adagios* of both the *D major* and (especially) the *A flat major* are gentle and touching, while the two closing movements of the early *B flat Sonata* have an engaging simplicity. Clear, realistic 1986 sound and not too much applause.

Piano Sonatas Nos. 20, Hob XVI/18; 30, Hob XVI/19; 31, Hob XVI/46; 32, Hob XVI/44.

(BB) **(*) Naxos 8.553364. Jandó.

Jandó continues his Haydn sonata series in his clean, direct style. The first movement of the *G minor Sonata* is particularly appealing, with its neat articulation and tight little runs, and the same might be said of the opening movement of the *A flat major* (No. 31), while its finale is similarly bright and sparkling. But first prize goes to the closing movement of the *D major*, which skips along delightfully and brings quite dazzling dexterity. The thoughtful *Adagio* of the *B flat major*, however, is just a little too studied; but this is not enough of a disadvantage to prevent a recommendation. The piano recording is very realistic.

Piano Sonatas No. 24, Hob XVI:26; 30, Hob XVI:19; 32, Hob XVI:44; 33, Hob XVI:20 ; 44, Hob XVI:29

🌑 *** EMI CDC5 56756-2. Andsnes.

Playing of great elegance and consummate artistry, the finest Haydn sonata record to have appeared for a long time. Very different in approach from Pletnev's 1989 recital (see below) – the repertoire does not overlap – but no less individual or persuasive. The young Norwegian pianist plays with rare imagination and keyboard colour, and the EMI sound is first class. The recordings are all made in Abbey Road, save for the *E flat* (No. 44) which was recorded in Oslo.

Piano Sonatas Nos. 29, Hob XVI/45; 33, Hob XVI/20; 34, Hob XVI/33; 35, Hob XVI/43.

(BB) *** Naxos 8.553800. Jandó.

Jandó is on very good form here. His style is a little plain and classical but never insensitive, and he is well recorded. A useful addition to a fine series.

Piano Sonatas Nos. 31 in A flat, Hob XVI/46; 45–47, Hob XVI/30–32.

(N) *** BIS CD 1094. Brautigam.

Piano Sonatas Nos. 32 in G min., Hob XVI/44; 34 in D, Hob XVI/33; 42–4, XVI/27–29.

(N) *** BIS CD 1093. Brautigam.

The two most recent recordings in Ronald Brautigam's ongoing Haydn cycle are devoted to the sonatas of 1776, and they are as refreshing and alive as earlier issues in this eminently collectable series. The high spirits are contagious, but nothing is ever driven too fast, and at no time does Brautigam step outside the sensibility of the period; the only reservation concerns the *A flat Sonata* (No. 31 Hob XVI/46), which is a shade judicious and without his usual sparkle. As in the earlier releases he uses a copy made in 1992 by Paul McNulty of a fortepiano by Anton Gabriel Walter from about 1795. Wonderful recorded sound.

Piano Sonatas Nos. 32, Hob XVI/44; 54, Hob XVI/40; 55, Hob XVI/41; 58, Hob XVI/48; 62, Hob XVI/52.

*** Decca (IMS) 436 454-2. S. Richter.

Richter's second Decca Haydn CD, made in Mantua in 1987, is undoubtedly the more attractive of the two, the playing no less direct but with less of a sense of classical austerity. The opening of the *G minor Sonata* is very winning indeed, and his softness of approach is carried over to the following *G major* work. Both the *C major* (Hob XVI/48) and the well-known *E flat major* (Hob XVI/52) are among Haydn's finest works for the piano – and that means very fine indeed – and Richter's playing is fully worthy of this marvellous music. Again the sound is vivid and immediate.

Piano Sonatas Nos. 33, Hob XVI/20; 47, Hob XVI/32; 53, Hob XVI/34; 50, Hob XVI/37; 54, Hob XVI/40; 56, Hob XVI/42; 58; 59; 60; 61; 62, Hob XVI/48–52; Adagio in F, Hob XVII/9; Andante with Variations in F min., Hob XVII/6; Fantasia in C, Hob XVII/4.

*** Ph. ADD/Dig. 416 643-2 (4). Brendel.

This collection offers some of the best Haydn playing on record – and some of the best Brendel, too. The eleven sonatas, together with the *F minor Variations* and the *C major Fantasia*, have been recorded over a number of years and are splendidly characterized and superbly recorded. The first is analogue, the remainder digital.

Piano Sonatas: 33, Hob XVI/20; 60, Hob XVI/50; 62, Hob XVI/52; Andante & Variations in F min., Hob XVII/6.

(BB) *** Virgin 2 x 1 VBD5 61881-2. Pletnev – *Piano Concertos, Hob XVIII/4, 7 & 11.* ***

Pletnev's reading of the *Sonatas* is full of personality and character. The *C major* is given with great elegance and wit, and the great *E flat Sonata* is magisterial. This playing has a masterly authority, and Pletnev is very well recorded. Now coupled with his equally memorable accounts of Haydn's three finest piano concertos, this reissue is a splendid bargain and one not to be missed.

Piano Sonatas Nos. 36, Hob XVI/21; 37, Hob XVI/22; 38, Hob XVI/23; 39, Hob XVI/24; 40, Hob XVI/25; 41, Hob XVI/26.

(N)(BB) *** Naxos 8.553127. Jandó.

The sonatas in Volume 5 of the Naxos series form a set of six, written in 1773 and dedicated to Prince Nikolaus

Esterhazy. They are all attractive works and they inspire Jandó to consistently fine performances, as the opening of No. 36 immediately shows. The finale of No. 37 is beautifully played, and the following two sonatas with their striking slow movements will not disappoint either. This is one of the most rewarding issues in this admirable series. Excellent piano sound.

Piano Sonatas Nos. 38, Hob XVI/23; 51, Hob XVI/38; 52, Hob XVI/39.

*** Mer. (ADD) CDE 84155. Cload.

Julia Cload's cool, unidiosyncratic style is heard at its best in her second group of sonatas. The piano image is bright and clear, with just a touch of hardness on *fortes*.

Piano Sonatas Nos. 42, Hob XVI/27; 43, Hob XVI/28; 44, Hob XVI/29; 45, Hob XVI/30; 46, Hob XVI/31; 47, Hob XVI/32.

(BB) *** Naxos 8.550844. Jandó (piano).

The last work here, in B minor, opens with perhaps the most striking idea of all and, after the gracious central Minuet, ends in a flurry of precocious virtuosity, with Jandó clearly in his element. He shows himself a complete master of this repertoire, and the recording, crisp and clean but not too dry, is first class.

Piano Sonatas Nos. 48, Hob XVI/35; 49, Hob XVI/36; 50, Hob XVI/37; 51, Hob XVI/38; 52 in G, Hob XVI/39.

(N)(BB) *** Naxos 8.553128. Jandö.

The sonatas in Volume 5 were part of a set of six published in 1780 and dedicated to the sisters Caterina and Marianna Auenbrugger, both proficient young players, admired by Leopold Mozart. Not all these works were newly written, and this shows in the writing; but their clear layout is obviously designed to attract talented amateurs. The opening movement of No. 49 and the memorable *Largo e sostenuto* of No. 50 (and its infectious finale) show Jandö in top form; in the other works his bright stylish playing is always responsive to Haydn's direct, lively manner. We underrated this disc on its first appearance. The recording is well up to the high standard of this series.

Piano Sonatas Nos. 48, Hob XVI/35; 49, Hob XVI/36; 50, Hob XVI/37; 51, Hob XVI/38; 52, Hob XVI/39.

*** BIS CD 992. Brautigam (fortepiano).

Piano Sonatas Nos. 53, Hob XVI/34; 54, Hob XVI/40; 55, Hob XVI/41; 56, Hob XVI/42; 57, Hob XVI/47; 58, Hob XVI/48.

*** BIS CD 993. Brautigam (fortepiano).

Piano Sonatas Nos. 59, Hob XVI/49; 60, Hob XVI/50; 61, Hob XVI/51; 62, Hob XVI/49–52.

*** BIS CD 994. Brautigam (fortepiano).

Ronald Brautigam plays a fortepiano by Paul McNulty in 1992, modelled on an instrument by Anton Gabriel Walter of *circa* 1795, and is recorded in the pleasing acoustic of Länna Church in Sweden. His first disc is given over to five of the so-called *Auenbrugger Sonatas*, Nos. 48–52 or Hob XVI/35–39, which derive their name from the dedicatees,

Katharina and Marianna Auenbrugger. Brautigam is hardly less vital and imaginative here than in Mozart. Apart from his technical virtuosity, his playing has tremendous flair and sparkle. This is spirited and life-loving music-making and almost ideally recorded. The second disc (CD993) includes the *Bossler Sonatas* (Nos. 54–6), so-called because they were published by the house of Bossler. Brautigam gives them with tremendous flair and, in the Presto of *G major* (No. 54, Hob XVI/40), great wit. The *B flat Sonata* (No. 55, Hob XVI/41) is played with conspicuous relish, and in fact the whole disc is a delight from beginning to end. The third (CD994) brings the *Genzinger Sonata* (No. 59), so named because Marianne von Genzinger was its dedicatee, and three *London Sonatas*, composed in 1794–5, when Haydn was in his early sixties. The *E flat Major* (No. 62, Hob XVI/52) is the biggest and most symphonic of all. Exhilarating playing which augurs well for the rest of the series.

Piano Sonatas Nos. 50, Hob XVI/37; 54, Hob XVI/40; 55, Hob XVI/41; Adagio in F, Hob XVII/9.

*** Mer. (ADD) ECD 84083. Cload.

Julia Cload's playing is fresh, characterful and intelligent, and will give considerable pleasure. She has the advantage of very truthful recorded sound.

Piano Sonatas Nos. 53, Hob XVI/34; 54, Hob XVI/40; 55, Hob XVI/41; 56, Hob XVI/42; 58, Hob XVI/48; Variations in F min. (Sonata, un piccolo divertimento), Hob XVII/6.

(BB) *** Naxos 8.550845. Jandó (piano).

These are appealing performances of the three *Sonatas*, Hob XVI/40–42, dedicated to Princess Marie Esterházy. All three are fine works and not as simple as they at first appear. Jandó also gives a splendid account of the more ambitious three-movement *Sonata in E minor*, Hob XVI/34. He is a true Haydn player, and this is in every way recommendable, particularly as the recording is so vivid and clean: just right for the repertoire.

Piano Sonatas Nos. 56, Hob XVI/41; 58; 59 in E flat; 60; 61; 62, Hob XVI/48–52.

(M) *(**) Sony SM2K 52623. Gould.

Glenn Gould's clean, classical style in Haydn is often refreshing, but after a while the squeaky-clean articulation, although quite remarkably crisp, becomes a little wearing and the ear craves a less staccato, less percussive approach to allegros. This is not a fortepiano imitation but a pianoforte played with the most sparing sonority. Gould undoubtedly makes a sensitively expressive response to slow movements, but an air of eccentricity remains in the overall shaping of phrases. The digital recording is clear, to match the playing.

Piano Sonatas Nos. 59; 60; 61; 62, Hob XVI/49–52.

(BB) *** Naxos 8.550657. Jandó.

Without allowing himself stylistic idiosyncrasies, Jandó here shows himself a thoughtfully imaginative player as well as a bold one, and the finale of the great *E flat Sonata* has splendid, unforced bravura. The recording, made in the Unitarian Church, Budapest, provides an attractive ambience without an excess of ecclesiastical resonance.

VOCAL MUSIC

Arianna a Naxos (cantata).

*** Decca 440 297-2. Bartoli, Schiff – BEETHOVEN: *Che fa il mio bene?* etc.; MOZART: *Ridente la calma;* SCHUBERT: *Da quel sembiante appresi* etc. ***

Arianna a Naxos; Fidelity; The mermaid's song; Pastoral song; Sailor's song; She never told her love; Spirit's song; Der verdienstvolle Sylvius.

*** DG 447 106-2. Von Otter, Tan (fortepiano) – MOZART: *Lieder.* ***

To declare a preference between Cecilia Bartoli and Anne Sofie von Otter in Haydn's extended scena is virtually impossible. With its double alternating recitative and aria, the first doubtful concerning a lover's faithfulness, the second expressing the despair and anger of known betrayal, Haydn's setting demands the widest range of mood and identification with the words; both singers rise to the occasion with passion and consummate artistry. Bartoli has the inestimable András Schiff as partner; Von Otter has Melvyn Tan's eloquent fortepiano. So in the end it depends on the couplings: the other Haydn songs on the DG disc are happily varied in mood, to bring either innocent simplicity (*A Pastoral song*), histrionics (*Fidelity*) – with Tan very much rising to the occasion – or touching, unexaggerated pathos (*She never told her love* and *Der verdienstvolle Sylvius*). By comparison, the *Sailor's song* is suitably robust and the melancholy *Spirit's song*, which ends the recital, pensively nostalgic. The recording balance is just about ideal.

The Creation (complete; in English).

*** EMI CDS7 54159-2 (2). Augér, Langridge, Thomas, CBSO & Ch., Rattle.

*** Decca 430 397-2 (2). Kirkby, Rolfe Johnson, George, New College, Oxford, Ch., AAM Ch. & O, Hogwood.

**(*) Telarc CD 80298 (2). Upshaw, Humphrey, Cheek, Murphy, McGuire, Chamber Ch. & SO, Shaw.

The English version may have its oddities – like the 'flexible tiger' leaping – but it is above all colourful, and Rattle brings out that illustrative colour with exceptional vividness: birdsong, lion-roars and the like. He has plainly learnt from period performance, not only concerning speeds – often surprisingly brisk, as in the great soprano aria, *With verdure clad* – but as regards style too. The male soloists sound none too sweet as recorded, but they characterize positively; and there is no finer account of the soprano's music than that of Arleen Augér. The weight of the Birmingham chorus is impressive, achieved without loss of clarity or detail in a full, well-balanced recording.

Hogwood defies what has become the custom in period performance and opts for large forces. The result, for all its weight, retains fine clarity of detail and an attractive freshness. The choir of New College, Oxford, with its trebles adds to the brightness of choral sound, and the trio of soloists is admirably consistent – Emma Kirkby brightly distinctive, and Anthony Rolfe Johnson sweet-toned. Hogwood may lack some of the flair and imagination of Rattle, but it would

be hard to find a period performance to match this. The sound has fine presence and immediacy.

Robert Shaw with his keenly disciplined chamber choir conducts a strong, clean-cut performance, using an English translation modified from the traditional one. Though Shaw's generally broad speeds show little influence from period performance, his concern for clarity of texture is very different from old-style performances, and the Telarc engineers help with full, immediate sound, bringing out sharp dynamic contrasts. Dawn Upshaw adopts too romantically expressive a manner, but the solo singing is good, with Heidi Grant Murphy and James Michael McGuire brought in for the Adam and Eve numbers of Part 3.

The Creation (Die Schöpfung; in German).

(M) *** DG (ADD) 449 761-2 (2). Janowitz, Ludwig, Wunderlich, Krenn, Fischer-Dieskau, Berry, V. Singverein, BPO, Karajan.

*** DG 449 217-2 (2). McNair, Brown, Schade, Finley, Gilfry, Monteverdi Ch., E. Bar. Sol., Gardiner.

*** Sony SX2K 57965 (2). Monoyios, Hering, Van der Kamp, Tölz Boys' Ch., Tafelmusik, Weil.

(B) *** DG Double (ADD) 453 031-2. Blegen, Popp, Moser, Ollman, Moll, Bav. R. Ch. & SO, Bernstein.

*** Decca (IMS) 443 445-2 (2). Ziesak, Lippert, Pape, Scharinger, Chicago Ch. & SO, Solti.

(M) **(*) DG (IMS) 445 584-2 (2). Battle, Winbergh, Moll, Stockholm R. Ch. and Chamber Ch., BPO, Levine.

(B) **(*) EMI double forte CZS5 69343-2 (2). Donath, Tear, Van Dam, Philh. Ch. & O, Frühbeck de Burgos.

(N) (BB) ** Erato Ultima 8573 85664-2 (2). Marshall; Branisteannu; Tappy; Rydl; Huttenlocher; SRO Ch., Lausanne Pro Arte Ch., Lausanne CO, Jordan.

(i) *The Creation (Die Schöpfung):* complete (in German);
(ii) *Salve regina.*

(B) *** Double Decca (ADD) 443 027-2 (2). (i) Popp, Hollweg, Moll, Döse, Luxon, Brighton Festival Ch., RPO, Dorati; (ii) Augér, Hodgson, Rolfe Johnson, Howell, L. Chamber Ch., Argo CO, Heltay.

Among regular versions of *The Creation* sung in German, Karajan's 1969 set remains unsurpassed and at mid-price is a clear first choice, despite two small cuts (in Nos. 30 and 32). The combination of the Berlin Philharmonic at its most intense and the great Viennese choir makes for a performance that is not only polished but warm and dramatically strong too. The soloists are an extraordinarily fine team, more consistent in quality than those on almost any rival version.

Characteristically, Gardiner takes a dramatic view, overtly expressive, vividly pointing the highlights of the Creation story. Gardiner may not always convey the relaxed joy of Weil's fresh and brisk version on Sony, but the exhilaration and power of Haydn's inspiration, as well as its lyrical beauty, have never been conveyed more tellingly in a period performance on disc, with the Monteverdi Choir singing with virtuoso clarity and phenomenal precision of ensemble. The soloists are outstanding too, though the silvery soprano, Sylvia McNair, does not always sing full out. A first choice among period performances.

Bruno Weil conducts a brisk, clean-cut reading, using the period instruments of Tafelmusik and a bright-toned chorus, augmented by the Tölz Boys' Choir. If the intimacy at times seems to reduce the scale of this masterpiece, and Weil at times is fussy over detail, the urgent exuberance of the performance is most winning, with an outstanding trio of cleanly focused soloists. The chorus is finely focused too, providing sharp, dramatic contrasts, and the orchestral sound is so clean that one can hear the fortepiano continuo even in tuttis.

Dorati, as one would expect, directs a lively and well-sprung account. The very opening is magnetic and its imaginative touches and joyfulness of spirit more than compensate for any minor lapses in crispness of ensemble. The soloists are a splendid team. The chorus is as gutsy as you like in *Die Himmel erzählen*, with the soloists nicely balanced. The set opens gloriously with Heltay's lovely 1979 recording of the *Salve regina*, an early work dating from 1771, comparable in its depth of feeling with his finest vocal music. The recording is most realistic and the CD transfer of *The Creation* is strikingly vivid and immediate.

Bernstein's DG version, recorded at a live performance in Munich, uses a relatively large chorus, encouraging him to adopt rather slow speeds at times. What matters is the joy conveyed in the story-telling, with the finely disciplined chorus and orchestra producing incandescent tone, blazing away in the big set-numbers, and the performance is compulsive from the very opening bars. Five soloists are used instead of three, with the parts of Adam and Eve sung by nicely contrasted singers, confirming this as an unusually persuasive version, well recorded in atmospheric sound.

Recorded live in the autumn of 1993, Sir Georg Solti's second recording, made (like the first) with Chicago forces, presents a striking difference. The influence of period performance means that not only does he adopt fast speeds, but his very choice of soloists reflects the new generation of light, clear singers, all excellent. Ornamentation and the use of a fortepiano continuo also give further indication of Sir Georg's changed stance on this work, which results in a crisp, buoyant reading, full of dramatic contrasts, which nevertheless is not out of scale with Haydn's vision. Splendid choral singing, captured in full, bright sound.

Though James Levine with his weighty forces is occasionally heavy-handed over both dynamics and rhythm, lacking rather in elegance, he conveys the joy of inspiration in this work with characteristic boldness. He is helped not just by the highly polished playing of the orchestra but by characterful singing from all three soloists and fresh, finely disciplined choral singing. The recording, made not in the Philharmonie but in the Jesus-Christus Kirche, is weighty and satisfyingly full, with ample bloom.

Rafael Frühbeck de Burgos directs a genial performance, recorded with richness and immediacy. The soloists are all excellent and, though Helen Donath has a hint of flutter in her voice, she is wonderfully agile in ornamentation, as in the bird-like quality she gives to the aria, *On mighty pens*. The chorus might gain from a more forward balance but their singing is impressive. An enjoyable set.

The glory of Jordan's version with the Lausanne Choir is the singing of Margaret Marshall in the first two parts with *Nun beut die Flur* sounding radiant at a very slow speed. There is much else to commend, though Kurt Rydl is a gruff bass soloist, and for all its discipline the chorus's words are unclear. Overall this cannot match the finest versions, despite cleanly balanced sound.

The Creation: highlights.

(B) *** DG (ADD) 439 454-2 (from above recording; cond. Karajan).

Anyone whose budget will not stretch to a complete version of Haydn's masterpiece will find that this 70-minute bargain Classikon highlights disc includes the key solos and choruses.

Masses

Masses Nos. (i–iii) 1 in F (Missa brevis), Hob XXII/1; (i; iii–vi) 1a in G (Rorate coeli desuper), Hob XXII/3; 3 in C: Missa Cellensis in honorem Beatissimae Virginis Mariae (Missa Santae Caecilae), Hob XXII/5; (i; iii; v–viii) 4 in E flat: Missa in honorem Beatissimae Virginis Mariae (Great Organ Mass), Hob XXII/4; (i; iii; vi; ix; x) 6 in G (Missa Sancti Nicolai), Hob XXII/6; (xi–xv) 7 in B flat: Missa brevis Sancti Joannis de Deo (Little Organ Mass); (xi; xiii–xviii) 8 in C: Mariazeller Messe, Hob XXII/8; (xiii–xvii; xix; xx) 9 in B flat: Missa Sancti Bernardi de Offida (Heligmesse), Hob XXII/10; (ix; xiii–xv; xix; xxi; xxii) 10 in C: Missa in tempore belli (Paukenmesse), Hob XXII/9; (xvi; xxiii–xxvi) 11 in D min.: Missa in augustiis (Nelson Mass), Hob XXII/11; (xiii–xv; xxv; xxvii–xxviii) 12 in B flat: Theresienmesse, Hob XXII/12; (xiii–xvii; xix; xxix) 13 in B flat: Schöpfungmesse (Creation Mass), Hob XXII/13; (xiii–xvi; xxvii; xxx) 14 in B flat (Harmoniemesse), Hob XXII/14.

(B) *** Decca (ADD) 448 518-2 (7). (i) Nelson; (ii) Kirkby; (iii) Christ Church Cathedral Ch., AAM; Preston; (iv) Cable; (v) Hill; (vi) Thomas; (vii) Watkinson; (viii); Hogwood (organ); (ix) Minty; (x) Covey-Crump; (xi) Smith; (xii) Scott (organ); (xiii) St John's College, Cambridge, Ch.; (xiv) ASMF; (xv) Guest; (xvi) Watts; (xvii) Tear; (xviii) Luxon; (xix) Cantelo; (xx) McDaniel; (xxi) Partridge; (xxii) Keyte; (xxiii) Stahlman; (xxiv) Wilfred Brown; (xxv) Krause; (xxvi) King's College, Cambridge, Ch., LSO, Willcocks; (xxvii) Spoorenberg; (xxviii) Greevy; Mitchinson; (xxix) Forbes Robinson; (xxx) Young, Rouleau.

Decca's survey of the complete Masses of Haydn, which appeared originally on the Argo and Oiseau-Lyre labels, omits only the newly discovered fragmentary *Missa Sunt bona mixta malis*, Hob XXII/2, of 1768. Overall this achievement stands alongside Dorati's complete recording of the symphonies (and the Beaux Arts' *Piano Trios*) as one of the landmarks of the gramophone during the analogue LP era.

Starting in 1962 with Sir David Willcocks's King's version of the *Nelson Mass*, the production team then moved down the road to St John's for the five remaining magnificent Mass settings which Haydn wrote between 1796 and 1802 for his patron, Prince Esterházy, after his return from London. With changing soloists, of generally consistent quality, George Guest directed a series of performances notable for their fresh directness and vigour, with his St John's Choir showing itself a ready match for the more famous choir at King's College and the sound even more vivid. The recordings were made between 1965 and 1969, with the *Little Organ Mass* and *Mariazellermesse* following in 1977. The project was completed over the next two years with the early Masses. But the 'authentic' era had arrived and the orchestra changed from the Academy of St Martin-in-the-Fields to the Academy of Ancient Music. Simon Preston took over, and he directed his Christ Church Cathedral Choir with a comparable freshness and spontaneity to that established at St John's. The engineering team excelled themselves throughout, to produce a well-balanced and spacious yet clearly detailed sound, boldly projected against a nicely resonant acoustic. As with the companion Decca box of the symphonies, H. C. Robbins Landon has provided the notes with his usual spirited scholarship.

Masses Nos. 1 in F (Missa brevis), Hob XXII/1; 11 in D min. (Nelson), Hob XXII/11; Ave Regina in A, Hob XXIIIb/3.

*** Chan. 0640. Gritton, Stephen, Padmore, Varcoe, Collegium Musicum 90, Hickox.

Masses Nos. 1a in G (Rorate coeli desuper), Hob XXII/3; (i) 13 in B flat (Schöpfungsmesse), Hob XXII/13 (with Haydn's alternative Gloria).

*** Chan. 0599. (i) Gritton, Stephen, Padmore, Varcoe; Collegium Musicum 90, Hickox.

Masses Nos. 2a: Sunt bona mixta malis; 3 in C: Missa Cellensis in honorem Beatissima Virginis Mariae.

(N) *** Chan. 0667. Gritton, Stephen, Padmore, Varcoe, CM 90, Hickox.

Masses Nos. 6 in G (Missa Sanctae Nicolai), Hob XXII/6; 9 in B flat (Missa Sancti Bernardi von Offida (Heiligmesse)), Hob XXII/10.

*** Chan. 0645. Anderson, Stephen, Padmore, Varcoe, Collegium Musicum 90, Hickox.

Masses Nos. 7 in B flat: Missa brevis Sancti Joannis de Deo (Little Organ Mass); 12 in B flat (Theresienmesse).

*** Chan. 0592. Watson, Stephen, Padmore, Varcoe, Collegium Musicum 90, Hickox.

Mass No. 10 in C: Missa in tempore belli (Paukenmesse), Hob XXII/9; Alfred, König de Angelsachsen (incidental music): Aria of the Guardian Spirit; Chorus of the Danes. 2 Te Deums in C, Hob XXIIIc/1–2.

*** Chan. 0633. Argenta, Denley, Padmore, Varcoe, Collegium Musicum 90, Hickox.

Mass No. 14 in B flat (Harmoniemesse); Salve regina in E.

*** Chan. 0612. Argenta, Stephen, Padmore, Varcoe, Collegium Musicum 90, Hickox.

In his superb series of Haydn recordings for Chandos, Richard Hickox offers performances which consistently bring out the freshness and originality of the writing, with crisp, bright singing from his excellent chorus, and first-rate soloists. The Chandos recording is well-scaled too, with chorus and soloists set in a natural balance, not spotlit, and with the lively acoustic giving agreeable bloom to the voices as well as a sense of space, while conveying ample detail.

Though some may prefer performances using boys' voices, the women singers of Collegium Musicum 90 are clear and youthful-sounding, allowing bitingly incisive attack in Haydn's many exuberant numbers, not least the settings of the final *Dona nobis pacem* in each mass, which so often joyfully reflect the motif which he had the habit of putting at the end of his scores, *Laudis Deo*, 'Praise to God'. Some of the earlier masses take a more conventional view, so that the *Missa brevis Sancti Joannis de Deo*, which comes as the coupling for the *Theresienmesse*, sets the *Dona nobis pacem* as simply an extended gentle cadence.

It is a great merit of this series that early masses and shorter choral works are included as couplings for the late, great masses written for the namedays of the Princess Esterházy, not least Haydn's last major work of all, the *Harmoniemesse* of 1802. Those extra items include some masterly works, and it is fascinating to hear Haydn's very first Mass – the coupling for the *Nelson Mass*, most popular of all – which he wrote in his teens, a wonderfully fresh, bright inspiration. It is good too as one of the couplings for the *Schöpfungsmesse* to have the alternative setting of the *Gloria*, with the quotation from Haydn's oratorio *The Creation* ('Schöpfung') removed in deference to an objection from the Austrian Empress.

The most recent issue includes the *Missa Cellensis* – not to be confused with the later *Missa Cellensis*, also associated with the Austrian pilgrimage town of Mariazell – is less confusingly known also as the *St Cecilia Mass*, Haydn's most expansive setting of the liturgy. Unlike his other masses this is a 'cantata mass' with 18 movements instead of six, presumably written for a grand occasion in Vienna. It is now known to date from 1766, surprisingly early, only five years after Haydn joined the court of Prince Esterházy. Consistently bold and imaginative, it has superb fugal writing, freshly and cleanly delivered by Hickox's choir. With a strong quartet of soloists, warmly led by Susan Gritton, this is even finer than Simon Preston's version on L'Oiseau-Lyre, and includes a fascinating bonus in the fragmentary *Missa sunt bona mixta malis*, with accompaniment only for organ and string continuo. This consists simply of a brief *Kyrie* and an impressive setting of the *Gloria* as far as *Gratias agimus tibi*. With full, warm recording which allows ample detail, this can be strongly recommended alongside the others in this splendid Chandos series.

Masses Nos. (i) 1 in F (Missa brevis), Hob XXII/1; (ii) 3 in C: Missa Cellensis in honorem Beatissimae Virginis Mariae (Missa Sanctae Caecilia), Hob XXII/5; (iii) 4 in E flat: Missa in honorem Beatissimae Virginis Mariae (Great Organ Mass), Hob XXII/4; (iv) 6 in G (Missa Sanctae Nicolai), Hob XXII/6.

(B) *** O-L Double (ADD) 455 712-2 (2). (i) Kirkby; (i–iv) Nelson; (ii) Cable; (ii–iii) Hill, (ii–iv) Thomas; (iii) Watkinson; (iv) Minty, Covey-Crump; Christ Church, Oxford, Cathedral Ch., AAM, Preston.

Haydn wrote the early *Missa brevis* when he was seventeen. The setting is engagingly unpretentious, some of its sections last for under two minutes and only the *Credo* takes slightly more than three and a half. The two soprano soloists, Judith

Nelson and Emma Kirkby, match their voices admirably and the effect is delightful. By contrast the *Missa Cellensis* (which is split between the two discs, after the *Gloria*), at 68 minutes, is Haydn's longest setting of the liturgy. Preston directs an excellent performance with fine contributions from choir and soloists, set against a warm acoustic. In the early *E flat Mass* Haydn followed the rococo conventions of his time, generally adopting a style featuring Italianate melody which to modern ears inevitably sounds operatic. The *Missa Sanctae Nicolai* has a comparable freshness of inspiration and the performance is first rate in every way, even finer than that of the earlier *Great Organ Mass*, beautifully sung, with spontaneity in every bar and a highly characterized accompaniment. Both are admirably recorded, and the CD transfers are first class.

Masses Nos. (i) *1a in G (Rorate coeli desuper), Hob XXII/3;* (ii) *8 in C: Mariazellermesse, Hob XXII/8;* (iii) *9 in B flat: Missa Sancti Bernadi de Offida (Heiligmesse), Hob XXII/ 10;* (iv) *13 in B flat: Schöpfungsmesse, Hob XXII/13.*

(B) *** Double Decca (ADD) 458 376-2 (2). (i) Christ Church Cathedral Ch., Oxford, AAM, Hogwood; (ii) Smith, Watts, Tear, Luxon; (iii) Cantelo, Minty, Partridge, Keyte; (iv) Cantelo, Watts, Tear, Forbes Robinson; (ii–iv) St John's College, Cambridge Ch., ASMF, Guest – Michael HAYDN: *Ave Regina.* ***

The little *Misa rorate coeli desuper* was written by Haydn when he was still a choirboy in Vienna, and it may well be his earliest surviving work, while the *Schöpfungsmesse* or *Creation Mass* was the last but one of this magnificent series that Haydn wrote for his patron, Prince Esterházy, after his return from London. The *Mariazellermesse* of 1782 was described by H. C. Robbins Landon as 'the most perfect large-scale work Haydn achieved', and the later *Heiligmesse* is one of the most human and direct in appeal of his religious works. The performances and recordings are all well up to the high standard of the Guest series, with Simon Preston directing a freshly authentic account of the earliest work.

Masses Nos. (i) *7 in B flat (Little Organ Mass): Missa brevis Sancti Joannis de Deo;* (ii) *10 in C (Paukenmesse): Missa in tempore belli;* (iii) *11 in D min. (Nelson);* (iv) *14 in B flat (Harmoniemesse).*

(B) *** Double Decca (ADD) 455 020-2 (2). (i) Smith, Scott (organ); (ii) I Cantelo, Watts, Tear, McDaniel; (iii) Stahlman, Watts, Brown, Krause; (iv) Spoorenberg, Watts, Young, Rouleau. (i–ii; iv) St John's College, Cambridge, Ch., ASMF, Guest; (iii) King's College Ch., LSO, Willcocks.

Three major Masses and one shorter work are combined here to make a very tempting Double Decca for those not wanting the complete set listed above.

(i; ii) *Mass No. 9 in B flat (Heiligmesse): Missa Sancti Bernardi von Offida, Hob XXII/10;* (ii) *Mare Clausum (fragment), Hob XXIVa/9; Motet: Insanae et varae curae, Hob XXI/1:13c; Motetti de Venerabili sacramento, Hob XXIIIc/5a–d; Te Deum for the Empress Marie Therese, Hob XXIIIc/2.*

*** Sony SK 66260. (i) Hering, (ii) Van de Kamp, Soloists from Tölz Boys' Ch., Tölz Ch., Tafelmusik, Weil.

Bruno Weil's inspired and inspiring new period-instrument version was recorded under the guidance of H. C. Robbins Landon, who provides the excellent notes. There could be no more thrilling version than this. The choral singing in the magnificent *Heiligmesse* has overwhelming momentum, yet is radiantly rich in expressive intensity, and the listener is carried through on a tide of exultant spiritual energy to a closing *Agnus Dei* of real grandeur. And in the *Credo* how touchingly the soloists from the Tölz Boys Choir enter, one by one, at the *Et incarnatus est*, with just a simple clarinet accompaniment. Then comes a surprise. The *Mare Clausum* brings a jolly patriot bass solo, sung in English, followed by a rousing chorus (all about preserving Britain's marine power!). The two affirmative sacred motets are hardly less vigorous, with the second using a solo group of trebles in alternation with the full chorus, and the programme ends with the even more dramatic Marie Therese *Te Deum*, which concludes with a thrilling, trumpet-laden climax. This is a superb collection, and the bright, spaciously resonant recording, with the words always clear, is in every way outstanding.

Mass No. 10 in C (Paukenmesse): Missa in tempore belli, Hob XXII/9; Salve Regina, Hob XXIIIb:2.

**(*) Teldec 0630 13146-2. Röschmann, Von Magnus, Lippert, Widmer, Arnold Schoenberg Ch., Harnoncourt.

Harnoncourt has the advantage of the gleaming-voiced Barbara Bonney and a really excellent tenor (Jörg Hering). The four soloists also show their fine tonal matching in the *Salve Regina*. The choral singing in the mass is excellent too and as it is a live recording there is an added dimension of concentration, so that Harnoncourt can afford to be more relaxed in his tempi. On its own terms, Harnoncourt's reading is satisfying, and at its finest in the *Agnus Dei*. The recording is spacious but the chorus, although vivid, lacks something in edge. In any case this is upstaged by the Sony disc, which offers an extra work and a very attractive one too.

Mass No. 11 in D min. (Nelson); Te Deum in C, Hob XXIIIc/2.

*** DG 423 097-2. Lott, Watkinson, Davies, Wilson-Johnson, Ch. & E. Concert, Pinnock.

Mass No. 11 in D min. (Nelson): Missa in augustiis, Hob XXII/11.

(M) *** Decca (ADD) 458 623-2. Stahlman, Watts, Brown, Krause, King's College, Cambridge, Ch., LSO, Willcocks – HANDEL: *Coronation Anthem: Zadok the Priest;* VIVALDI: *Gloria, RV 589.* ***

(i) *Mass No. 11 in D min. (Nelson): Missa in augustiis, Hob XXII/11;* (ii) *Arianna a Naxos (orchestral version), Hob XXVIb/2; Scena di Berenice (Berenice che fai?), Hob XXIVa/10.*

(B) *** Decca 448 983-2; 448 983-4. (i) Bonney, Howells, Rolfe Johnson, Roberts, L. Symphony Ch., Hickox; (ii) Augér, Handel & Haydn Society, Hogwood.

The *Nelson Mass* (*Missa in angustiis*: 'Mass in times of fear') brings a superb choral offering from Trevor Pinnock and the English Concert. With incandescent singing from the chorus and fine matching from excellent soloists, Pinnock brings home the high drama of Haydn's autumnal inspiration. Similarly, the *Te Deum* leaps forward from the eighteenth century all the more excitingly in an authentic performance such as this. Excellent, full-blooded sound, with good definition.

It was Sir David Willcocks who made Argo's pioneering recording of the *Nelson Mass* in 1962, a work that is clearly among Haydn's greatest music. The solo singing is uniformly good, Sylvia Stahlman negotiating her florid music with great skill, while Willcocks maintains quite remarkable tension throughout. The splendid recording is admirably remastered and the added Handel and Vivaldi bonuses for this reissue on Decca's Legends label make the reissue very competitive. It is characteristically well documented.

Hickox conducts a lively, well-sung reading of the most celebrated of Haydn's late Masses, most impressive in the vigorous, outward-going music which – with Haydn – makes up the greater part of the service; here the choral singing is little short of glorious. In serene moments the choral sound is slightly recessed, with inner parts less well defined than they might be. The soloists are very good, and Barbara Bonney's purity of line is impressive, although tonally she is a little thin. While in some ways the Willcocks version of 20 years earlier is even finer, in the work's more resplendent moments the London Symphony's choral focus is given greater impact by the more modern digital sound.

What makes Hogwood's version almost indispensable is the inclusion of Haydn's two major solo cantatas (a full half-hour of wonderful music) which he wrote for his two London visits in the 1790s. Arleen Augér was never more impressive in the recording studio than here. She is superbly dramatic in the cantata which tells of Ariadne abandoned by Theseus on Naxos, and – in melting voice – infinitely touching in the *Scena di Berenice*. Hogwood accompanies most sympathetically and the recording is perfectly balanced. Not to be missed.

(i) *Mass No. 12 in B flat (Theresienmesse), Hob XXII/12;* (ii) *Salve Regina in G min., Hob XXIIb/2;* (ii; iii) *Stabat Mater, Hob XX/bis.*

(B) *** Double Decca (ADD) 458 373-2 (2). (i) Spoorenberg, Greevy, Mitchinson, Krause, St John's College, Cambridge Ch., ASMF, Guest; (ii) L. Chamber Ch., Argo CO, Heltay; (iii) with Auger, Hodgson, Rolfe Johnson, Howell.

The *Theresienmesse* followed on a year after the *Nelson Mass*. It may be less famous, but the inspiration is hardly less memorable. George Guest injects tremendous vigour into the music and the St John's Choir is on top form throughout. The *Stabat Mater* was written in his early years at Esterháza. Scored for strings with oboes, the work is far bigger than that scale might suggest, and it is good that Heltay's reading conveys its essential greatness, helped by excellent soloists and vivid recording. The *Salve Regina* – another early work, comparable in its depth of feeling – is here given with full chorus; although solo voices were originally intended, the weight of the piece is better conveyed in this way. Excellent transfers throughout.

Mass No. 13 in B flat: Schöpfungsmesse (Creation mass), Hob XXII/13.

(N) *** Teldec 3984 26094-2. Oelze, Von Magnus, Lippert, Finley, Arnold Schoenberg Choir, VCM, Harnoncourt – SCHUBERT: *Magnificat, D.486; Offertorium in B flat, D.963 (Intende voci).* ***

Like the Schubert couplings, Harnoncourt's period performance of Haydn's *Schöpfungsmesse*, set in a warm church acoustic, was recorded live, making the music sound fresh and new. Marked by lightness, resilience and transparency, this is a reading that consistently demonstrates how far Harnoncourt has travelled since his early days with the Concentus Musicus. Speeds are moderate in both directions, easily flowing with rhythms well sprung. That is, until the final *Dona nobis pacem*, where Harnoncourt opts for a very fast speed, rounding off this celebration of the Mass in exhilaration – as Haydn himself used to put it, *Laus Deo*, 'Praise to God'. The four soloists are excellent, as is the chorus. The recording is warmly atmospheric, though the backward balance of the choir prevents it from having quite the impact its incisive singing deserves. An unexpected coupling, but an illuminating one.

The Seasons (complete; in English).

🔘 (B) *** Ph. Duo (ADD) 464 034-2 (2). Harper, Davies, Shirley-Quirk, BBC Ch. and SO, Davis.

Sir Colin Davis directs a tinglingly fresh performance of Haydn's last oratorio, which ranks alongside his great Haydn symphony performances (also on Philips Duo). The soloists are excellent and Davis's direction can hardly be faulted, even in our age of authentic enlightenment. This set makes a strong case for an English translation, and although no libretto is provided, the English generally comes over with clarity. The 1968 recording is exceptionally vivid and full, and this is another great bargain in the Philips Duo series.

The Seasons (*Die Jahreszeiten;* complete; in German).

*** DG 431 818-2 (2). Bonney, Rolfe Johnson, Schmidt, Monteverdi Ch., E. Bar. Sol., Gardiner.

(B) *** Ph. 438 715-2 (2). Mathis, Jerusalem, Fischer-Dieskau, Ch. & ASMF, Marriner.

(M) *** DG 457 713-2 (2). Janowitz, Schreier, Talvela, V. Singverein, VSO, Boehm.

(B) *** Double Decca (IMS) (ADD) 448 101-2 (2). Cotrubas, Krenn, Sotin, Brighton Festival Ch., RPO, Dorati.

(M) **(*) EMI CMS7 69224-2 (2). Janowitz, Hollweg, Berry, Ch. of German Op., BPO, Karajan.

Gardiner here more than ever rejects the idea prevalent among period performers that slow, measured speeds should be avoided, and almost always gets the best of both worlds in intensity of communication, whatever the purists may say. Even more than usual, this studio performance conveys the electricity of a live event. The silver-toned Barbara Bonney and Anthony Rolfe Johnson at his most sensitive are outstanding soloists, and though the baritone, Andreas

Schmidt, is less sweet on the ear, he winningly captures the bluff jollity of the role of Simon.

Marriner directs a superbly joyful performance of Haydn's last oratorio, effervescent with the optimism of old age. Edith Mathis and Dietrich Fischer-Dieskau are as stylish and characterful as one would expect, pointing the words as narrative. The tenor too is magnificent: Siegfried Jerusalem is both heroic of timbre and yet delicate enough for Haydn's most elegant and genial passages. The chorus and orchestra, of authentic size, add to the freshness. The recording, made in St John's, Smith Square, is warmly reverberant without losing detail. The CD transforms the sound, with added definition for both chorus and soloists. Highly recommended – a remarkable bargain by any standards.

Boehm's performance enters totally into the spirit of the music. The soloists are excellent and characterize the music fully; the chorus sing enthusiastically and are well recorded. But it is Boehm's set. He secures fine orchestral playing throughout, an excellent overall musical balance and real spontaneity in music that needs this above all else. The CD transfer of the 1967 recording is admirably managed.

Dorati brings to the work an innocent dedication, at times pointing to the folk-like inspiration, which is most compelling. This is not as polished an account as Boehm's in the same price-range but, with excellent solo singing and bright chorus work, is enjoyable in its own right. The choruses of peasants in Part 3, for instance, are boisterously robust. Textually there is an important difference in that Dorati has returned to the original version and restored the cuts in the introductions to *Autumn* and *Winter*, the latter with some wonderfully adventurous harmonies. This is all the more welcome at Double Decca price and competes strongly with the Boehm set now at mid-price.

Karajan's 1973 recording of *The Seasons* offers a fine, polished performance which is often very dramatic too. The characterization is strong, and in Karajan's hands the exciting Hunting chorus of Autumn (*Hört! Hört! Hört das laute Getön*) with its lusty horns anticipates *Der Freischütz*. The remastered sound is drier than the original but is vividly wide in dynamic range. Choruses are still a little opaque, but the soloists are all caught well and are on good form; and the overall balance is satisfactory.

Stabat mater.

**(*) Teldec 4509 95085-2. Bonney, Von Magnus, Lippert, Miles, Arnold Schoenberg Ch., VCM, Harnoncourt.

Harnoncourt's is a spacious and eloquent account of the *Stabat mater*, with a good solo team (although the tenor has moments of insecurity). But when the splendid bass, Alastair Miles, enters arrestingly at the *Pro peccatis* and the *Flammis orci ne succedar*, there are bursts of energy from Harnoncourt and the orchestra too, and one realizes that the overall tension has been lower than one expects with this conductor. Yet the penultimate *Quando corpus morietur* brings lovely singing from soprano and mezzo together, and the closing contrapuntal *Paradisi gloria* makes a telling close, even if here the soloists are not entirely comfortable in their sudden bravura entries.

Te Deum in C, Hob XXIIIc/2.

(BB) *** RCA Navigator (ADD) 74321 29238-2. V. Boys' Ch., Ch. Viennensis, VCO, Gillesberger – MOZART: *Requiem Mass*. ***

A fine, vigorous account of the *Te Deum* by these Viennese forces, very vividly recorded, coupled to a not inconsiderable account of Mozart's *Requiem*. At super-bargain price it makes excellent value.

OPERA

L'anima del filosofo (Orfeo ed Euridice) (complete).

*** O-L 452 668-2 (2). Bartoli, Heilmann, D'Arcangelo, Silvestrelli, AAM, Hogwood.

Haydn wrote his last and grandest opera for London in 1791 but, when the king refused to give the theatre a licence, it was never performed, and it was not until 1950 that the opera was heard complete.

Impressed by Handel oratorios and the English choral tradition, Haydn includes many choruses of comment. He also takes the opportunity of writing for a large orchestra, far beyond what he had been used to in Esterháza. Hogwood uses an enlarged Academy, with 12 first violins, and though at times his manner is severe, he paces the piece very effectively, making the most of the drama.

The very opening brings one of the most telling passages, a monologue when Euridice in distress flees into the forest. Cecilia Bartoli is in her element, passionately expressive, creating a larger-than-life character. Euridice's death scene, Orfeo's agony of lament (agitated, and very different from Gluck's *Orfeo* aria, *Che farò*), and a brilliant coloratura aria for the Sybil (dazzlingly done by Bartoli) bring other high points. Though Orfeo's death comes as an anticlimax, the final chorus for the Bacchantes is most memorable, in a minor key, dark and agitated, then fading away to the close. Uwe Heilmann is a most sympathetic Orfeo, musically stylish, even if the microphone catches the hint of a flutter, as it does too with the well-contrasted voices of Ildebrando d'Arcangelo as King Creonte, Euridice's father, and Andrea Silvestrelli as Pluto. The chorus, so important in this work, is fresh and well disciplined.

Armida (complete).

*** Ph. (IMS) (ADD) 432 438-2 (2). Norman, Ahnsjö, Burrowes, Ramey, Leggate, Rolfe Johnson, Lausanne CO, Dorati.

(N) **(*) Teldec 8573 81108 (2). Bartoli, Prégardien, Petibon, Schäfer, Weir, Widmer, VCM, Harnoncourt.

More than most of Haydn's works in this form, *Armida* presents a psychological drama, with the myrtle tree the most obvious of symbols. On CD it makes a fair entertainment, with splendid singing from Jessye Norman, even if she scarcely sounds malevolent. Claes Ahnsjö as the indecisive Rinaldo does better than most tenors in coping with the enormous range. The whole team of soloists is one of the most consistent in Dorati's Haydn opera series, with Norma Burrowes particularly sweet as Zelmira. As well as some advanced passages, *Armida* also has the advantage that there is little *secco* recitative. The 1978 recording quality is outstanding.

On Teldec, *Armida*, the last opera which Haydn wrote for the theatre at Esterháza, and arguably his finest, receives a period performance under Nikolaus Harnoncourt which brings out its freshness and vigour, helped by a strong cast. Cecilia Bartoli in the title role gives a seductive portrait of the sorceress, strongly and characterfully sung. The *tessitura* is high for her, which means that the warmth of her tone tends to disappear above the stave, yet unlike Jessye Norman on Antal Dorati's outstanding version for Philips (in 1978 using modern instruments), she does not transpose down the big fury aria in Act 2, *Odio furor.*

What seals the strength of her performance is the vitality of the recitatives, with word-meaning electrically conveyed. Christoph Prégardien gives a sensitive, stylish performance as Rinaldo, but the tone is sometimes thin, and Patricia Petibon as Zelmira, bright and agile, becomes a little shrill in high coloratura. With the others a good cast, though not as satisfying as Dorati's. Though the Concentus Musicus is not so abrasive as in its early days, and the full recording gives the players plenty of weight, there is still an edge on the sound that most period performance rivals have modified.

La fedeltà premiata (complete).

*** Ph. (IMS) (ADD) 432 430-2 (3). Terrani, Landy, Von Stade, Titus, Cotrubas, Alva, Mazzieri, Lövaas, SRO Ch., Lausanne CO, Dorati.

La fedeltà premiata shows its composer on his finest form. It was the first of Dorati's series of Haydn opera recordings for Philips, launched with characteristic effervescence, helped by an excellent Haydn-sized orchestra and a first-rate cast. The proud Aramanta is superbly taken by Frederica von Stade, while Haydn's unconventional allocation of voices brings a fine baritone, Alan Titus, to match her as the extravagant Count Perrucchetto. But the sweetest and most tender singing comes from Ileana Cotrubas as the fickle nymph, Nerina. The recording is intimate but with plenty of atmosphere. It is well transferred to CD, but at times one feels the cueing could be more generous.

(i) *L'incontro improviso* (complete). Arias for: (ii) *Acide e Galatea.* (iii) SARTI: *I finti eredi.* (iv) TRAETTA: *Ifigenia in Tauride.* (ii–iv) Terzetto from: PASTICCIO: *La Circe, ossia L'isola incantata.*

*** Ph. (ADD) 432 416-2 (3). (i; iv) Ahnsjö; (i) Zoghby, Trimarchi, Luxon, M. Marshall, Jones, Prescott; (ii) Devlin; (iii) Baldin; Lausanne CO, Dorati.

In eighteenth-century Vienna the abduction opera involving Moorish enslavement and torture became quite a cult. The greatest instance is Mozart's *Entführung*, but this example of the genre from Haydn is worthy of comparison, with its very similar story; the result is musically delightful. The most heavenly number of all is a trio for the three sopranos in Act I, *Mi sembra un sogno*, rather like *Soave sia il vento* in *Così fan tutte*. The tenor's trumpeting arias are beautifully crisp and the vigorous canzonettas for the two *buffo* basses include a nonsense song or two. Benjamin Luxon and Dom-

enico Trimarchi are delectable in those roles. Claes Ahnsjö is at his finest, resorting understandably to falsetto for one impossible top E flat; the role of the heroine is superbly taken by Linda Zoghby, and she is well supported by Margaret Marshall and Della Jones. The layout places each of the three Acts on a single CD and makes room on the third for two arias which Haydn devised for operas by other composers, plus one for his own *Acide e Galatea.*

L'infedeltà delusa (complete).

*** Ph. (ADD) 432 413-2 (2). Mathis, Hendricks, Baldin, Ahnsjö, Devlin, Lausanne CO, Dorati.

L'infedeltà delusa may not be dramatically the most imaginative of stage works, but by the standards of the time it is a compact piece, punctuated by some sharply noteworthy ideas. The opera brings many memorable numbers, such as a laughing song for Nencio (on Philips the admirable Claes Ahnsjö) and a song of ailments for the spirited and resourceful heroine, Vespina (Edith Mathis, lively and fresh). Dorati draws vigorous, resilient performances from everyone (not least from the delightful Barbara Hendricks). The Philips recording is splendidly full-blooded and neatly transferred on to a pair of CDs, with one Act complete on each.

L'isola disabitata (complete).

*** Ph. (IMS) (ADD) 432 427-2 (2). Lerer, Zoghby, Alva, Bruson, Lausanne CO, Dorati.

(N) *** Opus 111 OP 30319 (2). Kammerlohr, Hermann, Lee, Zinasi, Academia Montis Regalis, De Marchi.

(i) *L'isola disabitata* (complete); (ii) Cantata: *Arianna a Naxos.*

*** Ara. Z 6717-2 (2) Mentzer; (i) with Huang, Aler, Schaldenbrand, Padova CO, Golub; (ii) Golub (piano).

L'isola disabitata is a lightweight, relatively brief work, involving only four characters, performing seven arias and a final quartet, with copious recitative in between. The set numbers are typically fresh in their inspiration, and the final quartet is a delight in offering solo roles not just to the three singers but to a quartet of obbligato instruments echoing each character: violin and flute for the women, cello and bassoon for the men, with horns and timpani adding to the brilliance of the orchestra. The economy of scale was influenced by the fast that it was Haydn's first opera for Esterháza after the disastrous fire in the theatre in 1779.

L'isola disabitata, is described as an 'azione teatrale', more compact than most with seven solo numbers linked by orchestral recitative, and rounded off with a substantial quartet. David Golub and his orchestra from Padua give a warm, relaxed reading, with speeds consistently slower than on the rival Dorati version. The soloists are all first-rate, with Susanne Mentzer warm and firm as Costanza, Ying Huang fresh and girlish as Silvia and John Aler clear-toned as Gernando. Christopher Schildenbrand jibs at singing trills but is stylish otherwise. Well-balanced sound. *Arianna a Naxos* has Mentzer accompanied by Golub at the piano (unidentified in the booklet) to make a very welcome fill-up, to give a substantial advantage over the Dorati set.

Vocally, it is the second soprano on the Dorati set, Linda

Zoghby, who takes first honours, though the baritone, Renato Bruson, is splendid too. The piece ends with a fine quartet of reconciliation, only the eighth number in the whole piece. The direction of recitatives is unfortunately not Dorati's strong point – here, as elsewhere in the series, rather too heavy – but with excellent recording, very vividly transferred to CD, and with just the right degree of ambience, this makes a useful alternative to Golub's Arabesque version. The two acts are given a CD apiece.

De Marchi on Opus offers a fresh lively reading with period instruments, providing a useful alternative to the intermittently available Philips set in Dorati's Haydn series. As one would expect from a period performance, speeds are fast, sometimes hectic, and the strings are often edgy. With clear, young soloists, not specially characterful, it is hardly a strong recommendation.

(i) *Il mondo della luna* (complete). (ii) Arias for: Cantata: *Miseri noi, misera patria;* Petrarch's sonnet from *Il Canzoniere: Solo e pensoso.* BIANCHI: *Alessandro nell'Indie.* CIMAROSA: *I due supposti conti.* GAZZANIGA: *L'isola di Alcina.* GUGLIELMI: *La Quakera spiritosa.* PAISIELLO: *La Frascatana.* PASTICCIO: *La Circe, ossia l'Isola incantana.*

*** Ph. (IMS) (ADD) 432 420-2 (3). (i) Trimarchi, Alva, Von Stade, Augér, Mathis, Valentini Terrani, Rolfe Johnson, Lausanne CO, Dorati; (ii) Mathis, Lausanne CO, Jordan.

Il mondo della luna ('The World on the Moon') is better known (by name at least) than the other Haydn operas that the Philips series has disinterred. Written for an Esterházy marriage, it uses the plot of a naïve but engaging Goldoni comedy. Much of the most charming music comes in the brief instrumental interludes, and most of the arias are correspondingly short. That leaves much space on the discs devoted to *secco* recitative and, as on his other Haydn opera issues, Dorati proves a surprisingly sluggish harpsichord player. Nevertheless, with splendid contributions from the three principal women singers, this is another Haydn set which richly deserves investigation by anyone devoted to opera of the period. The 1977 recording is first class, as is the CD transfer; and the layout, with one Act allotted to each of the three CDs, leaves room for eight substitution arias (recorded three years later) on the last disc, stylishly sung by Edith Mathis.

Orlando paladino (complete).

*** Ph. (IMS) (ADD) 432 434-2 (3). Augér, Ameling, Killebrew, Shirley, Ahnsjö, Luxon, Trimarchi, Mazzieri, Carelli, Lausanne CO, Dorati.

Though long for its subject-matter, this is among the most delightful of all the Esterháza operas, turning the legend of Roland and his exploits as a medieval champion into something not very distant from farce. There are plenty of touches of parody in the music: the bass arias of the King of Barbary suggest mock Handel and Charon's aria (after Orlando is whisked down to the Underworld) brings a charming exaggeration of Gluck's manner. Above all the Leporello-like servant figure, Pasquale, is given a series of numbers which match Mozart, including a hilarious duet

when, bowled over by love, he can only utter monosyllables – cue for marvellous *buffo* singing from Domenico Trimarchi. The overall team is strong, with Arleen Augér as the heroine outstandingly sweet and pure. George Shirley as Orlando snarls too much in recitative, but it is an aptly heroic performance; and Elly Ameling and Gwendoline Killebrew in subsidiary roles are both excellent. The recitatives here, though long, are rather less heavily done than in some other Dorati sets, and the 1976 recording is first rate and splendidly transferred to three CDs, one for each Act.

La vera costanza (complete).

*** Ph. (IMS) (ADD) 432 424-2 (2). Norman, Donath, Ahnsjö, Ganzarolli, Trimarchi, Lövaas, Rolfe Johnson, Lausanne CO, Dorati.

Like Mozart's *Marriage of Figaro, La vera costanza* has serious undertones, if only because it is the proletarian characters who consistently inspire sympathy while the aristocrats come in for something not far short of ridicule. The individual numbers may be shorter-winded than in Mozart, but Haydn's sharpness of invention never lets one down, and the big finales to each of the first two Acts are fizzingly impressive, pointing clearly forward to *Figaro*. Overall, the opera is nicely compact. In every way bar one this is a delectable performance. The conducting of Dorati sparkles, Jessye Norman is superb as the virtuous fisher-girl, Rosina, while the others make up an excellent team, well cast in often difficult roles designed for the special talents of individual singers at Esterháza. The snag is the continuo playing of Dorati himself, heavy and clangorous, holding up the lively singing of the *secco* recitatives. Apart from some discrepancy of balance between the voices and a touch of dryness in the acoustic, the recorded sound is excellent.

HAYDN, Michael (1737–1806)

(i) *Horn Concertino in D;* (ii) *Violin Concertino in B flat. Symphonies: in E flat, P.1; A, P.6; D, P.11; C, P.12.* (ii; iii) *Duo for Violin & Viola No. 1 in C.*

(N) (B) *** Teldec Ultima 8573 87805-2 (2). Franz Liszt CO, Rolla or (ii) Zehetmair; (i) Clevenger; (ii) Zehetmair; (iii) Zimmerman.

Like some other issues in Warner's Ultima series, this might well have been entitled 'Meet the Composer', for it provides an admirable visiting card for Michael Haydn. His *Horn Concertino* is in the form of a French overture, beginning with a slow movement, followed by a fast one, and closing with a *Minuet* and *Trio*, in which the soloist is featured in only the middle section. The music is attractive, the second-movement allegro played with fine style by Dale Clevenger, whose articulation is a joy in itself. In the absence of the soloist in the elegantly played Minuet, an unnamed continuo player effectively embroiders the texture.

The *Violin Concerto* (written in 1760) is a fine piece with a lively first movement, rather briskly paced here, and a central *Adagio* of some depth. The finale is the weakest part, although not lacking in spirit. The performance, with Thomas Zehetmair combining the role of soloist and conductor, is strongly characterized. One's only reservation concerns a tendency for the phrasing – notably in the slow movement – to have squeezed emphases, though not as an alternative to vibrato, as in 'period' performances.

The four symphonies are all enjoyable: they contain at least one supremely beautiful inspiration: the elegiac *Andante* in A minor for strings with solo oboe from P.12 in C. With braying East European horns, the performances are lively and well recorded. The three-movement *Duo* was one of six commissioned by the Archbishop of Salzburg in 1808. Only four were completed by Haydn because of illness, and Mozart helped out the composer by writing the last two. The first of the set is offered here, a pleasing little work notable for its witty *Rondo* finale. It is very well played and recorded.

Symphonies Nos. 1 in C, P.35; 2 in C, P.2; 3 (Divertimento) in G; 4 in B flat, P.51; 5 in A, P.3; 6 in C, P.4; 7 in E, P.5; 8 in D, P.38; 9 in D, P.36; 10 in F, P.45; 11 in B flat, P.9; 12 in G, P.7; 15 in D, P.41; 16 in A, P.6; 18 in C, P.10; 25 in G, P.16; 26 in E flat, P.17; 27 in B flat, P.18; 28 in C, P.19. Sinfonia (Divertimento) in G, P.8.

**(*) CPO 999 591-2 (6). Slovak CO, Warchal.

Joseph Haydn's younger brother Michael worked first in Vienna, but gained security and a permanent post as Musical Director at the Salzburg court in 1763 where he remained until his death. His 41 symphonies were composed over three decades from 1760 until 1789. This is the first time they have been decently played on record and we owe a debt to CPO for allowing us to follow the composer's development from modest beginnings to considerable achievement in the later symphonies, the best of which ought to be much better known. The early works are comparatively straightforward and seldom adventurous, usually simply scored for oboes, horns and strings; sometimes flutes were added. The invention, too, though often quite endearing, is not particularly individual. Even so almost all the symphonies written in the 1760s have at least one memorable movement and sometimes two. No. 3 in G (subtitled Divertimento) has striking high horns in the outer movements and they trill spectacularly in the Minuet. The gracious *Andante* of No. 4 (*La confidenza*) alternates with quicker sprightly episodes. No. 6 opens like a familiar Handel chorus and has a wistful *Andante*, with the strings muted throughout; the *Minuet* acts as finale. No. 8 (1764) stands out and is most winning throughout. It is again drawn from a Divertimento, and scored for trumpets as well as horns. After a vigorous but light-hearted outer movement the *Andante* features pastoral flutes and introduces an aria on the bassoons, who return jocularly in the *Trio* of the *Minuet*, while the engaging finale even introduces clarinets. The concise No. 9, more like an Italian overture, produces one of the composer's loveliest tunes as its centrepiece. No. 10 is also a rather appealing three-movement work, with a charming *grazioso* slow movemet, and No. 11 has another delicate *Andantino* full of charm. The *Allegro molto* of No. 12 *in G* brings a light-hearted secondary theme on the violins worthy of Joseph, an *Andante* decorated with flutes, and a striking rondo finale. The horns are again used jovially in the dancing finale of No. 15.

With No. 18 we move into the 1770s and find the most ambitious work so far (36 minutes 34 seconds with repeats); its scoring includes a solo cor anglais. For a long time, No. 25 *in G* (1783) was attributed to Mozart, and with some justice – its slow movement is rather fine and the finale spirited and graceful. Nos. 26 to 28 all date from 1783–4 and show the composer at full stretch. All are in three movements and each has an outstanding slow movement. It is difficult to decide whether the *Adagietto affettuoso* of No. 26 or the *Poco Adagio* of No. 28 is the finer. Finales too are infectious and very neatly scored. No. 27 has an extended slow introduction, but it is No. 28 which caps the series so far. It is not for nothing that it is in *C major*, for its impressive fugato closing movement has much in common with the finale of Mozart's *Jupiter Symphony*. The Slovak Chamber Orchestra is an excellent modern instrument ensemble and performances throughout are lively in the traditional sense, warm and committed. Warchal phrases most musically, but generally observes repeats, which makes some slow movements seem rather long. Occasionally one might enjoy the brighter sound and brisker tempi of period-instrument manners, but overall this well-recorded set remains a fine achievement.

Symphonies: in A, P.6; in B flat, P.9; in G, P.16; in E flat, P.26; in F, P. 32.

*** Chan. 9352. LMP, Bamert.

Here are more performances of the Michael Haydn Symphonies that really do them full justice. P.6 and P.9 are both four-movement works but the others are in three-part Italian overture form. The elegance of the gentle *Andante* of the *A major Symphony* sets the seal on the playing, warm, polished and cultivated, while the *Allegro molto* finale, with its bold horns might almost be by Mozart. The charming *Andantino* of P.9 is no less engaging while the closing Rondo of P.16 has plenty of high spirits. None of this is great music, but all of it is enjoyable and the composer's penultimate F major work (1789) brings a strong, impressively constructed opening movement and a tender *Adagio* with muted strings. The well-detailed recording is pleasingly full and resonant.

Symphonies Nos. 21 in D, P.42; 30 in D, P.21; 31 in F, P.22; 32 in D, P. 23.

*** CPO 999 179-2. Deutsche CO, Neuss, Goritzki.

For the later symphonies Michael Haydn remains faithful to the three-movement format, jettisoning the minuet. Both Nos 21 and 30 have slow introductions. By now his orchestration has become much more sophisticated, using woodwind quite subtly for colouring and enriching the textures and in the *Andante* of No. 21 (a particularly impressive work) the horns too. His melodic material is more refined and musical arguments are developed with much greater assurance as in the quite excellent opening *Allegro assai* of No. 31 (1785). The following *Andante cantabile* uses orchestral soloists, including cor anglais, almost as in a sinfonia concertante. No. 32 (1786) is the only two-movement work in the series and very delightful it is. The playing of the Deutsche Chamber Orchestra is first rate.

Symphonies Nos. 34 in E flat, P.26; 35 in G, P.27; 36 in B flat, P.28; 37 in D, P. 29; 38 in F, P. 0; 39 in C, P.31.

*** CPO 999 379-2. Deutsche CO, Neuss, Goritzki.

Michael Haydn wrote these six symphonies in a continuing burst of inspiration in seven weeks, at the beginning of 1788. He again chose the three-movement format and his invention is fecund and concentrated: all but No. 39 are under ten minutes in overall length. But they bring a bubbling torrent of ideas; and how much more skilfully they are scored than the early symphonies!

The *Adagietto* of No. 34 introduces a dolorous bassoon solo and the closing fugato is skilfully and wittily contrived, with even surprise interjections from the solo horn. The outer movements of No. 35 sail along on a tide of rhythmic energy, yet with an underlying lyricism, and the unusal *Andante* brings a florid concertante oboe contribution. No 36 also buzzes along, and the *Andante con espressione* is full of galant charm, while the *Andantino* of No. 37 is songful. No. 38 opens with a spirited, gavotte-like rhythm, but is far more than a dance movement, and is most felicitously scored, including a horn solo. The slow movement brings a delightful cello and violin duet, with oboe echoes. The Joseph Haydnesque humour in the finale *Allegro scherzante*, with strong dynamic contrasts is most winning (one really smiles at the crisp, neat playing here). From its opening, No. 39 is strong and forward looking; the *Andante* uses the full orchestral palette, and in the final fugato there is mature use of counterpoint to knit the ideas convincingly together, with a brief, powerful coda. All these works are superbly played, conveying an exhilarating mixture of verve and elegance. Again first-class sound.

Ave Regina.

(B) *** Double Decca (ADD) 458 376-2 (2). St John's College, Cambridge Choir, ASMF, Guest – HAYDN: *Masses 1a, 8, 9, & 13.* ***

This lovely antiphon, scored for eight-part double choir, looks back to Palestrina, and the Venetian school of the Gabrielis and the young Monteverdi. It is beautifully sung and recorded.

HEADINGTON, Christopher

(1931–96)

(i) *Piano Concerto;* (ii) *The Healing Fountain;* (iii) *Serenade for Cello & String Orchestra.*

*** ASV CDDCA 969. Britten Sinfonia, Cleobury with (i) Fergus-Thompson. (ii) Carwood. (iii) Baillie.

The Healing Fountain was composed in 1978 'in memoriam Benjamin Britten' and is a 26-minute cycle for high voice and chamber orchestra comprising settings of Auden, Sassoon, Wilfred Owen, Thomas Moore and Shelley. It is expertly fasioned and often imaginative though it is perhaps a little too close for comfort to the Britten idiom – indeed it quotes from *Peter Grimes, Death in Venice* and the underrated *Nocturne*. The *Piano Concerto* was begun the following year but was put aside until 1991. Although it is not as haunting or

personal as the *Violin Concerto*, Headington's masterpiece, it is a strong piece, well structured and rewarding. The composer was an excellent pianist and his writing for the instrument is exhilarating and adroit. Those who respond to, say, Prokofiev or Britten will find much to admire here. The *Serenade* is the most recent work, and was commissioned by Juliam Lloyd Webber and premièred by him in 1995. Fine and committed performances and very good recording too.

Violin Concerto.

⚫ *** ASV CDDCA 780. Wei, LPO, Glover – R. STRAUSS: *Violin Concerto.* ***

The Headington *Violin Concerto* is a warmly lyrical, unashamedly tonal work in which a fiery central Scherzo is framed by two longer, more reflective movements. The finale is a spacious set of variations in which the last and longest acts as a movingly meditative summary. Xue Wei plays with a passionate commitment, with Jane Glover and the London Philharmonic providing warmly sympathetic accompaniments. Excellent sound. Those looking for twentieth-century music that is accessible and rewards familiarity need not hesitate.

HEATH, Dave (born 1956)

The Frontier.

(M) *** Virgin VM5 61851-2. LCO, Warren-Green – ADAMS: *Shaker Loops* *** ⚫; GLASS: *Company* etc. ***; REICH: *8 Lines.* ***

In *The Frontier* Heath's incisive rhythmic astringency is tempered by an attractive, winding lyrical theme which finally asserts itself just before the spiky close. The work was written for members of the LCO, and their performance, full of vitality and feeling, is admirably recorded.

HEBDEN, John (18th century)

6 Concertos for Strings (ed. Wood).

**(*) Chan. 8339. Cantilena, Shepherd.

These concertos are Hebden's only known works, apart from some flute sonatas. Although they are slightly uneven, at best the invention is impressive. The concertos usually feature two solo violins and are well constructed to offer plenty of contrast. The performances here are accomplished, without the last degree of polish but full of vitality.

HEINICHEN, Johann David

(1683–1729)

Dresden Concerti: in C, S 211; in G, S 213; in G (Darmstadt), S 214; in G (Venezia), S 214; in G, S 215; in F, S 217; in F, S 226, in F, S 231; in F, S 232; in F, S 233; in F, S 234; in F, S 235; Concerto movement in C min., S 240; Serenata di Moritzburg in F, S 204; Sonata in A, S 208.

*** DG 437 549-2 (2). Col. Mus. Ant., Goebel.

Dresden Concerti: in F, S 231; 233/5; in G, S 213; Concerto Movement in C min., S 240; Sonata in A, S 208.

*** DG 437 849-2. Col. Mus. Ant., Goebel.

Johann David Heinichen, a contemporary of Bach, was a Dresden court musician and the concertos here were intended for the (obviously excellent) Dresden court orchestra. It is the orchestral colour that makes these concertos so appealing rather than their invention, which is more predictable. Goebel's Cologne forces obviously relish the delicacy of Heinichen's wind scoring and his neat and busily vital allegros. The recording is freshly vivid, clean and realistic. One would be tempted to recommend the single-disc selection, but DG have cunningly not included therein the lollipop of the set. This is the *Pastorell* second movement of the *C major Concerto*, Seibel 211, with its piquant drone (track 5 of the second CD). It is immediately followed by a peaceful *Adagio* for flute and strings and a sparkling finale.

Dresden Concerti in A min., S 212; in E min., S 218; in E min., S 222; in D, S 225; in G min., S 237; in G min., S 238.

**(*) CPO 999 637-2. Fiori Musicale, Albert.

It is fortunate that the present issue from Thomas Albert and his Bremen group involves no duplication of items in the DG set, and so for those who have the Archive recordings, this will be a welcome supplement, though it must be said that the playing is by no means as accomplished or elegant as that of the Cologne group.

HELWEG, Kim (born 1956)

American Fantasy (A tribute to Leonard Bernstein).

** Chan. 9398. Safri Duo & Slovak Piano Duo – BARTOK: *Sonata for 2 Pianos & Percussion;* LUTOSLAWKI: *Paganini Variations.* ***

The *American Fantasy* is a four-movement sonata and at the same time a set of variations on Bernstein's song *America*, from *West Side Story*. But although it is obviously the work of a resourceful and intelligent musician, it is of insufficient individuality to reward repeated listening. Fine playing, stunning recording. The audience goes wild at the end of the performance.

HELY-HUTCHINSON, Victor
(1901–47)

Carol Symphony.

(M) ** EMI (ADD) CDM7 64131-2. Guildford Cathedral Ch., Pro Arte O, Rose – QUILTER: *Children's Overture;* VAUGHAN WILLIAMS: *Fantasia on Christmas Carols.* **

Hely-Hutchinson's *Carol Symphony* dates from the late 1920s. Hely-Hutchinson's first movement could do with a little judicious pruning, the Scherzo is quite effective and in the finale he gathers all the threads together and ends with a triumphal presentation of *O come, all ye faithful*. But it is the *Andante* that remains in the memory with its deliciously imaginative gossamer texture against which the solo harp embroiders *Nowell*. The performance here is lively and sensitive if not distinctive, but the close-miked recording is curiously dry and unexpansive, bearing in mind that the 1966 venue was Guildford Cathedral.

HEMING, Michael (1920–42)

Threnody for a Soldier Killed in Action.

(M) (***) EMI mono CDM5 66053-2. Hallé O, Barbirolli – BRITTEN: *Violin Concerto* (**); RUBBRA: *Symphony No. 5 etc.* (***)

Michael Heming was a kind of Second World War Butterworth and when he was killed at El Alamein, Anthony Collins concocted (to use Michael Kennedy's word) the *Threnody for a Soldier Killed in Action* from sketches that the young man had made. Barbirolli and the Hallé Orchestra recorded it in 1945. A moving piece in the English pastoral tradition and a welcome fill-up to this interesting disc.

HENSELT, Adolf von (1814–89)

Piano Concerto in F min., Op. 16; Variations de Concert on 'Quand je quittai la Normandie' from Meyerbeer's Robert le Diable, Op. 11.

*** Hyp. CDA 66717. Hamelin, BBC Scotish SO, Brabbins – ALKAN: *Concerti da camera.* ***

Henselt's *F minor Concerto* is fiendishly difficult (Egon Petri thought it one of the hardest pieces he had ever played) but it seems to present few problems for Marc-André Hamelin, who is more than equal to its challenges. The idiom, as one might expect, is much indebted to Mendelssohn and Chopin, but there is much to give delight quite apart from the virtuosity of the playing. Stunning playing throughout from this remarkable Canadian pianist, and very good recorded sound.

HENZE, Hans Werner (born 1926)

The DG Henze Collection

To mark the occasion of Hans Werner Henze's seventieth birthday, DG have issued a 14-CD set of the repertoire that the composer himself recorded in the heyday of his relationship with the company, plus a handful of others items. DG are wise to make the discs available separately as there are few who would necessarily want or could afford the whole package (now withdrawn).

For most collectors the best starting-point, perhaps, would be the symphonies, which come on a two-CD set. For R.L. the *Third* and *Fourth* remain the most haunting of the set, with the latter casting a particularly powerful spell, and its expressionist anguish is punctuated by moments of an all-pervasive melancholy which must spring from a deep personal experience. The *First Symphony* is also a delight. The *First Violin Concerto* (1947), recorded here with

Schneiderhan as soloist, is one of the most rewarding of Henze's early scores.

The other CDs which would make an excellent introduction to the set include the beautiful *Double Concerto for Oboe and Harp*, played by its dedicatees, Heinz and Ursula Holliger, coupled with one of his most haunting and affecting scores, the *Fantasia for Strings*. Likewise the beautiful *Five Neapolitan Songs* with the young Dietrich Fischer-Dieskau or the *Cantata della fiaba estrema*, expertly sung by Edda Moser, are wonderful pieces. The CD transfers, generally speaking, have an admirable clarity, but this is achieved at a certain cost: in comparison with the original LPs there is less depth and less space round the aural image.

(i) *2 Ballet Variations;* (ii) *Piano Concerto No. 2;* (iii) *Tristan* (preludes for piano, tapes and orchestra); (iv) *3 Tientos for guitar.*

(M) **(*) DG (ADD) mono/stereo 449 866-2 (2). (i) RIAS SO, Fricsay; (ii) Eschenbach, LPO; (iii) Francesch, Cologne RSO; (ii; iii) cond. composer; (iv) Behrend.

The *Piano Concerto* has great originality and poetry. Eschenbach, for whom the concerto was written in 1967, is the magnificent soloist. It is an interesting, often moving work, full of a sad eloquence that bursts into occasional bitter outcries of some violence. The brief *Ballet Variations* were written as music for a ballet without a narrative while Henze was strongly under the influence of the Stravinsky of the *Danses Concertantes*. The three *Tientos* for guitar, though brief, are very imaginatively conceived.

Tristan, the other extended work here, is an extraordinary montage with a kinship with Wagner's opera, yet is very much like a musical nightmare, originally deriving from an extraordinary mélange of extra-musical sounds, mixed together on tape in a studio in Putney, London. The resulting work is a six-part structure lasting just over 43 minutes, splicing in a quotation from the opening of Brahms's *First Symphony*, synthesized Chopin excerpts and more distorted Brahms. It is difficult to take seriously, but it certainly represents a new experience.

(i) *Concerto for Double-Bass;* (ii) *Violin Concerto No. 1;* (iii) *Ode to the West Wind* (for cello and orchestra).

(M) *** DG (ADD) 449 865-2. (i) Karr; (ii) Schneiderhan (iii) Palm; (i; iii) Bav. RSO; (ii) ECO; all cond. composer.

The *Violin Concerto* shows the influence of Hindemith, while the *Ode to the West Wind* was inspired by Shelley's poem. Both works contain pages of some beauty, though the later piece employs a more fragmented and complex style than the predominantly serial *Concerto*. The *Violin Concerto* is the more immediately appealing work and has an eloquent slow movement, and the performances, apart from having the composer's authority to commend them, are expertly recorded. The *Double-Bass Concerto* is not among the composer's most impressive pieces, though it fascinates by its resourceful treatment of an unpromising solo instrument. The performance is exemplary.

(i) *Double Concerto for Oboe, Harp & Strings. Fantasia for Strings; Sonata for Strings.*

(M) *** DG (ADD) 449 864-2. Zurich Coll. Mus., Sacher, with (i) Heinz and Ursula Holliger.

The language of the *Fantasia*, based on incidental music for a film, is more disciplined and diatonic than is often Henze's wont. It is a moving score with a vein of melancholy that is direct in utterance. The *Double Concerto* was inspired by the astonishing artistry and virtuosity of Heinz Holliger on the oboe, who performs it here with his wife, Ursula, on the harp. Highly inventive and resourceful, this performance is authoritative and is given an exemplary recording.

(i) *Piano Concerto No. 2; Telemanniana.*

(N) *** CPO 999 322-2. NWD PO, Markson, (i) Plagge.

Henze's *Second Piano Concerto* is a complex, intricate work. Rolf Plagge gives a good account of it, even if his recording must yield in authority to the Eschenbach version which features Henze himself. However, it is important that there should be new and alternative versions, and this newcomer has much going for it. Plagge has great fluency and an impressive technical address. The concerto has the benefit of being coupled with the appealing and beautifully written *Telemanniana*, which does for Telemann what Casella did for Paganini. While this does not displace the Eschenbach, which is still in circulation, it is a very good and recommendable alternative.

Symphonies Nos. (i) *1–5;* (ii) *6.*

(M) *** DG (ADD) 449 861-2 (2). (i) BPO; (ii) LSO; cond. composer.

The *First Symphony*, with its cool, Stravinskian slow movement, is a remarkable achievement for a 21-year-old. There is a dance-like feel to the *Third*, written while Henze was attached to the Wiesbaden Ballet. The *Fourth* is meant to connote 'an evocation of the living, breathing forest and the passing of the seasons'. There is at times an overwhelming sense of melancholy and a strongly Mediterranean atmosphere to its invention. The *Fifth* embraces the most violent angularity, with passages of exquisite poignancy and tranquillity; the language is strongly post-expressionist. The *Sixth Symphony* was composed while Henze was living in Havana. The performances are brilliant and the vivid recordings do not sound their age, those of the first five symphonies being over 35 years old.

Symphony No. 7; Barcarola.

*** EMI CDC7 54762-2. CBSO, Rattle.

The *Seventh Symphony* is not only the longest Henze has written, it is also the weightiest and most traditionally symphonic, Beethoven-like in four substantial movements. Rather belying its title, the *Barcarola* presents a similarly weighty and massive structure, an elegiac piece of over 20 minutes, inspired by the myth of the ferryman, Charon, crossing the Styx. The dramatic bite of both performances, recorded live in Symphony Hall, Birmingham, makes them instantly compelling. Full, colourful recording to bring out the richness of Henze's orchestral writing.

Symphony No. 9.

*** EMI CDC5 56513-2. Berlin R. Ch., BPO, Metzmacher.

Henze refers to his *Ninth Symphony* as a *summa summorum* of his musical output. Commissioned by the Berlin Philharmonic, it is choral throughout, a setting of seven poems by Hans-Ulrich Treichel based on Anna Seger's *The Seventh Cross*. It tells of seven prisoners condemned to be crucified who escape from a concentration camp and are hunted down and recaptured. Only one succeeds in eluding his pursuers. The poems and Henze's settings portray the most powerful and nightmarish emotions, and there is no doubt of the intensity and depth of feeling that lies behind this symphony. The recording derives from the première at the Philharmonie in 1997, and the singing of the Berlin Radio Choir is superb in every way. Powerful and impressive.

Undine (complete ballet).

⦿ *** DG 453 467-2 (2). L. Sinf, Knussen.

Here at last is a long overdue recording of Henze's wonderfully resourceful and strongly atmospheric ballet written for Covent Garden in 1958, choreographed by Ashton and starring the legendary Fonteyn. It is Henze's most approachable and attractive score. The scenario tells of the waternymph, Undine and her infatuation for a mortal. From the very opening note to the closing passacaglia, one is struck by the sheer profusion of invention, as well as the richness and subtlety of the orchestral palette. The evocation of the sea in Act II (CD1: track 22) is quite masterly. The score may not always bother to disguise Stravinskian touches, but if there is a bit of Stravinsky in it, there is so much more that is pure Henze, and richly imaginative Henze at that. With a totally committed and persuasive performance and recording of demonstration standard, this makes an ideal entry-point for the collector into Henze's world.

CHAMBER MUSIC

Piano Quintet.

*** Philips 446 710-2. Serkin, Guarneri Qt. – BRAHMS: *Piano Quintet.* ***

Henze's *Piano Quintet* was composed in 1990–91 for Peter Serkin and the Guarneri Quartet, and this recording emanates from 1995. It is a compact three-movement piece lasting some twenty minutes. In the composer's own words, 'each of the movements contrasts sharply from one another, and each evokes a world of its own [though] there is a distinct feeling of progression from the first movement to the last'. As always with Henze there is a highly imaginative creation of texture and a strong atmosphere. It shares some of its invention with the *Requiem* composed at roughly the same time. First-rate playing and recording.

INSTRUMENTAL MUSIC

Royal Winter Music: Guitar Sonatas Nos. 1 & 2.

*** MDG MDGL 3110. Evers.

These are 'sonatas on Shakespearean characters', the first ranging from Romeo and Juliet, Ariel, Ophelia and the malice and majesty of Richard III; the second encompassing Sir Andrew Aguecheek, Bottom's Dream from *A Midsummer Night's Dream* and a particularly compelling and effective portrait of Lady Macbeth. Henze exploits all the resources of the instrument with astonishing assurance, subtlety and imagination. Reinbert Evers despatches its many challenges with great virtuosity and brilliance. The 1983 recording still sounds first class.

Music for 2 guitars: Memorias se El Cimarrón; Minette (Canti e rimpianti ariosi); 3 Märchenbilder from the Opera Pollicino.

*** MDG 304 0881-2. Ruck, Càsoli.

Of the three pieces recorded here, *Memorias se El Cimarrón* (1995) is the most immediately striking. It retraces and paraphrases the course of his opera *El Cimarrón* and exploits an extraordinarily wide range of sonorities and expressive devices, which Jürgen Ruck and Elena Càsoli of the Ensemble Villa Musica bring vividly to life. Highly imaginative and resourceful writing, reproduced with exemplary subtlety and naturalness by the recording engineers. *Minette* (1997) returns to the theme of his opera *The English cat* and reworks, recreates and sometimes freshly composes its material. For the *Märchenbilder from Pollicino* Henze returns to the children's opera he composed for Montepulciano, 'a delightful self-immersion in simple music for the purpose of escorting the younger generation into the world of today's musical language', as the composer himself put it. The whole programme is played with effortless mastery and imagination.

VOCAL MUSIC

3 Auden Songs; 6 Songs from the Arabian.

(N) *** EMI CDC5 57112-2. Bostridge, Drake.

When Henze heard Ian Bostridge singing his *Three Auden Songs*, he embarked on the *Six Songs from the Arabian* specially for him and with his vocal qualities and timbre in mind. In recent years Henze has paid regular visits to the Arab world and drawn much inspiration from it. Henze's sensitivity to words is always in evidence and Bostridge and his fine pianist serve him well – as for that matter do the EMI recording team. A valuable addition to the composer's representation on disc.

(i) Being Beauteous; (ii) 5 Neapolitan Songs; (iii) Versuch über Schweine (Essay on Pigs); (iv) Whispers from Heavenly Death.

(M) *** DG (IMS) (ADD) mono/stereo 449 869-2. (i; iv) Moser; (i) RIAS Ch., BPO soloists; (ii) Fischer-Dieskau, BPO soloists, Kraus; (iii) Hart, Philip Jones Brass Ens., ECO; (iv) BPO soloists; (i; iii–iv) cond. composer.

The *Versuch über Schweine* ('Essay on Pigs') contains a voice-part that traverses an amazing range and which certainly encompasses an extraordinary variety of timbre. *Being Beauteous* is exquisite and quite moving, and *Whispers from Heavenly Death* is one of the composer's most fascinating works. The singing of Edda Moser is quite phenomenal both in purity of tone and in accuracy of intonation. The performances of all this repertoire could hardly be bettered, and the recording reproduces a wide dynamic range with admirable truthfulness of balance and quality of tone.

(i) *Cantata della fiaba estrema (Cantata of the Ultimate Fable);* (ii) *Moralitäten (Moralities);* (iii) *Musen Siziliens (Muses of Sicily).*

(M) *** DG (IMS) (ADD) 449 870-2. (i) Moser, RIAS Ch., Berlin Philh. CO; (ii) Schwarz, Leffler, Scheibner, Jäckel, Paspirgilis, Lang, Dresden Ch., Leipzig GO; (iii) Dresden Ch., Rollino, Sheftel, Dresden State O soloists; all cond. composer.

The *Cantata* is a setting of a Roman love-poem. With Edda Moser the soloist, it cannot fail to communicate vividly. *Moralities* (with narrator) is a setting of 'three scenic plays', which W. H. Auden devised from three of Aesop's fables. Its manner is not in the least intimidating and the result is potently ironic rather than lightly humorous in spirit. The *Muses of Sicily* opens with a *Pastorale* dialogue, and ends with the *Song of Silenus,* recounting the creation of the world from the elements of earth, air, sea and liquid. The work is entirely choral, with a vivid accompaniment for two pianos, wind instruments and timpani. Superb singing and very good recording.

El Cimarrón (autobiography of the runaway slave Esteban Montejo) (recital for four musicians).

(M) *** DG (IMS) (ADD) 449 872-2. Pearson, Zöller, Brouwer, Yamash'ta, cond. composer.

El Cimarrón uses the words of a former slave, born in Cuba over 100 years ago, a simple but moving story. The live performance was impressive for the antics of the Japanese percussionist, Stomu Yamash'ta; but on disc the impact of the work is even more intense, because the improvisatory passages have been considerably tightened up, and the story is after all best imagined in the mind's eye – the poetic passage where the runaway lives in the forest, the biting account of the Revolution, the scene of the swaggering Yankees where a four-letter word is inserted (in English) in an otherwise German text. The performance is as near definitive as one could expect, beautifully recorded.

Das Floss der Medusa (The Raft of the Medusa) (oratorio).

(M) *** DG (ADD) 449 871-2. Moser, Fischer-Dieskau, Regnier, RIAS Chamber Ch., Members of the St Nikolai Hamburg Youth Ch., N. German R. Ch. & O, cond. composer.

This is a vividly imaginative work and whatever the political bias, the message is both dramatic and moving as told in the tragic story of the crew of a shipwrecked frigate cast adrift and left to die by their officers. Henze has conceived the simple but effective idea of having the members of the crew as represented by the chorus move from one side of the stage to the other, one by one called from the land of the living, over to the side of Death (soprano soloist). A vivid experience, superbly realized.

Der langwierige Weg in die Wohnung der Natascha Ungeheuer (The Tedious Way to Natascha Ungueheuer's Apartment).

(M) **(*) DG (IMS) (ADD) 449 873-2. Pearson, Fires of London, Philip Jones Brass Quintet, Gunter Hampel Free Jazz Ens., Agostini, Yamash'ta, cond. composer.

It was unfortunate that the composer used the word 'tedious' in his title, for the writing here has the air of a political tract and comes from the period when the composer was rejecting opera. The work is an allegory: Natasha Ungeheuer is 'the siren of a false Utopia who constantly lures the leftist intellectual into the cosy situation of so many middle-class socialists, who preach revolution while meanwhile living more or less the same old comfortable life'.

Voices.

*** Berlin Classics (ADD) 2180-2 BC (2). Trexler, Vogt, Leipzig RSO Chamber Ens., Neumann.

This massive and wide-ranging song-cycle of 22 numbers, lasting over 90 minutes is among Henze's most inspired and characterful works, even including ironic songs echoing Kurt Weill, several of them setting poems by Bertolt Brecht. The wonder is that, so far from seeming too disparate a sequence, *Voices* gathers in richness as it progresses, with instruments including ocarina, accordion, mouth-organ and electric guitar, as well as a large percussion section. Some of the episodes are violent, but the work is rounded off with the most beautiful and most extended piece, a duet, *Blumenfest* ('Carnival of flowers'), which seems to suggest a final ray of hope, with bitterness gone. This analogue recording, made in Germany in 1980, presents a sharply focused performance, strong and dramatic, with two excellent, clean-cut soloists.

OPERA

Die Bassariden (The Bassarids).

*** Koch Schwann 314 006-2 (2). Tear, Schmidt, Armstrong, Riegel, Lindsley, Wenkel, Burt, Murray, Berlin RIAS Chamber Ch. & RSO, Albrecht.

Henze's *The Bassarids,* based on the *Bacchae* of Euripides, presents a contrast of rival philosophies between the Dionysiac and the Apollonian, the sensual and the intellectual and this fine account from Berlin amply confirms the work's power. The cast is first rate, including Kenneth Riegel, Andreas Schmidt, Robert Tear and Karen Armstrong, and the choral writing adds greatly to the impact, splendidly realized here by the RIAS Choir.

Elegie für junge Liebende (Elegy for Young Lovers) (scenes).

(M) *** DG (ADD) 449 874-2. Fischer-Dieskau, Driscoll, Dubin, Mödl, Berlin RSO & German Op. O, Berlin (members), cond. composer.

Elegie für junge Liebende is set in a mountain inn, from which the hero and heroine eventually go to their deaths in a storm; but the underlying psychology of the characters, their destinies dominated by the poet, Mittenhoffer, is most complex. So is the construction of the music, both in the variety of forms for the set pieces, and in the way each character is given his or her own musical personality by the individual use of specific instrumentation and note-groupings (intervals, rather than leitmotives). The composer shows his brilliant feeling for orchestral colour and, with Fischer-Dieskau as Mittenhoffer, Martha Mödl as a strong-voiced Carolina (the poet's patron) and Liane Dubin an appealing Elisabeth, the vocal writing is fully characterized. An excellent and enterprising issue.

Der junge Lord.

(M) *** DG (IMS) (ADD) 449 875-2 (2). Mathis, Grobe, McDaniel, Johnson, Driscoll, German Op., Berlin, Ch. & O, Dohnányi.

This 'opera buffa' is Henze at his most amiable, and it results for much of the time in his Stravinskian side dominating, though he also allows himself a warmer vein of lyricism than usual. The plot in its comedy is consciously cynical, involving a snobbish community duped by a titled Englishman. He introduces an alleged English lord who finally turns out to be an ape. There is an underlying seriousness to the piece, and in this excellent performance, recorded with the composer's approval, the full range of moods and emotions is conveyed. Very good (1967) sound.

HERBERT, Victor (1859–1924)

Auditorium Festival March; Columbus Suite; Irish Rhapsody; Natoma: excerpts.

(N) **(*) Marco Polo 8.225109. Slovak RSO (Bratislava), Brion.

The longest piece here, the *Columbus Suite* was also the composer's last major work and was premiered in 1903. Its four movements are all descriptive and have mild moments of interest (the *Murmurs of the Sea* bring nice orchestral effects), but it's all a bit thin really. The other works are more enjoyable. The *Irish Rhapsody*, with its haunting Irish folk-tunes running throughout and alternating pastoral and vigorous episodes, is really quite fun. The selections from *Natoma* – Herbert's one foray into grand opera – sounds like a mixture of Wagner and Hollywood, with a tango half way through! Its musical inspiration, the music of Native American Indians, gives it an additional dash of local colour, The *Auditorium Festival March* (1901) is an exuberant piece quoting extensively from *Auld Lang Syne*, and sounds ready made for a Hollywood film of the 1930s. Enthusiastic performances and acceptable recording.

Cello Concerto No. 2 in E min., Op. 30.

*** Sony (ADD) SK 67173. Ma, NYPO, Masur – DVORAK: *Cello Concerto*. ***

(M) ** Mercury (ADD) (IMS) [434 355-2]. Miquelle, Eastman-Rochester O, Hanson – GROFE: *Grand Canyon Suite; Mississippi Suite*. **(*)

The Victor Herbert concerto which sparked Dvořák into writing his masterpiece within the year makes an apt and unusual coupling for that superb work. Yo-Yo Ma gives a compelling, high-powered performance. Ma's use of rubato is perfectly judged, with that slow movement made the more tender at a flowing speed. The finale is then given a quicksilver performance, both brilliant and urgent.

Georges Miquelle is a very musical soloist, but his tonal image is modest and he is dynamically upstaged by the orchestra everywhere but in the slow movement. He plays the work sympathetically, but Ma's newest version is much more persuasive.

HÉROLD, Ferdinand (1791–1833)

La Fille mal gardée (ballet, arr. Lanchbery): complete.

(M) *** Decca 430 849-2 (2). ROHCG O, Lanchbery – LECOCQ: *Mam'zelle Angot*. ***

La Fille mal gardée: extended excerpts.

(M) *** Decca (ADD) 430 196-2. ROHCG O, Lanchbery.

Lanchbery himself concocted the score for this fizzingly comic and totally delightful ballet, drawing primarily on Hérold's music, but interpolating the famous comic *Clog Dance* from Hertel's alternative score, which must be one of the most famous of all ballet numbers outside Tchaikovsky. There is much else of comparable delight. Here, with sound of spectacular Decca digital fidelity, Lanchbery conducts a highly seductive account of the complete ballet with an orchestra long familiar with playing it in the theatre.

The alternative extended selection on Decca has a vintage Kingsway Hall recording. One cannot believe that it dates from 1962, for the combination of ambient bloom and the most realistic detail still places it in the demonstration bracket.The performance is also wonderfully persuasive and brilliantly played, displaying both affection and sparkle in ample quantity.

Overture: Zampa.

*** Chan. 9765. (i) RLPO Ch., BBC PO, Tortelier (with Concert: *French Bonbons* ***).

Hérold's famous bandstand overture is played here with fine panache and given first-class recording. The rest of the programme of 'French Bonbons' is equally diverting part of a concert of French orchestral lollipops.

HERRMANN, Bernard (1911–75)

(i) The Devil and Daniel Webster: suite; (ii) Obsession (abridged score); (i) Welles Raises Kane: suite.

(M) *** Unicorn (ADD) UKCD 2065. (i) LPO; (ii) Nat. SO; composer.

The *Devil and Daniel Webster* suite is not first-grade Herrmann; *Welles Raises Kane* is another matter. Beecham himself gave one of its first performances in New York during the war. The music is drawn from both Orson Welles's *Citizen Kane* and *The Magnificent Ambersons*, snappily and evocatively extrovert, showing a brilliant flair for orchestral colour. It is superbly played. For the reissue Unicorn have added a brilliant Decca recording of an abridged version of the music Herrmann wrote for *Obsession* (some 39 minutes overall). It offers some of his most spectacular and evocative writing, including choral effects.

Symphony; (i) The Fantasticks (song-cycle).

(M) *** Unicorn (ADD) UKCD 2063. (London) National PO, composer, (i) with Rippon, Dickinson, Amis, Gillian Humphreys, Thames Chamber Ch.

Underlying everything in this eclectic but enjoyable symphony the argument reflects the approach of a dedicated Sibelian and it is good to hear Herrmann extending himself and giving what is in effect a musical self-portrait. Admirable performance and very good recording. The coupled song-cycle – virtually a cantata – set to words by the Elizabethan poet Nicolas Breton, has more of the composer's own personality and is obviously deeply felt music. With its nicely spiced word-imagery, the music communicates readily, and it is a pity that Gillian Humphreys, who is very sympathetic, has such a close vibrato. Otherwise the soloists are excellent and the orchestral playing quite lovely. Most rewarding when the sound is so atmospheric.

HERTEL, Johann (1727–89)

Trumpet Concerto No. 1 in E flat.

*** EMI CDC5 55231-2. André, Franz Liszt O, Budapest, Rolla – HAYDN; HUMMEL: *Trumpet Concertos* ***. MARCELLO: *Concerto in D min.* **(*)

Hertel's *E flat Concerto* (the first of three) has a rather fine central *Larghetto*. André clearly relishes the work's high tessitura and plays it with aplomb.

Trumpet Concerto in D.

*** Ph. 420 203-2. Hardenberger, ASMF, Marriner – HAYDN ***; HUMMEL ***; STAMITZ: *Concertos.* ***

Johann Hertel's *D major Trumpet Concerto* is typical of many works of the same kind written in the Baroque era. Håkan Hardenberger clearly relishes every bar and plays with great flair. But the performance is also included on a Duo (464 028-3) of trumpet concertos, which is outstanding value.

HERZOGENBERG, Heinrich von (1843–1900)

Legends, Op. 62; Piano Quartet in B flat, Op. 95; String Trio in F, Op. 27/2.

(N) (M) *** CPO 999 710-2. Frölich, Belcanto Strings.

Von Herzogenberg was born in Vienna but was descended from French aristocrats. A connoisseur of Baroque music, a conductor of the Leipzig Bach-Verein, and then a professor of composition at the Berlin Hochschule, he features in biographies of Brahms and Clara Schumann. His wife, Elisabet, became a close confidant of Brahms in his later years. 2000 was the centenary of his death, and this CD serves to fill in our picture of him. These pieces are so indebted to Brahms in their musical language that they can only *just* be said to lead an independent life. They are played very well, and the recording is lifelike and well balanced.

HESS, Nigel (born 1953)

East Coast Pictures; Global Variations; Thames Journey; Scramble!; Stephenson's Rocket; (i) To the Stars!; The TV Detectives; The Winds of Power.

**(*) Chan. 9764. L. Symphonic Wind O, composer; (i) with children from Daubney Middle School, Bedford.

Nigel Hess is known primarily as a TV and theatre composer. He knows how to score and has a ready fund of melody, as demonstrated in *The TV Detectives*, five rather striking TV themes, including 'Dangerfield', 'Wycliffe' and 'Hetty Wainthrop Investigates'. Of the concert pieces here, the most impressive is the flamboyant *To the Stars!*, which gets a real lift-off from the vocal energy of the children of Daubney Middle School. *Thames Journey* has trickling woodwind at its source, like Smetana's *Vltava*, and a Wiltshire folk melody on the horn as its main theme, but overall is little more than a well-crafted pot-pourri, also introducing *Greensleeves* and *The Lass of Richmond Hill*. The three *East Coast Pictures* evoke the USA's Eastern seaboard, but curiously without any strong American colouring. *Stephenson's Rocket* is rugged and vigorous, but not much of a train imitation. *The Winds of Power* is more evocative, but rather loosely laminated. *Scramble!* is more succinct and celebrates the Battle of Britain vividly enough. Indeed, all these works have plenty of vitality, even if they are not really distinctive, and are brilliantly played here under the composer, with excellent Chandos sound.

HILDEGARD, of Bingen (1098–1179)

'900 Years' (1098–1998) Collection.

**(*) DHM/BMG ADD/Dig. 05472 77505-2 (8). Sequentia, Thornton.

Born almost exactly nine centuries ago, Abbess Hildegard of Bingen has over the last decade or so emerged as one of the great creative figures of medieval times; not just an inspired composer, but a poet, dramatist and theologian, a correspondent with emperors and popes. Her output is astonishing. In terms of the quantity of the music and religious poetry she left us, she stands head and shoulders above any other name in the twelfth or thirteenth centuries, and the quality and individuality of her writing are in no doubt. As many listeners have found, her melismas insinuate themselves into the consciousness and stay there. Following on Gothic Voices' best-selling disc for Hyperion (see below), the fine German group Sequentia has, under Barbara Thornton, made an eight-CD collected edition. The CDs are all available separately and are discussed below.

Canticles of Ecstasy.

✪ *** DHM/BMG 05472 77320-2. Sequentia, Thornton.

This first instalment makes a splendid introduction, a collection of Marian antiphons, sequences, and responsories, plus eulogies to the Holy Spirit where the poetic imagery is often drawn from nature. At speeds more spacious than those of the Gothic Voices, with women's voices alone, the elaborate monodic lines soar heavenwards even more sensuously, matching the imagery of Hildegard's poetry. For a meditative mood this outdoes Gregorian chant.

Voice of the Blood.

**(*) DHM/BMG 05472 77346-2. Sequentia, Thornton.

The sequence of music here is related to St Ursula who, in the company of a group of eleven virgin noblewomen, was reputedly slaughtered in Cologne on her return from a pilgrimage to Rome. (The telling of her story, in the course of time, increased the number of virgins to 11,000!) As leader of a spiritual community of women, Hildegard felt a strong identification with Ursula, and the opening lament of the cycle, *O rubor sanguinis*, immediately brings the imagery of flowing blood. It is sung unaccompanied, but the following responsory has a long instrumental pedal note over which the vocal melisma floats. The poetry draws on the natural world. *Favus distillans* pictures the saint as 'A honeycomb dripping honey' and later her purity is compared with apple-blossoms. After a reference to the Trinity, the fifth piece is an address to Ecclesia, a female personification of the heavenly community, and this symbolic (and vulnerable) figure is to return in the closing pieces, of which the antiphon *Nunc gaudeant* brings an extraordinary burst of spiritual energy. Two purely instrumental interludes (constructed by Elizabeth Gaver for fiddle and organ) add variety to a carefully planned collection which is, understandably, often rather sombre in its basic mood.

O Jerusalem.

*** DHM/BMG 05472 77353-2. Sequentia, Sons Thunder Men's Vocal Ens., Instrumental Ens., Bagby, Thornton.

On 1 May 1152 Hildegard's very own newly built church in Rupertsberg was dedicated, with considerable ceremony, to serve her personal Benedictine order, and this collection is devised as a conjectural programme of celebratory music to fit such an occasion. The bells of Bamberg Cathedral toll through the opening title piece, which also has the simple instrumental backing, and there is a more purely instrumental music here than in previous collections, joining flute, rebec, organ and vielle (hurdy-gurdy). There follows a lively *Magnificat* for St Rupert and two very touching (and typical) melismas extolling his virtues. The following music, beginning with *O tu illustrata*, soaringly evokes a radiantly mystical image of the Virgin Mary, to stand as symbol for the consecration of the women who were to renounce the physical world and join Hildegard's order; but for the hymn to the holy spirit a male group enters impressively, before the closing rapturous Marian testament from the women.

Symphoniae (Spiritual songs).

*** DHM/BMG (ADD) GD 77020. Sequentia, Thornton; with Tindemans, Babgy.

This is a reissue of Sequentia's very first collection, made in 1979. The collection divides into two groups – the first celebrating female divinities such as Mary, Ursula and her accompanying virgins, and even Wisdom, considered a type of feminine deity and for which Hildegard wrote one of her most eloquent tributes. The second group is of laudatory pieces – for the Apostles (a responsory, introduced with a plaintive flute solo), for the Holy Confessors, for the Patriarchs and Prophets, and for the Martyrs. In this last, remarkable piece the upper vocal line moves over a sustained lower note. The freshness of the singing here and the considerable instrumental interest makes this one of the most imaginatively conceived of the series.

Ordo virtutum (The Play of the Virtues).

*** DHM/BMG 05472 77394-2 (2). Sequentia Vox Feminae, Sons of Thunder Men's Vocal Ens., Instrumental Ens., Thornton, Bagby.

Ordo virtutum is a mystery play, and this 92-minute piece includes strikingly dramatic passages, with the Devil himself intervening. This was the second recording made by Sequentia – even more imaginatively theatrical than the first – and is superbly atmosperic and compelling as recorded here.

Saints.

**(*) DHM/BMG 05472 77378-2 (2). Sequentia Vox Feminae, Sons of Thunder Men's Vocal Ens., Instrumental Ens., Thornton, Bagby.

Apart from *Ordo virtutum*, the mystery play mentioned above, this two-disc set is Sequentia's most ambitious project so far. It covers a wide range of music created to be sung by monks as well as nuns in honour of the early Saints: Disibod, Eucharius and Maximin, Mattias (who joined the Apostles to replace Judas) and Saint Boniface. Sequentia's vigorous male group alternates with the Vox Feminae, sometimes with instrumental support. This is eloquent singing of stirring music, usually extrovert, with strong lyrical lines, more like Gregorian monody, less sensuous than much of Hildegard's output, except for the two tributes to Saint Ursula. It is all impressively sung, but a survey to be recommended to the Hildegard enthusiast rather than the general collector.

Other recordings

Hymns and sequences: *Ave generosa; Columba aspexit; O Ecclesia; O Euchari; O Jerusalem; O ignis spiritus; O presul vere civitatis; O viridissima virga.*

*** Hyp. CDA 66039. Gothic Voices, Muskett, White, Page.

This Hyperion CD by the Gothic Vices, was the disc which put Hildegard firmly on the map. It draws widely on the Abbess of Bingen's collection of music and poetry, the *Symphonia armonie celestium revelationum* – 'the symphony of the harmony of celestial revelations'. These hymns and sequences, most expertly performed and recorded, have excited much acclaim – and rightly so. A lovely CD.

'Heavenly Revelations': Hymns, sequences, antiphons, responds.

(BB) ** Naxos 8.550998. Oxford Camerata, Summerly.

The Oxford Camerata offer a simple presentation, alternating female and male voices in consecutive works. The opening female melisma, *O Euchari* ('*Eucharius, you walked in the paths of happiness when you remained with the son of God*') has a striking, recurring melodic line and establishes the group's unpretentious flowing style. Then follow two eulogies to the Virgin Mary, the first a rather dark *Alleluia* from the men, followed by a soaring female tribute, *Ave generosa* ('Hail noble one, shimmering and unpolluted girl'). There is no doubt that this music suits the Oxford females voices best (the later male praise for the Trinity here lacks any sense of euphoria), and the closing final accolade to the Virgin from the women certainly has a serene beauty. The conductor's restraint is palpable, there is very little feeling of ecstasy here.

Laudes of Saint Ursula.

*** HM HMC 901626. Ens. Organum, Pérès.

(B) *** HM Trio HMX 290891.93 (3) (as above) Ens.Organum, Pérès – MACHAUT: *Messe de Nostre Dame*; OCKGHEM: *Requiem*. ***

The sound of the Ensemble Organum directed by Marcel Pérès cannot fail to be stimulating. They sing at a lower than usual pitch, in a robustly vibrant style, darker than a normal West European vocal group. Pérès is concerned to present Hildegard's music alongside the Gregorian monody from which it springs, so it is heard in the context of a reconstruction of the liturgy for the office of Lauds (a celebration of the arrival of the sun and the end of night). The result is a great deal more chant than Hildegard, but the combination is certainly compelling. This CD additionally comes in a slip case as part of a Harmonia Mundi Trio at budget price which is highly recommendable, for the recordings of Machaut and Ockgehem are equally arresting.

Vision (The music of Hildegard; arranged and recomposed by Richard Souther).

*(**) EMI CDC5 55246-2. Van Evera, Sister Fritz (with chorus, instrumental contributions & synthesized rhythm).

Richard Souther's way-out recomposed versions are precociously and recklessly unauthentic, even including instrumental numbers (*The living light*, and *Only the Devil laughed* are typical titles). The sophisticated rock style amplifies the music's sensuous hypnotic melodic flow, adding all kinds of extra-instrumental vocal and synthesized nourishment, with echo chamber effects plus exotic live percussion. But Souther is obviously deeply involved in this very personal enterprise, and he has the advantage of the illustrious singing of Emily Van Evera, who really understands this repertoire, having also recorded it under authentic circumstances. Her beautiful voice is close-miked, 'pop style', unabashedly flattered with an acoustic halo. The programme opens with *O virga ac diadema purpure regis*, included on the Naxos disc, but the effect is extravagantly different. Certainly the emotional power of the music and its innate melodiousness projects vividly. The CD's title number, *Vision* (*O Euchari*) (also included in Jeremy Summerly's programme on Naxos) is heard twice, ending the programme in a more elaborate extended version. This is a disc to either wallow in or hate. Full translations are included.

HINDEMITH, Paul (1895–1963)

Concert Music for Strings & Brass; Violin Concerto; Symphonic Metamorphoses on Themes of Weber.

(N) *** Chan. 9903 (i) Kavakos; BBC PO, Y. P. Tortelier.

The *Concert Music for Strings and Brass* (1930) was commissioned by Koussevitzsky for the fiftieth anniversary of the Boston Symphony. It is superbly played here. The *Violin Concerto* of 1939 has been memorably recorded by David Oistrakh and the composer but this newcomer by Leonidas Kavakos is without doubt the best since then. A first-class account in every way, and coupled with and the post-war *Symphonic Metamorphoses on Themes of Weber* makes up a highly attractive and worthwhile programme.

Cello Concertos Nos. 1 in E flat, Op. 3; 2 (1940); Kammermusik No. 3, Op. 36/2.

(BB)*** CPO 999 375-2. Geringas, Queensland SO, Albert.

The *Cello Concerto*, Op. 3, comes from 1915–16 when the composer was entering his twenties. It is naturally a derivative piece with a lot of Reger and Strauss and not too much of the Hindemith we know. The 1940 *Concerto* is a fine piece, though not the equal of the *Violin Concerto* of the previous year, and the programme is completed by the little concerto from the *Kammermusik*. David Geringas is a generally impressive soloist and the orchestral response maintains the eminently respectable standard we have come to expect from this series.

Cello Concerto No. 2; (i) Clarinet Concerto.

*** Etcetera KTC 1006. De Machula; (i) Pieterson; Concg. O, Kondrashin.

The *Cello Concerto* is exhilarating and inventive, and Tibor de Machula proves an excellent protagonist. The *Clarinet Concerto* is lyrical and eventful. The recordings (made in the Concertgebouw, Amsterdam) are public performances and emanate from the Hilversum Radio archives.

(i) Cello Concerto No. 2; (ii) The Four Temperaments (theme and variations for piano and strings).

*** Chan. 9124. (i) Wallfisch; (ii) Shelley; BBC PO, Tortelier.

Both the *Cello Concerto* and *The Four Temperaments* are vintage Hindemith and well worth adding to your collection. The four variations of the latter are ingenious and subtle and are splendidly realized by Howard Shelley and the BBC Philharmonic under Yan Pascal Tortelier. Raphael Wallfisch is the eloquent soloist in the *Cello Concerto*. The Chandos recording is very good indeed. These recordings set new standards in both works.

Kammermusik Nos. 1 for 12 Instruments, Op. 24/1; (i) 2 (Piano Concerto), Op. 36/1; (ii) 3 (Cello Concerto), Op. 36/2; (iii) 4 (Violin Concerto), Op. 36/3; (iv) 5 (Viola Concerto), Op. 36/4; (v) 6 (Viola d'amore Concerto), Op. 46/1; (vi) 7 (Organ Concerto), Op. 46/2; Kleine Kammermusik for Wind Quintet, Op. 24/2.

*** Decca 433 816-2 (2). (i) Brautigam; (ii) Harrell; (iii) Kulka;

(iv) Kaskkashian; (v) Blume; (vi) Van Doeselaar; Concg. O, Chailly.

(B) *** Teldec Ultima 3984 21773-2 (2). (i) van Blerk;
(ii) Bylsma; (iii) Schröder; (iv) Doktor; (v) Vermeulen;
(vi) De Klerk; Concerto Amsterdam.

Kammermusik Nos. 1 (with finale) for 12 Solo Instruments, Op. 24/1; (i) 4 (Violin Concerto); (ii) 5 (Viola Concerto), Op. 36/3–4.

*** EMI CDC5 56160-2. BPO, Abbado, with (i) Blacher;
(ii) Christ.

(i) Kammermusik Nos. 2 (Piano Concerto); (ii) 3 (Cello Concerto), Op. 36/1–2; (iii) 6 (Viola d'amore Concerto); (iv) 7 (Organ Concerto), Op. 46/1–2.

*** EMI CDC5 56831-2. (i) Vogt; (ii) Faust; (iii) Christ;
(iv) Marshall; BPO, Abbado.

It is amazing what refinement and point Abbado and the Berlin Philharmonic bring to the *Kammermusik* The recording helps, with the chamber textures given transparency, where often – as in Chailly's set on Decca – the sound in its forwardness simulates a full orchestra. The soloists are excellent, with Lars Vogt giving an electrifying account of the piano part in No. 2, and in the *Violin Concertos* Kolja Blacher finds mercurial lightness in fast movements and warm expressiveness in the lovely *Nachtstuck*. Wayne Marshall as the organ soloist in No. 7 copes well with the thick textures, and Wolfram Christ, the orchestra's principal viola, finds beauty in the intractable writing for the viola d'amore in No. 6, with his cellist colleague a strong and positive soloist in No. 3. Abbado's control of rhythm and texture is masterly, helped by glowing EMI sound. He finds special inspiration in the slow movements, which bear the main emotional weight in these works, totally rebutting any idea of dryness in Hindemith's writing.

The Decca set also includes the delightful little *Wind Quintet (Kleine Kammermusik)*. The playing of the distinguished soloists and the members of the Concertgebouw is beyond praise and so is the Decca recording.

The Teldec performances come from the 1968 and are not only very expert but beautifully engineered. At their budget price, these may well be more tempting for the collector who wants an introduction to these engaging pieces than either of the admirable full price alternatives.

Kammermusik No. 2 for Piano & 12 Solo Instruments, Op. 36/1; Konzertmusik for Piano, Brass & Harps, Op. 49.

(N) (BB) **(*) CPO 999 138-2. Mauser, Frankfurt Radio SO, Albert.

Werner Andreas Albert's Hindemith survey continues to impress. The *Kammermusik No. 2* is well represented on disc but every newcomer serves to underline its originality of mind. Siegfried Mauser is the expert soloist, and he and his colleagues produce superb results in the imaginative second movement. The *Konzertmusik* is served less well (there is one alternative, albeit from the 1960s, on Supraphon with Panenka as pianist) and readers may well want this CD just for this. The work is as original as its instrumental setting might suggest. Good performances and clear studio

recording from the early 1990s. But even at mid-price it is perhaps short measure at 47 minutes.

(i) Kammermusik No. 4, Op. 36/3. Tuttifäntchen: Orchestral Suite; (i) Violin Concerto.

**(*) CPO 999 527-2. Queensland SO, Albert; (i) Dene with Olding.

The main work here is the *Violin Concerto* of 1939, in which Dene Olding acquits himself well. He is particularly impressive in the thoughtful and inward-looking slow movement. There is a good, truthful balance between soloist and orchestra, though on the *Kammermusik No. 4* the balance is too close and claustrophobic, and the results unpleasing. Hindemith's music needs all the help it can get from a flattering acoustic. Of good broadcasting standard rather than a first choice in the commercial record field.

Kammermusik No. 5, Op. 36/4; Konzertmusik for Viola & Orchestra, Op. 48; Viola Concerto (Der Schwanendreher).

*** ASV CDDCA 931. Cortese, Philh. O, Brabbins.

Paul Cortese is the accomplished soloist in all three works, including the fifth of the *Kammermusik*. The Philharmonia respond with some enthusiasm to Martyn Brabbins's direction, and although there are finer recordings of *Der Schwanendreher* to be had (above all, Tabea Zimmermann on EMI) this disc gives undoubted pleasure. The recording is very good indeed, with great presence and body.

Kammermusik No. 5, Op. 36/4 (for viola and large chamber orchestra); Konzertmusik (for viola and large chamber orchestra), Op. 48; Der Schwanendreher (Viola Concerto); Trauermusik (for viola and strings).

*** CPO 999 492-2. Dean, Queensland SO, Albert.

The viola was Hindemith's own instrument and he writes gratefully for it. The *Kammermusik No. 5* is generously represented on disc, while the *Konzertmusik*, Op. 48 (1929–30) (with no violins or violas in the string selection, hence its rich sonorities in the bass-baritone end of the spectrum) is relatively neglected, and undeservedly so, for it has a particularly engaging first movement and an imaginative and deeply felt slow movement. It operates at a higher level of inspiration than the oft-recorded *Der Schwanendreher*, good though that is, and the *Trauermusik* that Hindemith composed at high speed on the death of George V. The Australian violist and composer Brett Dean gives masterly accounts of all four pieces, and the Queensland Orchestra plays with excellent ensemble and precision for Werner Albert. Recommended with enthusiasm.

(i) Kammermusik No. 6 for Viola d'amore & Orch., Op. 46/1; (ii) Kammermusik No. 7 for Organ & Orch., Op. 46/2; Organ Concerto (1962).

(N) **(*) CPO 999 261-2 (i) Dean; (ii) Haas; Frankfurt Radio SO, Albert.

Although the *Kammermusik* are generously represented in the catalogue, the *Organ Concerto* of 1962, commissioned for the inauguration of the organ of the New York Philharmonic Hall, is a rarity. But to be frank, it is a rather manufactured piece, not by any means vintage Hindemith. The earlier

concerto, the *Kammermusik No. 7* written for another inauguration, that of the Frankfurt Radio instrument, on which
this performance was given, is infinitely more rewarding: its
austere contrapuntal slow movement is particularly impressive. The viola was Hindemith's own instrument and he
nursed a great affection for the viola d'amore, and the second
movement of his *Kammermusik No. 6* shows the quality of
feeling it aroused. Brett Dean plays with eloquence, as does
the organist Rosalinde Haas. Good recording, with well-
defined and transparent orchestral detail.

**(i) *Clarinet Concerto;* (ii) *Horn Concerto;* (iii) *Concerto for
Trumpet, Bassoon & Strings;* (iv) *Concerto for Woodwinds,
Harp & Strings.***

****(*) CPO 999 142-2. (i; iv) Mehlhart; (ii) Neunecker;
(iii) Friedrich; (iii–iv) Wilkening; (iv) Büchsel, Varcol,
Cassedanne; Frankfurt RSO, Albert.**

The *Clarinet Concerto* was written for Benny Goodman; the
Horn Concerto is comparatively familiar. The *Concerto for
Woodwinds, Harp and Strings* is the more rewarding of the
other two works and more varied in texture. The *Trumpet
and Bassoon Concerto* finds Hindemith in more routine
mode. The soloist is rather too forward in the *Clarinet
Concerto* and, though the recording quality is decent, it is
possible to imagine more transparent orchestral textures.
The performances throughout are eminently acceptable.

Horn Concerto.

**(***) EMI mono CDC7 47834-2. Brain, Philh. O, composer –
R. STRAUSS: *Horn Concertos Nos. 1–2.* (***) ✿**

The Hindemith *Concerto* is altogether drier than the Strauss
couplings, but has a hauntingly original, ruminative finale,
in which the soloist declaims a short poem – written by the
composer – in such a way that the note values match the
syllables of the words. Dennis Brain's performance is incomparable, and the first-class mono recording has been transferred expertly.

Piano Concerto.

****(*) First Edition (ADD) LCD 002. Luvisi, Louisville O, Smith
– (with LAWHEAD: *Aleost**(*)); ZWILICH: *Symphony
No. 2.* ****

Piano Concerto; The Four Temperaments.

(N) (BB) * CPO 999 078-2. Mauser, Frankfurt Radio SO,
Albert.**

The *Piano Concerto* (1945) is a rarity and has been grossly
and unjustly neglected, for it is an often inspired and beautifully lucid piece. The slow movement is one of the most
beautiful and imaginative of its period. The CPO recordings
emanate from the early 1990s, and even if you are normally
unattracted by Hindemith you should consider acquiring
this coupling, as *The Four Temperaments* is one of the
composer's most immediately approachable works and it is
equally successful here. In most respects this upstages the
earlier recording by Lee Luvisi and the Louisville Orchstra,
who nevertheless give a very good account of themselves
and are more than adequately recorded.

Viola Concerto (Der Schwanendreher).

***** EMI CDC7 54101-2. Zimmermann, Bav. RSO, Shallon –
BARTOK: *Viola Concerto.* *****

Everything about this performance is excellent – indeed it is
arguably the best now before the public. If you are prepared
to pay full price for such short measure, you will be well
rewarded in terms of both artistic and technical quality.

Violin Concerto.

(M) * Sony (ADD) SMK 64507. Stern, NYPO, Bernstein –
PENDERECKI: *Violin Concerto.* *****

**(i) *Violin Concerto;* (ii) *Mathis der Maler (Symphony);*
(iii) *Symphonic Metamorphoses on Themes of Weber.***

✿ (M) * Decca (ADD) 433 081-2. (i) Oistrakh, LSO,
composer; (ii) SRO, Kletzki; (iii) LSO, Abbado.**

David Oistrakh's Decca performance of Hindemith's *Violin
Concerto* is outstanding. The composer provides an overwhelmingly passionate accompaniment and the 1962
recording still sounds extraordinarily vivid and spacious.
The Rosette is for the concerto but the couplings are well
chosen, both also offering vintage late 1960s Decca sound.
Abbado's *Symphonic Metamorphoses on Themes of Weber* is
second to none. Kletzki's account of *Mathis der Maler* is also
impressive, very well prepared and with a similar attention
to detail. He, too, has the advantage of finely balanced and
truthful recording, and the Suisse Romande Orchestra still
plays very well for him.

If Oistrakh's performance under Hindemith has an
authority that no competitor can match, Stern plays with
eloquence, and Bernstein's accompaniment is always sympathetic and at times has something special to offer. In places
it scores over the composer's own (towards the end of
the slow movement, for example) but the recording is less
analytical than the Decca and detail is less in evidence. The
new coupling is admirably chosen

**Concerto for Winds, Harp & Orchestra; Konzertmusik for
Brass & Strings, Op. 50; Mathis de Maler: Symphony.**

*** Chan. 9475. Czech PO, Bělohlávek.

The *Concerto for Winds, Harp and Orchestra* has never been
heard to better effect on record. The *Konzertmusik for Brass
and Strings* is hardly less imposing. Bělohlávek takes a broad
and spacious view that is most impressive. Competition is
of course much keener in the *Mathis de Maler Symphony*
and here Bělohlávek is a little more detached and wanting
in intensity. The playing of the Czech Philharmonic is as
expert and responsive as one might expect, and the Chandos
engineers cope well with the reverberant acoustic.

Der Dämon; (i) Hérodiade (two versions).

(BB) * CPO 999 220-2. (i) Gicquel; Mauser, Frankfurt RSO,
Albert.**

Der Dämon (The Demon) (1922) is an early ballet has great
resource in matters of colour, and it is full of imaginative,
original textures. There is a prominent role for the piano,
brilliantly and sensitively played by Siegfried Mauser.
Hérodiade dates from 1944 and derives its inspiration from
Mallarmé's poem. It is an excellent idea to let us have it first

with the text, then again without it, and Annie Gicquel speaks it in exemplary fashion. *Hérodiade* is a beautiful score and Werner Andreas Albert gets excellent results from his Frankfurt forces. The Hessischer Rundfunk engineers produce recordings that are a model of good balance. Strongly recommended.

(i) *The Four Temperaments; Nobilissima visione.*

**(*) Delos D/CD 1006. (i) Rosenberger; RPO, De Preist.

The Four Temperaments, a set of variations, is one of Hindemith's finest and most immediate works. Carol Rosenberger gives a formidable reading of this inventive and resourceful score. James de Preist also secures responsive playing from the RPO strings and gives a sober, well-shaped account of the *Nobilissima visione* suite, doing justice to its grave nobility.

Mathis der Maler (symphony).

(M) *** EMI (ADD) CMS5 66109-2 (2). BPO, Karajan – BRAHMS: *Tragic Overture;* BRUCKNER: *Symphony No. 8.* ***

Mathis der Maler (symphony); *Nobilissima visione; Symphonic Metamorphoses on Themes by Weber.*

*** EMI CDC5 55230-2. Phd. O, Sawallisch.

Mathis der Maler (symphony); *Symphonic Metamorphoses on Themes by Weber; Trauermusik.*

*** Decca 421 523-2. San Francisco SO, Blomstedt.

It is good to hear the great Philadelphia Orchestra sounding itself again. Sawallisch draws a warm, rich-textured sound from them, and he also gives a performance of the *Nobilissima visione* that does justice to its breadth and dignity. Sawallisch's account of the *Symphonic Metamorphoses on Themes by Carl Maria von Weber* is not quite as sharp or fleet of foot as the older Bernstein version, but it is still very well characterized. The *Mathis* scores over the rival Blomstedt on Decca in depth of characterization and orchestral opulence and, all things considered, should probably be the preferred recommendation.

Blomstedt has a strong feeling for *Mathis der Maler* and presents a finely groomed and powerfully shaped performance, with lucid and transparent textures. The famous *Trauermusik* has an affecting quiet eloquence and dedication: the solo viola, Geraldine Walther, is exceptionally sensitive. Blomstedt's reading of the *Symphonic Metamorphoses on Themes of Carl Maria von Weber* is appropriately light in touch; and the recording is exemplary in the naturalness of its balance.

It is good to have Karajan's recording back in the catalogue. It dates from 1957, but it was made in the Berlin Jesus-Christus-Kirche and the sound is impressively spacious, the strings gloriously full. The warm, full-blooded performance is remarkably dramatic and convincing, the central movement very touching. Though Hindemith's markings may occasionally be ignored, Karajan is convincing in everything he does.

Nobilissima visione.

(M) *** RCA High Performance (ADD) 09026 63315-2.

Chicago SO, Martinon – BARTOK: *The Miraculous Mandarin: Suite;* VARESE: *Arcana.* ***

Jean Martinon delivers a splendid account of this finely conceived and often very beautiful score. *Nobilissima visione* is one of Hindemith's most approachable works and those who investigate it will be amply rewarded. The Chicago Orchestra play with tremendous attack and discipline and the recording, though it could be richer, has satisfactory sonority.

Nobilissima visione (suite).

(M) (**(*)) EMI (ADD) CDM5 67337-2. Philh. O, Klemperer – STRAVINSKY: *Symphony in 3 Movements;* WEILL: *Kleine Dreigroschenmusik* *** (with KLEMPERER: *Merry Waltz* **).

Klemperer recorded only the three-movement suite from *Noblissima visione*, but three movements incorporate music from all five numbers of the ballet. The Philharmonia play gravely and nobly (especially in the final *Passacaglia*). and Klemperer's rather austere style suits the music. The 1954 Kingsway Hall recording is made available in stereo here for the first time. The sound remains two-dimensional, dry, but vivid, and this disc is a worthwhile addition to EMI's 'Klemperer Legacy'.

Pittsburgh Symphony; Ragtime; Symphonic Dances.

*** Chan. 9530. BBC Philh. O, Tortelier.

The *Symphonic Dances* is one of Hindemith's most inventive and enjoyable works and its present neglect in the concert hall and in the recording studio quite unaccountable. Dating from 1937 it is full of resource and imagination and deserves to be as popular as the *Symphonic Metamorphoses on Themes of Weber*. The *Pittsburgh Symphony* is a rewarding piece – not as high-spirited or poetic as the *Symphonic Dances* but hard-edged and full of good ideas. Yan Pascal Tortelier and the BBC Philharmonic give meticulously prepared and committed performances and the Chandos sound is above reproach. Strongly recommended.

Sinfonia serena; Symphony (Die Harmonie der Welt).

⚙ *** Chan. 9217. BBC PO, Tortelier.

Sinfonia serena; Symphony (Die Harmonie der Welt).

*** Decca 458 899-2. Leipzig Gewandhaus O, Blomstedt.

The *Sinfonia serena* (1946) is a brilliant and inventive score, full of humour and melody. The scoring is inventive and imaginative. There is plenty of wit in the Scherzo, which paraphrases a Beethoven march from 1809. The *Symphony, Die Harmonie der Welt* (1951), is another powerful and consistently underrated score. These well-prepared and finely shaped performances are given state-of-the-art recording quality. An outstanding issue.

As his *Mathis der Maler* with the San Francisco Orchestra showed, Blomstedt has proved to be one of the most persuasive advocates of the composer and this newcomer confirms and enhances this impression. The clarity of his conception is well served by the lucidity of the Decca recording and the Leipzig Orchestra produces a finely cultured sound. There is formidable competition in this coupling from Yan Pascal Tortelier and the BBC Philharmonic on Chandos, but this newcomer can be recommended alongside it.

Symphony in E flat; Overture Neues vom Tage; Nobilissima visione.

*** Chan. 9060. BBC PO, Tortelier.

The *Symphony in E flat* is an inventive and resourceful score and is well worth investigating. Yan Pascal Tortelier gets excellent results from the BBC Philharmonic. Good, musicianly performances of *Nobilissima visione* and the much earlier *Neues vom Tage* Overture complete an admirable addition to the Hindemith discography.

CHAMBER MUSIC

(i) *Alto Saxophone Sonata;* (ii) *Bass Tuba Sonata;* (iii) *Bassoon Sonata;* (iv) *Morgenmusik;* (v) *Trio;* (vi) *Trombone Sonata;* (vii) *Trumpet Sonata.*

** BIS (ADD) CD 159. (i) Savijoki, Siirala; (ii) Lind, Harlos; (iii) Sonstevold, Knardahl; (iv) Malmö Brass Ens.; (v) Pehrsson, Jonsson, Mjönes; (vi) Lindberg, Pöntinen; (vii) Tarr, Westenholz.

(i) *Alto Horn Sonata in E flat;* (ii) *Bass Tuba Sonata;* (i) *Horn Sonata;* (iii) *Trombone Sonata;* (iv) *Trumpet Sonata.*

(M) ** Sony (ADD) SM2K 52671 (2). (i) Jones; (ii) Torchinsky; (iii) Smith; (iv) Johnson; Gould.

The *Alto Saxophone Sonata* and the *Alto Horn Sonata* are one and the same work. The BIS recordings are rather closely balanced though not disturbingly so. The Sony recordings are all from 1976 but unfortunately do not offer the *Recorder Trio,* expertly played on the BIS by Claes Pehrsson, Anders-Per Jonsson and Anders Mjönes, or the exhilarating *Morgenmusik* for brass – not to mention the inventive *Bassoon Sonata.* On the other hand, Sony's mid-price two-CD set gives you the *Alto Horn Sonata* with Mason Jones. Glenn Gould has great feeling for Hindemith and plays with strong personality and commitment throughout, even though the tiresome vocalise is a strain.

Bassoon Sonata; Harp Sonata; Horn Sonata; Sonata for 2 Pianos; Sonata for Piano 4 Hands.

*** MDG MDG 304 0694-2. Ens. Villa Musica with Thunemann, Storck, Vlatkovic, Piret and Kalle Randalu.

Hindemith had an unfailingly resourceful musical mind, even if inspiration at times takes second place to sheer facility. These are not only well fashioned but often very satisfying pieces. Klaus Thunemann is an expert and persuasive advocate of the *Bassoon Sonata* and its companions here receive highly accomplished performances. Throughout the Ensemble Villa Musica's Hindemith series we have heard so far, the recording is very faithful and lifelike.

(i) *Double-bass Sonata.* (ii) *Trombone Sonata.* (iii) *Tuba Sonata.* (iv) *Cello Sonata; Small Sonata for Violoncello; A Frog He Went A-courting.*

*** MDG MDG 304 0697-2. Randalu with (i) Güttler. (ii) Slokar. (iii) Hilgers. (iv) Ostertag.

This collection is both artistically rewarding and technically excellent. The sound is very vivid and present and the programme intelligently laid out. Hindemith was enormously prolific and often composed on automatic pilot but these pieces are fresh and inventive.

Kleine Kammermusik for Wind Quintet, Op. 24/2.

(BB) **(*) Naxos 8.553851-2. Thompson Wind Quintet – BARBER: *Summer Music* **(*); JANACEK: *Mládí***(*); LARSSON: *Quattro tempi.* **

The Michael Thompson Wind Quintet give an excellently spirited and alert performance with plenty of wit. The playing is wonderfully accomplished and sensitive but the close balance is a distinct handicap. If you think this would not worry you, it is worth the modest outlay.

Octet.

**(*) Nim. NI 5461. BPO Octet – BEETHOVEN: *Septet.* **(*)

The *Octet* is well fashioned but a bit manufactured, and many of the ideas find the composer at his most routine. The exception is the central slow movement, which has considerable eloquence. The playing is expert, but the recording is closely balanced and upfront.

Septet.

*** Virgin VC5 45056-2. Deutsche Kammerphilharmonie Wind – TOCH: *5 Pieces for Wind & Percussion;* WEILL: *Violin Concerto.* ***

The performance of Hindemith's *Septet* by the wind of the Deutsche Kammerphilharmonie is outstanding in every way. Hindemith's use of sonority is consistently imaginative and the invention fresher than in the later *Octet.* Exemplary recording. The Toch and Weill couplings are both excellent.

String Quartets Nos. 1 in C, Op. 2; 2 in F min., Op. 10; 3 in C, Op. 16; 4, Op. 22; 5, Op. 32; 6 in E flat; 7 in E flat.

(BB) *(*) CPO 999 287-2 (3). Danish Qt.

The Hindemith quartets are not generously represented in the catalogue, so this issue is on the face of it particularly welcome. It also includes an early quartet (Op. 2) composed in 1915 and not recognized in the published order of the scores. Accordingly, what we have always known as the *Sixth Quartet in E flat* of 1945 becomes the *Seventh,* and each of its predecessors adds one. Unfortunately, the Danish Quartet will not win over the unconverted; nor will they give much comfort and joy to those who like this repertory. Their playing lacks authority and is wanting in tonal finesse and colour.

String Quartet No. 3, Op. 22.

⊚ (***) Testament mono SBT 1052. Hollywood Qt – PROKOFIEV: *Quartet No. 2;* WALTON: *Quartet in A min.* (***) ⊚

The Hollywood Quartet possessed an extraordinary virtuosity and perfection of ensemble, and it is difficult to imagine more persuasive advocacy. The transfer is excellent and, although the mono sound is less than ideal, the performance still sweeps the board.

Viola Sonata in F, Op. 11/4.

(***) Biddulph mono LAB 148. Primrose, Sandromá – BAX: *Fantasy Sonata for Viola & Piano;* BLOCH: *Suite.* (***)

*(*) Olympia OCD 625. Bashmet, Richter – BRITTEN: *Lachrymae, Op. 48;* SHOSTAKOVICH: *Viola Sonata, Op. 147.* *(*)

The classic 1938 Primrose recording of Hindemith's most lyrical sonata, with Jesús María Sandromá, probably remains unsurpassed in sheer style and refinement of tone. Given the date, the sound is very acceptable.

Distinguished playing as you would expect from these artists who were recorded live in Germany in 1985. But the sound is distinctly unappealing, too close and hard.

(Unaccompanied) Viola Sonatas Nos. 1; 2, Op. 11/5; 3, Op. 25/1; 4, Op. 31/4.

*** ASV CDDCA 947. Cortese.

(i) Viola Sonatas (for viola and piano) Op. 11/4; Op. 25/4; (Unaccompanied) Viola Sonatas: Op. 11/5; Op. 25/1; Op. 31/4.

*** ECM 833 309-2 (2). Kashkashian, (i) Levin.

The solo sonatas are played with superb panache and flair – and, even more importantly, with remarkable variety of colour – by Kim Kashkashian, who has an enormous dynamic range. The performances of the sonatas with piano are hardly less imaginative and the recording is good.

Paul Cortese is a player of considerable accomplishments and he is persuasive in this somewhat forbidding repertoire. He is not perhaps always as imaginative or poetic as Kim Kashkashian, but the disc is certainly recommendable.

Violin Sonatas Nos. 1 in E flat, Op. 11/1; 2 in D, Op. 11/2; 3 in E; 4 in C.

*** BIS CD 761. Wallin, Pöntinen.

(N) **(*) Live Classics LCL 161 Kagan, S. Richter.

As with most Hindemith, both the Op. 11 sonatas are well crafted and inventive. The finest of the four is the last in C major, which is both individual and finely wrought. Ulf Wallin and Roland Pöntinen play this repertoire with real dedication and conviction, and the BIS recording is very lifelike and present. They include a fragment of an alternative finale for the E flat Sonata, Op. 11/1, that Hindemith subsequently discarded.

The Kagan/Richter performances were given in the Grand Hall of the Moscow Conservatory in May 1978. Some of the Soviet recordings of Oleg Kagan have suffered from inferior sound but this is acceptable without being anywhere near top-drawer. A tough programme for a live concert and there is the occasional minor blemish of intonation or colour to serve as a reminder that this great violinist was human. Admirers of Hindemith will want this.

PIANO MUSIC

Berceuse; In einer Nacht, Op. 15; Kleines Klavierstück; Lied; 1922 Suite, Op. 26; Tanzstücke, Op. 19.

**(*) Marco 8.223335. Petermandl.

Exercise in 3 Pieces, Op. 31/I; Klaviermusik, Op. 37; Series of Little Pieces, Op. 37/II; Sonata, Op. 17; 2 Little Piano Pieces.

** Marco 8.223336. Petermandl.

Ludus Tonalis; Kleine Klaviermusik, Op. 45/4.

** Marco 8.223338. Petermandl.

Piano Sonatas Nos. 1–3.

*** MDG 304 0693-2. Randalu.

Piano Sonatas Nos. 1–3; Variations.

** Marco 8.223337. Petermandl.

Hindemith's three piano sonatas, all written in quick succession in 1936 just before he fled from Hitler's Germany, are firmly in the grand German tradition. Long neglected but among the most satisfying piano sonatas of the century, they owe a direct debt not just to Beethoven but to Bach's *Well-Tempered Clavier.* Hindemith's crisply contrapuntal piano writing brings a strong consistency to the three contrasted works. No. 1 is the most challengingly ambitious, with the compact No. 2 more easily lyrical. Yet it is No. 3, directly echoing the first of Beethoven's late sonatas, Opus 101, which is the clearest masterpiece. Built on strikingly memorable themes, and ending with a formidable double fugue, it inspires the Estonian, Kalle Randalu, to a powerful performance, very well recorded.

Hans Petermandl is an expert guide in this repertoire and presents it with real sympathy for, and understanding of, the idiom; his performances are very persuasive. The textures in Hindemith's piano music are often unbeautiful and less than transparent and, although neither the piano nor the acoustic of the Concert Hall of Slovak Radio is outstanding, the sound is perfectly acceptable.

Ludus tonalis; Suite (1922), Op. 26.

**(*) Hyp. CDA 66824. McCabe.

Hindemith's *Ludus tonalis* – comprising 25 sections – is, in total, not far short of an hour in length. It has been recorded before, but not with more concentration and authority than it is on Hyperion by John McCabe. As if not wishing to compromise himself, instead of coupling it with something a little less formidably intellectual, he offers also the *Suite 1922* which, if anything, is thornier still. So if you are a Hindemith addict, this is surely a disc you will want to explore.

Organ Sonatas Nos. 1–3.

*** Chan. 9097. Kee – REGER: *4 Organ Pieces.* ***

Piet Kee plays on the Müller organ of St Bavo in Haarlem, an instrument more suited to Hindemith than the somewhat spacious acoustic in which it is recorded. This small point apart, Kee plays with his customary distinction and character. All three sonatas are rewarding, and no one investing in this disc is likely to be disappointed on either artistic or technical grounds.

VOCAL MUSIC

When Lilacs Last in the Dooryard Bloom'd (Requiem).

*** Telarc CD 80132. DeGaetani, Stone, Atlanta Ch. & SO, Shaw.

This 'Requiem for those we loved' is one of the composer's most deeply felt works and one of his best. Shaw gives a performance of great intensity and variety of colour and nuance. Both his soloists are excellent, and there is both weight and subtlety in the orchestral contribution. Splendid recording.

OPERA

Mathis der Maler (complete).

(M) *** EMI (ADD) CDS5 55237-2 (3). Fischer-Dieskau, Feldhof, King, Schmidt, Meven, Cochran, Malta, Grobe, Wagemann, Bav. R. Ch. & SO, Kubelik.

There is little doubt that the opera *Mathis der Maler* is Hindemith's masterpiece. Fischer-Dieskau proves the ideal interpreter of the central role, the painter Mathias Grüne-wald. The performance includes other fine contributions from James King as the Archbishop, Donald Grobe as the Cardinal, Alexander Malta as the army commandant and Manfred Schmidt as the Cardinal's adviser. The women principals are less happily chosen; Rose Wagemann as Ursula is rather squally. But with splendid playing and singing from Bavarian Radio forces under Kubelik, this is a highly enjoyable as well as an important set. Moreover the first-class (1977) analogue recording is just as kind to the voices as to the orchestra, with the balance between soloists, chorus and orchestra very natural. However, this set has just been deleted as we go to press.

(i; ii) *Sancta Susanna* (complete). *Das Nusch-Nuschi: Dances, Op. 20. Tuttifäntchen: Suite.* (i) *3 Songs, Op. 9.*

*** Chan. 9620. (i) Bullock; (ii) Jones, Gunson & Soloists, Leeds Fest. Ch.; BBCPO, Tortelier.

In the one-act opera *Sancta Susanna* Hindemith's musical language is distinctly expressionist, lyrical and atmospheric though with traces of Gallic influence (and in particular Debussy), and Puccinian elements happily intermingled. It is a far cry from the austere, monochrome contrapuntist of the later symphonies. Written immediately after the end of the First World War, it scandalized its first audiences by its erotic-cum-blasphemous character.

Susanna is a young nun (Susan Bullock), inflamed by the legend she is told by Sister Clementia (Della Jones) about a girl who comes to the altar naked to embrace the figure of Christ on the cross. For this blasphemy she is buried alive. Undeterred by this fate, Susanna strips off at the altar and rips the covering from Christ's torso. She is petrified when a huge spider falls on to her head from the crucifix and in a frenzy of remorse begs the other nuns to wall her up! The

opening is highly imaginative and full of atmosphere, closer indeed to Schreker or even Szymanowski than the Hinde-mith we know. It is a short piece some 23 minutes in length, but enormously intense and concentrated in feeling. The performance is gripping, splendidly sung and expertly played by Yan Pascal Tortelier and the BBC Philharmonic Orchestra.

The oriental elements in the *Nusch-Nuschi Dances* simply adorn a 1920s-style score, while the suite from the children's pantomime, *Tuttifäntchen*, of 1922 is delightful in its use of tunes from children's games, with ragtime introduced in the *Dance of the Dolls*. The Straussian *Drei Gesänge, Op. 3,* written earlier in 1917, are luxuriant and rich, and again unlike anything we know from the mature composer. Susan Bullock sings them with great conviction and flair. This is all music of outstanding interest, superbly performed, with Jan-Pascal Tortelier the most persuasive advocate, and beautifully recorded.

HODDINOTT, Alun (born 1929)

(i; ii) *Concertino for Viola & Small Orchestra, Op. 14;* (iii; iv) *Nocturnes & Cadenzas for Cello & Orchestra, Op. 62;* (v; ii) *Dives and Lazarus* (cantata), *Op. 39;* (vi; iv) *Sinfonia Fidei* (for soprano, tenor, chorus & orchestra), *Op. 95.*

*** Lyrita (ADD)/Dig. SRCD 332. (i) Erdélyi; (ii) New Philh. O, Atherton; (iii) Welsh; (iv) Philh. O, Groves; (v) Palmer, Allen, Welsh Nat. Op. Ch.; (vi) Gomez, Burrowes, Philh. Ch.

Csaba Erdélyi, the superb principal viola of the New Philhar-monia in the mid-1970s, makes an admirable advocate in the imaginatively conceived *Viola Concertino* of 1958, the point of the argument made sharper by the lightness of the string section against a normal woodwind group. By comparison the *Nocturnes and Cadenzas* is less easy to come to grips with, presenting a more withdrawn face, not helped by being based on an idea which rather limits the quota of fast music. Nevertheless Moray Welsh excels himself as the cello soloist, making his soliloquy seemingly improvisa-tional, and Sir Charles Groves draws excellent playing from the Philharmonia Orchestra. In the succinct and emotionally concentrated cantata, *Dives and Lazarus* the choral writing is highly individual, especially in the dramatic closing section, *When Lazarus Died*, with its exultant '*Allelujas*'. *Sinfonia Fidei* (1977) returns to a more conservative idiom and is one of the most impressive of Hoddinott's later works, purposeful and dramatic. Soloists, chorus and orchestra join to project all this music with the most ardent advocacy and the recordings, spaciously atmospheric, whether analogue or digital, are in every respect first rate.

Symphonies Nos. (i; ii) *2, Op. 29;* (i; iii) *3, Op. 61;* (iv) *5, Op. 81.*

*** Lyrita (ADD) SRCD 331. (i) LSO; (ii) Del Mar; (iii) Atherton; (iv) RPO, Davis.

The *Second Symphony* dates from 1962 and is clearly the work of a composer who, though a serialist, still retains an allegiance to tonal centres and who uses twelve-note technique as a spur rather than a crutch. Its arguments are not difficult to follow and there is a great outburst of passionate lyricism from the strings at the climax of the *molto adagio*. Del Mar directs the work confidently, and the LSO respond with eloquence. The *Third Symphony* is even more powerfully wrought, dark in colouring and deeply imaginative. It is well laid out for the orchestra and is perhaps the most completely effective of the three works offered here. Atherton's performance (again using the LSO) is wholly convincing. The *Fifth Symphony* is a more abrasive work than the *Third* and less immediately approachable. It is splendidly powerful, and it reinforces Hoddinott's representation in the catalogue when so impressively played. The vintage recordings of both the *Third* and *Fifth Symphonies* were made by a Decca engineering team in the early 1970s and are spectacularly vivid in their presence, range and definition.

HOFFMEISTER, Franz (1754–1812)

Flute Concertos: in D; in G.

(BB) **(*) ASV CDQS 6012. Dingfelder, ECO, Mackerras; Leonard – C. P. E. BACH: *Concerto*. **(*)

Franz Hoffmeister's two *Flute Concertos* are elegantly inventive, if not distinctive. They are well recorded and make pleasant late-evening listening. The performances are sprightly and polished, and the accompaniments have plenty of spirit. The sound is brightly lit, but not excessively so.

HOFMANN, Leopold (1738–93)

Sinfonias: in B flat; in C; in D; in F; in F.

(BB) **(*) Naxos 8.553866. N. CO, Ward.

Leopold Hofmann was one of the earliest composers who consistently wrote four-movement symphonies with both slow introduction and minuets. He preceded Haydn in this respect. Incidentally, for a brief period in 1791 Mozart acted as an assistant to him, doubtless in the hope of receiving preferment when Hofmann died. The five symphonies recorded here show him to be lively and fresh, though no one could pretend that his music plumbs great depths – or indeed is consistently interesting. The performances are very alert and sprightly but the recording, though distinguished by clarity and presence, is handicapped by a rather dry acoustic.

HOL, Richard (Rijk) (1825–1904)

Symphonies Nos. 1 in C min.; 3 in B flat, Op. 101.

*(**) Chan. 9796. Hague Residentie O, Bamert.

The son of an Amsterdam milkman, Richard (or Rijk) Hol was an influential figure in the second half of the nineteenth century, both as a conductor and as a teacher. He was prolific, and like Brahms he wrote four symphonies, but they are nearer to Schumann in their musical ethos, although the scoring owes more to Brahms and Mendelssohn, who provided the inspiration for the engaging Scherzo which is

the highlight of the later, B flat major work. The melodic invention is somewhat conventional, but is lyrical and pleasing throughout each symphony here. R. L. feels that whatever may be said of his originality or importance, Hol was a *real* symphonist who has total command over his material and has a sense of architecture and pace. For E. G. the orchestral writing is attractive, but the musical material hardly deserves such extended treatment, with too many passages depending on empty gestures, with trite repetitions and sequences, and melodies that turn back on themselves. For I. M. this is not music he would wish to return to very often. However, we are all agreed that the performances, from a first-class orchestra who are naturally at home in the repertoire, are warmly sympathetic and the full-bodied Chandos sound presents the composer's orchestration persuasively.

HOLBORNE, Antony (c.1560–1602)

Pieces for bandora: Almain: The Night Watch; Fantazia; A Ground; for cittern: A French Toy; A Horne Pype; The Miller; Praeludium; Sicke Sicke and Very Sicke; (i) for cittern with a bass: Galliard; Maister Earles Pavane; Queenes Galliard; for lute: Almains: Almaine; The Choice. Fantasia. Galliards: As it fell on a holie yve; The Fairy-rownde; Holburns passion; Muy linda; Responce; The teares of the muses. Pavans: Heres paternus; Pavan, and Galliard to the same; Posthuma; Sedet sola. A Toy. Variations: Il Nodo di gordio.

⊙ *** ASV CDGAU 173. Heringman, with (i) Pell.

An entirely delightful representation on CD of an Elizabethan lutenist, composer and poet, now totally overshadowed by Dowland. Indeed, his melancholy pavane *Posthuma* has as much 'dolens' as almost anything by Dowland. It is this meditative quality which Jacob Heringman catches to perfection and which makes this collection so appealing. He improvises his own divisions when needed, as was expected by the composer, and his playing is appealingly spontaneous. The thoughtful simplicity of a piece like *The Night watch* contrasts with the musing, improvisational extended *Fantazia*, both played on the more sonorous bandora, for which Holborne wrote more music than any of his contemporaries. But there is lively writing too, like *The Miller* and *A French toy*; and how well they sound on the cittern, a robust-timbred instrument mostly favoured by the lower classes, and which came to be much played in barber shops. The composer took especial care over the four duet pieces for cittern with bass viol. Jacob Heringman is beautifully recorded in a most suitable ambience, providing the ideal CD for a late evening reverie.

Lute pieces: Cradle Pavane; Countess of Ormond's Galliard; The fairy Round; Fantasia No. 3; Galliards Nos. 2 & 17; Heres Paternus; Muy Linda; The Night Watch; Last Will and Testament Pavans Nos. 2 & 11; Wanton.

(BB) **(*) Naxos 8.553974. Wilson (lute) – ROBINSON: *Lute Pieces & Duets*. ***

Christopher Wilson plays these pieces very well, notably the lively items like *The Fairy Round* and *Wanton*, with *Muy Linda* a highlight. But he does not penetrate the inner core of the ruminative pieces as touchingly as Jacob Heringman. However there is not too much duplication here and this inexpensive Naxos disc is well worth getting for the coupled repertoire (including duets) by Holborne's contemporary, Thomas Robinson.

HOLBROOKE, Joseph (1878–1958)

The Birds of Rhiannon, Op. 87; The Children of Don: Overture, Op. 56; Dylan: Prelude, Op. 53.

** Marco 8.223721-2. Ukraine Nat. SO, Penny.

In Holbrooke's opera, *The Children of Don* (the first of a trilogy), neither overture nor prelude offers particularly memorable or individual ideas and, generally speaking, inspiration is pretty thin. There are touches of Wagner in the former but the musical language is predominantly diatonic, particularly in the tone-poem *The Birds of Rhiannon*. The longest piece is the *Prelude* to *Dylan*, which is pretty undistinguished stuff. The performances sound a bit under-rehearsed but are adequate (some may find the horn vibrato a bit excessive), and the recording is decent.

Piano Concerto No. 1 (Song of Gwyn ap Nudd), Op. 52.

*** Hyp. CDA 67127. Milne, BBC Scottish SO, Brabbins – Haydn WOOD: *Piano Concerto.* ***

Joseph Holbrooke had the misfortune to develop his high romantic style just when it was being superseded on almost every front. It has taken a long time for his star to rise again, but this ambitious piano concerto provides a fair sample of his writing, presenting both its strengths and its weaknesses. The grandeur of the manner is not often enough matched by memorable material, and when a melody does emerge to catch in the mind it verges on the banal. The piano-writing too often suggests a popular idiom, making this an apt coupling for the fine concerto by a composer who did find his success in light music, Haydn Wood. What makes this recording of the concerto most enjoyable despite the weaknesses is not only the brilliance of the performance – with Hamish Milne masterly in finding poetry in the Chopinesque figuration – but also the presentation. As in the score, the twenty-two index-points are linked directly to the text of the poem which inspired the piece, telling the evocative story. Full, well-balanced recording.

(i) Piano Quartet in G min., Op. 21; (ii) String Sextet in D, Op. 43; (iii) Symphonic Quintet No. 1 in G min., Op. 44.

** Marco 8 223736. (i; iii) Hegedüs; (ii) Papp, Devich; New Haydn Qt.

Although the music here never falls below a certain level of melodic fluency and is expertly crafted, little of it remains in the memory. The *String Sextet* makes the most immediate and positive impact but, after the CD has come to an end, one realizes why Holbrooke has not stayed the course. The fine Hungarian ensemble play these pieces with appropriate conviction and ardour. Decent recording, much better than for the orchestral disc.

HOLLOWAY, Robin (born 1943)

Second Concerto for Orchestra, Op. 40.

*** NMC D015M. BBC SO, Knussen.

Holloway's *Second Concerto* is a richly imaginative score and shows a sensitivity of high quality, as well as a considerable mastery of instrumental resource. The *Concerto* is a work of substance that is well worth getting to know and is well served by the BBC Symphony Orchestra and Oliver Knussen. The engineers produce a better sound from the Maida Vale Studios than we have heard on any other occasion.

(i) Romanza for Violin & Small Orchestra, Op. 31; (ii) Sea-surface Full of Clouds, Op. 28.

*** Chan. 9228. (i) Gruenberg; (ii) Walmsley-Clark, Cable, Hill, Brett, Hickox Singers; City of L. Sinfonia, Hickox.

Both works recorded here show Holloway's sensitivity to colour and marvellous feeling for the orchestra. The *Sea-surface Full of Clouds* begins luminously, rather like Szymanowski, and has an at times magical atmosphere. There is an affecting and consuming melancholy about the *Romanza* for violin and orchestra. A composer of a refined intelligence and real sensibility.

HOLMBOE, Vagn (1909–96)

(i) Cello Concerto, Op. 120; (ii) Brass Quintet, Op. 79; (iii) Triade, Op. 123; (iv) Benedic Domino, Op. 59.

*** BIS ADD/Dig. CD 78. (i) Bengtsson, Danish RSO, Ferencsik; (ii) Swedish Brass Quintet; (iii) Tarr, Westenholz; (iv) Camerata Ch., Enevold.

Vagn Holmboe's magnificent *Cello Concerto* is given an excellent performance here, and the account of the choral piece, *Benedic Domino* has shows an austere beauty and elevation of feeling that are rare in contemporary music. The *Brass Quintet* is effective and stirring; and the *Triade* for trombone and organ is hardly less striking. Only the *Quintet* is a digital recording but its companions here are also strikingly good as sound.

(i) Chamber Concertos Nos. 1 for Piano Strings & Tympani, Op. 17; (ii) 2 for Flute, Violin, Strings & Percussion, Op. 20; (iii) 3 for Clarinet & Chamber Orchestra, Op. 21.

*** dacapo 8.224038. (i) Oland; (ii) Ostergaard, Futtrup; (iii) Tomsen; Danish R. Concert O, Koivula.

Chamber Concertos Nos. (i; ii; iv) 4 for Piano Trio & Chamber Orchestra, Op. 30; (iii) 5 for Viola & Chamber Orchestra, Op. 31; (ii) 6 for Violin & Chamber Orchestra, Op. 33.

*** dacapo 8.224063. (i) Oland; (ii) Futtrup; (iii) Fredericksen; (iv) Ullner, Danish R. Sinf., Koivula.

Chamber Concertos (i) Nos. 7, for Oboe, Op. 37; 8 (Sinfonia Concertante, Op. 38; (ii) 9 for Violin & Viola, Op. 39.

*** dacapo 8.224086. (i) Artved; (ii) Futtrup, Frederiksen; Danish R. Sinf, Koivula.

Chamber Concertos: No. 10 for Wood-brass-gut & Orchestra, Op. 40; (i) *No. 11 for Trumpet & Chamber Orchestra, Op. 44;* (ii) *No. 12 for Trombone & Orchestra, Op. 52;* (iii) *No. 13 for Oboe, Viola & Chamber Orchestra, Op. 67.*

*** dacapo 8.224087. (i) Antonsen; (ii) Mauger; (iii) Artved, Frederiksen, Danish R. Sinf., Koivula.

Vagn Holmboe began his series of *Chamber Concertos* way back in 1939 completing them in the mid-1950s. Many of them were composed for Lavard Friisholm and the Collegium Musicum, and are predominantly neoclassical in outlook. They are fresh, clean-textured pieces, full of musical interest and a zest for life. A good point to start is the third disc (Nos. 7–9) which covers the period 1944–6. The most substantial of the three being No. 8, the *Sinfonia Concertante* with its inventive set of variations, which (along with No. 11) is the only one that made any headway into the repertory outside Denmark in the 1950s. It is somewhat Hindemithian in its stance yet distinctive. Holmboe is always very much his own man. No. 11 has been the most widely recorded. Rewarding music, very well performed and decently recorded.

Chamber Concertos Nos. (i) *11 for Trumpet & Orchestra, Op. 44;* (ii) *12 for Trombone, Op. 52;* (iii) *Tuba Concerto, Op. 152. Intermezzo Concertante, Op. 171.*

*** BIS CD 802. (i) Hardenberger; (ii) Lindberg; (iii) Larsen; Aalborg SO, Hughes.

The noble neo-baroque *Concerto No. 11 for Trumpet* (1948) could hardly be better served than by Håkan Hardenberger's account with the Aalborg orchestra, and one is tempted to add that any newcomer will have to be pretty good to match Christian Lindberg's account of the *Twelfth Chamber Concerto.* These are inspiriting and inspiring pieces. The one-movement *Tuba Concerto* explores the virtuoso possibilities of this instrument as do few others as does the *Intermezzo Concertante.* These are dazzling performances and the orchestral support under Owain Arwel Hughes is first class. The recording is state of the art. Highly recommended.

Flute Concertos Nos. 1, Op. 126; 2, Op. 147; (i) *Concerto for Recorder, Strings, Celesta & Vibraphone, Op. 122.*

*** BIS CD 911. Wiesler; (i) Laurin; Aarhus SO, Hughes.

The *Flute Concertos* and the *Concerto for Recorder, Strings, Celesta and Vibraphone* are wonderfully inventive scores whose luminous, shining textures captivate the mind and reaffirm the conviction that Holmboe stands head and shoulders above his contemporaries in the North. Strong performances from all concerned and splendid recording too. Don't miss this.

Epilog, Op. 80; Epitaph (Symphonic Metamorphosis), Op. 68; Monolith, Op. 76; Tempo variabile, Op. 108.

✪ *** BIS CD 852. Aarhus SO, Hughes.

The first of Vagn Holmboe's *Symphonic Metamorphoses*

brings musical ideas that unfold, change shape, assume new identities without losing sight of their individuality, in much the same way as does, say, the *Seventh Symphony* of Sibelius. Three like-minded successors followed in the next few years, all of them works of great concentration, cogency and power. The playing of the Aarhus Orchestra is excellent and Owain Arwel Hughes in total sympathy with these magnificent scores. The recording is state-of-the-art.

Preludes for a Sinfonietta Ensemble: To a Dolphin; To a Living Stone, Op. 172C/5; To a Maple Tree, Op. 168/3; To the Unsettled Weather, Op. 188/10; To the Victoria Embankment, Op. 184/8.

(N) *** dacapo 8.224123. Copenhagen Athelas Sinf., Bellincampi.

The *Preludes* for a sinfonietta ensemble or chamber orchestra were composed over the period 1986–1991. They were to be Holmboe's last orchestral pieces and not all of them were performed in his lifetime. They are miniature tone poems, evocative and full of atmosphere and invention. These are dedicated performances from these Copenhagen musicians and their Italian-born conductor, and they are very well recorded too; so we eagerly await the release of the remaining five preludes.

Symphonies Nos. 1, Op. 4; 3 (Sinfonia rustica), Op. 25; 10, Op. 105.

*** BIS CD 605. Aarhus SO, Hughes.

The general outlook of the *First Symphony* (*Sinfonia da camera*) is neo-classical and its proportions are modest, but one recognizes the vital current of the later Holmboe, the lucidity of thinking and the luminous textures. The last movement has an infectious delight in life; so, too, has the exhilarating finale of the *Third* (*Sinfonia rustica*), the first of his three war-time symphonies. The *Tenth* is dark, powerful and imaginative; altogether one of the Danish composer's most subtle and satisfying works. The performances and recordings are altogether first class.

Symphony No. 2, Op. 15; Sinfonia in memoriam, Op. 65.

*** BIS CD 695. Aarhus SO, Hughes.

The *Second Symphony* with its imaginative middle movement and its vital companions is a splendid piece. The *Sinfonia in memoriam* is a dark work of striking power and imaginative breadth and is masterly in every way. Owain Arwel Hughes and the Aarhus orchestra give a performance that is in every way worthy of it, and the recording is in the demonstration bracket.

Symphonies Nos. (i) *4 (Sinfonia sacra), Op. 29. 5, Op. 35.*

**(*) BIS CD 572. (i) Jutland Op. Ch.; Aarhus SO, Hughes.

The *Fifth Symphony* makes a good entry point into Holmboe's world. The only word to describe its outer movements is exhilarating. The slow movement has a modal character, but an anguished outburst in the middle serves as a reminder that this is a wartime work, composed during the dark days of the Nazi occupation. The *Fourth* (*Sinfonia sacra*) is a six-movement choral piece dedicated to the memory of his brother who perished in a Nazi concentration camp. It encompasses a bracing vigour and underlying optimism alongside moments of sustained grief. Very good performances, though the strings are a little under-strength and the acoustic is on the dry side. But don't let this put you off this inspiriting music.

Symphonies Nos. 6, Op. 43; 7, Op. 50.

**(*) BIS CD 573. Aarhus SO, Hughes.

Holmboe's *Sixth Symphony* is a much darker piece than its predecessor. Its distinctively Nordic world is established by the brooding, slow-moving fourths of the long introduction; there is writing of great luminosity too. The one-movement *Seventh Symphony* is a highly concentrated score, individual in both form and content, which encompasses great variety of pace and mood. Owain Arwel Hughes acquits himself very well, and this is music that speaks with so strong and distinctive a voice that it is self-recommending.

Symphonies Nos 8, Op. 56 (1951); 9 (1968).

✪*** BIS CD 618. Aarhus SO, Hughes.

This conductor has real feeling for the composer and penetrates the spirit of the score of the *Eighth Symphony*. The *Ninth Symphony* is a dark, powerful work, among the finest Holmboe has given us. This is music which, one can feel with some certainty, future generations will want to hear. The Aarhus orchestra are equally persuasive in the *Ninth* as in the *Eighth*, and the recording is the best so far in the cycle.

Symphonies Nos. 11, Op. 141; 12, Op. 175; 13, Op. 192.

*** BIS CD 728. Aarhus SO, Hughes.

The *Thirteenth Symphony* is an astonishing achievement for a composer in his mid-eighties. It is a veritable powerhouse. The *Twelfth* is tautly structured and well argued, though less inspired than the *Eleventh Symphony*, which finds Holmboe at his most visionary. Every credit is due to Owain Arwel Hughes and the Aarhus Symphony Orchestra for their fervent advocacy of this music and to the splendid BIS engineers for the vivid and superbly natural sound.

String Quartets Nos. 1, Op. 46; 3, Op. 48; 4, Op. 63.

*** Danacord CDDC 9203. Kontra Qt.

String Quartets Nos. 2, Op. 47; 5, Op. 66; 6, Op. 78.

*** dacapo 8.224026. Kontra Qt.

These quartets have a certain reserve: nothing is overstated, everything is quietly but cogently argued and, once one has broken through its reticence, its rewards are rich. This is easily the finest post-war quartet cycle in Scandinavia. The *Second Quartet* has a particularly engaging main theme and these artists play it with conviction. The *Fifth* and *Sixth* are both finely argued works. What a rewarding composer Holmboe is, and how well played and recorded these quartets are!

String Quartets Nos. 10, Op. 102; 11, Op. 111 (Quartetto rustico); 12, Op. 116.

**(*) dacapo Dig 8.224101. Kontra Qt.

The *Tenth Quartet* in two movements is arguably the most concentrated in feeling and powerfully structured. Its suc-

cessor, the only one of his quartets to bear a subtitle, *Quartetto rustico*, is the most relaxed and smiling. The *Twelfth* is a five-movement piece whose central slow movement has great eloquence. Those who respond, say, to the Robert Simpson quartets should find this uncompromising music rewarding. The performances are excellent and the Danish Radio recording acceptable in quality though tone tends to harden a little above the stave.

String Quartets Nos. 13, Op. 124; 14, Op. 125; 15, Op. 135.

*** dacapo 8.224127. Kontra Qt.

The *Thirteenth Quartet* must be numbered among the most eloquent of Holmboe's works. Indeed, all three works here find him at the height of his intellectual powers. There is a certain severity and rigour about these pieces and the Kontras give them all with the concentration and dedication they require. The recordings made in 1997–8 are excellent and without hardness. Strongly recommended to admirers of this composer.

String Quartets Nos. 16, Op. 146; 18 (Giornata), Op. 153; Svrm, Op. 190b; Quartetto sereno, Op. 197 (completed Per Nørgård).

(N) *** dacapo 8.224131. Kontra Qt.

String Quartets Nos. 17 (Mattinata), Op. 152; 19 (Serata), Op. 156; 20 (Notturno), Op. 160.

(N) *** dacapo 8.224128. Kontra Qt.

With these two issues the Kontra Quartet completes its survey of the Holmboe string quartets. It was the medium with which Holmboe had a lifelong preoccupation and in which he felt most at home. In all he composed 20 quartets and the *Quartetto sereno*, on which he was working in the last year of his life and which he left incomplete. (It has been put into a performing version by his erstwhile pupil Per Nørgård.) In addition Holmboe wrote, but never published, at least ten other quartets during the 1930s and 1940s before his first official work (1949). As their titles show, the last four quartets form an entity on the theme of the times of the day from morning to evening. They were composed in quick succession: Nos. 17–19 all come from 1982, although *Mattinata* (No. 17) and *Serata* (No. 19) were revised a year or so later; *Notturno* (No. 20) comes from 1985. Apart from the *16th Quartet* (1981), which was recorded by the Copenhagen Quartet in the days of LP, these are all first recordings. Despite their titles these works are pure music and share the same distinction of mind that we find in their contemporaries. Along with the quartets of Robert Simpson and of course Shostakovich, this is the most notable twentieth-century quartet cycle after Bartók.

PIANO MUSIC

Romanian Suite; Sonatina Briosa (symphonic suite); Suono da bardo; Suite, Op. 4.

(N) *** Danacord DACOCD 502. Blyme.

Suono da bardo is Holmboe's most important piano piece and comes from the same period as the *Seventh Symphony*.

Subtitled *'Symphonic Suite'*, it is undoubtedly more symphonic than pianistic. Holmboe's composer—pianist colleague Niels Viggo Bentzon gave its first performance, and Anker Blyme made its first LP recording a few years later in 1956. He returned to it around four decades later to give this admirable account; the rest of the programme is equally impressive.

HOLMÈS, Augusta (1847–1903)

Andromeda (symphonic poem); *Ireland* (symphonic poem); (i) *Ludus pro patria: Night & Love. Overture for a Comedy; Poland* (symphonic poem).

*** Marco 8.223449. Rheinland-Pfalz PO, Friedmann;
  (i) Davin.

Augusta Holmès was from an Anglo-Irish family that had settled in France; She was a person of remarkable gifts for, apart from her musical talents, she was an accomplished painter and wrote well. Although the *Overture for a Comedy* (1876) is trite, *Andromeda* is quite striking. It is by far the best piece on the disc, and the best scored, though limitations in Augusta Holmès's technique are evident. But this is music of much interest – and its composer was obviously no mean talent. She has been well served by the Rheinland-Pfalz Philharmonic under Samuel Friedmann. The recordings too are eminently satisfactory.

HOLST, Gustav (1874–1934)

'The essential Holst': (i) *Egdon Heath, Op. 47;* (ii) *A Moorside Suite;* (iii) *The Perfect Fool, Op. 39;* (iv) *The Planets, Op. 32;* (v) *St Paul's Suite, Op. 29/2;* (vi) *Ave Maria, Op. 9b; Choral Hymns from the Rig Veda* (Group 3), *Op. 26/3; The Evening Watch, Op. 43/1;* (vii) *The Hymn of Jesus, Op. 37;* (vi) *This Have I Done for My True Love, Op. 34/1.*

(B) *** Double Decca ADD/Dig. 444 549-2 (2). (i; iii) LPO, Boult; (ii) Grimethorpe Colliery Band, Howarth; (iv) LPO, Solti; (v) St Paul CO, Hogwood; (vi) Purcell Singers, Imogen Holst; (vii) BBC Ch. & SO, Boult.

The brilliant Decca recording of Solti's Chicago version of the *Planets* combined with Boult's vintage accounts of *Egdon Heath* and *The Perfect Fool* ballet music is discussed below in its single-disc format. Boult's distinguished performance of the *Hymn of Jesus* is also available on another Double Decca, joined with music by Delius and Elgar. But if the present compilation is suitable, it could make a splendid basis for a Holst collection. The jolly, folksy *St Paul's Suite* for strings could hardly be done better. *A Moorside Suite* sounds splendid in its original, brass-band form, and it is superbly played by the Grimethorpe Colliery Band under Elgar Howarth, with recording approaching demonstration standard. Aptly, the first of the *Rig-Veda Choral Hymns* (taken from a Sanskrit source), the *Hymn to the Dawn*, brings echoes of *Neptune* from *The Planets*, while the fast and rhythmically fascinating *Hymn to the Waters* is even more attractive. The vocal music serves to balance the pic-

ture of Holst as a composer, to show the more mystical side of his musical character. Beautifully atmospheric recording to match intense and sensitive performances.

Beni Mora (oriental Suite); Egdon Heath; Fugal Overture; Hammersmith; (i) *Invocation for Cello & Orchestra. Somerset Rhapsody.*

*** Naxos 8.553696. RSNO, Lloyd-Jones; (i) with Hugh.

The six works here are neatly balanced, three dating from before the climactic period of *The Planets* and three after. So the generously lyrical *Somerset Rhapsody, Beni Mora* and the long-neglected *Invocation for Cello and Orchestra* (with Timothy Hugh a moving soloist) lead on to the tauter and more astringent post-war works: the Hardy-inspired *Egdon Heath*, the darkly intense prelude and fugue, *Hammersmith* and the *Fugal Overture*. Fresh and idiomatic performances, superbly recorded in full and brilliant sound.

(i) *Beni Mora (Oriental Suite), Op. 29/1; A Fugal Overture, Op. 40/1; Hammersmith – A Prelude & Scherzo for Orchestra, Op. 52;* (ii) *Japanese Suite;* (i) *Scherzo (1933/4); A Somerset Rhapsody, Op. 21.*

*** Lyrita (ADD) SRCD 222. (i) LPO; (ii) LSO; Boult.

Beni Mora (written after a holiday in Algeria) is an attractive, exotic piece. Boult clearly revels in its sinuosity. *The Japanese Suite* is not very Japanese, although it has much charm. The most ambitious work here is *Hammersmith*, far more than a conventional tone picture, intensely poetic. The *Scherzo*, from a projected symphony that was never completed, is strong, confident music. The *Somerset Rhapsody* is unpretentious but very enjoyable, and the brief, spiky *Fugal Overture* is given plenty of lift and bite to open the concert invigoratingly. As with other records in this Lyrita series the first class analogue recording has been splendidly transferred to CD.

Brook Green Suite for Strings; Capriccio for Orchestra; (i) *Double Violin Concerto, Op. 49;* (ii) *Fugal Concerto for Flute, Oboe & Strings, Op. 40/2. The Golden Goose* (ballet music, arr. Imogen Holst), *Op. 45/1;* (iii) *Lyric Movement for Viola & Small Orchestra. A Moorside Suite: Nocturne* (arr. for strings); *2 Songs Without Words, Op. 22.*

**(*) Lyrita (ADD) SRCD 223. ECO, Imogen Holst, with (i) Hurwitz, Sillito; (ii) Bennett, Graeme; (iii) Aronowitz.

The *Capriccio* proves an exuberant piece, with some passages not at all capriccio-like. *The Golden Goose* was written as a choral work for St Paul's Girls' School; these orchestral snippets were put together by Imogen Holst. The *Double Concerto*, with its bi-tonality and cross-rhythms, is grittier and with much less obvious melodic appeal, but it remains an interesting example of the late Holst. The first two movements of the *Fugal Concerto* are much more appealing with their cool interplay of wind colour, particularly when the soloists are so distinguished. The *Lyric Movement for Viola and Small Orchestra* is certainly persuasive in the hands of Cecil Aronowitz and is one of the most beautiful of Holst's later pieces. The concert is completed with the comparatively familiar *Brook Green Suite* and two *Songs without words*, early works that are tuneful and colourful. All the performances are sympathetically authentic and the recording is well up to Lyrita's usual high standard.

Brook Green Suite for String Orchestra; (i) A Fugal Concerto, Op. 40/2; (ii) Lyric movement for Viola & Small Orchestra; St Paul's Suite for String Orchestra, Op. 29/2. Arrangements of Morris Dance Tunes: Bean Setting; Constant Billy; Country Gardens; How d'ye do; Laudanum Bunches; Rigs o'Marlow; Shepherd's Hey.

*** Koch 3-7058-2. New Zealand CO, Braithwaite; with (i) Still, Popperwell; (ii) Yendoll.

The *Fugal Concerto* features concertante solos for flute and oboe and is a beautifully crafted triptych of miniatures; the rather more ambitious *Lyric Movement* is hardly less appealing and is warmly played here by Vyvyan Yendoll, who has a fine, rich timbre. The New Zealand Chamber Orchestra respond sensitively and persuasively to Nicholas Braithwaite who is thoroughly at home in this repertoire. The textures of the *Brook Green Suite* are pleasingly light and airy and in the *St Paul's Suite* the gutsy opening *Jig* makes a complete contrast with the pianissimo delicacy of the *Ostinati*. The set of country dances is agreeably spontaneous. The recording is in the demonstration bracket.

Brook Green Suite for String Orchestra; (i) Fugal Concerto for Flute & Oboe. The Perfect Fool (ballet suite), Op. 39; St Paul's Suite for String Orchestra, Op. 26/2; A Somerset Rhapsody, Op. 21/2.

(M) *** EMI CD-EMX 2227. ECO, Menuhin.

There are a number of collections of Holst's shorter orchestral works currently available on CD, but none better played or recorded than this and none less expensive. It includes warmly characterized performances of both the works Holst wrote for St Paul's Girls' School, not just the *St Paul's Suite* but also the *Brook Green Suite*, both sounding fresh, while the rarer *Somerset Rhapsody* is also very atmospherically presented. There is some delightful solo playing from Jonathan Snowden and David Theodore in the *Fugal Concerto*, and many will welcome Menuhin's vivid account of *The Perfect Fool*, Holst's most familiar orchestral suite after *The Planets*. If the programme suits, you need look no further.

Brook Green Suite; (i) Double Violin Concerto, Op. 49; (ii) Fugal Concerto for Flute, Oboe & Strings, Op. 40/2; (iii) Lyric Movement for Viola & Small Orchestra; 2 Songs Without Words, Op. 22; St Paul's Suite, Op. 29/2.

*** Chan. 9270. (i) Ward, Watkinson; (ii) Dobing, Hooker; (iii) Tees; City of L. Sinf., Hickox.

The most striking piece here, a fine example of Holst's later, sparer style, is the *Double Concerto* for two violins and small orchestra, very taut and intense. The delicacy of the solo playing in the central *Lament* of this fine work is matched by the ethereal pianissimo from Stephen Tees at the opening of the *Lyric Movement*. The woodwind playing is delightful here too, as is the gentle clarinet solo which opens the *Country Song*, the first of Holst's two *Songs Without Words*; the second, appropriately, is more robust. The *Brook Green Suite* is wonderfully fresh and there is a comparable lightness of touch at the opening of the delightful *Fugal Concerto*.

What matters throughout this programme is the surging warmth that Richard Hickox draws from his modest forces. The recording is superb – very real indeed.

Cotswolds Symphony in F, Op. 8; A Hampshire Suite, Op. 28/2 (orch. Gordon Jacob); The Perfect Fool (ballet suite); Scherzo for Orchestra (1933/4); Walt Whitman Overture.

*** Classico CLASSCD 284. Munich SO, Bostock.

We have had the *Cotswolds Symphony* before on Lyrita (see below), also the *Scherzo*, but it is good to hear fine, new, modern recordings of both. The work, completely new to CD is the *Walt Whitman Overture*, written as early as 1899. It is a vigorous but untypical piece, its scoring strong on trombones. The rather jolly *Cotswolds Symphony* immediately shows the Holstian flair for colourful orchestration and has a folksy influence. The melancholy slow movement (*An Elegy for William Morris*) brings a few slight hints of the later Holst; its scherzo has an attractive lumbering dance rhythm, and the finale brings quite a striking tune in 6/4 time. *A Hampshire Suite* is Gordon Jacob's orchestration of the *First Suite for Military Band*, and he skilfully ensures that wind and brass textures predominate. The independent *Scherzo* was the composer's final orchestral flourish. But it is the familiar suite from *The Perfect Fool* in which we hear the composer at his most inspired and, like the rest of the programme, is most vividly played and recorded, with the slow movement especially persuasive. It is remarkable how well this fine Munich orchestra takes to English music under the expert guidance of Douglas Bostock.

Cotswolds Symphony in F (Elegy: In Memoriam William Morris), Op. 8; Indra (Symphonic Poem), Op. 13; (i) Invocation (for cello and orchestra), Op. 19/2; (iii) The Lure (ballet music); The Morning of the Year: Dances, Op. 45/2. Sita: Interlude from Act III, Op. 23; (ii) A Song of the Night (for violin and orchestra), Op. 19/1; A Winter Idyll.

*** Lyrita Dig./ADD SRCD 209. (i) Baillie; (ii) McAslan; LPO or (iii) LSO; Atherton.

The earliest work here, *A Winter Idyll*, was written when Holst was in his early twenties. Both in this work and in the *Elegy*, which is a slow movement originally forming part of a *Cotswolds Symphony*, one can detect little of the mature Holst. The familiar fingerprints do surface, however, in *Indra* (1903) and *A Song of the night* (1905), which is among the scores Colin Matthews has edited. *The Lure* (1921) was written at short notice for Chicago and is characteristic, but the inspiration is not of the quality of *The Perfect Fool*.

(i) Egdon Heath; (ii) Fugal Concerto, Op. 40/2.

(N) (M) *** BBC mono/stereo BBCB 8007-2. (i) LSO, Britten; (ii) ECO, I. Holst – BRITTEN: *The Building of the House Overture*; BRIDGE: *Enter Spring; The Sea.*

Though the 1961 mono recording is dry, with the limited dynamic range sabotaging *pianissimos*, the concentration of Britten interpreting *Egdon Heath*, one of Holst's most inspired works, makes this well worth hearing, particularly with such excellent couplings.

Imogen Holst's urgent, robust reading of her father's *Fugal Concerto* comes from 1969 in much finer sound, also recorded at the Aldeburgh Festival. She brings out a bluff honesty in Holst's very English neo-classical writing. Fine solo work, too, from Richard Adeney on the flute and Peter Graeme on the oboe.

Hammersmith: Prelude & Scherzo, Op. 52; Marching Song, Op. 22; Military Band Suites Nos. 1 in E flat; 2 in F, Op. 28/ 1–2. Arr. of BACH (attrib.): Fugue à la gigue.

*** Chan. 9697. Royal N. College of Music Wind O, Reynish – VAUGHAN WILLIAMS: *English Folksongs Suite etc.* ***

Truly marvellous bravura playing from the Royal Northern College of Music's Wind Orchestra in the *Second Military Band Suite*. Timothy Reynish catches the jaunty quality of this attractive music and is especially perceptive in the way he sneaks the *Greensleeves* melody into the *Fantasia on the Dargason*. The only slight disappointment is the climax of the great *Chaconne*, at the opening of the *First Suite*, and the bass drum is submerged – not nearly as telling as on the Telarc recording. As a compensation we are given an inspired account of *Hammersmith*, the finest performance on record. The work's haunting atmosphere is fully captured. It is good too, to have Holst's effective arrangement of the spirited *Fugue à la gigue*. Apart from the matter of the bass drum, the vivid Chandos recording is demonstration worthy, with splendid range, detail and a rich underlying sonority. Most enjoyable!

Invocation for Cello & Orchestra, Op. 19/2.

(M) *** RCA (ADD) 74321 84112-2 (2). Julian Lloyd Webber, LPO, López-Coboz – BRUCH: *Kol Nidrei;* DELIUS: *Concerto; Hassan: Serenade;* LALO: *Concerto;* RODRIGO: *Concierto como un divertimento;* VAUGHAN WILLIAMS: *Fantasia on Sussex Folk Tunes.* *** (with Recital: *Celebration ***).

Holst's *Invocation* comes from 1911 and predates *The Planets*. Indeed, in her book on her father, Imogen Holst spoke of it as 'trying out' some of the ideas for the texture of *Venus*. It is a highly attractive and lyrical piece well worth reviving. Both the performance and the recording are of admirable quality and this is one of the most valuable items included this celebratory Double, reissued by RCA for Julian Bream's fiftieth birthday.

Military Band Suites Nos. 1 in E flat; 2 in F.

⬥ *** Telarc CD 80038. Cleveland Symphonic Winds, Fennell – HANDEL: *Royal Fireworks Music.* ***

Holst's two *Military Band Suites* contain some magnificent music. Frederick Fennell's Telarc versions have more gravitas though no less *joie de vivre* than his old Mercury set. They are magnificent, and the recording is truly superb – digital technique used in a quite overwhelmingly exciting way. The *Chaconne* of the *First Suite* makes a quite marvellous effect here. The playing of the Cleveland wind group is of the highest quality.

Military Band Suites Nos. 1–2. Hammersmith: Prelude & Scherzo, Op. 52.

(BB) *** ASV (ADD) CDQS 6021. L. Wind O, Denis Wick – VAUGHAN WILLIAMS: *English Folksong Suite etc.* ***

The London performances have great spontaneity, even if they are essentially lightweight, especially when compared with the Fennell versions. The sound is first class.

The Planets (suite), Op. 32.

*** DG 445 860-2. Monteverdi Ch. women's voices, Philh. O, Gardiner – GRAINGER: *The Warriors.* ***

(B) *** Penguin Decca 460 606-2. Montreal Ch. & SO, Dutoit.

(M) *** Decca (ADD) 452 303-2. VPO, Karajan – ELGAR: *Enigma Variations.* ***

(M) *** EMI (ADD) CDM7 64748-2. LPO, Boult (with G. Mitchell Ch.) – ELGAR: *Enigma Variations.* ***

(BB) *** DG (ADD) 439 446-2. Boston SO, Steinberg – ELGAR: *Enigma Variations.* ***

(N) (M) *** DG (ADD) 463 627-2. Boston SO, Steinberg – Richard STRAUSS: *Also sprach Zarathustra.* ***

*** DG 439 011-2. Berlin Ch., BPO, Karajan.

(N) (M) **(*) BBC (ADD) BBCM 5002-2. BBC SO, Sargent – ELGAR: *Enigma Variations.* **(*)

(M) **(*) EMI CDM7 64740-2. Philh. O, Rattle – JANACEK: *Sinfonietta.* ***

(N) (M) **(*) Chan. 6683. SNO & Ch., Gibson.

(M) **(*) Ph. (IMS) 442 408-2. Berlin R. Ch., BPO, Davis.

(M) (***) Cala mono CACD 0526. NBC SO, Stokowski (with DEBUSSY: *Prélude à l'après-midi d'un faune; La Cathédrale engloutie* (**(*)); GOULD: *2 Marches.* (***))

The Planets (suite); Egdon Heath, Op. 47.

(N) (BB) *** Warner Apex 8573 89087-2. BBC SO with women's chorus & organ, A. Davis.

(i) The Planets; (ii) Egdon Heath, Op. 47; (iii) The Perfect Fool (suite), Op. 39.

(M) *** Decca (ADD) 440 318-2. LPO, cond. (i) Solti, with LPO Ch.; (ii; iii) Boult.

(M) **(*) EMI (ADD) CDM5 66934-2. (i) New Philh. O, with Ch., Boult; (ii; iii) LSO, Previn.

(i) The Planets; (ii) The Perfect Fool (suite).

(B) *** Decca (ADD) 433 620-2. (i) LAPO, Mehta; (ii) LPO, Boult.

(BB) **(*) Virgin 2 x 1 Double VBD5 61510-2 (2). RLPO with Ch., Mackerras – ORFF: *Carmina Burana.* **(*)

With speeds never exaggerated, John Eliot Gardiner avoids vulgarity, yet with his rhythmic flair he gives *The Planets* a new buoyancy. Outstandingly enjoyable are the two most extrovert pieces: *Jupiter, the Bringer of Jollity* has rarely sounded so joyful, with a hint of wildness at the start, and the dancing rhythms of *Uranus* have a scherzando sparkle, with timpani and brass stunningly caught in the full, brilliant recording. The offstage women's chorus at the end of *Neptune* has seldom been more subtly balanced. Gardiner's *Planets* stands alongside the other current highly recommendable versions, whereas on DG the unusual Grainger coupling, typically rumbustious, pays tribute to the conductor's great-uncle, the composer Balfour Gardiner, who promoted the first performances of both works.

Charles Dutoit's natural feeling for mood, rhythm and colour, so effectively used in his records of Ravel, here results in an outstandingly successful version, both rich and brilliant, and recorded with an opulence to outshine almost all rivals. It is remarkable that, whether in the relentless build-up of *Mars*, the lyricism of *Venus*, the rich exuberance of *Jupiter* or in much else, Dutoit and his Canadian players sound so idiomatic. The final account of *Saturn* is chillingly atmospheric. This is one of the finest of Penguin's bargain-priced Classics, with a special note by Karen Armstrong in the UK, and in the USA by Ethan Canin.

With Karajan at his peak, this extraordinarily magnetic and powerful 1961 account of *The Planets* is uniquely individual, bringing a rare tension, an extra magnetism, the playing combining polish and freshness. The superb Decca recording – produced by John Culshaw in the Sofiensaal – is fully worthy of reissue in Decca's Classic Sound series. *Mars* is remorselessly paced and, with its whining Wagnerian tubas, is unforgettable, while the ravishingly gentle portrayal of *Venus* brings ardent associations with the goddess of love, rather than seeking a peaceful purity. The gossamer textures of *Mercury* and the bold geniality of *Jupiter* contrast with the solemn, deep melancholy expressed by the VPO strings at the opening of *Saturn*. *Uranus* brings splendid playing from the Vienna brass, given splendid bite.

With spectacularly brilliant and wide-ranging digital recording, engineered by Tony Faulkner, Andrew Davis's set of *Planets* is among the finest of modern recordings, and this Apex disc is a first choice among super-bargain versions. With a brilliant bite on the sound, and spectacular splashes from cymbals and tamtam, *Mars*, taken briskly, is both sinister and barbarous, followed by a transluscently chaste *Venus*, while *Mercury* has spritely daintiness and delicacy. *Jupiter* galumphs ruggedly, not as boisterously infectious as usual, with the central tune by contrast given a pastoral lyricism.

The highlight of the performance is *Saturn*, whose remorseless forward tread has remarkable sustained intensity, with the closing bass pedal notes (recorded by Davis on the organ at King's College) especially telling. The close of the ebullient *Uranus*, too, brings a magically evocative contrast, leading naturally into the ethereal atmosphere of *Neptune*, sustained by a celestially delicate contribution from the women of the BBC Chorus, and exquisite pianissimo orchestral tracery.

Egdon Heath then follows on very effectively, another intense performance, but here the spectacular recording at climaxes sounds more uninhibited, less in character than in the older Boult and Previn versions.

The Decca recording for Solti's Chicago version is extremely brilliant, with *Mars* given a vivid cutting edge at the fastest possible tempo. Solti's directness in *Jupiter* (with the trumpets coming through splendidly) is certainly riveting, the big tune red-blooded and with plenty of character. In *Saturn* the spareness of texture is finely sustained and the tempo is slow, the detail precise; while in *Neptune* the coolness is even more striking when the pianissimos are achieved with such a high degree of tension. The CD gives the orchestra great presence, and the addition of Boult's classic versions of *Egdon Heath* and *The Perfect Fool* ballet music makes this reissue very competitive.

Sir Adrian Boult with the LPO gives a performance at once intense and beautifully played, spacious and dramatic, rapt and pointed. The great melody of *Jupiter* is calculatedly less resonant and more flowing than previously but is still affecting, and *Uranus* as well as *Jupiter* has its measure of jollity. The spacious slow movements are finely poised and the recording still stands up well, with added presence and definition.

Mehta's set of *Planets* set a new standard for sonic splendour when it was first issued in 1971. The CD transfer still provides outstanding sound, but there is a touch more edge on the strings and the quality has lost just a little of its richness and amplitude; though definition is sharper, the background hiss is fractionally more noticeable. Even so, this is a superb disc and a strong bargain recommendation. As on the Solti *Planets*, Boult's splendid account of the ballet suite from *The Perfect Fool* has now been added. This was recorded a decade earlier, but the vintage Decca sound remains spectacular, with the LPO brass hardly less resplendent than their colleagues in Los Angeles.

Steinberg's Boston set of *Planets* is another outstanding version from a vintage analogue period. It remains one of the most exciting and involving versions and now sounds brighter and sharper in outline, though with some loss of opulence. *Mars* in particular is intensely exciting. At his fast tempo, Steinberg may get to his fortissimos a little early, but rarely has the piece sounded so menacing on record. The testing point for most will no doubt be *Jupiter*, and here Steinberg the excellent Elgarian comes to the fore, giving a wonderful *nobilmente* swagger.

Steinberg's version is also offered at mid-price, splendidly remastered as one of DG's Originals and coupled with an equally fine version of *Also sprach Zarathustra*.

Karajan's early (1981) digital DG recording is spectacularly wide-ranging, while the marvellously sustained pianissimo playing of the Berlin Philharmonic – as in *Venus* and the closing pages of *Saturn* – is very telling indeed. *Mars* has great impact, and the sound, full and firm in the bass, gives the performance throughout a gripping immediacy and presence. *Jupiter*, at its climax, still seems a bit fierce: ideally it needs a riper body of tone, yet the big melody has a natural flow and nobility. *Venus* brings sensuous string-phrasing, *Mercury* and *Uranus* have beautiful springing in the triplet rhythms, and the climax of that last movement brings an amazing glissando on the organ. In short this is a thrilling performance and highly recommendable, but it remains at full price and without a coupling.

For Simon Rattle EMI's digital recording provides wonderfully atmospheric sound, and the quality in *Venus* and *Mercury* is also beautiful, clear and translucent. Otherwise it is not as distinctive a version as one might have expected from this leading conductor; it is sensibly paced but neither so polished nor so bitingly committed as Karajan or Boult, and *Jupiter* is disappointing, lacking in thrust and warmth.

Sargent's BBC account of *The Planets* was recorded (like the coupled Elgar) in the Royal Albert Hall (in 1965), though the inner leaflet incorrectly suggests the Royal Festival Hall as the venue. One marvels that no one in the BBC's music production department noticed the three-second reverberation, confirming the point. Though this was a February performance, not one given at the Proms, the atmosphere is similarly electric, with the sequence of movements building warmly and atmospherically. As in the Elgar the playing may be a degree less polished than in Sargent's studio recording, but the excitement and tension are markedly greater, and for most that is what will matter. Good full-bodied if rather opaque sound.

Gibson's reading is characteristically direct and certainly well played. Other versions have greater individuality and are more involving, but there is no doubt that the Chandos recording has fine bite and presence, although there are moments when one would have expected a greater degree of transparency. With sound this vivid, the impact of such a colourful score is enhanced, and at mid-price this is much more competitive, a fine traditional account with plenty of character.

Sir Colin Davis's *Mars* is menacingly fast, with weighty Berlin brass and barbaric accents adding to the forcefulness. The resonant recording brings sumptuous textures to *Venus*, while even *Saturn* has a degree of opulence. *Mercury*, however, is infectiously spirited, and *Jupiter*, with a grand central tune, is bucolic in its amplitude. *Uranus* brings galumphing brass, and the closing *Neptune* is both ethereal and sensuous, an unusual combination, brought about partly by the warm reverberation. There are more subtle versions than this, but it is easy to enjoy. However, this reissue offers no coupling.

Mackerras's usual zestful approach communicates readily and the Liverpool orchestra bring a lively response, but the over-reverberant recording tends to cloud the otherwise pungently vigorous *Mars*, and both *Venus* and *Saturn* seem a little straightforward and marginally undercharacterized, while again in the powerful climax of *Uranus* there is some blurring from the resonance. *The Perfect Fool*, with its vivid colouring and irregular rhythms, has much in common with *The Planets* and makes a fine coupling, especially when played with such flair. This now comes on a bargain Virgin Double coupled with an excitingly vivid account of Orff's *Carmina burana*, rather let down by inadequate documentation.

Boult's New Philharmonia performance, recorded in Kingsway Hall in 1966 is brilliantly recorded but does not match his newer LPO version in imaginative detail. It has its moments of course: the beginning of the big string tune in *Jupiter* is a splendid example of truly British orchestral tone. But otherwise the transfer is not entirely flattering in the upper range. Previn gives a darkly intense performance of *Egdon Heath*, illuminatingly different from Boult's cooler, more detached approach. The rip-roaring ballet music from *The Perfect Fool* presents a colourful contrast, but the extremely vivid transfer has a hint of coarseness.

Stokowski's personality is stamped on every note of his individual and exciting reading of *The Planets*, taken from an NBC broadcast in February 1943. The tempi, with the exception of a few exaggerated examples, are remarkably similar to Holst's own, though the performance is very individual. Each planet is vividly characterized, with plenty of atmosphere running through each of the seven movements. The sound calls for some tolerance: although basically full – the opening of *Mars* (which makes a thrilling impact) is particularly effective – there is a fair amount of distortion at the climaxes and the surface noise can at times

make its presence felt. But not too much should be made of this as the performance tends to make one forget technical imperfections. As usual in Cala's Stokowski series, Edward Johnson provides a perceptively helpful essay.

The Planets (suite, including COLIN MATTHEWS: *Pluto and Neptune* with original ending); *Lyric Movement*.

(N) *** Hyp. CDA 67270. Hallé O, Elder.

Mark Elder conducts the Hallé Orchestra in a warm rather than bitingly dramatic reading of *The Planets*, which ends in Colin Matthews's extra movement, *Pluto – The Renewer*. That epilogue celebrates the outermost planet discovered after Holst wrote his suite, though not before he died. It was the idea of Kent Nagano as Elder's predecessor with the Hallé to add such a movement, with Matthews proving the ideal composer for a seemingly impossible task. Though he makes no attempt at writing Holst pastiche, his atmospheric movement inhabits very much the same sound-world as the suite, with colourful orchestration and high dynamic contrasts used dramatically. Though the tempo is very fast, the rapid scurrying seems to move round in circles, evoking an atmosphere of mystery apt for the smallest, remotest planet.

Since it emerges out of Holst's last movement, *Neptune*, involving a slight modification of the score, Elder conducts a second performance of that movement with the original ending of offstage women's choir fading into nothing. The tender, reflective *Lyric Movement*, with Timothy Pooley a fine viola soloist, makes a generous bonus.

Air & Variations; 3 Pieces for Oboe & String Quartet, Op. 2.

*** Chan. 8392. Francis, English Qt – BAX: *Quintet*; MOERAN: *Fantasy Quartet*; JACOB: *Quartet*. ***

The three pieces here are engagingly folksy, consisting of a sprightly little *March*, a gentle *Minuet* with a good tune, and a *Scherzo*. Performances are first class, and so is the recording.

The Planets (original version for 2 pianos); *Cotswolds Symphony: Elegy: In Memoriam William Morris* (original version for 2 pianos).

*** Olympia OCD 683. Goldstone and Clement – ELGAR: *String Serenade*; BAINTON: *Miniature Suite* *** (with Bury: *Prelude & Fugue in E flat* ***).

When one thinks of the brilliance and colour of Holst's orchestration it comes as a surprise to find how effective the score sounds on two pianos, and one often thinks of Ravel (especially so in the closing, very watery *Neptune*) who wrote first for piano, and scored his music afterwards. *Mars*, grumbling ominously in the bass certainly does not lack menace or power at its climax, *Venus* has remarkable translucence, and if nimble pianism cannot match a delicate string tracery in *Mercury*, *Saturn* is highly evocative.

Jupiter is ebullient enough although the performers here choose to play the famous central tune quite slowly and almost elegiacally, and to good effect. *Uranus* opens baldly and strongly, then is made to dance along spiritedly. Altogether a great success, partly because of the spontaneity of playing by a fine duo who obviously are very familiar with the orchestral version. The *Elegy*, part of the neglected *Cotswolds Symphony*, stands up well on its own. but is rather less effective in the composer's unpublished piano version, well played as it is.

VOCAL MUSIC

(i) *Ave Maria, H.49;* (ii–iv; viii) *A Choral Fantasia, Op. 51 (H.177);* (iii–iv; viii) *A Dirge for Two Veterans, H.121;* (v–viii) *The Cloud Messenger, Op. 30 (H.111);* (i) *The Evening Watch, H.159;* (vi–viii) *The Hymn of Jesus, Op. 37 (H.140);* (iv; vi; viii) *Ode to Death, Op. 38 (H.144);* (i) *4 Partsongs;* (ii–iv; viii) *7 Partsongs, H.162;* (i) *This have I done for my true love, H.128.*

(B) *** Chan. 2-for-1 241-6 (2). (i) Finzi Singers, Spicer; (ii) Rozario; (iii) Joyful Company of Singers; (iv) City of L. Sinfonia; (v) Jones; (vi) LSO Ch.; (vii) LSO Ch.; (viii) Hickox.

Richard Hickox proves a passionate advocate of the shorter choral works of Holst, demonstrating that the two Whitman settings, *A Dirge for Two Veterans* and *Ode to Death*, are among his finest pieces for voices: the *Dirge* written just after war had started in 1914, a grim processional for male voices, brass and percussion, and the *Ode* in 1919 when it was over and his disillusion was even more intense. That second work is in very much the same vein of inspiration as his masterpiece, the *Hymn of Jesus* and, with the larger forces of the London Symphony Chorus, brings the most powerful performance here. It easily outshines even Sir Adrian Boult's vintage version for Decca. Hickox secures tauter and crisper ensemble, as well as treating the sections based on plainchant with an aptly expressive freedom.

The long-neglected choral piece, *The Cloud Messenger*, may lack the concentration of the *Hymn of Jesus*, but it brings similarly incandescent choral writing. Warmly and positively realized by Hickox and his powerful forces, with Della Jones a fine soloist, it makes a major discovery. Both the later works, the *Seven Partsongs* of 1925 as well as the *Choral Fantasia* of 1930, set poems by Robert Bridges, with the choral writing fluently beautiful. Though Patricia Rozario is not on her finest form, the Joyful Company of Singers sing superbly in intense and moving performances, helped by rich and full Chandos sound.

A Choral Fantasia, Op. 51; Choral Symphony, Op. 41.

**(*) Hyp. CDA 66660. Dawson, Guildford Choral Society, RPO, Davan Wetton.

Though the ensemble of the Guildford Choral Society is not ideally crisp, and one really wants more weight of sound, the originality of Holst's choral writing and the purposeful nature of the argument are never in doubt in this surprisingly rarer coupling, with Lynne Dawson the radiantly beautiful soprano soloist in both works. Holst is nothing if not daring in using well-known texts of Keats in the *Choral Symphony*, adding a new dimension even to the 'Ode on a Grecian urn'.

(i) *A Choral Fantasia, Op. 51;* (ii) *Psalm 86.*

(M) *** EMI (ADD) CDM5 65588-2. (i) Baker; (ii) Partridge, Purcell Singers, ECO, Imogen Holst – FINZI: *Dies natalis;* VAUGHAN WILLIAMS: *5 Mystical Songs* etc. ***

In Holst's *Choral Fantasia* – a setting of words written by Robert Bridges in commemoration of Purcell – Dame Janet Baker once again shows her supreme quality as a recording artist. The recording, though not lacking ambient warmth, is admirably clear (indeed the organ pedals are only too clear). The sound could perhaps be more open, but there is no lack of projection and vividness. The setting of *Psalm 86*, with its expressive tenor part sung beautifully by Ian Partridge, is also included in this generous compilation. The recording here is outstanding, and the success of both these performances owes much to the inspired direction of the composer's daughter.

Choral Hymns from the Rig Veda (Groups 1–4), H. 97–100; 2 Eastern Pictures for Women's Voices & Harp, H. 112; Hymn to Dionysus, Op. 31/2.

**(*) Unicorn DKPCD 9046. Royal College of Music Chamber Ch., RPO, Willcocks; Ellis.

The *Choral Hymns from the Rig Veda* show Holst writing with deep understanding for voices, devising textures, refined, very distinctively his, to match atmospherically exotic texts. Though performances are not always ideally polished, the warmth and thrust of the music are beautifully caught. The *Hymn to Dionysus*, setting words from the *Bacchae* of Euripides in Gilbert Murray's translation, a rarity anticipating Holst's *Choral Symphony*, makes a welcome and substantial fill-up, along with the two little *Eastern Pictures*. Beautifully clean and atmospheric recording.

Choral Hymns from the Rig Veda (Group 3), H. 99, Op. 26/3.

(N) (B) *** Hyp. Helios CDH 55050. Holst Singers & O; Davan Wetton; Owen – BLISS: *Lie Strewn the White Flocks;* BRITTEN: *Gloriana: Choral Dances.* ***

The third group of *Choral Hymns from the Rig Veda*, like the whole series, reveals Holst in his Sanskritic period at his most distinctively inspired. In this responsive performance, it makes an excellent coupling for the attractive Bliss and Britten items, atmospherically recorded.

(i) *Choral Symphony, Op. 41;* (ii) *The Hymn of Jesus, Op. 37.*

(M) *** EMI (ADD) CDM5 65128-2. (i) Palmer, LPO Ch., LPO, Boult; (ii) St Paul's Cathedral Ch., L. Symphony Ch., LPO, Groves.

In the *Choral Symphony*, Boult and his performers in his totally unsentimental performance draw the whole work together. The 1974 recording remains richly atmospheric in its CD format, although the Scherzo could ideally be more sharply focused. The Groves recording of *The Hymn of Jesus* is on the whole finer than Boult's older, Decca account which has served collectors well over the years. Sir Charles Groves brings great sympathy and conviction to this beautiful and moving score, and the recording has transferred very well to CD.

The Evening Watch, H.159; 6 Choruses, H.186; Nunc dimittis, H.127; 7 Partsongs, H.162; 2 Psalms, H.117.

*** Hyp. CDA 66329. Holst Singers & O, Davan Wetton.

Hilary Davan Wetton's performancves of the comparatively austere but no less inspired *Evening Watch* creates a rapt, sustained pianissimo until the very closing bars, when the sudden expansion is quite thrilling. The *Six Choruses* for male voices show the composer at his most imaginative, while the comparable *Partsongs* for women often produce a ravishingly dreamy, mystical beauty. The final song, *Assemble all ye maidens*, is a narrative ballad about a lost love, and its closing section is infinitely touching. The performances are gloriously and sensitively sung and unerringly paced.

OPERA

(i) *At the Boar's Head, Op. 42* (complete); (ii) *The Wandering Scholar, Op. 50* (complete).

(M) *** EMI Dig./ADD CDM5 65127-2. (i) Langridge, Palmer, Ross, Tomlinson, Wilson-Johnson, Hall, Suart, George, RLPO, Groves; (ii) Burrowes, Tear, Rippon, Langdon, E. Op. Group, ECO, Bedford.

Finding that Shakespeare's lines went naturally to dances and tunes from Playford's collection, for his Falstaff opera, *At the Boar's Head*, Holst used that material on a libretto drawn entirely from the revelant scenes of *Henry IV, Parts I and II*. The result is busy-sounding in its emphasis on chattering comedy, and dramatically it is questionable. But on record the charm, colour and originality of the piece come over well. *The Wandering Scholar*, by contrast, works delightfully on stage, but on record its galumphing humour is less than sparkling. The recording comes from the mid-1970s, and the CD is something of a revelation in opening up the choral sound while still retaining the atmosphere and bloom of the analogue originals. An outstanding reissue in every way.

(i) *Savriti* (complete); (ii) *Dream City* (song-cycle, orch. Matthews).

(B) **(*) Hyp. Helios CDH 55042. (i) Langridge, Varcoe, Palmer, Hickox Singers; (ii) Kwella, City of L. Sinf., Hickox.

There are few chamber operas so beautifully scaled as Holst's *Savitri*. The simple story is taken from a Sanskrit source – Savitri, a woodcutter's wife, cleverly outwits Death, who has come to take her husband – and Holst with beautiful feeling for atmosphere sets it in the most restrained way. With light texture and many slow tempi, it is a work which can fall apart in an uncommitted performance, but the Hyperion version makes an excellent alternative to Imogen Holst's earlier recording with Dame Janet Baker, bringing the positive advantage of fine digital recording. Felicity Palmer is more earthy, more vulnerable as Savitri, her grainy mezzo well caught. Philip Langridge and Stephen Varcoe both sing sensitively with fresh, clear tone, though their timbres are rather similar. Hickox is a thoughtful conductor both in the opera and in the orchestral song-cycle arranged by Colin Matthews (with Imogen Holst's approval) from Holst's settings of Humbert Wolfe poems. Patrizia Kwella's soprano at times catches the microphone rather shrilly.

HOLT, Simon (born 1958)

. . . era madrugada . . .; Shadow Realm; Sparrow Night; (i) *Canciones.*

*** NMC D008. (i) Kimm; Nash Ens., Friend.

Regularly Simon Holt has found inspiration in Spanish sources, particularly Lorca, and two of these four pieces are fine examples – *. . . era madrugada*, a sinister evocation of a Lorca poem about a man found murdered in the hour just before dawn (*madrugada*). Like the other three pieces, it was written for the Nash Ensemble, who here under Lionel Friend respond superbly to Holt's virtuoso demands. Fiona Kimm is the formidable mezzo soloist in three Spanish settings, *Canciones*; but rather more approachable are the two highly atmospheric instrumental works, *Shadow Realm* and *Sparrow Night*, which round the disc off. These two also bring sinister nightmare overtones. The superb recording is engineered by Holt's fellow-composer, Colin Matthews.

HOLTEN, Bo (born 1948)

(i) *Clarinet Concerto* (1987); (ii) *Sinfonia Concertante for Cello & Orchestra* (1985–6).

*** Chan. 9272 (i) Schou; (ii) Zeuten; Danish National RSO; (i) Panula; (ii) Graf.

Bo Holten's *Clarinet Concerto* is certainly appealing. The *Sinfonia Concertante* comes from a broadcast of 1987 and is long on complexity (36 minutes 6 seconds) and short on substance, but there are sufficient moments of poetic vision to encourage one to return to it. It is played with great zest and conviction by Morten Zeuten (cellist of the Kontra Quartet), and the recording has exemplary presence and clarity.

HONEGGER, Arthur (1892–1955)

Cello Concerto.

** MDG 0321 0215-2. Schmid, NW German PO, Roggen – BLOCH: *Schelomo.* **

Honegger's delightful *Cello Concerto* is included in Rostropovich's retrospective anthology. Ulrich Schmid and the Nordwestdeutsche Philharmonie under the Swiss conductor Dominique Roggen give a dedicated account of it. All the same, at only 42 minutes' playing-time, this would be distinctly uncompetitive even at bargain price let alone premium rate.

(i) *Le Chant de Nigamon; Monopartita; Napoleon (film incidental music): Les Ombres.* (ii) *Mouvement symphonique No. 3; Pastorale d'été.* (i) *Phaedre: Prelude;*

Prélude, Fugue et postlude; The Tempest: Prélude. (iii) *Le Roi David.*

(B) *** Erato Ultima Dig./ADD 3984 24244-2 (2). (i) Monte Carlo PO, Constant; (ii) Bavarian RO; (iii) Eda-Pierre, Collard, Tappy, Desailly (narr.), Philippe Caillard Ch., Instrumental Ens; (ii; iii) Dutoit.

This Erato Ultima is outstanding value and highly recommendable. Charles Dutoit's *Le Roi David* (also available separately – see below) uses the original instrumental forces, not the full orchestra favoured by most of his rivals on record. It is a compelling performance of strong dramatic contrasts. Dutoit also gives an atmospheric and sympathetic account of *Pastorale d'été* and the *Mouvement symphonique No. 3*. The rest of the programme, directed by Marius Constant, is also well worth having. A warm welcome must be given to the music for *Phaedre*, which is highly imaginative and atmospheric. The earliest work included here is *Le Chant de Nigamon* (1917), a tone-poem concerning the fate of a native American chief who is burnt at the stake; and it is both graphic and powerful. The *Monopartita* is Honegger's last orchestral piece, coming from the same period as the *Fifth Symphony*. Again the invention is of the highest quality. Decent performances and acceptable, though not first-class digital sound.

Horace victorieux; Mermoz: La Traversée des Andes; Le Vol sur l'Atlantique; Pacific 231; Rugby; Pastorale d'été; La Tempête: Prélude.

*** DG (IMS) 435 438-2. Toulouse Capitole O, Plasson.

Horace victorieux is a noisy score but full of imaginative touches, as are the two scenes recorded here for the film *Mermoz*. We are also offered a beautifully languorous account of *Pastorale d'été*, among the best committed to disc, and Plasson's accounts of *Pacific 231* and *Rugby* are full of high spirits. His version of the *Prélude*, composed for a production of Shakespeare's *Tempest* in the late 1920s, is as fierce and violent as the composer's own pioneering Parlophone 78-r.p.m. disc. DG provide a realistic and natural sound-picture with plenty of detail. Strongly recommended.

Pacific 231; Pastorale d'été; Rugby; (i) *Christmas Cantata (Cantata de Noël).*

(M) **(*) EMI (ADD) CDM7 63944-2. O Nat. de l'ORTF, Martinon; (i) with Maurane & Ch. d'Oratorio Maîtrise de l'ORTF.

The Orchestre National de l'ORTF plays well for Jean Martinon, though we have heard more atmospheric accounts of *Pastorale d'été* (Martinon is not always responsive to pianissimo indications here). The *Cantata de Noël* is given a strong performance, though not even the expert French Radio choir manages the highly exacting demands of Honegger's difficult (and not always effective) choral writing. Generally these are good performances – although the programme offers short measure at 46 minutes.

Symphonies Nos. 1; 2 for Strings with Trumpet Obbligato; 3 (Symphonie liturgique); 4 (Deliciae Basilienses); 5 (Di tre re); 3 Symphonic Movements: Nos. 1, Pacific 231; 2, Rugby.

(B) *** Erato Ultima 3984 21340-2 (2). Bav. RSO, Dutoit.

Symphonies Nos. 1; 2 for Strings with Trumpet Obbligato; 3 (Symphonie liturgique); 4 (Deliciae Basilienses); 5 (Di tre re); 3 Symphonic Movements: Nos. 1, Pacific 231; 3. The Tempest: Prelude.

(M) *** Sup. (ADD) 11 1566-2 (2). Czech PO, Baudo.

Honegger's symphonies are currently much underrated. The *First* is a highly stimulating and rewarding piece: its level of energy is characteristic of the later symphonies. The *Second* is a probing, intense wartime composition that reflects something of the anguish Honegger felt during the German occupation. The *Third* (*Liturgique*) dates from the end of the war, while the *Fourth*, composed for Paul Sacher, makes use of Swiss folk material. Beneath its smiling surface there is a gentle vein of nostalgia and melancholy, particularly in the slow movement. The finale is sparkling and full of high spirits, though even this ends on a bitter-sweet note. The *Fifth* is a powerful work, inventive, concentrated and vital.

Although the performances are slightly uneven, Dutoit's Ultima Double is an appealingly economical way of acquiring excellent, modern, digital recordings (dating from the early 1980s). In Dutoit's hands the phrasing of the Bavarian orchestra in the beautiful slow movement of the *First* has both dignity and eloquence. He again produces very cultured string-playing in the dark, introspective *Symphony for Strings*, but here it is just a shade deficient in vitality and drive. The *Deliciae Basiliensis* also has rather measured tempi; however, this beautifully recorded performance serves to rekindle enthusiam for a much-underrated work whose sunny countenance and keen nostalgia bring unfailing delight. Dutoit then gives thoroughly idiomatic accounts of both the *Symphonie liturgique* and *Di tre re Symphonies*. In the *Fifth* he does not galvanize his orchestra into playing of the same volcanic fire and vitality that Serge Baudo secures from the Czech Philharmonic on Supraphon, but the Erato recording is fresher and more detailed. Room has been found for only two of the *Three Symphonic Movements*. Both *Pacific 231* and *Rugby* are well done; although the latter may be found a little genteel; the playing and recording are more than adequate compensation.

The Supraphon performances come from the 1960s, but they are more than merely serviceable. The sound comes up very well indeed and the playing of the Czech Philharmonic for Baudo is totally committed. The performance of the *Fifth Symphony* has never been surpassed (except possibly by the pioneering Munch recording) and has amazing presence and detail for its period.

Symphony No. 2 for Strings & Trumpet.

*** Delos DE 3121. Seattle SO, Schwarz – R. STRAUSS: *Metamorphosen;* WEBERN, arr. SCHWARZ: *Langsamer satz.* ***

In terms of recording quality, Schwarz's account can hold its own alongside the very best, and the playing of the Seattle strings is splendidly responsive. He is just a bit too slow at the very beginning, and the same reservation could be made against the slow movement, but there is plenty of atmosphere. Although it does not displace the Jansons or Karajan accounts or other recommendations, this performance is very fine indeed and will give much pleasure.

Symphony No. 2 for Strings & Trumpet Obbligato;
Monopartita; Mouvements symphoniques Nos. 1, Pacific
231; 2, Rugby; 3, Pastorale d'été.

*** Decca 455 352-2. Zurich Tonhalle O, Zinman.

David Zinman gets sensitive and subtly nuanced playing in
the symphony. *Monopartita* belongs to the period of the
Fifth Symphony. It was actually the composer's last orchestral
piece – and a powerfully concentrated one. The better known
orchestral evocations come off very well with a splendidly
powerful and purposeful *Pacific 231* which sounds as if it is
going to be in on time. Good performances, and though
Karajan remains a first choice for the symphony, the very
good Decca recording makes this disc thoroughly recommendable.

Symphonies Nos. 2 for Strings with Trumpet Obbligato; 3
(Symphonie liturgique).

⏺ (M) *** DG (ADD) 447 435-2. BPO, Karajan –
    STRAVINSKY: *Concerto in D.* ***

Symphonies Nos. 2 for Strings & Trumpet Obbligato; 3
(Liturgique); Pacific 231.

*** EMI CDC5 55122-2. Oslo PO, Jansons.

Karajan's accounts of these magnificent symphonies come
from 1973 and still remain in a class of their own. Not even
Munch's pioneering recording of the *Symphony No. 2* or its
successors comes near to it for sheer poetic intensity, and
the *Symphonie liturgique* has likewise never been surpassed.
It is luminous, incandescent and moving. The main rival is
the Jansons version with the Oslo Philharmonic on EMI,
but this is at full price. It certainly deserves its place as one
of DG's 'Legendary Originals'.

Jansons's account of these two symphonies has a virtuosity
and tonal sophistication that are almost the equal of the
Berliners' sumptuous string-tone in the *Symphony for*
Strings, and superb concentration and control. The
recording is magnificently rich and present, detail is splendidly focused. However, this has been withdrawn as we go
to press.

Symphonies Nos. 3; 5; Pacific 231.

*** Chan. 9176. Danish Nat. R. O, Järvi.

The *Symphonie liturgique* has stiff competition to meet in
the classic Karajan account, but Neeme Järvi and the Danish
orchestra serve it very well indeed, and the digital Chandos
recording is even more detailed and present, and certainly
fuller, than the DG version. Järvi's version of the *Fifth*
Symphony is also masterly, even if it does not match the
hell-for-leather abandon of Baudo's Supraphon set (see
above). But that is now over 30 years old and, though it still
sounds pretty amazing, this is undeniably superior.

Symphony No. 5 ('Di tre re').

(M) DG mono 449 748-2. Lamoureux O, Markevitch –
    MILHAUD: *Les Choéphores* (**); ROUSSEL: *Bacchus et*
    Ariane: Suite No. 2. **

Markevitch's account of the *Fifth Symphony* with the Orchestre Lamoureux was recorded in the Salle Wagram in
1957 – in mono. The sound has plenty of depth and good

perspective; it is a little set back, though there is no lack of
impact in tuttis, and there is plenty of space round the
instruments elsewhere. Markevitch generates plenty of atmosphere; his approach, which is lyrical, is strongly characterized but not a first choice.

Jeanne d'Arc au bûcher.

⏺ *** DG (IMS) 429 412-2. Keller, Wilson, Escourrou, Lanzi,
    Pollet, Command, Stutzman, Aler, Courtis, R. France Ch.,
    Fr. Nat. O, Ozawa.

(N) ** Cascavelle VEL 3024 (2) Petrovna, Lonsdale,
    Dominique, Maitrise des Haute-de-Seine, Ch. de
    Rouen-Haute-Normandie, O Symphonie Français,
    Petitgirard.

Honegger's 1935 setting of the Claudel poem is one of his
most powerful and imaginative works, full of variety of
invention, colour and textures. It is admirably served by
these forces, and in particular by the Joan of Marthe Keller.
The singers, too, are all excellent and the Choir and the six
soloists of the Maîtrise of Radio France are as top-drawer as
the orchestra. The DG engineers cope excellently with the
large forces and the acoustic of the Basilique de Saint-Denis.

Though strong on atmosphere, Laurent Petitgirard on
Cascavelle takes a rather more measured approach than
Ozawa. Petitgirard is a quarter-of-an-hour longer and although he gets generally good results from his forces and
has the benefit of first-rate recorded sound, the Ozawa is to
be preferred both artistically and as a recording.

The Cascavelle set offers two booklets, one in French, the
other in German, with 36 pages of artist and session photos
but no translations in English, Italian or Spanish. DG offered
a four-language booklet as well as an authoritative note by
Harry Hallbreich. That set also accommodates the work on
one CD, while this new version from Cascavelle runs to two.
Of course, this extraordinary piece still casts a strong spell
and if you can't find the Ozawa this is better than nothing.

Judith.

**(*) Van. 08 9054 71. Devrath, Christiansen, Milhaud (nar.),
    Salt Lake Symphonic Ch., Utah SO, Abravanel.

Judith is a dramatic vocal–orchestral concert work with
interspersed narration; some passages are marvellously
imaginative and atmospheric (the Choral invocation to pro-
tect Judith on her voyage through the valley of fear to cross
into the Assyrian lines is quite chilling). The performance
dates from 1964 and is totally committed; the only let-down
is in some of the choral singing, which could be stronger.
The work is short (just under 45 minutes) and it would have
added to the competitiveness of the issue to provide a fill-up.
But if it is short on quantity, it is long on musical and
dramatic interest.

Le Roi David (complete).

(M) *** Erato 2292 45800-2. Eda-Pierre, Collard, Tappy, Petel,
    Valere, Desailly, Philippe Caillard Ch., Instrumental Ens.,
    Dutoit.

(M) *** Van. 08.4038.71 [OVC 4038]. Davrath, Sorensen,
    Preston, Singher, Madeleine Milhaud, Utah University Ch.,
    Utah SO, Abravanel.

(BB) **(*) Naxos 8.553649. Martin, Fersen, Borst, Todorovitch, Ragon, Guedj, Ch. Régional Vittoria d'Ile de France, O de la Cité, Piquemal.

Both Dutoit's 1970 version and the Naxos set give us the original scoring of *Le Roi David* for seventeen instruments, the double-bass being the only string instrument. In 1923, Honegger scored it in the familiar concert version adding the narration which Naxos use here. Michel Piquemal's performance is a good one and though there are certain weaknesses (the tenor's vibrato will not be to all tastes), there is a good feeling for the dramatic shape of the work. Piquemal keeps a firm grip on the proceedings and the instrumentalists play with real commitment, while the recording is very adequate. However, now that Erato have restored the Dutoit set to the catalogue, that takes pride of place. It is a very compelling performance of strong dramatic coherence, and no one could guess that the excellent recording is thirty years old. It is also available as part of an Ultima collection – see above.

The Vanguard version using a full orchestration is remarkably vivid, well detailed and present, and the playing of the Utah Symphony under Maurice Abravanel is very fine. The recording also stands up well. Netania Davrath is excellent too, and so is Madeleine Milhaud, the composer's wife, as the Witch of Endor. Thoroughly recommendable.

HORNEMAN, Christian Frederik Emil (1840–1906)

Aladdin Overture; Ouverture héroïque: Helteliv; (i) *Gurre* (incidental music).

*** Chan. 9373. (i) Päevatalu, Danish R. Ch.; Danish RSO, Schønwandt.

Horneman is an altogether delightful composer, and the music recorded here deserves the widest dissemination. The incidental music to Holger Drachmann's play, *Gurre*, the major work on the disc is light-textured and full of charming, gracious invention and is beautifully scored. It is quite enchanting, particularly in such persuasive hands and the baritone, Guido Päevatalu, sings his simple strophic songs with great character. The other two pieces, *Helteliv* ('A Hero's Life') and the *Aladdin Overture* are the only purely orchestral works Horneman ever wrote: the *Aladdin Overture* is his first; it shows a real flair for colour. This is a most enjoyable disc, beautifully played and recorded. Strongly recommended.

HOTTETERRE, Jacques (1674–1763)

Pièces pour la flûte, Oeuvre II: *Echoes for Solo Flute; Suite in B flat for Recorder & Continuo; Suite in E min. for Transverse Flute & Continuo.* Oeuvre III: *Trio Sonatas: in C for 2 Oboes & Continuo; in D min. for 2 Recorders & Continuo; Suite in D for Transverse Flute & Continuo.* Oeuvre V: *Suite in E min. for Recorder & Continuo. Suite-Sonata in C for Oboe & Continuo.* Oeuvre VI: *Suite in G for 2 Transverse Flutes.* Oeuvre VII: *L'Art de Préluder:*

Préludes: for Recorder; for Transverse Flute; for Oboe; for Treble Viola da Gamba. Airs et brunettes: Arrangements of music by Mr Lambert, Lully, de Bousset etc.: *Fanfare et les Dieux for 3 Transverse Flutes.* (i) *Brunette: L'autre jour ma Cloris;* (i–ii) *Air de Mr Lambert: Goûtons un doux repos.* (iii) *Méthode pour La Musette;* Oeuvre X: *(Bourrée d'Achille; Contredanses: La Pharaonne; La Petite Janeton. Marche des dragons (Air); Musette de Mr. Clerambault; Menuet: La Badaut; Prélude et la Régence; Tes beaux yeux ma Nicole; Rigaudons).*

(B) *** Sony SB2K 62942 (2). Brüggen, Van Hauwe, Barthold Kuijken, Van Olmen, Haynes, Kuijken, Leonhardt, Gruskin; with (i) Kweksilber; (ii) Satoh (lute); (iii) Gruskin (musette).

The present pair of discs gathers together Hotteterre's complete wind music (written between 1708 and 1738). An original oboe and a musette, both made by the composer, are featured in their performance. The programme includes well over two hours of music and it should be approached with some caution. However, Hotteterre's invention is often resourceful, and the series of short dance-movements which make up the trio sonatas are certainly characterful. In his slow movements he languishes plaintively and with some individuality. The *Trio Sonatas* for a pair of oboes (with a bassoon featured in the continuo) and for two transverse flutes are texturally most diverting, and the latter also has some fine, expressive writing. The *Suite-Sonata* for oboe consists of five vignettes, none of which outlasts its welcome, and the similarly brief *Préludes* for various instruments have an attractive, improvisatory feeling. The closing surprise number for soprano (the sensitive Marjanne Kweksilber) and viola da gamba is quite haunting. Of the *Airs et Brunettes, L'autre jour ma Cloris* and the *Air de Mr Lambert* also feature the soprano voice, the latter with lute. They are both marked *Tendrement* and are genuinely touching. It is a pity the documentation does not include the words! The pieces for musette (which sounds like mini-bagpipes) are all piquant: they are offered as a series of interludes between the major works. The performances by a group of very distinguished soloists are of the highest calibre, and the recording is first class. It is very well, if rather closely, recorded.

(i) *6 Trio Sonatas, Op. 3;* (ii) *Suite for 2 Treble Recorders without Continuo in D min., Op. 4.*

(N) (M) ** Teldec (ADD) 3984 26797-2. (i) Boeke, Van Hauwe, Möller, Van Asperen; (ii) Brüggen, Boeke.

All the music gathered here was published in 1712. The *Trio Sonatas* are agreeable enough and are variously scored for pairs of treble recorders or voice flutes (Nos. 2 and 5), of which the latter works come off best here. Truth to tell, although the performances are authentic, complete with *notes inégales* (where the first note of two successive quavers is lengthened and the second correspondingly shortened), the sounds produced by Kees Boeke and Walter van Hauwe are somewhat pale. Their music-making is completely upstaged by the *Suite sans continuo*, where the far stronger personality of Frans Brüggen dominates the proceedings and brings this fine work vividly to life, especially its key movement – a splendid closing *Passacaille*. The recording is forward but truthful. This reissue would have been more enticing in Teldec's budget range.

HOVHANESS, Alan (born 1911)

(i) *Symphonies Nos. 1 (Exile), Op. 17/2;* (ii) *22 (City of Light), Op. 236;* (iii) *Bagatelles Nos. 1–4;* (i) *Fantasy on Japanese Woodprints, Op. 211;* (iv) *The Flowering Peach, Op. 125;* (i) *Prayer of St Gregory;* (v) *A Rose Tree Blossoms, Op. 246/4;* (iii) *String Quartet No. 4 (The Ancient Tree), Op. 208/2.*

(B) **(*) Delos Double DE 3700 (2). Seattle SO, (i) Schwarz; (ii) Hovhaness; (iii) Shanghai String Qt.; (iv) Ohio State University Concert Band, Brion; (v) St. John's Episcopel Cathedral Ch., Pearson.

The music on this CD is all melodic and easy to come to terms with. The persecution of Armenians in Turkey in the 1930s was the inspiration of the *Symphony No. 1:* its modal, oriental tonalities setting the scene quite hauntingly, while the violent outbursts sound distinctly gothic. *City of Light* is agreeable enough, if conventional, and the *Prayer of St Gregory,* essentially a chorale, has a certain innocent appeal. *The Flowering Peach* was a serio-comic retelling of the Noah's Ark story, performed on Broadway in 1954, for which Hovhaness wrote the incidental music; it has some atmosphere, but is not very interesting or memorable.

A Rose Tree Blossoms is a short but charmingly simple choral work, and the *Bagatelles* are unassuming, milk-and-water pieces. The *Fantasy on Japanese Woodprints* produces lots of bizarre sounds (horror-film-type noises), but to little effect. The performances and recordings are more than adequate and the two-for-the-price-of-one format makes this good value for the composer's admirers.

(i) *Symphonies Nos. 2 (Mysterious Mountain); 50 (Mount St Helens), Op. 360;* (ii) *53 (Star Dawn), Op. 377; Alleluia & Fugue; And God Created Great Whales; Celestial Fantasy; Meditation on Orpheus, Op. 155; Prelude & Quadruple Fugue;* (iii) *String Quartet No. 3 (Reflections on My Childhood), Op. 208/1; Suite from String Quartet No. 2.*

(B) *** Delos DE 3711 (2). (i) Seattle SO, Schwarz; (ii) Ohio State University Concert Band, Brion; (iii) Shanghai String Qt.

The *Symphony No. 2* begins with pastoral, modal writing, leading to a central fugal climax and returning to rich, expressive serenity. More action-packed is the extravagant *Mount St Helens Symphony,* with an awe-inspiring volcano eruption in the finale (with some quite shattering orchestral effects), as well as the genuinely evocative *Spirit Lake* central movement. The *Star Dawn Symphony,* evoking travelling in space towards heaven, is quite effectively depicted, though after the allegro climax, the following slow movement lets the listener down.

The *String Quartets* are attractive with some nice touches, without being really memorable. But the most sensational piece here is *And God Created Great Whales,* which reaches a hugely spectacular climax and interpolates tapes of actual song of the humpbacked whale. The effect is very grandiose indeed and everyone rises to the occasion, including both the whales and the recording engineers. The performances are dedicated and very well presented so this is excellent value if the musical scenario appeals.

HOWELLS, Herbert (1892–1983)

Concerto for String Orchestra; Elegy for Viola, String Quartet & Strings; Suite for String Orchestra; Serenade for Strings.

⚘ *** Chan. 9161. City of L. Sinf., Hickox.

These three splendid and inspired works are all in the great and ongoing tradition of English string-writing. The *Concerto* (1938) opens with a great burst of energy, but the secondary theme is hauntingly nostalgic, and the elegiac character of the slow movement establishes the music's character. That it owes a debt to Elgar is no accident, for the work is dedicated jointly to him and the composer's only son, whose loss is also remembered in the *Hymnus paradisi.* The viola *Elegy,* written much earlier (1917) is clearly modelled on Vaughan Williams's *Tallis Fantasia,* yet it is masterly in its own right and very moving. The delicate one-movement *Serenade,* which also features a solo quartet, dates from the same year. The *Allegro deciso* and *Rondo* which open and close the *Suite* (1938) are rhythmically extrovert in a Holstian 'St Paul's' manner, but then after a gentle, rapturous *Siciliano,* the Minuet opens with a deeper voiced pizzicato. The performances here are exemplary, superbly played and conducted by Hickox with deep commitment and understanding. The recording is warm, sonorous and clearly detailed.

(i) *Piano Concertos Nos. 1 in C min., Op. 4* (completed Rutter); *2 in C, Op. 39. Penguinski.*

(N) Chan. 9874. Shelley, BBC SO, Hickox.

Long buried, Herbert Howells's *First Piano Concerto,* with its final pages now restored by John Rutter, is a revelation. As one of Stanford's favourite pupils, Howells wrote this big bravura work in 1913, but a poor first performance put it in limbo. With Grieg and Rachmaninov among the models, the piano writing is bold and powerful, full of strong themes set in a warmly English idiom. Howard Shelley as soloist and Richard Hickox as conductor hold the expansive structure superbly together. The *Second Concerto* of 1925, more modest in scale but more advanced in idiom with its echoes of Debussy, Ravel and Stravinsky, is equally attractive, and the jolly occasional piece *Penguinski* makes a delightful encore.

(i) *Concerto for String Orchestra;* (ii) *Hymnus paradisi.*

(M) **(*) EMI (ADD) CDM5 67119-2. (i) LPO, Boult; (ii) Harper, Tear, Bach Ch., King's College Ch., New Philh. O, Willcocks.

Boult's understanding and vigorous performance of the *Concerto for Strings* – a work dedicated to him – is coupled here with the *Hymnus paradisi;* both were written in memory of the composer's son. It is a dignified and beautifully wrought piece but also, and more importantly, is both moving and powerful. Willcocks's performance is eloquent and warmly persuasive within the glowing Kingsway Hall acoustics, but even so it does not match Handley's later account on Hyperion (see below) in intensity of feeling.

(i) *3 Dances for Violin & Orchestra. Suite for Orchestra, the 5 'B's;* (ii) *In Green Ways* (song cycle).

*** Chan. 9557. (i) Mordkovitch; (ii) Kenny; LSO, Hickox.

The inspired suite *The Five 'B's* celebrates the composer's musician friends and colleagues at the Royal College of Music at the beginning of the 1914–18 war. As such it has something in common with Elgar's *Enigma Variations*, although Howells clearly identified each dedicatee. Two of them succumbed: Ivor Gurney, who was badly gassed and Frances 'Bunny' Warren, a viola player, who died at Mons. Gurney (nicknamed 'Bartholemew') is remembered with a movingly passionate *Lament*, and Bunny is personified in a delicate *Minuet/Mazurka*, at times disconsolate, but with as blithe pastoral counterpart. 'Blissy' (Arthur Bliss) inspires a dainty, chimerical *Scherzo* – with the piano an orchestral soloist – yet with a balancing touch of nostalgia reminiscent of Elgar. These shorter evocations are framed by an exuberant *Overture* with a *nobilmente* lyrical expansiveness representing the composer himself ('Bublum') and the finale ('Benjee' – Arthur Benjamin), which begins lightheartedly but ends grandiloquently, recalls the composer's own themes from the overture. The *Three Dances for Violin and Orchestra*, another wartime work (1915), are in the best English folk/pastoral tradition, with Lydia Mordkovitch as a brilliant violin soloist and the song-cycle, *In green ways*, with Yvonne Kenny – also include poignant elegies. The English countryside is strikingly evoked in this group of five songs, using lyrics by Shakespeare and Goethe. Yvonne Kenny sings the whole group most affectingly and Richard Hickox and the LSO are ardent and communicate advocates of all this fine music. A highly recommendable disc, very well recorded indeed.

(i) *Fantasia; Threnody* (both for cello and orchestra). *The King's Herald; Paradise Rondel; Pastoral Rhapsody; Procession.*

*** Chan. 9410. (i) Welsh; LSO, Hickox.

The most personal works here are the *Fantasia* and *Threnody*, both for cello and orchestra, together forming a sort of rhapsodic concerto. Howells was reflecting his anguish over the death of his ten-year-old son, with flashes of anger punctuating the elegiac lyricism. The *Threnody*, simpler in its lyricism, was probably planned as the slow movement of a three-movement *Cello Concerto*. The other major piece is the *Pastoral Rhapsody*, written in 1923. Similarly pastoral but predominantly vigorous, the *Paradise Rondel* of 1925 is full of sharp contrasts, with one passage offering clear echoes of the *Russian Dance* from *Petrushka*. The collection opens with the boldly extrovert *King's herald*, bright with Waltonian fanfares. *Procession* brings more echoes of *Petrushka*, again reflecting Howells's response to the Diaghilev Ballets Russes' appearances in London. Helped by rich, atmospheric sound, Richard Hickox draws performances that are both brilliant and warmly persuasive from the

LSO, with Moray Welsh a movingly expressive soloist in the concertante works.

CHAMBER MUSIC

Oboe Sonata.

(B) *** Hyp. Helios CDH 55008. Francis, Dickenson – BOUGHTON: *Pastoral;* HARTY: *3 Pieces;* RUBBRA: *Sonata.* ***

Howell's *Oboe Sonata* is a florid work, but Sarah Francis surmounts its complexities very musically, echoed by her pianist, Peter Dickenson. She provides a full, singing tone. The balance is forward, within a resonant acoustic, and it is important not to set the volume control too high.

In Gloucestershire (String Quartet No. 3).

(N) (B) *** Hyp. Helios CDH 55045. Divertimenti – DYSON: *3 Rhapsodies.* ***

Howells's *Third String Quartet* had a chequered history. The first 1916 version was lost on a train. A second version then also disappeared, but was reconstructed in the early 1960s. A third definitive version (full score and parts) was discovered in the Library of the Royal College of Music and is here recorded. The music is permeated with the spirit of Vaughan Williams; the opening movement, treating the first violin as a soloist, mistily yet radiantly evokes the Gloucester countryside. After the wind-swept *Scherzo*, the slow movement is elegiac; but the finale, jauntily alive and folksy in flavour, is drawn back eventually to the gently atmospheric mood of the work's opening. The performance by Divertimenti is deeply expressive and beautifully played and recorded.

PIANO MUSIC

The Chosen Tune; Cobbler's Hornpipe; Gadabout; Lambert's Clavichord: Lambert's Fireside (Hughes' Ballet; De la Mare's Pavanne; Sir Hugh's Galliard); Musica sine nomine; 3 Pieces, Op. 14; Sarum Sketches; Slow Dance (Double the Cape); Snapshots, Op. 30; Sonatina.

*** Chan. 9273. Fingerhut.

Howells has a good feeling for keyboard sonorities and the invention among these works is remarkably high. The high-spirited writing, as in *Gadabout* (1928) and *Jackanapes* (the third of the *Three Pieces*, Op. 14), has a Grainger-like rhythmic exuberance, while Howells can also be touchingly solemn, as in the dark processional which is the last item of Op. 14 or in the second of the *Sarum Sketches*. The *Sonatina* is astonishingly fresh, one of his very best works, spikily high-spirited and with a thoughtfully tender slow movement marked *serioso ma teneramente*, with something of Ravel in its thinking. Throughout this highly stimulating and enjoyable programme this fine pianist readily catches the composer's moods, light or grave, and she is most realistically recorded.

VOCAL MUSIC

3 Children's Songs (Eight o'clock, the postman's knock; The days are clear; Mother, shake the cherry-tree); 3 Folksongs (I will give my love an apple; The brisk young widow; Cendrillon); 4 French Chansons, Op. 29; A Garland for de la Mare (group of 11 unpublished songs); In Green Ways (song-cycle), Op. 43; Peacock Pie (song-cycle), Op. 33; 2 South African Settings (Loneliness; Spirit of freedom); 4 Songs, Op. 22 (There was a maiden; Madrigal; The widow bird; Girl's song). Miscellaneous songs: An old man's lullaby; Come sing and dance; Flood; Gavotte; Goddess of the Night; Here she lies; King David; The little boy lost; Lost love; Mally O!; The mugger's song; O garlands, hanging by the doors; O my deir hert; Old Meg; Old skinflint; The restful branches.

*** Chan. 9185/6 (2). Dawson; Pierard; Ainsley; Luxon; Drake.

This two-disc collection covers virtually all of Howells's completed songs. One of the driving forces behind the project is the pianist Julius Drake, who plays the accompaniments with a consistent rhythmic spring and a sense of fantasy. Two of the finest songs are among the best known, King David and Come sing and dance, and such a group of miniatures as Peacock Pie, settings of Walter de la Mare written early in Howells's career, have a characteristic point and charm. Far more searching are the 11 much longer settings of de la Mare poems. Among the other fascinating examples are two South African settings to words by the Afrikaans poet, Jan Celliers, including one still very topical, Spirit of freedom. The sopranos, Catherine Pierard and Lynne Dawson, both have aptly fresh, English-sounding voices, with John Mark Ainsley as the thoughtful tenor and Benjamin Luxon the characterful baritone, a fine team, even though the recording brings out some unevenness in the vocal production of both Ainsley and Luxon.

Chichester Service: Magnificat; Nunc dimittis. A Hymn for Saint Cecilia; Like as the hart desireth the waterbrooks; My eyes for beauty pine; O salutaris Hostia; Salve Regina.

(*) ASV CDDCA 851. Went, Ch. of The Queen's College, Oxford, Owens – LEIGHTON: Crucifixus pro nobis etc. *

Howells is nearly always at his best in his choral work and the pieces gathered here are all worth having. Neither in terms of ensemble nor intonation is The Queen's College, Oxford, choir in the first league, but the performances are committed and give pleasure, and they are well recorded. The disc has the advantage of coupling rarely heard music of quality by Kenneth Leighton.

Collegium regale: canticles; Behold, O God our defender; Like as the hart; St Paul's service: Canticles. Take him to earth for cherishing. (Organ): Psalm prelude: De profundis; Master Tallis's testament.

*** Hyp. CDA 66260. St Paul's Cathedral Ch., Scott; Dearnley.

All the music here is of high quality and the recording gives it resonance, in both senses of the word, with the St Paul's acoustic well captured by the engineers. A fine representation of a composer who wrote in the mainstream of English church and cathedral music but who had a distinct voice of his own.

Collegium Regale: Office of Holy Communion; Requiem. St Paul's Service: Magnificat; Nunc dimittis. Motets: Like as the hart; Long, long ago; Take him earth. Organ music: Paean; Rhapsody No. 3.

(BB) *** Naxos 8.554659. St John's College Ch., Robinson; Farrington.

No composer this century has surpassed Herbert Howells in the beauty and imagination of his Anglican church music. Naxos here offers a generous selection in seductive performances from the Choir of St John's College, Cambridge, that match and almost surpass any previous versions. This will have King's Choir down the road looking to its laurels, helped by immaculate sound at once atmospheric and cleanly focused.

Collegium regale: Te Deum & jubilate; Office of Holy Communion; Magnificat & Nunc dimittis. Preces & Responses I & II; Psalms 121 & 122; Take him, earth for cherishing. Rhapsody for Organ, Op. 17/3.

⊛ *** Decca 430 205-2. Williams, Moore, King's College, Cambridge, Ch., Cleobury.

Here is an unmatchable collection of the settings inspired by the greatest of our collegiate choirs, King's College, Cambridge, presented in performances of heartwarming intensity in that great choir's 1989 incarnation. The boy trebles in particular are among the brightest and fullest ever to have been recorded with this choir. The disc sensitively presents the sequence in what amounts to liturgical order, with the service settings aptly interspersed with responses, psalm-chants, anthems with organ introits and voluntaries all by Howells. Even those not normally attracted by Anglican church music should hear this.

Hymnus Paradisi, An English Mass.

*** Hyp. CDA 66488. Kennard, Ainsley, RLPO Ch., RLPO, Handley.

In Hymnus Paradisi Handley conveys a mystery, a tenderness rather missing from the previous recording, made by Sir David Willcocks for EMI (see above), strong as that is. Handley's soloists bring a moving compassion, as in the haunting setting of the 23rd Psalm which makes up the third movement. The Hyperion digital recording is warm, full and atmospheric. An English Mass is simpler yet also hauntingly beautiful.

Missa Sabrinensis.

*** Chan. 9348. Watson, Jones, Hill, Maxwell, L. Symphony Ch., LSO, Rozhdestvensky.

Rozhdestvensky here conducts a passionate account of what in many ways is the most powerful of all the composer's major works. There is little of the restraint that is typical of much of Howells' choral writing. Rather he exploits the lushest, most passionate elements in his richly post-impressionist style, and he hardly lets up over the whole span. It would be hard to imagine a more inspired performance than Rozhdestvensky's. Over the incandescent singing of the choir, the four excellent soloists give radiant performances, with the golden-toned soprano, Janice Watson, regularly crowning the mood of ecstasy in her solos. Full, glowing, atmospheric sound to match.

(i) (Organ): *Master Tallis's Testament; 6 Psalm-preludes, Set 1, Op. 32/1–3; Set 2 /1–3; 3 Rhapsodies, Op. 17/1–3;* (ii) Anthems: *Behold O God our defender; Like as the hart. Collegium regale: Jubilate & Te Deum. Motet: Take him, earth for cherishing. St Paul's Services: Magnificat & Nunc dimittis.*

(B) ** Hyp. Dyad CDD 22038 (2). Dearnley (organ); (ii) with St Paul's Cathedral Choir, Scott.

A good deal of the music here is for organ and there are only two items (about 12 minutes in all) from the *St Paul's Service*, which draws the eye as the heading on the frontispiece of this Dyad Double. Although the organ pieces provide contrast between the choral items, the *Psalm-preludes* are mostly gentle pieces, improvisatory in feeling (Op. 32/3 with its repeated bass is the most striking), and although the *Rhapsodies* are more flamboyant, their focus is not helped by the wide reverberation. The piece inspired by Tallis is the most individual, and some listeners may feel, like us, that the programme is a little overweighted with organ repertoire. Among the choral highlights are the two fine canticles associated with the *Collegium regale* and the eloquent motet, *Take him to earth* which was dedicated to John F. Kennedy. The anthems are splendid too, and all the choral music is of high quality. The recording gives it resonance in both sense of the word, with the St Paul's acoustic well captured by the engineers.

(Organ) *Psalm-prelude, Set 1/1; Paen; Prelude: Sine nomine. (Vocal): Behold, O God our defender; Here is the door; Missa Aedi Christi: Kyrie; Credo; Sanctus; Benedictus; Agnus Dei; Gloria. Sing lullaby; A spotless rose; Where wast thou?.*

(M) *** CRD 3455. New College, Oxford, Ch., Higginbottom (organ).

A further collection of the music of Herbert Howells, splendidly sung by Edward Higginbottom's fine choir, while he provides the organ interludes in addition. Among the shorter pieces, the carol-anthem *Sing lullaby* is especially delightful, and the programme ends with the motet *Where wast thou?*, essentially affirmative, in spite of the question posed at the opening. Beautifully spacious sound makes this a highly rewarding collection.

Requiem. Motets: The House of the Mind; A Sequence for St Michael.

*** Chan. 9019. Finzi Singers, Spicer – VAUGHAN WILLIAMS: *Lord thou hast been our refuge* etc. ***

Requiem; Take him, earth, for cherishing.

*** United Recordings 88033. Barber, Field, Johnstone, Angus, Vasari, Jeremy Backhouse – MARTIN: *Mass*. ***

Howells' *Requiem* is the work which prepared the way for *Hymnus Paradisi*, providing some of the material for it. For unaccompanied chorus, it presents a gentler, compact view

of what in the big cantata becomes powerfully expansive. The Finzi singers, 18-strong, give a fresh and atmospheric, beautifully moulded performance, well coupled with two substantial motets with organ by Howells as well as choral pieces by Vaughan Williams.

On United the soloists and Vasari, a choir conducted by Jeremy Backhouse, are absolutely first class and give a well-nigh exemplary performance, possibly finer than its immediate rival. Doubtless couplings will resolve the matter of choice. The present disc offers the *Requiem* in harness with another Mass from the inter-war years by Frank Martin.

Stabat Mater.

*** Chan. 9314. Archer, L. Symphony Ch., LSO, Rozhdestvensky.

The *Stabat Mater* was Howells' last major work. Though the ecstasy is not as consistently sustained as in the earlier *Missa Sabrinensis*, with many more passages of hushed devotion, one registers with new intensity the agony of St John the Divine at the foot of the Cross, the companion of the Virgin Mary. The saint is personified in the tenor solos, here sung superbly by Neill Archer with a clear, heady tone, starting with his first thrilling entry on *O quam tristis*. As in the *Missa*, Rozhdestvensky proves the most passionate advocate, magnetically leading one through the whole rich score. Though ensemble sometimes suffers, it is a small price to pay for such thrusting, spontaneous-sounding conviction. Glowing, rich sound.

HUME, Tobias (*c.* 1575–1645)

Captain Humes Poeticall Musick (1607) (music for viols, lute and voice).

(BB) *** Naxos 8.55416/7 (available separately). Les Voix Humains.

Tobias Hume was a mercenary who served in both the Swedish and Russian armies. Relatively little is known about him. The dedications of his two collections, the *First Part of Ayres* (1605) and the *Poeticall Musick* (1607), were designed to court favour, the first from the Earl of Pembroke and the second from Queen Anne. He was a champion of the viol as opposed to the lute, and the pieces recorded here vindicate him. It is obvious that he was an accomplished composer and this excellently recorded Canadian ensemble prove persuasive advocates. A most enjoyable and welcome addition to the catalogue.

HUMFREY, Pelham (1647–74)

Verse anthems: *By the waters of Babylon; Have mercy on me, O God; Hear, O Heav'ns; Hear my prayer, O God; Hear my crying, O God; Lift up your heads; Like as the hart; O give thanks unto the Lord; O Lord my God.*

*** HM HMU 907053. Deam, Minter, Covey-Crump, Potter, Thomas, Clare College, Cambridge, Ch., Romanesca, McGegan.

Pelham Humfrey (or Humphrey) was sent abroad at the

expense of the royal purse of Charles II to study in France and Italy. He brought back from Italy (and from Lully in France) a thorough absorption of the operatic style, and his verse anthems are remarkably dramatic and powerfully expressive, using soloists almost like operatic characters. Nicholas McGegan's fine performances reflect this histrionic dimension, helped by his soloists who at times approach stylistic boundaries in their performance of what is essentially devotional music, even if intensely felt. With a highly sensitive instrumental contribution from the excellent Romanesca, this collection (about half of Humfrey's surviving output) is very freshly recorded and is strongly recommended to the adventurous collector.

HUMMEL, Johann (1778–1837)

Bassoon Concerto in F.

*** Chan. 9656. Popov, Russian State SO, Polyansky –
  MOZART; WEBER: Bassoon Concertos. ***

A first-class modern recording of Hummel's genial *Bassoon Concerto* was needed, and Valeri Popov fits the bill, twinklingly good-natured and elegant, especially in the swinging 6/8 finale. His woody timbre (a French instrument perhaps) is most appealing, and Polyansky provides a warmly polished accompaniment, helped by the resonant, but not clouded, recording.

(i; ii) Mandolin Concerto in G; (iii) Trumpet Concerto in G; (iv; ii) Gesellschafts Rondo in D for Piano & Orchestra, Op. 117; (v; ii) Introduction, Theme & Variations in F for Oboe & Orchestra, Op. 102. (vi) Flute Sonatas Nos. 1–3; Grand rondo brillante in G, Op. 126.

(B) *** Erato Ultima Dig./ADD 3984 25596-2 (2).
    (i) Saint-Clivier, (ii) Pailliard CO, Paillard; (iii) André, O de Paris Ens., Wallez; (iv) Queffélec; (v) Chambon;
    (vi) Adoran, Lee.

The *Mandolin Concerto* is ingenuous but pleasing, dependent on a personable soloist and a felicitous recording balance, both of which are supplied here. The inestimable Maurice André has recorded the famous *Trumpet Concerto E flat* many times; this account dates from 1981, when his timbre was particularly warm, flattered by the comparatively resonant digital recording. The *Gesellschafts Rondo* is quite a find, a most impressive piece, played with flair by Anne Queffélec; the variations for oboe are comparatively facile, but also presented with agreeable brilliance. The *Flute Sonatas* are discussed below: the performances here are every bit as expert and pleasing as those on the separate Naxos anthology, and are well recorded (though the sound is analogue).

Piano Concertos: in A min., Op. 85; B min., Op. 89.

*** Chan. 8507. Hough, ECO, Thomson.
(B) *** Discover DICD 920117. Protopopescu, Slovak R. New PO, Rahbari.

The *A minor* is Hummel's most often-heard piano concerto, never better played, however, than by Stephen Hough on this prize-winning Chandos disc. The coda is quite stunning;

it is not only his dazzling virtuosity that carries all before it but also the delicacy and refinement of colour he produces. The *B minor*, Op. 89, is more of a rarity, and is given with the same blend of virtuosity and poetic feeling which Hough brings to its companion. He is given expert support by Bryden Thomson and the ECO – and the recording is first class.

At bargain price Discover offers an outstanding alternative coupling. Well accompanied by the Slovak Radio New Philharmonic, Dana Protopopescu, always sounding fresh and spontaneous, plays with lightness, point and poetry. On her smaller scale, she even rivals Stephen Hough , though Hough is more impulsive.

Trumpet Concerto in E.

*** Ph. 420 203-2. Hardenberger, ASMF, Marriner – HAYDN;
  HERTEL; STAMITZ: Concertos. ***

Trumpet Concerto in E flat.

(M) *** Sony SMK 37846. Marsalis, Nat. PO, Leppard –
  HAYDN: Concerto ***; L. MOZART: Concerto ***.
*** EMI CDC5 55231-2. André, Franz Liszt O, Budapest, Rolla –
  HERTEL; HAYDN: Trumpet Concertos ***. MARCELLO:
  Concerto in D min. ***

Hummel's *Trumpet Concerto* is usually heard in the familiar brass key of E flat, but the brilliant Swedish trumpeter, Håkan Hardenberger, uses the key of E, which makes it sound brighter and bolder than usual. Neither he nor Marriner miss the genial lilt inherent in the dotted theme of the first movement, and the finale captivates the ear with its high spirits and easy bravura. This is the finest version of the piece in the catalogue, but it is also available on a Duo (464 028-2) collection of trumpet concertos with the coupling listed here and many more besides.

Maurice André's latest digital recording dates from 1994. His playing has lost none of its charisma; the tone is noticeably more open (more 'trumpety') here than in the earlier Erato version (above), the phrasing and articulation if anything more stylish. He is helped by a warm but nicely scaled accompaniment from Rolla and his excellent Budapest orchestra.

Marsalis gives a fine account of Hummel's *Concerto*, but does not quite catch its full *galant* charm. In matters of bravura, however, he cannot be faulted; he relishes the sparkling finale.

Piano Quintet in E flat, Op. 87.

(B) **(*) Hyp. Dyad CDD 22008 (2). Schubert Ens. of L. –
  SCHUBERT: Trout Quintet; SCHUMANN: Piano Quintet;
  Piano Quartet. **(*)

A strong account of an impressive work from the Schubert Ensemble of London, who approach the piece as one in the classical mainstream rather than a *galant* entertainment. There is plenty of energy and commitment, and the brief *Largo* is made a touching interlude; only the finale (admittedly marked *Allegro agitato*) might seem too strongly driven and with not enough balancing elegance. The recording has fine immediacy.

Piano Trios Nos. 1–7.

*** MDG MDG 3307/8 (2). Trio Parnassus.

Piano Trios Nos. 1 in E flat, Op. 12; 2 in F, Op. 22; 3 in G, Op. 35; 7 in E flat, Op. 96.

*** Meridian CDE 84350. Triangulus.

Piano Trios Nos. 1, Op. 12; 3, Op. 35; 4, Op. 65; 7, Op. 96.

(B) *** Ph. 446 077-2. Beaux Arts Trio.

Piano Trios Nos. 1 in E flat, Op. 12; 5 in E, Op. 83; 7 in E flat, Op. 96.

*** Chan. 9529. Borodin Trio.

Hummel's *Piano Trios* span a period of two decades, the first was published in 1804, and the last in the early 1820s. All show the fluency, elegant craftsmanship and easy melodic flow for which he is admired in his better known concertos. Comparing the first with the last of the trios shows no marked development of style of the kind one expects with the very greatest composers, but all seven of these works are individually rewarding in their diverse ways, and the composer's fund of ideas never dries up for a moment. The Trio Parnassus play throughout with consistent zest and spontaneity and they obviously enjoy the simple lyrical melodies. They are admirably recorded and this box can carry a strong recommendation.

All these single-disc collections share the first and last of the Trios, each among the finest of the series, and each set of performances is enjoyable in different ways. Rostislav Dubinsky, leading the Borodin Trio, is a bolder, more temperamental player than Alison Kelly of Triangulus. Generally the Triangulus performance is more relaxed than the Borodin's, and we are inclined to prefer the stronger pulse of the latter's first movement; but in the finale they tend almost to rush, and here Triangulus score a point or two. The opening movement of the Op. 96 immediately produces the dotted rhythms which are Hummel's special trademark, while the simplicity of the melody at the heart of the *Poco Larghetto* is very winning in both performances; in the closing *Rondo alla Russe*, the Borodin account is that bit stronger. The finale of Op. 85 (only included by Chandos) is also very catchy; however Triangulus offer an extra work, and the closing Rondo of Op. 35 sparkles delightfully and shows the Meridian players at their most captivating.

However, the Philips performances have all the vitality and finesse we expect from the Beaux Arts team, and the recording is perfectly balanced and very real and present. The originals date from as recently as 1997, and this bargain reissue rather sweeps the board in this repertoire.

Septet in D min., Op. 74.

(M) *** CRD 3344. Nash Ens. – BERWALD: *Septet.* ***

Hummel's *Septet* is an enchanting and inventive work with a virtuoso piano part, expertly dispatched here by Clifford Benson. A fine performance and excellent recording make this a highly desirable issue, particularly in view of the enterprising coupling.

Flute Sonatas Nos. 1 in G, Op. 2/2; 2 in D, Op. 50; 3 in A, Op. 64; (i) Flute Trio in A, Op. 78. Grand rondeau brillant for Flute & Piano in G, Op. 126.

(BB) *** Naxos 8.553473. Daoust, Picard with (i) Dolin.

Hummel's elegant, easygoing melodic style seems custom-made for the flute, and his three lightweight sonatas are lacking in neither diversity nor charm. The *Grand rondeau brillant* is entertainingly like a Weber display piece. The performances on Naxos are both sunny and technically felicitous, and are warmly recorded. The *Trio* is an ingenuous set of variations on a Russian folk tune, which lends itself to sparkling divisions. Here there is plenty of bustle before the work ends peacefully.

String Quartets: in C; in G; in E flat, Op. 30/1–3.

*** Hyp. CDA 66568. Delmé Qt.

Hummel's three quartets are closer to Haydn than Beethoven, though the first of the set in C major with its impressive opening *Adagio e mesto* in the minor key, and fine *Adagio*, obviously leans towards the influence of the later composer, while the audacious quotation of *Comfort ye* from Handel's *Messiah* in the preceding *Andante*, brings yet another example of Hummelian sleight of hand. In short these are fascinating works, highly inventive, and crafted with the composer's usual fluent charm. They are splendidly played by the Delmé group, who provide plenty of vitality and warmth. The Hyperion recording is fresh and believable.

String Quartet in G, Op. 30/2.

*(*) Testament mono SBT 1085. Hollywood Qt – HAYDN: *Quartet No. 72*; MOZART: *Quartet No. 17.* **(*)

Hummel's charming *G major Quartet* comes with the first half of a 1957 Festival Hall concert. This performance was recorded two years earlier in a Hollywood studio and, though dazzlingly played, is a bit shrill.

Violin Sonatas: in E flat, Op. 5/3; in D, Op. 50; Nocturne, Op. 99.

*** Amon Ra (ADD) CD-SAR 12. Holmes, Burnett.

Ralph Holmes's violin timbre is bright and the Graf fortepiano under the fingers of Richard Burnett has plenty of colour and does not sound clattery. Burnett has a chance to catch the ear in the finale of the *D major Sonata* when he uses the quaintly rasping cembalo device (without letting it outstay its welcome). The *Nocturne* is an extended piece (nearly 16 minutes) in variation form. A thoroughly worthwhile issue, 'authentic' in the most convincing way, which shows this engaging composer at his most assured and inventive.

Piano Sonatas Nos. 1 in C, Op. 2/3; 2 in E flat, Op. 13; 3 in F min., Op. 20.

(BB) *(*) Discover DICD 920237. Protopopescu (piano).

Piano Sonatas Nos. 2 in E flat, Op. 13; 3 in F min., Op. 20; 5 in F sharp min., Op. 81.

(BB) *** Naxos 8.553296. Chang (piano).

Hummel's piano sonatas at their best can match those of Haydn, and the *E flat major* work (1805) in Hae-won Chang's hands makes an attractive introduction to the genre. The more thoughtful first movement of the *F minor Sonata* (1807) is interrupted by a recurring brief *Adagio*, the central

Adagio maestoso is more imposing, with the tension released in the bravura finale. The *F sharp minor Sonata* is a splendid work, nearer to Beethoven than Haydn, its kernel a memorable *Largo con molto expessione*, to be followed by a vigorous bravura finale. This is the first of a Naxos series, and very welcome it is when this accomplished Korean pianist is right inside the music, which she plays very persuasively indeed. She is excellently recorded.

Dana Protopopescu gives us the earliest sonata of all, from 1792, and begins very boldly and cleanly. Her approach is uncompromisingly classical and she begins the *F minor* with very crisp articulation verging on staccato. Throughout she presents these works in sharp focus rather than trying to coax the music or charm the listener. Unfortunately, the Discover recording does not help her: it is rather shallow and clattery.

Piano Sonata No. 2, Op. 13; La bella capricciosa (Polonaise), Op. 55, Caprice, Op. 49; La contemplazione (Una fantasia piccola), Op. 107/3; Hungarian Rondo, Op. 107/6; Rondo, Op. 11; Variations on a Theme from Gluck's Armide, Op. 57; Rondo Op.11.

(N) *** Chan. 9807. Shelley.

Starting with a wittily pointed account of the *Rondo, Opus 11*, Hummel's best-known piece, Howard Shelley gives the most persuasive accounts of piano music by this leading virtuoso of his time, a composer so well thought of that he succeeded Haydn as Kapellmeister to Prince Esterházy. He may never have developed towards free romanticism as Beethoven, Schubert and Weber did, but such stylish performances as Shelley's, beautifully recorded, bring many delights, as in the sparkling *Gluck Variations*, the well-constructed *Sonata Opus 13* and the late polka-like *Hungarian Rondo*.

Mass in B flat, Op. 77; Tantum ergo (after Gluck).

*** Koch 3-7117-2. Westminster Oratorio Ch., New Brunswick CO, Floreen.

Hummel wrote his *Mass in B flat* while working for the Esterházys. It is an unpretentious work of great charm and a real discovery. The Westminster Choir (from the College of that name in Princeton, New Jersey) give exactly the right kind of modest performance, emphasizing the work's warm lyricism; the conductor, while not lacking vigour, is careful not to be too forceful at climaxes. The orchestral accompaniment is nicely in scale, and the recording, though not crystal clear, has the most agreeable ambience.

HUMPERDINCK, Engelbert

(1854–1921)

Christmas Lieder: Altdeutsches Weihnachtslied; Christkindleins Wiegenlied; Das Licht der Welt; Der Stern von Bethlehem; Weihnachten.

⚙ *** EMI CDC5 56204-2. Bär, Deutsch (with Recital: *Christmas Lieder* *** ⚙).

These Christmas settings have all the character and charm one would expect from the composer of *Hänsel und Gretel*, and Olaf Bär's warmly flowing line consistently captures their easy lyricism. The closing *Weihnachten* has a Schubertian spontaneity of feeling and a lovely tune. Bär's relaxed, affectionate (yet at times dramatic) performances are perfectly judged, and he is beautifully accompanied by Helmut Deutsch. The recording too, is balanced most naturally. Unfortunately, as we go to press this issue has been deleted.

The Canteen Woman (Die Marketenderin): Prelude. The Merchant of Venice: Love Scene. Moorish Rhapsody: Tarifa (Elegy of Summer); Tangier (A Night in a Moorish Coffee-house); Tetuan (A Night in the Desert). The Sleeping Beauty: Suite.

**(*) Marco 8.223369. Slovak RSO (Bratislava), Fischer-Dieskau.

The Love scene from *The Merchant of Venice* ('On such a night') is beautiful but rather over-extended, and all three sections of the *Moorish Rhapsody* are much too long (the composite piece lasts some 32 minutes). The opening of the *Summer Elegy* begins with raptly ethereal writing for the violins, but the jolly Moorish coffee-house sequence sounds as if the restaurant has been leased from the owner of a Bavarian bier-keller. The Slovak performances under Martin Fischer-Dieskau (the famous Lieder singer's grandson) are not ideally polished but have freshness and vitality, while the Marco Polo recording is open and reasonably full.

Hänsel und Gretel (complete).

*** Teldec 4509 94549-2 (2). Larmore, Ziesak, Schwarz, Weikl, Behrens, Tölz Boys' Ch., Bav. RSO, Runnicles.

*** EMI CDS7 54022-2 (2). Von Otter, Bonney, Lipovšek, Schwarz, Schmidt, Hendricks, Lind, Tölz Boys' Ch, Bav. RSO, Tate.

(M) *** EMI mono CMS5 67061-2 [567145] (2). Schwarzkopf, Grümmer, Metternich, Ilsovay, Schürhoff, Felbermayer, Children's Ch., Philh. O, Karajan.

(M) **(*) RCA (ADD) 74321 25281-2 (2). Moffo, Donath, Fischer-Dieskau, Berthold, Ludwig, Augér, Popp, Bav. R. Ch. & RSO, Eichhorn.

(M) **(*) Decca 455 063-2 (2). Fassbaender, Popp, Hamari, Berry, Burrowes, Gruberová, Schlemm, V. Boys' Ch., VPO, Solti.

The success of the Teldec version of *Hänsel und Gretel* is largely due to Donald Runnicles, who has a lighter touch than his direct rivals. In the casting the emphasis more than ever is on fresh, youthful voices. So it was too with Barbara Bonney and Anne Sofie von Otter in the Tate set, but here the distinction between boy and girl is if anything even more sharply drawn. Ruth Ziesak as Gretel and Jennifer Larmore as Hänsel are above all natural-sounding, with little or no feeling of mature opera-singers pretending to be children, yet with no sense of strain and none of the edginess. Fresh clarity marks the other voices too, even that of the Witch as taken by Hanna Schwarz. Though aptly she uses a croaking voice, it makes the witch sharply sinister without being too frightening. Hildegard Behrens is strong and characterful, with Bernd Weikl firm and dark as the Father, while Rosemary Joshua makes a welcome recording début in opera as a bright-toned Sandman and Christine Schafer, fuller and firmer, is warmly contrasted as the Dew Fairy. On balance a first recommendation, the set brings incidentally a fascinating supplement in a brief orchestral coda, just over a minute long, which Humperdinck wrote in 1894 for a production of the opera in Dessau with Cosima Wagner as director. Ingeniously he has the Dessau national anthem set in counterpoint against various themes from the opera, with toy trumpets providing a commentary.

Tate brings a Brucknerian glow to the *Overture*, and then launches into a reading of exceptional warmth and sympathy, like Runnicles, at speeds generally faster than those in rival versions. The Witch of Marjana Lipovšek is firm and fierce, using the widest range of expression and tone. The chill that Lipovšek conveys down to a mere whisper makes one regret, more than usual, that the part is not longer. All the casting matches that in finesse, with no weak link. Barbara Bonney as Gretel and Anne Sofie von Otter as Hänsel are no less fine than the exceptionally strong duos on the rival sets. There is only a slight question mark over the use of the Tölz Boys' Choir for the gingerbread children at the end. Inevitably they sound what they are, a beautifully matched team of trebles, and curiously the heart-tug is not quite so intense as with the more childish-sounding voices in the rival choirs.

Karajan's classic 1950s set of Humperdinck's children's opera, with Schwarzkopf and Grümmer peerless in the name-parts, is enchanting; this was an instance where everything in the recording went right. The original mono LP set was already extremely atmospheric. In most respects the sound has as much clarity and warmth as rival recordings made in the 1970s. There is much to delight here; the smaller parts are beautifully done and Else Schürhoff's Witch is memorable. This has now been impressively remastered as one of EMI's 'Great Recordings of the Century'.

There are some fine solo performances on the mid-priced 1971 RCA set, notably from Helen Donath as Gretel and Christa Ludwig as the Witch; and Kurt Eichhorn's direction is vigorous, with excellent orchestral playing and full, atmospheric recording. It is a pity that a more boyish-sounding singer than Anna Moffo could not have been chosen for the role of Hänsel but, all told, this is a colourful and enjoyable account of a unique, eternally fresh opera, well worth considering.

Solti with the Vienna Philharmonic directs a strong, spectacular version, emphasizing the Wagnerian associations of the score. Solti does the *Witch's ride* very excitingly, and the VPO are encouraged to play with consistent fervour throughout. The result, though rather lacking in charm, is well sung, with the two children both engagingly characterized. Edita Gruberová is an excellent Dew Fairy and Walter Berry is first rate as Peter. Anny Schlemm's Witch is memorable if vocally unsteady, and there are some imaginative touches of stereo production associated with *Hocus pocus* and her other moments of magic. The recording is even more vivid in its CD transfer.

Königskinder (complete).

(*) Calig CAL 50968/70 (3). Moser, Schellenberger, Henschel, Schmiege, Kohn, Munich Boys' Ch., Bav. R. Ch. & O, Fabio Luisi.

The success of *Hänsel und Gretel* has completely over-shadowed this second fairy-tale opera of Humperdinck, which contains much fine music.

It is good to have a new recording of a rich score, generally well sung and warmly conducted by Fabio Luisi, who uses the same choir and orchestra as the earlier, EMI set, recorded in 1976, with sound rather more spacious but not so immediate. An incidental shortcoming is that the libretto comes in German only, with the Calig libretto omitting even the stage directions. The tenor of Thomas Moser, taking the central role of the Prince, is more heroic than that of his earlier EMI rival, Adolf Dallapozza, with the voice often shaded down beautifully. Though Dagmar Schellenberger as the Goosegirl lacks sweetness, hers is a feeling, well-characterized performance, and she finds a delicate *mezza voce* for the prayer to her parents. Marilyn Schmiege with her warm, firm mezzo makes rather a young Witch. All told, this is a performance marked by good teamwork, with the chorus bringing energetic echoes of Smetana's *Bartered Bride* in their brief contributions.

HURLSTONE, William (1876–1906)

The Magic Mirror: Suite; Variations on a Hungarian Air; Variations on an Original Theme.

*** Lyrita SRCD 208. LPO, Braithwaite.

As a glance at his dates shows, William Hurlstone only just reached thirty before the ill-health which dogged him during his life claimed him. The *Variations on an Original Theme* date from 1896, though the theme on which they are based comes from a *Trio*, written two years earlier. They show considerable inventive resource and although, like the *Variations on a Hungarian air*, there is also a certain debt to Brahms, they have a lightness of touch and a feeling for the orchestra which is marked. *The Magic Mirror Suite* of 1900 also offers reminders of the Elgar of *The Wand of Youth*. But it is not long before one can sense something quietly individual beginning to surface. The LPO and Nicholas Braithwaite give lively, cultured performances of this eminently well-crafted, immaculately scored and civilized music, and they are beautifully recorded.

Cello Sonata in D.

(M) ******* Dutton Epoch CDLX 7102. Fuller, Dussek – HARTY: *Butterflies; Romance & Scherzo, Op. 8; Wood-stillness;* PARRY: *Cello Sonata in A.* *******

Hurlstone's *Cello Sonata* is as well fashioned and musianly as you would expect from this gifted composer. It receives excellent advocacy from Andrew Fuller, who also writes the intelligent notes, and his fine pianist, Michael Dussek. At the same time it is not easy to discern a distinctive voice here beneath the Brahmsian veneer. The recording is excellent, well balanced and present.

HVOSLEF, Ketil (born 1937)

(i) *Antigone (1982);* (ii) *Violin Concerto.*

*** Aurora ACD4969. (ii) Saeverud; Bergen PO, cond.
(i) Eggen; (ii) Kitaienko.

Ketil Hvoslef is the son of Harald Saeverud and one of the brightest and most individual figures in the Norwegian musical firmament. He has the same craggy, salty quality as his father, the same rugged independence of personality and creative resource. This CD offers *Antigone*, which comes from the early 1980s, and the *Violin Concerto*, composed almost ten years later, in which the soloist is his son, Trond.

HYDE, Miriam (born 1913)

(i) *Piano Concertos Nos. 1 in E flat min.; 2 in C sharp min.;*
(ii) *Village Fair.*

(N) **(*) Australian Universal ABC Classics (ADD) 465 735-2.
(i) Hyde; Australian SO, Simon; (ii) Sydney SO, Franks.

Miriam Hyde is a well-respected composer and teacher in Australia, and we have here her early *Piano Concertos*, written in 1932/33 and 1934/5 respectively. They are unashamedly romantic in tradition, with bold writing and rich orchestration – Brahms and Rachmaninov being obvious models. The tunes are memorable and each work has many felicities, not least in the touches of folk-like melody and colour. The finale of the *First Concerto*, with its repeated figures on the strings with the timpani, sounds rather exotic, but soon becomes highly romantic, with flowing arpeggios, which at times reminds one of romantic film score of the 1940s. It is all very enjoyable and the music is instantly appealing. These are excellent performances, though the 1975 recording is a little thin. With an attractive fill-up in the form of *Village Fair*, once again with folk-like themes, this is a valuable addition to the catalogue. Miriam Hyde certainly deserves wider recognition.

IBERT, Jacques (1890–1962)

Bacchanale; Divertissement; Escales; Ouverture de fête; Symphonie marine.

(N) (BB) * Naxos 8.554222. LOP, Sado.

Sado's *Divertissement* is without the sheer champagne fizz of Martinon's old – but exceptionally vivid – Decca recording (currently withdrawn). *Escales* also suffers from comparison with more magical accounts already available (from Munch, and Paray), and while the *Symphonie marine* is a rarity, it is musically rather thin. The *Ouverture de fête* is enjoyable enough, but does rather outstay its welcome. The recording is quite good and the CD is cheap, but difficult to recommend even so.

La Ballade de la Geôle de Reading; Féerique; 3 pièces de ballet (Les Rencontres); (i) *Chant de folie; Suite elisabéthaine.*

**(*) Marco 8.223508. (i) Slovak Ph. Ch.; Slovak RSO (Bratislava), Adriano.

The *Suite elisabéthaine* is a nine-movement suite taken from the incidental music Ibert composed for Shakespeare's *A Midsummer Night's Dream*. It is largely pastiche and four of the movements draw on Blow, Purcell, Bull and Gibbons. More characteristic is *La Ballade de la Geôle de Reading*, an exercise in neo-impressionism and highly accomplished. The *Chant de folie* is an effective four-minute choral and orchestral piece inspired by the composer's experiences in the First World War.

Divertissement.

*** Chan. 9023. Ulster O, Tortelier – MILHAUD: *Le Boeuf; Création;* POULENC: *Les Biches.* ***

(M) *** Decca 448571-2. Paris Conservatoire O, Martinon (with Concert ***).

Divertissement; Escales.

(B) **(*) Sony (ADD) SBK 62644. Phd. O, Ormandy – FAURE: *Pelléas et Mélisande,* etc. **(*); ROUSSEL: *Bacchus et Ariane* ***.

Yan Pascal Tortelier provides at last a splendid, modern, digital version of Ibert's *Divertissement*. There is much delicacy of detail, and the coupled suite from Poulenc's *Les Biches* is equally delectable. Marvellous, top-drawer Chandos sound.

Martinon's 1960 Decca account has never been surpassed for fizzing energy and wit, although the recording now sounds a bit shrill.

Ormandy's 1960 *Divertissement* is enjoyable if without quite the unbuttoned *joie de vivre* that Yan Pascal Tortelier brings to it. In *Escales*, the Philadelphia strings produce a memorably sumptuous tone, and a noticeable intensity runs throughout the work. The sound is good considering its 1960 CBS provenance.

Escales (Ports of Call).

(M) *** RCA (ADD) 09026 61500-2. Boston SO, Munch – DEBUSSY: *La Mer* **(*); SAINT-SAENS: *Symphony No. 3.* *** ◉

(M) **(*) Mercury (IMS) 432 003-2. Detroit SO, Paray – RAVEL: *Alborada* etc. ***

Munch's *Escales* brings some ravishing textures from the Boston violins, and the finale, *Valencia*, has sparkling dance rhythms. The 1956 recording, if balanced rather closely, has brilliance and transparency, although it does not sound ideally rich and sumptuous.

Paray's recording catches the Mediterranean exoticism of *Escales* admirably, and the 1962 Mercury recording has plenty of atmosphere as well as glittering detail. The Ravel couplings are very impressive too.

Sinfonia Concertante for Oboe & Strings.

*** Koch C 130045. Schellenberger, Franz Liszt CO, Budapest, Peskó – LUTOSLAWSKI: *Double Concerto for Oboe & Harp;* MARTIN: *3 Danses for Oboe, Harp, String Quintet & String Orchestra.* ***

Like the other two works on this outstanding CD, the Ibert

Sinfonia Concertante was given its première (in 1951) by Paul Sacher. It is a complex piece, scored in the spirit of a concerto grosso, with soloists from all the string groups joining the oboist, and demands great virtuosity from the orchestra, which is certainly forthcoming here. The extended central *Adagio* has a wan, expressive poignancy. Schellenberger is a first-class soloist and Peskó and the Budapest strings provide a spirited backing, presenting the fugato writing of the finale with great energy and sharply focused detail. The recording is excellent.

Complete chamber music

Vol. 1: *Aria for Flute, Violin & Piano; Française* (for solo guitar); *Le Jardinier de Samos* (for flute, clarinet, trumpet, violin, cello & percussion); *Jeux (Sonatine for Flute & Piano); 2 Movements for Wind Quartet; Paraboles for 2 Guitars; Pastorale for 4 Pipes; 3 Pièces brèves for Wind Quintet; 5 Pièces en trio for Oboe, Clarinet & Bassoon; 6 Pièces for Harp.*

Vol. 2: *Ariette* (for solo guitar); *Caprilena for Solo Violin; Carignane for Bassoon & Piano; Chevalier errant: L'Age d'or* (for alto sax & piano); *Entr'acte for Flute & Guitar; Etude-caprice pour un tombeau de Chopin; Ghirlarzana* (both for solo cello); *Impromptu for Trumpet & Piano; 2 Interludes for Flute, Violin & Harpsichord; String Quartet; Trio for Violin, Cello & Harp.*

(B) *** Olympia Double OCD 707 A+B (2). Pameijer, Oostenejk, Colbers, Gaesterland, Bornkamp, Jeurissen, Masseurs, Stoop, Franssen, de Rijke, Grotenhuis, van Delft, Marinissen, New Netherlands Qt, Hulsmann, Biesta, Oldeman, Van Staalen.

This pair of Olympia discs (now attractively reissued as a 2 x 1 Double) offer music which is not only delightful but (for the most part) very little known, with the exception of the *Trois pièces brèves*, which are justly familiar. Yet the *Trio for Violin, Cello and Harp* is hardly less distinctive, while the *Cinq pièces en trio* have a winning pastoral flavour. French composers were especially good at writing Spanish music (Chabrier and Ravel spring immediately to mind), so it is not surprising that Ibert's music featuring the guitar has such southern Mediterranean feeling. But then so do the *Deux interludes* for flute, violin and harpsichord, another very winning trio and with something of a gypsy flamenco flavour. The two CDs, each lasting around 80 minutes, are arranged in order of composition, so the *Six pièces* for solo harp come at the beginning to entice the listener with their smooth melodic flow. But there is not a dull or unimaginative item here, and these excellent Dutch players have the full measure of the witty, piquant Poulenc manner. They are very well recorded. This is music to cheer you up on a dull day.

Trois pièces brèves.

(M) *** Chan. 6543. Athena Ens. – GOUNOD: *Petite symphonie in B flat;* POULENC: *Sextet.* ***

(N) (***) BBC mono BBCL 4066-2. Dennis Brain Wind Quintet (with instrumental recital (***)).

Ibert's *Trois pièces brèves* could hardly be played with more polish, wit and affection than in this brilliantly realized performance by the Athena group, the effect enhanced when they are recorded so realistically.

The characterful blend of Dennis Brain and his colleagues in his Wind Quintet (Gareth Morris, Leonard Brain, Stephen Waters and Cecil James) is fully captured in the BBC mono recording, and the warm, spirited geniality of their ensemble brings a delightful bonhomie to the music's wit – the pastoral opening is captivating.

4 Chansons de Don Quichotte.

(N) (M) *** Virgin VM5 61850-2. Van Dam, Lyon Nat. Op. O, Nagano – MARTIN: *6 Monologues from 'Jedermann';* POULENC: *Le Bal masque;* RAVEL: *Don Quichotte à Dulcinée.* ***

As with the coupled Ravel cycle, Kent Nagano creates a sultry Spanish backcloth for these highly atmospheric songs, which José Van Dam sings very movingly, especially the closing valedictory *Chanson de la mort de Don Quichotte*, which so perfectly suits his dark baritone colouring. Excellent, evocative recording and full text and translations make this a most desirable reissue.

INDIA, Sigismondo d' *(c. 1582–c. 1630)*

Duets, laments and madrigals: *Amico, hai vinto; Ancidetemi pur, dogliosi affanti; Che nudrisce tua speme; Giunto a la tomba; Langue al vostro languir; Occhi della mia vita; O leggiadr' occhi; Quella vermiglia rosa; Son gli accenti che ascolto; Torna il sereno Zefiro.*

(B) **(*) HM HMA 901011. Concerto Vocale – CESTI: *Cantatas.* **(*)

Sigismondo d'India was among the vanguard of the new movement founded by Monteverdi at the beginning of the seventeenth century, and his laments show him to be a considerable master of expressive resource. The performances are authoritative, though there are moments of slightly self-conscious rubato that hold up the flow. The recording is fully acceptable and the coupling is also of considerable interest; this is worth exploring.

Amico, hai vinto; Diana (Questo dardo, quest' arco); Misera me (Lamento d'Olympia); Piangono al pianger mio; Sfere fermate; Torna il sereno zefiro.

*** Hyp. CDA 66106. Kirkby, Rooley (chitarone) – MONTEVERDI: *Lamento d'Olympia* etc. ***

Sigismondo d'India's setting of the *Lamento d'Olympia* makes a striking contrast to Monteverdi's and is hardly less fine. This is an affecting and beautiful piece and so are its companions, particularly when they are sung as superbly and accompanied as sensitively as they are here. A very worthwhile CD début.

Il primo libro de madrigali (1606): *Interdette speranz'e van desio. Ottavo libro de madrigali: Il pastor fido, Act IV, Scene 9: Se tu, Silvio crudel, mi saetti* (five madrigal cycle).

⚫ (M) *** Virgin VER5 61165-2. Chiaroscuro, L. Baroque, Rogers – MONTEVERDI: *Madrigals*. *** ⚫

It is in the cycle from his Eighth Book of Madrigals, *Se tu, Silvio crudel, mi saetti*, that one experiences not only the composer's lyrical originality to the full but also his affinity with the operatic writing of his greater contemporary, Monteverdi. The vocal dialogue, which alternates solo and ensemble singing, is touching and dramatic by turns, and requires effortless vocal virtuosity. The quality of the performances is superlative, refined without a hint of preciosity, and always alive, while the accompaniments on theorbo and harpsichord are delicately balanced. An outstanding collection in every way.

INDY, Vincent d' (1851–1931)

(i) *Concerto for Piano, Flute & Strings, Op. 89*; (ii) *Jour d'été à la montagne, Op. 61*; (ii; iii) *Symphonie sur un montagnard français, Op. 25*; *Karadec* (incidental music), *Op. 34*; *Poème des montagnes, Op. 15*; (iv) *Suite in D, Op. 24*.

(N) (BB) **(*) Erato Ultima (ADD/DDD) 8573 85665-2 (2).
    (i) Rampal, André, Paillard CO, Paillard; (ii) R France PO, Janowski; (iii) Catherine Collard; (iv) Doyen.

The first CD is digital and is valuable for *Jour d'été à la montagne*, one of d'Indy's most inspired pieces. The well-known *Symphonie sur un montagnard français* is handicapped by a not altogether sympathetic accompaniment from Janowski and a synthetic balance which does not allow the sound to expand. The beautiful *Poème des montagnes* is more successful. The *Concerto for Piano, Flute, Cello and Strings* was d'Indy's last symphonic work. Written 'in the ancient style', is a kind of *septième brandenbourgeois*, and has delicacy and charm, especially with such distinguished soloists as Jean-Pierre Rampal and Maurice André. The *Karadec* music has a fair share of exotic flavourings. All the track listings on CD 2 are wrong, but the music is all there, and well worth exploring.

Diptyque méditerranéan; Poème des rivages (symphonic suite).

(M) **(*) EMI (ADD) CDM7 63954-2. Monte Carlo PO, Prêtre.

Apart from the influence of Franck, the *Soleil matinal* of the *Diptyque* has a blend of the Wagner of *Parsifal* and that quality of conservative impressionism which d'Indy made so much his own after the turn of the century. There are considerable beauties in this piece and in the *Poème* and, though the recording is not top-drawer, the sound does not lack allure. This is well worth investigating, for despite some unevenness of inspiration, Prêtre holds the music together impressively.

(i) *Fantasy on French Popular Themes* (for oboe and orchestra), *Op. 31. Saugelfleurie* (Legend after a Tale by Robert de Bonnières); *Tableaux de voyage, Op. 36*; *L'Etranger: Prelude to Act II. Fervaal: Prelude to Act I.*

** Marco 8.223659. (i) Cousu; Württemberg PO, Nopre or (i) Burfin.

The tone-poem, *Saugelfleurie*, based on a tale by Robert de Bonnières, the evocative *Tableaux de voyage* and the lovely *Prelude to Act I* of *Fervaal* all offer music of quality, and writing which also has the seeds of popularity. The *Fantaisie sur des thèmes populaires françaises* for oboe and orchestra has a fervent charm which is very winning. The performances of all these pieces are variable; they fall short of distinction but are more than routine. The recording, too, is eminently satisfactory and aficionados of French music need not hesitate.

Symphonie sur un chant montagnard français (Symphonie cévenole).

(BB) **(*) Naxos 8.550754. Thiollier, Nat. SO of Ireland, De Almeida – FAURE: *Ballade*; FRANCK: *Symphonic Variations*. **(*)

On Naxos the French-born but American-trained François-Joël Thiollier gives an intelligent performance, perfectly well accompanied and decently recorded, and with an interesting coupling. It is worth the money, but there are finer accounts to be had.

(i) *Symphonie sur un chant montagnard français*;
(ii) *Symphony No. 2 in B flat, Op. 57*.

(M) *** EMI (ADD) CDM7 63952-2. (i) Ciccolini, O de Paris, Baudo; (ii) Toulouse Capitole O, Plasson.

Symphony No. 2 in B flat, Op. 57; Souvenirs, Op. 52.

**(*) Koch 37280-2. Monte Carlo PO, DePreist.

Aldo Ciccolini gives a good account of himself in the demanding solo part of the *Symphonie*, and the Orchestre de Paris under Serge Baudo give sympathetic support. The recording is pleasing and with a convincing piano image. The *Second Symphony* remains one of the neglected masterpieces of turn-of-the-century French music. Michel Plasson proves a sympathetic and committed advocate, and his orchestra responds with enthusiasm and sensitivity to his direction. The recording too is spacious, full and well focused.

Choice between Plasson and DePreist is a matter of swings-and-roundabouts and should rest perhaps on the coupling. DePreist does not have as fine an orchestra as the Toulouse Capitole, though they play with plenty of commitment, but the recording is slightly more detailed and DePreist gives us the affecting *Souvenirs* which d'Indy composed on the death of his wife.

String Quartet No. 1.

(N) *** Hyp. CDA 67097. Chilingirian Qt. – CHAUSSON: *String Quartet* (completed D'INDY).

Among the string quartets which French composers wrote in the last years of the nineteenth century – generally prompted by the example of César Franck – those of Vincent d'Indy are the most unjustly neglected, as this outstanding performance of No. 1 demonstrates. It is a striking work, which in its bold thematic material often echoes Beethoven. A powerful first movement leads to an ecstatic slow movement, an elegant interlude and an exuberant finale. We now need the Chilingirians with their deep sympathy for the idiom to record d'Indy's other two quartets. The Chausson quartet makes a very apt coupling here, completed by d'Indy after the composer's tragic death in a road accident.

String Quartets Nos. 1 in D, Op. 35; 2 in E, Op. 45.

**(*) Marco 8.223140. Kodály Qt.

The *First Quartet* is a large-scale piece and beautifully crafted. The *Second* (1897) is hardly less ambitious and shows something of the composer's admiration for late Beethoven; it must also be said that greater variety of texture would be welcome. The excellent Kodály Quartet are recorded in the Italian Institute in Budapest, where the rather close balance tends to iron out dynamic extremes.

IPPOLITOV-IVANOV,
Mikhail (1859–1935)

Armenian Rhapsody, Op. 48; Caucasian Sketches, Set II: Iveria, Op. 42; Jubilee March (Voroshilov), Op. 67; (i) Mtsyri (symphonic poem), Op. 54; Turkish Fragments, Op. 62; Turkish March, Op. 55; (ii) Aria: Assya: I wonder if it is misfortune.

(N) *** ASV CDDCA 1102. Armenian PO, Tjeknavorian;
   (i) with Hatsagortsian; (ii) Vardouhi Khachaturian.

Tjeknavorian and ASV have turned up a second set of *Caucasian Sketches*, called *Iveria*, with a jubilant closing *Georgian March* that might become popular, like the *Procession of the Sardar*, given sufficient exposure. The sombre opening *Lamentation* is also rather telling, followed by a lazily sinuous *Berceuse* and a brightly scored, rhythmically catchy *Lezghinka*. The *Turkish Fragments* describe the progress of an Eastern caravan, opening with a processional, and including a nocturnal sequence with a sultry Rimskian oboe melody. The symphonic poem *Mtzyri* is mentioned below, and is most notable for its interpolated ballad from the nymph who finds the young hero of the story wounded by a leopard in the forest. This is touchingly sung by Hasmit Hatsagortsian, if with a very characteristic Russian vibrato. Vardouhi Khachaturian's performance of the mezzo scena from *Assya* has no lack of temperament or eloquence, and the other (*Turkish March*) is enjoyably ebullient. Very well recorded, this CD is worth exploring if you enjoy this kind of undemanding and tuneful Russian orchestral music.

Caucasian Sketches (suite), Op. 10.

*** Chan. 9321. BBC PO, Glushchenko – KHACHATURIAN:
   Symphony No. 3 etc. ***
*** ASV CDDCA 773. Armenian PO, Tjeknavorian –
   KHACHATURIAN: *Gayaneh etc.* **(*)

Once a popular repertory piece, the colourful *Caucasian Sketches* have fallen out of favour; only the final *Procession of the Sardar* is generously represented on CD. The present version by the BBC Philharmonic under Fedor Glushchenko is generally superior to the alternative on ASV.

The *Procession of the Sardar* is played by the Armenians with great brio. The other items rely mainly on picaresque oriental atmosphere for their appeal, which Tjeknavorian also captures evocatively in this brightly lit recording.

Symphony No. 1 in E min., Op. 46; Armenian Rhapsody, Op. 48; Caucasian Sketches, Op. 10; (i) Mtzyri, Op. 54. War March, Op. 42/4.

*** Conifer 75605 51317-2. Bamberg SO, Brain, (i) Barainsky.

Few will have encountered this *Symphony* in the concert hall. Although announced as No. 1, it remains the composer's only contribution to the genre and is as colourful as you would expect from a pupil of Rimsky-Korsakov. *Mtzyri* is a programmatic piece based on a Lermontov poem and has strong reminiscences of his master. No one would claim that any of these pieces is more than an effective example of Russian-national Romanticism without any great claims of originality, but it is all well worth recording and is splendidly played by the Bamberg Orchestra under Gary Brain.

IRELAND, John (1879–1962)

Concertino pastorale; A Downland Suite (arr. composer and Geoffrey Bush); Orchestral Poem; 2 Symphonic Studies (arr. Geoffrey Bush).

*** Chan. 9376. City of L. Sinfonia, Hickox.

The valedictory *Threnody* of the *Concertino pastorale* and the lovely *Elegy* from the *Downland Suite* show the composer at his most lyrically inspired, and the rapt playing here does them full justice. The early *Orchestral Poem* (1904) is a surprisingly powerful work as presented here with great passion, with splendid brass writing at its climax. The two *Symphonic Studies* come from film music Ireland wrote for *The Overlanders*, not incorporated into the concert suites: the brass chromatics in the first have a familiar ring, the second has a wild momentum, recalling the cattle stampede in the film, but both stand up well as independent concert pieces.

Piano Concerto in E flat.

*** Unicorn DKPCD 9056. Tozer, Melbourne SO, Measham –
   RUBBRA: *Violin Concerto.* ***

Piano Concerto in E flat; Legend for Piano & Orchestra; Mai-Dun (symphonic rhapsody).

*** Chan. 8461. Parkin, LPO, Thomson.

Eric Parkin gives a splendidly refreshing and sparkling performance and benefits from excellent support from Bryden Thomson and the LPO. They are no less impressive in *Mai-Dun* and the beautiful *Legend for Piano & Orchestra*.

Geoffrey Tozer conveys the poetic feel of the slow movement and, though he takes a rather measured tempo in the finale, the music loses none of its freshness. The recording is a little studio-bound, but too much should not be made of this. Doubtless the coupling will decide matters for most collectors.

A Downland Suite; Elegiac Meditation; The Holy Boy.

*** Chan. 8390. ECO, Garforth – BRIDGE: *Suite for
   Strings.* ***

A Downland Suite was originally written for brass band. However, the present version was finished and put into shape by Geoffrey Bush, who also transcribed the *Elegiac Meditation*. David Garforth and the ECO play with total conviction and seem wholly attuned to Ireland's sensibility. The recording is first class, clear and naturally balanced.

The Holy Boy.

(N) (M) *** EMI (ADD) CDM5 67431-2. Dilkes, E. Sinf. – FIELD: *Nocturnes;* HARTY: *John Field Suite;* LEIGH: *Harpsichord concertino.* ***

Ireland's most touching melody is heard here in his own arrangement for string orchestra of a carol which originated as a piano piece. It is presented with pleasing simplicity and very well recorded. A fine bonus for an attractive programme of British music.

Epic March; The Overlanders (film incidental music): Suite (arr. Mackerras).

(M) *** Unicorn UKCD 2062. W. Australian SO, Measham – VAUGHAN WILLIAMS: *On Wenlock Edge.* ***

The Overlanders is not the best of Ireland, but it contains some good ideas and it is persuasively presented here. The *Epic March* is jolly and rhythmically folksy, then presents an almost elegiac grand tune. This is all recommendable enough, for the CD transfers are first rate and the Vaughan Williams coupling is most appealing.

A London Overture.

(M) *** EMI (ADD) CDM5 65109-2. LSO, Barbirolli – VAUGHAN WILLIAMS: *London Symphony.* **(*)

One of Ireland's most immediately attractive works, and Barbirolli's performance of it is a great success, as is the remastering of an outstanding recording. The main theme (rhythmically conjuring up the bus conductor's call of 'Piccadilly!') is made obstinately memorable, and the ripe romanticism of the middle section is warmly expansive in Barbirolli's hands.

A London Overture; Epic March; The Holy Boy; (i–ii) Greater love hath no man; These things shall be; (i; iii) Vexilla Regis.

(M) *** Chan. Enchant 7074. LSO, Hickox, with (i) London Symphony Ch.; (ii) Terfel; (iii) Bott, Shaw, Oxley.

Richard Hickox is a sympathetic interpreter of Ireland's music and obtains sensitive results (and good singing) in *The Holy Boy* and *These things shall be* (surprisingly, the latter is not otherwise available on silver disc). The disc is of particular interest in that it brings a rarity, *Vexilla Regis*, for chorus, brass and organ, composed when Ireland was nineteen and still a student of Stanford. First-class recorded sound.

CHAMBER MUSIC

(i) Cello Sonata; (ii) Fantasy Sonata for Clarinet & Piano; (i) The Holy Boy (for cello and piano); (iii) Phantasie Trio; Piano Trios Nos. 2–3; (iv) Violin Sonatas Nos. 1–2.

*** Chan. 9377/8. (i; iii) Georgian; (i; iii–iv) Brown; (ii) De Peyer, Pryor; (iii–iv) Mordkovitch.

Few British composers have written with quite such easy lyricism as John Ireland. The first two of the *Piano Trios*, well contrasted, are warmly appealing, but the masterpiece is the four-movement *Piano Trio No. 3* of 1938, passionately intense. The two *Violin Sonatas* are both superb works too, masterfully played here by Lydia Mordkovitch with Ian Brown, who also accompanies Karine Georgian in the *Cello Sonata*. Completing the set, the recording of the *Fantasy Sonata* of 1943 for clarinet dates from earlier, with Gervase de Peyer and Gwenneth Pryor playing with equal commitment.

(i) The Holy Boy; (ii) Phantasie Trio in A min.; (iii) Violin Sonata No. 1 in D min.; (iv) Violin Sonata No. 2 in A min.

(M) (***) Dutton Epoch mono CDLX 7103. Hooton with (i) Pratt, (ii) Grinke, Taylor. Ireland with (iii) Grinke, (iv) Sammons.

We have long treasured Frederick Grinke's 78 r.p.m. set of the *Violin Sonata No. 1* with the composer at the piano, and can confirm that the Dutton transfer of this 1945 recording brings its sound to life with striking effect. It is possible that there have been better recordings but not a more vibrant or more authoritative performance. The *Violin Sonata No. 2*, on the other hand, again with John Ireland at the piano but with its dedicatee, the legendary Albert Sammons, recorded in 1930, still sounds very well for its age, as does the *Phantasie Trio*, in which Grinke is joined by Florence Hooton and Kenneth Taylor. An invaluable and self-recommending set which readers should cherish. Outstanding transfers.

String Quartets Nos. 1 in D min.; 2 in C min.; The Holy Boy.

**(*) ASV CDDCA 1017. Holywell Ens.

Both quartets come from 1897, when Ireland was eighteen, and were published posthumously. There is little sign of individuality but each work is beautifully crafted and gives much pleasure. The idiom is close to Dvořák and the ideas are fluent and pleasing. The Holywell Ensemble offer decent performances and are well recorded.

Violin Sonatas Nos. 1 in D min.; 2 in A min.; Bagatelle; Berceuse; Cavatina; The Holy Boy.

*** Hyp. CDA 66853. Barritt, Edwards.

Paul Barritt and Catherine Edwards make an effective partnership and give very persuasive accounts of both these fine sonatas. An excellent, well-balanced recording earns this a recommendation alongside Lydia Mordkovitch and Ian Brown's 2-CD set on Chandos coupled with the three *Piano Trios* and the *Cello Sonata*.

PIANO MUSIC

The Almond Tree; Decorations; Merry Andrew; Preludes (The Undertone; Obsession; The Holy Boy; Fire of Spring); Rhapsody; Sonata in E min.; Summer Evening; The Towing-Path.

*** Chan. 9056. Parkin.

Amberley Wild Woods; Ballad; The Darkened Valley; Equinox; For Remembrance; Greenways; In Those Days; Leaves from a Child's Sketchbook; London Pieces; 2 Pieces; Prelude in E flat; Sonatina.

*** Chan. 9140. Parkin.

Ballade of London Nights; Columbine; Month's Mind; On a Birthday Morning; 3 Pastels; 2 Pieces (February's Child; Aubade); 2 Pieces (April; Bergomask); Sarnia; A Sea Idyll; Soliloquy; Spring will Not Wait.

*** Chan. 9250. Parkin.

It goes without saying that Eric Parkin is completely inside Ireland's idiom and he brings both dedication and sympathy to this repertoire. Moreover, the sound is clean, well-rounded and pleasing.

Aubade; February's Child; The Darkened Valley; Decorations; April; Leaves from a Child's Sketchbook; Merry Andrew; 3 Pastels; Rhapsody; Sonatina; Summer Evening; The Towing-Path.

(BB) *** Naxos 8.553889. Lenehan.

Ballade; Columbine; In Those Days; London Pieces; Prelude in E flat; Sarnia.

(BB) *** Naxos 8.553700. Lenehan.

Few British composers have matched John Ireland in the point and individuality of his piano music, with its offbeat melodies and tangy dissonances. Making up for serious neglect, John Lenehan is making a complete survey for Naxos and he proves the most persuasive advocate, warmly expressive, using rubato in a totally idiomatic way. The four London Pieces are among his most colourful, not just Ragamuffin, played here with quicksilver lightness, but also the barcarolle-like Chelsea Reach, tenderly emotional. The most ambitious work is the three-movement suite, inspired by Guernsey, Sarnia, far more than a set of atmospheric colour pieces. This music shows Ireland's poetic imagination to particular advantage and its last movement has echoes of the Piano Concerto in E flat.

The second programme offers a score of miniatures, including two of Ireland's most hauntingly atmospheric pieces, The Towing-Path and The Darkened Valley, a Blake inspiration. The longest work here is the Sonatina in three short movements, with the opening Moderato bringing echoes of Ireland's colourful Piano Concerto, the second a dark meditation leading to a galloping finale. Impeccable performances vividly recorded.

VOCAL MUSIC

Songs: Disc 1: Earth's call; 5 Songs to Poems by Thomas Hardy; Great things; Hope the hornblower; If there were dreams to sell; If we must part; I have twelve oxen; Love is a sickness full of woes; Santa Chiara; Songs Sacred and Profane; Spleen; Spring Sorrow; 2 Songs; 3 Songs; 3 Songs to Poems by Thomas Hardy; Tryst; Tutto è sciolto; When I am old.

Songs: Disc 2: Bed in summer; The bells of San Marie; During music; 5 XVIth-Century Poems; The journey; Mother and child; The heart's desire; Ladslove; Remember; The sacred flame; Sea fever; Songs of a Wayfarer; 3 Songs; The vagabond; We'll to the woods no more; What art thou thinking of?; When I am dead, my dearest; When lights go rolling round the sky.

**(*) Hyp. CDA 67261/2 (2). Milne, Ainsley, Maltman, Johnson.

John Ireland's settings of English verse are among the most sensitive of the early twentieth century, as this welcome collection of sixty-eight songs makes plain. They include one of the best-known of all songs of the period, his setting of John Masefield's Sea fever, a haunting tune that completely transcends the genre of the drawing-room ballad. Mostly, Ireland's songs are more sophisticated, and his gift of writing distinctively for the piano is consistently revealed in the accompaniments with their ear-catching harmonies.

Graham Johnson relishes the felicity of the piano-writing, but the singing is less consistently satisfying. Lisa Milne uses her light, bright soprano very sympathetically in the women's songs, while John Mark Ainsley, if not in his sweetest voice, is similarly sensitive in the tenor songs, just over a dozen of them. But almost half of the selection features Christopher Maltman, who (as caught here by the microphones) sings with fluttery tone, often undistracting, but regularly under pressure, making the sound gritty and unfocused, as in the late setting of William Cornish's A thanksgiving. Clear, well-balanced recording. In the excellent documentation, the lively commentary of Andrew Green adds greatly to the value of the set.

ISAAC, Heinrich (c. 1450–1517)

Missa de apostolis. Motets: Optime pastor; Tota pulchra es; Regina caeli laetare; Resurrexi et adhuc tecum sum; Virgo prudentissima.

*** Gimell (ADD) GIMCD 923. Tallis Scholars, Phillips.

The German contemporary of Josquin des Pres, Heinrich Isaac has not until recently been widely appreciated. The Mass setting is glorious, culminating in an ethereal version of Agnus dei, flawlessly sung by the Tallis Scholars. Among the many striking passages is the opening of the six-part setting of Virgo prudentissima for two upper voices only, with women's rather than boys' voices all the more appropriate with such a text. Ideally balanced recording.

IVES, Charles (1874–1954)

Calcium Light Night; Country Band March; Largo cantabile: Hymn; Three Places in New England; Postlude in F; 4 Ragtime Dances; Set for Theatre Orchestra; Yale–Princeton Football Game.

*** Koch 37025-2. O New England, Sinclair.

This selection of shorter Ives pieces makes an ideal introduction for anyone wanting just to sample the work of this wild, often maddening, but always intriguing composer. Excellent performances and recording.

(i) *Central Park in the Dark;* (ii–iii) *Holidays Symphony;* (ii) *The Unanswered Question.*

(M) *** Sony (ADD) SMK 60203. NYPO, (i) Ozawa & Peress (under the supervision of Bernstein); (ii) Bernstein; (iii) with Lipkin (assistant conductor), Camerata Singers, Kaplan – CARTER: *Concerto for Orchestra.* ***

Central Park in the Dark, as the title implies, provides a brilliant collection of evening sounds, evocative yet bewildering. The first three sections of the so-called *Holidays Symphony*, with their still-startling clashes of impressionistic imagery, are well enough known. The fourth – full title: *Thanksgiving and/or Forefathers Day* – is more of a rarity, bringing in a full chorus to sing a single verse of a hymn at the close. The performance is red-bloodedly convincing yet has remarkably clear detail. *The Unanswered Question* is probably the most purely beautiful music Ives ever wrote, with muted strings (curiously representing silence) set against a trumpet representing the problem of existence. No need to worry about Ives's philosophy when the results are so naturally moving. Superb playing (the trumpeter is William Vacchiano) and vivid recording, but the forward balance means the lack of a true pianissimo, especially noticeable in *The Unanswered Question.*

Central Park in the Dark; New England Holidays Symphony; The Unanswered Question (original and revised versions).

*** Sony SK 42381. Chicago Symphony Ch. & O, Tilson Thomas.

The *New England Holidays Symphony* comprises four fine Ives pieces normally heard separately. The performance from Michael Tilson Thomas and his Chicago forces is in every way superb, while the wide-ranging CBS recording provides admirable atmosphere. This is now among the most impressive Ives records in the catalogue.

(i) *Central Park in the Dark;* (ii) *Three Places in New England;* (iii) *Piano Sonata No. 2 (Concord, Mass., 1840– 1860).*

(B) *** DG (ADD) 439 480-2. (i) Boston SO, Ozawa, or (ii) Tilson Thomas; (iii) Szidon (with Sonntag, flute).

Three Places in New England: The St. Gaudens in Boston Common; Putnam's Camp; The Housatonic at Stockbridge.

(N) (M) *** DG (ADD) 463 633-2. Boston SO, Tilson Thomas – PISTON: *Symphony No. 2;* RUGGLES: *Sun-treader.* ***

An outstanding and highly recommendable bargain anthology. The Boston Symphony Orchestra under Ozawa plays quite magnificently in the two orchestral works, so full of evocative atmosphere, and the DG engineers produce a most musical balance. Most remarkable of all is Roberto Szidon's unsurpassed account of the *Concord Sonata*, where the concentration of the performance here gives the reading enormous authority. Szidon is admirably recorded. In the last movement a brief melody is given to the flute. When questioned about this, Ives replied nonchalantly that the flute was right for that particular moment in the music and, as no one was likely to play the sonata anyway, there would be no performance difficulties!

Michael Tilson Thomas's eloquent and poetic account of Ives's pioneering and imaginative triptych – perhaps his finest work other than *The unanswered question* – is also available separately. This beautifully polished Boston performance, with its vintage 1970 analogue recording, is probably unsurpassed. It is good to have the original couplings restored, although the Ruggles work is pretty formidable.

(i) *Symphonies Nos. 1 in D min.; No. 2;* (ii) *No. 3;* (iii; iv) *No. 4;* (iii) *Orchestral Set No. 1;* (iii; iv) *Orchestral Set No. 2;* (iii) *Three Places in New England.*

(B) **(*) Double Decca (ADD) 466 745-2 (2). (i) LAPO, Mehta; (ii) ASMF, Marriner; (iii) Cleveland O, Dohnányi; (iv) Cleveland Ch.

Mehta's Los Angeles recordings of the first two symphonies are very well recorded indeed. The *First* is a charming work, much influenced by Dvořák and Tchaikovsky, but still with touches of individuality. It is superbly played, but the drawback here is a substantial cut in the last movement. The more uneven *Second Symphony* is given an equally committed performance, with the rich but brilliant Decca sound revealing every detail, though it is not over-lit or too analytical. Marriner's account of the *Third Symphony* is first rate in every way, just as successful as Bernstein's account, and much better recorded. For the *Fourth Symphony*, *Orchestral Set Nos. 1 & 2* and the masterly *Three Places in New England* we move into the digital era with Dohnányi's Cleveland forces: these performances are very fine, and the sound is superb. In short, if you don't mind about the cut mentioned above, this is an inexpensive way of making a representative collection of Ives's major works at a modest outlay.

Symphony No. 1 in D min.

*** Chan. 9053. Detroit SO, Järvi – BARBER: *Essays 1–3.* ***

Symphony No. 1 in D min.; Orchestral Set No. 2; Robert Browning Overture; The Unanswered Question.

(BB) **(*) RCA (ADD) Navigator 74321 29246-2. Chicago SO, Gould.

(i) *Symphony No. 1 in D min.;* (ii) *Robert Browning Overture;* (i) *Three Places in New England.*

(N) (B) **(*) Sony (ADD) SBK 89290. (i) Philadelphia. O, Ormandy; (ii) American SO, Stokowski.

Symphonies Nos. 1; 4.

*** Sony SK 44939. Chicago SO, Tilson Thomas.

This RCA recording, the very first recording of the *First Symphony*, was made by Morton Gould in Chicago in 1965; it has that special quality of freshness almost always found in recording premières, with the mercurial spirit of Ives emerging every so often, so that the result is very enjoyable indeed. The *Orchestral Set No. 2* is similarly vivid in colour and detail. The *Robert Browning Overture* (at 20 minutes) has some good ideas but rather outstays its welcome, while *The Unanswered Question* is one of the composer's most beautiful and imaginative pieces. Gould's performances are sympathetic and very well played, but they just lack the intensity that Bernstein and others brought to them, although they are still pretty magnetic. The mid-1960s recordings are basically warm and atmospheric, even if the violins are very brightly lit, and even fierce at times.

Neeme Järvi gives a very persuasive account of the *First Symphony*, and there is a fresh and unforced virtuosity from the Detroit orchestra. Excellent, very natural recorded sound, excellently balanced.

Tilson Thomas's strong and brilliant Chicago performances make a generous and apt coupling, the more valuable for providing first recordings of the revised editions of the composer's tangled scores, with bright, well-detailed sound and superb playing.

Stokowski brings out the often aggressive vigour of the *Robert Browning Overture*, but although it has several good ideas, he does not quite dispel the feeling that such a noisy piece – lasting over 22 minutes – is a bit over long. Ormandy secures a brilliant performance of Ives's Dvořákian *First Symphony*, as he does of the *Three Places in New England*, Ives's most compelling multi-movement work. Stokowski and Ormandy are both red-blooded Ivesians, and it shows in every bar. The recordings dates are not given (presumably from the 1960s) and are generally good, if a bit too present. A bargain just the same, with a playing time of just under 80 minutes.

Symphony No. 2.

*** Chan. 9390-2. Detroit SO, Järvi – CRESTON: *Symphony No. 2*. ***

Symphony No. 2; Central Park in the Dark; The Gong on the Hook and Ladder; Hallowe'en; Hymn for Strings; Tone Roads No. 1; The Unanswered Question.

*** DG 429 220-2. NYPO, Bernstein.

Symphony No. 2; Symphony No. 3 (The Camp Meeting).

(M) *** Sony (ADD) SMK 60202. NYPO, Bernstein (with talk: 'Leonard Bernstein discusses Charles Ives').

**(*) Sony SK 46440. Concg. O, Tilson Thomas.

Symphonies Nos. (i) 2; (ii) 4.

(M) **(*) RCA 09026 63316-2. (i) Phd. O, Ormandy. (ii) John Alldis Choir, LPO, Serebrier.

Ives composed his *Second Symphony* between 1897 and 1901. As the composer told us 'it expresses the musical feelings of the Connecticut country around here (Redding and Danbury) in the 1890s, the music of the country folk. It is full of tunes they sang and played then.' Indeed, it is full of all sorts of things, a mixture of nineteenth-century Romanticism and hymns, folk tunes, patriotic songs, college ditties – Ives's eclecticism already emerging strongly. It is an uneven work, perhaps, but very approachable. Ormandy offers a reasonably good account (1973), but there are more exciting and better recorded versions available.

The Chandos CD offers a very good performance, and has the great advantage of also offering Neeme Järvi's account of Paul Creston's vital and invigorating *Second Symphony*.

However, Bernstein's DG disc brings one of the richest offerings of Ives yet put on record, offering the *Symphony No. 2* plus six shorter orchestral pieces. They include two of his very finest, *Central Park in the Dark* and *The Unanswered Question*, both characteristically quirky but deeply poetic too. The extra tensions and expressiveness of live performance here heighten the impact of each of the works. The difficult acoustic of Avery Fisher Hall in New York has rarely sounded more sympathetic on record.

Bernstein's earlier CBS/Sony recordings have characteristic conviction and freshness. The remastered sound is amazingly improved over the old LPs, full and atmospheric. The balance is too close, but the dynamics of the playing convey the fullest range of emotion. This reissue includes Bernstein's illustrated lecture on Ives (recorded in 1966).

Tilson Thomas's performances may not have the fervour of a Bernstein in this music – perhaps reflecting the fact that this is not an American orchestra – but they are strong and direct, and in No. 3 the revised edition is used.

In the *Fourth Symphony* José Serebrier acted as subsidiary conductor for Stokowski when he conducted the world première in New York. In this English performance he managed to find his way through multi-layered textures which have deliberately conflicting rhythms. The players respond loyally. A vivid, gripping work, if perhaps not such great music as some American commentators thought at the time. For the CD collector it at least provides a storehouse of fantastic orchestral sound, and the recording is certainly vivid, if unrefined at times.

Symphony No. 3 (The Camp Meeting).

*** Argo 417 818-2. ASMF, Marriner – BARBER: *Adagio;* COPLAND: *Quiet City;* COWELL: *Hymn;* CRESTON: *Rumor.* ***

*** Pro Arte CDD 140. St Paul CO, Davies – COPLAND: *Appalachian Spring* etc. ***

Symphony No. 3; Three Places in New England.

(M) *** Mercury [432 755-2] . Eastman-Rochester O, Hanson – SCHUMAN: *New England Triptych* ***; MENNIN: *Symphony No. 5.* **(*)

Symphony No. 3; Three Places in New England; A Set of Pieces; The Unanswered Question.

(M) *** DG 457 911-2. Orpheus CO.

Marriner's account is first rate in every way. It does not have the advantage of a digital master, but the 1976 analogue recording has slightly sharper detail in this remastered format.

The Orpheus Chamber Orchestra never cease to amaze and their playing here is of their usual stunning order of accomplishment and artistry. Their account of the *Third Symphony* is as good as any in the catalogue, and the same goes for their evocative and imaginative accounts of the companion pieces. With first-class modern digital recording this is excellent value.

Russell Davies does not use the new edition of Ives's score; nevertheless, he too gives a fine account of this gentlest of Ives's symphonies, with its overtones of hymn singing and revivalist meetings, and the beauty of the piece still comes over strongly.

As Hanson readily shows, Ives's quixotic genius is at its most individual and harmonically daring in *Three Places in New England*. Both works here are most understandingly presented on Mercury, and Hanson proves equally at home in the folksy imagery of the *Third Symphony*. The acoustics of the Eastman theatre are less than ideally expansive, but the 1957 recording is remarkably full-bodied and vivid. This CD is available only in the USA.

Variations on America (orch. Schuman).

(N) (BB) *** Naxos 8.559083. Bournemouth SO, Serebrier –
  SCHUMAN: *Violin Concerto; New England Triptych*. ***

Ives's *Variations on America* is an apt coupling for two outstanding works of William Schuman, who proves an infinitely imaginative colourist in orchestrating the former's brilliant and sometimes whimsical variations on the national melody, which has quite different words and implications in the USA and England. Serebrier's performance with the excellent Bournemouth Orchestra has subtlety of detail as well as gusto and the recording is first class.

String Quartets Nos. 1–2.

*** DG 435 864-2. Emerson Qt – BARBER: *Quartet*. **(*)

The *First* of Ives's *String Quartets* comes from the composer's early twenties and makes liberal use of hymn-tunes in the first movement fugue. The *Second* is made of sterner stuff with its high norm of dissonance. It is undeniably an extraordinary musical document and is well worth study. The Emerson Quartet give it a performance of stunning efficiency and brilliance. Full-blooded and very present DG recording.

Songs: *Autumn; Berceuse; The cage; Charlie Rutlage; Down east; Dreams; Evening; The greatest man; The Housatonic at Stockbridge; Immortality; Like a sick eagle; Maple leaves; Memories: 1, 2, 3; On the counter; Romanzo di Central Park; The see'r; Serenity; The side-show; Slow march; Slugging a vampire; Songs my mother taught me; Spring song; The things our fathers loved; Tom sails away; Two little flowers.*

*** Etcetera KTC 1020. Alexander, Crone.

Roberta Alexander presents her excellent and illuminating choice of Ives songs in chronological order, starting with one written when Ives was only fourteen, *Slow march*, already predicting developments ahead. Sweet, nostalgic songs predominate, but the singer punctuates them with leaner, sharper inspirations. Her manner is not always quite tough enough in those, but this is characterful singing from an exceptionally rich and attractive voice. Tan Crone is the understanding accompanist, and the recording is first rate.

JACOB, Gordon (1895–1987)

Mini-Concerto for Clarinet & String Orchestra.

*** Hyp. CDA 66031. King, NW CO of Seattle, Francis –
  COOKE; RAWSTHORNE: *Concertos*. ***

Gordon Jacob in his eighties wrote this miniature concerto for Thea King, totally charming in its compactness. She proves the most persuasive of dedicatees, splendidly accompanied by the orchestra from Seattle and treated to first-rate 1982 analogue sound, splendidly transferred.

Symphony No. 2 in C; A Little Symphony; Festival Overture.

*** Classico CLASSCD 204. Munich SO, Bostock.

The *Second Symphony* (1944/5) is spirited and outgoing. The first movement, after its deceptively gentle introduction, is boisterously scored and full of energy, with a swinging string-melody for second subject. It is followed by an intense, searching *Adagio*, which opens plangently on high strings but later assumes the character of a threnody, reflecting not only the composer's recent wartime experience but also the 1914–18 conflict in which he lost a much-loved brother. The mood lightens with an engaging *Scherzo*, where gossamer strings and dainty woodwind are punctuated by more assertive brass. The final *Ground* is a passacaglia, which begins unostentatiously but reaches a boisterous, confident conclusion. The *'Little' Symphony* is perhaps an even finer work, more succinct and more introspective, but with a splendidly vigorous *Scherzo*, whose rhythmic character is arresting, and with a jaunty, light-hearted finale, full of good humour. The *Festival Overture*, written for the Essex Youth Orchestra, combines Waltonesque rhythmic exuberance with a characteristic Jacobian lyrical strain. The performances here by the excellent Munich orchestra under Douglas Bostock are alive and thoroughly persuasive and in no way unidiomatic; the recording is vivid and quite spacious.

Divertimento for Harmonica & String Quartet.

*** Chan. 8802. Reilly, Hindar Qt – MOODY: *Quintet; Suite*. ***

Gordon Jacob's set of eight sharply characterized miniatures shows the composer at his most engagingly imaginative and the performances are deliciously piquant in colour and feeling. The recording could hardly be more successful.

Oboe Quartet.

*** Chan. 8392. Francis, English Qt – BAX: *Quintet*; HOLST: *Air & Variations* etc.; MOERAN: *Fantasy Quartet*. ***

Gordon Jacob's *Oboe Quartet* is well crafted and entertaining, particularly the vivacious final Rondo. The performance could hardly be bettered, and the recording is excellent too.

JACQUET DE LA GUERRE, Elisabeth (1665–1729)

Pièces de clavecin: Premier livre (1687); Pièces de clavecin (1707): Suites: in D min.; G.

*** Metronome METCD 1026. Cerasi (harpsichord).

Elisabeth Jacquet de La Guerre emerges as a major musical talent of her time, composing music of very high quality which can compare with and match the output of her more famous contemporaries. Carole Cerasi's recital includes all her solo keyboard works, and her CD won the *Gramophone's* 1999 Award for baroque instrumental music. It received the special accolade of Stanley Sadie, who commented that Cerasi 'plays all this music with real command: she knows where in the passionate pieces to press forward and where to linger, how to let the rhythms flow in the dances, how to shape the extended chaconnes and how to make the most of Jacquet's expressive harmony.'

To this we would add her skill in giving an improvisatory impression in her freedom of line in the remarkable *Préludes*. We would add one proviso, and it is an important one. Her ornamentation is profuse and continuing, and it certainly affects the line of the music: some listeners may have problems with this, so an element of caution must accompany our otherwise strong recommendation. She plays a characterful seventeenth-century Ruckers harpsichord, rebuilt in 1763, and is excellently if fairly resonantly recorded.

JADIN, Hyacinthe (1775–1800)

String Quartets, Opp. 1/3; 2/1; 4/1.

*** ASV CDGAU 151. Rasumovsky Qt – VACHON:
   Quartets. ***

Jadin, of Belgian descent, obviously studied the quartets of Haydn and Mozart, for Op. 1/3 is dedicated to the former master. In F minor, it is the most strikingly individual work here. The chromatic flavour of the opening of Op. 2/1 has just a little in common with Mozart's *Dissonance Quartet*, and the amiable Op. 4/1 in two movements is attractively lightweight. The Rasumovsky Quartet have obviously lived with this music, and they play it with appealing simplicity and dedication. They are well recorded with plenty of presence and a nice ambient warmth.

JANÁČEK, Leoš (1854–1928)

Adagio for Orchestra; Ballad of Blaník; Cossack Dance; (i) *Danube Symphony. The Fiddler's Child* (ballad); *Idyll for Strings; Jealousy Overture; Lachian Dances;* (ii) *The Pilgrimage of the Soul (Violin Concerto);* (iii) *Schluck und Jau* (incidental music): excerpts: *Andante & Allegretto. Serbian Kolo; Sinfonietta; Suite, Op. 3; Suite for Strings; Taras Bulba* (rhapsody).

*** Sup. 11 1834-2 (3). Brno State PO, Jílek, with (i) Dvořáková; (ii) Zenatý; (i; iii) Beneš.

(i) *Danube Symphony. Sinfonietta;* (ii) *The Pilgrimage of the Soul (Violin Concerto);* (iii) *Schluck und Jau.*

*** Sup. 11 1422-2. Brno State PO, Jílek, with (i) Dvořáková; (ii) Zenatý; (i; iii) Beneš.

Jílek's performance of the *Sinfonietta* can hold its own with the best in terms of atmosphere and authority, though the recording is admittedly not in the demonstration bracket. There is some invention of great imagination in the *Danube Symphony*, as, indeed, there is in the *Violin Concerto (The Pilgrimage of the Soul)*. Ivan Zenatý is an aristocrat of the violin and his performance is poignantly affecting. The incidental music to *Schluck und Jau* is a two-movement piece about as long as the *Violin Concerto* and likewise full of characteristic ideas. Of the other two discs, the first, offering the *Lachian Dances*, the early *Suite for Strings* and its seven-movement companion, the *Idyll*, is well filled, and the other disc brings such valuable scores as *Blaník, The Fiddler's Child*

and *Taras Bulba*. Good, idiomatic performances and very good, though not demonstration-quality, recordings.

(i) *Capriccio for Piano & Wind; Concertino for Piano & Chamber Ensemble;* (ii) *Lachian Dances;* (iii) *Sinfonietta;* (iv) *Suite for String Orchestra;* (iii) *Taras Bulba;* (v) *Mládí* (suite for wind).

(B) *** Double Decca (ADD) 448 255-2 (2). (i) Crossley, L. Sinf., Atherton; (ii) LPO, Huybrechts; (iii) VPO, Mackerras; (iv) LACO, Marriner; (v) Bell, Craxton, Pay, Harris, Gatt, Eastop.

On this Double Decca Paul Crossley is the impressive soloist in the *Capriccio* and the *Concertino*, performances that can be put alongside those of Firkušný – and no praise can be higher. This account of *Mládí* is among the finest available; the work's youthful sparkle comes across to excellent effect here. In Mackerras's VPO coupling of the *Sinfonietta* and *Taras Bulba* the massed brass of the *Sinfonietta* has tremendous bite and brilliance as well as characteristic Viennese ripeness. *Taras Bulba* is also given more weight and body than usual, the often savage dance-rhythms presented with great energy. The performance of the *Lachian Dances* under the Belgian conductor, François Huybrechts, is highly idiomatic and effective, and he is helped by fine playing from the LPO. The *Suite for String Orchestra* was Marriner's first recording with the Los Angeles Chamber Orchestra, and the sound is characteristically ripe. The *Suite* is an early and not entirely mature piece but, when played as committedly as it is here, its attractions are readily perceived, and it certainly does not want character. Excellent sound throughout.

(i) *Capriccio for Piano & 7 Instruments; Concertino for Piano & 6 Instruments. (Piano) Sonata (1.X.1905); In the Mist; On an Overgrown Path I & II; Reminiscences; Zdenka Variations.*

(M) *** DG (ADD) 449 764-2 (2). Firkušný; (i) Bav. RSO (members), Kubelik.

Capriccio (for piano left hand & chamber ensemble); *Concertino* (for piano & chamber orchestra); *Mládí (Youth)* for wind sextet; *March of the Blue Boys* for piccolo and piano; (i) *Nursery Rhymes (Říkadla)* for chamber choir & chamber ensemble.

*** Chan. 9399. Berman, Netherlands Wind Ens., Fischer; (i) with Prague Music Ac. Ch.

Kubelik has a special feeling for this repertoire and partners Rudolf Firkušný in his thoroughly idiomatic earlier account of the *Concertino*. Now reissued in DG's series of 'Originals', this collection is eminently recommendable. It again offers Firkušný in a discerningly sympathetic account of the *Capriccio*. Firkušný has long been regarded as the most authoritative exponent of the piano music. He recorded these pieces in the early 1970s, and he produces seamless legato lines, hammerless tone and rapt atmosphere. Kubelik then partners him in the concertante works. The recordings are all of high quality.

Though Firkušný remains in a class of his own, Boris Berman is a good soloist in both the *Concertino* and *Capriccio*. The astonishing *Říkadla* are given with great character by the Netherlands Wind Ensemble and the Prague Academy

Choir. Thierry Fischer directs the proceedings impressively: the playing throughout is full of life and sensitivity. Vibrant recorded sound – every detail tells.

(i) *The Fiddler's Child;* (ii) *Idyll for String Orchestra;*
(i) *Jealousy: Overture; Sinfonietta;* (ii) *Suite for Strings;*
(i) *Taras Bulba; The Cunning Little Vixen: Suite.*

(B) *** Chan. 2-for-1 241-7 (2). (i) Czech PO, Bělohlávek;
    (ii) Jupiter O, Rose.

Idyll; Suite for String Orchestra.

⬤ *** Chan. 9816. Norwegian CO, Brown – BARTOK:
    Divertimento for Strings. *** ⬤
(N) (M) **(*) Panton 81 1437-2 131. Czech Chamber Soloists,
    Matyáš – MARTINU: *Sextet.*

The *Idyll* and the *Suite for Strings* are both from the late 1870s and are already available on Chandos. However, the Norwegian Chamber Orchestra and Iona Brown sweep the board. Their playing is vibrant, full of enthusiasm and vitality, and yet finding also a touching nostalgia in the slow sections of the *Idyll* and an even more subtle and haunting espressivo in the two lovely *Adagios* of the *Suite*. The ebb and flow of the performances is seemingly spontaneous, yet the ensemble of this splendid orchestra is that of a first-class string quartet, and they play with comparable integration of feeling. The recorded sound is absolutely state-of-the-art and the Bartók coupling quite outstanding.

The *Idyll* and the *Suite for Strings* are also ravishingly played by the Jupiter Orchestra under Gregory Rose, who shows himself completely at home in the lilting Czech idiom and who achieves rapt concentration in the touching slow movements. The rest of the programme is also very stimulating. There are more dramatic and fiery accounts available of *Taras Bulba*. Bělohlávek is perhaps less at home in this melodramatic piece than in the nature mysticism of the orchestral suite from *The Cunning Little Vixen* or the pathos of *The Fiddler's Child*. But his splendidly vivid account of the *Sinfonietta* is unsurpassed, and throughout all these performances the beauty of the orchestral playing, and opulence and detail of the recordings add, to the attractions of a very well-chosen compilation.

The Czech Chamber Soloists led by Ivan Matyáš deliver straightforward and well-played accounts of these early pieces for string orchestra, but they are no match for the stunningly recorded set by Iona Brown and the Norwegian Chamber Orchestra on Chandos which is coupled with the Bartók *Divertimento* and to which we accorded a rosette.

Sinfonietta.

(N) *** EMI (M) CDM5 66980-2 [566995]. Philh. O, Rattle –
    Glagolitic Mass. ***
(M) *** EMI CDM7 64740-2. Philh. O, Rattle – HOLST:
    Planets. **(*)
(M) *** DG 445 501-2. BPO, Abbado – BARTOK: *The
    Miraculous Mandarin* etc. ***
*** Chan. 8897. Czech PO, Bělohlávek – MARTINU:
    Symphony No. 6; SUK: *Scherzo.* ***
(B) *** EMI double fforte (ADD) CZS5 72664-2 (2). Chicago
    SO, Ozawa – BARTOK: *Concerto for Orchestra;*

LUTOSLAWSKI: *Concerto for Orchestra;* STRAVINSKY:
    Firebird Ballet. **(*)
(M) **(*) Telarc CD 82010. LAPO, Previn – BARTOK:
    Concerto for Orchestra. **(*)

Sinfonietta; Lachian Dances; Taras Bulba.

(BB) *** Naxos 8.550411. Slovak RSO (Bratislava), Lenárd.

(i) *Sinfonietta;* (ii) *Taras Bulba.*

(B) ** Sony (ADD) SBK 62404. (i) Cleveland O, Szell;
    (ii) Toronto SO, Davis – KODALY: *Dances of Galánta;
    Dances of Marosszék.* **(*)

Rattle gets an altogether first-class response from the orchestra and truthful recorded sound from the EMI engineers and his coupling with the *Glagolitic Mass* is very attractive indeed. It is also available with a less successful Holst coupling.

Abbado's later DG digital recording finds the Berlin Philharmonic Orchestra on splendid form. The Jesus-Christus Kirche provides a superbly spacious sonority for the brass. The opening brings a tautening of the pace, but the subtleties of colour are not diminished by the more robust body of the newer version.

Jiří Bělohlávek's exultant and imaginative account of the *Sinfonietta* is one of the best currently on offer and is coupled with an outstanding version of Martinů's *Sixth Symphony*; the recording, made in the Smetana Hall, Prague, is impressive.

On Naxos we have the normal LP coupling of the *Sinfonietta* and *Taras Bulba*, but with the *Lachian Dances* thrown in for good measure, all played by musicians steeped in the Janáček tradition – and all at a very modest cost. These are excellent performances; the recording, made in a fairly resonant studio, is natural and free from any artificially spotlit balance.

Ozawa's account too is brilliantly played and very well recorded (in 1969). The CD transfer is also very successful, full-bodied if not opulent. A useful alternative to Abbado, if the three coupings are suitable.

The amiability of Janáček's colourful and brassy work is what dominates Previn's performance rather than any more dramatic qualities. The Los Angeles Philharmonic has never been recorded with a warmer and more realistic bloom than here by Telarc. However, those looking for more bite and brilliance in this work will probably be happier with either Mackerras or Rattle.

Szell's 1965 recording of the *Sinfonietta* has long been admired for its orchestral virtuosity and control. It is a very spirited and colourful account, and the new transfer brings out the ambient effect of the Severance Hall recording, even if the dynamic range remains less expansive than it should be. But the real snag here is that Andrew Davis's *Taras Bulba* has an altogether lower voltage. What a pity that was included instead of Ormandy's *Háry János Suite!*

Suite for String Orchestra.

(BB) *** Discover DICD 920234. Virtuosi di Praga, Vlček –
    SUK: *Serenade for Strings* etc. ***

The expanded Virtuosi di Praga give an appropriately ardent and certainly a bravura account of Janáček's six-movement

Suite for String Orchestra, yet this group of seventeen players (including the leader/director, Oldřich Vlček) possess a vividly full sonority, and they do not miss the work's more subtle touches.

Taras Bulba.

(N) *** Australian Decca Eloquence 467 602-2. Cleveland O, Dohnányi – KODALY: *Concerto for Orchestra;* BARTOK: *Concerto for Orchestra.* ***

Dohnányi's warmly expressive reading of *Taras Bulba* is recorded in Decca's finest digital Cleveland style, and is imaginatively coupled on this excellent Australian Eloquence CD.

CHAMBER MUSIC

(i; iii) *Allegro; Dumka; Romance; Sonata* (for violin and piano); **(ii; iii)** *Pohádka (Fairy Tale); Presto* (for cello and piano); **(iii)** (Piano) *In the Mists; 3 Moravian Dances; On an Overgrown Path, Series I–II; Paralipomena; Reminiscence; Piano Sonata in E flat min. (I. X. 1905); Theme & Variations (Zdenka's Variations).*

**(*) BIS CD 663/664. (i) Wallin; (ii) Rondin; (iii) Pöntinen.

This excellent collection ranges from the *Romance* for violin and piano from the late 1870s, to the much later *Reminiscence* for piano. Pöntinen is an unfailingly intelligent player. Ulf Wallin proves a strong yet sensitive advocate of the *Violin Sonata*, and the cellist Mats Rondin is no less admirable in the *Pohádka (Fairy Tale)* and the *Presto* for cello and piano. Readers wanting this whole collection may rest assured that both playing and recording are of a generally high standard.

Mládí.

(BB) **(*) Naxos 8.553851-2. Michael Thompson Wind Quintet – BARBER: *Summer Music* **(*); HINDEMITH: *Kleine Kammermusik* **(*); LARSSON: *Quattro tempi.* **

Janáček's *Mládí* is superbly played by the Michael Thompson Wind Quintet, who are sensitive to every nuance of this glorious and haunting score. Wonderfully accomplished and sensitive though they are, they are let down by a close balance, which robs the music of atmosphere.

Pohádka.

(N) *** (M) Decca (ADD) 466 823-2. Rostropovich, Britten – SHOSTAKOVICH: *7 Blok Romances; Cello Sonata.* BRIDGE: *Phantasie Quartet.* ***

(BB) *** ASV CDQS 6218. Gregor-Smith, Wrigley – PROKOFIEV; SHOSTAKOVICH: *Cello Sonatas;* MARTINU: *Variations.* ***

Pohádka, described as a fairy-tale for cello and piano, makes a delightful extra item in this disc of performances from the Aldeburgh Festival. Characteristically, Rostropovich and Britten are prompted to take an improvisational approach, giving logic to the wayward, quirky element in Janáček's inspiration.

The husband-and-wife team of Bernard Gregor-Smith and Yolande Wrigley also gives a lively and sympathetic account of the three-movement *Pohádka*, which Janáček

composed in 1910. It makes an admirable makeweight for the Prokofiev and Shostakovich sonatas.

String Quartet No. 1 (Kreutzer Sonata).

✿ *** Koch 3-6436-2. Medici Qt –BRITTEN: *Quartet No. 3;* – RAVEL: *Quartet;* SHOSTAKOVICH: *Quartet No. 8;* SMETANA: *Quartet No. 1.* *** ✿

*** Testament (ADD) SBT 1074. Smetana Qt – DVORAK: *Piano Quintet etc.* ***

String Quartet No. 2 (Intimate Letters).

*** Testament (ADD) SBT 1075. Smetana Qt – DVORAK: *String Quartet No. 14 etc.* ***

(N) **(BB)** *** Arte Nova 74321 34036-2. Alexander Qt – SCHUBERT: *Quartetsatz;* SMETANA: *String Quartet No. 1.* ***

The Medici players grab the listener's attention in the very opening bars, and they give an unsurpassed performance which combines deep feeling with great subtlety of colour. The opening of the third movement is disarming yet gripping in its combination of poignant simplicity and spontaneous, passionate outbursts. The recording could not be more real and tangible.

The Smetana Quartet's account of the *First Quartet (Kreutzer Sonata)* is also one of the very best versions of the work ever committed to disc. There is a wonderful feeling that these players have lived with this music all their lives – and in fact live *for* it, so committed do they sound. Recommended with some urgency. Worth every penny of its full price.

Like its companion the Smetana account of the *Intimate Letters* appears in Britain for the first time. It deserves the same accolade. In terms of subtlety, tonal finish and technical polish, this is absolutely flawless – and the 1960s sound is superb, and not just for its period. Strongly recommended alongside its companion.

The *First Quartet*, like the Smetana an autobiographical work, also makes an excellent coupling in the Alexander Quartet's tough and powerful reading, which aptly brings out the composer's gritty, quirky originality. Vivid, immediate sound.

String Quartets Nos. 1 (Kreutzer); 2 (Intimate Letters).

*** ASV CDDCA 749. Lindsay Qt – DVORAK: *Cypresses.* ***

**(*) Ph. (IMS) 456 574-2. Guarneri Qt.

(B)**(*) HM (ADD) HMT 7901380. Melos Qt.

(i) *String Quartets Nos. 1–2;* **(ii)** *Mládí: Suite for Wind Sextet.*

**(*) Koch/Panton (ADD) 11203-2. (i) Vlach Qt; (ii) Foerster Wind Quintet, Horák.

(i) *String Quartets Nos. 1–2;* **(ii)** *On an Overgrown Path: Suite No. 1.*

*** Cal. CAL 9699. (i) Talich Qt; (ii) Kvapil.

(i) *String Quartets Nos. 1–2;* **(ii)** *Pohádka for Cello & Piano;* **(iii)** *Violin Sonata.*

(BB) *** Naxos 8.553895. (i) Vlach Qt; (ii) Ericsson; (ii–iii) Maly; (iii) Vlachová.

Pride of place must go to the Talich Quartet on Calliope,

not because their recording is the best, but because of their extraordinary qualities of insight. They play the *Intimate Letters* as if its utterances came from a world so private that it must be approached with great care. The disc's value is much enhanced by a fill-up in the form of the *First Suite, On an Overgrown Path*. Radoslav Kvapil is thoroughly inside this repertoire.

The Lindsays on ASV are also eminently competitive and have the right blend of sensitivity and intensity. Theirs must certainly rank very highly among current recommendations. They are played with the same concentration and sensitivity they bring to all they do, and recorded with great naturalness.

There are one or two finer performances of the two *Quartets* listed above, but the Vlach Quartet on Naxos give well-played, impassioned accounts of both and are warmly recorded. Moreover, the account of the *Violin Sonata* by Jana Vlachová and František Malý is very fine, and the *Pohádka for Cello and Piano* is given as touching and imaginative a performance by Mikael Ericsson as any in the catalogue. Good recordings and excellent value for money.

The Melos Quartet offer nothing in addition to the two *Quartets*, but theirs are performances of considerable character and fire and, though the playing-time is ungenerous and the recording a bit fierce, they are worth consideration. The performances are very idiomatic and appealing, the recording far from inferior, and this record will give pleasure. At least they are now offered at bargain price.

The account of the Janáček quartets from the Guarneri on Philips is a strong one: both are well characterized and well played, and the recording is truthful and well balanced. It would receive a strong recommendation, were it not handicapped by short measure (full price for 41 minutes is too much to ask these days, however enjoyable those may be). Many of its rivals are as good artistically and offer another major work.

The Koch/Panton coupling with the Vlach Quartet, recorded in 1969, and a 1970 version of *Mládí* should not automatically be dismissed on grounds of age. The performances are very idiomatic and appealing, the recording far from inferior; and this record will give pleasure.

Violin Sonata.

(N) *** Praga PRD 250 153. Remés, Kayahara – DVORAK: *Sonatina;* MARTINU, SMETANA: *Violin Sonatas.* ***

*** Ph. 462 621-2. Suwana, Berezovsky – BRAHMS: *Sonata, Op. 120/2, etc.;* DVORAK: *4 Romantic Pieces, Op. 75,* etc. ***

*** Virgin VC5 45122-2. Tetzlaff, Andsnes – DEBUSSY: *Sonata;* NIELSEN: *Sonata No. 2;* RAVEL: *Sonata.* ***

(*) DG 427 351-2. Kremer, Argerich – BARTOK: *Sonata No. 1;* MESSIAEN: *Theme & Variations.* *

This newest Praga account from Václav Remes and the rich-timbred Sachito Kayahara is fiercely intense, yet warmly affectionate, the questing closing *Adagio* highly dramatic, and with the closing pages creating a mood of tender intensity. The playing itself is superbly assured and characterful, and the recording first class. The couplings are equally fine.

In the hands of Akiko Suwana and Boris Berezovsky the sonata receives a most distinguished performance, among the finest in the catalogue. Both artists are completely natural and unaffected, and the recording is well nigh perfect. However, the Virgin version by Christian Tetzlaff and Leif Ove Andsnes offers perhaps more appropriate couplings. They play with commitment and dedication. Theirs is an eloquent – indeed at times inspired – performance, and they are accorded excellent recording.

The *Sonata* is also played with great imaginative intensity and power by Gidon Kremer and Martha Argerich, though there is some expressive exaggeration. Excellent DG recording.

(i) Violin Sonata; (ii) Piano Sonata (I.X.1905); On an Overgrown Path, Book 2; A Recollection.

(N) (BB) **(*) RCA Double 74321 84592-2 (2).(i) Korcia, Pludermacher; (ii) Firkus – MARTINU: *Cello Sonatas Nos. 1–2.* ***

Laurent Korcia and Georges Pludermacher make a thoroughly committed and sensitive reponse to the *Violin Sonata* and are well recorded, while Firkus brings a special authority and sensitivity to the piano repertoire. It is his selfless dedication to the music that again tells, and his basic approach has not changed since he recorded these pieces for DG twenty years earlier. His playing is as marvellous as ever, but the RCA digital recording does not give us the best piano quality: though it is perfectly acceptable it is a little biased towards the middle and bass registers. However this is an inexpensive reissue and the coupling is highly recommendable.

PIANO MUSIC

Along an Overgrown Path: Books 1 & 2; In the Mists; 3 Moravian Dances; A Recollection; Piano Sonata (1.X.1905).

*** EMI CDC7 54094-2. Rudy.

Along an Overgrown Path: Books I & II; In the Mists; A Recollection; Piano Sonata (1.X.1905).

(N) *(**) ECM 461 660-2. Schiff.

Along an Overgrown Path: Books I & II; In the Mists; Sonata (I.X.1905); Souvenir.

(N) **(*) HM HMC 901508. Planès.

Along an Overgrown Path: Suite No. 1; In the Mists; Piano Sonata (I.X.1905).

(N) (M) *** Virgin VM5 61839-2. Andsnes.

Mikhail Rudy proves a perceptive and sympathetic guide in this music. His is a fine account of the *Sonata*, and he succeeds in penetrating the world of the *Overgrown Path* miniatures to perfection. He conveys their acute sense of melancholy and their improvisatory character with distinction, but this has been deleted as we go to press.

Leif Ove Andsnes also gives us a very well-thought-out and imaginatively realized recital, including a highly sensitive account of *In the Mists*, which is second to none in conveying the pervasive melancholy and evocative atmosphere of these pieces. This is every bit as telling as Mikhail Rudy's EMI account, and beautifully recorded, and while it includes less music it has now been reissued at mid-price.

Alain Planès is a sensitive and intelligent artist whose sympathy with this repertoire is evident. All the same he is not quite as authoritative musically or as distinguished pianistically as Firkušný (DG) or Andsnes (Virgin).

András Schiff has great feeling for this repertoire and plays with enormous sensitivity and insight. But the recorded sound poses a real problem: there is a fair amount of reverberation which at times smudges detail and the instrument appears bass-heavy, ill-defined and thin on top. Readers should stick with Firkušný or Andsnes.

VOCAL MUSIC

Coz ta nase bríza (Our birch tree); Elegie na smrt dcery Olgy (Elegy on the death of daughter Olga); Hradcanske písnicky (Song of Hradcany); Holubicka (The dove); Kacena divoká (The wild duck); Kantor Halfar (Schoolmaster Halfar); Potulny silenec (The wondering madman); Ríkadla (Nursery Rhymes); Vlcí stopa (The wolf's trail).

*** Ph. (IMS) 442 534-2. Netherlands Chamber Ch., Schoenberg Ens., De Leeuw.

Janáček's choral music covers a wide range from such straightforward partsongs as *Our birch tree* or *The dove* to the ingenious, dazzling *Ríkadla* (*Nursery Rhymes*) of his last years. The affecting *Elegy on the death of daughter Olga* begins as if we are in the middle of *On an Overgrown Path* and is every bit as subtle. The Netherlands Chamber Choir and members of the Schoenberg Ensemble under Reinbert De Leeuw produce cultured, well-blended results, and the Philips recording is impressive in its clarity and presence. It is possible to imagine wilder and more passionate performances, particularly from Moravian choirs, but in an area of the repertoire which is not generously served this deserves a strong recommendation.

Glagolitic Mass (original version, ed. Wingfield).

*** Chan. 9310. Kiberg, Stene, Svensson, Cold, Danish Nat. R. Ch. & SO, Mackerras – KODALY: *Psalmus hungaricus.* ***

The added rhythmic complexities of this original version, as interpreted idiomatically by Mackerras, encourage an apt wildness which brings an exuberant, carefree quality to writing which here, more than ever, seems like the inspiration of the moment. The wildness is also reinforced by having the *Intrada* at the very beginning, before the Introduction, as well as at the end. The chorus sings incisively with incandescent tone, and the tenor soloist, Peter Svensson, has a trumpet-toned precision that makes light of the high tessitura and the stratospheric leaps that Janáček asks for. The soprano Tina Kiberg, also bright and clear rather than beautiful in tone, makes just as apt a choice, and only a certain unsteadiness in Ulrik Cold's relatively light bass tone prevents this from being an ideal quartet. Recorded sound of a weight and warmth that convey the full power of the music.

Glagolitic Mass.

(N) (M) *** EMI CDM5 66980-2 [566995]. Palmer, Gunson, Mitchinson, King, CBSO & Ch., Rattle – *Sinfonietta.* ***

*** Decca 460 213-2. Urbanová, Beňačková, Bogachov, Novák, Slovak Philharmonic Ch., VPO, Chailly – KORNGOLD: *Passover Psalm;* ZEMLINSKY: *Psalm 83.* ***

*** Australian Decca Eloquence (ADD) 466 902-2. Kubiak, Collins, Tear, Schöne, Brighton Festival Ch., RPO, Kempe – KODALY: *Laudes organi; Psalm 114.* ***

Rattle's performance of the standard published score, aptly paired with the *Sinfonietta*, is strong and vividly dramatic, with the Birmingham performers lending themselves to Slavonic passion. The recording is first class and is now reissued as one of EMI's 'Great Recordings of the Century'.

Chailly directs a strong and refined reading of the *Glagolitic Mass*, with fine detail brought out in the glowing Decca recording, though not as immediate as some. If the work's earthiness is a degree underplayed, the emotional depth is fully brought out, with fine idiomatic singing and a virtuoso display from Thomas Trotter in the final organ solo. Warmly recommended for those who fancy the rare couplings.

Kempe's interpretation and the singing of the Brighton Festival Chorus do not always have the snapping authenticity of Rattle's and Mackerras's versions. Instead Kempe stresses the lyrical elements of the score rather than going for outright fervour, but the orchestra and chorus are fully committed, and the solo singing is first rate too, with Teresa Kubiak particularly impressive. Everything is helped by the most realistic recording, which has transferred very well to CD. The unusual Kodály coupling is appropriate and adds to the interest of this reissue on Australian Decca's Eloquence label, which, however, becomes more expensive in the UK.

Mass in E flat; (i) Otčenáš (The Lord's Prayer).

(M) *** EMI CDM5 65587-2. King's College, Cambridge, Ch., Cleobury; Lane; (i) with Davies, Ellis – KODALY: *Missa brevis.* **(*)

The *Mass* comes from 1907–8 and was never completely finished. Janáček's pupil, Vilém Petrželka, discovered the *Kyrie* and *Agnus dei* and a part of the *Credo*, which he completed. It is a beautiful piece. *Otčenáš* (*The Lord's Prayer*) is earlier (1901), written originally for tenor, chorus and harmonium (or piano); accompaniment was replaced in 1906 by organ and harp. The singing is generally good, though the sound is (not unnaturally) English rather than Slavonic. There is no alternative version of either work, but, alas, this has been withdrawn as we go to press.

OPERA

The Cunning Little Vixen (complete); The Cunning Little Vixen (suite, arr. Talich).

*** Decca 417 129-2 (2). Popp, Randová, Jedlická, V. State Op. Ch., Bratislava Children's Ch., VPO, Mackerras.

*** Sup. SU (ADD) 3071/2 612 (2) (without suite). Tattermuschová, Zikmundová, Kroupa, Hlavsa, Prague Nat. Ch. & O, Gregor.

Mackerras's thrusting, red-blooded reading is spectacularly supported by a digital recording of outstanding, demonstration quality. The inspired choice of Lucia Popp as the vixen provides charm in exactly the right measure: sparkling and coquettish, spiteful as well as passionate. The supporting cast is first rate, too. Talich's splendidly arranged orchestral suite is offered as a bonus in a fine new recording.

Janáček's opera is given on Supraphon with plenty of idiomatic Slavonic feeling by the composer's compatriots, with the part of the little vixen here charmingly sung by Helena Tattermuschová. The recording is evocatively warm and atmospheric. While the digitally recorded Decca Mackerras set (with Lucia Popp) remains a more obvious first choice, this earlier Czech version can hold its own. While not missing the red-blooded nature of the composer's inspiration, Gregor also captures the woodland ambience with appealing warmth and colour.

(i) *The Cunning Little Vixen* (sung in English); (ii) *Taras Bulba.*

*** EMI (ADD) CDS7 54212-2 (2). (i) Watson, Tear, Allen, ROHCG Ch. & O; (ii) Philh. O; Rattle.

For anyone who wants the work in English, Simon Rattle's recording provides an ideal answer, with Rattle's warmly expressive approach to the score giving strong support to the singers. The cast is outstanding, with Lillian Watson delightfully bright and fresh as the Vixen and Thomas Allen firm and full-toned as the Forester. If Mackerras's Janáček style is more angular and abrasive, bringing out the jagged, spiky rhythms and unexpected orchestral colours, Rattle's is more moulded, more immediately persuasive, if less obviously idiomatic.

The Excursions of Mr Brouček (complete).

*** Sup. (ADD) 11 2153-2 (2). Přibyl, Svejda, Jonášová, Czech PO Ch. & O, Jílek.

This performance comes over with real charm, thanks to the understanding conducting of Jílek, but also to the characterization of the central character, the bumbling, accident-prone Mr Brouček (literally Mr Beetle). Vilém Přibyl portrays him as an amiable, much-put-upon figure as he makes his excursions. The big team of Czech singers (doubling up roles in the different parts, with Vladimir Krejčik remarkable in no fewer than seven of them) are outstanding, bringing out both the warmth and sense of fun behind the writing. The result is a delight, as sharp and distinctive as any Janáček opera. The analogue recording, made in Prague in 1980, is full and atmospheric with a fine sense of presence on CD.

(i) *From the House of the Dead;* (iii) *Mládí* (for wind sextet); (ii; iii) *Říkadla* (for chamber ch. & 10 instruments).

*** Decca Dig./ADD 430 375-2 (2). (i) Jedlička, Zahradníček, Zídek, Zítek, V. State Op. Ch., VPO, Mackerras; (ii) L. Sinf. Ch.; (iii) L. Sinf., Atherton.

With one exception, the Decca cast is superb, with a range of important Czech singers giving sharply characterized vignettes. The exception is the raw Slavonic singing of the one woman in the cast, Jaroslav Janska, as the boy Aljeja, but even that fails to undermine the intensity of the innocent relationship with the central figure, which provides an emotional anchor for the whole piece. The chamber-music items added for this reissue are both first rate.

Jenůfa (complete).

⬤ *** Decca 414 483-2 (2). Söderström, Ochman, Dvorský, Randová, Popp, V. State Op. Ch., VPO, Mackerras.

This is the warmest and most lyrical of Janáček's operas, and it inspires a performance from Mackerras and his team which is deeply sympathetic, strongly dramatic and superbly recorded. Elisabeth Söderström creates a touching portrait of the girl caught in a family tragedy. The two rival tenors, Peter Dvorský and Wieslaw Ochman as the half-brothers Steva and Laca, are both superb; but dominating the whole drama is the Kostelnitchka of Eva Randová. Some may resist the idea that she should be made so sympathetic but, particularly on record, the drama is made stronger and more involving.

Káta Kabanová (complete).

** Sup. SU 3291-2 632 (3). Vele, Straka, Randová, Kopp, Beňačková, Kundlak, Pecková, Harvánek, Bauerová, Burešová, Prague Nat. Theatre Ch., Czech PO, Mackerras.

(i) *Káta Kabanová* (complete); (ii) *Capriccio for Piano & 7 Instruments; Concertino for Piano & 6 Instruments.*

*** Decca (ADD) 421 852-2 (2). (i) Söderström, Dvorský, Kniplová, Krejčik, Márová, V. State Op. Ch., VPO, Mackerras; (ii) Crossley, L. Sinf., Atherton.

On Decca Elisabeth Söderström dominates the cast as the tragic heroine and gives a performance of great insight and sensitivity; she touches the listener deeply and is supported by Mackerras with imaginative grip and flair. The other soloists are all Czech and their characterizations are brilliantly authentic. But it is the superb orchestral playing and the inspired performance of Söderström that make this set so memorable. The recording is vividly transferred to CD, with a double bonus added in the shape of the two concertante keyboard works, in which Paul Crossley is the impressive soloist.

Though Mackerras's Supraphon set offers digital sound and has an excellent Czech cast, it cannot match his earlier Decca version in colour or bite. Though his speeds are a degree faster than before, the result is less violent and less involving, thanks partly to the low-level recording set in a reverberant acoustic. Beňačková, rich and vibrant, is an exceptionally characterful Káta, arguably more idiomatic than Söderström on Decca, and the other principals are first rate too, but at every point this pales before its rival.

(i) *The Makropulos Affair (Věc Makropulos)*: complete; (ii) *Lachian Dances.*

*** Decca (ADD) 430 372-2 (2). (i) Söderström, Dvorský, Blachut, V. State Op. Ch., VPO, Mackerras; (ii) LPO, Huybrechts.

Mackerras and his superb team provide a thrilling new perspective on this opera, with its weird heroine preserved by magic elixir well past her 300th birthday. Elisabeth Söderström is not simply malevolent: irritable and impatient rather, no longer an obsessive monster. Framed by richly colourful singing and playing, Söderström amply justifies that view, and Peter Dvorský is superbly fresh and ardent as Gregor. The recording, like others in the series, is of the finest Decca analogue quality. The performance of the *Lachian Dances* is highly idiomatic and makes a good bonus.

Osud (complete in English).

(M) *** Chan. 3029. Langridge, Field, Harries, Bronder, Kale, Welsh Nat. Op. Ch. & O, Mackerras.

Janáček's most unjustly neglected opera – richly lyrical, more sustained and less fragmented than his later operas –was for generations rejected as being unstageable, thanks to the oddities of the libretto; until, however, the English National Opera presented it at the Coliseum in London. Though this recording was made with Welsh National Opera forces, its success echoes the ENO production. Philip Langridge is again superb in the central role of the composer, Zivny, well supported by Helen Field as Mila, the married woman he loves, and by Kathryn Harries as her mother – a far finer cast than was presented on a short-lived Supraphon set. This performance, following ENO, uses Rodney Blumer's excellent English translation, adding to the immediate impact. Sir Charles Mackerras captures the full gutsiness, passion and impetus of the composer's inspiration, from the exhilarating opening waltz ensemble onwards, a passage that vividly sets the scene in a German spa at the turn of the century. The warmly atmospheric recording brings out the unusual opulence of the Janáček sound in this work written immediately after *Jenůfa*, yet it allows words to come over with fine clarity.

Sarka (complete).

(N) *** Sup. SU 3485-2. Urbanova, Straka, Kusnjer, Brezina, Prague P Ch., Czech PO, Mackerras

Sarka, written originally in 1887, was Janáček's very first opera, a piece that was put aside, when the author of the original play withheld his consent to its use. In 1916 Janáček rediscovered the score, was impressed, and made revisions until it was finally produced in 1925 in Brno. It was promptly dismissed as being inferior to Fibich's opera on the *Sarka*-legend. Though the idiom has more echoes of Dvořák and Smetana than anticipations of the mature Janáček, its dramatic point comes over strongly, with the legend reduced to bare essentials to give it a dream-like quality, making it a Freudian fantasy before its time. Though the three acts last little more than an hour, Janáček regarded this as his Wagnerian opera, ending as it does with the immolation of the formidable heroine, Sarka (an amazonian figure sworn to revenge herself on man) on the funeral pyre of Ctirad, the hero-figure with whom, against her will, she falls in love. It is not just an immolation, but a Liebestod, or love-death. This first stereo recording could hardly be finer, with Mackerras inspiring his Czech singers and players to give an incandescent performance, with Eva Urbanova and Peter Straka ideally cast, both characterfully slavonic and clean in

attack. First-rate sound, with atmospheric choral effects beautifully caught.

JANIEWICZ, Feliks (1762–1848)

Divertimento for Strings.

(B) *** EMI double fforte (ADD) CZS5 69524-2 (2). Polish CO, Maksymiuk – MENDELSSOHN: *String Symphonies;* ROSSINI: *String Sonatas;* JARZEBSKI: *Tamburetta; Chromatica.* ***

Feliks Janiewicz was an almost exact contemporary of Rossini, and this delightful work (one of six, written in London around 1805) might well have been another of Rossini's string sonatas, for the writing shares their brilliance and wit. The finale is a *tour de force* of bravura, relished here by this excellent Polish string band. A real find.

JÄRNEFELT, Armas (1869–1958)

Berceuse; Korsholm; Ouverture lyrique; Praeludium; The Promised Land (Det förlovade landet): Suite; The Song of the Crimson Flower (Sången om den eldröda blomman).

** Sterling CDS-1021-2. Gävle SO, Koivula.

Järnefelt is best remembered nowadays for two light classics, the *Berceuse* and *Praeludium*, which still delight music-lovers. He was one of the first Nordic composers to write for the cinema: *The Song of the Crimson Flower* dates from 1919. All this music is direct in feeling and has a touch of nobility. It is national-romantic in character, not dissimilar from, say, Sibelius's *King Christian II* music. It is appropriate that it should be played by a Swedish orchestra as he adopted Swedish nationality in the 1920s. Hannu Koivula's conducting disappoints. There is not enough charm in these performances. Worth hearing all the same.

JARZEBSKI, Adam (c. 1590–c. 1649)

Tamburetta; Chromatica.

(B) *** EMI double fforte (ADD) CZS5 69524-2 (2). Polish CO, Maksymiuk – MENDELSSOHN: *String Symphonies;* ROSSINI: *String Sonatas;* JANIEWICZ: *Divertimento.* ***

These two delightful lollipops show Adam Jarzebski to be a composer of real personality, the *Tamburetta* bouncing along joyously, with staccato bowing from the Polish strings adding to the rhythmic life, the second changing its mood from dance-like vivacity to stately yet slightly doleful elegance. Marvellous bravura playing from the Polish strings and vividly bright recording add to the music's projection.

JENKINS, John (1592–1678)

Consort Music: Divisions for 2 Bass Viols in D; Fantasias: a 4 in D; in F (2); a 5 in C min. (2); & D; a 6 in A min. & C min.; In nomines: a 6 in E min. & G min.; Pavan for 2 Bass Viols; Pavan a 6 in F; Pieces for Lyra Viol; Suites Nos.

4 in C for 2 Trebles, Bass & Organ; 7 in D min., for Treble, 2 Basses & Organ in D min.

*** Virgin VC5 45230-2. Fretwork with Nicholas.

Consort Music: Ayres a 4 in D min. & G min. (Ayre; Almaine; Couranto); Divisions for 2 Basses in C; Fantasia: in C min.; D; E min.; Fantasias in C min.(2); Fantasia in F (All in a Garden Green); Fantasy-suite in A min.; In nomine in G min.; Newarke Seidge: (Pavan; Galliard); Pavan in F.

(B) *** Naxos 8.550687. Rose Consort of Viols with Roberts.

John Jenkins spent his life in Norfolk and then lapsed into obscurity. Yet on the evidence of these two fine, complementary CDs his viol music is of high quality and well worth rediscovering. It does not seek great profundity, although the beautiful Pavane in F major, common to both discs, is memorable and all the Fantasias are well crafted – their invention appealingly immediate. Where there are several in the same key, each differs from the others, yet uses the same basic theme. In terms of colour, Jenkins's combination of viols with organ is quite ear-tickling.

Although they overlap, both collections are thoroughly recommendable with the difference between them accentuated by the difference in performance pitch, with Fretwork slightly higher, giving a brighter, fresher impression, whereas the Rose Consort have a somewhat warmer tonal blend, especially noticeable in that fine Pavane.

Consort Music for Violins in 6 Parts: Fantasies Nos. 1–11; Bell Pavan; In nomines Nos. 1–2.

(N) *** Astrée ES 9962. Hespérion XX, Savall.

Jenkins's set of six-part Fantasias appear to be early works. There is a twelfth, but it is not thought to be authentic and has been omitted here. The manuscripts include the pair of In nomines (based on plainsong), but the two Pavans have been added to give necessary variety to the programme, with the Bell Pavane, so called as it quotes a sequence of notes supposedly used (until the Great Fire of London) in the clock of St Mary-le-Bow.

The performances here are richly blended and bring out the full expressive depth of this music. At times one feels that the playing of the faster pieces could have produced a brighter projection, but viols are not violins and have a more limited dynamic range, so this remains a highly recommendable anthology. The recording itself, warm and full, and not too close, cannot be faulted.

JOACHIM, Joseph (1831–1907)

Hamlet Overture, Op. 4.

(N) *** Simax PSC 1206. Oslo PO, Jansons – BRAHMS: Symphony No. 1. ***

Though this first of Joachim's two Shakespearean overtures – the second being Heinrich IV – cannot compare in quality of material with the Brahms symphony, it makes an apt and enjoyable coupling, when the young Brahms admired it so much that he made a piano transcription. The Moderato introduction brings the main motif, but much of it is con-

ventional bogey music, and the main meat comes in the following Allegro, where a sharply rhythmic main subject leads to a lyrical second theme, presumably characterizing Ophelia. After that symphonic exposition the piece grows increasingly free on Lisztian lines, ending on a mysterious pianissimo. Excellent performance and fine sound.

Heinrich IV Overture, Op. 7.

(N) *** Simax PSC 1205. Olso PO, Jansons – BRAHMS: Symphony No. 4. ***

Joachim wrote the second of his Shakespearean overtures, based on Henry IV, over a prolonged period in 1853 and 1854, reacting to the adverse criticism of Schumann that it was too gloomy. Whether or not through Joachim's revisions, it is certainly not that, with its fanfares and marches a sharper, more inventive piece than the earlier Hamlet Overture, making an interesting coupling for the Brahms symphony, similarly well recorded.

JOHANSEN, David Monrad (1888–1974)

String Quartet, Op. 36.

(BB) *** Naxos 8.550879. Oslo String Qt – GRIEG: String Quartets. ***

David Monrad Johansen's String Quartet, composed in 1969 when in his early eighties, is persuasively played by the Oslo String Quartet and is impeccably recorded. It is a well-crafted piece but not as distinctively personal as Pan or the best of his mature works.

JOLIVET, André (1905–74)

Chant de Linos.

*** Koch 3-7016. Atlantic Sinf. – JONGEN: Concert; DEBUSSY: Sonata. ***

The Chant de Linos was originally composed for flute and piano, but Jolivet subsequently made this highly effective transcription for flute, violin, viola, cello and harp. It is played with exemplary taste and effortless virtuosity by Bradley Garner and his colleagues of the Atlantic Sinfonietta and is most beautifully recorded.

JONES, Daniel (1912–93)

Symphonies Nos. (i) 6; (ii) 9; (i; iii) The Country beyond the Stars.

*** Lyrita (ADD) SRCD 326. (i) RPO, Groves: (ii) BBC Welsh SO, Thomson; (iii) with Welsh Nat. Op. Ch.

Daniel Jones's facility in the use of the orchestra is striking and if his Sixth Symphony is eclectic in style, it is strong in personality, and the cogency of the argument (all six movements use the same basic material) is matched by an ability to communicate emotional experience. No. 9 too is finely crafted and has a particularly intense slow movement.

Both works show genuine integrity and power: they are the work of a real symphonist who has a sense of movement and a feeling for growth. Both are very well played by orchestras who show their commitment, and under conductors who respond naturally to the idiom. *The Country beyond the Stars* is a comparatively short cantata designed to suit the traditional qualities of Welsh Choirs, warm, relaxed writing, easy on the ear. Again, fine performance and a good sound balance, courtesy of the Welsh Arts Council.

String Quartets Nos. 1–8.

*** Chan. 9535 (2). Delmé Qt.

The *First Quartet* is a particularly impressive work, with a certain cosmopolitanism and a distinct French tinge to its atmosphere. But Jones is always his own man. No. 2 is exploratory and has a characteristically concentrated *Lento espressivo*. Nos. 3–5 are distinguished by seriousness of purpose and fine craftsmanship. And for the most part this is more than just expertly fashioned music: it is unflamboyant but all three works are of substance. The last three quartets are even more succinct (each lasting about a quarter of an hour). No. 6 marked the 250th birthday of Haydn, and uses two of that master's themes. Its mood is strongly focused, moving from a solemn introduction (and back again) via the Haydnesque scherzo and a simple slow movement. No. 7 is masterly, intensely concentrated: its central movement is marked *Penseroso*. The last quartet, full of memorable ideas, was left unfinished; it was skilfully completed from the composer's sketches by Giles Easterbrook. Appropriately, it has a hauntingly elegiac close. It is played here with enormous dedication and, like No. 7, holds the listener in a powerful emotional spell. A fitting conclusion to a splendid series, given definitive readings from a quartet closely identified with the music, and first-class Chandos sound.

JONES, Sidney (1861–1946)

The Geisha (complete).

*** Hyp. CDA 67006. Watson, Maltman, Walker, Suart, New London Light Opera Ch. & O, Corp.

The Geisha makes a delightful, innocent romp, helped by a sparkling performance under Ronald Corp. Jones and his librettist, Owen Hall, sought to follow up the success of Gilbert and Sullivan's *Mikado*. The formula worked so well that this Japanese musical play ran for two years. Granted that Jones cannot match Sullivan in finesse or tuneful memorability, this has a striking sequence of numbers with such off-beat titles as *The amorous goldfish* and *The interfering parrot*. The choruses too work splendidly. Though Lillian Watson's bright soprano grows edgy at the top, she is charming as the heroine Mimosa, and though Christopher Maltman's baritone grows gritty and uneven under pressure, he makes a dashing hero. Best of all is Sarah Walker, with her voice as rich and firm as ever, relishing the idiom, just as she does in cabaret songs. Richard Suart is ideal in the comic role of Wun-Hi.

JONGEN, Joseph (1873–1953)

(i) *Allegro Appassionato for Viola & Orchestra, Op. 79; Suite for Viola & Orchestra, Op. 48.* (ii) *Symphonie Concertante for Organ & Orchestra, Op. 81.*

**(*) Koch Schwann CD 315 012. (i) Gilissen, RTBF SO, Priestman; (ii) Schoonbroodt, Liège SO, Defossez.

Symphonie Concertante for Organ & Orchestra, Op. 81.

*** Telarc CD 80096. Murray, San Francisco SO, De Waart – FRANCK: *Fantaisie* etc. ***

Anyone who likes the Saint-Saëns *Third Symphony* should enjoy the Jongen *Symphonie Concertante*. Even if the music is on a lower level of inspiration, the passionate *Lento misterioso* and hugely spectacular closing *Toccata* make a favourable impression at first hearing and wear surprisingly well afterwards. Michael Murray has all the necessary technique to carry off Jongen's hyperbole with the required panache. He receives excellent support from Edo de Waart and the San Francisco Symphony Orchestra and Telarc's engineers capture all the spectacular effects with their usual aplomb. A demonstration disc indeed.

The Koch Schwann version comes from 1975 and has the advantage of being coupled with the *Suite for Viola & Orchestra, Op. 48*, whose first movement almost calls to mind the elegiac tone of Lekeu's *Adagio* for quartet and strings. Neither version is top-drawer, and the spectacular Telarc version by Michael Murray remains an easy first choice.

Concert à cinq.

*** Koch 3-7016-2. Atlantic Sinf. – DEBUSSY: *Sonata;* JOLIVET: *Chant de Linos.* ***

The three-movement *Concert à cinq* for flute, harp and string trio is a civilized piece very much in the post-impressionist style. It remains more pleasing than memorable, though these players do their utmost for it.

JOPLIN, Scott (1868–1917)

Elite Syncopations (ballet: Rags orch. for 11-piece ensemble by Günther Schüller).

(N) **(*) CRD (ADD) CRD 3329. Gammon (piano) with members of Royal Ballet O.

Kenneth Macmillan's ballet was danced to Günther Schüller's authentic arrangements and the disc includes also three extra rags not used in the ballet. Most of the favourites are included (though not *The Entertainer*), plus some novelties, and the scoring is nicely varied with the solo piano often left to play alone. The recording is excellent and Joplin fans will find this very enjoyable, although some might feel that the playing is *too* sophisticated.

Rags: *Bethena (Concert Waltz); Cascades Rag; Country Club (Ragtime Two-Step); Elite Syncopations; The Entertainer; Euphonic Sounds (A Syncopated Novelty); Fig Leaf Rag; Gladiolus Rag; Magnetic Rag (Syncopations classiques); Maple Leaf Rag; Paragon Rag; Pine Apple Rag;*

Ragtime Dance; Scott Joplin's New Rag; Solace (Mexican Serenade); Stoptime Rag; Weeping Willow (Ragtime Two-Step).

(M) *** None. Elektra 7559 79449-2. Rifkin.

Joshua Rifkin is the pianist whose name has been indelibly associated with the Scott Joplin revival, originally stimulated by the soundtrack music of the very successful film, *The Sting.* His relaxed, cool rhythmic style is at times remarkably subtle and, although the piano timbre is full, there is a touch of monochrome in the tone-colour. The current remastering gives the piano a natural presence.

JOSQUIN DESPREZ (died 1521)

Motets: *Absolom, fili mi; Ave Maria, gratia plena; De profundis clamavi; In te Domine speravi per trovar pietà; Veni, Sanctus Spiritus.* Chansons: *La Déploration de la mort de Johannes Ockeghem; El grillo; En l'ombre d'ung buissonet au matinet; Je me complains; Je ne me puis tenir d'aimer; Mille regretz; Petite camusette; Scaramella va alla guerra; Scaramella va la galla.*

(M) *** Virgin VER5 61302-2. Hilliard Ens.

The chansons recorded here have both variety of colour and lightness of touch, while the motets are sung with dignity and feeling by the Hilliard Ensemble. Indeed, these performances will kindle the enthusiasm of the uninitiated as will few others. The 1983 recording, made in London's Temple Church, is expertly balanced and eminently truthful.

Motets: *Ave Maria, gratia plena; Ave, nobilissima creatura; Miserere mei, Deus; O bone et dulcissime Jesu; Salve regina; Stabat mater dolorosa; Usquequo, Domine, oblivisceris me.*

*** HM HMC 901243. Chapelle Royale Ch., Herreweghe.

The Chapelle Royale comprises some nineteen singers, but they still produce a clean, well-focused sound and benefit from excellent recording. Their account of the expressive *Stabat mater* sounds thicker-textured than the New College forces under Edward Higginbottom, but there is a refreshing sense of commitment and strong feeling.

Antiphons, motets and sequences: *Inviolata; Praeter rerum serium; Salve regina; Stabat mater dolorosa; Veni, sancte spiritus; Virgo prudentissima; Virgo salutiferi.*

*** Mer. (ADD) ECD 84093. New College, Oxford, Ch., Higginbottom.

The Meridian anthology collects some of Josquin's most masterly and eloquent motets in performances of predictable excellence by Edward Higginbottom and the Choir of New College, Oxford. An admirable introduction to Josquin, and an essential acquisition for those who care about this master.

Chanson: *Fortuna desperata* (probably by BUSNOIS); *Missa Fortuna desperata; Adieu mes amours; Bererette savoysienne; Consideres mes incessantes (Fortuna); La plus des plus.*

(N) *** ASV CDGAU 220 Clerk's Group, Wickham (with

ISAAC: *Bruder Conrat/Fortuna;* SENFL: *Herr durch dein Bluet/ Pange lingua/Fortuna;* ANON: *Fortuna Zibaldone;* GRETTER: *Passibus anbiguis/Fortuna valubis errat* ***).

Josquin's *Missa Fortuna desperata,* as Edward Wickam points out in his excellent notes, is a surprisingly carefree setting, especially considering the translation of the title, ('Hopeless Fortune'). The polyphony only lightens the effect, although the closing *Agnus Dei* ends the work gravely, with the domination of the bass line.

But the fascination of the collection from the Clerk's Group is the inclusion of not just the *chanson* on which Josquin's mass was based, probably by Antoine Busnois (1430–92), but also eight further treatments and rearrangements of a song which in its time was obviously as popular as *L'Homme armé* – including four by Josquin himself. Both *Bergerette savoysienne* and *Adieu mes amours* are four-voiced extensions of monophonic originals, treated in canonic style.

Among the other variants Heinrich Isaac's version is touchingly doleful, for Bruder Conrat is lying ill and near to death. Senfl's *Herr durch dein Bluet* is an earnest petition to God, but Matthaes Greiter's *Passibus ambiguis* is livelier, and concerned with Fortune's unpredictability. Most striking of all is the anonymous Florentine *Fortuna Zibaldone,* in which one really needs the provided translation, for the four voices sing three different lighthearted texts simultaneously, together with the original *chanson,* with the whole performance taking just over a minute! As usual, the singing here is admirable in its blending and clarity of line, and the recording quite excellent.

Chanson: *L'Homme armé; Missa l'homme armé super voces musicales; Missa l'homme armé sexti toni.*

*** Gimmel GIMCD 919. Tallis Scholars, Phillips.

Missa l'homme armé sexti toni. Motets: *Absalom, fili mi; Ave Maria.*

◉ (BB) *** Naxos 8.553428. Oxford Camerata, Summerly – VINDERS: *Lament on the Death of Josquin.* ***

Josquin wrote two masses using *L'Homme armé* as the cantus firmus, but in the later (though not much later) *Sexti toni* (sixth mode), the last note of the cantus is different – F, instead of G as favoured by most other composers including Dufay (see above). The character of the melody is thus given a more positive character with the major key implied. The Tallis performances are in their usual impeccable flowing style, and the performance of the later work undoubtedly brings out its greater complexity, although the closing *Agnus Dei* has a hauntingly beautiful bare simplicity.

Another interesting feature of the Josquin setting is his interpolation of a trope (*Laeta dies*) following the *Credo* and before the *Sanctus* using a non-liturgical text. The effect is undoubtedly dramatic at the centre of a work where the flowing lines of the polyphony have such a rich harmonic implication. The long *Credo* breaks free, with the polyphony becoming more animated, and so becomes the central focus of the whole Mass – and what a beautiful Mass it is; very beautifully sung and recorded here. The *Ave Maria* is used to create a tranquil mood before the Mass itself begins, and the very touching motet, *Absalom, fili mi,* makes a poignant coda. This is followed by the radiant elegy of Josquin's contemporary, Jheronimus Vinders, with its soaring treble line, surely a fitting tribute. With full texts provided, this CD is one of the very finest of this distinguished Naxos series.

Missa pange lingua; Missa la sol fa re mi.

*** Gimell GIMCD 909. Tallis Scholars, Phillips.

The Gimell recording of the *Missa pange lingua* has collected superlatives on all counts and was voted record of the year in the *Gramophone* magazine's 1987 awards. The tone the Tallis Scholars produce is perfectly blended, each line being firmly defined and yet beautifully integrated into the whole sound-picture. Their recording, made in the Chapel of Merton College, Oxford, is first class, the best of the *Missa pange lingua* and the first of the ingenious *Missa la sol fa re mi*. Not to be missed.

KABALEVSKY, Dmitri (1904–87)

Colas Breugnon: Overture & Suite. The Comedians (Suite); Romeo and Juliet (Suite).

(N)*** ASV CDDCA 967. Armenian PO, Tjeknavorian.
(BB) *** Naxos 8.553411. Moscow SO, Jelvakov.

Kabalevsky speaks a patois akin to the language of Shostakovich and Prokofiev but without a scintilla of their depth and genius. The opera *Colas Breugnon* is based on Romain Rolland's novel *Le Maître de Clamécy* and dates from 1938, though it was revised twice after the war. The suite from *The Comedians*, music for a play called *The Inventor and the Comedian*, composed two years later, is cheap and cheerful, quite attractive and very well laid out for the orchestra – though, as in the score for *Romeo and Juliet* (which derives from 1956), some of its faster movements are tiresomely scatty. Still, there are others which are inventive and atmospheric.

However, Tjeknavorian's performances are more sharply characterized than Jelvakov's and in *Romeo and Juliet* these fine Armenian players find echoes of Prokofiev. Both *The Comedians* and *Colas Breugnon* are exceptionally vivid, for the ASV recording projects the orchestra in the brightest hues and with a striking presence.

The Comedians (suite), Op. 26.

(M) *** RCA (ADD) 09026 63302-2. RCA Victor SO, Kondrashin – KHACHATURIAN: *Masquerade Suite;* RIMSKY-KORSAKOV: *Capriccio espagnole;* TCHAIKOVSKY: *Capriccio italien.* *** ●

On the RCA collection the *Comedians' Galop* follows on almost immediately after the finale of Khachaturian's *Masquerade*, and the impetuous stylistic link is obvious. Kondrashin's performance is affectionate and colourful as well as lively, and the warm resonance of the recording helps to prevent the music from sounding too brash. The Tchaikovsky and Rimsky-Korsakov couplings are marvellous.

(i) Cello Concertos Nos. 1 in G min., Op. 49; 2 in C min., Op. 77. Spring (symphonic poem), Op. 65.

(BB) **(*) Naxos 8.553788. (i) Rudin; Moscow SO, Golovschin.

The enchanting *First Concerto in G minor* was written in 1949 for Knushevitzky, and it wears well. Alexander Rudin is a first-rate soloist who yields nothing to the majority of his full-priced rivals. The orchestral playing is decent and acceptable but falls short of distinction. Good recording; though Marina Tarasova, who couples the two concertos on Olympia (at slightly below full price), is even better, this Naxos disc is generally worth the money. The short, slight and charming symphonic poem is not otherwise available.

Cello Concerto No. 2, Op. 77.

*** Chan. 8579. Wallfisch, LPO, Thomson – GLAZUNOV: *Chant du ménestrel;* KHACHATURIAN: *Concerto.* ***
(BB) *** Virgin VBD5 61490-2 (2). Isserlis, LPO, Litton – BLOCH: *Schelomo (Hebraic Rhapsody)* for cello and orchestra; ELGAR: *Cello Concerto;* R. STRAUSS: *Don Quixote;* TCHAIKOVSKY: *Rococo Variations* etc. ***
**(*) BIS CD 719. Lindström, Gothenburg SO, Ashkenazy – KHACHATURIAN: *Cello Concerto.* **(*)

Steven Isserlis on Virgin gives as compelling and ardent an account of the concerto as does Wallfisch on Chandos and, since the LPO play as well for Andrew Litton as they did for Brydon Thomson, there is little to choose between them. As far as recorded sound is concerned, both are impressive; perhaps Virgin uses a slightly less resonant acoustic. The coupling will probably settle matters. Chandos offers two key Russian cello works; the Virgin bargain Double offers fine performances of concertante cello works by no fewer than five different composers.

Mats Lindström also proves an admirably sensitive soloist in Kabalevsky's *Second Concerto*. The recording is of high quality and well balanced but is a shade over-resonant, although the ear adjusts. Not a first choice, but an enjoyable performance, with no lack of spontaneity.

Violin Concerto in C, Op. 48.

*** DG 457 064-2. Shaham, Russian Nat. O, Pletnev – GLAZUNOV: *Concerto;* TCHAIKOVSKY: *Souvenir d'un lieu cher* etc. ***
*** Chan. 8918. Mordkovitch, SNO, Järvi – KHACHATURIAN: *Violin Concerto.* ***

Kabalevsky's *Violin Concerto* has never enjoyed the same popularity among players as either of the cello concertos. However, its effortless invention and Prokofievian charm lend it a genuine appeal. Gil Shaham's brilliant account of the piece with Mikhail Pletnev and the Russian National Orchestra should win it many friends.

Lydia Mordkovitch also plays with great flair and aplomb and is given first-class recording. This is coupled with an equally fine version of the Khachaturian concerto, which collectors who already have the Glazunov might prefer.

Symphonies Nos. 1 in C sharp min., Op. 18; 2 in C min., Op. 19.

** Olympia OCD 268. Szeged PO, Acél.

Kabalevsky's *First Symphony* unfolds naturally and the musical procedures have real dignity, even if some of the material of the finale is banal. The *Second Symphony* is both more individual and tautly argued. Good, though not first-class, performances from the Szeged Philharmonic Orchestra under Erwin Acél; however, the recording is handicapped by a rather cramped and constricted acoustic.

(i) *Symphony No. 4 in C min., Op. 54; (ii) Requiem, Op. 72.*

** Olympia (ADD) OCD 290 (2). (i) Leningrad PO; (ii) Levko, Valaitis, Moscow Artistic Educational Institute Ch., Moscow SO; Kabalevsky.

The *Fourth Symphony* is a rather conventional work which goes through the correct motions of sonata form, but the ideas are only intermittently engaging; indeed, many border on the commonplace. The *Requiem* is a more rewarding piece, even if much of it is hard work. But the longueurs are offset by some moving passages and a genuine, unforced dignity that grips the listener. The sound in the *Requiem* is very good indeed for the period – and the place.

Cello Sonata in B flat, Op. 71.

(N) *** Simax PSC 1146. Birkeland, Gimse – MARTINU: *Cello Sonata No. 1; Variations.* ***

Instead of giving us the remaining Martinů sonatas, Øystein Birkeland and Håvard Gimse offer a Kabalevsky rarity – his *Sonata in B flat* composed in 1962. It is one of Kabalevsky's better pieces. This new version beats off such recent competition as there is and is a first recommendation. Excellent, full-bodied and well-balanced sound as well as being artistically impeccable. A rewarding issue.

24 Preludes, Op. 38; Sonata No. 3, Op. 46; Sonatina in C, Op. 13/1.

**(*) Olympia OCD 266. McLachlan.

Murray McLachlan makes out a persuasive case for Kabalevsky's *24 Preludes*, Op. 38. Each of the preludes is based on a folk tune, mostly drawn from Rimsky-Korsakov's collection, and in *No. 13 in F sharp minor* we encounter the theme made famous by Stravinsky in the closing bars of *Firebird*. McLachlan does the set with great fluency and clarity of articulation. He also gives us two of Kabalevsky's best-known piano pieces, the *Sonatina* (1930) and the *Piano Sonata No. 3* (1946) with its Prokofievian middle movement. The piano-sound is decent but could do with greater transparency and bloom.

Colas Breugnon (complete).

*** Olympia (ADD) OCD 291 A/B (2). Boldin, Isakova, Kayevchenko, Maksimenko, Duradev, Gutorovich, Mishchevsky, Stanislavsky & Nemirovich-Danchenko Moscow Music Theatre Ch. & O, Zhemchuzhin.

This complete recording, made in Russia in the 1970s, confirms that the effervescent overture is not just a flash in the pan but part of an exceptionally winning piece, rhythmically inventive and full of good tunes, many of them drawn from French folksong. The snag is that between Acts I and II in the three-Act layout there is a story-gap of 40 years. Nevertheless the Russian performance and recording, made by members of the Moscow Music Theatre, is most convincing, with a cast superbly led by the baritone, Leonid Boldin, in the title-role. The other male singers are first rate too, with splendidly alert singing from the chorus. The women soloists are raw-toned in a very Russian way, and the whole performance under Georgy Zhemchuzhin reflects the confidence of experience on stage. The 1973 recording, rather dry but with fine presence, is a thoroughly worthwhile set.

KALINNIKOV, Vasily (1866–1901)

Intermezzos Nos. 1 in F sharp min.; 2 in G.

*** Chan. 8614. RSNO, Järvi – RACHMANINOV: *Symphony No. 3.* ***

These two colourful *Intermezzos* with a flavour of Borodin are charming.

Overtures: The Cedar and the Palm; Tsar Boris.

(M) *** Chan. 7093. RSNO, Järvi – RIMSKY-KORSAKOV: *Scheherazade* etc. ***

Kalinnikov's *Cedar and the Palm Overture*, his final work for orchestra, is an atmospheric piece (based on a Heine poem). It has eminently nostalgic Slavonic invention and, like its companion, *Tsar Boris*, vividly colourful scoring. Kalinnikov's portrayal of the Tsar, however, has none of the sombre desolation of Mussorgsky's opera and ends joyously with a resplendent fanfare. Järvi's performances with his responsive Scottish players are very sympathetic and the Chandos recording is in the demonstration class.

Symphonies Nos. 1 in G min.; 2 in A.

*** Chan. 9544. RSNO, Järvi.

Kalinnikov's *First Symphony* contains something akin to the flow and natural lyricism of Borodin, and the *Second* is also rewarding in a similar way if not quite as appealing as No. 1. Neeme Järvi and the Royal Scottish National Orchestra recorded these delightful works in 1987 and 1989 respectively. These are spacious, well-performed performances and exemplary recordings.

KALLSTENIUS, Edvin (1878–1963)

Clarinet Quintet, Op. 17.

(N) *** Phono Suecia PSCD 708. Andersen, Lysell Qt – FERNSTROM: *Wind Quintet.* von KOCH: *Piano Quintet.* ***

Edvin Kallstenius was ignored in his lifetime by the record companies and his neglect by Swedish Radio was almost total. After his studies in Germany he pursued a career as a conductor, and during the 1930s he was a music librarian of Radiotjänst, as the Swedish Radio was then known. The *Clarinet Quintet* was written in 1930 and is neo-Romantic in outlook, generally Brahmsian with a touch of Reger. It is a pleasing work but does not make a really strong impression in spite of an excellent performance by Niklas Andersen and the Lysell Quartet and a first-class recording.

KÁLMÁN, Emmerich (1882–1953)

Die Herzogin von Chicago (complete).

*** Decca 466 057-2 (2). Groop, Riedel, Wottrich, Polgate, Lindskog, Horn, Schoenberg Ch., Berlin RSO, Bonynge.

Kálmán was in good company in 1928 when this piece was first given in Vienna. That première was just after Krenek's jazz opera, *Jonny spielt auf*, had appeared and just before Weill's *Dreigroschenoper*, but Kálmán's aims were far less radical. Within the conventional operetta frame he introduced foxtrots and charlestons alongside his usual waltzes and csárdás numbers, and the wonder is that his melodies are just as catchy on whichever side of the fence he is working, especially the hit number, *Ein kleiner Slowfox mit Mary*. The piece is sparklingly directed by Richard Bonynge with forces from Berlin Radio. Endrik Wottrich as Prince Sándor may lack charm with his throaty baritonal tenor, but the others are a delight, notably Deborah Riedel, radiantly sweet as the heroine, Mary Lloyd, and the rich-toned Monica Groop as the poverty-stricken Princess Rosemarie. Full, warm, atmospheric recording with the excellent chorus nicely balanced.

KARAMANOV, Alemdar (born 1934)

Symphonies Nos. 20 (Blessed are the Dead); 23 (I am Jesus).

(M) ** Olympia OCD 486. USSR SO, Fedoseyev.

Alemdar Karamanov is another recent discovery among Russian composers. He is of a strongly religious temperament, and his music earned the allegiance of Shostakovich, who hailed him as 'one of the most original and unique composers of our time'.

The present symphonies come from a cycle of six (Nos. 18–23) on the theme of the Apocalypse, written between 1976 and 1980. The music has a certain ecstatic voluptuousness that is reminiscent of Scriabin, but there are also touches of Shostakovich, Rachmaninov and Glière. Karamanov is very imaginative, though a streak of sentimentality comes to the surface – fairly often in the case of No. 20. The USSR Symphony Orchestra produce rather crude tone at times and there are moments when the wind intonation is flawed. There is a certain pervading sameness about the hot-house atmosphere of this writing and the Szymanowski-like textures, and all three symphonies sound very similar. One wonders how well they will wear on repetition. There is, however, no question as to their interest.

KEISER, Reinhard (1674–1739)

Croesus.

(N) *** HM HMC 90174.6 (3). Röschmann, Trekel, Güra, Häger, Berlin RIAS Chamber Ch., Akademie für Alte Musik, Jacobs.

Reinhold Keiser, a short-lived contemporary of Bach and Handel, achieved great success early in his career as an opera-composer in Hamburg. He was acclaimed by some as the greatest opera-composer in the world, but his impresario went bankrupt, and in his absence from Hamburg his prime place was taken by the ever-inventive Telemann. In a surprisingly short time his operas were forgotten, which makes it timely that René Jacobs should demonstrate the delights of at least one Keiser opera.

Written in 1710/11 at the height of his popularity, this moral tale of Croesus, King of Lydia, fabulously rich, brings the message that money does not make men happy. It was revised 20 years later, an opera in German which, adventurously for the time, leavens the sequence of short arias and recitatives with the occasional duet and ensemble.

Even though this is hardly a match for the operas which Handel was writing (in Italian) for London at the time, it is full of lively and attractive invention, with one or two more serious arias longer than the rest, and with comic servant characters to provide further contrast.

Dorothea Roschmann is superb as the heroine, Elmira, whose minor-key aria in Act 1 sets the pattern for her rich sequence of arias and duets. The royal characters, not just Croesus of Lydia, but Cyrus, the invading King of Persia, are well taken by the basses Roman Trekel and Johannes Manov, the latter a sinister character who yet is given a jolly aria towards the end of Act 1. The rest make a first-rate team, with René Jacobs pacing arias and recitatives well, though it is strange that Keiser tended to end each act in mid-air, either on recitative or with the briefest of finales. A fascinating rarity, very well recorded.

KERN, Jerome (1885–1945)

Overtures: (i) *The Cat and the Fiddle; The Girl from Utah; Have a Heart; Leave It to Jane; O, Lady! Lady!;* (ii) *Show Boat;* (i) *Sitting Pretty; Sweet Adeline; Very Warm for May.* (i, iii) Film music: *Swing Time* (suite).

(B) ** EMI double fforte CZS5 68589-2 (2). (i) Nat. PO; (ii) L. Sinf.; (iii) Ambrosian Ch.; McGlinn – GERSHWIN: *Broadway & Film Music* **(*); PORTER: *Overtures.* ***

These Jerome Kern overtures, recorded from the original band-parts of musicals dating from between 1914 (*The Girl from Utah*) and 1939 (*Very Warm for May*), are musically unimpressive. They are all played with an infectious sense of style, but really memorable tunes are thin on the ground. In *Sweet Adeline*, instead of his own material, Kern uses a pot-pourri of period songs from the 1890s, including *Daisy, Daisy* and *The band played on*. By far the most attractive music comes in the film score from *Swing Time*, which includes *The way you look tonight*. For this reissue, the *Overture* from McGlinn's complete recording of *Show Boat* has been added, but that is not much more than a pot-pourri.

Songs from musicals: *Centennial Summer: All through the day. Cover Girl: Long ago and far away. High, Wide and Handsome: The folks who live on the hill. Lady be Good: The last time I saw Paris. Music in the Air: The song is you. Roberta: Yesterdays; Smoke gets in your eyes. Sally: Look for the silver lining. Show Boat: Can't help lovin' dat man. Swing Time: The way you look tonight. Very Warm for*

May: All the things you are. You were Never Lovelier: I'm old fashioned.

*** EMI CDC7 54527-2. Te Kanawa, L. Sinf., Tunick.

Kiri Te Kanawa proves completely at home in these luscious and life-enhancing Kern favourites. Her rich vocal line is matched by a nice feeling for the wittier lyrics. But it's the tunes that count, and she revels in them. So does Jonathan Tunick, who has scored the accompaniments; and the London Sinfonietta obviously enjoy themselves too, yet there is also a sense of sophistication and style. Excellent recording.

Show Boat (complete recording of original score).

❂ *** EMI CDS7 49108-2 (3). Von Stade, Hadley, Hubbard, O'Hara, Garrison, Burns, Stratas, Amb. Ch., L. Sinf., McGlinn.

In faithfully following the original score, this superb set at last does justice to a musical of the 1920s which is both a landmark in the history of Broadway and musically a work of strength and imagination hardly less significant than Gershwin's *Porgy and Bess* of a decade later. The original, extended versions of important scenes are included, as well as various numbers written for later productions. As the heroine, Magnolia, Frederica von Stade gives a meltingly beautiful performance, totally in style, bringing out the beauty and imagination of Kern's melodies, regularly heightened by wide intervals to make those of most of his Broadway rivals seem flat. The London Sinfonietta play with tremendous zest and feeling for the idiom; the Ambrosian Chorus sings with joyful brightness and some impeccable American accents. Opposite von Stade, Jerry Hadley makes a winning Ravenal, and Teresa Stratas is charming as Julie, giving a heartfelt performance of the haunting number, *Bill* (words by P. G. Wodehouse). Above all, the magnificent black bass, Bruce Hubbard, sings *Ol' man river* and its many reprises with a firm resonance to have you recalling the wonderful example of Paul Robeson, but for once without hankering after the past. Beautifully recorded to bring out the piece's dramatic as well as its musical qualities, this is a heart-warming issue.

KETÈLBEY, Albert (1875–1959)

The Adventurers: Overture; Bells across the Meadow; Caprice Pianistique; Chal Romano; The Clock and the Dresden Figures; Cockney Suite, excerpts: *Bank Holiday; At the Palais de Danse. In a Monastery Garden; In the Moonlight; In a Persian Market; The Phantom Melody; Suite Romantique; Wedgwood Blue.*

** Marco 8.223442. Slovak Philharmonic Male Ch., Slovak RSO (Bratislava), Leaper.

The Marco Polo collection has the advantage of modern digital recording and a warm concert-hall acoustic, and the effect is very flattering to *In a Monastery Garden.* Adrian Leaper's performance is romantically spacious and includes the chorus. If elsewhere his characterization is not always as apt as Lanchbery's, this is still an agreeable programme. It offers several novelties and, though some of these items (for

instance *The Adventurers Overture*) are not vintage Ketèlbey, there is nothing wrong with the lively Slovak account of the closing *In a Persian Market*, again featuring the chorus.

'Appy 'Ampstead; Bells across the Meadows; In a Chinese Temple Garden; In a Monastery Garden; In a Persian Market; In the Mystic Land of Egypt; The Phantom Melody; Sanctuary of the Heart; Wedgwood Blue.

(M) *** Decca (ADD) 444 786-2. RPO & chorus, Rogers – *Concert of Gypsy Violin Encores:* Sakonov, L. Festival O. ***

Eric Rogers and his orchestra present the more famous pieces with both warmth and a natural feeling for their flamboyant style, and the tunes throughout come tumbling out, vulgar but irresistible when played so committedly. The birds twittering in the monastery garden make perfect 'camp' but the playing is straight and committed, and the larger-than-life Phase Four recording suits the music admirably. Moreover, it was a happy idea to couple this programme with a collection of Hungarian gypsy fireworks and other favourite lollipops, played with great panache by Josef Sakonov – see Concerts section, below.

Bells across the Meadow; Chal Romano (Gypsy Lad); The Clock and the Dresden Figures; In a Chinese Temple Garden; In a Monastery Garden; In a Persian Market; In the Moonlight; In the Mystic Land of Egypt; Sanctuary of the Heart.

(B) *** CfP (ADD) CD-CFP 4637. Midgley, Temperley, Pearson (piano), Amb. S., Philh. O, Lanchbery – LUIGINI: *Ballet Egyptien.* ***

A splendid collection in every way. John Lanchbery uses every possible resource to ensure that, when the composer demands spectacle, he gets it. *In the Mystic Land of Egypt,* for instance, uses soloist and chorus in canon in the principal tune (and very fetchingly too). In the *Monastery Garden* the distant monks are realistically distant, in *Sanctuary of the Heart* there is no mistaking that the heart is worn firmly on the sleeve. The orchestral playing throughout is not only polished but warm-hearted – the middle section of *Bells across the Meadow,* which has a delightful melodic contour, is played most tenderly and loses any hint of vulgarity. Yet when vulgarity is called for, it is not shirked – only it's a stylish kind of vulgarity! The recording is excellent, full and brilliant.

KHACHATURIAN, Aram

(1903–78)

Cello Concerto in E min.

*** Chan. 8579. Wallfisch, LPO, Thomson – GLAZUNOV: *Chant du ménestrel;* KABALEVSKY: *Cello Concerto No.2.* ***

(*) BIS CD 719. Lindström, Gothenburg SO, Ashkenazy (with RACHMANINOV: *Vocalise* *) – KABALEVSKY: *Cello Concerto.* **(*)

Khachaturian's *Cello Concerto* of 1946 has some sinuous Armenian local colour for its lyrical ideas, but none of the thematic memorability of the concertos for violin and piano and the *Gayaneh Ballet* score, on which Khachaturian's reputation must continue to rest. Raphael Wallfisch plays with total commitment and has the benefit of excellent and sympathetic support. The recording is of the usual high standard we have come to expect from Chandos.

The combined concentration of Lindström and Ashkenazy prevents the writing from sounding too inflated. The recording is a bit over-resonant, but otherwise faithful and well balanced. As an encore we are given a fine if restrained account of Rachmaninov's *Vocalise*. An enjoyable if not, in the last resort, memorable coupling.

Cello Concerto in E min.; Concerto-Rhapsody for Cello & Orchestra in D min.

**(*) Olympia OCD 539. Tarasova, Russian SO, Dudarova.

Marina Tarasova plays both works with great eloquence and expressive vehemence; she has a big tone and impeccable technique. The orchestral playing is gutsy and sturdy without, perhaps, the finesse that might have toned down some of the garishness of the orchestral colours. The recording is bright and breezy – not worth a three-star grading and nor is the orchestral contribution, though Tarasova certainly is.

Piano Concerto in D flat.

✿ (N) (M) (***) Dutton Lab. mono CDEA 5506. Lympany, LSO, Fistoulari (with BALAKIREV: *Islamey* (**(*));
POULENC: *Novelette No. 1;* DOHNANYI: *Cappriccio in F min.;* MENDELSSOHN: *Capriccio & Rondo brillant.* (***))

(M) **(*) Hyp. CDA 66293. Servadei, LPO, Giunta –
BRITTEN: *Piano Concerto.* **(*)

(i) *Piano Concerto in D flat. Dance Suite; Polka & Waltz* (both for wind band).

*** ASV CDDCA 964. (i) Serviarian-Kuhn; Armenian PO, Tjeknavorian.

(i) *Piano Concerto in D flat. Gayaneh* (ballet) *Suite; Masquerade: Suite.*

**(*) Chan. 8542. (i) Orbelian; SNO, Järvi.

Moura Lympany premiered and pioneered the Khachaturian *Piano Concerto* in England in the 1940s and her superb 1945 Decca 78 rpm recording of it with Fistoulari has never been surpassed. The inspired partnership with Fistoulari brought a first movement of extraordinary zest and spontaneity, and a hauntingly beautiful *Adagio*, where apart from the poetic solo response, there is a memorably sinuous contribution from the orchestra's bass clarinet at the beginning and close of the movement. The finale has excitement and sparkle in plenty.

The competing American version by William Kapell and the Boston Symphony Orchestra under Koussevitzky is another incandescent account. Koussevitzky got stunning results from the orchestra and Kapell's virtuosity and delicacy are remarkable. This is also available in an alternative Dutton transfer (CDBP 9701, coupled with Beethoven and Shostakovich) but the Decca ffrr recording is far superior in this demonstration-worthy transfer. Indeed its combination

of vividness, inner definition and natural piano timbre is almost unbelievably realistic.

Lympany's brilliant account of Balakirev's famous pianistic showpiece *Islamey* is also worth having, but here the virtuosity seems rather more effortful. However, the two encores also show her in top form, and she is dazzling in the coupled Mendelssohn concertante pieces.

The Armenian partnership of Dora Serviarian-Kuhn and Loris Tjeknavorian provides a clear first recommendation for a modern version of Khachaturian's somewhat uneven *Piano Concerto*, easily the finest account to have appeared on disc since the pioneering versions of William Kapell and Moura Lympany. The Russian dance finale has plenty of dash, but what makes the performance individual is the sense of quixotic fantasy Serviarian-Kuhn brings to her cadential bravura. The bright piano-timbre and comparatively lean orchestral textures are not a disadvantage in a work that can too easily sound inflated. The other pieces on the ASV disc are very slight but lively enough; easily the most memorable item is the second *Uzbek Dance* in the *Dance Suite*, quite extended and touchingly atmospheric.

The Chandos recording is splendid technically, well up to the standards of the house. Constantin Orbelian, an Armenian by birth, plays brilliantly, and Järvi achieves much attractive lyrical detail. Overall it is a spacious account, and though the finale has plenty of gusto, the music-making seems just a shade too easygoing in the first movement. The couplings, sumptuously played, are both generous and appealing.

Annette Servadei makes up in clarity and point for a relative lack of weight in the outer movements, which she takes at speeds marginally slower than usual. The slow movement brings hushed and intense playing, sympathetically supported by the LPO under Joseph Giunta in a digital recording that is well balanced and unaggressive. However, ideally this work needs a stronger grip than these artists exert – the first movement in particular could do with greater thrust.

(i) *Piano Concerto in D flat;* (ii) *Violin Concerto in D min.;* (iii) *Masquerade Suite;* (iv) *Symphony No. 2.*

(B) **(*) Double Decca (ADD) 448 252-2 (2). (i) De Larrocha, LPO, Frühbeck de Burgos; (ii) Ricci, LPO, Fistoulari;
(iii) LSO, Black; (iv) VPO, composer.

The key performance here is the composer's own – of the *Second Symphony*. His advocacy is passionate and the recording is spectacular. The slow movement of the *Piano Concerto* as interpreted by a Spanish pianist and a Spanish conductor sounds evocatively like Falla, and the finale is also infectiously jaunty. Not so the first movement, which is disappointingly slack in rhythm at a dangerously slow tempo. Ricci is a good deal more consistent in the *Violin Concerto*. He does not supply quite the demonic energy which the outer movements ideally call for, but his lyrical approach has its own attractions, and the closing pages of the slow movement are wonderfully atmospheric. The late-1950s recording does not have the projection we would expect today, but Ricci's fine playing is well focused. The

Masquerade Suite is consistently alive and colourful and is vividly if forwardly recorded.

Violin Concerto in D min.

⚫ **(N) (M)** *** RCA [ADD] 09026 63708-2. Kogan, Boston SO, Monteux – PROKOFIEV: *Alexander Nevsky.* ⚫ ***

*** Chan. 8918. Mordkovitch, SNO, Järvi – KABALEVSKY: *Violin Concerto.* ***

(*) EMI CDC7 47087-2. Perlman, Israel PO, Mehta – TCHAIKOVSKY: *Méditation.* *

Leonid Kogan's powerfully direct approach to this once-popular concerto, aided by superlative playing from the Boston SO under Monteux, is electrifying. Together, they make it sound like an unqualified masterpiece, and the astonishingly vivid 1958 recording puts many digital recordings to shame with its vivid presence. This is the most exciting performance of Khachaturian's underrated concerto that you can buy.

Among recent performances of this attractively inventive concerto, Lydia Mordkovitch is probably the most competitive. She plays with real abandon and fire, and Chandos balance her and the orchestra in a thoroughly realistic perspective. This new version has far superior sound to Oistrakh on Melodiya (see below).

Perlman's performance sparkles too – indeed it is superb in every way, lyrically persuasive in the *Andante* and displaying great fervour and rhythmic energy in the finale. He is well accompanied by Mehta (who nevertheless does not match the composer's feeling for detail). However, on CD one's ear is drawn to the very forward balance of the soloist, and the generally bright lighting becomes rather fierce at the opening tutti of the finale – the comparatively dry Israeli acoustic does not provide an ideal bloom on the music-making. The coupling is attractive but offers very short measure.

(i; ii) Concert Rhapsody for Cello & Orchestra; (i; ii) Concert; Rhapsody for Piano & Orchestra; (i; iii) Violin Concerto in D min.; (iv) Gayaneh (ballet): excerpts. Spartacus (ballet): Adagio. Symphony No. 1 in E min.

(B) **(*) BMG/Melodiya Twofer (ADD) 74321 59056-2 (2).
(i) USSR RTV Large SO; with (ii) Georgian; Petrov; (iii) Oistrakh; (iv) USSR SO; all cond. composer.

The highlight here is, of course, the inspired *Violin Concerto* (1940) played by David Oistrakh, who gave the work its première and is its dedicatee. He is peerless in its performance, not only in projecting its very Russian bravura, but also in his melting phrasing and timbre in the sinuous secondary theme of the first movement (which returns in the exhilarating finale) and in the equally haunting melody of the *Andante*. Indeed, this performance is unlikely ever to be surpassed and fortunately the recording, if not entirely refined, is full, warmly atmospheric and well balanced.

Nicolai Petrov gives a barnstorming performance of the *Concert Rhapsody for Piano and Orchestra*, creating torrential energy at the opening and in the motoric, overextended finale. It is a very noisy piece, but no one could say this performance is without vitality. The *Concert Rhapsody for Cello* (1963) was written for Rostropovich and lends itself to

the kind of passionate playing it receives here from the forwardly balanced Karine Georgian, full-bodied in tone and a convincing substitute for its dedicatee. Again tuttis are at times dissonantly noisy, and the piece is overextended (nearly 25 minutes). The composer is a convincing advocate of his *First Symphony*, and brings out its full colouring, so that while the first movement is inflated, the work is not short of ideas. Here the recording is fully acceptable. The *Gayaneh* excerpts are also strongly characterized, and the famous *Spartacus Adagio* makes an ardently expansive encore.

Gayaneh (ballet): complete final score.

(B) **(*) BMG/Melodiya Twofer (ADD) 74321 63459-2 (2). USSR R & TV Large SO, Kakhidze.

Khachaturian's original full score for *Gayaneh*, dating from 1942, is perhaps his finest extended work. Fortunately Tjeknavorian made a complete recording of it for RCA, and this is in urgent need of reissue. The composer later reworked and added to the music in order to fit a new scenario (because the earlier narrative, with its ingenuous wartime moral tone, had become embarrassing to the Soviets). The fresh inspiration of the original is expanded and often vulgarized in the later version about love and jealousy among shepherds dwelling in the mountains. But plenty of striking ideas remain. This Russian recording from 1976 has great verve and energy but does not disguise the shallower invention and the inflation of the louder passages. Nevertheless the recording is vivid and, although brash, is not unacceptably so; and these performers know just how to present the folk dances. As a 'Twofer' it is good value.

Gayaneh (ballet): extended suite.

(M) **(*) Mercury 434 323-2. LSO, Dorati – SHOSTAKOVICH: *Symphony No. 5.* **(*)

Dorati understands this music as well as anyone, and his *Sabre Dance* has plenty of energy; and the other dances admirably celebrate Khachaturian's local colour. The 1960 Mercury recording is brilliant, with a tendency to fierceness in the strings, which suits the music well enough. There are eight items here; Dorati omits *Gayaneh*'s *Adagio*.

Gayaneh (ballet): excerpts; Spartacus (ballet): excerpts.

(M) *** Decca (ADD) 460 315-2. VPO, composer – GLAZUNOV: *The Seasons.* **(*)

(N) **(*) Chant du Monde RUS 288171. Bolshoi Theatre O, Svetlanov.

Gayaneh (ballet): Suite; Masquerade: Suite; Spartacus (ballet): Suite.

(*) ASV (ADD) CDDCA 773. Armenian PO, Tjeknavorian – IPPOLITOV-IVANOV: *Caucasian Sketches.* *

Gayaneh (ballet): Suite; Masquerade: Waltz & Mazurka. Spartacus (ballet): Suite.

(N) (BB) *** Warner Apex 8573 89237-2. Bolshoi SO, Lazarev.

Gayaneh (ballet): highlights; Spartacus (ballet): highlights.

(B) *** CfP CD-CFP. LSO, composer (with GLAZUNOV: *The Seasons: Autumn:* Philh. O, Svetlanov ***).

Khachaturian came to Vienna in 1962 to record these inspired performances of the most popular numbers from his two ballets, and this Decca record (reissued in Decca's Legends series) is the one to go for. It is superbly remastered to restore and even improve on the demonstration quality of the original LP, recorded in the Sofiensaal. Like the sound, the performances are very fresh. The Glazunov coupling, if not quite so fine, is very well played and shows Ansermet at his best. As usual in this series, good documentation and photographs of both conductors.

The composer's later EMI Classics for Pleasure selections from his two famous ballets offers one more item from *Gayaneh* than on his earlier Decca coupling. The EMI sound, obviously more modern than the Decca, is a shade reverberant for the more vigorous numbers, but the present remastering presents a firmer focus than on LP. The LSO play excitingly throughout. The inclusion of only *Autumn* from Glazunov's *Seasons* decreases the appeal of this CD, when the competing Decca disc offers the whole ballet.

At the opening of Alexander Lazarev's Bolshoi CD, the famous *Sabre Dance* bursts into the room spectacularly, with thumping drums and blazing percussion and the *Lezghinka* is similarly vibrant and exciting. Yet *Ayshe's awakening* could not be more evocative with its growling bass clarinet. The two best-known *Masquerade* items are brightly done, but with plenty of dynamic shading to counter the ebullience. Then Lazarev opens his *Spartacus* selection with the famous *Adagio*, and the gentle oboe solo and languorous Bolshoi strings soon expand passionately. The sparkling *Dances of the Greek Slave* and sinuous *Egypian Girl's Dance* provide similar contrast, and the *Bacchanalia* and closing *Victory of Spartacus* bring more exhilarating orchestral bravura. In short, with extremely spectacular, if reverberant, recording, this super-bargain reissue makes an easy first choice for those wanting a modern digital selection of this music.

The Armenians also clearly relish the explosive energy of this music. The *Masquerade Suite* relies rather more on charm for its appeal, but Tjeknavorian and his players bring a determined gusto, even to the *Waltz* and certainly to the ebullient closing *Galop*. Then the vibrant Spartacus and his ardent lover Phrygia come on stage with a great flair of passion in a melody that is justly famous. One wishes the recording were more sumptuous here, but for the most part its burnished primary colours suit the dynamic orchestral style.

Svetlanov's are brand-new recordings made as recently as January 2000, and both he and the Bolshoi Theatre Orchestra are in very good form. His ear for detail is as perceptive as ever and his handling of phrasing and dynamics is ever-senstive. The famous *Adagio* from *Spartacus* is both ardent and refined and the genre dances are beautifully played, a potent mixture of sinuosity and charm. There is plenty of rhythmic energy and vitality in the *Gayaneh lezginka* and the *Sabre Dance*, but both Tjeknavorian and the composer play this music more vibrantly and passionately still. Yet with excellent recording these Bolshoi performances do not lack appeal. They are certainly never dull.

Greeting Overture; Festive Poem; Lermontov Suite; Ode in Memory of Lenin; Russian Fantasy.

** ASV CDDCA 946. Armenian PO, Tjeknavorian.

Although it has plenty of characteristic Armenian colour, most of this music is routine Khachaturian, or worse: the *Festive Poem* (at nearly 20 minutes) is far too inflated for its content, and the *Ode to Lenin* is an all too typical Soviet tribute. The sub-Rimskian finale of the *Lermontov Suite* is by far the best movement. The *Russian Fantasy* uses an agreeable folk-like melody, but we hear it repeated too often before the final quickening. Good performances, but the resonant recording is acceptable rather than sparkling.

Masquerade Suite.

(M) *** RCA (ADD) 09026 63302-2. RCA Victor SO, Kondrashin – KABALEVSKY: *The Comedians Suite*; RIMSKY-KORSAKOV: *Capriccio espagnole*; TCHAIKOVSKY: *Capriccio italien*. *** ●

Kondrashin certainly knows how to play this music, with warmth as well as sparkle, and even a touch of romantic elegance when Oscar Shumsky plays the violin solo in the *Nocturne*. Yet the final *Galop* is as roisterous as one could wish. The resonant recording gives the orchestra a pleasing ambience.

Spartacus (ballet): *Suites Nos. 1–3.*

*** Chan. 8927. RSNO, Järvi.

The ripe lushness of Khachaturian's scoring in *Spartacus* narrowly skirts vulgarity. Järvi and the RSNO clearly enjoy the music's tunefulness and primitive vigour, while the warmly resonant acoustics of Glasgow's Henry Wood Hall bring properly sumptuous orchestral textures, smoothing over the moments of crudeness without losing the Armenian colouristic vividness.

Symphonies Nos. 1 in E min.; 3 in C (Symphonic Poem).

*** ASV CDDCA 858. Armenian PO, Tjeknavorian.

The *First Symphony* was Khachaturian's exercise on graduating from Miaskovsky's class in 1934. It is far from negligible and in some ways is superior to some of his later work – certainly to the bombastic *Third*. Now there is a modern account from Armenia under Boris Tjeknavorian, which enjoys the advantage of good digital recording. The Armenian orchestra play well for Tjeknavorian, and his is a safe recommendation.

Symphony No. 2 in E min. (The Bell); Battle of Stalingrad (suite).

**(*) ASV CDDCA 859. Armenian PO, Tjeknavorian.

Symphony No. 2 (original version); Gayaneh: Suite (excerpts).

*** Chan. 8945. RSNO, Järvi.

The *Second Symphony* comes from 1943 but the composer subsequently made a number of revisions, the last in 1969, which Tjeknavorian has recorded. It acquired its nickname, 'The Bell', because of a motive heard on tubular bells, and in the slow movement makes fascinating use of the *Dies irae*. Neeme Järvi and his Scottish forces give a very fine account of themselves and they enjoy the benefit of a superb recording. It runs to some 51 minutes, while Tjeknavorian's account of the final revision prunes the score down to 42 minutes 45 seconds. The suite from *The Battle of Stalingrad* is taken from a score composed for a patriotic film and is empty and inflated.

(i) Symphony No. 3 (Symphonic Poem). Triumphal Poem.

*** Chan. 9321. BBC PO, Glushchenko, (i) with Lindley –
IPPOLITOV-IVANOV: *Caucasian Sketches*. ***

If the *Third Symphony* was as strong on musical substance as it is on decibels, it would be something to reckon with. But, alas, it is garish and empty; there are no fewer than eighteen trumpets in all! Analgesics and earplugs will be in brisk demand in its vicinity. The BBC Philharmonic, spurred on by their Russian conductor, play as if they believe in it, and the Chandos recording is in the demonstration category. The three stars are for the performance and the recording – not for the music!

The Valencian Widow (incidental music): Suite; Gayaneh (ballet): Suite No. 2.

*** ASV CDDCA 884. Armenian PO, Tjeknavorian (with
TJEKNAVORIAN: *Danses fantastiques* **(*)).

Khachaturian's early suite from his incidental music to the Spanish comedy *The Valencian Widow* (1940) is probably his first major score and, brimming over with striking tunes as it is, one is surprised that it has not been discovered by the gramophone before this. This is the Khachaturian of *Gayaneh*, so the coupling of seven lesser-known excerpts from that fine ballet score is very appropriate. Tjeknavorian and his orchestra play this music with great spirit and relish its Armenian flavours; they are equally at home in Tjeknavorian's own suite of *Danses fantastiques*, full of energy and colour if essentially sub-Khachaturian. Splendidly vivid, yet spacious sound.

Clarinet Trio.

(B) *** HM HMA 1901419. Walter Boeykens Ens. –
PROKOFIEV: *Overture on Jewish Themes* etc. ***

Khachaturian's *Clarinet Trio* is a slight but pleasing work, full of sinuous, Armenian melodic lines. With a *Moderato* finale (in some ways the most striking movement, with the central dance section rather soberly framed), it is without the hyperbole which often distinguishes this composer's orchestral writing. It is very well played and recorded.

PIANO MUSIC

10 Children's Pieces; 2 Pieces; Poem; Sonata; Sonatina; Toccata; Waltz (from Masquerade).

**(*) Olympia OCD 423. McLachlan.

Apart from the *Toccata* (1932), which is a frequent encore, Khachaturian's piano music rarely features in piano recitals. At 80 minutes, this CD offers all of it with the exception of the *Scenes from Childhood* and the *Recitative and Fugues*. The early pieces, *Poem* (1927) and the *Valse-caprice* and *Dance* (1926), are much like the *Toccata*, pretty empty, but the later pieces including the *Sonatina* (1959), the *Ten Children's Pieces* (1964) and the *Sonata* (1961) are worth a hearing,

even though they are limited in range and rely on a small vocabulary of musical devices. Murray McLachlan is a persuasive guide. His recording, made at All Saints' Church, Petersham, is eminently serviceable, though there are times when the attentions of a tuner would not have come amiss (particularly in the garrulous first movement of the *Sonata*).

VOCAL MUSIC

Ballad of the Motherland (Maybe somewhere the sky is blue); 3 Concert Arias; Ode to Joy (The Spring Sun Rises); Poem; March of Zangezur.

(N) *(*) ASV CDDCA 1087. Amirkhanian, Hatsagortsian, Vardouhi Khachaturian, Armenian PO, Tjeknavorian.

Although the performances are adequate, none of this is first- or even second-class Khachaturian, although the three *Concert Arias* show a genuine operatic flair, essentially Armenian in flavour, but with a hint of Puccini too. Hasmik Hatsagortsian sings them passionately and convincingly. The *Ballad of the Motherland* was given its Russian première by six basses in unison! Here Mourad Amirkhanian sings alone, longing for his homeland. The 1936/7 *Ode to Stalin* is here revised and renamed innocuously *Poem*. It consists of a very long orchestral prelude followed by a brief patriotic chorus with quite a good tune. The *Ode to Joy* opens with a rather engaging 16-bar moto perpetuo on the violins; the mezzo soloist enters with an ardent soliloquy on the joys of spring; then the chorus enters and enthusiastically takes up the melody in popular Soviet style. Texts and translations are provided only for the *Concert Arias*.

KLAMI, Uuno (1900–61)

Kalevala Suite, Op. 23; Karelian Rhapsody, Op. 15; Sea Pictures.

**(*) Chan. 9268. Iceland SO, Sakari.

The *Kalevala Suite* is Klami's best-known work but, like the other two pieces on this disc, it is highly derivative. Ravel and Schmitt mingle with Falla, Sibelius and early Stravinsky; while there are some imaginative and inspired passages (such as the opening of the *Terheniemi* or Scherzo), there is some pretty empty stuff as well. The performances under Petri Sakari are very good indeed, and the recording has a good perspective and a wide dynamic range.

Lemminkäinen's Island Adventures; (i) Song of Lake Kuujärvi; Whirls: Suites Nos. 1 & 2.

*** BIS CD 656. (i) Ruuttunen; Lahti SO, Vänskä.

Klami was a master of orchestral colour. *Lemminkäinen's Island Adventures* dates from 1934 and is more Sibelian than is usual with this composer, but its musical substance does not really sustain its length. There is quite a lot of Prokofiev and Shostakovich in the ballet, *Whirls*, and in *Song of Lake Kuujärvi*, and greater depth in the orchestral song. The performances are good and Esa Ruuttunen is an excellent baritone, and the recording offers wide dynamic range and natural perspective.

Symphony No. 2, Op. 35; Symphonie enfantine, Op. 17.

** Ondine ODE 858-2. Tampere PO, Ollila.

Klami composed two symphonies, the second of which he finished at the war's end in 1945. If its tone is predominantly post-romantic in character, its musical coherence is less than impressive. It is stronger on rhetoric than on substance. The *Symphonie enfantine* is a slighter piece from the 1920s, heavily indebted to Ravel, and rather delightful. Tuomas Ollila and the Tampere Philharmonic are in good form, and the Ondine engineers produce sound of exemplary clarity and naturalness.

KNUSSEN, Oliver (born 1952)

Higglety Pigglety Pop!, Op. 21; Where the Wild Things Are, Op. 20.

(N) *** DG 469 556-2 (2) Buchan, Saffer, Hardy, Gillett, Wilson-Johnson, Richardson, King, London Sinf., Composer.

These two one-act operas based on the books of Maurice Sendak will please children of all ages, reflecting child-fantasies that so delight youngsters, while giving adult listeners many musical insights both witty and searching. Originally intended as a double-bill, they were written in reverse order between 1979 and 1985, with *Higglety-Pigglety Pop!* revised in 1999. It follows the idiosyncratic fortunes of the Sealyham, Jennie, delightfully characterized by Cynthia Buchan. It is the more complex of the two operas, leading to a play within a play, marked by colourful fanfares.

Where the Wild Things are, more compact, at times more violent, relates even more closely to the example of Ravel's *L'Enfant et les sortilèges*, involving Max, a boy in a wolf suit (Lisa Saffer excellent), who travels by boat to the land of the Wild Things and is there crowned king, only to return from his Rumpus-bound dream in time for supper. Oliver Knussen's evocation of a child-world is at once open and innocent in approach and charmingly sophisticated in expression. With consistently fine casts and brilliant playing from the London Sinfonietta he could not be more persuasive in performances recorded immediately after live concerts. Brilliant, atmospheric sound. The packaging adds to the charm of the issue.

KOCH, Sigurd Von (1889–1919)

Piano Quintet.

(N) *** Phono Suecia PSCD 708. Lucia Negro, Lysell Qt – FERNSTROM: *Wind Quintet.* KALLSTENIUS: *Clarinet Quintet, Op. 17.*

Little known outside Sweden, Sigurd von Koch was active as an author and painter as well as a composer. His *Piano Quintet* dates from 1916, and despite its length it is the least substantial work among these rarities. Its phrase structure tends to be square, and there is too much sequential repetition. It is played elegantly by Lucia Negro and the Lysell Quartet but is wanting in real personality and substance.

KODÁLY, Zoltán (1882–1967)

Concerto for Orchestra; Dances of Marosszék; Symphony in C; Theatre Overture.

(N) *** Chan. 9811. BBC PO, J. P. Tortelier.

Yan Pascal Tortelier and the BBC Philharmonic prove a superb partnership here, while the Chandos and BBC engineering team have surpassed themselves to produce demonstration quality. Kodály's *Concerto for Orchestra* was written for the Chicago Orchestra and Bartók actually took it with him to America in 1940. This, the *Dances of Marosszék* and the *Theatre Overture* leave no doubt that Kodály was a past-master of the orchestra, and these showpieces receive their full due on this highly recommendable issue.

Concerto for Orchestra; Dances of Galánta; Dances of Marosszék; Háry János: Suite; Symphony in C; Summer Evening; Theatre Overture; Variations on a Hungarian Folksong (The Peacock).

(B) *** Double Decca (ADD) 443 006-2 (2). Philh. Hungarica, Dorati.

Concerto for Orchestra.

(N) *** Australian Decca Eloquence (ADD) 467 602-2. Dorati – JANACEK: *Taras Bulba;* BARTOK: *Concerto for Orchestra.* ***

The more ambitious pieces like the *Concerto for Orchestra* and the three-movement *Symphony in C* are enjoyable even if they lack the sharpness of inspiration that pervades the music of Kodály's friend Bartók. The *Symphony* comes from the composer's last years and lacks real concentration and cohesion. Even so, in Dorati's hands the passionate *Andante* is strong in gypsy feeling and the jolly, folk-dance finale, if repetitive, is colourful and full of vitality. *Summer Evening*, too, is warmly evocative, but in the *Theatre Overture*, brightly and effectively scored, the invention is thin. The 1973 sound remains of vintage quality, and the CD transfers are first rate.

Dorati's warmly committed performance of Kodály's *Concerto for Orchestra* in fine analogue sound is also available in Australia with the more obvious coupling of Bartók's *Concerto*, while Janáček's *Taras Bulba* is equally worth having.

(i) *Dances of Galánta; Dances of Marosszék;* (ii) *Háry János Suite.*

(B) **(*) Sony (ADD) SBK 62404. Phd. O, Ormandy – JANACEK: *Sinfonietta; Taras Bulba.* **

(M) *** Mercury (ADD) 432 005-2. (i) Philharmonia Hungarica; (ii) Minneapolis SO; Dorati – BARTOK: *Hungarian Sketches* etc. ***

Dances from Galánta; Dances from Marosszék; Háry János Suite; (i) *Psalmus Hungaricus, Op. 13.*

(M) *** DG mono/stereo 457 745-2. Berlin R.I.A.S., Fricsay, (i) with Ernst Haefliger, St Hedwig's Cathedral Ch.

(i) *Dances of Galánta; Dances of Marosszék;* (ii) *Háry János Suite, Instrumental Excerpts & Singspiel;* (i) *Gergëly-Járás;* (ii) *Táncnóa; Túrót eszik a cigány.*

*** Ph. 462 824-2. Budapest Festival O, Fischer; with
(i) Children's Ch. Magnificat, Budapest; (ii) Children's Ch.
Miraculum, Kecskemét.

**Dances of Galánta; Dances of Marosszék; Háry János Suite;
Variations on a Hungarian Folksong (The Peacock).**

*** Decca (IMS) 444 322-2. Montreal SO, Charles Dutoit.

(i) *Dances of Galánta;* (ii) *Dances of Marosszék; Háry
János Suite;* (i) *Variations on a Hungarian Folksong (The
Peacock).*

**(*) BIS CD 875. (i) Brno State PO; (ii) SWF SO,
Baden-Baden; Serebrier.

Dances of Galánta; Háry János: Suite.

*** Delos DE 3083. Seattle SO, Schwarz – BARTOK:
Miraculous Mandarin. **(*)

**Dances of Galánta; Háry János Suite; Variations on a
Hungarian Theme (The Peacock).**

**(*) Telarc CD 80413. Atlanta SO, Levi.

Iván Fischer's Kodály is no less successful than his recent
Bartók records. His set has the advantage of totally idiomatic
playing from a very fine orchestra and superbly well-defined
recording from the Philips engineers. This is now the front-
runner in the Kodály discography, and the point from which
lovers of this genial composer should set out. The extra
items are very enticing.

Charles Dutoit offers the four most popular of Kodály's
orchestral works in richly resonant, purposeful performances, with rhythms crisply sprung and with superb playing
from the fine soloists of the Montreal orchestra. Though
Fischer and his Hungarian players sound more idiomatic,
Dutoit and his Montreal players gain in brilliance, helped
by recording of demonstration quality, outstanding even by
Montreal standards. The *Peacock Variations* benefit most of
all from the opulence of the Montreal sound.

From sneeze to finale, the Minneapolis orchestral playing
in the *Háry János Suite* is crisp and vigorous; given the
excellent 1956 Mercury stereo, Dorati went on to record the
other two sets of dances with the Philharmonia Hungarica
in 1958. The playing of the woodwind soloists in the slow
dances is intoxicatingly seductive, and the power and punch
of the climaxes come over with real Mercury fidelity. An
outstanding disc, since the Bartók couplings are equally
successful.

The Seattle Symphony Orchestra play Kodály's music
with great vividness and warmth. The *Háry János Suite* is
more spaciously romantic in feeling than some versions –
helped by the rich acoustics of Seattle Opera House – and
there is less surface glitter. But *The Battle and Defeat of
Napoleon* and the *Entrance of the Emperor and His Court*
have all the necessary mock-drama and spectacle, and it is
good to hear the cimbalom again balanced so effectively
within the orchestra. The *Galánta Dances* have splendid
dash. The recording is outstandingly real.

José Serebrier gets very good playing from the Brno
Orchestra in both the *Dances of Galánta* and the *Peacock
Variations*, and the remaining two works with the
Südwestfunk Orchestra in Baden-Baden are, if anything,
even better and the recording warmer. Iván Fischer remains

a clear first, but no one investing in the well-filled BIS disc
need feel short-changed. There is plenty of character in the
orchestral playing of both ensembles and the BIS recordings
are up to house standard.

Ormandy and the Philadelphia Orchestra play these well-
known sets of dances brilliantly and with characteristic panache. The 1962 recording too has been immeasurably
improved and it is pity that the reissue is let down by the
omission of the *Háry János Suite*, recorded around the same
time. Moreover, there is no internal cueing.

Robert Shaw in his Telarc recordings has repeatedly demonstrated what a fine orchestra the Atlanta Symphony is,
and here Yoel Levi carries on the good work in a coupling
of Kodály's three most popular orchestral works. The digital
recording is full and well balanced, and the performances
are brilliant and persuasive, with some fine, sensitive playing
from the wind principals in particular. The snag is that this
issue comes into direct competition with other versions that
offer the *Marosszék Dances*.

Fricsay's performances are crisp and exciting, the
orchestra superbly on its toes, a notable passage being the
beautifully managed horn solo in the central trio of the
intermezzo in *Háry János*. The mono recording was demonstration-worthy in its day and is still pretty remarkable.
The coupled performance of the *Psalmus Hungaricus* has
characteristic electricity, and with fine soloists is effortlessly
idiomatic and thrillingly alive. This disc is well chosen for
DG's 'Originals'.

Háry János Suite.

(B) *** Sony SBK (ADD) 48162. Cleveland O, Szell –
MUSSORGSKY: *Pictures at an Exhibition;* PROKOFIEV:
Lieutenant Kijé: Suite. ***
(BB) *** Naxos 8.550142. Hungarian State O, Mátyás Antal
(with Concert: 'Hungarian Festival' ***).

Szell – Budapest born – was in his element in *Háry János*.
Superb Cleveland polish matches the vitality of the playing,
with a humorous sparkle in Kodály's first two movements
and the mock pomposity of the Napoleon episode wittily
dramatized. The 1969 recording was one of the very finest
from this source, bold with a too-forward cimbalom, but the
engineers certainly capture the exhilaration of the playing in
this way.

The Naxos Hungarian performance of the *Háry János
Suite* is also wonderfully vivid, with the cimbalom – here
perfectly balanced within the orchestra – particularly telling.
The grotesque elements of *The Battle and Defeat of Napoleon*
are pungently and wittily characterized and the *Entrance of
the Emperor and His Court* also has an ironical sense of
spectacle. The brilliant digital sound adds to the vitality and
projection of the music-making, yet the lyrical music is
played most tenderly.

(i) *Hungarian Rondo. Summer Evening; Symphony.*

**(*) ASV CDDCA 924. (i) Warren-Green; Philh. O, Butt.

The *Summer Evening* is a beautiful piece – eminently well
served by Yondani Butt. It comes with a well-characterized
account of the *Symphony*, not more impressive than Dorati's

version but, of course, a more up-to-date recording. Very good indeed, albeit not quite three-star.

Variations on a Hungarian Folksong (The Peacock).

(M) ** RCA (ADD) 09026 63309-2. Boston SO, Leinsdorf – BARTOK: *Concerto for Orchestra.* *(*)
*** Decca 452 853-2. VPO, Solti – ELGAR: *Enigma Variations;* BLACHER: *Paganini Variations.* ***

Though Solti's interpretation of a fellow-Hungarian composer has altered less between recordings than the Elgar on this same fiftieth-anniversary disc, this performance too has extra warmth and subtlety, with the rhythmic verve just as sharply infectious as before, conveying joy. Vivid sound, capturing the warm acoustic of the Musikverein.

Leinsdorf is more successful in this work than in the Bartók coupling: this is a reading of genuine feeling and conviction. Helpfully, each individual variation has been separately cued. But it is a pity that instead of the Bartók the original coupling of the *Háry János Suite* was not chosen. Good up-front sound, but only a half-good disc.

(Unaccompanied) Cello Sonata, Op. 8; (i) Cello Sonata (for cello and piano), Op. 4.

(B) *** HM HMA 1901325. Claret, (i) with Cabestany.

(Unaccompanied) Cello Sonata, Op. 8; (i) Cello Sonata (for cello & piano), Op. 4; 3 Chorale Preludes (arr. from Bach, BWV 743, 747 & 762).

(BB) *** Naxos 8.553160. Kliegel, (i) with Jandó.

On the evidence of this record, the Andorran cellist Lluís Claret has a larger-than-life musical personality, and one is sorely tempted to use the word 'vintage' to describe his inspired performance of Op. 8. A memorably compulsive account of a work which, until now, Starker had made his own (see below). Moreover, the recording is real and tangible within a suitably open acoustic. Rose-Marie Cabestany joins Claret persuasively for the less ambitious but still impressive two-movement *Sonata for Cello and Piano*, Op. 4, and proves an excellent partner, so that this piece is by no means an anticlimax after the major work.

Maria Kliegel in Kodaly's magnificent solo *Cello Sonata* offers a warm and fanciful performance not quite as incisive as Claret's or Schiefen's on Arte Nova (see below) but just as powerful and rather more flowing. So in the long central slow movement Kliegel is not so daringly expansive or darkly tragic, but she is more easily lyrical. Jenö Jandó is an outstandingly sympathetic partner in the two-movement Op. 4 *Sonata*, a performance deeply introspective in the slow first movement and full of fantasy in the *Allegro con spirito* of the finale. The three *Chorale Preludes* are romantic arrangements – with the cello generally underlining the chorale melodies – of organ pieces attributed to Bach but now thought spurious.

(Unaccompanied) Cello Sonata, Op. 8; (i) Duo for Violin & Cello, Op. 7.

*** Delos D/CD 1015. Starker, (i) with Gingold.
(BB) *** Arte Nova 74321 51623-2. Schiefen, (i) with Strauss.

When, not long before the composer's death, Kodály heard Starker playing this *Cello Sonata*, he apparently said: 'If you

correct the ritard in the third movement, it will be the Bible performance.' The recording is made in a smaller studio than is perhaps ideal; the *Duo*, impressively played by Janos Starker and Josef Gingold, is made in a slightly more open acoustic. There is a small makeweight in the form of Starker's own arrangement of the Bottermund *Paganini Variations.*

Guido Schiefen gives a powerful, intense performance, fearless in attacking the bravura writing, with double-stopping clean and precise and with his full cello-tone made the more dramatic by the close recorded sound. Powerful and passionate as the outer movements are, the central *Adagio* at an exceptionally broad speed is particularly impressive in its hushed concentration. The *Duo*, written the previous year, receives an equally compelling performance, making the ideal coupling. It is astonishing what full and rich sounds Kodály draws from just two instruments. Another outstanding bargain.

Intermezzo for String Trio.

(N) (B) *** Virgin 2 x 1 VBD5 61904-2 (2). Domus – DOHNANYI: *Serenade for String Trio;* DVORAK: *Bagatelles;* MARTINU: *Piano Quartet No. 1* etc.; SUK: *Piano Quartet.* ***
*** ASV CDDCA 985. Lyric Quartet – DOHNANYI: *String Quartets Nos. 2 & 3.* ***

A short early piece from 1905 which shows a certain kinship with Dohnányi and has both elegance and charm. It comes on a Virgin Double in an eminently recommendable collection of predominantly Czech music, half of which is devoted to Martinů, with exemplary performances.

The *Intermezzo for String Trio* makes a perfectly acceptable and appropriate makeweight to the two Dohnányi quartets.

String Quartet No. 2, Op. 10.

*** DG (IMS) 419 601-2. Hagen Qt – DVORAK: *String Quartet No. 12* etc. ***
*** Testament (ADD) SBT 1072. Hollywood Qt – DVORAK; SMETANA: *Quartets.* (***)

The Hagen give a marvellously committed and beautifully controlled performance of the *Second* – indeed as quartet playing it would be difficult to surpass. In range of dynamic response and sheer beauty of sound, this is thrilling playing and welcome advocacy of a neglected but masterly piece. The recording is well balanced and admirably present.

Although American readers will know the Hollywood Quartet's account of this piece, it will be new to collectors on this side of the Atlantic. It was recorded in 1958 and, unlike the Dvořák and Smetana with which it is coupled, is in stereo. Once a frequent item on concert and radio programmes, the Kodály has become something of a rarity. The present performance can only be described as masterly, enhancing the attractions of an already excellent issue.

Laudes organi (Fantasia on a 12th-Century Sequence); Psalm 114 (from the Geneva Psalter).

*** Australian Decca Eloquence (ADD) 466 902-2. Brighton Festival Ch., Heltay, Weir – JANACEK: *Glagolitic Mass.* ***

These works were written towards the end of Kodály's career; they are richly rewarding and show that even when the composer took on dramatic subjects, his was a relatively gentle art (in contrast to his friend Bartók). Heltay directs persuasive performances, with Gillian Weir brilliant as the organ soloist (the *Laudes organi* performance receives its CD début here). The recording is excellent, and these works make a fine bonus for the Janáček coupling.

Missa brevis.

(M) **(*) EMI CDM5 65587-2. King's College, Cambridge, Ch., Cleobury; Lane – JANACEK: *Mass* etc. ***

The *Missa brevis*, as its subtitle *In tempore belli*, suggests, was composed at the height of the Second World War. It is one of Kodály's strongest and most deeply felt works, every bit as powerful as the *Psalmus Hungaricus*. Stephen Cleobury gives it in its earlier form, with organ, as did Laszlo Heltay in the 1970s. Some of the treble lines could be more secure, but for the most part this is a good performance, and it is sad that this fine coupling with Janáček has been deleted as we go to press.

Psalmus Hungaricus, Op. 13.

*** Chan. 9310. Svensson, Copenhagen Boys' Ch., Danish Nat. R. Ch. & SO, Mackerras – JANACEK: *Glagolitic Mass.* ***

*** Decca 458 929-2. Daróczy, Agache, Hungarian Radio and TV Ch. and Children's Ch., Schola Cantorum Budapestiensis, Budapest Festival O, Solti – BARTOK: *Cantata profana*; WEINER: *Serenade.* ***

As the unusual but refreshing coupling for the Janáček *Mass*, the *Psalmus Hungaricus* is infected by Mackerras with an element of wildness that sweeps away any idea of Kodály as a bland composer. As in the Janáček, the tenor Peter Svensson is an excellent, clear-toned and incisive soloist, if here rather more backwardly balanced. The glory of the performance lies most of all in the superb choral singing, full, bright and superbly disciplined, with the hushed pianissimos as telling as the great fortissimo outbursts. It is a mark of Mackerras's understanding of the music that the many sudden changes of mood sound both dramatic and natural. Full, warm and atmospheric recording, with plenty of detail.

Solti, in his very last recording sessions in Budapest, June 1997, paid tribute to all three of his principal teachers, Bartók, Kodály and Weiner. In representing Kodály with the *Psalmus Hungaricus* he was returning to a work he had first recorded right at the beginning of his recording career, offering a performance even warmer and more idiomatic, with incandescent choral singing, marred only by the unsteadiness of the tenor soloist.

KOECHLIN, Charles (1867–1961)

Les Heures persanes, Op. 65.

*** Marco 8.223504. Reinland-Pfalz PO, Segerstam.

Koechlin's powers as an orchestrator are evident in these 16 exotic mood-pictures which were originally composed for the piano in 1913. They evoke a journey recorded by Pierre Loti in 1900: 'He who wants to come with me to see at Isfahan the season of roses should travel slowly by my side,

in stages, as in the Middle Ages.' The work is generally slow-moving, but this music has tremendous atmosphere and exotic colours and the very titles of the movements (*Les Collines au coucher de soleil, A l'ombre près de la fontaine marbre*, for example) conjure up some idea of its character. In the hands of Leif Segerstam and the Reinland-Pfalz Orchestra this music casts a powerful spell. It is also beautifully recorded.

The Jungle Book (Le Livre de la jungle).

*** Marco 8.223484. Reinland-Pfalz PO, Segerstam.

(i) *The Jungle Book (Le Livre de la jungle);* (ii) *3 Songs (Seal Lullaby; Night-Song in the Jungle; Song of Kala Nag), Op. 18;* (iii) *Seven Stars Symphony, Op. 132; L'Andalouse dans Barcelone, Op. 13; 4 Interludes, Op. 214.*

(N)(B) *** RCA Double 74321 84596-2 (2). (i) Berlin RSO, Zinman; (ii) with Vermillion, Botha, Lukas & Ch.; (iii) Deutsches SO, Berlin, Judd.

Koechlin's lifelong fascination for Kipling's *Jungle Book* is reflected in this extraordinary four-movement tone-poem whose composition extended over several decades. *La Course de printemps*, Op. 95, the longest of them, is extraordinarily imaginative and pregnant with atmosphere: you can feel the heat and humidity of the rainforest and sense the presence of strange and menacing creatures. *La Loi de la jungle* is the most static and the least interesting. Leif Segerstam is excellent in this repertoire and with his refined ear for texture distils a heady atmosphere and is beautifully recorded. Anyone with a feeling for the exotic will respond to this original and fascinating music.

David Zinman and the Berlin Radio Symphony Orchestra also give a very well characterized performance, almost as atmospheric as their Marco Polo competitor, though the texture is more brightly lit and clearly defined. However, this RCA bargain Double not only includes the three Op. 18 *Songs* for soloists, chorus and orchestra, but also offers a very persuasive account under James Judd of the *Seven Stars Symphony*, the stars in question coming not from the heavens but from Hollywood. They include Douglas Fairbanks and Greta Garbo, who is cooly depicted by an *ondes martinot*; a brilliant *scherzando* represents Clara Bow; Marlene Dietrich is personified by a luscious melody using her name as its basis; and finally Chaplin is portrayed with considerable depth as well as humour. The *Four Interludes* (not orchestrated by the composer) were written as links intended to make the symphony into a ballet; the delightful *L'Andalouse dans Barcelone* was conceived as gypsy dance music for a film, but was never used. The recording is excellent – to match these highly persuasive performances.

Cello Sonata, Op. 66; Chansons bretonnes, Op. 115.

*** Hyp. CDA 66979. Lidström, Forsberg – PIERNE: *Cello Sonata.* ***

Koechlin's sonata is pensive and introspective, ruminative in character, and Mats Lidström and Bengt Forsberg give a cultured, finely controlled performance of compelling subtlety. The sound is natural and lifelike. In every respect this is a disc of quality.

Horn Sonata, Op. 70; 15 Pieces, Op. 180; Morceau de lecture (for horn); *15 Pieces, Op. 180; Sonneries.*

*** ASV CDDCA 716. Tuckwell, Blumenthal.

The *Sonata* is a richly conceived three-movement work, linked by its evocative opening idea. The *Morceau de lecture* is freer, more rhapsodic, immediately stretching up ecstatically into the instrument's higher tessitura. The 15 *Pieces* are delightful vignettes, opening with a rapturous evocation, *Dans la forêt romantique.* While some of them are skittish (notably the muted Scherzo (No. 4) or jolly *Allegro vivo* (No. 11), many explore that special solemn melancholy which the horn easily discovers in its middle to lower register, as in Nos. 10 and 12 (both marked *doux*). Two others are for hunting horns, and they robustly use the open harmonics which are naturally out of tune (an effect Britten tried more sparingly), while the 11 brief *Sonneries* are all written for cors de chasse in two, three or four parts, which Tuckwell plays by electronic means. This is a collection to be dipped into rather than taken all at once, but Tuckwell's artistry sustains the listener's interest and the fine pianist, Daniel Blumenthal, makes the most of his rewarding part in the *Sonata.* The recording is excellent.

KOKKONEN, Joonas (1921–96)

(i) *Sinfonia da camera; Il paesaggio;* (ii) *'. . . durch einen Spiegel . . .'* (iii) *Wind Quintet.*

*** BIS CD 528. (i; ii) Lahti SO; (i) Vänskä; (iii) Söderblom; (ii) with Tiensuu; (iii) Lahti Sinf. Wind Quintet.

Those coming new to Kokkonen's musical idiom, should try the pretentiously titled but resourceful and imaginative *'. . . durch einen Spiegel . . .',* subtitled *Metamorphosis* for twelve strings and harpsichord. There are some rewardingly individual sonorities. *Il paesaggio* is an evocative landscape study, and the earlier *Wind Quintet* is a lively piece. The early *Sinfonia da camera* is grey, general-purpose, modern music deriving from Bartókian–Hindemithian roots. Very good performances and splendid recording.

Symphony No. 1; Music for String Orchestra; (i) *The Hades of the Birds* (song-cycle).

*** BIS CD 485. Lahti SO, Söderblom; (i) Groop.

The *Music for String Orchestra* is a rather powerful piece lasting almost half an hour, well wrought and its invention finely sustained if slightly anonymous. The colourings are dark. *The Hades of the Birds* is a short song-cycle, which shows Monica Groop's talents to strong effect, but it is the *First Symphony* that is the strongest piece on the disc. It is serious in purpose and as far as the orchestra is concerned shows considerable mastery of colour.

Symphony No. 2; Inauguratio; Erekhtheion (cantata); *The Last Temptations* (opera): *Interludes.*

**(*) BIS CD 498. Vihavainen, Grönroos, Akateeminen Laulu Ch., Lahti SO, Vänskä.

The *Second Symphony* is a work of some eloquence and its invention has a certain freshness and quality, even if it

remains ultimately unmemorable. The interludes from his opera, *The Last Temptations,* make a strong impression. Not an essential purchase.

Symphony No. 3; (i) *Opus sonorum;* (ii) *Requiem.*

*** BIS CD 508. Lahti SO, Söderblom; with (i) Sivonen; (ii) Iskoski, Grönroos, Savonlinna Op. Festival Ch.

Söderblom's account of the *Third Symphony* has detail and atmosphere, and the same must be said of the *Requiem.* In the *Opus sonorum,* written in reaction to the sight of the vast battery of percussion so common in the 1960s, Kokkonen assigns all the percussion part to a piano, played with great delicacy here.

Symphony No. 4; (i) *Cello Concerto. Symphonic Sketches.*

*** BIS CD 468. (i) Thedéen; Lahti SO, Vänskä.

The *Fourth Symphony* is the strongest work here: its ideas are symphonic, its structure organic and its atmosphere powerful. The *Cello Concerto* is a lyrical and accessible piece, just a shade mawkish. The Swedish cellist Torleif Thedéen gives a performance of great restraint, mastery and sensitivity. Good orchestral playing and recording.

(i) *Piano Quintet. String Quartets Nos. 1–3.*

*** BIS CD 458. (i) Valsta; Sibelius Ac. Qt.

The *Quintet* is a slight but not unpleasing work; the *First Quartet,* which sounds like any chamber work of the period, has more gravitas. Like its companions it is very well played, but even such eloquent advocacy cannot disguise a certain facelessness. But three stars for the performers and the engineers.

The Last Temptations (opera): complete.

**(*) Finlandia 1576 51104-2 (2). Auvinen, Ruohonen, Lehtinen, Talvela, Savonlinna Op. Festival Ch. & O, Söderblom.

The Last Temptations tells of a revivalist leader, Paavo Ruotsalainen, from the Finnish province of Savo and of his inner struggle to discover Christ. The opera is dominated by the personality of Martti Talvela, and its invention for the most part has a dignity and power that are symphonic in scale. All four roles are well sung, and the performance under Ulf Söderblom is very well recorded indeed.

KOLESSA, Mykola (born 1903)

Symphony No. 1.

** ASV CDDCA 963. Odessa PO, Hobart Earle – SKORYK: *Carpathian Concerto* etc. **

Mykola Kolessa, now in his late nineties, is the grand old man of Ukrainian music. The *First* of his two symphonies was composed in 1950 in the immediate wake of the Zhdanov affair, when any sense of harmonic adventure was discouraged. This piece at times sounds like Glière or Arensky. It is expertly written and is easy to listen to, but it could just as well have been composed in the 1890s. Very well played and recorded. The pieces by Kolessa's pupil, Myroslav Skoryk, are more interesting.

KOMZÁK, Karel (1850–1905)

Edelweiss Overture; Der letzte Gruss Galopp; Louise de Lavallière (Air). Marches: Echtes Wiener Blut; Erzherzog Rainer; Thun-Hohenstein. Polkas: Am Gardasee; Heitere Stunden; Volapük. Waltzes: Bad'ner Mädl'n; Maienzauber; Neues Leben; Phantome.

(N) **(*) Marco 8.225175. Razumovsky SO, Pollack.

Czech composer Karel Komzák was not only an organist for a lunatic asylum in Prague but also founded, in the same city, an orchestra in which Dvořák played the viola. He then became a highly successful band-master travelling throughout Austria. He wrote around three hundred works, to which this CD is an ideal introduction. It includes a nice mixture of marches, waltzes and polkas, as well as a more substantial overture. Though not quite in the Johann Strauss league, it is all tuneful music of charm, and is well played and recorded here.

KOPPEL, Herman D. (born 1908)

Cello Concerto, Op. 56.

*** BIS (ADD) CD 80. Bengtsson, Danish Nat. RSO, Schmidt – NORHOLM: *Violin Concerto.* ***

Herman D. Koppel's idiom stems from Stravinsky and Bartók, but the opening of his *Cello Concerto* has something of the luminous quality of Tippett's *Midsummer Marriage*. Very good recording of an inventive and original piece that deserves to enter the wider international repertoire. It is more satisfying than either the Kokkonen or Sallinen concertos.

KOPYLOV, Aleksandr (1854–1911)

Concert Overture in D min., Op. 31; Scherzo in A, Op. 10; Symphony in C min., Op. 14.

*** ASV CDDCA 1013. Moscow SO, Almeida.

Aleksandr Kopylov, a pupil of Rimsky-Korsakov in St Petersburg, was more of a teacher than a composer, but all three of these works, the sum total of Kopylov's orchestral music, will delight devotees of the Russian Romantics. The *Concert Overture* has the strongest Russian flavour, with colourful themes and snapping rhythms in the main *Allegro*. The *Scherzo* too is fresh and open with well-contrasted themes. The *Symphony* is more like Balakirev watered down, beautifully made with clean-cut structures. Persuasive performances under Antonio de Almeida, in one of the last recordings he made before his untimely death.

KORNGOLD, Erich (1897–1957)

Baby Serenade, Op. 24; Sursum corda (Symphonic Overture), Op. 13; Der Schneemann: Prelude & Serenade. Die tote Stadt: Prelude. Das Wunder der Heliane: Interlude.

*** ASV CDDCA 1074. Bruckner O, Richter.

This is a delightful disc, centring on a work new to the catalogue, the *Baby Serenade*. Korngold wrote it in 1928 on the birth of his second son, George, a follow-up to Strauss's *Domestic Symphony* in providing a musical evocation of family life with a baby. Unlike the Strauss, the five movements here are miniatures, charmingly unpretentious. After a jolly overture, the slow movement, picturing a good baby, is built on a theme Korngold wrote at the age of seven. The *Overture, Sursum corda* is like Respighi with a German accent, and even the excerpts from *The Snowman*, an opera written when Korngold was only eleven, are rich and lush, though the orchestration is by Zemlinsky – a point not mentioned in the booklet. The other two operatic excerpts make up the warmly enjoyable programme, helped by excellent playing and recording.

(i) Cello Concerto in C, Op. 37; (ii) Piano Concerto in C sharp for the Left Hand, Op. 17. Symphonic Serenade for Strings, Op. 39; Military March in B flat.

*** Chan. 9508. (i) Dixon; (ii) Shelley; BBC PO, Bamert.

The more one hears of Korngold's lesser known music the more impressive he seems. The least interesting piece is the *Cello Concerto*, an adaptation of a short piece he composed in 1946 for the film *Deception* starring Bette Davis and Claude Rains. The *Concerto in C sharp for Piano Left Hand* (1924) is an altogether different matter. Composed, like Ravel's concerto, for the one-armed pianist Paul Wittgenstein, who had lost his right arm during the First World War, it is an extraordinarily imaginative and resourceful work. Although it springs from a post-Straussian world (Gary Graffman called it 'a keyboard *Salome*'), it is full of individual touches. Howard Shelley gives it a radiant performance and is given splendid support. To complaints that the *Military March* (1917) was rather fast, Korngold is said to have replied that it was intended to be played for the retreat! The *Symphonic Serenade for Strings* was composed after the Second World War. It is a very beautiful (as well as beautifully crafted) work with a highly inventive Scherzo and an eloquent, rather Mahlerian slow movement. First-rate playing and opulent, well-balanced recording. Well worth exploring.

Violin Concerto in D, Op. 35.

*** EMI CDC7 47846-2. Perlman, Pittsburgh SO, Previn – GOLDMARK: *Concerto.* ***

(BB) *** Naxos 8.553579. Tsu, Razumovsky Sinfonia, Yu Long – GOLDMARK: *Violin Concerto.* ***

(i) Violin Concerto; (ii) Much Ado about Nothing (suite), Op. 11.

*** DG 439 886-2. Shaham; (i) LSO, Previn; (ii) Previn (piano) – BARBER: *Violin Concerto.* ***

The Korngold was written within five years of the Barber *Concerto* and makes a desirable coupling for it. The Israeli violinist Gil Shaham gives a performance of effortless virtuosity and strong profile. Shaham may not have quite the flair and panache of the dedicatee, Jascha Heifetz, in his incomparable reading, but he is warmer and more committed than Itzakh Perlman in his Pittsburgh recording for EMI, again with Previn conducting. There is greater freshness and conviction than in the Perlman. The recording helps, far clearer and more immediate than Perlman's EMI. It is true that in his cooler way Perlman finds an extra tenderness in such passages as the entry of the violin in the slow movement, but Shaham and Previn together consistently bring out the work's sensuous warmth without making the result soupy. The suite from Korngold's incidental music to *Much Ado about Nothing* provides a delightful and apt makeweight, with Previn as pianist just as understanding and imaginative an accompanist and Shaham yearningly warm without sentimentality, clean and precise in attack.

Vera Tsu, born in Shanghai and trained in America, is an outstanding soloist in a coupling that directly challenges the EMI disc from Itzhak Perlman. In every way this ripely romantic version of the Korngold is a match for that and other full-price rivals, thanks to Tsu's rich, ample tone and her flawless intonation, as well as her fearless attack in bravura writing. In the quality of sound the recording outshines most other versions, rich and free, both immediate and atmospheric, with fine dynamic range and with the Chinese conductor, Yu Long, drawing beautiful, refined playing from the Bratislava orchestra.

Sinfonietta, Op. 5; Sursum corda, Op. 13.

*** Chan. 9317. BBC PO, Bamert.

Korngold's *Sinfonietta* is a four-movement symphony in all but name, betraying a prodigious expertise both in the organization of musical ideas and in the handling of the orchestra; and not only that, the ideas themselves are of real quality and individuality. At 43 minutes, it is an extraordinary achievement for a fourteen-year-old – an adolescent composer springing as it were fully equipped on to the musical scene. *Sursum corda*, an early virtuoso showpiece lasting 20 minutes, is finer than one might expect, an extraordinarily sumptuous piece that in its wide range of moods keeps suggesting that it will turn into the *Pines of Rome*. The present performance of the *Sinfonietta* is a clear frontrunner, and the Chandos recording is altogether superb in terms of definition and opulence. A ripely enjoyable disc of beautifully played performances, with a sumptuous soundpicture.

Symphony in F sharp, Op. 40; (i) Abschiedslieder, Op. 14.

*** Chan. 9171. (i) Finnie; BBC PO, Downes.

The *Symphony* is a work of real imaginative power. It is scored for large forces – a big percussion section including piano, celeste, marimba, etc., and the orchestra is used with resource and flair. The BBC Philharmonic play with enthusiasm and sensitivity for Edward Downes. The *Abschiedslieder* are much earlier and were completed in 1920; there is a great deal of Strauss, Mahler and Zemlinsky here. Linda

Finnie is a persuasive soloist, and the balance is eminently well judged. The Chandos recording is wide-ranging and lifelike.

CHAMBER MUSIC

(i) *Piano Quintet in E, Op. 15;* (ii) *Suite for 2 Violins, Cello & Piano Left Hand, Op. 23.*

*** ASV CDDCA 1047. (i) Schmolk; (ii) McFarlane; Schubert Ens. of London.

The *Piano Quintet* is powerfully wrought and superbly laid out for the medium, and rightly enjoyed much exposure in the 1920s. Its resurrection in this fine new recording is more than welcome, for it reaffirms the fertility of Korngold's imagination and the quality of his invention. The *Suite, Op. 23*, one of six works written for Paul Wittgenstein, has some splendid ideas: the third movement, *Grotesquerie* is particularly striking. This performance is less larger-than-life than the rival account from Sony.

String Quartet No. 2 in E flat, Op. 26.

*** Vanguard 99209. Brodsky Qt – KREISLER: *String Quartet in A min.* ***

The Brodsky Quartet are masterly in their control of expressive rubato in this richly post-romantic music, playing with flawless unanimity and fine balance. They capture nicely the hints of salon music in writing which only finds full weight in the third movement *Romanze*, but the finesse of the writing throughout is a delight. A fascinating coupling with the Kreisler *Quartet*.

String Sextet, Op. 10.

*** Hyp. CDA 66425. Raphael Ens. – SCHOENBERG: *Verklaerte Nacht.* ***

The Korngold *Sextet* is an amazing achievement for a seventeen-year-old. Not only is it crafted with musicianly assurance and maturity it is also inventive and characterful. The Raphael Ensemble play it with great commitment and the Hyperion recording is altogether first class.

Suite for 2 Violins, Cello & Piano Left Hand, Op. 23.

*** Sony SK 48253. Silverstein, Laredo, Ma, Fleischer – SCHMIDT: *Quintet for 2 Violins, Viola, Cello & Piano Left Hand.****

Having lain neglected for so long, the Op. 23 *Suite* for the unusual combination of two violins, cello and piano left hand, has been taken out of the deep freeze and given a virtuosic performance by these distinguished players. Their Schmidt coupling, another work written for Wittgenstein, enhances the attractions of this well-recorded issue.

VOCAL MUSIC

3 Lieder, Op. 18. Lieder: Alt-spanisch; Gefasster Abschied; Glückwunsch; Liebesbriefchen; Sonett für Wien; Sterbelied.

*** DG 437 515-2. Von Otter, Forsberg – BERG: *7 Early Songs;* R. STRAUSS: *Lieder.* ***

Inspired playing and singing in these rare and immediately attractive songs by Erich Korngold. Though a few date from his early, precocious years in Vienna, including some of the most sensuously beautiful, such a charming miniature as *Alt-spanisch* is taken from the film music he wrote in 1940 for the swashbuckling Hollywood film, *The Sea Hawk*. Singer and pianist draw out the intensity of emotion to the full without exaggeration or sentimentality. A fascinating programme.

5 *Lieder, Op. 38; Songs of the Clown, Op. 29.*

*** Sony SK 68344. Kirchschlager, Deutsch – MAHLER: *Lieder und Gesänge.* ***

These two song-groups, written after Korngold went to America – charming miniatures most of them – are tuneful in an innocent way. Even *Come away death* fails to draw from the composer a deep response (no doubt reflecting his title for the group), gravitating quickly to the major mode. With Op. 29 here receiving its first recording, they add a pointful element to the début recital of this talented, fresh-voiced singer; well worth exploring.

Passover Psalm.

*** Decca 460 213-2. Urbanová, Slovak Philharmonic Ch., VPO, Chailly – JANACEK: *Glagolitic Mass.* ZEMLINSKY: *Psalm 83.* ***

The *Passover Psalm*, commissioned by a rabbi in Hollywood in 1941, is Korngold's only religious work, a brief, warm-hearted piece that makes an unusual coupling for the Janáček. Very well recorded.

OPERA

Die Kathrin (complete).

*** CPO 999 602-2 (3). Diener, Rendall, Hayward, Watson, Jones, BBC Singers, BBC Concert O, Brabbins.

Erich Korngold composed *Die Kathrin*, his last opera, in summers spent back home in Austria, between Hollywood trips when he wrote his Oscar-winning film scores. Not so much grand opera as grand operetta, it is a far warmer and more relaxed piece than his other operas. The opulent scoring and ripe lyricism go with a novelettish story of Kathrin, a servant-girl, and her wandering minstrel of a sweetheart. With echoes of Strauss's *Arabella*, Puccini's *Suor Angelica* and even Humperdinck's *Hansel und Gretel*, Martyn Brabbins draws aptly sumptuous sounds from the BBC Concert Orchestra, in a recording taken from a BBC radio production. A characterful cast, including Della Jones and Lillian Watson in small roles, is headed by the radiant young German soprano, Melanie Diener, but with David Rendall rather strained as the hero, François.

Die tote Stadt (complete).

(M) *** RCA (ADD) GD 87767 (2). Neblett, Kollo, Luxon, Prey, Bav. R. Ch., Tölz Ch., Munich R. O, Leinsdorf.

At the age of twenty-three Korngold had his opera, *Die tote Stadt*, presented in simultaneous world premières in Hamburg and Cologne! The score includes many echoes of

Puccini and Richard Strauss, but its youthful exuberance carries the day. Here René Kollo is powerful, if occasionally coarse of tone, Carol Neblett sings sweetly in the equivocal roles of the wife's apparition and the newcomer, and Hermann Prey, Benjamin Luxon and Rose Wagemann make up an impressive cast. Leinsdorf is at his finest.

Das Wunder der Heliane (complete).

*** Decca 436 636-2 (3). Tomowa-Sintow, Welker, De Haan, Runkel, Pape, Gedda, Berlin R. Ch. & RSO, Mauceri.

Although the plot of this Korngold opera, with its tyrannical ruler, his wife and a mysterious stranger, is unconvincing, Decca's magnificent recording amply confirms the view that this is Korngold's masterpiece, musically even richer than his better known opera, *Die tote Stadt*. The opening prelude, with its exotic harmonies and heavenly choir, will seduce anyone with a sweet tooth, and though in three Acts of nearly an hour each it is overlong, Korngold sustains the story with a ravishing score. Puccini as well as Strauss is often very close, with one passage in the big Act I love-duet bringing languorous echoes of the end of *Fanciulla del West*. Korngold's lavish Hollywood scores of the 1930s are thin by comparison. John Mauceri draws glorious sounds from the Berlin Radio Symphony Orchestra, and the cast is headed by three outstanding singers, the soprano Anna Tomowa-Sintow at her richest, an impressive American Heldentenor, John David de Haan, as the Stranger and Hartmut Welker as the Ruler.

KOSMA, Joseph (1905–69)

Piano pieces: *Chants du ghetto; Danse des automates;.* Chansons: *Barbara; Faut pas m'en vouloir; Les enfants qui s'aiment; Les feuilles mortes; Friedhofstor; L'Hymne à la Résistance; Je ne veux que tes yeux; Jésus la Caille.* (Medley) *Le jour et la nuit; 3 Lieder vom Meer; Lueur dans la nuit Le merveilleux poème; Rue des Blancs-Manteaux; Rue de Seine; Sans coup férir* (cycle); *Si tu t'imagine; Les soutiers.*

(N) *** Decca 460 050-2. Le Roux, Matrix Ens. (members); Cohen (piano).

Who would have guessed that Decca's 'Entartete' series of music suppressed by the Third Reich would have produced an unmissable collection of chansons by the composer of one of the most haunting of all French popular songs, *Les feuilles mortes* ('Dead leaves'). This, like Kosma's other famous example of French nostalgia, *Barbara*, has lyrics by the composer's friend, Jacques Prévert, and it was he who helped Budapest-born Kosma to survive in Paris after in 1933 he had been forced to flee from Berlin. Prévert then introduced him to Jean Renoir, for whom he wrote his first film music.

Kosma survived the war to compose his most famous songs, many of which are included here. Particularly attractive is the mini-cycle *Sans coup férir*, where nearly all the ten (often whimsical) vignettes are only a minute long or less. At the conclusion there is a brief piano postlude and the singer suggests that listeners 'don't shoot the pianist'.

The three German Lieder about the sea are particularly evocative, as is *Je ne veux que tes yeux* with its memorable refrain, and the wordless *Lueur dans la nuit*. François Le Roux has the ideal light baritone timbre for these songs and he sings them with an innate feeling for their evocatively sentimental style. The atmospheric accompaniments are arranged by the pianist, Jeff Cohen, and feature a small intimate instrumental group. He also plays the two groups of piano miniatures very sensitively, revealing their individual flavour. Everything is beautifully recorded and full translations are provided. A wonderful record to generate a feeling of late-evening nostalgia.

KOZELUCH, Leopold (1747–1818)

Clarinet Concerto No. 2 in E flat.

*** ASV CDDCA 763. Johnson, RPO, Herbig – CRUSELL; KROMMER: *Concertos.* ***

Leopold Kozeluch's concerto is a highly agreeable work, especially when performed so magnetically by Emma Johnson. There is plenty of Johnsonian magic here to light up even the most conventional passage-work, and the 'naturally flowing melodies' (the soloist's own description), and she is well accompanied and admirably recorded, with the slow movement made to sound recessed and delicate.

Symphonies in D; F; & G min.

*** Chan. 9703. LMP, Bamert.

Kozeluch was born near Prague but established himself in Vienna in 1778, where he was appointed to the Imperial Court as official composer and director of the orchestra. These symphonies are pleasingly crafted, sub-Mozart, but each is distinguished by a graceful and appealing slow movement and a vigorous lighthearted finale. They are very well played here, and the fairly resonant Chandos recording ensures their weight and substance.

KRAMÁŘ, František – see
KROMMER, Franz

KRAUS, Joseph Martin (1756–92)

Symphonies: in A, VB 128; in F (Buffa), VB 129; in F, VB 130; C (Violin obbligato), VB 138.

(N) (BB) *** Naxos 8.554472. Swedish CO, Sundkvist.

Symphonies in C, VB 139; C min., VB 142; E flat, VB 144; Olympie Overture, VB 29.

(BB) *** Naxos 8.553734. Swedish CO, Sundquist.

Symphonies in C sharp min., VB 140; in E min., VB 141; in C min. (Funèbre), VB 148; Overture in D min., VB 147.

(N) (BB) *** Naxos 8.554777. Swedish CO, Sundkvist.

Born in the same year as Mozart, Kraus was dubbed the 'Swedish Mozart', but these lively symphonies, freshly performed by the Swedish Chamber Orchestra, suggest that his music has more in common with that of Haydn, above all the *Sturm und Drang* period. Haydn, who met Kraus in both Vienna and Esterházy, praised his music highly. Unlike Mozart, Kraus was drawn to minor keys, not just in the *C minor Symphony*, and the tough streak in the writing is emphasized by the sharpness of syncopated rhythms. The *Olympie Overture*, in three sections, slow–fast–slow, following the French pattern, dates from the year of Kraus's death, written for a stage production of Voltaire's play of that name. Full, warm sound and excellent performances, involving a substantial string section with first-rate wind and brass playing, notably from the horns. Well worth exploring.

The major-keyed symphonies are marginally less striking, although allegros still have plenty of vitality and VB 128 in C includes an important solo violin obbligato throughout all three movements. The hunting finales of the VB 128 and 130 dance along merrily, while the last movement of the *Sinfonia buffa* is strikingly ambitious, much varied in mood and with passages of concertante flute writing.

Most individual of all are the minor-key symphonies on the third disc, especially the remarkable work in C sharp minor (1782), a symphony fully worthy of Haydn. The first two movements are particularly searching, and the work is completed by a powerful driving finale. The E minor (VB 141) has another expressive Adagio and the strong, lively finale is by no means predictable. The *Symphonie funèbre*, written in the year of the composer's death is most remarkable of all in paying a dramatic tribute to King Gustav III (the composer's patron) who was assassinated at a masked ball. The work opens and closes with muffled beats on the side-drum: the first movement is a sombre march, the third a funeral chorale, the finale an expressive Adagio, which includes an eloquent central horn solo and an impressive double fugue. The *D minor Overture* (heard here in its original darker scoring for strings with bassoons) brings a solemn Largo followed by a dignified fugue. It shares the mood of Haydn's *Seven Last Words* and was often played on Good Friday.

KREBS, Johann Ludwig (1713–80)

Music for harpsichord: Preludes Nos. 2 in D min.; 3 in E min.; 5 in G; 6 in A min.; Suites in B min.; in C min.; Organ chorales: Allein Gott in der Höh' sei Ehr; Auf meinen lieben Gott (2 settings); Christ lag in Todesbanden; Jesu meine Freude (2 settings); Jesus meine Zuversicht (2 settings); Sei Lob und Ehr dem Höchsten Gut; Vater unser im Himmelreich; Von Gott will ich nicht lassen; Warum betrübst du dich, mein Herz?; Wass Gott will ich nicht lassen; Wass Gott tut, das ist wohlgetan (2 settings); Wer nur den lieben Gott lässt walten (2 settings).

*** Meridian (ADD) CDE 84306. Gifford (harpsichord or chamber organ).

The title of this collection, 'The best crayfish in the brook', is a pun on the composer's name, often attributed to his mentor. Krebs (which also covers the fish) was a favourite pupil of Bach (which also means brook). On the evidence of this highly attractive recital he was a very talented pupil too, who obviously absorbed much of his master's contrapuntal style in his organ chorale, even if their expressive and imaginative range is more limited. But Krebs's clavier music has a strong personality in its own right. His harpsichord dance *Suites* and *Preludes* demonstrate a lively mixture of French and Italianate manners, and their invention is consistently attractive. Gerald Gifford plays with a vividly communicative yet scholarly style, alternating harpsichord and organ music to make a stimulating and diverting programme. His harpsichord is a copy of a Hemsch, his organ a modern copy of a small eighteenth-century instrument in Nuremberg. Both are beautifully recorded. This is a disc you might easily pass by. But don't. Professor Gifford is a highly persuasive advocate and his two instruments are perfectly recorded.

ORGAN MUSIC
Complete organ music

Vol. 1: Chorales: *Ach Gott, erhör mein Seufzen; Ach Herr mich armer Sünder; Allein in Gott in der Höh' sei Her'; Sei Lob und Ehr dem höchsten Gut; Wer nur den lieben Gott lässt walten; Fantasia sopra 'Freu dich sehr, o meine Seele'; Prelude & Fugue in C; Toccatas & Fugues in A min.; E; Trio in E flat.*

(N) (BB) *** Naxos 8.553924. Gnann (Gabler organ, Weingarten Abbey).

Both Naxos and Priory are currently undertaking a complete survey of Kreb's organ music and this is likely to run to at least a half a dozen discs in each case. Fortunately both organists are players of calibre.

For Volume 1, Gerhard Gnann has chosen the Gabler organ in Weingarten Abbey, built between 1737 and 1750. It is a superb example of a large baroque organ, with throaty reeds (obvious from the very opening of the *Toccata in E*) and boldly powerful pedals, demonstrated splendidly in the *Prelude in C major*.

The organ's fine palette of colours is obvious in the slow chorales, where Gnann makes sure the cantus firmus is very clear (in *Ach Herr mich armer Sünder* he uses the Vox humana stop), and in the jaunty *Allein in Gott*, and the similar lightly registered *Wer nur den lieben Gott*, the effect is most engaging. Gnann's playing reveals the power and contrast inherent in the large-scale pieces, yet finds all the charm in the galante *Trio*. There are 65 minutes of music here, and if the Naxos series continues on this level it will be hard to beat.

Vol. 1: Chorales: *Ach Gott, erhör mein Seufzen; Ach Herr mich armen Sünder; Christ lag in Totesbanden; Herzlich lieb hab ich dich, o Herr; Nun freut euch, lieben Christen gmein; Sei Lob und Ehr dem höchsten Gut; Vom Himmel hoch; Was Gott tut, das ist wohlgetan. Fantasia à giusto italiano; Fugues: in A min.; C min.; F. Prelude in C; Prelude supra 'Sei Lob und Ehr dem höchsten Gut'; Prelude & Fugue in F min.; Prelude supra 'Christ lag in*

Todesbanden'; Prelude supra 'Was Gott tut, das ist wohlgetan'; Trios: E flat; 1 & 2 in F.

(N) *** Priory PRCD 734. Kitchen (organ of Canongate Kirk, Edinburgh).

The organ used by John Kitchen is a modern instrument, built by Frobenius of Denmark in the Canongate Kirk in Edinburgh. It, too, has character, its reeds slightly less pungent than the German instrument used on Naxos, but not lacking edge in fortissimo and glowing with colour in the chorales. When Kitchen registers *pro organo pleno*, the richness of texture is all but orchestral. The pedals have plenty of weight and are telling, even though they blend more smoothly into the overall texture than with the baroque instrument. And how vividly the *cantus firmus* stands out in the chorale *Vom Himmel hoch*.

In many cases Kitchen offers us two versions of the same chorale and in the *organo pleno* version of *Nun freut euch* the tutti is thrilling. One of the more striking pieces in Volume 1 is the enigmatically named *Fantasia à giusto italiano*, a very vocal melody simply ornamented. Like Gnann, Kitchen has planned each collection in the form of a recital and Volume 1 (78 minutes) ends with three fugues, of which the closing scalic piece in F makes a powerful coda.

Vol. 2: Chorales: *Freu dich sehr, o meine Seele; Jesu meine Zuversicht; Von Gott will ich nicht lassen; Wir glauben all an einen Gott, Vater; Wir glauben all an einen Gott, Schöpfer (3-verse setting) Fantasia & Fugue in F; Prelude supra 'Von Gott will ich nicht lassen'; Prelude & Fugue in C min.; Toccata & Fugue in E; Trios: in D min.; E flat; A min. Fantasia supra 'Freu dich sehr, o meine Seele'.*

(N) *** Priory PRCD 734. Kitchen (organ of St Salvator's Chapel, St Andrews University).

The St Andrews organ dates from 1974 and was built by Gregor Hradetzky. It has a slightly more baroque tang than the Edinburgh instrument, as John Kitchen demonstrates in the opening *Toccata and Fugue in E*. This opens with a virtuoso pedal solo and then exploits the antiphonal use of two manuals. The performance is properly grand, yet the instrument's pretty reed colouring comes to the fore in the three engaging Trios which are placed at strategic points in the programme. In several cases we are invited to enjoy different settings of the same cantus firmus. The contrast between the Chorale (*pro organo pleno*) and the lightly registered and nimbly played *Fantasia* on *Freu dich sehr* is very striking. The *Fantasia in F* is most diverting, followed by a perky fugue; the *Prelude and Fugue in C minor* are rather more sober. Kitchen ends with a three-verse chorale setting of *Wir glauben*, and although the third verse is jubilant and ends with a powerful *Amen*, one is left with the feeling that this is a less substantial (73 minute) programme than Volume 1, although it suits the organ in St Andrews very well.

Other organ music

Chorales: Herr Gott, dich loben alle wir; Herzlich lieb had ich dich, O Herr; Wir glauben all an einen Gott; Zeuch ein zu deinen Toren; Chorale fantasia sopra 'Wer nur den lieben Gott lässt walten'; Fantasia a giusto italiano; Fugue in B flat on B-A-C-H; Preludes & Fugues in C; in D; Trios in E flat; D min..

**(*) ASV CDGAU 125. Barber (organ of St Peter Mancroft, Norwich).

Graham Barber certainly catches the amiable quality of the Krebs style, and if this collection is perhaps less distinctive than Gerald Gifford's programme it includes much to divert, not least the opening *Fantasia a giusto italiano*. Yet the chorale *Herr Gott, dich loben alle wir*, with its powerful imitation in the pedals, is imposing, and the closing *D major Prelude and Fugue* also shows Krebs in his best Bach imitative style. Elsewhere the polyphony is often distinctly lightweight, as in the *C major Fugue* and the jolly finale of the *Trio in E flat*, while Barber's registration of the cantus firmus in the *Chorale Fantasia* is agreeably quirky. Krebs was one of the first composers to write a fugue based on the notes of Bach's name and he spells it out unequivocally at the opening with the close impressively full-blooded. The Norwich organ brings a bright, cleanly focused palette, which suits the music.

KREISLER, Fritz (1875–1962)

Arangements for Violin & Orchestra: Caprice viennoise; La gitana; Grave; Liebesfreud; Liebesleid; Praeludium & Allegro in the Style of Pugnani; La Précieuse, in the Style of Couperin; Rondino on a Theme by Beethoven; Scherzo in the Style of Dittersdorf; Schön Rosmarin; Sicilienne & Rigaudon in the Style of Francoeur. (Arr of: DVORAK: Slavonic Dances Nos. 1 in G min.; 2 in E min.. LECLAIR: Tambourin. GLUCK: Mélodie (Orfeo ed Euridice). WEBER: Larghetto. RAMEAU: Tambourin. TRAD.: Londonderry Air (all arr. for violin and orchestra by Peter Wolf)).

**(*) Sony SK 62692. Stern, with Franz Liszt CO.

These concertante arrangements serve to some extent to mask the fact that Stern's timbre is less sweet than it once was. If he can no longer match today's young lions in tonal sophistication, he still knows how to present this material with panache and *Schön Rosmarin* shows him at his most dashing. Gluck's famous theme from *Orfeo* too is beautifully phrased. The recording is forward but truthful.

Violin Concerto in the Style of Vivaldi.

*** DG 439 933-2. Shaham, Orpheus CO – VIVALDI: *The Four Seasons.* ***

An amiable pastiche, which sounds almost totally unlike Vivaldi as we experience his music performed today. It is warmly played and clearly enjoyed by its performers, and the sumptuousness of the sound is the more striking coming, as it does, immediately after Vivaldi's wintry winds.

Allegretto in the Style of Boccherini; Aucassin & Nicolette; Berceuse romantique; Caprice viennoise; La gitana; Liebesfreud; Liebesleid; Marche miniature viennoise; Menuett in the Style of Porpora; Polichinelle; Praeludium & Allegro in the Style of Pugnani; La Précieuse in the Style of Louis Couperin; Rondino on a Theme of Beethoven;

Schön Rosmarin; Sicilienne & Rigaudon in the Style of Francoeur; Syncopation; Tambourin chinois; Tempo di Minuetto in the Style of Pugnani; Toy-Soldiers' March.

*** Decca 444 409-2. Bell, Coker.

As readily shown by the opening *Praeludium & Allegro*, Joshua Bell refuses to treat this music as trivial, and there is a total absence of schmalz. *Tambourin chinois*, impeccably played, lacks something in charm, but not the neatly articulated *La Précieuse*. And what lightness of touch in *Schön Rosmarin*, what elegance of style in the *Caprice viennoise*, what panache in the paired *Liebesfreud* and *Liebesleid*, and how seductive is the simple *Berceuse romantique*, one of the novelties here, like the winning *Toy-Soldiers' March* and the unexpected, almost Joplinesque rag, *Syncopation*. The recording is completely realistic.

Allegretto in the Style of Boccherini; Caprice Viennoise; Chanson Louis XIII & Pavane; Liebeslied; Liebesfreud; Minuet; The Old Refrain; Praeludium & Allegro; Recitativo & Scherzo; Rondino on a Theme of Beethoven; Schön Rosmarin; Tambourin chinois; Tempo di Minuetto.

(M) *** Mercury (IMS) (ADD) 434 351-2. Szeryng, Reiner (with LECLAIR: *Violin Sonata No. 3 in D*; GLUCK, arr. KREISLER: *Mélodie*; LOCATELLI: *The Labyrinth* **).

It is good to have a reminder of the artistry of Henryk Szeryng. His playing of these occasional pieces of Kreisler – not all of them by any means trifles – is superb. The 1963 recording is firmly focused and truthful. The remaining items are played as virtuoso encores rather than showing any natural sympathy for the baroque style, although no one could fail to be impressed by the bravura of Locatelli's *Labyrinth*. However, in these pieces the Mercury sound brings rather more edge to the violin timbre.

Allegretto in the Style of Boccherini; Allegretto in the Style of Porpora; Caprice viennoise; Cavatina; La Chasse in the Style of Cartier; La gitana; Grave in the Style of W. F. Bach; Gypsy Caprice; Liebesfreud; Liebesleid; Praeludium & Allegro in the Style of Pugnani; Recitative & Scherzo; Schön Rosmarin; Shepherd's Madrigal; Sicilienne et Rigaudon in the Style of Francoeur; Toy-Soldiers' March; Viennese Rhapsodic Fantasia; arr. of Austrian National Hymn.

(BB) **(*) ASV CDQS 6039. Shumsky, Kaye.

Oscar Shumsky's combination of technical mastery and musical flair is ideal for this music; and it is a pity that the rather dry recording and forward balance – well in front of the piano – makes the violin sound almost too close.

Aucassin et Nicolette; Caprice viennois; La gitana; Marche miniature viennoise; 3 Old Viennese Dances (Liebesfreud; Liebesleid; Schön Rosmarin); Praeludium & Allegro in the Style of Pugnani; Preghiera in the Style of Martini; Sicilienne et Rigaudon in the Style of Francoeur; Slavonic Fantasie on Themes by Dvořák; Tambourin chinois.
Arrangements of: CHAMINADE: Sérénade espagnole.
DVORAK: Slavonic Dance, Op. 72/2. SCOTT: Lotus Land.
TCHAIKOVSKY: Chant sans paroles, Op. 2/3.
MENDELSSOHN: Songs without Words: Andante espressivo

in G, Op. 62/1. RACHMANINOV: *Rhapsody on a Theme of Paganini: Variation.* LEHAR: *Frasquita: Serenade.* ANON.: *Londonderry Air.* ALBENIZ: *España: Tango, Op. 165/2.* HEUBERGER: *Midnight Bells.*

(M) *** Classic fM 75605 57020-2. Hattori, Seiger.

Joji Hattori brings to these Kreisler trifles not only a brilliant technique and rich, firm violin-tone, but the rhythmic flair and naughty pointing of phrase which makes them sparkle. The 22 encores include not only original pieces by Kreisler, but his inspired violin arrangements of favourite pieces by such composers as Dvořák, Tchaikovsky, Rachmaninov, Lehár and others. Also a sequence of the pieces he wrote, originally attributing them to then-neglected eighteenth-century composers like Pugnani, Francoeur and Martini. The gently lyrical *Preghiera* after Martini inspires Hattori to hushed, meditative playing just as intense as his bravura fireworks in such pieces as *Tambourin chinois*. Joseph Seiger is a comparably inspired accompanist, relishing the glissando display in such a piece as *La gitana*. Warm, full recording. A best buy among mid-priced recordings of the repertoire.

Caprice viennoise; Chanson Louis XIII & Pavane in the Style of Couperin; La gitana; Liebesleid; Liebesfreud; Polinchinelle; La Précieuse in the Style of Couperin; Rondino on a Theme by Beethoven; Scherzo alla Dittersdorf; Tambourin chinois; Schön Rosmarin. Arrangements: BACH: *Partita No. 3 in E, BWV 1006: Gavotte.* BRANDL: *The Old Refrain.* DVORAK: *Humoresque.* FALLA: *La vida breve: Danza española.* GLAZUNOV: *Sérénade espagnole.* HEUBERGER: *Midnight Bells (Im chambre séparée).* POLDINI: *Poupée valsante.* RIMSKY-KORSAKOV: *Sadko: Chanson hindoue.* SCHUBERT: *Rosamunde: Ballet Music No. 2.* SCOTT: *Lotus Land.* TCHAIKOVSKY: *Andante cantabile from Op. 11.* WEBER: *Violin Sonata No. 1 in F, Op. 10: Larghetto.* TRAD.: *Londonderry Air.*

(M) (***) EMI mono CDH7 64701-2. Kreisler, Rupp or Rachelsein; or (in *Scherzo*) Kreisler String Qt.

Impeccable and characterful performances by Fritz Kreisler of his own lollipops, including those 'in the style of' pieces with which – until he owned up – he fooled his audiences into believing they were actually written by the composers in question. Most of the recordings were made with Franz Rupp in 1936 or 1938, and the transfers offer a convincingly realistic if studio-ish balance and are of excellent technical quality; a few (the *Polinchinelle*, the pieces in the style of Couperin, the Schubert *Rosamunde Ballet Music*, the Glazunov and Weber arrangements, *The Old Refrain* (especially) and an indulgent performance of Heuberger's *Im chambre séparée*) date from 1930 and here the piano balance is poor, the piano badly defined. However, these were recorded before Kreisler's accident and the violin timbre is noticeably more opulent. A valuable document.

String Quartet in A min..

*** Vanguard 99209. Brodsky Qt – KORNGOLD: *String Quartet No. 2.* ***

Kreisler is well known for his charming salon pieces but here he aims higher, and the result is not just skilled, but warmly imaginative and attractively varied. The quicksilver brilliance of the Scherzo, and the fantasy and sparkle of the finale, may reflect the salon-music composer we know, but there is a point and individuality that set them apart, and that is even more strikingly so in the other two, more ambitious movements. The Brodsky Quartet give a strongly characterized and beautifully refined reading.

KRENEK, Ernst (1900–91)

Symphonic Elegy for String Orchestra.

(M) (***) Sony mono MH2K 62759 (2). NYPO, Mitropoulos – BERG: *Wozzeck* (***); SCHOENBERG: *Erwartung.* (**(*))

Krenek wrote this powerful piece for strings as a direct response to hearing the news of the tragic death of his friend, Anton Webern. In homage he adopts full serial technique, but the result has little of the spareness of Webern; in its overtly emotional approach and lyrical warmth it comes nearer to Berg in style. Recorded in 1951, like *Wozzeck* and *Erwartung*, it makes an unexpected but valuable fill-up, very well played. (This set costs rather more than our usual upper-mid-price limitation.)

Jonny spielt auf (complete).

**(*) Decca 436 631-2 (2). Kruse, Marc, St Hill, Kraus, Posselt, Leipzig Op. Ch., Leipzig GO, Zagrosek.

Ernst Krenek's opera, *Jonny spielt auf* ('Jonny plays on'), was acclaimed as the first jazz opera, even though the composer always resisted that description. Yet it proved a flash in the pan. Paris was unimpressed, and back in Germany it was quickly banned by the Nazi regime, which condemned it as *Entartete Musik*, decadent music. Hearing the opera now in a fine recording, based on a 1990 Leipzig production – made just before the composer died at the age of ninety – it stands as more than a historical curiosity. Contradicting its reputation, it is a lyrical post-romantic piece. One's first disappointment is that it hardly matches the Kurt Weill operas. The idiom is far milder, with syncopations used more gently in the jazzy passages and with the instrumentation less abrasive. Though the Leipzig Gewandhaus Orchestra under Lothar Zagrosek does not always sound at home in the jazzy sequences, the recording provides the most convincing evidence yet that the piece deserves reappraisal. Heinz Kruse as Max sustains his long monologues impressively, and Krister St Hill as Jonny also sings well, even if the microphone catches an unevenness in their voices. It is Alessandra Marc as the heroine, Anita, who emerges as the main star, relishing lush Krenek melodies that yet never quite stick in the mind.

KREUTZER, Conradin (1780–1849)

Septet (for clarinet, horn, bassoon, violin, viola, cello & double-bass), *Op. 62;* (i) *Trio in E flat* (for piano, clarinet & bassoon), *Op. 43.*

♣ (BB) *** Arte Nova 74321 54462-2. Mithras Octet (members), (i) with Rivinius (piano).

A delightful performance to suggest that the *Septet* by Conradin Kreutzer is almost more infectiously enjoyable than the Beethoven *Septet* on which it was modelled (in 1824). The members of the Mithras Octet have the full measure of the music, playing with grace and elegance and an infectious charm, while the recording is excellent in every respect. The *Trio* is a similarly amiable and inventive work, if less distinctive. It has a doleful *Andante grazioso* and is capped by another memorably light-hearted finale. It is very well played here, but unfortunately the piano, recorded too resonantly, outbalances the pair of woodwind instruments, and this reduces the listener's enjoyment. The Rosette is for the *Septet*, which is not to be missed.

KREUTZER, Joseph (1778–1832)

Grand Trio for Flute, Clarinet & Guitar, Op. 16.

*** Mer. CDE 84199. Conway, Silverthorne, Garcia – BEETHOVEN: *Serenade;* MOLINO: *Trio.* ***

*** Koch 3-7404-2. Still, Alemany, Falletta – BEETHOVEN: *Serenade, Op. 8;* SCHUBERT: *Quartet for Flute, Guitar, Viola & Cello.* ***

Joseph Kreutzer, thought to be the brother of Rodolphe Kreutzer, dedicatee of Beethoven's *A major Violin Sonata*, wrote many works for the guitar, of which this is a delightful example. The guitar, given at least equal prominence with the other instruments, brings an unusual tang to the textures of this charming piece, ending with a rousing *Alla polacca*. A nicely pointed performance on Meridian, very well recorded in warm, faithful sound.

Equally stylishly played on Koch and very well recorded, it also makes an agreeable bonus for the more substantial pieces by Beethoven and Schubert.

KREUTZER, Rodolphe (1766–1831)

Grand Quintet in C.

(B) **(*) Hyp. Helios CDH 55015. Francis, Allegri Qt – CRUSELL: *Divertimento;* REICHA: *Quintet.* **(*)

This is the Kreutzer of the Beethoven sonata. The *Grand Quintet* is thought to date from the 1790s; it is rather bland but rather enjoyable when it is played as beautifully as it is here. This is part of an attractive triptych, now offered by Hyperion at bargain-price. However, the CD plays for under 50 minutes.

KROMMER, Franz (Kramař, František) (1759–1831)

Clarinet Concerto in E flat, Op. 36.

*** ASV CDDCA 763. Johnson, RPO, Herbig – CRUSELL: *Concerto No. 1;* KOZELUCH: *Concerto No. 2.* ***

Emma Johnson is at her most winning in this attractive concerto, which is made to sound completely spontaneous in her hands, particularly the engaging finale, lolloping along with its skipping main theme. The *Adagio* is darker in feeling, its mood equally well caught. Excellent accompaniments and warm, refined recording make this a most engaging triptych.

Clarinet Concerto in E flat, Op. 36; (i) Double Clarinet Concertos in A flat, Opp. 35 & 91.

(BB) ** Naxos 8.553178. Berkes; (i) Tsutsui; Nicolaus Esterházy Sinfonia.

Both the soloists here are good players and they blend very well together; but slow movements are rather deadpan and not all the music's sense of fun comes over. Neither clarinettists nor orchestra are helped by the reverberant recording which means a forward balance for the soloists and tends to coarsen the tuttis by spreading the sound. Even so, the *Double Concerto*, Op. 91, a winner if ever there was one, is very enjoyable, with the first movement swinging along merrily and the *Polacca* finale, with its jaunty duet theme introduced against orchestral pizzicatos, equally fluent.

Oboe Concertos in F, Opp. 37 & 52.

(N) (B) *** Hyp. Helios CDH 55080. Francis, LMP, Shelley – MOZART: *Oboe Concerto.* ***

These two concertos were published in 1803 and 1805 respectively, but were probably written some years apart. Op. 37 has a particularly charming first movement, scored for flute and trumpets as well as strings. The *Adagio* opens rather grandly, but then introduces a galant lyrical cantilena; the chirping *Rondo* finale is spirited and sparkling. The later concerto has a rather more expansive first movement tutti, but the solo writing has no less charm, and the slow movement is even more dramatic, with the solo melody very like a tragic operatic aria. The finale however throws solemnity to the winds and gambols along light-heartedly. Neeedless to say Sarah Francis winningly essays all these changes of mood and style: her exquisite timbre and elegant phrasing would surely have delighted this attractively inventive Bohemian composer as would Howard Shelley's polished accompaniments, delicate or full-blooded as necessary.

Partitas: in E flat; in B flat Op. 45/1–2; in E flat with 2 Horns, FVK 2d.

(BB) *** Naxos 8.553868. Michael Thompson Wind Ens.

Partitas: in F, Op. 57; E flat, Op. 71; B flat, Op. 78. Marches, Op. 31/3–5.

(BB) *** Naxos 8.553498. Budapest Wind Ens.

Franz Krommer specialized in music for wind instruments, of which the two *Partitas*, Op. 45, were always among his most popular works, exploiting the conventional wind band (or Harmonie) of flutes, oboes, horns and bassoons in pairs, plus trumpet on occasion. Even more striking – and not published till this century – is the third *Partita* here, with the two horns given virtuoso solo roles, a concerto in all but name. Vividly recorded, this Naxos issue offers masterly performances from the ensemble of leading London performers previously led by Barry Tuckwell.

This second Naxos disc is just as successful as its predecessor. The Budapest Wind, led by their exuberant clarinettist Kálmán Berkes, are a first-rate ensemble, full of spirit and personality. They yield nothing in terms of artistic excellence or recording quality to any rivals.

Symphonies Nos. 2 in D, Op. 40; 4 in C min., Op. 102.

*** Chan. 9275. LMP, Bamert.

Collectors who acquired the *Harmonien* on Naxos will know how infectiously high-spirited this composer is; and they will not be disappointed by the two symphonies played here by the London Mozart Players under Matthias Bamert. They present a different picture of him: the *D major Symphony* (1803) opens in something of the manner of *Don Giovanni*, while much else conveys a distinctly Beethovenian visage. The *C minor*, Op. 102, composed towards the end of the second decade of the nineteenth century, already has a whiff of the changing sensibility that we find in Schubert and Weber. Very interesting and refreshing music, played with evident enthusiasm and well recorded.

KROUSE, Ian (born 1956)

(i) *Rhapsody for Violin & Orchestra;* (ii) *Thamar y Amnon;* (iii) *Tientos;* (iv) *Cuando se abre en la mañana.*

(N) *** Koch 3-7482-2. (i) Bachmann, New Zealand SO, Sedares; (ii) Debussy Trio; (iii) Dinosaur Annex; (iv) Kim; Tennant.

Ian Krouse is another of the present generation of talented composers – in this instance from New Zealand – who has turned his back on serialism and returned to melody. His music is obviously strongly influenced ('through sheer empathy') by Spanish folk-song, with all four works here dating from 1990. The beautiful, warmly lyrical *Rhapsody for Violin and Orchestra* (with Maria Bachman the highly responsive soloist) memorably reveals him as a striking new voice.

The *Rhapsody* is an elliptical richly lyrical 21-minute piece ('a wordless motet') with a passionate climax and a virtuoso central cadenza. *Thamar y Amnon*, written for the present performers (Marcia Dickstein, harp, Angela Wiegand, flute, and Keith Greene, viola), is a chamber tone poem based on one of García Lorca's *Historical Ballads* and is both evocative and erotic, with Tamar's seductive role portrayed on the viola.

Tientos is inspired by and quotes from a sixteenth-century *villançio* and is scored for flute, violin, viola and cello. It is much more exotic, with a wild melismatic flamenco style. The result is ear-ticking, rhythmically pungent and highly imaginative.

Cuando se abre en la mañana, also inspired by García Lorca, comes from the incidental music Krouse wrote for one of his plays. Its simple refrain is exquisitely realized by Sun Young Kim, vibrantly yet delicately accompanied by Scott Tennant (guitar). All in all a thoroughly rewarding programme, excellently recorded.

KUHLAU, Friedrich (1786–1832)

(i) *Concertino for 2 Horns, Op. 45;* (ii) *Piano Concerto in C, Op. 7. Overture Elverhøj (The Elf's Hill), Op. 100.*

*** Unicorn DKPCD 9110. (i) Lansky-Otto, Wekre; (ii) Ponti; Odense SO, Maga.

The overture *Elverhøj* or *The Elf's Hill* is probably Kuhlau's best-known work and is certainly the finest piece on this disc. The *Piano Concerto in C*, Op. 7, is modelled on Beethoven's concerto in the same key. The *Concertino for Two Horns* (1821) is full of initially engaging, but eventually unmemorable, ideas. Very good performances from all concerned, and satisfactory recording.

Piano Concerto in C, Op. 7.

** Chan. 9699. Amalie Malling, Danish Nat. RSO, Schønwandt – GRIEG: *Piano Concerto.* *

Kuhlau's *C major Concerto* was composed in 1810, half a century before the coupled Grieg concerto. It is pretty nondescript in character, and little of it resonates in the memory. Amalie Malling is more persuasive here than in the Grieg, of which she gives a routine account, and Michael Schønwandt gets alert and crisp playing from the Danish Radio Orchestra. Excellent sound.

Overtures: *Elisa; Elverhøj (The Elf's Hill); Hugo and Adelheid; Lulu; The Magic Harp; The Robber's Castle; The Triplet Brothers from Damask; William Shakespeare.*

*** Chan. 9648. Danish National RSO, Schønwandt.

Lulu is a fairy-tale opera from the same source as *Zauberflöte*, while *William Shakespeare* is based on the Bard's youthful exploit (alleged) of poaching deer. This delightful disc, brilliantly played and recorded, offers all seven of Kuhlau's opera overtures, plus his most famous work, the overture to the classic Danish play, *Elverhøj* (*Elf's Hill*).

Flute Quintets Nos. 1–3, Op. 51.

(N) *** ASV CDDCA 979. Stinton, Prospero Ens.
(N)(BB) *** Naxos 8.553303. Rafn, Sjogren, Rasmussen, Andersen, Johansen.

Kuhlau's *Flute Quintets* are charmingly amiable works well crafted with fresh invention, the slow movements having surprising expressive depth. A choice between these two sets of performances is almost impossible. We are marginally inclined to prefer the playing of Jennifer Stinton, and she gets excellent support from the Prospero Ensemble, but their Scandinavian competitors are also first class, and Eyvind Raft is also a soloist of personality. Both recordings are vivid and present, though the ASV occasionally brings the lead violinist a fraction too close to the microphones. Of course, the Naxos disc has a considerable price advantage. But either disc will give much undemanding pleasure.

Violin Sonatas Nos. 1 in F min., Op. 33; 2 in E flat, Op. 64; 3 in F; 4 in F min.; 5 in C, Op. 79/1–3.

(N) (BB)*** CPO 999 363-2. Bratchkova, Meyer-Hermann.

This collection of Kuhlau's complete *Violin Sonatas* is a

delightful surprise. Written between 1820 and 1827, they have much in common with the violin sonatas of Beethoven, and it is surprising how often one is reminded of that master when listening to these attractive and in no way superficial works. The slow movement of the *F minor* and also the finale bring the most striking echoes, but the composer's own personality also emerges strongly, notably in the attractive variations on a Danish folksong which form the slow movement of the *E flat* work and in the *Rondo* finale. The three Opus 79 works are undoubtedly masterpieces, full of life and with invention of a consistently high order. The performances by the Bulgarian violinist Dora Bratchkova and Andreas Meyer-Hermann are in every way first rate, and they are most naturally balanced and realistically recorded. If you enjoy the Beethoven violin sonatas, you will certainly enjoy these.

Elverhøj (The Elf's Hill), Op. 100.

** Dacapo DCCD 8902. Gobel, Plesner, Johansen, Danish R. Ch. & SO, Frandsen.

Kuhlau's incidental music to J. L. Heiberg's play *Elverhøj* is endearingly fresh. Not so the recording however; this sounds really rather dryish, as if recorded in a fully packed concert hall. The music has great charm and the performance too under John Frandsen is very sympathetic.

Lulu (opera): complete.

*** Kontrapunkt/HM 32009/11. Saarman, Frellesvig, Kiberg, Cold, Danish R. Ch. & SO, Schønwandt.

This *Lulu* comes from 1824 and is surely too long: the spoken passages are omitted here – but, even so, the music takes three hours. The opening of Act II has overtones of the Wolf's Glen scene in *Der Freischütz* and the dance of the black elves in the moonlight is pure Mendelssohn – and has much charm. The invention is generally fresh and engaging, though no one would claim that it has great depth. The largely Danish cast cope very capably with the not inconsiderable demands of Kuhlau's vocal writing, the Danish Radio recording is eminently truthful and vivid, and Michael Schönwandt draws excellent results from the Danish Radio Chorus and Orchestra.

KUHN, Max (1896–1994)

Concierto de Tenerife for Piano & Large Orchestra.

(N) ** Guild GMCD 7206. Thew, Zürich Camerata, Tschupp – HAYDN: *Piano Concertos.* **

Max Kuhn studied with Philipp Jarnach, the Busoni pupil who completed *Doktor Faust*, and with Weingartner. He died in Ascona just a few weeks short of his 98th birthday. His *Piano Concerto* (1961–2) was composed in Santa Cruz in Tenerife – hence its title. It is a well-crafted work of modest dimensions and is pleasing, if not highly original. The opening has a touch of Reger about it, and the invention throughout shows the hand of a cultivated musician. Warren Thew is expert and sensitive, though neither the Camerata Zürich nor the recording (from 1976) are top drawer.

KUHNAU, Johann (1660–1722)

Der Gerechte kommt um (motet).

(M) *** O-L 443 199-2. Christ Church Ch., AAM, Preston – BACH: *Magnificat;* VIVALDI: *Nisi dominus* etc. ***

Kuhnau was Bach's predecessor in Leipzig. He wrote this charming motet with a Latin text; it was later arranged in a German version, and there are signs of Bach's hand in it. The piece makes an excellent makeweight coupling for the original version of Bach's *Magnificat.*

Magnificat in C.

*** BIS CD 1011. Persson, Tachikawa, Türk, Urano, Bach Collegium, Japan, Masaaki Suzuki – BACH: *Magnificat in D;* ZELENKA: *Magnificats in C & D.* ***

Johann Kuhnau died the year before the Bach *Magnificat* came into being in its first – E flat – incarnation. Kuhnau's own setting is his most ambitious work and calls for large forces (a five-part chorus, three trumpets, timpani, two oboes, strings including two viola parts and continuo) and is thought to have been composed for a Christmas Service at Leipzig. It is not otherwise available on CD and any rival will have to be pretty stunning to match this version from Masaaki Suzuki and his largely Japanese forces. It is not as consistently inspired as the Zelenka (let alone the Bach) but it is well worth hearing. Apart from the excellence of his singers and instrumentalists, the recorded sound is quite exemplary.

KULLAK, Theodor (1818–82)

Piano Concerto in C min., Op. 55.

*** Hyp. CDA 67086. Lane, BBC Scottish SO, Willén – DREYSCHOCK: *Piano Concerto in D min.* ***

Theodor Kullak, on the evidence of this most attractive concerto, was a very gifted composer, with melody coming easily to him. A strong march-like theme dominates the first movement and, when the piano enters, the glittering passage work lies somewhere between that in the Liszt and Chopin concertos, while the romantic secondary tune has a comparable heritage. The central movement is equally engaging, with bursts of energy, never languishing, and the glittering Weberian finale makes one smile with pleasure at the witty audacity of the main theme. The work is given a scintillating performance by Piers Lane, vigorously and sensitively supported by the BBC Scottish players under Niklas Willén. The recording is first class.

KURTÁG, György (born 1926)

Hommage à Mihály András (12 Microludes for String Quartet), Op. 13.

(N) *** DG 469 066-2. Hagen Qt. – DVORAK: *String Quartet No. 14;* SCHULHOFF: *5 Pieces.* ***

Kurtág's epigrammatic post-Webernesque *Microludes*, written in 1978 in memory of his compatriot Mihály András, are given with appropriate intensity though the sound strikes us as somewhat too well lit.

KUUSISTO, Jaakko (born 1974)

Between Seasons, Op. 7.

(N) *** Finlandia 8573 84714-2. Helsinki Strings, Csaba & Géza Szilvay – VIVALDI: *The Four Seasons.* **(*)

The Finnish composer and violinist, Jaakko Kuusisto, son and grandson of composers, wrote his suite of interludes so that they could either be performed in connection with the Vivaldi or on their own, prompting the eye-catching title of this disc, *The Seven Seasons.* The very titles of the movements bear out that role as links between each season – *May Day, Wind and Water* and finally *First Snow.* Partly designed to give the main violin soloist a rest, they make attractive, evocative interludes, with the harpsichord nicely integrated into the texture, with direct echoes mainly of Bartók but also of the Stravinsky of the string works. Vivid, immediate sound very well balanced.

LACHNER, Franz Paul (1803–90)

Symphony No. 5 in C min. (Passionata), Op. 52 (Preis-Symphonie).

**(*) Marco 8.223502. Slovak State PO (Košice), Robinson.

Franz Lachner's *Fifth Symphony* is. an ambitious work, lasting an hour, lyrical and well crafted. Its ideas unfold naturally and with a certain fluency; its scoring is effective and its idiom is close to the world of Schubert and Mendelssohn. It has more than mere curiosity value, and the Slovak orchestra under Paul Robinson play it with obvious enjoyment. Decent recording.

Septet in E flat.

*** Marco 8.223282. Ens. Villa Musica – FUCHS: *Clarinet Quintet.*

Lachner's *Septet* has an easygoing charm, which is quite winning. Here it is elegantly played and well recorded.

LAJTHA, László (1892–1963)

Hortobágy, Op. 21; Suite No. 3, Op. 56; Symphony No. 7, Op. 63 (Revolution Symphony).

**(*) Marco 8.223667. Pécs SO, Pasquet.

László Lajtha was one of the leading Hungarian composers and scholars to emerge after the generation of Bartók and Kodály. Indeed, as an exact contemporary of Honegger and Milhaud, he is separated from his compatriots by a mere decade. The *Seventh Symphony* is a well-wrought and eclectic score that is worth hearing, even if it does not possess the concentration or profile one expects of a major symphonist. The suite from *Hortobágy*, a memorable film set in the plains of Hungary, and the *Two Symphonic Portraits* are effectively scored but their material is insufficiently distinctive. Good performances and recording.

LALO, Edouard (1823–92)

Cello Concerto No. 1 in D min., Op. 33.

*** ASV CDDCA 867. Rolland, BBC PO, Varga – MASSENET: *Fantaisie;* SAINT-SAENS: *Cello Concerto No. 1.* ***

*** EMI (ADD) CDC5 55528-2. Du Pré, Cleveland O, Barenboim – R. STRAUSS: *Don Quixote.* *** ⊙

(B) *** Decca 448 712-2. Harrell, Berlin RSO, Chailly – SAINT-SAENS; SCHUMANN: *Concertos.* ***

(M) *** RCA (ADD) 74321 84112-2 (2). Lloyd Webber, LPO, López-Coboz – BRUCH: *Kol Nidrei;* DELIUS: *Concerto; Serenade;* HOLST: *Invocation;* RODRIGO: *Concierto como un divertimento;* VAUGHAN WILLIAMS: *Fantasia on Sussex Folk Tunes.* *** (with Recital: 'Celebration' ***).

(B) *** EMI Début CZS5 73727-2. Phillips, Bavarian Chamber O, Plasson – CAPLET: *Epiphany;* FAURE: *Elégie.* ***

*** Finlandia 4509 95768-2. Noras, Finnish RSO, Saraste – ELGAR: *Cello Concerto.* ***

*** DG (IMS) 427 323-2. Haimovitz, Chicago SO, Levine – SAINT-SAENS: *Concerto No. 1;* BRUCH: *Kol Nidrei.* ***

(M) *** DG (ADD) 457 761-2. Fournier, LOP, Martinon – BLOCH: *Schelomo;* BRUCH: *Kol Nidrei;* SAINT-SAENS: *Cello Concerto No. 1.* ***

(B) *** DG (ADD) 431 166-2. Schiff, New Philh. O, Mackerras – FAURE: *Elégie;* SAINT-SAENS: *Concerto No. 1.* ***

(M) **(*) Mercury (IMS) (ADD) 432 010-2. Starker, LSO, Skrowaczewski – SAINT-SAENS; SCHUMANN: *Concertos.* ***

(M) **(*) Sony (ADD) SBK 48278. Rose, Phd. O, Ormandy – BLOCH: *Schelomo;* FAURE: *Elégie;* TCHAIKOVSKY: *Rococo Variations.* ***

Sophie Rolland plays with effortless eloquence and is given responsive support from the BBC Philharmonic under Gilbert Varga, though he is a little brusque in the *Intermezzo.* An enjoyable and convincing performance. The excellence of the BBC/ASV recording makes for a strong recommendation.

Jacqueline du Pré's recorded repertory is thrillingly expanded in previously unpublished recordings of Strauss and Lalo. While the studio recording of *Don Quixote*, dating from 1968, has been pieced together from long-buried tapes, this recording of the Lalo *Concerto* was taken live from a broadcast in Cleveland in January 1973, right at the end of du Pré's playing career in one of her last remissions from multiple sclerosis. It is a masterly performance and is totally involving, even though the cello is balanced rather more backwardly than in du Pré's studio recordings. In spite of that, her fire at the opening grabs the attention, leading on to a performance that is both passionate and poetic.

Lynn Harrell's account is also highly recommendable. There is a yearning intensity in the *Intermezzo*, while the outer movements combine spontaneity and vigour. Chailly's accompaniment is attractively bold and the recording, made in the Berlin Jesus-Christus Kirche, has an attractively warm ambience.

Julian Lloyd Webber's account is played with style and feeling, and the RCA recording is of good quality. This comes as part of a celebratory reissue for Lloyd Webber's fiftieth birthday, which is worth having for the rare Holst work and his premiere recording of the Rodrigo concerto that he commissioned.

Emmanuel Plasson and his Bavarian Chamber Orchestra open Lalo's cello concerto with a bold dramatic flourish, and Xavier Phillips enters with a firm, full timbre, his line romantically strong. Yet he soon slips into gentle lyricism for Lalo's lovely secondary theme. The unusually clear (yet not unflattering) acoustic means that Lalo's scoring never congeals, and the cello focus is clean and truthful. In short this version of a much recorded work matches any of its competitors.

Arto Noras is an aristocrat among cellists, and he receives very responsive support from Saraste and excellent recording.

An outstandingly impressive début from Matt Haimovitz; the performance throughout combines vitality with expressive feeling in the most spontaneous manner. The recording is very well balanced indeed and highly realistic.

Fournier's performance has dignity and character and he is well supported by Martinon, who secures spirited playing from the Lamoureux Orchestra. The recording, from 1960, has never sounded better than in this new DG Originals transfer. Excellent value.

Heinrich Schiff's 1977 account is youthfully fresh and enthusiastic and very well recorded for its period. A fine bargain.

Janos Starker's 1962 recording with the LSO under Stanislaw Skrowaczewski sounds remarkably good for its age. Though the tutti chords are brutal and clipped, Starker plays splendidly, and the famous Mercury recording technique lays out the orchestral texture quite beautifully and with remarkable transparency.

Leonard Rose gives a strong, spontaneous account, bringing out the concerto's melodic character as well as its vitality of invention. Ormandy's accompaniment is wonderfully supportive and it is a pity that the orchestral sound has a hint of edginess in the violins and is a bit two-dimensional.

(i) *Concerto russe; Violin Concerto in F. Scherzo; Le Roi d'Ys Overture.*

*** Chan. 9758. (i) Charlier; BBC PO, Tortelier.

Yan Pascal Tortelier opens with a marvellously rumbustious account of *Le Roi d'Ys Overture*, with its melodramatic brass and luscious cello solo, and includes also an equally fine account of the orchestral *Scherzo*. But the main value of this disc is Olivier Charlier's seductive accounts of the two concertante works (both written for Sarasate). The *Violin Concerto* is engagingly songful and ought to be better known, but the real find is the *Concerto russe*, in essence a sister work to the *Symphonie espagnole*, but with Slavic rather than sultry Spanish inspiration. The *Intermezzo* has witty offbeat comments from the timpani and there is a sparkling finale introducing two more striking ideas. Charlier is obviously in his element throughout both works, relishing their lyricism. Tortelier – with the help of Lalo – provides a vivid orchestral backcloth and the opulent, well-balanced Chandos recording adds to the listener's pleasure.

Namouna (ballet): extended excerpts: *(Suites Nos. 1–2 & Allegro Vivace; Tambourin; La Gitane; Bacchanale).*

**(*) Audivis V 4677. Monte-Carlo PO, Robertson.

Namouna (ballet): *Suites Nos. 1–2; Valse de la cigarette.*

**(*) ASV CDDCA 878. RPO, Butt (with GOUNOD: *Mors et Vita: Judex*).

There is no complete version available of Lalo's ballet, but David Robertson has added four more items to the content of Lalo's two suites, plus the charmingly Gallic *Valse de la cigarette* (which the composer extracted as a separate number). He has also re-established the music in ballet-order, whereas in the suites Lalo reassembled the items for concert performance. Robertson secures sensitive, polished playing from his Monte Carlo orchestra, who resound with warmth, and the recording has plenty of colour and ambience.

Yondani Butt achieves performances of the suites and the *Valse de la cigarette* which have comparable colour and finesse, and the RPO play extremely well. Even so, they don't necessarily upstage their French competitors and they offer less music. Where they gain is in the *Prélude*, which is an unashamed crib from Wagner's *Das Rheingold*. The ASV disc offers a big *religieuse* Gounod tune as an encore, but more of *Namouna* would have been preferable.

Namouna: Suite No. 1. Overture: Le Roi d'Ys.

(M) **(*) Mercury [434 389-2]. Detroit SO, Paray – BARRAUD: *Offrande;* CHAUSSON: *Symphony.* **(*)

These 1958 recordings come up very well indeed, and the performances have sparkle and great lightness of touch. What delightful music it is, particularly in such authoritative hands.

Symphonie espagnole (for violin and orchestra), *Op. 21.*

*** EMI CDC5 55292-2. Chang, Concg. O, Dutoit – VIEUXTEMPS: *Violin Concerto No. 5.* ***

(N) (M) *** Virgin VM5 61910-2. Tetzlaff, Czech PO, Pešek – DVORAK: *Violin Concerto.* ***

(M) *** DG 445 549-2. Perlman, O de Paris, Barenboim – SAINT-SAENS: *Concerto No. 3;* BERLIOZ: *Rêverie et caprice.* ***

(M) *** Decca 460 007-2. Chung, Montreal SO, Dutoit – RAVEL: *Tzigane;* VIEUXTEMPS: *Violin Concerto No. 5.* ***

(M) *** Sony (ADD) SM2K 64501 (2). Stern, Phd. O, Ormandy (with Concert ***).

(M) **(*) Sony (ADD) SBK 48274. Zukerman, LAPO, Mehta – VIEUXTEMPS: *Concerto No. 5.* **(*)

(N) (BB) **(*) EMI Encore CDE5 74735-2. Mutter, O. Nat de France, Ozawa (with MASSENET: *Thaïs: Meditation*) – saraste: *Zigeunerweisen.* **(*)

Symphonie espagnole, Op. 21 (omitting *Intermezzo*).

(M) (**(*)) RCA mono 09026 61753-2. Heifetz, RCA Victor SO, Steinberg – CHAUSSON: *Poème* **(*); SAINT-SAENS: *Havanaise etc.;* SARASATE: *Zigeunerweisen.* (***)

(**(*)) APR Signature mono APR 5506. Huberman, VPO, Szell – BEETHOVEN: *Violin Concerto.* (***)

Sarah Chang's dazzling account of Lalo's five-movement

feast of Spanish dance-rhythms goes readily to the top of the list. Dutoit provides a vigorous backing and the soloist's seductive lilt in the shimmering malaguena of the first movement is matched by the sparkling seguidilla rhythms of the Scherzo and the bouncing habañera of the Intermezzo. The finale scintillates. The orchestra readily echoes Chang's sparkle, and the expansively resonant recording is ideally balanced.

Like his fine reading of the Dvořák *Violin concerto*, with which it is generously coupled, Tetzlaff's account of the Lalo is marked by playing of quicksilver lightness in passage-work, bringing out the element of fantasy. Equally the soloist's concentration makes for a sense of spontaneity, leading one on magnetically in this episodic work. He seems all the stronger for having a recording balance which does not spotlight the violin as sharply as in most other versions. As for Tetzlaff's accompanists – chosen no doubt specifically for the Dvořák – the Czech Philharmonic's playing under Pešek proves just as idiomatic in the Spanish dance-rhythms of Lalo as in Czech dances, with crisp ensemble and rhythms deliciously sprung. Characteristically Pešek makes orchestral textures clear, bringing out extra detail, despite the reverberant acoustic of the Dvořák Hall of the Rudolfinum in Prague, and the advantage of the resonant ambience is to give a more expansive warmth to the overall sound than in Perlman's DG version – which nevertheless remains highly recommendable at mid-price.

Although the lively digital sound remains a trifle dry, Perlman's performance easily maintains its place near the top of the list. For the reissue in the Masters series, the Berlioz *Rêverie et caprice* makes an attractive if brief bonus.

Kyung-Wha Chung has the advantage of a first-class Decca digital recording, with a highly effective, natural balance. Hers is an athletic, incisive account, at its most individual in the captivatingly light-weight finale, with an element almost of fantasy. Miss Chung does not have quite the panache of Perlman, but Charles Dutoit's accompaniment is first class and the orchestral characterization is strong throughout.

Stern's version from the late 1960s has all the rich, red-blooded qualities that have made this artist world-famous. Reservations concerning the close balance are inevitable (although Ormandy's fine accompaniment is not diminished), but the playing makes a huge impact on the listener and, although the actual sound-quality is far from refined, the charisma of this performance is unforgettable.

Heifetz's 1951 account has superb panache and there are no complaints about the mono recording. Alas, he omitted the *Intermezzo* (a practice curiously common in his time), which is our loss, but the performance of the rest, like all the music on this CD, is dazzling.

Zukerman's performance is outstandingly successful. He plays with great dash and fire yet brings a balancing warmth. His couplings are more generous than Perlman's, but the effect of the DG recording is to give Perlman's account slightly more romantic finesse.

Anne-Sophie Mutter's account brings a dazzling display of bravura in the outer movements. Many will find the delicacy of her phrasing in the second subject of the first movement refreshing, with its absence of schmaltz, though

Chang is more sinuously beguiling here, and similarly the opening of the slow movement is especially imaginative, with Ozawa's strong orchestral statement answered by the soloist with gentle, touching serenity. Both in the *Intermezzo* and the *Andante* there is solo playing of passionate eloquence, the timbre richly expansive. The balance, however, projects the violin well to the front, and the slightly-too-close microphones add a touch of shrillness to the upper range, while a degree of digital edge affects the orchestra too. As an encore Massenet's *Méditation* from *Thaïs* is played gently and dreamily, and here Karajan's accompaniment sounds more sumptuous.

When Huberman recorded the *Symphonie espagnole* in 1930, it was common practice to omit the central *Intermezzo*, and so it is here. Yet as a historic document this makes a welcome coupling for Huberman's classic reading of the Beethoven concerto with the same accompanists. Here more than in the Beethoven, Huberman indulges in surprising swoops of *portamento* – another sign of the times – though always with perfect control to match the sweetly expressive style.

Piano Trios Nos. 1 in C min., Op. 7; 2 in B min.; 3 in A min., Op. 26.

*** ASV CDDCA 899. Barbican Piano Trio.

As always with Lalo, this is the kind of unpretentious, inventive, well-crafted and delightful music which nineteenth-century civilization seemed able to foster and their composers to produce – and of which the late twentieth is conspicuously and lamentably bare. There is not much to say about the performances, except to note their excellence and poise.

LAMBERT, Constant (1905–51)

Aubade héroïque; (i) The Rio Grande; (ii) Summer's Last Will and Testament.

*** Hyp. CDA 66565. E. N. Philh. O, Lloyd-Jones; (i) with Gibbons; (ii) Burgess, Shimell, Ch. of Opera North & Leeds Festival.

The Rio Grande, Lambert's jazz-based choral concerto setting of a poem by Sacheverell Sitwell, is one of the most colourful and atmospheric works from the 1920s. The *Aubade héroïque* is an evocative tone-poem inspired by Lambert's memory of a beautiful morning in Holland in 1940 when, with the Nazi invasion, it was far from certain whether he and his colleagues would be able to get back to England. *Summer's Last Will and Testament* is a big, 50-minute choral work setting lyrics by the Elizabethan, Thomas Nashe, on the unpromising subject of the threat of plague. Lloyd-Jones and his outstanding team, mainly from Opera North, bring out the vitality and colour of the writing, with each of the nine substantial sections based on Elizabethan dance-rhythms. The recording in all three works is full, vivid and atmospheric.

The Bird Actors Overture; Pomona (ballet); Romeo and Juliet (ballet).

(N) *** Chan. 9865 Victoria State O, Lanchbery.

Pomona is well served by John Lanchbery and his Victoria State Orchestra even if it does not quite command the elegance of the David Lloyd Jones account on Hyperion. This present issue also brings *Romeo and Juliet*, which Lambert composed for Diaghilev, and which has not been recorded since Norman Del Mar's version on a Lyrita LP from the late 1970s (also coupled with *Pomona*). *The Bird Actors* is a short overture of some three minutes, originally intended for an earlier ballet called *Adam and Eve*. Recommended to all with a taste for this engaging composer.

(i) *Piano Concerto (1924). Merchant Seamen (Suite); Pomona; Prize Fight.*

(M) *** ASV CD WHL 2122. BBC Concert O, Wordsworth with (i) Owen Norris.

The *Piano Concerto* of 1924 is not to be confused with the later *Concerto for Piano and Seven Wind Instruments*. It was composed three years before *The Rio Grande*. Lambert's preferred scoring was for two trumpets, strings and timpani. It is very characteristic, with something of the spirit of Milhaud, jazzy and entertaining. *Prize Fight*, also from 1924, is Lambert's first ballet and his earliest surviving orchestral score. It is a rumbustious work for the same forces as the concerto and lasts a mere nine minutes. Lambert's score for the documentary *Merchant Seamen* dates from 1940 and he drew on this for a five-movement suite two years later. The most familiar of the pieces here is the ballet *Pomona*, which receives a most sympathetic performance at the hands of the excellent BBC Concert Orchestra and Barry Wordsworth. In fact, the playing throughout is very good indeed, and so is the ASV/BBC recording.

CHAMBER MUSIC

(i; ii) *Concerto for Piano & 9 Players;* **(i)** *Piano Sonata;* **(iii; i)** *8 Poems of Li-Po;* **(iv; i)** *Mr Bear Squash-you-all-flat.*

*** Hyp. CDA 66754. (i) Brown; (ii) Nash Ens., Friend; (iii) Langridge; (iv) Hawthorne.

Constant Lambert's remarkable qualities are in excellent evidence here in the Nash Ensemble's anthology which brings two of his most powerful works, the *Concerto for Piano and Nine Players* and the *Piano Sonata*, as well as one of his most delicately wrought, the *Eight Poems of Li-Po*, in a lovely performance from Philip Langridge. Ian Brown proves an equally exemplary advocate in the *Concerto* and the *Piano Sonata*, which is not generously represented on disc. *Mr Bear Squash-you-all-flat* is Lambert's first composition, an entertainment written at roughly the same time as Walton's *Façade*, when Lambert was still in his teens, and based on a Russian fairy story. Imaginative and accomplished but, hardly surprisingly, not first-class Lambert. It is not certain whether Lambert meant the text to be spoken, but Sir Nigel Hawthorne speaks it excellently; he is somewhat reticently balanced (a fault on the right side).

Horoscope (ballet): Suite.

⚘ *** Hyp. CDA 66436. E. N. Philh. O, Lloyd-Jones – BLISS: *Checkmate;* WALTON: *Façade.* ***

The music for *Horoscope* is sheer delight. David Lloyd-Jones is very sympathetic to its specifically English atmosphere. He wittily points the catchy rhythmic figure which comes both in the *Dance for the Followers of Leo* and, later, in the *Bacchanale*, while the third-movement *Valse for the Gemini* has a delectable insouciant charm. Excellent playing and first-class sound, perhaps a shade resonant for the ballet pit, but bringing plenty of bloom.

Pomona (ballet); Tiresias (ballet).

*** Hyp. CDA 67049. E. N. Philh. O, Lloyd Jones.

Pomona, written for Diaghilev in 1927, finds Lambert deftly echoing the neoclassical Stravinsky and Les Six, in his sequence of formal dances. *Tiresias*, completed not long before Lambert died, is more ambitious, the work of a composer steeped in the dramatic needs of ballet. The thematic material may not be so memorable as in Lambert's finest works, but with strong rhythmic invention and rich sounds – the piano often prominent – it is most attractive, only disappointing in the downbeat ending.

Salome (incidental music): suite.

(N) *** Hyp. CDA 67239. Nash Ens., Lloyd-Jones – WALTON: *Façade.* ***

The three items drawn from Constant Lambert's incidental music for Oscar Wilde's *Salome* make a pleasing extra for the excellent Hyperion version of Walton's *Façade* Entertainment. They were written for the first staging in English in 1931 of that controversial play, using four of the *Façade* instruments, clarinet, trumpet, cello and percussion. Long buried in the BBC Music Library, Lambert's score was discovered by Giles Easterbrook, who confected this suite of two atmospheric scene-setting fragments, followed by Salome's dance and sudden demise, a long way after Strauss. With Richard Hosford on clarinet and John Wallace on trumpet, the performance is exemplary and very well recorded.

The Rio Grande.

(M) **(*) Decca 452 324-2. Jones, Stott, BBC Singers, BBC Concert O, Wordsworth – ELGAR: *Sea Pictures* etc. **(*)

With bright, forward recording, this account of *The Rio Grande* is rather aggressive. Wordsworth is also literal, less than idiomatic in the interpretations of jazzy syncopations. The performance is not warmly expressive, but the power and the colour of the writing come across with fine bite and clarity.

LAMBERT, Michel *(c. 1610–96)*

Airs de cour: Admirons notre jeune et charmante Déesse; Ah! qui voudra desormais s'engager; C'en est fait, belle Iris; D'un feu secret je me sens consumer; Il faut mourir plutost que le changer; Iris n'est plus, mon Iris m'est ravie; Je suis aymé de celle que j'adore; Ma bergère est tendre et fidelle; Ombre de mon amant; Par mes chants tristes et touchants;

Pour vos beaux yeux, Iris; Le Repos, l'ombre, le silence; Tout l'univers obéit à l'amour; Trouver sur l'herbette.

(B) *** HM HMA 1901123. Les Arts Florissants, Christie.

Grove speaks of Michel Lambert's airs as models of elegance and grace, in which careful attention was paid to direct declamation. The 300 or so that survive show his artistry in characterization and dialogue to have been of the highest order. They are beautifully performed and expertly recorded by members of Les Arts Florissants and William Christie and are altogether delightful. Unlike some bargain issues, there is excellent documentation with the original texts and translation.

LAMPE, John Frederick (1702/3–51)

(i) *Pyramus and Thisbe* (A mock opera); (ii) *Flute Concerto in G (The Cuckoo).*

*** Hyp. CDA 66759. (i) Padmore, Bisatt, Opera Restor'd, Holman; (ii) Brown.

Pyramus and Thisbe, written in 1745, is a reworking of the entertainment given by the rude mechanicals in Shakespeare's *Midsummer Night's Dream*, with the role of the heroine, Thisbe, taken not by a man but by a soprano. The Opera Restor'd company, with Jack Edwards as stage director, here present it complete with spoken Prologue for several attendant characters. Following the overture come 16 brief numbers, with the score edited and completed by the conductor, Peter Holman. Mark Padmore is outstanding as Pyramus, with Susan Bisatt a fresh-toned Thisbe. The warm, immediate recording brings out the distinctive timbre of the period instruments, notably the braying horns. As an agreeable makeweight, the disc also offers Lampe's only surviving independent orchestral work, the *G major Flute Concerto*, with its three crisp movements lasting little more than 5 minutes.

LANDOWSKI, Marcel (born 1915)

(i) *Concerto for Ondes Martenot, Strings & Percussion;* (ii) *Piano Concerto No. 2;* (iii) *Concerto for Trumpet, Strings & Electro-Acoustic Instruments.*

*** Erato (ADD) 4509 96972-2. (i) Loriód, O de Chambre de Musique Contemporain, Rondon; (ii) D'Arco, ORTF, Martinon; (iii) André, Strasbourg PO, Lombard.

Marcel Landowski is little more than a name outside France, where he is much respected – and rightly so, if his symphonies are anything to go by. In the *Piano Concerto* of 1963 the balance places the soloist too prominently and the instrument itself sounds tubby. The musical invention is civilized and intelligent but remains ultimately unmemorable. The *Concerto for Ondes Martenot* of 1954 is stronger in atmosphere and invention, its idiom is a cross between Honegger and Shostakovich. Add Bartókian *Night Music* to that mix, and you have the opening of the *Trumpet Concerto* (1976). Scored for small forces (no oboes, two horns and one trombone), it also makes discreet use of magnetic tape. It is even finer than the *Concerto for Ondes Martenot*, and its

seriousness of purpose and powerful atmosphere make a strong impression. The 1978 Strasbourg recording is excellent, and Maurice André plays it with total commitment.

Symphonies Nos. (i) *1 (Jean de la peur); (ii) 2; (i) 3 (Des espaces); 4.*

*** Erato 4509 96973-2 (2). (i) French Nat. O, Prêtre; (ii) ORTF, Martinon.

The *First*, *Third* and *Fourth* of Landowski's symphonies were recorded in 1988. To them Erato have now added an analogue recording from 1970 of the *Second Symphony*, conducted by Jean Martinon. Like its companions the musical language and thought processes have their roots in Honegger; the musical argument is well sustained and has a certain dignity. Landowski has a powerful and fertile imagination, a resourceful sense of orchestration, and a commanding symphonic grip. He holds the listener from the first bar to the last. Generally excellent recorded sound.

LANGGAARD, Rued (1893–1953)

Symphony No. 1 (Klippepastoraler); Fra Dybet.

*** Chan. 9249. Danish Nat. RSO & Ch., Segerstam.

Rued Langgaard was a figure of undoubted but flawed talent, but as this banal, five-movement overblown sprawl slowly unwinds its 67 minutes, one realizes that the composer subjected this particular piece to no real critical scrutiny. There are some imaginative moments in the finale. *Fra Dybet* (*From the Deep*) comes from the other end of his career and was completed not long before his death: it opens rather bombastically but soon lapses into sentimentality at the entrance of the choir. Good recording.

Symphonies Nos. 4 (Løvfald: The Falling of the Leaf); 5 (Steppelands); 6 (Himmelrivende: Heaven Asunder).

*** Chan. 9064. Danish Nat. RSO, Järvi.

Rued Langgaard's *Fourth Symphony*, subtitled *The Falling of the Leaf*, has retained little more than a foothold on the repertoire. The *Sixth* (*Himmelrivende*, translated as *Heavens Asunder*) is another work that hovers on the periphery of the catalogue. What is lacking in Langgaard is any real sense of organic growth and ultimately, it must be said, a distinctive and original personality. However, Neeme Järvi makes out a strong case for this music and the Danish Radio Orchestra play with conviction and sympathy. They are given excellent recorded sound.

Symphonies Nos. 4 (Løvfald); 6 (Den Himmelrivende); (i) Sfrernas Musik.

**(*) Danacord (ADD) DACOCD 340/341. (i) Guillaume, Danish R. Ch.; Danish RSO, Frandsen.

Sfrernas Musik (*The Music of the Spheres*), written in 1918 between the two symphonies recorded here, is an extraordinary piece of undoubted vision and originality. It has a wild-eyed intensity and a quasi-mystical quality that is unusual in the Nordic music of its time. One has the feeling that it could equally stop earlier or go on longer, but formal coherence is not Langgaard's strong suit. The performances are good and the recording eminently satisfactory without being quite in the Chandos league.

Symphonies No. 6 (The Storming of the Heavens); 7 (1926 version); (i) 8 (Minder ved Amalienborg).

(N) * dacapo 8.224180. (i) Danish Nat. R. Ch; Danish Nat. R SO, Dausgaard.**

Much of the *Sixth Symphony* is ungainly and inexpert but, as with Charles Ives and Havergal Brian, to whom he has often been compared, there are glimpses of an original vision. It is the most often recorded of his sixteen symphonies, though Dausgaard holds his own with the best. The *Seventh* appears in its 1926 version, the autograph of which Bendt Viinholt Nielsen lists as missing in his vast 560-page *Annotated Catalogue*! However, a score which Langgaard had printed at his own expense has recently come to light and forms the basis of this première recording.

The *Eighth*, which occupied him for eight years (1927–34), honours the church at the Royal Palace at Amalienborg, where Langgaard made his debut as an organist in 1905. It recalls Mendelssohn and Gade, and even quotes from Bruckner's *Third Symphony*. There is little in the way of real symphonic coherence, but there is much to interest and stimulate, alongside much that is overblown. Fine performances and recording.

Symphonies Nos. 10 (Yon Dwelling of Thunder); 11 (Ixion); 12 (Helsingeborg); Sfinx (tone-poem).

**** Danacord DACOCD 408. Artur Rubinstein PO, Stupel.**

The *Eleventh* and *Twelfth* symphonies are shorter than they seem; in fact the *Eleventh* lasts less than six minutes but its main theme is of awesome vapidity. The Artur Rubinstein Philharmonic Orchestra turns in serviceable performances and are decently enough recorded, but do not dispel the impression that this is music of shadows rather than substance.

Symphonies Nos. 13 (Faithlessness); 16 (The Deluge of Sun); Anti-Christ (opera): Prelude.

**** Danacord DACOCD 410. Artur Rubinstein PO, Stupel.**

The *Sixteenth Symphony* opens rather like Strauss, then comes to an abrupt stop, before launching into a short, Schumannesque Scherzo of about 1 minute in the same key, and thence into a *Dance of Chastisement*. The *Elegy* which follows also has touches of Schumann and there is a short and unconvincing finale. In the *Thirteenth*, *Undertro* (*Faithlessness*), the composer returns to material he had first used in his *Seventh Symphony*, which he had in turn borrowed from his countryman, Axel Gade. What it lacks in substance it makes up for in bombast. Probably the best thing here is the *Prelude* to the opera, *Anti-Christ*, a much earlier piece dating from the 1920s. The performances and recordings are respectable rather than distinguished.

Humoresque (sextet for flute, oboe, cor anglais, clarinet, bassoon and snare drum); Septet for Flute, Oboe, 2 Clarinets, 2 Horns & Bassoon; String Quartet in A flat; (i) Lenau Moods; In Blossom Time.

(N) *(*) dacapo 8.224139. Randers CO; (i) Simonsen.

All the music on this CD belongs to Langgaard's twenties, the same period as his *Fourth Symphony*. By far the best is the *Lenau Moods*, which has poetic feeling and an appealing, gentle melancholy. The *Quartet in A flat* sounds like pastiche Haydn and is curiously awkward. The *Septet* is close to Dvořák or Brahms, although not particularly expert, and the *Humoresque*, with its angular wind and snare drum, was obviously influenced by Nielsen's *Fifth Symphony*, although it is something of a loose cannon with flashes of inspiration side by side with bizarre and ungainly writing. Subfusc performances except in the songs. Decent recorded sound.

VOCAL MUSIC

Sinfonia interna: Angelus; The Dream; Sea and Sun; Epilogue; The Star in the East, BVN 180.

*****(*) dacapo 8.22413. Dahl, Hansen, Jensen, Canzone Ch., Aarhus SO, Rasmussen.**

As always with Langgaard, one senses that he is content with the raw material of art and quite happy to pass it off as the finished article. All the same, there are some visionary moments in this amorphous but lush post-Wagnerian score, and Frans Rasmussen gets very good results from his singers and the Aarhus Orchestra. Good recorded sound.

LANGLAIS, Jean (born 1907)

(i) Messe solennelle; (i; ii; iii) Missa salve regina; (Organ): (i) Paraphrases grégoriennes, Op. 5: Te Deum. Poèmes évangéliques, Op. 2: La Nativité. Triptyque grégorien: Rosa mystica.

***** Hyp. CDA 66270. Westminster Cathedral Ch., Hill, (i) with O'Donnell; (ii) Lumsden; (iii) ECO Brass Ens.**

Jean Langlais's organ music owes much to Dupré's example, and the two Masses are archaic in feeling, strongly influenced by plainchant and organum, yet with a plangent individuality that clearly places the music in the twentieth century. The style is wholly accessible and the music enjoys fervent advocacy from these artists, who are accorded sound-quality of the high standard one expects from this label.

LANNER, Joseph (1801–43)

Badner Ring'ln (Baden Round Dance). Ländler: Dornbacher; Neue Wiener. Hofballtänze; Steyrische Tänze. Waltzes: Abend-Sterne; Die Kosenden; Pesther; Die Romantiker; Die Schönbrunner; Die Weber.

(N) (M) **(*) RCA (ADD) 74321 84145-2. Berlin SO or VSO, Stolz.

It was Joseph Lanner, rather than the Strausses, who fathered the Viennese waltz. Indeed, Johann Senior (who played the viola) joined Lanner's performing group when it was only a tavern trio – two violins and a guitarist; a cello was added soon afterwards. But it was not long before their success meant an expansion to a string orchestra, subsequently divided, to perform concurrently at different venues. Johann conducted the second orchestra, and not surprisingly he soon (1825) left to form his own orchestra.

This fascinating RCA collection dates from the beginning of the 1970s. Robert Stolz, using a full-bodied string section, conducts the whole programme liltingly and with gusto, and the reverberant recording, if not ideally refined, suggests the ambience of a large ballroom. The programme here is arranged in Opus number order and we can hear Lanner's ideas becoming more individual, his style more lyrically romantic. The more robust *Ländler* of Opp. 1 and 9 were peasant dances, which Stoltz makes clear by his bold rhythmic emphases. But we soon enter the Viennese upper-class ballroom with the much more sophisticated cyclic waltz, with an introducion and coda. *Die Weber*, for instance, begins with a fast introduction before the undulating waltz tune appears.

The *Baden Round Dance* is still in 3/4, but is more pointedly rhythmic, almost a polka. *Hofballtänze* opens in lively duple time and the brass enters before the coda. The *Styrian Dances* are particularly charming. *Pesther* opens with the brass in march time, but then lightens (with harp roulades) and the opening melody of *Abend-Sterne* ('Evening Stars') is quite seductive, sounding very like 'Under the lilac he played his guitar' while *Die Kosenden* ('The Lovers') has an agreeable rhythmic lift. The finale item, *Die Schönbrunner*, opens ruggedly on the brass, but the first waltz theme is the soul of delicacy, and this is another of Lanner's more sophisticated pieces, with a telling *rallentando* before the coda. All in all an excellent introduction to an underrated and very influential composer.

Galops: *Bruder Halt!; Neujahrs-Galopp; Tarantel-Galopp;* Waltzes: *Abend-Sterne; Dampf-Walzer und Galopp; Hofballtänze; Marien-Walzer; Pesther; Die Romantiker; Die Schönbrunner; Die Weber.*

(N)(M) **(*) EMI (ADD) CDM5 74372-2. Vienna Johann Strauss O, Boskovsky.

Boskovsky concentrates on the later works, and the more polished Viennese style of his orchestra produces greater elegance and finish than in Berlin. The recording, too (from the 1970s), though still warmly resonant, is better focused and wind detail emerges the more effectively, giving the scoring greater sophistication. All the music here is vivacious and elegant and the *Tarantelle-Galopp*, which opens with the horns, might readily be mistaken for a piece by one of the Strauss family. The *Dampf-Walzer and Galopp*, which closes the concert, is one of Lanner's most inventive numbers, and even more than with the RCA disc this selection demonstrates the musical background from which the masterpieces of Johann Strauss directly emerged.

LARSSON, Lars-Erik (1908–86)

(i; ii) *Folkvisenatt; Liten marsch;* (iii) *Little Serenade; Pastoral Suite, Op. 19;* (iv) *Variations for Orchestra;* (v) *Winter's Tale;* (vi) (Piano) *Croquisiers: Espressivo.*

(N) **(*) Swedish Society (ADD) SCD 1051. (i) Stockholm SO, Westerberg; (ii) Örrebro CO, Hedwall; (iii) Stockholm CO;

(iv) Swedish RO, Ehrling; (v) Stockholm PO, Westerberg; (vi) Larsson.

Most of these performances date from the 1960s, and this CD should be offered at a bargain price, particularly as the playing time is less than an hour. Best known is the celebrated *Pastoral Suite*, which Stig Westerberg recorded over forty years ago and which sounds fresher than ever. Probably the most substantial piece is the *Variations for Orchestra*, Larsson's flirtation with serialism from the 1960s, which is not just ingenious but full of fantasy and inspiration. Ehrling's account with the Swedish Radio Orchestra still comes up well, despite a rather dry acoustic. Much care has been taken over the transfers and the sound is excellent. The final item is Larsson himself playing one of his set of *Croquisiers*. An excellent introduction to this most likeable composer.

Förklädd Gud, Op. 24 (God in Disguise): Lyric Suite for Soprano, Baritone, Narrator, Chorus & Orchestra.

(N) **(*) Marco 8.225123. Inglebäck, Anders Larsson, Lindkvist, Amadel Chamber Ch., Swedish Chamber O, Sundkvist – ROSENBERG: *Den heliga natten (Holy Night).* ***

Förklädd Gud is a product of a collaboration between the poet Hjalmar Gullberg and Lars-Erik Larsson in the enlightened days when radio stations broadcast poems with accompanying specially commissioned music. It is a charming and lyrical piece with a Nielsenesque directness of utterance. Sundkvist's performance holds its own against earlier competition and can be recommended to all with a feeling for and interest in Swedish music.

Symphonies Nos. 1 in D, Op. 2; 2, Op. 17.

**(*) BIS CD 426. Helsingborg SO, Frank.

The *First Symphony* is derivative but a work of obvious promise, fluent and well put together. There are obvious echoes of the Russian post-nationalists as well as Nielsen and Sibelius. Much the same could be said of the more mature *Second Symphony* (1936–7), which is genial and unpretentious. Good performances and recording, but the music itself is not Larsson at his strongest.

Symphony No. 3 in C min., Op. 34; (i) *Förklädd Gud (A God in Disguise), Op. 24.*

** BIS (ADD) CD 96. (i) Nordin, Hagegård, Jonsson, Helsingborg Concert Ch.; Helsingborg SO, Frykberg.

A God in Disguise was a production for Swedish Radio. The choral suite for two soloists and narrator that Larsson fashioned from it has great freshness and charm. This 1978 performance has some fine singing from Håkan Hagegård, and the Helsingborg chorus and orchestra give a serviceable account of the score. The symphony is as diatonic as *A God in Disguise* and, though not completely successful, is strong enough to deserve rescue.

Quattro tempi (Divertimento for Wind Quintet).

(BB) ** Naxos 8.553851-2. Michael Thompson Wind Quintet – BARBER: *Summer Music* **(*); HINDEMITH: *Kleine Kammermusik* **(*); JANACEK: *Mládí.* **(*)

Lars-Erik Larsson's *Quattro tempi* are pleasing open-air pieces written in 1968 which have not made their way into the repertory. The Michael Thompson Wind Quintet give a most expert and sensitive performance, but the close balance is even more disturbing than in its couplings and seriously detracts from the pleasure this music should give. Disappointing.

Croquiser, Op. 38; 7 Little Fugues with Preludes in the Old Style, Op. 58; Sonatinas Nos. 1, Op. 16; 2, Op. 39; 3, Op. 41.

*** BIS CD 758. Pålsson.

Larsson's piano music is slight but far from insignificant. It is beautifully fashioned, always intelligent and often witty. Hans Pålsson serves it with exemplary taste and expertise. It is well recorded, and those who like Larsson's music need not hesitate.

LASSUS, Orlandus (c. 1532–94)

Chansons and Moresche: *Allala, pia Calia; Canta Giorgia Cathalina; Chi chilichi?; Elle s'en va; En un chasteau; Fuyons tous d'amour le jeu; Hai Lucia; Je l'ayme bien; Las! me faut-il; Lucescit jam o socii; Lucia, celu; O foible esprit; O Lucia; Mais qui pourroit estre celuy; La Nuict froide et sombre; Quand mon mary vient de dehors; Si du malheur; Une puce j'ay dedans l'oreille; Un triste coeur; Un jeune moine est sorti du couvent; Vignon, vignon, vignette.* Lute solos: *J'ay un mary; Quand mon mary; Le Tems peult bien.*

(B) *** HM HMC 90856.58 (3). Ens. Clément Jannequin, Visse
– BANCHIERI: *Barca di Venetia per Padova* ***;
MARENZIO: *Madrigals* **(*); VECCHI: *Madrigal Comedies.* ***

One tends to think of the madrigals of Lassus as of a predominantly dolorous nature, and indeed the opening number here, *Las! me faut-il* ('Alas must I needs bear so much woe'), and other settings like *Si du malheur* and *La Nuict froide et sombre* carry their full weight of expressive melancholy. They are sung simply and beautifully here. But this excellently varied collection shows another side to this remarkable composer: his sense of fun and the grotesque, and a ready response to the most ribald goings-on. The singers here enter fully into the boisterous spirit of this lively music and, led by their counter-tenor director, Dominique Visse, project the Rabelaisian texts with a characterful aplomb, remarkable precision and, at times, a very fitting slightly nasal tonal edge. Excellent recording, with fine presence. The disc is part of a Harmonia Mundi CD Trio of *'Comédies madrigalesques'*, worth exploring if you have a taste for such repertoire. Good documentation.

Le lagrime di San Pietro a 7.

(BB) *** Naxos 8.553311. Ars Nova, Holten.
*** HM HMC 901483. Kiehr, Koslowsky, Berridge, Türk, Lamy, Koay, Peacock, Ens. Voc. Européen, Herreweghe.

Le lagrime di San Pietro (*The Tears of St Peter*) is a late work, a setting of 21 verses of the poet, Luigi Transillo (1510–68), a Neapolitan best known for his lyrical love-sonnets. The music is rich in variety of expressive means: Howard Mayer Brown calls it a work of 'almost Baroque religious fervour'. The Naxos performance by a first-class Danish choir (6 sopranos, 2 altos, 2 counter-tenors, 4 tenors and 3 basses) is comparatively robust yet offers singing of great sensitivity and a wide dynamic range. The recording, made at the Copenhagen Grundtvigskirken, has a properly spacious ambience, yet is admirably clear.

The *Lagrime di San Pietro* is a work of great expressive purity and is also performed by Herreweghe's forces with dedication and perfection in the matter of intonation. Excellent recording.

9 lamentationes hieremiae.

*** HM HMC 901299. Paris Chapelle Royale Ens., Herreweghe.

(i) *9 lamentationes hieremiae.* (ii) *Missa pro defunctis (Requiem) for 4 voices.* (i) *Aurora lucis rutilat* (hymn for Lauds); *Magnificat on Aurora lucis rutilat.* Motets: *Christus resurgens; Regina coeli laetare; Surgens Jesus.*

(B) *** Hyp. Dyad CDD 22012 (2). Pro Cantione Antiqua, (i) Turner, (ii) Brown.

The competing Harmonia Mundi set of the *Lamentations* is available on an excellent single, premium-priced disc, whereas for approximately the same cost this Hyperion Dyad offers much more music. Within this set, Bruno Turner's 1981 digital recording of the *Lamentations* is also now accommodated on a single CD, while the second includes a selection of music for Easter Sunday, including the glorious *Aurora lucis rutilat* for two five-part choirs and the *Magnificat* based on the motet, plus Mark Brown's fine performance of the four-part *Requiem*. The performances under Bruno Turner are expressive and vital. The recording too is spacious and warm. So for that matter is the Harmonia Mundi recording for the Chapelle Royale and Philippe Herreweghe, whose performances of the *Lamentations* are hardly less admirable.

Missa bell'amfitrit'alterna.

(BB) *** Naxos 8.550836. Oxford Schola Cantorum, Summerly
– PALESTRINA: *Missa hodie Christus natus est* etc. ***

This magnificent Mass of Palestrina's great Flemish contemporary, Lassus, makes a superb coupling for the outstanding performances of Palestrina masterpieces on the Naxos disc. This is the full Schola Cantorum of Oxford, not just the smaller Camerata group, and arguably it is too large for the dedicated, intimate polyphony of Lassus; but the singing is superb and the recording is warm and atmospheric. Yet another outstanding Naxos issue of early music.

Missa osculetur me; Motets: *Alma redemptoris mater; Ave regina caelorum; Hodie completi sunt; Osculetur me; Regina caeli; Salve regina; Timor et tremor.*

*** Gimell CDGIM 918. Tallis Scholars, Phillips.

Lassus learned the technique of double-choir antiphonal music in Italy. The Mass is preceded by the motet, *Osculetur me* (*Let him kiss me with the kisses of his lips*), which provides much of its motivic substance and is glorious in its sonorities and expressive eloquence. The singing of the Tallis Scholars under Peter Phillips is as impressive as it was on their earlier records, and the recording is beautifully present.

St Matthew Passion; Exsultet; Visitatio.

**(*) HM HMU 907076. Elliot, Theatre of Voices, Hillier.

This is Lassus at his most austere and devotional, with more chant than polyphony; it is not the best entry-point into his music for those unfamiliar with its opulence. The *Visitatio* (*Easter Dialogue*), which uses the edition by John Stevens, and the *Exsultet* from the Paschal Vigil, are purely chant. In the *Passion* Paul Elliot sings the part of the Evangelist, Paul Hillier that of Christ. The recording, made in California, is exemplary.

LAWES, Henry (1596–1662)

Songs: *Amintor's welladay; The angler's song; Come sad turtle; Fairwell despairing hopes; Hark, shepherd swains; I laid me down; I prithee send me back my heart; The lark; My soul the great God's praises sings; O King of heaven and hell; Sing, fair Clorinda; Sitting by the streams; Slide soft you silver floods; Sweet stay awhile; Tavola; Thee and thy wondrous deeds; This mossy bank.*

*** Hyp. CDA 66315. Kirkby, Consort of Musicke, Rooley.

The Lawes songs were enormously popular in their time. Today their direct, declamatory style seems comparatively unsubtle alongside Purcell. The melancholy is tangible, but not overtly expressive. The brief but effective *Tavola* is like an arietta from an Italian opera. The Hyperion collection is fairly wide in its range: the title-number (*Sitting by the streams*) is a verse anthem. There are plenty of secular songs too, notably the engaging *Angler's song*, and admirers of Emma Kirkby – here in radiant voice – and Anthony Rooley's immaculately stylish Consort of Musicke will find much to enjoy.

LAWES, William (1602–45)

Consort Setts a 5: in A; C (2); F & G; Consort pieces a 4: 2 Aires in C; 2 Aires in C min.; Aire (Fantazy) in C; Fantazy in C min. (VdGS 108/113).

(N)*** Channel Classics CCS 15698. Phantasm.

These five-part viol *Consort Setts* show William Lawes as a thoughtfully inward-looking composer of individuality. They are usually in three movements and in each case the central *Paven* is both searching and touching in its expressive eloquence, particularly the sonorous example in the F major work and the two more melancholy examples in C major, the first of these drawing on Dowland's *Flow my tears*. The hauntingly withdrawn centrepiece of the G major work is based 'On the Playnsong' and all these slow movements make a striking contrast with the more playful *Aires*. The playing of Phantasm explores a wide dynamic range and is beautifully blended in its delicacy and warmth, in no way edgy or acerbic. The group is most naturally recorded and this disc is as fine an introduction to Lawes's consort music as any in the catalogue.

Fantasia Suites for 2 Violins, Bass Viol & Organ Nos. 1–8.

*** Chan. 0552. Purcell Qt.

Lawes studied with Coperario, and Lawes's own *Fantasia Suites* are based on those of his mentor but are simpler, usually more extrovert works than the *Consort Suites*. They are in three movements, in each case a *Fantazy* followed by two *Aires*, in essence dance movements, alman and galliard, later corant or saraband. The organ does not just play a continuo role but is important in its own right. The music itself is lively in invention and by no means predictable, with surprise moments of passing dissonance, and the composer's individuality comes out in his special brand of lyricism. The performances here have plenty of life, and the recording balance is very successful: the result is enjoyably fresh.

Royal Consorts Nos. 1–10.

*** Chan. 0584/5. Purcell Consort.

Royal Consorts Nos. 1 in D min.; 3 in D min.; 6 in D; 7 in A min.; 9 in F.

*** ASV Gaudeamus CDGAU 146. Greate Consort, Huggett.

Royal Consorts Nos. 2 in D min.; 4 in D; 5 in D; 8 in C; 10 in B flat.

*** ASV Gaudeamus CDGAU 147. Greate Consort, Huggett.

The ten *Royal Consorts*, even though they are in four rather than five or six parts like the *Sets*, in many ways represent Lawes's most ambitious undertaking. There is evidence that he conceived the works as simple quartets (two violins and two viols) around 1620, but a decade later theorbos (archlutes) were added to provide a basic continuo and increase the range of textural colour. Each suite is in six or seven movements, the first of which is the most extended, sometimes taking as long as the remaining charming *Aires* and increasingly lively *Almans*, *Corants* and *Sarabands*, all put together. Indeed, these opening expressive *Fantazys* or *Pavanes* offer the kernel of the arguments and contain the most adventurous music, combining nobility of feeling with ear-catching contrapuntal lines.

The playing of the Purcell Consort is notably sprightly, the recording fresh and vividly clear, but within an open acoustic of some depth. The brightness and transparency of the sound, without loss of sonority, means that the individual instruments are cleanly delineated, although blending well together, never better demonstrated than in the splendidly managed *Echo* movement that ends the first work of the series.

Monica Huggett and her Greate Consort are very slightly recessed; their sound is warmer and the expressive music is given a fuller texture by the resonance. Some will feel that, presented in this way, this music is afforded more atmosphere. They also play at a slightly lower pitch, which means that the effect is inevitably mellower when compared directly with the brighter Chandos sound, although on ASV detail is by no means unclear. Both sets of performances are very rewarding, and if we are inclined, marginally, to favour the bright projection and added transparency of Chandos, many collectors will surely respond differently.

COLLECTIONS

Consort Sets a 5: in A min. & C ; Divisions on a Pavan in G min. for 2 Bass Viols & Organ; Royal Consorts Nos. 1 in D min.; 6 in D; Set a 4 in G min. (with 2 theorbos); Lute duets: Alman; 2 Corants.

(BB) **(*) Naxos 8.550601. Rose Consort of Viols; Herigan, Miller (lutes), Roberts (organ).

Naxos provide an attractive cross-section of Lawes's instrumental music, using an all-viol texture for the string parts in the *Consorts* (with organ where appropriate). The group also include a fascinatingly bravura set of *Divisions for Viols and Organ* on the same *Pavane* which opens the four-part *Set in G minor*. The pieces for two lutes could have been given more lively projection, although they are well enough played. The excellent balance helps to make this inexpensive sampler recommendable, which readers might well try.

LECLAIR, Jean-Marie (1697–1764)

Flute Concerto in C, Op. 7/3; Violin Concertos: in F; in A, Op. 7/4 & 6; in A, Op. 10/2.

*** Chan. 0564. Brown; Standage, Coll. Mus. 90.

Violin Concertos: in D min., Op. 7/1; in D; F; G min., Op. 10/3–4 & 6.

*** Chan. 0589. Standage, Coll. Mus. 90.

Violin Concertos: Op. 7/2 in D; 7/5 in A min.; Op. 10/1 in B flat; 10/5 in E min.

*** Chan. 0551. Standage, Coll. Mus. 90.

The twelve concertos of Opp. 7 and 10 make up Leclair's complete orchestral output; generally speaking, they are underrated and their merits are considerable. Although one cannot include among these a strongly individual lyrical power, the *Aria gracioso* of No. 1 is quite ear-catching, while both the *Adagio* of Op. 7/4 and the *Largo* of Op. 7/5 are distinctly appealing. The *Andante* of Op. 10/3 could well have been written by Vivaldi. Finales too are sprightly in their invention. Op. 7/3 is optionally for flute or oboe, and Rachel Brown makes a pleasing case for the use of a baroque flute, especially in the rather winning slow movement. Simon Standage is a stylish soloist of impeccable technique and Collegium Musicum 90 (4.4.2.2.1) provide authentic, spirited accompaniments. The recordings were made either in St Jude's in north-west London or in All Saints', East Finchley, and textures are transparent and have good sonority.

Violin Concertos: in C & A min., Op. 7/3 & 5; in G min., Op. 10/6.

(BB) *** Teldec 4509 92180-2. Schröder, Concerto Amsterdam (with NAUDOT: *Recorder Concerto in G, Op. 17/5:* Brüggen, VCM, Harnoncourt **).

Distinguished playing from Jaap Schröder and his colleagues, who make outstanding advocates of these concertos. Leclair is a stronger composer than he is often given credit for. The *G minor Concerto*, Op. 10/6, is a work of real

sensibility and imagination, and one only has to sample the slow movements of both the other concertos to discover that Leclair's melodic lines are individual and pleasing. The performances are on period instruments or copies and can be recommended to *aficionados*, as the 1978 analogue sound is both flattering and vivid. The *Recorder Concerto* by Jacques-Christophe Naudot (*c.* 1690–1762), which is provided as a bonus, is less individual but very well played. However, here the sound of the supporting group is thin and less well focused. Nevertheless, this disc is well worth its modest cost.

Sonatas for 2 Violins without Basso Continuo, Op. 3/1–6; Op. 12/1–6.

(B) *** Erato Ultima 3984 24245-2 (2). Banchini, Holloway.

Leclair uses all the special devices of which the instrument's technique was capable in the early years of the eighteenth century, with sustained multiple-stopped chords (very effective in the opening of Op. 3/3), and even simulating a drone effect on one instrument while its companion ruminates melodically above (the *Adagio* of the same work). The sonatas of Op. 3 are written in a three-movement structure; four of the six sonatas of Op. 12 extend to four movements, yet the invention in the first set is if anything fresher than in the second. Leclair is always lighthearted, never austere, and his slow movements are often touchingly expressive. The performances here are first class in every way, and the recording is beautifully balanced, the violin timbres natural and never edgy or scratchy.

Trio Sonatas: in D (Première récréation de musique d'une exécution facile), Op. 6; in A, Op. 14; Double Violin Sonata in D, Op. 3/6.

**(*) Chan. 0582. Coll. Mus. 90 (Standage, Comberti, Coe, Parle).

The pair of *Trio Sonatas* prove to be elegant and tuneful French suites and, although the composer advertised the *D major* as making few technical demands on the players, it is by no means simplistic and the extensive decorated *Chaconne* with which it ends (splendidly played here) is hardly music for beginners! The *Double Violin Sonata* opens with a tenderly melancholy *Andante* but proves a lively and engaging work with a dancing finale, even though the central *Largo* is again rather doleful. In short this is all highly attractive music with a consistently high standard of invention, and it is played on period instruments with fine style and much vitality. The recording cannot be faulted. The sole reservation, and it is not unimportant, is that Simon Standage's timbre has a characteristic cutting edge which some ears may find wearing after a time.

LECOCQ, Alexandre (1832–1918)

Mam'zelle Angot (ballet, arr. Gordon Jacob).

(M) *** Decca (ADD) 430 849-2 (2). Nat. PO, Bonynge – HEROLD: *La Fille mal gardée.* ***

Mam'zelle Angot is a gay, vivacious score with plenty of engaging tunes, prettily orchestrated in the modern French style. Bonynge offers the first recording of the complete score, and its 39 minutes are consistently entertaining when the orchestral playing has such polish and wit. The Kingsway Hall recording is closely observed: the CD brings sharp detail and tangibility, especially at lower dynamic levels.

LECUONA, Ernesto (1895–1963)

Danzas Afro-Cubanas; Gardenia; Noche de Estrellas; Porcelana china (Danza de muñecos); Polka de los Enanos; (i) Rapsodia Cubana; Valses fantásticos; Vals del Nilo; Yo te quiero siempre.

** BIS CD 794. Tirino, (i) with Polish Nat. RSO, Bartas.

Ernesto Lecuona hailed from Cuba and made a career for himself outside Latin and Central America. With the exception of the *Rapsodia Cubana*, which is conspicuously slight in invention, this is light music in the Latin-American style but distinguished by an inventive and resourceful use of rhythm. Thomas Tirino is equal to its demands, although this recording – which emanates from New York and Katowice, not BIS's usual venues – is not three-star. Nor is the music; however, although it is all very limited, there are rewarding moments of sophistication.

Piano music: *Ante el escorial; La cardenese. Pièces caractéristiques: La Habanera; Mazurka glissando. Preludio en la noche. Diary of a Child: Canción de luna. Danzas Afro-Cubanas: La comparsa; La conga de media noche; Danza de los ñañigos; Danza lucumí; Danza negra; . . . Y la negra bailaba!. Ella y yo. Miniature No. 1: Bell-Flower. San Francisco el grande. Valses fantásticos: Valse apasionato; Valse arabesque; Valse brilliante; Valse maracilloso; Valse patéco; Valse poetico; Valse romantico. Yo te quiero siempre.*

*** EMI CDC5 56803-2. Stott.

Popular Cuban music has been the melting-pot for many ethnic influences, but the most famous rhythms – bolero, conga, habanera, guarache and rumba – have a shared Black and Spanish origin. Lecuona, best known for his songs, was also a virtuoso pianist, and for his piano pieces he fused these elements into a popular art form of considerable sophistication. His miniatures are not only tuneful, but well crafted. Evocations like *Ante el escorial* and *San Francisco el grande* are quite ambitious, while the romantic numbers like the sultry *Ella y yo* ('She and I') and *Yo te quiero siempre* ('I will always love you') in the sensitive hands of Kathryn Stott are gently seductive. The suite of *Valses fantásticos* shows her at her most stylish and sparkling. The *Valse arabesque* has an ongoing moto perpetuo flow which is played with the crispest delicacy; *Valse patéco* and *Valse poetico* bring a pleasingly subtle rhythmic feeling, and the others all have an engaging syncopated lilt. Though not to be taken all at once, this music has character and enjoyable individuality. Excellent recording, bright but not hard.

LE FLEM, Paul (1881–1984)

Symphony No. 4; (i) Le Grand Jardinier de France (film music). 7 Pièces enfantines; Pour les morts (Tryptique symphonique No. 1).

** Marco 8.223655. Rhenish PO, Lockhart, (i) with Nopre.

Paul Le Flem is another of the French composers who is emerging from the shadows into which he has been so prematurely cast. The *Fourth Symphony* bears witness to an amazing creative vitality, when one thinks that its composer was just ninety years young at the time (1971–2). (As his dates will show at a glance, he lived to be 103.) The *7 Pièces enfantines* is an orchestral transcription of a set of children's pieces for piano, and *Le Grand Jardinier de France* is a film score. Both have a certain charm and would have more, had the orchestra been allowed more rehearsal. Wind intonation is not always flawless. Le Flem is not, perhaps, a major personality, but the *Fourth Symphony* is in its way quite remarkable, and had the performance greater finesse, the disc would have rated a three-star recommendation.

LEHÁR, Franz (1870–1948)

Gold and Silver Waltz, Op. 79.

(N) *** BBC (ADD) BBCL 4038. Hallé O, Barbirolli – HAYDN: *Symphony No. 83 in G min. (La Poule);* JOHANN STRAUSS JNR: *Emperor Waltz* etc.; R. STRAUSS: *Der Rosenkavalier Suite.* ***

Lehár's finest waltz acts as an unforgettable encore for Barbirolli's 1969 Promenade Concert. He encourages the Prommers to hum along gently, yet not overwhelm the famous tune, and they even manage a pianopianissimo at the reprise. The result is magical.

Waltzes: *Eva; Gold and Silver; Gypsy Love. The Count of Luxembourg: Luxembourg. Giuditta: Where the lark sings. The Merry Widow: Ballsiren.*

(N)(BB) **(*) EMI Encore CDE5 74735-2. Vienna Johann Strauss O, Boskovsky.

Gold and Silver was Lehár's waltz masterpiece; the others are his arrangements, using melodies from the operettas. They are ravishingly tuneful, and given such warmly affectionate recordings and a digital recording which is sumptuous and has sparkling detail, this is easy to enjoy. Lehár's scoring is often imaginative, but in the last resort one misses the voices.

The Czarevitch (sung in English).

*** Telarc CD 80395. Gustafson, Hadley, Itami, Atkinson, Carl, ECO, Bonynge.

Though it lacks the really memorable melodies which make the finest Lehár operettas so winning, *The Czarevitch* is a delightful piece which, with Richard Bonynge as a most understanding conductor, is full of charm and sparkle, with Russian colour from balalaikas nicely touched in. Anyone wanting this in English translation will not be disappointed, with the second couple of principals readily matching up to Jerry Hadley and Nancy Gustafson.

Friederike (complete).

(M) *** EMI (ADD) CMS5 65369-2 (2). Donath, Dallapozza, Fuchs, Finke, Grabenhorst, Bav. R. Ch., Munich R. O, Wallberg.

The idea of Richard Tauber inspiring Lehár to write an operetta with the poet Goethe as the main character may sound far-fetched, but that is just what *Friederike* is, more ambitious than a genuine operetta and bringing the obvious snag for non-German speakers that there is a great deal of spoken dialogue, the more disruptive because there is no libretto, let alone an English translation. However, there is a track-by-track synopsis of each number, and in every other respect this is a delightful reissue, with Helen Donath charming and sensitive in the name-part. Dallapozza has a light, heady tenor, at times stressed by the weight of the part of Goethe but rising above all to the great Tauber number, *O Mädchen, mein Mädchen!*, based (like other numbers) on a Goethe poem, *Mailied*. Heinz Wallberg is a lively and persuasive director, but this set has been withdrawn as we go to press.

(i) *Giuditta* (complete). (ii) *Der Zarewitsch*: highlights.

(B) **(*) Double Decca (ADD) 458 552-2 (2). (i; ii) Gueden, Kmentt; (i) Loose, Dickie, Czerwenka, Berry; (i) Vienna State Op., Ch. & O., Moralt; (ii) Vienna Volksoper Ch. & O., Schönherr.

The classic Decca recording of *Giuditta* dates from 1958 and it is good to have this late and comparatively ambitious opera reissued complete. The performance is affectionately idiomatic in a Viennese way, very well sung and vividly presented. Hilde Gueden is in fresh, sparkling form, and Waldemar Kmentt makes an excellent Octavio: their duet, *Schön wie die blau' Sommernacht*, makes another attractive hit to put alongside Gueden's delightful *Mein' Lippen, sie küssen so heiss*. The score also has some more routine Lehár, but the infectious singing and bright, slightly garish sound injects it with plenty of life.

The highlights from *Der Zarewitsch* and *Der Graf von Luxemburg* (coupled with the *The Merry Widow* – see below) were recorded a decade later in the Sofiensaal. Although the offerings are not especially generous, the recording itself (produced by Christopher Raeburn) is splendid, as demonstrated by the atmospheric opening scenes, with lively support from the chorus and orchestra. The two principals are on top form so that the *Wolgalied* in *Der Zarewitsch* and the charming *Kosende Wellen* are matched by the delightful waltz-duet of *Der Graf von Luxemburg*. There are no librettos but good plot summaries detail individual numbers.

Das Land des Lächelns (The Land of Smiles) (complete).

(M) **(*) EMI (ADD) CMS5 65372-2 (2). Rothenberger, Gedda, Holm, Friedauer, Moeller, Bav. R. Ch., Graunke SO, Mattes.

This 1967 recording has on the whole transferred well to CD. Don't be put off by the sound of the overture, which seems thin because of the relatively small orchestra for the opening scene, but then has plenty of theatrical presence. The recording is atmospheric and real, not only in conveying the songs but also in the spoken dialogue, which is well produced. The cast is strong. Gedda is in excellent form and,

besides Anneliese Rothenberger, Renate Holm makes a charming contribution as Mi. The famous tunes, including *You are my heart's delight*, are splendidly done. Yet again there is no libretto, especially desirable in the operetta; but we are offered a track-by-track synopsis of each number.

The Land of Smiles (sung in English).

*** Telarc CD 80419. Gustafson, Hadley, Itami, Atkinson, ECO, Bonynge.

Richard Bonynge proves as warmly understanding of the Lehár idiom as he is in Bellini, while Jerry Hadley winningly takes the Tauber role of Prince Sou-Chong. He also provides a new translation, with the hit-number, 'You are my heart's delight', becoming *My heart belongs to you*, with diction commendably clear. Nancy Gustafson makes a bright heroine, and Lynton Atkinson sings with winning lightness in the second tenor-role. Recommended.

The Merry Widow (Die lustige Witwe; complete, in German).

*** DG 439 911-2. Studer, Skovhus, Bonney, Trost, Terfel, Monteverdi Ch., VPO, Gardiner.

(N) (M) *** EMI (ADD) CMS5 67370-2(2) [567367]. Schwarzkopf, Gedda, Waechter, Steffek, Knapp, Equiluz, Philh. Ch. and O, Matačić.

(***) EMI mono CDH7 69520-2. Schwarzkopf, Gedda, Kunz, Loose, Kraus, Philh. Ch. & O, Ackermann.

A single-disc version of *The Merry Widow*, with full text and ample dialogue, neatly packaged with libretto, makes an attractive recommendation ahead of any rival. John Eliot Gardiner has the bonus of the Vienna Philharmonic very much on home ground, playing not only with a natural feeling for the idiom but with unrivalled finesse and polish. As Hanna Glawari, the widow of the title, Cheryl Studer gives her most endearing performance yet. She may not have quite the vivacity of Elisabeth Schwarzkopf, but Studer's very first entry establishes her authority and charm, and the gentle half-tone on which she opens the soaring melody of the *Viljalied* is ravishing. Consistently she sings with sweeter, firmer tone than Felicity Lott on the Welser-Möst set and, though the Danish baritone, Boje Skovhus, as Danilo cannot match the velvet of Thomas Hampson's voice for Welser-Möst, he makes an even more animated, raffish hero. The second couple, Valencienne and Camille, are delectably taken by Barbara Bonney and Rainer Trost, clear and youthful-sounding, outshining all rivals. The rest make an outstanding team, with Bryn Terfel, ripely resonant, turning Baron Mirko into more than a *buffo* character, while the choristers of Gardiner's Monteverdi Choir, obviously enjoying their Viennese outing, bring to Lehár the point and precision they have long devoted to the baroque repertory.

Elisabeth Schwarzkopf was surely born to take the role of Hanna, and Matačić provides a magical set, guaranteed to send shivers of delight through any listener with its vivid sense of atmosphere and superb musicianship. It is one of Walter Legge's masterpieces as a recording manager, and the theatrical presence and ambience are something to marvel at, although at the very opening one might have welcomed a touch more sonic brilliance in the Decca manner. The new transfer certainly retains the full bloom of the original. This set is surely worthy of a place among EMI's 'Great Recordings of the Century', even if the famous *Merry Widow Waltz* appears only briefly (2 minutes 28 seconds) at the very end of the opera. However, the reissue, with an overall playing time of 79 minutes 40 seconds (the first CD, Act I, plays for just 29 minutes), is uneconomical, even at mid-price: it would surely have been possible to get the whole opera on a single disc, even if a line or two of the copious dialogue had to be cut. The documentation cannot be faulted, with a full translation included.

It was the mono set, of the early 1950s, which established a new pattern in recording operetta. Ten years later in stereo Schwarzkopf was to record the role again, if anything with even greater point and perception, but here she has extra youthful vivacity, and the *Viljalied* – ecstatically drawn out – is unique. Some may be troubled that Kunz as Danilo sounds older than the Baron, but it is still a superbly characterful cast. However, it has just been deleted.

(i) *Die lustige Witwe (The Merry Widow)* complete.
(ii) *Der Graf von Luxemburg*: highlights.

(M) *** Double Decca (ADD) 458 549-2 (2). (i; ii) Gueden, Kmentt; (ii) Grunden, Loose, Dönch, Equiluz, Klein, Rus; (i) Vienna State Op. O, Stolz; (ii) V. Volksoper Ch. & O, Schönherr.

As with *Giuditta*, the classic Decca *Merry Widow* dates from 1958, and was recorded in Vienna with characteristic engineering flair. After Robert Stolz's inflated but enjoyable overture, we are taken straight into the Pontevedrian Embassy with its multitude of guests, laughter and talk, clinking cocktail glasses and rustling dresses. This extraordinary ambient effect swirls into the room in the most spectacular manner and the *Polonaise* at the beginning of Act II and the entrance of the grisettes in Act III have similar startling presence. The recording itself has splendid atmosphere and sparkle throughout (one really feels oneself in the front stalls). Hilde Gueden gives a melting performance as the Widow and she sings the *Vilja-Lied* most seductively (helped at the close with an aura of resonance). Per Grunden makes Danilo a heady tenor role (it is usually sung by a baritone); Waldemar Kmentt is an appealing Camille de Rosillon and the other parts are well up to standard. Robert Stolz conducts an entirely authentic performance, missing not a whit of sparkle or allure, with the Vienna State Opera Orchestra adding a characteristic lilt to the music; indeed in its idiomatic Viennese inflection, this set in every way challenges the famous Schwarzkopf versions on EMI.

The coupled highlights from *Der Graf von Luxemburg* come first on disc 1, and immediately create a proper carnival atmosphere. The selection concentrates on four key excerpts, two from each act and the singing of the two principals is hardly less enjoyable. *Bist du's, lachendes Glück* is a hit, if ever there was one! Brief plot summaries place each number in narrative perspective.

Excerpts from: *Eva (Prelude); Das Fürstenkind; Frasquita (in English & German); Friederike; Giuditta; Das Land des Lächelns* (in German and English); *Die lustige Witwe; Paganini* (in German and English); *Der Rastelbinder;*

Schön ist die Welt; Der Zarewitsch; Zigeunerliebe.
Selections: '*Lehár memories I & II*'.

(N) (M) (*(*)) EMI mono CMS5 67652-2. Tauber (with var. orchestras and conductors).

Why is it that almost alone among singers who recorded in the 1920s and 1930s Richard Tauber's records suffer from so much distortion, insecurity and vocal blasting, immediately obvious in his famous opening number *Dein ist mein ganzes Herz* from *Das Land des Lächelns*, and which persists almost continually through all his German recordings. And the orchestral sounds are pretty appalling too (even when Franz Lehár himself conducts the *Vorspiel* from *Eva*).

Fortunately the English records from the 1940s, made at Abbey Road, emerge relatively unscathed, notably *You are my heart's delight* with a schmaltzy, gentle reprise; and many will relish the duets with Evelyn Laye from *Paganini*. For Tauber admirers there is much to treasure here, providing allowances are made for the sound; others should approach this set with caution.

LEIGH, Walter (1905–42)

Concertino for Harpsichord & String Orchestra.

(M) *** BBC BBCM 5025-2. Malcolm, ASMF, Marriner – FINZI: *Clarinet Concerto; Introit* *** (with Concert: *English Music* ***).

(N) (M) *** EMI (ADD) CDM5 67431-2. Dilkes, E. Sinf. – FIELD: *Nocturnes;* HARTY: *John Field Suite;* IRELAND: *The Holy Boy.* ***

Like George Butterworth, whose *Banks of Green Willow* is included on this disc, Walter Leigh was killed in action before his gifts could develop fully. His *Concertino for Harpsichord and String Orchestra*, with its heavenly slow movement, which dates from 1936, is an inventive and resourceful score, whose delights remain undimmed. It has surely never been played more winningly than it is here by George Malcolm. The balance with Marriner and his Academy is perfectly judged, so that the appearance of so lively a performance (from 1972), expertly engineered by the late James Burnett is most welcome. This is a highlight of a desirable bargain collection of English music, by Butterworth, Finzi, Vaughan Williams and Warlock.

EMI have now restored Neville Dilkes's pioneering 1971 recording to the catalogue. He takes the delightful *Andante* very gently and slowly, and while some may prefer this slightly more relaxed approach others may feel it is a shade too slow. But the finale is contrastingly crisp and vital and the Abbey Road recording is first class. The couplings are very enjoyable too.

Concertino for Piano & Orchestra.

(N)(BB) (***) Dutton CDBP 9714. K. Long (piano), Boyd Neel String O., Boyd Neel – FAURE: *Ballade in F sharp;* MOZART: *Piano Concerto No. 15, K.450; No. 24, K.491.* (***)

Though this charming *Concertino* was primarily designed for harpsichord, the piano is given as an option, chosen here for the premiere recording in 1946. In subtlety and feeling

Kathleen Long's reading has never been surpassed. It makes a fine supplement to the equally sensitive performances of Mozart and Fauré, which provide the greater part of this tribute to a superb pianist long under-appreciated. The transfer is excellent.

LEIGHTON, Kenneth (1929–88)

(i) Cello Concerto; (ii) Symphony No. 3 (Laudes musicae).

*** Chan. 8741. (i) Wallfisch; (ii) Mackie; SNO, Thomson.

The symphony is in part a song-cycle, and its glowing, radiant colours and refined textures are immediately winning. Raphael Wallfisch plays the *Concerto* as if his life depended on it, and the *Symphony* draws every bit as much dedication from its performers. The recording is very immediate, and has stunning clarity and definition.

Veris gratia (for cello, oboe and strings), Op. 9.

*** Chan. 8471. Wallfisch, Caird, RLPO, Handley – FINZI: *Cello Concerto.* ***

Finzi is the dedicatee of Kenneth Leighton's *Veris gratia*, and so it makes an appropriate coupling for his *Cello Concerto*, more particularly as its English pastoral style nods in his direction. The performance is highly sympathetic, George Caird the excellent oboist, and the naturally balanced recording is first class.

Conflicts, Op. 51; Fantasia contrappuntistica, Op. 24; Household Pets, Op. 86; Sonatina No. 1; 5 Studies, Op. 22.

**(*) Abacus ABA 402-2. Parkin.

Kenneth Leighton was one of the most musical of pianists and wrote beautifully for the instrument. The *Household Pets* is a sensitive piece, refined in craftsmanship, and the *Fantasia contrappuntistica* is comparably powerful. Eric Parkin plays it with total sympathy, and the recording is eminently serviceable.

Crucifixus pro nobis; Give me the wings of faith; O sacrum convivium; The second service: Magnificat; Nunc dimittis. Solus ad victimam.

*** ASV CDDCA 851. Went, Ch. of The Queen's College, Oxford, Matthew Owens – HOWELLS: *Chichester Service* etc. **(*)

A chorister in his youth, Kenneth Leighton wrote with an inborn sympathy for the voice and a natural feeling for line. These are beautiful pieces with an occasional reminder of Britten, and they are well sung, too, by the Choir of The Queen's College, Oxford, where Leighton was a student.

LEKEU, Guillaume (1870–94)

Adagio for Quartet & Orchestra (Les Fleurs pâles de souvenir . . .) arr. for quartet with piano by Gérard Inglésia; Molto Adagio for String Quartet (Commentaire sur les paroles du Christ); (i) Larghetto for Cello & Instrumental Septet; Piano Quartet (completed D'INDY). (ii) 3 Poèmes (Sur une tombe; Ronde; Nocturne).

(N) (B) *** HM HMA 901455. Ens. Musique Oblique; (i) with Veyrier; (ii) Yakar, Adler.

The Belgian composer Guillaume Lekeu left only a small number of works, all of which have a haunting post-Wagnerian *fin de siècle* atmosphere. Indeed, the slow movement of his unfinished *Piano Quartet*, the beautiful *Larghetto* for solo cello and instrumental septet with its voluptuous tenderness, and the (arranged) *Adagio* for string quartet and piano all resonate in the memory. In many ways the early extended *Molto Adagio for String Quartet*, with its strange 5/4 rhythmic pulse, inspired by Christ's lament in the Garden of Gethsemane, is most remarkable of all, not only in itself, but in having a germinal influence on the later works. The playing here by the Ensemble Musique Oblique catches the music's passionate feeling, and at times almost despairing intensity. The recording, though closely observed, has plenty of ambience. The collection ends with three delightful contrasting *Poèmes* for soprano (the sensitive Rachel Yakar) and piano, where the sombre mood melts away in the central *Ronde*, but is felt again in the closing *Nocturne*.

(i) Piano Quartet (2nd movt ed. D'INDY); (ii) Cello Sonata in F.

*** Koch Schwann 310 185. (i–ii) Blumenthal, (i) Adamopoulos, Desjardins, (i–ii) Zanlonghi.

Lekeu's *Cello Sonata* is a powerful, big-boned piece whose first movement alone takes well over 20 minutes (the whole work lasts just under 50). The *Piano Quartet*, composed at the instigation of Ysaÿe, was left incomplete when Lekeu succumbed to typhus; it was finished by d'Indy, who was a supportive figure after the death of Franck. The style is heavily indebted to these masters, but there is a dignity and melancholy at the heart of Lekeu's music which is moving. Excellent performances and vividly present recording.

Piano Trio in C min.

**(*) Koch Schwann 310 060. Blumenthal, Adamopoulos, Zanlonghi.

The *Piano Trio* has a secure grasp of form and is full of expressive intensity. Lekeu is a thoughtful composer and, though the slow movement perhaps outstays its welcome, there are relatively few *longueurs*. The performance is dedicated, and the only reservation is the quality of the piano-tone which is thick at the bottom end of the register; the acoustic is a bit over-reverberant.

LEMBA, Artur (1885–1960)

Symphony in C sharp min.

*** Chan. 8656. SNO, Järvi (with Concert: 'Music from Estonia': Vol. 2***).

Lemba's *Symphony in C sharp minor* was the first symphony ever to be written by an Estonian. It sounds as if he studied in St Petersburg: at times one is reminded fleetingly of Glazunov, at others of Dvořák (the scherzo) – and even of Bruckner (at the opening of the finale) and of Elgar. This is by far the most important item in an enterprising collection of Estonian music.

LEONCAVALLO, Ruggiero

(1858–1919)

I Pagliacci (complete).

(N) *** Decca 467 086-2. Cura, Frittoli, Alvarez, Keenlyside, Castronovo, Netherlands Radio Ch., R. Concg. O, Chailly.

(M) *** DG (ADD) 449 727-2. Carlyle, Bergonzi, Taddei, Panerai, La Scala, Milan, Ch. & O, Karajan.

*** DG (ADD) 419 257-2 (3) Cast as above, La Scala, Milan, Ch. & O, Karajan – MASCAGNI: *Cavalleria rusticana.* ***

(M) *** EMI (ADD) CMS7 63967-2 (2). Amara, Corelli, Gobbi, La Scala, Milan, Ch. & O, Von Matačić – MASCAGNI: *Cavalleria rusticana.* **(*)

(M) *** RCA (ADD) 74321 50168-2 (2) [09026 60865-2]. Caballé, Domingo, Milnes, John Alldis Ch., LSO, Santi

(***) EMI mono CDS5 56287-2 (2). Callas, Di Stefano, Gobbi, La Scala, Milan, Ch. & O, Serafin – MASCAGNI: *Cavalleria rusticana.* (***)

(M) **(*) EMI (ADD) CMS7 63650-2 (2). Scotto, Carreras, Nurmela, Amb. Op. Ch., Philh. O, Muti – MASCAGNI: *Cavalleria rusticana.* **(*)

(B) **(*) Naxos 8.660021. Gauci, Martinucci, Tumagian, Dvorský, Skovhus, Slovak Philh. Ch., Czech RSO, Rahbari.

(M) (**(*)) Nim. mono NI 7843/4. Gigli, Pacetti, Basiola, Nessi, Paci, La Scala Ch. & O, Ghione – MASCAGNI: *Cavalleria rusticana.*

It is surprising how in the digital era there have been so few really outstanding versions of this ever-popular opera, and many relatively disappointing. The first big merit of Chailly's recording is the glorious playing of the Royal Concertgebouw Orchestra under their long-time music director. The orchestral prelude instantly alerts you to the refinement of the playing, not just in the polished ensemble but in the subtle shading of tone and dynamic. The result is still totally natural and idiomatic in its phrasing and rubato, while letting one hear the piece with new clarity, making one marvel at the beauty and subtlety of Leoncavallo's orchestration. The very full dynamic range intensifies the dramatic bite of this story of blood and thunder, even if the acoustic is on the spacious side. The incisive singing of the Netherlands Radio Choir also has one marvelling afresh at the complexity of the choral writing in the sparkling ensembles which frame the piece.

If it was an experiment to use the Concertgebouw in a recording of Italian opera, it is a triumphant success. Happily Decca have lined up a first-rate cast to match. It is true that Jose Cura's tenor has not quite the glowing freshness it once had, having acquired something of a baritonal quality, but there is little of the roughness which mars other recent issues, and the feeling for detail as well as the heroic power make this a strong, intense reading, far more than a loud rant. *Vesti la giubba* is well shaped, moving without being lachrymose, and Cura reserves his finest singing of all for the climactic *No! Pagliaccio non son.*

Barbara Frittoli proves an excellent choice as Nedda, giving a finely detailed performance, with signs in almost every phrase that she has rethought the role, rather as Maria Callas did. Another rising star, Carlos Alvarez, with his big heroic baritone makes an impressive Tonio from the Prologue onwards, even if he does not sound as menacing as some. He is well contrasted in scale and timbre with Simon Keenlyside as Nedda's lover, Silvio, lighter and more lyrical. The pianissimo close to Silvio's big duet with Nedda could not be subtler from either singer, while Charles Castronovo as Beppe in the final Play scene sings with comparable refinement. Vintage versions may offer individual performances of each role which in various ways outshine these, but in the power, beauty and refinement of the Royal Concertgebouw's playing we have something incomparable, enhanced by Decca recording rich, spacious and brilliant.

Until now Karajan's *Pagliacci* has dominated the catalogue for three decades alongside its natural operatic partner, *Cavalleria rusticana*, so it is apt that DG have chosen it for separate reissue in their series of 'Originals', freshly remastered. Karajan does nothing less than refine Leoncavallo's melodrama, with long-breathed, expansive tempi and the minimum of exaggeration. Karajan's choice of soloists was clearly aimed to help that – but the passions are still there; and rarely if ever on record has the La Scala Orchestra played with such beautiful feeling for tone-colour. Bergonzi is among the most sensitive of Italian tenors of heroic quality, and it is good to have Joan Carlyle as Nedda, touching if often rather cool. Taddei is magnificently strong, and Benelli and Panerai could hardly be bettered in the roles of Beppe and Silvio. The combined set remains available, but on three records at premium price – although, as well as *Cav.*, DG provide a splendid set of performances of operatic intermezzi as a filler. However, the separate *Pagliacci* is something of a bargain.

The EMI (originally Columbia) recording under Von Matačić dates from the early 1960s and is especially notable for the contribution of the tenor, Franco Corelli, as Canio, which calls for some superlatives. He is not nearly as imaginative as some of the great tenors of the past, yet he shows a natural feeling for the phrases. It is not just a question of making a big, glorious noise – though of course he does that too – but of interpreting the music; and a performance like this puts several others, by more obviously starry names, in the shade. The coupled *Cav.* is dramatically not quite so striking, but this still makes a clear first choice in the mid-priced range for those who want the pairing with Mascagni.

For those who do not want that obvious coupling, the alternative RCA set is a first-rate recommendation, with fine singing from all three principals, vivid playing and recording, and one or two extra passages not normally included – as in the Nedda–Silvio duet. Milnes is superb in the Prologue.

It is thrilling to hear *Pagliacci* starting with the Prologue sung so vividly by Tito Gobbi. Di Stefano, too, is at his finest, but the performance inevitably centres on Callas and there are many points at which she finds extra intensity, extra meaning. Serafin's direction is strong and direct. The mono recording is greatly improved in the new transfer, with voices well forward, but this set is overpriced.

Under Muti's urgent direction both *Cav.* and *Pag.* represent the music of violence. In both he has sought to use the original text, which in *Pag.* is often surprisingly different, with many top notes eliminated and Tonio instead of Canio delivering (singing, not speaking) the final *La commedia è finita*. Muti's approach represents the antithesis of smoothness. Scotto's Nedda goes raw above the stave, but the edge is in keeping with Muti's approach, with its generally brisk speeds. Carreras seems happier here than in *Cav.*, but it is the conductor and the fresh look he brings that will prompt a choice here. The sound is extremely vivid.

Alexander Rahbari conducts his Slovak forces in a vigorous, red-blooded reading which with first-rate solo singing makes an excellent bargain recommendation, very well recorded, if with the chorus a little distant. Miriam Gauci is a warmly vibrant Nedda, with plenty of temperament, and Eduard Tumagian is an outstanding Tonio, not only firm and dark of tone but phrasing imaginatively. As Canio, Nicola Martinucci has an agreeable tenor that he uses with more finesse and a better line than many more celebrated rivals, even though his histrionics at the beginning and end of *Vesti la giubba* are unconvincing.

The Nimbus transfer of the classic 1934 recording with Gigli focuses the voices effectively enough, giving them a mellow bloom – though the orchestra, often rather recessed, is relatively muffled. Gigli is very much the centre of attention, with Iva Pacetti as Nedda clear and powerful rather than characterful.

I Pagliacci (in English; complete).

(M) *** Chan. 3003. Opie, Mannion, O'Neil, Bronder, Geoffrey Mitchell Ch., Peter Kay Children's Ch., LPO, Parry.

David Parry conducts a powerful performance in the Peter Moores Foundation's 'Opera in English' series, building the drama persuasively. The cast is one of the finest in the series yet, with Rosa Mannion a touching Nedda and Alan Opie and William Dazeley both outstanding and well contrasted in the baritone roles. Dennis O'Neill sings very well too as Canio, but faces greater problems with translating the tragic clown into an English-speaking hero. No longer *On with the motley* but 'Put on your costume'. Warm, atmospheric sound with voices beautifully focused.

I Pagliacci: highlights.

(M) **(*) EMI (ADD) CDM5 66048-2. Scotto, Carreras, Nurmela, Allen, Amb. Op. Ch., Philh. O, Muti – MASCAGNI: *Cavalleria rusticana*: highlights. **(*)

Muti uses the original text, which is often surprisingly different, with Tonio instead of Canio delivering (singing not speaking) the final *La commedia è finita*. It is an urgent performance and very involving, but the rendering of the Prologue by Kari Nurmela brings a coarse start to the proceedings.

LEONI, Franco (1884–1949)

L'Oracolo (opera): complete.

*** Decca (ADD) 444 396-2. Sutherland, Gobbi, Van Allan, Tourangeau, Davies, John Alldis Ch., Finchley Children's Music Group, Nat. PO, Bonynge.

L'Oracolo tells the lurid story of the wicked Cim-Fen, who finally gets strangled, to the delight of everyone, with his own pigtail. In the meantime the heroine goes mad after the murder of her beloved, and the whole drama is set against sound-effects which are superbly caught in this brilliant first recording, made in the Kingsway Hall in 1975. The very opening – three bangs on the bass drum, two crowings of a cockerel and a great jabber in Chinese from the chorus – might almost be a hi-fi demonstration.

The piece gives marvellous opportunities not only to the veteran Tito Gobbi (relishing the character's wickedness) but also to Joan Sutherland, specialist in mad scenes, and to Richard Van Allan as the doctor who finally dispatches Cim-Fen. If Leoni's actual idiom is rather too bland for so dark a story, and his melodies, although often lusciously attractive, never quite come up to Puccini standard, the piece makes a fine compact entertainment in such a performance as this, directed with passionate conviction by Richard Bonynge, with superb playing from the National Philharmonic. This enterprising set is well worth having: it grows more compelling on repeated hearings.

LEONIN (c. 1163–90)

Organa: *Alleluya, Epulemur Azamis; Gaude Maria; Propter veritatem; Viderunt omnes.*

*** Lyrichord LEMS 8002. Oberlin, Bressler, Perry –
PEROTINUS: *Organa.* ***

Over eight centuries have passed since the construction of the Cathedral of Notre Dame began and Leonin, the cathedral's composer, was writing this music. It is in two parts, with the top voice moving in unison or octaves, or over a sustained or only occasionally moving second part. Sometimes both voices sing in unison. The present performances are extraordinarily convincing and take us back in time to the very beginning of written music. Excellent recording.

Organa: *Alleluya, Dies sanctificatus; Alleluya, dulce lignum; Alleluja, inter natos mulierum; Alleluya, Pascha nostrum; Alleluja, Paraclitus Spiritus Sanctus; Alleluya, Spiritus Sanctus procedens; Priusquam te formarem; Vidernet omnes.*

(N) *** Hyp. CDA 66944. Red Byrd, Capella Amsterdam.

This is a more extensive selection of Leonin's organa than the Lyrichord disc above. The recordings include compositions for the main feasts from the first part of the liturgical year. Much of the music brings elaborate, rhapsodic melodic lines which are quite haunting in these atmospheric and confidently sung performances, admirably recorded. Full texts, translations and good documentation, as we expect from Hyperion.

LIADOV, Anatol (1855–1914)

Baba-Yaga, Op. 56; The Enchanted Lake, Op. 62; From the Apocalypse, Op. 66; Kikimora, Op. 63; Mazurka: Village Scene by the Inn, Op. 19; Polonaise, Op. 49; 8 Russian Folksongs, Op. 58; Scherzo in D, Op. 16.

(N) *** Chan. 9911. BBC PO, Sinaisky.

Russian composers at the end of the nineteenth century and beginning of the twentieth seem to possess the ability of evoke the world of the fairy-tale and of magic with unerring sympathy, and none more successfully than Liadov. *The Enchanted Lake* and *Kikimora* are wonderfully atmospheric and the performances by Vassily Sinaisky and the BBC Philharmonic are pure magic. Although they are the best known, a piece like *From the Apocalypse* is hardly less inspired. Commentators always speak of Liadov's expertise and beautiful craftsmanship, but he is a master, who creates a world quite unlike that of any other composer. The performances are matched by recording of equal richnes and luminosity.

(i) *Baba Yaga, Op. 56; The Enchanted Lake, Op. 62; Kikimora, Op. 63;* (ii) *8 Russian Folksongs.*

(BB) **(*) Naxos 8.550328. Slovak PO, (i) Gunzenhauser,
   (ii) Jean – Concert: 'Russian Fireworks'.

It is good to have inexpensive recordings of these key Liadov works, particularly the *Russian Folksongs*, eight orchestral vignettes of great charm, displaying a winning sense of orchestral colour. The performances are persuasive, and the digital recording is vivid and well balanced.

LIBERT, (or Liebert Reginaldus)

(born *c.* 1425/35)

Missa de Beata Virgine. Kyrie à 4.

*** Lyrichord LEMS 8025. Schola Discantus, Moll.

Libert's Marian Mass has the distinction of being – like Dufay's *Missa Sancti Jacobi* – one of the earliest to survive that includes settings of both the Ordinary and Proper. Moreover, the Mass is made cohesive by being based on a very striking, melismatic cantus firmus, which is always recognizable as it usually appears in the upper voice, decorated with ornamental notes. The three-voiced counterpoint is comparatively simple, with the third voice subordinate to the upper parts, enriching the sonority. Even so, the *Credo* is powerful and ambitious, followed by a particularly fine *Sanctus*. In short this is an appealing and memorable work, and the performance here is an eloquent one, with well-judged pacing. With the addition of the separate four-part *Kyrie* this disc includes all the music positively attributed to Libert. The recording is first class, made in a spacious acoustic and the documentation very good, except that for the text and translation of the *Kyrie* and *Gloria* we are referred to another Lyrichord issue (LEMS 8010), a curious proposition, as we are not told any more about this CD. The presentation also associates Libert's Mass with Jeanne d'Arc, and gives her biography, but although she was a contemporary of the composer and this music, there is no other connection.

LIGETI, György (born 1923)

(i) *Cello Concerto; Chamber Concerto;* (ii) *Piano Concerto.*

*** Sony SK 58945. (i) Perényi; (ii) Wiget; Modern Ens., Eötvös.

These three concertos span two decades of Ligeti's output. The *Cello Concerto* and the *Chamber Concerto*, for 13 instruments, are vivid in colour, complex in detail and undoubtedly full of energy. To some ears their content may not match their undoubted prolixity of surface comment. The *Piano Concerto* has five movements. The most striking movement is the second; perhaps the others, exuberant as they are, outlast their welcome. Dedicated Ligetians (are there many, we wonder) will welcome these obviously skilled and committed performances, well recorded, with Ueli Wiget a striking advocate of the demanding solo role in the concertante work for piano.

(i) *Cello Concerto;* (ii) *Piano Concerto;* (iii) *Violin Concerto.*

*** DG 439 808-2. (i) Queras; (ii) Aimard; (iii) Gawriloff; Ens. InterContemporain, Boulez.

This concertante triptych won the *Gramophone* magazine's Contemporary Music Award in 1996. The composer's imaginative inventiveness is never in doubt, but his musical purpose is not always easy to fathom. All the performers believe that this music has an underlying profundity; all three performances are musically and technically impressive and communicate strongly.

Bagatelles.

*** Crystal CD 750. Westwood Wind Quintet – CARLSSON: *Nightwings;* MATHIAS: *Quintet;* BARBER: *Summer Music.* ***

Ligeti's folk-inspired *Bagatelles* are highly inventive and very attractive; and they are played with dazzling flair and unanimity of ensemble by this American group.

Le Grand Macabre (complete opera).

*** Sony S2K 62312 (2). Ehlert, Clark, White, Nes, Ragin, Cole, Suart, L. Sinf. Voices, Philh. O, Salonen.

It is the revised version of *Le Grand Macabre* that is recorded here under supervision from the composer, using an English text. Set in Breughelland, this apocalyptic vision lightens its macabre theme – of the ending of the world – with humour, viciously satirical and anarchic, setting out from a witty prelude for tuned motor-horns, with tongue-in-cheek echoes of a baroque toccata. Salonen is a brilliant advocate, drawing colourful playing from the Philharmonia. Sibylle Ehlert is dazzling in the coloratura role of Gepopo, Graham Clark a characterful Piet the Pot, and Willard White aptly baleful as the *grand macabre* himself, the sinister Nekrotzar. This may be an off-beat piece, but as audiences have found, it has a sparkle which has one simultaneously laughing and thinking. Atmospheric sound, recorded live at the Theatre du Chatelet.

LILBURN, Douglas (born 1915)

Symphonies Nos. 1 (1949); 2 (1951); 3 in One Movement (1961).

*** Continuum 1069. New Zealand SO, Hopkins.

Douglas Lilburn is the doyen of New Zealand composers. The three symphonies collected here on this well-filled disc show an impressive musical mind at work. There is a strong affinity with Scandinavian music, induced perhaps by the similarities of latitude and landscape, and an imposing formal coherence. The opening of the *Third Symphony in One Movement* almost suggests an antipodean Holmboe. The musical invention shows a consistently high level of imagination, and the performances are thoroughly committed. Excellent, well-balanced recorded sound enhances the claims of this disc. Strongly recommended.

LINDBERG, Magnus (born 1958)

'Meet the Composer': (i) Action – Situation; Signification; (ii–iii) Kinetics; (i–ii; iv) Kraft; (v; iii) Rittrato; (vi–vii; iii) Zona; (Instrumental) (viii–ix) Ablauf; (x) . . . De Tartuffe, je crois (for piano quintet); (viii; xi) Linea d'ombra; (vi) Stroke; (Piano) (xii) Twine.

(B) *** Finlandia Double 0630 19756-2 (2). (i) Toimili Ens.; (ii) Finnish RSO; (iii) Salonen; (iv) Swedish RSO; (v) Avanti! CO; (vi) Karttunen; (vii) L. Sinf.; (viii) Krikku; (ix) Aaltonen, Ohenoja; (x) Endymion Ens., Witfield; (xi) Ferchen, Pohjola, Virtanen; (xii) Hakkila.

Magnus Lindberg belongs to the younger generation of Finnish composers now moving into their middle years. He studied with Paavo Heininen in Helsinki and with Bryan Ferneyhough at the Darmstadt summer courses in the early 1980s. He also studied with Franco Donati in Siena and with Vinko Globokar in Paris. His breakthrough as a composer came with *Kraft* (the second item on the first CD), which had its première in 1984 and brought him to international attention. This Finlandia *'Meet the Composer'* set of two CDs gives a good cross-section of his work during the 1980s, when he was still in his late twenties and early thirties. If you do not respond to avant-garde music, you may still find something to reward you here, for Lindberg is a composer of imagination and intelligence.

LINDBLAD, Adolf Fredrik (1801–78)

Symphonies Nos. 1 in C, Op. 19; 2 in D.

*** Marco 8.225105. Uppsala CO, Korsten.

Lindblad is best known for his songs, of which there are some 250. Indeed, he is generally spoken of as 'the father of Swedish song'. Mendelssohn thought highly enough of the *First Symphony* to conduct it at Leipzig with the Gewandhaus Orchestra. Gérard Korsten and the Uppsala Chamber Orchestra give splendid accounts of both symphonies, extremely vital and spirited with infectious high spirits in the first movement of the *C major Symphony*. And what

delightful pieces these are, not strong on individuality perhaps but like the Weber symphonies highly attractive. Quite a find and very good sound, warm and well focused.

LINKOLA, Jukka (born 1955)

'Meet the Composer': (i) Boogie Woogie Waltz; (ii–iii) Crossings; (iv) Trumpet Concerto; (i) Malaria; (v; iii) Ronia, the Robber's Daughter (5 movements); (vi; iii) The Snow Queen (film incidental music); (vii) Evoe!.

(B) *** Finlandia Double 0630 19808-2 (2). (i) Jukka Linkola Octet; (ii) Aaltonen, Helsinki PO; (iii) cond. composer; (iv) Harjanne, Finnish RSO, Segerstam; (v) Finnish Nat. Op. O; (vi) O; (vii) Helsinki University Ch., Hyökki, with Kristian and Laura Attila.

Jukka Linkola began life as a jazz musician, and it was an encounter with the music of Lutoslawski which turned him in the direction of serious contemporary music. Although his is not a voice of great individuality, he is obviously a composer of both sophistication and imagination. *Crossings* for tenor saxophone and orchestra from 1983 reveals traces of Messiaen and French music, as well as his past in the world of jazz. The excerpts from the ballet, *Ronia, the Robber's Daughter*, have more than the occasional reminder of Stravinsky and Prokofiev and the average Hollywood score. Even so, Linkola has the capability of taking the listener by surprise. Though not a major figure, he is far from negligible, and he is resourceful, rarely less than an entertaining aural companion and always intelligent.

LISZT, Franz (1811–86)

Piano Concertos Nos. 1–2; Fantasia on Hungarian Folksongs; Fantasia on Themes from Beethoven's 'Ruins of Athens'; Grande fantaisie symphonique on Themes from Berlioz's 'Lélio'; Malédiction; Polonaise brillante on Weber's Polonaise brillante in E (L'Hilarité); Totentanz (paraphrase on the Dies Irae); SCHUBERT/LISZT: Wanderer Fantasia.

(B) *** EMI (ADD) CZS5 69662-2 (2). Béroff, Leipzig GO, Masur.

Michel Béroff's 1977 account of the two concertos can hold its own with the best of the competition: here there is nothing routine or slapdash, but instead excitement, warmth and spontaneity, along with his remarkable technical prowess. The piano timbre has plenty of body and colour, as well as sparkle. This is an exhilarating and rewarding set which can be given a strong recommendation on all counts.

(i) Piano Concertos 1–2; Totentanz (paraphrase on the 'Dies irae'). Années de pèlerinage: Book 1: 1st Year: Switzerland; Book 2: 2nd Year (Italy); Book 3: 3rd Year (Italy) excerpts: Aux cyprès de la Villa d'Este; Sunt lachrimae rerum; Sursum corda (only). Sonata in B min.; Concert Paraphrase of 'Isolde's Liebestod' from Wagner's 'Tristan'. Csárdás macabre; En rêve (Nocturne); Harmonies poétiques et religieuses (Invocations;

Bénédiction de Dieu dans la solitude; Pensée des morts);
Funérailles. Klavierstück in F sharp; Légendes Nos. 1–2; La
Lugubre Gondola Nos. 1–2; Mosonyis Grabgeleit; Nuages
gris; Prelude & Fugue on the Name, 'bach'; RW (Venezia);
Schlaflos! Frage und Antwort; Unstern (Sinistre); Valse
oubliée No. 1; Vexilla regis prodeunt; Weinachtsbaum
(Christmas Tree) Suite (excerpts); Variations on 'Weinen,
Klagen, Sorgen, Zagen'.

(M) *** Ph. (ADD) 446 924-2 (5). Brendel, (i) LPO, Haitink.

Brendel's 1972 recordings of the *Concertos* and *Totentanz*
have long been among the key versions of these volatile
works, and Haitink is a persuasive accompanist. Brendel's
earlier set of the *Second Year* of the *Années de pèlerinage* was
recorded that same year and proved no less outstanding.
The performances are of superlative quality, the playing
highly poetic and brilliant, while the analogue recording
offers Philips's most realistic quality. The *First Year* (*Switzerland*) came 14 years later and was less successfully recorded
digitally. The four excerpts from the *Third Year* were
recorded as part of an outstanding (1979) analogue recital,
which included the extraordinary late pieces, many of whose
names are unfamiliar, and Brendel's presentation of them is
distinguished by a concentration and subtlety of nuance
that are wholly convincing, helped by extremely lifelike
recording. The *Prelude and Fugue on the Name 'bach'* and
the *Variations* on '*Weinen, Klagen, Sorgen, Zagen*' sound
impressive on the piano when played so masterfully, and
the *Harmonies poétiques et religieuses* are hardly less distinguished. However, the *Sonata* is something of a disappointment. Brendel has recorded this work three times and Philips
have chosen the most recent version, made in 1991. It was a
great pity that his second recording (also digital) was not
chosen. The newest account brings a similarly wide range of
colour, yet there is not the same spontaneity nor a comparable firmness of grip. There is much brilliant pianism, but
the overall purpose of the reading seems much less clear
and even the recording, though bright and clean, is less
impressive than either the 1983 version or even the analogue
record, made in the 1960s. But overall this box shows Brendel
as a superb Lisztian.

Piano Concertos Nos. 1–2.

(N)(M) *** Ph. (ADD) 464 710-2. S. Richter, LSO, Kondrashin
 – BEETHOVEN: *Piano Sonatas Nos. 10; 19–20.* ***

(i) *Piano Concertos 1–2*; (ii; iii) *Fantasia on Hungarian*
Folk Tunes; Malédiction; Totentanz; (ii; iv) Arr. of
Schubert: *Wanderer Fantasia* (all for piano and
orchestra).

(B) *** Double Decca (ADD) 458 361-2 (2). (i) Katchen, LSO,
Argenta; (ii) Bolet; (iii) LSO, Fischer; (iv) LPO, Solti –
DOHNANYI: *Variations on a Nursery Tune, Op. 25.* ***

Piano Concertos Nos. 1–2; Totentanz.

✪ *** DG 423 571-2. Zimerman, Boston SO, Ozawa.

(M) *** Ph. (ADD) 426 637-2. Brendel, LPO, Haitink.

Piano Concertos Nos. (i) 1 in E flat; (ii) 2 in A. Années de pèlerinage: Sonetto 104 del Petrarca. Hungarian Rhapsody No. 6; Valse oubliée.

(M) *** Mercury (ADD) [432 002-2]. Janis, (i) Moscow PO,

Kondrashin; (ii) Moscow RSO, Rozhdestvensky (also with
SCHUMANN: *Romance in F sharp; Novellette in F;*
FALLA: *Miller's Dance.* GUION: *The Harmonica*
Player ***).

Piano Concertos Nos. 1 in E flat; 2 in A; Hungarian Fantasia.

(***) BBC mono BBCL 4031-2. S. Richter, LSO, Kondrashin
(with CHOPIN: *Andante pianato & grande polonaise,*
Op. 22 (***)).

(i)Piano Concertos Nos. 1 in E flat; 2 in A., Piano Sonata in B min.

(M) *** Ph. (ADD) 446 200-2. S. Richter, (i) with LSO,
Kondrashin.

Krystian Zimerman's record of the two *Concertos* and the
Totentanz is altogether thrilling, and he has the advantage of
excellent support from the Boston orchestra under Ozawa. It
has poise and classicism and, as one listens, one feels this
music could not be played in any other way – surely the
mark of a great performance! This record is outstanding in
every way, and still remains a first choice for this repertoire.

Sviatoslav Richter's 1961 performances on Philips are very
distinguished indeed, and the recent remastering by Wilma
Cozart Fine makes the very most of the recording, originally
engineered by the Mercury team. It is good that both Wilma
and Robert Fine receive a credit in the insert notes for the
excellence of the original sound-balance. Richter's playing
is unforgettable and so is his rapport with Kondrashin and
the LSO, whose playing throughout is of the very highest
order. Richter's electrifying and highly poetic recording of
the *Sonata* has been added. The sound is vivid and present
but the acoustic is rather dry for full comfort. However,
given playing of this calibre, one soon adjusts.

As can be seen above, Richter's recording of just the pair
of concertos is also available as one of Philips's '50 Great
Recordings' curiously recoupled with three of Beethoven's
least ambitious early piano sonatas, beautifully played and
recorded.

The splendid Double combines sparkling pianism from
two of Decca's most distinguished keyboard lions, both of
whom died all too soon, at the peak of their form. Katchen
is superb in the *E flat Concerto*, only slightly less successful
with the changes of mood of the *Second*. But by any standard
these are commanding performances, and he found a fitting
partner in Ataulfo Argenta, who also died sadly young.
Bolet is no less masterful in the splendid triptych of shorter
concertante works, which thrillingly bring out all his characteristic bravura. The digital recording remains demonstration class. He and Solti also make out a fairly convincing
case for Liszt's concertante arrangement of Schubert's *Wanderer Fantasia*. With such a poetic response the central
Adagio loses nothing on the solo version, and the scintillating
pianism in the finale compensates for any moments of
un-Schubertian hyperbole in the orchestration.

Around the time they were recording Richter's Liszt *Concertos* for Philips in London (1961), the Mercury engineers
paid a visit to Moscow to record Byron Janis in the same
repertoire, and his is a comparably distinguished coupling.
Janis's glittering articulation is matched by his sense of

poetry and drama, and there is plenty of dash in these very compelling performances, which are afforded characteristically brilliant Mercury sound, although the piano is too close. The encores which follow the two *Concertos* are also very enjoyable.

Brendel's Philips recordings from the early 1970s hold their place at or near the top of the list and are discussed under the Brendel Liszt edition. The recording is one of Philips's best.

(i) *Piano Concertos Nos. 1 in E flat; 2 in A; Totentanz for Piano & Orchestra;* (ii) *Piano Sonata in B min.; Années de pèlerinage, 2nd Year: Après une lecture du Dante (Dante Sonata); Sonetti del Petrarca Nos. 104 & 123.*

(B) *** Teldec Ultima 3984 21092-2 (2). (i) Berezovsky, Philh. O, Wolff; (ii) Leonskaya.

Boris Berezovsky's thrillingly extrovert yet highly musical accounts of the two concertos and the rumbustious *Totentanz* are ideally balanced by Elisabeth Leonskaya's imaginative recital of solo piano music. Berezovsky plays throughout with enormous panach and bravura, yet with melting poetic feeling too. Hugh Wolff proves a splendid partner, and the Philharmonia Orchestra play with great gusto. The full-blooded, resonantly spacious recording was made at Aldeburgh in 1994.

Leonskaya then takes over for the *Sonata*, and she gives a very impressive reading indeed. She has a firm grip on this wayward piece, especially in the more reflective writing, where she displays much poetic feeling. The central *Allegro energico* is played superbly. The two *Petrarch sonnets* are played very freely, with flexible rubato which suits No. 123 particularly well. Even if you already have some of the music on record, this set is well worth investigating.

Piano Concerto No. 1 in E flat.

(M) *** DG (ADD) 449 719-2. Argerich, LSO, Abbado – CHOPIN: *Piano Concerto No. 1.* ***

(N) (M) **(*) RCA (ADD) 09026 63053-2. Rubinstein, RCA SO, Wallenstein – SAINT-SAENS: *Concerto No. 2;* SCHUMANN: *Concerto.* **(*)

(BB) **(*) Naxos 8.550292. Banowetz, Czech RSO, Bratislava, Dohnányi – CHOPIN: *Concerto No. 1.* **(*)

(i; ii) *Piano Concerto No. 1 in E flat;* (i) *Piano Sonata in B min.; Hungarian Rhapsody No. 6;* (iii) *Années de pèlerinage: Vallée d'Obermann; Les Jeux d'eau à la Villa D'Este.*

(B) **(*) DG (ADD) 439 409-2. (i) Argerich; (ii) LSO, Abbado; (iii) Berman.

Martha Argerich (in 1968) recorded only Liszt's *First Concerto* and not the *Second*. However, there is an excellent partnership between the pianist and Abbado, and this is a performance of flair and high voltage which does not ever become vulgar. It is very well recorded, and in this reissue, coupled with Chopin, it sounds better than ever. The performance is also available on DG's bargain Classikon label, coupled with the *Sonata*, which Argerich recorded three years later.

Rubinstein's performance, too, is quite splendid, full of panache, with an aristocratic command and glittering digital

dexterity. Wallenstein accompanies with gusto and the whole affair is like a live performance, gathering pace and excitement to give the finale fine dash and excitement. Astonishingly, the recording dates from 1956, yet it is bold and full-bodied, and the Carnegie Hall acoustics bring a fine resonance and bloom. The usual snag of the absence of any real pianissimo is less serious in an extrovert work like this, although it does affect the Schumann coupling.

A splendid, energetic account of the *First Concerto* from Joseph Banowetz, well coupled with Chopin, has the full measure of the work's flamboyance and its poetry. The wide-ranging sound is excellent, though the triangle solo in the scherzo is only just audible.

(i; ii) *Piano Concerto No. 1 in E flat;* (iii; iv) *Hungarian Fantasia;* (iv) *Hungarian Rhapsodies Nos. 2, 4 & i) 6;* (v) *Mephisto Waltz No. 1;* (iv) *Les Préludes;* (i) *Piano Sonata in B min.;* (vi) *Bénédiction de Dieu dans la solitude;* (vii) *Feux follets; Harmonies du soir.*

(N) (BB) ** DG Panorama [ADD] 469 151-2 (2). (i) Argerich; (ii) LSO, Abbado; (iii) Cherkassky; (iv) BPO, Karajan; (v) Ashkenazy; (vi) Arrau; (vii) Richter.

Argerich and Abbado are in very good form in the *E flat Concerto* (see above) and the recording is excellent. Equally compelling are Karajan's *Hungarian Rhapsodies Nos. 2 & 4* (the 6th is for piano solo, excitingly done by Argerich) and *Les Préludes* – all deservedly famous recordings. Cherkassky's glittering account of the *Hungarian Fantasia* is another highlight, and the solo items from Ashkenazy and Arrau are all worth having. The Richter performances are live and date from the late 1950s, but the much poorer sound and unbelievably noisy audience preclude much enjoyment.

Dante Symphony.

*** DG 457 614-2. Dresden State Op. Ch., and State O. Sinopoli (with BUSONI: *Doktor Faust; Saraband und Cortège* ***).

(i) *Dante Symphony;* (ii) *Années de pèlerinage, Book 2: Après un lecture du Dante (Fantasia Quasi Sonata).*

*** Teldec 9031 77340. (i) Women's Voices of Berlin R. Ch., BPO, Barenboim; (ii) Barenboim (piano).

(i) *Dante Symphony;* (ii; iii) *A Faust Symphony, G.108;* (ii; iv) *Les Préludes; Prometheus.*

(B) **(*) Decca-Double (ADD) 466 751-2 (2). (i) Voltaire College Ch., SRO, Lopez-Cobos; (ii) Solti; (iii) Jerusalem, Chicago Ch. & SO; (iv) LPO.

Liszt's *Dante Symphony* divides naturally into two very expansive, equally balanced halves – *Inferno* and *Purgatorio* – each lasting about 21 minutes, with a relatively short choral *Magnificat* as a finale. The work opens diabolically, with the rasping trombones evoking the gates of Hell, followed by a sustained frenzy of writing for strings and brass; later in a romantic interlude we meet Francesca da Rimini in all her grief. Interestingly, she is introduced by a bass clarinet in a not dissimilar way to her entrance on the clarinet in Tchaikovsky's symphonic poem. A blinding flash of harps introduces the malignant Scherzo, and the movement reaches a tremendous climax. The second movement is calming – some might say becalmed in its spacious paragraphs. Finally the heavenly chorus enters and lusciously proclaims salvation.

Sinopoli, on one of his very finest records, gives a grippingly inspired account. He draws a clear parallel, not only with Tchaikovsky's *Francesca da Rimini*, but also the *Manfred Symphony*. The refined and beautiful playing of the Dresden Orchestra easily sustains the long central *Purgatorio*, and the luminous and superbly sung choral entry in the finale creates a magical apotheosis. The DG recording is in the demonstration bracket, wonderfully spacious and clear. For an imaginative coupling we are offered the two pieces Busoni composed in 1918/19 as 'a reduced-size model' while working on his opera, *Doktor Faust*, well worth having when played so impressively.

Barenboim too really has the measure of this overextended but remarkable work and controls its rhapsodic structure admirably, holding the tension throughout the first movement and creating enormous visceral excitement at the close. He is helped by marvellous playing from the BPO, who really sound as if they believe in it all, and the radiant choral effects are superbly brought off. The resonant acoustic of Berlin's Schaulspielhaus lets everything expand with Wagnerian amplitude and the result is very impressive indeed. As an encore, Barenboim leaves the rostrum for the piano and offers the *Dante Sonata*, which has the same literary basis but offers a quite different musical treatment. The performance is flamboyantly arresting, but the piano recording is curiously shallow.

Lopez-Cobos's account of the *Dante Symphony* comes with Liszt's alternative conclusion, a sudden loud outburst of 'Hallelujahs' from the trebles after the usual *ppp* ending. It is most effective, crowning a performance which is more remarkable for its refinement of sound and balance than for its dramatic thrust. It is not underpowered, however, and the early digital recording is rich and full, while the SRO is on better form than it was in Ansermet's day. Solti's Liszt is almost always successful. His performance of the *Faust Symphony* is spacious, yet brilliant, with superb playing from his Chicago orchestra, though the bright recording underlines the fierce element in his reading and removes some of the warmth. The Mephistophelean finale brings the most impressive playing of all, with Solti's fierceness chiming naturally with the movement's demonic quality. The two tone poems, recorded in the 1970s, are brilliantly played and recorded. Even with the reservations expressed this is excellent value.

Fantasia on Hungarian Folk Tunes for Piano & Orchestra.

(M) *** Decca 430 726-2. Bolet, LSO, Fischer – ADDINSELL: *Warsaw Concerto* ***; GERSHWIN: *Rhapsody* **(*); GOTTSCHALK: *Grand Fantasia* ***; LITOLFF: *Scherzo.* ***

Bolet is a masterful soloist and he plays here with characteristic bravura. Like the pianist, the Hungarian conductor is an understanding Lisztian, and the accompaniment from the LSO is first rate, with a recording balance of demonstration quality.

(i) *Fantasia on Hungarian Folk Tunes; Malédiction; Totentanz;* (ii) Arr. of Schubert: *Wanderer Fantasia* (all for piano and orchestra). *Années de pèlerinage* (complete); *Ballade No. 2;* Concert paraphrases: *Bellini: Réminiscences de Norma; 12 Schubert Songs; Mozart: Réminiscences de Don Juan; Verdi: Rigoletto.* 2 Concert studies *(Waldesrauschen; Gnomenreigen);* 3 Concert studies *(Il lamento; La reggierezza; Un sospiro);* Consolations Nos. 1– 6; *12 Etudes d'exécution transcendente; Etudes d'exécution transcendente d'après Paganini: La campanella. Grand galop chromatique; Harmonies poétiques et religieuses: Funérailles. Hungarian Rhapsody No. 12; Liebesträume Nos. 1–3; Mephisto Waltz No. 1; Sonata; Valse impromptu.*

(N) (B) *** Decca 467 801-2. (9) Bolet; with (i) LSO, Iván Fischer; (ii) LPO, Solti.

The full range of the late Jorge Bolet's achievement for Decca in the music of Liszt is admirably surveyed in this bargain box, all splendidly recorded, and there are two other shorter surveys below. One or other should be in every representative collection.

(i) *Fantasia on Hungarian Folk Tunes. Hungarian Rhapsodies Nos. 2, 4–5; Mazeppa; Mephisto Waltz No. 2; Les Préludes; Tasso, lamento e trionfo.*

(B) *** DG Double (ADD) 453 130-2 (2). BPO, Karajan; (i) with Cherkassky.

Shura Cherkassky's glittering 1961 recording of the *Hungarian Fantasia* is an affectionate performance with some engaging touches from the orchestra, though the pianist is dominant and his playing is superbly assured. The rest of the programme is comparably charismatic. The cellos and basses sound marvellous in the *Fifth Rhapsody* and *Tasso*, and even the brashness of *Les Préludes* is a little tempered. *Mazeppa* is a great performance, superbly thrilling and atmospheric, with a riveting coda – worthy of a Rosette. A set showing Karajan and his Berlin orchestra at their finest.

Concert paraphrases (for piano and orchestra): *Fantasia on a Theme from Beethoven's 'Ruins of Athens'; Grande fantasie symphonique on Themes from Berlioz's 'Lélio'; Arr. of Schubert's Wandererfantasie; Arr. of Weber's Polonaise brillante.*

(N) *** Chan. 9801. Lortie, Hague Residentie O, George Pehlivanian.

In the 1940s Liszt's transcription of Schubert's *Wandererfantasie* for piano and orchestra was a familar item in the concert hall and on the radio, but it is now something of a rarity. It goes without saying that Louis Lortie is second to none; indeed his version would now be a first recommendation, particularly as the remainder of his programme – the *Fantasia on a Theme from Beethoven's Ruins of Athens*, the Weber *Polonaise brillante* and the *Grande fantasie symphonique on Berlioz's 'Lélio'* – is so desirable. Lortie's aristocratic pianism and the fine playing of the Residentie Orchestra of The Hague under George Pehlivanian make this an exhilarating record. Excellent Chandos recording.

A Faust Symphony.

*** Ph. 454 460-2. Blochwitz, Hung. Radio Ch., Budapest Fest. O, Fischer.

*** Teldec 3984 22948-2. Domingo, Ch. of German Op., BPO, Barenboim.

(M) *** DG (ADD) 447 449-2. Riegel, Tanglewood Festival Ch., Boston SO, Bernstein.

*** EMI CDC5 55220-2. Seiffert, Ernst-Senff Ch. Male voices, Prague Philharmonic Ch., BPO, Rattle.

(N) **(*) Chan. 9814. Elsner, Danish Nat. R. Ch. and SO, Thomas Dausgaard.

Iván Fischer's recording of *A Faust Symphony*, with the Budapest Festival Orchestra and Peter Blochwitz as the tenor soloist in the finale, is quite simply the best since Beecham. Obviously it has the advantage of exceptionally rich and present recording with great range and body. An additional point of interest is the ending: we are offered a choice between Liszt's original ending which is purely orchestral (preferred by Wagner) and the familiar more extended choral ending. An outstanding issue.

Barenboim's flamboyant account is at one with his fine companion version of the *Dante Symphony*. It has great gusto, especially in the choral finale, and his freely moulded spontaneous style suits the opening movement when the tension is so well sustained – as it is in the gentle portrayal of Gretel in the *Andante*, where there is most beautiful playing from the Berlin Orchestra. Another plus point is the ardent and memorable solo contribution from Placido Domingo in the last movement. Fine spacious recording make this an enjoyable alternative to Fischer on Philips, which remains first choice.

Bernstein on DG seems to possess the ideal temperament for holding together grippingly the melodrama of the first movement, while the lovely *Gretchen* centrepiece is played most beautifully. Kenneth Riegel is an impressive tenor soloist in the finale, there is an excellent, well-balanced choral contribution, and the Boston Symphony Orchestra produce playing which is both exciting and atmospheric. While Fischer's version remains first choice, the Bernstein account makes a fine, mid-priced alternative.

Rattle's début recording with the Berlin Philharmonic brings an exceptionally warm and persuasive reading, recorded live. Rattle's spontaneity of expression carries the ear on magnetically. He is helped by ravishing playing from the Berlin players, not least the strings, with the central movement, *Gretchen*, emerging as the high point of the performance. That the recording, made in the Philharmonie, sets the orchestra at a slight distance, notably the brass, prevents tuttis from biting as hard and as dramatically as they can. The impact of Bernstein's analogue version from Boston is more powerful, but Rattle is closer to Beecham's pioneering stereo set, and on its own terms one quickly adjusts to the balances of the Berlin sound, relishing its beauty. The performance culminates in a rapt account of the choral apotheosis, with Peter Seiffert singing radiantly, headily beautiful through the range.

Chandos offer a performance that brings together the tenor Christian Elsner and the Danish Radio Chorus and Orchestra under Thomas Dausgaard. This is a finely paced and intelligent reading which has a good deal going for it. It does not in any way displace Iván Fischer's masterly account on Philips but those investing in it are unlikely to be greatly disappointed.

Hungarian Rhapsodies Nos. 1–6.

(M) **(*) Mercury (ADD) 432 015-2. LSO, Dorati – ENESCU: *Roumanian Rhapsody No. 1.* ***

Hungarian Rhapsodies Nos. 1–6; Hungarian Battle March; Rákóczy March.

(M) **(*) EMI (ADD) CDM7 64627-2. Philh. Hungarica or LPO, Boskovsky.

Dorati's is undoubtedly the finest set of orchestral *Hungarian Rhapsodies*. He brings out the gypsy flavour and, with lively playing from the LSO, there is both polish and sparkle. The Mercury recording is characteristically vivid.

Boskovsky does not fully catch the mercurial element, the sudden changes of mood which is the gypsy heritage of these pieces, but the Philharmonia Hungarica (who play in Nos. 1, 4 and 6 – *Carnival in Pest*) are obviously at home; and the LPO clearly enjoy the famous No. 2. The freshly remastered recordings (from 1977/8) sound well and, though Dorati on Mercury takes pride of place in this repertoire, this EMI disc certainly gives pleasure.

Mephisto Waltz No. 1.

(N) *** BBC mono BBCL 4059-2. LSO, Stokowski – GABRIELI: *Sonata pian e forte.* NIELSEN: *Symphony No. 6.* TIPPETT: *Concerto for Double String Orchestra.*

Stokowski's zestful and vibrant account of the first *Mephisto Waltz* comes with two rarities of the Stokowski discography, Nielsen's *Sixth Symphony* and the Tippett *Double Concerto.*

SYMPHONIC POEMS

Symphonic poems: *Ce qu'on entend sur la montagne (Bergsinfonie); Festklänge; Hunnenschlacht; Die Ideale; Von der Wiege bis zum Grabe;* (i) *Dante Symphony.*

(B) *** EMI double fforte (ADD) CZS5 68598-2 (2). Leipzig GO, Masur; (i) with Arndt, Leipzig Thomaskirche Ch.

Symphonic poems: *2 Episodes from Lenau's Faust; Hamlet; Héroïde funèbre; Hungaria; Prometheus;* (i) *Faust Symphony.*

(N) (B) *** EMI double fforte (ADD) CZS5 68595.2 (2). Leipzig GO, Masur; (i) with König, Leipzig R. Ch.

On the whole, Masur's survey of Liszt's symphonic poems is the finest we have had so far. The performances have a dramatic vitality that eludes Haitink, and the Leipzig orchestra's playing is even finer than that of the LPO on Philips. Some of the earlier pieces, such as *Ce qu'on entend sur la montagne* and *Festklänge*, suffer not only from formal weakness but also from a lack of interesting melodic invention. However, these performances – and, whatever one may think of it, this music – cast a strong spell, and with rare exceptions Masur proves a most persuasive advocate. *Hamlet* has great dramatic intensity, and *Die nächtliche Zug*, the first of the *Two Episodes from Lenau's Faust*, strikes the listener immediately with its intent, brooding atmosphere. Masur's *Faust Symphony* can certainly hold its own against most of its rivals, although in the *Gretchen* movement he moves things on, though not unacceptably. It is the rich sonority of the lower strings, the dark, perfectly blended woodwind-tone and the fine internal balance of the Leipzig Gewandhaus Orchestra that hold the listener throughout.

Ce qu'on entend sur la montagne; Festklänge; Mazeppa; Orpheus; Les Préludes; Prometheus; Tasso, lamento e trionfo.

(B) **(*) Ph. (IMS) (ADD) Duo 438 751-2 (2). LPO, Haitink.

Hamlet; Héroïde funèbre; Hungaria; Hunnenschlacht; Die Ideale; Mephisto Waltz No. 1; Von der Wiege bis zum Grabe.

(B) **(*) Ph. (IMS) (ADD) Duo 438 754-2 (2). LPO, Haitink.

Haitink's set includes all the tone poems in two double-CD sets. They are fine performances and recorded in exemplary sound even if they perhaps lack the histrionic dimension and vulgarity that is part of Liszt's make-up. The recordings have never sounded better – far more vivid than on the original LPs. Liszt invented the symphonic poem; here is an inexpensive and, for the most part, rewarding way to sample his achievement overall. There is good documentation.

Symphonic poems: From the Cradle to the Grave (Von der Wiege bis zum Grabe); Hamlet; Die Ideale; Orpheus.

(BB) *(**) Naxos 8.553355. New Zealand SO, Halász.

Michael Halász gets a vital and sensitive response from his fine New Zealand Orchestra in these tone poems, with some beautiful string-playing at the opening of *From the Cradle to the Grave* – an elusive, extended work that he holds together very well – and the opening of *Orpheus* is most evocative. He does not shirk the melodrama in *Die Ideale*, and *Hamlet* too is powerfully done. Artistically this is very impressive, but the recorded sound brings problems that will worry some listeners more than others. There is no lack of vividness but the balance is too close, and while all is well in *piano* and pianissimo passages, tuttis are less comfortable, with a degree of glare and congestion and a lack of space round the climaxes. Impressive just the same, and good value.

(i) *Hunnenschlacht; Mazeppa; Orpheus;* (ii) *Les Préludes* (symphonic poems).

*** Australian Decca Eloquence 466 706-2. (i) LAPO; (i) VPO; Mehta.

Zubin Mehta is in his element here. The performances are red-blooded and tremendously exciting. Liszt's vulgarity is played up in a swaggeringly extrovert way, but there is plenty of character too. The rich, vibrant recording is an audiophile's delight – the staggered entries throughout the strings in *Mazeppa* are thrilling. Equally praiseworthy is the pastoral atmosphere Mehta creates in *Orpheus* – with real sensitivity from the Los Angeles orchestra. Although Karajan's Berlin Philharmonic account of *Mazeppa* is in a class of its own, those who like Liszt with all the stops out will

certainly enjoy this Australian reissue, especially when the CD transfer is so vivid.

Mazeppa; Les Préludes.

(M) * RCA (ADD) 09026 63532-2. Boston Pops O, Fiedler –
CHOPIN: *Les Sylphides* **; PROKOFIEV: *Love for 3 Oranges: Suite.* **(*)

These performances are too literal and clipped to make a positive recommendation. Moreover, the orchestral playing is sometimes sloppy (the opening of *Mazeppa* especially so) and the 1960 sound is coarse under pressure. Those wishing for these two works should go straight to Karajan's supreme readings (on DG 453 130-2), which are vastly superior in every way (see above under *Fantasia on Hungarian Folk Tunes*).

Mazeppa; Les Préludes; Prometheus; Tasso, lamento e trionfo (symphonic poems).

(BB) *** Naxos 8.550487. Polish Nat. RSO (Katowice), Halász.

Michael Halász has the full measure of this repertoire, and this is one of the most successful collections of Liszt's symphonic poems to have emerged in recent years. He draws some remarkably fine playing from the Katowice Radio Orchestra. The brass playing is very impressive throughout, especially the trombones and tuba, who have the epic main theme of *Mazeppa*, but its grandiloquence is no less powerful in *Les Préludes*, weighty and never brash. The recording is spacious, with full natural string textures, but it is the resounding brass one remembers most.

Les Préludes.

(N)(M) *** DG 463 650-2. BRSO, Fricsay – DVORAK:
Symphony No. 9 in E min. (New World); SMETANA: *Má vlast: Vltava.* ***

Though it is unfashionable to say so, *Les Préludes* is easily the best of Liszt's symphonuc poems, alongside *Mazeppa*, and Fricsay's performance is masterly. It has great impulse, coupled to engaging detail and freshness, and the climax has dignity, the vulgarity minimized.

Tasso, lamento e trionfo.

**(*) Testament mono SBT 1129. Philh. O., Silvestri –
TCHAIKOVSKY: *Manfred Symphony.* *(*)

Silvestri's version of *Tasso* was one of his best recordings (second only perhaps to his account of Elgar's *In the South*). It comes up well in this new transfer but the Tchaikovsky coupling does not show the Romanian maestro at his best.

COMPLETE PIANO MUSIC
Complete piano music

Vol. 1: *Albumblatt in Waltz Form; Bagatelle Without Tonality; Caprice-valses Nos. 1 & 2; Ländler in A flat; Mephisto Waltzes Nos. 1–3; Valse impromptu; 4 Valses oubliées.*

*** Hyp. CDA 66201. Howard.

Vol. 2: *Ballades Nos. 1–2; Berceuse; Impromptu*

(Nocturne); *Klavierstück in A flat; 2 Légendes; 2 Polonaises.*

**(*) Hyp. CDA 66301. Howard.

Vol. 3: *Fantasia & Fugue on B-A-C-H; 3 Funeral Odes: Les Morts; La notte; Le Triomphe funèbre du Tasse; Grosses Konzertsolo; Prelude on Weinen, Klagen, Sorgen, Sagen; Variations on a Theme of Bach.*

** Hyp. CDA 66302. Howard.

Vol. 4: *Adagio in C; Etudes d'éxécution transcendante; Elégie sur des motifs de Prince Louis Ferdinand de Prusse; Mariotte.*

** Hyp. CDA 66357. Howard.

Vol. 5: Concert paraphrases: BERLIOZ: *L'Idée fixe; Overtures: Les Francs-Juges; Le Roi Lear; Marche des pèlerins; Valse des Sylphes.* CHOPIN: *6 Chants polonais.* SAINT-SAENS: *Danse macabre.*

*** Hyp. CDA 66346. Howard.

Vol. 6: Concert paraphrases: AUBER: *3 Pieces on Themes from La Muette de Portici.* BELLINI: *Réminiscences de Norma.* BERLIOZ: *Benvenuto Cellini: Bénédiction et serment.* DONIZETTI: *Réminiscences de Lucia di Lammermoor; Marche funèbre et Cavatina (Lucia).* ERNST (Duke of Saxe-Coburg-Gotha): *Tony: Hunting Chorus.* GLINKA: *Ruslan and Ludmilla: Tscherkessenmarsch.* GOUNOD: *Waltz from Faust.* HANDEL: *Almira: Sarabande & Chaconne.* MEYERBEER: *Illustrations de L'Africaine.* MOZART: *Réminiscences de Don Juan.* VERDI: *Aida: Danza sacra & Duetto finale.* TCHAIKOVSKY: *Eugene Onegin: Polonaise.* WAGNER: *Tristan: Isoldes Liebestod.* WEBER: *Der Freischütz: Overture.*

*** Hyp. CDA 66371/2. Howard.

Vol. 7: Chorales: *Crux ave benedicta; Jesu Christe; Meine Seele; Nun danket alle Gott; Nun ruhen all Wälder; O haupt; O Lamm Gottes; O Traurigkeit; Vexilla Regis; Was Gott tut; Wer nur den Lieben; Via Crucis; Weihachtsbaum; Weihnachtslied.*

** Hyp. CDA 66388. Howard.

Vol. 8: *Alleluia & Ave Maria; Ave Marias 1–4; Ave Maria de Arcadelt; Ave Maris stella; Harmonies poétiques et religieuses (complete); Hungarian Coronation Mass; Hymnes; Hymne du Pape; In festo transfigurationis; Invocation; O Roma nobilis; Sancta Dorothea; Slavimo slavno slaveni!; Stabat Mater; Urbi et orbi; Vexilla regis prodeunt; Zum Haus des Herrn.*

** Hyp. CDA 66421/2. Howard.

Vol. 9: *6 Consolations; 2 Elégies; Gretchen (from Faust Symphony); Sonata in B min.; Totentanz.*

** Hyp. CDA 66429. Howard (piano).

Vol. 10: Concert paraphrases: bellini: *Hexaméron (Grand Bravura Variations on the March from I Puritani).* berlioz: *Symphonie fantastique. Un portrait en musique de la Marquise de Blocqueville.*

**(*) Hyp. CDA 66433. Howard.

Vol. 11: *Abschied (Russisches Volkslied); Am Grabe Richard Wagners; Carrousel de Madame P-N; Dem Andenken*

Petöfis; Epithalium; Klavierstück in F sharp; En Rêve; 5 Klavierstücke; Mosonyis Grabgeleit; Recueillement; Resignazione; Romance oubliée; RW (Venezia); Schlaflos! Frage und Antwort; Sospiri; Toccata; Slyepoi (Der blinde Sänger); Die Trauergondel (La Lugubre Gondola); Trauervorspiel und Trauermarsch; Trübe Wolken (Nuages gris); Ungams Gott; Ungarisches Königslied; Unstern: Sinistre; Wiegenlied (Chant de berceau).

**(*) Hyp. CDA 66445. Howard.

Vol. 12: *Années de pèlerinage, 3rd Year (Italy); 5 Hungarian Folksongs; Historical Hungarian Portraits.*

** Hyp. CDA 66448. Howard.

Vol. 13: Concert paraphrases: ALLEGRI/MOZART: *A la Chapelle Sitine: Miserere d'Allegri et Ave verum corpus de Mozart.* BACH: *Fantasia & Fugue in G min.; 6 Preludes & Fugues for Organ.*

** Hyp. CDA 66438. Howard.

Vol. 14: *Christus; Polonaises de St Stanislas; Salve Polonia; St Elizabeth.*

**(*) Hyp. CDA 66466. Howard.

Vol. 15: Concert paraphrases of Lieder: BEETHOVEN: *Adelaïde; An die ferne Geliebte; 6 Gellert Lieder; 6 Lieder von Goethe; An die ferne Geliebte.* DESSAUER: *3 Lieder.* FRANZ: *Er est gekommenin Sturm und Regen; 12 Lieder.* MENDELSSOHN: *7 Lieder including Auf Flügeln des Gesanges.* CLARA & ROBERT SCHUMANN: *10 Lieder including Frülingsnacht; Widmung.*

**(*) Hyp. CDA 66481/2. Howard.

Vol. 16: Piano transcriptions: DAVID: *Bunte Reihe (24 character pieces for violin and piano), Op. 30.*

*** Hyp. CDA 66506. Howard.

Vol. 17: Concert paraphrases: DONIZETTI: *Spirito gentil* from *La favorita; Marche funèbre* from *Don Sebastien.* GOUNOD: *Les Sabéennes (Berceuse)* from *La Reine de Saba.* GRETRY: *Die Rose (Romance)* from *Zémire et Azor.* MEYERBEER: *3 Illustrations du Prophète; Fantasia & Fugue on Ad nos, ad salutarem undam* on a theme from *Le Prophète.* MOSONYI: *Fantasy on Szép Ilonka.* WAGNER: *Spinning Song & Ballade* from *Der fliegende Holländer; Pilgrims' Chorus & O du, mein holder Abendstern* from *Tannhäuser; Valhalla* from *The Ring; Feierlicher Marsch zum heiligen Grail* from *Parsifal.*

**(*) Hyp. CDA 66571/2. Howard.

Vol. 18: Concert paraphrases: BEETHOVEN: *Capriccio alla turca; Fantasy* from *Ruins of Athens.* LASSEN: *Symphonisches Zwischenspiel zu Calderons Schauspiel über allen Zauber Liebe.* MENDELSSOHN: *Wedding March & Dance of the Elves* from *A Midsummer Night's Dream.* WEBER: *Einsam bin ich, nicht alleine* from *La preciosa.* HEBBEL: *Nibelungen.*

**(*) Hyp. CDA 66575. Howard.

Leslie Howard's ambitious project to record all the piano music of Liszt is now complete, and at least two of these earlier issues have already collected a Grand Prix du Disque in Budapest (Volumes 5 and 6). The performances are very capable and musicianly, and there are moments of poetic feeling, but for the most part his playing rarely touches distinction. The kind of concentration one finds in great Liszt pianists such as Arrau, Kempff and Richter (and there are many younger artists whose names also spring to mind) rarely surfaces. Howard's technical equipment is formidable, but poetic imagination and the ability to grip the listener are here less developed: his rushed account of the *Sonata* does not really stand up against the current competition. One of the most interesting issues is Volume 16, the *Bunte Reihe* of Ferdinand David (1810–70), a contemporary of Mendelssohn. These are transcriptions of music for violin and piano in which the violin seems hardly to be missed at all. Leslie Howard plays them beautifully. Certainly the coverage is remarkable and, if this playing rarely takes the breath away either by its virtuosity or poetic insights, it is unfailingly intelligent and the recordings are first class.

Vol. 19: *Die Lorelei; 3 Liebesträume; Songs for Solo Piano, Books 1–2.*

*** Hyp. CDA 66593. Howard.

Vol. 20: *Album d'un voyageur: Années de pèlerinage,* 1st, 2nd & 3rd Years (first versions); *Chanson du Béarn; Fantaisie romantique sur deux mélodies suisses; Faribolo pastour.*

*** Hyp. CDA 66601/2. Howard.

Vol. 21: ROSSINI: *Soirées musicales; Grande Fantaisie on Motifs from Soirées musicales; 2nd Fantaisie on Motifs from Soirées musicales.* DONIZETTI: *Nuits d'été à Pausilippe.* MERCADANTE: *Soirées italiennes. 3 Sonetti di Petrarca* (1st version); *Venezia e Napoli* (1st set).

*** Hyp. CDA 66661/2. Howard.

Vol. 22: Concert paraphrases of Beethoven symphonies: *Symphonies Nos. 1–9.*

** Hyp. CDA 66671/5. Howard.

Vol. 23: BERLIOZ: (i) *Harold in Italy.* LISZT: (i) *Romance oubliée.* GOUNOD: *Hymne à Sainte Cécile.* MEYERBEER: *Le Moine; Festmarsch.*

**(*) Hyp. CDA 66683. Howard, (i) with Coletti.

Vol. 24: Concert paraphrases: BEETHOVEN: *Septet, Op. 20.* MOZART: *Requiem Mass, K.626: Confutatis; Lacrimosa. Ave verum corpus, K.618.* VERDI: *Requiem Mass: Agnus Dei.* ROSSINI: *Cujus animam: Air du Stabat Mater; 3 Choeurs religieux: La Charité.* GOLDSCHMIDT: *7 Tödsunden: Liebesszene und Fortunas Kugel.* MENDELSSOHN: *Wasserfahrt und der Jäger Abschied.* WEBER: *Schlummerlied mit Arabesken; Leyer und Schwert-Heroïde.* HUMMEL: *Septet No. 1 in D min.*

** Hyp. CDA 66761/2. Howard.

Vol. 25: *San Francesco: Prelude: The Canticle of the Sun; Canticle of the Sun of St Francis of Assisi. Ave maris stella; Gebet; Ich liebe dich; Il m'aimait tant; O pourquoi donc; Ora pro nobis; O sacrum convivium* (2 versions); *Rezignazione – Ergebung; Salve regina; Von der Wiege bis zum Grabe; Die Zelle in Nonnenwerth.*

**(*) Hyp. CDA 66694. Howard.

Vol. 26: *Allegro di bravura; Apparitions; Berceuse; 12 Etudes; Feuilles d'album; Galop de bal; Hungarian Recruiting Dances; Impromptu Brillant on Themes of Rossini & Spontini; Klavierstücke (aus der Bonn Beethoven-Kantatej); 2 Klavierstücke; Marche hongroise; Notturno No. 2; Rondo di bravura; Scherzo in G min.; Variation on a Waltz of Diabelli; Variations on a Theme of Rossini; 5 Variations on a Theme from Méhul's Joseph; Waltz in A; Waltz in E flat.*

**(*) Hyp. CDA 66771/2. Howard.

Vol. 27: *Canzone napolitana* (2 versions); *La Cloche sonne; Gleanings from Woronince; God Save the Queen; Hungarian National Folk Tunes (Ungarische Nationalmelodien); Hussite Song; La Marseillaise; Rákóczi March; Szózat & Hungarian hymn; Vive Henri IV.*

*** Hyp. CDA 66787. Howard.

Vol. 28: *Bulow-Marsch; Heroischer Marsch im Ungarischer Geschwindmarsch; Csárdás; Csárdás macabre; Csárdás obstiné; Festmarsch zur Goethejubiläumsfeier; Festpolonaise; Festvorspiel; Galop in A min.; Grand galop chromatique; Huldigungsmarsch; Kunstierfestzug zur Schillerfeier; Marche héroïque; Mazurka brillante; Mephisto Polka; Petite valse; Rákóczy Marsch; Vorn Fels zurn Meer; La Favorite; Scherzo & March; Siegesmarsch; Ungarischer Marsch zur Krönungsfeier in Ofen-Pest; Ungarischer Stürmmarsch; Zweite Festmarsch.*

**(*) Hyp. CDA 66811/2. Howard.

The two Liszt *Songbooks* on Volume 19 offer 12 early Lieder in engagingly simple transcriptions. Leslie Howard plays them beautifully, as he does the three *Liebesträume*, of which only the third is really familiar. Volume 20 centres on what Leslie Howard prefers to call *Album d'un Voyager*, the early edition of what we know as the *Années de pèlerinage* (which the composer tried, unsuccessfully, to suppress). Book I includes a flamboyant extra item, *Lyon*, inspired by a workers' uprising, and only two of the pieces in Book II, *Fleurs mélodiques des Alpes*, were retained in the final set of *Années de pèlerinage*. Apart from the *Paraphrases* in Book III, this collection also includes an unknown major improvisatory work of the same period and inspiration, the 18-minute-long *Fantaisie romantique sur deux mélodies suisses*, with plenty of opportunities for bravura in the latter part. A fascinating collection, very well played indeed. Volume 21 is lightweight, opening with the Rossini *Soirées musicales*, which we know from the much later Britten orchestrations, and *Soirées italiennes*, based on rather less interesting music by Mercadante. For the second disc Howard returns to the initial versions of the *Années de pèlerinage*, including the *Petrarch Sonnets* and *Venezia e Napoli*. The second CD ends with a pair of *Grand Fantasias* on themes from the *Soirées* that began the recital.

Volume 22 brings us to Liszt's paraphrases of the nine Beethoven symphonies. Leslie Howard's 'interpretations' are sound throughout; he makes more of some movements than others (the first movement of the *Eroica* could be more compelling) and the resonance of the recording is not ideal for revealing detail. The *Ninth* works impressively, if not as earth-shaking as Katsaris's version on Teldec. Overall, this is surprisingly enjoyable to listen to; without the orchestral colour, one notices the more what is happening in the internal arguments of these inexhaustible works.

Volume 23 is an effective transcription of Berlioz's *Harold in Italy* for viola and piano, and Howard takes the opportunity to include Liszt's own *Romance oubliée* for the same combination. Here Paul Coletti joins the pianist, and the performances are well played and spontaneous, if not earth-shaking. The transcriptions of the Beethoven and Hummel *Septets* in Volume 24, however, do not really work at all. This music either needs the instrumental colour or a much more witty approach (and the resonant recording is not helpful). However, there are some other paraphrases here that are much more effective, notably the excerpts from Goldschmidt's *Die sieben Todsünden* and two transcribed Mendelssohn choruses.

The *Cantico del Sol di San Francesco d'Assisi* is pleasantly based on *In dulci jubilo*. Then comes the chrysalis of the symphonic poem, *From the Cradle to the Grave*, which was greatly expanded in its orchestral form. Volume 26 is almost entirely devoted to works written when Liszt was a teenager, and the *Variations* show his mettle. Volume 27 offers patriotic songs and airs in a much more interesting and varied programme than it looks at first glance. *God Save the Queen* was written for a British tour in 1840/41 and the tune is immediately interestingly varied in the opening bars. *La Marseillaise* starts off straightforwardly and the variants come later, but the tune reasserts itself strongly. The *Ungarische Nationalmelodien* is in effect a sketch for the *Sixth Hungarian Rhapsody*. But there are plenty of enticing ideas here, notably the three-part suite, *Glanes de Woronince*, and the delightful French folksong arrangements, *Vive Henry IV* and *La Cloche sonne*. Howard is at his most imaginative. Volume 28 is essentially a collection of marches and lively extrovert pieces, but they are very well presented.

Vol. 29: *Hungarian Themes & Rhapsodies, Nos. 1–22.*

** Hyp. CDA 66851/2. Howard.

Here is the source material for Liszt's *Hungarian Rhapsodies* and the *Hungarian Fantasia* in earlier, more earthy form, before the dances became sophisticated concert repertoire. There is even an early version (subsequently discarded) of the *Consolation No. 3*. Of course, not all the music here is equally interesting, but Leslie Howard brings it to life fluently. His playing has convincing rubato but lacks something in flair and adrenalin.

Vol. 30: Operatic fantasies, concert paraphrases and transcriptions: DONIZETTI: *Valse de concert on 2 Motifs of Lucia de Lammermoor & Parisina.* GOUNOD: *Les Adieux (Rêverie on a Theme from Roméo et Juliette).* ERKEL: *Schwanengesang & March to Hunyadi László.* MEYERBEER: *Réminscences de Robert le diable: Cavatine; Valse infernale.* MOZART: *Fantasy on Themes from Nozze di Figaro & Don Giovanni.* VERDI: *Ernani; Rigoletto; Il Trovatore: Miserere* (concert paraphrases); *Réminiscences de Simon Boccanegra.* WAGNER: *Lohengrin: Elsa's Bridal Procession; Wedding March; Elsa's Dream; Lohengrin's Reproof. Fantasy on Themes from Rienzi.* WEBER: overture: *Oberon.*

** Hyp. CDA 66861/2. Howard.

It is difficult for present-day music-lovers to appreciate that in Liszt's time even a piece as familiar as Weber's *Oberon Overture* was relatively inaccessible outside the opera house, though it must be said that Howard does not make a great deal of it – the allegros sound unpianistic. But, of course, his operatic paraphrases were designed both to entertain and to remind listeners not only of the tunes that made up the best-known operas of Mozart, Verdi and Wagner but those of lesser composers too. Some of this music ideally needs a Horowitz, but for the most part Leslie Howard is up to the display and pyrotechnics which Liszt's embellishments require. However, Mozart's *Là ci darem* is heavily romanticized and the Verdi paraphrases also need more impetus. The Wagner transcriptions are more successful.

Vol. 31: 'The Schubert transcriptions' (Vol. 1): *Ave Maria; Der Gondelfahrer; Erlkönig; Märche für das Pianoforte übertragen: Trauermarsch (Grande marche funèbre); Grande marche; Grande marche characteristique. Marche militaire*(concert paraphrase); *Mélodies hongroises; Die Rose; La Sérénade; Soirées de Vienne; 2 Transcriptions for Sophie Menter.*

** Hyp. CDA 66951/3. Howard.

Vol. 32: 'The Schubert transcriptions' (Vol. 2): *Die Forelle; Frühlingsglaube; Marche hongroise* (2 versions); *Meeresstille; 6 Mélodies favorites de la belle meunière; 6 Mélodies of Franz Schubert; 4 Sacred Songs; Schuberts Ungarische Melodien; Schwanengesang; 12 Songs from Winterreise; Ständchen (Leise flehen).*

** Hyp. CDA 66954/6. Howard.

Vol. 33: 'The Schubert transcriptions' (Vol. 3): *Die Forelle; Die Gestirne; 2 Lieder; 12 Lieder* (2 versions); *Marche hongroise; Meerestille* (2 versions); *Müllerlieder; Die Nebensonnen; Schwanengesang; Soirées de Vienne: Valse caprice No. 6; 12 Songs from Winterreise.*

** Hyp. CDA 66957/9. Howard.

Liszt obviously admired Schubert enormously and wanted to champion him as well as play his music. The songs were obvious candidates because of their sheer tunefulness, but he was also attracted to Schubert's lighter dance music. The *Soirées de Vienne* really suit Howard and are played with a pleasantly Schubertian feeling and nicely judged rubato, while the *Valse caprice* is quite charming. And what of the songs? The four *Geistliche Lieder* (*Sacred Songs*) which open the collection are made to seem unremittingly sombre, and Howard has a tendency to over-characterize the darker songs elsewhere. *Die Forelle* and some of the other most famous songs are not very imaginatively done, although *Erlkönig* comes off well. But not everyone will want two complete *Schwanengesangs* without a singer. Of course, the transcriptions are free – sometimes (but not often) very free – and there is more Liszt than Schubert. Leslie Howard plays them (as Liszt surely would have done) with comparable freedom in matters of phrasing and rubato, and for the most part he is convincing, if at times his tempi seem a little too indulgent.

Vol. 34: *12 Grandes études; Morceau de salon.*

*** Hyp. CDA 66973. Howard.

These *Grandes études* were the pilot version of the *Etudes d'exécution transcendente*, which appeared a quarter of a century later, in 1851. This (as with so much of this invaluable series) is their first recording, as the composer expressly forbade their performance. This music demands great bravura, and Leslie Howard surpasses himself in rising to the challenge with remarkable confidence. There is much to tickle the ear here, and all this music is Liszt's own and is not borrowed from others!

Vol. 35: *Arabesques (2 mélodies russes):* (ALABIEV: *Le rossignol.* P. BULAKHOV: *Chanson bohémienne*). Russian transcriptions: AN AMATEUR FROM ST PETERSBURG: *Mazurka.* (Liszt's) *Prelude à la Polka de Borodin.* BORODIN: (i) *Polka.* K. BULAKHOV: *Galop russe.* CUI; DARGOMIZHSKY: *Tarentelles.* WIELHORSKY: *Autrefois.* Hungarian transcriptions: *Rákóczi-March.* ABRANYI: *Flower Song.* FESTETICS: *Spanish Ständchen.* SZECHENYI: *Introduction & Hungarian March.* SZABADI/MASSENET: *Revive Szegedin!.* VEGH: *Valse de concert.* ZICHY: *Valse d'Adèle.*

*** Hyp. CDA 66984. Howard, (i) with Moore.

Liszt was especially enthusiastic about new Russian music and, as can by seen from the piece based on the *Mazurka* of 'An Amateur from St Petersburg', he didn't restrict his interest to famous names, although they are all here. He composed his own piano solo introduction to Borodin's engaging four-handed *Polka*, which is included here with the help of Philip Moore. Most of the Hungarian names are unfamiliar but the music itself, if slight, is often delightful. The two opening *Arabesques* are enticing; but everything tickles the ear, especially Abrányi's *Flower Song*, and no one can say that Leslie Howard does not relish its glittering colours. As usual, good recording. This is a most enjoyable collection.

Vol. 36: *Consolations Nos. 1–6; Elégie: Entwurf der Ramann; Excelsior! (Prelude to The Bells of Strasburg Cathedral); Fanfare for the Unveiling of the Carl August Memorial; Geharnischte Lieder; National Hymn (Kaiser Wilhelm!); Rosario Schlummerlied im Grabe; Die Zelle in Nonnenwerth (2 versions); Weimars Volkslieder Nos. 1–2.*

**(*) Hyp. CDA 66995. Howard.

The first version of the six *Consolations* misses out the most famous *Third in D flat* and substitutes a less memorable piece in *C sharp minor*, but in all other respects these earlier pieces are valid in their own right and are well worth having on disc, although the performances do tend to languish a bit. The rest of the programme consists of novelties, including cathedral bells (celebrated here by the two versions of *Die Zelle in Nonnenwerth* as well as by *Excelsior!*), all unknown, many of them occasional pieces and of no great interest except for *Rosario*, three gentle settings of *Ave Maria*, which are persuasively atmospheric.

Vol. 37: BULOW: *Tanto gentile e tanto onesta.* CONRADI: *Zigeuner-Polka.* ERNST: *Die Gräberinsel der Fürsten zu Gotha.* HERBECK: *Tanzmomente Nos. 1–8; No. 4 (alternative).* LASSEN: *Ich weil' in teifer Einsamkeit; Löse, Himmel meine Seele (2 versions).* LESSMAN: *3 Lieder from Julius Wolff's Tannhäuser.* LISZT/LOUIS FERDINAND: *Elégie sur des motifs du Prince Louis Ferdinand de Prusse.*

** Hyp. CDA 67004. Howard.

Liszt's interest in Johann Ritter von Herbeck reflects the latter's importance in Viennese musical life of the time. He was choirmaster as well as composer, and his *Tanzmomente* consists of eight dances, many of them waltzes of some charm. Liszt's transcriptions flatter them agreeably and he expands the finale considerably and to good effect. Otto Lessen was a journalist and theatre manager, and his songs also make agreeable transcriptions, as does Hans von Bülow's *Tanto gentile*. The closing *Zigeuner-Polka* of August Conradi was a pop hit in its day, and Liszt's arrangement adds a bit of spice to the melodic sequence. All this music is exceedingly rare, but its musical interest is frankly limited. The Lassen and Bülow pieces are the highlights.

Vol. 38: 'Concert études & Episodes from Lenau's Faust': *Les Préludes; 3 Etudes de concert; 2 Concert Studies; 2 Episodes from Lenau's Faust.*

*** Hyp. CDA 67015. Howard.

Volume 38 is a good deal more substantial than its predecessor, starting off with the popular *Les Préludes*, which anticipates the orchestral version fairly closely, with a few minor differences near the end. The transcription is made in pianistic terms and works well. The three *Etudes de concert* continue in familiar territory, especially the third, a Lisztian romantic blossoming better known as 'Un sospiro' (which Howard presents boldly). *Waldesrauschen* and *Gnomenreigen* (beautifully done) are equally welcome, as is the opportunity of hearing the two *Faust* pieces together in their piano versions, of which the *Mephisto Waltz* is easily the more famous. A rewarding collection, very well played and recorded.

Vol. 39: *Années de pèlerinage, 1st Year (Switzerland); 3 Morceaux suisses.*

** Hyp. CDA 67026. Howard.

With Volume 39, Leslie Howard moves on to the first year of the *Années de pèlerinage*, for the most part playing the second versions. But this is music we know well in the hands of artists like Wilhelm Kempff. Howard provides thoroughly musical performances, but without finding the degree of poetry and magic that these evocative pieces deserve. The three *Morceaux suisses* come off brightly and quite spontaneously. Liszt's descriptive powers are more literally used here, with a storm graphically depicted in the second, *Un soir dans la montagne.*

Vol. 40: *Ballade No. 2 (first version); Festmarsch zur Säkularfeier von Goethes Geburtstag; Seconde Marche hongroise; Nocturne (Impromptu); Concert paraphrases and transcriptions: Galop russe (Bulhakov); Gaudeamus igitur (2 versions: Paraphrase; Humoreske); Lyubila ya (Wielhorsky); La Marche pour le Sultan Abdul Médjid-Khan (Donizetti); Seconda Mazurka di Tirindelli; Le*

Rossignol-Air russe (Alyabiev); *Una stella amica-Valzer* (Pezzini).

** Hyp. CDA 67034. Howard.

This collection is described as *Pièces d'occasion*, and much of the music here is desperately trivial. Liszt's paraphrase on *Gaudeamus igitur* at nine minutes outlasts its welcome, while the second version, called *Humoreske*, is even less entertaining. Howard takes everything fairly seriously and, though his playing is secure technically, he seldom dazzles the ear, which is surely what the composer would have done.

Vol. 41: Recitations with piano: (i) *A holt költo szerelme (The Dead Poet's Love);*(ii) *Helge's Treue (Helge's Loyalty); Lenore; Der traurige Mönch (The Sad Monk);* (iii) *Slyepoi (The Blind Man).*

*(**) Hyp. CDA 67045. Howard, with (i) Eles; (ii) Kahler; (iii) Stepanov.

A real curiosity, but essentially a specialist compilation. While one is willing to follow an opera libretto alongside a recording, to have to listen to a spoken poetic narrative in German, Hungarian or Russian alongside its musical illustration while following the translation is a different matter. Certainly the ballades here are not lacking in melodrama. *Lenore*, whose lover fails to come back from the wars, cries out blasphemously against God. Night falls, and she hears the sound of hooves clip-clopping: there he is on his horse to take her to the bridal bed. They travel 'a hundred miles' through the night, later followed by demons, and at the end of the journey her lover is no more than a brittle skeleton. All the lurid tales here obviously excited Liszt's imagination, and Howard rises to the occasion. But one wonders how often one would want to return to a CD of this kind.

Vol. 42: Concert paraphrases: AUBER: *Tyrolean Melody* from *La Fiancée; Tarantelle di bravura* from *Masaniello.* BELLINI: *Réminiscences des Puritains; Introduction et Polonaise* from *I Puritani; Grosse Concert-fantaisie* on *La Sonnambula.* DONIZETTI: *Réminiscences de Lucrezia Borgia: Grandes fantaisies I & II.* MEYERBEER: *Réminiscences des Huguenots.* (i) MOZART: *Song of the Two Armed Men* from *Die Zauberflöte* (piano duet). RAFF: *Andante finale* and *Marsch* from *König Alfred.* VERDI: *Coro di festa e marcia funebre* from *Don Carlos; Salve Maria de l'opéra de Jérusalem* from *I lombardi* (two versions). WAGNER: *Pilgrims' Chorus* from *Tannhäuser; Am stillen Herd – Lied* from *Die Meistersinger.*

** Hyp. CDA 67101/2. Howard, (i) with Moore.

Liszt wrote his concert paraphrases in order to present his audiences with music they would hear but rarely in the opera house. To come off, they need to be played with dazzling virtuosity and – above all – real charisma. Leslie Howard is reliably equal to most of their technical demands but he does not titillate the ear, and much of this music tends to lose the listener's attention. These records have been praised elsewhere, but for us they did not prove very stimulating listening. For instance, Howard takes the *Pilgrims' chorus* from *Tannhäuser* unbelievably slowly; he is at his best in the Bellini items. As a sound document to demonstrate the range of Liszt's operatic interest this is valuable, but the playing is seldom very exciting in itself.

Vol. 43: *Années de pèlerinage, 1st Year, Switzerland: Au bord d'une source* (with coda for Sgambati). *Années de pèlerinage, 2nd Year, Italy; Supplement: Venezia e Napoli.*

**(*) Hyp. CDA 67107. Howard.

This is one of Howard's more spontaneous recitals. *Au bord d'une source* comes off delightfully, and the brief nine-bar additional coda, which Liszt wrote for his friend, the young composer/pianist Giovanni Sgambati, makes a charming (if superfluous) postlude. Howard is also at his best in the *Venezia e Napoli* Supplement, in which the closing *Tarantella* sparkles iridescently. The earlier pieces of the *Second Year* come off well enough, but the *Dante Sonata* needs more grip and fire than Howard finds for it. Excellent recording.

Vol. 44: Concert paraphrases: BEETHOVEN: *Symphonies Nos. 3 (Marche funèbre); 5–7* (complete) (first versions); *No. 6 (5th Movement)* (second version); *No. 7* (fragment); *Adelaïde* (two versions); *Fantasy* from *Ruins of Athens* (first version). BERLIOZ: *Marche au supplice* from *Symphonie fantastique* (second version). LISZT: *Cadenza for 1st Movement of Beethoven's Piano Concerto No. 3.*

** Hyp. CDA 67111/3. Howard.

Once again these recordings are valuable as documentation in showing how brilliantly Liszt transcribed Beethoven's orchestral works, preserving all the important detail. But Leslie Howard seems concerned to lay the music out before us with care for every bit of that detail, without seeking to create enough thrust to take the music onwards. The account of the *Fifth Symphony*, which opens the first disc, has almost no adrenalin whatsoever and proceeds onward as a very routine affair, while the *Marche funèbre* from the *Eroica* is similarly very literal in feeling. The *Pastoral Symphony* might be thought to work well with a simple, straightforward approach, especially when Howard's playing of the Scherzo and the storm sequence generates proper bravura. But then the *Shepherd's Hymn of Thanksgiving* is presented with little warmth of feeling. The opening of the *Seventh* has a false start, for we are first given only a fragment. When Howard begins again, the *Introduction* seems to go on for a long time but the allegro has momentum, and the other movements have more life than the other symphonies – especially the Scherzo, which really sparkles – although the articulation in the finale could be cleaner. The programme ends with excerpts from Berlioz's *Symphonie fantastique*, with first the *idée fixe* languorously turned into a 'nocturne' (which does not work especially well), followed by a bold, lively *Marche au supplice* which at least ends the programme vigorously. As with the rest of this series, the recording is excellent.

Vol. 45: *Feuille morte – Elégie d'après Soriano; Grand Concert Fantasia on Spanish Themes; Rapsodie Espagnole; La romanesca* (first and second versions); *Rondeau fantastique* on *El contrabandista.*

**(*) Hyp. CDA 67145. Howard.

Collecting virtually all of Liszt's Spanish-inspired solo piano music, this is one of Howard's more impressive discs. There is not quite all the necessary dash in the *Grand Concert Fantasia*, but there is some glittering fingerwork in the more familiar *Rapsodie Espagnole*. He does not find a great deal of inspiration in the alternative versions of *La romanesca*, but plays the *Feuille morte* beautifully, with just the right touch of romantic feeling. This comes as an interlude before the closing *Rondeau fantastique*, which produces arresting digital dexterity, but where one feels he could have let his hair down just a little bit more. He is excellently recorded.

Vol. 46: 'Meditations': *Responsories & antiphons.*

** Hyp. CDA 67161/2. Howard.

This set is in essence a series of simple chorales: settings of the matutinal plaintchant responsories from the Offices for Christmas (12) and Holy Week – Maundy Thursday (22), Good Friday (19), Holy Saturday (19) – and for the Office for the Dead (24), with ('for completeness' sake') eleven alternative harmonizations. The chants are accompanied for the most part in four and occasionally three parts. Liszt's harmony is innocently simple, reflecting the Lutheran hymn tradition, without frills. Howard plays them simply too, but dedicatedly and never didactically. However, with the average timing of each item around a minute, these are not collections to listen to in bulk, for monotony inevitably sets in after just a few of these essentially ingenuous arrangements.

Vol. 47: Music intended for a first cycle of *Harmonies poétiques et religieuses* (1847): *Litanies de Marie* (first and second versions); *Miserere* (first version); *Pater noster d'après la Psalmodie de l'Eglise* (first version); *Hymne de l'enfant à son réveil* (second version); *Prose des morts – De profundis* (second version); *La Lampe du temple* (first version); *Hymne; Bénédiction* (second version). Earlier related pieces: *Prière d'un enfant à son réveil; Prélude* (first version).

*** Hyp. CDA 67187. Howard.

This is surely one of the most valuable of Leslie Howard's pioneering series, and all Lisztians should have it. Almost all the music recorded here is unpublished, and none of it has been previously recorded. The *Harmonies poétiques et religieuses* is one of the composer's key works and its gestation in these earlier pieces is both fascinating and musically rewarding. Howard has never played better, and his account of the remarkable *Prose de morts – De profundis* is arresting, as are both versions of *Litanies de Marie*, sombre and commanding. He shows the composer at his most flamboyantly garrulous in the *Hymne*, with its cascades of notes. But his playing in the gentler pieces is even more memorable, notably the *Hymn* and *Prière de l'enfant* and *La Lampe du temple* while the *Bénédiction* is quite magical. Excellent recording.

Vol. 48: *Etudes d'exécution transcendante d'après Paganini* (complete); with *No. 1* (second version); *No. 5* (alternative); *Grandes études de Paganini* (complete); *Mazeppa* (intermediate version); *Technische Studien No. 62: Sprünge mit der Tremolo-Begleitung.*

**(*) Hyp. CDA 67193. Howard.

It would be a pity if Leslie Howard's glittering accounts of Liszt's *Grandes études de Paganini* escaped the attention of the general collector because they are 'hidden away' in this survey. He is clearly enjoying himself and his delectable digital dexterity is consistently ear-tickling, with the familiar numbers like *La campanella* sounding crisply minted. Rhythms are lifted spontaneously, even wittily, and these sparkling performances leap out of the speakers. He plays the more difficult *Etudes d'exécution transcendante d'après Paganini* with flair also, but here there are some technical smudges, although not enough to impair enjoyment; the alternative version of No. 1, incorporating a study by Schumann (Op. 10/2), is well worth having on disc. The 'intermediate' version of *Mazeppa* is structurally unconvincing yet demands enormous virtuosity; here it sounds flurried and overstressed, obviously reaching the outer limit of Leslie Howard's technique.

Vol. 49: '*Schubert & Weber Transcriptions*': SCHUBERT: *Impromptus in E flat; in G flat, D.899; Die Rose* (intermediate version); *Wanderer Fantasy in C.* WEBER: *Jubel Overture; Konzertstück; Polonaise brillante.*

**(*) Hyp. CDA 67203. Howard.

Liszt reorganized the pianistic layout of the Schubert *Wanderer Fantasy* with the excuse of taking advantage of the greater compass of the keyboard in the mid-nineteenth century and making the score more 'pianistic'. His own version involved considerable changes in the finale, which now sounds weightily orchestral, without using an orchestra. Leslie Howard gives a commanding and convincing account of the Liszt score, yet playing with real Schubertian feeling in the serenely lyrical *Adagio*. But the biggest surprise here comes in Liszt's shortened version of Schubert's famous *Impromptu in G flat*, where at the reprise of the main theme the melody is taken up an octave, with a much more elaborate accompaniment. The result is (enjoyably) highly romantic, but not at all Schubertian. Liszt's brilliant transcriptions of Weber's *Konzertstück* and *Jubel Overture* adhere fairly closely to the original texts, but demand great virtuosity, especially so in the concertante work, where the orchestral and piano parts are combined, to be played by two very busy hands. The *Polonaise brillante* (also originally for piano and orchestra) is more freely transcribed, with Weber's ideas further extended, notably in the introduction. Howard plays all this music with vigour and enthusiasm, and if at times bravura detail is lost in the pianistic stampedes, this is still impressive; the Lisztian flamboyance is well projected.

Vol. 50: 'Liszt at the opera V': Concert paraphrases: AUBER: *Souvenir de La Fiancée* (third version); *Tarantelle di bravura* from *Masaniello* (first version). BELLINI: *Fantaisie sur des motifs favoris* from *La sonnambula* (second version). DONIZETTI: *Fantaisie sur des motifs* from *Lucrezia Borgia.* HALEVY: *Réminiscences de La Juive.* MEYERBEER: *Réminiscences des Huguenots* (first version). PACINI: *Grande fantaisie sur des thèmes* from *Niobe.* ROSSINI: *William Tell Overture.* WAGNER: *Festspiel und Brautlied* from *Lohengrin; Einzug der Gäste auf der Wartburg* from *Tannhäuser.*

**(*) Hyp. CDA 67231/2. Howard.

This is discussed below with Volume 54.

Vol. 51: 'Paralipomènes': Après une lecture du Dante: Dante Sonata (first, second and third versions); A la chapelle Sixtine – Miserere d'Allegri et Ave verum de Mozart (first version); Elégie (Die Zelle in Nonnenwerth) (first version); Grand solo de concert (first version); Prelude & Fugue on B-A-C-H (first version); Ungarische National-Melodien Nos. 1–3 & Rákóczi marsch; Romance oubliée (draft); Sposalizio (first version); Weihnachtsbaum (Christmas Tree Suite).

*** Hyp. CDA 67233/4. Howard.

To have three different early versions of the *Dante Sonata* (altogether about an hour of music) might be thought by the average collector as being too much of a good thing, but Howard plays them all with prodigious virtuosity. This famous highlight of the second year of the *Années de pèlerinage* started life under the title *Paralipomènes à la Divina Commedia*, and originally had two distinct sections, the first of which comes to a full close. It has one thematic idea which the composer later deleted. The second revised single-movement version bears the familar title, *Après une lecture du Dante – Fantasia Quasi Sonata* and this resembles the final (fourth version) fairly closely. But the third version has more additions, including a hair-raising bravura section in the final peroration, which Liszt prudently later excised. Leslie Howard plays it with thrilling abandon, and in many ways this is the most exciting of the three accounts. But each interpretation is different in structural control and variations of dynamics, so that although there is much music common to all three scores, Howard achieves a feeling of fresh spontaneity with each – a remarkable achievement. The first version of *Sposalizio* and the solo *Elégie*, bring calmer waters, even if the *Grand solo de concert* again shows the composer at his most rhetoricallly flamboyant. The second disc opens with the piano transcription of the *B-A-C-H Prelude & Fugue* for organ (technically hair-raising but less effective than the original), and includes both the ingenuous *Christmas Tree Suite*, with its series of innocent chorales, and the ear-tickling conflation of Allegri and Mozart, in which Liszt characteristically misses the simple atmospheric beauty of the originals. The Hungarian pieces make a lively and colourful interlude. A formidable achievement, splendidly recorded.

Vol. 52: Hungarian romanzero Nos. 1–18 (complete); 2 Marches dans le genre hongrois.

** Hyp. CDA 67235. Howard.

Volume 52 has greater documentary than musical interest. The *Hungarian Romances* exist only in an unpublished manuscript dating from the early 1850s, held in the Wagner Museum in Bayreuth – a volume of Hungarian dance themes arranged for piano, sometimes simply, sometimes more elaborately. They are all quite short and appear to be a kind of detailed musical notebook for future use. (Liszt had already completed and published his set of *Hungarian Rhapsodies*.) Leslie Howard makes the most of relatively unpromising material, tickling the ear whenever he can. The two

unfinished *Hungarian Marches* date from ten years earlier, and have been edited and completed by Howard himself.

Vol. 53a: Music for piano and orchestra (Vol. 1): Piano Concerto No. 1; Piano Concerto in E flat, op. posth.; Concert Paraphrase on Weber's Polonaise Brillante; Fantasy on Motifs from Beethoven's Ruins of Athens; Grand solo de concert; Hexaméron; Lélio Fantasy; Malédiction (Concerto in E min. for Piano & Strings); Totentanz (2nd version).

*** Hyp. CDA 67401/2. Howard, Budapest SO, Rickenbacher.

Vol. 53b: Music for piano and orchestra (Vol. 2): Piano Concerto No. 2; Concerto pathétique (orch. Reuss); De profundis; Hungarian Fantasia; Totentanz (1st version). SCHUBERT, arr. LISZT: *Wanderer Fantasy.* WEBER, arr. LISZT: *Konzertstück.*

*** Hyp. CDA 67403/5. Howard, Budapest SO, Rickenbacher – MENTER: *Concerto in the Hungarian Style.* ***

Crowning his monumental project to record every note of piano music that Liszt ever wrote, Leslie Howard here tackles the concertante works; not just the handful of popular pieces but no fewer than fifteen works, sixteen if you count the two very different versions of *Totentanz*. Each of the two volumes centres round one of the numbered concertos, and then branches out to rarities. So after a bright and sparkling account of the *First Concerto*, Volume 1 offers a sequence of eight mid-length pieces. They include not just the final version of *Totentanz*, with its grim variations on the *Dies Irae*, but *Malédiction*, a concerto for piano and strings, and the *Fantasy on Themes from Beethoven's Ruins of Athens*. Rarer still, and even more interesting, are the works which Howard himself has helped to edit, usually from manuscript sources. Outstanding among these is the *Concerto in E flat*, written in the late 1830s, and reconstructed only recently after much detective work by the scholar, Jay Rosenblatt, a taut sequence of five sections introduced by unaccompanied timpani. The longest work is the *Grande fantaisie symphonique on Themes from Berlioz's Lélio*, which Berlioz himself conducted in 1834 with Liszt at the piano. It may be over-long for the material, but it is full of incident, and like much of this music, gives a clear idea of Liszt's style of improvisation.

Volume 2 follows up the *Second Concerto* (which Howard prefers to No. 1) with an extraordinary 36-minute piece, *De Profundis*, using a plainchant theme in a vastly expanded sonata-form. The *Concerto pathétique* is fascinating too, as not long before he died, Liszt added linking passages between sections in his late, spare style. Add to that the popular *Hungarian Fantasy* and Liszt's own distinctive versions of Schubert's *Wanderer Fantasy* and Weber's *Konzertstück*. On a third bonus disc (at no extra cost) comes the oddest item of all, a colourful concert piece based on Hungarian gypsy themes by Sophie Menter, which almost certainly Liszt helped to write. Howard's dedication is clear in all his playing here, with clear, crisp articulation vividly caught in finely balanced sound.

Vol. 54: 'Liszt at the opera VI': Concert paraphrases: AUBER: *Grande fantaisie on Tyrolean melodies from La*

Fiancée (first version). BELLINI: *Réminiscences des Puritains* (second version); *Fantaisie sur des motifs favoris* from *La sonnambula* (first version). DONIZETTI: *Valse à capriccio sur deux motifs de Lucia et Parisina* (first version). GLINKA: *Marche des Tcherkesses* from *Ruslan and Ludmilla* (first version). MERCADANTE: *Réminiscences de La Scala.* MEYERBEER: *Réminiscences des Huguenots* (second version). VERDI: *Ernani: Prière paraphrase de concert.* WAGNER: *Tannhäuser Overture.* WEBER: *Fantasie über Themen* from *Der Freischütz.*

*** Hyp. CDA 67406/7. Howard.

Both the two-disc selections of operatic paraphrases (see Volume 50 above) are entertaining, and in many cases they re-serve their original purpose – to disseminate operatic melodies to a public unlikely to hear them in the opera-house. Many of the operas here, by Auber, Donizetti, Merca-dante, Halévy, Pacini and even Meyerbeer, are either forgotten or seldom performed, and Liszt's selections are often as extended as they are elaborately set out and em-broidered. The more familiar Bellini pot-pourris are very characterful, and Leslie Howard clearly enjoys playing them. However, he has problems with the raging torrent of notes surrounding the Pilgrims' chorale in the closing section of the *Tannhäuser Overture*: surely this is only feasible in a four-handed version. The *William Tell Overture* on the other hand is a great success, as are the sparkling Auber *Tarantella* from *Masaniello*, and Glinka's March from *Ruslan and Lud-milla*. Howard's vitality, commitment and strong charac-terization here make up for any imprecisions in the thundering scalic passages. This is not music to hear all at once, but it tells us a great deal about popular operatic taste in the mid-nineteenth century.

Vol. 55: *Années de pèlerinage: Angelus! Prière aux anges gardiens* (4 drafts); *Den Cypressen der Villa d'Este – Thrénodie II; Le Lac de Wallenstadt* (early drafts). *Grand galop chromatique; Grande fantaisie di bravura* and *Grande fantaisie sur des thèmes de Paganini; Historische ungarische Bildnisse; Huldigungsmarsch; Hungaria; Legend: St Francis of Paola Walking on the Water* (simplified version); *Mélodie polonaise; Mephisto Waltz No. 4; Petite valse favorite; Rákóczi March; St Elizabeth* (excerpts); *Sunt lacrymae rerum; Valse-impromptu; Valse mélancolique* (2 versions); *Valse oubliée No. 3; Variations sur 'Le Carnaval de Venise' (Paganini).*

**(*) Hyp. CDA 67408/9/10. Howard.

Leslie Howard describes the contents of this three-disc set as 'first thoughts and second drafts' and indeed there is much here of interest which the composer discarded in later versions. And although the first draft of the *Mephisto Waltz* is surprisingly brief, there are many delights here, especially among the Valses, and notably among early drafts of pieces from the *Années de pèlerinage*. Howard plays the inter-mediate version of *Le Lac de Wallenstadt* beautifully, as he does the much less familiar transcription of *The Miracle of the Roses* from *St Elizabeth*. The *Historical Hungarian Por-traits* – the composer's last cycle of piano pieces, almost unknown in the recital room – is remarkable for the austerity of texture and feeling, while the rhetorical symphonic poem

Hungaria seems hopelessly inflated, for all Howard's powerful advocacy. Yet the *Huldigungsmarsch* is quite a find. The three extended *Paganini Fantasias*, using *La campanella*, the *Carnival of Venice* or both, are rather overextended, but Howard treats them thoughtfully and poetically, rather than as vehicles for mere display, and his performances have many felicities. Excellent recording as always in this series.

Vol. 56: '*Rarities, Curiosities, Fragments*' and 23 *Album Leaves. Andante sensibilissimo; Air cosaque; Années de pèlerinages: Canzonetta del Salvator; Il Penseroso* (1st versions). 2 *Cadenzas for Un sospiro;* Concert paraphrases: *Gaudeamus igitur* (2nd version). BACH: *Fantasia & Fugue in G min.* (1st version). CHOPIN: *Mes joies* (second version). DONIZETTI: *Marche pour le Sultan Abdul Medjid-Khan.* MEYERBEER: *Valse infernale.* NIVELLE: *La Mandragore* (ballad). RAFF: *Waltz in D flat.* ROSSINI: *La carità; Caritas; Harmonie on Carità La Serenata e l'orgia; Introduction & Variations on a March from the Siege of Corinth.* RUBINSTEIN: *Etude in D.* SCHUMANN: *Widmung.* (draft). SMETANA: *Polka.* JOHANN STRAUSS: *Waldstimmen (Valse-caprice). Le Bal de Berne (Grande valse); Dante Fragment; Dumka; En mémoire de Maximillian I (Marche funèbre* – 1st version); *Etude in F sharp* (fragment); *Fantasia on English Themes* (realized Howard); *Festklänge* (1st version); *Glasgow Fragment; Korrekturblatt* (for an earlier version of *La Lugubre Gondola); Künstlerfestzug* (1st version); *Hungarian Rhapsodies Nos. 2, 10, 15, 16, 18* (alternative versions); *Ländler in D; Magyar Tempo; March funèbre; Marie-poème* (incomplete); *Mazurka in F min.* (spurious); *Mazeppa; Mélodie in Dorian mode; Mephisto-Polka;* 3rd *Mephisto Waltz* (first draft); *Morceau in F; Operatic Aria & Sketched Variation; Orpheus* (1879 version); *Pásztor Lakodalmus (Mélodies hongroises); Petite Waltz* (completed Howard); *Polnisch* (sketch); *Prometheus: Schnitterchor* (1st version) & *Winzerchor. Rákóczi March* (1st version, incomplete); *St Stanislaus* (fragment); *Valse in A.*

(N) * Hyp. CDA 67414/7. Howard.

For his penultimate volume (of four CDs!) Leslie Howard clears his desk, as it were, offering all kinds of fascinating morsels, many incomplete or early drafts, and a great many fragmentary 'Album leaves', which the composer valued and often dedicated to his friends. Also, more sustantially, there are six important alternative versions of six of the *Hungarian Rhapsodies*, of which the final published works were to feature so successfully in Howard's last album, plus three complete symphonic poems prepared from manuscript sources. Standing out among the other major pieces is the fascinating *Fantasia on English Themes* (again assembled for performance by Howard himself), which combines excerpts from Handel's *Messiah* and *Judas Maccabaeus* with Arne's *Rule Britannia* and *God save the King*. Overall, this is perhaps a specialist set, but there is much here to interest any admirer of this remarkable and prolific composer. The playing con-sistently shows Howard at his best (especially the minia-tures) and the recording is well up to standard.

Vol. 57: *Hungarian Rhapsodies Nos. 1–19.*

*** Hyp. CDA 67418/2. Howard.

This splendid set represents a high artistic peak within Leslie Howard's distinguished survey, offering as it does the final version of material, much of which we have already heard in Volume 29. Clearly this is music which inspires the pianist and he plays every piece not only with great élan and virtuosity but also with an appealing sense of fantasy. His performances convey a spontaneity not always apparent in earlier volumes, and his readings are full of imagination. The second disc opens dramatically with a superb account of No. 10 in E major and Howard's rubato in No. 12 in C sharp minor is most seductive. The set concludes with one of the most impressive performances of all, No. 19, which is 'after the Csárdás nobles of Abrányi'. The recording is first class. In this repertoire György Cziffra's set (see below) remains memorable for its dazzling bravura, a remarkable achievement; but Leslie Howard's technical command and control of colour are always equal to the occasion, and in his hands much of this writing is shown to have an unexpected depth of feeling.

Music for piano duet

Concerto pathétique

*** EMI CDC5 56816-2. Argerich, Freire – BARTOK: *Contrasts;* PROKOFIEV: *Quintet.* ***

This performance, like the companion pieces on this CD, comes from live concerts at the Saratoga Arts Festival in 1998. The *Concerto pathétique* is marvellously played here and (although there is little opposition anyway) is unlikely to be superseded.

Other piano music

(i) *Années de pèlerinage: Book 1, 1st Year: Switzerland; Book 2, 2nd Year: Italy;* (ii) *Book 3, 3rd Year: Italy.*

(B) ** Philips Duo 462 312-2 (2). (i) Brendel; (ii) Kocsis.

Brendel made some of his finest conquests in the recording studio in this repertoire, and his 1959 analogue survey of the first book of the *Années de pèlerinage* was among the finest. This later digital set of both the first and second years has many impressive moments, but also some ugly *fortissimi* that are not wholly the responsibility of the engineers. Brendel plays the *First Book* segue, without pauses, and although there is some atmospheric playing in the set, the moments of magic are relatively few. Brendel is always to be heard with respect, but this playing is out of scale and over-projected. For *Book 3*, Kocsis takes over and he gives the most compelling account of these sombre and imaginative pieces; apart from beautiful pianism, he also manages to convey their character without exaggeration. He has impeccable technical control and can convey the dark power of the music without recourse to percussive tone. He is splendidly recorded and it is a pity that Philips decided to reissue his performances in harness with those of Brendel. Readers will note that the set omits the *Book 2* supplement (*Venezia e Napoli*).

Années de pèlerinage: 1st Year (Switzerland); 2nd (with supplement) & 3rd Years (Italy): complete. *Hungarian Rhapsodies Nos. 1–19* (complete).

(M) **(*) EMI (ADD) CMS7 64882-2 (4). Cziffra.

Cziffra's accounts of the complete *Années de pèlerinage* show the same prodigious virtuosity and keyboard command that make his set of *Hungarian Rhapsodies* unforgettable. His account of the *Dante Sonata* is enormously dramatic and produces the same fabulous digital dexterity that makes the *Tarantella* from the Italian Supplement, *Venezia e Napoli*, so breathtaking. In the more poetic pieces from Book 1, *Au lac de Wallenstadt* and *Au bord d'une source*, he finds more restrained romantic feeling, and in the Third Year *Les Jeux d'eau à la Villa d'Este* brings some most delicate articulation. He is not helped by a degree of hardness on piano timbre that is already somewhat dry. Remarkable pianism just the same. As can be seen below, the *Hungarian Rhapsodies* (in which he is in his element) are available separately.

Années de pèlerinage, 1st Year (Switzerland).

*** Decca 410 160-2. Bolet.

(BB) *** Naxos 8.550548. Jandó.

This recording of the Swiss pieces from the *Années de pèlerinage* represents Jorge Bolet at his very peak, with playing of magical delicacy as well as formidable power. The piano sound is outstandingly fine.

Even remembering his excellent Beethoven and Haydn recordings, Jandó's performances of the Liszt *Années de pèlerinage* are an impressive achievement. The solemn opening of *La Chapelle de Guillaume Tell* immediately shows the atmospheric feeling he can generate in this remarkable music, and its later, more grandiose rhetoric is handled with powerful conviction. First-class recording, and the feeling throughout is very much of the spontaneity of live music-making.

Années de pèlerinage, 2nd Year (Italy); Supplement: Venezia e Napoli.

(BB) *** Naxos 8.550549. Jandó.

Jandó offers Lisztian playing of the highest order, confirming the *Années de pèlerinage* as being among the supreme masterpieces of the piano. *Sposalizio* is superbly evoked, and the three contrasted *Petrarch Sonnets* bring the most imaginatively varied characterization, with No. 123 especially chimerical. But clearly Jandó sees the *Dante Sonata* as the climactic point of the whole series. His performance has tremendous dynamism and power. One has the sense of Liszt himself hovering over the keyboard. Again first-class recording and the feeling of a continuous live recital. This is the disc to try first, and we have awarded it a token Rosette.

Années de pèlerinage, 3rd Year (Italy) (complete).

(BB) *** Naxos 8.550550. Jandó.

The opening *Angelus* shows Jandó at his most imaginatively expansive and commanding, while *Les Jeux d'eau à la Villa d'Este* sparkles and glitters: this is playing of great appeal. The secret of Jandó's success is that he is deeply involved in every note of Liszt's music.

Années de pèlerinage: Au bord d'une source; Au lac de Wallenstadt; Les Jeux d'eau à la Villa d'Este. Harmonies poétiques et religieuses: Bénédiction de Dieu dans la solitude. Liebesträume No. 3; Mephisto Waltz No. 1; Hungarian Rhapsody No. 12; Variations on B-A-C-H.

(BB) *** Virgin 2 x 1 Double VBD5 61757-2 (2). Paik – *Recital of French Piano Music.* ***

Kun Woo Paik is an outstanding Lisztian. Whether in the delicacy of Liszt's watery evocations from the *Années de pèlerinage*, the devilish glitter of the upper tessitura of the *Mephisto Waltz*, or the comparable flamboyance of the *Hungarian Rhapsody*, this is playing of a high order. The famous *Liebestraum* is presented more gently, less voluptuously than usual and the wide range of the *Bénédiction* is controlled very spontaneously; it is only at the climax of the *B-A-C-H Variations* that perhaps a touch more restraint would have been effective. Fine recording and the coupled French repertoire is also very stimulating.

Années de pèlerinage, 1st Year: Au bord d'une source. 2nd Year: Sonetto del Petrarca No. 104. 2 Concert Studies: Waldesrauschen; Gnomenreigen. Mephisto Waltz No. 1; Rhapsodie Espagnole.

*** Sony SK 47180. Perahia – FRANCK: *Prélude, choral et fugue.* ***

Murray Perahia's Liszt shows all the keyboard distinction and poetic insight we associate with him. This is memorable and very distinguished Liszt playing, and the Sony engineers do full justice to him.

Années de pèlerinage, 2nd Year: 3 Sonetti di Petrarca (Nos. 47, 104 & 123). Concert Paraphrase on the Quartet from Verdi's Rigoletto; Consolations Nos. 1–5; Liebesträume Nos. 1–3.

(M) *** DG (ADD) 435 591-2. Barenboim.

Daniel Barenboim proves an ideal advocate for the *Consolations* and *Liebesträume*, and he is highly poetic in the *Petrarch Sonnets*. His playing has an unaffected simplicity that is impressive and throughout there is a welcome understatement and naturalness, until he arrives at the *Rigoletto Paraphrase*, which is played with plenty of flair and glitter. The quality of the recorded sound is excellent.

Recital I: *Années de pèlerinage, 3rd Year: Tarantella. Harmonies poétiques et religieuses: Pensées des morts; Bénédiction de Dieu dans le solitude; Legend: St Francis of Assisi Preaching to the Birds. Mephisto Waltz No. 1; Rhapsodie Espagnole.*

Recital II: *Années de pèlerinage, 2nd Year: Aux cyprès de la Villa d'Este; Après une lecture du Dante (Dante Sonata). 3rd Year: Aux cyprès de la Villa d'Este; Les Jeux d'eau à la Villa d'Este. Ave Maria; Ave Maria (Die Glocken von Rom); La Lugubre Gondola (2 versions); Recueillement.*

✪ (BB) *** Virgin 2 x 1 Double VBD5 61439-2. Hough.

Few pianists of the younger generation have quite such a magic touch as Stephen Hough, and this budget-priced Virgin Double rescues two of his finest recitals. The performances are all magnetic. On the first disc, he brings sparkle

and wit to the fireworks of the *Mephisto Waltz* and the *Tarantella* from the third year of the *Années de pèlerinage* with phenomenal articulation, and he plays the extended slow movement of the *Bénédiction* with velvety warmth. The second collection is mainly of rarer music and is imaginatively chosen to include two different versions of both *Aux cyprès de la Villa d'Este* and the darkly original *La Lugubre Gondola*, in each case with the second version longer and more elaborate than the first. The cascades of *Les Jeux d'eau à la Villa d'Este* make a glittering centrepiece. The recording is excellent, but the documentation is abysmal, and even the frontispiece (a detail from Giordano's *L'Archange Michel écrasant les anges rebelles*) seems far less appropriate than the pictures of the actual fountains and cypresses at the Villa d'Este that illustrated the second recital when it first appeared at full price. Nevertheless the concentration of the playing here is unforgettable.

Ave Marias in D flat; G; E; d'Arcadelt; 6 Consolations; Harmonies poétiques et religieuses, Nos. 7–10; Ungarns Gott (left-hand).

(BB) *** Naxos 8.553516. Thomson.

Concert paraphrase of sacred music: Alleluja; Ave maris stella; 11 Chorales; Hungarian Coronation Mass: Benedictus; Offertorium. L'Hymne du pape; In festo transfigurationis; O Roma noblis; Sancta Dorothea; Stabat Mater; Urbi et orbi; Weihnachtslied; Zum Haus des Herrn ziehen wir.

(BB) *** Naxos 8.553659. Thomson.

Harmonies poétiques et religieuses, Nos. 1–6; Les morts; Resignazione; Ungarns Gott (two-hand).

(BB) *** Naxos 8.553073. Thomson.

Philip Thomson is a Canadian pianist who has specialized in Liszt. He exhibits considerable artistry in the two discs listed above and commands not only the virtuosity which this repertoire calls for in abundance but also great poetic feeling. (He seems to be a remarkable all-rounder, having occupied teaching posts in both China and the United States, being an accomplished violinist, champion table-tennis player and even parachute jumper.) He commands a wide range of keyboard colour and refinement of pianissimo tone and has the benefit of very good recorded sound as well. All more of his Liszt recitals are touched by distinction and are a real bargain.

The transcriptions from the 1860s and 1870s are rarely heard in recital and, apart from Leslie Howard's survey, are seldom encountered on disc. Philip Thomson brings a wide dynamic range and a fund of keyboard colour to this repertoire. As in the earlier discs, the recording is eminently acceptable without being outstanding.

Ballades Nos. 1 in D flat; 2 in B min.; Christmas Tree (Weinachtsbaum) (suite).

(N) (M) **(*) Chan. 6629. Gillespie.

The *Christmas Tree Suite* is a charming rarity, which deserves recording, even if the music is simplistic by Lisztian standards. The composer wrote it for his granddaughter, Daniela von Bülow. Rhondda Gillespie plays with obvious dedication and is equally at home in the two very contrasted Ballades, the first chimerical, the second darker and more reflective. It is a pity that the piano recording of the suite is not out of Chandos's top drawer, though it is more impressive in the *Ballades*.

Ballade No. 2; Harmonies poétiques et religieuses: Bénédiction de Dieu dans la solitude. Mephisto Waltz No. 1; Sposalizio; En rêve; Schaflos!; Unstern!

(BB) *** Arte Nova 74321 67525-2. Perl.

The Chilean pianist Alfredo Perl tackles Liszt, making an imaginative choice of pieces, four of them substantial, three of them miniatures. In his rapt concentration Perl brings weight to Liszt's sequential arguments, underlining the link between the magnificent *Ballade* over its 15-minute span and Liszt's sonata in the same key. Even more expansive is the surgingly lyrical *Bénédiction*, with the first *Mephisto Waltz* bringing virtuoso fireworks at the end. Excellent, well-balanced sound.

Concert Paraphrases of Beethoven's Symphonies Nos. 2 & 5.

(BB) *** Naxos 8.550457. Scherbakov.

It is Scherbakov's achievement that he makes Liszt's piano transcriptions of these Beethoven symphonies sound so pianistic. With wonderfully crisp articulation and fluent passage-work, textures are clarified, and the freshness and energy of the writing are strongly brought out both in the exuberantly youthful No. 2 and the darkly dramatic No. 5. This is as imaginative as Cyprien Katsaris's Teldec accounts from the days of LP, and no one with a taste for keyboard heroism should overlook them. He is vastly superior to Leslie Howard's pedestrian set on Hyperion. He is, so to speak, more of a Weingartner than a Toscanini (as was Katsaris) but his *Fifth* still has that barnstorming quality that arrests your attention. At super-bargain price, well worth investigating even by those who shy away from transcriptions. Excellent, clear piano sound.

Concert paraphrases: BEETHOVEN: Symphony No. 5 in C min.; Symphony No. 6 (Pastoral): 1st movement.

(M) *(*) Sony (ADD) SMK 52636. Gould.

It is not easy to comment on Glenn Gould's Liszt–Beethoven transcriptions – or, for that matter, on anything by this artist. For his admirers he can do nothing wrong, while his detractors find him perverse. However, no one can deny his remarkable keyboard prowess and mastery – and even the most sceptical are impressed by his insights. These performances come from the 1960s and are handicapped by shallow recorded sound. Nor – even at mid-price – are they particularly generous on playing-time.

Concert paraphrase: BEETHOVEN: Symphony No. 6 (Pastoral).

(M) * Sony (ADD) SMK 52637. Gould.

Gould certainly holds your attention – but this is distinctly short measure. The sound is shallow and coarse.

Concert Paraphrases of Beethoven's An die ferne Geliebte; Mignon; Schumann Lieder: Widmung; Frühlingsnacht.

*** Chan. 9793. Lortie – SCHUMANN: *Fantaisie in C, Op. 17.* ***

Louis Lortie is an outstanding pianist who is rather taken for granted in this country. His latest Chandos recital appears under the title 'To the Distant Beloved', after Beethoven's song-cycle *An die ferne Geliebte*, which he plays in Liszt's transcription (together with a pair of Schumann Lieder) and very impressively too. But collectors will want this for the Schumann *Fantasy*, which is the centrepiece of the recital and is given an outstanding performance.

Concert paraphrases: BELLINI: Réminiscences de 'Norma'. VERDI: Rigoletto; Miserere du Trovatore. WAGNER: Tannhäuser Overture; Am stillen Herd from Die Meistersinger; Liebestod from Tristan und Isolde. Années de pèlerinage, 2nd Year: Sonetti del Petrarca Nos. 104 & 123; Consolation No. 3; Hungarian Rhapsody No. 12 in C sharp min.

(BB) **(*) CfP Double (ADD) CDCFPSD 4745 (2). Sheppard – *Sonata* etc. ***

Sheppard's playing of Liszt on this record is a fine tribute to his musicianship and technique, especially in the *Concert Paraphrases*. He does not manage to disguise the awkwardness of the *Pilgrims' Chorus* section of *Tannhäuser* where the pianist is expected to play the big tune and the swirling (string) accompaniment simultaneously with only two hands. But the *Trovatore* scene has fine, red-blooded melodrama, and the passion of the *Liebestod* is excitingly projected. The *Réminiscences de 'Norma'*, too, are stylishly done. The other items come from his début recital in 1973 and are almost equally compelling. The piano tone is bold and clear. It was a happy idea on this Silver Double reissue to couple these performances with a memorable account of the *Sonata* by another celebrated prizewinner, Bernard d'Ascoli, but this set has been deleted just as we go to press.

Concert Paraphrases: Faust Waltzes; Réminiscences de 'Don Juan' (Mozart); Réminiscences de 'Robert le Diable': Valse infernale (Meyerbeer); Concert Study: Gnomenreigen; Mephisto Polka; Mephisto Waltz No. 1.

(M) **(*) Van. 08.4035.71 [OVC 4035]. Wild.

The title of this recital is *The Demonic Liszt*, and as a display of brilliant piano playing it could hardly be bettered. Earl Wild's technique is prodigious. The articulation in *Gnomenreigen* has a fairy lightness, and the *Mephisto Polka* has a similar blithe delicacy of touch. The more sinister waltz which follows is played with formidable energy and power. There is glittering upper tessitura in the *Don Juan Fantasy*. But one ideally needs a programme designed to give more contrast, and the 1968 piano recording is on the dry side.

Concert paraphrases of Rossini: Soirées musicales; Overture William Tell.

(BB) *** Naxos 8.553961. Gekić.

Liszt made his Rossini transcriptions in 1836, and they are rarely heard in the recital room or on record. The only rival is Leslie Howard's set on Hyperion, and this performance by the Yugoslav-born Kemal Gekić at super-bargain price has infinitely more wit, lightness of touch and subtlety of articulation. Were the price-tags reversed, this would still be the preferred recommendation. In fact this is dazzling playing that sparkles when required and has an effortless brilliance that is quite captivating. Gekić has real flair and is very well recorded too, with natural, lifelike quality. One looks forward to returning to this disc.

Concert paraphrases of Schubert Lieder: *Auf dem Wasser zu singen; Aufenthalt; Erlkönig; Die Forelle; Horch, horch die Lerch; Lebe wohl!; Der Lindenbaum; Lob der Tränen; Der Müller und der Bach; Die Post; Das Wandern; Wohin.*

*** Decca (IMS) 414 575-2. Bolet.

Superb virtuosity from Bolet. He is not just a wizard but a feeling musician, though here he sometimes misses a feeling of fun. First-rate recording.

Concert paraphrases of Schubert Lieder: *Auf dem Wasser zu singen; Erlkönig; In der Ferne; Ständchen.*

⊛ *** Sony SK 66511. Perahia – BACH/BUSONI: *Chorales.* MENDELSSOHN: *Songs without Words.* *** ⊛

Murray Perahia brings to these transcriptions a poetic finesse that is very much his own. Impeccable artistry and taste are blended with a wonderful naturalness.

Concert paraphrases of Schubert Lieder: *Auf dem Wasser zu singen; Gretchen am Spinnrade; Der Müller und der Bach; Ständchen. Hungarian Rhapsody No. 12.*

(M) *** DG 445 562-2. Kissin – BRAHMS: *Fantasias;* SCHUBERT: *Wanderer Fantasia.* **(*)

There is – as always – much to admire in Kissin's playing, and he is in good form in these Liszt–Schubert transcriptions. Both *Der Müller und der Bach* and *Ständchen* are beautifully done. The Brahms and the *Wanderer Fantasia* find him in good rather than outstanding form.

Concert paraphrase of Verdi's *Rigoletto; Etudes d'exécution transcendante d'après Paganini: La campanella. Harmonies poétiques et religieuses: Funérailles. Hungarian Rhapsody No. 12; Liebestraum No. 3. Mephisto Waltz No. 1.*

*** Decca (IMS) 410 257-2. Bolet.

Bolet's playing is magnetic, not just because of virtuosity thrown off with ease, but because of an element of joy conveyed, even in the demonic vigour of the *Mephisto Waltz No. 1.* The relentless thrust of *Funérailles* is beautifully contrasted against the honeyed warmth of the famous *Liebestraum No. 3* and the sparkle of *La campanella.* First-rate recording.

3 Concert Studies; 2 Concert Studies; 6 Consolations; *Réminiscences de Don Juan (Mozart).*

*** Decca (IMS) (ADD) 417 523-2. Bolet.

In the *Concert Studies* the combination of virtuoso precision and seeming spontaneity is most compelling in the splendid account of the *Don Juan* paraphrase. The *Consolations* show

Bolet at his most romantically imaginative: he plays them beautifully.

12 Etudes d'exécution transcendante (complete).

*** Teldec 4509 98415-2. Berezovsky.

Boris Berezovsky shows astonishing flair and technical assurance, yet in *Feux follets* he plays with the utmost delicacy, and the ruminative poetry of *Ricordanza* is melting. The piano is recorded boldly and brilliantly, not as full and sonorous as with Arrau, but there is no lack of pianistic colour in the gentler lyrical writing. The colour portrait of Liszt on the back of the accompanying booklet demonstrates why so many women succumbed to his physical charms!

(i) 12 Etudes d'exécution transcendante; (ii) 6 Etudes d'exécution transcendante d'après Paganini; (i) 3 Etudes de concert (Il lamento; La leggierezza; Un sospiro); 2 Etudes de concert (Waldesrauschen; Gnomenreigen).

(B) **(*) Ph. (ADD) Duo 456 339-2 (2). (i) Arrau; (ii) Magaloff.

Arrau always played with great panache and musical insight, which more than compensates for the occasional smudginess in the recorded sound. He produced a wonderfully distinctive tone, and his enormous range of keyboard colour was splendidly captured by the Philips engineers of the day. Arrau's playing is most masterly and poetic, and the recording, if too reverberant, is admirably truthful and rich in timbre. The three *Etudes de concert,* too, are strongly characterized; indeed some might find Arrau's richly textured romanticism in *Un sospiro* a little overwhelming. However, his bravura in *Gnomenreigen* is riveting. So too is Nikita Magaloff's virtuosity in the *Paganini Studies,* and here the bright, less sumptuous piano-tone projects his digital dexterity with fine glitter. He gives scintillating accounts of *La campanella* and *Arpeggio* and tickles the ear with a delectably sparkling *La Chasse.* The set, of course, ends with variations on the famous theme used also by Brahms and Rachmaninov, also played with fine dash. Overall this is most impressive and can be recommended enthusiastically.

Etudes d'exécution transcendante d'après Paganini: Nos. 3 (La campanella); 5 (La Chasse). Etudes d'exécution transcendante: Feux follets; Polonaise No. 2 in E.

(M) *** Nim. NI 8810. Busoni (piano) – BACH: *Chaconne;* CHOPIN: *Preludes.* **

Very convincingly reproduced from a 1915 Duo-Art piano-roll, in first-class digital sound, this gives a stunning impression of Busoni's transcendental technique in music which calls for the kind of scintillating virtuosity this remarkable artist could so readily provide. Occasionally in *Feux follets* he seems somewhat wilful, but the bravura is prodigious, and the two *Paganini Studies* are superb, while there is some glittering upper tessitura in the central section of the characterful *Polonaise.* Fascinating.

Etudes d'exécution transcendante d'après de Paganini Nos. 1–8.

(BB) *** Koch Discover DICD 920423. Brancart – BRAHMS: *Paganini Variations.* ***

Evelyne Brancart displays a glittering technique, fine musicianship and a Lisztian sensibility. The recording is rather bright and forward but this is not ineffective in such repertoire. An enjoyable disc – though, even at super-bargain price, it is rather short measure at under 48 minutes.

Hexaméron (Grande bravura Variations on the March from I Puritani, by Liszt, Thalberg, Pixis, Herz, Czerny and Chopin).

(M) *** RCA (ADD) 09026 63310-2. Lewenthal – ALKAN: *Barcarolle; 12 Studies in all the Minor Keys, Op. 39, Nos. 4, 5, 6 (Symphonie), 7, 12 (Le Festin d'Esope), etc.* ***

Hexaméron was the brainchild of Princess Belgioioso, whose idea it was to have the six most famous pianists of the day perform at one of her glittering social occasions. Although the event never took place, she managed, after months of hounding, to extract each composer's assignment, with Liszt acting as the binding force. This musical curiosity became a favourite vehicle of Liszt because of its fiendish difficulty, yet is contrasted enough to be musically satisfying. Raymond Lewenthal's performance is as brilliant as can be imagined, and makes an enjoyable bonus to his flamboyant Alkan recital.

Hungarian Rhapsodies Nos. 1–15; Rhapsodie Espagnole.

(B) *** EMI (ADD) CZS5 69003-2 (2). Cziffra.

Hungarian Rhapsodies Nos. 1–19; Rhapsodie Espagnole.

(B) *** DG Double (ADD) 453 034-2 (2). Szidon.

Hungarian Rhapsodies Nos. 1–9 (Carnaval de Pesth).

(BB) ** Naxos 8.554480. Jandó.

Hungarian Rhapsodies Nos. 10–19.

(BB) ** Naxos 8.554481. Jandó.

Cziffra's performances are dazzling. They are full of those exciting spurts of energy and languorous rubato that immediately evoke the unreasonably fierce passions of gypsy music. Yet the control is absolute (try the delectably free opening of *No. 12 in C sharp minor*, or the *D minor* (No. 7)). There is plenty of power in reserve and poetry too. The high degree of temperament in the playing, with hardly two consecutive phrases at an even tempo, makes even Szidon (who has the full measure of the music) seem almost staid. Cziffra with coruscating brilliance sets every bar of the music on fire. Some might find him too impulsive for comfort (and they should turn to the DG alternative), but this is surely the way Liszt would have played them: the *Rákóczy March* (No. 15) is a *tour de force*. The recording, made in the Salle Wagram, Paris, in 1957/8 (or, in the case of Nos. 2, 6, 12 and 15, in the Hungaraton Budapest Studio a year earlier), is a little dry and close but otherwise truthful, and it does not lack sonority.

Roberto Szidon offers Liszt playing of the highest order. He has flair and panache, genuine keyboard command and, when required, great delicacy of tone. He is well recorded too, and this DG Double is not only inexpensive but also provides (as does Cziffra on EMI) an excellent version of the *Rhapsodie espagnole*. Cziffra's performances are from an artist of an even more volatile personality, but Szidon is by no means upstaged: his style is equally valid and his approach is always imaginatively illuminating.

This repertoire calls for great virtuosity and a musical personality of outsize stature. Jenö Jandó is not quite in that league but his performances are far from negligible. The price tag is attractive but Cziffra, who is also inexpensive, rivets the attention in a way that Jandó does not.

Hungarian Rhapsodies Nos. 2, 6, 8 (Capriccio), 9 (Carnival in Pest), 10 (Préludio), 12–15 (Rákoczy).

(N) (M) *** EMI (ADD) CDM5 67554-2 [567555-2]. Cziffra.

Hungarian Rhapsodies Nos. 2–3, 8, 13, 15 (Rákóczy March), 17; Csárdás obstinée.

(M) *** Van. 08.4024.71 [OVC 4024]. Brendel.

As can be heard in the most famous *C sharp minor Rhapsody* (No. 2), Cziffra's reckless impulsiveness is matched by his breathtaking bravura in the closing section, and it was an excellent idea to issue a selection from his complete set as one of EMI's 'Great Recordings of the Century'. The remastered recordings from the early 1970s have fine realism and presence.

Although the Vanguard recording is not a recent one, it sounds very good in this excellent CD transfer, and Brendel's playing is very distinguished indeed. There are few more charismatic or spontaneous accounts of the *Hungarian Rhapsodies* available, and there is no doubt about the brilliance of the playing nor the quality of musical thinking that informs it.

Piano Sonata in B min.

(B) *** EMI double fforte (ADD) CZS5 69527-2 (2). Anievas – CHOPIN: *Sonata No. 3* **; RACHMANINOV: *Preludes Nos. 1–24 etc.* **(*)

Piano Sonata; Années de pèlerinage, 1st Year: Vallée d'Obermann. Concert Studies Nos. 1: Waldesrauschen; 2: Gnomenreigen. Harmonies poétiques et religieuses: Bénédiction de Dieu dans le solitude.

(N)(M) *** Ph. (ADD) 464 713-2. Arrau.

Sonata in B min.; Années de pèlerinage, 1st Year: Vallée d'Oberman; Concert Paraphrase of Wagner: Isoldens Liebestod; Nuages gris; Variations on Weinen, Klagen, Sorgen, Zagen.

(N) (B) EMI *** Début CDZ5 74233-2. Papadiamandis.

Piano Sonata in B min.; Années de pèlerinage, 2nd Year: Après une lecture du Dante (Fantasia Quasi Sonata); Concert Study: Gnomenreigen; Harmonies poètiques et religieuses: Funérailles.

*** DG 457 629-2. Pletnev.

Piano Sonata in B min.; Berceuse; Concert Study: Gnomenreigen. Liebestraum No. 3 in A flat; Valse oubliée No. 1.

(M) *** Decca (ADD) 452 306-2. Curzon (with SCHUBERT: *Impromptu in A flat, D.935/2*).

Piano Sonata in B min.; Concert Paraphrase of Wagner: Isoldens Liebestod; La lugubra gondola No. 2; Mosonyis Grabgeleit; Romance oubliée; Variations on Weine, Klagen, Sorgen, Zagen.

(N) **(*) MDG 312 0957-2. Tanski.

Piano Sonata; 3 Concert Studies.

*** Chan. 8548. Lortie.

Piano Sonata; Concert Study No. 2 (La leggierezza).

(BB) *** CfP Double CDCFPSD 4745 (2). D'Ascoli – *Concert Paraphrases* etc. **(*)

Piano Sonata; Grand galop chromatique; Liebesträume Nos. 1–3; Valse impromptu.

*** Decca (IMS) 410 115-2. Bolet.

Piano Sonata; 2 Legends; Scherzo & March.

*** Hyp. CDA 66616. Demidenko.

Pletnev's earlier account of the *B minor Sonata*, made when he was in his twenties (briefly available on Olympia), had dazzling virtuosity and brilliance. This newcomer has even greater tonal finesse, articulation and control of keyboard colour; there is a tremendous grip, depth and majesty, and the breadth of the *Sonata* is deeply impressive. A performance of stature among the very best that this great pianist has yet given us. The remainder of the programme is hardly less gripping; reservations concerning the close balance do not obscure the artistry and distinction of this recital.

Nikolai Demidenko's is a keenly dramatic and powerfully projected account that has the listener on the edge of his or her seat. It must be numbered among the finest performances he has given us. The excitement and virtuosity are second to none and almost call to mind Horowitz: his playing can be measured against that of Brendel and Pletnev. He has the advantage of exceptionally vivid recorded sound, and the remainder of the recital goes equally well.

Curzon shows an innate understanding of the *Sonata*'s cyclic form, so that the significance of the principal theme is brought out subtly in relation to the music's structural development. There are only a few performances to compare with this and none superior, and Decca's recording matches the playing in its excellence. The shorter pieces too are imaginatively played. The excellent recording was made in the Sofiensaal in 1963, but the fairly close microphones create something of a studio effect.

Louis Lortie gives almost as commanding a performance of the Liszt *Sonata* as any in the catalogue; its virtuosity can be taken for granted and, though he does not have the extraordinary intensity and feeling for drama of Pletnev, he has a keen awareness of its structure and a Chopinesque finesse that win one over. The Chandos recording, though a shade too reverberant, is altogether natural.

Bernard d'Ascoli displays classical qualities in his refreshing and intense reading of this most romantic of sonatas. It is the sort of interpretation that one might have expected Wilhelm Kempff to have given, with articulation of pearly clarity, wonderful singing legato in the big melodies and an emphasis on control and concentration rather than thrusting urgency. Yet there is no lack of power, and the result is most satisfying. The delicate account of *La leggierezza* makes a fine encore. However, this set has been deleted as we go to press.

Arrau's performance of the *Sonata* has characteristic eloquence and power. His style, however, is somewhat deliberate, even pontifical, but this is still remarkable pianism. About the rest of the recital there are no reservations whatso-

ever. The *Bénédiction* is exceptionally imaginative and rewarding, the *Vallée d'Obermann* is hardly less fine, and the bravura in *Gnomenreigen* is riveting. The recording is resonant and full-blooded and makes a considerable impact.

The power, imagination and concentration of Bolet are excellently brought out in his fine account of the *Sonata*. With the famous *Liebestraum* (as well as its two companions) also most beautifully done, not to mention the amazing *Grand galop*, this is one of the most widely appealing of Bolet's outstanding Liszt series. However, the *Sonata* is also available in a Double Decca set – see below.

The young French pianist Matthieu Papadiamandis has made a considerable name for himself already as a winner of the Busoni Prize in Bolzano. He has dazzling technique (but then so have so many young players) and a refined musical intelligence. His *B minor Sonata* may not have the transcendental mastery of a Gilels, Richter, Pletnev or Brendel, but it is quite an achievement; you will be surprised how well it stands up to the most exalted rivals. His *Vallée d'Obermann* is quite something too, as is the Wagner transcription. Fine, lifelike recorded sound makes this a compelling and enjoyable recital, as well as a most auspicious début.

Claudius Tanski also possesses formidable technical prowess and fine musicianship. Although everything in his recital is musically satisfying and the claims of this well-recorded MDG version are quite strong. Unlike Matthieu Papadiamandis's recent account, however the Tanski recording is at full price, which will not enhance its competitive status.

Anievas gives a fine and memorable performance, notable for its thoughtfulness and its subtlety in the control of tension. The lyrical impulse is finely balanced to bring out the music's poetry as well as its fire and strength. The recording too is generally very good and, although the reverberation prevents absolute clarity in the bass in florid passages, the effect is firmer in the excellent CD transfer.

Miscellaneous recitals

Années de pèlerinage, 2nd Year: Après une lecture du Dante. Ballade No. 2 in B min.; Harmonies poétiques et religieuses: Andante lagrimoso. Mephisto Waltzes Nos. 1, 2 & 4; Valse oubliée No 4; Die Zelle in Nonnenwerth.

(N) *** EMI CDC5 57002-2 Leif Ove Andsnes.

Leif Ove Andsnes gives us an outstanding *Dante Sonata* and is hardly less impressive elsewhere, in a recital which strikes a good balance between well-known Liszt and the less familiar. There is no playing to the gallery and his virtuosity is always at the service of musical thought. He rarely puts a foot (or finger) wrong and he is aided by an eminently vivid and well-balanced recording.

Concert paraphrase of Wagner's Tannhäuser Overture; Etudes de concert, 1st Set, No. 3: Un sospiro; 2nd set, Nos. 1: Waldesrauschen; No.2 Gnomenreigen. Etudes d'éxécution transcendante d'après Paganini, No. 3: La campanella. Grand galop chromatique; Harmonies poétiques et religieuses: Funérailles; Liebestraum No. 3; Rhapsodie espagnole.

(N) *** RCA (ADD) 09026 63748-2. Bolet.

Here is a real find, a recital recorded by Jorge Bolet in the early 1970s, when he was at the very peak of his form, a decade before he made his series of digital recordings for Decca, and just before his Carnegie Hall debut in 1974. The playing in *Gnomenreigen* and the exuberant *Grand galop chromatique* is dazzling, while *La campanella* is articulated with crystal clarity, and there is more glittering fingerwork in the *Rhapsodie espagnole*.

The famous *Liebestraume* and *Un sospiro* are romantically charged, without a hint of sentimentality, while the darker atmosphere of *Funérailles* is powerfully caught. Even the almost unplayable finale of Liszt's arrangement of Wagner's *Tannhäuser Overture* is made coherent by the clear separation of the chorale from the decorative cascades – a *tour de force* of pianism. The analogue recording is excellent and the CD transfer faithful (perhaps a fraction hard) and gives him a most realistic presence.

Piano Sonata; Années de pèlerinage, 1st Year: Au bord d'une source; 2nd Year: Sonetto 104 del Petrarca; 3rd Year: Les Jeux d'eau à la Villa d'Este; Concert Paraphrases: Die Forelle; Erlkönig (Schubert); Réminiscences de Don Juan (Mozart); Rigoletto (Verdi). Consolation No. 3; Etudes d'exécution transcendante d'après Paganini: La campanella. Etudes de concert: Gnomenreigen; Un sospiro. Harmonies poétiques et religieuses: Funérailles. Hungarian Rhapsody No. 12 in C sharp min.; Liebestraum No. 3 in A flat; Mephisto Waltz No. 1.

(B) *** Double Decca 444 851-2 (2). Bolet.

The full range of Jorge Bolet's achievement for Decca in the music of Liszt is admirably surveyed here, ending with his commanding account of the *Sonata*. He can be romantic without sentimentality, as in the *Consolation*, *Un sospiro* or the most famous *Liebesträume*, yet can dazzle the ear with bravura or beguile the listener with his delicacy of colouring, as in the *Années de pèlerinage*. All the recordings here save the Mozart *Concert Paraphrase* are digital and are as clear and present as one could wish.

ORGAN MUSIC

Fantasia & Fugue on 'Ad nos, ad salutarem undam'; Prelude & Fugue on 'B-A-C-H; Variations on 'Weinen, Klagen, Sorgen, Zagen'.

(BB) *** ASV (ADD) CDQS 6127. Bate (Royal Albert Hall organ) – SCHUMANN: *4 Sketches.* ***

Jennifer Bate gives superb performances of the three major Liszt warhorses. The clarity and incisiveness of her playing go with a fine sense of line and structure, and there is plenty of exuberance in the *'Ad nos' Fantasia and Fugue*. Even making no allowance for the Royal Albert Hall's acoustic problems, the analogue recording captures an admirable combination of definition and atmosphere, well conveyed on CD. This makes a fine super-bargain alternative to the competing digital versions, which are only marginally more sharply defined.

VOCAL MUSIC

Lieder: Blume und Duft; Der drei Zigeuner; Der du von dem Himmel bist (2 settings); Ein Fichtenbaum steht einsam; Es muss ein Wunderbares sein; Es rauschen die Winde; Der Hirt; Ihr Auge; Ihr Glocken von Marling; Freudvoll und leidvoll; Die Loreley; O komm im Traum; Des Tages laute Stimmen schweigen; Uber allen Gipfeln ist Ruh; Vergiftet sind meine Lieder.

*** Cap. 10 294. Shirai, Höll.

There are only one or two collections of Liszt songs as searchingly persuasive as this, and none more beautiful. Provocatively the record starts with Shirai at her most vehement in *Vergiftet sind meine Lieder*, written when Liszt's long relationship with the Countess d'Agoult was breaking up. Regrettably, no English translations are provided with the text, only a commentary.

Lieder: Comment, disaient-ils; Es muss ein Wunderbares sein; Es rauschen die Winde; Go not happy day; Ihr Auge; Im Rhein, im schönen Strome; Oh, quand je dors; La tombe et la rose; Die Vätergruft; Vergiftet sind meiner Lieder; Wanderers Nachtlied.

*** EMI CDC5 55047-2. Hampson, Parsons – BERLIOZ; WAGNER: *Lieder.* *** ●

On his disc of romantic songs, Thomas Hampson ranges wide in his selection of 11 by Liszt, ending magically with one of the best known, his setting of Victor Hugo, *Oh, quand je dors*. Characteristic, in that he finds a wider range of expressiveness and dynamic than almost any of his rivals, building from the drawing-room charm of the opening to a tremendous climax. He is helped by Geoffrey Parsons's accompaniment and the fine, warm recording. Other fascinating songs include Liszt's setting of Tennyson in English, *Go not happy day*, with the words oddly stressed. There is also a still, hushed and intense setting of Goethe's *Wanderers Nachtlied*, best known from Schubert. Magnetic, rich-voiced performances.

Lieder: Du bist wie eine Blume; Die drei Zigeuner; Der du von dem Himmel bist; Es war ein König in Thule; Die Fischerstochter; Freudvoll und leidvoll; Im Rhein, im schönen Strome; Die Lorelei; S'il est un charmant gazon; Uber allen Gipfeln ist Ruh'; Die Vätergruft; Das Veilchen.

(B) *** EMI (ADD) Double fforte CZS5 73836-2 (2). Baker, Parsons – MENDELSSOHN: *Lieder;* SCHUMANN: *Liederkreis, Op. 39.* ***

Dame Janet Baker's selection of songs – starting with one of the most beautiful and the most ambitious, *Die Lorelei* – brings out the wide range of Liszt in this medium. His style is transformed when setting a French text, giving Parisian lightness in response to Hugo's words, while his setting of *King of Thule* from Goethe's *Faust* leaps away from reflectiveness in illustrating the verses. The glowing warmth of Dame Janet's singing is well matched by Geoffrey Parsons's keenly sensitive accompaniments. The recording is excellent, and the couplings admirably chosen, but there are no texts and translations.

LITOLFF, Henri (1818–91)

Concerti Symphoniques Nos. 2 in B min., Op. 22; 4 in D min., Op. 102.

*** Hyp. CDA 66889. Donohoe, Bournemouth SO, Litton.

The *Fourth Concerto Symphonique* is the source of the famous Litolff *Scherzo*, so often heard in the days of 78s. The first movement is rhetorical but opens with endearing flamboyance under the baton of Andrew Litton, while the passage-work scintillates in the hands of Peter Donohoe. The secondary material has both delicacy and charm. The famous *Scherzo* which follows is taken a fraction too fast and loses some of its poise, the articulation not always absolutely clean; but one adjusts to the breathless virtuosity, and it remains the work's finest inspiration. The *Adagio religioso* opens with some lovely horn-playing, its solemn mood nicely offset later by the pianistic decoration. The finale, marked *Allegro impetuoso*, is certainly all of that, with more twinkling bravura from Donohoe.

The *Second Concerto* is also well worth while. True, its opening *Maestoso* is hopelessly inflated, but in the Chopinesque secondary material Donohoe finds an engaging charm as well as brilliance. The second movement is another scintillating Scherzo, and if not quite as memorable as its more famous companion, it has a tripping centrepiece worthy of Saint-Saëns, especially as presented here. With a warm, naturally balanced recording, this entertaining Hyperion CD is very much worth having.

Concerti symphoniques Nos. 3 in E flat (National Hollandais), Op. 45; 5 in C min., Op. 123.

(N) *** CDA 67210. Donohoe, BBC Scottish SO, Litton.

Overall this pair of engaging works is much more consistently inspired than the more famous No. 4, and the story of the gestation of the *Concerto Symphonique No. 3* is in itself extraordinary. After unsuccessful divorce proceedings in London, Litolff was thrown into a debtor's prison, where he befriended the jailor's daughter, who aided his escape to Holland, where he was able to re-establish his career. Hence the work's subtitle, and Litolff gratefully incorporates two old Dutch tunes into his music. After an opening movement with a zestful military flavour, the rollicking *Scherzo* includes one of these; the following nocturnal *Andante* makes a touching, songful interlude before the dazzling finale, which is to introduce the second in the form of a patriotic chorale. The brilliant denouement is fully worthy of Liszt.

The opening mood of the *Fifth Concerto* seems darker, but the lyrical secondary theme is essentially nostalgic, and the second movement returns to a mood of poetic melancholy, dispelled by another jauntily memorable *Scherzo*. The finale opens with a whiff of Beethoven and has unexpected weight, with the contrasting lyrical material moving into a world somewhere between Liszt and Mendelssohn. There is to be an impressive fugue before the movement's dynamism finds its resolution. Both performances have great flair, with Donohoe playing brilliantly throughout, and Litton and his Scottish players giving splendid support. The recording is

first class. A most enjoyable and recommendable coupling, notable for its ready fund of memorable melody.

Concerto Symphonique No. 4: Scherzo.

(M) *** Decca (ADD) 466 376-2. Curzon, LPO, Boult – BRAHMS: *Piano Concerto;* FRANCK: *Symphonic Variations.* ***

*** Ph. 411 123-2. Dichter, Philh. O, Marriner (with Concert of concertante music ***).

(M) *** Decca 430 726-2. Ortiz, RPO, Atzmon – ADDINSELL: *Warsaw Concerto* ***; GERSHWIN: *Rhapsody* **(*); GOTTSCHALK: *Grand Fantasia* ***; LISZT: *Hungarian Fantasia.* ***

Curzon provides all the sparkle Litolff's infectious *Scherzo* requires, and the 1958 Walthamstow Town Hall recording makes a delightful encore for the Brahms *Concerto* and the Franck *Symphonic Variations* in this reissue in Decca's Classic Sound series. The fine qualities of the original sound, freshness and clarity, remain impressive.

Misha Dichter gives a scintillating account of Litolff's delicious *Scherzo*, played at a sparklingly brisk tempo. Marriner accompanies sympathetically and the recording is excellent.

Cristina Ortiz's version may lack extrovert brilliance but it has an agreeable elegance. The intimacy of this version is emphasized by the balance, which places the piano within the orchestral group, making the gentle central section especially effective. The Decca couplings are all appealing and the CD is impressively natural.

LLOYD, George (1913–98)

Concerto for Violin & Strings; Concerto for Violin & Winds.

*** Albany TROY 316. Anghelescu, Philh. O, Parry.

George Lloyd's *Concerto for Violin and Strings* is very much in the great English tradition of writing for string orchestra, with or without a soloist. Its plaintive opening develops a plangent melancholy in the first movement, yet towards the end of the first movement, after a period of angst, the main theme suddenly turns into a life-enhancing chorale on the full strings. The rhythmically quirky Scherzo which follows is more cheerful, but the clouds do not lift entirely. The apparently serene *Largo* opens with a sense of deep nostalgia and remains troubled; its tensions are not entirely resolved at the close. It is left to the dancing finale to round off the work but the closing bars are curiously equivocal. The *Concerto with Winds* is more robustly extrovert, neoclassical, acerbic, and brilliantly and originally scored. Its slow movement is bitter-sweet, very touching, but again producing an ambivalence of feeling, which strays into the initially light-hearted, dancing finale. In both works the Romanian soloist Cristina Anghelescu has just the right temperament for the music's quixotic changes of mood: her lyrical line is wholly persuasive while she revels in the spicy rhythms of the second work. David Parry directs, in partnership with his soloist, definitive recorded performances. The recording too is first class and most realistically balanced.

Piano Concerto No. 3.

**(*) Albany TROY 019-2. Stott, BBC PO, composer.

The *Third Piano Concerto* is very eclectic in style, with flavours of Prokofiev (with diluted abrasiveness) and even of Khachaturian – minus vulgarity – in outer movements which have a toccata-like brilliance and momentum. Kathryn Stott plays with a pleasing, mercurial lightness and makes the most of the music's lyrical feeling. But the slow movement is too long and its climax does not show Lloyd at his best. On the other hand, the wistful tune at the centre of the finale is rather appealing. The composer achieves a fine partnership with his soloist and the performance has undoubted spontaneity.

(i) *Piano Concerto No. 4; The Lily-Leaf and the Grasshopper; The Transformation of That Naked Ape.*

*** Albany AR 004. Stott; (i) LSO, composer.

The *Fourth Piano Concerto* is a romantic, light-hearted piece with a memorable 'long singing tune' (the composer's words), somewhat Rachmaninovian in its spacious lyricism contrasting with a 'jerky' rhythmic idea. The performance by Kathryn Stott and the LSO under the composer is ardently spontaneous from the first bar to the last. The solo pieces are eclectic but still somehow Lloydian. The recording is first rate.

Symphonies Nos. 1 in A; 12.

*** Albany TROY 032-2. Albany SO, composer.

The pairing of George Lloyd's first and last symphonies is particularly appropriate, as they share a theme-and-variations format. The *First* is relatively lightweight. The mature *Twelfth* uses the same basic layout but ends calmly with a ravishingly sustained pianissimo, semi-Mahlerian in intensity, that is among the composer's most beautiful inspirations. At the beginning of the work, the listener is soon aware of the noble lyrical theme which is the very heart of the *Symphony*. The Albany Symphony Orchestra gave the work its première and they play it with enormous conviction and eloquence, helped by the superb acoustics of the Troy Savings Bank Music Hall, which produces sound of demonstration quality.

Symphonies Nos. 2 & 9.

*** Albany TROY 055. BBC PO, composer.

Lloyd's *Second Symphony* is a lightweight, extrovert piece, conventional in form and construction, though in the finale the composer flirts briefly with polytonality, an experiment he did not repeat. The *Ninth* (1969) is similarly easygoing; the *Largo* is rather fine, but its expressive weight is in scale, and the finale, 'a merry-go-round that keeps going round and round', has an appropriately energetic brilliance. Throughout both works the invention is attractive, and in these definitive performances, extremely well recorded, the composer's advocacy is very persuasive.

Symphony No. 3 in F; Charade (suite).

*** Albany TROY 90. BBC PO, composer.

The *Third Symphony* dates from the composer's nineteenth year, its idiom undemanding but agreeable. Although it is described as a one-movement piece, it clearly subdivides into three sections and it is the central *Lento* which has *the* tune, a winding, nostalgic theme that persists in the memory. It is atmospherically prepared and eventually blossoms sumptuously. *Charade* dates from the 1960s and attempts to portray the London scene of the time, from aggressive *Student Power* and *LSD* to *Flying Saucers* and *Pop Song*. The ironic final movement, *Party Politics*, is amiable rather than wittily abrasive. The composer is good at bringing his music vividly to life, and he is very well recorded indeed.

Symphony No. 4.

*** Albany AR 002. Albany SO, composer.

George Lloyd's *Fourth Symphony* was composed during his convalescence after being badly shell-shocked while serving in the Arctic convoys of 1941/2. The first movement is directly related to this period of his life, and the listener may be surprised at the relative absence of sharp dissonance. After a brilliant scherzo, the infectious finale is amiable, offering a series of quick, 'march-like tunes', which the composer explains by suggesting that 'when the funeral is over the band plays quick cheerful tunes to go home'. Under Lloyd's direction, the Albany Symphony Orchestra play with great commitment and a natural, spontaneous feeling. The recording is superb.

Symphony No. 5 in B flat.

*** Albany TROY 022-2. BBC PO, composer.

The *Fifth Symphony* is a large canvas, with five strong and contrasted movements, adding up to nearly an hour of music. It was written during a happy period spent living simply on the shore of Lac Neuchâtel, during the very hot summer of 1947. In the finale, the composer tells us, 'everything is brought in to make as exhilarating a sound as possible – strong rhythms, vigorous counterpoints, energetic brass and percussion'. The symphony is played with much commitment by the BBC Philharmonic under the composer, who creates a feeling of spontaneously live music-making throughout. The recording is first class.

(i) *Symphonies Nos. 6; (ii) 10 (November Journeys);* (i) *Overture: John Socman.*

**(*) Albany TROY 15-2. (i) BBC PO; (ii) BBC PO Brass; composer.

The bitter-sweet lyricism of the first movement of *November Journeys* is most attractive, but the linear writing is more complex than usual in a work for brass. In the finale a glowing *cantando* melody warms the spirit, to contrast with the basic *Energico*. The *Calma* slow movement is quite haunting, no doubt reflecting the composer's series of visits to English cathedrals, the reason for the subtitle. The *Sixth Symphony* is amiable and lightweight; it is more like a suite than a symphony. Lloyd's performances are attractively spontaneous and well played, and the equally agreeable *John Socman Overture* also comes off well, although it is rather inconsequential.

Symphony No. 7.

*** Albany TROY 057. BBC PO, composer.

The *Seventh Symphony* is a programme symphony, using the ancient Greek legend of Proserpine. The slow movement is particularly fine, an extended soliloquy of considerable expressive power. The last and longest movement is concerned with 'the desperate side of our lives – "Dead dreams that the snows have shaken, Wild leaves that the winds have taken" –' yet, as is characteristic with Lloyd, the darkness is muted; nevertheless the resolution at the end is curiously satisfying. Again he proves an admirable exponent of his own music. The recording is splendid.

Symphony No. 8.

*** Albany TROY 230. Philh. O, composer.

After his severe depression and nervous breakdown, Lloyd gave up composing entirely for many years, earning his living instead as a mushroom farmer, only gradually turning back to composition. The *Eighth Symphony*, written in 1961 – the first to be heard in public – is a product of that long recuperative period, and in the openness of inspiration (passionately English) it both belies earlier depression and testifies to the success of composition as therapy. Linked by a six-note leitmotif, the work holds well together. Even if the scherzando finale is arguably a little too long for its material, the elliptical first movement (opening and closing atmospherically and with a richly memorable secondary theme) and the eloquently sustained *Largo* both show the composer at his finest. The recording, made in the spacious acoustics of Watford Town Hall, is first class.

Symphony No. 11.

*** Albany TROY 060. Albany SO, composer.

The urgently dynamic first movement of the *Eleventh Symphony* is described by the composer as being 'all fire and violence', but any anger in the music quickly evaporates, and it conveys rather a mood of exuberance, with very full orchestral forces unleashed. With the orchestra for which the work was commissioned, Lloyd conducts a powerful performance, very well played. The recording, made in the Music Hall of Troy Savings Bank near Albany, is spectacularly sumptuous and wide-ranging.

PIANO MUSIC

Music for piano duet

Aubade (fantasy suite); Eventide; The Road through Samarkand.

*** Albany Troy 248. Goldstone and Clemmow (piano duet).

Aubade, written in 1971, is a substantial suite of some 38 minutes' length. The composer describes it as a dream-like fantasy, with pictures flitting through his mind at dawn. Its evocations are impressionistic, its flavour distinctly Gallic. Included are *Charcoal Burners*, ghostly but robust *Tin Soldiers*, who gambol uninhibitedly after Waterloo, a Satie-esque *Love Duet* and quirkily ungainly *Waltz* (the imaginary participants are Lady Hamilton and the Duke of Well-

ington). There are tinkling *Bells, Monks and Lutherans*, a pair of *Moths*, who flit through a sparkling moto perpetuo, and a strong finale in which the bells return, now more dominant. It is all brilliantly imagined and its colourful imagery is vividly realized in a bravura performance by Anthony Goldstone and Caroline Clemmow. *Eventide* is a touching re-presentation and elaboration of a carol from the composer's youth – a simple melody which is charmingly ingenuous and not sentimentalized. *The Road through Samarkand* is a virtuoso toccata dominated by a simple motto theme. It is full of rhythmic interest, often syncopated, and the players clearly relish the virtuosity it demands. In short these are first-rate performances of highly communicative music which shows the composer at his most successfully spontaneous. The recording is vivid but somewhat over-reverberant.

An African Shrine; The Aggressive Fishes; Intercom Baby; The Road through Samarkand; St Anthony and the Bogside Beggar.

**(*) Albany AR 003. Roscoe.

The most ambitious piece here is *An African Shrine*, in which the composer's scenario is linked (not very dissonantly) to African violence and revolution. *The Road through Samarkand* (1972) has travellers from the younger generation leaving for the East; while *The Aggressive Fishes* are tropical and violently moody, changing from serenity to anger at the flick of a fin. The two most striking pieces are the picaresque tale of the *Bogside Beggar* and the charming lullaby written for a baby whose mother is in another room listening with the aid of modern technology. Martin Roscoe's performances are thoroughly committed and spontaneous, and the recording is first class.

VOCAL MUSIC

A Litany.

**(*) Albany TROY 200. Watson, White, Guildford Choral Soc., Philh. O, composer.

A Litany is a setting of 12 verses from the John Donne poem. If anything, the recording is more successful than the first performance, with the choir enthusiastically at home in music which communicates readily, even if the soloists are less than ideal, both having rather wide vibratos. *A Litany* is not as inspired as the *Symphonic Mass*. It is unfortunate that the very opening brings a curious reminder of *The Phantom of the Opera* and *Belshazzar's Feast* with a whiff of Ketèlbey for good measure. But the music soon settles down and there is much fine choral writing in the first two sections, even if it is the third, unaccompanied, section, 'a song of thanks to the Virgin', that is the heart of the piece. The spacious recording is well up to Albany's usual high standard.

A Symphonic Mass.

✹ *** Albany TROY 100. Brighton Festival Ch., Bournemouth SO, composer.

George Lloyd's *Symphonic Mass* is his masterpiece. Written

for chorus and orchestra (but no soloists) on the largest scale, the work is linked by a recurring main theme, a real tune which soon lodges insistently in the listener's memory, even though it is modified at each reappearance. It first appears as a quiet setting of the words *Christe eleison*, nearly four minutes into the *Kyrie*. The climax of the whole work is the combined *Sanctus* and *Benedictus*, with the latter framed centrally. To the words *Dominus Deus* the great melody finds its apotheosis in a passage marked *largamente con fevore*. Then the *Sanctus* reasserts itself dramatically and, after a cry of despair from the violins, the movement reaches its overwhelmingly powerful and dissonant denouement. Peace is then restored in the *Agnus Dei*, where the composer tells us the words *Dona nobis pacem* became almost unbearably poignant for him.

The performance is magnificent and the recording is fully worthy, spaciously balanced within the generous acoustic of the Guildhall, Southampton, and overwhelmingly realistic, even in the huge climax of the *Sanctus* with its shattering percussion.

The Vigil of Venus (Pervigilium Veneris).

*** Albany TROY 170. James, Booth, Welsh Nat. Op. Ch. & O, composer.

As in the symphonies, Lloyd thumbs his nose at fashion in a score that both pulses with energy and cocoons the ear in opulent sounds. Delian ecstasy is contrasted against the occasional echo of Carl Orff, an attractive mixture, even if – for all the incidental beauties – there is dangerously little variety of mood in the nine substantial sections. The composer was not entirely happy with what he was able to achieve in this first recording; even so, his performance certainly does not lack intensity and the recording (made by Argo engineers) is excellent, given the inherent problems of the recording venue in Swansea.

Iernin (opera; complete).

*** Albany TROY 121/3 (3). Hill Smith, Pogson, Herford, Rivers, Powell, BBC Singers & Concert O, composer.

George Lloyd was only 21 when in the early 1930s he wrote this ambitious opera, and there is an open innocence in the warmly atmospheric, lyrical score. The piece was inspired by an ancient Cornish legend about ten maidens turned into a circle of stones, one of whom, Iernin (pronounced Ee-er-nin), returns in human form. Though this is ostensibly an old-fashioned opera, it deserves revival, and on the recording – taken from a BBC Radio 3 presentation in 1988 – the composer conducts a red-blooded, warmly expressive reading. Though some of the ensemble writing is less distinguished, the offstage choruses of faery folk are most effective. As to the soloists, Marilyn Hill Smith sings brightly in the title-role with all the agility needed, and the tenor, Geoffrey Pogson, copes well with the hero's role, if with rather coarse tone. The most distinguished singing comes from the rich-toned contralto, Claire Powell, as Cunaide. The third disc includes a half-hour interview with the composer, which makes up in part for the absence of background notes in the booklet with the libretto. Excellent, well-balanced BBC sound.

LLOYD WEBBER, William
(1914–82)

(i) *Aurora (tone poem); Invocation; Lento; Serenade for Strings; 3 Spring Miniatures.* (ii) *Benedictus* (for violin and organ); (iii) *Nocturne* (for cello and harp); (iv) *Jesus, Dear Jesus;* (i; v) *Love divine, All Loves excelling; Mass (Princeps pacis).*

*** Chan. 9595. (i) City of L. Sinf., Hickox; (ii) Little, Watson; (iii) Julian Lloyd Webber, Kanga; (iv) Cook, Arts Educational School, London, Jones; Antrobus (organ); (v) Westminster Singers.

William Lloyd Webber demonstrates in ten short works that he wrote tunes every bit as fluently as his son, Andrew. Lloyd Webber senior, church organist and teacher, was yet an arch-romantic at heart, whose style sets English pastoral alongside Rachmaninov-like surges of passion. The most ambitious piece is the symphonic poem, *Aurora*, which starts like Bartók as smoothed over by Vaughan Williams, then develops in a colourfully orchestrated sequence of ideas. A forthright setting of the *Mass* written for Westminster Cathedral happily reconciles Roman and Anglican manners, yet every one of these unpretentious miniatures, beautifully performed and recorded, offers music of winning openness.

(i) *Air & Variations; Fantasy Trio; Frensham Pond (Aquarelle); The Gardens at Eastwell (A Late Summer Impression); Mulberry Cottage; Sonatina; A Song for the Morning; 3 Spring Miniatures.* (ii) Songs: *The call of the morning; The forest of wild thyme; How do I love thee; I looked out into the morning; Love, like a drop of dew; Over the bridge; Sun-Gold; To the Wicklow hills.*

*** Hyp. CDA 67008. (i) Nash Ens.; (ii) Ainsley, Brown.

Lloyd Webber's chamber and piano pieces span a far wider period than the songs, starting with the *Fantasy Trio* of 1936, written when the composer was 22. The pieces inspired by particular places, like his very last known work, *The Gardens at Eastwell* for flute, are as freely lyrical as the songs. Very English in idiom, this music echoes not just early Bridge but occasionally Ireland too, as in the brisk, chattering piano piece, *Tree Tops*. The Nash Ensemble soloists are all outstanding, with the pianist, Ian Brown, an inspired linchpin in every item. Again, the gift of melody revealed in the eight songs included here is a rare one. In idiom rather like early Frank Bridge they have tunes ready to latch in the mind, largely predictable but with unexpected twists. John Mark Ainsley is a most sensitive interpreter and again Ian Brown makes a fine contribution.

Aria; Chorale, Cantilena & Finale; Choral March; Elegy; Festal March; 3 Interludes on Christmas Carols; Intermezzo; Meditation on Stracathro; Prelude; Prelude on Winchester New; 3 Recital Pieces (Prelude; Barcarolle; Nuptial March); Slumber Song; Solemn Procession; Song without Words; Trumpet Minuet; Vesper Hymn.

*** Priory PRCD 616. Watts (Willis organ of Salisbury Cathedral).

Like other discs of William Lloyd Webber's music, the Priory issue of organ pieces consistently reveals his fluent tunefulness, even if this is much more a specialist issue, the first recording made on the refurbished Willis organ at Salisbury Cathedral. Roughly half the 22 pieces here are typical examples of hushed and meditative organ music designed to fill in discreetly between items in a service, with five more designed as bright and energetic voluntaries for speeding congregations out of church. There are Franckian echoes in the chromaticism of the *Chorale, Cantilena and Finale*, but generally the style is very similar to that of the orchestral pieces. Sympathetic performances, very well recorded.

(i) *Missa Sanctae Mariae Magdalenae;* (ii) Arias: *The divine compassion: Thou art the King. The Saviour: The King of Love. 5 Songs.* (iii; iv) *In the half light (soliloquy); Air varié (after Franck);* (iv) *6 Piano Pieces.*

*** ASV CDDCA 584. (i) Richard Hickox Singers, Hickox; Watson (organ); (ii) Hall, P. Ledger; (iii) Julian Lloyd Webber; (iv) Lill.

William Lloyd Webber was a distinguished academic who, in a few beautifully crafted works, laid bare his heart in pure romanticism. In his varied collection, the *Missa Sanctae Mariae Magdalenae* is both the last and the most ambitious of his works, strong and characterful. John Lill is a persuasive advocate of the *Six Piano Pieces*, varied in mood and sometimes quirky, and accompanies Julian Lloyd Webber in the two cello pieces, written – as though with foresight of his son's career – just as his second son was born. Graham Hall, accompanied by Philip Ledger, completes the recital with beautiful performances of a group of songs and arias. Recording, made in a north London church, is warm and undistracting.

LÔBO, Duarte (c. 1565–1646)

Missa pro defunctis.

(BB) *** Naxos 8.550682. Oxford Schola Cantorum, Summerly – CARDOSO: *Missa pro defunctis.* ***

Duarte Lôbo, Mestre de Capela at Lisbon Cathedral, was an almost exact contemporary of Manuel Cardoso, whose music we have already discovered and who provides an eloquent coupling for this splendid Naxos CD. As performed here, Lôbo's *Missa pro defunctis* for double choir is a work of beautiful flowing lines (following directly on from Palestrina), bold dramatic contrasts and ardent depth of feeling. The *Agnus Dei* is particularly beautiful. A solo treble briefly introduces each section except the *Kyrie*, which adds to the effect of the presentation. This is another triumph from Jeremy Summerly and his excellent Oxford group (38 singers), who catch both the Latin fervour and the underlying serenity of a work which has a memorably individual voice.

Motets: *Audivi vocem de caelo; Pater peccavi.*

(BB) *** Naxos 8.553310. Ars Nova, Holten (with Concert of Portuguese Polyphony ***) – CARDOSO: *Motets;* MAGALHAES: *Missa O Soberana luz etc.* ***

Lôbo's two beautiful motets, *Audivi vocem de caelo* ('I heard a voice from heaven') and *Pater peccavi* ('Father, I have

sinned'), confirm the individuality of his writing. They are part of an outstandingly sung collection which is among the most desirable records of its kind in the catalogue.

LOCATELLI, Pietro (1695–1764)

L'Art del violino (12 violin concertos), *Op. 3.*

*** Hyp. CDA 66721/3. Wallfisch, Raglan Bar. Players, Kraemer.

Pietro Locatelli was a younger contemporary of Handel and Vivaldi. It was in 1733 that he wrote the present set of concertos, each of which in its outer movements includes an extended *Capriccio* of enormous technical difficulty with fast, complicated, sometimes stratospheric upper tessitura. Elizabeth Wallfisch not only throws off the fireworks with ease but also produces an appealingly gleaming lyrical line. Although Locatelli has not as strong a melodic personality as his famous contemporaries, the invention here has rhythmic vitality (which at times mirrors Vivaldi) and, in the Largo slow movements, a series of flowing ideas that have an inherent Handelian grace. With excellent, vital and stylish support from Kraemer and his Raglan Baroque Players, this may be counted a stimulating authentic re-creation of a set of concertos which had a profound influence on the violin technique of the time. The very well-balanced recording (the soloist real and vivid) is admirably clear yet has plenty of ambience.

Concerti Grossi, Op. 1/1–12.

(BB) *** Naxos 8.553445/6. Capella Istropolitana, Jaroslav Kreček.

**(*) Hyp. CDA 66981/2. Raglan Bar. Players, Wallfisch, Kraemer.

Locatelli's Op. 1, although indebted to Corelli (with the eighth of the set ending with a Christmas *Pastorale*), has a style and personality of its own. The invention is vigorous, the expressive range appealing. The Capella Istropolitana play with crisp attack, plenty of sparkle and resilient rhythms; the style of the slow movements reveals a keen identity with the lessons of period performances, even though modern instruments are used and phrasing is unexaggerated by bulges. The recording is admirable, with textures clear and with attractive, light sonorities. Most enjoyable and highly recommended.

The performances on Hyperion are lively enough, but there is at times an element of routine, a feeling of jogging along, as if the players are not convinced that this is a very distinctive Opus. Elizabeth Wallfisch leads the concertino and is fully up to the bravura demands placed on her, though in the lyrical music her 'authentic' style of phrasing seems slightly more intrusive than usual. The recording is bright and vivid, the ambience spacious.

Concerti Grossi, Op. 1/2, 5 & 12; Il Pianto d'Arianna, Op. 7/ 6; Sinfonia in F min. (composta per le esequie della sua Donna che si celebrarono in Roma).

*** Opus 111 OPS 30-104. Europa Galante, Biondi.

The composer himself set great store by his Opus 1 and

they are remarkable works, full of individuality. The sonata subtitled *Il Pianto d'Arianna*, from Opus 7, is even more ambitious, with ten brief movements, an occasional whiff of Vivaldi, and plenty of drama. Perhaps most striking of all here is the *Sinfonia 'for the Funeral of his Lady which Took Place in Rome'*, which opens with an accented *Lamento* of rare intensity, in which the composer could be suggesting a heartbeat. The performances here are full of cleanly articulated, bouncing rhythmic vitality and are also persuasively expressive. Fabio Biondi, who really knows his way about this repertoire, uses a triple rather than a double layout, with the concertino, a further tutti group still made up of soloists, plus the real tutti or ripieno. The organ continuo adds subtle extra colour. The recording is most vividly clear yet not too close, with plenty of natural ambience. Highly recommended.

6 Introduttioni teatrali, Op. 4/1–6; 6 Concerti Grossi, Op. 4/7–12.

*** Hyp. CDA 67041/2. Raglan Bar. Players, Wallfisch.

There is simply no better introduction to the music of Locatelli than this superbly invigorating collection of his six *Theatrical Introductions*. They are essentially (highly inventive) small-scale concerti grossi, with a concertino of four players, written in the fast–slow–fast manner of an Italian overture. Indeed, the finale of No. 5 reminds one of the fifth concerto grosso of Handel's Op. 6.

The Raglan Baroque Players offer also the other six *Concerti Grossi* which make up the rest of Locatelli's Op. 4. They too show him on his finest form, particularly the *Concerto No. 8 in F à immitazione de Corni da caccia*, where the opening *Grave* is quite profound, and then in later movements the solo violin of the concertino uses double-stopping ingeniously to depict a pair of horns. The remaining works are not as novel as this, but No. 10 (*Da Camera*) is a reworking of the *Sixth Sonata* of Locatelli's Op. 8 (see below) and includes the remarkable *Minuetto* with extended bravura variations, which are superbly played here by Elizabeth Wallfisch. The final concerto of the set features four solo violins and was surely influenced by Vivaldi's famous work in this format which he included in *L'Estro armonico*. It deserves to be better known. The playing of the Raglan Baroque Ensemble, directed from the violin by the estimable Elizabeth Wallfisch, is supremely vital and expressively alive. The aural brightness is rather sharply etched, but the basic sonorities are full and the ambience is appealing.

CHAMBER MUSIC

12 Trio Sonatas, Op. 2.

(M) ** Van. 99099 (2). Wentz, Musica ad Rhenum.

The Vanguard set is fluent and highly musical, and the continuo group (including organ in Nos. 2, 4, 6, 9 and 11) is very effective; but Jed Wentz's period flute sounds a little pale. Even so, this is offered at mid-price and is very well recorded. Readers will note that the cueing goes wrong for the final double sonata (in which, presumably, Wentz plays a duet with himself), which starts at track 19 (not 18), since

the previous sonata has four sub-divisions, not the indicated three.

6 Trio Sonatas, Op. 5.

(M) **(*) Van. 99087. Wentz, Moonen, Musica ad Rhenum.

Locatelli's Op. 5 *Trio Sonatas* are full of agreeable, singing melody and have plenty of lively invention too. It is optional to use a pair of flutes or two violins in their performance, and it might have been a good idea to vary the instrumentation, as two flutes used continually can prove too much of a good thing. However, Jed Wentz and Marion Moonen play with style and they blend nicely together; the continuo group includes a bassoon for added colour. Good performances, without any of the acerbities one associates with period performance, nicely recorded.

Violin Sonatas (for 1 or 2 violins) and continuo, Op. 8/1–10.

*** Hyp. CDA 67021/2. Locatelli Trio.

Locatelli's Op. 8 consists of six works for solo violin, of which the last is the most impressive with its closing *Aria di minuetto* with eight variations, demanding considerable bravura from the soloist. All the sonatas start with a slow, expressive introduction, with faster movements following. The remaining works are *Trio Sonatas*; with their format of (usually) four (or sometimes five) movements, they offer the composer even greater opportunities for variety and he is obviously intending to please his cultivated listeners. But the invention in these later works is deft in imaginative touches, and the contrapuntal writing is genially spirited. Provided you don't respond adversely to Elizabeth Wallfisch's tendency in playing to bulge very slightly on expressive phrasing, the performances are admirable, crisply detailed and refreshingly alive. The Hyperion recording is well up to standard.

LOCKE, Matthew (c. 1621–77)

Consort of Fower Parts: Suites Nos. 1 in D min.; 2 in D min./maj.; 3 & 4 in F; 5 in G min.; 6 in G.

*** Astrée E 8519. Hespèrion XX.

Consorts of Fower Parts: Suites Nos. 1–6; Flatt Consort a 3 'for my cousin Kemble'.

(N) *** Global Music Network GMNC 0109. Phantasm.

Consort of Fower Parts: Suites Nos. 1–6. Duos for 2 Bass Viols Nos. 1 in C; 2 in D.

**(*) Virgin VC5 45142-2. Fretwork, with North and Nicholson.

Matthew Locke, born in Devon, was a choirboy at Exeter Cathedral. When Charles II was restored to the throne of England, Locke became Master of the King's Music at the royal court, but he probably wrote the *Consort of Fower Parts* earlier, in the 1650s. If they are not ambitious in instrumentation, they are much more so in musical achievement. Each suite opens with a *Fantazie* and then follows a standard sequence of *Courante*, *Ayre* and *Saraband*. Locke's suites were regarded at the time as being composed, 'after the old style', but the music itself is forward-looking and by no means predictable. It seems likely that they would have been performed with continuo, a practice followed sparingly in both the Fretwork and Hespèrion performances, the former using archlute and organ, the later preferring a double harp to the lute.

All three sets of performances are highly musical, scholarly and well recorded, but there is a first choice. In the dance movements there is a extra rhythmic vigour and buoyancy with Hespèrion, and in the *Ayres* of the *First* and *Second Suites*, for instance, there is an extra expressive warmth, compared with a faster tempo and relative austerity of feeling with Fretwork. The latter's playing brings somewhat more refined textures, and the Virgin Veritas programme includes two extra works: a pair of *Duos* (each in six movements) for two bass viols.

However, Phantasm also play this music delightfully. Their approach is intimate yet also reveals the music's expressive qualities as being considerable, while the dance movements are very sprightly. They are admirably recorded and they also include the ambitious suite of six movements which the composer wrote for his cousin which includes no fewer than three *Fantazies*.

The Tempest (incidental music); *Canon on a Plain Song by Mr William Brode of Hereford.*

**(*) Teldec 3984 21464-2. Il Giardino Armonico (with
ZEDENKA: *Fanfare*; ANON.: *Tune for the Woodlark*;
ONOFRI: *Ricercare for Viola da Gamba & Lute*) – BIBER:
Battaglia; *Passacaglia*; *Partita VII for 2 Viole d'Amore &
Continuo*; *Violin Sonata Representativa*. **(*)

Matthew Locke wrote only the instrumental pieces for the 1674 London performance of *The Tempest*, which was a hybrid work, almost an opera, with contributions from various composers in addition to spoken dialogue. However, this collection of lively dances (often strikingly English in spirit) and more expressive and sometimes piquant Act Tunes works well as a suite. It is presented with great vitality by Il Giardino Armonico, although they tend to overdramatize music intended to divert and their aggressive rhythmic and bowing style will appeal mainly to those totally won over to period-instrument practice. The recording is vivid but close.

LOEWE, Carl (1796–1869)

Ballads and Lieder: *Archibald Douglas; Canzonette; Die drei Lieder; Edward; Elvershöh; Erlkönig; Freibeuter; Frühzeitiger Frühling; Der getreue Eckart; Gottes ist der Orient!; Die Gruft der Liebenden; Gutmann und Gutweib; Der heilige Franziskus; Heinrich der Vogler; Herr Oluf; Hinkende Jamben; Hochzeitlied; Ich denke dein; Im Vorübergehen; Kleiner Haushalt; Lynkeus, der Türmer, auf Fausts Sternwarte singend; Meeresleuchten; Der Mohrenfürst auf der Messe; Der Nöck; Odins Meeresritt; Prinz Eugen; Der Schatzgräber; Süsses Begräbnis; Tom der Reimer; Der Totentanz; Trommelständchen; Turmwächter Lynkeus zu den Füssen der Helena; Die Uhr; Die wandelnde Glocke; Wandrers Nachtlied; Wenn der Blüten Frühlingsregen; Der Zauberlehrling.*

(M) *** DG (IMS) 449 516-2 (2). Fischer-Dieskau, Demus.

For the most part this set was recorded in 1968–9, with a second group of songs added a decade later. With the great German baritone consistently in fine voice, it makes an ideal selection of some of Loewe's most memorable songs and ballads. Fischer-Dieskau, admirably accompanied by Jörg Demus, gives performances which have the commitment and intensity of spontaneous expression while remaining flawlessly controlled and strongly thought through. This alternative setting of the *Erlkönig*, preferred by many in the nineteenth century, is in its way as dramatic as Schubert's, if musically less subtle. The following *Edward* is also extraordinarily dramatic, while the magnificent *Die Uhr* ('The Timepiece') opens lightly but develops an unexpected depth of feeling. It is an excellent feature of the set that the translations are provided in full. Splendidly vivid recording: if you enjoy Schubert, you can hardly fail to relish the best of Loewe.

LOMBARDINI, Maddelena Laura
– see SIRMEN, Maddelena Lombardini

LOPATNIKOFF, Nikolai (1903–76)

Concertino for Orchestra, Op. 30.

(M) (***) Sony mono SMK 60725. Columbia SO, Bernstein –
DALLAPICCOLA: *Tartiniana for Violin & Orchestra*;
SHAPERO: *Symphony*. (***)

Nikolai Lopatnikoff left Russia after the Revolution, proceeding first to Finland and then settling in America where he taught composition in Connecticut and Westchester, New York. His work includes four symphonies. Listening to the *Concertino for Orchestra* (1944) whets the appetite. Lopatnikoff was championed by Koussevitzky (like Bernstein) and the *Concertino* was commissioned by him. The music is neoclassical in outlook without being in the least arid, and the invention is bright, imaginative and lively. A most enjoyable piece, and the 1953 mono recording comes up well in this well-transferred and intelligently planned compilation.

LORTZING, Albert (1801–51)

Die Opernprobe.

(M) *** CPO/EMI (ADD) 999 557-2. Marheineke, Gedda,
Hirte, Litz, Lövaas, Berry, Bav. State Op. Ch. & O, Suitner.

Best known for his opera *Der Wildschütz*, still popular in Germany today, Lortzing wrote this light-hearted satire in 1851, his very last piece, given its first performance on the day before he died. As a singer and actor himself, writing his own librettos, he had the gift of composing operas which, helped by his easy tunefulness, work well. *Die Opernprobe* ('The opera rehearsal') involves disguises and confusions of identity in the household of a music-loving Count who encourages his servants to perform. In a sparkling overture and ten numbers, mostly brief, it tells a simple story of true love triumphant, ending with a substantial finale in Mozartian style. Otmar Suitner directs a lively performance, very well sung and well produced in its dialogue, with first-rate (1974) EMI sound.

LOTTI, Antonio (c. 1667–1740)

Crucifixus.

(B) *** Double Decca (ADD) 443 868-2 (2). St John's College, Cambridge, Ch., Philomusica, Guest – BONONCINI: *Stabat Mater ***; PERGOLESI: *Magnificat in C; Stabat Mater**(*); D. SCARLATTI: *Stabat Mater;* A. SCARLATTI: *Domine, refugium factus es nobis; O magnum mysterium;* CALDARA: *Crucifixus.* ***

(B) *** Double Decca (ADD) 455 017-2. St John's College, Cambridge, Ch., L. Philomusica, Guest – CALDARA: *Crucifixus ***; PERGOLESI: *Magnificat* etc. **(*)

This short *Crucifixus*, which takes less than four minutes, may well have inspired the noble Caldara setting with which it frames Bononcini's beautiful *Stabat Mater* in this highly desirable collection of choral music. The Lotti setting is less elaborate in texture than Caldara's but it is hardly less noble or affecting. Performance and recording are excellent. Alongside the Caldara setting, this fine piece also comes as a filler for Decca's alternative compilation which centres on Pergolesi.

LOURIÉ, Arthur (1892–1966)

(i) *Concerto da camera;* (ii) *A Little Chamber Music;* (iii) *Little Gidding.*

*** DG 437 788-2. (i & iii) Kremer; (ii) Klug; (iii) Riegel; Deutsche Kammerphilharmonie.

Arthur Lourié began his career in St Petersburg as a 'futurist', an advocate of all things modern. This DG record is an excellent introduction to his music. *A Little Chamber Music* has a strongly Russian feel to it and quite a bit of Stravinsky. While still in Russia, Lourié became a Catholic convert and wrote a good deal of music inspired by Gregorian chant. As a Jew, he was in great danger but succeeded in escaping to the USA, and the two remaining works come from his American years: the *Concerto da camera* and the setting of *Little Gidding* from Eliot's *Four Quartets* for tenor. By then, he had come to sympathize with Eliot's aesthetic as well as his conservative and classical values. Neither work is a masterpiece, but both are of genuine musical interest and value. First-rate performances from Kremer and the Deutsche Kammerphilharmonie and, in the *Little Gidding* setting, Kenneth Riegel. The recording is excellent.

(i) *String Quartets Nos. 1–3 (Suite);* (ii) *Duo for Violin & Viola.*

**(*) ASV CDDCA 1020. (i) Utrecht Qt; (ii) Koskinen, Raiskin.

The three quartets were composed in quick succession: the *First* is a two-movement piece lasting half an hour, whose first movement (nearly 20 minutes) is very amorphous and wanting in concentration. The *Second Quartet* (1923) is a much shorter, one-movement work with a hint of Stravinskian neoclassicism and humour. But it is the economical and well-wrought *Duo for Violin and Viola* that is most Russian. The *Third Quartet* (1924), subtitled *Suite* (its movements are called *Prélude, Choral, Hymne* and *Marche funèbre*), save for the last movement, does not make as strong an impression as *A Little Chamber Music* from the same year (see above). Nevertheless this is an interesting byway explored with great dedication by these players.

LOVENSKIOLD, Herman (1815–70)

La Sylphide (ballet) complete.

(M) *** Chan. 6546. Royal Danish O, Garforth.

La Sylphide (1834) predates Adam's *Giselle* by seven years. It is less distinctive than Adam's score, but it is full of grace and the invention has genuine romantic vitality – indeed, the horn writing in the finale anticipates Delibes. The wholly sympathetic playing is warm, elegant, lively and felicitous in its detailed delicacy, yet robust when necessary and always spontaneous. A most enjoyable disc, superbly recorded.

LUDFORD, Nicholas (1485–1557)

Masses; Magnificat benedicta & Motets (as listed below).

✪ (M) *** ASV CDGAX 426 (4). Cardinall's Musick, Carwood.

Nicholas Ludford is one of the least familiar of the Tudor masters; he never enjoyed the fame of his older contemporary, Fayrfax, or the much younger Tallis. This four-CD box gathers together the four splendid discs of Ludford's music performed by Andrew Carwood and his excellent group of singers, who are individually as impressive as in the blended whole. This is music of remarkably passionate feeling, and it brings to life a composer who spent much of his working life in St Stephen's Chapel at St Margaret's, Westminster. He was an ardent Catholic and was very happily married – he paid for his wife to have her own pew and gave her an elaborate ceremonial burial. He then married again, and his second wife was instructed to prepare something more modest for his interment alongside his beloved first spouse. His music is little short of extraordinary, and we hope our Rosette will tempt collectors to explore it, either through this comprehensive box, which will retail at just short of £40, or by trying one of the individual issues.

Missa Benedicta et venerabilis; Magnificat benedicta.

*** ASV CDGAU 132. Cardinall's Musick, Carwood.

Ludford uses the same plainchant for both works, but the voicing has a distinct emphasis at the lower end of the range, not only adding to the weight but also bringing a certain darkness to the sonority. The performance has the same spontaneous feeling that distinguishes this magnificent series throughout, and it confirms Ludford as one of the most emotionally communicative and original musicians of his age. The plainsong Propers relate the music to the Feast of the Assumption. Excellent, full recording.

Missa Christi Virgo dilectissima; Motet: Domine Ihesu Christie.

*** ASV CDGAU 133. Cardinall's Musick, Carwood.

This is music of great beauty, whose expressive eloquence and floating lines quite carry the listener away. Andrew Carwood proves an excellent advocate and the sound is also spacious and well balanced.

Missa Lapidaverunt Stephanum; Ave Maria ancilla trinitatis.

*** ASV CDGAU 140. Cardinall's Musick, Carwood.

This Mass, celebrating St Stephen the Martyr, is thought to have been written soon after he was appointed verger and organist there in 1527. In five-part polyphony the scale is formidable, culminating in a magnificent *Agnus Dei*. The performances, fresh and stylish, are punctuated by apt plainsong.

Missa Videte miraculum; Motet: Ave cuius conceptio.

*** ASV CDGAU 131. Cardinall's Musick, Carwood.

The six-part *Missa Videte miraculum* brings a remarkable double treble line running together, often in thirds. Overall this work is as fine as the others in the series, and it is gloriously sung.

LUIGINI, Alexandre (1850–1906)

Ballet Egyptien, Op. 12 (suite).

(B) *** CfP (ADD) CD-CFP 4637. RPO, Fistoulari –
KETELBEY: *Collection.* ***

Because of its bandstand popularity, Luigini's amiable and tuneful *Ballet Egyptien* has never been taken very seriously. However, the four-movement suite is highly engaging (both the two central sections have good tunes), especially when played as affectionately and stylishly as here under that master conductor of ballet, Anatole Fistoulari. The 1958 recording has come up remarkably freshly, and this makes an excellent bonus for an outstanding Ketèlbey concert.

LULLY, Jean-Baptiste (1632–87)

Petits motets: *Anima Christe; Ave coeli; Dixit Dominus; Dominum salvum fac Regem; Exaudi Deus; Laudate pueri; O dulcissime; Omnes gentes; O Sapientia; Regina coeli; Salve Regina.*

*** HM HMC 901274. Les Arts Florissants, Christie.

Lully's Italianate *Petits Motets* range in length from two to nine minutes. Recent scholarship has rejected several attributed works, but has confirmed the present group as authentic. They are written for three voices, usually sopranos – since the music was intended for a Paris Convent Choir, and the sopranos here are appealingly fresh-voiced. The continuo (with Christie himself at the organ) is tellingly and discreetly managed, and the performances have a pleasing sweetness of timbre and lightness of touch.

Motets: *Benedictus; Exaudi Deua; O dulcissime; Notus in Judaea Deus.*

(N) (BB) *** Naxos 8.554389. Concert Spirituel, Nicquet.

Master of the King's Music in the golden age of Louis XIV, Lully dominated French music for over thirty years, carefully keeping such composers as Charpentier in the background. Though in depth he may not quite match Charpentier, let alone Purcell, he was consistently lively and inventive. This excellent Naxos issue offers three of the larger-scale, multi-movement motets with choir and soloists, set against two of the best-known 'little' motets for soloists alone, including the beautiful *O dulcissime*. First-rate French performances with no singers individually named.

Dies irae; (i) *Te Deum.*

(M) **(*) Erato (ADD) 0630 11226-2. Smith, Devos; (i) Bessac, Vandersteene, Huttenlocher; Valence Vocal Ens., Paillard CO, Paillard.

The *Dies irae* is a noble piece encapsulating a mood of dark melancholy, and it makes a strong impression here, with a notably dedicated contribution from the two soloists. The effect has a striking, elegiac beauty. The sudden choral inter-jections at a faster pace are convincingly managed. Here the choral focus in the CD transfer could be cleaner, but the sound has plenty of body and a most attractive ambience. The better-known *Te Deum* dates from 1677. It opens regally with brilliant high trumpets and is a work of contrasting splendour and breadth rather than the general-purpose pomp often favoured by Lully and his followers. Paillard and his forces give a thoroughly committed and eloquent account of the piece, and the recording is richly expansive, with the choral sound cleaner. Incidentally, it was while conducting this work that Lully vigorously brought down the heavy stick that served to mark the beat on to his right foot; gangrene eventually set in, and a couple of months later he died!

Les Comédies Ballets: excerpts from: (i) *Les Amants magnifiques; L'Amour médecin; Le Bourgeois Gentilhomme; George Dandin (Le Grand Divertissement royal de Versailles); Monsieur de Pourceaugnac (Le Divertissement de Chambourd); Pastoral comique; Les Plaisirs de l'île enchantée.* (ii) *Phaëton (tragédie en musique; complete).*

(B) *** Erato Ultima 3984 26998-2 (2). (i) Poulenard, Mellon, Ragon, Laplénie, Verschaeve, Delétré, Cantor; (ii) Crook, Yakar, J. Smith, Gens, Thereul, Sagittarius Vocal Ens.; Musiciens du Louvre, Minkowski.

This immensely rewarding Ultima Double combines a selection of highlights from the comedies-ballets which Lully wrote in collaboration with Molière, with his 'tragédie en musique', *Phaëton*. One despairs at the absence of texts and translations – how can a major record company be so parsimonious in this way? – and the documentation provided instead is totally inadequate. (Otherwise this would have received a ✿.) But the music is so delightful, and the performances so alive and spirited, that this Ultima Double must be strongly recommended, even to those who are totally unfamiliar with this repertoire. The series of comédies-ballets represented here were written between 1663 and 1670, and their tuneful and often outrageous burlesque represents an unparalleled comic partnership between composer and playwright – French insouciance combined with wittily *bucolique* music which obviously reflects the influence of Italian comic opera, yet never loses its Gallic character, especially in the charming and often beautiful pastoral airs. The ensemble of ironic salutation to men of medicine (Lully despised doctors) in *L'Amour médecin* is matched by the robust *bouffe* male interchanges wallowing in the hedonistic pleasures of *L'Isle enchantée*, and there are similar comically boisterous ensembles in the divertissement, *George Dandin*, although they are perhaps capped by the extraordinary excerpt from *Monsieur de Pourceaugnac* which makes fun of polygamy. The two longest selections come from *Le Bourgeois Gentilhomme*, infectiously spirited, which includes one syncopated number which anticipates 'America' in Bernstein's, *West Side Story*, and finally, the masterly third *intermède* of *Les Amants magnifiques*, which combines a gentler humour with graceful lyricism. The team of soloists clearly relishes every ridiculous situation, and the presentation has consistent sparkle and spontaneity, while the lyrical music is most persuasively phrased by singers and orchestra alike.

Phaëton tells of the attempt of the son of the Sun God to drive across the heavens in his father's chariot. The horses bolt and this threatens to set fire to the earth, whereupon Jupiter strikes him dead, to the apparent rejoicing of everyone. When Libye can then be partnered by her beloved Epaphus, it is hardly a tragedy at all, with their love celebrated earlier in two brief, but intensely beautiful duets, punctuating the many solo airs. The cast is strong – Véronique Gens is most affecting as Libye, with Rachael Yakar and Jennifer Smith impressive too, and Howard Crook clean-focused and stylish in the name part. Throughout the two discs Marc Minkowski's direction is compellingly fresh and resilient. Both recordings are co-productions between Erato and Radio France and are strikingly vivid and immediate. Again one laments the appalling presentation, or lack of it, but this is still a set not to be missed.

Atys (opera): complete.

*** HM HMC 901257/9 (3). De Mey, Mellon, Laurens, Gardeil, Semellaz, Rime, Les Arts Florissants Ch. & O, Christie.

Christie and his excellent team give life and dramatic speed consistently to the performance of *Atys*, and there are many memorable numbers, not least those in the sleep interlude of Act III. Outstanding in the cast are the high tenor, Guy de Mey, in the name-part and Agnès Mellon as the nymph, Sangaride, with whom he falls in love.

Atys: highlights.

(M) *** HM HMX 291249 (from complete recording, with De Mey, Mellon, Les Arts Florissants, cond. Christie).

(B) *** HM HMX 290844/46 (3) (from complete recording, cond. Christie) – CAMPRA: *Idomenée:* highlights; RAMEAU: *Castor et Pollux:* highlights. ***

Atys remains one of Christie's greatest successes on record;

it is full of good things, and many of them are also included on the single-disc highlights selection (notably the delightful Sleep scene of Act III). With consistently fine singing and superb recording, this disc contains about a third of the opera (68 minutes).

This CD is also offered as part of one of Harmonia Mundi's enterprising 'Trios', in this case offering three discs of operatic highlights together in a slip-case at bargain price. But unlike its companions, *Idomenée* and *Castor et Pollux*, no translation is included for *Atys*. Taken as a package with its two companions, this collection of highlights costs only a fraction of the price of the three-disc complete set.

LUMBYE, Hans Christian (1810–74)

The complete orchestral works

Volume 1: *Amélie Waltz; Britta Polka; Artist Dreams Fantasia; Cannon Galop; Champagne Galop; Columbine Polka-mazurka; Copenhagen Steam Railway Galop; Dagma Polka; Deborah Polka Mazurka; King Christian IX's March-past; Otto Allin's Drum Polka; Queen Louise Waltz; Saecilie Waltz; Salute to August Bournonville Galop; A Summer Night at the Mön Cliffs Fantasia; (Berlin) Vauxhall Polka.*

** Marco 8.223743. Tivoli SO, Bellincampi.

Volume 2: *Amanda Waltz; Camilla Polka; Crinoline Polka-mazurka; The Dream after the Ball; Goodnight Polka; King Carl XV's March-past; A Little Ditty for the Party Galop; Master Erik's Polka; Military Galop; Minerva Polka; Regatta Festival Waltz; Rosa and Rosita Waltz; Salute to Capri Polka; Victoria Bundsen Polka-mazurka; Victoria Galop; Wally Polka.*

** Marco 8.223744. Tivoli SO, Bellincampi.

Volume 3: *Amager Polka, No. 2; Carnival Joys; Pictures from a Masquerade; Concert Polka for 2 Violins; Festival Polonaise in A; The Guardsmen of Amager: Finale-galop; New Year Greeting March; Ornithobolaia Galop; Sounds from Kroll's Dance Hall; Tivolis Concert Salon Galop; Tivoli Volière Galop; Torchlight Dance.*

** Marco 8.225122. Tivoli SO, Bellincampi.

Following on from their monumental Strauss Edition, Marco Polo now turn their attention to the 'Strauss of the North', Hans Christian Lumbye. The three volumes released at the time of writing are sympathetically and enjoyably played, but the recordings are not ideal: they are too reverberant and backwardly balanced, taking away some of the warm intimacy, as well as the sparkle, this music should ideally have. But collectors who wish to explore this composer's output in depth will find much to enjoy here. Like the Strausses, Lumbye's fund of melody is seemingly inexhaustible, and the various novelty pieces are often delightful. Much of the writing has a robust quality which is most infectious, and the orchestration is always colourful. These Marco Polo discs, despite the too-resonant sound, will certainly give pleasure.

Vol. 5: *Artist Carnival Locomotive Galop; Caroline Polka Mazurka; In the Dusk (Fantasy); Fountain Waltz; Hesperus Waltz; Jenny Polka; Marie Elisabeth Polka; Memories of Vienna, Waltz; The Night before New Year's Day (Polka Mazurka); Regards to the Ticket-Holders of Tivoli (March); Salute March of King Frederik VII; The Sleigh Ride (Galop); Telegraph Galop.*

(N) *** Marco 8.225171. Tivoli SO, Vetö.

We have not yet received Volume 4 but Volume 5 in Marco Polo's Lumbye edition seems to offer marginally richer sound than in earlier volumes, and the performances are excellent. There are plenty of things to delight here: the *Sleigh Ride* sounds suitably festive, with its dashing runs up and down the scale, whips and bells, while the full-length concert waltzes, such as *Memories from Vienna* and the *Hesperus Waltz*, provide more substantial fare as well as much charm and elegance. *The Night before New Year's Day* charmingly alternates between the major and minor keys, while *In the Dusk* is a charming pastoral evocation of a peaceful evening which gradually becomes more and more animated, though it ends, 'à la invitation to the dance', as peacefully as it began. There are some novelties here, too: the *Telegraph Galop*, reflecting rivalry between two orchestras, opens with a couple of wallops on the bass drum and is a communication between both groups, who 'telegraph melodies' to each other, sometimes in different keys, though finally coming together – an amusing idea skilfully realized. This is one of the best CDs in the series.

Amager Polka; Amelie Waltz; Champagne Galop; Columbine Polka Mazurka; Copenhagen Steam Railway Galop; Dream Pictures Fantasia; The Guard of Amager (ballet): Final Galop. Helga Polka Mazurka; Hesperus Waltz; Lily Polka (Dedicated to the Ladies); Queen Louise's Waltz; Napoli (ballet): Final Galop. Salute to August Bournonville; Salute to our Friends; Sandman Galop Fantastique.

⚘ *** Unicorn DKPCD 9089. Odense SO, Guth.

This superb Unicorn collection offers 75 minutes of the composer's best music, with wonderfully spontaneous performances demonstrating above all its elegance and gentle grace. It opens with a vigorous *Salute to August Bournonville* and closes with a *Champagne Galop* to rival Johann junior's polka. In between comes much to enchant, not least the delightful *Amelie Waltz* and the haunting *Dream Pictures Fantasia* with its diaphanous opening textures and lilting main theme. But Lumbye's masterpiece is the unforgettable *Copenhagen Steam Railway Galop*. This whimsical yet vivid portrait of a local Puffing Billy begins with the gathering of passengers at the station – obviously dressed for the occasion in a more elegant age than ours. The little engine then wheezingly starts up and proceeds on its journey, finally drawing to a dignified halt against interpolated cries from the station staff. Because of the style and refinement of its imagery, it is much the most endearing of musical railway evocations, and the high-spirited lyricism of the little train racing through the countryside, its whistle peeping, is enchanting. This is a superbly entertaining disc, showing the Odense Symphony Orchestra and its conductor, Peter Guth,

as naturally suited to this repertoire as are the VPO under Boskovsky in the music of the Strauss family. The recording has a warm and sympathetic ambience and gives a lovely bloom to the whole programme.

Amelie Waltz; Britta Polka; Champagne Galop; Columbine Polka Mazurka; Concert Polka (for 2 violins and orchestra); Copenhagen Steam Railway Galop; Dream Pictures (fantasy); The Lady of St Petersburg (polka); The Guards of Amager: Final Galop. My Salute to St Petersburg (march); Napoli (ballet): Final Galop. Polonaise with Cornet Solo; Queen Louise's Waltz; Salute to August Bournonville; St Petersburg Champagne Galop.

*** Chan. 9209. Danish Nat. RSO, Rozhdestvensky.

This 5 Chandos disc opens with an arresting fanfare and sets off into the *Champagne galop* with much brio. Throughout his programme, Rozhdestvensky's approach is altogether more extrovert than Guth's on Unicorn, and the Royal Danish Orchestra, without loss of finesse, play almost everything here with great gusto. The Copenhagen Steam Railway engine becomes a mainline express and reaches an exhilarating momentum before slamming on its brakes, to be vociferously welcomed by the Danish porters as it arrives at its destination. One cannot but respond to the energy and vivacity of the playing here, while the lovely *Dream Pictures* creates a total contrast and is most poetically done. The recording is spectacularly resonant and adds to the impact.

Britta Polka; Cannon Galop; Cecilie Waltz; Dancing Tune from Kroll Waltz; Indian War Dance; King Christian IX March of Honour; King George I March of Honour; Manoeuvre Galop; Memories from Vienna Waltz; Nordic Brotherhood; Pegasus Galop; Summernight at Møns Cliff Galop; Sophie Waltz; Velocipedes Galop; Victoria Quadrille; Welcome Mazurka; Les Zouaves Galop.

*** Unicorn DKPCD 9143. Odense SO, Guth.

A further, essentially energetic selection of sparkling Lumbye repertoire, splendidly played with much spirit by the excellent Odense orchestra under Guth. The *Velocipedes Galop* makes an engaging and vivacious opener, and the *Cannon Galop* which closes the concert has properly spectacular effects, plus a final bang to make the listener jump. The *Memories from Vienna Waltz* has a particularly winning lilt, but there is nothing here that quite matches the *Copenhagen Steam Railway Galop*.

LUTOSLAWSKI, Witold (1916–94)

(i) *Chain II. Chain III; Novelette; (i; ii) Partita.*

(M) *** DG (IMS) 445 576-2. (i) Mutter, (ii) Moll; (i; ii) BBC SO, composer.

Chain III; Novelette.

(B) *** DG 439 452-3. BBC SO, composer – LIGETI: *Chamber Concerto;* SCHNITTKE: *Concerto Grosso No. 1.* ***

Chain II, a 'dialogue for violin and orchestra', follows up the technique of *Chain I* (of which at present there is no really satisfactory recording), contrasting fully written sections with *ad libitum* movements, where chance plays its part within fixed parameters. *Chain III* then makes a sustained contrast with its ear-catching orchestral colours. The *Partita* is a development of a piece for violin and piano which Lutoslawski originally wrote for Pinchas Zukerman, with the first, third and fifth movements now scored for violin and orchestra. With Mutter and the composer the most persuasive advocates, both concertante pieces establish themselves as among the finest examples of Lutoslawski's late work. *Novelette*, an attractive, scherzo-like piece, full of incandescent energy, is common to both the main, mid-priced programme and the Classikon reissue, coupled with other stimulating works by Ligeti and Schnittke. DG here are obviously treading water to see if they can sell this kind of avant-garde music in a wider marketplace at budget price.

Cello Concerto.

*** EMI (ADD) CDC7 49304-2. Rostropovich, O de Paris, composer – DUTILLEUX: *Cello Concerto.* ***

The *Cello Concerto* was written in response to a commission by Rostropovich. As in some other Lutoslawski pieces, there are aleatory elements in the score, though these are carefully controlled. The sonorities are fascinating and heard to good advantage on the EMI CD. The soloist is rather forward, but in every other respect the recording is extremely realistic. Rostropovich is in his element and gives a superb account of the solo role, and the composer's direction of the accompaniment is grippingly authoritative.

(i; ii; iii) *Cello Concerto;* (i; ii; iv) *Concerto for Oboe, Harp & Chamber Orchestra;* (v) *Concerto for Orchestra;* (i; ii; ix) *Dance Preludes;* (i; vi; vii) *Les Espaces du sommeil;* (v) *Funeral Music;* (i; vii) *Symphony No. 3;* (viii) *Variations on a Theme by Paganini;* (v) *Venetian Games.*

(B) *** Philips Duo (ADD) 464 043-2 (2). (i) Composer; (ii) Bav. RSO; (iii) Schiff; (iv) H. and U. Holliger; (v) Nat. SO of Warsaw, Rowicki; (vi) Fischer-Dieskau; (vii) BPO; (viii) Argerich, Freire; (ix) Brunner.

This excellent introduction to Lutoslawski includes many of his most important works. The *Third Symphony* is given an authoritative performance under the composer, while *Les Espaces du sommeil* is performed by its dedicatee, Dietrich Fischer-Dieskau, and more definitive versions could hardly be imagined. Recorded around the same time in equally impressive performances was the *Cello Concerto* with Heinrich Schiff, a fine work, while the *Concerto for Oboe, Harp and Chamber Orchestra* was written for the Holligers, who perform it here; it mingles charm, irony and intelligence in equal measures. The *Dance Preludes* date from 1953 and were later scored for clarinet and orchestra, as recorded here. They are more folk-like in idiom and are attractively presented by Eduard Brunner (clarinet). The *Paganini Variations*, a piano duo from 1941, is exhilarating and played with great virtuosity by Martha Argerich and Nelson Freire. The Rowicki performances date from 1964. The *Funeral Music* is an angular work, which makes some impression, but is rather empty. *Venetian Games* is music of wider appeal, while the famous *Concerto for Orchestra* – a brilliant and highly

attractive work – is thoroughly idiomatic. All the Rowicki performances are excellently recorded and have transferred very well to CD. A bargain set in every way.

Concerto for Orchestra.

(B) **(*) EMI (ADD) double fforte CZS5 72664-2 (2). Chicago SO, Ozawa – BARTOK: *Concerto for Orchestra* **(*); JANACEK: *Sinfonietta* ***; STRAVINSKY: *Firebird Ballet.* **(*)

Concerto for Orchestra; Jeux vénitiens; Livre pour orchestre; Mi-parti; Musique funèbre; Symphonic Variations; Symphonies Nos. 1–2.

(B) *** EMI (ADD) double fforte CZS5 73833-2 (2). Polish Nat. RSO, composer.

Concerto for Orchestra; Mi-parti; Overture for Strings; 3 Poems by Henri Michaux.

(BB) *** Naxos 8.553779. Camerata Silesia, Szostak; Polish Nat. RSO, Wit.

(i) *Concerto for Orchestra;* (ii) *Paganini Variations* (for piano and orchestra); (iii) *Musique funèbre;* (iv) *Paroles tissées.*

(B) **(*) Double Decca (ADD) 448 258-2 (2). (i) SRO, Kletzki; (ii) Jablonski, RPO, Ashkenazy; (iii) Cleveland O, Dohnányi; (iv) Pears, LSO, composer – SZYMANOWSKI: *Violin Concerto No. 2; Symphonies Nos. 2–3.* **(*)

The eminently recommendable EMI set, conducted by the composer, is a 'retrospective', drawing many of the key orchestral works from an even more comprehensive six-LP set dating from the late 1970s. Opening with the enticing early *Symphonic Variations*, with their highly individual colouring and atmosphere (sparklingly recorded), the set includes not only the *Concerto for Orchestra* but also both symphonies. Even today some of this music, notably *Jeux vénitiens, Livre* and *Mi-parti*, sounds very avant-garde, but the latter piece is hauntingly atmospheric in the composer's hands. Indeed, with performances so obviously authoritative and of a high standard, and the recording exceptionally vivid, they show this composer's sound world to good advantage.

In the *Concerto for Orchestra* the Swiss orchestra on Decca 5 are no match for Ozawa's virtuoso players, and this EMI double fforte set is similarly priced and offers attractive couplings. The acoustics of Chicago's Medinah Temple posed problems for the engineers and the overall sound is somewhat two-dimensional and dryish.

Kletzki directs a brilliant account of the *Concerto for Orchestra*, and the Swiss orchestra play quite well for him; moreover they are given vintage Decca sound from 1968. Kletzki makes a small cut in the second movement, albeit with the composer's permission. *Musique funèbre* (not perhaps one of the composer's most inspired pieces) is very well played and recorded, but it does not generate the least degree of tension. The *Paganini Variations* for two pianos is very successful indeed, however: it is one of Lutoslawski's earliest and most readily appealing works. Peter Jablonski plays it in the much later transcription for piano and orchestra, and his pleasure and delight will surely be shared by the listener. The digital recording is first class. The *Paroles tissées* were written for Peter Pears, who sings the cycle here, and Lutoslawski's writing shows extraordinary understanding of that singer's special qualities and the colour of his voice. Performances and recording are ideal.

This fifth volume of Naxos's excellent Lutoslawski series provides an excellent cross-section for anyone wanting to sample this inspired composer's work. The settings of the surrealist poet, Henri Michaux, dating from the early 1960s are highly original in their use of choral textures, and *Mi-parti* in a single span, slow then fast, points forward in the brilliance and originality of its interplay of instruments to the later symphonies. Strong and purposeful performances vividly recorded in full, immediate sound.

Piano Concerto.

*** Koch 3-6414-2. Kupiec, Bamberg SO, Judd – SZYMANOWSKI: *Symphony No. 4.* **

(i) Piano Concerto. Chain 3; Novelette.

*** DG (IMS) 431 664-2. (i) Zimerman; BBC SO, composer.

(i) Piano Concerto. Little Suite; Symphonic Variations; Symphony No. 2.

(BB) *** Naxos 8.553169. (i) Paleczny; Polish Nat. RSO, Wit.

Ewa Kupiec gives a compelling performance of this difficult concerto, with its fragmentary writing in slow movements and chattering passage-work in the second-movement Scherzo. Even more than the dedicatee, Krystian Zimerman, or Piotr Paleczny, she finds fun in the Scherzo and, warmly supported by Judd and the Bamberg orchestra, gives point and purpose to the seemingly improvisatory writing of the other movements. Excellent sound. The Szymanowski symphony with its important piano part makes an interesting but ungenerous coupling.

The *Piano Concerto* is also marvellously played by Zimerman and the BBC Symphony Orchestra under the composer. It is beautiful to listen to, but for all its diversity of aural incident and activity here one is left wondering whether there is much of enduring substance. The two remaining works are also very convincingly presented. Absolutely first-rate recording.

The early, tonal *Symphonic Variations*, make an attractive introduction to the second of Naxos's discs in what aims to cover his complete orchestral music. The *Little Suite* is an approachable work too, before the much tougher and more substantial symphony and concerto, which make up the great part of the disc. In two massive movements, *Hesitant* and *Direct*, the *Symphony No. 2* is an uncompromising piece, and here is helped by a purposeful, very well-rehearsed performance. The *Piano Concerto* is even more elusive, often fragmentary, but again the performance is magnetic: Piotr Paleczny plays with a clarity and brilliance that sound totally idiomatic. Excellent sound, with good presence.

Double Concerto for Oboe, Harp & Chamber Orchestra.

*** Koch C 130045. Süss, Schellenberger, Franz Liszt CO, Budapest, Zoltán Peskó – IBERT: *Sinfonia Concertante;* MARTIN: *3 Danses for Oboe, Harp, String Quintet & String Orchestra.* ***

Lutoslawski develops the widest range of aurally intriguing colouristic patterns. The first movement opens with the strings buzzing like a hive of bees, with oboe and harp soon offering their own alternative mêlée. The central *Dolente* shimmers with pizzicato and other glistening sounds, yet the oboe melisma dominates; the finale is a piquant *Marciale e grotesco*. The concerto has brief aleatory elements, but they are framed within a carefully controlled structure. This is remarkable music and the performance and recording are in every way worthy of Lutoslawski's unpredictable progress.

Dance Preludes (for clarinet and orchestra).

*** Hyp. CDA 66215. King, ECO, Litton – BLAKE: *Clarinet Concerto;* SEIBER: *Concertino.* ***

*** Chan. 8618. Hilton, SNO, Bamert – COPLAND; NIELSEN: *Concertos.* ***

Lutoslawski's five folk-based vignettes are a delight in the hands of Thea King and Andrew Litton, who give sharply characterized performances, thrown into bold relief by the bright, clear recording. Janet Hilton also emphasizes their contrasts with her expressive lyricism and crisp articulation in the lively numbers. Excellent recording.

Symphony No. 3; (i) Variations on a Theme of Paganini; (ii) Les Espaces du sommeil; (iii) Paroles tissées.

(BB) *** Naxos 8.553423. (i) Glemser; (ii) Kruszewski; (iii) Kusiewicz; Polish Nat. RSO (Katowice), Wit.

Symphonies Nos. 3–4; (i) Les Espaces du sommeil.

*** Sony SK 66280. LAPO, Salonen; (i) with Shirley-Quirk.

The format of the *Fourth*, Lutoslawski's culminating symphony, is elliptical, its broodingly atmospheric opening building to an almost Waltonian lyrical cantilena and a darkly passionate climax. This slowly disintegrates until a brief, emphatically rhythmic coda produces a sudden resolution. Salonen gives deeply committed, passionate accounts of both this and the dramatic *Third Symphony*, also built in one continuous span. Here he challenges the composer's own interpretation, and in *Les Espaces du sommeil* Salonen provides a different slant from the composer himself, making it – with the help of John Shirley-Quirk as an understanding soloist – much more evocative and sensuous in full and well-balanced sound.

The earliest piece on Naxos, the *Paganini Variations* for two pianos, comes from 1941, but in 1978 the composer rearranged the piece for piano and orchestra. This and the *Third Symphony* from 1982 are well played and recorded. Less persuasive, perhaps, is *Les Espaces du sommeil* (the soloist is a bit forward, though he sings well). In the *Paroles tissées* the singer is less at ease both with the musical idiom and with the French language. All the same, this well-filled CD is recommendable in every other respect.

Symphony No. 4; (i) Chain II; Interlude; Partita. Musique funèbre.

(BB) *** Naxos 8.553202. (i) Bakowski; Polish Nat. RSO, Wit.

The *Symphony No. 4* is Lutoslawski's culminating masterpiece, which, in its concentration over two linked movements, seems to echo Sibelius's *Seventh*. The darkly intense *Funeral music* in memory of Bartók is another beautiful and concentrated work, while the two violin concertante works,

Chain II and *Partita*, here come with the separating *Interlude*, similarly thoughtful, which Lutoslawski wrote as a link. In almost every way, not least in the playing of the violinist, Krzysztow Bakowski, these Polish performances match and even outshine earlier recordings conducted by the composer, helped by full, brilliant sound.

Paganini Variations (arr. Ptasazynska).

*** Chan. 9398. Safri Duo & Slovak Piano Duo – BARTOK: Sonata for 2 Pianos & Percussion ***; HELWEG: American Fantasy. **

A slight piece from Lutoslawski's youth, dressed up by Marta Ptasazynska for the same forces as the Bartók *Sonata*. It is brilliantly played and no less remarkably recorded at a Danish Radio concert. There is enthusiastic applause, which is understandable, and whistling, which is unfortunate.

LYATOSHYNSKY, Boris (1895–1968)

Symphony No. 1 in A min., Op. 2; Overture on 4 Ukrainian Themes, Op. 20; Poem of Reunification, Op. 40.

*** Russian Disc RDCD 11055. Ukrainian State SO, Gnedash.

Symphonies Nos. 2, Op. 26; 3 in B min., Op. 50.

*** Marco 8.223540. Ukrainian State SO, Kuchar.

Symphonies Nos. 4 in B flat min., Op. 63; 5 in C ('Slavonic'), Op. 67.

*** Marco 8.223541. Ukrainian State SO, Kuchar.

Symphony No. 4 in B flat min., Op. 63; (i) On the Banks of the Vistula, Op. 59; (ii) Lyric Poem.

** Russian Disc RDCD 11062. Ukrainian State SO, Blazhkov; (i) Sirenko; (ii) Glushchenko.

Lyatoshynsky began writing his *First Symphony* immediately after the First World War, and it is a well-crafted, confident score that inhabits the world of Russian post-nationalism, Strauss and Scriabin. It abounds in contrapuntal elaboration and abundant orchestral rhetoric. The *Second Symphony* followed in 1936, but its air of pessimism did not sit well in post-*Lady Macbeth* Russia. Although the *Third Symphony* (1951) tries hard to be a good Soviet symphony, it does not wholly ring true.

The *Fourth Symphony* (1963) is more directly Shostako-vichian than its predecessors. Its middle movement depicts what must be a mysterious, chimerical city to a Ukrainian, namely, Bruges. There is striking use of bells and celesta, and at times a suggestion of Messiaen. The *Fifth (Slavonic)* certainly pays tribute to his master, Glière, in using the Rus theme, *Il'ya Mourametz*, as well as a wide variety of Russian, Bulgarian and Serbian liturgical melodies. It aspires to explore the common roots of the Slavonic peoples; hence its title. There are many touches of colour and some token modernity, but basically this looks back to earlier masters.

Those with exploratory tastes will find much to interest them in these symphonies, provided they are not expecting masterpieces. As far as performances are concerned, the Ukraine orchestra obviously is inside this music, and none of the playing is second rate. The Marco Polo recordings are more than marginally superior to the Russian Disc, and the

performances sound much better rehearsed than is usually the case with this label, while the odd fillers on the Russian Discs are not of sufficient interest to tip the scales in their favour.

MAAZEL, Lorin (born 1930)

(i) Music for Cello & Orchestra; (ii) Music for Flute & Orchestra; (iii) Music for Violin & Orchestra.

*** RCA 09026 68789-2. (i) Rostropovich; (ii) Galway; (iii) composer; Bav. RSO, Post.

The austere titles of these works of Lorin Maazel – products of his increased activity as a composer in the mid-1990s – belie the fact that Maazel is at root a late romantic, working to no formula but expressing what he feels, often lyrically, always with colour and fine feeling for orchestral timbres. The most outward-going of the three is the flute piece for James Galway, reflecting the dedicatee's flamboyant character as an artist. It ends with a big cadenza, accompanied by percussion, leading into a brilliant coda heightened by blatant brass. The cello piece written for Rostropovich is the most demanding of the three, an extended half-hour made up of eight contrasted sections, one developing from the other and ending, as the work began, with a darkly reflective coda. Maazel wrote the violin piece for himself to play, dedicating it to his wife, who inspired it. Again the music is largely reflective, ending on an epilogue marked 'tranquillo', which yet includes a pained climax. Excellent performances and recording.

MCCABE, John (born 1939)

(i) Flute Concerto. Symphony No. 4 (Of Time and the River).

*** Hyp. CDA 67089. BBC SO, Handley; (i) with Beynon.

Celebrating the composer's sixtieth birthday, this is the finest disc yet of the music of John McCabe. Completed in 1994, his *Fourth Symphony*, entitled *Of Time and the River* after Thomas Wolfe's novel, is a magnificent work in two substantial movements – fast to slow, then slow to fast. The idiom is warmer and more approachable than in McCabe's earlier music, echoing in its atmospheric orchestration and some of the melodic lines Britten on the one hand and Sibelius on the other, while remaining distinctive and new. Superb performances and vivid recording, not just of the *Symphony* but of the large-scale *Flute Concerto* McCabe wrote for James Galway. Ideal notes as well.

Edward II (ballet; complete).

*** Hyp. CDA 67135/6 (2). Royal Ballet Sinfonia, Wordsworth.

This full-length ballet, in two acts of nearly an hour each, is not only John McCabe's most ambitious work, it is among the most powerful as well as the most approachable of all his music. Taking as his starting point the Marlowe play *Edward II*, McCabe (in a scenario devised in collaboration with the choreographer David Bintley) has also drawn on Brecht's rethinking of that play, as well as the satirical fourteenth-century *Le Roman de Fauvel* (which was itself inspired by the story of the English king and his weaknesses). That last source has helped him to introduce a contrasting element of humour. McCabe's score is at once colourfully atmospheric as well as symphonic in its thinking, vividly telling the story in mood and action, drawing on medieval sources for themes and for the 'tuckets and alarums' which add point to such a plot. Having abandoned the more severely serial stance of his earlier music, McCabe as in his superb *Third Symphony* (also issued on Hyperion) adopts a tonal idiom which is yet distinctively his, not at all derivative. There have been few full-length ballet scores as impressive as this since Prokofiev and Britten, inspiring Barry Wordsworth and the Royal Ballet Sinfonia to a strong and colourful performance, vividly recorded.

(i) *Symphony No. 2;* (ii) *The Chagall Windows;* (i; iii) *Notturni ed alba.*

(M) *** EMI CDM5 67120-2. (i) CBSO, Frémaux; (ii) Hallé O, Loughran; (iii) Gomez.

The *Symphony*, in contrasted sections, fast and slow, within a single-movement framework, has an underlying bitterness to it, an expression of tension not entirely resolved. *Notturni ed Alba*, with its lovely writing for the soprano, is a setting of Latin words which yet inspire often passionate music, exciting sounds, a joy in sonorities. Fine committed performances of these two works, richly recorded. The commissioning of *The Chagall Windows* by the Hallé, his inspiration and composition were vividly depicted in a TV programme, and this colourful recording first appeared soon after. McCabe used the visual stimulus as his starting point, but the result, readily approachable, is satisfying on its own musical terms. Loughran's vigorous direction adds to the attractiveness of the piece.

String Quartets Nos. 3, 4 & 5.

*** Hyp. CDA 67078. Vanbrugh Qt.

Few twentieth-century string quartets have such a haunting opening as John McCabe's masterly *Third*, written in 1979; this indelibly simple phrase resonates throughout the *Variants* of the first movement, which alternate between intense slow sections and quixotic and sometimes aggressive faster passages. Two chimerical Scherzi frame the central *Romanza*, passionate and restless, and the work ends with a Passacaglia, which 'derives its overall shape and flow from the concept of a lakeland stream', tumbling down in irregular patterns until the return of that memorable opening motif leads to a wonderful sense of calm. The single-movement *Fourth Quartet* (1982) is hardly less compelling. It again uses variation form. Its treatment is at times serene, at others very vigorous indeed. Once again the close is comparatively peaceful, with an expressive cello soliloquy . The *Fifth Quartet* (1989) is programmatic and, as the very beginning makes plain, was inspired by a series of Graham Sutherland's aquatints called *The Bees*. We follow these small but energetic creatures through larval and hatching stages, the first flight, the partnership of bee and flower, a wild nest, the expulsion and killing of an enemy intruder, and finally a domestic fight between workers and drones, which ends

brusquely and positively. The aural results are most intriguing and require much virtuosity from the players, which is readily forthcoming. Indeed, these three remarkable works could hardly be presented with greater concentration or more commitment, and the recording is first class.

5 *Bagatelles; Haydn Variations; Studies Nos. 3 (Gaudi); 4 (Aubade); 6 (Mosaic); Variations, Op. 22.*

*** British Music Society BMS 424DC. Composer.

The British Music Society have here published a major survey of McCabe's piano music, from the early *Variations* (1963) to the much more complex *Haydn Variations* of 1983, while the pianistically exploratory *Studies* span the decade between 1970 and 1980. The early *Variations* are not difficult to follow, but the later *Haydn Variations* are much more complex and individual, and made less approachable for the listener in that the Haydn theme (from the *Piano Sonata in G minor*, Hob XVI:44) does not appear until more than halfway into the work. The *Bagatelles*, five brief vignettes, in the words of the composer 'were written to a request for not-too-difficult 12-notes pieces', but the third and sixth *Studies* are extended works, architecturally inspired. McCabe is a formidable pianist and is obviously an ideal exponent of his own music, which is highly atmospheric in pianistic terms, but intellectually stimulating rather than lyrical in the melodic sense. Excellent recording.

MacCUNN, Hamish (1868–1916)

Concert overture: *The Land of the Mountain and the Flood.*

(B) *** CfP (ADD) CD-CFP 4635. RSNO, Gibson – GERMAN: *Welsh Rhapsody;* HARTY: *With the Wild Geese;* SMYTH: *Wreckers Overture.* ***

Concert overture: *The Land of the Mountain and the Flood; The Dowie Dens o'Yarrow; The Ship o' the Fiend.* Cantata: (i) *The Lay of the Last Minstrel: Breathes There the Man; O Caledonia! Jeannie Deans (opera): excerpts.*

*** Hyp. CDA 66815. BBC Scottish SO, Brabbins; (i) with Watson, Milne, MacDougal, Sidholm, Gadd, Danby, Scottish Opera Ch.

Hamish MacCunn was the son of a Greenock ship-owner and proved something of a musical prodigy. For many years his name has been kept alive by Sir Alexander Gibson's dramatically sympathetic account of his colourful and melodramatic concert overture, *The Land of the Mountain and the Flood*, written when he was only eighteen. It is a very well-constructed piece, with a memorable tune, which became a signature tune for a Scottish TV series. Martin Brabbins and the BBC Scottish Orchestra, in a brilliant new performance, give it fresh life, and the Hyperion recording has more range and sparkle than the (fully acceptable) CfP version. *The Dowie Dens o' Yarrow* is a very similar piece, with comparable rhythmic impetus and another attractive secondary theme, given to the oboe. The even more atmospheric *Ship o' the Fiend* uses both solo horn and oboe most evocatively at the opening, then introduces another endearing lyrical cello theme reminiscent of *The Land of the*

Mountain and the Flood. Thus the three works are in many ways linked, and are all worth hearing in performances as committed and convincing as these.

MacCunn's opera *Jeanie Deans* is a tuneful and colourful piece with plenty of musical vitality. One thinks at times of a Scottish Edward German, but sometimes of Boughton too. Effie's aria, *Oh that I again could see* (she is imprisoned in the Tolbooth), and the following *Lullaby* are touchingly sung here by Janice Watson, and the choral contribution is very spirited. Some of the singing is vibrato-afflicted, but the performance is thoroughly alive and freshly enjoyable. The excerpt from the cantata *The Lay of the Last Minstrel* brings a suitably vigorous closing chorus, *O Caledonia!*

MacDOWELL, Edward (1861–1908)

Piano Concertos Nos. 1 in A min., Op. 15; 2 in D min., Op. 23.

*** Olympia OCD 353. Amato, LPO, Freeman.

(i) *Piano concertos Nos. 1–2. Witches' dance, Op.17/2;*
(ii) *Romance for Cello & Orchestra, Op. 35.*

(N) (BB) **(*) Naxos 8.559049 (i) Prutsman; (ii) Byrne; Nat. SO of Ireland, Fagen.

(i) *Piano concertos Nos. 1–2. Second Modern Suite, Op. 14.*

(N) *** Hyp. CDA 67165. Tanyel; (i) with BBC Scottish SO, Brabbins.

Of MacDowell's two *Piano Concertos* the *First* is marginally the lesser of the two: the melodic content, though very pleasing, is slightly less memorable than in the *Second*. This is a delightful piece, fresh and tuneful, redolent of Mendelssohn and Saint-Saëns. Donna Amato's scintillating performance is entirely winning, and she is equally persuasive in the *A minor*. This music needs polish and elegance as well as fire, and Paul Freeman's accompaniments supply all three. The recording, made in All Saints', Tooting, has an agreeable ambient warmth. A highly rewarding coupling in all respects.

Seta Tanyel also gives sparkling performances of these attractive works, relishing the pianistic fireworks typical of this lyrical American composer. Allegedly written in just two weeks to satisfy his composition teacher, Joachim Raff, the *First Concerto* reflects that genesis both in the improvisational quality of the writing and in the obvious exuberance of the composer in answering a challenge. There are echoes of Liszt in the structure and some of the piano writing, but the similarities with the Grieg concerto are more striking still, as they are in the more popular *Second Concerto* with its unconventional structure of a measured first movement leading to a central Scherzo and a finale with a substantial slow introduction.

The fill-up, involving piano alone, offers a sequence of six colourful and unpretentious genre pieces, squibs that allegedly were written largely on Macdowell's train journeys for composition lessons. Tanyel's characterful playing, full of sparkle and imagination, is well matched by the playing of the BBC Scottish Orchestra under Martyn Brabbins, helped by full-bodied, well-balanced recording.

Issued simultaneously with the excellent Hyperion ver-

sion, the Naxos issue offers a serviceable bargain alternative, if neither so characterfully played nor so beautifully recorded. Stephen Prutsman is a powerful pianist who relishes the challenge of Macdowell's virtuoso demands, never overtaxed, yet who misses the degree of characterful individuality brought to this music by Seta Tanyel. The coupling of two concertante works may not be as generous as that on Hyperion, but it is more apt, when the *Witches' Dance* is a delightful showpiece for piano and orchestra, and the *Romance*, rather less interesting, is a typically lyrical piece with cello. The Irish orchestra is most responsive, though not helped by sound which is slightly muffled at times.

2 Fragments after the Song of Roland, Op. 30: The Saracens; The Lovely Aldä. Hamlet/Ophelia, p. 22; Lancelot and Elaine, Op. 25; Lamia, Op. 29.

*** Bridge 9089. RPO, Krueger.

For the seven years between 1884 and 1890, MacDowell occupied himself with writing Lisztian symphonic poems. The two *Fragments from the Song of Roland* are the middle movements of what was intended as a programme-symphony, and *The Lovely Aldä* is a gentle portrait which has something in common with MacDowell's *Wild rose*, if not as melodically memorable. The portraits of *Hamlet* and *Ophelia* are highly romantic and, like both the symphonic poems, the lyrical writing is very appealing. There is a distinct flavour of Tchaikovsky, and Lisztian hyperbole is absent from the more vigorous passages. *Lancelot and Elaine* (drawing on Tennyson's *Idylls of the King*) is particularly evocative with a poignant theme portraying the heroine's unrequited love for Lancelot, and fine writing for the horns. *Lamia* is based on a poem by Keats. She is an enchantress in the form of a serpent, but changes into a lovely maiden in order to win the love of Lycius. MacDowell's music resourcefully varies the theme representing Lamia to indicate her changes of form and the events of the narrative, which ends badly for both characters. The performances here are very persuasive. Karl Krueger is a splendid and dedicated advocate and the RPO playing is warmly seductive and beautifully recorded.

Suite No. 1 for Large Orchestra, Op. 42.

(M) **(*) Mercury [434 337-2]. Eastman-Rochester O, Hanson – CHADWICK: *Symphonic Sketches* **(*); PETER: *Sinfonia.* **

Suites Nos. 1, Op. 42; 2 (Indian); Hamlet and Ophelia (tone poem), Op. 22.

(N) (BB) *** Naxos 8.559075. Ulster O, Yuasa.

It is good to see that at last the orchestral music of Edward MacDowell is being properly explored, and in Naxos's super-bargain 'American Classics' series. MacDowell may have been a musical conservative but, in spite of the European flavour of his music, he thought himself a true 'American' composer – favouring the influences of 'the manly and free rudeness of the American indian' rather than jazz, which he thought had too strong an eastern European, Bohemian inheritance.

The *Indian Suite* opens with a dramatic horn call and its

first movement (*Legend*) is a grandiose evocation of the 'once-great past of a dying race'. The delightful *Love Song* takes its melody from the Iowas, yet the rhythm has a Scottish snap. *In Wartime* is a lively country dance with a New England flavour, while the elegiac and touchingly powerful *Dirge* is drawn from the Kiowa tribe. The closing *Village Festival* opens with delicate pizzicatos and spirited flutes, but expands energetically in the brass, finally returning to the mood of the opening movement.

The *First Suite* (actually the second in order of composition) is a comparable series of genre evocations from the opening *In a Haunted Forest* to a brief, charming *Summer Idyll*. The lively hunting *October* sequence leads to a *Wild rose* reminder in the delightful *Shepherdess's Song*, and the suite ends with a winning dance from the *Forest Spirits*.

The brooding atmosphere of the portrait of *Hamlet and Ophelia* soon gives way to melodrama in the manner of a Lisztian symphonic poem. The music has a rich lyrical strain and later a doom-laden ambience; although it is Ophelia rather than Hamlet who dominates the touchingly lyrical close. The performances here are outstanding in every way, full of colour, warmth and vitality, and the recording is state-of-the-art. This would be worth getting at full price; in the Naxos range it is not to be missed.

The performance from Hanson is of high quality, as one would expect from this source; the 1961 recording is well up to Mercury standard, though the upper violin timbre is a bit tight.

PIANO MUSIC

Fireside Tales, Op. 61; New England Idylls, Op. 62; Sea Pieces, Op. 55; Woodland Sketches, Op. 51.

**(*) Marco 8.223631. Baragallo.

MacDowell's most famous piano piece opens this recital: *To a Wild Rose* (named by his wife) is the first of the ten *Woodland Sketches*. They are all pleasant if not distinctive vignettes, most lasting a little over a minute. The other three suites are very similar. Not a CD to listen to all at once but to be dipped into; one can appreciate that James Baragallo is a thoroughly sympathetic exponent, and he is well recorded.

MCEWEN, John Blackwood
(1868–1948)

Three Border ballads: Coronach; The Demon Lover; Grey Galloway.

*** Chan. 9241. LPO, Mitchell.

These three *Border Ballads*, written between 1906 and 1908, are symphonic poems, well-stocked with distinctive ideas, and with a strong Lisztian inheritance. *The Demon Lover*, the most ambitious in scale (some might feel too ambitious), has a kind of luscious melodramatic post-Wagnerian chromaticism that isn't too far from the world of Scriabin. Even the first to be written, *Coronach*, has a sensuous feeling that one associates with more southern climes, yet the nobility of its main theme also suggests links with Parry and Elgar.

The performances here are warmly sympathetic and very well played and recorded, and almost convince one that these works are masterpieces.

A Solway Symphony; (i) Hills o'Heather; Where the Wild Thyme Blows.

*** Chan. 9345. (i) Welsh; LPO, Mitchell.

McEwen's highly evocative *Solway Symphony* is a triptych of seascapes marked by magically transparent orchestration and crisply controlled argument. He was influenced by the folksong movement – notably here in *Hills o'Heather* with its hints of reels – but the flavour is quite individual, with occasional echoes of Sibelius in the sparer moments. Above all, this is warm-hearted music. The first of the three movements of the symphony, *Spring Tide*, is built on a striking motif, argued with clean-cut directness. The second movement, *Moonlight*, is developed, Sibelius-like, over a gently nagging ostinato, while the finale, *The Sou'west Wind*, opens with brassy exuberance in galloping compound time, and only later develops a stormy side, before ending darkly in F sharp minor. *Hills o'Heather* is a charming movement for cello and orchestra, while *Where the Wild Thyme Blows* uses slow pedal points to sustain harmonically adventurous arguments. The performances, conducted by Alasdair Mitchell, who edited the scores, are outstanding, a well-deserved tribute to a neglected composer who was far more than an academic. The recording is sumptuously atmospheric.

CHAMBER MUSIC

Violin sonatas Nos. 2; 5 (Sonata-Fantasia); 6; Prince Charlie – A Scottish Rhapsody.

(N) *** Chan. 9880. Charlier, Tozer.

McEwen was outward-looking and much drawn to the French school. His *Second Violin Sonata* (1913–14) was begun at Cap Ferrat outside Bordeaux and shows the influence of both Debussy and Chausson. All the works recorded here show him to be a polished craftsman and a composer of real culture. The *Fifth Sonata* (1921), written for Albert Sammons, said to be his finest in this genre, recalls John Ireland and like everything on this disc holds the listener. Very good playing from Olivier Charlier and Geoffrey Tozer, excellent and vivid sound from Chandos and informative notes by Bernard Benoliel.

MACHAUT, Guillaume de
(*c.* 1300–1377)

Ballades, rondeaux, virelais: Amours me fait desirer; Blauté qu toutes autres pere; Dame a qui; Dame, a vous sana retollir; Dame, de qui toute ma joie vent; Dame je sui cliz/Fins cuers doulz; Dame mon coeur en vous remaint; Douce dame jolie; Foy porter; Je vivroie liement; Rose, liz, printemps, verdure; Tuit mi penser; Motet: Inviolata genitrix/Felix virgo/Ad te suspiramus.

*** Hyp. CDA 66087. Kirkby, Gothic Voices, Page.

Although (until recently) primarily celebrated for his church music, Guilluame de Machaut, poet-composer, canon and lover (even in his sixties), led the fullest secular life. He was immensely successful on all levels, living in his later years in a large elegant house in Rheims. He finally assembled his own poetry and music and arranged to have it elaborately illustrated and copied into a permanent anthology. The ballades and virelais included here are written imploringly, and in elaborate admiration, to ladies of great beauty and of all other virtues, except apparently a willingness to respond. The fluid part-writing of the ensemble pieces is unique, but the solo pieces are very appealing, especially when sung, as two of them are here, by an artist of the calibre of Emma Kirkby. One wishes she had played a larger part in the programme, but Rogers Covey-Crump, Colin Scott-Mason, Emily Van Evera and Margaret Philpot all make sympathetic individual contributions. As a group the Gothic Voices certainly know how to shape the melancholy melismas of the concerted items: they blend beautifully together, giving effective unexaggerated tweaks to the passing moments of dissonance. The closing four-part motet, a Triplum, celebrates the Virgin Mary and is perhaps the most beautiful work on the disc. Excellent recording.

Ballades, motets, rondeaux & virelais: *Amours me fait desirer; Dame se vous m'estés lointeinne; De Bon Espoir – Puis que la douce rousee; De toutes flours; Douce dame jolie; Hareu! hareu! le feu; Ma fin est mon commencement; Mes esperis se combat; Phyton le mervilleus serpent; Quant j'ay l'espart; Quant je suis mis au retour; Quant Theseus – Ne quier veoir; Se ma dame m'a guerpy; Se je souspir; Trop plus est belle – Biauté paree – Je ne sui mie certeins.*

(M) *** Virgin (ADD) VED5 61284-2 (2). Early Music Cons. of L., Munrow (within Recital: 'The Art of Courtly Love' ***).

This collection is within 'Guillaume Machaut and His Age', which is itself part of David Munrow's wide-ranging collection, 'The Art of Courtly Love'. Treasures here include cantatas with James Bowman and Charles Brett beautifully matched as soloists. Everything reveals both the remarkable individuality of Guillaume de Machaut as a highly influential composer who spanned the first three-quarters of the fourteenth century, and the life and energy that Munrow consistently brought to early music. Excellent transfers.

Chansons (ballades, rondeaux, viralais): *Certes mon oueil; Comment peut on; De toutes flours; En amer a douce vie; En vipere; De Fortune; Hel dame de valour; Je ne cuit pas; Je puis trop bien; Liement me deport; Ma fin est mon commencement; Mors sui; Se quanque amours; Tant doucement.*

(*) DG 457 618-2. Orlando Consort.

The opening and closing four-part melismas here, *Tant doucement* ('So sweetly am I imprisoned') and *De toutes fleurs* ('If all the flowers'), are characteristic of Machaut's hypnotic flowing style. Moreover, the duet *Mors suis* ('I die if I do not see you') is a highlight, showing his writing at its most intensely melodic, while in *En amer a douce vie* ('In bitter love'), one of the composer's earliest four-part ballades, the twists of the melodic line and plangent touches in the part-writing have a remarkable emotional ambivalence.

The Orlando Consort blend beautifully together, led by Robert Harre-Jones whose richly coloured alto line is most appealing. But the snag is the basic sameness of colour inevitable with two, three or four unaccompanied male voices, however expressively they sing, and however pleasingly recorded. In that respect the Hyperion disc above is much more appealing.

Messe de Nostre Dame (with Plainsong for the Proper of the Mass of Purification for the Blessed Virgin (Candlemass).

(*) HM HMC 901590. Soloists, Ens. Organum, Pérès.
(B) *** HM Trio HMX 290891.93 (3) (as above) Ens. Organum, Pérès – OCKGEHEM: *Requiem;* HILDEGARD: *Laudes of Saint Ursula.* ***

Messe de Nostre Dame; Le Lai de la Fonteinne (The Lay of the Fountain); Rondeau: *Ma fin est mon commencement (My End is my Beginning).*

(*) Hyp. CDA 66358. James, Stafford, Covey-Crump, Potter, Padmore, Nixon, Hillier, George, Hilliard Ens., Hillier.

Messe de Nostre Dame. Le Livre dou Voir dit (excerpts): *Plourez dames; Nes qu'on porroit (ballades); Sans cuer dolens (rondeau); Le Lay de bonne esperance; Puis qu'en oubli (rondeau); Dix et sept cinq (rondeau).*

***(*) Naxos 8.553833. Oxford Camerata, Summerly.

With his *Messe de Nostre Dame* (dedicated to the Virgin Mary), Guillaume de Machaut wrote the first known complete setting of the Ordinary of the Mass: *Kyrie, Gloria, Credo, Sanctus* and *Agnus Dei*. He chose to finish with his own simple interpolation: *Ite missa est*, which very briefly tells us, 'The mass is ended; thanks be to God.' Machaut's writing is full of extraordinary, dissonant clashes and sudden harmonic twists which are immediately resolved, so the music is both serene and plangently stimulating: here is an epoch-making work of great originality. Both the Hilliard Ensemble and the Oxford Camerata present the Mass as it stands (and therefore they have room for extra items), whereas Marcel Pérès has inserted the plainsong for the Proper of the Mass, taken from the Candlemas liturgy for the Purification of the Virgin, which is presented in the same florid style as is Machaut's setting of the Ordinary.

Of the three performances here, Jeremy Summerly's account is undoubtedly the most eloquently serene; it is beautifully controlled and modulated, rather after the fashion of the famous Willcocks/King's College accounts of the Byrd Masses. The harmonic pungencies are cleanly presented but unexaggerated and – compared with Hillier and (especially) Pérès – the music's lines, although by no means bland, flow in relative tranquillity. The singers apparently experimented freely with plicas – notational signs indicating some kind of ornament – the meaning of which is uncertain but which appear frequently; but there is none of the audacious decoration which is so striking on the Harmonia Mundi version.

Hillier's approach certainly does not lack repose or linear beauty, but he presses the music onwards with a much greater sense of drama than obtains in Oxford. His *Kyrie* is three minutes shorter than Summerly's, and the *Gloria* brings freely passionate accelerandos, which are highly involving but may or may not be authentic. The Hilliard group is superbly recorded with a strong presence, and there is no doubt that the music's unexpected dissonances are more dramatically brought out here than on Naxos.

However, the boldness of effect produced by the Ensemble Organum under Marcel Pérès in every way dramatically upstages its two competitors. In his (confident and very interesting) notes, Pérès laments that 'The art of ornamentation is little practised by performers today, which is much to be regretted. Ornamentation is essential, for it creates the active force of the work.' And in this performance it certainly does – to an extraordinary degree. The Ensemble Organum bring a distinctly Arab flavour with the dark pungency of male timbre and twirling embellishments to the ornamentation. The singing itself is powerfully resonant and the dissonances ring out boldly. The recording is splendid. This CD additionally comes in a slip case as part of a Harmonia Mundi Trio at budget price which is highly recommendable, for the recordings of Hildegard and Ockeghem are equally arresting.

On Naxos the chansons were recorded, equally effectively, at the BBC's Maida Vale studio; they celebrate Machaut as poet/lover as well as composer and, at its modest price, the disc is worth having for these alone. Indeed *Le Livre dou voir dit* is one of the most remarkable cycles of poems of the Middle Ages, inspired by the passionate love between the elderly composer (Machaut was in his sixties when he wrote all the music here) and his adolescent student admirer, Péronne d'Armetières. The music itself is lighter in lyrical feeling than the Mass and its melodic and harmonic style, while recognizably similar, is far less plangent. This is one of Naxos's real bargains.

The solo singing in the extra items on the Hyperion disc is very impressive indeed. *Le Lai de la Fonteinne* is another elaborate poem of 12 stanzas in praise of the Virgin, six polyphonic, six monodic, beautifully sung by Mark Padmore, Rogers Covey-Crump and John Potter, while the shorter rondeau, an expressive piece if restlessly so, is ingeniously constructed, and is a 'crab' canon by inversion, in that the imitating part, instead of being presented straightforwardly, is written backwards and upside down – appropriately so, to fit the text: 'My End is my Beginning.'

MACHY, Sieur de (died c. 1692)

Pièces de viole (1685): Suites 1–3.

(N) (M) *(*) Astrée (ADD) ES 9946. Savall.

Little is known about Sieur de Machy (or Demachy) except that his published *Viol Suites* predated the first publication of the Marais suites by a year. They are the usual collection of Allemandes, Courantes, Sarabandes, Gavottes, Gigues and Minuets, but so freely improvisational is the style of Savall's performances that their rhythmic profile is often all but lost. This is simple music, and it needs a direct, clearly rhythmic approach. An interesting but essentially disappointing reissue (from the late 1970s).

MacKENZIE, Alexander (1847–1935)

Benedictus, Op. 37/3; Burns – 2nd Scottish Rhapsody, Op. 24; Coriolanus (incidental music): Suite, Op. 61; The Cricket on the Hearth: Overture, Op. 62; Twelfth Night (incidental music): Overture/Suite, Op. 40.

*** Hyp. CDA 66764. BBC Scottish SO, Brabbins.

Mackenzie wrote in the Stanford/Elgar/Parry tradition rather than showing any strong Scottish traits. However, in the *Burns Rhapsody* he uses three Scottish folk tunes quite felicitously, notably 'Scots! wha hae', which is very emphatic. The second movement has charm, and indeed Mackenzie's own lyrical gift is quite striking in the jolly, at times Sullivanesque *Cricket on the Hearth Overture* (which also shows his deft orchestral skill), and of course the *Benedictus* with a melody typical of its time. The incidental music for *Twelfth Night* is in the form of an overture, subdivided into six sections, with a Shakespeare quotation for each to identify its mood. These vignettes are attractively scored and have considerable character. The whole programme is presented with commitment and polish by the BBC Scottish Symphony Orchestra and makes a very agreeable hour and a quarter of not too demanding listening. The recording is excellent.

Scottish Concerto, Op. 55.

*** Hyp. CDA 67023. Osborne, BBC Scottish SO, Brabbins – TOVEY: *Piano Concerto in A.* ***

Hyperion's imaginative series of Romantic piano concertos here offers two works by composers associated with Scotland. Unlike Tovey, Sir Alexander Mackenzie was Scottish by birth. Built on Scottish themes, Mackenzie's *Concerto*, premiered by Paderewski, centres round its lyrical slow movement, framed by a rhapsodic first movement and a dance finale based on *Green Grow the Rushes O*. The young Scottish pianist Steven Osborne is a brilliant advocate, Brabbins a natural partner.

MacMILLAN, James (born 1959)

(i) As others see us; 3 Dawn Rituals; Untold; (ii) Veni, veni, Emmanuel (Concerto for Percussion & Orchestra); (iii) After the Tryst (Miniature Fantasy for Violin & Piano).

⬤ *** RCA 09026 61916-2. (i) Scottish CO (members), composer; (ii) Glennie, SCO, Saraste; (iii) Crouch, composer.

In *Veni, veni, Emmanuel* MacMillan has written a concerto for percussion that in its energy as well as its colour consistently reflects both the virtuosity and the charismatic personality of Evelyn Glennie. Taking the Advent plainsong of the title as his basis, he reflects in his continuous 26-minute sequence the theological implications behind the period between Advent and Easter. The five contrasted sections are in a sort of arch form, with the longest and slowest section in the middle. The very close of the work brings a crescendo of chimes intended to reflect the joy of Easter in the Catholic service and the celebration of the Resurrection. In this superb recording the orchestra as well as Evelyn Glennie play with both brilliance and total commitment, if not with quite the extra thrill that at the end is experienced in live performances. In the fill-up works – brief pieces marked by the same dramatic intensity – MacMillan himself as conductor inspires strong, positive performances from various groups of SCO players. With first-rate, atmospheric sound – *Veni, veni, Emmanuel* recorded in Usher Hall, Edinburgh, the rest in City Hall, Glasgow – this is outstanding in every way.

(i) *Clarinet Concerto (Ninian);* (ii) *Trumpet Concerto (Epiclesis).*

(N) *** BIS CD 1069. RSNO, Lazarev with (i) Cushing; (ii) Wallace.

Like most of his works, both these large-scale concertos owe their inspiration to MacMillan's profound Catholic faith, each of them involving a dramatic programme. *Epiclesis*, the *Trumpet Concerto*, was originally written in 1993 for John Wallace, the soloist here, and revised five years later. Meaning prayer or invocation, that title leads the composer to attempt a musical equivalent to the Eucharist, the act of communion, in what he describes as 'the transformation of musical substances'. As ever, the orchestral writing is colourful and brilliant, with elaborate use made of percussion, notably a thundersheet often played pianissimo. The free-flowing, almost improvisatory writing for the solo trumpet, with much fluttering figuration, is punctuated by big orchestral outbursts, leading at the most moving moment to a simple chorale, played pianissimo on the trumpet as though in purification. After that the jazzy syncopations of the final section sound almost like Charles Ives in brash contrast, leading finally to the most powerful climax and a fading away as the soloist departs.

The *Clarinet Concerto*, also played here by its dedicatee, John Cushing, first clarinet in the RSNO, dates from 1997, a celebration of the early Scottish Saint Ninian, with three of his miracles each inspiring a movement. The third and last, much the longest, brings another depiction of the Eucharist, with a joyful brassy chorale as a final climax. Again the soloist has a virtuoso role, but many of the most memorable moments come in hushed lyrical passages, with the clarinet bringing a resolution after orchestral violence. The performances of both works are not just brilliant but totally committed in bringing out the drama of this music, with BIS recording of demonstration quality.

Cumnock Fair; Sinfonietta; Symphony No. 2.

(N) *** BIS CD 1119. SCO, Composer.

MacMillan's *Second Symphony*, written in 1999, builds on ideas from an early piano sonata. A massive central movement is flanked by an evocative prelude, with bird-twittering ostinatos, a slow chorale and a reflective postlude, in which the chorale returns. The central movement is often violent, with sharp contrasts of mood and tempo. Typically full of striking ideas, it is brilliantly orchestrated.

The *Sinfonietta*, written in 1991 and dedicated to MacMillan's wife, Lynne, starts mysteriously with a hypnotic slow section, which is brutally interrupted by violent *fortis-*

simo chords. It is almost Ives-like in its terracing of contrasted ideas, while *Cumnock Fair* is even more so in its kaleidoscopic quotations of dances with a Scottish flavour, wilder and wilder. With a piano prominent in the texture, the mêlée finally fades away to common chords. Strong, intense performances flawlessly balanced.

The Confession of Isobel Gowdie; Tryst.

*** Koch/Schwann 3-1050-2. BBC Scottish SO, Maksymiuk.

Inspired by the horrific execution in 1662 of Isobel Gowdie, tortured into confessing herself a witch, MacMillan has used the story as a metaphor for twentieth-century witch-hunting, including what he sees as resurgent fascism today. The result is rather like Vaughan Williams's *Tallis Fantasia* updated and then invaded by Stravinsky's *Rite of Spring*. The other piece on the disc, *Tryst* – marginally longer at 28 minutes – has similar qualities. In juxtaposition it emerges as the obverse of *Isobel Gowdie*, similarly a massive single movement in arch form. This time the music works from violence at the beginning and end to a long slow meditation in the middle, again with echoes of ecclesiastical chant a basic element. Maksymiuk proves a dedicated interpreter.

(i) *I (A meditation on Iona); They Saw the Stone Had Been Rolled Away; Tryst;* (ii) *Adam's Rib for Brass Quintet.*

(N) *** BIS CD 101 (i) SCO, Swensen; (ii) SCO Brass.

The central piece in this fine collection is *Tryst*, inspired by a love poem in broad Scots by William Soutar. That poem has provided the source for a sequence of MacMillan's works, of which this is the most ambitious. Written in 1989, its five linked sections bring a kaleidoscopic sequence of striking ideas, brilliantly orchestrated, centring round a motto theme. *Adam's Rib* (1995) uses a brass quintet to produce dark and earthy sounds, underpinned by a growling tuba, and leading to a ritual built on sharp contrasts of timbres.

In *They Saw the Stone Had Been Rolled Away*, MacMillan conveys the exhilaration of Christ's resurrection with brilliant fanfares and ominous drumbeats, while *I* (pronounced 'ee'), written in 1996, in eight sections, is spare and less dissonant than the rest, evoking a mood of profound meditation. Dedicated performances, brilliantly recorded.

Triduum, an Easter Triptych, Part 1: (i) *The World's Ransoming* (for cor anglais and orchestra); Part 2: (ii) *Cello Concerto.*

*** BIS CD 989.(i) Pendrill; (ii) Wallfisch; BBC Scottish SO, Vänskä.

The World's Ransoming and the *Cello Concerto*, each self-contained, are the first two in a sequence of three related works representing MacMillan's response to Christ's Passion and the Easter story. *The World's Ransoming*, with its poignant writing for cor anglais set against violent interruptions, provides the emotional prelude and is intensely involving music, often wild in its expressionism. In its energy it mixes styles and idiom with abandon. This is religious inspiration at the farthest remove from that of John Tavener or Arvo Pärt, but just as likely to strike a chord with listeners of whatever faith, or none. Christine Pendrill is the superb soloist, and though Raphael Wallfisch is just as expressive as the soloist in the *Cello Concerto*, conveying Christ's agony, sadly the balance sets him at a distance. This three-movement work, a response to Good Friday and the Crucifixion, is even more violent – using thunder-sheet amid heavy brass and percussion, the embodiment of earthquake and storm, both physical and spiritual. Brilliant performances, spaciously recorded.

Triduum, an Easter Triptych, Part 3: *Symphony (Vigil)*.

*** BIS CD 900. Fine Arts Brass Ens., BBC Scottish SO, Vänskä.

The *Symphony (Vigil)* in three movements – *Light, Tuba insonet salutaris* and *Water* – forms the climax of the *Triduum* triptych, longer than either of the preceding works. Predictably it moves from darkness to light, with violence at the start of the first movement echoing the music of the *Cello Concerto*. The second movement brings fanfares spread spaciously, the last trump graphically portrayed, while the resolution of the final movement, longer than the other two put together, brings no easy salvation. Even the meditative close still implies the memory of pain, ever more pauseful, fading into nothing. Here too as in the companion disc Vänskä draws brilliant, warmly committed playing from the BBC Scottish Symphony orchestra, vividly recorded.

Veni, veni, Emmanuel; Tryst.

(BB) *** Naxos 8.554167. Currie, Ulster O, Yuasa.

With Colin Currie, the young prizewinning percussionist, matching his compatriot predecessor, Evelyn Glennie, in flair and panache, the Naxos version of the brilliant and dramatic percussion concerto, *Veni, veni, Emmanuel*, cannot be recommended too highly. Takuo Yuasa is a strong and persuasive conductor, not just in *Veni, veni, Emmanuel*, but in the earlier work, *Tryst*, an extended and colourful fantasy in five sections built on a setting of a Scottish song. Recorded in the helpful acoustic of the Ulster Hall, Belfast, the sound is exceptionally full and vivid, matching the excellent playing of the orchestra.

VOCAL MUSIC

Mass; A Child's Prayer; Changed; Christus vincit; A New Song; Seinte Mari moder milde; (i) *Gaudeamus.*

(N) *** Hyp. CDA 67219. Westminster Cathedral Ch, Baker; (i) Reid.

It would be hard to think of any recent music that so intensely conveys religious ecstasy as James MacMillan's *Mass*, a liturgical setting, with text (in English) expanded from the Ordinary of the Mass, which he wrote for Westminster Cathedral for the Millennium celebrations in 2000. Closer in style to Britten than to Tavener, MacMillan is yet distinctive in his brilliant use of choral effects, with surging crescendos up to glowing fortissimos to stir the blood.

Two of the extra sections, taken from the Eucharistic Liturgy, largely involve solo chanting, but the fervour of MacMillan's inspiration as a devout Catholic himself makes

for music of high voltage from first to last. Equally the shorter choral works on the disc, all written in the 1990s, have a rare freshness and concentration, often involving powerful slabs of sound.

The singing of the Westminster Cathedral Choir is electrifying, with Martin Baker directing his first recording as choirmaster. The solo singing, too, deserves special mention, with a solo treble negotiating a spectacular upward leap at the close of *Christus vincit*. *Gaudeamus* is a brief organ solo involving bird-noises, rather different from Messiaen's, beautifully played by Andrew Reid.

MACONCHY, Elizabeth (born 1907)

String Quartets Nos. 5–8.

*** Unicorn DKPCD 9081. Bingham Qt.

These works testify to the quality of Maconchy's mind and her inventive powers. She speaks of the quartet as 'an impassioned argument', and there is no lack of either in these finely wrought and compelling pieces. Even if there is not the distinctive personality of a Bartók or a Britten, her music is always rewarding. The Bingham Quartet play with total commitment and are well recorded.

MADETOJA, Leevi (1887–1947)

Symphonies Nos. 1 in F, Op. 29; 2, Op. 35; 3 in A, Op. 55; Comedy Overture, Op. 53; Okon Fuoko, Op. 58; Pohjolaisia Suite, Op. 52.

(M) *** Chan. 7097 (2). Iceland SO, Sakari.

Symphonies Nos. 1; (i) *2;* (ii) *3;* (iii) *Comedy Overture;* (iv) *Okon Fuoko; Pohjolaisia Suite;* (i) *Kullervo, Op. 15.*

(B) **(*) Finlandia Ultima 8573 81971-2 (2). Finnish RSO, Segerstam, (i) Saraste, (ii) Tampere PO, Rautio; (iii) Helsinki PO, Panula; (iv) Finnish RSO, Segerstam, Kamu.

Apart from Sibelius himself, with whom Madetoja briefly studied, there are many influences to be discerned in the *First Symphony* (1915–26) – figures like Strauss, the Russian post-nationalists, Reger and above all the French for whom Madetoja had a lifelong admiration. The *Second Symphony* (1917–18), composed at about the same time as Sibelius was working on the definitive version of his *Fifth*, is expertly fashioned and despite the obvious debts there is some individuality too. The *Third* was written in the mid-1920s while Madetoja was living in Houilles, just outside Paris. Gallic elements surface most strongly in this piece. The *Comedy Overture* (1923) is an absolute delight, and both the suite from the opera *Pohjalaisia (The Ostrobothnians)* and the ballet–pantomime *Okon Fuoko* show an exemplary feeling for colour and atmosphere. Now that the excellent Chandos set under Petri Sakari has been transferred to the Double format at mid-price, it deserves to carry our first recommendation. Both the performances and the spacious natural recordings are exemplary and Sakari gets imaginative and sensitive playing from his Rekjavik forces.

No real grumbles about the Finlandia performances, which are well worth the money and will give pleasure, but the Icelandic is the more distinguished of the two and worth the extra cost.

'Meet the Composer': Complete Songs for Male Voice Choir (52 songs).

(B) *** Finlandia Double 0630 19807-2 (2). Helsinki University Ch., Hyökki.

The present Finlandia Double assembles the contents of three previous issues, recorded 1990–91, devoted to Madetoja's output for male voice choir, and offers no fewer than 52 partsongs, many of them of signal quality. The male voice choir is a popular medium in both Finland and Sweden, and both countries have produced a rich repertory of songs and expert groups to sing them. The Helsinki University Choir is among the very finest, and they certainly sing these pieces with wonderful ensemble and fervour. The notes (by the conductor, Matti Hyökki) provide exemplary background information as well as the texts themselves. Many of the songs have something of the modal quality of Sibelius's output in this genre; and the later songs, which Madetoja composed in the 1940s when ill-health inhibited him from finishing a fourth symphony and a violin concerto, are striking. A rewarding set.

The Ostrobothnians (Pohjalaisa) (complete); Suite from the opera, Op. 52a.

(M) *** Finlandia 3984 21440-2 (2). Hynninen, Sirkiä, Groop, Auvinen, Finnish R. Ch; Finnish R. SO, Saraste.

Madetoja's opera dates from the early 1920s and is set in the western Finnish plains of Ostrobothnia which Madetoja knew well, and its central theme is the Bothnian farmer's love of personal liberty and his abhorrence of authoritarian restraints. Against this background of tension, there is a simple love story. Antti, one of the farmers, is imprisoned after a stabbing incident; the first act centres on his relationship with Maija, In the second Antti escapes, and the opera ends with Jussi's death at the sheriff's hands. The opera is also interspersed with humorous elements that lighten the mood and lend the work variety. Madetoja's language springs from much the same soil as most Scandinavian post-nationalists. However, the score makes often imaginative use of folk material and Madetoja's sense of theatre and lyrical gift is in good evidence. Pohjalaisa is effective theatre and this new recording completely supersedes the 1975 set under Jorma Panula – also with Hynninen as the hero – both artistically and technically. Like its predecessor it offers excellent teamwork from the soloists, and keen and responsive playing from the Finnish Radio forces under Saraste. The work lasts barely two hours, and the fill-up derives from a 1993 recording.

MAGALHÃES, Filipe de (1571–1652)

Missa O Soberana luz; Motets: Commissa mea pavesco; Vidi aquam.

(BB) *** Naxos 8.553310. Ars Nova, Holten – CARDOSO; LOBO Motets. ***

Filipe de Magalhães was the youngest of the three great Portuguese composers who all became pupils of Manuel Mendes (c. 1547–1605) at Evora in eastern Portugal. The others, Cardoso and Lobo, are also represented in this outstanding concert, but Magalhães was reputedly the favourite pupil. One can see why, listening to his highly individual writing in both the Mass O Soberana luz and the two hardly less memorable motets, Vidi aquam ('I beheld the water') and Commissa mea pavesco ('I tremble at my sins') with its instantly poignant opening. In the Mass the Sanctus soars radiantly and the lovely Benedictus is equally affecting, only to be capped by the Agnus Dei. The Danish performances are wonderfully eloquent and the recording, made at Kasterskirken, Copenhagen, has an ideal ambience and is beautifully clear.

MAGNARD, Albéric (1865–1914)

Symphonies Nos. 1 in C min., Op. 4; 2 in E, Op. 6.

*** Hyp. CDA 67030. BBC Scottish SO, Ossonce.

Symphonies Nos. 3 in B flat min., Op. 11; 4 in C sharp min., Op. 21.

*** Hyp. CDA 67040. BBC Scottish SO, Ossonce.

Symphonies Nos. 1–4; Chant funèbre; Hymne à la justice; Ouverture.

(B) *** EMI double forte (ADD) CZS5 72364-2 (3). Capitole Toulouse O, Plasson.

Symphonies Nos. 1 in C min., Op. 4; 3 in B flat min., Op. 11.

**(*) BIS CD 927. Malmö SO, Sanderling.

Symphonies Nos. 2 in E, Op. 6 ; 4 in C sharp min., Op. 21.

**(*) BIS CD 928. Malmö SO, Sanderling.

Of the four so-called Franckist symphonists (Vincent d'Indy, Chausson, Dukas and Albéric Magnard), it is clear that Magnard is not the least rewarding of them. The First Symphony (1889–90) was composed in the shadow of his friend and mentor, Vincent d'Indy, and follows more strictly cyclical principles. Yet its ideas still show individuality of character and, despite the debt to Wagner and Franck, the last two symphonies have distinct personalities; they are separated by seventeen years. The Fourth has an impressive intellectual power and is well crafted, with no shortage of ideas. For all the appearance of academicism, there is a quiet and distinctive personality here, and dignity too. The Chant funèbre is an earlier work that has a vein of genuine eloquence.

The superb Hyperion set of his four symphonies, neatly fitted on two separately available CDs, easily outshines earlier rivals, with warm, cleanly focused sound.

The Toulouse Capitole Orchestra under Michel Plasson also play this music as if they believe every note, as indeed they should, and the recording is sonorous and well defined. Plasson spreads to three CDs but offers extra items and the EMI set is at bargain price and is excellent value.

Generally speaking, Thomas Sanderling opts for broad tempi. Indeed, his leisurely tempi compel BIS to accommodate the Second and Fourth symphonies on a separate CD, retailing them for the price of one. In the *Fourth* Sanderling is almost five minutes longer than his two rivals. He is the best recorded of the three but both Plasson and Ossonce get a more powerfully concentrated response from their players. But in almost all respects the Hyperion set (using two full-priced discs) takes pride of place, with warm, cleanly focused sound.

MAHLER, Gustav (1860–1911)

Symphonies Nos. 1–9; 10 (Adagio).

(B) **(*) Ph. 442 050-2 (10). Concg. O, Haitink (with Ameling, Heynis & Netherlands R. Ch. in No. 2; Forrester, Netherlands R. Ch. & St Willibrord Boys' Ch. in No. 3; Ameling in No. 4; Cotrubas, Harper, Van Bork, Finnila, Dieleman, Cochran, Prey, Sotin, Amsterdam Choirs in No. 8).

(B) **(*) DG 463 738-2 (10). Arroyo, Mathis, Morison, Spoorenberg, Hamari, Procter, Marjorie Thomas, Grobe, Fischer-Dieskau, Crass, Bav. R. Ch., N. German R. Ch., W. German R. Ch., Regensburger Domchor, Munich Motteten Ch. Bav. RSO, Kubelik.

Symphonies Nos. 1–9.

(B) *** Decca Dig./ADD 430 804-2 (10). Buchanan, Zakai, Chicago Ch. (in No. 2); Dernesch, Ellyn Children's Ch., Chicago Ch. (in No. 3); Te Kanawa (in No. 4); Harper, Popp, Augér, Minton, Watts, Kollo, Shirley-Quirk, Talvela, V. Boys' Ch., V. State Op. Ch. & Singverein (in No. 8); Chicago SO, Solti.

Symphonies Nos. 1 (including Blumine); 2–9 (complete); 10 (Adagio).

** Chan. 9572 (12). Copenhagen Boys' Ch., Danish Nat. Ch. & RSO, Segerstam; (with Kilberg, Dolberg in Nos. 2 & 8; Gjevang in Nos. 3 & 8; Johansson in No. 4; Nielsen, Majken, Bonde-Hansen, Sirkiä, Hynninen, Stabell, BPO Ch. in No. 8).

Solti's achievement in Mahler has been consistent and impressive, and this reissue is a formidable bargain that will be hard to beat. Nos. 1–4 and 9 are digital recordings, Nos. 5–8 are digitally remastered analogue. Solti draws stunning playing from the Chicago Symphony Orchestra, often pressed to great virtuosity, which adds to the electricity of the music-making; if his rather extrovert approach to Mahler means that deeper emotions are sometimes understated, there is no lack of involvement; and his fiery energy and commitment often carry shock-waves in their trail. All in all, an impressive achievement.

Haitink's set of Mahler *Symphonies* offers characteristically refined and well-balanced Philips recording. The performances bring consistently fine playing from the Concertgebouw Orchestra, but Haitink is not by nature an extrovert Mahlerian. While he is always sensitive and thoughtful – and this works well enough in Nos. 1 (his earlier recording is included) and 4 (with Elly Ameling a freshly appealing soloist) and they have an attractive simplicity of approach – Nos. 2 and 8 lack the necessary sense of occasion, and No. 8 also needs greater overall grip and a more ex-

pansive recording. No. 5 is fresh and direct (the *Adagietto* a little cool) but No. 6 has more refinement than fire. The finest of the set are the deeply satisfying accounts of No. 3 (with fine contributions from both Maureen Forrester and the choristers) and the finely wrought and intensely convincing performance of No. 7. However, the series is capped by an outstanding performance of No. 9. Here Haitink is at his most inspirational and the last movement has a unique concentration, with its slow tempo maintained to create the greatest intensity of feeling. As usual from Philips, the original recordings are consistently enhanced by the CD transfers, and only No. 8 is technically disappointing.

Kubelik's is a fastidious and generally lyrical view of Mahler, most persuasive in the delightful performances of the least weighty symphonies, Nos. 1 and 4. In much of the rest these sensitive performances lack something in power and tension, tending to eliminate the neurotic in Mahler; but there is a fair case for preferring such an approach for relaxed listening. As can be seen he has excellent soloists and distinguished choral contributions in Nos. 2 and 8. Other sets more compellingly compass the full range of Mahler's symphonic achievement, but with good sound and in a bargain box, this is worth considering if Kubelik's less flamboyant view seems appealing. The new transfers are strikingly fresh.

The main advantages of the Chandos set are fine playing by a clearly committed and dedicated orchestra and superbly rich and expansive recording. Inner detail is not sharp, but it is not blurred either and the concert-hall feeling means that Mahler's most expansive sounds are superbly contained, notably the brass and chorus in the powerful finale of the *Resurrection Symphony*, although the vocal balance in No. 8, as so often, is less than ideal. Segerstam's is a very relaxed view of Mahler, and he takes us through the Mahlerian pastoral scenery as in an affectionate guided tour. Immediately in the *First Symphony* one notices a lack of grip in the opening evocation and throughout the series the relaxed tempi and Segerstam's lack of firmness mean that although the playing itself is committed and always sensitive there is a loss of sustained intensity. Inner movements are often delightfully coloured, and the famous *Adagio* of the *Fifth Symphony* is warmly atmospheric but very laid back. Similarly Segerstam opens the *Fourth* in the most coaxing manner, but remains very relaxed and the explosive fortissimo of the slow movement could be more biting. In the great *Adagio* of the *Ninth* there is the widest range of dynamic and some beautiful pianissimo playing, but the final pull of tension from the conductor which makes for a compellingly great performance is missing. The layout too is less than ideal, with the first five symphonies not coming in numerical order, so initially finding one's way about the twelve CDs takes some care.

(i) *Symphonies Nos. 1–9;* (ii) *Kindertotenlieder;*
(iii) *Kindertotenlieder; 3 Rückert Lieder; Das irdische Leben.*

(N) (B) **(*) Sony (ADD) SX12K 89499 (12). Spoorenberg, Annear, Procter, Mitchinson, Mcintyre, Venora, Tourel, Lipton, IPO, LSO or NYPO, Bernstein; (ii) J. Baker; (iii) J. Tourel.

This 12-disc compilation, neatly packaged, includes not only Bernstein's historic pioneering cycle of the Mahler symphonies for CBS but a number of valuable supplements. With the nine completed symphonies recorded between 1960 and 1967 and the *Adagio* from No. 10 added in 1975, the cycle has never sounded fresher or clearer, with sound less coarse than originally. The venues range between the St George Hotel in Brooklyn (surprisingly free in No. 4) to Walthamstow Assembly Rooms in London for No. 8, sounding more open than originally. The recordings made in the Philharmonic Hall, New York (now Avery Fisher Hall), vary between the relative dryness of No. 5, recorded in 1963, to the far fuller sound of Nos 6, 7 and 9, recorded later. Curiously the live recording of the first movement of No. 8, made at the opening of the hall in 1962, is more open in sound than the slightly disappointing No. 5.

Though Bernstein's later cycle for DG brings more refined sound, these earlier interpretations, all but No. 8 with the New York Philharmonic, are generally more thrustful and dramatic. The reading of No. 9 is far less expansive in the last movement, but still deeply meditative, so that the whole symphony can be fitted on to a single disc. The valuable supplements include a live recording of the *Adagietto* of No. 5 played at the funeral of Robert Kennedy and two versions of *Kindertotenlieder*, not just the one recorded in Israel in 1974 with Dame Janet Baker, but the earlier studio recording of 1960 with Jenny Tourel, a favourite singer with Bernstein, brisker, less reflective, as well as Tourel in three of the *Rückertlieder* and *Das irdische Leben* from *Des Knaben Wunderhorn*.

Symphony No. 1 in D (Titan).

(N) (M) *** Decca 458 622-2. LSO, Solti.

(B) *** CfP 573 5102. RLPO, Mackerras.

*** Decca 448 813-2. Concg. O, Chailly (with BERG: *Sonata, Op. 1*, orch. VERBEY). ***

*** DG 431 769-2. BPO, Abbado.

(M) *** Unicorn UKCD 2012. LSO, Horenstein.

** Koch 3-7405-2. Houston SO, Eschenbach.

Symphony No. 1 in D (Titan); (i) Lieder eines fahrenden Gesellen.

(B) **(*) DG Penguin 460 654-2. Bav. RSO, Kubelik, (i) with Fischer-Dieskau.

The London Symphony Orchestra play Mahler's *First* like no other orchestra. They catch the magical opening, with its bird sounds and evocatively distanced brass, with a singular ambience, at least partly related to the orchestra's characteristic blend of wind timbres. Throughout there is wonderfully warm string playing and the most atmospheric response from the horns. Solti's tendency to drive hard is felt only in the second movement, which is pressed a little too much, although he relaxes beautifully in the central section. Especially memorable are the poignancy of the introduction of the *Frère Jacques* theme in the slow movement and the exultant brilliance of the closing pages, helped by the wide range of dynamic and the wonderfully clear inner detail of the newly remastered 1964 Kingsway Hall recording. This is another disc produced by John Culshaw which is rightly included among Decca's 'Legends'.

Mackerras's version, now reissued on CfP, offers a performance that, with crisply sprung rhythms, brings out the youthful freshness of Mahler's inspiration. The natural warmth and spontaneity of the reading have one concentrating on Mahler's arguments rather than on points of interpretation. Speeds are consistently well chosen and though the finale is not quite so biting as the rest, the joy of the inspiration comes over winningly, so that the whole performance hangs magnetically together, making this an outstanding choice, irrespective of price.

Helped by immaculate playing from the Concertgebouw, meticulous on detail and with sound of demonstration quality, Chailly's direct, positive reading is magnetic in its control of the long line. More subjective interpretations may characterize more strongly, but this is consistently satisfying, and comes with an unusual coupling in an orchestration of the early Berg *Sonata* by the Dutch composer, Theo Verbey.

Abbado's Berlin reading, like others in his Mahler series, was recorded live and, though one or two coughs intrude, the sound is fresh and full, bringing out the beauty and clarity of the Berlin strings. Though Abbado occasionally exaggerates the pointing of rhythms and speed-changes (as in the Laendler), the high voltage of the whole performance makes it most compelling, if not an obvious first choice.

Horenstein's version has a freshness and concentration which put it in a special category among the many rival accounts. Fine recording from the end of the 1960s, though the timpani is balanced rather too close.

Kubelik gives an intensely poetic reading. He is here at his finest in Mahler and though, as in later symphonies, he is sometimes tempted to choose a tempo on the fast side, the result could hardly be more glowing. The rubato in the slow funeral march is most subtly handled. In its CD reissue (originally DG) the quality is a little dry in the bass and the violins have lost some of their warmth, but there is no lack of body. In the *Lieder eines fahrenden Gesellen* the sound is fuller, with more atmospheric bloom. No one quite rivals Fischer-Dieskau in these songs, and this is a very considerable bonus at Penguin Classics price. The essay is by Michael Dibdin.

Eschenbach's live recording, made in Vienna, brings a fresh, objective reading, very well played, though marred by audience noises and with sound that is not ideally clear in heavy tuttis.

Symphony No. 1 in D (Titan) (with Blumine).

**(*) HM HMU 907118-2. Florida PO, Judd.

(B) **(*) [EMI Red Line CDR5 69816]. Israel PO, Mehta.

** EMI CDC7 54647-2. CBSO, Rattle.

James Judd demonstrates the virtuoso qualities of the Florida Philharmonic in a warm, well-pointed, spontaneous-sounding performance, slightly marred by a slow and rather heavy reading of the second-movement Laendler, which yet includes a most delicate account of the central Trio. The atmospheric recording sets the orchestra at a slight distance, which may take away some of the bite but enhances the beauty of the string-tone, not least in a dedicated performance of *Blumine*, which comes as a supplement after the symphony.

Mehta's version with the Israel Philharmonic brings a hybrid – the regular four-movement version in its revised instrumentation, into which is inserted the lyrical *Blumine* movement from the original version, which Mahler later excised. Mehta's reading of the whole work, though not the most individual or illuminating, is satisfyingly warm and direct, helped by very full, forward recording, among the best in the difficult acoustic of the Mann Auditorium. A worthwhile reissue (available only in the USA).

Recorded live in Symphony Hall, Birmingham, Rattle's account with the CBSO is rather lacking in the spontaneity one expects. Speed-changes in the first movement sound self-conscious, as do the exaggerations of dotted rhythms in the Ländler movement. It remains an acceptable reading, well recorded, but hardly matches Rattle's achievement in other Mahler recordings. As a preface to the main work, the *Blumine* movement, is given with a freshness and spontaneity that rather shows up the rest.

Symphonies Nos. (i) 1; (ii) 2 (Resurrection).

(B) *** Double Decca (ADD) 448 921-2 (2). (ii) Harper, Watts,
  L. Symphony Ch.; LSO, Solti.

(N) (B) **(*) EMI double fforte (ADD) CZS5 74182-2 (2).
  (i) Mathis, Soffel, LPO Ch.; LPO, Tennstedt.

Solti's 1964 LSO account of No. 2 remains a demonstration of the outstanding results Decca were securing with analogue techniques at that time, although on CD the brilliance of the fortissimos may not suit all ears. Helen Watts is wonderfully expressive, while the chorus has a rapt intensity that is the more telling when the recording perspectives are so clearly delineated. Coupled with his outstanding version of No. 1, it makes a genuine bargain at Double Decca price.

Tennstedt's manner in the *First Symphony* is somewhat severe, with textures fresh and neat and the style of phrasing generally less moulded than under Solti. The concentration on precision and directness means that when the conductor does indulge in rubato or speed changes it does not sound quite consistent and comes as a surprise in the big string melody of the finale. Most Mahlerians will prefer a more felt performance than this, but the rich, warm Abbey Road recording is first class. Tennstedt's approach is more obviously dedicated in the *Resurrection Symphony*. The performance, if not quite as well played as the finest, conveys Mahlerian certainties in the light of day, underemphasizing neurotic tensions. The Kingsway Hall recording is excellent (with splendid perspectives), as are the soloists (especially Doris Soffel) and chorus, and both symphonies are given impressively full and clear new transfers. The snag is the absence of texts and translations.

Symphonies Nos. (i) 1 (Titan); (ii) 2 (Resurrection); (iii) Lieder eines fahrenden Gesellen.

(M) *** Sony (ADD) SMK 64447 (2). (i) Columbia SO;
  (ii) Cundari, Forrester, Westminster Ch., NYPO; (iii) Miller,
  Columbia SO; Walter.

Bruno Walter's stereo recordings of the *First* and *Second* symphonies are now economically coupled on a pair of discs together with the *Lieder eines fahrenden Gesellen*. The *First Symphony* was recorded in Hollywood in 1961, and in its remastered form the recording sounds better than ever, richer and fuller at the bottom end of the spectrum, and the dynamic range seemingly extended. Even more than the *First Symphony*, the 1958 set of the *Resurrection Symphony* is among the gramophone's indispensable classics. In the first movement there is a restraint and in the second a gracefulness which provide a strong contrast with a conductor like Solti. In the newest remastering, detail registers more clearly; while the sound is not sumptuous, in the finale the balance with the voices still gives the music an ethereal resonance, with the closing section thrillingly expansive. In the 1960 recording of the *Lieder eines fahrenden Gesellen* the superb orchestral detail glows as never before. Mildred Miller is perhaps not an inspirational soloist, but she sings well enough, and Walter ensures that the performance is dramatically alive.

Symphonies Nos. 1 in D (Titan); 3 in D min.

(B) ** RCA High Performance (ADD) 09026 63469-2 (2). BSO,
  Leinsdorf.

Neither of the Leinsdorf performances is completely recommendable. The *Titan* is hard driven, almost brutal, in no sense Viennese and lacking in atmosphere, yet one cannot deny that it is exciting at times. He is more successful in the *Third* where his straightforward approach makes for more convincing results. The recordings (from 1962 and 1966) are very up-front, brilliant in hi-fi terms, though not a genuine concert image.

Symphonies Nos. 1 in D; No. 5 in C sharp min.

(B) **(*) DG Double 459 472-2 (2). Philh. O, Sinopoli.

(i) *Symphonies Nos. 1 in D min. (Titan); (ii) No. 5 in C sharp min.; (ii; iii) Lieder eines fahrenden Gesellen. .*

(N) (BB) **(*) DG Panorama 469 154-2 (2). (i) Concg. O;
  (ii) VPO; Bernstein; (iii) with Hampson.

An inexpensive way to sample Bernstein's distinctive approach to Mahler. The *First* receives a vital performance with some splendidly alert and beautiful playing; the opening movement conveys the joys of spring with its *Wayfaring Lad* associations, while the second, with a relaxed Laendler tempo, sounds more rustic than usual. The finale has superb panache, and in all ways this performance is preferable to his 1966 Sony account. No allowances need be made for the live recording. The *Fifth* is hardly less compelling: it is a deeply personal account with the conductor's personal stamp apparent in every bar. The conception is certainly expansive, but it is utterly compelling, and ranks as one of his finest performances. Fine (live) recording.

Sinopoli's account of the *First Symphony* is warmly satisfying and passionately committed, with refined playing from the Philharmonia. He allows the fullest expressiveness with bold theatrical gestures thrust home purposefully. In the *Fifth* he draws a sharp distinction between the dark tragedy of the first two movements, and the relaxed *Wunderhorn* feeling of the rest. He seems intent in not overloading the big melodies with excessive emotion. This comes out more clearly in the central movements, where relaxation is the key-note, often with pastoral atmosphere. The celebrated *Adagietto* brings a tenderly wistful reading, songful and basically happy, not tragic. Warmly atmospheric recording throughout, though detail is not ideally clear in the *Fifth*, this is still a recommendable coupling.

Symphonies Nos. 1 in D; 9 in D min.; (i) Lieder eines fahrenden Gesellen.

(B) **(*) Teldec Ultima 3984 21339-2 (2). NYPO, Masur,
    (i) with Hagegård.

Masur's live Mahler recordings with the NYPO from the early 1990s are certainly worth considering. On the first disc the *Symphony No.1* and the related *Wayfaring Lad* song-cycle are given attractively fresh, unsentimental readings, even if ironic undertones are muted, with Hagegård a clear, firm, baritone soloist. The *Symphony No. 9*, complete on the second disc, is more variable. If the first movement establishes the directness of Masur's approach, the long, slow finale crowns the performance in a reading strong and purposeful rather than tenderly elegiac. The recording, made in Avery Fisher Hall (like that of the companion disc), has less air round it.

Symphonies Nos. 1 in D (Titan); 10 (Adagio).

(M) ** Sony (ADD) SMK 60732. NYPO, Bernstein.

Bernstein's is an excellent red-blooded version of the *First*, and the voltage is high, but when competition is so intense in this work it falls below a top recommendation if only because of the close-up mid-1960s sound, although the occasional self-indulgence in the interpretation (as in the trio of the *Ländler*) will not please the dedicated Mahlerian. In the *Tenth*, recorded a decade later in 1975, Bernstein uses the old fallible edition, but the passionate commitment of his performances is hard to resist, with contrasts underlined between the sharpness of the *Andante* passages and the free expressiveness of the main *Adagio*.

Symphonies Nos. (i) 1 in D (Titan); (ii) 10: Adagio (arr. Krenet, ed. Jokl).

(B) **(*) Sony Dig./ADD SBK 53259. (i) NYPO, Mehta;
    (ii) Cleveland O, Szell.

Mehta's Sony/CBS digital version of the *First Symphony*, successfully recorded in the Avery Fisher Hall in 1980, is far preferable to his later, Israeli, Decca CD. It has no less urgency and drama, but here Mehta's Viennese training comes out in the lilt of the *Ländler* second movement while his freely expressive rubato in the third, after the dark opening, is very appealing, and the reading overall has undoubted spontaneity. Many will also welcome the reissue of Szell's 1958 recording of the *Adagio* from the *Tenth Symphony* in Jokl's edition, the Cleveland orchestral playing stylish as well as eloquent. The sound, too, is very good.

Symphony No. 2 in C min. (Resurrection).

❀ *** EMI CDS7 47962-8 (2). Augér, Baker, CBSO Ch., CBSO, Rattle.

(M) *** EMI CDM5 57235-2 [567255]. Schwarzkopf, Rössl-Majdan, Philh. Ch. & O, Klemperer.

*** Ph. Dig 438 935-2 (2). McNair, Van Nes, Ernst Senff Ch., BPO, Haitink.

(M) *** Decca 446 992-2. Contrubas, Ludwig, V. State Op. Ch., VPO, Mehta.

(M) *** Chan. 6595/6. Lott, Hamari, Latvian State Ac. Ch., Oslo Philharmonic Ch., Oslo PO, Jansons.

**(*) DG 439 953-2 (2). Studer, Meyer, Arnold Schoenberg Ch., VPO, Abbado.

*** Conifer 76505 51337-2. Valente, Forrester, Ardwyn Singers, BBC Welsh Ch., Cardiff Philharmonic Ch., Dyfed Ch., L. Symphony Ch., LSO, Kaplan.

(i) Symphony No. 2 in C min. (Resurrection); (ii) Lieder eines fahrenden Gesellen; (iii) Lieder und Gesang aus der Jugendzeit: excerpts.

(M) *** DG (IMS) 445 587-2 (2). (i) Fassbaender, Plowright, Philh. Ch.; (ii) Fassbaender; (iii) Weikl; Philh. O, Sinopoli.

Simon Rattle's reading of Mahler's *Second* is among the very finest records he has yet made, superlative in the breadth and vividness of its sound and with a spacious reading which in its natural intensity unerringly sustains generally slow, steady speeds to underline the epic grandeur of Mahler's vision. The playing of the CBSO is inspired. The choral singing, beautifully balanced, is incandescent, while the heart-felt singing of Arleen Augér and Dame Janet Baker, is equally distinguished and characterful.

Klemperer's performance – one of his most compelling on record – comes back to the catalogue on a single CD as one of EMI's 'Great Recordings of the Century' sounding better than ever. The remastering of the Kingsway Hall recording is impressively full and clear, with a real feeling of spectacle in the closing pages. The first movement, taken at a fairly fast tempo, is intense and earth shaking, though in the last movement (which incidentally is generously cued) some of Klemperer's speeds are designedly slow, he conveys supremely well the mood of transcendent, heavenly happiness in the culminating passage, with the Philharmonia Chorus and soloists themselves singing like angels.

Bernard Haitink's 1993 version with the Berlin Philharmonic also brings one of his very finest Mahler recordings, weighty and bitingly powerful. The sound of the Berlin Philharmonic in the Philharmonie is caught with a vividness and sense of presence rarely matched. Above all Haitink conveys the tensions of a live occasion, even though this was a studio performance, leading up to a glorious apotheosis in the Judgement Day finale. The soloists are outstanding, and the chorus immaculately expands from rapt, hushed singing to incandescent splendour. Outstanding in every way, this can be placed alongside Rattle's superb CBSO set.

Sinopoli's version of the *Resurrection* has the advantage of including the *Lieder eines fahrenden Gesellen*, beautifully sung by Brigitte Fassbaender, and the *Songs of Youth* ('aus der Jugendzeit'), skilfully orchestrated by Harold Byrns and well sung by Bernd Weikl, bringing extra anticipations of the mature *Des Knaben Wunderhorn* songs. In the symphony Sinopoli has meticulous concern for detail, yet he still conveys consistently the irresistible purposefulness of Mahler's writing, fierce at high dramatic moments and intense too, rarely relaxed, in moments of meditation, with *Urlicht* beautifully sung with warmth and purity by Fassbaender. The recorded sound, though not quite as full and vivid as that for Rattle, is among the most brilliant of any in this work. Rosalind Plowright is a pure and fresh soprano soloist, contrasting well with the equally firm, earthier-toned mezzo of Fassbaender.

Mehta's account of the *Second Symphony*, if not quite in Klemperer's league, is far more impressive than one might have expected, and is indeed one of his most distinguished recording achievements. The refinement of the VPO playing, recorded with glorious richness and clarity, places it amongst the finest versions of this symphony available. At the very start, Mehta's fast tempi brings resilience, not aggressiveness, and later the *Wunderhorn* rhythms have a delightful lilt. The enormous span of the finale (which has Christa Ludwig in superb form) brings clarity as well as magnificence, with fine placing of the soloists and chorus; there is glorious atmosphere in such moments as the evocation of birdsong over distant horns, as heavenly moment as Mahler ever conceived. The performance on a single CD lasting just over 80 minutes, while not a first choice, is surely a very worthy addition on the Decca's Legends label.

The crisp attack at the start of the opening funeral march sets the pattern for an exceptionally refined and alert reading of the *Resurrection Symphony* from Jansons and his Oslo orchestra. During the first four movements, this may seem a lightweight reading, but the extra resilience of rhythm brings out the dance element in Mahler's *Knaben Wunderhorn* inspirations rather than ruggedness or rusticity, while at the finale the whole performance erupts in an overwhelming outburst for the vision of Resurrection. That transformation is intensified by the breathtakingly rapt and intense account of the song, *Urlicht*, which precedes it. In the finale, power goes with precision and meticulous observance of markings, when even Mahler's surprising diminuendo on the final choral cadence is observed. With the Oslo Choir joined by singers from Jansons's native Latvia, the choral singing is heartfelt, to crown a version which finds a special place even among the many distinguished readings on a long list.

Abbado's recording with the Vienna Philharmonic was made live in 1992 in the Musikverein, offering a predictably fine, beautifully paced performance, but one that rather suffers, compared both with his Berlin version of the *Fifth*, recorded live six months later, and with Haitink's Berlin account of the *Second*. The Vienna Philharmonic's ensemble is less refined than that of the Berliners, even in the strings, and the sound is less immediate and involving. Tensions are not helped when the audience is so noisy. Yet with powerful soloists and a superb choir, it is still a strong reading.

Kaplan's performance of the *Resurrection Symphony* is not only thoroughly idiomatic and full of enthusiasm but totally compelling. He gets keenly dramatic and highly responsive playing from the LSO, and the recording is of demonstration quality, indeed second to none. The performance runs to just over 83 minutes so it has been issued in a Double format to compete with other full-priced versions on a single CD.

Symphony No. 3 in D min.

*** Ph. 432 162-2 (2). Van Nes, Tölz Boys' Ch., Ernst Senff Ch., BPO, Haitink.

*** DG 410 715-2 (2). Norman, V. State Op. Ch., V. Boys' Ch., VPO, Abbado.

(N) *** Teldec 8573-82354-2 (2). Pecková, Women of Berlin R.

Ch. and Knabenchor Hannover, Berlin Deutsches SO, Nagano.

(M) *** Unicorn (ADD) UKCD 2006/7. Procter, Wandsworth School Boys' Ch., Amb. S., LSO, Horenstein.

**(*) BBC Legends BBCL 4004-7. Meyer, Ladies of Hallé Ch., Boys of Manchester Grammar School, Hallé O, Barbirolli.

(i) Symphony No. 3. Kindertotenlieder.

**(*) Chan. 9117/18. Finnie, RSNO, Järvi; (i) with R. Scottish Ch. & Junior Ch.

(i) Symphony No. 3 in D min.; (ii) Kindertotenlieder; Des Knaben Wunderhorn: Das irdische Leben; 3 Rückert Lieder: Ich atmet' einen linden Duft; Ich bin der Welt abhanden gekommen; Um Mitternacht.

(M) *** Sony (ADD) SM2K 61831(2). (i) Lipton, Schola Cantorum Ch., Boys' Ch. of the Church of Transfiguration; (ii) Tourel; NYPO, Bernstein.

(i) Symphony No. 3 in D min.; (ii) Des Knaben Wunderhorn: 8 Lieder.

*** EMI CDS5 56657-2 (2). (i) Remmert, CBSO Women's Ch.; (ii) Keenlyside; CBSO, Rattle.

Symphony No. 3; 5 Rückert Lieder.

(M) *** Sony (ADD) M2K 44553 (2). Baker, L. Symphony Ch., LSO, Tilson Thomas.

Rattle conducts an outstanding version of No. 3, magnetic from the very start, rich, bold and opulent and very well recorded with an exceptionally full bass. The subtlety of Rattle's phrasing and rubato not only brings out the work's deeper qualities, with the visionary intensity of the long finale superbly caught, but far more than most the joy and humour of the lighter movements. Simon Keenlyside's beautiful, finely detailed readings of the *Knaben Wunderhorn* songs makes a very welcome bonus, with an extra song, *Ablösung im Sommer* (which is quoted in the third movement of the *Symphony*) aptly included in an arrangement by Berio.

Michael Tilson Thomas inspires the orchestra to play with bite and panache in the bold, dramatic passages and to bring out the sparkle and freshness of the *Knaben Wunderhorn* ideas; but what crowns the performance is the raptness of his reading of the noble, hymn-like finale, hushed and intense, beautifully sustained. There is a formidable bonus in Janet Baker's searching performances of the five *Rückert Lieder*. Excellent CBS sound, both warm and brilliant.

With the Berlin Philharmonic producing glorious sounds, recorded with richness and immediacy, Haitink conducts a powerful, spacious reading. It culminates in a glowing, concentrated account of the slow finale, which gives the whole work a visionary strength often lacking. The mystery of *Urlicht* is then beautifully caught by the mezzo soloist Jard van Nes.

With sound of spectacular range, Abbado's performance is sharply defined and deeply dedicated. The range of expression, the often wild mixture of elements in this work, is conveyed with extraordinary intensity, not least in the fine contributions from Jessye Norman and the two choirs. The recording has great presence and detail on CD.

On its own merits Nagano's performance has much in its

favour: there is a good sense of drama, a well-judged balance between beauty of detail and the overall architecture of the piece, and impressively realistic sound – as good as any around now. Nagano has a real affinity with Mahler's pantheism and the middle movements come off splendidly. It is not easy these days to speak of a 'best' version but this is certainly impressive.

Horenstein is at his most intensely committed. The manner is still very consistent in its simple dedication to the authority of the score and its rejection of romantic indulgence; but with an extra intensity the result has the sort of frisson-creating quality one knew from live Horenstein performances and the recording quality is both full and brilliant. Fine vocal contributions from Norma Procter, the Ambrosian Singers and the Wandsworth School Boys' Choir.

Bernstein's 1961 account of Mahler's *Third Symphony*, strong and passionate, has few of the stylistic exaggerations that sometimes overlaid his interpretations. Here his style in the slow movement is heavily expressive but many will respond to his extrovert involvement. The recording, made in New York's Manhattan Center, the venue of so many of the best of his early records, has added spaciousness and body in this very successful remastering for CD. The vocal contributions from Martha Lipton and the two choirs contribute to the success of this venture and the generous Lieder coupling is well worth having, and Jennie Tourel is in excellent voice.

Barbirolli's BBC *Third Symphony* was recorded at a concert at the Free Trade Hall, Manchester, in May 1969, the same year as Sir John's celebrated *Fifth* with the New Philharmonia. There is much of the fervour and warmth that characterized all he did, which compensates for various shortcomings. The recording is generally very good, though the cellos and double-basses are wanting in weight. Kerstin Meyer displays artistry, but has an unwelcome and obtrusive vibrato. For some reason the engineers cut off the applause and the resulting edit on the last D major chord is ugly. The disc also includes an interesting conversation between Sir John and the critic, C. B. Rees.

Järvi conducts a warmly expressive, spontaneous-sounding reading which brings out the joy behind Mahler's inspiration rather than any tragedy. This makes light of the epic qualities in this massive work. Though the ensemble of the Royal Scottish Orchestra is not as immaculate as that of some distinguished rivals, the bite of communication is always intense, helped by full, atmospheric Chandos recording. Järvi brings out the folk-like elements in the second and third movements, and Linda Finnie is a dedicated soloist and gives a felt, expressive reading of the *Kindertotenlieder*.

(i) *Symphonies Nos. 3 in D min.; (ii) No. 4 in G.*

(N) (BB) *** EMI Double forte (ADD/Dig.) CZS 5 74296-2 (2). LPO, Tennstedt with (i) Wenkel, Southend Boys' Ch., Ladies of LPO Ch.; (ii) Popp.

The *Third Symphony* receives an eloquent performance under Tennstedt (1979), the spaciousness underlined with measured tempi. With Ortrun Wenkel a fine soloist and the

Southend boys adding lusty freshness to the bell music in the fifth movement, it is crowned by an impressively noble finale and splendid recording. The *Fourth* is similarly spacious yet conveys an innocence entirely in keeping with this most endearing of Mahler symphonies.

Tennstedt makes the argument seamless in his easy transitions of speed, yet he never deliberately adopts a coaxing, charming manner, and in that he is followed most beautifully by Lucia Popp, the pure-toned soloist in the finale. The peak of the work as this conductor presents it is in the long slow movement, here taken very slowly and intensely. The recording (1982) is splendid, and this is a fine bargain in EMI's 'Double Forte' series.

Symphony No. 4 in G.

*** EMI CDC5 56563-2. Roocroft, CBSO, Rattle.

(M) *** RCA (ADD) 09026 63533-2. Della Casa, Chicago SO, Reiner.

(BB) *** CfP 573 4372. Lott, LPO, Welser-Möst.

(M) *** DG (ADD) 419 863-2. Mathis, BPO, Karajan.

*** BBC (ADD) BBCL 4014-2. Harper, BBC SO, Barbirolli (with BERLIOZ: *Overture: Le Corsaire, Op. 21*).

(BB) *** Naxos 8.550527. Russell, Polish Nat. RSO, Wit.

(BB) *** Arte Nova 74321 46506-2. Kwan, Gran Canaria PO, Leaper.

(M) **(*) Van. (ADD) 08 6164 71 [OVC 4007]. Davrath, Utah SO, Abravanel.

(*) Decca 466 720-2. Bonney, Concg. O, Chailly – BERG: *7 Early Songs. *

(N) **(*) Australian Decca Eloquence 467 235-2. Israel PO, Mehta – WAGNER: *Lohengrin: Preludes. ***

(B) ** Ph. 442 394-2. Ameling, Concg. O, Haitink.

** DG 463 257-2. Banse, Cleveland O, Boulez.

(M) ** Sony (ADD) SMK 60733. Grist, NYPO, Bernstein.

Symphonies Nos. 4 in G; 5 (Adagietto).

(B) *** [EMI Red Line CDR5 69817]. Popp, LPO, Tennstedt.

(i) *Symphony No. 4 in G; (ii) Des Knaben Wunderhorn: Das irdische Leben; Wo die schönen Trompeten bläsen. Rückert Lieder: Ich atmet' einen linden Duft; Ich bin der Welt abhanden gekommen; Um Mitternacht.*

(M) **(*) EMI (ADD) CDM5 67035-2. (i) Schwarzkopf; (ii) Ludwig; Philh. O, Klemperer.

(i) *Symphony No. 4 in G; (ii) Lieder eines fahrenden Gesellen.*

✪ (M) *** Sony (ADD) SBK 46535. (i) Raskin, Cleveland O, Szell; (ii) Von Stade, LPO, A. Davis.

(i) *Symphony No. 4; (ii; iii) Lieder eines fahrenden Gesellen; (iii; iv) Des Knaben Wunderhorn: Das irdische Leben; Wer hat dies Liedlein erdacht?*

**(*) BBC mono/stereo BBCB 8004-2. (i) Carlyle, LSO; (ii) Reynolds; (iii) ECO; (iv) with Ameling, Britten.

(i) *Symphony No. 4 in G; (ii) Lieder und Gesang aus der Jugendzeit.*

(M) (***) Sony mono SMK 64450. Halban; (i) NYPO, Walter; (ii) Walter (piano).

Symphony No. 4 in G; 4 Early Songs.

*** RCA 75605 51345-2. Ziesak, RPO, Gatti.

George Szell's 1966 record of Mahler's *Fourth* represented his partnership with the Cleveland Orchestra at its highest peak and the digital remastering for CD brings out the very best of the original recording. The performance remains uniquely satisfying: the music blossoms, partly because of the marvellous attention to detail (and the immaculate ensemble), but more positively because of the committed and radiantly luminous orchestral response to the music itself. In the finale Szell found the ideal soprano to match his conception. An outstanding choice, generously coupled. In contrast with most other recorded performances, Frederica von Stade insinuates a hint of youthful ardour into her highly enjoyable account of the *Wayfaring Lad* cycle.

Daniele Gatti conducts a beautifully paced reading of the *Fourth* which is among the finest of recent digital versions, with the Royal Philharmonic playing superbly. It is a mark of Gatti's Mahlerian understanding that he can so perfectly time such a passage as the close of the first movement with its witty pay-off. That leads on to an account of the Scherzo which brings out its macabre humour, a dance of death. Gatti also paces the dedicated slow movement very impressively, with contrasts of tempo finely judged, and the finale too brings sharply defined contrasts, with Ruth Ziesak a sweetly girlish-sounding soloist. The *Four Early Songs* make an apt and generous coupling, also beautifully sung by Ziesak. Full, vivid sound.

Simon Rattle's performance begins with an idiosyncratic but valid reading of the opening bars, at first very slow then brisk for the main *Allegro*. It reflects the thoughtfulness on detail of his approach to Mahler, reflected in an unusually refreshing account, youthfully urgent, which rises to a spacious, songful reading of the long slow movement. Amanda Roocroft sings with warm, creamy tone in the finale. Refined recording to match. This also stands high among modern recordings of this beautiful symphony.

This remarkable new transfer of Reiner's 1958 recording has astonished us. The Chicago Hall ambience, warmth and bloom seem enhanced, yet the vividness of the detail is now so clear, and the bass response so naturally resonant, that one has a genuine illusion of sitting in the hall itself. Reiner's performance with its affectionate waywardness is undoubtedly further enhanced with everything sounding spontaneous. The glorious slow movement combines warmth with striking intensity, with its rapt closing pages leading on gently to the finale in which Lisa Della Casa, in ravishing voice, matches Reiner's mood. This must now rank alongside Szell's outstanding Cleveland performance.

Welser-Möst's outer movements are fresh and beautifully shaped, with Felicity Lott a youthful-sounding soloist, and the Ländler second movement clean-cut and crisp. It is the third movement *Adagio* that crowns the performance, hushed and intense from the start, with the emotional outbursts strongly controlled. At bargain-price with excellent modern digital sound, spacious like the performance, it makes an outstanding recommendation, a fine alternative to Szell.

Karajan's refined and poised, yet undoubtedly affectionate account remains among the finest versions of this lovely symphony, and Edith Mathis's sensitively composed contribution to the finale matches the conductor's meditative feeling. With glowing sound, this makes another outstanding mid-priced recommendation alongside Szell's renowned Cleveland CD.

With the orchestra very well drilled, responding warmly to the fluctations of Barbirolli's expressive Mahler style, this is an account to set alongside Barbirolli's classic studio recording of the *Fifth* in its passionate generosity. As in the *Fifth*, he tends to prefer broad speeds, but controls them masterfully with all the familiar warmth and conviction one expects from this conductor. The glowing, seamless reading of the slow movement leads on to a spacious account of the finale, with Heather Harper a radiant soloist. Full, warm, well-balanced sound to match. The Berlioz overture, dashingly done, and brilliantly played by this fine orchestra is a welcome makeweight.

Tennstedt's reading of the *Fourth Symphony* conveys spaciousness and strength, yet his agreeably light touch in the outer movements brings an innocence entirely in keeping with this most endearing of the Mahler symphonies, and in that he is followed most beautifully by Lucia Popp, the pure-toned soloist in the finale. The peak of the work as Tennstedt presents it lies in the long slow movement, here taken very slowly and intensely. The 1982 digital recording, made in the Kingsway Hall, is among EMI's finest, full and well balanced. Tennstedt's account of the *Adagietto* makes a worthwhile bonus.

Antoni Wit conducts a fresh, spontaneous-sounding reading, beautifully played and recorded, that can be warmly recommended at Naxos's bargain price. Lynda Russell is a pure-toned soprano soloist in the finale, both fresh and warm, with Wit giving a good lilt to the rhythm. Excellent sound, which gives a good bite and focus to the woodwind, so important in Mahler.

Spaciously recorded, the Arte Nova version offers a fresh, crisply paced reading from Adrian Leaper, demonstrating what polished ensemble the Gran Canaria Philharmonic can achieve. Woodwind soloists are most imaginative, and most striking of all is the refinement of the strings with the opening of the slow movement bringing the gentlest pianissimo, ravishingly sustained. The finale is then beautifully sprung, with the Korean soprano, Hellen Kwan, a golden-toned soloist, aptly young-sounding. Without being in the same class as the famous Szell version, this is thoroughly recommendable in the budget range.

Klemperer is slow in the first movement and, strangely, fractionally too fast in the slow movement. Yet the Philharmonia make some ravishing sounds, and one can easily fall under Klemperer's spell. The two highlights of the reading are the marvellously beautiful Laendler, which forms the central section of the second movement, and the simplicity of Elisabeth Schwarzkopf's singing in the finale. This is a record to enjoy, but perhaps not the one to buy as a single representation of Mahler's *Fourth* in a collection. In the Lieder other performers may find a deeper response to the words but the freshness of the singing, when Christa Ludwig's voice was in its early prime and at its richest, here gives much pleasure.

The *Fourth Symphony*, relatively lightweight, suits the Utah orchestra better than the weightier Mahler symphonies, and Abravanel directs a characteristically fresh and crisp reading, marked by some fine solo playing. The strings in the slow movement may not be quite as refined as in the finest rival versions, but the hushed intensity is most convincing, and the finale with Netania Davrath a firm, boyish soloist is light and urgent, bringing out the joy of the inspiration. Fair sound, fuller than in others in the Vanguard series. As with the other issues, no recording date is given.

With rich, immediate recording, Chailly draws brilliant playing from the Concertgebouw. The detail and clarity are extraordinary, with solos regularly highlighted, though at times too much so, as in the eerie *scordatura* violin solo of the Scherzo. Speeds are on the broad side both in the outer movements and the slow movement, with moulding of detail often meticulously underlined. Barbara Bonney is a delightfully girlish soloist in the *Wunderhorn* finale, both sweet and characterful, but she sounds even more appealing in the seven early Berg songs which come as a very generous coupling. Chailly, and the orchestra too, seem a degree more committed in Berg than in the Mahler.

Walter's glowingly radiant reading suffers from the fairly limited mono sound (especially at the climax of the slow movement). But the remastering of the 1945 recording has worked wonders, and orchestral textures are clear and yet warm. Desi Halban's contribution is refreshingly individual, dramatic as well as touching, and she is comparably impressive in the songs, which Walter accompanies discreetly at the piano. Her account of *Ich ging mit Lust durch einen grünen Wald* is enchanting.

Britten's mono account with the LSO recorded at Orford Church, Suffolk during the 1961 Aldeburgh Festival, brings a most distinctive reading. Britten is brisker, more classical in approach, yet his feeling for this music always shines through. Though the very opening threatens chaos, when he launches the main *Allegro* at a very fast tempo, it is still a revelatory account, in some ways neo-classical in its freshness, edgy and abrasive in the *Scherzo*, tender in the slow movement and light and jaunty in the child-heaven finale, with Joan Carlyle the boyish soloist. The fill-ups, both in stereo, come from two other Aldeburgh Festival concerts of a decade later, with Anna Reynolds rich and firm in the *Wayfaring Lad* cycle and Elly Ameling sweet and true, though not helped by the washy sound. The two songs from *Des Knaben Wunderhorn*, with Elly Ameling in radiant form, were recorded in 1969 and the *Lieder eines fahrenden gesellen* with Anna Reynolds three years later at Snape Maltings. No one with an interest in Britten as interpreter should neglect this issue.

Fresh and spontaneous-sounding, with an apt hint of rusticity, sums up Mehta's 1979 reading with the Israeli orchestra. The digital recording is cleanly defined and sounds better than many recordings from this source. The slow movement is expansive, but finely concentrated, and although Mehta occasionally indulges in exaggerated espressivo, it is a performance which holds together in its amiability, not least in the finale, where Barbara Hendricks brings a hint of boyishness to the solo. With two very well played *Preludes* from *Lohengrin* as fill-ups, this Australian release, while not a first choice, is worth considering, and has the interest that these performances appear on CD for the first time.

Haitink's earlier, late-1960s Concertegebouw recording now returns to the catalogue on Philips's Virtuoso bargain label. It is predictably well played and the recording still sounds very good. The performance is sober, but has an attractive simplicity, and Elly Ameling matches Haitink's approach in her serene contribution to the finale.

Nothing could be further removed from the warmth of Fritz Reiner than Pierre Boulez's account of the *Fourth Symphony* with the Cleveland Orchestra and Juliane Banse as soloist in the finale. It is a generally brisk, rather understated performance that takes a cool, analytical view of Mahler. The result lacks spontaneity except in the slow movement, where Boulez's simple dedication conveys a depth of feeling rather missing in the rest.

Bernstein's version, dating from 1960, brings a rather erratic reading, less controlled than his finest Mahler performances, and although well transferred, not really competitive in quality of sound.

(i) Symphonies Nos. 4 in G; (ii) 5 in C sharp min.

(B) ** Double Decca 458 383-2 (2). (i) Stahlman, Concg. O; (ii) Chicago SO; Solti.

Solti's earlier performance of the *Fourth Symphony* is disappointing. It is extremely well-balanced as a recording but the conductor is not altogether happy in the first movement and, besides a wilfulness of style, there are dull patches which he is unable to sustain with any richness of emotional expression. He does the finale best, and here Sylvia Stahlman sings charmingly. The opening *Funeral March* sets the tone of his reading of the *Fifth*. At a tempo faster than usual, it is wistful rather than deeply tragic, even though the dynamic contrasts are superbly pointed, and the string tone could hardly be more resonant. In the pivotal *Adagietto* too, Solti secures intensely beautiful playing, but the result lacks the 'inner' quality one finds so abundantly in Barbirolli's interpretation. Full-bodied if slightly over-reverberant recording.

Symphonies Nos. 1; (i) 4; 5: Adagietto (only).

(N) (BB) **(*) Royal Long Players Double DCL 70672-2 (2), Philh. O, Kletzki.

Cherishable recordings, made when the Philharmonia Orchestra was at its peak in the early 1960s. The Kingsway Hall acoustic produces glorious string textures and ripe horns, and the warmly atmospheric opening evocation of No. 1 is comparable to the Solti/LSO version in its spring-like glow. If later in the outer movements Kletzki's impulsive manner does not always knit the structure cohesively together, there is plenty of excitement.

Similarly in the *Fourth* there is radiant orchestral playing, especially in the elysian slow movement, and Emmy Loose's simplicity in the finale is enchanting. One's reservations here principally concern the opening movement, which Kletzki treats episodically, so that it tends to become a series of separate events rather than a carefully planned symphonic pattern. Yet the reading as a whole has a spontaneous individuality which is easy to enjoy. The lovely *Adagio* from the *Fifth Symphony* is slow and serene, unashamedly indulged, but ravishingly played.

Symphony No. 5 in C sharp min.

*** Decca 458 860-2. Concg. O, Chailly.

*** DG 437 789-2. BPO, Abbado.

✿ (M) *** EMI (ADD) CDM5 66910-2 [566962]. New Philh. O, Barbirolli.

*** Conifer 75605 51318-2. RPO, Gatti.

(M) *** EMI CD-EMX 2164. RLPO, Mackerras.

(B) *** DG (ADD) 439 429-2. BPO, Karajan.

(M) *** Decca Penguin 460 625-2. Cleveland O, Dohnányi.

(N) (B) ** Sony SBK 89289. VPO, Maazel.

Chailly excels himself in his strong, clear-sighted, but deeply felt reading of No. 5, with his concentration reflected in superlative playing from the Concertgebouw, caught with exceptional clarity in the full and brilliant Decca recording. The beauty of Mahler's orchestration has rarely been conveyed so vividly, with the hushed intensity of the *Adagio* the more moving for its reticence, and with the joyful finale dazzling in its crisp detail. Other, more personal readings may be more distinctive, but none is more widely recommendable.

Abbado's is an outstanding new version, recorded live in the Philharmonie, Berlin, with the dramatic tensions of a concert performance vividly captured. Abbado's view is clean-cut and taut, bringing out the high contrasts between movements, pointing rhythms not just precisely but with often-Viennese seductiveness. The great *Adagietto* is raptly done, wistful rather than openly romantic at a flowing tempo, and the *Wunderhorn* finale is at once refined and exuberant. With excellent sound, there are few versions to match this, presenting Abbado at his peak.

Barbirolli's famous analogue 1969 recording (made in Watford Town Hall) has now been splendidly remastered for EMI's 'Great Recordings of the Century' series and sounds fuller, clearer, more atmospheric than ever. On any count this is one of the greatest, most warmly affecting accounts ever committed to disc, expansive, yet concentrated in feeling: the *Adagietto* is very moving indeed. A classic version which many will prefer even to Abbado's newer digital account.

Daniele Gatti draws a colourful, impulsive reading of No. 5 from his RPO players, not as highly polished as some, and not so weightily recorded, but this is still an engagingly warm and relaxed performance to be recommended strongly.

Mackerras in his well-paced reading sees the work as a whole, building each movement with total concentration. There is a thrilling culmination on the great brass chorale at the end, with polish allied to purposefulness. Barbirolli in his classic reading may find more of a tear-laden quality in the great *Adagietto*; but Mackerras, with fewer controversial points of interpretation and superb modern sound, makes an excellent alternative choice at mid-price.

Karajan's 1973 version makes a very welcome reissue on DG's Classikon label. This is one of the most beautiful and intense versions available, starting with a highly compelling account of the first movement which brings biting funeral-march rhythms. Karajan's characteristic emphasis on polish and refinement goes with sharpness of focus. This is a performance of stature and, with excellent sound, a genuine bargain.

Dohnányi conducts the Cleveland Orchestra in an exceptionally high-powered reading, superbly played and recorded, which can still relax totally in expressive warmth. The toughness of the first two movements – with superb discipline bringing immaculate articulation in the second – gives way to an equally polished but nicely lilting Ländler in the third, finely shaded. Though the hushed *Adagietto* keeps a degree of reserve, the songful freshness and purity are very sympathetic, before the thrustful and dramatic finale. The brilliance of the Cleveland playing is matched by the vivid recorded sound. The descriptive essay is written by Hilary Spurling.

Maazel draws superb playing from the VPO. His is a direct, unexaggerated approach, refreshing and clear but, particularly in the slow movement, he misses the depth and emotional intensity which is an essential element in Mahler. A good recording, and it's inexpensive, but that's not enough in this fiercely competitive area.

(i) *Symphony No. 5;* (ii; iii) *Lieder eines fahrenden Gesellen;* (ii; iv) *Des Knaben Wunderhorn.*

(BB) ** Virgin 2 x 1 Double VBD5 61507-2 (2). (i) Finnish RSO, Saraste; (ii) Murray; (iii) RPO, Litton; (iv) Allen, LPO, Mackerras.

Saraste and the Finnish Radio Orchestra offer a refined and well-paced reading of the *Fifth*, which gives a relatively lightweight view of the symphony. Rhythms are beautifully sprung, and the *Adagietto* is the more tenderly moving for being a degree reticent and understated. The recording is refined to match, warm and naturally balanced. On the second disc Ann Murray gives a warmly responsive account of *Lieder eines fahrenden Gesellen*, and is particularly touching in the two outer songs. She is joined by Thomas Allen in *Des Knaben Wunderhorn*, directed with imagination and character by Mackerras. Two of the highlights are Allen's noble *Rheinlegendchen*, and Murray's ravishing performance of the closing song, *Wo die schönen Trompeten blasen*, here a solo rather than a duo. The recording is warmly resonant and spacious.

Symphony No. 6 in A min.

*** Ph. (IMS) 426 257-2. BPO, Haitink – *Lieder eines fahrenden Gesellen.* ***

*** DG 445 835-2. VPO, Boulez.

(M) *** Sony (ADD) SBK 47654. Cleveland O, Szell.

(M) **(*) Sony (ADD) SMK 60208. NYPO, Bernstein.

(B) *** Naxos 8.550529 (2). Polish Nat. RSO (Katowice), Wit.

(B) *** Double Decca (IMS) (ADD) 444 871-2 (2). Concg. O, Chailly – ZEMLINSKY: *Maeterlinck Lieder.* ***

(M) *** Unicorn (ADD) UKCD 2024/5. Stockholm PO, Horenstein.

(M) **(*) Decca (ADD) 425 040-2. Chicago SO, Solti.

(B) **(*) EMI double forte (ADD) CZS5 69349-2. New Philh. O, Barbirolli – R. STRAUSS: *Ein Heldenleben.* ***

**(*) EMI CDS5 56925-2. CBSO, Rattle.

**(*) Telarc CD 80444. Atlanta SO, Levi.

Symphony No. 6 in A min.; (i) Kindertotenlieder; 5 Rückert Lieder.

(M) *** DG (ADD) 457 716-2 (2). BPO, Karajan; (i) with Ludwig.

With superlative playing from the Berlin Philharmonic, Karajan's reading of the *Sixth* is a revelation, above all in the slow movement, which emerges as one of the greatest of Mahler's slow movements. Though the outer movements firmly stamp this as one of the darkest of the Mahler symphonies, in Karajan's reading their sharp focus makes them both compelling and refreshing. The fine mid-1970s DG recording, with its wide dynamic, adds enormously to the impact. This is well worthy of reissue as one of DG's Originals, especially as Christa Ludwig's moving account of the *Kindertotenlieder* has been added to the previously coupled *Rückert Lieder*; fine, positive performances with comparative distinction and refinement in the orchestral playing.

Haitink conducts a noble reading of this difficult symphony, underplaying the neurosis behind the inspiration, but, in his clean-cut concentration and avoidance of exaggeration, making the result the more moving in its degree of reticence, yet intensely committed. Jessye Norman's rich-toned account of *Lieder eines fahrenden Gesellen* makes a powerful bonus. Excellent sound, both full-blooded and refined.

Boulez conducts a performance of the most enigmatic symphony which in its power and sharpness of focus transcends almost any rival. Boulez's control of speeds is masterful, never rushed, even though this is a performance squeezed on to a single disc, and the slow movement brings hushed, ravishingly beautiful playing of a refinement it would be hard to match. The finale is rugged and weighty, with crisp pointing of rhythms, making this an outstanding recommendation alongside Karajan who, on two discs, also includes Christa Ludwig's five *Rückert Lieder*. Though R. L. found this a performance observed rather than felt at white heat, E. G. was totally involved.

Szell's powerful outer movements are masterfully shaped and unerringly paced, with the second-movement scherzo beautifully sprung to bring out the grotesquerie. The *Andante moderato* then brings a uniquely delicate and moving account, hauntingly wistful, tender without a hint of sentimentality. The CD transfer gives a fuller, more atmospheric impression of what the orchestra sounded like in Severance Hall, Cleveland, than most of the studio recordings of the time. At budget price, squeezed on to a single disc, this is buried treasure and a fine counterpart to Szell's classic reading of Mahler's *Fourth*.

It is good that Sony have now separated Bernstein's enormously gripping NYPO account of the *Sixth* from the *Eighth* (see below). Now on a single, mid-priced disc it is highly competitive. The remastering has further improved the sound; although the close balance remains a drawback, the actual sounds are impressive, and the performance itself is very compelling indeed.

The excellent quality of the Katowice Orchestra of Polish Radio is impressively demonstrated in all four movements of this difficult symphony. The ensemble can hardly be faulted, and the full, atmospheric recording enhances that quality with string-sound that is fresh and radiant. Wit conducts a spacious performance, clean and well sprung,

with the varying moods sharply contrasted. On two full discs it becomes less of a super-bargain than some Naxos issues, but it stands comparison with any rival.

Chailly's version with the Concertgebouw offers brilliant playing and spectacular sound in a reading remarkable for the broad, rugged approach in the outer movements. There is relentlessness in the slow speed for the first movement, with expressive warmth giving way to a square purposefulness, tense and effective. The third movement brings a comparably simple, direct approach at a genuine flowing *Andante*. In its open songfulness it rouses Wunderhorn echoes. Anyone fancying the unexpected but attractive Zemlinsky coupling need not hesitate.

In the first movement, Horenstein finds extra weight by taking a more measured tempo than most conductors. It is a sober reading that holds together with wonderful concentration, yet the slow movement brings the most persuasive rubato. The finale brings another broad, noble reading. Yet some will feel that 33 minutes is short measure for the second CD.

Solti draws stunning playing from the Chicago orchestra. The sessions were in March and April 1970, and this was the first recording he made with them after he took up his post as principal conductor; as he himself said, it represented a love-affair at first sight. The electric excitement of the playing confirms this, with brilliant, immediate but atmospheric sound. Solti's rather extrovert approach is here at its most impressive. His fast tempi may mean that he misses some of the deeper emotions, and the added brightness of the CD transfer perhaps emphasizes this, but it is still a very convincing and involving performance.

Barbirolli gives a characteristically expansive account of Mahler's *Sixth Symphony*, and there are many of the same fine qualities as in his version of the *Fifth*, recorded with the same orchestra a year later. But, particularly in the first movement, the slow tempo is allowed to drag a little, so that tension falls. Such wavering of concentration will not trouble everyone, but the 1967 Kingsway Hall recording has now lost some of its bloom. Moreover there is nothing like the same illusion of a live Barbirolli performance as there is with the *Fifth*. The pairing with *Ein Heldenleben* has a superior CD transfer.

At spacious speeds Rattle directs a thoughtful, finely detailed reading of what has become a favourite symphony for him. The performance yet lacks the electric tension which usually marks his work with this orchestra, with ensemble less crisp. One admires without being involved in the way Mahler demands, even in Rattle's tender and hushed account of the slow movement, which he places second in the scheme instead of third, following Mahler's last thoughts on the work rather than what is published. The sound is full and warm, but in its diffuseness it undermines tension further compared with the finest versions.

By dint of omitting the exposition repeat in the first movement Yoel Levi's version is squeezed on to a single disc, despite an exceptionally spacious reading of the finale. His is generally an extrovert approach to Mahler, leading occasionally to heaviness, though with finely disciplined playing from the Atlanta Orchestra, vividly recorded.

Symphony No. 7 in E min.

(M) *** Decca (ADD) 425 041-2. Chicago SO, Solti.

(M) *** DG 445 513-2. Chicago SO, Abbado.

(M) *** Sony (ADD) SMK 60564. NYPO, Bernstein.

*** RCA 09026 63510-2 (2). LSO, Tilson Thomas.

**(*) Telarc 2CD 80514 (2). Atlanta SO, Levi.

**(*) EMI CDC7 54344-2. CBSO, Rattle.

(BB) **(*) Naxos 8.550531. Polish Nat. RSO, Halász.

(**) BBC mono BBCL 4034-2 (2). Hallé O & BBC Northern O,
   Barbirolli – BRUCKNER: Symphony No. 9. (**)

In interpretation, Solti's version is as successful as his fine account of the *Sixth Symphony*, extrovert in display but full of dark implications. The tempi tend to be challengingly fast – at the very opening, for example, and in the Scherzo (where Solti is mercurial) and in the finale (where his energy carries shock-waves in its trail). The second *Nachtmusik* is enchantingly seductive, and throughout the orchestra plays superlatively. This is one of Solti's finest Mahler records and the recording is brilliant and full – the CD transfer increases the brightness.

Abbado's command of Mahlerian characterization has never been more tellingly displayed than in this most problematic of the symphonies; even in the loosely bound finale Abbado unerringly draws the threads together. The precision and polish of the Chicago orchestra go with total commitment, and the recording is one of the finest DG has made with this orchestra.

In 1965 Bernstein drew a performance of the *Seventh* of characteristic intensity and beauty from the New York Philharmonic; his love of the music is evident in every bar. The playing is fabulous, yet there are also reservations. His warmth of phrasing in the second subject makes Bernstein's pointing sound self-conscious and tense, and in the Night music of the second and fourth movements, where the New York orchestra produces playing of heavenly refinement, the same feeling is present. Even in the finale, where Bernstein's thrusting dynamism holds the disparate structure together, there is the feeling that he is unable to relax into simplicity. The recording, made in the Avery Fisher Hall, is vivid and forward.

Michael Tilson Thomas conducts a strong, purposeful reading of the *Seventh*, with polished and refined playing from the LSO and recording to match. His terracing of textures and dynamics is perfectly judged. The result may be less atmospheric and evocative than in some readings, but the relative coolness of the second *Nachtmusik*, for example, makes one appreciate the work the more keenly for its symphonic qualities. Although the fragmentary structure of the finale is in no way disguised, the pointedness of the playing holds it firmly together. A strong contender in a hotly competitive field.

Yoel Levi conducts a reading of the *Seventh* which gains in strength and purpose as it progresses. If the very slow tempo for the first movement makes it seem a degree subdued, the strong colouring of later movements, as in the nightmare quality he gives to the central Scherzo, makes an increasingly characterful impression, though the relatively fast tempo for the second *Nachtmusik* does not quite avoid

a jog-trot. The sound is close and brilliant, overpowering in big tuttis, if not ideally clear on detail.

Rattle, as ever, proves a sensitive and persuasive Mahlerian, in this most equivocal Mahler symphony. He made this recording live in The Maltings at Snape, disappointed with an earlier, studio version, which he did not want to have issued. Sadly, live or not, this performance does not have the biting tension and thrust that makes Rattle's recording of the *Second Symphony* so compelling, and the sound is not as full. The first movement suffers most, and the finale is the most successful. But as a single-disc version of the symphony – when most other versions take two CDs – this is still well worth considering.

Very well played and treated to refined and well-balanced digital recording, the Naxos version offers excellent value on a single disc at super-bargain price. With well-chosen speeds, often brisk but unhurried, with crisp ensemble and good rhythmic point, the only snag is that, by the standards of the finest versions, it is undercharacterized, lacking both flamboyance and tragic weight. Even there one has an advantage in the haunting melody of the second *Nachtmusik*, which is the more moving for being treated in a restrained way.

Sir John Barbirolli's performance received the accolade of Deryck Cooke no less, though his enthusiasm would probably not have extended to the somewhat primitive recorded quality. The playing of the combined BBC Northern and Hallé Orchestras was first class and already by this time Barbirolli was a fervent and committed Mahlerian and totally attuned to the composer's world. He is unhurried and expansive: indeed at 84 minutes, he is more leisurely than almost any other conductor, but paradoxically makes the overall performance seem more concentrated and convincing. Despite the poor sound this should be heard.

Symphony No. 8 (Symphony of 1000).

(M) *** Decca Legends (ADD) 460 972-2. Harper, Popp,
   Augér, Minton, Watts, Kollo, Shirley-Quirk, Talvela, V. Boys'
   Ch., V. State Op. Ch. & Singverein, Chicago SO, Solti.

(B) *** Sony (ADD) SBK 48281. Robinson, Marshall, Heichele,
   Wenkel, Laurich, Walker, Stilwell, Estes, Frankfurt Kantorei,
   Singakademie, Limburger Boys' Ch., Op. & Museum O,
   Gielen.

**(*) BBC (ADD) BBCL 4002-7. Barker, Hatt, Giebel, Meyer,
   Watts, Neate, Orda, Van Mill, BBC Ch. and Choral Soc.,
   Goldsmith's Ch. Union, Hampstead Ch. Soc., Emanuel
   School Boys' Ch., Orpington Junior Singers, LSO,
   Horenstein.

**(*) DG (IMS) 445 843-2 (2). Studer, McNair, Rost, Von
   Otter, Lang, Seiffert, Terfel, Rootering, Tölz Boys' Ch., Berlin
   R. & Prague Philharmonic Ch., BPO, Abbado.

** RCA 09026 68348-2 (2). Marc, Sweet, Norberg-Schulz,
   Kasarova, Liang, Heppner, Leiferkus, Pape, Bayerischen
   Rundfunks Ch., Berlin Rundfunkchor, Stuttgart Südfunk Ch.,
   Tölzer Knabenchor, Bayerischen Rundfunks SO, C. Davis.

(**) Orfeo mono C 519 992 B. Coertse, Zadek, West, Malaniuk,
   Zampieri, Prey, Edelmann, Konzertvereinigung, Singverein,
   Wiener Sängerknaben, VPO, Mitropoulos.

(i) *Symphony No. 8 (Symphony of 1000). Symphony No. 10: Adagio.*

(B) ***** DG Double 459 406-2 (2). (i) Studer, Blasi, Jo, Lewis, Meier, Nagai, Allen, Sotin, Southend Boys' Ch.; Philh. O, Sinopoli.

*(*) DG (IMS) (ADD) 435 102-2 (2). VPO, Bernstein, (i) with Price, Blegen, Zeumer, Schmidt, Baltsa, Riegel, Prey, Van Dam, V. Op. Ch., V. Boys' Ch.

Giuseppe Sinopoli gives a ripely passionate account of this most extravagant symphony, recorded with a richness and body that outshine any digital rival. In vividness of atmosphere it is matched only by Solti's magnificent analogue version, recorded in Vienna, which has the added advantage of now being available on a single CD – now reissued in Decca Legends series – which makes a strong alternative choice. Sinopoli, flexible in his approach to speed, here conveys a warmth of expression that brings joyful exuberance to the great outburst of the opening *Veni creator spiritus*. It builds into one of the most thrilling accounts ever, helped by a superb team of soloists and incandescent choral singing, recorded with fine weight and body. The *Adagio* from the *Tenth Symphony* makes a useful fill-up, but Sinopoli's very slow reading, with detail very heavily underlined, takes away the dark purposefulness of the argument.

Recorded live at the opening of the Alte Oper in Frankfurt in August 1981, Gielen's version offers a direct, fresh reading, full of atmosphere, in which brisk speeds allow ample weight. The analogue recording is less full than some, but it is naturally balanced with plenty of presence, if with brass a little distant. The chorus sings with heartfelt intensity, and the soloists make a distinguished team, except that the ringing Heldentenor, Mallory Walker, develops a beat in the voice under stress as Dr Marianus. On a single disc at budget price in Sony's Essential Classics series, it makes an outstanding bargain.

Bernstein's DG version of the *Eighth*, also coupled with the *Adagio* from the *Tenth*, is certainly compelling – and better recorded (in 1975) than his earlier CBS/Sony version. But at full price it is hardly a primary recommendation, even though the sound is quite full and atmospheric.

Horenstein's reading conveys a thrilling sense of occasion, and though it does not challenge some of the later commercial recordings, it is the feeling that they were engaged in something special that makes this so memorable. Though audience noises are intrusive at times, the atmosphere is vividly caught, with the conductor's unforced, firmly paced reading magnetic from beginning to end, always natural, never exaggerated. Other readings may have a higher voltage or present a more distinctive view, but this has a special place in the Mahler archive. The sound the BBC engineers get from the Festival Hall holds up very well. The second disc includes a conversation between Horenstein and the critic Alan Blyth.

Claudio Abbado's 1994 recording, keenly analytical and precisely balanced, fails to capture the very quality one would expect in a live account: a sense of atmosphere. Except in the final chorus, *Alles vergängliche*, where the tension and slow momentum are irresistible, making a magnificent climax, this is too often a detached-sounding reading, clear

and transparent rather than intense, relating the music more than usual to Mahler's *Knaben Wunderhorn* inspirations.

Sir Colin Davis has the benefit of the wonderful Bavarian Orchestra who play with great eloquence and commitment, and excellent engineering from his RCA team. There is some very fine choral singing and the sweep and grandeur of Mahler's vision comes over clearly. But the performance is flawed by some of the female singers. The soloists are too close to the microphone and are uneven, in what is otherwise a well-balanced sound picture. Alessandra Marc's vibrato is intrusive, and neither Sharon Sweet nor Ning Liang gives much pleasure.

Dimitri Mitropoulos's acclaimed 1960 account of the *Eighth Symphony*, with a fine line-up of soloists, choirs and the Vienna Philharmonic, will doubtless be sought after by Mahlerians and Mitropoulos admirers alike. This great conductor possessed a selfless dedication to whatever work he was performing and this certainly shines through. Artistic considerations aside, the ORF (Austrian Radio) recording lets it down. One has only to compare the sound their engineers achieved with the vivid stereo that BBC engineers produced for Horenstein in 1959 to realize how inadequate is the present engineering.

Symphony No. 9 in D min.

* DG 439 024-2 (2). BPO, Karajan.

* EMI CDS5 56580-2 (2). VPO, Rattle – R. STRAUSS: *Metamorphosen.* *****

* DG (IMS) (ADD) 435 378-2. BPO, Bernstein.

(M) ***** Sony (ADD) SMK 60597. NYPO, Bernstein.

(M) ***** EMI (ADD) CDM7 63115-2. BPO, Barbirolli.

(M) ***** EMI (ADD) CMS5 67036-2 (2). New Philh. O, Klemperer – R. STRAUSS: *Metamorphosen;* WAGNER: *Siegfried Idyll.* *****

(B) (*****) Dutton Lab. mono CDEA 5005. VPO, Walter.

** DG 457 581-2. Chicago SO, Boulez.

(M) ****** DG (ADD) 463 609-2 (2). Chicago SO, Giulini – SCHUBERT: *Symphony No. 8 (Unfinished).* ******

Symphony No. 9 (with rehearsal & conversation between Bruno Walter and Arnold Michaelis).

(M) ***** Sony (ADD) SMK 64452 (2). Columbia SO, Walter.

Symphony No. 9 in D (with separate talk by the conductor on performing and listening to the symphony).

(M) ****(*)** Telarc 3CD 80527 (3 for cost of 1). Philh. O, Zander.

Symphony No. 9; Symphony No. 10: Adagio.

(M) ***** Regis 2033 (2). Mahler-Jugend O or European Community Youth O, Judd.

Symphony No. 9; (i) *Kindertotenlieder; 5 Rückert Lieder.*

(B) ***** DG Double (ADD) 453 040-2 (2). BPO, Karajan; (i) with Ludwig.

Symphony No. 9; (i) *Des Knaben Wunderhorn.*

(N) (B) ***** Ph. (ADD) 464 714-2 (2). Concg. O, Haitink; (i) with Norman, Shirley-Quirk.

Symphony No. 9; (i) *Das Lied von der Erde.*

(B) ***** Ph. Duo (ADD) 462 299-2 (2). Concg. O, Haitink; (i) with Baker, King.

Fine as Karajan's other Mahler recordings have been, his two accounts of the *Ninth* transcend them. In the earlier analogue version (453 040-2) it is the combination of richness and concentration in the outer movements that makes for a reading of the deepest intensity, while in the middle two movements there is point and humour as well as refinement and polish. Helped by full, spacious recording, the sudden pianissimos that mark both movements have an ear-pricking realism such as one rarely experiences on record, and the unusually broad tempi are superbly controlled. In the finale Karajan is not just noble and stoic; he finds the bite of passion as well, sharply set against stillness and repose.

Yet within two years Karajan went on to record the work even more compulsively at live performances in Berlin. The major difference in that later recording (439024-3) is that there is a new, glowing optimism in the finale, rejecting any Mahlerian death-wish and making it a supreme achievement. The 'original-image' bit-processing has added to the projection, but the strings have plenty of body.

The earlier (1980) analogue performance makes a remarkable bargain alternative, reissued as a DG Double and costing half as much as the later, digital recording. Moreover the performances of the *Kindertotenlieder* and *Rückert Lieder* have a distinction and refinement of playing which stand out above all.

Haitink, too, is at his very finest in Mahler's *Ninth*, and the last movement, with its slow expanses of melody, reveals a unique concentration. Unlike most other conductors he maintains his intensely slow tempo from beginning to end. This is a great performance, beautifully recorded at the end of the 1960s, and this will be for many Mahlerians a primary recommendation, particularly as it now comes generously recoupled in Duo format with Haitink's famous set of *Das Lied von der Erde* with Baker and King or, alternatively, with his highly recommendable *Des Knaben Wunderhorn* with Jessye Norman and John Shirley-Quick (discussed below).

Rattle's reading, recorded live in the Musikverein in Vienna, consistently brings out the deeper qualities in No. 9, the hushed, tender intensity of the outer movements, erupting in monumental climaxes with dynamic contrast matched by emotional power. Equally the central movements are just as sharply characterized, with the fun and wit behind the writing conveyed with winning lightness, aptly Viennese. The sound is not as full or immediate as in some versions, but the beauty and subtlety of the Vienna Philharmonic's playing comes over vividly. Strauss's *Metamorphosen* makes an excellent fill-up.

Bernstein's Berlin version of Mahler's *Ninth*, made live in 1979, was the solitary occasion when he was permitted to conduct Karajan's own orchestra, and the response is electric, with playing not only radiant and refined but also deeply expressive in direct response to the conductor. Highly spontaneous, with measured speeds superbly sustained in a tautly concentrated reading. Bernstein conveys a comparably hushed inner quality.

Barbirolli greatly impressed the Berliners with his Mahler performances live, and this recording reflects the players' warmth of response. He opted to record the slow and intense finale before the rest, and the beauty of the playing makes it a fitting culmination. The other movements are strong and alert too, and the sound remains full and atmospheric, though now more clearly defined. An unquestionable bargain.

Bernstein's New York *Ninth* – a lucky symphony on record – is undoubtedly a great performance. Here Bernstein's sense of urgency has its maximum impact, though in the finale he does not quite achieve the visionary intensity of his later recording for DG with the Berlin Philharmonic. The recording made in the Avery Fisher Hall at the same time as his equally successful *Seventh* is forwardly balanced but has plenty of body.

Zander is a natural Mahlerian, and his is a powerful, red-bloodedly passionate, yet at times relatively intimate view of this visionary symphony. The concentration of the performance is immensely compelling throughout, with the hushed intensity of the final *Adagio* superbly caught, enhanced by an exceptionally spacious tempo, very well sustained. That said, while the orchestra is given great presence, the sound lacks full body as recorded in the difficult acoustic of the Barbican Hall. The illuminating and thoughtful extended talk on the third disc is a distinct bonus. The three discs come for the cost of one and, apart from the normal documentation, there is a folded facsimile of the first page of Mahler's score, with the conductor's markings.

Walter's Sony (originally CBS) performance was recorded in late January and early February 1961, and the producer, John McClure, took the opportunity to record a working portrait of the occasion. That is supplemented here by a 16-minute conversation between the conductor and Arnold Michaelis, dating from five years earlier. Walter's performance lacks mystery at the very start, but through the long first movement he unerringly builds up a consistent structure, controlling tempo more closely than most rivals, preferring a steady approach. The middle two movements similarly are sharply focused rather than genial, and the finale, lacking hushed pianissimos, is tough and stoically strong. A fine performance, quite different from his famous 1938 VPO account.

Klemperer's refusal to languish pays tribute to his spiritual defiance, and the physical power is underlined when the sound is full-bodied and firmly focused. The sublimity of the finale comes out the more intensely, with overt expressiveness held in check and deep emotion implied rather than made explicit. Now recoupled both with the Strauss *Metamorphosen* and Wagner's *Siegfried Idyll*, this is one of the more important reissues in EMI's 'Klemperer Legacy'.

Judd conducts the brilliant young players of the Mahler-Jugend Orchestra in a deeply moving account of the *Ninth*, recorded live in Bratislava in April 1990. With recording of spectacular range and vividness, this makes one of the most appealing of all versions. The searing emotional commitment of the players comes out consistently, and no allowance whatever need be made on technical grounds for their youth. The performance of the *Adagio* from the *Tenth* is not quite so distinguished, though warmly satisfying; it was recorded in August 1987 by the rival band from EEC countries, the European Community Youth Orchestra.

Bruno Walter's 1938 version with the Vienna Philharmonic was the first recording of this symphony ever issued.

The opening is not promising, with coughing very obtrusive; but then, with the atmosphere of the Musikvereinsaal caught more vividly than in most modern recordings, the magnetism of Walter becomes irresistible in music which he was the first ever to perform. Ensemble is often scrappy in the first movement, but intensity is unaffected; even at its flowing speed, the finale brings warmth and repose with no feeling of haste. The new Dutton transfer (transferred direct from 78-r.p.m. shellac discs) can do little about the audience noises, but the sound-balance is further enhanced over the EMI transfer (CDH7 63029-2), and the last movement in particular offers amazingly natural and believable string-sound.

Boulez's grasp of the work's architecture is impressive, and he charts this territory with unfailing clarity and intelligence without fully revealing its spiritual landscape. He seems determined to give us the facts without the slightest trace of hysteria, and his objectivity makes for a thought-provoking reading. He draws from the Chicago Orchestra the most powerful playing – strong, resonant and seamless – with DG's immediate recording adding to the impact.

Giulini's 1977 Chicago performance of the *Ninth Symphony* curiously lacks the very quality one expects from this conductor: dedication. It opens atmospherically, but the tempi are too measured for a sense of impetus to assert itself. The orchestral playing is of the highest standard, but the listener's interest is not consistently sustained, despite some fine moments. The sound is rather glamorized and this is a curious choice for DG's Originals label.

Symphony No. 10 in F sharp (revised performing edition by Deryck Cooke).

*** EMI CDC5 56972-2. BPO, Rattle.

(B) **(*) Double Decca 444 872-2 (2). Berlin RSO, Chailly – SCHOENBERG: *Verklärte Nacht.* **

In 1980, at the beginning of his recording career, Simon Rattle recorded this inspired realization of Mahler's five-movement concept. With the Bournemouth Symphony Orchestra, that remains an electrifying account, weightily recorded (CDC7 54406-2), but his new version with the Berlin Philharmonic, recorded live, transcends it in almost every way. It is not only the extra refinement of the Berliners but also the extra detail that Rattle brings out in almost every phrase, that goes with an even greater concentration. His interpretation remains broadly the same, though the slow outer movements are a shade more spacious than previously, with the finale and its brutal hammer blows – inspired by a funeral procession heard from afar – becoming a degree more consolatory than before, conveying hope after death. The contrast of the middle movements with their *Wunderhorn* echoes is also more strongly characterized.

Reissued at bargain price on this Double Decca, Chailly's Decca version is superbly recorded and his grasp of the musical structure is keen. The Berlin Radio Orchestra is highly responsive, although the internal tension of the music-making is not as high as in Rattle's version.

LIEDER AND SONG-CYCLES

7 frühe Lieder (with piano); *11 frühe Lieder* (arr. Berio); *Lieder eines fahrenden Gesellen.*

*** Teldec 9031 74002-2. Hampson, Lutz or Philh. O, Berio.

Thomas Hampson is in magnificent voice for his unusual collection of Mahler songs. He does the first seven of the early songs and the *Wayfaring Lad* songs with piano accompaniment by David Lutz. He then turns to the remaining early songs in the distinctive orchestral arrangements made by Luciano Berio. Though Berio follows Mahlerian practice in many of his orchestral colourings, his instrumentation overall is far thicker and weightier. Though these arrangements are far less 'authentic' than those made of a group of the same songs by Colin and David Matthews (see below), they have their fascination when sung as warmly and sensitively as by Thomas Hampson. First-rate sound.

7 early Lieder: Ablösung im Sommer; Frühlingsmorgen; Hans und Grete; Nicht Wiedersehen!; Selbstgefühl; Starke Einbildungskraft; Zu Strassburg Auf der Schanz' (orch. D. and C. Matthews).

*** Unicorn DKPCD 9120. Gomez, Bournemouth Sinf., Carewe (with MATTHEWS: *Cantiga, Introit; September Music*) ***.

David and Colin Matthews made this orchestration of Mahler's so-called 'Youth' songs, and, as is shown in this sensitive performance from Jill Gomez and the Bournemouth Sinfonietta under John Carewe, their feeling for the Mahler sound is unerring, making these a most rewarding addition to the tally of regular Mahler song-cycles with orchestra. It proves a very apt coupling for the warmly sympathetic works of David Matthews on the disc, notably the dramatic scena *Cantiga*, powerful and immediately attractive.

11 Lieder aus der Jugendzeit; Lieder eines fahrenden Gesellen; 4 Rückert Lieder.

(M) **(*) Sony (ADD) SMK 61847. Fischer-Dieskau, Bernstein (piano).

Both artists here respond to each other in an almost impressionistic way, producing a consistently expressive style. The Four *Rückert Lieder* inspire Fischer-Dieskau to a velvety legato, while *Scheiden und Meiden*, one of the eleven 'Youth' songs, is given an exhilarating bounce; *Nicht wiedersehen* from the same set is taken at half the normal speed, and evokes a totally different, magical world. The 1968 sound is excellent. This is one of the more impressive reissues in Sony's Bernstein Century edition.

Kindertotenlieder.

(M) (**) Decca mono 425 995-2. Ferrier, Concg. O, Klemperer – BRAHMS: *Liebeslieder Waltzes.* (***)

Kindertotenlieder; Des Knaben Wunderhorn: 3 songs; Leider eines fahrenden Gesellen; 4 Rückert Lieder.

**(*) Decca (IMS) 425 790-2. Fassbaender, Deutsches SO, Berlin, Chailly.

(i) *Kindertotenlieder; Lieder eines fahrenden Gesellen;* (ii) *5 Rückert Lieder.*

✹ (M) *** EMI (ADD) CDM5 66981-2 [566996]. Baker, Hallé or New Philh. O, Barbirolli.

(BB) *** Naxos 8.554156. Greevy, Nat. SO of Ireland, (i) Fürst; (ii) Decker.

Dame Janet Baker's collaboration with Barbirolli represents the affectionate approach to Mahler at its warmest, intensely beautiful, full of breathtaking moments. The spontaneous feeling of soloist and conductor for this music comes over as in a live performance and brings out the tenderness to a unique degree. An indispensable CD.

Bernadette Greevy uses her opulent mezzo, firm and even, to bring out the lyrical beauty of Mahler's writing in all three of these orchestral song-cycles. She may lack a degree of vitality in such a song as the second of the *Wayfaring Lad* cycle, the song that gave Mahler his first theme in his *First Symphony*, but her poise in such a great song as the Rückert setting, *Ich bin der Welt abhanden gekommen*, is most satisfying, readily compensating for any lack of emotional weight compared with the finest interpretations. The Irish National Symphony Orchestra play with rich, velvety tone in every section, helped by the warmly atmospheric recording, made in the National Concert Hall in Dublin.

Brigitte Fassbaender gives fearless, vividly characterized performances of Mahler's three shorter orchestral song-cycles, adding for good measure three songs from *Des Knaben Wunderhorn*, including *Urlicht*. In that last, her voice is not quite as even as usual, and the orchestra in *Kindertotenlieder* is slacker than elsewhere.

The Ferrier version with Klemperer is a live recording taken from a broadcast in July 1951, some two years after her EMI recording with Bruno Walter. Though the voice is caught vividly and the richness of her interpretation has, if anything, intensified, the surface-hiss is daunting. Unusually coupled with the Brahms in which Ferrier's role is only incidental.

(i) *Kindertotenlieder;* (ii) *Lieder eines fahrenden Gesellen;* (iii) Lieder: *Frühlingsmorgen; Hans und Grete; Liebst du um Schönheit; Des Knaben Wunderhorn:* excerpts.

(N) (BB) **(*) EMI Encore (ADD) CDE 574738-2. Ludwig, Philh. O, (i) Vandernoot; (ii) Boult; (iii) Moore (piano).

A valuable inexpensive compilation of Christa Ludwig's EMI recordings of Mahler, made when her voice was in its early prime and at its richest, whether in the orchestral items or the songs with piano. Other versions may find a deeper response to the words, but the freshness of the singing here gives much pleasure.

Kindertotenlieder; 5 Rückert Lieder. Das Lied von der Erde: Der Einsame im Herbst.

**(*) EMI CDC5 56443-2. Hampson, Rieger.

Thomas Hampson here sings with evenly beautiful tone and fine feeling for detail. With a male voice the *Rückert lieder* work better than *Kindertotenlieder*, with half-tones exquisitely shaded. The baritone version of the second song from *Das Lied von der Erde* makes a welcome bonus. Warm, well-balanced recording.

Das klagende Lied: complete (*Part 1, Waldmärchen; Part 2, Der Spielmann; Part 3, Hochzeitsstücke*).

*** EMI CDC5 66406-2. Döse, Hodgson, Tear, Rea, CBSO Ch., CBSO, Rattle.

Rattle brings out the astonishing originality of Mahler's cycle, but adds urgency, colour and warmth, not to mention deeper, more meditative qualities. So the final section, *Wedding Piece*, after starting with superb swagger in the celebration music, is gripping in the minstrel's sinister narration and ends in the darkest concentration on a mezzo-soprano solo, beautifully sung by Alfred Hodgson. The ensemble of the CBSO has a little roughness, but the bite and commitment could not be more convincing. Dating from 1983–4 this is one of Rattle's earliest Mahler recordings, but it sounds excellent in what appears to be a new transfer.

Des Knaben Wunderhorn.

(M) *** EMI CDM5 67236-2 [567256]. Schwarzkopf, Fischer-Dieskau, LSO, Szell.

Szell's 1968 Kingsway Hall recording of *Des Knaben Wunderhorn* was a primary recommendation for three decades at premium price. Now it rightly joins EMI's 'Great Recordings of the Century' and the careful remastering plus the lower price will surely extend its catalogue life for a considerable time to come. The superb singing of Schwarzkopf and Fischer-Dieskau is underpinned by wonderfully sensitive playing from the LSO under Szell, who matches and even surpasses his achievement with his own Cleveland Orchestra in the *Fourth Symphony*.

Des Knaben Wunderhorn (excerpts): *Verlor'ne Müh; Rheinlegendchen; Wo die schönen Trompeten blasen; Lob des hohen Verstandes; Aus! Aus!.* Lieder: *Erinnerung; Frühlingsmorgen; Ich ging mit Lust durch einen grünen Wald; Phantasie aus Don Juan; Serenade aus Don Juan.*

*** DG 423 666-2. Von Otter, Gothoni – WOLF: *Lieder.* ***

The Mahler half of Anne Sofie von Otter's brilliant recital is just as assured and strongly characterized as the formidable group of Wolf songs. Rolf Gothoni's sparkling and pointed playing makes this a genuinely imaginative partnership, bringing out the gravity as well as the humour of the writing. Excellent, well-balanced recording.

Lieder eines fahrenden Gesellen.

*** Ph. (IMS) 426 257-2. Norman, BPO, Haitink – *Symphony No. 6.* ***

(M) *** Orfeo C 522 991 B. Ludwig, VPO, Boehm – BEETHOVEN: *Symphony No. 4;* SCHUMANN: *Symphony No. 4.* ***

Jessye Norman is a joy to the ear, with Haitink, in his accompaniment for the jaunty second song, providing the necessary lightness. The stormy darkness of the third song fits the soloist more naturally, always a magnetic singer. It makes a valuable extra for Haitink's deeply satisfying version of the *Sixth Symphony*.

As the chosen soloist in an electrifying concert conducted by Karl Boehm in August 1969, Christa Ludwig excels herself in a deeply moving, strongly characterized reading of the

'Wayfaring Lad' songs. The spontaneity of the performance makes up for any incidental flaws of the moment, with the voice gloriously firm and rich. No texts or translations are given of the songs, but every word is clear in this helpfully balanced radio recording.

Lieder eines fahrenden Gesellen; Lieder und Gesänge (aus der Jugendzeit); Im Lenz; Winterlied.

⬤ *** Hyp. CDA 66100. Baker, Parsons.

Janet Baker presents a superb collection of Mahler's early songs with piano, including two written in 1880 and never recorded before, *Im Lenz* and *Winterlied*; also the piano version of the *Wayfaring Lad* songs in a text prepared by Colin Matthews from Mahler's final thoughts, as contained in the orchestral version. The performances are radiant and deeply understanding from both singer and pianist, well caught in atmospheric recording. A heart-warming record.

Lieder und Gesänge.

*** Sony SK 68344. Kirchschlager, Deutsch (with Alma
  MAHLER: *5 Lieder*) – KORNGOLD: *5 Lieder, Op. 38; Songs of the Clown.* ***

In Mahler's youth songs Angelika Kirchschlager may not have the subtlety of Janet Baker in the same repertory, with tonal contrasts far more limited, but the girlishness and direct approach are arguably more apt for these early songs with their folk flavours, often settings of *Des Knaben Wunderhorn*. The five additional songs by Alma Mahler were written in the early years of her marriage to Gustav: charming inspirations, tuneful and direct but full of subtle modulations, and quite unlike her husband's work. They make an attractive extra item in this impressive début recording.

Das Lied von der Erde.

(M) *** Ph. (ADD) 432 279-2. Baker, King, Concg. O, Haitink.
(M) *** DG (ADD) 419 058-2. Ludwig, Kollo, BPO, Karajan.
(M) *** BBC (ADD) BBCM 5012-2. Baker, Mitchinson, BBC N. SO, Leppard.
*** EMI CDC5 56200-2. Seiffert, Hampson, CBSO, Rattle.
*** DG (IMS) 413 459-2. Fassbaender, Araiza, BPO, Giulini.
(M) *** EMI (ADD) CDM5 66892-2 [566944]. Ludwig, Wunderlich, Philh. & New Philh. O, Klemperer.
(N) **(*) RCA 09026 67957-2. Meier, Heppner, Bavarian RSO, Maazel.
(M) **(*) Sony (ADD) SMK 64455. Miller, Haefliger, NYPO, Walter.
**(*) BBC (ADD) BBCL 4042-2. Hodgson, Mitchinson, BBC N. SO, Horenstein.
(M) **(*) DG (ADD) 463 682-2. Merriman, Haefliger, Concg. O, Jochum.
(N) (M) ** Orfeo C 494 001B. Jänicke, Elsner, Stuttgart Radio SO, Fischer-Dieskau.
(B) (*(**)) Naxos mono 8.110029. Ferrier, Svanholm, NYPO, Walter.
** Sony SK 60646. Domingo, Skovhus, LAPO, Salonen.

(i) *Das Lied von der Erde;* (ii) *Des Knaben Wunderhorn;* (iii) *Kindertotenlieder; Lieder eines fahrenden Gesellen.*

(B) *** Ph. Duo (ADD) 454 014-2 (2). (i) Baker, King; (ii) Norman, Shirley-Quirk; (iii) Prey; Concg. O, Haitink.

(i) *Das Lied von der Erde;* (ii) *5 Rückert Lieder.*

(B) **(*) Sony (ADD) SBK 53518. (i) Chookasian, Lewis, Phd. O, Ormandy; (ii) Von Stade, LPO, A. Davis.

Das Lied von der Erde; 3 Rückert Lieder.

(N) (M) (***) Decca mono 466 576-2. Ferrier, Patzak, VPO, Walter.

(i) *Das Lied von der Erde. 2 Rückert Lieder:* (ii) *Ich atmet' einen linden Duft;* (iii) *Ich bin der Welt abhanden gekommen.* (iv) *Symphony No. 5: Adagietto.*

(B) (***) Dutton Lab. mono CDEA 5014. (i; iii) Thorborg; (i–ii) Kullman; (i; iii–iv) VPO, Walter; (ii) O, Sargent.

The combination of Janet Baker, most deeply committed of Mahler singers, with Haitink, the most thoughtfully dedicated of Mahler conductors, produces radiantly beautiful and moving results, helped by refined and atmospheric recording. James King cannot match his solo partner, but his singing is intelligent and sympathetic. However, this version – vividly re-transferred – is now additionally offered on a Philips Duo set, coupled with Mahler's three other key song-cycles, and as such is very tempting. In *Des Knaben Wunderhorn* the singing of both Jessye Norman and John Shirley-Quirk brings out the purely musical imagination of Mahler at his finest, while Haitink's accompaniments are refined and satisfying, especially when the 1976 analogue sound is vividly atmospheric. Hermann Prey's performances of *Kindertotenlieder* and the *Lieder eines fahrenden Gesellen* are fresh and intelligent, and the colour of the baritone voice brings a darkness of timbre which is especially poignant, as in the third song of the *Wayfaring Lad* cycle.The Philips recording (from 1970) is of very high quality – the effect is most beautiful.

Taken from a performance for radio in the Free Trade Hall, Manchester, the Leppard version offers Baker at her very peak in 1977, giving one of the most moving and richly varied readings of the contralto songs ever. The final *Abschied* has a depth and intensity, a poignancy that set it alongside Dame Janet's earlier recording with Haitink. John Mitchinson may not have the most beautiful tenor, but his voice focuses ever more securely through the work, with many cleanly ringing top notes. Raymond Leppard draws fine playing from the orchestra, now renamed the BBC Philharmonic, though the body of strings is thin for Mahler. Acceptable BBC sound, with the voices naturally placed, not spotlit.

The latest remastering of the famous 1952 Ferrier/Patzak version of *Das Lied* is a revelation. At the very opening the orchestral strings are not ideally focused, but the edginess has been smoothed, and one is now made conscious of the ambience of the Grosser Saal of the Musikverein. Ferrier's voice is warmly and vividly caught as is the characterful Patzak. At last Walter's classic recording comes into its own. Even more remarkable is the transfer of the three Rückert songs recorded at the same time (*Ich bin der Welt abhanden gekommen, Ich armet' einen linden Duft* and *Um Mitternacht*). Here the recording is even more warm and atmospheric, and the richness of Ferrier's voice and the simplicity of her approach make for glorious listening. The brass at the close of *Um Mitternacht* is rather forward, but full-bodied. Full translations are provided.

Karajan presents *Das Lied* as the most seductive sequence of atmospheric songs, combining characteristic refinement and polish with a deep sense of melancholy. He is helped enormously by the soloists, both of whom have recorded this work several times, but never more richly than here. The sound on CD is admirably vivid and does not lack a basic warmth.

Rattle in a thoughtful, refined reading brings out the poetry of *Das Lied von der Erde*. Peter Seiffert makes an outstanding choice of tenor soloist, bringing together lyric and heroic qualities, singing with purity and refinement, with fine feeling for word meaning. What will decide choice more than anything is Rattle's preference for a baritone soloist instead of a mezzo. Thomas Hampson sings with both weight and refinement, using a wider dynamic range than most mezzos, not least in the final *Abschied*, where Rattle's concentration and depth of expression is matched by Hampson's singing.

Giulini conducts a characteristically restrained reading. With Araiza a heady-toned tenor rather than a powerful one, the line *Dunkel ist das Leben* in the first song becomes unusually tender and gentle, with rapture and wistfulness keynote emotions. In the second song, Fassbaender gives lightness and poignancy rather than dark tragedy to the line *Mein Herz ist müde*; and even the final *Abschied* is rapt rather than tragic, following the text of the poem; and the playing of the Berlin Philharmonic could hardly be more beautiful.

Klemperer's way with Mahler is at its most individual in *Das Lied von der Erde* – and that will enthral some, as it must infuriate others. With slower speeds, the three tenor songs seem initially to lose some of their sparkle and humour; however, thanks to superb expressive singing by the late Fritz Wunderlich – one of the most memorable examples of his artistry on record – and thanks also to pointing of rhythm by Klemperer himself, subtle but always clear, the comparative slowness will hardly worry anyone intent on hearing the music afresh, as Klemperer intends. As for the mezzo songs, Christa Ludwig sings them with a remarkable depth of expressiveness; in particular, the final *Abschied* has the intensity of a great occasion. Excellent digitally remastered recording.

Lorin Maazel and the Bavarian Radio Orchestra have the fine Waltraud Meier and Ben Heppner as their soloists. Indeed Heppner is magnificent and Meier sings eloquently, even if she is less penetrating in the *Abschied* than some rivals. The RCA sound is well detailed and refined and the orchestral playing is sumptuous, although Maazel sounds a little detached, even cool.

Though Bruno Walter's 1960 New York version does not have the tear-laden quality in the final *Abschied* that made his earlier Vienna account (in mono) with Kathleen Ferrier unique, that is the only serious shortcoming. Haefliger sparkles with imagination and Miller is a warm and appealing mezzo soloist, lacking only the last depth of feeling you find in a Ferrier or Janet Baker; and the maestro himself has rarely sounded so happy on record, even in Mahler. The

remastered recording has been freshly remastered for the Bruno Walter Edition and now has even more vivid detail.

As ever, Horenstein favours spacious speeds, sustaining them magnetically, not just over the meditative songs of the alto – with Alfreda Hodgson bringing echoes of Kathleen Ferrier, subtle and moving in her tonal shading – but in the tenor's lighter songs, at once relaxed and crisply pointed. John Mitchinson is here at his finest, contrasting his firm heroic tone in the first song against delicate half-tones, using his head-voice. Though the strings could be fuller and sweeter, the BBC Manchester recording is well balanced even if it now sounds rather opaque. In a brief interview Horenstein talks of his experience of the work.

Generally, Jochum avoided conducting Mahler – as a Brucknerian, underlining the point that these massive masters of symphony are totally contrasted. His reading of *Das Lied*, beautiful and compelling as it is, helps to explain why, for it speaks of the radiant calm of the Bruckner temperament rather than of Mahlerian tensions. Excellent solo singing and fine, clean recording, vivid and kind to the voices.

The Dutton Lab. CD offers the pioneering live recordings made in the mid-1930s by Bruno Walter with the Vienna Philharmonic. The soloists here are excellent, both with clear, firm voices that convey full expressiveness without strain. The recording is dry but voices are very well caught, and the Dutton transfer does wonders in improving the orchestral sound. The generous fill-ups are also welcome. *Ich bin der Welt abhanden gekommen* with Thorborg was recorded from the same concert as the main work, while the other Rückert setting – using an English translation – was recorded by Kullmann in 1938 with Sargent conducting. Walter's 1938 studio recording of the *Adagietto* from the *Fifth Symphony* is fascinating for being so much faster than latter-day readings, while still conveying total repose.

The account on Orfeo is of special interest in that Dietrich Fischer-Dieskau conducts rather than sings. The soloists are two German singers of the younger generation – Yvi Jänicke and one of Fischer-Dieskau's pupils, Christian Elsner – who are accompanied by the Stuttgart Radio Orchestra. It goes without saying that Fischer-Dieskau knows what this music is all about, but he is a little sluggish in *Der Einsame im Herbst*, though not as slow as the classic Bernstein version in which he sang. A good performance but not the outstanding experience one might have expected. Decent sound.

The historic recording from Naxos, taken from an NBC broadcast in January 1948, gives a valuable slant on Kathleen Ferrier's unique interpretation. She is even more deeply expressive than in her Decca studio recording of four years later, also with Walter conducting. Svanholm gives a powerful yet finely detailed reading of the tenor songs, yet many will find the scrubby orchestral sound a serious stumbling block to enjoyment, when the surface noise is often very intrusive. Even so, few will fail to note the desolation and poignancy of Ferrier in the final *Abschied*. An important historical document.

Ormandy conducts a purposeful, superbly played reading, dating from 1966, that may lack something in Mahlerian magic but which, with fine solo singing, carries you magnetically through to the final climax. Richard Lewis is by his standards sometimes a little rough in tone, but his perception is unfailing, and Lilli Chookasian's warm, weighty mezzo, with vibrato well controlled, brings poise and gravity to her songs, not least the final *Abschied*. Frederika von Stade makes a characterful soloist in the *Rückert Lieder*, sometimes colouring the voice too heavily; but, with fine bloom on the 1976 sound, she brings out ravishing tonal contrasts, helped by Andrew Davis's sympathetic accompaniment.

Salonen chooses speeds faster than usual, but gives a warmly sympathetic and sensitive reading which brings out the full emotion of the writing. There are good precedents on record for an all-male *Das Lied*. Plácido Domingo in Heldentenor mode produces a gloriously firm and full tone, but the subtler shadings required in Lieder-singing, even with orchestra, rather elude him. Bo Skovhus, following Mahler's option of using a baritone in place of the mezzo, has rarely sounded so clear and true on disc, subtly shading his tone, singing with perfect diction. The recording places the soloists well forward, with the orchestra in soft focus behind so that the violins, though refined, lack body.

Levine in what is claimed as a live recording conducts a heavyhanded account of *Das Lied*, weighty and often contrived, lacking flow. Neither soloist is helped by the very close balance. Jessye Norman sounds self-conscious in her detailing, missing the mystery of the final song, and Siegfried Jerusalem is less subtle than he can be (DG 439 948-2).

MALIPIERO, Gianfrancesco
(1882–1973)

La cimarosiana; Gabrieliana; Stradivario; Symphonic Fragments from 3 Goldoni Comedies.

(N)) **(*) Marco 8.225118. Swiss Italian O, Christian Benda.

Malipiero was an enormously prolific composer as well as a tireless scholar whose editions of Monteverdi served to re-awaken interest in that master. The present issue includes two pastiche suites, *La cimarosiana* made in 1921 and *Gabrieliana* written half-a-century later, both of which are well fashioned if inconsequential. The *Tre commedie goldoniane* (1925) have been described by John G. Waterhouse in his book on the composer as 'perhaps the richest expression of the comic side of his genius'. The ideas are drawn from episodes from the operas and are full of life and character.

The ballet *Stradivario* comes from 1947–8, when Malipiero was director of the Venice conservatory. It tells how in the silence of the night all the instruments from the collection come alive and dance. It is all pleasing and inventive, more than adequately played by the Orchestre della Svizzera Italiana under Christian Benda and decently recorded. None of this music sets the pulse racing but at the same time it is far from negligible. Not for nothing did Malipiero command respect both in the Italian musical world and internationally during his lifetime.

String Quartets Nos. 1–8.

*** ASV CDDCD 457 (2). Orpheus Qt.

Malipiero's eight *String Quartets* are all modest in length: the longest being the *First* (*Rispetti e strambotti*) (1920),

which runs to twenty minutes, while the *Eighth* (1963–4), written when the composer was in his early eighties, takes only twelve. None falls below a certain level of distinction, all are beautifully crafted and there is much freshness and fertility of invention. They are all played with expertise and conviction by the Orpheus Quartet, and very well recorded indeed.

MANFREDINI, Francesco
(1684–1762)

Concerti grossi, Op. 3/1–12.

⚙ (BB) *** Naxos 8.553891. Capella Istropolitana, Krček.

This splendid set of twelve concertos, published in Bologna in 1718, was dedicated to Prince Antoine I of Monaco, with whose court orchestra Manfredini was associated. The most famous of them is No. 12, a *Christmas Concerto* in the style of Torelli and Corelli, opening with a delightful *Pastorale* in siciliano rhythm. And if there are other influences here too, of Vivaldi in particular, and even anticipations of Handel, the music has its own individuality and is endlessly inventive. Allegros are vital and buoyant, slow movements tenderly touching, often featuring one or two solo violins. The performances here are both fresh and penetrating, with bouncing outer movements and expressive *Adagios*. Moreover the playing is perfectly in style, demonstrating how using modern instruments can be just as authentic as period manners in baroque music. The recording is absolutely natural, very much in the demonstration bracket.

MARAIS, Marin (1656–1728)

Pièces à violes: Suites for Viola da Gamba & Continuo: Book I: Tombeau de M. Meliton for 2 Viols; Book IV: Suite for 3 Viols in D.

*** Virgin VC5 45358-2. Hantaï, Uemura, Verzier, Hantaï –
    FORQUERAY: *Pièces for 3 Viols; Suite.* ***

These works were both part of a larger collection of solo viol pieces which Marais published in 1686. Their ethos is comparatively austere, yet the nine-movement *Suite* of dances has plenty of variety: the central *Sarabande* has a noble dignity followed by a lighter *Gigue* and an engaging *Petite paysanne*. The *Tombeau* for two bass viols – the composer's longest work in this form – sustains a mood of dark, profound melancholy and this fine performance holds the listener firmly in its spell. The recording is vividly real.

Pièces à violes: Suites for Viola da Gamba & Continuo: Book II: in E min.; Book III: in D; Book IV: Suite d'un goût étranger: Le Labyrinthe; Book V: in A min.

*** HM HMC 905248. Quintana, Costoyas, Cremonesi.

Juan Manuel Quintana plays the viola da gamba with superb assurance and virtuosity in these suites of dance movements, but when he comes to the deeply expressive *Plainte*, the penultimate movement, a degree more of expressive freedom would have been welcome. Even so it remains very affecting. He is heard at his finest in *Le Labyrinthe*, a continuing kaleidoscope of changing tempi describing the uncertainty of a man lost in a maze, but who eventually finds his way out, to the strains of a culminating chaconne. The final movement of the *E minor Suite* is a *Tombeau pour Monsieur de Sainte-Colombe* (Marais's revered teacher), eloquently and characterfully played, and this remains a highly recommendable collection.

Pièces à violes: Book 4 (1717): Suite d'un goût étranger (excerpts).

(N) (M) *** Astrée (ADD) ES 9932. Savall, Koopman, Smith.

Savall's selection of eleven items from Part II of the Marais Book 4 could not be more attractively chosen. The opening *Marche Tartare* is as bold as you could wish, contrasted with the charming *La Tartarine*. The swirling portrait of *Le Tourbillon* is matched by a lively Gigue and a fine Allemande – *La Superbe. La Rêveuse* is touchingly sombre. Most memorable of all is the superb account of the celebrated six-section fantasy *Le Labyrinthe*, played with spontaneous bravura, yet convincingly structured. Ton Koopman (harpsichord) and Hopkinson Smith (guitar) provide a discreet continuo.

La Gamme en forme de petit opéra; Sonata à la marésienne.

(B) *** HM (ADD) HMA 1901105. L. Baroque.

La Gamme is a string of short character-pieces for violin, viola de gamba and harpsichord that takes its inspiration from the ascending and descending figures of the scale. Although it is *en forme de petit opéra*, its layout is totally instrumental and the varied pieces and dramatic shifts of character doubtless inspire the title. The *Sonata à la marésienne* also has variety and character. The London Baroque is an excellent group, and they are well recorded too.

Collections

Pièces à violes: L'Arabesque; Le Badinage; Le Labyrinthe; Prélude in G; La Rêveuse; Sonnerie de Sainte-Geneviève du Mont de Paris; Suite in G; Tombeau pour Monsieur de Sainte-Colombe.

(BB) *** Naxos 8.550750. Spectre de la Rose – SAINTE-COLOMBE: *Le Retour* etc. ***

Naxos have stepped in enterprisingly and chosen a programme that is not only most attractive in its own right, but which also includes the key items used in the fascinating conjectural film about the relationship between Marin Marais and his reclusive mentor, Sainte-Colombe (*Tous les matins du monde*). Spectre de la Rose consists of a first-rate group of young players, led by Alison Crum, who plays in a dignified but austere style which at first seems cool but which is very effective in this repertoire. *Le Badinage* is perhaps a little stiff and unsmiling, but the key item, Marais' eloquent lament for his teacher, *Tombeau pour Monsieur de Sainte-Colombe*, is restrained and touching. Good, bright, forward recording, vividly declaiming the plangent viola da gamba timbre. But be careful not to play this record at too high a volume setting.

OPERA

Alcione: Suite des airs à joüer (1706).

(N) (M) *** Astrée ES 9945. Le Concert des Nations, Savall.

Marais is almost solely known as a performer/composer of viol music, and this collection of airs and dances from his opera *Alcione* is a revelation. The work was a great success in its day (1706). Its outrageous mythological plot has the gods intervening to rescue the pair of mortal lovers from the various disasters that continually befall them. Finally, Neptune rises out of the sea to provide a happy ending by bringing back to life the apparently drowned hero and his beloved (who has stabbed herself). He changes them into seabirds, commanding them to remain ever faithful in their love and calm the waves by charming the winds.

There is plenty of opportunity for divertissements, with dance music in the tradition of Lully, and Marais's delightfully elegant invention seems inexhaustible. There are dances for shepherds and shepherdesses, a Symphony of *Sleep*, a famous *Sailors' March* and a highly spectacular *Tempête*, in which a double bass was added to the score of a French opera for the first time. There is also a particularly fine closing *Chaconne for the Tritons*. Savall is here at his finest, directing the proceedings with great vitality, clearly relishing music's grace and colour, and the playing has an endearing vivacity and elegance. Excellent recording too.

MARCELLO, Alessandro (1669–1747)

6 Oboe Concertos (La cetra).

(M) *** DG (ADD) (IMS) 427 137-2. Holliger, Pellerin, Camerata Bern, Füri.

The six concertos of *La cetra* reveal a pleasing mixture of originality and convention; often one is surprised by a genuinely alive and refreshing individuality. These performances are vital and keen, full of style and character, and the recording is faithful and well projected.

Oboe Concerto in C min. (arr. Rothwell).

*** Dutton Lab./Barbirolli Soc. CDSJB 1016. Rothwell, Hallé O, Barbirolli – CORELLI; HAYDN: *Oboe Concertos* *** (with Recital: C. P. E. BACH; LOEILLET; TELEMANN: *Sonatas*, etc. ** – see Instrumental Recitals below).

Sir John's subtlety in matters of light and shade within an orchestral phrase brings this music immediately alive, and at the same time prevents the rather jolly opening tune from sounding square. The exquisitely beautiful *Adagio* is followed by a gay finale, both showing the soloist at her finest, and the well-balanced 1969 recording and excellent transfer add to one's pleasure.

Oboe Concerto in D min.

(BB) **(*) Naxos 8.550556. Kiss, Erkel CO – C. P. E. BACH: *Concertos.* **(*)

This enjoyable concerto, once attributed (in a different key) to Benedetto Marcello, is given a good performance here by József Kiss and is very well recorded. One might have preferred more dynamic contrast from the soloist, but his timbre is right for baroque music and he plays with plenty of spirit. This disc is well worth its modest cost for the C. P. E. Bach couplings.

10 Keyboard Sonatas, Op. 3; Laberinta sopra il clavicembalo; La stravaganza in C (ciaccona con variazione).

(N) *** Chan. 0671 (2). Loreggian (harpsichord).

Marcello's ten harpsichord sonatas, Op. 3, appear to date from between 1712 and 1717. As no complete set exists in print, Alessandro Boris, the editor of the edition recorded here, has drawn on five manuscripts held in the libraries of various European cities, centering on a Venetian source which appears to be the most reliable. He has chosen to group the movements of each sonata (using all five manuscripts) and the result is inevitably conjectural, yet always convincing.

Marcello's invention is usually common to all the movements of each sonata, and though infinitely varied in treatment the basic ideas remain intact and attractively recognizable throughout. They are nearly all four-movement works in sonata da camera layout (i.e. a slow introduction, followed by three faster sections). Two are condensed into three movements, while one of the finest of the series, No. 7 in C minor, has five. (Loreggian makes the point by playing its closing minuet using his lute stop.)

Clearly Marcello thought the harpsichord more suited to spirited than lyrical writing; even so the opening slow movements often have a thoughtful improvisatory feel, which Roberto Loreggian captures admirably. The *Labarinto* (in two sections) is a freer, fantasy-like piece, with the bold rhythms and repeated notes of the closing section catchily bizarre.

The C major ciaccona, *La stravaganza* was Marcellos's most famous harpsichord piece, and its thirty-eight variations produce an expansive fifteen-minute work which rather outstays its welcome. Not the fault of the performance, one hastens to say, for the playing here is full of life and sparkle. The instrument itself is a reconstruction of a late-seventeenth-century Italian harpsichord and it is vividly recorded.

Arianna (complete).

(N) **(*) Chan. 0656 (3). Chierichetti, Banditelli, Guadagnini, Foresti, Abete, Athesis Ch., Academia de li Musici, Bressan.

Benedetto Marcello, as a rich, dilettante composer, may treat the legend of Ariadne, Theseus and Bacchus rather casually, with little or no attempt to plumb the heroine's depths of feeling, but this 'Play in music for five voices' brings a sequence of fresh and lively numbers, predominantly brisk, starting with a vigorous overture. Though the strings of the Academia de li Musici are more abrasive than we now expect of period instruments, that is only obtrusive in slow music, and the conductor, Filippo Maria Bressan, inspires a well-sprung performance, with the singers sympathetically supported. The recording brings out some unevenness in the voices of both Anna Chierichetti as Ariadne (Arianna) and Mirko Guadagnini as Theseus (Teseo), but they are aptly fresh and youthful, and the mezzo Gloria Banditelli is outstanding as Phaedra (Fedra), with a resonant chest-voice, and Sergio Foresti as Bacchuas (Bacco) and Antonio Abete as Silenus are well-focused too. Clear, well-balanced sound.

MARCHAND, Louis (1669–1732)

Te Deum.

(BB) *** Arte Nova 74321 65413-2. Ens. Canticum, Erkens; Deutsch (Koenig organ, St Avold, France) – François COUPERIN: *Messe pour les couvents.* ***

Louis Marchand was a year younger than Couperin-le-grand and was among the most brilliant improvisers and virtuosi of the day. Like the Couperin organ masses, his *Te Deum* is interspersed with chant. A fine piece, it ends with a particularly magnificent *Grand jeu*. Helmut Deutsch plays with magisterial authority on the Koenig organ at the former St Nabor Abbey in St Avold, France. Very good and lifelike recordings and impressive playing. A most worthwhile issue.

MAREK, Czeslaw (1891–1985)

Meditations, Op. 14; Sinfonia, Op. 28; Suite for Orchestra, Op. 25.

*** Koch 36429-2. Philh. O, Brain.

Czeslaw Marek was a Polish-born Swiss composer who left a handful of finely crafted, warmly post-Romantic works which virtually no one had heard. This disc offers ripely convincing performances in spectacular sound of three richly orchestrated works. The *Suite*, Op. 25, consists of five colourful and atmospheric movements, with a hint of neo-classicism in the romantic mixture. Most rewarding of all is the inspired one-movement *Sinfonia* of 1929, over half an hour long, echoing Sibelius's *Seventh* in its formal control and concentration.

MARENZIO, Luca (1553–99)

Madrigals: Book VI: *Se quel dolor* (madrigal-cycle in 6 voices); Book VII: *Care mie selve; Cruda Amarilli; Questa vaghi concenti.*

(B) **(*) HM HMC 90856.58. Ens. Clément Jannequin, Visse – BANCHIERI: *Barca di Venetia per Padova;* LASSUS; VECCHI: *Madrigal Comedies.* ***

Marenzio's *Cruda Amarilli* is justly celebrated, but the other settings here also carry the aristocratic lines and eloquent pathos which are the hallmark of Marenzio's writing. The singing here is given added colour and warmth by a judicious instrumental accompaniment, but more subtlety in the matter of light and shade within the continually flowing lines would have been welcome. Good documentation with full translations.

Madrigals: *Come inanti de l'alba; Crudele acerba; Del cibo onde il signor; Giunto a la tomba; Rimanti inpace; Sola angioletta* (sestina); *Strider faceva; Tirsi morir volea; Venuta era; Vezzosi augelli.*

(B) *** HM (ADD) HMA 1901065. Concerto Vocale, Jacobs.

This record gives an altogether admirable picture of Marenzio's breadth and range. There are poignant and expressive pieces such as *Crudele, acerba*, which is harmonically daring, and lighter pastoral madrigals such as *Strider faceva* and the more ambitious sestina, *Sola angioletta*, which this excellent group of singers, occasionally supported by theorbo and lute, project to striking effect. Fine singing and recording and a modest price serve to make this a most desirable issue.

MARKEVITCH, Igor (1912–83)

Rébus; Hymnes.

*** Marco 8.223724. Arnhem PO, Lyndon-Gee.

Rébus was written in 1931 for Massine, though he never mounted or danced it. No less an authority than Henri Prunières hailed it as a work of genius: it is certainly an interesting piece of immense talent. *Hymnes* was completed in 1933, though the final section, *Hymne à la Mort*, was not added until 1936. There is much Stravinsky in the very imaginative *Prélude* and *Pas d'acier* in the first section, *Hymne au Travail*, and a strong sense of atmosphere in *Hymne au printemps*. This CD gave us much pleasure and is well worth investigating and good recorded sound too.

(i) *The Flight of Icarus;* (ii) *Galop;* (iii) *Noces;* (iv) *Serenade.*

*** Largo 5127. (i) Lyndon-Gee, Lang, Gagelmann, Haeger; (ii) Markevitch Ens., Köln; (i; iii; iv) Lessing; (iv) Meyer, Jensen.

Noces, for piano, was composed in 1925 when Markevitch was only thirteen, and it was on the strength of this and a *Sinfonietta* that Diaghilev was prompted to take him up. The young composer-conductor was only twenty when he composed *L'Envol d'Icare* which Lifar commissioned but subsequently never produced. It is heard here not in its orchestral form but in the transcription for two pianos and percussion. *Noces*, neatly played by Kolja Lessing, is close to the world of Poulenc and Satie, and it is obvious that Markevitch knew his Ravel. The *Serenade* is akin to the Milhaud of the *Petites symphonies*, and there is tremendous energy and a lot of Stravinsky in *L'Envol d'Icare*. This disc gives an insight into his talent and musicianship which will be of interest to all those who care about the Diaghilev years and Paris between the wars.

Vuca Lorenzo il Magnifico; Psaumes.

*** Marco 8.223882. Shelton, Arnhem PO, Lyndon-Gee.

Markevitch's vocal symphony *Lorenzo il Magnifico* sets poems by Lorenzo de' Medici. It is said to be his masterpiece, and it is not only highly imaginative but quite masterly in its variety of pace and feeling of growth. *Psaumes* comes from 1933 when Markevitch was twenty-one and enjoyed a *succès de scandale* at the time. It is powerful stuff, rather Milhaudesque at times, but at the same time evident of a distinctive and original mind. Lucy Shelton sings the demanding solo-part well in both scores and the playing and recording are eminently serviceable. Markevitch is a composer of substance and some distinction.

MARSH, John (1752–1828)

Symphonies Nos. 1 in B flat (ed. Robins); 3 in D; 4 in F; 6 in D; A Conversation Symphony for 2 Orchestras (all ed. Graham-Jones).

** Olympia OCD 400. Chichester Concert, Graham-Jones.

John Marsh was innovative: because of the continuing influence of Handel the symphony format was not fashionable in England at that time. For the most part they each consist of three short movements and, while the tunes sometimes have a whiff of Handel, there is a strong element of the English village green. The *Conversation Symphony* does not divide into two separate ensembles but makes contrasts between higher and lower instrumental groupings. Five of his works are presented here with enthusiasm by an aptly sized authentic Baroque group; they play well and are quite effectively recorded.

MARSHALL-HALL, G. W. L. (1862–1915)

Symphony in E flat; Symphony in C: Adagio.

(N) **(*) Move MD 3081. Queensland Theatre O, Bebbington.

Born in London, Marshall-Hall studied under Parry and Stanford and his first song cycle received an enthusiastic review from George Bernard Shaw. In 1892 he settled in Australia, where he became the first Professor of Music at Melbourne University. His *E flat Symphony* was premiered by Sir Henry Wood in London and Nikisch in Berlin, before lapsing into obscurity.

While highly eclectic, and often Brahmsian, it still remains very much his own, and has plenty of attractively flowing ideas. The first movement surges along, the central *Largamente* is appealingly lyrical and expertly scored and the rondo finale ends confidently. The *Adagio sostenuto* from the earlier *C minor Symphony* is gently elegiac, again attractively orchestrated. Both works are well played and quite persuasively directed by Warren Bebbington, although one feels at times that they need a stronger forward pulse. But this well-recorded CD is still enjoyable and appears on a bargain label in Australia. (Its publisher can be reached on www.move.com.au.)

MARTIN, Frank (1890–1974)

Ballades for: (i) *Cello & Small Orchestra;* (ii) *Flute, Strings & Piano;* (iii) *Piano & Orchestra;* (iv) *Saxophone & Small Orchestra;* (v) *Viola, Wind, Harpsichord, Timpani & Percussion;* (vi) *Trombone & Piano.*

*** Chan. 9380. (i) Dixon; (ii) Chambers; (ii, iii, v, vi) Elms; (iv) Robertson; (v) Dukes, Masters; (vi) Bousfield; LPO, Bamert.

The *Ballades* are among Martin's most personal utterances. Only three are otherwise currently available, so the present issue is a most valuable addition to the Martin discography, particularly in view of the excellence and commitment of the performances. Subtle, state-of-the-art recording with no false 'hi-fi' brightness, but a natural and unobtrusive presence. An indispensable disc for admirers of this subtle and rewarding master.

(i) Ballade for Piano & Orchestra. Piano Concertos Nos. 1; (ii) 2; (i; ii) Danse de la peur for 2 Pianos & Small Orchestra.

(N) ⊕ * ASV CDDCA 1082. (i) Sebastian Benda, (ii) Badura-Skoda; O della Svizzera Italiana, Christian Benda.**

The *Ballade for Piano and Orchestra* is a poignant and affecting score. Originally intended as a violin concerto, it was written in the immediate wake of a bereavement and its depth of feeling and imagination is never in doubt. The *First Piano Concerto* of 1933–4 is not quite as moving but anticipates many of the characteristic fingerprints of the *Petite symphonie concertante* and the *Concerto for Seven Wind Instruments*. The pale, haunting instrumental colourings of the slow movement evoke Martin's own special world. The ASV CD brings the *Danse de la peur*, also from the 1930s, a highly imaginative, dramatic and above all atmospheric score which is new to the Martin discography. Good performances, decently balanced recordings which are recommended with the strongest enthusiasm.

(i) Ballade for Piano & Orchestra; (ii) Ballade for Trombone & Orchestra; (iii) Concerto for Harpsichord & Small Orchestra.

(*) Jecklin-Disco (ADD) JD 529-2. (i) Benda; (ii) Rosin; (iii) Jaccottet; Lausanne CO, composer.

The *Harpsichord Concerto* is a highly imaginative and inventive piece, arguably the most successful example of the genre since the Falla *Concerto*. The orchestral texture has a pale, transparent delicacy that is quite haunting, and the atmosphere is powerful – as, indeed, it is in the fine *Ballade*. Christiane Jaccottet is a committed advocate and her performance has the authority of the composer's direction.

(i) Piano Concerto No. 2; (ii) Violin Concerto.

**** Jecklin-Disco (ADD) JD 632-2. (i) Badura-Skoda; (ii) Schneiderhan; Luxembourg RSO, composer.**

The *Violin Concerto* is a score of great subtlety and beauty. Don't be put off by the less than lustrous sound, for this is a masterpiece and has the benefit of having Martin himself at the helm. The *Second Piano Concerto* is not as lyrical as the *Violin Concerto* but is still worth investigation for its thoughtful slow movement.

Concerto for 7 Wind Instruments, Percussion & Strings; (i) Erasmi monumentum (for organ and orchestra); Etudes for Strings.

* Chan. 9283. (i) Pearson; LPO, Bamert.**

Erasmi monumentum is a substantial piece of some 25 minutes. The first movement, *Homo pro se* ('The Independent Man'), alludes to the name given to Erasmus by his contemporaries; the second is *Stulticiae Laus* ('In Praise of Folly'), and the third is *Querela Pacis* ('A Plea for Peace'). The outer movements are pensive and atmospheric; the

middle movement is less convincing. Matthias Bamert's account of the *Concerto for Seven Wind Instruments* is very assured, relaxed and animated; although thoroughly persuasive, he makes rather heavy weather of the *Etudes*.

3 Dances for Oboe, Harp, String Quintet & String Orchestra.

* Koch Campanella C 130045. Süss, Schellenberger, Franz Liszt CO, Budapest, Peskó – IBERT: *Sinfonia concertante*; LUTOSLAWSKI: *Double Concerto for Oboe & Harp*. ***

Like the other two concertante pieces on this enterprising Campanella CD, the *Trois danses* were commissioned by Paul Sacher. In Martin's triptych, a work with strong flamenco influences, the solo strings are not used concerto grosso style, but to provide haunting added textural colour against which the solo oboe, with his harpist partner, can weave his spell. The finale features a rumba rhythm, but the sound and rhythmic patterns soon become kaleidoscopic. It is a masterly piece, full of aural imagination, and it is superbly played, with equal virtuosity from soloists and orchestra. The vivid recording is admirably balanced.

The Four Elements; (i) In terra Pax.

* Chan. 9465. (i) Howarth, Jones, Hill, Williams, Roberts, Brighton Festival Ch.; LPO, Bamert.**

Les Quatre Eléments, written for Ansermet's eightieth birthday in 1967, is a highly imaginative work which exhibits to striking effect Martin's feeling for the orchestra and his subtle mastery of texture. *In terra Pax* is a noble work, and this makes a distinguished addition to the growing Martin discography. The singers are not perhaps quite as impressive as in the (deleted) Ansermet set, but in every other respect the new recording is superior.

Symphonie concertante (arr. of Petite symphonie concertante for full orchestra); Symphony; Passacaglia.

⊕ * Chan. 9312. LPO, Bamert.**

The *Symphony* is a haunting and at times quite magical piece. It has all the subtlety of colouring of the mature Martin and is a piece of great imaginative resource. The slow movement in particular has an other-worldly quality, suggesting some verdant, moonlit landscape. The two pianos are effectively used and although, as in the *Petite symphonie concertante*, lip service is paid to the twelve-note system, the overall effect is far from serial. Its main companion here is the transcription Martin made for full orchestra of the *Petite symphonie concertante* the year after its first performance. Harp and piano are used for colouristic effects but completely relinquish any hint of soloist ambitions. The *Passacaglia* is Martin's 1962 transcription for full orchestra of his organ piece. Sensitive playing from the LPO under Matthias Bamert and exemplary Chandos recording.

CHAMBER MUSIC

(i) Ballade for Cello & Piano; (ii) Ballade for Flute & Piano; Piano Quintet; (iii) Violin Sonata; (iv) 4 Sonnets à Cassandre.

*** ASV CDDCA 1010. Burnside, Pears–Britten Ens.;
(i) Watkins; (i–iv) Burnside; (ii) K. Jones; (iii) Jackson;
(iv) Rearick.

This rewarding issue brings us the rarely heard *Piano Quintet*, in which Martin's debts to Ravel and Fauré are clearly evident. The *Violin Sonata* is a three-movement piece, much indebted to the Debussy *G minor Sonata*. All these pieces, save for the *Ballades* for flute and cello, pre-date the period in which Martin found his true idiom – in such works as *Le Vin herbé* and *Der Cornet*. The performances are as alert and sensitive as one could wish, and the recordings are very good too.

Piano Quintet; String Quintet (Pavane couleur de temps); String Trio; Trio sur des mélodies populaires irlandaises.

*** Jecklin-Disco (ADD) JD 646-2. Zurich Ch. Ens.

The *Piano Quintet* has an eloquence and an elegiac dignity that are impressive; the short string quintet, subtitled *Pavane couleur de temps* (the title is taken from a fairy story in which a young girl wishes for 'a dress the colour of time'), is a beautiful piece. The *Piano Trio on Irish Popular Themes* is full of imagination and rhythmic life. The *String Trio* is a tougher nut to crack; its harmonies are more astringent and its form more concentrated. To summarize: altogether a most satisfying disc, offering very good performances and recordings.

Piano Trio on Irish Folktunes.

*** Simax PSC 1147. Grieg Trio – BLOCH: *3 Nocturnes*; SHOSTAKOVICH: *Piano Trios*. ***

The *Piano Trio* is expertly played here and the interest of the couplings further enhances the value of this issue, arguably the best the Grieg Trio has given us. The Simax recording is first rate.

VOCAL MUSIC

Der Cornet.

*** Orfeo S 164881A. Lipvšek, Austrian RSO, Zagrosek.

Der Cornet or, to give it its full title, *Die Weise von Liebe und Tod des Cornets Christoph Rilke* ('The Lay Song of the Love and Death of Cornet Christoph Rilke'), is one of Martin's most profound and searching works. It sets all but four of the 27 stanzas of Rainer Maria Rilke's poem, which tells of a youthful ensign who dies in 1660 'under the sabres of the Turks into an ocean of flowers'. Rilke's poem became a bestseller once the 1914–18 war broke out. Martin's setting for contralto and small chamber orchestra was written at the height of the war and in the immediate wake of *Le Vin herbé*, his oratorio on the Tristan legend. The shadowy, half-real atmosphere often reminds one of the world of *Pelléas*; and the restrained, pale colourings provide an effective backcloth to the vivid and poignant outbursts which mark some of the settings. The performance by Marjana Lipovšek is remarkable. Sensitive orchestral playing and faithfully balanced, well-recorded sound. This music casts a powerful spell and is strongly atmospheric.

(i) Golgotha (oratorio).(ii) Mass for Double Choir.

(B) *** Erato Ultima ADD/Dig. 3984 24237-2 (2). (i) Stampfli, De Montmollin, Tappy, Mollet, Huttenlocher, Faller Ch., Lausanne University Ch., SO, Faller; (ii) Midi Chamber Ch., D. Martin.

Martin's post-war oratorio, *Golgotha* is a work of power and substance. It has nobility and elevation of feeling, and its inspiration runs at a high level. Some have argued that it is possibly the greatest Passion since Bach but, in contradistinction to Bach, the narrative passes freely between the various soloists and the body of the choir. This is the only recording so far of *Golgotha* and it comes with a recommendable digital account of the *Mass for Double Choir*, not the equal of the Westminster version, but nonetheless eminently worthwhile.

Mass for Double Choir.

*** United Recordings (ADD) 88033. Vasari, Backhouse – HOWELLS: *Requiem* etc. ***

(*) Nim. NI 5197. Christ Church Cathedral Ch., Oxford, Darlington – POULENC: *Mass in G* etc. ***

(i) Mass for Double Choir; (ii) Passacaille for Organ.

⬤ *** Hyp. CDA 67017. Westminster Cathedral Ch., O'Donnell – PIZZETI: *Messa di requiem; De profundis*. *** ⬤

The *Mass for Double Choir* is one of Martin's purest and most sublime utterances. The latest version from the Westminster Cathedral Choir under James O'Donnell (Hyperion) is the most outstanding. The boys produce marvellously focused tone of great purity and expressive power, and the tonal blend that O'Donnell achieves throughout is little short of miraculous. This won *Gramophone* magazine's 'Record of the Year' award in 1998 and deservedly so. As a fill-up O'Donnell offers the *Passacaille* for organ, together with two magnificent Pizzetti works.

Irrespective of the above competition, the United Recordings version is also quite masterly in every respect and Vasari, a choir conducted by Jeremy Backhouse get remarkably fine results. A very convincing performance and an exemplary recording.

The Choir of Christ Church Cathedral, Oxford, under Stephen Darlington also give a good account of themselves: their tone is clean and beautifully balanced. The boys' voices are moving in a different way from that of the Frankfurt choir, but the English performance does not add up to quite as impressive or richly imaginative a musical experience. The Nimbus disc is eminently well recorded.

6 Monologues from 'Jedermann' (Everyman).

(N) (M) *** Virgin VM5 61850-2. Van Dam, Lyon Nat. Op. O, Nagano – IBERT: *4 Chansons de Don Quichotte*; POULENC: *Le Bal masqué*; RAVEL: *Don Quichotte à Dulcinée*. ***

(i) 6 Monologues from Everyman; (ii) Maria Triptychon; (i) The Tempest: 3 excerpts.

*** Chan. 9411. (i) Wilson-Johnson (ii) Russell; LPO, Bamert.

Kent Nagano directs powerfully sustained accompaniments for what is perhaps the most enterprising item in this imaginatively chosen quartet of French song groupings, all written around the third decade of the twentieth century. Van Dam has major rivals here, of course, notably Fischer-Dieskau, whom he does not quite match. But he comes pretty near to doing so: his singing, like Nagano's orchestral backcloth, is impressively felt, and his darkness of colour in the penultimate monologue prepares the way movingly for the ardently sombre closing prayer. A full text and translation is provided, and this collection can be strongly recommended.

As with Fischer-Dieskau's earlier (deleted) DG recording, Chandos couples the excerpts from *The Tempest* with the *Everyman Monologues*; it is a measure of David Wilson-Johnson's artistry here that in both instances one forgets the exalted comparison that the appearance of this new record invites. He sings with intense – but not excessive – dramatic feeling and total commitment and conviction. The extra rarity on this disc is the *Maria Triptychon*. The central movement, *Magnificat*, originally stood on its own, but Martin subsequently added the two outer movements, *Ave Maria* and *Stabat Mater*, and Linda Russell and the violinist Duncan Riddell give a totally dedicated account of it. Bamert and the LPO generate a keen sense of atmosphere, and the Chandos recording is every bit as good as the other issues in this splendid series.

Requiem.

*** Jecklin-Disco (ADD) JD 631-2. Speiser, Bollen, Tappy, Lagger, Lausanne Women's Ch., Union Ch., SRO, composer.

This is arguably the most beautiful *Requiem* to have been written since Fauré's and, were the public to have ready access to it, would be as popular. The recording, made at a public performance that the (then 83-year-old) composer conducted in Lausanne Cathedral, is very special. The analogue recording is not in the demonstration class, but this music and performance must have three stars.

Le Vin herbé (oratorio).

(N) *** Newport Classics NPD 85670 (2). Tharp, Whyte, Osborne, I Cantori di New York and Ens., Shapiro.

*(**) Jecklin-Disco (ADD) JD 581/2-2. Retchitzka, Tuscher, Comte, Morath, De Montmollin, Diakoff, De Nyzankowskyi, Tappy, Jonelli, Rehfuss, Vessières, Olsen, composer, Winterthur O (members), Desarzens.

Le Vin herbé was commissioned in 1938 by the Swiss-German conductor, Robert Blum, who wanted a piece for his madrigal choir. At the time Martin was occupied with the Tristan legend and so chose a section of Joseph Bédier's novel, *Le Roman de Tristan et Iseut*. The singers act both as a chorus and as soloists and are accompanied by two violins, violas, cellos, a double-bass and a piano, which as Martin put it were to play a secondary but not modest role and to serve as 'the scenery in a play'. It was finished in 1939 as *The Love Potion*, to which Martin eventually added two further sections as well as a short Prologue and Epilogue. It made a great impression on the young Hans Werner Henze when he heard it as a teenager in wartime Nazi Germany: 'So that's what 12-note music sounds like', he thought. 'So beautiful and so tender. And such ravishing sounds.' (Of course its

serialism is hardly even skin deep, like the *Petite symphonie*). It had been recorded only once, in 1961, with Swiss forces conducted by Victor Desarzens and with Martin himself playing the piano part. The colours are delicate in shade, pastel and half-lit and the whole piece strikes a strong, almost mesmeric spell. Commentators have stressed Martin's debt to *Pelléas* in its dramatic understatement and its fidelity to the intonations of French speech, yet the world it creates is intensely individual and the treatment of the drama is totally original. Although the Desarzens recording had the imprimatur as well as the participation of the composer, this new version – the first for almost forty years – is better in every respect. Both as soloists and as a choir the American singers are superior, as are the instrumentalists: there was some insecurity as well as vinegary tone in the 1961 set. The acoustic is warmer and more open, and the aural image better focused. *Le Vin herbé* is a haunting and powerful score, full of subtle beauties, and Mark Shapiro and his colleagues' love for this masterpiece is evident throughout.

On Jecklin-Disco there is some fine singing from Tuscher, Tappy and Rehfuss. The instrumental playing, though not impeccable, is dedicated (and the same must be said for the choral singing). The 1960s sound is much improved in the CD format. But this is now superseded.

MARTINI, Johannes (c. 1440–97/8)

Ave Maris stella; Magnificat terti toni; O beate Sebastiane; Salve regina.

*** ASV CDGAU 171. Clerks' Group, Wickham – OBRECHT: *Laudes Christo; Missa Malheur me bat.* ***

Though Martini cannot compare with Obrecht in imagination, the motets recorded here have a simple beauty made the more compelling by the dedicated performances of the Clerks' Group; atmospherically recorded.

MARTINŮ, Bohuslav (1890–1959)

La Bagarre; Half-Time; Intermezzo; The Rock; Thunderbolt.

*** Sup. (ADD) 001669. Brno State O, Vronsky.

La Bagarre and *Half-Time* are early evocations, the latter a Honeggerian depiction of a roisterous half-time at a football match that musically doesn't amount to a great deal. The three later works are much more interesting – *Intermezzo* is linked to the *Fourth Symphony* – and the collection as a whole will be of great interest to Martinů addicts, if perhaps not essential for other collectors. All the performances are alive and full of character, and the recording is vividly immediate.

Concerto grosso; (i) Sinfonietta la jolla; Toccata e due canzoni.

(N) *** Panton 71 0580-2. Prague CO, (i) with Hála.

The Prague Chamber Orchestra recorded the *Sinfonietta la jolla* and the *Toccata e due canzoni* initially in the days of mono LP and again in 1974. This version adds the *Concerto grosso* for chamber orchestra (1937), and two pianos to make a coupling that is both logical and rewarding. Even though there is some want of the nervous tension so characteristic of the composer, this latest recording is the most recommendable (and certainly the sunniest) of the three.

(i) *Concertino in C min. for Cello, Wind Instruments & Piano; (ii) Harpsichord Concerto; (iii) Oboe Concerto.*

*** Sup. 11 0107-2 031. (i) Večtomov, Topinka, members of Czech PO; (ii) Růžičková, Rehák; (iii) Krejči; (ii; iii) Czech Philharmonic Chamber O; (i, iii) Skvor; (ii) Neumann.

Zuzana Růžičková has made a number of recordings of the *Harpsichord Concerto* but this is her most successful. The sound is agreeably spacious, though the balance is synthetic and the piano has equal prominence with the solo harpsichord. However, the playing is spirited and sympathetic; and the *Oboe Concerto* is heard to excellent advantage too, with very good playing and a well-laid-out sound-picture. The early *Concertino for Cello with Piano, Wind and Percussion* is more than acceptably played and recorded.

Cello Concertos Nos. 1–2.

**(*) Sup. 1110 3901-2. May, Czech PO, Neumann.

Cello Concertos Nos. 1–2; Concertino in C min. for Cello, Wind Instruments, Piano & Percussion.

*** Chan. 9015. Wallfisch, Czech PO, Bělohlávek.

The *Cello Concerto No. 1* was composed in 1930 but has been revised twice. The *Cello Concerto No. 2* is the bigger of the two. It opens with a very characteristic and infectiously memorable B flat tune, and there is much of the luminous orchestral writing one associates with the *Fourth* and *Fifth* symphonies. It is a warm-hearted, lyrical score with a Dvořák-like radiance.

Angelica May, a Casals pupil, gives a good account of both scores and, in the absence of the Wallfisch, this is perfectly recommendable. But as both performance and recording, her version is outclassed by the Chandos, which has much greater definition and presence and also has the advantage of offering the *Concertino for Cello, Wind, Piano & Percussion* (1924).

(i; ii) Concerto for Double String Orchestra, Piano & Timpani; (iii) Concerto for String Quartet & Orchestra. 3 Frescoes of Piero della Francesca; (i; iv) 3 Ricercari (for chamber orchestra with 2 pianos). (i) Sinfonietta La Jolla; Toccata e due canzoni.

(B) ** Erato Ultima 3984 24238-2 (2). (i) Heisser; (ii) Camosi; (iii) Brandis Qt. (iv) Planès; O National de France, Conlon.

Concerto for Double String Orchestra, Piano & Timpani; Symphony No. 1.

*** Chan. 8950. Czech PO, Bělohlávek.

(i) Concerto for Double String Orchestra, Piano & Timpani, H. 271. Symphony No. 3, H 299.

(***) Sup. mono/stereo SU 1924-2 001. (i) Panenka, Hejduk; Czech PO, Sejna – DVORAK: *Suite in A, Op. 98b.* (***)

Karel Sejna's *Double Concerto* (recorded in 1958 and in stereo) is not the first recording, but the dark events that

inspired it were sufficiently close to be vivid in the minds of all Czechs. His account of the *Third Symphony*, made in 1947, was a first recording and there is the vivid, intense quality about the performance which you often find in premières. The frequency range is naturally limited, and much effort has been made to brighten the sound. It is a wonderful performance. Both performances on Supraphon have a dimension that is not always completely realized in more recent and better-recorded versions.

The *Double Concerto* is one of the most powerful works of the present century, and its intensity is well conveyed in Bělohlávek's vital, deeply felt performance. His dedicated and imaginative account of the *First Symphony* is very good indeed. Bělohlávek is totally inside this music, and the recording, made in the agreeably resonant Spanish Hall of Prague Castle, is very natural. Strongly recommended for both works.

On both the Erato discs the balance is close and unnatural. One soon becomes aware that the microphones are too near to the violins. There is plenty of impact and some vigorous, spirited playing from the strings of the Orchestre National, but overall this is not a match for the Czech Philharmonic and Jiří Bělohlávek on Chandos. The *Concerto for Quartet and Orchestra* is again very forwardly balanced and the perspective quite unnatural, though the performance by the Brandis Quartet with the orchestra under James Conlon certainly sounds convincing. Conlon also gets some very good playing from the Orchestre National in the *Frescoes*. In the *Toccata e due canzoni*, written at the same time as the *Fifth Symphony* in 1946, the piano is very prominent and the effect with close lower strings and percussion is bottom-heavy. The mix is again synthetic; the overall effect is over lit. The acoustic of Studio No. 104 in the Maison de la Radio in Paris is dryish and there is not enough space round the instruments. In the *Frescoes* the balance is more successful but there is still the aural equivalent of glare. These are marvellously evocative and tuneful scores, but the cramped acoustic diminishes the pleasure these performances would otherwise have given.

Oboe Concerto.

*** Nim. NI 5330. Anderson, Philh. O, Wright – FRANCAIX: *L'Horloge de flore;* R. STRAUSS: *Concerto.* ***

The account by John Anderson, principal of the Philharmonia, is outstanding in every way, with the *Andante* quite ravishing when the soloist's timbre is so rich. The recording is first class and the couplings particularly attractive.

Piano Concerto No. 5 in B flat (Fantasia concertante).

(M) *** DG (ADD) 463 085-2. Weber, Bav. RSO, Kubelik – TCHEREPNIN: *10 Bagatelles* ***; WEBER: *Konzertstück* **(*); FALLA: *Nights in the Gardens of Spain.* ***

Martinů's *Fantasia concertante* is a terse, cyclic work, aggressively brilliant in a twentieth-century manner, but with an underlying stream of lyricism. The performance is ideal, brash and extrovert, the performers glorying in the music's strong personality and willingness to wear its heart on its sleeve. The 1965 sound is excellent.

Violin Concertos Nos. 1–2; Rhapsody-Concerto for Viola & Orchestra.

(M) **(*) Sup. (ADD) 11 1969-2 Suk, Czech PO, Neumann.

The *Second Violin Concerto* is an appealing and inventive score and of greater substance than its predecessor from the 1930s, and it finds Martinů very much in concerto-grosso mode. By far the most poignant and eloquent of these three works is the *Rhapsody-Concerto* for viola and orchestra, in which Suk is also the soloist and which dates from the period of the *Fantaisies symphoniques*. Suk is a masterly player, of course, and the Czech Philharmonic play with obvious pleasure. The recordings are analogue and inner detail is not quite as sharply focused as in the very best discs from the 1970s.

3 Frescos of Piero della Francesca.

(**) Orfeo mono C 521 991 B. VPO, Kubelik – TCHAIKOVSKY: *Symphony No. 6.* (**)

Martinů dedicated the *Three Frescos of Piero della Francesca*, one of his most inspired and colourful scores, to Rafael Kubelik. This performance, recorded at the 1956 Salzburg Festival, was its première (Kubelik recorded them commercially on a mono HMV LP not long afterwards but that did not survive very long in the catalogue). His reading of the first movement is fractionally more measured than we often get nowadays and gains in its breadth. The mono sound is not bad for its period but this, of course, is a score which benefits from good modern sound.

Spalíček (ballet; complete); Dandelion (Romance); 5 Duets on Moravian Folksongs.

*** Sup. 11 0752-2 (2). Soloists, Kantilena Children's Ch., Kühn Mixed Ch., Brno State PO, Jílek.

The original of Martinů's engaging ballet *Spalíček* dates from 1931–2. The dances, familiar from the suites, are interspersed with vocal episodes, both solo and choral. For the most part this music is quite captivating, particularly given the charm of this performance. Two shorter works complete the set: *Dandelion Romance* for mixed chorus and soprano, and *Five Duets on Moravian Folksong Texts* for female voices, violin and piano, both of which come from his last years. All in all, a delightful addition to the Martinů discography.

Symphonies Nos. 1–6 (Fantaisies Symphoniques).

(M) *** Sup. 11 0382-2 (3). Czech PO, Neumann.

Symphonies Nos. 1; 3; 5.

*** Multisonic (ADD) 31 0023-2 (2). Czech PO, Ančerl.

Symphonies Nos. 1–4.

*** BIS CD 362-3. Bamberg SO, Järvi.

Martinů always draws a highly individual sound from his orchestra. On hearing the *First Symphony*, Virgil Thomson wrote, 'the shining sounds of it sing as well as shine', and there is no doubt this music is luminous and life-loving. The BIS recording is in the demonstration class yet sounds completely natural, and the performances under Neeme Järvi are totally persuasive and have a spontaneous feel for the music's pulse.

Neumann's set was recorded in the Dvořák Hall of the House of Artists, Prague, between January 1976 (No. 6) and 1978 (No. 5). The transfers to CD are excellently done: the sound is full, spacious and bright; it has greater presence and better definition than the original LPs.

Whether or not you have modern versions of these Martinů symphonies, you should obtain Ančerl's powerful, luminous performances; they come from Czech Radio recordings made in 1963, 1966 and 1962 respectively. They are such superb and convincing readings that readers should not hesitate. The music glows in Ančerl's hands and acquires a radiance that quite belies its date.

Symphonies Nos. 2 & 4.

(N) ** Naxos 8.553349. Nat. SO of the Ukraine, Fagen.

These are both radiant symphonies, life enhancing and infectious in their rhythmic vitality and luminous textures. The playing of the Ukraine Orchestra is lively, and the recording well lit and full of inner detail. All the same they are not in the same league as Järvi or, in the case of No. 4, Bělohlávek, which will give greater long-term satisfaction.

Symphony No. 4; Memorial to Lidice; (i) Field Mass.

*** Chan. 9138. (i) Kusjner, Czech Ph. Ch.; Czech PO, Bělohlávek.

There is a radiance about this work that is quite special, and Bělohlávek's account of it is quite the best that has appeared in recent years. The *Memorial to Lidice*, composed in response to a Nazi massacre, is a powerful and haunting piece, and so is the *Field Mass*, which receives its best performance until now – by far. An indispensable item in any Martinů discography.

Symphony No. 5.

(N) ** CBC Records (ADD) PSCD 2021. Toronto SO, Ančerl – BEETHOVEN: *Symphony No. 6.* **

Symphony No. 5; Les Fresques de Piero della Francesca; Memorial to Lidice; The Parables.

**(*) Sup. mono/stereo 11 1931-2. Czech PO, Ančerl.

Most of these are pioneering recordings. The *Fifth Symphony* comes from 1955 and the *Memorial to Lidice* from 1957 and, although the sound is naturally constricted in range, it never detracts for one moment from the stature of these performances. The *Three Frescoes* and *The Parables* are in stereo and are given a marvellously glowing performance and, though it has still not been possible to remove the slight glassiness and shrillness in the string-tone above the stave, there is rather more detail and body than in the LP. *The Parables*, never released in stereo on LP in the UK, sound better, and the performances have tremendous authority. An indispensable element in any Martinů collection.

A pity that another Martinů work could not have been found for this Canadian CD, as it would make a more logical coupling than Beethoven's *Pastoral Symphony*. Ančerl's Multisonic version of the Martinů is among the best recordings of the piece and has more breadth and sense of mystery than this Toronto account from 1971. The latter is rather fast: Ančerl takes 26'57'' as opposed 30'22'' in 1955. There is plenty of commitment and enthusiasm from the orchestra, and the CBC sound is decent if a little top heavy.

Symphonies Nos. 5; 6 (Fantaisies symphoniques).

*** BIS CD 402. Bamberg SO, Järvi.

Symphony No. 6 (Fantaisies symphoniques).

*** Chan. 8897. Czech PO, Bělohlávek – JANACEK: *Sinfonietta*; SUK: *Scherzo.* ***

The *Fifth* is a glorious piece and Järvi brings to it that mixture of disciplined enthusiasm and zest for life that distinguishes all his work. Wonderfully transparent, yet full-bodied sound, in the best BIS manner.

This Chandos version of No. 6 has great dramatic strength and is fully characterized; undoubtedly these players believe in every note. It is an outstanding performance that does full justice to the composer's extraordinarily imaginative vision and is very well recorded.

CHAMBER MUSIC

Cello Sonatas Nos. 1 (1939); 2 (1942); 3 (1952).

(N) (BB) *** RCA Double 74321 84592-2 (2). Starker, Firkušný – JANACEK:*Violin Sonata; Piano Sonata (I.X.1905)* etc. **(*).

*** Hyp. CDA 66296. Isserlis, Evans.

Cello Sonatas Nos. 1, H 277; 2, H 286; 3, H 340; 7 Arabesques, H 201a; Arietta, H 188b.

(BB) **(*) Naxos 8.554502. Sebastian and Christian Benda.

Martinů's three *Cello Sonatas* span the period 1939–52 and are full of rewarding musical invention. Steven Isserlis and Peter Evans offer very good playing and very acceptable recording, and this can be strongly recommended.

However, the RCA version with Starker and Firkušný is predictably even finer. Firkušný's authority in this repertoire is unchallenged, and Starker has a natural eloquence, though his tone is small. They are given the benefit of very good recorded sound and in the new super-bargain double format are to be preferred to their British rivals.

Christian Benda was a Fournier protégé and his playing, like that of his partner, is commendably direct in utterance, though these versions do not match the subtlety of Isserlis and Evans. Worth the money, but the performances are not as involving as those of their more expensive rivals.

Cello Sonata No. 1; Variations on a Theme of Rossini; Variations on a Slovak Theme.

(N) *** Simax PSC 1146. Birkeland, Gimse – KABALEVSKY: *Cello Sonata No. 2.* ***

Diverting though they are, the two sets of *Variations* are not top-drawer Martinů even if they do sound at their freshest and most charming in the hands of this Norwegian partnership. The powerful *Cello Sonata No. 1*, however, is another matter and Øystein Birkeland and Håvard Gimse play it wonderfully, with splendid rhythmic vitality, lyrical fervour and abundant imagination. The recorded sound is exceptionally truthful and lifelike, sonorous and marvellously balanced. A most rewarding issue in every way.

(i) Madrigal Sonata for Flute, Violin & Piano; (ii) 5 Madrigal Stanzas for Violin & Piano; (i) Promenades for Flute, Violin & Harpsichord; (iii) Scherzo for Flute & Piano; Sonata for Flute & Piano; (i) Sonata for Flute, Violin & Piano.

*** Fleurs de Lys FL 2 3031. (i) Dubeau, Hamelin, Marion; (ii) Dubeau, Hamelin; (iii) Marion, Hamelin.

The performances are as fresh and exhilarating as the music itself, delightfully inventive and vital. All three artists play with imagination and virtuosity, and the recording has exemplary clarity and presence. The jazz-like *Scherzo* from the late 1920s comes off particularly well.

4 Madrigals for Oboe, Clarinet & Bassoon; 3 Madrigals for Violin & Viola; Madrigal Sonata for Piano, Flute & Violin; 5 Madrigal Stanzas for Violin & Piano.

*** Hyp. CDA 66133. Dartington Ens.

These delightful pieces exhibit all the intelligence and fertility of invention we associate with Martinů's music. The playing of the Dartington Ensemble is accomplished and expert, and the recording, though resonant, is faithful.

Nonet; Trio in F for Flute, Cello & Piano; La Revue de cuisine.

*** Hyp. (ADD) CDA 66084. Dartington Ens.

Only one of these pieces is otherwise available on CD and all of them receive first-class performances and superb recording. The sound has space, warmth, perspective and definition. An indispensable issue for lovers of Martinů's music.

Oboe Quartet (for oboe, violin, cello & piano); Piano Quartet; String Quintet; Viola Sonata.

(BB) *** Naxos 8.553916. Artists of 1994 Australian Festival of Chamber Music.

The best thing here is the captivating *Oboe Quartet*, which is quite a discovery. Like the fine *Viola Sonata* and the early *String Quintet*, whose slow movement is crossed by the shadow of Martinů's master, Roussel, its appearance at budget price is doubly welcome in that the performances are lively and spirited and the recording eminently natural.

Piano Quartet No. 1; 3 Madrigals for Violin & Viola; String Trio No. 2.

(N) (B) *** Virgin 2 x 1 VBD5 61904-2 (2). Domus – DOHNANYI: *Serenade.* DVORAK: *Bagatelles, Op. 47.* KODALY: *Intermezzo.* SUK: *Piano Quartet, Op. 1.* ***

The *Second String Trio* comes from 1932, when Martinů was living in France, and the two remaining works come from his American years: the *First Piano Quartet* from 1942 and the *Madrigals for Violin and Viola* from 1947. The recordings of this vintage Martinů were made in 1989–90 and come in a bargain double entitled 'Czech Chamber Music'. (The news of their change of nationality might come as a surprise to Dohnányi and Kodály.) This is a rewarding programme with admirably alert and sensitive playing from Domus and eminently natural recorded sound.

Piano Quintet No. 2.

*** ASV CDDCA 889. Frankl, Lindsay Qt – DVORAK: *Piano Quintet*. ***

Martinů's *Second Piano Quintet* is a remarkably successful piece, characteristically original in its content and rhythmic style. The Lindsays with Peter Frankl have its full measure. The recording is lively and present, with the piano well integrated, although there is just a touch of thinness on the strings. An outstanding coupling.

(i) *Piano Trio No. 1 (5 Pièces brèves); 2 in D min.; 3 in C;* (ii) *Duo No. 2 for Violin & Cello.*

(BB) *** ASV CDQS 6230. (i) Angell Trio; (ii) Dvhmolvk, May.

Excellent performances of these engaging pieces recorded in very good sound. Anyone wanting the Martinů piano trios need really look no further.

Sextet for Strings.

(N) (M) **(*) Panton 81 1437-2 131. Czech Chamber Soloists, Matyáš – JANACEK: *Idyll; Suite.* **(*)

The *Sextet for Strings* (1932) is not one of Martinů's most inspired pieces. Even so it is played well enough by the Czech Chamber Soloists under the direction of Ivan Matyáš.

String Quartets Nos. 1–7.

**(*) Sup. (ADD) 110 994-2 (3). Panocha Qt.

The *First* of the quartets is both the longest and the most derivative; it is heavily indebted to the world of Debussy and Ravel. The *Third* is by far the shortest (it takes barely 12 minutes) and has the nervous energy and rhythmic vitality characteristic of the mature composer. The *Fourth* and *Fifth* are close to the *Double Concerto for Two String Orchestras, Piano and Timpani*. The *Fifth* is the darkest of the quartets and in its emotional intensity is close in spirit to Janáček's *Intimate Letters*. The *Sixth* – and in particular its first movement – is a powerful and disturbing piece, and there is a sense of scale and a vision that raise it above its immediate successor. The Panocha set is eminently recommendable, even though it is a bit steep to ask full price for it, and the recordings are a bit two-dimensional.

String Quartets Nos. 1–2; Tri jezdci (Three Horsemen).

(N) (BB) **(*) Naxos 553782. Martinů Qt.

The first two of Martinů's seven string quartets were written at an early stage in his career. Unlike the symphonies, which arrived at annual intervals over the five years 1942–6 with the *Sixth Symphony (Fantasies symphoniques)* following in the early 1950s, the quartets span the best part of three decades (1918–47). (There are two earlier attempts which were both lost, one from 1912 and another, in E flat, from 1917, as well as two quartet-movements, an *Andante* and *Nocturne*.) The *First Quartet* lasts almost 40 minutes and is known as the 'French' (the nickname was Martinů's own). It was only published in 1973, long after the composer's death, and its actual date could be nearer 1920 than 1918. It is heavily in debt to Debussy and Ravel, but what it lacks in individuality it makes up for in craftsmanship. The *Second Quartet* (1925) is more concentrated and more complex,

and its greater density of incident reflects the influence of Roussel, with whom Martinů was studying. The fill-up is a remarkably accomplished first recording of *Tri jezdci*, which was written when the composer was twelve. The Martinů Quartet play with spirit and the recording is decent – fresh and lifelike without being outstanding.

Violin Sonata No. 1, H 182; Sonatas in C, H 120; D min., H 152; Concerto, H 13; Elegy, H 3; Impromptu, H 166; 5 Short pieces, H 184.

(M) *** Sup. SU 3410-2 (2). Matoušek, Adamec.

Violin Sonatas Nos. 2, H 308; 3, H 303; Sonatina in G, H 262; 7 Arabesques, H 201A; Arietta, H 188A; Czech Rhapsody, H 307; Intermezzo, H 261; 5 Madrigal stanzas, H 297; Rhythmic études, H 202.

(M) *** Sup. SU 3412-2 (2). Matoušek, Adamec.

Violin Sonatas Nos. 2–3; 5 Madrigal Sonatas.

** Sup. 11 0099-2. Suk, Hála.

Enormously prolific in most genres and combinations, Martinů's output for violin and piano is fairly extensive – nineteen pieces in all. The two handsomely produced and well-recorded double-CD sets cover his whole output: from the age of nineteen when he composed the *Elegy*, and the *Concerto* from the following year, through to his mid-fifties and the *Sonata No. 3* (1944) and the *Czech Rhapsody* written for Kreisler (1945). At times, Martinů is given to self-imitation, and there are occasions when his muse is on autopilot but, for the most part, they are few and far between. The *Third Sonata* in particular is very impressive. Bohuslav Matoušek and Petr Adamec are completely inside the idiom, having played Martinů virtually from the cradle.

Josef Suk and Josef Hála give excellent accounts of all three pieces, though the 1987 recording is balanced less than appealingly. The sound is rather synthetic and too close.

Violin Sonata No. 3 in G, Op. 100.

(N) *** Praga PRD 250 153. Remés, Kayahara – DVORAK: *Sonatina;* JANACEK, SMETANA: *Violin Sonatas.* ***

Václav Remes and Sachito Kayahara combine to give a superb account of Martinů's passionate *Third Sonata*, fiery and intense, yet relaxing warmly for the composer's moments of gentler lyricism: the opening of the *Finale* has a lovely rapt serenity.

Sonata for 2 Violins & Piano.

(*) Hyp. CDA 66473. Osostowicz, Kovacic, Tomes – MILHAUD: *Violin Duo etc.* **(*); PROKOFIEV: *Violin Sonata.* *

Martinů's *Sonata for Two Violins and Piano* finds him full of invention and vitality. Krsyia Osostowicz, Ernst Kovacic and Susan Tomes play it with all the finesse and sensitivity you could want, and they are excellently recorded. The disc would be even more recommendable if it had a longer playing time than 46 minutes.

Variations on a Slovak Folksong.

(BB) *** ASV CDQS 6218. Gregor-Smith, Wrigley –

PROKOFIEV; SHOSTAKOVICH: *Cello Sonatas;* JANACEK: *Pohádka.* ***

The *Variations on a Slovak Folksong* are not top-drawer Martinů but the husband-and-wife team of Bernard Gregor-Smith and Yolande Wrigley gives a lively and persuasive account of it and, even if the piano is slightly too prominent, the recording is lively and fresh.

PIANO MUSIC

Bagatelle (Morceau facile), H 323; Dumka No. 3, H 285bis; Fantasia et toccata, H 281; The fifth day of the fifth moon, H 318; 8 Preludes, H 181; Piano Sonata, H 350.

** Chan. 9655. Bekova.

Martinuo's piano music has been well served in the past, but the uniquely authoritative RCA disc by Rudolf Firkušný is at present out of circulation, so Eleonora Bekova's set fills a gap. The playing is more than serviceable without being really distinguished, and the recording is eminently truthful.

VOCAL MUSIC

The Butterfly That Stamped (ballet): 5 scenes (arr. Rybár).

** Sup. 11 0380-2 Women's voices of Kühn Ch., Prague SO, Bělohlávek.

Martinů's choral ballet, *The Butterfly That Stamped,* is based on one of Kipling's *Just-So* stories. The five scenes have been put into a performing edition by Jaroslav Rybár. The score has a great deal of Gallic charm, and it is a pity that Supraphon market this slight but charming score (lasting only 41 minutes 47 seconds) at full price.

The Epic of Gilgamesh (oratorio).

*** Marco 8.223316. Depoltová, Margita, Kusnjer, Vele, Karpílšek, Slovak Ph. Ch. & O, Košler.

*** Sup. 11 1824. Machotková, Zahradníček, Zítek, Průša, Brousek, Czech Philh. Ch., Prague SO, Bělohlávek.

The Epic of Gilgamesh comes from Martinů's last years and is arguably his masterpiece. It evokes a remote and distant world, full of colour and mystery. Gilgamesh is the oldest poem known to mankind. The work abounds with invention of the highest quality and of consistently sustained inspiration. The Marco Polo performance is committed and sympathetic and the recording very natural in its balance.

Bělohlávek's version can hold its own artistically with the excellent Marco Polo account. It does not displace it but can certainly be recommended alongside it.

OPERA

Ariane (complete in French).

(N) *** Sup. SU 3524-2 6312. Lindsley, Phillips, Doležal, Burun, Novák (bass), Czech PO & Ch., Neumann.

As with his earlier operatic masterpiece, *Julietta,* Martinů based his one-act opera *Ariane* on a play, *Le Voyage de Thésée,* by his friend Georges Neveux. In making his adapta-

tion Martinů treats it as baroque monody, interspersed with three sinfonias, three self-contained dramatic sequences and a closing aria. The pastiche elements have great lightness of touch; it seems that the bravura of Ariane herself, sung excellently by the American soprano Celina Lindsley was inspired by Callas. Richard Novák's vibrato may be too wide for some, but generally speaking the performance is sung well (in French), and Václav Neumann gets alert and sensitive playing from the Czech Philharmonic. The recording (from 1987) is eminently serviceable. In order to accommodate its four-language libretto, the CD is housed in a jewel case that could happily encompass *Siegfried* or *Walküre* – somewhat bizarre as *Ariane* only runs to 43′44″. But the opera has both freshness and charm and devotees of Martinů need not hesitate.

The Greek Passion (original version).

(N) *** Koch Schwann 2-6590-2. Ventris, Stemme, Ruuttunen, Grigoris, soloists, Bregenz Musikhauptschuile Childrens' Ch., Moscow Chamber Ch. Vienna SO, Schirmer.

The Greek Passion has been acclaimed as the masterpiece of Martinů's last years. Its genesis however was somewhat fraught. Martinů was much drawn to Kazantzakis's novel *Christ Recrucified* and set about reducing it into four brief acts, no easy task at the best of times particularly as he was still writing in an alien tongue. Kazantzakis himself read and approved the results and Martinů worked on the score between 1954 and 1957. However, the piece was turned down by Covent Garden, in spite of the advocacy of its director, Martinů's fellow countryman Rafael Kubelik. His revisions for a production in Zurich were so comprehensive that the work took a further two years. Fortunately he gave away bits and pieces of the autograph to various friends, which enabled this reconstruction to be made. The Zurich version, which Mackerras has recorded for Supraphon, is almost a different piece. The plot is straightforward: Manolios, a shepherd, has been chosen to play Christ in the passion-play in a poor Greek village in the days of Ottoman rule; he comes to assume his chosen role, preaching charity towards the starving refugees whose village has been torched and who are destitute. Their pleas fall on deaf ears and so do his. He becomes an outcast, is excommunicated and finally murdered.

The production of *The Greek Passion,* on which this recording is based, was mounted in Bregenz in 1999 in collaboration with the Royal Opera House and reached Covent Garden in April 2000, ironically in the wake of tabloid agitation about Kosovan refugees. Those who saw the production will know how varied in technique and texture this music is and how powerful its dramatic impact can be. There is extensive use of *parlando,* 'speech melody' and *arioso:* it was this mixture plus the spoken dialogue that worried the Covent Garden panel in 1957. It does not completely convince as a dramatic entity even now: one misses the sense of the vital current that carries the action forward, which is perhaps why Martinů overhauled it. However, there is a great deal of imaginative and powerful invention such as the inspired landscape painting that opens the third act or the ecstatic life-enhancing music that accompanies the wedding in the fourth; both are glorious, though the effect of the latter is immediately dissipated by what seems an interminable spoken narrative. If it does not surpass late works like *The Prophecy of Isaiah*, *The Epic of Gilgamesh* and the *Fantaisies symphoniques*, there is music here that can register alongside them and which readers should investigate. Anyone who has Mackerras's set of the Zurich version will naturally want this earlier version. Esa Ruuttunen is an imposing Grigoris, and there is a fine sense of teamwork throughout. Ulf Schirmer holds everything together well. Like many off-air relays it is not ideally balanced, and there are the odd stage noises, but do not be put off: there is much imaginative and gripping music in this score.

The Greek Passion (sung in English).

*** Sup. 10 3611/2. Mitchinson, Field, Tomlinson, Joll, Moses, Davies, Cullis, Savory, Kuhn Children's Ch., Czech PO Ch., Brno State PO, Mackerras.

Written with much mental pain in the years just before Martinů died in 1959, this was the work he regarded as his musical testament. It tells in an innocent, direct way of a village where a Passion play is to be presented; the individuals – tragically, as it proves – take on qualities of the New Testament figures they represent. Mackerras makes an ideal advocate, and the recording is both brilliant and atmospheric. With the words so clear, the absence of an English libretto is not a serious omission, but the lack of any separate cues within the four acts is a great annoyance. Extraordinarily vivid recording.

Julietta (complete).

*** Sup. (ADD) 10 8176-2 (3). Tauberová, Zídek, Zlesák, Otava, Bednář, Mixová, Jedenáctík, Procházková, Hanzalíková, Soukupová, Jindrák, Veverka, Svehla, Zlesák, Lemariová, Berman, Prague Nat. Theatre Ch. & O, Krombholc.

Described by the composer as a Dreambook, *Julietta* was given first in Prague in March 1938. This vintage Supraphon recording, made in 1964, captures that surreal quality vividly, for the ear is mesmerized from the very start, when the howling of a high bassoon introduces the astonishingly original prelude. The voices as well as the orchestra are then presented with a bright immediacy which reinforces the power and incisiveness of Krombholc's performance. The sharpness of focus adds to the atmospheric intensity, as when in the first Act The Man in the Window plays his accordion. Ivo Zídek gives a vivid portrait of the central character, Michel, perplexed by his dream-like search, and there is no weak link in the rest of the cast. Informative notes and libretto come with multiple translations.

Les Larmes du couteau; The Voice of the Forest.

*** Sup. Dig SU 3386-3 631. Jonášová, Smidová, Janál, Prague Philharmonia, Bělohlávek.

The two one-act operas recorded here are both short, roughly half an hour each. With the Dadaist *Les Larmes du couteau* (or *The Knife's Tears*) we are close to the world of *L'Histoire du soldat*, Les Six and Kurt Weill. It is entertaining if insubstantial and diverts the listener. Good soloists and recording, with the musical and speech elements well balanced. *The voice of the forest* offers a more familiar Martinů. It is far more individual in style and like the ballet *Spalíček*, draws on Czech folklore and melody. In it, Martinů's invention is unfailingly fresh and although one can see why it has never made waves it has much to offer. The set is packaged as one disc in a box for two, so as to accommodate the copious and handsomely produced documentation.

MARTUCCI, Giuseppe (1856–1909)

(i) *Piano Concerto No. 1 in D min.;* **(ii)** *Le canzone dei ricordi.*

** ASV CDDCA 690. (i) Caramiello; (ii) Yakar; Philh. O, D'Avalos.

The *First Piano Concerto* (with Francesco Caramiello a capable soloist) is inevitably derivative, and it is the song-cycle that is the chief attraction here: Rachel Yakar sings beautifully and is particularly affecting in the Duparc-like *Cantavál ruscello la gaia canzone*. The recording is generally faithful.

(i) *Piano Concerto No. 2 in B flat, Op. 66;* **(ii)** *Le canzone dei ricordi.*

*** Sony SK 64582. (i) Bruno; (ii) Freni; La Scala, Milan, PO, Muti.

The *Second Piano Concerto in B flat* is a massively powerful work, Brahmsian in both its scope and scale; however, although it is indebted to him, there is far more to it than that: this is Brahms distilled through very individual filters, and there is no question of the mastery with which the composer unfolds his argument. Carlo Bruno is a commanding artist whom we would like to hear on more familiar terrain. The performance exhibits great authority and finesse, and it is recorded with subtlety and naturalness. Mirella Freni brings to *Le canzone dei ricordi* all the warmth and delicacy of feeling this lovely score calls for. Muti conducts with evident conviction and gets very fine results from the Milan orchestra. Strongly recommended.

Symphony No. 1 in D min., Op. 75; Notturno, Op. 70/1; Novelletta, Op. 82; Tarantella, Op. 44.

** ASV CDDCA 675. Philh. O, D'Avalos.

The *First Symphony* is greatly indebted to Brahms, but elsewhere there is a vein of lyricism that is more distinctive. The performances by the Philharmonia under Francesco D'Avalos are serviceable rather than distinguished, but the recording is very truthful and well balanced.

Symphony No. 2 in F, Op. 81; Andante in B flat, Op. 69; Colore orientale Op. 44/3.

** ASV CDDCA 689. Philh. O, D'Avalos.

The *Second Symphony* is a relatively late work. Though the performance falls short of distinction, it leaves the listener in no doubt as to Martucci's quality as a composer and the nobility of much of his invention. The *Colore orientale* is an arrangement of a piano piece; the beautiful *Andante*, a work of depth, has a Fauréan dignity. The recording is a bit too closely balanced.

Le canzone dei ricordi; Notturno, Op. 70/1.

*** Hyp. CDA 66290. Madalin, ECO, Bonavera – RESPIGHI: *Il tramonto.* ***

Le canzone dei ricordi is a most beautiful song-cycle, and its gentle atmosphere and warm lyricism are most seductive. At times Carol Madalin has a rather rapid vibrato, but she sings the work most sympathetically and with great eloquence. The *Notturno* is beautifully played. Recommended with all possible enthusiasm.

MARX, Joseph (1882–1964)

Quartetto chromatico; Quartetto in modo classico; Quartetto in modo antico.

*** ASV CDDCA 1073. Lyric Qt.

Joseph Marx viewed serial music with disdain, and in 1923, with the help of Korngold, Zemlinsky and others, he organized an 'alternative Salzburg Festival' representing the best of contemporary music, but music which stopped short of serial techniques. Yet the influence of early Schoenberg is strong in his music, especially the luscious *Quartetto chromatico*, which opens very like *Verklärte Nacht* and sustains its chromatic sensuality almost throughout. There is a sprightly Scherzo, but the third movement is particularly intense, although the passion is at least partly dispelled in the finale. By contrast the *Quartetto in modo antico* opens in spring-like pastoral mood, using the Mixolydian mode for its harmonic language. The touching *Adagio* has a lovely chorale-like theme in the Phrygian mode, and after an elegant neoclassical Minuet, the finale is light-heartedly fugal, with a song-like secondary episode. In the *Quartetto in modo classico* the sweetness of the lyricism is balanced by elegance, the Scherzo is light-hearted, the elegiac and beautiful *Adagio*, still rich in its harmonic palette, yet brings solo legato lines and is delicately refined in atmosphere. The dancing 6/8 finale introduces another fugato, but the movement closes expressively by recalling the work's opening. Marx's music may be conservative for its time, but it is rewardingly rich in lyrical feeling, and the performances here are persuasively committed and full of spontaneous feeling. The recording is warm, truthful and clear. Highly recommended.

MASCAGNI, Pietro (1863–1945)

L'amico Fritz (complete).

(N) (M) *** EMI CMS5 67376-2 [567373] (2). Pavarotti, Freni, Sardinero, ROHCG Ch. & O, Gavazzeni.

The haunting *Cherry Duet* from this opera whets the appetite for more, and it is good to hear so rare and delightful a piece, one that is unlikely to enter the repertory of our British opera houses. The performance could not be more refined, and Freni and Pavarotti were both at their freshest in 1969 when it was recorded. While the dramatic conception is at the opposite end of the scale from *Cavalleria rusticana*, one is easily beguiled by the music's charm. The Covent Garden orchestra responds loyally; the recording is clear, warm and atmospheric and has transferred beautifully to CD. Though perhaps not a 'Great Recording of the Century', this mid-priced reissue is very winning. The documentation includes a full libretto and attractive sessions photographs.

Cavalleria rusticana (complete).

(M) *** RCA (ADD) 74321 39500-2. Scotto, Domingo, Elvira, Amb. Op. Ch., Nat. PO, Levine.

(M) *** DG (ADD) 457 764-2. Cossotto, Bergonzi, Allegri, Guelfi, Martino, Ch. & O of La Scala, Milan, Karajan.

*** DG (ADD) 419 257-2 (3). Cossotto, Bergonzi, Guelfi, Ch. & O of La Scala, Milan, Karajan – LEONCAVALLO: *I Pagliacci* *** (also with collection of operatic intermezzi ***).

(***) EMI mono CDS5 56287-2 (2). Callas, Di Stefano, Panerai, Ch. & O of La Scala, Milan, Serafin – LEONCAVALLO: *I Pagliacci.* (***)

(M) **(*) Decca (ADD) 458 224-2. Tebaldi, Björling, Bastianini, Maggio Musicale Fiorentino Ch. & O, Erede.

(M) **(*) EMI (ADD) CMS7 63967-2 (2). De los Angeles, Corelli, Sereni, Rome Op. Ch. & O, Santini – LEONCAVALLO: *I Pagliacci.* ***

(M) **(*) EMI (ADD) CMS7 63650-2 (2). Caballé, Carreras, Hamari, Manuguerra, Varnay, Amb. Op. Ch., Southend Boys' Ch., Philh. O, Muti – LEONCAVALLO: *I Pagliacci.* **(*)

**(*) Decca (ADD) 444 391-2. Varady, Pavarotti, Bormida, Cappuccilli, Gonzales, Nat. PO, Gavazzeni.

(M) (***) RCA mono GD 86510. Milanov, Björling, Merrill, Shaw Chorale, RCA O, Cellini.

(B) **(*) Naxos 8.660022. Evstatieva, Aragall, Tumagian, Di Mauro, Michalková, Slovak Philh. Ch., Czech RSO, Rahbari – LEONCAVALLO: *I Pagliacci.* **(*)

(M) (**) Nim. mono NI 7843/4. Gigli, Bruna Rasa, Marcucci, Bechi, Simionato, La Scala Ch. & O, composer – LEONCAVALLO: *I Pagliacci.* (**(*))

Now reissued at mid-price (pleasingly presented in a slipcase with libretto), the Scotto/Domingo set now stands as a first recommendation for Mascagni's red-blooded opera, with Domingo giving a heroic account of the role of Turiddù, full of defiance. Scotto is strongly characterful too, and James Levine directs with a splendid sense of pacing, by no means faster than his rivals (except the leisurely Karajan) and drawing red-blooded playing from the National Philharmonic. The recording is vivid and strikingly present in its CD transfer.

It is good to see that Karajan's outstanding recording, hitherto linked to *Pagliacci*, is now available separately. Karajan pays Mascagni the tribute of taking his markings literally, so that well-worn melodies come out with new purity and freshness, and the singers have been chosen to match that. Cossotto quite as much as Bergonzi keeps a pure, firm line that is all too rare in this much abused music – not that there is any lack of bite (except that the original recording could have made the chorus better defined). However, it has never sounded more vivid than on this Originals CD – which manages to squeeze just under 81 minutes on a single disc – with texts and translations. The recording remains available at full price, coupled with *Pagliacci*.

Dating from the mid-1950s, Callas's performance as Santuzza reveals the diva in her finest form, with edginess and unevenness of production at a minimum and with vocal colouring at its most characterful. The singing of the other principals is hardly less dramatic and Panerai is in firm, well-projected voice.

The early (1957) Decca recording with Tebaldi offers a forthright, lusty account of Mascagni's piece of blood and thunder and has the distinction of three excellent soloists. Tebaldi is most moving in *Voi lo sapete*, and the firm richness of Bastianini's baritone is beautifully caught. As always, Björling shows himself the most intelligent of tenors, and it is only the chorus that gives serious cause for disappointment; they are very undisciplined. The CD sound is strikingly bright and lively.

Though not as vibrant as Von Matačič's *Pagliacci* coupling, this beautifully sung, essentially lyrical Santini performance could give considerable satisfaction, provided the bitterness of Mascagni's drama is not a first consideration. Like the coupling, it shows Corelli in good form; both he and de los Angeles are given scope by Santini to produce soaring, Italianate singing of Mascagni's richly memorable melodies. The recording is suitably atmospheric.

There are fewer unexpected textual points in Muti's EMI *Cav.* than in *Pag.*, but the conductor's approach is comparably biting and violent, brushing away the idea that this is a sentimental score, though running the risk of making it sound vulgar. The result is certainly refreshing, with Caballé – pushed faster than usual, even in her big moments – collaborating warmly. So *Voi lo sapete* is geared from the start to the final cry of *Io son dannata*, and she manages a fine snarl on *A te la mala Pasqua*. Carreras does not sound quite so much at home, though the rest of the cast is memorable, including the resonant Manuguerra as Alfio and the veteran Astrid Varnay as Mamma Lucia, wobble as she does. The recording is forward and vivid.

With Pavarotti loud and unsubtle as Turiddù – though the tone is often most beautiful – it is left to Julia Varady as Santuzza to give the 1976 Decca recording under Gavazzeni its distinction, the sharpness of pain in *Voi lo sapete* beautifully conveyed, the whole performance warm and authentic. Cappuccilli's Alfio is too noble to be convincing, and the main claim to attention lies in the brilliant forward recording. This set remains at full price.

Admirers of Milanov will not want to miss her beautiful singing of *Voi lo sapete*, and in the duet Merrill's dark, firm timbre is thrilling. Björling brings a good measure of musical and tonal subtlety to the role of Turiddù, normally belted out, while Cellini's conducting minimizes the vulgarity of the piece.

As in his parallel recording of *Pag.*, Alexander Rahbari conducts a red-blooded reading of *Cav.*, making it a first-rate super-bargain choice. Stefka Evstatieva is a warmly vibrant Santuzza, well controlled, no Slavonic wobbler, and Giacomo Aragall as Turiddù, not quite as fresh-sounding as he once was, yet gives a strong, characterful performance, with Eduard Tumagian excellent as Alfio, firm and dark. Well-focused digital recording.

EMI's vintage (1940) version of *Cav.*, conducted by the composer with Gigli as Turiddù, is again available from Nimbus, along with the curious little speech of introduction that Mascagni himself recorded. Yet the composer's sluggish

speeds mean that this opera has to start awkwardly at the end of the *Pag.* disc. Nimbus's transfer captures the voices well, giving them a mellow bloom, though the focus is not nearly as sharp as on the old EMI transfer.

Cavalleria rusticana: highlights.

(M) **(*) EMI (ADD) CDM5 66048-2 from above complete recording, with. Caballé, Carreras; cond. Muti – LEONCAVALLO: *I Pagliacci*: highlights. **(*)

Caballé is in good form here and receives good support from the rest of the cast. With Muti conducting strongly, this a recommendable sampler of a highly dramatic performance, vividly recorded.

Cavalleria rusticana (complete; in English).

(M) **(*) Chan. 3004 (2). Miricioiu, O'Neill, Joll, Montague, Bainbridge, Geoffrey Mitchell Ch., LPO, Parry.

David Parry gives a warmly atmospheric reading of the Mascagni score which, as well as bringing out its atmospheric beauty, brings home the high drama, as in the big duet between Turiddù and Santuzza at the very end. Nelly Miricioiu is an inspired choice to take the role of the heroine, her rich, vibrant voice firmly under control, with fine legato and passionately declaimed climaxes. Dennis O'Neill with his clear Italianate tone is also excellent as Turiddù, passionate and intense. It is good to hear the fruity and characterful Elizabeth Bainbridge as Mamma Lucia, and Diana Montague sings with creamy beauty in Lola's Song. The serious blot comes with the Alfio of Phillip Joll, most damagingly in the Carter's song, in which the voice is pitched so vaguely it is halfway to talking, with notes spreading under pressure. A pity, when the rest is so convincing.

Iris (complete).

*** Sony M2K 45526 (2). Domingo, Tokody, Pons, Giaiotti, Bav. R. Ch., Munich R. O, Patanè.

Musically, *Iris* brings a mixture of typical Mascagnian sweetness and a vein of nobility often echoing Wagner. With a strong line-up of soloists including Domingo, and with Giuseppe Patanè a persuasive conductor, this recording makes as good a case for a flawed piece as one is ever likely to get. Domingo's warm, intelligent singing helps to conceal the cardboard thinness of a hero who expresses himself in generalized ardour. The Hungarian soprano, Ilona Tokody, brings out the tenderness of the heroine, singing beautifully except when under pressure. Juan Pons, sounding almost like a baritone Domingo, is firm and well projected as Kyoto, owner of a geisha-house, and Bonaldo Giaiotti brings an authentically dark Italian bass to the role of Iris's father. Full, atmospheric recording.

MASSENET, Jules (1842–1912)

Le Carillon (ballet): complete.

(B) *** Double Decca 444 836-2 (2). SRO, Bonynge – DELIBES: *Coppélia*. ***

Le Carillon was written in the same year as *Werther*. The villains of the story who try to destroy the bells of the title are punished by being miraculously transformed into bronze jaquemarts, fated to continue striking them for ever! The music of this one-act ballet makes a delightful offering – not always as lightweight as one would expect. With his keen rhythmic sense and feeling for colour, Bonynge is outstanding in this repertory, and the 1984 Decca recording is brilliant and colourful. A fine bonus (37 minutes) for a desirable version of Delibes' *Coppélia*, at the cheapest possible price.

Le Cid: ballet suite.

(B) *** Double Decca (ADD) 448 095-2 (2). Nat. PO, Bonynge – DELIBES: *Sylvia* (complete). ***

(M) *** Decca (ADD) 444 110-2. Nat. PO, Bonynge – MEYERBEER: *Les Patineurs* (with DELIBES: *Naïla*, LSO, Bonynge; THOMAS: *Hamlet: Ballet Music* ***).

Over the years, Decca have made a house speciality of recording the ballet music from *Le Cid* and coupling it with Constant Lambert's arrangement of Meyerbeer (*Les Patineurs*). Bonynge's version is the finest yet, with the most seductive orchestral playing, superbly recorded, with the remastering for CD adding to the glitter and colour of Massenet's often witty scoring, and made the more attractive at Double Decca price. For the single-disc reissue in Decca's Ballet Gala series, Delibes' charming *Naïla Intermezzo* (a dainty little valse) and the lively, easily melodic – if less distinctive – ballet from Act IV of Thomas's *Hamlet* have been added, played with characteristic flair.

Piano Concerto in E flat.

*** Hyp. CDA 66897. Coombs, BBC Scottish SO, Ossonce – HAHN: *Piano Concerto in E.* ***

Massenet unexpectedly completed this substantial concerto at the age of sixty. It regularly reveals his love of the keyboard, and in a performance like Stephen Coombs's the result is a delight, the writing full of attractive ideas. That is so, even when in the Slovak dance of the finale the main theme barely skirts banality, providing an extra challenge for Coombs to magic it with sparkling articulation. As in the Hahn concerto – an apt coupling, when it occupies a similar place in that composer's career – Jean-Yves Ossonce is a most sympathetic accompanist, drawing idiomatic playing from the BBC Scottish Symphony, helped by warm, well-balanced sound.

Don Quichotte: 2 Interludes; Scènes alsaciennes; Scènes de féerie; Scènes dramatiques; Scènes pittoresques; La Vierge: The Last Sleep of the Virgin.

(B) **(*) Erato Ultima (ADD) 3484 26999-2 (2). Monte Carlo Op. O, Gardiner.

John Eliot Gardiner secures quite impressively characterized performances. The *Scènes pittoresques* are bright and fresh, the horns tolling in the *Angelus* with resonant impact. The *Scènes alsaciennes* also come off colourfully. The Monte Carlo Orchestra play well enough and the full recording has rather more presence than we remember from its last appearance; it is natural enough, although some ears will seek more sparkle. However the slight excess of resonance disguises any deficiencies, for the wind solos are well taken, and the orchestral response is generally persuasive. But the two discs only play for 45 and 41 minutes respectively, and the Naxos alternative below fits the four best-known suites comfortably on to one.

Fantaisie (for Cello & Orchestra).

*** ASV CDDCA 867. Rolland, BBC PO, Varga – LALO: *Cello Concerto*; SAINT-SAENS: *Cello Concerto No. 1.* ***

Massenet's *Fantaisie for Cello and Orchestra* is music for the sweet-toothed (and none the worse for that), though its ideas are not anywhere near as memorable as those of its two companions on this disc. The Canadian cellist, Sophie Rolland, and the BBC forces under Gilbert Varga play it with total commitment and fervour as if they believe every note. Excellent recording.

Hérodiade (ballet) Suite; Orchestral Suites Nos. 1; 2 (Scènes hongroises); 3 (Scènes dramatiques).

(BB) ** Naxos 8.553124. New Zealand SO, Ossonce.

The ballet suite from *Hérodiade* comes in the final scene of the opera and the five movements are nicely scored, including flutes and harp, delicate dancing strings, a luscious tune in the middle strings, decorated by chirpy woodwind, and a vigorous dance finale. The other orchestral suites are also well worth hearing, offering a further series of sharply memorable vignettes, demonstrating Massenet's ready store of tunes and his charmingly French orchestral palette. The playing of the New Zealand orchestra is first class, polished and vivid, though it is a pity that the microphones are somewhat close. The wind have plenty of colour, but the string tuttis are made to sound a bit tight and fierce.

Orchestral Suite No. 1, Op. 13; Cendrillon (opera): Suite. Esclarmonde (opera): Suite.

** Marco 8.223354. Hong Kong PO, Jean.

The delicate atmosphere of *L'Ile magique* and *Hymenée* from *Esclarmonde*, and the charming *Nocturne* from the *Suite*, Op. 13, is matched by the vigour of the finales from both, the *Marche et Strette* of Op. 13 and *La Chasse*, with its hunting horns in the operatic suite. The charming *Cendrillon* vignettes also have plenty of sparkle. The playing does not find the degree of Beechamesque finesse that makes for totally memorable results in such repertoire, but this remains an enjoyable collection.

Orchestral suites: Scènes alsaciennes; Scènes de féerie; Scènes napolitaines; Scènes pittoresques.

(BB) *** Naxos 8.553125. New Zealand SO, Ossonce.

Massenet's orchestral suites are in essence picture-postcard music, but they include plenty of tunes (perhaps not always first-rate ones) and the scoring has characteristic Gallic charm and colour. Best known are the somewhat ingenuous *Scènes pittoresques* and the *Scènes alsaciennes*. The most touching movement is the beautiful *Sous les tilleuls* ('Under the Lime Trees'), with its wilting dialogue between cello and clarinet, played here with an affectionate finesse worthy of a Beecham. With full, sparkling, yet warmly atmospheric recording, this is a first-class disc in every way. Why pay more?

(i) *Mélodie: Elégie* (arr. Mouton); *Les Erinnyes: Tristesse du soir*; (ii) *Thaïs: Méditation. La Vierge: Le Dernier Sommeil de la Vierge.*

*** Chan. 9765. (i) Dixon; (ii) Torchinsky; RLPO Ch.; BBC PO, Y. P. Tortelier (with Concert: *French Bonbons* ***).

This is Beechamesque material (especially *Le Dernier Sommeil de la Vierge*) and beautifully played and recorded too. It is part of a particularly delectable collection of French music including a number of familiar overtures – see Concerts below.

VOCAL MUSIC

Eve (mysterium in 3 parts).

(BB) ** Arte Nova 74321 58964-2. Geb, Kolczyk, Simos, Steidler, Three Nation Ch., Euregio SO, Faber.

Eve, described as a mysterium, is a compact oratorio lasting just under an hour. Written in 1875, it tells the story of the Fall of Man, bringing echoes of Mendelssohn and Gounod, as well as cross-references to Massenet's operas. The orchestration is often exotic, regularly including the harp, and with the impact of the Fall intensified on fortissimo timpani. The choruses in particular are most attractive, whether lyrical or dramatic. They are very well performed here under the energetic direction of Faber, by a chorus drawn from three nations – Germany, Austria and the Czech Republic. Sadly, the three soloists are all disappointing, singing with unsteady tone. Warmly atmospheric recording. The French text is given but no translation.

OPERA

Chérubin (complete)

✪ *** RCA 09026 60593-2 (2). Von Stade, Ramey, Anderson, Upshaw, Bav. State Op. Ch., Munich RSO, Steinberg.

What Massenet did in this delightful *comédie chantée* of 1903 (he was sixty at the time) was to follow up what happened to Cherubino after the *Marriage of Figaro*. The result is a frothy entertainment, one brimming with ear-tickling ideas, from the dazzlingly witty overture onwards. In this superb RCA recording the cast is both starry and ideal, with June Anderson powerful and flamboyant as the dancer with whom Cherubino has a fling, Dawn Upshaw sweet and pure as Nina, his faithful sweetheart, and Samuel Ramey warm and firm as the Philosopher. Yet finest of all is Frederica von Stade in the title-role. Cherubin is a perky figure, much more self-confident and pushy than in Mozart, master of his own household, though still full of youthful high spirits. What seals this as an exhilarating experience is the conducting of Pinchas Steinberg with the Munich Radio Symphony Orchestra, strong and thrustful yet responsive to the dramatic subtleties, plainly a conductor who should be used more often in recordings. The sound is fresh and atmospheric, bringing out the sparkle and fantasy of the piece.

Cléopâtre (complete).

**(*) Koch/Schwann 3 1032-2 (2). Harries, Streiff, Olmeda, Henry, Maurette, Hacquard, Festival Ch., Nouvel O de Saint-Étienne, Fournillier.

Cléopâtre has much of the easy opulence of a film spectacular. This première recording was taken from a live performance at the Massenet Festival in Saint-Etienne in 1990, with Patrick Fournillier conducting. The cast has no serious weakness, and the two principal roles are splendidly taken, with Didier Henry firm and responsive as Mark Antony and with Kathryn Harries demonstrating what a rich role for a singing actress this Cléopâtre is. Miss Harries with her rich mezzo should be used more on record, when her expressive intensity here in her big solos is magnetic. That is particularly so in the concluding scenes. Antony's death-throes bring first an extended love-duet leading to what becomes a Massenet equivalent of Isolde's *Liebestod*. The Koch live recording is not helped by the dryness of the orchestral sound, though only the brass is seriously affected, and the voices are vividly caught.

Don Quichotte (complete).

*** EMI CDS7 54767-2 (2). Van Dam, Fondary, Berganza, Toulouse Capitole Ch. & O, Plasson.

(i) *Don Quixote* (complete); (ii) *Scènes alsaciennes*.

(M) *** Decca (ADD) 430 636-2 (2). (i) Ghiaurov, Bacquier, Crespin, SRO Ch. & O, Kord; (ii) Nat. PO, Bonynge.

Massenet's operatic adaptation of Cervantes' classic novel gave him his last big success. There is genuine nobility as well as comedy in the portrait of the knight, and that is well caught here by Ghiaurov, who refuses to exaggerate the characterization. Bacquier makes a delightful Sancho Panza, but it is Régine Crespin as a comically mature Dulcinée, who provides the most characterful singing, flawed vocally but commandingly positive. Kazimierz Kord directs the Suisse Romande Orchestra in a performance that is zestful and electrifying, and the recording is outstandingly clear and atmospheric.

Michel Plasson conducts a sumptuous account of Massenet's charming Cervantes-based opera, with José van Dam singing gloriously as the Don, producing consistently firm and velvety tone. Alain Fondary as Sancho Panza is equally strong and firm vocally, shadowing and matching his master instead of contrasting, never indulging in exaggeratedly comic effects. Teresa Berganza as Dulcinée adds to the sensuousness of the performance, with the Toulouse acoustic bringing out the richness and beauty of Massenet's orchestral writing. No one will be disappointed, but the 1977 Decca set still has clear advantages. The Decca analogue sound is more clearly focused than the EMI digital, with the chorus full and immediate and with stage effects creating a vivid atmosphere. At mid-price the Decca set also comes with an attractive fill-up, the *Scènes alsaciennes*, brightly and colourfully presented by Bonynge and the National Philharmonic Orchestra.

Esclarmonde (complete).

(M) *** Decca (ADD) 425 651-2 (3). Sutherland, Aragall, Tourangeau, Davies, Grant, Alldis Ch., Nat. PO, Bonynge.

**(*) Koch Schwann 3-1269-2 (3). Gavazzeni-Daviola,

Sempere, Parraguin, Tréguier, Courtis, Gabelle, Massenet Festival Ch., Budapest Liszt SO, Fournillier.

Joan Sutherland is the obvious diva to encompass the demands of great range, great power and brilliant coloratura of the central role of *Esclarmonde*, and her performance is in its way as powerful as it is in Puccini's last opera. Aragall proves an excellent tenor, sweet of tone and intelligent, and the other parts are well taken too. Richard Bonynge draws passionate singing and playing from chorus and orchestra, and the recording has both atmosphere and spectacle to match the story, based on a medieval romance involving song-contests and necromancy.

Patrick Fournillier as a specialist interpreter of this composer persuades singers and players alike to perform with sympathy for the Massenet idiom. The Italian soprano, Denia Gavazzeni-Daviola, with a voice bright and clear at the top but which has fair weight down below, tackles here the weightiest of the Massenet roles and, though she cannot match Sutherland in the warmth and weight of her singing in this music, the element of vulnerability in the princess with magic powers is more readily conveyed than with Sutherland. The Spaniard, José Sempere, sings freshly and clearly as the hero, Roland, if less ringingly and with less warmth than Giacomo Aragall, the tenor who sings opposite Sutherland on her Decca recording. Reissued on CD at mid-price, that remains the first recommendation.

Grisélidis (complete).

*** Koch Schwann 3-1270-2. Command, Viala, Larcher, Desnoues, Courtis, Henry, Treguier, Sieyès, Lyon Ch., Franz Liszt SO of Budapest, Fournillier.

To suggest the medieval atmosphere and the purity of the heroine, Grisélidis, Massenet exceptionally dallies with modal writing, if not very consistently, and the introduction of the Devil as a comic figure, henpecked by his wife, gets in the way of one taking the threat to Grisélidis and her virtue seriously. Michèle Command sings warmly as the heroine and Jean-Luc Viala sings splendidly in the incidental tenor role of the shepherd, Alain, in love with Grisélidis, but pushed aside by the Marquis, who sweeps her off her feet, only to prove an over-possessive husband. As the Marquis, Didier Henry is in rather gritty voice, and it is a pity that Jean-Philippe Courtis does not bring out the comedy of the Devil's role more positively, though he sings well enough. Clear, generally well-balanced 1992 'live' recording.

Hérodiade (complete).

*** EMI CDC5 55378-2 (3). Studer, Denize, Heppner, Hampson, Van Dam, Capitole Toulouse Ch. & O, Plasson.

Massenet's opera about Salome and John the Baptist, completed in 1880, has little in common with either the Bible story or the violent Strauss opera based on Oscar Wilde's play, and the final scene, so far from involving Salome in asking for John's head, has an ecstatic duet for them both, 'hymning the chaste flame of their immortal love' – as the EMI synopsis graphically puts it. When John is executed, Salome then kills herself. What matters is that the opera offers five fat parts for well-contrasted voices.

Michel Plasson's studio recording offers well-balanced sound, opulent and firmly focused. His text is complete, using the final and fullest version of a work that Massenet revised several times. As Hérodiade herself, Nadine Denize sings with gloriously rich, firm tone, and Thomas Hampson's portrait of Hérode could hardly be richer either vocally or dramatically, with words brought out vividly. It would be hard to imagine a finer Phanuel than José van Dam, with his well-contrasted bass-baritone incisive in attack. As for Cheryl Studer as Salome, she has rarely sung with such expressive range and beauty of tone, with words crystal-clear. Sam Heppner as Jean confirms in his clear, firmly focused delivery earlier impressions of his development as a genuine heroic tenor with few rivals today. There are first-rate singers too in the small roles, and the Toulouse orchestra plays with glowing warmth and intensity, helped by the acoustic of the Halle-aux-Grains. A warmly enjoyable set from first to last, admirably filling a major gap in the catalogue.

Manon (complete).

(N) (***) Testament mono SBT 3203 (3) Los Angeles, Legay, Dens, Paris Opéra-Comique O, Monteux – BERLIOZ: *Les Nuits d'été*; DEBUSSY: *La Demoiselle élue*. (***)

**(*) EMI CDC7 49610-2. Cotrubas, Kraus, Quilico, Van Dam, Toulouse Capitole Ch. & O, Plasson.

(B) (**) Naxos mono 8.110003/5 (3). Sayao, Rayner, Bonelli, Metropolitan Chro. & O, Abravanel.

No one has recorded the role of Manon in Massenet's opera quite so bewitchingly as Victoria de los Angeles in this historic EMI recording of 1955, girlishly provocative at the start, conveying tragic depth later. The voice is at its most golden, and this vivid new transfer from Testament gives the mono sound extra warmth and immediacy. Henri Legay as Des Grieux also sings with honeyed tones, a believable young lover ensnared, and Pierre Monteux in one of his rare opera recordings is masterly in his timing and phrasing. As a splendid bonus you also have RCA recordings of Berlioz and Debussy, similarly persuasive, recorded in Boston also in 1955.

The Plasson Toulouse set is a stylish performance, well characterized and well sung. Ileana Cotrubas is a charming Manon, more tender and vulnerable than De los Angeles was on the earlier mono set but not so golden-toned and with a more limited development of character, from the girlish chatterbox to the dying victim. Alfredo Kraus betrays some signs of age, but his is a finely detailed and subtle reading. Louis Quilico has a delightfully light touch as Lescaut, and José Van Dam is a superb Comte Des Grieux. The warm reverberation of the Toulouse studio is well controlled to give bloom to the voices, and, although Plasson is rougher with the score than Monteux was on an older mono version, his feeling for French idiom is very good.

Taken from an NBC broadcast in 1937, the Naxos historic issue marked the début of the Brazilian, Bidu Sayao, whose light, bright soprano with a hint of rapid flutter in the tone exactly matches the role, perfectly conveying the provocative as well as the tender side of the heroine, totally at home in the French idiom. The American tenor, Sydney Rayner, makes a virile hero, using his rather baritonal voice stylishly if with occasional heaviness. Bonelli makes an excellent Lescaut too, but it is Maurice Abravanel, then in charge of the French repertory at the Met., who provides the impetus, drawing brilliant playing from the orchestra, recessed as it is behind the clearly focused voices.

La Navarraise (complete).

(M) *** RCA (ADD) 74321 50167-2. Horne, Domingo, Milnes, Zaccaria, Bacquier, Davies, Amb. Op. Ch., LSO, Lewis.

La Navarraise is a cross between Carmen and Cavalleria rusticana, with a touch of Il tabarro. To earn her dowry before marrying her beloved, the intrepid heroine penetrates the enemy lines in the Carlist wars and for money assassinates the royalist general's direct adversary. Following a misunderstanding, the hero follows her and is mortally wounded. In despair she promptly goes mad – a great deal of story for so short a piece. It says much for Massenet's dramatic powers that he makes the result as convincing as he does, and the score is full of splendid, atmospheric effects. Massenet originally had a heavyweight, 'Carmen' voice in mind, and Marilyn Horne seems an apt choice for the role of heroine. Even if her upper register is not as firm as it was, it remains an appealing performance, and Domingo is characteristically rich-toned. Henry Lewis conducts with a sense of the work's atmosphere and grandeur, and this is an opera ideally suited to the gramophone. The recording, made at Walthamstow in 1975, is appropriately spacious.

Le Roi de Lahore (complete).

✿ (M) *** Decca 433 851-2 (2). Sutherland, Lima, Milnes, Ghiaurov, Morris, Tourangeau, L. Voices, Nat. PO, Bonynge.

The characters in Le Roi de Lahore may be stock figures out of a mystic fairytale, but in the vigour of his treatment Massenet makes the result red-blooded in an Italianate way. This vivid performance under Bonynge includes passages added for Italy, notably a superb set-piece aria which challenges Sutherland to some of her finest singing. Sutherland may not be a natural for the role of the innocent young priestess, but she makes it a magnificent vehicle with its lyric, dramatic and coloratura demands. Luis Lima as the King is somewhat strained by the high tessitura, but his is a ringing tenor, clean of attack. Sherrill Milnes as the heroine's wicked uncle sounds even more Italianate, rolling his 'r's ferociously; but high melodrama is apt, and with digital recording of demonstration splendour and fine perspective this shameless example of operatic hokum could not be presented more persuasively on CD.

Thaïs (complete).

(M) ** EMI CMS5 65479-2 (2). Sills, Milnes, Gedda, Van Allan, John Alldis Ch., New Philh. O, Maazel.

Thaïs is an exotic period-piece, set in Egypt in the early Christian era. Sentimental as the plot is, it inspired Massenet to some of his characteristically mellifluous writing, with atmospheric choruses and sumptuous orchestration. Maazel's conducting is crisply dramatic (and he plays the violin solo himself most tastefully in the famous Meditation). The casting is good, except for the heroine. Beverly Sills has

a bright, almost brittle voice, and here it sounds neither seductive nor idiomatic. She is at her best as the reformed Thaïs in the later scenes. Sherrill Milnes is a powerful but conventional Athanaël, and, though Nicolai Gedda as Nicias sings with his usual intelligence, it is not a young enough voice for the role. A good, warm recording, well transferred on to CD, and with a complete text and translation.

Thérèse (complete).

*** Decca (ADD) 448 173-2. Tourangeau, R. Davies, Quilico, Linden Singers, New Philh. O, Bonynge.

This story of the French Revolution, depicting a conflict of love and loyalty, has so many parallels with Puccini's Tosca and Giordano's Andrea Chénier of the previous decade that it is surprising Massenet chose it. The result was this passionate score, compressed and intense, lacking only the last degree of memorability in the melodies that make Massenet's finest operas so gripping. Bonynge is a splendid advocate, amply proving how taut and atmospheric the writing is. There is some first-rate singing from the three principals. The vivid vintage recording is excellent, and the reissue now includes a libretto with a new translation.

Werther (complete).

*** EMI CDS5 56820-2 (2). Alagna, Gheorghiu, Hampson, Petibon, Tiffin School Children's Ch., LSO, Pappano.

*** Ph. 416 654-2 (2). Carreras, Von Stade, Allen, Buchanan, Lloyd, Children's Ch., ROHCG O, C. Davis.

*** RCA 74321 58224-2 (2). Vargas, Kasarova, Schaldenbrand, Kotoski, Berlin Knabenchor & Deutsche SO, Jurowski.

(M) *** Orfeo C4 64972 (2). Domingo, Fassbaender, Seibel, Nöcker, Bav. State Op. Ch., Bav. State O, López-Cobos.

*** Erato 0630 17790-2 (2). Hadley, Von Otter, Upshaw, Théruel, Lyon Opera Ch. & O, Nagano.

(M) **(*) EMI (ADD) CMS7 63973-2 (2). Gedda, De los Angeles, Mesplé, Soyer, Voix d'Enfants de la Maîtrise de l'ORTF, O de Paris, Prêtre.

It makes a formidable line-up to have the starry husband-and-wife team of Roberto Alagna and Angela Gheorghiu joined by the ever-responsive Antonio Pappano. Though Alagna with his French background is an ideal choice for Werther himself, Gheorghiu with her bright soprano is a less obvious one for the role of the heroine, Charlotte, normally given to a mezzo. But as a magnetic actress she conveys an extra tenderness and vulnerability, with no lack of weight in such a solo as Laisse couler mes larmes in Act III. Alagna makes a characterful Werther, using his distinctive tone-colours most sensitively, with Thomas Hampson outstanding as Albert and Patricia Petibon a sweet-toned Sophie. As in Puccini Pappano is subtle as well as powerful, using rubato idiomatically and with refinement to heighten the drama and point the moments of climax. Good warm sound.

Sir Colin Davis has rarely directed a more sensitive or more warmly expressive performance on record than his account of Werther, based on a stage production at Covent Garden. Frederica von Stade makes an enchanting Charlotte. Carreras uses a naturally beautiful voice freshly and sensitively. Thomas Allen as Charlotte's husband Albert and

Isobel Buchanan as Sophie, her sister, are excellent, too. The CD transfer on to a pair of discs has been highly successful, with a single serious reservation: the break between the two CDs is badly placed in the middle of a key scene between Werther and Charlotte, just before *Ah! qu'il est loin ce jour!*

The RCA set makes the perfect alternative to the EMI version. Here is casting of the two principals that in every way is centrally satisfying. With her vibrant mezzo, Vesselina Kasarova is a natural choice for Charlotte, full and intense at the big moments, even if the vibrancy, as caught by the microphone, turns into unevenness under pressure. Ramon Vargas with his clear, precise tenor is the perfect hero here. He may not be as distinctive as Alagna, but he sings such a solo as *Pourquoi me reveiller* with greater purity, shading the voice down most sensitively. The other principals are not so strongly cast, with Dawn Kotoski rather shrill as Sophie, but Jurowski's conducting is warm and dramatic, even if it lacks the distinctive subtleties of Pappano. The sound is brilliant and clear.

At mid-price the Bavarian Radio recording on Orfeo makes an excellent alternative choice, with Placido Domingo an ardent hero. Opposite him as Charlotte is Brigitte Fassbaender in peak form, rich and firm as well as passionately expressive. Marianne Seibel and Hans Günter Nöcker are first rate too, as Sophie and Albert. López-Cobos is an ardently red-blooded interpreter of Massenet's, and though, in this live recording, stage noises are obtrusive at times and balances are not always perfect, they hardly detract from the impact of the whole.

With an excellent cast, Kent Nagano conducts his Lyon Opera team in a warm, well-paced reading. With the orchestra backwardly placed, this is a relatively intimate performance, with the two principals, Jerry Hadley and Anne-Sofie von Otter, sounding youthful and characterizing well, with neurotic tensions implied. Dawn Upshaw is excellent too as a characterful Sophie.

Victoria de los Angeles's golden tones, which convey pathos so beautifully, are ideally suited to Massenet's gentle melodies and, though she is recorded too closely (closer than the other soloists), she makes an intensely appealing heroine. Gedda makes an intelligent romantic hero, though Prêtre's direction could be subtler.

Werther (complete; in English).

(M) *** Chan. 3033 (2). Brecknock, Baker, Wheatley, Blackburn, Roberts, Tomlinson, ENO Ch. & O, Mackerras.

Recorded live at the Coliseum in 1977 in vividly atmospheric sound, full of presence, Sir Charles Mackerras's version offers an exceptionally warm reading in English which is strong in dramatic thrust. The cast too is exceptionally strong, with John Brecknock clear, fresh and firm in the title role. Yet it is the performance of Janet Baker as Charlotte that provides the linchpin, rising to great heights in the tragedy of Act IV. This is Dame Janet at her very finest, singing with heartfelt fervour, using the full tonal range of her unique voice, always fresh and clear in attack. Joy Roberts is a bright, agile Sophie, and the other male singers can hardly be faulted. Remarkably, this was taken from a single performance, not edited from a series. Voices are close

enough for every word of Norman Tucker's excellent translation to be heard.

MATHIAS, William (1934–92)

(i) *Clarinet Concerto;* (ii) *Harp Concerto;* (iii) *Piano Concerto No. 3.*

*** Lyrita (ADD) SRCD 325. (i) De Peyer; (ii) Ellis; (iii) Katin; LSO or New Philh. O, Atherton.

Helped by vividly immediate recording, the *Clarinet Concerto* with its clean-cut, memorable themes sparks off an inspired performance from Gervase de Peyer, not just in the lively outer movements, but in the poignant *Lento espressivo* in the middle. The *Harp Concerto* (1970) is less outward-going, but it prompts Mathias to create evocative, shimmering textures, very characteristic of him. The harp, superbly played by the dedicatee, Osian Ellis, is set alongside exotic percussion, with the finale a snappy jig that delightfully keeps tripping over its feet. In the *Piano Concerto No. 3* of 1968 the outer movements bring jazzily syncopated writing, like Walton with a difference, here incisively played by Peter Katin. They frame an atmospheric central *Adagio* with echoes of Bartókian 'night music', like Bartók with a difference.

(i; ii) *Dance Overture, Op. 16;* (iii; ii) *Divertimento for String Orchestra, Op. 7;* (i; ii) *Invocation & Dance, Op. 17;* (iv; ii) 'Landscapes of the Mind': Laudi, Op. 62; Vistas, Op. 69. (iii; ii) *Prelude, Aria & Finale for String Orchestra, Op. 25;* (v) *Sinfonietta, Op. 34.*

*** Lyrita (ADD) SRCD 328. (i) LSO; (ii) Atherton; (iii) ECO; (iv) New Philh. O; (v) Nat. Youth O of Wales, Davison.

As this collection readily bears out, William Mathias was a composer of genuine talent, versatile as well as inventive. The joyful *Dance Overture* is vividly scored, rather after the manner of Malcolm Arnold, and the *Invocation and Dance* has genuine spontaneity. Undoubtedly the two most remarkable works here are the two pieces described by their composer as 'Landscapes of the mind'. *Laudi*, written in 1973, a 'landscape of the spirit', opens with temple bells and then contrasts bold cross-rhythms with gently voluptuous string sonorities, closing with a serene yet sensuous benediction, somewhat after the manner of Messiaen. The evocative *Vistas* was inspired by the composer's visit to the USA in 1975. Here an Ivesian influence is unmistakable. Performances throughout are of the highest calibre with Atherton at his most perceptive, and the recordings (engineered by Decca for the most part) are outstanding.

Summer Dances; Soundings.

*** Nim. NI 5466. Fine Arts Brass Ens. – HODDINNOTT: *Chorales, Variants & Fanfares* etc. ***

Mathias's seven *Summer Dances* (1990) bring witty rhythmic quirkiness but, if the writing is consistently skilful, the invention is at times rather conventional. His *Soundings* (commissioned by the Philip Jones Brass and first performed in 1988) is much more entertaining with its kinky *March* (its humour agreeably lugubrious), a darkly nostalgic *Elegy* and a catchy but unpredictable final *Capriccio*. Fine playing and splendid recording in an ideal acoustic that brings plenty of sonority but provides firmly focused detail.

String Quartets Nos. 1–3.

*** Metier MSVCD 92005. Medea Qt.

Spanning the years 1967–86, Mathias's three string quartets make a fine sequence, illuminating his whole achievement. The *First Quartet*, in a single 20-minute movement, pithily argued, has a Stravinskian directness. The idiom brings momentary echoes of Britten, but might best be described as music by a composer who has thoroughly digested the Bartók quartets. The *Second Quartet* dates from 1980–81, and in each of its four compact movements Mathias echoes medieval music in different ways. The result is stylistically as individual as the *First Quartet*, never sounding merely derivative. The *Third Quartet*, dating from 1986, brings together elements of both the earlier works, with the first of its three movements developing from a deceptively light opening into a taut, large-scale structure comparable with the *Quartet No. 1*. All three quartets, very well recorded, are outstandingly well performed by the young Medea Quartet, formed as recently as 1991 at the Royal Academy of Music.

Wind Quintet.

*** Crystal CD 750. Westwood Wind Quintet – CARLSSON: *Nightwings*; LIGETI: *Bagatelles*; BARBER: *Summer Music*. ***

Of the five movements of this spirited *Quintet* the Scherzo is particularly felicitous and there is a rather beautiful *Elegy*. The playing of the Westwood Wind Quintet is highly expert and committed, and the recording is very good indeed.

Lux aeterna, Op. 88.

*** Chan. 8695. Lott, Cable, P. Walker, Bach Ch., St George's Chapel Ch., Windsor, LSO, Willcocks; Scott (organ).

Just as Britten in the *War Requiem* contrasted different planes of expression with Latin liturgy set against Wilfred Owen poems, so Mathias contrasts the full choir singing Latin against the boys' choir singing carol-like Marian anthems, and in turn against the three soloists, who sing three arias and a trio to the mystical poems of St John of the Cross. Overall, the confidence of the writing makes the work far more than derivative, an attractively approachable and colourful piece, full of memorable ideas, especially in this excellent performance, beautifully sung and played and atmospherically balanced.

Missa brevis; Rex gloriae; Anthems: Ad majorem Dei gloriam; Angelus; Alleluia; Doctrine of Wisdom; Except the Lord build the house; Hodie Christus natus est; The Lord is my Shepherd; Veni sancte spiritus.

✪ *** Paraclete Press GDCD 026. Glori Dei Cantores, Patterson.

This splendidly sung programme comes from Glori Dei Cantores, a 44-voice choir from Cape Cod, Massachusetts, directed by Elizabeth Patterson. They have the advantage of the superb acoustics of the Methuan Music Hall and the use of its famous organ, which Mathias uses very orchestrally

– and often in the *Missa brevis* to provide 'instrumental' obbligatos. The thrilling opening of *Sanctus* establishes this as the emotional kernel of the work, with the organ then creating darker woodwind colours to introduce the very touching *Agnus Dei*. The anthems are hardly less individual and inspired. Trumpets and percussion annnounce the exultant setting of *Except the Lord build the house* while the celestial *Angelus* brings a surprisingly effective use of the piano. *The Lord is my shepherd* is very Welsh in feeling, a passionate declaration of faith; *The Doctrine of Wisdom* again uses the organ very atmospherically, and its melodic simplicity is telling. With singing of such commitment and intensity, yet exploiting the widest range of dynamics, every piece here is memorable. Mathias could hardly have hoped for more persuasive advocacy, nor finer recording. If you have difficulty in getting this disc the Choir's web-site address is: www.paraclete-press.com.

MATTEIS, Nicola (c. 1640–c. 1714)

Ayres for the Violin, Book I: Suite in C min.; Book II: Suite in G min.; Book IV: Suites in A; C; G min.; D min.

(N) (BB) *** HM HCX 3957067. Arcadian Academy.

Not a great deal is known about Nicola Matteis. Born in Naples, he apparently came to England in 1670 and later had considerable success as a solo violinist/guitar player, then married a wealthy widow and 'took a great house' in Norfolk. His *Suites of Ayres for the Violin* date from the 1670s and 1680s and are either solo or trio sonatas. Each suite is in essence a set of variations; for the same musical material undergoes many melodic and rhythmic transformations with diverting results. In every case there is an opening *Preludio*; then follows a series of brief vignettes exploiting various dance movements – Giga, Minuet, Ricercata, Corrent, Sarabanda – plus slow and fast sections, grounds, fugues and *Arie amarosi*. McGegan and his Arcadian Players respond with spontaneous vitality and revel in the music's undoubted fantasy. The recording although a bit edgy on top is otherwise vivid.

MAUNDER, John (1858–1920)

Olivet to Calvary (cantata).

(B) **(*) CfP (ADD) CD-CFP 4619. Mitchinson, Harvey, Guildford Cathedral Ch., Rose; Morse (organ).

It is easy to be patronizing about music like this but, provided one accepts the conventions of style in which it is composed, the music is effective and often moving. The performance has an attractive simplicity and genuine eloquence. Frederick Harvey is particularly moving at the actual moment of Christ's death; in a passage that, insensitively handled, could be positively embarrassing, he creates a magical, hushed intensity. The choir sing beautifully, and in the gentler, lyrical writing (the semi-chorus *O Thou whose sweet compassion*, for example) sentimentality is skilfully avoided. The 1964 recording is first class in every way, and it has been admirably transferred to CD.

MAW, Nicholas (born 1935)

Violin Concerto (1993).

*** Sony SK 62856. Bell, LPO, Norrington.

Maw here excels himself in a work specifically written for Joshua Bell, who responds superbly with playing of heartfelt warmth as well as brilliance. The opening *Moderato* movement has something of the fervour of the Walton *Violin Concerto*, with Maw firmly establishing his personal approach to tonality in seamless lyricism, leading up to a grinding climax. Coming second, the Scherzo is the longest movement, with Walton again brought to mind in the spiky brilliance, set against a central section with a ripe horn solo. The third movement, *Romanza*, is then a calm interlude before the carefree surging thrust of the finale, leading to a bravura conclusion, not the slow fade so often favoured latterly by concerto composers. Roger Norrington and the LPO are strong and sympathetic partners, with warm, full recording to match.

Flute Quartet: Night Thoughts for Solo Flute; (i) Roman Canticle for Mezzo-Soprano, Flute, Viola and Harp.

*** Koch 37355-2H1. Auréole Trio (i) Nessinger –
     R. R. BENNET: *Sonata after Syrinx etc.****

All these Maw pieces come from the 1980s and have been recorded before. The *Roman Canticle* for flute, viola and harp is sung here by a mezzo-soprano rather than a baritone. She is well balanced here and not too forward in the aural picture. In the inventive *Flute Quartet* there should ideally be a little more space round the players; the flautist is a bit upfront. However this should not put off collectors interested in this fine composer.

(i) Flute Quartet; (ii) Piano Trio.

*** ASV CDDCA 920. Monticello Trio; with (i) Pearce;
     (ii) Coletti.

Commissioned by the Koussevitzky Foundation, the *Piano Trio* was written in 1991 for the Monticello Trio, who here record it in a warmly expressive performance, fiery where necessary. The *Flute Quartet* of 1981 was written for Judith Pearce of the Nash Ensemble, who plays it most beautifully here; it is another fine example of Maw's broad romanticism, powerful and lyrical, often sensuous, approachable yet clearly contemporary. Though the central slow movement opens as a fugue, it develops emotionally to become an atmospheric nocturne, leading to a scurrying finale. Excellent performances and sound.

MAXWELL DAVIES, Peter
(born 1934)

Violin Concerto.

(M) *** Sony SMK 64506. Stern, RPO, Previn – BARBER:
     Violin Concerto. ***

Maxwell Davies wrote this massive *Violin Concerto* specifically with Isaac Stern in mind. The composer was inspired to draw on a more warmly lyrical side that he has displayed rarely. Davies claims to have been influenced by his favourite violin concerto, Mendelssohn's, but there is little of Mendelssohnian lightness and fantasy here; for all its beauties, this is a work which has a tendency to middle-aged spread, not nearly as taut in expression as the Walton. Stern, understandably, seems less completely involved here than in the inspired Barber coupling.

Sinfonia; Sinfonia concertante.

(M) *** Unicorn UKCD 2026. SCO, composer.

In his *Sinfonia* of 1962 Peter Maxwell Davies took as his inspiration Monteverdi's *Vespers* of 1610, and the dedication in this music, beautifully played by the Scottish Chamber Orchestra under the composer, is plain from first to last. The *Sinfonia Concertante* is a much more extrovert piece for strings plus solo wind quintet and timpani. In idiom this is hardly at all neo-classical and, more than usual, the composer evokes romantic images, as in the lovely close of the first movement. Virtuoso playing from the Scottish principals, not least the horn. Well-balanced recording.

CHAMBER MUSIC

Ave maris stella; Image, Reflection, Shadow; (i) Runes from a Holy Island.

(M) *** Unicorn (ADD) UKCD 2038. Fires of London, (i) cond.
     composer.

This is a CD compilation of key Maxwell Davies works. *Ave maris stella*, essentially elegiac, finds the composer at his most severe and demanding. The second piece, *Image, Reflection, Shadow*, is a kind of sequel. *Runes*, conducted by the composer, is much shorter yet just as intense in its rapt slowness. Ideal performances, well recorded, from the group for which all this music was written.

Renaissance and Baroque Realisations: PURCELL: *Fantasia & 2 Pavans; Fantasia upon One Note.* BACH: *Well-tempered Clavier: Preludes & Fugues in C sharp major & min. (i)* GESUALDO: *Tenebrae super Gesualdo.* DUNSTABLE: *Veni sancte – Veni creator spiritus.* KINLOCH: *His Fantaisie. 3 Early Scottish Motets.*

(M) *** Unicorn (ADD) UKCD 2044. Fires of London, (i) with
     Thomas; composer.

These pieces mainly represent the composer in the 1960s abrasively distorting into foxtrot and other dance rhythms pieces by Purcell, Bach, Dunstable and others. It is like painting a moustache on the Mona Lisa, only more fun.

(i) Vesalii Icones; The Bairns of Brugh; Runes from a Holy Island.

(M) *** Unicorn ADD/Dig. UKCD 2068. (i) Ward Clarke, Fires
     of London, composer.

Maxwell Davies has the great quality of presenting strikingly memorable visions, and *Vesalii Icones* is certainly one, an extraordinary cello solo with comment from a chamber group. It was originally written to accompany a solo dancer in a fourteen-fold sequence, each dance based on one of the horrifying anatomical drawings of Vesalius (1543) and each representing one of the Stations of the Cross. Characteristically, the composer has moments not only of biting pain and tender compassion but also of deliberate shock tactics – notably when the risen Christ turns out to be Antichrist and is represented by a jaunty fox-trot. This is difficult music, but the emotional landmarks are plain from the start, and that is a good sign of enduring quality. Jennifer Ward Clarke plays superbly, and so do the Fires of London, conducted by the composer. The 1970 recording is excellent. The two shorter pieces, digitally recorded more than a decade later, make a valuable fill-up, *The Bairns of Brugh* a tender lament (viola over marimba) and *Runes* a group of brief epigrams.

OPERA

The Martyrdom of St Magnus.

*** Unicorn DKPCD 9100. Dives, Gillett, Thomson, Morris, Thomas, Scottish Chamber Op. Ens., Rafferty.

With Gregorian chant providing an underlying basis of argument, Davies has here simplified his regular idiom. The musical argument of each of the nine compact scenes is summarized in the interludes which follow. The story is baldly but movingly presented, with St Magnus translated to the present century as a concentration camp victim, finally killed by his captors. Outstanding among the soloists is the tenor, Christopher Gillett, taking among other roles that of the Prisoner (or saint).

MAYER, Emilie (1812–83)

String Quartet in G min., Op. 14.

*** CPO 999 679-2. Basle Erato Qt – Fanny MENDELSSOHN: *String Quartet*; SIRMEN: *Quartets Nos. 2–3.* ***

We know comparatively little about Emilie Mayer. Op. 14 was the only string quartet included in her printed works and it was evidently valued, and rightly so. It is an ambitious, well-crafted work, romantic in feeling, with appealing ideas – the extended first movement opens with an engaging dialogue between violin and cello. The fine slow movement touchingly introduces the chorale, *Wer nur den lieben Gott lässt walten*, over a pizzicato accompaniment, before the reprise of the serene main theme. The busy finale has a Mendelssohnian lightness of touch, but overall the music has genuine individuality. The performance here is highly persuasive and naturally recorded.

MAYERL, Billy (1902–59)

Aquarium Suite; Autumn Crocus; Bats in the Belfry; Four Aces Suite: Ace of Clubs; Ace of Spades. 3 Dances in Syncopation, Op. 73; Green Tulips; Hollyhock; Hop-o'-my-thumb; Jill All Alone; Mistletoe; Parade of the Sandwich-board Men; Sweet William; White Heather.

*** Chan. 8848. Parkin.

Eric Parkin obviously enjoys this repertoire and plays the music with much sympathy and vivacious rhythmic freedom. His programme is well chosen to suit his own approach to Mayerl's repertoire, and this Chandos record is certainly very enjoyable as he is very well treated by the recording engineers.

MAYR, Giovanni (1763–1845)

Overtures: Adelasia e Aleramo; Alonso e Cora; Ginrevra di Scozia; Medea in Corinto; La rosa bianca e la rosa rossa; Il segreto; Sisara; Un pazzo ne fa cento; I virtuosi a teatro.

(N) **(*) Warner Fonit 8573 87134-2. O Stabile di Begamo, Renzetti.

This delightful collection of overtures is a real find. They are very Rossini-ish in character, and if Mayr's tuttis are more conventional and his manipulation of key changes less witty than with Rossini, the music itself is full of charming ideas and felicitous scoring. *Adelasia e Aleramo* is one of the most striking, opening with a fully scored melody in 6/8, after which the main string theme soon leads to a piquant march, reminiscent of Auber, which is introduced by a solo violin.

Sisara (which begins the programme) immediately brings a cute secondary theme on the strings and the jocular main theme of *Un pazzo ne fa cento* leads to a similarly dainty secondary idea. *Il segreto*, after a grand beginning, relents immediately with charming writing for the woodwind leading to a virtuoso bassoon solo.

These three overtures are all four-minute pieces, but the others are rather more ambitious, and still remarkably inventive. *Alonso e Cora* opens grandly and is more rumbustious than the rest, including dramatic timpani rolls, but still has an elegant secondary tune, while *La rosa bianca e la rosa rossa* brings pizzicati and a charming woodwind introduction leading to a succession of felicitous themes, with a rollicking clarinet solo as its highlight. The performances here by a modest-sized orchestra, using modern instruments, are nicely turned and quite well recorded. This is a disc with which to quiz your friends about the composer: they will almost certainly guess wrongly.

Medea in Corinto: highlights.

(N) *** Opera Rara ORR 215. Eaglen, Ford, Giménez, Miles, Kenny, Philh. O, Parry.

Recorded complete by Opera Rara in 1993, Mayr's Medea opera deserves to be more widely known, and this generous 76-minute selection of the highspots involving the heroine is very welcome. Since 1993 Jane Eaglen's international career has blossomed, not least on disc, but this relatively early recording reveals the voice at its freshest and firmest, with the big dramatic qualities that have made her reputation already in place. It is good to have not just the big solo numbers, but substantial sequences like the finale to Act 1, with excellent support from the other soloists, including the two fine high tenors Bruce Ford and Raul Gimenez. As ever, David Parry draws warmly idiomatic playing from the Philharmonia, with full, well-balanced recording. Unlike most Opera Rara issues, this one does not provide texts, only a summary of plot for each item.

MAZZOCCHI, Domenico

(c. 1592–1665)

Sacrae concertationes: *Concilio de' farisei;* (i–v) *Dialogo della cantica. Dialogo della maddalena; Dialogo dell'apocalisse; Dialogo di Lazaro;* (i; iv; v) *Gaudebunt labia mea; Jesu, dulcis memoria. Lamento di David.* (i; iii) *Miseris omnium, Domine;* (i; ii; v) *Peccantem me quotidie. Vide, Domine, afflictionem nostram.*

(M) *** HM (ADD) HMT 7901357. (i) Kiehr; (ii) Borden; (iii) Scholl; (iv) Türk; (v) Messthaler. Netherlands Chamber Ch., Jacobs, with Rousset, Swarts, Schröder.

Domenico Mazzocchi almost certainly studied music in Rome, and the present *Sacred Concertantes* form part of his last work to be published in 1664 though probably dating from much earlier. Whether writing for soloists, solo groups, chorus or a combination of them all, his part-writing is blended and interwoven with skill, and his invention is of high quality. His music includes deeply expressive solo melismas – as in the lovely *Peccantem me quotidie* ('Since daily I sin') – or chordal writing (*Jesu, dulcis memoria*), or both (the deeply touching *Dialogo della Maddalena*) alternated with bursts of Italianate exuberance. The *Lamento di David* has a remarkable closing section which includes all these features. Performances here are wonderfully sympathetic. The soloists include outstanding contributions from Maria Cristina Kiehr and the bass, Ulrich Messthaler, who has some splendidly resonant low notes to sing, while we should not underpraise the other members of the solo team here, or the excellent choir, admirably accompanied by a continuo led by Christophe Rousset, and directed very persuasively indeed by René Jacobs. The recording, too, is first class.

MEDTNER, Nikolai (1880–1951)

(i) *Piano Concertos Nos. 1 in C min., Op. 33; 2 in C min., Op. 50; 3 in E min. (Ballade), Op. 60.* (Piano) *Sonata-ballade in F sharp, Op. 27.*

*** Chan. 9040 (2). Tozer; (i) LPO, Järvi.

(i) *Piano Concerto No. 1; Sonata-ballade.*

*** Chan. 9038. Tozer, (i) LPO, Järvi.

(i) *Piano Concerto No. 1;* (ii) *Piano Quintet in C, Op. posth.*

**(*) Hyp. CDA 66744. Alexeev, with (i) BBC SO, Lazarev; (ii) New Budapest Qt.

Piano Concertos Nos. 1; 3.

(BB) *** Naxos 8.553359. Scherbakov, Moscow SO, Ziva.

(i) *Piano Concerto No. 2;* (ii) *Piano Quintet in C.*

(BB) *** Naxos 8.553390. Scherbakov, with (i) Moscow SO, Golovschin; (ii) Danel, Tedla, Bourová, Pudhoransk.

Piano Concertos Nos. 2–3.

*** Hyp. CDA 66580. Demidenko, BBC Scottish SO, Maksymiuk.

*** Chan. 9039. Tozer, LPO, Järvi.

Piano Concertos Nos. 2–3; Arabesque in A min., Op. 7/2; Tale in F min., Op. 26/3.

(***) Testament mono SBT 1027. Composer, Philh. O, Dobrowen.

Konstantin Scherbakov is highly sympathetic and offers very musical playing. He strikes us as more imaginative and subtle in both his range of dynamics and diversity of colour than any of his rivals. True, Geoffrey Tozer (Chandos) has the finer recording, but taken all round Scherbakov would make an eminently satisfactory first choice: artistically it is impeccable, as a recording it is very natural and well balanced and, not least, the price is right.

Geoffrey Tozer has obvious feeling for this composer and his playing has no lack of warmth and virtuosity. He has the advantage over his rivals of a richer, more transparent recording and a more sympathetic and responsive accompanist in Järvi and the London Philharmonic. Demidenko, on the other hand, has the greater fire and dramatic flair, and his performance with the BBC Scottish Orchestra under Jerzy Maksymiuk has one very much on the edge of one's chair. He is by no means as well recorded as Tozer: the sound of the piano is shallow and the orchestra lacks real transparency and is a bit two-dimensional in terms of front-to-back perspective.

Dmitri Alexeev also plays the *First Piano Concerto* with virtuosity, flair and sympathy, and the BBC Symphony Orchestra under Alexander Lazarev give excellent support. The recording is very good and generally well balanced, and overall gives better results than the coupling, the late *Piano Quintet in C major*. Alexeev plays it with dedication, but the New Budapest Quartet are conscientious rather than committed or inspired partners. The two-dimensional and rather congested recording does not help.

On Testament we have two of the celebrated set of Medtner concerto recordings which the Maharajah of Mysore funded in the late 1940s. Medtner was then in his sixties but his playing is still pretty magisterial. These two concertos and the early miniatures that make up the disc still possess an aristocratic allure and a musical finesse that it is difficult to resist. The performances were never reissued in the UK in the days of LP, and their reappearance at long last is as welcome as it is overdue. Good transfers.

(i) *Piano Quintet in C, Op. posth.;* (ii) *Violin Sonata No. 2 in G, Op. 44.*

** Russian Disc (ADD) RDCD 11019. Svetlanov, with (i) Borodin Qt; (ii) Labko.

The *Piano Quintet*, on which Medtner laboured for so long, is played with much greater variety of tone and dynamics by Svetlanov and the Borodin Quartet than in the more recent Hyperion issue (see above). The 1968 recording calls for tolerance, but it is worth extending for the sake of some fine music-making. Alexander Labko plays the *Second Violin Sonata* with conviction and eloquence. He is well partnered by Yevgeni Svetlanov, who proves a sensitive pianist. Unfortunately, the 1968 recording is not good, even for its age, and is wanting in frequency range.

Violin Sonatas Nos. 1 in B min., Op. 21; 2 in G, Op. 44.

*** Chan. 9293. Mordkovitch, Tozer.

The first two of Medtner's three *Violin Sonatas* come on a well-recorded Chandos release. Lydia Mordkovitch proves a most imaginative and thoughtful advocate of the sonata, betraying an effortless expressive freedom. Both she and her partner are well recorded.

Violin Sonata No. 3 (Sonata Epica), Op. 57.

*** Erato 0630 15110-2. Repin, Berezovsky – RAVEL: *Violin Sonata.* ***

Vadim Repin and Boris Berezovsky make a formidable partnership, and they give what is arguably the most sensitive and certainly the most persuasive account of the *Sonata Epica* since David Oistrakh and Alexander Goldweiser's celebrated Melodiya LP. They bring to it a wide range of colour and dynamics and infuse every phrase with life. Very natural recording-balance adds to the pleasure this CD gives.

PIANO MUSIC
Piano duet

Russian Round Dance; Knight Errant, Op. 58/1–2.

*** Hyp. CDA 66654. Demidenko, Alexeev – RACHMANINOV: *Suite etc.* ***

The Russian round-dance or *khorovod* was written in 1946 and Medtner and Moiseiwitsch recorded it the same year for EMI. Here it is given with great lightness of touch, though this partnership lose beauty of tone-production above fortissimo.

Canzona matinata, Op. 39/4; Canzona serenata, Op. 38/6; Dithyrambe, Op. 10/2; Fairy Tale, Op. 20/1; Sonata elegia in D min., Op. 11/2; Sonata reminiscenza in A min., Op. 38/ 1; Sonata tragica in C min., Op. 39/5; Theme & Variations in C sharp min., Op. 55.

** Hyp. CDA 66636. Demidenko.

In the solo pieces Nikolai Demidenko sounds posturing and self-regarding. As a guide to Medtner, the less glamorous Hamish Milne (CRD) remains the truer interpreter. The quality of the Hyperion recording has also been overpraised. It is good without being distinguished and there is a lack of transparency, particularly in the middle range.

Dancing Fairy Tale, Op. 48/1; Fairy Tale (1915); Fairy Tales in D min., Op. 51/1; in E min., Op. 34/2; in F min., Op. 26/ 3; in G sharp min., Op. 31/3. Funeral March, Op. 31/2; The Organ Grinder, Op. 54/3; Russian Fairy Tale, Op. 42/1; Sonata in G min., Op. 22; Sonata reminiscenza in A min., Op. 38/1.

*** Chan. 9050. Tozer.

Tozer takes much less time over the *Sonata reminiscenza* than Demidenko but creates the illusion of unhurried calm. He allows the music to speak for itself without recourse to ostentation or flamboyance. The lifelike recording enhances the claims of this issue and bodes well for the enterprise (a complete survey of the keyboard music) as a whole.

Fairy Tales, Op. 51; Forgotten Melodies, Op. 38; Sonata Triad, Op. 11.

**(*) Chan 9153. Tozer.

Forgotten Melodies, Op. 39–40; Sonata in A min., Op. 30.

**(*) Chan. 9692. Tozer.

Sonatas in B flat min. (Sonata romantica), Op. 53/1; in F min., Op. 5; in F min. (Sonata minacciosa), Op. 53/2.

**(*) Chan. 9691. Tozer.

Complete piano music (as above).

*** Chan. 9723 (4). Tozer.

Geoffrey Tozer has long championed Medtner, and his excellently recorded series for Chandos has put collectors in his debt. His playing is unfailingly reliable and scrupulously conscientious and often persuasive. Where, in the *Sonatas*, for instance, he duplicates repertoire recorded by Marc-André Hamelin, his imaginative and poetic limitations can be discerned. All the same he has good fingers and a keen musical intelligence. The Chandos discs are all available separately, as well as in a box at a slightly reduced price.

Dithyramb No. 3. Op. 10/3; 2 Elegies, Op. 59; Fairy Tales, Op. 20/1–2; Op. 26/1–4; Op. 48/2; Lyric Fragments, Op. 23; Theme & Variations, Op. 55.

(N) **(*) Chan. 9899. Tozer.

The most recent CD in Geoffrey Tozer's Chandos series includes a very attractive account of the delightful Op. 55 *Theme and Variations*, and more of the *Fairy Tales*, in which he readily displays their diversity. The recital ends with Medtner's final piano works, the two *Elegies*, both opening with the same music only in different keys. The recording was made at Snape Maltings concert hall with pleasing results.

Dithyramb, Op. 10/2; Elegy, Op. 59/2; Skazki (Fairy Tales): No. 1 (1915); in E min., Op. 14/2; in G, Op. 9/3; in D min. (Ophelia's Song); in C sharp min., Op. 35/4. Forgotten Melodies, 2nd Cycle, No. 1: Meditation. Primavera, Op. 39/ 3; 3 Hymns in Praise of Toil, Op. 49; Piano Sonata in E min. (The Night Wind), Op. 25/2; Sonata Triad, Op. 11/ 1–3.

(M) *** CRD (ADD) 3338/9. Milne.

Improvisation No. 2 (in Variation Form), Op. 47; Piano Sonata in F min., Op. 5.

(M) *** CRD 3461. Milne.

3 Novelles, Op. 17; Romantic Sketches for the Young, Op. 54; Piano Sonatas in G min., Op. 22; A min., Op. 30; 2 Skazki, Op. 8.

(M) *** CRD 3460. Milne.

Medtner's art is subtle and elusive. He shows an aristocratic disdain for the obvious, a feeling for balance and proportion, and a quiet harmonic refinement that offer consistent rewards. There is hardly a weak piece here, and Milne is a poetic advocate whose technical prowess is matched by first-rate artistry. The recording too is very truthful and vivid, and at mid-price is very competitive indeed.

Forgotten Melodies, Op. 39; 2 Skazki, Op. 48; Etude in C minor; I Loved Thee, Op. 32/4; Sonata minacciosa, Op. 53/2.

(M) *** CRD 3509. Milne.

4 Skazki, Op. 34; Sonata-Ballade in F sharp, Op.27; Sonata romantica in B flat min., Op. 53/1.

(N) (M) *** CRD 3498. Milne.

These are new performances, and such is the quality of Hamish Milne's playing that one is never tempted to think of this music as pale Rachmaninov. Milne has lived with Medtner for the best part of a lifetime and this tells. His playing has refinement and authority, and the transcription he has made of the Pushkin setting, *I Loved Thee*, is quite magical. In the *Sonata minacciosa*, though Milne's playing might be more mercurial and incandescent, he brings valuable insights of his own. The *Sonata-Ballet* and *Sonata Romantica* are also finely and perceptively played. Very good recording.

Forgotten Melodies, Opp. 38–39; 3 Marches, Op. 8; Sonata Ballada in F sharp, Op. 27; Sonata Idylle in G, Op. 56; Sonata Skazka in C min., Op. 25/1; Sonata Triad, Op. 11; Sonatas in A min., Op. 30; in B flat min. (Sonata romantica), Op. 53/1; in E min. (Night Wind), Op. 25/2; in F min., Op. 5; in F min. (Sonata minacciosa), Op. 53/2; in G min., Op. 22.

*** Hyp. CDA 67221-4 (4). Hamelin.

Marc-André Hamelin's artistry is to be found at its most consummate in this four-CD set of the sonatas and miscellaneous piano music. If you find Medtner just a little bland or predictable, then try this set, for in Hamelin's hands it is neither. Playing touched by distinction.

MÉHUL, Etienne-Nicolas (1763–1817)

Symphonies Nos. 1–4; Overtures: La Chasse de jeune Henri; Le Trésor supposé.

*** Nim. NI 5184/5. Gulbenkian Foundation O, Swierczewski.

The four symphonies recorded here come from 1808–10 (Nos. 3 and 4 have been discovered only in recent years by David Charlton, who has edited them) and are well worth investigating. The invention is felicitous and engaging, and in *No. 4 in E major* Méhul brings back a motif of the *Adagio* in the finale, a unifying gesture well ahead of its time. The performances are eminently satisfactory even if the strings sound a shade undernourished.

MELARTIN, Erkki (1875–1937)

(i) *Violin Concerto, Op. 60. Sleeping Beauty (Suite), Op. 22; Suite lyrique No. 3 (Impressions de Belgique).*

** Ondine (ADD) ODE 923-2. (i) Storgårds; Tampere PO, Segerstam.

Ten years younger than Sibelius, Erkki Melartin's music shows a considerable lyrical talent and expertise in writing for the orchestra. The *Violin Concerto* (1910–13) has a lot going for it and John Storgårds takes its formidable difficulties in his stride. At one point its slow movement even brings Delius to mind. The atmospheric *Suite lyrique* is a set of six impressionistic sketches inspired by a visit the composer made to Bruges in 1914, and the incidental music to Topelius's play, *The Sleeping Beauty*, dates from 1910. Decent recording, but the Tampere Orchestra is a bit too raw-toned and ill-tuned to do this music full justice. Worth hearing all the same.

MENDELSSOHN, Fanny (1805–47)

Piano Trio in D, Op. 11.

(N) (B) *** Hyp. Helios CDH 55078. Dartington Piano Trio – Clara SCHUMANN: *Trio in G min.* ***

Like Clara Schumann's *G minor Trio* with which it is coupled, the *Piano Trio* has impeccable craftsmanship and great facility. Its ideas are pleasing, though not strongly individual. The Dartington Piano Trio play most persuasively and give much pleasure. Excellent recording.

String Quartet in E flat.

*** CPO 999 679-2. Basle Erato Qt – Emilie MAYER: *Quartet No. 14*; SIRMEN: *Quartets Nos. 2 & 3.* ***

Fanny Mendelssohn's *String Quartet*, written in 1834, was influenced – notably in its layout and key sequence – by her brother's Op. 12, but the delectable Scherzo is the only movement that might be mistakenly assumed to be Felix's work; otherwise the music is wholly her own. The pervasive melancholy which permeates the opening movement and the *Romanze* is strikingly personal. But most remarkable of all is the forward-looking *Molto vivace* finale, with its determined energy, which is so like the finale of Tchaikovsky's *Souvenir de Florence* in its passionate forward impulse. The performance here is first class in every way, as is the recording; the couplings are stimulating too.

Lieder: Abenbild; Bergeslust; Du bist die ruh; Bitte; Dämmrung senkte sich von oben; Dein ist mein herz; Die ersehnte; Erwin; Ferne; Die Frühen graber; Frühling; Gondellied; Ich wandelte unter den bäumen; Im herbste; Italien; Der maiabend; Maienlied; Die mainacht; Morgenständchen; Nach Süden; Nachtwanderer; Der rosenkranz; Die schiffended; Schwanenlied; Suleika; Traum; Vorwurf; Wanderlied; Warum sind denn rosen so blass.

*** Hyp. CDA 67110. Gritton, Asti.

Fanny Mendelssohn's response to German poets from Goethe to Heine is at least the equal of her brother's, at once memorably tuneful and subtle in her illumination of the texts, adding distinctively to the Lieder tradition. Her writing is not just poetic but often vigorous, with fine accompaniments to match. Susan Gritton, sweet if just a little unvaried in tone, and Eugene Asti are refreshing, consistently sympathetic interpreters. They provide their own perceptive notes: Fanny's caustic comments on the poet Heine bring the man vividly to life.

MENDELSSOHN, Felix (1809–47)

Capriccio brillant for Piano & Orchestra, Op. 22.

(B) ** Sony (ADD) SBK 48166. Serkin, Phd. O, Ormandy –
BRAHMS: *Concerto No. 1;* SCHUMANN: *Introduction &
Allegro Appassionato.* **(*)

Serkin is on good form here. This is a brilliant performance,
not without panache, if not especially strong on charm. The
recording is a little shallow, but otherwise good.

*(i) Capriccio brillant in B min., Op. 22; (ii) Rondo brillant
in E flat, Op. 29.*

(N) (M) (***) Dutton Lab. mono CDEA 5506. Lympany, (i) Nat.
SO, Boyd Neel; (ii) LSO, Kisch (with BALAKIREV: *Islamey*
(**(*)); POULENC: *Novelette No. 1;* DOHNANYI:
Capriccio in F min.; KHACHATURIAN: *Piano Concerto in
D flat.* (***))

Dazzling playing from Moura Lympany at the peak of her
form in the mid-1940s. She is especially scintillating in the
Rondo brillant. Both recordings were made in the Kingsway
Hall, and the Dutton transfers are well up to form.

*(i; ii) Capriccio brillant in B min. for Piano & Orchestra,
Op. 22; (iii) Piano Concerto in A min. (for piano and
strings); (i; iv) Piano Concertos Nos. 1 in G min., Op. 25; 2
in D min., Op. 40; (iii; v) Double Piano Concerto in E (for
two pianos and strings); (i; ii) Rondo brillant in E flat for
Piano & Orchestra, Op. 29; (vi) Rondo capriccioso in E,
Op. 14.*

(B) *** Double Decca 452 410-2 (2). (i) Katin; (ii) LPO,
Martinon; (iii) Ogdon, ASMF, Marriner; (iv) LSO, Collins;
(v) with Lucas; (vi) Bolet.

Peter Katin's classic 1956 performances of the two best-
known solo concertos have come up very freshly on CD.
The two concertante pieces were recorded earlier (1954) and
find Katin in sparkling form. Here a mono master is used;
but this gives an impression of stereo. The ambitious and
successful *A minor Concerto* and the *Double Concerto* have
engaging ideas and are played with great verve and spirit by
John Ogdon and his wife. The orchestral playing is equally
lively and fresh throughout, and the vivid (originally Argo)
1969 Kingsway Hall recording has hardly dated. Jorge Bolet
(recorded digitally in 1985) offers the solo *Rondo Capriccioso*
as a closing encore with the lightest of touch.

*(i) Capriccio brillant, Op. 22; (i; ii) Double Concerto for
Violin & Piano. (i) Rondo brillant, Op. 29; Serenade &
Allegro Giocoso, Op. 43 (BIS CD 713); Piano Concertos
Nos. 1 in G min., Op. 25; 2 in D min., Op. 40; Piano
Concerto in A min. (BIS CD 718); (iii) Double Piano
Concertos: in A flat; E (BIS CD 688); (ii) Violin Concerto
in D min.; Violin Concerto in E min., Op. 64 (1844
version). Octet, Op. 20: Scherzo (orchestral version) (BIS
CD 935).*

(M) *** BIS CD 966/68. (i) Brautigam; (ii) Van Keulen;
(iii) Derwinger, Pöntinen, Amsterdam New Sinf., Markiz.

These are exemplary recordings of exemplary performances.
Indeed it is difficult to flaw them. They are available separ-

ately (the individual catalogue numbers are listed within the
titles above), but there is a price advantage in purchasing
them all together. The interesting account of the *E minor
Violin Concerto* in its original form (beautifully played by
Isabelle van Keulen) is of particular interest. Mendelssohn
spent seven years (1838–45) working over what is perhaps
his most successful concertante work and this is its earlier
draft. Its gestation is discussed in greater detail in the accompanying notes for the individual disc, but the notes here are
still pretty copious.

*(i) Piano Concerto in A min. (for piano and strings); (i; ii)
Double Piano Concerto in E.*

(N) (BB) *** Warner Apex 8573 89088-2. Katsaris; (i) Franz
Liszt CO, Rolla; (ii) Leipzig Gewandhaus O, Masur.

It was a happy idea to couple the early *A minor Concerto* at
budget price with the two major works in this form. The
former is an extended piece lasting over half an hour, far
longer than the two numbered concertos, an amazing work
for a thirteen-year-old and endlessly inventive. It is impossible not to respond to Katsaris's vitality, even if at times
there is a feeling of rushing his fences. He plays with enormous vigour in the outer movements and receives strong
support from Masur. There is nothing heavy, yet the music
is given more substance than usual, while the central slow
movements bring a relaxed lyrical *espresso* which provides
admirable contrast. The full, well-balanced recording has
attractive ambience and sparkle.

Piano Concertos Nos. 1–2; Capriccio brillant.

⊛ *** Chan. 9215. Shelley, LMP.

*Piano Concertos Nos. 1–2; Capriccio brillant; Rondo
brillant.*

(BB) *** Naxos 8.550681-2. Frith, Slovak State PO (Košice),
Stanovsky.

*Piano Concertos Nos 1–2; Capriccio brillant, Op. 22; Rondo
brillant, Op. 29; Serenade & Allegro Giocoso, in B min.,
Op.43.*

*** Hyp. CDA 66969. Hough, CBSO, Foster

*(i) Piano Concertos Nos. 1–2; Prelude & Fugue, Op. 35/1;
Rondo capriccioso, Op. 14; Variations sérieuses, Op. 54.*

(M) *** Sony (ADD) SMK 42401. Perahia; (i) ASMF, Marriner.

*(i) Piano Concertos Nos. 1–2; Songs without Words,
Op. 19/1, 2, & 6 (Venetian Gondola Song); Op. 30/4 & 6;
Op. 38/6; Op. 53/1; Op. 62/ 1 & 6 (Spring Song); Op. 67/4
(Spinning Song) & 6; Op. 85/6; Op. 102/5.*

(M) *** Decca 466 425-2. Schiff, with (i) Bav. RSO, Dutoit.

Stephen Hough treats these compact minor-key works with
a biting intensity. Yet with freer expressiveness and bigger
contrasts he also brings out extra poetry, and in the finales
a sparkling wit. He also has the advantage of the most
generous and very apt couplings, three other, rare concertante piano works by Mendelssohn. The point and delicacy of Hough's passage-work is a constant delight.

Howard Shelley offers marvellous playing in every respect:
fresh, sparkling and dashing in the fast movements, poetic
and touching in the slower ones. The London Mozart Players

are a group of exactly the right size for these works and they point rhythms nicely and provide the necessary lift. Shelley dispatches the *Capriccio brillant* with similar aplomb, and the recording-balance is admirably judged, with rich, truthful recorded sound.

Benjamin Frith on Naxos is a hardly less personable and nimble soloist: he is sensitively touching in the slow movements. The Slovak orchestra accompany with vigour and enthusiasm, and if the effect is at times less sharply rhythmic this is partly the effect of a somewhat more reverberant acoustic. What makes the Naxos disc very competitive is the inclusion of the *Rondo brillant*, which Frith dispatches with admirable vigour and sparkle. This disc is very good value indeed.

András Schiff plays both concertos marvellously, with poetry, great delicacy and fluency, while his virtuosity is effortless. He is given excellent accompaniments by Dutoit and the Bavarian players, and the Decca recording is first class. His simplicity of style suits the *Songs without Words*, although some might find his approach a little cool. Yet the famous *Spring Song* shows him at his best. The recording is again most natural and realistic.

Murray Perahia's playing catches the Mendelssohnian spirit with admirable perception. There is sensibility and sparkle, the slow movements are shaped most beautifully and the partnership with Marriner is very successful, for the Academy give a most sensitive backing. The recording could be more transparent but it does not lack body, and the piano timbre is fully acceptable. At mid-price, a very recommendable issue.

Double Piano Concertos: in A flat; in E.

*** Hyp. CDA 66567. Coombs, Munro, BBC Scottish SO, Maksymiuk.

(BB) *** Naxos 8.553416. Frith, Tinney, Dublin RTE Sinf., ODuinn.

Mendelssohn's *Double Concerto in A flat* is the most ambitious of all his concertante works, and the work in E brings an expansive first movement too; they provide formidable evidence of the teenage composer's fluency and technical finesse. Stephen Coombs and Ian Munro prove ideal advocates, playing with delectable point and imagination, finding a wit and poetry in the writing that might easily lie hidden, with even the incidental passagework magnetizing the ear. The recording of the pianos is on the shallow side, and the string-tone is thin too, but that is not inappropriate for the music.

The Naxos disc challenges the outstanding Hyperion issue coupling these same two charming double concertos. If the Irish players are not quite as persuasive as their Scottish counterparts on Hyperion, their playing is just as refined, and Frith and Tinney are a fair match for Coombs and Munro, less powerful but just as magnetic and even more poetic. The transparent recording helps, very appropriate for such youthful music.

Double Piano Concerto in E.

*** Chan. 9711. Güher and Süher Pekinel, Philh. O, Marriner –

BRUCH: *Double Piano Concerto in A flat min.*; MOZART: *Double Piano Concerto in E flat, K.365.* ***

**(*) Ph. 432 095-2. K. and M. Labèque, Philh. O, Bychkov – BRUCH: *Double Concerto.* **(*)

Mendelssohn wrote his *Double Piano Concerto* when he was only fourteen, yet it contains many ideas that are entirely characteristic of his mature style. In such a performance as this its freshness justifies the length, for unlike the rival version from the Labèque sisters on Philips – which has only the Bruch for coupling – this one brings an accompaniment from Marriner and the Academy, finely pointed, which does not inflate the piece. The Pekinel sisters, as in the other two works, give a fresh, alert performance with pin-point ensemble. Warm, full sound.

The Labèques play the ambitious *E major Double Concerto* with enthusiasm and flair, and Bychkov accompanies manfully. But, partly because of the resonant acoustic, the effect is rather inflated and the ear looks for more transparency and lightness of texture in such an amiable piece.

Piano Concerto in A min. (i) Double Concerto for Violin & Piano.

** Teldec 0630 13152-2. Staier, Concerto Köln; (i) with Kussmaul.

As these boyhood concertos were first heard in the Sunday salons of the composer's banker father, it is logical that they should be recorded here not just on period instruments but with a small band of strings – in places one instrument per part. What is less welcome is that the strings of Concerto Köln are too acid-sounding even by period standards. By contrast, the solo violinist, Rainer Kussmaul, plays with rare freshness and purity, allowing himself just a measure of vibrato, and if Staier takes second place, that is not just a question of balance between the violin and an 1825 fortepiano, but of the young composer's piano writing, regularly built on passage-work – often in arpeggios – rather than straight melodic statements. That also applies to the piano writing in the solo concerto, and it is striking that a clear progression is revealed between 1822, the date of the solo concerto, and March 1823, when the double concerto was completed in time for his 14th birthday.

Violin Concertos: in D min. (for Violin & Strings); in E min., Op. 64.

*** Ph. 432 077-2. Mullova, ASMF, Marriner.

(BB) **(*) Virgin 2 x 1 Double VBD5 61504-2 (2). Seiler, City of L. Sinf., Hickox – BEETHOVEN: *Concerto.* **(*)

Purity is the keynote of Mullova's fresh and enjoyable readings of both concertos, the early *D minor* as well as the great *E minor* which is tenderly expressive rather than flamboyant in the expression of emotion, yet with concentration keenly maintained. So the central *Andante* is sweet and songful and the finale, light and fanciful, conveys pure fun in its fireworks. The early work follows a similar pattern, with youthful emotions given full rein and with the finale turned into a headily brilliant Csardas. The Philips recording is admirably natural and beautifully balanced.

It is good to have a recommendable bargain pairing of Mendelssohn's youthful and mature concertos. Mayumi

Seiler is fresh and appealing in the one, and then gives a sparkling account of the famous *E minor* work with the slow movement serene in its simplicity, as with the coupled Beethoven concerto. Hickox is in good form and the recording is pleasingly balanced; although the timbre of the soloist is small, it is perfectly focused.

Violin Concerto in D min. (i) Double Concerto in D min. for Violin, Piano & Strings ; Violin Concerto in E min., Op. 64.

(BB) *** Naxos 8.553844. Bisengaliev, N. Sinfonia, Penney; (i) with Frith.

Two juvenilia are here dispatched with zest and freshness by these excellent musicians, even if in the *D minor Violin Concerto* Bisengaliev's final is a bit headlong. Spirited playing from the Northern Sinfonia under Andrew Pennet and a predictably stylish contribution from Benjamin Frith.

Violin Concerto in E min., Op. 64.

(M) *** Sony SMK 89715. Lin, Philh. O, Tilson Thomas – BRUCH: *Concerto;* VIEUXTEMPS: *Concerto No. 5.* ***

(M) *** Decca 460 976-2 Chung, Montreal SO, Dutoit – BRUCH: *Violin Concerto No. 1; Scottish Fantasy.* ***

(M) *** Decca 460 015-2. Chung, Montreal SO, Dutoit (as above) – ELGAR: *Violin Concerto.* ***

*** EMI CDC5 56418-2. Chang, BPO, Jansons – SIBELIUS: *Violin Concerto.* ***

*** Teldec 0630-15870-2. Perlman, Chicago SO, Barenboim – BRAHMS: *Double Concerto.* ***

(BB) *** Naxos 8.550153. Nishizaki, Slovak PO, Jean – TCHAIKOVSKY: *Concerto.* ***

(M) *** DG 445 515-2. Mutter, BPO, Karajan – BRAHMS: *Violin Concerto.* ***

(N) (M) *** DG 463 641-2. Mutter, BPO, Karajan – BRUCH: *Concerto No. 1.* ***

*** EMI CDC7 49663-2. Kennedy, ECO, Tate – BRUCH: *Concerto No. 1;* SCHUBERT: *Rondo.* ***

*** ASV (ADD) CDDCA 748. Xue-Wei, LPO, Bolton – BRAHMS: *Violin Concerto.* ***

(M) *** EMI (ADD) CDM5 66906-2 [CDM 66958]. Menuhin, Philh. O, Kurtz – BRUCH: *Concerto No. 1.* ***

(BB) *** Belart (ADD) 461 355-2. Campoli, LPO, Boult – BEETHOVEN: *Violin Concerto.* ***

(B) *** [EMI Red Line CDR5 69863]. Perlman, LSO, Previn – BRUCH: *Violin Concerto.* ***

(B) *** Penguin DG (ADD) 460 619-2. Milstein, VPO, Abbado – TCHAIKOVSKY: *Concerto.* ***

(B) *** DG Double (ADD) 453 142-2 (2). Milstein, VPO, Abbado – BEETHOVEN: *Concerto* ***; BRAHMS: *Concerto* **(*); TCHAIKOVSKY: *Concerto.* ***

**(*) RCA 09026 61743-2. Heifetz, Boston SO, Munch – TCHAIKOVSKY: *Concerto etc.* **(*)

(***) Testament mono SBT 1037. Martzy, Philh. O, Kletzki – BRAHMS: *Concerto.* (***)

(M) (***) EMI mono CDM5 66975-2 [CDM 66990]. Menuhin, BPO, Furtwängler – BEETHOVEN: *Concerto.* (***)

(***) Beulah (ADD) 1PD 10. Campoli, LPO, Boult – ELGAR: *Violin Concerto.* (***)

(M) **(*) Sony (ADD) SMK 66827. Stern, Phd. O, Ormandy – DVORAK: *Violin Concerto; Romance* **.

(B) **(*) Discover DICD 920122. Bushkov, Slovak New PO, Rahbari – TCHAIKOVSKY: *Concerto.* **

(M) **(*) Sup. (ADD) SU 1939-2 011. Suk, Czech PO, Ančerl – BERG: *Concerto* ***; BRUCH: *Concerto.* **

(N) **(*) Australian Decca Eloquence (ADD) 461 369-2. Ricci, LSO, Gamba – BRUCH: *Violin Concerto* **(*); SAINT-SAENS: *Havanaise, Op. 83, etc.* ***

(M) (**(*)) EMI mono CDH5 65191-2. Heifetz, RPO, Beecham – MOZART: *Concerto No. 5;* VIEUXTEMPS: *Concerto No. 5.* (***)

(N) (BB) (**(*)) Naxos mono 8.110941. Heifetz, RPO, Beecham – MOZART: *Violin Concertos Nos. 4, 5 (Turkish).* (**(*))

(N) (M) *(*) BBC (ADD) BBCL 4050-2. Menuhin, LSO, C. Davis – BACH: *Violin Concerto, BWV 1042.* BRAHMS: *Double Concerto.* *(*)

Cho-Liang Lin's vibrantly lyrical account is offered with the Bruch *G minor* plus the Vieuxtemps No. 5, to make an unbeatable mid-priced triptych. They are all three immensely rewarding and poetic performances, given excellent, modern, digital sound, and Michael Tilson Thomas proves a highly sympathetic partner in the Mendelssohn *Concerto.*

Kyung-Wha Chung favours speeds faster than usual in all three movements, and the result is sparkling and happy, with the lovely slow movement fresh and songful, not at all sentimental. With warmly sympathetic accompaniment from Dutoit and the Montreal orchestra, amply recorded, the result is one of Chung's happiest records. The Elgar coupling works well, but the alternative of Bruch's *G minor Concerto* and *Scottish Fantasy* in Decca's Legends series is more attractive still.

Unlike the Sibelius with which it is coupled, Sarah Chang's account of the Mendelssohn was recorded under studio conditions in the Philharmonie, Berlin. Here too she offers an astonishingly mature reading, more restrained than some, but still magnetic in its thoughtfulness and spontaneous poetry. Warm, atmospheric sound.

Perlman's 1993 Chicago version, strong and volatile, was recorded live and originally issued in coupling with the second Prokofiev. It makes an excellent, more generous coupling in the new format with the powerful Perlman/Ma version of the Brahms *Double Concerto.*

Takako Nishizaki gives an inspired reading of the concerto, warm, spontaneous and full of temperament. The central *Andante* is on the slow side, but well shaped, not sentimental, while the outer movements are exhilarating, with excellent playing from the Slovak Philharmonic. Though the forwardly placed violin sounds over-bright, the recording is full and warm. A splendid coupling at super-bargain price.

In the Mendelssohn *E minor*, the freshness of Anne-Sophie Mutter's approach communicates vividly to the listener, creating the feeling of hearing the work anew. Her gentleness and radiant simplicity in the *Andante* are very appealing, and the light, sparkling finale is a delight. Mutter is given a small-scale image, projected forward from the orchestral backcloth; the sound is both full and refined. This fine performance comes alternatively coupled with either Brahms or Bruch.

Kennedy establishes a positive, masculine view of the work from the very start, but fantasy here goes with firm control. The slow movement brings a simple, songful view of the haunting melody, and the finale sparkles winningly, with no feeling of rush. With a bonus in the rare Schubert *Rondo* and clear, warm recording, it makes an excellent recommendation.

Xue-Wei's version, clean and fresh if a little reticent emotionally, makes a generous and attractive coupling for his equally recommendable version of the Brahms. There are more strongly characterized readings than this but, with its pastel-shaded lyricism, this is undoubtedly satisfying, helped by first-rate recording.

The restrained nobility of Menuhin's phrasing of the famous principal melody of the slow movement has long been a hallmark of his reading with Efrem Kurtz, who provides polished and sympathetic support. The sound of the CD transfer is bright, with the soloist dominating but the orchestral texture well detailed.

Campoli's perfectly formed tone and polished, secure playing are just right for the Mendelssohn *Concerto*. A delightful performance, notable for its charm and disarming simplicity. The 1958 (originally Decca) recording is marred by a degree of roughness in the orchestral focus; but no matter, this very inexpensive record gives much pleasure and is a fine reminder of a superb violinist. This is also available in an alternative coupling with the Elgar concerto.

Perlman gives a performance of the Mendelssohn that is full of flair, superbly matched by the LSO under Previn, always an illuminating interpreter of this composer. Ripe recording quality.

Milstein's is a highly distinguished performance, very well accompanied. His account of the slow movement is more patrician than Menuhin's and his slight reserve is projected by DG sound which is bright, clean and clear in its CD remastering. This now comes either as a Penguin Classic (with an author's sleeve-note by Jan Morris) in its original coupling with Tchaikovsky, or on a DG Double which also includes the Beethoven and Brahms concertos.

As one might expect, Heifetz gives a fabulous performance. His speeds are consistently fast, yet in the slow movement his flexible phrasing sounds so inevitable and easy that it is hard not to be convinced. The finale is a tour de force, light and sparkling, with every note in place. The recording has been digitally remastered with success and the sound is smoother than before.

It is not just the perfect sweetness and purity of Martzy's tone that are so impressive, but also her freely flexible rubato, which always sounds spontaneous, and the hushed tenderness of her pianissimo playing is breathtaking, as in the central *Andante*. The performance is also remarkable for the quicksilver energy of the finale and, with the soloist well forward, the mono sound is full and clear.

Menuhin's unique gift for lyrical sweetness has never been presented on record more seductively than in his classic, earlier version of the Mendelssohn *Concerto* with Furtwängler. The digital transfer is not ideally clear, yet one hardly registers that this is a mono recording from the early 1950s.

Another totally memorable performance by Stern from the late 1950s. It has great bravura, culminating in a marvellously surging account of the finale. The slow movement too is played with great eloquence and feeling but, when pianissimos are non-existent – partly, but not entirely, the fault of the close recording-balance – the poetic element is diminished, even though there is a full flood of romanticism. Thisd is also available on a Super Audio CD compiled with Tchaikovsky (SR 6062).

Evgeny Bushkov is a pupil of Leonid Kogan, and he prepares and plays the secondary theme of the opening movement with appealing tenderness. The *Andante*, too, has a matching simplicity and the finale no lack of bravura and fire. He is well accompanied, and the recording, made in the Concert Hall of Slovak Radio, Bratislava, is full and well balanced. Not a first choice, however, for the coupled Tchaikovsky *Concerto* sounds less spontaneous.

Suk's small, sweet timbre is particularly suited to the Mendelssohn *Concerto*. This is a highly congenial performance, not as individual as some, with a straightforwardly lyrical slow movement and a finale which gains from not being rushed off its feet. An excellent CD transfer, firm and full. However, Suk's style is less suited to the Bruch *Concerto*.

Ricci's coupling of the Mendelssohn concerto is clean and sympathetic and technically brilliant even if his characteristic timbre and use of vibrato is rather intense. Gamba conducts with his usual vigour, and this 1958 performance, which sounds hardly at all dated, comes up fresh as paint in its new transfer. The couplings are equally charpertical.

Anything that Heifetz does is pretty well without compare, and his dazzling virtuosity is well in evidence in this 1948 performance of the Mendelssohn *Concerto* with the RPO and Beecham. However, there would seem to be less warmth and rapport between Heifetz and Sir Thomas than there was between the violinist and Barbirolli in the coupled Mozart *Concerto*.

Heifetz's 1949 version is among the most controversial of all his recordings, with breathtakingly fast accounts of the outer movements. If at first the impression is simply of rush for its own sake, there are contrasting passages where the Beecham influence brings total relaxation, as in the sweetness of the downward arpeggio leading into the second subject. In any case the results are undoubtedly exciting, and the sweet songfulness of the slow movement reveals Heifetz at his warmest. On Naxos, a good coupling with the two Mozart concertos, one also with Beecham, the other from 1934 – Heifetz's very first concerto recording.

In his BBC recording of the Mendelssohn concerto Menuhin is on rather better form than in the Brahms coupling with Rostropovich. All the same this is not one of the most successful of the BBC Legends series.

(i; ii) *Violin Concerto in E min., Op. 64;* (ii) *Hebrides Overture, Op. 26; Symphony No. 4 in A, Op. 90 (Italian);* (iii) *A Midsummer Night's Dream: Incidental Music;* (iv) *Octet;* (v) *Song Without Words: Op 38/6, 62/5 & 6, 67/4.*

(N) (B) *** DG Panorama (ADD) 469 157-2 (2). (i) Mutter;

(ii) BPO, Karajan; (iii) Mathis, Boese, Bavarian Radio SO, Kubelik (iv) ASMF Ch. Ens.; (v) Barenboim.

The finest of DG's Panorama double packs are proving invaluable providing that you haven't acquired the repertoire already in earlier incarnations. They are especially suitable for those starting a collection, and many of them offer performances that would be a first choice at any price level. Karajan and the Berlin Philharmonic playing the *Hebrides Overture* and the *Italian Symphony* is difficult to surpass and so is the *Violin Concerto* with a 19-year-old Anne-Sophie Mutter. On the companion disc Kubelik's much admired *Midsummer Night's Dream: Incidental Music* returns to the catalogue alongside the Academy of St Martin in the Fields' *Octet*. Given the blend of artistic excellence and good quality sound this is a bargain.

(i) *Violin Concerto in E min., Op. 64;* (ii) *Symphonies Nos. 3 (Scottish); 4 (Italian);* (iii) *A Midsummer Night's Dream: Overture & Incidental Music: Scherzo; Intermezzo; Nocturne; Wedding March.*

(B) *** Teldec/Erato ADD/Dig. Ultima 0630 18954-2 (2).
(i) Charlier, Monte Carlo Op. O, Foster; (ii) Leipzig GO, Masur; (iii) LPO, Leppard.

(i) *Violin Concerto in E min., Op. 64. Symphony No. 4 in A (Italian), Op. 90; Athalie, Op. 74: War March of the Priests; The Hebrides Overture, Op. 26.*

(M) ** Sony (ADD) SMK 61843. (i) Zukerman, NYPO, Bernstein.

(i) *Violin Concerto in E min.;* (ii) *Symphony No. 4 (Italian); Overtures: The Hebrides (Fingal's Cave); A Midsummer Night's Dream; Ruy Blas.*

(BB) *** EMI (ADD) Seraphim CES5 68524-2 (2). LSO, with
(i) Menuhin, cond. Frühbeck de Burgos; (ii) Previn –
BRUCH: *Violin Concerto No. 1.* ***

Menuhin's second stereo recording, with Rafael Frühbeck de Burgos, has its moments of roughness but it has magic too, at the appearance of the first movement's second subject and in the slow movement, even if the timbre itself is a little spare. The recording sounds fuller than the earlier account with Kurtz, and this makes a good bargain on EMI's new Seraphim label, coupled with the Bruch *Concerto* and Previn's 1979 version of the *Italian Symphony*, plus the three most popular overtures. Previn, always an inspired Mendelssohnian, gives exuberant performances. In the symphony the outer movements are urgent, without sounding at all breathless, and are finely sprung; the essential first-movement exposition repeat is included. Recording balance has the strings a little less forward than usual, but the overall effect is agreeably full.

Zukerman gives a sweet-toned but never cloying account of the *Violin Concerto*, and the support he receives from Bernstein and his orchestra is thoroughly sympathetic. An extremely fine performance, and one which would be a match for almost any, were it not for the 1969 recording, which is not as naturally balanced or as rich in tone as one would like. However, it is better than many of Bernstein's NYPO recordings and Sony have improved matters in this CD transfer. The snag with this release is the performance

of the *Italian Symphony*: it is a glossy reading lacking in charm and with some distracting mannerisms too. *The Hebrides Overture* too lacks the distinction of its best rivals.

Olivier Charlier's account of the *Violin Concerto* is warm, lyrically fresh, and nicely paced. Lawrence Foster accompanies persuasively and this is enjoyably spontaneous. So is Masur's highly recommendable coupling of Mendelssohn's two best-loved symphonies. He observes exposition repeats in both, and his choice of speeds brings out the freshness of inspiration judiciously, avoiding any suspicion of sentimentality in slow movements, which are taken at flowing tempi. However, the reverberant Leipzig recording tends to obscure detail in tuttis; the Scherzo of the *Scottish*, for example, becomes a blur, losing some of its point and charm. Otherwise, the sound of the orchestra has all the characteristic Leipzig bloom and beauty. Indeed the orchestral sound is glorious and the cultured playing always a joy to listen to, while at the climax of the first movement, by bringing out the timpani strongly, Masur finds a storm sequence almost to match *Fingal's Cave*. Leppard's suite from *A Midsummer Night's Dream* is also very sensitively played and well recorded.

2 Concert Pieces for Clarinet & Basset Horn: in F min., Op. 113; in D min., Op. 114.

(B) *** Hyp. Dyad CDD 22017 (2). King, Dobrée, LSO, Francis (with Concert – see below ***).

These Mendelssohn duets for clarinet and basset horn are most diverting, with their jocular finales; and they are played with a nice blend of expressive spontaneity and high spirits. Georgina Dobrée proves a nimble partner for the ever-sensitive Thea King. This is part of an excellent two-disc set, including other attractive concertante works by Max Bruch, Crusell, Spohr and other less familar names.

(i) *Overtures: Athalia; Calm Sea and a Prosperous Voyage; The Hebrides (Fingal's Cave); The Marriage of Camacho; A Midsummer Night's Dream; Ruy Blas;* (ii) *Symphonies Nos. 3 (Scottish); 4 (Italian); 5 (Reformation).*

(N) (BB) **(*) RCA Double 74321 84600-2 (2). (i) Bamberg SO, Flor; (ii) Boston SO, Munch.

Overtures: Athalia; Calm Sea and Prosperous Voyage; Fingal's Cave (The Hebrides); Ruy Blas. Symphonies Nos. 3 (Scottish); 4 (Italian); (i) *A Midsummer Night's Dream: Overture & Incidental Music* (complete).

(B) *** RCA Twofer 74321 34177-2 (2). Bamberg SO, Flor;
(i) with Popp, Lipovšek, Bamberg SO Ch.

Claus Peter Flor's collection of overtures (which received a Rosette from us in its original format) remains the most desirable the catalogue has ever offered. The magically evocative opening of *Calm Sea and Prosperous Voyage*, followed by an allegro of great vitality, is a demonstrable example of the spontaneous imagination of these performances, and there is no finer or more atmospheric version of *Fingal's Cave*. The bold *Ruy Blas* and the nobly contoured *Athalia* are also greatly enjoyable, especially when played with such freshness and polish. The recording, made in the Dominikanerbau, Bamberg, has splendid bloom, for the hall ambience is just right for this repertoire. The *Midsummer*

Night's Dream incidental music is recorded equally beautifully, glowing and radiant. The little melodramas are omitted, but the performance is otherwise complete. Flor's stylish yet relaxed control brings the kind of intimacy one expects from a chamber group. Again the Bamberg acoustic adds to the character of these performances, unforced and beaming.

Munch secures some outstanding bravura from his Boston players in the three symphonies: the *Scherzo* of the *Scottish* is particularly nimble, while the clean articulation means that the allegros of the outer movements of the *Italian* can be hard-driven without stress. However, some will feel that Munch's style is emotionally too fierce, and this applies especially to the *Reformation Symphony* which lacks any degree of charm. Nevertheless the excitement of these performances cannot be denied and the slow movements of both the *Scottish* and *Italian* are songful, although the omission of first-movement exposition repeats is another drawback. The RCA engineers have done wonders with the (1957/9) recordings, which sound much smoother and fuller than they did on LP.

The Hebrides (Fingal's Cave) Overture.

(N) (M) (**) Beulah mono 3PD12. BBC SO, Boult –
  SCHUBERT: *Symphony No. 9 in C (Great)* (**(*);
  WAGNER: *Die Meistersinger: Overture.* (**)

Boult, recording the *Hebrides Overture* in 1933 with the recently founded BBC Symphony Orchestra, takes a fresh, generally brisk view, which allows a degree of flexibility in the build-up of ostinatos and in the lovely reprise of the second subject, but with no romantic excess. The Beulah transfer is dry, with no added reverberation, not helped by a high but even surface hiss, but the body of sound makes one readily forget the limitations.

Symphonies for Strings Nos. 1–12; 13 in C min. (single movement).

*** BIS CD 938/940. Amsterdam New Sinf., Markiz.

Symphonies for Strings Nos. 1–12.

**(*) Teldec 0630 17433-2 (3). Concerto Köln.

Symphonies for String Orchestra Nos. 1–6.

(BB) *** Naxos 8.553161. N. CO, Ward.

Symphonies for String Orchestra Nos. 7–9.

(BB) *** Naxos 8.553162. N. CO, Ward.

Symphonies for String Orchestra Nos. 10–13 (Sinfoniesatz).

(BB) *** Naxos 8.553163. N. CO, Ward.

Mendelssohn's early symphonies for strings, lost for 150 years, were rediscovered in 1950. The first ten were student works and the last two, together with the virtually unknown *Symphony Movement in C minor* (No. 13), had all been completed before their young composer reached the age of fourteen. The playing of the Amsterdam New Sinfonietta is vibrant and alive, and the recording has a warmth and clarity that give the set the edge over almost all its current rivals. This music is full of charm, and the quality of Mendelssohn's youthful invention is little short of astonishing.

Nicholas Ward and the Northern Chamber Orchestra

match rivals at whatever price. The freshness and incisiveness of the performances are enhanced by bright, clean recording, made in the Concert Hall of Broadcasting House in Manchester. Not only does Ward bring out the exhilarating sparkle and vigour of the fast movements – with Mendelssohn, even at the age of eleven, giving clear anticipations of his mature style – but he also gives apt emotional weight to such beautiful lyrical movements as the *Andante* of No. 2 or the darkly slow introduction to the one-movement *No. 10 in B minor*. All three discs can be warmly recommended to everyone.

The Teldec three-CD set is made by the conductorless Concerto Köln. Although the usual original-instrument sonority is not to all tastes, those whose preference is for period instruments should consider these. The performances are very musical and the recorded sound is excellent.

Symphonies for String Orchestra Nos. 2 in D; 3 in E min.; 5 in B flat; 6 in E flat.

(B) *** EMI double forte CZS5 69524-2 (2). Polish CO,
  Maksymiuk, – JANIEWICZ: *Divertimento;* JARZEBSKI:
  Chromatica; Tamburetta; ROSSINI: *String Sonatas.* ***

This collection of four of the boy Mendelssohn's early *String Symphonies* is most invigorating. These earlier symphonies from the series of 13 may look to various models from Bach to Beethoven, but the vitality of the invention still bursts through. The slow movement of *Symphony No. 2*, for example, is a Bachian meditation that in its simple beauty matches later Mendelssohn. The Polish strings are set in a lively acoustic, giving exceptionally rich sound, but the playing also has plenty of dash.

Symphonies Nos. 1–5.

(M) *** DG (ADD) 429 664-2 (3). Mathis, Rebman, Hollweg,
  German Op. Ch., BPO, Karajan.

(B) **(*) RCA (ADD) 74321 20286-2 (3). Casapietra, Stolte,
  Schreier, Leipzig R. Ch. (in *No.* 2); Leipzig GO, Masur.

Symphonies Nos. 1 in C min., Op. 11; (i) 2 in B flat (Hymn of Praise), Op. 52. (ii) Die erste Walpurgisnacht, Op. 60.

(B) *** Double Decca (ADD) 460 236-2 (2). VPO, Dohnányi
  with (i) Ghazarian, Gruberová, Krenn, V. State Op. Ch.;
  (ii) Lilowa, Laubenthal, Krause, Sramek, V. Singverein.

Symphonies Nos. 3. (Scottish); 4 in A (Italian); 5 (Reformation); Athalie: Overture & War March of the Priests; Overtures: Calm Sea and Prosperous Voyage; The Hebrides (Fingal's Cave).

(B)*** Double Decca ADD/Dig. 460 239-2. VPO, Dohnányi.

Symphonies Nos. 1–5; Overture: The Hebrides.

(M) *** Chan. 7090 (3). Philh. O, Weller (with Haymon,
  Hagley, Straka, Philh. Ch. in *Symphony No.* 2).

Symphonies Nos. 1–5; Overtures: Fair Melusina, Op. 32; The Hebrides; A Midsummer Night's Dream; Octet, Op. 20: Scherzo.

*** DG 415 353-2 (4). LSO, Abbado (with Connell, Mattila,
  Blochwitz and L. Symphony Ch. in Symphony No. 2).

(i) *Symphonies Nos. 1;* (ii) *2 (Hymn of Praise);* (i) *3 (Scottish); Overture The Hebrides.*

(B) *** Ph. Duo (ADD) 456 071-2 (2). LPO; (i) Haitink; (ii) M. Price, Burgess, Jerusalem, LPO Ch., Chailly.

(i) *Symphonies Nos. 4 (Italian); 5 (Reformation); Calm Sea and Prosperous Voyage Overture; (ii–iii) Violin Concerto in E min.; (iii–iv) A Midsummer Night's Dream: Overture; Incidental Music.*

(B) *** Ph. Duo (ADD) 456 074-2 (2). (i) LPO; (ii) Grumiaux; (iii) Concg. O; (iv) with Woodland, Watts, Women of Netherlands R. Ch.; all cond. Haitink.

Abbado's is a set to brush cobwebs off an attractive symphonic corner; in the lesser known symphonies it is his gift to have you forgetting any weaknesses of structure or thematic invention in the brightness and directness of his manner. The toughness of the piece makes one marvel that Mendelssohn ever substituted the scherzo from the *Octet* for the third movement (as he did in London), but helpfully Abbado includes that extra scherzo, so that on CD, with a programming device, you can readily make the substitution yourself. Good, bright recording, though not ideally transparent. However, this set remains at full price.

Weller's set of the Mendelssohn symphonies can stand comparison with the finest alternatives, including Karajan and Abbado. Certainly it is the most beautifully recorded, the Chandos sound richly full-bodied, though not sharply defined. He plays the *First Symphony* as if it were a mature work, not the inspiration of a fifteen-year-old. The *Scottish* and *Italian Symphonies* convey the sense of live performances caught on the wing. These are warm, affectionate readings which include exposition repeats and build excitingly to climaxes. In the *Reformation Symphony* and in *Fingal's Cave*, which follows, there is an emotional thrust that is very involving, leading to a joyfully exultant conclusion in the finale. Again in the *Hymn of Praise* (No. 2) from the opening trombone solo onwards it is the warmth and weight of the recorded sound that tells, with a large chorus set against full-bodied, satisfyingly string-based orchestral sound. Though again speeds are often dangerously slow, the sense of spontaneity in the performance makes it compelling throughout. In the finale, Cynthia Haymon and Alison Hagley are warm-toned soloists, with Peter Straka an expressive if slightly fluttery tenor, but with a timbre which suits Mendelssohn. A considerable achievement.

Karajan's distinguished set of the Mendelssohn *Symphonies* was recorded in 1971/2 in the Berlin Jesus Christus Kirche. The early C minor work sounds particularly fresh, and the *Hymn of Praise* brings the fullest sound of all; the very fine choral singing is vividly caught. The soloists make a good team, rather than showing any memorable individuality; but overall Karajan's performance is most satisfying. The *Scottish Symphony* is a particularly remarkable account and the *Italian* shows the Berlin Philharmonic in sparkling form: the only drawback is Karajan's characteristic omission of both first-movement exposition repeats. There are few reservations to be made about the *Reformation Symphony*, and the sound has been effectively clarified without too much loss of weight.

When Bernard Haitink in 1980 was prevented from rounding off his planned Mendelssohn symphony cycle with the *Symphony No. 2* (*Lobgesang – Hymn of Praise*), Riccardo

Chailly stepped in to record it in his place. This compilation brings together what, despite the change of conductor, is an outstanding cycle, fresh and energetic, with a geniality that regularly puts a smile on Mendelssohn's face. Only in the first movement of the *Italian Symphony* does Haitink press too hard, and even then he has time to spring rhythms. Broadly, Chailly follows a similar pattern in the *Hymn of Praise*, another excellent performance with an outstanding trio of soloists, helped by full and vivid sound, though the fine chorus is backwardly balanced. The fourth disc contains Haitink's brilliant Concertgebouw version of the *Midsummer Night's Dream* incidental music – ten movements, including a dazzling account of the Overture – as well as the excellent Grumiaux version of the *Violin Concerto*, also with Haitink and the Concertgebouw, with 1960s sound still fresh and clear.

Dohnányi's pair of Double Deccas (which includes two key overtures, lesser-known *Athalie* items and a half-hour cantata, as well as the symphonies) brings performances which are fresh and direct, often relying on faster and more flowing speeds than in Abbado's full-price set. The most striking contrast comes in the *Hymn of Praise*, where Dohnányi's speeds are often so much faster than Abbado's that the whole character of the music is changed. Many will prefer Dohnányi in that, particularly when the choral sound is brighter and more immediate too. The *Reformation Symphony* comes off particularly well. The vintage recordings were made in the Sofiensaal between 1976 and 1978, and the two overtures and the *Italian Symphony* are digital, the Decca engineers producing sound which was among the finest of its period. The snag of the set is that Dohnányi, unlike Abbado, omits exposition repeats, which in the *Italian Symphony* means the loss of the substantial lead-back passage in the first movement. *Die erste Walpurgisnacht* makes an excellent contribution to the first of the two Doubles.

Recorded by Eurodisc in 1971/2, the earlier of Masur's two Mendelssohn *Symphony* cycles, reissued on RCA, makes an excellent bargain-priced alternative to the strongly characterized later set for Teldec. The recording is warmer and more immediate, and Masur's preference for flowing speeds in slow movements is not so marked, often with more affectionate moulding of phrase. The performances are often more vivid and more spontaneous-sounding, notably that of No. 2, the *Hymn of Praise*, where the forward focus of the voices adds to the impact of a most refreshing reading. Sadly, the two most popular symphonies, the *Scottish* and *Italian*, are the least successful, with generally slow speeds and slacker ensemble than in the rest. Masur here observes the exposition repeat in the *Italian* but not in the *Scottish*, but this is a case where Masur's mid-priced Teldec alternative coupling of these two key works is clearly preferable.

Symphonies Nos. 1; (i) 2 (Hymn of Praise); 5 (Reformation).

(B) **(*) Teldec Ultima 3984 21341-2 (2). Leipzig GO, Masur; (i) with Bonney, Schönheit, Leipzig R. Ch.

Masur's mastery in Mendelssohn is due in good measure to his ability to adopt relatively fast speeds and make them sound easy and relaxed, not hurried and breathless, and in all three symphonies here Masur is faster than his principal rivals on disc, not just in allegros but in slower movements too. In Nos. 1 and 5 that works very well indeed, bringing an alert freshness with no hint of sentimentality; but the fast speeds in the big choral symphony will for many be too extreme. Where Abbado on DG takes 29 minutes over the three instrumental movements which open the work, Masur takes only 21 minutes, an astonishing discrepancy. Nevertheless, as ever, Masur avoids breathlessness, and with excellent soloists and choir, freshly recorded with plenty of detail, the two-disc package is still competitive in bringing together Mendelssohn's three less popular symphonies.

Symphonies Nos. 1; 5 (Reformation); Octet, Op. 20: Scherzo.

(M) *** DG 445 596-2. LSO, Abbado.

The *First* and *Fifth* are Mendelssohn's least-played and least-recorded symphonies, so Abbado's coupling is very welcome. His version includes a sparkling version of the Scherzo from the Octet which Mendelssohn substituted for the original when he presented it in London, so that you can readily programme the substitution yourself. His direct manner suits the *Reformation Symphony* equally well. Brightly lit, early-digital recording (1984), but with the warm ambience of St John's, Smith Square, adding overall bloom.

Symphony No. 2 (Hymn of Praise).

*** DG (IMS) 423 143-2. Connell, Mattila, Blochwitz, L. Symphony Ch., LSO, Abbado.

(M) *** DG (ADD) 431 471-2 Mathis, Rebmann, Hollweg, German Op. Ch., BPO, Karajan.

*** Opus 111 OPS 30-98. Isokoski, Bach, Lang, Chorus Musicus Köln, Das neue Orchester, Spering.

We have already praised the 1972 Karajan recording of the *Hymn of Praise* within the context of his complete set of Mendelssohn symphonies above. In some ways Abbado's full-price digital version is even finer, if not more clearly recorded, brushing aside all sentimentality, both fresh and sympathetic and, though the recording is not ideally clear on inner detail, the brightness reinforces the conductor's view. The chorus, well focused, is particularly impressive, and the sweet-toned tenor, Hans-Peter Blochwitz, is outstanding among the soloists.

It is timely that Spering presents a performance of the *Hymn of Praise* in period style. With clean, crisp textures this is a most refreshing performance, full of incidental beauties. For example, the once-celebrated duet for the two soprano soloists, *Ich harrete des Herrn* ('I waited for the Lord'), is intensely beautiful in its simplicity, with Soile Isokoski (also in Herreweghe's *Elijah*) and Mechthild Bach both angelically sweet yet nicely contrasted. The tenor soloist, Frieder Lang, is also exceptionally sweet-toned, though his projection is keen enough to make the *Huter, ist die Nacht bald hin?* ('Watchman, what of the night?') episode very intense and dramatic. Though not always clear in inner definition, the freshness of the choral singing matches that of the whole performance.

Symphony No. 3 (Scottish); Overtures: Calm Sea and a Prosperous Voyage; The Hebrides; Ruy Blas.

(BB) **(*) Naxos 8.550222. Slovak PO, Dohnányi.

Symphony No. 3 in A min. (Scottish); (i) A Midsummer Night's Dream: Overture & Incidental Music.

✦ (M) *** Decca (ADD) 466 990-2. LSO, Maag; (i) with Vyvyan, Lowe, ROHCG female ch.

Maag's classic account of the *Scottish Symphony* rightly finds itself on the Legends label for it is indeed legendary, remarkable for its freshness and natural spontaneity. The opening cantilena is poised and phrased very beautifully and sets the mood for what is to follow. A pity that the exposition repeat is not included, and though in the last movement the final *Maestoso* is measured, the effect remains most compelling, almost Klemperian in manner, with superb horn-playing.

The *Midsummer Night's Dream* excerpts date from 1957 and sound equally fresh, and the character of the playing is again superb; while Maag's treatment of the *Overture*'s forthright second subject strikes the ear as rhythmically mannered, the recording includes a strong contribution from a fruity bass wind instrument (representing Bottom) which might possibly be Mendelssohn's ophicleide, but is probably a well-played tuba. The Kingsway Hall recording is warm, full and well-projected and this new Legends mastering includes the vocal and choral numbers on the original LP, which were not included on the previous reissue. Strongly recommended – a wholly delightful disc.

Oliver Dohnányi conducts a joyful account of the *Scottish Symphony* on Naxos, given the more impact by forward recording. Mendelssohn's lilting rhythms in all the fast movements are delightfully bouncy, and though the slow movement brings few hushed pianissimos, its full warmth is brought out without sentimentality. The three overtures, also very well done, not least the under-appreciated *Ruy Blas*, make an excellent coupling.

Symphonies Nos. 3 (Scottish); 4 (Italian).

*** Decca 433 811-2. San Francisco SO, Blomstedt.

*** Mer. CDE 84261. Apollo CO, Chernaik.

(M) *** DG 427 810-2. LSO, Abbado.

(BB) *** ASV (ADD) CDQS 6004. O of St John's, Lubbock.

(M) *** Virgin EMI VM5 61735-2. LCP, Norrington.

(B) *** Australian Decca Eloquence (ADD) 458 176-2. LSO, Abbado.

*** Teldec 9031 72308-2. COE, Harnoncourt.

(M) **(*) DG (IMS) (ADD) 439 980-2. Israel PO, Bernstein.

(i) Symphonies Nos. 3 (Scottish); (ii) 4 (Italian); (i) Hebrides Overture.

(M) *** DG (ADD) 449 743-2. BPO, Karajan.

(M) *** Classic fM 75605 57013-2. Ulster O, Sitkovetsky

Of all the many discs coupling Mendelssohn's two most popular symphonies, the *Scottish* and the *Italian*, there is none finer than Blomstedt's. Not only does he choose ideal speeds – not too brisk in the exhilarating first movement of the *Italian* nor sentimentally drawn out in slow movements – he conveys a feeling of spontaneity throughout, springing rhythms infectiously. The sound is outstandingly fine, outshining any direct rival.

Karajan's 1971 account of the *Scottish* is justly included among DG's 'Originals', as it is one of his finest recordings. The coupling was originally the *Fingal's Cave*, a characterful and evocative account, but now the *Italian Symphony* has been added, recorded two years later. This is also played very beautifully and brilliantly but, good though the performance is, it does not quite match that of the *Scottish* and it is just a shade wanting in spontaneity and sparkle.

Dmitry Sitkovetsky draws superb performances from the orchestra of both symphonies as well as the overture, helped by outstandingly full and rich recording, made in the Ulster Hall. With speeds beautifully chosen and with rhythms crisp and well sprung, his readings are full of light and shade, warmly dramatic, demonstrating an expressive freedom – notably in pressing ahead – which always sounds natural, never self-conscious. The strings in particular produce some magical pianissimos, reflecting Sitkovetsky's own mastery as an instrumentalist. A very generous and apt coupling, with the exposition repeat observed in the *Italian Symphony* but not in the *Scottish*.

The dynamic young American conductor, David Chernaik, gives performances of these two symphonies which in their vitality and freshness are second to none. Although the recording is live, the audience is notably quiet and shows its presence only by clapping perfunctorily at the end of each work, a distraction which could and should have been edited out. The London-based Apollo Chamber Orchestra, on its toes throughout, is exactly the right size for these two symphonies, and the recording (in St John's, Smith Square) has been beautifully balanced so that detail is transparently clear, yet a warm ambience remains. Chernaik includes the essential exposition repeats in both symphonies.

Abbado's fine digital recordings of the *Scottish* and *Italian Symphonies*, coupled together from his complete set, make a splendid mid-price bargain. The recording is admirably fresh and bright – atmospheric, too – and the ambience, if not absolutely sharply defined, is very attractive. Both first-movement exposition repeats are included.

As in his comparable Schumann coupling (see below), Norrington opts for unexaggerated speeds in the outer movements, relatively brisk ones for the middle movements. The results are similarly exhilarating, particularly in the clipped and bouncy account of the first movement of the *Italian*. The *Scottish Symphony* is far lighter than usual, with no hint of excessive sweetness. The Scherzo has rarely sounded happier, and the finale closes in a fast gallop for the 6/8 coda with the horns whooping gloriously. Good, warm recording, only occasionally masking detail in tuttis.

Lubbock's coupling of the *Scottish* and *Italian Symphonies* makes an outstanding super-bargain issue, offering performances of delightful lightness and point, warmly and cleanly recorded. The string section may be of chamber size but, amplified by a warm acoustic, the result sparkles, with rhythms exhilaratingly lifted. The slow movements are both on the slow side but flow easily with no suspicion of sentimentality, while the *Saltarello* finale of No. 4, with the flute part delectably pointed, comes close to Mendelssohnian fairy music.

It is good to have Abbado's outstanding 1968 coupling with the LSO back in the catalogue again on Australian Decca's Eloquence label. His *Scottish Symphony* is beautifully played and the LSO respond to his direction with the greatest delicacy of feeling, while the *Italian Symphony* has comparable lightness of touch, matched with lyrical warmth. The only drawback is the absence of the first-movement exposition repeat in the *Scottish* (though not in the *Italian*).

As in Beethoven and Schubert, Nikolaus Harnoncourt's happy relationship with the Chamber Orchestra of Europe brings performances which on modern instruments might be counted 'historically aware', with shortened phrasing, limited string vibrato, rasping horns and clean-cut timpani. The cleanness of texture is enhanced by Harnoncourt's generally relaxed speeds, which allow Mendelssohnian rhythms to have an infectious spring. Natural, well-balanced sound.

Bernstein's expansive tempi run the risk of overloading Mendelssohn's fresh inspiration, with heavy expressiveness making the slow introduction and slow movement sound almost Mahlerian. The rhythmic lift of the Scherzo and finale makes amends; but it is a performance to bring out for an interesting change, rather than a version to recommend for repeated listening. The recording is well balanced and full. The sparkling account of the *Italian* was made a year earlier in the Mann Auditorium, Tel Aviv, but remains convincingly atmospheric if not ideally clear. It is also available at bargain price, coupled with the *Midsummer Night's Dream* incidental music – see below.

Symphonies Nos. 3 (Scottish); 4 (Italian); 5 (Reformation); Overtures: Calm Sea and a Prosperous Voyage; The Hebrides.

*** Ph. 456 267-2. O of the 18th Century, Brüggen.

Even if you do not respond to period-instrument performances, this is worth investigating. The orchestral playing is splendidly uninhibited and at times virtuosic. The finale of the *Italian* is quite staggering. Textures are beautifully transparent and the only cause for reservation is the string tone, which though pure lacks the weight of sonority and the singing quality of modern instruments. Those who warm to period instruments will know what to expect, and will welcome these highly musical performances with enthusiasm. First-rate recording.

Symphony No. 4 (Italian).

(M) *** DG 445 514-2. Philh. O, Sinopoli – SCHUBERT: *Symphony No. 8*. *** ❂

(B) *** Decca Penguin 460 643-2. San Francisco SO, Blomstedt – SCHUBERT: *Symphony No. 8 (Unfinished)*. **

(***) Testament mono SBT 1173. Philh. O, Cantelli – BRAHMS: *Symphony No. 3*. (***)

Sinopoli's great gift is to illuminate almost every phrase afresh. His speeds tend to be extreme – fast in the first movement but with diamond-bright detail, and on the slow side in the remaining three. Only in the heavily inflected account of the third movement is the result at all mannered but, with superb playing from the Philharmonia and excellent Kingsway Hall recording, this rapt performance is most compelling. For refinement of detail, especially at lower dynamic levels, the CD is among the most impressive digital recordings to have come from DG.

Blomstedt's 1990 recording is also one of the very finest. Not only does he choose ideal speeds – not too brisk in the exhilarating first movement, nor sentimental in the slow one – he conveys a feeling of spontaneity throughout, springing the rhythms infectiously. The recording is outstanding, but it is a pity that the original coupling of an equally fine performance of the *Scottish Symphony* (still available at full price, see above) was replaced with Schubert's *Unfinished*, which is considerably less successful. The personal commentary is by John Guare.

Guido Cantelli recorded Mendelssohn's *Italian Symphony* twice with the Philharmonia. His later version of August 1955, originally published by EMI and long-admired, is already available on Testament (SBT 1034), but this 1951 version, the very first recording Cantelli made with the Philharmonia, was never issued. In fact, as close comparison reveals, it is even finer than the later version, a degree more biting and urgent in the first movement with more light and shade, more spontaneously expressive in the middle movements, and clearer and lighter in the *Presto* finale. In first-rate mono sound it makes a very welcome coupling for Cantelli's glowing account of the Brahms.

Symphonies Nos. 4 (Italian; original & revised versions); 5 (Reformation).

*** DG 459 156-2. VPO, Gardiner.

In both versions of the *Italian* and in the live recording of the *Reformation* – with all Victorian cobwebs blown away – John Eliot Gardiner brings out both the transparency and the urgency of Mendelssohn's inspiration, generally preferring fast but never breathless speeds. The *coup* is that the revised version of the last three movements of the *Italian* have never been recorded before. The composer made the revisions in the year following the London première. Surprisingly for so discriminating a composer, he undermined the exuberant inspiration of the original – smoothing over melodic lines (as in the *Pilgrim's March*) and extending linking passages. Even so, a fascinating insight into the creative process and the danger of second thoughts on what was originally white-hot inspiration.

Symphonies Nos. 4 (Italian); 5 (Reformation).

(M) (**(*)) RCA mono 74321 59480-2 (2). NBC SO, Toscanini
– SCHUBERT: *Symphonies Nos. 5; 8 (Unfinished); 9 in C (Great).* (**(*))

Though there is still an edge on high violins, this new RCA transfer of Toscanini's NBC performances offers fuller sound with plenty of body. The playing in this surprisingly rare coupling is characteristically brilliant, but not entirely without charm, and the *Reformation Symphony* is certainly arresting. With the three Schubert symphonies, this makes an attractive coupling.

Symphony No. 4 (Italian); A Midsummer Night's Dream: Overture; (i) Incidental Music (complete).

(M) *** EMI (ADD) CDM5 67038-2. Philh. O, Klemperer
   (i) with Harper, Baker, Philh. Ch.

(i) *Symphony No. 4 in A (Italian); Overture The Hebrides;* (ii) *A Midsummer Night's Dream: Overture; Scherzo; Nocturne; Wedding March.*

(B) *** DG (ADD) 439 411-2. (i) Israel PO, Bernstein; (ii) Bav. RSO, Kubelik.

(i) *Symphony No. 4 (Italian); Overtures: The Hebrides;* (ii) *Ruy Blas; A Midsummer Night's Dream: Overture; Scherzo; Intermezzo; Nocturne; Wedding March.*

(B) **(*) Decca 448 237-2. (i) VPO, Dohnányi; (ii) Montreal SO, Dutoit.

(i) *Symphony No. 4 (Italian); (ii) A Midsummer Night's Dream: Overture; Incidental Music: Scherzo; Intermezzo; Nocturne; Wedding March; Fanfare & Funeral March; Dance of the Rustics.*

(BB) *** LaserLight 15 526. (i) Philh. O, Sándor; (ii) Budapest PO, Kovacs.

Klemperer takes the first movement of the *Italian Symphony* substantially slower than we are used to, but this is no heavily monumental and humourless reading. The Philharmonia playing sparkles and has an incandescence which outshines many other versions with more surface sparkle. There is again a slowish speed for the second movement, but the way Klemperer moulds and floats the main theme over the moving bass defeats all preconceptions in its sustained beauty, and it is the beautiful shaping of a phrase that makes the finale so fresh and memorable. In the Overture and incidental music from *A Midsummer Night's Dream* the orchestral playing is again superb, the wind solos so nimble that even the *Scherzo*, taken more slowly than usual, has a light touch. The contribution of the celebrated soloists and the Philharmonia Chorus is first class and the quality of the remastered 1960 recording is full and fresh. This is another of the more notable reissues in the 'Klemperer Legacy'.

Bernstein's performance of the *Italian Symphony* (exposition repeat included) is sparkling and persuasive. The 1978 recording was made at a public concert and, though speeds are often challengingly fast in outer movements, they never fail to convey the exhilaration of the occasion. *Fingal's Cave* is also a live recording, made a year later, and while it has plenty of romantic warmth and Bernstein is slightly more indulgent, it too sounds spontaneously alive. In the items from *A Midsummer Night's Dream* the Bavarian orchestra are on top form, especially in the *Overture*, which is beautifully played. The recording, made in the Herkules-Saal, Munich, still sounds excellent, and this bargain Classikon CD would grace any collection.

Christoph von Dohnányi's is a refreshing account of the *Italian*, never pushed too hard, and with the *Saltarello* taken exhilaratingly fast. It is a pity that the first-movement exposition repeat is omitted so that one misses the extended lead-back passage. However, the CD is generously full for, besides Dohnányi's slow and romantic account of the *Hebrides Overture*, there is Dutoit's splendidly vital *Ruy Blas*. Indeed both this and the 32-minute selection from the *Midsummer Night's Dream* incidental music are marvellously recorded. However, the playing in the incidental music is altogether more routine: the very brisk *Scherzo* conveys little charm, although the *Wedding March* is grand without being pompous.

A first-class coupling in the super-bargain range from LaserLight. Sándor gives a fresh and exhilarating account of the *Italian Symphony*, with particularly elegant Philharmonia playing, and the digital sound is excellent. The performance of a generous selection from the *Midsummer Night's Dream* incidental music also shows the Budapest orchestra on top form: this is most beguiling and is recorded in a pleasingly warm acoustic which does not cloud detail.

Symphony No. 5 (Reformation).

(M) *** DG (ADD) 449 720-2. BPO, Maazel — FRANCK: *Symphony in D min.* ***

The *Reformation Symphony* springs grippingly to life in Maazel's hands. The Berlin Philharmonic brass make an immediate impact in the commanding introduction and the orchestral playing throughout continues on this level of high tension. The finale is splendidly vigorous, the chorale, *Ein' feste Burg is unser Gott*, ringing out resplendently. Maazel's interpretation was aptly chosen for reissue in DG's series of 'Originals', and the Franck coupling is hardly less impressive. The recording is spacious and has been vividly enhanced by the DG CD transfer.

CHAMBER AND INSTRUMENTAL MUSIC

Cello Sonatas Nos. 1 in B flat, Op. 45; 2 in D, Op. 58.

(N) (B) *** EMI (ADD) CZS5 74333-2 (2). Tortelier, De la Pau — CHOPIN; FAURE; RACHMANINOV: *Cello Sonatas.* ***

Cello Sonatas Nos. 1–2; Assai Tranquillo; Song Without Words, Op. 109; Variations concertantes, Op. 17.

(N) (B) *** Hyp. Helios CDH 55064. Lester, Tomes.

Cello Sonatas Nos. 1–2; Songs Without Words, Op. 19/1; Op. 109; Variations concertantes, Op. 17.

*** RCA 09026 62553-2. Isserlis, Tan (fortepiano).

Susan Tomes, the inspired pianist of the group Domus, and her cellist colleague, Richard Lester, give performances full of flair on this ideally compiled disc of Mendelssohn's collected works for cello and piano, brimming with charming ideas. As well as the works with opus number they include a delightful fragment *Assai tranquillo*, never previously recorded.

Steven Isserlis and Melvyn Tan also convey a freshness, delight and authenticity in music-making that rekindles enthusiasm for this delightful repertoire. They pace both sonatas expertly and are faithfully served by the RCA engineers. Like their colleagues, Richard Lester and Susan Tomes on Hyperion, they command poetry as well as virtuosity.

Tortelier is wholly in sympathy with these two sonatas, and even if he is partnered less expertly by his daughter Maria de la Pau this is still a thoroughly worthwhile collection. Good recording.

Cello Sonata No. 2 in D, Op. 58.

(M) *** Mercury (IMS) (ADD) 434 377-2. Starker, Sebök — BRAHMS: *Cello Sonatas.* ***

Starker and Sebök give an outstanding account of Mendelssohn's finest *Cello Sonata*, spontaneously full of ardour, yet with plenty of light and shade in the central movements, and topped by a sparkling finale, which yet retains the lyrical feeling. The 1962 recording is truthful and admirably balanced within a warm acoustic with a clear focus.

Octet in E flat.

(N) (B) *** Australian Decca Eloquence (ADD) 421 637-2. ASMF — BOCCHERINI: *Quintet for Cello & String Quartet.* ***

(N) (B) *** Hyp. Helios CDH 55043. Divertimenti — BARGIEL: *Octet.* ***

(i) Octet in E flat; String Quartet No.1 in E flat, Op. 12.

(N) (BB) ** Warner Apex (AAD) 8573 89089-2 Kreuzberger Qt; (i) with Eder Qt — SPOHR: *Double Quartet.* **

Octet in E flat, Op. 20; String Quintet No. 2 in B flat, Op. 87.

(B) *** Ph. 420 400-2. ASMF Chamber Ens.

The 1968 performance by the ASMF is fresh and buoyant, and the recording wears its years lightly. It offers fine judgement in matters of clarity and sonority, and it is coupled with a highly desirable and much less well-known work by Boccherini. This Australian Eloquence CD has full sleeve notes.

This Philips account comes from just over a decade after the Academy's earlier record of Mendelssohn's *Octet*, and the playing has greater sparkle and polish. The recorded sound is also superior and sounds extremely well in its CD format. The *Second Quintet* is an underrated piece and it too receives an elegant and poetic performance.

Divertimenti give a very natural and unforced account of the celebrated *Octet* which, though it may not be the most distinguished in the catalogue, still gives great pleasure. Excellent recorded sound.

The combined Kreuzberger and Eder Quartets give a vivacious account of the *Octet*, with the *Scherzo* the highlight, although the *Andante* is simply and affectionately played, treated like a *Song Without Words*. The *First Quartet* is also brightly presented, although here the neatly pointed *Andante* loses some of its delicate fairy atmosphere. The recording, from the early 1980s, is very good, but the transfer is not entirely flattering to the upper range of the string timbre at higher dynamic levels.

Octet in E flat, Op. 20; String Quintets Nos. 1 in A, Op. 18; 2 in B flat, Op. 87; String Quartet No. 2 in A min., Op. 13.

(N) (M) *** Virgin x 2 VBD5 61809-2 (2). Hausmusik.

A highly desirable bargain set, yet the effect of these period-instrument performances by Hausmusik on these two CDs is fascinatingly different. The *Octet* and *String Quintet No. 1* were recorded in the Concert Hall of York University in 1989, and the recording, balanced by Mike Hatch, is outstanding, clear and transparent, with an attractively warm ambience giving extra weight to the lower lines.

The performance of the *Octet*, with Monica Huggett leading the violins and Anthony Pleeth the cellos, is most refreshing, as is the account of the *Second String Quintet*, another miraculous masterpiece of Mendelssohn's boyhood. Most revealing of all is the way the last two movements of the *Octet*, the featherlight Scherzo and the dashing finale, with their similar figuration, are presented in contrast, the one slower and more delicately pointed than usual, the other more exhilarating than usual.

The coupling of the *Second Quartet* and *Second Quintet* was made four years later in an ecclesiastical acoustic, and the balance engineer, Mike Clements, had to put his microphones closer to the players. Paul Beznosiuk leads the violins, and the fine cellist is Richard Lester. While the overall sonority at lower dynamic levels is finely blended, the fortissimos sound somewhat thinner. Yet the textural transparency remains, and these are two very well-characterized readings. Playing is alert and articulate: the delicate *Intermezzo* of the *Second Quartet* contrasts most tellingly with the finale, and the *Andante scherzando* of the *Second Quintet* is delightfully done to offer a foil for the deeply felt *Adagio*, while the bustle of the finale is invigorating. Above all, these players communicate delight in all this music, and their account of the *Octet* is second to none.

Piano Quartet No. 1 in C min., Op. 1; Piano Sextet in D, Op. 110.

(BB) **(*) Naxos 8.550966. Bartholdy Piano Qt (augmented).

Piano Quartets Nos. 2 in F min., Op. 2; 3 in B min., Op. 3.

(BB) **(*) Naxos 8.550967. Bartholdy Piano Qt.

Piano Quartet No. 1 in C min., Op. 1.

(BB) *** ASV CDQS 6199. Schubert Ens. of London –
   BRAHMS: *Piano Quartet No. 2.* ***

Piano Quartet No. 2 in F min., Op. 2.

(N) (BB) *** ASV CDQS 6194. Schubert Ens. of London –
   BRAHMS: *Piano Quartet No. 2.* ***

Piano Quartet No. 3 in B min., Op. 3.

(BB) *** ASV CDQS 6198. Schubert Ens. of London –
   BRAHMS: *Piano Quartet No. 3.* ***

Musicianly and well-recorded performances on ASV that will give satisfaction at this (or any other) price level. Sensible tempi and very well-articulated phrasing. William Howard plays with great expertise and the instrumentalists are well balanced. The *F minor Quartet* was the product of a fourteen-year-old, yet there is no sign of immaturity: the *Adagio* is a song without words, the *Intermezzo* a delightful interlude before the slightly garrulous finale. The performance is admirably fresh, as is the recording.

The Bartholdy Quartet also have an excellent pianist in Pier Narciso Masi, and his mercurial style is just right for these early works. The string players are always fluent and show a light-hearted vivacity in Mendelelssohn's scherzos (especially in the very winning *Allegro molto* of No. 3) and finales, and they play the simple slow movements gracefully. The *Piano Sextet* also comes from the composer's youth and, like the other works, it has an engaging immediacy. The recording was made in the fairly resonant Clara Wieck

Auditorium in Heidelberg, which means that the microphones are fairly close to the strings and the balance is slightly contrived. Nevertheless the sound is good and the piano well caught.

Piano Trios Nos. 1 in D min., Op. 49; 2 in C min., Op. 66.

(M) *** HM HMT 7901335. Trio de Barcelona.
**(*) Chan. 8404. Borodin Trio.

Lovely music, and lovely performances of both works from the excellent Trio de Barcelona, as warm-hearted as they are fresh. Each *Andante* is beautifully played – and how sprightly they are in the two Scherzos. The pianist, Albert Attenelle, clearly holds the performances together, but the balance is admirable and he never dwarfs his fine string colleagues, Gérard and Lluis Claret. The one drawback is the acoustic, which is a bit too reverberant. It does not cloud detail, however; the players are given a realistic presence, and the ear soon adjusts when the music-making is so spontaneously enjoyable.

The Borodin Trio are also recorded in a very resonant acoustic and are rather forwardly balanced. They give superbly committed but somewhat overpointed readings. All the same, there is much musical pleasure to be found here.

String Quartets Nos. 1–6.

*** EMI (ADD) CDS7 54514-2 (3). Cherubini Qt.

String Quartets: in E flat; Nos. 1 in E flat, Op. 12; 4 in E min., Op. 44/2.

(BB) *** Naxos 8.550862. Aurora Qt.

String Quartets Nos. 2 in A min., Op. 13; 5 in E flat, Op. 44/3; Scherzo in A min., Op. 81/2; Theme & Variations in E, Op. 81/1.

(BB) *** Naxos 8.550863. Aurora Qt.

String Quartets Nos. 3 in D, Op. 44/1; 6 in F min., Op. 80; Capriccio in E min., Op. 81/3; Fugue in E flat, Op. 81/4.

(BB) *** Naxos 8.550861. Aurora Qt.

String Quartets: in E flat; Nos. 1–6; 4 Pieces, Op. 81.

*** Hyp. CDS 44051/3. Coull Qt.

At Naxos price, the new Aurora set of Mendelssohn's complete music for string quartet tends to sweep the board. The performances have a natural Mendelssohnian charm and elegance, but their strength and passion acknowledge the fact that the young composer in his teens wrote them under the influence of the Beethoven quartets. Indeed, the account of the *F minor* work, composed after his sister Fanny's death, is perhaps the highlight of the set. The allegros are full of passionate angst and the *Adagio* expresses the composer's pain. The engaging early *E flat Quartet* of 1823, with its confident closing *Fuga*, written when the composer was only fourteen is included, together with the four varied pieces of Op. 81 – notably the delightful *Scherzo in A minor*, here as light as thistledown. The very opening of the *First Quartet*, Op. 12, is invitingly persuasive and the charming 'fairy' *Canzonetta* which follows is delightfully crisp and pointed. Slow movements throughout are beautifully shaped and played with warmth and feeling, never sentimentalized; scherzi always sparkle; allegros have vivacity and bite. The recording is first class and, for those not seeking period-instrument performance, this is an easy first choice.

For those wanting a complete set, the Coull survey is also eminently satisfactory, the playing alive and spontaneous, well paced and musically penetrating. The quietly intense playing in slow movements shows the group's affinity with this repertoire. The recording is realistic and well balanced.

The young members of the Cherubini Quartet also consistently play with warmth as well as intensity. Here with a light touch they bring out the mercurial charm of Mendelssohn as well as his vigour and high spirits. However, unlike the Aurora and Coull sets, the Cherubini do not include two works from opposite ends of Mendelssohn's career that provide an extra insight into his development. However, this set has been deleted as we go to press.

String Quartets: in E flat; Nos. 1–2.

*** Audivis E 8622. Mosaïques Qt.

*** HM HMU 907245. Eroica Qt.

String Quartets Nos. 1–2; 2 Pieces, Op. 81.

*** Hyp. CDA 66397. Coull Qt.

String Quartet No. 2.

(M) *** Cal. (ADD) 6698. Talich Qt – BOCCHERINI: *Quartet, Op. 58/2;* HAYDN: *Quartet No. 74;* MICA: *Quartet No. 6.* ***

String Quartets Nos. 2; 4 in E min., Op. 44/2; 2 Pieces, Op. 81/1–2.

*(*) Chan. CHAN955 Sorrel Qt.

String Quartets Nos. 3–5, Op. 44/1–3.

(N) **(*) Cal. CAL 9302. Talich Qt.

For those wanting the first two *Quartets* only, the Coull Quartet give fresh and unaffected accounts of both and have the benefit of very good recorded sound. Tempi are well judged and everything flows naturally. The Coull offer the additional inducement of two of the *Four pieces*, Op. 81, which were published after Mendelssohn's death.

The Mosaïques Quartet apply their delicacy of style and subtle grading of texture with winning results to the *A minor Quartet*, particularly in the delectable *Intermezzo*, which is as light as thistledown. They open the *B flat major* with great concentration, and the *Canzonetta* has an airy fragility. Some ears might prefer the fuller, suaver quality of modern instruments in the *Andante espressivo* and finale, but certainly these performances have a character of their own, which aficionados will relish, and they are very well recorded.

The Eroica Quartet was formed in 1993 by four London period-instrument players who are committed to performing the nineteenth-century repertoire in nineteenth-century style. Their performances are distinguished by good ensemble, clean articulation and well-focused textures. Good recorded sound too.

Mendelssohn's *Quartet in A minor*, Op. 13, has a serene and remarkably searching slow movement, before its charmingly memorable 'Intermezzo', which is linked to the lively but lyrical *Presto* finale, which has something of the character of a Mendelssohn Scherzo. A most enjoyable work, played

with spirit, warmth and cultivated elegance by the Talich Quartet, who are most naturally recorded. The couplings are all equally recommendable.

The Sorrel Quartet do not produce a really beautiful sound or enough polish to be convincing candidates in these pieces. Excellent recording.

The Talich Quartet could not be more sympathetic, or warm more readily to the Mendelssohnian spirit in Op. 44, and they play brilliantly in the *Scherzi*. The snag is that though the recording is basically pleasing in an attractive ambience, the microphones are too near the leader and create a thinness of timbre more appropriate for a period-instrument performance.

String Quintets Nos. 1 in A, Op. 18; 2 in B flat, Op. 87.

*** Sony SK 60766. L'Archibudelli.

L'Archibudelli plays these two delightful works with much elegance and grace, and their lightness of touch and the transparency of texture characteristic of period instruments is revelatory, especially in the *Scherzo* of Op. 87 and the engaging *Andante scherzando* of Op. 87. The *Adagio e lento* of the latter work is played with warm expressive feeling. There are one or two passionate lunges, but these are fully acceptable as part of the overall period style and the recording is excellent.

PIANO MUSIC

Andante & Rondo capriccioso in E min., Op. 14; Prelude & Fugue in E minor/major, Op. 35/1; Sonata in E, Op. 6; Variations sérieuses in D min., Op. 53.

*** Sony MK 37838. Perahia.

Murray Perahia is perfectly attuned to Mendelssohn's sensibility and it would be difficult to imagine these performances being surpassed. The quality of the CBS recording is very good indeed.

Capriccio in F sharp min., Op. 5; 7 Characteristic Pieces, Op. 7; Fantasia (Sonata écossaise) in F sharp min., Op. 28; Prelude & Fugue in E min.; Sonata Movement in B flat.

(BB) *** Naxos 8. 553541. Frith.

This collection gives a very different idea of Mendelssohn's piano-writing from that in the *Songs Without Words*. The *Characteristic Pieces* present fascinating evidence of the influence of Bach on the young composer, with some impressive contrapuntal writing in fugues both brilliant and thoughtful. Also some echoes of Scarlatti. The three-movement *Fantasia* and the *Capriccio* as well, inspire Benjamin Frith to sparkling playing, vividly recorded.

Preludes & Fugues Nos. 1–6, Op. 35; 3 Caprices, Op. 33; Perpetuum mobile in C, Op. 33.

(BB) *** Naxos 8.550939. Frith.

Benjamin Frith offers a highly imaginative set of the Op. 35 *Preludes and Fugues*, full of diversity, from the flamboyant opening *Prelude in E minor* to the expansive *Prelude No. 6 in B flat*. The three *Caprices* are equally varied in mood and colour and are most sensitively presented. The *Perpetuum mobile* makes a scintillating encore. Acceptably full if not remarkable piano sound.

Scherzo from A Midsummer Night's Dream, Op. 61 (trans. Rachmaninov).

*** Hyp. CDA 66009. Shelley – RACHMANINOV: *Variations* etc. ***

Howard Shelley, with fabulously clear articulation and delectably sprung rhythms, gives a performance of which Rachmaninov himself would not have been ashamed.

Piano Sonata in G min., Op. 105; Capriccio in E, Op. 118; Etude in F min.; Fantasia on 'The Last Rose of Summer', Op. 15; 2 Pieces: Andante cantabile; Presto agitato. Scherzo a capriccio in F sharp min.; Variations in B flat, Op. 83.

(BB) *** Naxos 8.553358. Frith.

The *G minor Sonata*, Op. 105, is distinctly Haydnesque, and there is perhaps more charm than individuality. Although the *Fantasia on 'The Last Rose of Summer'* is pretty thin stuff, in such imaginative fingers, however, it sounds delightful and marvellously fresh. Naxos provide quite excellent recording and the series so far is touched with distinction.

Piano Sonata in B flat, Op. 106; Albumblatt, Op. 117; Andante cantabile e presto agitato in B; 3 Fantasies et Caprices, Op. 16; Rondo Capriccioso in E, Op. 14; Variations in E flat, Op. 82.

(BB) *** Naxos 8.553186. Frith.

The *B flat Sonata* has been called 'a comfortable and domestic' version of Beethoven's *Hammerklavier*. However, Benjamin Frith is so persuasive that he dispels this impression. His playing is nothing less than a delight, and in the celebrated *Rondo capriccioso* and the more conventional *Variations in E flat* of 1841 he is as light of touch as one could possibly wish.

Songs Without Words, Books 1–8 (complete); No. 49 in G min., Op. posth.

(B) **(*) Hyp. Dyad CDD 22020 (2). Rév.

Songs Without Words, Books 1–8 (complete); Albumblatt, Op. 117; Gondellied; Kinderstücke, Op. 72; 2 Klavierstücke.

(B) *** DG Double (ADD) 453 061-2 (2). Barenboim.

Songs Without Words (complete); Andante & Variations in E flat, Op. 82; Andante cantabile e presto agitato in B; Variations in B flat, Op. 83.

(B) *** Ph. Duo (IMS) (ADD) 438 709-2 (2). Alpenheim.

This 1974 set of Mendelssohn's complete *Songs Without Words*, which Barenboim plays with such affectionate finesse, has dominated the catalogue for nearly two decades. The sound is first class. At DG Double price this sweeps the board in this repertoire.

Ilse von Alpenheim's set of *Songs Without Words* may not have quite the distinctive character of Barenboim, but she plays this music with an appealing spontaneous simplicity. The (1980) recording of the piano is first class.

Lívia Rév's survey has charm and warmth, and she includes a hitherto unpublished piece. The set is handsomely presented and the recording is warm and pleasing. This might well now be seriously considered at its new price, especially by those who enjoy intimate music-making and want digital sound with its silent background.

Songs Without Words, Opp. 19/1, 3, 5; 30/2, 4, 6; 38/2, 3, 6; 53/4; 62/2; 67/1–2, 4; 103/5.

⚙ *** Sony SK 66511. Perahia – BACH/BUSONI: *Chorales*; LISZT: *Concert Paraphrases of Schubert Lieder*. *** ⚙

As his earlier records have so amply demonstrated, Murray Perahia has a quite unique feeling for Mendelssohn. He invests these pieces with a depth of poetic feeling that is quite special.

Songs Without Words, Opp. 19/1, 6; 30/6; 38/4, 6; 53/2–4; 62/1, 5–6; 67/3–4; 85/4, 6; 102/3, 5.

(M) (**) EMI mono CHS5 66775-2 (2). Gieseking – GRIEG: *Lyric pieces*. (**)

Gieseking's Mendelssohn recordings do not find him at his most inspired. Of course some are touched by his special poetry but others sound – dare one say it – a little 'casual'. The recorded sound is a little studio-bound.

ORGAN MUSIC

Organ Sonatas Nos. 1–6, Op. 65/1–6; Preludes & Fugues Nos. 1–3, Op. 37/1–3; Andantes in D & F; Allegro in B flat; Allegro, Chorale & Fugue in D; Allegro maestoso in C; Fugues: (Allegro) in E min.; (Lento) in F min.

(B) *(*) Hyp. Dyad CDD 22029 (2). Scott (organ of St Paul's Cathedral).

John Scott's survey of Mendelssohn's organ music is pretty comprehensive, but the choice of the St Paul's Cathedral organ was a mistake. The ample sounds and blurring resonance prevent any kind of bite – particularly striking in the *Allegro con brio* which opens the *Fourth Sonata*. He is undoubtedly a master of this repertoire technically speaking (witness the closing *Allegro, Choral and Fugue in D*, which pays direct homage to Bach) but his style seems embedded in Victorian tradition.

VOCAL MUSIC

Lieder: *Allnächtlich im Traume; Altdeutsches Liede; And'res Maienlied; An die Entfernte; Auf der Wanderschaft; Auf Flügeln des Gesanges ('On wings of song'); Bei deder Wiege; Der Blumenkranz; Da lieg' ich unter den Bäumen; Entelied; Erster Verlust; Das erste Veilchen; Es lauschte das Lamb; Frühlingslied* (3 versions: Lenau, Lichtenstein and Klingemann settings); *Grüss; Hirtenlied; Jagdlied; Minnelied* (Deutsches Volkslied); *Minnelied* (Tieck); *Der Mond; Morgengruss; Nachtlied; Neue Liebe; O Jugend; Pagenlied; Reiselied* (2 versions: Heine and Ebert); *Scheindend; Schiflied; Schlafloser Augen Leuchte; Tröstung; Venetianisches Gondellied; Volkslied (Feuchtersleben); Das Waldschloss; Wanderlied; Warnung vor dem Rhein; Wenn sich zwei Herzen scheiden; Winterlied.*

(M) **(*) EMI CMS7 64827-2 (2). Fischer-Dieskau, Sawallisch.

Though Mendelssohn generally reserved his finest song-like inspirations for the *Songs Without Words*, the lyrical directness of these settings of Heine, Eichendorff, Lenau and others assures him of a niche of his own among Lieder composers. Fischer-Dieskau conveys the joy of fresh discovery but in some of the well-known songs – *Grüss* or *On Wings of Song* – he tends to overlay his singing with heavy expressiveness. Lightness should be the keynote, and that happily is wonderfully represented in the superb accompaniments of Sawallisch. However, this set is now deleted.

Lieder: *Auf Flügeln des Gesanges; Der Blumenkranz; Der Blumenstrauss; Es weiss und rät es doch Keiner; Frage; Frühlingsglaube; Herbstlied; Hexenlied; Ich hör ein Vöglein; Im Grünen; Morgengruss; Nachlied; Neue Liebe; Reiselied; Scheidend; Die Sterne scheu'n in stiller Nacht.*

(B) *** EMI double forte (ADD) CZS5 73836-2 (2). Baker, Parsons – LISZT: *Lieder;* SCHUMANN: *Liederkreis, Op. 39.* ***

Mendelssohn's songs, often dismissed as trivial ballads, bring repeated revelations from Janet Baker, with Geoffrey Parsons a comparably perceptive accompanist. Whether in the airy beauty of the most famous of the songs, *Auf Flügeln des Gesanges* ('On wings of song'), the golden happiness of *Morgengruss*, the darkness of *Reiselied* or the expressive narrative of *Hexenlied*, Dame Janet sings not only with rare intensity and acute sense of detail, but also with an unexpected heightening of expression in tone-colours, beautifully contrasted. Mendelssohn's songs, she tells us, are not just tuneful, they can communicate with the resonance of Schubert Lieder. Well-balanced recording and fair documentation, but no texts or translations.

Motets: *Aus tiefer Noth schrei'ich zu dir; 2 Geistliche Choere: Beati mortui; Periti autem, Op. 115; Heilig; Mitten wir im Leben sind, Op. 23. (i) 3 Motets, Op. 39. 6 Sprüche, Op. 79.*

**(*) Paraclete Press GDCG 107. Gloria Dei Cantores, Patterson; (i) with Jordan (organ) – BRAHMS: *Motets.* **(*)

This excellent choir, based at Cape Cod, Massachusetts, is very much at home in Mendelssohn, and this rewarding repertoire is most persuasively presented and beautifully recorded in the ideal ambience of the Mechanics Hall in Worcester, Massachusetts, which shows the sonority and blend of this fine choir to moving effect. However, it is worth noting that the solo singing somewhat lets the side down, acceptable rather than distinguished, and in the three works for female voices with organ, Op. 39, the soloists (again from the choir) are insecure in *Surrexit pastor bonus*. But this is a relatively small blot on what remain eloquent performances and the six brief *Sprüche* ('Sayings') make a splendid closing group. With the reservations noted, this remains a most rewarding collection. Full texts and translations are included.

Elijah (oratorio), Op. 70.

*** Chan. 8774/5. White, Plowright, Finnie, A. Davies, L. Symphony Ch., LSO, Hickox.

(B) *** EMI double forte (ADD) CZS5 68601-2 (2). G. Jones, J. Baker, Gedda, Fischer-Dieskau, Woolf, Wandsworth School Boys' Ch., New Philh. Ch. & O, Frühbeck de Burgos.

**(*) Decca 455 688-2 (2). Terfel, Fleming, Bardon, Mark Ainsley, Edinburgh Festival Ch., OAE, Daniel.

**(*) Teldec 9031 73131-2 (2). Miles, Donath, Van Nes, George, Leipzig MDR Ch., Israel PO, Masur.

**(*) Ph. 432 984-2 (2). Kenny, Dawson, Von Otter, Rigby, Rolfe Johnson, Begley, Allen, Connell, Hopkins, ASMF Ch., ASMF, Marriner.

**(*) HM HMC 901463/4. Salomaa, Isokoski, Groop, Ainsley, Collot, La Chapelle Royale, Coll. Voc., O des Champs-Elysées, Herreweghe.

Richard Hickox with his London Symphony Chorus and the LSO secures a performance that both pays tribute to the English choral tradition in this work and presents it dramatically as a kind of religious opera. Willard White may not be ideally steady in his delivery, sometimes attacking notes from below, but he sings consistently with fervour. Rosalind Plowright and Arthur Davies combine purity of tone with operatic expressiveness, and Linda Finnie, while not matching the example of Dame Janet Baker in the classic EMI recording, sings with comparable dedication and directness in the solo, *O rest in the Lord*. The chorus fearlessly underlines the high contrasts of dynamic demanded in the score. The Chandos recording, full and immediate yet atmospheric too, enhances the drama.

Frühbeck de Burgos proves an excellent Mendelssohnian. The choice of Fischer-Dieskau as the prophet is more controversial. His pointing of English words is not always idiomatic, but his sense of drama is infallible and goes well with this Mendelssohnian new look. Gwyneth Jones and Nicolai Gedda similarly provide mixed enjoyment, but the splendid work of the chorus and, above all, the gorgeous singing of Dame Janet Baker make this a memorable and enjoyable set, very well recorded (in the late 1960s) and spaciously and realistically transferred to CD. Offered in EMI's double forte series, it makes a remarkable bargain.

The glory of Paul Daniel's Decca set is the fiercely dramatic portrayal of the central character by Bryn Terfel. This Elijah is the very personification of an Old Testament prophet. Renée Fleming sings most beautifully as the principal soprano, strong rather than reflective in *Hear ye, Israel*. There are no weak links among the others, even if there are no stars either, with Patricia Bardon's *O rest in the Lord* sounding rather matter-of-fact. Many will find it refreshing that with a period orchestra Paul Daniel takes a crisp, direct view of the work, helped by fresh, cleanly focused singing from the Edinburgh Festival Chorus. Yet Daniel is at times too metrical to conceal the squareness of some of the work's weaker passages. Clean, well-separated sound.

Masur as a Mendelssohnian consistently eliminates any hint of sentimentality, but in *Elijah* his determination to use a new broom involves many fast speeds that fail to let this dramatic music blossom, not least in the exuberant final chorus. Yet anyone wanting a fine, modern, digital recording using the German text, crisply and urgently done, should not be too disappointed, particularly when Alastair Miles sings so freshly and intelligently in the title-role.

Marriner in his line-up of soloists may look unmatchable, and there is much fine singing; but with the mellifluous Elijah of Thomas Allen balanced rather backwardly in the live recording, less dominant than he should be, the result is refined rather than dramatically powerful. Marriner and his splendid forces are in danger of sounding too well-mannered. He gives the quartets and double-quartets to the soloists, whereas Hickox, following the English tradition, has the chorus singing them.

Herreweghe's reading, using period forces, recorded live in Metz in February 1993, is predictably clean, fresh and light-textured. With a German text, this is as far removed from the English choral tradition as could be. Yet in its way it is quite compelling, thanks to the bright, clear choral singing. Petteri Salomaa is a lightweight Elijah, occasionally fluttery in timbre, and Soile Isokoski is less sweet-toned than in the Opus 111 recording of the *Hymn of Praise*, but John Mark Ainsley and Monica Groop are both excellent. Clear, atmospheric recording.

Hymne: Hor mein Bitten, Herr (Hymn of Praise); Motets: Ehre sei Gott in der Höhe; Herr, nun lässest du deinen Diener in Frieden fahren; Mein Gott, warum hast du mich verlassen; Mitten wir im Leben sind; Warum toben die Heiden; 6 Sprüche, Op. 79.

(B) *** HM (ADD) HMA 1901142. Paris Chapelle Royale, Coll. Voc. de Ghent, Herreweghe; Huys.

Herreweghe's motet performances are splendidly fresh and vital, bringing out the composer's acknowledged debt to earlier models. *Mitten wir im Leben sind* features antiphonal alternation of male and female choirs and uses a chorale previously used by Bach. The part writing is made admirably clear. Comparison with the recording by Gloria Dei Cantores of the *6 Sprüche*, Op. 79 shows the American choir rather more warmly expressive, but the slight reserve of the Herreweghe performances is enjoyable in a different way. Their account (in German) of the famous *Hymn of Praise* is very dramatic, shedding Anglican sentimental associations, with the excellent soloist, Greta de Reyghere, clear and true in the famous 'Oh for the wings of a dove'. The recording is excellent, cleanly focused within a non-blurring ecclesiastical ambience. The documentation is good, but the German texts and the English translations are not placed side by side.

Psalms Nos. 42: Wie der Hirsch schreit, Op. 42; 95: Kommt lasst uns anbeten, Op. 46; 98: Singet dem Herrn, Op. 91; 114: Da Israel aus Ägypten zog; 115: Nicht unserm Namen, Herr, Op. 31. Lass', o Herr, mich Hülfe finden, Op. 96; Lauda Sion, Op. 73.

(N) (B) *** Erato Ultima ADD/Dig. 8573 88048-2 (2). Baumann, Brunner, Silva, Stutzmann, Ihara, Blaser, Ramirez, Huttenlocher, Gulbenkian Ch & O, Lisbon, Corboz.

These recordings were made a decade apart, but although the digital versions of Op. 51 and Op. 96 are that bit more brightly defined, the recording throughout is very good.

Choral works like these may characteristically glide over the problems of religious faith in an easy and sweet setting (Psalm 42 begins with what is suspiciously close to a waltz), but in fine performances they are still worth hearing. Psalms Nos. 98 and 115 inspire Mendelssohn to some of his most effectively Bach-like writing. The text of No. 98 inspired Bach, too, and though austerity here periodically turns into sweetness both pieces are welcome in performances as fresh and alert as this. *Lauda Sion* is less varied in its expression, a persistent hymn of praise, but *Lass', O Herr, mich Hülfe finden* ('Let me find your help, O Lord'), a paraphrase of Psalm 13, is set in four contrasted sections, featuring contralto and chorus and ending with a fugue. There are good soloists and the Lisbon Choir responds to Corboz's dedicated direction.

Infelice; Psalm 47 (As pants the hart), Op. 42.

(BB) *** Virgin 2 x 1 Double VBD5 61469-2 (2). Baker, City of L. Sinf., Hickox – BERLIOZ: *Les Nuits d'été* etc.; BRAHMS: *Alto Rhapsody* etc.; RESPIGHI: *La sensitiva.* ***

The scena, *Infelice* – a piece that harks back to an earlier tradition – and the Psalm-setting both have the solos prescribed for soprano, but they suit Dame Janet well, here making a welcome foray out of official retirement for a recording. The voice is in superb condition, with the weight of expressiveness as compelling as ever. The Psalm sounds very like an extra item from *Elijah*.

A Midsummer Night's Dream: Overture, Op. 21; Incidental Music, Op. 61 (complete; with melodramas and text).

*** DG 439 897-2. Battle, Von Stade, Tanglewood Festival Ch., Boston SO, Ozawa (with excerpts from play spoken by Dame Judi Dench).

(i) *A Midsummer Night's Dream: Overture, Op. 21; Incidental Music, Op. 61 (including spoken passages with the melodramas); Symphony No. 4 (Italian).*

*** Sony SK 62826. (i) McNair, Kirchschlager, Branagh (speaker), Ch.; BPO Abbado.

Ozawa's virtually complete performance presents Mendelssohn's enchanting incidental music – which is most beautifully played throughout by the Boston Symphony Orchestra – complete with the Shakespearean text, which is spoken over the melodramas by Judi Dench. With two excellent soloists and a fine choral contribution, the only omission here is the brief excerpt which is No. 6 in the score; but the fragmentary reprise of the *Wedding March*, and the two little comic snippets, the Bergomask (*Dance of the Clowns*) and ironic little *Funeral March*, intended for the Rude Mechanicals' 'Pyramus and Thisbe' playlet, are included, whereas they are missing in the competing Sony version with Kenneth Branagh. Judi Dench speaks the Shakespeare text in the simplest way, without any of Branagh's occasional exuberance of style, and in her performance Shakespeare's words seem to glow as magically as Mendelssohn's music. The recording is first class, and the balance, with Dench's narration quite intimate but with every word clear, is very well judged indeed. This DG alternative has no coupling and plays for only 56 minutes, but every one of them is delightful.

It certainly makes an attractive package having Mendelssohn's *Midsummer Night's Dream* music dramatically presented (with Kenneth Branagh taking every role from Titania to Puck), and then very generously coupled with Mendelssohn's most popular symphony. Sony have managed to squeeze in 50 minutes of the incidental music. Some may resist Branagh's style – burring his 'r's for a Mummerset Puck, coming near to an Olivier imitation in Oberon's final speech – but in his versatility he is very persuasive. Abbado's performances are a delight, fresh and transparent in the fairy music, with generally fast speeds made exhilarating, never breathless. The chorus is balanced atmospherically, with the two excellent soloists, Sylvia McNair and Angelika Kirchschlager, set more forwardly. The recording, made live in the Philharmonie in Berlin, is rather more vivid, a degree less recessed than in the symphony, where Abbado's reading is fresh and beautifully sprung.

(i) A Midsummer Night's Dream: Overture, Op. 21; Incidental Music, Op. 61; (ii) Die erste Walpurgisnacht, Op. 60.

*** Teldec 9031 74882-2. (i) Coburn, Van Magnus, Bantzer (speaker); (ii) Remmert, Heilmann, Hampson, Pape; Arnold Schoenberg Ch., COE, Harnoncourt.

Harnoncourt gets the best of both worlds, simultaneously visiting both Mendelssohn's fairy kingdom and his not-too-serious evocation of satanic revelry and the traditional religious response. Soloists, chorus and a narrator for the Shakespearean text (translated into German) all participate in this vivid, condensed version of the *Midsummer Night's Dream* incidental music which manages to include the *Overture*, *Scherzo*, *Nocturne*, *Intermezzo* and *Wedding March*, plus the vocal numbers, including the finale. Harnoncourt is nothing if not dramatic in the *Overture*, with the featherlight violins opening *pianopianissimo* and the tuttis strong and rhythmic. The playing of the COE is of a virtuoso order and the *Scherzo* is wonderfully light and crisp in articulation. After the serene close, the atmosphere changes abruptly for Mendelssohn's Ballade, *Die erste Walpurgisnacht*, which has never before been performed so dramatically on record. He has an excellent team of soloists, with Thomas Hampson standing out, while the singing of the Arnold Schoenberg Choir is unforgettably vivid, helped by an exceptionally lively and spacious recording. This is one of Harnoncourt's very finest records.

A Midsummer Night's Dream: Overture, Op. 21; Incidental Music, Op. 61 (complete).

*** EMI (ADD) CDC7 47163-2. Watson, Wallis, Finchley Children's Music Group, LSO, Previn.

(B) *** CfP CD-CFP 4593; Wiens, Walker, LPO Ch. & O, Litton.

(i) A Midsummer Night's Dream: Overture, Op. 21; Incidental Music, Op. 61 (complete). (ii) Overtures: The Hebrides; Ruy Blas.

(BB) **(*) (ADD) Belart 461 345-2. (i) Van Bork, Hodgson, Amb. S., New Philh. O, Frühbeck de Burgos; (ii) SRO, Ansermet.

On EMI Previn offers a wonderfully refreshing account of the complete score; the veiled pianissimo of the violins at the beginning of the Overture and the delicious woodwind

detail in the Scherzo certainly bring Mendelssohn's fairies to life. Even the little melodramas which come between the main items sound spontaneous here, and the contribution of the soloists and chorus is first class. The *Nocturne* (taken slowly) is serenely romantic and the *Wedding March* resplendent. The recording is naturally balanced and has much refinement of detail.

Andrew Litton also includes the melodramas and, like Previn, he uses them most effectively as links, making them seem an essential part of the structure. He too has very good soloists; in the *Overture* and *Scherzo* he displays an engagingly light touch, securing very fine wind and string playing from the LPO. The wide dynamic range of the recording brings an element of drama to offset the fairy music. Both the *Nocturne*, with a fine horn solo, and the temperamental *Intermezzo* are good examples of the spontaneity of feeling that permeates this performance throughout and makes this disc a bargain.

Frühbeck de Burgos's 1969 recording is absolutely complete. The orchestral playing is very fine throughout – and notably so in the *Nocturne* and *Scherzo*. The performance of the *Overture* is not quite as magical as Flor's account (see above) and the Decca recording, though full-bodied and with plenty of bloom, is not as clear-cut and transparent. But this remains very good value at super-bargain price, for Ansermet's accounts of the two overtures are full of vitality and drama, while the romantic element in *Fingal's Cave* is not missed. The mid-1960s sound is excellent.

A Midsummer Night's Dream: Overture, Op. 21 (incidental music): suite.

(M) *** Sony (ADD) SBK 48264. Cleveland O, Szell – BIZET: *Symphony*; SMETANA: *Vltava*. ***

Seldom can Mendelssohn's score have been played so brilliantly on record as under Szell. The orchestral ensemble is superb, the fairies dance with gossamer lightness in the violins, yet the tension is high so that the listener is gripped from the first bar to the last of the *Overture*. The *Scherzo* is infectious, and in the *Nocturne* the solo horn is cool but very sensitive. This may not be everyone's idea of Mendelssohn, but of its kind it is first class, and the 1967 recording sounds smoother and fuller than on the old LP.

St Paul, Op. 36.

(N) *** Chan. 9882 (2). Gritton, Rigby, Banks, Coleman-Wright, BBC Nat. Ch. & O of Wales, Hickox.

(BB) *** Arte Nova 74321 59219-2 (2). Kwon, Ardam, Blochwitz, Lika, Bach-Ens. of Europa ChorAkademie, SWWR SO, Daus.

**(*) Ph. (IMS) (ADD) 420 212-2 (2). Janowitz, Lang, Blochwitz, Stier, Polster, Adam, Leipzig R. Ch. & GO, Masur.

Viciously attacked by Wagner and Bernard Shaw among others, *St Paul* – or *Paulus* in the original German, which is used here – has seriously suffered eclipse even in comparison with Mendelssohn's later and greater oratorio, *Elijah*. Yet Richard Hickox's version, recorded live in Cardiff with BBC Welsh forces, completely avoids sentimentality, finding a freshness in a score which effectively echoes the Bach Passions in punctuating the story of St Paul with chorales and the occasional 'turba' or crowd chorus. *St Paul* is not as dramatic as *Elijah*, but such a passage as the conversion of Paul (formerly Saul) on the road to Damascus is beautifully done, with the heavenly message bearing the words of Christ delivered by an ethereal women's chorus. The exuberance of the following chorus, like much else, then reflects the self-identification with Paul of a Jewish-born composer who was brought up as a Christian. In brushing any Victorian cobwebs away Hickox tends to favour speeds on the fast side, never sounding hurried as on occasion Kurt Masur can on his Philips version, but more importantly never sounding heavy or pompous as other German versions often do. Choral singing is excellent, and among the soloists Susan Gritton and Jean Rigby are first rate, though the tenor, Barry Banks, is a little strained, and Peter Coleman-Wright sounds rather gritty as recorded, though never wobbly as Theo Adam so often does on the Masur set. The warmth and clarity of the recording add to the freshness.

Joshard Daus's version is a fresh, sensitive reading with some lively choral singing and first-rate soloists, including the outstanding Helen Kwon and Hans-Peter Blochwitz. Kwon is appealingly girlish in the big aria, *Jerusalem*. The chorus is rather backwardly placed, lessening its impact, but adding to the impression of a performance rather more intimate than most. The German text is provided but no translation. Though in memorable ideas this earlier oratorio cannot match *Elijah*, it has a devotional intensity in a performance like this which is most compelling, with its echoes of Bach and Handel.

Masur, always a persuasive interpreter of Mendelssohn, here directs a performance which, without inflating the piece, conveys its natural gravity. Theo Adam is not always steady, but otherwise the team of soloists is exceptionally strong, and the chorus adds to the incandescence, although placed rather backwardly. The Leipzig recording is warm and atmospheric.

OPERA

Die beiden Pädagogen (complete).

(M) *** CPO/EMI (ADD) 999 550-2. Fuchs, Laki, Dallapozza, Fischer-Dieskau, Wewel, Hirte, Bav. Op. Ch. & O, Wallberg.

Mendelssohn wrote this jolly piece, *Die beiden Pädagogen* ('The Two Pedagogues'), when he was only twelve. Starting with a brilliant overture, remarkable for deft woodwind writing, the musical ideas are charming, the manner light and sparkling in a way astonishing from a boy, even one as talented as Mendelssohn. Solos are often superimposed on the choral writing with almost Mozartian skill. Under Heinz Wallberg, this CPO disc, very well recorded, offers a reissue of an EMI/Electrola recording made in 1978 with a first-rate cast. Fischer-Dieskau with great zest and style takes the *buffo* role of the schoolmaster, Kinderschreck, with Adolf Dallapozza clear and fresh in the principal tenor role of Carl, and with Krisztina Laki and Gabriele Fuchs well contrasted in the two soprano roles. A charming rarity. There is no libretto, only a detailed note and synopsis.

Die Heimkehr aus der Fremde (complete).

(M) *** CPO/EMI (ADD) 999 555-2. Donath, Schreier, Schwarz, Fischer-Dieskau, Kusche, Bav. Op. Ch. & O, Wallberg.

It was at the time of his first visit to England in 1829 at the age of twenty that Mendelssohn wrote this lighthearted little one-act *Singspiel*, *Die Heimkehr aus der Fremde* ('The Return from Abroad'). After the opening *Romanza* for the mother, a mezzo role, and a duet, the heroine Lisbeth is given a hauntingly beautiful aria in G minor, very sweetly sung here by Helen Donath. Hermann, the returning hero, also has a tender aria, more extended than the rest, with the young Peter Schreier perfectly cast. By that time an impostor, Kauz, has already made his mark in a jolly *buffo* aria referring to the *Dudelsack* (bagpipes), brilliantly sung by Fischer-Dieskau. The plot leads to a confrontation between the rivals, which brings an echo of Beethoven's *Fidelio*. A resolution is crisply achieved, leading to a mellifluous final ensemble very characteristic of the composer. Like *Die beiden Pädagogen*, this is a rarity well worth investigating in this vividly recorded, first-rate performance.

MENOTTI, Gian-Carlo (born 1911)

Apocalisse; (i) Fantasia for Cello & Orchestra. Sebastian: Ballet Suite.

(N) *** Chan. 9900. Spoleto Fest. O, Hickox; (i) with Wallfisch.

Richard Hickox as music director of the Spoleto Festival, having already recorded several of Menotti's operatic works for Chandos, here tackles three of his instrumental works, lyrical, colourful and communicative. The *Sebastian Ballet Suite* dates from 1944, an attractive sequence of genre pieces that gives little idea of the seedy side of the story. Hickox's reading is refined and spacious, helped by the first-rate Chandos sound, recorded live in Spoleto. The orchestral triptych, *Apocalisse*, was written for Victor de Sabata in 1951–2, with the ambitious first movement, *Improperia*, inspired by the conflict between the goodness of Christ and His suffering from mankind. The striking fanfare motifs bring echoes of Hollywood film music, and as in the *Sebastian Suite*, there are many echoes of Stravinsky ballet in ostinato rhythms. The other two movements are shorter and simpler and similarly approachable rather than darkly apocalyptic, while the *Fantasia* dating from 1976, is similarly full of striking ideas, with echoes of Walton in the virtuoso cello part, manfully tackled by Raphael Wallfisch. Good clear sound, giving no idea of the problems of live recording.

Piano Concerto in F.

(M) **(*) Van. (ADD) 08.4029.71 [OVC 4071]. Wild, Symphony of the Air, Mester – COPLAND: Concerto. ***

Menotti's *Piano Concerto*, like most of his music, is easy and fluent, never hard on the ear. Its eclectic style brings a pungent whiff of Shostakovich at the opening, and there are hints of Khachaturian elsewhere. Even if it is unlikely to bear repeated listening, the charisma and bravura of Earl Wild's playing make the music sound more substantial than it is.

Amahl and the Night Visitors (opera): **complete.**

*** That's Entertainment CDTER 1124. Haywood, Dobson,
Watson, Painter, Rainbird, ROHCG Ch. & O, Syrus.

Recorded under the supervision of the composer himself,
this is a fresh and highly dramatic performance, very well
sung and marked by atmospheric digital sound of striking
realism. Central to the success of the performance is the
astonishingly assured and sensitively musical singing of the
boy treble, James Rainbird, as Amahl, while Lorna Haywood
sings warmly and strongly as the Mother, with a strong trio
of Kings.

*Amahl and the Night Visitors: Introduction; March;
Shepherd's Dance. Sebastian* (ballet): **suite.**

*** Koch 3-7005-2. New Zealand SO, Schenck – BARBER:
Souvenirs. ***

The seven-movement suite from *Sebastian* is beautifully
crafted and expertly scored music whose attractions are
strong, as are the three movements from *Amahl and the
Night Visitors*. The players, under the late Andrew Schenck,
sound as if they are enjoying themselves, and are well
recorded.

The Consul (complete).

*** Chan. 9706 (2). Bullock, Otley, Kreitzer, Livengood,
Broadbent, 1998 Spoleto Festival O, Hickox.

This ripely red-blooded performance, recorded live at the
Spoleto Festival in 1998, finds Richard Hickox a passionate
interpreter of this early response to the cold war and the
human tragedies involved. In context today, it now emerges
as a positive strength that Menotti unashamedly echoes
Puccini in his emotional assault on the listener, whether in
dramatic coups such as the very opening, which echoes the
opening of *Tosca*, or in sweeping tunes that immediately
catch in the memory. Menotti also has room to heighten
tension in cunningly placed ensembles, as in the brilliant
quintet in Act I, based on a haunting tune, for those hopelessly waiting at the Consulate. Hickox builds the structure
masterfully, firmly controlling tension. He is helped by an
excellent orchestra and a good cast, led by Susan Bullock in
the central role of Magda. Her big outburst against bureaucracy at the end of Act II brings the emotional highpoint
of the whole opera, an overwhelming moment worthy of
Puccini. None of the others quite matches Bullock vocally,
with some voices rather unsteady. Jacalyn Kreitzer is warmly
affecting as the Mother, and Charles Austin sings strongly
as the Secret Agent, giving a rounded portrait. Full-toned
vivid recording, with ample detail.

(i) *Martin's Lie* (complete). (ii) *Canti della lontananza:
Impossible Lovers; The letter; Pegasus Asleep; Resignation;
The Seventh Glass of Wine; Snowy Morning; The Spectre.*
(iii) 5 songs: *The eternal prisoner; My ghost; The idle gift;
The longest wait; The swing.*

*** Chan. 9605. (i) Tees Valley Boy's Ch., Northern Sinfonia,
Hickox. (ii) Leggate, Martineau; (iii) Howarth, Martineau.

Martin's Lie was written as a follow-up to the children's
piece for TV, *Amahl and the Night Visitors*, a sinister medi-

eval story with a moral, fluently told in 45 minutes; warmly
involving singing and playing. Judith Howarth and Robin
Leggate are the singers in the two brief song-cycles, with
Menotti's writing all the richer in the Italian settings.

MERBECKE, John (c. 1505–c. 1585)

*Missa per Arma Iustitie; Antiphona per arma iustitie
(plainsong); Ave Dei patris filia; Domine Ihesu Christe; A
Virgin and Mother.*

*** ASV CDGAU 148. Cardinall's Musick, Carwood.

The Tudor composer John Merbecke was a polyphonic
master to bracket with his exact contemporary, Thomas
Tallis, but his Latin church music has largely disappeared,
perhaps destroyed by him after he became a devout Calvinist.
This disc brings together all the major items that survive, a
magnificent extended setting of the Mass and two splendid
anthems, one early and direct in its polyphony, the other
dauntingly complex. In the hands of Andrew Carwood and
his fine choral group, Cardinall's Musick, the disc proves as
revelatory and as beautiful as their previous, highly
acclaimed issues of earlier Tudor masters, Nicholas Ludford
and John Fayrfax.

MERCADANTE, Saverio (1795–1870)

Clarinet Concertos in B flat; E flat.

(BB) *** ASV CDQS 6242. Farrall, Britten Sinfonia, N. Daniel –
DONIZETTI: *Clarinet Concertino; Study;* ROSSINI:
Variations in B flat & C. ***

The Neapolitan composer Saverio Mercadante writes in the
galant style of Hummel, and these two *Clarinet Concertos*
are full of pleasing ideas. Indeed, the opening theme of the
better known B flat work is immediately inviting, providing
the soloist plenty of opportunities for sparkling bravura.
The three-movement *E flat Concerto* opens with classical
formality, but its secondary theme is most gracious. The
Andante is a melancholy aria, and then the sunny finale lifts
the spirits. Joy Farrall, with her lilting touch and luscious
roulades, plays both works with infectious, light-hearted
charm, and Nicholas Daniel and the Britten Sinfonia provide
elegant, neatly pointed accompaniments. With first-class
recording and equally diverting couplings, this disc is a
winner all the way.

Flute Concertos: in D; E; E min.

*** RCA 09026 61447-2. Galway, Sol. Ven., Scimone.

These three *Flute Concertos* show Mercadante to be an excellent craftsman with a nice turn for lyrical melody in the slow
movements with their simple, song-like cantilenas. Both the
Andante alla siciliana of the *D major Concerto* and the *Largo*
of the *E minor* are appealing, especially with Galway as
soloist, while the *Rondo Russo* or *Polacca* finales are inventively spirited. Scimone makes the most of the often exuberantly florid tuttis of the opening movements, and elsewhere
he accompanies Galway's silvery melodic line, sparkling

and delicate by turns, with style and polish. The sound is excellent.

Sinfonia caratteristica; Sinfonia fantastica; La danza; (i) *Fantasia on Lucia di Lammermoor for Cello & Orchestra; Fantasia on Themes from Rossini's Stabat Mater; Il lamento di Bardo.*

*(*) Fonit 8573 81472-2. O Philharmonia Mediterranea, De Filippi.

The *Sinfonia caratteristica* is delightful, very like a Rossini overture, and almost as tuneful and witty, even if Mercadante can't quite manage an authentic 'crescendo'. The episodic *Sinfonia fantasica* is less remarkable, and *Il lamento di Bardo* is melodramatic, if rather endearingly so. *La danza* is not nearly as infectious and catchy as Rossini's famous piece, and is rather like second-class ballet music; the two *Fantasias* need bolder advocacy than they receive here: the solo cello in *Lucia di Lammermoor* is wan and low-profiled. The orchestra play well-enough and are pleasingly recorded, but only in the first piece does Luigi De Filippi display the kind of flair the programme needs throughout.

MERIKANTO, Aarre (1893–1958)

Andante Religioso; 4 Compositions for Orchestra; Lemminkäinen, Op. 10; Pan, Op. 28; Scherzo.

** Ondine ODE 905-2. Tampere PO, Ollila.

Lemminkäinen comes from 1916, when Merikanto was finishing his studies in Moscow, and is derivative (Russian post-nationalism, Sibelius and a dash of Scriabin). *Pan* is more radical and is highly imaginative with an evocative and powerful atmosphere. The *Four Compositions for Orchestra* come from the 1930s as does the *Scherzo*. Good performances and decent recording, though the Tampere studio is a bit on the dry side.

(i) *Piano Concerto Nos. 2 & 3; 2 Studies for Small Orchestra; 2 Pieces for Orchestra.*

** Ondine ODE 915-2. (i) Raekallio; Tampere PO, Ollila.

Although neither of the piano concertos is the equal of the *Second Violin Concerto*, they are both inventive and rewarding. The middle movement of the *Third Piano Concerto*, with its strong evocation of nature, is one of Merikanto's most haunting inspirations. The orchestral pieces are less interesting. Matti Raekallio is a very capable player and the Tampere Orchestra, though obviously a provincial band, copes well under Tuomas Ollila. The sound is synthetic with little front-to-back perspective. Worth investigating all the same.

'Meet the Composer': (i) *Violin Concertos Nos. 2 & 4;* (ii) *Fantasy for Orchestra;* (iii) *Konzertstück for Cello & Orchestra;* (ii) *Largo misterioso;* (iv) *Notturno;* (ii) *Pan;* (iv) *10 Pieces for Orchestra;* (ii) *Symphonic Study;* (v) *Genesis (for soprano, chorus & orchestra).*

(B) *** Finlandia Double 4509-99970-2 (2). (i) Saarikettu, Helsinki PO, DePreist; (ii) Finnish RSO, Segerstam; (iii) Karttunen, London Sinf., Salonen; (iv) Avanti CO,

Angervo; (iv) Finnish RSO, Saraste; (v) Mattila, Savonlinna Op. Ch., Lahti SO, Söderblom.

Merikanto is the most rewarding of the Finnish composers after Sibelius, and this is undoubtedly a set of exceptional musical interest. Works like the *Fantasy for Orchestra* and *Pan* are searching in idiom and set great store by refinement of colour. The first of the *Ten Pieces, Largo misterioso,* also included in a fuller orchestration, is a haunting example of expressionism, highly original and powerful in its atmosphere. There are many reminders of Szymanowski in the *Second Violin Concerto,* never played during the composer's lifetime. The *Fourth Violin Concerto* opens with a Prokofiev-like ostinato figure and there is some lush and imaginative writing in the slow movement, which again comes close to Szymanowski. Kaija Saarikettu is a commanding and brilliant soloist, and she is well accompanied by the Helsinki Philharmonic and James DePreist. *Genesis,* too, is powerful and inspired music of high quality that enhances the claims of this composer on a wider public. Very strongly recommended.

(i) *Concerto for Violin, Clarinet, Horn & String Sextet;* (ii) *Nonet;* (iii) *Works for Male Choir.*

**(*) Ondine ODE 703-2. (i) Kagan, Brunner, Jolley, Erlich, Oramo, Hirvikangas, Mendelsson, Sariola, Karttunen, Söderblom; (ii) Ens., Söderblom; (iii) Polytech Ch., Länsiö.

Both the *Concerto for Violin, Clarinet, Horn and String Sextet* and the *Nonet* come from the mid-1920s. The concerto's atmosphere is quite heady, and there is little sense of it being Nordic in feeling. The *Nonet* (1926) for flute, cor anglais, clarinet, piano, violins, viola, cello and double-bass inhabits a similar world, and is an evocative piece with occasional reminders of the Ravel of the Mallarmé songs or *Aoua* from the *Chanson madécasses.* Good performances, but the recording is a trifle hard. The choral pieces are less adventurous in their harmonies except for *To the last living being,* but often quite haunting. Despite less than distinguished recording, this is strongly recommended for the sake of some extraordinary music.

MESSAGER, André (1853–1929)

Fortunio (complete).

(N) ☼ (M) *** Erato 2292 45983-2 (2). Dran, Alliot-Lugaz, Cachemaille, Dudziak, Tremplant, Rocca, Ch. & O de l'Opéra Lyon, Gardiner.

Dating from 1907, *Fortunio,* based on a play by Alfred de Musset, has all the effervescence and heady lyricism of an operetta, combined with the strength and subtlety of a full opera. The tuneful score has ravishing solos for the lovelorn hero – with the heady-toned Thierry Dran very well cast – which are beautifully woven into the through-composed structure in four compact acts.

Its story of the triumph of youthful love, and the outwitting of the older generation – husband and paramour alike – by a personable and essentially innocent hero was bound to appeal to the Parisian public. Gardiner is in his element, and the Lyon Opéra cast includes such outstanding singers as Collette Alliot-Lugaz, rich-toned and characterful as the vivaciously provocative heroine, Jacqueline, and Thierry Dran as Fortunio, with Pierre Cachemaille as the handsome Captain Clavaroche, rival suitor for the heroine's attention. On two mid-priced discs it makes an ideal rarity to recommend not just to opera-lovers but also to those normally limiting themselves to operetta.

MESSIAEN, Olivier (1908–92)

L'Ascension.

(N)* Häns CD 93.005 (2). Baden-Baden, Freiburg SWR SO, Cambreling – BERLIOZ: Roméo et Juliette. *

Messiaen's four symphonic meditations make an unusual supplement for Cambreling's version of the Berlioz, but similarly bring a performance conscientious rather than convincing, lacking tension. First-rate, refined recording.

Des canyons aux étoiles; Couleurs de la cité céleste; Oiseaux exotiques.

*** Sony MK 44762. Crossley, L. Sinf., Salonen.

The power of the writing in Messiaen's vast symphonic cycle, Des canyons aux étoiles, comes out vividly in Esa-Pekka Salonen's Sony version, with Paul Crossley as soloist both incisive and deeply sympathetic. Salonen's performance is not obviously devotional in the first five movements; but then, after Michael Thompson's virtuoso horn solo, in the sixth movement Salonen and his players increasingly find a sharper focus, with the playing of the London Sinfonietta ever more confident and idiomatic. Oiseaux exotiques finds Crossley in inspired form as soloist, with Couleurs de la cité céleste made tough rather than evocative. The recording is sharply focused, but has good presence and atmosphere.

(i) Colours de la cité céleste; (ii) Et exspecto resurrectionem mortuorum.

(M) ** Sony (ADD) SMK 68332. Groupe Instrumental à percussion de Strasbourg, with (i) Loriod; (ii) O du Domaine Musical; Boulez (with STRAVINSKY: Symphonies of Wind Instruments; with NYPO **).

In Messiaen's own words, his Colours de la cité céleste 'turns on itself like a rose-window', bringing together, with astonishing assurance, elements from plainsong, Greek and Hindu music, not to mention the persistent birdsong which runs through so much of this composer's writing. Boulez's account, helped by close microphones, centres on sharpness of detail rather than atmosphere; the result seems literal and fails to be seductive. Similarly, in the larger scale of Et exspecto resurrectionem the concentration of a series of clearly differentiated sounds and sonorities brings a negative effect. The Stravinsky encore makes a rather more positive impression, but this is essentially a reissue for Boulez aficionados rather than for the general collector.

Eclairs sur l'au-delà (Illuminations of the Beyond).

*** DG 439 929-2. Paris Bastille Opéra O, Chung.

Eclairs sur l'au-delà reveals an undoubted connection with the visionary Turangalîla Symphony especially so in the longest movement, a haunting adagio for strings, Demeurer dans l'Amour. This magical sequence returns to close the work in translucent radiance, portraying Le Christ, lumière du Paradis. Of course, the music features the composer's beloved birdsong. There are also evocations of constellations in the night sky 'in all their glory', and of 'seven angels with seven trumpets'. Myung-Whun Chung is at his most persuasive in holding this evocative score together, and this superbly played performance is even finer than his reading of Turangalîla; the DG sound is spaciously atmospheric yet beautifully clear.

(i) Et exspecto resurrectionem mortuorum; (ii) Quatuor pour la fin de temps.

(B) *** Ph. 446 578-2. (i) Concg. O, Haitink; (ii) Beths, Pieterson, Bijlsma, De Leeuw.

In Haitink's impressive performance, Messiaen's Et exspecto resurrectionem mortuorum exerts a hypnotic grip over the listener for much of the time. Its curiously inert yet strongly atmospheric world – as so often with this composer – draws liberally on birdsong as a source of inspiration, ranging from Brazil to New Zealand. It makes a generous coupling for a very fine performance of a greater work, Messiaen's visionary Quartet for the End of Time. As in the orchestral piece, the Dutch team are given the benefit of very good recording which has transferred well to CD; moreover their account has the merit of outstanding teamwork, and Reinbert de Leeuw has a keen sense of atmosphere, though he does not dominate the proceedings. There is also some superbly eloquent playing from George Pieterson (clarinet) and Anner Bijlsma (cello). A genuine bargain, with a playing time of 73 minutes.

Réveil des oiseaux; (i) Trois petites liturgies de la présence divine.

(N) ❂ *** Erato 0630 12702-2. Yvonne and Jean Loriod, Instrumental Ens.; O National de France, Nagano; (i) with Griffet & Maîtrise de R. France.

Réveil des oiseaux, as might be expected, centres on the composer's beloved bird song, and there is no question of his imaginative flair, with the music and recording vividly matching the plumage of the creatures which inspired him. Moreover, the notes include a written description by the composer of the events described in the four movements.

Opening at midnight with the introductory piano cadenza in essence a nightingale solo, the piece is climaxed at Four O'Clock in the Morning with the 'great tutti' of the dawn chorus. The documentation even gives a list of more than a hundred birds evoked by the composer, 'in order of appearance'!

The Trois petites liturgies (the composer tells us) 'is above all the music of colours' – multicolours – and the oriental atmosphere along with the introduction, in the middle section, of the gamelan from Bali and Java and the Chinese cymbals are intended to 'help accentuate these colours and their movements'.

But the music itself centres on the lusciously ecstatic singing of unison women's voices, and for all the jaunty syncopated rhythms and ostinato-like spoken passages, it is the 'rainbow of love' which is at the essence of this celestially sensuous music, gloriusly sung here. Try the haunting opening sequence and you surely won't be able to stop listening.

The choir is inspired by the passionate conviction of Kent Nagano, while the dedicated pianism of Yvonne Loriod dominates both works, with Jeanne Loriod playing the ondes martinot. In the birdsong an expert instrumental ensemble also contributes with distinction. The recording is both atmospheric and immensely vivid.

Turangalîla Symphony.

(B) *** EMI double forte (ADD) CZS5 69752-2 (2). Béroff, J. Loriod, LSO, Previn – POULENC: Concert Champêtre; Organ Concerto. ***

*** Decca 436 626-2. Thibaudet, Harada, Concg. O, Chailly.

*** DG 431 781-2. Y. and J. Loriod, Bastille O, Chung.

(N) (B) *** RCA 2-CD (ADD) 74321 84601-2 (2). Yvonne & Jeanne Loriod, Toronto SO, Ozawa – ROUSSEL: Symphonies Nos. 3–4; Bacchus et Ariane: Suite 2. ***

(N) *** Erato 8573 82043-2. Almard, Kim, BPO, Nagano.

**(*) Chan. 9678. Shelley, Hartmann-Claverie, BBC PO, Y. P. Tortelier.

(i) Turangalîla Symphony; (ii) Quartet for the End of Time.

*** EMI CDS7 47463-8 (2). (i) Donohoe, Murail, CBSO, Rattle; (ii) Gawriloff, Deinzer, Palm, Kontarsky.

Messiaen's Turangalîla Symphony is on an epic scale, seeking to embrace almost the totality of human experience. Turanga is Time and also implies rhythmic movement; Lîla is love, and with a strong inspiration from the Tristan and Isolde legend Messiaen's love-music dominates his conception of human existence. The actual love-sequences feature the ondes martenot with its 'velvety glissandi'. The piano obbligato is also a strong feature of the score. Previn's vividly direct approach, helped by spectacular recording, has much electricity. He is at his best in the work's more robust moments, for instance the jazzy fifth movement, and he catches the wit at the beginning of the Chant d'amour 2. The idyllic Garden of the Sleep of Love is both serene and poetically sensuous, and the apotheosis of the love theme in the closing pages is jubilant and life-enhancing. Chailly's full-priced Decca account may have the advantage of even finer, digital recording, and it costs about the same; being (just) fitted on to a single CD; however, it is without Previn's considerable bonus: outstanding versions of two of Poulenc's finest concertos.

Myung-Wha Chung's reading with the Bastille Orchestra was recorded in 1990 in the composer's presence, not long before he died. Messiaen's endorsement is confirmed when the soloists are his wife and his sister-in-law, at times less precise than rivals, but bringing a unique, expressive intensity. Their contributions, particularly the pointed piano-playing of Yvonne Loriod, heighten the natural warmth of Chung's reading, less high-powered and at times less precise than Chailly's rival one-disc version, and less cleanly recorded, but very persuasive.

Simon Rattle conducts a winning performance of Turangalîla, not only brilliant and dramatic but atmospheric and convincing. The recording is warm and richly co-ordinated

while losing nothing in detail. Peter Donohoe and Tristan Murail play with comparable warmth and flair. Led by Aloys Kontarsky, the performance of the Quartet for the End of Time provides a contrasting approach to Messiaen from Rattle's, where atmospheric warmth is only an incidental.

The Turangalîla Symphony has never sounded more turbulently spectacular than in the live Berlin recording from Nagano. He seems determined to emphasize all the bizarre qualities of the score, including glissando whoops among the brilliant percussive effects. The Joie du sang des étoiles is jazzily, joyously extrovert, and this high level of tension (and noise) persists throughout. The Final is almost overwhelming in its energetic flamboyance and its culmination certainly has the sense of absolute finality. It must have been very exciting to be there, and it will surely be a performance which will appeal to young listeners used to being blown away at rock concerts. But although the sensuous aspects of the score are fully realized in the Jardin du sommeil d'amour, the contrasting element of repose seldom surfaces, and such a consistent clamour for most of the 73 minutes needs a fair degree of stamina. The recording itself has remarkable range and vividness.

Ozawa's recording comes from 1967, but you would never guess that from the brilliantly atmospheric sound, which is just as vivid as Nagano's new Erato version (including glissandos) and has that bit more warmth and atmosphere. Yvonne Loriod's piano is placed too forward, but her contribution is undoubtedly important, and the overall balance is otherwise well managed. The performance itself is brilliantly played: it has plenty of electricity and a warm sensuality too. If you want the excellent Roussel couplings, this is well worth investigating.

Yan Pascal Tortelier's Chandos version falls between that of Chailly and Chung. It opens excitingly, has undoubted grip, and the recording is exceptionally vividly detailed, with Howard Shelley's piano contribution always crystal clear. But the very positive characterization seems to give the work a more episodic nature, less overtly sensuous than Chailly. The reading overall is not as warmly expressive as Chung's, partly the effect of the sound balance, and this is especially striking in the brilliant finale.

Quatuor pour la fin du temps.

(N) *** DG 469 052-2. Shaham, Meyer, Jian Wang, Myung-Whun Chung.

*** Decca 452 899-2. Mustonen, Bell, Isserlis, Collins – SHOSTAKOVICH: Piano Trio No. 2. ***

*** Delos D/CD 3043. Chamber Music Northwest – BARTOK: Contrasts. ***

(i) Quatuor pour la fin du temps; (ii) Le Merle noir.

(M) *** EMI (ADD) CDM7 63947-2. (i) Gruenberg, De Peyer, Pleeth, Béroff; (ii) Zöller, Kontarsky.

(i) Quatuor pour la fin du temps; (ii) Theme & Variations for Violin & Piano.

(B) **(*) DG (ADD) 445 128-2. (i) Yordanov, Tetard, Desurmont, Barenboim; (ii) Kremer, Argerich.

(i) Quatuor pour la fin du temps; (ii) Cinq rechants (for 12 voices).

(M) *** Erato 4509 91708. Fernandez, Deplus, Neilz, Petit;
   (ii) Solistes des Choeurs de l'ORTF, Couraud.

Messiaen's visionary and often inspired piece was composed during his days in a Silesian prison camp. Among his fellow-prisoners were a violinist, a clarinettist and a cellist, who, with the composer at the piano, made its creation possible.

The newest DG account of *Quatuor pour la fin du temps* must now take pride of place among its rivals. It is a performance of the highest quality, with a level of concentration and intensity that grips the listener from first to last, and is superbly recorded. There are notes both by Messiaen and the cellist Etienne Pasquier, who was interned with Messiaen and took part in the première at the German prisoner-of-war camp in January 1941.

The 1968 EMI account is also in the very highest class, the players meeting every demand the composer makes upon them, and the fine, clear Abbey Road recording gives the group striking presence while affording proper background ambience. The bonus, *Le Merle noir*, exploits the composer's love of birdsong even more overtly and is splendidly played and recorded here.

Undoubtedly the new Decca version is also among the finest recent digital recordings. All four artists distinguish themselves, and Messiaen's other-worldly piece is beautifully played and has great concentration and atmosphere. The one snag is the wide dynamic range of the recording, although the clarinettist, Michael Collins, makes the very most of it with his pianissimos. It is difficult (but not impossible) to find a volume setting in which the gentler passages register, yet fortissimos do not become just a shade fierce, and the ear is conscious that the microphones are fairly close. Nevertheless this is very fine, and as on the earlier EMI version, the Abbey Road ambience is well judged.

David Shifrin, like his colleagues, fully captures the work's sensuous mysticism, while the solos of Warren Lash (cello) and Williams Doppmann have a wistful, improvisatory quality: both *Louange à l'éternité de Jésus* and the closing *Louange à l'immortalité de Jésus* are played very beautifully. The Delos recording is naturally balanced and very realistic, while the ambience is suitably evocative.

The French Ensemble on Erato give a strong, powerfully integrated performance, well held together by the pianist, Marie-Madeleine Petit. The recording is very good, clear and well balanced. The coupling, *Cinq rechants*, is written for a choir of twelve soloists. The composer's inspiration of human passion brings both lyrical intensity and extraordinary irregular rhythmic effects (some of which have an Indian source) and the various bursts and cascades of vocal tone give the work a stimulatingly original vitality. The performance is remarkably assured and full of ardent spontaneity, and the group are vividly recorded. Excellent notes are provided by the composer.

Barenboim and his colleagues recorded the *Quatuor pour la fin du temps* in the presence of the composer. Barenboim is a strong personality who carries much of this vibrant and atmospheric performance in his own hands and inspired his colleagues with his own commitment to the music. There are fine contributions from the cellist Albert Tetard and the clarinetist Claude Desurmont. But the CD transfer has added

a degree of edginess to Luben Yordanoff's violin timbre, making this less attractive than the original LP from which the recording derives. The *Theme and Variations* (a digital recording from 1990) is something of a rarity on disc but is in every way successful. It is also available differently coupled (see below).

PIANO MUSIC
Music for two pianos

Visions de l'Amen.

*** EMI (ADD) CDC7 54050-2. Rabinovitch, Argerich.
*** New Albion NA 045 CD. Double Edge (Niemann and Tilles).

Messiaen's *Visions de l'Amen* for two pianos is a long, eloquent work in seven sections with a powerful sense of mystery, and is played with uncommon conviction by the Russian pianist-composer, Alexandre Rabinovitch, with Martha Argerich at the second piano.

The performance from Edmund Niemann and Nurit Tilles is hardly less spontaneous. They capture the work's colour and atmosphere powerfully and evocatively – it is Messiaen at his most compelling – and some may prefer the sound of the New Albion recording. The two pianists are set back in a fairly reverberant but not over-reverberant acoustic.

Solo piano music

Catalogue d'oiseaux (complete).

(N) (BB) ** Arte Nova 74321 72122-2 (3). Zehn.

Catalogue d'oiseaux (complete); *Petites esquisses d'oiseaux.*

(BB) *** Naxos 8.553532/4 (3). Austbø.

Catalogue d'oiseaux, Books 1–3.

*** Unicorn DKPCD 9062. Hill.

Catalogue d'oiseaux, Books 4–6: L'Alouette calandrelle; La Bouscarle; La merle de roche; La Rousserolle effarvatte.

*** Unicorn DKPCD 9075. Hill.

Catalogue d'oiseaux, Book 7; Supplement: La Fauvette des jardins.

*** Unicorn DKPCD 9090. Hill.

The seven books of the *Catalogue d'oiseaux* occupied Messiaen between 1956 and 1958. The *Petites esquisses d'oiseaux* are much later. Whatever one's reactions to Messiaen's music, he creates a world entirely his own. Håkan Austbø is completely attuned to this sensibility, and the recording is exemplary. Aficionados of Messiaen need not hesitate.

Peter Hill prepared this music in Paris with the composer himself and thus has his imprimatur. It evokes the wildlife pictured in this extraordinary music to splendid effect, and is recorded with the utmost clarity and definition. In addition to the *Catalogue d'oiseaux* we have here *La Fauvette des jardins*, which the sleeve annotator describes as the perfect parergon to the cycle. The composer himself has spoken with great warmth of this artist and, given what we hear on this disc, has every reason to.

Martin Zehn is a highly intelligent and dedicated player who brings considerable insight to this music, but unfortunately the overall sound he is given by the engineers is a little monochrome. Readers wanting a bargain *Catalogue d'oiseaux* are referred to the Norwegian Håkan Austbø on Naxos; his birds sing more spectacularly and have plumage of a greater diversity and richness of colour.

8 Préludes pour piano; Vingt regards sur l'Enfant Jésus.

(B) **(*) EMI (ADD) CZS5 69668-2. Béroff.

Vingt régards sur l'Enfant-Jésus.

*** Teldec 3984 26868-2 (2). Aimard (piano).

(B) *** Erato Ultima (ADD) 8573 8566-2 (2). Y. Loriod.

(BB) *** Naxos 8.550829/30. Austbø.

Pierre-Laurent Aimard has received the composer's praise for his 'magnifique technique, sonorité claire et timbrée, et interprétations d'une rare intelligence'. Aimard's performance on disc is technically remarkable (although the virtuosity is always at the service of the music) and atmospherically perceptive. Fascinatingly, he is very relaxed at the opening but evocation is in no doubt and the concentration steadily grows and with it the tension. The piano is very well recorded indeed, and this can be strongly recommended alongside the classic account of Yvonne Loriod and the fine super-bargain version on Naxos by Håkon Austbø.

The 1973 recording by Yvonne Loriod – the composer's second wife – of *Vingt regards* has long been considered very special in its understanding and feeling for the composer's musical sound-world. The piano recording is full but is otherwise acceptable rather than outstanding – yet the magnetism of the playing overcomes the lack of the sharpest focus.

Håkon Austbø has excellent credentials in this repertoire. His is an individual view, with a wider range of tempi and dynamic than Loriod. His account of the opening *Regard du Père* and the later *Regard du Fils sur le Fils* is paced much more slowly, but his playing has great concentration and evocative feeling so that he readily carries the slower tempo, and in *Par lui tout a été fait* articulation is bolder, giving the music a stronger profile, helped by the clearer, Naxos digital focus. This is undoubtedly a performance that grips the listener and can be strongly recommended as an alternative view.

The *Préludes* are early works but, like *Vingt regards*, they show Michel Béroff at his most inspired, generating the illusion of spontaneous creation. Clean, well-focused sound – but a little wanting in richness and sonority.

ORGAN MUSIC

Complete works for organ: *Apparition de l'Eglise éternelle; L'Ascension (4 Méditations); Le Banquet céleste; Le Corps glorieux (7 Visions de la vie des ressuscités); Diptyque (Essai sur la vie terrestre et l'éternité religieuse); Livre d'Orgue (Reprises par interversion; Première pièce en trio; Les Mains de l'abime; Chants oiseaux; Deuxième pièce en*

trio; Les Yeux dans les roues; Soixante-quatre durées). Messe de la Pentecôte; La Nativité du Seigneur (9 Méditations).

(M) *** EMI mono CZS7 67400-2 (4). Composer (Cavaillé-Coll organ de L'Eglise de la Sainte-Trinité, Paris).

In an intensive series of sessions which began at the end of May and continued through June and July 1956, Olivier Messiaen returned to the organ in Sainte-Trinité, with which all his music is associated, and recorded everything he had written and published before that date. These performances not only carry the imprint of the composer's authority, but also the inspiration of the occasion. The large-scale works have a concentration and compelling atmosphere that are unforgettable. No apologies at all need be made for the range, breadth and faithfulness of the recording, although some must be made for the organ itself, which is not always perfectly tuned. There is minor background hiss, which is not troublesome, and technically the CD transfers are a remarkable achievement.

La Nativité du Seigneur (9 meditations); Le Banquet céleste.

✪ *** Unicorn DKPCD 9005. Bate (organ of Beauvais Cathedral).

'*C'est vraiment parfait!*' said Messiaen after hearing Jennifer Bate's Unicorn recording of *La Nativité du Seigneur*, one of his most extended, most moving and beautiful works. For the CD issue, *Le Banquet céleste* also provides an intense comment on the religious experience which has inspired all of the composer's organ music. The recording of the Beauvais Cathedral organ is of demonstration quality.

OPERA

Saint François d'Assise (complete).

*** DG 445 176-2 (4). Van Dam, Upshaw, Aler, Krause, Arnold Schoenberg Ch., Hallé O, Nagano.

It was a labour of love over a full eight years, writing this massive four-hour opera. The live recording, made in the Felsenreitschule in Salzburg during the 1998 Festival, is astonishingly vivid, with voices and orchestra clear and immediate but with ample bloom in the helpful acoustic. The discs actually improve on the live experience not only in the extra clarity, but in the audibility of words, with the libretto an extra help in following the measured progress of a work that tells the story of St Francis in eight tableaux that fight shy of conventional dramatic design, predominantly meditative at measured speeds. In such a performance as this the result is magnetic, with Nagano drawing inspired playing from the Hallé, with José van Dam masterly in the title role, and Dawn Upshaw radiant in the role of the Angel. The rest of the cast is comparably strong. Messiaen himself regarded this as his greatest achievement, a synthesis of what he represented musically and a supreme expression of his Catholic faith. His characteristic use of birdsong here reaches its zenith – aptly so with such a subject – when in his hypnotic patterning he claims to have used every example he had ever notated.

MEYER, Edgar (born 1960)

Violin Concerto.

*** Sony SK 89029. Hahn, St Paul CO, Wolff – BARBER: *Violin Concerto*. ***

Edgar Meyer wrote this *Violin Concerto* specially for Hilary Hahn, providing an unusual but apt coupling for the Barber concerto, equally an example of American late romanticism. Unashamedly tonal and freely lyrical, it opens with a yearning folk-like melody that echoes Vaughan Williams, and there is also a folk-like pentatonic cut to some of the writing in both of the two substantial movements. The first is a free set of variations, leading to a virtuoso exercise in using a persistent pedal note, while avoiding monotony. The second movement, in clearly defined sections easily erupts at times into a rustic dance, and ends on a dazzling coda. Hahn plays with passionate commitment, amply justifying her choice of coupling.

MEYERBEER, Giacomo (1791–1864)

Les Patineurs (ballet suite, arr. & orch. Lambert).

(B) *** Decca 444 110-2. Nat. PO, Bonynge – MASSENET: *Le Cid* etc. ***

Les Patineurs was arranged by Constant Lambert using excerpts from two of Meyerbeer's operas, *Le Prophète* and *L'Etoile du nord*. Bonynge's approach is warm and comparatively easy-going and, with such polished orchestral playing, this version is extremely beguiling. The sound too is first rate.

Il Crociato in Egitto (complete).

*** Opera Rara (ADD) OR 10 (4). Kenny, Montague, D. Jones, Ford, Kitchen, Benelli, Platt, Geoffrey Mitchell Ch., RPO, Parry.

This was the sixth and last opera which Meyerbeer wrote for Italy. The musical invention may not often be very distinctive, but the writing is consistently lively, notably in the ensembles. With one exception – Ian Platt, ill-focused in the role of the Sultan – the cast is a strong one, with Diana Montague outstanding in the castrato role of the Crusader-Knight, Armando. Della Jones, too, in the mezzo role of Felicia, whom Armando has abandoned in favour of Palmide, the Sultan's daughter, sings superbly, with agile coloratura and a rich chest register. Yvonne Kenny is brilliant as Palmide. Bruce Ford, with his firm, heroic tone, and Ugo Benelli are very well contrasted in the two tenor roles. Though the chorus is small, the recording is clear and fresh.

Les Huguenots (complete).

(M) *** Decca (IMS) (ADD) 430 549-2 (4). Sutherland, Vrenios, Bacquier, Arroyo, Tourangeau, Ghiuselev, New Philh. O, Bonynge.

Sutherland is predictably impressive, though once or twice there are signs of a 'beat' in the voice, previously unheard on Sutherland records. The rest of the cast is uneven, and in an unusually episodic opera, with passages that are musically less than inspired, that brings disappointments. Gabriel Bacquier and Nicola Ghiuselev are fine in their roles and, though Martina Arroyo is below her best as Valentine, the star quality is unmistakable. The tenor, Anastasios Vrenios, copes with the extraordinarily high tessitura and florid diversions. Vrenios sings the notes, which is more than almost any rival could. Fine recording to match this ambitious project, well worth investigating by lovers of French opera. The work sounds newly minted on CD.

MIASKOVSKY, Nikolay (1881–1950)

Cello Concerto in C min., Op. 66.

*** Virgin VC5 45310-2. Mørk, CBSO, P. Järvi – PROKOFIEV: *Sinfonia Concertante*. ***

*** DG 449 821-2. Maisky, Russian Nat. O, Pletnev – PROKOFIEV: *Sinfonia concertante*. ***

(M) *** EMI CDM5 65419-2. Rostropovich, Philh. O, Sargent – TANEYEV: *Suite de concert*. ***

(i) *Cello Concerto;* (ii) *Cello Sonatas Nos. 1 in D, Op. 12; 2 in A min., Op. 81.*

*** Olympia OCD 530. Tarasova, with (i) Moscow New Op. O, Samoilov; (ii) Polezhaev.

The Miaskovsky *Cello Concerto* has an overwhelming sense of nostalgia and an elegiac atmosphere that is quite individual. Marina Tarasova earns praise for coupling it so logically with the two *Cello Sonatas*. The *Sonata in D major*, Op. 12 (1911, revised 1930), does not differ in idiom from its much later companion, *No. 2 in A minor*, Op. 81. Tarasova has a strong musical personality and produces a magnificent tone; she receives sympathetic support from her accompanists, and decent recording.

The Norwegian cellist Truls Mørk, with Paavo Järvi and the City of Birmingham Symphony Orchestra, couple the concerto with the Prokofiev *Sinfonia Concertante*. They enjoy superb and very balanced recorded sound Truls Mørk does not wear his heart anywhere near his sleeve and his restrained reading deserves a prime position among modern recordings.

Mischa Maisky shows admirable finesse and some restraint in Miaskovsky's elegiac concerto. Like the Prokofiev coupling, this is a strongly characterized performance. Pletnev keeps a firm grip on proceedings, and the Russian National Orchestra play with impeccable taste and aristocratic feeling. This will now probably be a first choice for many collectors. It is well recorded and, though the soloist is forwardly balanced, it is not at the expense of orchestral detail.

However, Rostropovich's pioneering account with Sir Malcolm Sargent is still in a class of its own. It could not be played with greater eloquence and restraint, and the (1956) Abbey Road recording is amazingly full and fresh. But it has been deleted as we go to press.

(i) *Lyric Concertino for Flute, Clarinet, Horn, Bassoon, Harp & String Orchestra, Op. 32/3; Salutation Overture in C, Op. 48; Serenade for Chamber Orchestra in E flat,*

Op. 32/1; Sinfonietta for String Orchestra in B min., Op. 32/2.

*** Olympia OCD 528. Moscow New Op. O, Samoilov.

The *Serenade* has great charm and strong lyrical appeal; the *Lyric Concertino*, and particularly its slow movement, has considerable harmonic subtlety. The performance under Yevgeny Samoilov is much finer than the earlier account by Vladimir Verbitzky, and he gives a sensitive reading of the *Sinfonietta for Strings*. These are endearing pieces; not so the *Salutation Overture*, written for Stalin's 60th birthday, which is worth giving a miss. Very good recording.

Sinfonietta for Strings in B min., Op. 32/2; Theme & Variations; 2 Pieces, Op. 46/1; Napeve.

*** ASV CDDCA 928. St Petersburg CO, Melia.

The *Sinfonietta for Strings* will appeal to anyone of a nostalgic disposition. The players give an affectionate, well-prepared account of it and convey the wistful, endearing nature of the slow movement to perfection. The *Theme and Variations* (on a theme of Grieg) also has the same streak of melancholy. The first of the *Two Pieces*, Op. 46, No. 1, is a transcription and reworking for strings of the inner movements, reversing their order, of Miaskovsky's *Symphony No. 19 for Military Band*, composed in 1939. The St Petersburg Chamber Orchestra is an expert and responsive ensemble, and the ASV recording does them proud.

Symphonies Nos. (i) 1 in C min., Op. 3; (ii) 19 in E flat for Wind Band, Op. 46.

**(*) Russian Disc (ADD) RDCD 11 007. (i) USSR MoC SO, Rozhdestvensky; (ii) Russian State Brass O, Sergeyev.

Miaskovsky's *First Symphony* is a student work, very much in the received tradition. It is obvious from the very start that Miaskovsky was a composer who could think on a big scale. The *Nineteenth Symphony in B flat* for military band is a slighter piece, worth hearing for its inner movements, a wistful *Moderato* and a well-written *Andante*. The *First Symphony* is well played by the Ministry of Culture Orchestra under Gennady Rozhdestvensky, though the brass sound a bit raw, as indeed do the upper strings. The *Nineteenth* is played with great brio and genuine affection. The less-than-three-star recording-quality should not deter collectors from investigating this work.

Symphonies Nos. 2 in C sharp min.; 10 in F min., Op. 30.

(N) **(*) Orfeo C496991A. Vienna RSO, Gottfried Rabl.

The *Second Symphony* comes from 1912, when Miaskovsky was still a student (he turned to music at a relatively late stage), and breathes much of the same air as Scriabin, Rachmaninov and Glière (he was a pupil of the latter). The *Tenth* (1927) is a more radical piece with greater contrapuntal density which in its level of dissonance shows the influence of his lifelong friend Prokofiev. The playing of the Austrian Radio Orchestra under Gottfried Rabl is serviceable rather than distinguished and the recording a bit resonant, but there are no alternative versions currently available.

Symphonies Nos. 5 in D, Op. 18; 9 in E min., Op. 28.

*** Marco 8.223499. BBC PO, Downes.

The *Fifth Symphony* is a sunny, pastoral score dating from 1918, very much in the tradition of Glazunov and Glière. Downes's recording with the BBC Philharmonic, recorded in an admittedly over-resonant venue in Derby, is to be preferred both artistically and sonically to its earlier rival by the USSR Symphony Orchestra under Ivanov on Olympia. The *Ninth Symphony* is somewhat better served than No. 5 so far as the sound is concerned. It is vintage Miaskovsky, more cogently argued and more interesting in thematic substance than the *Eighth*. Very good performances and good enough recording – just – to make three stars.

Symphony No. 6 in E flat min. (Revolutionary), Op. 23.

(**(*)) Russian Disc mono RDCD 15008. Yurlov Russian Ch., USSR SO, Kondrashin.

Here, at long last on CD, is the pioneering set of the mammoth *Sixth Symphony* with choral finale, which alerted many collectors to Miaskovsky's real stature. There are echoes of Miaskovsky's master, Glière, and also of Scriabin but, in the trio of the Scherzo, Miaskovsky strikes that note of nostalgia and lost innocence he was to make so much his own in the *Cello Concerto* – and the *Violin Concerto* too. It is a highly individual and often masterly score, although let down a little by its (somewhat inflated) choral finale, which employs folk and revolutionary songs, including the *Carmagnole*, which earned the symphony its nickname, *The Revolutionary*. Though the present recording dates from 1959, it is the one to have.

Symphony No. 8 in A, Op. 26.

** Marco 8.223297. Slovak RSO (Bratislava), Stankovsky.

Although the *Eighth* is not one of Miaskovsky's finest symphonies, it is still worth investigating. There are some characteristic ideas, and initially unfavourable impressions are soon dispelled as one comes closer to it. Neither the performance nor the recording is distinguished, but both are thoroughly acceptable; there is a lack of subtlety here, but not of vitality and commitment.

Symphony No. 12 in G min., Op. 35; Silence (symphonic poem after Poe), Op. 9.

**(*) Marco 8.223302. Slovak RSO (Bratislava), Stankovsky.

The *Twelfth Symphony* is endearingly old-fashioned and has strong appeal. Although some of the big rhetorical gestures of the *Sixth Symphony* are to be found in the second movement, there are also some pre-echoes of things to come in the later symphonies. It is highly enjoyable, particularly when it is as well played as it is here by the Bratislava Radio Orchestra under their gifted young conductor, Robert Stankovsky. The tone-poem *Silence* draws for its inspiration on Edgar Allan Poe's *The Raven* and has a strongly atmospheric quality with a distinctly *fin-de-siècle* air: if you enjoy Rachmaninov's *Isle of the Dead*, you should investigate it. The orchestra play with enthusiasm and they are decently recorded.

CHAMBER MUSIC

Cello Sonata No 1 in D, Op. 12.

*** Virgin VC5 45119-2. Mørk, Thibaudet — RACHMANINOV: *Cello Sonata etc.* ***

The Norwegian cellist Truls Mørk plays this lovely piece with both feeling and restraint. No doubt the most logical choice in this work is Marina Tarasova on Olympia, for she also offers its later companion in *A minor*, Op. 81, and the elegiac *Cello Concerto* (see above). For those wanting the present coupling, however, these artists give a very fine account both of the *Sonata* and of the Rachmaninov coupling. Well balanced recording.

String Quartets Nos. 1 in A min., Op. 33/1; 4 in F min., Op. 33/4.

(**) Russian Disc (ADD) RDCD 11013. Taneyev Qt.

The Taneyev Quartet of Leningrad recorded all the Miaskovsky *Quartets* on LP during the course of the 1980s, and their release on CD is warmly to be welcomed. The *First Quartet* finds him more among the avant-garde of Russian composers than the conservative figure he became, and it has a far higher norm of dissonance than we are used to. It is a surprisingly fascinating and powerful score. The *Fourth*, in F minor, is less challenging and more overtly lyrical and traditional in outlook. These imaginative and thought-provoking works are eminently well played, but the recording lets things down. The players are forwardly balanced, the sound is hard and vinegary and needs to be tamed above the stave. All the same, such is the interest of this disc that it must have a recommendation.

PIANO MUSIC

Piano Sonatas Nos. 1 in D min., Op. 6; 2 in F sharp min., Op. 13; 3 in C min., Op. 19; 6 in A flat, Op. 64/2.

**(*) Olympia OCD 214. McLachlan.

In its way, the *First Sonata* is an oddity; its opening, like that of the Balakirev *B flat minor Sonata*, written two years earlier, is fugal, but much of the second movement is more akin to the early Scriabin sonatas. So, too, is the *Second*, though Taneyev, Glazunov and Medtner also spring to mind. Murray McLachlan possesses a very considerable talent. An enterprising issue in every way and well recorded.

Piano Sonatas Nos. 4 in C min., Op. 27; 5 in B, Op. 64/1; Sonatine in E min., Op. 57; Prelude, Op. 58.

*** Olympia OCD 217. McLachlan.

The middle movement of the *Sonatine*, marked *Narrante e lugubre*, is dark and pessimistic, and quite haunting. McLachlan speaks of the 'enormous tactile pleasure' it gives to the performer, and his playing is both authoritative and persuasive. Perhaps this is the record to try first, since both *Sonatas*, not just the more 'radical' *Fourth*, are of interest and substance. Good recording.

Piano Sonatas Nos. 6 in A flat, Op. 62/2; 7 in C, Op. 82; 8 in D min., Op. 83; 9 in F, Op. 84.

**(*) Marco 8.223178. Hegedüs.

Piano Sonatas Nos. 7 in C, Op. 82; 8 in D min., Op. 83; 9 in F, Op. 84; Reminiscences, Op. 29; Rondo-sonata in B flat min., Op. 58; String Quartet No. 5: Scherzo (trans. Aliawdina): Yellowed Leaves, Op. 31.

**(*) Olympia OCD 252. McLachlan.

The sonatas on the Olympia disc are all from 1949. The music is of the utmost simplicity but has an endearing warmth. As in the earlier discs, McLachlan provides scholarly and intelligent notes. The recording is good though the acoustic ambience is perhaps not absolutely ideal.

The Marco Polo disc brings the last four sonatas. The young Hungarian pianist, Endre Hegedüs, is often the more imaginative interpreter: he colours the second theme of the *Barcarolle* section of the *Eighth Sonata* with greater tenderness and subtlety than Murray McLachlan on Olympia, though the latter has great freshness. The sound is a little wanting in bloom. On balance, then, honours are fairly even between these two artists.

MÍČA, Jan František Adam (1746–1811)

String Quartet No. 6 in C.

(M) *** Cal. (ADD) 6698. Talich Qt — BOCCHERINI: *Quartet, Op. 58/2;* HAYDN: *Quartet No. 74;* MENDELSSOHN: *Quartet No. 2.* ***

The Bohemian composer, Jan Míča (1746–1811), writes elegantly in the *galant* style, and this *C major Quartet* (his sixth) brings an enticing opening theme, then continues in a cultivated and courtly style. Throughout, the warmth and finesse of the Talich playing ensure our enjoyment of what is a slight but well-crafted little work.

MIELCK, Ernst (1877–99)

Symphony in F min., Op. 4; (i) Concert Piece in E min. for Piano & Orchestra, Op. 9.

** Sterling CDS 1035-2. (i) Pohjola; Turku PO, Lintu.

Ernst Mielck's *Symphony*, Op. 4, preceded Sibelius's *First* by two years, and its success is said to have acted as a spur to that great composer to complete his own. It is a four-movement work, some 40 minutes in length. Although it begins promisingly, neither of its main ideas can lay claim to any strong personality, though there is a genuine sense of form. Probably the best movement is the lyrical and endearing slow movement. By and large it offers promise rather than fulfilment. The Turku Orchestra under Hannu Lintu plays decently. The *Concert Piece*, Op. 9, is rather dreadful, though the central *Largo* has some poetic writing. A valuable release which will be of interest to Sibelians in deepening their historical perspective about his background, but Mielck is no Arriaga.

MILANO, Francesco Canova da

(1497–1543)

(i) Lute duets: *Canon; Fantasia quarta; Fantasia quinta; Fantasia sexta; Ricercar prima; Ricercar seconda; Ricercar terza; La spagna.* Pieces for solo lute: *Fantasias Nos. 30; 55–6; 63–7; 81–3; Ricercars Nos. 2; 10; 13; 69–70; 73; 76 & 79.*

(BB) *** Naxos 8.550774. Wilson, (i) with Rumsey.

During his lifetime Francesco Canova da Milano was known as 'Il Divino' and was, by all accounts, 'a miraculous lute player'. He was the most prolific lute composer of his day, even more so than his close contemporary, the Spanish vihuelist and composer, Luis de Milán. Christopher Wilson plays this collection of pieces, including duets with Shirley Rumsey, with a natural and unforced authority. Cultured playing of highly civilized music – recorded with admirable clarity, though it is advisable to reduce the level setting to get the most lifelike and natural result.

MILHAUD, Darius (1892–1974)

L'Apothéose de Molière, Op. 286; Le Boeuf sur le toit, Op. 58; (i) *Le Carnaval d'Aix, Op. 83b. Le Carnaval de Londres, Op. 172.*

*** Hyp. CDA 66594. (i) Gibbons; New L. O, Corp.

Le Carnaval d'Aix is a carefree work, full of high spirits and very expertly played by Jack Gibbons and the New London Orchestra under Ronald Corp. They also convey the Satie-like circus-music character of *Le Boeuf sur le toit* to excellent effect. What delightful music this is, and so expertly fashioned by this lovable composer. The Molière pastiche and the arrangement of melodies from *The Beggar's Opera* are not top-drawer Milhaud, but they are still worth having. Very good recording from the Hyperion team.

(i) *Ballade, Op. 61; Le Carnaval d'Aix, Op. 83b* (both for piano and orchestra); *Piano Concertos Nos. 1, Op. 127; 4, Op. 295; 5 Etudes for Piano & Orchestra, Op. 61;* (ii) *Le Boeuf sur le toit, Op. 58;* (ii–iii) *Harp Concerto, Op. 323;* (ii) *La Création du monde, Op. 81.*

(B) *** Erato Ultima Double 3984 21347-2 (2). (i) Helffer, O. Nat. de France, Robertson; (ii) Lyon Op. O, Nagano; (iii) with Cambreling.

This admirable Erato Ultima Double includes a great deal of Milhaud's most attractive music, very well recorded. The *Ballade* was composed for Roussel, and Milhaud made his piano début at its première in New York: its languorous opening seems to hark back to his days in Brazil. The first of the *Cinq Etudes* shows Milhaud in window-breaking, polytonal mode, as does the third. The *First Piano Concerto* is a relaxed, charming work not dissimilar to, though more complex in texture than, Jean Françaix's well-known *Concertino*. The *Fourth Piano Concerto*, Op. 295 (1949), is an inventive piece of some substance with a particularly imaginative, dream-like slow movement. Kent Nagano and the Orchestra of the Opéra de Lyon give a splendid account of

themselves in both the ballets. In *La Création* the playing is full of character (the jazz fugue comes off marvelously). The 1953 *Harp Concerto* is not top-drawer Milhaud; there is more activity than substance for much of the time, but the slow movement has many beautiful things and Cambreling makes out a very good case for the high-spirited finale.

Le Boeuf sur le toit.

(M) *** Mercury (ADD) [434 335-2]. LSO, Dorati – AURIC: *Overture;* FETLER: *Contrasts;* FRANCAIX: *Piano Concertino;* SATIE: *Parade.* ***

Le Boeuf sur le toit, Op. 58; La Création du monde, Op. 81.

*** Chan. 9023. Ulster O, Y. P. Tortelier – IBERT: *Divertissement;* POULENC: *Les Biches.* ***

(i) *Le Boeuf sur le toit;* (ii) *La Création du monde;* (iii) *Saudades do Brasil; Suite provençale;* (iv) *Scaramouche* (for 2 pianos).

(***) EMI mono/stereo CDC7 54604-2. (i) Champs-Elysées Theatre O; (ii) Ens. of 19 soloists; (iii) Concert Arts O, composer; (iv) Meyer, composer.

A most engaging account of *Le Boeuf sur le toit* from Yan Pascal Tortelier and his Ulster players, full of colourful detail, admirably flexible, and infectiously rhythmic. Perhaps *La Création du monde* is without the degree of plangent jazzy emphasis of a French performance, but its gentle, desperate melancholy is well caught, and the playing has plenty of colour and does not lack rhythmic subtlety. The Chandos recording, although resonant, is splendid in every other respect, and so are the couplings.

Dorati's reading, effervescent and light-hearted, catches the idiom splendidly and the music's lilt is infectiously conveyed. The LSO are obviously enjoying themselves and their playing, subtle as well as vivid, catches the audacious mood of a piece which is a trifle long for its content but which still entertains. The (1965) Mercury recording is perfectly judged, giving the music transparency, vibrant colour and its proper edge.

Milhaud's own account of *La Création du monde* has a certain want of abandon but is otherwise well played, and this *Scaramouche* has an altogether special charm. The Capitol mono LP coupling of the captivating *Suite provençale* and the carefree and catchy *Saudades do Brasil*, now appears for the first time in stereo, sounding very sprightly indeed. The 'Concert Arts' orchestra respond to the composer with evident delight, and they make this a most desirable issue. In addition there is *Le Boeuf sur le toit* that Milhaud made with a Champs-Elysées orchestra in 1958, which makes a welcome makeweight to an altogether delightful issue. However, it was curmudgeonly of EMI to put the disc in the full-price range.

(i; ii) *Le Carnaval d'Aix; Suite provençale; Suite française;* (iii; iv) *Le Bal martiniquais; Paris;* (iv) *Scaramouche.*

(N) (BB) **(*) EMI Encore CDE5 74741-2. (i) Béroff; (ii) Monte Carlo PO, Prêtre; (iii) Lee, Ivaldi; (iv) Béroff, Collard.

It is difficult to understand why Milhaud's *Le Carnaval d'Aix* does not enjoy greater popularity. It has immense charm and an engaging easy-going Mediterranean sense of gaiety that never ceases to captivate. However, the present account proves something of a disappointment. Béroff rattles off the solo part without a trace of charm and without the tenderness that is at times called for. It comes here with the endearing *Suite provençale* and *Suite française* as companions, but the orchestral playing under Prêtre is fairly brash too, and the digital sound does not help very much either: it is inclined to be dry and close. The charming music for two and four pianos fares much better. *Scaramouche* is the best-known piece and is extremely well played by Christian Ivaldi and Noël Lee, and they are joined by Béroff and Collard in the eight-handed *Paris* (for four pianos!). The recording here is fresh and lively. For all one's reservations this disc is more than worth its modest cost.

(i; ii) *Concertino de printemps* (2 versions); (iii) *Piano Concerto;* (ii) *Violin Concerto No. 2;* (iv) *Suite française;* (v) *Scaramouche* (suite for 2 pianos).

(N) (BB) (***) Dutton mono CDBP 9711. (i) Astruc with Orchestra; (ii) Kaufman, French R. O (members); (iii) Margueritte Long, O Nat. de France; NYPO; all cond. composer; (v) Sellick and Smith.

Milhaud regarded melody 'as the only living element in music' and turned all his resources towards to the expression of melodic ideas, often spring-like in their freshness and charm. No more so than in the vivacious *Concertino de printemps* which, in a Dutton scoop, is given here first in its brilliant 1933 première recording by Yvone Astrac, and also in an even more breathtaking later version (1949), dazzlingly played by Louis Kaufman. Yet both performances reveal the music's underlying expressive nostalgia and this is found again in the 'Slow and sombre' middle movement of the *Second Violin Concerto*, which Kaufman also plays superbly, then delivering the finale with sparkling virtuosity. He is recorded closely but truthfully.

Margaret Long (in 1935) scintillates in the small-scale *Piano Concerto*, and the composer delivers the full bonhomie of the *Suite française*, even if here the dated New York recording is brash and two-dimensional. For the most part however, the splendid Dutton transfers make one forget the early provenance of these always vivid recordings. The performance of *Scaramouche* by Cyril Smith and Phyllis Sellick is unsurpassed, with the lighthearted Braslian syncopations of the finale especially infectious, and here the 1948 Abbey Road recording sounds very realistic.

La Création du monde.

(M) *** EMI (ADD) CDM7 63945-2. Paris Conservatoire O, Prêtre – DUTILLEUX: *Le Loup;* POULENC: *Les Biches.* ***

Prêtre's recording of *La Création du monde* is unsurpassed in catching both the bitter-sweet sensuousness of the creation scene and the jazzy pastiche of the mating dance – the rhythmic touch is very much in the authentic spirit of 1920s' French jazz. The 1961 sound has been transformed in the CD remastering: it is fresh and vivid, yet admirably atmospheric. The couplings are no less attractive.

(i) *La Création du monde;* (ii) *Concertino de printemps;* (iii) *Piano Concerto No. 1;* (iv) *Suite française;* (v) 6 *Chants populaires hebraïques;* (vi) *String Quartet No. 7 in B flat.*

(N) (***) Pearl mono GEM 0124. (i) Orch. 19 soloists, Milhaud (ii) Yvonne Astruc, Milhaud; (iii) Marguerite Long, O. National; (iv) NYPO, Milhaud; (v) Martial Singher, Milhaud (piano); (vi) Galimir Qt.

Most of these performances are familiar from earlier transfers: both the *Concertino de printemps* and *La Création du monde* appeared on an earlier Pearl disc devoted to Milhaud and Honegger, and the *Seventh String Quartet*, which Milhaud supervised, appeared recently together with the Galimir Quartet's only other commercial records: the Berg *Lyric Suite* and the Ravel *Quartet* on Rockport. *La Création du monde* was recorded in 1931, the *Suite française* in 1946 and the remainder in the early 1930s in a rather dry studio acoustic. All the same this has great period flavour and is an indispensable part of the Milhaud discography.

Suite française.

(M) *** ASV (ADD) CDWHL 2067. L. Wind O, Wick – GRAINGER: *Irish Tune from County Derry* etc.; POULENC: *Suite française.*

Milhaud's *Suite française* for wind is an enchanting piece, full of Mediterranean colour and vitality. It would be difficult to imagine a more idiomatic or spirited performance than this one, which has excellent blend and balance. Vivid recording.

Suite provençale.

(N) (M) ** Chan. 6615. Detroit SO, Järvi – DEBUSSY: *La Mer;* RAVEL: *Boléro; La Valse.* **

Järvi's *Suite provençale* is very well played in Detroit and is well recorded too, but this captivating score needs greater lightness of touch if it is to charm the listener as it should. Not a first choice, and it must be conceded that neither *La Mer* nor the Ravel pieces are front-runners either, although all have their merits.

Symphonies for Chamber Orchestra Nos. 1 (*Le Printemps*); 2 (*Pastoral*); 3 (*Serenade*); 5 (*Dixtuor d'instruments*).

**(*) Koch 3-7067-2. Sinfonia O of Chicago, Faldner (with DEBUSSY: *Symphony in B min.;* GOUNOD: *Petite Symphonie for Winds* **).

Barry Faldner and his Chicago Sinfonia, drawn from principals and other winds of the Chicago Symphony, give expert accounts of four of the little symphonies Milhaud composed in the 1920s. It would have made better sense to have recorded all six rather than offering Faldner's orchestral transcription of Debussy's 10-minute symphony. The performances of the Milhaud are very alert, characterful and polished – and very well recorded indeed. They give much pleasure.

Symphonies Nos. 2, Op. 247; (i) 3 (*Te Deum*), Op. 271.

*** CPO 999 540-2. (i) Basel Theatre Ch.; Basel RSO, Francis.

Milhaud's first two symphonies come from his wartime exile in the United States. The central slow movement of the *Second Symphony* conveys some of the grief of the war years but elsewhere (particularly in the captivating fourth movement), the carefree atmosphere that distinguishes Milhaud's music and its Mediterranean light are much in evidence. The *Third* (1946) was commissioned by the French Radio to celebrate victory over the Nazis. Particularly effective is the atmospheric slow movement with its wordless chorus. Good performances and a natural and well-balanced recording that holds its own with rival versions.

Symphonies Nos. 7, Op. 344; 8 (Rhôdanienne), Op. 362; 9, Op. 380.

*** CPO 999 166-2. Basel RSO, Francis.

Alun Francis makes sense of the slow movement of the *Seventh*, holding it together at a realistic tempo. It is a powerful and often searching movement, even if there is a fair amount of note-spinning in its companions. For that matter, so there is in the *Ninth*, though it begins splendidly with a short and lively *Modérément animé*. If the *Eighth Symphony* is full of colour, the scoring is also open to the charge of being a bit too dense. The Basel Radio Orchestra is a far from second-rate ensemble and in the *Seventh Symphony* hold up well.

(i) Symphony No. 8 (Rhôdanienne), Op. 362; (i; ii) Scaramouche for Saxophone, Op. 165c; (iii) La Cheminée du Roi René, Op. 205; (iv) Organ Preludes, Op. 231b/3, 7–8; (v) Cantique du Rhône, Op. 155.

** Praga (ADD) PR 250 013. (i) Czech PO, Neumann, (ii) with Neidenbach-Rahbari, (iii) Mihule, Vaček, Hůlka, Uher, Svárovský; (iv) Tvrzský; (v) Czech R. Mixed Ch., Kühn.

The 1966 performance of the *Eighth Symphony* (*Rhôdanienne*) is worth acquiring. The *Cantique du Rhône* for *a cappella* choir, a setting of words by Claudel in praise of the Rhône, composed in Aix in 1936, is a beautiful piece, well sung here by the Pavel Kühn Choir and, like *Scaramouche*, recorded in 1987. The saxophone version of *Scaramouche* is played with plenty of character and a certain artful charm by Sohre Neidenbach-Rahbari and the Czech Philharmonic and was recorded at a live performance. *La Cheminée du Roi René* for wind quintet has an abundant charm, much of which is conveyed in this 1979 studio performance.

(i; ii) Symphony No. 10, Op. 382; (i; iii) Concertino d'hiver for Trombone & Strings, Op. 327; (iv) Music for Prague, Op. 415; (i; v) Hommage à Comenius, Op. 421.

** Praga (ADD) PR 250 012. (i) Prague R. O; (ii) Košler; (iii) Pulec, cond. Krombholc; (iv) Czech PO, composer; (v) Zikmundová, Jindrák, Hrnčíř.

The *Concertino d'hiver* comes from the set of 'Four Seasons' that Milhaud composed over a period of two decades and is given a very good performance by Zdenek Pulec and the Prague Radio Orchestra under Jaroslav Krombholc, as is the 1970 performance of the *Tenth Symphony* with Zdenek Košler conducting. *Musique pour Prague* under Milhaud's own baton on the whole is more rewarding than the symphony. Also associated with Prague is the cantata for soprano and baritone Milhaud composed in honour of the Czech philosopher and bishop Comenius (1592–1670), a pioneer

of universal education, which is new to the catalogue. This, like the symphony, is a studio performance from 1970; the soprano, Eva Zikmundová, has a characteristic Slavonic vibrato.

CHAMBER MUSIC

Caprice, Op. 335a; Duo concertant, Op. 351; Petit concert, Op. 192; Le Printemps, Op. 18; Violin Sonata No. 2, Op. 40; Sonatine, Op. 100; Le Voyageur sans bagage (suite) Op. 157b.

** Schwann 3-1310-2. Trio Bellerive.

Very bright, up-front recording in the suite from the music to *Le Voyageur sans bagage* (1936) for clarinet, violin and piano, though it is very well played. The sound is better in the *Violin Sonata No. 2* and *Le Printemps*, though the balance rather favours Robert Hairgrove's piano than Sandra Goldberg's violin. The pieces for clarinet and piano, the *Petit concert*, the *Sonatine*, Op. 100, and the two pieces from the mid-1950s (the *Caprice*, Op. 335a, and the *Duo concertant*, Op. 351) are played with spirit, but the close, unrelieved recording is a handicap.

La Cheminée du roi René.

(N) (***) BBC mono BBCL 4066-2. Dennis Brain Wind Quintet (with instrumental recital (***)).

The account by the Dennis Brain Wind Quintet of Milhaud's *Cheminée du roi René*, with its pastiche Provençal flavour, is sheer delight, making it seem like a minor masterpiece. How beguiling are the *Aubade*, *La Maousinglade* and the finale, a *Madrigal-nocturne*. The sound too has a pleasing ambient glow.

Music for wind: La Cheminée du Roi René, Op. 105; Divertissement en trois parties, Op. 399b; Pastorale, Op. 47; 2 Sketches, Op. 227b; Suite d'après Corrette, Op. 161b.

(M) **(*) Chan. 6536. Athena Ens., McNichol.

Though none of this is first-class Milhaud, it is still full of pleasing and attractive ideas, and the general air of easy-going, life-loving enjoyment is well conveyed by the alert playing of the Athena Ensemble. One's only quarrel is the somewhat close balance.

Duo for 2 Violins, Op. 243; (i) Sonata for 2 Violins & Piano, Op. 15.

(*) Hyp. CDA 66473. Osostowicz, Kovacic, (i) with Tomes – MARTINU: *Violin Sonata* **(*); PROKOFIEV: *Violin Sonata*. *

The *Sonata for Two Violins and Piano* of 1914 is beautifully crafted and has a charming slow movement but is very slight. Not as slight, though, as the *Duo*, the first two movements of which were composed at a dinner party; the finale was written the following morning. Elegant performances from Krysia Osostowicz and Ernst Kovacic – and in the *Sonata* Susan Tomes.

(i) *Oboe Sonatina, Op. 337;* (ii) *Suite d'après Corette, Op. 161b;* (iii) *Violin Sonata No. 1, Op. 240;* (iv) *4 Visages, Op. 238;* (v) *Organ pastorale, Op. 229;* (vi) *3 Chansons de Négresse, Op. 148b;* (vii) *2 Poems by Blaise Cendrars, Op. 113.*

*** Praga (ADD) PR 250 008. (i) Adamus, Bogunia;
  (ii) Hedba, Nechvatal, Zedník; (iii) Spelina, Friesl;
  (iv) Christ, Klánský; (v) Grubich; (vi) Fassbaender, Gage;
  (vii) Smíšený, Kühn Mixed Ch., Kühn.

All are live performances, made in Prague between 1981 and 1990, and are of decent to excellent quality. The two choral settings of poems by Blaise Cendrars are of striking quality and are very well sung by Pavel Kühn's choir. The *Trois Chansons de Négresse* hark back to Milhaud's years in Rio, and are sung with great character and charm by Brigitte Fassbaender. Wolfram Christ is the excellent soloist in the *Sonata No. 1*, based on eighteenth-century French tunes, and the *Quatre Visages* for viola and piano: this is a portrait of four ladies from California, Wisconsin, Brussels and Paris. Like Jean Françaix's *Cinq Portraits de jeunes filles* for piano, it has character and a winning charm. A valuable addition to the Milhaud discography.

String Quartets Nos. 1, Op. 5; 2, Op. 16.

(B) *** Discover DICD 920290. Arriaga Qt.

The *First Quartet* is among the most diatonic of all Milhaud's works, and is unusual in having two slow movements, both of which find him at his most serene. There are occasional hints of the Debussy *Quartet* and even a faint shadow of Franck in the *Grave* movement. The *Second* was composed during the first of the war years, and there are signs of an emergent fascination with polytonality. The Arriaga Quartet are very persuasive and communicate their feeling for the music.

String Quartets Nos. 1, Op. 5; 7 in B flat, Op. 87; 10, Op. 218; 16, Op. 303.

*** Cybella CY 804. Aquitaine National Qt.

The *Seventh Quartet* speaks Milhaud's familiar, distinctive language; its four short movements are delightful, full of melody and colour. The *Tenth*, too, is attractive; the *Sixteenth* was a wedding anniversary present for his wife: its first movement has great tenderness and warmth. The Aquitaine Quartet has excellent ensemble, intonation is good and their playing is polished. The recording has a wide dynamic range and a spacious tonal spectrum.

String Quartets Nos. 5, Op. 64; 8, Op. 121; 11, Op. 232; 13, Op. 268.

*** Cybella CY 805. Aquitaine National Qt.

The *Fifth Quartet* is not one of Milhaud's most inspired; the *Eighth*, on the other hand, has much to commend it, including a poignant slow movement. No. 11 has a splendid pastoral third movement and a lively jazzy finale; No. 13 has overtones of Mexico in its finale and a beguiling and charming *Barcarolle*. Both performance and recording are very good.

PIANO MUSIC

Music for 2 pianos: *Le Bal martiniquais, Op. 249; Le Boeuf sur le toit, Op. 58a; Carnaval à la Nouvelle-Orléans, Op. 275; Kentuckiana, Op. 287; La libertadora, Op. 236; Scaramouche, Op. 165b; Songes, Op. 237.*

*** Hyp. CDA 67014. Coombs, Pizarro.

Hyperion assemble the bulk of Milhaud's music for two pianos from the popular and irresistible *Scaramouche* through to the duet arrangement of *Le Boeuf sur le toit*. An entertaining and delightful issue which brings some high-spirited pianism from these fine players and very good recorded sound.

Piano Sonata No. 1; L'Automne; Printemps, Books 1 & 2; 4 Sketches (Esquisses); Sonatine.

(B) ** Discover DICD 920 167. Eidi.

Some of the music, such as the first book of *Printemps* or the *Quatre esquisses*, is charming; none of it makes great demands on either the pianist or the listener, and some of it is pretty inconsequential. All the same, there is much that gives pleasure – and would give more if the recording were not quite so bottom-heavy or wanting in transparency. Billi Eidi's playing is fluent, sensitive and totally committed.

VOCAL MUSIC

Les Choéphores, Op. 24.

*** Sony (ADD) MHK 62352. Zorina (narr.), Boatwright, Jordan, Babikian, NY Schola Cantorum, NYPO, Bernstein (with HONEGGER: *Rugby, Pacific 231* ** ROUSSEL: *Symphony No. 3.* **(*)

(M) (**) DG mono 449 748-2. Moizan, Bouvier, Rehfuss, Nollier, Chorale de L'Université, LOP, Markevitch – HONEGGER: *Symphony No. 5* (**); ROUSSEL: *Bacchus et Ariane: Suite No. 2.* **

Les Choéphores comprises seven scenes which cover the same events as are depicted in Strauss's *Elektra*. Milhaud scores the work for large forces, including a spoken role – effectively declaimed on Sony by Vera Zorina – plus soloists, chorus and orchestra. It marked a bold and radical departure in Milhaud's style, making use of polytonality, choral speech and arresting dramatic effects. Bernstein's 1961 performance is thrilling and the recording sounds excellent for the period. This is an important issue, much enhanced by the interest of the Roussel coupling and the excellence of the presentation.

Markevitch's 1957 recording has a lot going for it. The performance is strongly characterized, though less virtuosic than Leonard Bernstein's vivid stereo account. The mono recording is well balanced with plenty of front-to-back depth and good perspective, though it has the inevitable tonal frailty one might expect after 40 years. The soloists are generally good, but Bernstein scores with the superiority of the orchestral playing and the choral singing.

MINKUS, Léon (1826–1917)

La Bayadère (complete; arr. Lanchbery)

*** Decca 436 917-2 (2). ECO, Bonynge.

Lanchbery has provided the present score, and though officially he is only responsible for the orchestration, who knows, perhaps he also had a hand in its content, as in his vintage arrangement of Hérold's *La Fille mal gardée*. Whatever the case, the result is highly engaging. Unlike Adam's rather disappointing *Le Corsaire* (also recorded by the same forces), this work is full of attractive melody and sparkling orchestral effects. If you like late-nineteenth-century ballet music, then here is nearly two hours of it, played with much vivacity, elegance and drama, and given Decca's top-quality sound.

MOERAN, Ernest J. (1894–1950)

(i) *Cello Concerto;* (ii–iii) *Violin Concerto;* (iii) *2 Pieces for Small Orchestra: Lonely Waters; Whythorne's Shadow.*

(M) *** Chan. 7078. (i) Wallfisch, Bournemouth Sinf., Del Mar; (ii) Mordkovitch; (iii) Ulster O, Handley.

The *Cello Concerto* (1945) is a pastoral work with elegiac overtones, save in its rather folksy finale. Raphael Wallfisch brings an eloquence of tone and a masterly technical address to this neglected piece, and he receives very responsive orchestral support from Norman Del Mar and the Bournemouth players. The *Violin Concerto* is also strongly lyrical in feeling. The first movement is thoughtful and rhapsodic, its inspiration drawn from Moeran's love of the west coast of Ireland; the middle movement makes use of folk music; while the finale, a ruminative elegy of great beauty, is the most haunting of the three. Lydia Mordkovitch plays with great natural feeling for this music and, quite apart from his sensitive support in the *Concerto*, Vernon Handley gives an outstanding account of *Lonely Waters*. Superb recording.

Serenade in G (complete original score); (i) *Nocturne.*

*** Chan. 8808. Ulster O, Handley, (i) with Mackey, Renaissance Singers – WARLOCK: *Capriol Suite* etc. ***

The *Serenade in G* has a good deal in common with Warlock's *Capriol Suite*. Both use dance forms from a previous age and transform them with new colours and harmonic touches. Handley and the Ulster Orchestra present it with striking freshness and warmth in its original version. The *Nocturne*, a setting of a poem by Robert Nichols for baritone and eight-part chorus, much admired by Britten, receives a wholly sympathetic performance and recording here, and the resonant acoustics of the Ulster Hall, Belfast, provide a warmly atmospheric ambient glow.

Symphony in G min.; (i) *Rhapsody for Piano & Orchestra in F sharp.*

*** Chan. 7106. (i) Fingerhut; Ulster O, Handley.

Vernon Handley gives a bitingly powerful performance of a great British symphony, helped by superb playing from the Ulster Orchestra, totally committed from first to last. The *Rhapsody* is obviously more lightweight than the symphony, but is by no means insubstantial. Using three themes, the piece is melodically attractive (with a folksy touch) and well integrated. It is splendidly played here, and throughout the disc the Chandos recording is superb.

Fantasy Quartet for Oboe & Strings.

*** Chan. 8392. Francis, English Qt – BAX: *Quintet;* HOLST: *Air & Variations* etc.; JACOB: *Quartet.* ***

Moeran's folk-influenced *Fantasy Quartet*, an attractively rhapsodic single-movement work, is played admirably here, and the recording is excellent, well balanced too.

String Quartets Nos. 1 in E flat; 2 in A min.; String Trio.

(BB) *** Naxos 8.554079. Maggini Qt.

(i) *String Quartet No. 2 in A min.;* (ii) *Violin Sonata in E min.*

*** Chan. 8465. (i) Melbourne Qt; (ii) Scotts, Talbot.

The *String Quartet in A minor* (1921) has a certain pastoral quality, with Irish echoes in the dance rhythms and ending on a flamboyant Rondo. The *String Trio* of 1931, beautifully written with no feeling of thinness, is even subtler, with the pastoral idiom more equivocal in its tonal shiftings. The Naxos CD also offers something of a discovery in the form of an earlier *Quartet in E flat*. Although it is not a masterpiece, there are some quite inspired things in it and the Maggini play throughout with great dedication and commitment. The recording is very life-like and present. A first-class bargain.

Good performances and recording on Chandos, but the Naxos coupling is ideal.

MOLINO, Francesco (1775–1847)

Trio, Op. 45.

*** Mer. CDE 84199. Conway, Silverthorne, Garcia – BEETHOVEN: *Serenade;* JOSEPH KREUTZER: *Grand Trio.****

Italian-born, Molino first settled in Spain before going on to London and Paris, where he built a reputation as a violinist and guitarist. Undemanding music to complete a charming disc for a rare combination. First-rate playing and recording.

MOMPOU, Federico (1893–1987)

Cançons i danzas Nos. 1–12; 14; Cants màgics; Suburbis.

(N) (BB) *** Warner/Apex 8573 89228-2. Heisser.

Jean-François Heisser displays a natural sympathy for Mompou's elusive world, and besides the *Cançons i danzas* and *Cants màgics* he offers also the rarer early work *Suburbis* (1916/17), which evokes the suburbs of Barcelona. The second and third of the five pieces are concerned with the gypsies, followed by a touching portrait of a little blind girl (*La ceguetta*), while the last is a lively picture of a street organ player. At its modest cost and very well recorded this is well worth having.

Canciónes y danzas Nos. 1–12, 14; Charmes; Scènes d'enfants.

(BB) *** Naxos 8.554332. Masó.

In many ways Jordi Masó's excellent Naxos collection is not upstaged by the competition. Moreover this is to be the first of a continuing series. He gives us the complete *Canciónes y danzas* (except for No. 13 which is for guitar), plus the engagingly diverse, but at times almost mystical *Charmes*, and his playing is imbued with gentle poetic feeling. Masó's pianistic sensibility is never self-aware, always at the service of the composer, and the music's soft-hued colours are perceptively graduated. The unostentatious innocence of the *Scènes d'enfants* is beautifully caught. Excellent recording makes this a disc to recommend even if it cost far more than it does.

Canciónes y danzas No. 1, 3, 5, 7, 8–9; Cants mágics; Charmes; Dialogues Nos. I–II; Paisajes; Preludios Nos. 1, 5 (Palmier d'étoiles), 6 (for the left hand), 7, 9–10; 3 Variations.

✹ *** Hyp. CDA 66963. Hough.

This exceptionally generous (77 minute) and wide-ranging *Gramophone* Award-winning recital makes an obvious first choice for those wanting to explore, on a single CD, the fullest possible range of Mompou's piano music. Stephen Hough, who provides the illuminating notes, imaginatively describes this as 'the music of evaporation . . . There is no development of material, little counterpoint, no drama or climaxes to speak of; and this simplicity of expression – elusive, evasive and shy – is strangely disarming.' He is completely inside Mompou's fastidious, Satie-esque sound-world and understands the absorbed influences which make this music as much French as Spanish. The recording too is excellent if a little reverberant. Not even Mompou himself equalled, let alone surpassed Hough in this repertoire.

7 Canciones y danzas; Impresiones intimas; Música callada; Preludio a Alicia de Larrocha.

✹ (B) *** Double Decca ADD/Dig. 433 929-2 (2). De Larrocha – 'Música española' (Recital). ***

This is for the most part gentle, reflective music and its quiet ruminative quality finds an eloquent exponent in Alicia de Larrocha, to whom Mompou dedicated one of his preludes. The *Impresiones intimas* have absorbed some of the delicacy of Debussy in their poetic feeling, fine detail and well calculated proportions. Alicia de Larrocha plays these poetic miniatures *con amore*, and the Decca recording is superbly real. This is reissued economically as part of a Double Decca linked to a generous and stimulating recital of music by Mompou's Spanish contemporaries.

8 Canciones y danzas; Escenas de niños; Fiestas lejanas; Paisajes; Pessebres; Suburbis.

(M) *** EMI (ADD) CDM7 64470-2. Soriano or Bravo.

Gonzalo Soriano plays these reflective miniatures simply and with the right degree of restrained eloquence. Carmen Bravo also finds poetry in the rest of the programme and is charmingly perceptive in his portrayal – in *Suburbis* – of *L'home de l'aristo* (the *aristo* was a cross between a hand-held miniature barrel-organ and a hurdy-gurdy). A rewarding and generous recital, given remarkably good recording, even though it dates from the early days of stereo.

MONDONVILLE, Jean-Joseph Cassanéa de (1711–72)

6 Sonates en symphonies, Op. 3.

*** DG 457 600-2. Les Musiciens du Louvre, Minkowski.

This entirely captivating set of *Symphonies* confirms Mondonville as a great deal more than a historical figure. They originated as sonatas for violin and obbligato harpsichord in 1734, but the composer later skilfully orchestrated them. Each is in three movements, with an expressively tuneful centrepiece framed by sprightly allegros. Their invention is consistently fresh, and they are played here with great élan and spontaneity and are beautifully recorded. Highly recommended.

Pièces de clavecin avec voix ou violon, Op. 5/1-8.

(B) *** HM HMA 1901045. Nelson, Ritchie, Christie.

Mondonville is credited with developing the harpsichord sonata with obbligato violin, which he called *Pièces de clavecin en sonates* (Opus 3). But Mondonville experimented too with the voice as a chamber-music instrument alongside a stringed instrument. In his *Pièces de clavecin avec voix ou violon* the music was composed independently of any text. The composer then fitted religious Latin texts to the musical line. What is striking is how naturally vocal the music sounds. The fine balance and expert playing of Stanley Ritchie and William Christie's sensitive harpsichord contribution add much to this presentation. But the greater part of the credit must go to the lovely singing of Judith Nelson, whose many shakes and turns are a pleasure in themselves. The sequential lines of Mondonville's writing are followed most sensitively. Altogether an outstanding disc, and very well recorded.

VOCAL MUSIC

Grands motets: *De profundis; Venite exultemus.* Petits motets: *Benefac Domine; In decachordo psalterio; Regna terrae.*

(N) (B) *** Hyp. Helios CDH 55038. Fisher, Daniels, Varcoe, New Coll. Oxford Ch., L. Bar. Ens., Higginbottom.

Grand motets: *De profundis; Dominus Regnavit; In exitu Israel.*

(N) *** Erato 0630 17791-2. Daneman, Wieczorek, Agnew, Piolino, Koningsberger, Bazola, Les Arts Florissants, Christie.

Even more than his orchestral and instrumental music, Mondonville's vocal writing confirms that he was a major figure in eighteenth-century French music, comparable even with Rameau. His grands motets were modelled on those of Delalande, but are even finer and more individual. Both these outstanding CDs include his *De profundis*, a remarkably diverse setting of verses 1–8 of Psalm 129. The sublime opening chorus is followed by the flowing *Fiant aures*, a solo air in the form of a simple chaconne, sung by the bass over a delightful flute figuration; the second air, *Quia apud te*, is given to the haute-contre tenor. Then follows a dainty chorus, *A custodia matutina*, with the light, high voices suggesting a spring morning. The lovely *Quia apud Dominum* and the following lively *Et ipse redimet Israel* are paired soprano airs, with the chorus joining the latter and then providing the closing *Requiem aeternam*, which opens sombrely and majestically (the dark scoring remarkably forward-looking) and ends with a splendid fugue.

Both performances here are of very high quality. Christie uses female voices in the chorus to fine expressive effect, but with Higginbottom the opening *De profundis clamavi* is wonderfully ethereal, with boy trebles set back in the atmospheric Oxford acoustic. Their more refined approach is matched by the ravishingly pure soprano line of Gillian Fisher, while the closing *Requiem aeternam* floats celestially. Sophie Daneman is more extrovert in the Christie version, but not less expressive, and the counter-tenor and bass soloists are closely matched. Some will prefer the slightly more robust approach of Les Arts Florissants which makes the closing section darker, more powerful and more plangent.

The couplings are well contrasted. Christie offers two more grands motets. *Dominus Regnavit* (Psalm 92) follows the Delalande pattern closely by opening with a symphonie and closing with a grand polyphonic *Gloria Patri* and *Amen*. Characteristically the setting also includes both a trio (in the opening verse) and a delightful central duo, *Parata sedes* (marked *gratieusement*), for two sopranos accompanied by a pair of oboes and a violin. The vigorous following chorus, *Elevarunt flumina*, vividly depicts the rising floods of the text, then comes a lovely soprano air and slow recitative (Sophie Daneman at her finest).

In exitu Israel is even more dramatically pictorial. It opens imposingly with a march, and the following choral and orchestral sequence *Mare vite* and *Jordanus conversus est retsorum* first evokes the calm sea, then with rapid repeated notes from the chorus and rushing scales depicts the parting of the waters as 'Jordan was driven back'. A gentle counter-tenor air (*The mountains skipped like lambs*) then leads to the baritone call 'Tremble, thou earth' (string tremolandos) and later the chorus vigorously joins the soloist as the rock is changed to still water. The work closes with a thankful soprano aria and a chorus of praise, at first solemn and then exultant. It is a splendidly colourful work and Christie and his team rise to the occasion. They are spaciously and clearly recorded, although there is occasionally a curious hint of grittiness in the choral focus.

Higginbottom's Helios collection offers another rather less grand motet, but one which alongside *De profundis* was greatly popular and frequently performed in its day. It is more lyrical, less dramatic and textually simpler – a radiant expression of praise using three soloists, with the soprano opening delightfully in pastoral vein with flute and oboe,

and returning later for the similarly exquisite *Venite adoremus*, the *Quia ipse est Domnus* (with oboe obbligato) and the *Hodie si vocem*, in which she is joined by the chorus. Both the counter-tenor and bass have major contributions to make, which require virtuoso flexibility (notably Charles Daniels's *Quadraginta annis*), and the work closes with a radiant display of vocal agility from the trebles in the final *Gloria Patri*, which tests the Oxford Choir to their outer limits.

The three solo petits motets with their modest harpsichord and continuo accompaniments are altogether more intimate but no less valuable, each showing Gillian Fisher in glorious voice (indeed this CD is worth having for her contribution alone), while Edward Higginbottom exchanges his baton for the harpsichord keyboard. Altogether this is a delightful bargain collection, given state-of-the-art sound, and with only one grand motet duplicated (in a quite different performance) this is a case where collectors should consider purchasing both discs.

Titon et L'Aurore (complete).

*** Erato 2292 45715-2 (2). Fouchécourt, Napoli, Huttenlocher, Smith, Monnoyios, Les Musiciens du Louvre, Minkowski.

Described as a 'heroic-pastoral', *Titon et L'Aurore* tells of the mortal Titon who has the temerity to fall in love with Aurora, goddess of the dawn. Some of the instrumental effects are most vivid and the work is full of charming ideas, presented with freshness and vigour. Marc Minkowski proves an ideal interpreter, directing a performance of the highest voltage, which yet allows the singers a full range of expressiveness. Jean-Paul Fouchécourt proves an outstanding example of the French *haute-contre*, sustaining stratospheric lines with elegance and no strain. Catherine Napoli is bright and clear, if shallow at times as Aurore, while Anne Monnoyios sings with ideal sweetness as L'Amour.

MONTEMEZZI, Italo (1875–1952)

L'amore dei tre re (complete).

(M) **(*) RCA (ADD) 74321 50166-2 (2). Moffo, Domingo, Elvira, Siepi, Davies, Amb. Op. Ch., LSO, Santi.

Italo Montemezzi, one of Puccini's young successors, delivered this lurid melodrama based on a play by Sem Benelli, and the obvious dramatic echoes of *Tristan* and *Pelleas* combined with a red-blooded, lyrical score brought it success. What it lacks, compared to Puccini – let alone to Wagner or Debussy – are memorable ideas. Nevertheless, with colourful scoring and an economical structure it makes easy listening. This 1977 recording with Nello Santi a thrustful conductor makes as good a case for the piece as one is likely to get. Anna Moffo is an old-sounding if dramatic Fiora, but Plácido Domingo is in glowing form as Avito, and Cesare Siepi vividly heightens the melodrama as Archibaldo. As Manfredo, the baritone, Pablo Elvira, sings with firm, clean attack, as does Ryland Davies in the role of the castle guard, Flaminio. Full, warm, well-balanced sound.

Synopsis and libretto with translation are provided but no background information on the work or the composer.

MONTEVERDI, Claudio (1567–1643)

Madrigals, Book 2 (complete).

*** Opus 111 OPS 30-111. Concerto Italiano, Alessandro.

Rinaldo Alessandro and his superb Concerto Italiano are singing their sunny Italianate way through Monteverdi's complete madrigal sequence. Apart from being of Italian birth, all the performers here have studied early Italian and therefore bring a special idiomatic feeling to the words. The Second Book, about half of whose five-part settings are from Tasso, demands and receives a simpler style of presentation than the later works, and there is radiant freshness about the singing here which is particularly appealing. The recording has the most pleasing acoustic.

Madrigals, Book 4 (complete).

*** Opus 111 OPS 30-81. Concerto Italiano, Alessandro.

Madrigals, Books 4–5 (complete). Book 7: Con che soavità, labbra odorate; Tempro la cetra. Book 8: (Madrigali guerrieri et amorosi): Mentre vaga; Ogni amante è guerrier.

(B) *** O-L Double 455 718-2 (2). Consort of Musicke, Rooley.

Madrigals, Book 5 (complete).

✪ *** Opus 111 OPS 30-166. Concerto Italiano, Alessandro.

The Fourth Book, published in 1603 and again for five voices, marks an added richness of expressive feeling over Monteverdi's earlier settings, well recognized by Rinaldo Alessandro and his superbly blended vocal group. This series goes from strength to strength and can be strongly recommended. The recording continues to match the singing in excellence.

The Oiseau-Lyre Double offers exceptional value in including the whole of the contents of Book 4 (dating from 1603) and Book 5 (1605), plus four substantial accompanied madrigals which come from the composer's later, Venetian years. Under Anthony Rooley, the well-integrated singers of the Consort of Musicke, led by Emma Kirkby, give masterly performances of the fourth book, which suits their vocal style especially well. Book 5 marked a turning point in Monteverdi's madrigal output, for the last six works bring an obligatory continuo and are much freer in style than their predecessors, even semi-operatic in their use of freely individual vocal solos. It might be said that the change of style in the singing from the Consort of Musicke is less marked than in the competing (full-priced) collection of these works by the Concerto Italiano directed by Rinaldo Alessandro, whose singing is distinctly Italianate and more extrovert. Nevertheless the comparatively restrained approach of Rooley's group brings its own rewards, and their refinement is reflected in the delicate lute continuo in the later numbers. The later madrigals are even more successful, their quixotic mood-changes superbly caught. The recording is excellent throughout and full translations are provided.

However, the competing performances by Alessandro's

superb Italian vocal group, at one moment blending richly together, at another asserting solo individuality, cannot be praised too highly, and again they are beautifully recorded.

Madrigals from Books 7 and 8: Amor che deggio far; Altri canti di Marte; Chiome d'oro; Gira il nemico insidioso; Hor ch'el ciel e la terra; Non havea Febo ancora – Lamento della ninfa; Perchè t'en fuggi o Fillide; Tirsi e Clori (ballo concertato for 5 Voices & Instruments).

(B) *** HM (ADD) HMA 1901068. Les Arts Florissants, Christie.

The singing of this famous group is full of colour and feeling and, even if intonation is not absolutely flawless throughout, it is mostly excellent. Much to be preferred to the bloodless white tone favoured by some early-music groups. Good recording. A bargain.

Madrigals, Book 8: Madrigali guerrieri et amorosi (Madrigals of War and Love).

(BB) **(*) Virgin 2 x 1 Double VBD5 61570-2 (2). Soloists, Consort of Musicke, Rooley.

Madrigals, Book 8: Madrigali guerri et amorosi: Volume I: Sinfonia: Altri canti d'Amor; Lamento della Ninfa; Vago augelletto; Perchè t'en fuggi, o Fillide?; Altri canti di Marte; Due belli occhi fur l'ami; O gni amante è guerrier; Hor che'l ciel e la terra; Gira il nemico, insidioso Amore; Dolcissimo usignolo; Ardo, ardo avvampo.

*** Opus 111 OPS 30-187. Concerto Italiano, Alessandri.

Monteverdi published his Eighth Book after a long gap in his madrigal output. It is in two parts and one of the very greatest of his songs in the Madrigali amorosi is Lamento della ninfa in what Monteverdi called the stile rappresentativo or theatre style, and that is affectingly done here. The Madrigali guerrieri are also very theatrical and include Il ballo delle ingrate and Il combattimento di Tancredi e Clorinda, which are also available separately in other individual versions (see below). The performances here are distinctive, and anyone collecting Rooley's series should find this inexpensive Double well worth its modest cost. The cast list is strong, including Emma Kirkby and Evelyn Tubb, but Andrew King is the narrator in Il Combattimento and his approach is less than robustly full-blooded, while in both works the performances under Pickett and Christie are more dramatically arresting (see below).

Rinaldo Alessandri and his Concerto Italiano here continue their superlative series of recordings of Monteverdi's madrigals with the first part of Book 8, Madrigals of War and Love. As before, the singing combines Italianate fire and lyricism in ideal proportions and the instrumental accompaniments could hardly be finer. The present disc includes famous items like the three-part Lamento della Ninfa and the two-part Hor che'l ciel e la terra. The recording too is first class.

Madrigals, Book 8: Madrigali guerrieri et amorosi: Altri canti d'amor; Altri cante di marte; Il Gira il nemico; Hor ch'e ciel e la terra; Lamento della Ninfa; 2 Sinfonias; Volgendo il ciel movete al mio bel suon (Ballo).

(N) (M) *** Astrée ES 9944. Figueras, Tiso, Banditelli,

Climent, Carnovich, Garrigosa, Costa, La Capella Reial de Catalunya, Savall.

Savall's way with Monteverdi's Book VIII is, above all, theatrical and tremendously vital: his singers emphasize the strong rhythmic contrasts of the *Madrigali guerrieri*. There are some very fine voices in his team, none lacking individuality of character, yet blending splendidly, as at the opening of *Hor che'l ciel e la terra*. Montserrat Figueras, Lambert Climent (tenor) and Daniele Carnovich (bass) stand out, and Figueras is at her glorious best in the famous *Lamento della Ninfa*. This is an excellent anthology in all respects and full translations are included.

Madrigal collections

Madrigals & Motets (collection)

Disc 1: Madrigals: *Addio Florida bella; Ahi com'a un vago sol; E così a poco a poco torno farfalla; Era l'anima mia; Luci serene e chiare; Mentre vaga Angioletta ogn'anima; Ninfa che scalza il piede; O mio bene, a mia vita; O Mirtillo, Mirtill'anima mia; Se pur destina; Taci, Armelin deh taci; T'amo mia vita; Troppo ben può questo tiranno amore.*

Disc 2: Madrigals: *Bel pastor dal cui bel guardo; Lamento d'Arianna; Non è gentil cor; O come sei gentile; Ohimé, dov'é il mio ben; Zefiro torna* (with Benedetto FERRARI: *Queste pungenti spine* (cantata); (attributed FERRARI): Final duet for MONTEVERDI: *L'incoronazione di Poppea: Pur ti miro, pur ti godo*).

Disc 3: Motets for 1, 2 & 3 voices: *Confitebor tibi Domine* (solo); *Duo seraphim* (a 3); *Ego flos campi* (solo); *Fugge, anima mea* (a 2); *Jubilet; Laudate Dominum; Nigra sum* (all three solos); *O beata viae* (a 2); *O quam pulchra es* (solo); *Pulchra es, amica mea* (a 2); *Salve, O Regina* (solo).

(B) **(*) HM ADD/Dig. HMX 290841/3. Concerto Vocale, Jacobs.

One of Harmonia Mundi's bargain 'trios', this Monteverdi programme offers an admirable, inexpensive survey of Monteverdi's music, both his madrigals and his church music. The disc called *'Un concert spirituel'* is the highlight of the set and might have received a Rosette as an independent issue. It opens with the remarkable and beautiful *Duo seraphim*, suggesting angels' wings as well as a celestial chorale. Both the solo *Confitebor tibi Domine* and the duet *Fugge, anima mea* are in essence miniature cantatas, with complex parts followed by solos which additionally bring a violin obbligato. The dramatically expressive *Nigra sum* soon becomes lyrically quite sensuous, especially at the decorated closing section, and *O quam pulchra es* is very like one of the composer's operatic laments, and very touching. Both are set to words from the Song of Songs. Their dolorous feeling is well caught by Jacobs, whose decoration is very convincing. The *Laudate Dominum* and *Jubilet* are sung delightfully by Judith Nelson. An outstanding concert, with imaginatively varied continuo accompaniments (including organ as well as harpsichord). They are recorded in an

atmospheric acoustic, adding bloom to voices and instruments alike, without clouding detail.

The first madrigal collection is also available separately on a bargain Musique d'Abord CD (HMA 190184). It is a highly attractive collection of generally neglected items, briskly and stylishly performed, and, with continuo accompaniment, the contrasting of vocal timbres is achieved superbly. Again excellent recording.

The third programme offers more familiar repertoire, including the famous *Lamento d'Arianna*. Jacobs allots the lead vocal role to Helga Müller-Molinari, whose general approach is too redolent of grand opera, while her opulent voice does not blend readily with the instrumental support. The interest of this disc is also increased by the inclusion of music by Benedetto Ferrari, a Venetian composer of the generation following Monteverdi, and also a playwright and theorbo player. His *Queste pungenti spine* is a spiritual cantata and is accompanied on the CD by the final duet from *L'incoronazione di Poppea*, which has been attributed to him by some scholars. This collection is now also available separately in Harmonia Mundi's mid-price Suite series (HMT 7901129).

Madrigals: *Ab aeterno ordinata sum; Confitebor tibi, Domine* (3 settings); *Deus tuorum militum sors et corona; Iste confessor Domini sacratus; Laudate Dominum, O omnes gentes; La Maddalena: Prologue: Su le penne de venti. Nisi Dominus aedificaverit domum.*

⊛ *** Hyp. CDA 66021. Kirkby, Partridge, Thomas, Parley of Instruments.

There are few records of Monteverdi's solo vocal music as persuasive as this. The three totally contrasted settings of *Confitebor tibi* (Psalm 110) reveal an extraordinary range of expression, each one drawing out different aspects of word-meaning. Even the brief trio, *Deus tuorum militum*, has a haunting memorability – it could become to Monteverdi what *Jesu, joy of man's desiring* is to Bach – and the performances are outstanding, with the edge on Emma Kirkby's voice attractively presented in an aptly reverberant acoustic. The accompaniment makes a persuasive case for authentic performance on original instruments. The CD sounds superb.

Madrigals: *A Dio, Florida bella; Altri canti d'amor; Amor che deggio far; Hor che'l ciel e la terra; Presso un fiume tranquillo; Questi vaghi concenti; Qui rise, o Tirsi.*

(N) (BB) **(*) Teldec (ADD) 4509 9368-2. Jacobeit, Förster-Dürlich, Van t'Hoff, Runge, Villisech, Hamburg Monteverdi Ch., Leonhardt Consort, Jürgens.

This collection comes from the early 1960s, but the remastered sound confirms the high standard of Das Alte Werk recordings made during that period. On CD the choral sound is not sharply defined, but the acoustic is attractively spacious. The Hamburg Monteverdi Choir is a splendid ensemble and the soloists, while they are clearly not Italians, sing both eloquently and stylishly. Jürgen's direction and pacing is both lively and expressive. *Hor che'l ciel e la terra* is particularly fine, as indeed is *Qui rise, o Tirsi*. Full translations are provided. Value for money, even if the playing time is only 43'30''.

Madrigals: *Alcun non mi consigli; Ardo e scoprir Bel pastor; Eccomi pronta ai baci; Eri già tutta mia; Lamento d'Arianna; Lamento della Ninfa; Ohimè, ch'io cado; Tu dormi; Una donna fra l'altre.*

(B) **(*) Sony (ADD) SBK 60707. Kweksilber, Jacobs, Van Altena, Ten Houte de Lange, Rommerts, Leonhardt.

This is an attractive selection of ten of Monteverdi's very finest madrigals, including the famous five-voiced setting of the operatic *Lamento d'Arianna* and the companion four-part *Lamento della Ninfa*, with Marjanne Kweksilber singing exquisitely in '*Amor*', the lament itself. She also joins delightfully with Marius van Altena in the engaging dialogue of *Bel pastor*. René Jacobs is individually impressive in his two solos, *Ohimè ch'io cado*, and *Eri già tutta mia*. The balance with Gustav Leonhardt's harpsichord accompaniment is excellent, the recording is natural, and the only snag with an otherwise outstanding disc is the absence of translations, or any kind of guide to what the individual madrigals are about. The playing time is also short at 45 minutes, but the musical quality is very high.

Madrigals: '*Batto*', *qui pianse Ergasto; Gira, il nemico insidioso amore; Hor che'l ciel e la terra; O come sei gentile; Ogni amante è guerrir; Zefiro torna.*

⊛ (M) *** Virgin VER5 61165-2. Chiaroscuro, L. Baroque, Rogers – D´INDIA: *Madrigals.* *** ⊛

A hand-picked half-dozen of Monteverdi's finest madrigals, superlatively sung, consistently bringing out the expressive originality and the extraordinary variety of the settings, to say nothing of their inherent vocal bravura. *Zefiro torna* is justly famous, but '*Batto*', *qui pianse Ergasto* is hardly less remarkable, and the two *Madrigali guerrieri et amorosi* are very telling indeed. The engagingly lyrical *O come sei gentile* follows immediately after the d'India dramatized cycle from *Il pastor Fido* and makes a fascinating comparison. Accompaniments are nicely balanced and the recording has an exceptionally real and vivid presence.

Madrigals (duets and solos): *Chiome d'oro, bel thesoro; Il son pur vezzosetta pastorella; Non è di gentil core; O come sei gentile, caro augellino; Ohimè dov'è il mio ben?; Se pur destina e vole il cielo, partenza amorosa.* **Sacred music:** *Cantate Domino; Exulta, filia Sion; Iste confessoe II; Laudate Dominum in sanctis eius; O bone Jesu, o piissime Jesu; Sancta Maria, succurre miseris; Venite, siccientes ad aquas Domini.* (Opera) *Il ritorno d'Ulisse in patria: Di misera regina (Penelope's lament).*

(N) (M) *** Regis RRC 1060. Kirkby, Tubb, Consort of Musicke, Rooley.

Admirers of Emma Kirkby will surely revel in this collection, mostly of duets in which she is joined by Evelyn Tubb. The two voices are admirably matched and both artists ornament their lines attractively and judiciously. Evelyn Tubb is given a solo opportunity in Penelope's lament from *Il ritorno d'Ulisse*, which she sings dramatically and touchingly. Anthony Rooley's simple accompaniments with members

of the Consort of Musicke are also imaginatively stylish. We are pleased to report that the current reissue has been properly documented with notes and full translations.

Lamento d'Olympia; Maladetto sia l'aspetto; Ohimè ch'io cado; Quel sdengosetto; Voglio di vita uscia.

*** Hyp. CDA 66106. Kirkby, Rooley (chitarone) – D´INDIA: *Lamento d'Olympia* etc. ***

A well-planned recital from Hyperion contrasts the two settings of *Lamento d'Olympia* by Monteverdi and his younger contemporary, Sigismondo d'India. The performances by Emma Kirkby, sensitively supported by Anthony Rooley, could hardly be surpassed; this ranks among her best records.

Church music

Motets: (i) *Adoramus te, Christe; Cantate Domino; Domine, neinfurore tuo;* (ii; iii) *Exulta filia Sion;* (iv; i) *Exultent caeli;* (v; vi) *Laudate pueri Dominum I;* (ii; iii) *Laudate Dominum II;* (viii) *Laudate Dominum III;* (ix) *Magnificat* (1610); (x) *Messa da capella* (1640); *Messa da capella* (1650); (ii; iii) *Salve, o Regina;* (vii; iii) *Salve Regina; Sancta Maria;* (v; vi) *Ut queant laxis.*

(B) **(*) Double Decca 458 829-2 (2). (i) Monteverdi Ch., Gardiner; (ii) Rogers; (iii) AAM, Hogwood; (iv) Messana, Hill, Philip Jones Brass Ens.; (v) Turner, Odom; (vi) ASMF Strings, Guest; (vii) Kirkby, Nelson; (viii) Cooper, Leask, Magdalen College, Oxford, Ch., Rose; (ix) London Carmelite Priory Ch., Malcolm; (x) St John's College, Cambridge, Ch., Guest.

This is an ingeniously gathered miscellany rather than a planned collection. The chosen *Magnificat* is part of the 1610 *Vespers* but is the less elaborate version for six voices and organ. The refreshing performance by George Malcolm's Carmelite Priory Choir is excellent in every way. The four-part *Mass* from 1640 is full of remarkable passages in which the metre undergoes sudden changes and the harmony becomes expressive in an almost secular style. In both this and the later work, which is less innovatory, the part-writing comes over with eminent clarity. The singing under George Guest is extremely good, though the trebles (Michael Turner and Benjamin Odom) have a 'fluting' quality that is heard more effectively in the first, string-accompanied *Laudate pueri Dominum* (for six voices) and the *Ut queant laxis* (a hymn for St John the Baptist). Nigel Rogers is strong in the solo *Laudate Dominum*, and another excellent pair of trebles (Simon Cooper and Stuart Leask) suitably angelic in the third version, with contrasting sonorities from the Magdalen College Choir, plus sonorous brass. Following on agreeably, the voices of Emma Kirkby and Judith Nelson are a highlight in the Elysian *Salve Regina* and *Sancta Maria*.

Closing the collection, Gardiner's performances of the motets *Adoramus te, Christe, Cantate Domino* and *Domine, ne in furore tuo*, which also come from the *Selva morale et spirituale*, are also marked by excellent singing with firm tone and intonation. Dynamics and tempi are rather extreme, but there is no doubt that the music comes fully to life. In the *Exultent caeli* ('Let the heavens rejoice'), which ends the concert, the gentle central verses, which are concerned with the Virgin Mary and the conception of Jesus, are effectively framed by a jubilant opening and conclusion, where the singers are joined by the Philip Jones Brass Ensemble. The recording throughout is admirable, full translations are included, and there are adequate notes.

Motets: *Ego flos campi; Ego sum pastor bonus; Exulta, filia Sion; Fuge, fuge anima mea, mundum; Iusti tulerunt spolia; Lapidabant Stephanum; Lauda, Jerusalem; Laudate Dominum; Nigra sum; O bone Jesu, illumina oculos meos; O bone Jesu, O piissime Jesu; O quam pulchra es; Pulchra es; Salve regina; Spuntava al dì; Sugens Jesus, Dominus noster; Surge propera, amica mea; Veni in hortum meum* (with PICCININI: *Toccata X*).

*** Virgin VC7 59602-2. B. Lesne, G. Lesne, Benet, Cabré, Il Seminario Musicale, Tragicomedia.

The music on this disc encompasses all periods of Monteverdi's career; the earliest comes from his first published collection, the *Sacrae Canticulicae* (1582), composed when he was only fifteen. Other pieces, such as the *Salve Regina*, come from the *Selva Morale* (1640), while *Pulchra es* and *Nigra sum* are performed on instruments alone. The solo motet *O quam pulchra es* is preceded by a *Toccata* by Alessandro Piccinini about which the excellent notes are silent. The performances here are expert and totally committed. Excellent recording.

Missa de cappella a 4; Missa de cappella a 6 (In illo tempore); Motets: *Cantate domino a 6; Domine ne in furore a 6.*

*** Hyp. CDA 66214 [id]. The Sixteen, Christophers; Phillips.

Harry Christophers draws superb singing from his brilliant choir, highly polished in ensemble but dramatic and deeply expressive too, suitably adapted for the different character of each Mass-setting, when the four-part Mass involves stricter, more consistent contrapuntal writing and the six-part, in what was then an advanced way, uses homophonic writing to underline key passages. Vivid, atmospheric recording.

'Pianato della Madonna': Motets for solo voice: *Confitebor tibi Domini* (*Missa a 4 voci e salmi*, 1650). *Currite populi; Ecce sacrum paratum; O quam pulchra es* (*Ghirlanda sacra*, 1645). *Exulta, Filia Sion* (*Sacri canti*, 1629) *Jubilet a voce sola in dialogo; Lamento dell'Arianna: Pianato della Madonna; Laudate Dominum* (all from *Selva Morale e Spirituale*, 1640). *Salve, O Regina* (*Sacre canti*, 1624); *Venite, videte* (1625).

(M) ✪ *** HM HMX 2981680. Kiehr, Concerto Soava, Aymes (with MARINE: 2 *Sinfonias* (from *Church Sonatas*); Costanto ATEGNATI: *Ricercar*; Claudio MERULO: *Toccata con minute* ***).

Maria Cristina Kiehr's compilation is very beautiful. With the vocal items contrasted with short instrumental ritornellos by other musicians from the same period, we cannot praise this recital too highly. Every work is glorious and is ravishingly sung. *Currite populi* introduces a lovely flowing *Alleluia; O quam pulchra es* ('How fair thou art, my love') is

permeated with an exquisite melancholy, which returns in several later items, and especially the famous excerpt from the *Lamento dell'Ariana*, which give the CD its title. The fresh, spring-like *Jubilet* has a delightful echo effect, with a nice touch of added resonance, and *Exulta, Filia Sion* is another joyful song, with florid runs and a jubilant closing *Alleluia*. The closing *Laudate Dominum* makes a wonderful apotheosis, with alleluias and echoing phrases adding to its paean of praise. Superb music, superb singing and playing, and warmly atmospheric recording all here combine to bring the listener the very greatest musical rewards.

Selva morale e spirituale: excerpts: *Adoramus; Beatus vir a 6 voci; Chi vol che m'innamori; Confitebor terzo alla francese; Confitiebor tibi Domine; E questa vita un Iampo; Gloria a 7 voci; Laudate Dominum; O ciechi ciechi.*

*** HM HMC 901250. Les Arts Florissants, Christie.

Monte-verdi's *Selva morale e spirituale* (1640) is a huge collection of nearly 40 separate works, written over three decades. Christie's programme here gives an idea of its range, from *Beatus vir*, the vivid large scale psalm-setting for six voices and violins, and the splendid seven-voiced *Gloria*, with its burst of vocal virtuosity at the opening, to the succinct *Adoramus te*, and the more modest *Laudate dominum* for bass voice with continuo. All the performances here are imbued with a flowing vitality, and combine breadth and devotional feeling with vocal and instrumental refinement. As usual from this source the recording is admirably clear and spacious.

Vespro della Beata Vergine (Vespers).

✪ *** DG 429 565-2 (2). Monoyios, Pennicchi, Chance, Tucker, Robson, Naglia, Terfel, Miles, H.M. Sackbutts & Cornetts, Monteverdi Ch., London Oratory Ch., E. Bar. Sol., Gardiner.

(N) *** BIS CD 1071/2 (2). Midori Suzuki, Nonoshita, Hatano, Türk, Van Dyke, Taniguchi, MacLeod, Ogasawara, Bach Collegium Japan Ch. & O, Masaaki Suzuki.

(BB) *** Hyp. Dyad CDD 22028 (2). The Sixteen, Christophers.

**(*) DHM RD 77760. Zanetti, Fischer, Fordier, Elwes, Kendall, van der Meel, Kooy, Cantor, Stuttgart Ch Chor., Choralschola Niederalteich, Frieder Bernius.

(B) **(*) Teldec Ultima 0630 18955-2 (2). Marshall, Palmer, Langridge, Equiluz, Hampson, Korn, Tölz Boys' Ch., Soloists from V. Hofbur Ch., Arnold Schönberg Ch., VCM, Harnoncourt.

**(*) Erato/Warner 3984-23139-2 (2) Degor, Wieczorek, Stenowica, Schofrin, Agnew, Cornwell, Piolino, Felix, Bayley, Les Arts Florissants, Christie.

(M) **(*) Teldec (ADD) 4509 92175-2 (2). Hansmann, Jacobeit, Rogers, Van t'Hoff, Van Egmond, Villisech, V. Boys' Ch. soloists, Hamburg Monteverdi Ch., Plainsong Schola of Munich Capella Antiqua, VCM, Jürgens.

(i) *Vespro della Beata Vergine (Vespers);* (ii) Motet: *Exultent coeli.*

(B) *** Double Decca (ADD) 443 482-2 (2). (i) Gomez, Palmer, Bowman, Tear, Langridge, Shirley-Quirk, Rippon, Monteverdi Ch. & O, Salisbury Cathedral Boys' Ch., Philip

Jones Brass Ens., Munrow Recorder Consort;
(ii) Monteverdi Ch., Philip Jones Brass & Wind Ens.;
Gardiner (with (ii) Christmas motets: G. GABRIELI:
*Angelus ad pastores; Audite principes; O magnum
mysterium; Quem vidistis pastores?; Salvator noster.*
BASSANO: *Hodie Christus natus est ****).

*Vespro della Beata Vergine (Vespers); Selva morale e
spirituale: Beatus vir; Confitebor tibi Domine; Dixit
Dominus; Laudate pueri; Laudate Dominum; Salve
Regina.*

(BB) *** Virgin 2 x 1 VBD5 61662-2 (2). Kirkby, Rogers,
Thomas, Taverner Ch., Cons. and Players, Parrott.

Gardiner's second recording of the *Vespers* vividly captures
the spatial effects that a performance in the Basilica of
St Mark's, Venice, made possible. Gardiner made his earlier
recording for Decca in 1974 using modern instruments (see
below). Here, with the English Baroque Soloists and a team
of soloists less starry but more aptly scaled, all of them firm
and clear, he directs a performance even more compellingly
dramatic. It would be hard to better such young soloists as
the counter-tenor Michael Chance, the tenor Mark Tucker
and the bass Bryn Terfel. Without inflating the instrumental
accompaniment – using six string-players only, plus elaborate continuo and six brass from His Majesties Sackbutts
and Cornetts – he combines clarity and urgency with grandeur. Gardiner (as before) does not include plainchant antiphons and so has room on the two discs for the superb
alternative setting of the *Magnificat*, in six voices instead of
seven, in another dedicated performance.

Suzuki's fine set aims to include not just the *Vespers*,
complete with the grand *Magnificat* in seven voices, but the
other items in the collection which Monteverdi published
in 1610. Following the example of Andrew Parrott, Suzuki
has chosen to transpose the music down a fourth not only
for the two settings of the *Magnificat*, but for the *Mass* and
the *Lauda Jerusalem*, each written in a combination of high
clefs. He adds that this avoids the high scream of cornetts in
the two settings of the *Magnificat*.

It makes a satisfying and generous package, very well
performed and warmly recorded. The scale is not as grand
as in Gardiner's version recorded in St Mark's, Venice, nor
as intimate as Philip Pickett's or even Bernius's, which treats
the *Vespers* liturgically. The reverberation often obscures
detail in the big choral numbers, but the balance is excellent
between solo voices and choir, and the approach characteristically lively and well-sprung in the way one expects of
this fine choral conductor. A first-rate recommendation,
particuarly with such generous bonuses.

Gardiner's earlier, Decca recording was made before he
had been won over entirely to the claims of the authentic
school. Modern instruments are used and women's voices,
but Gardiner's rhythms are so resilient that the result is
exhilarating as well as grand. Singing and playing are exemplary, and the recording is one of Decca's most vividly atmospheric, with relatively large forces presented and placed
against a helpful, reverberant acoustic. Now issued as a
Double Decca, this set is well worth considering, with the
addition to the *Vespers* of a collection of Christmas motets,
mostly by Giovanni Gabrieli, first issued in 1972. The rich,

sonorous dignity of Gabrieli's *Sonata pian'e forte* sounds
resplendent, and in the choral numbers the vocal and instrumental blend is expert. The most impressive work here
is Gabrieli's glorious *Quem vidistis pastores?*. Monteverdi's
Exultent caeli is shorter, but one is again amazed by the
range of expressive contrast. Then there is Gabrieli's fine
Salvator noster, a motet for three five-part choirs, jubilantly
rejoicing at the birth of Christ. The CD transfer is admirable.

Although Parrott uses minimal forces, with generally one
instrument and one voice per part, so putting the work on
a chamber scale in a small church setting, its grandeur comes
out superbly through its very intensity. Far more than usual
with antiphons in Gregorian chant it becomes a liturgical
celebration, so that the five non-liturgical compositions or
concerti are added to the main Vespers setting as a rich
glorification. They are brilliantly sung here by the virtuoso
soloists, above all by Nigel Rogers, whose distinctive timbre
may not suit every ear but who has an airy precision and
flexibility to give expressive meaning to even the most taxing
passages. With fine all-round singing and playing, and a
warm atmospheric recording which, despite an ecclesiastical
ambience, allows ample detail through, this set is recommended. The other items, from the *Selva morale e spirituale*,
are not quite so impressive – this singing is a bit bloodless –
but are fully acceptable as a bonus. There are no texts or
translations and minimal notes, but this is very inexpensive.

The Sixteen's version of Monteverdi's 1610 *Vespers* on
Hyperion, beautifully scaled, presents a liturgical performance of what Graham Dixon suggests as Monteverdi's original conception. In practice the occasional changes of text
are minimal; the booklet accompanying the set even includes
an order of tracks if anyone wishes to hear the *Vespers* in
traditional form. As it is, with a liturgical approach, the
performance includes not only relevant Gregorian chant
but antiphon substitutes, including a magnificent motet of
Palestrina, obviously relevant, *Gaude Barbara*. The scale of
the performance is very satisfying, with The Sixteen augmented to 22 singers (7.4.6.5) and with members of the
group taking the eight solo roles. Christophers provides a
mean between John Eliot Gardiner's unashamedly grand
view and Andrew Parrott's vital, scholarly re-creation of an
intimate, princely devotion.

Bernius and his fine team, recorded in a modest-sized
chapel, present the vespers liturgically with antiphons before
each item. The extra clarity will please many, when the
sound remains vividly atmospheric. The snag is that the
six-part *Magnificat* is not offered as an alternative, making
rather short measure for the two discs, but because of the
scale and approach this for some will be a first choice, even
though Bernius is squarer rhythmically than most rivals.

Harnoncourt's admirers may well be attracted to his 1986
recording, particularly as it is now available as an Ultima
bargain Double. It was recorded live and gives a keen sense
of occasion, with the grandeur of the piece linked to a
consciously authentic approach. There is an entirely apt
ruggedness in the interpretation, which is lightened by the
characterful refinement of the solo singing from an exceptionally strong team of soloists, not to mention the fine
singing from all three choirs. Ample, atmospheric recording.

William Christie's version was recorded in 1997 following

a live performance given in Sicily, and simply follows the pattern of the live event. Imaginatively Christie punctuates the sequence with instrumental numbers – two *Sonatas* by Monteverdi's contemporary, Gioavnanni Paolo Clima, and presents the whole performance with flair and dedication. The reverberation of the recording venue in Paris makes for washy sound, and many will miss having the six-part *Magnificat* as an alternative, but Christie's admirers will not be disappointed.

Recorded in Vienna in 1966/67 the Jürgens set is scholarly yet not without warmth. The liturgical sequence is respectful, and authentic instruments are used. The continuo tends to be somewhat lightweight, but there is a sure sense of style. The opening chorus is vivid with the colour of renaissance trumpets and recorders, but the CD transfer cannot disguise a lack of sharpness of focus here and in the more complex analogue choral textures. At mid-price this is fair value, for the soloists are all fine artists and the choral singing is committed and polished. Documentation is excellent.

OPERA AND OPERA-BALLET

(i) *Il ballo delle ingrate;* (ii) *Il combattimento di Tancredi e Clorinda.*

*** Opus 111 OPS 30-196. (i) Ermolli, Dominguez, Carnovich, Franzetti; (ii) Franzetti, Ferrarini, Abbondanza; Concerto Italiano, Alessandrini.

(i) *Il ballo delle ingrate;* (ii) *Lamento d'Arianna.*

(M) **(*) Van. (ADD) 08.5063.71. (i) Deller, McLoughlin, Ward, Cantelo, Amb. S., L. Chamber Players, Stevens; (ii) Sheppard, Le Sage, Worthley, Todd, Deller, Bevan, Deller Consort, Deller.

Il combattimento di Tancredi e Clorinda.

(BB) *** HM Solo HM 926015. Semeliaz, Brand, Rovenq, Les Arts Florissants, Christie.

(i) *Il combattimento di Tancredi e Clorinda. Lamento della Ninfa; Mentre vaga Angioletta; Ogni amante e guerrier.*

(M) *** Teldec 4509 92181-2. (i) Equiluz, Schmidt, Hollweg, Murray, Langridge, Hartman, Perry, Palmer, Mühle, Franzden; VCM, Harnoncourt.

Il ballo and *Il combattimento* are drawn from Volume I of Monteverdi's Eighth Book of Madrigals. There is no more commandingly dramatic account of *Il combattimento* on record than this dramatic Italianate version with superb singing from all three principals. Roberto Abbondanza is a splendidly histrionic narrator, and in the death scene Elisa Franzetti, singing her farewell, is exquisitely moving. Franzetti returns at the end of *Il ballo delle ingrate* to bid an eloquent adieu on behalf of the ungrateful souls, condemned for rebelling against earthly love, to be echoed by Monteverdi's infinitely poignant closing chorus from her companions. The performance overall is cast from strength. Daniele Carnovich is a true basso profundo and makes a superb Pluto, but Francesca Ermolli and Rosa Dominguez are equally fine as Amor and Venus, respectively. The vivid recording is warmly atmospheric.

Denis Stevens's pioneering stereo version of Monteverdi's

Il ballo delle ingrate dates from 1956 and has an impressive cast, well backed up by the Ambrosian Singers and London Chamber Players. Although the orchestral sound seems rather ample to ears used to original instruments, this account rings true and there is much that is authentic, not least the decoration of the vocal line, by Deller himself who is most moving as Venus. Eileen McLoughlin makes a delightful Amor, and David Ward is suitably stentorian as Pluto. It is all emotively communicated here and the recording is vivid, if rather close. In addition Deller directs a performance of the famous *Lamento d'Arianna*, sung by a vocal sextet comprising Honor Sheppard, Sally le Sage, Max Worthley, Philip Todd, Maurice Bevan and Deller himself. Here the individual voices, while having plenty of character, do not always match ideally in consort. Nevertheless a thoroughly worthwhile reissue in the Alfred Deller Edition.

Like his companion CD of *Il ballo delle ingrate*, Christie's account of *Il combattimento* is very dramatic, with the storytelling vividly projected and with Françoise Semeliaz a touching Clorinda in the tragic closing scene. The recording is admirably vivid too. The libretto is in Italian and French only, but the narrative is easy enough to follow.

Harnoncourt also directs sharply characterized readings. The substantial scena telling of the conflict of Tancredi and Clorinda is made dramatic in a bald way. *Ogni amante e guerrier*, almost as extended, is treated with similar abrasiveness, made attractively fresh but lacking subtlety. The two *Canti amorosi* are treated quite differently, in a much warmer style, with the four sopranos of *Mentre vaga Angioletta* producing sensuous sounds. *Lamento della Ninfa*, perhaps the most celebrated of all Monteverdi's madrigals, brings a luscious performance with the solo voice (Ann Murray) set evocatively at a slight distance behind the two tenors and a bass. On CD the recording is extremely vivid, with voices and instruments firmly and realistically placed. The documentation is first class in every way, with full translations and the composer's own fascinatingly detailed instructions as to how *Il Combattimento* should be staged.

L'incoronazione di Poppea (complete).

*** DG 447 088-2 (3). McNair, Von Otter, Hanchard, Chance, D'Artegna, E. Bar. Sol., Gardiner.

(M) *** Virgin VM5 61783-2 (3). Augér, D. Jones, Hirst, Bowman, City of L. Bar. Sinfonia, Hickox.

(M) **(*) Teldec (ADD) 2292 42547-2 (4). Donath, Söderström, Berberian, Esswood, VCM, Harnoncourt.

With an exceptionally strong and consistent cast in which even minor roles are taken by star singers, Gardiner presents a purposeful, strongly characterized performance. He is helped by the full and immediate sound of the live recording, made in concert at the Queen Elizabeth Hall, London. Sylvia McNair is a seductive Poppea and Anne Sofie von Otter a deeply moving Ottavia, both singing ravishingly. Francesco d'Artegna, a robustly Italian-sounding bass, makes a stylish Seneca, and there are clear advantages in having a countertenor as Nero instead of a mezzo-soprano, particularly one with a slightly sinister timbre like Dana Hanchard. So in the sensuous duet which closes the opera, the clashing intervals of the voices are given a degree of abrasiveness, suggesting that, though this is a happy and beautiful ending, the characters still have their sinister side. The text has been modified with newly written ritornellos by Peter Holman, using the original, authentic bass line, and aiming to be 'closer to what Monteverdi would have expected' than the usual flawed text.

On Virgin the tender expressiveness of Arleen Augér in the title role of Monteverdi's elusive masterpiece combines with a performance from Richard Hickox and the City of London Baroque Sinfonia which consistently reflects the fact that it was recorded in conjunction with a stage production in 1988. Hickox daringly uses a very spare accompaniment of continuo instruments, but he overcomes the problems of that self-imposed limitation by choosing the widest possible range of speeds. The purity of Augér's soprano may make Poppea less of a scheming seducer than she should be, but it is Monteverdi's music for the heroine which makes her so sympathetic in this oddly slanted, equivocal picture of Roman history, and one that has seldom sounded subtler or more lovely on record than this. Taking the castrato role of Nero, Della Jones sings very convincingly with full, rather boyish tone, while Gregory Reinart is magnificent in the bass role of Seneca. James Bowman is a fine Ottone, with smaller parts taken by such excellent singers as Catherine Denley, John Graham-Hall, Mark Tucker, and Janice Watson. Linda Hirst sounds too raw of tone for Ottavia, making her a scold rather than a sympathetic suffering widow. Fitted on to three well-filled mid-priced CDs, the opera comes with libretto and translation and can be recommended alongside the Gardiner set.

Nikolaus Harnoncourt's well-paced and dramatic version makes a welcome reappearance at mid-price in Teldec's Harnoncourt series. First issued in 1974, it offers a starry cast, with Elisabeth Söderström as Nero (imaginative but not always ideally steady), Helen Donath pure-toned as Poppea and Cathy Berberian as the most characterful and moving Ottavia on disc. Others include Paul Esswood and Philip Langridge, and Harnoncourt's bold and brassy instrumentation adds to the bite. The snag is that, unnecessarily, the set stretches to four discs instead of three, which cancels out the price advantage over the excellent rival set from Richard Hickox.

(i) *L'incoronazione di Poppea* (abridged version, realized by Raymond Leppard); (ii) Madrigals: *Al lume delle stelle; A quest'olmo; Cor mio, mentre vi miro; Io mi son giovinetta; Lamento d'Arianna; Ohimè se tanto amaie; Volgendo il ciel* (ballo).

(B) **(*) EMI double forte (ADD) CZS5 73842-2 (2). (i) László, Bible, Lewis, Dominguez, Marimpietri, Cava, Alberti, Cuénod, Glyndebourne Festival Ch., RPO, Pritchard; (ii) Cantelo, Poulter, Watts, English, Tear, Keyte, ECO, Leppard.

Raymond Leppard's edition of this equivocal masterpiece will probably shock baroque purists with sounds that are sumptuous rather than spare, while he makes use of two harpsichords, two organs, two cellos, lute, guitar and harp for the continuo group – a most generous array of instruments which certainly serve to colour the score in the best baroque manner. Even in this cut version, the honeyed

warmth of the production comes over vividly, with Magda Laszlo and Richard Lewis fresh and dramatic. The bass, Carlo Cava, is a weighty Seneca, fully conveying the character of the noble and revered philosopher and statesman whose tragic suicide in this edition rounds off Act I. Throughout, his excellent low register never loses its flexibility. Nero's comic duet of rejoicing (with the unique Hugues Cuénod as Lewis's brilliant partner) could hardly be bettered as a musical picture of inebriation (hiccups and all), and this then sets the contrasted tone of Act II, leading to Nero and Poppea's ecstatic final duet. Frances Bible as Ottavia and Walter Alberti as Ottone portray the cast-off wife and lover with admirable skill. Vocally superior to these are Lydia Marimpietri, whose Drusilla is a marvel of characterization, and Orelia Dominguez, who plays the difficult and exacting role of Poppea's nurse and confidant. John Pritchard coaxes from the Royal Philharmonic Orchestra a truly Monteverdian sound, and the Glyndebourne Chorus makes brief but significant contributions, notably in the scene of Seneca's farewell. The stars of the piece, Richard Lewis and Magda László, are on top of their form and their final love duet comes as a magnificent end to a great opera. The recording is remarkably opulent.

This timely bargain issue is well supplemented by a collection of madrigals, recorded three years later with an entirely different cast. The singers here are all fine artists in their own right, but the choice of a group of soloists for this repertoire proves not to be the best way of ensuring a good blend between the parts, with individual voices tending to stick out at times from the overall texture. However, the performances certainly do not lack character and there are no complaints about the recording itself. In the opera no texts are given, but a detailed synopsis is related to the CD tracks, without however giving the Italian titles of each aria or excerpt, which are listed separately. There are no texts or translations for the madrigals.

Orfeo (opera): complete.

*** O-L 433 545-2 (2). Ainsley, Gooding, Bott, Bonner, George, Grant, New L. Cons., Pickett.

*** DG 419 250-2 (2). Rolfe Johnson, Baird, Dawson, Von Otter, Argenta, Robson, Monteverdi Ch., E. Bar. Sol., Gardiner.

(M) *** EMI CMS7 64947-2 (2). Rogers, Kwella, Kirkby, J. Smith, Chiaroscuro, L. Bar. Ens., L. Cornett & Sackbutt Ens., Medlam.

(M) ** Teldec (ADD) 2292 42494-2 (2). Kozma, Hansmann, Berberian, Katanosaka, Villisech, Van Egmond, Munich Cappela Antiqua, VCM, Harnoncourt.

(BB) ** Naxos 8.554094-2 (2). Carmignani, Pennichi, Frisani, Pantasuglia, Capella Musicale di San Petronio di Bologna, Vartolo.

Pickett has not tried to treat *Orfeo* with kid gloves but has aimed above all to bring out its freshness. So, in the dark *Sinfonia* with its weird chromatic writing, which at the opening of Act III represents Orfeo's arrival in the underworld, Pickett cuts out strings and uses brass instruments alone. As Orfeo, John Mark Ainsley may have a less velvety tenor than Anthony Rolfe Johnson on the Gardiner set, but his voice is more flexible in the elaborate decorations of *Possente spirto*, Orfeo's plea to Charon. Outstanding among the others is Catherine Bott. In *Orfeo* she not only sings the elaborate role given to La Musica in the Prologue, sensuously beautiful and seductive in her coloration, but also the part of Proserpina and the key role of the Messenger, who graphically describes the death of Euridice.

John Eliot Gardiner very effectively balances the often-conflicting demands of authentic performance – when this pioneering opera was originally presented intimately – and the obvious grandeur of the concept. So the 21-strong Monteverdi Choir conveys, on the one hand, high tragedy to the full, yet sings the lighter commentary from nymphs and shepherds with astonishing crispness, often at top speed. However, Gardiner is strong on pacing. This is a set to take you through the story with new involvement. Though editing is not always immaculate, the recording on CD is vivid and full of presence.

In the EMI version Nigel Rogers has the double function of singing the main part and acting as co-director. Rogers has modified his extraordinarily elaborate ornamentation in the hero's brilliant pleading aria before Charon and makes the result all the freer and more wide-ranging in expression. Euridice's plaint, beautifully sung by Patrizia Kwella, is the more affecting for being accompanied very simply on the lute. The other soloists make a good team, though Jennifer Smith as Proserpina, recorded close, is made to sound breathy. The brightness of the cornetti is a special delight, when otherwise the instrumentation used – largely left optional in the score – is modest. Excellent, immediate recording, making for a fine mid-priced alternative to Gardiner.

In Harnoncourt's version, the ritornello of the Prologue might almost be by Stravinsky, so sharply do the sounds cut. He is altogether more severe than John Eliot Gardiner. In compensation, the simple and straightforward dedication of this performance is most affecting, and the solo singing, if not generally very characterful, is clean and stylish. One exception is Cathy Berberian as the Messenger. She is strikingly successful and, though slightly differing in style from the others, she sings as part of the team. Excellent recording. The extra clarity and sharpness of focus – even in large-scale ensembles – add to the abrasiveness from the opening *Toccata* onwards, and the 1968 recording sounds immediate and realistic.

With some first-rate solo singing and a restrained, scholarly approach, there is much to enjoy in the Naxos version. However, Sergio Vartolo's speeds are consistently slow. Alessandro Carmignani is a fine, clear Orfeo, coping splendidly with all the technical problems, and his singing in the big solos has a dedicated intensity, but at such slow speeds there is a sleepwalking quality in the results, however beautiful. More seriously, the exchanges between characters never have the dramatic intensity needed. In the instrumental numbers the strings are often uncomfortably edgy. It is as well that full text and translation are provided, when the CD tracks on the disc are radically different from those indicated in the booklet. Clear, well-balanced sound, recorded in the Theatre of Puy-en-Velay in France.

Il ritorno d'Ulisse in patria (complete).

*** HM HMC 90 1427/9. Prégardien, Fink, Högeman, Hunt, Visse, Tucker, D. Thomas, Concerto Vocale, Jacobs.

(M) **(*) Teldec (ADD) 2292 42496-2 (3). Eliasson, Lerer, Hansen, Baker-Genovesi, Hansmann, Equiluz, Esswood, Wyatt, Walters, Van Egmond, Mühle, Junge Kantorei, VCM, Harnoncourt.

René Jacobs offers a scholarly performance that is not afraid of being expressive. Christoph Prégardien is splendid as Ulisse, firm and heroic but light enough to cope with the elaborate ornamentation. Bernarda Fink with her rich, firm mezzo gives full weight to Penelope's agony, and it is encouraging to find such excellent British singers as Martyn Hill, Mark Tucker and David Thomas taking character roles. Dominique Visse is also excellent, both as Human Frailty in the Prologue and as one of Penelope's suitors, with Guy de Mey in the comic role of the glutton, Iro. Jacobs explains that with the surviving manuscripts raising dozens of textual questions, he decided to return to the original five-Act division of the text, which, as he suggests, is better balanced. He also inserts music by Rossi and Caccini for the choruses included in the text but missing from the score.

Harnoncourt's 1971 recording of *Il ritorno d'Ulisse* brings a sympathetic performance, generally not quite as brisk as Jacobs in his recording from the Montpellier Festival, and rather more square in rhythm, but bringing a keener sense of repose, important in Monteverdi. The solo singing is not as characterful as that on the Jacobs set, nor as Harnoncourt's *Poppea*, though Norma Lerer makes a touching Penelope, with Sven Olaf Eliasson a stylish Ulisse, not ideally pure of timbre.

MOODY, James (born 1907)

(i) *Quintet for Harmonica & String Quartet*; (ii) *Suite dans le style français*.

*** Chan. 8802. Reilly; (i) Hindar Qt; (ii) Kanga – JACOB: *Divertimento*. ***

James Moody's *Suite in the French Style* may be pastiche but its impressionism is highly beguiling. The *Quintet* is more ambitious, less charming perhaps, but likely to prove even more rewarding on investigation, especially the very diverse theme and variations of the finale, the longest movement. The performance and recording are hardly likely to be bettered.

MORENO TORROBA, Federico (1891–1982)

Sonatina for Guitar & Orchestra; Interludes 1 & II.

*** Analekta Fleur de Lys FL 2 3049. Boucher, Amati Ens., Dessaints – ABRIL: *Concierto Mudéjar*. ***

Moreno Torroba's *Sonatina* was written in the early years of the twentieth century for Segovia; the composer made the concertante arrangement of the solo work not long before he died. The outer movements, with their Castilian atmosphere, are gay and engaging, and the Romance, which forms the central *Andante*, is quite captivating, especially when the performance has such a simple spontaneity and is not too overladen with expressive feeling. The two *Interludes* are also both highly evocative and they are most winning in their present format. Rémi Boucher is a splendid soloist, and Raymond Dessaints gives him affectionate support. The warmth of the truthful and very well-balanced recording adds to the listener's pleasure.

Luisa Fernanda (complete).

*** Valois V 4759. Domingo, Villaroel, Pons, Rodrigo, Madrid Univ. Ch., Madrid SO, Marba.

This is an ideal recommendation for anyone wanting to investigate the zarazuela, the Spanish genre of operetta. Moreno Torroba, best known for his guitar music, here offers in three compact acts a sequence of catchily tuneful numbers, brightly orchestrated. Led by Domingo in glowing form as the hero, Javier, an army colonel, the cast is as near ideal as possible, with Veronica Villaroel in the title role, and Juan Pons as Javier's rich rival. Bright, immediate sound.

MORLEY, Thomas (1557–1603)

Ayres and madrigals: *Absence, hear thou my protestation; Arise, awake; Besides a fountain; Deep lamenting; Fire and lightning; Hard by a crystal fountain; Hark! Alleluia; In every place; Mistress mine; No, no Nigelia; O grief ev'n on the bud; Phyllis I fain would die now; Singing alone; Sleep slumbr'ing eyes; Stay heart, run not so fast; With my love.*

(B) *** Double Decca (ADD) 458 093-2 (2) Consort of Musicke, Rooley – GIBBONS; WILBYE: *Madrigals.* ***

Morley is generally thought of as a lesser figure than his contemporaries, even though he was the pioneering English madrigalist. This collection should do something to modify the picture of him, for although the lighter canzonetti and balletti based on Italian model (and in particular Gastoldi) are in evidence, there are more searching and thoughtful pieces. *Deep lamenting* and *O grief ev'n on the bud* are very touching, while Rooley himself provides lute accompaniments for Emma Kirkby's lovely *Sleep slumb'ring eyes* and the ambitious *Absence, hear thou my protestation*, the longest song in the whole programme, sensitively sung by Andrew King. *Mistress mine* is unexpectedly precocious, and there are others that make one feel that the range of Morley's musical personality has not been adequately reflected before. This is a rewarding recital and has the benefit of well-projected performances and very good recording. Full texts are provided.

The First Booke of Ayres: A painted tale; Thyrsis and Milla; She straight he light greensilken coats; With my love; I saw my lady weeping; It was a lover; Who is it that this dark night?; Mistress mine; Can I forget; Love winged my hopes; What is my mistress; Come, sorrow, stay; Fair in a morn; Absence, hear thou; Will you buy a fine dog?; Sleep slumb'ring eyes.

(M) ** Teldec (ADD) 3984 21334-2. Rogers, Harnoncourt, Dombois.

This integral recording of Morley's *First Booke of Songs* first appeared at the beginning of the 1970s. The settings show the scope of the composer's imagination in his sensitivity to the words themselves, in the variety of style and metre, and in the diversity of manner of the accompaniments. The performances are fresh and direct and scholarly in the use of decoration.

MOSCHELES, Ignaz (1794–1870)

Piano Concertos Nos. 2 in E flat, Op. 56; 4 in E, Op. 64.

*** Zephyr Z 116-99. Hobson, Sinfonia da Camera.

A friend and contemporary of Beethoven, Moscheles was born in Prague but spent part of his later career in London. He was a well-liked man, and the character of his music comes over in both these concertos, with their debt to Hummel but with a clear anticipation of Chopin's concertos in the passage work. The *E flat Concerto* opens with the timpani setting the mood for an imposing march, with a Hummelian dotted rhythm, and they later set off the jolly *Polonaise* of the finale. The E major work has a more expansively ambitious opening tutti, and its slow movement centres on a romantic horn solo. The horns then announce the closing set of bold variations on 'The British Grenadiers', which gives Ian Hobson plenty of opportunities for glittering bravura. He plays spiritedly throughout both works, yet obviously relishes their *gallant* lyricism, while effectively directing the accompaniments from the keyboard. The recording is truthful and well balanced, and altogether this is a most enjoyable coupling.

MOSONYI, Mihály (1815–70)

(i) *Piano Concerto in E min.;* (ii) *Symphony No. 1 in D.*

** Marco 8.223539. (i) Körmendi, Slovak State Philh. O (Košice); (ii) Slovak RSO (Bratislava); Stankovsky.

Despite his English origins, Mosonyi is thought of as one of the most representative nineteenth-century Hungarian composers – apart, of course, from the more obvious major figures, Liszt and Erkel. The *Symphony No. 1 in D* is an early work, composed in his late twenties and modelled on the Viennese classics in general and Beethoven in particular. The *Piano Concerto in E minor*, which comes from about the same time, shows the influence of Chopin and Weber. If, like the symphony, it is not strong on individuality, it is at least well-crafted, well-bred music and well worth an occasional airing. Klára Körmendi is the fluent soloist and receives decent orchestral support from Robert Stankovsky and his Slovak forces.

MOSZKOWSKI, Moritz (1854–1925)

Piano Concerto in E, Op. 59.

*** Hyp. CDA 66452. Lane, BBC Scottish SO, Maksymiuk –
PADEREWSKI: *Piano Concerto.* ***

(i) *Piano Concerto in E, Op. 59. From Foreign Lands,
Op. 23.*

(BB) *** Naxos 8.553989. (i) Pawlik; Polish Nat. RSO
(Katowice), Wit.

Moszkowski is most often remembered for his dazzling
piano miniatures, but he is just as fluent in this big four-
movement concerto, written for the Polish virtuoso Josef
Hofmann. It was Piers Lane's performance of this concerto,
in partnership with the volatile Jerzy Maksymiuk, that inaugurated Hyperion's highly successful series, and anyone
fancying a coupling with Paderewski will not be disappointed by this brilliant version, certainly full of vitality
and both expressively sympathetic and subtle in detail. Excellent recording too.

The young German, Markus Pawlik, also proves a magnetic soloist, playing with the crispest articulation, readily
matching the fine version from Piers Lane in Hyperion's
parallel Romantic Piano Concerto series. The fill-up, a suite
of colourful orchestral pieces, is delightful.

MOURANT, Walter (born 1910)

The Pied Piper.

*** ASV CDDCA 568. MacDonald, N. Sinfonia, Bedford –
COPLAND; FINZI: *Concertos.* ***

Walter Mourant's *Pied Piper* is a catchy, unpretentious little
piece for clarinet, strings and celeste, which in a gently
syncopated style effectively contrasts 3/4 and 6/8 rhythms. It
makes an attractive filler after the Copland *Concerto.*

MOZART, Leopold (1719–87)

Cassation in G: Toy Symphony (attrib. Haydn).
(i) *Trumpet Concerto in D.*

*** Erato 2292 45199-2. (i) Touvron; Paillard CO, Paillard –
W. A. MOZART: *Musical Joke.* ***

One could hardly imagine this *Cassation* being done with
more commitment from the effects department directed by
Paillard, while the music itself is elegantly played. After this,
the more restrained approach to the excellent two-
movement *Trumpet Concerto* seems exactly right. The
recording has plenty of presence and realism.

Horn Concerto in D.

(N) *** Arabesque Z 6750. Rose, St Luke's Chamber Ens. –
FORSTER; HAYDN; TELEMANN: *Horn Concertos.* ***

Leopold Mozart virtually gave up composing to further his
young son's career, but the few works that have survived are
of quality. The *Horn Concerto* of 1755 is certainly one, but is
enormously demanding of its soloist – far more difficult

than the later concertos of Wolfgang Amadeus. The first
movement gambols in a sprightly 6/8, but soon takes the
horn up into its highest register, where it remains for the
expressive minor-key *Romanza.* The third movement then
sets off lustily and demands that the soloist trill his way up
a major arpeggio. Stewart Rose's trills, whether relaxed as in
the slow movement, or buoyant as here, are impressively
clean: he is a true virtuoso and establishes the difference
between this essentially classical work and the earlier baroque concerto of Telemann. A supplemental Minuet completes the piece traditionally and offers more opportunities
for bravura. This performance will be hard to surpass and
the recording is excellent.

MOZART, Wolfgang Amadeus
(1756–91)

Adagio & Fugue in C minor: see below, in VOCAL
MUSIC, under Complete Mozart Edition, Vol. 22.

Cassations, divertimenti and serenades

*Cassations Nos. 1, K.63; 2 K.99; Divertimenti for Strings
No. 1–3, K.136–8; Divertimenti Nos. 1 in E flat, K.113; 2 in
D, K.131; 7 in D, K.205; 10 in F, K.247; 11 in D K.251; 15 in
B flat, K.287; 17 in D, K.334. A Musical Joke, K.522.
Serenades Nos. 1 in D, K.100; 3 in D, K.185; 4 in D
(Colloredo), K.203; 5 in D, K.204; 6 in D (Serenata
notturna), K.239; 7 in D (Haffner), K.250; 8 in D, for 4
Orchestras, K.286; 9 in D (Posthorn), K.320; 13 in G (Eine
kleine Nachtmusik), K.525.*

(B) *** Decca (ADD) 458 310-2 (8). V. Mozart Ens., Boskovsky.

This set covers all Mozart's major divertimenti and serenades, except those for wind instruments alone. Even the
earliest works bring delight. Boskovsky's performances immediately set the manner for the whole series. The playing
is marvellously alive and stylish, investing comparatively
lightweight works with unexpected stature. The recording
balance is flawless. The three *String Divertimenti* sparkle, as
does the *Serenata notturna,* while *Eine kleine Nachtmusik* is
one of the freshest accounts on disc. And if the larger-scale
Divertimenti (K.247, K.287 and K.334 for instance) which
Mozart intended for solo instruments, are to be heard in
orchestral dress, none could be more elegant than this. The
large-scale *Haffner* and *Posthorn Serenades* combine vitality
with charm and elegance, and Boskovsky's own solo violin
contributions to the former are wholly admirable. The
recordings have been remastered and the bloom of Sofiensaal ambience now adds to one's aural pleasure.

Complete Bargain Mozart Edition, Vol. 2: (i) *Cassations;*
(ii) *Contredanses; German Dances & Marches;*
(ii) *Galimathias musicum; Marches (K.62, K.215, K.237,
K.189, K.335, Nos. 1 & 2);* (i) *Orchestral Serenades.*

(N) (B) *** Ph. (ADD) 464 790-2 (13). (i) ASMF, Marriner;
(ii) Vienna Mozart Ens., Boskovsky.

The Philips Complete Mozart Edition remains available in
its original format, but has also been reissued in a bargain

edition at a special price, much more simply packaged, and with limited documentation. The discs are in cardboard sleeves within seventeen boxes. This new 180-CD bargain set is available complete (on 464 660-2); but each of the new compilations is available separately. We have listed them concisely below alongside the original boxes, although in many cases (as in the case of the *Dances*, *Marches* and major orchestral *Serenades*) the new compilations involve more than one of the original collections.

Complete Mozart Edition, Vol. 3: *Cassations Nos. 1; 2; Divertimento No. 2; Galimathias musicum, K.32; Serenades Nos. 1 (with March, K.62); 3, (with March, K.189); 4 (Colloredo), K.203 (with March, K.237); 5, K.204 (with March, K.215); 6 (Serenata notturna), K.239; 7 (Haffner), K.250 (with March, K.249); 8 (Notturno), K.286; 9 (Posthorn), K.320 (with Marches, K.335/1–2); 13 (Eine kleine Nachtmusik), K.525.*

(M) *** Ph. 422 503-2 (7). ASMF, Marriner.

Marriner and his Academy are at their very finest here and make a very persuasive case for giving these works on modern instruments. The playing has much finesse, yet its cultivated polish never brings a hint of blandness or lethargy; it is smiling, yet full of energy and sparkle. In the concertante violin roles Iona Brown is an ideal soloist, her playing full of grace. Throughout this set the digital recording brings an almost ideal combination of bloom and vividness.

Cassations Nos. 1–3.

(BB) *** Naxos 8.550609. Salzburg CO, Nerat.

All three early *Cassations* are given lively, nicely turned performances, very well – if resonantly – recorded. This admirable disc is certainly worth its modest cost and nicely fills a gap in the catalogue.

CONCERTOS

Complete Mozart Edition, Vol. 9: (i) *Bassoon Concerto;* (ii) *Clarinet Concerto;* (iii) *Flute Concertos Nos. 1–2; Andante in C for Flute & Orchestra;* (iii; iv) *Flute & Harp Concerto;* (v) *Horn Concertos Nos. 1–4; Concert Rondo in E flat for Horn & Orchestra;* (vi) *Oboe Concerto. Sinfonia concertante, K.297b; Sinfonia concertante, K.297b* (reconstructed R. Levin).

(M) **(*) Ph. 422 509-2 (5). (i) Thunemann; (ii) Leister; (iii) Grafenauer; (iv) Graf; (v) Damm; (vi) Holliger; ASMF, Marriner (except (vi) Holliger).

Complete Bargain Mozart Edition, Vol. 5: *Concertos for Bassoon; Clarinet; Flute; Flute & Harp; Horn (including Rondos). Violin Concertos Nos. 1–5; 7 in D, K.271; Adagio in E, K.261; Rondo in B flat, K.269; Rondo in C, K.373; Concertone, K.190; Double Concerto in D for Violin, Piano & Orchestra, K.315f; Sinfonia concertantes, K.297b; K.320e; K.364.*

(N) (B) *** Ph. (ADD/DDD) 464 810-2 (9). Various soloists, ASMF, Marriner.

The principal wind concertos here are recent digital versions.

They are all well played and recorded. However, there is a slightly impersonal air about the accounts of the *Bassoon* and *Clarinet Concertos*, well played though they are; and there are more individual sets of the works for horn. The *Sinfonia concertante* is offered both in the version we usually hear (recorded in 1972, with the performance attractively songful and elegant) and in a more modern recording of a conjectural reconstruction by Robert Levin, based on the material in the four wind parts.

Bassoon Concerto in B flat, K.191.

*** Chan. 9656. Popov, Russian State SO, Polyansky – HUMMEL; WEBER: *Bassoon Concertos.* ***
*** Caprice CAP 21411. Sönstevold, Swedish RSO, Comissiona – PETTERSSON: *Symphony No. 7.* ***

Valeri Popov's playing has character and warmth. He is at his most personable in the Minuet Rondo finale. Polyansky's accompaniment is warmly supportive, and the Chandos recording is well up to standard.

Knut Sönstevold's performance of Mozart's concerto is a good, big-band performance which gives pleasure, and is very well recorded.

(i; ii) Bassoon Concerto; (iii; iv) Clarinet Concerto; (v) Flute Concerto No. 1 (vi; iv) Horn Concertos Nos. 1–4; (vii; ii) Oboe Concerto.

(B) Double Decca Dig./ADD 466 247-2 (2). (i) McGill; (ii) Cleveland O, Dohnányi; (iii) De Peyer; (iv) LSO, Maag; (v) Bennett, ECO, Malcolm; (vi) Tuckwell; (vii) Mack.

These recordings readily demonstrate the ongoing excellence of the Decca coverage of the Mozart wind concertos over three decades. Gervase de Peyer is admirable in the *Clarinet Concerto*, and his account remains as fine as any available, fluent and lively, with masterly phrasing in the slow movement and a vivacious finale. Barry Tuckwell at the time was proving a natural inheritor of the mantle of Dennis Brain. His easy technique, smooth, warm tone and obvious musicianship command allegiance and give immediate pleasure. William Bennett a decade later, but again in the Kingsway Hall, is hardly less impressive in the *G major Flute Concerto*. Throughout, the recording is clean and well detailed, with enough resonance to add bloom to the sound. The CD transfers are immaculate. For the *Bassoon* and *Oboe Concertos* we turn to Cleveland. The oboist, John Mack, has an appealingly sweet (but not too sweet) timbre; then David McGill, in the work for bassoon, immediately establishes his keen individuality. He does not overdo the humour in the finale. Both performances are beautifully recorded and attractively balanced. All-in-all very enjoyable music-making by musicians from both sides of the Atlantic who are equally at one with Mozart.

(i) Bassoon Concerto; (ii) Clarinet Concerto; (iii) Flute Concerto No. 1.

(M) *** DG 457 719-2. VPO, Boehm; with (i) Zeman; (ii) Prinz; (iii) Tripp.

These are meltingly beautiful accounts. All three soloists perform with the utmost distinction under Boehm, who lets the music unfold in an unforced way: relaxed yet vital.

Excellent mid-1970s sound makes this a highly recommendable DG Originals disc.

(i) *Bassoon Concerto;* (ii) *Clarinet Concerto;* (iii) *Oboe Concerto.*

(BB) **(*) Naxos 8.550345. (i) Turnovský; (ii) Ottensamer; (iii) Gabriel; V. Mozart Academy, Wildner.

In the *Oboe Concerto* the soloist on Naxos, Martin Gabriel, is excellent. The clarinettist, Ernst Ottensamer, is also a sensitive player, his slow movement is full of feeling; and there is an accomplished performance of the *Bassoon Concerto* from Stepan Turnovský, who has the measure of the work's character and wit. Recommendable.

(i) *Bassoon Concerto;* (ii) *Clarinet Concerto; Symphony No. 41 (Jupiter).*

(M) *** EMI (ADD) CDM5 67596-2. (i) Brooke; (ii) Brymer; RPO, Beecham.

Beecham's romantically expansive reading of the Mozart *Clarinet Concerto* with Jack Brymer is a 1958 classic recording, totally individual in every phrase, with conductor and soloist inspiring each other. The account of the *Bassoon Concerto* has equal magic, thanks to the comparable partnership between Beecham and Gwydion Brooke. This pair of concerto recordings has now been reissued as one of EMI's 'Great Recordings of the Century', coupled with Beecham's account of the *Jupiter Symphony*. This is an elegant rather than a magisterial reading, with the outer movements crisp, the slow movement gracious, and the Minuet a classic example of Beecham nuance.

(i) *Bassoon Concerto;* (ii) *Flute & Harp Concerto. Sinfonia concertante, K.297b.*

(M) *** Classic fM 76505 57038-2. (i) Andrews; (ii) Hill, Wakeford; soloists, Britten Sinfonia, Cleobury.

Julie Andrews gives Mozart's droll *Bassoon Concerto* a genial lift-off, while the flautist, Kate Hill, and the harpist, Lucy Wakeford, create winningly delicate tracery in the *Concerto for Flute and Harp*. Both slow movements are beautifully phrased, and the team of soloists is no less persuasive in the *Sinfonia concertante*, not least in the light-hearted finale. The recording and balance are altogether first class.

Clarinet Concerto in A, K.622

*** DG 457 652-2. Collins, Russian Nat. O, Pletnev –
  BEETHOVEN: *Clarinet (Violin) Concerto in D, Op. 61.* ***
*** EMI CDC5 56832-2. Meyer, BPO, Abbado – DEBUSSY:
  Première rapsodie; TAKEMITSU: *Fantasma/cantos.* ***

Michael Collins has here provided the weightiest, most challenging, if controversial, coupling in Mikhail Pletnev's arrrangement for clarinet of the Beethoven *Violin Concerto*. The result is a masterly disc in which Collins offers one of the finest versions of the Mozart ever. Collins uses a basset clarinet in that masterpiece, relishing the extra downward range and richness of timbre. Collins's speeds in the outer movements are fast, wonderfully agile and with the cleanest articulation and crisp rhythmic pointing as well as fine detail. It is a reading not just elegant but powerful too, as well as

deeply poetic in the slow movement. The playing of the Russian National Orchestra under Pletnev is refined and elegant to match.

Sabine Meyer's 1998 performance brings out how much her individual artistry has intensified even in the ten years between this and her first recording of this greatest of clarinet works, also for EMI (see below, where she chose to use the basset clarinet). She again opts for speeds faster than usual, but finds time to point phrasing and shade dynamics with keen imagination and a feeling of spontaneity. As before, where appropriate, she adds cadenza-like flourishes, as in the honeyed lead-back to the reprise in the central *Largo*.

(i) *Clarinet Concerto;* (ii) *Flute Concerto No. 1 in G;* (ii; iii) *Flute & Harp Concerto.*

(N) *** EMI CDC5 57128-2. (i) Meyer; (ii) Pahud; (iii) Langlamet, Berlin PO, Abbado.

Sabine Meyer's second recording of the *Clarinet Concerto* is available (above) in a mixed programme with pieces by Debussy and Takemitsu, which makes this recoupling very desirable. Recorded live, Meyer is even more inspired and imaginative than in her version of ten years earlier, with light, clear support from the orchestra which in the days of Karajan spurned her when she was proposed as principal clarinet. The two concertos with Pahud reveal him as an outstandingly individual artist, light and athletic, dominant over the rather reticent harpist in the Double concerto. Though the original issue also had the *Flute Concerto No. 2*, that is less important, being an arrangement of a work for oboe, so the present triptych is highly recommendable.

(i) *Clarinet Concerto;* (ii) *Flute Concerto No. 1;* (iii) *Oboe Concerto.*

(M) *** Classic fM 75605 57001-2. (i) Farrell; (ii) Hill; (iii) Daniel; Britten Sinfonia, Cleobury.

In the *Clarinet Concerto* Joy Farrell's solo style lies somewhere between the freely spontaneous manner of Emma Johnson and the flexible, classical directness of Thea King. Nicholas Daniel is equally appealing in the stylishly infectious account of the *Oboe Concerto*. Kate Hill's *Flute Concerto* is hardly less delectable. Excellent balancing and fine recording make this mid-priced triptych from Classic fM hard to beat.

(i) *Clarinet Concerto;* (ii) *Flute & Harp Concerto.*

*** ASV CDDCA 532. (i) Johnson; (ii) Bennett, Ellis; ECO, Leppard.
(N) (M) *** Regis RRC 1061. (i) Campbell; (ii) Davies, Masters, City of L. Sinf., Hickox.

Emma Johnson's account of the *Clarinet Concerto* has a sense of spontaneity and natural magnetism. There may be some rawness of tone in places, but that only adds to the range of expression, which breathes the air of a live performance. Leppard and the ECO are in bouncing form, as they are too for the *Flute and Harp Concerto*, though here the two excellent soloists are somewhat on their best behaviour, until the last part of the finale sends Mozart bubbling up to heaven. First-rate recording.

David Campbell's agile and pointed performance of the

clarinet work brings fastish speeds and a fresh, unmannered style in all three movements. His tonal shading is very beautiful. The earlier work for flute and harp is just as freshly and sympathetically done, with a direct, unmannered style sounding entirely spontaneous.

(i) *Clarinet Concerto;* (ii) *Flute & Harp Concerto;* (iii) *Serenade No. 13 (Eine kleine Nachtmusik).*

(M) **(*) Belart (ADD) 450 035-2. (i) Wright, Boston SO, Ozawa; (ii) Zöller, Zabaleta, BPO, Märzendorfer; (iii) VPO, Boehm.

Harold Wright's Boston performance of the *Clarinet Concerto* is thoroughly musical and well recorded. However, Ozawa's accompaniments are rather matter-of-fact, and the overall orchestral effect is accomplished rather than inspired. There are no strictures about the Zöller/Zabaleta account of the *Flute and Harp Concerto*, the phrasing a constant source of pleasure. Karl Boehm's 1976 performance of *Eine kleine Nachtmusik* is among the finest. Excellent value.

(i) *Clarinet Concerto;* (ii) *Oboe Concerto;* (i; ii; iii) *Sinfonia concertante, K.297b.*

*** ASV CDCDA 814. (i) Hosford; (ii) Boyd; (iii) O'Neill, Williams; COE, Schneider.

It would be hard to imagine a performance of the *Oboe Concerto* that conveys more fun in the outer movements. The wind soloists in this live recording of the *Sinfonia concertante* are four COE artists who each know when to take centre stage and when to hold back in turn. Richard Hosford in his reading of the *Clarinet Concerto* uses a basset clarinet. At slowish speeds he leans towards the lyrical rather than the dramatic, even in the first movement, and ends with a delightfully bouncy account of the finale. Full, atmospheric recording.

(i) *Clarinet Concerto;* (ii) *Clarinet Quintet, K.581.*

*** Hyp. CDA 66199. King, (i) ECO, Tate; (ii) Gabrieli Qt.
(M) **(*) Ph. (ADD) 442 390-2. Brymer, with (i) LSO, C. Davis; (ii) Allegri Qt.

Thea King's coupling brings together winning performances of Mozart's two great clarinet masterpieces. She steers an ideal course between classical stylishness and expressive warmth, with the slow movement becoming the emotional heart of the piece. The Gabrieli Quartet is equally responsive in its finely tuned playing. For the *Clarinet Concerto* Thea King uses an authentically reconstructed basset clarinet. With Jeffrey Tate an inspired Mozartian, the performance – like that of the *Quintet* – is both stylish and expressive, with the finale given a captivating bucolic lilt. Excellent recording.

Jack Brymer's (1964) Philips account of the *Clarinet Concerto* has an eloquent autumnal serenity and the reading a soft lyricism that is very appealing. However, the leisurely (1970) interpretation of the *Quintet* is more controversial. Generally the very slow tempi throughout are well sustained, although in the finale the forward flow of the music is reduced to a near-crawl. Good transfers.

(i) *Clarinet Concerto;* (ii) *Serenade No. 10, K.361: Adagio* (only).

*** EMI CDC5 55155-2. Meyer; (i) Dresden State O, Vonk; (ii) with Wind Ens. – STAMITZ: *Clarinet Concerto No. 10;* WEBER: *Clarinet Concerto No. 1.* ***

(i) *Clarinet Concerto;* (ii) *Sinfonia concertante, K.297b.*

(M) *** EMI CDM5 66897-2 [566949]. (i) Meyer, Dresden State O; (ii) cond. Vonk.

Using the original basset clarinet, Sabine Meyer gives a highly seductive performance of Mozart's beautiful concerto and at the same time accompanies herself by directing a rich-textured modern-instrument backing. The solo playing has much warmth and great finesse. Indeed, some listeners may feel that this music-making has an element of self-consciousness, especially at the gentle muted reprise of the *Adagio*. But the finale trips along gracefully, and it is good to have a performance of such individuality. She participates also in a sonorously solemn account of the *Adagio* from the *Grand Partita*. The couplings, too, are very impressive.

Meyer's performance has also been reissued paired with Vonk's persuasively stylish account of the *Sinfonia concertante*, with Meyer joining the team of soloists. The sound is excellent, but this coupling is a less than apt candidate for EMI's 'Great Recordings of the Century' series.

Flute Concertos Nos. 1–2; Andante, K.315.

(BB) **(*) Naxos 8.550074. Weissberg, Capella Istropolitana, Sieghart.

(i) *Flute Concertos Nos. 1–2; Andante, K.315;* (ii) *Flute & Harp Concerto, K.299;* (iii) *Sinfonia concertante, K.297b* (reconstructed R. Levin); (iv) *4 Flute Quartets.*

(B) **(*) Ph. Duo (ADD) 442 299-2. (i) Nicolet, Cong. O, Zinman; (ii) Barwahser, Ellis, LSO, C. Davis; (iii) Nicolet, Holliger, Baumann, Thunemann, ASMF, Marriner; (iv) Bennett, Grumiaux Trio.

Aurèle Nicolet's performances of the *Flute Concertos* and *Andante for Flute and Orchestra* are very positive, and the solo playing throughout is expert and elegantly phrased. Barwahser and Ellis give a sparkling account of the *Flute and Harp Concerto* and Sir Colin accompanies them with the greatest sprightliness and sympathy. If these are not a top choice in this repertoire, the William Bennett accounts of the four *Flute Quartets* with the Grumiaux Trio certainly are. The wind *Sinfonia concertante*, in which the oboe and clarinet parts are replaced by flute and oboe respectively, is an interesting conjectural experiment rather than an essential part of a Mozart collection. The recordings throughout are smoothly remastered and sound fine.

Herbert Weissberg does not have the outsize personality of some of his rivals, but he is a cultured player, and the quality of the recording is excellent. In short, good value for money and very pleasant sound.

Flute Concertos Nos. 1–2; (i) *Flute & Harp Concerto.*

*** RCA 09026 68256-2. Galway; (i) Robles; ASMF, Marriner.
(M) *** Decca (ADD) 440 080-2. (i) Bennett, ECO, Malcolm; (ii) Tripp, Jellinek, VPO, Münchinger.
(N) (B) **(*) DG 469 553-2. Zöller, (i) ECO, Klee; (ii) with Zabaleta, BPO, Märzendorfer.
**(*) EMI CDC5 56356-2. Pahud; (i) Langlamet; BPO, Abbado.

James Galway and Marisa Robles take an expansive, warmly expressive view of the slow movement of the *Flute and Harp Concerto*; she also matches him in a delightfully bouncy account of the finale, sharper in focus than the Pahud one. In the solo concertos, too, Galway takes an expansive, expressive view of the slow movements and a winningly relaxed one of the allegros.

William Bennett gives a beautiful account of the concertos, among the finest in the catalogue. Every phrase is shaped with both taste and affection, and the playing of the ECO under George Malcolm is fresh and vital. The earlier Vienna recording of the *Flute and Harp Concerto* has also stood the test of time. Refinement and beauty of tone and phrase are a hallmark throughout, and Münchinger provides most sensitive accompaniments.

Zöller is a superb flautist. K.313 is a little cool, but is played most elegantly, with pure tone and unmannered phrasing. The charming Minuet finale is poised and graceful. The performance of K.314 is more relaxed and smiling and the *Andante* is admirably flexible. Bernhard Klee provides adept accompaniments. Zöller favours the use of comparatively extended cadenzas whenever Mozart provided space for them, and one wonders whether they will not seem too much of a good thing on repetition. In the *Flute and Harp Concerto* Zabaleta's composure and sense of line knits the texture of the solo-duet together most convincingly. Märzendorfer conducts with warmth yet with a firm overall control. In short, with pleasing analogue sound from the 1970s, well transferred, this is highly successful.

The fast speeds in the Berlin performance have a light, taut touch, with the ever-imaginative Emmanuel Pahud set against a modest-sized Berlin Philharmonic. Next to Pahud, the harp soloist, Marie-Pierre Langlamet is rather reticent in the *Flute and Harp Concerto*, though always sensitive.

(i; ii) Flute Concertos Nos. 1–2; (i–iii) Flute & Harp Concerto; (iv) Divertimento for Strings No. 1, K.136; 2 Marches, K.335; Serenades Nos. 6 (Serenata notturna); 9 (Posthorn); (v) Symphonies Nos. 35 (Haffner); 36 (Linz); 38 (Prague); 39 in E flat, K.543; 40 in G min., K.550; 41 in C (Jupiter).

⚫ (BB) *** Virgin Classics 5 x 1 VBD5 61678-2 (5). (i) Coles; (ii) ECO; (iii) Yoshino; (iv) Lausanne CO; (v) Sinfonia Varviso; Menuhin.

In many ways this is the outstanding Mozartian CD bargain of all time – five discs for the price of one. Moreover, the set would be highly desirable if it cost several times as much. Both the flute concertos are stylishly and pleasingly played by Samuel Coles, and when Naoko Yoshino joins him in the delectable *Flute and Harp Concerto* the interplay is fluently appealing. No complaints about the sound either and there is no doubting the character of these performances. The *Serenata notturna* and the *Divertimento* are graceful and fresh, and so is the *Posthorn Serenade*. Menuhin's approach is above all elegantly light-hearted and Crispian Steele-Perkins has his brief moment of glory as the posthorn soloist in the Minuet.

Yet when we turn to the six last symphonies we encounter playing and interpretations of a very special order. The

Sinfonia Varviso responds warmly to Menuhin as the group's chosen President. Though modern instruments are used, the scale is intimate with textures beautifully clear, and the fresh, immediate sound highlights the refined purity of the string playing. In the last four symphonies speeds are on the fast side, yet he does not sound at all rushed. The *G minor* is especially memorable – among the finest ever recorded. With playing of precision, clarity and bite, one constantly has the feeling of live music-making. Exposition repeats are observed in both first and last movements of the *Jupiter* and this performance, like its partner, takes its place as a top recommendation for the two last symphonies, irrespective of cost. The five discs come in a pair of boxes (with accompanying booklet) in a slipcase, and are surely an essential purchase, even if some duplication is involved.

Flute Concerto No. 1; Andante , K.315; (i) Flute & Harp Concerto.

(B) *** Ph. 420 880-2. C. Monteux; (i) Ellis; ASMF, Marriner.

(M) *** Erato 2292 45832-2. Rampal, (i) VSO, Guschlbauer; (ii) Laskine, Paillard CO, Paillard.

First published in the early 1970s, these Philips performances with Claude Monteux as the principal soloist reappear on the bargain Virtuoso label. Exquisite playing from all concerned. The solo instruments sound larger than life as balanced, but in every other respect this splendidly remastered disc is highly recommendable.

Rampal and Lily Laskine create a genuine symbiosis in the *Flute and Harp Concerto*: their interplay has great charm and delicacy, and the slow movement is a delight. The solo concerto and *Andante* find Rampal in equally good form and he is well accompanied in both instances. With well-transferred recordings from the mid-1960s, this CD is well worth its mid-price.

Flute & Harp Concerto in C, K.299.

(N) (M) *** DG (ADD) 463 642-2. Zöller, Zabaleta, BPO, Märzendorfer – REINECKE: *Harp Concerto;* RODRIGO: *Concierto serenata.* *** ⚫

Karlheinz Zöller is a most sensitive flautist, his phrasing a constant source of pleasure, while Zabaleta's contribution is equally distinguished. Märzendorfer conducts with both warmth and lightness; the outer movements have an attractive rhythmic buoyancy. The 1963 recording is clear and clean, if not quite so rich as we would expect today. This performance is also available coupled with the solo flute concertos (see above).

(i) Flute & Harp Concerto in C, K.299; (ii) Oboe Concerto.

*** Chan. 9051. (i) Milan, Kanga; (ii) Theodore; City of L. Sinf., Hickox – SALIERI: *Double Concerto.* ***

A warmly elegant modern-instrument account of this beguiling concerto, with the delicate interweaving of flute and harp given a delightful bloom by the resonant recording. The *Oboe Concerto* is equally sensitive, again with the line of the *Adagio* delectably sustained by David Theodore, whose creamy tone is so enticing. Both soloists play their own cadenzas.

(i) *Flute & Harp Concerto; Sinfonia concertante, K.297b.*

(BB) *** Naxos 8.550159. (i) Válek, Müllerová; Capella Istropolitana, Edlinger.

Richard Edlinger's account of the *Flute and Harp Concerto* is thoroughly fresh and stylish, and the two soloists are excellent. Although the *Sinfonia concertante in E flat*, K.297b, is not quite so successful, it is still very impressive, and it gives much pleasure. Both performances are very decently recorded; in the lowest price-range they are a real bargain.

Horn Concertos Nos. 1 in D, K.412; 2–4 in E flat, K.417, 447 & 495.

(B) *** CfP 573 4392. Briggs, RLPO, Kovacevich – HAYDN: *Trumpet Concerto.* ***

*** Crystal CD 515. Cerminaro, Seattle SO, Schwarz.

(B) *** DG (ADD) 449 856-2. Seifert, BPO, Karajan.

(M) **(*) Teldec (ADD) 0630 17429-2. Baumann, VCM, Harnoncourt.

Horn Concertos Nos. 1 (with alternative versions of Rondo); 2–4; Allegro, K.370b & Concert Rondo in E flat (ed. Tuckwell); Fragment in E, K.494a.

(N) (B) *** Regis RRC 1007. Tuckwell, Philh. O.

Horn Concertos Nos. 1–4; Concert Rondo in E flat, K.371 (ed. Civil or E. Smith).

*** Chan. 9150. Lloyd, N. Sinfonia, Hickox.

(M) *** Ph. (ADD) 442 397-2. Civil, ASMF, Marriner.

(BB) *** Naxos 8.550148. Stevove, Capella Istropolitana, Kopelman.

Horn Concertos Nos. 1–4; Concert Rondo, K.371 (arr. Tuckwell).

(M) *** EMI CDM7 64851-2. Vlatkovic, ECO, Tate – R. STRAUSS: *Horn Concerto No. 1.* ***

Horn Concertos Nos. 1–4; Concert Rondo, K.371 (ed. Tuckwell); Fragment, K.494a.

(BB) *** Virgin 2 x 1 Double VBD5 61573-2 (2). Brown (hand-horn), OAE, Kuijken – Concert arias. ***

(M) *** EMI (ADD) CDM7 69569-2. Tuckwell, ASMF, Marriner.

Horn Concertos Nos. 1–4; Concert Rondos: in E flat, K.371 (completed John Humphries); in D, K.514 (completed Süssmayr); Fragment for Horn & Orchestra in E flat, K.370b (reconstructed Humphries).

(BB) *** Naxos 8.553592. Thompson, Bournemouth Sinf.

Horn Concertos Nos. 1 (including Rondo in D, K.514, completed Süssmayr); 2–4; Concert Rondos in E flat, K.371; in D (alternative finale to K.412, completed Humphries).

*** Häns. 98.316. T. Brown, ASMF, I. Brown.

Horn Concertos Nos. 1–4; Concert Rondo in E flat, K.371 (reconstructed Greer); Rondo in D, K.485 (reconstructed Jeurisson).

(N) (BB) *** HM HCX 3957012. Greer, Philh. Bar. O, McGegan.

Horn Concertos Nos. 1–4; Concert Rondo, K.371;

Fragments: in E, KAnh.98a; in E flat, K.370b; in D, K.524 (all ed. Tuckwell).

(M) *** Decca 458 607-2. Tuckwell, ECO.

As well as offering superb performances of the four regular concertos using revised texts prepared by John Humphries, the outstanding Naxos issue includes reconstructions of two movements designed for a horn concerto dating from soon after Mozart arrived in Vienna. The *Rondo* completed by Süssmayr is the version generally used as the second movement of K.412. The *Rondo* played here as the second movement of K.412 is Humphries's reconstruction from sources recently discovered. It is fascinating too to have extra passages in No. 4, again adding Mozartian inventiveness. Michael Thompson plays with delectable lightness and point, bringing out the wit in finales, as well as the tenderness in slow movements. He also draws sparkling and refined playing from the Bournemouth Sinfonietta, very well recorded in clear, atmospheric sound.

Another first-class super-bargain set comes from Lowell Greer, who uses a modern copy of a Raoux Parisian cor of 1818, which has a most attractive timbre. He plays with complete freedom, disguising the stopped notes skilfully and his Mozartian line is impeccable. Slow movements are phrased with appealing simplicity and the rondo finales have splendid buoyancy. McGegan and his chamber orchestra accompany very stylishly and the recording is excellent.

For Hänssler, Timothy Brown chooses a modern instrument, and his persuasive lyrical line, imaginative phrasing and neat use of cadenzas show him as a true Mozartian. Another of the memorable features of this fine Hänssler disc is the warmth and finesse of Iona Brown's stylish accompaniments. The recording too is most natural in balance and sound quality, and this CD stands high among modern versions of these ever-fresh concertos.

The Decca Ovation reissue (458 607-2) offers Barry Tuckwell's third set of the four concertos in excellent digital sound, recorded in the Henry Wood Hall in 1983. He plays as well as ever and also directs the accompanying ECO. The orchestra provides crisp, polished and elegant accompaniments to make a perfectly scaled backcloth for full-timbred solo playing which again combines natural high spirits with a warmly expressive understanding of the Mozartian musical line. This reissue now includes the rest of Mozart's concertante horn music. Added to the *Rondo*, K.371, are three fragments which Tuckwell presents as Mozart left them but edited for concert performance.

Barry Tuckwell's Regis (originally Collins) CD, his fourth recording of the Mozart *Horn Concertos*, remains a splendid alternative choice. They are fresh, without a suspicion of routine, and are played with rounded tone and consistently imaginative phrasing. Moreover the collection is complete. Besides the *Fragment*, K.494a, Tuckwell includes both the familiar *Concert Rondo*, K.371, plus an *Allegro* first movement which Mozart wrote to go with it. Tuckwell also includes his own alternative *Rondo* finale of the *Concerto in D*, K.412, based directly on Mozart's autograph, placing the two alternative finales side by side.

EMI have also effectively remastered Tuckwell's second set of the *Horn Concertos* with Marriner, and the 1972 recording sounds quite full and fresh. This mid-priced CD also includes the *Concert Rondo* and the *Fragment in E*.

In his earlier Virgin recording Timothy Brown uses an open hand-horn without valves. He uses stopped notes with especially smart effect in the Rondos, and more sparingly and more subtly in the lyrical music. In short, these performances sound delightfully fresh, and give constant pleasure. Timothy Brown includes the additional *Rondo* and also the *Fragment*, which he leaves in mid-air, at the point at which the composer abandoned his manuscript. Kuijken's accompaniments are also pleasingly smooth and cultivated. But it seems a strange idea to couple this repertoire (even as a super-bargain Virgin Double) with concert arias.

Among the more recent versions is a fine Chandros set by Frank Lloyd, an outstanding soloist of the new generation. He plays these works with great character and poetic warmth; his phrasing is supple and his tone full, though never suave. Like Tuckwell, he uses a modern German double horn with great skill and sensitivity. Hickox provides admirable accompaniments, and the Chandos recording is well up to the high standards of the house.

Claire Briggs also gives brilliant performances of all four *Concertos*, with the celebrated finale of No. 4 taken exceptionally fast. Even that is superbly articulated without any feeling of breathlessness, though it lacks some of the fun that others have brought. However, this is now deleted.

Alan Civil's Philips set was made in 1973. The recording is obviously modern and the performances are highly enjoyable, with Sir Neville Marriner's polished and lively accompaniments giving pleasure in themselves. The balance has the effect of making the horn sound slightly larger than life.

Miloš Stevove on Naxos uses the slightest trace of vibrato but it is never obtrusive, and one has only to listen to the *Larghetto* of K.447 or the *Andante cantabile* of K.495 to discover his naturally warm feeling for a Mozartian phrase. Allegros are lively and the Rondos have agreeable lift. In short, with excellent, stylish accompaniments from the Capella Istropolitana this is enjoyably spontaneous.

John Cerminaro, at present principal with the Seattle orchestra, is a splendid soloist. His tone is rich and glowing (a little plump as recorded), and the hints of vibrato add to the individuality of his supple phrasing, for he shows a warmly elegant feeling for the Mozartian line. One of the highlights is the outstanding account of the *First Concerto*, into which he interpolates a soaring account of the slow movement of the *Horn Quintet*. He is warmly and persuasively accompanied by Schwarz – himself a brass player of distinction. But at full price, and without the *Concert Rondo*, this can hardly be a top recommendation.

Gerd Seifert has been principal horn of the Berlin Philharmonic since 1964, and his velvety, warm tone is familiar on many records. His articulation is light and neat here, and his nimbleness brings an effective lightness to the gay Rondos. The 1969 recording now brings just a hint of overbrightness on the *forte* violins, but this adds to the sense of vitality without spoiling the elegance.

Hermann Baumann also successfully uses the original hand-horn, without valves, and he lets the listener hear the stopped effect only when he decides that the tonal change can be put to good artistic effect. In his cadenzas he also uses horn chords (where several notes are produced simultaneously by resonating the instrument's harmonics), but as a complement to the music rather than as a gimmick.

Radovan Vlatkovic's tone is very full; there is also at times the slightest hint of vibrato, but it is applied with great discretion and used mostly in the cadenzas. His performances are full of imaginative touches and he has the perfect partner in Jeffrey Tate, who produces sparkling accompaniments. Moreover, Vlatkovic includes both the *Concert Rondo*, K.371, and, very appropriately, a quite outstanding account of the *First Horn Concerto* of Richard Strauss. However, this coupling has been deleted at the time of going to press.

(i) *Horn Concertos Nos. 1–4;* (ii) *Piano & Wind Quintet in E flat, K.452.*

(M)(***) EMI mono CDM5 66898-2 [566950]. Brain; (i) Philh. O, Karajan; (ii) Horsley. Brain Wind Ens. (members).

Dennis Brain's famous (1954) mono record of the concertos with Karajan now rightly appears in EMI's 'Great Recordings of the Century' series. Brain's horn timbre was unique. As for the playing, Brain's glorious tone and phrasing – every note is alive – is life-enhancing in its warmth; the *espressivo* of the slow movements is matched by the joy of the Rondos, spirited, buoyant, infectious and smiling. Karajan's accompaniments, too, are a model of Mozartian good manners, and the Philharmonia at their peak play wittily and elegantly. Brain's distinguished earlier recording of the *Piano and Wind Quintet* has been added, with Colin Horsley making a fine contribution on the piano.

Oboe Concerto in C, K.314.

(N) (B) *** Hyp. Helios CDH 55080. Francis, LMP, Shelley –
   KROMMER: *Oboe Concertos*. ***
*** ASV CDCOE 808. Boyd, COE, Berglund – R. STRAUSS:
   Oboe Concerto. ***

Sarah Francis has already given us distinguished performances of oboe concertos by Handel and Telemann. Here she turns to Mozart with equal elegance and is persuasively accompanied by Howard Shelly and the London Mozart Players who, like their soloist, are completely satisfying in their stylish playing using modern instruments. The closing *Rondo* is particularly engaging.

Douglas Boyd is never afraid to point the phrasing individually, spontaneously and without mannerism. Others may be purer in their classicism, but this is a very apt reading next to Strauss. Recorded in Henry Wood Hall, the sound is full and vivid.

Piano concertos (with list of keys and Köchel nos.)

1 in F, K.37; 2 in B flat, K.39; 3 in D, K.40; 4 in G, K.41; 5 in D, K.175; 6 in B flat, K.238; 8 in C, K.246; 9 in E flat, K.271; 11 in F, K.413; 12 in A, K.414; 13 in C, K.415; 14 in E flat, K.449; 15 in B flat, K.450; 16 in D, K.451; 17 in G, K.453; 18 in B flat, K.456; 19 in F, K.459; 20 in D min., K.466; 21 in C, K.467; 22 in E flat, K.482; 23 in A, K.488; 24 in C, K.491; 25 in C, K.503; 26 in D, K.537 (Coronation); 27 in B flat, K.595; 2 Pianos:

E flat, K.365; 3 Pianos: F major, K.242; Concert Rondo in D, K.382; in A, K.386.

Complete Mozart Edition, Vol. 7: (i) *Piano Concertos, K.107/1–3;* (ii) *Nos. 1–4;* (iii) *5, 6, 8, 9, 11–27; Concert Rondos 1–2;* (iii; iv) *Double Piano Concertos, K.242 & K.365;* (v) *Triple Concerto in F, K.242.*

(M) **(*) Ph. ADD/Dig. 422 507-2 (12). (i) Koopman, Amsterdam Bar. O; (ii) Haebler, Vienna Capella Academica, Melkus; (iii) Brendel, ASMF, Marriner; (iv) Cooper; (v) K.and M. Labèque, Bychkov, BPO, Bychkov.

Complete Bargain Mozart Edition, Vol. 4: *Piano Concertos; Rondos 1–2; Double Piano Concertos, K.242 & K.365; Triple Piano Concerto in F, K.242.*

(N) (B) **(*) Ph. (ADD/Dig) 464 800-2 (12). Artists as above.

Piano Concertos Nos. 1–6; 8–9; 11–27; Rondo in D, K.382.

(M) *** EMI (ADD) CES5 72930-2 (10). Barenboim, ECO.
(N) (B) **(*) DG 469 510-2 (8). (without *Rondo*) Anda, Salzburg Mozarteum O.

Piano Concertos Nos. 5–6; 8–9; 11–27; Rondos Nos. 1–2, K.382 & 386.

⊛ (M) *** Sony ADD/Dig. SX10K 89500 (10). Perahia, ECO.

(i) *Piano Concertos Nos. 1–6; 8, 9, 11–27; Concert Rondos Nos. 1 in D, K.382;* (ii) *2 in A, K.386;* (iii) *Double Piano Concerto in E flat, K.365;* (iii; iv) *Triple Piano Concerto in F, K.242.*

(B) *** Decca ADD/Dig. 443 727-2 (10). Ashkenazy, with (i) Philh. O; (ii) LSO, Kertész; (iii) Barenboim, ECO; (iv) Fou Ts'ong.

Piano Concertos Nos. (i) *1–4;* (ii) *5;* (iii) *6;* (ii) *8–9;* (iv) *11;* (iii) *12;* (iv) *13–16;* (iii) *17;* (iv) *18;* (iii) *19;* (ii) *20;* (iii) *21;* (iv) *22;* (iii) *23;* (iv) *24;* (ii) *25;* (iii) *26;* (ii) *27; Concert Rondos in D, K.382; in A, K.386;* (ii; v) *Double Piano Concerto in E flat, K.365;* (ii; v; vi) *Triple Piano Concerto in F (Lodron), K.242.*

(B) **(*) Ph. 454 352-2 (10). Haebler ((i) fortepiano or (ii–iv) piano), with (i) V. Capella Academica, Melkus; (ii–vi) LSO; (ii) Galliera; (iii) Rowicki; (iv) C. Davis; (v) Hofmann; (vi) Bunge.

Piano Concertos No. 20 in D min., K.466; (ii) *21 in C, K.467.*

(BB) **(*) Belart (ADD) 450 055-2 (from above). Haebler, LSO; (i) Galliera; (ii) Rowicki.

By omitting the four early concertos after J. C. Bach, Sony have been able to reissue the Perahia set on ten mid-priced CDs. The cycle is a remarkable achievement; in terms of poetic insight and musical spontaneity, the performances are in a class of their own. There is a wonderful singing line and at the same time a sensuousness that is always tempered by spirituality. About half the recordings are digital and of excellent quality and, we are glad to report, the earlier, analogue recordings have been skilfully remastered with first-class results, both in this complete set and in the separate issues below. This is an indispensable set in every respect.

Ashkenazy's set with the Philharmonia appeared over more than a decade. The account of the *E flat Concerto*, K.365, with Barenboim and the ECO, and the *Triple Concerto*, with Fou Ts'ong to complete the trio, is earlier still (1972). These performances have won golden opinions over the years, and the clarity of both the performances and the recordings is refreshing: indeed, the fine Decca sound is one of their strongest features.

The sense of spontaneity in Barenboim's performances of the Mozart concertos, his message that this is music hot off the inspiration line, is hard to resist, even though it occasionally leads to over-exuberance and idiosyncrasies. These are as nearly live performances as one could hope for on record, and the playing of the English Chamber Orchestra is splendidly geared to the approach of an artist with whom the players have worked regularly. They are recorded with fullness, and the sound is generally freshened very successfully in the remastering. The set has been reissued in a handsomely produced super-bargain box, alongside his equally recommendable survey of the Beethoven piano sonatas. The recordings were made at Abbey Road between 1967 and 1974.

The Philips Mozart Edition *Piano Concertos* box is based on Brendel's set with the ASMF under Marriner. Throughout, his thoughts are never less than penetrating. The transfers are consistently of the very highest quality, as is the playing of the Academy of St Martin-in-the-Fields under Sir Neville Marriner. To make the set complete, Ingrid Haebler gives eminently stylish accounts of the first four *Concertos* on the fortepiano, accompanied by Melkus and his excellent Vienna Capella Academica; the sound is admirably fresh. However, on disc two the ear gets rather a shock when Ton Koopman presents the three works after J. C. Bach. Convincing though these performances are, it seems a strange idea to offer an authentic approach to these three concertos alone, particularly as at the end of the disc we return to a delightfully cultured performance on modern instruments of the alternative version for three pianos of the so-called *Lodron Concerto*, K.242, provided by the Labèque duo.

Were the competition not so fierce, Anda's often very fine performances could carry a stronger recommendation. They are beautifully poised and have excellent feeling for style; some are quite memorable for their unidiosyncratic freshness. The recordings, made between 1962 and 1969, do not quite match those of Barenboim (the violin timbre is more dated) and Anda is a less individual artist, but the sound is clean and well balanced and the set gives consistent enjoyment. Where none is available by Mozart, Anda plays his own cadenzas. DG have now managed to get three concertos on each disc (with only the second split after the first movement) so the whole set comes on eight CDs, and the economy is obvious.

Ingrid Haebler recorded the Mozart concertos with the LSO for Philips between 1965 and 1968, alternating among three different conductors, then completing the set in 1973 with eminently stylish accounts of the first four concertos played appropriately on the fortepiano, accompanied by Melkus and his excellent Vienna Capella Academica. Her readings of the remainder are distinguished by a singular poise, meticulous finger-control and great delicacy of touch.

She is less concerned with dramatic intensity; but with her carefully delineated boundaries she undoubtedly gives considerable pleasure by her restrained sensibility and musicianship. She is helped throughout by finely judged recordings, warm and spacious yet crystal clear, and the orchestral response is most sympathetic, particularly in the concertos conducted by Witold Rowicki and Colin Davis.

For those wanting a characteristic sample of the series, Belart have made available a super-bargain coupling of the two top favourite concertos, *Nos. 20 in D minor* and *21 in C major*, the latter with its 'Elvira Madigan' associations. The recordings are beautifully transferred.

Piano Concertos Nos. 5–6, 8–9, 11–27.

(M) *** Decca 448 140-2 (9). Schiff, Salzburg Mozarteum Camerata Academica, Végh.

Piano Concertos Nos. 5–6; 8–9; 11–27; Rondo in D, K.382.

**(*) Ph. 438 207-2 (9). Uchida, ECO, Tate.

Piano Concertos Nos. 5–6, 8–9, 11–27; (i) Double Piano Concerto, K.365; (i; ii) Triple Piano Concerto, K.242. Concert Rondos Nos. 1–2.

(B) *** DG 463 111-2 (9). Bilson (fortepiano), E. Bar. Sol., Gardiner; with (i) Levin; (ii) Tan.

András Schiff's cycle with the Salzburg Mozarteum Camerata Academica under Sándor Végh proves to be one of the most satisfying of recent years and – along with the new Shelley series on Chandos – arguably the finest since Murray Perahia's cycle of the late 1970s. Schiff plays a Bösendorfer piano, and its relatively gentle, cleanly focused timbre has something of the precision of a fortepiano without any loss of the colour which comes with a more modern instrument. The recording is consistently more beautiful than in Perahia's Sony set. For some listeners in certain works the warm resonance may offer a problem. This is agreeably relaxed music-making, though not in the least lacking in intensity or weight. Just occasionally Schiff dots his 'i's and crosses his 't's a little too precisely, but for the most part he is so musicianly and perceptive that this seems unimportant. In short, these are lovely performances, enhanced by the quality of the accompaniment under Végh, who is unfailingly supportive. For the most part Schiff plays his own cadenzas, but in the first movement of K.466 he uses a cadenza by Beethoven, and the finale of K.488 brings one by George Malcolm.

Malcolm Bilson's complete set of the piano concertos now appears in DG's Collector's Edition at bargain price, well documented. Bilson is an artist of excellent musical judgement and good taste and his survey is still the only one at present available on the fortepiano. The overall musical standard is very high, and the concentration and vitality of the music-making are very compelling – especially so in Nos. 20 in D minor and 21 in C (K.466–7), which received a ● for their separate issue.

Mitsuko Uchida, following up her stylish and sensitive accounts of the *Piano Sonatas*, began a cycle of the concertos in 1985 with Nos. 20 and 21, which set the style for the series (recorded over a period of nearly five years) with playing of considerable beauty and performances guaranteed never to

offend and most likely to delight. There is some lovely playing, although her cultured approach at times offers more than a glimpse of Dresden china. She is unfailingly elegant but a little over-civilized; some will find a faint hint of preciosity here and there. Uchida is eminently alive and imaginative, although at times one would welcome a greater robustness of spirit, a lively inner current, and this applies particularly to the last two concertos, K.537 and K.595. Throughout, Jeffrey Tate draws splendid playing from the ECO, and these artists have the benefit of exceptionally good recorded sound; although the perspective favours the piano, the timbre of the solo instrument is beautifully captured.

Piano Concertos Nos. 5, K.175; 6, K.238; 8, K.246.

***Teldec 3984 21483-2. Barenboim, BPO.

Barenboim continues his current Mozart cycle with the Berlin Philharmonic with these three early concertos. They sound very fresh and the orchestral sonority is pleasingly well nourished. The recording is full-blooded, a bit forward but not excessively so, and the whole disc radiates pleasure.

Piano Concertos Nos. 5, K.175/382 (1782 version); 14, K.449; 16, K.451.

*** O-L 458 285-2. Levin, AAM, Hogwood.

In this seventh issue in an ongoing series, the unusual point is that Levin and Hogwood have preferred the final version of K.175 to the one usually recorded. In this, the *Rondo*, K.382, written some nine years after the first version appeared in 1773, replaces the original finale. It is certainly a colourful, lively piece, but so is the original at half the length, which is stylistically more consistent. This version is different also in that Mozart reworked the wind parts of the first two movements. Compared with Malcolm Bilson's versions, the tinkly top of Levin's evidently smaller fortepiano gives one constant reminders of the harpsichord. Maybe as a result, Levin tends to favour speeds a fraction faster than Bilson's, and his own improvised cadenzas add to the freshness.

Piano Concertos Nos. 5, K.175; 25, K.503.

*** Sony SK 37267. Perahia, ECO.

Murray Perahia has the measure of the strength and scale of the *C major*, K.503, as well as displaying tenderness and poetry; while the early *D major*, K.175, has an innocence and freshness that are completely persuasive. The recording is good, but the upper strings are a little fierce and not too cleanly focused.

Piano Concerto No. 6, K.238.

(M) **(*) Decca (ADD) 448 598-2. Ashkenazy, LSO, Schmidt-Isserstedt – BACH: *Clavier Concerto No. 1* **(*); CHOPIN: *Piano Concerto No. 2.* ***

This is an eloquent performance of a charming work, beautifully accompanied. The 1968 recording is excellent for its period, though perhaps an unexpected choice for reissue in Decca's Classic Sound series. The coupled Chopin concerto is the highlight of this reissue.

Piano Concertos Nos. 6, K.238; 8, K.246; 19, K.459.

(BB) *** Naxos 8.550208. Jandó, Concentus Hungaricus, Antal.

No. 19 in F is a delightful concerto and it receives a most attractive performance, aptly paced, with fine woodwind playing, the finale crisply sparkling. No. 6 is hardly less successful; if No. 8 seems plainer, it is still admirably fresh. With excellently balanced recording this is a genuine bargain.

Piano Concertos Nos. 6, K.238; 13, K.415.

*** Sony (ADD) SK 39223. Perahia, ECO.

Perahia brings a marvellous freshness and delicacy to the *B flat Concerto*, K.238, but it is in the *C major*, with its sense of character and subtle artistry, that he is at his most sparkling and genial. Even if the acoustic ambience is less than ideally spacious, the CBS sound is still good.

Piano Concertos Nos. 6, K.238; 17, K.453; 21, K.467.

(M) *** DG (ADD) 447 436-2. Anda, Salzburg Mozarteum Camerata Academica.

Géza Anda's poetic account of the *C major Concerto*, K.467, is one of the most impressive from his cycle, notably for a beautifully poised account of the slow movement. In the *G major*, K.453, there is both strength and poetry, while the DG recording is excellent in both balance and clarity. The *B flat Concerto*, K.238, is played simply and eloquently. The recording is not quite so cleanly transferred in the early work, but this remains a most enjoyable triptych.

Piano Concertos Nos. 8 (Lützow), K.246; 9 (Jeunehomme), K.271; Concert Rondo No. 2, K.386.

🎵 (M) *** Decca (ADD) 443 576-2. Ashkenazy, LSO, Kertész.
(BB) *** Discover (ADD) DICD 920517. Kagan, Suk CO, Macecek.

Ashkenazy's earlier, 1966 coupling with Kertész, which includes the *A major Concert Rondo*, originally earned the LP a Rosette, and we see no reason not to carry it forward. Ashkenazy has the requisite sparkle, humanity and command of keyboard tone, and his readings can only be called inspired. He is very well supported by the LSO under Kertész, and they make an excellent case for a partnership with a sympathetic conductor, rather than having the soloist direct the proceedings from the keyboard.

These performances by the American performer and scholar Susan Kagan are notable for an appealingly direct simplicity of approach. These are not self-conscious interpretations, but Mozart played freshly and spontaneously. The recording, in an intimate, slightly dry acoustic, is real and immediate. Though without the experienced insights of a Perahia, of its kind this is first class.

Piano Concertos Nos. 9, K.271; 12, K.414; 21, K.467; 27, K.595.

(BB) **(*) Royal Long Players (ADD) DCL 70572-2 (2). Eschenbach, LPO.

Perhaps these readings lack the ultimate sparkle that Barenboim, Perahia, Kovacevich and Brendel have achieved over recent years; yet the *A major*, K.414, is particularly felicitous here, and in this lowest possible price range they are all still to be reckoned with. The recording is well balanced and natural and anyone wanting this particular group of concertos will surely not be disappointed. Eschenbach plays Mozart's cadenzas except in K.467 where he uses his own.

Piano Concertos Nos. 9, K.271; 14, K.449.

(N) (B) *** Regis (ADD) RRC 2008 [Van. 8.4015.71]. Brendel, I Solisti di Zagreb, Janigro.

Brendel's 1968 Vanguard performance of No. 9 is quite outstanding, elegant and beautifully precise. The classical-sized orchestra is just right and the neat, stylish string-playing matches the soloist. The performance of K.449 is also first rate, with a memorably vivacious finale. Altogether this is an outstanding Regis reissue with natural sound which hardly shows its age in the clean remastering.

Piano Concertos Nos. 9, K.271; 15, K.450; 22, K.482; 25, K.503; 27, K.595.

(B) *** Ph. Duo (ADD) 442 571-2 (2). Brendel, ASMF, Marriner.

A first-class follow-up to Brendel's first Duo collection of Mozart piano concertos (see below). The account of the opening *Jeunehomme* is finely proportioned and cleanly articulated, with a ravishing account of the slow movement. The finale has great sparkle and finesse and the recording has exemplary clarity. Brendel is hardly less fine in K.450, and the *E flat Concerto* has both vitality and depth. Brendel's first movement has breadth and grandeur as well as sensitivity, while the *Andante* has great poetry. No. 25 (there is well-deserved applause at the close) was recorded at a live performance and has life and concentration, and a real sense of scale. Here as elsewhere the playing of the ASMF under Marriner is alert and supportive. K.595 is also among Brendel's best Mozart performances, with a beautifully poised *Larghetto* and a graceful, spirited finale. Highly recommended.

Piano Concertos Nos. 9, K.271; 17, K.453.

(M) *** Chan. 9068. Shelley, LMP.

Piano Concertos Nos. 9 (Jeunehomme), K.271; 17, K.453; Rondo in D, K.382.

(M) *** DG (IMS) 447 291-2. Bilson (fortepiano), E. Bar. Sol., Gardiner.

Howard Shelley's playing is a delight and is possessed of a refreshing naturalness which should win many friends. There is spontaneity and elegance, a strong vein of poetic feeling and extrovert high spirits. His *G major Concerto* belongs in the most exalted company and can withstand comparison with almost any rival. But both performances are touched by distinction, and they are beautifully recorded too.

Malcolm Bilson shows himself a lively and imaginative artist, well matched by Gardiner. The CD catches the lightness and clarity of the textures, with the fortepiano sound not too twangy and with wind balances often revelatory. The darkness of the C minor slow movement of K.271 is eerily caught; K.453, as ever, is a delight, with Bilson allowing himself a natural degree of expressiveness, within the limits of classical taste. The lightness of the keyboard action encourages the choice of fast allegros, but never at the expense of Mozart.

(i) Piano Concertos Nos. 9 (Jeunehomme), K.271; 17, K.453; 20, K.466. Adagio & Fugue in C min., K.546.

**(*) ECM 1624/25. (i) Jarrett; Stuttgart CO, Russell Davies.

Admirers of Keith Jarrett should be well satisfied with his newest Mozartian venture, apart from the short measure. For the *Adagio and Fugue*, well played as it is, only lasts for just over seven minutes! Dennis Russell Davies and the excellent Stuttgart orchestra set the scene in each of the three concertos very impressively. Jarrett plays fluently and responsively throughout: only in the central *Romance* of the latter work does he seem not ideally relaxed. But the *Andante* of K.453, taken slowly and reflectively, shows him at his most thoughtful, while the finale is delightfully light-hearted. Excellent recording, well balanced, full bodied and clear.

Piano Concertos Nos. 9, K.271; 21, K.467.

*** Sony (ADD) SK 34562. Perahia, ECO.

(B) ** CfP 573 4402. Hough, Hallé O, Thomson.

Perahia's reading of K.271 is wonderfully refreshing and delicate, with diamond-bright articulation, urgently youthful in its resilience. The famous *C major Concerto* is given a highly imaginative performance. Faithful, well-balanced recording.

Stephen Hough plays with fine freshness, point and clarity; but here he tends to prettify two of Mozart's strongest concertos, minimizing their greatness. This delicate, Dresden-china treatment would have been more acceptable half-a-century ago, but now leaves out too much that is essential. However, this is now deleted.

Piano Concertos Nos. 9, K.271; 25, K.503.

*** None. 7559 79454-2. Goode, Orpheus CO.

Richard Goode, having given us an outstanding set of the Beethoven sonatas, is now embarking on a Mozart concerto series, like Murray Perahia before him, working with a first-class, modern-instrument chamber orchestra. The Orpheus Chamber Orchestra are consistently at one with him in matters of phrasing and style, and they immediately establish the boldly expansive character of the great *C major Concerto*, K.503. These are performances of much character, beautifully recorded. Mozart's cadenzas are used in K.271, but Goode uses his own in K.503.

Piano Concertos Nos. 11, K.413; 12, K.414; 13, K.415.

(B) *** EMI Debut CDZ5 72525-2. Dechorgnat, Henschel Qt.

The interplay between the stylish Patrick Dechorgnat and the polished and sympathetic Henschel Quartet is heard at its most appealing in the *Larghetto* of the *F major Concerto*, K.413, yet the touching *Andante* of K.414 is hardly less appealing, and the recording throughout is so expertly balanced that all three works are a great success. A first-rate début for soloist and string quartet alike.

Piano Concertos Nos. 11, K.413; 12, K.414; 14, K.449.

*** Sony (ADD) SK 42243. Perahia, ECO.

These performances remain in a class of their own. When it first appeared, we thought the *F major*, K.413, the most impressive of Perahia's Mozart concerto records so far, its slow movement wonderfully inward; and the *E flat Concerto*, K.449, is comparably distinguished. The current remastering is very successful.

Piano Concertos Nos. 12, K.414 (version for piano and string quartet); Piano Quartet No. 2 in E flat, K.493.

*** EMI CDC5 6962-2. Brendel, Alban Berg Quartet.

Breaking the bonds of his exclusive recording contract, Alfred Brendel joins the Alban Berg Quartet in live recordings made in the Konzerthaus in Vienna. Together they give electrifying performances to match the quartet, while the four string players respond to his example with Mozart-playing more flexible than usual, warmly expressive. The rapt *Andante* slow movement of the concerto brings playing of Beethovenian gravity, intensified still further on entry of the piano. The concerto works surprisingly well in this chamber version, in which Mozart makes no changes to the score, but simply points out that the wind parts can be omitted, and that those for strings can be played by four solo instruments. Brendel is here more relaxed than in his Philips recording of the full concerto, with delightful interplay between piano and quartet. The *Piano Quartet* brings a performance equally illuminating with Brendel at his most sparkling in the finale, playing with wonderfully clear articulation. The recording is bright, immediate and well balanced to match.

Piano Concerto No.12, K.414.

(M) (**(*)) Decca mono 458 869-2. Britten, Aldeburgh Festival O – HAYDN: *Symphonies Nos. 45 (Farewell); 55 (Schoolmaster).* (**(*))

Piano Concertos Nos. 12, K.414; 14, K.449; 21, K.467.

(BB) *** Naxos 8.550202. Jandó, Concentus Hungaricus, Ligeti.

Piano Concertos Nos. 12, K.414; 14, K.449; Rondo, K.382.

(BB) **(*) Arte Nova 74321 72117-2. Kirschnereit, Bamberg SO, Bermann.

In Jandó's hands the first movement of K.449 sounds properly forward-looking; the brightly vivacious K.414 also sounds very fresh here, and its *Andante* is beautifully shaped. The excellent orchestral response distinguishes the first movement of K.467: both grace and weight are here, and some fine wind playing. An added interest in this work is provided by Jandó's use of cadenzas provided by Robert Casadesus. Jandó is at his most spontaneous throughout these performances and this is altogether an excellent disc, well recorded.

The Westphalian pianist Matthias Kirschnereit is to record all Mozart's concertos for Arte Nova. This first disc makes an auspicious start. It opens with an engagingly fresh account of the well-known *D major Rondo* and follows with a warm and cultivated account of K.414, to which Frank Bermann's elegant and supportive accompaniment makes a very considerable contribution. K.449 is characterful and enjoyable too, though it is less individual than Barenboim's version. Mozart's cadenzas are used throughout. The recording is very good, the balance realistic, but Jandó's Naxos disc includes an extra concerto.

Decca's 'Britten in Aldeburgh' series is generally devoted to BBC radio recordings, but this one of K.414 was a live recording made by Decca at the Festival in 1956. It is a winningly spontaneous performance, with Britten as a light, sparkling soloist leading his players on at challengingly fast speeds in the outer movements, pressing ahead of the beat. The central slow movement similarly reveals Britten's magnetism as a pianist, warmly expressive at a slow tempo. Close, dry mono recording gives violins an acid edge, but the concentration of the performance makes one forget the sound.

Piano Concertos Nos. 12, K.414; 19, K.459.

(M) *** Chan. 9256. Shelley, LMP.

Another fine disc in Howard Shelley's musically rewarding and beautifully recorded series. Admirers of this artist need not hesitate in investing here, with the music's expressive range fully encompassed without mannerism, slow movements eloquently shaped and outer movements aptly paced and alive with vitality.

Piano Concertos Nos. 12, K.414; 20, K.466; Rondo in D, K.382.

*** RCA 09026 60400. Kissin, Moscow Virtuosi, Spivakov.

The D major Rondo, K.382, has an elegance and delicacy worthy of the greatest Mozart players of the day. The A major Concerto, K.414, shows the same immaculate technical finesse and musical judgement (save, perhaps, in the slow movement, which some could find a little oversweet). There are perhaps greater depths in the D minor Concerto than Kissin finds but, even so, the playing is musical through and through and gives unfailing pleasure. The recorded sound is very good and the disc as a whole deserves the attention of any Mozartian.

Piano Concertos Nos. 13, K.415; 20, K.466.

(BB) **(*) Naxos 8.550201. Jandó, Concentus Hungaricus, Ligeti.

These performances set a high standard in their communicative immediacy, and if they have not quite the individuality of Perahia or Ashkenazy, they are worth a place in any collection and are very modestly priced. Jandó uses Beethoven's cadenzas with impressive authority. The balance and recording are most believable and there is good documentation throughout this series.

Piano Concertos Nos. 13, K.415; 24, K.491.

(M) *** Chan. 9326. Shelley, LMP.

Howard Shelley has immaculate keyboard manners and his strong, natural musicianship is always in evidence. An instinctive yet thoughtful Mozartian whose consummate artistry places his cycle among the very finest now on the market.

Piano Concertos Nos. 14, K.449; 15, K.450; 16, K.451.

✪ *** Teldec 0630 16827-2. Barenboim, BPO.

These three delightful concertos were all composed within a few weeks of each other (beginning in February 1784) and they show Barenboim in his very finest Mozartian style, both at the keyboard and in directing the Berlin Philharmonic. Their contribution in opening movements is imposing without being too heavy, and they bring much grace to Andantes. Finales are no less engaging: witness the string playing at the opening of the superb Rondo of K.449. The B flat Concerto is a live performance, but the others are by no means studio-bound. Barenboim's keyboard articulation is a constant joy, as is his pearly tone, but it is the joyous spontaneity of the music-making that makes this triptych so cherishable.

(i) Piano Concertos Nos. 14, K.449; 15, K.450; 19, K.459; 21, K.467; 26 (Coronation), K.537; 27, K.595; (i; ii) Double Piano Concerto, K.365. Adagio in B min., K.540; Piano Sonatas Nos. 8 in A min., K.310; 11 in A, K.331; 13 in B flat, K.333; 14 in C min., K.457; Fantasia in C min., K.475; Rondo in A min., K.511.

(M) **(*) Ph. Brendel Edition ADD/Dig. 446 921-2 (5). Brendel, with (i) ASMF, Marriner; (ii) Cooper – HAYDN: Andante & Variations in F min.; Piano Sonatas. ***

Among Brendel's many fine recordings of the Mozart concertos, the E flat major, K.449, ranks highly, distinguished by beautifully clean and alive passage-work, while there is superb control and poise. He is hardly less impressive in K.450. In K.467 each detail of a phrase is meticulously articulated, every staccato and slur carefully observed. But there is so much to delight in these performances. In the Coronation Concerto, as always, Brendel's articulation and intelligence excite admiration. Only in the slow movement does one feel a trace of didacticism. There are no such reservations about No. 27, which is in every way distinguished and is beautifully recorded. Similarly the Double Concerto (with Imogen Cooper) is elegant and poised, combining vigour with tonal refinement, and here as elsewhere Marriner's accompaniments are comparably polished. The Sonatas, however, bring a few reservations. The pianism is masterly, as one would expect from this great artist, but in the performances of Nos. 8 and 14 the listener is all too aware of the mental preparation that has gone into the interpretations. The staccato markings in the slow movement of K.310 are exaggerated and the movement as a whole is unsmiling and strangely wanting in repose. Self-conscious playing, immaculately recorded. Both Nos. 11 and 13, however, are a joy, and beautifully recorded too.

Piano Concertos Nos. 14, K.449; 23, K.488; 24, K.491.

(M) *** DG 447 295-2. Bilson (fortepiano), E. Bar. Sol., Gardiner.

The much-loved A Major, K.488, is as fresh as you could wish for, with plenty of zing in outer movements – the horns ringing through the texture – the Adagio very poised. Gardiner and the English Baroque Soloists provide vigorous, large-scale orchestral tuttis, matching Bilson's expressiveness on the one hand, while on the other relishing the fast speeds he prefers in the finales and bringing wit to the last movement of K.488. The *C minor* is a performance that combines drama with poetry; here the tempo of the finale is a moderate *Allegretto*, allowing the detail to register admirably. Excellent recording, fresh and full-bodied, yet clear.

Piano Concertos Nos. 14, K.449; 27, K.595.

(M) *** Chan. 9137. Shelley, LMP.

Admirable performances, stylish and with a fine Mozartian sensibility. This is altogether most refreshing, and the recording is very good indeed.

Piano Concerto No. 15 in B flat, K.450; No. 24 in C min., K.491.

(N) (BB) (***) Dutton mono CDBP 9714. Kathleen Long, Nat. SO, Boyd Neel; Concg.O, Van Beinum – FAURE: *Ballade;* LEIGH: *Concertino.* (***)

These two vintage recordings of Mozart concertos, together with the works by Fauré and Walter Leigh, provide a superb memorial to a British pianist who has not been given credit for her inspired artistry. Born in 1896, she lived until 1968, but her recording career was all too short, even though she was very highly regarded in France above all, where the subtlety of her playing was much appreciated. In Mozart the pearly clarity of her articulation is a delight throughout, not least in the lilting finale of K.450. The natural, thoughtful gravity of her playing comes out in the slow movements of both works, with the C minor no less intense for being presented without Beethovenian grandeur on a deliberately limited scale, with Van Beinum and the Concertgebouw understanding partners. Excellent Decca ffrr sound superbly transferred.

(i) Piano Concerto No. 15; Symphony No. 36 (Linz).

(N) (M) **(*) Decca (ADD) 467 123-2. (i) Bernstein (piano); VPO, Bernstein.

An enjoyably light-hearted Mozartian coupling. In the performance of the *Linz* Symphony one relishes the carefree quality in the playing. The Concerto, even more than the *Symphony*, conveys the feeling of a conductor enjoying himself on holiday. Bernstein's piano playing may not be poised in every detail, but every note communicates vividly – so much so that in the slow movement he even manages to make his dual tempo convincing – faster for the tuttis than for the more romantic solos. The finale is taken surprisingly slowly, but Bernstein brings it off. The sound projects vividly enough, but it is not clear why Decca chose this reissue as one of their Legends series.

Piano Concertos Nos. 15, K.450; 16, K.451.

*** Sony SK 37824. Perahia, ECO.

Perahia's are superbly imaginative readings, full of seemingly spontaneous touches and turns of phrase very personal to him, which yet never sound mannered. His version of the *B flat Concerto*, K.450, has sparkle, grace and intelligence; both these performances are very special indeed. The recording is absolutely first rate, intimate yet realistic and not dry, with the players continuously grouped round the pianist.

Piano Concertos Nos. 15, K.450; 21, K.467; 23, K.488.

(M) *** Ph. (ADD) 464 719-2. Brendel, ASMF, Marriner.

Brendel's versions of Nos. 21 and 23 are already available (see below). Now Philips add his equally distinguished account of the *B flat Concerto*, K.450, with Brendel at his very finest in the noble slow movement and releasing the tension delightfully in the finale. Marriner's supportive accompaniments are admirable.

Piano Concertos Nos. 16, K.451; 25, K.503; Rondo in A, K.386.

(BB) *** Naxos 8.550207. Jandó, Concentus Hungaricus, Antal.

Jenö Jandó gives a very spirited and intelligent account of the relatively neglected *D major Concerto*, K.451, in which he receives sensitive and attentive support from the excellent Concentus Hungaricus under Mátyás Antal. The players sound as if they are enjoying themselves and, although there are greater performances of the *C major Concerto*, K.503, on record, few are at this extraordinarily competitive price.

Piano Concertos Nos. 17, K.453; 18, K.456.

*** Sony SK 36686. Perahia, ECO.
(BB) *** Naxos 8.550205. Jandó, Concentus Hungaricus, Antal.

The *G major Concerto*, K.453, is one of the most magical of the Perahia cycle and is on no account to be missed. The *B flat*, too, has the sparkle, grace and finesse that one expects from him. Even if you have other versions, you should still add this to your collection, for its insights are quite special.

This is also one of the finest in Jandó's excellent superbargain series. Tempi are admirably judged and both slow movements are most sensitively played. Jandó uses Mozart's original cadenzas for the first two movements of K.453 and the composer's alternative cadenzas for K.546. Excellent sound.

Piano Concertos Nos. (i) 17, K.453; 20, K.466; 21, K.467; 23, K.488; (ii) 24, K.491.

(N) (M) *** RCA (ADD) 09026 63061-2 (2). Rubinstein, RCA Victor SO, (i) Wallenstein; (ii) Krips.

Rubinstein's accounts of these favourite concertos are now reissued as part of RCA's complete edition of his performances. Their style could not be further removed from current period-instrument manners using the fortepiano. Here the orchestral sound is rich and glowing (almost lush), and Rubinstein has seldom been caught so sympathetically by the microphones. In each concerto the slow movement is the kernel of the intepretation, and Rubinstein's playing is meltingly lovely, notably in the three middle concertos, which are the finest of the set, where the hushed orchestral playing catches the intensity of the pianist's inspiration. K.488 is especially beautiful, while in K.491 crystal-clear articulation is allied to aristocratic feeling characteristic of vintage Rubinstein, and Krips's accompaniment acts as a foil to the tragic tone of this great and wonderfully balanced work. It is a pity, however, that K.467 had to be split between the two CDs.

Piano Concertos Nos. 17, K.453; 21, K.467.

*** DG 439 941-2. Pires, COE, Abbado.

Maria João Pires's playing, both in the mercurial *G major Concerto* and in its more ceremonial *C major* companion, is elegant, searching and intelligent. She has taste and fine musicianship, and the Chamber Orchestra of Europe under Abbado give excellent support. Good recording.

Piano Concertos Nos. 18, K.456; 19, K.459.

*** HM HMU 907138. Tan (fortepiano), Philh. Bar. O, McGegan.

No one is more convincing on the fortepiano than Melvyn Tan. The pointedly rhythmic main theme of the *F major Concerto* suits the fortepiano particularly well – which is not to say that the *Allegretto* isn't equally winning, with some delightful wind playing from these characterful period instrumentalists. The *B flat Concerto* is hardly less successful. McGegan and his players are clearly completely at one with their soloist. The recording is more intimate, slightly drier than in Malcolm Bilson's DG series, and the result is most persuasive.

Piano Concertos Nos. 18, K.456; 20, K.466.

(N) *** None. 7559 78439-2. Goode, Orpheus CO.

Yet another entirely captivating coupling in Richard Goode's outstanding series with the Orpheus Chamber Orchestra. The lightly sprung opening movement of the *B flat Concerto*, K.456, is sheer delight, and the interplay between soloist and orchestra in the central theme and variations wonderfully light-hearted, matched by the infectiously spirited *opera-buffa* closing *Rondo*. There is no finer performance in the catalogue.

The mood then changes completely for the dark opening of the *D minor Concerto*, at first ominously *sotto voce* but soon expanding with forceful rhythmic drama. The piano enters simply, but then engages in a dialogue which readily hints at the music's histrionic associations with *Don Giovanni*. After a serene opening, the central *Romance* brings comparable drama in its turbulent central section and the dynamic finale is suitably impassioned. Goode uses Mozart's second cadenza in the first movement of K.456 and Beethoven's in the equivalent movement of K.466, composing one of his own for the finale. A superb disc, splendidly balanced and recorded.

Piano Concertos Nos. 19–23.

(N) (B) **(*) Ph. Duo 468 540-2 (2). Uchida, ECO, Tate.

As we have said when discussing her more complete survey above, these are performances of grace and beauty, most naturally recorded. But on the highest level their degree of reticence – despite the superb orchestral work of the ECO under Tate, makes them at times less memorable than the very finest versions. The *F major* (No. 19) (here unfortunately divided over the two discs) is certainly very successful, with plenty of flowing lyrical momentum in outer movements, a thoughtful *Adagio* and lighthearted finale. Nos. 20 and 21, with which she begun her cycle, also provides much cultivated pleasure. But her thoughtful manner is shown at its very finest in Nos. *22 in E flat*, K.482 and its immediate successor, the beautiful *A major*, K.488. In balance, fidelity and sense of presence, few recordings can surpass these accounts, with outstanding playing from the ECO and its excellent wind soloists.

Piano Concertos Nos. 19, K.459; 20, K.466; 21, K.467; 23, K.488; 24, K.491; Concert Rondos Nos. 1–2, K.382 & 386.

⊛ (B) *** Ph. (ADD) Duo 442 269-2. Brendel, ASMF, Marriner.

This must be the Mozartian bargain of all time, five piano concertos and two concert rondos – all for the cost of one premium-price CD. A Rosette then for generosity, to say nothing of the distinction of the performances. Indeed, the playing exhibits a sensibility that is at one with the composer's world and throughout the set the Philips sound-balance is impeccable.

Piano Concertos Nos. 19, K.459; 23, K.488.

⊛ *** Sony SK 39064. Perahia, ECO.

Murray Perahia gives highly characterful accounts of both *Concertos* and a gently witty yet vital reading of the *F Major*, K.459. As always with this artist, there is a splendidly classical feeling allied to a keenly poetic sensibility. His account of K.488 has enormous delicacy and inner vitality, yet a serenity that puts it in a class of its own.

Piano Concertos Nos. 19, K.459; 25, K.503.

**(*) Erato 3984-23299-2. Fellner, Camerata Ac. Salzburg, Janiczek.

Till Fellner's fine musicianship, clean articulation and classical poise are heard to admirable effect in both works, and these performances are best described as fresh and light, with articulation of diamond-like precision, enhanced by the excellent Erato recording, cleanly separated. In slow movements he is at once poetic and unmannered. Alexander Janiczek draws clean, fresh playing from the fine Salzburg orchestra, yet on the cool side. Some may find both the first and last movements a shade too brisk, but generally speaking it is difficult to fault these performances. Taken in their own right they give considerable pleasure.

Piano Concertos Nos. 19 in F, K.459; 27 in B flat, K.595.

(N) *** None. 7559 79608-2. Goode, Orpheus CO.

Richard Goode follows up the success of his two earlier Mozart concerto discs with another nicely contrasted pair of works, superbly done. What shines out is the illusion of live performance, even though these come from the studio. Goode's approach is purposeful and direct, as well as magnetically individual, with natural weight and gravity reflecting his equivalent mastery as a Beethovenian. At such a moment as the hushed B minor opening of the development in the first movement of K.595, Goode has you marvelling afresh at a modulation that is quite extraordinary for a movement in B flat major. Not that Goode's Mozart has anything heavy about it, with the finales of both works marked by lightness, wit and sparklingly clear passage-work. The piano tone is firm and full, though the orchestra could be more forwardly placed after the opening tuttis.

Piano Concerto No. 20, K.466.

(N) (M) *** DG (ADD) 463 649-2. S. Richter, Warsaw PO, Wislocki – BEETHOVEN: *Piano Concerto No. 3; Rondo.* *(*)

(B) **(*) EMI double fforte CZS5 73329-2 (2). Egorov, Philh. O, Sawallisch – BEETHOVEN: *Symphony No. 9; Piano Concerto No. 5.* **(*)

Richter proves his virtuosity by restraint, and this is the quality running right through his extremely fine performance of the *D minor Concerto.* He lets Mozart's music speak for itself, but whether in the choice of tempo, a touch of rubato, or some finely moulded phrase, his mastery is always apparent. The slow movement is beautifully shaped, its opening theme phrased with perfect grace, and the closing pages are exquisite. The buoyancy of the finale is a joy. Wislocki and the Warsaw Orchestra provide an accompaniment of character, and although the recording sounds dated in the matter of string tone, the piano image remains realistic. This reissue is fully worthy to take a place among DG's 'Originals' and it is a pity that the coupling is so disappointing.

It seems a curious idea to couple this concerto (albeit inexpensively) with part of Sawallisch's Beethoven symphony cycle. But Egorov is stylish enough and Sawallisch finds plenty of drama in the outer movements, and the slow movement, too, is elegantly shaped. Good, bright 1985 recording, made at Abbey Road.

Piano Concertos Nos. 20, K.466; 21, K.467.

⚙ *** DG 419 609-2. Bilson (fortepiano), E. Bar. Sol., Gardiner.

These are vital, electric performances by Bilson and the English Baroque Soloists, expressive within their own lights, neither rigid nor too taut in the way of some period Mozart, nor inappropriately romantic. This is a disc to recommend even to those who would not normally consider period performances of Mozart concertos, fully and vividly recorded with excellent balance between soloist and orchestra – better than you would readily get in the concert hall.

(i) *Piano Concertos Nos. 20, K.466; 21, K.467; (ii) 22, K.482; 23, K.488.*

(BB) *** EMI Seraphim (ADD) CES5 68529-2 (2). Fischer, Philh. O; (i) Sawallisch; (ii) Boult.

Fischer's gentle, limpid touch, with its frequent use of half-tones, gives a great deal of pleasure. In the *C major Concerto* she uses cadenzas by Busoni and in the *E flat Concerto* the first-movement cadenza is by Hummel, which adds another point of interest to this coupling. In the *D minor Concerto* Boult's tempi are sensible and the orchestral playing is again felicitous, particularly from the wind. The reading perhaps misses the ultimate in breadth and dramatic fire, but it is a very good performance all the same. In K.488, Fischer plays with liveliness of feeling and refinement of touch. Beethoven's cadenzas are used in the *D minor Concerto.*

(i) *Piano Concertos Nos. 20, K.466; 21, K.467; 23, K.488; 24, K.491; 25, K.503.*

(B) *** Double Decca Dig./ADD 452 958-2 (2). Ashkenazy, Philh. O.

This Double Decca set, reissued for Ashkenazy's sixtieth birthday, now includes both the D minor and C minor masterpieces, but not K.595 (No. 27), which, however, remains available on a slightly different permutation at a similar cost – see below. K.491 and K.503 are among the finest in his series, so the present grouping is particularly attractive. The Kingsway Hall recordings cannot be faulted. They were made between 1977 and 1983; Nos. 20, 23 and 25 are digital.

(i) *Piano Concertos Nos. 20, K.466; 21, K.467; 23, K.488; 27, K.595. Piano Sonata No. 17 in D, K.576; Rondo in A min., K.511.*

(B) *** Double Decca ADD/Dig. 436 383-2 (2). Ashkenazy, Philh. O.

This alternative set, with slightly different contents, is also highly recommendable on all counts, with the three favourite Mozart piano concertos included, plus a splendid *Sonata* and a charming *Rondo.* Ashkenazy's performance of the *B flat Concerto* is as finely characterized as one would expect. The *Sonata* and *Rondo* were recorded earlier (in 1967); the playing is equally fine.

Piano Concertos Nos. 20, K.466; 21, K.467; 25, K.503; 27, K.595.

(B) **(*) DG Double (ADD) 453 079-2 (2). Gulda, VPO, Abbado.

Abbado had much greater luck in his Mozartian partnership with Gulda than he was to experience with Serkin a decade or so later. Gulda uses a Bösendorfer and in Nos. 20 and 21 his tone is crisp and clear with just a hint of a fortepiano about it, admirably suited to these readings, which have an element of classical restraint. In Nos. 25 and 27, however, Gulda is strangely cool, though he disciplines his responses impressively and there is no basic want of feeling or finesse, but overall there is a lack of charm. There are felicitous moments elsewhere, but the account of K.595 does not compare with the finest available, despite very good playing from the Vienna Philharmonic. The digital transfer is bright and clear, but there is also a certain shallowness of sonority.

Piano Concertos Nos. 20, K.466; 23, K.488.

(M) *** Chan. 8992. Shelley, LMP.
(B) **(*) Ph. (ADD) 422 466-2. Kovacevich, LSO, Davis.
**(*) Häns. CD 98.142. Moravec, ASMF, Marriner.

Those wanting this coupling with modern instruments will find Howard Shelley's performances immensely rewarding. Characterization is strong, yet the slow movement of K.488 is very beautiful and touching. Splendid Chandos recording.

If the coupling of the *D minor* and the *A major* from Kovacevich and Davis lacks some of the magic of their earlier pairing of the two *C major Concertos,* it is largely that the playing of the LSO is less polished. Nevertheless the minor-key seriousness of the outer movements of K.466 and the F sharp minor *Adagio* of K.488 come out superbly. The recording is full and clear in its new format, and in the bargain range this is very tempting.

Ivan Moravec gives fresh, thoughtful readings which never get in the way of Mozart, and Marriner and the Academy match him with playing of similar refinement. The *Romance* of the *D minor Concerto* and the *Adagio* of the *A major* are both on the slow side, sounding a little sluggish next to the outstanding performances of the same concertos with Howard Shelley as soloist–director, on Chandos. That also has a price advantage.

Piano Concertos Nos. 20, K.466; 24, K.491.

*** Ph. 462 622-2. Brendel, SCO, Mackerras.

(N) (M) **(*) Ph. (ADD) 464 718-2. Haskil, LOP, Markevitch.

Brendel recorded this coupling with Neville Marriner in 1974 and now, more than a quarter of a century later, he gives accounts that are hardly less thoughtful without being wanting in spontaneity and, if anything, are more searching and articulate. Moreover, in Mackerras he here has a partner who is one of the most experienced of Mozartians. This is a popular coupling: it is recorded with great realism, and can be accommodated among top recommendations.

Clara Haskil's recordings were made shortly before her death in 1960. The poise she brought to Mozart and her effortless sense of style, with no straining after effect, are still a source of wonder. Comparing these latest CD transfers with their last incarnation on LP, one finds much greater body and clarity of detail – and, of course, greater range. The image is firmly in focus and if the sound from the Lamoureux Orchestra is certainly beefier than we are used to nowadays, the solo playing remains rather special.

Piano Concertos Nos. 20, K.466; 27, K.595.

◉ (M) *** Decca (IMS) (ADD) 417 288-2. Curzon, ECO, Britten.

*** Sony (ADD) SK 42241. Perahia, ECO.

K.595, the last concerto of all, was always the Mozart work with which Curzon was specially associated, and anyone hearing this magical record, full of the glow and natural expressiveness which always went with Britten's conducting of Mozart, will recognize both performances as uniquely individual and illuminating, with Curzon at his very finest.

Perahia produces wonderfully soft colourings and a luminous texture in the *B flat Concerto*, yet at the same time he avoids underlining too strongly the valedictory sense that inevitably haunts this magical score. In the *D minor Concerto* none of the darker, disturbing undercurrents go uncharted, but at the same time we remain within the sensibility of the period. An indispensable issue, well recorded and excellently transferred. This is also available on one of Sony's Super Audio CDs (SR 42241) but you need a special player to reproduce it.

Piano Concertos Nos. 21, K.467; 22, K.482.

*** Chan. 9404. LMP, Shelley.

Howard Shelley's cycle continues to delight, and the *C major* has dignity, intelligence and poetic feeling. The *E flat* has poise and breadth, and the winds of the London Mozart Players are heard to good advantage. These performances can be confidently recommended alongside the very finest rivals.

Piano Concertos Nos. 21, K.467; 23, K.488.

(M) *** Virgin VM5 61852-2. Pommier, Sinfonia Varsovia.

(B) *** Penguin Ph. (ADD) 460 621-2. Brendel, ASMF, Marriner.

Piano Concertos Nos. 21, K.467; 23, K.488; Rondos for Piano & Orchestra Nos. 1 in D, K.382; 2 in A, K.386.

(M) *** Sony Dig./ADD SMK 64128. Perahia, ECO.

Both concertos capture Perahia's very special Mozartian sensibility and are beautifully recorded. The *C major*, K.467, is given delicacy and charm, rather than strength in the way of Brendel or Kovacevich, but the opposite is true of the exquisite slow movement (with very beautiful orchestral playing) and lively finale. The slow movement of K.488 has an elevation of spirit that reaffirms one's conviction that this is one of the classics of the gramophone. There is however a robust quality about the finale and a fresh but controlled spontaneity. The digital recording is particularly fresh and natural. This very generous collection is completed with the two *Concert Rondos*, which when recorded in 1983 incorporated for the first time on record the closing bars newly rediscovered by Professor Alan Tyson.

Both Virgin performances have plenty of sparkle in outer movements – the first movement of K.467 is particularly arresting – and both slow movements are played simply and beautifully. Jean-Bernard Pommier's *Adagio* in K.488 compares favourably with Brendel's, and the string playing at the famous opening of the *Andante* of K.467 is ravishing in its transparent delicacy and gentle warmth. The finale of the same work is brisk but never sounds rushed. The sound is first class.

Brendel's coupling has been issued as a Penguin Classic in the UK but, curiously, not in the USA. They are characteristically discerning performances, with No. 23 especially beautiful. Playing and recording are both immaculate. In K.467 Jean-Bernard Pommier is that bit more characterful. The Penguin disc comes with the usual author's essay, in this case by Tom Sharpe, who is a great admirer of Brendel as well as of Mozart. However by paying a little more, you can have additionally Brendel's fine account of No. 15, K.450 (see above).

Piano Concertos Nos. 21 in C, K.467; 24 in C min., K.491.

(N) (M) *** Regis RRC 1066. Shelley, City of L. Sinf.

Howard Shelley gives delightfully fresh and characterful readings of both the popular *C major* and the great *C minor* concertos, bringing out their strength and purposefulness as well as their poetry, never overblown or sentimental. His (originally Carlton, now Regis) disc is outstanding value, with accompaniment very well played and recorded.

Piano Concertos Nos. 21, K.467; 25, K.503.

(B) *** Ph. (ADD) 426 077-2. Kovacevich, LSO, C. Davis.

The partnership of Kovacevich and Colin Davis almost invariably produces inspired music-making. Their balancing of strength and charm, drama and tenderness, makes for performances which retain their sense of spontaneity but which plainly result from deep thought, and the weight of both these great C major works is formidably conveyed. The 1972 recording is well balanced and refined. A fine bargain.

(i) *Piano Concertos Nos. 21, K.467; 26 (Coronation), K.537;* (ii) *12 Variations on 'Ah, vous dirai-je, Maman', K.265.*

🌑 (B) *** Sony SBK 67178. (i) Casadesus, Columbia SO or Cleveland O, Szell; (ii) Previn (piano).

The ravishing slow movement of K.467 has never sounded more magical than here, and Robert Casadesus then takes the finale at a tremendous speed; but, for the most part, this is exquisite Mozart playing, beautifully paced and articulated. Casadesus's Mozart may at first seem understated, but the imagination behind his readings is apparent in every phrase.

Piano Concertos Nos. 21, K.467; 27, K.595.

*** Sony SK 46485. Perahia, COE.

Murray Perahia gives performances of characteristic understanding and finesse with the Chamber Orchestra of Europe. There are new and different insights into both works, though neither reading necessarily displaces his earlier accounts with the ECO, which may have a slight edge on the newcomer in terms of freshness and spontaneity.

(i) *Piano Concerto No. 22, K.482. Adagio & Fugue in C min., K.546;* (ii) *Sinfonia concertante, K.364.*

(M)*** BBC (ADD) BBCB 8010-2. (i) Richter; (ii) Brainin (violin), Schidlof (viola); ECO, Britten.

With Britten as partner Sviatoslav Richter gives an inspired reading of the Mozart concerto, for which Britten specially wrote new cadenzas, which are in use here. Though the sound is not so cleanly focused as in a studio recording, it is warmly atmospheric, as it is in the other two works. In the *Sinfonia concertante* Britten equally charms his two soloists from the Amadeus Quartet, making them relax in spontaneously expressive playing, with the lightness of the finale a special delight.

Piano Concertos Nos. 22, K.482; 24, K.491.

*** Sony SK 42242. Perahia, ECO.

Not only is Perahia's contribution inspired in the great *E flat Concerto*, K.482, but the wind players of the ECO are at their most eloquent in the slow movement. Moreover, the *C minor Concerto* emerges here as a truly Mozartian tragedy, rather than as foreshadowing Beethoven, which some artists give us. Both recordings are improved in focus and definition in the CD transfer.

Piano Concertos Nos. 22, K.482; 26 (Coronation), K.537.

(M) *** DG 447 283-2. Bilson (fortepiano), E. Bar. Sol., Gardiner.

The *Coronation Concerto* is presented strongly as well as elegantly, with the authentic timpani cutting dramatically through the textures in the first movement. Full and spacious recording in a helpful acoustic. The earlier concerto is hardly less vibrant and lyrically convincing, with the contrasts of the finale particularly effective.

Piano Concertos Nos. 22, K.482; 27, K.595.

(N) *** Ph.468 367-2. Brendel, SCO, Mackerras.

These are brand-new recordings made in September 2000. Brendel's playing is peerless, and the bold, big-boned orchestral tapestry against which he is admirably balanced ensures that the music-making looks forward, even while its Mozartean poise is secure. These are both concertos which were among the finest of Brendel's earlier recordings with Marriner. But many listeners will feel that these new readings have even greater breadth. His delightful performance of the finale of K.482 is wonderfully spirited and the slow movement of K.595 shows him at his most eloquent. Mackerras proves a splendid partner, vital and supportive, and the orchestral playing is consistently alive and elegant.

Piano Concertos Nos. 23, K.488; 24, K.491.

*** None. 7559 79489-2. Goode, Orpheus CO.
*** Virgin VC7 59280-2. Pletnev, Deutsche Kammerphilharmonie.
(M) **(*) Decca (ADD) 452 888-2. Curzon, LSO, Kertész.

Richard Goode gives an outstandingly fresh and satisfying account of Mozart's most lovable *A major Concerto*, the slow movement serenely beautiful and the finale delightfully vivacious. The opening tutti of K.491 is formidably strong and forward-looking, but the movement unfolds with a natural Mozartian flexibility, and Goode's playing in the *Larghetto* has a ravishing simplicity. The jaunty finale is nicely paced, and gets attractively bolder as it proceeds. Throughout both works, the ear notices the sensitive contributions of the Orpheus woodwind as well as the elegant finish and warmth of the strings. Goode uses Mozart's cadenza in K.488 and, enterprisingly, one by Paul Badura-Skoda in K.491. These recordings are being made at the Manhattan Center, and very good they are too, with a most attractive ambient bloom.

Pletnev and the Deutsche Kammerphilharmonie have obviously established a close rapport. In Pletnev's hands the slow movement of the *A major Concerto* is among the most beautiful on record, the finale the most rushed. In the *C minor Concerto* he is intensely dramatic, Beethovenian in feeling and powerful in conception: his own first-movement cadenza looks even more forward into the nineteenth century. There is nothing bland here: commanding playing from all concerned.

Curzon's account of these two concertos is immaculate and no connoisseur of the piano will fail to derive pleasure from them. Curzon has the advantage of sensitive support from Kertész and the LSO, and only an absence of the last ounce of sparkle and spontaneity prevents this from being strongly recommended.

Piano Concertos Nos. 23, K.488; 26 (Coronation), K.537.

(N) (BB) **(*) Warner Apex 8573 89091-2. Gulda, Concg. O, Harnoncourt.

Gulda discreetly participates in the orchestra ritornelli. The playing of the Concertgebouw Orchestra is careful in handling both balances and nuances, and Harnoncourt is particularly succesful in his direction of the *Coronation Concerto*. Gulda gives an admirably unaffected and intelligent account of the *A major*, which is most enjoyable – as is his reading of the *Coronation* – but it does not constitute a challenge to players such as Ashkenazy, Brendel or Perahia in K.488.

Piano Concertos Nos. 23, K.488; 27, K.595.

(M) *** Ph. (ADD) 442 391-2. Brendel, ASMF, Marriner.

These performances are included in Brendel's two Duo sets of Mozart concertos (one in each) and these represent marvellous value; the present disc remains of interest for those preferring uninterrupted performances as *Piano Concerto* No. 23 is split across the two discs in its Duo format.

Piano Concerto No. 24 in C min., K.491.

(N) (**(*) VAI mono VAIA 1192-2 (2). Tureck , Oslo PO, Güner-Hegge – BACH: *Clavier Concertos Nos. 1, 5 & 7; in D min.* **(*)

Needless to say Rosalyn Tureck's account, recorded live, is full of character, as is the accompaniment, although the actual orchestral playing could be more polished. Her style is both direct and flexible. She plays her own cadenzas and overall this is certainly an enjoyable account, the solo part beautifully articulated, if not as distinctive as her Bach. The finale is particularly strong. The mono recording is in every way excellent and well balanced too.

Piano Concertos Nos. 24, K.491; 27, K.595.

(B) *** DG 463 264-2. Anda, Salzburg Camerata Academica.

Géza Anda's Mozart is as sparkling and polished as one could wish for, and yet there is no sense that the tragic or prophetic overtones in the *C minor* are lost sight of. His account of K.595 is equally fresh, his playing deft and lively. The recordings, too, are excellent for their time, with clear sound, no lack of orchestral warmth and a natural image of the piano.

Piano Concerto No. 25, K.503.

**(*) EMI (ADD) CDC5 56974-2. Argerich, Netherlands CO, Goldberg – BEETHOVEN: *Piano Concerto No. 1.* **(*)

Martha Argerich is an inspirational pianist whose finest flights of imagination come in live performance. Like the Beethoven, recorded at the Concertgebouw fourteen years later, this 1978 live recording offers a performance of the weighty *C major Concerto* magnetic in its spontaneity. This is muscular, positive playing, which sparkles in the outer movements and finds a natural gravity in the central Andante. The recording is on the thin side, but never prevents one from enjoying a unique performance.

(i) Piano Concerto No. 25, K.503. Symphony No. 38 (Prague); (i; ii) Concert aria: Ch'io mi scordi di te.

*** MDG 340 0967-2. (i) Zacharias (piano); Lausanne CO, Zacharias; (ii) with Fink.

This is a delightful disc, offering a nicely balanced Mozart group of symphony, aria and concerto. Christian Zacharias, in consistently refreshing performances, relishes his multiple roles not just conducting a fresh and lively account of the *Prague Symphony*, but also acting as piano soloist; in the concerto, he directs the weighty K.503 from the keyboard,

and also provides a crisply pointed obbligato in the most taxing of Mozart's concert arias, *Ch'io mi scordi di te*. Bernarda Fink with her firm, creamy voice, officially a mezzo, is untroubled by the soprano tessitura, giving the most characterful interpretation, imaginatively pointing words and phrases. The sense of freedom and spontaneous enjoyment is here enhanced by the clarity of the recording, made in the Metropole, Lausanne.

Piano Concerto No. 26 (Coronation), K.537.

*** BBC (ADD) BBCL 4020-2. Curzon, BBC SO, Boulez – BEETHOVEN: *Piano Concerto No. 5 (Emperor).* ***

Curzon and Boulez in this 1974 Prom performance of the *Coronation Concerto* make rewarding partners. The combination of introspection and intellectual rigour results in an inspired reading of one of the more problematic Mozart piano concertos, fresh, bright and resilient in the outer movements with pearly passage work, and thoughtfully unmannered in the slow movement. Full-bodied sound set in the warm acoustic of the Royal Albert Hall.

Piano Concerto No. 27, K.595; (i) Double Piano Concerto, K.365.

✿ (M) *** DG (ADD) 463 652-2. Elena Gilels, VPO, Boehm, (i) E. Gilels (with SCHUBERT: *Fantasy in F min., D. 940*).

Gilels's is supremely lyrical playing that evinces all the classical virtues. No detail is allowed to detract from the picture as a whole; the pace is totally unhurried and superbly controlled. All the points are made by means of articulation and tone, and each phrase is marvellously alive, while Boehm and the Vienna Philharmonic provide excellent support. The performance of the marvellous *Double Concerto* is no less enjoyable. Its mood is comparatively serious, but this is not to suggest that the music's sunny qualities are not brought out. The quality on CD is first class, refining detail yet not losing ambient warmth. The Schubert bonus has been added for the CD's rightful re-issue as one of DG's 'Legendary Originals'.

(i; iv) Piano Concerto No. 27, K.595; (i; ii; iv) Double Piano Concerto, K.365; (i; iii) Double Piano Sonata in D, K.448.

(***) BBC (ADD) stereo/mono BBCL 4037-2. (i) Curzon; (ii) Barenboim (piano); (iii) Britten; (iv) ECO, Barenboim.

The two concertos, set in the warm Royal Albert Hall acoustic, come from a Prom concert in 1979, with Barenboim directing from the keyboard in the *Double Concerto* and conducting in Mozart's last piano concerto, K.595, Curzon's favourite. This is Mozart at his most joyous, with Curzon losing any of the inhibitions that sometimes dogged him in the studio, warmly supported by his younger colleague in both roles. Speeds in outer movements are broad enough to allow the most elegant pointing, not least in the jaunty finales. Slow movements are warmly expressive at broad speeds, concentrated and sustained. The *Duo Sonata* finds Curzon in 1960 in a partnership with Britten at Jubilee Hall, Aldeburgh, and though the mono sound is far drier, it is firm and immediate, letting one appreciate another exuberant performance, this time with the outer movements challengingly fast, and the middle movement bringing delectable interplay between the players.

(i) *Piano Concerto No. 27, K.595. Symphony No. 35 (Haffner); Overture: Marriage of Figaro.*

(B) (**) Naxos 8.110809. (i) Horszowski; NBCSO, Toscanini.

Toscanini's Mozart performances rarely have any charm. This concert, recorded in 1943, brings taut and refreshing but somewhat unyielding accounts of the symphony and the overture, but Toscanini responds much more illuminatingly to the classical poise and point of Horszowski's playing in Mozart's last *Piano Concerto*, allowing him surprising freedom. Typically dry, rough sound.

(i; ii) *Piano Concerto No. 27, K.595;* (iii) *Piano Quartet in G min., K.478;* (iv; ii) *Exsultate, jubilate, K.165.*

(M) *** BBC (ADD) BBCB 8005-2. (i) Richter; (ii) ECO, Britten; (iii) Britten, Sillito, Aronowitz, Heath; (iv) Ameling.

Elly Ameling has never sounded more sweetly radiant on disc than in this account of *Exsultate, jubilate*, technically immaculate. Britten as conductor in Richter's reading of K.595 is warmer in his Mozart style than his soloist, just as persuasive as he is in his recording with Clifford Curzon. Best of all is the *Piano Quartet*, where Britten's expressiveness even in the simplest scale passage has one magnetized, a great performance. Though the string sound in the concerto is a little thin, the other two recordings are excellent.

Double Piano Concerto in E flat, K.365.

*** Chan. 9711. G. and S. Pekinel, Philh. O, Marriner –
BRUCH: *Double Piano Concerto in A flat min.;*
MENDELSSOHN: *Double Piano Concerto in E.* ***

This unique coupling of double piano concertos, devised by the Pekinel sisters, is an inspired one, even though the Mozart is the only masterpiece among the three works. It receives a fresh, alert reading, marked by superb ensemble from the two soloists, helped by vivid Chandos sound.

Double Piano Concerto, K.365; (i) *Triple Piano Concerto, K.242;* (ii) *Piano Quartet in G min., K.478.*

(M)**(*) Sony (ADD) SMK 60598. Gold, Fizdale, NYPO, Bernstein; (i) with Bernstein also as pianist; (ii) Bernstein (piano), Juilliard Qt (members).

Bernstein's performance of the *Piano Quartet* – recorded in 1965 and sounding excellent – may not be as poised in every detail as some rival versions, but its power of communication more than makes amends. As for the *Double* and *Triple Concertos*, they are similarly relaxed and enjoyable accounts, romantic in approach, and if occasionally they miss that last ounce of sparkle, the quality of the music-making is never in doubt. The recordings, from the early 1970s, are a bit too closely miked but are acceptable.

(i) *Double Piano Concerto K.365;* (ii) *Sinfonia concertante, K.364.*

*** Chan. 9695. (i) Gimse, Anvik; (ii) Brown, Tomter; Norwegian CO, Brown.

Over the years since 1981, when she took over as music director, Iona Brown has built the Norwegian Chamber Orchestra into a superb body. It is good to welcome two brilliant young Norwegian pianists in K.365, light and agile, each articulating with refreshing clarity, relishing the antiphonal effects. In the elegant, spontaneously expressive account of the *Sinfonia concertante* the contrast between the soloists is far more extreme, when Iona Brown's clear, bright violin tone is set against the nut-brown warmth of Tomter's viola. Full, clear Chandos sound. Highly recommended.

Violin concertos

Complete Mozart Edition, Vol. 8: (i) *Violin Concertos Nos 1–5; 7 in D, K.271; Adagio in E, K.261; Rondo in B flat, K.269; Rondo in C, K.373;* (i; ii) *Concertone, K.190;* (iii; iv) *Double Concerto in D for Violin, Piano & Orchestra, K.315f;* (iii; v; vi) *Sinfonia concertante in A, for Violin, Viola, Cello & Orchestra, K.320e;* (iii; v) *Sinfonia concertante in E flat, K.364.*

(M) **(*) Ph. ADD/Dig. 422 508-2 (4). (i) Szeryng, (ii) with Poulet, Morgan, Jones; New Philh. O, Gibson. (iii) Brown, with (iv) Shelley; (v) Imai; (vi) Orton; ASMF, Marriner.

Philip Wilby has here not only completed the first movement of an early *Sinfonia concertante for Violin, Viola and Cello* (Mozart's only music with concertante cello) but also, through shrewd detective work, has reconstructed a full three-movement *Double Concerto* from what Mozart left as 'a magnificent torso', to use Alfred Einstein's description; it is for violin, piano and orchestra. The result here is a delight, a full-scale 25-minute work which ends with an effervescent double-variation finale, alternately in duple and compound time. That is superbly done with Iona Brown and Howard Shelley as soloists; and the other ASMF items are very good too, with Iona Brown joined by Nobuko Imai most characterfully on the viola in the great *Sinfonia concertante, K.364*. What is a shade disappointing is to have Henryk Szeryng's readings of the main violin concertos from the 1960s instead of the Grumiaux set. Szeryng is sympathetic but a trifle reserved and not as refreshing as Grumiaux.

Violin Concertos Nos. 1–5; Adagio in E, K.261; Rondo in C, K.373; Rondo Concertante in B flat, K.269.

(B) *** O-L Double 455 721-2 (2). Standage, AAM, Hogwood.
(N) (M) *** Virgin VM5 61841-2 (Nos. 1, 3 & 5); VM5 61842-2 (Nos. 2 & 4; *Adagio Rondos*). Tetzlaff, Deutsche Kammerphilharmonie.
(B) **(*) EMI double fforte CZS5 69355-2 (2). Zimmermann, Württemberg CO, Faerber.
(M) **(*) DG 445 535-2 (2). Perlman, VPO, Levine.
(BB) **(*) RCA Navigator (ADD) 74321 21277-2 (*Nos. 1–3 & Rondo, K.373*); 74321 21278-2 (*Nos. 4–5; Adagio, K.261 & Rondo K.269*). Suk, Prague CO, Hlaváček.

Violin Concertos Nos. 1–5; Adagio, K.261; Rondo, K.373; Rondo concertante, K.269.

(N) (BB) **(*) EMI Encore (ADD) CDE5 74743-2 (*Nos. 1–3; Rondo*); CDE5 74744-2 (*Nos. 4–5; Adagio; Rondo concertante*). D. Oistrakh, BPO.

Violin Concertos Nos. 1–5; Adagio in E, K.261; Rondo in C, K.373.

(B) **(*) Sony (ADD) SBK 46539/40. Zukerman, St Paul CO.

Violin Concertos Nos. (i) 1; (ii) 2; (iii) 3; (ii) 4; (i) 5 (Turkish); (ii) Adagio in E, K.261; Rondo in C, K.373. (iv) Concertone for 2 Violins & Orchestra in C, K.190; Sinfonia concertante, K.364.

(M) **(*) Sony (ADD) SM3K 66475 (3). Stern, with
(i) Columbia SO, Szell; (ii) ECO, Schneider; (iii) Cleveland O, Szell; (iv) Zukerman, ECO, Barenboim.

(i) Violin Concertos Nos. 1–5; (ii) Adagio in E, K.261; Rondo in C, K.373; (i; iii) Sinfonia concertante, K.364.

(B) *** Ph. (ADD) Duo 438 323-2 (2). Grumiaux, (i) LSO, C. Davis; (ii) New Philh. O, Leppard; (iii) with Pellicia.

Violin Concertos Nos. 1–5; Adagio in E, K.261; Rondo Concertante in B flat, K.269.

(BB) *** Virgin 2 x 1 Double VBD5 61576-2 (2). Huggett, OAE.

(i) Violin Concertos Nos. 1–5; (ii) Violin Sonatas Nos. 32 in B flat, K.454; 34 in A, K.526.

(N) (M) *** Ph. (ADD) stereo/mono. Grumiaux, (i) LSO, C. Davis; (ii) Haskil.

Violin Concertos Nos. 1–5; (i) Sinfonia concertante, K.364.

(BB) **(*) EMI Seraphim (ADD) CES5 68530-2 (2). Menuhin, Bath Festival O; (i) with Barshai.

Violin Concertos Nos. 1–5; Serenade in D (Haffner): Andante, Minuet & Rondo, K.250.

(BB) **(*) Arte Nova 74321 72104-2 (2). Frank, Zurich Tonhalle O, Zinman.

Grumiaux's accounts of the Mozart *Violin Concertos* come from the early 1960s and are among the most beautifully played in the catalogue at any price. The orchestral accompaniments have sparkle and vitality, and Grumiaux's contribution has splendid poise and purity of tone. For this generous reissue on their bargain Duo label, Philips have added the *Adagio*, K.261, and *Rondo*, K.373, recorded later in 1967, and also a fine performance of the great *Sinfonia concertante*, K.364, with Arrigo Pellicia proving a sensitive partner for Grumiaux, especially in the *Andante*. The new CD transfers are brightly lit but still faithful. Grumiaux's set comes alternatively with two late violin sonatas where he is admirably partnered by Clara Haskil. This was a celebrated partnership and these classic vintage accounts are of the highest calibre. The recordings from the late 1950s are mono, and although the sound is remarkably vivid and true, this is not made clear on the packaging. Nevertheless these are treasurable performances.

Anyone seeking period-instrument performances of Mozart's concertante music for violin and orchestra need look no further than Standage's superb Oiseau-Lyre set, which, for stylishness and spontaneity, can be ranked alongside the finest versions on modern instruments. Standage's beautifully focused, silvery tone is a constant joy. Hogwood's accompaniments are beautifully sprung, with no lack of warmth, the orchestral violins articulating neatly and gracefully to match the soloist, and the transparent textures revealing every detail of the orchestral scoring. The shorter

pieces are also given fine performances and are never just treated as encores. The 1990 Abbey Road recording is first rate throughout, beautifully balanced and with not a trace of edginess anywhere.

Monica Huggett provides an admirable alternative. She directs from the bow and she is a superb soloist: spontaneous, vital, warm and elegant. She plays her own cadenzas, and very good they are too. Orchestral textures are fresh and transparent, ensemble is excellent, and the solo playing is without even a drop of vinegar; indeed, the violin timbre, if not opulent, is firm, well focused and sparkling. The Virgin Double omits the *Rondo in C*, but costs somewhat less than its Oiseau-Lyre competitor.

It goes without saying that Stern's solo playing is always splendid; but he is not always as sensitive to detail as his rivals, and this especially applies to No. 1 and rather less so to No. 5 where the accompaniment is provided by the Columbia Symphony Orchestra under Szell. The great *Sinfonia concertante* stands among the finest available and is certainly the jewel in this set, presenting as it does two soloists of equally strong musical personality, and listening to the solo concertos again, so impressively remastered, is to relish the sheer beauty of Stern's tone and phrasing. The *Concertone* is attractive, but here the dryness of the acoustic rather detracts from the charm of a work which on any count goes on too long for its material. Stern, Zukerman and Barenboim pay the central *Andantino grazioso* the compliment of a really slow tempo, and though this makes a very long movement the concentration is superb. Whatever the shortcomings of the recording, the artistry of the soloists shines out through every bar.

Christian Tetzlaff is a first-class player and an equally first-class Mozartian. He plays all five concertos with great freshness and he simultaneously directs the Deutsche Kammerphilharmonie in polished and sympathetic accompaniments. His pacing of allegros is brisk, but exhilaratingly so, and his expressive phrasing in slow movements matches the clean, positive style of his contribution to faster movements. However, for a somewhat lower cost on a Philips Duo one can get Grumiaux, who is unsurpassed; and that set includes also the *Sinfonia concertante in E flat*.

Zukerman's set has the advantage of excellent digital recording and a good balance, the violin forward but not distractingly so. The playing of outer movements is agreeably simple and fresh, and in slow movements Zukerman's sweetness of tone will appeal to many, although his tendency to languish a little in his expressiveness, particularly in the *G major*, K.216, rather less so in the *A major*, K.219, may be counted a less attractive feature, and he is not always subtle in his expression of feeling. Nevertheless this is still enjoyably spontaneous and his admirers will certainly not be disappointed with K.219.

Frank Peter Zimmermann is also most impressive. His interpretations do not quite match those of Grumiaux (with whom, at the price, he comes into direct competition), Stern or Perlman; but they are distinguished by fine musicianship and an effortless technical command. Zimmermann uses cadenzas by Zukerman and Oistrakh in No. 2 and Joachim in No. 4. The digital recordings have agreeable warmth and freshness and are very well balanced. Jörg Faerber is an excellent partner and gets extremely alive playing from the Württemberg orchestra. Not a first recommendation then, but certainly worth considering,

Perlman gives characteristically assured, virtuoso readings with Levine, a fresh and undistracting Mozartian. The virtuoso approach sometimes involves a tendency to hurry, and the power is emphasized by the weight and immediacy of the recording. Warmth is here rather than charm; but Perlman's individual magic makes for magnetic results all through, not least in the intimate intensity of slow movements. Those of the first two concertos are particularly graceful, but at times (and notably in the two most popular concertos, Nos. 3 and 5) he treats the works rather more as bravura showpieces than is common. However, Perlman's virtuosity is effortless and charismatic, and the orchestral playing is first class. The DG recording is well balanced, with the soloist close but not too excessively so, and the perspective is on the whole well judged.

Josef Suk's recordings date from 1972. The solo playing has character, warmth and humanity, and its unaffected manner is especially suited to the first two concertos. The last three concertos have an agreeable simplicity and a freedom from histrionic gestures that is most welcome, and the recording, though not as vividly detailed as the DG, is agreeably smooth and natural. Hlaváček does not always make enough of the dynamic contrasts and, throughout, the music-making is dominated by Suk. This is partly a matter of the recording balance. But with any reservations noted, these are delightful performances and very good value.

Menuhin's recordings date from the early 1960s, a fruitful period for this fine artist, when he was closely associated with the Bath Festival. Most violinists use cadenzas by Joachim, but in all but No. 3 (where he chooses those by Franco) Menuhin uses cadenzas of his own, and many may feel that they are not Mozartian. Otherwise the style is sensibly exploited, and these performances give an engaging sense of musicians making intimate music together for the joy of it. One is always conscious that this is the phrasing of a master musician who can also provide the lightest touch in finales, which are alert and extrovert. In the *Sinfonia concertante* Menuhin and Barshai make a splendid team with happily similar views. Throughout, the stereo has a bright sheen and, with the remastering, the orchestral violins are made to sound glassy above the stave, but the ear adjusts when the music-making is so distinctive and the acoustic is basically warm.

David Oistrakh proves predictably strong and positive as a Mozartean, and he is well accompanied by the Berlin Philharmonic. But there are too many touches of unwanted heaviness to make this an ideal cycle. Needless to say, the performances have their fine moments. The slow movements of the *G major* and *D major* (Nos. 3 and 4) are memorably expressive, and the *Rondo concertante* is played with real sparkle. The recordings are consistently lively, with the soloist balanced well forward. Good value at Encore price.

The young American violinist Pamela Frank is a strong, imaginative artist, very well matched here by the Tonhalle Orchestra under David Zinman, who shows himself just as inspired an interpreter of Mozart as he is of Beethoven.

Outer movements are fresh and bright at speeds on the urgent side, while slow movements are spaciously expressive without sentimentality. As a super-bargain purchase, the two discs can be recommended, even if Frank's tone and the coloration she gives to the upper register are not ideally sweet and pure. First-rate sound. The three concertante movements from the *Haffner Serenade* provide an original and apt makeweight.

Violin Concertos Nos. 1; 2; Rondo in B flat, K.269; Andante in F (arr. Saint-Saëns from Piano Concerto No. 21, K.467).

(BB) **(*) Naxos 8.550414. Nishizaki, Capella Istropolitana, Wildner.

This was the last disc to be recorded of Takako Nishizaki's fine survey of the violin concertos. The opening movement of K.207 is brisk and fresh, although this is the least individual of Nishizaki's readings. The *Second Concerto*, K.211, has rather more flair, the *Andante* touchingly phrased, and the finale has a winning lightness of touch. The *Rondo* is also an attractively spontaneous performance, and as an encore we get Saint-Saëns's arrangement of the famous 'Elvira Madigan' theme from the *C major Concerto*, K.467.

(i) Violin Concertos Nos. 2; 4; (ii) Divertimento for Strings No. 1, K.136.

(B) *** [EMI Red Line CDR5 69865]. (i) Mutter, Philh. O; (ii) BPO; Muti.

Anne-Sophie Mutter is given very sensitive support from the Philharmonia under Muti. Her playing combines purity and classical feeling, delicacy and incisiveness, and is admirably expressive. Its freshness is also most appealing. The early digital recording is very good, the images sharply defined, but the balance satisfactory. The finest of Mozart's three string divertimenti makes a good bonus.

Violin Concerto No. 3.

(B) *** EMI double fforte (ADD) CZS5 69331-2 (2). Oistrakh, Philh. O – BEETHOVEN: *Triple Concerto;* BRAHMS: *Double Concerto;* PROKOFIEV: *Violin Concerto No. 2.* ***

*** EMI CDC5 55426-2. Zimmermann, BPO, Sawallisch – BRAHMS: *Violin Concerto.* **(*)

David Oistrakh's supple, richly toned yet essentially classical style suits the melodic line of this youthful work and gives it the stature of maturity. The orchestral contribution is directed by the soloist himself and is eminently polished. EMI provide admirably smooth yet vivid sound, and this is just one of four marvellous performances which make up this superb double forte compilation.

With the string complement of the Berlin Philharmonic aptly reduced, and with Sawallisch at his most sparkling, Zimmermann's studio recording of Mozart's *G major Concerto* is a delight, with a quicksilver lightness in the outer movements, very different from the traditional big bow-wow approach, and a compelling repose and concentration in the central *Adagio*. However, this coupling has just been deleted.

(i) Violin Concertos Nos. 3–4; (ii) Duo for Violin & Viola in G, K.423.

(M) **(*) DG 439 525-2. Kremer; (i) VPO, Harnoncourt;
   (ii) Kashkashian.

Harnoncourt is nothing if not eccentric. In the *G major*, K.216, the first movement flows at just the right pace, and then in the *Andante* a comma is placed to romanticize the climbing opening phrase of the main theme slightly. But with Kremer playing sweetly throughout, such individual touches may be found acceptable when there is plenty of vitality and Harnoncourt's tuttis are always strong. The *Duo* (quite substantial at 17 minutes) makes an interesting bonus, with skilful playing and a good balance between Kremer and Kashkashian. But there is more to this music than these players find.

(i) Violin Concertos Nos. 3–4; Serenade: Eine kleine Nachtmusik, K.525.

(M) **(*) Sony (ADD) stereo/mono SMK 64468.
   (i) Francescatti; Columbia SO, Walter.

Francescatti's coupling of the *Third* and *Fourth* Mozart *Concertos* is probably his best record. The playing is at times a little wayward, but Bruno Walter accompanies throughout with his usual warmth and insight and falls into line sympathetically with his soloist. Both slow movements are beautifully played, albeit with an intensity that barely stops short of romanticism. The whole atmosphere of this music-making represents the pre-authentic approach to Mozart at its most rewarding. The 1954 New York recording of the *Night Music* is no great bonus: the sound is harsh and ill-focused.

Violin Concertos Nos. 3–5.

(B) **(*) DG (ADD) 449 850-2. Schneiderhan, BPO.

Wolfgang Schneiderhan plays with effortless mastery and a strong sense of classical proportion. The Berlin orchestra plays well for him, although there is a slightly unsmiling quality at times. The *A major Concerto* was perhaps the finest of the set and makes a suitable coupling for his famous record of the Beethoven, made six years earlier (see below). The sound is realistically balanced.

Violin Concertos Nos. 3; 5 (Turkish).

(M) DG (ADD) 457 746-2. Mutter, BPO, Karajan.
(BB) *** Naxos 8.550063. Nishizaki, Capella Istropolitana,
   Gunzenhauser.

Extraordinarily mature and accomplished playing from Anne-Sophie Mutter, who was a mere fourteen years old when her recording was made. The instinctive mastery means that there is no hint of immaturity: the playing has polish, but fine artistry too and remarkable freshness. Karajan is at his most sympathetic and scales down the accompaniment to act as a perfect setting for his young soloist. The recording has been brilliantly transferred to CD, though some might feel that the orchestral strings are a shade too brightly lit.

This is the finest of Nishizaki's three discs of the Mozart violin concertos on Naxos. The readings are individual and possess the most engaging lyrical feeling and the natural response of the soloist to Mozartian line and phrase. A good

balance, the soloist forward, but convincingly so, and the orchestral backcloth in natural perspective. A real bargain.

Violin Concerto No. 4.

(M) (***) DG mono 457 720-2. Schneiderhan, BPO, Rosbaud
   – HAYDN: *Symphonies Nos. 92 & 104.* (***)

Wolfgang Schneiderhan plays very beautifully indeed, and there may be more points of detail in the orchestra which Rosbaud presents to the listener rather more clearly than in Schneiderhan's later, stereo version, where he directed the Berlin Philharmonic himself. Neverthless the (well-balanced) 1956 mono recording is marginally less flattering to his timbre than the stereo.

Violin Concerto No. 4; (i) Sinfonia concertante, K.364.

(BB) **(*) Naxos 8.550332. Nishizaki, (i) Kyselak; Capella
   Istropolitana, Gunzenhauser.

A fine account of No. 4, with Takako Nishizaki's solo playing well up to the high standard of this series and with Stephen Gunzenhauser's perceptive pacing adding to our pleasure. The *Sinfonia concertante* is very enjoyable too, if perhaps slightly less distinctive. The finale is infectious in its liveliness, its rhythms buoyantly pointed. Again, a good balance and excellent sound.

Violin Concertos Nos. 4, K.218; 5 (Turkish) K.219.

(N) (B) *** Nimbus NI 1735 (3). Shumsky, SCO, Tortelier –
   BACH: *Concertos;* YSAYE: *Sonatas.* ***
(N) (BB) (**(*)) Naxos mono 8.110941. Heifetz, (i) RPO,
   Beecham; (ii) LPO, Barbirolli – MENDELSSOHN: *Violin Concerto in E min.* (**(*))

Violin Concertos Nos. 4; 5 (Turkish); Adagio, K.261; Rondo concertante K.269.

(N) (B) **(*) EMI (ADD) Encore CDE5 74743-2. D. Oistrakh,
   BPO.

Shumsky's performances are of the highest calibre. They are totally unaffected, spontaneous, and full of character. He has an excellent rapport with Jan Pascal Tortelier, who secures a warm, very alive and musical response from the Scottish Chamber Orchestra, with the players themselves conveying enthusiasm and pleasure. The recording is natural and nicely balanced. This now comes as part of a memorial box to profile the three major recordings which Shumsky made for Nimbus before he died in 2000. It is inexpensive and with good documentation; it is well worth acquiring.

David Oistrakh's performances come from his complete set, recorded in 1970/71. The slow movement of K.219 is particularly fine, and so too is the finale. The two shorter concertante works also show the soloist at his finest; though the accompaniment for the *Adagio*, K.261, remains richly upholstered, this is played very beautifully.

It was not until February 1934 when he was already long established as the world's leading violin virtuoso, that Heifetz came to London to make his first concerto recording. The choice of the Mozart *A major* may seem surprising, but the flair and elegance of the playing, as well as the hushed purity of the slow movement reflect the violinist's devotion to the work, well matched by Barbirolli's beautifully sprung accompaniments with the recently founded LPO. The reading of the *D major Concerto*, recorded in 1947, has similar qualities, with Beecham's accompaniments intensifying the elegance. Well coupled with the Heifetz–Beecham Mendelssohn concerto. Good transfers, if with surface hiss at times intrusive.

Violin Concerto No. 5 (Turkish).

(M) *** DG (ADD) 447 403-2. Schneiderhan, BPO, Jochum – BEETHOVEN: *Violin Concerto.* *** ✿

(M) (***) EMI mono CDH5 65191-2. Heifetz, LPO, Barbirolli – MENDELSSOHN: *Concerto* (**(*)); VIEUXTEMPS: *Concerto No. 5.* (***)

This was perhaps the finest of the complete set of Mozart's violin concertos which Schneiderhan recorded with the Berlin Philharmonic in the late 1960s. The recording is realistically balanced, and this makes a generous coupling for his famous record of the Beethoven, made six years earlier.

Heifetz's EMI recording first appeared in 1934 and it is evident that there was a good rapport between him and the young John Barbirolli, whom Fred Gaisberg had chosen as partner. The playing has a commendable warmth and spontaneity which is less striking in the Mendelssohn coupling, where Beecham is at the helm.

(i) *Concertone in C, K.190;* (ii) *Sinfonia concertante, K.364.*

✿ *** DG (ADD) 415 486-2. Perlman, Zukerman, Israel PO, Mehta.

The DG version of the *Sinfonia concertante* is in a special class and is an example of 'live' recording at its most magnetic, with the inspiration of the occasion caught on the wing. Zubin Mehta is drawn into the music-making and accompanies most sensitively. The *Concertone* is also splendidly done; the ear notices the improvement in the sound-balance of the studio recording of this work. But the *Sinfonia concertante*, with the audience incredibly quiet, conveys an electricity rarely caught on record.

(i; ii) *Concertone in C, K.190; Sinfonia concertante, K.364;* (i) *Rondo in C, K.373.*

*** Virgin VC 545290-2. (i) Huggett; (ii) Beznosiuk; Portland Bar. O, Huggett.

Recordings of the great *Sinfonia concertante*, K.364, using period instruments, are surprisingly rare, and this warmly expressive one is welcome for being ideally coupled with the early *Concertone* as well as the *C major Rondo*. The Portland Baroque Orchestra offers sympathetic support for two soloists well known in Europe. Playing with period purity that avoids astringency, the style both of Monica Huggett (also the director) and of Pavlo Beznosiuk (on both viola and violin) is free rather than strictly controlled, with ensemble less crisp than in the earlier period performance on Cala. The outer movements of the *Concertone*, less complex, work extremely well – fresh and alert – and so does the *Rondo in C*. A welcome issue, when direct rivalry is limited.

Dances and marches

Contredanses: La Bataille, K.535; Das Donnerwetter, K.534; Les Filles malicieuses, K.610; Der Sieg vom Helden Koburg, K.587; Il trionfo delle donne, K.607. Gallimathias musicum (quodlibet), K.32; 6 German Dances, K.567; 3 German Dances, K.605; German Dance: Die Leyerer, K.611. March in D, K.335/1. A Musical Joke, K.522.

*** DG (IMS) 429 783-2. Orpheus CO.

A splendid sampler of the wit and finesse, to say nothing of the high quality of entertainment, provided by Mozart's dance music, which kept people on their feet till dawn at masked balls in the 1780s and early 1790s. The playing of the Orpheus group is winningly polished, flexible and smiling, and they bring off the *Musical Joke* with considerable flair, both in the gentle fun of the *Adagio cantabile*, which is exquisitely played, and in the outrageous grinding dissonance of the 'wrong notes' at the end. First-class sound, fresh, transparent and vividly immediate.

Complete Mozart Edition, Vol. 6: *La Chasse, KA.103/ K.299d; Contredanses, K.101; K.123; K.267; K.269b; K.462; (Das Donnerwetter) K.534; (La Bataille) K.535; 535a; (Der Sieg vom Helden Koburg) K.587; K.603; (Il trionfo delle donne) K.607; (Non più andrai) K.609; K.610; Gavotte, K.300; German Dances, K.509; K.536; K.567; K.571; K.586; K.600; K.602; K.605; Ländler, K.606; Marches, K.214; K.363; K.408; K.461; Minuets, K.61b; K.61g/2; K.61h; K.94, 103, 104, 105; K.122; K.164; K.176; K.315g; K.568; K.585; K.599; K.601; K.604; Minuets with Contredanses, K.463; Overture & 3 Contredanses, K.106.*

✿ (M) *** Ph. (ADD) 422 506-2 (6). V. Mozart Ens., Boskovsky.

Much of the credit for this remarkable undertaking should go to its expert producer, Erik Smith, who, besides providing highly stylish orchestrations for numbers without Mozart's own scoring, illuminates the music with some of the most informative and economically written notes that ever graced a record. The CD transfers preserve the excellence of the mid-1960s sound. The collector might feel that he or she is faced here with an *embarras de richesses* with more than 120 Minuets, nearly 50 German Dances and some three dozen Contredanses, but Mozart's invention is seemingly inexhaustible, and the instrumentation is full of imaginative touches.

12 German Dances, K.586; 6 German Dances, K.600; 4 German Dances, K.602; 3 German Dances, K.605.

(BB) *** Naxos 8.550412. Capella Istropolitana, Wildner.

Fresh, bright, unmannered performances of some of the dance music Mozart wrote right at the end of his life. The playing is excellent and the recording is bright and full. An excellent super-bargain.

Complete Mozart Edition, Vol. 45: *'Rarities and Curiosities': Contredanses in B flat & D* (completed Smith); *The London Sketchbook:* (i) *3 Contredanses in F; 2 Contredanses in G; 6 Divertimenti.* (ii) *Wind Divertimenti* arr. from operas: *Don Giovanni* (arr. Triebensee); *Die Entführung aus dem Serail* (arr. Wendt) & (i) *March, K.384.* (i; iii) *Rondo in E flat for Horn & Orchestra, K.371* (completed Smith); (iv) *Larghetto for Piano & Wind Quintet, K.452a;* (v) *Modulating Prelude in F/E min.* (vi) *Tantum ergo in B flat, K.142; in D, K.197;* (vii) *Idomeneo: Scene & Rondo.* (viii) *Musical Dice Game, K.516.*

(M) *** Ph. (ADD) 422 545-2 (3). (i) ASMF, Marriner;
(ii) Netherlands Wind Ens.; (iii) Brown; cond. Sillito;
(iv) Uchida, Black, King, Farrell, O'Neil; (v) Smith
(harpsichord); (vi) Frimmer, Leipzig R. Ch. & SO, Schreier;
(vii) Mentzler, Hendricks, Bav. RSO, Davis; (viii) Marriner & Smith.

Complete Mozart Bargain Edition, Vol. 17: *'Rarities & Surprises': Theatre Music:* Ballet music: *Idomeneo; Les Petits Riens;* Incidental music: *Thamos, King of Egypt.* Music for *Pantalon and Columbine; Sketches for a Ballet Intermezzo.*

(N) (B) *** Ph. (ADD) 464 940-2 (5). Artists as above and below.

The first CD includes the innocent little piano pieces from the child Mozart's *London Notebook.* Erik Smith has orchestrated them and, if the results may not be important, they charm the ear at least as much as Mozart's early symphonies, with many unexpected touches. Marriner and the Academy are ideal performers and the 1971 recording is warm and refined. Then come the arrangements for wind of selections from two key operas, elegantly played by the Netherlands Wind Ensemble. Finally come the rarities and curiosities, the *Rondo for Horn and Orchestra* with the missing 60 bars (discovered only in 1989) now added, and the other music made good by Erik Smith. There is a curious finale in which Erik Smith and Sir Neville Marriner participate (with spoken comments) in a *Musical Dice Game* to decide the order of interchangeable phrases in a very simple musical composition. The result, alas, is something of a damp squib. The theatre music is discussed below.

Divertimenti and serenades

Complete Mozart Edition, Vol. 4: *Divertimenti for Strings Nos. 1–3, K.136/8; Divertimenti for Small Orchestra Nos. 1 in E flat, K.113; 7 in D, K.205 (with March in D, K.290); 10 in F, K.247 (with March in F, K.248); 11 in D, K.251; 15 in B flat, K.287; 17 in D, K.334 (with March in D, K.445); A Musical Joke, K.622; Serenade (Eine kleine Nachtmusik), K.525.*

(M) *** Ph. 422 504-2 (5). ASMF CO.

This is one of the most attractive of all the boxes in the Philips Mozart Edition. The music itself is a delight, the performances are stylish, elegant and polished, while the digital recording has admirable warmth and realistic presence and definition.

Complete Mozart Bargain Edition, Vol. 3: (i) *Divertimenti for Strings & Wind;* (ii) *Serenades & Divertimenti for Wind.*

(N) (B) *** Ph. 464 790-2 (11). (i) ASMF, Marriner;
(ii) Hollinger Wind Ens.; NWE, De Waart; ASMF, Marriner or Laird.

Divertimenti for Strings Nos. 1–3, K.136–8; Serenades Nos. 6 in D (Serenata notturna), K.239; 13 in G (Eine kleine Nachtmusik), K.525.

(M) **(*) Classic fM 75605 57024-2. City of L. Sinfonia, Watkinson.

These are delightful performances from the City of London Sinfonia: fresh, warm and polished. *Eine kleine Nachtmusik* is elegant, graceful and nicely paced, and the same can be said of the three engaging *String Divertimenti.* The *Serenata notturna* features the leaders of each section (two violins, viola and double-bass) as a solo concertino group, and with the timpani not over-dominant. The resonance of the recording is rather excessive but if you don't mind that, this Classic fM programme is very recommendable.

Divertimenti Nos. 2 in D, K.131; 15 in B flat, K.287.

(BB)*** Naxos 8.550996. Capella Istropolitana, Nerat.

The playing of the Capella Istropolitana under Harald Nerat is beautifully turned and polished. They phrase elegantly; the sound is full and transparent, bringing the sweetest modern violin timbre, yet the effect is as refreshing as any period performance. The *D major Divertimento* is charmingly scored for flute, oboe, bassoon, four horns and strings, but it has a gracious second-movement *Adagio* cantilena of disarming simplicity for strings alone. The *B flat Divertimento* was written five years later, in Salzburg, and is scored more simply for two horns and strings.

Divertimenti Nos. 10 in F, K.247; 11 in D, K.331.

**(*) Cap. 10 203. Salzburg Mozarteum Camerata Academica, Végh.

The playing has striking freshness and vitality; these are chamber orchestral performances on modern instruments, but the scale is admirable and the resonance adds a feeling of breadth. Although slow movements tend to be on the slow side, while not lacking grace, allegros sparkle and have dash without ever seeming hurried, even if ensemble isn't always absolutely immaculate.

Wind divertimenti and serenades

Adagios: in F, K.410; in B flat, K.411; Divertimenti for Wind Nos. 3 in E flat, K.166; 4 in B flat, K.186; 8 in F, K.213; 9 in B flat, K.240; 12 in E flat, K.252; 13 in F, K.253; 14 in B flat, K.270; 16 in E flat, K.289; in E flat, K.Anh. 226; in B flat, K.Anh. 227. Serenades Nos. 10 in B flat, for 13 Wind Instruments, K.361; 11 in E flat, K.375; 12 in C min., K.488.

(B) **(*) Decca (ADD) 455 794-2 (3). L. Wind Soloists, Brymer.

Complete Mozart Edition, Vol. 5: *Divertimentos for Wind Nos. 3, K.166; 4, K.186; 6 , K.188; 8, K.213; 9, K.240; 12, K.252; 13, K.253; 14, K.270; 16, K.289; K.Anh. 226; K.Anh. 227; Divertimentos for 3 Basset Horns, K.439b/1–5; Duos for 2 Horns, K.487/1–12; Serenades for Wind Nos. 10 in*

B flat, K.361; 11 in E flat, K.375; 12 in C min., K.388; Adagios: in F; B flat, K.410–11.

(M) *** Ph. ADD/Dig. 422 505-2 (6). Holliger Wind Ens. (or members of); Netherlands Wind Ens., De Waart (or members of); ASMF, Marriner or Laird.

Divertimenti for Wind Nos. 3, K.166; 4, K.186; 8, K.213; 9, K.240; 12, K.252; 13, K.253; 14, K.270; Serenades Nos. 10, K.361; 11, K.375; 12, K.388.

(M) *** Audivis E 8627. Zefiro Ens.

Mozart's wind music, whether in the ambitious *Serenades* or the simpler *Divertimenti*, brings a naturally felicitous blending of timbre and colour unmatched by any other composer. It seems that even when writing for the simplest combination of wind instruments, Mozart is incapable of being dull. The playing on Philips of the more ambitious works is admirably polished and fresh, and it is interesting to note that Holliger's group provides a stylishly light touch and texture with the principal oboe dominating, while the blending of the Netherlanders is somewhat more homogeneous, though the effect is still very pleasing.

The Decca coverage is remarkably comprehensive and the playing here of the highest order, and the only drawback is the too-close balance for the large-scale *B flat major Serenade*. In this work the effect is rather dry; the digital remastering has taken much of the ambient bloom from the sound. However, Brymer's group gives a strong, stylish performance with plenty of imagination in matters of phrasing. Elsewhere there is presence and bloom in equal measure. There are countless felicities: all the finales have a wonderfully light touch, but one remembers especially the engaging three-movement *Divertimento in F*, K.253, with its charming first-movement theme and variations and its slow Minuet with its playful Trio.

Astrée Audivis offer a digital set at mid-price (three records for the cost of two), offering the same three major *Serenades* as Jack Brymer, plus seven of the *Divertimenti*, played on period instruments by a highly sensitive Italian group. The performances are very recommendable on all counts. The sounds of the period instruments are delightfully fresh and the blending of timbres most felicitous. The playing itself brings a characteristic Italianate sunny quality to Mozart yet is remarkably subtle in detail. The *Gran Partita* is particularly seductive, with only one tiny flaw. At the opening of its eloquent *Adagio* the initial oboe entry begins a little below the note: some ears might find this disturbing on repetition. Otherwise intonation is impeccable and the brilliant playing on natural horns by Raul Diaz and Dileno Baldin is most infectious. In the *C minor Serenade* with its darker sonorities, the Italians miss the sombre touch which the English players manage so adroitly, but overall the Zefiro group play with such glowing finesse and spontaneity that this Audivis set must marginally take pride of place.

Complete Mozart Edition, Vol. 25: (i) *Idomeneo* (ballet music), K.367; (ii) *Les Petits Riens* (ballet), K.299b; *Music for a Pantomime (Pantalon und Colombine)*, K.446 (completed and orch. Beyer); *Sketches for a Ballet Intermezzo*, K.299c (completed and orch. Erik Smith); (iii) *Thamos, King of Egypt* (incidental music), K.345.

(M) *** Ph. (ADD) 422 525-2 (2). (i) Netherlands CO, Zinman; (ii) ASMF, Marriner; (iii) Eickstädt, Pohl, Büchner, Polster, Adam, Berlin R. Ch. & State O, Klee.

Zinman and his Netherlanders give a neatly turned account of the ballet from *Idomeneo*, musical and spirited. Marriner takes over with modern digital sound for *Les Petits Riens* and the two novelties, and the ASMF playing has characteristic elegance and finesse. The *Sketches for a Ballet Intermezzo* survive only in a single-line autograph, but Erik Smith's completion and scoring provide a series of eight charming vignettes, most with descriptive titles, ending with a piquant *Tambourin*. The music for *Pantalon und Columbine* (more mime than ballet) survives in the form of a first violin part, and Franz Beyer has skilfully orchestrated it for wind and strings, using the first movement of the *Symphony*, K.84, as the overture and the last movement of *Symphony*, K.120, as the finale. Beautifully played as it is here, full of grace and colour, this a real find and the digital recording is first rate. *Thamos, King of Egypt* is marvellous music which it is good to have on record, particularly in such persuasive hands as these. The choral singing is impressive and the orchestral playing is excellent.

Masonic Funeral Music: see below, in VOCAL MUSIC, under Complete Mozart Edition, Vol. 22

A Musical Joke, K.522.

*** Erato 2292 45199-2. Paillard CO, Paillard – L. MOZART: *Cassation* etc. ***

Happily paired with a high-spirited version of Leopold Mozart's *Toy Symphony*, Paillard's account of Mozart's fun piece makes the most of its outrageous jokes, with the horns in the opening movement boldly going wrong and the final discordant clash sounding positively cataclysmic; yet it takes into account the musical values, too.

Notturno in D for 4 Orchestras, K.286; Serenade No. 6 (Serenata notturna), K.239; Symphony No. 32, K.318; Lucio Silla (Overture), K.135; Thamos, King of Egypt: 4 Interludes (Nos. 2–5), K.345; 6 German Dances, K.600/1, 2 & 5 (Der Kanarienvogel); K.602/3 (Der Leiermann); K.605/2 & 3 (Sleigh Ride).

(M) *** Decca (ADD) 466 500-2. LSO, Maag.

These performances are first class, stylish, full of vitality and grace, the *Serenata notturna* made the more elegantly attractive by a not too insistent contribution from the timpani. The *Notturno* is an ingenious Mozartian gimmick piece. It opens graciously (rather like Gluck) and is made interesting by a combination of left–right with forward–backward placements, to suggest the composer's four instrumental groups echoing each other. The rest of the programme is far finer music, with the *G major Symphony* given a fizzing performance with a quite lovely central *Andante*. The *Lucio Silla Overture* and *Thamos* incidental music are delightful and again played with the crisply pointed style at which this conductor is so adept. The *German Dances* have been added for the present reissue. They are played with enormous vigour, though some may feel that the uninhibited use of such a large orchestra is inappropriate for such simple material. However, the canary effect in K.600/5 is neatly done, and Maag similarly scales down for the gentle entry of the hurdy-gurdy in K.602/3. The *Sleigh Ride* swings along, urged on by a superb posthorn solo. The transfers of these vintage 1959 recordings (made in Kingsway Hall or Walthamstow) are most adept: the sound is remarkably full and natural and undated. Excellent documentation and session photographs.

Overtures: *Apollo et Hyacinthus; Bastien und Bastienne; La clemenza di Tito; Così fan tutte; Don Giovanni; Die Entführung aus dem Serail; La finta giardiniera; Idomeneo; Lucio Silla; Mitridate, re di Ponto; Le nozze di Figaro; Il re pastore; Der Schauspieldirektor; Die Zauberflöte.*

(BB) *** Naxos 8.550185. Capella Istropolitana, Wordsworth.

Barry Wordsworth follows up his excellent series of Mozart symphonies for Naxos with this generous collection of overtures, no fewer than 14 of them, arranged in chronological order and given vigorous, stylish performances. In Italian overture form, *Mitridate* and *Lucio Silla*, like miniature symphonies, have separate tracks for each of their three contrasted sections. Very well recorded, the disc is highly recommendable at super-bargain price.

Serenades Nos. 1, K.100; 6 (Serenata notturna), K.239; 7 (Haffner), K.250; 9 (Posthorn), K.320; 13 (Eine kleine Nachtmusik), K.525.

(B) **(*) Double Decca (ADD) 443 458-2 (2). V. Mozart Ens., Boskovsky.

Boskovsky and the Vienna Mozart Ensemble play with elegance and sparkle, and these performances still sound outstandingly bracing and vivid. The account of *Eine kleine Nachtmusik*, one of the freshest and most attractive on disc, here has a somewhat astringent treble, while Boskovsky's 1973 *Posthorn Serenade* seems rather dry in the matter of string-timbre, though the bloom remains on the wind and the posthorn is tangible in its presence. Like the *Haffner Serenade*, it is marvellously alive, full of the sparkle and elegance we associate with this group, with admirable phrasing and feeling for detail. The very engaging earliest *Serenade in D*, K.100, has the greatest glow of all, although it was recorded in 1970.

Serenades Nos. 3, K.185; 4 (Colloredo), K.203.

(BB) *** Naxos 8.550413. Salzburg CO, Nerat.

Well-played, nicely phrased and musical accounts on Naxos, recorded in a warm, reverberant acoustic, but one in which detail clearly registers. The Salzburg Chamber Orchestra has real vitality, and most readers will find these accounts musically satisfying and very enjoyable.

Serenades Nos. (i) 6 (Serenata notturna), K.239; 7 (Haffner), K.250; 9, K.320.

*** Telarc CD 80161. Prague CO, Mackerras.

Serenades Nos. (i) 6 (Serenata notturna), K.239; 7 (Haffner), K.250; 9 (Posthorn), K.320; (ii) 13 (Eine kleine Nachtmusik), K.525.

(B) ** DG (ADD) Double 453 076-2 (2). (i) BPO; (ii) VPO; Boehm.

Serenades Nos. 6 (Serenata notturna), K.239; 7 (Haffner), K.250 (with March in D, K.249); 9 (Posthorn), K.320 (with March in D, K.335/1); 13 (Eine kleine Nachtmusik), K.525.

⊛ (B) *** Ph. Duo Dig./ADD 464 022-2 (2). ASMF, Marriner.

There are plenty of fine recordings of Mozart's four key orchestral *Serenades*, but none to surpass those on this Philips Duo, which tends to sweep the board. Marriner's accounts of the *Haffner* and *Posthorn* are cultured, warm, spacious and marvellously played. Iona Brown makes a superb contribution in the concertante violin role of the *Haffner*. The performance of the *Serenata notturna*, too, is first class, crisply rhythmic in the first movement with the drums clearly focused. As for the most famous work of all, Sir Neville's polished and elegant account of *Eine kleine Nachtmusik* is clearly designed to caress the ears of traditional listeners wearied by period performance. Throughout, the Philips engineers provide a natural sound balance, with rich, full textures.

In Mackerras's coupling the playing is lively and brilliant, helped by warm recorded sound, vivid in its sense of presence, except that the reverberant acoustic clouds the tuttis a little. The violin soloist, Oldrich Viček, is very much one of the team under the conductor rather than a virtuoso establishing his individual line. By omitting repeats in the *Haffner*, Mackerras leaves room for the other delightful *Serenade*, just as haunting, with the terracing between the solo string quartet (in close focus) and the full string band aptly underlined.

On DG, characteristic Boehm performances from the early 1970s, the effect is warm and civilized (including the posthorn solos). There is a degree of suavity, although there is spirit in the allegros. In the *Posthorn Serenade* Boehm doesn't find much fun and sparkle in the music, although this is somewhat offset by Thomas Brandis's stylish solo violin contribution. The real snag is the sheer weight of sound, and on the first disc the string focus is not absolutely clean, not even in *Eine kleine Nachtmusik*, which lacks textural refinement, even though Boehm's reading is polished and spacious, with a neat, lightly pointed finale.

Serenades Nos. 6 (Serenata notturna), K.239; 13 (Eine kleine Nachtmusik), K.525; Serenade for Wind No. 12, K.388.

(M) **(*) DG (IMS) 439 524-2. Orpheus CO.

The *Serenata notturna*, which can easily sound bland, has a fine sparkle here. The famous *Night Music*, however, is rather lacking in charm with a very brisk opening movement, alert enough and very polished, but somewhat unbending. The *Wind Serenade* restores the balance of excellence, alert and sympathetic and full of character. The digital recording is first class throughout.

Serenade No. 7 (Haffner), K.250; March, K.249.

(BB) **(*) Naxos 8.550333. Nishizaki, Capella Istropolitana, Wildner.

The K.249 *March* is given twice, as both prelude and postlude to the main *Serenade* in the authentic manner. Wildner brings out the vigour rather than the charm of the fast movements, with the Minuets on the heavy side, but with the big final allegro superbly articulated and erupting in rustic jollity. The important violin solos in earlier movements are played superbly by Takako Nishizaki. Bright, full recording. Even with the above reservations, this is an excellent bargain.

Serenade No. 7 (Haffner), K.250; Symphony No. 35 (Haffner), K.385.

*** Häns. CD 98.173. ASMF, I. Brown.

The coupling of the *Haffner Symphony* and *Haffner Serenade*, especially apt, is surprisingly rare. In the *Symphony* Iona Brown, unlike Marriner, follows the autograph in omitting an exposition repeat. Brown herself is the virtuoso soloist in the *Serenade*, as she was in the Marriner version on Philips, lighter than ever in the moto perpetuo scurryings of the fourth movement *Rondo*. Hänssler describe this issue and the companion disc of the *Posthorn Serenade* as part of their Academy series, and such refreshing discs, vividly recorded, could not be more promising.

Serenades Nos. 9 (Posthorn); 13 (Eine kleine Nachtmusik), K.525.

**(*) Telarc CD 10108. Prague CO, Mackerras.

(i) Serenades Nos. 9 (Posthorn), K.320; 13 (Eine kleine Nachtmusik), K.525; (ii) 6 German Dances, K.509; Minuet in C, K.409.

(M) **(*) Sony (ADD) SBK 48266. (i) Cleveland O, Szell; (ii) LSO, Leinsdorf.

Serenade No. 9 (Posthorn), K 320; Symphony No. 33, K 319.

*** Häns. CD 98.129. ASMF, I. Brown.

Challenging earlier recordings by the Academy under Sir Neville Marriner, Iona Brown neatly offers another popular Serenade alongside a symphony contemporary with it. The sound is outstandingly good, with plenty of bloom but no excessive reverberation. These are attractively fresh Mozart performances, using modern instruments, which have concern for the crisper manners encouraged by period performance. Speeds are consistently brisker than those of the Marriner versions which we have used for comparison. The finale of *Symphony No. 33* for example, brings a hectic speed which does not sound at all breathless, with feather-light triplets, and similarly in the finale of the *Posthorn Serenade* with which it is coupled.

The Prague strings have great warmth and Mackerras gets vital results from his Czech forces. Rhythms are lightly sprung and the phrasing is natural in every way. The Telarc acoustic is warm and spacious with a wide dynamic range (some might feel it is too wide for this music), though most ears will find the effect agreeable.

Marvellously vivacious playing from the Clevelanders in the *Posthorn Serenade*, especially in the exhilarating *presto* finale, yet there is no lack of tenderness in the *concertante* third movement. *Eine kleine Nachtmusik* is similarly polished and vital, and in both works the Severance Hall acoustic provides a full ambience, but it is a pity that the close

balance means a reduced dynamic range. Even so, this is music-making of great character. Leinsdorf's *German Dances* make a lively bonus, if not as distinctive as the Szell performances.

Serenade No. 10 for 13 Wind Instruments, K.361.

**(*) Ph. 412 726-2. ASMF, Marriner.

**(*) Accent ACC 68642D. Octophorus, Kuijken.

Serenade No. 10 for 13 Wind Instruments, K.361; Divertimento in F, K.213.

(M) **(*) Chan. 6575. SNO Wind Ens., P. Järvi.

The Marriner version fits very stylishly in the Academy's series of Mozart wind works, characteristically refined in its ensemble, with matching of timbres and contrasts beautifully judged, both lively and graceful with rhythms well sprung and speeds well chosen, yet with nothing mannered about the result. Full, warm recording that yet allows good detail. However, there is no coupling.

On period instruments Barthold Kuijken directs his talented team in an authentic performance where the distinctive character of eighteenth-century instruments brings a sparer, lighter texture, as it should. Speeds tend to be on the cautious side but the liveliness of the playing makes up for that. The recording adds to the clarity but, again, there is no coupling.

The SNO Wind Ensemble's version under Paavo Järvi is enjoyably spontaneous-sounding, though ensemble is not quite as polished as in the finest versions. Speeds are well chosen, and the recording is warm, though the detail is sometimes masked by the lively acoustic. The little *Divertimento* makes an attractive bonus.

Serenades Nos. 10 in B flat for 13 Wind Instruments (Gran Partita), K.361; 11 in E flat, K.375; 12 in C min., K.388; Sinfonia concertante in E flat for Oboe, Clarinet, Bassoon, Horn & Orchestra, K.297b; (i) Concert Rondo for Horn & Orchestra in E flat, K.371.

(N) (B) *** ASV Double COS 242 (2). (i) Williams; COE, Schneider.

This new bargain double from ASV tends to sweep the board in this repertoire. The brilliant young soloists of the Chamber Orchestra of Europe, inspired by the conducting of Alexander Schneider, give performances of the three great wind serenades which are not only unusually positive, but which combine brilliance and warmth with a refreshing feeling of spontaneity. Right at the start of the *Gran Partita*, the flourishes from the first clarinet are far more effective when played as here: not literally, but with Schneider leading them on to the first forte chord from the full ensemble. The finale bubbles over with high spirits.

K.375 is a similar delight, as genial as it is charcterful, yet with a very touching central *Adagio*. K.388 might have been more menacing at the C minor opening, but the result is most persuasive, with the digital recording providing good detail, yet showing the succulent textural blending, set against a warm but not confusing acoustic. In the live recording of the *Sinfonia concertante* the four wind soloists are artists who each know when to take centre stage and when to hold back. The variations of the finale are pure joy.

The sparkling *Horn Rondo* comes as an engaging encore after K.361.

Serenades Nos. 10, K.361; 11, K.375; 12, K.388; Wind Divertimenti:K.240; K.252; K.253; K.270.

(B) *** Double Decca 458 096-2 (2). Amadeus Winds, Hogwood.

Anyone wanting period performances of Mozart's three supreme *Serenades for Wind* can safely have these Amadeus Winds versions recommended to them. Moreover, this collection offers a fascinating aural comparison. K.375 and K.388 were recorded first in 1985 in New York, and the effect is undoubtedly more plangent than in the later performances recorded in Boston in 1987 (K.361) and 1989 (the four *Divertimenti*). In the *C minor Serenade* the extra darkness of colour adds to the character of the music, although the blending is well matched and characterful. Both here and K.375 (similarly bold), where one might expect speeds faster than usual, these are on the leisurely side, except in the finales, though well lifted both rhythmically and in phrasing. The speeds are perhaps a recognition of the players' technical problems, coping with intonation and less sophisticated mechanisms, a point brought home in the clear, full digital recording, with much clicking of keys. By the time they came to record the *Gran Partita* two years later, the group's integration is much smoother and the effect is much more sophisticated. Indeed, this is an outstandingly characterful account, preferable to the Brymer version on modern instruments (see above), not lacking finesse, and making the strongest possible case for authenticity. Both the *Adagio* and *Romance* are lyrically mellow, and the *Theme and Variations* is almost Schubertian in its innocent charm. The jocular finale goes like the wind, pressed home with a virtuosity surmounting almost all difficulties. The four *Divertimenti* are also very successful, with the vivid colouring preventing any possible feeling of blandness.

Serenades Nos. 11, K.375; 12, K.388.

(**(*)) Testament mono SBT 1180. L. Bar. Ens., Haas – DVORAK: *Serenade.* (**(*))

Serenades Nos. 11, K.375; 12, K.388; Overtures: Le nozze di Figaro (arr. Vent); Don Giovanni (arr. Triebensee); Die Zauberflöte (arr. Heidenreich).

*** Hyp. CDA 66887. E. Concert Winds.

Hyperion offers one of the most enjoyable records of Mozart's wind music to appear for a long time. Fresh, spirited playing; firmly focused and well blended sound both from the players and from the engineers. A delight!

  This historic reissue of pioneering recordings from Karl Haas and the London Baroque Ensemble of three of the greatest of all wind works is valuable for performances that are ahead of their time in their brisk, no-nonsense manners and fast speeds, with the works often tackled impromptu. There is a brisk, military flavour in allegros, yet the mastery of individual players still defies the idea of over-rigid performances, with delectable interplay between the principals. Vivid and immediate transfers of recordings set in a dry acoustic.

Serenade No. 13 (Eine kleine Nachtmusik), K.525.

*** Ph. (IMS) 410 606-2. I Musici (with Concert of Baroque music ***).

(i) *Serenade No. 13 (Eine kleine Nachtmusik), K.525.*
(ii) *Allegro, K.121; 3 German Dances, K.605; Marches, K.249, 335; Minuet, K.409.*

(M) ** Mercury (IMS) (ADD) 434 398-2. (i) LSO, (ii) Festival CO; Dorati – HANDEL: *Fireworks Music; Water Music.* **(*)

I Musici play the music with rare freshness, giving the listener the impression of hearing the work for the first time. The playing is consistently alert and sparkling, with the *Romanze* particularly engaging. The recording is beautifully balanced.

  The LSO sparkle in Mozart's most famous *Serenade* and a similar spick-and-span rhythmic point gives a characteristic Dorati brightness to the other genre pieces, as played by the Festival Chamber Orchestra, whoever they may be! The Watford Town Hall recording is pleasingly warm but the Telefunken microphones give a somewhat glassy upper-range to the violins.

Sinfonia concertante in E flat, for Violin, Viola & Orchestra, K.364.

(M) *** RCA (ADD) 09026 63531-2. Heifetz, Primrose, RCA Victor SO, Izler Solomon – BACH: *Double Concerto;* BRAHMS: *Double Concerto.* ***
(***) BBC (ADD) BBCL 4019-2. D. and I. Oistrakh, Moscow PO, Menuhin – BEETHOVEN: *Violin Concerto in D, Op. 61.* (***)
(**(*)) Testament mono SBT 1157. Brainin, Schidlof, LMP, Blech – SCHUBERT: *String Quintet in C.* (**)
(M) ** EMI (ADD) CDM7 64632-2. D. and I. Oistrakh, BPO, D. Oistrakh – BRAHMS: *Violin Concerto.* **(*)

The Heifetz/Primrose partnership is too closely balanced and the brisk pace of the finale may not suit all tastes, but the crisp interchange is fresh and joyful, and in the slow movement the warmly responsive interchange between the two great soloists is genuinely moving, with the cadenza outstanding.

  With David Oistrakh playing the viola and his son, Igor, the violin, the Mozart *Sinfonia concertante* under Menuhin's baton is a most spontaneous and vivid performance, and the BBC recording gives us truthful and natural sound. Self-recommending.

  This Testament version of the *Sinfonia concertante* was recorded at Abbey Road in 1953. The studio recording, cleanly transferred, focuses the soloists sharply, giving warmth and body to the tone – exceptionally rich from Peter Schidlof on the viola. If the slow movement is a degree broad and heavy with Blech, the finale is jollier, at a marginally more relaxed tempo.

  On EMI, although the solo playing from the Oistrakhs is rich-timbred and beautifully matched, the orchestral accompaniment polished and the recording full and pleasing, there is a curiously literal approach to the music-making here, and the imaginative spark which can bring this glorious work fully to life is missing.

(i) *Sinfonia concertante, K.364;* (ii) *Sinfonia concertante, K.297b.*

*** DG 429 784-2. (i) Phillips, Gallagher; (ii) Taylor, Singer, Purvis, Orpheus CO.

(BB) **(*) ASV CDQS 6139. (i) McAslan, Inque; (ii) Anderson, Hacker, Gambold, Taylor; L. Festival O, Pople.

In the ideal coupling of Mozart's paired *Sinfonias Concertantes*, the performances from members of the Orpheus Chamber Orchestra have an appealing warmth and intimacy. The dialogue between the violin and viola soloists in K.364 is both lively and very sensitive, and the finale is buoyant. This is most satisfying, and the comparable work with wind soloists gives a similar feeling of a chamber performance. The recording is very truthful and the warm acoustic gives pleasing inner definition.

The outer movements of K.364 have a fine rhythmic spring on ASV, and the *Andante* is touchingly expressive in a pleasingly restrained manner. Lorraine McAslan is rather near the microphone, but the viola is not too backward, and the recording projects vividly. The account of K.297b brings a lively, alert performance with speeds relaxed enough to allow a winning lift to rhythms. Alan Hacker's distinctive reedy clarinet provides an extra tang, and the way the soloists appear in turn as protagonists in the variations finale is delightfully done. The sound is bright, firm and realistic. Good value.

Sinfonia concertante, K.297b;

(M) (***) Cala mono CACD 0523. Tabuteau, Portnoy, Schoenbach, Jones, Phd. O, Stokowski – BEETHOVEN: *Symphony No. 6 (Pastoral).* (***)

Stokowski recorded the *Sinfonia concertante* in December 1940; it was his first and only Mozart recording made in his quarter-century directing the Philadelphia Orchestra. The result is sheer joy. His graceful string phrasing may have romantic elements, but the warmth is ever persuasive. His expert group of orchestral soloists (balanced forwardly and clearly) blend well together – with the single proviso that the bassoonist at times produces a rather close vibrato. The transfer is excellent and the sound, though a bit subfusc, is always fully acceptable, with a wider dynamic range than on the coupled Beethoven. A disc to treasure for all Stokowskians.

(i) *Sinfonia concertante, K.297b;* (ii) *Piano & Wind Quintet in E flat, K.452.*

⚫ (***) Testament mono STB 1091. (i) Brain, James, Sutcliffe, Walton, Philh. O, Karajan; (ii) Gieseking, Philh. Wind Ens. – BEETHOVEN: *Piano & Wind Quintet.* (***) ⚫

The Mozart *Quintet* is one of the classic chamber-music recordings of all time. Gieseking and members of the Philharmonia Wind (Dennis Brain, Sidney Sutcliffe, Bernard Walton and Cecil James) recorded it over 40 years ago, and in terms of tonal blend and perfection of balance and ensemble it has few rivals. To the original quintet coupling Testament have added the *Sinfonia concertante* for wind, which these distinguished players recorded with Karajan in 1953, a performance of comparable stature. Not to be missed. The mono sound comes up wonderfully fresh in this Testa-

ment transfer. This is a full-price reissue and is worth every penny of the asking price.

Complete Mozart Edition, Vol. 21: (i) *Sonatas for Organ & Orchestra (Epistle Sonatas) Nos. 1–17 (complete). Adagio & Allegro in F min., K.594; Andante in F, K.616; Fantasia in F min., K.608.*

(M) **(*) Ph. 422 521-2 (2). Chorzempa (organs at Stift Wilhering, Linz, Austria; Schlosspfarrkirche, Obermarchtal, Germany – K.594; K.608); (i) with German Bach Soloists, Winschermann.

Complete Mozart Bargain Edition, Vol. 10: (i) *Epistle Sonatas for Organ & Orchestra and Solos. Masses and Requiem Mass (complete).*

(N) (B) **(*) Ph. (ADD/DDD) 464 860-2 (11). (i) as above; (ii) various artists (see below).

Sonatas Nos. 1–17 (Epistle Sonatas) .

(BB) **(*) Naxos 8.550512. Sebestyén, Budapest Ferenc Erkel CO.

The *Epistle Sonatas* derive their name from the fact that they were intended to be heard between the Epistle and Gospel in the Mass. Admittedly they are not great music or even first-class Mozart; however, played with relish they make a strong impression. The final *Sonata*, K.263, becomes a fully fledged concerto. The set is completed with the other works by Mozart which are usually heard on the organ, and here Chorzempa's registration is particularly appealing.

While it is understood that, apart from No. 16 in C, K.329, which has a specific solo part, the organ is not intended as a solo instrument in these *Chiesa Sonatas*, it seems perverse to balance the instrument so that it blends in completely with the orchestral texture, as the Naxos engineers have done. Otherwise these alert, polished and nicely scaled performances could hardly be improved on and, apart from the controversial matter of the relationship of the organ to the orchestra, the recording is first class.

SYMPHONIES
(with list of keys and Köchel nos.)

1 in E flat, K.16; 4 in D, K.19; 5 in B flat, K.22; 6 in F, K.43; 7 in D, K45; 8 in D, K.48; 9 in C, K.73; 10 in G, K.74; 11 in D, K.84; 12 in G, K.110; 13 in F, K.112; 14 in A; K.114; 15 in G, K.124; 16 in C, K.128; 17 in G, K.129; 18 in F, K.130; 19 in E flat, K.132; 20 in D, K.133; 21 in A, K.134; 22 in C, K.162; 23 in D, K.181; 24 in B flat, K.182; 25 in G min., K.183; 26 in E flat, K.184; 27 in G, K.199; 28 in C, K.200; 29 in A, K.201; 30 in D, K.202; 31 in D, K.297 (Paris); 32 in G, K.318; 33 in B flat, K.319; 34 in C, K.338; 35 in D, K.385 (Haffner); 36 in C, K.425 (Linz); 37 in G, K.444; 38 in D, K.504 (Prague); 39 in E flat, K.543; 40 in G min., K.550; 41 in C, K.551 (Jupiter).

Symphonies Nos. 1–47 (including alternative versions); K.35; K.38; K.42a; K.45b; K.46a (K.51); K.62a (K.100); K.74g (K.216); K.75; K.75b (K.110); K.111a; K.203, 204 & 196 (121); K.425a (K.444); Odense; New Lambacher.

(B) **(*) O-L ADD/Dig. 452 496-2 (19). AAM, Schröder, Hogwood.

With Jaap Schröder leading the admirably proportioned string group (9,8,4,3,2) and Christopher Hogwood at the keyboard, this was a remarkably successful joint enterprise. The playing has great style, warmth and polish, even if intonation is not always absolutely refined. The survey is complete enough to include No. 37 – in fact the work of Michael Haydn but with a slow introduction by Mozart. The *Lambacher* and *Odense Symphonies* are also here, plus alternative versions, with different scoring, of No. 40; while the *Paris Symphony* is given two complete performances with alternative slow movements. Hogwood's overall achievement is remarkable. The recording is well balanced and has plenty of ambience, the CD transfers are very successful, and the accompanying documentation is very good.

Complete Mozart Bargain Edition, Vol. 1: *Symphonies* **(complete).**

(N) (B) *** Ph. (ADD) 464 770-2 (12). ASMF, Marriner.

Symphonies Nos. (i) *1 in E flat, K.16; 4 in D, K.19; in F, K.19a; 5 in B flat, K.22; 6 in F, K.43; 7 in D, K.45; in G (Neue Lambacher); in G (Alte Lambacher), K.45a; in B flat, K.45b; 8 in D, K.48; 9 in C, K.73; 10 in G, K.74; in F, K.75; in F, K.76; in D, K.81; 11 in D, K.84; in D, K.95; in C, K.96; in D, K.97; 12 in G, K.110; 13 in F, K.112; 14 in A, K.114; 15 in G, K.124; 16 in C, K.128; 17 in G, K.129; 18 in F, K.130; 19 in E, K.132 (with alternative slow movement); 20 in D, K.133; in D, K.161 & 163; in D, K.111 & 120; in D, K.196 & 121; in C, K.208 & 102; Minuet in A, K.61g/1.* (ii) *21 in A, K.134; 22, K.162; 23 in D, K.181; 24 in B flat, K.182; 25 in G min., K.183; 26 in E flat, K.184; 27 in G, K.199; 28 in C, K.200; 29 in A, K.201; 30 in D, K.202; 31 in D (Paris), K.297 (with alternative slow movement); 32 in G, K.318; 33 in B flat, K.319; 34 in C, K.338; 35 in D (Haffner), K.385; 36 in C (Linz), K.425; 38 in D(Prague), K.504; 39, K.543; 40 in G min., K.550; 41 in C (Jupiter), K.551.*

(B) **(*) Ph. (ADD) 454 085-2 (12). (i) ASMF, Marriner; (ii) Concg. O, Krips.

Complete Mozart Edition, Vol. 1: *Symphonies Nos. 1, K.16; 4, K.19; K.19a; 5, K.22; 6, K.43; 7, K.45; (Neue Lambacher), G.16; (Alte Lambacher), K.45a; K.45b; 8, K.48; 9, K.73; K.74; 10, K.75; K.76; K.81; 11, K.84; K.95; K.96; K.97; 12, K.110; 13, K.112; 14, K.114; 15, K.124; 16, K.128; !7, K.129; 18, K.130; 19, K.132 (with alternative slow movement); 20, K.133; K.161 & 163; K.111 & 120;K.196 & 121; K.208 & 102 Minuet in A, K.61g/1.*

(M) *** Ph. (ADD) 422 501-2 (6). ASMF, Marriner.

The first half of this 12-CD box (also available separately in a 6-CD set) is a reissue of Volume 1 of the Philips Complete Mozart Edition. Marriner's recordings confirm the Mozartian vitality of the performances and their sense of style and spontaneity. The Philips engineers respond with alive and vivid recording. Except perhaps for those who insist on original instruments, the finesse and warmth of the playing here is a constant joy. The Dutch players for Krips also bring warmth, as well as proving characteristically stylish in phrasing and execution. Quick movements can be

bracingly vigorous. Both the previously underrated *No. 28 in C* and the first great masterpiece in A major, both aptly paced, are very persuasively done, with an almost ethereal delicacy from the strings in the beautiful *Andante* of No. 29 and the horns thrusting exuberantly in the coda of the finale. Although Krips's Mozartian sensibility never deserts him, the readings of some of the later symphonies are somewhat wanting in character, however, and do not do full honour to the fine Mozartian that Krips was, although No. 39 goes well enough. The ample Concertgebouw sound, with its resonant bass, emphasizes the breadth of scale of the music-making, yet the digital remastering gives an attractive freshness to the violins, although the Minuets sound well upholstered.

Symphonies Nos. 1–41.

(B) **(*) DG (ADD) 453 231-2 (10). BPO, Boehm.

All the earlier symphonies were recorded in intensive sessions in March and November 1968, a real voyage of discovery, with performances warm and genial, with bold contrasts of dynamic and well-sprung rhythms. This latest CD reissue, on ten discs instead of twelve, also brings the advantage of fuller and more forward transfers, with good body and presence. The new bargain box, unlike the previous one, has essays on Boehm as Mozartian by Peter Cosse and Mozart as symphonist by Heinz Becker. An excellent bargain, and not just for the historical specialist, but for all Mozartians.

Symphonies Nos. 1, K.16; 4, K.19; in F, K.19a; 5, K.22; K.45a; 6–36; 38–41.

(M) *** Telarc CD 80300 (10). Prague CO, Mackerras.

Mackerras's is an outstanding series, with electrifying performances of the early as well as the later symphonies. There is not a suspicion of routine, with the playing full of dramatic contrasts in rhythm, texture or dynamic. Mackerras has a keen feeling for Mozart style, not least in the slow movements and minuets, which he regularly takes faster than usual. His flowing andantes are consistently stylish too, with performances on modern instruments regularly related to period practice. An outstanding instance comes in the G minor *Andante* of No. 5 in B flat, K.22, where Mackerras, fastish and light, makes others seem heavy-handed in this anticipation of romanticism, underlining the harmonic surprises clearly and elegantly. Consistently Mackerras finds light and shade in Mozart's inspirations, both early and late, though some may feel that, with warm reverberation characteristic of this Prague orchestra's recording venue, the scale is too large, particularly in the early symphonies. Harpsichord continuo, where used, is usually well balanced.

Symphonies Nos. 13–36; 38–41.

(B) *** EMI CZS5 73631-2 (5). ECO, Tate.

Jeffrey Tate's performances are full of vitality, engagingly light in texture, with some lovely playing from individual members of the orchestra. Throughout, Tate provides a winning combination of affectionate manners, clean articulation and keen attention to detail, making for fresh results. In the *Paris Symphony*, the alternative *Andante* slow movement is included as well as the usual one, so you can programme which ever you prefer. The later symphonies can stand competition with any: the *Jupiter* has an apt scale, which allows the grandeur of the work fully to come out. On the one hand it has the clarity of a chamber orchestra, while on the other, with trumpets and drums, its weight of expression never underplays the scale of argument which originally prompted the unauthorized nickname. In both Nos. 40 and 41, exposition repeats are observed in the outer movements, particularly important in the *Jupiter* finale. With excellent recording quality (1984–93) – detailed with a pleasant reverberation – this set makes a fine bargain, especially in such attractive space-saving slimline packaging.

Symphonies Nos. 13–18.

(N) (B) **(*) DG 469 552-2. BPO, Boehm.

These 1968 recordings were part of Boehm's pioneering complete survey of the Mozart symphonies (see above). The playing is warm, elegant and polished, and has the freshness of new discovery by a great orchestra much more familiar with the later works. The recording was made in the Jesus-Christus-Kirche and wears its years lightly, the tranfers full-bodied and immediate. In spite of the changes brought about by period-instrument performances, this disc holds its place in the catalogue, for Boehm was a true Mozartian.

Symphonies Nos. 13; 14 & 20.

*** Teldec 0630 17110-2. VCM, Harnoncourt.

By observing repeats, Harnoncourt widens the scale of all three symphonies. Indeed, the first movement of No. 20 is extended to 10 minutes 44 seconds, but with lusty period horns it has great vitality in the outer movements, and the Andante does not lack charm. Harnoncourt gives vigorous readings of all three, as ever with a bold element of gruffness, but this certainly adds to their character. The *A major Symphony* comes off particularly well, with the Minuet not pressed as hard as with Mackerras's Prague account on the same label. Excellent, resonant recording.

Symphonies Nos. 14–18.

*** Telarc CD 80242. Prague CO, Mackerras.

No. 14 in A is a particularly fine work (as indeed are all Mozart's A major symphonies) and, like the others here, it receives an invigorating account with brisk Allegros and a strong, one-in-a-bar tempo for the Minuet (this suits the Minuet of *No. 18 in F* even better as it is very folksy). Slow movements, however, are very direct and are pressed onwards, slightly unbending; here some might find Mackerras's approach too austere. The bright recording is resonant, which prevents absolute clarity, but the clean lines of the playing ensure plenty of stimulating impact.

Symphonies Nos. 15–18.

(BB) **(*) Naxos 8.550874. N. CO, Ward.

Symphonies Nos. 19; 20; 37 in G Introduction only (with remainder of the symphony by Michael Haydn).

(BB) *** Naxos 8.550875. N. CO, Ward.

Nicholas Ward's stylish Mozart series here offers six sym-

phonies written in 1772. The orchestral string-phrasing is particularly elegant in slow movements (notably the wistful *Andante* of *No. 15 in G* and the charming melody which forms the centre-piece of No. 17), while the lively first movement of *No. 18 in F* effervesces neatly. Elsewhere allegros are alert and strong. Excellent, full and well-balanced recording, though not ideally sharply detailed. No. 19 is scored for four horns, two in E flat *alt*, and they give added weight and character to the orchestral texture in outer movements. No. 20 is given extra brightness by a pair of trumpets. But it is the delectable *Andante* that catches the ear with its charming flute solo over muted violins. Mozart contributed just the rather grand opening *Adagio maestoso* to the symphony once mistakenly regarded as his No. 37. It is played most persuasively: this disc is well worth having on all counts.

Symphonies Nos. 16–29.

*** DG 439 915-2 (4). E. Concert, Pinnock.

The playing here has polish and sophistication, fine intonation and spontaneity and great vitality, balanced by warm, lyrical feeling in slow movements. Indeed, the account of *No. 29 in A major* is among the finest available (on either modern or original instruments) and the earlier A major work (No. 21) is very impressive too, as is the G minor, K.183, and the very 'operatic' *No. 23 in D major*. Another clear first choice, and not only for authenticists.

Symphonies No. 19–23.

*** Telarc CD 80217. Prague CO, Mackerras.

Mackerras is equally lively in these early works from Mozart's Salzburg period. The surprising thing is how fast his speeds tend to be. In one instance the contrast is astonishing, when at a very brisk *Andantino grazioso* Mackerras turns the slow middle movement of No. 23 into a lilting Laendler, quite different from other performances. The recording is reverberant, as in the later symphonies, giving relatively weighty textures; with such light scoring, however, there is ample clarity, with braying horns riding beautifully over the rest.

Complete Mozart Edition, Vol. 2: *Symphonies Nos. 21–36; 37: Adagio maestoso in G, K.44 (Introduction to a symphony by M. Haydn); 38–41; Minuet for a Symphony in C, K.409.*

(M) **(*) Ph. (ADD) 422 502-2 (6). ASMF, Marriner.

As with the early works, the later symphonies in the Marriner performances are conveniently laid out on six mid-priced CDs, offered in numerical sequence. However, the over-resonant bass remains in the recording of No. 40 and the *Haffner* (both of which date from 1970, nearly a decade before the rest of the cycle was recorded). Otherwise the transfers are of Philips's best quality, and the performances generally give every satisfaction, even if their style does not show an awareness of the discoveries made – in terms of texture and balance – by the authentic school.

Symphonies Nos. 24, K.173; 26, K.161a; 27, K.161b; 30, K.202.

*** Telarc CD 80186. Prague CO, Mackerras.

Where in later symphonies Mackerras chooses more relaxed speeds, here he tends to be more urgent, as in the finale of No. 26 or the *Andantino grazioso* slow movement of No. 27, where he avoids the questionable use of muted strings. The reverberation of the recording gives the impression of a fairly substantial orchestra, without loss of detail, and anyone fancying this particular group of early Mozart symphonies need not hesitate.

Symphonies Nos. 24–27; 32, K.318.

(B) *** [EMI Red Line CDR5 69818]. ASMF, Marriner.

Symphonies Nos. 31 (Paris), K.297; 33, K.319; 34, K.338.

(B) *** [EMI Red Line CDR5 69819]. ASMF, Marriner.

Symphonies Nos. 40, K.550; 41 (Jupiter), K.551.

(B) **(*) [EMI Red Line CDR5 69820]. ASMF, Marriner.

Marriner's third set of Mozart symphony recordings, made for EMI, is the most beautifully recorded of all. The playing, too, is graceful and elegant. With bracing rhythms and brisker pacing than in his earlier, Philips set, these readings are positive yet unidiosyncratic. Phrasing is supple and the Mozartian spirit is always alive here. There is a degree of disappointment in the *Jupiter Symphony*, which is slightly undercharacterized. For the most part, however, this music-making will give a great deal of pleasure.

Symphonies Nos. 25, K.183; 29, K.201; 31 (Paris), K.297.

(M) **(*) DG (IMS) (ADD) 449 552-2. BPO, Boehm.

These three symphonies come from the complete box (see above) that Boehm recorded in the 1960s. The playing of the Berlin Philharmonic is quite superlative, but here enjoyment is occasionally marred by the want of spontaneity that sometimes distinguished Boehm's direction. The easy-going tempi are acceptable in No. 25 until the finale, which is very slow. The finales of Nos. 29 and 31 are more lively, but the weighty opening of the *Paris* will not appeal to everyone, although the violins articulate gracefully, and the Berlin wind phrase exquisitely throughout the disc. The mid-1960s recording does not sound too dated.

Symphonies Nos. 25, K.183; 32, K.318; 41 (Jupiter), K.551.

(BB) *** Naxos 8.550113. Capella Istropolitana, Wordsworth.

Symphonies Nos. 27, K.199/161b; 33, K.319; 36 (Linz), K.425.

(BB) *** Naxos 8.550264. Capella Istropolitana, Wordsworth.

Symphonies Nos. 28, K.200; 31 (Paris), K.297; 40, K.550.

(BB) *** Naxos 8.550164. Capella Istropolitana, Wordsworth.

Symphonies Nos. 29, K.201; 30, K.202; 38 (Prague), K.504.

(BB) *** Naxos 8.550119. Capella Istropolitana, Wordsworth.

Symphonies Nos. 34, K.338; 35 (Haffner), K.385; 39, K.543.

(BB) *** Naxos 8.550186. Capella Istropolitana, Wordsworth.

Symphonies Nos. 40, K.550; 41 (Jupiter), K.551.

(BB) *** Naxos 8.550299. Capella Istropolitana, Wordsworth.

The Capella Istropolitana consists of leading members of the Slovak Philharmonic Orchestra of Bratislava; though their string-tone is thinnish, it is very much in scale with the clarity of a period performance but tonally far sweeter. The

recording is outstandingly good, with a far keener sense of presence than in most rival versions and with less reverberation to obscure detail in tuttis. Wordsworth observes exposition repeats in first movements, but in the finales only in such symphonies as Nos. 38 and 41, where the movement particularly needs extra scale. In slow movements, as is usual, he omits repeats. He often adopts speeds that are marginally slower than we expect nowadays in chamber-scale performances; but, with exceptionally clean articulation and infectiously sprung rhythms, the results never drag, even if No. 29 is made to sound more sober than usual. In every way these are worthy rivals to the best full-priced versions, and they can be recommended with few if any reservations. Anyone wanting to sample might try the coupling of Nos. 34, 35 and 39 – with the hard-stick timpani sound at the start of No. 39 very dramatic. The *Linz* too is outstanding. For some, the option of having the last two symphonies coupled together will be useful.

Symphonies Nos. 25, K.183; 28, K.200; 29, K.201.

*** Telarc CD 80165. Prague CO, Mackerras.

If you want performances on modern instruments, these are as fine as any, fresh and light, with transparent textures set against a warm acoustic and with rhythms consistently resilient. Mackerras's speeds are always carefully judged to allow elegant pointing but without mannerism, and the only snag is that second-half repeats are omitted in slow movements, and in the finale too of No. 29.

(i) *Symphonies Nos. 25, K.183; 28, K.200; 29, K.201;* (ii) *35 (Haffner), K.385.*

(M) (***) Sony mono SMK 64473. (i) Columbia SO;
 (ii) NYPO; Walter.

'The Birth of a Performance' (recorded rehearsals of Symphony No. 36); (i) *Symphonies Nos. 36 (Linz) K.425;* (ii) *38 (Prague), K.504.*

(M) (***) Sony mono SM2K 64474 (2). (i) Columbia SO;
 (ii) NYPO; Walter.

Symphonies Nos. 39, K.543; 40, K.550; 41 (Jupiter), K.551.

(M) (**) Sony mono SMK 64477. NYPO, Walter.

Walter's recordings were made in the 1950s and have been impressively transferred. The early symphonies on the first CD show his touch at its lightest (especially in K.201) and there is some lovely playing, both graceful and delicate, from the New York violins in slow movements. The *Haffner* sparkles with vitality; this and the *Linz* (offered together with its justly famous rehearsal sequence) and the *Prague* all show Walter at his finest – stylish and vital yet always making the music sing. *No. 39 in E flat* is a strong performance, but the *G minor*, K.550, is curiously heavy and unspontaneous, while the *Jupiter*, more appropriately weighty, lacks incandescence.

Symphonies Nos. 25, K.183; 39, K.543.

**(*) Ph. (IMS) 454 443-2. VPO, Muti.

The very opening of the slow introduction to No. 39 makes it very clear that Muti has no thought of being influenced by latterday ideas of period performance. The result is big, bold and weighty, with a full and warm Philips recording which yet reveals good inner detail. In No. 25, the little *G minor*, Muti is fast and fierce in the first movement, with no sense that this is an early work, and in the second movement *Andante* he keeps the violins unmuted, bringing out more sharply the tonal contrasts with the woodwind in alternate phrases.

Symphonies Nos 26–28; 30; 32.

*** ASV CDDCA 762. LMP, Glover.

Glover's generous coupling of five early symphonies brings typically fresh and direct readings, marked by sharp attack and resilient rhythms, at speeds on the fast side. With tuttis a little weightier than with most rivals, these are brightly enjoyable performances.

Symphonies Nos. 28–29; 35 (Haffner), K.385.

*** Sony SK 48063. BPO, Abbado.

Abbado is never mannered and his phrasing and pointing of rhythm are delicately affectionate, conveying an element of fun and with speeds never allowed to drag. Slow movements are kept flowing, and finales are hectically fast, but played with such verve and diamond-bright articulation that there is no feeling of breathlessness. The Sony engineers have coped splendidly with the acoustic problems of the Philharmonie to give a full and forward sound, with good presence.

Symphonies Nos. 29; 31–36; 38–41.

**(*) Ph. 442 604-2 (5). E. Bar. Sol., Gardiner.

These period performances lean towards the nineteenth rather than the eighteenth century, with dark-toned, weighty tuttis set in high contrast to transparent treatment of lightly scored passages. Had Gardiner made the recordings a year or so later, he would probably have used fewer agogic hesitations and underlinings, for, by his standards, they sometimes lack a little in spontaneity. But anyone fancying late Mozart symphonies with a Beethovenian tinge and with extreme dynamic contrasts need not hesitate, for the playing avoids the abrasiveness of earlier period performances, and the recordings are generally full and weighty.

Symphonies Nos. 29; 31 (Paris); 34.

(BB) (***) Dutton Lab. mono CDEA 5008. LPO, Beecham.

These incomparable performances date from between 1937 and 1940. Beecham's are elegant and cultivated accounts which in many ways are unique, though No. 29 brings one of his most controversial readings, where the pace of the opening movement is eccentrically slow, even if Beecham is very persuasive in his pointing. In the finales, by contrast, Beecham prefers really fast speeds, exhilarating in all three here. The superb new transfers are fuller and have much finer presence, transparency and, above all, body than the earlier, EMI versions that appeared some years ago.

Symphonies Nos. 29; 32; 33; 35 (Haffner); 36 (Linz); 38 (Prague); 39; 40; 41 (Jupiter).

(M) *** DG 429 668-2 (3). BPO, Karajan.

With Nos. 29, 32 and 33 added to the original LP box (see below), these are beautifully played and vitally alert readings; and the recordings, made between 1966 and 1979, are well balanced and given full, lively transfers to CD.

Symphonies Nos. 29; 33; 34.

*** Ph. 462 906-2. VPO, Muti.

This is a total success, warmly recommendable to anyone who responds to Viennese Mozart. These earlier works find him and the orchestra at their most relaxed, with allegros which allow delicate pointing of rhythm and phrase, and with tenderly expressive slow movements. These are performances that follow tradition in full orchestral treatment, with few if any concessions to period practice, and none the worse for that. They are warmly recorded and the result is most enjoyable.

Symphonies Nos. 29; 35 (Haffner); 38 (Prague).

(***) BBC mono BBCL 4027-2. RPO, Beecham.

It is good to have these broadcast performances from the 1950s, with the characterful bonus of Beecham's spoken introductions to No. 29 and the *Prague*. Interpretatively, it is fascinating to note the contrasts between these performances and those he recorded for EMI with the LPO – No. 29 in 1937, the *Haffner* in 1938/9 and the *Prague* in 1940. The extra elegance of these later RPO performances – with playing more lightly sprung and a degree more refined (the odd mishap apart), with speeds less extreme than before – is what comes out most clearly. That impression is enhanced, when the BBC sound is rather more spacious and airy than the pre-war EMI.

Symphonies Nos. 25; 29; 31 (Paris); Adagio & Fugue., K.546; Overture: Così fan tutte.

(M) **(*) EMI (ADD) CDM5 67331-2. Philh. O or New Philh. O, Klemperer.

Symphonies Nos. 33; 34; 40; Masonic Funeral Music, K.477.

(M) **(*) EMI (ADD) CDM5 67332-2. New Philh. O or Philh. O, Klemperer.

Symphonies Nos. 35 (Haffner); 36 (Linz); 38 (Prague); Overture: Die Zauberflöte.

(M) **(*) EMI SFF CDM5 67333-2. Philh. O or New Phil. O, Klemperer.

Symphonies Nos. 39; 41 (Jupiter); Serenade No. 13 in G (Eine kleine Nachtmusik).

(M) **(*) EMI (ADD) CDM5 67334-2. Philh. O or New Philh. O; Klemperer.

Symphonies Nos. 38 (Prague); No. 39; Serenada notturna.

(***) Testament mono SBT 1094. Philh. O, Klemperer.

Symphonies Nos. 29; 41 (Jupiter); Serenade No. 13 (Eine kleine Nachtmusik).

(***) Testament mono/stereo SBT 1093. Philh. O, Klemperer.

Klemperer's recordings of the key Mozart symphonies, plus the orchestral works listed above, have never sounded fresher than in the present remastering, with fullness too and warmth. Of course, since they were made period-instrument practice has changed our view of symphonic Mozart, but not to the extent that these monumentally characterful readings cannot find and hold a place in the catalogue. If initially a Klemperer reading of, say, the first movement of the great *G minor Symphony*, No. 40, sounds heavy, rhythmic subtleties are there, so that the hidden power makes its impact. The account of No. 33 is strikingly fresh and No. 38 (the *Prague*) is among the greatest ever recorded. No. 39 has a strength and virility in the first movement that anticipates Beethoven, and Klemperer lifts the finale out of its usual Mendelssohnian rut and gives it a Beethovenian power without losing any of the instrumental charm. Almost all the allegros here are measured and meticulous, slow movements forthright rather than hushed, but power and purpose are never lacking. It is good that some of the shorter works are included, particularly the magnificent *Adagio and Fugue* and *Funeral Music*, while *Eine kleine Nachtmusik* is certainly not lacking in elegance, nor a lightness of touch in the finale.

Klemperer's 1954 Mozart symphony recordings of Nos. 29 and 41, unavailable for many decades, marked the turning-point in his accident-prone career. They were the very first recordings which he made with the Philharmonia Orchestra – from then on providing the focus of his work, belatedly establishing him as a central interpreter of the great German classics. Only the first movement of No. 29 bears out the later image of Klemperer as slow and rugged. After that, all is exhilaration, with superlative playing from the Philharmonia, with rhythms beautifully sprung and phrases elegantly turned. The *Jupiter* in particular is electrifying, one of the very finest versions on disc, both powerful and polished, while *Eine kleine Nachtmusik* (in stereo) for once is made to sound like late Mozart, both strong and elegant. Outstanding transfers.

The mono version of the *Prague Symphony* brings one of Klemperer's very finest Mozart performances, strong and rugged, but finely sprung and phrased, with the *Don Giovanni* relationship firmly established. This mono version of No. 39 too is fresher than the stereo remake, while the *Serenata notturna* brings a typical Klemperer contrast, with the orchestra providing rugged, four-square support for the soloists, who by contrast are allowed their measure of charm and elegance.

Symphonies Nos. 31 (Paris); 32–35 (Haffner); 36 (Linz); 38 (Prague); 39–41 (Jupiter).

*** DG 447 043-2 (4). E. Concert, Pinnock.

It is the joy and exhilaration in Mozart's inspiration that consistently bubble out from these performances, even from the dark *G minor* or the weighty *Jupiter*. The rhythmic lift which Pinnock consistently finds is infectious throughout, magnetizing the ear from the start of every movement, and few period performances are as naturally and easily expressive as these. Allegros are regularly on the fast side but never hectically so, and it is a measure of Pinnock's mastery that when in a slow movement such as that of the *Prague* he chooses an unusually slow speed, there is no feeling of dragging. Where Gardiner in these same works exaggerates the dynamic contrasts, Pinnock keeps them firmly in the eighteenth-century tradition, with textural contrasts more clearly integrated. Clear, well-balanced sound, with the orchestra in some symphonies set more distantly than in others.

Symphonies Nos. 31 (Paris); 33; 34.

**(*) Telarc CD 80190. Prague CO, Mackerras.

Mackerras and the Prague Chamber Orchestra give characteristically stylish and refined performances, clean of attack and generally marked by brisk speeds. As in their accounts of the later symphonies, all repeats are observed – even those in the *da capos* of minuets. However, the reverberant Prague acoustic, more than in others of the Telarc series, clouds tuttis: the Presto finale of the *Paris* brings phenomenal articulation of quavers at the start, which then in tuttis disappear in a mush.

(i) Symphonies Nos. 31 (Paris); 36 (Linz); (ii) Overture: Le nozze di Figaro.

(BB) *** ASV (ADD) CDQS 6033. (i) LSO; (ii) RPO; Bátiz.

After a sprightly account of the *Figaro Overture* from the RPO, the LSO under Bátiz provide two spirited and polished accounts of favourite named symphonies. Tempi in outer movements are brisk, but the *Presto* finale of the *Linz* (for instance) produces some sparkling playing from the strings; and in both slow movements the phrasing is warm and gracious. With excellent digital recording, this makes an enjoyable super-bargain pairing.

Symphonies Nos. 31 (Paris); 36 (Linz); 38 (Prague).

*** ASV CDDCA 647. LMP, Glover.

Jane Glover and the London Mozart Players offer a particularly attractive and generous coupling in the three Mozart symphonies associated with cities. Happily, exposition repeats are observed in the outer movements. The performances are all fresh and vital in traditional chamber style, with little influence from period performance. Tuttis are not always ideally clear on inner detail; but the result is nicely in scale, not too weighty, with the delicacy beautifully light and airy.

Symphonies Nos. 32–34.

(M) **(*) Teldec 4509 97487-2. Concg. O, Harnoncourt.

Symphonies Nos. 35 (Haffner); 36 (Linz).

(M) **(*) Teldec 4509 97488-2. Concg. O, Harnoncourt.

Symphonies Nos. 38 (Prague); 39.

(M) **(*) Teldec 4509 97489-2. Concg. O, Harnoncourt.

Nikolaus Harnoncourt's Mozart, for all its merits, is nothing if not wilful, turning to the glories of the Concertgebouw Orchestra and establishing his personality immediately, with strong, even gruff accents, yet at times with an approach which (notably in slow movements, with speeds rather slower than usual) is relatively romantic in its expressiveness. He constantly secured fine playing, and the Teldec engineers rewarded him with bright, clear, yet resonant recording. Overall, the results are of mixed appeal. Both the *Paris Symphony* and *No. 33 in B flat* are among Harnoncourt's most successful performances, with beautiful, cleanly articulated playing. In No. 33 Harnoncourt overdoes his slowness in the *Andante* but adds to the breadth of the finale by giving the repeats of both halves. The performances of Nos. 34 and the *Haffner* are refreshingly direct, certainly dramatic, marked by relatively unforced tempi; but charm is somewhat missing. *No. 32 in G* again shows Harnoncourt at his best, although it is made to sound weightier than usual. In the *Linz* he observes even more repeats than are marked in the regular scores, making it, like K.318, a more expansive work than usual. The *Prague* is generally very successful, superbly played, and Harnoncourt is again very generous with repeats (it runs for 38 minutes). Tempi are again erratic in No. 39 (the Minuet is rushed), although the first movement of this symphony is well judged.

Symphonies Nos. 32; 35 (Haffner); 36 (Linz); 39; 41 (Jupiter).

(BB) *** Virgin 2 x 1 Double VBD5 61451-2 (2). SCO, Saraste.

More than most other versions on modern instruments, Saraste's vividly alive accounts of the three earlier symphonies reflect the new lessons of period performance. These are more detached, less sostenuto than many modern-instrument chamber-orchestra versions and, with all repeats observed, are highly stimulating in their resilience. The recording, helpfully reverberant, yet gives lightness and transparency to textures, conveying an apt chamber scale for two of the finest accounts of the two late symphonies available on any disc. Wordsworth and the Capella Istropolitana may have more weight in these works, but Saraste has extra polish and refinement, with generally brisker speeds, notably in slow movements and Minuets.

Symphonies Nos. 32; 33; 35 (Haffner); 36 (Linz).

(M) *** DG (IMS) (ADD) 435 070-2. BPO, Karajan.

Symphonies Nos. 35 (Haffner); 36 (Linz); 38 (Prague); 39; 40; 41 (Jupiter).

(B) *** DG Double (ADD) 453 046-2 (2). BPO, Karajan.
(M) **(*) DG (ADD) 447 416-2 (2). BPO, Boehm.

Here on DG is Karajan's big-band Mozart at its finest. Although there may be slight reservations about the Minuet and Trio of the *Linz*, which is rather slow (and the other minuets are also somewhat stately), overall there is plenty of life here, and slow movements show the BPO at their most graciously expressive. The opening of the *G minor* may not be quite dark enough for some tastes. The *Jupiter*, although short on repeats, has power as well as surface elegance. The remastered sound is clear and lively, full but not over-weighted. The separate issue makes a good sampler.

Karl Boehm's way with Mozart in the early 1960s was broader and heavier in texture than we are used to nowadays, and the exposition repeats are the exception rather than the rule; but these Berlin Philharmonic performances are warm and magnetic, with refined and strongly rhythmic playing, and there is an attractive honesty and strength about them. The *Linz*, for instance, is an example of Boehm at his finest, with an agreeable, fresh vitality; but overall there is a comfortable quality of inevitability here, perpetuating a long Mozart tradition. The recordings sound full, vivid and well balanced in the new transfers.

Symphonies Nos. 32, K.318; 35 (Haffner), K.385; 39, K.543.

*** Telarc CD 80203. Prague CO, Mackerras.
(BB) *** ASV CDQS 6071. ECO, Mackerras.

On Telarc, Mackerras is fresh rather than elegant, yet with rhythms so crisply sprung that there is no sense of rush. His whirling one-in-a-bar treatment of Minuets may disconcert traditionalists, but brings exhilarating results. The third movements of both the *Haffner* and No. 39 become scherzos, not just faster but fiercer than regular minuets, and generally his account of No. 39 is as commanding as his outstanding versions of the last two symphonies. The clanging attack of harpsichord continuo is sometimes disconcerting, but this music-making is very refreshing.

Mackerras's ASV version was recorded digitally, in 1985, before he moved on to make his integral set for Telarc. Mackerras here anticipates the urgent style of the later recordings, especially in the Minuets and, with generally brisk speeds, the ASV readings are attractively fresh and full of momentum. Mackerras rarely seeks to charm, but unfussily presents each movement with undistractingly direct manners. The strong character of the music-making is in no doubt, and the sound is appealingly bright and vivid; at super-bargain price this undoubtedly remains competitive.

Symphonies Nos. 34; 35 (Haffner); 39.

*** ASV CDDCA 615. LMP, Glover.

Tackling three major works, Jane Glover provides freshly imaginative performances that can compete with any in the catalogue, given the most vividly realistic recorded sound; Nos. 34 and 39 are especially striking. This collection can be recommended with enthusiasm.

Symphonies Nos. (i) 34,; (ii) 39; 41 (Jupiter).

**(*) Testament mono/stereo SBT 1092. (i) PO, (ii) RPO; Kempe.

The Testament disc of Kempe in Mozart, very well transferred, offers 1956 stereo recordings of Nos. 39 and 41 previously unissued, as well as a 1955 mono account of No. 34. Though the results initially may seem smooth and soft-grained, the conductor's warmth and understanding magnetize the ear. No. 34 has an exhilarating account of the 6/8 finale. The only reservation is over the slowness of the *Minuets* in Nos. 39 and 41.

Symphonies Nos. 35–36; 38–41 – see also under Flute Concertos Nos. 1–2 (above).

Symphony No. 35 (Haffner).

(**) BBC mono BBCL 4016-2 (2). BBC SO, Toscanini –
  BEETHOVEN: *Missa solemnis; Symphony No. 7* (**(*));
  CHERUBINI: *Anacréon Overture*. ***

Mozart's *Haffner Symphony* was always a favourite with Toscanini, and this live performance, recorded in London, is warmer and more sympathetic than either his early version with the New York Philharmonic or his later performance with the NBC Symphony. Though the recording is rather rougher than on the rest of the two-disc set, it makes a valuable bonus to the Beethoven items.

Symphonies Nos. 35 (Haffner); 36 (Linz); 38 (Prague).

(BB) *** RCA Navigator (ADD) 74321 24198-2. ECO, Paillard.

Symphonies Nos. 35 (Haffner); 38 (Prague).

** Ph. 462 587-2. VPO, Muti.

Stylish, excellently paced performances from Paillard and the ECO, with warmly expressive slow movements – that for the *Linz* is particularly fine – and sparkling finales. Those enjoying these works in lively, traditional performances will find there is both polish and warmth here, and plenty of vitality. The recording is resonant but not so much as to obscure detail. An excellent bargain-basement triptych.

Immaculate playing from the VPO and opulent sound. But this is not one of the most recommendable of Muti's Mozart series with the Vienna Philharmonic, fierce in the outer movements at speeds that come to sound breathless.

Symphonies Nos. 35 (Haffner); 40; 41 (Jupiter).

(M) *** Sony (ADD) SBK 46333. Cleveland O, Szell.

As in his companion triptych of late Haydn symphonies, Szell and his Clevelanders are shown at their finest here. The sparkling account of the *Haffner* is exhilarating, and the performances of the last two symphonies are equally polished and strong. Yet there is a tranquil feeling to both *Andantes* that shows Szell as a Mozartian of striking sensibility and finesse. He is at his finest in the *Jupiter*, which has great vigour in the outer movements and a proper weight to balance the rhythmic incisiveness; in spite of the lack of repeats, the work's scale is not diminished. Here the sound is remarkable considering the early date (late 1950s), and the remastering throughout is impressively full-bodied and clean.

Symphonies Nos. 35 (Haffner); 41 (Jupiter).

(B) *** Penguin DG 460 615-2. VPO, Bernstein.

The *Jupiter* brings one of the very finest of Bernstein's Mozart recordings, edited together from live performances. Bernstein observes the repeats in both halves of the finale, and his powerful concentration sustains the length. The *Haffner* brings a similarly satisfying reading until the finale, when Bernstein in the heat of the moment breaks loose with a speed so fast that even the Vienna violins find it hard to articulate exactly. It remains very exciting, and with recording on CD only slightly cloudy in louder tuttis it makes an excellent recommendation, not so heavy in texture as most using regular symphony orchestras. The accompanying author's note, obligatory with this Penguin series, comes from Jane Smiley.

Symphony No. 36 in C (Linz), K.425.

(N) (M) ** BBC (ADD) BBCL 4055-2. LSO, Barbirolli –
    STRAUSS: *Ein Heldenleben, Op. 40.* **

From Barbirolli a big-band performance in the old manner – and none the worse for that! However, it must be admitted that Sir John was not in his usual robust form when this concert was recorded, and there is not much evidence of the elegance and élan which distinguished his finest work.

Symphonies Nos. 36 (Linz); 38 (Prague); 39; 40; 41 (Jupiter).

(B) *** Ph. (ADD) Duo 438 332-2 (2). ASMF, Marriner.

Symphonies Nos. 36 (Linz); 38 (Prague); 40; 41 (Jupiter).

(N) (B) *** EMI double fforte CZS5 74185-2 (2). ECO, Tate.

Tate directs characteristically strong and elegant readings of both the *Linz* and the *Prague Symphonies*, bringing out the operatic overtones in the latter, not just in the *Don Giovanni*-like progressions in the slow introductions, but also in the power of the development section and in the wonder of the chromatic progressions in the slow movement, as well as the often surprising mixing of timbres. In the *Linz*, Tate is again attractively individual, putting rather more emphasis on elegance and finding tenderness in the slow movement, taken like the *Adagio* of the *Prague* at a very measured speed. The last two symphonies are hardly less impressive, although those who prefer a plain approach may find the elegant pointing in slow movements excessive. Tate's account of the *Jupiter* has the clarity of a chamber performance, yet, with trumpets and drums, brings a full weight of expression which never underplays the scale of the argument. In both symphonies, exposition repeats are observed in outer movements and Tate's keen imagination in relation to detail, as well as over a broad span, consistently conveys the electricity of a live performance.

In terms of finesse and elegance of phrasing, the orchestral playing is of very high quality and Marriner's readings are satisfyingly paced, full of vitality and warmth. There is not a whiff of original-instrument style here, but those who enjoy the sound of Mozart in a modern orchestra of a reasonable size should be well satisfied.

Symphonies Nos. 36 (Linz); 39; Overtures: Così fan tutte; Le nozze di Figaro.

** Guild GMCD 7172. Bournemouth Sinf., Frazor.

These Bournemouth performances of a pair of favourite symphonies offer a model combination of warmth, elegance and finesse, though there is drama too, especially when the timpani open No. 39 so boldly. The recording is most naturally balanced. The overtures are neatly done, though they could have a shade more sparkle. But this is an enjoyable programme showing the conductor and orchestra as natural Mozartians.

Symphonies Nos. 37, K.444: Introduction (completed by M. Haydn); 40; 41 (Jupiter).

*** ASV CDDCA 761. LMP, Glover.

Jane Glover does not skimp on repeats, as she might have done. She omits them – as most versions do – in the slow movements, but includes exposition repeats in the finales as well as in first movements, particularly important in the *Jupiter*, with its grandly sublime counterpoint. There Glover's speed is exceptionally fast, with ensemble not quite so refined or crisp as in some rival versions, but still making for a strong and enjoyable reading.

Symphony No. 38 (Prague).

(M) (**) [Mercury mono 434 387-2.] Chicago SO, Kubelik –
DVORAK: *Symphony No. 9 (New World)*. (***)

Kubelik's 1953 account of the *Prague* is splendid: the outer
movements are alert and sparkling, the *Andante* is ideally
paced, gracefully phrased and beautifully played. The effect
is undoubtedly refreshing; the ambience of Chicago's
Orchestral Hall adds warmth, and the only snag is the
consistent edge imparted by the single Telefunken microphone to the violin timbre.

Symphonies Nos. 39–41 (Jupiter).

(B) (***) Dutton Lab. mono CDEA 5012. LPO, Beecham.

This generous coupling of the last three symphonies is made
possible by exposition repeats being omitted in Nos. 39 and
41. As ever, the rhythmic point of the playing, not least from
the LPO woodwind, is delectable so that, with brisk allegros
set against expressive slow movements, these readings seem
as fresh as ever. These always were among the best EMI
recordings of the 1930s, and the Dutton transfers are excellent.

Symphonies Nos. 39; 41 (Jupiter); (i) Concert arias: Si mostra la sorte, K.209; Per pietà, non ricercare, K.420.

(M) (**(*)) Decca stereo/mono 466 820-2. (i) Pears; ECO,
Britten.

The *Jupiter Symphony*, given in Blythburgh church in June
1966, is a strong, direct reading, with brisk outer movements
that bring out the power of the writing, even though the
second-half repeat in the finale is omitted – regular practice
in live performances. The slow movement by contrast is
beautifully moulded at a spacious tempo, with the opening
repeat observed. The stereo sound in a helpful church
acoustic is warmly atmospheric, where the BBC studio
recordings in mono for the other three works are drier, if
clear and well balanced. The bite of the cleanly focused
timpani in the slow introduction to No. 39 makes an aptly
dramatic opening gesture, then leads on to an easily relaxed
view of the main Allegro. The studio acoustic is not so
helpful to Peter Pears, whose voice sounds dry, with vibrato
exaggerated, though the poise and stylishness of the singing
cannot be faulted.

Symphonies Nos. 40; 41 (Jupiter).

✪ (M) *** DG 445 548-2. VPO, Bernstein.
*** Ph. (IMS) 426 315-2. E. Bar. Sol., Gardiner.
*** Telarc CD 80139. Prague CO, Mackerras.
(N) (M) ** Ph. (ADD) 464 721-2. Concg. O, Krips.

(i) Symphonies Nos. 40–41; (ii) Serenade: Eine kleine Nachtmusik.

(B) **(*) DG (ADD) 439 472-2. (i) BPO; (ii) VPO; Boehm.

Bernstein's electrifying account of No. 40 is keenly dramatic,
individual and stylish, with the finale delightfully airy and
fresh. If anything, the *Jupiter* is even finer: it is exhilarating
in its tensions and observes the repeats in both halves of
the finale, making it almost as long as the massive first
movement. Bernstein's electricity sustains that length, and
one welcomes it for establishing the supreme power of

the argument, the true crown in the whole of Mozart's
symphonic output. Pacing cannot be faulted in any of the
four movements and, considering the problems of making
live recordings, the 1984 sound is first rate, lacking only the
last degree of transparency in tuttis. This mid-price reissue
on DG's Masters label now takes its place again at the top
of the list of recommendations for this coupling.

Gardiner's coupling is also very impressive indeed and,
for those wanting period instruments, this is a clear first
choice. These are both large-scale conceptions with the
strings fuller and with less edge than usual, and there are no
eccentric tempi. The finale of the *Jupiter* has great vitality
and purpose. The second repeat is not taken here, which is
a pity; but these remain powerful and stimulating readings,
very well played and recorded.

On Telarc, with generally fast speeds, so brisk that he is
able to observe every single repeat, Mackerras takes a fresh,
direct view which, with superb playing from the Prague
Chamber Orchestra, is also characterful. On the question of
repeats, the doubling in length of the slow movement of
No. 40 makes it almost twice as long as the first movement,
a dangerous proportion – though it is pure gain having both
halves repeated in the magnificent finale of the *Jupiter*.

By its side Boehm sounds mellow and cultivated but still
magnetic and strong. He, of course, is much less generous
in the matter of repeats, but the Berlin Philharmonic play
very beautifully and the recording is agreeably warm and
full, the reissue inexpensive. *Eine kleine Nachtmusik* was
recorded a decade and a half later, and the VPO playing is
polished and fresh, with a neat, lightly pointed finale.

Josef Krips's coupling from 1972 is a very strange choice
for Philips's '50 Great Recordings'. The first movement of
the *G minor* is leisurely to the point of slackness, and although the symphony is predictably beautifully played, and
the finale has much more vitality, this would not be a first
choice. In the *Jupiter* Krips holds the tension even more
loosely, and overall there is something unmemorable and
wanting in character that does not do full honour to the fine
Mozartian Krips undoubtedly was. No complaints, however, about the recording or the excellent transfers. Curiously
the LP sleeve pictured on the frontispiece is of a coupling of
the *Jupiter* with the *Haffner Symphony*.

CHAMBER MUSIC

Adagio & Fugue in C min., K.546.

(N) (BB) (***) Dutton Lab. mono CDBP 9713. Griller Qt –
BLOCH: *String Quartet No. 2; Night*; DVORAK: *String
Quartet No. 12 (American)*.

Played by a string quartet, Mozart's masterly *Adagio and
Fugue* are if anything even tauter and stronger than when
played by full strings. The Griller Quartet, at the peak of
their form in 1948, give a fresh, purposeful reading, very well
recorded, a welcome supplement to the equally fine readings
of popular Dvořák and neglected Bloch.

(i)Adagio & Fugue in C min., K.546; (ii) Adagio & Rondo in C for Glass Harmonica, Flute, Oboe, Viola & Cello; (iii) Clarinet Quintet; (iv) String Quintets Nos. 4–6.

(B) **(*) Ph. (ADD) Duo 456 058-2 (2). (i) Italian Qt;
(ii) Hoffman, Nicolet, Holliger, Schouten, Decroos;
(iii) Brymer, Allegri Qt; (iv) Grumiaux Trio, Gérecz, Lesueur.

(i) *Horn Quintet;* (ii) *Piano & Wind Quintet;* (iii) *String
Quintets Nos. 1–3;* (iv) *Adagio in B flat for 2 Clarinets & 3
Basset Horns.*

(B) **(*) Ph. (ADD) Duo 456 055-2 (2). (i) T. Brown, ASMF
Chamber Ens.; (ii) Haebler, Bamberg Wind Qt (members);
(iii) Grumiaux Trio, Gérecz, Lesueur; (iv) Netherlands Wind
Ens.

Of the additional music above, the *Adagio and Fugue* is
splendidly played by the Quartetto Italiano. The *Adagio and
Rondo* for glass harmonica with Bruno Hoffman playing
that rare instrument, and the *Adagio in B flat* for clarinets
and basset horns, are delectable in these performances. Of
the other major works, Brymer's reading of the *Clarinet
Quintet* is warm and relaxed and very agreeable, if not
distinctive. Timothy Brown is a personable soloist and the
Horn Quintet is given a well-projected and lively account.
However, in spite of Ingrid Haebler's characteristically
stylish contribution to the *Piano and Wind Quintet*, the
Bamberg performance does not take flight, a straightforward
rather than an imaginative account. Throughout all four
CDs the recordings are admirably balanced and given high-
quality analogue sound.

Complete Mozart Edition, Vol. 14: (i) *Adagio for Glass
Harmonica, K.356;* (i; ii) *Adagio in C min. & Rondo for
Glass Harmonica, Flute, Oboe, Viola & Cello;* (iii) *Clarinet
Trio (Kegelstatt), K.498;* (iv; v) *Piano Quartets Nos. 1–2;*
(iv) *Piano Trios Nos. 1–6; Piano Trio in D min., K.442;*
(vi) *Piano & Wind Quintet.*

(M) *** Ph. Dig./ADD 422 514-2 (5). (i) Hoffmann; (ii) with
Nicolet, Holliger, Schouten, Decroos; (iii) Brymer,
Kovacevich, Ireland; (iv) Beaux Arts Trio, (v) with Giuranna;
(vi) Brendel, Holliger, Brunner, Baumann, Thunemann.

This compilation of Mozart's chamber music with piano has
no weak link. The last three discs contain the complete *Piano
Trios* recorded by the Beaux Arts Trio in 1987, a first-rate
cycle which includes not only the six completed trios but
also the composite work, put together by Mozart's friend,
the priest Maximilian Stadler, and listed by Köchel as K.442.
The Beaux Arts' teamwork brings consistently fresh and
winning performances, as it also does in the two great *Piano
Quartets* where they are joined by the viola-player, Bruno
Giuranna. The *Piano and Wind Quintet*, K.452, recorded in
1986, subtly contrasts the artistry of Alfred Brendel at the
piano with that of the oboist, Heinz Holliger, leading a
distinguished team of wind-players. The only non-digital
recordings are those of the *Kegelstatt Trio*, characterfully
done by Stephen Kovacevich with Jack Brymer and Patrick
Ireland, and of the two shorter works involving glass harmonica.

*Adagio & Rondo for Flute, Oboe, Viola, Cello & Piano,
K.617;* (i) *Clarinet Trio (Kegelstatt);* (ii) *Flute Quartets
Nos. 1–4;* (iii) *Horn Quintet;* (iv) *Oboe Quartet.*

(BB) *** Virgin 2 x 1 Double VBD5 61448-2 (2) [CVBD 61448].

Nash Ens., with (i) Collins; (ii) Davies; (iii) Lloyd;
(iv) Hulse.

This inexpensive Virgin Double offers two CDs which pair
naturally together. In the *Adagio and Rondo*, originally
written for glass harmonica, the wind instruments blend
together most felicitously. Michael Collins proves a winningly personable soloist in the *Clarinet Trio*. Gareth Hulse
plays exquisitely in the *Oboe Quartet* and the Nash Ensemble
blend in most sensitively, and give excellent support to Frank
Lloyd's warmly lyrical account of the *Horn Quintet*. The
second disc contains the four *Flute Quartets*, with Philippa
Davies both a nimble and a highly musical flautist. She is
very well balanced with her Nash colleagues and these are
pleasingly warm, intimate performances.

Canons for Strings; Canons for Woodwind: see below,
under VOCAL MUSIC: Complete Mozart Edition,
Vol. 23

Complete Mozart Edition, Vol. 10: (i; vi) *Clarinet Quintet;*
(ii) *Flute Quartets Nos. 1–4;* (iii; vi) *Horn Quintet;* (iv; vi)
Oboe Quartet; (v) *Sonata for Bassoon & Cello, K.292.*
(vi) Fragments: *Allegro in F, K.App. 90/580b for Clarinet,
Basset Horn & String Trio; Allegro in B flat. K.App. 91/
K.516c for a Clarinet Quintet; Allegro in F, K.288 for 2
Horns & Strings; String Quartet Movements: Allegro in
B flat, K.App. 72/464a; Allegro in B flat, K.App. 80/514a;
Minuet in B flat, K.68/589a; Minuet in F, K.168a;
Movement in A, K.App. 72/464a. String Quintet No. 1 in
B flat, K.174: 2 Original Movements: Trio & Finale. Allegro
in A min., K.App. 79, for a String Quintet. Allegro in G,
K.App., 66/562e for a String Trio* (completed, where
necessary, by Erik Smith).

(M) *** Ph. ADD/Dig. 422 510-2 (3). (i) Pay; (ii) Bennett,
Grumiaux Trio; (iii) Brown; (iv) Black; (v) Thunemann,
Orton; (vi) ASMF Chamber Ens.

Complete Bargain Mozart Edition, Vol. 6: *Clarinet
Quintet and Trio; Flute Quartets; Horn Quintet; Oboe
Quartet; Piano Quartets & Piano Trios;* 10 movements and
fragments for chamber ensemble.

(N) (B) *** Ph. (ADD/DDD) 464 820-2 (8), ASMF Chamber
Ens; Beaux Arts Trio, etc.

These are highly praised performances of the major chamber
works featuring modern wind instruments (Antony Pay uses
a normal clarinet). The rest of the items are by no means
inconsequential offcuts but provide music of high quality,
notably the *String Quartet Movement*, K.514a. The *Minuet in
B flat*, K.589a, in the rhythm of a polonaise and possibly the
first draft for the finale of the *Hunt Quartet*, is a real charmer
which, had it received more exposure, might well have
become a Mozartian lollipop like the famous and not dissimilar Minuet in the *D major Divertimento*, K.334. The
two pieces with solo clarinet are also very winning. The
performances here are all polished and spontaneous and
beautifully recorded.

Clarinet Quintet in A, K.581.

*** DG 459 641-2. Shifrin, Emerson Qt – BRAHMS: *Clarinet
Quintet.* ***

(B) *** HM HMN 911 691. Carbonare, Hery, Binder, Bone, Pouzenc – BRAHMS: *Clarinet Quintet.* ***

(B) *** Decca 448 232-2. Schmidl, V. Octet (members) – BEETHOVEN: *Septet in E flat, Op. 20.* ***

(BB) **(*) Belart (ADD) 450 056-2. Brymer, Allegri Qt – SCHUBERT: *Trout Quintet.* ***

David Shifrin achieves a particularly fine partnership with the Emerson Quartet and the recording balance is beautifully managed. The flowing opening movement has an appealing simplicity and the *Larghetto* is comparably songful and re-fined in feeling. Perhaps finest of all are the variations of the finale with the sunny solo-playing balanced with pleasing delicacy from the strings. The thoughtful central *Adagio* and return to the spirited opening mood are particularly successful. If you want a coupling with Brahms this can be strongly recommended.

With talented young performers in Harmonia Mundi's bargain series, Les Nouveaux Interprètes, this apt coupling is most welcome. Alessandro Carbonare, principal clarinet of the Orchestre Nationale of France, produces exceptionally beautiful, liquid tone-colours over the widest dynamic range. Clear and fresh as the outer movements are, the high point is the *Larghetto*, magically gentle and with the main melody tastefully elaborated on its reprise. The four string-players, also members of the Orchestre Nationale, are not quite so distinctive yet provide most sympathetic support.

Peter Schmidl, using a basset clarinet, is sometimes just a little cool, but his intimate approach has its own appeal. He phrases with imagination and much delicacy in matters of light and shade. Of course, these Viennese players use modern instruments, and the sound they make is consist-ently full and smooth. The 1989 Decca recording is state-of-the-art, and while this would not necessarily be a clear first choice for the *Quintet*, it is very distinguished, and the splendid Beethoven coupling makes this Eclipse reissue an outstanding bargain.

Brymer's interpretation of the *Clarinet Quintet* is warm and leisurely, and he chooses slow tempi throughout. With his tone so succulent, and with velvety support from the Allegri Quartet, he is almost entirely successful in sustaining them. The recorded sound is warm and flattering, and this is still very beguiling.

Clarinet Quintet; Clarinet Quintet Fragment in B flat, K.516c.

(*) ASV CDDCA 1079. Johnson, Takacs-Nagy, Hirsch, Boulton, Shulman – WEBER: *Clarinet Quintet.* *

Clarinet Quintet; Clarinet Quintet Fragment in B flat, K.516c; (i) Quintet Fragment in F for Clarinet in C, Basset Horn & String Trio, K.580b (both completed by Druce).

*** Amon Ra/Saydisc (ADD) CD-SAR 17. Hacker, Salomon Qt, (i) with Schatzberger.

This is a superb recording by Alan Hacker with the Salomon Quartet, using original instruments. Hacker's gentle sound on his period instrument is displayed at its most ravishing in the *Larghetto*. Tempi are wonderfully apt and the rhythms of the finale are infectious, the music's sense of joy fully projected. The recording balance is near perfect. Hacker includes a fragment from an earlier projected *Quintet* and a

similar sketch for a work featuring C clarinet and basset horn with string trio. Both are skilfully completed by Duncan Druce.

Clarinet Quintet in A, K.581; Allegro in B Flat for Clarinet Quintet, K.516c..

(*) ASV CDDCA 1079. Johnson. Takacs-Nagy, Hirsch, Boulton, Shulman – WEBER: *Clarinet Quintet.* *

The coupling of Weber's and Mozart's *Clarinet Quintets* is surprisingly rare, with Emma Johnson here offering a welcome, if brief, bonus in the fragment of a further quintet which Mozart wrote some time after 1790 just before his death, and which frustratingly breaks off just after the end of the exposition. Emma Johnson gives characterful readings, warmly expressive in the first movement of the main work, dashing in the last two movements. The close balance of the clarinet means that the slow movement is less poised than it can be, with some tonal unevenness. Sensitive support from four formidable chamber-players, but this is a less impressive account than the sparkling Weber coupling where the soloist returns to her most spontaneous form.

Clarinet Quintet in A, K.581; Clarinet Trio in E flat, K.498.

(B) **(*) HM HMA 1901384. Boeykens & Ens.

It is surprising that the Mozart *Clarinet Quintet* is not more often coupled with the *Trio*, a less inspired but still very enjoyable work. Both performances here are of high quality and beautifully recorded. Walter Boeykens's sensitive solo playing is well matched by his colleagues. Perhaps the *Larghetto* of the *Quintet* has been played even more imaginatively elsewhere, but here its gentle serenity is paramount. Excellent value.

(i) Clarinet Quintet; (ii) Flute Quartet No. 1; (iii) Oboe Quartet

(B) **(*) EMI CDZ5 69702-2. (i) Nicholas Carpenter; (ii) Jaime Martin; (iii) Jonathan Kelly; Brindisi Qt (members).

The three soloists introduced here in EMI's Debut series are all principals with various British orchestras. Each is a first-rate artist and all three performances are fresh and enjoyable, with the *Flute Quartet* the most successful of the three. In both the other works the slow movements, although played persuasively, are just a little plain; to make up for it, all three finales are sprightly, with that of the *Clarinet Quintet* being particularly successful. The members of the Brindisi Quartet provide admirable support, and the recording is excellent, vivid and transparent.

(i) Clarinet Quintet; (ii) Horn Quintet; (iii) Oboe Quartet, K.370.

(M) *** Ph. 422 833-2. (i) Pay; (ii) T. Brown; (iii) Black; ASMF Chamber Ens.

*** Nim. NI 5487. (i) Leister; (ii) Seifert; (iii) Koch; Brandis Qt.

Antony Pay's earlier account of the *Clarinet Quintet*, played on a modern instrument, with the Academy of St Martin-in-the-Fields players must be numbered among the strongest now on the market for those not insisting on an authentic basset clarinet. Neil Black's playing in the *Oboe Quartet* is distinguished, and again the whole performance radiates pleasure, while the *Horn Quintet* comes in a well-projected and lively account with Timothy Brown. The recording is of Philips's best.

We have heard these fine soloists on Nimbus before, all ex-principals of the Berlin Philharmonic. Karl Leister provides an essentially light-hearted account of the *Clarinet Quintet*, with the slow movement tranquil and beautifully poised. Gerd Seifert is just as lively and sensitive in the work for horn, even if his tone is a little plump. Koch is equally personable in the *Oboe Quartet*, although perhaps just a trifle studied in sustaining the *Adagio* (so beautifully opened by the Brandis Quartet). The recording, comparatively forward, is vividly present.

(i) *Clarinet quintet;* (ii) *Horn Quintet; String Quintet No. 3 in G min. K.516.*

(N) (BB) **(*) HM HCX 3957059. (i) Hoeprich; (ii) Greer; Music from Aston Magna.

Aston Magna offer very good period instrument performances of three of Mozart's best-loved quintets: for clarinet (here basset clarinet), horn (a well-played hand-horn, without valves), and the obvious favourite among the composer's string quintets, in G minor. Erich Hoeprich is a sensitive soloist with a lovely tone in the *Clarinet Quintet*. His performance is direct rather than subtle in inflection, but with plenty of light and shade, and very musical in phrasing. The *Horn Quintet* is robust and sprightly (a little lacking in solo finesse in the *Andante*), and the *String Quintet* comes off particularly well, especially the lovely *Adagio* which is beautifully transparent in texture. Excellent value, but not a first choice.

(i) *Clarinet Quintet;* (ii) *Oboe Quartet in F, K.370.*

(B) *** CfP (ADD/Dig.) 574 8832. (i) A. Marriner; (ii) Hunt; Chilingirian Qt (with *Clarinet Concerto.* ***)

Andrew Marriner's playing in the *Quintet* is wonderfully flexible; it reaches its apex in the radiantly beautiful reading of the slow movement, although the finale is also engagingly characterized. The *Oboe Quartet* is delectable too, with Gordon Hunt a highly musical and technically accomplished soloist. The *Clarinet Concerto* has been added for the reissue, beautifully played but rather less spontaneous.

(i) *Clarinet Quintet. String Quartet No. 18 in A, K.464.*

**(*) ASV CDDCA 1042. (i) Hilton; Lindsay Qt.

Janet Hilton gives a disarmingly simple, unaffected account of the *Clarinet Quintet* and gets excellent support from the Lindsays. The performance of the *A major Quartet* is characteristically perceptive and vital, with the *Andante* on the whole beautifully played, although some may find dynamics a little overstressed. The balance is forward and vivid.

(i) *Clarinet Quintet. String Quartet No. 19 (Dissonance), K.465.*

**(*) Cal. 6256. (i) Cuper; Talich Qt.

For their newest, digital recording of the *Clarinet Quintet* the Talich group have chosen Philippe Cuper, a fine and sensitive soloist. Both works here are immaculately played with many felicitous touches (notably the gentle reprise of

the slow movement of the *Quintet*). But neither performance has that extra dimension of spontaneous feeling that makes for true memorability.

(i) *Clarinet Quintet. String Quartet No. 20 in D (Hoffmeister), K.499.*

(M) **(*) Whitehall Associates MQCD 600l. (i) Brymer; Medici Qt.

The Medici String Quartet have set up their own label. Jack Brymer joins them for their first Mozart CD and has a benign influence in a fine, mellifluous performance of the *Clarinet Quintet*. He plays the *Adagio* as a sustained half-tone and conjures from the strings comparably soft playing. The finale is delightful; there is an attractive improvisational feeling in the lyrical variation before the main theme makes its joyful return. The recording is truthful, but the close balance is more noticeable in the coupled *Hoffmeister Quartet*, which is a lively, well-integrated performance.

(i) *Clarinet Quintet;* (ii) *Violin Sonatas in F, K.376; E flat, K.481.*

(M) *** Cal. 6628. (i) Zahradnik, Talich Qt; (ii) Messiereur, Bogunia.

The *Clarinet Quintet* is exquisitely done. Bohuslav Zahradnik's contribution has much delicacy of feeling and colour; he is highly seductive in the slow movement, and even in the finale the effect is gentle in the most appealing way without any loss of vitality. The recording balance is exemplary. The two *Violin Sonatas* are also beautifully played in a simple, direct style that is wholly persuasive. The recording is clearly detailed and well balanced, if slightly more shallow.

Complete Mozart Edition, Vol. 13: (i) *Divertimento in E flat for String Trio, K.563;* (ii) *Duos for Violin & Viola Nos. 1–2, K.423/4;* (i) *6 Preludes & Fugues for String Trio, K.404a;* (iii) *Sonata (String Trio) in B flat, K.266.*

(M) *** Ph. (ADD) 422 513-2 (2). (i) Grumiaux, Janzer, Szabo; (ii) Grumiaux, Pelliccia; (iii) ASMF Chamber Ens.

(B) *** Ph. Duo (ADD) 454 023-2 (2). As above.

Complete Mozart Bargain Edition, Vol. 8: (i) *Duos & String Trios;* (ii) *Violin Sonatas; Sonatinas,* etc. (complete).

(N) (B) *** Ph. (ADD/DDD) 464 840-2 (9). (i) Grumiaux Trio or ASMF Chamber. Ens., (ii) various artists.

Grumiaux's 1967 recorded performance of the *Divertimento in E flat* remains unsurpassed; he is here joined by two players with a similarly refined and classical style. In the *Duos*, which are ravishingly played, the balance is excellent, and Arrigo Pelliccia proves a natural partner in these inspired and rewarding works. The *Sonata for String Trio* is well played by the ASMF Chamber Ensemble and it has a modern, digital recording. Of the six *Preludes and Fugues*, the first three derive from Bach's *Well-tempered Clavier*, the fourth combines an *Adagio* from the *Organ Sonata*, BWV 527, with *Contrapunctus 8* from the *Art of Fugue*, the fifth is a transcription of two movements from the *Organ Sonata*, BWV 526, and the sixth uses music of W. F. Bach. The performances here are sympathetic and direct, the recorded sound bold, clear and bright.

Flute Quartets Nos. 1 in D, K.285; 2 in G, K.285a; 3 in C, K.285b; 4 in A, K.298.

*** EMI CDC5 56829-2. Pahud, Poppen, Schlicht, Queras.

(M) *** Van. (ADD) 08.4001.71. Robinson, Tokyo Qt (members).

*** Accent (ADD) ACC 48225D. Bernhard and Sigiswald Kuijken, Van Dael, Wieland Kuijken.

(i) *Flute Quartets Nos. 1–4;* (ii) *Andante for Flute & Orchestra in C, K.315.*

(B) *** DHM (ADD) 05472 77442-2. B. Kuijken; (i) Members of Coll. Aur.; (ii) La Petite Band.

(i) *Flute Quartets Nos. 1–4;* (ii) *Oboe Quartet in F, K.370.*

(M) *** DG (IMS) (ADD) 453 287-2. (i) Blau; (ii) Koch; Amadeus Qt (members).

Flute Quartets Nos. 1–4; Oboe Quartet (arr. for flute, Galway), *K.370.*

**(*) RCA 09026 60442-2. Galway, Tokyo Qt.

The Swiss flautist Emmanuel Pahud, the young principal flute of the Berlin Philharmonic, gives inspired performances of the four Mozart *Flute Quartets.* These are all early works, generally lightweight, but with one movement of deep emotional feeling, the B minor *Adagio* of the *First Quartet, K.285.* In that songful piece Pahud finds new mystery through his subtly shaded phrasing. Otherwise this is a fun disc, full of youthful high spirits, charming and witty. Even more than his earlier disc of Mozart concertos for EMI this signals the arrival of a new master flautist.

Andreas Blau is a fine artist and the Amadeus accompany him with subtlety and distinction. These performances are matched by the refinement of Koch in the *Oboe Quartet.* With creamy tone, nice embellishments (especially in the finale) and very stylish phrasing, he is splendid. The Amadeus accompany with sensibility and the balance is flawless.

James Galway is an impeccable soloist and the Tokyo Quartet provide admirable support. The recording too is fresh and well balanced and, if Galway dominates, that is partly the result of Mozart's writing and the use of a modern instrument. Some may feel that in slow movements his sweet, silvery timbre and individual vibrato are too much of a good thing. The transcription of the *Oboe Quartet* is more questionable, although it must be admitted that here the *Adagio* sounds refreshingly different on the flute, and the performance cannot be faulted.

The Vanguard recording of the *Flute Quartets* (presumably from the 1960s – no date is given) is most winning. Paula Robinson displays a captivating lightness of touch and her silvery timbre seems eminently suited to Mozart. Needless to say, the Tokyo Quartet provide polished accompaniments which combine warmth with much finesse, and the recording is most naturally balanced.

Readers normally unresponsive to period instruments should hear these performances by Bernhard Kuijken, for they have both charm and vitality; they radiate pleasure and bring one close to this music. This record is rather special

and cannot be recommended too strongly. The playing is exquisite and the engineering superb.

The Collegium Aureum set is the only bargain version using period instruments. Barthold Kuijken plays a beguilingly soft instrument from Dresden, made by August Grenser in 1789, and the effect has great charm. The playing of the three string instruments is also very smooth and accomplished, and the ensemble is beautifully recorded in a warm acoustic. The pitch is lower by a semitone, but few listeners will mind this. The *Andante for Flute and Orchestra* makes an engaging encore.

Horn Quintet in E flat, K.407.

(N) (BB) *** Warner Apex 8573 89080-2. Vlatkovic, Berlin Soloists – BEETHOVEN: *Septet, Op. 20.* ***

Radovan Vlatkovic is a most musical soloist, and his companions provide a warmly affectionate backing, most naturally recorded. The *Andante* is beautifully phrased by soloist and string group alike and the finale is appropriately perky. Excellent value.

Horn Quintet in E flat, K.407; Horn Duos in E flat, K.487/ 496a.

(B) *** EMI Debut CDZ5 72822-2. Clark (waldhorn); (i) Ens. Galant; (ii) Montgomery – BEETHOVEN: *Horn Sonata; Sextet, Op. 81b;* BRAHMS: *Horn Trio.* ***

On EMI's bargain Debut label Andrew Clark uses a waldhorn and displays considerable panache. As in the Brahms *Trio,* his virtuosity is well matched by his partners, also using period instruments. The two rare Mozart *Duos* are guaranteed to win the listener. Strongly recommended.

Horn Quintet; (ii) *Oboe Quartet in F, K.370; A Musical Joke, K.522.*

(BB) **(*) Naxos 8.550437. (i) Kiss; (ii) Keveházi; Kodály Qt.

Highly musical if not especially individual performances of the *Horn Quintet* and *Oboe Quartet;* in the latter the oboe is balanced forwardly and seems a bit larger than life; but no matter, the recordings have a pleasingly resonant bloom. The *Musical Joke* really comes off well: the horn players have a great time with their wrong notes.

Piano Quartets Nos. 1 in G min., K.478; 2 in E flat, K.493 **(see also above, under Complete Mozart Edition, Vol. 14).**

*** Sony SK 66841. Ax, Isaac Stern, Jaime Laredo, Yo-Yo Ma.

*** Ph. (IMS) 410 391-2. Beaux Arts Trio with Giuranna.

(BB) ** Naxos 8.554274. Menuhin Festival Piano Qt.

(N) (BB) *(*) Warner Apex (AAD) Ránki; Eder Qt (members).

(i) *Piano Quartets Nos. 1, K.478; 2, K.493. Rondo in A min., K.411.*

(N) (M) ** RCA (ADD) 09026 63075-2. Rubinstein, Guaneri Qt (members).

The grouping of star names by Sony offers performances of keen imagination and insight, with the line-up of three string soloists bringing extra individuality compared with members of a string quartet. Speeds are beautifully chosen and in both works the performances consistently convey a sense of happy spontaneity. It is striking that Emanuel Ax, in the many passages in which the piano is set against the strings, establishes the sort of primacy required, pointing rhythms and moulding phrases persuasively. The recording, made in the Manhattan Center, New York, in 1994, is a degree drier than in many previous versions, suggesting a small rather than a reverberant hall.

The Beaux Arts group provide splendidly alive and vitally sensitive accounts that exhilarate the listener, just as does the Curzon–Amadeus set (see below), and they have the advantage of first-class digital recording. The Beaux Arts play them not only con amore but with the freshness of a new discovery, and the sound (particularly that of the piano) is exceptionally lifelike.

The Menuhin Festival Piano Quartet is an international ensemble with an excellent German pianist, Friedemann Rieger, an American violinist, Nora Chastain, the Scottish-born violist Paul Coletti and a French cellist, Francis Gouton. They give very spirited accounts of both quartets, observing not only the exposition but also second-time repeats in the first movements, though the brilliant pianist is a little monochrome. They are not as tonally subtle as our first recommendations, but the acoustic in which they are recorded is a bit dry and so does not flatter them.

The pity is that Rubinstein's bright and invigorating playing and indeed the string timbre of the members of the Guarneri Quartet have been given added artificial brightness and their forwardness exaggerated by the recording balance. The mercurial re-creation of two of Mozart's most delectable chamber works is here in the hands of a pianist who is nothing if not an individualist and the liveliness of Rubinstein – even in his eighties enjoying himself with fellow-musicians – is ample reason for hearing this coupling, even if the string sound is not wholly congenial.

On Warner Apex Deszö Ránki and members of the Eder Quartet give polished accounts of these two engaging works, notable for their simplicity of approach and unostentatious musicianship. But the AAD remastering has left an edge on the timbre of Pál Eder's violin which spoils the otherwise smoothly balanced sound picture.

(i) Piano Quartets Nos. 1–2; (ii) Horn Quintet in E flat, K.407.

❂ (M) *** Decca mono 425 960-2. (i) Curzon, Amadeus Qt; (ii) Brain, Griller Qt.

All versions of the Mozart Piano Quartets rest in the shadow of the recordings by Clifford Curzon and members of the Amadeus Quartet. No apologies need be made for the 1952 mono recorded sound. The performances have a unique sparkle, slow movements are Elysian. One's only criticism is that the Andante of K.478 opens at a much lower dynamic level than the first movement, and some adjustment of the controls needs to be made. The Horn Quintet coupling was recorded in 1944 and the transfer to CD is even more miraculous. The slight surface rustle of the 78-r.p.m. source is in no way distracting and Dennis Brain's performance combines warmth and elegance with a spirited spontaneity, and the subtleties of the horn contribution are a continuous delight. A wonderful disc that should be in every Mozartian's library.

Piano Quartet No. 1 in G min., K.478.

*** Ph. 446 001-2. Brendel, Zehetmair, Zimmermann, Duven – SCHUBERT: Trout Quintet. ***

Brendel's performance of the G minor Piano Quartet has vigour and sensitivity and, not surprisingly, an admirable sense of style. It very well recorded too and, although most collectors will prefer a disc containing both piano quartets, this is a sizeable bonus for an outstanding account of Schubert's Trout Quintet.

Piano Trios Nos. 1–6 (see also above, under Complete Mozart Edition, Vol. 14).

Piano Trios Nos. 1 in B flat, K.254; 2 in G, K.496; 3 in B flat, K.502; 4 in E, K.542; 5 in C, K.548; 6 in G, K.564.

(N) (B) *** Teldec Ultima 8573 87794-2 (2). Trio Fontenay.
*** Chan. 8536/7 (2). Borodin Trio.
(B) **(*) EMI double fforte (ADD) CZS5 73350-2 (2). V. Trio.

Piano Trios Nos. 1–6; Piano Trio in D min., K.442.

*** Ph. (IMS) 422 079-2 (3). Beaux Arts Trio.

The Trio Fontenay have already given us excellent accounts of the Brahms and Dvořák Piano Trios and they are equally happy in the music of Mozart. As before, the splendid pianist Wolf Harden dominates the music-making by strength of personality, although the others are well in the picture, and the contribution of the cellist, Niklas Schmidt, is notable. The playing of this group is consistently fresh and spontaneous.

Indeed, these musicians are completely at one with Mozart and the recording is truthful and well balanced. Although the earlier Beaux Arts set remains very tempting on a Philips Duo (which throws in the Clarinet Trio for good measure), this Teldec set costs much less and has the advantage of modern digital recording.

Apart from including the D minor Trio completed by Stadler, the Beaux Arts are more generous with repeats, which accounts for the extra disc in their digital version. Their performances are eminently fresh and are no less delightful and winning. There is a somewhat lighter touch here compared with the Chandos alternative, thanks in no small degree to the subtle musicianship of Menahem Pressler. The Philips recording is strikingly realistic and present.

The Borodin Trio are slightly weightier in their approach and their tempi are generally more measured than the Beaux Arts, very strikingly so in the Allegretto of the G major. All the same, there is, as usual with this group, much sensitive playing and every evidence of distinguished musicianship. The balance in the Philips set tends to favour the piano a little; the Chandos, recorded at The Maltings, Snape, perhaps produces the more integrated sound.

Claus-Christian Schuster, the pianist on the EMI Vienna set, is a stylishly elegant player. He very much dominates his colleagues, but the recording itself is smooth and natural. These performances are lightweight, but they certainly give pleasure.

Piano & Wind Quintet in E flat, K.452.

(M) *** Sony SMK 42099. Perahia, members of ECO –
   BEETHOVEN: *Quintet.* ***

(N) *** CBC MCVD 1137. Kuerti, Campbell, Mason,
   Sommerville, McKay – MOZART; WITT: *Quintets.* ***

(N) **(*) Erato 4509 96359-2. Barenboim, Soloists of Chicago
   SO – BEETHOVEN: *Piano & Wind Quintet.* ***

An outstanding account (now at mid-price) of Mozart's
delectable *Piano and Wind Quintet* on Sony, with Perahia's
playing wonderfully refreshing in the *Andante* and a superb
response from the four wind soloists, and in particular
Neil Black's oboe. Clearly all the players are enjoying this
rewarding music, and they are well balanced, with the piano
against the warm but never blurring acoustics of The Maltings at Snape.

The performance by this excellent group of leading Canadian instrumentalists is hardly less captivating. They share
this wonderful music as a perfectly matched team. The
pianist, Anton Kuerti, sets the mood of the ravishing *Andante* with great poise with the finale hardly less captivating.
This is playing of great freshness and striking spontaneity,
given a perfectly balanced recording of vividness and presence. Moreover, the CBC issue scores by including also the
quintet of Friedrich Witt, closely modelled on the present
work.

Barenboim shares Mozart and Beethoven with members
of his Chicago Orchestra, and the result is undoubtedly fresh
and vital. But his comparatively brisk approach to the first
movement misses the feeling of relaxation that this music
ideally needs, and although the players work very well together elsewhere, and especially in the pert finale, this well
recorded performance is not a top choice.

Piano & Wind Quintet in E flat, K.452; Adagio in B flat, K.411; Adagio in C, K.580a; Adagio & Allegro in F min., K.594; Adagio & Rondeau in C min., K.617; Andante for a Small Organ Cylinder in F, K.616; Piece for Musical Clock in F min., K.608.

(N) *** BIS CD 1132. Hough, Berlin Philharmonic Wind
   Quintet.

The *Quintet for Piano and Wind* finds Stephen Hough and
the Berlin Philharmonic Wind Quintet in splendid form.
They have lightness and wit to commend them, as well as
an impeccable feeling for style. This recording is as good as
any in the catalogue and survives the most exalted comparisons. The remaining pieces are all sensitive arrangements
written by the flautist on this disc, Michael Hasel. However,
do not expect two clarinets and three basset-horns in K.411,
as there is a conventional wind quintet. Hough does his best
to sound like the musical glasses for which Mozart wrote
K.608. Good playing and recording throughout.

String quartets

Complete Mozart Edition, Vol. 12: String Quartets Nos. 1–23.

(M) *** Ph. (ADD) 422 512-2 (8). Italian Qt.

Complete Mozart Bargain Edition, Vol. 7: (i) String Quartets (complete); (ii) String Quintets (complete).

(N) (B) *** Ph. (ADD) 464 830-2 (11). (i) Italian Qt;
   (ii) Grumiaux, Gérecz, Janzer, Lesueur, Czako.

The earliest recordings by the Italians now begin to show
their age (notably the six *Haydn Quartets,* which date from
1966): the violin timbre is thinner than we would expect in
more modern versions. But the quality is generally very
satisfactory, for the Philips sound-balance is admirably
judged. As a set, the performances have seen off all chal-
lengers for two decades or more; one is unlikely to assemble
a more consistently satisfying overview of these works, or
one so beautifully played. They hold a very special place in
the Mozartian discography.

String Quartet No. 1, K.80.

(B) *** Discover DICD 920171. Sharon Qt – BEETHOVEN:
   Harp Quartet; RAVEL: *Quartet in F.* **(*)

The Sharon Quartet give an excellent account of Mozart's
First divertimento-like *Quartet,* which he wrote in Italy at
the age of fifteen. The playing has life and finesse and,
although the recording (made in a Cologne church) is reverberant, detail is clear; indeed the acoustic rather suits the
music.

String Quartets Nos. 8, K.168; 9, K.169; 10, K.170; 11, K.171; 12, K.172.

*** Cal. CAL 9247. Talich Qt.

The Talich are the soul of finesse and play with great expressive simplicity, while bringing vitality to allegros and
conveying a consistent feeling of spontaneous vitality
throughout. They are naturally if forwardly balanced, and
beautifully recorded. There are few records of Mozart's
earlier quartets to match this collection.

String Quartets Nos. 14, K.387; 15, K.421; 16, K.428; 17 (Hunt), K.458; 18, K.464; 19 (Dissonance), K.465 (Haydn Quartets); 20 (Hoffmeister), K.499; 21, K.575; 22 in B flat, K.589; 23 in F, K.590 (Prussian Quartets Nos. 1–3).

(M) *** Teldec 4509 95495-2 (4). Alban Berg Qt.

The Teldec recordings were made by the Alban Berg in the
latter half of the 1970s; the performances have not since been
surpassed, and now they make one of the most distinguished
sets of Mozart's late quartets currently available, with the
additional advantage of economy. The playing is thoroughly
stylish and deeply musical; it is entirely free from surface
gloss and there are none of the expressive exaggerations of
dynamics and phrasing that marred this group's later records
for EMI. The *Haydn Quartets* are consistently successful; the
Hunt (1979) is still possibly the finest on the market and the
Dissonance too is first class, with a wonderfully expressive
account of the slow movement.

String Quartets Nos. 14–19 (Haydn Quartets); 20 (Hoffmeister), K.499; 21–23 (Prussian Nos. 1–3).

(B) *** Nim. NI 1778 (5). Franz Schubert Qt of Vienna.

Among modern recordings this is outstanding in every way,
and for those wanting Mozart's last ten and – by general

consent – greatest quartets, this Nimbus bargain box rather sweeps the board. The Franz Schubert Quartet play with a refreshing lack of affectation, natural warmth, and great sweetness of tone. There is nothing narcissistic about their playing, and the listener is held from start to finish. In the six *Haydn Quartets* comparison with the Talich, and (at full price) the Chilingirians, is in no way disadvantageous to the Viennese group, who have the advantage of first-class, modern, digital recording (made between 1992 and 1994), most naturally balanced in a pleasing acoustic.

String Quartets Nos. 14–19 (Haydn Quartets).

(M) *** Audivis E 8596 (3) (*Nos. 14 & 15*: E 8843; *Nos. 16 & 17*: E 8844; *Nos. 18 & 19*: E 8845). Mosaïques Qt.

(M) *** CRD (ADD) 3362 (*Nos. 14–15*); 3363; (*Nos. 16–17*); 3364; (*Nos. 18–19*). Chilingirian Qt.

*** Hyp. CDS 44001/3. Salomon Qt.

(i) *String Quartets Nos. 14–19 (Haydn Quartets); also No. 3, K.156;* (ii) *Violin Sonata No. 18 in G, K.301.*

(M) *** Cal. 3241/3. (i) Talich Qt; (ii) Messiereur, Bogunia (with HAYDN: *String Quartet No. 74 in G min., Op. 74/3* **(*)).

String Quartets Nos. 14; 15.

(M) **(*) Whitehall Associates MQCD 6004. Medici Qt.

String Quartets Nos. 16; 19 (Dissonance).

(M) **(*) Whitehall Associates MQCD 6002. Medici Qt.

String Quartets Nos. 17 (Hunt); 18.

(M) **(*) Whitehall Associates MQCD 6003. Medici Qt.

Although we have long had a special liking for the mid-price Chilingirian performances on CRD, this new set by the Mosaïques Quartet must take pride of place, the more particularly as it too is offered at mid-price. As with their previous award-winning performances of Haydn, this is playing of great distinction which offers new insights in every one of the six quartets. Phrasing is wonderfully musical, textures are elegantly blended, there is great transparency yet a full sonority, and this music-making unfolds freshly and naturally. Slow movements have great concentration, yet allegros are alert and vital and finales are a joy. The recording is first class. The three CDs are separately packaged in a slip-case and now they are also available separately most attractively packaged.

For those wanting performances on modern instruments, the Chilingirian Quartet plays with unforced freshness and vitality, avoiding expressive mannerism but always conveying the impression of spontaneity, helped by the warm and vivid recording. The three CDs are packaged separately and offer demonstration quality.

The playing of the Salomon Quartet is highly accomplished and has a real sense of style; they do not eschew vibrato, though their use of it is not liberal, and there is admirable clarity of texture and vitality of articulation. There is no want of subtlety and imagination in the slow movements. The recordings are admirably truthful and lifelike, and those who seek 'authenticity' in Mozart's chamber music will not be disappointed.

The performances by the Talich Quartet are immaculate in ensemble and the performances have a special kind of shared intimacy which is yet immediately communicative. The analogue recordings are beautiful, very smooth on top, the balance slightly middle- and bass-orientated. The set has now been issued complete on three mid-priced discs with a pair of bonuses. The *Violin Sonata* comes after the *Dissonance Quartet*; the Haydn quartet, Op. 74/3, after the *Hunt*, K.458, at a disconcertingly higher level. This too is a fine performance – but be prepared!

The Medici provide a polished, well-integrated set of 'Haydn' quartets, fresh and alert, if without always the touch of extra individuality that appears in their account of the *Clarinet Quintet*. The studio recordings are rather closely balanced (although they are not airless) and the leader is obviously near the microphone. These records are competitively priced and certainly give pleasure.

String Quartets Nos. 14–15.

(N) ❂ (BB) *** Dutton mono CDBP 9702. Griller Qt –
HAYDN: *String Quartet No. 39.* *** ❂

(N) *** MDG 307 1035-2. Leipzig Quartet.

Even more than the *Adagio and Fugue* (above) the playing of Nos. 14, K.387, and 15, K.421, by the Grillers reveals their supreme musicianship in Mozart, their warmth and above all the spontaneous feeling of their playing. Moreover, the miraculous Dutton transfers of these superb Decca ffrr recordings are so natural and beautiful that the sound is preferable to many modern digital recordings. Just sample their fizzing account of the *Molto allegro finale* of K.387 or the simple beauty of the *Andante* of K.421 to discover quartet playing of a very rare calibre indeed.

Those preferring first-class digital recordings played on modern instruments with greater tonal warmth than afforded by the Mosaïques group will find the Leipzig Quartet second to none. As in their recordings of the three last quartets (see below), these performances also combine warmth and finesse with a natural spontaneity, and their music-making has much in common with the Grillers. They play repeats omitted on the earlier recordings. A lovely disc.

String Quartet No. 14; (i) *String Quintet No. 4 in G min., K.516.*

*** ASV CDDCA 923. Lindsay Qt, (i) with Ireland.

This is what chamber-music playing is about. The Lindsays radiate a delight in their music and judge the character of each piece of music exactly, and one has only to sample the finale of K.387, played with enormous vitality and sparkle, to sense immediately that the music-making is a world apart. The slow movement of the *G minor String Quintet* is very touching in its gentle intensity. These are among the finest modern recordings of either work. The disc must be recommended with enthusiasm.

String Quartets Nos. 15; 16; 18.

(***) Testament mono/stereo SBT 1117. Smetana Qt.

These are performances of a singular distinction, supremely classical in every way. The slow movement of K.428 has rarely sounded more affecting. This quartet appears in stereo for the first time. The *A major*, K.464, has not been issued before, and gives equal satisfaction. A very special record.

String Quartet No. 15; (i) String Quintet No. 5 in D, K.593.

**(*) ASV CDDCA 1018. Lindsay Qt. (i) Williams.

These are perceptive, highly musical and essentially dramatic accounts, very well played. But as with the other issues in this series, accents are strong, and in the *Andante* of the *D minor Quartet*, and the *Adagio* of the *Quintet* there are dynamic surges, which not all listeners will find quite comfortable. Alternative versions of the finale of the *Quintet* demonstrate how the main theme can either be presented as a descending chromatic scale, or a simplified 'zigzag' rhythmic pattern. With CD cueing you can take your choice. Vividly forward sound.

String Quartets Nos. 16–17 (Hunt) .

(B) **(*) Ph. (ADD) 422 832-2. Italian Qt.

The Italian players give a fine, unaffected account of the *Hunt Quartet*, although some may feel that is is a shade undercharacterized in places. K.428 however gives little cause for complaint, the playing unfailingly perceptive and most musical. In the present transfer, the ambient effect of the 1977 recording remains pleasing but the upper range is thinner, noticeably less smooth than the CRD recording of the Chilingirians.

String Quartet No. 17 (Hunt) .

(M) *** DG (IMS) (ADD) 449 092-2. Amadeus Qt – HAYDN: *String Quartets Nos. 77–78.* ***

**(*) Testament mono SBT 1085. Hollywood Qt – HUMMEL: *Quartet in G* *(*); HAYDN: *Quartet No. 76.* **(*)

The Amadeus, recorded in 1963, give a strikingly fine account of the *Hunt*, famous in its day. The reading is well characterized and, though there are some touches that will not have universal appeal, this is, generally speaking, a most satisfying version, notable for a finely blended and naturally balanced recording, which has been transferred beautifully to CD.

   The Hollywood Quartet's performance was recorded at a memorable concert in London's Royal Festival Hall in September 1957, and also included the Haydn coupling. The performance is as impeccable as one would expect from these artists and the sound astonishingly good for the period.

String Quartets Nos. 17 (Hunt); 19 (Dissonance).

(BB) **(*) Naxos 8.550105. Moyzes Qt.

The Moyzes Quartet come from Bratislava and are an accomplished ensemble, distinguished by a generally sweet and light tone, and decently recorded in the clean acoustic of the Concert Hall of Slovak Radio. The performances are very well prepared and neatly played, phrasing is musical and often sensitive, even if the overall effect is just a little bland. But the performances still have a lot going for them and can be recommended.

String Quartet No. 19 (Dissonance), K.465; (i) String Quintet No. 6 in E flat, K.614.

*** ASV CDDCA 1069. Lindsay Qt; (i) with Williams.

The Lindsays continue their combined series of Mozart's string quartets and quintets with one of the finest discs in the series so far. The striking harmonic atmosphere at the opening of K.465 immediately registers why it was nick-named 'Dissonance', yet the following allegro is sunny and the *Andante* has both serenity and depth of feeling to make a foil for the delightful Minuet and light-hearted finale. The *Quintet* is hardly less successful, with its witty finale brought off in a true Haydnesque spirit. The recording is real and immediate.

String Quartets Nos. 20 (Hoffmeister); 21–23 (Prussian Quartets Nos. 1–3).

(M) *** CRD (ADD) 3427/8. Chilingirian Qt.

The Chilingirian Quartet give very natural, unforced, well-played and sweet-toned accounts of the last four *Quartets*. They are very well recorded too, with cleanly focused lines and a warm, pleasing ambience; indeed, in this respect these two discs are second to none.

(i) String Quartets Nos. 20–21; (ii) Violin Sonata No. 17 in C, K.296.

*** Cal. 9244. (i) Talich Qt; (ii) Messiereur, Bogunia.

The Talich coupling of K.499 and K.575 is digital and the recording brighter and more present than in the *Haydn Quartets*. The playing has comparable sensibility and plenty of vitality.

String Quartets Nos. 20 (Hoffmeister); 22 (Prussian No. 2).

(N) **(*) Astrée E 8834. Mosaïques Qt.

The Mosaïques' performances of the *Hoffmeister* (No. 20) and the second of the *Prussian group*, while as discerning and characterful as ever, are let down a little by a closer recording balance than in their previous records. All are brightly lit, but here Erich Höbarth's first violin is made fierce at climaxes and this especially applies in the *Minuet* of the *Hoffmeister*, K.499.

String Quartets Nos. 20 (Hoffmeister); 23.

**(*) Arcana A 8. Festetics Qt.

These are fine, characterful performances, with splendid vigour and ensemble showing the Festetics Quartet in more relaxed form than in their coupling of K.575 and K.590. However, slow movements could still loosen up a bit more, they still sound very considered. Excellent recording.

String Quartets Nos. 21–23 (Prussian Quartets 1–3).

(B) *** MDG Double MDG 307 0936-2 (2). Leipzig Qt.

String Quartets Nos. 21–22 (Prussian).

*** Nim. NI 5351. Franz Schubert Qt.

String Quartets Nos. 21; 23 (Prussian).

*** Audivis E 8659. Mosaïques Qt.
**(*) Arcana A 9. Festetics Qt.

String Quartets Nos. 22–23 (Prussian).

*** Delos DE 3192. Shanghai Qt.

Although they use modern instruments – and with great finesse – the splendid Leipzig Quartet play with all the transparency of texture associated with period style, and in that they are helped by a recording that has clear separation and striking presence and realism. Their performances of Mozart's last three quartets are second to none and have all the spontaneity of live music-making. They fill up the rest of the space on the second CD by ingeniously creating a 'sampler' composite quartet. This combines the opening Allegro of Schubert's D.353 with the glorious *Lento assai* of Beethoven's Op. 135, followed by the *Scherzo* from Brahms's Op. 51/2 and the finale from Beethoven's Op. 59/3. In principle one would resist such an idea, but all four movements are superbly played, and the amalgam works astonishingly well.

The Franz Schubert Quartet play with refreshing lack of affectation and great sweetness of tone. There is perhaps more sweetness than depth in the slow movements; but at the same time it must be said that there is nothing narcissistic about the playing, and the listener is held from start to finish. They are very well recorded too.

Even those collectors who do not normally respond to period-instrument performances should be swayed by the warmth and finesse of the playing of the Mosaïques Quartet and by their lightness of touch in the finale of K.590. The closing *Allegretto* of K.575 is revealing in quite a different way, and both slow movements have a searching intensity; yet there is an underlying lyrical feeling, which often brings the sun out from behind the clouds. The thoughtful subtlety of this playing is matched by a spontaneous response to Mozart at his most penetrating. The recording is extremely lifelike.

The Hungarian Quatuor Festetics, who also play 'sur instruments d'époque', as the French so engagingly put it, approach Mozart with a degree of severity that not all will take to. The opening of K.575 is superbly poised, and the *Andante* is most eloquent. But never a suspicion of a smile until the arrival of the Minuet, and even this is very purposeful. Strong accents abound, and there is something a bit spare about the finale too, vital though it is. A record to be greatly admired, but not one to fall in love with.

The New York-based Shanghai Quartet, who use modern instruments, have won glowing opinions from the American press and elsewhere, and no wonder. Their accounts of Mozart's last two quartets are second to none. They create a beautifully blended sound, warm and refined. Slow movements have a natural expressive flow, and there is all the delicacy of articulation needed for the dancing finales. They are most naturally recorded in a pleasingly spacious ambience.

String quintets

Complete Mozart Edition, Vol. 11: *String Quintets Nos. 1–6.*

(M) *** Ph. (ADD) 422 511-2 (3). Grumiaux Trio, with Gerecz, Lesueur.

The Grumiaux ensemble's survey of the *String Quintets* offers immensely civilized and admirably conceived readings. Throughout the set the vitality and sensitivity of this team are striking, and in general this eclipses all other recent

accounts. The remastering of the 1973 recordings for CD is very successful indeed.

Complete Quintets: String Quintets Nos. 1 in B flat, K.174; 2 in C min., K406; 3 in C, K515; 4 in G min., K.516; 5 in D, K.593; 6 in E flat, K.614; (i) *Clarinet Quintet.*

🌑 (M) *** Cal. (ADD) 3231/3. Talich Qt, with Rehák, (i) Zahradnik.

String Quintets Nos. 1 (with original version of *Trio* of the *Minuet & Finale*); 2–6.

(BB) **(*) Naxos 8.553103 (Nos. 1–2); 8.553104 (Nos. 3–4); 8.553105 (Nos. 5–6). Eder Qt, with Fehérvári.

The six Mozart *String Quintets* played by the Talich Quartet and Karel Rehák are available in a mid-priced box, together with a radiant account of the *Clarinet Quintet* (with Bohyslav Zahradnik the sensitive soloist), on three Calliope discs, which cost approximately the same as the pair of Duos listed on pp. 886–7. The Calliope set will in the long run prove a far better investment.

The augmented Eder Quartet also offer a complete set of the *String Quintets*, and the first disc displays their unexaggerated Mozartian style, a fine blend of tone and musicianship. While not a match for the Talich, these performances are eminently recommendable to those with limited budgets. But after the success of the first disc, on the second the playing is still thoughtful and ensemble is clean, but there is an element of routine, and neither performance really takes off. It is not until the opening of the *Adagio* of the finale of the *G minor Quintet* that the Eder account achieves real concentration. The last two quintets come off very well indeed. The opening *Larghetto* of the *D major* is warmly intense, and the allegro immediately lifts off. The *Adagio* is beautifully played, the finale delightfully lighthearted. The *E flat major Quintet* is similarly well judged, with a poised *Andante* and another infectious closing movement. The recording is close but very realistic.

String Quintets Nos. 3–6.

(M) *** Virgin VCD 45169-2 (2). Hausmusik.

(B) **(*) Hyp. Dyad CDD 22005 (2). Salomon Qt, Whistler.

Those seeking period performances of the four finest of the Mozart *Quintets* should be more than satisfied with the playing of Hausmusik, even if, for some reason, the set was not completed. But as the very opening of the *C major* readily demonstrates, this playing brings a wonderfully light rhythmic touch and is remarkably airy in texture. The first movement of the *G minor* is managed no less beautifully, while the allegros of both the *D major* and *E flat major Quintets* burst with energy. Slow movements have a movingly restrained espressivo, withdrawn but without a feeling of austerity, and the *Adagio* of the *G minor* is hauntingly dark in its gentle melancholy. Finales bounce along joyfully and, although quite different in character, these performances are every bit as rewarding as those on modern instruments by the Talich. The EMI recording is very distinguished in its fine balance and naturalness.

The Salomon Quartet use period instruments and are at their very best in the *G minor Quintet*, with the beauty of the *Adagio* sensitively caught. The final work is also splendidly played, but the *C major* and *D major Quintets* are cooler. The Hyperion recording is excellent, and this Dyad costs the same as a single premium-priced CD; but on almost all counts Hausmusik, who are also most realistically recorded, find greater depth in this music.

String Quintets Nos. 3 & 4.

(M) **(*) HM Suite HMT 7901512. Ensemble 415.

Ensemble 415 (leader Chiara Banchini) couple the two favourite Mozart *String Quintets* and play them with warmth and the delicacy of texture possible from period instruments. Although one has to adjust to some linear swelling, this music-making is certainly enjoyable. Opening movements have plenty of rhythmic lift and slow movements are refined in feeling, although without quite the degree of rapt concentration found by Hausmusik. However, the finale of the *G minor* (which opens with a hushed *Adagio* and then finds its release in the following allegro) is very succesful. The recording is excellent.

Violin sonatas

Complete Mozart Edition, Vol. 15: *Violin Sonatas Nos. 1–34; Sonatinas in C & F, K.46d & 46e; Sonatina in F (for beginners), K.547; Sonata in C, K.403 (completed Stadler); Adagio in C min., K.396; Allegro in B flat, K.372; Andante & Allegretto in C, K.404; Andante in A & Fugue in A min., K.402 (completed Stadler); 12 Variations on 'La Bergère Célimène', K.359; 6 Variations on 'Hélas, j'ai perdu mon amant', K.360.*

(M) **(*) Ph. (ADD/DDD) 422 515-2 (7). Poulet, Verlet; Grumiaux, Klien; Van Keulen, Brautigam.

Violin Sonatas Nos. 1–16.

(B) *** Ph. Duo (IMS) (ADD) 438 803-2 (2). Poulet, Verlet.

The early sonatas, from K.6 through to K.31, were recorded in the mid-1970s by Gérard Poulet with Blandine Verlet on harpsichord. The various fragments, sonatinas, sonatas (K.46d, K.46e, K.403 and K.547) and variations by Isabelle van Keulen and Ronald Brautigam come from 1990. For the remaining four CDs, Philips have turned to the set by Arthur Grumiaux and Walter Klien, recorded digitally in the early 1980s. There is a great deal of sparkle and some refined musicianship in these performances, and pleasure remains undisturbed by the balance which, in the 1981 recordings, favours the violin. The later recordings, from 1982 and 1983, are much better in this respect.

Violin Sonatas Nos. 17–28; 32–4; Sonatina in F, K.547.

(B) *** DG 463 749-2 (4). Perlman, Barenboim.

(B) *** Decca (ADD) 448 526-2 (4). Goldberg, Lupu.

Violin Sonatas Nos. 17–25; 12 Variations in G on 'La Bergère Célimène', K.359.

(B) *** Ph. Duo (ADD) 462 185-2 (2). Szeryng, Haebler.

Violin Sonatas Nos. 17–20.

(BB) **(*) Naxos 8.553111. Nishizaki, Jandó.

Violin Sonatas Nos. 21–23; 25.

(BB) **(*) Naxos 8.553110. Nishizaki, Jandó.

Violin Sonatas Nos. 26–28.

(BB) **(*) Naxos 8.553112. Nishizaki, Jandó.

Violin Sonatas Nos. 32–33.

(BB) **(*) Naxos 8.553590. Nishizaki, Jandó.

It is good to have the Perlman/Barenboim Mozart violin sonatas in one nicely packaged bargain box. These artists form a distinguished team, with alert, vital playing, and a sense of spontaneous music-making which pervades these four CDs. There is much attention to detail (though never fussy sounding) which makes these come over as strikingly fresh accounts. Those who invest in this set will not be disappointed, and the recordings are vividly realistic.

These were among Radu Lupu's first recordings for Decca and he plays with uncommon freshness and insight, while Szymon Goldberg brings a wisdom, born of long experience, to these sonatas which is almost unfailingly revealing. Lupu gives instinctive musical support to his partner and both artists bring humanity and imagination to their performances. In short, very distinguished playing from both artists. The recordings were made in the Kingsway Hall in 1974 and expertly balanced by Christopher Raeburn. They have been most naturally transferred to CD, and this Decca bargain box can also be given the strongest recommendation.

Ingrid Haebler brings an admirable vitality and robustness to her part. Her playing has sparkle and great spontaneity. Szeryng's contribution is altogether masterly, and all these performances find both partners in complete rapport. The analogue recordings from the mid-1970s provide striking realism and truthfulness, and they have been transferred immaculately to CD. The *Variations* included in the set are managed with charm. The intimate atmosphere of these performances is particularly appealing.

The partnership of Takako Nishizaki and Jenö Jandó is very successful. In the earlier of the more mature sonatas, which date from 1778, the violin often takes a subsidiary role, and here the balance and Jandó's strong personality emphasize the effect. This is slightly less striking in K.379–80 (on the third disc) which are later (1781) and in which the part writing is more equal. On the fourth CD of the series we move on to K.454 and K.481, which date from 1785 and 1786, respectively. The two instruments now form a much more equal partnership. Nishizaki's tone is small and at times a little thin and uncovered (rather like a period instrument), but seems perfectly scaled for Mozart; her playing is highly musical and these artists strike a Mozartian symbiosis that is appealing in its fresh simplicity of approach.

(i) Violin Sonatas Nos. 18; 21; 32; (ii) Rondo in B flat for Violin & Orchestra, K.269.

**(*) EMI CDC5 56872-2. M.-E. Lott; with (i) Speidel (fortepiano); (ii) Salzburg Mozarteum O, Tomasi.

This collection should have been issued on EMI's Début bargain label rather than at premium price. However, there is a double interest in that Maria-Elisabeth Lott (11 years old at the time these recordings were made) is not only immensely talented – her playing was praised by Menuhin – but she uses here the violin on which Mozart performed as a child, which is smaller than half size. Yet she creates a warm full timbre, while in her spirited performances of fast movements her spick-and-span execution is ever stylish, although one would have liked a little more dynamic light and shade. Her older partner, Sontraud Speidel, gives her every support on a 1790 Viennese fortepiano which is a copy of one owned by Mozart. Lott is astonishingly mature for her age. The orchestral *Rondo* that opens the programme is full of charm.

Violin Sonatas Nos. 23 in D, K.306; 26 in B flat, K.378, No. 27 in G, K.379 & Sonata in B flat, K.372 (unfinished); Andante & Allegretto in C, K.404.

(N) (BB) **(*) EMI Double forte (ADD) CZS5 74292-2 (2). Kagaan, Richter – BEETHOVEN: *Violin Sonatas Nos. 4 & 5* **(*).

These live 1974 accounts have all the excitement of being present at a concert, with very few irritations. The sound is vivid – a little dry, but more than acceptable. These are strong, vibrant performances, never rushed, but always sparkling. A bargain with a fine coupling.

PIANO MUSIC
Complete works for piano

Complete Mozart Bargain Edition, Vol. 9: (i) *Complete Music for 2 Pianos and Piano Duets;* **(ii)** *Piano Sonatas Nos. 1–18; Fantasia in C min.;* **(iii)** *Variations, Rondos; miscellaneous music for keyboard.*

(N) (B) **(*) Ph. (ADD/DDD) 464 850-2 (12). Haebler, Hoffmann, Demus, Badura-Skoda; (ii) Uchida; (iii) Haebler, Koopman.

The highlight here is Uchuda's complete set of the *Piano Sonatas* – her finest achievement on record. Not all the other performances are of this calibre, but they are all discussed below.

Piano duet: (i–ii) *Andante & Variations, K.501; Sonatas, K.19d; K.381; K.357–8; K.497; K.521; 2 Pianos: Fugue, K.426; Sonata, K.448;* (iii) *Larghetto & Allegro in E flat* (reconstruction). Solo piano music: (i) *Sonatas Nos. 1–18;* (iv) *8 Variations in G, K.24; 7 Variations in D, K.25; 12 Variations in C, K.179; 6 Variations in G, K.180; 9 Variations in C, K.264; 12 Variations in C, K.265; 8 Variations in F, K.352; 12 Variations in E flat, K.353; 12 Variations in E flat, K.354; 6 Variations in F, K.398; 10 Variations in G, K.455; 12 Variations in B flat, K.500; 9 Variations in D, K.573; 8 Variations in F, K.613; Adagio in B min., K.540; Eine kleine Gigue in G, K.574; Fantasia in D min., K.397; Minuet in D, K.355; Rondos: in D, K.485; in A min., K.511; 21 Pieces for keyboard, K.1, K.1a–1d;1f; K.2–5; K.5a; K.33b; K.94; K.312; K.394–5; K.399–401; K.408/1; K.453a; K.460.*

(B) **(*) Ph. 456 132-2 (10). (i) Haebler; (ii) Hoffman; (iii) Demus and Badura-Skoda; (iv) Haebler (piano) or Koopman (harpsichord).

Ingrid Haebler with the help of several other artists gives us a complete ten-disc survey of Mozart's keyboard music for two and four hands. She has the solo sonatas to herself and, above all, she gets the scale right. In this repertoire it is quite wrong, on the one hand, to inflate or romanticize; on the other, it is equally unfair to miniaturize them. Haebler's classical approach avoids both these pitfalls. There is sparkle and lightness in the allegros, but also real thoughtfulness – without rhythmic exaggerations in slow movements. The early sonatas are very successful, while the well-known later works show a similar feeling for colour and atmosphere. Ton Koopman despatches various juvenilia with some brusqueness but he is not helped by the close balance of his harpsichord. The quality of the piano-sound, however, is very good indeed, beautiful and true in Philips's best analogue manner. The piano duet music is also available separately on a Philips Duo and is discussed below.

Piano duet

Adagio & Allegro in F min., K.594; Andante & 5 Variations in G, K.501. Fantasia in F min., K.608; Sonatas in: C, K.19d; B flat, K.358; D, K.381; F, K.497; C, K.521; Sonata for 2 Pianos in D, K.448.

(B) *** DG Double 459 475-2 (2). Eschenbach, Frantz.

(i) *Andante with 5 Variations, K.501; Fugue in C min., K.426; Sonatas for Piano Duet: in C, K.19d; D, K.381; G, K.357; B flat, K.358; F, K.497; C, K.521; Sonata in D for 2 Pianos, K.448;* (ii) *Larghetto & Allegro in E flat* (reconstructed Badura-Skoda).

(M) **(*) Ph. (ADD) 422 516-2 (2). (i) Haebler, Hoffmann; (ii) Demus, Badura-Skoda.

(B) **(*) Ph. ADD Duo 454 026-2 (2). (i) Haebler, Hoffmann; (ii) Demus, Badura-Skoda.

The Eschenbach/Frantz accounts of the Mozart piano duets were made between 1972 and 1975. They play with exemplary ensemble and fine sensitivity, and although finer performances of individual pieces may have come one's way, the standard maintained by these artists remains high throughout. The recordings are clean and well balanced, if occasionally a shade dry, but this is without doubt an excellent DG bargain Double.

The Philips two-CD set includes all the music Mozart composed for piano duet or two pianos, in elegant (if at times a little too dainty) performances by Ingrid Haebler and Ludwig Hoffmann in recordings dating from the mid-1970s. Also included is a Mozart fragment, the *Larghetto and Allegro in E flat*, probably written in 1782–3 and completed by Paul Badura-Skoda, who recorded it in 1971 for the Amadeo label with Jörg Demus. Despite the occasional distant clink of Dresden china, all these performances give pleasure and are very decently recorded.

Andante with 5 Variations, K.501; Sonata in D. K.448.

*** Chan. 9162. Lortie, Mercier – SCHUBERT: *Fantasia in F min.* ***

Sonata in D, K.448.

*** Sony SK 39511. Perahia, Lupu – SCHUBERT: *Fantasia in D min.* ***

With Perahia taking the primo part, his brightness and individual way of illuminating even the simplest passage-work dominate the performance, producing magical results and challenging the more inward Lupu into comparably inspired playing. Pleasantly ambient recording made at The Maltings, Snape, and beautifully caught on CD.

The Louis Lortie–Hélène Mercier partnership also gives one of the most sensitive accounts of the *D major Sonata*, K.448, currently available on disc, and their account of the *Andante and Variations* is equally fine. The Schubert coupling is also recommendable. Very good recording.

Sonatas in D, K.448; in C, K.521.

(N) (M) *** Decca (ADD) 466 821-2. Richter; Britten – SCHUBERT: *Andantino varié.* DEBUSSY: *En blanc et noir.* ***

Characteristically, Britten and Richter in these magnificent Mozart works adopt phenomenally fast speeds in outer movements, with the finale of K.448 almost beyond belief, wonderfully clean in articulation. The sparkle of those movements is then set against broad expressive treatment in the two slow movements. It is good to find the scale of the piano duet *Sonata* K.521 reinforced by the observance of every single repeat, including the second half of the first movement, and with minor-key passages given heightened intensity in all three movements.

Sonatas: in F, K.497; in C, K.521; Pieces for mechanical organ: Adagio & Allegro in F min., K.594; Adagio & Allegro in F min., K.608.

✿ *** Ottavio OTR C129242. Cooper and Quefféléc.

Above all, these performances convey a sense of joy in the music. The *Sonatas* – both highly inspired – are framed by the two works for mechanical clock, which here sound both thoughtful and unusually commanding: the opening *Adagio* of K.594 is wonderfully serene. The first movement of the *C major Sonata* sets off with great spirit, yet detail is always imaginatively observed. The slow movement of K.497 is a lovely, flowing melody, so persuasively presented, while the finale has a most engaging lilt. Altogether this is playing of great distinction. Everything is marvellously fresh. Very strongly recommended.

Solo piano music

Piano Sonatas Nos. 1–18 (complete).

(B) *** EMI (ADD) CZS7 67294-2 (5). Barenboim.

Piano Sonatas Nos. 1–18; Fantasia in C min., K.475; Variations, K.24–5; 54; 179–80; 264–5; 353–4; 398; 455; 500; 573; 613.

(N)(B) **(*) EMI CZS5 73915-2 [CDZZH] (8). Barenboim.

Complete Mozart Edition., Vol. 17: Piano Sonatas Nos. 1–18; Fantasia in C min., K.475.

✿ (M) *** Ph. 422 517-2 (5). Uchida.
(B) *** Decca (ADD) 443 717-2 (5). Schiff.
(M) ** Nim. (ADD) NI 1775 (6). Deyanova.

Piano Sonatas Nos. 1–18; Fantasias: in D min., K.397; C min., K.475.

*** DG 431 760-2 (6). Pires.

Piano Sonatas Nos. 1; 2; 9; 18.

*** DG (IMS) 435 882-2. Pires.

Piano Sonatas Nos. 3–4; 15: Andante & Allegro, K.533; Rondo, K.494.

*** DG (IMS) 437 546-2. Pires.

Piano Sonatas Nos. 5–6; 10.

*** DG (IMS) 437 791-2. Pires.

Piano Sonatas Nos. 7; 12; 17.

*** DG (IMS) 439 769-2. Pires.

Piano Sonatas Nos. 8; 13; 16.

*** DG (IMS) 427 768-2. Pires.

Piano Sonatas Nos. 11; 14; Fantasias: in C min., K.475; in D min., K.397.

*** DG (IMS) 429 739-2. Pires.

Piano Sonatas Nos. 1–18; Fantasia, K.475; Fantasia, K.396; Variations, K.353; Variations, K.398; Variations, K.460; Allegro, K.312; Minuet, K.355; Rondo, K.511; Adagio, K.540; Gigue, K.574.

(M) (***) Music & Arts mono (ADD) CD-1001 (5). Kraus.

Piano Sonatas Nos. 1–18; Sonatas in C, K.46d; in F, K.46e; Fantasia in C min., K.475.

(B) *** DG (ADD) 463 137-2 (5). Eschenbach.

Piano Sonatas Nos. 1–3.

*** BIS CD 835. Brautigam (fortepiano).

Piano Sonatas Nos. 4–6.

*** BIS CD 836. Brautigam (fortepiano).

Piano Sonatas Nos. 7–9.

*** BIS CD 837. Brautigam (fortepiano).

Piano Sonatas Nos. 10–12.

*** BIS CD 838. Brautigam (fortepiano).

Piano Sonatas Nos. 13–14; Fantasie in C min., KV.475.

*** BIS CD 839. Brautigam (fortepiano).

Piano Sonatas Nos. 15–18.

*** BIS CD 840. Brautigam (fortepiano).

Adagio in B min., K.540; Eine kleine Gigue, K.574; Prelude in C, K.284a; Prelude & Fugue in C, K.394; 12 Variations, K.354; 8 Variations, K.613.

*** BIS CD 896. Brautigam (fortepiano).

Fantasy-fragment in D min., K.397; Klavierstück in F, K.33b; Kleiner Trauermarsch, K, 453a; 8 Variations on Grétry's 'Dieu d'amour', K.352; 10 Variations in G on 'Unser dummer Pöbel meint', K.455; 12 Variations on a Minuet by J. C. Fischer, K.179.

*** BIS CD 895. Brautigam (fortepiano).

Modulation Prelude in F/E min.; Rondo, K.511; 6 Variations on 'Salve tu, Domine' from Paisiello's I filosofi immaginarii; 8 Variations on a Dutch song by C. E. Graaf, K.24; 12 Variations on 'Ah vous dirai-je maman', K.265; 12 Variations on an Allegretto, K.500; 12 Variations on a French song, 'La Belle Française', K.353.

*** BIS CD 894. Brautigam (fortepiano).

Rondo, K.485; Theme & 5 Variations, K.547; 2 Variations on the aria Come un' agnello by Sarti; 6 Variations on Salieri's Mio caro Adone, K.180; 7 Variations on the Dutch song, Willem van Nassau; 9 Variations on an ariette, Lison dormait, by Dezéde, K.264; 9 Variations on a Minuet by Jean Pierre Dupont, K.573.

*** BIS CD 897. Brautigam (fortepiano).

On Philips, Mitsuko Uchida's collection, with beautiful and naturally balanced digital recording made in the Henry Wood Hall, London, has now been reissued on 5 mid-priced CDs by omitting the shorter pieces, except for the *C minor Fantasia*. Uchida's set of the Mozart *Sonatas* brings playing of consistently fine sense and sound musicianship. There is every indication that this will come to be regarded as a classic series. Every phrase is beautifully placed, every detail registers, and the early *Sonatas* are as revealing as the late ones. The piano recording is completely realistic, slightly distanced in a believable ambience.

Maria João Pires is a stylist and a fine Mozartian, as those who have heard any of her cycle on Denon will know. But this splendid new DG set marks a step forward over her earlier interpretations. Pires is always refined yet never wanting in classical feeling, and she has a vital imagination. In these new readings there is even more life: she strikes an ideal balance between poise and expressive sensibility, conveying a sense of spontaneity in everything she does. Moreover, the DG recording is fuller, with greater depth than the Denon set, and the slight dryness to the timbre suits the interpretations, which are expressively fluid and calm without a trace of self-consciousness. With allegros always alert and vital yet never too predictable in their expressive contrasts, this is playing to stimulate the listener consistently – even the hackneyed *C major Sonata*, K.545, sounds freshly minted. While Uchida's much-praised versions are full of personal intimacy, Pires's more direct style with its tranquil eloquence is no less satisfying.

Ronald Brautigam's set is extraordinarily refreshing. It is bursting with life and intelligence. He uses a 1992 copy (made in his native Amsterdam) of a fortepiano by Anton Gabriel Walter from about 1795. It is a very good instrument and he is a very good player. Dip in anywhere in this set and you will be rewarded with playing of great imagination and sensitivity – not to mention sureness and agility of mind and fingers. At every turn he commands both delicacy and vitality, and he is completely inside the Mozartian sensibility of the period. Even if you prefer Mozart's keyboard music on the piano, you should investigate this set without delay. It brings Mozart to life in a way that almost no other period-instrument predecessor has done. It starts off very well from the early *C major Sonata*, K.279, with playing that sparkles and delights – and continues as it has begun. This series has given great pleasure as it has appeared over the last couple of years and it is beautifully recorded too.

Barenboim's distinguished set of the Mozart *Piano Sonatas* is reissued not only at bargain price but now on five CDs instead of the original six. Barenboim, while keeping his playing well within scale in its crisp articulation, refuses to adopt the Dresden china approach to Mozart's sonatas. Even the little *C major*, K.545, designed for a young player, has its element of toughness, minimizing its 'eighteenth-century drawing-room' associations. Though – with the exception of the two minor-key sonatas – these are relatively unambitious works, Barenboim's voyage of discovery brings out their consistent freshness, with the orchestral implications of some of the allegros strongly established. The recording, with a pleasant ambience round the piano sound, confirms the apt scale.

EMI now also offer an alternative choice of a complete coverage of *all* the important solo piano music. The *Variations* were recorded – more forwardly – in Munich in 1991. As before, Barenboim's positive, direct approach brings all this music fully to life. But compared with the sonatas the music is much more variable in interest, and this is a set to be dipped into with a degree of discretion, for Mozart occasionally seems almost on auto-pilot, writing for comparatively unsophisticated tastes.

András Schiff's earlier, Decca recordings now also reappear, in a bargain box. Schiff, without exceeding the essential Mozartian sensibility, takes a somewhat more romantic and forward-looking view of the music. His fingerwork is precise yet mellow, and his sense of colour consistently excites admiration. He is slightly prone to self-indulgence in the handling of some phrases, but such is the inherent freshness and spontaneity of his playing that one accepts the idiosyncrasies as a natural product of live performance. The piano is set just a little further back than in the Philips/Uchida recordings, and the acoustic is marginally more open, which suits his slightly more expansive manner.

Christoph Eschenbach gives consistently well-turned, cool and elegant performances without affectation or mannerism. Those looking for an unidiosyncratic, direct approach to Mozart should find this poised, immaculate pianism to their taste. The famous *Andante grazioso* variations which form the first movement of the *Sonata in A*, K.331, are entirely characteristic, played very simply and directly. Other pianists are gentler, more romantic, but Eschenbach's taste cannot be faulted. Reissued at bargain price in DG's Collector's Edition this is very competitive indeed, and the set is neatly packaged and well documented.

Lili Kraus, born in Budapest in 1905, recorded this cycle of the Mozart sonatas, as well as shorter pieces, in New York for the Haydn Society in 1954. Compared with her later recording, issued by Sony, the closeness of the sound allows one to appreciate more the diamond clarity of Kraus's playing with its high dynamic contrasts, even if pianissimos are not as hushed as they might be. The important point is that with Kraus one is never in danger – as so many commentators have been – of underprizing these sonatas. These earlier performances are not only more dramatic but more spontaneous sounding too, with firmer technical control. The mono sound is well transferred to make it firm and vivid. In both recordings Kraus omits the composite *Sonata in F*, K.533/494, which Mozart created by adding to two late movements an earlier *Rondo* in less complex style.

Marta Deyanova is an excellent Mozartian and she has her own distinct insights to offer in these sonatas: her style is crisp and clean, without artifice. There is an attractive sense of poise, as at the opening of the *F major*, K.289, while the *Adagio* of the same work is a fine demonstration of her thoughtful lyricism in slow movements, full of imaginative touches of light and shade, yet never precocious or out of style. But while we enjoyed these performances a great deal, the characteristically resonant recording which Nimbus seem to favour for their piano records slightly blurs the outlines of the playing, and the empty hall effect will not be to all tastes.

Piano Sonatas Nos. 3; 10; 13; Adagio, K.540; Rondo, K.485.

(M) *** DG 445 517-2. Horowitz.

Playing of such strong personality from so great an artist is self-recommending. With Horowitz there were astonishingly few reminders of the passage of time and the artistry and magnetism remain undiminished. The recordings were made in the pianist's last vintage period, between 1985 and 1989, in either a New York studio, the pianist's home, or an Italian studio in Milan (K.333). Remarkable playing, not always completely free from affectation; but for variety of articulation just sample the *Allegretto grazioso* finale of K.333 and, for simply expressed depth of feeling, the *Adagio*, K.540.

Piano Sonatas Nos. 8; 11; 13; 14; Adagio, K.540; Fantasia, K.475; Rondo, K.511; 9 Variations in D on a Minuet by Dupont, K.573.

(B) **(*) Ph. Duo ADD/Dig. 454 244-2 (2). Brendel.

The recordings of the *A major Sonata*, K.331, and the *B flat*, K.333, come from 1971 and 1975 respectively and they show Brendel at his very finest, while the *B minor Adagio* is also memorable. K.331, with its engaging opening theme and variations and justly famous *Alla turca* finale, is a joy. The analogue recording, too, is most realistic. However, the *A minor*, K.310, and the *C minor*, recorded digitally in the following decade, are more controversial. The first movement of the *A minor* has immaculate control but is more than a little schoolmasterly, particularly in the development. Brendel seems unwilling to seduce us by beauty of sound, and the result is self-conscious playing, immaculately recorded. Fortunately, he is back on form in the *Fantasia in C minor*, the *Rondo* and the *Variations*.

Piano Sonatas No. 8; 11; 15.

✪ *** Sony SK 48233. Perahia.

Such is Murray Perahia's artistry that one is never consciously aware of it. Nothing is beautified, nor does he shrink from conveying that hint of pain that fleetingly disturbs the symmetry of the slow movements. The Sony engineers provide excellent sound.

Piano Sonatas Nos. 10; 11; 16; Rondo, K.511.

*** Ph. 462 903-2. Brendel.

Although for the most part recorded 'live', Brendel's performances here have an appealingly thoughtful intimacy, as if he were hardly conscious of the audience. Yet one still has the sense of being in Brendel's presence. Interestingly, the studio recording of the *C major Sonata*, K.330, seems very slightly less spontaneous in feeling than the rest of the programme. But altogether this is playing of distinction. Audience noises are minimal (although applause is in-

cluded), and the recording, although fairly closely observed, is very natural.

Piano Sonata No. 17.

(***) Testament mono STB 1089. Gilels – CHOPIN: *Sonata No. 2*; SHOSTAKOVICH: *Preludes & Fugues Nos 1, 5 & 24.* (***)

The *B flat Sonata* was recorded in Paris at the Théâtre des Champs-Elysées in March 1954. The sound is a little dry and close, but the playing has a simplicity and poetry that completely transcend sonic limitations.

Complete Mozart Edition, Vol. 18: 8 Variations, K.24; 7 Variations, K.25; 12 Variations, K.179; 6 Variations, K.180; 9 Variations, K.264; 12 Variations, K.265; 8 Variations, K.352; 12 Variations, K.353; 12 Variations, K.354; 6 Variations, K.398; 10 Variations, K.455; 12 Variations, K.500; 9 Variations, K.573; 8 Variations, K.613; Adagio, K.540; Eine kleine Gigue, K.574; Fantasia, K.397; Minuet, K.355; Rondos: K.485; K.511; 21 Pieces for keyboard, K.1, K.1a–1d;1f; K.2–5; K.5a; K.33b; K.94; K.312; K.394–5; K.399–401; K.408/1; K.453a; K.460.

(M) ** Ph. ADD/Dig. 422 518-2 (5). Haebler or Uchida (both piano), Koopman (harpsichord).

Ingrid Haebler is an intelligent and perceptive artist who characterizes these variations with some subtlety. The quality of the sound is very good indeed: there is both warmth and presence. Mitsuko Uchida gives us various short pieces, such as the *A minor Rondo*, K.511, and the *B minor Adagio*, K.540, which she plays beautifully – though at less than 40 minutes her disc offers rather short measure. However, Haebler and Koopman make up for that, the latter offering 21 short pieces, including some juvenilia, which are very brightly recorded.

ORGAN MUSIC

Andante in F, K.616; Adagio & allegro in F min., K.594; Fantasia in F min. (Adagio & Allegro), K.608 (all for musical clock); Allegro in G (Veronese), K.72a; Gigue in G, K.574; (i) Epistle Sonatas: in F, K.244; in C, K.328.

(N) (BB) ** Teldec (ADD) 0630 17371-2. Tachezi (organ of Basilika Maria Treu, Vienna); (i) with Alice and Nicholas Harnoncourt and Walter Pfeiffer.

Mozart is never really thought of as a composer for the organ, but he loved its challenge and, whenever he travelled, always made a point of seeking out a local instrument. The problem for us was that he liked best of all to improvise and seldom wrote anything down. Until now, the only 'organ works' we have had on record have been the three pieces he wrote for Count Deym's mechanical organ attached to a clock. Mozart had no opinion of the mechanism for which his music was commissioned and is known to have wished the pieces were intended for a large instrument. To these Herbert Tachezi adds a brief *Allegro* and an attractive *Gigue*, plus two of the *Epistle sonatas*, in which he is joined by the Harnoncourt Trio. The performances overall are acceptable and well registered, but there is nothing distinctive about this record, although the sound is excellent.

VOCAL MUSIC

Complete Mozart Edition, Vol. 22: (i) *Adagio & Fugue in C min., K.546; Maurerische Trauermusik, K.477.* (ii) *La Betulia liberata* (oratorio), *K.118.* (iii) *Davidde penitente* (cantata), *K.469.* (iv) *Grabmusik (Funeral Music), K.42.* (v; i) Masonic music: *Dir, Seele des Weltalls, K.429; Ihr unsre neuen Leiter, K.484; Die ihr unermesslichen Weltalls Schöpfer, ehrt, K.619; Lasst uns mit geschlung'gnen Händen, K.623; Laut verkünde unsre Freude, K.623; Lied zur Gesellenreise, K.468; Lobgesang auf die feierliche Johannisloge, K.148; Die Maurerfreude, K.471; Zerfliesset heut, geliebte Brüder, K.483.* (vi) *Passionslied: Kommet her, ihr frechen Sünder, K.146.* (vii) *Die Schuldigkeit des ersten Gebots* (Singspiel), *K.35.*

(M) **(*) Ph. ADD/Dig. 422 522-2 (6). (i) Dresden State O., Schreier; (ii) Schreier, Cotrubas, Berry, Fuchs, Zimmermann, Salzburg Chamber Ch. & Mozarteum O., Hagen; (iii) M. Marshall, Vermillion, Blochwitz; (iv) Murray, Varcoe; (v) Schreier, Blochwitz, Schmidt, Leipzig R. Ch.; (vi) Murray; (vii) M. Marshall, Murray, Nielsen, Blochwitz, Baldin; (iii; iv; vi; vii) Stuttgart RSO, Marriner.

The two big oratorios are both early works, *La Betulia liberata* and (even earlier, dating from his twelfth year) *Die Schuldigkeit des ersten Gebots* ('The Duty of the First Commandment'). *Davidde penitente* is the cantata largely derived from the torso of the *C minor Mass*, while the sixth disc, in many ways the most inspired of all, contains the Masonic music, vividly done in Dresden under the direction of Peter Schreier. For convenience that disc also includes the purely instrumental Masonic music, the *Maurerische Trauermusik* and the *Adagio and Fugue in C minor*. Directed by Leopold Hager, *La Betulia liberata* is a plain, well-sung performance that does not quite disguise the piece's excessive length. Sir Neville Marriner is the conductor both of *Die Schuldigkeit* and of *Davidde penitente*, giving sparkle to the early oratorio and vigour to the cantata, a fine piece. Full texts are given, and informative notes on individual works.

Complete Mozart Bargain Edition, Vol. 11: *Ave verum corpus.* Cantatas, Oratorios: *La Betulia liberata; Davide penitente; Dixit et magnificat; Exultate jubilate; Grabmusik; Kyries; Litanies, Masonic music; Die Schuldigkeit des ersten Gebots; Masonic Music;* Short sacred works; *Apollo et Hyacinthus.*

(N) (B) *** Ph. (ADD/Dig) 464 870-2 (13). Soloists, Leipzig RO; LSO; Stuttgart RSO; Salzburg Mozart O; Kegel; C. Davis; Marriner; Hager.

Complete Mozart Edition, Vol. 20: (i) *Alma Dei creatoris, K.277;* (ii) *Ave verum corpus, K.618;* (i) *Benedictus sit Deus Pater, K.117; Cibavit eos ex adipe frumenti, K.44;* (iii) *Dixit et Magnificat, K.193;* (i) *Ergo interest, an quis, K.143;* (ii) *Exsultate, jubilate, K.165;* (i) *God is our refuge* (motet), *K.20; Inter natos Mulierum, K.72;* (iii) *Litaniae de BMV (Lauretanae), K.109 & K.195;* (i) *Kyries, K.33; K.90–91;*

K.322–3; (ii) *Kyrie, K.341;* (iii) *Litaniae de venerabili altaris sacramento, K.125 & K.243;* (i) *Miserere mei, Deus, K.85; Misercordias Domini, K.222; Quaerite primum regnum Dei, K.86; Regina coeli, laetare, K.108; K.127; K.276; Sancta Maria, mater Dei, K.273; Scande coeli limina, K.34; Sub tuum praesidium, K.198; Te Deum laudamus, K.141; Veni, Sancte Spiritus, K.47; Venite, populi, venite, K.260;* (ii) *Vesperae solennes de confessore, K.339;* (iii) *Vesperae solennes de Domenica, K.321.*

(M) *** Ph. (ADD) 422 520-2 (5). (i) Nawe, Reinhardt-Kiss, Schellenberger-Ernst, Selbig, Burmeister, Lang, Büchner, Eschrig, Ribbe, Pape, Polster; (ii) Te Kanawa, Bainbridge, Davies, Howell, L. Symphony Ch. & LSO, Davis; (iii) Frank-Reinecke, Shirai, Burmeister, Riess, Büchner, Polster; (i; iii) Leipzig R. Ch. & SO, Kegel.

It is fascinating to find that the boy Mozart's very first religious piece is an unaccompanied motet, written in London to an English text, *God is our refuge*. Herbert Kegel with the Dresden Staatskapelle and his Leipzig Radio Choir are responsible for the great majority of the pieces here, fresh and alert if on occasion rhythmically too rigid. The big exception is the great setting of the *Solemn Vespers, K.339,* for which Sir Colin Davis's 1971 version has understandably been preferred, when the young Kiri Te Kanawa sings the heavenly soprano setting of *Laudate Dominum* so ravishingly. She is also the soloist in the early cantata *Exsultate, jubilate* with its brilliant *Alleluia*. Those 1971 recordings, made in London, are bass-heavy, but the rest brings very fresh and clean recording, with the choir generally more forwardly placed than in the recordings of Mozart's Masses, made by the same forces.

Complete Mozart Edition, Vol. 23: (i) *2 Canons for Strings; 14 Canons for Woodwind; 10 Interval Canons for Woodwind;* (ii) *6 Canons for Female Voices; 3 Canons for Mixed Voices; 13 Canons for Male Voices; 4 Puzzle Canons for Mixed Voices.* (iii) *53 Concert Arias.* Aria (with ornamentation by Mozart) for: J. C. BACH: *Adriano in Siria.* (iv) *8 Vocal Duets, Trios & Quartets.* (v) Alternative arias and duets for: *Così fan tutte; Don Giovanni; Die Entführung aus dem Serail; La finta semplice; Idomeneo; Lucio Silla; Mitridate; Le nozze di Figaro.*

(M) *** Ph. (ADD) 422 523-2 (8). (i) Bav. RSO (members); (ii) Ch. Viennensis, Mancusi or Harrer; (iii) Moser, Schwarz, Popp, Mathis, Gruberová, Sukis, Araiza, Ahnsjö, Lloyd, Berry, Kaufmann, Blochwitz, Lind, Burrows, Eda-Pierre; (iv) Blochwitz, Schariner, Pape, Kaufmann, Lind, Jansen, Schreier; (v) Blochwitz, Szmytka, Wiens, Gudbjörnson, Vermillion, Schreier, Mathis, Burrows, Tear, Terfel, Kaufmann, Lind, Scharinger.

This Philips set offers not just a collection of a dozen or so ensembles and a whole disc of 35 canons (some of them instrumental) but also some fascinating alternative versions and substitute arias for different Mozart operas, from *La finta semplice* and *Mitridate* through to the three Da Ponte masterpieces. It is fascinating to have Bryn Terfel, for example, as Figaro in a varied recitative and slightly extended version of the Act I aria, *Non piu' andrai*. Eva Lind is vocally a less happy choice for the items involving Susanna and

Zerlina, and generally the sopranos chosen for this collection, stylish Mozartians as they are, have less sumptuous voices than those on the Decca set.

Complete Mozart Bargain Edition, Vol. 12: Canons; Concert arias; Vocal ensembles; Lieder; *Notturni*; Alternative opera arias.

(N) (BB) *** Ph. (ADD/DDD) 464 880-2 (10). Soloists; NWE; Salzburg Mozart O; ASMF; Dresden PO; Bav. RSO; Munich RO; Dresden State O; Hager; Marriner; Böem; Harrer; Mancusi; Schreier; Weigle; C. Davis.

Complete Mozart Edition, Vol. 24: (i) Lieder: *Abendempfindung; Als Luise die Briefe ihres ungetreuen Liebhabers; Die Alte; An Chloe; An die Freude; An die Freundschaft; Die betrogene Welt; Dans un bois solitaire; Geheime Liebe; Der Frühling; Gessellenreise; Die grossmütige Gelassenheit; Ich würd' auf meinem Pfad; Das Kinderspiel; 2 Kirchenlieder (O Gottes Lamm; Als aus Agypten); Des kleinen Friedrichs Geburtstag; Die kleine Spinnerin; Komm, liebe Zither, komm; Lied der Freiheit; Das Lied der Trennung; Un moto di gioia; Oiseaux, si tous les ans; Ridente la calma; Sehnsucht nach dem Frühling; Sei du mein Trost; Das Traumbild; Das Veilchen; Verdankt sei es dem Glanz der Grossen; Die Verschweigung; Warnung; Wie unglücklich bin ich nit; Der Zauberer; Die Zufriedenheit (2): (Was frag' ich viel nach Geld und Gut; Wie sanft, wie ruhig fühl' ich hier); Die Zufriedenheit im niedrigen Stande. (ii) 6 Notturni for Voices & Woodwind, K.346; K.436/9 & K.549.*

(M) *** Ph. (ADD) 422 524-2 (2). Ameling, (i) with Baldwin (piano or organ) or Ludemann (mandolin); (ii) with Cooymans, Van der Bilt, Netherlands Wind Ens. (members).

Elly Ameling is the ideal soprano for such fresh and generally innocent inspirations, with her voice at its purest and sweetest when she made the recordings in 1977. In the 1973 recordings of the *Notturni* (setting Italian texts by Metastasio) she is well matched by her soprano and baritone partners, though these are mostly plainer, less distinctive miniatures. Included are two hymns with organ and two tiny songs with mandolin, while aptly the very last of the series, K.598, is one of the lightest of all, *Children's Games*, sparklingly done. The recordings come up with fine freshness and presence.

Songs: *Abendempfindung; Als Luise die Briefe; An Chloe; Die betrogene Welt; Dans un bois solitaire; Komm, liebe Zither; Oiseaux, si tous les ans; Sehnsucht nach dem Frühling; Der Zauberer.*

*** DG 447 106-2. Von Otter, Tan (fortepiano) – HAYDN: *Songs.* ***

A delightful recital in all respects. There is a winning charm in the opening *Komm, liebe Zither*, and *Oiseaux, si tous les ans* is hardly less appealing. Melvyn Tan accompanies most sensitively and – as so often with this artist – makes one feel that nothing other than a fortepiano could have been used to give these songs the right lift. The balance seems just about ideal, and the Haydn couplings are equally pleasing.

51 Concert Arias.

(B) *** Decca ADD/Dig. 455 241-2 (5). Te Kanawa, Gruberová, Berganza, Laki, Hobarth, Winbergh; VCO, Fischer; or LSO, Pritchard; Fischer-Dieskau, V. Haydn O, Reinhard Peters; Corena, ROHCG, Quadri.

This very comprehensive coverage is based on a five-LP Decca set of the complete concert arias for female voice, published in 1981, to which those for male voice have subsequently been added. Berganza's collection includes the most demanding soprano aria of all, *Ch'io me scordi di te?*, recorded (with Pritchard and the LSO) a decade earlier than the rest. Te Kanawa opens the programme, and her items range from one of the very earliest arias, *Oh temerario Arbace!*, already memorably lyrical, to the late *Vado ma dove?* Gruberová's contribution is hardly less brilliant and charming, her singing full of sparkle and character, and superbly articulated. The others, Elfrieda Hobarth and Krisztina Laki, are less individual personalities but do not disappoint vocally. Laki shows impressive coloratura in her opening aria, the little-known *Fra cento affanni*, K.88, and she is equally impressive in the lyrical flow of *Non curo l'affetto*, which again demands comparable bravura. Elfrieda Hobarth's style is more operatic and she becomes a veritable Queen of the Night in tackling the fearsome upper tessitura of *Ma che vi fece, o stelle*, K.368, and *Mia speranza adorata!*, K.416, both of which are accomplished with confident bravado.

The digital recordings by Gösta Winbergh, an exceptionally stylish Mozart tenor, were added later; he rises splendidly to the challenges of such splendid arias as *Per pietà non ricercate*, K.420, and *Aura che intorno spiri*, K.431, using his clean, heady tenor very effectively if without the final degree of personal charisma. Fischer-Dieskau's contribution was a separate undertaking, recorded in 1969, and it includes a beautiful aria from 1787, *Mentre ti lascio*, which reveals Mozart's inspiration at its keenest. The other items too bring their delights. Fernando Corena's three contributions were among the first of any Mozart arias to be recorded in stereo, in 1960. In *Alcandro, lo confesso . . . Non so d'onde viene*, K.512, and *Per questa bella mano*, K.612, he is less than ideally stylish and in the latter not always absolutely secure in intonation. Admittedly, some of the florid passages are fiendishly difficult for a bass to cope with but, when strained, Corena has a tendency to slide between the notes to ungainly effect. Yet he is at his very finest in the *buffo* aria, *Rivolcete a lui lo sguardo*, K.584, originally written for *Così fan tutte* and later cut because of its length. It is a superb piece and it suits Corena's voice well, so that the full power is brought out magnificently. The CD transfers throughout are of high quality, and full translations are included, but the accompanying essay by Kenneth Chalmers documents the music only sketchily, because of limited space.

Concert arias: *Ah! lo previdi . . . Ah, t'invola, K.272; Alma grande e nobil core, K.578; A questo seno . . . Or che il cielo, K.374; Bella mia fiamma . . . Resta, o cara, K.528; Betracht dies Herz und frage mich, K.42; Misera, dove son! . . . Ah! non son io che parlo, K.369; Vado, ma dove? o Dei!, K.583.*

(M) *** DG (ADD) 449 723-2. Janowitz, VSO, Boettcher.

In 1966 when this recording was made (in the Grosser Saal of the Vienna Musikverein) Gundula Janowitz's voice combined a glorious tonal beauty with a surprising degree of flexibility so that Mozart's cruelly difficult divisions – usually written deliberately to tax the original ladies involved – present no apparent difficulty. Janowitz is helped by a flattering, reverberant acoustic, but there is no mistaking the singer's ability to shade and refine the tone at will. An excellent collection of delightful concert arias that are too often neglected nowadays, thanks to the vagaries of modern concert-planning.

Concert arias: *Ah! lo previdi . . . Ah t'invola, K.272; Bella mia fiamma . . . Resta oh cara, K.528; Chi sa, K.582; Nehmt meinen Dank, ihr holden Gönner, K.383; Non più, tutto ascolta . . . Non temer, amato bene, K.490; Oh temerario Arbace! . . . Per quel paterno amplesso, K.79/K.73d; Vado, ma dove?, K.583.* Opera arias: (ii) *Le nozze di Figaro: Porgi amor; E Susanna non vien! . . . Dove sono.* (iii) *Der Schauspieldirektor: Bester Jüngling!*

(M) *** Decca 440 401-2. Te Kanawa; (i) V. CO, Fischer; (ii) LPO, Solti; (iii) VPO, Pritchard.

Kiri Te Kanawa's Decca set of Mozart's concert arias for soprano, recorded in 1982, makes a beautiful and often brilliant recital. Items range from one of the very earliest arias, *Oh temerario Arbace!*, already memorably lyrical, to the late *Vado, ma dove?*, here sung for its beauty rather than for its drama. The arias from *Figaro* and *Schauspieldirektor* come from the complete Decca sets and show the singer at her finest.

Concert arias: *Alma grande e nobil core, K.578; Ch'io mi scordi di te?, K.505; Nehmt meinen Dank, K.383; Vado, ma dove?, K.583.* Lieder: *Abendempfindung; Als Luise die Briefe; Die Alte; An Chloë; Dans un bois solitaire; Im Frühlingsanfang; Das Kinderspiel; Die kleine Spinnerin; Das Lied der Trennung; Oiseaux, si tous les ans; Ridente la calma; Sehnsucht nach dem Frühling; Das Trumbild; Das Veilchen; Der Zauberer; Die Zuhfriedenheit.*

(M) *** EMI mono/stereo CDH7 63702-2. Schwarzkopf, Gieseking; Brendel; LSO, Szell.

Schwarzkopf's classic series of the Mozart songs with Gieseking includes the most famous one, *Das Veilchen*. As a generous coupling, the disc also includes Schwarzkopf's much later recordings, with Szell conducting four concert arias – including the most taxing of all, *Ch'io mi scordi di te?*, with Brendel playing the piano obbligato. Though the voice is not quite so fresh in the concert arias, the artistry and imagination are supreme, and stereo recording helps to add bloom.

Concert arias: *A questo seno deh vieni . . . Or che il cielo, K.374; Ah, lo previvi! . . . Ah, t'invola agl'occhi miei . . . Deh, non vacar, K.272; Bella mia fiamma . . . Resta, oh cara, K.528; Clarice cara, K.256; Miserero! O sogno . . . Aura che intorni spiri, K.431; Se ai labbro mio non credi, K.295; Si mostra la sorte, K.209; Va dai furor portata, K.211; Voi avete un cor fedele, K.217.*

(BB) *** Virgin 2 x 1 VBD5 61573-2 (2). Lootens, Prégardien, La Petite Bande, Kuijken – *Horn Concertos*. ***

This is a highly authentic collection of concert arias, several comparatively rare, divided between two fine artists, who not only have appealing voices, but understand about period style, and ornamentation. Lena Lootens produces nimble coloratura (as in the engaging *Voi avete un cor fedele*) and can be dramatic or provide a lovely legato line, and in both respects Christophe Prégardien is consistently her equal. The accompaniments are fresh, the recording is vivid; but it was a curious idea to couple this programme with the *Horn Concertos*, even though they are also first-rate period performances.

Concert aria: *Ch'io mi scordi di te?, K.505.*

(***) Testament mono SBT 1178. Schwarzkopf, Anda, Philh. O, Ackermann – BACH: *Cantatas 68: Aria; 199; 202; 208: Aria.* ***

As John Steane points out in his most illuminating note, there is a fascinating contrast between this account of *Ch'io mi scordi di te?* recorded in 1955 with Géza Anda playing the difficult piano obbligato and Schwarzkopf's classic recording with Alfred Brendel and George Szell of 1968. The voice may be fuller in the later one, but this is uniquely fresh and urgent, with Schwarzkopf's vehement side given freer rein. A splendid and valuable supplement to the Bach recordings, which have also remained unissued for far too long.

Concert arias: (i) *Ch'io mi scordi di te? Nehmt meinen Dank, ihr holden Gönner!, K.383; Voi, avete un cor fedele; Il re pastore: Aer tranquillo e di sereni;* (ii) *L'amerò sarò costante; Ah, lo previdi; Zaïde: Ruhe sanft, mein holdes Leben; Trostios schluchzet Philomele.*

(B) *** Double Decca (ADD) 458 084-2 (2). Kirkby, AAM, Hogwood; (i) with Lubin (fortepiano); (ii) Hirons (violin) – (with Recital. ***)

This delightful recital, recorded in 1988–9, is admirably suited to Emma Kirkby's sweetly confident line and dazzling coloratura. She is ideally cast as Amita (originally a castrato role) in *Il re pastore* and as the heroine of *Zaïde*. Indeed, her rapturous line in *L'amerò, sarò costante* is fully worthy of Mozart's imaginative accompaniment (including violin obbligato). She is a compellingly passionate Andromeda in projecting the pain and rage of *Ah, lo previdi*, and very touching in the equally ambitious, but more expressive *Ch'io mi scordi di te?* Here Stephen Lubin contributes the fortepiano accompaniment, which Mozart himself played at its first performance in Vienna by Nancy Storace (who created the role of Susanna in *Le nozze di Figaro*). Hogwood's accompaniments are both stylish and warmly, dramatically supportive, and the Walthamstow recording has a fine, spacious bloom. This is linked equally on Double Decca with a miscellaneous recital including music by Arne, Handel, Haydn and Lampe (see Vocal Recitals below).

Concert aria: *Ombra felice, K.255;* Opera arias: *Ascanio in Alba: Ah di si nobil alma; Mitridate: Venga pur, Gia dagli occhi.*

*** Virgin VC5 45365-2. Daniels, OAE, Bicket – GLUCK;
   HANDEL: *Arias*. ***

Under the title '*Sento amor*', David Daniels offers one of the
finest of counter-tenor recitals. In the arias from early
Mozart operas, the brilliance of his singing is what stands
out above all, giving beauty and energy to the florid writing,
as well as a deeper expressiveness to the lyrical passages than
one might expect. At once pure and warm, completely
avoiding the usual counter-tenor hoot, placing his voice
flawlessly, Daniels is exceptional even in an age which has
produced many outstanding rivals.

Concert aria: *Ridente la calma, K.152.*

*** Decca 440 297-2. Bartoli, Schiff – BEETHOVEN: *Che fa il
   mio bene?* etc.; HAYDN: *Arianna a Naxos;* SCHUBERT:
   Da quel sembiante appresi etc. ***

Ridente la calma is invested with much innocent charm by
Cecilia Bartoli within an interesting collection of Italian
songs by German composers.

Masonic music (see also above, in Complete Mozart
Edition, Vol. 22)

Masonic music: *Masonic Funeral Music (Maurerische
Trauermusik), K.477; Die ihr des unermesslichen Weltalls
Schöpfer ehrt (cantata), K.619; Die ihr einen neuen Grade,
K.468; Dir, Seele des Weltalls (cantata), K.429; Ihr unsre
neuen Leiter (song), K.484; Lasst uns mit geschlungnen
Händen, K.623a; Laut verkünde unsre Freude, K.623; O
heiliges Band (song), K.148; Sehen, wie dem starren
Forscherange, K.471; Zerfliesset heut', geliebte Brüder,
K.483.*

(M) *** Decca (ADD) 425 722-2. Krenn, Krause, Edinburgh
   Festival Ch., LSO, Kertész.

This Decca reissue contains the more important of Mozart's
masonic music in first-class performances, admirably
recorded. Most striking of all is Kertész's strongly dramatic
account of the *Masonic Funeral Music*; the two lively songs
for chorus, *Zerfliesset heut'* and *Ihr unsre neuen Leiter*, are
sung with warm humanity and are also memorable. Indeed,
the choral contribution is most distinguished throughout,
and Werner Krenn's light tenor is most appealing in the
other items, which he usually dominates.

SACRED VOCAL MUSIC

*Ave verum corpus, K.618; Exsultate, jubilate, K.165; Kyrie
in D minor, K.341; Vesperae solennes de confessore in C,
K.339.*

*** Ph. 412 873-2. Te Kanawa, Bainbridge, R. Davies, Howell,
   L. Symphony Ch., LSO, Davis.

This disc could hardly present a more delightful collection
of Mozart choral music, ranging from the early soprano
cantata, *Exsultate, jubilate*, with its famous setting of *Alleluia*,
to the equally popular *Ave verum*. Kiri Te Kanawa is the
brilliant soloist in the cantata, and her radiant account of
the lovely *Laudate Dominum* is one of the highspots of the

Solemn Vespers, here given a fine, responsive performance.
The 1971 recording has been remastered effectively, although
the choral sound is not ideally focused.

*(i–ii) Ave verum corpus, K.618; (iii–iv) Exsultate, jubilate,
K.165; Masses Nos. (i–iii; v) 10 in C (Missa brevis):
Spatzenmesse, K.220; (ii–iii; vi) 16 in C (Coronation),
K.317.*

(M) *** DG (IMS) (ADD) 419 060-2. (i) Regensburg Cathedral
   Ch.; (ii) Bav. RSO, Kubelik; (iii) Mathis; (iv) Dresden State
   O, Klee; (v) Troyanos, Laubenthal, Engen; (vi) Procter,
   Grobe, Shirley-Quirk, Bav. R. Ch.

Kubelik draws a fine, vivid performance of the *Coronation
Mass* from his Bavarian forces and is no less impressive in
the earlier *Missa brevis*, with excellent soloists in both works.
Then Edith Mathis gives a first-class account of the *Exsultate,
jubilate* as an encore. The concert ends with Bernard Klee
directing a serenely gentle account of the *Ave verum corpus*
(recorded in 1979).

*(i) Exsultate, jubilate, K.165; (ii) Litaniae Lauretanae in D,
K.195; Mass No. 16 (Coronation), K.317; (iii) Requiem Mass
(No. 19) in D min., K.626.*

(B) **(*) Double Decca (ADD) 443 009-2 (2). (i) Spoorenberg;
   (ii; iii) Cotrubas, Watts, Tear, Shirley-Quirk; (ii) Oxford
   Schola Cantorum; (iii) ASMF Ch; (i–iii), ASMF,
   Marriner.

It is good to have Marriner's 1971 (Argo) recordings of two
of Mozart's most appealing early choral works, the *Litaniae
Lauretanae* and the *Coronation Mass*, back in the catalogue
on this Double Decca set. The solo work is particularly
good (notably Ileana Cotrubas in the two lovely *Agnus Dei*
versions) and the Academy Choir is on its best form. Erna
Spoorenberg's impressive *Exsultate, jubilate* was recorded
earlier (1966). However, Marriner generates less electricity
than usual in the coupled (1977) *Requiem Mass*. It is interesting to have a version which uses the Beyer Edition and
a text which aims at removing the faults of Süssmyar's
completion. Solo singing is good, and some of the choruses
(the *Dies irae*, for instance) are vibrant, but at other times
they are less alert and the tension slackens. The sound is
excellent, well balanced and vivid.

*(i) Litaniae Lauretanae in D, K.195; (ii; iii) Litaniae de
venerabili altaris sacramento, K.243; (iii; iv) Mass No. 12 in
C (Spaur), K.258; (iii; iv) Vesperae solennes de confessore,
K.339; (ii; iii) Vesperae solennes de Domenica, K.321.*

(B) *** Double Decca (ADD) 458 379-2 (2). (i) Cotrubas,
   Watts, Tear, Shirley-Quirk, Oxford Schola Cantorum, ASMF,
   Marriner; (ii) Marshall, Cable, Evans, Roberts; (iii) St John's
   College, Cambridge, Ch., Wren O, Guest; (iv) Palmer, Cable,
   Langridge, Roberts.

Readers will note that Marriner's performance of the
Litaniae Lauretanae in D, K.195, is also available on another
Double Decca (see above). However, many collectors may
prefer the present programme. Mozart made four settings
of the Litany of which the *Litaniae de venerabili altaris
sacramento* is the last, written in 1776. It is ambitiously scored
and is Mozart at his most imaginative and vital; the artists

here rise to the occasion and give a highly responsive performance, with Margaret Marshall outstanding among the soloists. The *Spaur Mass* is not among Mozart's most inspired, but its directness is appealing and the *Benedictus* offers a fine Mozartian interplay of chorus and soloists. In Guest's vigorous performance it is very enjoyable. The vibrant *Vesperae solennes de Domenica* opens with a series of brilliant choral settings, Margaret Marshall is appropriately agile in the lively soprano solo of the *Laudate Dominum*, and the work closes with an ambitious *Magnificat*, in which all the participants are joined satisfyingly together. The collection is completed with the masterly *Vesperae solennes de confessore*, and although Guest's account does not always match Sir Colin Davis's Philips version (see above under *Ave verum corpus*) – with Felicity Palmer a less poised soloist than Kiri Te Kanawa – the Decca has the advantage of authenticity in the use of boys in the chorus. Moreover the CD transfer of these (originally Argo) recordings offers a brighter, sharper focus than the less well-defined Philips sound.

Masses: Nos. 1 in G (Missa brevis), K.49; 2 in D min. (Missa brevis), K.65; 3 in C (Dominicus), K.66; 4 in C min. (Waisenhaus), K.139; 5 in G (Pastoral), K.140; 6 in F (Missa brevis), K.192; 7 in C (Missa in honorem Ssmae Trinitas); 9 in D (Missa brevis), K.194; 10 in C (Spatzenmesse), K.220; 11 in C (Credo), K.257; 12 in C (Spaur), K.258; 13 in C (Organ Solo), K.259; 14 in C (Missa longa), K.262; 15 in B flat (Missa brevis), K.275; 16 in C (Coronation Mass), K.317; 17 in C (Missa solemnis), K.337; 18 in C min. (Great),K.427; 19 in D min. (Requiem), K.626. Alma Dei creatoris, K.72; Ave verum corpus, K.618; Benedictus sit Deus, K.117; Dixit et Magnificat, K.193; Ergo interest, an quis . . . Quaere superna, K.143; Exsultate, jubilate, K.165; Grabmusik, K.42; Hosanna, K.223; Iner natos mulierum, K.72; Kyries: K.33; K.89; K.90; K.322; K.323; K.341; Litaniae Lauretanae, K.195; Litaniae de venerabili altaris sacramento in B flat, K.125; Litaniae de venerabili altaris sacramento in E flat, K.243; Litaniae Lauretanae, K.109; Miserere in A min., K.85; Misericordias Domini, K.222; Quaerite primum regnum Dei, K.86; Regina coeli in C, K.108; Regina coeli in B flat, K.127; Regina coeli in C, K.276; Sancta Maria, mater Dei, K.273; Scande coeli limina, K.34; Sub tuum praesidium, K.198; Tantum ergo in B flat, K.142; Tantum ergo in D, K.197; Te Deum laudamus, K.141; Veni Sancte Spiritus, K.47; Venite populi, K.260; Vesperae de Domenica, K.321; Vesperae solennes de confessore, K.339.

(M) *** Teldec 3984 21885-2 (13). Bonney, Von Magnus, Margiono, McNair, Mei, Rodgers, Láki, Dénes, Blasi, Mei, Yakar, Wenkel, Equiluz, Hagegård, Hampson, Lippert, Prégardien, Protschka, Heilmann, Cachemaille, Van der Welt, Polgár, Holl, V. State Op. Konzertvereinigung, V. State Op. Ch., V. Hofburgkapelle Ch. Scholars, Arnold Schoenberg Ch., VCM, Harnoncourt.

Complete Mozart Edition, Vol. 19: *Masses Nos. 1–7; 9–19.*

(M) **(*) Ph. ADD/Dig. 422 519-2 (9). Mathis, Donath, M. Price, McNair, Montague, Shirai, Casapietra, Trudeliese Schmidt, Lang, Schiml, Markert, Burmeister, Knight, Schreier, Araiza, Heilmann, Baldin, Davies, Rolfe Johnson, Ude, Jelosits, Adam, Polster, Andreas Schmidt, Hauptmann, Rootering, Grant, Eder; Leipzig R. Ch.; Monteverdi Ch.; V. Boys' Ch.; John Alldis Ch.; Ch. Viennensis; Leipzig RSO; E. Bar. Sol.; Dresden State O; LSO; VSO; Dresden PO; Kegel; Davis; Gardiner; Schreier; Harrer.

Harnoncourt's consistently alive and superbly sung and played survey of Mozart's complete sacred works is a remarkable achievement and can be strongly recommended, with only the single reservation that the *Requiem* (No. 19), which came first in 1981, is a disappointment and ought to have been re-recorded for this complete edition. The bite of the singing is all but negated by the washiness of the recording of the voices. The sound is very over-resonant and though it flatters the fine team of soloists, it is a curious anomaly to have an orchestra of period instruments, clearly focused, set against such a flabby choral sound. But most collectors will own another version of Mozart's final masterpiece, and the rest of the survey earns the highest marks. As can be seen, there is an extraordinarily distinguished team of soloists, led by the splendid Barbara Bonney, which never lets the side down, either individually or grouped. Harnoncourt is at his very best in his fresh, vibrant accounts of the early *Missae breves*, but in the later works the soloists also distinguish themselves, and the choral and instrumental contributions are no less stimulating. There is not space here to detail individual accounts of this remarkable coverage; sufficient to say that Mozart's sacred music has a consistently high level of inspiration (with the lovely solo writing often reminding the listener of the opera house), and that Harnoncourt rises to the occasion. The recordings were mainly made over a decade from 1986 to 1996 and are consistently of the highest quality, well balanced within an attractively resonant acoustic.

In the Complete Mozart Edition only the *Great C minor Mass* has period performers. John Eliot Gardiner's inspired reading, with superb soloists as well as his Monteverdi Choir and English Baroque Soloists, has rightly been chosen, and the *Requiem* comes in another outstanding modern version, with the Dresden Staatskapelle and Leipzig Radio Choir conducted by Peter Schreier, as imaginative a conductor as he is a tenor. That same choir and orchestra under the choir's regular conductor, Herbert Kegel, is responsible for the great bulk of the rest of the Masses. With the chorus tending to be placed a little backwardly, it does not always sound its freshest, but performances – with consistently clean-toned soloists, including latterly Mitsuko Shirai – are bright and well sprung. Sir Colin Davis and the LSO in the earliest recording here, dating from 1971, take a weightier view than any in the *Credo Mass*, K.257, with sound bass-heavy, but again his vigour and freshness are very compelling. Two favourite Masses, the *Coronation Mass* and the *Spatzenmesse* (Sparrow Mass), come in performances conducted by Uwe Christian Harrer with the Vienna Symphony Orchestra and the Vienna Boys' Choir; boys also distinctively take the soprano and alto solos. Though Harrer's speeds tend to be slow, the rhythmic buoyancy is most compelling, with choral sound full and forward.

*Masses: Nos. 2 (Missa brevis), K.65; 3 (Dominicus), K.66; 4
(Waisenhaus), K.139; 7 (Missa in honorem Ssmae
Trinitas); 10 (Spatzenmesse), K.220; 11 (Credo), K.257; 12
(Spaur), K.258; 13 (Organ Solo), K.259; 16 (Coronation
Mass), K.317; 17 (Missa solemnis), K.337; 18 (Great), K.427;
19 (Requiem), K.626; Ave verum corpus, K.618.*

(BB) **(*) Virgin VBD5 61769-2 (5). Frimmer, Kwella,
Monoyios, Montague, Schlick, Graf, Groenewold, Chance,
Pfaff, Prégardien, Schäfer, Mertens, Selig, Cologne Chamber
Ch., Coll. Cartusianum, Neumann.

As can be seen from our comments about the Virgin Double
at Masses Nos. 16–18 below, Peter Neumann's performances
are fresh, stylish, and warmly enjoyable and very well sung.
Most importantly these artists give a very fine, dramatic
account of the *Requiem* (not included below), and the
recording here is excellent, clear and vivid. The soloists are
all very good throughout, and the other Masses, early and
late, have plenty of character. The backward balance of the
chorus is not enough of a problem to make this other
than a worthwhile collection of some of Mozart's finest
non-operatic vocal music for those not wanting to stretch
to the complete Harnoncourt edition.

Mass No. 3 in C (Dominicus), K.66; Vesperae de Domenica, K.321.

(M) *** Teldec 2292 46469-2. Margiono, Bonney, Von
Magnus, Heilmann, Cachemaille, Arnold Schoenberg Ch.,
V. Hofburgkapelle Choral Scholars, VCM, Harnoncourt.

Harnoncourt is at his finest in this splendidly lively Mass,
which the thirteen-year-old Mozart wrote for a personal
friend ten years his senior when he took holy orders, and
the direct Harnoncourt style, with its strong accents and
positive characterization, brings it vividly to life. The more
ambitious *Vesperae de Domenica*, written a decade later,
forms a neat and joyful *Missa brevis*, here refreshingly alive
and brimful of variety of invention. Again the singing of
chorus and soloists alike is highly stimulating, and Harnoncourt's affection brings a committed and vivacious approach
which is entirely successful. The recording is first rate.

Mass No. 4 in C min. (Waisenhausmesse), K.139.

(M) *** DG (IMS) (ADD) 427 255-2. Janowitz, Von Stade,
Moll, Ochman, V. State Op. Ch., VPO, Abbado.

(i; ii) Mass No. 4 in C min.; (i) Exsultate, jubilate, K.165.

(M) **(*) Teldec 2292 44180-2. (i) Bonney; (ii) Rappé,
Protschka, Hagegård, Arnold Schoenberg Ch.; VCM,
Harnoncourt.

By any standards this is a remarkably sustained example
of the thirteen-year-old composer's powers, with bustling
allegros in the *Kyrie, Gloria* and *Credo*, as well as at the end
of the *Agnus Dei*, while the *Gloria* and *Credo* end with
full-scale fugues. This far from negligible piece sounds at its
very best in Abbado's persuasive hands.

This work responds to strong characterization and, with
excellent soloists and vibrant choral singing, is another refreshing example of Harnoncourt's view of authenticity.
Barbara Bonney's *Exsultate, jubilate* is enjoyably bracing,
though it is sung a semitone lower than in modern instru-

ment performances. The sound is satisfactory. However, for
those not insisting on original instruments Abbado's DG
recording remains a more obvious first choice.

Masses Nos: (i–ii) 4 (Waisenhaus); (iii) 7 (Missa in honorem Ssmae Trinitas); (i–ii) 11 (Credo); (ii; iv) 16 (Coronation); 17 (Missa solemnis).

(B) **(*) Double Decca (ADD) 455 032-2 (2). (i) Mentzer,
Manca di Nissa, Mackie, Roberts; (ii) King's College,
Cambridge, Ch., ECO, Cleobury; (iii) V. State Op. Ch., VPO,
Münchinger; (iv) with Marshall, Murray, Covey-Crump,
Wilson-Johnson.

Mozart's early *C minor Mass* was composed for the dedication of a new orphanage church, the Waisenhausekirche
am Rennweg, in 1768, and it is notable both for its rich
choral writing and for the fine *Benedictus*, a dialogue between
soprano and chorus, with the trumpets entering resplendently for the *Amen*. It is presented here most effectively
by Cleobury and his team. The *Missa Trinitas*, written in
Salzburg five years later, is even more ambitious, using a
big orchestra with copious brass (four trumpets and three
trombones) as well as oboe, strings and organ. Münchinger
offers a strong, direct account, but the disappointment of
this 1974 recording, made in the Sofiensaal, is how little is
made of the trumpets, which, even in the *Credo*, are backwardly balanced. The other recordings are digital and were
made a decade later. Stephen Cleobury is perhaps at his
finest in the *Credo Mass* and, with the help of his excellent
soloists, gives a vividly exuberant performance of a work
that shows its composer at his most sunnily high-spirited
throughout. The *Missa solemnis in C major*, K.337, was the
very last of the 15 settings that Mozart wrote for Salzburg,
another work that is just as inspired as the better known
Coronation Mass. Though Cleobury's direction here could
be rhythmically more lively, both performances are of high
quality, with excellent soloists and fresh choral singing.

Masses Nos. (i) 10 (Spatzenmesse), K.220; (ii) 18 (Great), K.427; (iii) 19 (Requiem), K.626.

(B) **(*) DG Double ADD/Dig. 459 409-2 (2). (i) Mathis,
Troyanos, Laubenthal, Engen, Regensburg Cathedral Ch.,
Bav. RSO, Kubelik; (ii) Battle, Cuberli, Seiffert, Moll, V. State
Op. Konzertvereinigung, VPO, Levine; (iii) Tomowa-Sintow,
Baltsa, Krenn, Van Dam, V. Singverein, VPO, Karajan.

Kubelik's direct but lively account of the *Spatzenmesse* does
not disappoint: his soloists, led by Edith Mathis, make a
good team and the recording from the early 1970s is fresh
and clear. (This is also available coupled with the *Ave verum
corpus* and *Coronation Mass* – see above.) Karajan's 1975
analogue recording of the *Requiem* is outstandingly fine,
deeply committed, with incisive playing and clean-focused
singing from the chorus, not too large and set a little behind.
The fine quartet of soloists too is beautifully blended. The
reading has its moments of romantic expressiveness, but
nothing is smoothed over and with splendidly vivid
recording such a passage as the *Dies irae* has exceptional
freshness and intensity. Levine's recording of the *C Minor
Mass* is digital and dates from 1987. There are reservations
about the tremulous soprano line in the chorus, which

otherwise sings powerfully. The soloists are individually impressive (Kathleen Battle shines in the *Laudamus te*), but the ensemble of the *Quoniam* is less than ideally polished, and the performance overall is a little rough round the edges. Yet the music's emotional power is never in doubt, for Levine's reading has a compelling, spontaneous vigour. The recording, too, is very live and vivid.

Mass No. 16 in C (Coronation), K.317.

(M) ** (*) DG (ADD) 457 744-2. Stader, Dominguez, Haefliger, Roux, Brasseur Ch., LOP, Markevitch – CHERUBINI: *Requiem No. 2 in D min.*

(M) ** (*) DG 445 543-2 (2). Battle, Schmidt, Winbergh, Furlanetto, V. Singverein, VPO, Karajan – BEETHOVEN: *Missa solemnis.* ** (*)

(B) ** (*) DG Double (ADD) 453 016-2 (2). Tomowa-Sintow, Baltsa, Krenn, Van Dam, V. Singverein, BPO, Karajan – BEETHOVEN: *Missa solemnis.* ***

Markevitch's performance, though not always completely refined, is incisively brilliant and its sheer vigour is infectious. That is not to say that its lyrical moments are not equally successful. He has an impressive team of soloists and they are well matched in ensemble as well as providing very good individual contributions. The *Agnus Dei* is especially fine. The brightly remastered recording has plenty of life and detail, but it is the coupled Cherubini that makes this disc especially attractive.

Karajan's 1985 recording of Mozart's *Coronation Mass* is certainly vibrant, with fine choral singing and good soloists. Kathleen Battle sings beautifully in the *Agnus Dei*, and the recording is bright, if not ideally expansive.

Karajan's earlier (1976) recording is a dramatic reading, lacking something in rhythmic resilience perhaps; but, with excellent solo singing as well as an incisive contribution from the chorus, there is no lack of strength and the score's lyrical elements are sensitively managed. The current remastering has further improved the sound.

(i) *Masses Nos. 16 (Coronation); 17 (Missa solemnis);* (ii) *18 (Great); Kyrie in D min., K.341.*

(BB) ** (*) Virgin 2 x 1 VBD5 61665-2 (2). Cologne Chamber Ch., Coll. Cartusianum, Neumann, with (i) Kwella, Groenewold, Prégardien, Selig; (ii) Schlick, Frimmer, Prégardien, Mertens.

Masses Nos. (i; ii) *16 (Coronation);* (i; iii) *18 (Great);* (i; iv) *19 (Requiem).*

(B) ** (*) Ph. (ADD) Duo 438 800-2 (2). (i) Donath, R. Davies; (ii) Knight, Dean; John Alldis Ch., LSO; (iii) Harper, Dean, L. Symphony Ch., LSO; (iv) Minton, Nienstedt, Alldis Ch., BBC SO; C. Davis.

These very successful Philips CD transfers demonstrate the best features of the original Philips recordings, which date from between 1967 and 1971. Sir Colin Davis's vital account of the *Coronation Mass* is given with a fine team of soloists; and in the so-called 'Great' Mass in C minor the use of the Robbins Landon edition – which rejects the accretions formerly used to turn this incomplete torso of a work into a full setting of the liturgy – prompts him to a strong and intense performance which brings out the darkness behind

Mozart's use of the C minor key. Again he is helped by fine soprano singing from Helen Donath, and from Heather Harper too. The *Requiem*, with a smaller choir, is more intimate and the soloists are more variable, yet with his natural sense of style Davis finds much beauty of detail. While the scale is authentic and the BBC orchestra is in good form, this reading, enjoyable as it is, does not provide the sort of bite with which a performance on this scale should compensate for sheer massiveness of tone.

Neumann directs an enjoyable account of the *Coronation Mass*, as well as the much rarer *Missa solemnis*, which is on a similar scale and is also very well sung. The singers, a well-blended team, are balanced somewhat backwardly within an ecclesiastical acoustic, which takes a little of the bite from the chorus too, but the effect remains vivid. The *C minor Mass* has much to commend it: fine soloists – with Barbara Schlick always fresh and captivating in the *Laudamus te* – spacious choral singing (if, again, somewhat backwardly balanced) and excellent playing from an authentic-sized orchestra on original instruments. The only caveat is that the chorus again lacks the bite to make the performance really gripping, though the recording is partly to blame. The rather solemn *Kyrie* has plenty of character, with the performance darkly lyrical rather than dramatic. A good superbargain set (if without texts or translations), which has much to recommend it.

Masses Nos. (i) *16 in C (Coronation);* (ii) *19 in D min. (Requiem); Ave verum corpus.*

(N) (M) *** Ph. 464 720-2. (i) Price, Schmidt, Araiza, Adam; (ii) Mathis, Rappé, Blochwitz, Quasthoff; Leipzig Radio Choir, Dresden Staatskapelle, Schreier

It makes a generous and apt coupling in the Philips series of '50 Great Recordings' to have Schreier's 1982 version of the *Requiem* supplemented by the *Coronation Mass* and *Ave verum corpus*, recorded a decade later with the same choir and orchestra. By latterday standards the opening *Introitus* of the *Requiem* is rather heavy, but that is the exception in this intensely dramatic and purposeful reading, with Dame Margaret Price singing ravishingly. The quartet of soloists is impressive too in the *Coronation Mass*, and in both the Leipzig Radio Choir sings with superb attack, if occasionally resorting to an aspirated style. Full, well-refurbished sound.

Mass No. 18 in C min. (Great), K.427.

*** DG 439 012-2. Hendricks, Perry, Schreier, Luxon, V. Singverein, BPO, Karajan.

*** Ph. 420 210-2. McNair, Montague, Rolfe Johnson, Hauptmann, Monteverdi Ch., E. Bar. Sol., Gardiner.

(i) *Mass No. 18 (Great). Meistermusik* (1785 original choral version of *Masonic Funeral Music*), K.477.

** (*) HM HMC 901393. (i) Oelze, Larmore, Weir, Kooy; Chapelle Royale Coll. Voc., O of Champs Elysées, Herreweghe.

In his (1982) digital recording of the *C minor Mass* Karajan gives Handelian splendour to this greatest of Mozart's choral works and, though the scale is large, the beauty and intensity are hard to resist. Solo singing is first rate, particularly that of Barbara Hendricks, the dreamy beauty of her voice ravishingly caught. Woodwind is rather backward, yet the sound is both rich and vivid – though, as the opening shows, the internal balance is not always completely consistent.

John Eliot Gardiner, using period instruments, gives an outstandingly fresh performance of high dramatic contrasts, marked by excellent solo singing – both the sopranos pure and bright-toned and Anthony Rolfe Johnson in outstandingly sweet voice. With the recording giving an ample scale without inflation, this too can be warmly recommended.

Herreweghe directs a satisfying and very well-recorded period performance, if not as vital as those of Gardiner and Karajan. He opens somewhat squarely, but the performance soon opens out. The choral singing is always vivid, and both soprano soloists are outstanding: Christine Oelze sweetly nimble in the *Et incarnatus est* and Jennifer Larmore giving a brilliant and moving account of the *Laudamus te*. The fill-up is the original choral version of the *Masonic Funeral Music* and here Herreweghe achieves just the right feeling of sombre ceremonial.

Mass No. 19 (Requiem) in D min., K.626.

*** Sony SK 60764. Ulewicz, Hölzl, Hering, Van der Kamp, Tölz Boys' Ch., Tafelmusik, Weil.

*** DG 439 023-2. Tomowa-Sintow, Müller Molinari, Cole, Burchuladze, V. Singverein, VPO, Karajan.

*** Ph. 411 420-2. M. Price, Schmidt, Araiza, Adam, Leipzig R. Ch., Dresden State O, Schreier.

(BB) *** RCA Navigator (ADD) 74321 29238-2. Equiluz, Eder, V. Boys' Ch., V. State Op. Ch. & O, Gillesberger – HAYDN: *Te Deum.* ***

(M) **(*) Chan. 7059. Kenny, Walker, Kendall, Wilson-Johnson, St John's College, Cambridge, Ch., ECO, Guest.

(B) **(*) [EMI Red Line CDR5 69867]. Donath, Ludwig, Tear, Lloyd, Philh. Ch. & O, Giulini.

(B) **(*) Ph. (ADD) 420 353-2. Donath, Minton, R. Davies, Nienstedt, John Alldis Ch., BBC SO, C. Davis.

(B) **(*) Penguin (ADD) Ph. 460 607-2. (Soloists as above, with Alldis Ch., BBC SO, C. Davis.)

(N) (BB) ** Warner Apex (ADD) 8573 89421-2. Ameling, Scherler, Devos, Soyer, Gulbenkian Foundation, Lisbon Ch. & O, Corboz.

(i) Requiem Mass (No. 19); Adagio & Fugue, K.546.

(N) (M) ** DG (ADD) 463 654-2. BPO, Karajan; (i) with Lipp, Rössl-Majdan, Dermota, Berry, V. Singverein.

(i; ii) Mass No. 19 (Requiem) (ed. and revised Druce); (ii) Ave verum corpus. Maurerische Trauermusik, K.477.

(M) **(*) Virgin VM5 61520-2. (i) Argenta, Robbin, Mark Ainsley, Miles; (ii) L. Schütz Ch.; LCP, Norrington.

Mass No. 19 (Requiem); (i) Grabmusik, K.42: Beatracht dies Herz; Vesperae solennes de confessore, K.339: Laudate Dominum.

*** DG 463 181-2. (i) Harnisch; Mattila, Mingardo, Schade, Terfel, Swedish R. Ch., BPO, Abbado.

Mass No. 19 (Requiem); Kyrie, K.341.

*** HM HMC 901620. Rubens, Markert, Bostridge, Müller-Brachmann, La Chapelle Royale Coll. Vocale, O des Champs Elysées, Herreweghe.

*** Ph. 420 197-2. Bonney, Von Otter, Blochwitz, White, Monteverdi Ch., E. Bar. Sol., Gardiner.

(i) Mass No. 19 (Requiem). Maurerische Trauermusik, K.477.

(BB) Virgin 2 x 1 Double VBD5 61501-2 (2). (i) L Kenny, Hodgson, Davies, Howell, L. Sinf. Ch., N. Sinf. Ch. & O, Hickox – BRUCKNER: *Missa solemnis; Psalms.*

(B) *** Audivis ES 9965. Soloists, La Capella Reial de Catalunya; Le Concert des Nations, Savall.

Bruno Weil's splendid new period performance of Mozart's *Requiem* stands alone and distinctive in that it uses a completely new edition by H. C. Robbins Landon. In the accompanying notes he explains in detail how it was prepared, combining the work of Mozart's three pupils, Süssmayr, Eybler and Freystädler, which he suggests is 'nearer to the spirit of the torso than any twentieth-century reconstruction could be'. Weil conducts a highly dramatic, powerfully committed performance with a fine team of soloists, incisively vital choral singing, given excellent orchestral support. It is very well recorded indeed, in a spacious acoustic, and stands very high among current recorded performances, irrespective of the edition used. For many it could be first choice.

Recorded live in July 1999 in Salzburg Cathedral, Abbado's performance of the traditional score with the Berlin Philharmonic was given to commemorate the tenth anniversary of the death of Herbert von Karajan. The dedicated atmosphere of such an occasion is powerfully caught, with the DG engineers clarifying the sound to a remarkable degree, with fine detail as well as ample weight. With the brilliant Swedish Radio Choir singing with exceptionally clear focus, such choruses as the *Dies irae* are thrillingly intense, and the starry yet youthful line-up of soloists – none of whom Karajan would ever have heard – makes an outstanding team. In the two extra items, among Mozart's loveliest soprano solos, Rachel Harnisch sings with warmth and refinement. This can be recommended to those wanting a traditional, modern-instrument account of Mozart's choral masterpiece.

Herreweghe is arresting from the very dramatic opening bars, and in the work's central Sequenz (*Dies irae*; *Tuba mirum*; *Rex Tremendae*; *Recordare*; *Confutatis* and the moving *Lacrimosa*) he achieves a remarkable emotional thrust. The orchestra gives weighty support, and one is hardly aware that this is a period-instrument performance, with the horns and trumpets capping climaxes forcefully. The soloists make an excellent team, singing with individuality (especially Ian Bostridge) but also blending together. The sound is spacious, but there is no feeling that the choral impact is blunted.

Richard Hickox's excellent version of the *Requiem Mass* on the Virgin label matches any in the catalogue. With generally brisk speeds and light, resilient rhythms, it combines gravity with authentically clean, transparent textures in which the dark colourings of the orchestration, as with the basset horns, come out vividly. All four soloists are outstandingly fine, and the choral singing is fresh and incisive, with crisp attack. The voices, solo and choral, are placed rather backwardly; otherwise the recording is excellent. This now comes as part of a super-bargain Virgin

Double, aptly coupled with the rare Bruckner *Missa solemnis*, which is also very well sung, the only drawback being sparse documentation and an absence of texts.

John Eliot Gardiner with characteristic panache also gives one of the most powerful performances on record, for while the lighter sound of the period orchestra makes for greater transparency, the weight and bite are formidable. The soloists are an outstanding quartet, well matched but characterfully contrasted too, and the choral singing is as bright and luminous as one expects of Gardiner's Monteverdi Choir. The superb *Kyrie in D minor* makes a very welcome and generous fill-up, to seal a firm recommendation.

The performance by La Capella Reial de Catalunya and Le Concert des Nations directed by Jordi Savall is both gutsy and expressive; at times tempi have great urgency – witness the thrilling *Dies irae* and the strong accents of the opening of the *Confutatis*, then contrasted by the angelic soprano line, with Montserrat Figueras a blissfully serene soloist. The trombones make a remarkable contribution throughout, and especially in the *Benedictus* and *Agnus Dei*. The recording is absolutely first class and, certainly, no other version of the *Requiem* makes more impact on the listener. It is aptly introduced by the plangent timbres of the *Maurerische Trauermusik*.

Karajan's 1987 digital version of the *Requiem* is a large-scale reading, but one that is white-hot with intensity and energy. The power and bite of the rhythm are consistently exciting. The solo quartet is first rate, though Helga Müller Molinari is on the fruity side for Mozart. Vinson Cole, stretched at times, yet sings very beautifully, and so does Paata Burchuladze with his tangily distinctive, Slavonic bass tone. The close balance adds to the excitement.

Peter Schreier's is a forthright reading of Mozart's valedictory choral work, bringing strong dramatic contrasts and marked by superb choral singing and a consistently elegant and finely balanced accompaniment. The singing of Margaret Price in the soprano part is almost finer than any other yet heard on record, and the others make a first-rate team, if individually more variable. Only in the *Kyrie* and the final *Cum sanctis tuis* does the German habit of using the intrusive aitch annoy. Altogether this is most satisfying.

Norrington uses an entirely new score by Duncan Druce, rejecting Süssmayr and other additional editorial material. Druce's revisions are considerable, even presenting recomposed music, with alterations as early as the *Recordare* and *Sanctus*. The result is fascinating, and in its way is undoubtedly successful, once one adjusts to the changes. Norrington certainly believes in it, and his account is both vibrant and compelling, with unpredictable tempi at times, but never eccentric. The soloists too are very impressive and so is the recording. As bonuses Norrington offers a tranquil (though not dallying) *Ave verum corpus* and a strongly characterized version of the *Mauerische Trauermusik*, moved forward with more drive than usual. This acts as a rather effective prelude to the main work.

The surprise version is Gillesberger's. Using treble and alto soloists from the Vienna Boys' Choir, who sing with confidence and no little eloquence, this performance also has the advantage of a dedicated contribution from Kurt Equiluz. Gillesberger's pacing is well judged and the effect

is as fresh as it is strong and direct. The 1982 recording is excellent, vivid yet full, and the result is powerful but not too heavy.

Guest has the advantage of first-class singing from his St John's choristers, strong and eloquent, and an outstanding Chandos recording, full, vivid and clear. The performance is vigorous and positive, and well held together. The soloists, however, though making an excellent team and never letting the performance down, are not individually memorable, and altogether this cannot quite match Karajan or Hickox.

Giulini directs a large-scale performance which brings out both Mozartian lyricism and Mozartian drama, and anyone who fancies what by today's standards is an inauthentic approach may consider this version. The choir is in excellent, incisive form, and the soloists are a first-rate quartet. As one would expect, what Giulini's insight conveys is the rapt quality of such passages as the end of the *Tuba mirum* and the *Benedictus*. The recording is warm rather than brilliant.

Colin Davis gives a comparatively small-scale performance, but the choral sound itself is weighty and thick, and, while this account is enjoyable, in the last resort it is not memorable. Readers will note that this performance is also available on a Philips Duo, above, combined with the *Coronation* and *Great C minor Masses*, and overall that seems to be a rather more enticing proposition. As seen above, the Davis version is also available as one of the inexpensive Penguin Classics (with a note by D. M. Thomas). However, the Philips Virtuoso CD is the more economical proposition.

Karajan's earlier (1962) recording was a strange choice for reissue as one of DG's 'Originals'. There is nothing legendary here except Karajan's remarkably suave view of Mozart's valedictory work. Here detail tends to be sacrificed in favour of warmth and atmosphere. The solo quartet are wonderfully blended, a rare occurrence in this work above all, and though the chorus lacks firmness of line they are helped out by the spirited playing of the Berlin Philharmonic. However, both Karajan's later (1976) analogue and newest digital version are greatly preferable. The *Adagio and Fugue* offered as a makeweight, with glorious Berlin string tone, is both refined and expansive.

Michel Corboz, an excellent choral conductor, directs a nicely scaled performance and gets some fine, and often fervent, singing from his Lisbon Choir. His concern for detail is admirable. Elly Ameling is outstanding in a variable quartet of soloists, but the performance ultimately lacks the last degree of thrust, particularly in the closing *Lux aeterna*.

Requiem Mass (No. 19) in D min. (ed. Maunder).

(N) (M) **(*) O-L 464 720-2. Kirkby, Watkinson, Rolfe Johnson, Thomas, Westminster Cathedral Boys' Ch., AAM Ch. and O, Hogwood.

Hogwood's version cannot be compared with any other, using as it does the edition of Richard Maunder, which aims to eliminate Süssmayr's contribution to the version of Mozart's unfinished masterpiece that has held sway for two centuries. So the *Lacrimosa* is completely different, after the opening eight bars, and concludes with an elaborate *Amen*, for which Mozart's own sketches were recently discovered. This textual clean-out goes with authentic performances of

Hogwood's customary abrasiveness, very fresh and lively to underline the impact of novelty.

OPERA

Complete Mozart Edition, Vol. 26: *Apollo et Hyacinthus* (complete).

(M) *** Ph. (ADD) 422 526-2 (2). Augér, Mathis, Wulkopf, Schwarz, Rolfe Johnson, Salzburg Chamber Ch. & Mozarteum O, Hager.

The opera was written when Mozart was eleven, with all but two of the parts taken by schoolchildren. The style of the writing and vocalization is rather simpler than in other dramatic works of the boy Mozart, but the inspiration is still remarkable, astonishingly mature. The orchestration is assured and full of imaginative touches. The performance here is stylish and very well sung. Excellent, clear and well-balanced recording, admirably transferred to CD.

Complete Mozart Bargain Edition, Vol. 13: Early Italian Operas: *Ascanio in Alba; La finta semplice; Lucia Silla; Mitradate, Re di Ponte; Il sogno di Scipione.*

(N) (B) **(*) Ph. 464 890-2 (13). Soloists; CPE Bach Ch. O, Schreier; or Salzburg Mozart O, Hager.

Complete Mozart Edition, Vol. 30: *Ascanio in Alba* (complete).

(M) **(*) Ph. (ADD) 422 530-2 (3). Sukis, Baltsa, Mathis, Augér, Schreier, Salzburg Chamber Ch., Salzburg Mozarteum O, Hager.

Ascanio in Alba (complete).

(B) *** Naxos 8.660040-2 (2). Windsor, Chance, Feldman, Milner, Mannion, Paris Sorbonne University Ch., Budapest Concerto Armonico, Grimbert.

Mozart at the age of fifteen wrote this charming, ever-inventive 'festa teatrale' for the coronation of the Archduke Ferdinand to an Italian princess in Milan in 1771. A court entertainment rather than an opera proper, it designedly identifies characters in a classical story, with the bride and bridegroom taking part in a delightful and original closing trio. The Naxos version easily outshines previous recordings with a lightly sprung, stylishly conducted performance featuring an outstanding cast. The counter-tenor, Michael Chance, sings flawlessly in the castrato role of Ascanio, son of Venus, even-toned and brilliantly flexible. The others are fresh-toned too. Lorna Windsor, bright and clear as Venus, is nicely contrasted with the girlish-sounding Silvia of Jill Feldman, who sings with fine assurance in one of the two extended arias. The other, even more extended and demanding, is given to Fauno, with Rosa Mannion arguably the most accomplished soloist of all. The excellent tenor taking the role of Aceste is Howard Milner. Well recorded with transparent textures, if with chorus backwardly balanced, this makes an outstanding bargain in every way, rare Mozart that for most will be a delightful discovery.

Hager makes an excellent start with an exceptionally lively account of the delightful overture, but then the choruses seem relatively square, thanks to the pedestrian, if generally efficient, singing of the Salzburg choir. Hager's speeds are sometimes on the slow side, but the solo singing is excellent, with no weak link in the characterful cast, though not everyone will like the distinctive vibrato of Lilian Sukis as Venus. The 1976 analogue recording is full and vivid. But this set is now completely upstaged by the new Naxos version.

Bastien und Bastienne (complete). Concert arias: *Mentre ti lascio, o figlia, K.513; Misero! o sogno . . . Aura, che intorno spiri, K.431. Le nozze di Figaro: Giunse alfin il momento . . . Deh vieni; Un moto di gioia.*

*** Sony SK 45855. Gruberová, Cole, Polgar, Liszt CO, Leppard.

Complete Mozart Bargain Edition, Vol. 16: German Operas: *Bastien und Bastienne; Die Entführung aus dem Serail; Der Schauspieldirektor; Die Gärtnerin aus Liebe; Zaïde; Die Zauberflöte.*

(N) (B) *** Ph. (ADD/DDD) 464 930-2 11). Soloists; Vienna SO, Harrer; N. German RSO, Schmidt-Isserstedt; Dresden State O or LSO or ASMF, C. Davis.

Complete Mozart Edition, Vol. 27: *Bastien und Bastienne* (complete); Lieder: *Komm, liebe Zither, komm; Die Zufriedenheit.*

(M) *** Ph. 422 527-2. Orieschnig, Nigl, Busch, V. Boys' Ch., VSO, Harrer.

Leppard conducts a near-ideal performance of the eleven-year-old Mozart's charming little one-Acter, very well recorded. Edita Gruberová is delectably fresh and vivacious as the heroine, Vinson Cole is a sensitive and clean-voiced Bastien and Laszlo Polgar is full of fun in the buffo role of Colas. The Liszt Chamber Orchestra of Budapest plays with dazzling precision. As a generous fill-up, the three soloists sing Mozart arias, including the big scena for tenor, *Misero! o sogno*, and a replacement aria for Susanna, especially written for the 1789 production of *Le nozze di Figaro*: *Un moto di gioia.*

On Philips, the opera is performed by boy trebles instead of the soprano, tenor and bass originally intended. Members of the Vienna Boys' Choir give a refreshingly direct performance under Uwe Christian Harrer, missing little of the piece's charm. The two songs with mandolin accompaniment, also sung by one of the trebles, make an attractive fill-up. First-rate 1986 digital sound.

Complete Mozart Bargain Edition, Vol. 15: Late Italian Operas: *La clemenza di Tito; Così fan tutte; Don Giovanni; Le nozze di Figaro.*

(N) (B) *** Ph. (ADD) 464 920-2 (11). Soloists; BBC SO or ROHCG, C. Davis.

Complete Mozart Edition, Vol. 44: *La clemenza di Tito* (complete).

(M) *** Ph. (ADD) 422 544-2 (2). J. Baker, Minton, Burrows, Von Stade, Popp, Lloyd, ROHCG Ch. & O, C. Davis.

La clemenza di Tito (complete).

*** EMI CDS5 55489-2 (2). Winbergh, Vaness, Ziegler, Senn, Barbaux, V. State Op. Ch., VPO, Muti.

*** DG 431 806-2 (2). Rolfe Johnson, Von Otter, McNair,

Varady, Robbin, Hauptmann, Monteverdi Ch., E. Bar. Sol., Gardiner.

*** Teldec 4509 90857-2 (2). Langridge, Popp, Ziesak, Murray, Ziegler, Polgár, Zurich Op. Ch. & O, Harnoncourt.

**(*) O-L 444 131-2 (2). Heilmann, Bartoli, D. Jones, Montague, Bonney, Ch. & AAM, Hogwood.

Sir Colin Davis's superb set is among the finest of his many Mozart recordings. Not only is the singing of Dame Janet Baker in the key role of Vitellia formidably brilliant; she actually makes one believe in the emotional development of an impossible character, one who progresses from villainy to virtue with the scantiest preparation. The two other mezzo-sopranos, Minton as Sesto and Von Stade in the small role of Annio, are superb too, while Stuart Burrows has rarely if ever sung so stylishly on a recording as here. Davis's swaggering manner transforms what used to be dismissed as a dry *opera seria*. Excellent recording.

Recorded live on stage at the 1988 Salzburg Festival, Muti's version is vividly dramatic. The tension of the live performance is powerfully conveyed, underlining the emotional thrust. The cast is a strong one, with Carol Vaness as Vitellia and Delores Ziegler as Sesto intense and characterful, two singers who built their Mozartian reputations at Glyndebourne, although Vaness comes under strain by the end of this live event. Gösta Winbergh makes a noble Tito, heroic of tone and never strained, and the others are good if not always ideally sweet of tone. A good alternative to the Colin Davis version, if you want a recording on modern instruments, though in this Muti set live performance involves interruption from stage noises and audience applause. However, this set has been deleted as we go to press.

Again, with his vitality and bite, Gardiner turns the piece into a genuinely involving drama. Anthony Rolfe Johnson is outstanding in the title-role, matching the vivid characterization of both Anne Sofie von Otter as Sesto and Julia Varady as Vitellia. Sylvia McNair is an enchanting, pure-toned Servilia and Catherine Robbin a well-matched Annio, though the microphone catches an unevenness in the voice, as it does with Cornelius Hauptmann in the incidental role of Publio. More seriously, DG's vivid, immediate recording picks up a distracting amount of banging and bumping on stage in the Süssmayr recitatives.

Nikolaus Harnoncourt uses modern, not period, instruments. Even so, he has not forgotten his early devotion to period performance, making this a very viable account for anyone wanting a half-way approach. Though recorded in association with Zurich Opera, this is a studio, not a live, recording like Gardiner's. It gains from not having stage noises in recitative. Ann Murray is at her finest as Sesto, if not quite as firm or dominant as von Otter for Gardiner. Philip Langridge is a splendid Tito, and it is good to have Lucia Popp so affecting in her very last recording. Ruth Ziesak and Delores Ziegler complete a strong team which will not disappoint anyone, even if it cannot quite compare with Gardiner's, singer for singer.

With clean, crisp manners Hogwood draws transparent textures from the players in the Academy, pointing rhythms and phrases more lightly and almost as imaginatively as Gardiner. Sesto as portrayed by the characterful Cecilia

Bartoli is clearly established as the central figure in the drama, with Della Jones as Vitellia comparably positive. Diana Montague as Annio and Barbara Bonney as Servilia both weigh in favour of Hogwood, but Uwe Heilmann with his slightly fluttery tenor conveys nothing like the heroic strength of Anthony Rolfe Johnson in the title-role for Gardiner. Clean, well-balanced studio sound.

Complete Mozart Edition, Vol. 42: *Così fan tutte* (complete).

(M) *** Ph. (ADD) 422 542-2. Caballé, J. Baker, Cotrubas, Gedda, Ganzarolli, Van Allan, ROHCG Ch. & O, C. Davis.

Così fan tutte (complete).

(N) ✪ (M) *** EMI (ADD) CMS 5 67382-2 (3) [567379]. Schwarzkopf, Ludwig, Steffek, Kraus, Taddei, Berry, Philh. Ch. & O, Boehm.

*** Decca 444 174-2 (3). Fleming, Von Otter, Lopardo, Bär, Scarabelli, Pertusi, COE, Solti.

*** Ph. 422 381-2 (3). Mattila, Von Otter, Szmytka, Araiza, Allen, Van Dam, Amb. Op. Ch., ASMF, Marriner.

✪ (M) (***) EMI mono CMS5 67064-2 [567138] (3). Schwarzkopf, Otto, Merriman, Simoneau, Panerai, Bruscantini, Philh. Ch. & O, Karajan.

(B) **(*) Double Decca (ADD) 455 476-2 (2). Della Casa, Ludwig, Loose, Dermota, Kunz, Schoeffler, V. State Op. Ch., VPO, Boehm.

*** HM HMC 951663/5. Gens, Fink, Boone, Güra, G. Oddone, P. Oddone, Cologne Chamber Ch. & O, Jacobs.

*** DG 437 829-2 (3). Roocroft, Mannion, Gilfry, Trost, James, Feller, E. Bar. Sol., Gardiner.

*** EMI CDS7 47727-8 (3). Vaness, Ziegler, Watson, Aler, Duesing, Desderi, Glyndebourne Ch., LPO, Haitink.

(M) *** Erato (ADD) 4509 98494-2 (3). Te Kanawa, Stratas, Von Stade, Rendall, Huttenlocher, Bastin, Rhine Op. Ch., Strasbourg PO, Lombard.

**(*) EMI CDS5 56170-2 (3). Martinpelto, Hagley, Murray, Streit, Finley, Allen, OAE, Rattle.

Boehm's classic set has been splendidly remastered as one of EMI's 'Great Recordings of the Century' and remains a clear first choice, despite the attractions of the new Solti version. Its glorious solo singing is headed by the incomparable Fiordiligi of Schwarzkopf and the equally moving Dorabella of Christa Ludwig; it remains a superb memento of Walter Legge's recording genius and remains unsurpassed by any other recordings made before or since. The documentation is generous and includes a full libretto and sessions photographs.

Solti's digital *Così*, recorded live at the Royal Festival Hall in 1994, is as sparkling and full of humour as you could want. He takes a fast and light approach which yet has none of his old fierceness. The speeds may challenge the singers, notably in the many ensembles, but Solti gives his performers every consideration in moulding the arch of phrases or in allowing time for elaborate decorations. Though such meditative passages as the lovely little trio, *O soave sia il vento*, and the opening of Fiordiligi's aria, *Per pietà*, are taken at flowing speeds, faster than usual, they have a poise that holds one rapt. Much is owed to the superb playing of the Chamber Orchestra of Europe. Renée Fleming as

Fiordiligi, brought in as substitute at the last minute, sings with a firm, full voice that is yet brilliant and flexible, ranging down to a satisfyingly strong chest register. Dazzling as her *Come scoglio* is in Act I, *Per pietà* in Act II brings even greater emotional depth. Frank Lopardo too, as Ferrando, most sensitively uses his distinctive tenor over an unusually wide dynamic range, so that in the lovely aria, *Una aura amorosa*, he sings the reprise in a gentler, more beautiful half-tone than anyone else on disc. Anne Sofie von Otter predictably makes a characterful Dorabella, well contrasted with Fleming, and Olaf Bär a keenly intelligent Guglielmo, while two Italian singers, less well known but well chosen, Adelina Scarabelli and Michele Pertusi, complete the team in the manipulative roles of Despina and Alfonso. Altogether Solti's finest Mozart recording yet, outshining even his *Figaro*.

Marriner directs a fresh and resilient performance, beautifully paced, often with speeds on the fast side, and with the crystalline recorded sound adding to the sparkle. Though the women principals make a strong team, the men are even finer: Francisco Araiza as Ferrando, Thomas Allen as Guglielmo and José van Dam as Alfonso are all outstanding so that, though the reading is lighter in weight than those of Boehm, Karajan, Haitink or Davis, it has more fun in it, bringing out the laughter in the score.

Commanding as Schwarzkopf is as Fiordiligi in the 1962 Boehm set, the extra ease and freshness of her singing in the earlier (1954) version under Karajan makes it even more compelling. Nan Merriman is a distinctive and characterful Dorabella, and the role of Ferrando has never been sung more mellifluously on record than by Leopold Simoneau. The young Rolando Panerai is an ideal Guglielmo, and Lisa Otto a pert Despina; while Sesto Bruscantini in his prime brings to the role of Don Alfonso the wisdom and artistry which made him so compelling at Glyndebourne. Karajan has never sparkled more naturally in Mozart than here, for the high polish has nothing self-conscious about it. The recording has been impressively remastered for reissue as another of EMI's 'Great Recordings of the Century'.

Boehm's 1955 Decca stereo set is not as polished a performance as his later one for EMI, and the cutting of brief passages from the ends of arias may worry those who know the opera very well. But it remains a captivatingly spontaneous account of the frothiest of Mozart's comedies. Lisa della Casa is strong and sweet-toned, Christa Ludwig is admirably fresh-voiced, and the rest are sparklingly good, especially Emmy Loose's deliciously knowing portrayal of Despina. Paul Schoeffler in the role of Don Alfonso is most appealing. This was one of Decca's early stereo experiments, but the sense of the singers acting out the comedy just beyond the speakers is uncannily realistic. Decca's new-style synopsis – with the narrative first given briefly 'in a nutshell' followed by suggested highlights, and listener-friendly cueing of the action – is a distinct asset.

René Jacobs with the Concerto Köln directs an intimate period performance of *Così fan tutte*, often light and brisk, but occasionally marked by surprisingly slow speeds, extremely so in the Act I farewell quintet, *Di scrivermi*. Veronique Gens, golden-toned, makes a delightful Fiordiligi, scaling down *Come scoglio* to match the rest, with Bernarda Fink also singing with creamy beauty. Werner Güra is a charming, expressive Ferrando, but Marcel Boone is far less focused as Guglielmo. A thoroughly enjoyable set, well coordinated, though not a first choice.

For this comedy, John Eliot Gardiner controversially opted to get the engineers to record a live performance not in concert but on stage. Stage noises are often intrusive, with laughter and applause punctuating the performance, not always helpfully. Whatever the snags, the full flavour of *Così*, its effervescence as well as its deeper qualities, comes over the more intensely as a result. Though Amanda Roocroft and Rosa Mannion do not sound quite as sweet and even as they can, few tenors on disc can rival the German Rainer Trost in the heady beauty of his voice, above all in Ferrando's aria, *Una aura amorosa*. The poise and technical assurance of all the singers, not least Rodney Gilfry as Guglielmo, put this among the very finest versions of *Così*. DG offers the alternative of a video version (072 436-31), also made on stage, but at the Théâtre du Châtelet in Paris instead of Ferrara, and with Claudio Nicolai instead of Carlos Feller as Alfonso. The unscripted noises are here explained in the detail of Gardiner's own (sometimes excessive) staging, but with delectably pretty scenery. The crowning achievement on both CD and video is that the dénouement in the long Act II finale has a tenderness and depth rarely matched.

With speeds often more measured than usual, Haitink's EMI version is, above all, a sunny performance. Claudio Desderi as Alfonso helps to establish that Glyndebourne atmosphere, with recitatives superbly timed and coloured. If Carol Vaness and Delores Ziegler are rather too alike in timbre to be distinguished easily, the relationship becomes all the more sisterly when, quite apart from the similarity, they respond so beautifully to each other. John Aler makes a headily unstrained Ferrando, beautifully free in the upper register; and Lilian Watson and Dale Duesing make up a strong team. The digital recording gives fine bloom and an impressive dynamic range to voices and orchestra alike.

The energy and sparkle of Sir Colin Davis are set against inspired and characterful singing from the three women soloists, with Montserrat Caballé and Janet Baker proving a winning partnership, each challenging and abetting the other all the time. Cotrubas equally is a vivid Despina, never merely arch. Though Gedda has moments of rough tone and Ganzarolli falls short in one of his prominent arias, they are both spirited, while Richard van Allan sings with flair and imagination. Sparkling recitative and recording, which has you riveted by the play of the action.

On Erato, Kiri Te Kanawa's voice sounds radiant, rich and creamy of tone; she is commanding in *Come scoglio*, and tenderly affecting in *Per pietà*, which is more moving here than with Levine. Lombard is a sympathetic accompanist, if not always the most perceptive of Mozartians; some of his tempi are on the slow side, but his sextet of young singers make up a team that rivals almost any other, giving firm, appealing performances. With warm recording of high quality, this is most enjoyable and could be a first choice for any who follow the singers in question.

Sir Simon Rattle offers a sizzling account of *Così*, recorded live, with the period instruments of the Orchestra of the Age of Enlightenment. In its often hectic speeds from the overture onwards, it may miss some of the sparkle of the piece, but Rattle knows how to bring out the emotional high points, so that the superb Fiordiligi, Hillevi Martinpelto, at a measured speed sings with aching beauty in *Per pietà*. With less pointed playing, the set may not replace Gardiner, Boehm or Solti, but the cast is the most consistent of the three, including Thomas Allen as a masterly Alfonso, Kurt Streit a clear-toned Ferrando and Gerald Finley a youthfully ardent Guglielmo. It is refreshing too to have a soprano Dorabella, particularly when the lovely timbre of Alison Hagley's voice is clearly contrasted with the brighter tones of Martinpelto. As ever, Ann Murray is a characterful Despina. The acoustic of Symphony Hall, Birmingham, adds brightness to the sound, though this is not focused quite as well as Birmingham recordings made without an audience.

Così fan tutte (excerpts).

(***) Testament mono SBT 1040. Jurinac, Thebom, Lewis, Kunz, Borriello, Glyndebourne Festival O, Busch; Alda Noni, Philh. O, Susskind.

The superb Testament transfer of excerpts from *Così fan tutte* in the 1950 Glyndebourne production gives a vivid idea of the way that even in the first year when the re-established Glyndebourne Festival was recovering its pre-war format, standards were never higher. Sena Jurinac as Fiordiligi, clear and vibrant, provides the central glory, with both her two big arias included, as well as six of her ensemble numbers, and three substantial rehearsal 'takes'. Blanche Thebom too, as Dorabella, sings with clarity and freshness, and the others make a splendid team. Alda Noni, the Despina, was not recorded at the Glyndebourne sessions but later, at Abbey Road, with Susskind and the Philharmonia. The recording brings out a flutter in her voice, less steady than the others. As in pre-war days, a piano is used instead of harpsichord for recitatives.

Così fan tutte: highlights.

(BB) **(*) Belart (ADD) 450 114-2 (from complete recording, with Janowitz, Fassbaender, Prey, Schreier, Grist, VPO, cond. Boehm).

These Belart highlights come from Karl Boehm's third (DG) recording of the opera and, with 72 minutes of music included, it makes an attractive memento. It was recorded live during the Salzburg Festival performance on the conductor's eightieth birthday. It has a splendid cast, and the zest and sparkle of the occasion come over delightfully. Even if at times ensemble leaves a good deal to be desired, at super-budget price it makes a genuine bargain.

(i) Così fan tutte; (ii) Don Giovanni; (iii) Le nozze di Figaro.

(B) *** Ph. (ADD) 456 375-2 (9). (i–iii) Ganzarolli; (i) Caballé, J. Baker, Cotrubas, Gedda; (i–ii) Van Allan, ROHCG Ch. & O; (ii) Arroyo, Te Kanawa, Burrows, Roni; (ii–iii) Wixell, Freni; (iii) Norman, Minton, Casula, Grant, Tear, BBC Ch., BBC SO; all cond. C. Davis.

Philips wisely decided to omit Sir Colin Davis's recording of *Die Zauberflöte* from this very tempting bargain box; it was the least successful of his Mozart opera series and in any case is available separately and inexpensively on a Duo (see below). The other three performances are sheer delight. The sparkling *Così fan tutte* brings a superb female trio in Caballé, Janet Baker and Cotrubas, and the men fall only slightly short of this very high standard. In *Don Giovanni* the very consistency of the whole cast is its major asset, led by Kiri Te Kanawa as Donna Elvira and Mirella Freni's engaging Zerlina, while Ingvar Wixell and Wladimiro Ganzarolli strike sparks off each other as the Don and Leporello; and the same comment applies to *Nozze di Figaro*, where those same two male singers are equally successful in the comparable master and servant roles. Throughout all three operas Davis's lively pacing brings a flowing spontaneity as at live performances. The Philips sound, from clean CD transfers of recordings made between 1971 and 1974, is always fresh and immediate.

Complete Mozart Edition, Vol. 41: Don Giovanni (complete).

(M) *** Ph. (ADD) 422 541-2 (3). Wixell, Arroyo, Te Kanawa, Freni, Burrows, Ganzarolli, ROHCG Ch. & O, C. Davis.

Don Giovanni (complete).

*** EMI CDS7 47260-8 (3). Waechter, Schwarzkopf, Sutherland, Alva, Frick, Sciutti, Taddei, Philh. Ch. & O, Giulini.

*** DG 445 870-2 (3). Gilfry, Orgonasova, Margiono, James, d'Arcangelo, Prégardien, Clarkson, Silvestrelli, Monteverdi Ch., E. Bar. Sol., Gardiner.

✪ (M) *** Decca (ADD) 466 389-2 (3). Della Casa, Danco, Siepi, Corena, Dermota, V. State Op. Ch., VPO, Krips.

*** DG 419 179-2 (3). Ramey, Tomowa-Sintow, Baltsa, Battle, Winbergh, Furlanetto, Malta, Burchuladze, German Op. Ch., Berlin, BPO, Karajan.

*** EMI CDS7 47037-2 (3). Allen, Vaness, Ewing, Gale, Lewis, Van Allan, Rawnsley, Kavrakos, Glyndebourne Ch., LPO, Haitink.

(M) *** EMI (ADD) CMS7 63841-2 (3). Ghiaurov, Claire Watson, Ludwig, Freni, Gedda, Berry, Montarsolo, Crass, New Philh. Ch. & O, Klemperer.

(M) (***) EMI mono CHS5 66657-2 (3). Gobbi, Schwarzkopf, Welitsch, Seefried, Kunz, Dermota, Poell, Greindl, V. State Op. Ch., VPO, Furtwängler.

(M) (***) EMI mono CHS7 63860-2 (3). Siepi, Schwarzkopf, Berger, Grümmer, Dermota, Edelmann, Berry, Ernster, V. State Op. Ch., VPO, Furtwängler.

(M) **(*) Decca (ADD) 448 973-2 (3). Bacquier, Sutherland, Lorengar, Horne, Krenn, Gramm, Monreale, Grant, Amb. S., ECO, Bonynge.

(M) **(*) DG 463 629-2 (3). Fischer-Dieskau, Jurinac, Stader, Seefried, Haefliger, Kohn, Sardi, Kreppel, Berlin RIAS Chamber Ch. & R. O, Fricsay.

(M) (**(*)) Naxos mono 8.110013/14. Pinza, Novotna, Bampton, Sayão, Kullman, Kipnis, Harell, Cordon, NY Met. Op. Ch. & O, Walter.

(M) ** RCA 74321 57737-2 (3). London, Della Casa, Jurinac, Kunz, Dermota, Seefried, Berry, Weber, V. State Op. Ch. & O, Boehm.

** Decca 455 500-2 (3). Terfel, Fleming, Murray, Pertusi, Lippert, Groop, Scaltriti, Luperi, L. Voices, LPO, Solti.

(M) ** Virgin VMT5 61601-2 (3). Schmidt, Yurisich, Halgrimson, Dawson, Mark Ainsley, Argenta, Finley, Miles, Schütz Ch. of L., LCP, Norrington.

(N) (M) * Virgin VCD5 45425-2 (3). Mattei, Cachemaille, Remigio, Gens, Padmore, Larson, Fechner, Gudjon Oskarsson, Aix-le-Provence Acadmy Ch., Mahler CO, Harding.

The classic Giulini EMI set, lovingly remastered, sets the standard by which all other recordings have come to be judged. Elisabeth Schwarzkopf, as Elvira, emerges as a dominant figure to give a distinctive but totally apt slant to this endlessly invigorating drama. The young Sutherland may be relatively reticent as Anna but, with such technical ease and consistent beauty of tone, she makes a superb foil. Taddei is a delightful Leporello, and each member of the cast – including the young Cappuccilli as Masetto – combines fine singing with keen dramatic sense.

John Eliot Gardiner's set was recorded mainly live, and the result is vividly dramatic, beautifully paced and deeply expressive, with little or none of the haste associated with period practice. The performance culminates in one of the most thrilling accounts ever recorded of the final scene, when Giovanni is dragged down to hell. Gardiner opts for a text that is neither that of the original Prague version nor the usual amalgam of Prague and Vienna. Dramatically the result is tauter, and the numbers omitted are here included in an appendix. Sometimes lightness goes too far, as when Charlotte Margiono as Donna Elvira sings *Ah fuggi il traditor* in a half-tone, but increasingly Gardiner encourages his soloists, particularly Anna and Elvira, to sing expansively, bringing out the full weight of such arias as *Mi tradi* and Anna's *Non mi dir*. Fine as Margiono is, Luba Orgonasova is even more assured and characterful as Anna, and the agility of both is exemplary. Rodney Gilfry excels himself, on one side tough and purposeful, on the other a smooth seducer, with the clean-toned voice finely shaded. Ildebrando d'Arcangelo is suitably darker-toned as Leporello, lithe and young-sounding, hardly a *buffo*. Julian Clarkson makes a crotchety Masetto, and Eirian James a warmer, tougher Zerlina than usual, aptly so for her extra scene. The Commendatore of Andrea Silvestrelli, though recessed on the recording, is magnificently dark and firm, not least in the final confrontation. A recording that sets new standards for period performance and vies with the finest of traditional versions.

Sir Colin Davis has the advantage of a singing cast that has fewer shortcomings than almost any other on disc and much positive strength. Martina Arroyo controls her massive dramatic voice more completely than one would think possible, and she is strongly and imaginatively contrasted with the sweetly expressive Elvira of Kiri Te Kanawa and the sparkling Zerlina of Mirella Freni. As in the Davis *Figaro*, Ingvar Wixell and Wladimiro Ganzarolli make a formidable master/servant team with excellent vocal acting, while Stuart Burrows sings gloriously as Don Ottavio, and Richard Van Allan is a characterful Masetto. Davis draws a fresh and immediate performance from his team, riveting from beginning to end, and the recording is now better defined and more vivid than before.

Krips's version, recorded in 1955 for the Mozart bicentenary, has remained at or near the top of the list of recommendations ever since. Freshly remastered, it sounds better than ever. Its intense, dramatic account of the Don's disappearance into Hell has rarely been equalled, and never surpassed on CD, though there are many equally memorable sequences: the finale to Act I is also electrifying. As a bass Don, Siepi is marvellously convincing, but there is hardly a weak link in the rest of the cast. The early stereo recording is pretty age-defying, full and warm, with a lovely Viennese glow which is preferable to many modern recordings. It is good to see this set lovingly packaged on Decca's Legends label, and it ranks alongside the classic Giulini version on EMI.

Even if ensemble is less than perfect at times in the Karajan set and the final scene of Giovanni's descent to Hell goes off the boil a little, the end result has fitting intensity and power. Though Karajan was plainly thinking of a big auditorium in his pacing of recitatives, having Jeffrey Tate as continuo player helps to keep them moving and to bring out word-meaning. The starry line-up of soloists is a distinctive one. Samuel Ramey is a noble rather than a menacing Giovanni, consistently clear and firm.

Haitink's set superbly captures the flavour of Sir Peter Hall's memorable production at Glyndebourne, not least in the inspired teamwork. Maria Ewing comes in as Elvira, vibrant and characterful, not ideally pure-toned but contrasting characterfully with the powerful Donna Anna of Carol Vaness and the innocent-sounding Zerlina of Elizabeth Gale. Keith Lewis is a sweet-toned Ottavio, but it is Thomas Allen as Giovanni who – apart from Haitink – dominates the set, a swaggering Don full of charm and with a touch of nobility when, defiant to the end, he is dragged down to hell – a spine-chilling moment as recorded here. Rarely has the Champagne aria been so beautifully sung, with each note articulated – and that also reflects Haitink's flawless control of pacing, not always conventional but always thoughtful and convincing. Excellent playing from the LPO – well practised in the Glyndebourne pit – and warm, full recording. However, this set has been deleted as we go to press.

Most of the slow tempi that Klemperer regularly adopts, far from flagging, add a welcome breadth to the music, for they must be set against the unusually brisk and dramatic interpretation of the recitatives between numbers. Added to that, Ghiaurov as the Don and Berry as Leporello make a marvellously characterful pair. In this version the male members of the cast are dominant and, with Klemperer's help, they make the dramatic experience a strongly masculine one. Nor is the ironic humour forgotten with Berry and Ghiaurov about, and the Klemperer spaciousness allows them extra time for pointing. Among the women, Ludwig is a strong and convincing Elvira, Freni a sweet-toned but rather unsmiling Zerlina; only Claire Watson seriously disappoints, with obvious nervousness marring the big climax of *Non mi dir*.

The 1950 EMI set with Tito Gobbi in the title-role should not be confused with the later Furtwängler recording, also made at the Salzburg Festival and issued by EMI, with Schwarzkopf as Elvira. The speeds, spacious by most standards, are here a degree faster than they became four years later. Gobbi, not usually a Mozartian, yet gives a commanding, keenly characteristic portrayal of the Don, very much the centre of the drama, swaggering and snarling, a menacingly dangerous seducer. Schwarzkopf as ever is a comparably commanding and characterful Elvira, no wilting flower, and Ljuba Welitsch in 1950 was at her peak, a radiant Anna, with Irmgard Seefried a magical Zerlina and Anton Dermota a honeyed Ottavio. Erich Kunz is the vintage Leporello, and if neither Alfred Poell as Masetto nor Josef Greindl as the Commendatore can match the others vocally, the team could otherwise hardly be stronger. The sound is rough on the orchestra but improves after the overture, while voices are very well caught, though stage balances vary.

The alternative Furtwängler performance was recorded live by Austrian Radio at the 1954 Salzburg Festival, barely three months before the conductor's death. Though speeds are often slow by today's standards, his springing of rhythm never lets them sag. Even the very slow speed for Leporello's catalogue aria is made to seem charmingly individual. With the exception of a wobbly Commendatore, this is a classic Salzburg cast, with Cesare Siepi a fine, incisive Don, dark in tone, Elisabeth Schwarzkopf a dominant Elvira, Elisabeth Grümmer a vulnerable Anna, Anton Dermota a heady-toned Ottavio and Otto Edelmann a clear and direct Leporello. Stage noises often suggest herds of stampeding animals, but both voices and orchestra are satisfyingly full-bodied in the CD transfer, and the sense of presence is astonishing.

Richard Bonynge's reading of *Don Giovanni*, recorded in 1968 and originally dismissed as too lightweight, was in many ways ahead of its time. Though the overture is rather underpowered, tension never lapses after that, and the cast is exceptionally strong. Sutherland is commanding as Donna Anna, even finer than for Giulini on EMI. Gabriel Bacquier, at his peak as the Don, makes a vigorous hero, with Donald Gramm a firm if sober-sided Leporello and Werner Krenn an outstanding, heady-toned Ottavio, while Clifford Grant sings with thrillingly black tone as the Commendatore. Pilar Lorengar, with a hint of flutter in the voice, is a vulnerable rather than a biting Elvira, while the choice of Marilyn Horne as a full mezzo Zerlina, strange by latterday standards, follows historic precedent, with the singer scaling her powerful voice down.

As he has shown in his recording of *Die Zauberflöte*, Fricsay is a forceful, dramatic Mozart conductor, but here the absence of charm is serious. This is mainly felt in some ridiculously fast speeds. Seefried being the superb artist she is, her charm comes through. The cast is generally strong, but unfortunately there is a serious blot in the Donna Elvira of Maria Stader; she is made to sound shrill and some of her attempts to get round the trickier florid passages leave a good deal to be desired. Yet most of the singing is very stylish. Haefliger shows himself as one of the finest Mozart tenors of the time, Karl Kohn is a fine, incisive Leporello, Ivan Sardi an exceptionally rich-voiced Masetto, and Seefried a truly enchanting Zerlina. As so often on records, Sena Jurinac is not quite as thrilling here as one remembers her in the flesh. Fischer-Dieskau is a particularly interesting choice of Don; his characterization proves powerful and forwardly projected.

The vintage Bruno Walter recording, made live at the Met. in New York in March 1942, is one of the most desirable of the Naxos historic issues. Walter's brisk speeds may not allow the sort of detailed expressiveness one finds in either of the Furtwängler versions, but the bite of the drama is irresistible. Ezio Pinza is an engagingly characterful Don, a commanding performance vocally, matched by the rest of the cast. Few Annas equal Rose Bampton for her combination of purity and power, with every note cleanly in place; though Jarmila Novotna as Elvira is less polished, it is a strong performance, and Bidu Sayão makes a charming Zerlina. Charles Kullman is a clear-toned Ottavio, and though Alexander Kipnis as Leporello is not at his best in Act I, the biting clarity of his performance is magnetic. The 1942 sound, one of the better recordings from this source, has voices forwardly balanced. Elvira's aria *Mi tradi* is omitted.

The Boehm RCA version, recorded live by Austrian Radio and given in German, is a historic curiosity – a performance that in 1955 marked the reopening of the Vienna State Opera. Vocally, it is worth hearing for the contributions of the three women principals, with Lisa della Casa creamy-toned as Donna Anna, Sena Jurinac at her magical peak as Donna Elvira and Irmgard Seefried the most charming of Zerlinas. George London is a strong but sour-toned Giovanni. The others are not at their finest either, not helped by the dry acoustic and odd balances.

Recorded live at the Royal Festival Hall in London in October 1996, Solti's version is disappointing despite the promising cast list. It lacks the keen electricity that marks his live recording of *Così fan tutte*, and not one of the singers is on top form. Even Renee Fleming's beautiful voice sounds clouded, and Ann Murray as Elvira is seriously strained. Monica Groop as Zerlina, sweet enough in her arias, is edgy elsewhere, while Roberto Scaltriti is a gritty Masetto and Michele Pertusi often rough as Leporello. Bryn Terfel, so inspired a Leporello, proves an unpersuasive lover, with the tone tending to become unfocused. Dryish sound.

Sir Roger Norrington's version provides a period performance which ingeniously offers the alternative of playing the original Prague version or Mozart's revision for Vienna. This it does by having long sections on separate tracks, instead of tracking each individual number. The snag is that if you want to find a particular aria, it is far less convenient, and many numbers are duplicated when there are alternative sections for Prague or Vienna. Sadly, the singing cast cannot match that in the Gardiner set. Though Lynne Dawson as Elvira, John Mark Ainsley as Ottavio, Gregory Yurisich as Leporello and Alastair Miles as the Commendatore all sing impressively, they hardly outshine their DG opposite numbers, and most of the others fall seriously short, including Andreas Schmidt as an ill-focused Don and Amanda Halgrimson as a shrill Donna Anna. Good, well-balanced sound.

Recorded live at the 1999 Aix-en-Provence Festival, Daniel Harding's reading is an extraordinary exercise in speed. To describe it as perfunctory is to underestimate the impact of speeds that reduce the soloists to a gabble, and which prompt the Mahler Chamber Orchestra to produce sounds that would seem scrawny even from an unreconstructed period band, not helped by a recording that lacks body. The cast, mainly of promising young soloists, is almost completely defeated by such willfulness from the conductor, with even the stylish and characterful Véronique Gens sounding underpowered and uncomfortable. Only the experienced Gilles Cachemaille survives the experiment with any success, a winning and warm Leporello.

Don Giovanni: highlights.

(M) *** EMI (ADD) CDM5 65567-2 (from above complete recording, with Sutherland, Schwarzkopf, Waechter; cond. Giulini).

*** DG 449 139-2 (from above complete recording, with Gilfry, Orgonasova; cond. Gardiner).

(B) **(*) [EMI Red Line CDR5 69824] (from complete recording, with Shimell, Ramey, Studer, VPO, Muti).

*(*) Telarc CD 80442 (from complete set with Skovhus, Corbelli, Brewer; cond. Mackerras).

** Decca 466 065-2 (from above complete recording with Terfel, Fleming, Murray; cond. Solti).

Not surprisingly, the Giulini EMI selection concentrates on Sutherland as Donna Anna and Schwarzkopf as Donna Elvira, so that the Don and Leporello get rather short measure, but Sciutti's charming Zerlina is also given fair due. The selection from the Gardiner set is at full price but runs to 73 minutes.

Muti's *Don Giovanni* is on a big scale but is nevertheless refreshingly alert (using a fortepiano continuo). It is perhaps a set to sample rather than to have complete. Shimell makes a rather gruff Don, not as insinuatingly persuasive as he might be; like the others, he is not helped by the distancing of the voices. With Samuel Ramey convincinglytranslated here to the role of Leporello and Cheryl Studer an outstanding Donna Anna, the rest of the casting is strong and satisfying. The selection of highlights is not particularly generous but does include most of the key numbers.

Mackerras's 1995 recording of *Don Giovanni* is vividly dramatic and perfectly paced, with modern instruments echoing period practice. The teamwork is excellent, but individually the casting is flawed, so the performance is better approached through a highlights disc. This one is generous enough (77 minutes), although the booklet offers only historical notes on the opera and a synopsis which is uncued, which is surely unacceptable for a full-priced CD. In any case Bo Skovhus as the Don may be seductive in expression but his vocal focus too often grows woolly under pressure. Felicity Lott, as recorded, is in disappointing voice as Elvira, not nearly so sweet as usual and there is too much acid in the soprano tones of Christine Brewer as Donna Anna, though Christine Focile makes a characterful Zerlina. The sound has a pleasing ambience but does not provide much sparkle.

Solti's live recording is a disappointment in almost all respects, and this full-priced set of highlights (74 minutes), will be mainly of interest to collectors seeking a sampler of Bryn Terfel's assumption of the title-role, which is generously represented here. Full texts and translations are included.

Don Giovanni (complete in English).

(N) (M) **(*) Chan. 3057 (3). Magee, Cullagh, Shore, Tierney, Plazas, Banks, Robinson, Bayley, Geoffrey Mitchell Ch., Philh. O, Parry.

Vividly recorded, David Parry's well-paced reading breaks new ground in offering the masterpiece in English, and very successful it is, even though the casting is not as starry as in many versions. The lively translation of Amanda Holden is used, and particularly from the men every word is clear, with voices well-balanced against the full-bodied orchestra, set in the helpful acoustic of the Blackheath Concert Hall. David Parry, on the grounds of its greater cohesion, firmly opts for the original Prague version of the score, which may disappoint some when Elvira's *Mi tradi* and Ottavio's *Dalla sua pace* are omitted.

Garry Magee as the Don makes a believable virile lover, vigorous and youthful, articulating the *Champagne* aria cleanly at a crisp, well-chosen tempo. Andrew Shore also characterises well as Leporello, bringing out the comedy but not guying it. Clive Bayley as the Commendatore, Barry Banks as Ottavio, more heroic than usual, and Dean Robinson complete a strong team of men. Among the women the most satisfying performance comes from Mary Plazas as Zerlina, less soubrettish than usual but charming. Majella Cullagh is a warm-toned Donna Anna, only occasionally gusty, and Vivian Tierney a clear, reliable Elvira, whose voice is not flattered by the microphone.

Die Entführung aus dem Serail (complete).

*** DG 435 857-2 (2). Orgonasova, Sieden, Olsen, Peper, Hauptmann, Mineti, Monteverdi Ch., E. Bar. Sol., Gardiner.

(M) *** DG (ADD) 429 868-2 (2). Augér, Grist, Schreier, Neukirch, Moll, Leipzig R. Ch., Dresden State O, Boehm.

(BB) *** Arte Nova 74321 49701-2 (2). Habermann, Ellen, Bezcala, Kalchmair, Ringelhahn, Linz Landestheatre Ch., Linz Bruckner O, Sieghart.

*** Erato 3984 25490-2 (2). Schäfer, Petibon, Bostridge, Paton, Ewing, Les Arts Florissante, Christie.

(M) *** EMI (ADD) CMS7 63263-2 (2). Rothenberger, Popp, Gedda, Unger, Frick, V. State Op. Ch., VPO, Krips.

(M) *** Teldec 2292 44184-2 (2). Kenny, Watson, Schreier, Gamlich, Salminen, Zurich Op. Ch. & Mozart O, Harnoncourt.

(M) ** DG mono 457 730-2 (2). (i) Stader, Streich, Haefliger, Greindl, Vantin, Berlin RIAS Chamber Ch. & SO, Fricsay (with (i) *Exsultate, jubilate, K.165* ***).

(N) ** Telarc CD 80544 (2). Kodalli, Groves, Rancatore, Rose, Atkinson, Tobias, Scottish Ch. O, Mackerras.

Gardiner's *Entführung* was not recorded live but in the studio immediately after a concert performance. The overture immediately establishes the extra zest of the performance. So Konstanze's great heroic aria, *Martern aller Arten*, has tremendous swagger; thanks also to glorious singing from Luba Orgonasova, at once rich, pure and agile, the close is triumphant. Curiously, Gardiner exaggerates the *ad lib.* markings in the first half of that climactic aria. Orgonasova sounds far richer than Lynne Dawson for Hogwood; and in the other great aria, *Traurigkeit*, she is warmer too, less withdrawn. As Belmonte,

Stanford Olsen for Gardiner is firmer and more agile than the fluttery Uwe Heilmann for Hogwood, and though Cornelius Hauptmann, Gardiner's Osmin, lacks a really dark bass, he too is firmer and more characterful than the unsteady Günther von Kannen for Hogwood.

Boehm's is a delectable account, superbly cast and warmly recorded. Arleen Augér proves the most accomplished singer on record in the role of Konstanze, girlish and fresh, yet rich, tender and dramatic by turns, with brilliant, almost flawless coloratura. The others are also outstandingly good, notably Kurt Moll, whose powerful, finely focused bass makes him a superb Osmin, one who relishes the comedy too. The warm recording is beautifully transferred, to make this easily the most sympathetic version of the opera on CD, with the added attraction of being at mid-price.

With an excellent cast of young singers, the Arte Nova set offers an outstanding version to rival almost any in the catalogue. With Martin Sieghart a crisp and urgent conductor, stylistically impeccable, drawing fine playing from the Linz Bruckner Orchestra, the performance gains from having been recorded in conjunction with live performances on stage, a point consistently reflected in the interplay between the soloists. Ingrid Habermann is a formidable Konstanze, fresh and clear, bright in coloratura yet creamy of tone in lower registers, undaunted by the demands of *Martern aller Arten*. The American, Donna Ellen, is a lively Blonde with a clear, unstrained top register. The Polish tenor, Piotr Bezcala, is a stylish, honey-toned Belmonte, with power as well as lyric beauty, only occasionally lachrymose in attack, while Oliver Ringelhahn is a well-contrasted Pedrillo, though pushed to the limit in his big Act II aria, *Frisch zum Kampfe*. Best of all is the Osmin of Franz Kalchmair, whose firm, dark bass copes masterfully with every demand of the role, cleanly focused from top to bottom. Good sound, though the spoken dialogue (well edited) is not consistent. At super-bargain price, the set comes with full libretto, including English translation.

William Christie's speeds are consistently on the fast side, even imperilling articulation in the overture, and allowing less spring to rhythms than in the finest rival period performances. Christine Schäfer makes a ravishing Konstanze, powerful in *Martern aller Arten* and touchingly tender in *Traurigkeit*, though Christie's flowing speed prevents it from having the poignancy which more spacious treatment allows. Ian Bostridge, in the context of a light performance, is ideal as Belmonte, finely detailed in both words and musical treatment, always individual. Patricia Petibon is a light, bright, minxish Blonde, Iain Paton a clear Pedrillo. Most controversial is the choice of the velvet-toned Alan Ewing as Osmin, singing beautifully, but generally avoiding buffo characterization. The chorus is fresh and incisive, though at high speed the Janissaries at their entry are very rushed.

Recorded in 1966, the Krips EMI version brings an amiable and highly enjoyable performance with a formidable line-up of soloists. The team of Popp, Gedda, Unger and Frick could hardly be bettered at the time, each of them singing beautifully and with vivid characterization. Anneliese Rothenberger, potentially the weak link as Konstanze, not only sounds amply powerful as recorded, but sings with a purity and sweetness rarely caught on her discs. This is arguably her finest recording ever. The stereo sound is warm and well balanced, with spoken dialogue well presented. Act I comes on the first disc, with Acts II and III fitted complete on the second.

Harnoncourt's version establishes its uniqueness at the very start of the overture, tougher and more abrasive than any previous recording, with more primitive percussion effects than we are used to in his Turkish music. It is not a comfortable sound, compounded by Harnoncourt's often fast allegros racing singers and players off their feet. Slow passages are often warmly expressive, but the stylishness of the soloists prevents them from seeming excessively romantic. The men are excellent: Peter Schreier singing charmingly, Wilfried Gamlich both bright and sweet of tone, Matti Salminen outstandingly characterful as an Osmin who, as well as singing with firm dark tone, points the words with fine menace. Yvonne Kenny as Konstanze and Lilian Watson as Blonde sound on the shrill side, partly a question of microphones.

Though lacking in body, the mono sound for Fricsay's recording brings splendid detail, with voices well caught. Fricsay characteristically opts for fast, generally refreshing speeds and crisp attack, though Konstanze's great aria of lamentation, *Traurigkeit*, lacks tenderness. Maria Stader is appealing in that role, even though the sweet voice grows less secure on top. Haefliger as Belmonte brings weight but little lyrical beauty. Greindl is a strong but often gritty Osmin and Martin Vantin a boyish Pedrillo, while the finest singing comes from Rita Streich as Blonde. The dialogue is mainly spoken by actors. *Exsultate, jubilate*, with Stader, makes a welcome fill-up.

Recorded for the soundtrack of a film of *Entführung, Mozart in Turkey*, the Telarc version conducted by Sir Charles Mackerras offers lively conducting and a young sounding cast. The modest string band is set in contrast against prominent percussion, with wind and brass well to the fore too. As in his other Mozart with the Scottish Chamber Orchestra, Mackerras introduces elements of period practice in light, fast allegros, fierce at times, though in slow music he allows ample relaxation. Paul Groves is a fresh, clear-toned Belmonte, not quite free enough at the very top, and Yelda Kodalli a bright, clear Konstanze, as impressive in her tender account of *Traurigkeit* as in the bravura of *Martern aller Arten*. As Blonde, Desiree Rancatore is agile too, but as recorded, there is a distracting flutter in the voice. The Osmin of Peter Rose is vocally impressive, but sadly undercharacterised. There may be a point in making Osmin more serious than usual, but with the voice sounding far too young there is little or no comedy, and no feeling of anger in his rages. Lynton Atkinson makes a sparky Pedrillo, even if the voice is distractingly similar to that of Groves as Belmonte. Excellent singing from the chorus and lively playing from the orchestra. Clear recording, rather drier than some from this source. This is acceptable enough but hardly a primary recommendation.

Complete Mozart Bargain Edition, Vol. 14: Middle period Italian Operas: *La finta giardiniera; Idomeneo; L'oca del Cairo; Il re pastore; Lo sposo deluso.*

(N) (B) * Ph. (ADD/DDD) 464 910-2 (9). Soloists; Salzburg

Mozart O, Hager; ASMF, Marriner; Bav. RSO or LSO, C. Davis.

Complete Mozart Edition, Vol. 33: *La finta giardiniera* (complete).

(M) *** Ph. (ADD) 422 533-2 (3). Conwell, Sukis, Di Cesare, Moser, Fassbaender, Ihloff, McDaniel, Salzburg Mozarteum O, Hager.

Leopold Hager has a strong vocal team, with three impressive newcomers taking the women's roles – Jutta-Renate Ihloff, Julia Conwell (in the central role of Sandrina, the marquise who disguises herself as a garden-girl) and Lilian Sukis (the arrogant niece). Brigitte Fassbaender sings the castrato role of Ramiro, and the others are comparably stylish. It is a charming – if lengthy – comedy, which here, with crisply performed recitatives, is presented with vigour, charm and persuasiveness. The recording, made with the help of Austrian Radio, is excellent.

Complete Mozart Edition, Vol. 28: *La finta semplice* (complete).

(M) *** Ph. 422 528-2 (2). Hendricks, Lorenz, Johnson, Murray, Lind, Blochwitz, Schmidt, C. P. E. Bach CO, Schreier.

Schreier's version replaces the earlier, Orfeo full-priced set from Leopold Hager, particularly when it comes at mid-price on two discs instead of three. The digital recording is wonderfully clear, with a fine sense of presence, capturing the fun of the comedy. Ann Murray has never sung more seductively in Mozart than here as Giacinta, and the characterful Barbara Hendricks is a delight in the central role of Rosina.

Idomeneo (complete).

⬗ *** DG 431 674-2 (3). Rolfe Johnson, Von Otter, McNair, Martinpelto, Robson, Hauptmann, Monteverdi Choir, E. Bar. Sol., Gardiner.

*** DG 447 737-2 (3). Bartoli, Domingo, Vaness, Grant-Murphy, Hampson, Lopardo, Terfel, Met. Op. Ch. & O, Levine.

(M) *** DG 429 864-2 (3). Ochman, Mathis, Schreier, Varady, Winkler, Leipzig R. Ch., Dresden State O, Boehm.

*** Decca (IMS) 411 805-2 (3). Pavarotti, Baltsa, Popp, Gruberová, Nucci, V. State Op. Ch., VPO, Pritchard.

(B) (***) EMI double fforte mono CZS5 73848-2 (2). Lewis, Simoneau, Jurinac, Udovick, Milligan, McAlpine, Alan, Glyndebourne Festival Ch. & O, Pritchard.

With its exhilarating vigour and fine singing, Gardiner's aim has been to include all the material Mozart wrote for the original 1781 production, and he recommends the use of the CD programming device for listeners to select the version they prefer. Gardiner's Mozartian style is well sprung and subtly moulded rather than severe. The principals sing beautifully, notably Anne Sofie von Otter as Idamante and Sylvia McNair as Ilia, while Anthony Rolfe Johnson as Idomeneo is well suited here, with words finely projected. The electrifying singing of the Monteverdi Choir adds to the dramatic bite.

From the very opening of the overture it is clear what tense dramatic control James Levine has over this masterpiece of an *opera seria*, reflecting in the recording his experience in the opera house. It stands as his finest Mozart opera performance on disc. The text is roughly that of the Munich first performance, with Elettra given her culminating aria and Arbace both of his, and with recitatives given nearly complete – as satisfying and practical a solution to the textual problem as could be devised. The cast is not just starry but stylish, with Plácido Domingo a commanding Idomeneo, giving a noble, finely controlled performance, which makes it a pity that the shorter version of his big aria, *Fuor del mar*, is preferred. Carol Vaness is a powerful, dramatic Elettra, well focused, and Cecilia Bartoli characterizes well as Idamante, wonderfully pure-toned in the Trio, while Heidi Grant-Murphy is a charmingly girlish Ilia with a light, bright soprano. Completing this unrivalled team, you have Thomas Hampson as a superb Arbace and Bryn Terfel commanding in the brief solo given to the Oracle. The Met. chorus, like the orchestra, is incisively dramatic. For those who prefer modern rather than period instruments this is a clear choice.

Boehm's conducting is a delight, often spacious but never heavy in the wrong way, with lightened textures and sprung rhythms which have one relishing Mozartian felicities as never before. As Idomeneo, Wieslaw Ochman, with tenor tone often too tight, is a comparatively dull dog, but the other principals are generally excellent. Peter Schreier as Idamante also might have sounded more consistently sweet, but the imagination is irresistible. Edith Mathis is at her most beguiling as Ilia, but it is Julia Varady as Elettra who gives the most compelling performance of all, sharply incisive in her dramatic outbursts, but at the same time precise and pure-toned, a Mozartian stylist through and through.

In the Decca version, spaciously conducted by Sir John Pritchard, Pavarotti is the only tenor among the principal soloists. Not only is the role of Idamante given to a mezzo instead of a tenor – preferable, with what was originally a castrato role – but that of the High Priest, Arbace, with his two arias is taken by a baritone, Leo Nucci. The wonder is that though Pavarotti reveals imagination in every phrase, using a wide range of tone colours, the result remains well within the parameters of Mozartian style. Casting Baltsa as Idamante makes for characterful results, tougher and less fruity than her direct rivals. Lucia Popp as Ilia tends to underline expression too much, but it is a charming, girlish portrait. Gruberová makes a thrilling Elettra, totally in command of the divisions, as few sopranos are; owing to bright Decca sound, the projection of her voice is a little edgy at times.

The very first 'complete' recording of *Idomeneo*, made in 1955 with Glyndebourne forces under John Pritchard, makes a timely reappearance on EMI's double fforte label. Though it uses a severely cut text and the orchestral sound is rather dry, it wears its years well. The voices still sound splendid, notably Sena Jurinac as a ravishing Ilia, Richard Lewis in the title-role, and Léopold Simoneau so delicate he almost reconciles one to the casting of Idamante as a tenor (from Mozart's compromised Vienna revision). The cuts mean that the whole opera is fitted on to two discs instead of the usual three. A cued synopsis is provided, but as usual in this double fforte series there is no aria or ensemble title with each cue.

Complete Mozart Edition, Vol. 32: *Lucio Silla* (complete).

(M) *** Ph. (ADD) 422 532-3 (3). Schreier, Augér, Varady, Mathis, Donath, Krenn, Salzburg R. Ch. & Mozarteum Ch. & O, Hager.

Lucio Silla (slightly abridged).

*** Teldec 2292 44928-2 (2). Schreier, Gruberová, Bartoli, Kenny, Upshaw, Schoenberg Ch., VCM, Harnoncourt.

The sixteen-year-old Mozart wrote his fifth opera, on the subject of the Roman dictator Sulla (Silla), in double-quick time. On Philips the castrato roles are splendidly taken by Julia Varady and Edith Mathis, and the whole team could hardly be bettered. The direction of Hager is fresh and lively, and the only snag is the length of the *secco* recitatives. However, with CD one can use these judiciously.

What Harnoncourt has done is to record a text which fits on to two generously filled CDs, not just trimming down the recitatives but omitting no fewer than four arias, all of them valuable. Yet his sparkling direction of an outstanding, characterful team of soloists brings an exhilarating demonstration of the boy Mozart's genius, with such marvels as the extended finale to Act I left intact. As in the earlier set, Schreier is masterly in the title-role, still fresh in tone, while Dawn Upshaw is warm and sweet as Celia, and Cecilia Bartoli is full and rich as Cecilio. The singing of Edita Gruberová as Giunia and Yvonne Kenny as Cinna is not quite so immaculate, but still confident and stylish. The Concentus Musicus of Vienna has rarely given so bright and lightly sprung a performance on record. Excellent digital sound.

Complete Mozart Edition, Vol. 29: *Mitridate, re di Ponto* (complete).

(M) **(*) Ph. (ADD) 422 529-2 (3). Augér, Hollweg, Gruberová, Baltsa, Cotrubas, Salzburg Mozarteum O, Hager.

Mitridate, re di Ponto (complete).

*** Decca 460 772-2 (3). Bartoli, Dessay, Sabbatini, Asawa, Les Talens Lyriques, Rousset.

This Decca set is only the second recording to be issued, but it completely outshines the first (part of the Philips Mozart Edition). One big advantage is that Christophe Rousset conducts his period forces with a panache that disguises the weaknesses, pointing rhythms infectiously. Though the cast in the earlier set is an excellent one, the new line-up is even more characterful, with Cecilia Bartoli outstanding as the hero, Sifare, in love with Aspasia. In that prima donna role, Natalie Dessay is both rich of tone and brilliantly agile in coloratura, a match even for Arleen Augér on the earlier set. The counter-tenor, Brian Asawa, is firm and characterful as the predatory Farnace, and though in the title-role Giuseppe Sabbatini is overstrenuous at times, his is a heroic performance, clean in attack. The softer-grained Sandrine Piau as Ismene is well contrasted with the others. Vivid, well-balanced sound. An excellent set, unlikely to be easily supplanted.

Hager's fresh and generally lively performance (the rather heavy recitatives excepted) brings splendid illumination to the long-hidden area of the boy Mozart's achievement. Two of the most striking arias (including an urgent G minor piece for the heroine, Aspasia, with Arleen Augér the ravishing soprano) exploit minor keys most effectively. Ileana Cotrubas is outstanding as Ismene, and the soloists of the Salzburg orchestra cope well with the often important obbligato parts. The CD transfer is vivid and forward and a little lacking in atmosphere.

Complete Mozart Edition, Vol. 40: *Le nozze di Figaro* (complete).

(M) *** Ph. (ADD) 422 540-2 (3). Freni, Norman, Minton, Ganzarolli, Wixell, Grant, Tear, BBC Ch. & SO, C. Davis.

Le nozze di Figaro (complete).

*** Decca 410 150-2 (3). Te Kanawa, Popp, Von Stade, Ramey, Allen, Moll, Tear LPO & Ch., Solti.

(M) *** EMI (ADD) CMS7 63266-2 (2). Schwarzkopf, Moffo, Cossotto, Taddei, Waechter, Vinco, Philh. Ch. & O, Giulini.

(B) *** EMI double fforte (ADD) CZS5 73845-2 (2). Sciutti, Jurinac, Stevens, Bruscantini, Calabrese, Cuénod, Wallace, Sinclair, Glyndebourne Ch. & Fest. O, Gui.

*** DG 439 871-2 (3). Terfel, Hagley, Martinpelto, Gilfry, Stephen, McCulloch, Feller, Egerton, Backes, Monteverdi Ch., E. Bar. Sol., Gardiner.

(M) **(*) Decca (ADD) 466 369-2 (3). Gueden, Danco, Della Casa, Dickie, Poell, Corena, Siepi, V. State Op. Ch., VPO, Kleiber.

*** Teldec 4509 90861-2 (3). Scharinger, Bonney, Margiono, Hampson, Lang, Moll, Langridge, Netherlands Op. Ch., Concg. O, Harnoncourt.

(M) *** DG (ADD) 449 728-2 (3). Janowitz, Mathis, Troyanos, Fischer-Dieskau, Prey, Lagger, German Op. Ch. & O, Boehm.

(M) **(*) EMI (ADD) CMS7 63849-2 (3). Grist, Söderström, Berganza, Evans, Bacquier, Hollweg, Alldis Ch., New Philh. O, Klemperer.

**(*) DG 445 903-2 (3). McNair, Gallo, Studer, Skovhus, Bartoli, V. State Op. Ch., VPO, Abbado.

**(*) Telarc CD-80388 (3). Miles, Focile, Vaness, Corbelli, Mentzer, Murphy, R. Davies, R. Evans, SCO and Ch., Mackerras.

(M) (**(*)) EMI mono CMS7 69639-2 (2) [CMS5 67142]. Schwarzkopf, Seefried, Jurinac, Kunz, Majkut, London, V. State Op. Ch., VPO, Karajan.

(M) (**(*)) EMI mono CHS5 66080-2 (3). Kunz, Seefried, Schwarzkopf, Schoeffler, Gueden, V. State Op. Ch., VPO, Furtwängler.

Solti opts for a fair proportion of extreme speeds, slow as well as fast, but they rarely if ever intrude on the quintessential happiness of the entertainment. Samuel Ramey, a firm-toned baritone, makes a virile Figaro, superbly matched to the most enchanting of Susannas on record, Lucia Popp, who gives a sparkling and radiant performance. Thomas Allen's Count is magnificent too, tough in tone and characterization but always beautiful on the ear. Kurt Moll as Dr Bartolo sings an unforgettable *La vendetta* with triplets very fast and agile 'on the breath', while Robert Tear far outshines his own achievement as the Basilio of Sir Colin Davis's amiable recording. Frederica von Stade is a most attractive Cherubino, even if *Voi che sapete* is too slow; but crowning all is the Countess of Kiri Te Kanawa, challenged by Solti's spacious tempi in the two big arias, but producing ravishing tone, flawless phrasing and elegant ornamentation throughout. With superb, vivid recording this now makes a clear first choice for a much-recorded opera. However, in view of the strong competition, Decca should find a way of reducing its price.

Like others in EMI's series of Mozart operas, Giulini's set has been pleasingly re-packaged and has a cleanly printed, easy-to-read libretto, giving an advantage over the competing double fforte set. It remains a classic, with a cast assembled by Walter Legge that has rarely been matched, let alone surpassed. Taddei with his dark bass-baritone makes a provocative Figaro; opposite him, Anna Moffo is at her freshest and sweetest as Susanna. Schwarzkopf as ever is the noblest of Countesses, and it is good to hear the young Fiorenza Cossotto as a full-toned Cherubino. Eberhard Waechter is a strong and stylish Count. On only two mid-priced discs it makes a superb bargain, though – as in the other EMI two-disc version, the Gui – Marcellina's and Basilio's arias are omitted from Act IV.

Gui's effervescent Glyndebourne set has been promoted from Classics for Pleasure to EMI's own bargain double fforte label. It costs a little more, but is worth every penny. It remains a classic set with a cast that has seldom been bettered, and the only regret is that there is a (very minor) cut to fit the recording on to two discs. There is no libretto, but the cued synopsis follows the narrative in detail, yet not giving the Italian titles of each item, only telling the listener what the character or characters are singing about. A pity, for this makes the set less easy to dip into.

Gardiner's version was recorded live, and this brings disadvantages in occasional intrusive stage noises, but it also offers a vividly dramatic and involving experience. In one instance the effect of the moment goes too far, when Cherubino (Pamela Helen Stephen) sings *Voi che sapete* for the Countess in a funny, nervous voice. That is very much the exception, for Gardiner's approach is lively and often brisk, with period manners made more genial and elegant. One of the most consistent and characterful of modern casts is led superbly by Bryn Terfel as Figaro, already a master in this role, with the enchanting, bright-eyed Alison Hagley as Susanna. Rodney Gilfry and Hillevi Martinpelto are fresh and firm as the Count and Countess, aptly younger sounding than usual. Carlos Feller is a characterful *buffo* Bartolo, and Francis Egerton a wickedly funny Basilio. In Act III Gardiner adopts the revised order, suggested by Robert Moberly and Christopher Raeburn, with the Countess's aria placed earlier. More controversially, in Act IV he divides the recitative for Figaro's aria so that part of it comes logically before Susanna's *Deh vieni*.

Kleiber's famous set was one of Decca's Mozart bicentenary recordings of the mid-1950s. It remains a memorably strong performance with much fine singing. Few sets since have matched its constant stylishness. Gueden's Susanna might be criticized but her golden tones are certainly characterful and her voice blends with Della Casa's enchantingly.

Danco and Della Casa are both at their finest. A dark-toned Figaro in Siepi brings added contrast and, if the pace of the recitatives is rather slow, this is not inconsistent within the context of Kleiber's overall approach. The closing scene of Act II is marvellously done.

The pacing of Sir Colin Davis has a sparkle in recitative that directly reflects experience in the opera house, and his tempi generally are beautifully chosen to make their dramatic points. Vocally the cast is exceptionally consistent. Mirella Freni (Susanna) is perhaps the least satisfying, yet there is no lack of character and charm. It is good to have so ravishingly beautiful a voice as Jessye Norman's for the Countess. The Figaro of Wladimiro Ganzarolli and the Count of Ingvar Wixell project with exceptional clarity and vigour, and there is fine singing too from Yvonne Minton as Cherubino, Clifford Grant as Bartolo and Robert Tear as Basilio. The 1971 recording has more reverberation than usual, but the effect is commendably atmospheric and on CD the voices have plenty of presence.

Harnoncourt on Teldec makes the Royal Concertgebouw Orchestra produce fresh, light and transparent sounds close to period style. The excellent cast has Thomas Hampson as a dominant Count, Charlotte Margiono as a tenderly sweet Countess, with Barbara Bonney a charmingly provocative Susanna and Anton Scharinger a winning Figaro, both tough and comic. Recitative at flexible speeds conveys the dramatic confrontations and complications vividly. A version that gets the best of both interpretative worlds, new and old.

Boehm's version of *Figaro* is also among the most consistently assured performances available. The women all sing most beautifully, with Janowitz's Countess, Mathis's Susanna and Troyanos's Cherubino all ravishing the ear in contrasted ways. Prey is an intelligent if not very jolly-sounding Figaro, and Fischer-Dieskau gives his dark, sharply defined reading of the Count's role. All told, a great success, with fine playing and recording, here impressively re-mastered.

A clue to the Klemperer approach comes near the beginning with Figaro's aria *Se vuol ballare*, which is not merely a servant's complaint about an individual master but a revolutionary call, with horns and pizzicato strings strongly defined, to apply to the whole world: 'I'll play the tune, sir!' Sir Geraint Evans is masterly in matching Klemperer; he is superb here, singing and acting with great power. Reri Grist makes a charming Susanna and Teresa Berganza is a rich-toned Cherubino. Gabriel Bacquier's Count is darker-toned and more formidable than usual, while Elisabeth Söderström's Countess, though it has its moments of strain, gives ample evidence of this artist's thoughtful intensity. However, this set has just been deleted as we go to press.

Claudio Abbado adopts a surprisingly metrical, unyielding approach, failing to bend rhythms and phrases to suit the needs of words or plot or the natural expressiveness of singers. Sylvia McNair as Susanna, Cheryl Studer as the Countess and Cecilia Bartoli as Cherubino are all characterful and musically imaginative enough to overcome much of the dulling effect of this, but the character-roles of Dr Bartolo, Marcellina and Basilio are all displayed colourlessly, with young voices unable to present the characters convincingly. Lucio Gallo is a dark-voiced Figaro who finds it hard to point comedy, similar in tone to the Count of Boje Skovhus, who however has a less pleasing, grittier voice. Most disappointing of all are the big ensembles, where with unexpectedly slow speeds and metrical rhythms the comedy evaporates. Happily, the final resolution on *Contessa perdono* is done ravishingly, with Cheryl Studer crowning a totally radiant performance. McNair also sings enchantingly and Bartoli is ideally cast. It is worth hearing the set for these three alone. The recording, faithful to voices, is slightly cavernous.

The big advantage of the Telarc version is that Sir Charles Mackerras with the Scottish Chamber Orchestra provides some 34 minutes of alternative items and variants. It is fascinating, for example, to have two alternative versions of the Count's Act III aria, with the difficult triplets largely removed, and there is also a heavily ornamented version of Cherubino's *Voi che sapete*. Mackerras also encourages his singers to provide ornamentation in their arias and, more than his rivals, he inserts appoggiature, avoiding 'blunt endings'. Orchestrally, this is an exceptionally characterful reading, more so than for the singing of the arias and ensembles. Alastair Miles as Figaro sings superbly with clean focus but, next to his main rivals, he is straight-faced, and similarly the Susanna of Nuccia Focile is a little lacking in charm and humour, while Carol Vaness as the Countess is perhaps stressed by Mackerras's slow speeds (an exception) for her two big arias. The Count of Alessandro Corbelli is rather rough in tone, and Alfonso Antoniozzi is too light and unsteady as Bartolo, but Ryland Davies is a superb Basilio and Susanne Mentzer a strong Marcellina, both given their arias in Act IV, which comes complete on disc 3, along with the appendices.

Recorded in 1950, Karajan's first recording of *Figaro* offers one of the most distinguished casts ever assembled; but, curiously at that period, they decided to record the opera without the secco recitatives. That is a most regrettable omission when all these singers are not just vocally immaculate but vividly characterful – as for example Sena Jurinac, a vivacious Cherubino. The firmness of focus in Erich Kunz's singing of Figaro goes with a delightful twinkle in the word-pointing, and Irmgard Seefried makes a bewitching Susanna. Schwarzkopf's noble portrait of the Countess – not always helped by a slight backward balance in the placing of the microphone for her – culminates in the most poignant account of her second aria, *Dove sono*. The sound, though obviously limited, presents the voices very vividly.

Furtwängler's vintage recording of *Figaro* from the Salzburg Festival was made by Austrian Radio in 1953, and at the conductor's insistence the performance is in German, reverting to the pre-war custom in Salzburg. It is a revelation to compare his reading of *Figaro* with Karajan's in the EMI studio recording made only a year earlier with the same orchestra, the Vienna Philharmonic, and with three of the same principals: Elisabeth Schwarzkopf as the Countess, Irmgard Seefried as Susanna and Erich Kunz as Figaro. Next to Furtwängler, Karajan sounds stiff and plain, surprisingly lacking in humour. By contrast, many of Furtwängler's speeds are very broad, though, even at their most extreme, there is always a lift to the rhythm to give Mozartian sparkle.

The result is an exceptionally warm and relaxed reading, in which all the principals joyfully bring out the comedy, Kunz and Seefried above all. Schwarzkopf is in superb voice, rich and full, more creamy-toned than with Karajan, though her later performance on Giulini's 1959 recording is finest of all. Hilde Gueden as Cherubino and Paul Schoeffler as the Count are also most characterful, even if Schoeffler no longer sounds young. The snag is that, even with Basilio's and Marcellina's arias cut in the last act – as habitually they were in those days – the performance stretches to three CDs. Also, as with other EMI historic issues, no libretto is provided, just a detailed synopsis.

Le nozze di Figaro: highlights.

(M) *** EMI (ADD) CDM5 66049-2 (from above complete recording, with Schwarzkopf, Moffo, Cossotto; cond. Giulini).

(M) **(*) Decca (ADD) 458 225-2. (from complete recording with Tomowa-Sintow, Cotrubas, Von Stade, Van Dam, Krause; cond. Karajan).

(B) *** DG (ADD) 439 449-2 (from above complete recording, with Janowitz, Mathis, Prey, Fischer-Dieskau; cond. Boehm).

**(*) Telarc CD 80449 (from above set with Miles, Focile, Vaness; cond. Mackerras).

The Giulini CD makes a clear first choice for a highlights CD from *Nozze di Figaro*. The selection may play for only 62 minutes but every item is treasurable, not least *Non più andrai*, the Countess's two arias, and the long excerpt from the Act II finale. The new transfer is extremely vivid, and the synopsis relates the excerpts to the narrative.

The Karajan set of highlights is exceptionally generous (73 minutes), and very well documented, with full translation. The complete set would not be a first choice – Karajan's approach is rather too smooth and polished – but the singing, especially from the ladies, is often very fine and this gives an impressive overall survey of Mozart's inspired score, and is very well recorded.

Boehm's selection includes many of the key numbers, but with a little over an hour of music it is less than generous and inadequately documented; but the singing is first class and the sound vivid.

A well-selected 77 minutes from the Mackerras Scottish set, with most of the key items, will be useful as this is not likely to be a first choice for the complete opera, except for those with a special interest in the singers or the additional items which Mackerras includes (but which are not offered here). There is a good synopsis, but it is not cued.

Complete Mozart Edition, Vol. 39: *L'oca del Cairo* (complete).

(M) *** Ph. 422 539-2. Nielsen, Wiens, Coburn, Schreier, Johnson, Fischer-Dieskau, Scharinger, Berlin R. Ch. (members), C. P. E. Bach CO, Schreier – *Lo sposo deluso*. ***

We owe it to the Mozart scholar and Philips recording producer, Erik Smith, that these two sets of Mozartian fragments, *L'oca del Cairo* and *Lo sposo deluso*, have been prepared for performance and recorded. *L'oca del Cairo*

('The Cairo goose'), containing roughly twice as much music as *Lo sposo deluso*, involves six substantial numbers, most of them ensembles, including an amazing finale to the projected Act I, with contrasted sections following briskly one after the other. It is very well conducted by Peter Schreier, who also takes part as one of the soloists. Dietrich Fischer-Dieskau takes the *buffo* old-man role of Don Pippo, and Anton Scharinger is brilliant in the patter aria in tarantella rhythm for the major-domo, Chichibio, bringing a foretaste of Donizetti. Fresh, bright digital recording.

Complete Mozart Edition, Vol. 35: *Il re pastore* (complete).

(M) **(*) Ph. 422 535-2 (2). Blasi, McNair, Vermillion, Hadley, Ahnsjö, ASMF, Marriner.

Il re pastore (complete).

(M) **(*) RCA (ADD) 74321 50165-2 (2). Grist, Popp, Saunders, Alva, Monti, O of Naples, Vaughan.

Il re pastore is not exactly a music drama but it is still a splendid example of Mozart's youthful genius at work, the more enchanting for being performed here with real style and verve. Denis Vaughan – once a Beecham protégé – is a lively advocate. Among the singers, Lucia Popp is wonderfully sweet-toned, and her high legato phrases never concede even a momentary blemish. Reri Grist's voice is harder, less smooth, but in a way that is fitting enough in the castrato role of Aminta, and her singing of the most famous number, *L'améro*, is expressively beautiful. Arlene Saunders is a graceful Tamiri, and Nicola Monti and Luiga Alva make a quite stylish pair of tenors, even if their florid singing is not always quite immaculate. Not the least important quality of Vaughan's direction is his editing, with a plentiful sprinkling of appoggiature smoothing the blunt phrase-endings. He also plays the continuo in the recitatives most effectively. The one slight snag is the CD transfer, which has brightened what was a pleasingly full and lively analogue sound: the voices now have a degree of added edge and the orchestral tuttis bring some rough moments. However, this remains a vivid musical experience, and a full libretto is provided.

The alternative version by Marriner and the Academy, with a first-rate cast and with plenty of light and shade, and superbly played, does not efface memories of the 1979 DG version conducted by Leopold Hager, which offered even purer singing. Here Angela Maria Blasi, despite a beautiful voice, attacks notes from below, even in *L'améro*. Excellent sound.

Complete Mozart Edition, Vol. 36: *Der Schauspieldirektor* (complete).

(M) **(*) Ph. (ADD) 422 536-2 (2). Welting, Cotrubas, Grant, Rolfe-Johnson, LSO, C. Davis – *Zaïde*. ***

There is no contest whatsoever between the two rival prima donnas presented in the Philips recording. *Ich bin die erste Sängerin* ('I am the leading prima donna'), they yell at each other; but here Ileana Cotrubas is in a world apart from the thin-sounding and shallow Ruth Welting. Colin Davis directs with fire and electricity a performance which is otherwise (despite the lack of spoken dialogue) most re-freshing and beautifully recorded (in 1975) in a sympathetic acoustic.

Complete Mozart Edition, Vol. 31: *Il sogno di Scipione* (complete).

(M) *** Ph. (ADD) 422 531-2 (2). Popp, Gruberová, Mathis, Schreier, Ahnsjö, Moser, Salzburg Chamber Ch. & Mozarteum O, Hager.

Il sogno di Scipione.

(N) (*) Astreé E 8813 (2). Hartelius, Larsson, Brandes, Ford, Workman, Ovenden, Cremonesi, Louvre Ch. & O, Freiburger Bar. O, Goltz.

Il sogno di Scipione presents an allegorical plot with Scipio set to choose between Fortune and Constancy. Given the choice of present-day singers, this cast could hardly be finer, with Edita Gruberová, Lucia Popp and Edith Mathis superbly contrasted in the women's roles (the last taking part in the epilogue merely), and Peter Schreier is joined by two of his most accomplished younger colleagues. Hager sometimes does not press the music on as he might, but his direction is always alive. With fine recording, vividly and atmospherically transferred to CD, the set is not likely to be surpassed in the immediate future.

Described as an 'azione teatrale', *Il sogno di Scipione* was first performed at the installation of Hieronimus Colloredo as Prince-Archbishop of Salzburg in 1772, having first been conceived as a celebratory piece for his predecessor, who promptly died. Like most early Mozart operas, it is an attractive trifle, that only occasionally reveals the full individuality of the genius who was emerging. Sadly, this live recording made in the Stravinsky Auditorium in Montreux in September 2000, is far too flawed to recommend beside the existing set in the Philips Mozart Edition. This new one uses period instead of modern instruments, but the style is rough and abrasive, and made worse by the unpleasantly dry acoustic. That also affects the voices, with only two of the soloists rising above the elimination of bloom, the radiant Malin Hartelius as Costanza and Christine Brandes as Licenza. All the others, including the distinguished tenor Bruce Ford, sound gritty or unsteady. The lumpish conducting of Gottfried von der Goltz does not help.

Complete Mozart Edition, Vol. 39: *Lo sposo deluso*.

(M) *** Ph. (ADD) 422 539-2. Palmer, Cotrubas, Rolfe Johnson, Tear, Grant, LSO, C. Davis – *L'oca del Cairo*. ***

The music presented here from *Lo sposo deluso* is the surviving music from an unfinished opera written in the years before *Figaro*, and it contains much that is memorable. The *Overture*, with its trumpet calls, its lovely slow middle section and recapitulation with voices, is a charmer, while the two arias, reconstructed by the recording producer and scholar, Erik Smith, are also delightful: the one a trial run for Fiordiligi's *Come scoglio* in *Così*, the other (sung by Robert Tear) giving a foretaste of Papageno's music in *The Magic Flute*.

Complete Mozart Edition, Vol. 36: *Zaïde*.

(M) *** Ph. (ADD) 422 536-2 (2). Mathis, Schreier, Wixell, Hollweg, Süss, Berlin State O, Klee – *Der Schauspieldirektor*. **(*)

Zaïde, written between 1779 and 1780 and never quite completed, was a trial run for *Entführung*. Much of the music is superb, and melodramas at the beginning of each Act are strikingly effective and original, with the speaking voice of the tenor in the first heard over darkly dramatic writing in D minor. Zaïde's arias in both Acts are magnificent: the radiantly lyrical *Ruhe sanft* is hauntingly memorable, and the dramatic *Tiger aria* is like Konstanze's *Martern aller Arten* but briefer and more passionate. Bernhard Klee directs a crisp and lively performance, with excellent contributions from singers and orchestra alike – a first-rate team, as consistently stylish as one could want.

Die Zauberflöte (complete).

*** Ph. 426 276-2 (2). Te Kanawa, Studer, Lind, Araiza, Bär, Ramey, Van Dam, Amb. Op. Ch., ASMF, Marriner.

*** DG 449 166-2 (2); Video VHS 072 447-3. Oelze, Schade, Sieden, Peeters, Finley, Backes, Monteverdi Ch., E. Bar. Sol., Gardiner.

*** Erato 0630 12705-2 (2). Mannion, Blochwitz, Dessay, Hagen, Scharinger, Les Arts Florissants, Christie.

⊛ (M) (***) DG mono 459 497-2 (2). Stader, Streich, Fischer-Dieskau, Greindl, Haefliger, Berlin RIAS Ch. & SO, Fricsay.

(N) (M)*** EMI (ADD) CMS5 67388-2 (2) [567385]. Janowitz, Putz, Popp, Gedda, Berry, Frick, Schwarzkopf, Ludwig, Hoffgen (3 Ladies), Philh. Ch. & O, Klemperer.

(M) *** EMI mono CMS5 67071-2 [567165] (2). Seefried, Lipp, Loose, Dermota, Kunz, Weber, V. State Op. Ch., VPO, Karajan.

*** EMI CDS7 47951-8 (3). Popp, Gruberová, Lindner, Jerusalem, Brendel, Bracht, Zednik, Bav. R. Ch. & SO, Haitink.

*** Telarc CD-80302 (2). Hadley, Hendricks, Allen, Anderson, Lloyd, SCO & Ch., Mackerras.

(B) *** Naxos 8. 660030/31 (2). Norberg-Schulz, Kwon, Lippert, Leitner, Tichy, Rydl, Hungarian Festival Ch., Failoni O, Budapest, Halász.

(M) **(*) DG (ADD) 449 749-2 (2). Lear, Peters, Wunderlich, Fischer-Dieskau, Crass, Hotter, BPO, Boehm.

(B) (***) Dutton mono 2CDEA 5011 (2). Lemnitz, Roswaenge, Hüsch, Berger, Strienz, BPO, Beecham.

**(*) O-L 440 085-2 (2). Bonney, Jo, Streit, Cachemaille, Sigmundsson, Drottningholm Court Theatre Ch. & O, Ostman.

(M) **(*) RCA (ADD) 74321 32240-2 (2). Donath, Geszty, Schreier, Adam, Hoff, Leib, Vogel, Leipzig R. Ch., Dresden State O, Suitner.

(B) ** Double Decca 448 734-2 (2). Gueden, Lipp, Simoneau, Berry, Böhme, Schoeffler, V. St. Op. Ch., VPO, Boehm.

Marriner directs a pointed and elegant reading of *Zauberflöte*, bringing out the fun of the piece. It lacks weight only in the overture and finale, and the cast is the finest in any modern recording. Dame Kiri lightens her voice delightfully, while Olaf Bär, vividly characterful, brings the Liedersinger's art to the role of Papageno. Araiza's voice has coarsened since he recorded the role of Tamino for Karajan, but this performance is subtler and conveys more feeling. Cheryl Studer's performance as Queen of the Night is easily

the finest among modern recordings; and Samuel Ramey gives a generous and wise portrait of Sarastro.

John Eliot Gardiner rounds off his outstanding series for DG Archiv of Mozart's seven great mature operas with an electrifying account of *Zauberflöte*, even though the generally inspired casting is marred by the underpowered and uneven Sarastro of Harry Peeters. The recording was made in studio conditions over the same period as staged performances at the Ludwigsburg Festival, getting the best of both worlds. Gardiner is helped enormously by his choice of singer as Pamina, a young German soprano with a ravishingly pure and sweet voice, flawlessly controlled, Christiane Oelze. In the agonized Act II aria, *Ach, ich fühl's*, she conveys a depth of emotion rarely matched. Also superb is the American soprano who takes the role of Queen of the Night, with a voice as full and silvery as it is flexible, Cyndia Sieden. The Tamino of Michael Schade has youthful freshness combined with keen imagination; though there are more characterful Papagenos than Gerald Finley, few sing as freshly and cleanly as he. With recording clear and well balanced, the set offers an incidental practical advantage in putting the spoken dialogue on separate tracks.

Based on a production at the Aix-en-Provence Festival, and recorded in 1995 in collaboration with Radio France, William Christie's Erato set otherwise sweeps the board for recordings using period instruments, with Les Arts Florissants firm and full. More than his rivals, Christie wears his period manners easily and amiably, with fast speeds crisp and light, and with some numbers – such as Papageno's first aria – relaxedly expansive. There is no weak link in the cast, with Rosa Mannion a warm, touching Pamina, able to bring out deeper feelings as in *Ach, ich fühl's*, and Blochwitz is an imaginative, sweetly expressive Tamino, while Natalie Dessay as Queen of the Night is unusually warm-toned for the role, not so much a frigid figure as a fully rounded character, with the coloratura display dazzlingly clear. Scharinger is a genial, rich-toned Papageno, and Hagen a Sarastro satisfyingly clean of focus. Above all, the joyful vigour of Mozart's inspiration captures one from first to last.

From the early LP era Fricsay's is an outstandingly fresh and alert *Die Zauberflöte*, marked by generally clear, pure singing and well-sprung orchestral playing at generally rather fast speeds. Maria Stader and Dietrich Fischer-Dieskau phrase most beautifully, but the most spectacular singing comes from Rita Streich as a dazzling Queen of the Night, and the relatively close balance of the voice gives it the necessary power such as Streich generally failed to convey in the opera house. Ernst Haefliger, too, is at his most honeyed in tone as Tamino, and the excellent, strongly characterised Sarastro of Josef Greindl sings with a satisfyingly dark resonance. This was the first version to spice the musical numbers with brief sprinklings of dialogue, just enough to prevent the work from sounding like an oratorio. Even including that, DG has managed to put each of the Acts complete on a single disc.

Klemperer's conducting of *The Magic Flute* is one of his finest achievements on record; indeed, he is inspired, making the dramatic music sound more like Beethoven in its breadth and strength. The dialogue is omitted, but he does not miss the humour and point of the Papageno passages, and he gets the best of both worlds to a surprising degree. The cast is outstanding – look at the distinction of the Three Ladies alone – but curiously it is that generally most reliable of all the singers, Gottlob Frick as Sarastro, who comes nearest to letting the side down. Lucia Popp is in excellent form, and Gundula Janowitz sings Pamina's part with a creamy beauty that is just breathtaking. Nicolai Gedda too is a firm-voiced Tamino. The new transfer is managed expertly, and like Klemperer's set of Beethoven's *Fidelio*, this recording has reverted to mid-price and has been repackaged for its reissue as one of EMI's 'Great Recordings of the Century'. The documentation is first class, with a full libretto and plenty of sessions photographs included.

The Vienna State Opera cast of Karajan's mono version of 1950 has not since been matched on record: Irmgard Seefried and Anton Dermota both sing with radiant beauty and great character, Wilma Lipp is a dazzling Queen of the Night, Erich Kunz as Papageno sings with an infectious smile in the voice, and Ludwig Weber is a commanding Sarastro. There is no spoken dialogue; but on two mid-priced CDs instead of three LPs, it is a Mozart treat not to be missed, with mono sound still amazingly vivid and full of presence.

Haitink directs a rich and spacious account of *Zauberflöte*, superbly recorded in spectacularly wide-ranging digital sound. The dialogue – not too much of it, nicely produced and with sound effects adding to the vividness – frames a presentation that has been carefully thought through. Popp makes the most tenderly affecting of Paminas and Gruberová has never sounded more spontaneous in her brilliance than here as Queen of the Night: she is both agile and powerful. Jerusalem makes an outstanding Tamino, both heroic and sweetly Mozartian; and though neither Wolfgang Brendel as Papageno nor Bracht as Sarastro is as characterful as their finest rivals, their personalities project strongly and the youthful freshness of their singing is most attractive. The Bavarian chorus too is splendid.

Though the recording puts a halo of reverberation round the sound, Mackerras and the Scottish Chamber Orchestra find an ideal scale for the work. His speeds are often faster than usual, not least in Pamina's great aria of lament, *Ach, ich fühl's*, but they always flow persuasively. Jerry Hadley makes a delightfully boyish Tamino, with Thomas Allen the most characterful Papageno, singing beautifully. Robert Lloyd is a noble Sarastro, and though June Anderson is a rather strenuous Queen of the Night, it is thrilling to have a big, dramatic voice so dazzlingly agile. Barbara Hendricks is a questionable choice as Pamina, not clean enough of attack, but the tonal quality is golden.

The Naxos set offers a very satisfying performance, well conducted and well recorded, with some very stylish solo singing and with a fair measure of German dialogue included (but on separate tracks to allow it to be programmed out if preferred). As Tamino, Herbert Lippert is a good, clean-cut Germanic tenor, hardly ever strained, with fine legato in *Dies Bildnis*. The young Norwegian, Elisabeth Norberg-Schulz, is a bright, girlish Pamina, who sustains a slow speed for *Ach, ich fühl's* very effectively, tenderly making it an emotional high point. Rydl is a powerful Sarastro, if not always perfectly steady, and Tichy is a delightful Papageno, defying Halász's

uncharacteristically stodgy tempo for his first aria, and from there consistently conveying characterful humour without vocal exaggeration. Hellen Kwon is an outstanding Queen of the Night, using full, firm tone with bright attack in her two big arias. The recording is clear and well balanced, with the Queen's thunder vividly caught.

One of the glories of Boehm's DG set is the singing of Fritz Wunderlich as Tamino, a wonderful memorial to a singer much missed. Fischer-Dieskau, with characteristic word-pointing, makes a sparkling Papageno on record and Franz Crass is a satisfyingly straightforward Sarastro. The team of women is well below this standard – Lear taxed cruelly in *Ach, ich fühl's*, Peters shrill in the upper register (although the effect is exciting), and the Three Ladies do not blend well – but Boehm's direction is superb, light and lyrical, but weighty where necessary to make a glowing, compelling experience. Fine recording, enhanced in this new transfer.

Beecham's magical pre-war set of *Zauberflöte* has had three earlier CD transfers, all of them seriously flawed, which makes it especially welcome that Mike Dutton comes up with a transfer which at last does justice to the original sound, full and vivid; and the two discs are offered at bargain price. There is glorious singing from Tiana Lemnitz as Pamina, brilliant coloratura from Erna Berger as Queen of the Night, and sharp characterization from Gerhard Hüsch as Papageno. Helge Roswaenge is a Germanic Tamino and Wilhelm Strienz a firm but lugubrious Sarastro. No spoken dialogue, but much warmth and sparkle.

In contrast with his earlier Drottningholm recordings of Mozart operas, often rushed and brittle, Ostman in his Oiseau-Lyre series offers a far more sympathetic set of *Zauberflöte*. It may lack weight but it rarely sounds rushed, for consistently Ostman gives a spring to the rhythms and his cast has no weak link. Barbara Bonney is a charming Pamina, with Kurt Streit a free-toned Tamino and with Gilles Cachemaille as Papageno both finely focused and full of fun. Sumi Jo is a bright, clear Queen of the Night and, though the Sarastro of Kristian Sigmundsson is lightweight, that matches the overall approach.

The RCA (originally Eurodisc) set is well cast, directed with breadth and spirit, and vividly recorded. There are no real flaws here. The finest performances come from Peter Schreier, an outstanding Tamino, ardent and stylish; Sylvia Geszty's Queen of the Night is fierce to the point of shrillness, but it is a forceful projection and balances with Donath's somewhat ingenuous portrayal of Pamina, prettily sung. Theo Adam is a commanding Sarastro and Renata Hoff and Günther Leib make an attractive team as Papagena and Papageno; while the orchestral playing is first rate, the contribution of the Leipzig Radio Choir is less impressive. There is a minimum of dialogue and it is separately cued. Not a top choice, but enjoyable just the same. The accompanying libretto is in German with no translation.

The principal attraction of this Double Decca reissue from the earliest days of stereo, apart from its modest cost, is the conducting of Karl Boehm. That might well be counted recommendation enough, in spite of the absence of dialogue, particularly when the Tamino of Léopold Simoneau and the Papageno of Walter Berry are strongly and sensitively sung and Wilma Lipp proves an impressive Queen of the Night. But the rest of the singing is variable, with Hilde Gueden a pert, characterful Pamina, unhappy in the florid divisions, and Kurt Böhme a gritty and ungracious Sarastro. The new cued synopsis is a great improvement on the previous reissue and includes new documentation intended to offer a helpful guide for the newcomer to the opera.

Die Zauberflöte: highlights.

*** Ph. 438 495-2 (from above complete recording, with Te Kanawa, Studer, Araiza, Bär, Ramey; cond. Marriner).

(M) *** EMI (ADD) CDM5 65568-2 (from above complete recording, with Janowitz; Putz, Popp, Gedda cond., Klemperer).

(B) *** [EMI Red Line CDR5 72098] (from above complete recording, with Popp, Gruberová, Lindner; cond. Haitink).

(M) (***) EMI mono CD-EMX 2220 (from above complete recording with Seefried, Lipp; cond. Karajan).

(B) **(*) DG (ADD) 449 845-2 (from above complete recording, with Lear, Peters, Wunderlich, Fischer-Dieskau, Crass; cond. Boehm).

(M) **(*) Decca (ADD) 458 213-2 (from complete recording, with Lorengar, Deutekom, Burrows, Talvela, Prey, Stoltze, V. State Op. Ch., VPO, Solti).

First choice goes to Marriner with his outstanding cast and first-class, modern, digital recording. The selection includes the *Overture* and plays for 69 minutes. Otherwise, those looking for a first-rate set of highlights from *Die Zauberflöte* will find the mid-priced Klemperer disc hard to beat. It makes a good sampler of a performance which, while ambitious in scale, manages to find sparkle and humour too. A synopsis details each individual excerpt, and in this case the inclusion of the *Overture* is especially welcome. The remastered sound has plenty of presence, but atmosphere and warmth too.

This selection from the full-priced Haitink set is well made to include many favourites, with the Papageno/Papagena music well represented to make a contrast with the lyrical arias and the drama of the Queen of the Night. The gravitas of Haitink's approach does not miss the work's elements of drama and charm, though nothing is trivialized. Superb recording in spectacularly wide-ranging, digital sound.

The Karajan Vienna State Opera selection on Eminence will be a good way for many to sample a highly enticing mono set with a superb cast, all on the top of their form. The selection lasts 68 minutes, but seven of these are taken up by the Overture, a less than sensible idea, even if it is superbly played. It is disgraceful, though, that the front of this CD – aimed at a popular market – does not make it absolutely clear that the sound is mono.

The hour of excerpts from Boehm's recording is not obviously directed towards bringing out its special qualities, although there would have been room on the CD (which includes the *Overture*) for at least another quarter of an hour of music. One would have liked more of Wunderlich's Tamino, one of the great glories of the set. This is now on DG's bargain Classikon label, which means that the synopsis is not cued.

Solti's highlights, which come from his earlier (1970) analogue set, are certainly worth sampling. On the male side the cast is very strong indeed, with Stuart Burrows a stylish, rich-toned Tamino. Martti Talvela is a bold Sarastro and Hermann Prey rounds out the character of Papageno with intelligent pointing of words. Pilar Lorengar's Pamina is sweetly attractive as long as your ear is not worried by her intrusive vibrato, while Cristina Deutekom's Queen of the Night is technically impressive, though the coloratura has a curious colouristic flaw. Solti's reading is tough and brilliant, but it is arguable that in highlights this is less worrying than in a complete set, even if the almost total absence of charm is disconcerting. The selection is generous (73 minutes) and the disc is handsomely packaged in Decca's Opera Gala series, with a full translation included.

Recitals

'The Mozart Experience': Arias from *Ascanio in Alba; Così fan tutte; Die Entführung aus dem Serail; Le nozze di Figaro; Die Zauberflöte; Zaïde.*

**(*) Conifer 75605 55031-2. Dawson; Dam-Jensen; D. Jones; Rolfe Johnson; Le Roux; ROHCG O, McGegan.

This is a mixed bag of a Mozart compilation, starting with the Overture to *La clemenza di Tito*, and then presenting a variable collection of arias early and late. Inger Dam-Jensen is disappointingly edgy in her two items from *Zaïde*, but the other soprano, Lynne Dawson, sings ravishingly both in *Ascanio in Alba* and as the Countess in *Figaro*. Della Jones is strong and characterful in a range of items, and Anthony Rolfe Johnson too sings with immaculate point and style in the great tenor arias from *Entführung, Così* and *Zauberflöte*. François Le Roux is disappointingly variable, until the Papageno items at the end find him at his most winningly characterful. Clear, well-balanced sound.

Arias from: *La clemenza di Tito; Così fan tutte; Don Giovanni; Die Entfürung aus dem Serail; Le nozze di Figaro; Il re pastore; Zaïde; Die Zauberflöte.*

(M) *** Decca ADD/Dig. 458 233-2. with Burrows, Evans, Horne, Te Kanawa, Ramey, Popp, Prey, Siepi, Von Stade, Sutherland.

A typically expert collection of Mozart arias on Decca's well-planned Opera Gala series. Many obvious items are here, some taken from complete sets: Solti's *Magic Flute* and *Marriage of Figaro*, Krips's *Don Giovanni*, etc., while others are from recital discs, including Sutherland's splendid *Marten aller Arten* from *Die Entführung*. What makes this particularly worthwhile is the inclusion of lesser-known arias from *La clemenza di Tito, Il re pastore* and *Zaïde*, and they have been arranged most judiciously. The recordings all are excellent and, with full texts and translations, this is as good a Mozart aria compilation as any available. It is far preferable to the Penguin Classics disc below, which costs only a little less.

Arias from: *La clemenza di Tito; Così fan tutte; Don Giovanni; Le nozze di Figaro; Il re pastore; Zaïde; Die Zauberflöte.*

(B) ** Decca Penguin Classics 460 651-2. Bacquier, Berganza, Burrows, Deutekom, Ghiaurov, Krause, Lorengar, Krenn, Popp, Tomowa-Sintow (with various orchestras and conductors).

With the star-studded collection of singers contributing to this collection, there is little here really to disappoint. The performances range from good to excellent, and there are a couple of rarities thrown in as well. Some may find the collection a bit piecemeal, but for anyone wanting just over an hour of Mozart arias, this CD fits the bill. The personal note is by Antonia Fraser, but there are no texts or translations.

Arias: *La clemenza di Tito: S'altro che lagrime. Così fan tutte: Ei parte . . . Sen . . . Per pietà. La finta giardiniera: Crudeli fermate . . . Ah dal pianto. Idomeneo: Se il padre perdei. Lucio Silla: Pupille amate. Il re pastore: L'amerò, sarò costante. Zaïde: Ruhe sanft, mein holdes Leben. Die Zauberflöte: Ach ich fühl's es ist verschwunden.*

*** Ph. (IMS) 411 148-2. Te Kanawa, LSO, C. Davis.

Kiri Te Kanawa's is one of the loveliest collections of Mozart arias on record, with the voice at its most ravishing and pure. One might object that Dame Kiri concentrates on soulful arias, ignoring more vigorous ones; but with stylish accompaniment and clear, atmospheric recording, beauty dominates all.

Arias from: *La clemenza di Tito; Idomeneo; Lucio Silla; Le nozze di Figaro.*

(N) *** Erato 8573 85768-2. Graham, OAE, Bickett – GLUCK: Arias from *Iphigénie en Tauride; Orphée et Eurydice; Paride e Elena.* ***

This is a glorious recital of Mozart and Gluck, with Susan Graham radiant and characterful in arias she has sung on stage, highlighting the distinctive points of each character. So from *La clemenza di Tito* she contrasts Sesto's purposeful first aria with the far gentler second, producing a breathtaking pianissimo on the reprise. Cherubino's two arias from *Figaro* are made to sound new and intense, with the last and longest item, Cecilio's big, taxing number from *Lucio Silla*, *Il tenero momento*, providing the title of the whole recital, making a superb climax. Fine, sympathetic accompaniment and perfect sound.

Arias from: *Così fan tutte; Don Giovanni; La clemenza di Tito; Idomeneo; Lucio Silla; Mitridate; Le nozze di Figaro.*

*** RCA 09026 68661-2. Kasarova, Dresden State O, C. Davis.

The young Bulgarian, Vesselina Kasarova, with her tangy, sharply projected mezzo, is both characterful and magnetic. Here in a formidable collection of Mozart arias, much enhanced by Colin Davis's accompaniment, she demonstrates not only her stylishness and technical prowess – with not a single intrusive aitch allowed – but her musical flair. At the very start, she launches into the recitative before Dorabella's aria in *Così fan tutte* with a vehemence that takes the breath away, and vehemence is a quality that draws many of these portrayals together, whether as Donna Elvira in *Don Giovanni* (giving way to tenderness when required), Vitellia in

Clemenza or a whole range of trouser roles, including those in the early *Mitridate* and *Lucio Silla.*

Arias from: *Don Giovanni; Die Entführung aus dem Serail; La finta giardiniera; Il re pastore; Le nozze di Figaro; Il sogno di Scipione; Zaïde; Die Zauberflöte. Concert aria: Nehmt meinen Dank.*

*** Decca 452 602-2. Fleming, O of St Luke's, Mackerras.

Renée Fleming has rarely sounded quite so beautiful on disc as in this wide-ranging collection of Mozart arias, one of the finest available. If it is disappointing not to have her singing the role of the Countess in *Figaro*, the two Susanna items are both welcome – *Deh vieni* bringing out her most golden tone and the big alternative aria, *Al desio*, challenging her to her most brilliant singing. Her account of La Fortuna's aria from *Il sogno di Scipione* is commanding too, and her ornamentation is phenomenally crisp and brilliant throughout, not least in *Ach ich liebte* from *Entführung*. The only reservations come with the brisk treatment, period-style, of Pamina's *Ach, ich fühl's* and the lovely aria from *Zaïde*, both of which could be much more tenderly expressive. Excellent, stylish accompaniment and first-rate recording.

Arias: *Don Giovanni; Die Entführung aus dem Serail; Idomeneo; Le nozze di Figaro; Die Zauberflöte.*

(M) (***) EMI mono CDH7 63708-2. Schwarzkopf (with various orchestras & conductors, including John Pritchard).

Just how fine a Mozartian Schwarzkopf already was early in her career comes out in these 12 items, recorded between 1946 and 1952. The earliest are Konstanze's two arias from *Entführung*, and one of the curiosities is a lovely account of Pamina's *Ach ich fühl's*, recorded in English in 1948. The majority, including those from *Figaro* – Susanna's and Cherubino's arias as well as the Countess's – are taken from a long-unavailable recital disc conducted by John Pritchard. Excellent transfers.

ANTHOLOGIES

'*Fifty Years of Mozart Singing on Record*': (i) *Concert Arias;* Excerpts from: (ii) *Mass in C min., K.427;* (iii) *La clemenza di Tito;* (iv) *Così fan tutte;* (v) *Don Giovanni;* (vi) *Die Entführung aus dem Serail;* (vii) *La finta giardiniera;* (viii) *Idomeneo;* (ix) *Le nozze di Figaro;* (x) *Il re pastore;* (xi) *Zaïde;* (xii) *Die Zauberflöte.*

(M) (***) EMI mono CMS7 63750-2 (4). (i) Rethberg, Ginster, Francillo-Kaufmann; (ii) Berger; (iii) Kirkby-Lunn; (iv) V. Schwarz, Noni, Grümmer, Hahn, Kiurina, Hüsch, Souez, H. Nash; (v) Vanni-Marcoux, Scotti, Farrar, Battistini, Corsi, Leider, Roswaenge, D'Andrade, Pinza, Patti, Maurel, Renaud, Pernet, McCormack, Gadski, Kemp, Callas; (vi) Slezak, L. Weber, Tauber, Lehmann, Nemeth, Perras, Ivogün, Von Pataky, Hesch; (vii) Dux; (viii) Jurinac, Jadlowker; (ix) Stabile, Helletsgruber, Santley, Gobbi, Lemnitz, Feraldy, Schumann, Seinemeyer, Vallin, Rautawaara, Mildmay, Jokl, Ritter-Ciampi; (x) Gerhart; (xi) Seefried; (xii) Fugère; Wittrisch; Schiøtz, Gedda, Kurz,

Erb, Kipnis, Galvany, Hempel, Sibiriakov, Frick, Destinn, Norena, Schöne, Kunz.

This is an astonishing treasury of singing, recorded over the first half of the twentieth century. It begins with Mariano Stabile's resonant 1928 account of Figaro's *Se vuol ballare*, snail-like by today's standards, while Sir Charles Santley in *Non più andrai* a few tracks later is both old-sounding and slow. The stylistic balance is then corrected in Tito Gobbi's magnificently characterful 1950 recording of that same aria. Astonishment lies less in early stylistic enormities than in the wonderful and consistent purity of vocal production, with wobbles – so prevalent today – virtually non-existent. That is partly the result of the shrewd and obviously loving choice of items, which includes not only celebrated marvels like John McCormack's 1916 account of Don Ottavio's *Il mio tesoro* (breaking all records for breath control, and stylistically surprising for including an appoggiatura), but many rarities. The short-lived Meta Seinemeyer, glorious in the Countess's first aria, Germaine Feraldy, virtually unknown, a charming Cherubino, Johanna Gadski formidably incisive in Donna Anna's *Mi tradi*, Frieda Hempel incomparable in the Queen of the Night's second aria – all these and many dozens of others make for compulsive listening, with transfers generally excellent. There are far more women singers represented than men, and a high proportion of early recordings are done in languages other than the original; but no lover of fine singing should miss this feast. The arias are gathered together under each opera, with items from non-operatic sources grouped at the end of each disc. Helpfully, duplicate versions of the same aria are put together irrespective of date of recording, and highly informative notes are provided on all the singers.

MUDARRA, Alonso (1510–80)

Music in Tablature for Vihuela & Voice, Book 3 (1546)

(N) (M) *** Astrée ES 9941. Figueras, Hopkinson Smith.

The music here (taken from the last of from Mudarra's set of three Books) is also the third known collection of music for vihuela (following publications by Luis Milán and Luis de Nárvaez). In this repertoire Montserrat Figuerras is in her element, singing these simple but beautiful melodies without artifice. She is accompanied by what many music reference books have described as an obsolete instrument, the guitar's lute-like predecessor. But Hopkinson Smith plays four vihuelas (all modern reproductions) to accompany these captivating folk-like *romances* and *villancicos*. The singing is quite lovely. A cherishable disc, beautifully recorded and with full translations included.

MULDOWNEY, Dominic (born 1952)

(i) *Piano Concerto;* (ii) *Saxophone Concerto.*

(M) *** EMI (ADD) CDM5 66528-2. (i) Donohoe, BBC SO, Elder; (ii) Harle, L. Sinf., Masson.

Dominic Muldowney has been music director at the National Theatre since 1976. These two colourful and dramatic concertos are excellent examples of his more recent style, far more approachable than his earlier work. His *Piano Concerto* is a formidable work in a continuous half-hour span of many different sections. It uses Bachian forms, along with tough Bachian piano figuration, to move kaleidoscopically in a kind of musical collage of references to different genres, including jazz and the popular waltz. With Peter Donohoe giving one of his finest performances on record, and with colourful playing from the BBC Symphony Orchestra under Mark Elder, the piece emerges powerfully, with occasional gruff echoes of Hindemith. The *Saxophone Concerto* (written for the outstanding virtuoso of the instrument, John Harle, who plays it on the record) is a more compact, strongly characterized work in three movements, each throwing up a grateful number of warm, easy tunes without any sense of compromise or incongruity. Warm, well-balanced recording.

MUNDY, William (c. 1529–c. 1591)

Vox Patris caelestis.

*** Gimell CDGIM 939. Tallis Scholars, Phillips – ALLEGRI: *Miserere;* PALESTRINA: *Missa Papae Marcelli.* ***

Mundy's *Vox Patris caelestis* was written during the short reign of Queen Mary (1553–8). The work is structured in nine sections in groups of three, the last of each group being climactic and featuring the whole choir, with solo embroidery. Yet the music flows continuously, like a great river, and the complex vocal writing creates the most spectacular effects, with the trebles soaring up and shining out over the underlying cantilena. The Tallis Scholars give an account which balances linear clarity with considerable power. The recording is first class and the digital remastering for CD improves the focus further.

MUSSORGSKY, Modest (1839–81)

The Capture of Kars (Triumphal March); St John's Night on the Bare Mountain (original score); *Scherzo in B flat. Khovanshchina: Prelude to Act I;* (i) *Introduction to Act IV. The Destruction of Sennacherib.* (i; ii) *Joshua.* (i)*Oedipus in Athens: Temple Chorus. Salammbô: Priestesses' Chorus* (operatic excerpts all orch. Rimsky-Korsakov).

(M) *** RCA (ADD) 09026 61354-2. (i) L. Symphony Ch.; (ii) Zehava Gal; LSO, Abbado.

It is particularly good to have so vital and pungent an account of the original version of *Night on the Bare Mountain,* different in all but its basic material from the Rimsky-Korsakov arrangement. Mussorgsky's scoring is so original and imaginative that the ear is readily held. Best of all are the four choral pieces; even when they are early and untypical (*Oedipus in Athens,* for example), they are immediately attractive and very Russian in feeling, and they include such evocative pieces as the *Chorus of Priestesses* (intoning over a pedal bass) from a projected opera on Flaubert's novel. The recording is first rate, and this is one of the most attractive

Mussorgsky records in the catalogue. But see under Vocal Music below for Abbado's even finer collection.

Night on the Bare Mountain (orch. Rimsky-Korsakov).

(M) *** Mercury (ADD) [432 004-2]. LSO, Dorati – PROKOFIEV: Romeo and Juliet Suites. ***

Dorati's fine 1960 account of Night on the Bare Mountain comes as an encore for Skrowaczewski's outstanding Prokofiev, and it is interesting at the end of Romeo and Juliet to note the subtle shift of acoustic from the Minneapolis auditorium to Wembley Town Hall.

A Night on the Bare Mountain (arr. Rimsky-Korsakov); Pictures at an Exhibition (orch. Ravel).

*** DG (IMS) 429 785-2. NYPO, Sinopoli – RAVEL: Valses nobles et sentimentales. **(*)

*** Telarc CD 80042. Cleveland O, Maazel.

(M) *** RCA (ADD) 09026 61958-2. Chicago SO, Reiner – Concert of Russian Showpieces. ***

(B) **(*) Decca 448 233-2; Montreal SO, Dutoit – RIMSKY-KORSAKOV: Capriccio espagnol etc. **(*)

(BB) ** Virgin Classics 2 x 1 VBD5 61751-2 (2). RLPO & Ch., Mackerras – BORODIN: Prince Igor: Overture & Polovtsian Dances ***; RIMSKY-KORSAKOV: Scheherazade **(*); TCHAIKOVSKY: The Tempest. ***

Sinopoli's electrifying New York recording of Mussorgsky's Pictures at an Exhibition again displays the New York Philharmonic as one of the world's great orchestras, performing with an epic virtuosity and panache that recall the Bernstein era of the 1960s. The playing of violins and woodwind alike is full of sophisticated touches, but it is the brass that one remembers most, from the richly sonorous opening Promenade to the malignantly forceful rhythms of The Hut on Fowl's Legs, with the playing of the trombones and tuba often assuming an unusual yet obviously calculated dominance of the texture. The finale combines power with dignified splendour. A Night on the Bare Mountain is comparably vibrant, with the Rimskian fanfares particularly vivid and the closing pages full of Russian nostalgia. The splendid digital recording was made in New York's Manhattan Center.

The quality of the Telarc Cleveland recording is apparent at the very opening of A Night on the Bare Mountain in the richly sonorous presentation of the deep brass and the sparkling yet unexaggerated percussion. With the Cleveland Orchestra on top form, the Pictures are strongly characterized; this may not be the subtlest reading available, but each of Mussorgsky's cameos comes vividly to life. The closing Great Gate of Kiev is overwhelmingly spacious in conception and quite riveting as sheer sound, with the richness and amplitude of the brass which make the work's final climax unforgettable. Unfortunately, the Pictures are not cued separately.

Reiner's RCA Pictures (recorded in 1957) is another demonstration of vintage stereo. The sound-balance is full and atmospheric and Reiner's approach is evocative to match – the sombre picture of The Old Castle, the lumbering Ox-wagon, the unctuous picture of Samuel Goldenberg

(powerfully drawn in the strings) and the superb brass playing in the Catacombs sequence are all memorable. The final climax of The Great Gate of Kiev is massively effective. The Chicago brass is again very telling in A Night on a Bare Mountain, a performance just as strongly characterized.

Dutoit's A Night on the Bare Mountain is strong and biting. His Pictures have each movement strongly characterized and there is a sense of fun in the scherzando movements, but overall this is less involving than with Reiner, and the brilliant recording is not as sumptuous as some other versions, although it has the bloom characteristic of the Montreal sound.

Mackerras's characterization of Mussorgsky's picture gallery comes over at a lower voltage than expected. The opening Promenade is fairly brisk, but the first few pictures, although well played, are almost bland, and while Bydlo reaches a fairly massive climax, it is not until Limoges that the performance springs fully to life; then The Hut on Fowl's Legs is powerfully rhythmic, with an impressive tuba solo. The Great Gate of Kiev is not as consistently taut as some versions, but is it properly expansive at the close, with the recording, always full-bodied, producing an impressive breadth of sound. A Night on the Bare Mountain, although vivid enough, lacks Satanic bite and its closing pages fail to wrench the heartstrings.

A Night on the Bare Mountain; Pictures at an Exhibition; Khovanshchina, Act IV: Entr'acte. Boris Godunov: Symphonic Synthesis (all arr. and orch. Stokowski).

*** Chan. 9445. BBC PO, Bamert.

A Night on Bald Mountain (the correct title, and nearer the original Russian meaning) was scored for Disney in 1940. Mussorgsky's satanic conception makes a spectacularly sinister impact, with the coda by contrast sumptuously romantic. (One wonders why Matthias Bamert chose not to tack on Schubert's Ave Maria, as Stokowski did for the film.) The sombre power of the operatic synthesis from Boris Godunov, with its Kremlin bells and chanting monks, and the haunted portrait of Boris himself, are also gripping, while the Entr'acte from Khovanshchina is even finer, one of Stokowski's most telling transcriptions, rich in its sonorities and played very tellingly under Bamert. We like the vividness of Stokowski's Pictures too, while to choose a cor anglais for the main theme in The Old Castle is every bit as telling as Ravel's saxophone, perhaps more so. The one moment when Ravel's orchestration is truly inspired is the interchange between Goldenberg and Schmuyle; Stokowski has the solo trumpet echoed by the woodwind and the effect is mockingly bizarre, but less bleatingly obsequious than Ravel's version. However, the Catacombs sequence makes a sumptuously weighty impact, and Baba-Yaga is grotesquely pointed with imaginative orchestral comments. Two numbers are omitted: Tuileries and Limoges; according to Edward Johnson's authoritative notes, Stokowski considered them 'too French' and 'not Mussorgskian'. The Great Gate of Kiev, massively scored, including tolling bells and organ, makes a huge final apotheosis. In all, this record is a great success, for the Chandos sound is fully worthy.

(i) *A Night on the Bare Mountain* (arr. Rimsky-Korsakov); *Pictures at an Exhibition* (arr. Funtek). (ii) *Songs & Dances of Death* (arr. Aho).

*** BIS CD 325. (i) Finnish RSO, (i) Segerstam; (ii) Järvi, with Talvela.

This CD offers an orchestration by Leo Funtek, made in the same year as Ravel's (1922). The use of a cor anglais in *The Old Castle* mirrors Stokowski, while the soft-grained wind scoring makes the portrait of *Samuel Goldenberg and Schmuyle* more sympathetic, if also blander. The performances by the Finnish Radio Orchestra under Leif Segerstam both of this and of the familiar Rimsky *Night on the Bare Mountain* are spontaneously presented and very well recorded. The extra item is no less valuable: an intense, darkly Russian account of the *Songs and Dances of Death* from Martti Talvela with the orchestral accompaniment plangently scored by Kalevi Aho.

A Night on a Bare Mountain (trans. Tchernov).

⬤ *** Teldec 4509 96516-2. Berezovsky – BALAKIREV: *Islamey.* *** ⬤

This remarkable transcription by Konstantin Tchernov sounds hardly less dazzling in Berezovksy's hands than the outstanding *Islamey* with which it is coupled. The engineers capture very good piano sound.

Pictures at an Exhibition (orch. Ravel).

(M) *** DG (ADD) 447 426-2. BPO, Karajan – DEBUSSY: *La Mer;* RAVEL: *Boléro.* ***

(B) *** Sony (ADD) SBK 48162. Cleveland O, Szell – KODALY: *Háry János Suite;* PROKOFIEV: *Lieutenant Kijé Suite.* ***

⬤ (M) *** RCA (ADD) 09026 61401-2. Chicago SO, Reiner – RESPIGHI: *The Fountains of Rome; The Pines of Rome.* *** ⬤

*** DG Gold (IMS) 439 013-2. BPO, Karajan – RAVEL: *Boléro* etc. ***

(B) *** DG Penguin 460 633-2. LSO, Abbado – RAVEL: *Boléro.* ***

(M) *** DG (IMS) (ADD) 415 844-2. Chicago SO, Giulini – RAVEL: *Ma Mère l'Oye; Rhapsodie espagnole.* ***

(N) (BB) *** EMI Encore CDE5 74742-2. Phd. O, Muti – STRAVINSKY: *Rite of Spring.* ***

(M) *** Decca 417 754-2. Chicago SO, Solti – BARTOK: *Concerto for Orchestra.* ***

(M) (***) Mercury mono [434 378-2]. Chicago SO, Kubelik – BARTOK: *Music for Strings, Percussion & Celesta.* (***)

(**(*)) BBC mono BBCL 4023-2. Philh. O, Giulini – TCHAIKOVSKY: *Symphony No. 6 (Pathétique).* (**(*))

(N) ** RCA 74321 72788-2. NDR SO, Wand – DEBUSSY: *Le Martyre de Saint Sébastien.* **

Among the many fine versions of Mussorgsky's *Pictures* on CD, Karajan's 1966 record stands out. It is undoubtedly a great performance, tingling with electricity from the opening *Promenade* to the spaciously conceived finale, *The Great Gate of Kiev*, which has real splendour. The remastered analogue recording still sounds marvellous, and this reissue, in DG's 'Originals' series of legendary recordings, includes a uniquely evocative performance of Debussy's *La Mer* as well as a very exciting account of Ravel's *Boléro.*

Szell's 1963 Cleveland performance also remains among the greatest of all recordings of Ravel's vividly inspired orchestration. Even if the recording has a somewhat less expansive dynamic-range, the character of each portrait is firmly drawn with vivid strokes of orchestral colour. The portrayal of *Goldenberg and Schmuyle* brings superbly full articulation from the lower strings and *Baba-Yaga* makes the most incisive impact. Whether in the cheeping and chattering of the unhatched chicks, the bravura swirl of the *Limoges Market*, or the dignified grandiloquence of that final great gateway of Kiev, the controlled brilliance of the recording projects everything with extraordinary vividness.

With the advantage of the rich acoustics of Symphony Hall, the RCA sound-balance of Reiner's 1957 Chicago performance is highly atmospheric, if less sharply focused. The finale climax of *The Great Gate of Kiev* shows the concentration of the playing. The remastering is fully worthy, and there is excellent documentation.

Karajan's 1986 recording is one of the most impressive of DG's digital recordings. The tangibility of the sound is remarkable, with the opening brass *Promenade* and the massed strings in *Samuel Goldenberg and Schmuyle* notable in their naturalness of sonority. With superb Berlin Philharmonic playing and the weight of the climaxes contrasting with the wit of *Tuileries* and the exhilaration of *The Market at Limoges*, this is certainly now among the top recommendations. Even the spacious finale, if not quite as electrifying as his earlier, analogue version, is given greater impact by the added weight and makes a fittingly grandiose culmination.

Abbado takes a straighter, more direct view of Mussorgsky's fanciful series of pictures than usual. He is helped by the translucent and naturally balanced digital recording. Abbado's speeds tend to be extreme, with *Tuileries* taken very fast and light, while *Bydlo* and *The Great Gate of Kiev* are slow and weighty. This now reappears on Penguin Classics at mid-price, coupled with Ravel. The author's essay is by Richard Ford.

Giulini's 1976 Chicago recording has always been among the front-runners. He is generally more relaxed and often more wayward than Karajan, but this is still a splendid performance and the finale generates more tension than Karajan's most recent, digital version, though it is not as overpowering as the earlier, analogue recording.

Muti's reading, given the excellence of its recorded sound, more than holds its own, although the balance is forward and perhaps not all listeners will respond to the brass timbres at the opening. The lower strings in *Samuel Goldenberg and Schmuyle* have extraordinary body and presence, and *Baba-Yaga* has an unsurpassed virtuosity and attack, as well as being of a high standard as a recording. The coupling is no less thrilling.

Solti's performance is fiercely brilliant rather than atmospheric or evocative. He treats Ravel's orchestration as a virtuoso challenge, and with larger-than-life digital recording it undoubtedly has demonstration qualities, and the transparency of texture, given the forward balance, provides quite startling clarity.

Kubelik's famous (1951) mono version of Ravel's masterly scoring was the Mercury recording which coined the term 'Living Presence'. The realism of the recording (in spite of some thinness in the top range of the strings) still has the power to astonish. It still conveys much of the splendid acoustic of Chicago's Orchestral Hall. The success of the record is not just technical, but musical too. The performance has great freshness with not a hint of routine anywhere; there are many subtleties, particularly as one picture or promenade is dovetailed into another.

Though the initial impact of the dry mono sound of 1961 is disconcerting, made striking by the unhelpful acoustic of the Usher Hall, Edinburgh, there are ample compensations for losing the full beauty of Ravel's orchestration in this characterful BBC version. The bite and impact of a performance under Giulini at his most electrifying is intensified, so that in such a movement as *The Hut on Fowl's Legs* one even begins to think of this as a precursor of the *Rite of Spring*. The fast, light articulation of *Limoges* is very exciting, and the *Catacombs* brass fiercely sepulchral. Solo playing is immaculate too, despite the lack of bloom, and the closing *Great Gate of Kiev* makes a spectacularly spacious impact, with a fine contribution from the tam-tam. A generous coupling.

Günter Wand's account comes from a concert performance given in 1999 at the Musikhalle in Hamburg and must be addressed primarily to his wide circle of admirers. It is undoubtedly good but comes somewhat illogically with the four fragments from Debussy's *Le Martyre*. At 54 minutes this strikes us as a non-starter: it would not be really competitive at the price of a Naxos issue.

Pictures at an Exhibition (incomplete; orch. Ravel).

(N) (**(*)**) Naxos mono 8.110105. Boston SO, Koussevitzky – BARTOK: *Concerto for Orchestra.* (***)

Koussevitzky's 1943 reading of *Pictures* is an exciting one, prompting wild applause at the end. This is a performance white-hot with passion, with Koussevitzky challenging his players to the very limit, as in the hectic account of the *Tuileries* movement. Even with limited radio sound it makes an attractive supplement to the historic performance of the Bartók, though, sadly, Koussevitzky omits the two most evocative movements, the *Old Castle* and *Bydlo* (the Polish ox-cart), together with the *Promenades* that frame them.

(i) Pictures at an Exhibition (orch. Ravel); **(ii) Boris Godunov** (original version): highlights (including *Death Scene*).

(M) *** Sony SMK 60008. (i) BPO, Giulini; (ii) Ghiaurov, Ghiuselev, Petrov, Frank, Sofia Nat. Op. Ch., Bodra Smyana Children's Ch., Sofia Festival O, Tchakarov.

It was a splendid idea to reissue Giulini's newest (1989) Sony account of Mussorgsky's *Pictures* with highlights from Tchakarov's Sofia *Boris Godunov*. Ghiaurov gives a magnificent performance as Boris and Tchakarov brings out the reflective side of the score well. But the opening chorus of wandering minstrels from the *Prologue* makes a fine impact and the intensity of Boris's monologue *I have achieved power*, and above all the death scene (both included here), with Ghiaurov singing beautifully, make this set of excerpts particularly valuable. Nicola Ghiuselev is magnificent as Pimen

in his Act I aria, *Just one last story*, and this is a thoroughly worthwhile and unusual coupling.

(i) Pictures at an Exhibition (orch. Ravel); **(ii) Pictures at an Exhibition** (original piano version).

(N) **(*) Australian Decca Eloquence (ADD) 467 127-2. (i) Los Angeles PO, Mehta; (ii) Ashkenazy.
(M) **(*) Ph. 442 650-2. (i) VPO, Previn; (ii) Brendel.

Zubin Mehta's Decca recording of *Pictures at an Exhibition* is brilliantly played and exciting, if not quite as imaginative as the very best. The sound has few rivals – it is exceptionally vivid and still packs a punch: the bass drum knocks spots off many modern digital recordings, and the whole orchestra sounds rich and full, with all departments clearly defined, within a realistic balance. Ashkenazy's account of the original piano version is distinguished by a strong poetic feel, if not with the extrovert flair pianists like Richter or Berman brought to this music.

Obviously the Philips engineers had problems with the acoustics of the Musikvereinsaal, as the bass is noticeably resonant and inner definition is far from sharp. Otherwise the balance is truthful; but the performance, though not lacking spontaneity, is not distinctive, and there is a lack of the kind of grip which makes Karajan's version so unforgettable.

Brendel's performance of the original piano score has its own imaginative touches and some fine moments. Brendel keeps the music moving but effectively varies the style of the Promenades. The closing pages, however, need to sound more unbuttoned: Brendel is weighty, but fails to enthral the listener. The recording is faithful.

Pictures at an Exhibition (orch. Cailliet).

(***) Biddulph mono WHL 046 Phd. O, Ormandy – TCHAIKOVSKY: *Symphony No. 6.* (***)

This 1937 recording offers the only version yet of Lucien Cailliet's orchestration of *Pictures*, specially commissioned by Ormandy from the orchestra's 'house arranger' and principal bass clarinet. Surprisingly for a wind-player, Cailliet uses full strings markedly more than Ravel in his orchestration, so that the result is more conventional. One bonus is that Cailliet includes the long *Promenade*, after *Goldenberg* and before *Limoges*, which Ravel omits. The transfer is clear and fresh, with remarkably little feeling of limitation.

(i) Pictures at an Exhibition (arr. Leonard for piano and orchestra). *3 Pictures from the Crimea* (orch. Goehr); *A Night on the Bare Mountain* (arr. & orch. Rimsky-Korsakov); *Scherzo in B flat* (orch. Rimsky-Korsakov); *From my Tears* (orch. Kindler); *Khovanshchina: Prelude* (orch. Rimsky-Korsakov); *Golitsyn's Journey* (orch. Stokowski) *Sorochinsky Fair: Gopak* (orch. Liadov).

(M) *** Cala CACD 1030. (i) Ungár; Philh. O, Simon.

Lawrence Leonard's arrangement of Mussorgsky's *Pictures* for piano and orchestra is remarkably effective and very entertaining. The concertante format works admirably, especially powerful in *Gnomus* and *The Hut on Fowl's Legs*, charmingly depicting the *Unhatched Chicks* (a piquant mixture of keyboard and woodwind, spiced with xylophone).

There are many added touches of colour. The other pieces are all well worth having, notably Rimsky's chimerical scoring (following the composer's orchestral sketch) of the *Scherzo in B flat*. The three *Pictures from the Crimea* are darkly nostalgic, and the lively *Gopak*, like the *Khovanshchina* excerpts (Stokowski's arrangement of *Golitsyn's Journey* is sombrely characterful), is very welcome. All Geoffrey Simon's performances have plenty of life, and Tamás Ungár makes an exciting contribution and is fully equal to all the technical demands of the revised piano-part. The recording is warm, full and expansive, but not always sharply defined.

Pictures at an Exhibition (original piano version)

(N) (M) (***) Ph. mono 464 734-2. S. Richter – (with 1958 live recital of CHOPIN; LISZT; RACHMANINOV; SCHUBERT (***).

* Hyp. CDA 67018. Demidenko – PROKOFIEV: *Romeo & Juliet: 10 Pieces; Toccata, Op. 11.* **

This Philips reissue offers Sviatislav Richter's 1958 Sofia recital rightly included among their '50 Great Recordings'. The mono recital has been remastered using the latest background noise reduction technology. While this cannot suppress the audience's bronchial afflictions, the previously very troublesome tape roar has been considerably mitigated. It has never before sounded as vivid as this: the magnetism of Richter's playing comes over splendidly, and his enormously wide dynamic range brings a riveting final climax. The piano is backwardly positioned, and some of the pianissimo playing could ideally be more present; but the focus is improved, the piano timbre itself has more body and substance than previously, and does not lack colour. One can certainly forget the technical limitations and respond to this marvellous, indeed uniquely charismatic performance, which has never been surpassed on record.

Besides the Mussorgsky the 76-minute recital offers a generous programme including two Schubert *Impromptus* (D 899/2 & 4) and the *C major Moment musical* (D.780/1), Chopin's *E major Etude*, Op. 10/3, two Liszt *Valses oubliées* plus a pair of *Transcendental Studies (Feux follets)* and *Harmonies du soir*, where there is more fabulous virtuosity. The recital closes with Rachmaninov's *Prelude in G sharp minor*, Op. 32/13. An indispensible disc for all lovers of great pianism.

No doubts about Demidenko's virtuosity and keyboard command here, or the excellence of the Hyperion sound. There are doubts however about many of the highly idiosyncratic touches that are so pervasive that he attracts more attention to himself than to Mussorgsky!

Pictures at an Exhibition (piano version, ed. Horowitz).

(N) (B) (***) RCA 2-CD mono 74321 84594-2 (2). Horowitz – (with CLEMENTI: *Sonatas, Op. 14/3; Op. 34/2; Op. 47/2: Rondo* (***); – SCRIABIN: *Etudes; Preludes; Sonatas.* (***)

Horowitz's famous 1951 recording, made at a live performance at Carnegie Hall, is as thrilling as it is perceptive. Mussorgsky's darker colours are admirably caught and the lighter, scherzando evocations are dazzlingly articulated. In *The Great Gate of Kiev* Horowitz embellishes the texture to make the result even more spectacular. The performances of the Clementi *Sonatas*, also from the 1950s, are hardly less electrifying, and though the piano sound is again shallow, the quality is a great improvement on their previous vinyl transfers.

VOCAL MUSIC

(i; ii) *St John's Night on the Bare Mountain* (version for bass soloist, chorus and orchestra); *Intermezzo symphonique in modo classico; Scherzo in B flat min.;* **(ii; iii)** *Khovanshchina: Prelude* and excerpts, including *Dance of the Persian Slave Girls. Mlada Festive March.*

(N) ● ******* Sony SK 62034. BPO, Abbado with (i) Berlin R Ch., South Tirol Children's Ch. (ii) Kotcherga; (iii) Tarakova.

Mussorgsky arranged a choral version of *St John's Night on the Bare Mountain* for his opera *Sorochinsky Fair* and Rimsky-Korsakov then elaborated it to include a bass soloist. The result in this superb account from Anatole Kotcheraga and the Berlin Choirs and Philharmonic Orchestra is thrillingly diabolic, far more spectacular than either of the orchestral versions. All the rest of Mussorgsky's orchestral music is here, plus some splendidly performed excerpts from *Khovanshchina* with Kotcherga and Marianna Tarasova richly colloquial soloists. The performance of the lovely orchestral *Prelude* is the finest on record, richly evocative, with gorgeous playing from the Berlin Philharmonic strings. The *March* from *Mlada* makes a festive close to a disc which cannot be too highly recommended, and is given demonstration sound quality.

Songs

The Complete Songs.

● **(M) (***)** EMI mono CHS7 63025-2 (3). Christoff, Labinsky, Moore, French R. & TV O, Tzipine.

Boris Christoff originally recorded these songs in 1958; they then appeared in a four-LP mono set with a handsome book, generously illustrated with plates and music examples, giving the texts in Russian, French, Italian and English, and with copious notes on each of the 63 songs. Naturally the documentation cannot be so extensive in the CD format – but, on the other hand, one has the infinitely greater ease of access that the new technology offers. The Mussorgsky songs constitute a complete world in themselves, and they cast a strong spell: their range is enormous and their insight into the human condition deep. Christoff was at the height of his vocal powers when he made the set with Alexandre Labinsky, his accompanist in most of the songs; and its return to circulation cannot be too warmly welcomed. This was the first complete survey, and it still remains the only really recommendable set. Alas, it has been deleted just as we go to press.

OPERA

Boris Godunov ((i) 1869 & (ii) 1872 versions)).

(M) *** Ph. 462 230-2 (5). (i) Putilin, Lutsuk, (ii) Vaneev, Galusin; (i; ii) Ohotnikov, Kuznetsov, Trifonova, Bulycheva, Pluzhnikov, Akimov, Kirov Opera Ch. & O, Gergiev.

It makes a fascinating contrast in Gergiev's St Petersburg set – five discs for the price of three – to have the original 1869 version of seven scenes set against the 1872 revision with its amplification in the extra Polish act and elsewhere. Gerviev's incisive, keenly dramatic readings bring out the differences very effectively, and the casting of Boris in each heightens that. In 1869 the character is more direct, more of a villain, less of a victim – reflected in Nikolai Putilin's virile and firm singing – where in the expanded 1872 portrait the character is more equivocal, more self-searching, clearly verging on madness, and there you have Vladimir Vaneev bringing out the element of thoughtfulness and mystery over a wider expressive range. The role of Grigory, the Pretender, brings alternative casting too, but it is only in the 1872 version that the character plays a full part, very well taken by the ringing and clear, very Russian-sounding tenor, Vladimir Galusin. The others make a first-rate team, individually strong and idiomatic, and all enhancing the drama, obviously experienced on stage. Outstanding are Olga Borodina as Marina and Konstantin Pluzhnikov as a sinister Shuisky. The sound is fresh and forward, with voices set in front of the orchestra, more powerful in wind and brass than in the strings. The Abbado set on Sony (see below) offers a starrier cast and a more spacious reading, often more warmly expressive, but the practical advantages of the Gergiev set make it even more recommendable.

Boris Godunov (original version; complete).

*** Sony S3K 58977 (3). Kotcherga, Leiferkus, Lipovšek, Ramey, Nikolsky, Langridge, Slovak Philharmonic Ch., Bratislava, Tölz Boys' Ch., Berlin RSO, Abbado.

**(*) EMI (ADD) CDS7 54377-2 (3). Talvela, Gedda, Mróz, Kinasz, Haugland, Krakow Polish R. Ch., Polish Nat. SO, Semkow.

Claudio Abbado recorded *Boris Godunov* in its original version with speeds that regularly press ahead, and the urgency of the composer's inspiration is conveyed without reducing the epic scale of the work or its ominously dark colouring. Abbado inserts the beautiful scene in front of St Basil's at the start of Act IV, but then omits from the final Kromy Forest scene the episode about the Simpleton losing his kopek, which would otherwise come in twice – as it does in the Semkow (EMI) set. Vocally, the performance centres on the glorious singing of Anatoly Kotcherga as Boris. Rarely has this music been sung with such firmness and beauty as here. Kotcherga may not have as weighty a voice as Talvela on EMI, but the darkly meditative depth of the performance is enhanced without loss of power. The other principal basses, Samuel Ramey as the monk, Pimen, and Gleb Nikolsky as Varlaam, are well contrasted, even if Ramey's voice sounds un-Slavonic. The tenor, Sergei Larin, sings with beauty and clarity up to the highest register as the Pretender,

not least in the Polish act, while Marjana Lipovšek is a formidably characterful Marina, if not quite as well focused as usual. Having Philip Langridge as Shuisky and Sergei Leiferkus as Rangoni reinforces the starry strength of the team. The sound is spacious, more atmospheric than usual in recordings made in the Philharmonie in Berlin, and allowing high dynamic contrasts, with the choral ensembles – so vital in this work – full and glowing.

The EMI version offers (at full price) an analogue recording of 1977, but its warmth and richness go with a forward balance and a high transfer level. The voices have an extra bite, not least the firm, weighty bass of Martti Talvela as Boris or of Aage Haugland, magnificent as Varlaam. Nicolai Gedda is excellent as the Pretender, if not as free on top as Larin in the Abbado set. The other soloists, as well as the chorus, make up a formidable Polish team, with hardly a weak link. Bozena Kinasz as Marina is particularly impressive. Jerzy Semkow may not convey such bite and beauty as Abbado, but in his rugged, measured way he conveys more intensity at moments of high drama than the other Sony rival, Tchakarov, helped by the firm, full sound. However, this set has been deleted just at the time of going to press.

Boris Godunov (arr. **Rimsky-Korsakov**).

*** Decca (IMS) (ADD) 411 862-2 (3). Ghiaurov, Vishnevskaya, Spiess, Maslennikov, Talvela, V. Boys' Ch., Sofia R. Ch., V. State Op. Ch., VPO, Karajan.

With Ghiaurov in the title-role, Karajan's superbly controlled Decca version, technically outstanding, comes far nearer than previous recordings to conveying the rugged greatness of Mussorgsky's masterpiece. Only the Coronation scene lacks something of the weight and momentum one ideally wants. Vishnevskaya is far less appealing than the lovely non-Slavonic Marina of Evelyn Lear on EMI, but overall this Decca set has much more to offer. However, Abbado's Sony recording of the original version now makes a clear first choice for this opera, and Decca need to reissue the Karajan at mid-price, when it would still be competitive.

Boris Godunov (original, 1869 version): excerpts: *Coronation Scene; Varlaam's Song; Apartment Scene; St Basil Scene; Death Scene* (sung in English).

⚫ (M) *** Chan. 3007. Tomlinson, Kale, Bayley, Rodgers, Best, Opera N. Ch., E. N. Philh. O, Daniel.

This generous, 75-minute selection of excerpts from *Boris Godunov* is highly recommendable even when compared with current Russian versions of Mussorgsky's masterpiece. John Tomlinson has never been in finer voice on disc than here, with his dark bass-baritone perfectly focused. This is an exceptionally lyrical view of the self-tortured tsar, both dramatically powerful and warmly expressive, letting one appreciate the beauty of Mussorgsky's melodies. Tomlinson is helped by Paul Daniel's inspired direction and opulent recorded sound, with excellent support from singers in the vintage Opera North production, including Stuart Kale as Prince Shuisky, Clive Bayley as Varlaam, Joan Rodgers as Xenia and Matthew Best as Pimen. Anyone who supports the idea of opera sung in English should not miss this highly compelling disc.

Khovanshchina (complete).

*** DG 429 758-2 (3). Lipovšek, Burchuladze, Atlantov, Haugland, Borowska, Kotscherga, Popov, V. State Op. Ch. & O, Abbado.

**(*) Ph. 437 147-2 (3). Minjelkiev, Galusin, Steblianko, Ohotnikov, Borodina, Kirov Theatre Ch. & O, Gergiev.

Abbado's live recording brings the most vivid account of this epic Russian opera yet on disc. He uses the Shostakovich orchestration (with some cuts), darker and harmonically far more faithful than the old Rimsky-Korsakov version. Yet Abbado rejects the triumphant ending of the Shostakovich edition and follows instead the orchestration that Stravinsky did for Diaghilev in 1913 of the original subdued ending as Mussorgsky himself conceived it. When the tragic fate of the Old Believers, immolating themselves for their faith, brings the deepest and most affecting emotions of the whole opera, that close, touching in its tenderness, is far more apt. Lipovšek's glorious singing as Marfa, the Old Believer with whom one most closely identifies, sets the seal on the whole performance. Aage Haugland is a rock-like Ivan Khovansky and, though Burchuladze is no longer as steady of tone as he was, he makes a noble Dosifei. Stage noises sometimes intrude and voices are sometimes set back, but this remains a magnificent achievement.

Gergiev does not disguise the squareness of much of the writing and his performance lacks the flair and brilliance of Abbado. He stays faithful to the Shostakovich version of the score to the very end. There he simply adds a loud version of the *Old Believers' Chorale* on unison brass – hardly a subtle solution! The Kirov soloists make a fine team, but on almost all counts Abbado is more persuasive.

MUSTONEN, Olli (born 1967)

(i) Triple Concerto for Violins & Orchestra. Frogs Dancing on Water Lilies. (ii) Petite Suite for Cello & Strings. Nonets Nos. 1 & 2.

*** Ondine ODE 9742. (i) Pekka & Juaakko Kuusisto, Batiashvili; (ii) Rousi; Tapiola Sinfonietta, Composer.

The Finnish pianist Olli Mustonen has made a name for himself as a gifted if somewhat idiosyncratic composer. His *Triple Concerto* for three violins and orchestra is a neo-Baroque pastiche. There is a strong element of pastiche too in the *Nonet No. 1*, whose *Scherzo* trips along like Mendelssohn with great delicacy and lightness. The *Petite suite for Cello and Strings* has something of the naturalness and charm of Gunnar de Frumerie's *Pastoral Suite*.

Mustonen does not have a strongly individual voice (to put it mildly) and limits himself to a limited range of musical devices, but the naïveté and directness of it all is undoubtedly likeable. Very good playing and recording.

MYSLIVEČEK, Josef (1737–81)

Violin Concerto in C.

(B) *** Discover DICD 920265. Zenaty, Virtuosi di Praga, Vlček (with DVORAK: *Romance; Mazurka* ***) – VANHAL: *Violin Concerto.* ***

Born in Bohemia almost a generation before Mozart, Mysliveček wrote fresh, vigorous music, of which this violin concerto is a fine examples, its central slow movement a brief, gentle interlude. The Vanhal coupling is a comparable work, equally attractive. On this well-recorded bargain issue Ivan Zenaty with his clean, full tone proves an outstanding advocate, with the Virtuosi di Praga providing lively support on modern instruments. In the two shorter concertante works of a century later, Zenaty and the orchestra readily adapt their style to the romanticism of Dvořák, tender in the *Romance*, flamboyant in the *Mazurka*.

Octets Nos. 1 in E flat; 2 in E flat; 3 in B flat.

**(*) EMI CDC5 55512-2. Sabine Meyer Wind Ens. – DVORAK: *Serenade in D min.* **(*)

The Sabine Meyer Wind Ensemble offer three charming *Octets* by Mysliveček as their fill-up to an eminently satisfying if laid-back account of the Dvořák *Wind Serenade*. Too many claims should not be made for this music, which is of no great substance but is nevertheless genuinely charming, particularly in the slow movements. However, this has been deleted as we go to press.

NEPOMUNECO, Alberto

(1864–1920)

Galhofeira, Op. 13/4; Improviso, Op. 27/2; Nocturnes: Nos. 1 in C; 2 in G (for the left hand); 5 Pequenas peças (for the left hand); Nocturne, Op. 33; Sonata in F min., Op. 9; Suite antiga, Op. 11.

** Marco 8.223548. Guimarães.

Alberto Nepomuceno has every right to be called the father of Brazilian music. He was active as a teacher and for a time director of the National Institute of Music in Rio da Janeiro, helping the youthful Villa Lobos. Although he composed in most genres, little of his output has been recorded, so this disc of his piano music is welcome. Much of it is derivative – Brahmsian or Schumannesque – but it shows him to be far from negligible. Morever there is a trace of the kind of popular Brazilian music that fascinated Milhaud in his *Saudades do Brasil*. The *Cinco Pequenas peças* and the *Nocturnes* of 1919 were both written for Nepomuceno's daughter, who was born without a right arm. Maria Inês Guimarães is not the most imaginative of pianists and is somewhat wanting in finesse, but those with a taste for off-beat repertoire may find this worth investigating.

NEVIN, Arthur (1871–1943)

From Edgeworth Hills.

*** Altarus AIR-CD 9024. Amato – A. NEVIN: *A Day in Venice* etc. ***

Arthur Nevin was without his older brother's melodic individuality, but he wrote spontaneously and crafted his pieces nicely. The most striking number of *From Edgeworth Hills* is the tripping *Sylphs*, very characteristic of its time, while *As the Moon Rose* has an agreeably sentimental tune, and the picaresque *Firefly* sparkles nicely here. *Toccatella* is rhythmically a bit awkward but is quite a showpiece, and Donna Amato plays it with real dash. Excellent recording.

NEVIN, Ethelbert (1862–1901)

A Day in Venice (suite), Op. 25; *Etude in the Form of a Romance; Etude in the Form of a Scherzo, Op. 18/1–2; May in Tuscany* (suite), Op. 21; *Napoli (En passant), Op. 30/3; Mighty Lak' a Rose* (after the transcription by Charles Spross); *O'er Hill and Dale* (suite); *The Rosary* (arr. Whelpley); *Water Scenes, Op. 13.*

*** Altarus AIR-CD 9024. Amato – A. NEVIN: *From Edgeworth Hills.* ***

Ethelbert Nevin was born in Edgeworth, Pennsylvania, scored his first great success when *Narcissus* became a worldwide hit, and *The Rosary* was Nevin's other succes, with the sheet music selling over a million copies in the decade following its publication in 1898. Donna Amato grew up in the area where he was born, and she takes care not to sentimentalize these genre pieces, which can be just a little trite but also quite engaging. *Mighty Lak' a Rose*, another favourite, retains all its charm. The recording is clear and natural in a pleasing acoustic.

NICOLAI, Carl Otto (1810–49)

The Merry Wives of Windsor (Die lustigen Weiber von Windsor): complete.

(B) *** Double Decca (ADD) 460 197-2 (2). Ridderbusch, W. Brendel, Malta, Donath, Schmidt, Bav. R. Ch. & SO, Kubelik.

(M) **(*) EMI (ADD) CMS7 69348-2 (2). Frick, Gutstein, Engel, Wunderlich, Lenz, Hoppe, Putz, Litz, Mathis, Ch. & O of Bav. State Op., Heger.

Kubelik's performance may be slightly lacking in dramatic ebullience, but its extra subtlety has perceptive results – as in the entry of Falstaff in Act I, where Kubelik conveys the tongue-in-cheek quality of Nicolai's *pomposo* writing. Ridderbusch portrays a straight and noble Falstaff. Although as an opera this may not have the brilliant insight of Verdi or all the atmosphere of Vaughan Williams, it has its own brand of effervescence which is equally endearing and is well caught here. The dialogue is crisply edited, and the recording, while fairly reverberant, is vividly atmospheric. *Faute de mieux*, it should receive a strong recommendation.

This is particularly welcome as a Decca Double, although the documentation includes only a cued synopsis.

As Falstaff, Gottlob Frick is in magnificent voice, even if he sounds baleful rather than comic. It is good too to have the young Fritz Wunderlich as Fenton opposite the Anna Reich of Edith Mathis. Though the others hardly match this standard – Ruth-Margret Putz is rather shrill as Frau Fluth – they all give enjoyable performances. The effectiveness of the comic timing is owed in great measure to the conducting of the veteran, Robert Heger. From the CD transfer one could hardly tell the age of the recording, with the voices particularly well caught.

NIELSEN, Carl (1865–1931)

Aladdin (suite); *A Fantasy-Journey to the Froes* (rhapsodic overture); *Helios Overture; Maskarade: Overture; Prelude to Act II, Dance of the Cockerels. Pan and Syrinx; Sagadrøm.*

*** DG 447 757-2. Gothenburg SO, Järvi.

Of the anthologies of Nielsen's orchestral music other than the symphonies, this is now the best on offer. The performances are vital and affectionate, with the orchestra playing with their usual finesse and enthusiasm. Both *Pan and Syrinx* and *Saga-drøm* are atmospheric. One minor reservation: the *Helios Overture* is too swiftly paced (the sun rises over the Aegean in fast-forward mode). The recording is very fine indeed.

At the Bier of a Young Artist; Little Suite for Strings, Op. 1.

*** Virgin VC5 45224-2. Norwegian CO, Iona Brown – GRIEG: *At the Cradle* etc. ***

The Norwegian Chamber Orchestra are an excellent group and their account of Nielsen's first opus, the *Little Suite for Strings*, is about the best in the catalogue. His moving elegy, the *Andante lamentoso* (*At the Bier of a Young Artist*), is equally eloquent in their hands. The recording, made in the glorious acoustic of Eidsvoll Church in Norway, is very real and tangible. Very strongly recommended.

Clarinet Concerto, Op. 57.

*** Chan. 8618. Hilton, SNO, Bamert – COPLAND: *Concerto;* LUTOSLAWSKI: *Dance Preludes.* ***

Janet Hilton gives a highly sympathetic account of the Nielsen *Concerto*, but it is characteristically soft-centred and mellower in its response to the work's more disturbing emotional undercurrents than Olle Schill's splendid account on BIS – see below. The Chandos recording is first class.

(i) *Clarinet Concerto;* (ii) *Flute Concerto;* (iii) *Violin Concerto, Op. 33.*

*** Chan. 8894. (i) Thomsen; (ii) Christiansen; (iii) Sjøgren; Danish RSO, Schønwandt.

Niels Thomsen's powerfully intense account of the late *Clarinet Concerto* is completely gripping. Michael Schønwandt gives sensitive and imaginative support, both here and in the two companion works. Toke Lund Christiansen is hardly less successful in the *Flute Concerto*. Kim

Sjøgren and Schønwandt give a penetrating and thoughtful account of the *Violin Concerto*; there is real depth here, thanks in no small measure to Schønwandt. The recording is first class.

(i) *Clarinet Concerto;* (ii) *Flute Concerto;* (iii) *Violin Concerto. An Imaginary Journey to the Faeroe Islands (Rhapsodic Overture); Helios Overture, Op. 17; Pan and Syrinx, Op. 49; Saga-drøm, Op. 39; Symphonic Rhapsody.*

(B) *** EMI double forte (ADD) CZS5 69758-2 (2).
  (i) Stevennson; (ii) Lemmser; (iii) Tellefsen; Danish RSO, Blomstedt.

Arve Tellefsen is a first-class soloist in the *Violin Concerto* and Kjell-Inge Stevennson is pretty stunning in the remarkable and other-worldly *Clarinet Concerto*. The charm and subtleties of the *Flute Concerto* are hardly less well realized by Frantz Lemmser's nimble and sensitive account. Moreover, since the orchestra is Danish, the other works (such as the marvellous *Pan and Syrinx* and the atmospheric *Helios Overture*) are played with authentic accents. The collection also includes a novelty in the *Symphonic Rhapsody* (1889), composed before the *First Symphony*. Throughout the EMI engineers secure a natural sound-balance. In its economical new format this is a most attractive proposition, and the recordings still sound very warm and fresh.

(i) *Clarinet Concerto. Overture: Amor og digteren (Love & the Poet), Op. 54; Little Suite for Strings; Pan and Syrinx.*

(M) *** HM HMT 7901489. (i) Boeykens; Beethoven Academie, Caeyers.

Walter Boeykens gives a remarkably perceptive account of the *Clarinet Concerto*, one which gets to the heart of this often elusive and other-worldly score. There is always an undercurrent of tenderness and poetic feeling. The make-weights include a rarity in the late overture, *Amor og digteren* (1930). Jan Caeyers has as genuine a feeling for Nielsen as has Boeykens in the concerto, and *Pan and Syrinx* comes off very well indeed.

(i) *Clarinet Concerto;* (ii) *Symphony No. 3 (Sinfonia espansiva). Maskarade Overture.*

*** BIS CD 321. (i) Schill; (ii) Raanoja, Skram; Gothenburg SO, Chung.

Olle Schill brings brilliance and insight to what is one of the most disturbing and masterly of all modern concertos. The young Korean conductor secures playing of great fire and enthusiasm from the Gothenburgers in the *Third Symphony* and he has vision and breadth – and at the same time no want of momentum. Two soloists singing a wordless vocalise are called for in the pastoral slow movement, and their contribution is admirable. Myung-Whun Chung also gives a high-spirited and sparkling account of the *Overture* to Nielsen's comic opera, *Maskarade*. The BIS recording is marvellous, even by the high standards of this small company.

(i) *Clarinet Concerto;* (ii) *Serenata in Vano;* (iii) *Wind Quintet, Op. 43.*

(***) Clarinet Classics mono CC 002. (i) Cahuzac,

Copenhagen Op. O, Frandsen; (ii) Oxenvad, Larsson, Sorensen, Jensen, Hegner; (iii) Royal Chapel Wind Quintet.

These are pioneering recordings. The *Clarinet Concerto* was to have been recorded by its dedicatee, Aage Oxenvad, who is heard in both the *Quintet* and the *Serenata in Vano*, but death intervened and the eminent French clarinettist Louis Cahuzac filled the breach. This lovely performance of the *Quintet* is so full of character that in some ways it remains unsurpassed. These transfers are a great improvement on the earlier ones on Danacord LPs, a bit dry but eminently clean and well detailed in the case of the *Concerto*, which Cahuzac plays with great feeling.

(i) *Flute Concerto; Symphony No. 1; Rhapsody Overture: An Imaginary Journey to the Faeroe Islands.*

*** BIS CD 454. (i) Gallois; Gothenburg SO, Chung.

The *Flute Concerto* is given a marvellous performance by Patrick Gallois, and Myung-Whun Chung and the Gothenburg orchestra have an instinctive feeling for Nielsen. They play with commendable enthusiasm and warmth, and Chung shapes the *Symphony* with great sensitivity to detail and a convincing sense of the whole. The *Rhapsody Overture: An Imaginary Journey to the Faeroe Islands* is not the composer at his strongest, but it has a highly imaginative opening.

Violin Concerto, Op. 33.

(N) ✪ (M) *** Sony SMK 89748. Lin, Swedish RSO, Salonen – SIBELIUS: *Violin Concerto.* *** ✪

(N) ** EMI CDC5 56906-2. Znaider, LPO, Lawrence Foster – BRUCH: *Violin Concerto No. 1.* **

(i) *Violin Concerto. Symphony No. 5.*

*** BIS CD 370. (i) Kang; Gothenburg SO, Chung.

Cho-Liang Lin brings as much authority to Nielsen's *Concerto* as he does to the Sibelius and he handles the numerous technical hurdles with breathtaking assurance. His perfect intonation and tonal purity excite admiration, but so should his command of the architecture of this piece; there is a strong sense of line from beginning to end. Salonen is supportive here and gets good playing from the Swedish Radio Symphony Orchestra. A superb bargain.

Dong-Suk Kang is more than equal to the technical demands of this concerto and is fully attuned to the Nordic sensibility. He brings tenderness and refinement of feeling to the searching slow movement and great panache and virtuosity to the rest. The *Fifth Symphony* is hardly less successful and is certainly one of the best-recorded versions now available. Myung-Whun Chung has a natural feeling for Nielsen's language and the first movement has real breadth.

Nikolaj Znaider comes from Denmark but is of Russian parentage and made a very strong impression at the 1999 Ysaÿe Competition in Brussels, taking the first prize in a very strong field. His Nielsen concerto is very well thought out and fervent, though it lacks the total conviction and white-hot inspiration that Cho-Liang Lin and Salonen bring to it. He has very good support from Lawrence Foster and the LPO, but he is slightly self-aware and reluctant to let go.

En aften paa Giske: Prelude (1889); Bøhmiske-dansk folketone; Helios, Overture, Op. 17; Paraphrase on 'Nearer my God, to thee', for Wind Band; Rhapsodic Overture: An Imaginary Journey to the Faeroe Islands; Saga-drøm, Op. 39; Symphonic Rhapsody (1888).

**(*) Chan. 9287. Danish Nat. RSO, Rozhdestvensky.

The *Paraphrase on the Psalm, 'Nearer, my God, to thee', for Wind Band* is both noble and individual. Rozhdestvensky gives musicianly, well-prepared and often poetic accounts of the more familiar pieces, though his *Helios Overture* must be the slowest ever – over 14 minutes! His account of *Saga-drøm* ('The Dream of Gunnar') is also spacious. Very good recording, but in the last analysis these performances are a little deficient in zest.

Symphonies Nos. 1–4; Bohemian-Danish Folk Tune; At the Bier of a Young Artist.

(N)(B) **(*) EMI double fforte (ADD) CZS5 74188-2 (2). Danish RSO, Blomstedt.

Symphonies Nos. (i) 1 in G min. Op. 7; 2 in B min., Op. 16; (i – ii) 3 (Espansiva), Op. 27; (iii) 4 (Inextinguishable), Op. 29; (i) 5, Op. 50; (iii) 6 (Sinfonia semplice); (i; iv) Clarinet Concerto; (i; v) Flute Concerto; (i; vi) Violin Concerto.

(M) *** BIS CD 614/6 (4). Gothenburg SO, (i) Chung; (ii) with Raanoja, Skram; (iii) Järvi; (iv) with Schill; (v) Gallois; (vi) Kang.

Symphonies Nos. 1; 2 (Four Temperaments); (i) 3 (Sinfonia espansiva); (ii) Aladdin (Suite). Maskarade Overture.

(B) *** Double Decca 460 985-2 (2). San Francisco SO, Blomstedt (i) with Kromm, McMillan ; (ii) San Francisco SO Ch.

(i)*Symphonies Nos. 4 (Inextinguishable); 5; 6 (Sinfonia semplice); (ii) Little Suite; (ii; iii) Hymnus amoris, Op. 12.*

(B) *** Double Decca 460 988-2 (2). (i) San Francisco SO, Blomstedt; (ii) Danish Nat. RSO, Schirmer; (iii) with Bonney, Pedersen, Ainsley, M. & B. Hansen, Danish Nat. R. Ch., Copenhangen Boys' Ch.

Symphonies Nos. (i) 1; (ii) 2; (iii) 3; 4; (i) 5; (iii) 6.

*** Chan. 9163/5. RSNO, Thomson.

(B) *** RCA 74321 20290-2 (3). Royal Danish O, Berglund (with soloists in *No. 3*).

(**(*)) Danacord mono DACOCD 351/3. Danish RSO; (i) Tuxen; (ii) Grøndahl; (iii) Jensen.

Blomstedt's complete Decca set of the symphonies is pretty well self-recommending. All six performances are among the finest available: the *First Symphony* has vitality and freshness, and there is a good feel for Nielsen's natural lyricism. Nos. 2 and 3 are possibly the finest of the cycle: Blomstedt finds just the right tempo for each movement. The two soloists are good and the orchestra play with all the freshness and enthusiasm one could ask for. The opening of Blomstedt's *Fourth* has splendid fire: this must sound as if galaxies are forming. The *Fifth Symphony*, too, is impressive: it starts perfectly and is almost as icy in atmosphere as those pioneering recordings of the 1950s. In the *Sixth Symphony* there is no want of intensity, though a broader tempo would

have helped generate greater atmosphere in the first movement. However, the performance is undeniably impressive and like the rest of the series enjoys the advantage of first-class recording.

The fill-ups are also very recommendable. Blomstedt is an eminently reliable guide to the *Aladdin Suite*. Ulf Schirmer, too, shows a natural affinity for Nielsen. On the second of the two Doubles, he gives us Nielsen's early cantata, *Hymnus amoris*, one of his warmest and most open-hearted scores, and there is a also persuasive account of Nielsen's first published opus, the endearing *Little Suite for Strings*. To put it briefly, this remains the best all-round modern set of the symphonies and can be purchased with confidence.

Myung-Whun Chung's accounts of the *First* and *Second* symphonies can hold their own against the best, and his version of the *Sinfonia espansiva* is one of the *very* best – and can be recommended alongside Blomstedt (Decca). The concertos are all excellent – some may even prefer them to the rival collection on Chandos. The package as a whole with four records for the price of three is eminently competitive.

Generally speaking Bryden Thomson's Nielsen symphonies are eminently sound and straightforward, without the extra ounce of finish that we find with the Blomstedt set. They have the merit of being totally unmannered and unfussy, with generally well-chosen tempi. Thomson's version of the *Sixth* is arguably the best now on the market, and his *Fourth* has great fire.

Berglund's set with the Royal Danish Orchestra was recorded between 1987 and 1989. The ever-fresh *First Symphony* is given a thoroughly straightforward account and the *Sinfonia espansiva* (No. 3) is perhaps the finest of his cycle. His two soloists, though unnamed, are very good and the general architecture of the work is well conveyed. The *Fourth* (*Inextinguishable*) is more problematic. In his desire to convey the sense of drama and urgency, Berglund tends to be impatient to move things on, particularly in the closing paragraphs. The *Fifth* opens with a strong sense of atmosphere and the second movement's complex structure is well controlled and satisfyingly resolved. In the *Sinfonia semplice* (No. 6) Berglund again proves a perceptive guide. Here as elsewhere, the playing of the Royal Danish Orchestra is beautifully prepared and full of vitality and the RCA engineers produce a recording of splendid body and presence.

Blomstedt's EMI Nielsen symphony cycle was originally issued in 1975 as part of an 8-LP quadraphonic compilation, also including much of the orchestral music. Now it is reappearing, piecemeal, and comes into direct competition with Blomstedt's later and superior Decca series. These earlier accounts of the symphonies are variable. At the time it was issued No. 1 was arguably the best since Jensen's Decca mono version, with tempi excellently judged. Nos. 2 and 3 are less well characterized, yet are thoroughly alive. No. 4 is very successful, full of vitality, with a thrilling finale, and there is some fine wind playing from the Danish orchestra. The elegiac *Andante lamentoso, At the Bier of a Young Artist*, makes a touching epilogue. The recording is well balanced and clear, but lean-textured – nothing like the quadraphonic LPs.

The Danacord set of three CDs tells us more about Nielsen

than almost any later performances. Only one commercial disc is included: Thomas Jensen's masterly account of the *Sixth Symphony*. Launy Grøndahl's version of the *Second Symphony* (*The Four Temperaments*) has tremendous fire, and Jensen's accounts of the *Third* (*Sinfonia espansiva*) and *Fourth* (*Inextinguishable*) are pretty electrifying. Although allowances must be made for the poor quality of sound in some instances, these performances radiate an authenticity of atmosphere and love of the scores that is quite infectious.

Symphonies Nos. 1; 2 (The 4 Temperaments).

*** Chan. 8880. RSNO, Thomson.

Strong, vigorous accounts of both symphonies from the Royal Scottish Orchestra under Bryden Thomson, with a particularly well-characterized reading of *The Four Temperaments*. The second movement is perhaps a shade too brisk, but in most respects these performances are difficult to fault.

(i) Symphonies Nos. 1; 5; (ii) Helios Overture, Op. 17.

⚫ (M) *** Dutton Lab. mono CDLXT 2502. Danish State RSO; (i) Jensen; (ii) Tuxen.

These are exemplary transfers of the première recording of the *First Symphony* and the first LP recordings of the *Fifth* (the very first was on 78s under Tuxen) and the *Helios Overture*. Jensen and Tuxen both played under Nielsen, and their performances have a special authenticity. The quality of these Decca recordings is captured with absolute fidelity in these stunning transfers; the engineers of the day, working in the pleasingly warm yet crisp acoustic of the Danish Radio concert hall, produced remarkably truthful results. An indispensable issue that belongs in every Nielsen collection.

Symphonies Nos. 1; 6 (Sinfonia semplice).

(N) *** dacapo 8.224169. Danish Nat. R. SO, Schønwandt.
(BB) **(*) Naxos 8.550826. Nat. SO of Ireland, Leaper.

Michael Schønwandt's account of the *Sixth Symphony* is among the most powerful and convincing in the catalogue. He has a good grasp of structure, and in the inspired first movement he is particularly successful in conveying its atmosphere and sense of mystery. The *First* does not come off quite so well: it is sound and well proportioned, but does not carry all before it on an irresistible forward current. Both recordings have excellent sound with a wide dynamic range and vivid detail. As in earlier issues the new Carl Nielsen Edition is used. The *First* is recommendable, but the *Sixth* is now a first recommendation.

Very good performances indeed of Nielsen's first and last symphonies from Adrian Leaper and the National Symphony Orchestra of Ireland. The sound is exceptionally well balanced, with exemplary detail and good perspective. The playing is well prepared, full of vitality, and phrasing is always intelligent. Blomstedt on Decca and Berglund with the Danish Orchestra on RCA are finer still (these players have the music in their blood), but the Naxos disc remains very good value for money.

Symphony No. 2 (Four Temperaments); Aladdin Suite.

*** BIS CD 247. Gothenburg SO, Chung.

Symphonies Nos. 2 (Four Temperaments); (i) 3 (Espansiva).

(BB) *** Naxos 8.550825. Nat. SO of Ireland, Leaper.
*** dacapo 8.224126. Danish Nat. SO, Schønwandt; (i) with Elming.

Symphonies Nos. 2 (Four Temperaments); 5.

*** Classico CD296. RLPO, Bostock.

Myung-Whun Chung has a real feeling for this repertoire and his account of the *Second Symphony* is among the best, while the *Aladdin Suite* is particularly successful. The Gothenburg Symphony Orchestra proves an enthusiastic and responsive body of players. The recording is impressive, too, and can be recommended with enthusiasm.

Adrian Leaper gets vibrant and involving playing from the Dublin orchestra in *The Four Temperaments*, which is as good as any in the catalogue (save for the Jensen), and the *Espansiva* is well paced, with tempi well judged throughout. The orchestra sounds better rehearsed and more accustomed to the Nielsen idiom than they did in their earlier disc, and they are certainly well enough recorded. Not necessarily a first choice but highly competitive.

Both Michael Schønwandt and Douglas Bostock use the new scholarly Complete Edition. In the *Second Symphony*, Nielsen made minor corrections in the orchestral parts after the first printing and these are restored. Schønwandt gets very cultured playing from his fine orchestra, and judges tempi to excellent effect. There is breadth and nobility in *The Four Temperaments* and his account of the *Espansiva* is equally well paced. Its attractions are greatly enhanced by the fine singing of both soloists. This can hold its own with the best.

Bostock's account of *The Four Temperaments* has tremendous character. In the *Fifth*, he really inspires his players, who convey enthusiasm and freshness. Bostock has real identification with Nielsen and though the playing has some rough edges and does not match the finesse or bloom of Blomstedt's San Francisco orchestra, it more than compensates in fire and intensity.

(i) Symphonies Nos. 3 (Espansiva); (ii) 5.

*** Chan. 9067. (i) Bott, Roberts; RSO, Thomson.
(M) **(*) Sony (ADD) SMK 47598-2. (i) Guldbaeck, Moller, Royal Danish O; (ii) NYPO; Bernstein.

Symphonies Nos. (i) 3 (Sinfonia epansiva); 5; Saul and David – Prelude to Act II.

⚫ (M) (***) Dutton Lab. mono CDK 1207. (i) Hasing, Sjøberg; Danish State Radio SO, Tuxen.

Erik Tuxen introduced Nielsen to British audiences after the war. The *Sinfonia epansiva* was recorded as long ago as 1946 for Decca. It shows just how advanced Decca engineering was. It is a vibrant, beautifully judged performance, which casts a stronger spell than many of its successors. The *Fifth Symphony*, recorded in 1950, was another pioneering recording though it was soon eclipsed by Thomas Jensen's LP. In many respects it is its equal and brings us close to this extraordinary score. The Dutton transfer has great detail and presence.

Bryden Thomson's chosen tempi in the *Sinfonia espansiva*

are just right, particularly in the finale. In the slow movement Catherine Bott and Stephen Roberts are excellent, and the performance has a refreshing directness that is most likeable. The *Fifth Symphony* is equally committed and satisfying. The recordings are very good indeed.

Bernstein's genial *Espansiva* with the Royal Danish Orchestra has a lot going for it. And yet, for all the excellence of the orchestral playing, this performance misses something of the music's innocence. Bernstein is at his finest in the *Fifth*, giving an immensely powerful reading, and the passion of the string cantilena and the following movement through into the finale are indicative of the spontaneous feeling which pervades the whole symphony. The well-detailed, resonant recording adds to the impact of the performance.

Symphony No. 4 (Inextinguishable), Op. 29.

(M) *** DG (IMS) 445 518-2. BPO, Karajan – SIBELIUS: *Tapiola.* ***

(N) (B) ** Australian Decca Eloquence (ADD) 466 904-2. LAPO, Mehta – SCRIABIN: *Le Poème de l'extase.* ***

Symphony No. 4 (Inextinguishable); Amor og digteren (Cupid and the Poet) (extracts); Symphonic Rhapsody; (i) Genrebillede (Genre Picture), Op. 6/1; Ariel's Song; Hjemlige Jul.

(N) *** Classico CD298. RLPO, Bostock; (i) Jan Lund.

Symphony No. 4 (Inextinguishable); Pan and Syrinx.

(M) *** EMI (ADD) CDM7 64737-2. CBSO, Rattle – SIBELIUS: *Symphony No. 5.* ***

Symphonies Nos. 4 (Inextinguishable), Op. 29; 5, Op. 50.

(N) *** dacapo 8.224156. Danish RSO, Schønwandt.

(i) Symphonies Nos. 4 (Inextinguishable); 5, Op. 50; (i; ii) Clarinet Concerto; (iii) Violin Concerto; (v) Aladdin: Oriental March; (vi) At the Bier of a Young Artist; Bohemian-Danish Folk Tune.

(B) *** Finlandia Ultima 8573-81966-2 (2). (i) Finnish RSO, Saraste; (ii) Kojo; (iii) Hannisdal, Norwegian R. O, Mikkelsen; (v) Royal Stockholm O, A. Davis;
(vi) Ostrobothnian Chamber O, Kangas.

Symphonies Nos. 4 (Inextinguishable); 6 (Sinfonia semplice).

❀ *** Chan. 9047. RSO, Thomson.

One of the very finest performances of Nielsen's *Fourth* comes from Karajan. The orchestral playing is altogether incomparable; there is both vision and majesty in the reading and a thrilling sense of commitment throughout. The wind playing sounds a little over-civilized – but what exquisitely blended, subtle playing this is. It is also excellently recorded, although there is an editing error in the finale.

Simon Rattle's version of the *Inextinguishable* dates from the late 1970s and is also very fine indeed: it deserves a strong recommendation, particularly given the fact that it comes with an altogether outstanding account of *Pan and Syrinx* (the best ever on record) and his classic account of Sibelius's *Fifth Symphony*. Excellent sound.

In the *Fourth Symphony* Douglas Bostock uses the newly published score in the Complete Nielsen Edition. The orchestral playing is not as polished as in Blomstedt's or Schønwandt's versions, but the reading has tremendous character, and both tempos and phrasing are just right. Bostock includes the early *Symphonic Rhapsody* (1888), using a new scholarly edition, as well as various songs and the Overture and four new excerpts from the incidental music to *Amor og digteren*; this late work, which was written in 1930 for the 125th anniversary of Hans Christian Andersen, is slight but rewarding nonetheless. The orchestral version of the *Genrebillede (Genre Picture)* is also new to the catalogue. Although the *Fourth Symphony* is not a first recommendation, it is certainly among the most fiery and committed accounts to have appeared in recent times. Good, though not outstanding sound.

There can be no doubting the extraordinary energy of Mehta's performance of the *Fourth Symphony* nor the brilliance of the 1974 Decca recording. Though he fails to penetrate the music's fullest depths and disclose all its subtleties, this is still an exciting performance, and the coupling is superb.

The glory of the Ultima set is Saraste's coupling of the *Fourth* and *Fifth Symphonies* – both among the best performances to have appeared in recent years. Saraste and his Finnish orchestra capture the explosive character of the opening of *No. 4* to perfection, and although there are moments when one feels the current could flow with a higher charge, for the most part this performance is splendidly shaped and impressively executed. The *Fifth* is hardly less successful: the conception is spacious yet there is no want of movement. The recorded sound has clarity, though the acoustic is a shade dry. Henrik Hannisdal's account of the *Violin Concerto* is a good one, though not the finest available. The Norwegian orchestra do not match the excellence of the Oslo Philharmonic, but under their conductor, Terje Mikkelsen, they turn in an appealingly unaffected account, and the recording is good. The *Clarinet Concerto*, with Kullervo Kojo, is a strong performance and thoroughly recommendable. With three highly attractive, lighter fill-ups (two of which are quite rare), this Ultima Double is good value.

Michael Schønwandt continues his fine survey of the Nielsen symphonies in the newly published Carl Nielsen Edition with a magisterial *Fifth*. The orchestral playing is sensitive and cultured, but in fire and spirit Schønwandt's *Fifth* must yield pride of place among modern versions to Donald Bostock's rougher but wonderfully characterized account from Liverpool; this also draws on the new Nielsen Edition.

The late Bryden Thomson's coupling of the *Fourth* and *Sixth Symphonies* is by far the most successful of his Nielsen cycle and possibly the finest recording of his career. The *Fourth Symphony* has great sweep and excitement and this account of the *Sixth Symphony* is quite simply the finest version now before the public, and arguably the most penetrating since Thomas Jensen's first recording. Indeed no one brings us closer to the spirit of this music than Thomson, and the recording is very good too. Recommended with enthusiasm.

(i) *Symphonies Nos. 5, Op. 50; 6 (Sinfonia semplice);*
(ii) *Hymnus amoris, Op. 12; Sleep, Op. 18; (iii) Wind Quintet.*

(N)(BB) **(*) EMI Double forte (ADD) CZS 5 74299-2 (2).
(i) Danish RSO, Blomstedt, (ii) Schultz, Göbil, Landy, Norup, Johansen, Anderson, Copenhagen Boys' Ch., Danish RSO, Wöldike; (iii) Melos Ens.

Blomstedt's 1970s Nielsen recordings have been admired by us over the years and stand the test of time, though the symphonies are generally eclipsed by his later Decca accounts. However, the sound in these EMI recordings is more than acceptable and the performances will not disappoint. Neither of the lovely choral cantatas is otherwise available at mid-price and both are eminently worth acquiring. The performances have an appealing freshness. They are not superior to the Chandos accounts, but both are perfectly acceptable. The 1960s Melos account of the *Wind Quintet* still ranks among the best and is also very well recorded.

Symphony No. 6 (Sinfonia semplice).

(N) *** BBC mono BBCL 4059-2. NPO, Leopold Stokowski –
GABRIELI: *Sonata pian e forte;* LISZT: *Mephisto Waltz No. 1;* TIPPETT: *Concerto for Double String Orchestra.* ***

Although Stokowski conducted the *Second Symphony* in Copenhagen, he never recorded any of the symphonies commercially. This account comes from the celebrated centenary series that Robert Simpson mounted in his days as a BBC producer, in which the major works of Sibelius and Nielsen were broadcast. This studio performance from Maida Vale makes one think again about this absorbing and in some ways puzzling score. The first movement comes off marvellously, not that its companions fare less well. Meticulous playing, expertly prepared and thought through, which leaves one regretting that Stokowski never recorded the *Fifth*. The sound is very good and balanced beautifully.

CHAMBER MUSIC

Canto serioso; Fantasias for Oboe & Piano, Op. 2; The Mother (incidental music), Op. 41; Serenata in vano; Wind Quintet, Op. 43.

**(*) Chan. 8680. Athena Ens.

This reissue gathers together Nielsen's output for wind instruments in chamber form, with everything played expertly and sympathetically. The recording is balanced very close; nevertheless much of this repertoire is not otherwise available, and this is a valuable disc.

String Quartets Nos. 1 in G min., Op. 13; 2 in F min., Op. 5.

(BB) *** Naxos 8.553908. Oslo Qt.

String Quartets Nos. 3 in E flat, Op. 14; 4 in F, Op. 44.

(BB) *** Naxos 8.553907. Oslo Qt.

String Quartets Nos. 1–4. . (i) String Quintet in G (1888); (ii) Andante lamentoso (At the Bier of a Young Artist) (1910).

*** BIS CD 503/4. Kontra Qt, (i) Naegele; (ii) Johansson.

String Quartets Nos. 1–4. 5 Quartet Movements, FS2.

*** Kontrapunkt 32150-1. Danish Qt.

String Quartets Nos. 1 ; 4; Little Suite for Strings (arr. Zapolski).

* Chan. 9635. Zapolski Qt.

String Quartets Nos. 2 in F min., Op. 5; 3 in E flat, Op. 14.

(N) *(*) Chan. 9817. Zapolski Qt.

The performances by the Oslo Quartet are spirited, sensitive and very alive. There is a touch of fierceness in the recording quality (they are rather closely balanced) but artistically they are a first recommendation. They also enjoy a hefty price advantage over their Danish rivals.

The Danish Quartet are sensitive to the shape of the phrase, they produce a wide dynamic range, including really soft pianissimo tone when required. They are not always the last word in polish, but everything they do is musical, which makes one forgive the occasional rough edge and the somewhat dry quality and rather close balance of the recording. The set also includes five short movements that Nielsen wrote in his late teens and early twenties.

There is an ardour and temperament to the playing by the Kontra Quartet, which most listeners will find very persuasive. In addition we are given the finest account yet recorded of the *G major String Quintet*, where they are joined by the American violist Philipp Naegele, and the only current account of the *Andante lamentoso (At the Bier of a Young Artist)* in its chamber form. The BIS recordings, made in the Malmö Concert Hall, have plenty of presence and clarity, and are rather forwardly (but not unpleasingly) balanced.

The Zapolski Quartet is so concerned with projecting Nielsen's ideas that the music is never allowed to speak for itself. Those who know these delightful works will view both performances with some impatience, though the playing as such is accomplished and the recording more than acceptable. Just try the scherzo movement of the *E flat Quartet* and you can see for yourself. The directness of utterance of Nielsen's ideas is undermined by over-sophisticated expressive exaggeration. Perhaps the group is not quite as intrusive as it was in the *F major Quartet, Op. 44* but it is still too studied and self-aware. Fortunately the Oslo Quartet is available at a third of the price.

String Quintet in G (1888), FS5.

*** Chan. 9258. ASMF Ens. – SVENDSEN: *Octet.* ***

The *String Quintet in G major* is very well fashioned and owes more to Svendsen, under whose baton the composer was to play, than to his teacher, Gade. It makes both an agreeable and an appropriate companion for Svendsen's early and delightful *Octet*. It receives a three-star performance and recording.

Violin Sonata No. 2 in G min., Op. 35.

*** Virgin VC5 45122-2. Tetzlaff, Andsnes – DEBUSSY; JANACEK; RAVEL: *Sonatas.* ***

Nielsen's *G minor Sonata* is a transitional work in which Nielsen emerges from the geniality of the *Sinfonia espansiva* into the darker and more anguished world of the *Fourth Symphony*. It has much of the questing character of the latter and much of its muscularity. Christian Tetzlaff and Leif Ove Andsnes give a very distinguished – at times inspired – performance, and are accorded excellent recording.

PIANO MUSIC

Chaconne; Dream of Merry Christmas; Festival Prelude; Humoresque-bagatelles, Op. 11; Piano Pieces for Young and Old, Op. 53; 3 Pieces, Op. 59; 5 Pieces, Op. 3; Luciferian Suite, Op. 45; Symphonic Suite, Op. 8; Theme & Variations, Op. 40.

(B) ** Danacord DACOCD 498/499. Miller.

Chaconne; Humoresque-bagatelles; Luciferian Suite; Piano Music for Young and Old, Books I–II; 5 Pieces, Op. 3; 3 Pieces, Op. 59; Symphonic Suite, Op. 8; Theme & Variations, Op. 40.

*(*) dacapo 8.224095/6 (2). Koppel.

Chaconne, Op. 32; Humoresque-bagatelles, Op. 11; 5 Pieces, Op. 3; 3 Pieces, Op. 59; Suite luciferique, Op. 45.

🟢 *** Virgin VC5 45129-2. Andsnes.

Nielsen's piano music is unmissable! The early pieces have great charm and the later *Suite* and the *Three Pieces*, Op. 59, great substance. Although their finest exponent up to now, the Danish pianist Arne Skjold Rasmussen, committed them to disc, he never enjoyed the international exposure to which his gifts entitled him. But now at last they have found a princely interpreter in the Norwegian, Leif Ove Andsnes, who has a natural feeling for and understanding of this music. Indeed these are performances of eloquence and nobility that are unlikely to be surpassed for some years to come, and the recorded sound is vivid and lifelike.

Mina Miller is an American academic who edited the texts of the piano music for the Wilhelm Hansen Edition in 1981 and subsequently recorded them for Hyperion in 1986, of which this is a Double reissue. She really understands what this music is about but does not command the keyboard authority or range of sonority of an Andsnes.

Apart from his distinction as a composer, Herman Koppel's interpretations of Nielsen provide a link with the composer, for as a young man of 21, he played for him. He recorded the *Chaconne* and the *Theme and Variations* in 1940, and again in 1952, in the early days of LP, when he also committed the *Suite*, the *Three Piano Pieces*, Op. 59, and other important works to disc. The present set was recorded in 1982–3, when he was in his mid-seventies and beyond his prime. There is insufficient subtlety in tonal colour and dynamic shading.

VOCAL MUSIC

Amor and the Poet; An Evening at Giske; Cosmus; Sir Oluf He Rides; Tove; Willemoes (incidental music).

**(*) BIS CD 641 Bonde-Hansen, Persson; Lund; Vigant, Danish Nat. Op. Ch.; Aalborg SO, Vetö.

The music to *Herr Oluf han rider* (*Sir Oluf He Rides*) was written at high speed (in one number Nielsen even presses one of his early piano pieces, Op. 3, into service). The overture is very imaginative and deserves to enter the repertoire, but for the most part the music is slight. *An Evening at Giske* (*En aften paa Giske*), the earliest piece on the disc, is well held together. The Overture, *Love and the Poet* (*Amor og Digtaren*), is not dissimilar in style or quality to *An Imaginary Journey to the Færoe Islands*. More engaging than the Kontrapunkt collection with *Hagbarth og Signe*, but of specialist rather than general interest.

(i) *Hymnus amoris;* (ii) *3 Motets, Op. 55; The Sleep, Op. 18;* (iii) *Springtime in Fünen, Op. 43.*

*** Chan. 8853. Soloists; (i) Copenhagen Boys' Ch.; (ii–iii) Danish Nat. R. Ch.; (iii) Skt. Annai Gymnasium Children's Ch., Danish Nat. RSO; (i; iii) Segerstam; (ii) Parkman.

Hymnus amoris is full of glorious music whose polyphony has a naturalness and freshness that it is difficult to resist, and which is generally well sung. The harsh dissonances of the middle *Nightmare* section of *Søvnen* ('The Sleep') still generate a powerful effect. Segerstam gets very good results both here and in the enchanting *Springtime in Fünen*, and the solo singing is good. The three motets actually contain a Palestrina quotation. Generally excellent performances and fine recorded sound.

6 Songs, Op. 10.

*** Virgin VC5 45273-2. Kringelborn, Martineau – GRIEG; RANGSTROM; SIBELIUS: *Songs.* ***

Solveig Kringelborn's anthology includes a half-dozen songs by four composers from each of the Nordic countries. The most neglected are Nielsen's, perhaps because of their uniformly strophic folk-like character. The Op. 10 set is among the most delightful and she sings them with great purity and does them full justice. Only in *Lake of Memory* does she falter. (She is a little under the note.) But this apart, this is a lovely group and we are not well endowed with alternative readings. Malcolm Martineau is superb throughout. Excellent recorded sound too.

(i) *Springtime in Fünen. Aladdin Suite, Op. 34.*

*** Unicorn DKPCD 9054. (i) Nielsen, Von Binzer, Klint, Lille Muko University Ch., St Klemens Children's Ch.; Odense SO, Vetö.

Springtime in Fünen is one of those enchanting pieces to which everyone responds when they hear it, yet which is hardly ever performed outside Denmark. The engaging *Aladdin* orchestral suite is well played by the Odense orchestra. This disc is a little short on playing time – but no matter, it is well worth its cost and will give many hours of delight.

STAGE WORKS

Aladdin (complete incidental music), *Op. 34*.

*** Chan. 9135. Ejsing, Paevatalu, Danish R. Chamber Ch. & SO, Rozhdestvensky.

Until now the *Aladdin* music has been known only from the 20-minute, seven-movement suite, but the complete score runs to four times its length. Some numbers are choral, and there are songs and a short piece for solo flute. Thirteen of the movements are designed to accompany spoken dialogue and, although not all of it is of equal musical interest and substance, most of it is characteristically Nielsenesque, and much of it is delightful. The two soloists, Mette Ejsing and Guido Paevatalu, are very good and the Danish Radio forces respond keenly to Rozhdestvensky's baton. This is not top-drawer Nielsen but, given such a persuasive performance and excellent recording, one is almost lulled into the belief that it is.

OPERA

Maskarade (complete).

*** Decca 460 227-2 (2). Haugland, Resmark, Henning Jensen, Skovhus, Kristensen, Ravn, Bonde-Hansen, Rørholm, Danish Nat. R. Ch. & SO, Schirmer.

It is sad that so brilliant and delightful an opera as *Maskarade* has so far failed to get a foothold in the international repertory, but this superb recording should help to change that, an ideal work for enjoying on disc. The plot is the classic one of young lovers being coerced into arranged marriages by heavy-handed fathers, with the masquerade as the symbol of freedom. The result in the opera is a charming mixture, with echoes of Verdi's *Falstaff* as well as of Johann Strauss's *Fledermaus*. With eighteenth-century flavours invading the idiom, Nielsen has also learnt from Mozart's da Ponte operas. Central to the success of the recording is the weighty performance of the bass, Aage Haugland, as the heavy father, Jeronimus. Though the tenor, Gert Henning Jensen, is light-weight as the son, he characterizes well, as do the rest of the cast, including Susanne Resmark as the wife, Henriette Bonde-Hansen as the heroine, Leonora (who appears only in the second half of the opera), and above all, Bo Skovhus as the servant, Henrik, a key commentator. Ulf Schirmer draws sparkling and idiomatic playing from the Danish Radio Orchestra, recorded in warm, opulent sound.

Saul and David (complete).

⚫ *** Chan. 8911/12. Haugland, Lindroos, Kiberg, Westi, Ch. & Danish Nat. RSO, Järvi.

Nielsen's first opera is here sung in the original language, which is as important with Nielsen as it is with Janáček, and it has the merit of an outstanding Saul in Aage Haugland. The remainder of the cast is very strong and the powerful choral writing is well served by the Danish Radio Chorus. The opera abounds in wonderful and noble music, the ideas are fresh and full of originality. It convinces here in a way that it rarely has before, and the action is borne along on an

almost symphonic current that disarms criticism. A marvellous set.

NIELSEN, Ludolf (1876–1939)

Symphony No. 1 in B min. Op. 3; Fra Bjrgene (From the Mountains: Symphonic Suite), Op. 8.

** dacapo 8.224093. Danish PO, Cramer.

Ludolf Nielsen was eleven years younger than his famous namesake, and like his exact contemporary, Hakan Børresen, a pupil of Svendsen. His *First Symphony* (1903) has real symphonic feeling and a natural grasp of form. The ideas have a touch of Bruckner and of Carl Nielsen too, and it is obvious that Ludolf possessed an original mind. The Danish Philharmonic is the South Jutland Orchestra, based at Odense, and the playing under the German conductor, Frank Cramer, is perfectly acceptable though the recording is not top-drawer. Both the symphony and the suite, Op. 8, are well worth investigating.

Symphony No. 3 in C, Op. 22; Hjortholm, Op. 53.

(N) ** dacapo 8.224098. Bamberg SO, Frank Cramer.

There are six Nielsens other than the famous Carl in the record catalogues, and even one who shares his first name. Like his colleague Hakon Børresen, who has been receiving attention of late, Carl Henrik Ludolf Nielsen was 11 years younger than his celebrated countryman. With him he shares a rural upbringing: he was born in Nørre Tvede, a village near Nstved, where he learned the violin. After studying in Copenhagen and Leipzig, he settled in Hellerup, a quiet suburb of the Danish capital. He was both eclectic and prolific, with some two hundred works to his credit, and served for a time in the viola section of the Tivoli Orchestra and later as its conductor. From 1926 until his death in 1939 Nielsen was with the Danish Radio, planning the programmes of its newly founded orchestra. Whatever his limitations, he has the breadth of a symphonist. His *Third Symphony* (1913) is generally post-romantic with touches of Bruckner and the occasional reminder of the late Dvořák tone poems and of Wagner. However, the work is overlong and not free from bombast. Nielsen was not a great original, but his craftsmanship is expert and his discourse civilised. The tone-poem *Hjortholm*, written in the early 1920s, does not fulfil the promise of its opening. Well-prepared performances and acceptable recording, even if it is wanting the last ounce of transparency.

NORBY, Erik (born 1936)

The Rainbow Snake.

*** BIS (ADD) CD 79. Danish Nat. RO, Frandsen –
BENTZON: *Feature on René Descartes;* JORGENSON: *To Love Music.* **

The Rainbow Snake is an American Indian fable which tells how drought had produced infertility in the land. The snake heard of this and let itself be thrown, coiled up, into the sky where it uncoiled until it touched the earth at both ends. It then arched its back and scraped down the blue ice which had given rise to the drought, thus restoring life to the earth. Every time the sun and rain meet, the snake stretches its luminous body across the heavens. The scoring is highly colourful, the harmonic language impressionist. All highly atmospheric, with kaleidoscopic changes of harmony against an almost static rhythmic background. It is very well played and recorded.

NØRGÅRD, Per (born 1932)

Symphony No. 1 (Sinfonia austera); Symphony No. 2.

*** Chan. 9450. Danish Nat. RSO, Segerstam.

Per Nørgård is the leading Danish composer of his generation. The *Sinfonia austera*, Nørgård's *First Symphony*, comes from 1955 and has a strong atmosphere with something of Holmboe's sense of power and forward movement; impressive and compelling. The *Second* (1970) is different in kind, static in feeling and hypnotic in effect. The 'infinite series' which shaped his *Voyage into the Golden Screen* dominates the whole piece. There are some striking and imaginative effects here. Very good performances too from Leif Segerstam and the Danish National Radio Symphony Orchestra.

NØRHOLM, Ib (born 1931)

Violin Concerto, Op. 60.

*** BIS (ADD) CD 80. Hansen, Danish Nat. RSO, Blomstedt – KOPPEL: *Cello Concerto.* ***

Ib Nørholm's *Violin Concerto* not only evinces considerable imaginative powers but contains some music of real beauty and is expertly laid out for the orchestra. The Danish Radio recording, while not state of the art, is more than acceptable, and it comes with a rewarding coupling.

(i) Symphonies Nos. 4 (Décreation), Op. 76. 5 (The 4 Elements), Op. 80.

** Kontrapunkt CD 32212. (i) Pavlovski, Dahlberg, Høyer, Nørholm, Danish Nat. R. Ch.; Danish Nat. RSO, Serov.

The *Fourth Symphony* (*Décreation*) is highly self-conscious – the sub-title itself, *Moralities* or *There may be many miles to the nearest spider*, puts you in the picture, although there are many imaginative touches during its course. Sadly, inspiration is intermittent and the work as a whole is deficient in thematic vitality. There is a lot going on but very little actually happens. The *Fifth Symphony* (*The Four Elements*) is better, though again its neo-expressionism outstays its welcome. The performances under Eduard Serov are obviously committed, and in the *Fourth* the composer himself is the narrator. Decent recording.

NORMAN, Ludwig (1831–85)

Symphonies Nos. 1 in F min., Op. 22; 3 in D min., Op. 58.

*(*) Sterling CDS 1038-2. Nat. SO of South Africa, Eichenholz.

Ludwig Norman was an interesting figure in Swedish musical life. A champion of Berwald, whose influence can be discerned in the *First Symphony*, he was much drawn to the world of Schumann and Mendelssohn. The former remains the dominant influence not only here but elsewhere in his output. Unfortunately the orchestral playing is wanting in finish and the strings are particularly scruffy. There is little space in which the tutti can expand and the texture lacks transparency.

NOSYREV, Mikhail (1924–81)

(i) Capriccio for Violin & Orchestra; (ii) Piano Concerto; Skazka (Fairy Tale): symphonic poem; (iii) 4 Preludes for Harp.

(N) *** Olympia OCD 696. (i) Gantvang; (ii) Uyash, with Mussorgsky Op. & Ballet O, St Petersburg, Anikhanov; (iii) Donskaya.

Mikhail Nosyrev spent his professional career as a theatre conductor in Voronezh, a major provincial city in Southern Russia. In his early student life he was a victim of Soviet politics: he was arrested at the age of nineteen for 'counter-revolutionary agitation' and imprisoned for ten years in Siberia. There, apparently, the library of the Gulag contained a copy of Rimsky-Korsakov's book on orchestration! Equally amazingly, Nosyrev later became a respected member of the Soviet Composers' Union.

The earliest work here, *Skazka* (1947), which in atmosphere is nearer to Scriabin and Tchaikovsky of *The Tempest* than Rimsky-Korsakov, has a striking but simple principal motif, introduced magically on the oboe, and shows an amazing command of the orchestra. The *Capriccio for Violin* (1957), opening in a mood of dark nostalgia, is in even more traditional style, with a distinctly Russian lyrical melody, but ends in a burst of bravura. The *Piano Concerto* of 1974 is – not surprisingly – more self-consciously avant-garde, with percussive writing for the soloist in the first movement, leading to a brilliant toccata-like *Scherzo* with touches of both irony and lyricism. The elliptical finale, however, begins and ends peacefully.

The harp was the composer's main instrument, and his *Four Preludes* are essentially reflective, exploiting the instrument's full range of colour; the final section is described enigmatically as *Reflections of the Sun*. The performances here are all first class and the recording is excellent. This disc is well worth exploring.

The Song of Triumphant Love (ballet).

(N) *** Olympia OCD 684. Kondina, Voronezh State SO, Verbitsky.

The Song of Triumphant Love is the composer's most successful work. First performed in 1971 it was immensely popular in Voronezh, but the composer's fame did not reach as far as Moscow until after his death. Based on a story by Turgenyev, the ballet is in the Russian romantic tradition, reminiscent of Rimsky-Korsakov, Tchaikovsky and Stravinsky. Beginning with a harp solo, followed by the orchestra then a wordless voice, the scene is immediately set, with characteristic orchestral mastery. There is much extrovert and dramatic writing, as well as subtle colouring, and the large orchestra is used to maximum effect. This music is worth getting to know, and the performance is excellent. The sound is good, though not in the demonstration class.

NOVÁK, Vitězslav (1870–1949)

(i) **Symphonic poems:** *About the Eternal Longing, Op. 33; In the Tatras, Op. 26;* (ii) *Moravian-Slovak Suite, Op. 32.*

*** Virgin VC5 45251. RLPO, Pešek.
(M) **(*) Sup. (ADD) 11 0682-2. (i) Czech PO; (ii) Brno State PO, Sejna.

In the Tatras (1902), an opulent Straussian tone-poem, and *About the Eternal Longing* (1903/4) were inspired by unrequited love for a beautiful young pupil, Růžna. The *Slovak Suite* is a heavenly score. *Two in Love*, its third movement, could well become as widely popular as any piece of music you care to think of. *In the Church*, the opening movement, has something in common with Mozart's *Ave verum corpus*, though more obviously romantic, and the closing *At Night* is beguilingly atmospheric. Libor Peček and the Liverpool orchestra put us firmly in their debt with this Virgin issue. Both performance and recording are first rate. All three works here are also persuasively played on Supraphon. The recording of the two symphonic poems is atmospheric and clear but a bit pale in the more expansive tuttis; the suite has slightly more body and colour.

De profundis, Op. 67; Overture: Lady Godiva, Op. 41; Toman and the Wood Nymph, Op. 40.

(N) *** Chan. 9821. BBC PO, Pešek.

De profundis, Op. 67; Overture: Lady Godiva, Op 41; South Bohemian Suite, Op. 64.

(***) Sup. mono 11 1873-2 011. Brno State PO, Vogel.

Anyone familiar with *The Storm* should be in no doubt as to Novák's stature. A contemporary of Suk, he has been overshadowed understandably by Janáček and Martinů. Not even such an enchanting a work as the *South Bohemian Suite* is heard in the concert hall. *Lady Godiva* and *Toman and the Wood Nymph* come from 1906–7. There is a lot of Dvořák in these pieces and a considerable debt to both Strauss and Mahler, plus an obvious awareness of French musical culture. *Lady Godiva* has something of the opulence of Strauss or the Elgar of *In the South*. It is full of dramatic fire, and its ideas are bold and orchestrated marvellously. Both *Lady Godiva* and *De profundis* are already available, but *Toman and the Wood Nymph* is new to the catalogue. It has the same lush orchestral palette and rich harmonic language. The dark and anguished *De profundis* was written in 1941 at the height of the Nazi occupation for a large orchestra with piano and organ. Stunning recorded sound from Chandos and admirably vivid and idiomatic playing from the BBC Philharmonic under Libor Pešek.

The classic Supraphon performances all come from 1960, except for the *De profundis*, which Jaroslav Vogel recorded two years later. The recordings still sound very good for their period and the performances are very fine. What attractive music it is, too. Recommended.

Pan (symphonic poem), *Op. 43.*

*** Marco 8.223325. Slovak PO, Bílek.

Novák's five-movement symphonic poem, *Pan*, has some lovely music in it, and there is a pantheistic sensibility here. The scoring has great delicacy and imaginative resource, and there is a distinctly Gallic feeling to much of it. Lyrical, often inspired (occasionally a bit overlong – particularly the last movement) and rewarding, this score is beautifully played by the Slovak Philharmonic under Zdenk Bílek, and no less beautifully recorded.

The Storm, Op. 42.

(M) *** Sup. (ADD) SU 3088-2 211. Soloists, Czech PO Ch. & O, Košler.

The Storm is a work of great beauty and imagination, scored with consummate mastery and showing a lyrical gift of a high order. It has warmth and genuine individuality; the idiom owes something to Richard Strauss as well as to the Czech tradition, and there is an impressive command of both melody and structure. The performance is fully worthy and has splendid dramatic feeling, helped by good soloists and a fine chorus. The recording, too, is admirably balanced, and there is depth, and plenty of weight, even if the soloists are rather too forward. This is one of the best Supraphon reissues for some time.

NYMAN, Michael (born 1948)

(i) *Piano Concerto;* (ii) *MGV.*

*** Argo 443 382-2. (i) Stott, RLPO; (ii) Nyman Band, O; composer.

Michael Nyman's brand of minimalism has been most effective in illustrating a whole sequence of films, including the Oscar-winning *The Piano*, in which this concerto was evocatively used. Kathleen Stott's account of the concerto is as fine as one would expect, and the coupling on the Argo CD, *Musique à grande vitesse*, was commissioned for the inauguration of the high-speed TGV train from Paris to Lille. Not surprisingly, it relies on train rhythms, with all their unexpected syncopations. The Michael Nyman Band, heavily amplified, is set as a ripieno group alongside the orchestra, giving the piece what the composer thinks of as concerto grosso associations. Powerful, forward recording.

Noise, Sounds & Sweet Airs.

*** Argo 440 842-2. Bott, Summers, Bostridge, Ens. Instrumental de Basse-Normandie, Debart.

The musical material here is drawn from his opera-ballet, *La Princesse de Milan*, with new vocal lines superimposed over the top, setting a text drawn from Shakespeare's *The Tempest*, 'very heavily and idiosyncratically edited', as Nyman says himself. The oddest idiosyncrasy is that the three different voices keep switching roles, so that the words of Prospero, Miranda and other characters are divided among all three singers. The performance and recording are superb, as vivid as any Nyman on disc, giving the result a hypnotic fascination. The three soloists in particular sing magnificently, each with clear, firm, richly focused voice. Catherine Bott, always compelling, is well matched by the alto, Hilary Summers and the clear-toned young tenor, Ian Bostridge.

NYSTEDT, Knut (born 1915)

Canticles of Praise: Kristnikvede. A Song as in the Night.

** Simax PSC 1190. Bergen Cathedral Ch. and O, Magnersnnes.

At eighty-five, Knut Nystedt is the doyen of Norwegian composers. The *Kristnikvede* or *Canticles of Praise* was commissioned in 1995 to commemorate Olav Trygvason's arrival in Norway in ᵃᵈ 995 and its conversion to Christianity; *A Song as in the Night* was written for a Swedish choral society in the university city of Uppsala. Nystedt's musical language is very direct in utterance, diatonic and well written. He knows exactly what voices can do. There is a faint wisp of Stravinsky and Honegger too. Worthwhile music decently performed, though the choir is not in the first flight and neither is the orchestra. But Nystedt is a composer of substance.

NYSTROEM, Gösta (1890–1966)

(i) *Viola Concerto (Hommage à la France). Ishavet (Arctic Sea);* (ii) *Sinfonia concertante for Cello & Orchestra.*

*** BIS CD 682. (i) Imai; (ii) Ullner; Malmö SO, P. Järvi.

Niels Ullner is a fine cellist with an opulent tone and eloquent phrasing and his is a thoughtful, well-integrated performance of the *Sinfonia concertante*, and the music has both quality and depth. The *Viola Concerto* has a neo-classical and eminently Gallic *joie de vivre*, as well as poignancy. Nobuko Imai plays it superbly and, throughout the whole programme, the Malmö orchestra are in excellent form under Neeme Järvi's son, Paavo. The recording is transparent and has excellent presence and definition.

(i) *Sinfonia del mare; Sånger vid havet (Songs by the Sea);* (ii) *The Tempest: Prelude.*

(N) *** Phono Suecia CD 709. (i) Hellekant; (ii) Swedish R. Ch. & SO, Svetlanov.

All these pieces are inspired by the sea. Nystroem was a gifted painter and was a great admirer of the cubists and Matisse. The *Sinfonia del mare* (1948) is for a large orchestra and includes a wordless role for soprano which is beautifully sung here by the Swedish-born, America-trained mezzo-soprano Charlotte Hellekant. It was quite in vogue in Sweden during the early 1950s, although this performance under Evgeni Svetlanov has a stronger atmosphere and greater concentration than any of his previous recordings. The symphony itself is distinctly short on thematic invention, and its main semitone idea overstays its welcome. *Songs by the Sea* is much stronger and more rewarding. Honegger was a major influence on Nystroem, and his *Tempest* prelude

no doubt acted as a model for Nystroem's own *Prelude* (1934), although the Honegger work was written for women's voices as well as large orchestral forces. Those who warm to the *Sinfonia del mare* should get this dedicated performance under Svetlanov. It supersedes its predecessors and has excellent and natural recorded sound.

Sinfonia espressiva; Sinfonia seria.

*** BIS CD 782. Malmö SO, P. Järvi.

Along with the *Sinfonia concertante* for cello and orchestra, the *Sinfonia espressiva* is probably Nystroem's finest work; finely crafted and purposeful. The fires of inspiration burn less brightly in the *Sinfonia seria* of 1963, though its opening, which recalls Honegger a little, has a certain promise. Paavo Järvi and the Malmö orchestra give committed accounts of both pieces and the BIS engineers produce excellent results.

OBRADORS, Fernando Jaumandreu (1897–1945)

Symphonic Suite: El Poema de la jungla.

*** ASV CDDCA 1043. Gran Canaria PO, Leaper – RODO: *Symphony No. 2.* ***

Fernando Obradors is best known for his collection of classical Spanish songs. *El Poema de la jungla* was begun at the outset of the Spanish civil war and shows his remarkable skill as an orchestrator. It is less imaginative and resourceful than Koechlin's *Le Livre de la jungle*, but colourful and atmospheric all the same. Good performances and excellent recorded sound too.

OBRECHT, Jacob (1457–1505)

Laudes Christo; Missa Malheur me bat.

*** ASV CDGAU 171. Clerks' Group, Wickham – MARTINI: *Motets & Magnificat.* ***

The Dutch composer, Jacob Obrecht, was one of the pioneers in developing a new, more closely organized polyphonic style, notably in his use of segmentation. This is well illustrated in this fine *Mass*, with the theme on which the work is based successively fragmented. There is a sublime summation at the end when the theme is restored to its original form, radiantly performed by the Clerks' Group, and warmly atmospheric sound. The coupling is apt – Obrecht ended up as *Maestro di capella* at the court of Ferrara, where Martini had spent his career.

Missa Caput; Salve Regina: in 4 parts; in 6 parts. Venit ad Petrum.

(BB) *** Naxos 8.553210. Oxford Camerata, Summerly.

The *Missa Caput* survives in a manuscript at the court of Ferrara but could possibly have been compiled in Bruges. Both of the *Salve Regina* settings are based on plainchant melody and are *alternatim* settings, the music alternating between a polyphonic treatment of the chant and the unadorned chant itself. Jeremy Summerly and his Oxford

Camerata, recorded in the Chapel of Hertford College, Oxford, give expert and committed accounts of this music and they are accorded first-class sound.

OCKEGHEM, Johannes (c. 1410–97)

Alma redemptoris mater; Missa Mi-Mi; Salve Regina.

*** ASV CDGAU 139. Clerks' Group, Wickham (with motets by BUSNOIS, ISAAC and OBRECHT).

Ockeghem's *Salve Regina*, the motet *Alma redemptoris mater* and the *Missa Mi-Mi* are contrasted here with motets by three of his contemporaries. The *Missa Mi-Mi* is so named because of the recurring descending fifth, both named 'mi' in the natural and soft hexachords. These performances have a refreshing enthusiasm and the approach to rhythm is remarkably free. The Clerks' Group and Edward Wickham, who specialize in the music of the late Middle Ages and early Renaissance, promise us more Ockeghem, including the *Requiem* – and if the others are as good as this, readers can invest in the series with confidence.

Ave Maria; Intemerata Dei Mater; Missa ecce ancilla Domina.

(N) *** ASV CDGAU 223. Clerk's Group, Wickham (with OBRECHT: *Salve Regina;* JOSQUIN DES PREZ: *Déploration sur la mort de Ockeghem.* ***)

Ecce ancilla Domina is a middle-period mass (*c.* 1470), but its polyphonic richness and unpredictable rhythmic impetus make for compelling listening in a performance so aptly paced and involvingly spontaneous. The *Ave Maria* is relatively familiar (see below), but *Intemerata Dei Mater* (from the 1480s) has a poignant atmosphere all its own which matches the expressive power of Obrecht's six-part *Salve Regina* from the same period. Josquin's valedictory musical farewell in the plaintive Phrygian mode also has links to Ockeghem's moving supplication to the mother of God. This beautifully recorded disc is well up to the high standard of ASV's admirable series.

Missa caput; Ma Maistresse; Missa Ma Maistresse: Kyrie & Gloria.

*** ASV CDGAU 186. Clerks' Group, Wickham (with ANON: Hymn: *O solis ortus cardine;* Motets: *O sidus Hispanie; Gaude Marie.* SARUM CHANT: Antiphon: *Venit ad Petrum*).

Only two movements survive of the *Missa Ma Maistresse*, but very fine they are, bright and extrovert in feeling, making ingenious use of the song material. The song itself is solo-led, ravishingly sung: Ockeghem's lovely setting is fully worthy of the words: '*My mistress and my greatest love, perfect in attributes as ever woman was*'. The cantus firmus of the *Missa Caput* is derivied from the long melisma on the word 'caput' which we have already heard at the end of the Sarum Antiphon, *Venit ad Petrum*. It is perhaps an awkward basis for a mass, but Ockehem's polyphony rises to the challenge, and the work is both texturally and aurally intriguing, yet moves forward on a seemingly inevitable course, in spite of Ockgehem's frequent use of cadences. The three anonymous

motets can be found in the same manuscript which is the earliest source of this mass and it is possible that *O sidus Hispanie*, an eulogy for St Anthony of Padua, was written by Du Fay, who greatly admired this Saint. All the performance here are of the highest order and the recording is first-class too.

Missa De Plus en Plus; Missa Fors seulement.

*** Lyrichord LEMS 8029. Schola Discantus, Moll.

This Lyrichord disc joins the beautiful middle-period four-part *Missa De Plus en Plus* with a later five-part work, *Missa Fors seulement*, based on one of the composer's own chansons, which is unfortunately not included here as it is on Edward Wickam's ASV disc (see below). However the performances are finely sung and blended here and have an appealing simplicity. Ken Moll's varied pacing is convincing. The *Missa Fors seulement* (which only consists of a *Kyrie, Gloria* and *Credo*) is especially striking for its use of two basses, which darkens the texture very strikingly, although Moll takes care not to provide an exaggerated balance.

Missa l'homme armé; Alma redemptoris mater; Ave Maria.

✿ (BB) *** Naxos 8.554297. Oxford Camerata, Summerly (with JOSQUIN DESPREZ: *Memor esto veri tui* ***).

Missa l'homme armé; Missa Sine nomine; Salve Regina (probably by Philippe Basiron).

*** ASV CDGAU 204. Clerks' Group, Wickham (with MORTON (attrib.): *Rondeau: Il sera pour vous (L'Homme armé)* ***).

On Naxos the soaring opening *Ave Maria*, gloriously sung, immediately sets the seal on the inspirational power of Ockeghem's music. It is followed by the plainchant, *Alma redemptoris mater*, and then its polyphonic setting, simple and flowing and harmonically rich. The robust ballad, *L'Homme armé*, follows ('The armed man must be feared'), sounding vigorously jolly, like a carol. It must have been hugely popular in its day since so many composers used it as a basis for a Mass. While the polyphony in the *Gloria* and *Credo* moves onward inventively, the work's dramatic and emotional peak is readily found in the extended *Sanctus* (by far the longest section) and resolved in the sublime melancholy of the *Agnus Dei*. In short, this is a work of striking individuality and beauty, and it is sung superbly here, and marvellously paced. Josquin's setting of sixteen verses from Psalm 119, *Memor esto verbi tui*, with its expressively fertile imitative devices, makes an eloquent postlude, and the recording, made in the Chapel of Hertford College, Oxford, could hardly be bettered. It dates from February 1997, thus aptly celebrating the 500th anniversary of Ockeghem's death.

Ockeghem's striking *L'Homme armé* mass is always easy to follow as its cantus firmus is so characterful. On ASV it is quoted first in a rondeau, attributed to Ockeghem's contemporary, Robert Morton, where it is used mockingly; it is surprising that no translation is given, although it is provided for the other music. Both the *Missa sine nomine* and the *Salve Regina* are dubiously attributed to Ockeghem, but he would surely have been glad to acknowledge the rich polyphony of the latter.

The *Sine nomine mass* for three voices, however, is much less characteristic, although to our ears its flowing lines are very attractive. The performances here are well up to the standard of this excellent group, but the Naxos recording of the *Missa l'homme armé* by the Oxford Camerata is even more attractively coupled.

Missa Prolationum.

*** ASV CDGAU 143. Clerks' Group, Wickham – with BUSNOIS: *Gaude coelestis Domina; In hydraulis.* JOSQUIN DESPREZ: *Illibata dei Virgo nutrix.* OBRECHT (attrib.): *Humilium decus.* PULLOIS: *Flos de spina* ***.

Missa Prolationum; Alma redemptoris mater; Ave Maria; Intemerata Dei Mater; Salve Regina (2 settings).

(M) **(*) Virgin VER5 61484-2. Hilliard Ens.

Missa Prolationum; Requiem; Intemerata Dei Mater.

(BB) **(*) Naxos 8.554260. Musica Ficta, Holten.

Ockeghem was a mathematician as well as a composer, and his *Missa Prolationem* is famous for its intellectually complex polyphony based on double canons, while the rhythmic discipline is also carefully calculated. To all but the most analytical listener this will not matter too much, for the resulting music has a seemingly effortless flow, although the eight-voiced Clerks' Group, without losing melismatic sonority, certainly don't miss the special rhythmic relationships. They support the mass with five diverse motets by Ockeghem's contemporaries (nearly all set to Marian texts), to make a stimulating introduction to other Franco-Netherlands composers of this period. Excellent recording.

The performances by this first-class Danish Choir under Bo Holten on Naxos use a larger group (fourteen in all) and one in which the rich-voiced women singers refine their tone to sound very like boy-trebles when required. The account of the *Missa Prolationem* is particularly rich-textured, and beautifully balanced: the *Sanctus* and *Benedictus* strikingly so. The *Requiem* is also superbly sung, if with the rough edges smoothed off. The *Intemerata Dei Mater* opens the programme. It is sung with considerable feeling and immediately shows the splendid inner blend commanded by this group. Holten moves the polyphony forward with just the right degree of momentum. The choir is very beautifully recorded, but the disc (unusually for Naxos) is let down a little by the absence of English translations.

When this Hilliard collection first appeared (on EMI in 1989) its authenticity and the smoothness of execution were widely praised. The Mass, famous for its polyphonic complexities, is sung with perfect vocal blend and immaculate ensemble, but the characteristic austerity of the Hilliard approach now sounds a little cool alongside the newer version by the Clerks' Group under Edward Wickham on ASV. However, the added attraction of the Hilliard programme is that it also includes similarly flowing accounts of all the known motets of Ockeghem, although the shorter of the two *Salve Regina* settings is now re-attributed to Philippe Basiron. Full texts and translations are provided, so this remains a valuable reissue.

Masses for 3 voices: Missa Sine nomine; Missa Quinti toni.

*** Lyrichord LEMS 8010. Schola Discantus, Moll.

The very austerity of Ockeghem's part-writing, with its serenely flowing polyphony, adds to the potency of his music for modern ears. It is very beautifully sung by a vocal quartet of high quality whose tonal matching and fine tuning are ideal. The recording, too, is clear yet has a perfectly judged ambience.

Requiem (Missa pro defunctis).

*** HM 901441. Ens. Organum, Pages de la Chapelle, Pérès.
(B) *** HM Trio HMX 290891.93 (3) (as above) Ens. Organum, Pérès – MACHAUT: *Messe de Nostre Dame;* HILDEGARD: *Laudes of Saint Ursula.* ***

Requiem; Motet and Missa Fors seulement.

*** ASV CDGAU 168. Clerks' Group, Wickham.

Requiem (Missa pro defunctis); Missa Mi-Mi (Missa Quarti toni).

(M) *** Virgin VER5 61219-2. Hilliard Ens., Hillier.

Ockeghem's *Requiem* remains one of the riddles of medieval liturgical music. Its various surviving movements are very different in style, notation and part-writing, and (rather like the Du Fay *St Anthony Mass*) it was long thought that the manuscript might be a collection of fragments from a number of different works. Even so the *Requiem* holds together with a convincing unity. Of all the available recordings, that by Marcel Pérès and the Ensemble Organum carries the darkest medieval feeling. The conductor's reconstruction is a quite arbitrary one. He even sings the solo plainchants himself, lugubriously but resonantly. Later he adds the (missing) *Sanctus* and *Communion* from a Mass by Antonius Divitis, emphasizing the change by the inclusion of trebles (Les Pages de la Chapelle). Inevitably this must be a controversial account, but it is both gripping and aurally stimulating. This CD additionally comes in a slipcase as part of a Harmonia Mundi Trio at budget price which is highly recommendable, for the recordings of Hildegard and Machaut are no less stimulating.

Certainly every bar of the music is memorable in such a dedicated performance as we have from the Clerks' Group under Edward Wickham, who offer fine blending and tuning, clearly detailed inner parts and a richly flowing line which is seemingly ideally paced. In addition we are offered the *Kyrie*, *Gloria* and *Credo* of the *Missa Fors seulement*, plus the rondeau on which it is based, and further arrangements of the latter by Pierre de la Rue and Antoine Brumel, which offer more splendid music to intrigue the inquisitive ear.

The performances reissued on Virgin Veritas have the expertise, secure intonation, blend and ensemble that one expects from these singers, and the music itself has an austere and affecting simplicity. Although alongside the account of the *Requiem* by the Clerks' Group it has a certain blandness, it would be curmudgeonly not to welcome such generally persuasive accounts of both works.

OFFENBACH, Jacques (1819–80)

Gaîté parisienne (ballet, arr. Rosenthal): complete.

⊛ (M) *** RCA 09026 61847-2. Boston Pops O, Fiedler – ROSSINI/RESPIGHI: *Boutique fantasque.* ***

(M) ** EMI (ADD) CDM7 63136-2. Monte Carlo Op. O, Rosenthal – WALDTEUFEL: *Waltzes.* ***

Gaîté parisienne (ballet: complete); *Offenbachiana* (both arr. Rosenthal).

(BB) ** Naxos 8.554005. Monte-Carlo PO, Rosenthal.

Fiedler's *Gaîté parisienne* is irresistible – one of his very finest records. The orchestra are kept exhilaratingly on their toes throughout and are obviously enjoying themselves, not least in the elegantly tuneful waltzes and in the closing *Barcarolle*, which Fiedler prepares beautifully and to which the generous acoustic of Symphony Hall affords a pleasing warmth without in any way blunting or coarsening the brilliance. The percussion, including bass drum in the exuberant *Can-Can*, adds an appropriate condiment and John Pfeiffer's superb new transfer makes the recording sound remarkably fresh and full. Unbelievably it dates from 1954, one of the very first of RCA's 'Living Stereo' records and still one of the finest.

Maurice Rosenthal's absolutely complete EMI version from the mid-1970s has now been restored to the catalogue. The performance, though often idiomatically persuasive, has not the verve and glamour of that by Fiedler and Karajan. The sound, however, has been greatly improved, with the original excess resonance considerably tempered.

Naxos must have felt that it was quite a feather in their cap to get Manuel Rosenthal to record his own arrangements of these two Offenbach ballets. But alas, as he proved with his previous recording for EMI, he is a less inspiring conductor than he is an arranger. He obviously chooses ballet dance tempi and while the orchestra responds with playing of elegance and polish, and the wind soloists are all very good, the absence of uninhibited zest is a great drawback, especially in the famous final *Can-can*.

(i) *Gaîté parisienne* (ballet, arr. Rosenthal; complete); (ii) *Overtures & Suites* from: *Orpheus in the Underworld* (1874 version, with *Pastoral Ballet*); *Le Voyage dans la lune* (with *Snowflakes Ballet*).

(M) *** Ph. (ADD) 442 403-2. (i) Pittsburgh SO, Previn; (ii) Philh. O, Almeida.

An outstanding coupling. In *Gaîté parisienne* Previn realizes that tempi can remain relaxed and the music's natural high spirits will still bubble to the surface. The orchestral playing is both spirited and elegant, with Previn obviously relishing the score's delightful detail. The *Snowflakes Ballet* from *Le Voyage dans la lune* is a charmer, and the ballet from *Orpheus in the Underworld* is hardly less delectable. The other surprise is the *Orpheus Overture*, not the one we know but a more extended work in pot-pourri style, with some good tunes. Almeida is no less high-spirited than Previn, and the Philharmonia's response is both polished and elegant. Excellent recording too.

Gaîté parisienne (ballet, arr. Rosenthal): extended excerpts.

(B) *** DG (ADD) 429 163-2. BPO, Karajan – CHOPIN: *Les Sylphides* *** ⊛; DELIBES: *Coppélia:* suite. ***

Karajan's selection is generous. On the DG disc, only Nos. 3–5, 7 and 19–21 are omitted. The remastering of the 1972 recording is highly successful; textures have been lightened to advantage, and the effect is to increase the raciness of the music-making, while its polish and sparkle are even more striking.

Gaîté parisienne (ballet: excerpts); *Orpheus in the Underworld: Overture.*

(M) ** Sony (ADD) SMK 61830. NYPO, Bernstein – BIZET: *Symphony in C* **; SUPPE: *Beautiful Galathea: overture.* ***

Bernstein's quite enjoyable performance of excerpts from *Gaîté parisienne* dates from 1969, and would be more recommendable if the ballet were recorded complete and the sound was less brash. The *Orpheus in the Underworld* overture comes off well, and the (1967) recording is richer here than in *Gaîté parisienne*.

Overtures: *La Belle Hélène; Bluebeard; La Grande-Duchesse de Gérolstein; Orpheus in the Underworld; Vert-vert.* Barcarolle from *Contes d'Hoffmann.*

**(*) DG (IMS) 400 044-2. BPO, Karajan.

Other hands besides Offenbach's helped to shape his overtures. Most are on a pot-pourri basis, but the tunes and scoring are so engagingly witty as to confound criticism. Karajan's performances racily evoke the theatre pit. The Berlin playing is very polished and, with so much to entice the ear, this cannot fail to be entertaining; however, the compact disc emphasizes the dryness of the orchestral sound; the effect is rather clinical, with the strings lacking bloom.

Overture: *La Belle Hélène* (arr. Haensch); (i) *Les Contes d'Hoffmann: Entr'acte et Barcarolle.*

*** Chan. 9765. (i) RLPO Ch.; BBC PO, Y. P. Tortelier (with Concert: *French bonbons* ***).

Haensch's *Overture La Belle Hélène* is a far better piece than the more famous overture to *Orpheus in the Underworld*. A stylish pot-pourri, it includes two of the opera's best tunes, the disarmingly seductive waltz, and a delightfully songful siciliano given to the oboe; it then ends with a brief, infectious can-can. Tortelier has its full measure, shaping it with great style and affection, and reminding us of Martinon's justly famous LPO mono Decca version (which needs a Dutton Lab. reissue). The *Barcarolle*, too, is very seductive, and both are given state of the art recording. This is part of an unmissable concert of '*French bonbons*'.

Le Papillon (ballet; complete).

(B) *** Double Decca (ADD) 444 827-2 (2). Nat. PO, Bonynge – TCHAIKOVSKY: *Nutcracker.* ***

Le Papillon is Offenbach's only full-length ballet and it dates from 1860. The quality of invention is high and the music sparkles from beginning to end. In such a sympathetic performance, vividly recorded (in 1972 in the Kingsway Hall), it cannot fail to give pleasure.

Cello Duos, Op. 54: Suites Nos. 1–2.

(B) *** HM 1901043. Pidoux, and Péclard.

Offenbach was himself a very accomplished cellist, and these two works are tuneful and imaginatively laid out to exploit the tonal possibilities of such a duo. Offenbach's natural wit is especially apparent in the *First Suite in E major*. The performances are excellent and so is the recording.

OPERA

La Belle Hélène (complete).

***EMI (ADD) CDS7 47157-8 (2). Norman, Alliot-Lugaz, Aler, Burles, Bacquier, Lafont, Capitole Toulouse O, Plasson.

The casting of Jessye Norman in the name-part of *La Belle Hélène* may seem too heavyweight, but the way that great soprano can lighten her magisterial voice with all the flexibility and sparkle the music calls for is a constant delight, and her magnetism is irresistible. John Aler, another American opera-singer who readily translates to the style of French operetta, makes a heady-toned Paris, coping superbly with the high tessitura in the famous Judgement couplets and elsewhere. The rest of the cast is strong too, not forgetting Colette Alliot-Lugaz as Oreste, who had such a dazzling success in the central role of Chabrier's *L'Etoile* in John Eliot Gardiner's brilliant recording. Michael Plasson here produces similarly fizzing results, with excellent ensemble from the chorus and orchestra of the Capitole. Excellent, lively recording.

Les Brigands (complete).

**(*) EMI CDS7 49830-2 (2). Raphanel, Alliot-Lugaz, Raffalli, Trempont, Le Roux, Lyon Opera Ch. & O, Gardiner.

Les Brigands has a Gilbertian plot about brigands and their unlikely association with the court of Mantua, with the *carabinieri* behaving very like the police in *The Pirates of Penzance*. The tone of the principal soprano, Ghislaine Raphanel, is rather edgily French, but the rest of the team is splendid. Outstanding as ever is the characterful mezzo, Colette Alliot-Lugaz, in another of her breeches roles. Warm, well-balanced recording. (This recording has been deleted as we go to press.)

Les Contes d'Hoffmann (The Tales of Hoffmann): complete.

⊕ *** Decca (ADD) 417 363-2 (2). Sutherland, Domingo, Tourangeau, Bacquier, R. Suisse Romande and Lausanne Pro Arte Ch., SRO, Bonynge.

**(*) Ph. (IMS) 422 374-2 (3). Araiza, Lind, Studer, Norman, Von Otter, Ramey, Dresden Ch. & State O, Tate.

On Decca Joan Sutherland gives a virtuoso performance in four heroine roles, not only as Olympia, Giulietta and Antonia but also as Stella in the *Epilogue*. Bonynge opts for spoken dialogue, and puts the Antonia scene last, as being the more substantial. His direction is unfailingly sympathetic, while Sutherland is impressive in each role, notably as the doll Olympia and in the pathos of the Antonia scene. As Giulietta she hardly sounds like a *femme fatale*, but still produces beautiful singing. Domingo gives one of his finest performances on record, and so does Gabriel Bacquier. It is a memorable set, in every way, much more than the sum of its parts.

Jeffrey Tate in this textually troubled work uses a new expanded edition prepared by Michael Kaye, where dialogue replaces all the recitatives written by Ernest Guiraud. The Prologue is more extended, showing the transformation of the Muse into Nicklausse, with extra material in the Olympia and Antonia Acts too. Jessye Norman, the Antonia of the new set, cunningly lightens her voice, making it sound as girlish as she can, but it is still hard to imagine her as the fragile young girl destined to die. Tate's determination to adopt an authentic text leads him to reject the wonderful septet, based on the *Barcarolle* theme, not even including it in an appendix. Nor is Dapertutto's *Scintille, diamant* included, drawn originally from another Offenbach work, when the authentic *Tourne, tourne miroir* is restored at that point. Samuel Ramey sings very well in all four villainous roles, with satisfyingly firm, dark tone, but principal vocal honours go to Anne Sofie von Otter as a superb Muse and Nicklausse, making one relish all the extra music given the character in this version. Eva Lind is bright and clear, if a little edgy and shallow, as Olympia, perfectly doll-like in fact; and Cheryl Studer is technically very strong and confident, even if she does not quite sound in character. Francisco Araiza makes an agreeable Hoffmann, but he lacks the flair of his finest rivals.

Les Contes d'Hoffmann: highlights.

(M) *** Decca (ADD) 458 234-2 (from above set, cond. Bonynge).

The newly compiled Decca highlights disc is one of the finest set of excerpts of its kind from any opera. With about 70 minutes of music, it offers a superbly managed distillation of nearly all the finest items and is edited most skilfully, including both the vocal and orchestral versions of the famous *Barcarolle*.

Orphée aux enfers (Orpheus in the Underworld; 1874 version).

*** EMI (ADD) CDS7 49647-2 (2). Sénéchal, Mesplé, Rhodes, Burles, Berbié, Petits Chanteurs à la Croix Potencée, Toulouse Capitole O, Plasson.

Plasson recorded his fizzing performance – the first complete set in French for 30 years – using the far fuller four-act text of 1874 instead of the two-act version of 1858, so adding such delectable rarities as the sparkling *Rondo* of Mercury and the Policemens' chorus. Mady Mesplé as usual has her shrill moments, but the rest of the cast is excellent, and Plasson's pacing of the score is exemplary. The recording is brightly atmospheric and the leavening of music with spoken dialogue just enough. The newer recording by Minkowski of the alternative version is a disappointment (in spite of an impressive cast), over-driven and without the effervescence of the Plasson set.

Orpheus in the Underworld: highlights of English National Opera production (in English).

**(*) That's Entertainment CDTER 1134. Kale, Watson, Angas, Squires, Bottone, Pope, Belcourt, Styx, Burgess, E. Nat. Op. Ch. & O, Elder.

The sparkling English National Opera production depends a lot for its fun on the racy new adaptation and translation by Snoo Wilson and the ENO producer, David Pountney. Offenbach devotees should be warned: there is little of Parisian elegance in this version and plenty of good knock-about British fun, brilliantly conveyed by the whole company, including Bonaventura Bottone's hilariously camp portrait of a prancing Mercury. Bright, vivid recording to match the performance.

La Périchole (complete).

(M) *** Erato (ADD) 2292 45686-2 (2). Crespin, Vanzo, Bastin, Lombard, Friedmann, Trigeau, Rhine Op. Ch., Strasbourg PO, Lombard.

**(*) EMI CDS7 47362-8 (2). Berganza, Carreras, Bacquier, Sénéchal, Trempont, Delange, Toulouse Capitole Ch. & O, Plasson.

Though both Régine Crespin in the title-role and Alain Vanzo as her partner, Piquillo, were past their peak at that time, their vocal control is a model in this music, with character strongly portrayed but without any hint of vulgar underlining. Crespin is fresh and Vanzo produces heady tone in his varied arias, some of them brilliant. Jules Bastin is characterful too in the subsidiary role of Don Andres, Viceroy of Peru. Lombard secures excellent precision of ensemble from his Strasbourg forces, only occasionally pressing too hard. The recorded sound is vivid and immediate.

Though the sound in Toulouse is over-reverberant, the CD remastering has sharpened the impact, and diction is surprisingly clear against the full orchestral sound. The incidental roles are superbly taken, but it is odd that Spaniards were chosen for the two principal roles. José Carreras uses his lovely tenor line to fine effect but is often unidiomatic, while Teresa Berganza – who should have made the central character into a vibrant figure, as Régine Crespin used to – is surprisingly heavy and unsparkling. The CD disc-break is well placed between the Acts, but cueing might have been more generous.

Robinson Crusoe (sung in English).

*** Opera Rara ORC 7 (3). Brecknock, Kenny, Kennedy, Hartle, Hill Smith, Oliver, Browne, Geoffrey Mitchell Ch., RPO, Francis.

More ambitious than Offenbach's operettas, *Robinson Crusoe* offers a sequence of fresh and tuneful numbers with many striking ensembles. The plot is derived less from Daniel Defoe than from the British pantomime tradition. Characterization is strong and amusing, with a secondary couple shadowing Crusoe and his beloved Edwige. The casting is also from strength, with John Brecknock and Yvonne Kenny outstanding as Crusoe and Edwige, while Man Friday, as in the original Paris production, is sung by a mezzo, Sandra Browne. On the three discs are 3 hours of music, covering numbers which the composer cut even from the original production. The witty English translation, very freely adapted from the French text, with some changes of plot, is by Don White, and words are admirably clear.

La Vie parisienne (complete)

*** EMI (ADD) CDS7 47154-8 (2). Crespin, Mesplé, Masson, Sénéchal, Trempont, Benoit, Chateau, Lublin, Toulouse Capitole Ch. & O, Plasson.

Hardly less effervescent than the parallel version of *Orpheus in the Underworld*, also conducted by Michel Plasson for EMI, *La Vie parisienne* is a scintillating example of Offenbach's work, an inconsequential farce around the heady days of the International Exhibition in Paris. Though the EMI recording is not quite as consistent as the one of *Orphée aux enfers*, the performance and presentation sparkle every bit as brilliantly, with the spoken dialogue for once in a special attraction. Régine Crespin, in a smaller role, is most commanding and, though the cast lacks the excellent Vanzo and Massard, the style is captivatingly authentic. The CD transfer is vivid, without loss of ambient atmosphere.

'The World of Offenbach': Overtures: (i–ii) La Belle Hélène; (iii–iv) La Fille du tambour-major; (i–ii) Orpheus in the Underworld; (iii–iv) Le Papillon: Pas de deux (excerpt); Valse des rayons. Les Contes d'Hoffmann: (v; i; iv) Ballad of Kleinzach; O Dieu! De quelle ivresse (vi; i; iv) Doll song (vi–vii; i; iv) Barcarolle (2 versions). La Grande Duchesse de Gérolstein: (viii–x) Portez armes . . . J'aime les militaires. La Périchole: (viii; i; x) O mon cher amant (Air de lettre); Ah! quel dîner. (vi; i; iv) Robinson Crusoé: Conduisez-moi vers celui que j'adore (Waltz song). (xi; iv) Valse tyrolienne.

🎵 (M) *** Decca ADD/Dig. 452 942-2. (i) SRO; (ii) Ansermet; (iii) LSO; (iv) Bonynge; (v) Domingo; (vi) Sutherland; (vii) Tourangeau; (viii) Crespin; (ix) V. Volksopernorchester; (x) Lombard; (xi) Jo, ECO.

This 'lucky-bag' of Offenbachian goodies which Decca have expanded for CD from the original LP selection is bursting with lollipops to make a marvellously entertaining 74 minutes. The programme now opens and closes with the *Barcarolle*. Ansermet and Bonynge offer much character in the overtures; even if the former takes the famous can-can which closes the *Orpheus* overture more slowly than usual, he invests it with much rhythmic vigour. Bonynge has another scintillating can-can to offer in *La Fille du tambour-major*, which opens with an arresting side-drum, and he now also includes two items from Offenbach's only ballet, *Le Papillon*. The various excerpts from Bonynge's complete *Contes d'Hoffmann* are matched by Régine Crespin's delightful contribution as *La Périchole*, and Sutherland returns to sing the *Waltz song* from *Robinson Crusoé*. The other additional item is Sumi Jo's sparkling *Valse tyrolienne*. With splendidly vivid recording this is an unmissable sampler, to match and even surpass 'The World of Borodin'.

ORFF, Carl (895–1982)

Carmina Burana.

*** EMI CDC5 55392-2. Dessay, Hampson, Lesne, Choeur d'enfants de Midi-Pyrénées, Orféon Donostiarra, Toulouse Capitole O, Plasson.

*** Decca 430 509-2. Dawson, Daniecki, McMillan, San Francisco Boys' & Girls' Choruses, San Francisco Symphony Ch. & SO, Blomstedt.

(M) *** Ph. 464 725-2. Gruberová, Aler, Hampson, Shinyukai Ch., Knaben des Staats & Berlin Cathedral Ch., BPO, Ozawa.

✿ (M) *** Sony (ADD) SBK 47668. Harsanyi, Petrak, Presnell, Rutgers University Ch., Phd. O, Ormandy.

(N) *** Guild GMCD 7227. Herrera, Holt, Kelly, Guadalope Basilica Boys' Ch., Mineria Academy of Music Ch. & O, De La Fuente.

*** EMI (ADD) CDM5 66899-2 [566951]. Armstrong, English, Allen, St Clement Danes Grammar School Boys' Ch., L. Symphony Ch., LSO, Previn.

(M) *** DG 447 437. Janowitz, Stolze, Fischer-Dieskau, Schöneberger Boys' Ch., Berlin German Op. Ch. & O, Jochum.

(BB) *** RCA Navigator 74321 17908-2. Hendricks, Aler, Hagegård, St Paul's Cathedral Boys' Ch., L. Symphony Ch., LSO, Mata.

(BB) **(*) Virgin 2 x 1 Double VBD5 61510-2 (2). Watson, Bowman, Maxwell, Highcliffe Junior Ch., Waynflete Singers, Bournemouth Symphony Ch. & SO, Hill – HOLST: *The Planets; Perfect Fool* (suite). **(*)

**(*) Teldec 9031 74886-2. Jo, Kowalski, Skovhus, LPO Ch., Southend Boys' Ch., LPO, Mehta.

(N) (BB) **(*) EMI Encore (ADD) CDE5 74742-2. Popp, Unger, Wolansky, New Philh. Ch. & O, Frühbeck de Burgos (with STRAVINSKY: *Circus Polka; Fireworks.* **(*)

(N) **(*) Arte Nova 74321 34048-2. Liebeck, Hill, Barrell, New L. Children's Ch., Tallis Chamber Ch., L. Fest O, Pople.

(B) **(*) [EMI Red Line CDR5 69868]. Augér, Van Kesteren, Summers, Southend Boys' Ch., Philh. Ch. & O, Muti.

(B) ** Decca Penguin (ADD) 460 646-2. Burrows, Devos, Shirley-Quirk, Brighton Festival Ch., RPO, Dorati.

Carmina Burana is very well served on CD, but Michel Plasson's EMI performance, recorded in Toulouse, is rather special. It is sumptuously packaged, as CDs seldom are, and not only is the choral singing extraordinarily vivid, it is as seductively warm in pianissimos as it is incisively vibrant in fortissimos. The three soloists are the finest on record. Thomas Hampson's tender first entry, *Omnia sol temperat* ('The sun rules over all'), is matched by his great vigour in the *Tavern scene*, and Gérard Lesne's alto timbre is uniquely suited to the *Song of the roast swan*. The trebles open *Amor volat undique* with knowing Gallic delicacy, and Lesne and Hampson combine to make the sequence *Si puer cum puella* ('If a boy with a girl') quite delectable, topped by Natalie Dessay's tenderly ravishing *Stetit puella*. The choral *Tempus est iocundum* brings the fullest expression of sexual rapture, into which the trebles from the Midi-Pyrénées enter with enthusiasm, if without quite the knowing exuberance which

English boy-trebles bring to it. But Plasson's closing *Ave formosissima – O Fortuna* has splendid grandeur, and this outstandingly recorded new version must go straight to the top of the list.

Blomstedt's is also among the finest modern versions of Orff's exhilaratingly hedonistic cantata. Throughout the choral singing, men, boys, and girls all enjoy themselves hugely – as they should, with such stimulating words to sing. They generate great passion and energy and all three soloists are equally outstanding. John Daniecki's use of vocal colouring is entertainingly diverse, while Kevin McMillan is a splendidly unctuous Abbot, and Lynne Dawson portrays the girl in the red tunic with sensuous innocence. Blomstedt's reading is full of imaginative touches of light and shade, yet the flow of passionate energy is paramount. He is helped by the remarkable range and sonority of the Decca recording, very much in the demonstration bracket.

Ozawa's digital recording of Orff's justly popular cantata carries all the freshness and spontaneity of his earlier successful Boston version. The *Cours d'amours* sequence is the highlight of his reading, with the soprano, Edita Gruberová, highly seductive; Thomas Hampson's contribution is also impressive. Ozawa's infectious rubato in *Oh, oh, oh, I am bursting out all over*, interchanged between male and treble chorus towards the end of the work, is wonderfully bright and zestful, with the contrast of the big *Ave formosissima* climax which follows made to sound spaciously grand. Taken overall, this Philips version holds its position near the top of the list alongside Ormandy, and it has the additional advantage of spectacular digital recording.

Ormandy and his Philadelphians have just the right panache to bring off this wildly exuberant picture of the Middle Ages by the anonymous poets of former days, and there is no more enjoyable analogue version. It has tremendous vigour, warmth and colour and a genial, spontaneous enthusiasm from the Rutgers University choristers, men and boys alike, that is irresistible. The soloists are excellent, but it is the chorus and orchestra who steal the show; the richness and eloquence of the choral tone is a joy in itself. This is quite splendid, one of Ormandy's most inspired recordings and, even if you already have the work in your collection, this exhilarating version will bring additional delights. (This is also available as a Super Audio CD: SS6163.)

It is surprising that Orff's *Carmina Burana* has not been recorded live more often, for the presence of an audience can stimulate an extra tautness, immediately apparent on the Guild version in the genial vigour with which the chorus welcomes spring (*Ecce gratum*). The warm ambience of the Sala Mezahualcoyotl in Mexico City has already enveloped the listener, providing a sense of space and perspective. Even if the quieter choral enunciation is less sharp than it would be in the studio, the rich orchestral tapestry, capped with percussion, makes a splendid backcloth, while Herrera de la Fuente's zestful pacing ensures a vigorously spontaneous forward flow. The singing of the Mineria Chorus is first class, with the boys' voices especially fresh and full of bounce in *Veni, veni, venias*. The Mineria Academy Orchestra, too, add characterful wind and brass colours: their comments lacing the tenor's *Tale of the Roasted Swan* are engagingly grotesque. Ben Holt gives a spirited personification of the

Abbot, and the male tavern chorus follows on with gleeful, uninhibited impetus. However, it is the soprano, Gabriella Herrera, who stands out, nostalgically chaste in *Siqua sine socio*, radiantly feminine in *Stetit puella*, and soaringly celestial in *Dulcissime*, her rapturous moment of submission. The closing choral *Ave formossima* has exultant grandeur, and the tension builds to a remarkable final climax (helped by a splendid bass drum). No wonder the audience bursts into applause even before the final words have died away.

Previn's 1975 analogue version, vividly recorded, is even more sharply detailed than Ozawa's. It is strong on humour and rhythmic point. The chorus sings vigorously, the men often using an aptly rough tone; and the resilience of Previn's rhythms, finely sprung, brings out a strain not just of geniality but of real wit. This is a performance which swaggers along and makes you smile. Among the soloists, Thomas Allen's contribution is one of the glories of the music-making, and in their lesser roles the soprano and tenor are equally stylish. The digital remastering is wholly successful: the choral bite is enhanced, yet the recording retains its full amplitude.

Jochum's 1968 recording of *Carmina Burana* has never sounded better than it does in this reissue. The choral pianissimos lack the very last degree of immediacy, but the underlying tension of the quiet singing is very apparent. Fischer-Dieskau's singing is refined but not too much so, with the kind of tonal shading that a great Lieder singer can bring; he is suitably gruff in the Abbot's song – so much so that for the moment the voice is unrecognizable. Gerhard Stolze too is very stylish in his falsetto *Song of the roasted swan*. The soprano, Gundula Janowitz, finds a quiet dignity, rather than an overt sensuality for her contribution and this is finely done. The closing scene is moulded by Jochum with wonderful control, most compelling in its restrained power.

Mata's splendid 1980 digital recording now comes at super-bargain price and is highly recommendable on all counts. It is a joyously alive and volatile reading, not as metrical in its rhythms as most; this means that at times the London Symphony Chorus is not as clean in ensemble as it is for Previn. The choristers of St Paul's Cathedral sing with purity and enthusiasm but are perhaps not boyish enough, though the soloists are first rate (with John Aler coping splendidly, in high, refined tones, with the Roast Swan episode). There is fine warmth of atmosphere and no lack in the lower range; indeed in almost every respect the sound is superb. This is unbeatable value for those wanting a bargain-priced version.

David Hill's Bournemouth recording has a choral bite and an exhilarating rhythmic zest that carries the music thrustfully forward. Among the soloists Donald Maxwell makes a strenuously boisterous Abbot, his solo punctuated with spectacular percussion; but one wonders whether a counter-tenor was a good choice for the song about the roasting swan. Here a falsetto can have a more piquant edge. Janice Watson sings with enticing femininity: her red shift is obviously just a temporary covering. The boys' chorus are as pubescently eager as you could wish. This is excitingly vivid, and it is a pity that this reissue is so poorly documented. There are no texts or translations included, indeed virtually no information whatsoever to inform the listener of the meaning of the Latin titles of the work's twenty-five cued sections.

Mehta's newest Teldec version is often enjoyably vigorous, it has good soloists and an excellent choral response, with the Southend boys throatily enjoying their pubescent spree. Sumi Jo is a seductive and rather knowing Girl in the Red Shift who submits willingly, rising nimbly up her ascending scale to a spectacularly floated pianissimo. But Boje Skovhus makes a strongly vibrant rather than a subtle contribution. The recording, made at The Maltings, Snape, is resonantly spectacular, especially in the matter of the orchestral percussion, but the quieter choral passages are a little recessive. In the last resort this is not a first choice, for Mehta's direction is not as imaginative or as spontaneously exuberant as that of his finest competitors.

While the New Philharmonica performance under Burgos has no lack of vitality, it is in the more lyrical pages that Burgos scores, with his imaginative care for detail and obvious affection. The sheer gusto of the singing is the more remarkable when one considers the precision from both singers and orchestra alike. The brass, too, brings out the rhythmic pungency which is such a dominating feature of the work, helped by a very bright CD transfer. Lucia Popp's soprano solo, *Amor volat*, is really ravishing and Gerhard Unger, the tenor, brings a Lieder-like sensitivity to his lovely singing of the very florid solo in the tavern scene. The new coupling of early works by Stravinsky is hardly apt, but they are well played and this Encore disc is certainly worth its very modest cost.

With brilliant and atmospheric modern digital recording, Ross Pople's super-bargain version has a lot going for, it including vibrant singing and clear enunciation from the modest-sized but excellent Tallis Chamber group and the highly animated New London Children's Choir. Much of it is very enjoyable, but in *Tempus es iocundum* Pople's constant fluctuations of tempi detract from the feeling of unbuttoned sexual abandon. Among the solo contributions, Martin Hill's *Tale of the Roasted Swan* is suitably bizarre, and David Barrell makes an unctuous Abbot. The soprano, Anne Liebeck, sings sweetly and with virginal freshness, though her *Dulcissima* leap is dramatic rather than rapturous, and when the chorus follows, their *Ave formossima* is very broad indeed. It is certainly jubilant, but Pople almost loses the forward impetus, fortunately regaining it in the closing *O Fortuna*. However, this account does not have the overwhelming impact of the new Mexican version. And it was a pity that Arte Nova have supplied the Latin texts only – without translation.

Muti's is a reading which underlines the dramatic contrasts, both of dynamic and of tempo, so the nagging ostinatos as a rule are pressed on at breakneck speed; the result, if at times a little breathless, is always exhilarating. The soloists are first rate; the Philharmonia Chorus is not quite at its most polished, but the Southend Boys are outstandingly fine. However, the digital remastering of the 1980 analogue recording is disappointing. The chorus and soloists seem to have lost a degree of immediacy.

Dorati's version was recorded in the Kingsway Hall in 1976 in Decca's Phase Four system. The result is a beefy, vibrant account with good singing and playing. Despite some eccentric speeds, Dorati shows a fine rhythmic sense, but the performance cannot match the best available. The remastered recording brings a bold impact in fortissimos, but the quieter, more atmospheric passages are less cleanly defined. Now reissued on the bargain Penguin Classics label with an essay by John Berendt, it hardly makes a primary choice.

Catulli Carmina.

(M) *** DG (IMS) (ADD) 449 097-2. Augér, Ochman, Berlin Op. Ch., 4 pianos & percussion, Jochum – EGK: *The Temptation of St Anthony.* ***

(B) **(*) Sony (ADD) SBK 61703. Blegen, Kness, Temple University Ch., Phd. O, Ormandy – STRAVINSKY: *Symphony of Psalms.* ***

Catulli Carmina; Trionfo di Afrodite.

✪ *** EMI CDC5 55517-2. Schellenberger, Odinius, Linz Mozart Ch., Munich R. O, Welser-Möst.

Orff's sequel to *Carmina Burana* (using much the same formula, but with the accompaniment scored for four pianos and percussion) cannot match its predecessor in memorability, but for anyone hypnotized by the composer's vital rhythmic ostinatos this is the work to recommend next, and certainly so in Franz Welser-Möst's vibrant performance, complete with enthusiastic crowd noises and superlative choral singing that in its sharpness and precision lifts the music clear of banality. The soloists, too, are excellent, the soprano, Dagmar Schellenberger, revelling in the sensuous upper tessitura which is so like the music for the Girl in the Red Tunic in *Carmina Burana*.

Trionfo di Afrodite is scored for large orchestra, including three pianos and plentiful percussion; with more nagging rhythmic repetitions it pays its hedonistic tribute to the pleasures of love in a similarly exhilarating manner. The vibrant *Invocation to Hymenaeus* brings a curious reminder of *Petrushka* but stirringly returns us to Orff's world of ostinatos until the arrival of the bride at the wedding chamber brings a series of spoken exhortations by the leader of the guests with vehement choral interruptions. The work ends dramatically with a vision of Aphrodite, which brings an immensely bold closing chorus and a final explosion of enthusiasm from the assembled guests. It is an extraordinary dramatization, and it is brought thrillingly to life by Welser-Möst and his combined soloists, singers and orchestra, working splendidly as a team and superbly recorded.

Until the arrival of the Welser-Möst version, Jochum's performance of *Catulli Carmina* was never surpassed. His chorus sings with sharp, rhythmic point and, if imagination is called for in such music, Jochum matches flexibility with a spark of humour in his control of mechanistic rhythms. His soloists are individual and sweet-toned. The recording is very fine, although even on CD evocative pianissimos sound a little recessed.

The exotic colours and rhythmic ostinatos are also well brought out by the Temple University Choir, and Ormandy's vigorous performance produces an altogether rougher experience than Jochum's version, for all the virtuosity of the players and singers. But the bluff humour of the piece comes out boldly. The 1967 recording is generally good,

a little thin by modern standards, particularly at the top end, but nothing too serious. An undoubted CD bargain with the excellent Stravinsky coupling.

(i) Die Kluge; (ii) Der Mond.

(M) *** EMI (ADD) CMS7 63712-2 (2). (i) Cordes, Frick, Schwarzkopf, Wieter, Christ, Kusche; (ii) Christ, Schmitt-Walker, Graml, Kuen, Lagger, Hotter; Philh. Ch. & O, Sawallisch.

Sawallisch's pioneering Orff recordings of the mid-1950s are vivid and immediate on CD, with such effects as the thunderbolt in *Der Mond* impressive still. Elisabeth Schwarzkopf is characterful and dominant as the clever young woman of the title in *Die Kluge*. It is good too to hear such vintage singers as Gottlob Frick and Hans Hotter in unexpected roles. Musically, these may not be at all searching works, but both short operas provide easy, colourful entertainment, with Sawallisch drawing superb playing from the Philharmonia. No texts are provided, but the discs are very generously banded.

PACINI, Giovanni (1796–1867)

Maria, Regina d'Inghilterra (complete).

(N) *** Opera Rara ORC 15. Miricioiu, Ford, Fardilha, Plazas, Miles, Bickley, Geoffrey Mitchell Ch., Philh. O, Parry.

With an outstanding cast, full, well-balanced recording and powerful, well-paced conducting, this long-neglected opera about Mary Tudor emerges as a surprisingly strong and enjoyable piece, far finer than most conventional Ottocento operas from the contemporaries of Donizetti and Bellini. The admittedly improbable story is loosely based on a Victor Hugo play, centring on the love of Mary for Fenimoore (high tenor), her scheming favourite, also loved by Clotilde, who in turn is loved and protected by Ernesto (baritone). Add to that the Chancellor (bass), who is determined to unmask Fenimoore's evil-doing, and you have an operatic plot that gives ample scope for confrontation in duets and ensembles, skillfully and imaginatively exploited by Pacini.

Nelly Miriciou sings with warmth and character as the suffering Queen, not least in her final agonized aria on Fenimoore's execution. She is well contrasted with the lighter Mary Plazas as Clotilde, with José Fardilha as Ernesto, distinctive with his flickering vibrato. Alastair Miles sings powerfully as the Chancellor, but it is the prowess of Bruce Ford in the demanding role of Fenimoore that more than anything holds the piece together, from his first evocative off-stage entry in Act 1. David Parry draws strong, idiomatic playing from the Philharmonia, with the Geoffrey Mitchell Choir intensifying the big ensembles.

PACIUS, Fredrik (1809–91)

Kung Karls Jakt (King Charles's Hunt) (opera): complete.

(M) *** Finlandia 1576 51107-2. Törnqvist, Lindroos, Krause, Grönroos, Jubilate Ch., Finnish Nat. Op. O, Söderblom.

Fredrik Pacius became known as 'the father of Finnish

music', for he brought the Finnish capital, then a provincial backwater, into contact with the mainstream of European music. His opera *King Charles's Hunt* brings pretty simple musical ideas. Some are pleasant but there is little evidence of much individuality. There is some fine singing from Pirkko Törnqvist as the fisherman's daughter, Leonora, Peter Lindroos as her fiancé, and from Walton Grönroos as the coup leader, Gustaf Gyllenstjerna. The young King is a speaking role. Much care has been lavished on the production and Ulf Söderblom holds things together admirably. No masterpiece is uncovered but it will be of interest to collectors with a specialist interest in the beginnings of opera in the northern countries.

PADEREWSKI, Ignaz (1860–1941)

Piano Concerto in A min., Op. 17.

*** Hyp. CDA 66452. Lane, BBC Scottish SO, Maksymiuk – MOSZKOWSKI: *Piano Concerto.* ***

Paderewski's *Piano Concerto* opens with strong thematic promise, and the secondary lyrical material is attractive too. The central *Romanza* brings another very winning theme, and throughout the invention has genuine vitality. Even if some of the passage-work is relatively conventional, the work is well worth having back in the catalogue, especially when Piers Lane gives a performance that is poetic and subtly coloured, as well as vivacious. In that he has an accompaniment from the BBC Scottish Orchestra under Maksymiuk that is as alert as it is spirited.

Symphony in B min. (Polonia), Op. 28.

**(*) Hyp. CDA 67056. BBC Scottish SO, Maksymiuk.

Paderewski's *Symphony in B minor* is a mammoth affair. Its first movement alone takes half an hour, and the finale is almost as long. It occupied him for five years (1903–8) and runs to 74 minutes. It would have been longer had he added a scherzo as he had originally planned. Although some of the ideas are unmemorable and the symphony is undoubtedly overblown, it is far from negligible. Moreover it has a certain sweep and is very well laid out for the orchestra. It is far more interesting than the admittedly much earlier *Piano Concerto.* If, for example, you enjoy the Glière symphonies, you should try it. The BBC Scottish Symphony Orchestra play well for Jerzy Maksymiuk and the only minor reservation is the recording quality, which is a bit opaque.

PAGANINI, Niccolò (1782–1840)

Andante amoroso; Balletto campestre (Variations on a Comic Theme) (orch. Tamponi); *Larghetto con passione; Moto perpetuo in C, Op. 11; Polacca with Variations in A; Sonata for Grand Viola; Sonata Maria Luisa in E; Sonata Varsavia; Variations on The Carnival of Venice; Variations on a Theme from Rossini's Mosè.*

(B) *** EMI (ADD) CZS7 67567-2 (2). Accardo, COE, Tamponi.

Salvatore Accardo here explores the by-ways of Paganini's concertante music for violin and orchestra (with one piece for viola), and much of the virtuosity is stunning – sample the *Moto perpetuo.* As can be seen from the listing, Paganini's favourite device was a set of variations on a simple, often ingenuous theme, alternating *galant* lyricism with fiendish bravura. Accardo is equally at home in both. The orchestral accompaniments are of minimal interest but they are warmly supportive; the flattering ambience of the recording and the good balance ensure that the sounds reaching the listener are pleasingly believable. There are, however, no notes about the music.

Violin Concertos Nos. 1–6; 24 Caprices, Op. 1; Duo merveille; Introduction & Variations on 'Di tanti palpiti' from Rossini's Tancredi; Introduction & Variations on 'Nel cor più non mi sento' from Paisiello's La molinara; Maestoso scnata sentimentale; Perpetuela; La primavera; Sonata with Variations on a Theme by Joseph Weigl; Sonata Napoleone; Le streghe (Variations on a Theme by Süssmayr), Op. 8; Variations on 'God save the King'; Variations on 'Non più mesta' from Rossini's La Cenerentola.

(B) *** DG 463 754-2 (6). Accardo, LPO, Dutoit.

A self-recommending set. The Accardo/Dutoit Paganini cycle remains a secure first choice: the concertos are brilliantly and imaginatively played and well recorded accounts which do not fall down in any department. The individual discs are contained in an excellently packaged DG bargain box.

Violin Concertos Nos. 'o' in E (orch. Mompellio); 2 in B min.

(N) (M) *(**) EMI CDC5 57150-2. Accardo, O da Camera Italiana.

Violin Concertos Nos. 1 in D, Op. 6; 3 in E.

(N) (M) *(**) EMI CDC5 57151-2. Accardo, O da Camera Italiana.

Violin Concertos Nos. 4 in A min.; 5 in A min. (orch. Mompellio).

(N) (M) *(**) EMI CDC5 57152-2. Accardo, O da Camera Italiana.

Phonè Italia have prevailed on Accardo to re-record the Paganini concertos and have provided what is described as an additional work, discovered in London as recently as 1972. The manuscript for the so-called No. 'o' was scored for guitar accompaniment which has been filled out and orchestrated very convincingly by Federico Mompiello. However, this is in fact the same concerto as the posthumous No. 6 included by DG. It almost certainly dates from just before the first concerto, and it might be regarded as a model for that familiar piece, for it has a rather similar (if not so memorable) lyrical secondary theme in the first movement and plenty of solo display in the finale.

Accardo's consummate technique and his persuasive musical response are as impressive as ever, as are his dazzling fireworks. The finales of Nos. 1 and 2 have great flair. He also directs the orchestral accompaniments, and very impressively too. The snag is the recording, which spotlights the solo violin, and brings an unwanted excess of digital brilliance to the orchestra which fiercens the orchestral strings in all the fortissimos. There is plenty of weight but the upper range is often unagreeably shrill. The DG set is the one to go for.

Violin Concertos Nos. (i; ii) 1 in D, Op. 6; (iii; iv) 2 in B min., Op. 7; (v) 3 in E; (i; ii) 4 in D min.; (i; vi) Introduction & Variations on 'Di tanti palpiti' (arr. Kreisler); Le streghe, Op. 8 (arr. Kreisler); (iii; vii) Caprices, Op. 1, Nos. 13 & 20 (arr. Kreisler); 24 (arr. Auer); (viii) Moto perpetuo, Op. 11.

(B) ** Ph. (ADD) Duo 462 865-2 (2). (i) Grumiaux; (ii) Monte Carlo Op. O, Bellugi; (iii) Gitlis; (iv) Warsaw Nat. Philharmonic SO, Wislocki; (v) Szeryng, LSO, Gibson; (vi) Castagnone (piano); (vii) Janopoulo (piano); (viii) ASMF, Marriner.

This set is a mixed success. The first CD contains Grumiaux's 1972 recordings of the *First* and *Fourth Concertos*, which are extremely good performances, full of bravura, yet highly musical. Grumiaux really comes into his own in the slow movements, and the outer movements tingle with excitement. The orchestra plays with passion, and the recording, albeit within the characteristic Monte Carlo acoustic, is warm and full. In the *Third Concerto*, Szeryng is not so well recorded, and Gibson's accompaniments, whilst fully acceptable, lack flair. The snag with this set is the *Second Concerto*: the performance is undistinguished and the sound thin. At bargain price, the set is worth considering for Grumiaux's readings alone, and the various fill-ups are a bonus.

Violin Concerto No. 1 in D, Op. 6.

*** EMI (ADD) CDC7 47101-2. Perlman, RPO, Foster –
  SARASATE: *Carmen Fantasy.* ***
*** DG (IMS) 429 786-2. Shaham, NYPO, Sinopoli –
  SAINT-SAENS: *Concerto No. 3.* ***
**(*) EMI CDC5 55026-2. Chang, Phd. O, Sawallisch –
  SAINT-SAENS: *Havanaise; Intro. & Rondo capriccioso.* **(*)

(i) Violin Concerto No. 1. Caprices for Solo Violin Nos. 1, 3–4, 9–11, 14, 16–17, 24.

(B) *** DG (ADD) 439 473-2. Accardo; (i) LPO, Charles Dutoit.

(i) Violin Concerto No. 1 in D, Op. 6; Introduction & Variations on 'Nel cor più non mi sento' (from Paisiello's La molinara); (ii) Cantabile; La campanella; Moses Fantasia.

✿ *** BIS CD 999. Gringolts; with (i) Lahti SO, Vänskä; (ii) Ryumina.

Violin Concerto No. 1 in D, Op. 6; I palpiti; Perpetuela; Sonata Napoleone.

(M) *** DG (ADD) 439 981-2. Accardo, LPO, Dutoit.

The seventeen-year-old Russian violinist Ilya Gringolts plays the Paganini *D major Concerto* and the remainder of this recital not only with quite astonishing virtuosity but also with impeccable taste. Like Salvatore Accardo in the 1970s, he brings a refinement and noblesse to this repertoire, and indeed manages to make some of these display pieces really sound like music. There is an ardent quality to the playing,

and a natural finesse that silences criticism. In the *Violin Concerto* and the *Introduction and Variations on 'Nel cor più non mi sento'* (from Paisiello's *La molinara*), the Lahti orchestra under Osmo Vänskä give excellent support, and the BIS recording is in the highest traditions of the house – natural and lifelike.

Itzhak Perlman demonstrates a fabulously clean and assured technique and, with the help of the EMI engineers, he produces a gleamingly rich tone, free from all scratchiness. Lawrence Foster matches the soloist's warmth with an alive and buoyant orchestral accompaniment. Provided one does not feel strongly about Perlman's traditional cuts, there has been no better record of the *D major Concerto*.

Accardo's account is second to none in its sense of lyrical style, finesse and easy bravura. The selection of solo *Caprices*, too, is well made, including the most famous of all, which so many other composers have used for variations of their own. Accardo presents his selection with an eloquence far beyond mere display. Excellent recording.

Accardo's account is also available recoupled at mid-price with attractive, shorter concertante pieces, of which the *Perpetuela* is quite dazzling and *I Palpiti* is like an operatic air with variations.

Gil Shaham's technical ease in the histrionics of Paganini's stratospheric tessitura, harmonics and all, is breathtaking, and he can phrase an Italianate lyrical melody – and there are some good ones in this concerto – with disarming charm and ravishing timbre. His dancing spiccato in the finale is a joy and, however high he ascends, there is never a hint of scratchiness. Sinopoli's finely graduated and often dramatic accompaniment could hardly be more sympathetic.

Sarah Chang recorded this famous bravura concerto in Philadelphia. The slow movement is fresh and direct rather than romantic, but she knows how to charm the ear gently. The finale is dazzling. Chang can bounce her bow with aplomb and never fails to entice the ear. Sawallisch gives her admirable support, but the recording is flattering neither to soloist (balanced close) nor to orchestra, which lacks sumptuousness.

Violin Concertos Nos. 1; 2 in B min. (La campanella), Op. 7.

(BB) *** Naxos 8.550649. Kaler, Polish Nat. RSO, Gunzenhauser.
(B) *** DG (ADD) 429 524-2. Ashkenazy, VSO, Esser.

Ilya Kaler is fully equal to Paganini's once-devilish technical demands and the phrasing of warm Italianate melody. In every respect his technique is commandingly secure. Stephen Gunzenhauser is a sympathetic accompanist throughout, and the Polish Radio Orchestra play with suppleness and bring a sense of elegance and style to this music. There is no lack of dazzle in the fireworks, and no damp squibs here. With very good notes, this is an excellent example of a Naxos super-bargain at its best.

Ashkenazy's coupling of the two favourite Paganini concertos is also good value. He surmounts all the many technical difficulties in an easy, confident style and, especially in the infectious *La campanella* finale of No. 2, shows how completely he is in control. The microphone is close, but his timbre is sweet and the high tessitura and harmonics are always cleanly focused.

Violin Concertos Nos. 3 in E; 4 in D min.

(N) (BB) **(*) Naxos 8.554396. Rózsa, Slovak RSO, Dittrich.

Ernö Rózsa is a first class soloist, fully equal to all Paganini's pyrotechnical demands, and on his bow the characteristic cantabile tunes (often over pizzicato accompaiments) sing out very winningly. He also plays his own cadenzas, which are perhaps rather too much of a good thing when these two concertos are quite long enough already! Michael Dittrich opens the first movement of No. 3 at an agreeable jog-trot, but then follows his soloist who relaxes for the lyrical passages. The result is that the movement lasts for just over 22 minutes, and the bass-heavy orchestral tuttis do not help to give a music a great deal of lift. The acoustic is not ideal but the recording of the orchestra (and the scoring) in No. 4 seems fresher, and the performance cannot be faulted when the soloist plays so enticingly and with such easy bravura, especially in the attractive *Rondo* finale.

CHAMBER MUSIC

Allegro di concert (Moto perpetuo) in C, Op. 11; Cantabile in D, Op. 17; Centone si sonate: in D; in A, Op. 64/2 & 4; Guitar & Violin Sonatas: in A; A min.; E min., Op. 3/1, 4 & 6; Grand Sonata for Violin & Guitar in A, Op. posth.; Sonata concertata in A, Op. 61; Sonata a preghiera (arr. Hannibal).

*** DG 437 837-2. Shaham, Söllscher.

The atmosphere of much of this repertoire is comparatively intimate, something these artists readily appreciate, and their playing is immaculate and amiably easy-going. Perhaps at times here the style of performance could with advantage have been more extrovert, but the present hour-long recital will make attractive late-evening entertainment (not taken all at once, of course). The recording has a realistic balance and fine presence.

Cantabile & Valse; 6 Sonatas for Violin & Guitar, Op. 2; Sonata for Grand Viola & Guitar; Variations di bravura on Caprice No. 24.

(B) **(*) Naxos 8.550759. St John, Wynberg.

Cantabile in D; 6 Sonatas for Violin & Guitar, Op. 3; Sonata concertata in A; Variations on Barucabà, Op. 14.

(B) **(*) Naxos 8.550690. St John, Wynberg.

Scott St John plays with flair and considerable virtuosity: his approach has more extrovert dazzle and rather less charm than the performances on DG, and he dominates the performances strongly. The recording venue is resonant, which means close microphones, but the violin timbre is bright without being edgy.

Centone di sonate for Violin & Guitar, Nos. 1–12.

(BB) **(*) Naxos 8.553141 (Nos. 1–6); 8.553142 (Nos. 7–12) (available separately). Hammer, Kraft.

Moshe Hammer plays with plenty of character and an agree-able cantabile line: his style lies somewhere between those of Scott St John and Terebesi on Teldec. He is truthfully recorded in a resonant ecclesiastical acoustic, and the effect is slightly smoother in Volume 2 (*Sonatas Nos. 7–12*), made three months after Volume 1. But both records reproduce realistically and offer enjoyable music-making.

Grand Sonata; Sonata concertata (both for violin and guitar).

(N) (BB) *** H.M. HCX 3957116. Huggett, Savino –
    GIULIANI: *Duo concertante for Violin & Guitar, Op. 25.* ***

Monica Huggett and Richard Savino create a winning partnership in these intimate and amiable works. The *Romanza* of the *Grand Sonata* (a siciliano) is played very gently and persuasively, to be followed by an ingenuous Theme and Variations introduced by the guitar. The *Sonata* is slightly more ambitious in its writing for the latter instrument, but remains essentially an agreeable dialogue. The performances are attractively elegant and most naturally recorded.

24 Caprices, Op. 1.

(M) *** DG 429 714-2. Accardo.
(M) *** EMI CDM 67237-2 [567257]. Perlman.
(BB) *** Naxos 8.550717. Kaler.
(M) *** Decca (IMS) (ADD) 440 034-2. Ricci.
*** Telarc CD 80398. Ehnes.
(M) **(*) Teldec 9031 76259-2. Zehetmair.

Accardo succeeds in making Paganini's most routine phrases sound like the noblest of utterances and he invests these caprices with an eloquence far beyond the sheer display they offer. There are no technical obstacles and, both in breadth of tone and in grandeur of conception, he is peerless. He observes all the repeats and has an excellent CD transfer.

Perlman's superbly played 1972 set now returns to the catalogue at mid-price as one of EMI's 'Great Recordings of the Century'. The transfer is immaculate, the violin image very real and vivid, and this can now be recommended without reservation alongside Accardo on DG.

Those looking for a bargain will surely not be disappointed with the Russian fiddler, Ilya Kaler, on Naxos. A pupil of Leonid Kogan, his playing is technically very assured, the lyrical bowing vibrant in a Slavic way, and, like Ricci, he projects a strong profile. The 1992 Naxos recording is truthful and real.

Ricci's Decca recording dates from 1959 but it is remarkably vivid and present. Ricci's playing often offers a breathtaking display of bravura and, oddly enough, his very occasional imperfections (usually minor slips of intonation) come at points where they are least expected – in the easier rather than the more difficult parts. The playing has great personality and the quicksilver articulation is often dazzlingly precise, conveying enormous dash, for instance in *No. 5 in A minor*. However, Perlman and Accardo are even more polished.

James Ehnes is Juilliard-trained and has technique to burn. He tosses off these pieces with great bravura and aplomb. His playing has real personality, even if others have managed to find greater subtlety and delicacy. All the same, there is much to relish in his youthful ardour and the splendid sound the Telarc engineers give us.

Thomas Zehetmair has a somewhat more reticent personality and seems to want to avoid virtuosity for its own sake. His style of articulation in the faster passages at times has an almost throwaway quality, but he soars most agreeably in the lyrical writing and his timbre above the stave is richly caught by the recording. There is much to appreciate and enjoy in these performances, but in the last resort Zehetmair projects less charisma than his competitors.

Caprice No. 24, Op. 1/24; Grand Sonata in A.

(B) *** Sony (ADD) SBK 62425. Williams (guitar) –
  GIULIANI: *Variations on a Theme by Handel;*
  D. SCARLATTI: *Sonatas;* VILLA-LOBOS: *5 Preludes.* ***

Grand sonata in A.

(B) **(*) Decca 448 709-2. Fernández – GIULIANI; VIVALDI: *Concertos.* **(*)

John Williams is in excellent form in the *Grand Sonata*, with its charming central *Romanza* and ingenuous closing *Andantino variato* (originally a duo for guitar and violin), and the famous *Caprice*, for violin solo, both arranged by Williams. The recording is only marginally balanced too forwardly and is otherwise truthful. Most enjoyable.

Fernández's playing is rightly much admired by fellow guitarists. His technique is immaculate and his somewhat self-effacing approach always puts the composer first. He is beautifully recorded and the effect is engagingly intimate to suit the gentle, improvisatory nature of his playing, especially the pensive central *Romanza*. Some might feel that the finale needs more extrovert feeling, but there is certainly no lack of dash or bravura.

PAINE, John Knowles (1839–1906)

Symphony No. 1 in C min., Op. 23; Overture, As You Like It.

*** New World NW 374-2. NYPO, Mehta.

Paine's symphonies were milestones in the history of American music, and it is good that at last Mehta's fine recordings of both of them will allow them to be appreciated more widely. Paine consciously inspires echoes of Beethoven, with little feeling of dilution – though, after his dramatic C minor opening, he tends to relax into sweeter, more Mendelssohnian manners for his second subject and the three other movements. What is striking is the bold assurance, and the overture is also full of charming ideas. Mehta is a persuasive advocate, helped by committed playing and full, well-balanced recording.

Symphony No. 2 in A, Op. 34.

*** New World NW 350-2. NYPO, Mehta.

Written four years after the *First Symphony*, this magnificent work is both more ambitious and more memorable than its predecessor and, far more remarkably, anticipates Mahler. The idiom is notably more chromatic than that of the *First*, and the other movements – introduced by an extended slow introduction – bring an element of fantasy, as in the fragmented rhythms and textures of the Scherzo. Mehta draws a strongly committed performance from the New York Philharmonic, and the sound is first rate.

PAISIELLO, Giovanni (1740–1816)

Piano Concertos Nos. 1–8.

**(*) ASV CDDCS 229 (2). Monetti, ECO, Gonley.

Piano Concertos Nos. 1 in C; 5 in D; 7 in A; 8 in C.

*** ASV CDDCA 873. Monetti, ECO, Gonley.

Piano Concertos Nos. 2 in F; 3 in A; 4 in G min.; 6 in B flat.

**(*) ASV CDDCA 872. Monetti, ECO, Gonley.

Mariaclara Monetti reveals herself to be an artist who can produce a silk purse out of more humble material, for her playing here is both sparkling and elegant. Paisiello obviously was primarily an opera composer, and these concertos, though not wanting grace or fluency, are often very conventional in most other respects. But with a ready facility Paisiello could certainly spin an expressive cantilena. No complaints about the recording, and on the whole the first of the two discs is the one to go for. As can be seen, the eight concertos are also available as a boxed set, though with no saving in cost.

PALESTRINA, Giovanni Pierluigi da (1525–94)

Ave Regina Caelorum; Lamentations of Jeremiah I–III; Gloriosi principes terrae; Missa in duplicibus minoribus II.

*** DHM 05472 77317-2. Maîtrise de Garçons de Colmar, Ens. Binchois, Cantus Figuratus, Vellard.

This ensemble produce singing of exceptional purity and quality. The Marian antiphon, *Ave Regina Caelorum*, is for two choruses, one high and one low, and was printed in 1575. The *Missa in duplicibus minoribus*, which belongs to the Mantuan repertoire, was discovered in Milan as late as 1950 and is not otherwise available. All this material is sung with impressive control, a wonderfully integrated balance and great beauty of tone. Those who find Palestrina too bland should investigate this eloquent and beautifully recorded disc.

Canticum canticorum Salomonis (Fourth Book of Motets for 5 voices from the Song of Songs).

*** Hyp. CDA 66733. Pro Cantione Antiqua, Turner.

The *Canticum canticorum Salomonis* is one of Palestrina's most sublime and expressive works, possibly wider in its range than anything else he composed, and certainly as deeply felt. His disclaimer in the dedication to Pope Gregory XIII, which Bruno Turner quotes at the beginning of his notes ('There are far too many poems with no other subject than love of a kind quite alien to the Christian faith'), cannot disguise the fervour which he poured into these 29 motets. The ten members of the Pro Cantione Antiqua under Bruno

Turner bring an appropriate eloquence and ardour, tempered by restraint. They are accorded an excellently balanced and natural-sounding recording. This music is not generously represented on disc, but no one acquiring this is likely to be disappointed.

Canticum canticorum; Madrigals for 5 voices, Book I: 8 Madrigali spirituali.

(M) *** Virgin VED5 61168-2 (2). Hilliard Ens., Hilliard.

The Hilliard Ensemble provide beautifully shaped performances, with refined tonal blend and perfect intonation, but they are more remote and ultimately rather cool in emotional temperature. The second CD includes eight Petrarch settings from the First Book of Madrigals. Excellent recording.

Lamentations of Jeremiah

(N)(M) *** Regis RRC 1038. Cantione Antiqua, Turner.

Many composers have set the Lamentation Lessons for the Tenebrae services on Maundy Thursday, Good Friday and Holy Saturday but, remarkably, Palestrina did so on five different occasions, the present (fourth) setting was discovered only at the beginning of the nineteeth century, and it is recorded here complete for the first time. The music has a serene but poignant simplicity, which Bruno Turner captures admirably with spacious tempi. The concentration is obvious and the quality of the singing from a group of eight (including several famous names) is of a high order. So is the recording, which is very well balanced in the warm acoustic of St Alban's Church, Brook Street, London.

Masses

'The Palestrina 400 collection': Missa Assumpta est Maria (with Plainchant: Assumpta est Maria); Motet: Assumpta est Maria. Missa Benedicta es (with Plainchant: Benedicta es. JOSQUIN: Benedicta es). Missa brevis; Missa Nasce la gioia mia (with PRIMAVERA: Madrigal: Nasce la gioia mia). Missa Nigra sum (with Plainchant: Nigra sum. LHERITIER: Nigra sum). Missa Papae Marcelli. Missa Sicut lilium inter spinas; Motet: Sicut lilium inter spinas.

(M) *** Gimell ADD/Dig. CDGIM 890 (4). Tallis Scholars, Phillips.

This highly recommendable and well-documented box gathers together four CDs recorded by the Tallis Scholars between 1981 and 1989. As is their practice, this group records the Masses together with the motets on which they are based, even if they are by other composers. Their account of the most famous of Palestrina's works, the Missa Papae Marcelli, brings a characteristically eloquent performance.

Missa Aeterna Christi munera; Missa Papae Marcelli.

(BB) **(*) Naxos 8.550573. Oxford Camerata, Summerly.

Summerly's are bold, flowing performances, lacking something in mysticism and ethereal dynamics, but sung very confidently, with textures clear and the performances alive and compelling. The Oxford Camerata consists of twelve singers, of whom a third are female, and the blend is impressive. The account of the lesser-known Missa Aeterna Christi munera is particularly compelling. The recording was made in Dorchester Abbey, so the ambience is flattering, although the balance is fairly close.

Missa Assumpta est Maria; Missa Sicut lilium.

*** Gimell CDGIM 920. Tallis Scholars, Phillips.

After the Missa Papae Marcelli, the Missa Assumpta est Maria is one of Palestrina's most sublime works. Its companion on this CD is based on the motet, Sicut lilium inter spinas ('Like a lily among thorns'). As is their practice, the Tallis Scholars record the Masses together with the motets on which they are based, and sing with their customary beauty of sound and well-blended tone. They are superbly recorded in the Church of St Peter and St Paul in Salle, Norfolk.

Mass & Motet: Assumpta est Maria. Motets: Ave Maria; Beata es, Virgo Maria; Hodie gloriosa semper Virgo Maria; Regina coeli; Magnificat septimi toni.

(B) **(*) EMI CDZ5 69703-2. Clare College, Cambridge, Ch., Brown.

This is an exceptionally well-chosen collection, mainly of shorter works, but also including the splendid Missa Assumpta est Maria. The programme ends with an equally fine Magnificat setting. We are familiar with the excellent Clare College Choir and their rich sound, partly achieved by using women's voices, from earlier recordings. This EMI Debut CD introduces their new conductor, Timothy Brown, and the choir responds expressively to his melismatic direction. The choir is beautifully recorded, and the only minor criticism is the relatively restricted dynamic range. But this remains a thoroughly worthwhile bargain disc, although it is a pity that the documentation has so little to say about the music.

Missa Beata Mariae virginis II; Missa Descendit angelis Domini; Jubilate Deo (for double choir); Motets: Ad te levavi oculos meos; Miserere nostri Domine; Sitivit anima mea; Super flumina Babylonis.

** Paraclete Press GDCD 106. Gloria Dei Cantores, Patterson; Chant conductor: Pugsley.

This fine American choir sing and blend beautifully and those looking for an essentially serene approach to these two Palestrina Masses will find much to enjoy. However, there is a distinct lack of Latin fervour, and the different sections, Kyrie, Gloria and Credo are sung in much the same somewhat bland style. The motets fare better, for one can sense the underlying intensity in Super flumina Babylonis and Miserere nostri Domine. The concert ends with Jubilate Deo, and this has more momentum, but even here the joy could be more unbuttoned. The recording is outstandingly fine.

Missa: Benedicta es (with Plainchant).

*** Gimell CDGIM 901. Tallis Scholars, Phillips (with JOSQUIN: Motet: Benedicta es).

Palestrina's Mass is coupled with the Josquin motet, Benedicta es, on which it is based, together with the plainchant sequence on which both drew. It would seem that this Mass was the immediate predecessor of the Missa Papae Marcelli and was composed while the music of *Benedictus es* was still at the forefront of the composer's mind. The Tallis Scholars and Peter Phillips sing with impressive conviction and produce an expressive, excellently blended sound.

Missa Ecce ego Johannes; Cantantibus organis; Laudate pueri; Magnificat quarti toni; Peccantem me quotidie; Tribulationes civitatum; Tu es Petrus.

*** Hyp. CDA 67099. Westminster Cathedral Ch., O'Donnell.

Even among the Westminster Cathedral Choir's superb records this disc stands out. Perfect chording and ensemble, natural and musical phrasing, spot-on intonation and a glorious tonal blend, make this issue one to treasure. The recording serves the choir well and there are scholarly notes by Ivan Moody.

Masses: *Ecce ego Johannes; Sine nomine.*

(BB) *** Belart (ADD) 461 018-2. Thomas, Allister, Fleet, Keyte, Carmelite Priory Ch., London, McCarthy — VICTORIA: Mass & Motet: *O quam gloriosum.* ***

The two works offered here make a good foil for each other, for they are contrasted in style and texture. The Mass 'without name' is a small-scale work, whereas *Ecce ego Johannes* is more ambitious and dramatic. Both are beautifully sung and very well recorded. With the availablity of this record so inexpensively and with extra works by Victoria (not on the original LP) included for good measure, one hopes that more music-lovers will be tempted to sample this wonderfully expressive and rewarding music.

Missa Hodie Christus natus est; Motet: Hodie Christus natus est; Stabat Mater.

(BB) *** Naxos 8.550836. Oxford Schola Cantorum, Summerly — LASSUS: *Missa Bell' Amfitrit' alterna.* ***

Where in their account of Palestrina's *Missa aeterna Christi munera*, Summerly's group are restrained in their devotional manner, this celebrated Mass for Christmas has them joyful and exuberant. The choir, over 30 strong, brings out both the beauty and the drama of the writing, and equally so in the brief motet setting the Christmas words. The magnificent *Stabat Mater* is wisely given to a smaller group of 16 singers, two to a part, with added clarity in the complex polyphony. Well coupled with one of Lassus's best-loved Masses, representing the work of Palestrina's close contemporary from Flanders, the two supreme polyphonic masters who died in the same year.

Missa brevis; Missa: Nasce la gioia mia (with PRIMAVERA: *Madrigal: Nasce la gioia mia*).

*** Gimell CDGIM 908. Tallis Scholars, Phillips.

The *Missa: Nasce la gioia mia* is a parody Mass, modelled on the madrigal, *Nasce la gioia mia* by Giovan Leonardo Primavera. The Tallis Scholars and Peter Phillips give expressive, finely shaped accounts of both the *Missa brevis* and the *Mass*, which they preface by the madrigal itself. A most rewarding disc: no grumbles about the recording.

Missa: Nigra sum (with motets on *Nigra sum* by LHERITIER; VICTORIA; DE SILVA).

*** Gimell CDGIM 903-2. Tallis Scholars, Phillips.

Palestrina's *Missa: Nigra sum* is another parody Mass, based on a motet by Jean Lheritier, and follows its model quite closely; its text comes from the Song of Solomon. On this record, the plainchant and the Lheritier motet precede Palestrina's *Mass*, plus motets by Victoria and Andreas de Silva, a relatively little-known Flemish singer and composer who served in the Papal chapel and later in Mantua. The music is inspiring and the performances exemplary. This is a most beautiful record and the acoustic of Merton College, Oxford, is ideal.

Missa Papae Marcelli.

*** Gimell (ADD) CDGIM 939-2. Tallis Scholars, Phillips — ALLEGRI: *Miserere;* MUNDY: *Vox Patris caelestis.* ***

Missa Papae Marcelli; Alma redemptoris Mater; Magnificat 1 toni; Nunc dimittis; Stabat mater; Surge illuminare.

(*) Gimell CDGIM 994-2. Tallis Scholars (with ALLEGRI: *Miserere* *).

Missa Papae Marcelli; Alma redemptoris Mater (antiphon); *Peccantem me quotidie* (motet); *Stabat Mater.*

(BB) **(*) ASV (ADD) CDQS 6086. L. Pro Cantione Antiqua, Turner.

Missa Papae Marcelli; Missa brevis.

*** Hyp. CDA 66266. Westminster Cathedral Ch., Hill.

Missa Papae Marcelli; Tu es Petrus (motet).

*** DG (IMS) (ADD) 415 517-2. Westminster Abbey Ch., Preston (with ANERIO: *Venite ad me omnes;* NANINO: *Haec dies;* GIOVANNELLI: *Jubilate Deo* ***) — ALLEGRI: *Miserere.* **(*)

David Hill and the Westminster Cathedral Choir give an imposing and eloquent *Missa Papae Marcelli* that many collectors may prefer to the finely sung Gimell issue from the Tallis Scholars. They, too, have the advantage of a spacious acoustic and excellent recording.

The account by the Westminster Abbey choristers is a performance of great fervour, married to fine discipline, rich in timbre, eloquent both at climaxes and at moments of serenity. The singing is equally fine in the hardly less distinctive motet, *Tu es Petrus*. Felice Anerio, Giovanni Bernardino Nanino and Ruggiero Giovannelli represent the following generation of composers. Their contributions to this collection are well worth having, particularly Giovannelli's *Jubilate Deo* which makes a splendid closing item. The digital recording is first class.

The earlier Gimell alternative is an analogue recording from 1980. The singing has eloquence, purity of tone, and a simplicity of line which is consistently well controlled.

For their second, digital recording, the Tallis Scholars were recorded in the Basilica of Maria Maggiore in Rome, where Palestrina was a choirboy and, later, master of the choristers. The most celebrated of Palestrina's Masses, *Missa Papae Marcelli*, receives as eloquent a performance as any in the catalogue. The Tallis Scholars have wonderful fluidity and the sense of movement never flags in this finely tuned, well-paced reading. Much the same goes for the remaining motets here and, of course, for the Allegri *Miserere*, which had a unique association with the Sistine Chapel. As the recording was made before an audience, there is applause, which is quite inappropriate and very tiresome. In every other respect this is a first-class issue and can be warmly recommended.

Bruno Turner uses small forces throughout his well-conceived programme, and these are most beautiful performances of all four pieces, offering both intelligence and sensitivity in the handling of each line. Partly because of the recording balance, which is rather forward, one can hear the inner parts with uncommon clarity and, although this is not achieved at the expense of the overall sonority, some might feel that the clear and precise acoustic robs the music of some of its mystic atmosphere.

Officium defunctorum: Ad Dominum cum tribularer clamavi; Domine quando veneris; Heu mihi Domine; Libere me, Domine (with Plainchant taken from Graduale Romanum).

**(*) ECM 1653. James, Covey-Crump, Potter, Jones – VICTORIA: *Responsories.* **(*)

This CD combines music by Palestrina and Victoria, for the Office and Matins for the Dead and the Burial service, including one text, *Libera me Domine*, set by both composers. These 'composed pieces' are surrounded by the appropriate plainchant, of which there is a great deal. But it could hardly be more convincingly or beautifully sung. Indeed the four singers blend their voices beautifully and sing with eloquence, and are beautifully recorded. However the pervasive mood of doom and gloom will not suit all tastes!

Veni sponsa Christi.

(M) *** EMI CD-EMX 2180. St John's College, Cambridge, Ch., Guest – ALLEGRI: *Miserere*; LASSUS: *Missa super bella.* **(*)

Veni sponsa Christi is a parody Mass – which means that it uses pre-existing music, here an earlier Palestrina motet based on Gregorian chant, and this impressive work ends with two *Agnus Dei* settings, the second with an additional tenor part. It receives an eloquent, imaginatively detailed and finely shaped performance here, and the relative restraint of the Anglican choral tradition suits Palestrina's flowing counterpoint better than it does the Lassus Venetian coupling.

COLLECTIONS

Hodie Beata Virgo; Litaniae de Beata Virgine Maria in 8 parts; Magnificat in 8 parts (Primi Toni); Senex puerum portabat; Stabat Mater.

(M) *** Decca (ADD) 466 373-2. King's College Ch., Willcocks – ALLEGRI: *Miserere.* ***

The flowing melodic lines and serene beauty which are the unique features of Palestrina's music are apparent throughout this programme, and there is no question about the dedication and accomplishment of the performance.

The recording is no less successful, sounding radiantly fresh and clear as remastered for Decca's Legend series.

PALMGREN, Selim (1878–1951)

'Meet the Composer': Piano Concertos Nos. (i–ii) 1, Op. 13; (iii; ii) 2 (The River), Op. 33; (iv; ii) 3 (Metamorphoses), Op. 41; (iii; ii) 4 (April), Op. 85; (v; ii) 5, Op. 99; (ii) Pictures from Finland, Op. 24; (vi) Piano Sonata in D min., Op. 11; Piano pieces: Raindrops, Op. 54/1; Preludes Nos. 12 (The Sea); 24 (The War), Op. 17/12 & 24; Spring: Dragonfly; May Night, Op. 27/3–4; Dusk, Op. 47/1.

(B) *** Finlandia Ultima Double 3984 28171-2 (2).
(i) Heinonen; (ii) Turku PO, Mercier; (iii) Lagerspetz; (iv) Raekallio; (v) Kerppo; (vi) Tateno.

At one time in Finland Palmgren was even thought to threaten Sibelius's pre-eminence, but his music is limited in its emotional range. This valuable Double in Finlandia's 'Meet the Composer' series collects the five *Piano Concertos*, which range in the composer's career from 1903 to 1941, and some of his piano miniatures, as well as the early *Sonata in D minor*, Op. 11, of 1900. There is poetic feeling here, tinged at times by a certain gentility. Palmgren was influenced by impressionism, though his melancholic sensibility is undoubtedly Nordic. All the soloists are persuasive in the concertos and are well supported by the Turku orchestra under Jacques Mercier. The orchestra gives an eminently acceptable account of the *Pictures from Finland*, Op. 24, from 1908. In the *Sonata* and the solo miniatures the pianist is the Japanese-born Izumi Tateno, who has lived in Finland since his student days. He plays these pieces with great sympathy and is very well recorded. A useful survey of Palmgren's music, recorded in very decent sound.

PIANO MUSIC

Barcarolle, Op. 14; Finnish Rhythms, Op. 31; Illusion, Op. 1/2; Intermezzo, Op. 3/4; 3 Piano Pieces, Op. 54; Snowflakes, Op. 57/2; Sonette, Op. 4/3; Spring, Op. 27; Spring, Op. 47: 2 Pieces; Youth, Op. 28.

*** Finlandia 4509-98991-2. Tateno.

Palmgren will be remembered here by the older generation of piano students brought up on pieces like *May Night* and *Moonlight*. He was spoken of as the 'Chopin of the north' for he wrote more idiomatically for the piano than Sibelius; but his music is limited in its repertoire of pianistic devices. The present disc collects some of his early and middle-period music, from *Illusion* (which comes from his first published collection of 1899) through to the *Three Piano Pieces*, Op. 54, of 1918. There is a certain poetic feeling, tinged at times by a hint of gentility.

24 Preludes, Op. 17; Piano Sonata in D min., Op. 11.

*** Finlandia 4509 95868-2 (2). Tateno.

These are early works. The *Sonata* is modestly imposing, at its best in the rhapsodical finale. Tateno makes the most of it, without inflation. The *24 Preludes* are a homage to Chopin, although the piano technique they exploit is much narrower, and they also have a French influence at times. The opening two pieces are characteristic, appealing in their simplicity, and many of them have charm, such as the chattering *Bird song* (No. 19). They are played very pleasingly and are truthfully recorded.

PANDOLFI MEALLI, Giovanni Antonio *(fl. 1620–69)*

Violin Sonatas, Op. 3, Nos. 1 (La stella); 2 (La cesta); 3 (La melana); 4 (La castella); 5 (La clemente); 6 (La sabbatina); Op. 4, Nos. 1 (Labernabea; 2 (La viviana); 3 (La monella romanesca); 4 (La biancuccia); 5 (La stella); 6 (La vinciolina).

(N) *** HM HMU 907241. Manze, Egarr.

Apart from being registered as an employee at the Hapsburg Court, nothing is known of Pandolfi. The manuscripts of his Opp. 3 and 4 were found in the Civico Museo of Bologna. These twelve sonatas (published in 1660) are written in a highly individual and certainly unpredictable improvisatory style which moves from gentle expressive lyricism to bursts of more plangent virtuosity, allowing the kind of latitude in performance ('a Pandora's box of possibilities') which Andrew Manz and Richard Egarr obviously relish. *La biancuccia* and the passionate final sonata *La vinciolina* (the only work dedicated to a woman) are particularly remarkable. They are named after their dedicatees, who range from composers to Kapellmeisters, violinists and even castrati.

These remarkably spontaneous re-creative period-instrument performances won a *Gramophone* Baroque Music Award, and no wonder. They are superbly recorded. But in his notes Andrew Manz offers good advice: 'Only the more discerning palates will be able to appreciate more than one or two (sonatas) at a sitting. Indulge the chef by not over-indulging.'

Violin Sonatas: La cesta; La castella; La clemente; La sabbatina, Op. 3/2, 4, 5 & 6; La bernabea; La biancuccia; La vinciolina, Op. 4/1, 4 & 6; (i) Anon.: Harpsichord Suites in A, C & D.

*** Channel CCS 5894. Manze, (i) Egarr, Jacobs.

Giovanni Antonio Pandolfi Mealli's reputation rests on a single surviving copy of two sets of violin sonatas, six sonatas in each. Seven are recorded here, interspersed with three anonymous, French-influenced harpsichord suites, very different in style. These are all rewarding and interesting scores, marvellously played by all concerned, and very well recorded too.

PANUFNIK, Andrzej *(1914–91)*

(i) Autumn Music; Heroic Overture; (i, ii) Nocturne; (iii) Sinfonia rustica; (i) Tragic Overture.

(M) *** Unicorn (ADD) UKCD 2016. (i) LSO, Horenstein; (ii) with Peebles; (iii) Monte Carlo Op. O, composer.

The *Autumn Music* and *Nocturne* may strike some listeners as musically uneventful, but the opening of the *Nocturne* is really very beautiful indeed and there is a refined feeling for texture and a sensitive imagination at work here. The *Sinfonia rustica* is the most individual of the works recorded here and has plenty of character. The performance under the composer is thoroughly committed. The LSO under Horenstein play with conviction and they are very well recorded.

Cello Concerto.

*** NMC Single D 0105. Rostropovich, LSO, Wolff.

Panufnik's *Cello Concerto* was his very last work, completed only days before his death in September 1991. The recording is even more successful at conveying the purposefulness of the writing than the first performance, bringing out the tautness of the palindromic structure, with the two movements, each in arch form, a mirror-image of the other, slow then fast. The result is not a drily schematic work, as one might expect, but a piece that in its warmth reflects the player who inspired it, strong and eventful with a more open lyricism than in many previous Panufnik compositions.

(i) Concerto festivo; (ii) Concerto for Timpani, Percussion & Strings; Katyn Epitaph; Landscape; (iii) Sinfonia sacra (Symphony No. 3).

(M) *** Unicorn (ADD) UKCD 2020. (i) LSO, (ii) with Goedicke & Frye; (ii) Monte Carlo Op. O, composer.

This splendidly recorded collection might be a good place for collectors to begin exploring Panufnik's output. The *Concertos* are both readily communicative and the *Katyn Epitaph* is powerfully eloquent. The best of this music is deeply felt. The *Sinfonia sacra* serves to demonstrate the spectacular quality of the vividly remastered recording, with its compelling introductory 'colloquy' for four trumpets, followed by a withdrawn section for strings alone. In the finale of the second part of the work, Hymn, the trumpets close the piece resplendently.

Symphony No. 8 (Sinfonia votiva).

*** Hyp. CDA 66050. Boston SO, Ozawa – SESSIONS: *Concerto for Orchestra.* ***

The *Sinfonia votiva* has a strongly formalistic structure, but its message is primarily emotional. Though Panufnik's melodic writing may as a rule reflect the formalism of his thought rather than tapping a vein of natural lyricism, the result is most impressive, particularly in a performance of such sharp clarity and definition as Ozawa's. Very well recorded.

PARAY, Paul *(1886–1979)*

Mass for the 500th Anniversary of the Death of Joan of Arc.

(M) **(*)** [Mercury (ADD) 432 719-2]. Yeend, Bible, Lloyd, Yi-Kwei-Sze, Rackham Ch., Detroit SO, Paray – SAINT-SAENS: *Symphony No. 3.* ***

Paray's *Mass*, much admired by the composer, Florent Schmitt, could hardly have a more eloquent performance.

The soloists are good and the choir are inspired to real fervour by their conductor, who at the close (in a brief recorded speech) expresses his special satisfaction in the singing of the closing, very romantic *Agnus Dei*. Excellent (1957) Mercury stereo, using the Ford Auditorium in Detroit.

PARRY, Hubert (1848–1918)

(i) *The Birds: Bridal March;* (ii) *English Suite; Lady Radnor's Suite* (both for strings); *Overture to an Unwritten Tragedy; Symphonic Variations.*

*** Lyrita (ADD) SRCD 220. (i) LPO; (ii) LSO; Boult.

The *Bridal March* comes from Parry's equivalent to Vaughan Williams's *Wasps*, a suite of incidental music for *The Birds*, also by Aristophanes. Here the rich, *nobilmente* string melody asserts itself strongly over any minor contributions from the woodwind aviary. The two *Suites* of dances for strings have some charming genre music and the *Overture* is very strongly constructed. But best of all is the *Symphonic Variations*, with its echoes of Brahms's *St Anthony* set and its foretastes of *Enigma*. Boult's advocacy is irresistible and the CD transfer demonstrates the intrinsic excellence of the analogue recordings, with gloriously full string sound.

Piano Concerto in F sharp min.

*** Hyp. CDA 66820. Lane, BBC Scottish SO, Brabbins – STANFORD: *Piano Concerto.* ***

The *Piano Concerto in F sharp minor* may at first seem rather naïve in the way it embraces a grand manner but, written in 1880, it is a relatively early work which appeals openly with its directness and lyricism. The Brahmsian echoes are supplemented in the finale by clear if momentary echoes of Bizet's *Carmen*, then a very new work. Piers Lane plays with feeling and brilliance, helped by beautiful sound.

Concertstück in G min.; Elegy for Brahms; From Death to Life; Symphonic Variations.

(N) (M) *** Chan. 6610. LPO, Namert.

The eloquent *Concertstück*, literally a 'concert piece' without a soloist and with a strong Wagnerian flavour, is the least known work here. The *Elegy for Brahms* conveys grief, but its vigour rises above passive mourning into an expression of what might almost be anger. *From Death to Life* consists of two connected movements – hardly Lisztian as the title implies but exuberantly melodic, with a theme in the second that echoes Sibelius's *Karelia* and is at the same time Elgarian in its sweep. But the finest work of all is the *Symphonic Variations*, with its echoes of Brahms's *St Anthony* set and its foretastes of *Enigma*. Shorter than either, it does not waste a note: a big work in a small compass. The performances could hardly be more sympathetic, and the Chandos sound is suitably rich and clear.

An English Suite; Lady Radnor's Suite.

(M) *** EMI CDM5 66541-2. City of L. Sinfonia, Hickox – ELGAR: *Elegy for Strings* etc. **(*)

Parry's two elegant and beautifully crafted suites make an unusual and very apt coupling for the Elgar string music.

The combination of straightforward, warm expression with hints of melancholy below the surface is very Elgarian. Both suites were written later than the Elgar *Serenade*, with *An English Suite* published only after the composer's death. The Bach tributes in *Lady Radnor's Suite* are surface-deep; the slow minuet for muted strings is particularly beautiful. Refined playing and first-rate recording.

Lady Radnor's Suite.

*** Nim. NI 5068. E. String O, Boughton – BRIDGE: *Suite;* BUTTERWORTH: *Banks of Green Willow* etc. ***

Parry's charming set of pastiche dances, now given an extra period charm through their Victorian flavour, makes an attractive item in an excellent and generous English collection, one of Nimbus's bestsellers. Warm, atmospheric recording, with refined playing set against an ample acoustic.

Symphonies Nos. 1–5; Symphonic Variations in E min.

*** Chan. 9120-22. LPO, Bamert.

Bamert takes us convincingly through the symphonic terrain of a highly influential composer about whom Elgar declared, 'He is our leader – no cloud of formality can dim the healthy sympathy and broad influence he exerts upon us. Amidst all the outpourings of modern English music the work of Parry remains supreme.' Bamert's set, discussed in detail below, is offered here complete on three CDs and includes also Parry's best-known orchestral work, the *Symphonic Variations*.

Symphony No. 1 in G; Concertstück in G min.

*** Chan. 9062. LPO, Bamert.

Bamert immediately demonstrates his response to the composer's muse in the way the opening *Con fuoco* sails off with a powerful thrust in the first movement. His control of the overall structure with its interrelated thematic material is most convincing, through the eloquent *Andante* and the Scherzo with its double trio, until he brings the finale to an impressively up-beat conclusion. He also offers the earlier *Concertstück for Orchestra*, though here the Wagnerian influences remain incompletely absorbed. The spacious Chandos recording seems exactly right for this pre-Elgarian opulence of symphonic thought.

Symphony No. 2 in F (Cambridge); Symphonic Variations.

*** Chan. 8961. LPO, Bamert.

Symphony No. 2 (Cambridge); Overture to an Unwritten Tragedy; Symphonic Variations.

(BB) **(*) Naxos 8.553469. RSNO, Penny.

The *Second Symphony* opens confidently (with distinct Mendelssohnian associations) and Brahms's influence appears in the main lyrical idea of the finale. In between there are reminders of Dvořák and Schumann but for all its eclecticism and occasional longwindedness, notably in the finale, Parry finds his own voice and the music has a genuinely vital flow. Bamert's advocacy certainly holds the listener's attention and the orchestra responds with obvious relish. The *Symphonic Variations* makes an admirable makeweight. Excellent, full-bodied sound of the best Chandos vintage.

Naxos here offers a very acceptable alternative to the

Symphony No. 2, similarly coupled with the *Symphonic Variations* and with an extra item in the *Overture*. The playing of the Royal Scottish National Orchestra is just as polished as that of the LPO on Chandos, but Penny's manner is less warmly expressive at speeds generally a little faster, and the recorded sound is rather less opulent.

Symphonies Nos. 3 in C (English); 4 in E min.

*** Chan. 8896. LPO, Bamert.

No. 3 is the most immediately approachable of the symphonies, with its bold melodies, often like sea-shanties, and its forthright structure. Yet it is No. 4 which proves the more rewarding, a larger-scale, ambitious work. The bold opening, in its dark E minor, echoes that of Brahms's *First Piano Concerto*, leading to an ambitious movement lightened by thematic transformation that can take you in an instant into infectious waltz-time. The elegiac slow movement and jolly and spiky scherzo lead to a broad, noble finale in the major key. Bamert again proves a masterly interpreter, bringing out the warmth and thrust of the writing. The sound is rich and full to match the outstanding playing.

Symphony No. 5 in B min.; Symphonic Variations; Elegy for Brahms; (i) Blest Pair of Sirens.

(M) *** EMI (ADD) CDM5 65107-2. LPO, Boult, (i) with LPO Ch.

Symphony No. 5; Elegy for Brahms; From Death to Life.

*** Chan. 8955. LPO, Bamert.

The *Fifth* and last of Parry's symphonies is in four linked movements, terser in argument than the previous two, and often tougher, though still with Brahmsian echoes. After the minor-key rigours of the first movement, *Stress*, the other three movements are comparably subtitled *Love*, *Play* and *Now*, with the Scherzo bringing echoes of Berlioz and the optimistic finale opening with a Wagnerian horn-call. The *Elegy for Brahms* conveys grief, but its vigour rises above passive mourning into an expression of what might almost be anger. *From Death to Life* consists of two connected movements, exuberantly melodic, with a theme in the second which echoes Sibelius's *Karelia*. It would be hard to imagine finer, more committed performances than those on Chandos, or richer sound.

This was the last record made by Sir Adrian Boult, whose recording of the slow movement is particularly beautiful here. Equally impressive is the *Elegy*, not merely an occasional piece but a full-scale symphonic movement which builds to a powerful climax. Recording and performances are exemplary, a fitting coda to Sir Adrian's recording career. To make the CD even more representative, it is good to welcome so enjoyably professional a motet as Parry's *Blest Pair of Sirens*.

Cello Sonata in A.

(M) *** Dutton CDLX 7102. Fuller, Dussek – HARTY: *Butterflies; Romance & Scherzo, Op. 8; Wood-Stillness;* HURLSTONE: *Cello Sonata in D.* ***

Parry's *Cello Sonata* is finely wrought, though it does not wear its debt to Brahms lightly – understandably, perhaps, since it is a fairly early piece dating from 1879. It is designed on an almost symphonic scale – particularly the sinewy *Allegro* first movement. A splendid performance and recording.

Nonet in B flat.

(N) (BB) *** Hyp. Helios CDH 55061. Capricorn – STANFORD: *Serenade (Nonet)*. ***

Parry's *Nonet* is for flute, oboe, cor anglais and two each of clarinets, bassoons and horns. Although the finale is perhaps a little lightweight, it is a delight from beginning to end. If one did not know what it was, one would think of early Strauss, for it is music of enormous accomplishment and culture as well as freshness. An excellent performance and recording, the more attractive at bargain price.

(i) Piano Quartet in A flat; Piano Trio No. 1 in E min.

**(*) Mer. CDE 84248. Deakin Piano Trio, (i) with Inoue.

The *E minor Piano Trio* is both shorter and more direct than the *Piano Quartet*, which is more ambitious, with a darkly meditative slow introduction echoing late Beethoven. Though the performance on the disc is not as polished as one would like, Parry's melodic writing is more than distinctive enough to rebut the charge of mere imitation, with such a movement as the dashing tarantella-like Scherzo of the *Piano Quartet* very effective indeed. The recording balances the piano rather behind the rest, which is a pity when Catherine Dubois so often takes the lead.

Piano Trios Nos. 2 in B min.; 3 in G.

*** Mer. CDE 84255. Deakin Piano Trio.

In the two *Piano Trios* the English element in Parry's invention is more clearly identifiable, with some themes bringing anticipations of Elgar. Equally, the healthy outdoor feel of the triple-time main themes of the finales of both trios has a hint of English folk-music. Both works are richly enjoyable, with the warm, open lyricism of the slow movement of No. 2 particularly attractive. The players of the Deakin Piano Trio seem more happily adjusted to the rigours of recording than in the first volume, with rather better matching and intonation.

Violin Sonata in D, Op. 103; Fantasie-sonata in B, Op. 75; 12 Short Pieces.

*** Hyp. CDA 66157. Gruenberg, Vignoles.

The *Fantasie-sonata* provides a fascinating example of cyclic sonata form, earlier than most but also echoing Schumann. The three-movement *Sonata in D* is another compact, meaty piece, the strongest work on the disc. The *Twelve Short Pieces*, less demanding technically, are delightful miniatures. Gruenberg and Vignoles prove persuasive advocates, and the recording is first rate.

PIANO MUSIC

Hands Across the Centuries (suite); 10 Shulbrede Tunes; Theme & 19 Variations in D min.

*** Priory PRCD 451. Jacobs.

Shulbrede Priory was the remains of a substantial twelfth-century Augustinian settlement, turned into a country house, where the composer's married daughter lived with her family. Parry was captivated by its charm and atmosphere and he published a set of ten delightful miniatures which showed this affection and the strong spell the house wielded over him. The mock-baroque *Hands Across the Centuries (suite)* is hardly less diverting, and its invention equally varied. The more ambitious *Theme and Variations* is rather prolix but is very well organized. Peter Jacobs, obviously enjoying himself, plays all this music with flair and there is never a dull bar here. Excellent natural recording, too.

VOCAL MUSIC

Blest Pair of Sirens; I Was Glad (anthems).

*** Chan. 8641/2. L. Symphony Ch. & LSO, Hickox – ELGAR: *Dream of Gerontius.* ***

Parry's two finest and most popular anthems make an attractive coupling for Hickox's fine, sympathetic reading of Elgar's *Dream of Gerontius*. The chorus for Parry is rather thinner than in the main work but is very well recorded.

Evening Service in D (Great): Magnificat; Nunc dimittis. Hear my words, ye people; I was glad when they said unto me; Jerusalem; Songs of Farewell.

*** Hyp. CDA 66273. St George's Chapel, Windsor, Ch., Robinson; Judd (organ).

Everyone knows *Jerusalem*, which highlights this collection resplendently. In the *Songs of Farewell* trebles are used and the effect is less robust than in Marlow's version, but undoubtedly with trebles affecting. Perhaps the stirring coronation anthem, *I was glad*, needs the greater weight of an adult choir, but it is still telling here. The excerpts from the *Great Service in D* are well worth having on record, as is the anthem, *Hear my words, ye people*. Excellent recording, the chapel ambience colouring the music without blunting the words.

Job (oratorio).

**(*) Hyp. CDA 67025. Coleman-Wright, Spence, Davies, Hitchcock, Guildford Choral Soc., RPO, Davan Wetton.

Though Parry, as a Victorian, sidesteps the problem of conveying the pain and bitterness in the story of Job, this is a warm, beautifully written oratorio which is most welcome on disc, very English and optimistic. It would be even better, had Hilary Davan Wetton drawn a more biting response from the chorus and had Peter Coleman-Wright in the title role, clear and direct as he is, sounded less respectful. The other soloists are first-rate, notably Toby Spence in the tenor part of Satan, and the recording is warm and atmospheric, though with the chorus rather backwardly placed. For all its limitations a highly enjoyable curiosity.

The Soul's Ransom (sinfonia sacra); The Lotos Eaters.

*** Chan. 8990. Jones, Wilson-Johnson, LPO and Ch., Bamert.

Using a biblical text *The Soul's Ransom*, with its sequence of solos and choruses, forms a broadly symphonic four-movement structure with references back not only to Brahms and the nineteenth century but to much earlier choral composers, notably Schütz. This 45-minute piece is generously coupled with *The Lotos Eaters*, a setting for soprano, chorus and orchestra of eight stanzas from Tennyson's choric song of that name, with Della Jones again the characterful soloist. Full and atmospheric recording to match the incandescent performances.

PÄRT, Arvo (born 1935)

(i) *Arbos* (two performances); (ii) *Pari Intervallo*; (iii) *An den Wassern zu Babel; De Profundis*; (iv; v) *Es sang vor langen Jahren*; (iii) *Summa*; (iii; v; vi) *Stabat Mater*.

*** ECM 831 959-2. (i) Brass Ens., Stuttgart State O, Davies; (ii) Bowers-Broadbent; (iii) Hilliard Ens., Hillier; (iv) Bickley; (v) Kremer, Mendelssohn; (vi) Demenga.

All the music recorded here gives a good picture of Pärt's musical make-up with all its strengths and limitations. *Arbos*, which is heard in two different versions, 'seeks to create the image of a tree or family tree'. It does not modulate and has no development, though pitch and tempi are in proportional relationships. The *Stabat Mater* (1985) for soprano, counter-tenor, tenor and string trio is distinguished by extreme simplicity of utterance and is almost totally static. This music relies for its effect on minimal means and invites one to succumb to a kind of mystical, hypnotic repetition rather than a musical argument. The artists performing here do so with total commitment and are excellently recorded.

(i) *Cantus in Memory of Benjamin Britten; Festina lente; Summa*; (i; ii) *Tabula rasa*; (ii) *Fratres; Spiegel im Spiegel*.

(M) *** CfP 573 117-2. (i) Bournemouth Sinf., Studt; (ii) Little, Roscoe.

An admirable and enterprising compilation Classics for Pleasure to tempt those who have not yet sampled this composer's highly individual sound-world with its tintinnabulation. *Summa* is another version of the vocal *Creed* and is certainly effective, if not superior in its new costume. In the two chamber works Tasmin Little holds the listener's attention by the intensity of her commitment and the powerful projection of her playing. But most striking of all is the ambitious *Tabula rasa* with strong contrasts between the erupting energy of the opening *Ludus* and the aptly named second-movement *Silentium* which, of course, is not silent but spins a compulsive atmospheric web. Fine performances and evocative sound, spread within an ecclesiastical acoustic, and first-rate recording combine to give this programme persuasive advocacy.

Fratres (6 versions); *Cantus in Memory of Benjamin Britten; Festina lente*.

*** Telarc CD 80387. Manning, Springuel, Gleizes, I Fiamminghi, Werthen.

For all the repetitions involved in Pärt's minimalist progressions there are no more hypnotic examples of his curiously compelling, ritualistic writing than this sequence of six settings of a very simple monastic chorale which he calls *Fratres*. We hear it first slowly swelling up from a *piano-pianissimo* on strings, with unobtrusive decorative percussion, then sinking away again. Then follow variants featuring first a solo violin, then for a carefully blended wind octet, for eight cellos used in their higher register, then returning to a string group and quickening to achieve the flavour of an elegant baroque dance, further adapted to the more economical texture of a string quartet, and finally rustling on the cello with the piano tolling a bell-like accompaniment until a closing climax builds and abates. The Britten tribute and *Festina lente for Strings and Harp ad libitum* are used as interludes. The playing here has great atmosphere and concentration, while Telarc's glowing sound adds to the sensuous physical beauty.

(i) *Fratres*; (ii) *Magnificat; 7 Magnificat Antiphons*.

*** Sony SK 61753. (i) Welsh, Blayden, Stirling; Tavener Ch., Parrott – TAVENER: *Canticle; etc.* ***

It may be considered an advantage or a disadvantage that in coupling the hypnotic and often static music of Pärt and Tavener, the ear is drawn to the similarity of the style of the two composers. *Fratres*, which exists in many versions, is heard here in its comparatively spare instrumental scoring to make a centrepiece in what is essentially a choral programme. The simplicity of the *Magnificat* setting is its prime virtue, but the *Antiphons* are more varied, although still very compelling when so beautifully sung and recorded.

Fratres; Summa (string quartet versions).

*** Virgin VC5 45023-2. Chilingirian Qt – TAVENER: *Last Sleep of the Virgin* etc. ***

Like the Tavener works with which they are generously coupled on this 74-minute CD, these are both atmospheric works with a liturgical basis, using sparse basic material, which try to convey a sense of eternity. The performances here, obviously felt, make an interesting comparison with the alternative versions discussed above. But it must be admitted that, as music, they are less potent than the Tavener pieces.

And One of the Pharisees; (i) The Beatitudes; Cantate Domino (Psalm 95); (ii) De Profundis (Psalm 129); Magnificat; 7 Magnificat Antiphons; (i) Missa Sillabica; Solfeggio; Summa (Credo).

*** HM HMU 907182. Theatre of Voices, Hillier; (i) with Bowers-Broadbent (organ); Kennedy (percussion).

The cover of this CD indicates that it includes just *De Profundis*, whereas this 76-minute collection covers a very wide range of Pärt's choral output, from the short *Solfeggio* of 1964, which seems to float in space, to *The Beatitudes* (1990) of which this is the recording première. This work opens in stillness and calm but, as so often with this composer, leads on to a great climax, here over an organ pedal; then, after an exultant 'Amen', the organ has a brief but prolix postlude. *De Profundis* (1980) brings a similarly elliptical structure, based on a simple climbing phrase in the bass; it again uses an organ pedal to underpin the climax. The *Missa Sillabica* (1977), heard here in a slightly revised

version, is a fine example of Pärt's use of the simplest means to communicate his expression of the liturgical text, the repetitions within the 'Credo' a characteristic example. *And One of the Pharisees* is a setting for three voices of a text from Chapter 7 of St Luke's Gospel and its powerful medieval atmosphere, including solo chants, reminds us of the link which Pärt's litugical music has with the distant past. The performances here could hardly be more powerful or atmospheric, yet they are firmly controlled. They are magnificently recorded.

Passio Domini Nostrum Jesu Christi secundum Joannem.

*** ECM 837 109-2. George, Potter, Hilliard Ens., Western Wind Chamber Ch. (Instrumental group), Hillier.

Pärt's '*Passion of Our Lord Jesus Christ According to St John*' was composed in a bleak narrative style that reminds one of a mixture of Stravinsky and Schütz. It repeats the same scraps of ideas over and over again; it takes 70 minutes and never seems to leave the Aeolian mode, and it ought to be intolerable; yet in its way it is a strangely impressive experience, albeit not a wholly musical one. Impeccable recording and a dedicated performance.

PATTERSON, Paul (born 1947)

Concerto for Orchestra, Op. 45; Europhony, Op. 55; (i) Missa brevis, Op. 54.

(M) *** EMI CDM5 66529-2. LPO, Arwel Hughes; (i) with LPO Ch.

This disc offers representative examples of Patterson's recent work, much more approachable in idiom than his earlier music. The gem of the collection is the *Missa brevis*, using a seemingly simple style boldly and freshly. It must be as welcome for the singers as it is for the listener, with moments of pure poetry as in the *Benedictus*. The two orchestral pieces, though less individual, are colourful and immediately attractive. Their openness of idiom conceals the ingenuity of their construction, with *Europhony* clearly developing on variation form. Vigorous performances and wide-ranging recording.

PENDERECKI, Kryszstof (born 1933)

(i) Anaklasis; (ii; iii) Capriccio for Violin & Orchestra; (iii; iv) Cello Concerto; (iii) De natura sonoris I & II; The Dream of Jacob; Emanationen for 2 String Orchestras; Fonogrammi; (iii; v) Partita for Harpsichord & Orchestra; (iii) Threnody for the Victims of Hiroshima; (i) Symphony; (vi) Canticum canticorum Salomonis.

(N) (B) *** EMI double forte (ADD) CZS 5 74302-2 (2). (i) LSO; (ii) Wilkomirska; (iii) Polish Nat. RSO; (iv) Palm; (v) Blumenthal (vi) Kraków Phil. Ch., all cond. Composer.

For those who admire such athematic music, this inexpensive anthology, in authoritative performances under the composer's own direction, makes a splendid introduction to Penderecki's music.

Anaklasis is an inventive piece for strings and percussion and *De natura sonoris* is also brilliant in its use of contrasts. Wilkomirska proves a superb soloist in the *Capriccio* and so does Palm in the *Cello Concerto*. The beautiful and touching *Threnody* for 53 strings is the composer's best-known piece, and it is here given a magnificent performance. *The Dream of Jacob* of 1974 is as inventive as the rest, but sparer and more cogent.

Penderecki's music relies for its appeal on its resourceful use of sonorities and his sound world is undoubtedly imaginative, albeit limited. The choral work is a setting of a text from the *Song of Solomon* for large orchestra and sixteen solo voices. But the *Symphony* is the most ambitious work here. It was commissioned by a British engineering firm and first performed in Peterborough Cathedral. That setting influences the range of sumptuous orchestral colours devised by the composer, though you could argue that this work is a series of brilliant orchestral effects rather than a symphonic argument. However, with such a committed performance, it is certainly memorable. The 1970s recordings are excellent, and this EMI Double forte is an undoubted bargain.

Violin Concerto.

(M) *** Sony (ADD) SMK 64507. Stern, Minnesota O, Skrowaczewski – HINDEMITH: *Violin Concerto*. ***

This concerto, written for Isaac Stern in 1977, marked Penderecki's return to a more conservative idiom. Even so, his fingerprints are clearly identifiable and the compression of thematic material, combined with spare, clean textures, makes for memorable results. The single movement, which lasts nearly 40 minutes, contains within it the traces of a funeral march, a Scherzo and a meditative adagio. The performance here is passionately committed, with Stern at his most inspired, and the recording is splendidly detailed. With its hardly less valuable Hindemith coupling, this is a key reissue in Sony's Stern Edition.

CHORAL MUSIC

Benedictus; Benedicamus Domine; Magnificat: Sidcut locutus est. Polish Requiem: Agnus Dei. Saint Luke's Passion: Stabat Mater; In pulverem mortis; Miserere. Veni creator; Song of Cherubim.

(N)(BB) *** Warner Apex 8573 88433-2. Tapiola Chamber Ch., Kulvanen.

This superbly sung collection inexpensively monitors Penderecki's changing style of vocal writing beginning with the excerpts from the *St Luke's Passion* (1962) for three mixed choruses, using dramatic spoken utterance as well as powerfully sustained block choral sonorities. The *Sidcut locutus est* from the *Magnicat* (1974) works in a similar way. Then with the lovely, plaintive *Agnus Dei* (for eight-part mixed chorus) of 1981 there is much more movement, and a surge of romantic feeling, with a dissonant climax of real angst. The new, freer romantic style reaches its peak in the powerful and often seraphic *Song of Cherubim* (1986) with its gentle closing Alleluias, the finest work here. But the remarkable setting of *Veni creator* (1987) returns to the

spoken murmurings and interjections, while climaxing with a passionate affirmation, before the ethereality of the closing Amen. By 1992 the *Benedictus Domine* for five-part male choir is looking back to organum, and the closing *Benedictus*, based on the text of the medieval *Sanctus* trope is linked to liturgical chant, yet romanticised and brought into our own time. The Tapiola Choir sings passionately, with fine blending and a bright firm line in an atmospheric but never blurring acoustic. With texts and translations included, this is a real bargain.

PENELLA, Manuel (1880–1939)

El gato montes (The Wild Mountain Cat).

(B) *** DG Double 459 427-2 (2). Domingo, Villarroel, Pons, Berganza, Nat. Lyrical Theatre Zarzuela Ch., Madrid SO, Roa.

This is a red-blooded performance of a melodramatic piece half-way between opera and zarzuela, which Plácido Domingo has a special affection for. He sings the role of the bullfighter, Rafael, in love with the heroine, Soleá, who still keeps her affection for the bandit, Juanillo, *El gato montes*, 'The wildcat'. The highly coloured plot ends with the death of all three, Rafael gored to death in the ring, Soleá dying of a broken heart and *El gato montes* cornered by the police. The writing is fluent and lyrical, with scenes punctuated by attractive orchestral pieces, notably the most celebrated, a paso doble. The musical invention may not be distinguished, but in such beefy performances, with Juan Pons in the title-role a genuine rival for Domingo, it is certainly attractive. The casting of the women principals is strong too, with Veronica Villarroel fresh and bright as the heroine and Teresa Berganza as characterful as ever as the Gypsy. Full, forward sound.

PERGOLESI, Giovanni (1710–36)

(i) *Magnificat in C;* (ii) *Miserere II in C min.;* (iii) *Salve Regina in C min.;* (iv) *Stabat Mater* (revision and organ part by M. Zanon).

(B) **(*) Double Decca (ADD) 455 017-2 (2). (i) Vaughan, J. Baker, Partridge, Keyte, King's College Ch., ASMF, Marriner, Willcocks; (ii) Wolff, James, Covey-Crump, Suart, Magdalen Coll., Oxford, Ch., Wren O, Rose; (iii) Kirkby, AAM, Hogwood; (iv) Raskin, Lehane, O Rossini di Napoli, Caracciolo – CALDARA: *Crucifixus;* LOTTI: *Crucifixus*. ***

This more ambitious if slightly uneven collection of Pergolesi's choral music (although only the *Salve Regina* and the *Stabat Mater* are almost certainly authentic) makes a useful alternative to the Double Decca set below, with the Willcocks performance of the *C major Magnificat* common to both. The *Stabat Mater* is modest in its demands, requiring originally two castrati plus strings and continuo. The orchestral accompaniment is spirited and the warm acoustic of the Naples Conservatorio adds richness to a fairly small body of strings. The *Miserere*, whether authentic or not, is undoubtedly moving. The singers here are all of quality, particularly Richard Suart; Bernard Rose secures expressive and persuasive results from the Magdalen College choir and the Wren Orchestra. The (originally Argo) recording sounds magnificently real and vivid. Last but not least comes Emma Kirkby's radiantly expressive and spirited *Salve Regina*, the finest solo contribution to this collection. Here period instruments enter the sound-picture, and the accompaniment from Hogwood's Academy matches Kirkby's depth of feeling, particularly in the touching closing '*O clemens*'.

(i) *Magnificat in C;* (ii) *Stabat Mater.*

(B) **(*) Double Decca 443 868-2 (2). (i) Vaughan, J. Baker, Partridge, Keyte, King's College Ch., ASMF, Willcocks; (ii) Palmer, Hodgson, St John's College, Cambridge, Ch., Argo CO, Guest – BONONCINI: *Stabat Mater;* D. SCARLATTI: *Stabat Mater;* A. SCARLATTI: *Domine, refugium factus es nobis; O magnum mysterium;* CALDARA: *Crucifixus;* LOTTI: *Crucifixus.* ***

This well-planned Double Decca collection centres on three different settings of the *Stabat Mater dolorosa.* Pergolesi's version dates from 1735 and, subsequently, settings were made by many other composers, including Vivaldi and Haydn. Pergolesi conceived a work which has secular and even theatrical overtones, and its devotional nature is un-exaggerated. George Guest directs a sensible, unaffected performance, simple and expressive, with relaxed tempi, not overladen with romantic sentiment. The *Magnificat* – doubtfully attributed, like so much that goes under this composer's name – is a comparatively lightweight piece, notable for its rhythmic vitality. The King's College Choir under Willcocks gives a sensitive and vital performance, and the recording matches it in intensity of atmosphere.

Stabat Mater.

⚫ *** Opus OPS 30-160. Bertagnolli, Mingardo, Concerto Italiano, Alessandrini – A. SCARLATTI: *Stabat Mater.* ***
*** DG 415 103-2. Marshall, Terrani, LSO, Abbado.

(M) **(*) DG 459 454-2 (2). Freni, Berganza, soloists from the Scarlatti O of Naples – A. SCARLATTI: *Concerti grossi; Stabat Mater.* **(*)

(B) (**) Dutton 2CDAX 2005 (3). Taylor, Ferrier, Oriana Ch., Henderson – BACH: *St Matthew Passion.* (**(*))

(i; ii) *Stabat Mater;* (ii) *In coelestibus regnis;* (i) *Salve Regina in A.*

*** Hyp. CDA 66294. (i) Fisher; (ii) Chance; King's Consort, King.

(i; ii) *Stabat Mater;* (ii) *Salve Regina in A min.;* (i) *Salve Regina in F min.*

*** Decca 466 134-2. Scholl, Bonney, Les Talens Lyriques, Rousset.

Both the soprano, Gemma Bertagnolli, and the contralto, Sara Mingardo (with her remarkably resonant lower register) have extraordinarily colourful voices, which blend beautifully at the work's sustained opening, but which only display their full richness in their solos, notably *Cujus animam gementem* and *Fac ut portem Christi mortem.* This is a

totally Italianate performance of both high drama and moving pathos. The closing *Quando corpus morietur*, in which both singers join in sustained legato, is very moving indeed, followed by a passionately final affirmation of faith. Alessandrini's instrumental support could not be more telling and the recording is made in an ideal acoustic.

Abbado's account brings greater intensity and ardour to this piece than almost any rival, and he secures marvellously alive playing from the LSO – this without diminishing religious sentiment. The DG recording has warmth and good presence and the perspective is thoroughly acceptable. But there is no coupling.

The combination of Andras Scholl's alto and Barbara Bonney's soprano makes a well-matched and certainly individual tonal blend and they often sing exquisitely, both solo and in tandem. Their *Stabat Mater* has plenty of drama as well as a fine expressive intensity and the closing *Quando corpus* is movingly restrained and beautiful. Both settings of the *Salve Regina* are authentic: Andras Scholl sings the *A minor*, Barbara Bonney the *F minor*. Throughout, Christophe Rousset's period-instrument accompaniments are outstandingly fine and full of life, and the Decca recording is splendidly real. But this version of the *Stabat Mater* needs to be sampled before purchase: you may be captivated by it or not. Our vote still goes to the Bertagnolli/Mingardo account mentioned above.

The Hyperion recording also makes a very good case for authenticity in this work. The combination of soprano and male alto blends well together yet offers considerable variety of colour. Gillian Fisher's *Salve Regina* is quite a considerable piece in four sections, whereas Michael Chance's motet is brief but makes an engaging postlude. Excellent sound.

The DG reissue involves a pair of discs. In the vocal works there is fine, eloquent singing from both soloists, and they match their close vibratos skilfully. They are well accompanied and naturally recorded, and this performance is certainly affecting.

The 1946 Decca recording of the *Stabat Mater* makes a welcome fill-up to the Bach *St Matthew Passion*, thanks to the contribution of Kathleen Ferrier. The rest is less distinguished, with Joan Taylor a fluttery soprano soloist.

(i; ii) *Stabat Mater;* (iii) *Salve Regina;* (i; iv) *Cantatas: Chi non ode e chi non vede; Dalsigre, abi, mia Dalsigre; Luce degli occhi mei; Nel chiuso centro (Orfeo)* (ADD).

(B) **(*) Erato Ultima (ADD) 3984 28172-2 (2).
 (i) Ticinelli-Fattori; (ii) Minetto; (iii) Retchitzka; (i; ii) Societa Camerista di Lugano, Loehrer; (iii) Nuovo Concerto Italiano, Gallico.

The cantatas were (very well) recorded in the late 1960s, and the *Stabat Mater* and *Salve Regina* come from 1972. Erato have understandably reissued them, for although none of the soloists have familiar names, their singing is of a high standard and the modern-instrument accompaniments are pleasingly stylish and nicely scaled. In the famous *Stabat Mater*, Luciano Sgrizzi's harpsichord continuo comes through the strings clearly, and the two voices – both pleasing in tone and line – blend well; each singer makes a strong solo contribution, dramatically open-voiced and meditative by turns. The small, sweet-timbred Basia Retchitzka is genuinely touching in the *Salve Regina*. The four little-known cantatas are in many ways even more demanding and Ticinelli-Fattori, articulating lightly, but singing with rich espressivo, rises to the occasion, especially in the most ambitious of the four, *Nel chiuso centro*, a most beautiful work. Three out of the four have a string quartet to support the keyboard accompaniment and very effective it is. With truthful, well-balanced recording this would have received a stronger recommendation had the set included texts and translations. Even so it is worth exploring.

PEROTINUS, Magister (c. 1160–1225)

Organa: *Alleluya, Nativitas; Sederunt principes.*

*** Lyrichord (ADD) LEMS 8002. Russell Oberlin, Bressler, Perry, Barab – LEONIN: *Organa.*

Perotinus extended the simple polyphony of Leonin from two to three and four parts, and the ear is very aware of the intervals which characterize the organum: unison, octave, fourths and fifths. This music is more florid, freer than the coupled works written several decades before. The performances here are totally compelling and the recording excellent.

PETER, Johann (1746–1813)

Sinfonia.

(M) ** Mercury [434 337-2]. Eastman-Rochester O, Hanson – CHADWICK: *Symphonic Sketches;* MACDOWELL: *Suite for Large Orchestra, Op. 42.* **(*)

The Dutch composer Johann Peter copied and studied the scores of symphonies by Abel, J. S. Bach and others. But instead of writing symphonies himself, he gave us six string quintets, of which this is the *Third*, here presented by a chamber orchestra as a *Sinfonia*. The music is graceful and has something of the charm of Boccherini, but sounds more like pastiche. Agreeable enough, it is very neatly played, but not memorable enough to return to very often.

PETERSON-BERGER, Wilhelm (1867–1942)

Symphony No. 1 in B flat (The Banner); Last Summer (suite).

*** CPO 999 561-2. Saarbrücken RSO, Jurowski.

The Swedish composer Wilhelm Peterson-Berger is essentially a miniaturist, a watercolourist, whose ideas are not ideally suited to the symphonic canvas. His *First Symphony* (*Banéret* or *The Banner*) is heavily indebted to Grieg and Wagner, and has some appealing moments. As a symphony it is pretty flimsy in structure. In the quieter, pastoral moments the scoring is fresh but elsewhere it is far from expert. The suite, *Last Summer*, is the better piece. Both receive sympathetic and persuasive performances, and excellent recording.

Symphony No. 3 (Lapland); The Doomsday Prophets: Chorale & Fugue. Earina Suite.

(N) *(**) CPO 999 632-2. Norrköping SO, Jurowski.

In the *Third Symphony* the ideas are still pretty thin but Peterson-Berger scores with some skill. His is a modest talent whose strengths lie in his songs and piano pieces, which are permeated by Swedish folk music and Grieg-like harmonies. The Norrköping Orchestra and Mikhail Jurowski give a very good account of themselves. One star only for the music but three for the performers.

Flowers from Frösö: Book I, Op. 16; Book II; Book III (Humoresques & Idylls for Piano).

*** BIS CD 925. Ogawa.

(BB) *** Naxos 8.554343. Sivelöv.

Frösöblomster is variously described on these discs as *Frösö-flowers* and *Flowers from Frösö Island* but they are the same pieces, and these miniatures, though not earth-shattering in any way, have a pallor and charm that is all their own. Norika Ogawa plays them with charm, grace and much sensitivity – and the BIS recording is exemplary.

Niklas Sivelöv is hardly less successful in conveying the fineness of these pieces. There is a Grieg-like salon quality about them redeemed by a certain freshness, and Sivelöv plays with style and elegance, He is recorded in St George's, Brandon Hill, Bristol and the sound is excellent. Price apart, there is nothing to choose between his set and Norika Ogawa on sonic or artistic grounds.

PETTERSSON, Allan (1911–80)

(i) *Viola Concerto. Symphony No. 5.*

*** BIS CD 480. (i) Imai; Malmö SO, Atzmon.

Allan Pettersson's *Fifth* is a one-movement work and begins well. However, invention flags and the brooding, expectant atmosphere and powerful ostinatos arouse more promise of development than fulfilment. The *Viola Concerto* comes from the last year of Pettersson's life and is pretty amorphous. Both pieces lack the concentration and quality of Tubin or Holmboe. The three stars are for the performers and the recording team.

Symphony No. 7.

*** Caprice CAP 21411. Swedish RSO, Comissiona – MOZART: *Bassoon Concerto.* ***

Symphonies Nos. 7; 11.

*** BIS CD 580. Norrköping SO, Segerstam.

Symphonies Nos. 7; (i) No. 16.

(N) **(*) Swedish Soc. (ADD) SCD 1002. Stockholm PO, Doráti; (i) Ahronovitch.

To some extent the success of Allan Pettersson's *Seventh Symphony* in Sweden was a reaction against the unremitting diet of serial and post-serial music. It enjoyed something of a cult following in the 1970s. Here was a tonal work which sounded much more human than Blomdahl and had a certain cumulative effect for all its debt to Mahler. Doráti is a persuasive advocate and achieves a good performance from the fine Stockholm Orchestra. The *16th Symphony* is not among his best works, although Yuri Ahronovitch does his best with it.

The *Seventh Symphony* is a long, dark work which wears an anguished visage and packs a considerable emotional punch. Its musical substance is less weighty than appears to be the case on first acquaintance, and the ideas seem static and thinly spread; but it has a strong emotional appeal for many music-lovers and its atmosphere is quite powerful. Sergiu Comissiona gives a dedicated and sensitive account of the score that is every bit as fine as Dorati's première recording. The rather bizarre coupling is unlikely to sway the collector one way or the other.

Segerstam and his fine Norrköping players bring great feeling to the *Seventh* and give the somewhat shorter *Eleventh Symphony* the most sympathetic advocacy. If you want to explore further, you could try the *Fifth Symphony*, but the BIS disc seems the best possible place to start.

Symphonies Nos. 8; 10.

*** BIS CD 880. Norrköping SO, Segerstam.

The *Eighth Symphony* is long, often static, at times powerful and at others totally wanting in any kind of symphonic coherence. The *Tenth* is shorter but good though this performance is, it does not dispel the impression made by an earlier LP account that it is still essentially empty: the music of gesture not substance, and deficient in thematic vitality. Those who are on Pettersson's wavelength need not have any hesitations about either the performances or recordings on this BIS CD.

Symphony No. 9.

*** CPO 999 231-2. Berlin RSO, Francis.

Pettersson's *Ninth Symphony* (1970) was composed in the valley of the shadow of death. Life being short and sweet, one can only say that the 70 minutes which it takes to unfold seem an eternity. The three stars are for the performance and recording, so that admirers of the composer can proceed accordingly.

(i; ii) 7 Sonatas for 2 Violins; (i; iii) Andante espressivo; 2 Elegies; Romanza (all for violin & piano); (iii) Lamento (for piano).

(N) *** BIS CD 1028. Duo Gelland: (i) Martin Gelland & (ii) Cecilia Gelland; (iii) L. Wallin.

Pettersson wrote the *Seven Sonatas for 2 Violins* in 1951, after years in the viola section of the Stockholm Philharmonic, at roughly the time when he was studying in Paris with René Leibowitz. The music is indebted to Bartók, who was a cult figure in the Sweden during the 1950s, and to folk music. Although expertly conceived for this demanding medium, it is somewhat anonymous. The performances are exemplary, as is the splendid BIS recording.

Barfota sånger (Barefoot Songs); 6 Songs.

** CPO 999499-2. Groop, Garben.

These songs come from the war years when Pettersson was working as an orchestral player. The *Barefoot Songs* precede

any of his seventeen symphonies and are of the utmost simplicity. They are all strophic, and few last more than a couple of minutes. They are superbly sung by Monica Groop but not even she and her expert pianist can disguise their naïvety and in some cases emptiness. Admirers of the composer may not find their charms so eminently resistible or the melodic invention so unmemorable.

PFITZNER, Hans (1869–1949)

Das Herz: Liebesmelodie (Love theme). Das Kaethchen von Heilbronn: Overture. Palestrina: Preludes to Acts I, II & III.

**(*) DG 449 571-2. German Opera, Berlin, O, Thielemann –
  R. STRAUSS: *Capriccio* etc. ***

Thielemann believes passionately in Pfitzner, and in the three *Preludes* the playing is passionate yet at the same time restrained. The *Love Theme* from Pfitzner's last opera, and the extended prelude to his early opera, *Das Kaethchen von Heilbronn*, if overlong, are more sparkling than the rest. Both add to a fairly persuasive portrait. The Orchestra of the Berlin Deutsches Oper does not possess the opulent string-tone found at the *Philharmonie* but they play with conviction. The DG recording is very good without being state of the art.

String Quartets: in D, Op. 13; in C min., Op. 50.

(BB) *** CPO 999 072-2. Franz Schubert Qt.

We think of Pfitzner primarily as a composer of opera and Lieder, but this first-class CPO string quartet coupling serves to show him as a composer of fine chamber music in the mainstream of the German romantic tradition. Altogether these are two thoroughly rewarding works, finely crafted, with a ready flow of appealing variations and subtly individual harmonic progressions. They are splendidly played by the richly blended Schubert Quartet, whose chording is immaculate and who respond to the bittersweet, *fin de siècle* flavour of the writing. Excellent, realistic recording.

Palestrina (opera) complete.

(M) *** DG (ADD) 427 417-2 (3). Gedda, Fischer-Dieskau, Weikl, Ridderbusch, Donath, Fassbaender, Prey, Tölz Boys' Ch., Bav. R. Ch. & SO, Kubelik.

Though Pfitzner's melodic invention hardly matches that of his contemporary, Richard Strauss, his control of structure and drawing of character through music make an unforgettable impact. It is the central Act, a massive and colourful tableau representing the Council of Trent, which lets one witness the crucial discussion on the role of music in the church. The outer Acts – more personal and more immediately compelling – show the dilemma of Palestrina himself and the inspiration which led him to write the *Missa Papae Marcelli*, so resolving the crisis, both personal and public. At every point Pfitzner's response to this situation is illuminating, and this glorious performance with a near-ideal cast, consistent all through, could hardly be bettered in conveying the intensity of an admittedly offbeat inspiration. This CD reissue captures the glow of the Munich recording superbly and, though this is a mid-price set, DG has not skimped on the accompanying booklet.

PHILIPS, Peter (c. 1561–1640)

Motets: *Ave verum corpus; Ave Maria gratia plena; Ecce vicit Leo; Factum est silentium; Gaudent in coelis; Hodie nobis de coelo; O bone Jesu; O crux ave spes unica; O quam suavis.*

**(*) EMI CDM5 66788-2. King's College, Cambridge, Ch., Cleobury – DERING: *Motets.* **(*)

Both Peter Philips and his younger contemporary, Richard Dering, were Catholics and spent much of their lives on the Continent. This CD contrasts and compares the two composers' beautiful and expressive settings of the same texts. The performances are faithful, but the actual sound is not always perfect in either focus or blend, partly but not solely due to the recording.

PIERNÉ, Gabriel (1863–1937)

Cello Sonata in F sharp min., Op. 46.

*** Hyp. CDA 66979. Lidström, Forsberg – KOECHLIN: *Cello Sonata* etc. ***

Pierné was an interesting and cultured composer. His sonata is finely wrought with touches of real individuality, and well worth getting to know. Mats Lidström and Bengt Forsberg play with great intelligence and refinement and are well served by the engineers.

(i; iii) *Piano Quintet in E min., Op. 41;* (i; ii) *Violin Sonata, Op. 36;* (iv) *Les Enfants à Bethléem* (mystère for narrator, soloists and children's chorus).

(B) **(*) Erato Ultima Double (ADD) 3984 24239-2 (2).
(i) Hubeau; (ii) Charlier; (iii) Viotti Qt; (iv) Deiber (narr.), Chamonin, Schaer, Orliac, Frémeau, Ansellem, Hazard, French R. Maîtrise & PO, Lasserre de Rozel.

The *Piano Quintet* is quite a powerful piece, Franckian in influence, but with its own voice. Its Scherzo seductively borrows the rhythms of a Basque dance. The *Violin Sonata* is impressive too, with a most engaging central *Andante tranquillo*. Both are well played; the digital sound is a bit reverberant, but acceptable. *Les Enfants à Bethléem* is a work of great charm, for narrator (who sets the scene and closes the work, but does not outstay his welcome), adult and child soloists, and children's chorus. It sees the Nativity through the eyes of a child and could hardly be better presented: the performance has an engaging enthusiasm and innocence. The recording too is admirably atmospheric. Alas, the documentation is poor and there is no text for the cantata.

PIJPER, Willem (1894–1947)

String Quartets Nos. 1–5.

*** Olympia OCD 457. Schönberg Qt.

Willem Pijper was a dominant force in Dutch music between the wars. This CD collects all five of his *String Quartets*. The post-war *Fifth Quartet* (1946) was left unfinished at his death, though two movements were completed. Pijper's music is concentrated and thoughtful, eminently civilized and predominantly gentle in outlook, even if it falls short of having that unmistakable and distinctive voice betokening a great composer. The Schönberg Quartet is one of the finest Dutch ensembles, and they are beautifully recorded. A rewarding disc, well worth investigating.

PINTO, George Frederick (1785–1806)

Fantasia & Sonata in C min. (completed Joseph Woelfl); *Grand Sonatas Nos. 1 in E flat; 2 in A, Op. 3/1–2; in C min.; Minuetto in A flat; Rondo in E flat; Rondo on an Irish Air, 'Cory Owen'.*

*** Chan. 9798. O'Rorke (piano).

This unmissable Chandos collection reveals another forgotten composer of distinction, who might have become a very considerable figure had he not died prematurely at the age of twenty-one. He was born in London within a musical family and began playing in public at the age of eleven. His first two *Grand Sonatas* were published in 1801 when Pinto was sixteen and already a very accomplished composer indeed, with a distinct individuality, yet writing in a forward-looking lyrical style, that sometimes reminds us of the young Schubert. The *C minor Sonata*, however, is dedicated to John Field and delightfully identifies with that composer's melodic simplicity. But most striking of all is the *Fantasia and Sonata in C minor*, left unfinished at the composer's death, the opening quite worthy of Mozart, with a following *Adagio – Fugato* which has all the serenity of Bach, followed by a Beethovenian finale, which yet still has a personality of its own. Míceál O'Rorke plays all this music very persuasively indeed and is beautifully recorded.

PISTON, Walter (1894–1976)

(i; ii) *Capriccio for Harp & Strings;* (ii) *3 New England Sketches;* (iii) *Serenata;* (ii) *Symphony No. 4.*

✪ *** Delos DE 3106. (i) Wunrow; (ii) Seattle SO; (iii) NY CO; Schwarz.

Piston's *Fourth* is arguably the finest American symphony, as powerful in its forward sweep as the Harris *Third* and better held together than either Barber's *First* or Copland's *Third*. The remaining pieces, not only the *New England Sketches* but also the inventive *Capriccio for Harp and Strings*, are well worth seeking out. The fine recording and Gerard Schwarz's natural and unforced direction make this a most desirable CD. The slow movement of the *Serenata*, equally well played by New York forces, is quite inspired.

Violin Concertos Nos. 1–2; Fantasia for Violin & Orchestra.

✪ (BB) *** Naxos Dig. 8.559003. Boswell, Ukraine Nat. SO, Kucher.

It is quite extraordinary that a work as inspired as Piston's

First Violin Concerto (1939) is not already in the standard repertoire alongside the Barber, with which it has much in common, including a comparable profusion of individual, lyrical melody. The second subject of the first movement persists in the memory until, most engagingly, it is rhythmically transformed to become the secondary theme of the riotous Rondo finale. The *Second Concerto* is more elusive, but its opening is no less haunting. The first movement is a two-part structure, developing two ideas, one sinuously 'expressible', the other pungently rhythmic and angular. The extended *Adagio* introduces a calm and very beautiful theme which is later to form a canonic duet with the flute. The *Fantasia* is a late work, first performed in 1973. Ruminative and searching, its language is more dissonant. It may seem remarkable that these works should be given their CD début by a Russian orchestra, but they play the music with security, splendid commitment and feeling. James Boswell, who studied at Juilliard, is a superbly accomplished, dedicated and spontaneous soloist, and the recording is first class.

Symphony No. 2.

(N) (M) *** DG (ADD) 463 633-2. Boston SO, Tilson Thomas
– IVES: *Three Places in New England*; RUGGLES: *Sun-treader*. ***

Walter Piston's wartime *Second Symphony* (1943) makes a good entry point if you are starting to collect his music. It is more than finely crafted: it has a generosity of melodic invention and in the slow movement possesses a nobility that makes a strong impression. Michael Tilson Thomas and the Boston Symphony are very persuasive in its advocacy and the excellent recording from the early 1970s has been most effectively transferred to CD.

(i) Symphonies Nos. 2; 6; (ii) Sinfonietta.

*** Delos DE 3074. (i) Seattle SO; (ii) NY CO, Schwarz.

Gerard Schwarz's coupling of the *Second* and *Sixth Symphonies* is a welcome addition to the Piston discography. The sound has amplitude and warmth, and the playing of the Seattle Orchestra has plenty of enthusiasm and vitality. The *Sinfonietta* of 1942 is neoclassical in outlook – fresh and inventive with a touch of Hindemith about it.

Symphonies Nos. 5; (i) 7 & 8.

** Albany AR 011. Louisville O, Whitney, (i) Mester.

The *Fifth Symphony* has a sureness of purpose and feeling for organic growth that are the hallmark of the true symphonist. The *Seventh* and *Eighth Symphonies*, though not quite the equal of the finest Piston, are powerful and rewarding works which will speak to those who are more concerned with substance than with surface appeal. The Louisville performances are thoroughly committed and good, without being outstanding. The recordings sound better than they did on LP.

(i) Piano Quintet. Passacaglia; Piano Sonata; Toccata.

**(*) Northeastern/Koch NR 232-CD. Hokanson; (i) Portland Qt.

The *Piano Quintet* must be numbered among the finest post-Second World War piano quintets; it is a work of great vitality and integrity. These artists give a more than respectable account of it, and Leonard Hokanson proves no less convincing and responsive in the early *Piano Sonata*. The recording is fully acceptable.

String Quartets Nos. 1–3.

** Northeastern/Koch NR 9001-CD. Portland Qt.

Piston's three *String Quartets* are finely crafted pieces, sinewy and Hindemithian at times (the first movement of No. 1), thoughtful and inward-looking at others (the Lento opening of No. 2 and the slow movement of No. 3). His music never wears its heart on its sleeve, but if its emotional gestures are restrained there is no real lack of warmth. The Portland Quartet play well and the recordings are clear, although the acoustic is a little on the small side.

PIZZETTI, Ildebrando (1880–1968)

(i) Piano Concerto. Preludio per Fedra; (ii) Sinfonia del fuoco (for the film Cabiria).

** Marco Polo 8.225058. Schumann Phil. O, Caetani; with (i) Stefani; (ii) Statsenko, Städtischer Opera Ch., Chemnitz.

The present issue brings the eloquent Act I *Prelude* to the opera Pizzetti composed with Gabriele d'Annunzio, plus the *Sinfonia del fuoco*, drawn from the incidental music Pizzetti wrote in 1914 for an elaborate production of *Cabiria* (again with d'Annunzio) in which silent film was used. But the most substantial work is the *Piano Concerto*, 'Song of the High Seasons', of 1930. It is a little overripe perhaps, and at times even rather like Rachmaninov. The soloist Susanna Stefani acquits herself well. The *Fedra* prelude is the finest thing here and the Robert Schumann Philharmonie of Chemnitz give decent, serviceable performances. However, at less than 50 minutes' playing time this CD is over-priced.

La pisanella; 3 Preludii sinfonici (per L'Edipo Re); Preludio a un altro giorno; Rondò Veneziano.

**(*) Hyp. CDA 67084. BBC Scottish SO, Vänskä.

This well-filled programme makes an excellent introduction to Pizzetti. The *Rondò Veneziano* of 1929 was first performed by Toscanini; the three preludes from the opera *L'Edipo Re* are full of interest and *La pisanella* is a sunny and glorious work, which dates from 1913. Osmo Vänskä plays all these pieces with appropriate feeling but the string sound lacks real body and richness, particularly at the bass end of the spectrum.

Messa di requiem. De profundis.

❀ *** Hyp. CDA67017. Westminster Cathedral Ch., O'Donnell
– MARTIN: *Mass for Double Choir etc.* *** ❀

Messa di Requiem. Due composizioni corali: Il giardino dia Afrodite; Piena sorgeva la luna. Tre composizioni corali: Cade la sera; Ululate; Recordare, Domine.

**(*) Chan. 8964. Danish Nat. R. Chamber Ch., Parkman.

Pizzetti's 'serene and lyrical Requiem' (as his biographer, Guido Gatti puts it) is a work of surpassing beauty which will be a revelation to those who have not encountered it before, particularly in this fervent and inspired performance. It comes with the *De profundis* he composed in 1937 to mark the healing of his breach with Malipiero. Fine though the performance by the Danish Radio Chamber Choir under Stephen Parkman is coupled with other Pizzetti choral pieces, this Westminster Cathedral version completely supplants it.

PLATTI, Giovanni Benedetto

(1697–1763)

Solo for Oboe & Continuo in C min.; Sonata for Oboe, Cello & Continuo in G min.; Sonata in D for Violin, Oboe & Continuo; Sonata a tre in G for Violin or Oboe, Cello & Continuo; Trio for Flute, Violin or Oboe & Continuo in G; Trio for Oboe, Bassoon Obbligato & Continuo in D min.

*** Tactus TC 691601. J. M. Anciuti Ens.

Giovanni Benedetto Platti was prolific, and besides his vocal music he established a reputation with twelve harpsichord sonatas, published in Nuremberg between 1742 and 1746. This attractive collection of chamber sonatas reveals him as a musician of resource, skill and imagination. Where there is a choice in instrumentation, the excellent baroque oboeist Paollo Palastri takes the lead, and a period bassoon (Alberto Santi) is used as the continuo in the *C minor* solo as well as in the *Trio in D minor*. With the flute leading in the *Trio in G major*, there is plenty of colour, and as Platti's invention is always appealing – particularly the plaintive slow movements – this collection gives much pleasure. The recording is intimate and naturally balanced.

PLEYEL, Ignaz (1757–1831)

(i) *Sinfonia concertante for Violin, Cello & Strings in D. Symphony in A; Flute Quartet in B.*

(BB) ** Discover DICD 920130. (i) Bushkov, Kozodov; Moscow Concertino (members), Bushkov.

Pleyel's writing here is a bit like Boccherini without the pathos. The *Flute Quartet* (for flute, violin, viola and cello) has surface charm and the *Symphony* is fluent, if rather too long. The *Sinfonia concertante* – easily the best work here, and half as long as the *Symphony* – is full of neat invention and has an engaging finale. The whole programme is given persuasive advocacy by this excellent Russian group who are thoroughly within the style of the music and play with expert precision and much vitality. They are forwardly balanced and rather dryly recorded, but this inexpensive disc gives a fascinating glimpse of an interesting and distinctly talented musician.

Symphonies in C min. (Ben 121), C (Ben 128); F min. (Ben 138).

(N) (BB) *** Naxos 8.554696. Capella Istropolitana, Grodd.

Symphonies in D min. (Ben 147); C, Op. 66 (Ben 154); G, Op. 68 (Ben 156).

*** Chan. 9525. LMP, Bamert.

It was Pleyel who gave the series of London concerts to rival Haydn and Solomon in 1792. He later settled in Paris, founding the celebrated Playel piano factory. The earliest of the three symphonies on the Naxos disc was composed in 1778, when the composer was twenty-one; it is actually in C major but has a dramatic C minor introduction leading to a very lively allegro with trumpets and drums lacing the tuttis. The *Adagio* is rather fine, with horns echoing the string theme, but the trumpets and drums return in the bold minuet and add zest to a spirited moto perpetuo finale.

The other two symphonies date from 1786 and follow a similar pattern, but Pleyel's minor-key works are the most strikingly inventive, and the *F minor* has an *Andante grazioso* of Boccherinian charm, using gently muted strings against a persistent repeated accompanying figure in the second violins.

The fast *Minuet* with its Laendler-like *Trio* is no less individual. The performances from the excellent Capella Istopolitana are crisply stylish, expressively persuasive, and very well recorded.

On the companion Chandos disc the playing of the London Mozart Players under Matthew Bamert has much charm and grace, and the recording is in the best traditions of the house. The earliest of this second group of symphonies, the *D minor*, has hints of *Don Giovanni* and the *C major* has Rossinian undertones. In short, both these CDs explain why Pleyel, pupil of Haydn from the age of fifteen to twenty (under the patronage of Count Erdödy), was such a successful composer in the early years of the nineteenth century.

PLUMMER, John (died *c.* 1487)

Missa Sine nomine.

*** Signum SIGCD 015. Clerks' Group, Wickham (with BEDYNGHAM: *Myn hertis lust; Fortune alas; Mi verry joy;* ANON.: *Kyrie; Song; Pryncesse of youthe* ***) – FRYE: *Missa Flos Regalis*, etc. ***

We know very little about the English composer, John Plummer, whose mass only survives in a Brussels manuscript. His setting is rather bare and primitive in its part writing, less inspired than its coupling by Walter Frye, but it makes a fascinating aural glimpse into an unfamiliar period of English polyphony. The coupled songs by Bedyngham are delightful and this whole collection, beautifully sung and recorded, is treasurable.

PONCE, Manuel (1882–1948)

Folia de España (Theme & Variations with Fugue).

(M) *** Sony (ADD) SBK 47669. Williams (guitar) – BARRIOS: *Collection.* ***

Ponce's *Variations on 'Folia de España'* are subtle and haunting, and their surface charm often conceals a vein of richer, darker feeling. The performance is first rate and the sound admirably clean and finely detailed, yet at the same time warm.

PONCHIELLI, Amilcare (1834–86)

La Gioconda (complete).

*** Decca 414 349-2 (3). Caballé, Ghiaurov, Baltsa, Pavarotti, Milnes, Hodgson, L. Op. Ch., Nat. PO, Bartoletti.

*** EMI (ADD) CDS5 56291-2 (3). Callas, Cossotto, Ferraro, Vinco, Cappuccilli, Companeez, La Scala, Milan, Ch. & O, Votto.

(M) (***) Fonit mono 3984 29355-2 (3). Callas, Barbieri, Amadini, Silveri, Neri, Poggi, Turin R. Ch. & O, Votto.

The colourfully atmospheric melodrama of this opera gives the Decca engineers the chance to produce one of their most vivid opera recordings. Caballé is just a little overstressed in the title-role but produces glorious sounds. Pavarotti has impressive control and heroic tone. Commanding performances too from Milnes as Barnaba, Ghiaurov as Alvise and Baltsa as Laura, firm and intense all three. Bartoletti proves a vigorous and understanding conductor, presenting the blood and thunder with total commitment but finding the right charm in the most famous passage, the *Dance of the Hours*.

Maria Callas gave one of her most vibrant, most compelling, most totally inspired performances on record in the title-role of *La Gioconda*, with flaws very much subdued. The challenge she presented to those around her is reflected in the soloists – Cossotto and Cappuccilli both at the very beginning of distinguished careers – as well as the distinctive tenor Ferraro and the conductor Votto, who has never done anything finer on record. The recording still sounds well, though it dates from 1959.

Like the companion Callas set of *La Traviata*, this Fonit set was recorded (for Cetra in 1952) very early in the diva's career. She was to re-record the opera in 1959, again with Votto, but, as in the remake, the present set shows her dramatic powers at their peak and the voice fresher than ever. The famous *Suicidio* is sung with an intensity that has rarely if ever been equalled and the closing scenes of both Acts I and IV (with Maria Amadini and Paolo Silveri respectively) are memorable. Barbieri and Neri also make fine contributions and Poggi's contribution is suitably ardent. Votto conducts with understanding, maintaining a spontaneous dramatic flow and the remastering of the old mono recording is surprisingly good.

POPOV, Gavril (1904–72)

(i) *Symphonies Nos. 1, Op. 7*; (ii) *2 (Motherland), Op. 39.*

**(*) Olympia Dig./ADD OCD 576. (i) Moscow State SO; (ii) USSR R. & TV SO; Provatorov.

An accomplished all-round musician and a pupil of Vladimir Shcherbachov in Leningrad, Popov was a prolific composer for the cinema, providing music for 38 films, including some by Eisenstein. He gave us six symphonies in all, plus a good deal of chamber music as well as an opera on *Alexander Nevsky*. His *First Symphony* occupied him during 1928–34. The first movement is over 20 minutes long, inventive and powerful, though indebted to Shostakovich,

his junior by two years. The wartime *Second Symphony* (1943) opens with a long and expansive slow movement, not without overtones of the cinema, while the lively *Presto* sounds as if it has strayed out of *Petrushka*. Perhaps the most eloquent movement is the third, a soulful and powerfully sustained threnody. The performances under Gennady Provatorov are totally committed, though the recordings are not wholly satisfactory. This should not, however, deter readers from investigating this interesting music.

Symphony No. 5 in A, 'Pastoral', Op. 77; (i) *Symphonic Suite No. 1.*

**(*) Olympia OCD 598. USSR State SO, Karapetian; (i) Glushkova, Polyakov, Moscow R. & TV SO, Chivzhel.

The *Symphonic Suite No. 1* derives from the score Popov composed in 1933 for the film *Komsomol is the Chief of Electrification*, an early example of Socialist-Realist cinema! The *Fifth Symphony*, on the other hand, is much later – composed in 1956, three years after Shostakovich's *Tenth*. It is certainly well structured, the first and last of the five movements are subtitled 'Pastorale' and the intervening three are inventive, with an excellent sense of orchestral colour. The performances are thoroughly committed even if the sound is a bit raw in climaxes.

PORTER, Cole (1891–1964)

Overtures: *Anything Goes; Can-Can; Gay Divorce; Kiss Me, Kate. Night and Day* (from *Gay Divorce*).

(B) *** EMI double forte CZS5 68589-2 (2). L. Sinf., McGlinn – GERSHWIN: *Broadway & Film Music* **(*); KERN: *Overtures.* **

These overtures were not put together or scored by the composer but by the professionals of the day. As *Gay Divorce* does not include the most famous number from the show, a separate arrangement of *Night and Day* has been included, richly scored. The performances here are definitive and the bright recording fits the music like a glove.

Song arrangements for orchestra: *Anything goes; Begin the beguine; Blow, Gabriel blow; In the still of the night; It's de-lovely; I've got you under my skin; My heart belongs to Daddy; Night and day; It's all right with me; Ridin' high; So in love; You'd be so nice to come home to* (all orch. Ray Wright).

(M) **(*) [Mercury 434 327-2]. O, Fennell – GERSHWIN: *Song Arrangements.* **(*)

The lyrics are missed more than most with orchestral arrangements of Cole Porter songs and, though Ray Wright's scoring is imaginative and admirably sophisticated, this is essentially a CD to use as a pleasing background for a dinner party, rather than for concentrated listening. Unusually for this label, the recording is multi-miked, so the stereo effects are unashamedly directional. But the sound is silky-smooth as well as being clearly defined and, of its kind, this is very good indeed.

Kiss Me, Kate (musical).

*** EMI CDS7 54033-2 (2). Barstow, Hampson, Criswell, Dvorsky, Burns, Evans, Amb. Ch., L. Sinf., McGlinn.

Having two opera-singers, Josephine Barstow and Thomas Hampson, in the principal roles of the ever-argumentative husband-and-wife team who play Kate and Petruchio in *The Taming of the Shrew* works excellently, both strong and characterful. Kim Criswell is delectable as Lois Lane, brassy but not strident in *Always true to you, darling, in my fashion*. Strong characterization too from George Dvorsky, Damon Evans and Karla Burns, with the London Sinfonietta playing their hearts out. However, this has been deleted just as we go to press.

Songs: *Begin the beguine; Bring me back my butterfly; Bull dog; Don't fence me in; Drink; Easy to love; A fool there was; How's your romance?; I concentrate on you; In the still of the night; It was written in the stars; I've got you under my skin; My cozy little corner in the Ritz; Night and day; Two little babes in the wood; When I had a uniform on; When my baby goes to town; Who said gay Paree?.*

*** EMI CDC7 54203-2. Hampson, Amb. Ch., LSO, McGlinn.

Thomas Hampson proves an ideal baritone for this repertoire, totally inside the idiom, yet bringing to it a gloriously firm, finely controlled voice. The selection is a delightful one, including not just popular 'standards' but unexpected rarities. Excellent sound.

Let's do it; Miss Otis regrets; My heart belongs to Daddy; The physician; Night and day.

(*) Unicorn DKPCD 9138. Gomez, Jones, Instrumental Ens. – BRITTEN: *Songs.* *

Though the accompanist, Martin Jones, is too stiff and deadpan in these five classic Cole Porter songs, Jill Gomez is so warmly expressive a singer that the dry backing serves to add to the poignancy of songs like 'Miss Otis regrets'. Despite the reservations, a good coupling for the Britten items.

POTTER, A. J. (1918–80)

Finnegans Wake; Fantasia Gaelach No. 1; Overture to a Kitchen Comedy; Sinfonia de profundis; Variations on a Popular Tune.

(N) ✸ *** Marco 8.225158. National SO of Ireland, Houlihan.

Archibald James Potter's imaginative gift for enlivening folksongs might be compared to that of Percy Grainger. But he also had the ability to work on a larger canvas, and his five-movement *Sinfonia de profundis* is very impressive indeed. Although it is based on a serial theme (heard at the very outset), one would hardly suspect it, for the music is clearly tonal. Written in 1968 the opening movement reflects in its angst a very desperate period in the composer's life. Then comes a touchingly wan little *Waltz* which slowly gathers energy and passion, and collapses into a double bassoon growl.

The eloquent and moving *Adagio* brings powerful writing for strings and then a trumpet solo heralds a popular march-like scherzo combined with a gossamer Irish jig on the violins, and Malcolm Arnold-like groans from the brass. The *Sinfonia* closes with an ethereal *Epilogue*, resolved with a chorale of affirmation over hammering timpani. It is an altogether remarkably communicative work, well worth getting to know.

Among the folksongs, *Finnegans Wake*, which is brilliantly scored for wind and percussion, reminds one a little of Vaughan Williams's *Folksongs Suite*, only it is far wittier. The *Fantasia Gaelack No. 1*, which features both *My Lagan love* and *The fair child*, makes a ravishing lyrical contrast. The seven *Variations on a Popular Tune (The Wild Colonial Boy)*, given out first by a solo violin, are brilliantly diverse and most entertaining, especially when Potter lapses into boisterous, trumpet-led vulgarity.

The *Overture to a Kitchen Comedy* (1956) was the composer's first orchestral work and bustles with energy and orchestral exuberance, but also has a nice lyrical strain. It is perhaps a trifle over-extended, but still very enjoyable. First-class performances and splendid recording make this CD unmissable.

POULENC, Francis (1899–1963)

EMI Centenary Edition, Vol. 1: Concertos, orchestral and sacred music: (i–iii) *Aubade (Concerto choréographique);* (ii; iii) *Les Animaux modèles;* (iv; v; iii) *Les Biches* (ballet; complete); (iv; iii) *Bucolique;* (vi; ii; vii) *Concert champêtre (for Harpsichord & Orchestra);* (viii; ii; iii) *Concerto in G min. for Organ, Strings & Timpani;* (i–iii) *Piano Concerto in C sharp min.;* (ix; ii; vii) *Double Piano Concerto in D min.;* (x) *Gnossienne No. 3* (Satie, orch. Poulenc); (xi; iii) *2 Marches et un intermède (for chamber orchestra);* Les Mariés de la Tour Eiffel; (iv; iii) *Matelote provençale; Pastourelle;* (xi; iii) *Suite française; Sinfonietta.* (Vocal): (xii) *Ave verum corpus; Exultate Deo;* (xiii; xiv; iii) *Gloria;* (xv) *Laudes de Saint Antoine de Padoue;* (xvi) *Litanies à la Vierge Noire;* (xvii) *Mass in G; 4 Motets pour le temps de Noël;* (xiv; xviii) *4 Motets pour un temps de pénitence;* (xix) *4 Petites prières de Saint François d'Assise;* (xx; iii) *7 Répons des ténèbres;* (xii) *Salve Regina;* (xxi; ii; iii) *Stabat Mater.*

(M) **(*) EMI stereo/mono ADD/Dig. CMS5 66837-2 (5).
(i) Tacchino; (ii) Paris Conservatoire O; (iii) Prêtre; (iv) Philh. O; (v) Amb. S.; (vi) Van der Wiele; (vii) Dervaux; (viii) Duruflé; (ix) Février, composer; (x) Toulouse Capitole O, Plasson; (xi) O de Paris; (xii) Groupe Vocal de France, Alldis; (xiii) Cateri; (xiv) French R. & TV Ch. & O; (xv) The Sixteen, Christophers; (xvi) French R. Children's Ch., Joineau; Roget; (xvii) Winchester Cathedral Ch., Neary; (xviii) Resnel; (xix) The King's Singers; (xx) Carpentier, various choirs, New PO of R. France; (xxi) Crespin, René Duclos Ch.

The composer's own recording of the *Double Piano Concerto* with Jacques Fevrier goes back to 1957, a high-spirited account, at times unpolished; and so does the *Concert champêtre* with Aimée van der Wiele, made all the more effective thanks to a clangorous Pleyel harpsichord of the kind intended by the composer. The *Organ Concerto*, with the original soloist, Maurice Duruflé, brings some suspect intonation, but the performance is lively and dramatic. *Les Biches* comes in the full ballet version with chorus, not the usual suite. Readers will note that this, and much of the other orchestral and concertante music, are also available separately on the two-disc set below. In the religious music, the choral singing is variable, with the British choirs and groups generally setting a higher standard than the French, although the Groupe Vocal de France under John Alldis is the exception. For all the unevenness and occasional roughness of sound, a valuable and enjoyable collection. As in the rest of the series, the five CDs come in stout cardboard inners within a stylish box. There are excellent notes, with original texts provided (in French or Latin), but no translations.

EMI Centenary Edition, Vol. 2: Chamber and piano music: (i; ii) *Bagatelle for Violin & Piano*; (ii; iii) *Cello Sonata*; (ii; iv) *Clarinet Sonata*; (iv; v) *Sonata for 2 Clarinets*; (iv; vi) *Sonata for Clarinet & Bassoon*; (ii; vii) *Elégie for Horn & Piano*; (ii; viii) *Flute Sonata*; (vii; ix) *Sonata for Horn, Trumpet & Trombone*; (x) *3 Mouvements perpétuels for chamber ensemble*; (xi) *Sarabande for Guitar*; (ii; xii) *Oboe Sonata*; (ii; xiii) *Sextet for Piano, Flute, Oboe, Clarinet, Bassoon & Horn*; (xiv) *Suite française for Cello & Piano*; (ii; xv) *Trio for Piano, Oboe & Bassoon*; (xvi) *Villanelle for Flute & Piano*; (xvii) *Violin Sonata*. Piano duet: (xviii; ii) *Capriccio; Elégie; L'Embarquement pour Cythère; Sonata for Piano, 4 Hands; Sonata for 2 Pianos*. Solo piano: (xviii) *Badinage; Bourrée au Pavillon d'Auvergne; 3 Feuillets d'album; Française; Humoresque; 5 Impromptus; 15 Improvisations; 3 Intermezzi; Mélancolie; Pastourelle; 3 Mouvements perpétuels;* (ii) *Napoli;* (xviii) *8 Nocturnes; 3 Novelettes; 3 Pièces; Pièce brève; Presto in B flat; Promenades;* (ii) *Les Soirées de Nazelles;* (xviii) *Suite française; Suite in C;* (ii) *Thème varié;* (xviii) *Valse in C; Valse improvisation; Villageoises*.

(M) ** EMI ADD/Dig. CMS5 66831-2 (5). (i) Grimal;
(ii) Février; (iii) Fournier; (iv) Portal; (v) Gaal; (vi) Wallez;
(vii) Civil; (viii) Debost; (ix) Wilbraham, Iveseon;
(x) Members of O de la Garde Républicaine, F. Boulanger;
(xi) Ghiglia; (xii) Bourgue; (xiii) Wind Ens.; (xiv) Phillips,
Strosser; (xv) Casier, Faisandier; (xvi) Pottier, Strosser;
(xvii) Zimmermann, Lonquich; (xviii) Tacchino.

This is a pretty comprehensive collection of Poulenc's chamber music, but not all the performances are equally distinguished. It is good to have Fournier's elegant account of the *Cello Sonata* and Zimmermann's more recent one of the *Violin Sonata*; Bourgue's performance of the *Oboe Sonata* is also very enjoyable, and the other wind sonatas are effective enough, if less individual. Both the *Trio for Piano, Oboe and Bassoon* and the *Sextet* are rather dryly recorded; however, although the playing could have more elegance, there is a high-spirited, knockabout quality here that is eminently likeable. The brass trio is one of the highlights, very entertainingly played and given good sound. Most of the recordings date from the 1970s but one or two are more

modern. Jacques Février's pianism, both in the sonatas and the two-piano works, does not always have the finish such repertoire ideally demands. Tacchino's playing of the solo piano music is often technically brilliant and strongly characterized (perhaps at times a shade too strongly), but it does not have the degree of charm or the gamin quality which are ideally required. The recording too, closely balanced, is a bit hard and lacking bloom.

EMI Centenary Edition, Vol. 3: Mélodies and chansons: *Airs chantés; A sa guitare; Banalités; Le Bestiare ou Cortège d'Orphée* (with unpublished supplement: *La colombe; Le serpent; La puce*). *Calligrammes* (cycle); *Bleuet; Ce doux petit visage; Chanson à boire; 3 Chansons de Federico Garcia Lorca; Chansons gailliardes; 7 Chansons for mixed choir, a cappella; 8 Chansons françaises; 8 Chansons polonaises; 4 Chansons pour enfants; Une chanson de porcelaine; Chansons villageoises; Les Chemins de l'amour; Cocardes; Colloque; La Courte Paille* (cycle); *Dernier poème; Le disparu; Epitaphe; Fancy; Fiançailles pour rire; La Fraîcheur et le feu* (cycle); *La grenouillère; Hymne; Main dominée par le coeur; Mazurka; 2 Mélodies: (Le souris; Nuage); 2 Mélodies de Guillaume Apollinaire; Métamorphoses; Miroirs brûlants; Nos souvenirs qui chantent; Paul et Virginie; Petites voix* (cycle); *Pierrot; 2 Poèmes de Guillaume Apollinaire* (2 sets); *Poèmes de Guillaume Apollinaire; 3 Poèmes de Louise Lalanne; 3 Poèmes de Louis de Vilmorin; 4 Poèmes de Max Jacob; 5 Poèmes de Max Jacob; 2 Poèmes de Louis Aragon; 5 Poèmes de Paul Eluard; 5 Poèmes de Pierre de Ronsard; Le portrait; Priez pour la paix; Rapsodie nègre; Rosamonde; Tel jour telle nuit* (cycle); *Toréador; Le Travail du peintre* (cycle); *Vive Nadia; Vocalise*.

(M) *** EMI stereo/mono ADD/Dig. CMS5 66849-2 (5).
Benoit, Rivenq, Fouchécourt, La Roux, Van Dam, Streich,
Souzay, Ameling, Gedda, Mesplé, Bernac, Berton, Sénéchal,
Parker, Bacquier, Norman, Develiereau, French R.
Children's Ch., Besson, The Sixteen, Christophers,
Stockholm Chamber Ch., Erikson. Accompanists include
Collard, Baldwin, Parsons, Tacchino, Francis Poulenc,
Février.

A fine gallery of singers is presented here, in vintage performances covering the full span of Poulenc's work as a song composer, with his cabaret style happily set alongside deeper songs. There is an immense variety here and though there have been more refined performances on rival discs, there are none more idiomatic than these, with each singer characterizing vividly. Rita Streich, Jessye Norman and Elly Ameling are very well represented alongside native French singers ranging back to the composer's friend and associate, Pierre Bernac. The close-up sound, transferred with fine immediacy, hardly shows its age. Entirely new are the a cappella choral recordings, very well performed by The Sixteen and the Stockholm Chamber Choir. An indispensable collection.

EMI Centenary Edition, Vol. 4: Vocal works ('*Oeuvres lyriques*'): (i) *Le Bal masqué;* (ii) *Les Chemins de l'amour;* (iii) *La Dame de Monte-Carlo;* (iv) *Dialogues des Carmélites;* (v) *Esquisse pour une fanfare;* (vi) *Figure humaine;* (vii) *Le Gendarme incompris;* (viii) *L'Histoire de*

Babar le petit éléphant; (ix) *L'Invitation au château;*
(x) *Les Mamelles de Tirésias;* (xi) *Sécheresses;* (vi) *Un soir
de neige;* (xii) *La Voix humaine.*

(M) (***) EMI mono/stereo ADD/Dig. CMS5 66843-2 (5).
   (i) Benoit, Charpentier, Paris Conservatoire O (Soloists),
   Prêtre; (ii) Printemps, O, Cariven; (iii) Mesplé, Monte-Carlo
   PO, Prêtre; (iv) Duval, Crespin, Scharley, Berton, Gorr,
   Depraz, Finel, Paris Op. O, Dervaux; (v) Toulouse O
   (members), Cardon; (vi) The Sixteen, Christophers;
   (vii) Rivenq, Fouchécourt, Benoit, Garde Républicaine
   Soloists' O, F. Boulanger; (viii) Peter Ustinov, Paris
   Conservatoire O, Prêtre; (ix) Strosse, Grimal, Guyot;
   (x) Duval, Giraudeau, Opéra-Comique Ch. & O, Cluytens;
   (xi) New O of R. France, Prêtre; (xii) Duval, Opéra-Comique
   O, Prêtre.

Although not everything here has been satisfactorily re-
recorded, the vintage performances in this collection of
Poulenc's stage works may not measure up to more recent
rivals in opulence of recording, but the immediacy, intensity
and feeling for idiom have never been surpassed, and the
singers are all well chosen, firm and true even in face of the
close-up sound favoured by the French EMI engineers. So
the *Dialogues des Carmélites,* much the longest work, lacks
atmospheric beauty, but makes its dramatic point with overwhelming force, and Poulenc's favourite soprano, Denise
Duval, could not be more characterful, both there and in
Les Mamelles de Tirésias and *La Voix humaine.* Peter Ustinov
narrates the story of *Babar the Elephant* charmingly in
French. Totally new and beautifully done by The Sixteen
under Harry Christophers are the secular cantatas at the
end, *Figure humaine* and *Un soir de neige.* Texts in French
are provided but no translations.

ORCHESTRAL MUSIC

(i) *Les Animaux modèles: suite.* (iii) *Aubade. La Baigneuse
de Trouville; Les Biches (ballet): suite. Les Mariés de la
Tour Eiffel: Discours du général. Matelote provençale
(from La Guirlande de Campra). Pastourelle (from
L'Eventail de Jeanne); 2 Préludes posthumes et une
Gnossienne* (SATIE, orch. POULENC); *Valse;* (from *Album
des six*) (452 937).

(i) *Bucolique; Fanfare; 2 Marches et un intermède; Pièce
brève sur le nom d'Albert Roussel; Sinfonietta; Suite
française;* (iii) *Concert champêtre* (for harpsichord and
orchestra) ✪ (452 665).

(ii; iv) *Concerto in G min. for Organ, Strings & Timpani;*
(ii; iii) *Piano Concerto;* (ii; iii; v) *Double Piano Concerto in
D min.* (436 546).

Complete Orchestral Music & Concertos (as above).

*** Decca 452 937-2; 452 665-2; 436 546-2 (3) (CDs available
   separately.) (i) O Nat. de France, or (ii) Phil. O; Dutoit; with
   (iii) Rogé (piano or harpsichord); (iv) Hurford; (v) Deferne.

This Decca set makes a clear first choice for those wanting a
complete survey of Poulenc's concertante and orchestral
works. The discs are available separately for those wanting

to fill in gaps in a collection. The first disc is new and well
up to the standard of the others, with the *Aubade* particularly
delightful, and the richly coloured orchestral arrangement
of Satie's *Gnossiennes* ending the disc magnetically. The only
slight proviso concerns the suite from *Les Biches.* It is a pity
the complete ballet was not chosen (as on the EMI Rouge et
Noir set below). Dutoit readily catches the music's languid
warmth and veiled eroticism, notably in the beautiful *Adagietto,* but the opening *Rondeau,* with its pert, jazzy trumpet
solo, might have had more bite, partly the fault of the warm
resonance of the recording.

The major works on the second disc are the *Sinfonietta,*
which comes off marvellously, and the *Concert champêtre,*
where Pascal Rogé proves as fine a clavecinist as pianist and
his account, equally strong on charm and elegance, ranks
very highly indeed. The smaller pieces greatly enhance the
already strong attractions of this disc. The excellence of
the performances is matched by first-rate and meticulously
balanced Decca sound.

Rogé's playing in the third collection (the first to be
issued, in 1993) is hardly less captivating, so it will be no
surprise that his accounts of the *Piano Concerto* (with its
moments of tenderness and gamin-like *joie de vivre*) and the
delightful D minor *Concerto for Two Pianos* (partnered by
Silvia Deferne) are completely attuned to the sensibility and
spirit of this still underrated master. One of Poulenc's most
extraordinary qualities is his ability to effect an abrupt
change of mood from the highest of spirits to a sudden
glimpse of melancholy and desolation, which is mirrored
here. Hurford is hardly less successful in the *Organ Concerto*
and the Philharmonia Orchestra produces a cultivated
sound for Dutoit, marginally less characterful and idiomatic
perhaps than the French orchestra on the companion discs,
but warmly elegant. The recording is excellent.

(i) *Les Animaux modèles;* (ii; iii) *Les Biches (complete
ballet);* (ii) *Bucolique;* (i; iv) *Concert champêtre (for
harpsichord & orchestra);* (i; v) *Double Piano Concerto in
D min.;* (vi) *2 Marches et un intermède (for chamber
orchestra); Les Mariés de la Tour Eiffel (La Baigneuse de
Trouville; Discours du général).* (ii) *Matelote provençale;
Pastourelle;* (vi) *Sinfonietta; Suite française.*

(B) *** EMI Rouge et Noir ADD/Dig. CZS5 69446-2 (2).
   (i) Paris Conservatoire O; or (ii) Philh. O; (iii) with Amb. S.;
   (iv) with Van der Wiele, or (v) composer and Février; (vi) O
   de Paris; all cond. Prêtre.

Les Biches comes here in its complete form, with the choral
additions that Poulenc made optional when he came to
rework the score. The music is a delight, and so too is the
group of captivating short pieces, digitally recorded at the
same time (1980): *Bucolique, Pastourelle* and *Matelote
provençale.* High-spirited, fresh, elegant playing and sumptuous recorded sound enhance the claims of all this music.
The *Suite française* is another highlight. It is well played and
recorded in a pleasing, open acoustic. Poulenc himself was
a pianist of limited accomplishment, but his interpretation
with Jacques Février of his own skittish *Double Concerto* is
infectiously jolly. In the imitation pastoral concerto for
harpsichord, Aimée van der Wiele is a nimble soloist, but

here Prêtre's inflexibility as a conductor comes out the more, even though the finale has plenty of high spirits. The *Sinfonietta*, too, could have a lighter touch. *Les Animaux modèles* is based on the fables of La Fontaine, with a prelude and a postlude, but here the recording is rather lacking in bloom, and the *Deux Marches* are also a trifle overbright. With nearly 156 minutes' playing time, these CDs are well worth exploring.

(i) *Aubade (Concerto choréographique);* (ii) *Concert champêtre for Harpsichord & Orchestra;* (iii) *Organ Concerto in G min.;* (i) *Piano Concerto in C sharp min.;* (i; iv) *Double Piano Concerto in D min.*

(B) *** Erato Ultima 3984 21342-2 (2). Rotterdam PO, Conlon; with (i) Duchable; (ii) Koopman; (iii) Alain; (iv) Collard.

The Erato Ultima Double is one of the most attractive of all Poulenc issues. The *Aubade* is an exhilarating work of great charm. The *Piano Concerto* evokes the faded charms of Paris in the 1930s. The performances of two of the solo works by François-René Duchable and the Rotterdam orchestra have a certain panache and flair that are most winning. The *Double Concerto* too captures all the wit and charm of the Poulenc score, and the 'mock Mozart' slow movement is particularly elegant. Perhaps in these two solo works Duchable is a shade too prominent, but not sufficiently so to disturb a strong recommendation, for the sound is otherwise full and pleasing. The *Organ Concerto*, too, has never come off better on record than in Marie-Claire Alain's performance using the excellent Flenthrop organ in Rotterdam's concert hall, the Doelen. The *Concert champêtre* always offers problems of balance as it is scored for a full orchestra, but the exaggerated contrast was clearly intended by the composer. The performance is most perceptive, with a particularly elegant and sparkling finale. James Conlon provides admirable accompaniments throughout a highly recommendable pair of discs.

(i) *Aubade;* (ii) *Double Piano Concerto in D min.; Sinfonietta.*

(M) *** Virgin VM5 61907-2. (i–ii) Pommier, with (ii) Queffélec; City of L. Sinf., Hickox.

Jean-Bernard Pommier gives a thoroughly idiomatic and incisive account of the *Aubade*, and both he and Anne Queffélec play the *Concerto for Two Pianos* to the manner born. They have the measure of the pastiche Mozart slow movement and the quasi-Gamelan first. Good though the Duchable–Collard performance is, this has the better recording. Hickox gives an affectionate and charming account of the *Sinfonietta* that matches – almost – the splendid account from the Orchestre National under Dutoit. Very recommendable, especially at mid-price.

Aubade; Sinfonietta.

*** Hyp. CDA 66347. Evans, New London O, Corp – HAHN: *Le Bal de Béatrice d'Este.* ***

The *Sinfonietta* is a fluent and effortless piece, full of resource and imagination, and Ronald Corp and the New London Orchestra do it proud. Julian Evans is an alert soloist in the *Aubade*: his is a performance of real character and, though

less well balanced than the *Sinfonietta*, his account can hold its own artistically with the competition. The Hahn rarity with which it is coupled enhances the interest and value of this release.

Les Biches (ballet suite).

*** Chan. 9023. Ulster O, Y. P. Tortelier – IBERT: *Divertissement;* MILHAUD: *Le Boeuf; La Création.* ***

(M) *** EMI (ADD) CDM7 63945-2. Paris Conservatoire O, Prêtre – DUTILLEUX: *Le Loup;* MILHAUD: *Création du Monde.* ***

Yan Pascal Tortelier and the Ulster Orchestra give an entirely winning account of Poulenc's ballet suite. Here the opening has delightfully keen rhythmic wit, and the playing is equally polished and crisply articulated in the gay *Rag-Mazurka* and infectious *Final*. The lovely *Adagietto* is introduced with tender delicacy, yet reaches a suitably plangent climax. Top-drawer Chandos sound and splendid couplings ensure the overall success of this admirable compilation.

Prêtre has re-recorded *Les Biches* digitally in its complete format (see above). This 1961 recording of the suite, omitting the chorus, is well worth having in its own right: the racy style of the orchestral playing is instantly infectious in the opening *Rondeau* with its catchy trumpet solo. The remastered sound-picture is much better focused than in its old LP format; and this is one example where the bright vividness of CD is entirely advantageous, for there is just the right degree of ambient atmosphere. With excellent couplings this is a most desirable triptych.

Concert champêtre (for harpsichord); *Concerto in G min. for Organ, Strings & Timpani.*

(B) *** EMI (ADD) double forte CZS5 69752-2 (2). Preston, LSO, Previn – MESSIAEN: *Turangalîla Symphony.* ***

On EMI double forte each of the recordings is realistically balanced, and Simon Preston, who plays the solo parts in both concertos, produces readings of great fluency and authority, to say nothing of wit in the work for harpsichord. Previn too has a genuine feeling for the music: the orchestral playing is always musical, often sparkling, and the recording is first class. It set new standards in its day (1977).

Concerto in G min. for Organ, Strings & Timpani.

(*) Chan. 9271. Tracey (organ of Liverpool Cathedral), BBC PO, Y. P. Tortelier – GUILMANT: *Symphony No. 1;* WIDOR: *Symphony No. 5.* *

(N) ** René Gailly CD 87 162. Michiels, Brugense Collegium, Peire – FAURE: *Requiem, Op. 48.* **

The wide reverberation period of Liverpool Cathedral produces gloriously plushy textures (the orchestra strings are radiantly rich in colour) but little plangent bite, and some may feel that the effect is too overwhelmingly sumptuous for Poulenc's *Concerto*. Yet it is easy to wallow in the gloriously full sounds, and the performance itself, spacious to allow for the resonance, is certainly enjoyable.

Ignace Michiels is an excellent soloist for the Brugense performance, and the orchestra has plenty of fire. However, it is obvious that there are few players, and there is a want of body and weight. Not a first choice, although the Fauré is not unappealing.

Double Piano Concerto in D min.

(M) *** Teldec 4509 97445-2. Güher and Süher Pekinel, French R. PO, Janowski – SAINT-SAENS: *Carnival of the Animals*. ***

The Pekinel Duo come from mixed Spanish/Turkish parentage and their account of Poulenc's *Double Concerto* is given with great dash and sparkle. Janowski provides a lively and thoroughly supportive accompaniment, and the recording balance is excellent. But even at mid-price 38 minutes is short measure even if the Saint-Saëns zoological fantasy is equally enticing and attractive.

The Story of Babar the Elephant (orch. Jean Françaix).

⬤ (BB) *** Naxos 8.554170. Humphries, Melbourne SO, Lanchbery – BRITTEN: *Young Person's Guide to the Orchestra;* PROKOFIEV: *Peter and the Wolf.* ***

Barry Humphries adopts an engagingly cultivated male persona to tell *The Story of Babar* with an elegance and a sense of innocence which make the narrative seem completely believable, within a children's world where elephants can assume human vanities and aspirations. He is genial, gently touching and animated by turns, but always stylish; and so is Lanchbery's matching orchestral accompaniment, which catches the moments of nostalgia and joy with equal sensitivity and flair. The dance after the wedding (in Jean Françaix's uninhibited scoring) momentarily recalls *Les Biches.* The effect here is infinitely more involving than the composer's rather bald, original piano version. Jean de Brunhoff's tale has never been presented more effectively on record, or better recorded. A delight and very highly recommended, as the couplings are first rate too.

Suite française.

(M) *** ASV (ADD) CDWHL 2067. L. Wind O, Wick – GRAINGER: *Irish Tune from County Derry* etc.; MILHAUD: *Suite française.* ***

This engaging suite is based on themes by the sixteenth-century composer, Claude Gervaise. Poulenc scored them for a small ensemble of wind instruments and they come up very freshly in these artists' hands. Excellent recording and couplings. Thoroughly recommended.

CHAMBER MUSIC

Complete chamber music: *Cello Sonata; Clarinet Sonata; Sonata for 2 Clarinets; Sonata for Clarinet & Bassoon; Elégie for Horn & Piano (in Memory of Dennis Brain); Flute Sonata; Oboe Sonata; Sarabande for Guitar; Sextet for Piano, Flute, Oboe, Clarinet, Bassoon & Horn; Sonata for Horn, Trumpet & Trombone; Trio for Piano, Oboe & Bassoon; Villanelle for Piccolo (pipe) & Piano; Violin Sonata.*

*** Hyp. CDA 67255/6. Nash Ens. with Brown.

Poulenc's delightful chamber music has done well in recent years: the set by various British artists on Cala has strong claims on the collector, and so has the Decca account with Patrick Gallois, Maurice Bourgue, Pascal Rogé and friends. Poulenc (or 'Poolonk', as he is called on BBC Radio 3 these days) is quintessential Nash territory and their Hyperion survey is of predictable excellence. Common to most of these works is the pianist Ian Brown, a stylist if ever there was one, whose playing lends such character to the proceedings. There are few performances that fail to delight and fewer that are surpassed elsewhere. Very good recorded sound makes this an excellent recommendation.

(i) Elégie for Horn & Piano; (ii) Violin Sonata; Music for 2 pianos: Le Bal masqué (Capriccio); Elégie; L'Embarquement pour Cythère; Sonata; Sonata for Piano (4 hands).

*** Decca 443 968-2. (i) Cazalet; (ii) Juillet; Rogé, Collard.

Poulenc has the capacity to charm and enchant. His lightness of touch and elegance often mask a vein of deeper feeling into which he can briefly move to striking and original effect. No one is more closely attuned to Poulenc's world than Pascal Rogé, and his presence ensures the authenticity of feeling that distinguished his earlier Poulenc. His masterly compatriot, Jean-Philippe Collard, is no less superb. In the *Elégie* for horn, written in memory of Dennis Brain, André Cazalet is an eloquent player and so, too, is Chantal Juillet in the *Violin Sonata.* An outstanding issue.

(i) L'Invitation au château (for clarinet, violin & piano); (ii) Mouvements perpétuels for Flute, Oboe, Clarinet, Bassoon, Horn, Violin, Viola, Cello & Bass; (iii) Rapsodie nègre for Flute, Clarinet, String Quartet, Baritone & Piano; (iv) Sextet for Flute, Oboe, Clarinet, Bassoon, Horn & Piano; (v) Sonata for Clarinet; Sonata for Clarinet & Bassoon; (vi) Sonata for 2 Clarinets; (vii) Sonata for Flute & Piano; (viii) Oboe Sonata; (ix) Trio for Oboe, Bassoon & Piano; (x) Villanelle for Piccolo & Piano.

(B) *** Cala CACD 1018 (2). (i–vi) Campbell; (i–ii) Carter; (i) York; (ii–iv; vii; x) Bennett; (ii; iv; viii; ix) Daniel; (ii; iv–v; ix) Gough; (ii; iv) Watkins; (ii) Tapping, Schrecker, West; (iii) Allegri Qt, Sidhom; (iii; viii–ix) Drake; (iv; vii; x) Benson; (vi) Campbell – RAVEL: *Introduction & Allegro* etc. ***

These Cala discs are a terrific bargain. The Poulenc accounts for the bulk of the two CDs (two hours' music in fact), all of it full of sparkle and freshness of invention. The discs comprise the complete chamber music for woodwind by Ravel and Poulenc, with the exception of works written primarily for the voice. The performances have great elegance and finesse. Poulenc has this rare gift of being able to move from the most flippant high spirits to the deepest poignancy, as in the *Oboe Sonata,* expressively played by Nicholas Daniel. His pianist, Julius Drake, is highly sensitive, though the piano is not always ideally focused in the excessively resonant acoustic. Elsewhere, in the captivating incidental music to a play by Jean Cocteau and Raymond Radiguet, *L'Invitation au château,* the playing is expert, tasteful and stylish. The *Mouvements perpétuels,* the *Sextet* and the various wind sonatas are beautifully played with great relish and spirit. This is a most attractive set, which deserves the widest dissemination.

Sextet (for piano and wind).

(M) *** Chan. 6543. Brown, Athena Ens. – GOUNOD: *Petite Symphonie in B flat;* IBERT: *3 Pièces brèves.* ***

From Ian Brown and the Athena Ensemble a bravura and responsive performance of Poulenc's many-faceted *Sextet*, catching its high spirits as well as its wit, and the gentle melancholy which intervenes at the close of the boisterous finale. The recording is excellent, slightly dry, yet with a nice ambience. Even though the programme is short measure, every minute is enjoyable.

Sextet for Piano & Wind; Trio for Piano, Oboe & Bassoon; (i) Le Bal masqué; Le Bestiaire.

(M) *** CRD 3437. (i) Allen; Nash Ens., Friend.

Thomas Allen is in excellent voice and gives a splendid account of both *Le Bal masqué* and *Le Bestiaire*. The Nash play both the *Trio* and the *Sextet* with superb zest and character. The wit of this playing and the enormous resource, good humour and charm of Poulenc's music are well served by a recording of exemplary quality and definition. Not to be missed.

(i) 3 Mouvements perpétuels; (ii) Le Bal masqué; (iii) Le Bestiaire; Cocarde; (iv) Le Gendarme incompris; (iii) 4 Poèmes de Max Jacob; (ii) Rapsodie nègre (1919).

*** Decca 452 666-2. (i–ii) Rogé; Fr. Nat. O (members); (ii– iv) Le Roux; (iv) Visse, Wilson; Dutoit.

Most of these pieces are early (1917–21) settings of Apollinaire, Cocteau and Max Jacob and are offered together with the later, better-known and always captivating *Le Bal masqué*. Such was the popularity of the *Trois Mouvements perpétuels* that Poulenc made an arrangement for nine instruments. *Le Bestiaire* is recorded in its original form for baritone and a small instrumental ensemble without piano. *Le Gendarme incompris* ('The misunderstood policeman') is a spoken entertainment, a *comédie-bouffe*, lasting about 20 minutes, a curtain-raiser interspersed with some songs for boarding schools to words by Cocteau and Raymond Radiguet (1903–23). As always with Poulenc there is a lot of charm, but an undercurrent of deeper feeling too. Elegant and polished performances, expertly balanced by the Decca engineers.

Violin Sonata

(B)*** CfP 573 115-2. Little, Lane – DEBUSSY: *Violin Sonata;* RAVEL: *Violin Sonata; Tzigane.*

In this well-designed collection of violin-and-piano music, Tasmin Little and Piers Lane give outstanding performances, very well recorded, aptly and subtly changing style for each composer, as here in Poulenc's *Sonata*, longer but generally lighter in tone than the other works included. In the slow movement Little produces her sweetest, warmest tone, and she relishes the virtuoso demands of the *Moto perpetuo* finale.

PIANO MUSIC
Piano duet

Capriccio; Elégie; L'Embarquement pour Cythère; Sonata for Piano, 4 Hands; Sonata for 2 Pianos.

*** Chan. 8519. Tanyel, J. Brown.

These two artists have a very close rapport and dispatch this repertoire with both character and sensitivity. The Chandos recording is excellent, very vivid and present.

Solo piano music

Badinage; Bourrée, au Pavillon d'Auvergne; Feuillets d'album; 5 Impromptus; Mélancolie; Napoli; 3 Pastorales; Pièce brève sur le nom d'Albert Roussel; Promenades; Suite française d'après Claude Gervaise; Valse-improvisation sur le nom de Bach.

*** Decca 460 329-2. Rogé.

This CD (72 minutes) completes Rogé's distinguished coverage of Poulenc's piano music, and it is just as delightful and wide-ranging in mood as its two companions. Who but Poulenc would have written a frivolous *Valse-improvisation* to celebrate the name of B-A-C-H, and his light-hearted manner is equally felicitous in the delicious *Third Impromptu* or the gentle melancholy of *Badinage*. But he is perhaps at his most touching in his suite of pieces paying a tribute to Claude Gervaise, which is thoroughly imbued with personal nostalgia. As before, Rogé is beautifully recorded.

Humoresque; Improvisations Nos. 4, 5, 9–11 & 14; 2 Intermezzi; Intermezzo in A flat; Nocturnes; Presto in B flat; Suite; Thème varié; Villageoises.

*** Decca 425 862-2. Rogé.

Pascal Rogé's second Poulenc recital is every bit as captivating as his earlier disc (see below). The acoustic is somewhat reverberant but not excessively so. Elegant playing, responsive to all the rapidly changing shifts of tone in Poulenc's music, and strongly recommended.

Improvisations Nos. 1–3; 6–8; 12–13; 15; Mouvements perpétuels; 3 Novelettes; Pastourelle; 3 Pièces; Les Soirées de Nazelles; Valse.

*** Decca 417 438-2. Rogé.

This music is absolutely enchanting, full of delight and wisdom; it has many unexpected touches and is teeming with character. Rogé is a far more persuasive exponent of it than any previous pianist on record; his playing is imaginative and inspiriting, and the recording is superb.

Badinage; Bourrée, au pavillon d'Auvergne; Humoresque; Française d'après Claude Gervaise; 15 Improvisations; 5 Impromptus; Intermède en ré mineur; 3 Intermezzi; Pastourelle; Presto en si bémol; Mélancholie; 3 Mouvements perpétuels; Napoli (suite); 8 Nocturnes; 3 Novellettes; 3 Pièces; Les Soirées de Nazelles; Suite; Suite française; Valse; Valse improvisation sur le nom de Bach.

(N) (B) *** RCA 2 CD 74321 84603-2 (2). Eric le Sage.

Erid le Sage is a virtuoso of a high order, as he immediately demonstrates in the opening *Presto en si bémol* (marked by Poulenc to be played as fast as possible), and later with the most precisely delicate articulation in *Les Soirées de Nazelles*, and in the second disc the amazingly varied *Improvisations* and the *Impromptus*, which are presented with great élan.

Sometimes his tempi seem a fraction fast, as in the most famous of the *Mouvements perpetuelles*, but he can readily charm the ear, as in the lovely *Pastourelle*, the *Novellettes* and *Suite française*. There is wit, too, and the flimsy little *Valse* is most delicate. In short, the playing here is full of character and certainly does not lack spontaneity of variety of style and timbre. The closing group of *Nocturnes* are exquisite. The recording is very real and vivid. Excellent value.

Badinage; Les Biches: Adagietto; Intermezzo No. 3 in A flat; 3 Mouvements perpétuels; Napoli; 3 Pièces; Les Soirées de Nazelles; Suite in C; Valse-improvisation sur le nom de Bach.

*** Chan. 8637. Parkin.

Humoresque; 15 Improvisations; Intermezzi Nos. 1 in C; 2 in D flat; Mélancolie; 3 Novelettes; Presto in B flat; Suite française d'après Claude Gervaise; Thème varié; Villageoises (Petites pièces enfantines).

*** Chan. 8847. Parkin.

Eric Parkin is an artist of instinctive taste and a refined musical intelligence who is completely inside this idiom: he has plenty of spirit and character and abundant sensitivity. Perhaps Rogé has the greater pianistic finesse plus a gamin-like charm, but Parkin too has charm and, in many of the pieces where they overlap, there is often little to choose between them. The Chandos recording is rather more resonant, though not unacceptably so.

CHORAL MUSIC

Ave verum corpus; Exultate Deo; Figure humaine; 4 petites prières de Saint François d'Assise; Un soir de neige; 4 Motets pour le temps de Noël; Salve Regina; Sept Chansons.

** ASV CDDCA 1067. Joyful Company of Singers, Broadbent.

Poulenc's choral music is very well represented on disc. This newcomer from the Joyful Company of Singers and Peter Broadbent is not without merit but, in terms of ensemble, chording and tonal blend it does not outclass the recommendations listed there.

Ave verum corpus; Exultate Deo; Laudes de Saint-Antoine de Padoue; (i) Litanies à la Vierge Noire; 4 Motets pour le temps de Noël; 4 Motets pour un temps de pénitence; Salve Regina.

(M) *** EMI (ADD) CDM5 65165-2. Groupe Vocal de France, Alldis; (i) with Alain.

An outstanding collection. This is music that ideally needs French voices, and John Alldis has trained his French group splendidly so that they combine precision and fervour with a natural feeling for the words. The soaring *Ave verum* is matched by the exhilaration of the *Exultate Deo* and the originality of the *Litanies* with its stabbing bursts of organ tone. The *Salve Regina* is very fine too, and the four *Christmas Motets* have the right extrovert joyfulness and sense of wonder. However, this has just been deleted at the time of going to press.

Le Bal masqué (cantata).

(N)(M) *** Virgin VM5 61850-2. Van Dam, Lyon Nat. Op. O, Nagano – IBERT: *4 chansons de Don Quichotte;* MARTIN: *6 Monologues from 'Jedermann';* RAVEL: *Don Quichotte à Dulcinée.* ***

Kent Nagano and the Lyon Orchestra set the scene vivaciously for Poulenc's 'cantata profana', and present the *Intermède* and reckless *Bagatelle* with the sharpest rhythmic felicity. José Van Dam is in his element, singing with all the necessary point in the opening *Préambule* and entering fully into the unpredictably changing moods of *Malvina*, with its touching lyrical strain. The spirited finale, with a prominent solo piano role (and even a momentary burst of falsetto from Van Dam), confirms the feeling that this is a kind of 'Divertissement' with vocal obbligato. It could hardly be more winningly presented. The accompanying notes do not include a translation, suggesting instead that Max Jacob's poems are 'best appreciated in their original French, as they rely for much of their effect on word associations – those of sound and suggestion rather than sense'. First-rate recording.

(i) Figure humaine; (ii) Laudes de Saint Antoine de Padoue; (i) Mass in G; (ii) 4 Motets pour un temps de Pénitence; (i) Petites prières de Saint François d'Assise, (iii) La Voix humaine.

(B) *** Erato Ultima ADD/ Dig. 3984 25598-2 (2). (i) Mellnäs, Sunnegärdh, Uppsala Academic Chamber Ch., Kfum Chamber Ch., Stenlund; (ii) Chamonin, Caillat, Vocal Ens., Caillat; (iii) Migenes,O Nat. de France, Prêtre.

Figure humaine is perhaps Poulenc's most substantial and deeply felt work in this medium and these Swedish forces convey its eloquence to good effect. The pre-war *Mass in G major* is less intense but contains a moving soprano solo, which is beautifully done here. The four male-voiced *Prières* are post-war and are effectively projected by these fine Uppsala singers. For this reissue the more familiar *Laudes* and *Motets* have been added in ardent and idiomatic accounts from the Stephen Caillat Ensemble. Good atmospheric analogue sound throughout.

The second CD contains Julia Migenes's dramatic and moving performance of Poulenc's theatrical telephone monologue, *La Voix humaine*, a setting of Cocteau. She conveys the utter despair of a woman brought to the verge of suicide by the desertion of her lover, at first pathetically hoping he will call her back, and the final hopeless resignation. The lyrical writing is both Puccinian but Ravelian too in its moments of tenderness. Prêtre holds the piece together admirably, but then he conducted the work's première. The digital sound could not be more vivid. This is the finest modern version on record.

Figure humaine; Laudes de Saint Antoine de Padoue; 4 Motets pour le temps de Noël; 4 Motets pour un temps de pénitence; 4 petites prières de Saint François d'Assise.

*** Virgin VC7 59192-2. The Sixteen, Christophers.

A lovely record which assembles the cantata for double choir, *Figure humaine*, with some of the composer's most celebrated *a cappella* motets. These performances can be recommended strongly, both on artistic grounds and for the excellence of the sound.

Gloria.

(B) *** Decca (ADD) 448 711-2. Greenberg, SRO Ch., Lausanne Pro Arte Ch., SRO, López-Cobos – DURUFLE: *Requiem;* FAURE: *Pavane.* ***

The *Gloria* is one of Poulenc's last compositions and is among his most successful. López-Cobos gives a fine account, expansive yet underlining the Stravinskian elements in the score. The recording is first class, full-bodied and with clean definition.

(i; ii) *Gloria; Ave verum corpus; Exultate Deo;* **(ii)** *Litanies à la Vierge Noire; 4 Motets pour le temps de Noël; 4 Motets pour un temps de pénitence; Salve Regina.*

*** Coll. (ADD) COLCD 108. (i) Deam, Cambridge Singers; (ii) City of L. Sinfonia, Rutter.

A generous selection of Poulenc's choral music, much of it of great beauty and simplicity, in very fresh-sounding performances and well-focused sound.

(i) *Gloria; Litanies à la Vierge noire;* **(i)** *Stabat mater.*

(N)(M) *** Virgin VM5 61843-2. (i) Dubosc; Westminster Singers, City of L. Sinf., Hickox.

Richard Hickox's quite outstanding version of Poulenc's *Gloria* brings singing of great freshness and bite. The ear is immediately struck, not only by the security of the Westminster Singers and the excellent playing of City of London Sinfonia, but also by the remarkably well-judged balance and detail of the recording. The *Stabat mater* is hardly less memorable, intensely dramatic and movingly lyrical by turns. Catherine Dubosc, who has already sung ravishingly in the *Dominus Deus* of the *Gloria*, is ethereally radiant in *Vidit suum* and soars heavenwards in *Fac ut portem*. The Westminster Singers are heard at their most subtle in the expressive contrasts of the *Litanies à la Vierge noire*, singing of much clarity and delicacy of feeling. Throughout this splendid disc the recording is demonstration-worthy, with the orchestral woodwind glowing luminously. Full translations are included.

(i) *Mass in G. Exultate Deo;* **(ii)** *Litanies à la Vierge Noire. Salve Regina.*

(B) *** Double Decca (ADD) 436 486-2 (2). St John's College, Cambridge, Ch., Guest; (i) with Bond; (ii) Cleobury – FAURE; DURUFLE: *Requiems.* ***

Mass in G; 4 petites prières de Saint François d'Assise; Salve Regina.

*** Nim. NI 5197. Christ Church Cathedral Ch., Oxford, Darlington – MARTIN: *Mass for Double Choir.* **(*)

The *Mass in G* is a work of strong appeal and greater dramatic fire than the *Salve Regina* or the more intimate *Quatre petites prières de Saint François d'Assise* for men's voices. The choir of Christ Church Cathedral, Oxford, under Stephen Darlington sing with clean tone and excellent balance, and the Nimbus recording is very good indeed.

As an extraordinarily generous bonus for the two great *Requiems* of Fauré and Duruflé, this Double Decca set offers the Poulenc *Mass in G* together with two motets, *Exultate Deo* and *Salve Regina*, finely wrought pieces in performances of great finish. Then, together with Stephen Cleobury, they give us the cool, gently dissonant *Litanies à la Vierge Noire*, a dialogue between voices and organ in which the voices eventually take dominance. It is beautifully done and the St John's College forces cope with the delicacy and sweetness of Poulenc's chromatic harmony throughout. The (originally Argo) recording is eminently realistic and truthful.

Stabat Mater; Litanies à la Vierge Noire; Salve Regina.

*** HM HMC 905149. Lagrange, Lyon Nat. Ch. and O, Baudo.

In the *Stabat Mater* Serge Baudo certainly makes the most of expressive and dynamic nuances; he shapes the work with fine feeling and gets good singing from the Lyon Chorus. Michèle Lagrange has a good voice and is an eminently expressive soloist. The coupling offers the short *Salve Regina* and the *Litanies à la Vierge Noire*, an earlier and somewhat more severe work.

SONGS

Mélodies: Airs chantés; Bleuet; La courte paille; Fancy; La grenouillère; Montparnasse; Monsieur Sans-Souci, il fait tout lui-même; Nous voulons une petite soeur; Le petit garçon trop bien portant; 2 Poèmes de Louis Aragon; 3 Poèmes de Louise Lalanne; 5 Poèmes de Max Jacob; Le portrait; Priez pour paix; Toréador; La tragique histoire du petit René.

*** Decca 458 859-2. Lott, Rogé.

Felicity Lott is a stylist par excellence and her sympathy for and affinity with the songs of Poulenc is long standing. This recital with Pascal Rogé whose understanding of this repertoire is *sans pareil* centres on the theme of childhood, and ranges from *La courte paille* – written for Denise Duval, Poulenc's favourite soprano, to sing for her young son – the *Cinq poèmes de Max Jacob* which evoke childhood memories of Brittany. Dame Felicity is in excellent form throughout and brings the right blend of feeling and style to everything here. *Hier*, the third of the *Trois poèmes de Louise Lalanne*, is marvellously characterized and quite haunting. Excellent recording.

Mélodies: Disc 1: A sa guitare; Le bestiaire (unpublished): La colombe; La puce; Le serpent; Calligrammes; Une chanson de porcelaine; Cocardes; Poèmes de Ronsard; Tel jour telle nuit; Le travail du peintre; Vive Nadia (460 327). *Disc 2: 3 Chansons de F. Garcia-Lorca; Epitaphe; Mazurka; Paul et Virginie; Pierrot; 5 Poèmes de Paul Eluard; Chansons villageoises; Dernier poème; Le disparu; Le*

fraîcheur et le feu; Hymne; . . . mais mourir; Nuage;
Parisiana; 2 Poèmes de Guillaume Apollinaire; 4 Poèmes
de Guillaume Apollinaire; Rosemonde; (v) 8 Chansons
polonaises (460 328). *Melodies.*

**(*) Decca 460 326-2 (2). Le Roux, Cachemaille, Kryger, Rogé.

This two-disc collection, most sensitively sung by fine
French singers of today, concentrates on cycles and sequences of Poulenc songs, mainly from the later years of his
life. François le Roux, a high baritone who can cope with the
demanding tessitura of the songs written for the composer's
friend, Pierre Bernac, takes on the major share, including all
the songs on the first disc – notably the fine cycle, *Tel jour,*
telle nuit. He also sings superbly the three extra songs for *Le*
bestiaire, only recently published. On the second disc, Gilles
Cachemaille, a warmer but less versatile baritone, and
Urszula Kryger provide contrast in an equally varied selection. Throughout the series Pascal Rogé is the intensely
poetic accompanist.

Banalités; Les Chemins de l'amour; 2 Mélodies de
Guillaume Apollinaire.

*** Virgin VC5 45360-2. Gens, Vignoles – DEBUSSY; FAURE:
  Mélodies. ***

Véronique Gens possesses a delightful voice of much beauty,
and is very much at home in Poulenc's world. As with
the Debussy, she is both imaginative and characterful. She
receives sensitive support from Roger Vignoles, and Virgin
give her excellent and natural sound.

Mélodies: Banalités: Hôtel; Voyage à Paris. Bleuet.
Calligrammes: Voyage. 4 Chansons pour enfants: Nous
voulons une petite soeur. Les Chemins de l'amour;
Colloque; Hyde Park; Métamorphoses; Miroirs brûlants:
Tu vois le feu du soir. Montparnasse; 2 Poèmes de Louis
Aragon; 3 Poèmes de Louise Lalanne; Priez pour paix; Tel
jour, telle nuit; Toréador.

*** Hyp. CDA 66147. Songmakers' Almanac: Lott, Rolfe
  Johnson, Murray, Jackson.

Felicity Lott sings the great majority of the songs here, joyful
and tender, comic and tragic by turns. The other soloists
have one song apiece, done with comparable magnetism,
and Richard Jackson joins Felicity Lott (one stanza each) in
Poulenc's solitary 'song for two voices', *Colloque.* First-rate
recording, though Lott's soprano is not always as sweetly
caught as it can be.

OPERA

Dialogue des Carmélites (complete).

*** Virgin VCD7 59227-2 (2). Dubosc, Gorr, Yakar, Fournier,
  Van Dam, Viala, Dupuy, Lyon Op. O, Nagano.

The opening of Poulenc's *Dialogue des Carmélites* with its
very Stravinskian ostinatos for a moment suggests a minimalist opera, written before its time. Much is owed to the
dynamic Nagano, who gives an extra momentum and sense
of contrast to a work that with its measured speeds and
easily lyrical manner can fall into sameness. That the male

casting is so strong, with the principal roles taken by José
van Dam and the tenor, Jean-Luc Viala, compensates for
any lack of variety in having women's voices predominating
in an opera about nuns. Catherine Dubosc in the central
role of the fear-obsessed, self-doubting Blanche is fresh and
appealing, with Brigitte Fournier charming as the frivolous
nun, Constance, and the veteran Rita Gorr as the old Prioress
and Rachel Yakar as the new Prioress both splendid. The
vivid recording, helped by a stage production in Lyon, culminates in a spine-chilling rendering of the final execution
scene, with the sound of the guillotine ever more menacing.

(i) *Les Mamelles de Tirésias* (opéra-bouffé); (ii) *Le Bal*
masqué (cantata).

** Ph. 456 504-3. (i–ii) Holzmair; (i) Bonney, Fouchécourt,
  Lafont, Oswald, Clark, Gietz, Griffey, Sakamoto, Tokyo Op.
  Singers; Saito Kinen O, Ozawa.

With the help of a fine team of soloists from the West, Seiji
Ozawa conducts his Japanese forces in refined, polished
performances of both works, with rhythms crisply sprung.
With refined recording to match, this gives a muted idea of
the witty Poulenc. In *Le Bal masqué,* a 'cantata profana',
Wolfgang Holzmair sings beautifully, but the necessary
sharpness in this 1920s piece for voice and chamber group
is largely missing. *Les Mamelles de Tirésias* dates from much
later, 1944, but the same satirical spirit is still there in this
romp. There too the impact is muted, in a performance not
quite idiomatic.

POWER, Leonel (d. 1445)

Missa, Alma redemptoris mater. Motets: *Agnus Dei; Ave*
Regina; Beata viscera; Credo; Gloria; Ibo michi ad
montem; Quam pulchra es; Salve Regina; Sanctus.

(M) *** Virgin VER5 61345-2. Hilliard Ens., Hillier.

Power was a contemporary of Dunstable and was born
probably in the mid-1370s. One of the leading composers
represented in the Old Hall MS. (some 20 pieces are attributed to him), Power spent the last years of his life at Canterbury, but the music on this disc is earlier, coming from the
period before 1413. The *Missa, Alma redemptoris mater* is
probably the earliest, in which all the Mass sections are
linked by a common cantus firmus and there is also a
complex mathematical design. The music is of an austere
beauty that is quite striking, as indeed is the remarkable
singing of the Hilliard Ensemble. The digitally remastered
recording comes from the early 1980s and is vivid and
present. Strongly recommended.

PRAETORIUS, Michael (1571–1621)

Dances from Terpsichore (extended suite).

(M) *** Decca 414 633-2. New L. Cons., Pickett.

Terpsichore is a huge collection of some 300 dance tunes
used by the French-court dance bands of Henri IV. They
were enthusiastically assembled by the German composer,
Michael Praetorius, who also harmonized them and

arranged them in four to six parts; however, any selection is conjectural in the matter of orchestration. Philip Pickett's instrumentation is sometimes less exuberant than that of David Munrow before him; but many will like the refinement of his approach, with small instrumental groups, lute pieces and even what seems like an early xylophone! There are also some attractively robust brass scorings (sackbuts and trumpets). The use of original instruments is entirely beneficial in this repertoire; the recording is splendid.

Dances from *Terpsichore: Ballet des coqs; Ballet des feus; Ballet des matelotz; Ballet du Roy pour sonner après; La Bourrée; Bransle de villages; La Canarie; 3 Courantes; Pavane de Spaigne; La Sarabande; Spagnoletta.*
Arrangements: CAROUBEL: *Bransles.* VALLET: *Suite of Dances.* CAROUBEL: *Bransle simple.* BESARD: *Ballo des Gran Duca; Bransles de village; Une jeune fillette.*
DOWLAND: *Courante;* CAMPION: *Courante.* ANON: *Ballet; Ballet des Baccanales; 2 Courantes.*

(N) *** Hyp. CDA 67240. Parley of Instruments, Renaissance Violin Band, Holman.

This seventy-minute collection from Peter Holman and his various instrumental groups must be regarded as the most authentic and comprehensive now available. Praetorius makes it clear in the preface to *Terpsichore* that he regards these as French dances, and Holman convincingly suggests that they were intended primarily for performances on a French-style violin band, or a lute combination (a group of four lutes play together here), and that is the instrumentation that he very refreshingly offers.

A good deal of the music is attributed to Praetorius himself, but that implies that he was arranging tunes, rather than composing them. Among his discoveries are a particularly lively group of *Courantes*, which he did not realize had an English source, of which the most attractive is Thomas Campion's *I care not for these ladies.*

The programme here is very enjoyable in its undemanding way, even if the instrumentation itself is comparatively restricted. However, two engaging exceptions are Praetorius's own *Bransle de villages*, which are exotically scored for five-part violin band, pipe, tabor and bagpipe, and the Anonymous *Courante* (*Battaglia*), which closes the programme in an very rhythmic arrangement for violins, lutes, guitar and – when it enters – a dominating drum. Excellent recording and documentation.

Dances from *Terpsichore (Suite de ballets; Suite de voltes).*
(i) Motets: *Eulogodia Sionia: Resonet in laudibus; Musae Sionae: Allein Gott in der Höh sei Ehr; Aus tiefer Not schrei ich zu dir; Christus der uns selig macht; Gott der Vater wohn uns bei; Polyhymnia Caduceatrix: Erhalt uns, Herr, bei deinem Wort.*

**(*) Virgin (ADD) VER5 61289-2. Early Music Cons. of L., Munrow; (i) with boys of the Cathedral and Abbey Church of St Alban.

Munrow's instrumentation is imaginatively done: the third item, a *Bourrée* played by four racketts (a cross between a shawm and comb-and-paper in sound), is fascinating. The collection is a delightful one. After this stimulating aural

feast, Munrow offers six of the composer's eloquent motets, the finest of which is *Erhalt uns, Herr, bei deinem Wort* for four choirs, each with its own accompanying instrumental group, although the shorter *Gott der Vater wohn uns bei* for double choir is hardly less resplendent, and the joyful *Allein Gott in der Höh sei Ehr* (for counter-tenor and triple choir) is also most stimulating, with crumhorns added to the third accompanying group. The only snag is the lack of a really clean focus in the CD transfer, especially in the exultant closing *Christus der uns selig macht.* The Abbey Road acoustic is reverberant, creating a wide amplitude, and the remastering has not altogether been a success in trying to sharpen up the focus. But the result remains rich in amplitude, and this inspired music, which often reminds the listener of Giovanni Gabrieli, is sung superbly by the choir.

Christmas motets and chorale concertos: *In dulci jubilo; Joseph, lieber Joseph mein; Der Morgenstern ist aufgedrungen; Nun komm der Heiden Heiland; Omnis mundus jocundetur; Psalitte; Puer natus: Ein Kind geborn zu Bethlehem; Singet und klinget; Vom Himmel hoch; Wachet auf, ruft uns die Stimme; Wie schön leuchtet der Morgenstern. Missa gantz Teudsch: Kyrie eleison.*

**(*) MDG 614 0660-2. Hassler Consort, Rami.

The skill of Praetorius as a polyphonist is readily demonstrated in the more ambitious works here, with the settings varying within the chorale concertos between three and fifteen parts. Indeed the busy contrapuntal textures of the opening *Wachet auf* stretch up to nineteen different lines. They are full of interest, and *Nun komm der Heiden Heiland* is similarly lively and inventive. *Puer natus est* (à 3, 7 and 11) alternates slow and jolly, energetic sections very appealingly, while the two movements from the *Mass* show the composer at his most unconventionally individual. But it is the simpler and more lyrical settings that one remembers most affectionately. *In dulci jubilo* for double choir with solo lines simply embellished is quite delightful, and *Joseph, lieber Joseph mein* is equally lovely. *Der Morgenstern* is first heard in a simple evocative presentation and then in the chorale variations which follow. Of the two closing items *Omnis mundus jocundetur* is appealingly carol-like, pastoral in feeling, in spite of its complexity of texture. *Singet und klinget* reintroduces the melody, so associated with this composer, which we have heard before as the basis for *Joseph, lieber Joseph mein.* The performances here are on a chamber scale, with solo voices well matched and blended, if lacking something in individuality. But the freshness of the music-making is never in doubt and, although the balance is immediate, the recording is very good.

Lutheran Mass for Christmas Morning (1620).

(N) *** DG 439 250-2. Soloists, Boys' Ch. and Congregational Ch. of Roskilde Cathedral, Gabrieli Consort and Players, McCreesh.

Following on after Paul McCreesh's hypothetical re-creation of Schütz's *Christmas Day Vespers* of 1664 (see below), this is an even more stimulating and enjoyable liturgical Feast-day celebration. It is also a most attractive way to present a great deal of Praetorius's music within a Lutheran Mass, as it might have been heard at one of the churches in central Germany around 1620.

Opening with a choral processional to a simply harmonized Lutheran melody, we pass straight into the *Introit, Puer natus in Bethlehem*, for three soloists and three choirs; and after the *Alleluia* comes a spectacularly fast choral entry, *Singet jubilliret triumphant'*. The *Kyrie* follows, set for pairs of soloists, and then the brilliantly florid *Gloria*, where the singers (solo and choral) are again joined by brass and organ.

This alternation sets the pattern for much that is to follow. The congregation participates richly in the *Gradual* hymn, *Vom Himmel hoch*, and as the Mass proceeds, there are also organ interludes and even a five-part brass sonata by Schein. After the jaunty closing hymn, *Puer nobus nascitur*, the Mass ends with the thrillingly exultant setting of *In dulci jubilo* for five choirs, including organ, six trumpets and drums, which is also used by the Taverner Consort to close their collection of Christmas music (see below). But here, magnificently sung and played in the echoing acoustic of Denmark's Roskilde Cathedral, the effect is even more spectacular.

COLLECTIONS

Christmas music: *Polyhymnia caduceatrix et panegyrica Nos. 9–10, 12 & 17. Puericinium Nos. 2, 4 & 5. Musae Sionae VI, No. 53: Es ist ein Ros' entsprungen. Terpsichore: Dances Nos. 1; 283–5; 310.*

*** Hyp. CDA 66200. Westminster Cathedral Ch., Parley of Instruments, Hill.

Praetorius was much influenced by the polychoral style of the Gabrielis; these pieces reflect this interest. The music is simple in style and readily accessible, and its performance on this atmospheric Hyperion record is both spirited and sensitive.

Christmas music: *Polyhymnia caduceatrix et panegyrica Nos. 10, Wie schön leuchtet der Morgenstern; 12, Puer natus in Bethlehem; 21, Wachet auf, ruft uns die Stimme; 34, In dulci jubilo.*

(M) *** Virgin (ADD) VM5 61353-2. Taverner Cons. Ch. & Players, Parrott – SCHUTZ: *Christmas Oratorio.* ***

This is the finest collection of Praetorius's vocal music in the current catalogue. The closing setting of *In dulci jubilo*, richly scored for five choirs and with the brass providing thrilling contrast and support for the voices, has great splendour. Before that comes the lovely, if less ambitious *Wie schön leuchtet der Morgenstern*. Both *Wachet auf* and *Puer natus in Bethlehem* are on a comparatively large scale, their combination of block sonorities and florid decorative effects the very essence of Renaissance style. The recording is splendidly balanced, with voices and brass blending and intertwining within an ample acoustic, and all the more welcome in this mid-priced Veritas reissue.

PREVIN, André (born 1929)

(i) *Diversions for Orchestra;* (ii) *3 Emily Dickinson Songs; The Giraffes Go to Hamburg;* (iii) *Sallie Chisum Remembers Billy the Kid;* (iii; iv) *Vocalise.*

(N) *** DG 471 028-2 (i) VPO, Previn; (ii) Fleming, Previn (piano) (iii) Bonney, LSO, Previn; (iv) with Welsh

'Diversions' is an apt title for this winning demonstration of André Previn's astonishing versatility as composer, conductor and pianist. The opening item, *Diversions*, written for the Vienna Philharmonic, is a compact four-movement work which with brilliant orchestration aims to exploit the solo talents of a range of the orchestra's leading players – woodwind, including piccolo, and trumpet and horn. The jaunty lighthearted mood of the *Prologue* leads finally to a deeply expressive slow finale which echoes Previn's opera, *A Streetcar Named Desire*. The two works for Renée Fleming come with Previn at the piano. *The Giraffes Go to Hamburg* sets an improbable passage from Karen Blixen's *Out of Africa*, a surreal prose-poem, strangely affecting, while the Emily Dickinson settings find Previn at his most warmly lyrical and approachable, lovely songs exactly reflecting the masterly innocence of the poems. Barbara Bonney earlier recorded the two vocal works written for her in the original piano versions, but the orchestral versions are even more richly expressive, particularly the *Vocalise* with Moray Welsh as cello soloist. Excellent sound.

(i) *Peaches for Flute & Piano; Trio for Piano, Oboe & Bassoon;* (ii) *Triolet for Brass;* (i) *Wedding Waltz for 2 Oboes & Piano;* (iii) (Piano) *Variations on a Theme by Haydn.*

*** Ara. Z 6701. (i) Previn (piano) with Mann, Taylor, Godburn, Field; (ii) Brass En.; (iii) Han.

These works bring out the fluency of Previn's writing in a lighter vein. The *Trio for Piano, Oboe and Bassoon* begins and ends as fun music, with a deeply emotional slow movement between. The *Triolet* is a display piece written for the Philip Jones Brass ensemble, and the piano *Variations*, using the slow movement theme from Haydn's *Symphony No. 82 (The Bear)*, set grittily purposeful writing against two warmly expressive slow variations. The two little occasional pieces, *Peaches* and the *Wedding Waltz* also bring out Previn's lyrical side. A charming collection, very well performed and recorded.

Violin Sonata (Vineyard).

*** DG 453 470-2. Shaham, Previn – BARBER: *Canzone;* COPLAND: *Violin Sonata; Nocturne;* GERSHWIN: *3 Preludes.* ***

The inspired collaboration between Previn and Gil Shaham is crowned in their formidable performance of Previn's own *Violin Sonata*, one of the most ambitious of his chamber works. If there are echoes of Walton's writing in the mixture of rhythmic energy and warm lyricism, the idiom is distinctively Previn's own, over the broad span of three substantial movements. Part of a fine, attractive survey of twentieth-century American violin music.

A Streetcar Named Desire (complete).

*** DG 459 366-2 (3). Fleming, Futral, Gilfry, Griffey, San Francisco Op. Ch. & O, Previn.

This live recording, conducted by Previn himself, confirms this as by far his most powerful score yet, not just colourful and atmospheric but agonizingly intense in its portrait of the central character, Blanche. That role was specifically created for the soprano, Renée Fleming, and in the recording she responds magnificently. The inbred tensions created by Blanche's arrival in the home of her sister and the coarse Stanley Kowalski, build up relentlessly over the first two acts. They erupt in Act III in a sequence of solos for Blanche as she loses her mind, that have an overwhelming impact, at once sensuous and sinister. The final solo, as beautiful as it is moving, leads on to the chill of the final scene of Blanche's departure for the asylum. The whole is a great operatic concept, brilliantly achieved, distinctive in its lyricism and subtle in its orchestration. Fleming gives a heart-rending performance, well supported by Elizabeth Futral as Blanche's sister (if rather too close in timbre to Fleming), Rodney Gilfry as Stanley and Anthony Dean Griffey as the wimpish Mitch. Warm, atmospheric recording, with voices well caught and good detail in the orchestral sound.

PRICE, Florence (1887–1953)

The Oak; Mississippi River Suite; Symphony No. 3.

(N) **(*) Koch 3-7518-2. Women's PO, Apo Hsu.

Florence Beatrice Price was born in Little Rock, Arkansas. Her musical talents soon became obvious and she studied under George Chadwick at the New England Conservatory of Music, and was to become the first African-American woman composer to earn recognition in the concert hall. The score of *The Oak* is not dated, but is shows considerable orchestral skill and opens atmospherically, establishing a theme that is to dominate the piece throughout. The *Mississippi River Suite* dates from 1934 and, like the river it describes, it is lengthy, detailing a series of images and events on the banks, and quoting popular tunes as varied as *Deep River*, *Go Down Moses* and *Steamboat Bill*. Its scoring is effective, but less sophisticated than the tone poem and it is very loose-structured.

The *Third Symphony* dates from 1938, and uses more indigenous material: the first movement includes a theme not unlike that of the slow movement of Dvořák's *New World Symphony*. The *Andante* is pleasingly fresh in its scoring, and has an innocent pastoral quality; the Scherzo, entitled *Juba Dance*, is full of ragtime syncopations; the finale has plenty of energy too, and a vigorous coda draws the music together flamboyantly. This is hardly one of the great American symphonies, but it is a fascinating attempt, and the performances from this all-female orchestra conducted by Apo Hsu certainly have the full measure of the music. Good recording, too.

PROKOFIEV, Serge (1891–1953)

Andante for Strings, Op. 50 bis; Autumn (symphonic sketch), Op. 8; Lieutenant Kijé: Suite, Op. 60; The Stone Flower: Suite, Op. 118; Wedding Suite, Op. 126.

*** Chan. 8806. SNO, Järvi.

The *Andante* is a transcription for full strings of the slow movement of the *First String Quartet*, and its eloquence is more telling in this more expansive format. *Autumn*, on the other hand, is an early piece, much influenced by Rachmaninov and full of imaginative touches. Järvi takes it at a fairly brisk tempo but it remains appropriately atmospheric. The *Wedding Suite* is drawn from *The Stone Flower* and complements the Op. 118 suite from Prokofiev's last full-length ballet. The performances and recording are in the best traditions of the house.

Boris Godunov, Op. 70 bis: Fountain Scene; Polonaise. Dreams, Op. 6. Eugene Onegin, Op. 71: Minuet, Polka, Mazurka. 2 Pushkin Waltzes, Op. 120. Romeo and Juliet (ballet): Suite No. 2, Op. 64.

*** Chan. 8472. SNO, Järvi.

Järvi's second suite from *Romeo and Juliet* has sensitivity, abundant atmosphere, a sense of the theatre, and is refreshingly unmannered. A fuller selection of the music Prokofiev wrote for a production of *Eugene Onegin* is available – see below – but what is offered here, plus the *Two Pushkin Waltzes*, are rather engaging lighter pieces. The performances are predictably expert, the balance finely judged and detail is in exactly the right perspective.

Chout (ballet): Suite, Op. 21a; The Love for Three Oranges: Suite, Op. 33a; Le Pas d'acier: Suite, Op. 41a.

*** Chan. 8729. SNO, Järvi.

Järvi has a natural affinity for this repertoire and gets splendid results from the SNO; and the recording is pretty spectacular.

Cinderella (ballet; complete), Op. 87.

(B) *** Double Decca 455 349-2 (2). Cleveland O, Ashkenazy – GLAZUNOV: *The Seasons.* ***

(N) ** CPO 999610-2. Cologne WDR SO, Jurowski.

Cinderella (ballet; complete), Summer Night: Suite, Op. 123.

❀ *** DG 445 830-2 (2). Russian Nat. O, Pletnev.

Cinderella (ballet; complete), Symphony No. 1 in D (Classical), Op. 25.

(B) *** EMI Dig./ADD double forte CZS5 68604-2 (2). LSO, Previn.

Pletnev produces playing of terrific life, lightness of touch, poetic feeling and character. Quite simply the best-played, most atmospheric and affecting *Cinderella* on disc. We found its effect tremendously exhilarating, and have had difficulty in stopping playing it! Don't hesitate – on every count this is one of the best recordings of the 1990s.

Otherwise artistic honours are very evenly divided between the Ashkenazy and Previn recordings. Some dances come off better in Previn's EMI version and there is an element of swings and roundabouts in comparing them. Ashkenazy gets excellent results from the Cleveland Orchestra. On CD, the recording's fine definition is enhanced, yet not at the expense of atmosphere, and the bright, vivid image is given striking projection. The appeal of the Double Decca is greatly increased by the inclusion of Ashkenazy's splendid account of Glazunov's finest ballet score. However, the EMI engineers have a more spacious acoustic within which to work and yet lose no detail. Moreover the CD reissue adds a splendid account of the *Classical Symphony*, sunlit and vivacious and hardly less well recorded five years previously.

Michail Jurowski's recording of *Cinderella* is in no sense the equal of his account of *The Tale of the Stone Flower* with the Hanover Radio Philharmonic Orchestra, which was distinguished by refined orchestral playing and a pleasingly natural sound. It is soon evident that the characterisation and the quality of the orchestral playing do not begin to approach either Pletnev or Previn. This is a studio performance with no sense of the footlights or atmosphere. Good though the Cologne Orchestra is, the Russian Orchestra and the LSO outclass it in every way, as do the Cleveland Orchestra for Ashkenazy. Moreover all these competitors offer more music.

Cinderella: Suite No. 1, Op. 107; Lieutenant Kijé (suite); The Love for Three Oranges: March; Scherzo; The Prince and Princess. Romeo and Juliet: Madrigal; Dance of the Girls with Lilies.

(BB) *** Naxos 8.550381. Slovak State PO, (Košice), Mogrelia.

The calibre of this excellent Slovak orchestra is well demonstrated here, and its perceptive conductor, Andrew Mogrelia, is at his finest in his gently humorous portrait of *Lieutenant Kijé*, the three 'best bits' from *The Love for Three Oranges* and the charming items from *Romeo and Juliet*. Excellent recording.

Cinderella: Ballet Suite; 2 Pushkin Waltzes, Op. 120; The Stone Flower (ballet), Op. 118: 2 Waltzes; Waltz Suite, Op. 110.

(M) *** Chan. 7076. RSNO, Järvi.

Prokofiev chose three suites from *Cinderella*, and the selection here draws on the First and Third, opening with the ballet's yearning Introduction, moving on to the *Quarrel* between the Ugly Sisters and including the Courtiers' elegant *Pavane* and the *Adagio* danced by Cinderella and the Prince. The *Waltz Suite*, Op. 110, is drawn from various works, including *Cinderella* and the opera, *War and Peace*, while the final *Mephisto Waltz* comes from incidental music for the film, *Lermontov*. The pair of excerpts from *The Stone Flower* include the *Waltz of the Diamonds*, and the two equally engaging *Pushkin Waltzes*, one passionate, the other more delicate, are part of the music Prokofiev wrote for a production of *Eugene Onegin*. The variety of the composer's invention and his often piquant scoring negate any suggestion that a succession of pieces in triple time could be too much of a good thing. The orchestral playing throughout is very persuasive. The recording is first class.

Concertino in G min. for Cello & Orchestra (original version); *Cello Concerto in E min., Op. 58.*

(N) *** Chan. 9890. Ivashkin, Russian State SO, Polyanski.

This Chandos disc is called 'The Unknown Prokofiev' and offers the *Cello Concerto* in its original form, before Prokofiev reworked it for Rostropovich. Starker's record from the 1960s was cut, whereas this is complete. Chandos's claim that this is its first recording is not strictly speaking true: Roger Aubin recorded it in the late 1950s and Rostropovich has recorded the *Cello concertino in G minor*, albeit not in this edition by Vladimir Blok and the cellist himself. These quibbles apart, the performances are very good indeed and splendidly recorded. There is much to be said for the original version of this piece: Prokofiev's second thoughts were not in every case improvements and he cut some inventive ideas.

(i) *Concertino in G min. for Cello & Orchestra, Op. 132* (completed and orch. Kabalevsky & Rostropovich); *Sinfonia concertante in E min. for Cello & Orchestra, Op. 125;* (ii) *Cello Sonata in C, Op. 119.*

(M) (**) Revelation mono RV10102. Rostropovich, (i) USSR SO, Rozhdestvensky; (ii) Richter.

Concertino in G min. for Cello & Orchestra; Symphony-Concerto in E min. for Cello & Orchestra, Op. 125; 2 Pushkin Waltzes, Op. 120.

(BB) *** Naxos 8.553624. Rudin, Ukraine Nat. SO, Kuchar.

Rostropovich's performances of this coupling were made at public concerts in 1964 and 1960 respectively (the performance is a composite one). Some allowance must be made for the sound here and in the 1951 recording of the *Cello Sonata*, once briefly available on the Monitor label, but what a performance!

The Russian cellist, Alexander Rudin, proves a powerful interpreter of these two concertante works. Rudin can match and even outshine most other rivals, not least in the beauty of his half-tones, as in the slow movements of both works. He and the conductor, Theodore Kuchar, inspire the Ukraine orchestra to play with similar incisiveness, helped by vivid, immediate sound. The two charming Pushkin-based *Waltzes* make an attractive fill-up, winningly pointed.

Piano Concertos Nos. 1–5.

(B) *** Double Decca (ADD) 452 588-2 (2). Ashkenazy, LSO, Previn.

*** Ph. 462 048-2 (2). Toradze, Kirov O, Gergiev.

*** Chan. 8938 (2). Berman (in Nos. 1, 4 & 5); Gutiérrez (in Nos. 2 & 3), Concg. O, Järvi.

(B) **(*) Teldec Ultima 3984 21038-2 (2). Krainev, Frankfurt RSO, Kitaenko.

Piano Concertos Nos. 1 in D flat, Op. 10; 3 in C, Op. 26; 4 in B flat, Op. 53.

(BB) *** Naxos 8.550566. Paik, Polish Nat. RSO (Katowice), Wit.

Piano Concertos Nos. 2 in G min., Op. 16; 5 in G, Op. 55.

(BB) *** Naxos 8.550565. Paik, Polish Nat. RSO (Katowice), Wit.

(i) *Piano Concertos Nos. 1–5;* (ii) *Overture on Hebrew Themes. Visions fugitives, Op. 22.*

(B) **(*) EMI (ADD) CZS5 69452-2 (2). Béroff; (i) with Leipzig GO, Masur; (ii) with Portal, Parrenin Qt.

Ashkenazy is a commanding soloist in both the *First* and *Second Concertos,* and his virtuosity in the *First* is quite dazzling. If he is curiously wayward in the opening of the *Second,* there is no question that this too is a masterly performance. The *Third Concerto* is keen-edged and crisply articulated, and the only reservation here concerns the slow movement which at times is uncharacteristically mannered. Ashkenazy is authoritative in No. 4 and gives an admirable account of No. 5: every detail of phrasing and articulation is well thought out, and yet there is no want of spontaneity or any hint of calculation. Throughout, Previn and the LSO accompany sympathetically, and the recently remastered recording makes the most of the vintage mid-1970s Kingsway Hall sound.

The merits of the Berman single discs are discussed below. As a package, their claims are strong, both artistically and in terms of recording quality.

Kun Woo Paik's playing throughout these five concertos has exhilarating bravura. Tempi are dangerously fast at times and occasionally he has the orchestra almost scampering to keep up with him, but they do, and the result is often electrifying. The famous theme and variations central movement of the *Third Concerto* is played with great diversity of mood and style and the darkly expressive *Larghetto* of No. 5 is very finely done. The *First Concerto,* which comes last on the first CD has great freshness and compares well with almost any version on disc. In short, with vivid recording in the Concert Hall of Polish Radio, which has plenty of ambience, this set is enormously stimulating and a remarkable bargain. It has far better sound than the remastered Decca recording for Ashkenazy.

Alexander Toradze is a powerful pianist in whose musical armoury virtuosity is not in short supply. Superb recorded sound of impressive clarity and presence enhances the appeal of these performances, which are spirited, big-boned and powerful. As in the Scriabin *Prometheus* (coupled with Stravinsky's *Firebird*), this is a formidable partnership.

Vladimir Krainev and the Frankfurt Radio Orchestra under Dmitri Kitaenko are also formidable contenders in their Ultima Double format. The recordings were made in 1992 and offer sound of considerable warmth and naturalness. Krainev is a virtuoso of the first order and, apart from the *Third,* which has greater brilliance than poetic feeling, his accounts of these concertos have much to recommend them. Though not quite the equal of Ashkenazy, these are eminently worthwhile accounts that will give pleasure.

A satisfying Rouge et Noir set from Michel Béroff, who plays masterfully and is a pianist of genuine insight where Prokofiev is concerned; Masur gives him excellent support. Béroff is free from some of the agogic mannerisms that distinguish Ashkenazy in the slow movement of the *Third,* and he has great poetry. The balance is good; although the overall sound-picture is not wholly natural, it is certainly vivid, and the timbre of the piano is captured sympathetically. However, in the transfer to CD, a degree of hardness and opaqueness has crept in.

(i) *Piano Concerto No. 1. Suggestion diabolique, Op. 4/4.*

(M) *** EMI (ADD) CDM7 64329-2. Gavrilov, (i) LSO, Rattle – BALAKIREV: *Islamey;* TCHAIKOVSKY: *Piano Concerto No. 1.* ***

A dazzling account of the *First Piano Concerto* from Andrei Gavrilov. This version is second to none for virtuosity and sensitivity. Simon Rattle provides excellent orchestral support and the EMI engineers offer most vivid recording, while the *Suggestion diabolique* makes a hardly less dazzling encore after the concerto.

Piano Concertos Nos. 1; 3.

*** DG (IMS) 439 898-2. Kissin, BPO, Abbado.
**(*) EMI CDC5 56654-2. Argerich, Montreal SO, Dutoit – BARTOK: *Piano Concerto No. 3.* **(*)

(i) *Piano Concertos Nos. 1; 3. Piano Sonata No. 7 in B flat, Op. 83.*

*** ASV CDDCA 786. Kodama, (i) with Philh. O, Nagano.

Yevgeni Kissin gives a virtuosic, dashing account of both concertos and is given highly sensitive and responsive support from the Berlin Philharmonic under Abbado. It is unfailingly brilliant, aristocratic in feeling and wonderfully controlled pianism, and the recording is very good. It is a pity that DG did not offer a fill-up, as this CD offers only 42 minutes 27 seconds of playing time.

Mari Kodama is a vital and imaginative player and the performances are wonderfully alert and fresh-eyed; there is splendid rapport between soloist and conductor (not surprisingly since they are husband and wife) and they benefit from first-class recording. A strong recommendation not only for newcomers to Prokofiev but for the experienced collector.

Argerich is pretty dazzling in the *First Concerto,* though there is perhaps more grace than fire. Indeed some will find it just a shade underpowered. The *Third,* too, has many felicitous touches and great refinement though it does not supersede the earlier version she made in Berlin for DG with Abbado (see below).

Piano Concertos Nos. 1; 4 for the Left Hand; 5.

*** Chan. 8791. Berman, Concg. O, Järvi.
*(*) Hyp. CDA 67029. Demidenko, LPO, Lazarev.

Boris Berman has established an enviable reputation in this repertoire, and he plays with great panache and dazzling virtuosity. He holds the music on a taut rein and has the nervous energy and ebullience this music needs. The superb recording quality will sway many collectors in his favour.

Nikolai Demidenko possesses formidable technical address but his musical personality is too intrusive for this to be the kind of recommendation his virtuosity should ensure. Tone above *forte* is not always beautiful, pianissimo markings are not always observed, and though there is much to admire, it is the pianist rather than the composer to whom one's attention is too often drawn.

Piano Concerto No. 3 in C, Op. 26.

(M) *** DG (ADD) 447 438-2. Argerich, BPO, Abbado –
RAVEL: *Piano Concerto in G* etc. ***

(M) *** Mercury (IMS) (ADD) 434 333-2. Janis, Moscow PO,
Kondrashin (with PROKOFIEV: *Toccata;* SCHUMANN:
Sonata No. 3; MENDELSSOHN: *Songs Without Words,
Op. 61/1;* PINTO: *3 Scenes from Childhood* ***) –
RACHMANINOV: *Piano Concerto No. 1.* ***

(BB) **(*) Belart (ADD) 450 081-2. Margalit, New Philh. O,
Maazel (with MUSSORGSKY: *Pictures*). **(*)

(N) *(**) Chan. 9913. Judd, Moscow PO, Lazarev –
TCHAIKOVSKY: *Piano Concerto No. 1.* *(**)

Martha Argerich made her outstanding record of the Prokofiev *Third Concerto* in 1968, while still in her twenties. There
is nothing ladylike about the playing, but it displays countless
indications of sensuous feminine perception and subtlety,
and Abbado's direction underlines that from the very first,
with a warmly romantic account of the ethereal opening
phrases on the high violins. This is a much more individual
performance of the Prokofiev than almost any other available and brings its own special insights. The 1967 recording,
always excellent, sounds even more present in this new
transfer.

Byron Janis's account of the Prokofiev *Third Concerto*
is outstanding in every way, soloist and orchestra plainly
challenging each other in a performance full of wit (particularly in the delightfully managed slow-movement variations), drama and warmth. Even though it was made three
decades ago, the Mercury recording sounds amazingly clean
and faithful. The recital (recorded in Russia the following
year – except for the Schumann, which was made in the USA)
is comparatively low-key, except perhaps for the captivating
Scenes from Childhood of Octavio Pinto, which combine
charm with glittering yet unostentatious bravura.

The performance by Israela Margalit and Maazel has a
splendid feeling of spontaneity and enjoyment, and there is
no lack of wit in the central theme and variations. The
recording balance is somewhat contrived, but the end-result
is unfailingly vivid and the piano image is tangible.

Recorded live when the late Terence Judd was competing
in the 1978 Moscow Tchaikovsky Competition, this urgent
and dynamic account of the Prokofiev *Third Concerto* makes
up in impulse and conviction for what it lacks in refinement.
The recording favours the piano. Like the coupled Tchaikovsky performance this is a valuable and compelling reminder of a talent tragically cut off. Limited sound, and while
this reissue is welcome it ought to have been at mid-price.

(i) *Piano Concerto No. 3;* (ii; iii) *Violin Concerto No. 1 in
D, Op. 19;* (iii) *Lieutenant Kijé (suite), Op. 60.*

(B) *** DG ADD/Dig. 439 413-2. (i) Argerich, BPO; (ii) Mintz;
(iii) Chicago SO; all cond. Abbado.

Martha Argerich's highly individual performance of Prokofiev's *C major Concerto* (see above) is here coupled with the
First Violin Concerto, which also has a magical opening,
and once again Abbado's accompaniment is peerless, while
Mintz phrases with imagination and individuality. *Lieutenant Kijé* is hardly less successful and also sounds splendid.

This compilation is one of the very finest reissues on DG's
bargain Classikon label.

(i) *Piano concerto No. 3 in C, Op. 26;* (ii) *Symphony No. 5
in B flat, Op. 100.*

(N) (BB) (***) Dutton Lab mono CDBP 9706. (i) Composer,
LSO, Coppola; (ii) Boston SO, Koussevitzky.

Two classic performances from the days of shellac, Prokofiev's own pioneering and exhilarating account of his then
relatively new *Third Piano Concerto* from 1932 coupled with
the superb 1946 Boston version of the *Fifth Symphony* under
Koussevitzky. Both are indispensable and both have never
sounded better.

(i) *Piano Concerto No. 5. Piano Sonata No. 8 in B flat,
Op. 84; Visions fugitives, Op. 22/3, 6 & 9.*

(M) *** DG (ADD) 449 744-2. S. Richter, (i) with Warsaw PO,
Rowicki.

Richter's account of the *Fifth Piano Concerto* is a classic. It
was recorded in 1959, yet the sound of this excellent CD
transfer belies the age of the original in its clarity, detail and
vividness of colour. Richter then plays the *Eighth Sonata* and
the excerpts from the *Visions fugitives* with comparable
mastery, the latter deriving from a live recital. In both cases
the recording is surprisingly good.

Violin Concertos Nos. 1, Op. 19; 2, Op. 63

⚫ *** Sony SK 53969. Lin, LAPO, Salonen – STRAVINSKY:
Concerto. ***

(BB) *** Virgin 2 X 1. VBD5 61633-2 (2). LSO, C. Davis –
SHOSTAKOVICH: *Concertos.* ***

(M) *** Decca 425 003-2. Chung, LSO, Previn –
STRAVINSKY: *Concerto.* ***

*** Chan. 8709. Mordkovitch, RSNO, Järvi.

**(*) EMI CDC7 47025-2. Perlman, BBC SO, Roshdestvensky.

(M) **(*) Sony SMK 64503. Stern, NYPO, Mehta – BARTOK:
Rhapsodies. **

The two Prokofiev concertos are among the composer's
most richly lyrical works, and Cho-Liang Lin brings out their
romantic warmth as well as their dramatic bite. Salonen's
understanding support – helped by sound more refined than
this orchestra usually gets, if with weighty bass – culminates
in ravishing accounts of the outer movements of No. 1 and
the central slow movement of No. 2. The Stravinsky coupling
is another more powerful and warmly expressive reading,
although here Chung is in some ways even more stimulating.

The Virgin two-for-one Double makes an amazing bargain in offering first-class versions of both the paired concertos of Prokofiev and Shostakovich. Dmitri Sitkovetsky
conveys the demonic side of the *First Concerto* more effectively than any other player, without losing sight of its
lyricism or sense of line. His version of the Scherzo touches
an ironic, almost malignant nerve, while he has the measure
of the ice-maiden fairy-tale element at the opening. He has
a sympathetic collaborator in Sir Colin Davis and the *Second
Concerto* is hardly less powerful, and the internal orchestral
balance is very natural.

Kyung Wha Chung's performances emphasize the lyrical
quality of these concertos with playing that is both warm

and strong, tender and full of fantasy. Previn's accompaniments are deeply understanding, while the Decca sound has lost only a little of its fullness in the digital remastering, and the soloist is now made very present. The Stravinsky coupling is equally stimulating.

Perlman's performances bring virtuosity of such strength and command that one is reminded of the supremacy of Heifetz. Though the EMI sound has warmth and plenty of bloom, the balance of the soloist is unnaturally close, which has the effect of obscuring important melodic ideas in the orchestra behind mere passage work from the soloist. Apart from the balance, the recording is a fine one.

Lydia Mordkovitch enters a hotly contested field and gives readings of strong personality and character. She is well supported by the RSNO and Järvi, and more than holds her own with rival versions. There are some splendidly malignant sounds in the Scherzo of No. 1, and both performances make a very satisfying alternative and have first-class sound.

In his digital recordings, made in the Avery Fisher Hall in 1982, Stern's are warm and boldly extrovert readings, a degree freer in expression and more spontaneous-sounding than his 1965 versions, recorded in Philadelphia, even if Ormandy offered riper accompaniments than Mehta does here. Stern may here lack the depth of poetry of Chung, and the fearless brilliance of Perlman, but his accounts are full of character and not without distinction in their own right.

(i) *Violin Concertos Nos. 1–2. Symphony No. 5 in B flat, Op. 100; Romeo and Juliet, Op. 64: Suite (Nos. 1–10); Scythian Suite, Op. 20.*

(M) **(*) Decca (ADD) 466 996-2 (2). (i) Ricci; SRO, Ansermet.

Ansermet's Prokofiev is always characterful, and if one accepts the less than ideally polished playing of the Swiss orchestra, there is much to enjoy here. The *Fifth Symphony* was one of Ansermet's finest performances, straight and unaffected, and the recording as brilliant as you could wish. The *Scythian Suite* comes off very well too: it is a grossly underrated score because of its parallels with *The Rite of Spring*. The aggressive passages are particularly threatening, largely due to the brilliant recording (wonderful timpani and bass drums), though the performance as a whole is not quite forceful enough. The *Romeo and Juliet Suite* is also rather impressive, though it is the conductor's attention to detail, rather than orchestral virtuosity, which impresses. The *Violin Concertos* are new to CD – and how good they sound. They are hardly top recommendations (intonation on the part of the soloist as well as the orchestra is not immaculate), but they have plenty of character and are not dull. A collection which will be of particular interest to Ansermet admirers, particularly as the vintage sound has been so vividly transferred to CD.

Violin Concertos Nos. (i) *1;* (ii) *2. Solo Violin Sonata in D, Op. 115; Sonata for 2 Violins in C, Op. 56.* (iii) *Violin Sonatas Nos. 1–2; 5 Melodies, Op. 35b; The Love for Three Oranges: March* (arr. Heifetz).

(M) **(*) EMI CMS5 66605-2. Zimmermann; (i) BPO, Maazel; (ii) Philh. O, Janssons; (iii) Longquich.

If Frank Peter Zimmermann does not quite compete with the finest rivals in the two concertos, the solo and duo sonatas are outstanding performances. Otherwise Zimmermann offers finely crafted performances, marked by poetry in the lyrical movements and quicksilver lightness in such a movement as the central *Scherzo* of the *First Concerto*, which is taken exceptionally fast. Though that means there is a lack of bite and spikiness in the concertos and the violin-and-piano sonatas, it works very well in the *Cinq mélodies*, transcribed from the *Songs Without Words*. In the *Sonatas* Zimmermann is not helped by the slightly distant recording-balance, and the pianist is sometimes rhythmically a little square, not as responsive as his partner. Nevertheless the set is well worth considering.

Violin Concerto No. 1 in D, Op. 19.

*** Teldec 4509 92256-2. Vengerov, LSO, Rostropovich – SHOSTAKOVICH: *Violin Concerto No. 1.* ***
*** Erato 0630 17722-2. Mutter, Nat. SO, Rostropovich – GLAZUNOV: *Violin Concerto, Op. 82;* SHCHEDRIN: *Stihira.* ***

Maxim Vengerov's magnetism in both concertos is in no doubt; his playing is full of life and spontaneous feeling, helped by Rostropovich's highly supportive accompaniments. In the Prokofiev, Mintz displays rather more poetic subtlety but his pairing is Tchaikovsky's *Third Piano Concerto*, and many will feel that Vengerov's coupling is even more appropriate, while his performance has its own special character and insights. The recording is excellent too.

As in the Glazunov, Anne-Sophie Mutter gives a warmly sympathetic account, responding to the inspirational direction of Rostropovich. The great melodies of the outer movements are tenderly expressive and the central *Scherzo* delightfully witty. The Washington recording, airy and spacious, has the soloist forwardly balanced.

(i) *Violin Concerto No. 1. Symphony No. 1 (Classical); Visions fugitives* (orch. Barshai).

* Chan. 9615. (i) Grubert; Moscow CO, Orbelian.

All these pieces date from 1917, but the *Classical Symphony* apart, they receive pretty lacklustre performances. Ilya Grubert undergoes too close a scrutiny from the recording engineers and in the *Visions fugitives*, their American conductor sets somewhat slow tempi. Subfusc recording.

Violin Concerto No. 2 in G min., Op. 63.

(M) *** RCA (ADD) 09026 61744-2. Heifetz, Boston SO, Munch – GLAZUNOV; SIBELIUS: *Concertos.* ***
(B) *** EMI double forte (ADD) CZS5 69331-2 (2). D. Oistrakh, Philh. O, Galliera – BEETHOVEN: *Triple Concerto;* BRAHMS: *Double Concerto;* MOZART: *Violin Concerto No. 3.* ***
*** Teldec 4509 98255-2. Perlman, Chicago SO, Barenboim – STRAVINSKY: *Violin Concerto.* ***
(N) (BB) (***) Naxos mono 8.110942. Heifetz, Boston SO, Koussevitzky – GRUENBERG: *Violin Concerto, Op. 47.* (**)

In the *arioso*-like slow movement, Heifetz chooses a faster speed than is usual, but there is nothing unresponsive about his playing, for his expressive rubato has an unfailing inevitability. In the spiky finale he is superb, and indeed his playing is glorious throughout. The recording is serviceable merely, though it has been made firmer in the current RCA remastering. But no one is going to be prevented from enjoying this ethereal performance because the technical quality is dated.

David Oistrakh's is a beautifully balanced reading which lays stress on the lyricism of the concerto, and the orchestral support he receives could hardly be improved upon. The 1958 recording is admirably spacious and atmospheric, with finely focused detail and great warmth. The CD transfer is immaculate. An altogether marvellous performance, and this double forte compilation of four very distinguished recordings is extraordinary value for money.

Though Perlman's coupling of Prokofiev's *Second Concerto* and the Stravinsky is most ungenerous, this performance, recorded live, is more compelling than his earlier studio recording, with Barenboim adding to the urgency and energy.

Heifetz's 1937 recording of the second Prokofiev concerto has extraordinary bite and intensity, tough and purposeful in the outer movements, flowing and lyrical in the lovely central slow movement, despite a recording that does not allow a true pianissimo. Otherwise the sound is good, well transferred in this Naxos edition. It is a pity that here it is coupled with the empty and overlong Gruenberg concerto.

Divertimento, Op. 43; The Prodigal Son, Op. 46; Symphonic Song, Op. 57; Andante (Piano Sonata No. 4).

*** Chan. 8728. RSNO, Järvi.

The *Divertimento* is a lovely piece: its first movement has an irresistible and haunting second theme. Its long neglect is puzzling since it is highly attractive and ought to be popular. So, for that matter, should *The Prodigal Son*, some of whose material Prokofiev re-used the following year in the *Fourth Symphony*. Another rarity is the *Symphonic Song*, a strange, darkly scored piece. The recording is first class – as, indeed, are the performances. An indispensable item in any Prokofiev collection.

The Gambler: 4 Portraits, Op. 49; Semyon Kotko: Symphonic Suite, Op. 81 bis.

*** Chan. 8803. RSNO, Järvi.

Prokofiev's *Four Portraits* enshrine the best of the opera and are exhilarating and inventive. *Semyon Kotko*, though not top-drawer Prokofiev, is still thoroughly enjoyable. Järvi gives a thoroughly sympathetic reading in vivid and present sound.

Lieutenant Kijé (incidental music): Suite, Op. 60.

(B) *** Sony (ADD) SBK 48162. Cleveland O, Szell – KODALY: *Háry János Suite;* MUSSORGSKY: *Pictures at an Exhibition.* ***

(M) **(*) RCA (ADD) 09026 61957-2. Chicago SO, Reiner – HOVHANESS: *Mysterious Mountain Symphony;* STRAVINSKY: *Le Baiser de la fée.* ***

(i) *Lieutenant Kijé: suite, Op. 60;* (ii) *The Love of Three Oranges: suite, Op. 33a;* (iii) *Romeo and Juliet: excerpts from Suites Nos. 1, Op. 64a & 2, Op. 64b.*

(N) (B) **(*) Sony (ADD) SBK 89287. (i) Cleveland O, Szell; (ii) Philadelphia O, Ormandy; (iii) NYPO, Mitropoulos.

Lieutenant Kijé (Suite); The Love for Three Oranges (Suite); Symphony No. 1 (Classical).

(B) **(*) Ph. 426 640-2. LSO, Marriner.

Szell is on his highest form. Seldom on record has the *Lieutenant Kijé* music been projected with such drama and substance, and Szell is wonderfully warm in the *Romance* without a suggestion of sentimentality. The recording, like the couplings, is balanced too closely, but the orchestral playing is so stunning one hardly minds, for the opening and closing trumpet-calls are properly distanced.

Mitropoulos's 1958 *Romeo and Juliet* excerpts generate tremendous passion with some electrifying playing from the NYPO, as well as equally compelling moments of tenderness. Szell, too, is on top form in his 1969 recording of the *Lieutenant Kijé suite*: the music is presented with fine drama, but also much warmth in the *Romance* without suggesting sentimentality. Ormandy's 1963 *Love of Three Oranges* is not quite as gripping, but is still very impressive. The up-front sound is vivid, very good for its period.

Reiner's *Lieutenant Kijé* is very well played and sounds astonishingly good for 1959, but is just a bit too straight-faced to bring out all the humour in the music. Still, all Reiner performances have authority, and this is no exception.

This bargain Philips disc offers good playing and recording and there is nothing to disappoint. Individually these works are available in other versions that are as good as (or better than) this compilation, but these are lively performances, and the remastered sound is fresh and open.

The Love for Three Oranges: Suite, Op. 33.

(N) *** BBC (ADD) BBCL 4056-2. BBC SO, Kempe – BEETHOVEN: *Overture: Leonore No. 3.* DVORAK: *Symphony No. 9.* *** ●

(M) **(*) RCA (ADD) 09026 63532-2. Boston Pops O, Fiedler – CHOPIN: *Les Sylphides* **; LISZT: *Les Préludes; Mazeppa.* *

(B) ** Sony SBK 53621. Phd. O, Ormandy – SHOSTAKOVICH: *Symphony No. 5* etc. **(*)

(i) *The Love for Three Oranges: Suite;* (ii) *Le Pas d'acier: suite, Op. 41 bis;* (i) *Scythian Suite, Op. 20.*

(B) (**) EMI mono CZS5 69674-2 (2). (i) French Nat. R. O; (ii) Philh. O; Markevitch – STRAVINSKY: *Le Baiser de la fée* etc. (***)

(i) *The Love for Three Oranges Suite; Scythian Suite;* (ii) *Symphony No. 5, Op. 100.*

(M) **(*) Mercury (IMS) 432 753-2. (i) LSO; (ii) Minneapolis SO; Dorati.

The Prokofiev suite, strikingly intense, finds Kempe at home in a sharply characterized performance full of grotesquerie. With well-defined contrasts of light and shade, bite and tenderness, it becomes more than a sequence of genre pieces.

Vivid transfer of the 1975 radio recording, with high dynamic contrasts.

Dorati's account of Prokofiev's powerful and atmospheric *Scythian Suite* was recorded at Watford Town Hall in 1957; the remastering confirms the excellence of the original engineering. The suite from the *Love for Three Oranges* is similarly striking in its characterization and vivid primary colours, with the resonance not blunting the rhythms. The CD is worth considering for these two performances; but the *Fifth Symphony*, recorded in Minneapolis two years later, is less successful. Dorati's reading is similarly forceful but the effect is hard and often unsympathetic.

Fiedler is on top form, full of life and character – the *Scène infernale* is especially effective, with some electrifying string-playing. The 1961 recording is generally impressive too – brilliant in the 'Living Stereo' manner, with splendid definition set in the Boston Symphony Hall acoustic (the bass drum sounds particularly realistic). The only fault is some slight distortion, but that is soon forgotten in the vitality of the playing.

Superb orchestral playing in Philadelphia of course, but Ormandy's view of the score is larger than life, spectacle seemingly more important than subtlety, which the close recording tends to emphasize. The excitement is undeniable, but the famous *March* seems rather inflated and heavy.

Sharply characterized performances from Markevitch, brilliantly played. No apologies need be made for the mono sound, which is both brilliant and atmospheric and is transferred to CD without added edge or thinness. However, it is the Stravinsky coupling which makes this reissue distinctive. The pair of CDs are now offered in EMI's French 'two for the price of one' series.

Peter and the Wolf, Op. 67.

(BB) *** Naxos 8.554170. Dame Edna Everage, Melbourne SO, Lanchbery – BRITTEN: *Young Person's Guide* ***; POULENC: *The Story of Babar.* *** ✪

(BB) *** ASV (ADD) CDQS 6017. RPO, Hughes – SAINT-SAENS: *Carnival.* ***

(M) * Sony SMK 60175. NYPO, Bernstein (cond. and narr.) – SAINT-SAENS: *Carnival of the Animals* *; BRITTEN: *Young Person's Guide.* (*)

(M) Virgin VM5 61782-2. Henry, RLPO, Pešek – BRITTEN: *Young Person's Guide* **(*); SAINT-SAENS: *Carnival of the Animals* (chamber version). ***

(i) *Peter and the Wolf;* (ii) *Lieutenant Kijé* (suite).

(M) **(*) Decca Phase Four (ADD) 444 104-2. (i) Connery (nar.), RPO; (ii) Netherlands R. PO; Dorati – BRITTEN: *Young Person's Guide.* **(*)

(i; ii) *Peter and the Wolf;* (iii) *Lieutenant Kijé: Suite;* (iv) *The Love for Three Oranges: Suite;* (ii) *Symphony No. 1 in D (Classical).*

✪ (B) *** Decca (ADD) 433 612-2. (i) Richardson, (ii) LSO, Sargent; (iii) Paris Conservatoire O, Boult; (iv) LPO, Weller.

Sir Ralph Richardson brings a great actor's feeling for words to the narrative; he dwells lovingly on their sound as well as their meaning, and this genial preoccupation with the manner in which the story is told matches Sargent's feeling exactly. Sir Malcolm Sargent's direction of the accompaniment shows his professionalism at its very best. The original coupling, Sargent's amiable, polished account of the *Classical Symphony*, has now been restored. All the tempi, except the finale, are slow but Sir Malcolm's assured elegance carries its own spontaneity. The sound is vivid. Boult's Paris recording of *Lieutenant Kijé* offers more gusto than finesse, but the result is exhilaratingly robust and the very early (1955) stereo comes up remarkably well. Weller's *Love for Three Oranges* is a first-class performance, given top-drawer 1977 recording. But our Rosette is for *Peter and the Wolf.*

If you react adversely to Dame Edna Everage's exuberantly eccentric persona, the Naxos version cannot be recommended. But for those willing to be included among her possums it is a highly entertaining and very dramatic narrative, with the orchestral accompaniment splendidly paced to match the gripping onward flow of the story. The wolf-horns positively snarl, the flute-bird chirps merrily and the cat-clarinet has a certain elegant insouciance, while the hunter's guns are like thunder. There are twee moments, but children will readily respond to Dame Edna's very positive involvement with her characters, and so will most parents. At the close she throws away the humour of Grandfather's grumble but not the childish delight on discovering that the duck is still alive after all, inside the wolf. The couplings are equally splendid.

Angela Rippon narrates with charm yet is never in the least coy; indeed she is thoroughly involved in the tale and thus also involves the listener. The accompaniment is equally spirited, with excellent orchestral playing, and the recording is splendidly clear, yet not lacking atmosphere. This makes an excellent super-bargain recommendation.

Sean Connery uses a modern script by Gabrielle Hilton which brings a certain colloquial friendliness to the narrative and invites a relaxed style, to which the actor readily responds. If you can accept such extensions as 'dumb duck' and a pussy cat who is 'smooth, but greedy and vain', you will not be disappointed with Connery's participation in the climax of the tale, where Dorati supports him admirably. Both *Peter and the Wolf* and *The Young Person's Guide to the Orchestra* start with the orchestra tuning up, to create an anticipatory atmosphere, and the introductory matter is entirely fresh and informal. In *Lieutenant Kijé* Dorati is characteristically direct, with everything boldly characterized, and he secures excellent playing from the Netherlands orchestra. As with *Peter and the Wolf*, the extremely vivid Decca Phase Four recording (not unnaturally balanced but ensuring every detail is clear) gives the performance a strong projection.

Bernstein opens his narration with a kind of quiz on which instrument represents which character. The effect is mildly patronizing, as is his narration throughout. If you are a Bernstein *aficionado* you may well take to it. The playing is excellent, though the performance lacks charm. Vivid, 1960 sound.

Lenny Henry's colloquial narration is enthusiastic, clear and communicative. Children will certainly respond to his individual 'voices' for the characters in the tale and also his additional vocalized effects. But the record's appeal is reduced to virtually nil by the extraordinarily inept new instrumental characterization for each of the characters in the tale. The piece was specifically designed by Prokofiev to introduce young listeners to the orchestral palette, and the dumbing-down here robs his score of its primary purpose, plus almost all its elegance and wit. Peter stays with the strings; but, instead of a flute, the bird is portrayed by a Chinese 'mouth organ', the duck is a squealing Catalan 'tiple'. Even more unfortunately, the wolf is represented by three very bland accordions; and, worst of all, the engagingly feline clarinet with which Prokofiev identified the cat is changed to an oboe d'amore in order to produce a semblance of a 'miaow'.

Romeo and Juliet (ballet), Op. 64 (complete).

(M) *** Double Decca (ADD) 452 970-2 (2). Cleveland O, Maazel.

(B) *** EMI double forte (ADD) CZS5 68607-2 (2). LSO, Previn.

(N) (B) **(*) Ph. 464 726-2 (2). Kirov O, Gergiev.

Almost simultaneously in 1973 two outstanding versions of Prokofiev's complete Romeo and Juliet ballet appeared, strongly contrasted to provide a clear choice on grounds of interpretation and recording. Previn and the LSO made their recording in conjunction with live performances at the Royal Festival Hall, and the result reflects the humour and warmth which went with those live occasions. Previn's pointing of rhythm is consciously seductive, whether in fast, jaunty numbers or in the soaring lyricism of the love music. The Kingsway Hall recording quality is full and immediate, yet atmospheric too.

Maazel by contrast will please those who believe that this score should above all be bitingly incisive. The rhythms are more consciously metrical, the tempi generally faster, and the precision of ensemble of the Cleveland Orchestra is little short of miraculous. The recording is one of Decca's most spectacular, searingly detailed, but atmospheric too. With the reissue of the Maazel set as a Double Decca, honours are even between both sets: if you want the finest sound and a gripping sense of drama, choose Maazel; if you prefer a more genial manner, Previn is your man.

Gergiev secures beautifully polished playing from the Kirov Ballet Theatre Orchestra. Indeed it is graceful to the point of being over-cultivated. There is much delicacy of effect, rhythms are crisp and clean and there is plenty of energy, while the brass sonorities are without the rough edges one expects from Russian orchestras. But this is a very romantic view, at its finest in the captivating portrayal of The young Juliet, and Juliet alone, while the picaresque numbers like the engaging Dance with mandolins and the charming Aubade and Dance of the girls with lilies are beautifully played. The Death of Mercutio certainly brings a moment of red-blooded drama, but when it come to the Balcony scene the lovers' ardour has little sexuality and elsewhere Prokofiev's pungency is muted. The opening of Act III is powerful, but the anguish and tragedy of the climax of the story has intensity without stark despair. The recording, made on location in Leningrad by a Philips team, is of the very highest quality, so this is a performance to enjoy primarily for the lyricism of Prokofiev's inspiration.

Romeo and Juliet (ballet), Op. 64: highlights.

*** Sony SK 42662. BPO, Salonen.

(N) (M) *** Virgin VM5 61977-2. RLPO, Pešek.

With magnificent playing from the Berlin Philharmonic Orchestra, Esa-Pekka Salonen's set of excerpts seems marginally a first choice for those wanting a full-priced disc of highlights from Prokofiev's masterly score. The Berlin Philharmonic playing has an enormous intensity and a refined felicity in the score's more delicate evocations. One is touched and deeply moved by this music-making, while the selection admirably parallels the ballet's narrative. The recording, made in the Philharmonie, matches sumptuousness with a potent clarity of projection, and the dynamic range is dramatically wide.

Pešek's selection follows the narrative line, and one feels that the conductor and his players are highly involved in the course of events; in the closing numbers Pešek tightens the screws so that the Death of Juliet is devastating. The Royal Liverpool Philharmonic Orchestra play very well indeed and achieve great freshness and spontaneity; they are given a satisfying concert-hall balance. This Virgin CD offers 71 minutes from Prokofiev's inspired score, and every minute is stimulating and enjoyable.

Romeo and Juliet (ballet): excerpts (including Suites Nos. 1–3).

** DG 453 439-2. BPO, Abbado.

Romeo and Juliet (ballet): excerpts (including Suite No. 2).

(M) *** Classic fM 75605 57047. RPO, Gatti –
TCHAIKOVSKY: Romeo and Juliet (Fantasy Overture)

Romeo and Juliet (ballet): Suites Nos. 1 & 2, Op. 64.

(M) *** [Mercury 432 004-2]. Minneapolis SO, Skrowaczewski
– MUSSORGSKY: Night. ***

(B) **(*) Double Decca (ADD) 440 630-2 (2). SRO, Ansermet
– TCHAIKOVSKY: Swan Lake. **(*)

Romeo and Juliet: Suites Nos. 1 & 2: excerpts.

*** Telarc CD 80089. Cleveland O, Levi.

After a bitingly pungent opening (Montagues and Capulets), Daniele Gatti's 50-minute selection effectively encapsulates the ballet's dramatic narrative in nine key numbers. The RPO characterizes very strongly indeed and, with generally brisk tempi, the strongest contrast is made between the bold, pungent rhythms of the more vigorous dances and the exquisite delicacy of the gentler, romantic evocation with its wonderfully translucent orchestral colouring. The portrait of Friar Laurence is touchingly gentle, but the ballet's passionate climax could not be more heart-rendingly plangent. The recording is superb, very much in the demonstration bracket, and the coupling with Tchaikovsky's fantasy overture is made the more apt by Gatti's highly romantic approach to that quite different response to Shakespeare's tragedy.

Skrowaczewski's recording of the two ballet suites was made in 1962. The playing of the Minneapolis orchestra is on a virtuoso level. The crystal-clear acoustic of the hall in Edison High School, with its backing ambience, seems ideally suited to the angular melodic lines and pungent lyricism of this powerful score, to underline the sense of tragedy without losing the music's romantic sweep. The fidelity and spectacle of the Mercury engineering reach a zenith in the powerful closing sequence of *Romeo at Juliet's tomb*. At mid-price this is highly recommendable.

Ansermet's performances have both atmosphere and passion (notably *Romeo with Juliet before his departure*). After the ominous introduction, the playing is rhythmically a bit sluggish. But *Juliet As a Young Girl* and the *Madrigal* are charming, and the love scene of *Romeo and Juliet* is genuinely touching; the *Death of Tybalt* bursts with energy, and *Masks* is nicely pointed. If the Suisse Romande Orchestra in 1961 was not one of the world's greatest ensembles, Ansermet was very persuasive and he brings everything vividly to life. The dramatically vibrant recording is well up to Decca's vintage standard of the early 1960s.

Yoel Levi also seems to have a special affinity with Prokofiev's score, for pacing is unerringly apt and characterization is strong. There are some wonderfully serene moments, as in the ethereal introduction of the flute melody in the first piece (*Montagues and Capulets*). The quicker movements have an engaging feeling of the dance and the light, graceful articulation in *The Child Juliet* is a delight; but the highlights of the performance are the *Romeo and Juliet Love Scene* and *Romeo at Juliet's before Parting*, bringing playing of great intensity, with a ravishing response from the Cleveland strings. The rich Telarc recording is in the demonstration class, but this offers less music than several of its competitors.

Abbado's selection from *Romeo* has some exemplary playing from the Berlin Philharmonic and the DG engineers offer us very well-balanced recorded sound. This 70-minute anthology is assembled from the three published concert suites, as well as the ballet itself. Everything is well shaped and finely characterized, but Daniele Gatti's shorter RPO selection has greater atmosphere and dramatic flair. The problem is that it offers much less music!

Russian Overture, Op. 72; Summer Night: suite from *The Duenna, Op. 123; War and Peace* (suite, arr. Palmer).

*** Chan. 9096. Philh. O, Järvi.

The *Russian Overture* is determinedly popular in appeal, and it teems with ideas, both lyrical and grotesque, and has plenty of vitality. The *Summer Night Suite* is notable for its delicate *Serenade* and a charmingly romantic movement called *Dreams*. But the finest music here is Christopher Palmer's suite of interludes from *War and Peace*, full of splendid ideas. It ends triumphantly with the magnificent patriotic tune associated with Marshal Kutuzov, the architect of the Russian victory. Järvi and the Philharmonia Orchestra are thoroughly at home in these scores, and the Chandos recording is characteristically spectacular.

Sinfonia concertante for Cello & Orchestra, Op. 125 (see also above under *Concertino*).

*** Virgin VC5 45310-2. Mørk, CBSO, P. Järvi – MIASKOVSKY: *Cello Concerto, Op. 66*. ***

*** DG 449 821-2. Maisky, Russian Nat. O, Pletnev – MIASKOVSKY: *Cello Concerto*. ***

Virgin bring the Norwegian Truls Mørk and the Bir-mingham Orchestra under Paavo Järvi in an exhilarating and masterly performance that, as far as the solo playing is concerned, certainly matches if not surpasses its DG rival. So, too, does the Virgin recording, which is both richer and more present. It is unique in offering the alternative version of the finale on a second CD.

Mischa Maisky is often over-emotional, but in Prokofiev's masterpiece his intensity is not misplaced. Pletnev and the Russian National Orchestra give a superb account of themselves and produce a real Prokofievian sonority, full of the mordant flavour the composer commands and with a splendid rhythmic spring.

The Stone Flower (ballet): complete.

(M) *** CPO 999385-2 (3). Hanover R. PO, Jurowski.

(B) *** Melodiya Twofer 74321 63458-2 (2). Bolshoi Theatre O, Rozhdestvensky.

There is much that is imaginative in this score. The new version from Hanover under Michail Jurowski has a lot going for it. The orchestral playing is polished and characterful, and the CPO recording is fresh and well detailed. Indeed, it must now be a first recommendation, though it is much the more expensive on three mid-price discs, when the Russian recording has been reissued as a 'Twofer'. Incidentally, the 1991 Kirov video production (Teldec 9031-76401-3) is not to be missed: a joy to the eye, very well danced and well worth buying; but the score is not complete.

Rozhdestvensky's Bolshoi performance dates from 1968 and still sounds pretty good on CD.

SYMPHONIES

Symphonies Nos. 1–7.

*** Chan. 8931/4. RSNO, Järvi.

Symphonies Nos. 1–7; Lieutenant Kijé (Suite).

(B) * DG 463 761-2 (4). BPO, Ozawa.

Symphonies Nos. 1–7; Overture russe, Op. 72; Scythian Suite, Op. 20.

(B) **(*) Decca (ADD) 430 782-2 (4). LSO or LPO, Weller.

These Chandos recordings from the mid-1980s are of the highest quality. They have been shorn of their couplings in this box, the only important loss being the delightful *Sinfonietta*. Both versions of the *Fourth Symphony* are included: the 1947 revision appears with the *Classical* on the first disc, while the 1930 original is coupled with the *Third*. Nos. 2 and 6 are on the third disc, and 5 and 7 on the last, so no side-breaks are involved. As performances, these are the equal of the best.

Weller's performances are polished and very well played, though at times they are emotionally a little earthbound. Transfers are well managed, though there is some loss of naturalness in the upper range. The finest of the set is No. 2. Elsewhere, the bitter tang of Prokofiev's language is again toned down and the hard-etched lines smoothed over. The *Seventh* suits Weller's approach readily and he catches the atmosphere of its somewhat balletic second movement particularly well. The *Russian Overture* has plenty of energy but the *Scythian Suite*, too, needs more abrasiveness.

Ozawa's BPO set of Prokofiev symphonies is a non-starter. The performances are well played, but are very routine: without looking at the documentation, it would be hard to recognize this celebrated orchestra, which here produces a general-purpose sonority which Karajan would never have countenanced in his day. *Lieutenant Kijé* is sadly lacking in sparkle.

Symphonies Nos. 1–4; Hamlet, Op. 77 (incidental music).

(B) **(*) Melodia Twofer (ADD) 74321 66979-2 (2). USSR RTV Grand SO, Rozhdestvensky.

Rozhdestvensky's set begins with a brilliant performance of the *Classical Symphony* (one of the finest available in its day) with sparkling outer movements, while the slow movement and Minuet are admirably paced. The *Second Symphony*, with its unremittingly loud first movement, must be among the noisiest music Prokofiev ever wrote. However, the second movement, with its beautiful set of variations and some highly imaginative writing, occupies quite another world, and Rozhdestvensky and his orchestra adapt well to the conflicting demands of both. The *Third Symphony* receives a fiery performance, though the powerful atmosphere of the slow movement is not entirely realized. The *Fourth Symphony* receives a similarly committed performance. All four were recorded in the 1960s and, though the sound is a little dated, and the Russian brass will not be to everyone's liking, Rozhdestvensky's total commitment makes up for any minor reservations. The *Hamlet* incidental music was recorded in 1988 and makes a rare and enjoyable fill-up. All in all, this is excellent value.

Symphony No. 1 in D (Classical), Op. 25.

*** DG 423 624-2. Orpheus CO – BIZET: *Symphony;* BRITTEN: *Simple Symphony.* ***

The Orpheus performance has freshness and wit – the droll bassoon solo in the first movement against sparkling string figurations is delightful. In the cantilena of the *Larghetto*, some ears might crave a greater body of violin tone; but the playing has a fine poise, and the minuet and finale have equal flair. Excellent, truthful recording to make this a highly desirable triptych.

Symphonies Nos. 1 (Classical); 4 in C, Op. 112 (revised, 1947 version).

*** Chan. 8400. RSNO, Järvi.

Järvi succeeds in making out a more eloquent case for the revision of the *Fourth Symphony* than many of his predecessors. He also gives an exhilarating account of the *Classical Symphony*, one of the best on record. The slow movement has real douceur and the finale is wonderfully high-spirited. On CD in the *Fourth Symphony* the upper range is a little fierce in some of the more forceful climaxes.

Symphonies Nos. 1 (Classical); 5, Op. 100.

(M) *** DG (ADD) 437 253-2. BPO, Karajan.

(M) *** Ph. (IMS) 442 399-2. LAPO, Previn.

(M) **(*) Sony SBK 53260. Phd. O, Ormandy.

(BB) **(*) Naxos 8.550237. Slovak PO, Gunzenhauser.

Karajan's 1969 recording of the *Fifth* is in a class of its own. The playing has wonderful tonal sophistication and Karajan judges tempi to perfection so that proportions seem quite ideal. It is coupled with Karajan's 1982 digital recording of the *Classical Symphony*, in which his performance is predictably brilliant and the playing beautifully polished, with grace and eloquence distinguishing the slow movement.

In the first movement of the *Fifth*, Previn's pacing seems exactly right: everything flows so naturally and speaks effectively; and in the slow movement he gets playing of genuine eloquence from the Los Angeles orchestra. He also gives an excellent account of the perennially fresh *Classical Symphony*. The recording is beautifully natural, with impressive detail, range and body.

The Philadelphia Orchestra play superbly and with much wit in the *Classical Symphony*. Ormandy's expansive warmth in the *Adagio* and the easy brilliance of the orchestral articulation in the second and fourth movements make for splendid results in the *Fifth*. Although the early stereo recording could be more opulent and less brightly lit, it still conveys impressively the ample body of tone this great orchestra was creating in the late 1950s.

The Naxos coupling is very good value indeed. The recording is altogether first class: there is splendid detail and definition, and the balance is extremely well judged. Moreover the American conductor, Stephen Gunzenhauser, gets very good playing from the excellent Slovak Philharmonic and the performances have the merit of being straightforward and unaffected. The first movement of the 'Classical' Symphony is a bit sedate and wanting in sparkle; the finale comes off best.

Symphonies Nos. 1 (Classical); 7, Op. 131; The Love for Three Oranges: Suite.

(B) *** CfP (ADD) CD-CFP 4523. Philh. O, Malko.

(i) Symphony No. 1 (Classical); (ii) Romeo and Juliet (ballet): highlights.

(B) *** DG 439 492-2. (i) Orpheus CO; (ii) Boston SO, Ozawa.

All the performances on CfP are quite excellent, and the *Seventh Symphony*, of which Malko conducted the UK première, is freshly conceived and finely shaped. What is so striking is the range and refinement of the 1955 stereo recording: the excellence of the balance and the body of the sound are remarkable.

An outstanding coupling on DG. The Orpheus performance (see above) of the *Classical Symphony* is first class in every way while *Romeo and Juliet* was one of Ozawa's finest recordings. The playing has elegance and an attractive rhythmic lightness and point. There is no lack of drama or feeling, but it is the stylishness and beauty of the playing one remembers, together with the conductor's obvious affection for the score. The sound throughout is of DG's best, warm yet transparent and with a most attractive ambience.

Symphony No. 2 in D min., Op. 40; Romeo and Juliet (ballet): Suite No. 1.

**(*) Chan. 8368. RSNO, Järvi.

The *Second Symphony* reflects Prokofiev's avowed intention of writing a work 'made of iron and steel'. Neeme Järvi produces altogether excellent results from the Scottish National Orchestra and the Chandos recording is impressively detailed and vivid. The *Romeo and Juliet* suite comes off well; the SNO play with real character.

Symphonies Nos. 3; 4 in C, Op. 47 (original, 1930 version).

*** Chan. 8401. RSNO, Järvi.

Neeme Järvi's account of the *Third* is extremely successful. In many ways the original of the *Fourth Symphony* seems more like a ballet suite than a symphony: its insufficient tonal contrast tells – yet the Scherzo, drawn from the music for the Temptress in *The Prodigal Son* ballet, is particularly felicitous.

Symphony No. 4 in C (revised, 1947 version), Op. 112; The Prodigal Son (ballet; complete), Op. 46.

(BB) *** Naxos 8.553055. Ukraine NSO, Kuchar

It makes an ideal coupling having the *Symphony No. 4* alongside the ballet score from which Prokofiev drew most of the material. The 1947 revision of the symphony, now generally preferred, is richer in both structure and instrumentation. Kuchar's readings are both powerful and idiomatic, with crisply disciplined playing from the Ukraine orchestra bringing home the weight and violence of much of the writing. These are performances to match and even outshine current rivals at whatever price; the Naxos recording is satisfyingly full-bodied, not least in vivid brass and percussion sounds, with the piano both clear and well integrated in the symphony.

Symphony No. 5 in B flat, Op. 100.

(M) *** DG (ADD) 463 613-2. BPO, Karajan – STRAVINSKY: *Rite of Spring*. **(*)

*** Chan. 8576. Leningrad PO, Jansons.

Symphony No. 5; Romeo and Juliet: excerpts.

** Teldec 4509 96301-2. NYPO, Masur.

Symphony No. 5; Scythian Suite, Op. 20.

*** EMI CDC7 54577-2. CBSO, Rattle.

Symphony No. 5; Waltz Suite, Op. 110.

*** Chan. 8450. RSNO, Järvi.

Karajan's reading of the *Fifth Symphony* is outstanding in every way. It is a totally unaffected, beautifully played account, with the Berlin Philharmonic on top form, and the DG engineers at their best. The recording is a model of its kind, allowing all the subtleties of the orchestral colouring to register without any distortion of perspective. It has splendid range and fidelity and is wholly free from any artificial balance. It is here paired with his highly individual version of *The Rite of Spring* to make an intriguing coupling in DG's Originals series.

Rattle's *Fifth Symphony* with the CBSO is very fine indeed, full of fire and vitality; given the quality of the sound, it must rank along with the best now available. The slow movement comes off particularly well – though perhaps it is invidious to single out one particular movement, for these are really stimulating performances with many imaginative touches. Thoroughly recommendable.

Jansons goes for brisk tempi – and in the slow movement he really is too fast. The Scherzo is dazzling and so, too, is the finale, which is again fast and overdriven. An exhilarating and exciting performance, eminently well recorded, recommended to those willing to accept the ungenerous measure.

Järvi's direction is unhurried, fluent and authoritative. His feeling for the music is unfailingly natural. The three *Waltzes* which derive from various sources are all elegantly played. The Chandos recording is set just a shade further back than some of its companions in the series, yet at the same time every detail is clear.

In Kurt Masur's live account, the playing is eminently cultured, and the performance would be enjoyable in the concert hall were it not for the abrupt hiatus at the *l'istesso tempo* section (fig. 48) of the Scherzo which will rule it out of court for many collectors. The recording is very full-bodied and well detailed. The six movements from *Romeo and Juliet* are studio recordings and paradoxically enough, sound more spontaneous.

Symphony No. 6 in E flat min., Op. 111; Romeo and Juliet (ballet): excerpts.

**(*) Decca 458 190-2. NHK SO, Dutoit.

Symphony No. 6. Waltz Suite, Op. 110/1, 5 & 6.

*** Chan. 8359. RSNO, Järvi.

The *Sixth Symphony* goes much deeper than any of its companions; indeed it is perhaps the greatest of the Prokofiev cycle. Neeme Järvi shapes its detail as skilfully as he does its architecture as a whole. These artists have the measure of the music's tragic poignancy more than almost any of their predecessors on record. The fill-up is a set of waltzes, drawn and adapted from various stage works.

Dutoit gives warmth to one of Prokofiev's most elusive works, but misses some of the darker qualities. Warm, full recording. The excerpts from *Romeo and Juliet* were recorded in Tokyo, again with warmth in both the sound and performance, making the focus less sharp than it might be.

Symphony No. 7 in C sharp min., Op. 131; Sinfonietta in A, Op. 5/48.

*** Chan. 8442. SNO, Järvi.

Neeme Järvi's account of the *Seventh Symphony* is hardly less successful than the other issues in this cycle. He draws very good playing from the SNO and has the full measure of this repertoire. The early *Sinfonietta* is a highly attractive coupling (what a sunny and charming piece it is!). The digital recording has great range and is excellently balanced.

CHAMBER AND INSTRUMENTAL MUSIC

Music for cello and piano: *Adagio (Cinderella), Op. 97; Ballade in C min., Op. 15; Cello Sonata Op. 119; Solo Cello Sonata, Op. 133; 5 Mélodies, Op. 35 bis* (arr. Wallfisch); *The*

Love for Three Oranges: March. The Tale of the Stone Flower: Waltz.

*** Black Box Music BBM 1027. Wallfisch, York.

Adagio (Cinderella); Ballade, Op. 15; Cello Sonata, Op. 119.

*** Chant du Monde LDC 2781112. Hoffman, Bianconi –
SHOSTAKOVICH: *Cello Sonata; Moderato.* **(*)

Cello Sonata in C, Op. 119.

*** Virgin VC5 45274-2. Mørk, Vogt – SHOSTAKOVICH: *Cello Sonata;* STRAVINSKY: *Suite italienne.* ***

*** Chan. 8340. Turovsky, L. Edlina – SHOSTAKOVICH: *Sonata.* ***

(BB) *** ASV CDQS 6218. Gregor-Smith, Wrigley – MARTINU: *Variations;* JANACEK: *Pohádka;* SHOSTAKOVICH: *Cello Sonata.* ***

(BB) **(*) Arte Nova 74321 27805-2. Klein, Beldi – SHOSTAKOVICH: *Cello Sonata.* **(*)

Truls Mørk and Lars Vogt give a perceptive and thoughtful account of the *Sonata* and are expertly recorded in the Eidsvoll Church, Norway. This is among the best of recent versions and in addition to the Shostakovich has the advantage of an additional item, the Stravinsky *Suite italienne.*

In addition to the *Cello Sonata* Raphael Wallfisch and John York give us the early *Ballade,* Op. 15, as well as Wallfisch's own transcription of the enchanting *Cinq Mélodies,* Op. 35, and the solo sonata which Prokofiev began just before his death and whose first movement Vladimir Blok put into shape some years later. Wallfisch plays with superb golden tone and with great expressive eloquence. John York is a sensitive and intelligent partner. Their sonata can rank with the best.

Gary Hoffman and Philippe Bianconi are hardly less fine than their distinguished rivals and are every bit as well recorded. Indeed, there is more air round the aural image in their recital. They opt for the more traditional Shostakovich coupling but do offer the early *Ballade.* Not too much to choose between the two newcomers, though their Shostakovich may not be to all tastes.

Yuli Turovsky and Luba Edlina are also eloquent advocates of this *Sonata* and the balance is particularly lifelike.

Of the two budget versions Bernard Gregor-Smith and Yolande Wrigley have the benefit of the better recording: there is greater bloom and a more lively acoustic. They are more relaxed and thoughtful in approach than the Romanian partnership.

However, Emil Klein and Cristian Beldi give a very well-characterized account of the *Sonata,* tautly held together and vital in feeling. The balance between cello and piano is better judged, even if the timbre of the latter is less realistic.

Flute Sonata in D, Op. 94.

*** EMI CDC5 56982-2. Pahud, Kovacevich – DEBUSSY: *Syrinx; Bilitis,* etc.; RAVEL: *Chansons madécasses.* ***

(M) *** RCA (ADD) 09026 61615-2. Galway, Argerich – FRANCK; REINECKE: *Sonatas.* ***

Prokofiev's *Flute Sonata* (1943) is one of his sunniest and most serene wartime compositions. Played as it is on EMI, it is quite captivating. Emmanuel Pahud and Stephen Kovacevich set ideal tempi in each movement and their charac-

terization is perfect as a result. The familiar ideas sound completely fresh and novel. Easily a first recommendation. A perfectly balanced recording.

With its combination of effortless virtuosity and spontaneity of feeling, every detail of the Galway/Argerich version falls naturally into place. The RCA recording is most sympathetic.

Overture on Hebrew Themes (for clarinet, piano & string quartet), *Op. 34; Quintet* (for oboe, clarinet, violin, viola & cello), *Op. 39.*

(B) *** HM HMA 1901419. Walter Boeykens Ens. (with KOKAI: *Clarinet Quartettino* ***) – KHACHATURIAN: *Clarinet Trio.* ***

Prokofiev composed his *Overture on Jewish Themes* in 1919 at the request of a Jewish commission from a small ensemble of musical refugees in New York. The *Quintet* was written to accompany a ballet commissioned by a Russian dancer whom the composer had met while working with Diaghilev. It has a wide range of moods it also brings clear rhythmic influences from Stravinsky. Both works are performed here with vigour, affection and wit; indeed they are beautifully played and recorded. The *Quartettino* (for clarinet and string trio) by Rezsö Kókai (1906–62) provided as a bonus is deliciously flimsy in texture (suggesting Françaix with Hungarian inflexions) but with a touching folk-tune-like *Canzonetta* for its slow movement.

Quintet.

*** EMI CDC5 56816-2. Woodhams, Collins, Juillet, Van Keulen, Robinson – BARTOK: *Contrasts;* LISZT: *Concerto pathétique.* ***

A pretty flawless account of a haunting and often poignant work from EMI. Impeccable playing by all concerned and good, well-balanced sound.

String Quartets Nos. 1 in B min., Op. 50; 2 in F, Op. 92.

*** Olympia OCD 340. American Qt.

(i) *String Quartets Nos. 1–2;* (ii) *Cello Sonata.*

(BB) *** Naxos 8.553136. (i) Aurora Qt; (ii) Grebanier, Guggenheim.

String Quartets Nos. 1–2; (i) *Overture on Hebrew Themes.*

(B) **(*) Hyp. Helios CDH 55032. Coull Qt. (i) with Malsbury, Pettit.

The American Quartet play the *First Quartet* far more persuasively than any earlier version. The *Second* incorporates folk ideas from Kabarda in the Caucasus, to highly characteristic ends. Although the performance does not have quite the bite and zest of the Hollywood Quartet, it does not fall far short of it, and the recording is absolutely first class.

The Aurora Quartet give thoroughly straightforward, unaffected accounts of both *Quartets.* They are recorded in a warm, resonant acoustic. The *Cello Sonata* is a thoroughly musical account, not perhaps as strongly characterized as some, but eminently satisfying, and well recorded. This CD is well worth the money.

Good, well-recorded performances on Hyperion whose attractions are enhanced by the competitive price. At the same time, they are not a first recommendation, given the excellence of the competition.

String Quartet No. 2 in F, Op. 92.

⚙ (***) Testament mono SBT 1052. Hollywood Qt — HINDEMITH: *Quartet No. 3*; WALTON: *Quartet in A min.* *** ⚙

The pioneering Hollywood Quartet version of the *Second Quartet* is a stunning performance which has an extraordinary precision and intensity (as well as repose when this is required). The transfer sounds excellent.

Violin Sonata (for solo violin), Op. 115; Sonata for 2 Violins.

*** Chan. 8988. Mordkovitch, Young — SCHNITTKE: *Prelude*; SHOSTAKOVICH: *Violin Sonata.* ***

Violin Sonata (for solo violin) Op. 115; (i) Violin Sonatas Nos. 1 & 2; 5 mélodies, Op. 33b; Cinderella: 5 Dances (arr. Fichtenholz).

(N) (B) *** Virgin 2 x 1 VBD5 61887-2 (2). Sitkovetsky,
  (i) Gililov (with Recital: DVORAK: *Slavonic Dance Op. 72/ 2.* BRAHMS: *Hungarian Dance No. 6.* BARTOK: *Rumanian Folk Dances.* WIENAWSKI: *Polonaise in D.* KREISLER: *Liebesfreud; Liebesleid; Schön Rosmarin.* GRANADOS: *Spanish Dance No. 5.* ALBENIZ: *Malagueña, Op. 71/6.* RAVEL: *Valses nobles et sentimentales Nos. 6–7.* KHACHATURIAN: *Gayaneh: Aisha's Dances; Sabre Dance*).

Sonata for 2 Violins, Op. 56.

*** Hyp. CDA 66473. Osostowicz, Kovacic — MARTINU: *Violin Sonata*; MILHAUD: *Violin Duo* etc. **(*)

The solo *Violin Sonata in D*, Op. 115, is a crisply characteristic piece in three short movements. The *Sonata in C for Two Violins*, written much earlier, is just as effective. The warmth of Lydia Mordkovitch is well matched by her partner, Emma Young.

The *Sonata for Two Violins* gives the impression of being vintage Prokofiev, as performed by Krysia Osostowicz and Ernst Kovacic. The slow movement is played with exceptional imagination and poetry.

The two *Violin Sonatas* with Dmitri Sitkovetsky and Pavel Gililov on Virgin were recorded in 1990 and ranked among the best. With the *5 mélodies* and the *Sonata for Solo Violin* they occupy the first disc – as they did originally. It is a pity that they were not coupled with the award-winning account of the two violin concertos that Sitkovetsky recorded with Sir Colin Davis, which would have greatly enhanced the value of the present set. The other virtuoso pieces and arrangements come from 1988; they are eminently well played but are not in any way more than *bonne bouches*.

Violin Sonatas Nos. 1–2.

(M) *** DG 445 557-2. Mintz, Bronfman — RAVEL: *Violin Sonata in G.* ***

Violin Sonatas Nos. (i) 1 in F min., Op. 80; (ii) 2 in D, Op. 94; (iii) Sonata for 2 Violins, Op. 56.

*** Finlandia 3984 23399-2. Kuusisto, with (i) Paananen;
  (ii) Kerppo; (iii) Kuusisto.

Violin Sonata No. 1 in F min., Op. 80.

*** Orfeo (ADD) C489981B. D. Oistrakh, S. Richter — BRAHMS: *Sonata No. 2.* ***

Shlomo Mintz made a great impression with his coupling of the two *Concertos*, and his recording of the *Sonatas* is hardly less successful. Mintz has a wonderful purity of line and immaculate intonation, and his partner, Yefim Bronfman, is both vital and sensitive. These are commanding performances, imaginative in phrasing and refined in approach. The DG recording is excellent. This is a clear first choice.

Pekka Kuusisto's playing has a youthful ardour and vitality that is refreshing and ranks among the best, with excellent modern recording. No one investing in it is likely to be disappointed.

This Orfeo disc records the Oistrakh–Richter partnership in a live concert at the 1972 Salzburg Festival in the very top of their form. The playing, as one might expect, silences criticism and the recording from ORF (Austrian Radio) is perfectly serviceable.

PIANO MUSIC

Cinderella: 3 Pieces, Op. 95; 3 Pieces, Op. 97; Romeo and Juliet: 10 Pieces, Op. 75; War and Peace: 3 Pieces, Op. 96.

(N) (BB) *** HM HCX 3957150. Chiu.

Prokofiev's transcriptions of the ballet music from *Romeo and Juliet* are better known than *Cinderella* or the three pieces from the opera *War and Peace* (which include the delectable *Grand Waltz*). Frederic Chiu, who has already given us a first class set of the sonatas, plays with vivid colouring, often dazzling with his bravura. He is rather closely balanced, but the bright piano image is real enough, and this can be strongly recommended. Excellent value for money.

10 Pieces from Romeo and Juliet, Op. 75; Toccata in D min., Op. 11.

** Hyp. CDA 67018. Demidenko — MUSSORGSKY: *Pictures.* *

No doubts about Demidenko's virtuosity and keyboard command, particularly in the *Toccata*, or the excellence of the Hyperion sound. His playing in the *Romeo and Juliet* often delights, but there are exasperating mannerisms that attract attention to the pianist rather than Prokofiev.

Piano Sonatas 1–9 (complete); Lieutenant Kijé (suite, transcribed Chiu).

**(*) HM HMU 907086/8 (3). Chiu.

Piano Sonata No. 1 in F min., Op. 1; 4 Pieces, Op. 4; Prelude & Fugue in D min. (Buxtehude, arr. Prokofiev); 2 Sonatinas, Op. 54; Gavotte (Hamlet, Op. 77 bis); 3 Pieces, Op. 96.

*** Chan. 9017. Berman.

Piano Sonata No. 2 in D min., Op. 14; Cinderella: 3 Pieces, Op. 102; Dumka; 3 Pieces, Op. 69; Waltzes (Schubert, arr. Prokofiev).

*** Chan. 9119. Berman.

Piano Sonata No. 3 in A min., Op. 28; Cinderella: 6 Pieces, Op. 95; 10 Pieces, Op. 12; Thoughts, Op. 62.

*** Chan. 9069. Berman.

Piano Sonata No. 4, Op. 29; Music for Children, Op. 65; 6 Pieces, Op. 52.

*** Chan. 8926. Berman.

Piano Sonata No. 5 in C, Op. 38/135; 4 Pieces, Op. 32; The Love for Three Oranges: Scherzo & March. Romeo and Juliet: 10 Pieces, Op. 75.

*** Chan. 8851. Berman.

Piano Sonatas Nos. 5 in C, Op. 38; 6 in A, Op. 82; 10 in E min., Op. 137 (fragment); Gavotte (Classical Symphony, Op. 25); Juvenilia; Toccata, Op. 11.

*** Chan. 9361. Berman.

Piano Sonata No. 7; Sarcasms, Op. 17; Tales of an Old Grandmother, Op. 31; Visions fugitives, Op. 22

*** Chan. 8881. Berman.

Piano Sonata No. 8; Cinderella: 10 Pieces, Op. 97; 4 Pieces, Op. 3

*** Chan. 8976. Berman.

Piano Sonata No. 9; Choses en soi, Op. 45; Divertissement, Op. 43 bis; 4 Etudes, Op. 2.

*** Chan. 9211. Berman.

Boris Berman always plays with tremendous concentration and control. He commands a finely articulated and vital rhythmic sense as well as a wide range of keyboard colour. In the *Second Sonata in D minor* Berman is quite magnificent and full of panache. The *Third* remains one of the most desirable of the set. The *Fourth Sonata*, like its predecessor, takes its inspiration from Prokofiev's earlier notebooks. The Op. 52 *Pieces* are transcriptions of movements from other works. Berman plays them incisively, with marvellous articulation and wit. He plays the post-war revision of the *Fifth Sonata*, and its crisp, brittle inner movement is heard to splendid advantage. The other works are presented with equal perception.

Of course with the *Sixth Sonata* Berman is traversing hotly contested ground. Yet his cooler and more collected reading remains eminently recommendable. He then gives us the original (1923) version of the *Fifth Sonata* (generally to be preferred to the revision) but also the minute or so that survives of a *Tenth Sonata*. Berman is completely inside the astringent idiom and subtle character of the *Seventh Sonata*, and his playing in the *Sarcasms* could scarcely be bettered.

In the expansive *Eighth Sonata*, there is more pianistic refinement in Berman's account than in the Lill reviewed below, though it is in the ten numbers from *Cinderella* and the Op. 3 *Pieces* that Berman's command of atmosphere and character tells most.

Berman plays the *Ninth Sonata* with tremendous concentration and control. The *Choses en soi* ('Things in themselves') come from the period of the *Third Symphony*, though there is a momentary hint of *The Prodigal Son*. The *Divertissement* is a delightful piece in Prokofiev's most acerbic manner which derived from the ballet, *Trapeze*.

Berman couples them with the brilliant Op. 2 *Etudes* of 1909. First class recording throughout.

Exciting playing too from Frederic Chiu. His tempi can be a little extreme, and there are greater extremes of dynamics and colours. The *Seventh* is brilliant and can be ranked along with the best, and the *Sixth*, though not superior to either of the Kissin accounts, is pretty dazzling. Throughout the cycle he impresses with his marvellous fingers, abundant energy and good musical taste. Unfortunately the recording lets him down: the tone is shallow and the balance a bit too close. Otherwise this would have been a strong three-star recommendation.

Piano Sonatas Nos. 2; 7 & 8

*** DG 457 588-2. Pletnev.

Pletnev's 1997 account of the *Seventh Sonata* seems broader and deeper than his earlier version, and it is the mastery of pacing and characterization that gives this impression. The variety of keyboard colour and the control of voicing is stunning both here and in the *Eighth Sonata*. Stunning playing and good recording.

Piano Sonata No. 6 in A, Op. 82.

✿ *** DG 413 363-2. Pogorelich – RAVEL: *Gaspard de la nuit.* ***

Pogorelich's performance of the *Sixth Sonata* is quite simply dazzling; indeed, it is by far the best version of it ever put on record. It remains Pogorelich's most brilliant record so far and can be recommended with the utmost enthusiasm in its CD format.

Piano Sonata No. 7 in B flat, Op. 83.

(M) *** DG (ADD) 447 431-2. Pollini – *Recital.* ***

This is a great performance by Pollini, well in the Horowitz or Richter category. It is part of a generous CD of twentieth-century music.

Piano Sonatas Nos. 7–9.

*** ASV CDDCA 755. Lill.

This disc, coupling the last three *Sonatas*, offers exceptionally good value, and the excellent ASV recording was made in Henry Wood Hall. All three performances are of high quality, and John Lill is never less than a thoughtful and intelligent guide in this repertoire.

VOCAL MUSIC

Alexander Nevsky (cantata), Op. 78 (in English).

(N) ✿ (M) *** RCA (ADD) 09026 63708-2. Elias, Chicago SO & Ch., Reiner – KHACHATURIAN: *Violin Concerto.* ***

Reiner's gripping account of *Alexander Nevsky* offer astonishingly vibrant and atmospheric sound from 1959. Even now these early stereo Chicago recordings can astonish the listener, while Reiner's performance is among the most exciting accounts available, with the music for the Teutonic invaders as sinister as the *Battle on the Ice* is thrilling. No less effective is the scherzando-like middle section of the battle music, which Reiner points in the most sparkling manner. The fervour of the choral singing is matched by the eloquence of Rosalind Elias's *Lament*.

(i) *Alexander Nevsky* (cantata), *Op. 78*; (ii) *Ivan the Terrible, Op. 116* (film music, arr. in oratorio form by Stasevich).

(B) *** EMI double forte (ADD) CZS5 73353-2 (2). (i) Reynolds, LSO & L. Symphony Ch., Previn; (ii) Arkhipova, Mokrenko, Morgunov (narr.), Amb. Ch., Philh. O, Muti – RACHMANINOV: *The Bells*.

(i) *Alexander Nevsky, Op. 78*; (ii) *Lieutenant Kijé, Op. 60*; *Scythian Suite, Op. 20*.

(M) *** DG (ADD) 447 419-2. (i) Obraztsova; L. Symphony Ch., LSO; (ii) Chicago SO; Abbado.

(i) *Alexander Nevsky, Op. 78. Scythian Suite, Op. 20.*

*** Chan. 8584. (i) Finnie, RSNO Ch.; RSNO, Järvi.

Abbado's performance of *Alexander Nevsky* culminates in a deeply moving account of the tragic lament after the battle (here very beautifully sung by Obraztsova), made the more telling when the battle itself is so fine an example of orchestral virtuosity. The chorus is as incisive as the orchestra. The digital remastering of the 1980 recording has been all gain, and the sound is very impressive indeed. A fine account of *Lieutenant Kijé* and what is probably the best version of the *Scythian Suite* to appear in many years make this a very desirable reissue.

The bitter chill of the Russian winter can be felt in the orchestra at the very opening of Järvi's reading and the melancholy of the choral entry has real Slavic feeling. His climactic point is the enormously spectacular *Battle on the ice*, with the recording giving great pungency to the bizarre orchestral effects and the choral shouts riveting in their force and fervour. Linda Finnie sings the final lament eloquently and Järvi's apotheosis is very affecting. As coupling, Järvi also chooses the *Scythian Suite*.

Previn's direct and dynamic manner ensures that the great *Battle on the ice* scene is powerfully effective. Anna Reynolds sings the lovely *Lament for the dead* most affectingly. The sound is sharply defined, with plenty of bite. Like Rostropovich, Muti uses the version of *Ivan the Terrible* with spoken narration (in Russian), and this could well prove irritating on repetition when no texts are provided. Nevertheless, with fine playing and choral singing, there is much here to relish, not least those broad, folk-like melodies. The Kingsway Hall recording is admirably spacious and though the histrionic style of the narrator, Boris Morgunov, is unappealing, the two other soloists are excellent in their limited roles. The remastering has been successful and the effect is often thrillingly vivid, with the chorus especially telling.

Cantata for the 20th Anniversary of the October Revolution, Op. 74.

*** Chan. 9095. Rozhdestvensky (speaker), Philh. Ch. & O, Järvi – *Stone Flower Suite*. ***

Even Prokofiev rarely wrote so wild and totally original a piece as this cantata. The key movement, centrally placed and the longest, uses such exotic percussion as rattles and sirens, with shouting from the chorus, in a graphic description of the revolution in St Petersburg. Järvi, here with his fellow-conductor Gennadi Rozhdestvensky as narrator, has made a first complete recording with the Philharmonia Chorus and Orchestra. As a valuable fill-up comes a suite of excerpts from the folk-tale ballet of 1948, *The Stone Flower*.

Ivan the Terrible (complete film score).

(N) *** Ph. 456 645-2. Sokolova, Putilin, Kirov Op. Chor., Rotterdam PO, Gergiev.

Prokofiev's vividly colourful music for the Eisenstein film of *Ivan the Terrible* has never sounded quite so bitingly dramatic on disc as under Gergiev – as electrifying as any of his opera recordings with the Kirov Company. Here he has the advantage of excellent sound, recorded in the Rotterdam hall, De Doelen, with his 'other' orchestra, thrustful and earthy. Like competing versions, this one is based on Abram Stasevich's editing of the music into an 'oratorio', but without the spoken narration – hardly necessary on disc, when notes and text are provided. The two soloists, Liubov Sokolova and Nikolai Putilin, vibrantly Slavonic, add to the drama, as do the Kirov Chorus.

On Guard for Peace, Op. 124.

*** RCA 09026 68877-2. Rjavkin (nar.), Bulitcheva, Rjavkin, Glinka College Boys' Ch., St Petersburg Ch. & PO, Temirkanov – SHOSTAKOVICH: *Song of the Forests*. ***

Prokofiev was required by the Soviet authorities to write his quota of propaganda pieces. The writing is inventive, even if it lacks distinctive Prokofiev melody, while the use of a reciter (in Russian) is questionably effective. Nonetheless in coupling with the fine Shostakovich work, strongly and persuasively performed and recorded, it is very welcome.

5 Poems of Anna Akhmatova, Op. 27; 2 Poems, Op. 9; 5 Poems of Konstantin Balmont, Op. 36; 3 Romances, Op. 73.

**(*) Chan. 8509. Farley, Aronov.

The Akhmatova settings are quite beautiful. The *Three Romances*, Op. 73, to words of Pushkin, are full of the wry harmonic sleights of hand that are so characteristic of his musical speech. The American soprano, Carole Farley, responds to the different moods and character of the poems and encompasses a rather wide range of colour and tone, although at times her voice is rather edgy and uneven in timbre. The accompaniments of Arkady Aronov are highly sensitive and perceptive. The recording is completely truthful.

OPERA

L'Amour des trois oranges (The Love for Three Oranges): complete. (See also below, The Love for Three Oranges – Russian version.)

**(*) Virgin VCD7 59566-2 (2). Bacquier, Bastin, Dubosc, Gautier, Viala, Lyon Opéra Ch. & O, Nagano.

French inevitably brings a degree of softening in vocal texture, but the brilliant young conductor, Kent Nagano, and his Lyon Opera House team make up for any loss in knife-edged precision of ensemble. Gabriel Bacquier as the King and Jules Bastin as the monstrous Cook, guardian of the three oranges, are well matched by the others, including Jean-Luc Viala as an aptly petulant Prince and Catherine Dubosc as a sweetly girlish Princess Ninette. The recorded sound is not ideally focused so that the commenting chorus – very much a part of the action in *commedia dell'arte* style – is not always clear. Happily, the solo voices are better served. However, it is irritating that there are so few cueing points on the CDs (just one for each scene).

Betrothal in a Monastery.

*** Ph. 462 107-2 (3). Gassie, Netrebko, Gergalov, Diadkova, Akimov, Tarassova, Alexashkin, Kirov Opera Ch. & O, Gergiev

(M) **(*) Melodiya 74321 60318-2 (2). Maslennikov, Sergienko, Redkin, Borisova, Mishenkin, Shutova, Krutikov, Verestnikov, Bolshoi Theatre, Moscow, Ch. & O, Lazarev.

Betrothal in a Monastery is based on Sheridan's play, *The Duenna*, using all the conventional trappings of *opera buffa* – secret lovers, comic old father pressuring the heroine, rich suitor thwarted and so on. This is wittily pointed in its comic writing, but regularly giving foretastes of the ripe lyricism that was to blossom in his last, most masterly opera, *War and Peace*. The Philips set from the Kirov, St Petersburg, follows up the success of Gergiev's earlier opera sets, with stage performances recorded live and edited together. Stage noises and odd balances are only occasionally distracting, and the dry, intimate acoustic suits the scale of the comedy, even if voices are not helped, with the orchestra a little cloudy. Outstanding in the cast – outshining her fruity opposite number in the rival Bolshoi set – is the sweet and youthful-sounding Anna Netrebko as the heroine, Louisa. The male soloists are relatively light-toned, with a sharp contrast between the two principal tenors, the buffo Don Jerome and the lightweight Don Antonio. The big advantage is that Philips's three-disc set offers a full libretto, translation and excellent background notes.

The Bolshoi version, recorded for Melodiya in 1990, presented on two mid-priced discs has the merit of a strong cast headed by the characterful Maslennikov, with a first-rate Duenna and a powerful team of male soloists. With a reverberant studio recording, there is plenty of bloom on the voices, with the beauty of the orchestral writing evocatively brought out. Lazarev's well-chosen speeds, generally a little broader than those of Gergiev on the Kirov set, allow an extra infectious spring to Prokofiev's repetitive rhythms. The snag is that at mid-price no libretto is offered, only a detailed synopsis.

The Fiery Angel (complete).

⊕ *** Ph. 446 078-2 (2) (Video 070 198-3; LD 070 198-1). Gorchakova, Leiferkus, Pluzhnikov, Ognovanko, soloists; Kirov Op. Ch. & O, Gergiev.

*** DG 431 669-2 (2). Secunde, Lorenz, Zednik, Moll, Gothenburg SO, Järvi.

Impressive as Neeme Järvi's 1990 recording for DG of this elusive but powerful opera is, Gergiev's with Kirov forces is even finer. From the very outset the style is declamatory in a way that recalls Mussorgsky. The vocal line is largely heightened speech, but Prokofiev does provide a series of leitmotivs which are identified with characters or situations in the opera. Indeed, in terms of fantasy and sheer imaginative vision, *The Fiery Angel* reaches heights which Prokofiev never surpassed, and its atmosphere resonates for a long time. This Philips live recording, with full, forward sound, avoids most of the snags of a recorded stage-performance. Above all, it offers in the singing and acting of Elena Gorchakova in the central role of Renata, the hysterical woman obsessed by demons, one of the most compelling operatic performances in years, with the timbre of the voice often sensuously beautiful, even when stretched to the limit. Sergei Leiferkus as Ruprecht with his clear, firm baritone is also ideally cast; the remainder of the cast, from the Landlady of Evgenia Perlasova to the resonant Inquisitor of Vladimir Ognovanko, are absolutely first class, while the Kirov team provides outstanding, always idiomatic and individual performances in smaller roles. Gergiev proves an inspired conductor who secures orchestral playing of great dramatic eloquence. There are the inevitable stage noises, but any snag is quickly forgotten.

The presence of vision in the finely directed video tape and laser disc serves to underline an implicit ambiguity in the opera – whether Madiel and the spirits conjured up in Act II are real or are just Renata's paranoid delusions. Here the use of mimed figures, unseen by the protagonists but perceived by the audience, was a brilliant solution. The frenetic, highly charged atmosphere of the final Convent scene benefits by vision particularly in this splendid production. The sound in the laser disc version has marvellous presence and detail.

The Love for Three Oranges (complete in Russian).

(N) *** Ph. 462 913-2 (2). Akimov, Kit, Diadkova, Morozov, Pluzhnikov, Gerello, Shevchenko, & Soloists, Kirov Op. Ch. & O, Gergiev.

Gergiev adds to his formidable Kirov series of Russian opera recordings with a brilliant reading of this fantasy fairy-tale. It was recorded not in St Petersburg but live in concert performances at the Concertgebouw in Amsterdam, with warmer, more consistent sound. Using the Russian text this is earthier, tougher and more biting than the smoother French version offered on Virgin by Kent Nagano and his Lyon Opera team. The satirical element of the piece with its wry humour comes over the more sharply, with more sparkle, and though not all the Kirov cast can quite match their Lyon counterparts in vocal beauty, they are on balance more characterful, notably the formidable mezzo, Larissa Diadkova, as Princess Clarissa. In practical layout too the Philips set is preferable, with many more tracks for different sections.

Semyon Kotko (complete).

(N) *** Ph. 464 605-2 (2). Lutsiuk, Pavlovskaya, Savoya, Bezzubenkov, Nikitin, Chernomortsev, Solovieva, Markova-Mikhailenko, Karasev, Akimov, Kirov Ch. & O, Gergiev.

Those who saw the production of *Semyon Kotko* by Valery

Gergiev and the Kirov at Covent Garden in 2000 will know what a strong work it is. Well paced, inventive and full of imaginative touches, it grips the listener from start to finish. It was composed in the immediate wake of his score for Eisenstein's *Alexander Nevsky* and features numerous Soviet propaganda stereotypes: the loyal hero returning to his village at the end of the First World War; invading Germans who burn the village and break up the hero's wedding preparations; the collaborating father-in-law (very well played by Gennady Bezzubenkov) and so on. The characters are one-dimensional as one would expect from this period, and the anti-German tenor of the work was suddenly an embarrassment when the Nazi–Soviet pact was signed in 1939. All the same there is a lot of good music, not counting the orchestral excerpts already in the catalogue, and although there are no big numbers, there is some consistently inventive writing. Viktor Lutsiuk as Semyon and Tatiana Pavlovskaya as his fiancée Sofya are both first class; however, the real hero is Gergiev who phrases sensitively and paces the music with all his dramatic expertise and gets an enthusiastic response from his Kirov forces. The recording is excellent.

War and Peace (complete).

*** Chan. 9855 (4). Morozova, Roderick Williams, Justin Lavender, Balashov, Dupont, Stephen, Ionova, Ewing, Opie, Russian State Symph. Cap., Spoleto Fest.O, Hickox.

⚫ (M) *** Erato (ADD) 2292 45331-2 (4). Vishnevskaya, Miller, Ciesinski, Tumagian, Ochman, Ghiuselev, Smith, Paunova, Petkov, Toczyska, Zakai, Gedda, Fr. R. Ch. & Nat. O, Rostropovich.

*** Ph. 434 097-2 (3). Gergalov, Prokina, Gregoriam, Borodina, Gerelo, Bogachova, Okhotnikov, Morozov, Kirov Theatre Ch. & O, Gergiev.

War and Peace is not just epic in scale but warmly approachable, with a fund of melody rarely matched this century. In Rostropovich's powerful reading one revels – thanks also to the lively Erato recording – in the vividness of the atmosphere, both in the evocative love scenes and ball scenes of the first half (Peace) and in the high tensions of the battle scenes in the second (War). The opera culminates in a great patriotic chorus, using the most haunting tune of all, earlier sung by General Kutuzov after the Council of Fili, and the emotional thrust is overwhelming. The French Radio Choir sings that chorus with real Russian fervour. It was natural that Rostropovich's wife, Galina Vishnevskaya, should sing the central role of Natasha, as she did in the earlier, much-cut, Bolshoi recording. It is extraordinary how convincingly this mature soprano in her early sixties characterizes a young girl; there may be raw moments, but she is completely inside the role. The Hungarian baritone, Lajos Miller, not flawless either, is a clear-voiced Andrei, and Wieslaw Ochman is a first-rate Pierre, with the veteran, Nicolai Gedda, brought in as Kuragin. Katherine Ciesinski is a warm-toned Sonya, but Dimiter Petkov is disappointingly unsteady as Natasha's father, Count Rostov. The small role of Napoleon is strongly taken by Eduard Tumagian, while Nicola Ghiuselev is a noble Kutuzov, in some ways the most impressive of all. The libretto contains French and English

translations, but no Russian transliteration, only the Cyrillic text in a separate section.

Recorded live at the 1999 Spoleto Festival in full and open Chandos sound, Richard Hickox's formidable version of Prokofiev's epic opera offers a strong, thrustful alternative performance with a cast more consistent than those on rival sets. With a warm understanding of the idiom, helped by a substantial Russian element among the singers, not least the chorus, Hickox keeps the thirteen scenes moving well at speeds often on the fast side. Pointing the dramatic contrast between personal tragedy and great public events, the surging lyricism of Prokofiev's inspiration is sharply set against bitingly rhythmic writing, whether in the party scenes of the first part or the wartime scenes of the second half. The glorious tunefulness of the patriotic numbers has just the gulp-in-throat quality needed, whether General Kutuzov's big aria, nobly sung by Alan Ewing, or the big choruses fervently sung by the Russian choir.

Ekaterina Morozova is a moving Natasha, Slavonic in timbre, weighty but still girlish enough, with an edge to the voice that rarely turns squally. She is well matched in the beautiful opening scene by Pamela Helen Stephen as her cousin, Sonya, while Roderick Williams is a fresh, virile Andrei, and Justin Lavender a vulnerable-sounding Pierre, who convincingly erupts in anger

Alan Opie is a characterful Napoleon, with the battle scene of Borodino thrillingly vivid, not least in shattering cannon shots. Other versions may have starrier individual contributions, but this one has no weak link, and the recording is not just full and brilliant, but, beautifully balanced, captures the sweetness of the Spoleto strings very persuasively. The four-disc layout (for the price of three) means breaks come at the ends of scenes.

The Kirov performance under Valery Gergiev, at rather more urgent speeds than Rostropovich's, may be less warmly expressive and atmospheric, but it brings the advantage of having in the principal roles younger voices. Many will prefer the Kirov Natasha, Yelena Prokina, to the controversially cast Vishnevskaya on the Rostropovich set. The voice is fresher as well as younger-sounding, though the tone becomes hard under pressure, losing any sweetness. Alexander Gergalov, Prince Andrei in the Kirov performance, is attractively young-sounding too, lighter and more lyrical than Rostropovich's principal, also good, the Hungarian baritone, Lajos Miller. Otherwise the Kirov principals, including Nikolai Okhotnikov as Kutuzov, are almost all as characterful and assured as their generally starrier rivals on Erato, and the sense of purpose from a very large company, well drilled in the music, counterbalances in part, though not entirely, the unhelpful dryness of the sound. The economical layout on three CDs may seem to favour Philips, but there is no price-advantage, when Rostropovich's Erato comes at mid-price in the Libretto series.

PUCCINI, Giacomo (1858–1924)

Capriccio sinfonico; Crisantemi; Minuets Nos. 1–3; Preludio sinfonico; Edgar: Preludes, Acts I & III. Manon

Lescaut: Intermezzo, Act III. Le Villi: Prelude; La Tregenda (Act II).

(M) *** Decca 444 154-2. Berlin RSO, Chailly.

In a highly attractive collection of Puccinian juvenilia and rarities, Chailly draws opulent and atmospheric playing from the Berlin Radio Symphony Orchestra, helped by outstandingly rich and full recording. The CD is of demonstration quality. The *Capriccio sinfonico* of 1876 brings the first characteristically Puccinian idea in what later became the opening Bohemian motif of *La Bohème*. There are other identifiable fingerprints here, even if the big melodies suggest Mascagni rather than full-blown Puccini. *Crisantemi* (with the original string quartet scoring expanded for full string orchestra) provided material for *Manon Lescaut*, as did the three little *Minuets*, pastiche eighteenth-century music.

Crisantemi for String Quartet.

(M) *** CRD (ADD) 3366. Alberni Qt – DONIZETTI: *Quartet No. 13;* VERDI: *Quartet.* ***

Puccini's brief essay in writing for string quartet dates from the late 1880s; three years later he used the main themes in his first fully successful opera, *Manon Lescaut*. The piece is given a warm, finely controlled performance by the Alberni Quartet and makes a valuable makeweight for the two full-scale quartets by fellow opera-composers. The sound is excellent.

Crisantemi; Fugues 1–3; Minuets 1–3; Scherzo in A min.; String Quartet in D.

*** ASV CDDCA 909. Puccini Qt. – CATALANI: *String Quartet in A etc.* ***

Puccini's three *Fugues* and the *Quartet Movement in D* (with the jolliest, most trivial of main themes) are mere student exercises, technically adept and charming but with no stylistic personality. The *Minuets*, more developed, are hardly identifiable as by Puccini. Then suddenly the full Puccini emerges in the beautiful *Crisantemi* of 1890, which provided key material for the final death scene in *Manon Lescaut*. It is strange that though Puccini's musical personality began to emerge early in his choral and orchestral works, this sparer genre found him more anonymous, even in his melodies. Nonetheless, a delightful disc, warmly played and atmospherically recorded, with Catalani's quartet music providing an ideal coupling.

Messa di gloria.

(M) *** Erato 4509 96367-2. Carreras, Prey, Amb. S., Philh. O, Scimone.

(M) *** Ph. (ADD) 434 170-2. Lövaas, Hollweg, McDaniel, West German R. Ch., Frankfurt RSO, Inbal (with MOZART: *Vesperae solennes, K.339: Laudate Dominum:* Te Kanawa, LSO, C. Davis ***).

Messa di Gloria; Preludio sinfonico; Crisantemi.

(N) *** EMI CDC5 57159-2. (i) Alagna, Hampson, LSO Ch., LSO, Pappano.

Puccini's *Messa di gloria*, by far the most ambitious of his early works, is much more than a student exercise, full of anticipations of the mature opera-composer. He even uses material from the *Agnus Dei* in *Manon Lescaut*, yet the piece has been unfairly neglected on disc, when particularly the extended setting of the *Gloria* is so memorable, starting with a swaggering march such as Rossini might have put into a religious work.

Antonio Pappano easily outshines his two rivals on disc, enhancing the operatic element, including obvious echoes not just of the Verdi *Requiem*, but of *Otello*. Ideal soloists in Alagna and Hampson, with the London Symphony Chorus and LSO in incandescent form. The two bonuses are welcome, aptly chosen and very well played.

The return of Scimone's second (1983) digital recording at mid-price makes this version much more competitive, even though it has no fill-up. He and a fine team are brisker and lighter than their predecessors on record, yet effectively bring out the red-bloodedness of the writing. José Carreras turns the big solo in the *Gratias* into the first genuine Puccini aria. His sweetness and imagination are not quite matched by the baritone, Hermann Prey, who is given less to do than usual, when the choral baritones take on the yearning melody of *Crucifixus*. Excellent, atmospheric sound.

The 1975 Philips version has stylish soloists, a fine choral contribution and clean, well-balanced recording. Kiri Te Kanawa's ravishing account of the *Laudate Dominum* from Mozart's *Solemn Vespers* is thrown in as an enticing encore.

OPERA

La Bohème (complete).

🌑 *** EMI CDS5 56120-2. Vaduva, Alagna, Swenson, Hampson, Keenlyside, Ramey, L. Voices, boys from L. Oratory School, Philh. O, Pappano.

(***) EMI mono CDS7 47235-8 (2). De los Angeles, Björling, Merrill, Reardon, Tozzi, Amara, RCA Victor Ch. & O, Beecham.

*** Decca (ADD) 421 049-2 (2). Freni, Pavarotti, Harwood, Panerai, Ghiaurov, German Op. Ch., Berlin, BPO, Karajan.

*** Decca 466 070-2 (2). Gheorghiu, Alagna, Scano, Keenlyside, D'Arcangelo, La Scala, Milan, Verdi Ch. & O, Chailly.

(B) *** Double Decca (ADD) 448 725-2 (2). Tebaldi, Bergonzi, Bastianini, Siepi, Corena, D'Angelo, St Cecilia Ac. Ch. & O, Serafin.

(B) (***) Double Decca mono 440 233-2 (2). Tebaldi, Prandelli, Gueden, Inghilleri, Corena, Arié, Luise, Santa Cecilia Ac., Rome, Ch. & O, Erede.

(***) EMI mono CDS5 56295-2 (2). Callas, Di Stefano, Moffo, Panerai, La Scala, Milan, Ch. & O, Votto.

(M) **(*) EMI (ADD) CMS7 69657-2 (2). Freni, Gedda, Adani, Sereni, Mazzoli, La Scala, Milan, Ch. & O, Schippers.

(M) **(*) RCA (ADD) 74321 39496-2 (2) [09026 61725-2]. Caballé, Domingo, Milnes, Raimondi, Alldis Ch., Wandsworth School Boys' Ch., LPO, Solti.

(M) ** RCA (ADD) 09026 63179-2 (2). Moffo, Tucker, Costa, Merrill, Tozzi, Rome Opera Ch. & O, Leinsdorf.

(B) ** Naxos 8.660003/4. Orgonasova, Welch, Gonzales, Previati, Senator, Slovak Philharmonic Ch., Slovak RSO (Bratislava), Humburg.

(M) ** Nim. mono NI 7862/3. Albanese, Gigli, Oili, Menotti, Baracchi, Baronti, La Scala, Milan, Ch. & O, Berrettoni.

Pappano's recording of *Bohème* is the finest in over 20 years or even longer – sumptuously played and recorded, and characterfully sung by a starry cast. Above all, it is conducted with ever-fresh imagination by Antonio Pappano, who brings out not just subtle emotions alongside high passion, but also the fun of the piece in lightly sprung rhythms. Yet the exchanges when Mimì arrives have the most moving intimacy at the gentlest pianissimo, with the singers given full expressive freedom within a purposeful frame. The great set-piece numbers at the end of Act I, *Che gelida manina*, *Mi chiamano Mimì* and *O soave fanciulla*, then have the freshness of genuine emotion swelling in a radiant, towering crescendo. Alagna's tenor may not be velvety, but it has a fine tonal range with a heroic ring and Adriva is similarly characterful rather than just sweet. The others make a superb team, virtually incomparable today – Ruth Swenson using her dramatic timbres most delicately even in the outburst of the waltz song, Thomas Hampson a swaggering Marcello, with Samuel Ramey and Simon Keenlyside characterfully contrasted as the other two Bohemians, all relishing the fun. With the Philharmonia inspired to playing of consistent flair, notably the woodwind soloists, this is a version to stand alongside the classics of the past.

Beecham's is a uniquely magical performance with two favourite singers, Victoria de los Angeles and Jussi Björling, challenged to their utmost in loving, expansive singing. The voices are treated far better by the CD remastering than the orchestra, though as ever the benefits of silent background are very welcome in so warmly atmospheric a reading. With such a performance one hardly notices the recording, but those who want fine modern stereo can turn readily to Pappano. No doubt this will shortly be reissued at mid-price as one of EMI's 'Great Recordings of the Century'.

Karajan takes a characteristically spacious view of *La Bohème*, but there is an electric intensity which holds the whole score together as in a live performance. Pavarotti is an inspired Rodolfo, with comic flair and expressive passion, while Freni is just as seductive as Mimì. Elizabeth Harwood is a charming Musetta. Fine singing throughout the set. The reverberant Berlin acoustic is glowing and brilliant in superb Decca recording, with the clean placing of voices enhancing the performance's dramatic warmth.

The husband-and-wife partnership of Gheorghiu and Alagna is formidably demonstrated in Decca's most recent recording, though with Chailly in taut control and speeds consistently on the fast side, this is a performance that misses some of the tenderness in the score, as well as some of the fun. Gheorghiu's glorious singing is powerfully matched by the heroic tones of Alagna, culminating in a deeply moving death scene. Angela Gheorghiu stands out, with the creamy sound of her soprano never more sensuously caught on disc, so that she dominates the performance whenever she appears. With voices well forward and with words exceptionally clear, in an acoustic more open than in most Milan recordings, the brilliance of Chailly's reading is enhanced. Roberto Alagna as Rodolfo is more impulsive here than in EMI's Pappano recording, made four years earlier, re-

sponding no doubt to Chailly's fast speeds, but the manner is less affectionate. His is a heroic reading rather than a tender one, just as Gheorghiu's Mimì is a fully tragic heroine, not just a Puccinian 'little woman'. These are performances for a big opera-house, with shading less subtle than with Pappano. The notable casting among the rest is that of Simon Keenlyside, promoted to Marcello this time from Schaunard in the EMI set, again consistently responsive and alert. Elisabetta Scano is a light, bright Musetta, strongly contrasted with Gheorghiu, if a little shrill on top. Roberto di Candia makes a positive Schaunard, but Ildebrando d'Arcangelo as Colline is not helped by the close vocal balance, with a flutter emerging in the Act IV Coat Song.

Tebaldi's Decca set with Bergonzi dominated the catalogue in the early days of stereo, and it still sounds astonishingly vivid, with a very convincing theatrical atmosphere. At Double Decca price, it is one of the great operatic bargains in the current catalogue. Vocally the performance achieves a consistently high standard, with Tebaldi as Mimì the most affecting. Carlo Bergonzi is a fine Rodolfo; Bastianini and Siepi are both superb as Marcello and Colline, and even the small parts of Benoit and Alcindoro (as usual taken by a single artist) have the benefit of Corena's magnificent voice. The veteran Serafin was more vital here than on some of his records. The set comes with a perfectly adequate cued synopsis, for *La Bohème* is an exceptionally easy opera to follow.

The 1951 Decca set immediately won glowing praise, above all for Tebaldi's radiant and rich-voiced portrayal of Mimì. The effect is still extraordinarily atmospheric in its sense of stage perspective. The one drawback was the whistly sound of the violins. The CD transfer has improved the violin focus, but the effect is still emaciated above the stave. Yet one soon adjusts to this, for the acoustic is basically warm and evocative. It is still a lovely performance, and there are no appreciable weaknesses in the cast: Gueden an exceptionally characterful Musetta (a part that fitted her like a glove), Prandelli a most likeable Rodolfo, engagingly light-voiced yet stirring at climaxes. Erede keeps the music flowing; he controls the great love duet of Act I spaciously. The atmospheric opening of Act III at the Paris toll-gate is remarkably evocative. Indeed, at times here one could almost think stereo had already arrived.

Callas, flashing-eyed and formidable, may seem even less suited to the role of Mimì than to that of Butterfly, but characteristically her insights make for a vibrantly involving performance. Though Giuseppe di Stefano is not the subtlest of Rodolfos, he is in excellent voice here, and Moffo and Panerai make a strong partnership as the second pair of lovers. Votto occasionally coarsens Puccini's score but he directs with energy. The comparatively restricted dynamic range means that the singers appear to be 'front stage', but there is no lack of light and shade in Act II, and the sound of the new transfer is greatly improved.

In the Schippers version, the beauty of Freni's voice is what one remembers, with a supremely moving account of the Death scene. Nicolai Gedda's Rodolfo is not rounded in the traditional Italian way, but there is never any doubt about his ability to project a really grand manner of his own. Schippers quickly shows his genuinely Italianate sense of pause, giving the singers plenty of time to breathe and allowing the music to expand. The resonant, 1964 recording has transferred vividly to CD and the set has been attractively re-packaged with an excellently printed libretto.

The glory of Solti's set of *La Bohème* is the singing of Montserrat Caballé as Mimì, an intensely characterful and imaginative reading, the voice at its most radiant. Domingo is unfortunately not at his most inspired. *Che gelida manina* is relatively coarse, though here as elsewhere he produces glorious heroic tone, and he never falls into vulgarity. The rest of the team is strong, but Solti's tense interpretation of a work he had never conducted in the opera house does not quite let either the full flexibility of the music or the full warmth of romanticism have their place. The recording, however, is both vivid and atmospheric.

On the Leinsdorf set Anna Moffo is an affecting Mimì, Mary Costa a characterful Musetta, while Merrill and Tozzi provide strong support. Tucker gives a positive characterization as Rodolfo, though he has lachrymose moments. Sadly, Leinsdorf's rigid direction, with speed fluctuations observed by instruction and never with natural expression, sets the singers against a deadpan, unsparkling accompaniment. Dated recording, impressively remastered.

Well played and atmospherically recorded, the Naxos version of *La Bohème* offers an outstanding performance by Luba Orgonosova as Mimì. The creamy quality of the voice, coupled with her warm expressiveness and her vocal poise, brings out the tenderness of the character to the full; and it is a pity that none of the others matches her. Jonathan Welch as Rodolfo and Fabio Previati as Marcello are both strained and unsteady at times, while Carmen Gonzales tries too hard as Musetta.

It is good to have the classic recording with Gigli restored to the catalogue in Nimbus's Prima Voce series. The Nimbus transfer process works well here, with plenty of body in the sound, without too much masking of reverberation, and with a bloom on the voices. The glory of the set is Gigli's Rodolfo, with a chuckle in the voice bringing out the fun, while Gigli uses his pouting manner charmingly, with the occasional sob adding to the charm. He adds little touches, as when he murmurs '*Prego*' when ushering Mimì out, before she discovers she has lost her key. He dwarfs the others, with even Albanese a little shrill as Mimì.

La Bohème: highlights.

(B) ** Penguin Decca 460 617-2 (from above complete recording with Tebaldi, Bergonzi; cond. Serafin).

(M) (**) EMI mono CDM5 66670-2 (from above complete recording with Callas, di Stefano; cond. Votto).

The sets of excerpts from the Tebaldi and Callas recordings are little more than samplers. Although both include the Love duet from Act I, and the closing scene, the overall playing time is only 54 minutes for the EMI disc, and a minute or so more for the Decca. There is a cued synopsis for Callas, but the Decca selection offers merely a very brief cued narrative summary. However, the one compensation here is the usual Penguin Classics author's note and it is written most engagingly by Rabbi Lionel Blue.

La Bohème: (highlights). Arias from: *Gianni Schicchi; Manon Lescaut; Turandot; Suor Angelica.*

(N) (M) *** Decca (ADD) 458 248-2. Tebaldi, Bergonzi, d'Angelo, Bastianini, St Cecilia Ac. Ch. & O, Serafin.

This is a well-chosen if not particularly generous selection of Serafin highly involving 1959 *Bohème*, retaining all the fine qualities for which that set is famous. The handsomely packaged Opera Gala CD (texts and translations included) contains five primarily solo tracks of famous Puccini arias featuring Tebaldi, taken from Decca's complete opera recordings (from 1955 to 1962) and make an enjoyable bonus. The sound generally is astonishingly warm and vivid. The overall playing time is nearly 70 minutes.

La Bohème (complete; sung in English).

*** Chan. 3008 (2). Haymon, O'Neill, McLaughlin, Miles, Dazeley, Geoffrey Mitchell Ch., Peter Kay Children's Ch., Philh. O, Parry.

The magic mixture of humour and pathos in this unsinkable masterpiece is brought all the closer for having it in translation, even if the occasional line may ring false. Dennis O'Neill reinforces his high reputation as the regular tenor in the series, despite some intrusive vibrato under pressure, and Cynthia Haymon as a touching Mimi has never sounded more beautiful on disc, with the widest range of expression and tone. Marie McLaughlin is a warm-toned Musetta, temperamental rather than just flighty, and the other three Bohemians are ideally cast. Voices are vividly caught in the atmospheric recording, with the crowd scenes of Act II beautifully clarified. Highest praise too for David Parry who knows how to relax in tenderness, as well as when to press home hard. Warm, refined playing from the Philharmonia. Highly recommended to all who enjoy opera in English.

Edgar (complete).

(M) ** Sony (ADD) M2K 79213 (2). Scotto, Bergonzi, Sardinero, Killibrew, NY Schola Cantorum and Op. O, Queler.

Edgar, Puccini's second opera, is a work which took him in the wrong direction, away from realism towards medieval fantasy in which the knightly hero has to choose between the loves of the symbolically named Fidelia and Tigrana (a Carmen figure without the sparkle). However, as this recording makes plain, there is much to enjoy. The melodies are not quite vintage Puccini, but Scotto as Fidelia, Killibrew as Tigrana, and Bergonzi as Edgar give them compelling warmth. Eve Queler proves a variably convincing conductor, with Act III in need of more rehearsal. But this set, edited from live performances at Carnegie Hall, and commendably well recorded, makes a welcome stop-gap.

La Fanciulla del West (The Girl of the Golden West: complete.

(M) *** Decca (IMS) (ADD) 421 595-2 (2). Tebaldi, Del Monaco, MacNeil, Tozzi, St Cecilia Ac., Rome, Ch. & O, Capuana.

**(*) DG (ADD) 419 640-2 (2). Neblett, Domingo, Milnes, Howell, ROHCG Ch. and O, Mehta.

Tebaldi here gives one of her most warm-hearted and understanding performances on record, and Mario del Monaco displays the wonderfully heroic quality of his voice to great – if sometimes tiring – effect. Cornell MacNeil as the villain, Sheriff Rance, sings with great precision and attack, but unfortunately has not a villainous-sounding voice to convey the character fully. Jake Wallace's entry and the song *Che faranno i viecchi miei* is one of the high spots of the recording, with Tozzi singing beautifully. Capuana's expansive reading is matched by the imagination of the production, with the closing scene wonderfully effective in spectacular sound.

On DG, Mehta's manner – as he makes clear at the very start – is on the brisk side, even refusing to let the first great melody, the nostalgic *Che faranno i viecchi miei*, linger into sentimentality. Sherrill Milnes as Jack Rance makes that villain into far more than a small-town Scarpia, giving nobility and understanding to the first-Act arioso. Domingo, as in the theatre, sings heroically, disappointing only in his reluctance to produce soft tone in the great aria *Ch'ella mi creda*. The rest of the team is excellent, not least Gwynne Howell as the minstrel who sings *Che faranno i viecchi miei*; but the crowning glory of a masterly set is the singing of Carol Neblett as the Girl of the Golden West herself, gloriously rich and true and with formidable attack on the exposed high notes. Full, atmospheric recording to match, essential in an opera full of evocative offstage effects, but the slight drying-out process of the digital sound adds some stridency in tuttis, readily acceptable with so strong a performance.

Gianni Schicchi (complete).

(M) *** RCA 74321 25285-2. Panerai, Donath, Seiffert, Bav. R. Ch., Munich R. O., Patanè.

(N) (M) ** Orfeo (ADD) C546 001B. Fischer-Dieskau, Schary, Mödl, Ahnsjö, Thaw, Fahberg, Auer, Engen, Grumbach, Wewezow, Bav. State Ch. & O., Sawallisch.

The RCA (formerly Eurodisc) recording of *Gianni Schicchi* brings a co-production with Bavarian Radio, and the recording is vivid and well balanced. Central to the performance's success is the vintage Schicchi of Rolando Panerai, still rich and firm. He confidently characterizes the Florentine trickster in every phrase, building a superb portrait, finely timed. Peter Seiffert as Rinuccio gives a dashing performance, consistently clean and firm of tone, making light of the high tessitura and rising splendidly to the challenge of the big central aria. Helen Donath would have sounded even sweeter a few years earlier, but she gives a tender, appealing portrait of Lauretta, pretty and demure in *O mio babbino caro*. Though Italian voices are in the minority, it is a confident team.

Gianni Schicchi recorded live in German makes little sense outside Germany, but this is well worth hearing for the powerful contribution of Dietrich Fischer-Dieskau in the title-role. He takes a freer view than you would expect of so meticulous a musician, resorting to parlando at times, but in that he is responding to the joy of the piece as a member of a strong team. The trouble is that Gunther Rennert's lively production involves stage noises – often sounding louder than the music. The balance of voices is very variable,

too, with the orchestra set behind. One result of the dryness and Sawallisch's incisive conducting is that the dissonant modernity of Puccini's writing in places is brought out the more.

Fischer-Dieskau is well supported by a delightful pair of young lovers. As Lauretta, Elke Schary is fresh and girlish, ending her celebrated aria (in German *O du, mein lieber Vater*) with a tender diminuendo. As Rinuccio, the Swedish tenor Claes-Haakan Ahnsjö sings with a bright, clear tone. Among the others one cherishes most of all the characterful contribution of Martha Mödl, then over sixty, as a formidable Zita.

Madama Butterfly (complete).

*** Decca (ADD) 417 577-2 (3). Freni, Ludwig, Pavarotti, Kerns, V. State Op. Ch., VPO, Karajan.

*** DG 423 567-2 (3). Freni, Carreras, Berganza, Pons, Amb. Op. Ch., Philh. O, Sinopoli.

(B) *** Double Decca (ADD) 452 594-2 (2). Tebaldi, Bergonzi, Cossotto, Sordello, St Cecilia, Rome, Ac. Ch. & O., Serafin.

(M) *** EMI (ADD) CMS7 69654-2 (2). Scotto, Bergonzi, Di Stasio, Panerai, De Palma, Rome Op. Ch. & O., Barbirolli.

(***) Testament mono SBT 2168 (2). De los Angeles, Di Stefano, Gobbi, Rome Opera Ch. & O., Gavazzeni.

(M) **(*) EMI (ADD) CMS7 63634-2 (2). De los Angeles, Björling, Pirazzini, Sereni, Rome Op. Ch. & O., Santini.

(***) EMI mono CDS5 56298-2 (2). Callas, Gedda, Borriello, Danieli, La Scala, Milan, Ch. & O., Karajan.

(B) (**(*)) Double Decca mono 440 230-2 (2). Tebaldi, Campora, Inghilleri, Rankin, St. Cecilia Ac., Rome, Ch. & O., Erede.

Karajan's set is extravagantly laid out on three discs instead of two as for most of the rival sets – slow speeds partly responsible. However, he inspires singers and orchestra to a radiant performance which brings out all the beauty and intensity of Puccini's score, sweet but not sentimental, powerfully dramatic but not vulgar. Freni is an enchanting Butterfly, consistently growing in stature from the young girl to the victim of tragedy, sweeter of voice than any rival on record. Pavarotti is an intensely imaginative Pinkerton, actually inspiring understanding for this thoughtless character, while Christa Ludwig is a splendid Suzuki. The recording is one of Decca's most resplendent, with the Vienna strings producing glowing tone.

However expansive his speeds, Sinopoli is never sentimental or self-indulgent. Puccini's honeyed moments are given, not sloppily, but with rapt intensity, through to the final aria, tough and intense. As she was for Karajan in his classic Decca set, Freni is a model Butterfly; though the voice is no longer so girlish, she projects the tragedy even more weightily than before. José Carreras is similarly presented as a large-scale Pinkerton. Juan Pons is a virile Sharpless and Teresa Berganza an equally positive, unfruity Suzuki.

Serafin's sensitive and beautifully paced reading finds Tebaldi at her most radiant. Though she was never the most deft of Butterflies dramatically, her singing is consistently rich and beautiful. The excellence of the Decca engineering in 1958 is amply proved in the CD transfer, the current remastering now providing full, atmospheric sound from the very beginning, opening out further as the orchestration grows fuller, with voices very precisely and realistically placed. At Double Decca price this is a pretty formidable bargain.

Under Sir John Barbirolli, players and singers perform consistently with a dedication and intensity rare in opera recordings made in Italy, and the whole score glows more freshly than ever. There is hardly a weak link in the cast. Bergonzi's Pinkerton and Panerai's Sharpless are both sensitively and beautifully sung; Anna di Stasio's Suzuki is more than adequate, and Renata Scotto's Butterfly has a subtlety and perceptiveness in its characterization that more than make up for any shortcoming in the basic beauty of tone-colour.

The *Butterfly* set with Victoria de los Angeles on Testament is her mono recording, made in 1954, when the voice was at its fullest and most golden, meltingly beautiful, bringing out the tender vulnerability of Puccini's heroine. Giuseppe di Stefano is also at his very finest as Pinkerton, with Tito Gobbi giving unexpected depth to the role of Sharpless, and Gavazzeni's timing heightening the pathos. The superb transfer is clearer and more forward than EMI's earlier CD version.

Victoria de los Angeles' 1960 recording also displays her art at its most endearing, her range of golden tone-colour lovingly exploited. Opposite her, Jussi Björling produces a flow of rich tone to compare with that of the heroine. Mario Sereni is a full-voiced Sharpless, but Miriam Pirazzini is a disappointingly wobbly Suzuki; Santini is a reliable, generally rather square and unimaginative conductor who rarely gets in the way.

Callas's view, aided by superbly imaginative and spacious conducting from Karajan, gives extra dimension to the Puccinian little woman, and with some keenly intelligent singing too from Gedda as Pinkerton this is a set which has a special compulsion. The performance projects the more vividly on CD, even though the lack of stereo in so atmospheric an opera is a serious disadvantage. and the new transfer is full and fairly spacious. However, it is at full price.

The Decca mono set was made in 1951. In the last resort she lacks temperament but there is much magnificent singing. Campora is a fine Pinkerton and the fresh young voices of the two lovers are particularly convincing in Act I. Erede's conducting is stong and dramatic, and there is much to relish, not least the amazingly atmospheric Decca recording, which is very kind to the voices. The orchestra sounds thinner. The two CDs come in a single jewel-case with an independent plot summary unrelated to the 40 cues.

Madama Butterfly: highlights.

(M) *** Decca (ADD) 458 223-2. (from above complete set, with Tebaldi, Bergonzi, cond. Serafin).

(M) *** EMI (ADD) CDM5 65580-2 (from above complete set, with Scotto, Bergonzi, Di Stasio; cond. Barbirolli).

The Decca selection is quite generous (68 minutes), and singing and recording are splendid; moreover, a full translation is included. But for only a little extra one can get this version of the complete opera on a Double Decca, which seems a far more sensible investment.

The EMI selection (54 minutes) does include the essential *Humming Chorus*. For those owning another complete set, it offers a fine sampler of Barbirolli's deeply felt performance with its admirably consistent cast. Scotto's Butterfly was one of her finest recorded performances. The transfer does reveal the age of the 1966 recording in the orchestral sound, but the voices are full and vividly projected.

Madame Butterfly: highlights (sung in English).

(B) **(*) CfP (ADD) CD-CFP 4600. Collier, Craig, Robson, Griffiths, Sadler's Wells O, Balkwill.

This 1960 recording lets the listener hear almost every word, and this is achieved without balancing things excessively in favour of the voices. Marie Collier got inside the part very well; she has a big, full voice and she sings most movingly. Charles Craig is a splendid Pinkerton: his singing achieves international standards and he was in particularly fresh voice when this record was made. As to the choice of extracts, the one omission which is at all serious is the entry of Butterfly. As it is, the duet of Pinkerton and Sharpless cuts off just as she is about to come in. The recording wears its years lightly; just occasionally the bright CD transfer brings a touch of peakiness in the vocal climaxes. However, this has been deleted just as we go to press.

Manon Lescaut (complete).

*** Decca 440 200-2 (2). Freni, Pavarotti, Croft, Taddei, Vargas, Bartoli, NY Met. Op. Ch. & O, Levine.

*** DG 413 893-2 (2). Freni, Domingo, Bruson, ROHCG Ch., Philh. O, Sinopoli.

(B) *** Double Decca 460 750-2 (2). Te Kanawa, Carreras, Coni, Tajo, Matteuzzi, Ch. & O of Teatro Cumunale di Bologna, Chailly.

*** Naxos 8.660019/20 (2). Gauci, Sardinero, Kaludov, BRT Philh. Ch. & O, Rahbari.

(***) EMI mono CDS5 56301-2 (2). Callas, Di Stefano, Fioravanti, La Scala, Milan, Ch. and O, Serafin.

(M) **(*) EMI (ADD) CMS7 64852-2 (2). Caballé, Domingo, Amb. Op. Ch., New Philh. O, Bartoletti.

(N) (BB) (**(*)) Naxos mono 8.110123/24 (2). Kirsten, Björling, Valdengo, Baccaloni, Hayward, Met. Op. Ch. & O, Antonicelli.

** DG 463 186-2 (2). Guleghina, Cura, Gallo, Roni, La Scala, Milan, Ch. & O, Muti.

With Luciano Pavarotti as a powerful Des Grieux, James Levine conducts a comparably big-boned performance of *Manon Lescaut*, bringing out the red-blooded drama of Puccini's first big success, while not ignoring its warmth and tender poetry. The impact is enhanced by exceptionally full, vivid sound, with the voices balanced close, well in front of the orchestra, and, though the closeness of balance exposes some inevitable blemishes of age in the voice, its fullness and warmth are more faithfully captured in a performance even warmer and more relaxed.

Pavarotti tackles his little opening aria challenging the girls to make him fall in love, *Tra voi belle*, with a beefy bravado that misses the subtlety and point of Domingo, for example. But then he characteristically points word-meaning with a bright-eyed intensity that compels attention, and there is little harm in having so passionate a portrait of Des Grieux as Pavarotti's. The rest of the cast is strong too, with Dwayne Croft a magnificent Lescaut who brings out the character's wry humour. The veteran Giuseppe Taddei is superbly cast as Geronte, very characterful and still full-throated, while Cecilia Bartoli makes the unnamed singer in the Act II entertainment into far more than a cipher.

Plácido Domingo's portrait of Des Grieux on DG is far subtler and more detailed, with finer contrasts of tone and dynamic, than in his earlier, EMI recording opposite Caballé. Freni proves an outstanding choice: her girlish tones in Act I rebut any idea that she might be too mature. Of the others, who represent a first-rate team, Renato Bruson nicely brings out the ironic side of Lescaut's character, and having Brigitte Fassbaender just to sing the *Madrigal* adds to the feeling of luxury, as does John Tomlinson's darkly intense moment of drama as the ship's captain. The voices are more recessed than is common, but they are recorded with fine bloom, and the brilliance of the orchestral sound comes out impressively.

The digital Chailly set dates from as recently as 1988 and makes a splendid bargain as a Decca Double. It comes with Decca's new reissue documentation including a 'listening guide' which offers good documentation and a simple cued synopsis. Dame Kiri gives an affecting characterization of Manon, at times rather heavily underlined but passionately convincing in the development from innocent girl to fallen woman. The playing from Chailly's Bologna orchestra cannot quite match that of the Philharmonia for Sinopoli, yet Chailly is a degree more idiomatic in his pacing. Carreras is in good form, but sounds a little strained at times. The Decca sound, with the voices well forward is characteristically vivid.

On the bargain Naxos issue, Miriam Gauci gives one of the most sensitive performances of this role on any set. The young Bulgarian, Kaludi Kaludov, is a clean-cut, virile Des Grieux, opening up impressively in his big moments. Vincente Sardinero makes a powerful Lescaut, and Rahbari is a red-blooded interpreter of Italian opera, generally pacing well, even if at the very start he is disconcertingly hectic. This is the least expensive *Manon Lescaut* in the catalogue but, even if it cost more, it would still be very recommendable.

It is typical of Maria Callas that she turns the final scene into the most compelling part of the opera. Serafin, who could be a lethargic recording conductor, is here electrifying, and Di Stefano too is inspired to one of his finest complete opera recordings. The cast-list even includes the young Fiorenza Cossotto, impressive as the singer in the Act II *Madrigal*. The recording, which is still in mono – not a stereo transcription – minimizes the original boxiness and gives good detail.

The EMI version conducted by Bartoletti is chiefly valuable for the performance of Montserrat Caballé as the heroine, one of her most affecting, with the voice alluringly beautiful. Otherwise the set is disappointing, with Plácido Domingo unflattered by the close acoustic, not nearly as perceptive as in his much later, DG performance under Sinopoli. The new transfer to CD, however, has improved the sound.

Dorothy Kirsten was a favourite lyric soprano at the Met in New York for over thirty years, yet with hardly any commercial recordings to her name she is little known outside the United States. That makes this brilliant, well-cast version of *Manon Lescaut* especially welcome, recorded live on Christmas Eve, 1949. Kirsten's may not be a specially distinctive voice, but it is a pure, clear, beautiful one, perfectly controlled, as her portrayal here makes plain in her tender, affecting accounts of Manon's big moments. It is a pity that her final solo, *Sola, perduta, abbandonata* is severely cut. Björling as Des Grieux is even more ardent here than he is in his commercial recording opposite Albanese on RCA, a great tenor ideal for the role, and Giuseppe Valdengo is a powerful Lescaut, with Salvatore Baccaloni a characterful Geronte. Antonicelli sometimes rushes the fast music, Toscanini-style, but draws out the lyrical warmth perfectly. Clear, if limited sound, only occasionally marred by surface noise.

The problems of recording live at La Scala weigh heavily in the Muti recording for DG. The stage noises are often intrusive; the orchestral sound lacks body, and choral ensemble is often poor. Muti too is encouraged to underline too heavily such big dramatic moments as the end of Act III. Though Maria Guleghina sings affectingly as the heroine, the lovely soprano tone tends to spread under pressure in the upper register. José Cura sings strenuously from his very first aria, *Tra voi belle*, onwards, though he too characterizes well and is occasionally persuaded to modify his strong, heroic tone.

Manon Lescaut: highlights.

(N) (B) *** DG 469 589-2 (from above complete recording, with Freni, Domingo; cond. Sinopoli).

Most of the key items are included in this well-chosen Classikon bargain-price selection of highlights from the brilliant Sinopoli set which is a strong alternative recommendation for this opera. An adequate synopsis with track cues is provided in lieu of a libretto. The playing time is 66 minutes.

'The Puccini Album': Manon Lescaut: Intermezzo; Act IV (complete). Tosca: Recondita armonia. Act I: Love Duet; Vissi d'arte; Act III (complete).

**(*) Ph. 456 586-2. Gorchakova, Shicoff, Maggio Musicale Fiorentino O, Ozawa.

The title is misleading when this offers simply substantial extracts from only two operas, concentrating on scenes rather than arias, with incidental voice-parts all included. Both Gorchakova and Shicoff sing powerfully, but the overall impression is rather generalized. Gorchakova, in splendid voice, rises superbly to the challenge of Manon's big monologue, *Sola perduta, abbandonata*, the climax of the whole disc.

La Rondine (complete).

*** Sony M2K 37852 (2). Te Kanawa, Domingo, Nicolesco, Rendall, Nucci, Watson, Knight, Amb. Op. Ch., LSO, Maazel.

(i) *La Rondine* (complete). (ii) *Le Villi: Prelude,*

L'abbandono; La tregenda; Ecco la casa . . . Torna al felice.
(iii) Song: *Morire!.*

*** EMI CDS5 56338-2 (2). (i–iii) Alagna; (i) Gheorghiu,
Mula-Tchako, Matteuzzi, Rinaldi; (i–ii) L. Voices, LSO,
Pappano; (iii) Pappano (piano).

Pappano on this EMI issue transforms the work, revealing
it to be another masterpiece. He is aided by the partnership
of Angela Gheorghiu, most moving in the Violetta-like role
of the heroine, Magda, and of Alagna as the ardent young
student she falls in love with. Pappano consistently brings
out the poetry, drawing on emotions far deeper than are
suggested by this operetta-like subject, thanks also to
Gheorghiu's superb performance, tenderly expressive, as in
Magda's first big solo, *Che il bel sogno di Doretta*. Consistently she makes you share the courtesan's wild dream of
finding her young student. As Ruggero, the hero, Alagna
winningly characterizes the ardent young student, singing
in his freshest voice. What will specially delight Puccinians
in this set is that he is given an extra aria about Paris,
Parigi e un citta, which transforms his otherwise minimal
contribution to Act I. The role of the poet, Prunier, is also
transformed thanks to the casting of the clear-toned William
Matteuzzi in what is normally a comprimario role. Inva
Mula-Tchako is equally well cast in the soubrette role of
Lisette, bright, clear and vivacious, with Alberto Rinaldi
making the sugar-daddy, Rambaldo, the dull dog intended.
The excerpts from *Le Villi*, warm and dramatic, include two
orchestral showpieces. Alagna also gives a ringing account
of Roberto's aria, as he does of the song, *Morire!* – with
Pappano at the piano – the source of the extra aria for
Ruggero included in the main opera.

Maazel's is a strong, positive reading, crowned by a superb
and radiant Magda in Dame Kiri Te Kanawa, mature yet
glamorous. Domingo, by age too mature for the role of
young hero, yet scales his voice down most effectively in the
first two Acts, expanding in heroic warmth only in the final
scene of dénouement. Sadly, the second pair are far less
convincing, when the voices of both Mariana Nicolesco and
David Rendall take ill to the microphone.

Suor Angelica (complete).

(M) **(*) RCA (ADD) 74321 40575-2. Popp, Lipovšek, Schiml,
Jennings, Bav. R. Ch., Munich R. O, Patanè.

Suor Angelica (complete); *Tosca: Vissi d'arte.*

(M) *** Decca (ADD) 458 218-2. Sutherland, Ludwig, Collings,
L. Op. Ch., Finchley Children's Music Group, Nat. PO,
Bonynge.

Puccini's atmospheric picture of a convent is superbly captured in the Decca version, with sound of spectacular depth.
Bonynge's direction is most persuasive, and Sutherland rises
superbly to the big dramatic demands of the final scenes.
With Sutherland, Angelica is a formidable match for the
implacable Zia Principessa, here superbly taken by Christa
Ludwig. The supporting cast is outstanding, and the pity is
that Sutherland did not record the piece rather earlier, before
the beat developed in her voice. The recording is attractively
re-packaged, with full translation included, plus an encore,
Vissi d'arte from *Tosca*, recorded six years earlier in 1972.

Patanè's performance is idiomatic and consistently well
played. Neither Lucia Popp as Angelica nor Marjana Lipovšek as the vindictive Zia Principessa is ideally cast – the
one overstressed, the other sounding too young – but these
are both fine artists who sing with consistent imagination,
and the recording is pleasingly atmospheric. There is a
libretto/translation provided, and the only snag is the lack
of cueing: only two tracks are indicated, one 28 minutes into
the opera and the second 12 minutes later.

Il Tabarro (complete).

(M) *** RCA (ADD) 74321 40581-2. Nimsgern, Tokody,
Lamberti, Pane, Bav. R. Ch., Munich R. O, Patanè.

Patanè in his larger-than-life direction may at times run the
risk of exaggerating the melodrama, but the result is richly
enjoyable. Ilona Tokody, already well known from Hungaroton opera sets, makes a powerful, strongly projected Giorgetta, somewhat showing up the relative weakness of the
tenor, Giorgio Lamberti, as her lover, Luigi. His over-
emphatic underlining mars his legato, but the main love-
duet comes over with gusty strength. Siegmund Nimsgern
makes a powerful Michele, making the character more sinister. The full and brilliant recording has voices set convincingly on a believable stage, well balanced against the
orchestra, the effect appealingly atmospheric. There is a
libretto/translation and the reissue is much more generously
cued than before, providing ten tracks in all.

Tosca (complete).

✪ *** EMI mono CMS5 66444-2. Callas, Di Stefano, Gobbi,
Calabrese, La Scala, Milan, Ch. and O, De Sabata.

(M) *** Decca (ADD) 466 384-2 (2). L. Price, Di Stefano,
Taddei, V. State Op. Ch., VPO, Karajan.

*** DG 431 775-2 (2). Freni, Domingo, Ramey, Terfel, ROHCG
Ch., Philh. O, Sinopoli.

(N) (B) *** Ph. (ADD) 464 729-2 (2). Caballé, Carreras, Wixell,
ROHCG Ch. & O, Davis.

(M) *** RCA (ADD) 74321 39503-2 (2). Price, Domingo,
Milnes, Plishka, Alldis Ch., Wandsworth School Boys' Ch.,
New Philh. O, Mehta.

*** DG (ADD) 413 815-2 (2). Ricciarelli, Carreras, Raimondi,
Corena, German Op. Ch., BPO, Karajan.

**(*) Decca 414 597-2 (2). Te Kanawa, Aragall, Nucci, Welsh
Nat. Opera Ch., Nat. PO, Solti.

(M) **(*) EMI CMS5 66504-2 (2). Scotto, Domingo, Bruson,
Amb. Op. Ch., St Clement Danes School Boys' Ch., Philh.
O, Levine.

(M) ** RCA mono 09026 63305-2 (2). Milanov, Björling,
Warren, Rome Op. Ch. & O, Leinsdorf.

There has never been a finer recorded performance of *Tosca*
than Callas's first, with Victor de Sabata conducting and Tito
Gobbi as Scarpia. Gobbi makes the unbelievably villainous
police chief into a genuinely three-dimensional character,
and Di Stefano as the hero, Cavaradossi, was at his finest.
The conducting of De Sabata is spaciously lyrical as well
as sharply dramatic, and the mono recording is superbly
balanced in Walter Legge's fine production. Though there
is inevitably less spaciousness than in a stereo recording, the
voices are caught gloriously.

Karajan's 1962 Vienna *Tosca* is rightly now assigned its place in Decca's Legends series. It was previously available on a Double Decca and now costs more, but as it includes a libretto/translation is well worth its mid-price bracket. Karajan deserves equal credit with the principal singers for the vital, imaginative performance, recorded in Vienna. Taddei himself has a marvellously wide range of tone-colour, and though he cannot quite match the Gobbi snarl he has almost every other weapon in his armoury. Leontyne Price is at the peak of her form and Di Stefano sings most sensitively. The sound is quite marvellous in its digitally remastered format, combining presence with atmosphere.

Even more than the Puccini operas he had previously recorded – always with spacious, finely moulded treatment – *Tosca* seems to match Sinopoli's musical personality, helped by DG recording of spectacular weight and range. Ramey's is not a conventional portrait of the evil police-chief, but the role has rarely been sung with more sheer beauty, with such a climax as the *Te Deum* at the end of Act I sounding thrilling in its firmness and power. Domingo's heroic power is formidable too, and unlike many of his opera recordings for DG this one presents him in close-up, not distanced. Freni's is not naturally a Tosca voice, but it is still a powerful, heartfelt performance.

Pacing the music naturally and sympathetically, Sir Colin Davis proves a superb Puccinian, one who not only presents Puccini's drama with richness and force but gives the score the musical strength of a great symphony. Davis rarely if ever chooses idiosyncratic tempi, and his manner is relatively straight; but it remains a strong and understanding reading, as well as a refreshing one. In this the quality of the singing from a cast of unusual consistency plays an important part. Caballé may not be as sharply jealous a heroine as her keenest rivals, but with the purity of *Vissi d'arte* coming as a key element in her interpretation, she still presents Tosca as a formidable siren-figure ('*Mia sirena*' being Cavaradossi's expression of endearment). Carreras reinforces his reputation as a tenor of unusual artistry as well as of superb vocal powers. Though Wixell is not ideally well focused as Scarpia, not at all Italianate of tone, he presents a completely credible lover-figure, not just the lusting ogre of convention. The 1976 analogue recording is full as well as refined, bringing out the beauties of Puccini's scoring. It is given a strikingly successful CD transfer, with three-dimensional placing of voices. An unexpected but worthy choice for the Philips selection of '50 Great Recordings'.

Leontyne Price made her second complete recording of *Tosca* (for RCA) ten years after the first under Karajan, and the interpretation remained remarkably consistent, a shade tougher in the chest register – the great entry in Act III a magnificent moment – and a little more clipped of phrase. That last modification may reflect the relative manners of the two conductors – Karajan more individual in his refined expansiveness, Mehta more thrustful. On balance, taking Price alone, the preference is for the earlier set, but Mehta's version also boasts a fine cast, with the team of Domingo and Milnes at its most impressive. The recording, too, is admirable, even if it yields to the Decca in atmosphere and richness.

On Karajan's DG version the police chief, Scarpia, seems to be the central character, and his unexpected choice of singer, a full bass, Raimondi, helps to show why, for this is no small-time villain but a man who in full confidence has a vein of nobility in him. Katia Ricciarelli is not the most individual of Toscas, but the beauty of singing is consistent. Carreras gives a powerful, stylish performance. The recording is rich and full, with the stage picture clearly established and the glorious orchestral textures beautifully caught.

Rarely has Solti phrased Italian melody so consistently *con amore*, his fiercer side subdued but with plenty of power when required. Even so, the timing is not always quite spontaneous-sounding, with transitions occasionally rushed. But the principal *raison d'être* of the set must be the casting of Dame Kiri as the jealous opera-singer. Her admirers will relish the glorious sounds, but the jealous side of Tosca's character is rather muted.

Levine directs a red-blooded performance which underlines the melodrama. Domingo here reinforces his claim to be the finest Cavaradossi today, while the clean-cut, incisive singing of Renato Bruson presents a powerful if rather young-sounding Scarpia. Renata Scotto's voice is in many ways ideally suited to the role of Tosca, certainly in its timbre and colouring; as caught on record, however, the upper register is often squally. The digital recording is full and forward.

At mid-price Leinsdorf's version will be of principal interest to admirers of the veteran singer in the cast. Jussi Björling was at the peak of his fame as Cavaradossi. Though Zinka Milanov was past her best and was sometimes stressed by the role, there is much beautiful singing here from a great soprano who recorded all too little. Leonard Warren was another characterful veteran, but the furry edge to the voice makes him a less-than-sinister Scarpia.

Tosca: highlights.

(B) *** DG (ADD) 439 461-2 (from above complete recording, with Ricciarelli, Carreras, Raimondi; cond. Karajan).

(M) ** EMI (ADD) CDM5 66666-2 (from complete recording with Callas, Bergonzi, Gobbi, Paris Op. Ch., Paris Conservatoire O, Prêtre).

The breadth of Karajan's direction is well represented in the longer excerpts; there is also Tosca's *Vissi d'arte* and Carreras's two famous arias from the outer Acts. Now in this 70-minute selection Scarpia's music in Act II is much better represented, essential when Raimondi is such a distinctive Scarpia with his dark, bass timbre.

Even to Callas admirers her stereo remake of Tosca must be a disappointment when it fails so obviously to match the dramatic tension of the first version under de Sabata. This is another sampler-length selection with only 56 minutes of music.

Tosca (complete; in English).

(M) *** Chan. 3000 (2). Eaglen, O'Neill, Yurisich, Mitchell Ch., Kay Children's Ch., Philh. O, Parry.

David Parry with Jane Eaglen, in one of her finest performances on disc, directs a gripping account of Puccini's red-blooded drama, sung in English. With the help of opulent, atmospheric Chandos sound, the bite and energy of the Philharmonia bring out the expressive warmth of the score, not least in the love music, whether in the power of the big tuttis or in magical, whispered pianissimos. What above all seals the success of the set is the power and command of Jane Eaglen as Tosca. The confident sureness with which she attacks every top note is a delight, so that in Act I she expresses her jealousy with the vehemence of a Wagnerian, while singing with warm, rounded tone. She is well matched by Dennis O'Neill as Cavaradossi, aptly Italianate, and Gregory Yurisich makes a powerful Scarpia, younger-sounding than most and therefore a plausible lover. The others are well cast too, notably Peter Rose as a fresh-voiced Angelotti. The Geoffrey Mitchell Choir and children's choir are superb in the crowd scenes of Act I.

Tosca: highlights (sung in English).

(N) (M) *** Chan. 3066. (from above complete recording with Eaglen, O'Neill, Yuriisich; cond. Parry

A generous selection (74 minutes), centring on Jane Eaglen's magnificently sung portrayal of Tosca. The recording is superbly rich and this singing can stand alongside any inter-national competition. A hugely enjoyable disc.

Il Trittico: (i) *Il Tabarro;* (ii) *Suor Angelica;* (iii) *Gianni Schicchi.*

*** EMI CDS5 56567-2 (3) (i; iii) Gheorghiu, Alagna; (i) Guelfi, Guleghina, Shicoff; (ii) Gallardo-Domas, Manca di Nissa; (ii–iii) Palmer; (iii) Van Dam, Roni; (i–ii) L. Voices; (ii) Tiffin School Boys' Ch., LSO or Philh. O, Pappano.

(M) *** EMI mono/stereo CMS7 64165-2 (3). (i; iii) Gobbi; (i) Pradelli, Mas; (ii–iii) De los Angeles; (ii) Barbieri; (iii) Canali, Del Monte, Montarsolo; Rome Op. Ch. & O; (i) Bellezza; (ii) Serafin; (iii) Santini.

No previous recordings of the three one-acters in Puccini's triptych bring quite such warmth or beauty or so powerful a drawing of the contrasts between each – in turn Grand Guignol melodrama, pure sentiment and high comedy. Pacing each opera masterfully, Pappano heightens emotions fearlessly to produce at key moments the authentic gulp-in-throat, whether for the cuckolded bargemaster, Michele, for sister Angelica in her agonized suicide and heavenly absolution, or for the resolution of young love at the end of *Gianni Schicchi.*

Angela Gheorghiu and Roberto Alagna, as well as making a tiny cameo appearance in *Il Tabarro* as the off-stage de-parting lovers, sing radiantly as Lauretta and Rinuccio in *Gianni Schicchi,* with the happy ending most tenderly done. Maria Guleghina, well known for her fine Tosca, makes a warm, vibrant Giorgetta, and the touch of acid at the top of the voice adds character. Even more remarkable is the singing of the young Chilean soprano, Cristina Gallardo-Domas as Sister Angelica. This is a younger, more tender, more vulnerable Angelica than usual. As with Gheorghiu, the dynamic shading brings pianissimos of breathtaking delicacy, not least in floated top-notes. The casting in the middle opera is as near flawless as could be. The Zia Prin-cipessa is sung with chilling power by Bernadette Manca di Nissa, her tone firm and even throughout. Felicity Palmer

with her tangy mezzo tone is well contrasted as the Abbess, and she is just as characterful as the crabby Zita in *Gianni Schicchi.* Among the men, Carlo Guelfi makes a superb Michele in *Il Tabarro,* incisive, dark and virile. Neil Shicoff makes a fine Luigi, his nervy tenor tone adding character. As Gianni Schicchi, José van Dam is in fine voice, with his clean focus bringing out the sardonic side of Schicchi, and his top Gs wonderfully strong and steady still. The recording is comfortingly sumptuous and atmospheric, very wide in its dynamic range, with magical off-stage effects.

The classic EMI set of *Il Trittico* has dominated the cata-logue since the earliest days of LP, with Tito Gobbi giving two of his ripest characterizations. The central role of the cuckolded bargemaster, Michele, in the mono *Il Tabarro* inspires him to one of his very finest performances on record. The central leaf of the triptych, *Suor Angelica,* brings a glowing performance from Victoria de los Angeles, giving a most affecting portrayal of Angelica, with Fedora Barbieri formidable as her unfeeling aunt, the Zia Principessa. De los Angeles reappears, charmingly girlish as Lauretta, in *Gianni Schicchi,* where the high comedy has never fizzed so de-liciously outside the opera house. Though Gobbi's incom-parable baritone is not by nature comic-sounding, he is unequalled as Schicchi. Only *Gianni Schicchi,* recorded last in 1958, is in genuine and excellent stereo; *Il Tabarro* (1955) and *Suor Angelica* (1957) are mono, but all the transfers are expert, clear and convincingly balanced.

Turandot (complete).

*** Decca (ADD) 414 274-2 (2). Sutherland, Pavarotti, Caballé, Pears, Ghiaurov, Alldis Ch., Wandsworth School Boys' Ch., LPO, Mehta.

(M) *** EMI (ADD) CMS7 69327-2 (2). Nilsson, Corelli, Scotto, Mercuriali, Giaiotti, Rome Op. Ch. & O, Molinari-Pradelli.

*** DG 423 855-2 (2). Ricciarelli, Domingo, Hendricks, Raimondi, V. State Op. Ch., V. Boys' Ch., VPO, Karajan.

(***) EMI mono CDS5 56307-2 (2). Callas, Fernandi, Schwarzkopf, Zaccaria, La Scala, Milan, Ch. & O, Serafin.

(M) **(*) EMI (ADD) CMS5 65293-2 (2). Caballé, Carreras, Freni, Plishka, Sénéchal, Maîtrise de la Cathédrale, Ch. of L'Opéra du Rhin, Strasbourg PO, Lombard.

*(*) RCA 74321 60617-2 (2). Casolla, Larin, Frittoli, Maggio Musicale Fiorentino Ch. & O, Mehta.

Joan Sutherland gives an intensely revealing and appealing interpretation, making the icy princess far more human and sympathetic than ever before, while Pavarotti gives a performance equally imaginative, beautiful in sound, strong on detail. To set Caballé against Sutherland was a daring idea, and it works superbly well; Pears as the Emperor is another imaginative choice. Mehta directs a gloriously rich and dramatic performance, superlatively recorded, still the best-sounding *Turandot* on CD, while the reading also re-mains supreme.

The EMI set brings Nilsson's second assumption on record of the role of Puccini's formidable princess. As an interpretation it is very similar to the earlier, RCA perform-ance, but its impact is far more immediate, thanks to the conducting of Molinari-Pradelli. Corelli may not be the most sensitive prince in the world, but the voice is in glorious condition. Scotto's Liù is very beautiful and characterful too. With vividly remastered sound, this makes an excellent mid-priced recommendation, though the documentation, as yet, does not include an English translation.

In Karajan's set, Hendricks is almost a sex-kitten with her seductively golden tone, and one wonders how Calaf could ever have overlooked her. This is very different from the usual picture of a chaste slave-girl. Ricciarelli is a far more vulnerable figure than one expects of the icy princess, and the very fact that the part strains her beyond reasonable vocal limits adds to the dramatic point, even if it subtracts from the musical joys. By contrast, Plácido Domingo is vocally superb, a commanding prince; and the rest of the cast present star names even in small roles.

With Callas, the character seems so much more believably complex than with others, and this 1957 recording is one of her most thrillingly magnetic performances on disc. Schwarzkopf provides a comparably characterful and distinctive portrait as Liù, far more than a Puccinian 'little woman', sweet and wilting. Eugenio Fernandi sounds relatively uncharacterful as Calaf, but his timbre is pleasing enough. By contrast, Serafin's masterly conducting exactly matches the characterfulness of Callas and Schwarzkopf, with colour, atmosphere and dramatic point all commandingly presented. With such a vivid performance, the 1957 mono sound hardly seems to matter, and the sound is much more expansive in the new transfer.

From the very start Caballé conveys an element of mystery while Freni underlines the dramatic rather than the lyrical side of Liù's role. The pity is that the EMI recording is unflattering to the voices – allowing Caballé less warmth and body of tone than usual, while setting Freni so close that a flutter keeps intruding. Lombard, so alert and imaginative in French music, proves a stiff and unsympathetic Puccinian so that the tenor, José Carreras, for example is prevented from expanding as he should in the big arias. A good CD transfer and excellent back-up documentation.

The RCA recording offers a strong performance under Zubin Mehta in beefy, if at times abrasive, sound, with ample space round the voices. The casting of the principals is seriously flawed. Sergei Larin sings with fine dramatic thrust, though his voice grows strained towards the end. Giovanna Casola has a big voice with a pronounced flutter, so that the tone grows sour, and at the top pitching becomes vague under stress, so that *In questa reggia* ends with a squeal. Barbara Frittoli is even less well cast as Liù, with her heavy vibrato and reluctance to sing softly.

Turandot: highlights.

(M) *** Decca (ADD) 458 202-2 (from above complete recording, with Sutherland, Pavarotti, cond. Mehta).

A generous and shrewdly chosen 70-minute collection of excerpts from the glorious full-priced Decca set of *Turandot*. *Nessun dorma*, with Pavarotti at his finest, is here given a closing cadence for neatness. The vintage Decca sound is outstandingly full and vivid. The reissue in Decca's Opera Gala series is neatly packaged in a slipcase and includes a full translation.

Le Villi: complete.

*** Sony (ADD) MK 76890. Scotto, Domingo, Nucci, Gobbi, Amb. Op. Ch., Nat. PO, Maazel.

Maazel directs a performance so commanding, with singing of outstanding quality, that one can at last assess Puccini's first opera on quite a new level. Scotto's voice tends to spread a little at the top of the stave but, like Domingo, she gives a powerful performance, and Leo Nucci avoids false histrionics. A delightful bonus is Tito Gobbi's contribution reciting the verses which link the scenes; he is as characterful a reciter as he is a singer. The recording is one of CBS's best.

COLLECTIONS

(i) *Crisantemi; Minuets Nos. 1–3; Quartet in A min.: Allegro moderato; Scherzo in A min.;* (ii) *Foglio d'album; Piccolo tango;* (iii; ii) Songs: *Avanti Urania; E l'uccellino; Inno a Diana; Menti all'avviso; Morire?; Salve regina; Sole e amore; Storiella d'amore; Terra e mare.*

*** Etcetera KTC 1050. (i) Raphael Qt; (ii) Crone; (iii) Alexander.

It is fascinating to find among early, rather untypical songs like *Storiella d'amore* and *Menti all'avviso* a charming little song, *Sole e amore*, written jokingly for a journal, 'Paganini', in 1888, which provided, bar for bar, the main idea of the Act III quartet in *La Bohème* of eight years later. The two piano pieces are simple album-leaves; among the six quartet pieces, *Crisantemi* is already well known; the rest are student pieces, including a delightful fragment of a Scherzo. Performances are good, though Roberta Alexander's soprano is not ideally Italianate. The recorded sound is vivid and immediate against a lively hall ambience.

'The Essential Puccini': Preludio sinfonico; Famous arias, duets and choruses from: *La Bohème; La fanciulla del West; Gianni Schicchi; Madama Butterfly; Manon Lescaut; La Rondine; Suor Angelica; Tosca; Turandot.*

(B) **(*) Double Decca ADD/Dig. 444 555-2 (2). Caballé, Chiara, Freni, Te Kanawa, Sutherland, Tebaldi, Bergonzi, Bjoerling, Carreras, Pavarotti, Corena, Ghiaurov, Krause, Milnes, Siepi (with various orchestras & conductors).

Many collectors will welcome a sampler of the vintage set of *La Bohème* with Tebaldi and Bergonzi at the height of their powers. Five items are included here, including the love scene from Act I. Tebaldi is also at her most seductive in *Madama Butterfly*, which is generously represented with well over half an hour of excerpts, including the whole of the Act I Love duet. She also provides the key arias from *Gianni Schicchi* and *La Rondine*, while Suor Angelica's ravishing *Senza mamma, o bimbo, tu sei morto* comes from Maria Chiara's glorious 1971 début recital. Dame Kiri gives a movingly passionate if comparatively unsubtle characterization of *Manon Lescaut*; with three numbers included, her partner, Carreras, recorded just before his illness, sounds a little strained. It was a pity that Rescigno's recording was chosen for the 30 minutes or so of *Tosca* excerpts. Freni as Tosca is below her best form and, though Sherrill Milnes does not disappoint as Scarpia, Pavarotti's *E lucevan le stelle* is the high point. Joan Sutherland's assumption of the role of the formidable *Turandot* is justly esteemed, as is Caballé's melting Liù, while Pavarotti delivers a splendid *Nessun dorma*. With Bjoerling on hand to provide a superb *Ch'ella mi creda* from *Fanciulla del West*, this is something of a (143-minute) Puccini feast, with the ripely expansive Decca sound fairly consistent throughout. The snag is that the documentation is totally inadequate.

Arias: *La Bohème: Quando m'en vo' soletta. Gianni Schicchi: O mio babbino caro. Madama Butterfly: Un bel dì. Manon Lescaut: In quelle trine morbide. La Rondine: Chi il bel sogno di Doretta; Ore dolci e divine. Tosca: Vissi d'arte. Le Villi: Se come voi piccina.*

(M) *** Sony (ADD) SMK 60975. Te Kanawa, LPO, Pritchard, or LSO, Maazel – VERDI: Arias *** (with MOZART: *Don Giovanni: Ah! fuggi il traditor; In quali eccessi . . . Mi tradì;* HUMPERDINCK: *Der kleine Sandmann bin ich;* DURUFLE: *Requiem: Pie Jesu* ***).

In a recital recorded in 1981 the creamy beauty of Kiri Te Kanawa's voice is ideally suited to these seven lyrical Puccini arias including the little waltz-like song from *Le Villi*. The other excerpt from this opera comes from the complete set made around the same time. Throughout, expressive sweetness is more remarkable than characterization, but in such music it is difficult to complain. Kiri was also in top form in her 1978 assumption of the role of Elvira in Mozart's *Don Giovanni* (again with Maazel), and the delightful Sandman aria from *Hänsel und Gretel* and Duruflé's beautiful, serene *Pie Jesu* again show the voice at its most appealing.

'Gala': *La Bohème:* (i) *Che gelida manina; Si, mi chiamano Mimi;* (ii) *Quando m'en vo;* (iii) *Donde lieta usci.* (iv) *La fanciulla del West: Ch'ella mi creda.* (v) *Gianni Schicchi: O mio babbino caro.* (i) *Madama Butterfly: Un bel dì; Addio fioriti asil.* (iii) *Manon Lescaut: In quelle trine morbide;* (vi) *Donna non vidi mai.* (v) *La Rondine: Sogno di Doretta.* (iii) *Suor Angelica: Senza mamma.* (vii) *Tosca: Recordita armonia; Vissi d'arte; E lucevan le stelle.* (viii) *Turandot: Signore ascolta!; Non piangere Liù!; Ah! Per l'ultima volta!; In questa reggia; Tu che di gel sei cinta; Nessun dorma!*

(M) *** Decca (ADD) 458 212-2. (i) Freni, Pavarotti; (ii) Harwood; (iii) Chiara; (iv) Milnes; (v) Tebaldi; (vi) Carreras; (vii) Corelli, Nilsson; Sutherland, Caballé, Pavarotti, Ghiaurov.

This generous (71-minute) 'Gala' collection, with 22 items, opens predictably with Freni and Pavarotti in the Act I love scene from Karajan's 1972 *La Bohème*, and they sing again Karajan's 1974 *Butterfly*. The programme closes ambitiously, with six major excerpts from Mehta's *Turandot* with Sutherland, Caballé, and Pavarotti. Tebaldi is at her most ravishing in arias from *La Rondine* and *Gianni Schicchi*, and imaginatively, the 1966 Nilsson/Corelli/Maazel recording is chosen for the three items from *Tosca*. Decca are skilled at this kind of anthology, and particularly welcome is the inclusion of three arias from Maria Chiara's magical 1971 début recital, including lyrically very beautiful accounts of 'In quelle trine

morbide' (*Manon Lescaut*) and 'Senza mamma' (*Suor Angelica*), recorded when her voice sounded wonderfully young and fresh. The documentation is excellent and full translations are included.

'Sole e amore': Arias and Duets: *La Bohème: Donde lieta usci; Si,mi chiamano Mimi.* (i) *Canto d'anime. Gianni Schicchi: O mio babbino caro. Madama Butterfly: Intermezzo Atto II, Parte seconda; Un bel di vedremo. Manon Lescaut: In quelle trine morbide; Intermezzo Act III; Sola perduta, abandonnata.* (i) *Morire. La Rondine: Ch'il bel sogno di Doretta.* (i) *Sole e amore. Suor Angelica: Senza Mamma, o bimbo. Tosca: Vissi d'arte. Turandot: Signore ascolta; Tu che di gel sei cinta. Le Villi: Se come voi.*

*** Erato 0630 17071-2. Te Kanawa, (i) Vignoles; with Nat. Op. O de Lyon, Nagano.

This is a Puccini recital disc with a difference. The title,'*Sole e amore*' (Sunshine and love), is taken not from an aria but from one of the three Puccini songs included. Rightly, Dame Kiri sings it not as an opera excerpt *manqué* but – encouraged by Roger Vignoles's imaginative accompaniment – as the trivial album-leaf intended. Those three songs with piano provide a welcome variety in a Puccini collection which, avoiding Minnie and Turandot, might have lacked contrast. Tosca's *Vissi d'arte* comes as an introduction, but then the ordering is chronological. The orchestral interludes from *Manon Lescaut* and *Butterfly* are beautifully done, but more songs with piano would have been preferable. With a recording lacking in bloom on top, the voice is not quite as creamy as it once was, if still very beautiful.

Arias: *La Bohème; Sì, mi chiamano Mimì; Donde lieta usci. Gianni Schicchi: O mio babbino caro. Madama Butterfly: Un bel dì; Tu, tu piccolo Iddio. Manon Lescaut: In quelle trine morbide; Sola, perduta, abbandonata. La Rondine: Chi il bel sogno di Doretta. Tosca: Vissi d'arte. Turandot: Signore, ascolta!; Tu che di gel sei cinta. Le Villi: Se come voi piccina.*

*** EMI (ADD) CDC7 47841-2. Caballé, LSO, Mackerras.

Montserrat Caballé uses her rich, beautiful voice to glide over these great Puccinian melodies. The effect is ravishing, with lovely recorded sound to match the approach. This is one of the loveliest of all operatic recital discs and the comparative lack of sparkle is compensated for by the sheer beauty of the voice. The CD transfer is extremely successful, vivid yet retaining the full vocal bloom.

Arias: *La Bohème: Si, mi chiamano Mimì; Donde lieta usci. Gianni Schicchi: O mio babino caro. Madama Butterfly: Un bel dì; Con onor muore. Manon Lescaut: In quelle trine morbide; Sola, perduta. Suor Angelica: Senza mamma. Turandot: Signore acolta!; In questa reggia; Tu che di gel sei cinta.*

(M) (***) EMI mono CDM5 66463-2. Callas, Philh. O, Serafin.

This collection of Puccini arias was Callas's first EMI recital, recorded in mono in Watford Town Hall in September 1954. Now reissued as part of EMI's Callas Edition, it brings a classic example of her art. She was vocally at her peak. Even when her concept of a Puccinian 'little woman' has eyes controversially flashing and fierce, the results are unforgettable, never for a moment relaxing on the easy course, always finding new revelation, whether as Turandot or Liù, as Manon, Mimì or Butterfly. Well-balanced recording, with the voice vividly projected by the transfer and with plenty of depth and detail in the orchestra.

Arias: *Madama Butterfly: Un bel dì; Tu? tu? piccolo Iddio! (Death of Butterfly). La Rondine: Che il bel sogno di Doretta. Tosca: Vissi d'arte. Turandot: Signore ascolta; Tu che di gel sei cinta.*

(M) ✱✱(✱) RCA (ADD) 09026 68883-2. L. Price, Rome Op. O, De Fabritiis or Basile – VERDI: *Arias.* ✱✱✱

There is some glorious singing in this recital from the beginning of the 1960s. Perhaps Leontyne Price does not always get right inside each heroine at this stage in her career, but *Un bel dì* is thrilling, with a sharp contrast of tone between the incisiveness of the opening and the delicacy of *Chi sarà, Chi sarà*. In *Vissi d'arte* she forces a little too hard so that her vibrato becomes a wobble, but the two *Turandot* arias are very beautiful. Most welcome of all is Magda's aria from *La Rondine*, sweet, charming and lyrical. The recording was always very good indeed, and it sounds even more vivid in this CD transfer, without any loss of bloom.

PURCELL, Henry (1659–95)

INSTRUMENTAL MUSIC

Chaconne in G min.; Overtures in D min.; G; & G min.; 3 Parts on a Ground in D; 2 Pavans in A; Pavan in A min.; 2 Pavans in B flat; 2 Pavans in G min.; Sonatas Nos. 6 in G min.; 7 in E min.; 12 in D; Suite in G.

(B) ✱✱(✱) HM HMT 7901 327. L. Baroque.

Most of the music here was composed at the same time as his well-known four-part *Fantasias* (see below), and shows the young composer exploring the various instrumental styles available to him. The *Three Parts on a Ground* has some quite unexpected harmonies, while the *Pavan à 4 in G minor* uses some haunting and forward-looking minor-keyed progressions. But all these overtures, suites and sonatas are rewardingly inventive. The London Baroque perform them well, though lacks a little in dynamic range. It may also have been better to have arranged the programme differently (with four pavans playing one after another), but one can reprogramme the order, and this bargain CD is certainly worth having.

3 Fantasias for 5 viols; 9 Fantasias for 4 viols; Fantasia on one note for 5 viols; In nomine for 6 viols; In nomine for 7 viols.

✱✱✱ Virgin VC5 45062-2. Fretwork.

Purcell wrote these *Fantasias* in 1680 at the time of his twenty-first birthday, consciously adopting what was then considered an archaic style, but displaying not only an astonishing contrapuntal skill but also a harmonic and structural adventurousness which leaps the centuries, sounding to us amazingly modern still in its daring chromaticisms. The players of Fretwork use viols with a concern for matching, tuning and balance which is quite exceptional, and their natural expressiveness matches the deeper implications of these masterpieces in microcosm.

(i) 3 Fantasias for 3 viols; 9 Fantasias for 4 viols; Fantasia on one note for 5 viols; In nomine for 6 viols; In nomine for 7 viols; (ii) Chacony in G min.

(M) ✱✱(✱) DG (ADD) 447 153-2. (i) VCM, Harnoncourt; (ii) E. Concert, Pinnock.

The Purcell *Fantasias* and *In nomines* are among the most searching and profound works in all music, and the 1963 Vienna Concentus, led by Alice Harnoncourt (with Nikolaus at the time playing 'second fiddle'), provide a set of performances of these wonderful pieces, darkly sombre in colour, using original instruments with a minimum of vibrato. Then at track 16 there is a splash of cold water in the face as Trevor Pinnock and his English Concert (recorded two decades later) demonstrate modern ideas of authenticity of style and pitch with a brightly astringent and strikingly vital account of the famous *Chacony in G minor*. This transition is not entirely comfortable, and it is better to listen to this piece as a separate item.

Sonatas in 3 Parts: Nos. 1–12 (complete).

(M) ✱✱✱ HM HMT 7901439. L. Baroque.

Purcell's set of 12 *Sonatas in 3 Parts* was published in 1683. The Italian influence is undeniable but they remain very much Purcell's own in their contrapuntal interest, their deeply expressive harmonic richness and their English seriousness of purpose. The period performances from London Baroque are full of vitality and warmth. The full resonance of the recording is helpful, but that in itself brings the one drawback: the effective dynamic range is reduced, although there is no lack of light and shade in the playing itself; and the continuo, featuring both harpsichord and organ (as was the practice at the time), comes through as it should, beautifully.

Sonatas of 3 Parts Nos. 1–12, Z.790/801; Sonatas of 4 Parts Nos. 1–10, Z.802/810; Chacony in G min., Z.730; Pavans, Z.438/52; 3 Parts upon a Ground in D, Z.731.

✱✱✱ Chan. 0572/3. Purcell Qt.

Sonatas of 3 Parts Nos. 1–7, Z.790–6; Pavans: in A min.; B flat; G min., Z.749, Z.750, Z.752.

✱✱✱ Chan. 8591. Purcell Qt.

Sonatas of 3 Parts Nos. 8–12, Z.797–801; Sonatas in 4 Parts Nos. 1–2, Z.802–3; Chacony in G min., Z.751; Fantasia on a Ground in D & F; Pavans in A, Z.748; G min., Z.751.

✱✱✱ Chan. 8663. Purcell Qt.

Sonatas of 4 Parts Nos. 3–10, Z.804–811; Prelude for Solo Violin in G min., Z.773; Organ Voluntaries Nos. 2 in D min.; 4 in G, Z.718 & 710.

✱✱✱ Chan. 8763. Purcell Qt.

In these *Sonatas* Purcell turned to the new, concerted style which had been developed in Italy. Interspersed among the *Sonatas* are three earlier and highly chromatic *Pavans*, composed before Purcell embraced the sonata discipline. If anything, the second volume is more attractive than the first, for it includes the indelible *Chacony in G minor*. The third leaves room for a solo violin *Prelude* and two organ *Voluntaries*, both admirably presented and, like the *Sonatas*, offering very realistic sound. The Purcell Quartet give a first-class account of themselves: their playing is authoritative and idiomatic, and the artists are firmly focused in a warm but not excessively reverberant acoustic. Strongly recommended. These authoritative and thoroughly enjoyable accounts of Purcell's *Sonatas* have also been gathered together on two CDs without the miscellaneous items which filled out a third. Whichever format is chosen, this set can be thoroughly recommended.

VOCAL MUSIC

Anthems & Services, Vol. 1: *It is a good thing to give thanks; Let mine eyes run down with tears; My beloved spake; O give thanks unto the Lord; O praise God in his holiness; O sing unto the Lord; Praise the Lord, O Jerusalem.*

*** Hyp. CDA 66585. Witcomb, Finnis, Hallchurch, Bowman, Daniels, George, Evans, King's Cons., King.

Anthems & Services, Vol. 2: *Behold now praise the Lord; Blessed are they that fear the Lord; I will give thanks unto Thee, O Lord; My song shall be alway; Te Deum & Jubilate.*

*** Hyp. CDA 66609. Bowman, Covey-Crump, George, New College, Oxford, Ch., King's Cons., King.

Anthems & Services, Vol. 3: *Begin the song, and strike the living lyre; Blessed Virgin's expostulation: Tell me, some pitying angel. Blow up the trumpet in Zion; Hear my prayer, O Lord; Hosanna to the highest; Lord, I can suffer thy rebukes; The Lord is King, be the people never so impatient; O God, Thou has cast us out; O Lord, our governor; Remember not Lord our offences; Thy word is a lantern unto my feet.*

*** Hyp. CDA 66623. Dawson, Bowman, Daniels, George, Evans, King's Cons. Ch., King's Cons., King.

Anthems & Services, Vol. 4: *Awake ye dead; Behold I bring you glad tidings; Early, O Lord, my fainting soul; The earth trembled; Lord, not to us but to thy name; Lord, what is man?; My heart is inditing of a good matter; O all ye people, clap your hands; Since God so tender a regard; Sing unto God; Sleep, Adam and take thy rest; The way of God is an undefiled way.*

*** Hyp. CDA 66644. Witcomb, Finnis, Hallchurch, Kennedy, O'Dwyer, Gritton, Bowman, Covey-Crump, Daniels, George, Varcoe, R. Evans, New College, Oxford, Ch., King's Cons., King.

Anthems & services, Vol. 5: *Awake, and with attention hear; How long, great God; Let the night perish (Job's Curse); O God, the king of glory; O God, Thou art my God; O, I'm sick of life; O Lord, rebuke me not; Praise the Lord,*

O my soul, and all that is within me; Rejoice in the Lord alway; We sing to him, whose wisdom form'd the ear; When on my sick bed I languish; With sick and famish'd eyes.

*** Hyp. CDA 66656. Witcomb, Finnis, Hallchurch, Kennedy, Gritton, Bowman, Covey-Crump, Daniels, George, Evans, King's Cons. Ch., King's Cons., King.

Anthems & Services, Vol. 6: *Great God and just; Hear me, O Lord, the great support; I will love Thee, O Lord; Lord, who can tell how oft he offendeth?; My heart is fixed, O God; O Lord, grant the King a long life; O praise the Lord, all ye heathen; Plung'd in the confines of despair; Thou wakeful shepherd that dost Israel keep; Who hath believed our report?; Why do the heathen so furiously rage together?*

*** Hyp. CDA 66663. Witcomb, Kennedy, O'Dwyer, Bowman, Covey-Crump, Daniels, Agnew, George, New College, Oxford, Ch., King's Cons., King.

Anthems & Services, Vol. 7: *Beati omnes qui timent; In the black dismal dungeon of despair; I was glad (2 settings: coronation anthem & verse anthem); Jubilate in B flat; O consider my adversity; Music for the funeral of Queen Mary; Save me O God; Te Deum in B flat; Thy way O God is holy.*

❁ *** Hyp. CDA 66677. Kennedy, O'Dwyer, Goodman, Gritton, Bowman, Short, Covey-Crump, Daniels, Milhofer, George, R. Evans, King's Cons. Ch., King's Cons., King.

Anthems & Services, Vol. 8: *Be merciful unto me; Benedicte in B flat; Blessed is the man that feareth the Lord; Bow down thine ear, O Lord; Full of wrath, his threatening breath; In Thee, O Lord, do I put my trust; Jehova, quam multi sunt hostes mei; Magnificat & Nunc Dimittis in G min.; They that go down to the sea in ships.*

*** Hyp. CDA 66686. O'Dwyer, Kennedy, Bowman, Covey-Crump, Daniels, Padmore, Milhofer, George, King's Cons. Ch., King's Cons., King.

The different categories of work here, Services, Verse Anthems, Motets (or Full Anthems) and devotional songs, cover the widest range of style and expression, with Robert King's own helpful and scholarly notes setting each one in context. Generally the most adventurous in style are the Full Anthems, with elaborate counterpoint often bringing amazingly advanced harmonic progressions. Yet the Verse Anthems too include some which similarly demonstrate Purcell's extraordinary imagination in contrapuntal writing. So though Volume 6 is confined to Verse Anthems and devotional songs, they too offer passages of chromatic writing which defy the idea of these categories as plain and straightforward. As the title suggests, the devotional song, *Plung'd in the confines of despair*, is a particularly fine example. Although all the earlier volumes are full of good things, Volume 7 (to which we award a token Rosette for the extraordinary achievement of this series) is the one to recommend first to anyone simply wanting to sample Purcell's church music. Not only does it contain the *Music for the Funeral of Queen Mary* in 1695, with drum processionals, the solemn *March* and *Canzona* for brass and *Funeral sentences*, it has the *B flat Morning service*, two settings of the Coronation anthem, *I was glad*, (one of them previously unrecorded), a magnificent Full Anthem, three Verse Anthems and two splendid devotional songs. Volume 8, too, is full of fine music. The opening Verse Anthem, *In Thee, O Lord, do I put my trust*, opens with a very striking, slightly melancholy *Sinfonia*, with a six-note figure rising up from a ground bass, which sets the expressive mood. The closing anthem, so appropriate from an island composer, *They that go down to the sea in ships*, is characteristically diverse, with Purcell helping the Lord 'maketh the storm to cease' and at the end providing a joyful chorus of praise. King's notes and documentation closely identify each item, adding to one's illumination. An outstanding series, full of treasures, with King varying the scale of forces he uses for each item. Often he uses one voice per part, but he regularly expands the ensemble with the King's Consort Choir or turns to the full New College Choir, which includes trebles.

Anthems: *Blow up the trumpet in Sion; My heart is inditing; O God, thou art my God; O God, thou hast cast us out; Rejoice in the Lord alway; Remember not, Lord, our offences; Chacony in G min.*

(N) (BB) * Teldec (ADD) 2292 43548-2. Bowman, Rogers, Van Egmond, King's College Ch., Cambridge; Leonhardt Consort, Leonhardt.

An attractive concert from the beginning of the 1970s which blends scholarship and spontaneity. The period-instrument playing style is very distinctive. Not all these anthems have instrumental accompaniments but they are all very well sung with the characteristic King's penchant for tonal breadth and beauty. The *Chaconne* makes a stimulating interlude, placed midway through the recital. Excellent 1970 recording, very well-transferred, and full texts are provided.

Anthems: *Man that is born of woman; O God, thou has cast us out; Lord, how long wilt thou be angry?; O God, thou art my God; O Lord God of hosts; Remember not, Lord, our offences; Thou knowest, Lord, the secrets of our hearts. Verse anthems: My beloved spake; My heart is inditing; O sing unto the Lord; Praise the Lord, O Jerusalem; They that go down to the sea in ships. Morning Service in B flat: Benedicte omnia opera; Cantate Domino; Deus miscreatur; Magnificat; Nunc dimittis. Evening service in G min.: Magnificat; Nunc dimittis. Latin Psalm: Jehovah, quam multi sunt hostes mei. Te Deum & Jubilate in D.*

(B) * DG Double (ADD) 459 487–2 (2). D. Thomas, Christ Church Cathedral, Oxford , Ch., E. Concert, Preston.

Recorded in the Henry Wood Hall in 1980, this admirable collection of Purcell's church music is self-recommending. Apart from David Thomas's fine contribution (in the verse anthems) the soloists come from the choir, and very good they are too, especially the trebles. The performances are full of character, vigorous, yet with the widest range of colour and feeling, well projected in a recording which is both spacious and detailed. The sound is excellent in its current transfer, and as a DG Archiv Double this is even more attractive.

Odes & Welcome Songs Vols. 1–8 (complete).

*** Hyp. CDS 44031/8. Soloists, New College, Oxford, Ch., King's Cons., King.

Odes & Welcome songs, Vol. 1: *Arise my muse (1690); Now does the glorious day appear (1689) (Odes for Queen Mary's birthday); Ode for St Cecilia's Day: Welcome to all pleasures (1683).*

*** Hyp. CDA 66314. Fisher, Bonner, Bowman, Chance, Daniels, Ainsley, George, Potts, King's Cons., King.

Odes & Welcome songs, Vol. 2: *Ode on St Cecilia's Day (Hail! bright Cecilia!) (1692). Ode for the birthday of the Duke of Gloucester: Who can from joy refrain (1695).*

*** Hyp. CDA 66349. Fisher, Bonner, Bowman, Covey-Crump, Ainsley, George, Keenlyside, New College, Oxford, Ch., King's Cons., King.

Odes & Welcome songs, Vol. 3: *Ode for Queen Mary's birthday: Celebrate this festival (1693). Welcome song for Charles II (1683): Fly, bold rebellion (1683). Welcome song for James II: Sound the trumpet, beat the drum (1687).*

*** Hyp. CDA 66412. Fisher, Bonner, Bowman, Kenny, Covey-Crump, Müller, George, Pott, King's Cons., King.

Odes & Welcome songs, Vol. 4: *Ode for Mr Maidwell's School: Celestial music did the gods inspire (1689). Ode for the wedding of Prince George of Denmark & Princess Anne: From hardy climes and dangerous toils of war (1683). Welcome song for James II: Ye tuneful muses (1686).*

*** Hyp. CDA 66456. Fisher, Bonner, Bowman, Kenny, Covey-Crump, Daniels, George, Pott, King's Cons., King.

Odes & Welcome songs, Vol. 5: *Ode for the birthday of Queen Mary: Welcome, welcome, glorious morn (1691). Ode for the Centenary of Trinity College, Dublin: Great parent, hail to thee (1694). Welcome song for King Charles II: The Summer's absence unconcerned we bear (1682).*

*** Hyp. CDA 66476. Fisher, Tubb, Bowman, Short, Covey-Crump, Ainsley, George, Pott, King's Cons., King.

Odes & Welcome songs, Vol. 6: *Ode for Queen Mary's birthday: Love's goddess sure was blind (1692). Ode for St Cecilia's Day: Laudate Ceciliam (1683). Ode for St Cecilia's Day: Raise, raise the voice (c. 1685). Welcome song for Charles II: From those serene and rapturous joys (1684).*

*** Hyp. CDA 66494. Fisher, Seers, Bowman, Short, Padmore, Tusa, George, Evans, King's Cons., King.

Odes & Welcome songs, Vol. 7: *Welcome song for Charles II: Swifter Isis, swifter flow (1681). Welcome song for the Duke of York: What shall be done in behalf of the man? (1682). Yorkshire feast song: Of old, when heroes thought it base (1690).*

*** Hyp. CDA 66587. Fisher, Hamilton, Bowman, Short, Covey-Crump, Daniels, George, Evans, King's Cons., King.

Odes & Welcome songs, Vol. 8: *Ode for the birthday of Queen Mary: Come ye sons of Art, away (1694). Welcome song for Charles II: Welcome, viceregent of the mighty king (1680). Welcome song for King James: Why, why are all the Muses mute?*

*** Hyp. CDA 66598. Fisher, Bonner, Bowman, Chance, Padmore, Ainsley, George, Evans, Ch. of New College, Oxford, King's Cons., King.

Just what a wealth of inspiration Purcell brought to the occasional music he wrote for his royal and noble masters comes out again and again in Robert King's splendid collection of the Odes and Welcome songs. It is sad that for three centuries this fine music has been largely buried, with just a few of the Odes achieving popularity. In those, King's performances do not always outshine the finest of previous versions, but with an outstanding team of soloists as well as his King's Consort the performances achieve a consistently high standard, with nothing falling seriously short. Being able to hear previously unrecorded rarities alongside the well-known works sets Purcell's achievement vividly in context, helped by informative notes in each volume, written by King himself. Volume 1 includes the shorter of the two *St Cecilia odes* and immediately – among the fine team of soloists – it is a delight to hear such superb artists as the counter-tenors James Bowman and Michael Chance in duet. Volume 3 with the 1693 *Birthday ode* and Volume 7 with the fascinating *Yorkshire feast song* are two more CDs that would make good samplers. Those who want to dive in at the deep end should invest in the complete set, where all eight CDs are offered in a slip-case. First-rate sound throughout.

Ode for Queen Mary's Birthday: Celebrate This Festival (1693).

(N) (M) Decca/BBC Analogue 466 819-2. Harper, Veasey, Watts, Pears, Fischer-Dieskau, Shirley-Quirk, Ambrosian Singers, ECO, Britten – BACH: *Cantatas Nos. 102–151.* ***

This account of the Purcell Birthday Ode of 1693 is taken from the concert which inaugurated the Queen Elizabeth Hall in March 1967, a happy choice. It was also the London debut of the countertenor, James Bowman, already very distinctive. Harper is superb, as is John Shirley-Quirk, with Josephine Veasey firm and clear in her minor-key aria with its tricky ornamentation. Peter Pears is the constant among the soloists, wonderfully assured, with the juxtaposition of Bach and Purcell bringing out the extra ease he has in Purcell, partly because the vocal figuration often relates to Britten's own music. Any discrepancies in the sound have been well ironed out.

(i) *Odes for Queen Mary's Birthday: Come ye sons of art; Love's Goddess sure.* **(ii)** *Funeral Music for Queen Mary (March; Canzone; Funeral sentences: Man that is born of woman; In the midst of life; Thou knowest, Lord; March; Anthems: Hear my prayer, O Lord; Remember not, Lord, our offences).* **Anthems:** *Blessed are they that fear the Lord; My beloved spake; Rejoice in the Lord alway.* **(iii) (Organ)** *The Queen's doleur; Trumpet minuet in C (including March from The Married Beau); Trumpet tunes in C & D; Voluntary in A.*

(B) *** EMI (ADD) CZS5 69270-2 (2). (i) Burrowes, Bowman, Lloyd, Brett; Ch.; York Skinner, Hill, Shaw, Lloyd; L. Early Music Cons., Munrow; (ii) Cockerhan, King, Hayes, Chilcott, Morell, Castle, Byram-Wigfield, Robarts, Grier, King's College Ch., ASMF, Philip Jones Brass Ens., Ledger;

(iii) Brosse (organ of Cathedral of Sainte Marie de Saint Bertrand de Comminges).

Of Purcell's series of ceremonial odes for the birthdays of Queen Mary *Come ye sons of art* is the richest, with its magnificent overture or symphony. Such memorable pieces as the duet, *Sound the trumpet,* and *Love's goddess sure,* though not quite so grand, bring more Purcellian delights. David Munrow gives sensitive, intelligent performances of both works, which deliberately opt for an intimate scale, using old instruments and an authentic style of string playing; the results are entirely congenial to the ear. The intimacy clearly detracts from the sense of grandeur and panoply which are apt for this music but, with refined yet full sound to match, this alternative approach is equally satisfying. As can be seen from the listing above, *Queen Mary's Funeral Music* consists of far more than the unforgettable *March* for lugubrious trombones (sackbuts) with punctuating timpani (later repeated without timpani), which still sounds so modern to our ears. Here Philip Ledger has the advantage of spacious sound and his account of the *March* is darkly memorable. The anthems are well sung too, if slightly less alertly. The organ pieces, very well played, are particularly characterful heard on a comparatively pungent French organ. They are used as a postlude for the two birthday odes, while the voluntary (on disc 2) becomes an overture to introduce the three great verse anthems. The trumpet ayres are jolly, with a hurdy-gurdy effect in the Minuet framing a march from *The Married Beau;* the *Voluntary in C* is dark in timbre to match the dolorous piece specifically dedicated to the Queen.

Odes for Queen Mary's Birthday: Come Ye Sons of Art; Love's Goddess Sure was Blind; Now Does the Glorious Day Appear.

(N)(M) ** Virgin VM5 61844-2. Gooding, Bowman, Robson, Crook, Wilson-Johnson, George, Ch. & O of Age of Enlightenment, Leonhardt.

A happy triptych on Virgin, but Leonhardt's personality is firmly stamped on all three works here. The orchestral texture has the less than fully-nourished sound of period stringed instruments, and Leonhardt's jogging rhythm at the opening of *Now Does the Glorious Day Appear* seems a little too circumspect for that joyful ode. Indeed, his sobriety tends to override the music's character. He has a splendid chorus and superb soloists, and they are in excellent voice. James Bowman stands out, as does Julia Gooding (most winning, both in *Love's Goddess Sure* and in her lovely duet with the oboe, *Bid the virtues,* in *Come Ye Sons of Art*). But Leonhardt's restraint prevents Purcell's inspired settings from taking the fullest flight.

Alfred Deller Edition: (i) Come ye Sons of Art (Ode on the birthday of Queen Mary, 1694); Anthems: (ii) My beloved spake; (iii) Rejoice in the Lord alway (Bell anthem); (iv) Welcome to all the pleasures (Ode on St Cecilia's Day, 1683).

(M) **(*) Van. (ADD) 08.5060 71. Deller, Deller Consort; (i) Deller, Thomas, Bevan, Oriana Concert Ch. & O; (ii) Cantelo, English, Bevan; (iii) (iv) Kalmar O; (iii) Thomas,

Sheppard, Tear, Worthley; Oriana Concert O; (iv) Cantelo, McLoughlin, English, Grundy, Bevan.

An enjoyable anthology, now reissued as part of the Alfred Deller Edition, showing Deller at his finest. The other soloists are good too, especially the tenor, Gerald English. The two anthems make a fine centrepiece. The warm, expressively played accompaniments are rather different from the effect one would achieve today with original instruments. The recording is closely balanced; although made at either Walthamstow or Cricklewood Church, the effect is not quite as spacious as one would expect, though pleasingly full.

Come, ye Sons of Art Away (Ode on the birthday of Queen Mary, 1694); Funeral Music for Queen Mary (1695); Funeral Sentences; Odes for St Cecilia's day: Hail! bright Cecilia; Welcome to all the pleasures.

(BB) *** Virgin 2 × 1 VBD5 61582-2 (2). Kirkby, Chance, K. Smith, Covey-Crump, Elliott, Grant, George, Thomas, Taverner Ch. & Players, Parrott.

Come, ye Sons of Art, Away; Ode for St Cecilia's Day: Welcome to all the pleasures. Of old when heroes thought it base (The Yorkshire Feast song).

(B) *** DG 449 853-2. J. Smith, Chance, Wilson, Richardson, Ainsley, George, E. Concert Ch., E. Concert, Pinnock.

A most inexpensive collection of key Purcell works on Virgin with many individual touches in Andrew Parrott's performances. His speeds are generally slower and rhythms less alert than those of Trevor Pinnock, but these are still very fine performances, sounding more intimate as recorded. Parrott takes the view that Purcell would have used a high tenor and not a second counter-tenor in *Sound the trumpet*, and it works well, with John Mark Ainsley joining the counter-tenor, Timothy Wilson. In his pursuit of authenticity Parrott has eliminated the timpani part from the well-known solemn march for slide trumpets (performed here on sackbutts) in the *Queen Mary Funeral Music* – a pity when it becomes far less effective. The central anthem is beautifully done, and it is good also to have the three *Funeral Sentence Anthems*, written a few years earlier. *Hail! bright Cecilia* is also relatively reticent, but brings another performance full of incidental delights, particularly vocal ones from a brilliant array of no fewer than twelve solo singers, notably five excellent tenors. With pitch lower than usual, some numbers that normally require counter-tenors can be sung by tenors. Interestingly, Parrott includes the *Voluntary in D minor* for organ before the wonderful aria celebrating that instrument and St Cecilia's sponsorship of it, *O wondrous machine*. And, if you feel it holds up the music's flow on, it can easily be omitted.

Pinnock directs exuberant performances of all three works. The weight and brightness of the choral sound go with infectiously lifted rhythms, making the music dance, as in the first chorus of *Welcome to all pleasures*, the best-known of the Queen Mary *Odes*, the one for 1694. There the line, 'to celebrate this triumphant day', could not come over more catchingly. The soloists are all outstanding, with the counter-tenor duetting of Michael Chance and Timothy Wilson for *Sound the trumpet* delectably pointed. The neglected *Yorkshire Feast song* (composed in 1690 for 'an other-wise obscure gathering of York nobility') is full of wonderful inspirations, like the tenor and counter-tenor duet, *And now when the renown'd Nassau* – a reference to the new king, William III.

Come, ye Sons of Art Away; Funeral Music for Queen Mary (1695); Ode on St Cecilia's Day (Hail! bright Cecilia).

(M) *** Erato Ultima 8573 88044-2 (2). Soloists: Monteverdi Ch. & O, Equale Brass Ens., Gardiner.

Come, ye Sons of Art is splendidly paired here with the unforgettable funeral music he wrote on the death of the same monarch. With the Monteverdi Choir at its most incisive and understanding the performances are exemplary, and the recording, though balanced in favour of the instruments, is clear and refined. Among the soloists Thomas Allen is outstanding, while the two counter-tenors give a charming performance of the duet, *Sound the Trumpet*. The *Funeral Music* includes the well-known *Solemn march* for trumpets and drums, a *Canzona* and simple anthem given at the funeral, and two of Purcell's most magnificent anthems setting the *Funeral sentences*. Recording made in 1976 in Rosslyn Hill Chapel, London.

Gardiner's characteristic vigour and alertness in Purcell also come out superbly in the 1692 *St Cecilia Ode* – not as well known as some of the other odes he wrote, but a masterpiece. Soloists and chorus are outstanding even by Gardiner's high standards, and the recording excellent. Recording made in 1982 in the Barbican Concert Hall, London.

Jubilate Deo in D; The noise of foreign wars; Ode for St Cecilia's Day; Raise, raise the voice; Te Deum; (i) Trumpet sonata.

(BB) *** Naxos 8.553444. Bern, Bisatt, Robson, Purefoy, Honeyman, Guthrie, The Golden Age Ch. & O, Glenton; (i) with Staff.

These superb examples of Purcell's choral music, both church music and secular cantatas, as well as a brief, joyful trumpet sonata, make an attractive collection, well recorded. The singing is excellent from a group which includes such distinguished singers as the counter-tenor, Christopher Robson, though the instrumental group is lacking in bite in the string section, hardly matching the wind. But this is not enough to detract from the pleasure of the music-making overall. David Staff on the trumpet is outstanding, in both the sonata and the choral works too. Specially fascinating is the première recording of the *Noise of foreign wars*, a substantial fragment of a cantata only recently identified as being by Purcell.

Funeral Music for Queen Mary: March, Anthem & Canzona; 3 Funeral Sentences; 2 Elegies; 2 Coronation Anthems; Anthem for Queen Mary's Birthday, 1688: Now does the glorious day appear.

*** Sony SK 66243. Kirkby, Tubb, Chance, Bostridge, Richardson, Birchall, Westminster Abbey Ch., New L. Consort, Neary (with music by TOLLETT; PAISIBLE; MORLEY; BLOW).

Funeral Music for Queen Mary (with (i) Queen's

epicedium); *March & Canzona on the Death of Queen Mary.* Funeral sentences: *Man that is born of a woman; In the midst of life are we in death; Thou knowest, Lord, the secrets of our hearts.* Anthems: *Hear my prayer; Jehova quam multi sunt.* (ii) *3 (Organ) Voluntaries: in D min.; in G; in C.*

(BB) *** Naxos 8.553129. Oxford Camerata, Summerly; with (i) Lane; (ii) Cummings.

In the ample acoustic of Westminster Abbey, where the music was first performed in 1695, Martin Neary restores the original sequence of musical numbers given at the funeral of Queen Mary. The well-known *March* and *Canzona*, as well as the beautiful anthem, *Thou know'st, Lord, the secrets of our hearts,* are presented along with the settings of the remaining funeral sentences by Thomas Morley, equally inspired, as well as marches by James Paisible and Thomas Tollett. He adds a generous collection of other works inspired by Queen Mary. The result is not ideally clear, with the sound of traffic murmuring in from outside, but is undeniably atmospheric, conveying a weighty devotional intensity. One has a genuine sense of a great ceremonial, not just in the funeral music but in the other works too, including the glorious 1688 Birthday ode, *Now does the glorious day appear,* the first that Purcell composed for the new Queen. The boy trebles of the Abbey Choir are authentic and beautifully tuned. The soloists are outstanding, notably the counter-tenor, Michael Chance, and the tenor, Ian Bostridge.

The Naxos CD follows a similar sequence. This glorious, darkly intense funeral music is here given an outstandingly fresh and clear rendition, vividly recorded, matching even the finest rival versions. The sharpness of focus in the sound means that Purcell's adventurous harmonies with their clashing intervals are given extra dramatic bite in these dedicated performances, marked by fresh, clear soprano tone in place of boy trebles. The choice of extra items – full anthems with their inspired counterpoint rather than verse anthems – is first rate, including as it does the magnificent *Jehova, quam multi sunt* and the wonderfully compressed *Hear my prayer,* both beautifully done. Aptly, the extended solo song for soprano (with simple organ accompaniment), *The Queen's epicedium,* is also included with the funeral music, sung with boyish tone by Carys-Ann Lane.

In Guilty Night (Saul and the Witch of Endor); Man that is born of woman (Funeral sentences); Te Deum & Jubilate Deo in D.

(B) **(*) HM HMA 190207. Deller Cons., Stour Music Festival Ch. & O, Deller.

In Guilty Night is a remarkable dramatic scene depicting Saul's meeting with the Witch of Endor. The florid writing is admirably and often excitingly sung by Alfred Deller himself as the King and Honor Sheppard as the Witch. The *Te Deum and Jubilate* are among Purcell's last and most ambitious choral works; the *Funeral sentences* from early in his career are in some ways even finer in their polyphonic richness. The chorus here is not the most refined on record but, with sensitive direction, this attractive collection is well worth hearing. The recording is good.

SONGS

Songs: *Ah! How sweet it is to love; The earth trembled; An evening hymn; If music be the food of love; I'll sail upon the dog star; I see she flies me ev'rywhere; Let the night perish; Lord, what is man; Morning hymn; A new ground.* Arias: *Birthday ode for Queen Mary: Crown the altar. Bonduca: Oh! Lead me to some peaceful gloom. History of Dioclesian: Since from my dear Astrea's sight. The Indian Queen: I attempt from love's sickness to fly. The Mock marriage: Man that is for woman made. Oedipus: Music for a while. Pausanias: Sweeter than roses. The Rival sisters: Take not a woman's anger ill.*

(BB) *** ASV CDQS 6172. I. Partridge, J. Partridge –
BRITTEN: *Winter words.* ***

Appropriately entitled 'Sweeter than Roses', this is a warmly sympathetic collection of favourite Purcell songs from a tenor whose honeyed tones are ideally suited to recording. With ever-sensitive accompaniment from George Malcolm, who also contributes one brief solo, this is an excellent recommendation for those who resist the pursuit of authenticity. Atmospheric recording, with the voice well forward and the harpsichord image believable and nicely focused.

Songs: *An Evening hymn; Not all my torments; O solitude.* Arias: *Bonduca: O lead me to some peaceful gloom. Don Quixote: From rosy bow'rs. The Fairy Queen: The Plaint; Thrice happy lovers. History of Dioclesian: Since from my dear Astrea's sight. The Indian Queen: I attempt from love's sickness to fly. King Arthur: Fairest isle. Gentleman's Journal of June: If music be the food of love. Oedipus: Music for a while. Pausanias: Sweeter than roses. The History of the Sicilian usurper: Retired from any mortal's sight.*

**(*) HM HMC 190249. Deller, with continuo led by Christie.

Alfred Deller opens here with a touching account of *The Plaint* and is heard at his best in *I attempt from love's sickness to fly, Fairest isle,* and especially the ravishing *Music for a while,* which he made his own. Although in the late 1970s, his voice was no longer quite as smooth on top as on his earlier Vanguard discs, his artistry is if anything even more penetrating, and the stylish accompanying continuo group with Christie at the harpsichord is a great asset.

Songs: *The fatal hour comes on apace; Lord, what is man?; Love's power in my heart; More love or more disdain I crave; Now that the sun hath veiled his light; The Queen's epicedium; Sleep, Adam, sleep; Thou wakeful shepherd; Who can behold Florella's charms.* Arias: *History of Dioclesian: Since from my dear Astrea's sight. Indian Queen: I attempt from love's sickness to fly. King Arthur: Fairest isle. Oedipus: Music for a while. Pausanias: Sweeter than roses. The Rival Sisters: Take not a woman's anger ill. Rule a wife and have a wife: There's not a swain.*

*** Etcetera KTC 1013. Dalton, Uittenbosch, Borstlap.

Andrew Dalton has an exceptionally beautiful counter-tenor voice, creamy even in its upper register to make the extended 'Hallelujahs' of *Lord, what is man?* and *Now that the sun* even more heavenly than usual. A delightful disc, well recorded.

Songs and duets for counter-tenor: *Bonduca: Sing, sing ye Druids. Come, ye sons of art: Sound the trumpet. Elegy on the death of Queen Mary: O dive custos Auriacae domus. The Maid's last prayer: No, resistance is but vain. Ode on St Cecilia's Day: In vain the am'rous flute. O solitude, my sweetest choice. The Queen's epicedium: Incassum, Lesbia rogas. Timon of Athens: Hark how the songsters.*

*** Hyp. CDA 66253. Bowman, Chance, King's Cons., King –
   BLOW: *Ode* etc. ***

A sparkling collection of solos and duets which show both the composer and these fine artists in inspirational form. The performances are joyous, witty and ravishing in their Purcellian melancholy, with often subtle response to word meanings, and King's accompaniments have plenty of character in their own right. Excellent recording.

Songs and dialogues: *Go tell Amynta; Hence fond deceiver; In all our Cinthia's shining sphere; In some kind dream; Lost is my quiet; Stript of their green; What a sad fate is mine; What can we poor females do; Why my poor Daphne, why complaining.* Theatre music: *Amphitryon: Fair Iris and her swain.* Dioclesian: *Tell me why.* King Arthur: *You say 'tis love; For love every creature is formed by his nature.* The Old Bachelor: *As Amoret and Thyrsis lay.*

(N) (B) *** Hyp. Helios CDH 55065. Kirkby, Thomas, Rooley.

This nicely planned Hyperion collection has one solo apiece for each of the singers, but otherwise consists of duets, five of them from dramatic works. These near-ideal performances, beautifully sung and sensitively accompanied on the lute, make a delightful record, helped by excellent sound. Now reissued on the bargain Helios label, this disc is more attractive than ever.

Songs and Duets: *Here let my life; In vain the am'rous flute; Music for a while; Sweetness of nature.*

**(*) Virgin VC5 45342-2. Lésne, Dugardin, La Canzona –
   BLOW: *An Ode on the Death of Mr Henry Purcell* etc. **(*)

It makes an illuminating programme to have John Blow's moving tribute to his former pupil, Purcell, set alongside some of Purcell's songs and duets, even more striking in their ideas. Though the recorders of La Canzona are on the abrasive side, Gérard Lesne and his counter-tenor colleague are stylish singers, well attuned to this repertory. Though *Music for a while* is the best-known item here, such a duet as *In vain the am'rous flute* is just as memorable with its side-slipping chromatics over a ground bass. Close recording.

Other collections

Pavans 1–4; Beati omnes qui timent Dominum; In Guilty Night (Saul and the Witch of Endor); Jehova, quam multi sunt hostes mei; My beloved spake; Te Deum & Jubilate (for St Cecilia's Day, 1694); Te Deum; When on my sick bed I languish.

*** Virgin VC5 45061-2. Taverner Ch., Cons. & Players, Parrott.

Starting with an exceptionally brisk and compelling account of the *Te Deum and Jubilate*, Parrott and his team provide a refreshing and illuminating survey of Purcell's vocal music, punctuated by four of the adventurous, intense *Pavans* which Purcell wrote in his youth, at about the same time as the great sequence of string *Fantasias*. In the relatively brief span of 70 minutes Parrott ranges wide, with the elaborately contrapuntal Latin anthem, *Jehova, quam multi sunt*, one of Purcell's finest, made the more moving, if less grand, with one voice per part, and with the scena about the Witch of Endor, *In Guilty Night*, thrillingly dramatic. Well-matched singing and playing, atmospherically recorded.

(i) *Abdelazar: Suite; (i; ii) Cibell for Trumpet & Strings;* (i) *Dioclesian: Dances from the Masque; Overtures: in D min.; G min.; (i; ii) Sonata for Trumpet & Strings;* (i) *Staircase Overture; Suite in G, Z.770; Timon of Athens: Curtain Tune; (Keyboard): (iii) New Irish Tune; New Scotch Tune; Sefauchi's Farewell; Suite No. 6 in D; Songs:* (iv; i) *Hark how all things; If Love's sweet passion; (iv; iii) If music be the food of love; Lord what is man (Divine hymn); (iv; i) See even night is here; Thus the ever grateful Spring.*

*** Chan. 0571. (i) Purcell Qt; (ii) Bennett; (iii) Woolley; (iv) Bott.

Catherine Bott opens this 72-minute concert with a glorious account of one of Purcell's most famous Shakespearean settings, most artfully decorated: *If music be the food of love*; if anything, the later song, *See, even Night herself is here*, is even more ravishing, given an ethereal introduction by the string group. The instrumental items are most rewarding, notably the attractive unpublished suite of dances in G, while the three Overtures are full of plangent character. Robert Woolley's harpsichord contribution is most infectious (the *New Irish tune*, incidentally, is 'Lilliburlero') and he is beautifully recorded, the harpsichord set back in an intimate acoustic and perfectly in scale. There are few better Purcell anthologies than this, and overall the CD gives an ideal introduction to the music of one of the very greatest English composers. The Chandos recording is first class, well up to the standards of the house.

'Music for England, my England': *Sonata for Trumpet & Strings in D; Abdelazar: Rondeau. The Married Beau: Overture. Come ye Sons of Art (Birthday Ode, 1694): Sound the Trumpet. Music for Funeral of Queen Mary: March; Canzona; 3 Funeral Sentences. Saul and the Witch of Endor. Dido and Aeneas: Dido's Lament. The Indian Queen: Adagio. King Arthur: Fairest Isle; Upon a Quiet Conscience; Act III (complete).*

*** Erato 0630 10700-2. Chance, Bowman, Dawson, Graham, Argenta, Varcoe, Monteverdi Ch., E. Bar. Sol., Gardiner.

Tony Palmer's film on Purcell to a provocative script by the late John Osborne prompted John Eliot Gardiner to make these fine recordings of music for the sound-track. This generous selection provides an excellent sampler of the composer's work.

'Pocket Purcell': *Fantasia VIII; 3 Parts upon a Ground;* Anthem: *Rejoice in the Lord, alway.* Funeral sentences: *Man that is born of woman; In the midst of life; Thou knowest Lord.* (Keyboard) *Ground in Gamut; Organ voluntary in D min.* Songs: *Close thine eyes; If music be the food of love;* Duets: *Close thine eyes; Of all the instruments. Suite of theatre music.*

**(*) Virgin VC5 45116-2. Taverner Cons. Ch. & Players, Parrott.

This attempt at an authentic 'Pocket Purcell' nearly comes off. If perhaps it tries to do too many different things in the space of one 66-minute CD, it certainly shows the composer's breadth and variety of achievement. Opening with a four-movement *Suite of Theatre Music* brightly played (and including the inevitable *Rondeau* from *Abdelazar* which Britten borrowed for his *Young Person's Guide*). There is also a touching *Fantasia for Viols*, a delightful set of keyboard divisions on a *Ground in Gamut*, admirably played by John Toll, and an equally engaging joke-duet for two tenors, *Of all the instruments that are.* Fine, vivid recording; but this would be far more attractive at mid-price.

Ayres, Theatre music and Sacred songs: *Awake awake, ye dead (Hymn for the Day of Judgement); Birthday ode for Queen Mary: Strike the viol.* Dioclesian: *O how happy's he; Chaconne. The earth trembled (A hymn on our Saviour's Passion). The Fairy Queen: One charming night. How plaisant is this flow'ry plain and grove* (ode). *The Indian Queen: Ye twice ten hundred deities; Wake Quivera. Ode for St Cecilia: Raise, raise the voice; Oedipus: Hear, ye sullen pow'rs below; Come away, do not stay. The Old Bachelor: Thus to a ripe consenting maid. Olinda: There ne'er was so wretched a lover as I* (duet). *Timon of Athens: Hark how the songsters. Pavane & Trio.*

(B) **(*) HM HMA 190214. Deller Cons. & Ens., Deller.

Deller has put together what one might regard as a sampler of Purcell's vocal music, a varied collection which includes some of his finest inspirations. Always fresh and often lovely performances, given good if not outstanding recording.

STAGE WORKS AND THEATRE MUSIC

Instrumental suites from: *Dioclesian; The Fairy Queen; The Indian Queen; King Arthur.*

**(*) Sony SK 66169. Tafelmusik, Lamon.

Although Purcell's standard of invention is high and these period performances are vital and alive, if not always strong on expressive charm, it seems perverse to offer 71 minutes of mostly instrumental snippets from essentially vocal works. When the trumpets enter, there is an element of grandeur, certainly, but this is not a disc to play all at once. The bright recording has great immediacy.

Dido and Aeneas (complete).

☻ (M) *** Decca (ADD) 466 387-2. Baker, Herincx, Clark, Sinclair, St Anthony Singers, ECO, Lewis.

*** Erato 4509-98477-2. Gens, Berg, Marin-Degor, Brua, Fouchécourt, Les Arts Florissants, Christie.

(N) (BB) *** Teldec 4509 91191-2. Della Jones, Harvey, Dean Bickley, Murgatroyd, St James's Singers & Bar. Playres, Bolton.

*** Chan. 0586. Ewing, Daymond, MacDougall, R. Evans, Burgess, Bowman, Coll. Mus. 90, Hickox.

*** Ph. 416 299-2. Norman, McLaughlin, Kern, Allen, Power, ECO and Ch., Leppard.

*** Chan. 0521. Kirkby, Thomas, Nelson, Noorman, Rees, Taverner Ch. & Players, Parrott.

(N) **(*) HM HMC 901683. Dawson, Joshua, Finley, Bickley, Clare Col. Chapel Ch., OAE, Jacobs.

(M) (***) EMI mono CDH7 61006-2. Flagstad, Schwarzkopf, Hemsley, Mermaid Theatre Singers & O, Jones.

(BB) **(*) Naxos 8.553108. Scholars Bar. Ens.

(N)(BB) ** Warner Apex 8573 89242-2. Troyanos, Stilwell, Johnson, Ch. & CO, Leppard.

Janet Baker's 1962 recording of *Dido* is a truly great performance. The radiant beauty of the voice is obvious enough, but the opening phrase of *When I am laid in earth* and its repeat a few bars later is a model of graduated mezza voce. Then with the words *Remember me!*, delivered in a monotone, she subdues the natural vibrato to produce a white tone of hushed, aching intensity. Anthony Lewis and the ECO (Thurston Dart a model continuo player) produce the crispest and lightest of playing, which never sounds rushed. Herincx is a rather gruff Aeneas, but the only serious blemish is Monica Sinclair's Sorceress. She overcharacterizes in a way that is quite out of keeping with the rest of the production. Like most vintage Oiseau-Lyre recordings, this was beautifully engineered, and it is a welcome reissue on the Decca Legends label.

On Erato the scale is intimate, with one instrument per part, and one voice per part in choruses, yet Christie cunningly varies the pace to intensify the drama. Though speeds are generally fast, he points an extreme contrast in Dido's two big arias, giving them full expressiveness at measured speeds. In the final exchanges between Dido and Aeneas the hastening speed of the recitative directly reflects the mounting tensions. What then sets this above other period performances is the tragic depth conveyed by Veronique Gens in Dido's great *Lament*, taken very slowly, with the voice drained and agonized in a way that Janet Baker supremely achieved. The young Canadian baritone, Nathan Berg, dark and heroic of tone, is outstanding as Aeneas, making this thinly drawn character for once more than a wimp. Textually this version is interesting for supplying two very brief extra numbers to fill in the music missing from the end of Act II, as indicated in the suriviving libretto. Together they last less than 90 seconds.

Ivor Bolton and the St James's Singers and Players present a period performance, intimately scaled, which avoids the snags of earlier versions, with Della Jones as Dido giving one of her finest recorded performances yet. She has a weightier mezzo than her rivals in other period performances, yet her flexibility over ornamentation is greater, and Dido's lament is the more moving when, unlike Von Otter on DG Archiv, she is restrained over expressive gestures, keeping a tender simplicity. She shades her voice tonally very much as Dame Janet Baker did in her classic recording with Sir Anthony Lewis.

Ivor Bolton's team, recorded with bright immediacy, has no weak link, with Peter Harvey as Aeneas, Susan Bickley as a clear-toned Sorceress, Donna Dean as a characterful Belinda, and Andrew Murgatroyd as the Sailor, a tenor who plays no stylistic tricks. Setting the seal on the performance's success, the choir is among the freshest and liveliest, and the use of the guitar continuo, as well as brief guitar interludes (suggested by the original libretto), enhances the happy intimacy of the presentation. Moreover, this reissue is very reasonably priced.

Richard Hickox's version was linked to a striking television presentation revolving round the magnetically characterful portrayal of the central role by Maria Ewing. In the event her performance, as recorded, is both distinctive and stylish. Combined with Hickox's lively direction, unmarred by intrusive re-allocation of voices, it makes an impressive version, with Karl Daymond making Aeneas a more complex character than usual, with Rebecca Evans a radiant Belinda, matching Ewing in emotional intensity, and with Sally Burgess a characterful, unexaggerated Sorceress. Add the excellent contributions of James Bowman and Jamie MacDougall, and it makes a strong contender, certainly for admirers of Maria Ewing.

Authenticists should keep away, but the security and dark intensity of Jessye Norman's singing make for a memorable performance, heightened in the recitatives by the equally commanding singing of Thomas Allen as Aeneas. The range of expression is very wide – with Norman producing an agonized whisper in the recitative just before *Dido's Lament*. Marie McLaughlin is a pure-toned Belinda, Patrick Power a heady-toned Sailor, singing his song in a West Country accent, while Patricia Kern's performance as the Sorceress uses conventionally sinister expression. Leppard's direction is relatively plain and direct, with some slow speeds for choruses. Excellent recording.

Andrew Parrott's concept of a performance on original instruments has one immediately thinking back to the atmosphere of Josias Priest's school for young ladies where Purcell's masterpiece was first given. The voices enhance that impression, not least Emma Kirkby's fresh, bright soprano, here recorded without too much edge but still very young-sounding. It is more questionable to have a soprano singing the tenor role of the Sailor in Act III; but anyone who fancies the idea of an authentic performance need not hesitate. The sound is well focused, with analogue atmosphere yet with detail enhanced.

René Jacobs directs a characterful and dramatic reading of *Dido and Aeneas*, with Lynne Dawson a pure and refined heroine leading an excellent cast. Speeds tend to be extreme in both directions, with Dido's *Lament* and final chorus very slow indeed, with some heavy underlining. Happily Dawson sustains her line very well in the *Lament*, deeply affecting in her noble dedication. What is more controversial is Jacobs's tendency in choruses not just to underline individual notes – as in the final chorus – but to pull the tempo around outrageously, particularly in the Witches' choruses. So both *Harm's our delight* and *Destruction's our delight* start very slowly indeed, and then have sudden bursts at high speed, with phrasing pulled around too. Many will accept such quirks as part of a characterful experience, particularly when the Sorceress (Susan Bickley) and the two countertenors who take the roles of the first two witches (Dominique Visse and Stephen Wallace) are hilariously characterful in a way that Purcell would certainly have relished. Rosemary Joshua as Belinda, golden in tone, and Gerald Finley as a virile Aeneas are also ideally cast. Well-balanced recording, if with a reverberation that gives some of the choruses a religious flavour.

Though Flagstad's magnificent voice may in principle be too weighty for this music, she scales it down superbly in her noble reading, which brings beautiful shading and masterly control of breath and tone. Schwarzkopf is brightly characterful as Belinda, and though Thomas Hemsley is not ideally sweet-toned as Aeneas, he sings very intelligently; even in this age of period performance, this traditional account under the late Geraint Jones sounds fresh and lively still, not at all heavy. The mono sound, obviously limited, yet captures the voices vividly, and this above all is Flagstad's set. Alas, it has just been deleted.

Using minimum forces, with one-to-a-part strings, the Scholars Baroque Ensemble offer an intimate view of Purcell's compressed epic. Though the instrumental sections are rather rough in ensemble, the performance is vigorous and compelling, with Dido's two great ground-bass arias both given necessary emotional weight. Kym Amps is a warmly expressive heroine, singing with moving restraint in the *Lament*, while Anna Crookes as Belinda sings with fresh, clear tone, and Sarah Connolly with her rich mezzo makes an impressive Sorceress. Though David van Asch is a dry-toned Aeneas, he compensates by his expressiveness. Two improvised guitar dances and an interlude for two violins are added to the surviving musical text where the libretto suggests. Clear, immediate recording.

On the Apex/Erato reissue, Leppard directs a consistently well-sprung and well-played performance, as one would expect, but the overall impression is disappointing, largely because the climax of the opera fails to rise in intensity as it should. Tatiana Troyanos, stylish elsewhere, misses the tragic depth of the great lament of Dido, and without that the focus the impact of the rest falls away. However, it is interesting to have a baritone (Richard Stilwell), instead of a tenor, singing the *Sailor's song*. The recording is excellent.

(i) *Dido and Aeneas* (ed. Britten; complete). (ii) Evening hymn: *When night her purple veil had softly spread*.

(**(*)) BBC mono/stereo BBCB 8003-2. Watson, Pears, J. Sinclair, Mandikian, Clark, Allister, Phillips, Hahessy, Ronayne, Purcell Singers, EOG O, Britten;
(ii) Fischer-Dieskau; Davies; Pople; Britten.

Britten's own performance of *Dido and Aeneas*, using the edition he and Imogen Holst prepared for the English Opera Group, was recorded in mono in the Maida Vale studio in 1959. The distinctive point about the text is that three brief Purcell items are added at the end of Act II, setting the passage in the libretto missing from the score. Britten's direction is alert, with rhythms crisply articulated and speeds on the slow side only in choruses. Though the EOG's strings are relatively sumptuous, he is ahead of his time in use of ornamentation. What is disappointing is the casting. Claire Watson is a reliable soprano but hardly a characterful one, even though she puts great feeling into the *Lament*. Peter Pears is an expressive Aeneas, treating recitative in a Lieder-like way, though in a low-lying role his tone is sometimes gritty. Arda Mandikian repeats the performance she gave earlier as the Witch in the Flagstad recording, characterful but at times ungainly, and Jeannette Sinclair, a fresh, bright Belinda, has moments of shrillness. Following the Britten edition, boy-trebles are used for the roles of Spirit and the Sailor, with often disconcerting results. Britten's edition of Purcell's extended *Evening hymn* makes a valuable bonus, triumphing over current stylistic fashion when it inspires Fischer-Dieskau to give such a moving and intense performance.

(i) *Dido and Aeneas* (arr.Britten/Holst); *The Fairy Queen* (adapted Britten).

(N)(B) *** Double Decca (ADD) 468 561-2 (2). (i) Baker, Pears, Burrowes, Reynolds, Lott, Palmer, Hodgson, Tear, L. Op. Ch., Aldeburgh Fest. Strings, Bedford; (ii) Vyvyan, Bowman, Pears, Wells, Partridge, Shirley-Quirk, Brannigan, Amb. Op. Ch., ECO, Britten.

Both these productions were planned by Britten, but in the event it was Steuart Bedford who stepped in to conduct the Decca recording of the Britten/Holst edition of *Dido and Aeneas*, with Dame Janet Baker returning (in 1975) to the area of her earliest major success in the recording studio. Her portrait of Dido is even richer than before, with more daring tonal colouring, and challengingly slow tempi for the two big arias.

Many will prefer the heartfelt spontaneity of her youthful performance under Anthony Lewis, but the range of expression on the newer version is unparalleled, and the richer, more modern Kingsway Hall recording adds to the vividness of the experience. With Norma Burrowes a touchingly youthful Belinda, with Peter Pears using Lieder style in the unexpected role (for him) of Aeneas, with Anna Reynolds an admirable Sorceress, and other star singers in supporting roles, there is hardly a weak link, and the London Opera Chorus relishes Bedford's often unusual tempi (that suggest earlier consultation with Britten).

Britten's edition of *The Fairy Queen* grouped Purcell's music into four sections, *Oberon's Birthday*, *Night and Silence*, *The Sweet Passion* and *Epithalamium*. This version was first heard at the Aldeburgh Festival in 1967, and here the authentic glow of a Maltings performance (1971 vintage) is beautifully conveyed in the playing, the singing and the recording. Philip Ledger's imaginative harpsichord continuo is placed too far to one side, but otherwise the sound can hardly be faulted. The cast is consistently satisfying, with Peter Pears and Jennifer Vyvyan surviving from an earlier 'complete' mono recording directed by Anthony Lewis. At Double Decca price this is well worth exploring.

Dido and Aeneas: Dido's Lament (arr. Stokowski).

(M) *** EMI (ADD) CDM5 66760-2. RPO, Stokowski –

DVORAK: *String Serenade;* VAUGHAN WILLIAMS: *Fantasia on a Theme by Thomas Tallis.* ***

Stokowski's indulgent arrangement of Purcell's famous *Lament* is certainly not for purists. But Stokowski feels this music deeply: it is beautifully played and recorded, and the lovely melody is genuinely touching.

Dioclesian; Timon of Athens (Masque).

(M) *** Erato 4509 96556-2 (2). Dawson, Fisher, Covey-Crump, Elliott, George, Varcoe, Monteverdi Ch., E. Bar. Sol., Gardiner.

*** Chan. 0569/70. Pierard, Bowman, Ainsley, George, Coll. Mus. 90, Hickox.

Dioclesian; Timon of Athens: Masques only.

*** Chan. 0568. (as above).

The martial music, shining with trumpets, is what stands out in *Dioclesian*, adapted from a Jacobean play first given in 1622. Gardiner is such a lively conductor, regularly drawing out the effervescence in Purcell's inspiration, that the result is delightfully refreshing, helped by an outstanding team of soloists. The incidental music for *Timon of Athens* offers more buried treasure, including such enchanting inventions as *Hark! how the songsters of the grove*, with its 'Symphony of pipes imitating the chirping of birds', and a fine *Masque for Cupid and Bacchus*, beautifully sung by Lynne Dawson, Gillian Fisher and Stephen Varcoe. Excellent Erato sound.

Following John Eliot Gardiner on Erato, both Trevor Pinnock on DG Archiv and Richard Hickox on Chandos offer the same apt coupling of *Dioclesian* and *Timon of Athens* (see above), both sets of theatre music involving masques. Hickox takes a lighter view, at times more detached, often adopting faster speeds and using on balance the most consistent team of soloists, including in smaller roles such outstanding younger singers as Ian Bostridge and Nathan Berg. On the other hand, he does not include the overture to *Timon* which Gardiner does offer. The single Chandos CD contains the masque music only.

The Fairy Queen (complete).

*** DG 419 221-2 (2). Harrhy, J. Smith, Nelson, Priday, Penrose, Stafford, Evans, Hill, Varcoe, Thomas, Monteverdi Ch., E. Bar. Sol. Gardiner.

*** HM HMC 901308/9. Argenta, Dawson, Daniels, Loonen, Correas, Les Arts Florissants, Christie.

(B) *** Naxos 8.550660-1 (2). Atherton, Amps, Davidson & Soloists, Scholars Bar. Ens., Van Asch.

(B) **(*) HM HMA 190257/8. Sheppard, Knibbs, Bevan, Platt, A. Deller, Jenkins, M. Deller, Buttrey, Clarke, Stour Music Ch. & O, A. Deller.

**(*) Erato 4509 98507-2 (2). Bott, Thomas, Schopper, Amsterdam Bar. Ch. & O, Koopman.

Purcell's setting of Shakespeare's *Midsummer Night's Dream*, written in 1692, takes the form of five masques, each symbolizing one aspect of the play. Gardiner's performance is a delight from beginning to end, for, though authenticity and completeness reign, scholarship is worn lightly and the result is consistently exhilarating, with no longueurs whatever. The fresh-toned soloists are first rate, while Gardiner's regular choir and orchestra excel themselves, with Purcell's sense of fantasy brought out in each succeeding number. Beautifully clear and well-balanced recording.

William Christie uses a far bigger team of both singers and instrumentalists than Gardiner, allowing a wider range of colours. The bite of the performance is increased by the relative dryness of the recorded sound. Among Christie's soloists, Nancy Argenta and Lynne Dawson are outstanding, and the whole team is a strong one. The number of singers in solo roles allows them to be used together as chorus too – an authentic seventeenth-century practice. This makes a vigorous and refreshing alternative to the fine Gardiner set; but the Harmonia Mundi booklet is inadequate.

For Naxos at bargain price the Scholars Baroque Ensemble offer an outstanding version, stylishly presented with a refreshing vigour in its scholarly approach. The recording too is exceptionally bright and immediate, regularly giving the illusion of a dramatic entertainment on stage. Logically this version, unlike previous ones, presents the purely instrumental numbers designed as interludes for *A Midsummer Night's Dream* as an appendix, rather than including them during the course of the musical entertainment of five separate masques. The humour of the Scene of the Drunken Poet is touched on delightfully without exaggeration, thanks to David van Asch, as is the Dialogue between Corydon and Mopsa, though the counter-tenor, Angus Davidson, has a flutter in the voice that the recording exaggerates. Outstanding among the sopranos are Diane Atherton, singing most beautifully in the Night solo of Act II, and Kym Amps, not only bright and agile in *Hark! The ech'ing air* but making the plaint, *O ever let me weep*, of Act V into the emotional high-point of the whole performance. Instrumental playing on period instruments is first rate, and the chorus sings consistently with bright, incisive attack.

Deller's set was recorded – very well too – at the Stour Music Festival in 1972. All the solo singing is of a high standard, with Honor Sheppard particularly memorable as Night in Act II, well matched by Jean Knibbs's Mystery in some of Purcell's most evocative writing. Norman Platt is a suitably bucolic Drunken Poet in Act I and becomes one of a pair of West Country haymakers (Alfred Deller obviously enjoying himself as his companion, Mopsa) in Act III. The many ensembles are eloquently sung, and its robust warmth and Deller's considerable concern for detail make for an enjoyable entertainment, well worth its modest price when so smoothly and vividly transferred to CD.

Ton Koopman's version is generally rather mellower than its period-performance rivals. Koopman's approach to each successive number is strongly characterized, at times idiosyncratic, but always convincing, and he offers some fine solo singing from the three billed soloists, notably from Catherine Bott whose accounts of *Ye gentle spirits*, taken very slowly, and of *Hark! The ech'ing air* have an unsurpassed richness and intensity. The soloists billed in small print are less consistent, but Koopman's understanding of this enigmatic Purcell masterpiece is never in doubt. He is helped by excellent singing and playing from the Amsterdam Choir and Orchestra.

The Indian Queen (incidental music; complete).

(M) *** Erato (ADD) 4509 96551-2. Hardy, Fisher, Harris, Smith, Stafford, Hill, Elwes, Varcoe, Thomas, Monteverdi Ch., E. Bar. Soloists, Gardiner.

The Erato version is fully cast and uses an authentic accompanying baroque instrumental group. The choral singing is especially fine, with the close of the work movingly expressive. John Eliot Gardiner's choice of tempi is apt and the soloists are all good, although the men are more strongly characterful than the ladies; nevertheless the lyrical music comes off well. The recording is spacious and well balanced. However the *Masque of Hymen* is not included.

The Indian Queen (complete; with Daniel PURCELL (c. 1661–1717): The Masque of Hymen).

*** O-L 444 339-2. Kirkby, Bott, Ainsley, D. Thomas, Finley, Williams, AAM Ch. & O, Hogwood.

(BB) **(*) Naxos 8.553752. Soloists, Ch., Scholars Bar. Ens.

Hogwood's recording of Purcell's fourth and last semi-opera, left incomplete at his death, is the first to include the Wedding cantata which the composer's brother, Daniel, wrote to round off the entertainment. It makes an attractive if inconsistent addition to a score which contains vintage Purcell inspirations, notably the solo with chorus, *All dismal sounds*, which was the last part of the work completed by Purcell himself. The elaborate chromatics in that confirm the continuing vigour of Purcell's genius to the end. With John Mark Ainsley, Emma Kirkby and Catherine Bott all making outstanding solo contributions, and with clean-cut period playing from the orchestra, this performance on a relatively grand scale is consistently convincing, by turns lively and moving.

The Naxos version also comes with the added bonus of the concluding *Masque of Hymen*, which Daniel Purcell added after his brother's death, and that makes for a celebratory instead of a tragic conclusion. The work overall suits the lively style of the Scholars Baroque Ensemble admirably, on a scale that is rather more intimate than will be found on most rival versions, with one instrument per part. There is bright, clear recording to match, with dances and trumpet-tunes well sprung. The choral work is first rate; but when the singers come to their solos, the voices (mostly unidentified as to who sings what) are uneven, and the delivery is often rather unsteady. The fresh-toned soprano, Anna Crookes, makes an honourable exception. Yet solos are usually short, and what matters is the overall freshness, vigour and intensity.

King Arthur (complete).

✪ *** Erato 4509 98535-2 (2). Gens, McFadden, Padmore, Best, Salomaa, Les Arts Florissants, Christie.

(M) *** Erato 4509 96552-2 (2). J. Smith, Fischer, Priday, Ross, Stafford, Elliot, Varcoe, Monteverdi Ch., E. Bar. Sol., Gardiner.

*** DG 435 490-2 (2). Argenta, Gooding, Perillo, MacDougal, Tucker, Bannatyne-Scott, Finley, Ch. & E. Concert, Pinnock.

Christie's Erato recording of the musical numbers consistently reflects stage experience. Some may not like the crowd noises in the more rollicking numbers but, more than his rivals, Christie brings out the jollity behind much of the piece. Even the pomposo manner of some of the Act Tunes (or interludes) has fun in it, with the panoply of the ceremonial music swaggering along genially. Few will resist the jollity of *Your hay it is mow'd* when the chorus even includes 'gentlemen of the orchestra' in the last verse. Christie's soloists are generally warmer and weightier than Pinnock's, notably Véronique Gens as Venus, sustaining Christie's exceptionally slow speed for *Fairest isle*. Otherwise speeds are generally on the fast side, with *Shepherd, shepherd, cease decoying* deliciously light and brisk. The vigour of Purcell's inspiration in this semi-opera has never been more winningly conveyed in a period performance on disc, with full-bodied instrumental sound set against a helpful but relatively dry acoustic, giving immediacy to the drama.

Gardiner's solutions to the textual problems carry complete conviction, as for example his placing of the superb *Chaconne in F* at the end instead of the start. Solo singing for the most part is excellent, with Stephen Varcoe outstanding among the men. *Fairest isle* is treated very gently, with Gill Ross, boyish of tone, reserved just for that number. Throughout, the chorus is characteristically fresh and vigorous, and the instrumentalists beautifully marry authentic technique to pure, unabrasive sounds.

Pinnock opens with the *Chaconne*, which is placed before the *Overture*. His performance is consistently refreshing and can be recommended alongside, though not in preference to Christie's. Linda Perillo makes a charming Philidel. Brian Bannatyne-Scott is superb in Aeolus's *Ye blust'ring brethren*, and in his *Frost aria* he achieves an unusual if controversial effect by beginning his series of shakes from slightly under the note. Not surprisingly, Nancy Argenta sings beautifully in the double roles of Cupid and Venus and her *Fairest isle* will not disappoint; both chorus and orchestra sing and play throughout with consistent vitality. The DG recording is first class, but why no coupling? The second CD plays for only 39 minutes.

The Tempest (incidental music).

(M) *** Erato (ADD) 4509 96555-2. J. Smith, Hardy, Hall, Elwes, Varcoe, Thomas, Earle, Monteverdi Ch. & O, Gardiner.

Whether or not Purcell himself wrote this music for Shakespeare's last play (the scholarly arguments are still unresolved), Gardiner demonstrates how delightful it is, a masterly collection, in performances both polished and stylish and with excellent solo and choral singing. At least the overture is clearly Purcell's, and that sets a pattern for a very varied collection of numbers, including three da capo arias and a full-length masque celebrating Neptune for Act V.

Theatre Music (collection).

Disc 1: *Abdelazar: Overture & Suite. Distressed Innocence: Overture & Suite. The Gordian Knot Untied: Overture & Suite; The Married Beau: Overture & Suite. Sir Anthony Love: Overture & Suite.*

Disc 2: *Bonduca: Overture & Suite. Circe: Suite. The Old Bachelor: Overture & Suite. The Virtuous Wife: Overture & Suite.*

Disc 3: *Amphitrion: Overture & Suite; Overture in G min.; Don Quixote: Suite.*

Disc 4: *Overture in G min. The Double Dealer: Overture & Suite. Henry II, King of England: In vain, 'gainst love, in vain I strove. The Richmond Heiress: Behold the man. The Rival Sisters: Overture; 3 Songs. Tyrannic Love: Hark my Damilcar! (duet); Ah! how sweet it is to love. Theodosius: excerpts. The Wives' Excuse: excerpts.*

Disc 5: *Overture in D min.; Cleomenes, the Spartan Hero: No, no, poor suff'ring heart. A Dialogue between Thirsis and Daphne: Why, my Daphne, why complaining?. The English Lawyer: My wife has a tongue: excerpts. A Fool's Preferment: excerpts. The History of King Richard II: Retir'd from any mortal's sight. The Indian Emperor: I look'd and saw within. The Knight of Malta: At the close of the ev'ning. The Libertine: excerpts. The Marriage-hater Match'd: As soon as the chaos . . . How vile are the sordid intregues. The Massacre of Paris: The genius lo (2 settings). Oedipus: excerpts. Regulus: Ah me! to many deaths. Sir Barnaby Whigg: Blow, blow, Boreas, blow. Sophonisba: Beneath the poplar's shadow. The Wives' Excuse: excerpts.*

Disc 6: *Chacony; Pavans Nos. 1–5; Trio Sonata for Violin, Viola de Gamba & Organ. Aureng-Zebe: I see, she flies me. The Canterbury Guests: Good neighbours why?. Epsom Wells: Leave these useless arts. The Fatal Marriage: 2 songs. The Female Virtuosos: Love, thou art best. Love Triumphant: How happy's the husband. The Maid's Last Prayer: excerpts. The Mock Marriage: Oh! how you protest; Man is for the woman made. Oroonoko: Celemene, pray tell me. Pausanius: Song (Sweeter than roses) & duet. Rule a Wife and Have a Wife: There's not a swain. The Spanish Friar: Whilst I with grief.*

(M) *** O-L (IMS) (ADD) 425 893-2 (6). Kirkby, Nelson, Lane, Roberts, Lloyd, Bowman, Hill, Covey-Crump, Elliott, Byers, Bamber, Pike, Thomas, Keyte, Shaw, George, Taverner Ch., AAM, Hogwood.

Most of the music Purcell wrote for the theatre is relatively little heard and much of the music comes up with striking freshness in these performances using authentic instruments. As well as the charming dances and more ambitious overtures, as the series proceeds we are offered more extended scenas with soloists and chorus, of which the nine excerpts from *Theodosius*, an early score (1680), are a particularly entertaining example. Before that, on Disc 3 we have already had the highly inventive *Overture and Incidental Music* for *Don Quixote*, with much enchanting singing from both the soprano soloists, Emma Kirkby and Judith Nelson. Disc 4 also includes a delightful duet from *The Richmond Heiress*, representing a flirtation in music. There are other attractive duets elsewhere, for instance the nautical *Blow, blow, Boreas, blow* from *Sir Barnaby Whigg*, which could fit admirably into *HMS Pinafore* (Rogers Covey-Crump and David Thomas) and the jovial *As soon as the chaos* from *The*

Marriage-hater Match'd. In *Ah me! to many deaths* from *Regulus,* Judith Nelson is at her most eloquent while, earlier on Disc 5, she sings charmingly the familiar *Nymphs and shepherds,* which comes from *The Libertine,* a particularly fine score with imaginative use of the brass. The equally famous *Music for a while,* beautifully sung by James Bowman, derives from *Oedipus.* The last disc also includes a splendidly boisterous *Quartet* from *The Canterbury Guests.* The collection is appropriately rounded off by members of the Academy giving first-class performances of some of Purcell's instrumental music, ending with the famous *Chacony.* The discs are comprehensively documented and with full texts included.

QUANTZ, Joseph Joachim (1697–1773)

Flute Concertos: in C; in D (For Potsdam); G; G min.

*** RCA RD 60247. Galway, Württemberg CO, Heilbron, Faerber.

Quantz was a skilled musician and all four concertos here are pleasing, while their slow movements show a genuine flair for melody. Quantz also wrote well-organized allegros, and the opening *Allegro assai* of the *G major* shows him at his most vigorous, even if perhaps the *Potsdam Concerto* is overall the best of the four works here. The thoroughly musical James Galway is most winning in the lyrical cantilenas, and the Württemberg group accompany with polish and much vitality. Excellent sound.

QUILTER, Roger (1877–1953)

A Children's Overture.

(M) ** EMI (ADD) CDM7 64131-2. Light Music Society O, Dunn (with TOMLINSON: *Suite of English Folk Dances*) – HELY-HUTCHINSON: *Carol Symphony;* VAUGHAN WILLIAMS: *Fantasia on Christmas Carols.* **

The neglect of this charming overture, skilfully constructed from familiar nursery rhymes, is inexplicable. Sir Vivian Dunn gives a good if not remarkable performance and the recording too is pleasing rather than outstanding. But the music itself is a delight. Ernest Tomlinson's suite of six folk-tunes, simply presented and tastefully scored, makes an attractive bonus. Again the sound is acceptable but could be richer.

A Children's Overture; Country Pieces; 3 English Dances; As You Like It: Suite; The Rake: Suite; Where the Rainbow Ends: Suite.

**(*) Marco 8.223444. Slovak RSO (Bratislava), Leaper.

Adrian Leaper plays the enchanting *Children's Overture* with the lightest touch, and the transparency of the recording ensures that all the woodwind detail comes through nicely, even if his performance could ideally have had a shade more momentum. One might also have wished for a bigger band with a more opulent string sheen, but the texture here well suits the suites of incidental music, an agreeable mixture of the styles of Edward German (especially the *Country Dance*

from *As You Like It*), Eric Coates and sub-Elgar of the *Nursery Suites.* All this nicely scored and amiably tuneful music is freshly and spontaneously presented and the recording is nicely resonant.

RABAUD, Henri (1873–1949)

Divertissement sur des chansons russes, Op. 2; Eglogue, Op. 7; Mârouf, savetier du Caire: dances; Symphonic Poem after Lenau's Faust (Procession nocturne), Op. 6; Suites anglaises Nos. 2–3.

** Marco 8.223503. Rheinland-Pfalz PO, Segerstam.

The *Eglogue* was Rabaud's first orchestral piece and derives its inspiration from the first *Eclogue* of Virgil. The dances from *Mârouf, savetier du Caire* have an appropriately oriental flavour since the opera itself is based on an episode from the *Arabian Nights.* The *Procession nocturne* is a tone-poem based on the same Lenau poem which inspired Liszt's *Nächtlige Zug* and is the most atmospheric of the pieces on this disc. The *Suites anglaises* are arrangements of Byrd, Farnaby and other Elizabethan composers that Rabaud made for a 1917 production of *The Merchant of Venice.* Like Roger-Ducasse, Rabaud's music is not strongly personal, but it is distinctly Gallic and well worth investigating. Segerstam and his orchestra show a real sympathy with this turn-of-the-century French repertoire, and they are decently recorded too.

RABE, Folke (born 1935)

Sardinsarkofagen (Sardine Sarcophagus).

(N) *** BIS CD 1021. Hardenberger, Malmö SO, Varga – BORTZ: *Trumpet Concerto.* SANDSTROM: *Trumpet Concerto No. 2.* ***

The Swedish composer Folke Rabe is now in his mid-60s and writes effectively for brass, though such earlier pieces as we have heard leave us unpersuaded that his is a notable creative gift. His *Sardinsarkofagen* alludes to the fact that in Seville a sardine is buried as part of the passion ritual, so rather appropriately the piece was commissioned by the Music Factory in Bergen, a lively group based in an old sardine factory! Despite Håkan Hardenberger's electrifying performance, the music remains pretty feeble, and the rather pointless quotes from Mahler serve to highlight the emptiness of the surroundings. The stars are for the performance and recording.

RACHMANINOV, Sergei (1873–1943)

Piano Concertos Nos. (i) 1; (ii) 2 (2 versions); (i) 3–4; (ii) Rhapsody on a Theme of Paganini; (iii) The Isle of the Dead; Symphony No. 3; Vocalise. (piano, 4 hands): (iv) Polka italienne. (Solo piano): Barcarolle, Op. 10/3; Daisies (song transcription); Etudes-tableaux, Op. 33/2 & 7 & Op. 39/6; Humoresque, Op. 10/5; Lilacs (song transcription; 2 versions); Mélodie, Op. 3/3; Moment musical, Op. 16/2; Oriental sketch; Polichinelle, Op. 3/4; Polka de W. R. (3 versions). *Preludes: in C sharp min., Op. 3/2* (3 versions); *in G min.; in G flat, Op. 23/5 & 10; in E, G, F min., F, G sharp, Op. 32/3, 5–7, 12; Serenade, Op. 3/5* (2 versions); (v) BEETHOVEN: *Violin Sonata No. 8 in G, Op. 30/3.* SCHUBERT: *Violin Sonata in A, D.574.* GRIEG: *Violin Sonata in C min., Op. 45.* BACH: *Partita No. 4, BWV 828: Sarabande.* HANDEL: *Suite No. 5: Air & Variations (The Harmonious Blacksmith).* MOZART: *Piano Sonata in A, K.331: Theme & Variations; Rondo alla Turca.* BEETHOVEN: *32 Variations in C min. WoO 80.* LISZT: *Concert Paraphrase of Chopin: Polish Songs (Return home; The maiden's wish). Concert Paraphrases of Schubert: Das Wandern; Serenade. Polonaise No. 2; Concert Study: Gnomenreigen; Hungarian Rhapsody No. 2.* MENDELSSOHN: *Song without Words: Spinning Song, Op. 67* (2 versions). *Etudes, Op. 104b/2–3.* SCHUBERT: *Impromptu in A flat, Op. 90/4.* GLUCK: *Orfeo ed Euridice: Mélodie.* SCHUMANN: *Der Kontrabandiste* (arr. Tausig); *Carnaval, Op. 9.* PADEREWSKI: *Minuet, Op. 14/1.* CHOPIN: *Sonata No. 2 (Funeral March); Nocturnes, Op. 9/2; Op. 15/2; Waltzes: Op. 18 (Grand valse brillante), Op. 34/3; Op. 42; Op. 64/1* (2 versions); *Op. 64/2; Op. 64/3* (2 versions); *Op. 69/2; Op. 70/1; in E min., Op. posth.; Ballade No. 3; Mazurkas, Op. 63/3, Op. 68/2; Scherzo No. 3.* BORODIN: *Scherzo in A flat.* TCHAIKOVSKY: *The Seasons: November (Troika; 2 versions). Humoresque, Op. 10/2; Waltz, Op. 40/8.* SCRIABIN: *Prelude, Op. 11/8.* Johann STRAUSS Jnr: *Man lebt nur einmal (One lives but once;* arr. Tausig). DAQUIN: *Le Coucou.* SAINT-SAENS: *Le Cygne* (arr. Siloti). GRIEG: *Lyric Pieces: Waltz; Elfin Dance.* DOHNANYI: *Etude, Op. 28/6.* HELSELT: *Etude, Op. 2/6 (Si oiseau j'étais).* MOSZKOWSKI: *Etude, Op. 52/4 (La Jongleuse).* DEBUSSY: *Children's Corner: Dr Gradus ad Parnassum; Golliwog's Cakewalk.* Domenico SCARLATTI: *Pastorale* (arr. Tausig). Transcriptions: KREISLER: *Liebesfreud* (3 versions). BACH: *(Unaccompanied) Violin Partita No. 3, BWV 1003: Preludio; Gavotte & Gigue.* MENDELSSOHN: *A Midsummer Night's Dream: Scherzo.* SCHUBERT: *Wohin?.* MUSSORGSKY: *Gopak.* TCHAIKOVSKY: *Lullaby, Op. 16/1.* RIMSKY-KORSAKOV: *Flight of the Bumble-Bee.* BEETHOVEN: *Ruins of Athens: Turkish March.* BIZET: *L'Arlésienne: Minuet.* TRAD.: (vi) *Powder and Paint.*

(M) (***) RCA mono 09026 61265-2 (10). Composer (piano); with Phd. O, (i) Ormandy; (ii) Stokowski; (iii) cond. composer; (iv) with Rachmaninov; (v) Kreisler; (vi) Plevitskaya.

Spurred by the 50th anniversary of Rachmaninov's death, RCA has issued a ten-disc box at mid-price collecting all the recordings the composer made from 1919, the time he arrived in America, until 1942, the year before his death. These include all four of his *Piano Concertos* (No. 3 with the cuts Rachmaninov himself made) as well as the *Paganini Rhapsody*, the *Third Symphony* and the tone-poem, *The Isle of the Dead.* Among Rachmaninov's many solo piano recordings it is fascinating to compare his different readings of the most celebrated piece of all, the *Prelude in C sharp minor.* The stiff performance of 1919 (made for Edison) leads

to a much freer and subtler reading in 1921, while the 1928 version, using the new electrical process, remains free and subtle but is emotionally less charged. The acoustic recordings, made between 1920 and 1925, are on balance the most cherishable of all, with the sound astonishingly full and the readings sparkling and spontaneous. That is true even of his 1924 recording of the *Piano Concerto No. 2,* now for the very first time issued complete. As in his classic electrical recording of five years later, he is partnered by Stokowski and the Philadelphia Orchestra, but the earlier one has a more volatile quality, with the fingerwork even clearer. Interpreting Chopin, Rachmaninov was also at his freshest and most imaginative in the early recordings, yet dozens of items here bear witness to the claim often made that he was the greatest golden-age pianist of all, bar none. The delicacy of his playing in Daquin's little piece, *Le Coucou,* shows how he was able to scale down his block-busting virtuosity and, though in Beethoven's *32 Variations in C minor* he omitted half-a-dozen variations so as to fit the piece on two 78 sides, it is full of flair. There is magic too in his collaborations with Fritz Kreisler, not just in Beethoven but also in the Grieg and Schubert sonatas, and in the private recordings, when he accompanies a gypsy singer in a traditional Russian song or plays a piano duet, the *Polka italienne,* with his wife, Natalie. Transfers are commendably clean but with high background hiss. The ten discs come in a box at mid-price.

Piano Concertos Nos. 1–4.

(B) *** Double Decca (ADD) 444 839-2 (2). Ashkenazy, LSO, Previn.

(BB) *** EMI CZS5 73765-2 (3). Rudy, St Petersburg PO, Jansons – TCHAIKOVSKY: *Piano Concerto No. 1.* ***

(B) *** EMI (ADD) CZS7 67419-2 (2). Collard, Capitole Toulouse O, Plasson.

(M) *** Chan. 7114 (2) Wild, RPO, Horenstein.

Piano Concertos Nos. (i) 1 in F sharp min.; (ii) 2 in C min.; (iii) 3 in D min.; (i) 4 in G min.; (iv) Rhapsody on a Theme of Paganini, Op. 43.

(B) *** BMG/Melodiya Twofer 74321 40068-2 (2). Eresko; (i–iii) USSR SO, Provotorov; (iv) Leningrad PO, Ponkin.

(B) **(*) EMI double forte (ADD) CZS5 68619-2 (2). Anievas, New Philh. O; (i) Frühbeck de Burgos; (i; iv) Atzmon; (iii) Ceccato.

The Double Decca set of the four Rachmaninov concertos tends to sweep the board. The current transfers are admirable, fully capturing the Kingsway Hall ambient warmth yet not lacking brilliance and clarity, and with the *Third Concerto* better focused than when it first appeared on LP. The vintage 1972 performances, with their understanding partnership between Ashkenazy and Previn, have achieved classic status. The *Second Concerto's* slow movement is particularly beautiful; it is almost matched by the close of the first movement of the *Third* and the restrained passion of the opening of the following *Adagio.* The individuality and imagination of the solo playing throughout, combined with the poetic feeling of Previn's accompaniments and the ever-persuasive response of the LSO, provide special rewards. An outstanding bargain in every way.

Mikhail Rudy and the St Petersburg Philharmonic under

Mariss Jansons consistently demonstrate that extrovert bravura is not everything in Rachmaninov piano concertos, and that poetry and refinement can offer exceptionally rewarding results in works which emerge here as far more than conventional warhorses. There is plenty to admire and relish. The results are fresh and unhackneyed from first to last, with Rudy's light, clean articulation adding sparkle. Not that he lacks weight, and the strong support of Jansons and the St Petersburg Philharmonic intensifies the idiomatic warmth, with mystery alongside passion in Rachmaninov's writing. This account of the *Fourth Concerto* is especially valuable in offering the original, uncut version of the finale, as well as the usual revised text. On their last appearance, we underestimated these versions, but now the three discs (each originally issued at full price), come repackaged at super-budget price to make an excellent recommendation, even if you already have a set of the concertos, for the Tchaikovsky coupling is similarly enticing.

Issued as a 'Twofer', the Melodiya digital versions of the four Rachmaninov *Piano Concertos* (1984) plus the *Paganini Rhapsody* (1983) make another excellent bargain in performances full of flair. Victor Eresko proves a formidable virtuoso who in No. 3 opts for the weightier and more difficult of Rachmaninov's two cadenzas. Eresko plays with the crispest definition, not just in bravura passage-work, but magically in the light, quicksilver skeins of notes so characteristic of Rachmaninov, and in such movements as the finales of Nos. 3 and 4 he points rhythms with a sparkle of wit, making most others seem a little plain. He also brings off the virtuoso codas to each of these works with splendid panache, to set this up as a most attractive set, well recorded and a first-rate bargain.

Collard too is completely at home in this repertoire; his account of the *First* has splendid fire and can hold its own with all comers (even Pletnev and Ashkenazy); and much the same goes for its companions. Perhaps the *Third Piano Concerto* is the least incandescent in his hands, but readers wanting an alternative, inexpensive set (all four concertos for the price of one CD) need look no further, for this is playing of real quality, and the recording, though not outstanding, is fully acceptable.

The Earl Wild set with Horenstein was recorded at the Kingsway Hall in 1965. They worked marvellously together, with Horenstein producing an unexpected degree of romantic ardour from the orchestra. Earl Wild's technique is prodigious and sometimes (as in the first movement of the *Fourth Concerto*) he almost lets it run away with him. What is surprising is how closely the interpretations here seem to be modelled on the composer's own versions – not slavishly, but in broad conception. This applies strikingly to the *First Concerto* and the *Rhapsody*. In terms of bravura, the *Third Concerto* is in the Horowitz class. However, he makes the three cuts Rachmaninov sanctioned, one in the second movement and two in the third, a total of 55 bars. All in all, this is a first-class and very rewarding set, and the sumptuousness of the sound belies the age of the recording.

Anievas cannot match Ashkenazy as a searching and individual interpreter of Rachmaninov, but his youthful freshness makes all these concerto performances highly enjoyable. With three Mediterranean conductors to help him, and with bright, vivid EMI recording, not as atmospheric as the quality Decca provide for Ashkenazy, the result brings a combination of brilliance and romanticism which never lets go, even if it rarely produces the moments of magical illumination that mark the most inspired interpretations. Like Ashkenazy, Anievas gives the *Third Concerto* absolutely uncut and uses the longer, more difficult version of the first-movement cadenza. It is a strong, direct interpretation, though at the very end of the finale the presentation of the big melody nearly goes over the top.

(i) *Piano Concertos Nos. 1–4; Rhapsody on a Theme of Paganini, Op. 43.* (ii) (2 Pianos): *Suites Nos. 1–2, Opp. 5 & 17; Russian Rhapsody; Symphonic Dances, Op. 45.* (Piano) *Etudes-tableaux, Opp. 33 & 39; 24 Preludes* (complete); *Piano Sonata No. 2 in B flat min., Op. 36; Variations on a Theme by Corelli, Op. 42.*

⬤ (B) *** Decca ADD/Dig. 455 234-2 (6). Ashkenazy; (i) LSO, Previn; (ii) with Previn (piano).

All these performances are very distinguished indeed. The vintage Decca recordings (made over a decade and a half between 1971 and 1986, mostly in the Kingsway Hall, but also at Walthamstow and All Saints', Petersham) are fully worthy of the quality of the music-making. Ashkenazy's readings, with Previn an admirable partner (whether conducting or at the keyboard), are unsurpassed on CD, except by the composer's own historic versions; while they are also available on a series of Double Deccas, any collector not involved in too much duplication will find this bargain box will make an ideal linchpin for a Rachmaninov collection.

Piano Concerto No. 1 in F sharp min., Op. 1.

(M) *** Mercury (IMS) (ADD) 434 333-2. Janis, Moscow PO, Kondrashin – PROKOFIEV: *Piano Concerto No. 3.* ***

As in the Prokofiev coupling, soloist and orchestra plainly challenged each other to the limit, and the American technical team brilliantly captured the warmly romantic and charismatic interpretation which resulted. The solo playing stands alongside that of Horowitz in this repertoire, scintillating in the finale, yet never offering virtuosity simply for its own sake. Even now the recording is impressive for its clarity of texture and subtle detail within a warm acoustic. The CD is one of Wilma Cozart Fine's most successful transfers.

(i) *Piano Concerto No. 1 in F sharp min., Op. 1;* (ii) *Rhapsody on a Theme of Paganini, Op. 43.*

(N) (M) *** Virgin VM5 61976-2. Pletnev, Philh. O, Pešek.

Mikhail Pletnev's accounts of the *F sharp minor Concerto* and the *Rhapsody on a Theme of Paganini* with the Philharmonia Orchestra under Libor Pešek are very fine indeed. The *Paganini Rhapsody* is distinguished not only by quite stunning virtuosity and unobtrusive refinement but also by great feeling. This is playing of classic status, strong in personality and musicianship, and with especially vivid sound.

Piano Concertos Nos. (i) 1; (ii) 3 in D min., Op. 30.

(M) *** RCA (ADD) 09026 68762-2. Janis; (i) Chicago SO, Reiner; (ii) Boston SO, Munch.

Byron Janis in his late twenties (in March 1957) gives a

dashing account of the *F sharp minor Concerto*, freshly charismatic. With Reiner at the helm the performance cannot help but be commanding: how beguilingly warm and relaxed is the phrasing of the lyrical string-melody in the finale! Then in December of the same year Janis went to Boston to record the greater *D minor* work, with Munch an equally perceptive partner; here it is the acoustics of Boston's Symphony Hall which cast a glow over the proceedings and the piano balance is very well judged. Janis's tempo for the main theme of the first movement is brisk (he tells us the reason for his choice in the accompanying notes); but the contrast with the second subject is nicely made and Munch's orchestral backcloth reveals much subtlety of colour-shading. He is an excellent partner. Janis was to go on to re-record both works for Mercury, but the present coupling has a youthful spontaneity which is hard to resist.

Piano Concertos Nos. 1; 4 in G min.; Rhapsody on a Theme of Paganini.

(BB) *** Naxos 8.550809. Glemser, Polish Nat. RSO, Wit.

Bernd Glemser has a boldly impetuous way with Rachmaninov and, with excellent support from the Polish National Radio Orchestra under Antoni Wit, he generates plenty of excitement and expressive fervour in all three works here. If Janis and Reiner are that bit more characterful in the *F sharp minor Concerto*, and Pletnev is even more charismatic in the *Rhapsody*, Glemser is by no means unimaginative or wanting in poetic feeling, and he gives a very enjoyable account of the more elusive *Fourth Concerto*.

Piano Concerto No. 2 in C min., Op. 18.

*** Hänssler CD 98.932. Ohlsson, ASMF, Marriner – TCHAIKOVSKY: *Piano Concerto No. 1.* ***

(M) *** DG (ADD) 447 420-2. S. Richter, Warsaw PO, Wislocki – TCHAIKOVSKY: *Piano Concerto No. 1.* (**)

(B) *** Decca 448 221-2.. Ortiz, RPO, Atzmon – TCHAIKOVSKY: *Piano Concerto No. 1.* *(*)

Ohlsson and Marriner combine to give a satisfyingly romantic account of this favourite concerto. The climax of the first movement is broad and very powerful, and the finale, while not lacking brilliance, makes the very most of Rachmaninov's great secondary melody with a gorgeously expansive final presentation. The *Adagio* is equally persuasive with the reprise tenderly beautiful, rapt in its gentle concentration. The recording is full-bodied and natural and is admirably balanced. If you want a modern, digital recording of this coupling, this Hänssler CD is hard to beat.

With Richter the long opening melody of the first movement is taken abnormally slowly, and it is only the sense of mastery that he conveys in every note which prevents one from complaining. The slow movement too is spacious – with complete justification this time – and the opening of the finale lets the floodgates open the other way, for Richter chooses a hair-raisingly fast allegro, so this is a reading of vivid contrasts. The sound is very good. It's a great pity that the performance chosen as the new coupling should be Tchaikovsky's *First Concerto*, with Karajan and the Berlin Philharmonic, an example of a performance where two great artists pull simultaneously in different directions.

Cristina Ortiz's account has the advantage of rich Decca digital sound. The performance is warmly romantic, the first-movement climax satisfyingly expansive and the *Adagio* glowingly poetic, while the finale brings sparklingly nimble articulation from Ortiz and a fine expressive breadth from the strings in the famous lyrical melody. However, the Postnikova version of the Tchaikovsky *B flat minor Concerto* which acts as coupling is too eccentric to be recommendable.

Piano Concertos Nos. (i) 2; (ii) 3.

(M) **(*) Decca (ADD) 466 375-2. Ashkenazy, (i) Moscow PO, Kondrashin; (ii) LSO, Fistoulari.

(M) **(*) Erato 0630 18411-2. (i) Duchable, Strasbourg Philh. O, Guschlbauer; (ii) Berezovsky, Philh. O, Inbal.

** BIS CD 900. Ogawa, Malmö SO, Arwel Hughes.

Piano Concertos Nos. (i) 2 ; (ii) 3. Preludes: in C sharp min., Op. 3/2; in E flat, Op. 23/6.

(M) *** Mercury (ADD) 432 759-2. Janis; (i) Minneapolis SO; (ii) LSO, Dorati.

Byron Janis has the full measure of this music: his shapely lyrical phrasing and natural response to the ebb and flow of the melodic lines is a constant source of pleasure. In the finale there is all the sparkling bravura one could ask for, but the great lyrical tune is made beguilingly poetic. Although the 1960 recording has plenty of ambience, the Minneapolis violins lack the richness of the LSO strings, recorded at Watford in 1961. The simple opening of the *Third Concerto* benefits from the extra warmth, and Janis lets the theme unwind with appealing spontaneity, and in the great closing climax of the finale the passion is built up – not too hurriedly – to the greatest possible tension. Janis makes two cuts (following the composer's own practice), one of about ten bars in the second movement and a rather longer one in the finale. Two favourite *Preludes*, with the *E flat* coming first, most persuasively played, make some compensation.

Ashkenazy's first (1963) recording of the *C minor Concerto* is more successful than his much later, digital account with Haitink, but less compelling than his version with Previn, which remains uniquely beautiful. But the performance with Kondrashin offers superb Walthamstow sound and, though Kondrashin does not hold the first movement at a consistent level of tension, the close of the *Andante* is ravishing and no one should be disappointed with the passionate climax of the finale. The *Third Concerto* is another matter. Anatole Fistoulari proved a splendid partner, and this reading is the freshest and most spontaneous of Ashkenazy's four recordings. Both CD transfers are outstandingly successful and the vintage (again Walthamstow) sound-balance is very satisfying.

Duchable's 1985 performance of the *Second Concerto* with Theodor Guschlbauer and the Strasbourg Orchestra is well paced and involving, though for all his keyboard mastery, this would not be a first choice. Boris Berezovsky's aristocratic performance of the *Third* with the Philharmonia Orchestra under Eliahu Inbal is an admirable example of his elegant pianism and artistic finesse. There is playing of great delicacy though he does at times seem a little reluctant to let himself go. In the finale he cuts from two bars after fig 52 through to 54 (an excision which Rachmaninov himself made but which is unusual nowadays). Very good recording balance.

Norika Ogawa is a cultured and musical artist but she does not have quite the tempestuous, barnstorming brilliance that any pianist aspiring to the *Third Piano Concerto* must command if he or she is to convince. She gives us the bigger cadenza, which seems to have replaced the more exhilarating one that Rachmaninov and Horowitz recorded. This is all rather low voltage though the Malmö Orchestra under Owain Arwel Hughes are very supportive and the BIS recording is first-class.

Piano Concertos Nos. (i) *2;* (ii) *3* (transfers use alternative takes).

(***) Biddulph mono LHW 036. (i) Composer, Phd. O, Stokowski; (ii) Horowitz, LSO, Coates.

Two classics of the Rachmaninov discography: the 1929 account of the *C minor Concerto* the composer recorded with the Philadelphia Orchestra, coupled with the first (and in some ways most exciting) of Horowitz's recordings of the *Third,* made in London the following year with Albert Coates conducting. An electrifying performance. The Biddulph transfers made by Mark Obert Thorn are first-rate and in the *C minor,* use is made of alternative takes made at the original sessions. An invaluable supplement to RCA's Complete Rachmaninov Edition and a mandatory purchase for collectors of this repertoire.

(i) *Piano Concerto No. 2;* (ii) *Rhapsody on a Theme of Paganini.*

(B) *** Decca Penguin (ADD) 460 632-2. Ashkenazy, LSO, Previn.

(BB) *** Naxos 8.550117. Jandó, Budapest SO, Lehel.

(B) *** CfP CD-CFP 9017. Tirimo, Philh. O, Levi.

(M) *** Decca (ADD) 448 604-2. Katchen; (i) LSO, Solti; (ii) LPO, Boult – DOHNANYI: *Variations on a Nursery Tune.* ***

For those not investing in the Double Decca, which includes all four concertos played by the same artists, Decca's re-coupling of Ashkenazy's earlier recordings with Previn is a very desirable CD indeed. At mid-price on Penguin Classics it makes a first choice. In the *Concerto,* the gentle, introspective mood of the *Adagio* is among the most beautiful on record. The finale is broad and spacious rather than electrically exciting, but the scintillating, unforced bravura provides all the sparkle necessary. The *Rhapsody* too is outstandingly successful. The Kingsway Hall sound is rich and full-bodied in the best analogue sense. Detail is somewhat sharper in the *Rhapsody*; in the *Concerto,* however, atmosphere rather than clarity is the predominating factor. The commentary is by Reynolds Price.

Katchen's performances of both works offer drama and excitement in plenty – the outer movements of the *Concerto* reach the highest peak of excitement, with bravura very much to the fore. Solti makes a splendid partner here; Boult sees that the *Rhapsody* is superbly shaped and has diversity and wit as well as romantic flair. With three works offered, this reissue can be recommended very highly.

Jandó has the full measure of the ebb and flow of Rachmaninov's musical thinking, and the slow movement is romantically expansive and the finale has plenty of dash and ripe, lyrical feeling. The *Rhapsody* is as good as almost any around. The digital recording is satisfyingly balanced, with a bold piano image and a full, resonant orchestral tapestry.

Concentrated and thoughtful, deeply expressive yet never self-indulgent, Tirimo is outstanding in both the *Concerto* and the *Rhapsody,* making this another of the most desirable budget versions. Speeds for the outer movements of the *Concerto* are on the fast side, yet Tirimo's feeling for natural rubato makes them sound natural, never breathless, while the sweetness and repose of the middle movement are exemplary. The digital recording is full, clear and well balanced.

(i, iii) *Piano Concerto No. 2;* (ii, iii) *Rhapsody on a Theme of Paganini;* (iv) *Suite No. 2 in C, Op. 17.*

(M) (***) Dutton Lab. mono CDCLP 4004. Cyril Smith, with (i) Liverpool PO; (ii) Philh. O; (iii) Sargent; (iv) Sellick.

Cyril Smith's version of the *C minor Concerto,* made with the Liverpool Philharmonic in the Abbey Road Studios in 1947, has the real Rachmaninov sound and a great deal of feeling (Sir Malcolm Sargent too is an exemplary and supportive accompanist). Well worth investigating – as are the *Paganini Rhapsody,* again with Sargent, and the Op. 17 *Suite* which Cyril Smith recorded with his wife the following year. The sound is remarkably good for its day and the transfer in the best traditions of the house.

(i) *Piano Concertos Nos. 2–3; Rhapsody on a Theme of Paganini. Preludes: in C sharp min., Op. 3/2; in B flat & G min., Op. 23/2 & 5; in B min. & D flat, Op. 32/10 & 13; Etudes-tableaux, Op. 39/1, 2 & 5.*

(B) *** Double Decca (ADD) 436 386-2 (2). Ashkenazy, (i) LSO, Previn.

This pair of Decca CDs includes outstanding performances of Rachmaninov's three greatest concertante works for piano and orchestra, plus five favourite *Preludes* and three of the Op. 39 *Etudes-tableaux.* The digital remastering offers first-class transfers, full and well-balanced, with the Kingsway Hall ambience casting a pleasing glow over the proceedings. This is very highly recommendable.

(i) *Piano Concerto No. 2; Etudes-tableaux, Op. 39/1–2, 4–6 & 9.*

*** RCA 07863 57982. Kissin, (i) LSO, Gergiev.

Evgeny Kissin phrases intelligently and resists the temptation to play to the gallery in any way. He produces a beautiful sound throughout and it is a compliment to him that any comparisons that spring to mind are with great pianists. The LSO under Valentin Gergiev give him every support. The six *Etudes tableaux* are imaginatively played and impressively characterized. The recording is well balanced and truthful.

(i) *Piano Concerto No. 2 in C min., Op. 19;* (ii) *Rhapsody on a Theme of Paganini;* (iii) *Symphony No. 2 in E min., Op. 29; Vocalise;* (iv) *The Bells. Op. 30.*

(N) **(*) DG (ADD) Panorama 469 178-2 (2). (i) Richter,

Warsaw PO, Wislocki; (ii) Ashkenazy, LSO, Previn; (iii) BPO, Maazel; (iv) Soloists, Concg. O, Ashkenazy.

This DG Panorama compilations collection brings together Richter's classic performance of the *Second Piano Concerto*, made on his visit to Warsaw in 1959, and Ashkenazy's reading of the *Paganini Rhapsody* from the early 1970s and his Amsterdam recording of *The Bells*. Less successful is Lorin Maazel's recording from 1983 of the *Second Symphony*, in which less than justice is done to the sumptuous tone of the Berlin Philharmonic.

Piano Concerto No. 3 in D min., Op. 30.

*** Ph. 446 673-2. Argerich, Berlin RSO, Chailly – TCHAIKOVSKY: *Piano Concerto No. 1.* ***

(***) Testament mono SBT 1029. Gilels, Paris Conservatoire O, Cluytens (with SHOSTAKOVICH: *Prelude & Fugue in D*) – SAINT-SAENS: *Piano Concerto No. 2.* (***)

(*(**)) VAI mono VAIA IPA 1027. Kapell, Toronto SO, MacMillan – KHACHATURIAN: *Piano Concerto.* (**)

(i) *Piano Concerto No. 3. Barcarolle in G min., Op. 23/5; Mélodie in E, Op. 3/3; Preludes: in C sharp min., Op. 3/2; in G min., Op. 23/5; in G sharp min., Op. 32/12.*

*** Decca 448 401-2. Cherkassky, (i) with RPO, Temirkanov.

(i) *Piano Concerto No. 3. Elegy, Op. 3/1; Polichinelle; Preludes: in C sharp min., Op. 3/2; in B flat; G min.; E flat, Op. 23/2, 5 & 6; in G; G sharp min., Op. 32/5 & 12.*

✿ *** Elan CD 82412. Rodriguez; (i) with Lake Forest SO, McRae.

(i) *Piano Concerto No. 3. Prelude in B flat, Op. 23/2; Vocalise, Op. 34/14.*

** RCA 09026 61548-2. Kissin; (i) Boston SO, Ozawa.

(i) *Piano Concerto No. 3;* (ii) *Suite for 2 Pianos No. 2, Op. 17.*

(N) (M) *** Ph. 464 732-2. Argerich; (i) Berlin RSO, Chailly; (ii) Freire.

Santiago Rodriguez is Cuban by birth but like Bolet has made his home in the United States. There is no doubt from the opening bars of the *Third Concerto* that he is a Rachmaninov interpreter of outstanding calibre, whose playing withstands the most exalted comparisons. Indeed, as one plays this disc, one's thoughts turn only to the greatest exponents of this repertoire – Horowitz, Rachmaninov himself and William Kapell. Rodriguez, too, has dazzling virtuosity at his command and also fine musicianship and a rare keyboard authority. He plays the first-movement cadenza (and how!) that Rachmaninov himself favoured rather than the alternative one that came into fashion with Vladimir Ashkenazy. The eight remaining pieces are of the same exalted standard. A most exciting issue.

There are few finer examples of live recording than Martha Argerich's electrifying performance of Rachmaninov's *Third Concerto*, recorded in Berlin in 1982. Her volatility and dash are entirely at one with the romantic spirit of this music, and her interpretation is so commanding that individual eccentricities seem a natural part of the musical flow. Moreover she plays with great tenderness (well supported by Chailly) in the *Adagio* and the lyrical theme of the finale.

Throughout the concerto her bursts of scintillating bravura are quite hair-raising (comparison with Horowitz is not to her disadvantage), and the rush of romantic adrenalin at the close is thrilling and brings forth a well-deserved response from the audience in which the listener is tempted to join. The overall sound-picture satisfyingly demonstrates the skill of the Philips engineering team.

Those not wanting the coupling with Tchaikovsky will find the performance of the *Second Suite* for two pianos equally exciting. Argerich and Nelson Freire give it a dazzling virtuoso account, rushing the waltzes off their feet (the movement is marked *presto* but they play it *prestissimo*). They are as fresh, idiomatic and thoughtful as their Decca rivals (Ashkenazy and Previn – see below) and their performance is thoroughly exhilarating and well recorded too.

Shura Cherkassky's playing could always be relied on for both individuality and finesse. His account of the Rachmaninov *Third Piano Concerto* appeared at about the same time as his version of the Rubinstein *Fourth*. It is something of a *tour de force* for an octogenarian and, although there are others with greater fire and zest, this has a poetic grace which in its way is rather special. Nothing Cherkassky did was without its special musical insights, and readers who respond to Cherkassky's pianism should snap up this last opportunity of hearing him, for he made no more records after this.

Gilels's classic account of the *Concerto* with André Cluytens and the Paris Conservatoire Orchestra comes from 1955 and belongs among the 'greats'. The piano-sound is a bit shallow and at times the balance favours the soloist unduly – but what lovely playing. This should still be in the collections of all who have an interest in Rachmaninov and piano playing.

During his short life William Kapell was closely identified with this concerto, and this performance was recorded in Toronto at a public concert in 1948. He is one of the very few pianists who can be compared to Horowitz and Rachmaninov himself. He plays the same cadenza as they did. The sound is very poor indeed, but the playing is absolutely electrifying.

Kissin's opening is very measured and at low voltage. The pianism is superbly elegant, and one can easily feel that it is curiously judicious, given the incandescence this artist can command. Yet there are a number of poetic insights which almost persuade the listener that the slow tempo is justified. The record is assembled from live performances and the piano timbre is at times discoloured. Ozawa gets decent rather than distinguished results from the orchestra, which, as recorded, is curiously veiled and badly wanting in transparency at the top.

(i) *Piano Concerto No. 3. Piano Sonata No. 2, Op. 36.*

(N) (M) *** RCA 09026 63681-2. Horowitz; (i) NYPO, Ormandy.

Horowitz's most celebrated record, the *D minor Piano Concerto*, was made in partnership with Fritz Reiner and dates from 1951. It is now withdrawn. In 1978 Horowitz re-recorded the work in stereo with Ormandy and the New York Philharmonic Orchestra, this time at a live concert.

Perhaps just a little of the old magic is missing in the solo playing, but it remains prodigious, and Horowitz's special insights, which the composer acknowledged, are very apparent.

The recording was made in Carnegie Hall, but certain portions of the work were remade following the concert. The result is that the sound is not completely stable; at times it seems to recede. But one adjusts when the music-making is so magnetic and the newest transfer makes the most of the sound and captures the hall ambience faithfully. The *Sonata* comes from two live recitals in 1980 and is also pretty electrifying. Horowitz plays the conflation he made (and which Rachmaninov approved) of the 1913 original and the 1931 revision, plus a few further retouchings he subsequently added. This disc is an indispensable part of any Rachmaninov collection, although we hope the Reiner version will also be reissued.

Piano Concertos Nos. 3; 4.

(B) *** Penguin Decca 460 608-2. Ashkenazy, LSO, Previn.

(M) **(*) Van. 99091. Lugansky, Russian State Ac. SO, Shpiller.

Ashkenazy's performances with Previn are thoroughly recommendable. But for only a little more outlay one can get a Double Decca including all four concertos. The author's note here is provided by William Boyd.

Nikolai Lugansky produces a wonderful sound, allows phrases to breathe naturally and the music to unfold freely. In short he is content to serve Rachmaninov rather than his own ego. He plays the cadenza that Rachmaninov himself recorded, and in the *Fourth Concerto* his playing is wonderfully fluid. There is ample virtuosity, but it takes second place to poetic fantasy. There are drawbacks, however, for the orchestral playing is not of comparable distinction and the recording is not in the very first flight, though it is far from inadequate.

Piano Concerto No. 4 in G min., Op. 40.

⊕ (M) *** EMI (ADD) CDM5 67238-2 [CDM5 67258]. Michelangeli, Philh. O, Gracis – RAVEL: *Piano Concerto in G*. *** ⊕

There are few records in the catalogue more worthy of being described as a 'Great Recording of the Century' than Michelangeli's superb coupling of Rachmaninov and Ravel. It has been with us for four decades and time has not diminished its unique appeal from the commanding opening onwards. The current remastering has been expertly managed and at mid-price it should be included in even the most modest collection.

The Isle of the Dead, Op. 29; Symphonic Dances, Op. 45.

(M) *** Decca 430 733-2. Concg. O, Ashkenazy.

(BB) **(*) Naxos 8.550583. RPO, Bátiz.

Ashkenazy's is a superb coupling, rich and powerful in playing and interpretation, *The Isle of the Dead* relentless in its ominous build-up, while the *Symphonic dances* have extra darkness and intensity too. The splendid digital recording highlights both the passion and the fine precision of the playing.

Bátiz gives the *Symphonic Dances* an attractively spontaneous performance, full of lyrical intensity, with some splendid playing from the RPO strings. The vivid recording helps give the feeling that Bátiz almost goes over the top in his extremely passionate climax for *The Isle of the Dead*. The performance certainly does not lack darker feelings, and at super-bargain price this remains well worth considering.

(i) Rhapsody on a Theme of Paganini, Op. 43..

(M) *** RCA (ADD) 09026 68886-2. Rubinstein, Chicago SO, Reiner – with CHOPIN: *Andante spianato & Grand polonaise;* FALLA: *Nights in the Gardens of Spain.* ***

Rubinstein's early stereo (1956) account of Rachmaninov's romantic showpiece is new to the British catalogue. There is no finer version. Rubinstein's playing is dazzling and it continually delights with its poetic sensibility and flair. Reiner is with him in every bar, orchestral detail persuasively delineated, and the warm Chicago acoustic ensures a glorious blossoming of string-tone at the *Eighteenth*. Both pianist and conductor relish the *Dies irae* each time it appears, and the closing pages reach a high pitch of excitement. The recording, with the piano forward but not unattractively so, sounds little short of ideal in Richard Mohr's splendid new remastering.

(i) Rhapsody on a Theme of Paganini, Op. 43. Etudes-tableaux, Opp. 33 & 39; Piano Sonata No. 2, Op. 36; Moment musical, Op. 16/3; Preludes: Op. 3/2; Op. 23/1, 2 & 4; Op. 32/12; Variations on a Theme of Corelli, Op. 42.

(B) *** EMI (ADD) CZS5 69677-2 (2). Collard; (i) Capitole Toulouse O, Plasson.

In the *Rhapsody on a Theme of Paganini* Collard can hold his own with the finest, though he is not as well recorded as Ashkenazy. His account of the *Variations on a Theme of Corelli* is exemplary and the *Second Sonata* is no less powerful. Collard plays the 1913 version but, like Horowitz, incorporates elements of the revision. Playing of real distinction and very competitively priced.

Symphonic Dances, Op. 45; (i) The Bells, Op. 35.

(M) **(*) Melodiya (ADD) 74321 32046-2. (i) Shumskaya, Dovenman, Bolshakov, Russian State Chamber Ch. Moscow PO, Kondrashin.

**(*) Chan. 9759. (i) Lutsiv-Ternovskaya, Bomstein, Pochapsky, Russian State Cappella; Russian State SO, Polyansky.

Kondrashin's classic 1969 performance with the Moscow Philharmonic returns in a less than distinguished transfer. One wonders whether the impression, that our LPs sounded better, is deceptive – until you hear them side by side. All the same, this is an electrifying performance and, like *The Bells*, which comes from 1966, shines through all sonic limitations.

Valeri Polyansky is a bit self-indulgent in the *Symphonic Dances* and lingers, particularly in the middle movement, while the *Lento assai* section of the finale nearly crawls to a stop. The playing of the Russian State Orchestra is very fine and the recording is little short of spectacular in its clarity, definition and warmth. Artistically this is not a first choice.

However, *The Bells* comes off well and is much helped by good soloists and the glorious recorded sound.

SYMPHONIES

Symphonies Nos. 1–3.

(M) **(*) Double Decca 448 116-2 (2). Concg. O, Ashkenazy.

Symphonies Nos 1–3; The Isle of the Dead, Op. 29; Symphonic Dances, Op. 45; Vocalise, Op. 34/14; Aleko: Intermezzo & Women's Dance.

(M) *** EMI (ADD) CMS7 64530-2 (3). LSO, Previn.

Symphonies Nos. 1–3; The Isle of the Dead; Symphonic Dances; (i) The Bells, Op. 35.

(B) *** Decca 455 798-2 (3). Concg. O, Ashkenazy; (i) with Troitskaya, Karczykowski & Concg. Ch.

Symphonies Nos 1–3; The Rock, Op. 7.

(M) **(*) DG (IMS) 445 590-2 (2). BPO Maazel.

Symphonies Nos 1–3; Vocalise, Op. 34/14.

(B) *** Sony SB2K 63257 (2). Phd. O, Ormandy.

Ormandy pioneered the recording of the three Rachmaninov symphonies in stereo, and in many ways his performances remain unsurpassed. Certainly they have never sounded as good as they do in these splendid new transfers. The *Second Symphony* has great intensity of feeling and passion. The *First Symphony* was the work's first stereo version, an exceptionally strong performance it is too. Ormandy's thrustful view of the outer movements is supported by superbly committed Philadelphia playing, with the orchestra on top form. The balance has woodwind solos spotlighted, but the spacious acoustic of Philadelphia Town Hall provides the necessary ambient warmth. In some ways the *Third Symphony* is even more distinguished and now that the artificial brilliance of the old LP has been tamed one can at last appreciate the body of tone this great orchestra commanded in its heyday. The playing itself is marvellous, and this warmth of feeling carries over into the touchingly shaped *Vocalise* which acts as a final encore. A bargain set not to be missed, even if you have more modern versions of these splendid works.

The Ashkenazy digital set of the three symphonies now comes either as a Double Decca or in a bargain box of three discs, one symphony to each CD and coupled respectively with *The Isle of the Dead, Symphonic Dances* and the dramatic cantata, *The Bells*, outstanding in every way. The performances of the symphonies, passionate and volatile, are intensely Russian; the only possible reservation concerns the slow movement of the *Second*, where the clarinet solo is less ripe than in some versions. Elsewhere there is drama, energy and drive, balanced by much delicacy of feeling, while the Concertgebouw strings produce great ardour for Rachmaninov's long-breathed melodies. The vivid Decca sound within the glowing Concertgebouw ambience is ideal for the music.

Previn's LSO set at mid-price offers some alternative couplings. His 1973 account of the *Second Symphony* – a passionately committed performance, with a glorious response from the LSO strings – has been remastered for CD again, with great improvement in the body of the string timbre. No. 1 is a forthright, clean-cut performance, beautifully played and very well recorded. It may lack some of the vitality that one recognizes in Russian performances (Ashkenazy is more volatile and remains first choice in this work) but is still very enjoyable. Previn's account of the *Third*, however, is outstanding: the LSO's playing again has enormous bravura and ardour, and the performances of the two shorter works have plenty of atmosphere and grip. With the *Aleko* excerpts and the *Vocalise* also included, this EMI box remains very competitive.

Maazel's set offers superb playing from the Berlin Philharmonic. However, the DG engineers secured a less sumptuous sound in the Berlin Philharmonie than their Decca colleagues in Amsterdam. The climaxes of the *Second Symphony* in particular would have been enhanced by a warmer middle and lower range. Maazel's readings are not to be dismissed: the *First Symphony* is particularly fine, with Rachmaninov's often thick orchestration beautifully transparent. The *Third* too is distinctive, unusually fierce and intense. The result is sharper and tougher than one expects, less obviously romantic, and the finale for all its brilliance lacks joyful exuberance.

Symphony No. 1 in D min., Op. 13; Caprice bohémien, Op. 12.

(BB) ** Naxos 8.550806. Nat. SO of Ireland, Anissimov.

Symphony No. 1; The Isle of the Dead.

(N) ● DG 463 075-2. Russian Nat. O, Pletnev.
*** EMI CDC5 56754-2. St. Petersburg PO, Jansons.

Symphony No. 1; The Rock; Vocalise, Op. 34/14; Aleko: Intermezzo.

(B) *** DG 449 854-2. BPO, Maazel.

Both Robert Simpson in his two-volume *The Symphony* (Pelican, 1967) and Professor David Brown in the *Guide to the Symphony* speak of the *First* as the finest of the three Rachmaninov symphonies. 'Had he followed it', wrote Simpson, 'with advancing successors he would have been one of the great symphonists of the first half of the twentieth century', a view which Brown endorses roundly. The *First* is wonderfully integrated and explores a world of feeling to which Rachmaninov never subsequently returned. (This is not to say that Nos. 2 and 3 are not tremendous pieces.) In the *First Symphony* Mikhail Pletnev produces a range of sonority and clarity of articulation that we recognize from his keyboard playing, and there is poetic vision alongside a splendid command of architecture. The symphony is quite outstanding in his hands and so is *The Isle of the Dead* which has the sense of inevitability and forward movement that recall Rachmaninov himself, Koussevitzky and Reiner.

Mariss Jansons and his St Petersburg musicians do not wear their hearts on their sleeves but give a totally committed and finely shaped performance of the *First Symphony*. Jansons maintains a firm hold over the architecture of the piece and produces playing of great poetic feeling. *The Isle of the Dead* is highly atmospheric, a convincing and indeed haunting performance. The recording is beautifully natural, with transparent string sound and plenty of space round the instruments, and no want of presence. A very satisfying issue and now first choice among separate recordings of the symphony.

Maazel's is a superb performance, beautifully transparent and consistently clarifying detail. He lacks something in Slavonic passion but, with generous fill-ups, the positive strength of the reading stands up well. The 1984 recording is drier than Ashkenazy's Decca.

Taken on its own merits, the budget account from Alexander Anissimov and the National Symphony Orchestra of Ireland is more than adequate. Were none of the excellent alternatives available, this could be recommended. The recording is very good.

Symphony No. 2 in E min., Op. 27.

⊛ (M) (***) DG mono 449 767-2. Leningrad PO, K. Sanderling.

(BB) *** ASV (ADD) CDQS 6107. Philh. O, Tung.

(M) **(*) Chan. 6606. SNO, Gibson.

**(*) Ph. 438 864-2. Kirov O, Gergiev.

Symphony No. 2; The Rock.

**(*) DG 439 888-2. Russian Nat. O, Pletnev.

(N) (BB) * Naxos 8.554230. Nat. SO of Ireland, Anissimov.

Symphony No. 2; (i) 3 Russian Songs, Op. 41.

*(*) Chan. 9665. Russian State SO, Polyansky; (i) with Russian State Symphonic Capella.

Symphony No. 2; Scherzo in D min.; Vocalise.

*** EMI CDC5 55140-2. St Petersburg PO, Jansons.

Symphony No. 2; (i) Vocalise.

**(*) Telarc CD 80312. (i) McNair; Baltimore SO, Zinman.

Symphony No. 2; Vocalise, Op. 34/14; Aleko: Intermezzo & Women's Dance.

(M) *** EMI (ADD) CDM5 66982-2 [CDM 566997]. LSO, Previn.

Previn's 1973 recording of the *Second Symphony* dominated the catalogue for over a decade in the analogue era. Now it has been vibrantly and richly remastered for CD as one of EMI's 'Great Recordings of the Century'. Its passionate intensity combines freshness with the boldest romantic feeling, yet the music's underlying melancholy is not glossed over. With vividly committed playing from the LSO and a glorious response from the strings, this remains a classic account, not even surpassed by Sanderling's, now that the recording has such opulence and weight in the bass. The addition of the engaging *Aleko* excerpts, plus a fine lyrical account of the *Vocalise*, makes for a generous reissue playing for nearly 75 minutes.

Kurt Sanderling's famous mono recording dates from 1956, but one would never guess, so voluptuously full is the sound of this current DG re-transfer and so remarkably refined the detail. Here is a great Russian orchestra at their very peak, obviously inspired by their conductor, Kurt Sanderling, and carried away on a tide of passion, underpinned by the very Russian melancholy of the slow movement, and especially at its close. The string playing throughout is glorious, reaching its apotheosis in the tremendous climaxes

of the finale. A great performance and, astonishingly, the mono sound is fully worthy of it.

Jansons's newest St Petersburg account offers a strong, warm reading in which climaxes are thrust home powerfully, with full dramatic impact. Phrasing is warmly idiomatic, even if occasionally over-moulded, and the recording gives fine body and immediacy to the sound, outshining most latter-day rivals. In Russian fashion the clarinet in the slow movement sounds like an organ stop. A warm, exciting reading which stands among the best modern versions. The coupling in addition to *Vocalise*, beautifully done, offers the early orchestral *Scherzo* of 1887.

Ling Tung's reading is refined but he knows just how to mould the sweeping lines necessary to bring out the rapture inherent in this lovely symphony, notably at the climax of the slow movement and at the very satisfying close. One needs to play back at a fairly high level, then the Philharmonia strings emerge with a warmly natural, radiant sheen of tone. At super-bargain price this is well worth considering.

Gibson and the Scottish National Orchestra have the advantage of an excellent digital recording. The brass sounds are thrilling, but the slightly recessed balance of the strings is a drawback. But this is a freshly spontaneous performance and overall the sound is admirably natural, even if it includes some strangely unrhythmic thuds at climaxes (apparently the conductor in his excitement stamping on the podium).

Pletnev brings a fresh mind to this symphony, with his approach very much controlled, giving a strong sense of onward current and producing none of the heart-on-sleeve emotion in the slow movement. The clarity and lightness of articulation that distinguish his piano playing seem to be in ample evidence and, throughout the work, feeling is held in perfect control. It is a performance of quality, though the recording, while good, could be cleaner-detailed in the lower end of the range. Ensemble is endangered by some frenetically fast speeds – as in the finale. *The Rock* makes a generous coupling.

As in his opera recordings, Gergiev gives a strong and well-paced reading, if lacking a little in individuality. Although he takes what one might think of as a more traditional approach, he brings an appropriate warmth and also possesses considerable command of the architecture.

After a slack start Zinman builds the symphony persuasively, if with less character than some, helped by first-rate playing from the Baltimore orchestra. Good, clean sound. The coupling is an attraction when, unlike most rivals, Zinman has *Vocalise* with soprano soloist, the radiant Sylvia McNair. Even with that extra, Zinman manages to observe the exposition repeat in the first movement of the symphony.

Valéry Polyansky's account is far from negligible, but it is equally far from distinguished. The most attractive feature of the disc is the Op. 41 set of *Three Russian Songs*, a glorious triptych, full of character, which are given decent, full blooded performances.

Though the Naxos version is well-played and recorded, the conductor, Alexander Anissimov, tends to make heavy weather of the outer movements, with boldly underlined rubato in the big melodies and with a final climax in the fourth movement which fails to lift as it should. Even in the super-bargain category there are preferable, more idiomatic versions, including the earlier Naxos issue with Gunzenhauser, which also boasts *The Rock* as a coupling.

Symphony No. 3 in A min., Op. 44.

*** Chan. 8614. LSO, Järvi – KALLINIKOV: *Intermezzos.* ***

Symphony No. 3; Symphonic Dances.

(M)*** EMI (ADD) CDM5 73475-2. LSO, Previn.
DG 457 598-2. Russian Nat. O, Pletnev.

Symphony No. 3; Vocalise.

(M) *** EMI (ADD) CDM5 66759-2. Nat. PO, Stokowski.

(i) *Symphony No. 3;* (ii; iii) *Spring* (cantata), *Op. 20;* (iii) *3 Unaccompanied Choruses.*

*** Chan. 9802. (i) Russian State SO; (ii) Martyrosyan;
   (iii) Russian State Symphonic Capella, Polyansky.

It was Stokowski who in 1936 in Philadelphia conducted the first performances of Rachmaninov's last symphony. Nearly 40 years later he re-recorded it with Sydney Sax's fine group of selected orchestral players, and the result is very rewarding and exciting. There are idiosyncrasies aplenty, not least a tempo for the finale that whirls one along in exhilarating danger; but this is a splendid example of Stokowski's energy in old age, his ability to inspire players to a totally individual and riveting performance, full of romantic warmth and fervour, not directly comparable with others. The recording, made at West Ham Central Mission, has a wide dynamic range and good definition and it produces the richest patina of string-tone.

Previn's EMI CD brings another outstanding performance; the digital remastering brings plenty of body alongside the sharpened detail. Previn conveys the purposefulness of the writing at every point, revelling in the richness, but clarifying textures. The LSO has rarely displayed its virtuosity more brilliantly in the recording studio, and, with its generous Shostakovich coupling, this is a first choice for this symphony.

A splendid, very Russian account of the *Third Symphony* from Polyansky, volatile but convincingly so, with some glorious playing from the strings, especially in the lovely, nostalgic secondary theme of the first movement which is so very Slavic in feeling. The choral works too are superbly done, with the widest range of dynamic in the masterly unaccompanied choruses, while Tigram Martyrosyan is a richly resonant bass soloist in the cantata. The singers are helped by the resonant acoustic which creates the richest vocal sonorities. For the symphony, competition is strong, with Stokowski and Previn vying for position at mid-price, but with state-of-the-art Chandos sound this new version is well worth considering.

The Russian National Orchestra and Mikhail Pletnev couple the symphony with the late *Symphonic Dances.* If you have acquired Pletnev's CD of the *Second Symphony* you will know that he has a special feeling for this composer and is completely steeped in his spiritual climate. Thus, he can persuade you that his interpretative idiosyncrasies – the very slow tempo he adopts for the interlude in the finale, just about seven minutes in, or his phrasing of the second subject of the first movement – are right. The opulent sound world of this wonderful score is beautifully served by his players

(and in particular the strings). However this is not a first choice.

Järvi in his weighty, purposeful way misses some of the subtleties of this symphony, but with superb playing from the LSO – linking back to André Previn's unsurpassed reading with them – the intensity is magnetic, with even a very slow *Adagio* for the outer sections of the middle movement made to sound convincing, and with the finale thrusting on at an equivalently extreme tempo.

CHAMBER AND INSTRUMENTAL MUSIC

Cello Sonata in G min., Op. 19.

(N) (B) *** EMI (ADD) CZS5 74333-2 (2). Paul Tortelier,
   Ciccolini – CHOPIN; FAURE; MENDELSSOHN: *Cello
   Sonatas.* ***

*Cello Sonata in G min., Op. 19; Lied (Romance) in F min.;
Mélodie in D; 2 Pieces, Op.2; Romance in F, Op. 4/3;
Vocalise.*

(BB) *** Naxos 8.550987. Grebanier, Guggenheim.

*Cello Sonata in G min., Op. 19; 2 Pieces, Op. 2; Vocalise,
Op. 34/14.*

*** Virgin VC5 45119-2 Mørk, Thibaudet – MIASKOVSKY:
   Cello Sonata No. 1. ***

Rachmaninov's *Cello Sonata*, written at the same period as such masterpieces as the *Second Symphony* and the *Second Piano Concerto*, is one of the greatest in the repertory. Michael Grebanier gives it a powerful, richly expressive reading, with Janet Guggenheim an incisive partner, very clearly focused if not always as warm. The slow movement is most moving, the headlong finale thrilling in its clarity. The shorter pieces make up an excellent bargain disc to match rivals at premium price.

Tortelier is at his finest here: Rachmaninov's passionate lines are shaped with the right degree of nervous tension, and if Ciccolini sounds rather more like an accompanist than a full participant, his playing is technically secure. Excellent recording.

The gifted Norwegian cellist Truls Mørk plays with a restrained eloquence that is totally compelling. The demanding (and commanding) piano part is given with authority and conviction by Thibaudet, and they handle the companion pieces excellently. The value of this well-recorded and well-balanced issue is enhanced by the attractive Miaskovsky coupling.

Trios élégiaques Nos. 1 in G min., Op. 8; 2 in D min., Op. 9.

*** Chan. 8431. Borodin Trio.

The *Trios* are both imbued with lyrical fervour and draw from the rich vein of melancholy so characteristic of Rachmaninov. The performances by the Borodin Trio are eloquent and masterly, and the recording is admirably balanced.

PIANO MUSIC
Piano duet

Music for 2 pianos: (i) *Suites Nos. 1–2, Opp. 5 & 17;*
Symphonic Dances, Op. 45; Russian Rhapsody; (Solo
piano) *Etudes-tableaux, Op. 33; Variations on a Theme by
Corelli, Op. 42.*

(B) *** Double Decca (ADD) 444 845-2 (2). Ashkenazy,
(i) with Previn.

Suites Nos. 1–2; Symphonic Dances.

*** Hyp. CDA 66375. Shelley, Macnamara.

*Suite No. 2; Russian Rhapsody, Op. posth.; Symphonic
Dances.*

**(*) Hyp CDA 66654. Demidenko, Alexeev – MEDTNER:
Russian Round Dance etc. **(*)

The colour and flair of Rachmaninov's writing in the two
Suites (as inspired and tuneful as his concertos) are captured
with wonderful imagination. The two-piano version of the
Symphonic Dances is masterly and dazzling, and they are
hardly less persuasive in the early *Russian Rhapsody*. Ashkenazy's superb solo performances of the *Etudes-tableaux*
and the *Corelli Variations* (a rarity and a very fine work) cap
the appeal of this bargain Double. The recording throughout
is superb, with a natural presence and a most attractive
ambience.

Howard Shelley and Hilary Macnamara give strong performances of both *Suites* and the *Symphonic Dances*. In the
Suites their responses are not quite as imaginative as those
of Ashkenazy and Previn, but there is plenty of dramatic fire
in the *Symphonic Dances* in this generously filled disc.

There are some beautiful things on the Aleev – Demidenko disc. They shape the second group of the first of the
Symphonic Dances with exquisite sensitivity and colour, and
there are many other felicities elsewhere. However, even
allowing for the hazards of two pianos, there is some ugly
fortissimo tone. All the same there is much to delight the
listener, even though Previn and Ashkenazy are to be preferred in this repertoire.

Solo piano music

*Andante ma non troppo in D min.; Canon in E min.;
Fragments (1917); Fughetta; Lento in D min. (Song without
words) (1866–7); Moment Musical, Op. 16/2 (rev. version,
1940); Morceau de fantaisie in G min.; Oriental Sketch
(1917); Prelude in F (1891); Variations on a Theme of
Chopin, Op. 22.*

(BB) *** Naxos 8.554426. Biret.

Idil Biret's Rachmaninov recital here brings a powerful yet
poetic reading of the *Chopin Variations*, one of Rachmaninov's finest piano works, coupled with miniatures and
rarities including many rare early pieces. Biret's reading of
the *Variations*, a work seriously neglected, brings out the
high dramatic contrasts, cleanly establishing the character
of each section and setting the whole structure (overall
almost sonata-like) in relief. The fill-ups include an unpretentious little piece, *Lento*, that Rachmaninov wrote at thir-

teen, and demonstrations of his prowess in writing
counterpoint, untypical but crisply refreshing. Excellent
sound to bring out the subtleties of Biret's tonal shading.

*Etudes-tableaux, Opp. 33 & 39; Fragments; Fughetta in F;
Mélodie in E; Moments musicaux; Morceaux de fantaisie;
Morceaux de salon; 3 Nocturnes; Oriental sketch; 4 Pieces;
Piece in D min.; 25 Preludes (complete); Sonatas Nos. 1–3
(including original & revised versions of No. 2); Song
without words; Transcriptions (complete); Variations: on a
Theme of Chopin; on a Theme of Corelli.*

(M) *** Hyp. CDS 44041/8 (8). Shelley.

Hyperion have collected Howard Shelley's exemplary survey
of Rachmaninov into a mid-price, eight-CD set, and very
good it is, too. Shelley can hold his own against most rivals
not only in terms of poetic feeling but in keyboard authority
and virtuosity. The recordings are variable in quality but are
mostly excellent.

*Elégie, Op. 3/1; Etudes-tableaux, Op. 39/3 & 5; Moments
musicaux, Op. 16/3–6; Preludes, Op. 23/1, 2, 5 & 6; Op. 32/
12.*

(B) *** [EMI (ADD) Red Line CDR5 69869 Gavrilov (with
RAVEL: *Gaspard de la nuit*)]

There is some pretty remarkable playing here, especially in
the stormy *B flat major Prelude*, while the *G sharp minor*
from Op. 32 has a proper sense of fantasy. More prodigious
bravura provides real excitement in the *F sharp minor Etude-
tableau*, Op. 39/3, and in the *E minor Moment musical*,
while Gavrilov relaxes winningly in the *Andante cantabile* of
Op. 16/3 and the *Elégie*. Sometimes his impetuosity almost
carries him away, and the piano is placed rather near the
listener so that we are nearly taken with him, but there is no
doubt about the quality of this recital.

Etudes-tableaux, Opp. 33 & 39.

*** Hyp. CDA 66091. Shelley.

The conviction and thoughtfulness of Shelley's playing,
coupled with excellent modern sound, make this convenient
coupling a formidable rival to Ashkenazy's classic versions,
which in any case are not coupled together on CD.

Moments musicaux; Morceaux de salon, Op. 10.

*** Hyp. CDA 66184. Shelley.

Howard Shelley has a highly developed feeling for Rachmaninov and distinguishes himself here both by masterly
pianism and by a refined awareness of Rachmaninov's
sound-world. The recording is eminently realistic and
natural.

*Morceaux de fantaisie, Op. 3; Sonata No. 2 in B flat min.,
Op. 36 (revised, 1931 version); Variations on a Theme of
Corelli, Op. 42.*

*** Danacord DACOCD 525. Marshev.

Oleg Marshev possesses the grand manner, and has won
golden opinions for his Russian repertoire. Listening to his
Rachmaninov, one can see why, for, apart from flawless
technical address and sensitivity, he has an innate feeling for

this repertoire. His account of all three pieces belongs up there with the finest, though in the *Corelli Variations* Pletnev is in a class of his own. The dryish recording, if not ideal, is perfectly serviceable and should not deter readers from investigating some superbly idiomatic Rachmaninov playing.

24 Preludes (complete); Piano Sonata No. 2 in B flat min., Op. 36.

(M) *** Decca (ADD) 467 685-2. Ashkenazy.

24 Preludes; Preludes in D min. & F; Morceaux de fantaisie, Op. 3.

*** Hyp. CDA 66081/2 (available separately). Shelley.

(i) *24 Preludes (complete);* (ii) *Suite No. 2 for 2 pianos, Op. 17.*

(B) **(*) Erato Dig./ADD Ultima 3984 25599-2 (2).
  (i) Lympany; (ii) K. and M. Labèque.

There is superb flair and panache about Ashkenazy's playing and his poetic feeling is second to none. For its Legends reissue the whole get has been accommodated on such a single mid-priced CD playing for just over 80 minutes, and as such sweeps the board, for the new transfer offers a most realistic piano image.

Shelley is a compellingly individual interpreter of Rachmaninov. Each one of the *Preludes* strikes an original chord in him. These are very different readings from those of Ashkenazy but their intensity is well caught in full if reverberant recording.

Moura Lympany is at her finest in the lyrical preludes, which truly blossom in her hands. The whole set moves forward spontaneously and the piano recording is full and vivid. The snag is that the Labèques' performance of the Opus 17 *Suite for 2 Pianos*, offered as a bonus, is much less appealing, partly because the analogue recording (from 1974) is somewhat shallow.

Piano Sonatas Nos. 1 in D min., Op. 28; 2 in B flat min., Op. 36 (revised 1931).

*** Hyp. CDA 66047. Shelley.

Piano Sonata No. 2 in B flat min., Op. 36 (original version); Fragments in A flat; Fughetta in F; Gavotte in D; Mélodie in E; Morceau de fantaisie in G min.; Nocturnes Nos. 1–3; Oriental Sketch in B flat; Piece in D min.; 4 Pieces; Prelude in E flat min.; Romance in F sharp min.; Song without words in D min.

*** Hyp. CDA 66198. Shelley.

Piano Sonata No. 2 in B flat min., Op. 36 (original version); Etudes-tableaux, Op. 33/1, 39/4 & 7; Morceaux de fantaisie, Op. 3/3 & 5; Preludes, Op. 23/1 & 7; 32/2, 6, 9 & 10.

⚫ *** Ph. 446 220-2. Kocsis.

Piano Sonata No. 2, Op. 36 (original version); Etudes-tableaux, Op. 39; (with Kreisler's Liebesleid, trans. Rachmaninov).

*** BIS CD-1042. Kempf.

On CDA 66047, Howard Shelley offers the 1931 version of the *B flat Sonata*. He has plenty of sweep and grandeur

and an appealing freshness, ardour and, when required, tenderness. He is accorded an excellent balance by the engineers.

Shelley then on CDA 66198 gives us the original version of Op. 36 and his performances here show unfailing sensitivity, intelligence and good taste. They have the merit of excellent recorded sound.

Be it in the smaller, reflective pieces or in the bigger-boned *B flat minor Sonata*, Zoltán Kocsis's piano speaks with totally idiomatic accents, effortless virtuosity and keen poetic feeling. A most distinguished offering and is recommended with enthusiasm. Excellent recording.

Freddy Kempf has a real feeling for this composer, and the authority and technical prowess to go with it. He is also a narrative pianist – from the very beginning he has you in the palm of his hand. The *Second Sonata* in the original, 1913 version is as good as any now before the public, and the *Etudes-tableaux* come off equally well. Vivid, realistic piano sound.

Transcriptions: *Daisies; Lilacs; Polka de W. R.; Vocalise.* BACH: *Prelude; Gavotte; Gigue.* BIZET: *Minuet from L'Arlésienne.* KREISLER: *Liebesleid; Liebesfreud.* MENDELSSOHN: *Midsummer Night's Dream: Scherzo.* MUSSORGSKY: *Sorochinsky Fair: Gopak.* RIMSKY-KORSAKOV: *Flight of the Bumble-Bee.* SCHUBERT: *Wohin?.* TCHAIKOVSKY: *Lullaby.*

*** Hyp. CDA 66486. Shelley.

Shelley plays with an authority and sensitivity that is wholly persuasive and dispatches the virtuoso transcriptions to the manner born. The transcription of the *Vocalise* is by Zoltán Kocsis, but otherwise all are Rachmaninov's own.

Variations on a Theme of Chopin, Op. 22; Variations on a Theme of Corelli, Op. 42; Mélodie in E, Op. 3/3.

*** Hyp. CDA 66009. Shelley – MENDELSSOHN: *Scherzo.* ***

Howard Shelley gives dazzling, consistently compelling performances, full of virtuoso flair. First-rate piano sound.

VOCAL MUSIC

Songs: *All passes; All was taken from me; At my window; Before the icon; By a fresh grave; Christ is risen; Fate; The fountain; Night; Fragments from A. Musset; How pained I am; How peaceful; I am again alone; I am not a prophet; I beg for mercy; Lilacs; Let us leave, my sweet; Melody; Night is sorrowful; On the death of a siskin; The ring; There are many sounds; They replied; To my children; Twilight; Two farewells; We shall rest; Yesterday we met.*

*** Chan. 9451. Rodgers, Popescu, Naoumenko, Leiferkus, Shelley.

Fluent in Russian, Joan Rodgers with her richly expressive voice makes a perfect interpreter of Rachmaninov songs, ideally partnered by the pianist, Howard Shelley. This generous selection of those for soprano ranges through the whole of the composer's songwriting career up to his exile from Russia in 1917, when in rejection of his roots he stopped completely. Loveliest of the songs is the extended wordless *Vocalise*, here set against its neighbour in Op. 34, the dramatic song, *Dissonance*. Most distinctive are the six forward-looking songs, Op. 38, to words by symbolist poets.

Songs: *The answer; Believe it or not; Beloved let us fly; By the grave; The fountains; Let me rest here alone; The little island; The moon of life; The muse; Night is mournful; No prophet I; O never sing to me again; The Pied Piper; The pity I implore; The quest; To her; To the children.*

(BB) ** Belart (ADD) 461 626-2. Tear, Ledger – CHOPIN: *Songs.* **

Robert Tear is always sensitive and musical, shows a good understanding of the Russian poetry, and only occasionally seems to suffer strain on top notes. Ledger accompanying and the Decca (originally Argo) recording from the mid-1970s are of a good standard; the artists are not too closely balanced and there is a pleasing ambience. At super-bargain price this is a more than acceptable way of discovering some fine Rachmaninov songs. But there are no texts and translations.

The Bells, Op. 35.

⊕ (N) **** DG 471 029-2. Mescheriakov, Larin, Chernov, Moscow State Ch.O, Russian Nat. O, Pletnev – TANEYEV: *John of Damascus.* ***

(B) *** EMI (ADD) double forte CZS5 73353-2 (2). Armstrong, Tear, Shirley-Quirk, LSO & Ch., Previn – PROKOFIEV: *Alexander Nevsky; Ivan the Terrible.* ***

*** Telarc CD 80363. Fleming, Dent, Ledbetter, Atlanta Ch. & SO, Shaw – ADAMS: *Harmonium.* ***

From Pletnev comes a performance and recording that shows *The Bells* in an entirely new light. He has his finger on the composer's pulse and always has special insights to bring to his music. He goes beyond the music's vivid colours and lush sonorities, and without in any way indulging in over-characterization gets singing and playing of impressive quality, much subtlety and intensity. With Rachmaninov, as with Tchaikovsky, Pletnev seems to have great affinity of temperament and spirit. The recording is first class.

The late Robert Shaw conducts a colourfully expansive performance of Rachmaninov's cantata. The special melancholy of the finale is touchingly conveyed, with a fine orchestral response as well as an ardent contribution from the choir. All three soloists are impressive and if Renée Fleming, who sings beautifully, is not especially Slavonic, in the closing *Lento lugubre* the baritone, Victor Ledbetter, catches the darkly expressive mood admirably. Anyone wanting the spectacular Adams work should be well satisfied with Shaw's Rachmaninov.

In *The Bells*, Previn's concentration on purely musical values as much as on evocation of atmosphere produces powerful results, even when the recording has lost just a little of its original ambient warmth in favour of added presence and choral brilliance. The soloists are excellent.

Liturgy of St John Chrysostom, Op. 31.

⊕ (B) *** EMI double forte (ADD) CZS5 68664-2 (2).

Maximova, Zorova, Vidov, Stoytsov, Petrov, Bulgarian R. Ch., Milkov.

*** Hyp. CDA 66703. Corydon Singers, Best.

Rachmaninov's *Liturgy of St John Chrysostom*, written in 1910, is an even fuller setting than Tchaikovsky's of 1878, and listening to this glorious performance by the Chorus of Bulgarian Radio, recorded in the spacious acoustics of the Alexander Nevsky Memorial Cathedral in Sofia, one can be in no doubt that the work's powerful expressive feeling has an underlying deep spirituality, while the performance itself conveys great religious fervour. Apart from the continuing dialogue between cantor (Ivan Petrov) and chorus (in which the soloists also participate), there are moments of overwhelming simple beauty, as in the sublime, sustained *Cheroubikon* ('Cherubic hymn'). It would be difficult to imagine this superbly recorded performance being bettered and, although the spacious tempi (which are sustained with continuing concentration) mean that the work runs to 97 minutes, the set is offered in EMI's forte series so that the two discs are offered for the price of one. It is a pity that a full text with translation is not included, but the presentation is otherwise fully acceptable.

The fine Hyperion alternative is a sharper, more cleanly enunciated account – the choral sound is without that misty focus which is so much part of the character of Slavic *a capella* singing. It is immensely stimulating, and very well recorded and documented. However, the Corydons curiously omit the prayer dialogue which is the centrepiece of the *Cherubic hymn* and which in Sofia brings such a strikingly exhilarating response from the chorus. There are various other versions in the catalogue, including a superbly sung and deeply moving account from the St Petersburg Chamber Choir under Nikolai Korniev (Philips 442 776-2). But this has been cut to fit on to a single CD. If you have already succumbed to the *Vespers*, you won't be disappointed with *St John Chrysostom's Liturgy*.

Vespers, Op. 37.

⊕ (M) *** HM Chant du Monde RUS 788050. St Petersburg Capella, Chernuchenko.

(M) *** Virgin VM5 61845-2. Emman, Björsund, Höglund, Swedish R. Ch., Kaljuste.

*** Hyp. CDA 66460. Corydon Singers, Best.

*** EMI CDC5 56752-2. King's College Ch., Cleobury.

Rachmaninov's *Vespers* – more correctly the 'All-night vigil' – rank not only among his most soulful and intensely powerful music but are also the finest of all Russian choral works. The St Petersburg Capella is in fact the Mikhail Glinka Choir and their lineage goes back to the fifteenth century. Their earlier recording of the piece was pretty impressive. Even so, this newcomer surpasses it and offers singing of an extraordinarily rapt intensity. The dynamic range is enormous, the perfection of ensemble and blend and the sheer beauty of tone such as to exhaust superlatives. The recording does them justice and is made in a suitably atmospheric acoustic.

Under Tönu Kaljuste the Swedish Radio Choir's account of the *Vespers* shows that they have lost nothing of their sensitivity or command of sonority. They can produce a wonderful range of colour from the darkest to the most luminous. Their Russian sounds totally authentic too. This is undoubtedly one of the finest versions available, with its own special character.

Though Matthew Best's British choir, the Corydon Singers, lacks the dark timbres associated with Russian choruses and though the result could be weightier and more biting, theirs is still a most beautiful performance, very well sung and recorded in an atmospheric, reverberant setting.

It also makes a moving experience having the Anglican tradition, as ideally represented by the choir of King's College, Cambridge, meeting the Russian Orthodox tradition, represented by Rachmaninov's supremely beautiful setting of the *All-night Vigil*. Against the warm acoustic of King's College Chapel, beauty and refinement are the keynotes. The precision of ensemble and subtlety of dynamic shading – remarkable from a choir of young singers – are given extra freshness with the high dramatic contrasts. However, of the English versions, Matthew Best has the more authentic ring.

OPERA

Aleko (complete).

(N) *** DG 453 453-2. Leiferkus, Levitsky, Kotscherga, Guleghina, Von Otter Gothenburg Op. Ch., & SO, Järvi.

Rachmaninov wrote this one-acter based on Pushkin when still a teenager, completing it (with orchestration) in only seventeen days. It is rather like a Russian-flavoured *Cavalleria rusticana*, with the hero murdering his unfaithful sweetheart and her lover, but musically it brings echoes of Borodin, notably in evocative choruses like Polovtsian dances. Distinctive Rachmaninov fingerprints are few, but the result is most attractive, particularly in a performance like this, ideally cast, with Serge Leiferkus a commanding Aleko and Neeme Järvi a warmly persuasive conductor. This fine version, originally in a package with Rachmaninov's two other one-act operas, is welcome on its own, at full price.

(i) Monna Vanna (incomplete opera: Act I, orch. Buketoff); (ii) Piano Concerto No. 4 (original version).

**(*) Chan. 8987. (i) Milnes, McCoy, Walker, Karoustos, Thorsteinsson, Blythe; (ii) Black; Iceland SO, Buketoff.

Monna Vanna is the fragment of an opera based on Maeterlinck. Rachmaninov thought so well of the fragment that it was the one score he brought away from Russia after the Revolution. Igor Buketoff, who knew the composer, has rescued this Act I score and orchestrated it very sensitively to make an interesting curiosity. In its ripely romantic manner the writing has lyrical warmth and flows freely, thrusting home climactic moments. Buketoff's performance with the Iceland Symphony is warmly convincing, but the singing is flawed, with Sherrill Milnes, as Monna Vanna's jealous husband, standing out from an indifferent team, otherwise thin-toned and often wobbly. Buketoff's resurrection of the original score of the *Fourth Piano Concerto* is rather more expansive than the text we know. William Black

is the powerful soloist, though the piano sound, unlike that of the orchestra, lacks weight.

RAFF, Joachim (1822–82)

Symphony No. 1 in D (An das Vaterland), Op. 96.

** Marco 8.223165. Rhenish PO, Friedman.

Symphony No. 2 in C, Op. 140; Overtures: Macbeth; Romeo and Juliet.

** Marco 8.223630. Slovak State PO (Košice), Schneider.

Symphonies Nos. 3 in F (Im Walde), Op. 153; 10 in F min. (Zur Herbstzeit), Op. 213.

** Marco 8.223321. Slovak State PO (Košice), Schneider.

Symphonies Nos. 3; 4 in G min., Op. 167.

(B) **(*) Hyp. Helios CDH 55017. Milton Keynes City O, Davan Wetton.

Symphonies Nos. 4; 11 in A min. (Winter), Op. 214.

*(*) Marco 8.223529. Slovak State PO (Košice), Schneider.

Symphony No. 5 in E (Lenore), Op. 177; Overture, Ein' feste Burg ist unser Gott, Op. 127.

*(*) Marco 8.223455. Slovak State PO (Košice), Schneider.

Raff enjoyed enormous standing during his lifetime though nowadays he is best remembered for a handful of salon pieces. However, he composed no fewer than eleven symphonies between 1864 and 1883, some of which have excited extravagant praise. Yet generally speaking Raff's music is pretty bland, though far from unambitious. The *First Symphony* (*An das Vaterland*), takes itself very seriously and runs to over 70 minutes. To be frank, it places some strain on the listener's concentration. Although the well-played and -recorded *Symphony No. 2 in C* has a certain charm, it is predominantly Mendelssohnian and, although outwardly attractive, it remains pretty insubstantial.

Of the eleven symphonies it is the *Fifth* (*Lenore*) which has captured the imagination of many. No doubt this can be accounted for by the somewhat macabre programme that inspired its finale. Although the symphony itself is more inspired than some of its companions (it has a particularly eloquent slow movement), it does need rather better advocacy than it receives from the Slovak State Philharmonic Orchestra under Urs Schneider. The Overture, *Ein' feste Burg ist unser Gott*, is hardly sufficient to tip the scales in its favour.

The *Eleventh Symphony in A minor* was left incomplete on Raff's death in 1882 and is not otherwise available; the *Fourth* of 1871, available on the Hyperion version under Hilary Davan Wetton, is insufficiently persuasive. This music has moments of charm but is essentially second-rate and must have the most expert advocacy and opulent recorded sound if it is to be persuasive; neither of these two versions is really first class. One needs a Beecham to work his magic on these scores. In these performances they are merely amiable but insignificant.

RAID, Kaljo (born 1922)

Symphony No. 1 in C min.

*** Chan. 8525. SNO, Järvi – ELLER: *Dawn; Elegia* etc. ***

Raid's *First Symphony* shows a genuine feel for form and a fine sense of proportion, even though the personality is not fully formed. Well worth hearing. Neeme Järvi gets very committed playing from the Scottish National Orchestra and the recording is warm and well detailed.

RAMEAU, Jean Philippe (1683–1764)

Overtures: Acante et Céphise, ou La Sympathie; Castor et Pollux; Dardanus; Les Fêtes de l'Hymen et de l'amour, ou Les Dieux d'Egypte; Les Fêtes de Polymnie; Hippolyte et Aricie; Les Paladins; Naïs; Pigmalion; Platée; Les Surprises de l'amour: Prologue (le retour d'Astrée); Act I (L'Enlèvement d'Adonis); Les Talens lyriques (Les Fêtes d'Hébé); Le Temple de la Gloire; Zaïs; Zoroastre.

*** O-L 455 293-2. Les Talens Lyriques, Rousset.

This collection of overtures is well nigh comprehensive. It covers three decades from 1733 (*Hippolyte et Aricie*) through to *Les Paladins* of 1761. The familiar, such as *Platée, Dardanus, Les Indes galantes* and so on, is leavened by the unfamiliar, *Acante et Céphise*. Rameau's mastery of instrumental colour is little short of amazing and completely original. Try *Platée* or *Zaïs* or the *Feu d'artifice* section of *Acante* with its cannon fire. Christophe Rousset and his accomplished musicians play with flair and imagination and are superbly recorded. One of the best discs of its kind for the last three years.

Les Boréades: Orchestral Suite; Dardanus: Orchestral Suite.

*** Ph. 420 240-2. O of 18th Century, Brüggen.

The orchestral suite from *Les Boréades* occupies the larger part of the disc. The invention is full of resource and imagination, and the playing here of both this and *Dardanus* is spirited and sensitive and will provide delight even to those normally unresponsive to authentic instruments.

6 Concerts en sextuor (for strings).

(M) ** Cal. (ADD) CAL 6838. Caen CO, Dautel –
  BOISMORTIER: *Première suite de clavecin.* **

The anonymous arrangement of Rameau's five suites of *Pièces de clavecin en concert* for string sextet is a novelty and a pleasing one. The arranger used Rameau's instrumental version for harpsichord and two violins and the music becomes a true sextet only when the bass has a separate part. The additional *Sixth Suite* is a further transcription of four pieces taken from the third book for the harpsichord, published in 1728, and is very effective, including the famous *La Poule* (clucking realistically on violins to anticipate Saint-Saëns). The music is played spiritedly on modern instruments by the Caen Chamber Orchestra under Jean-Pierre Dautel; if, as recorded, the violins seem a shade pallid, this approaches the sound (if not always the degree of polish) we expect from a period group.

Dardanus: suite; *Les Indes galantes:* suite.

(B) *** DHM/BMG 05472 77420-2. Coll. Aur.

Any abrasiveness here deriving from the use of original instruments is countered by the generous acoustics of the Cedernsaal in the Schloss Kirchheim. But the playing has both life and elegance and the sound, though warm and full, is by no means bland: the flutes and oboes (and trumpets in *Les Indes galantes*) bring plenty of added colour. The selection from *Les Indes galantes* is shorter than Herreweghe's, but many will welcome the coupling with *Dardanus*. At super-bargain price this is very recommendable.

Ballet music: Les Fêtes d'Hébé; Hippolyte et Aricie.

*** Erato 3984 26129-2. Les Arts Florissants, Christie –
  MARC-ANTOINE CHARPENTIER: *La Descente d'Orphée aux Enfers* etc. ***

These extended selections from two of Rameau's ever-inventive and charmingly scored opera ballets were recorded to celebrate the twenty-fifth anniversary of William Christie and Les Arts Florissants. This is all delightfully fresh and inventive music and Rameau's scoring is ever-resourceful and as presented here constantly sparkling and ear-tickling. Most entertaining and beautifully recorded.

Les Indes galantes: suites for orchestra.

(B) *** HM (ADD) HMA 1901130. Chappelle Royale O,
  Herreweghe.

Besides the harpsichord arrangements listed below, Rameau also arranged his four 'concerts' of music from *Les Indes galantes* for orchestra. The result makes nearly three-quarters of an hour of agreeable listening, especially when played so elegantly – and painlessly – on original instruments, and very well recorded (in 1984) by Harmonia Mundi.

Naïs: orchestral suite. Le Temple de la Gloire: orchestral suite.

*** HM HMU 907121. Philh. Bar. O, McGegan.

There is much delightful music here and the playing by the Philharmonia Baroque Orchestra has ravishing finesse, showing original instruments at their most persuasively delicate, textures always transparent; the ear is continually beguiled by this warm and polished playing, beautifully recorded. A quite lovely disc.

CHAMBER MUSIC

Pièces de clavecin en concert Nos. 1–5.

(N) (BB) *** Virgin 2 x 1 VBD5 61872-2 (2). Trio Sonnerie –
  FORQUERAY: *Harpsichord Suites.* ***

The Trio Sonnerie (Monica Huggett, Mitzi Meyerson and Sarah Cunningham) are perfectly attuned to the sensibility of the period and its requirements. Theirs is a performance which exhibits a sense of style and a quality of feeling that outweigh any shortcomings. The most notable of these is the fact that they choose to limit the instrumental colours available to them by confining themselves to string instruments, excluding the flute which is usual in this repertoire.

The Virgin recording is of great naturalness and presence and this reissue, with its excellent coupling, is a strong contender.

KEYBOARD MUSIC

Les Indes galantes: excerpts (harpsichord transcriptions).

*** HM (ADD) HMC 1901028. Gilbert.

These transcriptions are Rameau's own, including not only dance numbers and orchestral pieces but arias as well. Kenneth Gilbert, playing a fine instrument in contemporary tuning, reveals these miniatures as the subtle and refined studies they are. He could not be better served by the recording engineers.

Music for Harpsichord: *Book 1* (1706); *Pièces de clavecin* (1724); *Nouvelles suites de pièces de clavecin* (c.1728); *La Dauphine.*

(N) (B) **(*) Double Decca (ADD) 468 555-2 (2). Malcolm (harpsichord) – FRANÇOIS COUPERIN: *Pièces de clavecin.* ***

George Malcolm gives secure and brilliant performances, but purists – and even the general listener – should approach them with some caution. His ornamentation is imaginative, but departs from the original in places, and his handling of *notes inègales* does not always carry conviction.

Music for harpsichord: *Book 1* (1706); *Pièces de clavecin* (1724); *Nouvelles suites de pièces de clavecin* (c. 1728); 5 *Pièces* (1741); *La Dauphine* (1747).

*** O-L 425 886-2 (2). Rousset (harpsichord).

Rousset's playing is marvellously persuasive and vital, authoritative and scholarly, yet fresh and completely free from the straitjacket of academic rectitude. He plays a Hemsch in a perfect state of preservation and a 1988 copy of a 1636 Ruckers harpsichord, modified by Hemsch. The sound is excellent.

Pièces de clavecin: Suite (No. 1) in A min.; L'Agaçante; La Dauphine; L'Indiscrète; La Livri; La Pantomime: La Timide.

(M) *** CRD (ADD) CRD 3320.. Pinnock.

Harpsichord Suites: in A min. (1728); *in E min.* (1724).

(M) *** CRD (ADD) CRD 3310. Pinnock.

Harpsichord Suites: in D min./maj. (1724); *in G maj./min.* (1728).

(M) *** CRD (ADD) CRD 3330. Pinnock.

Trevor Pinnock chose a mellow instrument here, making his stylish, crisply rhythmic performances even more attractive. The first selection includes *La Dauphine*, the last keyboard piece which Rameau wrote, brilliantly performed. Pinnock is restrained in the matter of ornamentation, but his direct manner is both eloquent and stylish. The harpsichord is of the French type and is excellently recorded.

Pièces de clavecin, Book I: Suite in A min. (1706); *Suites in E min.; D min.* (1724, rev. 1731).

(N) *** Chan. 0659. Yates (harpsichord).

Sophie Yates gives us Book I complete and plays it very persuasively indeed. Her ornamentation has flair and she is especially winning in the named pieces (notably the delightful *Vénétienne* in the *A minor* suite and the cascading *La Joyeuse* in the *D minor*). She uses a copy by Andrew Garlick of a 1749 Goujon harpsichord which has a most attractive palette, and she is very well recorded.

Suite de clavecin in E min. (1724).

(BB)*** HM Solo HMS 926018. Christie (harpsichord).

Rameau's *E minor Suite* is one of this most inventive from the bursting birdsong of *Le Rappel des oiseaux* to the charming portrait of *La Villageoise*, while the penultimate movement, a tender *Musette en rondeau*, is splendidly contrasted with the rumbustious closing *Tambourin*. William Christie plays the whole suite with infectious spontaneity and in fine style, and his Goujon-Swanen harpsichord is vividly recorded.

Grand motets: *In convertendo; Quam dilecta. Laboravi.*

(B) *** HM (ADD) HMA 1901078. Gari, Monnaliu, Ledroit, De Mey, Varcoe, Chapelle Royale Ch., Ghent Coll. Voc., Herreweghe.

These two motets are among Rameau's finest works. The Ghent Collegium Vocale is stiffened by forces from La Chapelle Royale in Paris. They produce excellent results, and the soloists are also very fine indeed. The instrumental ensemble includes several members of La Petite Bande, so its excellence can almost be taken for granted. The brief *Laboravi* makes an appealing little encore. This CD is even more attractive at bargain price.

OPERA-BALLET AND OPERA

(i) *Anacréon* (opéra-ballet; complete); (ii) *Le Berger fidèle* (cantata).

*** DG (IMS) 449 211-2. (i–ii) Gens; (ii) Félix, Massis, Del Pozo, Ch.; Musiciens du Louvre, Minkowski.

Rameau's *Acte de ballet Anacréon* has both vivacity and charm, and they are fully revealed in this splendidly alive, DG Archiv performance from Minkowski and his excellent Choeur and Musiciens du Louvre, who are given first-class recording. The plot asks the question: can love and wine coexist? There is real drama at the opening of Scene 2 when Anacreon's unremitting wining and dining is interrupted by the angry arrival of Bacchus's Priestess (the excellent Véronique Gens) to destroy a statue of Cupid and abduct Anacreon's neglected lover, Lycoris. Scene 3 opens with an atmospheric evocation reminiscent of Vivaldi: *Sommeil-Pluie* (delicate pizzicati) *-Orage*; here as elsewhere the ear is caught by the contributions from the petites flûtes (transverse baroque piccolos), which return piquantly in the closing *Contredanse* after the problem has been resolved with the very happy compromise: wine should be one of the joys of lovers, not alternative diversion! As an encore, Véronique Gens sings very affectingly an equally inspired 15-minute solo cantata which juxtaposes happiness and sacrifice with all the drama of the operatic stage. Once again the power of love wins out and tragedy is averted. This fine coupling now replaces Christie's earlier, Harmonia Mundi version of *Anacréon* with Les Arts Florissants (HMC 90190).

Les Boréades (complete).

(M) *** Erato (ADD) 2292 45572-2 (3). Smith, Rodde, Langridge, Aler, Lafont, Monteverdi Ch., E. Bar. Sol. Gardiner.

Though the story – involving the followers of Boreas, the storm god – is highly artificial, the music, involving many crisp and brief dances and arias, is as vital and alive as anything Rameau ever wrote. Gardiner here directs an electrifying performance with generally first-rate singing, except that Jennifer Smith's upper register, in the central role of Alphise, Queen of Baltria, is not sweet. Chorus and orchestra are outstanding and the recording excellent. Bizarre copyright problems prevented a libretto from being included, which makes it hard to follow the plot because the synopsis is not cued. However, the set is very welcome.

Castor et Pollux (complete).

*** HM HMC 901435/7. Crook, Corréas, Mellon, Gens, Schirrer, Brua, Piau, Les Arts Florissants Ch. & O., Christie.

(M) **(*) Erato 4509 95311-2 (2). Jeffes, Huttenlocher, Smith, Buchan, Wallington, Parsons, Rees, E. Bach Festival Singers & Bar. O, Farncombe.

William Christie's performance of Rameau's second *tragédie en musique* uses the original 1733 text, quite different from the 1754 text recorded by Charles Farncombe. Christie's performance consistently benefits from the dramatic timing, not least in the fluently alert and idiomatic exchanges in recitative, as well as in the broad, expressive treatment of set numbers like Telaire's lament, *Tristes apprets*, beautifully sung by Agnès Mellon. With such fine sopranos as Véronique Gens and Sandrine Piau in relatively small roles, the cast has no weakness. Howard Crook has the clear tenor needed for the role of Castor (who appears very late in the drama), with Jérôme Corréas a stylish Pollux. The sound is fresh and immediate and has plenty of body, with military percussion beautifully caught. This is now a clear first choice.

Farncombe, after a brisk and refreshing account of the Overture, fails to spring rhythms brightly enough. But this is an admirable mid-priced set, marked by an agreeably authentic orchestral contribution and some stylish singing, notably from Huttenlocher as Pollux, who was not in the stage performances. Excellently clear, 1982 digital recording with a most attractive ambience, made at All Saints', Tooting. The documentation, too, is admirable.

Castor et Pollux: highlights.

(B) *** HM HMX 290844/46 (3) (from above set; cond. Christie) – CAMPRA: *Idomenée*: highlights; LULLY: *Atys*: highlights. ***

(B) *** HM HMA 1901501 (as above).

This is one of Harmonia Mundi's enterprising 'Trios', compiling three discs of operatic highlights at bargain price, in this case with full documentation, including translation. *Castor et Pollux* is a masterpiece, vividly recorded, and this 70-minute selection, if taken with its two companions, costs

but a fraction of the price of the three-disc complete set. As can be seen, this is now also available as a separate Musique d'abord disc, also including full texts and translations.

Dardanus (complete).

(N) *** DG 463 476-2. Ainsley, Gens, Naouri, Delunsch, Courtis, Smythe, Kozená, Masset, Bindi, Ch. & O of the Louvre, Minkowski.

(M) **(*) Erato (ADD) 4509 95313-2 (2). Gautier, Eda-Pierre, Von Stade, Devlin, Teucer, Soyer, Van Dam, Paris Op. Ch. & O, Leppard.

Strongly cast and characterfully conducted, Minkowski's version offers a magnetic, lively reading of one of Rameau's finest *tragédies lyriques*. For reasons Minkowski explains, he opts for the earlier 1739 version of the score, but includes the most inspired passage from the 1744 revision, incompatible when its second half involves quite a different plot. So Dardanus's extended prison monologue, *Lieux funestes*, from 1744 is included as a moving prelude to Act IV. The striking combination of thrustful vigour and refinement in Minkowski's direction is instantly established in the Overture, and marks the whole performance, including the colourful dance movements which round off each act. The soloists are excellent, with Mireille Delunsch singing with beauty and biting dramatic power as Venus, and with Veronique Gens similarly beautiful yet subtly contrasted as the heroine, Iphise. In the title role John Mark Ainsley is in exceptionally sweet voice, light and clear, while Russell Smythe as Teucer, Iphise's father, is similarly fresh and well focused, with no weak link among the others. This was recorded live from a French Radio studio broadcast, with the double advantage of studio conditions and the flow of adrenalin from a live occasion. The storm sequence of Act IV could hardly be more dramatic, with vivid stage effects. The complete opera in prologue and five acts is neatly fitted on two very well-filled discs.

Though the French chorus and orchestra (using modern instruments) here fail to perform on Erato with quite the rhythmic resilience that Leppard usually achieves on record, the results are refreshing and illuminating, helped by generally fine solo singing and naturally balanced (if not brilliant) 1980 analogue recording, smoothly transferred to CD, with the choral sound quite vivid. José van Dam as Ismenor copes superbly with the high tessitura, and Christiane Eda-Pierre is a radiant Venus. The story may be improbable (as usual), but Rameau was here inspired to some of his most compelling and imaginative writing. Well documented and well worth exploring.

(i) Dardanus: extended orchestral suite; (ii) Les Fêtes d'Hébé: 3rd Entreé : La Danse (Acte de ballet).

(B) *** Erato Dig./ADD Ultima 3984 27002-2 (2). (i) E. Bar. Sol.; (ii) Gomez, Rode, Orliac, Monteverdi Ch. & O, Gardiner.

Dardanus (orchestral suite); Platée (orchestral suite).

*** Conifer 75605 51313-2. Philh. Bar. O, McGegan.

Gardiner offers a substantial selection (58 minutes) from the orchestral music of both versions of *Dardanus*. There is plenty of variety here, from lightly orchestrated dance music to the powerful closing *Chaconne*. The third Act of *Les Fêtes d'Hébé* (which is given here) is a pastoral interspersed with dances in which Mercury courts the shepherdess, Eglé. The music is inventive and delightful. As in *Dardanus*, Gardiner's performance is distinguished by an alive sensitivity: he secures excellent singing and playing from his first-rate team. Here the analogue recording is smoothly transferred, with lovely textures, the soloists most naturally balanced. All in all this makes an ideal and inexpensive introduction to the music of Rameau.

McGegan offers rather less music from *Dardanus* than Gardiner (about half-an-hour), but includes a charmingly Beechamesque *Air gracieux pour les Plaisirs*, omitted in the Erato suite. This makes room for the more extended suite from *Platée*, a 'ballet bouffon' dating from 1745 written as an entertainment at a royal wedding between the king's son and a princess noted for her plain appearance! Platée herself is an unlovely nymph who rules over a swamp full of frogs and insects (we hear them croaking in the *Passepieds* and *Tambourins*). However, she fancies herself as a catch for the roving eye of the amorous Jupiter. The mock nuptials are finally interrupted by Folie and Momus (the God of Ridicule). McGegan and his period-instrument orchestra are if anything more crisply resilient than Gardiner and not a whit less graceful. Moreover the Conifer recording is first-class and the suite from *Dardanus* is given a warmer ambience, notably in the lovely *Le Sommeil*. The music for *Platée* has plenty of character and charm and, like *Dardanus*, ends with a memorable *Chaconne* for which – as it is interrupted in the ballet – McGegan provides a concert ending.

La Guirlande; Zéphyre.

(N) *** Erato 8573 85774-2 (2). Daneman, Méchaly, Agnew, Bazola, Ockended, Decaudaveine, WDR Capella Coloniensis, Les Arts Florissants Ch. & O, Christie.

Rameau, as he was growing old in the 1740s, turned to writing such short operas, or ballets as they were called, as these. On classical pastoral themes, they have been described as 'Dresden-china Rameau', but that is to underestimate the bubbling inventiveness and warmth of expression which Rameau brought to these artificial stories. *La Guirlande*, the tale of a shepherd and shepherdess whose love is restored, appeared in 1751, but *Zéphyre*, telling the story of the Wind God, infatuated with the wood nymph Cloris, seems never to have been performed in Rameau's lifetime.

Though it is more limited in scale, in having only soprano soloists, it is even more inventive musically, with a sequence of striking numbers, as when the Goddess, Diana, briefly appears at the denouement, accompanied by braying horn-fanfares.

The duet which follows, with the voices of Zephyr and Cloris interweaving, is also one of the loveliest in this double bill. Not that *La Guirlande* is at all lacking in invention, with extended monologues and dialogues punctuated by brief set numbers not just for the soloists but for the chorus. In all this Christie and his team are at their most inspired, consistently fresh and lively, though the Capella Coliniensis of West German Radio is not quite as polished a period band as Christie's own in Paris. With excellent soloists,

notably Sophie Daneman and the pure 'haute-contre', Paul Agnew, this is a delightful set, giving new perspectives on the composer.

Hippolyte et Aricie (complete).

*** Erato (ADD) 0630 15517-2 (3). Padmore, Panzarella, Hunt, Naouri, James, Les Arts Florissants, Christie.

*** DG (IMS) 445 853-2 (3). Gens, Fouchécourt, Fink, Feighan, Massis, Naouri, Smythe, Sagittarius Vocal Ens., Les Musiciens du Louvre, Minkowski.

Christie has the benefit of using the text specially prepared for the complete Rameau Edition by Sylvie Bouissou, restoring fully the original (1733) edition. Marc Minkowski in his fine, crisply alert DG Archiv recording uses a text substantially similar, and both of them include the Prologue. The contrasts with Minkowski are striking, for Christie, using rather larger forces to produce warmer textures and timbres, consistently brings out the sensuous beauty of much of the writing as well as its dramatic point. At speeds fractionally broader, he bounces rhythms more infectiously and allows himself more flexible phrasing without undermining the classical purity of style. Though Anne-Maria Panzarella as Aricie is not as golden in tone as Véronique Gens for Minkowski, she is fresh and bright, responding immediately to Christie's timing which more consistently seems geared to stage presentation, with a conversational quality given to passages of recitative. Mark Padmore is a more ardent Hippolyte than his opposite number and Lorraine Hunt a weightier, more deeply tragic Phèdre, with Eirian James a warm Diana and Laurent Naouri as Thésée weightier than Russell Smythe. The Erato sound too is warmer and more immediate than the DG Archiv.

Mark Minkowski is helped by an excellent cast, with the two young lovers of the title ideally taken by the sweet, silver-toned Véronique Gens, enchantingly girlish, and the light, very French-sounding tenor, Jean-Paul Fouchécourt, similarly conveying depth of feeling in formal melodic lines. Also central to the set's success is the powerful performance of Bernarda Fink as Phèdre, firm and rich, well contrasted with Gens, as memorable in its way as Dame Janet Baker's on the original Argo set conducted by Anthony Lewis. Though in the other major role of Thesée Russell Smythe's baritone is not always sweet, he sings with clear focus and expression, with Luc Coadou aptly sinister as Tisifone and Laurent Naouri sepulchral as Pluton. In the formal scheme the longest, most sustained aria which comes at the very end, celebrating the nightingale, is given to an incidental character, a shepherdess, and is sung here sweetly and charmingly by Annick Massis. Minkowski also draws crisp, alert performances from his chorus and well-tuned orchestra.

Les Indes galantes (complete).

(M) *** Erato (ADD) 4509 95310-2 (3). Smith, Hartman, Elwes, Devos, Huttenlocher, Ens. Vocale à Coeur Joie de Valence, Paillard O, Valence, Paillard.

The plot of *Les Indes galantes* is complicated but brings opportunities for a splendid tempest and sailors' chorus in Act I, which is set in Turkey. Act II moves to Peru, with a Sun Festival and a volcano erupting (admittedly not as spectacular as the tempest), and Act III with its floral festival is appropriately pastoral and picturesque. Finally we are taken to an Amazonian forest, where the two principal European characters are courting an Indian girl, Zima. She chooses one of her own tribe instead, but a pipe of peace ensures a final reconciliation; there are spectacular trumpets and a triumphant aria from the heroine before the closing ballet. The work is full of lyrical inspiration, and Jennifer Smith sings ravishingly in the roles of Phani, Fatime and Zima, while John Elwes as Tacmas and Adario brings a headily beautiful light-tenor response. Gerda Hartman as Hébé, Emilie and Zaire is charmingly lightweight, if not always quite as secure as Smith, and Philippe Huttenlocher sings all his roles with distinction. Paillard directs the proceedings with much flair and warmth, and the 1974 recording is vividly atmospheric. With first-class documentation and a full translation, this is a set to cherish.

Naïs (complete).

(M) *** Erato (ADD) 4509 98532-2 (2). Russell, Caley, Caddy, Tomlinson, Jackson, Parsons, Ransome, E. Bach Festival Ch. and Bar. O, McGegan.

Rameau's opera Naïs tells of Neptune's courtship of the water-nymph Naïs and is full of bold invention. The overture has some astonishing dissonances and syncopations, and the opening battle scenes in which the Heavens are stormed by the Titans and Giants are quite striking. The performance, based on the 1980 English Bach Festival production, is full of spirit and uses authentic period instruments to good effect. The work is not long, and the rewards of the music are such as to counterbalance any reservations one might have as to imperfections in ensemble or the like. Admirers of Rameau will need no prompting to acquire this attractive reissue. The unconverted should sample the opening, which will surely delight and surprise. The sound of this 1980 recording is strikingly well balanced, vivid and present. Highly recommended.

Platée (complete).

** Erato 2292 45028-2 (2). Ragon, Smith, De Mey, Le Texier, Gens, Ens. Vocale Françoise Herr, Musiciens du Louvre, Minkowski.

Platée, written in 1745 and described as a 'ballet bouffon', is in fact a comic opera, based on a classical theme. With such a send-up of classical tradition, the performers here understandably adopt comic expressions and voices, which in a recording, as opposed to a stage performance, become rather wearing on the listener. Also almost all the soloists aspirate heavily in florid passages. Within that convention this is a lively, brisk performance, very well conducted by Marc Minkowski, but marred by the dryness of the recording.

La Princesse de Navarre (complete).

(M) *** Erato (ADD) 0630 12986-2 (3). Hill-Smith, Harrhy, Chambers, Rees, Goldthorpe, Caddy, Wigmore, Savidge, E. Bach Festival Singers and Bar. O, McGegan.

La Princesse de Navarre is a collection of dance movements which Rameau used in other works, as well as interludes for the Voltaire comédie. The finest is a chaconne of some magnificence, in which dancers and singers participate. This edition is the first to incorporate all the music Rameau composed for the work. There is some altogether delightful music here and a cued CD recording gives one the opportunity to pick and choose. Very good performances, and excellent recording too.

(i) Pygmalion (Acte de ballet); (ii) Nélée et Myrthis (Acte de ballet).

⊛ (M) *** HM HMT 7901381. (i) Crook, Piau; (i; ii) Mellon, Michel-Dansach; (ii) Corréas, Semellaz; (ii) Pelon; Ch. & O, Les Arts Florissants, Christie.

Pygmalion (Acte de ballet). Le Temple de la gloire (excerpts): Air gay; Ces oiseaux par leur doux ramage.

(M) **(*) Virgin VM5 61539-2. Fouchécourt, De Reyghere, Fournié, Piau.

In the story of Nélée and Myrthis the heroine, Myrthis, is put to the test by her lover, who encourages her to think his attentions are roving elsewhere. This is balanced by the famous legend of Pygmalion, who falls in love with a female statue he has sculpted. The statue is then (by the courtesy of Venus) brought to life by that very love – a moment of sheer orchestral magic in Rameau's delightful score. Both works have happy endings. The performances under Christie are comparatively intimate, giving the effect of chamber-operas, and are ideally cast. Howard Crook is a most sympathetic Pygmalion, and Agnès Mellon charming as Céphise. But then Donatienne Michel-Dansac is a soaringly sweet-voiced statue. The celebrated scene where the Statue learns to dance (in various different tempi) brings delightfully elegant and sprightly playing from the orchestra, where the piccolos are very telling. In the hardly less appealing companion piece, Mellon is equally well cast as a touching Myrthis, as is Françoise Semellaz as her apparent rival, Corinne. Beautifully balanced recording and a fully translated libretto earns this coupling the highest recommendation. The only slight snag is the comparatively meagre allotment of cues.

The alternative Virgin Veritas version is more robustly operatic, immediately obvious in the Overture, with its boldly repeated notes, superbly articulated which may (or may not) have been intended by Rameau to simulate the sculptor's chisel. Jean-Paul Fouchécourt gives a strong characterization of Pygmalion, but most listeners will find Howard Crook more sympathetic, and apart from Sandrine Piau as the Statue, her two female colleagues are more histrionic but less sweet-voiced than their rivals on Harmonia Mundi. Moreover, the excerpts from Le Temple de la gloire are quite brief (about 8 minutes), and while the Virgin reissue includes good notes and a libretto in French, there is no English translation.

RANGSTRÖM, Ture (1884–1947)

Symphonies Nos. 1 (August Strindberg in memoriam); 2 in D min. (My Country); 3 in D flat (Song under the Stars); (i) 4 (Invocation) – Symphonic Improvisations for

Orchestra & Organ; Dithyram; Intermèzzo drammatica; Vårhymn (Spring Hymn).

(N) (B) **(*) CPO 999 748-2 (3). Norrköping SO, Jurowski;
(i) Fahlsjö.

We discuss the individual issues of Nos. 1, 3 and 4 separately below, and the performances by the Norrköping Symphony Orchestra under Michail Jurowski are eminently acceptable. The package comes at a discount and those who enjoy the symphonies of Alfvén or Atterberg may well be tempted to investigate this set, although it must be said that neither as a symphonist nor as a man of the orchestra is Rangström their equal.

Symphony No. 1 in C sharp min. (August Strindberg in memoriam); Dithyramb; Spring Hymn.

**(*) CPO 999 367-2. Norrköping SO, Jurowski.

Symphonies Nos. 1; (i) 3 (Song under the stars).

** Sterling (ADD) CDS 1014-2. Swedish RSO, Segerstam;
(i) Helsingborg SO, Fürst.

Rangström's *First Symphony* dates from 1914, two years after the death of Strindberg, to whose memory it is dedicated, as indeed is the *Vårhymn* (*Spring Hymn*) of 1942 on the CPO disc. This also includes his very first orchestral work, the *Dithyramb* of 1909. Rangström was basically self-taught, and the prime influences are Franck and early Sibelius. There are some individual things in the slow movement but elsewhere, and particularly in the finale, the rhetoric is overblown and the ideas second-rate. It is strange that a composer who could write with such artlessness and inspiration in his songs or in the *Divertimento elegiaco* should exhibit such lapses of taste.

Of the two performances, Michail Jurowski is the more persuasive and he gets very good playing from the Norrköping orchestra. Leif Segerstam draws an accomplished performance from his players and is decently recorded in good analogue sound. It is difficult to work up much enthusiasm for the Sterling coupling, the *Third Symphony* ('Song under the stars'), which is also rather corny. No grumbles about the playing of the Helsingborg Symphony Orchestra under Janos Fürst.

Symphonies Nos. 3; (i) 4 in E flat (Invocatio).

** CPO 999 369-2. (i) Fahlsjö; Norrköping SO, Jurowski.

The *Third Symphony* (1929) takes one of his songs, *Bön till natten* ('Prayer to the night') as its starting point, but the result is terribly inflated. The *Fourth Symphony* (1933–6) is best described as a suite for orchestra and organ. Its invention is very uneven, though there is a charming *Intermezzo*, which forms the central movement. Good performances and recordings, but neither work is remotely convincing symphonically.

The Girl under the New Moon (Flickan under nymånen); Melody; The Only Moment; Pan; Prayer to the Night (Bön till natten); Villemo.

*** Virgin VC5 45273-2. Kringelborn, Martineau – GRIEG;
NIELSEN; SIBELIUS: *Songs.* ***

Rangström is Sweden's leading *romans* composer and the simplicity and eloquence of his best songs – and the present half dozen are among his very finest – are affecting. Although Solveig Kringelborn does not eradicate memories of Söderström or von Otter, she does these lovely songs justice and her pianist Malcolm Martineau is superb throughout. Excellent recorded sound too.

RATHAUS, Karol (1895–1954)

Symphony No. 1, Op. 5; Der letzte Pierrot.

*** Decca 455 315-2. Deutsches SO, Berlin, Yinon.

Karol Rathaus, born in Poland, left Germany just before the Nazis came to power, before settling in the USA. His music's language is distinctly expressionist, albeit not atonal, and is expertly laid out for the orchestra. The *First Symphony* is a striking and arresting score, which can be strongly recommended. The ballet *Der letzte Pierrot* is also rewarding, full of variety and interesting ideas. There are jazz elements and the motivic organization is skilful. The performances under Israel Yinon are very good indeed and the recording quite outstanding.

RAUTAVAARA, Einojuhani

(born 1928)

Anadyomene (Adoration of Aphrodite); (i) Flute Concerto, Op. 63; (ii) On the Last Frontier.

*** Ondine ODE 921-2. Helsinki PO, Segerstam; with
(i) Gallois; (ii) Finnish Philharmonic Ch.

Anadyomene or the *Adoration of Aphrodite* comes from 1969, and is highly atmospheric and compelling. The *Flute Concerto*, subtitled *Dances with the Winds*, employs bass flute, alto flute and piccolo. It is one of Rautavaara's most imaginative and resourceful scores, and its many hurdles are effortlessly despatched by the distinguished French soloist, Patrick Gallois. *On the Last Frontier*, a fantasy for chorus and orchestra, is inspired by Edgar Allan Poe's description of Antarctica, at the end of *The Narrative of Arthur Gordon Pym*. Vaughan Williams occasionally comes to mind in its pages. All three pieces are expertly performed by the Helsinki Philharmonic Orchestra under Leif Segerstam and superbly recorded.

(i) Angel of Dusk (Concerto for Double Bass & Orchestra); (ii) Cantos I–III for String Orchestra; (iii) Cantus arcticus (Concerto for Birds & Orchestra); (iv) Epitaph for Béla Bartók; Hommage à Ferenc Liszt; Hommage à Zoltán Kodály; (v) A Requiem in Our Time for Brass Ensemble; (vi) Clarinet Sonata; (vii) String Quartet No. 2.

(B) *** Finlandia Dig./ADD Ultima 3984 27003-2 (2).
(i) Kosonen, Finnish RSO, Segerstam; (ii) Tapiola Sinf., Lamminmäki; (iii) Klementi Institute SO, Pekkanen;
(iv) Helsinki Strings, Csaba & Géza Szilvay; (v) Helsinki PO, Panula; (vi) Kojo, Lagerspetz; (vii) Sibelius Qt.

This generously full Finlandia Ultima Double seems an ideal way of entering Rautavaara's highly individual sound world. The *Angel of Dusk* is a hauntingly unconventional way of writing a darkly atmospheric yet bravura concertante work for double bass and orchestra, with the Angel's 'closing appearance', a plaintive blending of toccata and threnody, finally fading into silence. In the *Cantus arcticus* the taped Arctic birds are full throated and equally balanced with the warmly sinuous orchestral melismas. The kernel of the searchingly restless *String Quartet* is the concentrated and deeply felt Adagio; the yearning finale is ambivalent, but curiously satisfying. The performance by the Jean Sibelius Quartet is deeply felt and well recorded.

Angels and Visitations; (i) Violin Concerto. Isle of Bliss.

✿ *** Ode ODE 881-2. (i) Oliveira; Helsinki PO, Segerstam.

Rautavaara's wholly original *Violin Concerto* is hauntingly accessible and grips the listener completely. It moves from an ethereal opening cantilena, through a series of colourful events and experiences until, after a final burst of incandescent energy, it makes a sudden but positive homecoming. The lively opening of the *Isle of Bliss* is deceptive, for the music centres on a dreamy, sensual romanticism and creates a rich orchestral tapestry with a sense of yearning ecstasy, yet overall it has a surprisingly coherent orchestral structure. *Angels and Visitations* is close to the visions of William Blake and (as the composer tells us) brings a sense of 'holy dread'. The extraordinary opening evokes a rustling of angels' wings, which is then malignantly transformed, becoming a ferocious multitude of bumblebees. It is a passage of real imaginative power, in some ways comparable to the storm sequence in Sibelius's *Tapiola*. The work is in a kind of variation form and moves from the ethereal nature of angels to demons quite readily, while later taking on board forceful rhythmic influences from Stravinsky's *Rite of Spring* and *Petrushka*. Its orchestration and impact are spectacular, hardly music for a small flat! Elmar Oliveira is the inspired soloist in the *Violin Concerto*, floating his line magically and serenely in the opening *Tranquillo* and readily encompassing the work's adventurous shifts of colour and substance. Segerstam provides a shimmering backing and directs a committed and persuasively spontaneous orchestral response throughout all three works. The recording is superbly balanced, spacious and vivid in detail.

Cantus arcticus (Concerto for Birds & Orchestra), Op. 61; (i) Piano Concerto, Op. 45; Symphony No. 3, Op. 20.

(BB) *** Naxos 8.554147. (i) Mikkola; RSNO, Lintu.

The *Cantus arcticus* (1972) uses taped Arctic bird-cries against an evocative orchestral background. The *Third Symphony* (1959–60) has genuine breadth and space. Rautavaara speaks of it as being 'freely constructed and emphatically tonal'. It has a strong feeling for nature. The later *Piano Concerto No. 1* (1969) has a certain neo-romantic feel to it. Laura Mikkola is a fervent exponent of it, and the Royal Scottish National Orchestra under Hannu Lintu play with real commitment and are well recorded.

Piano Concerto No. 3 (Gift of Dreams); Autumn Gardens.

*** Ondine 950-2. Helsinki PO, Ashkenazy.

The *Third Piano Concerto* is predominantly meditative and unconcerned with conventional bravura. It gets its subtitle from a Baudelaire setting, *La Mort des pauvres*, which Rautavaara made in the late 1970s and in which the words '*le don des rêves*' appear. *Autumn Gardens*, from 1999, also has a dreamlike feel to it. The performances are exemplary and the recording is in the demonstration class. The disc also includes a conversation between Rautavaara and Vladimir Ashkenazy.

Symphonies Nos. 1–3.

*** Ondine ODE 740-2. Leipzig RSO, Pommer.

Einojuhani Rautavaara is a symphonist to be reckoned with. Ideas never outstay their welcome and there is a sense of inevitability about their development. Those with a taste for Shostakovich or Simpson should find these pieces congenial. Good performances by the Leipzig Radio Orchestra under Max Pommer and very decent recorded sound too.

Symphony No. 6 (Vincentiana); (i) Cello Concerto, Op. 41.

*** Ondine ODE 819-2. (i) Ylönen; Helsinki PO, Pommer.

The *Sixth Symphony* draws on material from the opera, *Vincent* (1985–7), based on the life of van Gogh. There is, appropriately enough, no lack of colour, though the score tends to be both eclectic and amorphous. The orchestral scoring itself is quite sumptuous and there is no lack of incident. It comes with a much earlier and more cogently argued piece, the *Cello Concerto* of 1968, which is expertly played by Marko Ylönen. The recording is very impressive, well detailed and present, and is in the demonstration bracket.

Symphony No. 7 (Angel of Light); (i) Annunciations.

*** Ondine ODE 869-2. (i) Jussila; Helsinki PO, Segerstam.

Symphony No. 7; Cantus arcticus; (i) Dances with the Winds (Concerto for Flutes & Orchestra).

*** BIS CD 1038. (i) Alanko; Lahti SO, Vänskä.

The *Seventh Symphony* is the more substantial piece and is both powerful and atmospheric. There is a good deal of Sibelius in its first movement and there is a pervasive sense of nature. Rautavaara betrays some affinities with the minimalists but offers greater musical substance. *Annunciations* for organ, brass quintet, winds and percussion, written in 1976–7, strikes a more dissonant note but it is brilliant and well thought out. Kari Jussila is the virtuoso soloist, and the Helsinki orchestra under Segerstam are eminently well served by the Ondine engineers.

The new BIS version of the *Seventh Symphony* is every bit as good as its Ondine competitor, both artistically and as a recording. The sound is pretty state-of-the-art, though its rival has the deeper perspective. But Vänskä's performance has impressive power and atmosphere; he keeps the music moving and casts the stronger spell. Both shorter pieces, the familiar *Cantus arcticus* and the *Dances with the Winds*, a concerto in which the solo flautist plays four members of the flute family (though not at the same time), are from the 1970s, and these fine performances have appeared before in other couplings.

PIANO MUSIC

Etudes, Op. 42; Icons, Op. 6; Partita, Op. 34; Preludes, Op. 7; Piano Sonatas Nos. 1 (Christus und die Fischer), Op. 50; 2 (The Fire Sermon), Op. 64.

(BB) *** Naxos 8.554292. Mikkola.

These admirably lucid performances by Laura Mikkola fill an important gap. The *First Sonata* (*Christus und die Fischer*) comes from 1969, the same year as the *First Piano Concerto*, which this artist has also recorded with such success, and the *Second* (1970) is also most convincingly done. She is given first-class recorded sound. An excellent and economical way of filling in your picture of this fine composer.

VOCAL MUSIC

Ave Maria; Magnificat; Canticum Mariae Virginis; Missa Duodecanonica.

*** Ondine ODE 935-2. Finnish R. Chamber Ch, Nuoranne.

The *Ave Maria* (1957) for male voices and the *Missa Duode-canonica* (1963) for female voices are both serialist, albeit in much the same way as was Frank Martin's at one time. The *Magnificat* of 1979, the first Finnish setting of the text, has dignity and eloquence. The singing of the Finnish Radio Chamber Choir under Timo Nuoranne has security of pitch, subtle colouring and purity of tone. Expert, well-balanced Ondine recording.

Hymnus; Independence Fanfare; Octet for Winds; Playgrounds for Angels; Requiem in our Time, Op. 3; A Soldier's Mass; Tarantara.

(N) *** Ondine ODE 957-2. Soloists, Finnish Brass Symphony, Lintu.

A *Requiem in our Time* for brass and percussion put Rauta-vaara on the map. While he was in his mid-20s, before he began his studies with Copland, it won an American competition (1953). Rautavaara speaks of *A Soldier's Mass* (1968) as 'a companion work', although the forces involved are larger (it demands a full wind section) and the mood lighter. The *Octet for Winds* (1962) is mildly serial, but in no way inaccessible. Both the *Requiem* and the ingenious *Playgrounds for Angels*, the virtuoso piece written for the Philip Jones Brass Ensemble, are also available in a stunning BIS anthology by the German group, Brass Partout (BIS CD 1054 – see the Penguin 2000/1 Yearbook) which is not easily eclipsed. The rest of the programme is not otherwise available: *Hymnus*, for trumpet and organ was written recently for the Wagner scholar and critic, Barry Millington; *Tarantara* is for solo trumpet and played brilliantly by Pasi Pirinen, as for that matter is the rest of the programme. The Ondine recording is of demonstration quality.

RAVEL, Maurice (1875–1937)

Alborada del gracioso; Un barque sur l'océan; Boléro; Daphnis et Chloé (complete ballet); L'Eventail de Jeanne:

Fanfare; Introduction & Allegro for Harp, Flute, Clarinet & String Orchestra; Ma Mère l'Oye (complete ballet); Menuet antique; Pavane pour une infante défunte; Shéhérazade: Ouverture de féerie; Le Tombeau de Couperin; Trio in A min. (orch. Tortelier); Tzigane (for violin and orchestra); La Valse; Valses nobles et sentimentales. (Vocal): Don Quichotte à Dulcinée; Shéhérazade (song-cycles).

(N) (M) **(*) Chan. 7100 (4). Ulster O, Yan Pascal Tortelier; with Renaissance Singers, Belfast Philharmonic Soc.; Masters; Roberts; Finnie.

These are fine performances, and all with the advantages of excellent Chandos engineering. Tortelier's *Daphnis et Chloé* soon puts you under its spell: he conveys much of the sense of ecstasy and magic of this score and colours so richly hued and vivid that they belong to the world of the imagination rather than reality. Phrasing is sensitive, and there are some gorgeous sounds throughout. All the same, this version does not have quite the ecstatic quality of the old Munch version or Dutoit on Decca.

Ma Mère l'Oye has a more balletic feel that usual to it, bringing out the affinities with *Daphnis et Chloé*. The exotic orchestration associated with *Laideronnette, Empress of the Pagodas* glitters vividly, yet the lovely closing *Jardin féerique*, opening serenely, moves to a joyous climax. Tortelier's *Rapsodie espagnole* is not quite as gripping as some celebrated accounts (Reiner, Karajan, for instance), but it is highly atmospheric all the same.

Whether or not Ravel approved of full strings, the *Introduction and Allegro* loses some of its ethereal quality when given in this form, although the playing of the harpist, Rachel Masters, is impeccable. The validity of Tortelier's own transcription of the *Piano Trio* begs the question that Ravel was himself rather good at orchestration, and had he thought it worthwhile he might have had a shot at it himself! Some of the orchestral effects are idiomatic, but others (particularly the climax in the finale) are more questionable.

To most ears something quite essential is lost in the process; the soul as well as the scale of this music lies in the sonorities Ravel chose, and although Tortelier's skill and musicianship are not in question, this transcription is not one to which many will want to return. Tortelier directs the *Tzigane* from the bow, as it were, and plays very well, and this and the performance of *Le Tombeau de Couperin*, *La Valse* and *Valses nobles* have plenty of appeal.

The Ulster Orchestra certainly plays consistently well, and the top quality Chandos sound is a considerable bonus. The *Ouverture de féerie* is impressive, as is Linda Finnie's account of the *Shéhérazade* song-cycle, although it must be admitted that in neither vocal beauty not interpretative insight does it challenge classic accounts by Crespin or Baker. No grumbles about Stephen Roberts's fine singing in the *Don Quichotte* songs, but overall this set has uneven appeal and will best suit those for whom outstanding recorded quality is paramount.

Alborada del gracioso; Une barque sur l'océan; Boléro; Daphnis et Chloé (ballet: suite No. 2. L'Eventail de Jeanne: Fanfare. Menuet antique; Ma Mère l'Oye (complete); Pavane pour une enfante défunte; Rapsodie espagnole; Le

Tombeau de Couperin; La Valse; Valses nobles et sentimentales.

⚙ *** Double Decca 460 214-2 (2). Montreal SO, Dutoit.

Anyone beginning a Ravel collection, or coming fresh to most of this repertoire and willing to duplicate, will find this Double Decca unbeatable value, including as it does all the key orchestral works, though not the piano concertos (by no means a disadvantage, when there is plenty of choice available). The orchestral playing is wonderfully sympathetic and the recording ideally combines atmospheric evocation with vividness. The balance is most musically judged and very realistic; indeeed the sound remains in the demonstration class.

(i) *Alborada del gracioso; Une barque sur l'océan; Boléro;* (ii) *Daphnis et Chloé* (ballet) *suite No. 2;* (i) *L'Eventail de Jeunne: Fanfare; Menuet antique; Pavane pour une infante défunte; Rapsodie espagnole; Shéhérazade: Ouverture de féerie. Le Tombeau de Couperin; La Valse; Valses nobles et sentimentales.*

(B) *** DG Double Dig./ADD 459 439-2 (2). (i) LSO;
(ii) Boston SO, with New England Conservatory Ch., Abbado.

Abbado's feeling for the music's atmosphere is matched by his care for detail, and the glowing analogue recording was one of the best made in Symphony Hall in the analogue era. *Ma Mère l'Oye* is omitted, yet the early overture to *Shéhérazade* is included alongside the *Alborada* and *Une barque sur l'océan*. Abbado gets delicious sounds in all three, as he does in the *Valses nobles et sentimentales*. The sultry atmosphere of *Rapsodie espagnole* is very evocative, the *Pavane* has a grave, withdrawn melancholy and the characteristically polished and refined playing is matched by sound with a wide dynamic range, a fine focus, and yet plenty of ambience and warmth. *Boléro* and the exquisitely played *Le Tombeau de Couperin* are also included on another single-disc anthology, below.

(i) *Alborada del gracioso;* (ii) *Une barque sur l'océan; Boléro;* (i; iii) *Piano Concerto for the Left Hand;* (ii; iv) *Daphnis et Chloé* (complete ballet); (ii) *Fanfare pour L'Eventail de Jeanne; Menuet antique; Ma Mère l'Oye* (complete ballet); (i) *Pavane pour une infante défunte; Rapsodie espagnole;* (ii) *Shéhérazade: Ouverture de féerie. Le Tombeau de Couperin; Valses nobles et sentimentales.*

(M) **(*) Sony (ADD) SM3K 459 439-2 (2). (i) Cleveland O;
(ii) NYPO; Boulez; (iii) with Entremont; (iv) Camerata Singers.

Boulez's distinguished Sony set offers a glitteringly iridescent account of the *Ouverture de féerie*, which is omitted by Dutoit. Entremont's account of the *Left-hand Concerto* is strong and characterful and not lacking in colour; but the rather fierce CBS sound does not flatter the piano timbre. On the whole, however, the remastering makes the most of recordings which were originally among the best of their period (1972–5). Boulez allows all the music ample time to breathe; gentler textures have the translucence for which this conductor is admired. There is no doubt that this music-making with its cleanly etched sound is immensely

strong in character, and many listeners will respond to it very positively.

Alborada del gracioso; Une barque sur l'océan; Boléro; Ma Mère l'Oye (complete); *Menuet antique; Ouverture de féerie; Pavane pour une infante défunte; Rapsodie espagnole; Le Tombeau de Couperin; La Valse; Valses nobles et sentimentales.*

(B) *** EMI double forte (ADD) CZS5 68610-2 (2). O de Paris, Martinon.

Like his version of *Daphnis et Chloé*, Martinon's *Ma Mère l'Oye* is exquisite, among the finest ever put on record. Although the *Valses nobles et sentimentales* and *La Valse* do not eclipse the 1961 Cluytens versions (see below) and the present *La Valse* has a rather harsh climax, there is much ravishing delicacy of orchestral playing, notably in *Le Tombeau de Couperin* and the rare *Ouverture de féerie* (*Shéhérazade*). The sound is warm and luminously coloured and the refined virtuosity of the Orchestre de Paris is a constant source of delight. Excellent value.

Alborada del gracioso; Une barque sur l'océan; Boléro; Ma Mère l'Oye (complete ballet); *Menuet antique; Pavane pour une infante défunte; Rapsodie espagnole; Le Tombeau de Couperin; La Valse; Valses nobles et sentimentales.*

(M) *** EMI (ADD) CZS7 67897-2 (2). Paris Conservatoire O, Cluytens.

These 1961 performances, made in the Salle Wagram, Paris, are as good as any in the catalogue. They have a strongly idiomatic and atmospheric feel; the *Rapsodie espagnole*, *La Valse* and the *Valses nobles* are exceptionally good, and so too is the complete *Ma Mère l'Oye*. The only snag is the wide vibrato of the horn in *Pavane pour une infante défunte*. The recordings still sound remarkably realistic, and not just for the period: they are very good by present-day standards.

(i) *Alborada del gracioso; Boléro;* (ii) *Daphnis et Chloé: Suite No. 2; Rapsodie espagnole;* (i) *La Valse.*

(M) **(*) Sony (ADD) SMK 60565. (i) O Nat. de France;
(ii) NYPO; Bernstein.

This is repertoire at which Bernstein excels: *La Valse* has a genuinely intoxicating quality, *Alborada del gracioso* glitters as it should, and the *Boléro* is most effective. These French recordings were made in 1975 and are very good, though not in the demonstration class. The *Daphnis Suite* dates from 1961, and is excellent too, with an immensely exciting finale (the recording is not quite so satisfactory though), and the 1973 *Rapsodie espagnole*, if a little indulgent here and there, has atmosphere and imagination. An enjoyable collection.

(i) *Alborada del gracioso;* (ii) *Boléro;* (i) *Pavane pour une infante défunte; Rapsodie espagnole;* (ii) *Le Tombeau de Couperin; La Valse.*

(M) *** Sony (ADD) SMK 60303. (i) Cleveland O; (ii) NYPO;
Boulez.

These recordings come from the three-disc Boulez anthology above, showing him at his very finest, securing top-class performances from both orchestras. Atmosphere is not sacrificed to detail, and the concentration of the playing is remarkable. The recordings from the early 1970s have all been impressively remastered.

Alborada del gracioso; Boléro; (i) *Daphnis et Chloé* (complete). *Ma Mère l'Oye* (complete); *Pavane pour une infant défunte; Rapsodie espagnole; La Valse; Valses nobles et sentimentales.*

(N)(B) **(*) Double Decca (ADD) 468 564-2 (2). SRO, Ansermet (i) with Lausanne R. Ch.

Any comprehensive stereo Ravel discography would be incomplete without Ansermet's pioneering recordings, made between 1957 and 1965 in the excellent acoustics of the Victoria Hall, Geneva. But although Ansermet's ear for detail brought undoubted insights, the playing of the Suisse Romande Orchestra was distinctly variable in quality, and seldom matched the superb contribution of the Decca recording team, which included as producers James Walker and Michael Bremner, and as balance engineers Roy Wallace and, later, James Lock.

It was the vividness of the Decca sound which made these recordings famous; nevertheless two of the earliest works to be recorded, the *Rapsodie espagnole* and *Ma Mère l'Oye*, both from 1957, earned our praise in their day when we commented (concerning the latter) on the 'gauze-like textures of the quieter music, spun with the utmost delicacy, the sound at once vivid and iridescent'.

The strings sound impressive now the recordings have been remastered, but the ambient glow remains. Ansermet's coolness suits the *Pavane*, while *La Valse* was a piece which roused him and he always did well, spectacular and atmospheric. The outstanding *Boléro*, one of the last works to be recorded (in 1965), has held its place as top recommendation up to the present day.

But the complete *Daphnis and Chloé*, from the same sessions, although again magnificently served by the engineers, misses the rapture and magic which Monteux for one so readily found, and the Swiss orchestra does not play with the virtuosity and sensitivity that this masterly score demands. Ansermet aficionados will surely want this generously full Double Decca, but the general collector would do better to invest in Abbado, Dutoit or Martinon (not necessarily in that order).

(i) *Alborado del gracioso; Boléro; Rapsodie espagnole; Le Tombeau de Couperin;* (ii) *Valses nobles et sentimentales.*

(B) **(*) Sony (ADD) SBK 48163. Phd. O, (i) Ormandy; (ii) Munch.

Ormandy was a first-class Ravel conductor. These performances are eminently well worth the money at bargain price, even if the recording is not three-star by present-day standards.

Alborada del gracioso; Daphnis and Chloé: suite No. 2; Introduction & Allegro for Harp, Flute, Clarinet & String Quartet; Ma Mère l'Oye (suite); Rapsodie espagnole.

(N) (M) *** RCA (ADD) 09026 63683-2. Chicago SO, Martinon.

These are fresh, vital accounts. The opening of the *Rapsodie espagnole* may strike the listener as a bit fast, but overall

Martinon's conception is sound, and the result – as with the rest of the programme – is undoubtedly idiomatic. The *Introduction and Allegro* is a chamber orchestral version using a fairly full body of violins which fill out the climaxes, and this detracts a little from the music's sublime textural delicacy. However with excellent 1960s sound and brilliant playing from the Chicago SO, this is a distinctive reissue on RCA's High Performance label. Bizzarely, the sleeve note concentrates only on *Daphnis and Chloé*, though a note by Martinon about Ravel is included.

Alborada del gracioso; Daphnis et Chloé (Suite No. 2); Rapsodie espagnole; Le Tombeau de Couperin; La Valse.

** DG (ADD) 453 194-2 (3 + 1). Stuttgart RSO, Celibidache – DEBUSSY: *Images etc.* (**)

For Celibidache, refinement of sonority is the *sine qua non* of his music-making. And he does produce a beautiful sound from the Stuttgart orchestra, though the affected phrasing is tiresome. The middle section of the *Alborada* has great mystery and atmosphere, though it is still terribly slow. The recordings come from the 1970s and are not always as successfully balanced as is usual from Südwestfunk.

Alborada del gracioso; Fanfare for L'Eventail de Jeanne; Ma Mère l'Oye (complete ballet); Miroirs: La Vallée des cloches (arr. Grainger); La Valse; (i) Shéhérazade (song-cycle).

*** EMI CDC7 54204-2. (i) Ewing; CBSO, Rattle.

The recording of the CBSO, made in the Arts Centre of Warwick University, is spectacular, with a state-of-the-art sound-balance of the widest range and amplitude. The orchestral playing is superb. Rattle captures the lambent allure of Percy Grainger's orchestration of the last of the *Miroirs* and gives an equally glowing account of *Ma Mère l'Oye*. At the beginning of the programme, Maria Ewing's *Shéhérazade* is matched in voluptuous intensity by Rattle and his players; in the aching yearning of *La Flûte enchantée* the atmosphere becomes more impressionistic. But it is essentially a dramatic performance, and the shimmering *Alborada* is well placed to follow on afterwards.

Alborada del gracioso; Pavane pour une infante défunte; Rapsodie espagnole; Le Tombeau de Couperin; La Valse.

(M) *** Mercury (IMS) (ADD) 432 003-2. Detroit SO, Paray – IBERT: *Escales.* **(*)

Paray's *Rapsodie espagnole* can be spoken of in the same breath as the Reiner/RCA and Karajan/EMI versions, with its languorous, shimmering textures and sparkling *Feria*. His *Alborada* glitters and the *Pavane* is glowingly elegiac. *La Valse*, too, is impressively shaped and subtly controlled. *Le Tombeau de Couperin* has great refinement and elegance: the solo oboist plays beautifully. All have been excellently remastered.

Alborada del gracioso; Pavane pour une infante défunte; Rapsodie espagnole; Valses nobles et sentimentales.

(M) *** RCA (ADD) GD 60179. Chicago SO, Reiner – DEBUSSY: *Ibéria.* ***

These performances are in an altogether special class. In

the *Rapsodie espagnole*, the *Prélude à la nuit* is heavy with fragrance and atmosphere; never have the colours in the *Feria* glowed more luminously, while the *Malagueña* glitters with iridescence. In the three and a half decades since it first appeared, this is the recording we have turned to whenever we wanted to hear this work for pleasure. No one captures its sensuous atmosphere so completely as did Reiner, and the recorded sound with its natural concert-hall balance is greatly improved in terms of clarity and definition.

Alborada del gracioso; Boléro; Pavane pour une infante défunte; La Valse; (i) Shéhérazade (song-cycle); Vocalise en forme de habanera (orch. Hoérée).

(BB) *** Virgin 2 x 1 VBD5 61742-2 (2). (i) Augér; Philh. O, Pešek – CANTELOUBE: *Chants d'Auvergne.* ***

This is a particularly attractive programme, brilliantly recorded. The Philharmonia are in exuberant form. The *Alborada* glitters, the *Boléro* is built steadily to a splendid climax, and among the solos the flamboyant trombone is particularly memorable. The *Pavane* has a noble dignity and *La Valse* liltingly generates plenty of adrenalin. Arleen Augér's lovely voice is ideally suited to a languorous account of *Shéhérazade*, which she makes entirely her own, opening *Asie* gently and seductively but expanding to a passionate climax, while *La Flûte enchantée* is more intimate, with some delicately refined playing from the Philharmonia solo flute. If you also want the (excellent) coupling, this is a fine bargain.

Boléro.

(M) *** DG (ADD) 447 426-2. BPO, Karajan – DEBUSSY: *La Mer;* MUSSORGSKY: *Pictures.* ***

Boléro; Daphnis et Chloé: Suite No. 2.

(M) *** DG (ADD) 427 250-2. BPO, Karajan – DEBUSSY: *La Mer; Prélude.* ***

Karajan's 1964 *Boléro* is a marvellously controlled, hypnotically gripping performance, with the Berlin Philharmonic at the top of its form. It is available either with a superb suite from *Daphnis et Chloé*, or among DG's Legendary Recordings series of 'Originals'; the couplings on both discs show Karajan at his very finest.

Boléro; (i) Daphnis et Chloé (complete ballet). Ma Mère l'Oye (suite); Pavane pour une enfante défunte; Rapsodie espagnole; La Valse.

(N) (B) *** RCA 2-CD (ADD) 74321 84604-2 (2). Boston SO, Munch; (i) with New England Conservatory & Alumni Ch. (with DUKAS: *L'Apprenti sorcier.* **(*))

We have a special affection for these Ravel performances, which include the first stereo recordings RCA made with Munch and his great Boston Orchestra in the incomparable acoustics of Symphony Hall. The complete *Daphnis et Chloé*, (unbelievably) dates from 1955, and is discussed more fully below under its separate issue. *Ma Mère l'Oye* and *La Valse* came in 1958 and the rest in 1962.

The translucent quality of the recording of *Ma Mère l'Oye* gives a pure and lovely sound to the orchestral texture, and Munch and his players are caught up in its shimmering

radiance. He then uses the *Rapsodie espagnole* to show off the orchestra's prowess in the many sparkling and highly coloured effects.

The percussion section, every department, is marvelously captured and the string glissandi also, while the ear is seduced by the sultry atmosphere and the exquisite recorded tone of the quiet muted strings. *La Valse* is both voluptuous and exciting with the orchestra driven almost to a frenzy at the climax. The *Pavane*, elegantly played, is rather too forwardly balanced, but *Boléro* generates plenty of tension, and here the range of dynamic here is enough to make a properly graduated climax. Dukas's *L'Apprenti sorcier* (1957) also sounds pretty marvellous and is played with élan to produce a spectacular if somewhat driven climax.

(i) Boléro; Daphnis et Chloé: Suite No. 2; Ma Mère l'Oye: Suite; (ii) Rapsodie espagnole; La Valse.

**(*) Australian Decca Eloquence 466 667-2. (i) LAPO, Mehta; (ii) LSO, Monteux.

Mehta's Ravel is very high powered, but the visceral excitement he produces is most compelling. *La Valse* is full of tension, and the *Daphnis suite* builds up to a splendid climax. *Ma Mère l'Oye* is brilliantly played too, although here the music's sense of gentle rapture is less fully realized. Not surprisingly, *Boléro* is a great success. Throughout, one marvels at the vivid Decca sound and the brilliance of the playing of the Los Angeles orchestra, and one feels that this period (late 1960s and 1970s) was Mehta's golden recording era. Monteux's LSO account of the *Rapsodie espagnole* is justly famous; it is a memorably glowing account, drenched in atmosphere, and, despite some tape hiss, it still sparkles.

Boléro; (i) Daphnis et Chloé: Suite No. 2; Ma Mère l'Oye (suite); Valses nobles et sentimentales.

(BB) *** Naxos 8.550173. (i) Slovak Philharmonic Ch.; Slovak RSO (Bratislava), Jean.

The Slovak Radio Orchestra, which is a fine body and is superbly recorded, respond warmly to Kenneth Jean. At the price, this is very good value indeed; the *Ma Mère l'Oye* can hold its own alongside all but the most distinguished competition: indeed *Les Entretiens de la belle et de la bête* is as keenly characterized as Dutoit at mid-price, and *Le Jardin féerique* is enchanting. For those wanting these pieces this is a real bargain.

Boléro; Jeux d'eau (orch. Viacava); Ma Mère l'Oye: Suite; (i) Tzigane. La Vallée des cloches (orch. Grainger); La Valse; (ii) 5 Mélodies populaires grecques.

(M) **(*) Cala CACD 1004. (i) Chase; (ii) Burgess; Philh. O, Simon.

The test of good orchestration is to convey the illusion that the music could have existed in no other form, and it is a tribute to Viacava's cunning and expertise that he succeeds as well as he does (albeit not completely) to disguise the keyboard origins of *Jeux d'eau*. Percy Grainger's *La Vallée des cloches* is quite remarkable, calling as it does on an exotic array of glockenspiel, vibraphone, marimba, celeste and dulcitone plus the strings of a piano struck by a mallet. It is not perhaps wholly Ravel in sensibility, but it is highly effective in its own right. Geoffrey Simon directs good performances from the Philharmonia: his two soloists in the *Cinq mélodies populaires grecques* and *Tzigane* are excellent, and the recording is very good indeed.

Boléro; Ma Mère l'Oye (complete); Pavane pour une infante défunte; Rapsodie espagnole; La Valse.

(N) (M) *** Ph. (ADD) 464 733-2. LSO, Monteux.

For this Philips reissue Polygram have taken the opportunity to combine recordings from two separate sources. Monteux's 1964 version of the complete *Ma Mère l'Oye* is a poetic, unforced reading, given naturally balanced sound. *La Valse* is impressive too, and *Boléro* has well-sustained concentration, even though some will raise an eyebrow at the slight quickening of pace in the closing pages. These three recordings are taken from a Philips original which has responded well to its digital remastering, retaining its warmth while obtaining a clearer profile. The *Pavane* and *Rapsodie espagnole*, however, come from a Decca source and date from two years earlier, yet the sound has strikingly more range and an added lustre. The *Pavane* is warm and poised; the *Rapsodie espagnole* can be spoken of in the same breath as Reiner's version. Monteux moves naturally and spontaneously from the exotic nocturnal atmosphere of the opening *Prélude à la nuit* to the flashing brilliance of the closing *Feria*.

Boléro; Rapsodie espagnole.

*** DG 439 013-2. BPO, Karajan – MUSSORGSKY: *Pictures.* ***

Karajan's later versions of *Boléro* and *Rapsodie espagnole* find the Berlin Philharmonic in characteristically brilliant form, recorded in very wide-ranging digital sound; the thrust of *Boléro* and the sensuousness of the *Rapsodie* are conveyed with unerring power and magnetism, and the close of the *Feria* of the *Rapsodie espagnole* is spectacular indeed!

Boléro; Rapsodie espagnole; La Valse.

(B) *** DG Penguin 460 633-2. LSO, Abbado – MUSSORGSKY: *Pictures at an Exhibition.* ***

Boléro; La Valse.

(N) (M ** Chan. 6615. Detroit SO, Järvi – DEBUSSY: *La Mer;* MILHAUD: *Suite provençale.* **

Abbado has impeccable taste in this repertoire, and it goes without saying that the LSO plays superbly throughout. No complaints about the 1986 digital recording. The author's essay is by Richard Forde.

Järvi's *La Valse* opens atmospherically but is fairly brisk and not without its moments of exaggeration – indeed, affectation unusual in this conductor. There is no lack of tension, either here or in *Boléro*, although this is not a first choice for either piece. Very natural recorded sound.

Piano Concerto in G.

✿ (M) *** EMI (ADD) CDM5 67238-2 [CDM5 67258]. Michelangeli, Philh. O, Gracis – RACHMANINOV: *Piano Concerto No. 4.* *** ✿

Piano Concerto in G; Piano Concerto in D for the Left Hand.

(N)(BB) *** Warner Apex (ADD). 8573 89232-2. Quéffelec, Strasbourg PO, Lombard – DEBUSSY: *Fantaisie for Piano & Orchestra.* ***

(*) Chan. 8773. Lortie, LSO, Frühbeck de Burgos – FAURE: *Ballade.* *

(M) *(*) EMI CDM5 66905-2. François, Paris Conservatoire O, Cluytens.

(i) Piano Concerto in G; Piano Concerto for the Left Hand. Une barque sur l'océan; L'Eventail de Jeanne: Fanfare; Menuet antique.

**(*) Decca 410 230-2. (i) Rogé; Montreal SO, Dutoit.

(i–ii) Piano Concerto in G; Piano Concerto for the Left Hand; (ii) La Valse; (i) (Piano) Valses nobles et sentimentales.

(B) *** CfP (ADD) CD-CFP 4667. (i) Fowke; (ii) LPO, Baudo.

(i) Piano Concerto in G; Piano Concerto for the Left Hand. Jeux d'eau (ii) La Valse (for 2 pianos).

(N) (BB) *** EMI Encore CDE5 74749-2. Collard (i) O Nat. de France, Maazel; (ii) Béroff.

(i; ii) Piano Concerto in G; (i; iii) Piano Concerto for the Left Hand; (ii) Valses nobles et sentimentales.

*** ✿ DG 449 213-2. (i) Zimerman; (ii) Cleveland O; (iii) LSO; Boulez.

(i) Piano Concerto in G; Gaspard de la nuit.

(M) *** DG (ADD) 447 438-2. Argerich, (i) BPO, Abbado – PROKOFIEV: *Piano Concerto No. 3.* ***

Piano Concerto for the Left Hand in D.

(BB) *** ASV CDQS 6092. Osorio, RPO, Bátiz – FRANCK: *Symphonic Variations* **(*); SAINT-SAENS: *Wedding-Cake* ***; SCHUMANN: *Concerto.* ***

Ravel's masterpiece is well served on CD but this reissue in EMI's 'Great Recordings of the Century' is second to none. Michelangeli's slow movement is ravishing, and the sparkle of the outer movements is underpinned by a refined Ravelian sensitivity. The remastering of the early stereo master (1957) is wholly beneficial, the sound full yet remarkably transparent in revealing detail.

Zimerman's *G major Concerto*, the *Valses nobles et sentimentales* and the *Left-hand Concerto* are also well nigh perfect in every respect. Boulez's account of the *Valses nobles* is quite wonderfully atmospheric, indeed magical, and in the concertos the delicacy and finesse of Krystian Zimerman's pianism is dazzling, his refinement of nuance and clarity of articulation a source of wonder. Beautifully balanced and finely detailed recording.

Argerich's half-tones and clear fingerwork give the *G major Concerto* unusual delicacy, but its urgent virility – with jazz an important element – comes over the more forcefully by contrast. The compromise between coolness and expressiveness in the slow minuet of the middle movement is tantalizingly sensual. Her *Gaspard de la nuit* abounds in character and colour. The remastered recordings sound first class.

When Jean-Philippe Collard's coupling of the two concertos first arrived on LP in the 1980s we gave it the highest praise. It offers splendidly vivid recording quality, and Collard gives a meticulously refined and sparkling account of the *G major Concerto* and a brilliant and poetic account of the *Left-Hand Concerto*. He brings great *tendresse* to the more reflective moments and there is real delicacy of feeling throughout. Maazel's thoroughly sympathetic support shows how keenly attuned he is to this composer, and the Orchestre National play superbly. The solo account of *Jeux d'eau* is touched with the same sensitivity, and the other bonus is a rare two-piano version of *La Valse* in which Collard is admirably partnered by Michel Béroff. This is a real bargain.

Anne Quéffelec's accounts of both Ravel concertos are less extrovert than Collard's, thoughtful and imaginative and often bringing an enticing languor, yet without loss of sparkle in the outer movements of the *G major*. She is a thorough musician with a considerable technique and no mean sense of poetry and her approach is refreshing. The excellent Strasbourg Orchestra under Alain Lombard give her admirable support, and the recording is well balanced in a warm acoustic. Again excellent value and proof that there are different ways of approaching these highly engaging works.

The performances of both the *Concertos* by Philip Fowke with Baudo and the LPO are particularly attractive in the way they bring out the jazzy side of Ravel's inspiration with winning results. In the slow movement of the *G major Concerto* the Spanish overtones also come out strongly, and Fowke's solo playing in the *Valses nobles et sentimentales* is clean, bright and rhythmic in a muscular way, without ever becoming brutal or unfeeling; nor does he lack poetry. Baudo and the orchestra also give a strongly characterized reading of *La Valse*. Excellent 1988 recording; is irresistible at bargain price.

Pascal Rogé brings both delicacy and sparkle to the *G major Concerto*, which he gives with his characteristic musical grace and fluency. He brings great poetry and tenderness to the slow movement; but in the *Left-Hand Concerto* he is a good deal less dynamic, even though there is much to admire in the way of pianistic finesse – and charm. The Decca recording offers excellent performances of three short orchestral pieces as a makeweight, but this remains at full price.

Louis Lortie's account of the two *Concertos* on Chandos has the advantage of altogether outstanding recording. In the *G major* he is often highly personal without becoming unduly idiosyncratic, with a fastidious sense of colour at his command. In the *Left-Hand Concerto* he really takes his time over the cadenzas and his agogic hesitations are sometimes over-indulgent. Immaculate playing as such, and superb recording.

Samson François has good analogue sound in his favour. But the choice of this pairing for EMI's 'Great Recordings of the Century' series is surely misguided, however much affection the French may feel for the soloist. François was not always a particularly sensitive player and there is little to recommend in his efficient but prosaic performance of one of Ravel's most magical works. Fortunately his spirited account of the *Left-Hand Concerto* is more competitive. The piano is forwardly balanced, but not at the expense of orchestral detail.

Jorge Federico Osorio's account of the *Left-Hand Concerto* can hold its own with the best and it is very well recorded. With its tempting bargain couplings, about which there are only minor reservations, this disc is a genuine bargain. He also gives a crisp and colourful performance of the *Alborada* in an alternative, full-price coupling with Prokofiev.

(i) *Piano Concerto in G; Piano Concerto for the Left Hand in D. A la manière de Borodine; A la manière de Chabrier; Gaspard de la nuit; Jeux d'eau; Menuet antique; Menuet sur le nom de Haydn; Miroirs; Pavane pour une infante défunte; Prélude; Sonatine; Le Tombeau de Couperin; Valses nobles et sentimentales.*

(B) **(*) Ph. Duo (ADD) 438 353-2 (2). Haas; (i) Monte-Carlo Opéra O, Galliera.

Werner Haas has a genuine Ravel sensibility and he plays with delicacy and a fine feeling for the music's colour and its moments of gentle rapture. The performances of the two *Concertos* match the rest, refined and satisfying. Perhaps the playing here is a little strait-laced (elsewhere Haas is often pleasingly flexible) but Galliera's fine accompaniments add to the authority of these performances, and the 1968 recording is well balanced. These are performances one could live with.

Daphnis et Chloé (ballet; complete).

⚫ (M) *** RCA (ADD) 09026 61846-2. New England Conservatory & Alumni Ch., Boston SO, Munch.
*** Decca 443 934-2. Groot Ch., Conc. O, Chailly – DEBUSSY: *Khamma.* ***
*** Testament (ADD) SBT 1128. Choeurs René Duclos, Paris Conservatoire O, Cluytens – FRANCK: *Psyché.* (***)

Daphnis et Chloé (complete); *Boléro*.

(BB) *** EMI Encore CDE5 74750-2. CBSO & Ch., Rattle.

Daphnis et Chloé (complete); *Pavane pour une infante défunte; Rapsodie espagnole*.

(M) *** Decca (ADD) 448 603-2. ROHCG Ch., LSO, Monteux.

Daphnis et Chloé (complete); *Pavane pour une infante défunte; La Valse*.

(M) *** Decca 458 605-2. Montreal SO & Ch., Dutoit.

Charles Munch's Boston account is one of the great glories of the 1950s. The playing in all departments of the Boston orchestra is simply electrifying. The sound here may not be as sumptuous as the Dutoit on Decca, but the richness of colour lies in the playing, and there is a heady sense of intoxication that at times sweeps you off your feet, and the integration of the chorus is impressively managed. Try the *Danse de supplication de Chloé* (track 15) and the ensuing scene in which the pirates are put to flight, and you will get a good idea of how dazzling this is, with the ballet ending in tumultous orchestral virtuosity.

Dutoit adopts an idiomatic and flexible style, observing the minute indications of tempo change but making every slight variation sound totally spontaneous. The final *Danse générale* finds him adopting a dangerously fast tempo, but the Montreal players – combining French responsiveness with transatlantic polish – rise superbly to the challenge, with the choral punctuations at the end adding to the sense of frenzy. The digital recording is wonderfully luminous, with the chorus ideally balanced at an evocative half-distance, fully worthy of Decca's Legends series. The CD is now generously cued.

Monteux conducted the first performance of *Daphnis et Chloé* in 1912; Decca's 1959 recording, a demonstration disc in its day, captured his poetic and subtly shaded reading in vivid colours in the most agreeably warm ambience. The performance was one of the finest things Monteux did for the gramophone. Decca have added his 1962 recording of the *Pavane*, wonderfully poised and played most beautifully, and the highly spontaneous *Rapsodie espagnole*.

Riccardo Chailly conducts a remarkably fine *Daphnis*. The excellence of the orchestral playing can be taken for granted, and the same goes for the luminous Decca recording, perhaps the finest the work has received. Not necessarily a first recommendation, but a choice that is unlikely to disappoint.

With André Cluytens's 1962 version with the Paris Conservatoire Orchestra you are confronted with the orchestral tradition that Ravel himself would have known; they have a voluptuousness all their own. The *Danse de Pan* is wonderfully atmospheric (and marvellously played) and the stereo recording beautifully open and natural. This was before the days when naturalness became a casualty in the engineers' desire to astonish us with *their* own brilliance.

Simon Rattle conducts the CBSO in a most warmly expressive reading of Ravel's great ballet score. The sensuous beauty of the slow sequences is enhanced by the mistily evocative recording, though the dynamic range is extreme. Such showpiece numbers as the *Danse guerrière* and the final *Danse générale* have a winning resilience and energy. *Boléro* is relatively slow and easily expressive, not as hard-edged as it can be. Excellent value.

Daphnis et Chloé: suite No. 2.

(N) **(*) BBC (ADD) BBCL 4039-2. PO, Boult – BIZET: *Jeux d'enfants*; SCHUBERT: *Symphony No. 8 (Unfinished)*; SIBELIUS: *Symphony No. 7.* **(*)

RL recalls hearing Sir Adrian conduct *Daphnis* in the early 1950s and being astonished by his slow tempo in *Lever du jour*. He subsequently learnt that Boult had adopted Ravel's tempo, after Boult had heard the composer conduct the piece in the 1920s. It really feels too slow all the same, but his account has a finely controlled sensuousness that is very persuasive. Excellent sound.

Daphnis et Chloé: Suite No. 2; Pavane pour une infante défunte.

(N)(M) *** Häns. CD 93013. Stuttgart SW RSO, Prêtre – BIZET: *Symphony in C.* ***

(***) Testament mono SBT1017. Philh. O, Cantelli – CASELLA: *Paganiniana*; DUKAS: *L'Apprenti sorcier*; FALLA: *Three-Cornered Hat.* (***)

Prêtre shapes the opening of *Daybreak* with an ecstatic richness of line, the Stuttgart strings gloriously expansive. There is some radiant woodwind playing too in the *Pantomime* and the principal flute of this fine orchestra plays his famous solo with scintillating brilliance leading on to a thrillingly zestful *Danse générale*. *La Valse* rises out of the mists and Prêtre's string phrasing is again passionately seductive, the final climax thrillingly impulsive yet still controlled. This is 'live' music-making at its finest, and the warm ambience of the digital recording is just right for it.

Cantelli's account of *Daphnis* was among his last – and finest – records. It sounds remarkably good in this splendid transfer and has classic status.

(i) Introduction & Allegro for Harp, Flute, Clarinet & Strings (orchestral version); (ii) Ma Mère l'Oye (ballet suite); (iii) Pavane pour une infante défunte; (iv) La Valse.

(B) *** Sony (ADD) SBK 63056. (i) Cleveland O, Lane; (ii) Philh. O, Tilson Thomas; (iii) Cleveland O, Szell; (iv) Phd. O, Ormandy – DEBUSSY: *Petite suite*; SATIE: *Gymnopédies Nos. 1 & 3.* ***

The orchestral version of Ravel's haunting *Introduction and Allegro* is less delicately textured than the chamber version, but as played by the splendid Cleveland Orchestra under Louis Lane it does not lose its magic or its refinement of feeling. Michael Tilson Thomas is wholly attuned to the sensibility of Ravel's ravishing *Ma Mère l'Oye*. Szell takes over the Cleveland podium for the *Pavane*, which brings more first-class playing, particularly from the orchestra's principal horn. Finally Ormandy and the Philadelphia Orchestra give a sensuous, exciting, bravura account of *La Valse*, with the 1963 sound suitably spacious and with plenty of atmosphere.

Ma Mère l'Oye (complete ballet).

(B)*** Ph. (ADD) 462 938-2. Pittsburgh SO, Previn – SAINT-SAENS: *Carnival of the animals*; DUKAS: *L'Apprenti sorcier* ***

Ma Mère l'Oye: suite.

(M) *** Mercury (IMS) (ADD) 434 343-2. Detroit SO, Paray – DEBUSSY: *Ibéria* etc. ***

(B) *** CfP (ADD) 574 9472 (with *Boléro*). SNO, Gibson – BIZET: *Jeux d'enfants*; SAINT-SAENS: *Carnival.* ***

Ma Mère l'Oye: suite; Rapsodie espagnole.

(M) *** DG (IMS) (ADD) 415 844-2. LAPO, Giulini – MUSSORGSKY: *Pictures.* ***

In Previn's version, played and recorded with consummate refinement, the quality of innocence shines out. The recording is superb, with the Philips engineers presenting a texture of luminous clarity. Now at bargain price this is very competitive indeed, particularly as Philips have added Zinman's attractive version of Dukas's narrative masterpiece.

Paray's gently evocative *Ma Mère l'Oye* is most beautifully played and recorded. The score's calm innocence with its undercurrent of quiet ecstasy is caught perfectly. So lustrous is the sound that it is almost impossible to believe the early recording date: 1957.

The Giulini Los Angeles performance conveys much of the sultry atmosphere of the *Rapsodie espagnole*. Indeed some details, such as the sensuous string responses to the cor anglais tune in the *Feria*, have not been so tenderly caressed since the intoxicating Reiner version. The *Ma Mère* l'*Oye* suite is also sensitively done; though it is cooler, it is still beautiful.

Gibson is highly persuasive, shaping the music with obvious affection and a feeling for both the innocent spirit and the radiant textures of Ravel's beautiful score. The orchestral playing is excellent and, with excellent couplings, this is very recommendable.

Ma Mère l'Oye (ballet): Suite (with narration).

(BB) *** Naxos 8.554463. Morris (nar.), Slovak RSO, Jean – DUKAS: *L'Apprenti sorcier;* SAINT-SAENS: *Carnival of the Animals* **(*).

Ma Mère l'Oye is exquisite music and it is most beautifully played by the Slovak orchestra under Kenneth Jean. Johnny Morris provides a friendly spoken introduction for each fairy-tale number which has been admirably and concisely written by Keith and Anthony Anderson. To link them with Ravel's music is surely a marvellous way of familiarizing younger children with the music.

Ma Mère l'Oye: Suite; La Valse

** Chan 9799. Danish Nat. RSO, Termirkanov – TCHAIKOVSKY *The Nutcracker* ** (with GADE: *Tango: Jalousie*)

It is difficult to know quite for whom this recording is designed. Recordings of the *Ma Mère l'Oye* suite and *La Valse* are hardly in short supply and most collectors will want a more logical coupling than bits of Act II of *Nutcracker.* Including the Gade item was a curious idea. No complaints about the sound.

Le Tombeau de Couperin; La Valse.

(B) *** Decca Penguin 460 649-2. Montreal SO, Dutoit – DEBUSSY: *Nocturnes;* SATIE: *3 Gymnopédies.* ***

Dutoit's account of Ravel's delightful *Tombeau de Couperin* is wonderfully sensitive and sympathetic, and the recording offers demonstration quality, transparent and refined, with the textures beautifully balanced and expertly placed. Jonathan Cope, who provides the author's note, should be very happy with this performance which will surely rekindle his nostalgic memories of that first heady discovery of this wonderful music. *La Valse* too is a model of its kind, and again the playing of the Montreal orchestra is absolutely first class, while the Decca recording has a clarity, range and depth of perspective that is equally satisfying. But what a pity room was not found for Dutoit's exquisite account of *Ma Mère l'Oye.*

Tzigane (for violin and orchestra).

(M) *** EMI (ADD) CDM5 66058-2. Perlman, O de Paris, Barenboim – SAINT-SAENS: *Havanaise;* VIEUXTEMPS: *Violin Concertos Nos. 4 & 5.* ***

*** EMI CDC7 47725-2. Perlman, O de Paris, Martinon – CHAUSSON: *Poème;* SAINT-SAENS: *Havanaise* etc. ***

(M) *** DG 447 445-2. Perlman, NYPO, Mehta – BERG; STRAVINSKY: *Concertos.* ***

(M) *** Decca 460 007-2. Chung, RPO, Dutoit – LALO: *Symphonie espagnole;* VIEUXTEMPS: *Violin Concerto No. 5.* ***

(B) **(*) Ph. 420 887-2. Szeryng, Monte Carlo Op. O, Remoortel – SAINT-SAENS: *Violin Concerto No. 3* etc. **(*)

Perlman's classic (1974) account of Ravel's *Tzigane* for EMI is marvellously played; the added projection of the CD puts the soloist believably at the end of the living-room and the orchestral sound retains its atmosphere. As can be seen this is offered in alternative couplings.

Perlman's later digital version is very fine and the recording is obviously modern. But the earlier, EMI performance has just that bit more charisma.

With its seemingly improvisatory solo introduction, *Tzigane* is a work which demands an inspirational artist, and Kyung Wha Chung is ideally cast, catching the atmosphere of this elusive piece with natural affinity.

Szeryng was at the height of his powers when he recorded his splendidly strong and committed account of Ravel's *Tzigane,* flexible and responsive as well as brilliant in execution. The recording spotlights him so that the rather less distinguished orchestral contribution emerges less strongly.

Valses nobles et sentimentales.

(*) DG (IMS) 429 785-2. NYPO, Sinopoli – MUSSORGSKY: *Night* etc. *

With Sinopoli, Ravel's *Valses nobles et sentimentales* is perhaps a shade too idiosyncratic, even though it is played superbly by the New York Philharmonic.

CHAMBER MUSIC

Berceuse; Pièce en forme de habanera; Tzigane.

*** DG (IMS) 445 880-2. Dumay, Pires – DEBUSSY; FRANCK: *Violin Sonatas.* ***

Polished and elegant performances of these Ravel pieces. There would, of course, have been room on this disc for the 1922 *Sonata,* which at premium price would have made better sense as well as value for money. However, no complaints about these performances or the recording quality.

Introduction & Allegro for Harp, Flute, Clarinet & String Quartet.

(***) Testament mono SBT 1053. Gleghorn, Lurie, Stockton, Hollywood Qt – CRESTON: *Quartet;* DEBUSSY: *Danse sacrée* etc. TURINA: *La oración del torero;* VILLA-LOBOS: *Quartet No. 6.* (***)

(i) Introduction & Allegro; (ii) Pièce en forme de habanera.

(B) *** Cala CACD 1018 (2). Campbell; (i) Bennett, Jones, Allegri Qt; (ii) York – POULENC: *L'Invitation au château* etc. ***

The Cala performances are recommendable in their own right, but they come in a particularly valuable two-CD set for the price of one, which includes over two hours of music for wind instruments by Poulenc. It is sheer delight from start to finish and cannot be too strongly recommended.

The Hollywood Quartet's version of the *Introduction and allegro* gives us an example of the exquisite flute playing of Arthur Gleghorn as well as the artistry of Mitchell Lurie and Ann Mason Stockton. A fine performance, sounding remarkably fresh for a 1951 recording.

(i; ii) Introduction & Allegro for Harp, Flute, Clarinet & String Quartet; (ii; iii; iv) Piano Trio; (v) String Quartet; (ii; iii) Violin Sonata; (vi) Sonata for Violin & Cello; (vii) Chansons madécasses.

(M) ** Calliope (ADD) CAL 3822.4 (3). (i) Jamais & Ens.; (ii) Barda; (iii) Carracilly; (iv) Heitz; (v) Talich Qt; (vi) Hanover String Duo; (vii) Herbillon, Larde, Degenne, Paraskivesco – DEBUSSY: *Chamber Music.* **(*)

The *String Quartet* was recorded in 1972 and very good it is too. The remaining performances in the repertoire date from 1974 and are decent rather than distinguished. The recordings are all analogue – and none the worse for that! But this is serviceable rather than special.

Piano Trio in A min.

*** Ph. 411 141-2. Beaux Arts Trio – CHAUSSON: *Piano Trio.* ***

*** Hyp. CDA 67114. Florestan Trio – DEBUSSY; FAURE: *Piano Trios.* ***

*** Chan. 8458. Borodin Trio – DEBUSSY: *Violin & Cello Sonatas.* ***

(BB) **(*) Naxos 8.550934. Joachim Trio – DEBUSSY: *Piano Trio in G*; SCHMITT: *Piano Trio: Très lent.* **(*)

The most recent Beaux Arts account of the Ravel *Trio* is little short of inspired and is even finer than their earlier record of the late 1960s. The recording, too, is of high quality, even if the piano is rather forward.

Led by the masterly pianist Susan Tomes, the Florestan Trio also give an outstanding account of the Ravel masterpiece. They generally adopt speeds on the fast side, but with no feeling of haste, thanks to playing at once highly polished and flexibly expressive. The couplings are unique and apt, with each composer represented at a different period of his career. Vivid sound.

The Borodin Trio are excellently recorded and their playing has great warmth and is full of colour. Some may find them too hot-blooded by the side of the Beaux Arts.

The Naxos version by the Joachim Trio who comprise Rebecca Hirsch, Caroline Dearnley and the pianist John Lenehan is worth any collector's notice. They play with sensitive musicianship and finesse. Their performance is imaginative and beautifully recorded, and it is far from uncompetitive.

Piano Trio in A min.; Sonata for Violin & Cello; (i) Chansons madécasses; 3 Poèmes de Stéphane Mallarmé (song-cycle).

(BB) **(*) Virgin 2 x 1 Double VBD5 61427-2 (2). Nash Ens. (members), (i) with Walker – DEBUSSY: *Chamber Music.* **

The *Sonata for Violin and Cello* is expertly played by Marcia Crayford and Christopher van Kampen – as good an account as any – and in the *Piano Trio* Ian Brown joins them in a performance of real stature and eloquence. In the *Chansons madécasses* and the exquisite *Trois poèmes de Stéphane Mallarmé* Sarah Walker is *primus inter pares* rather than a soloist,

though she is not balanced as reticently by Andrew Keener's team as is Delphine Seyrig in the Debussy *Chansons de Bilitis*. This is a pity, but it is not an insuperable obstacle to an apt and inexpensive Ravel collection.

(i) Piano Trio in A min.; (ii) String Quartet in F; (iii) Violin Sonata in G.

(M) **(*) Ph. (ADD) 454 1342-2. (i) Beaux Arts Trio; (ii) Italian Qt; (iii) Grumiaux, Hajdu.

Ravel's *String Quartet* is offered here as part of a triptych of Ravel's key chamber-works. The performance by the Quartetto Italiano has long been praised by us. The Beaux Arts give a predictably fine account of the *Trio*, though the violinist, Daniel Guilet, is a shade wanting in charm. In the *Violin Sonata* Grumiaux's playing has great finesse and beauty of sound. The recordings date from 1966 and are very naturally balanced, but the CD transfer demonstrates their age by a degree of shrillness of the fortissimo string-timbre.

String Quartet in F.

❀ *** Koch 3-6436-2. Medici Qt – BRITTEN: *Quartet No. 3*; JANACEK: *Quartet No. 1*; SHOSTAKOVICH: *Quartet No. 8*; SMETANA: *Quartet No. 1.* ***

*** DG (IMS) 437 836-2. Hagen Qt – DEBUSSY; WEBERN: *Quartets.* ***

*** Sony SK 52554. Juilliard Qt – DEBUSSY; DUTILLEUX: *Quartets.* ***

(N) (BB) *** EMI Début CDZ5 74020-2. Belcea Qt – DEBUSSY: *String Quartet in G min.* DUTILLEUX: *Ainsi la nuit.* ***

(M) *** DG (ADD) 463 082-2. Melos Qt – DEBUSSY: *String Quartet in G min.* *** ❀

(N) (B) *** DG (ADD) 469 591-2. LaSalle Qt. – DEBUSSY: *Quartet.* ***

(N) (M) *** Ph. 464 699-2. Italian Qt – DEBUSSY: *Quartet.* ***

(B) *** CfP CD-CFP 4652. Chilingirian Qt – DEBUSSY: *Quartet.* ***

(*) ASV CDDCA 930. Lindsay Qt – DEBUSSY: *String Quartet* **(*); STRAVINSKY: *3 Pieces.* *

(N) (M) **(*) EMI CDM5 67550-2 [567551]. Alban Berg Qt – DEBUSSY: *String Quartet* **(*); STRAVINSKY: *Concertino; Double Canon; 3 Pieces.* ***

(B) **(*) Discover DICD 920171. Sharon Qt – BEETHOVEN: *Harp Quartet* **(*); MOZART: *Quartet No. 1.* ***

(B) **(*) Sony (ADD) SBK 62413. Tokyo Qt – DEBUSSY: *Quartet* **(*); FAURE: *Piano Trio.* (*)

(N) (BB) ** Warner Apex 8573 89231-2. Keller Qt – DEBUSSY: *Quartet.* **

String Quartet in F; (i) Introduction & Allegro for Harp, Flute, Clarinet & String Quartet.

(BB) *** Naxos 8.550249. Kodály Qt, (i) with Maros, Gyöngyössy, Kovács – DEBUSSY: *Quartet.* **(*)

In the hands of the Medici players the opening of the Ravel *Quartet* is utterly magical, its subtlety of atmosphere caught with a perfection rare in the concert hall, let alone on record. This is a great performance of a masterly work, for the stillness at the opening of the *Très lent* make one hold one's breath at the music's *tendresse*. The recording is completely tangible: it is as if these players were at the end of one's room.

The Hagen Quartet give a performance of great finesse and tonal refinement, and are beautifully recorded to boot, very well served by an excellent balance from one of DG's best engineers, Wolfgang Mitelehner.

The Juilliard are very impressive too, not quite so youthful, elegant and fresh in their approach but eminently polished and sensitive. This Sony disc is to be recommended primarily to those attracted to the fine Dutilleux bonus. However, the earlier (and less expensive) versions remain very competitive.

The Belcea Quartet sounds as if it is completely inside the music, but its responses are still fresh and felt keenly. As in the Debussy, it is scrupulous in detail and tempos could not be judged better. A performance of real finesse that can be recommended along with the best; at budget price it also enjoys a strong competitive edge.

The Melos playing is perfect in ensemble, has fine attack and great beauty of tone. The slow movement offers the most refined and integrated matching of timbre; in terms of internal balance and blend it would be difficult to surpass, and the reading has great poetry. In both the Scherzo and finale the Melos players evince the highest virtuosity, with complete identification with Ravel's sensibility. The (1979) sound remains excellent in its Galleria transfer, and this disc remains among the primary mid-priced recommendations for this coupling.

There is little to choose between the DG LaSalle perform-ance and the Italian Quartet on Philips. If the latter have perhaps the greater immediacy and sense of vitality, the former create a superb feeling of atmosphere and bring great freshness and delicacy to this score. The DG transfer of the early 1970s recording is excellent and this Classikon disc now has a price advantage.

For many years the Italian Quartet held pride of place in this coupling. Their playing is perfect in ensemble, attack and beauty of tone, and their performance remains highly recommendable, one of the most satisfying chamber-music records in the catalogue. However, it has now reverted to mid-price from its previous bargain incarnation.

The Chilingirian recording has plenty of body and pres-ence, and also has the benefit of a warm acoustic. The players give a thoroughly committed account, with well-judged tempi and very musical phrasing. The Scherzo is vital and spirited, and there is no want of poetry in the slow move-ment. At mid-price this is fully competitive and the sound is preferable to that of the Italian Quartet on Philips.

The Naxos version can more than hold its own. Artistically and technically this is a satisfying performance which has the feel of real live music-making. The *Introduction and Allegro* is not as magical or as atmospheric as that of the Melos Ensemble from the 1960s, nor is it as well balanced (the players, save for the harp, are a bit forward), but it is still thoroughly enjoyable.

A highly accomplished and finely etched performance from the Lindsays, who play with their usual aplomb and panache. There are splendid things here, notably the youthful fire of the opening movement and the vivid finale. They do not always match the poetic feeling and the *douceur*

which some rivals find, but this is not a neglible account, and it is well recorded.

Superb, indeed incomparable playing from the Alban Berg Quartet, and splendidly full and sonorous recording from the EMI engineers. Yet while this is marvellously polished and has such excellence in terms of ensemble and tonal blend, there is a want of spontaneity that ultimately weighs against it, so that one is unable to forget the physical aspects of the music-making and become totally absorbed in the music itself.

The Sharon Quartet are completely at home in this music and play with ardour and sensitivity. The resonant acoustic (a Cologne church) suits the work better than the Beethoven coupling. It certainly does not cloud the Scherzo or the energetic account of the finale (which also has much delicacy of feeling) and adds warmth and atmosphere to the *très lent*. Very good playing: if the couplings are suitable, this is a bargain.

The Tokyo Quartet play with great finesse and tonal beauty, especially in the warm yet refined account of the *très lent*. They certainly observe the marking of the finale, *vif et agité* and perhaps elsewhere there could be a touch more poise. But their music-making is thoroughly alive. The sound is very good.

The Keller Quartet are tauter and more dramatic than some of their rivals, but for all its merits their performance does not match those rivals in terms of subtlety and tonal finesse.

Violin Sonata in G.

*** Virgin VC5 45122-2. Tetzlaff, Andsnes – DEBUSSY: *Sonata;* JANACEK: *Sonata;* NIELSEN: *Sonata No. 2.* ***
*** Erato 0630 15110-2. Repin, Berezovsky – MEDTNER: *Sonata No. 3 (Sonata epica).* ***

Violin Sonata; Tzigane.

(B) *** CfP 573 1152. Little, Lane – DEBUSSY; POULENC: *Violin Sonatas.* ***

(i; ii) *Violin Sonata (1897); Violin Sonata in G; Tzigane; (i;iii) Sonata for Violin & Cello; (i;ii) Berceuse sur le nom de Gabriel Fauré; Kadish; Pièce en forme de habanera; Tzigane.*

*** Decca 448 612-2. (i) Juillet; (ii) Rogé; (iii) Mørk.

The performance from Christian Tetzlaff and Leif Ove Andsnes proves as characterful and imaginative as any avail-able, and an additional attraction is the interest of the couplings, in particular the Nielsen *Second Sonata*. Excellent recording too.

Chantal Juillet and Pascal Rogé present a *Tzigane* with a difference in that Rogé uses a piano luthenal (an instrument modified to sound like a cimbalom, which was used in the first performance in 1922) and Juillet sounds more zigeuner-like than most of her rivals. Their accounts of the two *Sonatas* are predictably cultured and beautifully recorded. Pascal Rogé scores over Cho-Liang Lin's partner in terms of sheer responsiveness, and Chantal Juillet and Truls Mørk are first rate in the *Duo Sonata*. Strongly recommended, if this programme is suitable.

In their well-designed collection of violin-and-piano

music, Tasmin Little and Piers Lane also give outstanding performances, very well recorded, aptly and subtly changing style for each composer, equally bringing out the contrast of tone in the two Ravel works here, the *Sonata* fleeting and elusive, the *Tzigane* more rhetorical and extrovert. Pointing of rhythm could hardly be more persuasive, with Little relishing the colour-changes in the central Blues movement of the *Sonata*. Excellent sound.

Vadim Repin and Boris Berezovsky on Erato offer an unusual coupling. These two artists command a wide range of colour and dynamics, infuse every phrase with life, and have the full measure of the 'Blues' movement. Repin plays the Guarneri with which Isaac Stern delighted us for almost half a century and it sounds magnificently responsive in his hands. Very good and completely natural recording.

PIANO MUSIC
Piano duet

Boléro; Introduction & Allegro; Ma Mère l'Oye; Rapsodie espagnole; La Valse.

⊛ *** Chan. 8905. Lortie and Mercier.

Louis Lortie's recital for piano (four hands and two pianos) with his Canadian partner, Hélène Mercier, is quite magical; these artists command an exceptionally wide range of colour and dynamic nuance. The acoustic is that of The Maltings, Snape, and the result is quite outstanding sonically: you feel that you have only to stretch out and you can touch the instruments. Ravel's transcriptions are stunningly effective in their hands, even, surprisingly, *Boléro*.

Ma Mère l'Oye.

*** Ph. 420 159-2. K. & M. Labèque – FAURE: *Dolly;* BIZET: *Jeux d'enfants.* ***

The Labèque sisters give an altogether delightful performance of Ravel's magical score, which he later orchestrated and expanded. The recording could not be more realistic and present.

Solo piano music

Complete solo piano works: *A la manière de Borodine; A la manière de Chabrier; Gaspard de la nuit; Jeux d'eau; Menuet antique; Menuet sur le nom de Haydn; Miroirs; Pavane pour une infante défunte; Prélude; Sérénade grotesque; Sonatine; Le Tombeau de Couperin; La Valse; Valses nobles et sentimentales.* (i) *Sites auriculaires; Ma Mère l'Oye* (i–ii) *Frontispièce.*

(B) *** EMI (ADD) CES5 72376-2 (3). Collard, with (i) Béroff; (ii) K. Labèque – DEBUSSY: *En blanc et noir* etc. ***

Jean-Philippe Collard's Ravel playing never falls below distinction. What a beautiful sense of line he achieves in *Ondine*, the first of the *Gaspard de la nuit*, though it must be admitted that the right-hand ostinato is far from the pianopianissimo which Ravel marks. The recording, made in the Salle Wagram, is not wholly sympathetic; there is a shallow quality, particularly in the upper part of the spectrum.

A la manière de Borodine; A la manière de Chabrier; Gaspard de la nuit; Jeux d'eau; Menuet antique; Menuet sur le nom de Haydn; Miroirs; Pavane pour une infante défunte; Prélude; Sérénade grotesque; Sonatine; Le Tombeau de Couperin; Valses nobles et sentimentales.

*** Decca 433 515-2 (2). Thibaudet.

(M) *** CRD 3383/4 Crossley.

(M) *** Chan. 7004/5. Lortie.

(BB) **(*) Virgin 2 x 1 Double VBD5 61489-2 (2). Queffélec.

Jean-Yves Thibaudet's collected Ravel is quite outstanding playing on all counts; Thibaudet exhibits flawless technique, perfect control, refinement of touch and exemplary taste. He distils just the right atmosphere in *Oiseaux tristes* and *Une barque sur l'océan* – but then, one might as well choose any other piece from *Miroirs*, and his *Gaspard* can hold its own with any in the catalogue. The recording is of real distinction too.

Paul Crossley's accounts of all these works are aristocratic, with an admirable feeling for tone-colour and line, and rarely mannered. His version of *Le Tombeau de Couperin* has a classical refinement and delicacy that are refreshing. The CRD recording is very good indeed.

Chandos have now put Louis Lortie's two Ravel discs together. We found his *Gaspard de la nuit* with its chilling and atmospheric account of *Le Gibet* particularly impressive. The Chandos sound, which emanates from The Maltings, Snape, is very realistic and truthful.

No quarrels with Anne Queffélec's playing. There are some masterly and enjoyable interpretations here, but it is all far too closely observed, as if one were in the front row of the concert hall; as a result not all the atmosphere registers to full effect, once the dynamics rise above *mf*. However, this is now the least expensive way of collecting a complete digital survey of the solo piano music in really distinguished performances.

A la manière de Borodine; A la manière de Chabrier; Menuet antique; Menuet sur le nom de Haydn; Miroirs; Pavane pour une infante défunte; Prélude; Sérénade grotesque; Sonatine.

**(*) ASV CDDCA 809. Fergus-Thompson.

Gaspard de la nuit; Jeux d'eau; Le Tombeau de Couperin; Valses nobles et sentimentales.

**(*) ASV CDDCA 805. Fergus-Thompson.

Turning to Gordon Fergus-Thompson's Ravel immediately after Thibaudet is to enter a different imaginative world. There is an ample and rich colour-palette, and he exhibits considerable personality and imagination. Not to be preferred to the Decca set, but readers considering it can be assured that it is very well recorded.

A la manière de Borodine; A la manière de Chabrier; Menuet antique; Prélude; Le Tombeau de Couperin; Valses nobles et sentimentales.

**(*) Nim, (ADD) NI 5011. Perlemuter.

Gaspard de la nuit; Jeux d'eau; Miroirs; Pavane.

**(*) Nim. (ADD) NI 5005. Perlemuter.

Though Perlemuter's technical command is not as complete

as it had been, he gives delightful, deeply sympathetic readings; the sense of spontaneity is a joy. There may be Ravel recordings which bring more dazzling virtuoso displays, but none more persuasive. Nimbus's ample room acoustic makes the result naturally atmospheric on CD.

Gaspard de la nuit.

*** DG 413 363-2. Pogorelich – PROKOFIEV: *Sonata No. 6.* *** ✿

Pogorelich's *Gaspard* is out of the ordinary. In *Le Gibet*, we are made conscious of the pianist's refinement of tone and colour first, and Ravel's poetic vision afterwards. But for all that, this is piano playing of astonishing quality. The control of colour and nuance in *Scarbo* is dazzling and its eruptive cascades of energy and dramatic fire have one sitting on the edge of one's seat.

VOCAL MUSIC

(i) Alcyone; (ii) Alyssa; (iii) Myrrha (Rome Cantatas).

(N) EMI *** CDC5 57032-2. (i) Delunsch, Uria-Monzon; (ii) Gens, Beron, Tézler; (iii) Amsellem, Grives, Barrard, Toulouse Capitole O, Plasson.

Ravel applied for the prestigious *Prix de Rome* no fewer than five times and on two occasions his entries were not deemed worthy even to reach the final round! The present three did: *Myrrha* in 1901, and *Alcyone* and *Alyssa* in the subsequent years. The competition involved writing a cantata to a given text on a classical subject, and the wonder is that these long-buried settings, rejected by the judges – who included Massenet, Saint-Saëns and Fauré – are so sensuously beautiful, as this disc amply demonstrates. There is little to identify the distinctive Ravel style, but the young composer, seeking to ingratiate himself with his judges, provides many echoes of Massenet, Saint-Saëns, Gounod, Chabrier and others, often with masterly orchestration, particularly in the last of the three, *Alyssa*, dating from 1904, by which time Ravel had already written such works as his *String Quartet* and the *Sonatine*.

His final rejection in 1905, by which time he was an established composer, caused outrage and led to the resignation of the director of the Conservatoire. None of the three cantatas has the purity of style with which we associate him, and we feel something of the fascination Ravel and his contemporaries felt with Rimsky-Korsakov. However, the real Ravel shines through from time to time, and it would be difficult to surpass the present accounts. With soloists who represent a formidable selection of rising stars among young French singers, notably the superb artistry of Véronique Gens, and with Plasson drawing sumptuous sounds from his Capitole Orchestra, this is a delightful disc for anyone with a sweet tooth, despite the banal texts. Warmly atmospheric recording.

Mélodies: Ballade de la Reine; Morte d'Aimer; Canzone italiana; Chanson du rouet; Chanson espagnole; Chanson française; Chanson hébraïque; Chansons madécasses; 5 mélodies populaires grecques; 2 Epigrammes de Clément Marot; 2 Mélodies hébraïques; Don Quichotte à Dulcinée; Un grand sommeil nuit; Les grands vents venus d'outremer; Histoires naturelles; Manteau de fleurs; Noël des jouets; Rêves; Ronsard à son âme; Sainte; Scottish song; Shéhérazade (complete); Si mornel; Sur l'herbe; Tripatos; 3 Poèmes de Stéphane Mallarmé; Vocalise en forme de Habanera.

(B) *** EMI CZS5 69299-2 (2). Norman, Mesplé, Lott, Berganza, Van Dam, Bacquier, Capitole Toulouse O or Paris CO, Plasson; Baldwin (piano).

Teresa Berganza as well as singing *Shéhérazade* has two songs inspired by Spain, the *Vocalise in the form of a Habanera* and the *Chanson espagnole* from the set of five *Chants populaires*, each of which is allotted to a different singer. Felicity Lott's *Chanson écossaise* is a rarity, *Ye Banks and Braes* sung in a convincing Scots accent. For all the shallowness of Mady Mesplé's voice, it works well in the *Mélodies populaires grecques*, while Jessye Norman, rich-toned if not quite as characterful as usual, has the *Chansons madécasses* as well as lesser-known songs. It is the contribution of the two men that provides the sharpest illumination: José van Dam magnificently dark-toned in the *Don Quichotte* songs and the *Mélodies hébraïques* (making *Kaddish* thrillingly powerful in its agony of mourning), while Gabriel Bacquier twinkles in Figaro tones in the point songs. Excellent sound, and the pair of CDs particularly generous (136 minutes).

3 Chansons.

*** Ph. 438 149-2. Monteverdi Ch., ORR, Gardiner – FAURE: *Requiem*; DEBUSSY; SAINT-SAENS: *Choral Songs.* ***

With his superb choir, Gardiner lightly and crisply touches in the wit and humour behind the two outer songs with their sixteenth-century overtones, and he draws out the lyrical beauty of the central one. A welcome addition to the fascinating group of works chosen by Gardiner as coupling for his expressive reading of the Fauré *Requiem*.

Chansons madécasses.

*** EMI CDC5 56982-2. Karnéus, Pahud, Mørk, Kovacevich – DEBUSSY: *Syrinx; Bilitis*, etc.; PROKOFIEV: *Flute Sonata, Op. 94.* ***

(i) Chansons madécasses; (ii) 5 Mélodies populaires grecques; Histoires naturelles; (i) 3 Poèmes de Stéphane Mallarmé.

(BB) **(*) Belart 461 624-2. Palmer; with (i) Nash Ens., Rattle; (ii) Constable – FAURE: *Mélodies.* **(*)

This EMI version of *Chansons madécasses* is primarily a vehicle for the virtuosity – or rather artistry – of Emmanuel Pahud, for there is no egotism in his playing, the virtuosity is merely by the by. He and Kovacevich are joined by Katerina Karnéus and Truls Mørk. Great sensitivity, powerful atmosphere, lucidity of diction and clarity of texture. This is an outstanding recital.

Felicity Palmer has revealed herself a sensitive performer of French songs, and so she is here, even if the microphone brings out a slight beat to her voice rather distractingly and the interpretations are less characterful than the finest currently available. Yet the atmospheric accompaniments from the Nash Ensemble under Simon Rattle and from the equally sensitive John Constable are a strong plus point. There is no comparable collection available in this budget price range and the grouping of these four evocative cycles with songs by Fauré is pleasingly apt. Outstanding mid-1970s (originally Argo) recording, but no texts or translations.

'Chant d'amour': 4 Chansons populaires; 2 Mélodies hébraïques; Tripatos; Vocalise-étude en forme de Habanera.

*** Decca 452 667-2. Bartoli, Chung – BIZET; BERLIOZ; DELIBES: Mélodies. ***

Cecilia Bartoli is just as much at home in the music of Ravel as she is with the songs of the other composers represented in this outstanding recital of French songs. Myung Whun-Chung, too, proves himself a natural accompanist.

Don Quichotte à Dulcinée (song cycle).

(N)(M) *** Virgin VM5 61850-2. Van Dam, Lyon Nat. Op. O, Nagano – IBERT: 4 Chansons de Don Quichotte; MARTIN: 6 Monologues from 'Jedermann'; POULENC: Le Bal masqué. ***

José Van Dam's approach to Ravel's Quichotte triptych has an operatic flair, yet he closes the opening eulogy to Dulcinée very touchingly, while the central Epic song has poignant nobility of line to contrast with the lighter closing number. Kent Nagano makes the very most of the scintillating orchestration, setting the scene admirably, and in the final song finding ready parallels with the Rapsodie espagnole. Excellent atmospheric recording, and full texts and translations make this imaginative collection more than the sum of its parts.

Shéhérazade (song-cycle).

◉ (M) *** Decca 460 973-2. Crespin, SRO, Ansermet – BERLIOZ: Les Nuits d'été *** (with Recital of French Songs ***).

(M) **(*) Sony SMK 60031. Von Stade, Boston SO, Ozawa – BERLIOZ: Nuits d'été; DEBUSSY: La Demoiselle élue. *(*)

Crespin is right inside these songs and Ravel's magically sensuous music emerges with striking spontaneity. She is superbly supported by Ansermet who, aided by the Decca engineers, weaves a fine tonal web round the voice. Her style has distinct echoes of the opera house; but the richness of the singer's tone does not detract from the delicate languor of The Enchanted Flute, in which the slave-girl listens to the distant sound of her lover's flute playing while her master sleeps. The new transfer of the 1963 recording adds to the allure of the remarkably rich and translucent Decca sound.

Ozawa is an experienced and sympathetic advocate of Ravel, and he and the Boston orchestra provide a seductive web of sound for von Stade's beguiling account of this most sensuous of French song-cycles. The centrepiece, La Flûte enchantée, is particularly ravishing; as the recording is warm and atmospheric, it is a pity that the Berlioz and Debussy couplings are so much less successful.

OPERA

L'Enfant et les sortilèges (complete).

◉ (***) Testament mono SBT 1044. Sautereau, Vessières, Michel, Scharley, Le Marc'Hadour, Peyron, Angelici, French Nat. R. Ch. and O, Bour.

(i) L'Enfant et les sortilèges (complete). Ma Mère l'Oye (complete ballet).

*** DG 457 589-2. (i) Stephen, Owens, Lascarro, Johnson, Soloists New L. Children's Ch., LSO Ch.; L. Symphony, Previn.

With opulent recording heightening the sumptuousness of Ravel's orchestration, and with Previn infectiously pointing rhythms at generally spacious speeds, this evocative one-acter could not be more persuasive, with the atmospheric magic beautifully captured. Though a French-speaking cast might have sounded more idiomatic, characterizations here are exceptionally vivid, with Pamela Helen Stephen as the Child easily outshining her predecessor on Previn's EMI version, and the others making a strong team. The apt and substantial fill-up, the complete Mother Goose ballet, also beautifully done, makes a welcome bonus.

Testament here offer a superlative transfer of the unsurpassed first 1947 recording of Ravel's charming one-Acter under Ernest Bour. There is a magic about this performance that completely captivates the listener. Each part, from Nadine Sautereau's Child, Yvon Le Marc'Hadour's Tom-Cat and Clock and Solange Michel's touching squirrel, to Denise Scharley as the Dragonfly and the Mother, could not be improved upon in character, subtlety and style. The singing and playing of the French Radio forces are vital and imaginative. Ravel's exquisite score is heard to best advantage in this extraordinary transfer with voices firm and immediate. With no stars but with no weak link, the singers make an outstanding team, helped by sound which, with background hiss eliminated, has astonishing presence. No other version casts quite such a strong spell.

(i) L'Enfant et les sortilèges; (ii) L'Heure espagnole (both complete).

(M) *** DG (ADD) 449 769-2 (2). (i) Ogéas, Collard, Berbié, Sénéchal, Gilma, Herzog, Rehfuss, Maurane, RTF Ch. & Boys' Ch., RTF Nat. O; (ii) Berbié, Sénéchal, Giraudeau, Bacquier, Van Dam, Paris Opera O, Maazel – RIMSKY-KORSAKOV: Capriccio espagnol; STRAVINSKY: Le Chant du rossignol. *** ◉

Maazel's recordings of Ravel's two one-Act operas were made in the early 1960s and, though the solo voices in L'Enfant are balanced rather closely, the remastered sound in both operas is wonderfully vivid and atmospheric and each performance is splendidly stylish. The singing is delightful: neo-classical crispness of articulation goes with refined textures that convey the ripe humour of one piece, the tender poetry of the other. The inclusion of Maazel's superb early stereo accounts of Rimsky's Capriccio (with the Berlin Philharmonic) and Le Chant du rossignol glitteringly played by the Berlin Radio Orchestra, two classics of the gramophone, is particularly welcome.

L'Heure espagnole (complete).

(M) (***) EMI mono CDM5 65269-2. Duval, Giraudeau,
Vieuille, Herent, Clavensy, O du Théâtre Nat. de
l'Opéra-Comique, Cluytens.

(i) *L'Heure espagnole. Rapsodie espagnole.*

*** DG 457 590-2. (i) Barber, Gautier, Ollman, Wilson
Johnson, Ainsley; LSO, Previn.

Just as in his companion recording of *L'Enfant*, Previn, with
his subtle pointing of rhythm at spacious speeds, heightens
the atmospheric beauty, so in this charming farce he brings
out the wit of the score, not least in Ravel's Spanish dance
rhythms and parodies. Again the casting is strong and
characterful, with commendably clear French from mainly
non-French singers. Kimberly Baker is a seductive Concepcion and Kurt Ollman a fine forthright Ramiro. Warm, full
sound. Again the coupling is very apt, if less generous.

The EMI version, with Denise Duval as Concepcion and
Jean Giraudeau as Gonzalve, was recorded at the Théâtre
des Champs-Elysées in 1952. Denise Duval is altogether superb, as is the rest of the cast for that matter. Apart from the
quality of the singing, the artists of this period understood
the importance of diction and acting. The sound comes up
very well indeed. However, the set has just been deleted.

RAWSTHORNE, Alan (1905–71)

Clarinet Concerto.

*** Hyp. CDA 66031. King, NW CO of Seattle, Francis –
COOKE: *Concerto*; JACOB: *Mini-Concerto*. ***

Though the *Clarinet Concerto* is an early work of Rawsthorne's it already establishes the authentic flavour of his
writing, the more obviously so in a performance as persuasive as this from soloist and orchestra alike. Excellent
recording.

(i) *Concertante pastorale for Flute, Horn & Strings;
Concerto for String Orchestra; Divertimento for Chamber
Orchestra; Elegiac Rhapsody for String Orchestra; Light
Music for Strings* (based on Catalan tunes); (ii) *Suite for
Recorder & String Orchestra* (orch. McCabe).

(BB) *** Naxos 8.553567. Northern CO, Lloyd-Jones; with
(i) Marshall, Goldberg; (ii) Turner.

Though the melodic writing is rarely as memorable as that
of, say, Walton, all the works here are beautifully crafted,
not least the *Concerto for String Orchestra*, with two dark
movements followed by lightness and open intervals. The
Concertante is most evocative with beautiful solos for flute
and horn. The neoclassical *Recorder Suite* has been deftly
arranged by John McCabe from an original with piano.
Finest of all is the *Elegiac Rhapsody*, written in memory of
the poet Louis MacNeice, touching a deeper vein, erupting
from lamentation into anger. Outstanding performances,
vividly recorded.

(i) *Cello Concerto*; (ii) *Oboe Concerto; Symphonic Studies.*

(N) (BB) *** Naxos 8.554763. RSNO, Lloyd-Jones; (i) Baillie;
(ii) Rancourt.

The *Cello Concerto* of 1966 is both imaginative and resourceful, though perhaps a little amorphous. Its first two
movements are rewarding, though the finale sounds a bit
manufactured. The post-war *Oboe Concerto* is less ambitious
but full of good things. Alexander Baillie gives a masterly
account of the *Cello Concerto*, and Stéphane Rancourt is
hardly less persuasive in its companion. First-class orchestral
playing under David Lloyd-Jones and excellently balanced
and vividly present recording.

The *Symphonic Studies* is arguably Rawsthorne's masterpiece and one of the most ingenious works of its period.
Astonishingly, apart from Constant Lambert's pioneering
set with the Philharmonia Orchestra, there has been only
one other recording, by Nicholas Braithwaite on Lyrita. All
Rawsthorne's music is crafted superbly and highly personal,
so that the idiom is immediately recognizable as his.

Piano Concertos Nos. 1–2; (i) *Double Piano Concerto.*

*** Chan. 9125. Tozer, (i) with Cislowski; LPO, Bamert.

Piano Concertos Nos.(i) *1;* (ii, iii) *2.* (iv) *Practical Cats.*
(ii) (Piano) *Bagatelles.*

(M) *** EMI stereo/mono CDM5 66935-2. (i) Lympany, Philh.
O, Menges; (ii) Matthews; (iii) BBC SO, Sargent; (iv) Donat,
Philh. O, composer.

The *First Piano Concerto* was a wartime work and the *Second*
was composed for the Festival of Britain and is also rewarding. The *Concerto for Two Pianos* is likewise stimulating.
Geoffrey Tozer gives a good account of the concertos. The
opening of No. 1 is a bit rushed; Tamara-Anna Cislowski is
an excellent partner in the 1968 concerto. Matthias Bamert
and the LPO are very supportive and the recording is in the
best traditions of the house.

Moura Lympany's account of the *First Piano Concerto*
with the Philharmonia Orchestra under Herbert Menges
also uses the revision for larger orchestra of 1943 and – like
Denis Matthews's recording with Sir Malcolm Sargent of
the *Second* – has the benefit of stereo. Of particular interest
is *Practical Cats*, which has long been out of circulation and
has the advantage of Robert Donat's impeccable reading and
the composer's own direction. Great care has been taken
over the transfers.

(i) *Violin Concertos Nos. 1–2. Fantasy Overture: Cortèges.*

(BB) *** Naxos 8.554240. (i) Hirsch; BBC Scottish SO, Friend.

The Naxos recording brings the accomplished Rebecca
Hirsch as soloist, with excellent orchestral support from the
BBC Scottish Symphony under Lionel Friend. Her performances hold their own, and the value of the disc is enhanced by
another première recording that of Rawsthorne's *Cortèges*. It
is an imaginative and at times haunting piece, very well
played and recorded here.

Film music: *Burma Victory* (suite). *The Captive Heart*
(suite) (both arr. Gerard Schurmann). *The Cruel Sea:
Main Titles & Nocturne. The Dancing Fleece: 3 Dances*
(both scores arr. & orch. Philip Lane). *Lease of Life: Main
Titles & Emergency. Saraband for Dead Lovers: Saraband
& Carnival* (both arr. Schurmann). *Uncle Silas: Main
Titles & Opening Scene; Valse Caprice; End Titles. West of*

*Zanzibar: Main Titles. Where No Vultures Fly:
Introduction; Main Titles & Opening Scene. Surveying the
Game* (all arr. and orch. Philip Lane).

*** Chan. 9749. BBC PO, Gamba.

Between 1937 and 1964 Rawsthorne wrote music for twenty-
seven British films. He was not a ready melodist like Malcolm
Arnold, but he could write memorable paragraphs, imaginatively and powerfully scored, and Gerard Schurmann's two
suites from *The Captive Heart* and the fine documentary
Burma Victory demonstrate his remarkable ability to characterize situations in music.

He is very good at flamboyant, Hollywoodian title music,
yet the charming delicacy of the *Valse caprice* from *Uncle
Silas* shows the other side of his musical nature and makes
for a number well worth preserving independently. Gerard
Schurmann had worked with the composer in preparing the
original scores, and Philip Lane demonstrates his skills of
reconstruction using the original soundtracks when the
manuscripts are missing. The music is splendidly played and
given Chandos's top-quality sound.

Symphonies Nos. (i) *1*; (ii) *2 (Pastoral)*; (iii) *3*.

*** Lyrita ADD/Dig. SRCS 291. (i–ii) LPO; Pritchard; or
(ii) Braithwaite, with Chadwell; (iii) BBC SO, Del Mar.

The *First Symphony* is played with evident enjoyment by the
LPO under Sir John Pritchard. But, of the three, the *Second
(Pastoral) Symphony* is the most readily approachable, since
its thematic material catches the ear, especially in the expressive ideas of the *Poco lento* and the gay country-dance
Scherzo. Rawsthorne uses a soprano soloist in the finale,
with a succinct text by Henry Howard, Earl of Surrey (1516–
47), giving brief impressions of three of the four seasons:
spring, summer and winter. The music has a powerful atmosphere, and Tracey Chadwell copes successfully with the
rather angular vocal-line to catch the essential melancholy
of the poem. All three works receive superb performances
and the recording is outstanding with the sense of space and
splendid detail we expect from Lyrita.

Clarinet Quartet.

*** Redcliffe RR 010. Cox, Redcliffe Ens. – BLISS; ROUTH:
Clarinet Quintets. ***

Rawsthorne's *Clarinet Quartet* is more ambivalent in feeling
than the Bliss *Quintet*, but its quirky opening movement is
appealing and the darker *Poco lento* hardly less striking. With
Nicholas Cox a most winning soloist, the performance here
could hardly be improved upon, and the recording is first
class.

*4 Bagatelles; Ballade; 4 Romantic Pieces; Sonatina; Theme
& 4 Studies.*

**(*) Paradisum PDS-CD2. Clegg – LENNOX BERKELEY: *6
Preludes.* **(*)

On this CD John Clegg presents the whole of Rawsthorne's
output for the piano (apart from the two concertos). Inventive and civilized music, every bar bearing his personal
stamp, and persuasively played. The only snag is the rather
claustrophobic acoustic in which it is recorded.

REBEL, Jean-Féry (1661–1747)

*Les Caractères de la danse; Les Elémens; Le Tombeau de M.
de Lully.*

*** Erato 2292 45974-2. Les Musiciens du Louvre, Minkowski.

The eloquent trio sonata, *Le Tombeau de M. de Lully* was
written on the death of the great French composer whose
pupil Rebel had become as a boy of eight and *Les Elémens* is
one of the most original works of the period. With its
representation of chaos in which all the notes of the harmonic scale are heard simultaneously, it is certainly quite
astonishing in effect. The performance and recording are of
the highest quality.

REGER, Max (1873–1916)

*Ballet Suite, Op. 130; 4 Böcklin Tone-Pictures, Op. 128;
Variations & Fugue on a Theme by Beethoven, Op. 86.*

*** BIS CD 601. Norrköping SO, Segerstam.

Segerstam gets a very good response from the Norrköping
Orchestra and obviously cares for this music and makes the
most of it without succumbing to the expressive exaggeration which spoils some of his other work. Both the *Ballet
Suite* and the *Beethoven Variations* are well served, and very
well recorded.

(i) *Ballet Suite, Op. 130; Variations & Fugue on a Theme
by Mozart, Op. 132;* (ii) *Variations & Fugue on a Theme by
Hiller, Op. 100.*

(B) ** Teldec Ultima Double stereo/mono 3984 28175-2 (2).
(i) Hamburg Philharmonic State O; (ii) Bamberg SO,
Keilberth.

Reger had a genuine talent for the variations form and if his
Mozart set immediately takes the winsome theme
(composed for the keyboard) soaring into the voluptuous
textures of Richard Strauss and early Schoenberg, there is
no denying the attractive qualities of some of the later
sections, particularly the *Fifth* and *Sixth Variations*. The
closing fugue is taken fairly sedately by Keilberth, but on
the whole these are impressive accounts, very well played,
especially the engaging *Ballet Suite*. In the Hiller (mono) set
one notices Reger's debt to Brahms, but this too is agreeably
presented. The recordings are of good quality, with plenty
of ambience, but show their age in a certain fierceness in the
fortissimo upper strings.

*4 Böcklin Tone-Pictures, Op. 128; Variations on a Theme
by Hiller, Op. 100.*

*** Chan. 8794. Concg. O, Järvi.

Of the four *Tone Poems* on Chandos, textures in *Der geigende
Eremit* ('Hermit playing the violin') are unexectedly transparent, and *Im Spiel der Wellen* has something of the sparkle
of the *Jeu de vagues* movement of *La Mer* photographed in
sepia; while the *Isle of the Dead* is a lovely and often very
touching piece. The *Hiller Variations* are gloriously inventive. These works are beautifully recorded and Neeme Järvi's

performances have the combination of sensitivity and virtuosity that this composer needs.

(i) *Concerto in Olden Style, Op. 123;* (ii) *Sinfonietta, Op. 90.*

**(*) Koch 31354-2. (i) Orlovsky; (i; ii) Rosenberg; Bamberg SO, Stein.

The *Concerto in Olden Style* is Reger's tribute to the great Baroque masters, though his Op. 123 is scored for somewhat larger forces! The *Sinfonietta in A major* is an ambitious work, full of luxuriant invention, and richly and at times thickly scored; at others, it is a model of delicacy. The *Largo* is absolutely inspired. Horst Stein gets very good playing from the Bamberg orchestra and the recording is very warm and sonorous, perhaps not transparent enough at the top end of the spectrum.

Piano Concerto in F min., Op. 114.

*** RCA 09026 68028-2. Douglas, French R. PO, Janowski – R. STRAUSS: *Burleske.* ***

Reger's *Piano Concerto* is a remarkable and powerful composition. The slow movement is a contemplative, rapt piece that touches genuine depths. Barry Douglas receives exemplary recording from the RCA/Radio France engineers, and this is its best recording and certainly Barry Douglas's best disc so far.

(i) *Symphonic Prologue to a Tragedy, Op. 108;* (ii) 2 *Romances for Violin & Orchestra, Op. 50.*

**(*) Schwann (ADD) CD311 076. (i) Berlin RSO, Albrecht; (ii) with Maile; cond. Lajovic.

The tragedy in question is Sophocles' *Oedipus Rex*, and Reger's *Symphonic Prologue* is one of his very finest and most powerful works. Inspiration runs consistently high. The violin *Romances* are beautiful pieces and are very well played by Hans Maile and the Berlin Radio Orchestra. Strongly recommended, even if the 1982 recording is serviceable rather than distinguished.

Symphonic Prologue to a Tragedy; Variations & Fugue on a Theme of Mozart.

*** BIS CD 771. Norrköping SO, Segerstam.

Segerstam's obvious dedication to the spirit and the letter of these scores rises to their challenge admirably. The BIS recording is of demonstration standard.

Serenade in G for Orchestra, Op. 95; Suite im alten Stil, Op. 93.

*** Koch Schwann 3-1566-2. Bamberg SO, Stein.

Reger's beautiful *Serenade in G major* is one of the loveliest, most lyrical scores of the twentieth century. However, it is never heard in the concert hall and is a rarity both in broadcast concerts and on CD. Horst Stein's performance of it is full of eloquence. The pastiche *Suite in the Olden Style*, originally a *Duo* for violin and piano, which Reger scored later in life, has much charm. But it is the *Serenade* which is essential listening in this persuasive and well-recorded account.

Variations & Fugue on a Theme of Beethoven, Op. 86.

(N) (M) *** Chan. 7080 (2). LPO, Neeme Järvi – BRUCKNER: *Symphony No. 8.* **(*)

Terminally ill, in his last years Reger concentrated on composition, here orchestrating eight of the twelve variations of a work he originally scored for two pianos. The result is a brilliant, sharply characterized piece with obvious echoes of Brahms, a fine companion for Reger's two better-known sets of variations on themes of Mozart and Hiller, and an attractive coupling for Järvi's warm-hearted reading of the Bruckner, now at mid-price. Rich 1986 Chandos sound.

CHAMBER MUSIC

Cello Suites Nos. 1 in G; 2 in D min.; 3 in A min., Op. 131c.

(BB) *** Arte Nova 74321 65428-2. Schiefen.

Guido Schiefen proves an authoritative and persuasive advocate of the three Reger *Cello Suites*, Op. 131c. These were modelled on Bach, whom they at times paraphrase. Not essential listening perhaps, but played like this they are quite impressive, and they are well recorded too.

(i) *Clarinet Quintet in A, Op. 146. String Quartet in E flat, Op. 109.*

*** Nim. NI 5644. (i) Leister; Vogler Qt.

The mellifluous *Clarinet Quintet*, his very last work, has never found its rightful place in the concert hall or the record catalogues. Karl Leister's artistry and eloquence are very persuasive, as indeed are those of the wonderful Vogler Quartet. The Nimbus engineers place us rather too close to the artists and we would welcome rather more space round the sound, but there is no doubt that these are very distinguished performances that call for a strong recommendation.

Piano Trios in B min., Op. 2; E minor, Op. 102.

(N) *** MDG 303 0751-2 Trio Parnassus.

The *B minor Trio* is for piano, violin and viola and is very derivative. There are faint hints of things to come, but for the most part Brahms is the pervasive influence. The *E minor Trio* is another matter: there are some striking harmonic sleights of hand and a reminder of the first of the *Böcklin Portraits*, which bear a slightly later opus number. Fine performances, very well recorded too, and well worth taking the trouble to hear.

ORGAN WORKS

Aus tiefer Not schrei ich zu dir, Op. 67/3; Intermezzo in F min., Op. 129/7; Introduction & Passacaglia in D min., Op. posth.; Prelude in D min., Op. 65/7.

*** Chan. 9097. Kee – HINDEMITH: *Organ Sonatas.* ***

The Müller organ of St Bavo in Haarlem seems ideally suited to this repertoire, as is the slightly reverberant acoustic which rather softens the textures and contours of the Hindemith.

Piet Kee plays with his customary authority and distinction. A rewarding and satisfying issue.

Chorale fantasia on Straf' mich nicht in deinem Zorn, Op. 40/2; Chorale Preludes, Op. 67/4, 13, 28, 40, 48; Introduction, Passacaglia & Fugue in E min., Op. 127.

*** Hyp. CDA 66223. Barber (Klais organ of Limburg Cathedral).

The *Introduction, Passacaglia and Fugue* is bold in conception and vision and is played superbly on this excellently engineered Hyperion disc by Graham Barber. The five *Chorale Preludes* give him an admirable opportunity to show the variety and richness of tone-colours of this instrument.

PIANO MUSIC

5 Humoresques, Op. 20; Improvisations, Op. 18; In der nacht; Träume am Kamin, Op. 143.

(BB) *** Naxos 8.553331. Pawlik.

5 Humoresques; Variations & Fugue on a Theme of Johann Sebastian Bach, Op. 81; Variations & Fugue on a Theme of Georg Philipp Telemann, Op. 134.

✿ *** Hyp. CDA 66996. Hamelin.

Variations & Fugue on a Theme of Bach, Op. 81.

(BB) **(*) Naxos 8.550469. Harden – SCHUMANN: *Humoreske.* **(*)

Like Brahms, Reger was one of the greatest masters of the variation form. The Bach and Telemann sets are generally acknowledged to be among his finest keyboard works, and Marc-André Hamelin's playing has enormous eloquence and imagination as well as a wide range both of dynamics and tonal colour. This has an elegance and refinement that never calls attention to itself. Superbly natural recorded sound too.

Markus Pawlik is a most musical and sensitive player who captures the intimacy of the *Träume am Kamin* to perfection. They are predominantly poetic and gentle pieces, but elsewhere in the *Humoresques* he shows formidable virtuosity. Very acceptable sound – and those with a taste for music off the beaten track will find this well rewards the modest outlay.

Wolf Harden's account of the Reger *Variations and Fugue on a Theme of Bach*, Op. 81, is also very fine. The piano sounds much drier here than in the Schumann coupling. Yet the compelling quality of his playing is in no doubt.

VOCAL MUSIC

Christmas Lieder: Christkindleins Wiegenlied; Ehre sei Gott in der Höhe! Maria am Rosenstrauch; Morgengesang; Uns ist geboren ein Kindelein.

✿ *** EMI CDC5 56204-2. Bär, Deutsch (with Recital: '*Christmas Lieder*' *** ✿).

Max Reger's Christmas Lieder sustain the most serious mood of any of the songs in Olaf Bär's superb recital, especially the closing *Ehre sei Gott in der Höhe!* But the imagination of Bär's word-colouring and his wide range of dynamic pre-

vents any feeling of heaviness. The opening *Morgengesang*, 'morning song', brings a delightfully fresh spontaneity, and *Mary in the Rosebower* has a gentle, rocking lyricism, beautifully realized in Helmut Deutsch's flowing accompaniment. Unfortunately, this issue is now deleted.

REICH, Steve (born 1936)

8 Lines.

(N) (M) *** Virgin VM5 61851-2. LCO, Warren-Green – ADAMS: *Shaker Loops* *** ✿; GLASS: *Company* etc. ***; HEATH: *Frontier.* ***

Steve Reich's *8 Lines* is minimalism in its most basic form, and, although the writing is full of good-humoured vitality, the listener without a score could be forgiven for sometimes thinking that the music was on an endless loop. The performance is expert.

Music for 18 Musicians.

*** RCA 09026 68672-2. Ens. Modern.

Dating from 1974–6, *Music for 18 Musicians* derives from and returns to a pulsing eleven-chord cyclic 'theme', framing twelve connected sections, which have comparatively simple additional material superimposed upon them, as the music proceeds. As the recording is cued into fourteen separate tracks, the listener can readily isolate the changes within the basic structure. In his accompanying notes, Frank Oteri draws a parallel between Reich's sonic architecture and Beethoven's *Eroica Symphony*. This is going a bit far, but there is no doubt that this is a hypnotic performance of a key work in Reich's continuing odyssey in musical minimalism.

(i) 6 Pianos; (ii) Music for mallet instruments; (iii) Variations for Winds, Strings & Keyboards.

(B) *** DG ADD/Dig. 439 431-2. (i–ii) Chambers, Preiss, Hartenberger, Becker, Velez, composer; (ii) Ferchen, Harms, Jarrett, LaBarbara, Clayton; (iii) San Francisco SO, De Waart.

Both the first two pieces exploit the composer's technique of endlessly repeating a very brief fragment which gradually becomes transformed, almost imperceptibly, by different emphases being given to it. The recording throughout is of high quality.

Tehillim.

** ECM 827 411-2. Composer & musicians, Manahan.

Steve Reich is listed among the percussion players in *Tehillim*, with George Manahan conducting. The central focus, in this Hebrew setting of Psalms 19 and 18 (in that order), is on the vocal ensemble of four voices. The result – with clapping and drumming punctuating the singing – has an element of charm rare in minimalist music. With jazzy syncopations and Cuban rhythms, the first of the two movements sounds like Bernstein's *Chichester Psalms* caught in a groove. The second starts slowly but speeds up for the verses of praise to the Lord and the final *Hallelujahs*. Clear, forward, analogue recording.

Variations for Winds, Strings & Keyboard.

(B) *** Ph. 412 214-2. San Francisco SO, De Waart – ADAMS: *Shaker Loops.* ***

Reich's *Variations*, written for the San Francisco orchestra in 1980, marked a new departure in the writing of this leading minimalist, using a large orchestral rather than a small chamber scale. The repetitions and ostinatos, which gradually get out of phase, are most skilfully used to produce a hypnotic kind of poetry, soothing rather than compelling.

REICHA, Antonín (1770–1836)

(i) *Sinfonia concertante in G for Flute, Violin & Orchestra. Symphony in E flat, Op. 41; Overture in D.*

*** MDG 335 0661-2. (i) Bieler, Gérard; Wuppertal SO, Gülke.

The first movement of Reicha's *Sinfonia concertante* brings engaging textures but is otherwise relatively conventional.The galant *Andante* however, brings a charming little violin melody over a tick-tock flute accompaniment; later the two instruments change roles. The *Overture in D minor* is, remarkably, in 5/8 time and its nagging ostinato main theme is at first quite catching. The snag is that, despite its variety of colour, it is a shade over-long. The *Symphony* is a different matter. Its main allegro is very confidently constructed. The *Andante un poco adagio* doesn't disappoint, while in the lively finale the composer keeps a card or two up his sleeve until the very end. A real discovery, which invites repeated hearings. The orchestra is a fine ensemble and, with two first-class soloists here, offers a rewarding collection, well recorded.

Flute Quartets Nos. 1 in E min.; 2 in A; 3 in D, Op. 98/1–3.

*** MDG 311 0630-2. Hünteler, Rainer and Jürgen Küssmaul, Dietiens.

In the opening *Quartet*, a particularly fine piece, one thinks often of Mozart, and Reicha's invention is seldom inferior. The piquant opening of the *Second Quartet* has a charming insouciance, and in the *Third Quartet* the quaint little tune, marching along slowly and elegantly is again Bohemian in spirit. Throughout all three works the solo flute part demands, and receives, the utmost virtuosity from its performer, here Konrad Hünteler, who either dominates or blends with his colleagues, all excellent players. The vivid recording completes the listener's pleasure.

Oboe Quintet in F, Op. 107.

[B] *** Hyp. Helios CDH 55015. Francis, Allegri Qt – CRUSELL: *Divertimento;* (with R. KREUTZER: *Grand Quintet).* ***

Antonín Reicha's *F major Quintet* is unmemorable but always amiable. The present performance is of high quality and very well recorded.

Wind Quintets: in F (1811); in E flat; in B flat, Op. 88/2 & 5; in D; in A, Op. 91/3 & 5.

(B) *** Hyp. Dyad CDD 22006 (2). Academia Wind Quintet of Prague.

Czech wind-playing in Czech wind music has a deservedly high entertainment rating, and the present performances are no exception. The music itself has great charm and geniality; it is ingenuous yet cultivated, with some delightful, smiling writing for the bassoon. The players are clearly enjoying themselves, yet they play and blend expertly. The sound too is admirable.

REINCKEN, Johann (1623?–1722)

(i) *Partitas Nos. 1–6 (Hortus musicus): excerpts; Keyboard pieces:* (ii) *Ballet (Partite diverse) in E min.; Toccata in G; Suite in G.*

(N) *** Chan. 0664. (i) Purcell Qt; (ii) Woolley.

Johann Reincken reigned over Hamburg's musical scene before Telemann. He was organist at the Katharinenkirche from 1663 onwards, and his improvisational skills were greatly admired. Indeed, the young Bach came to hear him play; on a second visit in 1720 and improvising himself on the great organ, he received in return Reincken's admiration. These six *Partitas* (for two violins, viola da gamba and continuo) juxtapose movements in the styles of Italian church and chamber sonatas. It seems that Reincken did not intend that each partita should be played through in its entirety, so in these admirable performances the Purcell Quartet have selected movements from each of them. Reincken's invention is lively and his expressive writing quite touching. But what makes this collection especially attractive is the harpsichord music, full of winningly attractive ideas. Sample, for instance, the delightful closing *Gigue* of the *Suite in G major*. Most entertaining of all is the *Toccata in G*, a virtuosic piece, alternating free and fugal textures. It reminds one of Bach's bouncing *Fugue à la gigue*: the improvisatory sections use the *stylus phantasicus*, and Robert Woolley clearly revels in the dashing opportunities he is offered. Excellent recording.

REINECKE, Carl (1824–1910)

Harp Concerto in E min., Op. 182.

(N)(M) *** DG (ADD) 463 642-2. Zabaleta, BPO, Märzendorfer – MOZART: *Flute & Harp Concerto;* REINECKE: *Harp Concerto;* RODRIGO: *Concierto serenata.* *** ✸

This is an attractive work, Zabaleta's performance is an outstanding one, and it is truthfully recorded. If the couplings are suitable this is a highly recommendable disc.

Fantasiestücke, Op. 43.

*** EMI CDC5 55166-2. Caussé, Duchable – BEETHOVEN: *Notturno ***;* SCHUBERT: *Arpeggione Sonata.* **

Reinecke's musical language is Schumannesque and the *Fantasiestücke*, Op. 43, owe an obvious debt to Schumann's *Märchenbilder.* They are very slight, but Caussé and Duchable make out the best possible case for them.

Flute Sonata (Undine), Op. 167.

(M) *** RCA (ADD) 09026 61615-2. Galway, Argerich –
FRANCK; PROKOFIEV: *Sonatas.* ***

Some of Reinecke's invention here is quite striking (as in
the sonata's first movement). His writing, which has sudden
florid bursts, makes an engaging vehicle for an artist of
Galway's calibre, and this makes a fine bonus for the coupling of two masterly works by Prokofiev and Franck.

String Trio in C min., Op. 249.

*** MDG 634 0841-2. Belcanto Strings – FUCHS: *Trio in A,
Op. 94.* ***

This *C minor Trio* comes from around 1898 and is conservative in style, finely crafted and cultured music, superbly
played and recorded.

RESPIGHI, Ottorino (1879–1936)

(i) *Adagio con variazioni* (for cello and orchestra); *The
Birds; 3 Botticelli Pictures;* (ii) *Il tramonto.*

*** Chan. 8913. (i) Wallfisch; (ii) Finnie; Bournemouth Sinf.,
Vásáry.

Raphael Wallfisch is very persuasive in Respighi's *Adagio.
The Birds* brings lovely playing and the luminous recording
give much pleasure. The lambent Italianate evocation of the
Three Botticelli Pictures is also aurally bewitching. But what
caps the success of this Chandos Respighi anthology is Linda
Finnie's ravishing account of *Il tramonto*, even finer than
Carol Madalin's on Hyperion – see below. Again very responsive orchestral playing and the recording is in the demonstration class throughout this CD.

(i) *Ancient Airs & Dances: Suites Nos. 1–3;* (ii) *Belfagor:*
Overture; (iii) *The Birds* (suite); (ii) *The Fountains of
Rome; The Pines of Rome;* (iii) *3 Botticelli Pictures
(Trittico botticelliano).*

(B) **(*) EMI double forte CZS5 69358-2 (2). (i) LACO, or
(iii) ASMF; Marriner; (ii) LSO, Gardelli.

(i) *Ancient Airs & Dances: Suites Nos. 1–3; The Birds (Gli
uccelli); 3 Botticelli Pictures (Trittico botticelliano);*
(ii) *Feste romane; The Fountains of Rome; The Pines of
Rome.*

(B) *** Teldec Ultima 0630 18970-2 (2). (i) St Paul CO, Wolff;
(ii) LPO, Rizzi.

*Ancient Airs & Dances: Suites Nos. 1–3; 3 Botticelli Pictures
(Trittico botticelliano).*

*** Telarc CD 80309. Lausanne CO, López-Cobos.

Marriner's account of the suites of dances is attractively
light and gracious, offering an almost French elegance, with
pleasingly transparent textures. *The Birds* and *Trittico botticelliano* are no less delightful, and they are beautifully
recorded. So far so good; but Lamberto Gardelli's performances of *The Pines* and *Fountains of Rome*, though warmly
sympathetic and finely played, bring less of a feeling of
drama, and generate neither the atmospheric magic nor
electricity experienced in the competing versions from Re-

iner or Karajan. The *Belfagor Overture* is an acceptable
bonus, a dramatic and lively piece, strongly characterized
and vivid.

The playing of the St Paul Chamber Orchestra in the first
group of works on this Ultima Double is excellent: they are
responsive equally to dynamic contrasts and to changes of
colour. Hugo Wolff gets a sympathetic and spirited response
throughout and the *Ancient Airs and Dances* are beautifully
played; the recording is bright but spacious. Carlo Rizzi's
vivid acount of the Roman triptych is hardly less impressive.
The recording is immensely spectacular and its moments of
hyperbole are thrilling in a very physical way, as at the huge,
overwhelming climax of *The Pines of the Via Appia* and, in
Feste Romane, the crude spectacle of *Circuses* with its distant
brass effects. The *Fountains* too are brilliantly pictorial, while
Respighi's gently luminous evocation of *The Pines of the
Janiculum* and the heady, sensuous nostalgia of *Villa Medici
at Sunset* are drawn with subtle colours. The LPO respond
with superb virtuosity and dash, balanced by warm sensitivity.

Opening brightly and comparatively robustly, the Lausanne performance of the *Ancient Airs* yet has both warmth
and finesse. The rhythmic pulse is lively without being heavy,
and there is much engaging woodwind detail; at the graceful
beginning of the *Third Suite* textures are agreeably light and
transparent. The Telarc recording is first rate and even
more impressive in the *Botticelli Pictures*, with *La primavera*
burgeoning with the extravagantly exotic spring blossoming,
and *The Birth of Venus* rapt in its radiantly expansive ecstasy.

(i; ii) *Ancient Airs & Dances: suite No. 3;* (iii) *The Birds
(Gli uccelli);* (iv; ii) *Brazilian Impressions;* (v; vi) *Feste
romane;* (vii; viii) *The Fountains of Rome;* (vii; vi) *The
Pines of Rome;* (ix) *Il tramonto.*

(N) (B) *** DG Panorama (ADD/DDD) 469 181-2 (2).
    (i) Philharmonia Hungarica; (ii) Dorati; (iii) Orpheus CO;
    (iv) LSO; (v) Cleveland O; (vi) Maazel; (vii) BPO;
    (viii) Karajan; (ix) Seefried, Lucerne Fest. Strings,
    Baumgarter.

In this cunningly contrived Panorama compilation DG have
drawn also on the Decca, and Mercury back catalogues.
Karajan's *Fountains of Rome* represents the Berlin Philharmonic at their peak, but they play brilliantly for Maazel too,
and he also conducts the Cleveland Orchestra in a superbly
engineered *Feste romane* (see below). The Orpheus Chamber
Orchestra are exhilaratingly songful in *The Birds*, and Dorati's vivid (LSO) *Brazilian Impressions* are balanced by the
delicacy and refinement of the playing of the Philharmonia
Hungarica in the *Suite No. 3* for strings, from the *Ancient
Airs and Dances*. If one laments the absence of the the first
two suites, the compensation is the encore – Irgard Seefried's
lovely 1960 recording of *Il tramonto* (*The Sunset*), which is
new to the CD catalogue and very welcome indeed.
Throughout both, the recordings and CD transfers are of a
very high standard, and this would form a splendid basis for
any collection of Respighi's enticingly colourful and tuneful
music.

*Ancient Airs & Dances: Suite No. 3 for Strings; The
Fountains of Rome; The Pines of Rome.*

(M) *** DG (ADD) 449 724-2. BPO, Karajan (with
  BOCCHERINI: *Quintettino;* ALBINONI: *Adagio in G min.*
  (arr. Giazotto) ***).

In the symphonic poems Karajan is in his element, and the
playing of the Berlin Philharmonic is wonderfully refined as
well as exciting. The opening of the *Ancient Airs* brings
ravishing tone from the strings, and they sound even more
lavish in Giazotto's famous arrangement of Albinoni's *Adagio*, while Boccherini's *Quintettino* makes an engaging additional lollipop.

Le astuzie di Colombina; La pentola magica; Sèvres de la vieille France.

*** Marco 8.223346. Slovak RSO (Bratislava), Adriano.

Sèvres de la vieille France is based on seventeenth- and
eighteenth-century airs, scored with great elegance and
charm; *La pentola magica* makes use of Russian models. *Le
astuzie di Colombina*, described as a 'Scherzo Veneziano',
uses popular Venetian melodies among other things. The
scores contain some winning and delightful numbers. Decent performances and good recording.

Ballata delle Gnomidi; (i) Concerto gregoriano; Poema autunnale.

*** Chan. 9232. (i) Mordkovitch; BBC PO, Downes.

The *Concerto gregoriano* is a meditative, lyrical outpouring
making free use of Gregorian modes. Apart from some
moments of brilliant display, the slightly later *Poema autun-
nale* for violin and orchestra is also predominantly lyrical and
has moments of a Delius-like mysticism. Lydia Mordkovitch
gives most affecting accounts of both pieces and is very
well supported by Downes and the BBC Philharmonic. The
Ballata delle Gnomidi (1920) finds Respighi in his most exotic
Roman Trilogy mode: it is a dazzling exercise in colour and
orchestration.

Belfagor Overture; 3 Corali; (i) Fantasia slava for Piano & Orchestra; Toccata for Piano & Orchestra.

*** Chan. 9311. (i) Tozer; BBC PO, Downes.

The best thing here is the *Toccata for Piano and Orchestra*.
It is better argued and structured, more inventive and novel,
as well as more musically rewarding, than either of the piano
concertos, and Tozer plays it with considerable bravura
and panache and the BBC Philharmonic under Sir Edward
Downes are admirably supportive. The *Fantasia slava* is
shorter and less interesting, and the same goes for the three
chorale arrangements. The *Belfagor* is a re-composition
based on themes from his opera, and not the curtain-raiser
heard in the theatre. Excellent in every way, and with
recording of first-class quality.

Belkis, Queen of Sheba: Suite. Metamorphoseon modi XII.

*** Chan. 8405. Philh. O, Simon.

The ballet-suite *Belkis, Queen of Sheba*, is a score that set
the pattern for later Hollywood biblical film music; but
Metamorphoseon is a taut and sympathetic set of variations.
It has been ingeniously based on a medieval theme, and
though a group of cadenza variations relaxes the tension of

argument in the middle, the brilliance and variety of the
writing have much in common with Elgar's *Enigma*. Superb
playing from the Philharmonia, treated to one of the finest
recordings that even Chandos has produced, outstanding in
every way.

(i) The Birds (suite); Brazilian Impressions; (ii) The Fountains of Rome; The Pines of Rome.

(M) **(*) Mercury (ADD) 432 007-2. (i) LSO; (ii) Minneapolis
  SO, Dorati.

In Dorati's hands the opening and closing evocations of the
Fountains of Rome have a unique, shimmering brightness
which certainly suggests a sun-drenched landscape, although
in Minneapolis the turning-on of the Triton fountain brings
a shrill burst of sound that almost assaults the ears. The
tingling detail in the companion *Pines of Rome* is again
matched by Dorati's powerful sense of atmosphere, while
the finale has an overwhelming juggernaut forcefulness. The
coupling of *The Birds* and *Brazilian Impressions* was made
in the smoother, warmer acoustics of Watford Town Hall
in 1957, and here the vividness of detail particularly suits
Dorati's spirited account of *The Birds*, bringing pictorial
piquancy of great charm and strongly projected dance-
rhythms. *Brazilian Impressions* certainly glitters in Dorati's
hands even if overall this work does not represent Respighi
at his finest.

The Birds (Gli uccelli); Church Windows (Vetrate di chiesa).

(B) **(*) Sony (ADD) SBK 60311. Phd., Ormandy –
  SCARLATTI: *The Good-Humoured Ladies.* **(*)

In *Church Windows* the picture of the baby Jesus in *The
Flight into Egypt* has a Latin intensity of feeling which suits
Ormandy and the rich-textured Philadelphia sound, while
the following evocation of St Michael, sword in hand, is
spectacularly painted with broad strokes of the orchestral
brush. The finale, a papal blessing scene, is on the largest
scale. Ormandy rises to the occasion and the spectacular
recording is a match for the Philadelphia big guns – although
subtlety is not the keynote here and the listener is all but
overwhelmed. *The Birds* is slighter, but the playing is full of
charm, especially the delicate tracery of the final cuckoo
evocation.

Brazilian Impressions; Church Windows (Vetrate di chiesa).

*** Chan. 8317. Philh. O, Simon.

Geoffrey Simon is sympathetic and he secures very fine
playing from the Philharmonia. On CD, the wide dynamic
range and a striking depth of perspective create the most
spectacular effects.

Burlesca; Overture Carnevalesca; Prelude, Chorale & Fugue; Suite in E; Symphonic Variations.

**(*) Marco 8.223348. Slovak RSO (Bratislava), Adriano.

The *Symphonic Variations*, an early work, is very well crafted,
with a lot of Brahms and Franck – though the scoring already
betrays Respighi's future expertise. In the *Suite in E major*
the influences are mainly Slavonic; primarily Dvořák and

Rimsky-Korsakov, but in the *Burlesca* of 1906 with its whole-tone scale one can discern a whiff of Debussy. The release discovers no masterpieces but does afford a valuable insight into Respighi's creative development. Good performances from Adriano and the Slovak Radio Orchestra and decent recording.

Piano Concerto in A min.; Concerto in modo misolidio.

**(*) Chan. 9285. Tozer, BBC PO, Downes.

In Respighi's *Piano Concerto in A minor* of 1902, the influences of Rachmaninov and Grieg are strong. It is aptly coupled with a much later and more ambitious concertante work with piano, the *Concerto in modo misolidio* ('in the mixolydian mode'), which reflects Respighi's fascination with early Church music which is rather too diffuse a work for its material. The impact of Geoffrey Tozer's playing in both works is undermined by the backward balance of the piano, with only the A minor work taking fire.

Piano Concerto in A min.; Fantasia slava; Toccata for Piano & Orchestra.

(BB) *** Naxos 8.553207. Scherbakov, Slovak RSO (Bratislava), Griffiths.

Concerto in modo misolidio; (i) Concerto a cinque.

(BB) *** Naxos 8.553366. Scherbakov, Slovak RSO, Griffiths; (i) Capella Istropolitana, Danel.

The first Naxos CD misses out the *Concerto in modo misolidio* and includes instead the much finer if rather extended *Toccata* and the concise and rather engaging *Fantasia slava*. The Russian pianist, Konstantin Scherbakov, is a persuasive and at times dazzlingly brilliant soloist and he is accompanied persuasively by the Slovak Radio Symphony Orchestra (Bratislava) under Howard Griffiths. The recording is excellent and this disc is well worth its modest cost.

Scherbakov's account of the *Concerto in modo misolidio* is superior in every way (except recorded quality) to Tozer's on Chandos – and a third of the price. The *Concerto a cinque* makes a delightful and inventive makeweight.

The Fountains of Rome.

(***) Testament mono SBT 1108. St Cecilia Ac., Rome, O, De Sabata – DEBUSSY: *La Mer; Jeux; Nuages; Fêtes.* (***)

Victor de Sabata's 1947 account of *The Fountains of Rome* was the earliest post-war set and superseded Albert Coates's early 1930s version with the LSO also on HMV. It is a magical performance with many touches that, though different from Reiner, Toscanini and Karajan, are of comparable subtlety and atmosphere.

Feste romane; The Fountains of Rome; The Pines of Rome (symphonic poems).

*** EMI CDC5 55600-2. Oslo PO, Jansons.
(BB) *** Naxos 8.550539. RPO, Bátiz.
(M) *** Decca 430 729-2. Montreal SO, Dutoit.
*** EMI CDC7 47316-2. Phd. O, Muti.
(B) **(*) Sony (ADD) SBK 48267. Phd. O, Ormandy.

The Fountains of Rome; The Pines of Rome.

● (M) *** RCA (ADD) 09026 (ADD) 61401-2. Chicago SO, Reiner – MUSSORGSKY: *Pictures at an Exhibition.* *** ●
● (M) *** RCA (ADD) 09026 68079-2. Chicago SO, Reiner – DEBUSSY: *La Mer.* ***

In the Oslo recording *Feste romane*, *The Pines* and *The Fountains* are equally magnificent: Jansons has their full measure. There is more to this music than just colour, Mediterranean atmosphere and virtuoso orchestration. There is a sense of longing and nostalgia that are beautifully realized here. The orchestral playing is of the first order, marvellous wind and brass throughout; and the Oslo recording scores over its immediate rival in having the deeper and more sumptuous acoustic ambience. However, as we go to press this issue has just been deleted.

Reiner's legendary recordings of *The Pines* and *Fountains of Rome* were made in Symphony Hall, Chicago, on 24 October 1959, and the extraordinarily atmospheric performances have never been surpassed since for their sultry Italian warmth. Yet the turning on of the Triton fountain brings an unforced cascade of orchestral brilliance. RCA's new generation of transfer engineers have put it all on CD with complete fidelity. Reiner's performances are available with two alternative couplings, Debussy's *La Mer* and his equally riveting (1957) recording of the Mussorgsky/Ravel *Pictures at an Exhibition.*

The Naxos recording, engineered by Brian Culverhouse in St Barnabas, Mitcham, is also in the demonstration bracket. The climax of *The Fountain of Trevi at Midday*, when Neptune parades across the heavens, is enormously spectacular, and here a computer organ was used to provide the underlying sustained pedal. The *Pines* and *Fountains* bring extremely fine playing with much warmth and finesse from the RPO. The sharp focus of the Naxos recording brings an extra degree of brazen splendour to the tumultuous popular crowd sequences in the *Circus* and *Jubilee* scenes of the *Feste romane*, while at the close of the *October Festival* the mandolin serenade emerges more tangibly.

Dutoit, as in other brilliant and colourful pieces, draws committed playing from his fine Montreal orchestra. Where many interpreters concentrate entirely on brilliance, Dutoit finds a vein of expressiveness too, which – for example in the opening sequence of *The Pines of Rome* – conveys the fun of children playing at the Villa Borghese. The recorded sound is superlative on CD, where the organ pedal sound is stunning. At mid-price, this is now very competitive, especially for those who enjoy the Montreal ambience.

Muti gives warmly red-blooded performances of Respighi's Roman trilogy, captivatingly Italianate in their inflexions. With brilliant playing from the Philadelphia Orchestra and warmly atmospheric recording, these are exceptional for their strength of characterization.

Ormandy's Sony *Feste romane* has great electricity and enormous surface excitement, and it is a pity that the sound-quality is fiercely brilliant. In the other two works the effect is more opulent, and the Philadelphia playing is fabulous, while the recording has come up astonishingly well. This is still a very exciting example of the Ormandy/Philadelphia regime at its most spectacularly compelling.

Feste romane; The Pines of Rome.

(M) *** Decca (ADD) 466 993-2. Cleveland O, Maazel –
RIMSKY-KORSAKOV: *Le Coq d'or Suite* ***.

In its day (the mid-1970s) Maazel's Decca Cleveland *Feste romane* was something of a revelation: the Decca recording is extremely sophisticated in its colour and detail, and Respighi's vividly evocative sound picture is brought glitteringly to life. The orchestral playing shows matching virtuosity, and the final scene (*The Night before Epiphany in the Piazza Navona*), with its gaudy clamour of trumpets and snatches of melody from the local organ grinder, is given a kaleidoscopic imagery exactly as the composer intended. *The Pines of Rome* is given a strong, direct characterization, undoubtedly memorable, though it does not efface memories of Karajan's classic account. But this whole CD has a breathtaking, demonstration vividness.

The Fountains of Rome; The Pines of Rome; Metamorphosen (Modi XII): Theme & Variations for Orchestra.

*** Telarc CD 80505. Cincinnati SO, López-Cobos.

This impressive new Telarc disc springs a surprise in making a new pairing with the *Theme and Variations for Orchestra*. This suffers from the somewhat ungainly title of *Metamorphosen Modi XII*, but as those who know the earlier Chandos recording will testify, it is a marvellously inventive and resourceful score. Expert and sympathetic playing by the excellent Cincinnati orchestra under Jesús López-Cobos and (not unexpectedly from Telarc) altogether excellent recording which is spectacular, but also both natural in perspective and impressively detailed, with splendid range.

The Pines of Rome.

*** BBC Legends (ADD) BBCL 1007-2. Bournemouth SO,
Silvestri – TCHAIKOVSKY: *Manfred Symphony.* **(*)

Silvestri's account of the *Pines* comes from the Colston Hall, Bristol and 1967. It sounds remarkably good technically and the performance is very fine indeed. Atmospheric and evocative, and well worth considering. Not as subtle nor as masterly as Reiner but far from negligible. Unfortunately the *Manfred Symphony* is not so competitive, given the outstanding versions now available.

Sinfonia drammatica.

*** Chan. 9213. BBC PO, Downes.

Respighi's *Sinfonia drammatica* (1914) is a work of ambitious proportions: epic in scale, it lasts just over an hour, the first movement alone taking 25 minutes. Yet it proves rich in incident and lavish in its orchestral colours and virtuosity; even if it is not organic in conception or symphonic in the classical sense, it is an immensely worthwhile addition to the catalogue. If you enjoy the *Alpine Symphony*, you should try this. An excellent performance and outstanding recording.

String Quartet in D; Quartetto dorico; (i) Il tramonto (The Sunset).

(N) ✪ (M) *** Vanguard 99216. Brodsky Qt; (i) with von
Otter.

Il tramonto, a setting of Shelley, is relatively familiar: a number of great singers have recorded it. Anne Sofie von Otter is a match for any of them. However, the little-known early *Quartet in D major* and the *Quartetto dorico* are quite a find. Respighi was in his late twenties when he wrote the *D major*. His facility as a muscian was legendary: he played the viola in the Imperial Orchestra in St Petersburg, took composition lessons from Rimsky-Korsakov and was also a violin maker! He was still a member of the Quartetto Mugellini at the time of this piece, so one would expect the music to be crafted beautifully. There is the occasional whiff of Brahms and even Debussy and at the beginning of the slow movement a fleeting suggestion of late Strauss, and there are moments of serene beauty throughout. The *Quartetto dorico*, which is hardly less rewarding, comes from the 1920s, when Respighi was at the height of his enthusiasm for Gregorian melody. Sensitive playing, finely-blended tone and a magisterial authority distinguish the playing, and the recording team deserves congratulation on its truthfully balanced and natural sound.

Violin Sonata in B min.

*** DG 427 617-2. Chung, Zimerman – R. STRAUSS:
Sonata. ***

A splendid disc. Kyung Wha Chung is at her best and Krystian Zimerman brings an enormous range of colour and dynamics to the piano part – the clarity of his articulation in the *Passacaglia* is exceptional. This is undoubtedly the finest performance to appear on record since the Heifetz version. This coupling won a *Gramophone* Award and no wonder!

PIANO MUSIC

Ancient Airs & Dances; 6 Pieces; 3 Preludi sopra melodie gregoriane; Sonata in F min.

(BB) *** Naxos 8.553704. Scherbakov.

Respighi followed his famous orchestral set of *Antiche danze ed arie*, (transcriptions from lute tablature), with some for the piano. He also transcribed others: the first by the Genovese, Simone Molinaro, *Balletto detto il Conte Orlando* bears a strong resemblance to the first movement of *The Birds*, as does the *Gagliarda* by Vincenzo Galilei (father of the famous scientist). Of the other pieces, the *Notturno* from the *Six Pieces* has a distinctly Rachmaninovian feel. The *F minor Sonata* (1897–8) is a rarity, and it is difficult to imagine a performance that is more persuasive than this – at any price level. Konstantin Scherbakov is a pianist of quality, combining the highest musicianship with sensitivity and refinement. He is excellently recorded too.

VOCAL MUSIC

(i) Deità silvane; (i; ii) Lauda per la Natività del Signore. 3 Botticelli pictures (Trittico botticelliano).

(B) *** Double Decca (ADD) 444 842-2 (2). (i) Tear;

(ii) Gomez, Dickinson; L. Chamber Ch.; Argo CO, Heltay –
ROSSINI: *Petite messe solennelle*. **

The two rarities here are most appealing. The *Lauda per la Natívitá del Signore* is a setting of words attributed to Jacapone da Todi, a Franciscan of the thirteenth century, and is ingeniously scored for two flutes, piccolo, oboe, cor anglais, two bassoons, piano (four hands) and triangle, while the voices are wonderfully handled. The *Deità silvane* is scored for single wind, horn, percussion, harp and strings – to great effect. All this music, including the much better-known *Botticelli Pictures*, shows great skill in the handling of pastel colourings, and the performances reflect credit on all concerned, including the recording team. It is a pity that the coupling is less readily recommendable.

La primavera; (i) 4 Liriche su poesie popolari armene (1921) (arr. Adriano).

**(*) Marco 8.223595. Lednárová, Valásková, Geriová, Dvorsky, Haan, Kubovčic, Slovak Ph. Ch., Slovak RSO (Bratislava); (i) Slepkovská, Ens., Adriano.

La primavera is an ambitious cantata for six soloists, chorus and orchestra. It takes 45 minutes and is not vintage Respighi. But, although it has moments of bombast and periodically finds his muse on automatic pilot, it has some music of real quality and in particular the sixth of the seven movements; there are evocative and opulently scored orchestral interludes. The *Quattro liriche su poesie popolari armene* are simple and affecting. They are given here in Adriano's arrangement for flute, oboe, clarinet, bass clarinet, bassoon, trombone and harp. The performances throughout are more than adequate and are acceptably recorded.

La sensitiva.

(BB) *** Virgin 2 x 1 Double VBD5 61469-2 (2). Baker, City of L. Sinf., Hickox – BERLIOZ: *Les Nuits d'été* etc.; BRAHMS: *Alto Rhapsody* etc.; MENDELSSOHN: *Infelice* etc. ***

Tautly structured over its span of more than half an hour, Respighi's setting of Shelley's poem, *The Sensitive Plant* (in Italian translation), is a most beautiful piece which Janet Baker and Richard Hickox treat to a glowing first recording. The vocal line, mainly declamatory, is sweetly sympathetic and the orchestration is both rich and subtle. Altogether this makes a quite outstanding anthology.

Il tramonto.

*** Hyp. CDA 66290. Madalin, ECO, Bonavera – MARTUCCI: *Le canzone dei ricordi; Notturno*. ***

Respighi's *Il tramonto* (*The Sunset*) is a glorious work which at times calls to mind the world of late Strauss. A most lovely record. Recommended with all possible enthusiasm.

REZNIČEK, Emil von (1860–1945)

Symphonies Nos. 3 in D; 4 in F min.

**(*) Koch Schwann 3 1203-2. Philh. Hungarica, Wright.

Rezniček is known only by his enchanting, irresistible *Donna Diana* Overture (available in a fine collection on favourite

Overtures from the Cincinnati Pops Orchestra with Erich Kunzel on Telarc CD80116). Those expecting anything approaching its inventiveness will be disappointed here. The symphonies are well crafted and expertly fashioned, even if originality is not their strong suit. All the same there are some delightful ideas, the minuet of the *D major Symphony* begins like Haydn or Schubert and there are overtones of Mahler, and some of the humour of *Donna Diana*. Elsewhere in the *F minor Symphony* there are echoes of Mahler, Bruckner, Wagner and Dvořák. Well worth trying, decently performed, and recorded.

RHEINBERGER, Joseph (1839–1901)

Organ Concerto No. 1 in F, Op. 137.

*** Telarc CD 80136. Murray, RPO, Ling – DUPRE: *Symphony*. ***

Rheinberger's *Concerto* is well made, its invention is attractive and it has suitable moments of spectacle that render it admirable for a coupling with the Dupré *Symphony*, with its use of the massive Albert Hall organ. The performance here is first rate. A fine demonstration disc.

Masses: in E flat (Cantus missae), Op. 109 in G min., for Female Voices & Organ, Op. 187; in F for Male Voices & Organ, Op. 190; Hymn: Tribulationes. Motets: Anima nostra; Laudate Dominum; Meditabor.

(N) **(*) Paraclete Press Gloria de Cantores GDCD 108. Gloria Dei Cantores, Patterson.

Having given us a stimulating collection of the music of William Matthias, the Cape Cod-based choir Gloria Dei Cantores turn their attention to Reinberger, best known for his oratorio, *The Star of Bethlehem*. But he composed his first Latin Mass in 1847, when he was just eight years old.

The finest work here is the E flat *Cantus missae* for double chorus, dating from 1878. It is eloquently performed, with the sequence of *Credo, Sanctus Bendictus* and *Agnus Dei* inspiring the singers to considerable expressive fervour. Among the motets the Offertory for Lent in D minor, *Meditabor*, is the most appealing.

The divided choirs seem slightly less confident, although the men are on the whole impressive in the *F major Mass*, with the rather sombre *Credo* the highlight. The women, however, have occasional moments of insecurity in the *G minor* work (dedicated to Brahms) although they still convey its linear beauty. Excellent recording (made in 1994) and an enterprising programme that deserves support. (Your supplier can obtain the disc via: www.paraclete-press.com.)

RICHAFORT, Jean (c.1480–c.1547)

Requiem Mass.

*** Signum SIGCD 005. Chapelle du Roi, Dixon (with GUERRERO: *Gradual & Tract*. GOMBERT: *Dicite in magni*. INFANTAS: *Domine ostende*. JOSQUIN DESPRES: *Nimphes nappés*. LOBO: *Versa est in luctum; Libera me*).

This superbly recorded collection is entitled '*Music for Philip*

[II] of Spain', and it gathers together music that might have been sung at the spectacular Royal Exequies which was celebrated at San Jerónimo, Madrid on 18th October 1598, five weeks after the King had died. It is not certain which music accompanied the celebrations, but scholarly detective work suggests that the *Missa pro defunctis* for six voices, composed by Jean Richefort around 1532, might have been chosen, supplemented here by Guerrero's *Gradual* and *Tract*. As a prelude, Alistair Dixon presents Gombert's motet written to celebrate Philip's birth in 1527, and he has also interpolated Josquin's great song of mourning, *Nimphes nappés*. Richafort's setting of the *Missa pro defunctis* is in a darkly solemn, chordal polyphonic style which has a grave beauty. So when, after the *Sanctus* we hear Alonso Lobo's radiant motet *Versa est in luctum* (for the elevation of the Host) it is like a light shining down from heaven, and it is Lobo's equally beautiful Respond, *Libera me* which concludes this remarkable vocal memento of the death of a long-dead monarch. Whether or not these actual settings were used in 1598, this enterprise achieves a satisfying linking together of some remarkable music, all sung with devotion and with the beautiful tonal blending for which the Chapelle du Roi are renowned.

RIES, Ferdinand (1784–1838)

Symphonies Nos. 1 in D, Op. 23; 2 in C min., Op. 80.

(N) *** CPO 999 716-2. Zürich CO, Griffiths.

Ferdinand Ries was a pupil and protégé of Beethoven. The latter entrusted the second performance of his *Third Piano Concerto* to the youngster and also allowed him to write his own cadenza. Ries was in his mid-twenties when he wrote the first of his eight symphonies in 1809 (the year of the Siege of Vienna) and the *Second in C minor* was written and first given in 1814 in London, where Ries spent the best part of a decade. It enjoyed much exposure during Ries's lifetime and although the shadow of his master (and especially the *Eroica*) is strikingly in evidence, it is by no means wanting in quality.

Ries is a fine craftsman and has good taste and an inventive lyrical vein. This music serves to show that if Beethoven loomed head and shoulders above his contemporaries, they were still far from negligible. Both symphonies are the product of a fine musical intelligence and offer civilized discourse. Persuasive performances and decent recording from the Zürich orchestra under Howard Griffiths.

RIHM, Wolfgang (born 1952)

Gesungene Zeit (Time Chant).

*** DG 437 093-2. Mutter, Chicago SO, Levine – BERG: *Violin Concerto*. ***

Under the title *Gesungene Zeit* ('Time Chant'), Rihm has written what in effect is an extended lyrical meditation for the soloist, heightened and illustrated by the orchestra in the most discreet way. As in the Berg, Mutter is inspired,

playing with an inner hush that used only rarely to mark her recordings.

RIISAGER, Knudåge (1897–1974)

(i) *Concertino for Trumpet & Strings, Op. 29. Darduse, Op. 32; Slaraffenland (Fools' Paradise): Suites Nos. 1 & 2; Tolv med Posten, Op. 37.*

*** Marco 8.224082. (i) Hardenberger; Hälsingborg SO, Dausgaard.

Knudåge Riisager is best known for his neoclassic works from the 1930s, and all the music on this CD comes from that decade. *Fools' Paradise* has a fair amount of circus-like music *à la manière de* Satie and Milhaud but the touching lyricism of *Prinsesse Sukkergodt* ('Princess Sweets') is captivating. The whole work has bags of charm and deserves the widest currency. Håkan Hardenberger is in good form in the *Concertino*, though the orchestral support could have greater lightness of touch and finesse. *April* from *Tolv med Posten*, on the other hand, has much elegance. Readers who investigate this CD will find little depth, but much to entertain them. Generally good performances under Thomas Dausgaard but rather bass-light sound.

Erasmus Montanus Overture, Op. 1; Etudes (ballet; complete); Qarrtsiluni, Op. 36.

*** Chan. 9432. Danish Nat. RSO, Rozhdestvensky.

Both the *Etudes* and *Qarrtsiluni* are classics of the Danish ballet. Knudåge Riisager's admiration for *Les Six* is evident in the elegance and wit that distinguish the *Etudes* (1948), a pastiche based on Czerny, and *Qarrtsiluni* (1938). There is a zest and sparkle about his music, though it neither aims for nor has any great depth. The attractive *Erasmus Montanus Overture* is a highly accomplished first opus, neatly performed and superbly recorded.

RILEY, Terry (born 1935)

The Heavenly Ladder, Book 7; The Walrus in memoriam.

*** Telarc CD 80513. Cheng-Cochran – ADAMS: *China Gates; Phrygian Gates*. ***

The five pieces which make up *The Heavenly Ladder* were written in 1994 and represent the composer's move away from an aleatory improvisational style into written 'paper music'. The jazz element remains and is never more effectively interpolated than in the third piece, the polyponic *Ragtempus fugatum*. *Venus in '94* is a bizarre waltz-scherzo and the *Fandango on the Heavenly Ladder* (the most extended movement) intriguingly combines melancholy with energy. Its three themes are then gently re-explored in the closing *Simone's Lullaby*, a set of variations marked pianissimo throughout, and dedicated to the composer's newly arrived granddaughter. *The Walrus in memoriam* is a witty ragtime encore piece ending more reflectively, as it is intended as a memorial to John Lennon. The performances here are persuasive: Gloria Cheng-Cochran is very sensitive to the composer's eclectic but very personal pianistic excursions, and with the stimulating Adams couplings (dating from the late 1970s) this is an important issue for those interested in the way mimimalism is developing.

RIMSKY-KORSAKOV, Nikolay
(1844–1908)

Capriccio espagnol, Op. 34.

(M) *** RCA (ADD) 09026 63302-2. RCA Victor SO, Kondrashin – KABALEVSKY: *The Comedians Suite*; KHACHATURIAN: *Masquerade Suite*; TCHAIKOVSKY: *Capriccio italien.* *** ●

(M) *** DG (ADD) 449 769-2 (2). BPO, Maazel – RAVEL: *L'Heure espagnole; L'Enfant et les sortiléges* ***; STRAVINSKY: *Le Chant du rossignol.* *** ●

Kondrashin's 1958 performance is among the finest ever recorded, ranking alongside Maazel's famous Berlin Philharmonic account, but with the advantage of slightly more sumptuous string textures. Like the coupled Tchaikovsky *Capriccio* it has great flair and excitement, with glittering colour and detail in the variations and the *Scena e canto gitana*. The orchestral zest is exhilarating, yet there is warmth too and the resonant recording still sounds very good indeed.

Maazel's 1960 recording of the *Capriccio espagnol* is memorable in every way, and remains one of his finest recorded performances. With gorgeous string and horn playing and a debonair, relaxed virtuosity in the *Scene e canto gitano*, leading to remarkable bravura in the closing sequence, every note in place, this is unforgettable. The remastering has restored the recording's analogue allure and, although the fortissimo violins are a little thin above the stave, the ear readily adjusts when the playing is so exciting.

(i) *Capriccio espagnol;* (ii) *Le Coq d'or: Suite; Dubinushka;* (iii) *May Night Overture;* (iv) *Russian Easter Festival Overture; Scheherazade;* (ii) *Snow Maiden: Suite;* (v) *Tsar Saltan: Suite;* (i) *Flight of the Bumble-Bee.*

(B) **(*) EMI (ADD) CZS5 69680-2 (2). Philh. O, with (i) Cluytens; (ii) Kurtz; (iii) Silvestri; (iv) Von Matačič; (v) Kletzki.

These recordings were made at Abbey Road between 1956 and 1963, and although some of the allure in the treble has been lost with the CD remastering, the bright colouring remains, and the Philharmonia are on top form, as they immediately demonstrate in an exciting *Scheherazade*. Matačič's direction has plenty of drive in the opening movement, and the silky strings in the slow movement are matched by the lustre of the woodwind solos. The finale is really exciting. The *Russian Easter Festival Overture* wrings every ounce of colour from the music, and the famous trombone solo is played with great dignity. Efrem Kurtz is thoroughly at home in *Le Coq d'or* and *The Snow Maiden*, and Kletzki is vibrant in *Tsar Saltan*. Cluytens closes the first disc and opens the second with virtuoso accounts of the *Capricio espagnol* and *Flight of the Bumble-Bee* respectively; in the former the sound is brilliant but lacking in voluptuousness.

Capriccio espagnol, Op. 34; Le Coq d'or: Suite; Russian Easter Festival Overture, Op. 36.

(M) *** Mercury (IMS) (ADD) 434 308-2. LSO, Dorati – BORODIN: *Prince Igor: Polovstian Dances.* **(*)

Dorati's 1959 *Capriccio espagnol* brings glittering bravura and excitement from the LSO players, and the *Russian Easter Festival Overture*, recorded at Walthamstow at the same sessions, is equally dynamic and colourful. Even more remarkably, the rich-hued and vibrant *Le Coq d'or* dates from as early as 1956, yet hardly sounds dated. The playing has plenty of allure in its evocation of Queen Shemakha, yet has drama and well defined detail.

(i; ii) *Capriccio espagnol;* (iii) *Le Coq d'or: Suite; Russian Easter Festival Overture, Op. 36;* (i; iv) *Scheherazade, Op. 35;* (v) *Symphony No. 2, Op. 9 (Antar);* (vi) *Tsar Saltan: Suite Op. 57; The Flight of the Bumble-Bee.*

(N) (BB) **(*) DG Panorama (ADD) 469 187-2 (2). (i) BPO; (ii) Maazel; (iii) LOP, Markevitch; (iv) Karajan; (v) Gothenburg SO, Järvi; (vi) PO, Ashkenazy.

On the whole, a good Panorama selection here. You get Karajan's exciting, and superbly played (if uneven) *Scheherazade*; vibrant accounts of the *Russian Easter Festival Overture* and *Le Coq d'or Suite* from Markevitch (from the late 1950s, and sounding slightly dated in the matter of string timbre); Ashkenazy's beautifully played and sumptuously recorded (Decca) *Tsar Saltan Suite*, and an excellent reading of *Antar* by Järvi (even if it could do with a bit more Russian bite). Best of all is Maazel's glittering *Capriccio espagnol*, a classic account which shows just how this repertoire should be played.

Capriccio espagnol; Russian Easter Festival Overture.

(B) **(*) Decca Eclipse 448 233-2. Montreal SO, Dutoit – MUSSORGSKY: *Night on the Bare Mountain* etc. **(*)

Dutoit's *Capriccio espagnol* is comparatively genial and relaxed; the *Russian Easter Festival Overture* is strong, with a fine climax . In both works the Montreal recording is full, with iridescent detail.

Christmas Eve (Suite); Le Coq d'or: Suite; Legend of the Invisible City of Kitezh: suite; May Night: overture; Mlada: suite; The Snow Maiden: suite; The Tale of the Tsar Saltan: suite.

*** Chan. 8327/9 (3). SNO, Järvi.

Apart from the feast of good tunes here, the composer's skilful and subtle deployment of the orchestral palette continually titillates the ear. Neeme Järvi draws the most seductive response from the SNO; he consistently creates orchestral textures which are diaphanously sinuous. Yet the robust moments, when the brass blazes or the horns ring out sumptuously, are caught just as strikingly and the listener is assured that here is music which survives repetition uncommonly well.

Christmas Eve: Suite; Le Coq d'or: Suite; The Tale of Tsar Saltan: Suite; Flight of the Bumble-Bee.

*** ASV CDDCA 772. Armenian PO, Tjeknavorian.

Tjeknavorian and his fine Armenian orchestra are completely at home in Rimsky's sinuous orientalism, with its glittering, iridescent wind-colouring. The racy vigour and sparkle of the playing brings a jet-setting bumble-bee and the carolling horns and bold brass add to the vividness. The Tchaikovskian *Polonaise* music from *Christmas Eve* exudes similar sparkling vitality within a glowing palette. In short this is one of the most desirable and generous Rimsky-Korsakov collections in the current catalogue, and only a degree of thinness in the violin timbre above the stave prevents the use of the adjective sumptuous. In all other respects this is in the demonstration bracket.

Christmas Eve (Suite); Dubinushka, Op. 62; May Night Overture; Russian Easter Festival Overture, Op. 36; Sadko (musical picture), Op. 5; (i) Scheherazade, Op. 35; The Snow Maiden (Suite). Tsar Saltan (Suite), Op. 57; Tsar Saltan (opera): The Flight of the Bumble-Bee.

(B) **(*) Double Decca (IMS) (ADD) 443 464-2 (2). SRO, Ansermet, (i) with Geneva Motet Ch.

This is all repertoire for which Ansermet was famous in the early stereo era, and *Scheherazade* must be counted a historic recording. It dates from 1960, and the sound still offers quality regarded as demonstration standard in its day and not very far short of it now. Ansermet's skill as a ballet conductor comes out persuasively. The outer movements with their undoubted sparkle are the finest: the first is dramatic and the last is built steadily to a climax of considerable impact. The music's sinuous qualities are not missed and every bar of the score is alive. *May Night* was recorded a year earlier and the strings have far less lustre; but the *Tsar Saltan Suite*, also made in 1959, shows Ansermet and the Decca engineers in glittering form, especially in the recording of brass and woodwind. The *Flight of the Bumble-Bee* is rather leisurely, but Ansermet is at his finest in the *Christmas Eve Suite*, played with much affection, plus that mixture of spontaneity and a remarkably graphic orchestral palette which made Ansermet's performances special. *Dubinushka* has some typical brass fanfare writing and Ansermet is (again in 1958) well served here by the engineers, as he is in *Sadko*, an exotic fairy-tale handled with characteristic aplomb. The earliest recording offered here is *The Snow Maiden Suite* (1957) and once again the sound is remarkably warm and richly coloured. This set can certainly be recommended at Double Decca price, especially to Ansermet aficionados.

Concert Fantasy on Russian Themes for Violin & Orchestra in B min., Op. 33.

**(*) Globe GLO 5174. Lubotsky, Estonian Nat. SO, Volmer – ARENSKY; TCHAIKOVSKY: *Violin Concertos.* **(*)

The *Concert Fantasy in B minor on Two Russian Themes* is a slight but colourful piece, and it is persuasively performed here. It makes an admirable fill-up to Arensky's endearing *Violin Concerto* and the Tchaikovksy which inspired it. Good orchestral playing under Arvo Volmer and naturally balanced sound.

Piano Concerto in C sharp min., Op. 30.

*** Hyp. CDA 66640. Binns, E. N. Philh. O, Lloyd-Jones – BALAKIREV: *Concertos Nos. 1–2.* ***

Malcolm Binns proves a sensitive and intelligent exponent in the Rimsky-Korsakov concerto, which comes aptly coupled with Balakirev's two essays in the form. The Northern Philharmonia under David Lloyd-Jones give excellent support and the Hyperion recording is first class.

Le Coq d'or: Suite.

(M) *** Decca (ADD) 466 993-2. Cleveland O, Maazel – RESPIGHI: *Feste romane; Pines of Rome.* ***

Le Coq d'or; The Maid of Pskov; Pan Voyevoda: suites.

✪ *** Kontrapunct 32247. Odense SO, Serov.

A sumptuously played and recorded account of sumptuously exotic music: Maazel wallows in the luxuriant aural magic of Rimsky-Korsakov's scoring, but his warmth of affection strongly communicates, and he creates a superb climax with *The Marriage Feast and the Lamentable End of King Dodon.* The sound is as brilliant as could be imagined on this fine Decca Legends CD.

Serov is also complete master of the repertoire, and the playing of the Odense orchestra is glorious, the glowing woodwind palette matched by the most seductive and transparent string textures Serov's performance of *Le Coq d'or* is every bit as fine as Maazel's, and the recording here is even more luxuriant. Indeed it is very much in the demonstration bracket. In *The Maid of Pskov,* suite *The Tsar Hunting in the Wood and Tempest* has much of the imaginative pictorial evocation and imagery of Berlioz's *Royal Hunt and Storm.* Again it is superbly presented, as is the hardly less attractive *Pan Voyevoda* which opens with a pastoral evocation rather like Wagner's *Forest Murmurs,* and includes three brilliantly scored *Russian Dances.*

Fairy Tale (Skazka), Op. 29; Fantasia on Serbian Themes, Op. 6; Legend of the Invisible City of Kitzh (symphonic suite); The Maid of Pskov (Ivan the Terrible): Suite.

(N) (BB) ** Naxos 8.553513. Moscow Symphony O, Golovchin.

This is a very attractive compilation containing some of Rimsky's lesser-known music, often languorous in feeling and displaying a characteristically glowing orchestral palette. The Moscow Symphony Orchestra are obviously at home in this repertoire and they play it very beguilingly (apart from occasional rasping trombones), and the recording is warmly atmospheric. But the effect is very relaxed and in music which is atmospherically sustained one needs more internal tension. The narrative of *Skazka,* too, lacks a positive momentum. Even so this is still desirable and worth its modest price.

Scheherazade (symphonic suite), Op. 35.

(N) (M) *** Ph. (ADD) 464 735-2. Concg. O, Kondrashin – BORODIN: *Symphony No. 2.* *(*)
(M) *** EMI CDM5 66983-2 [CDM 566998]. RPO, Beecham (with BORODIN: *Polovtsian Dances* ***).
*** DG (IMS) 437 818-2. O de l'Opéra Bastille, Chung – STRAVINSKY: *Firebird Suite.* ***

**(*) Decca (IMS) 443 703-2. Concg. O, Chailly (with
STRAVINSKY: *Scherzo fantastique*).

(N) (BB) **(*) EMI Encore CDE5 74751-2. Phd. O, Muti –
TCHAIKOVSKY: *1812*. **(*)

(M) **(*) Mercury (ADD) 462 953-2. Minneapolis SO, Dorati
(with LSO: LISZT: *Les Préludes*; SIBELIUS: *Valse triste*;
SMETANA: *Vltava*) **.

(BB) **(*) Virgin 2 x 1 VBD5 61751-2 (2). LPO, Litton –
BORODIN: *Prince Igor: Overture & Polovtsian
Dances* ***; MUSSORGSKY: *Night on the Bare Mountain*;
Pictures at an Exhibition **; TCHAIKOVSKY: *The
Tempest*. ***

(M) **(*) DG (ADD) 463 614-2. BPO, Karajan –
TCHAIKOVSKY: *Capriccio italien*; *1812 Overture*. **(*)

(B) ** EMI double forte (ADD) CZS5 69361-2 (2). LSO,
Svetlanov – ARENSKY: *Variations on a Theme by
Tchaikovsky*; GLAZUNOV: *The Seasons*; *Concert
Waltzes*. ***

(**) Testament mono SBT 1139. Philh. O, Stokowski –
STRAVINSKY: *Petrushka*. (***)

Scheherazade; Capriccio espagnol, Op. 34.

🌑 *** Telarc CD 80208. LSO, Mackerras.

(M)*** Classic fm 74605 57055-2. LPO, Lazarev.

**(*) Australian Decca Eloquence 466 907-2. (i) LAPO;
(ii) Israel PO; Mehta.

**(*) EMI CDC5 55227-2. LPO, Jansons.

(B) **(*) DG ADD/Dig. 439 443-2. (i) Boston SO, Ozawa;
(ii) Gothenburg SO, Järvi.

*(i–ii) Scheherazade; (iii–iv) Capriccio espagnol; (i; iv)
Russian Easter Festival Overture, Op. 36.*

(M) *** Ph. (ADD) 442 643-2. (i) Concg. O; (ii) Kondrashin;
(iii) LSO; (iv) Markevitch.

*Scheherazade,; Capriccio espagnol, Op. 34; Tsar Saltan:
Flight of the Bumble-Bee.*

** Teldec 0630 17125-2. NYPO, Masur.

*Scheherazade; Dubinushka, Op. 62; Tale of Tsar Saltan:
Flight of the Bumble-Bee.*

(M) *** Chan. 7093. RSNO, Järvi – KALINNIKOV:
Overtures. ***

(i) Scheherazade; (ii) Fairy Tale (Skazka).

(N) (BB) (**) Dutton mono CDBP 9712. (i) Paris Conservatoire
O, Ansermet; (ii) Philh. O, Lambert (with BORODIN arr.
RIMSKY-KORSAKOV: *Polovtsian Dances* (**)).

*Scheherazade; Fairy Tale (Skazka), Op. 29; Sadko, Op. 5;
Song of India, from Sadko (arr. Tjeknavorian).*

*** ASV CDDCA 771. Armenian PO, Tjeknavorian.

Scheherazade; Russian Easter Festival Overture.

(N) ** Telarc CD 80568. Atlanta SO, Spano.

*Scheherazade; Russian Easter Festival Overture; The Maid
of Pskov: Hunt and Storm.*

(M) (***) Biddulph mono WHL 010. Phd. O, Stokowski.

Scheherazade; Tsar Saltan: Orchestral Suite.

(BB) *** Naxos 8.550726. Philh. O, Bátiz.

Mackerras's reading combines gripping drama with romantic ardour, subtlety of colour with voluptuousness; he

is helped by a wonderfully beguiling portrait of Scheherazade
herself, provided by his orchestral leader, in this case Kees
Hulsmann. After an appropriate pause, Mackerras then delivers a thrilling bravura account of *Capriccio espagnol*, lushly
opulent in the variations, glittering in the exotic *Scena e
canta gitano*, and carrying all before it in the impetus of the
closing *Fandango asturiano*. Telarc's digital recording is very
much in the demonstration class.

Kondrashin's version of *Scheherazade* with the Concertgebouw Orchestra has the advantage of splendidly glowing
(1980) analogue recorded sound. Hermann Krebbers' exquisitely seductive portrayal of Scheherazade is cleverly used
by Kondrashin to provide a foil for the expansively vibrant
contribution of the orchestra as a whole, and he creates an
irresistible forward impulse, leading to a huge climax at the
moment of the shipwreck. Markevitch gives an excellent
account of the *Russian Easter Festival Overture* with the same
orchestra; the *Capriccio espagnol*, too, is brilliantly played by
the LSO, and in both the sound also has considerable allure,
with the present CD transfer much more vivid than the
original LP.

Kondrashin's account is also available alternatively
coupled with an unrecommendable account of Borodin's
Second Symphony.

Beecham's 1957 *Scheherazade* is a performance of extraordinary drama and charisma. Alongside the violin contribution of Stephen Staryk, all the solo playing has great
distinction; in the second movement Beecham gives the
woodwind complete metrical freedom. The sumptuousness
and glamour of the slow movement are very apparent and
the finale has an explosive excitement, rising to an electrifying climax. Now finally reissued at mid-price, as one of
EMI's 'Great Recordings of the Century' this could well be
first choice for some collectors, although the fortissimo
massed strings in the first movement are on the thin side
and show the age of the recording (1957).

The striking digital coupling from Alexander Lazarev on
Classic fm is very successful indeed. The recording, made at
Watford Colosseum, combines brilliance and lustre, with
body and warmth . The LSO are consistently on top form,
with seductive horn and string playing in the *Variazioni* of
the *Capriccio*, sparkling detail in the *Scena e canto gitano* and
a highly zestful closing *Fandango asturiano*. Lazarev opens
Scheherazade very boldly, but the heroine's entry (Jaokim
Svenheden, the violin soloist) is sharply contrasted, delicately
alluring. The first movement is spacious, but the tension is
built up steadily to a powerful climax. Lazarev's idyllic languor in the slow movement then brings the most glowingly
seductive response from the LPO, strings and woodwind
alike, to contrast with a thrillingly uninhibited finale.

On ASV a refreshing and totally gripping *Scheherazade*
from Eastern Russia. Yuri Boghosian immediately presents
a seductively slight and sinuous image for the heroine-
narrator and throughout the central movements one is made
aware of the lustrous oriental character of Rimsky's melodies. The finale, with its spectacular storm and shipwreck,
has exhilarating animation and bite. Tjeknavorian shows
great imaginative flair in the two shorter folk tales and also
offers his own gently luscious arrangement of the *Chant
hindue*, which caresses the ear beguilingly. The brilliant

recording has great vividness and projection, but relatively little sumptuousness. But it suits the performances admirably.

There is a certain freshness about the newest Paris account under Myung-Whun Chung; nothing is routine and the playing has a certain enthusiasm. Very fast and effective tempo in the finale. The sound has warmth and perspective, though the timpani resonate perhaps a bit too much. All the same, a very enjoyable newcomer.

Järvi's version of *Scheherazade* with the RSNO is given one of Chandos's most sumptuous and spectacular digital recordings and, as with Kondrashin, Järvi's reading generates a vivid narrative feeling. The playing is no less fine, and this is well worth considering, and it offers a smiliarly brilliant account of the colourful *Dubinushka*, plus a buzzing, convincingly scaled *Bumble-Bee*. The coupled overtures by Kalinnikov are also well worth having.

Bátiz's reputation for spontaneity in the recording studio is demonstrated at its most telling. His performance is impulsive, full of momentum and seductively volatile. David Nolan's picture of Scheherazade is rhapsodically evanescent and in the key second movement the lilting Philharmonia wind solos are a constant pleasure. The slow movement combines refinement with its sensuous patina, and the finale has fine zest and excitement. The colourful *Tsar Saltan Suite* is comparably dramatic and vivid. In short, with first-class recording, both clear in detail and full-bodied, at super-bargain price this is hard to beat.

Mehta's *Scheherazade* was considered a demonstration disc in its day (mid-1970s) and still sounds impressive. Though it is a high-powered performance, there is affection too, and despite the odd mannerism, it is very enjoyable, and the orchestral leader, Sydney Harth, offers a sinuously seductive image for Scheherazade herself. The Israeli version of *Capriccio espagnol* is not quite so successful in terms of sound or performance, but still entertains, and makes a fair bonus for the main work, which is more exciting than many more recent digital versions.

Jansons gives us a very well-played and warmly distinctive version with much to recommend it. What comes out in all four movements is the way he points rhythms, lilting, bouncy and affectionate, to distinguish this from most other versions, bringing a satisfying resolution at the great climax towards the end of the finale, with Joakim Svenheden a warmly expressive soloist. The *Capriccio espagnol* brings a similar combination of expressive warmth and exuberance. But the recorded sound has less bloom and transparency than others made in Abbey Road Studio No. 1. However, this Janson CD has just been withdrawn.

Chailly's newest Decca *Scheherazade* has sound out of Decca's top drawer, with all the glowing lustre one expects from the Concertgebouw acoustics, but Jaap van Zweden's assumption of the role of voluptuous storyteller, though sweetly sinuous, does not have a strong enough profile to dominate the narrative, especially at the opening and close of the work. But it is in the sensuous grace of the two central movements, with their translucent detail, that the performance is at its most appealing. The brief Stravinsky encore is beautifully played and has never been recorded more richly.

Muti's reading is colourful and dramatic in a larger-than-life way that sweeps one along. The bravura has one remembering that this was the orchestra which in the days of Stokowski made this a party-piece. The great string theme of the slow movement has all the voluptuousness one expects of Philadelphia strings in one of the best of HMV's latter-day Philadelphia recordings, more spacious than usual, though not ideally balanced. There is a glare in the upper range to which not all ears will respond, even if the racy finale, with its exciting climax, carries all before it. However, the brightness in the treble, especially in climaxes, is much less congenial than the Philips sound for Kondrashin.

Litton's first movement brings strong dramatic contrasts and the violin soloist, David Nolan, plays seductively. The *Andantino* has a Beechamesque languor and the freedom given to the woodwind soloists also recalls the Beecham version, which is also coupled with the Borodin *Polovtsian Dances*. Litton's finale is less than overwhelming, indeed less exciting than Beecham's, and although the Virgin recording is opulent as well as brilliant, the RPO performance brings a greater sense of spontaneity, although Litton's version has more modern sound and is certainly enjoyable in its spaciousness.

In Karajan's account it is the brilliance and prowess of the Berlin Philharmonic which is immediately apparent from the sensitive opening violin solo from Michel Schwalbé onwards. The recording is full-blooded and vivid, but is a little light on bass – although in the preset remastering this is less obvious. The first movement is hard driven but has plenty of excitement; the finale (a resounding success) has even more, but the inner movements do not glow as you would ideally expect them to. A typically individual Karajan account then, and if he is not quite on his best it is still impressive.

Mercury *aficionados* will be glad to have this very well remastered CD transfer of Dorati's fine 1958 Performance, which sounds much better than the old LP. The Minneapolis orchestra play very well for him and, if the first movement is not especially arresting, the finale is very brilliant indeed. The encores were recorded two years later in the more flattering ambience of Wembley Town Hall, though the massed violins still reveal the recording date. Liszt's *Les Préludes* is outstandingly successful, with dignity and warm romantic feeling as well as excitement. *Valse triste* is sombrely characterful, and only Smetana's *Vltava* brings a measure of disappointment when the flowing opening string tune fails to lift off as much as it can.

Ozawa's earlier (1977) Boston *Scheherazade* is an attractive performance, richly recorded; if the last degree of vitality is missing from the central movements, the orchestral playing is warmly vivid. The reading as a whole has plenty of colour and atmosphere, however, and is certainly enjoyable. Moreover Järvi's digital *Capriccio espagnol* is a distinctive and worthwhile bonus, brilliantly recorded.

The collection of Leopold Stokowski's recordings of Rimsky-Korsakov on Biddulph centres on the first of his five versions of *Scheherazade*. Made in 1927, it is wilder and more passionate than later ones; fascinatingly, an alternative version of the first movement, never issued before, is included as a supplement. At a slightly broader speed, spreading to an extra 78-r.p.m. side, it is even more persuasive. Equally impressive is Stokowski's intense, volatile account of the *Russian Easter Festival Overture*, dating from 1929, while the *Hunt and Storm* sequence from the *The Maid of Pskov* comes from ten years later, with the sound drier and marginally less full. The Biddulph transfers are excellent, with plenty of body.

Though Ansermet's 1948 recording of Scheherazade cannot match his later stereo version with the Suisse Romande Orchestra in power or polish, let alone in sound, its lighter manner gives it an attractively balletic quality, building up gradually rather than packing a punch. The usual reservations need mentioning about the playing of the Paris orchestra – with brass vibrato and a sugary solo violin among them. As transferred, this is not one of the most vivid of early Decca mono ffrr recordings. The rarity, *Skazka*, conducted by Constand Lambert, is taken from a 1946 EMI recording, here transformed, with Gregor Fitelberg's reading of the *Polovtsian Dances* a welcome bonus.

Svetlanov's 1978 version with the LSO is disappointing, despite John Georgiadis's subtly seductive image of Scheherazade herself. The broad, powerful opening movement, taken very spaciously indeed, is balanced by a finale which is almost aggressively brilliant. The inner movements are extremely volatile and less contrasted than usual. The LSO wind solo playing is impressive, but the strings sometimes have an almost febrile timbre which is less than glamorous.

Robert Spano in his first recording as music director draws clean, polished playing from the Atlanta Orchestra, which yet lacks the forward thrust and improvisatory freedom needed in the episodic structure of *Scheherazade*. The violin soloist, Cecylia Arzewski, similarly plays with precision but too stiffly. The *Russian Easter Festival Overture*, too, brings a note of caution. The Telarc recording is unobtrusively brilliant, with brass very well caught.

Though Masur's *Scheherazade* was recorded live, there is little or no rush of adrenalin. Ensemble is phenomenally precise, with the cleanest articulation, and Masur's control is so complete that even the rhapsodic solos, both from the solo violin and from the woodwind, have little feeling of freedom. The approach is similar in the *Capriccio espagnol*, fast and fierce, missing jollity. Some may find the results of Masur's approach refreshing, and the *Flight of the Bumble-Bee* does bring a dazzling performance full of wit and fun, but there is a missing dimension here.

Stokowski's 1950s Philharmonia recording of the *Scheherazade* on Testament offers some superb playing – what performances under his baton did not! – but it is actually less likeable than his pre-war Philadelphia set. His rubati are intrusive in the slow movement and he pulls phrases out of shape elsewhere. Good sound and an excellent transfer.

Symphonies Nos. 1 in E min., Op. 1; 2 (Antar), Op. 9; 3 in C, Op. 32; Capriccio espagnol, Op. 36; (i) Piano Concerto in C sharp min., Op. 30. Russian Easter Festival Overture, Op. 36; Sadko, Op. 5.

(N) (M) **(*) Chan. 6613 (2). (i) Tozer; Bergen PO, Kitaienko.

Whatever Rimsky-Korsakov's symphonies may lack in symphonic coherence they make up for in colour and charm.

Some of the material is a little thin but there is some highly attractive invention as well. *Antar* is not quite as strong as some of its protagonists would have us believe, but it should surely have a stronger presence in the concert and recorded repertoire than it has. Kitaienko draws very good playing from the Bergen Philharmonic throughout and the first two symphonies are generally successful. In the *Third Symphony* the lustrous colours of the secondary material glow appealingly, but the Scherzo lacks sparkle. He gets very lively results in the *Capriccio espagnol*, but *Sadko* takes a while to warm up, although it has a spectacular close. With Tozer at the keyboard he shares a warmly lyrical view of the *Piano Concerto* but, partly because of the resonant sound, the finale lacks something in sparkle, and Malcolm Binns on Hyperion (see above) is preferable. However, this Chandos set is value for money.

Tsar Saltan: Suite

*** Belair BAM 9724. New Russian O, Poltevsky – BORODIN: *Symphony No. 2 in B min.* *(*)

The young Russian, Oleg Poltevsky, conducts this handpicked Russian orchestra in an electrifying account of the colourful *Tsar Saltan* music, well recorded. An excellent, if ungenerous coupling for a rather ponderous reading of the Borodin.

Piano & Wind Quintet in B flat.

*** Hyp. CDA 66163. Capricorn – GLINKA: *Grand Sextet*. ***
(M) *** CRD (ADD) 3409. Brown, Nash Ens. – ARENSKY: *Piano Trio No. 1.* ***

Rimsky-Korsakov's youthful *Quintet for Piano, Flute, Clarinet, Horn and Bassoon* is a thoroughly diverting piece. It is like a garrulous but endearing friend whose loquacity is readily borne for the sake of his charm and good nature. The main theme of the finale is singularly engaging, and the work as a whole leaves a festive impression. Capricorn's account has great vivacity and is very well recorded.

The Nash Ensemble also give a spirited and delightful account of it on CRD that can be warmly recommended for its dash and sparkle and full, naturally balanced sound.

OPERA

Kashchey the Immortal (complete).

*** Ph. 446 704-2. Pluzhnikov, Shaguch, Gergalov, Diadkova, Morozov, Kirov Op. Ch. & O, Gergiev.

With its prominent use of the exotic whole-tone scale and other devices, this one-act fairy-tale opera of 1901 puzzled and surprised early audiences, the most radical of Rimsky's operas up to that time. Gergiev with a strong, characterful cast from his Kirov company proves a persuasive interpreter of this rich, colourful piece. The first of the three tableaux has Kashchey in dialogue with the Princess he has imprisoned, with Konstantin Pluzhnikov darkly incisive in the title-role and Marina Shaguch bright and clear if edgy as the Princess. The oddity of the casting is that there is no tenor soloist, with Alexander Gergalov as Prince Ivan an aptly heroic-sounding baritone and Alexander Morozov equally well-focused as the Storm Knight, father of the Princess. Most characterful of all is the mezzo, Larissa Diadkova, as Kascheyevna, at once rich-toned and sinister. Recorded in concert at the Philharmonic Hall in St Petersburg, the sound is clear and generally well-balanced.

The Legend of the Invisible City of Kitezh (complete).

*** Ph. 462 225-2 (2). Gorchakova, Galuzin, Putilin, Ohotnikov, Marusin, Minjilkiev, Ognovienko, Kirov Opera Ch. & O, Gergiev.

Recorded live at the Mariinsky Theatre in St Peterburg, this long fairy-tale piece (lasting almost three hours) relies above all on the cadences of Russian folk-song. As usual with Russian folk-tales the plot brings a curious mixture of jollity and bitterness. Though the Prince dies in battle in the middle of Act III – illustrated in an interlude – he is resurrected in Act IV, when the disappearing City of Kitezh is magically transformed into Paradise, with hero and heroine united in life after death. What adds spice to the plot is the equivocal character of the drunkard, Grishka, comic only in part, who initially is prompted to attack Fevroniya, but who later is befriended by her. Galina Gorchakova sings powerfully as Fevroniya and Yuri Marusin is a strong, idiomatic Prince, whose distinctive tenor is well contrasted with that of Vladimir Galuzin as an incisive Grishka, characterizing splendidly. Despite moments of strain, the rest of the Kirov cast makes an excellent team. Live recording inevitably brings intrusive stage noises and odd balances, but this is another warmly recommendable set in Gergiev's excellent Philips series.

The Maid of Pskov.

*** 446 678-2 (2). Gorchakova, Ognovienko, Galusin, Filatova, Kirov Op. Ch. & O, Gergiev.

Much has been made by commentators of the parallels between The Maid of Pskov and Mussorgsky's Boris. Both tackle serious historic themes and concerned tormented monarchs; both have sumptuous crowd scenes and splendid bell-ringing (the Coronation Scene in Boris is matched by the council summons in Act II of The Maid of Pskov); both aspire to naturalistic declamation and to a kind of 'formlessness' in the name of realization, though both operas have set-pieces. The characterization of his Tsar Ivan may not equal Mussorgsky's Tsar in Boris either in depth or psychological understanding, but there is no lack of effective characterization elsewhere. Olga, marvellously sung by Gorchakova, is in fact an illegitimate daughter of Ivan, whom his vice-regent Prince Tokmakov has brought up. Her abduction and subsequent death enable him to show the more human side of his personality in much the same way as did Boris in Mussorgsky's opera. The well-known orchestral interlude from the third Act, the Hunt and Storm was written under the influence of Berlioz's Royal Hunt and Storm from Les Troyens. The cast is strong and Gergiev gets very good singing from the chorus and orchestra. There is a lot of striking music here and the Philips team do it proud.

Sadko (complete).

*** Ph. 442 138-2 (3). Galusin, Tsidipova, Tarassova, Minjelkiev, Gergalov, Grigorian, Alexashin, Diadkova, Boitsov, Bezzubenkov, Ognovenko, Gassiev, Putilin, Kirov Op. Ch. & O, Gergiev.

Whatever its dramatic weaknesses, Sadko is full of glorious musical invention, sumptuously orchestrated, which puts the listener completely under its spell. Vladimir Galusin's assumption of the name role is very good, though his handling of dynamic nuance is not always subtle. The vibrato to which one is long accustomed in Russian sopranos is not worrying in Valentina Tsidipova's portrayal of the Sea Princess, Volkhova. Indeed most of the roles are well sung, with the possible exception of Gegam Grigorian's rather tight-throated Hindu merchant. Valery Gergiev brings great warmth and feeling for colour to the opera. The recording is very good, though there are some stage noises, inevitable in stage performances. There is an excellent video (070 439-1 for the laserdisc; 070 439-3 for the VHS cassette), well directed for the cameras by Brian Large; both sound and vision are particularly impressive on Laserdisc. Thoroughly recommended.

The Tsar's Bride (complete).

*** Ph. 462 618-2 (2). Bezzuhenkov, Shaguch, Hvorostovsky, Alexashlin, Akinov, Borodina, Kirov Ch. & O, Gergiev.

Gergiev firmly establishes The Tsar's Bride as a most richly enjoyable opera, full of outstanding set numbers, such as the banqueting song in the party scene of Act I, which uses the Tsar's Hymn in opulent counterpoint. The story itself, set at the time of Ivan the Terrible, is a curious mixture of darkness and light, of fairy-tale fantasy and melodramatic realism. Jealousy is the dominant emotion, when the sinister adventurer, Gryaznoy, and the scheming Lyubasha take priority over even the hero and heroine. In the casting here, that priority is a great source of strength, when Dmitri Hovorostovsky as Gryaznoy and Olga Borodina as Lyubasha give superb performances, not just singing with rich, firm tone but characterizing powerfully. Marina Shaguch is fresh and clear as Marfa the heroine, if edgy under pressure, and Evgeny Akimov with his typically Slavonic tenor sings idiomatically if with forced tone. In Act IV, with the plot turning sour, Rimsky is prompted to round the work off with a sequence of remarkable numbers, including a splendid quintet with chorus, when Gryaznoy stabs Lyubasha to death, and a mad-scene for Marfa. A rich offering, strongly recommended.

ROBINSON, Thomas (fl.1589–1609)

Lute pieces: Bonny Sweet Boy; A Galliard; A Gigue; Go from My Window; A Toy. Lute duets: (i) A Fantasy for 2 Lutes; Pazzamezzo Galliard; A Plaine Song for 2 Lutes; The Queen's Goodnight; A Toy for 2 Lutes; Twenty Ways upon the Bells.

(BB) *** Naxos 8.553974. Wilson (lute); (i) with Rumsey – HOLBORNE: Lute Pieces. **(*)

Thomas Robinson taught the future Queen Anne in Denmark before she married King James. He liked to write and play duets with his pupils and the 'Goodnight' here is obviously addressed to her. All the duets here are delightful, particularly *Twenty Ways upon the Bells* with its two players ingeniously ringing the changes. The solo pieces, too, are full of character, notably the melancholy solo *Toy*, worthy of Dowland. But Robinson has a personality in his own right and it is good to have his music rediscovered. Christopher Wilson and his pupil Shirley Rumsey play everything intimately and spontaneously, readily conveying their pleasure in the music. They are truthfully recorded (not too close) in a pleasant acoustic.

RODGERS, Richard (1902 – 1979)

Carousel (film musical).

(N) *** EMI (ADD) CDC5 27352-2. Film soundtrack recording with MacRae, Jones, Mitchell, Ruick, Turner, Rounseville, Christie, 20th Century Fox Ch. & O, Newman.

The King and I (film musical).

(N) *** EMI (ADD) CDC5 27351-2. Film soundtrack recording with Marni Nixon/Kerr, Brynner, Leona Gordon/Moreno, Saunders, Fuentes/Rivas, 20th Century Fox Ch. & O, Newman.

Oklahoma! (film musical).

(N) *** EMI (ADD) CDC5 27351-2. Film soundtrack recording with MacRae, Jones, Greenwood, Grahame, Nelson, Steiger, 20th Century Fox Ch. & O, Newman.

In these days when so many twentieth-century composers of so-called 'serious' music and opera seem unwilling, or unable, to write hummable melodies, it seems worth while to celebrate again the achievement of three great Rodgers and Hammerstein musicals of the 1940s and early 1950s. The sheer tunefulness of the music is of the kind which, once lodged in the memory, is impossible to erase. And Richard Rodgers had the good fortune to collaborate with a librettist who not only showed a natural feeling for a melodic line, but also an inspired ear for the vernacular. The Rodgers and Hammerstein love songs communicate directly and universally, while in the case of *I cain't say no* and *With me its all er nothin* (from *Oklahoma!*) there is an attractive colloquial realism.

When Carrie Pipperidge (Barbara Ruick) in *Carousel* sings her charming song about her beloved fisherman, Mr Snow, she tells us engagingly 'my heart's in my nose', while *June is bustin' out all over* coveys the burgeoning fecundity of spring with an elemental exuberance seldom matched elsewhere.

In *The King and I* author and composer were faced with a seemingly unromantic widow-heroine, who had become an impecunious school teacher. Yet in *Hello young lovers* (with its graceful shifts between duple and waltz time) they triumphed over the problem with one of their loveliest songs, as Anna remembers and communicates her past happiness with her husband, Tom. Later, the underlying tension between Anna and the King underpin the apparently lighthearted number *Shall we dance*.

In short, these are masterly scores, with masterly lyrics and, as the recent outstanding National Theatre revival of *Oklahoma!* demonstrated, this is a work of classic stature, with much greater depth of characterization than had been hitherto realized.

We discussed the original Capitol soundtrack LPs of these three spectacular wide-screen movies in the very first volume of our hardback *Stereo Record Guide* (1960), where our response was mixed. In spite of often surprisingly good stereo effects the sound was often coarse, and unnecessary musical cuts were made. The new digital transfers show how extraordinarily rich and vivid was the quality of the original film tracks, and what gorgeous sounds were made by the superb 20th Century Fox studio orchestra under Alfred Newman. The chorus is pretty good too.

The dubbing of Deborah Kerr's songs in *The King and I* by the sweet-voiced Marni Nixon, and Tuptim's *We kiss in the shadow* by the sultry Leonora Gordon (originally undisclosed) is now part of the current documentation, although Rita Moreno herself narrates the highly dramatic ballet sequence *The small house of Uncle Tom*. In *Carousel* and *Oklahoma!* Gordon Macrae and Shirley Jones make a delightfully fresh-voiced pair of lovers, and the smaller parts are all full of character.

Much that was previously omitted has now been restored, including items which did not appear in the final edited films. This means that there is a good deal of repetition and reprises. Never mind, these three discs are very enjoyable, and you may even find yourself humming along. The documentation is excellent, so a final word from Oscar Hammerstein about the gestation of the famous *Carousel Waltz* seems appropriate:

'I'd become weary – and am still weary – of the sound that comes out of an orchestral pit during the 'Overture'. All you can hear is the brass, because you never have a sufficient number of strings; and the audience must make a concerted effort to pick up any melody that is not blasted. I wanted to avoid this. I wanted people to start paying attention to what came out of the pit with the very first sound they heard.' He did.

**'*Rodgers & Hammerstein Songs*' from: *Allegro; Carousel; The King and I; Me and Juliet; Oklahoma!; The Sound of Music; South Pacific; State Fair.*

*** DG 449 163-2. Terfel, Opera North Ch., E. N. Philh., Daniel.

Bryn Terfel masterfully embraces the Broadway idiom, projecting his magnetic personality in the widest range of songs, using a remarkable range of tone, from a whispered head voice (as he does magically at the end of *Some enchanted evening*) to a tough, almost gravelly fortissimo at climaxes, from the biting toughness of *Nothing like a dame* or Billy Bigelow's big soliloquy in *Carousel* (using a very convincing American accent) to the warmth of *If I loved you* and *You'll never walk alone* (with chorus). Specially welcome are the rarities, including one number from *Me and Juliet* and four from the stylized and underprized *Allegro*, including the powerfully emotional *Come home*. With excellent sound and fine playing from Opera North forces under Paul Daniel, this is a wide-ranging survey. It deserves the widest circulation.

RODÓ, Gabriel (1904–63)

Symphony No. 2.

*** ASV CDDCA 1043. Gran Canaria PO, Leaper –
OBRADORS: *El poema de la jungla.* ***

Gabriel Rodó was a cellist and conductor who spent his last years (1951–62) as conductor of the Gran Canaria Filarmónica and subsequently as first cellist in Bogotá where he died. His *Second Symphony* was composed in 1957 following the death of Sibelius. It is a powerful and well-argued piece and though not highly individual, it is well worth investigating, particularly in such a good performance and recording.

RODRIGO, Joaquín (1902 – 99)

A la busca del más allá; (i) *Concierto Andaluz* (for 4 guitars);* (ii) *Concierto de Aranjuez* (for guitar); (iii) *Concierto de estío* (for violin); (iv) *Concierto en modo galante* (for cello); (v) *Concierto heroico* (for piano); (vi) *Concierto madrigal* (for 2 guitars); (vii) *Concierto pastoral* (for flute); (viii) *Concierto serenata* (for harp). (ii) *Fantasia para un gentilhombre. Música para un jardín; Per la flor del Iliri blau; 5 Piezas infantiles; Soleriana; Zarabanda lejana y villancico.*

(M) *** EMI CDZ7 67435-2 (4). (i) Moreno, Garibay, López,
Ruiz; (ii) Moreno; (iii) Léo Ara; (iv) Cohen; (v) Osorio;
(vi) Moreno, Mariotti; (vii) Hansen; (viii) Allen; LSO;
Mexico State PO; RPO, Bátiz.

The present EMI recordings are of excellent quality, although the early digital technique often brings an overlit sound to the treble, perhaps appropriate for music drenched in Spanish sunshine. The *Summer Concerto* for violin ('conceived in the manner of Vivaldi') it was the composer's own favourite, and Augustin Léo Ara catches its neo-classical vitality admirably. The *Cello Concerto* is given a masterly performance by Robert Cohen; the *Concierto serenata* for harp has both piquancy and charm. Nancy Allen consistently beguiles the ear with her gentleness. The opening of *Concierto pastoral* is far from pastoral in feeling, but Rodrigo's fragmented melodies soon insinuate themselves into the consciousness. Rodrigo's *Piano Concerto* has a programmatic content, with the four movements written 'under the sign of the Sword, the Spur, the Cross and the Laurel'. The performers give a strong, extrovert account of the piece. The *Concierto Andaluz* has its weaknesses but remains engaging if a trifle inflated. A similar comment might be made about the effect of the duo *Concierto madrigal*, but the four guitar soloists here do not achieve the strongest profile, and this is also one reason why Alfonso Moreno's account of the famous *Concierto de Aranjuez*, though bright and sympathetic, is in no way outstanding.

The symphonic poem, *A la busca del más allá*, is evocative and powerfully scored; *Música para un jardín* is a quartet of cradle songs. The *Five Children's Pieces* are equally delightful, while the two neo-classical evocations of eighteenth-century Spain (*Soleriana*) are also unostentatiously appealing. *Per la flor del Iliri blau* is based on a Valencian legend, and Rodrigo is more impressive in moments of gently atmospheric detail than in the melodrama. The *Zarabanda lejana* was Rodrigo's first work for guitar. He later orchestrated it and added the *Villancico* to make a binary structure, the first part nobly elegiac, the second a gay dance movement.

(i) *Concierto Andaluz* (for 4 guitars); (ii) *Concierto de Aranjuez;* (ii; iii) *Concierto madrigal* (for 2 guitars); (ii) *Concierto para una fiesta; Fantasia para un gentilhombre.* Solo guitar pieces: *Bajando de la Meseta; En los trigales; Fandango; Junto al Generalife; 3 Little Pieces; Romance de Durandarte; Sonata a la española; Tiento antiquo.*

(M) *** Ph. (ADD) 432 581-2 (3). (i) Los Romeros; (ii) Pepe
Romero; (iii) Angel Romero; ASMF, Marriner.

This distinguished set gathers together all Rodrigo's major concertante guitar works in first-class performances and adds a rewarding recital of solo works as a postlude, all played with natural spontaneity and complete authority by an artist who feels this music from his innermost being. The *Sonata* is no less strongly Spanish in character and the genre pieces are comparably picturesque in evoking Mediterranean atmosphere and local dance-rhythms. Throughout, Marriner and the Academy provide accompaniments which are thoroughly polished and have much warmth, and the Philips sound is most natural and beautifully balanced.

(i) *Concierto Andaluz* (for 4 guitars); (ii) *Concerto de Aranjuez* (for guitar); (ii; iii) *Concierto madrigal* (for 2 guitars); (ii) *Concierto para una fiesta; Fantasia para un gentilhombre; Sones en la Giralda;* (iv) *Concierto serenata* (for harp).

(B) *** Ph. Duo (ADD) 462 296-2 (2). (i) Los Romeros;
(ii) Pepe Romero; (iii) Angel Romero; (i–iii) ASMF,
Marriner; (iv) Catherin Michel, Monte Carlo Op. O,
Almeida.

This Duo includes all Rodrigo's splendid concertante guitar works, plus the *Concierto serenata* for harp and orchestra, a delectable and unaccountably neglected work in which Catherine Michel is a seductive soloist, neatly accompanied by Almeida. La Giralda, the ancient tower of Seville Cathedral, obviously stimulated Rodrigo's imagination so that the first of its two sections is eerily atmospheric; then the clouds clear away and the finale sparkles with the flamenco dance rhythms of the *Sevillanas*. Pepe Romero and Marriner show an immediate response to its evocation and spirit, and the result is memorable, helped by the first-class recording which pertains throughout these two generously filled CDs.

(i) *Concierto Andaluz;* (ii; iii) *Concierto de Aranjuez;* (ii; iii; iv) *Concierto madrigal;* (v) *Concierto pastoral;* (vi) *Concierto serenata;* (ii; vii) *Fantasía para un gentilhombre;* (ii) *Entre olivaras.*

(N) (B) ** DG Panorama (ADD/DDD) 469 190-2 (2). (i) Los
Romeros, San Antonia SO, Alessandro; (ii) Yepes;
(iii) Philh. O, Navarro; (iv) with Monden; (v) Gallois, Philh.
O, Marin; (vi) Zabaleta, Berlin RSO, Märzendorfer;
(vii) ECO, Navarro.

The duet *Concerto madrigal*, with Yepes and Monden, is most enjoyable, with each of the twelve miniatures which make up the work springing readily to life. Yet Yepes's account of the *Concierto de Aranjuez* – the most famous piece here – lacks sparkle in the outer movements, and the DG sound is rather lack-lustre. Yepes's *Fantasia para un gentilhombre* has more character and refinement, and the *Concierto Andaluz* for four guitars, recorded much earlier, is immediately more vivid and open, if a bit astringent, the performance more spontaneous. The *Concierto pastoral* is brilliantly played and recorded (digitally), but the highlight of the set is the delightful *Concierto serenata* given an ideal performance and recording. Fortunately it is available separately – see below.

Concierto de Aranjuez (for guitar and orchestra).

🌑 (M) *** Decca 430 703-2. Bonell, Montreal SO, Dutoit – FALLA: *El amor brujo* etc. *** 🌑

(M) *** RCA (ADD) 09026 61598-2. Bream, Melos Ens., Davis – ARNOLD: *Concerto*; BENNETT: *Concerto* ***.

*** EMI CDC7 54661-2. Bream, CBSO, Rattle – ARNOLD: *Concerto*; TAKEMITSU: *To the Edge of Dream*. ***

(M) *** Sony (ADD) SMK 60022. Williams, ECO, Barenboim – CASTELNUOVO-TEDESCO; VILLA-LOBOS: *Guitar Concerto*. ***

*** Guild GMCD 7176. Jiménez, Bournemouth Sinf., Frazor – ANGULO: *Guitar Concerto No. 2 (El Alevín)*; VILLA-LOBOS: *Guitar Concerto*. ***

(BB) *** Naxos 8.550729. Kraft, N. CO, Ward – CASTELNUOVO-TEDESCO: *Concerto* ***; VILLA-LOBOS: *Concerto*. **(*)

Concierto de Aranjuez; (i) Concierto madrigal (for 2 guitars); Fantasia para un gentilhombre.

(M) *** Ph. (ADD) 432 828-2. P. Romero; (i) A. Romero; ASMF, Marriner.

(i; ii) Concierto de Aranjuez; (i; iii) Fantasia para un gentilhombre.

🌑 (B) *** Decca Penguin 460 638-2. Bonell, Montreal SO, Dutoit – FALLA: *The Three-Cornered Hat: 3 Dances*. ***

(B) *** Decca 448 243-2. Bonell, Montreal SO, Dutoit – ALBENIZ: *Rapsodia española*; TURINA: *Rapsodia sinfónica*. ***

(M) *** Decca 417 748-2. Bonell, Montreal SO, Dutoit (with FALLA: *Three-Cornered Hat* ***).

(BB) *** Virgin Classics 2 x 1 VBD5 61627-2 (2). Isbin, Lausanne CO, Foster – SCHWANTER: *From Afar* (fantasy) **; Recital: 'Latin Romances'. ***

(B) **(*) Sony (ADD) SBK 61716. Williams; (i) Philadelphia O, Ormandy; (iii) ECO, Groves – DODGSON: *Concerto*, etc. **(*)

(i) Concierto de Aranjuez; Fantasia para un gentilhombre. Guitar pieces: En los trigales; Fandango; Hommage à Falla.

(M) *** Sony Dig./ADD SMK 64129. Williams; (i) with Philharmonia O, Frémaux.

(i) Concierto de Arajuez; Fantasia para un gentilhombre. Piezas españolas: Fandango; Zapateado. (ii) Tonadilla (for guitar duo).

(N) (BB) **(*) Warner Apex 8573 89243-2. Santos; (i) Monte Carlo Op. O, Scimone; (ii) Caceres.

(i) Concierto de Aranjuez; (ii) Fantasia para un gentilhombre. Invocation & Dance (Hommage à Manuel de Falla); 3 Piezas españolas.

(M) *** RCA 09026 61611-2. Bream, (i) COE, Gardiner; (ii) RCA Victor CO, Brouwer.

The Bonell/Dutoit *Concierto* was originally paired with the *Fantasia para un gentilhombre*. Decca made this issue even more attractive by adding a bonus of three dances from Falla's *Three-Cornered Hat* (taken from Dutoit's complete set). In the *Fantasia*, the balance between warmly gracious lyricism and sprightly rhythmic resilience is no less engaging. Their latest incarnation is on the Penguin Classics label and graced by a personal essay by Victoria Glendinning. There is a third, even more generous coupling on Decca's Eclipse bargain label which is well worth considering, as the Albéniz and Turina concertante works for piano are given dazzling, sultry performances by De Larrocha and Frühbeck de Burgos.

The differences between Bream's two earlier RCA readings of the *Concierto*, the first (analogue) with Colin Davis in 1963, the second (digital) with Gardiner in 1982, are almost too subtle to analyse and perhaps depend as much on the personalities of the two conductors as on that of the soloist. Certainly neither account is upstaged by the most recent version with Rattle. Colin Davis's direction is at its best in the opening movement, as crisply rhythmic as you could like, and in the slow movement Bream is raptly inspirational. Maybe the Gardiner version has a little extra dash and, for those who prefer an all-Rodrigo programme, this could be a good choice and the famous *Adagio* is played in a very free, improvisatory way, with some highly atmospheric wind solos in the orchestra. In the *Fantasia para un gentilhombre* Leo Brouwer, himself a guitarist, brings plenty of orchestral vitality to the later sections of the score. The *Tres piezas españolas* add to the value of the disc, and both this and the *Hommage to Falla* show Bream at his most inspirationally spontaneous.

The later, EMI recording of the *Concierto* with Rattle is also very enjoyable in a slightly more relaxed way. This is not to suggest a lack of point and alertness but, with warmer, somewhat more modern digital sound, the effect is more opulent, although Bream maintains his ruminative, improvisatory style convincingly. The finale is engagingly spirited and lighthearted. In the end choice will depend on couplings.

Sharon Isbin's recordings of Rodrigo's two most popular works with the Lausanne Chamber Orchestra under Lawrence Foster received the imprimatur of the composer before he died, and justly so. They are both played with flair and the orchestral detail could not be more vivid, while the famous slow movement of the *Concierto* is most atmospherically done. The recording is in the demonstration bracket. The snag is that the Schwanter coupling is a good deal less tangible.

Williams's third version of the *Concierto*, with Frémaux (SMK 64129), is very successfully recorded, and the performance is even finer than his previous analogue partnership with Barenboim. The slow movement is wonderfully atmospheric with the soloist's introspective yet inspirational mood anticipated and echoed by Frémaux. The finale is light and sparkling with an element of fantasy and much delicacy of articulation in the accompaniment. The performance of the *Fantasia* is no less memorable, with much subtlety of detail and colour from both orchestra and conductor.

John Williams's 1974 recording of the *Concierto de Aranjuez* with Barenboim is superior to his earlier version with Ormandy. The playing has marvellous point and spontaneity, the famous *Adagio* played with poetic spontaneity. The balance is characteristically forward, but the result is extremely vivid and clearly focused.

Pepe Romero's performance of the *Concierto de Aranjuez* has plenty of Spanish colour, the musing poetry of the slow movement beautifully caught. The account of the *Fantasia* is warm and gracious, with the Academy contributing quite as much as the soloist to the appeal of the performance. Angel joins Pepe for the Renaissance-inspired duet, *Concierto madrigal*, which is very attractive indeed, making this a very viable alternative to the Decca couplings.

Rafael Jiménez and the Bournemouth Sinfonietta under Terence Frazor make a fine partnership. The slow movement brings an appealing, ruminative intimacy to contrast with its bold, passionate climax, and the finale also has a neat delicacy of touch from the soloist, with buoyant rhythmic pointing from the orchestra. The recording is very good too.

Norbert Kraft is a soloist of personality and he receives spirited, sensitive accompaniments from the Northern Chamber Orchestra under Nicholas Ward. Indeed the work sounds remarkably fresh using a smaller-sized orchestral group. This Naxos CD deserves a place very near the top of the list. The recording is very well balanced, with the guitar given a most convincing relationship with the orchestra and the sound itself vividly realistic.

With Ormandy providing a rich orchestral tapestry Williams's earlier version is a distinctly romantic reading of the *Concierto*. If the later recording is maturer and has greater subtlety of detail, this performance, taken a little bit faster, remains fresh and enjoyable. Groves and the ECO take over for the *Fantasia*, and once again, the interpretation is a shade brisker than the later, digital version.

Santos does not project as strongly individual a personality as Bonell, Bream or Williams, but he is a very musical player and his thoughtfully improvisatory approach to the *Adagio* is not unappealing. The resonant Erato recording gives the whole proceedings a pleasing glow, and if inner detail is less sharply focused than on Decca, it brings a sumptuously rich quality to the opening string melody in the *Fantasia*. For his encores Santos not only dances a lilting solo *Fandango* and lively *Zapateado*, but joins with a colleague, Oscar Caceres, in the more relaxed three-part *Tonadilla*, where the engaging central *Minuetto pomposo* leads to the busy interweave of the finale. Good value.

Concierto de Aranjuez (arr. for harp).

(B) *** Double Decca (ADD) 433 938-2 (2). Robles, Philh. O, Dutoit – Recital: *Música española for harp*; SARASATE: *Music for Violin & Piano*. ***

Marisa Robles is so convincing an advocate that for the

moment the guitar original is almost forgotten, particularly when, with inspirational freedom, she makes the beautiful slow movement sound like a rhapsodic improvisation. It is a haunting performance, and coupled not only with a hardly less magical solo recital of Spanish music, but also with some comparatively rare Sarasate, played with panache by Campoli and Ricci.

Concierto como un divertimento (for cello and orchestra).

(M) *** RCA (ADD) 74321 84112-2 (2). Julian Lloyd Webber, LPO, López-Coboz – BRUCH: *Kol Nidrei*; DELIUS: *Concerto; Serenade*; HOLST: *Invocation*; LALO: *Concerto*; VAUGHAN WILLIAMS: *Fantasia on Sussex Folk Tunes*. *** (with Recital 'Celebration' ***)

One suspects that Julian Lloyd Webber, in commissioning this concerto, may not have known of the existence of Rodrigo's earlier *Concierto en modo galante* (written in 1949). If so, the gain is considerable, for the present work, here appearing on CD for the first time, is delightful and even more sinuously Spanish in feeling than the old. The style of writing is familiar, with a sultry, atmospheric *Adagio* sandwiched between sparkling outer movements. The moto perpetuo finale has an engaging lyrical strain, and the first movement, too, has a catchy main theme. It is all characteristically friendly music and Lloyd Webber is obviously attuned to its spirit and completely equal to its technical demands. The sound is first class – clear, yet warmly atmospheric.

Concierto serenata (for harp and orchestra).

⚙ (N) (M) *** DG (ADD) 463 642-2. Zabaleta, BPO, Märzendorfer – MOZART: *Flute & Harp Concerto*; REINECKE: *Harp Concerto*. ***

We have always had a special regard for Zabaleta's pioneering version of Rodrigo's *Concierto serenata*, which has an unforgettable piquancy and charm both in its invention and in its felicity of scoring. The performance has great virtuosity and flair, and our ⚙ is carried over from the original LP. It is excellently recorded, with the delicate yet colouful orchestral palette tickling the ear in charming contrast to the beautifully focused timbre of the harp. A worthy addition to DG's series of legendary 'Originals'.

SOLO GUITAR MUSIC

3 Piezas españolas.

⚙ (BB) *** RCA (ADD) Navigator 74321 17903-2. Bream (guitar) – ALBENIZ: *Collection*; GRANADOS: *Collection*. *** ⚙

Rodrigo's *Three Spanish Pieces* are characteristically inventive, the central *Passacaglia* quite masterly and the closing *Zapateado* attractively chimerical in Julian Bream's nimble figers. This 1983 recording has been added to what was already one of the finest of all recorded guitar recitals of Spanish music. An outstanding bargain in every way.

PIANO MUSIC

Music for 2 pianos: (i) *5 Piezas infantiles* (piano, 4 hands): *Atardecer; Gran marcha de los subsecretarios; Sonatina para dos Muñecas;* (solo piano): *Air de ballet sur le nom d'une jeune fille; Album de Cecilia; A l'ombre de Torre Bermeja; Bagatela; Berceuse d'automne; Berceuse de printemps; Danza de la Amapola; 3 Danzas de españa; 4 Estampas andaluzas; 3 Evocaciones; Pastorale; 4 Piezas (Caleseras: Homenaje a Chueca; Fandango del Ventorrillo; Plegaria de la Infanta de Castilla; Danza Valenciana); Preludio de Añoranza; Preludio al gallo mañanero; Serenata española; Sonada de adiós (Hommage à Paul Dukas); 5 Sonatas de Castilla, con toccata a modo de Pregón: Nos. 1–2 in F sharp min.; 3 in D; 4 in B min. (como un tiento); 5 in A. Suite: Zarabanda lejana.*

🏵 *** Bridge BCD 9027 A/B. Allen (i) with Nel.

Rodrigo's keyboard music is all but unknown and, as this first-class and comprehensive survey shows, for all its eclecticism it is well worth exploring. In his earliest piano work, the *Suite* of 1923, with its sprightly *Prelude*, cool *Sicilienne* and Satie-ish minuet, the link with the French idiom is obvious, while the glittering brilliance of the *Preludio al gallo mañanero* is unmistakably Debussian. The *Cinq sonatas de Castilla* look back further in time and draw continually on the keyboard writing of Scarlatti. But they are spiced with piquant dissonances which the Italian composer would have disowned. The *Serenata española* marks Rodrigo's positive adoption of an overtly Andalusian style, while the *Cuatro piezas* and the *Cuatro estampas andaluzas* are as sharply Spanish in character as any of the similarly picaresque miniatures of Granados or Albéniz. Rodrigo's children's pieces have especial charm. The darker side of Rodrigo's nature, sometimes brooding, sometimes nostalgic, is at its most expressive in the nocturne, *Atardecer*, an ambitious piece for two players; but it also colours some of the miniatures, not least the austere yet deeply felt *Plegaria de la Infanta de Castilla* from the *Cuatro piezas*. The recording is uncommonly real and has great presence. In the duo works Gregory Allen is admirably partnered by Anton Nel.

ROGER-DUCASSE, Jean-Jules
(1873–1954)

Au jardin de Marguérite: Interlude; Epithalame; Prélude d'un ballet; Suite française.

*** Marco 8.223641. Rheinland-Pfalz Philh. O, Segerstam.

Le Joli Jeu de furet: Scherzo; Marche française; Nocturne de printemps; Orphée: 3 Fragments symphoniques; Petite suite.

*** Marco 8.223501. Rheinland-Pfalz Philh. O, Segerstam.

The music of Roger-Ducasse has both elegance and atmosphere. The *Nocturne de printemps* and the fragmentary but imaginative *Prélude d'un ballet* show a post-impressionist, Debussy-like figure with a refined feeling for the orchestra; elsewhere, in *Orphée* for example, the influence of d'Indy

can be discerned. There are touches of Ravel and in the *Epithalame* something of the high spirits of Les Six. Segerstam has a good feeling for this repertoire and gets atmospheric and sensitive performances from his Baden-Baden forces and good, serviceable recordings from the Marco Polo and radio engineers.

ROMAN, Johan Helmich (1694–1758)

(i) *Violin Concertos: in D min.; E flat; F min. Sinfonias: in A; D & F.*

*** BIS CD 284. (i) Sparf; Orpheus Chamber Ens.

Of the five *Violin Concertos*, the three recorded here are certainly attractive pieces, particularly in such persuasive hands as those of Nils-Erik Sparf and the Orpheus Chamber Ensemble, drawn from the Stockholm Philharmonic. None of the *Sinfonias* have appeared on disc before. Very stylish and accomplished performances that are scholarly in approach.

Drottningholm Music; Little Drottningholm Music.

(BB) *** Naxos 8.553733. Uppsala CO, Halstead.

Little Drottningholm Music; Sjukmans Music; (i) *Piante amiche.*

*** Musica Sveciae MSCD 417. (i) Nilsson; Stockholm Nat. Museum CO, Génetay.

In 1744 Johan Helmich Roman wrote 24 pieces celebrating the marriage of the future King of Sweden to a daughter of Frederick the Great of Prussia. From first to last they are full of delightful invention, starting with a swaggering *Allegro* which, like other movements, owes something to the example of Handel's *Water Music*, and ending with a bouncy *vivace Jig*. Halstead also includes eight extra pieces, written to be used in reserve at the wedding, under the title *Little Drottningholm Music*. Unlike the recording on Musica Sueciae, Halstead's Naxos version – just as exhilarating, often at brisker speeds – uses period instruments to bring out the great variety of instrumental colour. Fresh, lively performances and excellent sound.

Génetay offers all 17 dances of the *Little Drottningholm Music* plus the somewhat earlier *Sjukmans-musiquen* which has no less appeal. The performances by the Stockholm National Museum Orchestra convey real pleasure in the music-making. The disc includes a short cantata probably (but not certainly) by Roman, *Piante amiche*, which is attractive whatever its authenticity, and nicely sung too by Pia-Maria Nilsson. The recorded sound is well balanced and truthful.

6 Assaggi (solo violin).

(N) *** Nytorp 9902. Ringborg.

As a young violinist in the Swedish Royal Orchestra, Roman was sent to study in England, where he played briefly in Handel's opera orchestra at the King's Theatre. He possessed much individuality and resource, even though here he is much indebted to Geminiani, Tartini and above all Handel. Tobias Ringborg is the first to record all six of the *Assaggi* ('essays' or 'attempts') for solo violin, which leave no doubt as to his familiarity with and mastery of contemporary technique, multiple stopping etc. Technical matters apart, he reveals the extent of his inventive resource and imagination. He plays with great authority, and we doubt that his compelling accounts of these suites will be surpassed easily. They are excellently recorded.

(i) *Assaggi for Violin in A, in C min. & in G min., BeRI 301, 310 & 320;* (i; ii) *Violin & Harpsichord Sonata No. 12 in D, BeRI 212;* (ii) *Harpsichord Sonata No. 9 in D min., BeRI 233.*

*** Cap. (ADD) 21344. (i) Schröder; (ii) Sönnleitner.

The *Assaggi* (essays) recorded here often take one by surprise, particularly when played with such imagination as they are by Jaap Schröder. The harpsichord sonata is also more inward-looking than many others of Roman's pieces, and the only work that one could possibly describe as fairly predictable is the opening *Sonata for Violin and Continuo.* Excellent performances and recording, as well as exemplary presentation.

ROMBERG, Andreas (1767–1821)

String Quartets, Op. 1/1–3.

(N) **(*) DGM 307 0963-2. Leipzig Qt.

String Quartets, Op. 2/2; Op. 16/2; Op. 30/2.

(N) *** MDG 307 1026-2. Leipzig Qt.

Romberg was a celebrated violinist, admired by both Haydn and Beethoven. His three Opus 1 quartets date from between 1794 and 1796 and are very much after the style of Haydn. Although they leave no doubt as to his expertise, next to the Viennese masters this is small talk – amiable and pleasing, but unmemorable. The Leipzig Quartet is such a superb ensemble and so thoroughly musical that the disc gives pleasure nonetheless.

The Op. 2 *Quartets* come from 1797–9 and show an intimate knowledge of and admiration for Haydn's quartets, and indeed are dedicated to *'l'homme de génie à l'immortel Haydn'.* The Op. 16 *Quartets* come from 1804–6 and the Op. 30 set from 1806–10. After Romberg's death, his quartets fell into oblivion, for they do not blaze a trail as those of Haydn and Beethoven did. But they are none the less urbane, inventive and civilized, and well worth getting to know, particularly in these unforced and musical performances. Exemplary recording.

ROPARTZ, Joseph Guy (1864–1955)

Symphony No. 3 (for soloists, chorus and orchestra).

(M) *** EMI CDM7 64689-2. Pollet, Stutzman, Dran, Vassar, Orféon Donostiarra Ch., Toulouse Capitole O, Plasson.

The *Third Symphony* of Ropartz has much nobility, there is a sense of scale and grandeur, and some felicitous harmonic invention. There is a personality here, and all lovers of French music will find it rewarding. Even if the recording (and some of the solo singing) is not of the very highest

order, the orchestral playing under Michel Plasson is thoroughly committed. But this is now deleted.

(i) *Le Miracle de Saint-Nicolas.* (ii) *Psalm 136; Dimanche; Nocturne; Les Vêpres sonnent.*

(N) (BB) *** Naxos 8. 555656. (i) Solistes de la Maîtrise de R. France, Lebrun (organ); (ii) Papis, Henry, Le Texier, Ile de France Vittoria Regional Ch., O Symphonique et Lyrique de Nancy, Piquemal.

Ropartz has been rather overshadowed by Magnard, and while neither is in the front rank of French masters, both are rewarding. The longest piece on the disc is *Le Miracle de Saint-Nicolas* of 1905 for soloists, children's voices (here the excellent *Solistes de la Maîtrise de Radio-France*), organ, piano and orchestra. The *Psalm 136* dates from 1897 and the *Nocturne* and *Les Vêpres sonnent* from 1926–7. They are dignified and rather beautiful pieces with more than a touch of d'Indy and Fauré to commend them, and in the case of *Les Vêpres sonnent* echo the *Sirènes* of Debussy's *Nocturnes.* This recording from the mid-1990s first appeared on Marco Polo but its competitive price renders it much more attractive. The performances are eminently serviceable, though the Choeur Régional Vittoria d'Ile de France is at times a little vulnerable in terms of focus and blend. The repertoire will be new to most readers and will delight many that do not realize how touching and appealing this music is.

RORE, Cipriano da (c. 1515–65)

Missa Praeter rerum seriem. Motets: *Ave regina; Descendit in hortum meum; Infelix ego; Parce mihi.*

*** Gimell CDGIM 920. Tallis Scholars, Phillips (with JOSQUIN DESPRES: Motet: *Praeter rerum seriem* ***).

Cipriano da Rore was Josquin's successor at the Italian Court d'Este at Ferrara. His *Missa Praeter rerum seriem* is appropriately preceded by the richly textured six-part Josquin motet based on the same melodic sequence. Rore's piece was intended as a tribute to his illustrious predecessor and is a worthy accolade, lyrically powerful, contrapuntally fascinating, spiritually serene and beautifully sung by these highly experienced singers, whose director knows just how to pace and inflect its linear detail and shape its overall structure. The four motets are hardly less impressive, and Gimell's recording, as ever, is virtually flawless.

ROREM, Ned (born 1923)

Violin Concerto.

*** DG 445 186-2. Kremer, Israel PO, composer – BERNSTEIN: *Serenade after Plato's Symposium;* GLASS: *Violin Concerto.* ***

Ned Rorem is a great character among American composers. So the six brief movements in this concerto, beautifully played by Gidon Kremer with Bernstein conducting in the year before he died, start with a gritty first movement, but by the Romance of the third movement he has veered towards lyrical sweetness, following that with a longer, more thoughtful slow movement, *Midnight*. An interesting coupling for the other two American concertante works.

Songs: *Alleluia; Clouds; Do I love you more than a day?; Early in the morning; Little elegy; Far far away; Ferry me across the water; For Poulenc; For Susan; I am rose; I will always love you; I strolled across an open field; A journey; Jeannie with the light brown hair; Look down fair moon; The Lordly Hudson; Love; Now sleeps the crimson petal; Ode; O do not love too long; O you, whom I often and silently come; Orchids; Santa Fé, Op. 101: Nos. 2, 4, 8 & 12; The serpent; The tulip tree; Sometimes with one I love; Stopping by woods on a snowy evening; To a young girl; That shadow, my likeness.*

*** Erato 8573 80222-2. Graham, Martineau.

Ned Rorem spent many of his formative years in Paris during the 1950s, when he came to know Poulenc and Auric, but he never lost the American flavour that makes his style so distinctive. This recital, encompassing settings of English, American and French verse, gives a good idea of his melodic resource and feeling for words. His songs, such as the *Santa Fe* series and the setting of Tennyson's *Now sleeps the crimson petal*, bear witness to a rich imagination and a marvellous feel for both the voice and the piano. Susan Graham does them all proud, and Malcolm Martineau gives impeccable support.

ROSENBERG, Hilding (1892–1985)

Piano Concertos Nos. 1 & 2.

*** Daphne DR 1006. Widlund, Swedish RSO, Sundkvist.

The *First Piano Concerto* is a recent discovery. When the *Second* (1950) was premièred, Rosenberg hinted at the existence of an earlier concerto. The two movements of the *First* were then discovered together with sketches for the finale. One can understand Rosenberg's doubts: the orchestral writing occasionally swamps the texture, and the range of keyboard devices is very limited. The *Second Concerto* is the more rewarding and the keyboard writing more interesting with some highly imaginative invention. There is some particularly atmospheric writing for strings and wind in the central *Andante tranquillo*. The score is rewarding and serves to fill in our picture of an underrated composer. Mats Widlund is the excellent soloist and Petter Sundkvist impresses with his sensitivity and musicianship. The recordings have good definition and the balance between soloist and orchestra is very well judged.

Concertos for Strings Nos. 1, 4; Suite on Swedish Folk Tunes for Strings, Op. 36.

*** CPO 999 573-2. Deutsche Kammerakadmie, Neuss, Goritzki.

The *First Concerto* for strings is, one of Rosenberg's most inventive and engaging scores. Johannes Goritzki and his superb Deutsche Kammerakademie Neuss couple it with the early and often charming *Suite on Swedish Folk Songs* from 1927 and the much later *Fourth Concerto* also for strings from 1966. The latter is persuasively played here by these

artists and the balance is eminently truthful. Those who are on Rosenberg's wavelength need not hesitate.

Louisville Concerto; Orpheus in Town (suite); Symphony No. 3.

(N) *** Finlandia 3984 29719-2 R. Stockholm PO, A. Davis.

Hilding Rosenberg was enormously prolific and not averse to note-spinning! However, *Orpheus in Town* is one of his most inventive and engaging scores and the *Third Symphony* (1939) one of his very finest. The work was originally based on Romain Rolland's *Jean Christophe*, each movement being prefaced by a narration. Later, Rosenberg decided that he wanted to remove any literary programme and he also excised a fugal section in the scherzo movement. Caprice once issued a broadcast from the 1940s of the original. The slow movement is of great beauty and the second group of the first movement, with its muted colours and transparent scoring, is one of his most delicately-imagined inspirations. The symphony has been recorded by Tor Mann in the early 1950s on mono LP and Herbert Blomstedt in the mid-1960s, both by the present orchestra, but this is its first recording since – and very fine it is too. Andrew Davis is an intelligent advocate of the piece and gets excellent results throughout. He does *Orpheus in Town* with great lightness of touch and the Louisville Concerto, also a good piece, comes off brilliantly. Recommended with much enthusiasm.

Orfeus i sta'n (Orpheus in Town): ballet suite; (i) Sinfonia concertante for Violin, Viola, Oboe, Bassoon & Orchestra; (ii) Violin Concerto No. 1. Symphony Nos. 3 (The Four Ages of Man; 1939 version); (iii) 4 (Johannes Uppenbarelse: The Revelation of St John the Divine): excerpts; (iv) 5 (Ortagårdsmästaren); (v) Den heliga natten (The Holy Night); (vi) Suite in D: Pastorale.

(***) Caprice mono CAP 21510 (3). Swedish RO or Stockholm PO, composer; with (i) Barter, Berglund, Lännerholm, Lavér; (ii) Barkel; (iii) De Wahl, Swedish R. Ch.; (iv) Lail, Swedish R. Ch.; (v) Björker, Lail, Lindberg-Torlind, Nilsson, Ohlson, Saedén, Widgren, Chamber Ch.; (vi) Andriesson.

The majority of these Archive recordings were made between 1940 and 1947. The suite from the ballet, *Orpheus in Town*, shows the sophisticated man-about-town side of the composer and is inventive and witty, while his inspiration in the oratorio, *The Holy Night*, is spread rather thin – despite some memorable singing from the baritone, Erik Saedén. There is nothing thin about the *Third Symphony*, based on Romain Rolland's *The Four Ages of Man* and interspersed with narration before each of the four movements, read by the composer. His pacing, particularly in the first movement, is expansive and, above all, convincing, and the same measured style emerges in the excerpts from the *Fourth Symphony* (*The Revelation of St John the Divine*), recorded in 1940 with narrator rather than baritone. The *Fifth Symphony*, for soprano, chorus and orchestra, has a serenity, eloquence and strength which are very striking. The *Sinfonia concertante* is a good piece in neo-classical idiom (sounding like a Swedish Martin) but the *Violin Concerto No. 1* is of lesser interest and finds the composer in manufactured mode. It is good to hear him as pianist, accompanying Lotte Andriesson in 1935 in the *Pastorale* movement from his *Suite in D* for violin and piano. The documentation could not be more comprehensive or researched more scrupulously. A valuable issue of great interest.

(i) Symphonies Nos. 3; (ii) 6 (Sinfonia semplice).

*** Phono Suecia (ADD) PSCD 100. Stockholm PO, Blomstedt; (ii) Stockholm SO, Westerberg.

The *Third Symphony* originally bore the subtitle, *The Four Ages of Man* and was inspired by Romain Rolland's novel, *Jean Christophe*. Originally there was narration between each of the four movements. After this Rosenberg had second thoughts about the symphony, withdrawing the literary programme and excising a fugal section in the scherzo. It is strong, purposeful music and its slow movement shows the composer at his best. Blomstedt and the Stockholm Philharmonic are persuasive advocates and the 1966 recording sounds well. The *Sinfonia semplice* radiates the poetic feeling and sense of melancholy that pervade the Swedish summer nights. The 1960 recording made by the augmented Swedish Radio Orchestra, here called the Stockholm Symphony, under Sixten Ehrling is very good and the performance excellent. It would be more competitive at midrather than full price but nevertheless this CD is strongly recommended.

Symphony No. 4 (Johannes Uppenbarelse: The Revelation of St John the Divine).

*** Caprice CAP 21429. Hagegård, Swedish R. Ch., Pro Musica Ch., Rilke Ens., Gothenburg SO, Ehrling.

Rosenberg's remarkable 80-minute symphony-oratorio to texts from the Bible and by the Swedish poet, Hjalmar Gullberg, is for large forces and is a powerful work of real vision. Its opening fourths recall the world of Walton's *Belshazzar's Feast* or of Hindemith, and one's thoughts occasionally turn to Honegger's *King David*. The biblical text inspires the most vividly expressive music, while the Gullberg poems are in an archaic and often serene style. Despite occasional longueurs, the overall impact of this score is very powerful. A splendid performance, very well recorded.

Christmas Oratorio: Den heliga natten (The Holy Night).

(N) ** Marco 8.225123. Inglebäck, Anna & Anders Larsson, Elby, Amadel Chamber Ch., Swedish Chamber O, Petter Sundkvist – LARSSON: *Förklädd gud, Op. 24 (God in Disguise).* **

Rosenberg's *Christmas Oratorio* was composed in 1938, the year before the *Third Symphony*, and was recorded both in the days of 78s and again by Eric Ericsson and Swedish Radio forces in the 1960s. Like Lars-Erik Larsson's *Forklädd Gud*, it is a setting of poems by Hjalmar Gullberg, who enjoyed much standing in the 1930s and 1940s. At one time it was a regular fixture in the Swedish Radio Christmas schedules but has fallen out of favour in recent years.

Understandably perhaps, since it is not one of Rosenberg's strongest or most inventive pieces, and in many of its sections his muse seems to be on auto-pilot. There are, of course, good things (*Herod's Song* is one) and Petter Sundkvist gets good results from his chorus and orchestra. Not essential listening and by no stretch of the imagination as rewarding as the *Third Symphony* listed above.

PIANO MUSIC

Improvisationer; Plastiska Scener; Små föredragsstudier; Sonatas Nos. 1 & 3.

** Daphne 1001. Widlund.

Sonatas Nos. 2 & 4; Sonatina; Suite; Tema con variazioni.

** Daphne 1003. Widlund.

The musical quality of Rosenberg's piano music is variable: the cosmopolitan influences are obvious and Rosenberg is at his best in the smaller-scale miniatures such as the *Små föredragsstudier* ('Small Performing Studies'). He obviously knew his Ravel and Honegger, and in the *Largamente* from the *Plastiska Scener* there are hints of Schoenberg. The *Third Sonata* in particular is arid and its companions are not uniformly rewarding. But the smaller pieces are well worth having and like the sonatas are new to the catalogue. Mats Widlund is a dedicated advocate and the recordings are very natural.

ROSETTI, Antonio (c. 1750–1792)

(i) Clarinet Concertos Nos. 1–2; (i) Double Horn Concerto in F.

**(*) CPO 999 621-2. (i) Klöcker; (ii) Wallendorf, Willis; SW R SO, Baden-Baden & Freiburg, Schröter-Seebeck.

These two clarinet concertos are very Bohemian in flavour; both are melodically quite attractive, with the *Rondo* of the *First* and the *Romanze* and *Rondo scherzante* of the *Second* all equally striking. Dieter Klöcker certainly finds the lighthearted Bohemian spirit of this music and is a sympathetic soloist with a luscious tone. The *Double Horn Concerto* is less memorable musically, but demands considerable virtuosity in its solo interplay and certainly receives it here, especially in the buoyant finale. With sympathetic accompaniments and a pleasing recording this is all enjoyable, if not distinctive.

Sinfonias: in D, K.I:12; in C, K.I:21; in G, K.I:22; in A, K.I:24.

**(*) Chan. 9567. LMP, Bamert.

Sinfonias: in D (La Chasse), K.I:18; in C, K.I:21; in G, K.I:22 in D, K.I:30.

*** Teldec 0630 18301-2. Concerto Köln.

Sinfonias: in E flat, K.I:23; in B flat, K.I:25; in G min., K.I:27; in E flat, K.I:32.

*** Teldec 4509 98420-2. Concerto Köln.

As a court composer, first in South and later in North Germany, Rosetti composed a fair number of symphonies, and those recorded here come from the 1780s. In the hands of the London Mozart Players under Matthias Bamert they are amiable works, engagingly melodic and nicely scored for the normal classical orchestra. The Chandos recording is well up to standard, as is the playing of the London Mozart group, polished and nicely turned. But when one turns to the period-instrument Concerto Köln, the music springs to life with far greater zest and vitality, Kaul I:21 and 22 there is no doubt that the Cologne performances give the music a much stronger profile. The first Teldec disc opens with the most striking symphony of all, *La Chasse*.

In the splendidly vigorous account from the Concerto Köln, the outer movements, with rasping horns and brilliant brass, certainly convey a picture of the hunt in full cry, and to bring contrast the central movements are a lyrical *Romance*, with pleasing writing for woodwind, and a maestoso Minuet. The recording is vivid to match.

ROSLAVETS, Nikolai (1881–1944)

Cello Sonatas Nos. 1 & 2; Dance of the White Girls; Meditation; 5 Preludes for Piano.

(N) *** Chan. 9881. Ivashkin, Lazareva.

Roslavets was one of the leading avant-garde figures in the 1920s Soviet Union and the first to experiment with atonality. He soon fell foul of official orthodoxy and while his work was known in specialist quarters, he never gained wide recognition either in the Soviet Union or the West. In fact he is known for his reputation rather than the music itself.

The *Dance of the White Girls* is an early piece with a strong whiff of impressionism, while the two one-movement *Cello Sonatas* and the *Meditation* come from the early 1920s. Alexander Ivashkin speaks of the *Second* as a mixture of late Scriabin and early Messiaen, and the *Five Preludes for Piano* are certainly indebted to Scriabin's Op. 74. Both the cellist and pianist make out a strong case for this music and they are well served by the recording.

Piano Trios Nos. 2–4.

(N) ** Teldec 8573 82017-2. Fontenay Trio.

The Fontenay give a strong account of the three *Trios* but interesting though this music is, it conveys little real feeling of mastery.

ROSSI, Luigi (1597–1653)

Orfeo (opera; complete).

(B) **(*) HM HMX 2901358.60 (3). Mellon, Zanetti, Piau, Favat, Fouchécourt, Salzmann, Corréas, Deletré, Les Arts Florissants, Christie.

Luigi Rossi's *Orfeo* has a much more complex classical story than the Monteverdi, yet in its artificial way it is less effectively dramatic. Even so, it offers such incidental delights as a slanging match between Venus (enemy of Orfeo, when he represents marital fidelity) and Juno. That hint of a classical send-up adds sparkle, contrasting with the tragic emotions conveyed both in Orfeo's deeply expressive solos and in magnificent Monteverdi-like choruses. William Christie

draws characteristically lively and alert playing from Les Arts Florissants, but his cast is not as consistent as those he usually has in his Harmonia Mundi recordings. Too many of the singers sound fluttery or shallow, and even Agnès Mellon as Orfeo is less even and sweet of tone than usual. Nevertheless this remains a most welcome recording of an important rarity, and at bargain price, with full libretto and translation included, it is well worth considering.

ROSSINI, Gioachino (1792–1868)

Ballet music from: Mosè; Otello; Le Siège de Corinthe; William Tell.

(B) **(*) Ph. (IMS) (ADD) Duo 442 553-2 (2). Monte Carlo Op. O, Almeida – DONIZETTI: *Ballet Music.* ***

Not all these items are lightweight, and Almeida draws positive and vigorous performances from the Monte Carlo orchestra. The strings often play with finesse, notably in the famous *William Tell Ballet*, but the orchestra cannot quite provide the colour and degree of zestful brilliance which makes the Philharmonia Donizetti coupling so attractive. The sound in Monte Carlo, although agreeable, is less vivid than in London. Even so, this is very enjoyable.

La Boutique fantasque (ballet, arr. Respighi) complete.

(B) **(*) Decca 448 984-2. Nat. PO, Bonynge – CHOPIN: *Les Sylphides.* **(*)

Bonynge goes for sparkle and momentum above all in Respighi's brilliant and sumptuous rescoring of Rossini, a magical ballet if ever there was one. The Decca compact disc has great brilliance and the orchestral colours glitter and glow within the attractive resonance of Kingsway Hall, although there is a degree of digital edge on the treble. Bonynge's exuberance is certainly exhilarating when the sound is so spectacular.

La Boutique fantasque: extended suite.

(M) *** RCA (ADD) 09026 61847-2. Boston Pops O, Fiedler – OFFENBACH: *Gaîté parisienne.* *** ❂

Fiedler offers nearly half an hour of the ballet, not missing out much of importance. The performance sparkles, the playing has warmth and finesse and the Boston acoustics add the necessary atmosphere at the magically evocative opening. John Pfeiffer's remastering of this 1956 recording leaves little to be desired and the coupling is indispensable.

La Boutique fantasque (ballet, arr. Respighi): Suite.

(M) **(*) Chan. 6503. SNO, Gibson – DUKAS: *L'Apprenti sorcier;* SAINT-SAENS: *Danse macabre.* **(*)

(M) **(*) Sony (ADD) SBK 46340. Phd. O, Ormandy (with TCHAIKOVSKY: *Sleeping Beauty:* highlights. **)

Gibson's version of the suite is strikingly atmospheric. Helped by the glowing acoustics of Glasgow's City Hall, the opening has much evocation. The orchestra is on its toes and plays with warmth and zest, and the 1973 recording has transferred vividly to CD.

Ormandy presents Respighi's glittering orchestration with much brilliance and dash, and the Philadelphia Orchestra has all the sumptuousness one could ask for. This is more extrovert music-making than Gibson's and it is undoubtedly exhilarating, matched by the sumptuously glossy and generous Tchaikovsky coupling.

Introduction, Theme & Variations in B flat; Variations in C (for clarinet and orchestra).

(BB) *** ASV CDQS 6242. Farrall, Britten Sinfonia, Daniel – DONIZETTI: *Clarinet Concertino; Study;* MERCADANTE: *Clarinet Concertos.* ***

Joy Farrall chortles her way through Rossini's characteristically witty sets of variations, playing with a smiling charm, and a lovely lyrical line and winningly beautiful tone in the introductions (that in B flat is for all the world like an operatic aria). She is stylishly accompanied and most naturally recorded. A highly recommendable disc that is more than the sum of its parts.

Introduction, Theme & Variations in C min. for Clarinet & Orchestra.

*** ASV CDDCA 559. Johnson, ECO, Groves – CRUSELL: *Concerto No. 2* *** 🌑; BAERMANN: *Adagio ***;* WEBER: *Concertino.* ***

As in all her recordings, Emma Johnson's lilting timbre and sensitive control of dynamic bring imaginative light and shade to the melodic line. Brilliance for its own sake is not the keynote, but her relaxed pacing is made to sound exactly right. Vivid recording.

String Sonatas Nos. 1–6 (complete).

(BB) *** Double Decca 443 838-2 (2). ASMF, Marriner (with CHERUBINI: *Etude No. 2 for French Horn & Strings* (with Tuckwell); BELLINI: *Oboe Concerto in E flat* (with Lord) ***) – DONIZETTI: *String Quartet.* ***

(BB) *** Arte Nova 74321 30480-2. St Petersburg Soloists, Gantvarg.

*** ASV (ADD) CDDCA 767. Serenata of L. (members).

*** Hyp. CDA 66595. OAE (members).

(B) *** EMI double forte ADD/Dig. CZS5 69524-2 (2). Polish CO, Maksymiuk – MENDELSSOHN: *String Symphonies;* JANIEWICZ: *Divertimento;* JARZEBSKI: *Chromatica; Tamburetta.* ***

(i) Sonatas for strings Nos. 1–6; (ii) Overtures: Il barbiere di Siviglia; (iii) L'Italiana in Algeri; Otello; Maometto II; Semiramide; Le Siège de Corinthe.

(B) **(*) Erato Ultima Double (ADD) 3984 24242-2 (2). (i) I Solisti Veneti; (ii) Lausanne CO; (iii) Philh. O; (i; iii) Scimone; (ii) López-Coboz.

String sonatas Nos. 1–3; (i) Andante & Theme with Variations in E flat for Clarinet & Orchestra; (ii) Une larme for Double Bass.

(BB) ** Naxos 8.554418. Hungarian Virtuosi, Benedek, with (i) Szepesi; (ii) Buza.

String Sonatas Nos. 4–6; (i) Variations in C for Violin & Small Orchestra.

(BB) ** Naxos 8.554419. Hungarian Virtuosi, Benedek, with (i) Szenthelyi.

We have a very soft spot for the sparkle, elegance and wit of these ASMF performances of the Rossini *String Sonatas,* amazingly accomplished products for a twelve-year-old. Marriner offers them on full orchestral strings but with such finesse and precision of ensemble that the result is all gain. The 1966 recording still sounds remarkably full and natural, and the current CD transfer adds to the feeling of presence. The new Double Decca format has other music added. Apart from the Donizetti *Quartet,* which has an appropriately Rossinian flavour, the two minor concertante works are well worth having, with both Barry Tuckwell (in what is in essence a three-movement horn concertino) and Roger Lord in excellent form.

But on Arte Nova comes a really first-class super-bargain set of the Rossini *String Sonatas,* played with elegance, wit and polish, and often fizzing virtuosity by a superb Russian string group of fifteen players – an ideally sized ensemble for this ever-fresh repertoire written with precocious charm by the twelve-year-old Rossini. The ensemble may not be quite as immaculate as that of the famous ASMF set under Marriner, but the playing has finesse and affection, yet sparkles with life. And the double-bass contribution is pretty impressive too. The recording, made in a warm acoustic, is absolutely real and natural.

The Serenata of London, working as a string quartet, and a comparably sized group from the Orchestra of the Age of Enlightenment, playing period instruments, each manage to include all six of the *String Sonatas* on one CD. As might be expected, the Serenata, playing modern instruments and led by the easily brilliant Barry Wilde, give the warmer, more sunny bouquet to Rossini's string textures; their competitors, led by the dazzling Elizabeth Wallfisch, offer a slightly drier vintage, though their approach is by no means unsmiling. On both discs the recording is truthful and naturally balanced.

Jerzy Maksymiuk with the Polish Chamber Orchestra consistently chooses challengingly fast speeds, and the playing is bracingly brilliant. Though some of the fun is lost, the wit remains, and these virtuoso performances are still most enjoyable for the exhilarating dash, and made the more attractive by the couplings, notably the Janiewicz *Divertimento,* so like Rossini in style, and also the two Jarzebski lollipops which stand out for their strength of personality.

Scimone gives affectionate and nicely turned performances of the *String Sonatas,* their geniality not missed. The overtures are also played with enthusiasm and polish in London and more resonantly recorded (*Il barbiere* in Lausanne is rather more intimate). Although Marriner's set of the sonatas remains in a class of its own, if the programme appeals this Ultima Double is certainly worth considering.

The Naxos performances are very well played, warm and elegant enough, but surprisingly, with a Hungarian virtuoso group, have neither fizz not wit. Of the extra items the *Variations* for clarinet has an attractively jocular finale. No complaints about the recording.

String Sonatas Nos. 1 in G; 2 in A; 3 in C; 6 in D.

(M) **(*) DG (ADD) 457 914-2. BPO, Karajan – BOCCHERINI: *Quintet: La ritirada di Madrid.* ***

Rossini's delightful string sonatas cannot fail to entertain, and nor do they here. Karajan's examples are sumptuously played, but are too suave to bring out all the wit and sparkle of Rossini's youthful inspiration. The 1972 recording is as rich as can be imagined.

VOCAL MUSIC

Cantata: *Giovanna d'Arco.* Songs: *L'âme délaissée; Ariette à l'ancienne; Beltà crudele; Canzonetta spagnuola (En medio a mis colores); La grande coquette (Ariette pompadour); La légende de Marguerite; Mi lagnerò tacendo* (5 settings including *Sorzico* and *Stabat Mater); Nizza; L'Orpheline du Tyrol (Ballade élégie); La pastorella; La regata veneziana* (3 songs in Venetian dialect); *Il risentimento; Il trovatore.*

*** Decca 430 518-2. Bartoli, Spencer.

The songs of Rossini's old age were not all trivial, and this brilliantly characterized selection – with the pianist as imaginative as the singer – gives a delightful cross-section. Bartoli's artistry readily encompasses such a challenge, a singer who, even at this early stage of her career, is totally in command both technically and artistically. The recording, too, has splendid presence.

(i) *Cantata in onore del Sommo Pontefice Pio Nono;* (ii) *La morte di Didone.*

**(*) Decca 458 843-2. (i; ii) Devia; (i) Kelly, Pertusi, Piccoli, La Scala Philharmonic Ch. & O., Chailly.

La morte di Didone comes from 1811, not long after Rossini had abandoned his studies in Bologna, while the *Cantata in onore del Sommo Pontefice Pio Nono* was written for the accession of Pope Pius IX in 1847. The latter is significantly longer, and was more of a compilation, since Rossini recycled material from *Ermione, Armide* and *Ricciardo e Zoraide,* operas that had by this time fallen into obscurity. Neither work is top-drawer Rossini by any manner of means but Chailly gives lightly articulated and well-sprung accounts of both and draws excellent singing from his splendid team. Mariella Devia, the soloist in the early cantata, brings a splendid ardour to her part. The Decca recording is very good without being in the first flight.

Petite messe solennelle.

(M) **(*) Decca 444 134-2 (2). Dessì, Scalchi, Sabbatini, Pertusi, Bologna Teatro Comunale Ch. & O., Chailly.

(i) *Petite messe solennelle;* (ii) *Stabat Mater.*

(B) **(*) EMI double forte CZS5 68658-2 (2). (i) Popp, Fassbaender, Gedda, Kavrakos, King's College Ch., Katia & Marielle Labèque, Briggs, Cleobury; (ii) Malfitano, Baltsa, Gambill, Howell, Maggio Musicale Fiorentino Ch. & O., Muti.

Rossini's *Petite messe solennelle* must be the most genial contribution to the church liturgy in the history of music. Sawallisch's recording of Rossini's original score of this work – originally Ariola, later Eurodisc – remains the finest on record, but perversely it remains out of the catalogue. The use of the refined trebles of King's College Choir brings a timbre very different from what Rossini would have expected from boys' voices – but, arguably, close to what he would have wanted. That sound is hard to resist when the singing itself is so movingly eloquent. The work's underlying geniality is not obscured, but here there is an added dimension of devotional intensity from the chorus which, combined with outstanding singing from a fine quartet of soloists and beautifully matched playing from the Labèque sisters, makes for very satisfying results. The recording, too, attractively combines warmth with clarity. Rossini loses nothing of his natural jauntiness in his setting of the coupled *Stabat Mater,* but Muti's view is a dramatic one, and it is sad that he did not record it with the Philharmonia or with the Vienna Philharmonic. As it is, the Florence Festival forces are sometimes rough – notably the orchestra – and the singing at times unpolished, though the solo quartet is a fine one. Warm but rather unrefined recording.

Chailly chooses Rossini's orchestral version (made in 1867), although Rossini himself preferred his original, as do we. Nevertheless, with a fine solo team, Daniella Dessì and Gloria Scalchi both singing beautifully (and ravishing in their *Qui tollis* duet), and with the bass rising to the occasion in the *Quoniam tu solus sanctus,* this is a very considerable account. The Bologna Chorus are not helped by a somewhat backward balance which, within the warmly resonant acoustic, does not provide an ideal sharpness of focus. But they sing with much ardour, especially in the *Gloria* and *Credo,* and Chailly ensures that the *Et resurrexit* caps the performance ebulliently. Apart from the choral balance (and that is not a real problem when the performers are so committed), the recording is glowing and vivid.

Soirées musicales (excerpts); *La partenza; La pesca; La promessa; La regatta veneziana.*

*** BBC (ADD) BBCB 8001-2. Harper, Baker, Britten – BRAHMS: *Liebeslieder Waltzes, Op. 52;* TCHAIKOVSKY: *4 Duets.* ***.

Both the tongue-in-cheek humour and the outright fun (as in the gondolier race of *La regatta veneziana*) are vividly caught in this BBC recording from the 1971 Aldeburgh Festival. Heather Harper and Janet Baker match beautifully, while remaining characterfully distinct, yet Britten at the piano remains master of ceremonies in family music-making idealized.

Stabat Mater.

✪ *** Chan. 8780. Field, D. Jones, A. Davies, Earle, L. Symphony Ch., City of L. Sinfonia, Hickox.

(B) (***) DG Double mono 439 684-2 (2). Stader, Radev, Haefliger, Borg, Berlin RIAS Chamber Ch., St Edwige's Cathedral Ch., Berlin RIAS SO, Fricsay – VERDI: *Requiem.* (***).

Richard Hickox rightly presents Rossini's *Stabat Mater* warmly and with gutsy strength. All four soloists here are first rate, not Italianate of tone but full and warm, and the London Symphony Chorus sings with fine attack as well as producing the most refined pianissimos in the unaccompanied quartet, here as usual given to the full chorus rather than to the soloists. Full-bodied and atmospheric sound.

It is also the vitality and drama that come over most strongly in Fricsay's strong and spontaneous account of a work that can easily sound lightweight. Even the tenor's *Cujus animam*, jaunty as the rhythm may be, has a warm, lyrical resilience, the fervour of the choral singing is matched by the soloists and this makes a worthy coupling for Fricsay's electrifying account of the Verdi *Requiem*. The mono recording from the mid-1950s has astonishing vividness.

OVERTURES

Overtures: *Armida; Il barbiere di Siviglia; Bianca e Faliero; La cambiale di matrimonio; La Cenerentola; Demetrio e Poblibio; Edipo a Colono; Edoardo e Cristina; (i) Ermione. La gazza ladra; L'inganno felice; L'Italiana in Algeri; Maometto II; Otello. (i) Ricciardo e Zoraide. La scala di seta; Semiramide; Le Siège de Corinthe; Il Signor Bruschino; Tancredi; Il Turco in Italia; Torvaldo e Dorliska; Il viaggio a Reims; William Tell. Sinfonia al Conventello; Sinfonia di Bologna.*

(M) *** Ph. (IMS) (ADD) 434 016-2 (3). ASMF, Marriner;
   (i) with Amb. S.

Marriner's three discs span all Rossini's overtures, but one must remember that the early Neapolitan operas, with the exception of *Ricciardo e Zoraide* and *Ermione*, make do with a simple Prelude, leading into the opening chorus. *Ricciardo e Zoraide*, however, is an extended piece (12 minutes 25 seconds), with the choral entry indicating that the introduction is at an end. *Maometto II* is on a comparable scale, while the more succinct *Armida* is an example of Rossini's picturesque evocation, almost like a miniature tone-poem. Twenty-four overtures plus two sinfonias make a delightful package in such sparkling performances, which eruditely use original orchestrations. Full, bright and atmospheric recording, spaciously reverberant, admirably transferred to CD, with no artificial brilliance.

Overtures: *Il barbiere di Siviglia; La cambiale di matrimonio; La Cenerentola; La gazza ladra; L'Italiana in Algeri; La scala di seta; Semiramide; Il Turco in Italia; William Tell.*

(M) *** Classic fM 75605 57031-2. Sinfonia Varsovia, Menuhin.

Mehuhin and his Polish group, the Sinfonia Varsovia, present a stylishly enjoyable collection of nine favourite Rossini overtures. There is a nice balance between wit and finesse, geniality and grace. Tempi are often brisk, but when there is a surge of vivacity there is no loss of poise. The wind solos are elegantly done and the string phrasing combines neatness with graceful warmth. Above all there is spontaneity here, and even at times a Beechamesque twinkle. The recording, made in the No. 1 Studio of Polish Radio in Warsaw, is full and resonant but not excessively so.

Overtures: *Il barbiere di Siviglia; La cambiale di matrimonio; La gazza ladra; L'Italiana in Algeri; Otello; La scala di seta; Semiramide; Le Siège de Corinthe; Il signor Bruschino; Tancredi; Torvaldo e Dorliska; Il Turco in Italia; Il viaggio a Reims; William Tell.*

(B) *** Double Decca 443 850-2 (2). Nat. PO, Chailly.

In 1981 Chailly and the National Philharmonic made the first compact disc of Rossini overtures and these performances are here combined with their further compilation, recorded in 1984, to make a desirable bargain double. At times on the first disc there is a degree of digital edge on tuttis, but the bustle from the cellos is particularly engaging. The solo playing is fully worthy of such clear presentation demonstrating that this is an orchestra of London's finest musicians. Under Chailly the spirit of the music-making conveys spontaneous enjoyment too. Incidentally, *Il viaggio a Reims* had no overture at its first performance, but one was cobbled together later, drawing on the ballet music from *Le Siège de Corinthe*. The other novelties, *Otello* – played with great dash – and *Torvaldo e Dorliska*, with its witty interchanges between woodwind and strings, are among the highlights, and overall the performances are undoubtedly as infectious as they are stylish.

Overtures: *Il barbiere di Siviglia; La Cenerentola; La gazza ladra; L'Italiana in Algeri; La scala di seta; Semiramide; Il Signor Bruschino; Il Turco in Italia; William Tell.*

(M) *** Ph. (ADD) 446 196-2. ASMF, Marriner.

All the performances here are vivacious and for *Il barbiere*, *L'Italiana in Algeri*, *La scala di seta*, *Il Signor Bruschino* and *Il Turco in Italia* Marriner resurrected the original and lighter orchestrations (*sans* heavy brass and bass-drum). They emerge the more sparkling, and *Il Signor Bruschino* brings the tapping of a triangle stick, not the usual bows. However, no one need fear that *William Tell* is minus trombones or lacks an enthusiastic closing *galop*. There is no shortage of recommendable anthologies of Rossini overtures at mid- and bargain-price, but this is certainly among them.

Overtures: *Il barbiere di Siviglia; La Cenerentola; La gazza ladra; L'Italiana in Algeri; Le Siège de Corinthe; Il Signor Bruschino.*

(M) *** DG (IMS) (ADD) 419 869-2. LSO, Abbado.

Brilliant playing, with splendid discipline, vibrant rhythms and finely articulated phrasing – altogether invigorating and bracing. There is perhaps an absence of outright geniality here, but these are superb performances and this remains one of the very finest collections of Rossini overtures ever, for the wit is spiced with a touch of acerbity, and the flavour is of a vintage dry champagne which retains its bloom, yet has a subtlety all its own.

Overtures: *Il barbiere di Siviglia; La Cenerentola; La gazza ladra; La scala di seta; L'Italiana in Algeri; Semiramide; Il Signor Bruschino; William Tell.*

(N) **(*) Australian Decca Eloquence 460 590-2. Montreal SO, Dutoit.

From Dutoit a good collection of popular Rossini overtures, very well played, and decently recorded, though it lacks something in character and sparkle.

Overtures: *Il barbiere di Siviglia; La gazza ladra; L'Italiana in Algeri; La scala di seta; Semiramide; William Tell.*

(B) **(*) DG (ADD) 439 415-2. BPO, Karajan.

Karajan's virtuoso performances are polished like fine silver. The main allegro of *La scala di seta* abandons all decorum when played as fast as this, and elsewhere bravura often takes precedence over poise. However, with the Berlin Philharmonic on sparkling form, there is wit as well as excitement; but the remastering casts very bright lighting on the upper range, which makes sonic brilliance approach aggressiveness in some climaxes.

Overtures: *Il barbiere di Siviglia; La gazza ladra; L'Italiana in Algeri; La scala di seta; Il Signor Bruschino; Semiramide; William Tell.*

(N) 🔘 (M) *** Virgin VM5 61900-2. L. Classical Players, Norrington.

It is the drums that take a star role in Norrington's Rossini collection. They make their presence felt at the beginning and end of an otherwise persuasively styled reading of *Il barbiere*; at the introduction of *La gazza ladra*, where the snares rattle spectacularly and antiphonally; creating tension more distinctly than usual at the beginning of *Semiramide*, and bringing tumultuous thunder to the Storm sequence in *William Tell*. Of course the early wind instruments are very characterful too, with plenty of piquant touches: the oboe colouring is nicely spun in *L'Italiana in Algeri* and properly nimble in *La scala di seta*, a particularly engaging performance, mainly because of the woodwind chirpings. The brass also make their mark, with the stopped notes on the hand horns adding character to the solo quartet in *Semiramide*, and both horns and trumpets giving a brilliant edge to the announcement of the galop in *William Tell*. The strings play with relative amiability and a proper sense of line and are obviously determined to please the ear as well as to stimulate; altogether these performances offer a very refreshing new look over familiar repertoire. The recording is first-class and this is one of the most characterful of all available collections of Rossini overtures, and irresistible at mid-price.

Overtures: *La gazza ladra; L'Italiana in Algeri; Semiramide; Il Signor Bruschino; William Tell.*

(B) **(*) EMI double forte (ADD) CZS5 69364-2 (2). RPO, C. Davis – BEETHOVEN: *Symphony No. 7* *** 🔘; SCHUBERT: *Symphony No. 9.* ***

Sir Colin Davis's 1962 collection, recorded at Abbey Road, brings playing that is admirably stylish with an excellent sense of nuance. *Semiramide* is superb, reminding one of Beecham, as does the spunky opening of *The Thieving Magpie*. *William Tell* is pretty good too, the opening beautifully played. In *Il Signor Bruschino* it seems as if the bow-tapping device is done by the leader alone, which is rather effective. The CD transfer is vivid, but very brightly lit, with some loss of the body of the original; but the orchestral balance is natural.

Semiramide: Overture.

(***) Testament mono SBT 1015. BBC SO, Toscanini –

BRAHMS: *Symphony No. 2* (***); MENDELSSOHN: *Midsummer Night's Dream* excerpt. (**)

Toscanini's famous concerts with the BBC Symphony Orchestra were obviously very special. This overture from a 1935 concert has one on the edge of one's seat. Quite electrifying. The sound calls for tolerance – but what playing!

OPERA

Armida (complete).

*** Koch Europa 350211. Gasdia, Merritt, Matteuzzi, Ford, Furlanetto, Workman, Amb. Op. Ch., I Sol. Ven., Scimone.

Armida brings some marvellous fire-eating moments of display, particularly in the last act, when the knight, Rinaldo, finally manages to resist the heroine's magic and escape. Her realization of defeat, dramatically conveyed on a repeated monotone, is intensely human. As Armida, Cecilia Gasdia may not be strikingly characterful (Maria Callas knew the role) but her singing is both powerful and agile, firm and bold in Rossini's brilliant coloratura. As for the problem of finding three high *bel canto* tenors capable of tackling elaborate ornamentation, William Matteuzzi and Bruce Ford more than match Chris Merritt as Rinaldo. Though the principal, he is the least gainly of the three, but still impressive, notably in the love duets with Armida. Ferruccio Furlanetto is excellent in two bass roles, and a fourth tenor, Charles Workman, might well have stood in for any of the others. The booklet includes an introduction in English, but no translation of the Italian libretto.

L'assedio di Corinto (*The Siege of Corinth*; complete).

(M) **(*) EMI (ADD) CMS7 64335-2 (3). Sills, Verrett, Diaz, Theyard, Howell, Lloyd, Amb. Op. Ch., LSO, Schippers.

Thomas Schippers here encourages the coloratura prowess of the prima donna, Beverly Sills, at the expense of the composer's final thoughts, with display material from Rossini's earlier version. Some of the most striking passages are the patriotic choruses, recognizably Rossinian but not at all in the usual vein. Sills, as so often on record, is variable, brilliant in coloratura but rarely sweet of tone, and she is completely upstaged by Shirley Verrett, singing magnificently as Neocle. Some strong singing too among the others, though not all the men are very deft with ornamentation. The recording, made at All Saints', Tooting, has plenty of atmosphere. However, this issue has just been deleted.

Il barbiere di Siviglia (complete).

*** Decca 425 520-2 (3). Bartoli, Nucci, Matteuzzi, Fissore, Burchuladze, Ch. & O of Teatro Comunale di Bologna, Patanè.

*** Ph. 446 448-2 (2). Baltsa, Allen, Araiza, Trimarchi, Lloyd, Amb. Op. Ch., ASMF, Marriner.

*** Teldec 9031 74885-2 (2). Larmore, Hagegård, Giménez, Corbelli, Ramey, Lausanne CO, López-Cobos.

*** EMI CDS5 56310-2 (2). Callas, Gobbi, Alva, Ollendorff, Philh. Ch. & O, Galliera.

(M) *** EMI CMS7 64162-2 (2). De los Angeles, Alva, Cava, Wallace, Bruscantini, Glyndebourne Festival Ch., RPO, Gui.

(***) Testament mono SBT 2166 (2). De los Angeles, Monti, Bechi, Rossi-Lemeni, Milan Ch. & SO, Serafin.

(B) *** Naxos 8.660027/29. Ganassi, Serville, Vargas, Romero, De Grandis, Hungaria R. Ch., Failoni CO, Budapest, Humburg.

**(*) DG 435 763-2 (3). Battle, Domingo, Lopardo, Raimondi, Ch. & COE, Abbado.

(B) **(*) Double Decca (ADD) 452 591-2 (2). Berganza, Ausensi, Benelli, Corena, Ghiaurov, Rossini Ch. & O of Naples, Varviso.

(M) ** DG (ADD) 457 733-2 (2). Berganza, Prey, Alva, Dara, Montarsolo, Amb. Ch., LSO, Abbado.

Cecilia Bartoli's rich, vibrant voice not only copes brilliantly with the technical demands but who also gives a winningly provocative characterization. Like the conductor, Bartoli is wonderful at bringing out the fun. So is Leo Nucci, and he gives a beautifully rounded portrait of the wily barber. Burchuladze, unidiomatic next to the others, still gives a monumentally lugubrious portrait of Basilio, and the Bartolo of Enrico Fissore is outstanding, with the patter song wonderfully articulated at Patanè's sensible speed. The snag is that this Decca set is on three CDs; other recommended versions manage with two.

Sir Neville finds a rare sense of fun in Rossini's witty score. His characteristic polish and refinement – beautifully caught in the clear, finely balanced recording – never get in the way of urgent spontaneity, the sparkle of the moment. Thomas Allen as Figaro – far more than a *buffo* figure – and Agnes Baltsa as Rosina – tough and biting too – manage to characterize strongly, even when coping with florid divisions, and though Araiza allows himself too many intrusive aitches he easily outshines most latter-day rivals, sounding heroic, not at all the small-scale tenorino, but never coarse either. Fine singing too from Robert Lloyd as Basilio.

López-Cobos conducts a scintillating performance, helped by brilliant ensembles, generally taken at high speed, with rhythms sprung delectably. Though Håkan Hagegård is a dry-toned Figaro, the recording sets him in a helpful ambience, which equally helps to enhance the comic atmosphere, with the interplay of characters well managed. Raúl Giménez, though his voice is not as youthful as some, brings musical imagination which goes with fine flexibility and point. As for Jennifer Larmore, she is an enchanting Rosina, both firm and rich of tone and wonderfully agile. This is a strong contender among modern digital versions, even next to the delectable Decca version featuring Cecilia Bartoli, particularly when it comes (like Marriner's Philips version) on two discs instead of three.

Gobbi and Callas were here at their most inspired and, with the recording quality nicely refurbished, the EMI is an outstanding set, not absolutely complete in its text, but so crisp and sparkling it can be confidently recommended. Callas remains supreme as a minx-like Rosina, summing up the character superbly in *Una voce poco fa*. The early stereo sound comes up very acceptably in this fine new transfer, clarified, fuller and more atmospheric, presenting a uniquely characterful performance with new freshness and immediacy.

Victoria de los Angeles is as charming a Rosina as you

will ever find: no viper this one, as she claims in *Una voce poco fa*, and that matches the gently rib-nudging humour of what is otherwise a 1962 recording of the Glyndebourne production. It does not fizz as much as other Glyndebourne Rossini on record but, with a characterful line-up of soloists, it is an endearing performance which in its line is unmatched. The recording still sounds well and the documentation is freshly printed.

The Testament issue, superbly transferred, brings out of EMI's archive the long-buried set which Victoria de los Angeles recorded with Serafin in mono in 1952, when her voice was at its fullest and most golden. Though the orchestral playing is often rough, and Serafin is relaxed rather than sparkling, the performance of de los Angeles could not be more seductive. Not as light as her later account with Gui in stereo, this is even sunnier and more glowing. Gino Bechi is a strong if gruff Figaro, Nicola Monti a heady-toned Almaviva and Nicola Rossi-Lemeni a characterful Basilio.

Though the cast is not as starry as with most full-price rivals, the Naxos set makes a first-rate bargain. The singing is hardly less stylish, with Sonia Ganassi a rich-toned Rosina, controlling vibrato well, and with Ramon Vargas an agile and attractively youthful-sounding Almaviva. Roberto Serville as Figaro conveys the fun of the role brilliantly. The *buffo* characters are strongly cast too, with Basilio's *La calunnia* (Franco de Grandis) delightfully enlivened by comments from Bartolo (Angelo Romero), both very much involved in their roles. Will Humburg's often brisk speeds, with crisp recitative matched by dazzling ensembles, never prevent the music (and the singers) from breathing.

With Claudio Abbado conducting the Chamber Orchestra of Europe, Domingo is the set's biggest success. Abbado is free and spontaneous-sounding, but his touch, as conveyed in dry, close-up sound, is much heavier-handed than in his earlier DG set, with ensemble-work surprisingly rough. Even Raimondi as Basilio in his big aria, *La calunnia*, is relatively undisciplined, if spontaneous-sounding, and the big bangs at the climax are completely miscalculated. Kathleen Battle makes a minx of a Rosina, coy but full of flair, and Frank Lopardo is a stylish Almaviva, though not well contrasted with Domingo.

Vocally, the Double Decca set with Teresa Berganza an agile Rosina, is very reliable, and Silvio Varviso secures electrifying effects in many of Rossini's high-spirited ensembles. Manuel Ausensi as Figaro himself is rather gruff but Ugo Benelli is charming as the Count, a free-voiced 'tenorino', though he sounds nervous in his first aria. Corena's fine Dr Bartolo is justly famous, and Ghiaurov sings with characteristic richness as Basilio. The Decca 1964 sound is well up to standard and the reissued set comes with a good cued synopsis and is listener-friendly in its documentation. Good value.

Abbado's earlier recording of *Il barbiere* is a clean, satisfying performance, but one which lacks the last degree of sparkle. Berganza's interpretation of the role of Rosina remains very consistent with her earlier performance on Decca, but the Figaro here, Hermann Prey, is more reliable, and the playing and recording have an extra degree of polish. The text is not absolutely complete, but the omissions are of minimal importance. With fresh recorded sound and plenty of immediacy, this remains competitive, but hardly a primary recommendation.

Il barbiere di Siviglia: highlights.

(M) *** EMI (ADD) CDM5 66671-2 (from above complete recording, with Gobbi, Callas; cond. Galliera).

(M) ** DG (ADD) 463 086-2 (from above complete recording, with Berganza, Prey, Abbado).

The EMI highlights disc offers most of the key solo numbers from Act I, while in Act II it concentrates on Rossini's witty ensembles, including the extended Second Act *Quintet*. The *Overture* is included and, while it is stylishly played, it would have been better to have offered more of the vocal music. The overall playing time is only 57 minutes 26 seconds.

DG offer a generous 70-minute highlights CD which reflects the merits of the complete performance: Teresa Berganza's Rosina is agile and reliable, as is the Figaro of Hermann Prey, and the rest of the cast is generally excellent. At mid-price, and with good (1971) sound, it is good value, but the packaging, with no texts and translations, is parsimonious compared with Decca's Opera Gala series.

The Barber of Seville (in English).

(M) **(*) Chan. 3025 (2). Jones, Ford, Opie, Rose, Shore, ENO Ch. & O, Bellini.

Chandos here offers at mid-price this *Barber* in English, using the bright translation of Amanda and Anthony Holden. Strongly cast, it is a genial performance, very well played and recorded. The only reservation is over the relaxed conducting of Gabriele Bellini which lacks dramatic bite. Compensating for that, the principal singers not only characterize vividly but together form a lively ensemble. Alan Opie is a strong, positive Figaro, while Della Jones as Rosina both exploits her rich mezzo tones and brings sparkle to the coloratura. It is good too to have so accomplished a Rossini tenor as Bruce Ford singing Almaviva. Peter Rose as Basilio and Andrew Shore as Dr Bartolo, both young-sounding for these roles, are fresh and firm too. Excellent documentation includes a full English libretto.

La cambiale di matrimonio (complete).

* Claves CD 50-9101. Praticò, Rossi, Comencini, De Simone, Facini, Baiano, ECO, Viotti.

Here, while the voices have fair bloom on them, the recessed orchestra sounds washy, a significant flaw in such intimately jolly music, with ensembles suffering in particular. Viotti is a relaxedly stylish Rossinian, drawing pointed playing from the ECO, but the singing is poor. The tenor Maurizio Comencini sounds unsteady and strained, while Alessandra Rossi as the heroine, agile enough, is too shrill for comfort. The best singing comes from the buffo baritone, Bruno Praticò, as the heroine's father.

La Cenerentola (complete).

*** Decca 436 902-2 (2). Bartoli, Matteuzzi, Corbelli, Dara, Costa, Banditelli, Pertusi, Teatro Comunale (Bologna) Ch. & O, Chailly.

*** Teldec 4509 94553-2 (2). Larmore, Giménez, Quilico, Corbelli, Scarabelli, ROHCG Ch. & O, Rizzi.

(M) (***) EMI mono CMS7 64183-2 (2). Gabarain, Oncina, Bruscantini, Noni, Glyndebourne Festival Ch. & O, Gui.

(B) ** DG Double (ADD) 459 448-2 (2). Berganza, Alva, Montarsolo, Capecchi, Scottish Op., Ch., Abbado.

Cecilia Bartoli makes an inspired Cenerentola. Her tone-colours are not just more sensuous than those of her rivals: her imagination and feeling for detail add enormously to her vivid characterization, culminating in a stunning account of the final rondo, *Non più mesta*. William Matteuzzi is an engaging prince, sweeter of tone and more stylish than his direct rivals, while the contrasting of the bass and baritone roles is ideal between Alessandro Corbelli as Dandini, Michele Pertusi as the tutor, Alidoro, and Enzo Dara as Don Magnifico. Few Rossini opera-sets have such fizz as this, and the recording is one of Decca's most vivid. The video was recorded more recently at the Houston Grand Opera with Bartolli, Corbelli, Dara and Pertusi continuing in the principal roles and Bruno Campanella conducting with fine spirit. Visually the production is a delight. Subtitled in English, this is very highly recommended (Decca 071 444-3).

On Carlo Rizzi's Teldec version with Covent Garden forces, Jennifer Larmore makes an enchanting heroine, with her creamily beautiful mezzo both tenderly expressive in cantilena and flawlessly controlled through the most elaborate coloratura passages. She may not be the fire-eating Cenerentola the vibrant Cecilia Bartoli is on Chailly's outstanding Decca version, but this is a more smiling character, not least in the final exuberant rondo, *Non più mesta*, which sparkles deliciously, more relaxed than with Bartoli. As Ramiro, Raúl Giménez sings with a commanding sense of style, less youthful but more assured than his rival, while Alessandro Corbelli is far more aptly cast here as Don Magnifico than as Dandini in the Decca set. Here the Dandini of Gino Quilico is youthful and debonair, and Alastair Miles is a magnificent Alidoro. Though the Covent Garden forces cannot quite match the close-knit Bologna team in underlining the comedy as in a live performance, as directed by Carlo Rizzi they are consistently more refined, with more light and shade, bringing out the musical sparkle all the more. Excellent, well-balanced sound.

Gui's 1953 recording of *Cenerentola* has mono sound of amazing clarity and immediacy. Sadly the text is seriously cut, but the effervescence of Gui's live performances at Glyndebourne has been infectiously caught. Juan Oncina produces the most sweet-toned singing as the Prince, with the vintage baritone, Sesto Bruscantini, a vividly characterful Dandini, almost another Figaro. The title role is sung by the Spanish mezzo, Marina de Gabarain, a strikingly positive singer with a sensuous flicker in the voice, very much in the style of the legendary Conchita Supervia. However, as we go to press this set has been deleted.

Abbado's 1971 DG set lacks the extrovert bravura and sparkle of an ideal performance. The atmosphere in places is almost of a concert performance, helped by fine analogue recording. Berganza, agile in the coloratura, seems too mature, even matronly, for the fairy-tale role of Cinderella. Alva sings well enough but is somewhat self-conscious in the florid writing. Abbado, although hardly witty in his direction, inspires delicate playing throughout.

Le Comte Ory (complete).

🌑 (M) (***) EMI mono CMS7 64180-2 (2). Oncina, Roux, Jeannette and Monica Sinclair, Glyndebourne Festival Ch. & O, Gui.

🌑 *** Ph. 422 406-2 (2). Jo, Aler, Montague, Cachemaille, Quilico, Pierotti, Lyon Op. Ch. & O, Gardiner.

Gui's classic recording of Le Comte d'Ory, with the same Glyndebourne forces who gave this sparkling opera on stage, brings pure delight. In limited but clearly focused mono sound, Gui conveys an extra sparkle and resilience, even over Gardiner's brilliant Philips version. There is a natural sense of timing here that regularly has you laughing in joy, as in the dazzling finale of Act I, one of the most infectiously witty of all recordings of a Rossini ensemble. Juan Oncina in his prime as the Count, the Hungarian Sari Barabas as the Countess Adèle and Michel Roux as the Count's friend are superbly matched by Monica Sinclair as the Countess's housekeeper and Ian Wallace as the Count's tutor. Some 10 minutes of text have been cut, but that allows the complete opera to be fitted on two CDs, each containing a complete act.

On Philips, Gardiner tends to be rather more tense than Gui was, with speeds on the fast side, and he allows too short a dramatic pause for the interruption to the Nuns' drinking choruses. But the precision and point are a delight. Though John Aler hardly sounds predatory enough as the Count, the lightness of his tenor is ideal, and Sumi Jo as Adèle and Diana Montague as the page, Isolier, are both stylish and characterful. So is the clear-toned Gino Quilico as the tutor, Raimbaud. With the cuts of the old Glyndebourne set opened out and with good and warm, if not ideally crystal-clear, recording, this set takes its place as a jewel of a Rossini issue.

La donna del lago (complete).

*** Sony M2K 39311 (2). Ricciarelli, Valentini Terrani, Gonzalez, Raffanti, Ramey, Prague Philharmonic Ch., COE, Pollini.

Maurizio Pollini, forsaking the keyboard for the baton, draws a fizzing performance from the Chamber Orchestra of Europe. Katia Ricciarelli in the title-role of Elena, Lady of the Lake, has rarely sung so stylishly on record, the voice creamy and very agile in coloratura. Lucia Valentini Terrani is no less impressive in the travesti role of Elena's beloved, Malcolm; while Samuel Ramey as Elena's father, Douglas, with his darkly incisive singing makes you wish the role was far longer. Of the two principal tenors, Dalmacio Gonzalez, attractively light-toned, is the more stylish; but Dano Raffanti as Rodrigo Dhu copes with equal assurance with the often impossibly high tessitura. The recording is clear and generally well balanced and given added immediacy in the new format.

Elisabetta Regina d'Inghilterra (complete).

(M) *** Ph. (ADD) 432 453-2 (2). Caballé, Carreras, Masterson, Creffield, Benelli, Jenkins, Amb. S., New Philh. O, Masini.

The overture, which turns out to be the one which we know as belonging to Il barbiere di Siviglia, is one of a whole sequence of self-borrowings which add zest to a generally delightful score. In a well-sprung performance like this, with beautiful playing from the LSO and some very fine singing, it is a set for any Rossinian to investigate. Of the two tenors, José Carreras proves much the more stylish as Leicester, with Ugo Benelli, in the more unusual role of a tenor-villain, singing less elegantly than he once did. Caballé produces some ravishing sounds, though she is not always electrifying. Lively conducting and splendid recording.

Ermione (complete).

(M) **(*) Erato 2292 45790-2 (2). Gasdia, Zimmermann, Palacio, Merritt, Matteuzzi, Alaimo, Prague Philharmonic Ch., Monte Carlo PO, Scimone.

Ermione begins very strikingly with an off-stage chorus, introduced in the slow section of the overture, singing a lament on the fall of Troy. The use of dramatic declamation, notably in the final scene of Act II, also gives due weight to the tragedy; however, not surprisingly, Rossini's natural amiability keeps bursting through, often a little incongruously. Though the three tenors in this Monte Carlo set from Erato are good by modern standards – Ernesto Palacio (Pirro), Chris Merritt (Oreste) and William Matteuzzi (Pilade) – they are uncomfortably strained by the high tessitura and the occasional stratospheric top notes. Cecilia Gasdia makes a powerful Ermione, not always even enough in her production but strong and agile; while Margarita Zimmermann makes a firm, rich Andromaca. Scimone, not always imaginative, yet directs a strong, well-paced performance. The recording is rather dry on the voices, but the hint of boxiness is generally undistracting and this set is a must for true Rossinians.

Guglielmo Tell (William Tell: complete, in Italian).

*** Decca (IMS) (ADD) 417 154-2 (4). Pavarotti, Freni, Milnes, Ghiaurov, Amb. Op. Ch., Nat. PO, Chailly.

Rossini wrote his massive opera about William Tell in French, but Chailly and his team here put forward a strong case for preferring Italian, with its open vowels, in music which glows with Italianate lyricism. Chailly's is a forceful reading, particularly strong in the many ensembles, and superbly recorded. Milnes makes a heroic Tell, always firm, and though Pavarotti has his moments of coarseness he sings the role of Arnoldo with glowing tone. Ghiaurov too is in splendid voice, while subsidiary characters are almost all well taken, with such a fine singer as John Tomlinson, for example, ripely resonant as Melchthal. The women singers too are impressive, with Mirella Freni as the heroine Matilde providing dramatic strength as well as sweetness. The recording, made in 1978 and 1979, comes out spectacularly, with the Pas de six banded into its proper place in Act I.

Guillaume Tell (William Tell) (sung in French).

(M) *** EMI (ADD) CMS7 69951-2 (4). Bacquier, Caballé, Gedda, Mesplé, Amb. Op. Ch., RPO, Gardelli.

The interest of the 1973 EMI set is that it is sung in the original French. Gardelli proves an imaginative Rossini interpreter, allying his formidable team to vigorous and sensitive performances. Bacquier makes an impressive Tell, developing the character as the story progresses; Gedda is a model of taste, and Montserrat Caballé copes ravishingly with the coloratura problems of Mathilde's role. While Chailly's full-price Decca set puts forward a strong case for using Italian with its open vowels, this remains a fully worthwhile alternative, with excellent CD sound. Indeed the current re-mastering is first class in every way and the choral passages, incisively sung, are among the most impressive; moreover the set now comes with full translation.

L'inganno felice (complete).

*(*) Claves CD 50-9211. De Carolis, Felle, Zennaro, Previato, Serraiocco, ECO, Viotti.

L'inganno felice is stylishly and energetically conducted by Viotti with sprung rhythms and polished playing, but with a flawed cast. As the heroine, Amelia Felle is agile but too often raw-toned, even if on occasion she can crown an ensemble with well-phrased cantilena. As the hero, Bertrando, Iorio Zennaro has an agreeable natural timbre, but his tenor is not steady enough and strains easily. The buffo, Fabio Previato, is the soloist who comes closest to meeting the full challenge. The recorded sound has a pleasant bloom on it, but the orchestra is too recessed, and though the recitatives are briskly done, with crisp exchanges between the characters, the degree of reverberation is a serious drawback.

L'Italiana in Algeri (complete).

✹ *** DG (ADD) 427 331-2 (2). Baltsa, Raimondi, Dara, Lopardo, V. State Op. Konzertvereinigung, VPO, Abbado.

(M) *** Erato 2292 45404-2 (2). Horne, Palacio, Ramey, Trimarchi, Battle, Zaccaria, Prague Ch., Sol. Ven., Scimone.

Abbado's brilliant version was recorded in conjunction with a new staging by the Vienna State Opera, with timing and pointing all geared for wit on stage to make this the most captivating of all recordings of the opera. Agnes Baltsa is a real fire-eater in the title-role, and Ruggero Raimondi with his massively sepulchral bass gives weight to his part without undermining the comedy. The American tenor, Frank Lopardo, proves the most stylish Rossinian, singing with heady clarity in superbly articulated divisions, while both buffo baritones are excellent too. This uses the authentic score, published by the Fondazione Rossini in Pesaro.

Scimone's highly enjoyable version is beautifully played and recorded with as stylish a team of soloists as one can expect nowadays. The text is complete and alternative versions of certain arias are given as an appendix. Marilyn Horne makes a dazzling, positive Isabella, and Samuel Ramey is splendidly firm as Mustafa. Domenico Trimarchi is a delightful Taddeo and Ernesto Palacio an agile Lindoro, not coarse, though the recording does not always catch his tenor timbre well. Nevertheless the sound is generally very good indeed.

Maometto II (complete).

*** Ph. (IMS) 412 148-2 (3). Anderson, Zimmermann, Palacio, Ramey, Dale, Amb. Op. Ch., Philh. O, Scimone.

Claudio Scimone's account of Maometto II has Samuel Ramey magnificently focusing the whole story in his portrait of the Muslim invader in love with the heroine. The other singing is less sharply characterized but is generally stylish, with Margarita Zimmermann in the travesti role of Calbo and June Anderson singing sweetly as Anna. Laurence Dale is excellent in two smaller roles, while Ernesto Palacio mars some fresh-toned singing with his intrusive aitches. Excellent recording.

Mosè in Egitto (complete).

(M) *** Ph. (ADD) 420 109-2 (2). Raimondi, Anderson, Nimsgern, Palacio, Gal, Fisichella, Amb. Op. Ch., Philh. O, Scimone.

Scimone here justifies his claim that the 1819 version is dramatically more effective than both the earlier Italian one and the later Paris one. Rossini's score brings much fine music and, among the soloists, Raimondi relishes not only the solemn moments like the great invocation in Act I and the soaring prayer of Act III, but also the rage aria in Act II, almost like Handel updated if with disconcerting foretastes of Dr Malatesta in Donizetti's Don Pasquale. The writing for the soprano and tenor lovers (the latter the son of Pharaoh and in effect the villain of the piece) is relatively conventional, though the military flavour of their Act I cabaletta is refreshingly different. Ernesto Palacio and June Anderson make a strong pair, and the mezzo, Zehava Gal, is another welcome newcomer as Pharaoh's wife. Siegmund Nimsgern makes a fine Pharaoh, Salvatore Fisichella an adequate Arone (Aaron). The well-balanced recording emerges most vividly on CD.

L'occasione fa il ladro (complete).

(M) ** Claves CD 50-9208/9. Bayo, De Carolis, Zennaro, Provvisionato, Previati, Massa, ECO, Viotti.

On two discs, this is one of the longer one-Acters in the Claves series, bringing one of the more recommendable performances, with Viotti at his most relaxed. Maria Bayo as the heroine sings warmly and sweetly, with no intrusive aspirates in the coloratura. The soubrette role of Ernestina is also charmingly done, and the buffo characters sing effectively, though the tenor, Iorio Zennaro, is hardly steady enough for Rossinian cantilena. The two discs come in a single hinged jewel-box at upper mid-price.

Otello (complete).

*** Opera Rara ORC 18 (3). Ford, Futral, Matteuzzi, D'Arcangelo, Lopera, Philh O, Parry.

Otello (abridged).

(M) *** Ph. (ADD) 432 456-2 (2). Carreras, Von Stade, Condò, Pastine, Fisichella, Ramey, Amb. S., Philh. O, López-Cobos.

Justifiably overshadowed by Verdi's masterpiece, this early opera of Rossini, written in 1816 for Naples, is a piece very much of its time, with the changes in Shakespeare's story making the drama more conventional: a love-letter is substituted for the fatal handkerchief, and Desdemona is stabbed instead of being smothered, while she also acquires a new father, Elmiro. Even so, Rossini is inspired by a serious subject to produce a striking series of arias and ensembles, which culminate in what was then a revolutionary course in

Italian opera, a tragic ending. Significantly, later, in 1820 and pressured by the authorities, Rossini provided a happy ending, when Otello is finally convinced of Desdemona's innocence. That alternative close is the first of three important appendices included in this very well-documented set. Where the previous Philips recording, more starrily cast, provided a badly cut text on two CDs merely, this one stretches to three very well-filled discs.

It is a credit to Opera Rara that three formidable Rossini tenors are here involved, not just Bruce Ford in the title role, strong and stylish if a little gritty as recorded, but also Juan José Lopera as Iago, who is also impressive, and, singing even more sweetly, William Matteuzzi as Rodrigo, here given a relatively big role. Elizabeth Futral is a strong, dramatic heroine, rising superbly to the challenge of the final Act, which, coming closer to Shakespeare, brings the most memorable music, including a lovely *Willow Song*. Enkeljda Shkosa sings most beautifully as Emilia, as she does too in the alternative Malibran version of the Act II duet, in which she sings Otello, transformed into a breeches-role. David Parry excels himself in drawing powerful, sensitive playing from the Philharmonia, dramatically paced, with some outstanding solo work from the wind. Vivid, well-balanced sound.

In the Philips performance, superbly recorded, and brightly and stylishly conducted by López-Cobos, the line-up of tenors is again turned into an asset, with three nicely contrasted soloists. Carreras is here at his finest – most affecting in his recitative before the murder, while Fisichella copes splendidly with the high tessitura of Rodrigo's role, and Pastine has a distinct timbre to identify him as the villain. Frederica von Stade pours forth a glorious flow of beautiful tone, well-matched by Nucci Condò as Emilia. Samuel Ramey is excellent too in the bass role of Elmiro.

La pietra del paragone (complete).

(M) **(*) Van. 08 9031 73 (3). Carreras, Wolff, Bonazzi, Elgar, Reardon, Foldi, Diaz, Murcell, Clarion Concerts Ch. & O, Jenkins.

This 1972 recording presents the young José Carreras in an incidental role, just one in an attractively fresh-voiced cast of soloists. It is given a vigorous, if occasionally hard-pressed performance under Newell Jenkins. The plot of disguises and deceit is a throwback to artificial eighteenth-century conventions, involving a house-party with a couple of poets and a venal critic brought in. For modern performance the problem is the length, though on disc that evaporates when Rossini's invention is at its peak in number after number.

La scala di seta (complete).

*** Claves 50-9219/20. Corbelli, Ringholz, Vargas, De Carolis, Provvisionato, Massa, ECO, Viotti.

The overture is among the best known of all that Rossini wrote, and here Viotti establishes his individuality with an unusually expansive slow introduction leading to a brisk and well-sprung allegro, scintillatingly played by the ECO. The cast here is stronger vocally than those in the rest of the Claves series, with Teresa Ringholz delightful as the heroine,

Giulia, warm and agile, shading her voice seductively. She and the *buffo*, sung by Alessandro Corbelli, have the biggest share of the solo work, and he is also first rate. The tenor Ramon Vargas sings without strain – rare in this series – and the mezzo, Francesca Provvisionato, sings vivaciously as the heroine's cousin, with a little aria in military rhythm a special delight. Warm sound with good bloom on the voices.

Semiramide (complete).

*** DG (IMS) 437 797-2 (3). Studer, Larmore, Ramey, Lopardo, Amb. Op. Ch., LSO, Marin.

Semiramide (complete, but with traditional cuts).

(M) *** Decca (IMS) (ADD) 425 481-2 (3). Sutherland, Horne, Rouleau, Malas, Serge, Amb. Op. Ch., LSO, Bonynge.

Rossini concentrates on the love of Queen Semiramide for Prince Arsace (a mezzo-soprano), and musically the result is a series of fine duets, superbly performed here by Sutherland and Horne (in the mid-1960s when they were both at the top of their form). In Sutherland's interpretation, Semiramide is not so much a Lady Macbeth as a passionate, sympathetic woman and, with dramatic music predominating over languorous cantilena, one has her best, bright manner. Horne is well contrasted, direct and masculine in style, and Spiro Malas makes a firm, clear contribution in a minor role. Rouleau and Serge are variable but more than adequate, and Bonynge keeps the whole opera together with his alert, rhythmic control of tension and pacing.

On the DG version, Ion Marin opens out many traditional cuts, notably in the role of the tenor, Idreno. Lopardo sings Idreno's splendid Act I aria magnificently, a scene omitted on Decca; and the newer performance, even at speeds generally faster, altogether lasts almost 40 minutes longer, though most of the extra material – recitative, repeats, introductions – is not of major importance. Though Cheryl Studer cannot match Sutherland in command or panache as the Babylonian queen, hers is still a strong, aptly agile performance. Jennifer Larmore sings superbly in the breeches role of Arsace, less powerful than Marilyn Horne but even more convincing in character, with the voice more youthfully fresh. What above all prevents Semiramide and Arsace's great duet, *Serbami ognor*, from sounding so seductively idiomatic is the conducting of Ion Marin, strong and purposeful but often too mechanical, generally missing the helpful rubatos that mark the Bonynge reading. The role of Assur is strongly sung by Samuel Ramey, but he gives little idea of the character's villainous side. The digital DG recording provides extra brilliance and range.

Il Signor Bruschino (complete).

*** DG (IMS) 435 865-2. Battle, Ramey, Lopardo, Desderi, Larmore, ECO, Marin.

(N) (BB) **(*) Arte Nova 74321 80783-2. Ruggeri, Kouda, Tisi, Saudelli, Tirol Fest. O, Kuhn.

You could hardly devise a starrier cast for this 'comic farce in one act' than that assembled by DG, with even the tiny role of the maid, Marianna, taken by Jennifer Larmore. Ion Marin springs rhythms very persuasively, with the first Cavatina of Gaudenzio, the tutor, so delectably pointed in the introduction that one registers the character even before Samuel Ramey enters. Kathleen Battle makes a provocative heroine and the tenor, Frank Lopardo, sings sweetly and freshly as Sofia's lover, Florville. He is delightfully agile in his patter duet with Filiberto, the innkeeper, taken by Michele Pertusi. Excellent, well-balanced sound. The single disc (76 minutes) comes complete with libretto, translation and notes in a double-disc jewel-case.

Il Signor Bruschino is the one-act comic opera best remembered for the quirky overture, in which the string players tap their bows on their music stands. As this live recording, made at the Tirol Festival in August 2000, demonstrates, it is a piece full of fun, with a sequence of lively numbers including a sparkling patter duet for the hero, Florville (ably taken by Patrizio Saudelli) and his friend, Filiberto. Each principal in turn has at least one moment of glory, with the role of the heroine, Sofia, brightly and freshly sung by Hiroko Kouda. The two principal *buffo* roles are characterfully sung by Gianpiero Ruggeri and Ezio Maria Tisi, though with voices of uneven quality. With lively playing from the Tirol Festival Orchestra under Gustav Kuhn, cleanly recorded, it makes an excellent and welcome bargain.

Tancredi (complete).

(B) *** Naxos 8.660037/8. Podles, Jo, Olsen, Spagnoli, Di Micco, Lendi, Capella Brugensis, Brugense Coll. Instrumentale, Zedda.

This Naxos set completely displaces the previous versions from Sony and RCA, and the eminent Rossini scholar and conductor, Alberto Zedda, proves a far more resilient, generally brisker and lighter Rossini interpreter than his predecessors. Sumi Jo is superb as the heroine, Amenaide, in dazzlingly clear coloratura, as well as imaginative pointing of phrase, rhythm and words. The mezzo, Ewa Podles, is less characterful, yet the voice is firm and rich as well as flexible; but it is the tenor, Stanford Olsen, previously heard as Belmonte on John Eliot Gardiner's recording of *Entführung*, who offers some of the freshest, most stylish and sweetly tuned singing from a Rossini tenor in recent years. The recording is a little lacking in body, but that partly reflects the use of a small orchestra, and the voices come over well. An Italian libretto is provided but no translation. Instead, a helpful synopsis is geared to the different tracks on the discs; had there been a libretto, this could well have received a Rosette.

Il Turco in Italia (complete).

*** Ph. 434 128-2 (2). Jo, Alaimo, Fissore, Giménez, Mentzer, Corbelli, Bronder, Amb. Op. Ch., ASMF, Marriner.

**(*) Decca 458 924-2 (2). Bartoli, Corbelli, Pertusi, Vargas, La Scala, Milan, Ch. & O, Chailly.

(***) EMI mono CDS5 56313-2 (2). Rossi-Lemeni, Callas, Gedda, Stabile, Ch. & O of La Scala, Milan, Gavazzeni.

On Philips, Sumi Jo as Fiorilla, the sharp-tongued heroine, unhappily married to old Don Geronio, is no fire-eater, as Callas was in her vintage recording, but she sparkles delightfully, a most believable young wife. What seals the success of the Philips version is the playing of the St Martin's Academy under Sir Neville Marriner, consistently crisp and light, wittily bringing out the light and shade in Rossini's score and offering a full text. As for the rest of the Philips cast, Simone Alaimo as the visiting Turkish prince, Selim, may lack sardonic weight, but it is a fine voice, and the *buffo* role of Geronio finds Enrico Fissore agile and characterful in his patter numbers. Raúl Giménez is the stylish tenor in the relatively small role of Narciso, which happily acquires an extra aria. Altogether a most welcome follow-up to Marriner's excellent set of the *Barber*.

Chailly's Decca version centres round the brilliantly characterful singing of Cecilia Bartoli as a fire-eating Fiorilla. The tessitura is high for a mezzo, but she copes with sparkling confidence. Chailly paces the many ensembles most effectively, with a first-rate team of soloists to back up Bartoli. Even so, the Marriner's version on Philips with Sumi Jo as Fiorilla remains preferable, when the sound is so much clearer and more immediate than in this rather mushy Milan recording. Though Sumi Jo has a lighter voice than Bartoli, she is no less positive and just as agile and sparkling.

Callas was at her peak when she recorded this rare Rossini opera in the mid-1950s. As ever, there are lumpy moments vocally, but she gives a sharply characterful performance as the capricious Fiorilla, married to an elderly, jealous husband and bored with it. Nicola Rossi-Lemeni as the Turk of the title is characterful too, but the voice is ill-focused, and it is left to Nicolai Gedda as the young lover and Franco Calabrese as the jealous husband to match Callas in stylishness. It is good too to have the veteran Mariano Stabile singing the role of the Poet in search of a plot. Walter Legge's production has plainly added to the sparkle. On CD the original mono recording has been freshened and given added bloom, despite the closeness of the voices. It is a vintage Callas issue, her first uniquely cherishable essay in operatic comedy.

Il viaggio a Reims (complete).

⊛ *** DG 415 498-2 (2). Ricciarelli, Terrani, Cuberli, Gasdia, Araiza, Giménez, Nucci, Raimondi, Ramey, Dara, Prague Philharmonic Ch., COE, Abbado.

This DG set is one of the most sparkling and totally successful live opera recordings available, with Claudio Abbado in particular freer and more spontaneous-sounding than he generally is on disc, relishing the sparkle of the comedy, and the line-up of soloists here could hardly be more impressive, with no weak link. Apart from the established stars the set introduced two formidable newcomers in principal roles, Cecilia Gasdia as a self-important poetess and, even finer, Lella Cuberli as a young fashion-crazed widow. Abbado's brilliance and sympathy draw the musical threads compellingly together with the help of superb, totally committed playing from the young members of the Chamber Orchestra of Europe.

Zelmira (complete).

*** Erato 2292 45419-2 (2). Gasdia, Fink, Matteuzzi, Merritt, Amb. S., Sol. Ven., Scimone.

Scimone takes a generally brisk view of both the arias and the ensembles of this underrated opera, but never seems to race his singers. In this performance the choice of singers underlines the contrast between the two principal tenor-roles. Chris Merritt combines necessary agility with an almost baritonal quality as the scheming Antenore, straining only occasionally, and William Matteuzzi sings with heady beauty and fine flexibility in florid writing as Ilo. Star of the performance is Cecilia Gasdia in the name-part, projecting words and emotions very intensely in warmly expressive singing. She is well matched by the mezzo, Barbara Fink, as her friend, Emma, and only the wobbly bass of José Garcia as the deposed Polidoro mars the cast.

COLLECTIONS

'Rossini Gala': Arias from: *Armida; Aureliano in Palmira; Bianca e Falliero; Elisabetta Regina D'Inghilterra; Mosè in Egitto; Semiramide; Vallace; Zelmira.*

(N) *** Opera Rara ORR 211. Miricioiu, Ford, Magee, Banks, ASMIF, Parry.

Nelly Miriciou, Romanian-born and British-based, is a soprano who deserves to be recorded far more. This wide-ranging, imaginatively devised recital of rare Rossini arias admirably fills a gap with Miriciou strongly supported by a range of singers, including the Rossini tenors Bruce Ford and Barry Banks. Miriciou's is a warm, characterful voice, which she uses with a fine feeling for dramatic point, bringing to life even the most conventional of operatic numbers. She also has the merit, very necessary in Rossini, of coloratura flexibility, which she relishes brilliantly in the cabalettas to arias. Strong support from David Parry and the Academy, with full, brilliant recording.

'Serious Rossini': excerpts from: *Armida; Mosé in Egitto; Otello; Ricciardo e Zoraide; Ugo Re d'Italia.*

(N) *** Opera Rara ORR 218 Ford, Miricioiu, Matteuzzi, Kelly, & Soloists, Geoffrey Mitchell Ch., Phil. O or ASMF, Parry.

Here is a further glorious recital of Rossini excerpts, this time centring on the excellent tenor Bruce Ford, but including many memorable ensemble items. All are vividly projected by this outstanding cast of singers. Highlights include the duet of Agorante and Ricciardo (William Matteuzzi) in *Riccardo e Zoraide*, and the quintet from the finale of Act I. The trio *In quale aspetto imbello* (from *Armida*) and the quartet *Mi manca la voce* (from *Mosè in Egitto*) also stand out, as does the supremely dramatic finale of Otello, where Bruce Ford is powerfully partnered by Nelly Miricioiu. David Parry keeps the tension high and the chorus and orchestra give admirable support. The recording is splendidly vivid.

Arias: *L'assedio di Corinto: L'ora fatal s'appressa . . . Giusto ciel! Avanziam . . . Non temer, d'un basso affetto . . . I destini tradir ogni speme! . . . Signor che, tutto puoi . . . Sei tu che stendi, o Dio! La Cenerentola: Nacqui all'affanno . . . Non più mesta. La donna del lago: Mura felici; Tanti affetti. L'Italiana in Algeri: Cruda sorte! Semiramide: Bel raggio lusinghier. Tancredi: Di tanti palpiti.*

🌓 (M) *** Decca (ADD) 458 219-2. Horne, SRO or ROHCG O, Lewis.

Marilyn Horne's famous Rossini recital disc is one of the most cherishable of all Rossini aria records ever issued. Moreover full translations are included, which is especially valuable in the long 25-minute scene from *L'assedio di Corinto* which (with the excerpts from *La donna del lago*) dates from 1972. The rest of the selection derives from two recitals the great mezzo also recorded with her then husband, Henry Lewis, in 1964–6 when she was at the zenith of her powers. The voice is in glorious condition, rich and firm throughout its spectacular range, and is consistently used with artistry and imagination, as well as brilliant virtuosity in coloratura. By any reckoning this is thrilling singing, the more valuable for the inclusion of the rarities – which, with Horne, make you wonder at their neglect. The sound is full and brilliant, hardly showing its age at all.

Arias from: *Il barbiere di Siviglia; La cambiale di matrimonio; La Cenerentola; Gugliemo Tell; L'Italiana in Algeri; Otello; Semiramide.*

(M) **(*) Decca ADD/Dig. 458 247-2. Nucci, Sutherland, Horne, Pavarotti, Berganza, Ghiaurov, Tebaldi.

A generally fine Rossini anthology: Sutherland glitters in her coloratura, whilst Horne's bravura is a marvel. Berganza is engaging in her numbers from *Cenerentola* and *L'Italiana*, whilst Pavarotti and Ghiaurov keep the men's side up. A good collection, but it does not quite maintain the very highest standards of Decca's always reliable Opera Gala series, which come with full texts and translations.

Arias from: *Il barbiere di Siviglia; La Cenerentola; La donna del lago; L'Italiana in Algeri; Maometto II; Semiramide; Tancredi.*

(BB) *** Naxos 8.553543. Podles, Hungarian State Op. Ch. & O, Morandi.

The Hungarian mezzo, Ewa Podles, earlier the star singer in the complete set of Rossini's *Tancredi* on Naxos, is here even more impressive in one of the finest Rossini recitals in years. Hers is a rich and even voice which is not only weighty throughout its range but is also extraordinarily agile, dazzling in the elaborate divisions in all these coloratura numbers. She may find it hard to convey the fun and sparkle in Rossini, but the bright-eyed intensity provides fair compensation even with Cinderella or Rosina, and the cabaletta of Cinderella's final aria is breathtaking in its bravura at a formidably fast tempo. By contrast, this great voice is an ideal vehicle for the *opera seria* arias here, with the male characters very well characterized. First-rate accompaniment too.

Arias: *La Cenerentola: Nacqui all'affano. Guglielmo Tell: S'allontano alfin!; Selva opaca. Semiramide: Bel raggio lusinghier.*

(M) **(*) EMI (ADD) CDM5 66464-2. Callas, Paris Conservatoire O, Rescigno – DONIZETTI: *Arias.* **

If these performances from 1963–4 show a degree of cautiousness that rarely marked Callas's earlier work, this only goes to show how conscious she was of all the criticisms and how she did her utmost to avoid any real blots. In general she succeeds, often producing golden tone. Yet there is something less positive about the end result than in her earlier recordings of this repertory, and, more seriously, the performances do not have that refinement of detail which at her peak lit up so many phrases and made them unforgettable. Good documentation and full translations are provided.

Arias: *La Cenerentola: Non piu mesta. La Donna del Lago: Mura felici . . . Elena! O tu, che chiamo. L'Italiana in Algeri: Cruda sorte! Amor tiranno! Pronti abbiamo . . . Pensa all patria. Otello: Deh! calma, o ciel. La Pietra del Paragone: Se l'Italie contrade . . . Se per voi lo care io torno. Tancredi: Di tanti palpiti. Stabat Mater: Fac ut portem.*

*** Decca 425 430-2. Bartoli, A. Schoenberg Ch., V. Volksoper O, Patanè.

Cecilia Bartoli's first recital of Rossini showpieces brings a formidable demonstration not only of Bartoli's remarkable voice but of her personality and artistry, bringing natural warmth and imagination to each item without ever quite making you smile with delight. Yet there are not many Rossini recitals of any vintage to match this. Vocally, the one controversial point to note is the way that Bartoli articulates her coloratura with a half-aspirate, closer to the Supervia 'rattle' than anything else, but rather obtrusive. Accompaniments are exemplary, and Decca provided the luxury of a chorus in some of the items, with hints of staging. Full, vivid recording. Recommended.

'Rossini Heroines': Arias from: *La donna del lago; Elisabetta, Regina d'Inghilterra; Maometto II; Le nozze di Teti e Peleo; Semiramide; Zelmira.*

*** Decca 436 075-2. Bartoli, Ch. & O of Teatro la Fenice, Marin.

Cecilia Bartoli follows up the success of her earlier Rossini recital-disc with this second brilliant collection of arias, mostly rarities. The tangy, distinctive timbre of her mezzo goes with a magnetic projection of personality to bring to life even formal passage-work, with all the elaborate coloratura bright and sparkling. The rarest item of all is an aria for the goddess Ceres from the classically based entertainment, *Le nozze di Teti e Peleo*, making a splendid showpiece. The collection is crowned by a formidably high-powered reading of *Bel raggio* from *Semiramide*, with Bartoli excitingly braving every danger.

ROTA, Nino (1911–79)

Piano Concertos in C; E (Piccolo mondo antico).

*** EMI CDC5 56869-2. Tomassi, La Scala PO, Muti.

The *First Piano Concerto* (1959–60) was composed for Michelangeli, and the neo-romantic *E major (Piccolo mondo antico)* from 1978 was Rota's last composition. Even if they are too prolix, they are both inventive and expertly crafted works in the received tradition with reminders of Prokofiev and Rachmaninov. Giorgia Tomassi is a formidable soloist

who skilfully negotiates the extreme difficulties of the keyboard role while Muti secures sumptuous tone from the fine La Scala orchestra. Good recording too. Not great music, but worth investigating.

Piano Concertos in C; E min.

**(*) Chan. 9681. Palumbo, I Virtuosi Italiani, Boni.

Disconcertingly for the collector, the *C major Concerto* is also on the EMI disc above, but the *E minor Concerto* (1960) is new to the catalogue. It begins (*Allegro tranquillo*) in an attractively melancholy way, somewhere between film music and Rachmaninov, and goes on in a similar vein for some 16 minutes, with occasional lively outbursts. It is all attractive, but goes on too long; it doesn't help that another melancholy movement follows, lacking the necessary contrast. The finale is lively enough and brings the work to a jolly conclusion. The performances and recording are good, but not quite as polished or as vivid as the EMI disc above.

Concerto for Strings; The Leopard: Dances; La strada: Ballet Suite.

*** Sony SK 66279. La Scala PO, Muti.

The ballet *La strada* (1960) was inspired by Fellini's celebrated picture of the same name. It is a highly attractive score, drawing heavily from Rota's own film music, and is full of colour as well as atmosphere (it also has good tunes – rare for a new ballet at that time). The *Concerto for Strings* was written in the mid 1960s and revised in 1977. It has a meltingly beautiful beginning, and a dream-like quality which is quite haunting. In the Scherzo, the atmosphere of dance forms is evoked – waltzes and minuets – which are divided by more vibrant passages. The following *Aria* is rather more serious in nature, and the finale is a lively quirky galop – a most enjoyable work. The *Dances* from the film *The Leopard* (1963) are actually arrangements of unpublished dance music by Verdi. They are exhilaratingly tuneful (very much like Verdi's own ballet music) and have been delightfully orchestrated by Rota. This is a most entertaining disc and, with such splendid playing and vivid sound, is strongly recommended.

Symphonies Nos. 1 in G; 2 in F (Tarantina – Anni di pellegrinaggio).

** BIS CD 970. Norrköping SO, Ruud.

The *First Symphony* (1935–9) shows the imprint of Stravinsky, Copland, Hindemith and even Sibelius. It is well scored and often inventive. The *Second* (subtitled *Tarantina – Anni di pellegrinaggio*, alluding to the period he spent in Taranto, southern Italy, as a teacher) is even more indebted to Copland. They are thoroughly accessible pieces which engage the interest not only of the listener but also the Norrköping players and their Norwegian conductor. Good sound.

ROTT, Hans (1858–84)

Symphony in E.

*** Hyp. CDA 66366. Cincinnati Philh. O, Samuel.

It is astonishing to encounter in Hans Rott's *Symphony* ideas that took root in Mahler's *First* and *Fifth* symphonies. Structurally the work is original, each movement getting progressively longer, the finale occupying nearly 25 minutes. But the music is full of good ideas and, anticipations of Mahler apart, has a profile of its own. The Cincinnati Philharmonia is a student orchestra who produce extraordinarily good results under Gerhard Samuel. The recording is good. Readers should investigate this issue without delay.

ROUSE, Christopher (born 1949)

(i) *Flute Concerto; Phaeton; Symphony No. 2.*

*** Telarc CD 80452. (i) Wincenc; Houston SO, Eschenbach.

The remarkable five-movement *Flute Concerto*, commissioned by the present soloist, followed two years after Rouse's *Trombone Concerto* (see below). The beautiful first and last movements, with their serene, soaring solo line, are connected thematically, and share the Gaelic title *Anhran* ('Song'). They frame two faster, much more dissonant and rhythmically unpredictable movements. The kernel of the work is the gripping central *Elegia*, written in response to the terrible murder of the two-year-old James Bulger by two ten-year-old schoolboys. Rouse introduces a rich, Bach-like chorale, which moves with a wake-like solemnity towards a central explosion of passionate despair. Throughout, the solo writing demands great bravura and intense emotional commitment from the flautist, which is certainly forthcoming here.

The *Second Symphony* is a three-part structure, with the outer movements again using identical material to frame the anguished central slow movement. In the composer's words that forms a 'prism' through which the mercurial opening material is 'refracted' to yield the angry, tempestuous finale. The desperately grieving *Adagio* is another threnody for a personal friend and colleague, Stephen Albert, killed in a car accident in 1992. *Phaeton* is a savage, explosive early work (1986), which could hardly be more different from the tone poem of Saint-Saëns. Helios's sun chariot, immediately out of his son's control, charges its way across the heavens with horns roistering, and is very quickly blown out of the sky by Zeus's thunderbolt. Performances here are excellent, very well played and recorded, and the *Flute Concerto* is unforgettable.

(i) *Trombone Concerto. Gorgon; Iscariot.*

✪ *** RCA 09026 68410-2. (i) Alessi; Colorado SO, Alsop.

Rouse's Pulitzer-prize winning *Trombone Concerto*, dedicated to the memory of Leonard Bernstein, is a stunning piece and this, its dynamic recording première, is unlikely to be surpassed. Joseph Alessi's solo performance is breathtaking, and the sheer electricity Marin Alsop generates in the orchestra is equally astonishing. The listener is gripped from the very opening, when the soloist emerges from the profoundest depths, through the central eruptions to the sombre, elegiac finale, where the trombone returns to its lowest register after a valedictory intonation of the solemn

Kaddish from Bernstein's *Third Symphony*. A masterly work, given a masterly performance.

Gorgon, written a decade earlier, pictures the hideous female creatures of Greek myth, producing ferocious music that in its continuing rhythmic ostinatos outguns the Stravinsky of the *Rite of Spring*, with the percussive volume of Rock drumming, yet with slithery interludes to suggest snakes in the hair.

The composer describes *Iscariot* (1989), dedicated to John Adams, as 'a symbol of betrayal'. It primarily depends on intense, concentrated string sonorities, taking its sound and ethos from Ives's *Unanswered Question*, yet is much more complex and remains individual, closing with a brief but riveting quotation of Bach's chorale *Es ist genug* ('It is enough'). The continuing dynamism of Alsop's performances of both works is matched by a virtuoso and intensely committed response from the Colorado players and sound of the most spectacular demonstration quality with the widest dynamic range.

ROUSSEAU, Jean-Jacques (1712–78)

Le Devin du village (complete).

(M) *** CPO/EMI CPO 999 559-2. Micheau, Gedda, Roux, Ch. Raymond St-Paul, Louis de Froment CO, Froment.

The one-act Intermezzo, *Le Devin du village* (*The Village Soothsayer*), is Rousseau's most celebrated musical work, written in 1752, an unpretentious piece in what he conceived as the Italian style of the day, which he vigorously supported against the French, even though he here uses a French text. Starting with an overture in the Italian style, fast–slow–fast, it is charming in a plain and straightforward style, hardly original, and the baldness of the writing is rather underlined in this performance with continuo in bare chords. The 25 sections, mostly very short indeed, last well under an hour, offering a simple story of the soothsayer reconciling the estranged lovers, for a price. All three soloists are first rate, with Micheau at her most seductive, and the young Gedda heady-toned.

ROUSSEL, Albert (1869–1937)

(i; ii) *Aeneas* (ballet), *Op. 54*; (iii) *Bacchus et Ariane* (complete ballet); (i) *Le Festin de l'araignée* (complete); (i) *Petite suite, Op. 39*; (i) *Pour une fête de printemps, Op. 22*; (iv) *Sinfonietta, Op. 52*; (iii) *Suite in F, Op. 33*.

(B) *** Erato Ultima ADD/Dig. 3984 24240-2 (2). (i) O Nat. de l'ORTF, Martinon (ii) Ch. de l'ORTF; (iii) O de Paris, Dutoit; (iv) Paillard CO, Paillard.

The quintessential Roussel is all assembled on this two-CD set. Performances are at best excellent, and always good. Martinon's beautifully played account of the complete *Le Festin de l'araignée* is particularly welcome, and there is currently no alternative version of his later ballet, *Aeneas* with chorus (not identified in the documentation but that of the French Radio). This is a rarity dating from 1935. Neither recording is digital but none the worse for that –

indeed most of these come from the late 1960s early 1970s – save for the *Suite en fa* and *Bacchus* which are from 1986 and digital. Abundant testimony to the musical resource and richly endowed imagination Roussel possessed, and very much worth getting.

Bacchus et Ariane (complete ballet), *Op. 43; Le Festin de l'araignée (The Spider's Feast), Op. 17.*

⚫ *** Chan. 9494. BBC PO, Y. P. Tortelier.

Tortelier offers the best *Bacchus et Ariane* yet – and what a marvellously inventive and resourceful score it is. The BBC Philharmonic play with tremendous zest and give a sensitive and atmospheric account of *Le Festin de l'araignée*. They offer us the complete banquet, not just the chosen dishes on the set menu! Splendid recording and performances of rewarding and colourful music that deserves to be more widely heard.

The EMI recording, made in the generous acoustic of the Salle Wagram, is a shade too reverberant at times, but no essential detail is masked. Georges Prêtre obtains an excellent response from the Orchestre National de France in both scores. The CD freshens detail a little, although the resonance means that the improvement is relatively limited.

Bacchus et Ariane: Suite No. 2

(M) ** DG 449 748-2. LOP, Markevitch – HONEGGER: *Symphony No. 5;* MILHAUD: *Les Choéphores.* (**)

Markevitch's spirited and atmospheric account of the secound suite from *Bacchus et Ariane* is very well played and recorded, with plenty of space round the aural image, but the sound naturally lacks the body and focus of a modern recording, although it is fully acceptable.

Suite in F, Op. 33.

(M) **(*) Mercury (ADD) 434 303-2. Detroit SO, Paray – CHABRIER: *Bourrée fantasque* etc. ***

The outer movements of Roussel's *Suite in F* have a compulsive drive which also infects the harmonically complex, bittersweet central *Sarabande*. The scoring is rich (some might say thick), and the resonance of the Detroit Ford Auditorium makes it congeal a little. It is well played and alive, with Paray at his best in the closing *Gigue*.

Symphonies Nos. 1 in D min. (Le Poème de la forêt), Op. 7; 2 in B flat, Op. 23; 3 in G min., Op. 42; 4 in A, Op. 53.

(B) *** Erato Ultima 3984 21090-2 (2). French Nat. O, Dutoit.

Dutoit gets first-class playing from the Orchestre National, who are in excellent form, while the CD transfers do particular justice to the richness of Roussel's scoring and are particularly imposing in the definition at the bottom end of the register. So, with any minor reservations, this is certainly a recommendable set and splendid value for money.

Symphony No. 3 in G min., Op. 42.

(M) **(*) Sony (ADD) MHK 62352. NYPO, Bernstein (with HONEGGER: *Rugby; Pacific 231* ** – MILHAUD: *Les Choéphores.* ***

(M) **(*) DG (IMS) 445 512-2. O Nat. de France, Bernstein – FRANCK: *Symphony.* **(*)

On Sony Heritage, a vividly characterized and enormously vital account of Roussel's magnificent *Third Symphony*. It was Bernstein's mentor, Koussevitzky, who commissioned the work for the fiftieth anniversary of the Boston Symphony Orchestra, and Bernstein's reading is as highly charged as one could wish for. The Sony performance comes from 1961 and in the original LP format was shrill and reverberant. The present transfer has tamed some though not all of its ferocity and cleaned up some of the detail. Though the recording is not perfect, this is still the best performance of the symphony in the current catalogue, and it comes with a Milhaud rarity new to these shores.

In his later, DG version, Bernstein again compulsively brings out all its energy and pungent dissonance, and yet he lightens the mood attractively for the high-spirited finale. The 'live' recording is extremely vivid if a shade harsh. But his Sony account is even finer,

(i) *Symphonies Nos. 3-4; (ii) Bacchus et Ariane: suite 2.*

(N) (B) **(*) RCA 2-CD (ADD) 74321 84601-2 (2). (i) R. France PO, Janowski; (ii) Boston SO, Munch – MESSIAEN: *Turangalîla Symphony.* ***

Symphonies Nos. 3; 4 in A, Op. 53; Bacchus et Ariane, Suite No. 2; Sinfonietta for String Orchestra, Op. 52.

**(*) Chan. 7007. Detroit SO, Järvi.

Neeme Järvi's account of the *Third Symphony* has an engaging vitality and character, and the playing of the Detroit orchestra is highly responsive. In the slow movement he indulges in a rather steep *accelerando* after the fugal section. Likewise his finale feels too fast. But it is a committed performance. Some may find the acoustic a shade too resonant, but the overall balance is very natural and pleasing and this is certainly very recommendable, given the superior sound and Järvi's obvious enthusiasm for this repertoire.

Janowski has a natural feeling for the Roussel idiom, and his performances of the symphonies are well worth having. Perhaps the *Scherzo* of the *Third* is a shade too fast, but in all other respects his readings cannot be faulted. The digital recording has plenty of presence, body and detail and this coupling is definitely preferable to Järvi on Chandos. As for the new transfer of Munch's 1952 mono account of the second suite from Roussel's ballet, the sound is little short of amazing in its colour and ambient bloom. The Boston Orchestra was still under Koussevitzky's spell at the time and the playing is quite electrifying. Munch re-recorded it twice during the 1960s, but never with greater brilliance and luminosity than here. A few bars are missing, perhaps due to the original tapes being damaged, or Munch himself may have made a cut in performance.

Symphony No. 4 in A, Op. 53.

⚫ (M) (***) EMI mono CDM5 66595-2. Philh. O, Karajan – BALAKIREV: *Symphony No. 1.* (***) ⚫

Karajan's pioneering version of Roussel's marvellous *Fourth Symphony* was recorded in November 1949, yet it still sounds exceptionally fresh. Having treasured this in its 78-r.p.m. form and on LP and in its brief CD incarnation, it is good to have it back again. What a performance! It is vastly superior to most of its successors. Unfortunately, as we go to press it has been deleted.

CHAMBER MUSIC

Andante & Scherzo for Flute & Piano, Op. 51; Andante from an Unfinished Wind Trio for Oboe, Clarinet & Bassoon; Aria No. 2 for Oboe & Piano; Divertissement for Wind Quintet & Piano, Op. 6; Duo for Bassooon & Double Bass; Impromptu for Harp Solo, Op. 21; Joueurs de flûte for Flute & Piano, Op. 27; Music from Elpénor (poème radiophonique) for Flute & String Quartet, Op. 59; Piano Trio in E flat, Op. 2; Pipe for Piccolo & Piano; 2 Poèmes de Ronsard for Flute & Soprano, Op. 25; Segovia for Guitar, Op. 29; Sérénade for Flute, String Trio & Harp, Op. 30; String Quartet, Op. 45; String Trio, Op. 58; Trio, Op. 40 for Flute, Viola & Cello; Violin Sonatas Nos. 1 in D min., Op. 11; 2, Op. 28.

(M) *** Olympia OCD 706 ABC (3). Verhey; Röling; Roerade; Van den Brink; De Lange; Jeurissen; Van Altena; Waarsenburg, Schoenberg Qt (members); Kantorow; Jan Stegenga; Maessen; Goodswaard.

These are good performances, well presented here by these fine Dutch artists. This is eminently civilized music and, without going into too much detail, artistically these would carry a three-star rating. The recordings are eminently serviceable. The *Sérénade* for flute, string trio and harp, a lovely piece – and very well played indeed – is not as finely focused as on the old Melos recording (Decca), and the piano in the *Joueurs de flûte* seems to be in a slightly more resonant acoustic than the flute. All the same this is as economical a way as any of exploring this interesting repertoire. The three discs are not now available separately, but if you respond to Roussel, this set is well worth considering, especially at mid-price.

ROUTH, Francis (born 1927)

Clarinet Quintet.

*** Redcliffe RR 010. Redcliffe Ens. – BLISS: *Clarinet Quintet;* RAWSTHORNE: *Clarinet Quartet.* ***

Routh's *Quintet* was written for Nicholas Cox, who plays it with great skill and understanding. Its variety of mood makes up for the melodic fragmentation, and its invention is lively throughout. Excellent recording.

ROYER, Pancrace (1705–55)

Pièces de clavecin (1746).

(B) *** HM HMA 901037. Christie (harpsichord).

Royer's *Pièces de clavecin*, his only collection to appear in print, had their origins in his stage works but, unlike Rameau, who transcribed instrumental dances for the keyboard, Royer drew on arias and choral pieces as well. William Christie's Harmonia Mundi recording, made in the 1980s, is very fine and at bargain price deserves an enthusiastic recommendation.

RÓZSA, Miklós (1907–94)

(i)Cello Concerto, Op. 32; (ii) Violin Concerto, Op. 24; (i; ii) Theme & Variations for Violin, Cello & Orchestra, Op. 29a.

(N) *** Telarc CD 80518. Atlanta SO, Levi; with (i) Harrell; (ii) McDuffie.

These are splendid new recordings of Rózsa's highly romantic *Violin* and *Cello Concertos*, plus an enjoyable set of variations in which both soloists join. The performances are superb and the recording is warm and detailed. Recommendable in every way.

Symphony in 3 Movements, Op. 6a (ed. Palmer); The Vintner's Daughter, Op. 23a.

*** Koch 37244-2. New Zealand SO, Sedares.

Rózsa's early attempt in 1930 to write a large-scale symphony proved abortive, and the present structure, minus a Scherzo and heavily edited by Christopher Palmer, relies on an incomplete manuscript. However, as we know from his film scores, Rózsa had no difficulty finding memorable musical ideas and in the first movement uses them cogently and with intensity. The second-movement *Andante* is highly evocative and the finale does not lack fire and energy, even if structurally it remains the least convincing part of the work. *The Vintner's Daughter*, a picturesque set of variations, again shows the composer's melodic appeal, and again he uses the orchestral palette as seductively as in his film music. James Sedares and his New Zealand players are obviously caught up in the music and present it persuasively, with the conductor showing a notably firm grip on the first movement of the symphony. The recording has plenty of body and colour.

(i) String Quartets Nos. 1, Op. 22, 2, Op. 38; (ii) Sonata for 2 Violins, Op. 15a.

(N) *** ASV CDDCA 1105. (i) Flesch Qt; (ii) Ibbotson, Gibbs.

The *First String Quartet* was written in the late 1940s and revised and shortened in 1950. It is dedicated to Peter Ustinov, who was playing Nero in the film *Quo vadis* for which Rósza composed the score. It is a rewarding score, finely wrought and civilized, which improves as you get to know it better. There are reminders of Rózsa's kinship with Bartók and with Debussy in the slow movement. The *Second Quartet* is much later, completed in 1981, again the product of a cultured musical mind. Perhaps not as distinctively individual as, say, the Kodály *Second Quartet* but again eminently well worth getting to know. The *Sonata for Two Violins* is an early piece from 1933, which Rosza overhauled in 1973 and which the leader and violist of the Flesch play with spirit. Altogether an interesting and worthwhile issue, very well played and well if perhaps forwardly recorded.

RUBBRA, Edmund (1901–86)

Sinfonietta (for strings), Op. 163; 4 Medieval Latin Lyrics, Op. 32; 5 Spenser Sonnets, Op. 42; Amoretti: 5 Spenser Sonnets, 2nd series, Op. 43.

(M) *** EMI CDM5 66936-3. Hill, Wilson-Johnson, Endellion Qt, City of L. Sinfonia, Schönzeler.

The *Sinfonietta for Strings* is Rubbra's last work and alone is worth the price of the record. It is short but concentrated and is eloquently played by the City of London Sinfonia under Hans-Hubert Schönzeler. The songs are all much earlier and are rewarding pieces, the settings are strikingly melodic and full of atmosphere with each collection very distinct in character, and a certain pastiche period flavour imbuing the music of each group.

Symphonies Nos. 1–8; 9 (Hommage à Teilhard de Chardin); (i) 9 (Sinfonia Sacra); 10–11.

(N) *** Chan. 9944 (5). BBC Nat. O of Wales, Hickox; (i) with Dawson, Della Jones, Roberts, BBC Nat. Ch. of Wales.

As can be seen, Chandros have collected all eleven Rubbra symphonies in a box of five CDs offered for the price of four, which can be strongly recommended to those collectors who have not already begun investing in the individual records. No doubt the couplings on those earlier issues will also reappear separately.

Symphony No. 1, Op. 44; (i) Sinfonia concertante for Piano & Orchestra, Op. 38; A Tribute, Op. 56.

*** Chan. 9538. BBC Nat. O of Wales, Hickox; (i) with Shelley.

The first movement of the symphony is fiercely turbulent; a French dance tune, a *Perigourdine*, forms the basis of the middle movement, but the pensive, inward-looking finale, which is as long as the first two movements put together, is the most powerful and haunting of the three. The *Sinfonia concertante* is no less symphonic in character and substance. The opening *Fantasia* begins with a reflective lento passage which anticipates the tranquility of the *G major Piano Concerto*, though it is the final *Prelude and Fugue*, composed in memory of his teacher, Gustav Holst, which lingers longest in the memory. Howard Shelley is an inspired soloist and the sometimes thick textures of the symphony sound remarkably lucid in Richard Hickox's hands. The BBC National Orchestra of Wales play splendidly and the Chandos sound is in the best traditions of the house.

Symphonies Nos. 2 in D, Op. 45; 6, Op. 80.

*** Chan. 9481. BBC Nat. O of Wales, Hickox.

Symphonies Nos. (i) 2; (ii) 7 in C, Op. 88; (i) Festival Overture, Op. 62.

*** Lyrita (ADD) SRCD 235. (i) New Philh. O, Handley; (ii) LPO, Boult.

Richard Hickox and his fine players do make the score of the *Second Symphony* more lucid than Handley's Lyrita recording from the 1970s. The performance is meticulously prepared and yet flows effortlessly, and the slow movement speaks with great eloquence. The heart of the *Sixth Symphony*

is the serene *Canto* movement which is not dissimilar in character to the *Missa in honorem Sancti Dominici* It is arguably the finest of the cycle after No. 9, and Hickox and his fine players do it proud. So, too, do the Chandos engineers.

The *Seventh Symphony* is a very considerable piece. The longest and most ambitious of its three movements – perhaps the most enigmatic, too – is the finale, an extended passacaglia and fugue displaying the composer's naturally contrapuntal mode of thought at its most typical. The first movement brings a cogent argument based on a simple four-note motif, and the second a rhythmic Scherzo that leads to a more lyrical, noble climax. Boult's performance is outstandingly successful. A good performance too from Handley of both the *Second Symphony* and the overture which bears an adjacent opus number to the *Fifth*. Both recordings, from the 1970s, are up to the high standards of realism one expects from this label.

Symphonies Nos. 3, Op. 49; 4, Op. 53; Resurgam Overture, Op. 149; A Tribute, Op. 56.

*** Lyrita SRCD 202. Philh. O, Del Mar.

Symphonies Nos. 3; 7 in C, Op. 88.

✿ *** Chan. 9634. BBC Nat. O of Wales, Hickox.

The *Third Symphony* (1939) once enjoyed repertory status – at least in BBC programmes – but completely fell out of establishment favour from the 1960s through to the late 1980s. It has a pastoral character and a certain Sibelian feel to it (woodwind in thirds), though Rubbra is always himself. In the final movement there is even a hint of Elgar in the fourth variation. Hickox's is a more eloquent and ultimately more convincing account than the fine Philharmonia version under Norman Del Mar on Lyrita.

The opening of the *Fourth Symphony* is of quite exceptional beauty and has a serenity and quietude that silence criticism; there is a consistent elevation of feeling and continuity of musical thought. Rubbra's music is steeped in English polyphony and it could not come from any time other than our own.

The *Seventh Symphony* (1956) receives a performance of real power from Hickox and his Welsh orchestra. This is music that speaks of deep and serious things and its opening paragraphs are among the most inspired that Rubbra ever penned. Noble performances and excellent recorded sound.

Symphonies Nos. 4; 10 (Sinfonia da camera), Op. 145; 11, Op. 153.

*** Chan. 9401. BBC Nat. O of Wales, Hickox.

Richard Hickox offers a particularly imaginative account of the *Eleventh Symphony* in one movement (1979), which is new to the catalogue. Like so much of Rubbra's music, it has an organic continuity and inner logic that are immediately striking. And in common with the *Tenth Symphony*, also in one movement, its textures are spare and limpid. Hickox's account of the *Fourth Symphony* is totally convincing. The Chandos recording is excellent in every respect, with plenty of warmth and transparency of detail.

Symphony No. 5 in B flat, Op. 63.

(M) *** Chan. 6576. Melbourne SO, Schönzeler – BLISS:
Checkmate ***; TIPPETT: *Little Music.* **(*)

*Symphonies Nos. 5; 8 (Hommage à Teilhard de Chardin),
Op. 132; (i) Ode to the Queen, Op. 83.*

*** Chan. 9714. BBC Nat. O of Wales, Hickox; (i) with Bickley.

*Symphony No. 5; Loth to Depart (Improvisations on
virginal pieces by Giles Farnaby), Op. 50/4.*

(M) (***) EMI mono CDM5 66053-2. Hallé O, Barbirolli –
BRITTEN: *Violin Concerto* (**); HEMING: *Threnody for a
Soldier Killed in Action.* (***)

Barbirolli's was the very first recording of any Rubbra symphony. Made in 1950, it originally appeared on seven 78-r.p.m. discs with the haunting *Loth to Depart* as a fill-up. It has never sounded as fresh and 'present' as it does in Andrew Walter's exemplary transfer. Barbirolli's spacious and affectionate reading stands up well, nearly half a century after its composition.

However, Richard Hickox's reading is easily the finest and most penetrating; the slow movement has depth and, thanks to a magnificent recording, a greater clarity than either of its predecessors. Tempi are unerringly judged and he brings great breadth and gravitas to the very opening of the work. He gives, too, a more intense account of the *Eighth (Hommage à Teilhard de Chardin)* than we have had before. *Ode to the Queen*, commissioned by the BBC for the Coronation in 1953 is a setting of three poems, variously by Richard Crashaw, Sir William d'Avenant and Thomas Campion, for mezzo-soprano and full orchestra and is strong in inspiration. Excellent performances and outstanding recorded sound from the Chandos/BBC team.

Although the Melbourne orchestra is not in the very top division, they play this music for all they are worth, and the strings have a genuine intensity and lyrical fervour that compensate for the opaque effect of the octave doublings. Altogether, though, this is an imposing performance which reflects credit on all concerned. The recording is well balanced and lifelike; but the ear perceives that the upper range is rather restricted.

*(i) Symphonies Nos. 6, Op. 80; 8; (ii) Soliloquy for Cello &
Orchestra, Op. 57.*

*** Lyrita (ADD) SRCD 234. (i) Philh. O, Del Mar; (ii) De
Saram, LSO, Handley.

In Norman Del Mar's hands Rubbra's music speaks here with directness and without artifice; the Philharmonia play marvellously and the composer's sound-world is very well served by the recording balance. The *Soliloquy* has a grave beauty of which exerts a strong appeal. Rohan de Saram plays with a restrained eloquence that is impressive and he has excellent support from the LSO under Vernon Handley.

*(i) Symphony No. 9 (Sinfonia sacra), Op. 140. The
Morning Watch for Chorus & Orchestra, Op. 55.*

✪ *** Chan. 9441. (i) Dawson, Jones, Roberts; BBC Nat. Ch.
of Wales, BBC Nat. O of Wales, Hickox.

The *Ninth Symphony*, arguably Rubbra's greatest work, is an unqualified masterpiece. Subtitled *The Resurrection*, it

was inspired by a painting of Donato Bramante and has something of the character of the Passion, which the three soloists relate in moving fashion. *The Morning Watch*, a setting of Henry Vaughan for chorus and orchestra, which was originally to have formed part of a choral fifth symphony, is another score of great nobility, which has taken even longer (half a century) to be recorded. Both works are superbly served here by all these fine musicians, and the Chandos recording is no less magnificent.

*Symphony No. 10 (Sinfonia da camera), Op. 145;
Improvisations on Virginal Pieces by Giles Farnaby,
Op. 50; A Tribute to Vaughan Williams on his 70th
Birthday (Introduction & danza alla fuga), Op. 56.*

(M) *** Chan. 6599. Bournemouth Sinf., Schönzeler.

Rubbra's *Tenth Symphony* is a short, one-movement work, whose opening has a Sibelian seriousness and a strong atmosphere that grip one immediately. Schönzeler is scrupulously attentive to dynamic nuance and internal balance, while keeping a firm grip on the architecture as a whole. The 1977 recording has been impressively remastered. It has a warm acoustic and reproduces natural, well-placed orchestral tone. The upper range is crisply defined. The *Farnaby Variations* is a pre-war work whose charm Schönzeler uncovers effectively, revealing its textures to best advantage. *Loath to Depart*, the best-known movement, has gentleness and vision in this performance. Strongly recommended. Even though this CD plays for only 40 minutes, it remains indispensable.

CHAMBER MUSIC

*The Buddha (incidental music: suite, arr. Croft); Duo for
Cor Anglais & Piano, Op. 156; Meditazioni sopra 'coeurs
désolés', Op. 67b; Phantasy for 2 Violins & Piano; Oboe
Sonata in C, Op. 100; Piano Trios Nos. 1, Op. 68 (one
movement); 2, Op 138.*

(N) (M) *** Dutton Lab. CDLX 7106. Endymion Ens
(members).

Rubbra had a lifelong interest in the East, and his incidental music for Clifford Bax's radio play on the life of the Buddha makes a strong impression; it has a cleansing simplicity. The *Duo for Cor Anglais and Piano* is a late work, written in 1980 after the *Eleventh Symphony*, with a deeply-felt, elegiac and valedictory character. The *Meditazioni sopra 'coeurs désolés'* (1949), originally for recorder and harpsichord, is a set of variations on Josquin's chanson. The wonderful *Oboe Sonata*, written in 1958 for Evelyn Rothwell (Lady Barbirolli), is the best known of the seven pieces on this disc, and Melinda Maxwell and Michael Dussek successfully capture its nobility of spirit. The *Phantasy for Two Violins and Piano* (1927) was Rubbra's first published work and is finely wrought in every way. The *First Piano Trio* was written in 1950 and has the quiet seriousness of late Fauré and the same naturalness of speech; there is no trace of rhetoric or expressive emphasis, qualities which hold true of this dignified and selfless performance. *No. 2* was composed 20 years later and is sparer than its predecessor. A thoroughly recommendable anthology, admirably recorded.

Oboe Sonata in C, Op. 100.

(B) *** Hyp Helios CDH 55008. Francis, Dickenson –
BOUGHTON: *Pastoral;* HARTY: *3 Pieces;* HOWELLS: *Sonata.* ***

Rubbra's *Oboe Sonata in C, Op. 100* has a songful, rhapsodic opening movement, which leads naturally into the soulful central *Elegie;* the fluent finale is rondo with a semi-oriented melodic line. The performance here is of quality, but these artists are not helped by the forward balance and the background resonance. It is important not to have the volume level set too high.

(i) Violin Sonatas Nos. 1, Op. 11; 2, Op. 31; 3, Op. 135; 4 Pieces, Op. 29. Variations on a Phrygian Theme for Solo Violin, Op. 105.

(M) *** Dutton Lab. CDLX 7101. Osostowicz; (i) with Dussek.

The *Second Violin Sonata,* with Albert Sammons and Gerald Moore, was the first Rubbra work to reach the gramophone. Although Frederick Grinke and the composer himself recorded it for Decca in the early days of LP, there has been no decent modern recording. Krysia Osostowicz and Michael Dussek are worth waiting for, since not only the recording but also, surprisingly, the performance eclipses both its distinguished predecessors. The *First Sonata,* Op. 11, from the 1920s, is heavily indebted to Debussy and Rubbra's teacher, Gustav Holst. The *Third* is a sinewy work from 1963, formidably argued and finely laid out for the medium. The Op. 29 *Pieces* are really teaching material, as is the set of variations for violin alone.

PIANO MUSIC

Fantasy Fugue, Op. 161; Fukagawa (Deep River); Introduction & Fugue, Op. 19; Introduction, Aria & Fugue, Op. 104; Invention on the Name of Haydn, Op.160; Nemo Fugue; Prelude & Fugue on a Theme of Cyril Scott, Op. 69; 8 Preludes, Op. 131; 4 Studies, Op. 139; (i) 9 Teaching Pieces, Op. 74.

(N) (M) *** Dutton CDLX 7112. Michael Dussek (i) with Rachel Dussek.

Considering that he was an outstanding pianist, Rubbra wrote relatively little for his instrument. Apart from the seraphic *Piano Concerto in G major,* of which we badly need a new recording, and the *Sinfonia concertante* the present disc contains the lot. Although all these pieces do exist in various other versions, Michael Dussek's fine survey is undoubtedly the one to have. Artistic matters apart, it also has the benefit of vivid and truthful recorded sound.

VOCAL MUSIC

(i) Advent Cantata: natum Maria virgine, Op. 136. Inscape, Op. 122; (i) 4 Mediaeval Latin Lyrics, Op. 32; Song of the Soul, Op. 78; Veni, creator spiritus, Op. 130.

(N) ⊛ *** Chan. 9847. ASMF Ch., City of L. Sinf., Hickox; (i) with Varcoe.

Having put us in their debt with their survey of the symphonies, Richard Hickox and Chandos now turn to the choral music. Three of the pieces here are first recordings. *Natum Maria virgine* comes from the late 1960s when Rubbra was working on the *Sinfonia sacra.* As with all his vocal music it is beautifully crafted, its polyphony growing effortlessly and inevitably. *Song of the Soul* comes from 1951, the year of the *Second String Quartet,* and has dipped under the horizon as far as both concert and recorded performances are concerned, as has the *Veni, creator spiritus,* another late and inspiring piece. The only work otherwise available, now that John Carol Case's Decca account of *Inscape* (1966) has disappeared from view, is the *Four Mediæval Latin Lyrics* with David Wilson-Johnson as soloist and the late Hans-Hubert Schönzeler conducting (EMI). Although that has done sterling service, Stephen Varcoe and Hickox are to be preferred. The Abelard setting, the fourth of the *Medivel Latin Lyrics,* sound more beautiful. *Inscape,* which is set to the words of Gerard Manley Hopkins, has a quiet eloquence and depth that puts it among Rubbra's most memorable works in any genre. Hickox has real feeling for the mystical side of Rubbra and conveys his elevation of feeling. The recording has amplitude yet clarity and is expertly and naturally balanced. A very special disc.

The Beatitudes, Op. 109; 4 Carols; Lauda Sion, Op. 110; 5 Madrigals, Op.51; 2 Madrigals, Op. 52; Mass in Honour of St Teresa of Avila; Missa à 3 voci, Op. 98; 5 Motets, Op. 37.

(N) *** ASV CDDCA 1093. Voces Sacrae, Martin.

This CD is devoted to Rubbra's *a cappella* music and ranges from the early Motets of 1934, settings of Herrick, Donne and Vaughan, through to his last Mass, the *Mass in Honour of St Teresa of Avila,* which was composed in 1981, five years before his death. It also includes the spare and austere *Missa à 3 voci* from the early 1960s; both these Masses are new to the catalogue. When you think that Rubbra belongs to the same generation as Tippett, Walton, and Shostakovich, you realize just how original a voice he has. His music is not of our time but could come from any other, and the two Masses recorded here have a sense of the eternal verities. The most important work here is the *Mass in Honour of St Teresa of Avila,* a work of haunting beauty and directness. The *Lauda Sion* (1960) is another work that leaves one feeling cleansed. Judy Martin and Voces Sacrae give sympathetic and idiomatic accounts of all these pieces, and the sound is natural and present.

Songs: (i & ii) A hymn to the virgin; The jade mountain; Jesukin; Mystery; Orpheus with his lute; Rosa mundi. Instrumental pieces: (ii & iii) Discourse, Op. 127; (iii) Fukagawa; Improvisation, Op. 124. (ii) Harp pieces: Pezzo ostinato, Op. 102; Transformations, Op. 141.

*** ASV CDDCA 1036. (i) Chadwell, (ii) Perrett, (iii) Gill (with LENNOX BERKELEY: *Nocturne for Harp;* HOWELLS: *Prelude* ***)

The CD reflects Rubbra's lifelong interest in the Orient from the early *Fukagawa* (1929), an arrangement of a Japanese melody, to *The Jade Mountain* songs (1962). The two pieces for harp, the *Pezzo ostinato* and the *Transformations*, both reflect the fascination that Indian music exercised. They are both impressive – indeed, exalted is the word that springs to mind. Some of the very early pieces reflect the spell cast by Holst and Cyril Scott but the bulk of the music here finds him at his most individual. Tracy Chadwell sings ethereally though there is perhaps a little too much echo round her voice, but the harp pieces are both exquisitely played and could hardly be more authoritative. A most rewarding and recommendable issue.

Magnificat & Nunc dimittis, Op. 65; Missa Cantuariensis, Op. 59; Missa in honorem Sancti Dominici; Tenebrae Motets, Op. 72: Nocturns 1–3; (i) (Organ) Meditation, Op. 79; Prelude & Fugue, Op. 69.

(N) (BB) * Naxos 8.555255. Ch. of St John's College, Cambridge, Robinson; (i) Houssart.

In his remarkable study *Counterpoint* (1960) Rubbra argued that the whole of Western music grew out of melody and in particular the interaction of independent melodic lines. As a student he received a thorough grounding in 16th-century contrapuntal technique from one of the greatest theoreticians of the day, R. O. Morris, and his mastery is demonstrated in his symphonies and his choral works. The present inexpensive recording by Christopher Robinson and the Choir of St John's College, Cambridge, makes an excellent entry point into his sacred music. The *Missa Cantuariensis* was composed for Canterbury Cathedral, whereas the *Missa in honorem Sancti Dominici* (1948) was written for the Catholic Rite. Both are crafted beautifully and elevated in feeling. The first *Nocturn* (which comprises three motets) of the *Tenebrae* was written in 1951, and a further two *Nocturns* followed ten years later. They are anguished and eloquent expressions of faith. Do go on to explore the *Mass in Honour of St Teresa of Avila* and the *Mass for Three Voices* (on ASV) as they are among the most inspired works he wrote. This deeply satisfying recording is completed by the *Meditation* for organ, which was written for James Dalton, and Bernard Rose's transcription of the *Prelude and Fugue on a Theme of Cyril Scott*, a seventieth birthday tribute to Rubbra's first teacher. The performances are quite outstanding and well recorded.

(i) Magnificat & Nunc dimittis in A flat, Op. 65. Missa in honorem Sancti Dominici, Op. 66; 3 Hymn Tunes, Op. 114; 3 Motets, Op. 78.

*** ASV CDDCA 881. Gonville & Caius College, Cambridge, Ch., Webber; (i) Phillips (organ) – HADLEY: *Lenten Cantata* etc. ***.

The most important work here is the *Missa in honorem Sancti Dominici* (1948), written at about the time of the *Fifth Symphony* and one of the most beautiful of twentieth-century *a cappella* choral pieces written in this or any other country. None of the other works on the disc is its equal. The performance by the Choir of Gonville & Caius College, Cambridge, under Geoffrey Webber is dedicated and sensitive. Excellent balance, though the organ is obtrusive, particularly so in the first of the Op. 78 *Motets*.

RUBINSTEIN, Anton (1829–94)

Piano Concertos Nos. 1 in E, Op. 25; 2 in F, Op. 35.

** Marco 8.223456. Banowetz, Czech State PO, A. Walter.

Piano Concertos Nos. 3 in G, Op. 45; 4 in D min., Op. 70.

** Marco 8.223382. Banowetz, Slovak State PO (Košice), Stankovsky.

Piano Concerto No. 5 in E flat, Op. 94; Caprice russe, Op. 102.

**(*) Marco 8.223489. Banowetz, Slovak RSO (Bratislava), Stankovsky.

Rubinstein was the first composer of concertos in Russia and was enormously prolific. His *First Piano concerto in E major*, dating from 1850, is greatly indebted to Mendelssohn though it is more prolix. The *Third Piano Concerto in G* (1853–4) is more concentrated, and there is a recording of the *Fourth in D minor* (1864) by his pupil, Josef Hofmann; no later pianist has equalled that. By the mid-1860s Rubinstein's perspective had broadened (rather than deepened), and the *Fifth Piano Concerto in E flat* (1874) is an ambitious piece, longer than the *Emperor* and almost as long as the Brahms *D minor*. No doubt its prodigious technical demands have stood in the way of its wider dissemination. It has all the fluent lyricism one expects of Rubinstein, though most of its ideas, attractive enough in themselves, overstay their welcome.

Joseph Banowetz has now recorded all the concertos for Marco Polo and, although the orchestral support and the recording do not rise much above routine, there is nothing ordinary about Banowetz's pianism. The *Fifth*, at least, is worth investigating (for the *Fourth*, one should turn to Cherkassky.) The *Caprice russe* was written four years after the concerto, but the fires were obviously blazing less fiercely. All the same, this is an issue of some interest, and the solo playing has conviction.

Symphony No. 1, Op. 40; Ivan the Terrible, Op. 79.

(N) (BB) *(*) Naxos 8.555476 Slovak State PO (Košice), Stankovsky.

Naxos are presumably going to reissue on their bargain label all six of the Rubinstein symphonies previously available at full-price on Marco Polo (They were originally discussed in our 1996 edition). The *First* – a young man's work – comes from 1850 and is coupled with the tone-poem *Ivan the Terrible* of 1869, which draws its inspiration from the same source as did Rimsky-Korsakov's opera of the same name (also known as *The Maid of Pskov*). Tchaikovsky, incidentally, made the piano score of it. Rubinstein's language is completely and utterly rooted in Mendelssohn, and David Brown's verdict on the *Second Symphony* (*Ocean*) as 'watery and Mendelssohnian' applies equally here. Music of lesser stature calls for interpreters of quality and flair if it is to have the slightest chance of success and neither of these performances are much more than routine. However, given the modest outlay involved, readers may be inclined to give these pieces a try.

Piano Sonatas Nos. 1 in E min., Op. 12; 2 in C min., Op. 20; 3 in F, Op. 41; 4 in A min., Op. 100.

(B) *** Hyp. Dyad CCD 22007 (2). Howard.

Leslie Howard proves highly persuasive in all four works. The 1981 recordings sound excellent, and this set is more enticing as a Dyad, with two discs offered for the price of one. Returning to these works, one is surprised to find how enjoyable the music is, with some good lyrical ideas, phrased romantically, to balance the arrestingly flamboyant rhetoric which Leslie Howard obviously relishes.

RUDERS, Poul (born 1949)

(i) Concerto for Clarinet & Twin Orchestra; (ii) Violin Concerto No. 1; (iii) Drama Trilogy No. 3 for Cello & Orchestra 'Polydrama'.

*** Unicorn DKPCD 9114. (i) Thomsen; (ii) Hirsch; (iii) Zeuten; Odense SO, Vetö.

This Violin Concerto is a tribute to the sunny atmosphere of Italian baroque music in general and Vivaldi's Four Seasons in particular. Apart from its neo-classicism there is a whiff of minimalism about much of it. The Clarinet Concerto is strong stuff; to quote Ruders himself, the soloist is a 'Pierrot-like vox humana caught in a vice of orchestral on-slaught', and the effect is often disturbing and almost sur-realistic. He is an imaginative composer with a vein of lyrical feeling and melancholy that surfaces in the Cello Concerto. A rewarding and interesting figure.

RUGGLES, Carl (1876–1971)

Sun-Treader.

(N) (M) *** DG (ADD) 463 633-2. Boston SO, Tilson Thomas – IVES: Three Places in New England; PISTON: Symphony No. 2. ***

Carl Ruggles belongs to the same generation as Ives, whose exploratory outlook he shares, though not his carefree folksiness. Ruggles's music is impressionistic and powerful, assured in structure and finish. Sun-Treader takes its inspi-ration from Browning and, like so much of Ruggles's music, is uncompromising. There are moments of wild dissonance here, which make tough but rewarding listening. Tilson Thomas and the Boston orchestra make out a very good case for the work, as do the DG engineers.

RUTTER, John (born 1943)

(i; ii) Suite antique (for flute and orchestra); (iii) 5 Childhood Lyrics (for unaccompanied choir); (ii; iii) Fancies; When Icicles Hang (for choir and orchestra).

(N) *** Collegium COLCD 117. (i) Dobing, Marshall (ii) City of L. Sinf.; (iii) Soloists, Cambridge Singers; Composer.

This whole collection is imbued with Rutter's easy melodic style and the touches of offbeat rhythm which he uses to give a lift to his lively settings. The Antique Suite (for flute, harpsichord and strings) opens with a serene Prelude, but includes a typically catchy Ostinato, a gay Waltz and a chirpy closing Rondeau. Fancies has a delightful Urchins' Dance, after the fairy style of Mendelssohn, and its Riddle song has a most appealing lyrical melody. But the mood darkens for the closing Bellman's song. Among the Childhood Lyrics, the settings of Edward Lear's Owl and the pussy-cat and Sing a song of sixpence are particularly endearing.

The evocative When Icicles Hang brings characteristically winning scoring for the orchestral woodwind (Rutter loves flutes) and another fine melody in Blow, blow thou winter wind. The work ends happily in folksy style. Splendid per-formances throughout. Rutter is currently the most per-formed (by amateur choirs) of any living English composer, and no wonder. The performances here are excellent and so is the recording.

(i; ii) The Falcon; (ii) 2 Festival Anthems: O praise the Lord in Heaven; Behold, the Tabernacle of God; (ii; iii) Magnificat.

*** Coll. COLCD 114. (i) St Paul's Cathedral Choristers; (ii) Cambridge Singers, City of L. Sinfonia; (iii) with Forbes; all cond. composer.

The Falcon was Rutter's first large-scale choral work. Its inspiration was a medieval poem, which is linked to the Crucifixion story, but the core of the piece is the mystical central Lento. The Magnificat has the usual Rutter stylistic touches, with a syncopated treatment of the opening Magni-ficat anima mea, and a joyous closing Gloria Patri. The two anthems are characteristically expansive and resplendent with brass. Fine performances and recording in the best Collegium tradition.

(i) Gloria; (ii) Anthems: All things bright and beautiful; For the beauty of the earth; A Gaelic blessing; God be in my head; The Lord bless you and keep you; The Lord is my Shepherd; O clap your hands; Open thou my eyes; Praise ye the Lord; A prayer of St Patrick.

*** Coll. COLCD 100; Cambridge Singers, (i) Philip Jones Brass Ens.; (ii) City of L. Sinfonia, composer.

Rutter has a genuine gift of melody and his use of tonal harmony is individual and never bland. The resplendent Gloria is a three-part piece, and Rutter uses his brass to splendid and often spectacular effect. The anthems are di-verse in style and feeling and, like the Gloria, have strong melodic appeal – the setting of All things bright and beautiful is delightfully spontaneous. It is difficult to imagine the music receiving more persuasive advocacy than under the composer, and the recording is first class in every respect.

3 Musical Fables: (i) Brother Heinrich's Christmas; (ii) The Reluctant Dragon; The Wind in the Willows.

**(*) Coll. COLCD 115; City of L. Sinf.; with (i) Kay, Cambridge Singers, composer; (ii) Baker, King's Singers, Hickox.

Brother Heinrich's Christmas is a musical narrative, with choir, telling the story of how one of the most famous of all carols was introduced late at night by the angels to Brother Heinrich, just in time for it to be included in the monks' Christmas Day service. It is all highly ingenuous but engagingly presented, and should appeal to young listeners who have enjoyed Howard Blake's *The Snowman*. The settings of the two famous Kenneth Grahame stories are no less tunefully communicative and include simulations of pop music of the 1940s (among other derivations), notably a Rodgers-style ballad which sentimentalizes the end of *The Wind in the Willows* episode, after Toad's escape from prison. All the music is expertly sung and played and blends well with the warmly involving narrative, splendidly done by Richard Baker.

Gloria; As the bridegroom to his chosen; Clare benediction; Come down, O Lord divine; Go forth into this world; I my best-beloved's am; Lord make me an instrument of Thy peace; Psalmfest: I will lift up mine eyes; The Lord is my light and my salvation; Praise the Lord O my soul. Te Deum; To everything there is a season.

(N) *** Hyp. CDA 67259. Polyphony, Wallace Collection, City of L. Sinf., Layton.

Framed by superb accounts of the *Gloria* and *Te Deum*, each with a magnificent brass contribution from the Wallace Collection, and given demonstration-standard sound quality, this is one of the most attractive Rutter collections yet. Brass are used again to introduce the first of the three psalm settings taken from the nine-movement *Psalmfest*, followed by *I will lift up my eyes* introduced serenely by woodwind, which has much in common with Vaughan Williams's *Serenade to Music*. The third, *The Lord is my light and my salvation*, opens with a clarinet solo and has one of Rutter's most beguiling melodies. But everywhere here there is melody. *As the bridegroom to his chosen* has a chaste lyrical beauty and *Thy perfect love* soars gently, like one of Rutter's carols. Polyphony sing rapturously, with lovely blended tone, and the warmly persuasive accompaniments are ideally balanced within a pleasingly resonant but not blurring acoustic.

(i) Requiem; (ii) Magnificat.

(M) *** Collegium CSCD 504. (i) Ashton, Dean; (ii) Forbes; Cambridge Singers, City of L. Sinfonia, composer.

(i) Requiem. Cantata Domino; (ii) Cantus. Hymn to the Creator of light; Veni sancta spiritis; What Sweeter Music; (ii)Te Deum.

*** EMI CDC5 56605-2. King's College, Cambridge, Ch., Cleobury; with (i) Saklatvala, Harries, City of L. Sinfonia; (ii) The Wallace Collection.

(i) Requiem. Cantata Domino; Choral fanfare; Draw on sweet night; (ii) Gaelic blessing. God be in my head; Hymn to the Creator of light; My true love hath my heart; (ii) The Lord bless you and keep you. Open thou mine eyes; A prayer for Saint Patrick.

*** Hyp. CDA 66947. Polyphony, Layton; with (i) Manion; (ii) Bournemouth Sinf.

John Rutter's melodic gift, so well illustrated in his carols, is used in the simplest and most direct way to create a small-scale *Requiem* that is as beautiful and satisfying in its English way as the works of Fauré and Duruflé. The penultimate movement, a ripe setting of *The Lord is my Shepherd* with a lovely oboe obbligato, sounds almost like an anglicized Song of the Auvergne. On Collegium Caroline Ashton's performance of the delightful *Pie Jesu* is wonderfully warm and spontaneous, most beautifully recorded on CD, with the equally glorious *Magnificat* setting (see above) making a superb bonus on this mid-priced reissue.

Both the EMI and Hyperion recordings are of high quality and both bring first-class digital sound. On EMI there is something special about hearing this music within the King's acoustic, and using boy trebles in the choir as well as for the two solos. At times there is an ethereal resonance here, although climaxes emerge strongly.

Polyphony uses women's voices (as does Rutter himself) in a choir of 25 voices. The balance is slightly more forward, and the result brings a radiant richness of sound which is hardly less enjoyable. Both choirs complete their programmes with some of Rutter's shorter choral works. Three of them – the memorable *Veni sanctus spiritus*, *What sweeter music* and the *Cantus*, with its resonant brass accompaniment – were written for King's, but both choirs give us the refreshingly lively *Cantate Domino* and the remarkable *Hymn to the Creator of Light* for double chorus, which was written in memory of Herbert Howells but reminds one also of Tavener. The King's programme ends with the exultant *Te Deum*; Polyphony include the lovely *Gaelic blessing* and *Draw on sweet light*, plus Rutter's beautiful setting of the *Benediction*, which introduces one of his friendliest tunes.

RYBA, Jakob Jan (1765–1815)

Czech Christmas Mass; Missa pastoralis.

(BB) *** Naxos 8.554428. Soloists, Czech Madrigalists Ch. & O, Thuri.

The Czech composer, Jakob Jan Ryba, contemporary with Mozart, wrote these *Christmas Masses* – one long, one short – as seasonal cantatas. With only token references to the liturgy, obvious enough in the *Gloria*, they relate the story of the shepherds visiting the baby Jesus to the various sections of the Mass. Understandably, with their simple folk-like tunes and harmonies, they have long been part of traditional Czech celebrations at Christmas, and they here receive winningly fresh and direct performances, atmospherically recorded.

SABATA, Victor de (1892–1967)

Gethsemani; Juventus; La notte di Plàton.

(N) *** Hyp. CDA 67209. LPO, Ceccato.

Most conductors from Furtwängler to Pletnev compose, though few reach the record catalogues. As you might expect, Victor de Sabata shows himself a master of the orchestra and these scores have the opulence and extravagance of Respighi and Strauss. The three pieces recorded here comprise the bulk of his orchestral output. *Juventus* (1919) was championed by Toscanini and its two companions are also virtuoso orchestral showpieces. *La notte di Plàton* (1923) is an evocation of Plato's last feast and its opening portrayal of night is highly imaginative. So is *Gethsemani* (1925), which makes some use of Gregorian melody. The LPO under Aldo Ceccato respond well to these scores, as will those who take the trouble to investigate this impressively recorded disc.

SÆVERUD, Harald (1897–1992)

(i) *Cello Concerto, Op. 7; Symphony No. 8, (Minnesota) Op. 40.*

(N) *** BIS CD 972. (i) Mørk; Stavanger SO, Ruud.

From a position of almost total neglect in the mid-1980s, when he barely had a foothold in the catalogue, Harald Sæverud has at last come in from the cold. This is the fifth volume in the BIS survey of his work. The *Cello Concerto*, first performed in April 1999, dates from the years 1930–31, although the original autograph score does not survive. Sæverud had intended to revise it: a copy on which he was working in 1954 indicates various changes, but he never got round to finishing it. The present score has been prepared by Robert Rennes who collaborated with the composer on the revision of his *Bassoon Concerto*. Although Sæverud writes gratefully for the cello, the invention is less memorable or imaginative than in the *Lucretia* or *Peer Gynt* suites.

The *Eighth Symphony* was commissioned by the State of Minnesota to mark its centenary in 1958. It is full of imaginative things, particularly the mysterious opening pages, and the invention often takes you by surprise. Its four movements all have their rewards though the whole is ultimately less than the sum of its parts. There is little of the concentration or the continuity of thought that we find in the *Sixth*, *Seventh* or *Ninth* symphonies. Nevertheless this is a world well worth exploring and to which you will want to return. Sæverud has a strong personality and creates his own distinctive sound world. In the concerto Truls Mørk is masterly and plays with a glorious tone, and the Stavanger Orchestra does well throughout. The recording is superb.

Peer Gynt Suites Nos. 1 & 2, Op. 48.

*** Finlandia 0630 17675-2. Eikaas, Norwegian R. O, Rasilainen – GRIEG: *Peer Gynt Suites*. ***

This disc contrasts the two scores for Ibsen's *Peer Gynt*: Grieg's romantic setting of 1874 on which he later based his two orchestral suites, and Harald Sæverud's anti-Romantic, altogether rougher, incidental music of 1947. The Norwegian Radio Orchestra under their Finnish conductor, Ari Rasilainen, give a stimulating account of the piece, every bit as enjoyable and full of character as the Stavanger account on BIS listed below. Excellent recording.

Symphony No. 6 (Sinfonia dolorosa), Op. 19; Galdreslåtten, Op. 20; Kjæmpevise-slåtten, Op. 22; Peer Gynt Suites Nos. 1 & 2.

*** BIS CD 762. Stavanger SO, Dmitriev.

The *Sixth Symphony* (*Sinfonia dolorosa*) is a short but intense piece from the war years, dedicated to a close friend who perished in the resistance, and the *Kjæmpevise-slåtten* ('Ballad of Revolt') comes from the same years. It is an inspiriting work, an outraged, combative reaction to the sight of the Nazi occupation barracks near his Bergen home. The *Peer Gynt* music, written for a post-war production of Ibsen's play, could not be further removed from Grieg's celebrated score. It is earthy and rambunctious and it makes Grieg sound positively genteel. So, too, does the delightful, inventive and wholly original *Galdreslåtten*. Eminently satisfactory performances from the Stavanger orchestra under Alexander Dmitriev, brought vividly to life by the BIS recording team.

Symphony No. 7 (Salme), Op. 27; (i) Bassoon Concerto, Op. 44. Lucretia (suite), Op. 10.

*** BIS CD 822 (i) Rønnes; Stavanger SO, Dmitriev.

The one-movement *Seventh* (1945) is the last of Sæverud's wartime symphonies, *Salme-symfoni*, a deeply-felt work, a hymn of thanksgiving for peace. It has never sounded better than it does in this recording. The *Lucretia Suite* derives from the incidental music Sæverud wrote in 1936 for André Obey's play. Much of it is highly imaginative (the evocation of night in the fourth movement, for example) and the charming middle movement, *Lucretia Sleeping*. The second movement portrays Lucretia spinning. The *Bassoon Concerto* (1965) was revised towards the end of his long life in collaboration with Robert Rønnes, the soloist here. Absolutely first-class performances and recordings.

Symphony No. 9, Op. 45; (i) Piano Concerto, Op. 31. Fanfare & Hymn, Op. 48.

*** BIS CD 962. Stavanger SO, Dmitriev (i) with Ogawa.

Alexander Dmitriev and the Stavanger Orchestra are very persuasive in the *Ninth Symphony*. There is a strong sense of the Norwegian landscape here and the BIS recording conveys it all with striking clarity and presence. The *Piano Concerto* of 1950 is a delightful piece, full of quirky, robust humour. It is a work that haunts and fascinates, and the farmyard noises of the finale together with the strongly atmospheric slow movement linger in the memory. Norika Ogawa is an alert, sensitive player who has the measure of this piece, and Alexander Dmitriev and the Stavanger Orchestra are eminently supportive. The short *Fanfare and Hymn* was commissioned by the City of Bergen to celebrate its 900th anniversary. The sound is in the demonstration bracket.

SAINTE-COLOMBE (died c . 1700)

Concerts à deux violes: Bourrasque; La Dubois; La Raporté; Le Retour; Tombeau 'les regrets'.

(B) *** Astrée E 9968. Savall, Kuijken.

Concerts à deux violes: La Conférence; Dalain; Le Figuré; La Rougeville; Le Tendre.

*** Astrée Audivis E 8743. Savall, Kuijken.

Le Retour; Tombeau 'les regrets'.

*** Naxos 8.550750. Spectre de la Rose – MARAIS: *Tombeau pour M. de Sainte-Colombe etc.* ***

The success of the film (*Tous les matins du monde*) about this reclusive composer and his relationship with his pupil,

Marin Marais, has led to the soundtrack becoming a best-seller. However, this enterprising and inexpensive Naxos recital includes the 'hits' from the film. The two Saint-Colombe works included are austerely but certainly touchingly played by a fresh-sounding 'authentic' group led by Alison Crum (viola da gamba) and Marie Knight (baroque violin). The Naxos recording is vivid, but its forward balance means that for a realistic effect a modest setting of the volume control should be chosen.

Those who are then tempted to explore the music of Saint-Colombe further might invest in the pair of excellent Audivis CDs featuring Jordi Savall, who was associated with the film. They are performed by artists who have this music in their bones, and the playing is more subtle and has even greater emotional depth. The two CDs are excellently recorded and are available separately the first at bargain price; the second duplicates nothing on the Naxos CD.

SAINT-SAËNS, Camille (1835–1921)

(i) *Africa Fantasy for Piano & Orchestra, Op. 89. Ascanio: Valse-finale; Parysatis: Airs de ballet. Sarabande et Rigaudon, Op. 93; Suite algérienne, Op. 60: Marche militaire française.* (ii) *Tarantelle for Flute, Clarinet & Orchestra, Op. 6;* (iii) *Messe de Requiem, Op. 54.*

(M) **(*) Cala CACD 1015. LPO, Simon, with (i) Mok; (ii) Milan, Campbell; (iii) Olafimihan, Wyn-Rogers, Roden, Kirkbride, Hertfordshire Ch., Harlow Ch., East London Ch.

La jota aragonesa, Op. 64; (i) *La Muse et le poète. La Princesse jaune: Overture;* (ii) *Symphony No. 3 in C min.;* (iii) *Danse macabre (original vocal version). Grande fantaisie on Themes from Samson et Dalila (arr. Luigini).*

(M) ** Cala CACD 1016. LPO, Simon, with (i) Chase, Truman; (ii) O'Donnell; (iii) Roden.

Geoffrey Simon is an amiably persuasive advocate of these Saint-Saëns novelties and his affectionate approach emphasizes the music's surface elegance. The resonant acoustics of All Hallows Church, Gospel Oak, cast a warm glow over the proceedings, and detail could be sharper. However, the nicely scored *Airs de ballet*, which come from the incidental music for *Parysatis*, are certainly enticing. But it is the lively and charming *Tarantelle* for flute, clarinet and orchestra which is the vivacious highlight of the first CD. It is winningly played by Susan Milan and James Campbell. The rich sonority of the sound suits the melodically catchy *Marche militaire française*, with its resplendent brass, but the exotically oriental *Africa Fantasy for Piano and Orchestra* loses some of its point and glitter when the acoustic is so resonant. Even so, the performance is full of charm, and Gwendolyn Mok plays with flair. The *Messe de Requiem* is a real find, even if here the focus of the choral sound needs to be sharper. Pretty good choral singing, a well-matched team of soloists, and the recording gives the work a fine, sonorous impact, even if more bite is needed.

The undoubted highlight of the second disc is the fascinating original vocal version of *Danse macabre*, very much shorter than the familiar tone-poem. The effect is semi-operatic, interrupted by the cock-crow. *La Muse et le poète*

is an extended duo for violin and cello with orchestra. It opens dreamily, but as it becomes more passionate it also becomes technically demanding. Stephanie Chase and, especially, the cellist Robert Truman are good if not distinctive soloists. The *Jota aragonesa* is very like the Glinka fantasy and needs a recording with more glitter. The *Grande Fantaisie on Samson et Dalila* arranged by Luigini is rather inflated but is not helped by Geoffrey Simon's very leisurely tempo for *Softly Awakes My Heart*, even though there is some lovely warm string-playing. The *Overture: La Princesse jaune* is presented with real charm but Geoffrey Simon then chooses to end his second CD with the *Organ Symphony* – an agreeable account, but no more than that.

Carnival of the Animals.

(M) *** Teldec 4509 97445-2. Güher and Süher Pekinel, French R. PO, Janowski – POULENC: *Double Piano Concerto.* ***

(B)*** Ph. (ADD) Virtuoso 462 938-2. Villa, Jennings, Pittsburgh SO, Previn – RAVEL: *Ma Mère l'Oye* (complete) (with DUKAS: *L'Apprenti sorcier;* Rotterdam PO, Zinman ***).

(B) *** CfP (ADD) CD-CFP 4086. Katin, Fowke, SNO, Gibson – BIZET: *Jeux d'enfants;* RAVEL: *Ma Mère l'Oye.* ***

(BB) *** ASV (ADD) CDQS 6017. Goldstone, Brown, RPO, Hughes – PROKOFIEV: *Peter.* ***

Güher and Süher Pekinel make a sparklingly spontaneous contribution to Saint-Saëns's zoological fantasy, readily dominating the performance with their scintillating pianism. Janowski and the French Radio Orchestra provide admirable support, and Saint-Saëns's portrait gallery comes vividly and wittily to life. The performance is beautifully recorded and naturally balanced within an attractively warm ambience; although the playing time is short, this mid-priced CD remains highly recommendable.

Previn's version makes a ready alternative. The music is played with infectious rhythmic spring and great refinement. It is a mark of the finesse of this performance – which has plenty of bite and vigour, as well as polish – that the great cello solo of *Le Cygne* is so naturally presented. Fine contributions too from the two pianists, although their image is rather bass-orientated, within a warmly atmospheric recording.

On CfP the solo pianists, Peter Katin and Philip Fowke, enter fully into the spirit of the occasion, with Gibson directing his Scottish players with affectionate, unforced geniality. The couplings are attractive and the CD transfer confirms the vivid colourfulness and presence of the mid-1970s recording.

The two pianists on ASV also play with point and style, and the accompaniment has both spirit and spontaneity. *The Swan* is perhaps a trifle self-effacing, but otherwise this is very enjoyable, the humour appreciated without being underlined. The recording is excellent, and this makes a good super-bargain CD recommendation.

Carnival of the Animals (with narration).

(BB) **(*) Naxos 8.554463. Morris (nar.), Slovak RSO, Lenárd – DUKAS: *L'Apprenti sorcier;* RAVEL: *Ma Mère l'Oye.*

This Naxos collection is clearly aimed at younger children, and many adults could find Johnny Morris's very personal (and often eccentric) descriptions and rhymes, which adorn this performance, too much to take. But the playing of the Slovak orchestra, with a persuasively spontaneous contribution from the two anonymous pianists, is most attractive. If Morris's friendly delivery and the lazy timing of his own text bring children to the music, all to the good, especially if they remember the musical association past childhood. They will surely not mind Morris's singing along in a quavery fashion with the Tortoise, and in the Aquarium, even though he drowns the music.

'The Essential Saint-Saëns': (i) *Carnival of the Animals;* (ii) *Piano Concerto No. 2 in G min., Op. 22;* (iii) *Violin Concerto No. 3 in B min., Op. 61;* (iv) *Danse macabre, Op. 40;* (v) *Havanaise, Op. 83; Introduction & rondo capriccioso, Op. 28;* (vi) *Symphony No. 3 in C min. (Organ), Op. 78. Samson et Dalila:* (vii) *Air et danse bacchanale;* (viii) *Mon coeur s'ouvre à ta voix.*

(B) **(*) Double Decca (ADD) 444 552-2 (2). (i) Ortiz; (i; ii) Rogé; (iii) Bell; (v) Chung; (vi) Priest; (viii) Horne; (i) L. Sinf.; (ii; v) RPO; (iii; vii) Montreal SO; (iv) Philh. O; (i–v; vii) cond. Dutoit; (vi) LAPO, Mehta.

(i) *Carnival of the Animals;* (ii) *Le Cygne; Piano Concertos Nos.* (iii) *2;* (iv) *4 in C min., Op. 44;* (v) *Violin Concerto No. 3;* (vi) *Danse macabre;* (v) *Introduction & rondo capriccioso;* (vii) *Symphony No. 3 in C min. (Organ).*

(B) **(*) Ph. Duo (ADD) 442 608-2 (2). (i) Villa, Jennings, Pittsburgh SO, Previn; (ii) Gendron, Gallion; (iii) Davidovich, Concg. O, Järvi; (iv) Campanella, Monte Carlo Op. O, Ceccato; (v) Szeryng, Monte Carlo Op. O, Remoortel; (vi) Concg. O, Haitink; (vii) Chorzempa, Rotterdam PO, Edo de Waart.

Mehta's Los Angeles account of the *Third Symphony* is among the more recommendable versions of this much-recorded work, for he draws a well-disciplined and exuberant response from all departments of the orchestra. Joshua Bell's performance of the *Violin Concerto* is very attractive indeed: the pianissimo opening is full of atmosphere and the *Andantino* has a pleasingly lyrical simplicity. The disappointment is Dutoit's *Carnival of the Animals* – in a crisp, clean, digital recording with very bright sound – which is lacking characterization and charm. *The Swan* is played in a very matter-of-fact way. Dutoit shows himself in a better light in his deft account of the *Danse macabre,* while Kwung Wha Chung is on top form, playing with flair in both the famous violin showpieces. Marilyn Horne's ripe characterization of Saint-Saëns's most famous aria, 'Softly awakes my heart', will not disappoint, and nor will the excerpts from *Samson et Dalila.* Pascal Rogé's account of the favourite Saint-Saëns *Second Piano Concerto* is second to none.

The inexpensive Duo collection is described as 'The Best of Saint-Saëns'. Notable here is Previn's 1980 *Carnival of the Animals,* as fine as almost any available (see above). (Philips have also included a second performance of *Le Cygne* , by the inestimable Maurice Gendron.) Bella Davidovich gives a most sympathetic account of the *G minor Piano Concerto*

and draws pleasing tone-quality from the instrument, even if she lacks the last degree of brilliance and flair. She has the advantage of excellent orchestral support from the Concertgebouw Orchestra, who also give a lively account of the *Danse macabre* under Haitink. In the *C minor Concerto* (which is analogue) the effect is harder, partly because Michele Campanella is a more boldly extrovert soloist; but this account has undoubted vitality and no lack of *espressivo.* Henryk Szeryng gives clean, immaculate performances of the *B minor Violin Concerto* and the *Introduction and Rondo capriccioso.* His approach is aristocratic rather than seductive. The contribution of the Monte Carlo orchestra is adequate. De Waart's 1976 recording of the *Organ Symphony* is not among the most exciting versions available but, with polished orchestral playing and refined Philips sound, it is certainly enjoyable.

(i) *Carnival of the Animals;* (ii) *Danse macabre, Op. 40; Suite algérienne, Op. 60: Marche militaire française. Samson et Dalila: Bacchanale.* (ii; iii) *Symphony No. 3 in C min., Op. 78.*

(M) *** Sony (ADD) SBK 47655. (i) Entremont, Gaby Casadesus, Pasquier, Tortelier, Caussé, Ma, Lauridon, Marion, Arrignon, Cals, Cerutti; (ii) Phd. O, Ormandy; (iii) with E. Power Biggs.

(i) *Carnival of the Animals;* (ii) *Danse macabre;* (iii) *Symphony No. 3;* (iv) *Wedding-Cake* (caprice-valse for piano and orchestra), *Op. 76.*

**(*) ASV Dig CDDCA 665. (i) Guillermo Salvador Snr & Jnr, Mexico City PO; (ii) Mexicana State SO; (iii) Rawsthorne, LPO; (iv) Osorio, RPO; Bátiz.

It would be churlish to bracket the third star for the generous Sony collection because the opening of the *Carnival of the Animals,* performed in its original chamber version, is a bit lacklustre. The ear adjusts to the rather dry effect. It is a starry cast: Yo-Yo Ma personifies *The Swan* gently and gracefully. Ormandy and his splendid orchestra play the other orchestral lollipops with fine panache. No complaint about the 1962 sound in the *Symphony.* The performance is fresh and vigorous, with Ormandy at his most involved.

The *Carnival of the Animals* and *Danse macabre* also have plenty of genial vitality on ASV but are less strong on finesse, and the forwardly balanced recording adds to the robust feeling. Jorge Federico Osorio, however, dispatches the charming *Wedding-Cake caprice-valse* with a winning sparkle. Bátiz's version of the spectacular *Organ Symphony* was the first digital success for this work. The orchestral playing is exhilarating in its energy, while the organ entry is an impressive moment and the sense of spectacle persists in the closing pages.

Cello Concertos Nos. 1 in A min., Op. 33; 2 in D min., Op. 119; Allegro appassionato in B min., Op. 43; Suite in D min., Op. 16; Carnival of the Animals: The Swan (orch. Vidal).

(BB) **(*) Naxos 8.553039. Kliegel, Bournemouth Sinf., Monnard.

Maria Kliegel proves a most sympathetic soloist, technically immaculate, undeterred even by the relatively ungrateful writing for the cello in the *Second Concerto*, so much less striking a work than No. 1. It is good to have the early *Suite*, a colourful collection of genre pieces, and the dashing *Allegro appassionato*, both originally with piano accompaniment and here arranged by the composer himself. Saint-Saëns's most celebrated cello piece, *The Swan*, makes an attractive supplement, played in an orchestral arrangement by Paul Vidal, which adds strings to the usual harp accompaniment.

Cello Concerto No. 1 in A min., Op. 33.

*** EMI CDC5 56126-2. Han-Na Chang, LSO, Rostropovich – BRUCH: *Kol Nidrei* ***; FAURE: *Elégie* ***; TCHAIKOVSKY *Rococo Variations.* *** ✪

(N) *** Teldec 8573-85340-2. Du Pré, Phd. O, Barenboim – DVORAK: *Cello Concerto.* ***

*** ASV CDDCA 867. Rolland, BBC PO, Varga – LALO: *Cello Concerto in D min.;* MASSENET: *Fantaisie.* ***

(B) *** Decca 448 712-2. Harrell, Cleveland O, Marriner – LALO; SCHUMANN: *Concertos.* ***

(M) *** DG (ADD) 457 761-2. Fournier, LOP, Martinon – BLOCH: *Schelomo;* BRUCH: *Kol Nidrei;* LALO: *Cello Concerto.* ***

(B) *** DG (ADD) 431 166-2. Schiff, New Philh. O, Mackerras – FAURE: *Elégie;* LALO: *Cello Concerto.* ***

(M) *** Mercury (IMS) (ADD) 432 010-2. Starker, LSO, Dorati – LALO: *Concerto* **(*); SCHUMANN: *Concerto.* ***

(i) *Cello Concerto No. 1, Op. 33;* (ii) *The Swan;* (iii) *Allegro appassionato, Op. 43; Cello Sonata No. 1, Op. 32; Chant saphique, Op. 91; Gavotte, Op. posth.; Romances Nos. 1 in F, Op. 36; 2 in D, Op. 51;* (iv) *Prière* (for cello & organ).

*** RCA 09026 61678-2. Isserlis; (i) LSO, Tilson Thomas; (ii) Tilson Thomas, Dudley Moore; (iii) Devoyon; (iv) Grier.

(i) *Cello Concerto No. 1; Suite, Op. 16;* (ii) *Allegro appassionato, Op. 43; Carnival of the Animals: The Swan Romance No. 1 in F; Cello Sonata No. 1.*

** DG 457 599-2. Maisky, (i) Orpheus CO; (ii) Hovora.

Han-Na Chang's delicacy of feeling, natural sense of line and wide range of dynamic show an instinctive musicianship and a mastery of her instrument that recall the young Menuhin, while the sophistication of the performance is extraordinarily mature, helped in no small part by Rostropovich's always supportive accompaniment and the superb playing of the LSO. The EMI Abbey Road recording is first class in every way and beautifully balanced.

The Saint-Saëns, recorded live in Philadelphia in 1971, makes a good coupling for du Pré's warmly expressive account of the Dvořák with Celibidache. Though this came right at the end of du Pré's playing career, before the onset of multiple sclerosis, the performance is typically magnetic in its high-powered intensity, full of manic energy, faster and wilder than her studio account, if not quite so cleanly recorded.

Sophie Rolland takes its technical hurdles in her effortless stride and is very well supported by the BBC Philharmonic under Gilbert Varga. Perhaps their opening is marginally too fast for an *Allegro non troppo*, but the performance is in every respect a highly enjoyable one. The excellence of the BBC/ASV recording makes for a strong recommendation.

Harrell's reading of the Saint-Saëns, altogether more extrovert than Yo-Yo Ma's, makes light of any idea that this composer always works on a small scale. The opening is positively epic, and the rest of the performance is just as compelling, with the minuet-like *Allegretto* crisply neoclassical. The addition of the Lalo *Concerto* makes this reissue very competitive.

Steven Isserlis's account of the *Cello Concerto in A minor* is among the best on record. Of particular interest too is the *Cello Sonata No. 1 in C minor*, composed in the same year, in which he is accompanied with elegance and finesse by Pascal Devoyon. Isserlis himself plays with the musicianship and virtuosity one has come to expect from him. Most of the remaining pieces are both worthwhile and entertaining, particularly the *Allegro appassionato*. The *Prière*, Op. 159, for cello and organ, is a small but affecting addition to the Saint-Saëns discography. The recorded sound is very good indeed.

Fournier brings his customary nobility to the concerto, and is well supported by Martinon, who provides stylish support with the Lamoureux Orchestra. The recording from 1960 has never sounded better than on this new DG Originals transfer, and the collection is excellent in every way.

Schiff gives an eloquent account of this concerto as any available. He sparks off an enthusiastic response from Mackerras, and the recorded sound and balance are excellent. At bargain price, this deserves the strongest recommendation.

Starker plays the Saint-Saëns *A minor* with charm and grace, and Dorati provides first-class support. The 1964 recording comes up amazingly well and is excellently (and naturally) balanced.

Mischa Maisky plays with great virtuosity and brings splendid vitality as well as brilliance to the quicker movements of the *A minor Concerto*. But for all his virtuosity and beauty of tone, expressive exaggeration is not alien to his nature and he is prone to emote heavily at the slightest pretext. Of course, he makes a glorious sound and the Orpheus Chamber Orchestra play with splendid attack. One longs for the finesse and understatement of a Fournier.

(i) *Cello Concerto No. 1;* (ii) *Piano Concerto No. 2;* (iii) *Violin Concerto No. 3.*

✪ (M) *** Sony SMK 66935. (i) Ma, O Nat. de France, Maazel; (ii) Cécile Licad, LPO, Previn; (iii) Lin, Philh. O, Tilson Thomas.

Three outstanding performances from the early 1980s are admirably linked together in this highly desirable CBS midprice reissue. Yo-Yo Ma's performance of the *Cello Concerto* is distinguished by fine sensitivity and beautiful tone, while Cécile Licad and the LPO under Previn turn in an eminently satisfactory reading of the *G minor Piano Concerto* that has the requisite delicacy in the Scherzo and seriousness elsewhere. Cho-Liang Lin's account of the *B minor Violin Concerto* with the Philharmonia Orchestra and Michael Tilson Thomas is exhilarating and thrilling; indeed, this is the kind of performance that prompts one to burst into applause; his version is arguably the finest to have appeared for years.

Cello Concerto No. 2, Op. 119; La Muse et le poète, Op. 132; Cello Sonata; Romance, Op. 67.

(N) *** RCA 09026 68928-2. Isserlis, Bell, NDR SO, Hamburg, Eschenbach; or Devoyon.

The *Second Cello Concerto* and *Sonata* come from the end of the composer's long career, not so hauntingly lyrical as the *First*, but equally strong and purposeful. With Isserlis masterly in bringing rarities back to life, they draw dedicated playing from him, full of high contrasts, so that the *Sonata* here rivals Brahms's *Second* in heroic power and scale. Loveliest of all is the concertante piece, *La Muse et le poète*, inspired by de Musset's *La Nuit de mai*, a haunting piece for violin (Joshua Bell), cello and orchestra, which has an affecting directness of utterance. Warmly sympathetic playing too from the violinist, Joshua Bell, and the pianist, Pierre Devoyon.

Piano Concertos Nos. 1 in D, Op. 17; 2 in G min., Op. 22; 3 in E flat, Op. 29; 4 in C min., Op. 44; 5 in F ('Egyptian').

(B) *** Double Decca (ADD) 443 865-2 (2); 443 865-4. Rogé, Philh. O, RPO or LPO, Dutoit.

(B) *** EMI (ADD) CZS5 69258-2 (2). Ciccolini, O de Paris, Serge Baudo.

Piano Concertos Nos. 1–5; Africa Fantaisie, Op. 89; Wedding-Cake Caprice-valse, Op. 76.

✹ *** Hyp. CDA 67331/2 (2). Hough, CBSO, Oramo (with *Allegro appassionato; Rhapsodie d'Auvergne*).

(B) *** EMI double fforte CZS5 73356-2 (2). Collard, RPO, Previn.

(i) *Piano Concertos Nos. 1–5;* (ii) *Septet in E flat, Op. 65.*

(B) (***) EMI mono CZS5 69470-2 (2). Darré, with (i) French Nat. RO, Fourestier; (ii) Delmotte, Logerot, Pascal Qt.

Marvellous performances from Stephen Hough, full of joy, vigour and sparkle, with Oramo and the CBSO accompanying spiritedly and with the lightest touch. The recording is in the demonstration bracket and this Hyperion set includes no fewer than four encores. An easy first choice.

As always with Collard there is splendid character and a dazzling technique. He brings panache and virtuosity to these concertos, as well as impressive poetic feeling. At one point in the *Fifth (Egyptian) Concerto* Collard exploits Saint-Saëns's genius in manipulating the piano to suggest Eastern sonorities, and makes his instrument sound exactly like an Arab *qunan* or zither. Throughout, Previn and the Royal Philharmonic Orchestra are sensitive accompanists.

Although in many respects allegiance to Pascal Rogé on Decca remains strong, Collard with his greater dynamic range and authority often makes even more of this music. The digital sound is very good too.

Pascal Rogé brings delicacy, virtuosity and sparkle to the piano part and he receives expert support from the various London orchestras under Dutoit. Altogether delicious playing and excellent piano-sound from Decca, who secure a most realistic balance.

The performances from Ciccolini and Baudo on EMI are admirably spirited and emerge freshly on CD. The vibrant,

at times slightly brash, 1970 sound gives the music-making strong character and projection.

Jeanne-Marie Darré's recordings of the Saint-Saëns *Piano Concertos* enjoy classic status. The performances come from the 1950s and are wonderfully high-spirited and vivacious. Both in the concertos and in the delightful *Septet*, in which Roger Delmotte is the trumpeter, she sparkles and glitters. Well worth considering even if you have a good modern set, for the sound is very good.

(ii) *Piano Concertos Nos. 1 in D, Op. 17; 2 in G min., Op. 22;* (i) *Orchestral Suite in D, Op. 49.*

(N) *** BIS CD 1040. (i) Tapiola Sinf., Kantorow; (ii) with Ogawa.

BIS couples the *First* and *Second* piano concertos, which are played with great charm and grace by Norika Ogawa and the Tapiola Sinfonietta under Jean-Jacques Kantorow. As a make-weight it has added the *Suite in D major, Op. 49*, which was originally conceived for the harmonium and later arranged for orchestra. It is all attractive and engaging and excellently recorded too. Ms Ogawa's many admirers can proceed with confidence. All the same it is well worth remembering that you can get all five Saint-Saëns piano concertos for the same money in Pascal Rogé's elegant and refreshing performances on Decca.

Piano Concerto No. 2 in G min., Op. 22.

(N) (M) *** RCA (ADD) 09026 63053-2. Rubinstein, Symphony of the Air, Wallenstein – LISZT: *Concerto No. 1;* SCHUMANN: *Concerto.* **(*)

(M) *** RCA (ADD) 09026 63070-2. Rubinstein, Phd. O, Ormandy – FALLA: *Nights in the Gardens of Spain* etc. **(*); FRANCK: *Symphonic Variations for Piano & Orchestra.* ***

(***) Testament mono SBT 1029. Gilels, Paris Conservatoire O, Cluytens (with SHOSTAKOVICH: *Prelude & Fugue in D, Op. 87/5)* – RACHMANINOV: *Piano Concerto No. 3.* (***)

(B) **(*) BMG/Melodiya (ADD) 74321 40721-2. Grigory Sokolov, USSR SO, Neeme Järvi – TCHAIKOVSKY: *Piano Concerto No. 1.* **(*)

(M) ** Chan. 6621 (2). Margalit, LSO, Thompson (with MENDELSSOHN: *Capriccio brillant* **) – BRAHMS: *Concerto No. 1;* SCHUMANN: *Concerto.* **

Rubinstein, understandably, had a soft spot for the Saint-Saëns *Second Piano Concerto*. He chose it for his debut in Berlin in 1900 and played it finally on his last TV show in 1979. Rubinstein's secret is that, though he appears at times (especially in the *Toccata* finale) to be attacking the music, his phrasing is full of little fluctuations so that his playing never sounds stilted.

Of these two recordings the earlier 1958 account with Wallenstein has marginally the greater sparkle. The newer recording with Ormandy is technically rather more satisfactory and has a warmer acoustic, although the earlier version still sounds pretty good in its current remastering. The *Scherzo* scintillates in both, so you can safely choose according to preferred couplings.

Gilels's celebrated account of the Saint-Saëns *G minor*

Concerto comes from 1954 and is masterly in every respect. Its delicacy and refinement still come across in spite of the limitations of the recording, and Gilels gets marvellous support from the Paris orchestra under André Cluytens. Excellent transfers.

Grigory Sokolov was a mere sixteen when he gave his dazzling account of the Saint-Saëns *G minor Concerto*, with which he won the Tchaikovsky Piano Competition in 1966. A remarkable response from both the young soloist and from the USSR Symphony Orchestra and Neeme Järvi. The recording may be pretty rough-and-ready but what playing!

Israela Margalit's version of the concerto has no want of abandon, but it lacks the aristocratic distinction that Rubinstein brings to it. The recording is resonant, but the piano is rather forward in the rural picture. The two-CD format does not enhance the attractions of this reissue.

Piano Concertos Nos. 2 in G min.; 4, Op. 44.

(BB) **(*) Naxos 8.550334. Biret, Philh. O, James Loughran.

Idil Biret makes rather heavy weather of the opening of the *G minor Concerto* and her performance sounds just a little portentous and wanting in charm, though the scherzo is played with delicacy and character. The accompaniment by the Philharmonia Orchestra under James Loughran is very good and the recording is very good indeed. There are performances of greater subtlety to be had – albeit not at this price.

Violin Concertos Nos. 1 in A, Op. 20; 2 in C, Op. 58; 3 in B min., Op. 61; Caprice andalou, Op. 122; Le Déluge, Op. 45: Prélude. Havanaise, Op. 83; Introduction & Rondo capriccioso, Op. 28; Morceau de concert, Op. 62; Romances: in D, Op. 37; in C, Op. 48; (i) La Muse et le poète, Op. 132. (Also includes: YSAŸE: Caprice d'après l'étude en forme de valse, Op. 52/6.)

(BB) **(*) EMI (ADD) CZS5 72001-2 (2). Hoelscher, New Philh. O, Dervaux; (i) with Kirshbaum.

This two-CD box collects all Saint-Saëns's music for violin and orchestra (with a short bonus from Ysaÿe) in performances of excellent quality. Ulf Hoelscher is an extremely accomplished soloist who plays with artistry as well as virtuosity. The *Second Concerto* has a most attractive *Andante* and a catchy *Allegro scherzando* finale, while the first of the two *Romances* deserves to be much better known. The *Morceau de concert* is most engaging, as is the relatively ambitious extended duo concertante piece, *La Muse et le poète*, in which Hoelscher is admirably partnered by Ralph Kirshbaum, seems much more substantial here than usual. In this EMI set Pierre Dervaux directs excellent accompaniments, and the recording (made at Abbey Road in 1977) is basically of excellent quality even though the forward balance of the soloist does not enhance Hoelscher's timbre in the upper range.

Violin Concertos Nos. 1–3.

*** Hyp. CDA 67074. Graffin, BBC Scottish SO, Brabbins.

Violin Concertos Nos. (i) 1; (ii) 3; (iii) Havanaise; Introduction & rondo capriccioso.

(M) *** Decca (ADD) 460 008-2. Kyung Wha Chung, (i) Montreal SO, Dutoit; (ii) LSO, Lawrence Foster; (iii) RPO, Dutoit.

Violin Concerto No. 1; Havanaise in E, Op. 83; Introduction & rondo capriccioso, Op. 28; Morceau de concert, Op. 62; Romance in C, Op. 48; Sarabande, Op. 93/1.

*** BIS CD 860. Kantorow, Tapiola Sinf.

Though Saint-Saëns's *Third Concerto* is relatively well known, with its charming central *Andantino* set between two bravura movements, and the *First Concerto*, in a single movement, has not been neglected either, the *Second Concerto* is the earliest and longest, yet arguably the most memorable – full of the youthful exuberance of a 23-year-old. The French violinist Philippe Graffin, with, rich, firm tone, gives performances full of temperament, warmly supported by Martyn Brabbins and the BBC Scottish Symphony Orchestra, and the recording cannot be faulted.

Kyung Wha Chung presents Saint-Saëns's *First Violin Concerto* delightfully and receives admirable support from Dutoit. She gives a passionate account of the *B minor Concerto*, so intense that even a sceptical listener will find it hard not to be convinced that this is a great work. Such music needs this kind of advocacy, and Miss Chung is splendidly backed up by the LSO under Lawrence Foster. The 1975 analogue recording is slightly less flattering than the 1980 digital sound in Montreal, but it remains full and clear.

It is a pleasure also to welcome this BIS collection which brings the short and early *First Violin Concerto* with such rightly popular display pieces as the *Introduction and Rondo capriccioso* and the *Havanaise*. Everything is expertly played and Kantorow has the right blend of panache and spontaneity. First-class sound, as one expects from this source.

Violin Concerto No. 3 in B min., Op. 61.

(M) *** DG 445 549-2. Perlman, O de Paris, Barenboim – LALO: *Symphonie espagnole*; BERLIOZ: *Rêverie et caprice*. ***

*** DG 429 786-2. Shaham, NYPO, Sinopoli – PAGANINI: *Concerto No. 1*. ***

*** ASV CDDCA 680. Xue Wei, Philh. O, Bakels – BRUCH: *Concerto No. 1*. ***

Violin Concerto No. 3; Havanaise; Introduction & Rondo capriccioso.

(B) **(*) Ph. (ADD) 420 887-2. Szeryng, Monte Carlo Op. O, Remoortel – RAVEL: *Tzigane*. **(*)

(i) Violin Concerto No. 3; (ii) Introduction & rondo capriccioso, Op. 28.

(M) *** Sony (ADD) SM2K 64501 (2). Stern, with (i) O de Paris, Barenboim; (ii) Philadelphia O, Ormandy (with Concert ***).

On DG, Perlman achieves a fine partnership with Barenboim, in a performance that is both tender and strong, while Perlman's verve and dash in the finale are dazzling. The forward balance is understandable in this work, but orchestral detail could at times be sharper. The Berlioz *Rêverie et caprice* has been added for this reissue.

One only has to sample the delectable way Gil Shaham presents the enchanting *Barcarolle*, which forms the principal theme of Saint-Saëns's *Andante*, to discover the distinction of his performance, which balances elegant *espressivo* with great dash and fire: neither the soloist nor the conductor lets even the slightest suspicion of routine into a reading which dazzles and charms in equal measure. The recording is first class.

Stern's violin is for once balanced naturally against the orchestra, and paradoxically it gives his splendid performance of the Saint-Saëns more strength than close-up sound does. Though this is not as persuasively affectionate as with Gil Shaham, it remains among the finest versions, and the *Introduction and Rondo capriccioso* is dazzling.

Xue Wei's account is full of flair from the very first entry onwards. The orchestral accompaniment is strongly characterized as well, while the soloist creates an ideal mixture of ruminative lyricism and dash, especially in the slow movement. The sound is vivid, even if the balance, within a church acoustic, seems artificially contrived.

Clean and immaculate performances from Szeryng, whose approach is aristocratic rather than indulgent. The orchestral contribution, adequate rather than distinguished, is not helped by the balance of the recording, which spotlights the violin and does not add a great deal of lustre to the accompaniment. However, the present remastering has improved the orchestral presence while the ambience remains pleasing.

Danse macabre, Op. 40; (i) Havanaise; Introduction & rondo capriccioso. La Jeunesse d'Hercule, Op. 50; Marche héroïque, Op. 34; Phaéton, Op. 39; Le Rouet d'Omphale, Op. 31.

(M) *** Decca (ADD) 425 021-2. (i) Kyung Wha Chung, RPO; Philh. O; Dutoit.

The symphonic poems are beautifully played, and the 1979 Kingsway Hall recording lends the appropriate atmosphere. Charles Dutoit shows himself an admirably sensitive exponent, revelling in the composer's craftsmanship and revealing much delightful orchestral detail in the manner of a Beecham. Decca have now added Kyung Wha Chung's equally charismatic and individual 1977 accounts of what are perhaps the two most inspired short display-pieces for violin and orchestra in the repertoire.

Danse macabre; Le Rouet d'Omphale.

(M) *** Decca (ADD) 448 571-2. Paris Conservatoire O, Martinon – BIZET: *Jeux d'enfants* ***; BERLIOZ: *Overtures* **(*); IBERT: *Divertissement.* ***

Martinon's are delightful, Beechamesque performances, offering excellent orchestral playing and a characteristic sense of delicacy and style. The 1960 recording is excellent, and this collection of French music, reissued in Decca's 'Classic Sound' series, is well worth exploring.

Havanaise, Op. 83.

(M) *** EMI (ADD) CDM5 66058-2. Perlman, O de Paris, Barenboim – RAVEL: *Tzigane*; VIEUXTEMPS: *Violin Concertos Nos. 4 & 5.* ***

Havanaise; Introduction & Rondo capriccioso Op. 28.

*** EMI CDC7 47725-2. Perlman, O de Paris, Martinon – CHAUSSON: *Poème*; RAVEL: *Tzigane.* ***

(M) (***) RCA mono 09026 61753-2. Heifetz, RCA Victor SO, Steinberg – CHAUSSON: *Poème* **(*); LALO: *Symphonie espagnole* **(*)); SARASATE: *Zigeunerweisen.* (***)

(N) (BB) *** Australian Decca Eloquence (ADD) 461 369-2. Ricci, LSO, Gamba – BRUCH; MENDELSSOHN: *Violin Concertos.* **(*)

**(*) EMI CDC5 55026-2. Sarah Chang, Phd. O, Sawallisch – PAGANINI: *Violin Concerto No. 1.* **(*)

Perlman plays these Saint-Saëns warhorses with splendid panache and virtuosity on EMI; his tone and control of colour in the *Havanaise* are ravishing. The digital remastering brings Perlman's gorgeous fiddling right into the room, at the expense of a touch of aggressiveness when the orchestra lets rip; but the concert-hall ambience prevents this from being a problem.

The Heifetz performances have quite extraordinary panache: his bowing in the coda of the *Havanaise* is utterly captivating. Indeed, this dazzling playing is unsurpassed on record and the 1951 mono recording, if closely balanced, is very faithful. Even if you have these works in more modern versions, this marvellous disc should not be passed by.

These famous violin showpieces are superbly played by Ricci, who has dash and sparkle in plenty, helped by Gamba's lively conducting. The 1959 recording is full and vivid, only just hinting at its age. A fine bonus for Ricci's very individual performances of the two concertos.

Although she misses some of the sultry seductiveness in the *Havanaise*, the twelve-year-old Sarah Chang still captures the gleaming Spanish sunshine. She is well supported by Sawallisch but is not flattered by the close recording-balance.

Henry VIII: ballet music.

(BB) *** Naxos 8.553338/9. Razumovsky Sinfonia, Mogrelia – DELIBES: *Sylvia.* ***

This ballet-divertissement, described as a '*fête populaire*', comes in Act II of the opera, and in the outer movements Saint-Saëns wittily introduces first a Scottish reel then an Irish jig with Gallic insouciance. But all six numbers, which are enjoyably tuneful, unashamedly incorporate a great many airs from both countries, and Mogrelia presents them affectionately and vividly. With excellent recording, this is a genuine bonus to a pleasing account of Delibes's *Sylvia*.

Introduction & rondo capriccioso.

(M) *** DG 457 896-2. Mintz, Israel PO, Mehta – LALO: *Symphonie espagnole*; VIEUXTEMPS: *Violin Concerto No. 5.* ***

(M) (***) Dutton Lab. mono CDK 1204. Ida Haendel, Nat. SO, Basil Cameron – DVORAK: *Violin Concerto* (***); TCHAIKOVSKY: *Violin Concerto in D.* (***) ◉

Mintz dazzles the ear with Saint-Saëns's fireworks, while always playing with elegance and finesse. If the couplings are suitable, this is highly recommendable.

Ida Haendel recorded the Saint-Saëns display piece at the same time as her superb account of the Tchaikovsky concerto and it has a comparable freshness and sparkle.

The recording is amazingly lifelike and the transfer most natural.

Symphonies: in A; in F (Urbs Roma); Symphonies Nos. 1–3.

(B) *** EMI (ADD) CZS5 69683-2 (2). French Nat. R. O., Martinon (with Gavoty, organ of the Église Saint-Louis des Invalides in *No. 3*).

The *A* and *F major* works were totally unknown and unpublished at the time of their recording and have never been dignified with numbers. Yet the *A major*, written when the composer was only fifteen, is a delight and may reasonably be compared with Bizet's youthful work in the same genre. More obviously mature, the *Urbs Roma Symphony* is perhaps a shade more self-conscious, and more ambitious too, showing striking imagination in such movements as the darkly vigorous Scherzo and the variation movement at the end.

The first of the numbered symphonies is a well-fashioned and genial piece, again much indebted to Mendelssohn and Schumann, but with much delightfully fresh invention. The *Second* is full of excellent ideas. Martinon directs splendid performances of the whole set, well prepared and lively. The account of the *Third* ranks with the best: freshly spontaneous in the opening movement, and the threads knitted powerfully together at the end of the finale. Here the recording could do with rather more sumptuousness. Elsewhere the quality is bright and fresh, with no lack of body.

Symphony in F (Urbs Roma); Symphony No. 2 in A min., Op. 55; (i) Africa for Piano & Orchestra, Op. 89

*** BIS CD 790. (i) Mikkola; Tapiola Sinfonietta, Kantorow.

The *F major 'Urbs Roma' Symphony* and the delightful *Second Symphony in A minor* are played with great spirit and zest by the Tapiola Sinfonietta and Jean-Jacques Kantorow. *Africa*, a fantasy for piano and orchestra, is a later piece, written after Saint-Saëns had returned from a trip to Ceylon (as Sri Lanka was then known) and Egypt. Laura Mikkola is the excellent pianist. If the coupling is suitable, these intelligent and well-recorded performances can be recommended.

(i) Symphonies Nos. 1 in E flat, Op. 2; 2; (ii) Piano Concerto No. 4; (i) La Jeunesse d'Hercule; (iii) Le Rouet d'Omphale.

(B) ** Erato Ultima ADD/Dig. 3984 24236-2 (2). (i) VSO, Prêtre; (ii) Duchable, Strasbourg PO, Lombard; (iii) O Nat. de l'ORTF, Martinon.

This Ultima double is attractive in assembling very serviceable performances of the composer's two lesser-known published symphonies (useful for those who already have No. 3), plus one of the most attractive of the piano concertos, and the seldom-heard *La Jeunesse d'Hercule*. Prêtre does not quite match Martinon's flair in the symphonies, but he gets some refined playing from the VPO in the central movements (the two scherzi are highlights), and finds a pleasing energetic lightness for the first movement fugato and the tarantella-finale of the *Second*. Duchable then opens the *C minor Concerto* pleasingly (what a seductive work it is!) and the solo playing is never thoughtless or slipshod. Yet his bold assertiveness later in the work brings a hint of

agressiveness to music which should above all captivate the listener with its charm. *La Jeunesse d'Hercule* is quite strongly characterized if a bit melodramatic; then Martinon's extremely vivid *Le Rouet d'Omphale, Op. 31* shows us what the earlier performances lacked in spontaneity and panache.

Symphony No. 2; Phaéton, Op. 39; Suite algérienne, Op. 60.

*** ASV CDDCA 599. LSO, Butt.

Symphonies Nos. 2; (i) 3 in C min., Op. 78.

*** Chan. 8822. Ulster O, Tortelier; (i) with Weir.

If you want the *Second Symphony*, it is particularly well played by the LSO under Butt, with the freshness of a major orchestra discovering something unfamiliar and enjoying themselves. The companion pieces are also thoroughly enjoyable and are just as attractively presented. The recording is warmly atmospheric.

Yan Pascal Tortelier's performance of the *Second* is also very attractive and very well recorded; but Yondani Butt's account of this work has greater freshness, and the slightly less reverberant ASV recording contributes to this. If, however, your main interest lies with the *Third Symphony*, this extra resonance proves no disadvantage and the Tortelier version is a 'best buy', both for the appeal of the performance overall and for the state-of-the-art Chandos recording.

Symphony No. 2 in A min., Op. 55; Symphony in F (Urbs Roma). (i) Africa for Piano & Orchestra, Op. 89.

*** BIS CD 790. Tapiola Sinf., Kantorow; (i) with Mikkola.

Jean-Jacques Kantorow gives lively, well-shaped and splendidly musical accounts of both the *Symphony No. 2 in A minor* and the early F major *Urbs Roma*. Very bright and well-detailed recording too, both here and in the vital – indeed vibrant – performance of *Africa for Piano and Orchestra* in which Laura Mikkola is the expert soloist. Those for whom this coupling is suitable could regard this as a primary recommendation.

Symphony No. 3 in C min., Op. 78.

✿ (M) *** RCA (ADD) 09026 61500-2. Zamkochian, Boston SO, Munch – DEBUSSY: *La Mer* **(*); IBERT: *Escales*. ***

*** DG 419 617-2. Preston, BPO, Levine – DUKAS: *L'Apprenti sorcier*. ***

(B) **(*) DG 439 494-2. Litaize, Chicago SO, Barenboim – FRANCK: *Symphony*. *(*)

**(*) Teldec 4509 98416-2. Chorzempa BPO, Mehta – FRANCK: *Symphony in D min.* **(*)

Symphony No.3; (i) Carnival of the Animals.

(N) (BB) **(*) EMI Encore (ADD) CDE5 74753-2. Paris Conservatoire O, Prêtre; (i) with Ciccolini, Weissenberg (with POULENC: *Les Animaux modèles* **).

(i; ii) Symphony No. 3; (ii) Danse macabre, Op. 40; Samson et Dalila: Bacchanale; (i) 3 Rhapsodies sur des cantiques bretons, Op. 7.

*** BIS CD 555. (i) Fagius; (ii) Royal Stockholm PO, DePreist.

(i) *Symphony No. 3; Cyprès et lauriers, Op. 156. La Foi, 3 Tableaux symphoniques, Op. 130.*

(M) *** EMI CDC5 55584-2 (2). Toulouse Capitole O, Plasson; (i) with Eisenberg.

(i) *Symphony No. 3. Danse macabre, Op. 40; Phaéton, Op. 39; Samson et Dalila: Danse bacchanale.*

*** Sony SK 53979. (i) Newman; Pittsburgh SO, Maazel.

Symphony No. 3; Phaéton, Op. 39; Le Rouet d'Omphale, Op. 31.

(B) *** [EMI Red Line CDR5 69833]. O de France, Ozawa.

(i) *Symphony No. 3;* (ii) *Danse macabre; Le Déluge: Prélude, Op. 45; Samson et Dalila: Bacchanale.*

(M) *** DG (ADD) 415 847-2. (i) Litaize, Chicago SO, Barenboim; (ii) O de Paris, Barenboim.

Maazel's new Sony recording must go to the top of the list for audacious spectacle in the finale. The recording, rich and spacious, was made in the Heinz Hall in Pittsburgh, employing similar microphone techniques to those used by the RCA engineers in the late 1960s for Reiner's Symphony Hall recordings in Chicago. The organ part, admirably played by Anthony Newman, was recorded in the Church of St Ignatus Loyola in New York City, and laminated on afterwards. It makes a superb impact. Maazel presses the music onwards thrillingly to its close, the trombones very much to the fore, as in the climax of the first movement, and the organ pedals underlining the whole edifice, while his accelerando in the coda tautens the excitement even further. *Phaéton* and *Danse macabre* come off splendidly and there is real abandon at the close of the *Bacchanale* from *Samson and Dalila*.

Munch's Boston recording dates from 1960, yet in its currently remastered form it still sounds spectacular. The performance is stunning, full of lyrical ardour and moving forward in a single sweep of great intensity. The couplings, showing Munch and his Bostonians at their peak, are equally valuable, if not quite so outstandingly recorded.

With the Berlin Philharmonic in cracking form, Levine's is a grippingly dramatic reading, full of imaginative detail. The great thrust of the performance does not stem from fast pacing: rather it is the result of incisive articulation, while the clarity of the digital recording allows the pianistic detail to register crisply. The thunderous organ entry in the finale makes a magnificent effect, and the tension is held at white heat throughout the movement. The Dukas coupling is equally memorable, and this remains among the first choices for modern, digital versions of the symphony.

DePreist is straight and unmannered, completely at the service of the music, and proves very persuasive. Hans Fagius plays the Stockholm Concert Hall organ so that, unlike some performances in which the organist is tacked on afterwards, this is a genuine performance. He plays the *Trois rhapsodies sur des cantiques bretons* on the splendid Marcussen instrument of St Jakobs Kyrka in Stockholm to striking effect. The recording of all these items is full-blooded and has plenty of impact yet it is beautifully and naturally balanced.

Michel Plasson's account of the *Symphony No. 3*, made in the Basilique Notre-Dame La Daurade, Toulouse, with Matthias Eisenberg, is first rate and the recording first class,

although brightly lit. The plangent, reedy sound of the Puget organ, very French and somewhat harsh, will not appeal to all ears. But its spectacular impact cannot be denied. The symphony comes in a two-for-the-price-of-one format with two rarities, *Cyprès et lauriers* and *La Foi*, three symphonic tableaux drawn from incidental music for Eugène Brieux's play, *False Gods. Cyprès et lauriers* is extravagantly scored: its first movement (*Cyprès*) is for organ solo, and here the organ sounds just right. The second (*Lauriers*) brings trumpet fanfares and a general sense of spectacle. *La Foi*, which runs for just over 30 minutes, comes on the second CD and has some of the fey, oriental charm that characterizes the *Egyptian Piano Concerto* (No. 5). However, this has just been deleted as we go to press.

Barenboim's inspirational 1976 performance of the *Symphony* glows with warmth from beginning to end. The digital remastering is not wholly advantageous: while detail is sharper, the massed violins sound thinner and the bass is drier. In the finale, some of the bloom has gone, and the organ entry has a touch of hardness. It is now also available in a bargain Classikon disc, but here the Franck coupling is not an asset.

Ozawa's version is coupled with attractive performances of two of Saint-Saëns's most colourful symphonic poems, in which the conductor is in his element. The *Symphony* too is very enjoyable, and this performance certainly wears well. Ozawa's finale makes a splendidly opulent effect. The sound is in the demonstration class.

Under Mehta, the first-movement allegro of the symphony immediately takes wing. The *Poco adagio* makes a serene, cantabile contrast, its climactic ardour affecting. The bustling energy of the Scherzo is well caught, with the detail of the piano figurations sparkling, and Daniel Chorzempa's powerful organ entry certainly makes one sit up. The tension is well held, and the BPO produces a characteristically full body of sound. Sonically this is spectacular too, though not quite as impressive as Maazel's recent Pittsburgh recording for Sony, which also has the edge as a performance. But then that does not offer the Franck symphony as well.

At super-bargain price Prêtre's reading has much to recommend it. The recording is open to the charge of being over-reverberant, but the overall sound is vivid enough and the performance has vigour and commitment. In the refreshingly brilliant account of the *Carnival of the Animals* Ciccolini and Weissenberg make a contribution of some distinction. It opens a little heavily, but the characterisation is nicely managed, with some very good orchestral playing. As Poulenc's *Les Animaux modèles* is based on the fables of La Fontaine, it makes a rather apt bonus, although here the sound is drier.

Wedding-Cake (Caprice-valse), Op. 76.

(BB) *** ASV CDQS 6092. Osorio, RPO, Bátiz – FRANCK: *Symphonic Variations* **(*); RAVEL: *Left-Hand Concerto* ***; SCHUMANN: *Concerto.* **(*)

A delightfully lightweight performance of Saint-Saëns's frothy but engaging *morceau de concert*, infectious and sparkling. Nicely recorded, too.

CHAMBER MUSIC

Bassoon Sonata, Op. 168; Clarinet Sonata, Op. 167; Caprice on Danish & Russian Airs for Flute, Oboe, Clarinet & Piano, Op. 79; Feuillet d'album, Op. 81 (arr. Taffanel); Oboe Sonata, Op. 166; Odelette for Flute & Piano, Op. 162; Romance in D flat for Flute & Piano, Op. 37; Tarantelle for Flute, Clarinet & Piano, Op. 6.

(B) *** Cala CACD 1017 (2). Bennett, Daniel, Campbell, Gough, & Ens. – DEBUSSY: Chamber Music. ***

The Sonatas for Clarinet, for Oboe and for Bassoon are elegantly finished but surprising pieces, with an unaccustomed depth of feeling. The Caprice is a diverting kind of potpourri, inspired by the composer's visit to Russia in 1876. Paul Taffanel's arrangement of the Feuillet d'album, Op. 81, for flute, oboe and two each of clarinets, bassoons and horns, is a first recording and, like almost everything on this record, refreshing and elegant. That goes for the performances too, which are well recorded, though the piano is occasionally overpowering. Strongly recommended – and outstanding value.

Carnival of the Animals (chamber version).

(M) *** Virgin VM5 61782-2. Nash Ens. – BRITTEN: Young Person's Guide to the Orchestra **(*). PROKOFIEV: Peter and the Wolf.

Carnival of the Animals (chamber version); Piano Trio in F, Op. 18; Septet in E flat for Trumpet, Strings & Piano, Op. 65.

(BB) *** Virgin 2 x 1 VBD5 61516-2 (2). Nash Ens. – DVORAK: Piano Quintet, Op. 81; Piano Trio No. 4 (Dumky). ***

In the sparkling Nash chamber version of the Carnival of the Animals, Ian Hobson is joined by Susan Tomes. Its humour is nicely captured without clumsiness, and these players make sure the listener does not miss the composer's witty quotations, with delightful results. The Septet too is presented with a similar geniality and lightness of touch, and the account of the first of Saint-Saëns's two piano trios is similarly persuasive. The acoustic has warmth and the balance between the instruments, particularly in the Grande fantaisie zoologique, is admirably judged. Coupled with fine performances of two of Dvořák's most appealing chamber works, this inexpensive Virgin Double is self-recommending.

However, the alternative coupling of Peter and the Wolf is a non-starter.

Cello Sonatas Nos. 1 in C min., Op. 32; 2 in F, Op. 123; Le Cygne (trans. Godowski).

*** Hyp. CDA 67095. Lidström, Forsberg.

Written thirty years apart, the two Cello Sonatas have an abundant and fluent invention, and are captivating when played with such fervour and polish. These artists radiate total conviction and a life-enhancing vitality and sensitivity.

Piano Trio No. 1 in F, Op. 18.

(*) Ara. Z 6643. Golub–Kaplan–Carr Trio – DEBUSSY; FAURE: Trios. *

Piano Trios Nos. 1 in F, Op. 18; 2 in E min., Op. 92.

(BB) *** Naxos 8.550935. Joachim Trio.

No quarrels with the playing of the Joachim Trio (Rebecca Hirsch, Caroline Dearnley and John Lenehan). The pianist in particular has elegance and charm. This is delightful and inventive music, well recorded – and well worth the money.

David Golub, Mark Kaplan and Colin Carr also give a very good account of themselves in the Piano Trio in F major. They are intelligent and imaginative. The piano dominates in the right way, and David Golub makes a particularly strong and vital impression. They are very well recorded too.

String Quartets Nos. 1 in E min., Op. 112; 2 in G, Op. 153.

*** Conifer 75605 51291-2. Miami Qt – FAURE: String Quartet. ***

** Koch Schwann 364842. Medici Qt.

The quartets are products of Saint-Saëns's maturity. They are both splendidly fashioned, the product of a cultured musical mind, though his invention, always fertile and finely shaped, is not quite as distinguished here as in his very best music. Of the two ensembles, the Miami quartet score both in terms of polish and technical finesse, and musical insight, though the Medici play very well and are accorded excellent sound, rich and well balanced. The Miami score in also giving us an excellent bonus, Fauré's glorious E minor Quartet.

Violin Sonata No. 1 in D min., Op. 75.

*** Essex (ADD) CDS 6044. Accardo, Canio – CHAUSSON: Concert. ***

(BB) *** Arte Nova 74321 59233-2. Contzen, Rogatchev – DEBUSSY; FRANCK: Violin Sonatas. ***

Violin Sonatas Nos. 1; 2 in E flat, Op. 102; Berceuse, Op. 38; Introduction & rondo capriccioso, Op. 28 (arr. Bizet).

**(*) ASV CDDCA 892. Xue-Wei, Lenehan.

Of Saint-Saëns's two Violin Sonatas the second is especially appealing with its simple Andante and closing Allegro grazioso, in which Xue-Wei seems thoroughly at home. He is also delightfully nimble in the Scherzo (as is his fine partner, John Lenehan) and he manages the moto perpetuo finale of the First Sonata with equal facility. Before that comes the lovely Berceuse, which shows Xue-Wei's tone at its most appealing, but in the opening Introduction and Rondo capriccioso, played with real sparkle, the close microphones are unflattering to the violin's upper range.

The performance of the D minor Sonata by Accardo and Canio is marvellously played, selfless and dedicated. The recording too is very good, and this can be recommended strongly, if the coupling is suitable.

Mirijam Contzen uses her rich, warm tone to give a compelling, purposeful performance, passionate in the first movement, poised and intense in the inner meditation of the second, light and sparkling in the Scherzo and brilliant in the exuberant finale. With sensitive accompaniment this makes an outstanding bargain, very well recorded.

VOCAL MUSIC

Choral songs: *Calme des nuits; Des pas dans l'allée; Les Fleurs et les arbres.*

*** Ph. 438 149-2. Monteverdi Ch., ORR, Gardiner — FAURE: *Requiem;* DEBUSSY; RAVEL: *Choral Works.* ***

Three charming examples of Saint-Saëns's skill and finesse in drawing inspiration from early sources in a way remarkable at the time he was writing. Gardiner and his team give ideal performances, adding to the valuable list of rarities which he provides as coupling for the Fauré *Requiem.*

Mass, Op. 4.

(N) (BB) *** Warner Apex. 8573 89235-2. Lausanne Vocal Ens., Corboz; Alain; Fuchs (organ) — GOUNOD: *Messe Chorale.* ***

The Op. 4 *Mass* of Saint-Saens, like its Gounod coupling, is an early work (1855) but although it still draws on the alternation tradition of the French organ mass, the addition of soloists and orchestral accompaniment makes for a more modern larger-scale work, with only the organ preserving the plainsong tradition. Here the *Mass* is performed with the orchestral music transcribed for a second organ by Léon Rogues, which is less than ideal. Nevertheless this is generally a fine performance. Even if the soloists are not as impressive as the chorus, the choral alternation with the main organ (magnificently played by Marie-Claire Alain) in the *Sanctus* is very impressive, while the *O Salutaris* brings a memorable floating choral line against a gently pointed organ accompaniment, leading to a romantically seraphic *Agnus Dei.* At its modest cost this disc is well worth having.

OPERA

Samson et Dalila (opera): complete.

*** EMI (ADD) CDS7 54470-2 (2). Domingo, Meier, Fondary, Courtis, L'Opéra-Bastille Ch. & O, Myung-Whun Chung.

(M) **(*) DG (ADD) 413 297-2 (2). Obraztsova, Domingo, Bruson, Lloyd, Thau, Ch. & O de Paris, Barenboim.

(M) (**(*)) EMI mono CMS5 65263-2 (2). Luccioni, Bouvier, Cabanel, Cambon, Medus, Paris Opéra Ch. & O, Fourestier.

In the newer, EMI set, Domingo with Chung gives a deeper, more thoughtful performance than on DG, broader, with greater repose and a sense of power in reserve. When the big melody appears in Dalila's seduction aria, *Mon coeur s'ouvre,* Chung's idiomatic conducting encourages a tender restraint, where others produce a full-throated roar. Meier may not have an ideally sensuous voice for the role, with some unwanted harshness in her expressive account of Dalila's first monologue, but her feeling for words is strong and the characterization vivid. Generally Chung's speeds are on the fast side, yet the performance does not lack weight, with some first-rate singing in the incidental roles from Alain Fondary, Samuel Ramey and Jean-Philippe Courtis. Apart from backwardly placed choral sound, the recording is warm and well focused.

Barenboim proves as passionately dedicated an in-terpreter of Saint-Saëns here as he did in the *Third Symphony,* sweeping away any Victorian cobwebs. It is important, too, that the choral passages, so vital in this work, be sung with this sort of freshness, and Domingo has rarely sounded happier in French music, the bite as well as the heroic richness of the voice well caught. Renato Bruson and Robert Lloyd are both admirable too; sadly, however, the key role of Dalila is given an unpersuasive, unsensuous performance by Obraztsova, with her vibrato often verging on a wobble. The recording is as ripe as the music deserves.

EMI's 1946 recording from the Paris Opéra provides a formidable showcase for outstanding singers, little known outside France. José Luccioni was a favourite in Paris, his voice combining lyric beauty with heroic timbre that made him an outstanding choice as Samson. His diction and command of style are as sure as his vocal production, and so it is with Hélène Bouvier, boasting a rich mezzo, rock-steady throughout its range, and again a perfect command of style. Sadly, her career was cut short by polio. Paul Cabanel as the High Priest was also at the end of his career but is impressive too. Choral singing and orchestral playing are often ragged, and the sound from 78-r.p.m. discs is very limited; but this is a performance with plenty of feeling, well worth investigating.

SALIERI, Antonio (1750–1825)

Overtures: *L'Angiolina, ossia Il matrimonio per sussurro; Armida; Axur, re d'Ormus; Cesare in Farmacusa (Tempesta di mare); Les Danaïdes; Don Chisciotte alle nozze di Gamace; Eraclito e Democrito; La grotta di Trofonio; Il moro; Il ricco d'un giorno; La secchia rapita; Il talismano.*

(N) ** Marco Polo 8.223381. Czech-Slovak RSO (Bratislava), Dittrich.

In his day Salieri was a highly successful opera composer in both Vienna and Paris, and this collection of overtures covers his output from the one-act opera-ballet *Don Chisciotte* of 1770 to *L'Angiolina, ossia Il matrimonio per sussurro* of 1800, of which a complete recording exists (see below). The overtures are often dramatic, *Armida* and *Les Danaïdes* especially so, while *La grotta di Trofonio* begins by depicting the magician's cave where the two male heroes are put under a spell to interchange their characters, much to the annoyance of their prospective brides. *Cesare in Farmacusa* is entirely taken up by the standard opening storm sequence. Elsewhere there are plenty of bustle and vigour, and some agreeable lyrical ideas, but also much that is conventional. The performances are lively and well played but not distinctive, and the recording is more than acceptable. But this cannot match the Chandos collection below and would have been more attractive as a budget Naxos issue.

Overtures: *Angiolina, ossia Il matrimonio per sussuro; Cublai, gran kan de'Tartari; Falstaff, ossia Le tre burle; La locandiera. Sinfonia Il giorno onomastico; Sinfonia Veneziana; 26 Variations on La follia di Spagna.*

(N) *** Chan. 9877. LMP, Bamert.

A fascinating disc demonstrating just why Salieri was such a successful composer in his day. The music here brings a profusion of ear-tickling ideas and the secondary themes for his concise and lively overtures are most engaging (especially a fast, tripping figure on the strings in *Cublai, grand kan de' Tartari*). Tuttis, with trumpets, are invariably bright and rather grand, but the lighter scoring shows a nice feeling for woodwind colour and there is much elegant phrasing for the violins. The *Larghetto* of the four movement *Sinfonia Il giorno onomastico* is deliciously delicate, opening with gossamer strings over a pizzicato bass followed by delicate writing for flutes and oboes. The *Allegretto* finale brings an equally charming moto perpetuo, and this work could easily be mistaken for a ballet. Indeed the sinfonias are interchangeable with the overtures in their insubstantial but very agreeable content, well crafted but hardly symphonic. Perhaps the most striking work is the kaleidoscopic set of *26 Variations on 'La folia'* which occupies eighteen minutes, continually changing colour and mood, often dramatically, sometimes bizarrely, but usually entertainingly (although there is an element of repetition). Among other combinations, Salieri scores for harp, solo violin, a trombone chorale with flute decoration, and he uses the woodwind most engagingly. This piece dates from 1815 and deserves to be better known. The London Mozart Players play all this music most winningly, with vigour, polish and charm and the Chandos recording is state of the art.

Double Concerto in C for Flute & Oboe.

*** Chan. 9051. Milan, Theodore, City of L. Sinf., Hickox –
   MOZART: *Flute & Harp Concerto; Oboe Concerto.* *******

Salieri's innocently insubstantial *Double concerto* is quite transformed by the charisma and sheer style of the solo playing from Susan Milan and David Theodore. The exquisite playing of Theodore in the simple melody of the *Largo* and the perfect blending of the two soloists turn it into a really memorable slow movement, and the flute and oboe chase each other round engagingly in their winning decorations of the nicely poised Minuet finale. Hickox's accompaniment is both polished and genial, and the recording casts a pleasing glow over the whole proceedings.

Falstaff, or The Three Tricks (complete).

*** Chan. 9613 (2). Franceschetto, Myeounghee, De Filippo, Chialli, Luis Ciuffo, Bettoschi, Valli, Milan Madrigalists & Guido Cantelli, O, Veronesi.

Like Verdi, Salieri and his librettist ignore the Falstaff of the histories. They tell the story within the framework of the conventional two-act opera of the period with crisp and brief numbers leading to extended finales. Though Fenton and Anne (Nannetta) are omitted, Mistress Page (here renamed Slender) is given her husband. Though it never comes near to matching Mozart, it is all great fun, particularly in performances as fresh and lively as these. The Chandos version takes priority over the Hungaroton (HCD 21789/91) – which in any case is currently not easily obtainable – when thanks to the brisk, alert pacing of Veronesi the opera is squeezed on to two discs instead of three. Though Romano Franceschetto in the title role is not so firmly commanding

as Joszef Gregor in the Hungarian performance, he does sing characterfully. As for the rest, the Italian cast on Chandos is fresher and more idiomatic than the Hungarian, with fuller sound an added advantage.

SALLINEN, Aulis (born 1935)

(i; ii) *Cello Concerto, Op. 44;* (iii) *Chamber Music I, Op. 38;* (i; iii) *Chamber Music III, Op. 58;* (iii) *Some Aspects of Peltoniemi Hintrik's Funeral March;* (iv) *Sunrise Serenade* (for 2 trumpets and chamber orchestra), *Op. 63;* (ii) *Shadows, Op. 52; Symphonies Nos. 4, Op. 49; 5 (Washington Mosaics), Op. 57.*

(B) ******* Finlandia Ultima 8573 81972-2 (2). (i) Noras;
   (ii) Helsinki PO, or (iii) Finland Sinfonietta, Kamu;
   (iv) Harjanne, Välimäki, Avanti CO.

This Ultima set brings an extensive survey of Sallinen's music, and provides an inexpensive entry into the composer's world. Apart from the symphonies, the *Cello Concerto* of 1976 is the most commanding piece here. Sallinen's ideas resonate in the mind. Artos Noras has its measure and plays with masterly eloquence. *Shadows* is an effective short piece which reflects or 'shadows' the content of the opera *The King Goes Forth to France. Some Aspects of Peltoniemi Hintrik's Funeral March* is a transcription for full strings of the *Third Quartet* (1969), a one-movement work in five variations that never loses sight of its basic folk-inspired idea; not one of the composer's strongest works, but persuasively presented here. The middle movement of the *Fourth Symphony* is marked *Dona nobis pacem;* throughout the finale, bells colour the texture, as is often the case with Sallinen's orchestral writing. *Washington Mosaics* is a five-movement work in which the outer movements form the framework for three less substantial but highly imaginative intermezzi. There are Stravinskian overtones in the first movement and the intermezzi cast a strong spell. The work has a feeling for nature and a keen sense of its power. The performances, under Okko Kamu, are very impressive and the recording quite exemplary. Overall, excellent value.

(i) *Violin Concerto, Op. 18;* (ii) *Nocturnal Dances of Don Juanquixote, Op. 58. Some Aspects of Peltoniemi Hintrik's Funeral March, Op. 19; Variations for Orchestra (Juventas variations), Op. 8.*

*** BIS CD 560. (i) Koskinen; (ii) Thedéen; Tapiola Sinf., Vänskä.

The *Variations for Orchestra* is an imaginative and inventive piece which shows remarkable command of the orchestra. It is tonally ambiguous without being serial; indeed at one point there is a reminder of Britten. The *Violin Concerto* is also rewarding and in the slow movement often beautiful but its lyrical impulse is not strong enough for it to enter the standard repertoire. It has a powerful advocate in Eeva Koskinen. Excellent playing from Torleif Thedéen and the Tapiola Sinfonietta under Osmo Vänskä and a vivid, well-lit but not overbright BIS recording.

(i) *Symphonies Nos. 1; 3;* (ii) *Chorali;* (iii) *Cadenze for Solo Violin;* (iv) *Elegy for Sebastian Knight;* (v) *String Quartet No. 3.*

*** BIS (ADD) CD 41. (i) Finnish RSO, Kamu; (ii) Helsinki PO, Berglund; (iii) Paavo Pohjola; (iv) Frans Helmerson; (v) Voces Intimae Qt.

The *First Symphony*, in one movement, is diatonic and full of atmosphere, as indeed is the *Third*, a powerful, imaginative piece which appears to be haunted by the sounds and smells of nature. The performances under Okko Kamu are excellent. *Chorali* is a shorter piece, persuasively done by Paavo Berglund; and there are three chamber works, albeit of lesser substance. The recordings are from the 1970s and are all very well balanced. Highly recommended.

Symphonies Nos. 2 (Symphonic Dialogue for Solo Percussion Player & Orchestra), Op. 29; 6 (From a New Zealand Diary), Op. 65; Sunrise Serenade, Op. 63.

*** BIS CD 511. Malmö SO, Okko Kamu.

The *Second Symphony*, like the *First*, is a one-movement affair lasting a quarter of an hour. Its sub-title, *Symphonic Dialogue for Solo Percussion Player and Orchestra*, gives an accurate idea of its character, pitting the fine soloist, Gerd Mortensen, against the remaining orchestral forces. The main work is the ambitious *Sixth Symphony*. Like the *Third Symphony*, it is powerfully evocative of natural landscape; indeed, it is one of the strongest and most imaginative of all Sallinen's symphonies. Okko Kamu gets very responsive playing from the Malmö Symphony Orchestra in both symphonies and in the slight but effective *Sunrise Serenade*. The recording is excellent.

Symphonies Nos. 4, Op. 49; 5 (Washington Mosaics), Op. 57; Shadows (Prelude for Orchestra), Op. 52.

*** BIS CD 607. Malmö SO, James DePreist.

Suffice it to say that these performances by the Malmö Symphony Orchestra under James DePreist are every bit as good as the Helsinki rivals listed above; if anything, the recording has more impressive range and definition.

Chamber Music Nos. I, Op. 38; (i) *II, for Alto Flute & Strings, Op. 41;* (ii) *III, for Cello & Strings (The Nocturnal Dances of Don Juanquixote), Op. 58. Some Aspects of Peltoniemi Hintrik's Funeral March (Quartet No. 3 arr. for strings); Sunrise Serenade for 2 Trumpets, Piano & Strings, Op. 63.*

(BB) *** Naxos 8.553747. Finnish CO, Kamu, with (i) Juutilainen; (ii) Rondin.

Aulis Sallinen's string music is tonal and accessible ('audience friendly'), and in no way forbidding. However, to our ears it is insubstantial, the invention thin and repetitive. Others may respond more warmly to this music, and those who do will find the playing and recording very good indeed.

Kullervo (opera).

*** Ondine ODE 780-3T. Hynninen, Sallinen, Jakobsson, Silvasti, Vihavainen, Finnish Nat. Op. Ch. & O., Söderblom.

Although the theme will be familiar from Sibelius's early symphony of the same name, Sallinen has based his *Kullervo* on the play by Aleksis Kivi and he wrote the libretto himself. The plot emerges from a mixture of narration, in which the chorus plays a central role, and dreams. The opera is a compelling musical drama. Sallinen's musical language has debts to composers as diverse as Britten (shadows of the 'Sunday morning' interlude in *Peter Grimes* briefly cross the score in Kullervo's Dream at the beginning of Act II), Puccini, Debussy even, though they are synthesized into an effective vehicle for a vivid theatrical imagination. There is impressive variety of pace and atmosphere, and the black voices of the Finnish Opera Chorus resonate in the memory. So, too, do the impressive performances of Jorma Hynninen as Kullervo and Anna-Lisa Jakobsson as the smith's young wife and, indeed, the remainder of the cast and the Finnish National Opera Orchestra under Ulf Söderblom. While *Kullervo* may not be a great opera, it is gripping and effective musical theatre, and the Ondine recording has excellent presence and detail.

SAMMARTINI, Giovanni Battista (1700–75)

Symphonies in D; G; String Quintet in E.

(B) *** HM (ADD) HMA 1901245. Ens. 145, Banchini – IUSEPPE SAMMARTINI: *Concerti grossi* etc. ***

Giovanni Battista was the younger of the two Sammartini brothers; he spent his whole life in Milan. On this record, the Ensemble 145, led by Chiara Banchini, offer two of his symphonies; although neither attains greatness, they have genuine appeal. Good recording.

SAMMARTINI, Giuseppe (c. 1693–1750)

Concerti grossi Nos. 6 & 8; (i) *Recorder Concerto in F.*

(B) *** HM (ADD) HMA 901245. (i) Steinmann; Ens. 145, Banchini – GIOVANNI SAMMARTINI: *Symphonies* etc. ***

Giuseppe settled in England in the 1720s and he was a refined and inventive composer. The Ensemble 145 is a period-instrument group; they produce a firmly focused sound, even though the textures are light and the articulation lively. Excellent playing from Conrad Steinmann in the *Recorder Concerto*.

SANDSTRÖM, Jan (born 1954)

Trumpet Concerto No. 2.

(N) *** BIS CD 1021. Hardenberger, Malmö SO, Varga – BORTZ: *Trumpet Concerto.* RABE: *Sardinsarkofagen.* ***

Jan Sandström is in his mid-40s and the youngest of the three Swedish composers on this disc. His concerto, with its pert, if occasionally predictable syncopations, is often diverting and at times in the slow movement even touching. Bright and lively in every way, stunningly played and recorded.

SANTOS, Joly Braga (1924–88)

Symphonies Nos. 3 & 6.

*** Marco 8.225087. Neves, São Carlos Theatre Ch., Portuguese SO, Cassuto.

José Manuel Joly Braga Santos is the leading Portuguese symphonist of his day. His *Third Symphony*, composed in 1949, when he was in his mid 20s, is strongly modal in idiom, with a strong sense of forward movement and a powerful feeling for architecture. It is imaginatively scored and at times suggests Vaughan Williams, and even at one point in the slow movement (about two and a half minutes in) the Shostakovich of the *Fifth Symphony*. The *Sixth Symphony* (1972) is a one-movement work with a closing choral section. The first two-thirds are purely orchestral and more expressionist in their musical language, non-tonal but without being dodecaphonic, the choral part being tonal. Very good performances and recordings.

SARASATE, Pablo (1844–1908)

Carmen Fantasy, Op. 25.

*** EMI CDC7 47101-2. Perlman, RPO, Foster – PAGANINI: *Concerto No. 1.* ***

Played like this on EMI, with superb panache, luscious tone and glorious recording, Sarasate's *Fantasy* almost upstages the concerto with which it is coupled. The recording balance is admirable, with the quality greatly to be preferred to many of Perlman's more recent digital records.

Carmen Fantasy, Op. 25; Zigeunerweisen, Op. 20.

(N) *** Ph. 464 531-2. Suwanai, Budapest Fest. O, Ivan Fischer – DVORAK: *Violin Concerto; Masurek.* ***

It takes a magnetic violinist like Akiko Suwanai – the youngest ever winner of the Tchaikovsky Competition in Moscow in 1990 – to bring off Sarasate's brilliant showpieces, particularly the *Zigeunerweisen*, which can easily outstay its welcome. Suwanai's virtuoso flair comes out not just in bold bravura playing, but in the daring range of dynamic, with Suwanai communing with herself in extreme, hushed pianissimos. An unexpected if attractive coupling for the Dvořák concerto, very well recorded.

Zigeunerweisen, Op. 20.

*** DG 431 815-2. Shaham, LSO, Foster – WIENIAWSKI: *Violin Concertos Nos. 1 & 2 etc.* ***

(M) (***) RCA mono 09026 61753-2. Heifetz, RCA Victor SO, Steinberg – CHAUSSON: *Poème* **(*); LALO: *Symphony espagnole* (**(*)); SAINT-SAENS: *Havanaise etc.* (***)

(M) (***) EMI mono CDH7 64251-2. Heifetz, LPO, Barbirolli – SAINT-SAENS: *Havanaise etc.*; VIEUXTEMPS: *Concerto No. 4*; WIENIAWSKI: *Concerto No. 2.* (***)

(N)(BB) **(*) EMI Encore CDE5 74735-2. Mutter, O Nat. de France, Ozawa (with MASSENET: *Thaïs: Meditation*) – LALO: *Symphonie espagnole.* **(*)

(B) **(*) [EMI Red Line CDR5 69861]. Mutter, O Nat. de France, Ozawa – BIZET: *Carmen: Suites* etc; LALO: *Symphonie espagnole.* **(*)

(B) **(*) EMI Debut CDZ5 73501-2. Shapira, ECO, Hazlewood – BLOCH: *Baal Shem* ***; BRUCH: *Violin Concerto No. 1 in G min., Op. 26* **; BUNCH: *Fantasy.* **

Gil Shaham plays Sarasate's sultry and dashing gypsy confection with rich timbre, languorous ardour and a dazzling display of fireworks at the close.

What can one say about the Heifetz performances except that they are unsurpassed: they are dazzling in the fireworks and with the most luscious tone and sophisticated colouring in the lyrical melody. The recording is dry but faithful. This is a marvellous disc.

A sparkling performance of Sarasate's gypsy pot-pourri from Anne-Sophie Mutter, given good support from Ozawa. There are some dazzling fireworks, but some may feel her playing in the famous principal lyrical melody too chaste. The balance places the solo violin well forward, and the timbre is very brightly lit. This comes with alternative couplings in the USA.

Ittai Shapira is a twenty-four-year-old Israeli violinist, whose début recording this is. The closing part of the *Zigeunerweisen* shows that EMI's confidence in him is not misplaced, as does the splendid *Baal Shem*.

INSTRUMENTAL MUSIC

'Música española': (i; vi) *Capricho vasco, Op. 24; Introducción y tarantela, Op. 43;* (ii; iv) *8 Danzas españolas, Op. 22/1–2; Op. 22/1–2; Op. 23/1–2; Op. 26/1–2;* (i; v) *Jota aragonesa, Op. 27;* (ii; iii; iv) *Navarra for 2 violins, Op. 33.*

(B)*** Double Decca stereo/mono 433 938-2 (2). (i) Ricci; (ii) Campoli; (iii) Bunt; (iv) Ibbott; (v) Lush; (vi) Persinger – Robles Instrumental recital. ***

One of the most attractive of Decca's *'Música española'* series, this restores to the catalogue Campoli's charismatic set of Sarasate's *Danzas españolas*, plus *Navarra*, in which he is joined by Belinda Blunt. Campoli is in excellent form and he has never been so truthfully recorded. With the art that disguises art he makes these dances sound effortless yet brilliant, and infinitely stylish. Ricci takes over for three other genre pieces and plays with stunning bravado in the *Tarantella, Op. 43*. This and the *Capricho* are mono but one would hardly guess. Popular light music this may be, but it is all so thoroughly enjoyable when the playing is of this quality. The recording is at times rather close (especially the Ricci items), but never troubling.

SARMANTO, Heikki (born 1939)

'Meet the Composer': (i–ii) *Kalevala Fantasy: Return to Life.* (iii) *Max and the Enchantress; Sea of Balloons;* (iv–v; ii) *Suomi (A Symphonic Jazz Poem for Orchestra);* (iii; vi) *The Traveller: Northern Atmosphere.* (Instrumental): (iv; vii) *Distant Dreams: Tender Wind. Pan Fantasy: The Awakening; In the Night.* (Vocal) (viii) *Carrousel;*

(ix) *Light of Love;* **(x)** *New England Images;* **(xi; iii)** *New Hope Jazz Mass: Have Mercy on Us.* **(x)** *Northern Pictures.*

(B) ✱✱ Finlandia 0630 19809-2 (2). (i) UMO Jazz O; (ii) dir. composer; (iii) Heikki Sarmanto Ens.; (iv) with Juhani Aaltonen; (v) with O; (vi) with Vasile Pantir, Tom Rainey; (vii) composer (keyboards); (viii) Helen Merrill, Tapiola Sinf., Torrie Zito; (ix) Karen Parks, Samuel McKelton, Opera Ebony, Kyösti Haatanen; (ix–x) Sarmanto Jazz Ens.; (x) Finnish Chamber Ch., Eric-Olof Söderström; (xi) Maija Hapuoja, Gregg Smith Vocal Qt, Long Island Symphonic Choral Assoc., Gregg Smith.

Heikki Sarmanto firmly 'eludes all attempts at categorization', writes Antti Suvanto in his notes for this set. Sarmanto was a theory pupil of Joonas Kokkonen and he went on to further studies in the United States. The main influence on the music that represents him here is Duke Ellington, though few of the pieces here rival his model. He is accomplished and inventive, though the choral pieces really do strike us as having more facility than taste. There is some good playing from the various artists involved, and Sarmanto is obviously a skilled as well as a prolific musician. On the whole, however, his music strikes us as deeply unappealing.

SARUM CHANT

Missa in gallicantu; Hymns: A solis ortus cardine; Christe Redemptor omnium; Salvator mundi, Domine; Veni Redemptor omnium.

✱✱✱ Gimell CDGIM 917. Tallis Scholars, Peter Phillips.

Filling in our knowledge of early church music, the Tallis Scholars under Peter Phillips here present a whole disc of chant according to the Salisbury rite – in other words *Sarum Chant* – which, rather than the regular Gregorian style, was what churchgoers of the Tudor period and earlier in England heard at their devotions. The greater part of the record is given over to the setting of the First Mass of Christmas, intriguingly entitled *Missa in gallicantu* or *Mass at Cock-Crow.* Though this is simply monophonic (the men's voices alone are used), it is surprising what antiphonal variety there is. The record is completed with four hymns from the Divine Offices of Christmas Day. The record is warmly atmospheric in the characteristic Gimell manner.

SATIE, Erik (1866–1925)

Les Aventures de Mercure (ballet); *La Belle Excentrique: Grande ritournelle. 5 Grimaces pour 'Un songe d'une nuit d'été'; Gymnopédies Nos. 1 & 3; Jack-in-the-box* (orch. Milhaud); *3 Morceaux en forme de poire; Parade* (ballet); *Relâche* (ballet).

(M) ✱✱(✱) Van. 08.4030.71. Utah SO, Abravanel.

A generous mid-priced collection of Satie's orchestral music, well played and given full, vivid recording from the early 1970s; if Abravanel fails to throw off some of the more pointed music with a fully idiomatic lightness of touch, these are still enjoyable performances; the ballet scores have plenty of colour and rhythmic life.

Gymnopédies Nos. 1 & 3 (orch. Debussy).

(B) ✱✱✱ Sony (ADD) SBK 63056. Cleveland O, Louis Lane – DEBUSSY: *Petite suite;* RAVEL: *Introduction & Allegro* etc. ✱✱✱

Satie's *Gymnopédies,* heard in Debussy's orchestration, are beautifully played by the excellent Cleveland band. Louis Lane has the full measure of the languorous melancholy of these haunting pieces, and his chosen tempi are admirably judged. The sound too is warmly atmospheric.

Parade.

(M) ✱✱✱ Mercury [434 335-2]. LSO, Dorati – AURIC: *Overture;* FETLER: *Contrasts;* FRANCAIX: *Piano Concertino;* MILHAUD: *Le Boeuf sur le toit.* ✱✱✱

Satie's *Parade* is the most audacious piece in an excellent Mercury compilation of (mostly) twentieth-century French music, its scoring including several extra-musical effects. Dorati makes it all fit together wittily and entertainingly and the necessary atmosphere and colour are given to the more restrained sections of the score. The Mercury recording team excel themselves in presenting Satie's kaleidoscopic circus colours with the utmost vividness.

(i) *Choses vues à droite et à gauche (sans lunettes)* for violin and piano; **(ii)** Music for piano, 4 hands: *Aperçus désagréables; La Belle Excentrique; En habit de cheval; 3 Morceaux en forme de poire; Parade; 3 Petites pièces montées.* Piano pieces: *Pièces de la période Nos. 1, Désespoir agréable; 6 Songe-Creux. 3rd Sarabande.*

(N) ✱✱✱ Decca 455 401-2. Rogé with (i) Chantal Juillet; (ii) Collard.

Good to have a follow-up to Pascal Rogé's excellent Satie discs. The *Choses vues à droite et à gauche (sans lunettes)* is his only piece for violin and piano, which finds Chantal Juillet at her stylish best. The *Trois petites pièces montées* are given with cool elegance and Rogé and Jean-Philippe Collard despatch the duet version of *Parade* with undoubted relish and abandon – perhaps too much of the latter. The excellent recording was made in St George's, Brandon Hill, Bristol in 1996, and for some reason Decca have taken four years to issue it.

PIANO MUSIC

Piano, 4 hands: **(i)** *La Belle Excentrique; 3 Morceaux en forme de poire.* Solo piano: *Caresse; Croquis et agaceries d'un gros bonhomme en bois; Danse de travers; Descriptions automatiques; Fantaisie valse; Passacaille; Les Pantins dansent; Première pensée Rose + Croix; Petite ouverture à danser; Pièces froides I: Airs à faire fuir. II: Danse de travers. Poudre d'or; Prélude de la porte héroïque du ciel; Prélude en tapisserie; Valse ballet; 3 Valses distinguées du précieux dégoûté.*

(M) ✱✱✱ Virgin VCT 59296-2. Anne Queffélec; (i) with Catherine Collard.

Although we think Pascal Rogé is very special in this repertoire, Anne Queffélec has strong claims too. She can be quirky, as in the opening *Croquis et agaceries d'un gros bonhomme en bois* or, more particularly, the satirical *Valse ballet*; she is engagingly cool in the *Pièces froides*; her accounts of the *Caresse* and *Les Pantins dansent* are quite haunting, while the *Petite ouverture à danser* has much charm. In the *Trois morceaux en forme de poire* and the lively *La Belle Excentrique* she is partnered by the late lamented Catherine Collard, and how brilliantly they end the concert with that final quartet of sparkling vignettes, opening with the dazzling *Grande ritournelle* and ending with the irrepressible *Can-can 'grand-mondain'*. The recording is excellent.

Piano, 4 hands: (i) *La Belle Excentrique; 3 Morceaux en forme de poire.* **Solo piano:** *Descriptions automatiques; Embryons desséchés; 3 Gnossiennes; 3 Gymnopédies; 2 Valses.*

(N) (M) *** Virgin VM5 61846-2. Queffélec; (i) with Catherine Collard.

This reissue also includes solo items from an earlier recital, dating from 1988, notably the celebrated *Gymnopédies* and *Gnossiennes*. All the music here is dispatched with great character and style, and these artists are exceptionally well served by the engineers. While this would have been an ideal opportunity to pair both the original CDs as a Virgin Double, the present collection cannot be recommended too highly.

Aperçus désagréables; La Belle Excentrique (fantaisie sérieuse) (both for 4 hands); *Croquis et agaceries d'un gros bonhomme en bois; Descriptions automatiques; Embryons desséchés; En habit de cheval* (for 4 hands); *Le Fils des étoiles, wagnerie kaldéenne du Sar Peladan; 6 Gnossiennes; 3 Gymnopédies; Jack-in-the-box; 3 Mouvements en forme de poire* (for 4 hands); *3 Nocturnes; Peccadilles importunes; 3 Petites pièces montées* (for 4 hands); *Pièces froides; Préludes flasques (pour un chien); Première pensée et sonneries de la Rose Croix; 3 Sarabandes; Sonatine bureaucratique; Sports et divertissements; 3 Valses distinguées du précieux dégoûté.*

(B) **(*) EMI (ADD) CZS5 68994-2 (2). Ciccolini.

Music for Piano, 4 hands: (i) *La Belle Excentrique; 3 Morceaux en forme de poire.* **Solo Piano Music:** *Avant-dernières pensées; Embryons desséchés; 6 Gnossiennes; Croquis et agaceries d'un gros bonhomme en bois; 3 Gymnopédies; 5 Nocturnes; Sonatine bureaucratique; Véritables préludes flasques (pour un chien).*

(M) *** EMI CDM5 67239-2 [567260]. Ciccolini; (i) with Tacchino.

Aldo Ciccolini is widely praised as a Satie interpreter and in this 2-CD recital he plays with unaffected sympathy. He certainly understands the *douloureux* feeling of the famous *Gymnopédies* and finds the '*conviction et tristesse rigoureuse*' of the *Gnossiennes*. *La Belle Excentrique* is thrown off with great dash and élan. In the works where (by electronic means) Ciccolini provides all four hands, the percussive edge of the pianism seems somewhat accentuated by the recording, but generally the analogue piano recording is very acceptable, and the CD transfer has plenty of colour and sonority.

Aldo Ciccolini recorded the selection on the single disc again during the 1980s and he is completely in sympathy

with their style. He is totally inside this music and makes the most of its (not particularly wide) contrasts of mood and atmosphere. The recorded sound, harder in outline and not as rich as afforded to Pascal Rogé in his complete survey on Decca, is still very good. And some may feel that the slight edge given to the sharply articulated pieces (the *Embryons desséchés* and the *Sonatine bureaucratique* for instance) adds to their witty vitality. Gabriel Tacchino joins his colleague for the four-handed pieces. In many ways this is one of the most distinctive Satie collections in the catalogue.

Avant-dernières pensées; Chapitres tournés en tous sens; Croquis et agaceries d'un gros bonhomme en bois; Descriptions automatiques; Deux rêveries nocturnes; Heures séculaires et instantanées; Nocturnes Nos. 1–3, 5; Nouvelles pièces froides; Pièces froides; Prélude de la porte héroïque du ciel; 3 Valses distinguées du précieux dégoûté; Véritables préludes flasques.

*** Decca 421 713-2. Rogé.

Pascal Rogé's choice of repertoire on this well-filled disc ranges from the Rose-Croix pieces through to the *Nocturnes*. As with the earlier recital, his playing has an eloquence and charm that are altogether rather special, and the recorded sound is very good indeed.

(i) *Avant-dernières pensées; Embryons desséchés; Gnossiennes Nos. 1–5; Gymnopédies Nos. 1–3; Nocturne No. 1; Sarabandes Nos. 1–3; Sonatine bureaucratique; 3 Valses distinguées du précieux dégoûté;* **(ii)** *Croquis et agaceries d'un gros bonhomme en bois; Descriptions automatiques; Je te veux; Poudre d'or.*

(B) **(*) Sony (ADD) SBK 48283. (i) Varviso; (ii) Entremont.

Both recitals here were recorded in 1979. Daniel Varviso has the measure of these pieces and plays admirably. Perhaps the first of the *Embryons desséchés* could have greater delicacy and wit, and there could be greater melancholy in the second of the *Gymnopédies*. But one's main reservation concerns the closely balanced recording of the piano and the slightly dry sound. Entremont, too, is placed forwardly, but he brings some charm to *Je te veux* and *Poudre d'or*, while the *Descriptions automatiques* are engagingly crisp and witty.

Avant-dernières pensées; Embryons desséchés; 6 Gnossiennes; 3 Gymnopédies; Pièces froides; Sarabande No. 3; Sonatine bureaucratique; 3 Valses distinguées du précieux dégoûté; 3 Véritables préludes flasques (pour un chien).

*** BIS CD 317. Pöntinen.

Roland Pöntinen seems perfectly in tune with the Satiean world, and his playing is distinguished by sensibility and tonal finesse. He is very well recorded too.

Berceuse; Caresse; 6 Gnossiennes; 3 Gymnopédies; Nocturne No. 4; 2 Oeuvres de jeunesse; Peccadilles importunes; Petit prélude à la journée; Le Piccadilly; Poudre d'or; Prélude de la porte héroïque du ciel; Rêverie du pauvre; Sonatine bureaucratique.

*** Decca 458 105-2. Rogé.

This generous compilation, taken from Rogé's uniquely

distinguished Decca coverage of Satie's piano music, is entitled (reasonably enough) 'Piano Dreams'. The selection concentrates on the composer's gentler, haunting evocations, including – besides the *Gymnopédies* and *Gnossiennes* – several highlights from the third disc, which we especially enjoyed. The mood livens up towards the close, with the ragtime valse from the *Oeuvres de jeunesse*, and finally the cakewalk, *Le Piccadilly*. With first-class recording, this could well be a first choice for those wanting a single disc Satie collection.

Caresse; Carnet d'esquisses et de croquis; Danse de travers; La Diva de l'Empire; Enfantillages pittoresques; Esquisses et sketch montmartoise; Le Fils des étoiles: Preludes to Acts I & II. 2 Oeuvres de jeunesse; Les Pantins dansent; Peccadilles importunes; Petite musique de clown triste; Petite ouverture à danser; Le Piège de Méduse; Première pensée Rose + Croix; Rêverie du pauvre; Sports et divertissements.

*** Decca 455 370-2. Rogé.

There is some exquisite playing here, particularly in the *Enfantillages pittoresques*, the delicately sensuous and infinitely brief *Caresse*, and the two serene *Préludes* for *Le Fils des étoiles*. The waltzes of *Deux oeuvres de jeunesse* and the little dance movements of *Le Piège de Méduse* are delectably pointed, and there is both wit and charm in the *Esquisses et sketch montmartrois* and the twenty snippets which make up the *Sports et divertissements* after the opening *Choral inappétissant*. The final piece here, *Rêverie du pauvre*, has a haunting stillness. The recording, in an ideal acoustic, could not be more real.

Chapitres tournés en tous sens; Croquis et agaceries d'un gros bonhomme en bois; Le Fils des étoiles; Gymnopédies; Je te veux (valse); Prélude et tapisserie; Le Piccadilly; Pièces froides; Le Piège de Méduse; Poudre d'or; Sonata bureaucratique; Sports et divertissements; Véritables préludes flasques pour un chien; Vexations.

(N) *** Olympia OCD 695. Dickinson.

Peter Dickinson has made Satie's music a centrepoint of his repertoire, and his thoughtful approach to this highly rewarding music is all his own, often more withdrawn than usual. By his side Ciccolini sounds almost brittle. The *Trois Gymnopédies*, taken very slowly, have a grave dignity, and Dickinson finds a captivating delicacy of feeling for the *Chapitres tournés en tous sens*. The *Sonata bureaucratique* is playful rather than ironic, its *Andante* most delicate, while the *Pièces froides* have a distinct air of nostalgia.

Of the two *valses*, *Je te veux* is attractively intimate, *Poudre d'or* more populist, though not without refined light and shade. *Piccadilly* is as perky as ever, and the charming rhythmic diversity of the dance vignettes which make up *Le Piège de Méduse* is matched by the *Sports et divertissements*, which have a much wider range of character and feeling here than in most performances. Throughout, Dickinson's variety of articulation and colour is fully at the service of the composer, and he departs in an air of mystery with his gentle account of the enigmatic *Vexations*. The recording, made at the Maltings in 1989, and engineered by the late Bob Auger, is very real indeed.

Embryons desséchés; 6 Gnossiennes; 3 Gymnopédies; Heures séculaires et instantanées; Nocturnes Nos. 1–5; Sonatine bureaucratique; Sports et divertissements.

*** Hyp. CDA 66344. Seow.

The Singapore-born pianist Yitkin Seow is a good stylist; his approach is fresh and his playing crisp and marked by consistent beauty of sound. Seow captures the melancholy of the *Gymnopédies* very well and the playing, though not superior to Rogé or Queffélec in character or charm, has a quiet reticence that is well suited to this repertoire. The recording is eminently truthful.

Embryons desséchés; 6 Gnossiennes; 3 Gymnopédies; Je te veux; Nocturne No. 4; Le Piccadilly; 4 Préludes flasques; Prélude en tapisserie; Sonatine bureaucratique; Vieux séquins et vieilles cuirasses.

*** Decca 410 220-2. Rogé.

Rogé has real feeling for this music and conveys its grave melancholy as well as he does its lighter qualities. He produces, as usual, consistent beauty of tone, and this is well projected by the recording. Very well recorded, too.

3 Gymnopédies.

(B) *** Decca Penguin 460 649-2. Rogé – DEBUSSY: *Nocturnes;* RAVEL: *Le Tombeau de Couperin; La Valse.* ***

Those wanting just the three famous *Gymnopédies* will find that Pascal Rogé captures their bitter-sweet melancholy to perfection.

Gymnopédies; Ogives; Sarabandes.

(B) ** Ph. 420 472-2. De Leeuw.

Reinbert de Leeuw is a sensitive pianist who is thoroughly attuned to Satie's personality; he takes the composer at his word by playing *très lent*, though at times one feels a little more movement would be an advantage. The recording is good, but not exceptional; the playing time of less than 50 minutes is ungenerous, but the reissue is at bargain price.

SAUER, Emil von (1862–1942)

Piano Concerto No. 1 in E min.

*** Hyp. CDA 66790. Hough, CBSO, Foster – SCHARWENKA: *Piano Concerto No. 4.* ***

This potent coupling of Sauer and Scharwenka surely combines every feature of the 'Romantic concerto', from flamboyant display to beguiling lyricism. As a greatly admired virtuoso, Emil von Sauer was an able exponent of the Scharwenka concerto; and his own work, although lighter in feeling, makes comparable demands on the dexterity of the soloist. Its delightful melodic vein and style have much in common with Saint-Saëns. Stephen Hough sparkles his way through its glittering upper tessitura. Altogether this makes a perfect foil for the more ambitious concerto with which it is paired. Splendid recording, with a nice sense of scale.

SAUGUET, Henri (1901–89)

Mélodie concertante for Cello & Orchestra.

*** Russian Disc (ADD) RDCD 11108. Rostropovich, USSR SO, composer – BRITTEN: *Cello Symphony.* **(*)

Sauguet belongs at the heart of the Gallic tradition, and the opening of his *Mélodie concertante* has a dream-like, pastoral. Its source of inspiration was an old, persistent memory of a young cellist from Bordeaux. It is an extended improvisation, based on a haunting, introspective theme heard at the beginning of the piece. The performance is, of course, authoritative in every way, and the 1964 analogue recording sounds every bit as good as it did in its fine LP format.

SAXTON, Robert (born 1953)

(i) *Chamber Symphony (Circles of Light);* (ii) *Concerto for Orchestra; The Ring of Eternity;* (i) *The Sentinel of the Rainbow.*

(M) *** EMI CDM5 66530-2. (i) L. Sinf.; (ii) BBC SO; Knussen.

The *Concerto for Orchestra* was first given at the Proms in 1984. Its four linked sections broadly follow a symphonic shape, as do those of the *Chamber Symphony* of 1986, which uses smaller forces, with solo strings. That later work has the title *Circles of Light* and was inspired by a quotation from Dante, when in the *Divine Comedy* he looks into the eyes of his beloved, Beatrice, and links what he sees to the movement of the heavens. The other two works are linked in the composer's mind to the *Concerto for Orchestra* to form a sort of trilogy. Oliver Knussen draws intense, committed playing both from the BBC Symphony Orchestra in the *Concerto for Orchestra* and *The Ring of Eternity*, and from the London Sinfonietta in the chamber-scale works. Full, warm recording.

SCARLATTI, Alessandro (1660–1725)

(i) *Concerti grossi Nos. 1–6;* (ii) *Stabat Mater.*

(M) **(*) DG (ADD) 459 454-2 (2). (i) Solisti from Scarlatti Orchestra of Naples, Gracis; (ii) Freni, Berganza, Paul Kuenz CO, Mackerras – PERGOLESI: *Stabat Mater* **(*).

Ettore Gracis's recording of these six fine *Concerti grossi* was made in the 1960s. The first three act as a postlude to Scarlatti's memorably searching setting of the *Stabat Mater*; the remainder are used in a similar way for the coupled Pergolesi setting. In the vocal work, recorded a decade later, there is fine singing from both soloists, and the beauty of the writing is never in doubt, even if the balance unduly favours the voices, while the orchestral playing could be more resilient. The accounts of the *Concerti grossi* are alive and workmanlike, but not as fresh or accomplished as those by I Musici.

Concerti grossi Nos. 1–3; (i) *Sinfonie di concerti grossi for Flute & Strings Nos. 7–12.*

(M) *** Ph. (IMS) Dig./ADD 434 160-2. (i) Bennett; I Musici.

I Musici give performances of much eloquence and warmth and great transparency; the latter is welcome in the fugal movements, especially as the 1979 analogue recording is of the very first rank. The *Sinfonie di concerti grossi* feature a flute soloist, in this instance the excellent William Bennett, who plays fluently and in fine style. The performances are lively and attractive, and eminently freshly recorded in Philips's best digital sound.

Cantatas: Clori e Mirtillo; E pur vuole il cielo e amore; Ero e Leandro; Filli che esprime la sua fede a Fileno; Marc'Antonio e Cleopatra; Questo silenzio ombroso.

(N) ᵇ**(*) Virgin VBD 561803-2 (2). Lesne, Piau, Il Seminario Musicale – HANDEL: *Italian Cantatas.* **(*)

As so often with this repertoire, the texts dramatize the problems of lovers who are unable to be together or who destiny insists must part. The most dramatic of these is the dialogue between Antony and Cleopatra at the moment when he has to leave for Rome. The opening, much shorter, pastoral cantata here, *Questa silenzio ombroso* ('This shady quietude'), is a deeply expressive duet which lightens as the soprano line describes the sweetly lamenting nightingale. *Filli che esprime la sua fede a Fileno*, an expression of steadfast love, has a long instrumental introduction for violin and flute which comes off well. Both vocal artists are on top form, and the simple continuo accompaniments are admirably played by Il Seminario Musicale. This is specialized repertoire, perhaps not to all tastes; but Lesne and Piau are exceptional artists. This disc now comes as a Virgin Double coupled inexpensively with *Italian Cantatas* by Handel. The snag is the absence of texts and translations.

Cantata per la Notte di Natale: Abramo, il tuo sembiante (Christmas Eve cantata).

*** Opus 111 OPS 30-156. Bertini, Fedi, Cavina, Naglia, Foresti, Concerto Italiano, Alessandrini – CORELLI: *Christmas concerto grosso in G min., Op. 6/8.* ***

This delightful semi-operatic cantata presents the Nativity through the eyes of five figures from the Old Testament, Abraham (bass), Ezekiel (soprano), Isaiah (tenor), Jeremiah (alto) and Daniele (soprano), who are all together in Limbo, where they await the Messiah. There is splendid music for all the soloists, and especially the excellent male alto, Claudio Cavina, who as Jeremiah foresees and laments the coming suffering and death of Christ. The whole performance bursts with life under Rinaldo Alessandrini, and makes a fine entertainment, touching, but never solemn. Corelli's most famous concerto grosso, with its *Pastorale* closing movement, is used as a vivacious introduction. The recording sparkles and this is very highly recommended.

Missa, Ad usum Capellae Pontificale. Motets: Ad te, Domine, levavi; Domine vivifica me; Exaltabo e Domine quoniam; Exultate Deo adjutori; Intellige clamorem meum; Salvum fac populum tuum.

(M) **(*) Erato (ADD) 0630 11229-2. Lausanne Vocal Ens.,
Corboz.

The *Missa, Ad usum Capellae Pontificale* is a fine example of
Scarlatti's ready homage to the *stilo antico*. The atmosphere
is restrained, never overtly dramatic. Overall, if not ambitious, the Mass is a moving work, never austerely withdrawn, and Corboz's refined performance catches its
restrained mood; even if perhaps he could have produced
more dramatic contrast at times, the peaceful atmosphere is
very affecting. Each of the six *a capella* motets is short. The
first four, with their gentle linear flow and serene atmosphere, are again very much in the inherited Palestrina tradition. In the fifth, *Ad te, Domine, levavi*, the composer more
strongly asserts his own harmonic style; but all five are
beautiful and Corboz's performances are worthy of them.
The final motet, *Exultate Deo adjutori*, understandably
brings a change of mood, and the result is quite light-hearted,
very like a madrigal. The reissue is well documented, but it
is a pity there are no translated texts.

Motets: *De tenebroso lacu; Infirmata, vulnerata;* (i) *Salve
Regina. Totus amore languens.*

(M) *** Virgin (ADD) VC5 45103-2. Lesne; (i) Gens; Il
Seminario Musicale.

Alessandro Scarlatti wrote about a hundred motets. Often
strikingly original, in many ways they are like vocal concerti
grossi, contrasting slow and fast movements to suit the text;
at the same time they combine an Italianate expressive
melodic cantilena with an operatic feeling for drama. Lesne
is right inside the music's expressive world and it is difficult
to imagine this being better sung. In the setting of *Salve
Regine* he is joined by Véronique Gens, and their voices blend
admirably. Throughout, the accompaniments are creative,
vital and warmly supportive – stimulating and beautiful in
their own right. This is period-instrument performance at
its most revealing. The recording is vivid, yet has just the
right degree of warmth and spaciousness. Full translations
are provided.

Motets: *Domine, refugium factus es nobis; O magnum
mysterium.*

(B) *** Double Decca (ADD) 443 868-2 (2). Schütz Ch. of L.,
Roger Norrington – BONONCINI: *Stabat Mater* ***;
PERGOLESI: *Magnificat in C; Stabat Mater* **(*);
D. SCARLATTI: *Stabat Mater;* CALDARA: *Crucifixus;*
LOTTI: *Crucifixus.* ***

These two motets are fine pieces that show how enduring
the Palestrina tradition was in seventeenth-century Italy.
They are noble in conception and are beautifully performed
here and, given first-class sound, make a fine bonus for this
enterprising Double Decca collection of Italian baroque
choral music.

Cantatas: *Il rossignuolo se scioglie il volo; Clori vezzosa e
bella.*

(N) **(*) Australian Decca Eloquence (ADD) 461 596-2. Watts,
Dupré, Dart – HANDEL: *Italian Cantatas.* ***

Very attractive performances dating from the late 1950s in
warm, vivid sound. The only curious thing is a low rumble

which effects these two cantatas from time to time which
is noticeable with only viola de gamba and harpsichord
accompaniments. The main Handel items (with orchestra)
are unaffected.

(i) *Salve Regina;* (i; ii) *Stabat Mater;* (iii) Motet: *Quae est
ista.*

**(*) Virgin VC5 45366-2. (i) Lesne; (ii) Piau; (i–iii) Novelli; Il
Seminario Musicale.

Gérard Lesne is heard at his finest in Scarlatti's eloquent A
minor setting (one of five) of the *Salve Regina*, expressive
and dramatic by turns. But when he joins with Sandrine
Piau for the *Stabat Mater* the combination of voices is
charracterful in its contrast rather than a vocal symbiosis.
Sandrine Piau's singing is pure, and tenderly touching, Lesne
is more dramatic and brings a wider range of vocal colour,
but his contribution is less moving. The two singers are
successfully joined by the tenor Jean-François Novelli for
the attractive closing motet, *Quae est ista*, which is widely
varied in style; but again it is the soprano who stands out. Il
Seminario give pleasing authentic support and this is a
stimulating collection, but collectors primarily interested in
the *Stabat Mater* will find that the performance by Gemma
Bertagnolli and Sara Mingardo with the Concerto Italiano
remains unsurpassed (see below).

St Cecilia Mass.

(B) *** Double Decca (ADD) 458 370-2 (2). Harwood,
Eathorne, Cable, Eans, Keyte, St John's College Ch., Wren
O, Guest – J. C. BACH: *Magnificat;* J. S. BACH:
Magnificat. ***

This is far more florid in style than Scarlatti's other Masses
and it receives from Guest a vigorous and fresh performance.
The soloists cope with their difficult fioriture very confidently and they match one another well. This now comes
as part of a Decca Double offering excellent accounts of
Magnificats by Bach, father and son.

Stabat Mater.

*** Opus 111 OPS 30-160. Bertagnolli, Mingardo, Concerto
Italiano, Alessandrini – PERGOLESI: *Stabat Mater.* *** ⊙

If somewhat less theatrical than Pergolesi's setting, Scarlatti's
music brings continual bursts of vitality to contrast with the
rich flowing polyphonic lines when the soprano and alto
voices are combined. There are memorably expressive solos
for both singers and, as in the companion work, they combine touchingly for the work's closing benediction before
the tension lifts at the coda. Once again both the radiant
soprano, Gemma Bertagnolli, and the dark-voiced contralto,
Sara Mingardo, rise fully to the challenge of this remarkable
music, and Alessandrini's instrumental support could not
be more persuasive or authentic.

SCARLATTI, Domenico (1685–1757)

The Good-Humoured Ladies (ballet suite; arr.
Tommasini).

(M) *** EMI (ADD) CDM5 65911-2. Concert Arts O, Irving –
GLAZUNOV: *The Seasons;* WALTON: *Wise Virgins.* ***

(B) **(*) Sony (ADD) SBK 60311. Cleveland O, Lane –
RESPIGHI: *The Birds; Church Windows.* **(*)

Scarlatti's music in Tommasini's witty arrangement chatters
along very like a group of dear old ladies gossiping over tea.
Irving points this up most beautifully and (especially in the
finale) offers some very brilliant orchestral playing, while the
Andante (from the *Sonata in B minor,* Kk. 87) is touchingly
tender. The EMI recording is first class and completely belies
its age (1961). Alas, this disc has just been deleted.

Louis Lane directs freshly an enjoyable account of this
delightfully light-hearted music, so wittily scored. The Clevelanders respond with style and delicacy, and the 1970 Severance Hall recording is warm and pleasing, even if ideally it
could be a little more transparent. However, the so-called
'Cats' Fugue' is neatly and clearly articulated, and Lane scores
a bonus point by including the *Overture.*

Keyboard Sonatas (complete).

*** Erato 2292 45309-2 (34). Ross, Huggett, Coin, Henry,
Vallon.

The tercentenary of Domenico Scarlatti's birth prompted
the production of an integral recording of Scarlatti's 555
Keyboard Sonatas, including the three intended for organ,
others for violin and continuo, and two for the unlikely
combination of violin and oboe in unison. Scott Ross, who,
with the participation of Monica Huggett (violin),
Christophe Coin (cello), Michel Henry (oboe) and Marc
Vallon (bassoon), is primarily responsible, plays five different harpsichords plus the organ, and he is very well
recorded throughout in varying acoustics. Scarlatti's invention shows an inexhaustible resourcefulness, and Ross's
playing is fully worthy: he is lively, technically assured,
rhythmically resilient and, above all, he conveys his enjoyment of the music, without eccentricity. We cannot claim
to have heard all thirty-four CDs, but all the evidence of
sampling suggests that for the Scarlatti addict they will prove
an endless source of satisfaction. The documentation is
ample, providing a 200-page booklet about the composer,
his music and the performers. The overall cost of this set is
somewhere in the region of £200.

Keyboard Sonatas, Kk. 1, 3, 8–9, 11, 17, 24–5, 27, 29, 87, 96, 113, 141, 146, 173, 213–14, 247, 259, 268, 283–4, 380, 386–7, 404, 443, 519–20, 523.

(BB) *** Virgin 2 x 1 VBD5 61961-2 (2). Pletnev (piano).

This carefully chosen selection of some of Scarlatti's finest
and most adventurous sonatas, stretches over two CDs,
giving the fullest opportunity to demonstrate the extraordinary range of this music in a recital-length programme
playing for 140 minutes. In the opening *D major Sonata,* Kk.
443, Pletnev establishes a firm pianistic approach, yet the
staccato articulation reminds us that the world of the harpsichord is not so far away. However, in the *G major Sonata,*
Kk. 283, and in the following Kk. 284 his fuller piano sonority
transforms the effect of the writing. The second CD opens
with the almost orchestral Kk. 96 *in D,* with its resonant
horn calls, and later the lovely, flowing *C minor Sonata* and

the even more expressive Kk. 11 *in F sharp minor* bring a
reflective poetic feeling, which could not have been matched
in colour by the plucked instrument. The performances
throughout are in the very front rank.

Keyboard Sonatas, Kk. 1, 8–9, 11, 13, 20, 87, 98, 119, 135, 159, 380, 450, 487 & 529.

*** DG 435 855-2. Pogorelich (piano).

Pogorelich plays with captivating simplicity and convinces
the listener that this is music which sounds far more enjoyable on the piano than on the harpsichord. His dazzling
execution, using the lightest touch, consistently enchants
the ear with its subtle tonal colouring, and the music emerges
ever sparkling and fresh. These performances can be
measured against those of Horowitz and not found wanting.
Moreover Pogorelich is beautifully recorded in an ideal
acoustic, and the hour-long programme is admirably chosen
to provide maximum variety.

Keyboard Sonatas, Kk. 1, 27, 39, 87, 266, 298, 299, 366, 367, 374, 377, 379, 400, 417, 426, 484, 518, 519, 526, 545.

*** Sanctus SCS 016. Demidenko (piano).

Demidenko's are modern pianistic performances, fully
coloured, neatly decorated, but with plentiful use of the
pedal, judicious enough, but especially noticeable in Kk. 367,
where there is a degree of blurring. Yet the very opening *D
major Sonata,* Kk. 298, with its crisp bursts of staccato
repeated notes, is most engaging, as is the simpler *B flat
major,* Kk. 266, and the flightier Kk. 1. Demidenko has not
followed the often suggested grouping in pairs, but has
chosen his own order and effectively so. Excellent recording.

Keyboard Sonatas, Kk. 3, 52, 184–5, 191–3, 208–9, 227, 238–9, 252–3.

(B) *** Sony (ADD) SBK 60099. Leonhardt (harpsichord).

Very distinguished playing from Gustav Leonhardt, who
often plays with dash and exuberance, as in the first sonata
here, Kk. 3 *in A minor.* He uses a copy of a Dulcken harpsichord, and these are consistently characterful performances
which project direct to the listener in well-focused, clean
sound, recorded in a pleasant acoustic.

Complete Keyboard Sonatas, Vol. 1: Kk. 8, 13, 44, 184, 246, 402, 421, 427, 430, 434, 446, 450, 487, 523, 531, 533, 544.

(BB) (***) Naxos 8.553061. Andjaparidze (piano).

Naxos have planned their Scarlatti survey to include different pianists, and the Georgian pianist Eteri Andjaparidze,
the youngest prize-winner in Moscow's Tchaikovsky competition, proves an excellent choice for the first collection. She
plays with finesse, elegance and style, and is at her finest in
the reflective minor-key sonatas. The snag is that this recital
was recorded over three days in June 1994, and for some
reason the piano pitch is not consistent and changes disconcertingly between some items. Otherwise the recording is of
high quality.

Keyboard Sonatas, Kk. 8, 20, 32, 107, 109, 124, 141, 159, 234, 247, 256, 259, 328, 380, 397, 423, 430, 440, 447, 481, 490, 492, 515 & 519.

(M) (***) EMI mono CHS7 64934-2. Landowska (harpsichord).

Landowska led the revival of interest in the harpsichord at a time when it was a relative rarity both in the recital room and in the recording studio. She used a thunderous Pleyel that was specially built to withstand the rigours of 1920s and '30s travel; but her playing has more character than most other modern players put together; it is electrifying in its sheer vitality and imagination. Lionel Salter's excellent notes quote her as saying she was 'sensitive to Scarlatti's bucolic mind, his rustic jauntiness ... the elemental strength, the richness of his rhythmical power, as well as all that is Moorish in them. He has the genuine nobility, the heroism and the audacity of Don Quixote.' The first batch of sonatas was recorded in 1934 and the others in 1939 and 1940. Indispensable.

Keyboard Sonatas, Kk. 10, 46, 54, 69–70, 105, 119, 126, 201, 203, 212, 261, 444, 447, 525, 537.

(N)(BB) ** Naxos 8. 555047. Jandó (piano).

Jenö Jandó's Scarlatti style is brisk, crisp and clean. His articulation at times offers remarkable bravura (witness K. 10 in D minor or K. 212 in A major). The E minor K. 203 and G major K. 105 are certainly characterful, while the C minor K. 126 has an appropriate pensive quality. Yet other performers find more diversity of colour and delicacy of feeling in this music. He is very well recorded.

Keyboard Sonatas, Kk. 12, 25, 27, 45, 118, 183, 187, 197, 201, 213, 233, 409, 239, 340, 517, 545. Essercizi: 'Cats' Fugue' in G min., Kk. 30.

**(*) Lyrichord LEMS 8043. Comparone (harpsichord).

It was Clementi who nicknamed the last of Scarlatti's Essercizi the 'Cats' Fugue', which gives this Lyrichord collection its sobriquet. Fortunately Elaine Comparone is not tempted to overdo such a pictorial suggestion.

She uses a modern Hubbard copy of a 1646 Ruckers harpsichord, enlarged in 1780 by Taskin, which she plays with bold, clear articulation and plenty of rhythmic lift. However, we would have liked a little more relaxation at times in some of the minor-key works, where she makes little attempt to seduce the ear with a more gentle approach. The recording is real and vividly present.

Keyboard Sonatas, Kk. 25, 33, 39, 52, 54, 96, 146, 162, 197–8, 201, 303, 466, 474, 481, 491, 525, 547.

**(*) Sony (ADD) SK 53460. Horowitz (piano).

Provided you are prepared to accept sometimes less than flattering and often rather dry recorded sound, this is marvellous playing which sweeps away any purist notions about Scarlatti having to be played on the harpsichord. The eighteen sonatas were chosen by Horowitz after he had recorded nearly twice as many throughout 1964. The very opening, staccato D major, Kk. 33, is made to sound very brittle by the close balance, but in the following A minor, Kk. 54, the pianist's gentle colouring is fully revealed. Here, as in the two slow F minor Sonatas, Kk. 466 and Kk. 481, the music is particularly beautiful in a way not expected of Scarlatti. The

playing time has been extended to 72 minutes by the addition of six more sonatas to the content of the original CD.

Keyboard Sonatas, Kk. 32, 64, 69, 87, 133, 146, 160, 198, 208, 213, 380, 429, 466, 481, 511, 517; Toccata in D min.

(B) **(*) Cal. CAL 6670. Södergren (piano).

Inger Södergren gives an appealing recital of 16 well-contrasted *Sonatas* plus a brilliant account of the highly individual *Toccata in D minor*. Some might feel that her gentle, almost wistful treatment of the lyrical sonatas errs towards being too romantic but her keen sensitivity and crisp articulation in the lively pieces are unimpeachable, and she is very well recorded.

Keyboard Sonatas, Kk. 46, 87, 99, 124, 201, 204a, 490–92, 513, 520–21.

(M) *** CRD (ADD) CRD 3368. Pinnock (harpsichord).

No need to say much about this: the playing is first rate and the recording outstanding in its presence and clarity. There are few better harpsichord anthologies of Scarlatti in the catalogue, although the measure is not particularly generous.

Keyboard Sonatas: Kk. 115–16, 144, 175, 402–3, 449–50, 474–5, 513, 516–17, 544–5.

**(*) Decca 421 422-2. Schiff (piano).

Exquisite and sensitive playing, full of colour and delicacy. As always, András Schiff is highly responsive to the mood and character of each piece. At times one wonders whether he is not a little too refined: in some, one would have welcomed more abandon and fire. However, for the most part this is a delightful recital, and the Decca recording is exemplary in its truthfulness.

Keyboard Sonatas, Kk. 213–14; 318–19; 347–8; 356–7; 380–81; 454–5; 478–9; 524–7.

(B) *** DG (ADD) 439 438-2. Kirkpatrick (harpsichord).

These performances have all the panache and scholarship one would expect from this artist, in addition to a welcome degree of freedom and poetry. Some of his Bach playing has seemed pedantic, so it is a pleasure to welcome this brightly recorded bargain collection back to the catalogue without reservation.

Keyboard Sonatas, Kk. 159, 175, 208, 213, 322 & 380 (arr. for guitar).

(B) *** Sony (ADD) SBK 62425. Williams (guitar) –
   GIULIANI: *Variations on a Theme by Handel;*
   PAGANINI: *Caprice; Grand Sonata;* VILLA-LOBOS: 5
   Preludes. ***

Guitar arrangements of Scarlatti sonatas have their charms when played by an artist as imaginative as John Williams. He manages by percussive plucking to sound at times almost like a harpsichord, while his gentle playing is always beguiling , especially in the delightful *D major Sonata*, Kk. 159. The recording is faithful, somewhat close and larger than life, but never unacceptably so. This diverse and well-planned recital (76 minutes) is very enjoyable indeed.

VOCAL MUSIC

Dixit Dominus.

*** DG (IMS) 423 386-2. Argenta, Attrot, Denley, Stafford, Varcoe, Ch. & E. Concert, Pinnock – VIVALDI: *Gloria.* ***

Pinnock, as so often, inspires his performers to sing and play as though at a live event. This Scarlatti psalm-setting, very well recorded, makes an attractive coupling for the better known of Vivaldi's settings of the *Gloria.*

Stabat Mater.

(B) *** Double Decca (ADD) 443 868-2 (2). Schütz Ch. of L., Norrington – BONONCINI: *Stabat Mater* ***; PERGOLESI: *Magnificat in C; Stabat Mater* **(*); A. SCARLATTI: *Domine, refugium factus es nobis; O magnum mysterium;* CALDARA: *Crucifixus;* LOTTI: *Crucifixus.*

(B) **(*) Sony (ADD) SBK 48282. BBC Singers, John Poole – VIVALDI: *Stabat Mater; Dixit Dominus.* **(*)

Norrington's performance is admirable, though not always impeccable in matters of tonal balance; and the recording is very good. Overall this well-designed Double Decca set combines three fine *Stabat Mater* settings with other comparable baroque choral music, all well performed and impressively recorded.

A thoroughly musical, if not distinctive, performance from the BBC Singers, who blend well together and are realistically recorded. An attractive coupling for two enjoyable period performances of Vivaldi.

SCHARWENKA, Franz Xaver
(1850–1924)

Piano Concerto No. 4 in F min., Op. 82.

*** Hyp. CDA 66790. Hough, CBSO, Foster – SAUER: *Piano Concerto No. 1.* ***

Scharwenka wrote four piano concertos; this, his finest, was very famous in its time. It is ambitiously flamboyant and on the largest scale. Its invention, which manages a potent mix of bravura and lyricism, readily holds the attention, with plenty of interest in the bold orchestral tuttis. The second-movement *Allegretto* has much charm and is very deftly scored; a full flood of romanticism blossoms in the *Lento* slow movement. The stormy *con fuoco* finale combines a touch of wit and more robust geniality with glittering brilliance and power; and all four movements make prodigious technical and artistic demands on the soloist, to which Stephen Hough rises with great technical aplomb and consistent panache; he also plays with fine poetic sensibility. He is given vigorously committed support by Lawrence Foster and the CBSO and a first-class Hyperion recording. Winner not only of the *Gramophone* Concerto Award, this was also that magazine's Record of the Year in 1996, and deservedly so.

SCHEIDT, Samuel (1587–1654)

Ludi musici (Hamburg, 1621): excerpts.

*** Audivis ES 8559. Hespèrion XX, Savall.

Samuel Scheidt published four collections of instrumental music between 1621 and 1624 under the title *Ludi musici* but only the First Book survives, and all these pieces are drawn from it. For all its good nature, his music has a melancholy streak and has much in common with Dowland's *Lachrimae.* Scheidt actually draws on Dowland in his spirited *Battle galliard,* so characteristic of its time. Other English tunes are featured in his canzons, notably in the delightful five-part *Canzon* (from Cantus XXVI). All this music is played with characteristic finesse, nicely judged espressivo and plenty of vitality by the superb Jordi Savall and Hespèrion XX, and the viol sound is smooth and pleasingly natural, with none of that scratchiness which comes from too close microphones.

SCHEIN, Johann Hermann (1586–1630)

Banchetto musicale (1617): Nos. 2, Suite a 5 in D; 6, Suite a 5 in D; 16, Suite a 5 in A; 20, Suite a 5 in E; 26, Canzon a 5 in A (Corollarium). Venus Kräntzlein (1609): Nos. 17, Intrada a 5 in D; 20, Intrada a 5 in G; 22, Gagliarda a 5 in D; 23, Canzon a 5 in A.

(M) *** Virgin VM5 61399-2. Hespèrion XX, Savall.

Johann Hermann Schein's instrumental music has much in common with that of his Italian contemporary, Giovanni Gabrieli, although the interplay between various groups, usually brass and strings (or recorder), is much less spectacular. The *Canzon in A major* (*Corollarium*), however, is a more ambitious piece, very much in the contrapuntal Gabrieli manner The *Banchetto musicale* is intended as a background for meals, although the sonorous brass writing with occasional bravura roulades would suggest that the banqueting hall would have needed to be very spacious. However, the very pleasing expressive music (especially the *Padouanas*) invites lower dynamic levels. The *Intradas* open with a drum-beat, suggesting the musicians marching in to the feast. The performances here are stylish and pleasing, responding to the music's dolorousness. Perhaps they could have been more robust, but the result is very suitable for domestic listening and is very well recorded.

SCHIERBECK, Poul (1888–1949)

The Chinese Flute, Op. 10.

(**(*)) Bluebell mono ABCD 075. Nilsson, Swedish Radio O, Mann – BARTOK: *Bluebeard's Castle.* (**(*))

The Chinese Flute, Op. 10; Queen Dagmar; The Tinder-Box, Op. 61.

*** dacapo 224104. Dam-Jensen, Dolberg, Larsen, Van Hal, Dreyer, Odense SO, Giordano Bellincampi.

Schierbeck belongs to the generation midway between Nielsen and Vagn Holmboe. Until recently he was unrepresented in the catalogue, now no fewer than three versions of his charming songs *The Chinese Flute*, to poems by Hans Bethge, which inspired many composers, not least Mahler in *Das Lied*, are available and the present issue also brings the cantata *Dronning Dagmar* ('Queen Dagmar'). The melodrama *Fyrtøjet* ('The Tinder-box'), based on Hans Andersen, is both inventive and imaginative. This is an excellent introduction to a gifted minor master. Inger Dam-Jensen is excellent in the Bethge settings and the orchestral playing and recording are first class.

Nilsson's first recording was in 1946 of an aria from Berwald's *Estrella di Soria*, and this recording of *The Chinese Flute* comes from a Swedish Radio broadcast two years later. What a voice! It comes with a haunting but unaccountably cut *Bluebeard's Castle* under Fricsay.

(i) *In Denmark I was born;* (ii) *Capriccio, Op. 5* (for wind quintet); (iii; iv) *Violin Sonata, Op. 3;* (iv) (Piano) *2 Fantasie-études, Op. 4; Sou'wester, Sweater and Shag, Op. 31;* (v) *The Chinese Flute.*

(*) Classico CLASSCD 290. (i) Copenhagen Younger Strings, Sørensen; (ii) Jensen, Fredericksen, Thorsten, Gottschalk, Andersen; (iii) Granvig; (iv) Bevan; (v) Johansen, Hokkerup.

The *Violin Sonata* is very Brahmsian, the Op. 4 *Etudes* show the influence of Nielsen, and the *Capriccio*, a wind piece from the war years, is full of character and is decently played. The other performances are pretty ordinary and unimaginative and the soprano in *The Chinese Flute* barely adequate. Readers who enjoyed the dacapo should not go on to explore this.

SCHILLINGS, Max von (1868–1933)

(i) *Violin Concerto, Op. 23. King Oedipus* (tone-poem), *Op. 11; Moloch: Harvest Festival Scene.*

*** Marco 8.223324. (i) Rozsa; Czecho-Slovak RSO (Kosice), Alfred Walter.

Max von Schillings' *Violin Concerto* is a beautifully crafted and highly accomplished score in the post-Romantic. Although it reveals no strong individuality, it has a certain rhetorical command and lyrical warmth to commend it, and its masterly handling of the orchestra will make a strong appeal to those with a taste for turn-of-the-century music. The eloquent soloist plays marvellously and inspires the Kosice Orchestra under Alfred Walter to great heights. Neither the excerpt from the opera *Moloch* (1906) nor the *Symphonic Prologue to the Oedipus Tyrannus of Sophocles* (1900) makes anywhere near as strong an impression. The Marco Polo recording is very well detailed and has plenty of warmth and presence.

SCHMELZER, Johann (c. 1620–80)

Balletto di centauri, ninfe e salvatici; Balletto di spiritelli; Sacro-Profans concentus musicus: Sonata I a 8; Sonata a 7 flauti; Sonata con arie der kaiserlichen Serenade.

(B) *** Double Decca (ADD) 458 081-2 (2). New L. Consort,

Pickett – BIBER: *Ballettae; Sonate; Serenade; Requiem.* ***

Johann Schmelzer was apppointed Vice-Kapellmeister to the Viennese Imperial Court, and in 1679 he became Kapellmeister – almost too late, for he died of the plague a year later. One of his tasks was the provision of ballet music for use in pageants, and much of this survives. The *Balletto di spiritelli* is scored for recorders and curtal (an ancester of the bassoon), violins and viols, and the *Balletto di centauri* uses cornetts and sackbuts, as well as recorders, strings and continuo. The even more robust *Sonata con arie zu der kaiserlichen Serenada* (with three trumpets, timpani plus a string ensemble and continuo) has six movements, including two *Arias* and a *Canario*, but still only lasts seven minutes. Philip Pickett himself leads the consort of recorders in the *Sonata a 7*, which is a fairly ambitious continuous piece, longer than either of the ballets, and the *Sonata a 8* highlights a trumpet duo against a group of violins and viols. This is agreeably inventive music, which is brought refreshingly to life by Pickett's instrumetal ensemble, using original instruments to persuasive effect. The recording is both clear and spacious.

SCHMIDT, Franz (1874–1939)

Symphonies Nos. 1–4.

*** Chan. 9568 (4). Detroit SO, Järvi.

Chandos have now boxed their individual releases of the symphonies into a 4-CD set, discarding the fill-ups. The *First Symphony* was composed during Schmidt's early to mid 20s and, as one might expect, is derivative, even if his orchestration is masterly. Right from the start, one is left in no doubt that Schmidt is a born symphonic composer with a real feeling for the long-breathed line and the natural growth flow of ideas. He began work on the *Second Symphony* on leaving the Vienna Philharmonic in 1911 and finished two years later. The *Third* (1927–8) is a richly imaginative score in the romantic tradition, though it yields pride of place among the symphonies to the elegiac, valedictory *Fourth* (1933–4), whose nobility and depth of feeling shine through every bar. The Detroit Symphony Orchestra under Neeme Järvi play with a freshness and enthusiasm which is totally persuasive. They almost sound Viennese and the recording are very good indeed.

Symphony No. 4 in C.

(B) *** Double Decca (ADD) 440 615-2 (2). VPO, Zubin Mehta – MAHLER: *Symphony No. 2 (Resurrection).* ***

Symphony No. 4 in C min.; Variations on a Hussar's Song.

*** EMI CDC5 55518-2. LPO, Welser-Möst.

This neglected symphony is in one long movement, whose material all derives from the inspired, long-breathed trumpet theme with which it opens. Schmidt's music has an elegiac feel to it and the chromaticism, though occasionally reminiscent of Reger, is never cloying. Mehta's impressive recording of it with the Vienna Philharmonic from the early 1970s, easily one of his most memorable discs, has recently been reissued by Decca as the coupling for his Mahler *Second* (see above); but the EMI set from the LPO and Franz Welser-Möst completely supersedes it. Like many Austrians, Welser-Möst obviously has great feeling for the composer and manages to convey this to his players. The delightful *Variations on a Hussar's Song* comes off with equal conviction. Unfortunately, this disc has just been deleted.

(i) Quintet in B flat for Clarinet, Piano & Strings; (ii) 3 Fantasy Pieces on Hungarian National Melodies. (Piano) Romance in A; Toccata in D min..

** Marco 8.223415. Ruso, with (i) Janoska, Török, Lakatos; (i; ii) Slávik.

The *Quintet*, like so much of Schmidt's music with piano, was composed with the left-handed pianist Paul Wittgenstein (brother of the philosopher) in mind. The piano part was subsequently rearranged for two hands by Friedrich Wührer. Its character is predominantly elegiac; it was composed after the death of Schmidt's daughter, and can best be described as having something of the autumnal feeling of late Brahms, the subtlety of Reger, and the dignity and nobility of Elgar or Suk. The players sound pretty tentative at the very start but soon settle down, though their tempo could with advantage have been slower. All the same it is a thoroughly sympathetic, recommendable account. The *Drei Phantasiestücke* and the two piano pieces, the *Romance* and the *D minor Toccata*, are earlier and less interesting, though they are well enough played.

Clarinet Quintet No. 2 in A (for clarinet, piano & strings).

*** Marco 8.223414. Jánoska, Mucha, Lakatos, Slávik, Ruso.

The *Quintet in A major for Clarinet, Piano and Strings* is unusual: it begins like some mysterious other-worldly scherzo which immediately introduces a pastoral idea of beguiling charm. The second movement is a piano piece in ternary form; there is a longish scherzo, full of fantasy and wit, and there is an affecting trio, tinged with the melancholy of late Brahms. The fourth movement sets out as if it, too, is going to be a long, meditative piano piece, but its nobility and depth almost put one in mind of the Elgar *Quintet*. The fifth is a set of variations on a theme of Josef Labor, and is sometimes played on its own. The recording has freshness and bloom, though it could benefit from a bigger recording venue. This is a glorious work.

Quintet for 2 Violins, Viola, Cello & Piano Left Hand.

*** Sony SK 48253. Fleischer, Silverstein, Smirnoff, Tree, Ma — KORNGOLD: *Suite, Op. 23*. ***

An impressive account in every way, aptly coupled with the Op. 23 *Korngold Suite*, also written for Paul Wittgenstein. All in all an unusual and stimulating disc.

Das Buch mit sieben Siegeln (The Book with Seven Seals).

*** EMI Dig CDS5 56660-2. Oelze, Kallisch, Andersen, Odinius, Pape, Reiter, Bav. R. Ch. & SO, Welser-Möst; Friedemann Winkelhofer (organ).

(N) **(*) Teldec 8573 81040-2 (2) Röschmann, Lipovšek, Lippert, Hawlata, Tachezi; Vienna Singverein, VPO, Harnoncourt.

** Calig CAL 50 978/9. Fontana, Hintermeier, Azesberger, Büchner, Holl, Hollzer, V. Singverein, VSO, Stein; Haselböck (organ).

After finishing the *Fourth Symphony* in 1933, Schmidt devoted his remaining creative years to this setting of the *Revelation of St John the Divine*, completing it in 1937. The newest version was recorded by EMI in the Herkulessaal, Munich, and is played by the magnificent Bavarian Radio Orchestra under Franz Welser-Möst, who shows great sympathy for the score. This supplants the Calig version recorded live at the Grosser Musikvereinsaal in Vienna in May 1996, which also has the advantage of modern recorded sound.

The newcomer from Nikolaus Harnoncourt with the Wiener Singverein and Philharmoniker has a lot going for it: very good and full-bodied choral singing, fine soloists and impressive orchestral playing. Were it not for some didactic and intrusive expressive over-emphases from Harnoncourt, it would represent a serious challenge to the Welser-Möst. As it is, the latter remains a safe first choice.

SCHMITT, Florent (1870–1958)

Symphony No. 2, Op. 137; La Danse d'Abisag, Op. 75; (i) Habeyssée (suite for violin and orchestra), Op. 110. Rêves, Op. 65.

*** Marco Polo 8.223689. (i) Segerstam; Rheinland-Pfalz PO, Segerstam.

La Danse d'Abisag, like the much earlier *Tragédie de Salomé*, has a biblical theme: unlike Salome, Abisag, despite her erotic dancing, fails to arouse the ageing monarch (King David). The *Symphony No. 2* was no mean achievement for a composer in his eighty-eighth year! In terms of orchestral expertise and flair, it is second to none, and the opulence of its palette and its imaginative vitality are remarkable. *Rêves* is an early piece, inspired by a poem by Léon-Paul Fargue and appropriately atmospheric; and *Habeyssée*, said to be inspired by an Islamic legend, is a three-movement suite for violin and orchestra. This is a rewarding issue which offers some good playing from the Rheinland-Pfalz Orchestra under Segerstam, who excels in this repertoire. Good recording too.

La Tragédie de Salomé (ballet; complete).

*** Marco 8.223448. Fayt, Rheinland-Pfalz PO, Davin.

Schmitt's skill as an orchestrator is such that the heady, exotic draft he prepared is hardly less potent than the more sumptuously scored, 1908 version. The piece is as long again as the more familiar ballet, and much of the music that was lost in the process is every bit as atmospheric and colourful. Patrick Davin and the Rheinland-Pfalz Philharmonic Orchestra cast a strong spell, and Marie-Paule Fayt is the off-stage nymphet. The Marco Polo recording has a good, spacious acoustic and plenty of detail. The documentation is of unusual interest and gives a detailed account of the action of the ballet.

Piano trio: Très lent.

(BB) **(*) Naxos 8.550934. Joachim Trio – DEBUSSY; RAVEL: *Piano Trios.* **(*)

This three-minute fragment, about which the notes are uninformative, is rather haunting and, like the rest of the programme, beautifully played and recorded.

(i; ii) *Psalm 47, Op. 38;* (i) *La Tragédie de Salomé, Op. 50;* (iii) *Janiana, Op. 52;* (iv) *Lied et Scherzo, Op. 54;* (v) *Suite en Rocaille, Op. 84.*

(N) (B) **(*) Erato Ultima (ADD/DDD) 8573 85636-2 (2).
   (i) French Radio PO, Janowski; (ii) Sweet, French R Ch., Gil (organ); (iii) Jean-François Paillard O, Paillard; (iv) Vescovo, Hubeau; (v) Marie-Claire Jamet Qt.

Florent Schmitt's colourful and highly atmospheric music deserves the strongest advocacy. His two most well-known works – the exotic ballet *La Tragédie de Salomé* and the imposing *Psalm 47* (which begins and ends in the most spectacular manner imaginable) receive splendid performances here. The digital recordings are very good, though not quite in the demonstration class. The second CD of his chamber music is just as diverting – and rarer. The recording of *Janiana* and the *Suite* date from the early 1960s and sound a little rough around the edges, but acceptable. The former, written for strings alone, begins rather agitatedly, but soon becomes infused with more lyrical passages. The following *Musette* is quite charming, as is the beautiful *Chorale* which follows; the finale is tremendous fun and should alone persuade string orchestras to take it into their repertoire. The *Suite* for flute, string trio and harp, is delightfully piquant and full of imaginative touches: the opening has a child-like fantasy which is quite haunting. The *Lied et Scherzo* for horn and piano makes an unusual and entertaining bonus. Well worth having.

SCHNITTKE, Alfred (born 1934)

Concerto grosso No. 1; Quasi una sonata; Moz-Art à la Haydn; A Paganini.

(M) *** DG (IMS) 445 520-2. Kremer, Smirnov, Grindenko, COE, Schiff.

If you want to jump in at the deep end of the Schnittke repertoire, the present collection offers the formidable, at times even ferocious, *Quasi una sonata* with its extraordinary scratchings and abrasions, the pastiche *Moz-Art à la Haydn*, which is almost humorous, and the virtuoso solo violin piece, *A Paganini*. The performances here are expert, very committed and brilliantly recorded.

(i) *Cello Concerto No. 2. In Memoriam . . .*

*** Sony SK 48241. (i) Rostropovich; LSO, Ozawa.

Schnittke has a strong feeling for the cello, and his *Second Cello Concerto* is conceived on a large scale, the main emotional weight residing in the fifth and last movement, a passacaglia lasting a quarter of an hour. Its powerful, concentrated atmosphere resonates long in the mind. So, for that matter, does *In Memoriam . . .*, a transcription and re-

working of the *Piano Quintet*, written on the death of his mother, where there are gains in colour in the highly imaginative use of the orchestra. The recording has exceptional richness, detail and depth and the performance of the concerto has all the authority and panache one might expect.

Violin Concertos Nos. 1–2.

*** BIS CD 487. Lubotsky, Malmö SO, Klas.

The *First Violin Concerto* inhabits a post-romantic era. Its lyricism is profoundly at variance with its successor of 1966, commissioned by Mark Lubotsky, the soloist on this record. Here the central concept is what Schnittke calls 'a certain drama of tone colours', and there is no doubt that much of it is vividly imagined and strongly individual. The double-bass is assigned a special role of a caricatured 'anti-soloist'. There is recourse to the once fashionable aleatoric technique, but this is all within carefully controlled parameters. The Malmö orchestra under Eri Klas play with evident feeling in both works and are very well recorded. This is an altogether highly satisfactory coupling.

(i) *Gogol Suite* (compiled Rozhdestvensky); *Labyrinths.*

*** BIS CD 557. Malmö SO, Markiz; (i) with Kontra.

There is a surrealistic quality to the *Gogol Suite* reminiscent of Gogol's own words quoted in Jürgen Köchel's note, 'The world hears my laughter; my tears it does not see nor recognize.' *Labyrinths* is a ballet score composed in 1971, thin in development and musical ideas but sufficiently strong in atmosphere to survive the transition from stage to concert hall. The Malmö Orchestra under Lev Markiz play very well and the recording is in the demonstration class.

Symphony No. 1.

*** Chan. 9417. Russian State SO, Rozhdestvensky.

Schnittke's *First Symphony* is a huge radical canvas lasting some 68 minutes. In his essay on 'The Symphony in the Soviet Union' in *A Guide to the Symphony*, David Fanning writes that it 'contains a whole lexicon of advanced devices – the theatricality of American happenings with the players entering one by one and leaving at the end only to enter again as if to restart the whole process, the aleatory (chance) elements of the Polish school, and the multiple quotations of Berio's *Sinfonia* plus a cadenza for jazz violin'. It is essentially a musical gesture, a tirade rather than a symphony of protest and anger which sounds pretty thin now. Rozhdestvensky's performance is committed, and the recording, made at a public performance in the Moscow Conservatoire in 1988, is well detailed. There is more rhetoric than substance here. The three stars are allotted for the performance and recording; for the composition the stars can be aleatoric!

(i) *Symphony No. 4;* (ii) *3 Sacred Hymns.*

*** Chan. 9463. (i) Zdorov, Pianov; (i–ii) Russian State Symphonic Cappella; (i) Russian State SO; Polyansky.

The *Fourth Symphony* draws on Christian (Catholic, Lutheran and Russian Orthodox) and Jewish chant and is avowedly religious in programme, reflecting episodes in the life of the Virgin Mary. It lasts 40 minutes and is scored for two singers, one a counter-tenor, chorus and orchestra; it also makes inventive and colourful use of keyboard sonorities. Both the performance and the recording are of high quality, but the piece seems too concerned with gesture and essentially empty of musical substance. The *Three Sacred Hymns* for *a cappella* choir from 1983 are both eloquent and beautiful.

Cello Sonata.

*** BIS CD 336. Thedéen, Pöntinen – STRAVINSKY: *Suite italienne;* SHOSTAKOVICH: *Sonata.* ***

The *Cello Sonata* is a powerfully expressive piece, its avant-garde surface enshrining a neo-romantic soul. Torleif Thedéen is a refined and intelligent player who gives a thoroughly committed account of this piece with his countryman, Roland Pöntinen.

Piano Trio.

*** Nim. NI 5572. V. Piano Trio – SHOSTAKOVICH: *Trios, Opp. 8 & 67.* ***

Schnittke's *First Sonata* is a well-argued piece that seems to unify his awareness of the post-serial musical world with the tradition of Shostakovich. On this version it is linked with a pastiche of less interest, dating from 1977. Excellent playing from both artists, and very good recording too.

Prelude in Memoriam Shostakovich (for 2 solo violins).

*** Chan. 8988. Mordkovitch, Young – PROKOFIEV; SHOSTAKOVICH: *Violin Sonatas.* ***

Schnittke's *Piano Trio* has its origins in a string trio written in 1985. In 1987 it was transcribed as the *Trio Sonata for Chamber Orchestra* and then in 1992 put into its present form. The Vienna Piano Trio give as convincing a performance as you are ever likely to hear, and they certainly get superb recorded sound.

Violin Sonata No. 1; Sonata in the Olden Style.

*** Chan. 8343. Dubinsky, Edlina – SHOSTAKOVICH: *Violin Sonata.* ***

Berman gives as persuasive an account of Schnittke's *Piano Sonata* as it is possible to imagine. He is very well recorded, too, and the three Stravinsky pieces with which it comes are also given with great pianistic elegance.

Piano Sonata.

*** Chan. 8962. Berman – STRAVINSKY: *Serenade etc.* ***

The Schnittke *Prelude* for two solo violins is the shortest of the works on Lydia Mordkovitch's excellent disc of Soviet violin music, but it is among the most moving in its intense, elegiac way. She is well matched by her partner, Emma Young.

SCHOECK, Othmar (1886–1957)

(i) *Horn Concerto, Op. 65. Prelude for Orchestra, Op. 48;* (ii) *Serenade for Oboe, Cor Anglais & Strings, Op. 27. Suite in A flat for Strings.*

** CPO CPO 999 337-2. (i) Schneider; (ii) Zabarella, Zuchner; Coll. Musik, Winterthur, Albert.

The major work here is the five-movement *Suite in A flat for Strings*, which Schoeck composed in 1945. Although it is not quite as poignant as *Sommernacht*, there is some imaginative and expressive writing. The second movement, *Pastorale tranquillo*, has that sense of melancholy and nostalgia so characteristic of Schoeck. In it he imagined 'the peace and deep stillness of the forests'. The slightly later *Concerto for Horn and Strings* (1951) is well played by Bruno Schneider and is an appealing piece that will strike a responsive chord among all who care for late Strauss. The *Serenade for Oboe, Cor Anglais and Strings* is a five-minute interlude which Schoeck composed for a much-truncated production of his opera, *Don Ranudo*, at Leipzig in 1930. The *Prelude for Orchestra* serves as a reminder that Schoeck was at one time a pupil of Reger. Its textures lack transparency, but this is in part due to the rather opaque recording, made in a radio studio. It is perfectly acceptable, but the strings could do with more bloom and tuttis need to open out a little more.

Violin Sonatas: in D, Op. 16; in E, Op. 46; in D, WoO22; Albumblatt, WoO70.

** Guild GMCD7142. Barritt, Edwards.

The two *D major Violin Sonatas* come from the first decade of the present (soon to be last) century. The student essay of 1905 is of lesser interest, but Op. 16 has a strong vein of lyricism and a characteristic warmth of invention. The *Sonata in E major*, Op. 46, of 1931 inhabits a totally different world. Its musical language is less immediate, and in this respect could possibly be compared with late Fauré, though there is no resemblance in idiom. Paul Barritt and Catherine Edwards give very capable and sensitive performances and were the recording a little more spacious and less forward, this would gain the three stars.

Elegie (song cycle), Op. 36.

❂ *** CPO CPO 999 472-2. Schmidt, Winterthur Music Collegium, Albert.

The *Elegie, Op. 36* has been described as 'a narrative of a dying love' and to some extent charts the turbulent course of the composer's affair with the pianist Mary de Senger. The cycle comprises twenty-four short but concentrated settings of poems by Lenau and Eichendorff, and is for baritone and a small instrumental ensemble, used with great subtlety and resource. The songs are powerfully evocative and beautifully fashioned; each one immediately establishes its own atmosphere within a bar or two, and draws the listener completely into its world. Almost any would serve as an example but particularly potent is the third, *Stille Sicherheit*, which is extraordinarily concentrated in feeling, or the wonderfully haunting *Vesper*, with its tolling bells and almost tangible half lights. This is deeply felt music with a wonderful sense of line, and Andreas Schmidt sings with tremendous conviction. Werner Andreas Albert gets very sensitive and supportive playing from the Winterthur ensemble and the CPO recording is first class.

3 Lieder, Op. 35; 6 Lieder, Op. 51; Das Wandsbecker Liederbuch, Op. 52; Im Nebel; Wiegenlied.

** Jecklin JD677-2. Banse, Henschel, Rieger.

Das Wandsbecker Liederbuch is a latterday equivalent of the Hugo Wolf Songbooks; they offer a portrait of a poet (in this case Mathius Claudius) rather than a thematically connected cycle, and the songs, though highly conservative in idiom, are full of subtleties and depth, as indeed are the remaining songs on this CD. They are decently sung and recorded, and admirers of Schoeck's art need not hesitate.

Der Sänger (The Singer), Op. 57.

** Koch-Schwann 310921. Lang, Lang-Oester.

Der Sänger is a setting of twenty-six poems by the nine-teenth-century Swiss poet, Heinrich Leuthold, to whose work Schoeck's friend, Hermann Hesse, had introduced him. Its sentiment harmonized with Schoeck's own feelings of melancholia and the feeling that he had been denied the recognition to which his talents entitled him. Like the other late song-cycles *Unter Sternen* (*Under the Stars*) and *Das stille Leuchten* (*The Silent Light*) it contains songs of great beauty.

OPERA

Venus (complete).

*** MGB Musikszene Schweiz CD 6112 (2). Lang, Popp, O'Neal, Fassbender, Skovhus, Alföldi, Heidelberg Kammer Ch., Basle Boys' Ch., Swiss Youth PO, Venzago.

Venus is based on a libretto by Schoeck's school-friend, Armin Rüeger. The basic argument is simple and comes from Ovid, though Rüeger sets the action in a country castle in the south of France. The tenor role is particularly demanding and may have hampered the work reaching the international stage. Venzago's conducting radiates total dedication, and so does the playing of the young Swiss orchestra. The opening scene almost prompts one's thoughts to turn to the Strauss of *Ariadne*, but as the opera unfolds Venzago's view of the work as partly 'an enormous orchestral poem (exposition, development, Scherzo and recapitulation) with obbligato voices' seems more and more valid. The sheer quality of the invention is notable and many of the ideas, particularly the Venus motive, have great tenderness and delicacy. Schoeck's scoring is superb, and those who know *Penthesilea* should lose no time in acquiring this glorious score. The performance may not be absolutely ideal vocally, but it is worth putting up with that for the sake of such beautiful music. Good and atmospheric recording.

SCHOENBERG, Arnold (1874–1951)

'The Early Tonal Years': (i) *Chamber Symphony No. 1, Op. 9;* (ii) *Verklaerte Nacht (String sextet), Op. 4;* (iii) *Friede auf Erden, Op. 13;* (iv) *Gurrelieder: Song of the Wood-Dove.*

(M) *** Sony (ADD) SMK 62019. (i) Marlborough Festival O (members); (ii) Trampler, Ma, Juilliard String Qt; (iii) BBC

Singers; (iv) Jessye Norman, Ens. InterContemporain (members), Boulez.

This disc, not unexpectedly, opens with Schoenberg's post-Wagnerian *Verklaerte Nacht* with its erotically potent, Tristanesque chromaticism, written in 1902. The Juilliard performance of what is in effect a symphonic poem for string sextet is highly charged but rather over-characterized. Nevertheless, technically it is marvellously played and richly and atmospherically recorded. In 1906 Schoenberg took a new path with the polyphonically complex *First Chamber Symphony* for 15 instruments. The Marlborough performance is committed and highly spontaneous. *Friede auf Erden* ('Peace on earth') for unaccompanied chorus was written the following year, its part-writing even more thornily complex. Here its vocal difficulties, which inhibited early performances, are readily surmounted by the BBC Singers under Boulez and they make it sound almost mellifluous. In the lovely *Lied der Waldtaube* ('Song of the wood-dove') from *Gurrelieder*, Jessye Norman is a radiant soloist, crowning her performance with a thrilling top B flat.

'The Expressionist Years': (i) *String Quartet No. 2 in F sharp min., Op. 10;* (ii) *6 Small Pieces for Piano, Op. 19;* (iii) *Pierrot lunaire, Op. 21;* (iv) *Die glückliche Hand, Op. 18.*

(M) **(*) Sony (ADD) SMK 62020. (i) Valente, Juilliard String Qt; (ii) Glenn Gould; (iii) Minton (reciter), Debost, Pay, Zukerman, Harrell, Barenboim; (iv) Nimsgern, BBC Singers and SO; (iii; iv) Boulez.

The *Second String Quartet* (1907–8) is individual and powerful; its last two movements (both slow) are intensified by the contribution of the soprano Benita Valente. The Juilliards are less sympathetic than they were in *Verklaerte Nacht*: there is no lack of intensity but there is a want of real pianissimo, intensified by the close balance. Glenn Gould displays a ready grasp of the six minuscule piano *Pieces* (1911). But the key work here is *Pierrot lunaire* (1912). As can be seen from the cast-list here, the performance gathers together a distinguished group of instrumentalists, but the result is lacking in the expressive intensity one expects of Boulez in this music. With Yvonne Minton eschewing sing-speech, the vocal line is too precisely pitched. Boulez's approach places Schoenberg's score within the mainstream of vocal writing, and many listeners will relish the comparative lack of difficulty in coming to terms with its highly original language. *Die glückliche Hand* (which the composer translated as 'The hand of Fate') is much more successful, with Nimsgern an impressive bass soloist. The disc ends with a six-minute interview with Halsey Stephens, 'Schoenberg the painter', recorded in 1949.

'Dodecaphony': (i) *Variations for Orchestra, Op. 31;* (ii) *Suite for Piano, Op. 25;* (iii) *Moses und Aron: Act II, scene 3.*

(M) ** Sony (ADD) SMK 62021. (i; iii) BBC SO, Boulez; (ii) Gould; (iii) Palmer, Knight, Manning, Watts, Cassilly, Winfield, Hermann, Orpheus Boys' Ch.

Boulez's strong, compulsive account of the orchestral *Variations* is also available coupled with a matching orchestral

version of *Verklaerte Nacht* (see below). Here it is supplemented by a recorded talk by the composer, made by
Radio Frankfurt in 1931. Gould's 1964 recording of the piano
Suite, Op. 25, has the expected concentration. But it was a
curious idea to select just the third scene of the second Act
of *Moses und Aron* (1932), effective though it is, when the
complete recording of the opera from which it comes is
readily available. It is certainly well performed and recorded.

'Schoenberg in America': (i) *Piano Concerto in C, Op. 42;*
(ii) *Phantasy for Violin with Piano Accompaniment,*
Op. 47; (iii) *String Trio, Op. 45;* (iv) *Dreimal tausend*
Jahre, Op. 50a; (v) *Kol Nidre, Op. 39;* (vi) *Psalm 130,*
Op. 50b; (vii) *A Survivor from Warsaw, Op. 46.*

(M) *** Sony (ADD) SMK 62022. (i) Ax, Philh. O, Salonen;
(ii) Menuhin, Gould; (iii) Juilliard Qt (members); (iv; vi)
BBC Singers; (vii) Günther Reich; (v; vii) Shirley-Quirk, BBC
Ch. & SO; (iv–vii) Boulez.

Schoenberg's *Piano Concerto* is a work which consciously
echoes the world of the romantic concerto in twelve-note
serial terms, but the thick and (at times) glutinous textures
favoured by the composer tend to obscure the focus of the
argument rather than making it sweeter on the ear. The
soloist, Emanuel Ax, immediately displays an engaging
lyrical feeling at the opening, and his performance is warmly
sympathetic (the *Giocoso* finale very attractively handled).
But despite flatteringly luminous (1992) recording, made in
Watford Town Hall, Salonen does not convince the listener
that the work is orchestrally a complete success. Of Schoenberg's final two chamber works, the intractable *String Trio*
was begun in 1946 when the composer was in hospital,
recovering from a heart attack; Schoenberg suggested that
its restless progress reflected the course of his illness, treatment and convalescence. It is confidently played by the
Juilliard group and the 1985 recording is very well balanced.
The *Phantasy for Violin and Piano* (1949), though not
opening very invitingly, is perhaps marginally more approachable. This distinguished account by Menuhin and
Gould is a mono recording from 1965, made by CBC in
Toronto, and it is of first-class quality. But perhaps the most
striking music here, apart from *A Survivor from Warsaw*
with its extraordinary opening so vividly and dramatically
projected, is the remaining triptych of vocal pieces from
the BBC Singers. In such choral works, particularly when
inspired by a Jewish theme, as in the magnificent *Kol Nidre*
of 1938 for narrator, mixed chorus and orchestra, the
composer's full romanticism broke out. Fine performances
and excellent sound.

(i) *Accompaniment to a Motion Picture Scene, Op. 34;*
(ii) *Chamber Symphony No. 1, Op. 9;* (i; iii) *Die*
Jakobsleiter (oratorio fragments, completed Zillig).

(M) *** Sony (ADD) SMK 48462. (i) BBC SO; (ii) Ens.
InterContemporain (members); (iii) Nimsgern, Bowen,
Partridge, Hudson, Shirley-Quirk, Rolfe Johnson, Wenkel,
Mesplé, BBC Singers; Boulez.

The performance of the film scene is as atmospheric as one
would expect, if not as emotionally involved as the *Chamber*
Symphony, given a strong, warmly enjoyable account. *Die*

Jakobsleiter is an ambitious oratorio, which he left fully
sketched out. It was completed and orchestrated by Winif-
ried Zillig, revealing an exceptionally powerful piece.
Strongly cast, the performance has passion and commitment
and the recording projects it vividly.

Chamber Symphonies Nos. 1–2; (i) *Piano Concerto, Op. 42.*

*** Ph. (IMS) 446 683-2. (i) Brendel; SW German RSO,
Baden-Baden, Gielen.

Alfred Brendel has been a lifelong champion of the *Piano*
Concerto: this is his third recording and it is undoubtedly
the most telling, partly because the knotty orchestral textures
are brightly revealed in a recording which is admirably clear
yet does not lack fullness, while the balance with the piano
is admirable. The performance is strong, impassioned in the
Adagio, with the mixtures of *grotesquerie* and *giocoso* nicely
juxtaposed in the finale, where Brendel's contribution is
quite brilliant. Michael Gielen is a committed partner, subtle
in his rhythmic inflexions and bringing plenty of vitality to
the accompaniment, matching Brendel's dash in the last
movement. The two *Chamber Symphonies* have never been
more enjoyable on record, their diverse moods and amazing
range of colouring caught with lyrical warmth and detail
finely and affectionately observed. The orchestral playing is
of the very highest calibre. Again first-rate recording. A
major addition to the Schoenberg discography.

(i) *Chamber Symphony No. 1 , Op. 9;* (ii) *5 Pieces for*
Orchestra; (i) *Variations, Op. 31; Verklaerte Nacht;*
(iii) *Erwartung, Op. 17; 6 Songs, Op. 8.*

(B) **(*) Double Decca ADD/Dig. 448 279-2 (2). (i) LAPO,
Mehta; (ii) Cleveland O, or (iii) VPO, with Silja, Dohnányi.

The *First Chamber Symphony* is given a rich performance
under Mehta, arguably too fast at times but full of understanding for the romantic emotions which underlie much
of the writing. The Op. 31 *Variations* somehow reveal their
secrets and their unmistakable greatness more clearly when
the performance has such a sense of drive. Mehta's *Verklaerte*
Nacht has warmth and intensity yet is free of schmalz; it is
sympathetically recorded and the Los Angeles strings play
with great virtuosity and opulence of tone. The Cleveland
Orchestra are comparably at home in Schoenberg's seminal
Five Pieces. Their perfection of ensemble goes with a remarkable depth of feeling. Schoenberg's searingly intense monodrama, *Erwartung*, makes an apt bonus. Silja is at her most
committed. The sound under pressure may be raw, but the
self-tortured questionings of the central character come over
grippingly; again the digital sound is outstandingly vivid.

(i) *Chamber Symphony No. 1, Op. 9;* (ii; iii) *Erwartung;*
(iii) *Variations for Orchestra, Op. 31.*

*** EMI CDC5 55212-2. (i) Birmingham Contemporary Music
Group; (ii) Bryn-Julson; (iii) CBSO; Rattle.

In the *Chamber Symphony No. 1* Rattle, with fifteen players
from the Birmingham Contemporary Music Group, springs
rhythms infectiously, relaxedly bringing out the thrust of
argument. The playing may not be as bitingly crisp as in
some rival versions but it has far more character, thanks to
both conductor and players. By contrast, he is daringly

expansive in the *Variations* of 1928, even more so than Karajan in his classic recording with the Berlin Philharmonic. The Birmingham players may not always be quite so refined as the Berliners, but they play with even greater emotional thrust and with a keener sense of mystery, while heightened dynamic contrasts add to the dramatic bite. Equally in Schoenberg's taxing atonal vocal lines, Phyllis Bryn-Julson sings with a clarity and definition to coax the ear instead of assaulting it. Bright and clear, she gives a more vulnerable portrait, tender and compelling, with Rattle more urgent than James Levine for Norman. Superb sound.

Chamber Symphony No. 1, Op. 9 (arr. Webern); (i) Ode to Napoleon. Verklaerte Nacht (string sextet version), Op. 4.

(BB) **(*) Virgin 2 x 1 VBD5 61760-2 (2) [CDVB 61760]. Nash Ens.; (i) with Allen – SHOSTAKOVICH: *Piano Quintet; Piano Trio No. 2; 4 Waltzes.* ***

The Nash Ensemble give us Webern's arrangement of the *Chamber Symphony*, Op. 9, reduced to the same group of five instruments used in the *Ode to Napoleon*. Contrapuntal detail is certainly clarified, but the Nash players ensure that the work's emotional content comes over expressively in spite of the less opulent textures. Thomas Allen provides a congenial, characterful narration for the strange *Ode* and although the close balance in *Verklaerte Nacht* is less than ideally alluring, throughout the Nash Ensemble play with easy virtuosity, intensity and fine blending. As so often with bargain reissues, no text is provided for the *Ode*, and the notes are sparse. An intriguing issue, just the same, for the Shostakovich couplings are first class.

Piano Concerto, Op. 42.

*** Chan. 9375. Malling, Danish Nat. RSO, Schønwandt – SCHUMANN: *Piano Concerto.* *(*)

Amalie Malling proves an intelligent and sympathetic soloist who, if not more persuasive than some of her better-known rivals such as Pollini and Brendel, is every bit as convincing. Michael Schønwandt gets very good results from the Danish orchestra and the texture is lucid and transparent, and splendidly recorded. The coupling is, however, not completely logical or particularly successful. This needs a reissue with the pairing better thought out.

(i) Piano concerto, Op. 42; Klavierstücke, Opp. 11 & 19.

(N) *** Ph. 468 033-2. Uchida, (i) Cleveland O, Pierre – BERG: *Piano Sonata;* WEBERN: *Variations.* ***

Mitsuko Uchida is logically coupled, and she and Boulez and the Cleveland Orchestra give us a keenly articulate account of the *Piano Concerto* that may well reach home to a wider audience than before. There is both delicacy and lyrical feeling. Surprisingly, William Glock once asked way back in the 1960s, 'Why is it that Schoenberg's music always sounds so ugly?' But in Uchida's hands it doesn't. She is also very persuasive in the Opp. 11 and 19 *Klavierstücke* (not, incidentally, the same performance of the former that Philips included in her *Great Pianists of the Century* set). The Philips recording has both clarity and warmth. Those who have not responded even to the Brendel account should try this beautifully recorded piece.

(i; ii) Piano Concerto, Op. 42; (ii; iii) Violin Concerto, Op. 33; (iv) Pelleas und Melisande, Op. 5; Variations, Op. 31.

(B) *** Erato/Ultima 3984 24241-2 (2). (i) Peter Serkin, (ii) LSO; (iii) Amoyal; (iv) Chicago SO; Boulez.

A good and inexpensive introduction to Schoenberg ranging from the early, lush *Pelleas und Melisande* to the intractable yet rewarding *Violin Concerto* and the masterly *Variations for Orchestra*, in authoritative performances and exemplary recordings.

Concerto for String Quartet & Orchestra after Handel's Concerto grosso, Op. 6/7.

*** Ara. Z 6723. San Francisco Ballet O, Lark Qt, Le Roux – HANDEL: *Concerto grosso in B flat, Op. 6/7;* ELGAR: *Introduction & Allegro for Strings;* SPOHR: *Concerto for String Quartet & Orchestra.* ***

Schoenberg virtually recomposed Handel's Op. 6/7 for string quartet and large modern orchestra, adding a plentiful spicing of dissonance and special effects, even string harmonics. The result, inflated to nearly twice the length of the original, is at times grotesque, but always aurally fascinating and entertaining, for Handel's underlying tunefulness keeps bursting through. The performance has plenty of edge, vitality and colour and it was a bright idea to include also Handel's original (in a performance for full modern strings) so the listener can switch back and forth between the two utterly different sound worlds.

Pelleas und Melisande (symphonic poem), Op. 5.

*(*) Koch 3-7316-2 Houston SO, Eschenbach – WEBERN: *Passacaglia.* *(*)

(N) *(*) DG 469 008-2. Berlin Deutsche Op. O, Thielemann – WAGNER: *Siegfried Idyll.* *(*)

It was Richard Strauss who suggested to Schoenberg the subject of Maeterlinck's drama as an opera. Schoenberg opted for a Straussian symphonic poem, and this he completed before he ever knew that Debussy had turned the same subject into an opera. Christoph Eschenbach and the Houston Symphony were recorded at concert performances but strangely enough they sound strangely cautious and careful.

Christian Thielemann is an outstanding conductor but sometimes an intrusive interpreter who is loth to allow the music to unfold naturally. There is too much expressive exaggeration here, and although the playing of the Orchestra of the Deutsche Oper is fine, this mannered account does not begin to challenge the classic Karajan account.

Pelleas und Melisande; Variations for Orchestra, Op. 31; Verklaerte Nacht (orchestral version), Op. 4.

(M) *** DG (ADD) 427 424-2 (3). BPO, Karajan – BERG: *Lyric Suite; 3 Pieces;* WEBERN: *Collection.* ***

Pelleas und Melisande; Verklaerte Nacht.

(M) *** DG 457 721-2. BPO, Karajan.

The Straussian opulence of Schoenberg's early symphonic poem has never been as ravishingly presented as by Karajan and the Berlin Philharmonic in this splendidly recorded version. The gorgeous tapestry of sound is both rich and full of refinement and detail, while the thrust of argument is powerfully conveyed. These are superb performances which present the emotional element at full power but give unequalled precision and refinement. The Op. 31 *Variations*, the most challenging of Schoenberg's orchestral works, here receives a reading which vividly conveys the ebb and flow of tension within the phrase and over the whole plan. Superb recording, excellently remastered.

Karajan's unsurpassed performances of the two early Schoenberg masterpieces, taken from the above set, make an ideal candidate for separate reissue in DG's series of Originals.

(i) *Pelleas und Melisande, Op. 5;* (ii) *Verklaerte Nacht* (string sextet version).

(B) **(*) Ph. (ADD) Duo 462 309-2. (i) Rotterdam PO, Zinman; (ii) augmented New Vienna Qt – FAURE: *Pelléas et Mélisande; Pavane, Op. 50* ***; SIBELIUS: *Pelléas et Mélisande; Swan of Tuonela.* **(*)

Zinman's reading of Schoenberg's somewhat inflated symphonic poem is strongly characterized and very well played, finding warmth and refinement as well as passion. If the Rotterdam orchestra cannot quite match Karajan's Berlin Philharmonic version, they are richly recorded in a glowing acoustic which flatters Schoenberg's sometimes pungent scoring. The inclusion of Schoenberg's other most famous early work seems apt and if the choice of the string sextet rather than the orchestral version is less appropriate, it is passionately played, and though the matching of the members of the augmented New Vienna Quartet is not flawless, they produce a full body of tone and the performance remains very persuasive.

3 Pieces for Chamber Orchestra (1910); Suite, Op. 29; Verklaerte Nacht (string sextet version).

(M) *** Sony ADD/Dig. SMK 48465. Ens. InterContemporain (members), Boulez.

Boulez first recorded *Verklaerte Nacht* in the version for full strings – see below – but this beautifully played account for solo strings is even more impressive. The neo-classical *Suite* – with Boulez this time conducting a mere seven players – reveals a totally different side of the composer, a spiky piece presented at its sharpest in this reading. The *Three Pieces for Chamber Orchestra* were found after Schoenberg had died and date from 1910. They are atonal and the third piece was unfinished. This is an earlier analogue recording but of good quality.

5 Pieces for Orchestra, Op. 16.

*** EMI CDC7 49857-2. CBSO, Rattle – BERG: *Lulu: Suite;* WEBERN: *6 Pieces.* ***

Rattle and the CBSO give an outstanding reading of this Schoenberg masterpiece, bringing out its red-blooded strength, neither too austere nor too plushy. With sound of demonstration quality and an ideal coupling, it makes an outstanding recommendation.

(i) 5 Pieces for Orchestra, Op. 16; (ii) Ode to Napoleon Buonaparte, Op. 41 (for string quartet, piano and reciter); (iii) Serenade, Op. 24 (for clarinet, bass clarinet, mandolin, guitar, violin, viola, cello and bass voice).

*** Sony SMK (ADD) 48463. (i) BBC SO; (ii) Wilson-Johnson; (iii) Shirley-Quirk; (ii; iii) Ens. InterContemporain (members) Boulez.

With Boulez, the *Five Pieces for Orchestra* emerge as colourfully expressive, hardly more elusive than Debussy when played as strongly as this. The Abbey Road recording has plenty of body and atmosphere. The *Serenade* finds Schoenberg in rather crustily neo-classical mood, and even Boulez with his team (including Shirley-Quirk) cannot bring out all the lightness the composer seems to have intended. With David Wilson-Johnson a characterfully ironic narrator, the Byron setting of the *Ode to Napoleon* is more warmly memorable. Both are very clearly recorded and, if the balance is close, there is plenty of ambient warmth.

A Survivor from Warsaw, Op 46.

(N) (M) **(*) RCA (ADD) 09026 63682-2. Milnes, Boston SO, New England Cons. Ch., Leinsdorf – BEETHOVEN: *Symphony No. 9.* **

This startling work from 1947 is for narrator, chorus and full orchestra; its seven minutes have the narrator describing the courage of Jews on their way to the gas chamber yet singing the *Shema Yistoel* (the command to love God). Milnes narrates it very dramatically, and the performance and sound are certainly both vivid enough. However, it makes a curious filler for an ordinary but well-recorded Beethoven *Nine*.

Variations for Orchestra, Op. 31.

(M) *** DG (ADD) 457 760-2. BPO, Karajan – BERG: *Lyric Suite,* etc.; WEBERN: *Passacaglia.* ***

Variations for Orchestra; Verklaerte Nacht.

*** DG (ADD) 415 326-2. BPO, Karajan.

(i) Variations for Orchestra; (ii) Verklaerte Nacht; (i; iii) Die glückliche Hand, Op. 18.

(M) **(*) Sony (ADD) SMK 48464. (i) BBC SO; (ii) NYPO; (iii) Nimsgern, BBC Singers; Boulez.

The *Variations* receives a reading under Karajan which vividly conveys the ebb and flow of tension within the phrase and over the whole plan. The recording is superb and it is part of an equally impressive programme of twentieth-century music (see above), reissued on DG's Originals label.

Karajan's version of *Verklaerte Nacht* too is altogether magical and very much in a class of its own. There is a tremendous intensity and variety of tone and colour: the palette that the strings of the Berlin Philharmonic have at their command is altogether extraordinarily wide-ranging.

Boulez's BBC account of the *Variations* and the New York performance of *Verklaerte Nacht* may lack the warmth, final polish and subtlety of Karajan's celebrated versions, but Boulez's earthiness, unrelentingly forceful, is compelling in the former, while in the latter he has the full measure of Schoenberg's poetry and secures responsive playing from the New York strings. The Sony recording is vivid but not as richly beautiful as the Berlin sound. There is also a bonus here in the 'psychological pantomime', *Die glückliche Hand,* which is sharply observed, with Nimsgern a fine soloist.

Verklaerte Nacht.

(BB) *** Navigator (ADD) 74321 29243-2. Georgian State CO, Isakadze – BERG: *Violin Concerto;* WEBERN: *Passacaglia for Orchestra.* ***

(i) *Verklaerte Nacht; 5 Orchestral Pieces, Op. 16;*
(ii) (Piano): *3 Pieces, Op. 11; 6 Little Pieces, Op. 19.* arr.
BUSONI: *Piece, Op. 11/2 (Konzertmässige interpretation).*

*** Teldec 4509 98256-2. (i) Chicago SO, Barenboim;
(ii) Barenboim (piano).

On the evidence of this Navigator CD, the Georgian State Chamber Orchestra has a first-class string section, and they play Schoenberg's sensuous string work with a uniquely Slavonic ardour to grip the listener in the intensity of the final climax. Isakadze controls the emotional ebb and flow unerringly, and there is refinement here as well as passion. The recording is admirably full and vivid, and this comes at the lowest possible price with two other key twentieth-century works.

Barenboim's Teldec reading of *Verklaerte Nacht* is weighty and passionate, with the Chicago strings playing superbly, while the *Five Orchestral Pieces* are comparably purposeful and sharply characterized. They lead naturally to the miniatures for piano, which Barenboim interprets with persuasive warmth, treating them rather like Brahms 'with the wrong notes'. He concludes with a fascinating rarity, an elaborate rearrangement of the second of the Op. 11 *Pieces* which Busoni made in 1909, turning it into something close to late Liszt. Warm sound, if not ideally detailed in the orchestral works.

CHAMBER MUSIC

String Quartets Nos. 1 in D min., Op. 7; (i) 2 in F sharp min., Op. 10. 3, Op. 30; 4, Op. 37.

(***) Archiphon ARC mono 103/4. Kolisch Qt, (i) with C. Gifford.

String Quartets Nos. 1–4.

(B) ** Ph. Duo (ADD) 464 047-2 (2). (i) Lear; New Vienna Qt.

String Quartet (1897); String Quartet No. 1, Op. 7.

*** MDG MDG 307 0919-2. Leipzig Qt.

String Quartets Nos. (i) 2, Op. 10. 4, Op. 37.

*** MDG MDG 307 0935-2. (i) Oelze; Leipzig Qt.

No quartet has ever been more closely associated with these pieces than the Kolisch, and the present recordings were made at the turn of 1936–7. They were straight performances with no re-takes, though the Kolisch always played these works (and other repertoire) by heart – with the exception of the *Fourth*, which was new. It is well worth putting up with surface noise (which one soon barely notices anyway) for the sake of *real* music-making. Indeed, given phrasing of this quality there is more to the rigorously disciplined *Third* and *Fourth Quartets* than most later ensembles have found;

and never have the two earlier *Quartets* sounded so eloquent. The set contains a short speech of thanks by Schoenberg.

MDG and the Leipzig Quartet do go in for extravagant layout. Their Schoenberg runs to three CDs – No. 3 is coupled with *Verklaerte Nacht* on a third disc which we have not heard. It is difficult to fault them in the two early quartets or for that matter in the *Second*, Op. 10, in which Christiane Oelze sings beautifully. They phrase with great naturalness, their ensemble is perfect and they have great warmth, richness and tonal beauty, though nothing is overstated or projected. If any ensemble or recording could win doubting listeners over to this repertoire, this is it. The recording balance is perfect.

The New Vienna recordings on Philips come from 1969. They are far from negligible performances – indeed, they are more than adequate – but by no means as persuasive as the Leipzig Quartet. Of course, they enjoy a distinct price advantage which may tempt some readers but they don't give us the early *D major Quartet* of 1897. The Leipzig set is well worth the extra outlay.

Verklaerte Nacht, Op. 4 (string sextet version).

⊛ (***) Testament mono SABT 1031. Hollywood Qt, with Dinkin, Reher – SCHUBERT: *String Quintet.* (***) ⊛
*** Hyp. CDA 66425. Raphael Ens. – KORNGOLD: *Sextet.* ***
*** Nim. NI 5614. Brandis Qt, with Küssner, Schwalke –
R. STRAUSS: *Metamorphosen; Capriccio: Prelude.* ***

(i) *Verklaerte Nacht (string sextet version); (ii) String Quartet No. 2 in F sharp min., Op. 10.*

(B) **(*) DG (ADD) 439 470-2 [(M) id. import]. LaSalle Qt, with (i) McInnes and Pegis; (ii) Price – WEBERN: *6 Bagatelles etc.* ***

The 1950 Hollywood account was the first version of *Verklaerte Nacht* in its original sextet form ever to appear on records, and arguably it remains unsurpassed and possibly unequalled. This almost flawless performance enjoyed the imprimatur of Schoenberg himself, who supplied the sleeve-note for it (reproduced in the excellent booklet), the only time he ever did so. The sound is remarkably good and very musical. Recommended with enthusiasm.

For those wanting a modern, digital version, the Raphael Ensemble have the advantage of very good recorded sound and give a fine account of Schoenberg's score. They also have the advantage of a rarity in their coupling, the youthful *Sextet* of Korngold.

The Brandis Quartet with two colleagues from the Berlin Philharmonic are in excellent form. They possess an unforced eloquence and expressive beauty that is impressive. The Nimbus recording is well balanced and very lifelike and can be recommended alongside the Raphael version.

The LaSalle Quartet give a virtuosic account with no lack of expressive feeling. At times they are inclined to rush things, but the digital recording, if rather bright, is faithful enough. It is good also to have on this bargain disc the rather later *Second Quartet*. Its last two movements (both slow) are intensified by the contribution of a soprano, here the secure and sympathetic Dame Margaret Price. Unfortunately the back-up notes (which are otherwise adequate) omit the words of her two songs, settings of poems by Stefan George

– *Litanei* and *Entrückung* ('Transport') – particularly as they are important in establishing the composer's intentions. The 1969 analogue recording, however, cannot be faulted, and the couplings are well chosen and generous.

Piano music: *3 Pieces, Op. 11; 6 Little Pieces, Op. 19; 5 Pieces, Op. 23; 2 Pieces, Op. 33a & b; Suite, Op. 25.*

(M) *** DG (IMS) (ADD) 423 249-2. Pollini.

(BB) *** Naxos 8.553870. Hill – BERG: *Piano Sonata;* WEBERN: *Variations, Op. 27.* ***

This CD encompasses Schoenberg's complete piano music. Pollini plays with enormous authority and refinement of dynamic nuance and colour, making one perceive this music in a totally different light from other performers. He is accorded excellent sound (very slightly on the dry side), extremely clear and well defined.

Peter Hill may not challenge Pollini's magisterial survey of the Schoenberg canon but his is highly intelligent, thoughtful playing, acutely sensitive to dynamic and tonal shading. In some ways he is more persuasive than Pollini in that one feels more completely drawn into this musical world. In any event, given the low price tag and the high quality of the recorded sound, this is self-recommending.

VOCAL MUSIC

Choral works: *Dreimal Tausend Jahre; 3 Folksongs; Friede auf Erden; 4 Pieces, Op. 27; 6 Pieces, Op. 35; Psalm 130, Op. 50b; 3 Satires, Op. 28.*

(BB) *** Arte Nova 74321 27799-2. South German R. Ch., Stuttgart, Huber.

Schoenberg's writing for choir was often taxing, but it drew from him some of his most warmly expressive music, whether he was employing his serial technique or relaxing in a more conventional tonal idiom. Though this disc does not – as is claimed on the cover – contain the complete choral works, omitting those with orchestra for example, it offers most of the finest in superlative performances, beautifully recorded. Comparing these readings with those of Pierre Boulez in his pioneering recordings for Sony with the BBC Chorus, the Stuttgart choir is consistently crisper in ensemble and more clearly confident in matching and pitching. So much so that Rupert Huber, the conductor, can readily and without serious problem adopt faster, more flowing speeds, which give the performances greater impact. It is astonishing to find the early *Friede auf Erden* ('Peace on earth'), once thought to be unperformable, sung here with an expressive ease and confidence such as you might find in a Bach performance. At super-bargain price, an issue to suggest to anyone hitherto daunted by this bogeyman composer, as well as to his regular admirers.

Erwartung, Op. 17.

*** Decca 417 348-2 (2). Silja, VPO, Dohnányi – BERG: *Wozzeck.* ***

(M) (**(*)) Sony Heritage mono MH2K 62759 (2). Dow, NYPO, Mitropoulos – BERG: *Wozzeck;* KRENEK: *Symphonic Elegy.* (***)

(i) *Erwartung.* (ii) Cabaret Songs: *Arie aus dem Spiegel von Arcadien; Einfältiges Lied; Galathea; Der genügsame Liebhaber; Jedem das Seine; Mahnung; Nachtwandler* (with trumpet, piccolo & snare drum).

*** Ph. 426 261-2. Norman; (i) Met. Op. O, Levine; (ii) Levine (piano).

Jessye Norman herself has said that *Erwartung* is 'technically the most difficult thing I have ever sung' but that, having learnt it, she found it 'immensely singable'. That clearly accounts for the warmth, intensity, range of expression and sheer beauty that she and Levine bring to this score. Levine draws ravishing sounds from the Metropolitan Opera Orchestra; Jessye Norman's singing, beautiful and totally secure over the widest range of expression and dynamic, is a revelation too. Compare this with Anja Silja, and the extra depth, range of emotion and refinement of the New York performance come out at every point. Then accompanied by Levine at the piano – a sparkily individual partner – Jessye Norman sings all eight of the cabaret songs that Schoenberg wrote when he was working in Berlin. In these witty, pointed, tuneful songs Schoenberg was letting his hair down in a way that to his detractors must be almost unimaginable and Jessye Norman projects her personality as masterfully as a latterday Marlene Dietrich.

Schoenberg's searingly intense monodrama makes an apt and generous coupling for Dohnányi's excellent version of Berg's *Wozzeck*. As in the Berg, Silja is at her most passionately committed, and the digital sound is exceptionally vivid.

Mitropoulos recorded Schoenberg's sinister monodrama in 1951, the same year as his recordings of *Wozzeck* and the Krenek piece. Unlike the Berg opera, this was recorded in the studio and, though the performance does not crackle with quite such high-voltage electricity, it has similar clarity and purposefulness. Dorothy Dow tackles the formidable vocal line with freshness and clarity, though the timbre of her voice does not provide the central character's soul-searching on finding the body of her lover. The result is not as chilling as it can be, though satisfying musically. As with the Berg, full libretto and translations are provided, but this CD is comparatively expensive.

(i) *Erwartung;* (ii) *Pierrot lunaire, Op. 21.*

** Teldec 3984 22901-2. (i) Castellani, Lucchesini, members of Dresden State O; (ii) Marc; Dresden State O, Sinopoli.

Sinopoli, a sympathetically persuasive interpreter of Schoenberg who brings out any underlying romanticism, offers an apt coupling not otherwise available – but the results are flawed. The live recording of *Erwartung* has Alessandra Marc as a warm-toned soloist with a rich chest register, who sings well, but conveys little of the horror behind this monodrama. Luisa Castellani in *Pierrot lunaire* is intimately confidential in her sing-speech recitations, but too often is masked by the instruments, which are balanced too far forward.

Gurrelieder.

*** Teldec 4509-98424-2 (2). Moser, Voigt, Larmore, Weikl, Riegel, Brandauer, Saxon State Op. Ch., Dresden, Leipzig R. Ch., Prague Male Ch., Dresden State O, Sinopoli.

*** DG 439 944-2 (2). Sweet, Jerusalem, Lipovšek, Wekler,

Langridge, Sukowa, Vienna State Op. Ch., Schoenberg Ch., Slovak Phil Ch., BPO, Abbado.

*** Decca 430 321-2 (2). Jerusalem, Dunn, Fassbaender, Brecht, Haage, Hotter, St Hedwig's Cathedral Ch., Berlin, Düsseldorf State Musikverein, Berlin RSO, Chailly.

(i) *Gurrelieder;* (ii) *Chamber Symphony No. 1, Op. 9b; No. 2, Op. 38.*

(B) **(*) Ph. Duo (ADD) 464 736-2 (2). McCracken, Norman, Troyanos, Klemperer, Tanglewood Festival Ch., Boston SO, Ozawa.

(i) *Gurrelieder;* (ii) *Suite for Strings.*

(N) (B) **(*) EMI double fforte (ADD) CZS5 74194-2 (2). (i) Arroyo, Young, Janet Baker, Woltad, Möller, Patzak, Danish State R. Ch., SO & Concert O, Ferencsik.

(i) *Gurrelieder;* (ii) *4 Orchestral Songs.*

(M) *** Sony (ADD) SM2K 48459 (2). (i) Jess Thomas, Napier, Nimsgern, Bowen, Reich, BBC Singers & Ch. Soc., Goldsmith's Ch. Union, Men's voices of LPO Ch.; (i; ii) Yvonne Minton, BBC SO; Boulez.

In his highly compelling live recording, Sinopoli conducts the most sensuous reading of *Gurrelieder* on record, bringing out all its high romantic voluptuousness. Speeds are spacious, thanks in part to his expressive freedom, and anyone who has ever thought of Schoenberg as cold should certainly hear this, magnetic from first to last, helped by rich, immediate sound. The soloists are excellent, even if Thomas Moser as Waldemar is gritty at times in a Wagnerian way. While the Abbado and Chailly versions are by no means upstaged (the latter with a superb Decca recording) and Boulez, too, has his own special insights to offer, this new Sinopoli set could well be first choice for many collectors.

Recorded live in the Philharmonie, Berlin, Abbado's version begins magnetically with the most delicate tracery of sound, immediately capturing both atmosphere and dramatic intensity. Though Siegfried Jerusalem as Waldemar is not quite as firmly focused as he was on Riccardo Chailly's Decca set, he conveys more passion, and regularly Abbado's reading is freer and more volatile than Chailly's, with a sense of wonder enhanced by the very atmosphere of a concert. Susan Dunn as Tove in Chailly's version is firmer and truer than Abbado's Sharon Sweet, whose tight vibrato is often intrusive, but this is a strong, characterful reading, and Marjana Lipovšek is deeply moving as the Wood-dove, with the hushed tension behind her big solo tellingly conveyed. Philip Langridge is outstanding as Klaus-Knarr and Hartmut Welker makes a bluff if slightly unsteady Peasant. The only soloist who is controversial is the woman speaker, Barbara Sukowa, whose use of sliding *Sprech-Stimme*, chattering in the style of *Pierrot lunaire*, comes near to being comic. With the Berlin Philharmonic's playing richly and atmospherically caught, this must now stand as a first choice among live recordings, though the extra weight and detail of the sound in Chailly's studio version will for many make that still preferable.

Chailly's magnificent recording of Schoenberg's massive *Gurrelieder* remains highly recommendable. Siegfried Jerusalem as Waldemar is not only warm and firm of tone, but imaginative too. Susan Dunn makes a sweet, touchingly vulnerable Tove, while Brigitte Fassbaender gives darkly baleful intensity to the message of the Wood-dove. Hans Hotter is a characterful Speaker in the final section. The impact of the performance is the more telling with sound both atmospheric and immediate, bringing a fine sense of presence, not least in the final choral outburst.

Boulez's warm, expressive style using slow, luxuriating tempi brings out the operatic quality behind Schoenberg's massive score. With Boulez, the Wagnerian overtones are richly expressive and, though Marita Napier and Jess Thomas are not especially sweet on the ear, they show the big, heroic qualities which this score ideally demands, while Yvonne Minton is magnificent in the *Song of the Wood-dove.* Boulez builds that beautiful section to an ominous climax and, at mid-price, remains competitive, for the CBS/Sony recording has attractively vivid and atmospheric sound, and this set also offers a generous coupling of Yvonne Minton's fine account of the *Orchestral Songs.*

Ozawa directs a gloriously opulent reading of *Gurrelieder.* The playing of the Boston SO has both warmth and polish and is set against a resonant acoustic; among the soloists, Jessye Norman gives a performance of radiant beauty, reminding one at times of Flagstad in the burnished glory of her tone colours. As the Wood-dove, Tatiana Troyanos sings most sensitively, though the vibrato is at times obtrusive; and James McCracken does better than most tenors at coping with a heroic vocal line without barking. The live 1979 recording is good, though obviously not up to studio standards, and the absence of a libretto will be a drawback for some. However, at bargain price this Duo is good value.

Though the 1968 HMV recording of a live performance given in Copenhagen is less precise of ensemble than the studio versions, it is very dynamic musically, the forward movement of the writing very effectively presented, whether in the lyrical or the dramatic passages of this extraordinarily rich and evocative score. Janet Baker (as she was then) was in glorious voice as the Wood Dove, giving expressive weight to every word, and although Alexander Young may seem too light a tenor for a Heldentenor role, the result as heard on record is the more beautiful. Martina Arroyo as Tove is also impressive, and it is good to hear the veteran Patzak in the non-singing role of the narrator. But above all it is the dramatic thrust of the performance that comes over, with Ferencsik creating consistent tension and spontaneity. The vividly atmospheric recording, well balanced, and clear in every detail, is here admirably transferred to CD for the first time, with the closing chorus, *Seht die Sonne,* quite resplendent.

Norman Del Mar then gives a polished and vibrantly expressive account of the leonine *Suite for Strings,* the first product of Schoenberg's American years and an attractive example of his later style at its richest and most inventive. This was recorded four years earlier at Abbey Road and is equally successful in its CD format. The great snag is the absence of texts and translations.

Pierrot lunaire, Op. 21.

(M) *** Chan. 6534. Manning, Nash Ens., Rattle — WEBERN: *Concerto.* ***

(i) *Pierrot lunaire; Herzgewächse, Op. 20.* (ii) *Ode to Napoleon Buonaparte.*

*** DG 457 630-2. (i) Schäfer; (ii) Pittman-Jennings; Soloists of Ensemble Intercontemporain, Boulez.

Jane Manning is outstanding among singers who have tackled this most taxing of works, steering a masterful course between the twin perils of, on the one hand, actually singing and, on the other, simply speaking; her sing-speech brings out the element of irony and darkly pointed wit that is an essential. Rattle draws strong, committed performances from the members of the Nash Ensemble and, apart from some intermittently odd balances, the sound is excellent.

For *Pierrot lunaire*, Boulez imaginatively chooses a sweet-toned soprano and the result is the more revealing, in an element of beauty and mystery usually missing while the dramatic point of this cabaret-like sequence is never underplayed. Balance is excellent, with the Ensemble Intercontemporain playing with warmth and brilliance, as they do in the brief *Herzgewächse* (Schäfer again radiant) and in the *Ode to Napoleon*. David Pittman-Jennings takes an idiosyncratic view of the narration, reciting in a stylized way as though English is a foreign language, but it is good to have this neglected work so well played and recorded.

OPERA

Moses und Aron.

*** Decca 414 264-2 (2). Mazura, Langridge, Bonney, Haugland, Chicago SO and Ch., Solti.

(i) *Moses und Aron* (complete); (ii) *Chamber Symphony No. 2, Op. 38.*

(M) *** Sony SM2K 48456 (2). (i) Reich, Cassilly, Palmer, Knight, BBC Singers, Orpheus Boys' Ch., BBC SO; (ii) Ens. InterContemporain; Boulez.

Solti gives Schoenberg's masterly score a dynamism and warmth which set it firmly – if perhaps surprisingly – in the grand romantic tradition, yet finds an element of fantasy and, in places – as in the *Golden Calf* episode – a sparkle such as you would never expect from Schoenberg. The Moses of Franz Mazura may not be as specific in his sing-speech as was Gunter Reich in the two previous versions – far less sing than speech – but the characterization of an Old Testament patriarch is the more convincing. As Aron, Philip Langridge is lighter and more lyrical, as well as more accurate, than his predecessor with Boulez, Richard Cassilly. Aage Haugland with his firm, dark bass makes his mark in the small role of the Priest; Barbara Bonney too is excellent as the Young Girl. Above all, the brilliant singing of the Chicago Symphony Chorus matches the playing of the orchestra in virtuosity. More than ever the question-mark concluding Act II makes a pointful close, with no feeling of a work unfinished. The brilliant recording has an even sharper focus on CD.

Pierre Boulez is helped not just by the passionately committed singing and playing (with Günter Reich expansive in his fully rounded characterization of Moses) but also by the rich, atmospheric recording, so that the operatic qualities are allowed to blossom. It is typical of Boulez that in the final scene Moses' mounting frustration in the face of the glib, articulate Aron is superbly built up, so that the final words – *O Wort, du Wort das mir fehlt* – come with a compelling sense of tragedy. Though the composer planned a third Act, such a moment makes a telling conclusion. Richard Cassilly makes a big-scaled Aron, a worthy brother-adversary to the central tragic figure. The *Second Chamber Symphony*, given an equally committed performance, follows the end of the opera to make a good bonus on the second CD.

SCHOENFIELD, Paul (born 1947)

Piano Concerto (Four Parables).

** Athene CD 21. Boyde, Dresden SO, Nott – DVORAK: *Piano Concerto.* **

The American composer Paul Schoenfield is now in his early fifties and has made few inroads into the concert hall outside the USA. This CD is of the 1998 European première of his *Piano Concerto (Four Parables)*, which draws on a variety of styles – popular music, vernacular and folk traditions and 'the normal historical traditions of cultivated music often treated with sly twists'. It has some degree of flair but from the multiplicity of styles, no distinctive personality emerges. Very brilliant playing from the talented Andreas Boyde but this is not music which arouses enthusiasm.

SCHREKER, Franz (1878–1934)

(i) *Chamber Symphony for 23 Solo Instruments;* (ii) *Nachtstück;* (i) *Prelude to a Drama;* (ii) *Valse lente.*

**(*) Koch CD 311 078. Berlin RSO, (i) Gielen, (ii) Rickenbacher.

Schreker's *Chamber Symphony* is quite magical, scored with great delicacy and feeling for colour. The other works are not quite so seductive but they, too, have a heady art-nouveau atmosphere. A most rewarding disc, with good performances and very acceptable, though not out of the ordinary, recording. But don't miss this issue.

Ekkehard (Symphonic Overture), Op. 12; Fantastic Overture, Op. 15; Interlude from Der Schatzgräber; Nächtstuck (from Der ferne Klang); Prelude to a Drama; Valse lente.

*** Chan. 9797. BBC PO, Sinaisky.

Schreker reused material from his stage works to produce concert pieces such as the ones here, all demonstrating his gift for drawing sumptuous sounds from the orchestra. This sequence of six pieces presents a good cross-section of his output, demonstrating Schreker's development from the *Symphonic Overture, Ekkehard*, and the charmingly unpretentious *Valse lente*, to the later works, which remain sumptuously late-romantic but which were regarded as daringly modern by early audiences. Both the *Nachtstück* from *Der ferne Klang* (1909) and the *Prelude to a Drama* (1913) – the drama in question being the opera *Die Gezeichneten* – are powerfully imaginative. Perhaps the most seductive piece is the *Valse lente*. Schreker had a wonderful sense of fantasy, a feeling for colour, and impressive mastery of the orchestra. The textures are lush and overheated. Sinaisky draws seductively beautiful playing from the BBC Philharmonic, heightened by gloriously rich Chandos sound, and the whole disc serves to advance Schreker's cause.

Der Geburtstag der Infantin.

** Edition Abseits ED A013-2. Berlin Kammersymphonie,
  Bruns – TOCH: *Tanz-Suite, Op. 30.* **

This is a first recording of the original 1910 version of Schreker's dance pantomime on Oscar Wilde's short story, *The Birthday of the Infanta*. It surfaced during the 1980s in a Vienna Archive, having been misfiled. Good playing and recording.

Der ferne Klang (opera; complete).

(N) (BB) *** Naxos 8.660074/5 (2). Grigorescu, Harper,
  Haller, Hagen Op.Ch. & PO, Halász.

Schreker started *Der ferne Klang* in or around 1901 but put it on one side, returning to the score in 1910. It was staged in Frankfurt am Main two years later, and put him firmly on the operatic map. Its central character is an ambitious young dramatist, Fritz, who pursues his creative ambitions and his search for *Der ferne Klang* ('the distant sound') at the expense of his love for Grete, whom he abandons and who turns to prostitution.

Schreker scores with chamber-like delicacy and has a Puccini-like finesse in the handling of colour, and great imagination in his handling of harmonic resource. And like Puccini, he was also aware of developments in French music. The skill with which he handles the orchestras in the pit and on the stage in the Venetian scene is impressive and obviously influenced Berg in *Wozzeck*. Anyone coming afresh to this opera will find the modest outlay this set entails well worth while. The score is quite gripping, its sound world at times astringent in its harmonies, at others lush and intoxicating. Good soloists, though it is a pity that the voices are rather prominently balanced in this 1989 recording and that the subtlety of Schreker's lavish scoring is not always heard to best advantage. Strongly recommended.

Die Gezeichneten (opera): complete.

*** Decca 444 442-2 (3). Kruse, Connell, Pederson, Muff,
  Berlin R. Ch. & O, Zagrosek.

The opening prelude of this opera with its magic, shimmering sounds, using the most exotic orchestration, establishes the hothouse atmosphere of a story which in its melodrama can indeed be regarded as decadent, if hardly more so than Strauss's *Salome*. What Zagrosek's gloriously recorded version demonstrates is the range of atmospheric beauty in the score. Ripe echoes of composers from Scriabin to Puccini intensify the story of a dying woman painter, Carlotta, who deserts her faithful, ugly lover, Alviano, in favour of the physical love of Tamare, finally giving herself to him with fatal consequences. The Decca cast has no weak link, with Heinz Kruse fresh and clear-toned in the taxing tenor role of Alviano and Elizabeth Connell conveying with sharp clarity the positive yet vulnerable character of the

heroine. Monte Pederson in cleanly focused singing conveys the animal quality of Tamare, while Alfred Muff is well contrasted as the older figure of Duke Adorno. Zagrosek draws dedicated playing and singing from the massive ensemble, and the beautifully balanced sound is of demonstration quality. This supersedes the earlier Marco Polo set.

Der Schatzgräber (opera): complete.

**(*) Capriccio 60010-2 (2). Protschka, Schnaut, Stamm,
  Haage, Hamburg State O, Albrecht.

The attractions of Schreker's sweet-sour treatment of a curious morality fairy-story are fairly well conveyed in this first recording, made live at the Hamburg State Opera in 1989, though there are very few signs of the audience's presence, with no applause, even at the end. Josef Protschka sings powerfully as Elis, hardly ever over-strenuous, but Gabriele Schnaut finds it hard to scale down her very bright and powerful soprano and seems happiest when she is scything your ears with loud and often unsteady top notes; yet she is certainly dramatic in this equivocal role. Outstanding among the others is Peter Haage as the court jester. *Der Schatzgräber* may be hokum, but it is enjoyable hokum, and, with Albrecht drawing committed performances from the whole company, this well-made recording is most welcome.

SCHUBERT, Franz (1797–1828)

ORCHESTRAL MUSIC

(i) *Konzertstück in D, D.345; Rondo, D.438;* (ii) *Duo in A, D.574; Fantasy in C, D.934.*

(M) *** DG ADD/Dig. 453 665-2. Kremer, with (i) LSO,
  Tchakarov; (ii) Afanassiev.

All four works here have that freshness and (at times) innocence of invention which make Schubert's instrumental music so engaging, yet Kremer and Afanassiev (a splendid partnership) treat the *Duo* as a major sonata by observing the first-movement exposition repeat. They also show imaginative flair in the *Fantasy*, especially in its chimerical *Allegretto*. The concertante pieces are equally successful, the recording is excellent, and this was an excellent choice for including within DG's special bicentenary collection.

Rondo in A for Violin & Strings, D.438.

*** EMI CDC7 49663-2. Kennedy, ECO, Tate – BRUCH;
  MENDELSSOHN: *Concertos.* ***

The ideas in Schubert's *Rondo* flow very sweetly with Kennedy, making this an attractive bonus to the usual Bruch–Mendelssohn coupling.

Symphonies Nos. 1–6; 8–9.

*** RCA 09026 62673-2 (4). Dresden State O, Davis.

(BB) *** Arte Nova 74321 54458-2 (4). Putbus Festival O,
  Keitel.

**(*) Teldec 4509 91184-2 (4). Concg. O, Harnoncourt.

(BB) **(*) Brilliant 99587 (4). Hanover Band, Goodman.

Symphonies Nos. 1–6; 8–9; Grand Duo in C, D.812 (orch. Joachim); Rosamunde Overture (Die Zauberharfe).

*** DG 423 651-2 (5). COE, Abbado.

Symphonies Nos. 1–6.

(B) **(*) EMI double fforte (ADD) CZS5 73359-2 (2). Menuhin Festival O, Menuhin.

Symphonies Nos. 8 (Unfinished); 9 (Great); Overtures: Alfonso and Wstrella; in C & in D in the Italian Style; Die Zwillingsbrüder.

(B) **(*) EMI double fforte (ADD) CZS5 73362-2 (2). Menuhin Festival O, Menuhin.

Symphonies Nos. 1–6; 8 (Unfinished); 9 (Great); Overtures: Fierrabras; In the Italian Style in C; Des Teufels Lustschloss.

(B) **(*) Decca (ADD) 430 773-2 (4). VPO, Kertész.

Symphonies Nos. 1 in D, D.82; 2 in B flat, D.125.

(M) **(*) EMI (ADD) CDM5 66102-2. BPO, Karajan (with WEBER: *Der Freischütz: Overture* **(*)).

Symphonies Nos. 3 in D, D.200; 4 in C min. (Tragic), D.417; Rosamunde: Ballet Music 1–2.

(M) ** EMI (ADD) CDM5 66103-2. BPO, Karajan.

Symphonies Nos. 5 in B flat, D.485; 6 in C, D.589; Rosamunde: Overture (Die Zauberharfe), D.644.

(M) **(*) EMI (ADD) CDM5 66104-2. BPO, Karajan.

Symphonies Nos. 8 in B min. (Unfinished), D.759; 9 in C (Great), D.944.

(M) **(*) EMI (ADD) CDM5 66105-2. BPO, Karajan.

Symphonies Nos. 1–6; 8 (Unfinished); 9 (Great).

(N) (B) **(*) DG (ADD) 471 307-2 (4). BPO, Boehm.

Symphonies Nos. 1–2; Rosamunde: Overture (Die Zauberharfe).

(M) **(*) DG (ADD) 453 661-2. BPO, Boehm.

Symphonies Nos. 3; 4 (Tragic); Rosamunde: Ballet Music Nos. 1–2, D.797.

(M) ** DG (ADD) 453 662-2. BPO, Boehm.

Symphonies Nos. 5–6.

(M) *** DG (ADD) 453 663-2. BPO, Boehm.

Symphonies Nos. 8 (Unfinished); 9 (Great).

(M) *** DG (ADD) 453 664-2. BPO, Boehm.

Abbado's is an outstanding set. Rarely has he made recordings of the central Viennese classics which find him so naturally sunny and warm in his expression. Speeds are often on the fast side but never feel breathless, and the recording is refined, with fine bloom on the string-sound. Textually too, the Abbado set takes precedence over its rivals and there are certain fascinating differences from what we are used to. The five CDs are now also available separately – see below.

Sir Colin Davis's Dresden cycle of the Schubert symphonies (on four discs for the price of three), despite observing all repeats, makes a glowing tribute that regularly reveals Davis drawing magnetic and intense playing from the Dresden orchestra, with the polish of the ensemble adding to the impact, never making the results sound self-conscious. In the youthful symphonies, Nos. 1–3, Davis refuses to regard them as just elegantly Mozartian, but genuinely Schubertian. In the middle symphonies Davis seems happier bringing out the elegance and charm, but then crowns the cycle with a radiant reading of the *Unfinished*, marked by high dynamic contrasts. In the *Great C major* tensions are not quite so keen. This is a most distinguished cycle, helped by glowing sound.

In full, immediate, yet open sound the inexpensive Arte Nova performances are as fresh and direct as any you will find. Keitel follows period practice to the extent of favouring fast speeds. Light, crisp articulation also helps to bring transparent textures, with dynamic contrasts dramatically brought out and Scherzo-like Minuets given extra bite, thanks to sharp observance of accented cross-rhythms. If the earlier symphonies up to No. 6 are remarkable above all for their freshness, the *Unfinished* then brings the one idiosyncratic interpretation, with the first movement taken very slowly and steadily. The *Great C major Symphony* – with all repeats observed – brings steady speeds, again on the brisk side, and a fresh, direct manner. With any reservations noted, this set is worth the money.

Karajan presents a most polished and beautiful set of Schubert symphonies, recorded in the latter part of the 1970s in the Philharmonie. The point and elegance of the Berliners' playing in the early symphonies is most persuasive, yet the results are never mannered. The reverberant acoustic gives the impression of a band rather large for Schubert, lacking in brightness and transparency, and the *Fourth Symphony*, the *Tragic*, finds Karajan less compelling. The *Unfinished*, dating from 1975, with Berlin refinement at its most ethereal, has an other-worldly quality, rapt and concentrated. The *Great C major* (1977) is also compelling, but here some may find that the reverberant acoustic gives the impression of too much weightiness. However, as we go to press this set has been withdrawn, as also have the individual discs except for the coupling of Nos. 8 and 9.

Boehm does not smile as often as Schubert's music demands – especially by the side of Beecham in Nos. 3 and 5, but he is always sympathetic. Certainly the Berlin wind are a joy to listen to, and it is only in the early symphonies that he does not quite capture the youthful sparkle of these delightful scores, although in its way No. 1 is brightly and elegantly done and No. 2 also is characteristically strong; both are classical in spirit. No. 4 offers splendidly disciplined playing, but this is not one of the more characterful interpretations of the set. Boehm's warmly graceful account of No. 5 and the glowing performance of No. 6, coupled together, show Boehm at his best, taking an easy-going view, with relaxed tempi that never grow heavy.

Boehm capped his series with an outstanding account of the *Unfinished Symphony* and one of the finest of all recorded performances of the *Great C major*, to make an excellent coupling. The recording is very good indeed and in its CD transfer sounds fresh, warm and full. One notes, however, that on its last appearance this coupling appeared on DG's bargain Classikon label, so now it costs more. However, the CDs are also available together in a budget box in DG's Collector's Edition.

Kertész began his Schubert cycle with Nos. 8 and 9 and the overtures, and these two symphonies are the finest performances in the cycle. The *Ninth* is fresh, dramatic and often very exciting, the *Unfinished* highly imaginative and comparably dramatic in its wide dynamic contrasts. In the two early symphonies Kertész scores with the spirited VPO playing and a light touch, and this also applies to Nos. 3 and 6, even if they are without the last ounce of character and distinction. The playing of the VPO is beyond reproach throughout, and it has a pervading freshness, helped by the transparent yet full Decca sound.

Harnoncourt takes a relatively severe view, and significantly he is at his finest in the darkness of the *Tragic Symphony*. There is little of Schubertian charm here, with his eccentrically slow tempo for the finale of No. 6 in its lumbering gait missing the pure sunlight of the piece. Harnoncourt's preference for short phrasing also tends to make slow movements less songful, though equally it adds to the bite and intensity of other movements, notably Scherzos with their sharp cross-rhythms. Though the reverberance of the Amsterdam Concertgebouw hall obscures detail in tuttis, as well as reinforcing the weight of sound, the recording is warm and otherwise helpful. Harnoncourt, like Abbado, has used specially prepared texts, but they avoid the radical changes that spice the Abbado set.

Goodman draws lively, beautifully sprung performances from the players of the Hanover Band. For anyone wanting an inexpensive set of period performances of these symphonies, they can be warmly recommended with the reservation that the (originally Nimbus) sound balance is very reverberant. The strings are attractively caught in a warm acoustic, but the resonance tends to obscure detail in tuttis, with the woodwind set very backwardly, and even the rasp of the natural horns is underplayed. However this Brilliant reissue is in the lowest possible price range (cheaper than Naxos), although documentation is non-existent. The four discs are in individual jewel-boxes within a slip case.

Youthful ardour burns in most of Menuhin's performances. Some will find them too thrustful, not gentle enough, but the result is always refreshing. The Menuhin approach shows the music's underlying strength, and although the gaiety in the early symphonies sometimes becomes a little relentless the string playing is graceful, and the energy is never in doubt. The approach to Nos. 4 and 5 is unsentimental and direct, although the finale of No. 5 is comparatively leisurely; a greater degree of expressiveness in slow movements would have been welcome. No. 6 is a delicious performance and the affectionate touch in the *Andante* brings a glow of warmth. The *Unfinished* returns to the mood of Nos. 4 and 5, and here a little more relaxation would have been ideal. But, as in the overtures which are offered as a sizeable bonus, the playing is unmannered and fresh. With No. 9 Menuhin has preferred to retain the smaller (and authentic) scale. The performance has plenty of character; brisk, lightweight and refreshing, it is very enjoyable in its way, even though it leaves one remembering more searching interpretations. The CD transfers retain the analogue warmth and bloom, yet with the extra clarity adding to the bite of the music-making.

Symphonies Nos. 1–3; 4 (Tragic); 5–7; 8 (Unfinished); 9 in C (Great); 10 in D, D.936a; Symphonic Fragments in D, D.615 & D.708a (completed and orch. Newbould).

*** Ph. (IMS) 412 176-2 (6). ASMF, Marriner.

Marriner's excellent set gathers together not only the eight symphonies of the regular canon but two more symphonies now 'realized', thanks to the work of Professor Brian Newbould of Hull University. For full measure, half a dozen fragments of other symphonic movements are also included, orchestrated by Professor Newbould. The set brings sparkling examples of the Academy's work at its finest, while the bigger challenges of the *Unfinished* (here completed with Schubert's Scherzo filled out and the *Rosamunde B minor Entr'acte* used as finale) and the *Great C major* are splendidly taken. These are fresh, direct readings, making up in rhythmic vitality for any lack of weight. The recordings, all digital, present consistent refinement and undistractingly good balance. But this set now seems expensive.

Symphonies Nos. 1 in D, D.82; 2 in B flat, D.125.

*** DG 423 652-2. COE, Abbado.

(BB) **(*) Naxos 8.553093. Failoni O of Budapest, Halász.

The coupling of the two earliest *Symphonies* on DG brings bright and sparkling performances, reflecting the youthful joy of both composer and players. Abbado brings out the sunny relaxation of the writing, most exhilaratingly of all in the light-hearted finales. The recording of both captures the refined playing of the COE very vividly.

Michael Halász and the Failoni Orchestra are affectionately easy-going rather than overtly dramatic, but they play both these works most winningly. The recording too is full and naturally balanced, although the resonance of the Italian Institute in Budapest makes the tuttis spread and lose some of the sharpness of focus. But this is a most enjoyable disc nevertheless and well worth its modest cost.

(i) Symphony No. 1; (ii) Marche militaire, Op. 51/1; (iii) Overtures: Fierrabras; Des Teufels Lustschloss; (iv) 4 Waltzes & 4 Ecossaises (2 sets).

** Australian Decca Eloquence 466 908-2. (i) Israel PO, Mehta; (ii) VPO, Knappertsbusch; (iii) VPO, Kertész; (iv) Boskovsky Ens.

Mehta is no Beecham, but his account of the *First Symphony* is a fresh, straightforward account which gives pleasure. The Israeli orchestra lacks something in polish. But there are no such problems for the ensuing Viennese recordings, which give this bargain disc its appeal. Knappertsbusch's noble and trusty account of the *Marche militaire*, and the little-known overtures under Kertész are always a joy to hear. *Des Teufels Lustschloss* is a juvenile work. *Fierrabras* is more melodramatic, but lively in invention. To cap an imaginative programme, Boskovsky gives delectable accounts of the charming dance pieces, and all are well recorded.

Symphonies Nos. 3; 4 (Tragic).

*** DG (IMS) 423 653-2. COE, Abbado.

Crisp, fast and light, No. 3 is given a delectable performance by Abbado. In No. 4, the *Tragic*, Abbado makes the slow

C minor introduction bitingly mysterious before a clean, elegant *Allegro*, and with this conductor the other movements are also elegant and polished as well as strong. Textually, No. 4 eliminates the extra bars in the slow movement which had been inserted originally by Brahms. The slow movement is outstandingly beautiful, with the oboe solo – presumably COE's Douglas Boyd – most tenderly expressive.

Symphonies Nos. 3; 5; 6.

✪ (M) *** EMI (ADD) CDM5 66984-2 [566999]. RPO, Beecham.

Beecham's are magical performances in which every phrase breathes. There is no substitute for imaginative phrasing and each line is shaped with affection and spirit. The *Allegretto* of the *Third Symphony* is an absolute delight. The delicacy of the opening of the *Fifth* is matched by the simple lyrical beauty of the *Andante*, while few conductors have been as persuasive as Beecham in the *Sixth* 'little' *C major Symphony*. The sound is now just a shade drier in Nos. 3 and 6 than in their last LP incarnation but is generally faithful and spacious. This is an indispensable record for all collections and a supreme bargain in the Schubert discography, now rightly reissued as one of EMI's 'Great Recordings of the Century'.

Symphonies Nos. 3 in D, D.200; 6 in C, D.589.

(BB) *** Naxos 8.553094. Failoni O of Budapest, Halász.

These are delightful performances, fully capturing the innocent charm of these youthful symphonies. Michael Halász is most sensitive and in the *Allegretto* second movement of No. 3 the conductor's style is Beechamesque in its affectionate elegance. The economy of Schubert's scoring means that the resonant acoustic affects the clarity of the tuttis only marginally and it certainly lends an attractive bloom to the proceedings.

Symphonies Nos. 3; 8 (Unfinished).

(M) **(*) DG (ADD) 449 745-2. VPO, Kleiber.

Carlos Kleiber is a refreshingly unpredictable conductor, turning at times towards quirkiness, as in the slow movement of No. 3, which is rattled through jauntily at breakneck speed. The Minuet too becomes a full-blooded Scherzo, and there is little rest in the outer movements. The *Unfinished* brings a more compelling performance, but there is unease in the first movement, where first and second subjects are not fully co-ordinated, the contrasts sounding a little forced. The recording brings out the brass sharply, and is of wide range.

Symphony No. 4 in C min. (Tragic), D.417.

(M) (***) DG mono 457 705-2. BPO, Markevitch – BERWALD: *Symphonies Nos. 3 & 4.* (***)

Although it derives from a (very fine) mono LP, first issued in the mid-1950s, Markevitch's remains a hotly competitive version, perhaps not as introspective as might be – but then, despite the label 'Tragic', this is a fresh, early work. The Berlin Philharmonic plays with its characteristic warmth and brilliance, and the reverberant recording hardly sounds its age at all.

Symphony No. 4 (Tragic); Grand Duo in C, D.812 (orch. Joachim).

(BB) **(*) Naxos 8.553095. Failoni O of Budapest, Halász.

Halász presents the *Tragic Symphony* sympathetically and, though this is not a strongly dramatic reading, the resonant acoustic adds a certain weight, and the *Andante* is warmly and expressively played. This inexpensive disc is valuable for its coupling, the orchestration of the large-scale *Grand Duo* for piano duet by Joachim. The work is convincingly played, with gravitas and freshness nicely balanced. The warm resonancy of the Budapest Italian Institute suits this work very well.

Symphony No. 5 in B flat, D.485.

(M) *** DG (ADD) 447 433-2. VPO, Boehm – BEETHOVEN: *Symphony No. 6.* ***

(*) BBC (ADD) BBCL 4003-2. BBC SO, Kempe – BRAHMS: *Symphony No. 4.*(*)

(M) (***) Dutton Lab. mono CDK 1208. Concg. O, Van Beinum (with BEETHOVEN: *Creatures of Prometheus: Overture* (LPO)) – BERLIOZ: *Symphonie fantastique, Op. 14* (***).

**(*) DG (ADD) 445 471-2 (4). Stuttgart SW RSO, Celibidache – BRUCKNER: *Symphonies Nos. 7–9.* *(**)

Boehm's VPO recording of the *Fifth Symphony* dates from the very end of his career. In his eighties he preferred a tauter, more incisive view than he had given in his 1967 Berlin performance, weightier, but still with a light rhythmic touch, while the slow movement is not lacking grace. The finale is strong and purposeful and this is Boehm at his finest, with superbly polished and responsive VPO playing in repertoire they know and love. The 1980 recording is full and warm, a live performance and rightly reissued now in DG's 'Legendary Recordings' series of 'Originals'.

Kempe's *Fifth Symphony* comes as a makeweight to an excellent 1974 concert performance of the Brahms *Fourth*. The Schubert was recorded at a Promenade Concert three years earlier, and is a delight from start to finish. Very musicianly, enjoyable, natural and full of life. Small wonder that Beecham thought so highly of Kempe. Very decent sound too.

From Eduard van Beinum and the Concertgebouw Orchestra cultured playing and well-balanced sound. An enjoyable reminder of the fine results Eduard van Beinum achieved in Amsterdam.

Celibidache is surprisingly brisk in the opening movement, and his affectionately indulgent reading is at its most individual in the lovely *Andante*. Admirers of this conductor will want this alongside the Bruckner couplings, but for others there are more obvious recommendations. The recording is very good.

Symphonies Nos. 5 in B flat; 6 in C.

*** DG 423 654-2. COE, Abbado.

Abbado brings out the happy songfulness of the slow movements in these works, as well as the rhythmic resilience of the *Allegros*. As in No. 4, so also in No. 6 Abbado eliminates the extra bars added by Brahms in his original Schubert

Edition. Excellent recording, with fine bloom and good, natural contrasts.

Symphonies Nos. 5 in B flat; 8 (Unfinished).

(M) *** Sony (ADD) SMK 64487. Columbia SO or NYPO, Bruno Walter (with: BEETHOVEN: *Overture Leonora No. 3* ***).

Bruno Walter brings special qualities of warmth and lyricism to the *Unfinished*. Affection, gentleness and humanity are the keynotes of this performance; while the first movement of the *Fifth* is rather measured, there is much loving attention to detail in the *Andante*. The 1961 recording emerges fresh and glowing in its CD format and, like the rest of the Walter series, completely belies its age. The sound is richly expansive as well as clear, and the CD is in every way satisfying.

Symphonies Nos. 5; 8 (Unfinished); 9 (Great).

(B) *** Double Decca 448 927-2 (2). VPO, Solti.
(M) (**(*)) RCA mono 74321 59480-2 (2). NBC SO, Toscanini – MENDELSSOHN: *Symphonies Nos. 4–5.* (**(*))

Symphonies Nos. 5; 8 in B min. (completed by Brian Newbold); 9 (Great); Rosamunde (Ballet Music), D.797: No. 2 in G.

(B) *** Virgin 2 x 1 Double VBD5 61806-2(2). OAE, Mackerras.

This Double Decca coupling three favourite Schubert symphonies is one of the most attractive of all Solti's many reissues on the Decca label. There have been more charming versions of No. 5 but few that so beautifully combine freshness with refined polish. The *Unfinished* has Solti adopting measured speeds but with his refined manner keeping total concentration. The *Great C major Symphony* is an outstanding version, among the very finest, beautifully paced and sprung in all four movements, and superbly played. It has drama as well as lyrical feeling, but above all it has a natural sense of spontaneity and freshness. The recordings all confirm the Vienna Sofiensaal as an ideal recording location, and the glowing detail, especially in No. 9, is a source of consistent pleasure.

Mackerras was the first to use period instruments in Schubert's *Ninth*. The characterful rasp on the period brass instruments and the crisp attack of timpani are much more striking than any thinness of string-tone. It is a performance of outstanding freshness and resilience. The *Fifth* is not quite as magnetic as the *Ninth*, but still has comparable qualities. Tempi are only marginally brisker than conventional performances, and the slow movement has grace if not quite the degree of warmth that Boehm and Walter finds. The special claim of this second disc is the inclusion of the *Unfinished Symphony* heard here as 'finished' by Brian Newbold. Mackerras opens in the mysterious depths with the darkest pianopianissimo, and the plangent period timbres bring a real sense of *Sturm und Drang*, with powerful contrasts and strong, forceful accents in the second movement. The recording is excellent throughout.

To have all three of the Schubert symphonies that Toscanini recorded, in a single package, makes an attractive bargain, particularly when the new transfer gives extra body to the sound, with the original dry acoustic given fair ambi-

ence. Toscanini's Schubert may lack charm, but the symphonic power is made all the clearer.

Symphonies Nos. 5; 9 in C (Great).

(B) *** Penguin Decca (ADD) 460 634-2. VPO, Kertesz.

A good choice for a Penguin Classics coupling from the Kertesz/VPO series. No. 5 offers attractive, stylish playing. Kertesz does not always find the smile in Schubert's writing, but here he is at his freshest, and the playing of the Vienna Philharmonic is exemplary. The *Ninth* is perhaps the finest performance in the whole cycle. Like the *Fifth*, it is remarkably well recorded, with an appealing overall warmth yet plenty of bite and clarity. One is made conscious that the symphony is scored for trombones as well as horns, something that does not emerge clearly in some recordings. The performance is fresh, dramatic and often very exciting. Kertesz's springlike approach counteracts any feeling that each movement is just a shade too long.

Symphonies Nos. (i) 6 in C; (ii) 9 in C (Great).

(M) **(*) Mercury 434 354-2. (i) LSO, Schmidt-Isserstedt; (ii) Minneapolis SO, Skrowaczewski.

A unique coupling of the two C major symphonies – each completely different in character – and two most interesting readings. The *Sixth* with Schmidt-Isserstedt is a little matter-of-fact, but helped by the warm, glowing ambience of Watford Town Hall, he underlines the bubbling gaiety of the work. All is joy until the finale, when the *Allegro moderato* is a little too moderate. In the *Ninth* Skrowaczewski is attractively straightforward and animated. He manages to maintain a steady speed through the whole of the coda in the first movement without sounding ruthless and, after a sympathetic *Andante*, the Scherzo and finale have compelling impetus. The 1961 Minneapolis recording is full-bodied but (as so often in the Northtrop Auditorium) the violins are made to sound fierce.

Symphony No. 8 in B min. (Unfinished), D.759.

⚫ (M) *** DG 445 514-2. Philh. O, Sinopoli – MENDELSSOHN: *Symphony No. 4 (Italian).* ***
(N) **(*) BBC (ADD) BBCL 4039-2. PO, Boult – BIZET: *Jeux d'enfants;* RAVEL: *Daphnis et Chloé: Suite No. 2;* SIBELIUS: *Symphony No. 7.* **(*)
(M) ** DG (ADD) 463 609-2 (2). Chicago SO, Giulini – MAHLER: *Symphony No. 9.* **
(B) ** Decca Penguin 460 643-2. San Francisco SO, Blomstedt – MENDELSSOHN: *Symphony No. 4 in A (Italian).* ***

Symphony No. 8 (Unfinished); Grand Duo (orch. Joachim).

*** DG 423 655-2. COE, Abbado.

Sinopoli secures the most ravishingly refined and beautiful playing; the orchestral blend, particularly of the woodwind and horns, is magical. It is a deeply concentrated reading of the *Unfinished*, bringing out much unexpected detail, with every phrase freshly turned in seamless spontaneity. The contrast, as Sinopoli sees it, is between the dark tragedy of the first movement, relieved only partially by the lovely second subject, and the sunlight of the closing movement, giving an unforgettable, gentle radiance. The exposition repeat is observed, adding weight and substance. Warmly atmospheric recording, made in Kingsway Hall.

Abbado's outstandingly refined and sensitive version comes with a valuable coupling. The second subject in the *Unfinished* brings some slightly obtrusive agogic hesitations at the beginning of each phrase; but with such responsive playing they quickly sound fresh and natural.

Showmanship and flamboyance were alien to Sir Adrian's personality, which is perhaps why he remains under represented on CD and under rated by the wider public. In his BBC days he pioneered a varied repertoire that included Berg's *Wozzeck*, Schoenberg's *Variations for Orchestra* and Busoni's *Doktor Faust*, not to mention Bax, Vaughan Williams and many young British composers. This recording serves as a reminder of his stature and the quiet, natural dignity that informed his music-making. The Bizet, Schubert and Ravel come from a Promenade Concert in 1964 and the Sibelius from a Festival Hall concert given the preceding year. In the *Unfinished* there is the unforced eloquence that distinguished his famous *Great C major*.

There are some very good things in Giulini's deeply felt 1978 reading of the Unfinished, with much carefully considered detail. But the Mahler coupling is not a prime recommendation.

Blomstedt's account of the *Unfinished* is beautifully played, but only in the second movement does the performance glow as it should – the first movement is rather uneventful. The recording is excellent. The accompanying essay in the Penguin Classics CD is by John Guare.

Symphonies Nos. 8 (Unfinished); 9 in C (Great).

(B) *** RCA Twofer 09026 68314-2 (2). BPO, Wand.

*** Telarc CD 80502. Sc CO, Mackerras.

(B) *** DG (ADD) 439 475-2. BPO, Boehm.

(M) **(*) Sony (ADD) SBK 48268. Cleveland O, Szell.

(M) **(*) EMI (ADD) CDM5 67338-2. Philh. O, Klemperer.

(M) **(*) Erato Ultima 0630 18960-2. Lyon Op. O, Gardiner – Mass No. 6. ***

(M) ** Sony (ADD) SMK 61842. NYPO, Bernstein.

Günter Wand offers visionary performances of both works, superbly played in live Berlin performances and glowingly recorded. Consistently he makes the playing sound spontaneous, even in the tricky problems of speed-changes in the *Great C major*. In the manner of his generation he does not observe exposition repeats in the outer movements or second-half repeats in the Scherzo, but this is a beautifully co-ordinated, strong and warm reading. The *Unfinished* is just as magnetic, again with no exaggeration, but with every interpretative problem solved as though it did not exist. An outstanding issue if you want this coupling.

Having earlier recorded both these symphonies for Virgin with the period instruments of the OAE (see above), Mackerras here gives his revised thoughts using modern instruments. The results are both intense and refreshing, with the benefits of period performance consistently apparent in the clarity of texture, but with warmer, sweeter string sound, which yet on a chamber-scale has the necessary freshness. In the finale of the *Great C major* this time the sound is

even more transparent, but where in the Scherzo he omits second-half repeats this time, he does include the exposition repeat in the finale, omitted before. Broadly, Mackerras's readings remain the same but with more of the mystery of the *Unfinished* revealed than before.

Boehm's mid-1960s version of the *Unfinished Symphony* with the Berlin Philharmonic combines deep sensitivity and great refinement, and the points of detail as well as the overall warmth keep this version among the very finest on record. Boehm's performance of the *Ninth*, recorded three years earlier, stands in the lyrical Furtwängler tradition rather than in the forceful Toscanini stream, but it is the balance between the conflicting interests in this symphony which distinguishes Boehm's reading. The recording is very good indeed and in its CD transfer sounds fresh, warm and full.

Szell's, too, is a splendid performance of the *Unfinished*. Phrasing and general discipline are immaculate, but Szell never lacks warmth here, and drama and beauty walk hand in hand in the second movement. Apart from the lack of a real pianissimo, the 1960 recording is very good for its time. The *Ninth* dates from the previous year. Szell's control of tempo in the first movement brings a convincing onward flow, and the performance is notable for the alertness and rhythmic energy of the playing, yet there is no lack of resilience in the *Andante*. In the brilliant finale few rivals can match the precision of the hectic triplet rhythms. The sound is fuller in this remastered form than it was originally on LP.

Klemperer's *Unfinished* is seen as a massive two-part symphonic structure, with keen, alert playing that never lets the attention flag. The quiet opening is deliberately purposeful, but when the second subject finally arrives there is no attempt to beautify the melody and it acquires an unusual purity. So it is at the opening of the second movement and through the whole performance and it remains an outstanding example of Klemperer's interpretative genius. The *Ninth Symphony* is deliberately literal, but also rather heavy, particularly in the first movement. Yet once the speeds and severe approach are accepted, the power of the performance is matched by its fascination and there is some glorious playing from the Philharmonia. The Kingsway Hall recording from the early 1960s is rich and full and most realistically balanced.

Gardiner made these recordings in 1986 and 1987, with modern instruments. In the opening movement of the *Great C major* he negotiates all the problems inherent in the tempo changes with consummate ease: indeed the coda of the first movement is particularly satisfying. The *Andante* is certainly *con moto* but is elegantly handled, and it is surprising, considering that the performance was recorded live, that the reading overall lacks the last degree of compulsive zest. The *Unfinished* is most impressive and dramatic, yet with the second movement glowingly lyrical. This now comes on an Ultima double coupled with Schubert's last and finest *Mass* (see below).

Bernstein gives a dramatic account of the *Unfinished*, with a great surge of energy in the first-movement development. Yet there is lyrical warmth too and at times a sense of mystery. The playing of the NYPO is first class and the recording from 1963 is acceptable. The account of the *C major Symphony* is less consistent. There is plenty of vitality, but it lacks the unforced spontaneity which can make this symphony so exhilarating. The finale charges along like a runaway express train, exciting and brilliant, yes, but a bit charmless too.

(i) *Symphonies Nos. 8 (Unfinished); 9 (Great);* (ii; iii) *Piano Quintet in A (Trout), D.667;* (ii) *Impromptu in G flat, D.899/3; Moment Musical, D.780/3; Rosamunde:* (iv) *Jägerchor; Ballet Music in G.* Lieder: (v) *An Sylvia;* (vi) *Ave Maria;* (vii) *Die Forelle;* (v) *Heidenröslein.*

(B) *** Double Decca ADD/Dig. 444 546-2 (2). (i) VPO, Solti; (ii) Curzon; (iii) V. Octet (members); (iv) V. State Op. Ch., VPO, Münchinger; (v) Prey, Engel; (vi) Price, VPO, Karajan; (vii) Fontana, Fischer.

The *Unfinished* and *Great C major* symphonies are indispensable to any collection, and Solti does these marvellous works full justice (see above). Both bring superb VPO playing. The Decca recording too is outstanding. Clifford Curzon's vintage recording of the *Trout* is hardly less distinguished, a good-natured reading with an admirable rapport between the pianist and the excellent Viennese players. Again vigour and freshness go hand in hand. Curzon's performances of the most beautiful of Schubert's *Impromptus* and a favourite *Moment Musical* are hardly less winning, while Hermann Prey and Gabriele Fontana (who is delightfully innocent-sounding in *Die Forelle*) give fine accounts of three famous songs. The inclusion of the *Hunting Chorus* from *Rosamunde* alongside the familiar *Ballet Music* is a pleasant surprise, and this is still a thoroughly worthwhile set, playing for 148 minutes.

Symphony No. 9 in C (Great), D.944.

❂ (M) *** Decca Legends (ADD) 460 311-2. VPO, Solti – WAGNER: *Siegfried Idyll.* ***

(M) (***) DG mono 447 439-2. BPO, Furtwängler – HAYDN: *Symphony No. 88.* (***) ❂

(B) *** EMI fforte (ADD) CZS5 69364-2 (2). Cleveland O, Szell – BEETHOVEN: *Symphony No. 7* *** ❂; ROSSINI: *Overtures.* **(*)

(M) **(*) Ph. (IMS) 442 646-2. ASMF, Marriner.

(N) (M) (**(*)) Beulah mono 3PD12. BBC SO, Boult – MENDELSSOHN: *Hebrides Overture;* WAGNER: *Die Meistersinger: Overture.* (**)

(N) (M) ** Sup. (ADD) SU 3468–2 011. Czech PO, Konwitschny.

Symphony No. 9 in C (Great); Rosamunde: Overture (Die Zauberharfe), D.644.

*** DG 423 656-2. COE, Abbado.

Symphony No. 9 in C (Great); Rosamunde: Overture; Ballet Music; Entr'acte No. 3.

(M) **(*) Sony (ADD) SMK 64478. Columbia SO, Bruno Walter.

Symphony No. 9 in C (Great); (i) *Gesang der Geister über den Wassern.*

*** DG 457 648-2. VPO, Gardener; (i) with Monteverdi Ch.

Solti's superb recording with the Vienna Philharmonic Orchestra (one of his finest records) is also available as part of a Double Decca, which includes Nos. 5 and 8 (see above). Decca have rightly chosen it for reissue in their 'Legends' series, coupled with Wagner's *Siegfried Idyll.* Both performances have comparable distinction and show that Solti could relax in music which he loved, without sacrificing concentration and drama.

Though the COE is by definition an orchestra of chamber scale, the weight of Abbado's version, taken from his complete cycle, is ample, while allowing extra detail to be heard, thanks also to the orchestra's outstandingly crisp ensemble. Speeds are very well chosen, and the expressive detail is consistently made to sound natural. This version is important too for including textual amendments, and the Scherzo has four extra bars that were originally cut by Brahms in his early edition. The sound is beautifully refined, to match the point and polish of the playing. The *Rosamunde (Zauberharfe) Overture* makes a valuable and generous fill-up.

Gardiner's DG reading was recorded live at the Salzburg Festival in 1997, representing a most refreshing meeting-point between period performance and traditional Viennese. The result is strong and weighty, with expressive rubato encouraged, but within a tauter frame than usual in this orchestra's performances, and with generally fast speeds. Clarity is here combined with sweetness, and that also applies to the dedicated performance of the beautiful motet, which was given at the same concert with Gardiner's Monteverdi Choir imported for the occcasion. Highly recommendable with good, clear sound, and far finer than Gardiner's earlier recording of the *Great C major* for Erato.

As with the coupled Haydn, Furtwängler gives the *Great C major* a glowing performance, if a highly individual one. The first movement brings an outstanding example of his wizardry, when he takes the recapitulation at quite a different speed from the exposition and still makes it sound convincing. In the beautifully played *Andante*, his very slow tempo is yet made resilient by fine rhythmic pointing. The mono recording dates from 1951 and the sound is remarkably fresh and very well balanced, with the dynamic range in the slow movement strikingly wide.

Szell's Cleveland account was his second in stereo with that orchestra (the first is discussed above, paired with the *Unfinished*). It has the hallmarks of an HMV recording from the beginning of the 1970s, with a wider dynamic range than Szell usually enjoyed and better overall balancing. Szell's powerful reading provides a reminder that the parallels between him and another great disciplinarian conductor, Toscanini, were sometimes significant. Szell's approach is similarly direct, but lyrical feeling underlies the surface brightness and the crisply sprung rhythms are exhilarating. In the hectic triplets of the finale that the orchestra is unmatched in precision, with a sparkling lightness of articulation that is a joy to the ear.

Marriner's account of the *Great C major* makes up for any lack of weight with the fresh resilience of the playing, consistently well sprung. All repeats are observed, bringing the timing of the *Symphony* to over an hour; however, the fill-up offered with the full-priced issue has now been omitted and, although the recording is first rate, this makes the present reissue much less tempting in a competitive market-place.

Bruno Walter's 1959 CBS recording has less grip than Furtwängler's, while Solti shows greater spontaneity; but in the gentler passages there are many indications of Walter's mastery, not least in the lovely playing at the introduction of the second subject of the *Andante*. There is much to admire, even if this never quite achieves the distinction of the conductor's earlier recordings of this symphony. The *Rosamunde* music makes an endearing bonus.

When in 1934 Sir Adrian Boult recorded the *Great C major Symphony*, it was only one of three versions then available, yet this classic reading, fresh and direct, certainly stands the test of time, a work specially close to Boult's heart. Not surprisingly, speeds are a shade brisker than in his well-known stereo version with the LPO of almost 40 years later, yet in a similar way he solves the speed changes just as subtly, concealing problems with natural ease. Like the two overtures which come as fill-ups, the playing of the BBC Symphony, founded only in 1930, is a splendid tribute to Boult's genius as an orchestral trainer. Reflecting the limitations of short-playing 78 records, there are no repeats in the outer movements, and only the very first one in the Scherzo. The Beulah transfer involves a high but even surface hiss, which is generally easy to ignore when the sound has plenty of body, with fine presence and good detail, set against a dry acoustic, evidently with no added reverberation.

Konwitschny's *Ninth* dates from 1962. It is a straightforward, simple and warmly relaxed reading, Viennese in feeling. In that, it has a good deal in common with Krips's early Decca version with the VPO, although without the level of concentration that makes that performance so totally compelling. Konwitschny is more easygoing, The first movement's development has a pleasing jaunty progress and the return to the opening theme is deftly managed. The *Andante* is beautifully played (the principal oboe's contribution a highlight). Only the Scherzo, with all repeats included, brings a nagging suggestion of 'heavenly length', and the finale, although not pressed hard, makes an agreeable conclusion. The analogue recording is warm and naturally balanced.

CHAMBER AND INSTRUMENTAL MUSIC

Arpeggione sonata, D.821 (arr. for cello) (see also under Trout Quintet).

*** Ph. 412 230-2. Maisky, Argerich – SCHUMANN: *Fantasiestücke* etc. ***

(BB) *** Naxos 8.550654. Kliegel, Merscher – SCHUMANN: *Adagio & Allegro* etc. ***

(M) **(*). Decca (ADD) 443 575-2. Rostropovich, Britten – BRIDGE: *Cello Sonata.* ***

(M) **(*) Decca Legends (ADD) 460 974-2. Rostropovich, Britten (as above) – DEBUSSY: *Sonata*: SCHUMANN: *5 Stücker in Volkston.* ***

(*) EMI CDC5 55166-2. Caussé, Duchable – BEETHOVEN: *Notturno*; REINECKE: *Fantasiestücke.* *

Mischa Maisky and Martha Argerich make much more of the *Arpeggione Sonata* than any of their rivals. Their approach may be relaxed, but they bring much pleasure through their variety of colour and sensitivity. The Philips recording is in the very best traditions of the house.

At super-bargain price, Maria Kliegel and Kristin Merscher are highly competitive. The performances are well shaped and sensitive, though perhaps lacking the last ounce of character you find in, say, the Rostropovich–Britten account. All the same, neither the Schubert nor the Schumann coupling will disappoint at this price, given the general high standard of playing and recording.

Rostropovich gives a curiously self-indulgent interpretation of Schubert's amiable *Arpeggione Sonata*. The playing of both artists is eloquent and it is beautifully recorded, but it will not be to all tastes. The first reissue is part of Decca's Classic Sound series, and there is an alternative coupling with Debussy and Schumann in Decca's Legend series.

Gérard Caussé gives a refined account of the *Arpeggione Sonata* with François-René Duchable. His viola sounds closer to the original instrument than does the modern cello. Though he is sensitive, Duchable is not always the most imaginative partner. However, this is now deleted.

Arpeggione Sonata; Cello Sonatinas Nos. 1–3, D.384–5 & D.408.

*** Channel Classics CCS 9696. Wispelwey, Giacometti.

The highly musical Pieter Wispelwey has the full measure of Schubert's innocent lyricism, and the pianist's light touch in the finale is especially persuasive. Paolo Giacometti makes a most convincing case for the use of the fortepiano in Schubert, and the restored has a remarkable range of colour. Pieter Wispelwey's tone, using gut strings, always sings and, even using a minimum of vibrato, he constantly cajoles the ear, while his phrasing has an appealing simplicity. Thus the three violin *Sonatinas* are made to sound convincing in these cello transcriptions, especially the *G minor*, D.408, in which the *Andante* and finale are endearing. The recording is forwardly but truthfully balanced. Recommended.

(i) Arpeggione Sonata; (ii) Piano Quintet in A (Trout). Adagio in E flat ('Notturno') (for piano trio), D.897.

(M) **(*) DG (ADD) 453 667-2. (i) Fournier, Fonda; (ii) Eschenbach, Koeckert Qt.

Pierre Fournier gives this a wholly persuasive account of the *Arpeggione Sonata*. He is beautifully balanced and recorded. Alongside it comes an enjoyably alert performance from Christoph Eschenbach and members of the Koeckert Quartet of the *Trout*. The variations are given plenty of individual interest, the outer movements striking momentum, with Eschenbach playing elegantly. The recording acoustic is clear and rather dry. The *Notturno* has the advantage of a warmer acoustic and is played most sympathetically.

Arpeggione Sonata, D.821 (arr. in G min. for clarinet & piano).

*** Chan. 8506. De Peyer, Pryor – SCHUMANN: *Fantasiestücke; 3 Romances*; WEBER: *Silvana Variations.* ***

So persuasive is the performance of Gervase de Peyer and Gwenneth Pryor that the listener is all but persuaded that the work was actually written for this combination.

(i) Fantasia in C for Violin & Piano, D.934. Fantasia in C (Wanderer Fantasia), D. 760.

**(*) ECM 464 320-2. Schiff; (i) with Shiokawa.

As might be expected, András Schiff's account of the *Wanderer Fantasia* is finely paced and highly sensitive, and entirely free from expressive exaggeration. He has the advantage of lifelike and full-bodied recorded sound. The coupling is another *C major Fantasy*, for violin and piano, with Yuuko Shiokawa, his partner in previous recordings. However the piano is very dominant, and Shiokawa very backwardly placed. At 50 minutes the disc is short measure anyway. A pity, since this is a distinguished *Wanderer*.

(i) Fantasy in C, D.934; (i; ii) Piano Trio No. 2 in E flat, D.929; (iii) String Quartets Nos. 8 in B flat, D.112 (Op. 168); 14 in D min. (Death and the Maiden), D.810; 15 in G, D.887 (Op. 161).

(***) Pearl mono GEMMCDS 9141 (2). (i) Adolf Busch, Serkin; (iii) with Hermann Busch; (iii) Busch Qt.

Some have spoken of the Busch Quartet's Schubert as the greatest ever committed to disc. Certainly the *G major Quartet* has never had so searching and powerful a reading, and the early *B flat Quartet*, which used to be known as Op. 168, sounds every bit as captivating as one remembers it from the days of shellac. The *E flat Trio* and the *C major Fantasy* are also in the highest class, and the Pearl transfers are very good indeed. These two CDs, packed economically in one jewel-case, encompass three LPs and are really excellent value for money. A lovely set.

Flute Quartet (after Matiegka, for flute, guitar, viola and cello).

*** Koch 3-7404-2. Still, Falletta, Neubauer, Thomas –
BEETHOVEN: *Serenade, Op. 8;* KREUTZER: *Grand Trio.* ***

Schubert himself played the guitar, and the present quartet is a reworking of a *Notturno* by Matiegka, originally for flute, viola and guitar, with a cello part added for Schubert's father to play. However, only two and a half variations (out of eight) were completed of Matiegka's finale. Much later, the guitarist JoAnn Falletta returned to Matiegka's original and finished off the transcription – very effectively as can be heard here. The result is charmingly ingenuous, and with fine playing and recording makes very agreeable lightweight listening.

Octet in F, D.803.

❀ (M) *** Decca (ADD) 466 580-2. Vienna Octet – SPOHR: *Octet in E.* ***

*** Chan. 8585. ASMF Chamber Ens.

*** ASV CDDCA 694. Gaudier Ens.

Octet in F, D.803; Eine kleine Trauermusik (for wind nonet), D.79.

*** Praga PR 250 087. Czech Nonet.

(i) Octet in F, D.803; (ii) Introduction & Variations for Flute & Piano on 'Trock'ne Blumen' from Die schöne Müllerin, D.802.

(M) *** DG (ADD) 453 666-2. (i) V. Chamber Ens.; (ii) Nicolet, Engel.

Octet in F, D. 803; Wind octet, in F. D.72.

(BB) **(*) Naxos 8.550389. Budapest Schubert Ensemble.

The Vienna Octet's 1958 recording of the Schubert *Octet* has stood the test of time. It has a magical glow with the group at its peak under the leadership of Willi Boskovsky. The horn has a Viennese fruitiness which helps to make the performance more authentic, and these fine players never put a foot wrong throughout. The recording only betrays its age in the upper registers, but is basically full and modern sounding. The delightful and unusual Spohr coupling makes this a fine addition to Decca's Legends series.

The Chandos version brings a performance just as delightful as the earlier one by the ASMF, less classical in style, a degree freer in expression, with Viennese overtones brought out in Schubert's sunny invention. It has the benefit of excellent modern digital sound, cleaner on detail than before.

The members of the Czech Nonet give an engagingly infectious performance, never more so than in the finale which, after a dramatic opening, continues with rustic high spirits, often winningly bucolic in feeling. But the playing throughout combines refinement of blending and ensemble with spirited warmth. The *Trauermusik*, which opens with solemn horns, makes an unusual prelude for the main work. The recording is beautifully balanced within a spacious but not over-resonant acoustic.

The Gaudier Ensemble give an entirely winning account of the *Octet*, essentially spontaneous yet very relaxed and catching all the ingenuous Schubertian charm. Excellent sound, vivid yet well balanced within a pleasing acoustic which gives a feeling of intimacy. An ideal record for a warm summer evening.

The Vienna Chamber Ensemble do not overlap in personnel with the New Vienna Octet, who have recorded this work for Decca, though their performance has a similar polish and urbane Viennese warmth. This is mellifluous Schubert, and very engaging it is: fresh and elegant. This dates from 1980, and the CD transfer maintains the smoothness and realism of the LP. Very enjoyable. The innocent set of variations on a melancholy little tune makes a slight but pleasing encore.

A vivacious-enough account from the Schubert Ensemble on Naxos provides a more than viable super-bargain version, particularly as the bonus, a little *Wind Octet* in the same key, has a particularly winning finale. Good playing and lively recording ensure that this disc gives pleasure, although it is worth paying the extra money for the Decca Vienna version.

(i) Octet, D.803; (i–ii) Piano Quintet in A (Trout); (iii) Violin Sonatinas Nos. 1–3, D.384/5 & D.408.

(B) *** O-L Dig./ADD Double 455 724-2 (2). (i) AAM Chamber Ens.; (ii) Lubin (fortepiano); (iii) Schröder, Hogwood (fortepiano).

We have long praised the Academy's 1988 recording of the *Octet* using period instruments for bringing out the open joyfulness of Schubert's inspiration, with excellent matching and vivid recording. The reading is not at all stiff or pedantic, but personal and relaxed. Lightness is the keynote, with speeds never eccentrically fast. The vibrant account of the *Trout*, from three years later, is even more successful. At first the opening tempo may seem brisk, but the lyrical flow is impetuous rather than hurried. Stephen Lubin leads zestfully from his fortepiano and there is also a nice rhythmic spring in the *Andante*, while the variations bring the most engaging and sparkling pianism of all. The recording, made in the Henry Wood Hall, is perfectly balanced, the sound both warm and transparent, so that the ear relishes the interplay and never seeks the fuller sonority of a modern piano. The present pairing makes a clear choice for those wanting these favourite works played on period instruments, and the three *Violin sonatinas*, which (with repeats included) offer a further 55 minutes of Schubertian delights. Schröder plays with fine artistry, and both artists are truthfully recorded (in 1978). The CD transfers cannot be faulted.

(i) Octet in F, D.803; String Quintet in C, D.956.

(N) (BB) **(*) Teldec Ultima 8573 87803-2 (2). (i) Berlin Soloists; (ii) Berlin Brandis Qt with Boettscher.

An enterprising coupling of two of Schubert's greatest, yet utterly different, chamber works, the one full of bonhomie, the other with an extraordinary profundity of inner feeling. The Berlin soloists give a strong and stylish account of the first, on a bigger scale than most. Every single repeat is observed, and with such distinguished playing that length is readily sustained. The characterization is strong, not just in the large-scale 'symphonic' movements, but in the charming *Andante Variations* too. Though the sound is not always ideally sweet on string tone, the recording is full and clear.

The augmented Brandis Quartet also give a very considerable account of the more elusive *Quintet*. In the first movement they include the exposition repeat, but miss the opportunity of a real pianissimo for the haunting second subject. Yet the slow movement brings a very wide range of dynamic to create considerable intensity. The *Scherzo* is gutsy, but the strong contrast of the central section immediately recalls the withdrawn atmosphere of the *Adagio*, and the control of mood and tempo in the finale is again very successful. Good, full-bodied sound and a pleasing acoustic.

Piano Quintet in A (Trout), D.667.

*** BBC (ADD) BBCL 4009-2 (2). Curzon, Amadeus Qt, Merret – BRAHMS: *Piano Quintet in F min., Op. 34*. ***

*** Ph. 446 001-2. Alfred Brendel, Thomas Zehetmair, Tabea Zimmermann, Richard Duven, Peter Riegelbauer – MOZART: *Piano quartet No. 1*. ***

(BB) *** Belart (ADD) 450 056-2. Haebler, Grumiaux, Janzer, Czako, Cazauran – MOZART: *Clarinet Quintet*. **(*)

(M) **(*) Decca (ADD) 448 602-2. Curzon, Vienna Octet (members) – DVORAK: *Piano Quintet*. ***

(B) **(*) Hyp. Dyad CDD 22008 (2). Schubert Ens. of L. –

HUMMEL: *Piano Quintet;* SCHUMANN: *Piano Quintet; Piano Quartet*. **(*)

**(*) Decca 460 034–2 Haefliger, Takács Qt (with MOZART: *Serenade: Eine kleine Nachtmusik* **; WOLF: *Italian Serenade* **(*)).

Piano Quintet in A (Trout); Adagio & Rondo concertante in F, D.487.

(BB) **(*) Naxos 8.550658. Jandó, Kodály Qt, with Tóth.

Piano Quintet in A (Trout); Adagio & Rondo concertante; Notturno in E flat, D.897.

(M) **(*) Classic fm 75605 570062. Berezovsky, Soloists of ROHOCG.

(i; ii; iii) Piano Quintet in A (Trout); (i; iii) Arpeggione Sonata, D.821; (iv; i). Die Forelle.

**(*) Sony SK 61964. (i) Ax; (ii) Frank, Young, Meyer; (iii) Ma; (iv) Barbara Bonney.

(i) Piano Quintet in A (Trout); (ii) String Quartet No. 14 (Death and the Maiden).

(B) *** Decca Penguin (ADD) 460 650-2. (i) Curzon, Vienna Octet (members); (ii) VPO String Qt.

(M) *** Ph. (ADD) 442 656-2. (i) Beaux Arts Trio with Rhodes & Hörtnagel; (ii) Italian Qt.

(M) **(*) Sony (ADD) SBK 46343. (i) Horszowski, Budapest Qt (members), Julius Levine; (ii) Juilliard Qt.

(M) **(*) DG (ADD) 449 746-2. Amadeus Qt, with (i) Gilels, Zepperitz.

(i) Piano Quintet in A (Trout); (ii) String Trios, D.471 & D.581.

(M) *** Ph. 422 838-2. (i) Haebler, Grumiaux, Janzer, Czako, Cazauran; (ii) Grumiaux String Trio.

(i) Piano Quintet in A (Trout); (ii) Die Forelle; (iii) Der Hirt auf dem Felsen.

**(*) ASV CDDCA 684. (i) Seow, Prometheus Ens.; (ii; iii) Mackay; (iii) Craker.

(i) Piano Quintet in A (Trout); Fantasia in C (Wanderer), D.760.

(B) *** [EMI Red Line CDR5 72567]. Richter, (i) with Borodin Qt.

(i) Piano Quintet in A (Trout), D.667. Moments musicaux, D.780.

(M) *** Decca 458 608-2. Schiff; (i) Hagen Qt.

(i) Piano Quintet in A (Trout); (ii) Der Hirt auf dem Felsen.

(N) (M) **(*) Regis RRC 1027. (i) Ian Brown, Nash Ens.; (ii) Lott, Brown, Collins.

András Schiff and the Hagen Quartet give a delectably fresh and youthful reading of the *Trout Quintet*, full of the joys of spring, but one which is also remarkable for hushed concentration, as in the exceptionally dark and intense account of the opening of the first movement. The *Scherzo* brings a light, quick and bouncing performance, and there is extra lightness too in the other middle movements. Alongside Brendel and Haefliger (but no other current rivals), this version observes the exposition repeat in the finale, and with such a joyful, brightly pointed performance one welcomes that. The *Moments musicaux* are also beautifully played and recorded, and make a considerable bonus.

Like the Brahms *Quintet*, with which it is coupled on a bonus disc, Curzon's live BBC recording of the *Trout Quintet* with the augmented Amadeus Quartet, made at the Royal Festival Hall in 1971, amply compensates in warmth and power for what it may lack in high studio polish, with all five artists at their most spontaneous. The Trout variations may be on the slow side, but the rhythmic pointing is a delight. Good radio sound, smoother on top than Curzon's famous Decca version.

Curzon's Decca *Trout* has been swimming for over forty years, and still remains near the surface of the stream. It is a memorable performance, with a distinguished account of the piano part and splendidly stylish support from the Vienna players. If the violin tone – a bit thin sounding – betrays the age of the recording (1958), the ear quickly adjusts. The Vienna Philharmonic players treat the *Death and the Maiden Quartet* with comparable affection, yet bring out all the music's vitality. Indeed, the playing is peerless: Boskovsky, the leader, shows his fine musicianship throughout the work, and in the variations in particular. The 1963 sound is as fresh as paint, and the specialist essay is by Dan Jacobson. The *Trout* is also available with a Dvořák coupling on Decca's 'Classic Sound' label, but this Penguin Classics disc is probably a preferable choice, if both works are wanted.

The later Brendel performance is superbly recorded, the imagery rich and tangible, especially the piano, with Thomas Zehetmair's violin sweetly caught and the string bass gently resounding at the bottom. Like Brendel's previous Cleveland performance, which it easily displaces, this lacks something in traditional Viennese charm, but it has a compensating warmth and weight and certainly plenty of natural impetus, with Brendel consistently persuasive. The inclusion of a substantial Mozart coupling gives this Philips account an advantage over the competing Decca version, which is in some ways even more endearing.

From the augmented Beaux Arts Trio comes another of the most delightful and fresh *Trouts* now available. Every phrase is splendidly alive, there is no want of vitality and sensitivity, and a finely judged balance and truthful (1976) recording make it a most desirable version. The Italian Quartet's version of the *Death and the Maiden* dates from a decade earlier, but the recording was first class in its day, and this sounds every bit as good as the *Trout*. The performance remains one of the finest available. The slow movement is particularly eloquent.

Richter dominates the EMI digital recording of the *Trout Quintet*, not only in performance but in balance. Yet this account has marvellous detail, with many felicities drawn to the attention that might have gone unnoticed in other versions. The first movement is played very vibrantly indeed, while the second offers a complete contrast, gently lyrical, and the variations have plenty of character. This is very satisfying, even though other versions are stronger on Schubertian charm. The performance of the *Wanderer Fantasia* comes from as long ago as 1963 but still sounds well. It is very distinguished indeed and makes a superb bonus, even if the piano-timbre is a shade hard.

There is some admirably unassertive and deeply musical playing from Ingrid Haebler and from the incomparable Grumiaux. These artists do not try to make 'interpretative points' but are content to let the music speak for itself. The quality of the recorded sound is good. Philips have added a pair of *String trios*, given characteristically refined performances by Grumiaux and his companions, delightful music superbly played. This is available on Belart attractively coupled with Mozart's *Clarinet Quintet*.

Horszowski's contribution to the *Trout* is most distinguished and his clean, clear playing dominates the performance which, although full of imaginative detail, is a little on the cool side – though refreshingly so, for all that. The Juilliard Quartet are far from cool in the *Death and the Maiden Quartet*, the unanimity of ensemble consistently impressive. In both works the sound is a little dry, but not confined.

In the 1975 DG recording of the *Trout* there is a masterly contribution from Gilels, and the Amadeus play with considerable freshness. The approach is very positive, not as sunny and spring-like as in some versions, but rewarding in its seriousness of purpose. The recording balance is convincing and the remastering creates a firm and vivid soundimage. The Amadeus's account of the *Death and the Maiden Quartet* was their first analogue recording of this work in 1959. The unanimity of ensemble is remarkable. The quartet play as one in dealing with the finer points of phrasing, for example at the very beginning of the variations. The early DG stereo, too, is very good.

On Classic fm, Boris Berezovsky leads a direct, spontaneous account, in which he makes a memorable contribution to the famous variations. If the performance (which includes the exposition repeat) had been imbued with the added expressive intensity which appears at the beginning of the *Adagio and Rondo concertante*, it would have been even more recommendable; but it is certainly fresh and well recorded. The *Notturno* also opens (and closes) with rapt concentration (and one recalls the slow movement of the *String Quintet*), but the playing is also just a little mannered.

A lively, immediate account from the Schubert Ensemble of London, strongly led by the pianist, William Howard. The first movement is brisk but committed, and the famous variations are well characterized. There are more touching accounts on record but few more vivaciously spontaneous, with a vivid recording to match.

Emanuel Ax leads an impressive ensemble in this invigorating Sony account of the *Trout Quintet*. But, alas, there is a constant tendency to move onwards too quickly. This does not affect the famous theme and variations, which is done most imaginatively, but the Scherzo is very fast indeed, and the finale sounds rushed. A pity, as Yo-Yo Ma's performance of the *Arpeggione Sonata* is totally endearing, with all the warmth, joy and innocent Schubertian charm one could ask for. Barbara Bonney's account of the famous song is direct rather than innocently beguiling. No complaints about the recording balance.

The Jandó/Kodály *Trout* is above all bracing. The first movement is soon moving along briskly and at a concert one could well be swept along by the momentum of the performance, for there is relaxation in the *Andante* and the famous *Variations* are mellow and strongly characterized. The polish and impetus of this playing is never in doubt and the recording is excellent, but this account obviously comes from east of Vienna. The *Adagio and Rondo concertante* sounds a stronger work here than usual and the rondo is spirited and jolly.

Andreas Haefliger joins the Takács Quartet for another of the breeziest accounts of the *Trout Quintet* on record, with the first-movement exposition repeat made an integral part of the forward flow. The sense of briskness comes as much from the players' style as the actual tempi, although the finale certainly wings its way along with an irresistible impulse. Some of the music's relaxed charm is lost, partly the effect of the recording balance which makes the violin timbre sound somewhat thin. Mozart's *Eine kleine Nachtmusik* is effective enough, though not memorable, but the Wolf *Italian serenade* certainly doesn't lack sparkle.

The account by the Nash Ensemble, previously on Carlton, now on Regis, brings a fill-up in the shape of *The Shepherd on the Rock*. They are rather forwardly recorded here, and their account is just a little wanting in the spontaneity that distinguishes the finest of current versions. Ian Brown is, as always, a sensitive artist, and Michael Collins provides an admirable clarinet obbligato for one of Schubert's most engaging songs.

(i; ii) *Piano Quintet in A (Trout); (i; iii) Piano Trios Nos. 1–2; Notturno, D.897; Sonata in B flat, D.28.*

(B) **(*) EMI (ADD) CZS7 62742-2 (2). (i) H. Menuhin; (ii) Amadeus Qt, J. Edward Merrett; (iii) Y. Menuhin & Gendron.

The 1958 Hephzibah Menuhin/Amadeus *Trout* has a pleasingly domestic sense of scale and considerable charm, even though the bright recording creates a balance in favour of the upper register of the piano and the upper strings. The Amadeus Quartet play with nicely judged feeling. Intimacy is also the keynote of the works for piano trio, and in the *Trios* Menuhin relaxes with his pianist sister and cellist friend to produce delightfully spontaneous-sounding performances. The atmosphere of the *Second Trio* is well caught, and the unassertive music-making captures the music's spirit very appealingly. These recordings are cleanly remastered; the sound lacks something in fullness but the focus is natural and the balance realistic.

(i) *Piano Quintet in A (Trout). String Quartets Nos. 13 in A min., D.804; 14 (Death and the Maiden); 15 in G, D.887; (ii) String quintet in C, D.956.*

(M) ** EMI (ADD) CMS5 66144-2 (4). Alban Berg Qt, with (i) Leonskaja, Hörtnagel; (ii) Schiff.

The Alban Berg *Trout* (in which the quartet are joined by Elisabeth Leonskaja and Georg Hörtnagel) brings keen disappointment. Despite the excellence of the recording and some incidental beauties, it remains a curiously uninvolving performance with routine gestures. The *A minor Quartet*, however, is beautifully managed, though the slow movement is very fast indeed. The exposition repeat is omitted in the first movement of *Death and the Maiden* but otherwise this, too, is a very impressive performance. The playing is

breathtaking in terms of tonal blend, ensemble and intonation throughout both these works; if one is not always totally involved, there is much to relish and admire. In the *G major* the Alban Berg players are most dramatic. They are strikingly well recorded, and beautifully balanced; but the sense of over-projection somehow disturbs the innocence of some passages.

In the great *C major Quintet*, where they are joined by Heinrich Schiff, they produce a timbre which is richly burnished and full-bodied. Once more there is no first-movement exposition repeat, but theirs is still a most satisfying account, strongly projected throughout. The recording is admirable. But as a collection this is a mixed success.

Piano Trios Nos. 1 in B flat, D.898; 2 in E flat.

(B) **(*) Decca 455 685-2 (2). Ashkenazy, Zukerman, Harrell.

Piano Trios Nos. 1–2; Adagio in E flat ('Notturno') (for piano trio), D.897; Sonata in B flat (for piano trio), D.28.

(B) **(*) Teldec Ultima 8573 87796-2 (2). Trio Fontenay.

(i–iii) *Piano Trios Nos. 1–2; Notturno in E flat, D.897; Sonata Movement, D.28; (i, ii) Grand Duo in A, D.574.*

(N)(B) **(*) EMI double fforte CZS5 74197-2. (i) Jean-Philippe Collard; (ii) Dumay; (iii) Lodéon.

(i) *Piano trios Nos. 1–2; Notturno, D.897; Sonata in B flat, D.28; (ii) String Trios: in B flat (in one movement), D.471; in B flat, D.581.*

(B) *** Ph. Duo (ADD) 438 700-2 (2). (i) Beaux Arts Trio; (ii) Grumiaux Trio.

The Beaux Arts set of the Schubert *Piano Trios* from the late 1960s is another of the extraordinary bargains now offered on the Philips Duo label. The performances provide impeccable ensemble with the pianist, Menahem Pressler, always sharply imaginative and the cellist, Bernard Greenhouse, bringing simple dedication to such key passages as the great slow-movement melody of the *Trio No. 2 in E flat*. The *Notturno*, played here with great eloquence, recalls the rapt, hushed intensity of the glorious slow movement of the *String Quintet*. What makes the set doubly attractive is the inclusion of the two much rarer *String Trios*, also early works from 1816/17. Given such persuasive advocacy, both pieces cannot fail to make a strong impression.

Jean-Philippe Collard, Augustin Dumay and Frédéric Lodéon, all splendid performers in their own right, here create a fully integrated ensemble that sounds as if the players enjoy chamber music at home. All these performances sparkle, and there is a true Schubertian spirit in the *Grand Duo*. The one reservation concerns the first movement (and to a lesser extent the finale) of the *Second Trio in E flat*. The balance here is rather dominated by the piano and Collard adopts very brisk tempi. There is plenty of charm elsewhere, but this is a less easily recommendable performance than those of the *B flat Trio*, the *Notturno* and the *Sonatensatz*, where the balance is better integrated and the pacing can hardly be faulted. The recordings were made in a concert-hall acoustic (the Salle Wagram in Paris), and the early digital sound is bright and clearly focused, if a touch dry.

There are many felicities of detail in the performances

from the Trio Fontenay and their affectionate lyricism certainly does not lack warmth. But at times they over-dramatize and at others there is a feeling that phrasing is indulgent, as for instance with Niklas Schmidt's beautifully timbred yet almost sensuous cello solo in the *Andante* of the *B flat Trio*. The rapt opening of the *Notturno* needs a greater feeling of Schubertian innocence: a serenity without too much *espressivo*. The first movement of the *B flat Trio* has a strong impulse, and the Scherzo is treated as an opportunity for extrovert virtuosity. Excellent recording, but these performances lack the springlike freshness of the competing Viennese group, or indeed the famous Beaux Arts set on Philips.

Ashkenazy, Zukerman and Harrell give strong performances of both works, full of impetus and there is much subtlety of detail. But although the concentration of the playing in the slow movement of the *E flat Trio* is in no doubt and Ashkenazy produces scintillating passage work, in the last result the innocent charm which informs Schubert's inspiration is all but missed. The players are not helped by a vividly forward recording which tends to sound aggressive in fortissimos, though some reproducers will register this more strikingly than others. These are new digital recordings but the two discs are offered as a Double Decca.

Piano Trio No. 1 in B flat, D.898.

(B) *** EMI fforte (ADD) CZS5 69367-2 (2). Oistrakh, Knushevitzky, Oborin – BEETHOVEN: *Archduke Trio* ***; BRAHMS: *Violin Sonatas Nos. 1–2.* **(*)

Schubert's music needs warmth and humanity, and this well-integrated Russian team on the bargain forte reissue give both these qualities in abundance. They imbue the music with just that essence of clarity and warmth that it demands by right. The tempi are sensitively chosen, and the Scherzo is handled in masterly fashion by all three players. Excellent piano-tone and a good round sound from the strings. The encores are beautifully played and, if the couplings are suitable, this makes a fine bargain.

Piano Trio No. 2 ; Notturno, D.897.

*(*) ECM 453 300-2. Schneeberger, Thomas Demenga, Dähler.

These fine players do not help themselves by choosing an all too leisurely tempo in the first movement. They are just a shade ponderous and heavy-handed at times in both pieces, though the actual quality of the recorded sound is more than serviceable.

Rondo in B min. (for Violin & Piano), D.895.

(N) (M) *** EMI Debut CDZ5 74017-2 Batiashvili, Chernyavska – BACH: *Partita No. 1;* BRAHMS: *Violin Sonata No. 1 in G., Op. 78.*

A pupil of Mark Lubotsky, the Georgian-born Elisabeth Batiashvili came to international attention when at the age of sixteen she won second prize at the Sibelius Competition in Helsinki. Now twenty-two, she makes her EMI debut with a mixed programme. She gives a vital and lyrical account of this Schubert piece and is expertly partnered by Milana Chernyavska.

String quartets

String Quartets Nos. 1–15; Quartet Movement in C min., D.103.

(B) **(*) DG (ADD) 463 151-2 (6). Melos Qt of Stuttgart.

String quartets Nos. 1 in G min./B flat, D.18; 2 in C, D.32; 3 in B flat, D.36; 4 in C, D.46; 5 in B flat, D.68; 9 in G min., D.173; 10 in E flat, D.87; 12 in C min. (Quartettsatz), D.703; 15 in G, D.887; in C min. (Overture), D.8a.

*** CPO CPO 999 410-2 (3). Auryn Qt.

String Quartets Nos. 6 in D, D.74; 7 in D, D.94; 8 in B flat, D.112; 11 in E, D.353; 13 in A min., D.804; 14 in D min. (Death and the Maiden), D.810. 5 Minuets & 5 German Dances, D.89.

**(*) CPO CPO 999 409-2 (3). Auryn Qt.

String Quartets Nos. 1; 13; Overture in B flat, D.470.

*** MDG MDG 307 0602-2. New Leipzig Qt.

String Quartets Nos. 2; 11; Overture in C min. (for quintet), D.8; Fragment, D. 87a.

*** MDG MDG 307 0609-2. New Leipzig Qt.

String Quartets Nos. 4; 5 (including 1st & 2nd versions of Allegro maestoso); 2 Ländler for 2 Violins in D, D.354.

*** MDG MDG 307 0608-2. New Leipzig Qt.

String Quartets Nos. 5; 10; in C min. (fragment), D.103.

*** MDG 307 0605-5. New Leipzig Qt.

String Quartets Nos. 6; 8; in B flat (fragment), D.470.

*** MDG 307 0606-5. New Leipzig Qt.

String Quartets Nos. 7; 9; Quartet movement in C min., D. 703.

*** MDG 307 0607-2. New Leipzig Qt.

String Quartet No. 14 (Death and the Maiden); Minuet, D.86; Minuets & German Dances, D.89.

*** MDG 307 0604-2. New Leipzig Qt.

String Quartet No. 15; Fragment, D.2c; String Trio, D.472.

*** MDG 307 0601-2. New Leipzig Qt.

(i) *String Quintet in C, D.956. Fragment, D.3; Overture, D.8a.*

*** MDG 307 0603-2. (i) Sanderling; New Leipzig Qt.

The New Leipzig Quartet offer an ideal approach. They have great sweetness of tone, yet they are not sugary; they give us a wide dynamic range without drawing attention to themselves, and they seem totally inside the Schubert tradition. They have much greater warmth than the Melos of Stuttgart on DG and are far removed from the overpowering jet-setting quartet-machines. Theirs is humane music-making which conveys some sense of period and naturalness of expression. The *Quintet* may not be as intense as some versions but it is still very rewarding. The recordings are very good and the set has the merit of including various less familiar fragments. A thoroughly musical and well-recorded series.

The Auryn quartet also give eminently satisfactory accounts of the Schubert *quartets* adding also some early minuets and trios, D.89. They are at their happiest in the earlier quartets which they play with an unforced fluency which will delight listeners. They may not always penetrate the depths of the *G major*, D.887, as some of their rivals do, but generally speaking both performances and recordings are more than just serviceable. The package is far more economical than Leipzig Quartet on Dabringhaus and Grimm, which stretches to nine CDs – and just as comprehensive. Those looking for a complete ready-made Schubert quartet cycle could find this a worthwhile investment. Not every performance is competitive with the finest, but they are all eminently musical.

The Melos Quartet give us an inexpensive survey. The early works have a disarming grace and innocence and some of their ideas are most touching (witness the *Adagio* introduction of No. 4 in C). The Melos Quartet give impressive, unmannered accounts of all these works, finding the drama as well as the music's inner tensions. They are let down by the recording which, although faithful, is rather too closely balanced. The remastering provides good presence, and conveys a wide dynamic range, but fortissimos can be a little fierce. Nevertheless this well-documented set is value for money and worth considering when the full-priced competition costs twice as much.

String quartets Nos. 7–15; Quartettsatz; (i) String quintet in C, D.956.

(BB) **(*) EMI (ADD) CDZ4 71943-2 (5). Heutling Qt; (i) Hungarian Qt with Varga.

All the Heutling Quartet performances were recorded in 1968–71 and the Hungarian Quartet's account of the sublime *C major String Quintet* with Lazlo Varga as second cello comes from 1970. The Heutling give us very musical performances full of affection and charm. They may strike some listeners as a little too sweet but the depths of the *D minor* and *G major* quartets do register. The *C major Quintet* is eminently well served by these distinguished players and the recordings sound well for their age. At their very competitive price (they were offered for £15 last year), they can be recommended as an excellent and inexpensive introduction to these great works.

String Quartet No. 8 in B flat, D.112.

(M) (***) EMI mono CHS5 65308-2 (4). Busch Qt (with MENDELSSOHN: *Capriccio in E min.*) – BEETHOVEN: *String Quartets.* *** ◉

The excellence and lightness of spirit the Busch communicate in this quartet is exhilarating. There is an alternative transfer available on Pearl (see above, under *Fantasy in C major*.)

String Quartets Nos. 8; 13 in A min., D.804.

*** ASV CDDCA 593. Lindsay Qt.

In the glorious *A minor* the Lindsays lead the field. It would be difficult to fault their judgement in both these works on tempi and expression, and dynamics are always the result of keen musical thinking. Excellent recording.

String Quartets Nos. 10 (7); 13, D.804.

◉ *** Audivis E 8580. Mosaïques Qt.

Above all these period-instrument performances, so notable for their points of closely observed detail, are highly spontaneous. The very opening of the *E flat Quartet* (published posthumously as No. 10) is warmly inviting, and the players have the full measure of the songful serenity of its lovely *Adagio*. The profundities of the *A minor* are fully understood by this highly sensitive group, and the recapitulation is particularly memorable. There is dramatic intensity as well as charm in the famous (*Rosamunde*) *Andante*, with the finale following gracefully: the delicacy of the shading of the playing here is a marvel. A superb disc, beautifully recorded.

String Quartet No. 12 (Quartettsatz).

(N) (BB) *** Arte Nova 74321 34036-2. Alexander Qt – JANACEK: *String Quartet No. 1*; SMETANA: *String Quartet No. 1.* ***

In an urgent and fresh reading, this inspired quartet movement makes an unexpected but welcome bonus with the Alexander Quartet's powerful readings of the two autobiographical Czech quartets.

String Quartets Nos. 12 (Quartettsatz); 13; 14 (Death and the Maiden); 15 D.887.

(B) *** Ph. (ADD) Duo 446 163-2 (2). Italian Qt.
**(*) DG 459 151-2 (3). Emerson Qt. with (i) Rostropovich.

String Quartets Nos. 12–15; (i) String Quintet in C, D. 956.

(M) *** Nim. NI 1770. Brandis Qt, (i) with W.-S. Yang.

The Brandis Quartet, a fine Central European group, have warmth and they bring a natural eloquence to all these quartets which are all the more potent for being free of interpretative point-making. In the great *C major Quintet*, with beautiful matching, they again convey spontaneous expressiveness, and they are not afraid to linger a little over the first movement's lovely second-subject melody. Their slow movement, played freely, has rapt tension but, again, also conveys warmth, rather an ethereal, withdrawn atmosphere which communicates in a quite individual way. They are very naturally recorded.

The Italian Quartet's 1965 coupling of the *Quartettsatz* and the *Death and the Maiden Quartet* was counted the finest available in its day, with the famous variations played with great imagination and showing a notable grip in the closing pages. Technically the playing throughout is remarkable. These players' understanding of Schubert is equally reflected in their performance of the *A minor Quartet*, recorded a decade later. The familiar 'Rosamunde' slow movement is beautifully paced, with an impressive command of feeling. The 1976 sound, too, is first class. The *G major Quartet* is, if anything, even finer. And the recording is extremely vivid, making this one of the most thought-provoking accounts of the *Quartet* ever. Excellent CD transfers throughout.

The Emersons certainly have an amazing technical address and are among the finest quartets playing now. Their attack and ensemble are impeccable; their tonal blend and finesse disarm criticism. Their approach is distinctly late twentieth-century Manhattan, rather than early nineteenth-century Europe with its gentler colours. Yet they spring from a different culture and have no want of intelligence and insight. There is tenderness at times and, in the *C major Quintet* with Rostropovich as second cello, an abundant eloquence. Good recording.

String Quartets Nos. 12 (Quartettsatz); 14 (Death and the Maiden).

*** ASV CDDCA 560. Lindsay Qt.

(BB) **(*) Naxos 8.550221; 4550221. Mandelring Qt.

The Lindsays' intense, volatile account of the *Death and the Maiden Quartet* is played with considerable metrical freedom and the widest range of dynamic, and the *Quartettsatz*, which acts as the usual filler, is unusually poetic and spontaneous in feeling. The recording is excellent.

The Mandelring Quartet are very good indeed. The performances are sensitively and sensibly played and very decently recorded, and anyone tempted by this Naxos disc will not be disappointed for so modest an outlay.

String Quartets Nos. 13 in A min., D.804; 14 in D min. (Death and the Maiden), D.810.

(B) *** Ph. (ADD) 426 383-2. Italian Qt.

This separate bargain issue, taken from the above Duo, is most welcome. The sound is excellent.

String Quartet No. 14 in D min. (Death and the Maiden).

(BB) *** CfP Double (ADD) CDCFPSD 4772 (2). Gabrieli String Qt – BORODIN: *String Quartet No. 2* ***; BRAHMS: *Clarinet Quintet* **(*); DVORAK: *String Quartet No. 12.* ***

Like the other performances on this Classics for Pleasure Silver Double, the Gabrielis give a direct, sensitive and polished account of Schubert's great *D minor Quartet*, not wearing their hearts on their sleeves but genuinely touching in the slow movement. The recording, from the beginning of the 1970s, is first class and has been smoothly transferred to CD. However, this has just been deleted.

String Quartets Nos. 14 (Death and the Maiden); 15 in G.

(M) (***) EMI (mono) CDH7 69795-2. Busch Qt.

The Busch Quartet's account is more than fifty years old, but it brings us closer to the heart of this music than almost any other. The slow movement of the *Death and the Maiden Quartet* is a revelation, and the same must be said of the *G major*, which has great depth and humanity. For its age, the sound is still amazing.

String Quartet No. 15 in G, D.887.

*** DG 457 615-2. Hagen Qt – BEETHOVEN: *String Quartet No. 11 in F min., Op. 95.* **(*)

String Quartet No. 15; (i) Notturno, D. 897.

*** Decca 452 854-2. Takács Qt, (i) with Haefliger.

As in their performance of the *String Quintet* (see below), the Takács Quartet play very freely, using the widest range of dynamic, with the leader often dropping to a withdrawn pianissimo with seeming spontaneity, so that the result does

not seem mannered or self-conscious. The opening of the *Andante* brings the most delicate entry from the cello, gentle and restrained, and the Scherzo, too, opens with a gossamer touch, while the finale dances with joyful vigour. In the *Notturno* Andreas Haefliger weaves his piano figurations with comparable finesse. The top-quality recording has fine presence, yet the quartet image is set slightly back.

The Hagen Quartet also give a thoughtful and perceptive account of the great *G major Quartet*, D.887. They have dramatic intensity (indeed, they are a shade too intense at times) and an impressive virtuosity. Dynamic extremes are scrupulously projected but do not draw excessive attention to themselves, save perhaps in the opening of the slow movement. As quartet-playing it is masterly and thoroughly compelling. As with the Beethoven coupling, there is an aggressive feel in tutti at times, as in the impassioned outbursts in the slow movement. All the same the DG recording has exemplary warmth and clarity.

String Quintet in C, D.956.

(M) *** EMI CDM5 66890-2 [566942]. Alban Berg Qt with Schiff.

⊕ (***) Testament mono SBT 1031 Hollywood Qt, Kurt Reher – SCHOENBERG: *Verklaerte Nacht.* (***) ⊕

*** Channel Classics CCS 6794. Orpheus Qt, Wispelwey.

(***) Biddulph mono LAB 093. Pro Arte Qt, Pini – BRAHMS: *String Sextet No. 1.* (***)

(M) **(*) DG (ADD) 453 668-2. Melos Qt, Rostropovich.

(**) Testament mono SBT 1157. Amadeus Qt, Pleeth – MOZART: *Sinfonia concertante, K.364.* (**(*))

String Quintet in C; String Quartet No. 14 (Death and the Maiden); Quartettsatz, D. 703.

(N) ⊕ (M) *** ASV CDDCS 243(2). The Lindsays.

String Quintet in C; String Trio in B flat, D.581.

(BB) *** ASV CDQS 6207. Locrian Ens.

(BB) *** Naxos 8.550388. Villa Musica Ens.

(i) String Quintet in C, D.956; (ii) Auf der Strom, D.943; (iii) Gretchen am Spinnrade; Nacht und Träume; Rastlose Liebe.

(M) *** Sony SMK 60032. (i) Cleveland Qt, Ma; (ii) Valente, Bloom, Serkin; (ii) Te Kanawa, Amner.

The Lindsay version gives the impression that one is eavesdropping on music-making in the intimacy of a private concert. They observe the first-movement exposition repeat and the effortlessness of their approach does not preclude intellectual strength. In the ethereal *Adagio* they effectively convey the sense of it appearing motionless, suspended, as it were, between reality and dream, yet at the same time never allowing it to become static. Their reading must rank at the top of the list; it is very well recorded. It now comes coupled at mid price with an equally memorable version of the *Death and the Maiden Quartet* – a virtually unbeatable pairing, with the *Quartettsatz* thrown in for good measure.

The Cleveland Quartet and Yo-Yo Ma are scrupulous in observing dynamic markings (the second subject is both restrained and pianissimo) and they also score by observing all repeats. Their performance has feeling and eloquence, as well as a commanding intellectual grip. Moreover they are admirably recorded and thus present a strong challenge at mid-price. For the reissue, some Schubert Lieder have been added. A fine performance from Benita Valente of *Auf der Strom* is made memorable by Myron Bloom's glorious horn obbligato. Of the following three songs from Kiri Te Kanawa, *Gretchen am Spinnrade* has a delightful simplicity and *Nacht und Träume* is tonally ravishing. So this vocal music makes a considerable bonus.

Few ensembles offer timbre as full-bodied or as richly burnished as that produced by the Alban Berg and Heinrich Schiff, whose recording has impressive sonority, although there is just a touch of digital fierceness on top. This group has the advantage of wonderfully homogeneous tone, even in their raptly sustained pianissimo in the *Adagio*. Given the sheer polish and full sound that distinguishes their playing, this must rank high among current recommendations. However, unlike the Lindsays, they do not observe the first movement exposition repeat. This CD now returns to the catalogue in EMI's 'Great Recordings of the Century' series.

The Hollywood Quartet's 1951 version of the *Quintet* with Kurt Reher as second cello stands apart. Over 40 years on, its qualities of freshness and poetry, as well as an impeccably confident technical address, still impress as deeply as ever. This is the product of consummate artistry and remains very special indeed.

The recording of the *Quintet* on ASV by members of the Locrian Ensemble is for the 1990s what the famous old Saga version was for the 1960s. It has polish, warmth and deep feeling. The hushed pianissimo playing in the *Adagio* is magnetic, rapt in its intensity, and the players have the advantage of a silent background and excellent, truthful recording in a pleasing acoustic. The lighter, single-movement *Trio in B flat* is also played most persuasively, its nostalgic feeling nicely caught.

The Villa Musica players tackle the great *C major Quintet* with a freshness and concentration that are consistently compelling, even if the finale is neat and clean rather than urgently dramatic. The little *String Trio* makes an attractive and generous fill-up, another assured and stylish performance. With clear, well-balanced recording this super-budget issue makes another outstanding bargain.

The Orpheus Quintet offer a performance of communicated warmth and feeling, both in the slow movement and in the remarkable *Andante* central section of the Scherzo. The playing is fresh and feels alive, and the recording has striking body and realism.

Rostropovich plays as second cello in the Melos performance, and no doubt his influence from the centre of the string texture contributes to the eloquence of the famous *Adagio* which, like the performance as a whole, is strongly, even dramatically, characterized. The emphasis on the rhythmic articulation of the outer movements leaves no doubt as to the power of Schubert's writing, and there is no lack of atmosphere in the opening and closing sections of the slow movement. The recording is live and immediate. A fine version, but not a first choice.

The Pro Arte Quartet's 1935 account of the Schubert *Quintet*, with Anthony Pini as second cello, dominated the pre-war catalogues. Its humanity and warmth still tell, particularly in the slow movement. It comes with a fine account

of the Brahms *B flat Sextet*, made in the same year. Needless to say, some allowance has to be made for the recording, eminently well transferred though it is.

EMI made their Amadeus Quartet's recording of the great *C major Quintet* before their long-term contract with DG. If the first movement is a degree warmer and more purposeful than in the later versions, the slow movement at a more flowing speed lacks the inner intensity of the later recordings, partly a question of pianissimos not being registered so gently. Also the finale at a marginally broader speed lacks the exuberance of later recordings, but the youthful freshness and strength of the whole performance are most winning, helped by an excellent transfer.

(Duo) in A, D.574; Fantaisie in C, D.934; Violin Sonatinas Nos. 1–3, D.384–5, & D.408. (ii) Arpeggione Sonata.

(N) **(B)** *** Double Decca stereo/mono (ADD) 466 748-2 (2)
(i) Goldberg, Lupu; (ii) Gendron, Françaix.

Violin Sonatinas, Nos. 1–3; Fantasy in C, D.934.

(BB) *(**) Naxos 8.550420. Dong-Suk Kang, Devoyon.

Violin Sonatinas Nos. 1–3; Rondo in B min., D.895; Duo in A (Grand Duo), D.574; Fantasie in C, D.934.

(M) *** Sony IV Dig./ADD SM2K 64528 (2). Stern, Barenboim
(with: HAYDN: *Violin Concerto in C, Hob VIIa/1* with Chamber O **).

Szymon Goldberg and Radu Lupu give us the complete violin and piano music (except for one small piece) in beautifully played and well-recorded performances, which have an unaffected Schubertian feeling. Indeed, Goldberg's account of the *Fantasy* is particularly intimate and appealing. The presence of Lupu ensures that these performances give pleasure, and his playing has a vitality and inner life that are undoubtedly rewarding. These recordings date from the end of the 1970s, but the *Arpeggione Sonata*, which has a comparable intimacy and Schubertian affinity, is hardly less appealing even though the recording is mono (but very truthful mono) and dates from 1954.

These 1988 Stern performances have a natural warmth and plenty of character, yet there is an unaffected simplicity and directness of style which suits the three early *Sonatinas*, written in 1816 but not published until two decades later. The *Grand Duo* dates from little more than a year later, but both artists provide the necessary added flair (especially in the Scherzo) for this rather more ambitious piece. The gentle, mysterious opening of the *Fantasie* is superbly caught and the lilting *Allegretto* makes a perfect foil for the songful *Andantino* (which readily takes wing on Stern's bow). The finale is a joy. The Haydn *Concerto*, excellently recorded in mono in 1947, is a very acceptable bonus. Stern directs the work himself and the highlight of the performance is his touching account of the *Adagio*.

Korean-born Dong-Suk Kang plays with style and panache and is given excellent support by Pascal Devoyon. Neither is well served by the recording, however, made in a cramped studio that robs the piano-tone of some of its timbre, while the close balance does less than complete justice to the sound this fine violinist makes in the flesh.

Nevertheless it still gives pleasure. Performances three star; the recording one.

PIANO MUSIC
Piano music for four hands

Allegro moderato & Andante, D.968; Divertissement on Original French Themes, D.823; 2 Ecossaises, from D.783; Fantaisie, D.48; Marche héroïque in C, D.602/2.

** Olympia OCD 677. Goldstone, Clemmow (with SCHUMANN: *Polonaises Nos. 7 in G min.; 8 in A flat **).

16 Deutscher Tänze from D.783; Fugue in E min., D.952; Grande marche et trio in B min., D.819/3; Marche héroïque in B min., D.602/1; Overture in G min., D.668; 2 Polonaises in D min., D.824/1 & D.599/1; Sonata in B flat, D.617; Variations on a Theme from Hérold's Opera Marie, D.908.

** Olympia OCD 676. Goldstone, Clemmow (with SCHUMANN: *Polonaise No. 6 in E **).

Deutscher Tanz in C, D.783/9; Fantaisie, D.9; Grande marche héroïque, D.885; 2 Marches caractéristiques, D.886; Duo in A min. (Lebensstürme), D.947; Polonaise in E, D.824/6; D.599/3; Variations on a French Song, D.624.

** Olympia OCD 675. Goldstone, Clemmow (with SCHUMANN: *Polonaise No. 5 in B min. **).

Fantaisie, D.1; Grande marche funèbre in C min., D.859; Grande marche et trio in D, D.819/4; 2 Ländler in C min. & C, D.814/3 & D.814/4; March in G (Kindermarsch), D.928; Polonaise in D, D.824/4; Variations on an original theme in A flat, D.813.

** Olympia OCD 674. Goldstone, Clemmow (with SCHUMANN: *Polonaise No. 4 in B flat **).

Deutscher Tanz in E flat, D.783/8; Divertissement à la hongroise, D.818; Grande marche et trio in G min., D.819/2; 2 Ländler in E flat & A flat, D.814/1 & D.814/2; 3 Marches militaires, D.733; Polonaises in A, D.824/5; B flat, D.618a, sketches (realized by Goldstone); Rondo in A, D.951.

** Olympia OCD 673. Goldstone, Clemmow (with SCHUMANN: *Polonaise No. 3 in F min. **).

Allegro in A min. (Lebensstürme), D.947; Divertissement à la française in E min., D.823; Divertissement à la hongroise in G min., D.818; Fantasia in F minor, D.940; Grand duo in C, D.812; 4 Ländler, D.814.

(B) *** EMI double fforte (ADD) CZS5 69770-2 (2). Eschenbach and Frantz.

German Dance in G min., D.818; Grande marche funèbre, D.859; Grande marche héroïque, D.885; 6 Grandes marches et trios, D.819; Grand rondeau (allegretto quasi andantino), D.951; Kindermarsch in G min., D.928; 2 Ländler in E, D.618; 2 Marches caractéristiques, D.886; 2 Marches héroïques, D.602; 3 Marches militaires, D.733.

(B) *** EMI double fforte (ADD) CZS5 69764-2 (2). Eschenbach and Frantz.

Christoph Eschenbach and Justus Frantz made their extensive survey of Schubert's four-handed piano music in 1978 and 1979, and the Abbey Road recording was of high quality. The EMI transfers occasionally bring a touch of hardness in the treble, but the underlying sound is full and well rounded and has plenty of colour. The opening of the *F minor Fantasia* here may suggest that the performance is too reticent, but that is deceptive and this is as powerful a reading as any available with its rhythms well sprung; and the same comment applies to *Grand Duo*, while the wide range of mood in the *Lebensstürme* is encompassed impressively. The delicate interplay between the two pianists is a constant delight, whether in the simple *Ländler*, the charming central *Andantino varié* of the *Divertissement à la française* or the cimbalom imitations in the companion Hungarian-style *Divertissement*, both extended three-movement works showing the composer at his most felicitously inventive and presented here joyfully.

The second collection includes a great many marches, but their expressive range is very much wider than might be expected. Much of it is jolly and extrovert, but there is delicacy and lyricism too. In the hands of Eschenbach and Frantz the third *Marche héroïque* of D.602 is quite charming, more like an impromptu. The *German Dance in G minor* opens with appealing restraint and the *Kindermarsch* brings a delightful, child-like simplicity, while the two *Marches caractéristiques* sparkle with brilliance. Most remarkable of all are the *Grande marche funèbre* and the *Grande marche héroïque*. The first is highly eloquent, but it is the second, in A minor, which is the more extended (17 minutes), with a characteristic lyrical strain as its centerpiece. The closing *Grand rondeau*, most touchingly played, was written in June 1828, only five months before the composer's death at the age of thirty-one. Overall Eschenbach and Frantz score in sheer freshness, but the EMI sound at times has a bright edge.

The Anthony Goldstone and Caroline Clemmow partnership are a husband-and-wife team who give eminently musical and shapely accounts with plenty of sensitive observation. They can be confidently recommended (save for the recorded sound which is not of uniform quality) but not in preference to their EMI rivals which have the advantage of also being less expensive. The Schumann *Polonaises* are rarer repertoire and make acceptable bonuses for each disc.

Allegro moderato & Andante, D.968; Fantasy in G min., D.9; 3 Marches militaires D.733; 4 Polonaises, D.599; Variations on 'Marie' by Herold.

(BB) **(*) Naxos 8.553441. Jandó, Kollar.

This disc of some of Schubert's lesser works for piano duet begins most temptingly with the most famous of his *Marches militaires*, played by the Hungarian duo with crispness and vigour. Ranging from the very early *Fantasy* to the late *Allegro & Andante*, this well-recorded collection may be a little short on charm, but is winningly fresh throughout.

Andante varié in B min., D.823.

(N) (M) *** Decca (ADD) 466 821-2. Richter, Britten – MOZART: *Piano Sonata in C, K521, etc.* DEBUSSY: *En blanc et noir.*

This inspired account of the Schubert *Divertissement* – labelled *Andantino varié* – was recorded at the same Jubilee Hall concert as the *Fantasie* and *Grand Duo*, also available in the Britten at Aldeburgh series. It may be just a charming trifle, but in their hands it is magnetic, revealing deeper expression.

Andante varié, D.823; Duo, D.947; Fantasia in F min.; Grand Duo, D.812; 3 Marches militaires, D.733; 6 Polonaises, D.824; Rondo, D.951; Variations on an Original Theme in A flat, D.813.

(M) *** Erato Ultima (ADD) 8573 85670-2 (2). Quefférec & Cooper.

The playing of Anne Quefférec and Imogen Cooper is hardly less eloquent than any of their rivals', and they also offer a commanding account of the *Grand Duo Sonata*. The slighter pieces also come off well: the *Variations* are beautifully played and have an engaging innocence, while the most famous *Marche militaire*. Its two lesser-known companions are also worth having on disc when played (like the six *Polonaises*) so brightly and spontaneously. The 1978 analogue recording is well balanced, clear and natural, the acoustic neither over-reverberant nor too confined.

There can be no doubting that this Ultima CD set is a bargain in every way: these are excellent performances, well recorded, and provide an inexpensive way to explore Schubert's delightful piano music for four hands.

Fantasia in F min., D.940.

*** Sony SK 39511. Perahia, Lupu – MOZART: *Double Piano Sonata*. ***

*** Chan. 9162. Lortie, Mercier – MOZART: *Andante with Variations* etc. ***

(N) (M) *** DG (ADD) 463 652-2. Emil & Elena Gilels – MOZART: *Piano Concerto No. 27; Double Piano Concerto*. *** ◉

Recorded live at The Maltings, the performance of Lupu and Perahia is full of haunting poetry, with each of these highly individual artists challenging the other in imagination. Warmly atmospheric recording.

The Louis Lortie–Hélène Mercier partnership is as impressive here as it is elsewhere. The Schubert holds its own even against such illustrious competition as the Lupu–Perahia recording on Sony, also coupled with Mozart. Very good recording.

On DG an apt and finely played bonus for a treasurable Mozart coupling.

Fantasia in F min.; Grand Duo; Variations, D.813.

(M) *** Decca (ADD) 466 822-2. Richter, Britten.

As these electrically intense performances demonstrate, Richter and Britten favoured fast speeds, which yet allowed crisply sprung rhythms and warmly lyrical phrasing, with phenomenally crisp articulation from both players. The two major works were recorded in 1965 in Jubilee Hall, Aldeburgh, the *Variations* in the Parish Church a year earlier, both with clear, immediate stereo-sound balanced for radio by BBC engineers.

(i) **Piano duet:***Fantasy in F min., D.940.* (ii) *Impromptus 1–4, D.899; Piano Sonatas Nos. 18 in G, D.894;* (iii) *20 in A, D.959.*

(B) **(*) Erato/Warner Ultima ADD/Dig. 3984 27004-2 (2). Pires with (i) Sermet; (ii) Quefférec; (iii) Dalberto.

Maria João Pires and Huseyin Sermet are perfectly attuned in the *F minor Fantasy* and the recording from 1989 is very good. The four D.899 *Impromptus* are sensitively played by Anne Quefférec and the analogue recording wears very well. Maria João Pires lingers long and lovingly over the first movement of the *G major Sonata*, D.894. It is a finely musical pout that may not appeal to all listeners. But the set can be warmly recommended to her admirers.

(i) **Piano duet:** *Fantasy in F min.; Introduction & Variations on an Original Theme, D.603; 2 Marches caractéristiques in C, D.886; Rondo (for piano duet) in D, D.608.* (Piano) *6 German Dances, D.783; Impromptus Nos. 1–4, D.899; 5–8, D.935; 6 Moments musicaux, D.780; Piano Sonatas Nos. 3, D.459; 4, D.537; 7, D.568; 9, D.575; 13, D.664; 14, D.784; 16, D.845; 17, D.850; 18, D.894; 19, D.958; 20, D.959; 21, D.960.*

(B) **(*) Ph. (ADD) 456 367-2 (7). Haebler, (i) with Hoffmann.

Ingrid Haebler has been criticized for reticent playing. But her *Moments musicaux* can be ranked with the finest available. Her stereo survey of the *Sonatas* was incomplete and somewhat uneven but she has special insights to offer, and the disarming simplicity of her Schubertian style cannot fail to give pleasure when she is so well recorded. The music for piano duet was among the first to be recorded (in 1961) but one would not guess this from the excellent quality with which it reproduces. The playing is very good indeed and finds Miss Haebler and her partner in top form. As is immediately apparent at the sensitive opening of the *F minor Fantasy*, this is relaxed and spontaneous playing that should give much pleasure.

Solo piano music

Adagio in E major, D.612; Adagio & Rondo in E, D.506; Allegretto in C minor, D.915; 3 Klavierstücke, D.946; 12 Ländler, D.790; Variations on a Theme by Anselm Hüttenbrenner, D.576.

(N) *** Chan. 9860. Edlina.

Luba Edlina is better known as a chamber-music player than a soloist – she is the pianist of the Borodin Trio – although she has made a handful of very good solo recordings, including Russian repertoire and Mendelssohn's *Songs Without Words*. Her Schubert recital is satisfying and unaffected, and the searching *3 Klavierstücke* are well served. The Chandos recording is natural, and readers attracted to the repertoire need not hesitate.

Allegretto, D.915; Impromptus Nos. 1–4, D.899; 5–8, D.935; 3 Klavierstücke, D.946.

**(*) DG 457 550-2 (2). Pires.

Maria João Pires proves as impressive a Schubertian as she is a Mozart interpreter. The presentation reproduces various quotes from Goethe and does not tell us too much about Schubert, but Pires does! Despite the odd touch of prettification, this is satisfying playing and eminently well recorded. However the set is uneconomically laid out on a pair of full-priced CDs, the first of which only plays for 35 minutes 20 seconds!

Fantasia in C (Wanderer), D.760.

*** Sony MK 42124. Perahia – SCHUMANN: *Fantasia in C.* ***

(N) (M) *** EMI (ADD) CDM5 66895-2 [566947]. S. Richter – DVORAK: *Piano Concerto.* ***

⚫ (M) *** Decca mono 466 498-2. Curzon – SCHUMANN: *Fantasia in C, Op. 17; Kinderszenen, Op. 15.* *** ⚫

(M) *** Ph. (ADD) 420 644-2. Brendel – *Sonata No. 21.* ***

(M) *** DG (ADD) 447 451-2. Pollini – SCHUMANN: *Fantasia, Op. 17.* ***

(M) **(*) DG 445 562-2. Kissin – BRAHMS: *Fantasias* **(*); LISZT: *Concert Paraphrases of Schubert Lieder etc.* ***

Murray Perahia's account of the *Wanderer* stands alongside the finest. In his hands it sounds as fresh as the day it was conceived, and its melodic lines speak with an ardour and subtlety that breathe new life into the score. The recording is more than acceptable.

Richter's 1963 performance is masterly in every way. The piano timbre is real and the remastering gives the great pianist a compelling presence; the coupling is hardly less outstanding.

Curzon's famous account of the *Wanderer Fantasia* dates from 1949 and the clear, dry recording emphasizes his dramatic approach to the outer movements, putting his infinitely touching account of the sadly yearning central *Adagio* into bold relief. It is this movement which expresses the message of the song on which the work is based: *Dort, wo du nicht bist, dort ist das Glück!* ('Happiness is where you are not!').

Brendel's playing is of a high order, and he is truthfully recorded and coupled with what is perhaps Schubert's greatest *Sonata*, so this is excellent value at mid-price.

Pollini's account is outstanding and, though he is not ideally recorded and the piano timbre is shallow, the playing still shows remarkable insights. Moreover the Schumann coupling is equally fine.

Kissin, the amazing young Russian, gives a fine account of the *Wanderer*, though it is not quite as persuasive (perhaps he himself is not quite as persuaded by the music) as the finest rivals. Of course there is some very fine pianism, but other artists, Kempff for instance, find greater depths. Good DG recording.

Fantasia in C (Wanderer), D.760; Piano Sonata No. 21 in B flat, D.960; Impromptus D 899/3–4.

(N) ⚫ (M) *** RCA 09026 63054-2. Rubinstein.

This CD is among the very finest of all the Rubinstein reissues from the 1960s. He plays the *Wanderer fantasia* with sure magnificence. The extended structure needs a master to hold it together and, particularly in the variations section, Rubinstein is electrifying. He compels attention as though he is improvising the work himself, but even so avoids any

sentimentality. The 1965 recording sounds surprisingly full, and it is even better in the two *Impromptus*, played with the most subtle shading of colour and delectable control of rubato, and in the superb account of the *Sonata*. Unaccountably, this has never been issued before, yet it shows Rubinstein as a magically persuasive Schubertian. The first movement is very relaxed (14 minutes 17 seconds as against Curzon's 13 minutes 18 seconds) yet the effect is wonderfully luminous, and a similar inspired and ruminative spontaneity infuses the essentially gentle *Andante*. Then the articulation in the final two movements is a joy, light and crisp in the Scherzo, bolder but never heavy in the finale. Throughout, the great pianist conveys his love for the music, and the playing is wonderfully refined in detail. The sound is remarkably real, with fine presence and almost no shallowness.

Impromptus Nos. 1–8 (including original draft of No. 1); Moments musicaux Nos. 1–6; 3 Klavierstück D.946 (including original version of No. 1).

(N) (B) *** Virgin 2 x 1 VBD5 61797–2 (2). Orkis (fortepiano).

Those who think they are allergic to Schubert on the fortepiano in this repertoire should try this inexpensive set from Lambert Orkis. Both the *Impromptus* and the *Moments musicaux* are vital and fully attuned to the Schubertian sensibility, and the three *Klavierstück* are full of character. This is exceptional playing in every way – living and responsive to every nuance – and although it is not a sole recommendation for either the *Impromptus* or *Moments musicaux*, it is certainly a set that all Schubertians should consider as a supplement to modern grand piano recordings. It is made the more fascinating by the inclusion of Schubert's original version of the stormy first *Klavierstück*, and more strikingly the pencil draft for the *C minor Impromptu*, in which the original arresting opening chord is omitted. The timbre of the fortepiano here certainly does not lack sonority or colour.

Impromptus Nos. 1–4, D.899; 5–8, D.935; 3 Klavierstücke, D.946; Moments musicaux Nos. 1–6, D.780; Allegretto in C min., D.915; 6 German Dances, D.820; Grazer Galopp, D.925; Hungarian Melody in B min., D.817; 12 Ländler, D.790.

(B) *** Double Decca 458 139-2 (2). Schiff.

Impromptus Nos. 1–4, D.899; 5–8, D.935; 3 Klavierstücke (Impromptus), D.946; 6 Moments musicaux, D.780; 12 German Dances, D.790; 16 German Dances, D.783.

⚫ (B) *** Ph. (ADD) Duo 456 061-2 (2). Brendel.

Brendel's analogue set of the *Impromptus* is magical, and the *Moments musicaux* are among the most poetic in the catalogue. It is difficult to imagine finer Schubert playing than this; to find more eloquence, more profound musical insights, one has to go back to Edwin Fischer – and even here comparison is not always to Brendel's disadvantage. The *Klavierstücke* are searching, and in his hands the *German Dances*, although retaining their underlying charm, sound anything but trivial. The recordings offer Philips's very finest analogue quality.

András Schiff's playing is idiomatic, intelligent and humane, and the recording is more than acceptable. It is impossible to recommend his *Impromptus* in preference to those of Brendel, but no one will be disappointed with them. Schiff has the advantage of very natural digital recording, the effect lighter-textured than with Brendel.

Impromptus Nos. 1–4, D.899; 5–8, D.935; Moments musicaux Nos. 1–6, D. 780; Piano Sonatas Nos. 13 in A, D.664; 21 in B flat, D.960.

🅒 (B) *** DG Double (ADD) 459 412-2. Kempff.

Predictably fine playing, of course, and the magic is obvious from the gentle opening of the first *C major* work. The D.899 set is beautifully done, with all the pieces perceptively characterized. The two *Sonatas* are cherishable: neither performance has been surpassed and here the piano timbre is fully coloured and resonant in the bass. It is a tribute to Kempff's artistry that with the most relaxed tempi he conveys such consistently compulsive intensity. In his account of Schubert's greatest sonata, the long-breathed expansiveness is hypnotic so that here, quite as much as in the *Great C major Symphony*, one is bound by the spell of heavenly length. Rightly, Kempff repeats the first movement exposition repeat, with the important nine bars of lead-back, and though the overall manner is less obviously dramatic than is common, the range of tone-colour is magical. Though very much a personal utterance this interpretation is no less great for that. Both this and the equally warm and concentrated account of the *A Major*, again with a hauntingly rapt *Andante*, belong to a tradition of pianism that has almost disappeared. The *Moments musicaux* were recorded in the summer of the same year and the sound is very good, if not so full in timbre as the sonatas. Kempff characteristically gives intimate performances of pieces which range so much farther than one expects from their name and scale. All in all this is a treasurable set, indispensable to any collector who cares about Schubert or indeed the art of the piano.

Impromptus Nos. 1–4, D. 899; 5–8, D.935.

*** Sony SK 37291. Perahia.
*** DG 435 788-2. Gavrilov.
(M) *** Decca 460 975-2. Lupu.
(BB) **(*) Naxos 8.550260. Jandó.

Perahia's account of the *Impromptus* is very special indeed. Directness of utterance and purity of spirit are of the essence here, with articulation of sparkling clarity. The CBS recording is very good, truthful in timbre.

Andrei Gavrilov's playing has something of the divine simplicity for which this music calls. No expressive excesses and a wide dynamic range. Surprisingly, perhaps, this is quite selfless playing which serves Schubert well. So, too, does the admirably balanced DG recording. One of the best, even in a strongly competitive field, and highly recommendable.

Lupu's account of the *Impromptus* is of the same calibre as the Brendel analogue version, and he is most beautifully recorded on CD. Indeed, in terms of natural sound this is a most believable image.

Though his set of the *Impromptus* is not ideally recorded (the microphones are rather too close, with unpleasing re-

sults in fortissimo passages), Jandó is a very musical player and his unaffected (and often perceptive) readings are more than acceptable.

Impromptus Nos. 1–4, D.899; Piano Sonata No. 21 in B flat, D.960.

*** Cal. CAL 6689. Södergren.

Inger Södergren's account of the first four *Impromptus* belongs in exalted company, and the *B flat Sonata* is hardly less fine. Her playing is marked throughout by sensitivity and a selfless and unostentatious dedication to Schubert. The recording is acceptable rather than outstanding.

4 Impromptus, D.899; Impromptu in B flat, D.935/3; Moments musicaux, D.780/1, 2 & 6.

(B) *** LaserLight 15609. Jandó.

Jenö Jandó is here heard recorded in an acoustic that does justice to his talent. The sound, at least in the opening *B flat major Impromptu* of D.935, is fresh and truthful, the ambience is warm, and the playing is very good. The balance is not as good in the three *Moments musicaux* or in the D.899 *Impromptus*: it is closer and marginally drier.

Moments musicaux Nos. 1–6, D.780; 3 Klavierstücke, D.946; Allegretto in C min., D.915.

(BB) **(*) Naxos 8.550259. Jandó.

Though the venue is the Italian Institute in Budapest, Jandó is much better recorded here than he often has been. He proves a thoroughly sympathetic and sensitive Schubertian, but he is still too upfront. The opening of the *Drei Klavierstücke* is a shade too fast (Jandó does not completely convey its dark, disturbing overtones) but the middle section is beautifully judged. Thoughtful and intelligent music-making, acceptably recorded, and very good value for money.

Moments musicaux, D.780; 2 Scherzi, D.593; Piano Sonata No. 14 in A min., D.784.

*** DG (IMS) 427 769-2. Pires.

Maria João Pires gives masterly accounts of the *Moments musicaux* and the *A minor Sonata*, distinguished throughout by thoughtful and refined musicianship, and she is fully aware of the depth of feeling that inhabits the *Moments musicaux*, without ever indulging in the slightest expressive exaggeration. The digital recording is exceptionally present and clear.

Piano sonatas

Piano Sonatas Nos. 1 in E, D.157; 2 in C, D.279; 3 in E, D.459; 4 in A min., D.537; 5 in A flat, D.557; 6 in E min., D.566; 7 in E flat, D.568; 9 in B, D.575; 11 in F min., D.625; 13 in A, D.664; 14 in A min., D.784; 15 in C, D.840 (Relique); 16 in A min., D.845; 17 in D, D.850; 18 in G, D.894; 19 in C min., D.958; 20 in A, D.959; 21 in B flat, D.960.

(B) *** DG 463 766-2 (7). Kempff.

Piano Sonatas Nos. 1 in E, D.157; 2 in C, D.279; 3 in E,

D.459; 4 in A min., D.537; 5 in A flat, D.557; 6 in E min., D.566; 7 in E flat, D.568; 9 in B, D.575; 11 in F min., D.625; 13 in A, D.664; 14 in A min., D.784; 15 in C, D.840 (Relique); 16 in A min., D.845; 17 in D, D.850; 18 in G, D.894; 19 in C min., D.958; 20 in A, D.959; 21 in B flat, D.960.

(M) *** Decca 448 390-2 (7). Schiff.

Wilhelm Kempff's cycle was recorded over a four-year period (1965–9) and has been much admired over the years. These are among the most consistently satisfying accounts of the sonatas, with a wisdom that puts them in a category of their own. Indeed their insights are very special indeed. The recording has a touch of shallowness, but is generally excellent. All seven CDs are now available in a convenient, inexpensive bargain box, and represent exceptional value.

With Schiff's collection (like Kempff's survey) including the *First Sonata*, D.157 (written when the composer was eighteen), and also the fragment of the *Eighth* (which Kempff omits), Schiff sets the seal on his seven-CD survey for Decca which has excited golden opinions. In his note he calls them 'among the most sublime contributions written for the piano' – and he plays them as if they are, too. Yet Schiff's is a survey that blends pianistic finesse with keen human insights. He has a good feeling for the architecture of these pieces and he invests detail with just the right amount of feeling. Good modern, digital recordings, made in the Brahms-Saal of the Musikverein in Vienna. The CDs come conveniently packaged in a mid-priced box, and are still available separately at full price.

Other sonata recordings

Piano Sonatas Nos. 14–21; German Dances; Impromptus; Moments musicaux; Wanderer fantasia.

*** Ph. 426 128-2 (7). Brendel.

Piano Sonatas Nos. 14 in A min., D.784; 17 in D, D.850.

*** Ph. 422 063-2 Brendel.

Piano Sonatas Nos 15 in C (Relique), D.840; 18 in G, D.894.

*** Ph. 422 340-2. Brendel.

Piano Sonata No. 16 in A min., D.845; 3 Impromptus, D.946.

*** Ph. (IMS) 422 075-2. Brendel.

Piano sonata No. 19 in C min., D.958; Moments musicaux Nos. 1–6, D.780.

*** Ph. 422 076-2. Brendel.

Piano Sonata No. 20 in A, D.959; Allegretto in C min., D.915; 16 German dances, D.783; Hungarian Melody in B min., D.817.

**(*) Ph. (IMS) 422 229-2. Brendel.

Piano Sonata No. 21 in B flat, D.960; Wanderer fantasia, D.760.

*** Ph. 422 062-2. Brendel.

Brendel's later digital set is more intense than his earlier cycle of recordings for Philips, though there was a touching freshness in the earlier set, and he has the benefit of clean, well-focused sound. These are warm performances, strongly

delineated and powerfully characterized, which occupy a commanding place in the catalogue. They are separately available, and all of them can be confidently recommended to Brendel's admirers.

'The Last Six Years, 1823–1828': Vol. 1: *Piano Sonatas Nos. 14 in A min., D.784; 18 in G, D.894; 12 German Dances (Ländler), D.790.*

*** Priory/Ottavo OTR C68608. Cooper.

Vol. 2: *Piano Sonatas Nos. 15 in C, D.840; 20 in C, D.959; 11 Ecossaises, D.781.*

*** Priory/Ottavo OTR C58714. Cooper.

Vol. 3: *Piano Sonata No. 16 in A min., D.845; 4 Impromptus, D.935.*

*** Priory/Ottavo OTR C88817. Cooper.

Vol. 4: *Piano sonata No. 17 in D, D.850; 6 Moments musicaux, D.780.*

*** Priory/Ottavo OTR C128715. Cooper.

Vol. 5: *Piano Sonata No. 21 in B flat, D.960; Allegretto in C min., D.915; 3 Impromptus (Klavierstücke), D.946.*

*** Priory/Ottavo OTR C88821. Cooper.

Vol. 6: *Piano sonata No. 19 in C min., D. 958; 4 Impromptus, D.899.*

*** Priory/Ottavo OTR C78923. Cooper.

Imogen Cooper, in her outstanding set on the Dutch Ottavo label has a true Schubertian sensibility; her feeling for this composer's special lyricism is second to none, yet her playing has both strength and a complete understanding of the music's architecture. The recordings were made in the London Henry Wood Hall over a period of three years, between June 1986 and July 1989, using a Steinway for the first three volumes and a fine-sounding Yamaha for the later records. The balance is admirable and the sound full, with a convincing natural resonance. The playing has the spontaneity of live music-making, and the warm colouring and fine shading of timbre are as pleasing to the ear as the many subtle nuances of phrasing, which are essentially based on a strong melodic line. These performances can be recommended alongside those by artists with the most illustrious names, and they do not fall short. With their fine, modern, digital recording these CDs will give much delight and refreshment.

Piano Sonatas Nos. 1; 14, D.784; 20, D.959.

(M) *** Decca (ADD) 425 033-2. Lupu.

Lupu is sensitive and poetic throughout. In the *A major* work he leaves one with the impression that the achievement is perfectly effortless, with an inner repose and depth of feeling that remain memorable long after the record has ended. Excellent vintage Decca recording, made in the Kingsway Hall in the late 1970s.

Piano Sonata No. 4 in A min., D.537.

(M) ** DG 457 762-2. Michelangeli – BEETHOVEN: *Piano Sonata No. 4 in E flat, Op. 7 ***; BRAHMS: *Ballades.* ***

Michelangeli rushes the opening theme of the *A minor*

Sonata and rarely allows the simple ideas of the first movement to speak for themselves. Elsewhere his playing, though aristocratic and poised, is not free from artifice, and the natural eloquence of Schubert eludes him. Fine 1981 digital recording, but on this CD only the Brahms finds this artist at his best.

Piano Sonatas Nos. 4; 13; 14; 15 (Relique); 16; 19; 20; 21; Allegretto, D.915; 11 Ecossaises, D.781; Fantasia in C (Wanderer), D.760; 12 German Dances, D.790; 16 German Dances, D.783; Hungarian Melody, D.817; 6 Moments musicaux, D.780.

(M) *** Ph. (ADD) 446 923-2 (5). Brendel.

Four out of the five records here come from Brendel's earlier, analogue set of Schubert recordings, but the first, pairing Nos. 4 and 13, is digital. Here Brendel's account of the *A minor Sonata*, D.537, sounds a little didactic: the gears are changed to prepare the way for the second group, and this sounds unconvincing on the first hearing and more so on the repeat. He also broadens on the modulation to F major towards the end of the exposition, only to quicken the pulse in the development. The result is curiously inorganic. The *A major*, D.664, is also given with less simplicity and charm than one expects from this great artist. Both in *Sonatas 14 in A minor* and *15 in C major* he manages to convey romantic feeling within a relatively taut framework; indeed in the *C major* his eloquence and poetry leave nothing to be desired. No. 16, D.845, is one of the very finest of the series, with a searching reading of the first movement, free in expression, but direct too. The variations of the slow movement are given heavenly length, while the Scherzo and finale have strength and urgency. *No. 20 in A major*, however, suffers from rather more agogic changes than is desirable, and the *C minor Sonata*, D.958, is also not free from this charge. Brendel's performance of the final *B flat major Sonata* is as impressive and full of insight as one would expect; his playing of the *Wanderer Fantasia* is also of a high order, and throughout he is truthfully recorded. The *German Dances* are delightful and particularly beautifully played, while the *Moments musicaux* are given wonderfully poetic performances and rank very highly indeed in Brendel's Schubert discography. The slightly soft-grained recording is exemplary.

Piano Sonata No. 5 in A flat, D.557; 2 Scherzi, D.593.

(M) *** Decca (ADD) 448 129-2. Lupu – BRAHMS: *Piano sonata No. 3.* ***

In the little three-movement *A flat Sonata* Lupu strikes the perfect balance between Schubert's classicism and the spontaneity of his musical thought. The *Andante* unfolds with appealing delicacy and the finale combines delicacy with strength. The two *Scherzi* are hardly less successful. The analogue recording from the mid-1970s is as natural and fresh as the performances themselves.

Piano Sonatas Nos. 9; 11; 13; Moment Musical, D.780/1.

*** BBC (ADD) BBCL 4010-2. Richter.

This disc comprises a Schubert recital Richter gave at the Royal Festival Hall in 1979, and the dryish sound is perfectly

acceptable. Richter recorded all three sonatas for EMI in Japan three years later, and there is little significant difference in approach between the two accounts. As always his playing is magisterial and eloquent. Thoroughly recommendable.

Piano Sonatas Nos. 9 in B, D.575; 18 in G, D.894; 20 in A, D.959; 21 in B flat, D.960.

(N) **(*) Ph. 456 573-2 (2). Brendel.

Issued to celebrate Brendel's 70th birthday in January 2001, these inspired Schubert performances were all recorded live, unlike his previous Schubert on disc. Brendel describes them as 'correctives, alternatives or supplements to my previous studio recordings', but they are more than that. Though Brendel's approach to Schubert remains broadly the same as in his 1971 series of late sonatas and the more individual digital versions of the late 1980s, there is an extra magnetism in these live accounts, intensifying the depth of what he has to say. He is more freely expressive than before, with speeds more flexible, and with rhythms given an extra lift. At times he seems improvisational in his flights of fantasy, while the depth of concentration conveyed in pianissimos is consistently greater than in his studio performances.

Three of the four last and greatest sonatas are included, with the early *B major Sonata* of 1817 as a supplement, a sonata not previously recorded by Brendel and one that, as he sees it, points forward to the late works. The opening of the great *B flat Sonata* is marred by intrusive coughing from a woman in the Festival Hall audience, but otherwise the sound is excellent, bright and full-toned, with acoustic differences between four different venues ironed out – the Alte Oper in Frankfurt, the Concertgebouw in Amsterdam, the Snape Maltings and the Royal Festival Hall.

Piano Sonatas Nos. 13 in A; 14 in A min.; Hungarian Melody, D.817; 12 Waltzes, D.145.

⚫ (M) *** Decca (ADD) 443 579-2. Ashkenazy.

A magnificent record in every respect. Ashkenazy is a great Schubertian who can realize the touching humanity of this giant's vision as well as his strength. There is an astonishing directness about these performances and a virility tempered by tenderness. This matches Ashkenazy's own high standards, and Decca have risen remarkably to the occasion. The 1966 analogue recording, reissued in Decca's Classic Sound series, has splendid range and fidelity.

Piano Sonatas Nos. 13 in A, D.664; 17 in D, D.850.

(N) ** HM HMC 901713. Planès.

The French pianist Alain Planès is currently embarked on a project to record all the Schubert sonatas. A sensitive and perceptive artist, he proves an authoritative guide and holds the right balance between beauty of detail and the overall architecture. The sunny *A major Sonata* comes from 1819, the same year as the *Trout* quintet, and the *D major* of 1825 paves the way for the big late sonatas. Planès is handicapped by his recording acoustic, so that the piano seems dry and brittle. However, it is worth making allowances for there are real musical rewards here. Planès is a Schubertian of real quality, and his interpretations are far more satisfying than some of his more celebrated rivals.

Piano sonatas Nos. 13, D.664; 21 in B flat.

*** Decca (IMS) 440 295-2. Lupu.

Radu Lupu's is one of the most searching of all his Schubert recordings and finds this masterly pianist at his most eloquent and thoughtful.

Piano Sonata No. 14 in A min., D.784; Moments musicaux, D789; 12 Grazer Walzer, D.924.

*** Erato 0630 17869-2. Fellner.

Till Fellner more than justifies his growing reputation in this fine Schubert recital. His playing is totally unaffected and completely natural, and at the same time is distinguished by great finesse and sensitivity. He never fusses over detail and shows both a freshness and spontaneity of feeling and a command of the architecture of the music. One of the finest Schubert recitals in the current lists.

Piano Sonatas Nos. 14 in A min., D.784; 17 in D, D.850.

(N) **(*) Philips 464 480-2. Uchida.

Wonderful pianism and great delicacy of sound from Mitsuko Uchida and recording quality of great naturalness. This artist is occasionally an intrusive interpreter and does not always allow Schubert to speak for himself in the way that Kempff did. Some may find that her insights enhance their feeling for these wonderful pieces, but others may see them as a barrier. Recommended without qualification to Ms Uchida's admirers, but with caution to others.

Piano Sonatas Nos. 15 (Reliquie); 18, D.894.

*** Philips 454 453-2. Uchida.

The unfinished torso of the *Reliquie Sonata* is given an eloquent, inward-looking reading of great tonal beauty. The *G major Sonata* is masterly, combining careful thought with emotional depth. Another of the best Schubert sonata discs of the last few years. The Philips recording is excellent in every way.

Piano Sonatas Nos. 15; 19; 16 German Dances, D.783.

(M) *** Regis (ADD) RRC 1009. Brendel.

Brendel was at his finest and most spontaneous in the l960s. The *C minor Sonata* is particularly fine, with a thoughtful, improvisatory feeling in the slow movement which is consistently illuminating. The two-movement *C major Sonata* also has a memorable *Andante*, and the *German Dances* are an endless delight. The recording is full and bold.

Piano Sonata No. 17; Impromptus, D.899/3–4; Moments musicaux Nos. 1–6.

(M) *** Decca (ADD) 443 570-2. Curzon.

Curzon could hardly be more convincing – the spontaneous feeling of a live performance captured better than in many earlier discs. Curzon also gives superb performances of the *Moments musicaux*. These readings are among the most poetic in the catalogue, and the recording throughout is exemplary. The *Impromptus* make an attractive bonus (the

G flat major particularly magical) in this reissue in Decca's Classic Sound series, and they too are beautifully played. The recording remains of Decca's finest analogue quality.

Piano Sonatas Nos. 17; 20; 21; March in E, D.606; Moments musicaux, D.780.

(M) (***) EMI mono CHS7 64259-2 (2). Schnabel.

It was thanks to Schnabel's championship that the *Piano Sonatas* re-entered the repertory. Neither the *A major* and *B flat Sonatas* was state-of-the-art piano-sound, but the *Moments musicaux* sound remarkably full-bodied. The playing is full of characteristic insights, and as always with this artist there is imagination of a remarkable order. These recordings are now fifty years old, but some of the playing Schnabel offers – at the opening of the *B flat* and in the slow movements of all three *Sonatas* – will never be less than special.

Piano Sonata No. 19; Moments musicaux, D.780.

(M) *** Decca (IMS) 417 785-2. Lupu.

Lupu's performance has a simple eloquence that is most moving. His *Moments musicaux* are very fine indeed. The Decca recording is very natural and, at mid-price, this is extremely competitive.

Piano Sonatas Nos. 19; 20 in A, D.959.

(M) *** DG (ADD) 453 673-2. Kempff.
*** DG 427 327-2. Pollini.

Kempff is never less than illuminating in Schubert, and these highly spontaneous performances are nicely turned and well shaped, as one would expect from so authoritative a Schubertian, and there are numerous imaginative insights. The recording gives pleasingly realistic sound, even if is not of DG's very finest.

In Pollini's hands these emerge as strongly structured and powerful sonatas, yet he is far from unresponsive to the voices from the other world with which these pieces resonate. Perhaps with his perfect pianism he does not always convey a sense of human vulnerability, as have some of the greatest Schubert interpreters.

Piano Sonatas Nos. 19–21; 3 Klavierstücke, D. 946/1–3.

(B) **(*) Ph. Duo (ADD) 438 703-2. Brendel.

Brendel's analogue recording of the *A major* suffers from rather more agogic changes than is desirable. Some listeners may find these interferences with the flow of the musical argument a little too personal. The *C minor Sonata* is not free from this charge but it remains an impressive performance. Brendel's account of the *B flat Sonata* is characteristically imposing and full of insight, as one would expect. Here his mood is both serious and introspective, and he is not unduly wayward; moreover he is at his very finest in the *Klavierstücke*. This is eloquent and profoundly musical playing. Throughout, the recording is well up to Philips's high standard of realism.

Piano Sonata No. 20 in A, D.959.

*** Sony MK 44569. Perahia – SCHUMANN: *Piano Sonata No. 2.* ***

Perahia's combination of intellectual vigour and poetic insight shows that awareness of proportion and feeling for expressive detail which distinguish the greatest interpreters. As always with this artist, every phrase speaks and each paragraph breathes naturally.

Piano Sonatas Nos. 20, D.959; 21, D.960.

(M) *** Virgin VER5 61272-2. Tan (fortepiano).

Melvyn Tan uses a fortepiano that was much admired by Beethoven. He is a compelling artist of keen musical intelligence who makes you listen, even when you might not agree with every expressive or agogic hesitation. Generally speaking, tempi are well judged, though the *Andantino* of the *A major* and the slow movement of the *B flat* are far too fast, if surprisingly persuasive. His account of this sonata is very impressive: there is depth of feeling as well as many felicities of sonority. These performances will make you think afresh about this music. The recording is first class.

Piano Sonata No. 21 in B flat, D.960.

(M) *** Decca (ADD) 448 578-2. Curzon – BRAHMS: *Piano Sonata No. 3 etc.* ***

(M) *** Ph. (ADD) 420 644-2. Brendel – *Wanderer Fantasia.* ***

Piano Sonata No. 21 in B flat, D.960; Allegretto in C min., D.915; 12 Ländler, D.790.

⁂ *** EMI CDC5 55359-2. Kovacevich.

Piano Sonata Nos. 21; 3 Klavierstücke, D.946.

*** Ph. 456 572-2. Uchida.

Stephen Kovacevich made a memorable recording of the great *B flat major Sonata* for Hyperion which (in our 1988 edition) we called 'one of the most eloquent accounts on record of this sublime sonata and one which is completely free of expressive point-making. It is an account which totally reconciles the demands of truth and the attainment of beauty.' One could well say the same of the present version, though, if anything, it explores an even deeper vein of feeling. With excellent, truthful recording, it earns the strongest and most enthusiastic recommendation.

Curzon's is among the finest accounts of the *B flat Sonata* in the catalogue. Tempi are aptly judged and everything is in fastidious taste. It is beautifully recorded, and the piano sounds very truthful in timbre. For the reissue in Decca's 'Classic Sound' series, the Brahms *F minor Sonata* has been added, an equally perceptive account, plus a pair of *Intermezzi*, to make this quite outstanding value.

Brendel's earlier analogue performance is as impressive and full of insight as one would expect. He is not unduly wayward, for there is room for the *Wanderer Fantasy* as well, and he is supported by excellent Philips sound.

Mitsuko Uchida couples the last Sonata with the *Drei Klavierstücke*. Hers is a performance of considerable stature; she allows Schubert to speak for himself. There is a rapt concentration and an almost other-worldly quality about her playing that will repay the attentive listener. Some may feel that she lingers a little too long in the slow movement and allows the onward flow of the music to stagnate – and they will doubtless prefer Curzon or Brendel. In any event

there is no doubt whatever as to the excellence of the Philips recording.

VOCAL MUSIC

Lieder on Record (1898–1952): Vol. 1, 1898–1929 (all with piano unless otherwise indicated): *Ave Maria* (1898) Edith Clegg; sung in English. *Ungeduld* (1901) Paul Knüpfer. *Heidenröslein* (1902) Minnie Nast. *Litanei* (1901); *Ständchen: Zögernd leise* – with Hofoper Ch. & O, Bruno Seidler (1908) both Marie Götze. *Ständchen* (sung in English): *Hark, hark! the lark* (1902) David Bispham. *Die schöne Müllerin: Der Neugierige* (1902) Franz Naval. *Rastlose Liebe* (1902); *Die Allmacht* (1910) both Edyth Walker. *Erlkönig* (1906); *Du bist die Ruh; Die Liebe* (1907) all three Lilli Lehmann. *Der Wanderer* (1902) Ernst Wachter. *Schwanengesang: Abschied* (1904); *Winterreise: Der Leiermann* (1934) both Harry Plunket-Greene; sung in English. *An die Leier* (1909) Pauline Cramer. *Die Forelle* (1902) Leopold Demuth. *Schwanengesang: Am Meer* (1904) Gustav Walter. *Die junge Nonne* (1907) Susan Strong (with orchestra). *Der Wanderer* (1906); *Schwanengesang: Aufenthalt* (1912); *Winterreise: Der Leiermann* (1910) all three Lev Sibiriakov; sung in Russian. *Frühlingsglaube* (1910) Heinrich Hensel. *Der Kreuzzug* (1905) Wilhelm Hesch. *Schwanengesang: Ständchen* (1907 with orchestra) & *Liebesbotschaft* (1909) both Leo Slezak. *An die Musik; Du bist die Ruh* (1911 – both with Arthur Nikisch, piano); *Suleika II* (1929 – with Coenraad V. Bos, piano); *Ellens Gesang* (1939 – with Gerald Moore, piano) all four Elena Gerhardt. *Die schöne Müllerin: Das Wandern* (1914); *Winterreise: Der Leiermann* (1928) both Sir George Henschel (accompanying himself on the piano). *Die schöne Müllerin: Der Müller und der Bach* (1911) Elise Elizza. *An die Musik; Gruppe aus dem Tartarus* (1910) both Ottilie Metzger. *Sei mir gegrüsset* (1921) Friedrich Brodersen. *Die schöne Müllerin: Undgeduld & Wohin?* (1922–3) both Frieda Hempel. *Gruppe aus dem Tartarus* (1924); *Erlkönig* (1936, with Gerald Moore) both Alexander Kipnis. *Du bist die Ruh* (1924); *Die Liebe hat gelogen* (1927, with Edwin Schneider) both John McCormack. *Im Abendrot; Verklärung* (1929) both Aaltje Noordewier-Reddingius. *Winterreise: Rückblick; Frühlingstraume & Mut!* (1927) all three Richard Tauber, with Mischa Spoliansky. *Gretchen am Spinnrade; Mignon II* (1928) both Meta Seinemeyer, with O, Frieder Weissmann. *Die Forelle; Lachen und Weinen* (1928); *Winterreise: Der Lindenbaum* (1931) all three Vanni Marcoux, with Piero Coppola; sung in French. *An die Musik* (1926) Ursula van Diemen, with Arpád Sándor. *Memnon* (1932) Harold Williams, with Herbert Dawson. *Das Lied im Grünen* (1930) Sigrid Onegin, with Clemens Schmalstich. *Schwanengesang: Der Doppelgänger. Der Tod und das Mädchen* (1930 with O, Eugene Goossens) both Feodor Chaliapin (sung in Russian). *Schwanengesang: Aufenthalt; Ihr Bild. Die schöne Müllerin: Pause* (1928) all three Hans Duham, with Ferdinand Foll. *Sei mir gegrüsset; Auf dem Wasser zu singen; Geheimes* (1927) all three Lotte Lehmann with O,

Manfred Gurlitt. *Winterreise: Der Lindenbaum. Der Tod und das Mädchen* (1926) both Julia Culp, with Fritz Lindemann.

(M) (***) EMI mono CHS5 66150-2 (3).

The first item in this fascinating historical survey offers a frisson to the listener, even though it is a very swoopy account of *Ave Maria* sung in English. It is what is thought to be the very first recording of a Schubert song, delivered in 1898 by Edith Clegg, a contralto known only for having sung at Covent Garden in 1909. From then on the focus grows ever clearer, both in sound and in vocal technique, with even the second item, *Ungeduld* from *Die schöne Müllerin*, recorded by the German bass, Paul Knüpfer, in 1901 with a forwardness and clarity that defy the years.

Each item brings its revelations, with the American, David Bispham, singing *Hark, hark! the lark* in 1902 in a prim D'Oyly Carte English accent; the soprano, Lilli Lehmann, in 1906 giving an intensely dramatic account of *Erlkönig*; Harry Plunket-Greene (born 1865), vivid in 1934 electrical recording, characterfully giving *Der Leiermann* from *Winterreise* in English, every word clear, but with an Irish accent, the narrative effect like a folksong; Lev Sibiriakov transforming the same song to become intensely Russian (again extraordinarily vivid recording, made in St Petersburg by Fred Gaisberg); and Sir George Henschel (born 1850) at 78 recording that same song in the original German with a firmness and point for any modern singer to envy. It is amazing to think that the tenor, Gustav Walter, who was recorded in a ringing account of *Am Meer* at the age of 70, was born in 1834, within six years of Schubert's death.

It is a set which telescopes history and tells, among much else, what store all these vintage singers set by firm, clear delivery with not a hint of a wobble among them. Quite apart from such starry names as Chaliapin, Tauber and McCormack, Alexander Kipnis (who gives another memorable account of *Erlkönig*), the brilliant Frieda Hempel and the golden-toned Meta Seinemeyer demand special mention. Anyone listening to these 65 items, lasting 3 hours, will be amazed at the riches, with freshness the keynote, stylistically flawed only occasionally in sentimental *rallentandos*. Texts are given in the booklet but, alas, none of the potted biographies from the original LP set nor (worse still) an index of songs. However, this set is now deleted.

Lieder on Record, 1898–1952: Vol. 2, 1929–52: *Schwanengesang: Der Atlas* (1930); *Erlkönig* (orch. Berlioz); *Schwanengesang: Der Doppelgänger* (1934) all three Charles Panzéra, with O, Piero Coppola (sung in French). *Die Forelle* (1927); *Der Hirt auf dem Felsen* (1929) both Lotte Schöne, the second with Berlin State Op. O, Leo Blech); *Schwanengesang: Am Meer* (1929) Friedrich Schorr, with Robert Jäger. *Gretchen am Spinnrade* (1929) Dusolinna Giannini, with Michael Raucheisen. *Erlkönig* (1930) Georges Thill, with Henri Etcheverry (baritone), C. Pascal (treble) & O. *Der Tod und das Mädchen* (1929) Maria Oiszewska, with George Reeves. *Nachtviolen; An die Geliebte; Das Heimweh* (1938) all three Elisabeth Schumann, with Leo Rosenek. *Der Jüngling an der Quelle* (1936) Elisabeth Schumann, with Elizabeth Coleman. *An*

die Nachtigall (1933); *Der Schmetterling* (1937) both Elisabeth Schumann, with George Reeves. *Der Musensohn* (1932) Therese Behr-Schnabel, with Artur Schnabel. *An die Laute; Am See* (1932); *Der Wanderer an den Mond* (1937) all three Karl Erb, with Bruno Seidler-Winkler. *Schwanengesang: Frühlingssehnsucht* (1937) Karl Erb, with Gerald Moore. *Auflösung; Schwanengesang: Liebesbotschaft* (1935); *Wiegenlied: Schlafe, schlafe; Wiegenlied: Wie sich der Auglein* (1933) all five Ria Ginster, with Gerald Moore. *Ganymed; Rosamunde: Der Vollmond strahlt. Winterreise: Das Wirthaus* (1938); *Schwanengesang: Kriegers Ahnung* (1937) all four Herbert Janssen, with Gerald Moore. *Mignon I; Nachtstücke; Die junge Nonne* (1937) all three Susan Metcalfe-Casals, with Gerald Moore. *Erlkönig* (1937) Marta Fuchs, with Michael Raucheisen. *Schwanengesang: Die Taubenpost* (1937) both Gerhard Hüsch, with Gerald Moore. *Lied eines Schiffers; Widerschein* (1939) both Gerhard Hüsch, with Hanns Udo Müller. *Auf dem Wasser zu singen* (1943) Frida Leider, with Michael Raucheisen. *Die schöne Müllerin: Halt!; Eifersucht und Stolz* (1945); *Schäfers Klagelied* (1949) all three Aksel Schiotz, with Gerald Moore. *Die Vögel; Liebhaber in allen Gestalten* (1948) both Elisabeth Schwarzkopf, with Gerald Moore; *Seligkeit* (1946) Elisabeth Schwarzkopf, with Karl Hudez. *Im Frühling; Auf der Bruck* (1950) both Peter Pears, with Benjamin Britten. *Der Hirt auf dem Felsen* (1947) Margaret Ritchie, with Reginald Kell (clarinet) & Gerald Moore. *Schwanengesang: Ihr Bild* (1947) Julius Patzak, with Hermann von Nordberg. *Auf dem Wasser zu singen* (1948) Irmgard Seefried, with Gerald Moore. *Heidenröslein* (1947) Irmgard Seefried, with Hermann von Nordberg. *Am Bach im Frühling; Gruppe aus dem Tartarus; Meerstille; Wandrers Nachtlied I–II* (1949) all five Hans Hotter, with Gerald Moore. *An die Leier* (1949) Flora Nielsen, with Gerald Moore. *Prometheus* (1949) Bernhard Sönnerstedt, with Gerald Moore. *Aus Heliopolis I* (1949) Endré Koréh, with Hermann von Nordberg. *Die schöne Müllerin: Am Feierabend; Trock'ne Blumen. Nacht und Träume. Schwanengesang: Das Fischermädchen* (1951) all four Dietrich Fischer-Dieskau, with Gerald Moore. *Die Allmacht; Frühlingsglaube; Wandrers Nachtlied II* (1952) Kirsten Flagstad, with Gerald Moore.

(M) (**(*)) EMI mono CHS5 66154-2 (3) [CDHC 66154].

This second volume in EMI's historic survey of Schubert song on record brings almost comparable delight, even if there are fewer surprises when many, if not most, of the singers are already familiar from their recordings. The 64 items lead up to the two great exponents of Lieder in our time, Schwarzkopf and Fischer-Dieskau, here both vividly characterful at the start of their recording careers. In timbre the charming Lotte Schöne might almost be mistaken for the even more sparkling Elisabeth Schumann, here represented in five brief songs. Naturally German singers predominate, but some of the most cherishable items are from non-German singers: Charles Panzéra and Georges Thill from France (heard in a version of *Erlkönig*, sung very dramatically in French as a trio with Henri Etcheverry and a boy treble), Peter Pears and Margaret Ritchie from Britain, as well as transatlantic singers like Dusolina Giannini (fresh and powerful in *Gretchen am Spinnrade*), Flora Nielsen and Susan Metcalfe-Casals, whose very rare recordings, privately made for her by EMI, are a revelation. The only disappointments are the recordings of Therese Behr-Schnabel (accompanied by her husband), recorded when she was 58, and Herbert Janssen, whose rapid flutter in the voice is distracting among performances of immaculate firmness. The programme ends with three songs from Kirsten Flagstad, in 1953 past her prime but still commanding. Excellent transfers, as in the first volume, with the same reservations over documentation. However, this set is also now deleted.

Dietrich Fischer-Dieskau: The EMI Recordings

The First Recital (1951): *Der Atlas; Ihr Bild; Fischermädchen; Die Stadt; Am Meer; Der Doppelgänger; Erlkönig; Nacht und Träume; Du bist die Ruh; Ständchen.*

Vol. I (1955): *Der Wanderer an den Mond; Uber Wildemann; Der Einsame; Auflösung; Der Kreuzzug; Totengräbers Heimweh; Nachtviolen; Frühlingssehnseht; Geheimnes; Rastlose Liebe; Liebesbotschaft; Im Abendrot; Abschied.*

Vol. II (1957): *Dem Unendlichen; Die Sterne; An die Musik; Wehmut; Kriegers Ahnung; Der Zwerg; Der Wanderer; Frühlingsglaube; Die Taubenpost; An Silvia; Im Frühling; Auf der Bruck.*

Vol. IIIa (1958): *Ständchen; Alinde; Nähe des Geliebten; Normanns Gesang; In der Ferne.*

Vol. IIIb (1958): *Aufenthalt; Lied des gefangenen Jägers; Greisengesang; Erlkönig; Nachtstück.*

(all with Gerald Moore).

Vol. IV (1959): *Gruppe aus dem Tartarus; Die Götter Griechenlands; Ewartung; Sehnsucht; Der Taucher.*

Vol. V (1959): *Der Sänger; Die Bürgschaft; Der Fischer; Einsamkeit.*

Vol. VIa (1959): *Am Strome; Der Alpenjäger; Erlafsee; Wie Ulfru fischt; Beim Winde; Trost; Auf der Donau (1959).*

Vol. VIb (1959): *Abendstern; Liedesend; Sehnsucht; Heliopolis; Zum Punsche; Der Sieg; An die Freunde.*

(Vols. IV–VIb with Karl Engel).

Vol. VII (1962): *Der Atlas; Ihr Bild; Das Fischermädchen; Die Stadt; Am Meer; Der Doppelgänger; Lachen und Weinen; Dass sie hier gewesen; Sei mir gegrüsst; Du bist die Ruh; Im Walde (Waldesnacht).*

Vol. VIII (1965): *Seligkeit; Heidenröslein; Ständchen; Des Fischers Liebesglück; Fischerweise; Der Jüngling an der Quelle; An die Laute; Die Forelle; Auf der Riesenkoppe.*

Vol. IX (1965): *An die Entfernte; Auf dem Wasser zu singen; Der Schiffer; Der Wanderer; Nachtgesang; Das Zügenglöcklein; Der Jüngling und der Tod; Das Heimweh; Das Lied im Grünen; Der Tod und das Mädchen; Der*

Winterabend; Der zürnende Barde; Der Strom; Litanei auf das Fest Aller Seelen.

(all with Gerald Moore).

(M) *** EMI mono/stereo CMS5 65670-2 (6). Fischer-Dieskau, Moore or Engel.

This HMV set makes an admirable survey of Fischer-Dieskau's Schubert recordings for EMI over a decade and a half before he moved to Deutsche Grammophon to make the extensive survey listed below. It is particularly interesting to compare the earliest recordings (the first in mono), with the voice and manner still youthfully fresh, to the second generation, again with Gerald Moore but also with Karl Engel. The contrast is fascinating, with the voice still younger than on DG. The transfers are superbly managed and full translations are provided to make this an indispensable supplement to the DG sets.

Lieder, Vol. 1 (1811–17); Vol. 2 (1817–28); Song cycles: *Die schöne Müllerin; Schwanengesang; Die Winterreise.*

(B) *** DG (ADD) 437 214-2 (21). Fischer-Dieskau, Moore (as below).

Fischer-Dieskau's monumental survey of all the Schubert songs suitable for a man's voice (some of the longer ones excepted) was made over a relatively brief span, with the last 300 songs concentrated on a period of only two months in 1969, yet there is not a hint of routine. The two big boxes of nine discs come at bargain price, whereas the smaller box, containing the song-cycles, comes at mid-price. Nor has the background information been skimped. Each box contains complete German texts and English translations (plus summaries in French) as well as introductory essays. The one serious omission is an alphabetical list of titles. It makes it unnecessarily hard to find a particular song – much the most likely way of using so compendious a collection.

This collection of 21 CDs is offered at bargain price, as are the two separate 9-disc collections of Lieder listed below. The three great song-cycles – also included here – cost more if purchased separately.

Lieder, Vol. I (1811–17): *Eine Leichenfantasie; Der Vatermörder* (1811); *Der Jüngling am Bache* (1812); *Totengräberlied; Die Schatten; Sehnsucht; Verklärung; Pensa, che questo istante* (1813); *Der Taucher* (1813–15); *Andenken; Geisternähe; Erinnerung; Trost, An Elisa; Die Betende; Lied aus der Ferne; Der Abend; Lied der Liebe; Erinnerungen; Adelaide; An Emma; Romanze: Ein Fräulein klagt' im finstern Turm; An Laura, als sie Klopstocks Auferstehungslied sang; Der Geistertanz; Das Mädchen aus der Fremde; Nachtgesang; Trost in Tränen; Schäfers Klagelied; Sehnsucht; Am See* (1814); *Auf einen Kirchhof; Als ich sie erröten sah; Das Bild; Der Mondabend* (1815); *Lodas Gespenst* (1816); *Der Sänger* (1815); *Die Erwartung* (1816); *Am Flusse; An Mignon; Nähe des Geliebten; Sängers Morgenlied; Amphiaraos; Das war ich; Die Sterne; Vergebliche Liebe; Liebesrausch; Sehnsucht der Liebe; Die erste Liebe; Trinklied; Stimme der Liebe; Naturgenuss; An die Freude; Der Jüngling am Bache; An den Mond; Die Mainacht; An die Nachtigall; An die Apfelbäume; Seufzer; Liebeständelei; Der Liebende; Der Traum; Die Laube;*

Meeres Stille; Grablied; Das Finden; Wandrers Nachtlied; Der Fischer; Erster Verlust; Die Erscheinung; Die Täuschung; Der Abend; Geist der Liebe; Tischlied; Der Liedler; Ballade; Abends unter der Linde; Die Mondnacht; Huldigung; Alles um Liebe; Das Geheimnis; An den Frühling; Die Bürgschaft; Der Rattenfänger; Der Schatzgräber; Heidenröslein; Bundeslied; An den Mond; Wonne der Wehmut; Wer kauft Liebesgötter? (1815); Der Goldschmiedsgesell (1817); Der Morgenkuss; Abendständchen: An Lina; Morgenlied: Willkommen, rotes Morgenlicht; Der Weiberfreund; An die Sonne; Tischlerlied; Totenkranz für ein Kind; Abendlied; Die Fröhlichkeit; Lob des Tokayers; Furcht der Geliebten; Das Rosenband; An Sie; Die Sommernacht; Die frühen Gräber; Dem Unendlichen; Ossians Lied nach dem Falle Nathos; Das Mädchen von Inistore; Labetrank der Liebe; An die Geliebte; Mein Gruss an den Mai; Skolie – Lasst im Morgenstrahl des Mai'n; Die Sternenwelten; Die Macht der Liebe; Das gestörte Glück; Die Sterne; Nachtgesang; An Rosa I: Warum bist du nicht hier?; An Rosa II: Rosa, denkst du an mich?; Schwanengesang; Der Zufriedene; Liane; Augenlied; Geistes-Gruss; Hoffnung; An den Mond; Rastlose Liebe; Erlkönig (1815); Der Schmetterling; Die Berge (1819); Genügsamkeit; An die Natur (1815); Klage; Morgenlied; Abendlied; Der Flüchtling; Laura am Klavier; Entzückung an Laura; Die vier Weltalter; Pflügerlied; Die Einsiedelei; An die Harmonie; Die Herbstnacht; Lied: Ins stille Land; Der Herbstabend; Der Entfernten; Fischerlied; Sprache der Liebe; Abschied von der Harfe; Stimme der Liebe; Entzückung; Geist der Liebe; Klage: Der Sonne steigt; Julius an Theone; Klage: Dein Silber schien durch Eichengrün; Frühlingslied; Auf den Tod einer Nachtigall; Die Knabenzeit; Winterlied; Minnelied; Die frühe Liebe; Blumenlied; Der Leidende; Seligkeit; Erntelied; Das grosse Halleluja; Die Gestirne; Die Liebesgötter; An den Schlaf; Gott im Frühling; Der gute Hirt; Die Nacht; Fragment aus dem Aeschylus (1816); An die untergehende Sonne (1816/ 17); An mein Klavier; Freude der Kinderjahre; Das Heimweh; An den Mond; An Chloen; Hochzeitlied; In der Mitternacht; Trauer der Liebe; Die Perle; Liedesend; Orpheus; Abschied; Rückweg; Alte Liebe rostet nie; Gesänge des Harfners aus Goethes Wilhelm Meister: Harfenspieler I: Wer sich der Einsamkeit ergibt; Harfenspieler II: An die Türen will ich schleichen; Harfenspieler III: Wer nie sein Brot mit Tränen ass. Der König in Thule; Jägers Abendlied; An Schwager Kronos; Der Sänger am Felsen; Lied: Ferne von der grossen Stadt; Der Wanderer; Der Hirt; Lied eines Schiffers an die Dioskuren; Geheimnis; Zum Punsche; Am Bach im Frühling (1816); An eine Quelle (1817); Bei dem Grabe, meines Vaters; Am Grabe Anselmos; Abendlied; Zufriedenheit; Herbstlied; Skolie: Mädchen entsiegelten; Lebenslied; Lieden der Trennung (1816); Alinde; An die Laute (1827); Frohsinn; Die Liebe; Trost; Der Schäfer und der Reiter (1817); Lob der Tränen (1821); Der Alpenjäger; Wie Ulfru fischt; Fahrt zum Hades; Schlaflied; Die Blumensprache; Die abgeblühte Linde; Der Flug der Zeit; Der Tod und das Mädchen; Das Lied vom Reifen; Täglich zu singen; Am Strome; Philoktet; Memnon; Auf dem See; Ganymed; Der Jüngling und der Tod; Trost im Liede (1817).

(B) *** DG (ADD) 437 215-2 (9). Fischer-Dieskau, Moore.

This remarkable project, with Volume 1 recorded between 1966 and 1968 and Volume 2 over two months of intensive sessions in 1969, is an astonishing achievement in bringing together the greatest Schubertian of our time and the finest accompanist in a wide survey of the Lieder for solo voice. Already in 1811, as a boy in his early teens, Schubert was writing with astonishing originality, as is shown in the long (19 minutes) opening Schiller setting, a *Funeral Fantasy* with its rough, clashing intervals of a second and amazing harmonic pointers to the future. Drama comes very much to the fore in the second song here, *Der Vatermörder* ('A father died by his son's hand'), while the composer's endearing, flowing lyricism makes both *Der Jüngling am Bache* and *Die Schatten* sound remarkably mature. *Totengräberlied* ('Dig, spade, dig on!') brings a characteristically light touch to a gravedigger's soliloquy as he reflects that rich and poor alike, handsome and noble, are all in the end reduced to bones. Throughout these nine well-filled CDs the diversity of Schubert's imagination holds the listener, and his melodic gift almost never disappoints, especially when the performances are so completely at home with the music. The songs are presented in broadly chronological order and the arrangement of items ensures that each disc of the nine makes a satisfying recital in its own right. The CD transfers are impeccable, adding a little in presence to what were originally very well-balanced recordings.

Lieder, Vol. II (1817–28): *An die Musik; Pax vobiscum; Hänflings Liebeswerbung; Auf der Donau; Der Schiffer; Nach einem Gewitter; Fischerlied; Das Grab; Der Strom; An den Tod; Abschied; Die Forelle; Gruppe aus dem Tartarus; Elysium; Atys; Erlafsee; Der Alpenjäger; Der Kampf; Der Knabe in der Wiege (1817); Auf der Riesenkoppe; An den Mond in einer Herbstnacht; Grablied für die Mutter; Einsamkeit; Der Blumenbrief; Das Marienbild (1818); Litanei auf das Fest Allerseelen (1816); Blondel zu Marien; Das Abendrot; Sonett I: Apollo, lebet noch dein Hold verlangen; Sonett II: Allein, nachdenken wie gelähmt vom Krampfe; Sonett III: Nunmehr, da Himmel, Erde schweigt; Vom Mitleiden Mariä (1818) ; Die Gebüsche; Der Wanderer; Abendbilder; Himmelsfunken; An die Freunde; Sehnsucht; Hoffnung; Der Jüngling am Bache; Hymne I: Wenige wissen das Geheimnis der Liebe; Hymne II: Wenn ich ihn nur hab; Hymne III: Wenn alle untreu werden; Hymne IV: Ich sag es jedem; Marie; Beim Winde; Die Sternennächte; Trost; Nachtstück; Prometheus; Strophe aus Die Götter Griechenlands (1819); Nachthymne; Die Vögel; Der Knabe; Der Fluss; Abendröte; Der Schiffer; Die Sterne; Morgenlied (1820); Frühlingsglaube (1822); Des Fräuleins Liebeslauschen (1820); Orest auf Tauris (1817); Der entsühnte Orest; Freiwilliges Versinken; Der Jüngling auf dem Hügel (1820); Sehnsucht (1817); Der zürnenden Diana; Im Walde (1820); Die gefangenen Sänger; Der Unglückliche; Versunken; Geheimnes; Grenzen der Menschheit (1821); Der Jüngling an der Quelle (1815); Der Blumen Schmerz (1821); Sei mir gegrüsst; Herr Josef Spaun, Assessor in Linz; Der Wachtelschlag Ihr Grab; Nachtviolen; Heliopolis I: Im kalten, rauhen Norden; Heliopolis II: Fels auf Felsen hingewälzet; Selige Welt; Schwanengesang: Wie*

*klage'ich's aus; Du liebst mich nicht; Die Liebe hat gelogen;
Todesmusik; Schatzgräbers Begehr; An die Leier; Im Haine;
Der Musensohn; An die Entfernte; Am Flusse; Willkommen
und Abschied (1822); Wandrers Nachtlied: Ein Gleiches;
Der zürnende Barde (1823); Am See (1822/3); Viola; Drang
in die Ferne; Der Zwerg; Wehmut; Lied: Die Mutter Erde;
Auf dem Wasser zu singen; Pilgerweise; Das Geheimnis;
Der Pilgrim; Dass sie hier gewesen; Du bist die Ruh;
Lachen und Weinen; Greisengesang (1823); Dithyrambe;
Der Sieg; Abendstern; Auflösung; Gondelfahrer (1824);
Glaube, Hoffnung und Liebe (1828); Im Abendrot; Der
Einsame (1824); Des Sängers Habe; Totengräbers
Heimwehe; Der blinde Knabe; Nacht und Träume;
Normans Gesang; Lied des gefangenen Jägers; Im Walde;
Auf der Bruck; Das Heimweh; Die Allmacht; Fülle der
Liebe; Wiedersehn; Abendlied für die Entfernte; Szene I aus
dem Schauspiel Lacrimas; Am mein Herz; Der liebliche
Stern (1825); Im Jänner 1817 (Tiefes Leid); Am Fenster;
Sehnsucht; Im Freien; Fischerweise; Totengräberweise; Im
Frühling; Lebensmut; Um Mitternacht; Über Wildemann
(1826); Romanze des Richard Löwenherz (1827); Trinklied;
Ständchen; Hippolits Lied; Gesang (An Silvia); Der
Wanderer an den Mond; Das Zügenglöcklein; Bei dir
allein; Irdisches Glück; Wiegenlied (1826); Der Vater mit
dem Kind; Jägers Liebeslied; Schiffers Scheidelied;
L'incanto degli occhi; Il traditor deluso; Il modo di prender
moglie; Das Lied im Grünen; Das Weinen; Vor meiner
Wiege; Der Wallensteiner Lanznecht beim Trunk; Der
Kreuzzug; Das Fischers Liebesglück (1827); Der
Winterabend; Die Sterne; Herbst; Widerschein (1828);
Abschied von der Erde (1825/6).*

(B) *** DG (ADD) 437 225-2 (9). Fischer-Dieskau, Moore.

Volume II of this great project brings the mature songs; performances and recording are just as compelling as in Volume 1. In their Berlin sessions Fischer-Dieskau and Moore adopted a special technique of study, rehearsal and recording most apt for the project. The sense of spontaneity and new discovery is unfailing, since each take was in fact a performance. On a later occasion, both artists might have taken a different view but, using the ease of access possible with CD, this collection is a unique way of sampling the many different aspects of Schubert's genius. The collection opens appropriately with *An die Musik* of 1817 and, as before, the songs in this volume are laid out chronologically with certain obvious exceptions – on disc 4, for instance, *Orest auf Tauris* (1817) is placed alongside the highly contrasted *Der entsühnte Orest*, 'Orestes purified' (1820) – and the closing recital on disc 9 is suitably concluded with *Abschied von der Erde* ('Farewell to the Earth'), dating from 1825/6. Once again there is much unfamiliar repertory to discover: the four *Hymnes* grouped together on the second disc are little known but show the composer's imaginative diversity in a specifically religious connotation, while the unexpected song dedicated to *Herr Josef Spaun, Assessor in Linz*, which closes the fourth CD, is strikingly operatic. Both booklets offer full translations and each includes also brief essays by Fischer-Dieskau and Walther Dürr on the composer.

Lieder, Vol. III: Song-cycles: *Die schöne Müllerin;
Schwanengesang; Die Winterreise.*

(M) *** DG (ADD) 437 235-2 (3). Fischer-Dieskau, Moore.

Fischer-Dieskau and Moore had each recorded these great cycles of Schubert several times already before they embarked on this set in 1971/2 as part of DG's Schubert song series. It was no mere repeat of earlier triumphs. If anything, these performances – notably that of the darkest and greatest of the cycles, *Winterreise* – are even more searching than before, with Moore matching the hushed concentration of the singer in some of the most remarkable playing that even he has put on record. As in the extensive recitals listed above, Fischer-Dieskau is in wonderfully fresh voice, and the transfers to CD have been managed very naturally.

Lieder: *Abendbilder; Am Fenster; Auf der Bruck; Auf der
Donau; Aus Heliopolis; Fischerweise; Im Frühling;
Liebeslauschen; Des Sängers Habe; Der Schiffer; Die Sterne;
Der Wanderer; Wehmut; Das Zügenglöcklein.*

(M) *** DG (ADD) 445 717-2. Fischer-Dieskau, Richter.

Recorded live in 1977, this beautifully balanced selection of Schubert songs displays the singer's enormous range of expression, as well as the acute sensitivity of the pianist in responding. The songs have been grouped almost in a cycle, starting with a biting expression of self-torment (*Des Sängers Habe*. This is sung aggressively here (understandably so) but gradually the mood lightens from melancholy (*Wehmut*) to brighter thoughts (*Das Zügenglöcklein* – 'The little bell'). Not many of these songs are well known, but it is a programme to delight aficionado and newcomer alike, atmospherically recorded with remarkably little interference from audience noises.

Elly Ameling Collection ('The Early Years'): Disc 1: *An die
Laute; An die Nachtigall* (2 settings); *An Sylvia; Der
Blumenbrief; Du bist die Ruh'; Du Liebst mich nicht; Das
Lied im Grünen; Der Einsame; Fischerweise; Die Gebüsche;
Im Abendrot; Im Freien; Im Haine; Die Liebe hat gelogen;
Der liebliche Stern; Das Mädchen; Die Männer sind
méchant; Minnelied; Nacht und Träume; Nachtviolen;
Rosamunde: Romanze. Schlummerlied; Der Schmetterling;
Seligkeit; Die Sterne; Die Vögel; Der Wachtelschlag.* Disc 2:
*Ave Maria; Gretchen am Spinnrade; Gretchens Bitte;
Heidenröslein; Jäger, ruhe von der Jagd; Der König in
Thule; Die junge Nonne; Die Liebende schreibt; Liebhabner
in allen Gestalten; 4 Mignon Lieder (Kennst du das Land;
Nur wer die Sehnsucht kennt; Heiss mich nicht reden; So
lass mich scheinen); Nähe des Geliebten; Raste, Krieger!;
Scene aus Faust; Suleika I & II.* Disc 3: *Abendbilder; An die
Musik; An den Mond; Bertas Lied in der Nacht; Die
Blumensprache; Erster Verlust; Frülingssehnsucht; Der
Knabe; Nachthymne; Schwestergruss; Sei mir gegrüsst; Die
Sterne; Wiegenlied.* Disc 4: *Am Bach im Frühling; An den
Tod; An die Entfernte; An die untergehende Sonne; Auf
dem Wasser zu singen; Die Forelle; Fülle der Liebe;
Ganymed; Die Götter Griechenlands; Im Abendrot; Im
Frühling; Der Musensohn; Der Schiffer; Schwanengesang:
Sehnsucht; Sprach der Liebe.*

(M) *** Ph. ADD/Dig. (IMS) 438 528-2 (4). Ameling, Baldwin (CDs 1–3); Jansen (CD 4).

Elly Ameling appeared on the international scene in the mid-1960s. These records cover her period of maturity from 1972 until 1984. Her lovely voice with its diamond purity is consistently appealing and she is a persuasive interpreter, whether in the engaging *Mignon* songs or in the most familiar favourites: the poised freshness of *Nacht und Träume*, the innocence of *Nachtviolen* or the more emotionally fraught *Die Liebe hat gelogen*. These, like so much else, are most affecting; the analogue recordings on the first two discs show her at the peak of her form, with Dalton Baldwin most sensitive in support. The third disc, digitally recorded in 1982, had the distinction of being the first Lieder recital to appear on compact disc and readily deserved its accolade. It is a typically characterful and enchanting collection, starting with *An die Musik* and including other favourites like the *Cradle song* as well as lesser-known songs that admirably suit the lightness and sparkle of Ameling's voice. The fourth CD offers a 1984 digital recital with Rudolf Jansen accompanying. It brings more delights, even if the voice is not quite as fresh and agile as in the earlier collections, notably the 1972 recordings included on the second disc. Yet she is able to bring new depths to such a song as *An die Entferne* and her breath control remains immaculate – as in the opening *Ganymed* – while she still brings delightful bounce to the ever-popular *Der Musensohn*. Her voice is caught naturally by the engineers and the balance is excellent. A treasurable collection, marred only by the absence of translations: only the German texts are given.

The Graham Johnson Schubert Lieder Edition

When it comes to background information, Graham Johnson's Schubert Lieder Edition for Hyperion using some of the greatest singers of the day – is unmatchable. With each disc devoted to a group of songs on a particular theme, Johnson provides notes that add enormously to the enjoyment, heightening the experience of hearing even the most familiar songs.

Lieder Vol. 1: *Der Alpenjäger; Amalia; An den Frühling; An den Mond; Erster Verlust; Die Ewartung; Der Fischer; Der Flüchtling; Das Geheimnis; Der Jüngling am Bache; Lied; Meeres Stille; Nähe des Geliebten; Der Pilgrim; Schäfers Klagelied; Sehnsucht; Thekla; Wanderers Nachtlied; Wonne der Wehmut.*

*** Hyp. CDJ 33001. Baker, Johnson.

Hyperion's complete Schubert song edition, master-minded by the accompanist, Graham Johnson, this first volume sets the pattern of mixing well-known songs with rarities. Dame Janet's whole collection is devoted to Schiller and Goethe settings, above all those he wrote in 1815, an exceptionally rich year for the 18-year-old; one marvels that, after writing his dedicated, concentrated setting of *Wanderers Nachtlied*, he could on that same day in July write two other equally memorable songs, *Der Fischer* and *Erster Verlust* (*First loss*). Dame Janet is in glorious voice, her golden tone ravishing in a song such as *An den Mond* and her hushed tone caressing

the ear in *Meeres Stille* and *Wanderers Nachtlied*. Presented like this, the project becomes a voyage of discovery.

Lieder Vol. 2: *Am Bach im Frühling; Am Flusse; Auf der Donau; Fahrt zum Hades; Fischerlied* (two settings); *Fischerweise; Der Schiffer; Selige Welt; Der Strom; Der Taucher; Widerschein; Wie Ulfru fischt.*

*** Hyp. CDJ 33002. Varcoe, Johnson.

Graham Johnson with the baritone, Stephen Varcoe, devises a delightful collection of men's songs, culminating in the rousing strophic song, *Der Schiffer*, one of the most catchily memorable that Schubert ever wrote, here exhilaratingly done. Otherwise the moods of water and wave, sea and river, are richly exploited. The last 28 minutes of the collection are devoted to the extended narrative, *Der Taucher* (*The Diver*), setting a long poem of Schiller which is based on an early version of the Beowulf saga. Varcoe and Johnson completely explode the long-accepted idea that this is overextended and cumbersome, giving it a thrilling dramatic intensity.

Lieder Vol. 3: *Abschied; An die Freunde; Augenlied; Iphigenia; Der Jüngling und der Tod; Lieb Minna; Liedesend; Nacht und Träume; Namenstagslied; Pax vobiscum; Rückweg; Trost im Liede; Viola; Der Zwerg.*

*** Hyp. CDJ 33003. Murray, Johnson.

This is one of Ann Murray's finest records with the intimate beauty of the voice consistently well caught and with none of the stress that the microphone exaggerates on record. Like the songs that Johnson chose for Ann Murray's husband, Philip Langridge, these too represent Schubert in his circle of friends, with their poems his inspiration, including a long flower ballad, *Viola*, by his close friend, Franz von Schober, which Murray and Johnson sustain beautifully.

Lieder Vol. 4: *Alte Liebe rostet nie; Am See; Am Strome; An Herrn Josef von Spaun (Epistel); Auf der Riesenkoppe; Das war ich; Das gestörte Glück; Liebeslauschen; Liebesrausch; Liebeständelei; Der Liedler; Nachtstück; Sängers Morgenlied* (2 versions); *Sehnsucht der Liebe.*

*** Hyp. CDJ 33004. Langridge, Johnson.

Philip Langridge brings a collection to illustrate Schubert's setting of words by poets in his immediate circle, ending with *Epistel*, a tongue-in-cheek parody song addressed to a friend who had left Vienna to become a tax collector, extravagantly lamenting his absence. It is Johnson's presentation of such rarities that makes the series such a delight. Langridge has rarely sounded so fresh and sparkling on record.

Lieder Vol. 5: *Die Allmacht; An die Natur; Die Erde; Erinnerung; Ferne von der grossen Stadt; Ganymed; Klage der Ceres; Das Lied im Grünen; Morgenlied; Die Mutter Erde; Die Sternenwelten; Täglich zu singen; Dem Unendlichen; Wehmut.*

*** Hyp. CDJ 33005. Connell, Johnson.

Thanks in part to Johnson's choice of songs and to his sensitive support at the piano, Connell has rarely sounded so sweet and composed on record, yet with plenty of temperament. The collection centres round a theme – this one,

Schubert and the countryside, suggested by the most popular song of the group, *Das Lied im Grünen*. As ever, the joy of the record is enhanced by Johnson's brilliant, illuminating notes.

Lieder Vol. 6: *Abendlied für die Entfernte; Abends unter der Linde* (two versions); *Abendstern; Alinde; An die Laute; Des Fischers Liebesglück; Jagdlied; Der Knabe in der Wiege (Wiegenlied); Lass Wolken an Hügeln ruh'n; Die Nacht; Die Sterne; Der Vater mit dem Kind; Vor meiner Wiege; Wilkommen und Abschied; Zur guten Nacht.*

*** Hyp. CDJ 33006. Rolfe Johnson, Johnson (with chorus).

The theme of Anthony Rolfe Johnson's contribution is 'Schubert and the Nocturne'. Two items include a small male chorus, a group of individually named singers. *Jagdlied* is entirely choral, and the final *Zur guten Nacht*, a late song of 1827, has the 'Spokesman' answered by the chorus, ending on a gentle *Gute Nacht*. Rolfe Johnson's voice has never sounded more beautiful on record, and the partnership of singer and accompanist makes light even of a long strophic song (using the same music for each verse) like *Des Fischers Liebesglück*, beautiful and intense.

Lieder Vol. 7: *An die Nachtigall; An den Frühling; An den Mond; Idens Nachtgesang; Idens Schwanenlied; Der Jüngling am Bache; Kennst du das Land?; Liane; Die Liebe; Luisens Antwort; Des Mädchens Klage; Meeres Stille; Mein Gruss an den Mai; Minona oder die Kunde der Dogge; Naturgenuss; Das Rosenband; Das Sehnen; Sehnsucht* (2 versions); *Die Spinnerin; Die Sterbende; Stimme der Liebe; Von Ida; Wer kauft Liebesgötter?.*

*** Hyp. CDJ 33007. Ameling, Johnson.

An extraordinarily rewarding sequence of 24 songs, all written in the composer's *annus mirabilis*, 1815. With Ameling both charming and intense, Johnson's robust defence in his ever-illuminating notes of the first and longest of the songs, *Minona*, is amply confirmed, a richly varied ballad. Here too is a preliminary setting of *Meeres Stille*, less well-known than the regular version, written a day later, but just as clearly a masterpiece, sung by Ameling in a lovely intimate half-tone at a sustained pianissimo. It is fascinating too to compare the two contrasted settings of Mignon's song, *Sehnsucht*, the first of five he ultimately attempted.

Lieder Vol. 8: *Abendlied der Fürstin; An Chloen; An den Mond; An den Mond in einer Herbstnacht; Berthas Lied in der Nacht; Erlkönig; Die frühen Gräber; Hochzeitslied; In der Mitternacht; Die Mondnacht; Die Nonne; Die Perle; Romanze; Die Sommernacht; Ständchen; Stimme der Liebe; Trauer der Liebe; Wiegenlied.*

*** Hyp. CDJ 33008. Walker, Johnson.

For Sarah Walker, with her perfectly controlled mezzo at its most sensuous, the theme is 'Schubert and the Nocturne', leading from the first, lesser-known version of the Goethe poem, *An den Mond*, to two of the best-loved of all Schubert's songs, the delectable *Wiegenlied*, 'Cradle-song', and the great drama of *Erlkönig*, normally sung by a man, but here at least as vividly characterized by a woman's voice.

Lieder Vol. 9: *Blanka; 4 Canzonen, D.688; Daphne am Bach; Delphine; Didone abbandonata; Gott! höre meine Stimme; Der gute Hirt; Hin und wieder Fliegen Pfeile;* (i) *Der Hirt auf dem Felsen. Ich schleiche bang und still (Romanze). Lambertine; Liebe Schwärmt auf allen Wegen; Lilla an die Morgenröte; Misero pargoletto; La pastorella al prato; Der Sänger am Felsen; Thekla; Der Vollmond strahlt (Romanze).*

*** Hyp. CDJ 33009. Augér, Johnson; (i) with King.

'Schubert and the Theatre' is the theme of Arleen Augér's contribution, leading up to the glories of his very last song, the headily beautiful *Shepherd on the rock*, with its clarinet obbligato. The *Romanze, Ich schleiche bang* – adapted from an opera aria – also has a clarinet obbligato. Notable too are the lightweight Italian songs that the young Schubert wrote for his master, Salieri, and a lovely setting, *Der gute Hirt* ('The good shepherd'), in which the religious subject prompts a melody which anticipates the great staircase theme in Strauss's *Arabella*.

Lieder Vol. 10: *Adelwold und Emma; Am Flusse; An die Apfelbäume, wo ich Julien erblickte; An die Geliebte; An Mignon; Auf den Tod einer Nachtigall; Auf einen Kirchhof; Harfenspieler I; Labetrank der Liebe; Die Laube; Der Liebende; Der Sänger; Seufzer; Der Traum; Vergebliche Liebe; Der Weiberfreund.*

*** Hyp. CDJ 33010. Hill, Johnson.

Graham Johnson here correlates the year 1815 with what has been documented of his life over those twelve months, which is remarkably little. So the songs here form a kind of diary. The big item, overtopping everything else, is the astonishing 38-stanza narrative song, *Adalwold and Emma*, with Hill ranging wide in his expression. It is almost half an hour long, from the bold march-like opening to the final happy resolution.

Lieder Vol. 11: *An den Tod; Auf dem Wasser zu singen; Auflösung; Aus 'Heliopolis' I & II; Dithyrambe; Elysium; Der Geistertanz; Der König in Thule; Lied des Orpheus; Nachtstück; Schwanengesang; Seligkeit; So lasst mich scheinen; Der Tod und das Mädchen; Verklärung; Vollendung; Das Zügenglöcklein.*

*** Hyp. CDJ 33011. Fassbaender, Johnson.

Starting with a chilling account of *Death and the Maiden*, the theme of Brigitte Fassbaender's disc is 'Death and the Composer'. Fassbaender's ability precisely to control her vibrato brings baleful tone-colours, made the more ominous by the rather reverberant, almost churchy, acoustic. So in *Auf dem Wasser zu singen* the lightly fanciful rippling-water motif presents the soul gliding gently 'like a boat' up to heaven, and the selection ends astonishingly with what generally seems one of the lightest of Schubert songs, *Seligkeit*. This, as Johnson suggests, returns the listener from heaven back to earth. In this, as elsewhere, Fassbaender sings with thrilling intensity, with Johnson's accompaniment comparably inspired.

Lieder, Vol. 12: *Adelaide; An Elise; An Laura, als sie Klopstocks Auferstehungslied sang; Andenken; Auf den Sieg* *der Deutschen; Ballade; Die Betende; Don Gayseros I, II, III; Der Geistertanz; Lied an der Ferne; Lied der Liebe; Nachtgesang; Die Schatten; Sehnsucht; Trost; Trost in Tränem; Der Vatermörder.*

** Hyp. CDJ 33012. Thompson, Johnson.

Adrian Thompson's disc brings the only disappointment in Graham Johnson's outstanding Schubert series. As recorded, the voice sounds gritty and unsteady, with the tone growing tight and ugly under pressure, yet this collection of early songs, all teenage inspirations, still illuminates the genius of Schubert at this earliest period of his career.

Lieder, Vol. 13: (i) *Eine altschottische Ballade. Ellens Gesang I, II & III (Ave Maria); Gesang der Norna; Gretchen am Spinnrade; Gretchens Bitte; Lied der Anna Lyle; Die Männer sind méchant; Marie; Das Marienbild;* (i) *Normans Gesang; Szene aus Faust. Shilrik und Vinvela; Die Unterscheidung.*

*** Hyp. CDJ 33013. McLaughlin, Johnson; (i) with Hampson.

The theme for Marie McLaughlin's contribution to the Hyperion Schubert edition is broadly a survey of Schubert's inner conflicts and contradictions. The Goethe settings are crowned by one of the most celebrated of all Schubert songs, *Gretchen am Spinnrade*. McLaughlin gives a fresh and girlish portrait, tenderly pathetic rather than tragic. Fascinatingly the selection also includes *Gretchens Bitte*, an extended song that Schubert left unfinished and for which Benjamin Britten in 1943 provided a completion of the final stanzas. The translations of Scottish ballads cover a wide range. *Eine altschottische Liede* is one of the three dramatic items involving the baritone, Thomas Hampson, which also include a sinister dialogue for Gretchen and an evil spirit, *Szene aus Faust*. McLaughlin's voice comes over sweetly, with brightness and much charm.

Lieder, Vol. 14: *Amphiaraos; An die Leier;* (i) *Antigone und Oedip. Der entsühnte Orest; Freiwilliges Versinken; Die Götter Griechenlands; Gruppe aus dem Tartarus; Fragment aus dem Aeschylus;* (i) *Hektors Abschied. Hippolits Lied; Lied eines Schiffers an die Dioskuren; Memnon; Orest auf Tauris; Philoktet; Uraniens Flucht; Der Zürnenden Diana.*

*** Hyp. CDJ 33014. Hampson, Johnson; (i) with McLaughlin.

Thomas Hampson's theme here is 'Schubert and the Classics', mainly Ancient Greece. Matching the hushed intensity of the opening song, *Die Götter Griechenlands*, singer and accompanist give a rapt performance, and Hampson's ecstatically sweet tone, with flawless legato, contrasts with the darkly dramatic timbre – satisfyingly firm and steady – that he finds for later songs and dialogues, including the finale *Hektors Abschied*. In that dialogue Marie McLaughlin sings the part of Andromache to Hampson's Hector.

Lieder, Vol. 15: *Am Fenster; An die Sonne; An die untergehende Sonne; Der blinde Knabe; Gondelfahrer; Im Frieien; Ins stille Land; Die junge Nonne; Klage an den Mond; Kolmas Klage; Die Mainacht; Der Mondabend; Der Morgenkuss; Sehnsucht; Der Unglückliche; Der Wanderer an den Mond; Der Winterabend.*

✿ *** Hyp. CDJ 33015. Price, Johnson.

In the fifteenth disc of his Hyperion series, Graham Johnson, accompanying Dame Margaret Price in songs on the theme of 'Night', achieves a new peak. One winning rarity is *Klage an den Mond* ('Lament to the Moon'), gloriously fresh and lyrical. Price and Johnson find here a distinctive magic so that its simple melody rings through the memory for hours. The other Holty setting on Margaret Price's disc is of *Die Mainacht*, much better known in Brahms's raptly beautiful setting. The young Schubert simply lets his lyricism flower as no one else could. Johnson and Dame Margaret match that with folk-like freshness, concealing art. In the best-known song, *Der Wanderer an den Mond*, Price is light and crisp, but she finds extra mystery in the moonlight scene of *Am Fenster*, poignantly reflecting the lover's sadness.

Lieder, Vol. 16: *An die Freude; An Emma; Die Bürgschaft; Die Entzückung an Laura I & II; Das Geheimnis; Der Jüngling am Bache; Laura am Clavier; Leichenfantasie; Das Mädchen aus der Fremde; Die vier Weltalter; Sehnsucht; Der Pilgrim.*

*** Hyp. CDJ 33016. Allen, Johnson.

Following the pattern of Graham Johnson's unique Schubert series, Thomas Allen in Schiller settings is challenged to some of his most sensitive singing, using the widest tonal range. They include two extended narrative songs that are a revelation, one of them, *Leichenfantasie* ('Funereal fantasy'), written when Schubert was only fourteen. As before, Johnson's notes and commentaries greatly heighten one's understanding both of particular songs and of Schubert generally.

Lieder, Vol. 17: *Am Grabe Anselmos; An den Mond; An die Nachtigall; An mein Klavier; Aus 'Diego Manazares' (Ilmerine); Die Einsiedelei; Frühlingslied; Geheimnis; Der Herbstabend; Herbstlied; Die Herbstnacht; Klage; Klage um Ali Bey; Lebenslied; Leiden der Trennung; Lied; Lied in der Absehenheit; Litanei; Lodas Gespenst; Lorma; Minnelied; Pflicht und Liebe; Phidile; Winterlied.*

*** Hyp. CDJ 33017. Popp, Johnson.

It was fitting that one of the last recordings which Lucia Popp made, only months before her tragic death in the autumn of 1993, was her contribution to Graham Johnson's Schubert series. These songs, written in 1816 and almost all of them little known, inspire all her characteristic sweetness and charm. They include an extended narrative song to a text from Ossian, *Lodas gespent*, which, like others resurrected by the indefatigable Johnson, defies the idea that long equals boring. She also relishes two of Schubert's rare comic songs, pointing them deliciously. As ever, Johnson's notes are a model of fascinating scholarship.

Lieder, Vol. 18: *Abendlied; An den Schlaf; An die Erntfernte; An die Harmonie; An mein Herz; Auf den Tod einer Nachtigall; Auf der Bruck; 'Die Blume und der Quell'; Blumenlied; Drang in die Ferne; Erntlied; Das Finden; Das Heimweh* (2 versions); *Im Frühling; Im Jänner 1817 (Tiefes Lied); Im Walde; Lebensmut; Der Liebliche Stern; Die Nacht; Uber Wildemann; Um Mitternacht.*

*** Hyp. CDJ 33018. Schreier, Johnson.

This eighteenth disc in Graham Johnson's masterly series represents the halfway point, with Peter Schreier providing a keenly illuminating supplement to his prize-winning recordings with András Schiff of the great Schubert song-cycles for Decca. The challenge is just as great here, when this particular group centres on strophic songs. The first nine songs are all early ones, dating from 1816, leading to just one extended non-strophic song, *Das Heimweh*, D.851, of 1825. Its weight and complexity come over the more powerfully after such a preparation. Johnson then delivers a master-stroke by devising for Schreier what amounts to a new Schubert song-cycle, presenting in sequence ten settings of poems from the *Poetisches Tagebuch* ('Poetic Diary'), by the obsessive, unstable poet, Ernst Schulze, all written in 1825 and 1826. Quoting the first song, Johnson calls the cycle *Auf den wilden Wegen* ('On the wild paths'), with the sequence following the poet's madly fanciful love-affair with a beloved who in real life rejected him as a mere stranger. Schreier and Johnson in their imaginative treatment present clear parallels with *Winterreise*, offering one momentary haven of happiness, instantly shattered. That comes in the best-known song, *Im Frühling*, among the most haunting that even Schubert ever wrote. Johnson's comprehensive notes, as in previous discs of the series, intensify enjoyment enormously.

Lieder, Vol. 19: *Abendlied; Am See; Auf dem See; Auf dem Wasser zu singen; Beim Winde; Der Blumen Schmerz; Die Blumensprache; Gott im Frühling; Im Haine; Der liebliche Stern; Nach einem Gewitter; Nachtviolen; Die Rose; Die Sterne; Suleika I & II; Die Sternennächte; Vergissmeinicht.*

*** Hyp. CDJ 33019. Lott, Johnson.

Graham Johnson's theme for Felicity Lott's disc is 'Schubert and Flowers', prompting a sequence of charming, ever-lyrical songs, mostly neglected but including such a favourite as *Nachtviolen* (raptly sung) and – less predictably – *Auf dem Wasser zu singen*, all enchantingly done. Lott's soprano is not caught quite at its purest, but the charm and tender imagination of the singer consistently match the inspired accompaniments. In his detailed notes Johnson manages to include a 'Schubertian florilegium', listing several hundred of the songs inspired by particular flowers.

Lieder, Vol. 20: 'Schubertiad' (1815) Songs and part-songs: *Abendständchen (An Lina); Alles um Liebe; Als ich sie errötten sah; Begräbnislied; Bergknappenlied; Der erste Liebe; Die Frölichkeit; Geist der Liebe; Grablied; Heidenröslein; Hoffnung; Huldigung; Klage um Ali Bey; Liebesrausch; Die Macht der Liebe; Das Mädchen von Inistore; Der Morgenstern; Nachtgesang; Ossians Lied nach dem Falle Nathos; Osterlied; Punschlied (Im Norden su singen); Schwertlied; Schwangesang; Die Tauschung; Tischerlied; Totenkranz für ein Kind; Trinklied (2 versions); Trinklied vor der Schlacht; Wiegenlied; Winterlied; Der Zufriedene.*

*** Hyp. CDJ 33020. Rozario, Mark Ainsley, Bostridge, George, Johnson; L. Schubert Ch., Layton.

The twentieth volume of the Hyperion Schubert series brings

a different kind of recital disc, with a range of singers performing no fewer than 32 brief songs and ensemble numbers, all written in 1815. Johnson conceives that this might well have been the sort of Schubertiad to take place towards the end of that year and, aptly for the opening and closing numbers, chooses drinking songs. In between, the vigorous and jolly songs are effectively contrasted with a few darker ones, such as a burial song. The team of singers has the flair one expects of Johnson as founder of the Songmakers' Almanac, with the young tenor, Ian Bostridge, appearing in one of his first recordings. More Schubertiads are planned for later on in the Hyperion series.

Lieder, Vol. 21: Songs from 1817–18: *Die abgeblühte Linde; Abschied von einem Freunde; An die Musik; An eine Quelle; Erlafsee; Blondel zu Marien; Blumenbrief; Evangelium Johannes; Der Flug der Zeit; Die Forelle; Grablied für die Mutter; Häbflings Liebeswerbung; Impromptu; Die Liebe; Liebhaber in allen Gestalten; Lied eines Kind; Das Lied vom Reifen; Lob der Tränen; Der Schäfer und der Reiter; Schlaflied; Schweizerlied; Sehnsucht; Trost; Vom Mitleiden Mariä.*

*** Hyp. CDJ 33021. Mathis, Johnson.

Instead of adopting a particular theme for this sequence, sung with characteristic sweetness by the Swiss soprano, Edith Mathis, Graham Johnson has devised a delectable group of 24 songs written in 1817–18, including a high pro-portion of charmers. Two of them are among the best known of all Schubert's songs, *Die Forelle* ('The trout') and *An die Musik*, here sung with disarming freshness and given extra point through Johnson's inspired playing. The songs in swinging compound or triple time are particularly delightful, as are the often elaborately decorative accompaniments which Johnson points with winning delicacy.

Lieder, Vol. 22: 'Schubertiad II': *Der Abend; Das Abendroth; An die Sonne; An Rosa I & II; An Sie; Das Bild; Cora an die Sonne; Cronnan; Die drei Sänger; Die Erscheinung; Furcht der Geliebten; Gebet wahrend der Schlacht; Genugsamkeit; Das Grab; Hermann und Thusnelda; Das Leben ist ein Traum; Lob des Tokayers; Lorma; Das Mädchen aus der Fremde; Morgenlied; Punschlied; Scholie; Selma und Selmar; Die Sterne; Trinklied; Vaterlandslied.*

*** Hyp. CDJ 33022. Anderson, Wyn-Rogers, MacDougall, Keenlyside; Johnson.

The year 1815 was an *annus mirabilis* for Schubert, and Graham Johnson here, from the wealth of songs written in those twelve months, devises a sequence such as the composer might have performed with friends in an intimate Schubertiad. So the solo items are punctuated by three male-voice quartets and one trio for female voices in which the main soloists, listed above, are joined by four other distinguished singers: Patricia Rozario, Catherine Denley, John Mark Ainsley and Michael George. Though most of the 28 items are brief, they include one more-extended song, *Die drei Sänger* ('The three minstrels'), in which Schubert adventurously illustrates the narrative in an almost operatic way. The final page is missing from the manuscript, which is here sensitively completed by Reinhard von Hoorickx.

Lieder, Vol. 23: Songs from 1816: *Abendlied; Abschied von der Harfe; Am ersten Maimorgen; An Chloen; Bei dem Grabe meines Vater; Edone; Der Entfernten; Freude der Kinderjahre; Die frühe Liebe; Geist der Liebe; Gesänger des Harfners aus 'Wilhelm Meister' (Wer sich der Einsamkeit ergibt; Wer nie sein Brot mit Tränen ass; An die Türen will ich schleichen); Das Grab; Der Hirt; Julius an Theone; Der Jüngling an der Quelle; Klage; Die Knabenzeit; Der Leidende (2 versions); Die Liebesgötter; Mailied; Pflügerlied; Romanze; Skolie; Stimme der Liebe; Der Tod Oscars; Zufriedenheit.*

*** Hyp. CDJ 33023. Prégardien, Johnson.

The German lyric tenor, Christoph Prégardien, uses his lovely voice with its honeyed tone-colours through a wide expressive range in a very varied selection of songs from 1816. It is his artistry as well as Johnson's that makes the opening item so riveting, a long narrative song to words by Ossian in translation, which Prégardien's feeling for word-meaning helps to bring to life. That is followed by a brief chorus, *Der Grab*, sung by the London Schubert Chorale, which Johnson intends as a comment on that narrative. The poet is Johann von Salis-Seewis, who is also represented by four solo songs, including the ravishing *Der Jungling an der Quelle*, one of the most haunting that Schubert ever composed. In that year Schubert was expanding the range of poets he chose to set, including Johann Mayrhofer for the first time, here represented by the little-known *Der Hirt* ('The shepherd'). The selection of 19 items is rumbustiously rounded off by a drinking-song, *Skolie*.

Lieder, Vol. 24: *Goethe Schubertiad: An Mignon; An Schwager Kronos; Bundeslied; Erlkönig; Ganymed; Geistes-Gruss; Gesang der Geister über den Wassern (2 versions); Der Goldschmiedsgesell; Der Gott und die Bajadere; Hoffnung; Jägers Abendlied (2 versions); Mahomets Gesang; Mignon (So lasst mich scheinen); Rastlose Liebe; Der Rattenfänger; Schäfers Klagelied; Der Schatzgräber; Sehnsucht (2 versions); Sehnsucht (Nur wer die Sehnsucht kennt); Tischlied; Wer nie sein Brot mit Tränen ass.*

*** Hyp. CDJ 33024. Schäfer, Mark Ainsley, Keenlyside, George, L. Schubert Ch., Layton; Johnson.

This collection, drawn from Schubert's many settings of Goethe, aims to celebrate the important role the poet's works played in the composer's life. Graham Johnson in his notes makes high claims: 'It was the collaboration between Schubert and Goethe which allowed song with piano to become an enduring and valid means of musical expression on a large emotional scale.' Sadly, Goethe himself was indifferent to the inspired efforts of this then-obscure composer, but it did not affect the intensity of Schubert's response to the words. This selection, like that of Volume 28, devoted to Schiller, is related to the life of the poet and includes many fascinating items, not least those in which Schubert set a text more than once. There are half a dozen of them here, including two quite different settings of *The Song of the Spirits over the Waters*, each completed by other hands.

The second, for male chorus, is particularly powerful. Also fascinating is the version of *Erlkönig* here, with three singers taking part, characterizing the different voices in the story, a practice which Schubert himself sanctioned. (This is also included in Volume 2 of EMI's historical Lieder collection, with Georges Thill leading a performance in French.) All the singers here are ideally responsive, with Michael George reining in a voice weightier than the rest.

Lieder, Vol. 25: (i) *Die schöne Müllerin* **(song-cycle); (ii) with additional poems by Wilhelm Müller.**

✿ *** Hyp. CDJ 33025. (i) Bostridge, Johnson; (ii) read by Fischer-Dieskau,

For this first of the big song-cycles in his comprehensive Schubert edition for Hyperion, Graham Johnson could not have chosen his singer more shrewdly. It is a delight to have in Ian Bostridge a tenor who not only produces youthfully golden tone for this young man's sequence but who also gives an eagerly detailed account of the 20 songs, mesmeric at the close, to match even the finest rivals. With the help of Johnson's keenly imaginative accompaniment, Bostridge's gift for changing face and conveying mood makes the story-telling exceptionally fresh and vivid. The bonus is also to have Dietrich Fischer-Dieskau (now retired from singing) reciting the Müller poems which Schubert failed to set. Johnson is at his most inspired too in his detailed notes, which will be a revelation even to experienced Schubertians.

Lieder, Vol. 26: 'An 1826 Schubertiad': 2 Scenes from *Lacrimas (Schauspiel); 4 Mignon Lieder* **of Wilhelm Meister. Lieder:** *Abschied von der Erde; An Sylvia; Das Echo; Der Einsame; Grab und Mond; Mondenschein; Nachthelle; Des Sängers Habe; Ständchen; Totengräberweise; Trinklied; Der Wanderer an den Mond; Widerspruch; Wiegenlied.*

*** Hyp. CDJ 33026. Schäfer, Mark Ainsley, Jackson. L. Schubert Ch., Layton; Johnson.

Starting with *Der Einsame*, sung by Richard Jackson, one of the most haunting of Schubert songs, here is a Schubertiad that brings its measure of darkness, relying entirely on Lieder which Schubert wrote in 1825 and 1826. By then he was writing fewer songs than before, but was hitting the mark every time. It ends in sombre tones with *Abschied von der Erde* ('Farewell to the Earth'), not a song at all but a melodrama for reciter and piano, which Richard Jackson narrates as effectively as one could imagine. Christine Schäfer and Richard Jackson between them perform most of the programme, with John Mark Ainsley contributing just one or two, including *To Sylvia*. That is one of the three Shakespeare settings which come as a lightweight interlude. Schäfer's contributions shine the most brightly, not least the hypnotic *Wiegenlied*, to words by Seidl. Graham Johnson's notes include a survey of Schubert's career in 1825–6, a list of the songs written then, and his brilliant analysis of each item.

Lieder, Vol. 27: *Abendröte cycle of Friedrich von Schlegel* **(complete). Other settings of Friedrich von Schlegel:** *Blanka; Fülle der Liebe; Im Walde; Der Schiffer.* **Settings of**

August von Schlegel: *Lebensmelodien; Lob der Tränen; Sonnets I–III; Sprache der Liebe; Wiedersehn.*

*** Hyp. CDJ 33027. Görne, Schäfer, Johnson.

When the young German baritone, Matthias Görne, made his début at Wigmore Hall, deputizing on a gala occasion, it was instantly obvious that here was a major new Lieder singer. He makes an inspired choice for this fine disc in Graham Johnson's collected edition of the Schubert songs, firmly established as one of the most important recording projects of the nineties. With a masterly feeling for words and vocal line Görne brings out the full charm of these settings of poems by the von Schlegel brothers, Friedrich as well as August, the translator of Shakespeare. The seven songs to words by August are rounded off with three settings of his translations of Petrarch sonnets, while Johnson, prompted by circumstantial evidence, has ingeniously assembled a cycle of 11 Friedrich von Schlegel settings, *Abendröte* ('Sunset'), with Christine Schäfer as soloist in three of them, though not in the best-known of them, *Die Vogel* ('The Bird'), a favourite with both Elisabeth Schumann and Elisabeth Schwarzkopf. Görne and Johnson regularly demonstrate what masterpieces even some of the least known and briefest songs are. Johnson's notes are, as ever, a model, explaining why belated publication of particular songs has unfairly brought about neglect.

Lieder Vol. 28: *'Schubertiad' (1822): Am Flusse; An die Entferntel; Du liebst mich nicht; Frülingsgesang; Geheimes; Geist der Liebe; Ihr Grab; Im Gegenwärtigen Vergangenes; Johanna Sebus; Die Liebe hat gelogen; Mahomets Gesang; Mignon (Heiss mich nicht reden); Der Musensohn; Die Nachtigall; Schatzgräbers Begehr; Sei mir gegrüsst!; Selige Welt; Des Tages Weihe; Todesmusik; Versunken; Der Wachtelschlag; Willkommen und Abschied.*

*** Hyp. CDJ 33028. Schäfer, Mark Ainsley, Koningsberger, Ch., Johnson.

Described as an 1822 Schubertiad, this volume offers an attractively varied collection of items, not just songs from the principal tenor and baritone, both sensitive singers, but concerted numbers, ending with a solemn quartet, a miniature cantata, *Des Tages Weihe*. Settings of Goethe predominate, with Christine Schäfer a very welcome contributor in the first version of *Der Musensohn*, made to sparkle in a higher key than usual. The sound between items is not always consistent, when the chorus is set in a more reverberant acoustic.

Lieder Vol. 29: *Abendbilder; Blondel zu Marien; Einsamkeit* (cantata); *Frühlingsglaube; Himmelsfunken; Hoffnung; Hymne I – IV; Im Walde (Waldesnacht); Der Jüngling auf dem Hügel; Die Liebende schreibt; Morgenlied; Nachthymne; Trost.*

*** Hyp. CDJ 33029. Lipovšek, Berg, Johnson.

Though Marjana Lipovšek with her warm, velvety mezzo, is the central soloist in this collection of songs from 1819 and 1820, the young Canadian baritone, Nathan Berg, takes on the biggest challenge here. That is the cantata, *Einsamkeit*, in twelve sections, setting words by Mayrhofer, with whom Schubert at that time shared a small room. The beauty and range of tone, with flawless legato, make one want to hear more of Berg, but Lipovšek's contribution is equally persuasive in a wide range of songs including five settings of metaphysical poems by Novalis, distinctive in Schubert's oeuvre. Like his playing, Johnson's sleeve notes are revelatory, both on the music and Schubert's life and character.

Lieder, Vol. 30: *Winterreise* (song cycle), D.911.

*** Hyp. CDJ 33030. Goerne, Johnson.

For this greatest of song-cycles Graham Johnson has boldly turned not to a staid, long-experienced artist but to Matthias Goerne, the young baritone who is rapidly proving himself the most exciting and inspired Lieder-singer since Dietrich Fischer-Dieskau. Goerne movingly brings out the point that this is the tragedy of a young lover, not an old one. He sings not just with velvety beauty of tone in every register but with a rapt dedication that forces you to rethink each poem in the cycle, ending with a chill that is all-involving. At every point Graham Johnson heightens the experience with his subtly pointed playing. His commentary in a massive booklet not only illuminates the musical inspiration, but invaluably puts the work in its historical context, showing how profoundly Schubert's reordering of the songs, different from that of the poet, Müller, heightens their tragic impact.

Lieder, Vol. 31: *Die Allmacht* (2nd version for chorus); *Die gestirne; Hagars Klage; Himmelsfunken; Im Abendrot; Das Mädchens Klage* (1st version); *Mirjams Siegergesang; Psalms Nos. 13; 23* (both trans. Mendelssohn); *Psalm 92* (unaccompanied in Hebrew); *Dem Unendlichen.*

*** Hyp. CDJ 33031. Brewer, Holst Singers, Layton; Johnson.

In Graham Johnson's superb series covering all of Schubert's songs, this disc devoted to sacred songs is quite distinct from previous issues, offering not only those for solo voice, but some with chorus too. With the sensitive and powerful American soprano, Christine Brewer, as the central soloist, joined by the Holst singers and other soloists in the concerted numbers, this provides a fascinating survey of Schubert's equivocal approach to religious inspiration, too individual to follow Catholic dogma precisely. Schubert may not have been devout, but the plight of Hagar and Ishmael in the desert, as told in Genesis, led him as a mere 14-year-old to write an extended 16-minute sequence. It is good to have this big religious narrative piece – *Hagars Klage* and *Mirjams Siegesgesang*, a cantata on the Exodus story of Miriam, from the last year of his life – so strongly and persuasively performed, defying length. There is also some electrifying chorus work from the Holst Singers in the Psalm settings, The first two come in translations by Moses Mendelssohn, grandfather of the composer, while Schubert set the third in the original Hebrew, responding sensitively to a commission from a Jewish friend. The solo songs, often simple and hymn-like, are also beautifully sung by the rich-toned mezzo, Christine Brewer. As ever in this series, Johnson's brilliant notes are an inspiration.

Lieder, Vol. 32: *'An 1816 Schubertiad': An die Sonne; Beitrag zur Fünfzigjährigen Jubelfeier des Herrn von Salieri: Der Entfernten; Entzückung; Der Geistertanz; Gott* *der Weltschöpfer; Gott im Ungewitter; Grablied auf einen Soldaten; Das grosse Halleluja; Licht und Liebe; Des Mädchens Klage; Naturgenuss; Ritter Toggenburg; Schlachtgesang; Vedi quanto adoro (Dido Abbandonata); Die verfehlte Stunde; Der Wanderer; Das war ich; Zufriedenheit; Zum Punsche.*

*** Hyp. CDJ 33032. Dawson, Schäfer, Murray, Mark Ainsley, Daniel Norman, Prégardien, Schade, Spence, Maltman, Varcoe, L. Schubert Chorale & Soloists, Layton; Johnson.

With the exception of *Der Wanderer*, few items in this '*1816 Schubertiad*' are well known yet it makes for fascinating listening, with Graham Johnson's illuminating notes providing an ideal commentary. Solitary but substantial contributions from such artists as Christine Schäfer and Christoph Prégardien come as bonuses from earlier sessions in the series, and the collaborations of various artists on ensemble pieces brings just the right atmosphere for a Schubertiad. A trivial but charming sequence of four items was written in celebration of the 50th anniversary of the arrival in Vienna of Schubert's evidently much-loved teacher, Salieri. The brief, trivial canon, *Unser aller Grosspapa* is a special delight. Full, warm sound.

Lieder, Vol. 33: (i) *Lebenstraum (Gesang in C min.); Lebenstraum; Pensa, che questo istante; Totengräberlied;* (ii) *Entra l'uomo allor che nasce (Aria di Abramo); L'incanto degli occhi; Misero pargoletto; O combats, o désordre extrême!; Ombre amene, amiche piante (La serenata); Quelle' innocente figlio (Aria dell' Angelo); Rien de la nature; Son fra l'onde;* (iii) *Klaglied;* (iv) *Entra l'uomo allor che nasce (Aria di Abramo); Erinnerungen; Geisternähe;* (v) *Serbate o dei custodi;* (vi) *Die Befreier Europas in Paris;* (vii) *Der abend;* (viii) *Ammenlied; Die Nacht;* (ix) *Dithyrambe; Trinklied; Viel tausend Sterne prangen.*

*** Hyp. CDJ 33033. McLaughlin, Murray, Wyn-Rogers, Langridge, Norman, Thompson, Koningsberger, Varcoe and soloists, L. Schubert Ch., Layton; Johnson.

Entitled 'The Young Schubert', this volume brings together a mixed bag of songs from the years of the composer's boyhood, 1810–14, which for various reasons have not been included in previous volumes. Thanks to Graham Johnson and his powers of coordination, the result is intensely compelling; it even offers what, through scholarly detective work, is now thought to be the very first Schubert song: probably written before 1810, an extended piece of 394 bars, previously described simply as 'Gesang in C minor', when the words were unknown. Now, as *Lebenstraum*, 'Life's dream', it has been persuasively fitted with words from a poem by Gabriele von Baumberg, which Schubert also used in another song on the disc. It is fascinating too to find the boy Schubert doing arrangements of arias by Gluck, and no fewer than ten of these early songs set Italian words. Standing out among the original songs is the tenderly beautiful *Klaglied* lament of 1812, magically sung by Marie McLaughlin. Though the recordings were made from a whole sequence of sessions between 1990 and 1999, Johnson and his chosen singers offer performances of consistent excellence, very well recorded.

Lieder, Vol. 34: (i) *Abend;* (ii) *Das Abendrot;* (iii) *Der Alpenjäger;* (iv) *Atys;* (v) *Kantate zum Geburtstag des Sängers Michael Vogl;* (vi) *Das Dörfchen;* (vii) *Die Einsiedelei;* (viii) *Frohsinn;* (ix) *Die gefangenen Sänger;* (x) *Die Geselligkeit (Lebenslust);* (xi) *Das Grab;* (xii) *Grenzen der Menschheit; Der Kampf;* (xiii) *Das Mädchen;* (vi) *La pastorella al prato;* (xiv) *Prometheus;* (xv) *Sing-Ubungen;* (xvi) *Uber allen Zauber Liebe;* (iii) *Wandrers Nachtlied II.*

*** Hyp. CDJ 33034. Anderson, Dawson, Lozario, Lipovšek, Hill, Langridge, Norman, Schade, Finley, Gorne, Hampson, Keenlyside, Loges, Maltman, Davies (with Denley, Mark-Ainsley, Bostridge, MacDougall, George); Johnson; L. Schubert Ch., Layton.

It is one of the great merits of Graham Johnson's inspired method of presenting the collected Schubert songs that he gives such a clear perspective on Schubert's career over each year of his short working life. This thirty-fourth Volume brings together the songs that Schubert wrote between 1817 and 1821 not previously included in the Edition. As Johnson explains, the years 1815 and 1816 were the most productive for songs, leading to the present years when other commitments left him with fewer opportunities for songwriting. The nineteen items here, presented in chronological order, offer a wide range of pieces, including several vocal quartets, one of them the delectable *Die Geselligkeit*, 'Zest for Life', and a ten-minute cantata written for the birthday of his singer-friend and advocate, Michael Vogl. Other jewels include some fine Goethe settings, notably the dramatic *Prometheus*, and the second version of the *Wandrers Nachtlied*, a miniature of just a few bars that delves astonishingly deep. Consistently fine performances from sessions recorded between 1991 and 1999.

Lieder, Vol. 35: (1822–25): *Bootgesang; Coronach; Dass sie hier gewesen!; Du bist die Ruh; Gebet (Du Urquell aller güte); Gondelfahrer; Gott in der Natur; Greisengesang; Lachen und Weinen; Lied des gefangenen Jägers; Lied eines Kriegers; Pilgerweise; Schwestergruss; Der Sieg; Der Tanz; Totengräbers Heimwehe; Die Wallfahrt; Der zürnende Barde.*

*** Hyp. CDJ 33035. Dawson, McGreevy, Langridge, Thoas Hampson, Konigsberger, Maltman; Johnson

Rounding off his magnificent project of recording all Schubert's songs, Graham Johnson gathers together what might have seemed loose ends, concentrating on songs from the years of the composer's late twenties. It was a period which, as Johnson explains in his ever-informative notes, brought more extreme highs and lows in the composer's life than ever before.

Central to the scheme are the five settings of poems by Rückert, four of them masterpieces including two of the best-known songs here, the playful *Lachen und weinen* (lightly touched by in by Geraldine McGreevy, and the glorious *Du bist die Ruh*, with Lynne Dawson rapt and dedicated in its soaring vocal line.

Also from the Rückert group the tenor song, *Dass sie hier gewesen*, winningly sung by Philip Langridge, and a fine sixteen-bar fragment only recently discovered. Another song to note is *Totengräbers Heimwehe*, a baritone song which in its marching tread seems to anticipate *Winterreise*, powerfully sung by Christopher Maltson if with gritty tone on sustained notes.

Rarities that prove a revelation include the poised *Schwestergruss* (McGreevy again), with four fine ensemble pieces framing the collection, starting with *Gott in der Natur*, written at the time of the *Unfinished Symphony*, and ending with the exuberant quartet, *Der Tanz*, 'The Dance'. Recordings from different periods are all beautifully balanced.

Lieder, Vol. 36: 'Am 1827 Schubertiad': Cantata zur Feier der Genesung der Irene Kiesewetter; Fröhliches Scheiden; Frühlingslied; Heimliches Lieben; Der Hochzeitsbraten; Il mondo di prender moglie; Il traditor deluso; L'incanto degli occhi; Jägers Liebeslied; Der Kreuzzug; Romanze des Richard Löwenherz; Schiffers Scheidelied; Sie in jedem Liede; Die Sterne; Das Wallensteiner Lanzknecht beim Trunk; Das Weinen; Wolke und Quelle.

(N) *** Hyp. CDJ 33036. Banse, Schade, Finley, Dawson; Johnson; Holst Singers, Layton; Asti.

This penultimate volume brings together miscellaneous songs from the year preceding the composer's death, ending with one of his very rare pieces, an extended comic dialogue for three singers, *Der Hochzeitsbraten*, 'The Wedding Roast', designed to raise a laugh. That is just the sort of item which might have rounded off a Schubertiad in that year, leading to a final brief chorus from the Holst Singers, misleadingly entitled *Cantata*.

The major vocal contribution here comes from the baritone, Gerald Finley, in magnificent voice, clear, firm and dark. As well as the comic trio, he sings eight of the songs, three of them settings of Italian, sounding very Schubertian rather than Italianate. Juliane Banse with her light, bright soprano sings five songs and Michael Schade just two. Though none of them is well known, Johnson and his colleagues make them magnetic, also thanks to his detailed, revelatory notes. Excellent sound.

Lieder, Vol. 37: 'The final year': Schwanengesang, Parts I & II. (i) Auf der Strom. Bei dir allein!; Herbst; Irdisches Glück; Lebensmut.

*** Hyp. CDJ 33037. Mark Ainsley, Rolfe Johnson, Schade; (i) with Pyatt.

Graham Johnson here rounds off his comprehensive Schubert Edition with a magnificent final offering. Whether in scholarship, breadth of musical imagination no single recording project can quite match it, covering every one of the many hundreds of songs. Not only does it include the last song-cycle, *Schwanengesang*, presented by Johnson with new insight, but a carefully chosen group of other songs from 1828, the year Schubert died. Poignantly after the darkness of the final songs of *Schwanengesang* – with *Der Döppelganger* stark and bare as though in anticipation of death – comes the last song that Schubert ever composed, *Die Taubenpost* ('Pigeon post'), seemingly trivial. Here finally happy lyricism blossoms gloriously over an exhilarating accompaniment, representing the clip-clopping of a horse.

As in the previous 36 volumes Johnson's notes (112 pages)

are both searching and original, exploiting with daunting scholarship themes which bring the composer vividly to life. So the extended first song on the disc, *Auf dem Strom* ('On the river'), with opulent horn obbligato from David Pyatt, was written for a memorial concert exactly a year after Beethoven died, with Schubert both paying a heartfelt tribute to that master, and laying claim to be his successor. Johnson then explores the way that many of these songs echo the theme of Beethoven's late song-cycle, *An die ferne Geliebte* ('To the distant beloved'), ever more intensely pursuing an aching realization that true love is all too seldom encountered this side of the grave.

It was shrewd to choose three fine Lieder-tenors as the soloists here. So after Michael Schade's refreshing and thoughtful singing of the introductory songs Johnson divides the *Schwanengesang* cycle between the two other tenors, for once using Schubert's original keys – John Mark Ainsley, ardent in the seven Rellstab settings (the hackneyed *Serenade*sounding totally new at a broad tempo), and Anthony Rolfe Johnson, weightier and darker-toned in the six Heine settings. All three singers – who together give a joint performance of the bizarre *Glaube, Hoffnung und Liebe* ('Faith, Hope and Love') – excel themselves in bringing out word-meaning and in tonal shading, while Johnson in his accompaniments consistently revels in Schubert's joyfully original piano writing. Few series of recordings so richly repay detailed study, and no disc from it more than this culminating issue.

'The Songmakers' Almanac Schubertiade': I, 'Lebensmut': Die junge Nonne; Der zürnende Diana; Vom Mitleiden Mariä; Lachen und Weinen; Selige Welt; Mignon und der Harfner; Auflösung; Lebensmut; Willkommen und Abschied. II, 'Nacht und Träume': An die Laute; Wiegenlied; Ellens Gesang II; Nacht und Träume; Licht und Liebe; Ständchen (Horch! horch! die Lerch); Der Tod und das Mädchen; Der Winterabend; Abschied von der Erde. III, 'Das Lied im Grünen': Fischerweise; Das Lied im Grünen; Der Schiffer; Nähe des Geliebten; Frühlingsglaube; Wandrers Nachtlied; Im Frühling; Wehmut; Auf der Bruck. IV, 'An mein Klavier': An mein Klavier; Zum Punsche; Geheimnis; Viola; Der Hochzeitsbraten.

(B) **(*) Hyp. Dyad CDD 22020 (2). Lott, Murray, Rolfe Johnson, Jackson; Johnson.

Recorded in 1983, this two-disc collection presents over two hours of songs arranged by related groups – 'The Romantic Struggle', 'Serenades and Lullabies', 'Nature and Love', 'At home with the Schubertians'. That was the way Graham Johnson devised his immensely popular Songmakers' Almanac concerts, making this a forerunner of his brilliantly conceived recorded edition of the complete songs. Johnson's notes, including comments on individual items and full texts, observe a similar pattern to that adopted in the main edition, though a song like the Seidl *Wiegenlied* is allowed only three of its stanzas, not all five. The analogue recording, given an AAD transfer to CD, is not quite as clean as in the main edition, not quite sharply focused enough. Such inspired performance give a delightful impression of just such live events as the original Schubertiads. Left to the end are the two items which are by far the longest: the poignant *Viola*, a ballad telling of an abandoned flower, with Ann Murray a charming soloist, and the convivial *Hochzeitsbraten* ('Wedding dish'), featuring the other three soloists. All four singers are at their freshest, with Ann Murray in particularly fine voice, taking on many of the most challenging songs.

Hyperion Schubert Edition sampler. Lieder: (i) *Die Allmacht;* (ii) *Alinde;* (iii) *Als ich sie erröten sah;* (iv) *Am Bach im Frühling;* (v) *Am See;* (vi) *Am Strome;* (vii) *An den Frühling;* (viii) *An die Sonne;* (ix) *An Emma;* (x) *An Silvia;* (xi) *Auflösung;* (xii) *Blondel zu Marien;* (xiii) *Erlkönig;* (xiv) *Jüngling an der Quelle;* (xv) *Der liebliche Stern;* (xvi) *Lied, D.284;* (xvii) *Lied eines Schiffers an die Dioskuren;* (xviii) *Lob der Tränen;* (iii) *Mein;* (xix) *Romanze;* (xx) *Rückweg;* (xxi) *Sehnsucht;* (xxii) *Seufzer;* (xiii) *Ständchen;* (xxiii) *Tost im Tränen;* (xxiv) *Unterscheidung.*

(BB) *** Hyp. HYP 200. (i) Connell; (ii) Rolfe Johnson; (iii) Bostridge; (iv) Varcoe; (v) Lott; (vi) Langridge; (vii) Ameling; (viii) Price; (ix) Allen; (x) Mark Ainsley; (xi) Fassbaender; (xii) Mathis; (xiii) Walker; (xiv) Prégardien; (xv) Schreier; (xvi) Baker; (xvii) Hampson; (xviii) Görne; (xix) Augér, King; (xx) Murray; (xxi) Schäfer; (xxii) Hill; (xxiii) Thompson; (xxiv) McLaughlin; all with Johnson.

This is a delightful sampler, featuring the widest range of the fine Lieder singers whom Graham Johnson has assembled for his magnificent project, which is covered in depth in our main *Guide*. Dame Janet Baker, Dame Margaret Price and Dame Felicity Lott are on the list, with Peter Schreier, Christoph Prégardien, Brigitte Fassbaender, Elly Ameling and the late Arleen Augér among the distinguished singers from outside Britain. Inspired newcomers include Christine Schäfer, Matthias Görne and, in some ways most striking of all, Ian Bostridge, who contributes three songs. Sarah Walker has the longest item, a serenade, *Ständchen*, quite different from the famous one, with male chorus as backing. What – understandably – are missing are the texts and detailed notes which Johnson provides for the individual discs, but the booklet includes full details of each of the first 27 discs.

Secular vocal music

Secular vocal music and part-songs: *Die Advocaten; An den Frühling; Andenken; Bardengesang; Bergknappenlied; Bootsgesang; Coronach; Die Entfernten; Dessen Fahne; Donnerstürme wallte; Das Dörfchen; Dreifach ist der Schritt der Zeit* (2 versions); *Ein jugendlicher Maienschwung; Eisiedelei; Erinnerungen; Ewige Liebe; Fischerlied; Flucht; Frisch atmet des Morgens lebendiger Hauch; Frühlingsgesang; Frühlingslied* (2 versions); *Geist der Liebe; Der Geistertanz; Gesang der Geister über den Wassern; Goldner Schein; Der Gondelfahrer; Gott in der Natur; Grab und Mond; Hier strecket; Hier unarmen sich getreue Gatten; Im Gegenwärtigen Vergangenes; Jünglingswonne; Klage um Ali Bey; Lacrimosa son io* (2 versions); *Leise, leise, lasst uns singen; Liebe; Liebe säusein die Blätter; Lied im Freien; Lutzows wilde Jagd; Mailied* (3 versions); *Majestät'sche Sonnenrose; Mirjams Siegesgesang; Mondenschein; Der Morgernstern; Die Nacht; Nachtgesang im Walde; Nachthelle; Die Nachtigall; Nachtmusik; Naturgenuss; Nur wer die Sehnsucht kennt; La pastorella al prato; Punschlied; Räuberlied; Ruhe, schönstes Glück der Erde; Schlachtegesang; Der Schnee zerrinnt; Selig durch die Liebe; Ständchen (Zögernd leise); Das stille Lied; Thronend auf erhab'nem Sitz; Totengräberlied; Trinklied* (4 versions); *Trinklied aus dem 16 (Jahrhundert); Trinklied im Mai; Trinklied im Winter; Unendliche Freude* (2 versions); *Vorüber die stöhnende Klage; Wehmut; Wein und Liebe; Wer die steile Sternenbalm; Widerhall; Widerspruch; Wilkommen, lieber schöner Mai; Zum Rundetanz; Zur guten Nacht; Die zwei Tugendwege.*

(M) *** EMI (ADD) CMS5 66139-2 (4). Behrens, Fassbaender, Schreier, Fischer-Dieskau, Capella Bavariae, Bav. R. Ch. & SO, Sawallisch.

Schubert's part-songs make up a sizeable proportion of his total output, and this outstanding four-disc collection, superbly performed and recorded with Sawallisch the most understanding guide, both as pianist and conductor, brings out many rare treasures. Many are jolly ballads to celebrate life's simple pleasures, like the opening 'Song in the open air'; others are more expressively eloquent, such as *Ruhe, schönstes Glück der Erde* ('Rest, greatest earthly blessing'), the joyous *Gott in der Natur*, and the evocative male-voice chorale, *Nachtmusik*. On the other hand, *Die Advocaten* is a light-hearted trio in which a pair of lawyers wonder whether their fees are going to be paid; their client, Mr Sempronius, then arrives to do so, if reluctantly, and they are all bewitched by the clink of coins. The longest item, *Miriam's Song of triumph, on a Biblical subject*, is almost a miniature oratorio. Two striking Psalm-settings and the *Hymn to the Holy Ghost* (with brass accompaniment) have been omitted from the original LP collection but are now included on Sawallisch's EMI set of Schubert's religious music. Another substantial piece to cherish here is the version of *The Song of the Spirits over the Waters* with eight-part chorus and strings, as well as the atmospheric *Nachtgesang im Walde*, with horns accompanying a male-voice ensemble. Not surprisingly, horns also provide a lively opening for the gleeful and much briefer *Lützows wilde Jagd*, which begins the fourth disc. The highly imaginative setting of *Wehmut*, which comes near the end of the collection, has a haunting tolling bell effect, achieved in the voices alone. The tiny songs designed for Schubert and his friends to sing together, many of them drinking songs, add to the delight of the collection. Highly recommended to any Schubertian eager for new discovery. The transfers to CD could hardly have been managed more naturally. However, this set has now been deleted.

Miscellaneous vocal recitals

Abendlied der Fürstin; An die Nachtigall; An die Sonne; Blanca (Das Mädchen); Du bist die Ruh; Ellens Gesang I, II & III; Gesang der Norna; Gretchen am Spinnrade; Im Freien; Der Hirt auf dem Felsen; Die junge Nonne; Klage der Ceres; Klaglied; Die Liebende schreibt; Lied de Anne Lyle; Lied der Mignon I, II & III; Das Mädchens Klage; Die Männer sind méchant; Mignons Gesang; Suleika I & II; Wiegenlied.

(B) *** DG Double (ADD) 453 082-2 (2). Janowitz, Gage.

This attractive DG Double is self-recommending. Many of the songs here are favourites, although there are some novelties. They come from a comprehensive survey of Lieder suitable for female voice, originally issued on five LPs and recorded in 1976–7. They receive persuasive handling from Janowitz and, with a voice so naturally beautiful and used with such musical intelligence, the results are consistently compelling, helped by the sympathetic, concentrated accompaniments of Irwin Gage. If *Gretchen am Spinnrade*, which comes near the beginning of the recital, is somewhat idiosyncratic in its speed variations, Janowitz makes it very much her own, and her *Die junge Nonne*, which opens the second CD, is similarly appealing. Perhaps the most ravishing singing comes in the *Wiegenlied* and *Du bist die ruh* and, most memorably of all, the first Suleika song (*Was bedeutet die Bewegung?*) with its gentle closing pianissimo as the singer reflects that the soft whisper of the wind suggests the breath of love. The recital ends with the famous *Shepherd on the rock* with its clarinet obbligato well played by Ulf Rodenhäuser, although it has been presented more seductively elsewhere. The recording is first rate and full translations are included.

Lieder: *Berthas Lied in der Nacht; Fischerweise; Der Fluss; Die Forelle; Die gefangenen Sanger; Gretchen vor der Mater dolorosa; Hagars Klage; Heimliches Lieben; Im Frühling; Iphigenia; Kolmas Klage; Der König in Thule; Lambertine; Liebe schwarmt auf allen Wegen; Lilla an die Morgenrote; Des Mädchens Kläge (2 versions); Die Rose; Schwestergruss; Szene der Delphine; Thekla, eine Geisterstimme; Vergissmeinnicht; Vom Mitleiden Marias; Wiegenlied.*

(B) *** DG Double (ADD) 453 139-2 (2). Janowitz, Gage.

This second collection from Janowitz and Gage, taken from their 1976–7 survey, starts with what is probably Schubert's first vocal work, written when he was fourteen, *Hagars Klage*. Many of the earlier items are extended works, complete scenas or songs of many stanzas. They require persuasive handling, and Janowitz is greatly helped by the sympathetic, concentrated accompaniments of Irwin Gage. With a voice so naturally beautiful, and used with such easy musical intelligence, the results are consistently compelling, whether in the rarities or the popular songs such as *Die Forelle*. The recording is first rate.

'A Schubert Evening': (i) *Abendstern; Am Grabe Anselmos; An die Nachtigall; An die untergehende Sonne'; Berthas Lied in der Nacht; Delphine; Ellen's Gesang* from *The Lady of the Lake (Raste Krieger; Jäger von der Jagd; Ave Maria); Epistel an Herrn Josef von Spaun; Gondelfahrer; Gretchen am Spinnrade; Hin und wieder; Iphigenia; Die junge Nonne; Kennst du das Land; Liebe schwärmt; Das Mädchen; Das Mädchens Klage; Die Männer sind méchant; Mignon Lieder I–III (Heiss mich nicht reden; So*

lasst mich scheinen; Nur wer die Sehnsucht kennt); Schlummerlied; Schwestergruss; Strophe von Schiller (Die Götter Griechenlands); Suleika songs I–II (Was bedeutet die Bewegung; Ach, um deine feuchten Schwingen); Wiegenlied; Wiegenlied (Schlafe, schlafe). 'Favourite Lieder': (ii) *An die Musik; An Sylvia; Auf dem Wasser zu singen; Du bist die Ruh'; Die Forelle; Frühlingslaube; Heidenröslein; Litanei; Der Musensohn; Nacht und Träume; Rastlose Lied; Der Tod und das Mädchen.*

⦿ (B) *** EMI fforte (ADD) CZS5 69389-2 (2). Baker, with (i) Moore; (ii) Parsons.

This very generous collection combines a pair of recitals recorded by Dame Janet at two different stages in her career, in 1970 and a decade later. The first collection ranges wide in an imaginative *Liederabend* of Schubert songs that includes a number of comparative rarities. They move from the delectably comic *Epistel* to the ominous darkness of *Die junge Nonne*. The two cradle songs are irresistible, the Seidl setting even more haunting than the more famous one; and throughout Baker consistently displays the breadth of her emotional mastery and her range of tone-colour. With Gerald Moore (who returned to the studio out of retirement especially for the occasion) still at his finest, this is a rarely satisfying collection. Only the opening *Gretchen am Spinnrade* brings a performance which one feels Baker could have intensified on repetition, but the rest could not be more treasurable. A very high proportion of favourite Schubert songs is included in the 1980 group. With a great singer treating each with loving, detailed care, the result is a charmer of a recital. The very first item, Dame Janet's strongly characterized reading of *Die Forelle*, makes it a fun song, and similarly Parsons' naughty, springing accompaniment to *An Sylvia* (echoed later by the singer) gives a twinkle to a song that can easily be treated too seriously. One also remembers the ravishing *subito piano* for the second stanza of *An die Musik*. The later recording is of fine EMI vintage and catches the more mature voice naturally and with rather more presence than a decade earlier. It is a pity that, because the set is so economically priced, there are no translations, but this remains an unmissable reissue.

Lieder: *Abendstern; An die Entfernte; Atys; Auflösung; Ganymed; Der Musensohn; Nähe des Geliebten.*

(B) (***) BBC (ADD) BBCB 8015-2. Pears, Britten – BRITTEN: *On this island;* WOLF: *7 Mörike Lieder* ***; (with ARNE: *Come Away death; Under the Greenwood Tree;* QUILTER: *O Mistress Mine;* WARLOCK: *Take, O Take Those Lips Away;* TIPPETT: *Come unto These Yellow Sands* (***)).

Britten as accompanist in Lieder regularly conveyed a sense of spontaneity and here – in a shrewdly chosen group of songs, not all well known – he seems almost to be improvising. The lightness and agility of his accompaniment in the best-known songs, *Der Musensohn*, is a marvel. Fine, sensitive singing from Pears in these 1969 performances.

Lieder: *Alinde; Am Tage aller Seelen; An die Entfernte; An die Laute; Auf dem Wasser zu singen; Auf der Riesenkoppe; Die Bürgschaft; Du bist die Ruh'; Der Fischer; Der Fischers Liebesglück; Fischerweise; Die Forelle; Die Götter*

Griechenlands; Greisengesang; Heidenröslein; Das Heimweh; Im Walde; Der Jüngling an der Quelle; Der Jüngling und der Tod; Lachen und Weinen; Lied des gefangenen Jägers; Das Lied im Grünen; Nachtgesang; Nachtstück; Nähe des Geliebten; Normans Gesang; Der Schiffer; Sei mir gegrüsst; Seligkeit; Das sie hier gewesen; Ständchen; Strophe aus Die Götter; Der Strom; Der Tod und das Mädchen; Der Wanderer; Der Winterabend; Das Zügenglöcklein; Der zürnende Barde.

(M) *** EMI (ADD) CMS7 63566-2 (2). Fischer-Dieskau, Moore; Engel.

Dating from 1965, most of the items in this collection of Schubert songs superbly represent the second generation of Fischer-Dieskau recordings with Gerald Moore, deeper and more perceptive than his mono recordings, yet with voice and manner still youthfully fresh. The contrast is fascinating, if subtle, between that main collection and the last nine songs on the second disc: they were recorded six years earlier, with three of them accompanied by Karl Engel, and with the voice still younger. However, this set is now withdrawn.

Lieder: *Die Allmacht; An die Natur; Auf dem See; Auflösung; Erlkönig; Ganymed; Gretchen am Spinnrade; Der Musensohn; Rastlose Liebe; Suleika I; Der Tod und das Mädchen; Der Zwerg.*

*** Ph. 412 623-2. Norman, Moll.

Jessye Norman's characterization of the four contrasting voices in *Erlkönig* is powerfully effective, with none of the reticence which marked her Lieder singing early in her recording career. The poignancy of *Gretchen am Spinnrade* is exquisitely touched in, building to a powerful climax; throughout, the breath control is a thing of wonder, not least in a surpassing account of *Ganymed*. Fine, sympathetic accompaniment from Philip Moll, and first-rate recording.

(i) *Am grabe Anselmos; An die Musik; An die Nachtigall; An Sylvia; Auf dem See; Auf dem Wasser zu singen; Dass sie hier gewesen; Die Forelle; Die junge Nonne; Du bist die Ruh'; Ganymed; Geheimes; Gretchen am Spinnrade; Heidenröslein; Lachen und Weinen; Der Musensohn; Rastlose Liebe; Sei mir gegrüsset; Seligkeit; Ständchen; Suleika I & II; Wiegenlied.* (ii) *Winterreise* (song-cycle), D.911.

(BB) **(*) Virgin Double VBD5 61457-2 (2). (i) Augér, Orkis (fortepiano); (ii) Allen, Vignoles (piano).

This Virgin Double joins up Arleen Augér's collection of favourite Lieder with Thomas Allen's *Winterreise*, dating from 1991 and 1994 respectively. The distinctive point about Arleen Augér's collection of Schubert songs – which includes a high proportion of favourites – is that the accompaniment is played by Lambert Orkis on a fortepiano. Though Augér's voice is caught most beautifully, with the tone consistently sweet and pure, the scale of the accompaniment intensifies a lightweight feeling, with beauty of tone given higher priority than word-meaning.

On the second disc Thomas Allen, understandingly supported by Roger Vignoles, tackles this Everest of the Lieder repertory with a beauty of tone and line that sets his reading apart. Allen's concentration on purely musical qualities, far from watering down word-meaning, is used to intensify the tragic emotions of the wandering lover. Allen uses a wider dynamic range than most of his direct rivals, shading the voice down to a half-tone for intimate revelations, then expanding dramatically, using the art of the opera-singer. In the two final songs, *Die Nebensonnen* and *Der Leiermann*, he is very restrained, keeping them hushed instead of underlining expressiveness. The poignancy of Schubert's inspiration is allowed to speak for itself. The one serious reservation here is the lack of translations.

Lieder, Vol. 1: *An den Mond; An die Musik; Auf dem Wasser zu singen; Du bist die Ruh; Erlkönig; Erster Verlust; Der Fischer; Fischerweise; Die Forelle; Ganymed; Frühlingsglaube; Heidenröslein; Im Frühling; Im Haine; Litanei auf das Fest Allerseelen; Der Musensohn; Nacht und Träume; Seligkeit; An Silvia; Wandrers Nachtlied I & II; Der Zwerg.*

*** EMI CDC5 56347-2. Bostridge, Drake.

Few discs of favourite Schubert songs match this for sheer beauty. As in his prizewinning recording of *Die schöne Mullerin* for Hyperion, Ian Bostridge here not only sings with ravishing tenor tone but, with German words heightened, offers fresh revelation in even the best-known songs. So, with Julius Drake matching him in insight, *Die Forelle* ('The Trout'), opens the sequence in youthful eagerness, light and brisk, and lightness is also the keynote in such songs as *Heidenroslein*. The contrast is all the keener when in darker songs such as *Wandrers Nachtlied*, Bostridge sings with such rapt intensity, the legato lines perfectly sustained on a mere thread of sound.

Lieder, Vol. II: Goethe Lieder: *Am Flüsse; An die Entfernte; Geheimes; Schäfers Klagelied; Versunken; Wilkommen und Abschied; Maryrehoderlieder: Abendstern; Auf der Donau; Auflösung; Lied eines Schiffers; Nachtstuck; Lieder: Die Götter Griechenlands; An die Leier; Am See; Alinde; Wehmut; Uber Wildemann; Auf der Riesenkoppe; Sei mir gegrüsst; Dass sie hier gewesen; Geistertanz.*

(N) *** EMI CDC5 57141-2. Bostridge, Drake

This second volume of Schubert songs from Ian Bostridge and Julius Drake on EMI is divided neatly between songs to poems by Goethe and Mayrehoder, and miscellaneous songs, some of them favourites like *Die Götter Griechenlands* and *An die Leier*, but many less well known. In this wide-ranging selection Bostridge reveals his expanding mastery in the widest variety of expression, with the subtlest range of tone, and with a deliberate hardening of the characteristically sweet voice in some of the more dramatic songs, effectively so when the sense of strain adds to the intensity. In all this Drake is the perfect partner, ranging wide in his tonal palette too. Natural, beautifully balanced sound.

Goethe Lieder: *An den Mond; An die Türen; An Mignon; Auf dem See; Erster verlust; Erlkönig; Der Fischer; Ganymed; Heidenröslein; Meeres Stille; Der Musensohn; Nachtgesang; Nahe des Gelibten; Prometheus; Rastlose Liebe; Schäfers Klaglied; Schwager Kronos; Versunken;*

Wandrers Nachtlied; Wer nie sein Brot mit Tränen ass; Wer sich der Einsamkeit ergibt.

*** Decca 452 917-2. Goerne, Haefliger.

Matthias Goerne here confirms his mastery as a Lieder-singer, already revealed in his account of *Winterreise* and other Schubert songs in Graham Johnson's collected edition on Hyperion. With Andreas Haefliger a deeply under-standing accompanist – challenging as well as matching his partner – Goerne here tackles a beautiful sequence of Goethe settings, thrillingly powerful in *Prometheus*, youthfully exuberant in such a favourite as *Der Musensohn*, finding a rapt gravity rare in a young singer in such visionary songs as *Meeres Stille*. Even the understatement of his *Erlkönig* brings bonuses in extra beauty. Outstanding in every way.

Goethe Lieder:(i) *An den Mond; An schwager Kronos; Auf dem See; Erster Verlust; Ganymed; Gesänge des Harfners: Harfenspieler I, II, & III Jägers Abendlied; Meeres Stille; Der Musensohn; Prometheus; Wandrers Nachtlied I & II.* (ii) *Am Flusse; Erlkönig; Geheimes; Grenzen des Menschheit; Heidenröslein; Der König in Thule; Nähe des Geliebten; Rastlose Liebe; Wilkommen und Abscheid.*

(M) *** DG (ADD) 457 747-2. Fischer-Dieskau; (i) Demus; (ii) Moore.

This reissued collection draws on three sets of recordings: Fischer-Dieskau's first stereo DG Goethe LP, recorded with Demus in 1960, and two subsequent groups with Gerald Moore dating from a decade later. Some of the very finest Goethe settings are here and Fischer-Dieskau is on top of his form, but the partnership with Demus is less than ideal. He proves a capable but not highly imaginative accompanist, although his artistry is not to be denied. But as for the singing, the spectrum of emotion takes on a new glow as each song begins. The two settings of *Wandrers Nachtlied* are particularly fine, as are the joyous *Der Musensohn* and the fiery *An schwager Kronos*. Needless to say the partnership with Gerald Moore is much more of a symbiosis, and these later performances are outstanding in every way. The recording too, is warmer and has a more pleasing ambience. A treasurable disc, just the same, well worthy of DG's Originals.

Lieder: *An den Mond* (2 versions); *Der Einsame; Erlkönig; Der Fischer; Ganymed; Im Abendrot; Die junge Nonne; Der Musensohn; Nachtstück; Nacht und Träume; Nachtviolen; Rastlose Liebe; Schäfers Klagelied; Die Sterne; Suleika I & II; Wandrers Nachtlied; Der Zwerg.*

(N)(M) *** CRD 3464. Walker, Vignoles.

Sarah Walker's début Lieder recital was made not long before she joined Graham Johnson for her contribution to Hyperion's Schubert Lieder Edition. Only *An den Mond* and *Erlkönig* are duplicated, and the CRD recital includes many favourites. Here she is accompanied by Roger Vignoles on a period piano of 1864. The attractive selection of songs, with many favourites, consistently draws warm, easily confident singing from her, full of charm, yet she is dramatic when required as in *Erlkönig*. There she is not helped by the balance with the piano, which slightly favours the accom-panist, masking the full intensity of her characterization,

with power kept in reserve until the end. That contrasts beautifully with her easy-going lightness in such a song as *Der Einsame* and the poise of *Nacht und Träume*, with phrases sustained on a mere thread of sound. Despite the balance, words are clear thanks to the singer's fine diction and feeling for word-meaning. Roger Vignoles accompanies persuasively, full translations are included, and the playing-time is generous too: 74 minutes.

Goethe Lieder, Vol. 1: *An den Mond* (1st and 2nd versions); *An schwager Kronos; Bundeslied; Der Fischer; Ganymed; Geistes-Gruss; Gesang des Harfners* (1st, 2nd, and 3rd versions); *Der Gott und die Bajadere; Grenzen der Menschheit; Harfenspieler* (1st and 2nd versions); *Heidenröslein; Der König in Thule; Mahomets Gesang; Meeres Stille; Prometheus; Der Rattenfänger; Der Schatzgräber; Wandrers Nachtlied* (1st and 2nd versions).

(BB) *** Naxos 8.554665. Bästlein, Laux.

This fine Goethe collection is one of the first of a proposed series of Schubert Lieder discs masterminded for Naxos by the pianists Stefan Laux and Ulrich Eisenlohr. They aim to choose only German-speaking singers from the younger generation, and Ulf Bästlein certainly qualifies. His is a firm, warm baritone which he uses most sensitively, shading tone and dynamic with fine feeling for words, as in his rapt account of *Meeres Stille*, 'Becalmed'. Though the selection includes the popular favourite *Heidenröslein*, and such mas-terly songs as *An den Mond* (both settings) and *Ganymed*, the choice is imaginative, and it is good to have such multiple settings of the same words, sensitively contrasted by singer and pianist. Unlike many bargain discs of Lieder, this offers full texts and translations.

Lieder: *An die Entfernte; Auf dem Wasser zu singen; Du bist die Ruh'; Der Erlkönig; Die Forelle; Heidenröslein; Das Heimweh; Der Jüngling an der Quelle; Der Jüngling und der Tod; Das Lied im Grünen; Litanei auf das Fest Allerseelen; Nachtgesang; Der Schiffer; Sei mir gegrüsst!; Ständchen; Der Strom; Der Tod und das Mädchen; Der Wanderer; Der Winterabend; Das Zügenglöcklein; Der zürnende Barde.*

(N) (BB) *** EMI Encore (ADD) CDE5 74754-2. Fischer-Dieskau, Moore.

EMI's Encore collection of vintage Fischer-Dieskau record-ings makes an ideal sampler of favourite Schubert songs. Early in his career the voice was at its freshest and most beautiful and, though the comparatively early stereo recording is less atmospheric than on later issues, there is a face-to-face immediacy which with such an artist could not be more revealing. With Gerald Moore at the piano this is a supreme bargain among Schubert Lieder recitals.

Lieder: (i) *An die Freunde; Auf der Donau; Aus Heliopolis; Fischerweise; Freiwilliges Versinken; Gruppe aus dem Tartarus;* (ii) *Der Hirt auf dem Felsen;* (i) *Prometheus; Der Strom; Der Wanderer; Der Wanderer an den Mond.*

(B) *** BBC (ADD) BBCB 8011-2. (i) Fischer-Dieskau; (ii) Harper, King; Britten – WOLF: *3 Christmas Songs; 3 Michelangelo Lieder.* ***

Fischer-Dieskau has rarely if ever been more inspired in his recordings of Schubert than here, in live performances given with Britten at the Snape Maltings in 1972 – the last year Britten was able to take an active part in the Aldeburgh Festival. The great baritone, then at his peak, was plainly inspired by the inspirational quality of his accompanist's playing, and the selection of songs, well contrasted, brings together an attractive mixture of rare and well known. Similarly, in the *Shepherd on the Rock*, with Thea King producing honeyed tone in the clarinet obbligato, the magnetism is irresistible. The Wolf songs from Pears and Shirley-Quirk make an attractive bonus.

Lieder: *An die Laute; An die Leier; An die Musik; An Silvia; Auf der Bruck; Du bist die Ruh'; Erlkönig; Das Fischermädchen; Die Forelle; Ganymed; Gruppe aus dem Tartarus; Heidenröslein; Lachen und Weinen; Litanei auf das Fest; Meeres Stille; Der Musensohn; Rastlose Liebe; Schäfers Klagelied; Ständchen; Die Taubenpost; Der Tod und das Mädchen; Der Wanderer; Wandrers Nachtlied.*

*** DG 445 294-2. Terfel, Martineau.

Bryn Terfel's DG disc of Schubert was one of his first recordings to confirms his exceptional gift of projecting his magnetic personality with keen intensity, in Lieder, not just in opera. Terfel emerges as a positive artist, giving strikingly individual and imaginative readings of these 23 favourite songs. As you immediately realize in three favourite songs common to both collections, *Heidenröslein, An Silvia* and *Du bist die Ruh*, Terfel is daring in confronting you face to face, very much as the young Fischer-Dieskau did, using the widest range of dynamic and tone. You might argue that Terfel's characterization of the different characters in *Erlkönig* is too extreme, but it is a measure of his magnetism that the result is so dramatically compelling. Full, firm sound.

An die Laute; An die Musik; An Silvia; Der Einsame; Im Abendrot; Liebhaber in allen Gestalten; Lied eines Schiffers an die Dioskurern; Der Musensohn; Ständchen (Leise flehen meine Lieder).

(M) *** DG (ADD) 449 747-2. Wunderlich, Giesen –
BEETHOVEN: *Lieder;* SCHUMANN: *Dichterliebe.* ***

Few tenors have matched the young Wunderlich in the freshness and golden bloom of the voice. The open manner could not be more appealing here in glowing performances, well coupled with other fine examples of this sadly short-lived artist's work. A very apt addition to DG's series of 'Legendary Performances'.

Lieder: *An die Musik; An Sylvia; Auf dem Wasser zu singen; Ave Maria; Du bist die Ruh'; Die Forelle; Ganymed; Gretchen am Spinnrade; Heidenröslein; Im Frühling; Die junge Nonne; Litanei; Mignon und der Harfner; Der Musensohn; Nacht und Träume; Sei mir gegrüsst; Seligkeit.*

(N)(M) *** Regis RRC 1052. Lott, Johnson.

At mid-price, Felicity Lott's collection brings an ideal choice of songs for the general collector. With Graham Johnson the most imaginative accompanist, even the best-known songs emerge fresh and new, and gentle songs like *Litanei* are raptly beautiful.

Lieder: (i) *An die Musik; An Sylvia; Auf dem Wasser zu singen; Ganymed; Gretchen am Spinnrade; Im Frühling; Die junge Nonne; Das Lied im Grünen; Der Musensohn; Nachtviolen; Nähe des Geliebten; Wehmut. 6 Moments musicaux, D.780.*

(M) (***) EMI mono CDH5 67494-2. (i) Schwarzkopf, Fischer.

Elisabeth Schwarzkopf at the beginning of her recording career and Edwin Fischer at the end of his make a magical partnership, with even the simplest of songs inspiring intensely subtle expression from singer and pianist alike. Though Fischer's playing is not immaculate, he left few records more endearing than this, and Schwarzkopf's colouring of word and tone is masterly. So are his performances of the *Moments musicaux*.

Choral songs: *An die Sonne; Gebe; Gesang der Geister über den Wassern; Gondelfahrer; Gott in der Naur; Mondenschein; Nachtgesang im Walde; Nachthelle; Die 23 Psalm; Sehnsucht; Ständchen; Des Tages Weihe.*

*** Ph. Monteverdi Ch., Gardiner.

In a wide-ranging and illuminating choice of choral songs from deeply philosophical to trivial, Gardiner and his Monteverdi Choir offer performances at once immaculate and intense, using the widest range of tone and dynamic. Period accompaniments on the fortepiano from Malcolm Bilson, with a fine quintet of horns accompanying *Nachtgesang im Walde* and with accompaniment for lower strings in the longest item, *Gesang der Geister uber den Wassern*. Refined recording to match.

(i; ii) Duets: *Antigone und Oedip; Cronnan; Hektors Abschied; Hermann und Thusnelda; Licht und Liebe (Nachtgesang); Mignon und der Harfner; Selma und Selmar; Sing-Ubungen;* (vi) *Szene aus Goethes Faust.* (ii; iii; iv; v) Trios: *Die Advokaten; Gütigster, Bester, Weisester; Die Hochzeitsbraten; Kantata zum Geburtstag des Sängers Johann Michael Vogl; Punschlied; Trinklied; Verschwunden sind die Schmerzen (a cappella).* (i–iv) Quartets: *An die Sonne; Gebet; Die Geselligkeit (Lebenslust); Gott der Weltschöpfer; Gott im Ungewitter; Hymne an den Undenlichen; Nun lasst uns den Leib begraben (Begräbnislied); Des Tages Weihe; Der Tanz.*

(M) *** DG (IMS) (ADD) 435 596-2 (2). (i) Baker;
(ii) Fischer-Dieskau; (iii) Ameling; (iv) Schreier;
(v) Laubenthal; Moore; (vi) with Berlin RIAS Chamber Ch.

Not all these duets are vintage Schubert – some of the narrative pieces go on too long – but the artistry of Baker and Fischer-Dieskau makes for magical results. Gerald Moore, who is at his finest throughout the set, relishes the magic too. The trios are domestic music in the best sense. Specially delightful are the two contrasted drinking songs, but *The wedding feast (Die Hochzeitsbraten)* is even more remarkable, a 10-minute scena in the style of *opera buffa*. The quartets, like the trios, were written for various domestic occasions, but the use of four voices seems to have led the composer regularly to serious or religious subjects. These are sweet and gentle rather than intense inspirations, but one could hardly ask for more polished and inspired performances than these. Fine recording from 1973/4, giving the singers a vivid presence on CD.

Lieder: *Auf dem Wasser zu singen; Ave Maria; Die Forelle; Du bist die Ruh; Ganymed; Gretchen am Spinnrade; Gretchens Bitte; Heidenröslein; Heiss mich nicht reden; (i) Der Hirt auf dem Felsen; Im Abendrot; Kennst du das Land; Liebhaber in allen Gestalten; Nahe des Geliebten; Nur wer die Sehnsucht kennt; So lasst mich scheinen; Ständchen.*

*** Teldec 4509 90873-2. Bonney, Parsons; (i) with Kam.

Barbara Bonney here is at her freshest, and who better to accompany her than Geoffrey Parsons? The generous programme (well over an hour) includes many firm favourites, and Bonney not only sings with much beauty of tone and a flowing Schubertian line but with keen concern for word-meanings. Songs like *Die Forelle, Auf dem Wasser zu singen* and the lovely *So lasst mich scheinen* sound especially fresh; and it is always good to have 'The shepherd on the rock' (*Der Hirt auf dem Felsen*) with its fluid obbligato clarinet (here the persuasive Sharon Kam). Spontaneous-sounding expressiveness in a natural partnership between fine artists.

Auf der Riesenkoppe; Der blinde Knabe; Du bist die Ruh'; Die Forelle; Das Geheimnis; Gretchen am Spinnrade; Heidenröslein; (i) Der Hirt auf dem Felsen; Der König in Thule; La pastorella; Schwanengesang; Die Wehmut.

(B) **(*) CfP (ADD) CD-CFP 6040. Price, James Lockhart; (i) with Brymer.

Dame Margaret Price was in fine voice when she made this record in 1971. Her singing of Schubert is full-throated in style, although she successfully fines down the tone for a song like *Du bist die Ruh*. The opening recitative of *Auf der Riesenkoppe* takes us straight into the opera house; *La pastorella* (a charming song) reminds us of Rossini, and in *The Shepherd on the rock* the sheer breadth of the singing tends to dwarf even Jack Brymer's beguiling clarinet obbligato. *Die Forelle* is very attractively done, and *Der König in Thule* is serenely beautiful. *Heidenröslein* has a simple, affecting charm and in *Gretchen am Spinnrade* the soaring line is sensitively controlled, but Price's involvement is obvious. James Lockhart accompanies most sensitively but, maybe because of the recording balance, like Brymer he tends to be dwarfed by the voice. No translations are provided, but the notes give a synopsis of each song. Short measure, but anyway this is now deleted.

Italian songs: *Da quel sembiante appresi; Guarda, che bianca luna; Io vuo'cantar di Cadmo; Mi batte'l cor!; Mio ben ricordati; Non t'accostar all'urna; La pastorella; Pensa, che questo istante; Se dall'Etra; Vedi quanto adoro ancora ingrato!.*

*** Decca 440 297-2. Bartoli, Schiff – BEETHOVEN: *Che fa il mio bene?* etc.; HAYDN: *Arianna a Naxos;* MOZART: *Ridente la calma.* ***

Bartoli is at her finest here in *Dido's lament*, but the other rare songs are also fresh and enjoyable, helped by sensitive accompaniments from András Schiff.

Song-cycles

Die schöne Müllerin (song-cycle), *D.795* (see also above, under Graham Johnson Schubert Lieder Edition, Vol. 25).

*** DG (ADD) 415 186-2. Dietrich Fischer-Dieskau, Moore.

*** Cap. 10 082. Protschka, Deutsch.

(M) *** CfP CD-CFP 4672. Ian and Jennifer Partridge.

Die schöne Müllerin (complete); *Die Forelle; Frühlingsglaube; Heidenröslein.*

(M) ** DG 447 452-2. Fritz Wunderlich, Hubert Geisen.

Fischer-Dieskau's classic 1972 version on DG remains among the very finest ever recorded, combining as it does his developed sense of drama and story-telling, his mature feeling for detail and yet spontaneity too, helped by the searching accompaniment of Gerald Moore. It is a performance with premonitions of *Winterreise*.

Josef Protschka gives an intensely virile, almost operatic reading, which is made the more youthful-sounding in the original keys for high voice. As recorded, the voice, often beautiful with heroic timbres, sometimes acquires a hint of stridency, but the positive power and individuality of the performance make it consistently compelling, with all the anguish behind these songs caught intensely. The timbre of the Bösendorfer piano adds to the performance's distinctiveness, well if rather reverberantly recorded.

Fritz Wunderlich had one of the most headily beautiful voices among German tenors and that alone makes his record cherishable. But when he recorded the cycle (and the three favourite songs which are also included here), he had still to develop as a Lieder singer, and for so subtle a cycle the performance lacks detail. He was not helped either by a rather unimaginative accompanist, and the recording is unflattering to the piano.

Die schöne Müllerin, D.795 (with spoken Prologue & Epilogue), D.795.

(M) *(**) EMI CDM5 66907-2 [CDM5 66959]. Fischer-Dieskau, Moore.

EMI have understandably chosen Fischer-Dieskau's 1961 recording of *Die schöne Müllerin* (which includes spoken versions in German of the *Prologue* and *Epilogue*) for their 'Great Recordings of the Century' series. But alas all their current remastering skill has not been able to improve the sound: the voice remains unpleasingly edgy. The later DG recording (also with Gerald Moore) remains far preferable.

Die schöne Müllerin; An die Musik; Du bist die Ruh; Erlkönig; Heidenröslein; Der Musensohn.

⊙ (M) *** DG (ADD) 453 676-2. Fischer-Dieskau, Moore.

Though Fischer-Dieskau had made several earlier recordings, this is no mere repeat of previous triumphs, now combining his developed sense of drama and story-telling, his mature feeling for detail and yet spontaneity too, helped by the searching accompaniment of Gerald Moore. It is a performance with premonitions of *Winterreise*. With extra

Lieder added to fill out the recital, this is one of the most cherishable of Fischer-Dieskau's many superb Schubert CDs.

Song-cycles: *Die schöne Müllerin, D.795; Schwanengesang, D.957; Winterreise, D.911.* **Lieder:** *Du bist die Ruh'; Erlkönig; Nacht und Träume.*

(M) (***) EMI mono CMS7 63559-2 (3). Fischer-Dieskau, Moore.

Fischer-Dieskau's early mono versions may not match his later recordings in depth of insight, but already the young singer was a searching interpreter of these supreme cycles. Gerald Moore was, as ever, the most sympathetic partner.

Song-cycles: (i) *Die schöne Müllerin, D.795* (with spoken *Prologue* and *Epilogue*); *Schwanengesang, D.957; Winterreise, D.911.* (ii) *Einsamkeit, D.620.*

(M) **(*) EMI (ADD) CMS5 66146-2 (3). Fischer-Dieskau, (i) Moore; (ii) Engel.

Fischer-Dieskau's EMI recordings of the three song-cycles were made in 1961–2, around the time of the great baritone's fortieth birthday, and they represent the second wave of his Schubert interpretations. He was to re-record them, again with Gerald Moore, for DG with even greater thought and refinement, but the direct power of expression here is superb, too. For *Die schöne Müllerin*, he also included spoken versions of the *Prologue* and *Epilogue* (taken from the songs in Wilhelm Müller's cycle) which Schubert did not set. The snag is that in the case of *Die schöne Müllerin* the 1985 digital remastering has caused the voice to sound edgy, although the other cycles, transferred later, are altogether smoother.

As an added bonus, following after *Schwanengesang*, we are offered a rarity: Schubert's 1818 setting of Johann Mayrhofer's poem in twelve stanzas, *Einsamkeit* ('Solitude'). At nearly 19 minutes, this is almost a mini-cycle in itself. Moving on from its thoughtful opening, Fischer-Dieskau follows the poet's mood-changes dramatically and with characteristic sensitivity, and the listener is thoroughly involved. The sound is excellent, and it is a pity that for this reissue EMI did not cue the individual verses. However, full translations are included. But this set is now deleted.

Song-cycles: *Die schöne Müllerin; Schwanengesang* (with also: *Im Freien; Der Wanderer an den Mond; Das Zügenglöcklein); Winterreise.* **Lieder:** *Alinde; An den Monde; An die Leier; An die Laute; An die Musik; An Silvia; Dass sie hier gewesen; Der Einsame; Die Forelle; Frühlingsglaube; Im Frühling; Der Schiffer; Schwanengesang; Sei mir gegrüsset.* **Goethe Lieder:** *Ganymed; Geheimes; Heidenröslein; Liebhaber in allen Gestalten; Der Musensohn; Rastlose Liebe; Wandrers Nachtlied.*

(M) *** EMI (ADD) CMS5 66145-2 (4). Bär, Parsons.

Die schöne Müllerin was the first of the cycles which Olaf Bär recorded, in 1986 in Dresden, with the voice fresher and more velvety than later, especially when the digital recording is so flattering to Bär's warmly beautiful lyrical flow. In *Winterreise*, recorded two years later, again with Geoffrey Parsons a masterful accompanist, Bär again finds a winning

beauty of line and tone in singing both deeply reflective and strongly dramatic, if without quite the power of Fischer-Dieskau's poetic projection or the sheer intensity of Britten and Pears (see below). The third disc, recorded in 1989, amplifies the collection of late songs, posthumously published as *Schwanengesang*, with three well-chosen extra items from the same period. The singing throughout is characteristically sensitive and dramatic, with *Ständchen* strong and passionate rather than light and charming. The fourth disc offers 21 miscellaneous songs, most of them favourites, including 7 Goethe settings. Recorded in 1991–2, they show the voice grittier than earlier, but still searchingly expressive, with Geoffrey Parsons again the most understanding accompanist. However, this set too is now deleted.

Schwanengesang – see also under Lieder Edition Vol. 37

Schwanengesang, D.957.

(N) *** Amphion/Priory (ADD) PHI CD157. Hemsley, Wilde.

Schwanengesang, D.957; Lieder: Am Bach in Frühling; An die Musik; Geheimes; Gruppe aus dem Tartarus; Im Abendrot; Im Frühling; Meeresstille; Sei mir gegrüsst; Wandrers Nachtlied I & II.

(M) (***) EMI mono CDH5 65196-2. Hotter, Moore.

(i) *Schwanengesang, D.957;* (ii) **Lieder:** *An die Laute; An die Musik; An Silvia; Auflösung; Der Einsame; Fischerweise; Die Forelle; Der Schiffer; Der Wanderer an den Mond; Wandrers Nachtlied.*

(BB) *** ASV (ADD) CDQS 6171. (i) Shirley-Quirk, Bedford; (ii) Ian Partridge, Jennifer Partridge.

Schwanengesang. Am Fenster; Bei dir allein; Herbst; Der Wanderer an den Mond.

*** Decca 425 612-2. Schreier, Schiff.

Schwanengesang; 5 Lieder: Am Fenster; Herbst; Sehnsucht; Der Wanderer an den Mond; Wiegenlied, D.867.

⚫ *** DG 429 766-2. Fassbaender, Reimann.

Schwanengesang, D.957. **Lieder:** (i) *Auf dem Strom. Herbst; Lebensmut.*

(BB) ** Naxos 8.554663. Volle, Eisenlohr; (i) with Scott.

Schwanengesang, D.957; Lieder: Du bist die Ruh; Erlkönig; Nacht und Träume; Ständchen.

(N) (M) (***) EMI mono CDM5 67588-2 [567559]. Fischer-Dieskau, Moore.

Brigitte Fassbaender gives a totally distinctive and compelling account of *Schwanengesang*, proving stronger and more forceful than almost any rival. She turns what was originally a relatively random group of late songs into a genuine cycle, by presenting them in a carefully rearranged order and adding five other late songs. Her magnetic power of compelling attention is intensified by the equally positive accompaniment of Aribert Reimann. The celebrated Schubert *Serenade* to words by Rellstab is far more than just a pretty tune, rather a passionate declaration of love; and Fassbaender builds her climax to the cycle round the final Heine settings, heightening their dramatic impact.

As in his darkly searching account of *Winterreise*, also recorded in mono with Gerald Moore in the 1950s, this

Schubert collection coupling *Schwanengesang* with other favourite songs reveals Hotter at his peak. The voice as recorded may not always be beautiful, but the gravity and intensity of the singing reveal a master Lieder-singer, as commanding here as in his Wagner interpretations.

It is curious that EMI have selected the early Fischer-Dieskau Schubert collection for inclusion in their 'Great Recordings of the Century'. Although the voice showed a ravishing lyrical beauty in the 1950s (especially striking in the famous *Ständchen*, of which two versions are included) and the artistry is not in doubt, the great baritone was to re-record most of these songs with even greater insight. *Erlkönig*, for instance, almost goes over the top in its bold dramatisation. However, the closing *Nacht und Träume* and *Du bist die Ruh* (from 1951) are melting in their simple melodic flow, and throughout Gerald Moore's accompaniments are an artistic bedrock. The mono recording is most naturally transferred.

Schreier's voice may no longer be beautiful under pressure, but the bloom on this Decca recording and the range of tone and the intensity of inflexion over word-meaning make this one of the most compelling recordings ever of *Schwanengesang*. Enhancing that are the discreet but highly individual and responsive accompaniments of András Schiff. Schreier includes not just the 14 late songs published together as *Schwanengesang*, but four more, also from the last three years of Schubert's life. The recording is vividly real.

The ASV reissue happily combines Schubert interpretations from two fine British artists, John Shirley-Quirk and Ian Partridge, recorded in the late 1970s. John Shirley-Quirk's special success is in creating a feeling of unity over the whole group. Steuart Bedford provides equally imaginative accompaniments and Ian Partridge then takes over for a well-chosen group of ten of the composer's most popular songs, and the fresh lyrical flow of his tenor voice gives much pleasure. The intelligence of the interpretations complements the tonal beauty of the voice, with Jennifer Partridge a sensitive accompanist. The one drawback to this otherwise enjoyably generous (77-minute) collection is the absence of texts with translations – but they *are* available on request and without charge by writing to ASV.

Thomas Hemsley spent much of his career in opera houses in Germany and made few commercial Lieder records. This *Schwanengesang* from 1976 derives from live performances with David Wilde and serves as a welcome reminder of the artistry of this master singer.

In Naxos's enterprising Schubert Lieder Edition, Michael Volle adds three settings of poems by Ludwig Rellstab to the seven which come in the late collection of songs, *Schwanengesang*. It is an imaginative bonus, when they include the extended song with horn obbligato, *Auf dem Strom*, 'On the River'. Volle is as yet a rather cautious Lieder singer, not always avoiding the squareness that can overtake strophic songs, and he seems unable to convey a smile in his voice, with the tone growing plaintive at the top. Yet with his clear diction, this is still a disc worth hearing and, as in the rest of the series, full words and translations are provided.

Winterreise (song cycle), *D.911.*

*** DG 415 187-2. Fischer-Dieskau, Moore.

*** Ph. 464 739-2. Fischer-Dieskau, Brendel.

(M) *** DG 447 421-2. Dietrich Fischer-Dieskau, Joerg Demus.

◉ (M) *** Decca (ADD) 466 382-2. Pears, Britten.

(B) *** DG Classikon (ADD) 439 432-2. Fischer-Dieskau, Barenboim.

*** Hyp. CDJ 33030. Goerne, Johnson.

**(*) Decca (IMS) 436 122-2. Schreier, Schiff.

*** EMI CDC7 49846-2. Fassbaender, Reimann.

(M) (***) EMI mono CDM5 66985-2 [567000]. Hotter, Moore.

(M) **(*) DG 453 987-2. Schmidt, Jansen.

** EMI CDC5 56445-2. Hampson, Sawallisch.

(BB) ** Naxos 8.554471. Trekel, Eisenlohr.

In the early 1970s Dietrich Fischer-Dieskau's voice was still at its freshest, yet the singer had deepened and intensified his understanding of this greatest of song-cycles to a degree where his finely detailed and thoughtful interpretation sounded totally spontaneous, and this DG version is now freshened on CD. However on Philips, the collaboration of Fischer-Dieskau with one of today's great Schubert pianists, Alfred Brendel, brings endless illumination in the interplay and challenge between singer and pianist, magnetic from first to last. With incidental flaws, this may not be the definitive Fischer-Dieskau reading, but in many ways it is the deepest and most moving he has ever given. This has been re-issued as one of Philips's '50 Great Recordings' at mid-price.

There are those who regard Fischer-Dieskau's third recording of *Winterreise* as the finest of all, such is the peak of beauty and tonal expressiveness that the voice had achieved in the mid-1960s, and the poetic restraint of Demus' accompaniment. The recording still sounds well, and as a mid-price reissue in DG's Legendary Recordings series it certainly makes an excellent alternative recommendation.

What is so striking about the Pears performance is its intensity. One continually has the sense of a live occasion and, next to it, even Fischer-Dieskau's beautifully wrought singing sounds too easy. As for Britten, he re-creates the music, sometimes with a fair freedom from Schubert's markings, but always with scrupulous concern for the overall musical shaping and sense of atmosphere. The sprung rhythm of *Gefror'ne Tränen* is magical in creating the impression of frozen teardrops falling, and almost every song brings similar magic. The recording and the CD transfer are exceptionally successful in bringing a sense of presence and realism, and this is certainly a proper candidate for reissue on Decca's Legends label.

Fischer-Dieskau's fifth recording of Schubert's greatest cycle, made in 1979, has now appeared on DG's Classikon bargain label, with the voice still in superb condition. Prompted by Barenboim's spontaneous-sounding, almost improvisatory accompaniments, it is highly inspirational. In expression this is freer than the earlier versions, and though some idiosyncratic details will not please everyone the sense of concentrated development is irresistible. The recording is very natural and beautifully balanced, and full translations are included.

Matthias Goerne's outstanding performance is discussed above as Volume 30 of Graham Johnson's Schubert Lieder

Edition and is among the most magnetically perceptive of recent versions.

As in *Die schöne Müllerin* and *Schwanengesang*, the partnership of Schreier and Schiff brings much new revelation, with the pianist as individual in his imagination as the singer, rather as Britten is with Pears. Schreier's voice is not always perfectly steady, but the focus is clean, and only occasionally is there a roughening of tone, and that to intensify the drama. With Schreier's facial expression instantly apparent, this is an intensely involving reading, with changes of mood vividly conveyed, positive, electrifying, often confidential, though the full, immediate recording does not help pianissimos.

Brigitte Fassbaender gives a fresh, boyishly eager reading of *Winterreise*, marked by a vivid and wide range of expression; she demonstrates triumphantly why a woman's voice can bring special illumination to this cycle, sympathetically underlining the drama behind the tragic poet's journey rather than the more meditative qualities. Reimann, at times a wilful accompanist, is nevertheless spontaneous-sounding like the singer. However, this has been deleted.

Hans Hotter's 1954 mono recording of *Winterreise* has been reissued as one of EMI's 'Great recordings of the century'. It brings an exceptionally dark, even sepulchral performance, lightened by the imagination of Gerald Moore's accompaniment. Hotter scales down his great Wagnerian baritone so that only occasionally is the tone gritty. His concern for detail brings many moments of illumination, but the lack of animation makes this an unrelievedly depressing view.

Andreas Schmidt with Rudolf Jansen offers a beautifully sung, thoughtfully presented version of the greatest and most demanding of all song-cycles. With forwardly balanced sound on this 1990 digital recording, words are strikingly clear, enhancing Schmidt's use of dramatic contrast, with the voice, generally smooth and even, acquiring the necessary bite at climaxes. Everything is perfectly controlled, almost too much so: it means that the poignant dénouement at the end, conveying even greater tragedy than on the surface it seems, is to a degree underplayed, leaving one dry-eyed.

Though Thomas Hampson produces a stream of distinctively velvety tone, his account of this challenging song-cycle is too easy and undetailed, even bland, with Wolfgang Sawallisch uncharacteristically square and unimaginative in his playing. The experience is observed in detachment, where above all it should be involving.

Roman Trekel's baritone is more remarkable for sensitive inflection than for beauty, and though the tone grows fluttery under pressure of emotion, as in the last two songs of this supreme song cycle, the concentration and intelligence of the performance are considerable compensation. This may not rival the finest available versions of this challenging work, but it is good to hear a German singer towards the beginning of his career giving a young man's view. Ulrich Eisenlohr, one of the two pianists who have masterminded the Naxos series, does not always help with accompaniments that are too square at times. Full texts and translation as in the rest of the series.

(i) *Winterreise* (complete); Lieder: (ii) *An die Musik; An Sylvia; Auf dem See; Auf dem Wasser zu singen; Der Einsame;* (iii–iv) *Ellens Gesang III (Ave Maria);* (ii) *Erster verlust;* (iii–iv) *Die Forelle;* (ii) *Frühlingsglaube;* (iii–iv) *Ganymed;* (ii) *Gretchen am Spinnrade;* (iii; v–vi) *Der Hirt auf dem Felsen;* (iii; v) *Der Jüngling und der Tod;* (ii) *Der König in Thule; Lachen und Weinen; Der Musensohn; Nähe des Geliebten; Rastlose Liebe; Seligkeit;* (iii–iv) *Ständchen;* (ii) *Die Sterne.*

(B) **(*) EMI (ADD) CZS5 72004-2. (i) Souzay, Baldwin; (ii) Fassbaender, Werba; (iii) Ameling; (iv) Demus; (v) Gage; (vi) with Pieterson.

There are splendid things here. Souzay's 1976 account of the *Winterreise* does not find him in such fresh voice as his earlier (1962) version on Philips. But Souzay is still an imaginative artist, and the Fassbaender and Ameling interpretations are memorable. Alas, this is now deleted.

Church music

6 Antiphons for the Blessings of the Branches on Psalm Sunday; Auguste jam coelestium in G, D.488; Deutsche Messe, D.872 (with Epilogue, The Lord's Prayer); Graduale in C, D.184; Hymn to the Holy Ghost, D.964; Kyries: in D min., D.31; F, D.66; Lazarus, D.689; Magnificat in C, D.486; Offertorium (Totus in corde) in C, D.136; Offertorium (Tres sunt) in A min., D.181; 2 Offertoriums (Salve Regina) in F, D.223 & A, D.676; Psalm 23, D.706; Psalm 92, D.953; Salve Reginas: in B flat, D.106; in C, D.811; Stabat Mater in G min., D.175; Tantum ergo (3 settings) in C, D.460/1 & D.739; Tantum ergo in D, D.750.

(M) *** EMI Dig./ADD CMS7 64783-2 (3). Popp, Donath, Rüggerberg, Venuti, Hautermann, Falk, Fassbaender, Greindl-Rosner, Dallapozza, Araiza, Protschka, Tear, Lika, Fischer-Dieskau, Capella Bavariae, Bav. R. Ch. & SO, Sawallisch.

Volume two of Sawallisch's great and rewarding Schubertian survey has much glorious music, sung with eloquence and richly recorded in the Munich Hercules Hall. Even some of the shortest items – such as the six tiny *Antiphons*, allegedly written in half an hour – have magic and originality in them. Plainer, but still glowing with Schubertian joy, is the so-called *Deutsche Messe*. The *Magnificat*, too, is a strongly characterized setting, and even the three settings of St Thomas Aquinas's *Tantum ergo* (all in C) have their charm. There are other surprises. The lovely setting of the *Offertorium in C (Totus in corde)* is for soprano, clarinet and orchestra, with the vocal and instrumental lines intertwining delectably, while the no less appealing *Auguste jam coelestium* is a soprano–tenor duet. The *Salve Regina in C*, D.811, is written for four male voices, *a cappella*, and they again contribute to the performance of *Psalm 23*, where Sawallisch provides a piano accompaniment. The religious drama, *Lazarus*, has the third CD to itself. Schubert left it unfinished and, though no more dramatic than his operas, it contains much delightful music. With Robert Tear in the name-role, Helen Donath as Maria, Lucia Popp as Jemima, Maria Venuti as Martha, Josef Protschka as Nathanael and Fischer-Dieskau as Simon, it is very strongly cast and the performance is splendid; the singing is outstanding from chorus and soloists alike throughout this set. Warm, well-balanced recording. But this is another of EMI's deletions.

Choruses: *Chor der Engel, D.440; Das Dörfchen, D.598; Gesang der Geister über den Wassern, D.714; Glaub, Hoffnung und Liebe, D.954; Gondelfahrer, D.809; Jägerlied, D.201; Kantate für Irene Kiesewetter, D.936; Klage um Ali Bey, D.140; Lützows wilde Jagd, D.205; Die Nacht, D.983C; Die Nachtigall, D.724; 23rd Psalm, D.706; (i) 92nd Psalm, D.953.*

(M) **(*) DG (ADD) 453 679-2. Austrian R. Ch., ORF SO (members), Preinfalk, with (i) Katzböck.

An enjoyable and well-planned programme of Schubert's shorter choral works, including the engaging *Song of the Spirits over the waters*, the *Jägerlied* and *Lützows wilde Jagd* (complete with horns) and a pair of fine Psalm settings. Sympathetic if not distinctive performances, flattered by the warm recording acoustic.

Lazarus (cantata); *Mass No. 3 in G, D.167.*

(N) (B) *** Erato Ultima (ADD) 8573 88045-2 (2). Armstrong, Welting, Chamonin, Rolfe Johnson, Hill, Egel, R. France Ch., & Nouvel PO, Guschlbauer.

Lazarus is a rarity, both on the gramophone and in the concert hall. Schubert put the score on one side in February 1820 and never returned to it; perhaps he realized that it was too wanting in contrast and variety. About eighty minutes or so survive, and then the work comes to an abrupt ending in the middle of a soprano solo. Yet for all its uniformity of mood and pace, *Lazarus* is well worth having on record. Some of it is as touching as the finest Schubert and other sections are little short of inspired; there are some thoroughly characteristic harmonic colourings and some powerful writing for the trombones.

Though it would be idle to pretend that its inspiration is even or sustained, no Schubertian will want to be without it, for the best of it is quite lovely. The soloists here and the French Radio forces are thoroughly persuasive and it would be difficult to fault Theodore Guschlbauer's direction or the warm quality of the sound achieved by the Erato engineers.

The *G major Mass*, an earlier piece, written when Schubert was only eighteen, has less depth and subtlety than the best of *Lazarus*. But there are some endearing moments, and the *Agnus Dei* is poignant. Again the performance and recording here are a good deal more than acceptable.

Magnificat, D.486; Offertorium in B flat, D.963 (Intende voci).

(N) *** Teldec 3984 26094-2. Oelze, von Magnus, Lippert, Finley, Arnold Schoenberg Ch., VCM, Harnoncourt –
HAYDN: *Mass No. 13 in B flat: Schöpfungsmesse*. ***

These period performances, set in a warm church acoustic, were recorded live, like the Haydn Mass with which they are coupled, sounding similarly fresh and new. The *Magnificat* is relatively well known, with Christiane Oelze ravishingly beautiful in the central *Deposuit* section. By contrast the offertorium *Intende voci* for tenor soloist, choir and orchestra, written in 1828 within weeks of the composer's

death, is surprisingly a rarity. Though the formalised style harks back to Haydn and Mozart, the gravity of the inspiration is clear. The recording is warmly atmospheric, even if the balance of the choir, slightly backward, prevents it from having quite the impact its incisive singing deserves. An unexpected coupling, but an illuminating one.

Magnificat, D.486; Offertorium, D.963; Stabat Mater, D.383.

(M) *** Erato 4509 96961-2. Armstrong, Schaer, Ramirez, Huttenlocher, Goy, Lausanne Vocal Ens. & CO, Corboz.

Schubert's strikingly fresh setting of the *Stabat Mater* dates from the composer's nineteenth year, yet it shows him at the height of his early powers and has many anticipations of later music, especially in the Terzetto for soprano, tenor, bass and chorus (No. 11) and the fine chorus, *Wer wird Zähren sanflen Mitleids* (No. 5), with its superb horn-writing. There is a lovely, Bach-like tenor aria, with oboe obbligato, stylishly sung by Alejandro Ramirez, and a bass aria, *Sohn des Vaters*, recalling the Mozart of *Die Zauberflöte*, sung by Philippe Huttenlocher. The chorus is incisive, both in counterpoint in Schubert's lively fugues, and in the simple chordal writing. The other, lesser pieces make a good coupling, also persuasively directed by Corboz, and the recording, although not crystal clear, has transferred vividly.

Masses Nos. 1–6 (complete); Kyries in B flat, D.45; D min., D.49; Offertorium in B flat, D.963; Salve Reginas: in F, D.379; in B flat, D.386; Stabat Mater in F min., D.383; Tantum ergo in E flat, D.962.

(M) *** EMI Dig./ADD CMS7 64778-2 (4). Popp, Donath, Fassbaender, Dallapozza, Schreier, Araiza, Protschka, Fischer-Dieskau, Bav. R. Ch. & SO, Sawallisch.

Sawallisch's highly distinguished survey of Schubert's church music was recorded in the early 1980s. This first volume is centred on his major Mass settings, especially his masterpiece in this form, the *E flat Mass*. Though the chorus is not flawless here, the performances are warm and understanding. The earlier Mass settings bring superb, lively inspirations, not to mention the separate *Kyries* and *Salve Reginas*. Excellent, cleanly focused sound, for the most part digital, with the benefit of the ambience of the Munich Herkules-Saal. However, this is now deleted.

Masses Nos. 1 in F, D.105; 2 in G, D.167.

*** Sony SK 68247. Nader, Puchegger, Leskovich, Hering, Azesberger, Van der Kamp, V. Boys' Ch., Ch. Viennensis, OAE, Bruno Weil.

(i) *Mass No. 5 in A flat, D.678 (2nd version); Deutsche Messe, D.872.*

*** Sony SK 53984. (i) Treble soloists from V. Boys' Ch. (Stefan Preyer, Thomas Weinnhappel), Hering, Van der Kamp; V. Boys' Ch., Ch. Viennensis, OAE, Bruno Weil.

Bruno Weil draws incandescent performances of Schubert's *Masses* from his fine team, helped by sound that is clearer and more detailed than on direct rival recordings. The combination of Viennese choirs – with the trebles of the Vienna Boys' Choir outstandingly full and fresh – and of a British period orchestra works superbly, making one appreciate, even more than with the Sawallisch versions, how seriously this area of Schubert's oeuvre has been underappreciated. In the earlier *Masses* and in the simple chordal writing of the *Deutsche Messe* the presence of boys adds to the impression of liturgical performances, fresh and dedicated. The one snag is the relatively short measure compared with the Sawallisch set, but for such music-making that is relatively unimportant. Those looking for a place to start might choose SK 53984, which couples the delightful *Deutsche Messe*, with its simple chordal settings of German words, with the A flat masterpiece which is Schubert's *Missa Solemnis*. It helps that Weil uses the second version of the work, with the *Credo* more compact. As ever, he draws inspired playing and singing from his Austro-British team, with the bright, full treble sound of the Vienna Boys cleanly set against the period instruments of the OAE, both beautifully balanced in a recording with plenty of bloom on the sound, yet with good detail.

Masses Nos. (i–iv) 4 in C, D.452; (ii; iv–vi) 5; 6. (iii; vii) Offertorium, D.963; (i–ii; iv; vii) Tantum ergo, D.962.

(B) *** EMI double fforte ADD/Dig. CZS5 73365-2 (2).
(i) Popp; (ii) Fassbaender; (iii) Dallapozza;
(iv) Fischer-Dieskau; (v) Donath; (vi) Araiza; (vii) Schreier;
Bav. R. Ch. & SO, Sawallisch.

This inexpensive reissue from Sawallisch's excellent choral series combines three settings of the Mass including the two finest, *in A flat* and the masterly work *in E flat*; while the *Tantum ergo* (*in C*) also undoubtedly has its charm. These performances have stood the test of time, containing some outstanding singing from soloists and chorus, although the latter is not flawless in D.950. Sawallisch proves to be a warmly understanding Schubertian and the recordings are both vivid and atmospheric.

Mass No. 6 in E flat, D.950.

*** BBC (ADD) BBCL 4029-2 (2) Scottish Festival Ch., New Philh. O, Giulini – VERDI: Requiem. ***
(N) (B) *** Erato Ultima 0630 18960-2 (2). Michael, Baileys, Baldin, Homberger, Brodard, Swiss R. Chamber Ch., Lausanne Pro Arte Ch., SRO, Jordan – Symphonies Nos. 8 (Unfinished); 9 (Great). **(*)
(M) **(*) DG 453 680-2. Mattila, Lipovšek, Hadley, Pita, Holl, V. State Op. Ch., VPO, Abbado.

Schubert's last and most ambitious setting of the Mass makes a generous coupling for Giulini's inspired account of the Verdi *Requiem*. It was recorded at the Edinburgh Festival in 1968 with radio sound remarkably free and full for a performance in Usher Hall. As in the Verdi Giulini directs a dedicated performance, again with incandescent choral singing from the Scottish Festival Chorus.

The Swiss and Lausanne Choirs blend well together and sing with ardour and discipline. The digital sound is well focused, the acoustic expansive, and the results are powerful and satisfying. The soloists, too, are a good team, although in this work they are less important than the chorus. This was originally coupled with a rare Schumann mass, and the present re-coupling with Gardiner's performances of the *Unfinished* and *Great C major Symphonies* seems less apt.

Abbado takes a spacious rather than a dramatic view of Schubert's most popular setting of the Mass, making the music look forward to Bruckner. This is quite unlike the performance from Bruno Weil on Sony (see below) but is intriguing in its way. With first-rate singing from soloists and chorus it is certainly stimulating, with well-balanced digital sound, but it would not be a prime choice.

OPERA AND INCIDENTAL MUSIC

Alfonso und Estrella (complete).

*** Berlin Classics BC2156-2 (3). Schreier, Mathis, Prey, Adam, Fischer-Dieskau, Berlin R. Ch. & State Op. O, Suitner.

It is strange that Schubert, whose feeling for words in lyric poetry drew out emotions which have natural drama in them, had little or no feeling for the stage. Had his operas been produced, no doubt he would have learnt how to use music more positively; as it is, this tale of royal intrigue in medieval times never quite captures the listener as an opera should. Even so, it contains a stream of delightful music, Schubert at his most open and refreshing; under Suitner's direction it here receives a sparkling performance, excellently cast. Edith Mathis makes a sweet heroine, and Peter Schreier sings radiantly, as if in an orchestrated *Schöne Müllerin*. The reconciliation of the two principal male characters, Froila and Mauregato, is most touching as sung by Fischer-Dieskau and Prey. The recording is richly atmospheric and is splendidly transferred to CD. A full translation is included.

Fierrabras (complete).

*** DG (IMS) 427 341-2 (2). Protschka, Mattila, Studer, Gambill, Hampson, Holl, Polgár, Schoenberg Ch., COE, Abbado.

Schubert may often let his musical imagination blossom without considering the dramatic effect, but there are jewels in plenty in this score. Many solos and duets develop into delightful ensembles, and the influence of Beethoven's *Fidelio* is very striking, with spoken melodrama and offstage fanfares bringing obvious echoes. A recording is the ideal medium for such buried treasure, and Abbado directs an electrifying performance. Both tenors, Robert Gambill and Josef Protschka, are on the strenuous side, but have a fine feeling for Schubertian melody. Cheryl Studer and Karita Mattila sing ravishingly, and Thomas Hampson gives a noble performance as the knight, Roland. Only Robert Holl as King Karl (Charlemagne) is unsteady at times. The sound is comfortably atmospheric, outstanding for a live recording.

Rosamunde Overture (Die Zauberharfe, D.644) & Incidental Music, D.797 (complete).

*** DG 431 655-2. Von Otter, Ernst Senff Ch., COE, Abbado.
*** Australian Decca Eloquence (ADD) 466 677-2. Yachmi, Vienna State O Ch., VPO, Münchinger.

Abbado and COE give joyful performances of this magical incidental music. It is a revelation to hear the most popular of the entr'actes played so gently: it is like a whispered meditation. Even with a slow speed and affectionate phrasing, it yet avoids any feeling of being mannered. Glowing recording to match. Anne Sofie von Otter is an ideal soloist.

Münchinger's performance of the delightful *Rosamunde* music glows with an affectionate warmth and understanding which places this as one of his very best records. Its unavailability on CD until this Australian disc appeared is unaccountable: there is an unforced spontaneity, as well as strength here, and the 1970s recording is rich and naturally balanced. The vocal numbers are superbly done, and the VPO is at its magnificent best. A real bargain.

Die Verschworenen (complete).

(M) *** CPO/EMI (ADD) 999 554-2. Moser, Fuchs, Dallapozza, Schary, Moll, Finke, Bav. R. Ch., Munich RO, Wallberg.

Die Verschworenen ('The Conspirators') is a variant on the old theme of Aristophanes' *Lysistrata*, with the wives of returning crusaders withholding their favours from their menfolk. Though the heroine's lovely minor-key *Romance* near the beginning with clarinet obbligato points to serious emotions, and there is a Weber-like storm sequence, this is predominantly light-hearted, with ensemble passages which for the Anglo-Saxon listener will recall Gilbert and Sullivan, as in the fourth number, a chorus in which men are set against women. Much the longest number is the extended finale, structured like a Mozart operatic finale and here, as in Schubert's other one-act operas, there are hints that he had studied Beethoven's *Fidelio*. In this very well-made recording there is no weak link in the Munich cast, with the bass, Kurt Moll, outstanding as Count Heribert. As in other issues in this CPO series of recordings originally made by EMI, there is no libretto but a good synopsis linked to the CD tracks.

Der vierjährige Posten (complete).

(M) *** CPO/EMI (ADD) 999 553-2. Donath, Schreier, Fischer-Dieskau, Brokmeier, Lenz, Bav. R. Ch. & O, Wallberg.

Schubert wrote this one-act piece ('The Four-Year Post') in 1815 at the age of eighteen. With little more than half an hour of music, including a substantial overture, its eight numbers have many characteristically Schubertian touches, not just in the flowing tunes but in foretastes of the *Rosamunde* music. Apart from the overture, the only extended number (and the only real aria) is the prayer of Kätchen, the heroine, which in its calm beauty seems to anticipate Agathe's aria, *Und ob die Volke*, in Weber's *Der Freischütz* of six years later. The cast in this recording, originally made by EMI–Electrola, is an outstanding one, with star singers forming a splendid team. Highly recommended, though the piece offers short measure for a whole disc. No libretto is provided, only a synopsis.

Die Zwillingsbrüder (complete).

(M) *** CPO/EMI (ADD) 999 556-2. Donath, Gedda, Moll, Fischer-Dieskau, Munich State Op. Ch., Bav. RSO, Sawallisch.

Die Zwillingsbrüder ('The Twin Brothers'), completed in 1819, deftly tells the story of twin brothers, strikingly contrasted, both returning from serving in the army, the one a rough-diamond of a soldier, the other – thought to be dead – the devoted lover. Inevitably this leads to confusion, resolved only at the end in a conventional but winning way. When Fischer-Dieskau takes the roles of both twins – who never appear on stage together – the result is delightful, with Schubert inspired to sparkling music, and with the brothers' contrasting characters well conveyed in their respective arias. With Sawallisch drawing superb playing and singing from the whole team, this comes near to being an ideal performance, not just starrily cast but very well recorded.

Opera arias from Adrast; Alfonso und Estrella; Die Bürgschaft; Die Freunde von Salamanka; Der Graf von Gleichen; Des Teufels Lustschloss; Die Zwillingsbrüder.

(N) *** Hyp. CDA 67229. Widmer, Hungarian Nat. PO, Jan Schultz.

This collection of arias from operas composed at various periods in Schubert's career points the contrast with his song-writing. Lively as these items are, with the two from the mature *Alfonso und Estrella* the most elaborate, they are generally less individual than his songs. Even so, there is much to enjoy, helped by the lively, characterful singing of the Swiss baritone Oliver Widmer, with sympathetic accompaniment from the Hungarian orchestra. Just occasionally one of the items will offer a magical orchestral effect, as in the second of the *Alfonso und Estrella* excerpts, with airy harp arpeggios in 3/4 time, nearly but not quite a waltz song. The two contrasted arias from the comic *Die Zwillingsbrüder*, 'The Twins', are relatively well known, but most of the rest are rarities, some of them from operas not otherwise recorded. The collection is rounded off with five arias from the incomplete opera *Die Bürgschaft*, 'The Bond', four of them for the character Möros, one less serious for Dionysos, a comic tyrant like Mozart's Osmin in *Entführung*. Good characterization and clear recording.

SCHULHOFF, Erwin (1894–1942)

5 Pieces (for string quartet.)

(N) *** DG 469 066-2. Hagen Qt. – DVORAK: *String quartet No. 14*; KURTAG: *Hommage à Mihály András*. ***

These five pieces are very slight indeed, witty and inventive but not the kind of music to which you would often want to return, even given the excellence of the performance and recording.

Flammen (opera; complete).

*** Decca 444 630-2 (2). Westi, Eaglen, Vermillion, Prein, Wolff, Soloists, Berlin RIAS Chamber Ch., Deutsches SO, Berlin, John Mauceri.

Flammen is a curiosity, a rich and exotic score inspired by a stylized story and characters, with long, purely instrumental passages which in a stage presentation would involve ballet and mime. The central figure is Don Juan, condemned to eternal life amid the hell-flames of the title, loved by the symbolic figure of Death (a woman) who is yet unable to claim him. The other principal women's roles are taken by a single singer (here the rich-voiced and formidable Jane Eaglen), with Donna Anna turning into Margarethe when the stylized story implies that Don Juan and Faust are linked. Dramatically, it is variably successful, but the concluding scenes are most moving. The performance is outstanding in every way, with John Mauceri drawing bitingly intense playing and singing from his excellent team. Kurt Westi is superb in the central role of Don Juan, clear, firm and fresh, and both Jane Eaglen and Iris Vermillion as Death sing with power and passion. Recording of demonstration quality.

SCHULZ, Johann Abraham (1747–1800)

(i; ii; iii) *The Death of Christ (Christe Dod). Overture, The Harvest Festival (Höstgilder).* (iii) (Keyboard): *Allegretto in C; Andante Sostenuto in A, Op. 1/1.* (i; iv) Songs: *Abendlied; An die Natur; Mailied; Neujahrslied.* (ii; iii) Motet: *Denk ich Gott an deine Güte* (arr. from Haydn's Symphony No. 104).

*** Chan. 9553. (i) Dam-Jensen, Halling, Zachariassen, Mannov; (ii; iii) Danish National Ch. & RSO, Hogwood; (iv) Hogwood (fortepiano).

Born in north Germany in 1747, Johann Abraham Peter Schulz established himself in Copenhagen as the pioneer of Danish national music, dying in 1800. *The Death of Christ* is a 35-minute cantata, both moving and dramatic, which in its linked sequence of 13 sections moves from total darkness, mourning Christ's death, to blazing light in the exhilarating final chorus, *He lives!* In style Schulz echoes both Haydn and C. P. E. Bach with a fascinating anticipation of Beethoven's *Pastoral Symphony* in the storm music. Excellent performance under Hogwood, who also plays two fortepiano pieces as interludes. Inger Dam-Jensen, Cardiff Singer of the World, is outstanding among the soloists, both in the cantata and in the songs *Abendlied* and *Mailied*.

SCHUMAN, William (1910–92)

American Festival Overture.

(B) *** DG (ADD) 445 129-2 [(M).import]. LAPO, Bernstein – BARBER: *Adagio for Strings.* BERNSTEIN: *Candide Overture;* COPLAND: *Appalachian Spring;* ***

Schuman's *Overture* is the least known of the four representative works making up this attractive Classikon disc. It is rather like a Walton comedy overture with an American accent, and is played here with tremendous panache. Close, bright, full recording.

(i) *Violin Concerto. New England Triptych.*

(N) (BB) *** Naxos 8.559083. (i) Quint; Bournemouth SO, Serebrier – IVES: *Variations on America.* ***

Schuman's powerfully expressive *Violin Concerto* (1959) underwent more than one transformation in its gestation, with the original three movements becoming two. After a strong, rhythmically angular opening (with the soloist immediately introducing the work's dominating motif) the first movement soon slips into a magically lyrical *molto tranquillo.* Later there is a sparkling scherzando section and an extended cadenza before the brilliant conclusion. Lyrical feeling also seeps through the finale, although there is plenty of vigour and spectacle too, and a fugue, before the bravura *moto perpetuo* display of the closing section. Altogether a splendidly rewarding work, given a first-rate performance here by Philip Quint and the strongly involved Bournemouth players under Serebrier.

They are no less persuasive in the *New England Triptych*, a folksy, immediately communicative work inspired by and drawing on the music of William Billings. The central movement, *When Jesus Wept,* in the form of a round, is warmly, sonorously expressive and the piquant, spirited finale surges forward with quick-marching energy, yet at the same time Schuman remembers the hymn on which the piece is based. First-class recording in an attractively spacious acoustic. The coupling, which Schuman orchestrated, could not be more apt.

In Praise of Shahn (Canticle for Orchestra); (i) *To Thee Old Cause (Evocation for Oboe, Brass, Timpani, Piano & Strings).*

(M) *** Sony (ADD) SMK 63088. (i) Gomberg (oboe); NYPO, Bernstein – BARBER: *Adagio for Strings; Violin Concerto.* ***

Both of these works are commemorative. *To Thee Old Cause* is dedicated to the memory of Dr Martin Luther King, and the score quotes from Walt Whitman ('Thou peerless, passionate, good cause, Thou stern, remorseless, sweet idea'). It features an oboe obbligato within its string textures which are reinforced by brass sonorities. In a single movement, its *Larghissimo* opening is intense and evocative, although poignant lyrical feeling predominates. *In Praise of (Ben) Shahn* remembers the New York artist. It is in two sections, both (drawing on Eastern European Jewish folk material) include dynamic and expressive writing. This is music which in its atmosphere and use of dissonance often looks back to Charles Ives, although Schuman's own individual voice is never submerged. Bernstein is in his element and neither piece could receive more passionate advocacy. The (1970) Avery Fisher Hall recording is very immediate but has plenty of atmosphere too.

Judith; New England Triptych; Symphony for Strings; Variations on America.

*** Delos DE 3115. Seattle SO, Gerard Schwarz.

The composer himself heard these performances and spoke of their combination of 'intellectual depth, technical superiority and emotional involvement'. The *Symphony for Strings,* his Fifth, is one of his strongest and most beautiful works. This Seattle account has the advantage of fresh recorded sound. The ballet, *Judith,* was written for Martha Graham. Powerful and atmospheric music, here given a performance with both these qualities. The *New England Triptych* makes use of New England themes by the Bostonian, William Billings (1746–1800), whose music served to fuel the cause of the American Revolution. This present account is superior to the version by Howard Hanson on Mercury.

New England Triptych.

(M) *** Mercury [432 755-2]. Eastman-Rochester O, Hanson –
IVES: *Symphony No. 3 etc. ***; MENNIN: Symphony
No. 5. **(*)*

Each of these three pieces is an orchestral anthem, the first
a thrustingly vibrant *Hallelujah*; the second is in the form of
a round, and the finale features a marching song. Splendidly
alive playing and excellent (1963) Mercury recording, admirably transferred to CD.

Symphonies Nos. 3; 5 (for strings); 8.

(M) *** Sony SMK 63163. NYPO, Leonard Bernstein.

The *Third* (1941) is (to quote Bernstein) 'alive, radiant and
optimistic', and it is without question a masterpiece. It has
the sweep and power of Harris, the freshness of Copland
and an entirely individual and compelling atmosphere.
Bernstein's 1960 performance is superb, and superior to his
later remake for DG. The *Symphony for strings* comes from
1943 and is consistently imaginative, with a highly developed
and sophisticated harmonic vocabulary. The *Eighth Symphony*, on the other hand, was commissioned by the New
York Philharmonic in 1962. Its inspiration gives the impression of being manufactured rather than composed, except
in the impressive and beautiful *Largo* movement; but make
no mistake, its two companions on this record are among
the finest symphonies to come out of America. The performances are terrific and the recordings, all emanating from the
1960s are expertly restored, sounding much fresher and
better defined than the LP originals.

String Quartets Nos. 2, 3 & 5.

*** HM HMU 907114. Lydian String Qt.

The *Third Quartet* (1939) serves as a reminder of what a
powerful composer William Schuman is. Less accessible,
perhaps, than Aaron Copland or his exact contemporary,
Samuel Barber, Schuman's music has sinew and a toughness
that is bracing. It demands persuasive and committed
playing from its interpreters, which it receives from the fine
Lydian Quartet, and concentration from its listeners. The
Second Quartet (1937) is slighter than the *Third* but is a
strong piece nevertheless. The latter has something of the
volcanic energy and drive of the *Third Symphony*, Schuman's
best-known work, as well as its sense of line and momentum;
it is one of the great American quartets. The *Fifth Quartet* is
a relatively late piece, coming from 1987, and its opening is
among Schuman's most inward and searching inspirations.
Some may find his quartets a hard nut to crack but they are
well worth taking trouble over. All three are beautifully
played and recorded.

SCHUMANN, Clara (1819–96)

Piano Trio in G min., Op. 17.

(N) (B) *** Hyp. Helios CDH 55078. Dartington Piano Trio –
Fanny MENDELSSOHN: *Trio*. ***

Piano Trio, Op.17; 3 Romances for Violin & Piano, Op. 22.
Piano music: Romanze, Op. 21; 2 Romances, Op. 11;

Scherzo, Op. 14; Toccatina, Op. 11; Variations on a Theme by Robert Schumann, Op. 1; 20.

(N) (BB) *** Arte Nova 74321 72106-2. Krsti, Haack, Gelius.

Clara's *Piano Trio* moves within the Mendelssohn–
Schumann tradition with apparently effortless ease and,
when played as persuasively as it is here, makes a pleasing
impression. If it does not command the depth of Robert, it
has a great deal of charm to commend it. Excellent recording.

The Arte Nova disc of Clara Schumann's two chamber
works – the *Piano Trio* and the *Opus 22 Romances* for violin
and piano – plus a good selection of solo piano pieces
provides a winning portrait of this key figure not just in the
life of her husband, Robert, but of Brahms too. Her love of
the keyboard and her delight in virtuosity come out in all
the piano pieces, magnetically played by Micaela Gelius. The
style is very close to that of her husband, warmly romantic
if marginally less radical, with the *Piano Trio* beautifully
crafted to make one regret that she concentrated on miniatures and wrote so little after her husband died.

Hyperion Schumann Edition

Lieder Edition, Vol. 5: Ihr Bildnis; Lorelei; Sie liebten sich beide; Volkslied.

(N) *** Hyp. CDJ 33105. Maltman, Johnson – Robert
SCHUMANN: *Lieder*. ***

It adds to the value of this searching collection of Heine
settings by Robert Schumann that four rival settings by his
wife are appended, simpler and less distinctive in style as
they are. As in the rest of the disc Maltman is at his finest,
with Graham Johnson ever-illuminating both as accompanist and annotator.

SCHUMANN, Robert (1810–56)

Cello Concerto in A min., Op. 129.

*** BIS CD 486. Thedéen, Malmö SO, Markiz – ELGAR:
Concerto. ***

(M) **(*) Mercury (IMS) (ADD) 432 010-2. Starker, LSO,
Skrowaczewski – LALO: *Concerto* **(*); SAINT-SAENS:
Concerto. ***

(BB) *** Naxos 8 550 938. Kliegel, Nat. SO of Ireland,
Constantine – BRAHMS: *Double Concerto*. ***

(B) *** Decca 448 712-2. Harrell, Cleveland O, Marriner –
LALO; SAINT-SAENS: *Concertos*. ***

(M) *** Sony SMK 60151. Ma, Bav. RSO, Davis – DVORAK:
Cello Concerto. ***

(M) *** EMI (ADD) CDM5 66913-2 [CDM5 66965]. O Nat. de
France, Bernstein – R. STRAUSS: *Don Quixote*. ***

The young Swedish virtuoso, Torleif Thedéen, is splendidly
recorded on BIS, and the Malmö orchestra give him sympathetic support. He plays with a refreshing ardour, tempered by nobility and a reticence that is strongly appealing.
He couples it with an account of the Elgar that is every bit
as attuned to the latter's sensibility as any in the catalogue.
Strongly recommended.

Janos Starker gives a persuasive account of it that is

thoroughly sensitive to the letter and spirit of the score. Skrowaczewski accompanies with spirit and without the rather explosive, clipped tutti chords that somewhat disfigure the Lalo with which it is coupled. The 1962 recording is amazing for its age: people make great claims for these early Mercury recordings and, judging from this expertly engineered disc, rightly so!

The Schumann *Cello Concerto* makes an apt coupling for the Brahms *Double Concerto* and is the more attractive for coming on the Naxos super-budget label in a warmly spontaneous-sounding performance, very well recorded. Kliegel takes a spacious, lyrical view of the first movement, using a soft-grained tone at the start, with wide vibrato. The simple, dedicated approach to the central *Langsam* also brings dedicated playing, while the finale is wittily pointed, not least in the second subject.

Harrell's is a big-scale reading, strong and sympathetic, made the more powerful by the superb accompaniment from the Cleveland Orchestra. Its controversial point is that he expands the usual cadenza with a substantial sequence of his own. The digital recording is outstandingly fine.

As always, Yo-Yo Ma's playing is distinguished by great refinement of expression, and his account of the *Concerto* is keenly affectionate, although at times he carries tonal sophistication to excess and drops suddenly into *sotto voce* tone and near-inaudibility. Both he and Sir Colin Davis are thoroughly attuned to the sensibility of this composer. The balance, both between soloist and orchestra and within the various departments of the orchestra, blends perfectly.

Except in the finale where energy triumphs, the collaboration of Rostropovich and Bernstein sounds disappointingly self-conscious. The great Russian cellist is at his most indulgent, not least in the lovely slow section, which is pulled about wilfully at a very slow basic tempo. The Strauss coupling is in an altogether different class, so this is a strange choice for EMI's 'Great Recordings of the Century' series.

(i) *Cello Concerto.* **(ii)** *Adagio & Allegro, Op. 70; 3 Fantasiestücke; 5 Stücke im Volkston; Romanze No. 1 in A min., Op. 94/1; Marchenbilder, Op. 113/1.*

(N) **(*) DG 469 524-2. Maisky; (i) Orpheus CO; (ii) Argerich.

Mischa Maisky has never been an artist for half measures. It was he who earlier recorded the Schumann *Cello Concerto* with Leonard Bernstein, a big-scale reading, often wayward and self-indulgent. His new version, recorded with the conductorless Orpheus Chamber Orchestra brings a more purposeful reading, faster and marginally less wilful in the first movement, but with the slow movement pulled around even more than before, with exaggerated rubato. Like the first movement the finale gains in bite from the close-up sound. The concerto comes last on the disc as the culmination of Schumann's cello music. Maisky also offers the other shorter pieces with piano which Schumann either wrote specifically for cello (the *Adagio & Allegro* and the *5 Stücke im Volkston*) or suggested the cello as an option. Unlike his rivals he adds two extra pieces, the *Romance* and the *Marchenbilder* movement as bonuses in his own adaptations, though that hardly compensates for the wilfulness. Maisky is well part-

nered by another great individualist, Martha Argerich. The sound is full and bright.

(i) *Cello Concerto in A min.;* **(ii)** *Piano Concerto in A min.*

(M) **(*) DG (IMS) (ADD) 449 100-2. (i) Rostropovich, Leningrad PO, Rozhdestvensky; (ii) Argerich, Nat. SO of Washington, Rostropovich.

Rostropovich's DG performance of the *Cello Concerto* is superbly made, introspective yet at the same time outgoing, with a peerless technique at the command of a rare artistic imagination. The sound is vivid. In the *Piano Concerto* Rostropovich moves to the rostrum and Argerich takes on the role of soloist. The partnership produces a performance which is full of contrast – helped by a recording of wide dynamic range – and strong in temperament. There is an appealing delicacy in the *Andantino* and the outer movements have plenty of vivacity and colour. Yet in the last analysis the work's special romantic feeling does not fully blossom here, although the playing is not without poetry. The recording is admirably lifelike and well balanced.

(i) *Cello Concerto;* **(ii)** *Piano Concerto; Introduction & Allegro appassionato, Op. 92.*

(N) (BB) ** EMI (ADD) CDE5 74755-2.(i) Du Pré, New Philh. O, Barenboim; (ii) Barenboim, LPO, Fischer-Dieskau.

The most attractive performance here is Jacqueline du Pré's 1968 recording of the *Cello Concerto*. Her spontaneous style is strikingly suited to this most recalcitrant of concertos and the slow movement is particularly beautiful. She is ably assisted by Daniel Barenboim and the only snag is the rather faded orchestral sound, unflattered by the present transfer, though the cello timbre is realistically focused.

The coupling was recorded in the mid-1970s; the sound is somewhat firmer and the balance lets the piano dominate but, with the LPO below its best under Fischer-Dieskau (a good but not outstanding conductor), this is probably just as well. Barenboim is brisk and not particularly poetic, and these performances lack what he usually achieves on record: a sense of spontaneity, a simulation of live performance.

(i) *Cello Concerto;* **(ii)** *Piano Concerto in A min.;* **(iii)** *Violin Concerto in D min.;* **(ii)** *Introduction & Allegro appassionato;* **(iv)** *Konzertstück in F for 4 Horns & Orchestra, Op. 86.*

(B) **(*) EMI (ADD/DDD) CZS7 67521-2 (2). (i) P. Tortelier, RPO, Y. P. Tortelier; (ii) Barenboim, LPO, Fischer-Dieskau; (iii) Kremer, Philh. O, Muti; (iv) Hauptmann, Klier, Kohler, Seifert, BPO, Tennstedt.

This is a useful collection of Schumann's concertante works and it is a pity that it is let down somewhat by Barenboim's rather too direct account of the works for piano. Tortelier's is a characteristically inspirational performance of the *Cello Concerto*, at its most concentrated in the hushed rendering of the slow movement. The *Violin Concerto* comes off pretty well in the hands of Gidon Kremer and he has good support from the Philharmonia under Riccardo Muti. What makes this two-disc set well worth it is the inclusion of the exuberant *Konzertstück* with its brilliant horn playing. The four soloists from the Berlin Philharmonic play with superbly ripe virtuosity and Tennstedt's direction is both urgent and expansive. The 1978 recording is admirably full-blooded.

(i) *Cello Concerto in A min., Op.129;* (ii; iii) *Piano Concerto in A min., Op.54;* (iv) *Symphony No. 1 in B flat (Spring);* (ii) *Arabeske in C, Op. 18; Fantasia in C, Op. 17;* (iii) *Kinderszenen, Op. 15.*

** DG Panorama ADD/Dig. 469 199-2. (i) Rostropovich, Leningrad PO, Rozhdestvensky (ii) Pollini; (iii) BPO, Abbado; (iv) VPO, Bernstein. (v) Pollini; (v) Kempff.

This Panorama Schumann compilation is drawn exclusively from Deutsche Grammophon. The earliest recording is the *Cello Concerto* performed by Rostropovich and Rozh-destvensky in 1960, and the most recent is the *A minor Piano Concerto,* which Pollini made almost 30 years later. It is difficult to flaw DG's choice of the former, but the *Piano Concerto* is more questionable. It makes only intermittent contact with Schumann's sensibility. Pollini's recording of the *C major Fantasia* enjoys classic status. The *Kinderszenen* comes from 1973 when Kempff was in his late seventies. From the symphonies DG's choice has fallen on the *Spring Symphony;* here Kubelik or Karajan would surely have stronger musical claims than Bernstein, who is intrusive at times and pushes the first movement rather hard.

Piano Concerto in A min., Op. 54.

[M] *** Ph. (ADD) 464 702-2. Kovacevich, BBC SO, C. Davis – GRIEG: *Concerto;.* ***

*** EMI CDC7 54746-2. Vogt, CBSO, Rattle – GRIEG: *Concerto.* ***

*** Sony SK 44899. Perahia, Bav. RSO, C. Davis – GRIEG: *Concerto.* ***

(N) (M) *** Decca (ADD) 458 628-2. Ashkenazy, LSO, Segal – TCHAIKOVSKY: *Concerto No. 1.* **(*)

(M) *** Decca (ADD) 466 383-2. Lupu, LSO, Previn – GRIEG: *Piano Concerto.* ***

(N) (M) **(*) RCA (ADD) 09026 63053-2. Rubinstein, Chicago SO, Giulini – LISZT: *Concerto No. 1;* SAINT-SAENS: *Concerto No. 2.* **(*)

(**(*)) EMI CDM5 66597-2. Gieseking, Philh. O, Karajan – FRANCK: *Symphonic Variations;* GRIEG: *Piano Concerto* (**(*)).

(B) **(*) Decca (ADD) 433 628-2. Gulda, VPO, Andrae – FRANCK: *Symphonic Variations* *** 🟢; GRIEG: *Concerto.* ***

(B) **(*) [EMI Red Line CDR5 69859]. Ousset, LPO, Masur – GRIEG: *Piano Concerto.* **(*)

(BB) **(*) ASV CDQS 6092. Osorio, RPO, Bátiz – FRANCK: *Symphonic Variations* **(*); RAVEL: *Left-Hand Concerto* ***; SAINT-SAENS: *Wedding-Cake.* ***

(N) (BB) (***) Naxos mono 8.110612. Cortot, LPO, Ronald – CHOPIN: *Piano Concerto No. 2 in F min., Op. 21.*

(N) (M ** Chan. 6621 (2). Margalit, LSO, Thompson (with MENDELSSOHN: *Capriccio brillant* **) – BRAHMS: *Concerto No. 1;* SAINT-SAENS: *Concerto No. 2.* **

Piano Concerto in A min.; Concert-allegro with Introduction in D min., Op. 134. Introduction & Allegro appassionato, Op.92.

(N) **(*) MDG 340 1033-2. Zacharias, Lausanne Chamber O.

(i; ii) *Piano Concerto in A min.;* (i; iii) *Introduction & Allegro appassionato, Op. 92. Novellette in F, Op. 21/1; Toccata in C, Op. 7; Waldszenen, Op. 82.*

(M) **(*) DG stereo/mono 447 440-2. Richter, with (i) Warsaw Nat. PO, (ii) Rowicki, (iii) Wislocki.

(i) *Piano Concerto in A min.; Arabeske; Etudes Symphoniques, Op. 13.*

(M) **(*) DG (ADD) (IMS) 445 522-2. Pollini; (i) BPO, Abbado.

(i) *Piano Concerto in A min.; Carnaval; Kinderszenen (Scenes from Childhood), Op. 15.*

(B) **(*) DG (ADD) 439 476-2. Kempff; (i) Bav. RSO, Kubelik.

Although Pires should not be forgotten (coupled with the *Piano Quartet*), our primary recommendation for this favourite Romantic concerto remains with the successful symbiosis of Stephen Kovacevich and Sir Colin Davis, who give an interpretation which is both fresh and poetic, un-exaggerated but powerful in its directness and clarity, and the spring-like element of the outer movements is finely presented by orchestra and soloist alike. This is now rightly placed among the Philips '50 Great Recordings'.

Lars Vogt's sensitivity, an innate sense of style, and a keen imagination, are strongly in evidence in this account of the Schumann, in which he is well supported by Simon Rattle and the CBSO. There is stiff competition, of course, but among modern recordings Vogt acquits himself with honour.

Perahia's 1988 version also benefits from having the guiding hand of Sir Colin Davis directing the orchestra. The recording is live. Perahia is never merely showy, but here he enjoys displaying his ardour and virtuosity as well as his ability to invest a phrase with poetry and magic. With its full and spacious sound, the Perahia is among the finest recent versions of this favourite coupling.

Ashkenazy's performance, balancing the demands of drama against poetry, comes down rather more in favour of the former than one might expect, but it is a refined reading as well as a powerful one, with the finale rather more spa-cious than usual. The recording, from the late 70s, is of vintage quality and has been remastered most successfully. However, Ashkenazy is less obviously attuned to the rhetoric of the Tchaikovsky coupling.

The Lupu/Previn performance suits the music admirably, with the piano lucidly and truthfully caught against a natural orchestral backcloth. Lupu's clean boldness of approach in the outer movements is appealingly fresh, with the finale brilliant yet unforced, while the *Intermezzo* has both warmth and the necessary tender delicacy. This reissue in Decca's Legends series must move up to stand high alongside other current mid-priced recommendations.

Kempff, after a rather positive account of the opening chords of the *Piano Concerto,* proceeds characteristically to produce an unending stream of poetry. The dialogue of the *Intermezzo* is like an intimate conversation overheard. Tempi are generally leisurely, notably so in the finale where there is fine support from the Bavarian Radio Orchestra under Kubelik. Good early-1970s recording. But of the solo recordings neither is among Kempff's more compelling Schumann performances.

Rubinstein gives a truly melting performance, his playing is consistently beautiful and the use of Chicago's Orchestral Hall has brought a warm orchestral sound and a pleasingly real piano image. The snag is that the forward balance means that everything, apart from the big orchestral tuttis, has a limited range of dynamic, and his interchange both with the wind soloists in the first movement and with the strings in the *Intermezzo* seems to lack light and shade as a result (although one can hear it in the playing). Even so Rubinstein and Giulini have the work's full measure and it is difficult not to respond to a performance so persuasive in its warm, gently romantic feeling.

Gieseking's 1953 recording with Karajan and the Philharmonia was overshadowed at the time by Lipatti's version. There is much to relish in Gieseking's refined performance – and in particular the exquisite intermezzo. However, this has been deleted as we go to press.

Gulda's account is refreshingly direct yet, with light, crisp playing, never sounds rushed. The *Intermezzo* remains delicate in feeling, with nicely pointed pianism. The finale is just right, with an enjoyable rhythmic lift, and the early stereo (1956), though a little dated, is fully acceptable. Cécile Ousset, with sympathetic support from Masur, gives a spirited account of the Schumann *Concerto*, like the Grieg coupling rather weightier than one might have expected but not lacking sparkle, while the central dialogue with the orchestra is delightfully done.

Pollini's account of the concerto is not without tenderness and poetry, but he is at times rather business-like and wanting in freshness. He is handicapped by rather unventilated recording and an inconsistent balance. The coupling is every way successful: the *Symphonic Studies* has a symphonic gravitas and concentration; it also has the benefit of excellent recorded quality.

Zacharias, with chamber forces, offers a comparatively small-scale approach, with textures exceptionally transparent, and with his crisp articulation consistently adding sparkle in the most elaborate passage-work. His speeds are fast in the first two movements of the *Concerto*, and this emphasizes the *Andantino* as an Intermezzo rather than a full slow movement. But both in the finale and in the two rarer concertante works he takes a broad view, avoiding pomposity in the rhetorical gestures of Opus 134, and springing rhythms lightly, never letting the music drag, the effect carefree if lacking flamboyance. With exceptionally clear recording it makes a refreshing and distinctive view, certainly poetic.

Richter's reissue in DG's 'Originals' series does not always represent him at his very finest. Perhaps the sluggishness of the orchestral playing affected his concentration. Not that the concerto or the *Introduction & Allegro appassionato* lack style but the tension could be greater. The focus of the late-1950s Polish recording has been improved in the concerto but in Opus 92 remains a little fuzzy around the edges, not quite up to the standard one expects from DG. The *Novellette* and *Toccata* are fabulous performances, full of hair-raising virtuosity, but shaped with an unerring sense of style and musical as well as technical control. The piano

tone is dry but clear. The *Waldszenen* is a mono recording from 1956 and beautifully played.

Jorge Federico Osorio's account of the Schumann *Concerto* is boldly romantic yet in no way lacking in poetry. The central *Intermezzo* is beautifully in scale, but in the first movement, with Bátiz bringing strong support in the tuttis, he presses on impulsively, and the finale has similar urgency. Some may prefer a more relaxed romanticism, but there is no lack of spontaneity here and the result is undoubtedly fresh and involving. Excellent recording and recommendable couplings make this disc a genuine bargain.

In all Cortot made three recordings of the Schumann *A minor Concerto*, all with Sir Landon Ronald, including an acoustic set with the Royal Albert Hall Orchestra and a 1927 version with the LSO. This listed account was the standard version when the present authors were growing up, and though it was soon challenged by a less expensive plum-label version from Myra Hess, and superseded technically by Lipatti, Lupu, Kovacevich and so many others, there is something quite special about Cortot. There is lyrical warmth, poetic feeling and a wonderful freshness and individuality. Mark Obert-Thorn gets a very good sound from the shellac originals.

Israela Margalit brings no lack of warmth or poetic feeling to the concerto, but she is somewhat idiosyncratic. The central A flat section of the first movement is very measured, and she is not averse to point-making by means of rubati. The recording is resonant with the piano well forward. This offers no serious challenge to the front-runners in the catalogue, and the two-disc format is uneconomical.

(i) *Piano Concerto in A min., Op. 54;* (ii) *Abendlied; Adagio & Allegro in A flat; Fantasiestücke; 3 Romances; 5 Stücke im Volkston.* (Piano) *Etudes symphoniques. Fantasia in C; Fantasiestücke; Kinderszenen; Kreisleriana.*

(M) *** Ph. (IMS) (ADD/DDD) 446 925-2 (5). Brendel, with
(i) LSO, Abbado; (ii) Holliger – BRAHMS: *Piano Concertos; Ballades* etc. ***

Brendel's is a fresh, thoughtful account of the *Piano Concerto*, though missing something of the work's delicate romantic feeling in the slow movement. Neither the orchestral response under Abbado nor the Philips recording will seriously disappoint. It was a curious idea to include the series of pieces with oboe, beautifully though Holliger plays. They are available separately – see below. But the piano music is all well chosen. The very opening of the *Fantasiestücke*, Op. 12, demonstrates magically spontaneous playing; both this and the *Fantasia in C* are full of imaginative touches of colour, strong as well as poetic. The digital sound serves Brendel well and truthfully conveys the depth of timbre. *Kinderszenen* and *Kreisleriana* bring more thoughtful and poetically characterized playing from Brendel, while the *Etudes symphoniques* are ardent and yet beautifully controlled, again given first-class digital sound.

(i) *Piano Concerto in A min., Op. 54;* (ii) *Piano Quintet in E flat, Op. 44.*

*** DG 463 179-2. Pires; (i) COE, Abbado; (ii) Dumay, Capuçon, Caussé, Wang.

It makes an excellent if unusual coupling to have the Schumann *Piano Concerto* alongside the most heroic of his chamber works. In both Pires is inspired to give freely spontaneous performances, at once powerfully persuasive and poetic. In the *Quintet* the interplay between musicians is delightful, each distinguished individually but who plainly enjoy working together. Consistently Pires leads the team to play with natural, unselfconscious rubato in all four movements, with speeds perfectly chosen and the structure firmly held together.

In the *Concerto* Pires is also at her most persuasive. With the ever-responsive Chamber Orchestra of Europe, Abbado matches the volatile quality in Pires's performance with beautifully transparent accompaniment. Two beautifully judged performances, both very well recorded.

Piano Concerto in A minor, Op. 54; (i) *Carnaval, Op. 9; Waldszenen: Vogel als Prophet* (only).

(N) (BB) (***) Naxos mono 8.110604. Hess; (i) O, Goehr.

Dame Myra Hess was admired particularly for her Schumann, which was both authoritative and sensitive. Nothing is ever overstated, and she is completely inside Schumann's poetic world. Virtuosity and display are bi-products of her dedication to the letter and spirit of the score. Her rubato seems completely right and tempos are judged perfectly. The recording of the *Piano Concerto* (in the 78 era, the preferred choice of most collectors) is a little dry, but the performance is fresher than her mono account with Rudolf Schwarz and the Philharmonia. Decent transfers.

Violin Concerto in D min.

***** Decca 444 811-2. Bell, Cleveland O, Dohnányi − BRAHMS: *Violin Concerto.* *****

(N) **(*) CBC SMCD 5197. Kang, Vancouver SO, Comisiona − WIENIAWSKI: *Violin Concerto No. 2 in D min.; Légende in G min.* **(*)**

With Dohnányi and the Cleveland Orchestra adding to the weight and drama, Joshua Bell in a commanding performance defies the old idea of this concerto as flawed: he brings out its charm as well as power. The central slow movement has rapt intensity and the dance-rhythms of the finale have fantasy as well as jauntiness and jollity. Full-bodied, well-balanced recording.

It is a measure of the artistry of the young Canadian violinist Juliette Kang, winner of the Yehudi Menuhin International Competition, that she conceals the problems of the Schumann concerto, so much less grateful for the soloist than the Wieniawski. Playing with dazzlingly clean articulation even in the most taxing bravura passages, she gives a smaller-scale reading than most, which compensates for any lack of weight in fiery brilliance and thoughtful expressiveness. The slightly recessed CBC recording plays its part in giving that impression, with orchestral sound also less full-bodied than most.

Introduction & Allegro appassionato in G, Op. 92.

(B) **(*) Sony (ADD) SBK 48166. Serkin, Phd. O, Ormandy − BRAHMS: *Concerto No. 1* **(*)**; MENDELSSOHN: *Capriccio brillant.* ****

(N) (BB) ** Naxos 8.554089. Biret, Polish Nat. R. SO, Wit − BRAHMS: *Piano Concerto No. 2.* ****

Serkin plays with his accustomed panache and he is given excellent support from Ormandy. The piano-tone could be fuller in timbre but the overall effect has considerable warmth, and those looking for a recording of this relatively unfamiliar piece will find much here to arrest them. The Brahms coupling shows Serkin at his finest.

As with the companion work below, Biret's playing is romantically full-blooded, and she receives warm support from Wit and the Polish Orchestra. However, a tighter overall grip would have made the performance even more effective. No complaints about the recording, which is resonantly full and well balanced.

Introduction & Concert-allegro, Op. 134.

(N) (BB) ** Naxos 8.554088. Biret, Polish Nat. R. SO, Wit − BRAHMS: *Piano Concerto No. 1 in D minor, Op. 15.* ****

Idil Biret plays with no mean virtuosity and brilliance, and this performance is more successful than its coupling. The recording is spacious.

SYMPHONIES

Symphony in G min. (Zwickau); Symphonies Nos. 1–3 (Rhenish), Op. 97; Symphony No. 4: original 1841 version and revised 1851 version; (i) *Konzertstück for 4 Horns & Orchestra in F, Op. 86.*

⚫ DG 457 591-2 (3). ORR, Gardiner.

Symphonies Nos. 1–3 (Rhenish); 4 (original version).

***** Teldec 0630 12674-2(2). COE, Harnoncourt.

With his brilliant orchestra of period instruments Gardiner offers not just the four regular symphonies but a complete survey of Schumann as symphonist. He seeks specifically to explode the myth that Schumann was a poor orchestrator, pointing out how quick he was to learn from his own mistakes. Gardiner makes an exception over the 1851 revision of the *Fourth Symphony*, in which Schumann thickened the woodwind writing with much doubling. Illuminatingly, both versions of that symphony are included, with the contrasts well brought out. Gardiner himself, like Brahms, prefers the slimmer, more transparent first version, suggesting that the 1851 changes made it safer and less original. Yet paradoxically, in performance Gardiner is even more inspired in the later version, which here emerges as bitingly dramatic, working up to a thrilling coda. Like other cycles this one offers the *Overture, Scherzo and Finale* of 1841 as a necessary extra, but still more fascinating is the *Konzertstück* of 1849 for four horns, with the ORR soloists breathtaking in their virtuosity on nineteenth-century instruments. Also included is the early, incomplete *Symphony in G minor* of 1832 (named after Schumann's home town of Zwickau). Under Gardiner the two completed movements emerge as highly original in their own right.

Typically, Harnoncourt takes a distinctive view of Schumann in his symphony cycle, drawing fine playing from the COER, even though the slightly distanced recording with a relatively small string band reduces the impact. Those devoted to Harnoncourt's rethinking will find much to admire, not least in the original version of No. 4, but too often his point-making draws attention to itself distractingly, with fussy detail in obtrusive rallentandos or a reluctance to phrase over a melody as in the slow movement of No. 1. It is surprising too to find him trivializing the Cologne Cathedral fourth movement of the *Rhenish*.

Symphonies Nos. 1–4.

(M) *** DG 429 672-2 (2). BPO, Karajan.

(M) *** RCA 74321 61820-2 (2). NDR SO, Eschenbach.

(B) **(*) DG Double 453 049-2 (2). VPO, Bernstein.

(N) (B) ** Teldec Ultima 8573 85191- (2). LPO, Masur.

Symphonies Nos. 1–4: Manfred Overture, Op. 115.

(M) **(*) Sony (ADD) MH2K 62349 (2). Cleveland O, Szell.

Symphonies Nos. 1 in B flat (Spring), Op. 38; 2 in C, Op. 61.

(B) *** Sony (ADD) SBK 48269. Bav. RSO, Kubelik.

Symphonies Nos. 3 in E flat (Rhenish), Op. 97; 4 in D min., Op. 120; Overture Manfred, Op. 115.

(B) *** Sony (ADD) SBK 48270. Bav. RSO, Kubelik.

Symphonies Nos. 1–4; Overture, Scherzo & Finale, Op. 52.

(M) *** EMI CMS7 64815-2 (2). Dresden State O, Sawallisch.

Symphonies Nos. 1–4; Overture: Julius Caesar, Op. 128; Overture, Scherzo & Finale, Op. 52.

(B) **(*) Double Decca (ADD) 448 930-2 (2). VPO, Solti.

Symphonies Nos. 1–2 in C; Genoveva Overture.

**(*) Australian DG Eloquence 463 200-2. BPO, Kubelik.

Symphonies Nos. 3–4; Manfred Overture.

**(*) Australian DG Eloquence 463 201-2. BPO, Kubelik.

Karajan's interpretations of the Schumann *Symphonies* stand above all other recordings on modern instruments. No. 1 is a beautifully shaped performance, with orchestral playing of the highest distinction; No. 2 is among the most powerful ever recorded, combining poetic intensity and intellectual strength in equal proportions; and No. 3 is also among the most impressive versions ever commited to disc: its famous fourth-movement evocation of Cologne Cathedral is superbly spacious and eloquent, with quite magnificent brass playing. No. 4 can be classed alongside Furtwängler's famous record, with Karajan similarly inspirational, yet a shade more self-disciplined than his illustrious predecessor. However, the reissued complete set brings digital remastering which – as with the Brahms symphonies – has leaner textures than before, while in tuttis the violins above the stave may approach shrillness.

The Dresden CDs of the Schumann *Symphonies* under Sawallisch are as deeply musical as they are carefully considered; the orchestral playing combines superb discipline with refreshing naturalness and spontaneity. Sawallisch catches all Schumann's varying moods, and his direction has splendid vigour. These recordings have dominated the catalogue, alongside Karajan's, for some years. Although the reverberant acoustic brought a degree of edge to the upper strings, the sound-picture has the essential fullness which the Karajan transfers lack, and the remastering has cleaned

up the upper range to a considerable extent. The set now appears in a mid-priced box.

Christoph Eschenbach's set with the North German Radio Symphony Orchestra is among the finest to have appeared for many years. There is a consistent feeling for line and a firm yet flexible pulse. Tempi are sensible, phrases shaped with natural feeling and without any hint of the fussy intrusive touches that attract attention to the interpreter rather than the composer. Moreover Eschenbach is most responsive to the textures, so often written off as thick. He brings a warmth and above all clarity that almost dispels the traditional view of Schumann's orchestration as opaque. As one recalls from his performances as a pianist earlier in his career, he has a keen affinity with the Schumann sensibility. Good, clean recording too. This is the first modern set that can be recommended alongside the classic Sawallisch and above all Karajan recordings, and it offers probably the best sound of all.

Kubelik's fine Sony set also remains fully competitive. The recording was made in the Hercules-Saal, Munich, in 1979, and the advantages of that glowing acoustic can be felt throughout. The orchestral playing is generally very fine (if not quite as polished as the Berlin Philharmonic) and is especially eloquent in the spacious slow movements. These are strongly characterized readings with plenty of vitality which display the same bright and alert sensitivity to Schumann's style as did his earlier set for DG. But the Sony recording is obviously more modern, and the latest CD transfer brings plenty of body to the sound and a better focus to the violins than in the Sawallisch set. That more logically includes the *Overture, Scherzo and Finale*, but many will count the *Manfred Overture* an equally desirable alternative.

No. 2, with which Szell began his cycle in October 1958, proves to be a thrilling performance of great power and strong forward thrust, yet the eloquent *Adagio* expands gloriously and brings the most ardent response from the Cleveland strings. Szell is at his most incisive and the orchestra are at their warmest in No. 1. The account of the *Rhenish* is even finer, marvellously full of life. The playing is breathtaking, with the horns gloriously full-blooded. No. 4 is strong and dramatic, not as weighty as some, but equally convincing. Szell proves himself an outstanding exponent of Schumann, able to stand alongside the finest interpreters of his day, and, were it not for the reduced range of dynamic, this set would have been even more recommended.

Kubelik's earlier accounts of the symphonies are beautifully played and well recorded. The readings have not the drive of Karajan, notably in No. 4, but they undoubtedly have both eloquence and warmth. They are straightforward and unmannered and recorded in a spacious acoustic with good CD transfers. Kubelik's ear for balance removes all suspicions of heaviness in the orchestration, and the recordings, dating from the mid-1960s, still sound good. Two enjoyable overtures are offered as a bonus.

Bernstein's VPO recordings from 1984–5 have the extra voltage which comes with live music-making at its most compulsive, though he seems reluctant to let the music speak for itself. The first movement of the *Spring Symphony* is pushed very hard, and the *Second Symphony* also brings the same larger-than-life projection. Slow movements are obviously deeply felt and have both warmth and humanity. In the *Rhenish Symphony* Bernstein's expressive indulgences are less disruptive. The outer movements of the *Fourth* are not allowed to move forward at a steady pace, but the *Romanze* has warmth and charm, even if the phrasing at the opening has an element of self-consciousness. Even so, with splendid orchestral playing and much engaging detail, there is a great deal to admire throughout these performances, and the resonant acoustic of the Grossersaal of the Musik-verein gives the music-making a robust immediacy.

Solti's Schumann interpretations are full of his personal brand of lyrical intensity. The most compelling performance of the cycle is the *Second Symphony*, with its passionate slow movement. And with a feeling of spontaneous lyricism paramount, this is a most compellingly individual reading. The performance of the *Spring Symphony* is played well enough but is just a shade disappointing. However the *Rhenish* is another memorable performance. Here Solti's sense of rhythm is strikingly alert so that the first movement hoists one aloft on its soaring melodies and, comparably, the drama of the *Fourth Symphony* is given full force without ever falling into excessive tautness: there is always room to breathe. The *Julius Caesar Overture* is no masterpiece, but makes an enjoyable bonus and the *Overture, Scherzo and Finale* is very successful. The late 1960s recordings are slightly dry, bright and forward, but one cannot complain that Schumann's scoring sounds too thick!

The Masur set, well played as it is, and given full-blooded digital sound, is less convincing. The performances have boldness and strength, but the slow movements lack something in romantic expansiveness and the second movement of the *Rhenish* is comparatively brusque. In the *Fourth Symphony* Masur uses the original 1841 Leipzig version of the score favoured by Brahms, where the differences are most marked in the finale.

Symphony No. 1 in B flat (Spring), Op. 38.

(M) *** DG (ADD) 447 408-2. BPO, Karajan – BRAHMS: *Symphony No. 1*. ***

Karajan is totally attuned to Schumann's sensibility and he provides a strong yet beautifully shaped performance of the *Spring Symphony*. The very opening is electrifying with the Berlin Philharmonic giving of their finest. The sound is an obvious improvement on the previous CD incarnation of this well-balanced analogue recording from the early 1970s, adding body and weight to the clear, fresh detail.

Symphonies Nos. 1; 3 in E flat (Rhenish), Op. 97.

(BB) *** ASV CDQS 6073. RLPO, Janowski.

Janowski's pairing of the *Spring* and *Rhenish symphonies* is particularly successful. The pacing throughout both sym-phonies is most convincing, with a good deal of the inspi-rational pull that makes the Karajan readings so telling. In the Cologne Cathedral evocation of the *Rhenish*, the Liverpool brass rise sonorously to the occasion and the recording is altogether first class, bright, clear and full, with a concert hall ambience. At super-bargain price, this is strongly competitive.

Symphonies Nos. 1; 4 in D min..

(M) *** DG (IMS) 445 718-2. BPO Karajan.

Karajan's recording of the *Spring Symphony* is additionally available coupled with the splendid account of the *Fourth Symphony* at mid-price, in which the current transfer seems somewhat fuller than in the boxed set.

Symphony No. 2; Konzertstück for 4 Horns; Manfred Overture, Op. 115.

*(*) DG 453 480-2. Philh. O, Thielemann.

Christian Thielemann is obviously a major talent, and made a strong impression both at the Met and at Covent Garden when he conducted Richard Strauss's *Elektra* and Pfitzner's *Palestrina*. Alas, his Schumann proves a great disappoint-ment. He produces a superb sound from the Philharmonia but he pulls the *Second Symphony* mercilessly. The sublime slow movement is never allowed to speak for itself. The same goes for the *Manfred Overture*, though he is less intrusive in the *Konzertstücke*. Good recording but a write-off all the same.

Symphonies Nos. 2 in C, Op. 61; 3 in E flat (Rhenish), Op. 97.

(b)*** DG 469 030-2. BPO, Levine.

(N)(M) **(*) DG (ADD) 469 554-2. Chicago SO, Barenboim.

Levine conducts warm and positive readings of both *Sym-phonies*, drawing superb playing from the Berlin Philhar-monic. Though the Berlin recording is warm and full to match – allowing thrilling crescendos in the Cologne Ca-thedral movement of the *Rhenish* – the inner textures are not ideally clear. The compensation is that the modern digital recording gives a satisfyingly full body to the sound.

Barenboim's exhilarating account of the *Second Symphony* stood out in his late 1970s cycle with the Chicago Orchestra, not only for the brilliance of the playing but also for the sense of purpose conveyed from beginning to end, even if in the slow movement he adopts a more heavily expressive style in the radiant opening melody than some will approve. His account of the *Rhenish* strongly brings out the long-established German sympathies of the Chicago Orchestra. Richly impressive with superb horn playing, the perform-ance is above all weighty, with the first movement less lightly sprung than usual, but the more powerful for that and with the Cologne Cathedral movement taken slowly and heavily. The originally very opulent recording has been freshened in the present transfers, but has lost some of its richness of sonority in consequence.

Symphony No. 2 in C, Op. 61; 4 Pieces from Carnaval, Op. 9 (arr. Ravel); 6 Pieces from Kinderjahr, Op. 68 (arr. Adorno).

**(*) BIS CD 1055. RPO, Joeres.

Dirk Joeres offers an idiomatic and sensitive account of the *Second Symphony*. He has the advantage of excellent playing from the Royal Philharmonic and this is a performance of some quality. The extra items are undeniably enterprising: there are four fragments that survive from Ravel's orchestra-tion of *Carnaval*, never before recorded, which only came to light in the 1970s; with *Kinderjahr*, there is a transcription by the philosopher and once-composer Theodor Wiesengrund Adorno of six of the Op. 68 *Album for the Young*.

Symphony No. 3 in E flat (Rhenish), Op. 97.

(M) *** DG (IMS) 445 502-2. LAPO, Giulini – BEETHOVEN: *Symphony No. 5.* ***

Symphony No. 3 (Rhenish); (i) Des Sängers Fluch, Op. 139.

*** Chan. 9760. Danish Nat. RSO, Schonwandt; (i) with Fischer, Rorholm, Wagenführer, Henschel, Hansen, Danish Nat. R. Ch.

Symphony No. 3 (Rhenish); Overture, Scherzo & Finale; Overture Genoveva.

*(*) DG 459 680-2. Philh. O, Thielemann.

Giulini's *Rhenish* is completely free of interpretative exaggeration and its sheer musical vitality and nobility of spirit are beautifully conveyed. The Los Angeles players produce a very well-blended, warm and cultured sound that is a joy to listen to in itself. The 1980 recording is also extremely fine and, with its superb Beethoven coupling, this is very highly recommendable.

Schonwandt and the fine Danish orchestra also give a fresh, spontaneous-sounding, well-paced reading of Schumann's warmest symphony. Schonwandt lifts rhythms infectiously in a performance full of light and shade, giving rapt intensity to the inner meditation of the *Cologne Cathedral* movement. The playing of the fine Copenhagen Orchestra is unfailingly cultured. A strongly competitive and compelling account, beautifully recorded by the Danish Radio engineers. The rare and generous coupling is most welcome, the 40-minute long choral ballad *The Minstrel's Curse*. A late work, it comes from 1852 and is a setting of Ludwig Uhland's ballad, which Schumann's collaborator Richard Pohl interspersed with other Uhland poems. No less a Schumann authority than Joan Chissell rates it well above the companion choral pieces of the period, and it has some delightful moments. It may lack the lyrical freshness of the symphony, but in this dedicated performance it impressively reveals Schumann's dramatic side, with foretastes even of Wagner. Not all the soloists are ideally steady, but the chorus is outstanding. First-rate sound.

Once again here Thielemann draws glowing sounds from the Philharmonia in the *Rhenish Symphony*, helped by a weighty recording marked by opulent horn tone. Yet for all its power, the reading is too often self-conscious in moulding of phrases and changes of speed, while the *Cologne Cathedral* movement is taken surprisingly fast, making it a casual perambulation rather than a meditation.

Symphonies Nos. 3 (Rhenish); 4, Op. 120.

(M) *** Virgin VM5 61734-2. L. Classical Players, Norrington.

With Schumann's orchestration usually accused of being too thick, there is much to be said for period performances like this. Norrington not only clarifies textures, with natural horns in particular standing out dramatically, but, at unexaggerated speeds for the outer movements – even a little too slow for the first movement of No. 3 – the results are often almost Mendelssohnian. Middle movements in both symphonies are unusually brisk, turning slow movements into lyrical interludes. Warm, atmospheric recording.

Symphony No. 4 in D min., Op. 120.

⚙ (M) (***) DG mono 457 722-2 (2). BPO, Furtwängler – FURTWANGLER: *Symphony No. 2.* (***)

*** Orfeo (ADD) C 522 991 B. VPO, Boehm – MAHLER: *Lieder eines fahrenden Gesellen;* BEETHOVEN: *Symphony No. 4.* ***

(M) *** EMI (ADD) CDM5 67336-2. Philh. O, Klemperer – TCHAIKOVSKY: *Symphony No. 6 (Pathétique).* **(*)

(N) *** BBC BBCL4058-2. BBC SO, Monteux – BRAHMS: *Symphony No. 3* *** (with ROSSINI: *L'italiana in Algeri Overture.* **(*)).

Furtwängler's legendary account of the *Fourth Symphony* with the Berlin Philharmonic comes from 1953, the year before his death. It has long enjoyed classic status, and deservedly so. It is a really great performance and conveys the illusion that the musicians are spontaneously composing or improvising this music. The 'Wagnerian' preparation for the finale is quite electrifying, and for all the fluctuations of tempo, throughout at the same time there is a commanding musical grip on the proceedings. The sound is remarkably warm and vivid for its period.

Boehm's thrilling account of Schumann's *Fourth*, incandescent from first to last, crowns what was a very special Salzburg Festival concert in August 1969. In his studio recordings Boehm was rarely so fiery as here, with biting attack and strong rhythmic emphasis from the Vienna Philharmonic in superb form. The second-movement *Romanze* is set in sharp contrast: the deeply meditative opening theme gives way to lightness and transparency. The mystery of the slow introduction to the finale maintains the high voltage too, and though the close is something of a scramble with its successive accelerandos, the result could not be more exciting. Good radio sound, if with some edge on high violins.

Klemperer's too is a masterly performance. His slow introduction has a weight and consequence that command attention, and the slow tempo for the allegro is equally weighty and compelling, even if initially one disagrees with it. The Scherzo with its striking main theme packs enormous punch and the brief slow movement is exquisitely played. For the finale Klemperer's speed is faster than many, and he makes the conclusion most exciting. Plainly the Philharmonia players were on their toes throughout. The 1961 Kingsway recording is full, rounded and fresh in EMI's best manner and the new coupling for the Klemperer Legacy is most generous.

Monteux recorded the *Fourth Symphony* in his San Francisco days but this did not enjoy wide currency outside the United States. Those who remember the BBC Symphony Orchestra in the early 1960s when it had been in the hands of Sir Malcolm Sargent and Rudolf Schwarz will recall that strong though its wind section was, the string sonority was generally opaque and thick. By comparison, Monteux produces a lighter, more transparent sound, given the constraints of Schumann's much criticised scoring. Rhythmic accents are lighter and there is a sense of drama without any histrionics. A valuable memento of Monteux in repertoire that is not associated with him.

CHAMBER MUSIC

Abendlied, Op. 85/2; Adagio & Allegro in A flat, Op. 70; Fantasiestücke, Op. 73; 3 Romances, Op. 94; 3 Pieces in Folk Style, Op. 102/2–4.

(M) *** Ph. (IMS) (ADD) 426 386-2. Holliger, Brendel.

Adagio & Allegro, Op. 70; Fantasiestücke, Op. 73; 5 Stücke im Volkston, Op. 102.

(BB) *** Naxos 8.550654. Kliegel, Merscher – SCHUBERT: *Arpeggione Sonata.* ***

The three *Romances* are specifically for oboe, but Holliger suggests that the others too are suitable for oboe, since the composer himself gave different options. One misses something by not having a horn in the *Adagio and Allegro*, a cello in the folk-style pieces, or a clarinet in the *Fantasiestücke* (the oboe d'amore is used here); but Holliger has never sounded more magical on record and, with superbly real recording and deeply imaginative accompaniment, the result is an unexpected revelation.

Maria Kliegel and Kristin Merscher couple these charming Schumann miniatures with the Schubert *Arpeggione* and turn in fresh and musical performances and are recorded in very clean and well-focused sound.

Fantasiestücke, Op. 73.

*** Decca (ADD) 430 149-2. Cohen, Ashkenazy – BRAHMS: *Clarinet Sonatas.* ***

Fantasiestücke, Op. 73; 3 Romances, Op. 94.

*** Chan. 8506. De Peyer, Pryor – SCHUBERT: *Arpeggione Sonata*; WEBBER: *Silvana Variations.* ***

Fantasiestücke; 5 Stücke in Volkston.

*** Ph. 412 230-2. Maisky, Argerich – SCHUBERT: *Arpeggione Sonata.* ***

With warmth of tone and much subtlety of colour, Gervase de Peyer gives first-class performances and is well supported by Gwenneth Pryor. The recording is most realistic.

A thoroughly recommendable alternative account by Franklin Cohen and Vladimir Ashkenazy of these lovely pieces; if you want them on clarinet, this version is as good as any. It is well recorded, too.

Mischa Maisky on cello and Martha Argerich give relaxed, leisurely accounts of these pieces that some collectors will find a bit self-indulgent. Others will luxuriate in the refinement and sensitivity of their playing.

Märchenbilder, Op. 113.

*** Virgin VC7 59309-2. Tomter, Andsnes – BRAHMS: *Viola Sonatas.* *** ●

**(*) Chan. 8550. Imai, Vignoles – BRAHMS: *Viola Sonatas.* **(*)

The young Norwegian duo bring great sensitivity and freshness to bear on the *Märchenbilder*, and their playing gives great pleasure, as does the Brahms coupling.

The *Märchenbilder* are also persuasively played here by Nobuko Imai and Roger Vignoles. The recording acoustic is not ideal, but this does not seriously detract from the value of this coupling.

Märchenerzählungen, Op. 132; Kinderszenen: Träumerei.

*** RCA 09026 63504-2. Collins, Isserlis, Hough – BRAHMS; FRUHLING: *Clarinet Trios.* ***

It makes a delightful coupling on an outstandingly successful disc having Schumann's *Fairy-tale Suite* – an association not explained in the booklet, which leaves you simply with the daunting German title – with Steven Isserlis on the cello taking the original viola part. *Träumerei*, offered as an encore to the three main works on the disc, comes in an arrangement for the same forces by Stephen Hough.

Piano Quartet in E flat, Op. 47; Piano Quintet in E flat, Op. 44.

(M) **(*) Berlin Classics (ADD) 0094032BC. Rösel, Gewandhaus Qt.

(B) **(*) Hyp. Dyad CDD 22008 (2). Schubert Ens. of L. – HUMMEL: *Piano Quintet*; SCHUBERT: *Trout Quintet.* **(*)

(M) **(*) CRD (ADD) CRD 3324. Rajna, members of the Alberni Qt.

These Leipzig performances both sound very good, though a little more amplitude round the aural image would perhaps be welcome. The playing of Peter Rösel and the Gewandhaus Quartet is keenly alive and very musical. Tempi are fairly brisk but phrasing is affectionate and sensitive. This is playing of quality and good value at mid-price.

Lively, committed performances from the Schubert Ensemble of London led by their excellent pianist, William Howard. There are more individual versions of both works but if this inexpensive Dyad compilation seems tempting, the overall standard of musicianship is commendable and their playing enjoyable. Good if not outstanding recording.

Though not flawlessly polished in their playing, Thomas Rajna and the Alberni give performances that in their way are urgent and enjoyable. The recording is brighter and crisper, which gives an extra (and not unlikeable) edge to the performances.

Piano Quartet, Op. 47; Piano Quintet, Op. 44; Adagio & Allegro, Op. 70; Andante & Variations, Op. 46; Fantasiestücke, Op. 73; Märchenbilder, Op. 113; Violin Sonata No. 2 in D min., Op. 121.

*** EMI CDS5 55484-2 (2). Argerich, Schwarzenberg, Hall, Imai, Maisky, Neunecker, Gutman, Rabinovitch.

These recordings were made at a series of informal concerts at Nijmegen, and they radiate a spontaneity and life that are more difficult to capture under studio conditions. The *Piano Quintet* with Martha Argerich, Dora Schwarzenberg, Lucy Hall, Nobuko Imai and Mischa Maisky must be numbered among the most vibrant on record, and the *Piano Quartet*, with Natalia Gutman replacing Maisky and with Alexandre Rabinovitch at the piano, is hardly less fine. Although this is an arbitrary collection, those whose needs are met by this particular compilation will not be disappointed.

(i) *Piano Quartet, Op. 47; Piano Quintet, Op. 44. Piano Trios Nos. 1 in D min., Op. 63; 2 in F, Op. 80; 3 in G min., Op. 110.*

(B) *** Ph. Duo (ADD) 456 323-2 (2). Beaux Arts Trio, (i) with Bettelheim and Rhodes.

Once again Philips have compiled a particularly generous measure for this Duo of Beaux Arts Schumann performances from the 1970s. This illustrious trio (with associates) give splendid readings of the *Piano Quartet* and *Quintet*. The vitality of inspiration is brought out consistently, and with that goes their characteristic concern for fine ensemble and refined textures. They are also probably the safest bet for the three *Piano Trios*. Not that competition is exactly legion, but none that we have heard can outclass the Beaux Arts in terms of musicianship and finesse. Throughout, the set offers cultured and concentrated music-making, matched by truthful and present analogue recording.

Piano Quintet in E flat, Op. 44.

(BB) *** Naxos 8.550406. Jandó, Kodály Qt – BRAHMS: *Piano Quintet.* ***

(***) Testament mono SBT 3063. Aller, Hollywood Qt – BRAHMS: *Piano Quartets* etc. (***)

(BB) **(*) ASV CDQS 6217. Bradbury, Silvestri String Qt – BARTOK: *Piano Quintet.* **(*)

A strongly characterized performance of Schumann's fine *Quintet* from Jenö Jandó and the Kodály Quartet. This is robust music-making, romantic in spirit, and its spontaneity is well projected by a vivid recording, made in an attractively resonant acoustic. An excellent bargain.

Exhilarating and masterly, the Hollywood Quartet and Victor Aller on Testament comes from the compilation of Brahms chamber music, recorded in the mid-1950s. A performance of some stature which transcends sonic limitations.

Suzanne Bradbury and the Silvestri Quartet give eminently satisfactory performances of the Schumann *Quintet* and, although they would not necessarily be a first choice, they deserve a recommendation, not least on account of the enterprising Bartók coupling.

Piano Trios Nos. 1–3; Fantasiestücke, Op. 88.

*** Ph. 432 165-2 (2). Beaux Arts Trio.
**(*) Chan. 8832/3 (2). Borodin Trio.

Piano trio No. 1 in D. min., Op. 63; Bilder aus Osten, Op. 66; Phantasiestücke, Op. 88.

(N) *** MDG 303 0921-2. Trio Parnassus.

Piano Trios Nos. 2 in F, Op.80; 3 in G min., Op.110; 6 Pieces in the Form of a Canon, Op. 56.

(N) *** MDG 303 0922-2. Trio Parnassus.

Piano Trio No. 1 in D min., Op. 63.

(M) **(*) CRD (ADD) CRD 3433. Israel Piano Trio – BRAHMS: *Piano Trio No. 2.* **(*)

Piano Trios Nos. 2 in F, Op. 80; 3 in G min., Op. 110; Fantasiestücke, Op. 88.

(M) ** CRD (ADD) CRD 3458. Israel Piano Trio.

Piano Trios Nos. 1, Op. 63; 2, Op. 80.

(BB) *** Naxos 8.553836.Vienna Brahms Trio.

The Beaux Arts are probably the safest choice in this repertoire, an instance of the most obvious recommendation being the best. Not that competition is exactly legion, but none that we have heard can outclass them in terms of musicianship and finesse. Cultured playing, matched by truthful and present recording.

The Trio Parnassus are a very good ensemble and give characterful and sensitive accounts of the three *Piano Trios* and the other repertoire included here. The MDG recording is very natural and well focused, and although they are not to be recommended in preference to the Beaux Arts, they can be considered alongside them.

On Chandos are full-hearted performances that give undoubted pleasure – and would give more, were it not for some swoons from Rostislav Dubinsky who, at the opening of the *D minor Trio*, phrases with a rather ugly scoop. While too much should not be made of this, greater reticence would have been more telling throughout. The Chandos recording is vivid and faithful.

The Israel Piano Trio give a powerfully projected account of the *D minor Trio*; the pianist is at times rather carried away, as if he were playing a Brahms concerto. There are, however, some sensitive and intelligent touches, and the recording is first class. Nos. 2 and 3 are much the same: lively, articulate playing with a sometimes over-forceful pianist.

The Vienna Brahms Trio give eminently musical accounts of both scores and are satisfactorily recorded. The Beaux Arts Trio on Philips, however, are every bit as competitive.

Piano Trio No. 3 in G min.; Piano Quartet in E flat, Op. 47; Fantasiestücke, Op.88.

(N) *** Hyp. CDA 67175. Florestan Trio (augmented).

The Florestan Trio is first rate in every way and gives thoughtful and spirited accounts of all three of these Schumann pieces. It is joined effectively in the *E flat Piano Quartet* by the violist Thomas Riebl.

String Quartets Nos. 1–3, Op. 41/1–3.

(N) *** HM HMU 907270. Eroica Qt.

String Quartets Nos. 1 in A min.; 2 in F, Op. 41/1–2.

*** CRD (ADD) CRD 3333. Alberni Qt.

The Eroica is the only ensemble so far to have squeezed all three Schumann quartets onto a single CD. Schumann's writing benefits from the transparency of tone produced by the group's early instruments. Tempos are judged well, and the overall impression is fresh and enjoyable.

The well-recorded and sympathetic performances by the Alberni Quartet have plenty of finesse and charm and are guided throughout by sound musical instinct. However, only two of the *Quartets* are included.

Violin Sonatas Nos. 1 in A min., Op. 105; 2 in D min., Op. 121; 3 in A min., Op. posth.

(N) **(*) CPO 999 597-2. Faust, Avenhaus.

Violin Sonatas Nos. 1; 2 in D min., Op. 121.

*** DG 419 235-2. Kremer, Argerich.

Violin Sonata No. 1 in A min., Op. 105.

(***) Biddulph mono LAB 165. Busch and Serkin – BRAHMS: *String Quartets Nos. 1–2* (**(*)) (with REGER: *Violin Sonata No. 5, Op. 84: Allegretto* (***)).

The *Violin Sonatas* both date from 1851 and are 'an oasis of freshness' in Schumann's last creative period. Kremer and Argerich are splendidly reflective and mercurial by turn and have the benefit of an excellent recording.

The Biddulph sleeve-note hails the 1937 Busch–Serkin account of the *A minor Sonata*, Op. 105, erroneously billed as No. 2 on both the label and sleeve, as 'never having been equalled for its intensity and romantic ardour'. This is absolutely right. The disc throws in the only Reger that Busch recorded, the *Allegretto* from the *F sharp minor Sonata*, Op. 84.

Isabelle Faust and Silke Avenhaus are not household names but both are accomplished players. The *Third Sonata* was composed on the brink of Schumann's breakdown and began life in October 1853 as a collaborative piece with Brahms and Albert Dietrich. Schumann provided the *Intermezzo* and *Finale*, but a few days later he replaced the others' movements with two of his own. It was the last music he ever wrote, but was not published until the centenary year in 1956. In character the first movement is close to its D minor predecessor, but as a whole the piece is far from negligible. The *A minor* is still the finest of the three. The performances are a little assertive and not always prepared to let Schumann speak for himself but this should not deter the reader from considering this well-recorded disc.

Fünf Stücke in Volkston (for cello and piano).

(M) *** Decca (ADD) .452 895-2. Rostropovich, Britten – BRITTEN: *Sonata*; DEBUSSY: *Cello Sonata in D min.* ***
(M) *** Decca 460 974-2. Rostropovich, Britten (as above) – DEBUSSY: *Sonata* ***; SCHUBERT: *Arpeggione Sonata.* **(*)

Though simpler than either the Britten or Debussy sonatas with which it is coupled, this is just as elusive a work. Rostropovich and Britten show that the simplicity is not as square and solid as might at first seem and that, in the hands of masters, these *Five Pieces in Folk Style* have a rare charm, particularly the last with its irregular rhythm. The excellent recording justifies the reissue under the Classic Sound logo, and is also available with Schubert instead of Britten in Decca's Legend series.

PIANO MUSIC

Abegg Variations, Op. 1; Davidsbündlertänze, Op. 6.

*** Ottavio OTRC 39027. Cooper – BRAHMS: *Fantasias, Op. 116.* ***

Imogen Cooper plays the *Abegg Variations* with a rare combination of iridescent brilliance and poetic feeling, and she characterizes the *Davidsbündlertänze* with consistent imagination and colour. Her playing is spontaneous from first to last, and the recording most realistic.

Abegg Variations, Op. 1; Kreisleriana, Op. 16; 3 Romances, Op. 28.

(N) **(*) CPO 999 598-2. Banfield.

Volker Banfield provides a thoughtfully musical account of *Kreisleriana* (although the ending of the third section is a bit scrambled and overpedalled) as well as the *Abegg Variations* and the three *Romances*. No challenge to the likes of Perahia or Lupu, but intelligent playing all the same.

Albumblätter, Op. 99; Arabeske, Op. 18; Etudes symphoniques, Op. 13.

(BB) *** Naxos 8.550144. Vladar.

Stefan Vladar intersperses the additional studies that Schumann published as an appendix into the *Etudes symphoniques*. His account is quite simply superb in every respect and deserves recording of comparable excellence. The *Albumblätter* is hardly less masterly. Artistically this rates three stars, with the compelling quality of the playing transcending the sonic limitations of the recording.

Allegro, Op. 8; Gesänge der Frühe, Op. 133; Novelletten, Op. 21; 3 Fantasiestücke, Op. 111.

**(*) Olympia OCD 436. Brautigam.

As the opening *Allegro* shows, this is strong, spontaneously impulsive playing, though in the *Novelletten* some might wish for less passion and more poise. However, there is poetry too: the second and, especially, the third of the *Fantasiestücke* are very appealing. The *Gesänge der Frühe* ('Morning Songs') brings the most responsive playing of all and is most touchingly done. Clear, bold piano recording.

Arabeske in C, Op. 18; Blumenstück, Op. 19; Carnaval, Op. 9; Davidsbündlertänze, Op. 6; Fantasia in C, Op. 17; 8 Fantasiestücke, Op. 12; 3 Fantasiestücke, Op. 111; Faschingsschwank aus Wien, Op. 26; Humoresque in B flat, Op. 20; Kinderszenen, Op. 15; 4 Nachtstücke, Op. 23; Novelletten, Op. 21; Papillons, Op. 2; 3 Romances, Op. 28; Piano Sonatas Nos. 1 in F sharp min., Op. 11; 2 in G min., Op. 22; Waldszenen, Op. 82.

(M) **(*) Ph. (IMS) (ADD) 432 308-2 (7). Arrau.

Claudio Arrau's playing has warmth, poise and the distinctive, aristocratic finesse that graced everything this artist touched. Arrau has the measure of Schumann's impulsive temperament and is almost always perfectly attuned to his sensibility. Not all the rubati ring true and there are moments that seem a little self-conscious. But there is a very great deal to admire in this compilation, and few collectors will be greatly disappointed.

Arabeske, Op. 18; Bunte Blätter, Op. 99; Carnaval, Op. 9; Kreisleriana, Op. 16; Novelletten, Op. 21/1 & 8; Papillons, Op. 2; Toccata, Op. 7.

(N)(B) *** EMI double fforte (ADD) CZS5 74191-2 (2). Egorov.

Yuri Egorov has the kind of temperament that makes him a highly volatile but always perceptive Schumann advocate. His playing offers many insights as well as superb pianism. There is no lack of delicacy in the *Arabeske*, a winningly flowing account, and he brings out the wide range of colour and attractive ideas in the elaborate set of *Bunte Blätter* (*Various Leaves*). His are among the finest versions of

Carnaval and *Kreisleriana*, the latter full of poetic and dynamic contrast, to say nothing of impulsive bravura. *Papillons*, too, has a great deal to commend it. Egorov does it with real imagination and much sensitivity, and although artistically his version is not superior to Murray Perahia's Sony account, the EMI recording is incomparably better. Indeed, the piano is given full sonority and fine presence throughout.

Arabeske, Op. 18; Carnaval, Op. 9; Davidsbündlertänze, Op. 6; Fantasie in C, Op. 17; Humoreske, Op. 20; Kinderszenen; Kreisleriana, Op. 16; Nachtstücke, Op. 23; Novelette, Op. 99/9; Papillons, Op. 2; 3 Romances, Op. 28; Sonata No. 2 in G min., Op. 22; Symphonic Studies, Op. 13; Waldszenen, Op. 21.

(N)(B) *** DG (ADD) 471 312-2 (4). Kempff.

Kempff began recording the major Schumann piano works in 1967 with *Papillons* and *Davisbündlertänze*, and he completed his survey in the early 1970s. Not all the music suits him equally well. He is in his element in pieces like the *Arabeske*, the relatively little-known first and third *Romances*, and the *Novelette*, where he inspires an element of fantasy, of spontaneous re-creation, and he is at his most inspirational in the *Fantasie in C major*. The reading is wayward and personal, but the poetry of the playing is never in doubt. *Davidsbündlertänze*, the *Nachtstücke* and *Papillons* are all extremely fine.

On the other hand the comparatively extrovert style of *Carnaval* suits him less well. It certainly does not lack life, but there is no special degree of illumination, and the performance even seems to lack absolute technical assurance. The recording too – hitherto very good – in *Carnaval* is clear but a little lacking in richness of sonority.

It might also be argued that Kempff's thoughtful, intimate readings of two of Schumann's most ambitious piano works, the *Etudes symphoniques* and *Kreisleriana*, are in danger of missing some of the heroism of the music, yet they are still marvelously persuasive, giving a clear illusion of live performances, spontaneously caught and again well recorded. Similarly if the sharper contrasts of the *Humoreske* are toned down by charm and geniality, the *Waldszenen* are glowingly relaxed and both are comparably personal and individual. Neither the *Kinderszenen* or the *Piano Sonata No. 2* are among Kempff's more compelling Schumann performances, but both are enjoyable, and the sound is improved in the current transfers.

The last time these recordings were gathered together they occupied six LPs, issued to commemorate Kempff's eightieth birthday, and we commented at the time that they were fully worthy of the occasion. The reissues still are, and on four bargain-priced CDs they are even better value.

Arabeske, Op. 18; Carnaval, Op. 9; Humoresque, Op. 20; Toccata in C, Op. 7.

*** Bis CD-960. Freddy Kempf.

A debut recital from Freddy Kempf. His Schumann blends the right amount of intelligence and intuitive feeling. He is at his best in the reflective and inward moments and his *Humoresque* is particularly successful. He has remarkable

technical prowess and refined musicianship. The recorded sound is very lively and natural, and the disc as a whole gives much satisfaction.

Carnaval; Faschingsschwank aus Wien, Op. 26; Kinderszenen, Op. 15.

(B) *** DG (ADD) 448 855-2. Barenboim.

Barenboim's 1979 reading of *Carnaval* is one of his finest recording achievements as a pianist. His lively imagination lights on the fantasy in this quirkily spontaneous sequence of pieces and makes them sparkle anew. *Carnival Jest from Vienna* is more problematic, but the challenge inspires Barenboim, and here too he is at his most imaginative and persuasive, bringing out the warmth and tenderness, as well as the brilliance. The recording is bold and truthful.

Davidsbündlertänze, Op. 6; Sonata No. 2 in G min., Op. 22; Toccata, Op. 7.

*** Teldec 9031 77476. Berezovsky.

Boris Berezovsky is a keyboard lion of the first order. Everything we have so far heard of his has been of exceptional artistry and great finesse. His formidable musicianship is allied to a technique of magisterial calibre, and this coupling is very impressive indeed.

Etudes symphoniques.

(B) *** EMI double forte CZS5 69521-2 (2). Alexeev –
    BRAHMS: *Fantasias* etc. ***

Dimitri Alexeev combines the virtuoso technique which the work demands with supreme musicality and poetic feeling, the performance providing a structural cohesion not always in evidence. The digital recording, made several years later than that of the coupling, is excellent in bringing out the warmth of the piano-tone. A first-rate bargain.

Fantasia in C, Op. 17.

(M) *** DG (ADD) 447 451-2. Pollini – SCHUBERT: *Wanderer Fantasia.* ***
*** Sony MK 42124. Perahia – SCHUBERT: *Wanderer Fantasia.* ***
*** Chan. 9793. Lortie – LISZT: *Concert Paraphrases of Beethoven's An die ferne Geliebte; Mignon; Schumann Lieder.* ***

This is among the most distinguished Schumann performances in the catalogue. Pollini's playing throughout has a command and authority on the one hand and deep poetic feeling on the other that hold the listener spellbound. The recording is good but not outstanding. A welcome mid-priced reissue in DG's series of 'Originals'.

Murray Perahia's account of the *C major Fantasy* is a performance of vision and breadth, immaculate in its attention to detail and refinement of nuance. The recording is good, even if it does not wholly convey the fullest range of sonority and dynamics.

Lortie is an unfailingly thoughtful and thought-provoking artist of compelling utterance, who always has something new to say – and whose expressive eloquence is always at the service of the composer. This newcomer ranks alongside the finest and most satisfying versions of the *C major Fantasia* now around. And it is *very* well recorded.

Fantasia in C; Faschingsschwank aus Wien, Op. 26; Papillons, Op. 2.

(M) *** EMI (ADD) CDM7 64625-2. S. Richter.

Richter's 1961 account of the *C major Fantasy* is a wonderfully poetic performance. Richter's phrasing, his magnificent control of dynamics, his gift for seeing a large-scale work as a whole – all these contribute towards the impression of unmatchable strength and vision. The recording is faithful, with genuine presence. The other two works included on this CD were recorded live during Richter's Italian concert tour a year later. The piano sound inevitably is somewhat less sonorous, shallower at fortissimo level, but fully acceptable. The account of *Papillons* is beguilingly subtle in control of colour.

Fantasia in C, Op. 17; Kinderszenen, Op. 15.

◉ (M) (***) Decca mono 466 498-2. Curzon – SCHUBERT: *Wanderer Fantasia.* (***) ◉

The *Fantasia* is a work indelibly associated with the composer's love for Clara and the spell that she cast over him. Curzon's extraordinarily chimerical and romantic reading of the first movement is matched by the depth of poetic feeling and passion he finds in the finale. Surely in this instance, to use his own metaphor, he perfectly succeeded in 'catching the butterfly on the wing' in a performance which is so 'live' and spontaneous in feeling, that it is difficult to believe it was made in the studio. The gentle *Kinderszenen* (also inspired by Clara) are equally magical. The recording is dry but faithful.

Fantasia in C, Op. 17; Kreisleriana, Op. 16.

(N) (M) *** RCA (ADD) 09026 63052-2. Rubinstein.

Rubinstein's account of the *Fantasia in C* is one of his finest Schumann performances on record. It is a wonderfully subtle in its control of tempo and colour, and the poetry of the outer sections is quite magical, while the centrepiece is arrestingly bold. In spite of the close balance, Rubinstein achieves exquisite graduations of tone; the recording made in 1965 ia among the best he received during this period. The CD opens with a hardly less compelling account of *Kreisleriana* in which the great pianist is at his most aristocratic. The impetuous opening is commanding and here the 1965 recording has been further enhanced by the new transfer which gives greater fullness and colour at all dynamic levels.

Fantasiestücke, Op. 12.

(N) (M) *** RCA (ADD) 09026 63071-2. Rubinstein, Phd. O, Ormandy – BRAHMS: *Piano Concerto No. 2.* ***

Rubinstein's high reputation as a Schumann interpreter is again well borne out here. His performance of the *Fantasiestücke* is unsurpassed, not even by Perahia. He shows the same control of colour and rubato that makes his Chopin playing so distinctive, yet there is nothing Chopinesque about the music-making itself; the changes of mood, so perfectly caught, are Schumann at his most poetic and chimerical. The 1976 recording has been greatly enhanced by the current remastering and has fine sonority and bloom.

Fantasiestücke, Op. 12; Kinderszenen, Op. 15; Kreisleriana, Op. 16.

(M) *** Ph. 434 732-2. Brendel.

Fantasiestücke is strong as well as poetic. The *Kinderszenen* is also one of the finest performances of the 1980s and is touched with real distinction. Brendel's *Kreisleriana* is intelligent and finely characterized. He is better recorded (in 1981/2) than most of his rivals and the overall impression is highly persuasive.

Fantasia in C; Piano Sonata No. 1 in F sharp min., Op. 11.

◉ *** EMI CDC5 56414-2. Andsnes.

The young Norwegian pianist gives us the freshest and most vibrant account of the *C major Fantasy* since Murray Perahia, coupled with as fine an account of the *F sharp minor Sonata* as you could find. It is beautifully paced and shaped. This is both magisterial and subtle playing, and well served by the engineers.

Humoreske in B flat, Op. 20.

(BB) **(*) Naxos 8.550469. Harden – REGER: *Variations.* **(*)

Wolf Harden's performance of the Schumann *Humoreske* is highly imaginative, idiomatic and full of sensitive touches. There is plenty of air round the aural image.

Humoreske, Op. 20; Kinderszenen, Op. 15; Kreisleriana, Op. 16.

*** Decca 440 496-2. Lupu.

Lupu is one of the few artists whose understanding of the composer can be measured alongside that of Murray Perahia. His account of the *Humoreske*, Op. 20, is both poetic and hardly less magical than the *Kreisleriana*. This is playing of great poetry and authority. The recording is excellent, albeit resonant.

Impromptus on a Theme of Clara Wieck, Op. 5; Variations on a Theme of Beethoven; Variations on an Original Theme (Geistervariationen); Variations on a Theme of Schubert.

** Athene ATHCD 23. Boyde – BRAHMS: *Variations on a Theme of Schumann.* **

An intelligently planned recital, which brings repertoire little-known even to those who know their Schumann. The ten *Impromptus on a Theme of Clara Wieck* of 1833 are well represented in the catalogue but the remainder are relatively neglected. The Beethoven variations of 1830 are based on the slow movement of the *Seventh Symphony*. The *Geistervariationen* was Schumann's very last work. Andreas Boyde has reconstructed the *Variations on a Theme of Schubert* which Schumann began in 1829 and to which he returned five years later. Accomplished but not highly sensitive playing, though this impression may in part be due to the close and two-dimensional recording.

Kinderszenen, Op. 15.

(N) (BB) *** Naxos 8.550885. Biret – DEBUSSY: *Children's*

Corner Suite **(*); TCHAIKOVSKY: *Album for the Young.* ***

Idil Biret was a pupil of Kempff and is completely at home in the delightful children's pieces of Schumann. The characterization is strong, sensitive and often touching, as in *Träumerei* and the lovely closing movement, *The Poet Speaks*. The piano recording, made in the Clara Wieck Auditorium, is forward but realistic.

Kinderszenen, Op. 15; Kreisleriana, Op. 16; Novelette in F, Op. 21/1.

(M) *** DG 445 599-2. Horowitz.

The subtle range of colour and articulation in *Kreisleriana* is remarkable, but then Horowitz plays in the studio just as if he were in front of a live audience, and the freshness and accuracy would be astonishing if we had not heard him repeating the trick. He was over eighty when he recorded the *Novelette* but the playing betrays remarkably little sign of frailty, and the recording given him by the DG engineers was among the finest he ever received. *Kinderszenen*, however, comes from a live recital, recorded in the Vienna Musikverein in 1987, a delightfully innocent performance never making pianistic points but letting the music speak for itself. The recording is good, but the audience's bronchial afflictions are inevitably a nuisance, even during the early spring of the year! An unmissable collection, just the same.

Kinderszenen, Op. 15; Kreisleriana, Op. 16; Waldszenen, Op. 82.

(N) (B) *** DG (ADD) 469 555-2. Kempff.

Nothing that Kempff does is without insight and the simplicity of his approach to the *Kinderszenen* is disarming. Even the famous *Träumerei* has an innocence to match the suite's overall conception. The *Waldszenen* too are delightfully evoked, especially the famous *Prophet Bird*; and if Kempff's thoughtfully intimate reading of the more ambitious *Kreisleriana* misses the element of heroism in the music, the playing is still marvellously persuasive, giving a clear illusion of live performance. The new transfers of recordings from the early 1970s have never sounded more natural and present.

Kinderszenen, Op. 15; Papillons, Op. 2.

(B) ** EMI Début CDZ5 73500-2. Slobodyanik – CHOPIN: *Piano Sonata No. 3; Polonaise No. 6.* **(*)

Alex Slobodyanik's accounts of *Papillons* and *Kinderszenen* are undoubtedly sensitive and distinguished by great beauty of touch. There are many imaginative touches but the performance is somewhat marred by moments of affectation, from which the Chopin is relatively free.

Piano Sonata No.1 in F min., Op. 14 (2nd version); Studies after the Caprices of Paganini, Op. 3/1–6; Op. 10/1–6.

(N) **(*) MDG 604 0941-2. Lee.

The Korean pianist Mi-Joo Lee gives us the 1853 version of the *F minor Sonata* which had a complicated gestation, although she restores two of the variations which Schumann finally excised. She also performs the two sets of *Paganini*

Studies, more rarities that Schumann lovers will want to investigate. Good playing and decent recording.

Piano Sonata No. 2 in G min., Op. 22.

*** Sony MK 44569. Perahia – SCHUBERT: *Piano Sonata No. 20.* ***

Perahia's account of the Schumann *G minor Sonata* is fresh, ardent and vital; every phrase is beautifully moulded yet somehow seems spontaneous in feeling – and spontaneity was the essence of Schumann's youthful genius. The recording places the listener fairly near the piano but is eminently truthful.

ORGAN MUSIC

4 Sketches, Op. 58 (ed. Bate).

(BB) *** ASV (ADD) CDQS 6127. Bate (Royal Albert Hall organ) – LISZT: *Organ Music.* ***

The *Four Sketches* were originally written for a piano with pedal attachment and are here arranged for organ by E. Power Biggs. Each of the pieces is in 3/4 time, but the writing is attractively diverse; they are pleasant trifles. Rich, atmospheric recording with fair detail, impressively transferred to CD. Generously coupled with Liszt's three major organ warhorses, this makes a very tempting super-bargain reissue.

VOCAL MUSIC

The Graham Johnson Lieder Edition

Following up his monumental Schubert song series for Hyperion, Graham Johnson here sets out on his parallel Schumann project with the same inspired combination of scholarship and artistry.

Lieder Vol. 1: *6 Gedichte und Requiem, Op. 90; 6 Gesänge, Op. 107; Aufträge; Die Blume der Ergebung; Er ist's; Heiss' mich nicht reden; Ihr Stimme; Mädchen-Schwermut; Melancholie; Die Meersee; Mignon (Kennst du das Land?); Nachtlied; Nur wer die Sehnsucht kennt; Röslein, Röslein!; Sängers Trost; Singet nicht in Trauertönen; So lasst mich scheinem; Das verlassene Mägdelein; Warnung; Zigeunerliedchen I & II..*

*** Hyp. CDJ 33101. Schäfer, Johnson.

For volume 1, Christine Schäfer is chosen to sing a collection of late songs, written between 1849 and 1852, which reflect the increasing disturbance of the composer's mind in bouts of depression. Though these songs – generally with writing more chromatic than earlier – have been seriously neglected, Schäfer and Johnson consistently show that Schumann's inspiration remained undiminished. The recording, forward and well-balanced, does not always bring out the full sweetness of Schäfer's voice, though the subtlety and beauty of her tonal shading is faithfully caught, in unfailingly sensitive response to word-meaning.

Lieder Vol. 2: *3 Gedichte von Emanuel Geibel, Op. 30; 12 Gedichte von Justinus Kerner, Op. 35; 4 Husarenlieder,*

Op. 117; An die Türen will ich schleichen; Ballade des Harfners; Die Löwenbraut; Wer nie sein Brot mit Tränen ass; Wer sich der Eisamkeit ergibt.

*** Hyp. CDJ 33102. Keenlyside, Johnson.

The virility of Simon Keenlyside's strongly projected singing is thrilling. This selection of songs concentrates on four poets, starting with four powerful settings of Goethe from late in Schumann's career, contrasting with light, ballad-like *Hussar songs*, also late, to words by Lenau. The other two groups of early songs, including *Der Hidalgo* to words by Geibel, with sparkling Spanish dance rhythms, and the substantial set of 12 settings of Justinus Kerner, a figure who links the other three poets. Johnson's notes as ever, like his playing, could not be more illuminating.

Lieder Vol. 3: *Frauenliebe und Leben, Op. 42* with poem; *Traum der eignen Tage, 7 Lieder of Elisabeth Kulmann, Op. 104; Songs of Mary Queen of Scots, Op. 135*. Lieder: *Blonde Lied; Geisternähe; Gesungen!; Himmel und Erde; Jasminenstrauch; Die Kartenlegerin; Loreley; Sag'an, o lieber Vogel mein; Schneeglöckchen; Die Soldatenbraut; Stiller Vorwuf..*

*** Hyp. CDJ 33103. Banse, Johnson.

The young German soprano Juliane Banse, with her warm, vibrant voice beautifully controlled, makes an imaginative choice of artist for this third volume of Graham Johnson's Schumann series. The selection concentrates mainly on songs on the subject of women's life and loves, not just in the ever-popular *Frauenliebe und Leben*. In that cycle, the strong tonal contrasts in Banse's singing heighten the drama throughout, but most of all in the final tragic song. As an epilogue, Banse recites the final poem in Chamisso's cycle, which wisely Schumann did not set. She also reads the composer's superscriptions before touching songs to poems by Elisabeth Kulmann, a poet who died tragically at 17. Rounding off the disc is the late set of five poems to words by Mary Queen of Scots – as Johnson points out, another 'Frauenliebe' without the 'Leben'. Fine recording and excellent notes.

Lieder, Vol. 4: *5 Lieder und Gesange, Op. 51; 6 Romanzen und Balladen, Op. 45* including *O weh des Scheidens, das er tat* by Clara SCHUMANN; *20 Poems from Liebesfrühling, Op. 37* (including 4 settings by Clara SCHUMANN).

**(*) Hyp. CDJ 33104. Doufexis, Widmer, Johnson.

In his fourth selection for the Hyperion Schumann Edition, Graham Johnson offers as centrepiece a sequence of twenty settings of poems from Rückert's *Liebesfrühling*, including four by Schumann's wife, Clara. Other Rückert settings are included too, as well as settings of Heine, Eichendorff and Goethe, all presented with the compelling scholarship with was associated with his monumental Schubert series. This time, instead of well-known singers, he has chosen to work with two sensitive artists relatively little known.

The German mezzo, Stella Doufexis, has a bright, girlish voice, which suits the songs for a woman's voice well, including those of Clara Schumann. The voice of the Swiss baritone, Oliver Widmer, is more problematic when, for all his feeling for word-meaning and musical shaping, it with a

hint of flutter grows unpleasantly uneven under pressure, most notably in the first song of all, *Sehnsucht*, making an unpromising start. Otherwise, clear, well-balanced sound.

Lieder, Vol. 5: *Dichterliebe, Op. 48; Lieder: Der arme Peter* (2 settings); *Auf ihrem Grab da steht eine Linde; Die beiden Grenadiere; Belsatzar; Dein Angesicht si lieb; Entflieh' mit mir und sei mein Weib; Es fiel ein Relf in der Frühlingsnacht; Es leuchtet meine Liebe; Die feindlichen Brüder; Der Hans und Grete tanzen; In meiner Brust; Lehn deine Wang' an mein Wang'; Die Lotosblume* (2 settings) ; *Mein Wagen rollet langsam; Die Minnesïnger; Tragödie.*

(N) *** Hyp. CDJ 33105. Maltman, Polyphony, Johnson –
CLARA SCHUMANN: *Lieder*. ***

Christopher Maltman's expressive baritone is not easy to capture gracefully on disc, with the microphone inclined to bring out an unevenness of production. It says much for Graham Johnson as inspirer as well as accompanist that he prompts Maltman to give his finest, best-focused recorded performances yet, not only in the sixteen well-loved songs of *Dichterliebe*, but in a score of others mostly little known. They include two which Schumann originally planned for that cycle, but which he excised – *Dein Angesicht so lieb* and *Lehn deine Wang'*. Over the whole range of songs Maltman uses a sharp contrasts of tone and dynamic, with diction crystal clear. *Die beiden Grenadiere*, the best known of the non-*Dichterliebe* songs, with its portrait of the two Napoleonic veterans, is powerfully and movingly dramatic, leading up to the quotation of the 'Marseillaise'. Johnson's notes, as in his Schubert series for Hyperion, are a model of scholarly insight, bringing extra illumination on every level, as in his analysis of Schumann's own contacts with Heine, as well as those of his wife, Clara, four of whose songs are also included. It is also illuminating to have two a capella choral settings of Heine poems, beautifully sung by Polyphony, including *Die Lotosblume*, a poem also set as a solo song. Excellent, beautifully balanced sound.

Lieder from *Album für die Jugend, Op. 79; Gedichte der Königen Maria Stuart, Op. 135; Myrthen Lieder, Op. 25:* excerpts. *Abends am Strand; Die Kartenlegerin; Ständchen; Stille Tränen; Verratene Liebe.*

(M) *** CRD (ADD) CRD 3401. Walker, Vignoles.

Sarah Walker's 1982 Schumann collection is most cherishable, notably the five Mary Stuart songs which, in their brooding darkness, are among Schumann's most memorable. With superb accompaniment and splendid recording, this is an outstanding issue.

Dichterliebe, Op. 48.

(M) *** DG (ADD) 449 747-2. Wunderlich, Giesen –
BEETHOVEN; SCHUBERT: *Lieder*. ***

(i) *Dichterliebe, Op. 48; (ii) Frauenliebe und Leben, Op. 42.*

(B) ** DG ADD/Dig 439 417-2. (i) Fischer-Dieskau, Eschenbach; (ii) Fassbaender, Irwin Gage.

Dichterliebe, Op. 48; Liederkreis, Op. 39.

*** Ph. (IMS) 416 352-2. Fischer-Dieskau, Brendel.

Dichterliebe (song-cycle), *Op. 48; Liederkreis* (song-cycle), *Op. 39; Myrthen Lieder, Op. 25.*

*** DG (ADD) 415 190-2. Fischer-Dieskau, Eschenbach.

Fischer-Dieskau's earlier DG *Dichterliebe* (415 190-2 – recorded between 1973 and 1977) is not quite as emotionally plangent as his later, digital version on Philips, but the contrasts between expressive warmth and a darker irony are still apparent. Eschenbach is always imaginative and the recording has fine presence. Fassbaender's account of *Frauenliebe und Leben* is certainly strongly characterized, with a wide range of expression and fine detail, but she conveys little sense of vulnerability. If the underlying sentimentality of the poems is here concealed, so is much else. Irwin Gage is an excellent accompanist and the digital recording is very vivid.

On Philips in inspired collaboration with Alfred Brendel, Fischer-Dieskau brings an angry, inconsolable reading, reflecting the absence of fulfillment in the poet's love. The Op. 39 *Liederkreis* also brings inspired, spontaneous-sounding performances, with the voice here notably fresher.

Yet another outstandingly fine *Dichterliebe* comes at bargain price on DG plus the magnificent Op. 39 *Liederkreis*, made the more attractive on CD by the generous addition of seven of the *Myrthen* songs. Eschenbach is imaginative without ever being intrusive. Very good sound for the period.

Wunderlich, had he lived, would no doubt have surpassed this early recording of a favourite Schumann song-cycle but, even with an often unimaginative accompanist here, his freshness is most endearing, irresistible with so golden a voice.

Frauenliebe und Leben, Op. 42; 5 Lieder, Op. 40 (Märzveilchen; Muttertraume; Der Soldat; Der Spielmann; Verratene Liebe). Lieder: *Abendlied; Dein Angesicht; Die Kartenlegerin; Die Löwenbraut; Lust der Sturmnacht; Mein schöner Stern; Die Meersee; Rose, Meer und Sonne; Der Schätzgräber ;Schneeglöckchen; Des Sennen Abscheid; Die Soldatenbraut; Stille Liebe; Volksliedchen; Vom Schlaraffenland.*

*** DG 445 881-2. Von Otter, Forsberg.

Anne Sofie von Otter characterizes the contrasting songs in *Frauenliebe* with exceptional intensity, presenting a character, as in an opera, developing from youthful, eager girl to bereaved widow. By creating a character outside herself, von Otter may for some seem a shade detached compared with other, more personally involved singers, but that strengthens the cycle, minimizing the sentimentality of the poems. This is an exceptionally generous recital (79 minutes) and other songs on the disc are then characterized commandingly, with dramatic contrasts heightened. Try the beautiful Heine setting, *Dein Angesicht* ('Your face'), sung with poise and flawless legato. Excellent sound and fine accompaniment from Forsberg. Highly recommended.

Frauenliebe und Leben, Op.42; Liederkreis, Op. 39; Aus den östlichen Rosen; Kennst du das Land; Meine Rose; Der Nussbaum; Requiem; Die Soldatenbraut; Widmung.

(N)(M) *** Regis RRC 1051. Lott, Johnson.

There are several versions of Schumann's *Frauenliebe und Leben* that command our allegiance, yet Felicity Lott and Graham Johnson are highly distinguished. Felicity Lott is a connoisseur's artist, far greater than many more illustrious and publicized rivals, and she sings here with great poise and a completely unaffected artistry. The recording comes from 1990 and is not new, but the finesse and musicianship of this partnership, as well as the intelligence which guides everything they do, make it treasurable. The sound, too, is very good indeed.

12 Gedichte, Op. 35; Liederkreis, Op. 39.

*** Decca 460 797-2. Goerne, Schneider.

Matthias Goerne's coupling of the Op. 39 *Liederkreis* and the twelve songs of Op. 35 is very fine. Goerne's silken, soft-grained tone and his elegant phrasing will win him and his partner Eric Schneider many new friends. There are times when some may feel he underprojects, favouring an almost whispered delivery but his intelligence and discernment are never in doubt. Good Decca recording.

Liederkreis, Op. 39.

(B) *** EMI Double fforte (ADD) CZS5 73836-2 (2). Baker, Barenboim – LISZT; MENDELSSOHN: *Lieder.* ***

With Barenboim an endlessly imaginative if sometimes reticent accompanist, this song-cycle is a classic example of Dame Janet Baker's art, the centrepiece in a superb recital which contrasts the high romantic and sometimes tragic world of Schumann with fine collections of hardly less fine settings of Liszt and Mendelssohn.

Liederkreis, Op. 39; 4 Husarenlieder. Other Lieder: *Aus der hebräischen Gesängen; Aufträge; Die beiden Grenadiere; Dein Angesicht; Du bist wie eine Blume; Die fiendlichen Brüder; Geständnis; Der Kontrabandiste; Meine Wagen roller langsam; Melancholie; Der Nussbaum; Myrthen (Widmung); Der Schätzgräber; Talismane;* (i) *Tragödie. Venetianisches Lied I–II.*

**(*) DG 447 042-2. Terfel, Martineau; (i) with Anderson, Robinson.

For DG, this is among the most characterful discs that even Bryn Terfel has yet recorded, with the great Welsh bass tackling no fewer than thirty-four songs with an electrifying spontaneity and a fearless range of expression. Some may feel that his emphasis on the dramatic element is too great, straying from Lieder to opera, and R.L. suggests that, while this is a glorious voice, not everyone will feel comfortable with Terfel's tendency to over characterize and overproject in a way that can detract from, rather than enhance, the emotional impact of the songs.

But we are agreed that it is thrilling to hear singing of such spontaneous intensity, as though the singer himself, superbly aided by his pianist, was in the instant creating each song afresh. The range of expression in Terfel's account of the Eichendorff *Liederkreis* is very wide indeed, so that he seems to relate the encounter with the Lorelei in *Waldesgesprach* directly to the very similar story in Schubert's *Erlking*.

Bitingly dramatic as most of the songs are, with the military songs standing out, including the best known, *Die beiden Grenadiere*, Terfel's honeyed tone is gloriously caught in *Mondnacht*, hushed and tender, and in the best-known song of all, *Der Nussbaum*. In spite of any reservations this is an outstanding collection in every way. The two other singers appear only in a brief duet, which comes as the third item in *Tragödie*.

Liederkreis, Op. 39; 12 Kerner Lieder, Op. 35.

(B) *** Hyp. Helios CDH 55011. Price, Johnson.

As a spin-off from Graham Johnson's Schubert recording with Dame Margaret Price (No. 15 in the series), Johnson partners her here in a superb Schumann disc, coupling the sequence of 12 *Settings of Justinus Kerner*, Op. 35, with the Eichendorff *Liederkreis*, Op. 39. The singer's presence, magnetism and weight of expression are superbly caught, and the tonal beauty and immaculate sense of line go with detailed imagination in word-pointing. Price may underplay the horror of such a song from Opus 39 as *Waldesgespräch* about meeting the Lorelei, but the moment of confrontation is sharply pointed when legato is suddenly abandoned. The lesser-known *Kerner Lieder* also contain many treasures. First-rate sound. Full notes and texts with translations are included in this bargain reissue.

Der Rose Pilgerfahrt, Op. 112.

*** Chan. 9350. Nielsen, Van der Walt, Møller, Paevatalu, Danish Nat. R. Ch. and SO, Kuhn.

Schumann wrote his cantata, *Der Rose Pilgerfahrt* ('The Pilgrimage of the Rose'), in 1851 towards the end of his career. The very opening has the lyrical openness of Schubert, its freshness enhanced by the interplay of solo voices and women's chorus. The idiom, as well as recalling Schubert, often suggests the folk-based writing of Humperdinck in *Hänsel und Gretel*, similarly innocent-seeming, but in fact subtle. Gustav Kuhn conducts an aptly bright and atmospheric performance, very well recorded, with Inga Nielsen and Deon van der Walt in the two principal roles. The chorus and orchestra are first rate and the recording, sponsored by Danish Radio, is full-bodied and atmospheric. A valuable rarity. Sadly, the booklet contains no translation alongside the German text, though Richard Wigmore's note and summary are very helpful.

Scenes from Goethe's Faust.

✿ (M) *** Decca (ADD) 425 705-2 (2). Harwood, Pears, Shirley-Quirk, Fischer-Dieskau, Vyvyan, Palmer, Aldeburgh Festival Singers, ECO, Britten.

**(*) Sony SK 66308 (2). Terfel, Mattila, Rootering, Bonney, Wottrich, Vermillion, Poschner-Klebel, Graham, Blochwitz, Peeters, BPO, Abbado.

Though the episodic sequence of scenes is neither opera nor cantata, the power and imagination of much of the music, not least the delightful garden scene and the energetic setting of the final part, are immensely satisfying. In 1972, soon after a live performance at the Aldeburgh Festival, Britten inspired his orchestra and his fine cast of singers to vivid performances, which are outstandingly recorded against the warm Maltings acoustic. This is magnificent music, and readers are urged to explore it – the rewards are considerable.

Abbado's recording was taken live from concert performances in June 1994, using a cast, headed by Bryn Terfel in the title-role and with Karita Mattila as Gretchen, that could hardly be bettered at the time. Abbado's direction is strong and sympathetic, and the singing good; but one has only to go back to Benjamin Britten's inspired Decca recording to find even keener imagination, not just in the conducting but in the singing too. Bryn Terfel is thoughtful and expressive as Faust, but Fischer-Dieskau was far more illuminating and detailed; Elizabeth Harwood as Gretchen sang even more radiantly than Mattila, bringing out the heroine's tenderness and vulnerability; and Jan-Hendrik Rootering as Mephistopheles is not as characterful as John Shirley-Quirk. The analogue 1972 sound is also rather cleaner than the 1994 digital, but, were the Decca set to become unavailable, this Sony will always provide a most enjoyable recording of an all-too-rare work.

SCHURMANN, Gerard (born 1928)

6 Studies of Francis Bacon for Large Orchestra; Variants for Small Orchestra.

*** Chan. 9167. BBC SO, composer.

Inspired by the fantastic, often violent or painful paintings of Francis Bacon, Schurmann here writes a virtuoso orchestral showpiece, full of colourful effects. The vigour of the writing is admirably caught both in this performance and in the often spiky writing of the *Variants* for a rather smaller orchestra, set against passages of hushed beauty. First-rate 1979 recording, made in the warm acoustics of All Saints', Tooting, and admirably transferred to CD.

SCHÜTZ, Heinrich (1585–1672)

Christmas Day Vespers 1664 (including: Christmas Story; Magnificat with Christmas Interpolations; O bone Jesu, fili Mariae (Sacred Concerto); Warum toben die Heiden).

*** DG 463 046-2. (i) Daniels, Boys Ch. & Congregational Ch. of Roskilde Cathedral, Gabrieli Consort and Players, McCreesh.

As in his earlier hypothetical recreation of Vespers, at St Mark's, Venice, Paul McCresh here celebrates *Christmas Vespers* as it might have been heard at the Dresden Court in 1664. The result is an immensely varied vocal and instrumental tapestry, ranging from congregational hymns, to Schütz's glorious *Magnificat* setting including such familiar Christmas interpolations as the chorales *Lobt Gott, ihr Christen all zugleich* and *In dulci jubilo*, and ending with a burst of magnificence in the organ postlude, *Benedicamus Domino* by Samuel Scheidt. The centrepiece is a very fine performance of Schütz's *Christmas Story* with Charles Daniels a lyrical rather than a dramatic Evangelist. Other soloists are drawn from the Gabrieli Consort and the instrumental groups include wind instruments, cornetts and sackbutts, strings and a widely varied palette of continuo. The cathedral ambience adds to the sense of occasion and the variety of the music here is matched by the colourful and dedicated response of the performers. A remarkable achievement.

Christmas Story (Weihnachthistorie).

(M) *** Virgin VM5 61353-2. Kirkby, Rogers, Thomas, Taverner Cons., Taverner Ch., Taverner Players, Parrott –
PRAETORIUS: *Christmas Motets.* ***

Christmas Story (Weihnachthistorie); 3 Cantiones sacrae (1625); Psalm 100.

(BB) *** Naxos 8.553514. Agnew, Crookes, MacCarthy, Oxford Camerata, Summerly.

Virgin Veritas's version has the advantage of three first-class soloists, all of whom are in excellent voice. One is soon gripped by the narrative and the beauty and simplicity of the line. There is no sense of austerity here, merely a sense of purity, with the atmosphere of the music beautifully captured by these forces under Andrew Parrott. Apart from a rather nasal edge on the violin tone, it is difficult to fault either this moving performance or the well-balanced and refined recording.

On Naxos Summerly with his talented group of 10 singers – two of them doubling as soloists – also give a compelling reading of Schütz's vivid and compact telling of the *Christmas Story*. Aptly austere in its overall manner, with clear instrumental accompaniment, it yet brings out the beauty and vigour of the numbers depicting the different groups, in turn the angels, the shepherds and the wise men. The scholarly credentials are impeccable, with excellent notes provided, and the recording, made in Hertford College, Oxford, is full and vivid. The motets and the psalm-setting make a welcome fill-up.

(i) Christmas Story (Weihnachthistorie); (ii) Easter Oratorio (Historia der Auferstehung Jesu Christi); Cantiones sacrae: Quid commisisti (cycle of five 4-part motets); (iii) Deutsches Magnificat; Motets for Double Choir: Ach, Herr, straf mich nicht (Psalm 6); Cantate Domino (Psalm 96); Herr unser Herrscher (Psalm 8); Ich freu mich des, das mir geredt ist (Psalm 122); Unser Herr Jesus Christus.

(B) *** Double Decca (ADD) 452 188-2 (2). Heinrich Schütz Ch.; with (i) Partridge, Palmer, Soloists, Instrumental Ens., Philip Jones Brass Ens.; (ii) Pears, Tear, Langridge, Elizabethan Consort of Viols, L. Cornett & Sackbut Ens.; (iii) Symphoniae Sacrae Chamber Ens.; Norrington.

The Decca *Christmas Story* offers some extremely fine singing from Ian Partridge as the Evangelist, while Peter Pears shows impressive authority and insight as well as singing beautifully in the same role for its companion work. The Heinrich Schütz Choir phrases with great feeling and subtlety; indeed, some may feel that their singing is a little too self-consciously beautiful for music that is so pure in style. The *Deutsches Magnificat* is given with admirable authority and is one of the best things in this very generous collection. Indeed, this set offers much to admire, and the vintage recordings, made between 1969 and 1975, have fine sonority, with the ambitious double motets given a proper sense of spectacle.

Italian Madrigals (complete)

(B) *** HM (ADD) HMA 1901162. Concerto Vocale, Jacobs.

Schütz's first and only *Book of Italian Madrigals* reflects his encounter with the music of Giovanni Gabrieli and Monteverdi. The Concerto Vocale, led by the counter-tenor, René Jacobs, employ a theorbo which provides added variety of colour, and at times they offer great expressive and tonal range. They omit the very last of the madrigals, the eight-part *Vasto mar*.

Motets: Auf dem Gebirge; Der Engel sprach; Exultavit cor meum; Fili mi Absolon; Heu mihi Domine; Hodie Christus natus est; Ich danke Dir, Herr; O quam tu pulchra es; Die Seele Christi, helige mich; Selig sind die Todten.

(BB) *** ASV (ADD) CDQS 6105. Pro Cantione Antiqua, L. Cornett & Sackbut Ens., Restoration Ac., Fleet.

An eminently useful and well-recorded super-bargain anthology of Schütz motets that offers such masterpieces as *Fili mi Absolon* (for bass voice, five sackbuts, organ and violone continuo) and the glorious *Selig sind die Todten* in well-thought-out and carefully prepared performances under Edgar Fleet. These accounts have a dignity and warmth that make them well worth considering. Moreover the CD transfer is excellently managed, the sound rich and clear.

Musicalische Exequien. Motets: Auf dem Gebirge; Freue dich des Weibes Jugend; Ist nicht Ephraim mein teurer Sohn; Saul, Saul, was verfolgst du mich.

*** DG 423 405-2. Monteverdi Ch., E. Bar. Soloists, His Majesties Sackbutts & Cornetts, Gardiner.

Schütz's *Musical Exequien* contains music that is amazing for its period. The Monteverdi Choir respond with fiery intensity, making light of the complex eight-part writing in the second of the three *Exequies*. Four more superb motets by Schütz make an ideal coupling, with first-rate recorded sound.

O bone Jesu, fili Mariae.

(M) *** DG (IMS) 447 298-2. Monteverdi Ch., E. Bar. Soloists, Gardiner – BUXTEHUDE: *Membra Jesu nostri.* ***

A wonderfully eloquent performance of this *Spiritual Concerto* by one of the greatest of baroque masters. Schütz juxtaposes stanzas of a poem ascribed to St Bernard of Clairvaux with prose passages of Latin devotional literature, treating the latter as recitative and the former set homophonically, and ending the cantata in *concertato* style. Beautifully recorded.

Psalm 150.

(B) **(*) EMI double forte (ADD) CZS5 68631-2 (2). Cambridge University Musical Soc., Bach Ch., King's College Ch., Wilbraham Brass Soloists, Willcocks – G. GABRIELI: *Motets* etc. **(*); MONTEVERDI: *Vespers.* *(*)

Schütz's setting of *Psalm 150* is for double choirs and soloists, each used in juxtaposition against the others, with built-in antiphony an essential part of the composer's conception.

The majesty of Schütz's inspiration certainly comes over vividly here, the closing *Alleluja* having remarkable weight and richness, though the overall focus of the recording is not absolutely clean. In the coupled Monteverdi *Vespers* there is actual distortion and the performance is disappointing.

The Resurrection (Easter Oratorio); Meine Seele erhebt den Herren.

(M) *** HM HMT 7901311. Concerto Vocale, Jacobs.

René Jacobs's account of Schütz's *Historia der Auferstehung Jesu Christi* with the Concerto Vocale is a performance of great accomplishment and taste, and quite beautifully recorded. This performance still gives great pleasure, as does the lively account of *Meine Seele erhebt den Herren* from the second Book of the *Symphoniae sacrae* (1647).

Der Schwanengesang (Opus ultimum; reconstructed by Wolfgang Steude).

(M) *** Virgin VED5 61306-2 (2). Hannover Knabenchor, Hilliard Ens., L. Bar., Hennig.

Schütz's *Opus ultimum* is a setting of Psalm 119, the longest psalm in the psalter, which he divides into 11 sections. He finishes off this 13-part motet cycle with his final setting of Psalm 100, which he had originally composed in 1662, and the *Deutsches Magnificat*. Wolfram Steude's note recounts the history of the work, parts of which disappeared after Schütz's death; and his reconstruction of two of the vocal parts is obviously a labour of love. The performance is a completely dedicated one, with excellent singing from all concerned and good instrumental playing, and the conductor, Heinz Hennig, secures warm and responsive singing from his Hannover Knabenchor. The acoustic is spacious and warm and the recording balance well focused. The sound is firm, clear and sonorous.

The Seven Words of Jesus on the Cross. Magnificat; Motets: Ach Herr, du Schöpfer aller Ding; Adjuro vos; Anima mea; Die mit Tränen säen; Erbarm dich mein, o Herre Gott; Meine Seele erheben den Herren; Quemadmodum desiderat.

(N) (B) ** HM HMA 1951255. Soloists, Clément Janequin Ens., Les Saqueboutiers de Toulouse, Visse.

Schutz's *Seven Last Words* is a comparatively short work (17 minutes) and takes up only a small part of this programme, although the front of this Musique d'abord CD does not make this clear. After the *Introitus*, seven sentences of text (taken from Schuruck's *Book of Saints and Martyrs* of 1617) are given meditatively to a tenor, alternated with the four Evangelists (different solo voices), who briefly narrate the Gospel story, with brass accompaniment.

The concert opens with a Latin *Magnificat* setting, again alternating brass and solo voices, but sounding more like a secular madrigal than a religious celebration. The madrigal spirituel, *Ah, Herr du Schöpfer aller Ding*, is also sung slowly and serenely. The excerpts from the *Symphoniae sacrae* too, might again have been more spirited, although the closing concerted number from, the *Psalmen Davids* is livelier. The actual singing here is of a high standard, and the brass-

playing superb, but one feels that the music-making could have been more eloquently extrovert. The recording is excellent, but only texts and no translations are provided. A fascinating disc, just the same.

SCHWANTER, Joseph (born 1943)

From Afar . . . (Fantasy for Guitar and Orchestra).

(BB) ** Virgin 2 x 1 VBD5 61627-2 (2). Isbin, Saint Paul CO, Hugh Wolf – RODRIGO: *Concierto de Aranjuez; Fantasia para un gentilhombre ***;* Recital: *'Latin Romances'*. ***

Sharon Isbin commissioned Schwanter's *From Afar . . .* and the insert note describes it as 'an intense fantasy which unfolds in a combination of brilliant passages and lyrical episodes'. So it does, but well played as they are, they are neither remarkably cohesive nor memorable, and the best part of the work by far is the cadenza, which the soloist sustains with brilliant playing and personal magnetism.

SCOTT, Cyril (1879–1970)

Aubade, Op. 77; 3 Symphonic Dances, Op. 22; 2 Passacaglias on Irish Themes; Suite fantastique.

(N) **(*) Marco 8.223485. South Africa Broadcasting Corporation Nat. SO, Marchbank.

Cyril Scott, born in Birkenhead, studied composition in Frankfurt at the Hoch Conservatoire. In 1895 his fellow students included Percy Grainger, Balfour Gardiner and Roger Quilter, and the group subsequently became known as the 'Frankfurt Group'. But Scott eventually went his own musical way.

Now he is best remembered for his piano piece *Lotus Land*, but at the very beginning of the last century his *First Symphony* was performed in Manchester and Liverpool under Hans Richter (who admired it) and the *Second* by Sir Henry Wood at the London Promenade Concerts. This was subsequently to be reworked as the *Three Symphonic Dances*.

The first of these opens with appealingly English pastoral flair, but its ideas become repetitive; the second (*Andante sostenuto e sempre molto cantabile*) is already anticipating the languorous, sequence-laden style of his later music, especially when the rather lovely winding main tune is reprised on the oboe, and rapturously taken up by the violins.

By the time he came to write his *Aubade* for large orchestra in 1911, Scott's feeling for voluptuous colour and translucent textures had developed further, and although this very telling evocation is very like Debussy, it is most impressively scored. At the close one is also reminded of Delius, and the latter's influence is also to reappear in the *Neapolitan Rhapsody*.

If the ideas themselves are rather amorphous in the *Suite fantastique*, the 'Spectres', 'Goblins' and 'Elves' of the two final movements are imaginatively pictured, and in the two *Passacaglias* Scott effectively decorates and re-orchestrates the themes on which they are based, rather than developing them organically. These are all excellent, sympathetic performances, well recorded in a warm acoustic.

Piano Sonata No. 1, Op. 66; 3 Danses tristes, Op. 74; Over the Prairie: 2 Impressions; 2 Pieces, Op. 47; 2 Pierrot Pieces, Op. 35; Pierrette; Poems.

(N) **(*) Australian ABC Eloquence 465 737-2. Henning.

Cyril Scott's piano music is at times Debussian, and if without that composer's genius it is certainly individual, atmospheric and attractive. The performances are good and the recording acceptable, if a touch brittle, and this Eloquence CD comes with helpful notes by the pianist.

SCRIABIN, Alexander (1872–1915)

(i) Piano Concerto in F sharp min., Op. 20; (ii) Poème de l'extase, Op. 54; (i) Prometheus.

*** Decca (ADD) 417 252-2. (i) Ashkenazy, LPO; (ii) Cleveland O; Maazel.

(i) Piano Concerto; (i; ii) Prometheus; (i) Preludes, Op. 11/6, 10, 15, & 17; Fragilité, Op. 51/1; Sonata No. 1, Op. 6: Marche funèbre (orch. Rogal-Levitsky).

(BB) *** Naxos 8.550818. (i) Scherbakov; (ii) Russian State TV and R. Ch.; Moscow SO, Golovschin.

Piano Concerto in F sharp min., Op. 20; Fantasy (arr. Rozhdestvensky); (i) Prometheus.

**(*) Chan. 9728. Postnikova; Residentie O, Rozhdestvensky, (i) Hague Ch.

(i) Piano Concerto in F sharp min., Op. 20; Le Poème de l'extase, Op. 54; (i–ii) Prometheus.

** DG 459 647-2. (i) Ugorski; (ii) Chicago S Chorus; Chicago SO, Boulez.

Piano Concerto; Le Poème de l'extase; Symphonies Nos. 2; 3 (Le Divin Poème).

**(*) BMG/Melodiya Twofer ADD/Dig. 74321 66980 (2). (i) Nasedkin; USSR SO, Svetlanov.

Ashkenazy plays the *Piano Concerto* with great authority. *Prometheus* too, powerfully atmospheric and curiously hypnotic, is given a thoroughly poetic and committed reading and Ashkenazy copes with the virtuoso obbligato part with predictable distinction. Maazel's 1979 Cleveland recording of *Le Poème de l'extase* is a shade too efficient to be really convincing. The playing is often brilliant and the recording is very clear but the trumpets are rather forced and strident. However, it can be regarded as a bonus for the other two works.

On Naxos Konstantin Scherbakov gives a most poetic account of the Chopinesque *F sharp minor Concerto*, which is as good as any in any price range. The improvisatory musings of the slow movement come over beautifully, and *Prometheus* is no less characterful. Of course, the Moscow Symphony are not in the same league as the Cleveland Orchestra but they play with ardour, and the sound is very natural without being in the demonstration category.

Victoria Postnikova and her husband, Gennadi Rozhdestvensky, replace *Le Poème de l'extase* with a transcription of the early *Fantasy*. The Chandos sound is exemplary and the performance of the *Piano Concertos* both sensitive and poetic. A good account of *Prometheus* even if it does not displace Ashkenazy.

On BMG/Melodiya, the *Second* and *Third Symphonies* are full-blooded and idiomatic performances recorded way back in the 1960s. They have conviction and authority and are unlikely to disappoint, with the Russian sound, while not ideally sumptuous, coming up very well for the period. *Le Poème de l'extase* is later (taken from a live concert in 1977). It receives the passionate direction needed to sustain such a work, although with no want of atmosphere. Only the *Piano Concerto in F sharp minor* is digital, coming from 1990, but here the sound is rather vague compared with the earlier recordings. A good, well-shaped account, though Alexander Nasedkin is by no means as sensitive a player as Konstantin Scherbakov on Naxos.

Boulez's second recording of *Le Poème de l'extase* is short on ecstasy and not too strong on poetry either; ultimately it is analytical and detached. Boulez does restrain Anatole Ugorski's propensity to pull things out of shape, and both the *Piano Concerto* and *Prometheus* receive straightforward and at times elegant performances with excellent recorded sound. All the same this is not a first choice for any of these pieces.

Le Poème de l'extase, Op. 54.

*** BBC (ADD) BBCL 4018-2. New Philh. O, Stokowski (and conversation with Deryck Cooke) – BERLIOZ: *Symphonie fantastique.* **(*)

(N) *** Australian Decca Eloquence (ADD) 466 904-2. LAPO, Mehta – NIELSEN: *Symphony No. 4.* **

(M) **(*) Sony (ADD) SM2K 64100 (2). NYPO, Boulez – BARTOK: *Wooden Prince* etc. **(*)

Stokowski conducted the American première of *Le Poème de l'extase* in 1917 and it is difficult to imagine a performance of greater luminosity and energy from an octogenarian over half a century later. This account comes from a 1968 Festival Hall concert with the New Philharmonia Orchestra. Orgiastic, no holds barred, totally abandoned and wonderfully dedicated playing. Boulez's DG recording sounds tame and prosaic alongside this, which is still rather special even if the BBC sound is less than ideally transparent in its handling of detail.

This is Mehta on top form in his vintage Decca years. Recorded in the mid-1960s, it is still sonically very impressive, with the engineers doing ample justice to the complexity and opulence of this lavishly self-intoxicated and orgasmic score. It remains one of the most gripping performances available today, but is coupled with an extrovert and less recommendable account of Nielsen's *Fourth Symphony*.

Boulez's Sony account of *Le Poème de l'extase* has ardour and splendid control. The all-important trumpet part emerges from within a texture that is inherently voluptuous, even if the sound-quality itself could be more alluring.

Prometheus (The Poem of Fire), Op. 60.

*** Ph. 446 715-2. Toradze, Kirov Op. Ch. & O, Gergiev – STRAVINSKY: *Firebird* (complete ballet). ***

(***) Music & Arts mono CD 967. VPO, Mitropoulos –
  SCHOENBERG: *Pelleas und Melisande, Op. 5a.* (***)

On Philips an *echt*-Russian account of *Prometheus*, with a suitably inflammable pianist in the person of Alexander Toradze. This is the only current recording by a Russian orchestra and under Gergiev's masterly direction they given an outstanding account of this voluptuous and gloriously decadent score. The recording, too, is in the demonstration class even if the pianist is perhaps slightly too forwardly placed in the aural picture. It comes with an appropriately incandescent *Firebird*, marvellously played and recorded.

The Mitropoulos is a fine account not quite as well recorded as his unavailable New York version. Despite its sonic limitations, this is well worth considering.

Symphonies Nos. 1–3; Le Poème de l'extase;
(i) *Prometheus.*

(N) (M) *** EMI ADD CMS5 67720-2 (3). Toczyska, Myers, Westminster Ch. (in *No. 1*), Phd. O, Muti, (i) with Alexeev.

(i) *Symphonies Nos. 2;* (ii) *3 (Le Divin Poème);* (iii) *Le Poème de l'extase;* (i) *Rêverie, Op. 24.*

(B) *** Chan. 2-for-1 241-5 (2). (i) RSNO; (ii) Danish Nat. RSO; (iii) Chicago SO; Järvi.

(B) **(*) Double Decca 460 299-2 (2). (i) Berlin Deutsche SO; Ashkenazy; (ii) Balleys, Larin, Berlin R. Ch.; (iii) Berlin RSO.

(i; ii) *Symphonies Nos. 1 in E, Op. 26;* (i) *2 in C min., Op. 29;* (iii) *3 (Le Divin Poème); Le Poème de l'extase.*

(B) **(*) Double Decca 460 299-2 (2). (i) Berlin Deutsche SO; Ashkenazy; (ii) Balleys, Larin, Berlin R. Ch.; (iii) Berlin RSO.

(B) ** Ph. Duo 454 271-2 (2). Frankfurt RSO, Inbal.

Muti's complete set of the Scriabin symphonies can be recommended almost without reservation; overall the sound is as vivid and richly coloured as the performances. With the two later symphonies-cum-symphonic poems (*Le Poème de l'extase* white-hot with passionate intensity, yet masterfully controlled) now added, this is an impressive achievement.

The Philips Frankfurt recordings are full, smooth and clear and the orchestral playing is refined and committed, albeit less intoxicatingly vivid than in Muti's full-priced EMI set, which is distinctly superior. The *Poème de l'extase* is beautifully played and has plenty of atmosphere and, if it is not as passionately voluptuous as in Muti's hands, it makes a considerable impression and is pleasingly lacking in vulgarity.

The splendid account of the *Second Symphony* from Järvi, with its richly detailed recording, can be recommended strongly. There is something refreshingly unforced and natural about Järvi's version of the *Third*, which puts this score in a far better light than those conductors who play it for all they are worth. Järvi's version of *Le Poème de l'extase*, played superbly and recorded vividly and resonantly in Chicago's Orchestral Hall, emphasizes Scriabin's primary colours, with the trumpet solo penetrating boldly through the voluptuous texture and skirting vulgarity by a small margin. There have been more subtle performances, but this one certainly makes a strong impact.

Decca have now put together Ashkenazy's Berlin perform-ances of the three Scriabin symphonies, plus *Le Poème de l'extase*, and by breaking the *Second* halfway they have managed to get all three on a pair of discs, making a pretty formidable bargain Double. If recording were the sole criterion, these performances would be a first choice. The sound is extraordinarily well detailed in the *First Symphony*, with both allure and presence, and only slightly less well defined in the *Second*. But in the *First Symphony* one misses that wild-eyed demonic fire that is so strong an ingredient in Scriabin's make-up. The *Second Symphony* is more impetuously volatile and has a good deal more vigour and sense of internal combustion. There is an atmosphere of simmering passion in the *Andante*, which often wells ardently to the surface. The *Third* brings an even more highly charged feeling from the Berlin forces, which carries through into *Le Poème de l'extase*. Again the Decca engineers rise to the occasion and the recording is very impressive. Yet overall the performances do not have the sheer grip of Muti's Philadelphia accounts.

Symphony No. 3 (Le Divin Poème), Op. 43; Le Poème de l'extase, Op. 54.

*** DG 459 681-2. Russian Nat. O, Pletnev.

Mikhail Pletnev's account of the *Third Symphony* is gripping and commanding, and its architecture every bit as well held together as in Muti's 1988 Philadelphia account (EMI). Everything is always beautifully shaped and there is an expressive freedom. The playing has ardour but the lushness and delicacy of the orchestral textures are finely conveyed. Pletnev is as profoundly inside these symphonies as he is in the piano music. In *Le Poème de l'extase* he has masterly control of pace and secures sumptuous orchestral sound. The brass are particularly impressive and have real nobility. Excellent sound and now a first recommendation for the symphony.

Symphony No. 3 (Le Divin Poème); Le Poème de l'extase (arr. Konyus for piano, 4 hands).

(N) (BB) ** Naxos 8.555327. Prunyi, Falvai.

In the early years of the twentieth century, piano reductions were the only way for most music lovers to get to know the repertoire. Nowadays such arrangements of complex orchestral scores seem much less useful. As transcriptions go this is expert enough, and the playing and recording is fully acceptable, but it is far more sensible to get a coupling of the real thing!

PIANO MUSIC

Etudes (complete): *Etude in C sharp min., Op. 2/1; 12 Etudes, Op. 8; 8 Etudes, Op. 42 (1903); Etude in E flat, Op. 49/1; Op. 56/4 (1908); 3 Etudes, Op. 65.*

**(*) Hyp. CDA 66607. Lane.

Piers Lane makes light of the various technical problems in which these pieces abound and he plays with an admirable sense of style. Yet he does not give us the whole picture. He has sensibility and produces a good sonority, aided in no small measure by an excellently balanced recording; but one misses the nervous intensity, the imaginative flair and the feverish emotional temperature that the later pieces call for.

Etudes, Op. 8/7 & 12; Op. 42/5; Preludes, Op. 11/1, 3, 9–10, 13–14, 16; Op. 13/6 Op. 15/2; Op. 16/1 & 4; Op. 27/1; Op. 48/ 3; Op. 51/2; Op. 59/2; Op. 67/1; Sonatas Nos. 3, Op. 23; 5, Op. 53; 9 (Black Mass), Op. 68.

(N) (B) (***) RCA 2-CD mono 74321 84594-2 (2). Horowitz –
   (with CLEMENTI: *Sonatas, Op. 14/3; Op. 34/2; Op. 47/2: Rondo* (***); – MUSSORGSKY: *Pictures at an Exhibition* (***).

The engineers have done wonder to these recordings from the 1950s, though some of the original shallowness and clatter remains. The *Preludes* and the legendary accounts of the *Third* and *Ninth* sonatas come from 1956, the *Fifth* is much later, coming from 1976, and has more bloom. The performances form an essential part of any good Horowitz collection and the Mussorgsky and Clementi couplings are equally indispensable.

10 Mazurkas, Op. 3; 9 Mazurkas, Op. 25; 2 Mazurkas, Op. 40.

(N) *** ASV CDDCA 1066. Fergus-Thompson.

Another impressive instalment of Scriabin's complete piano music from Gordon Fergus-Thompson, a masterly and underrated artist. Even when put alongside native Russian pianists he can hold his own.

Preludes: Op. 2/2; Prelude for the Left Hand, Op. 9/1; 24 Preludes, Op. 11; 6 Preludes, Op. 13; 5 Preludes, Op. 15; 5 Preludes, Op. 16; 7 Preludes, Op. 17; 4 Preludes, Op. 22; 2 Preludes, Op. 27; 4 Preludes, Op. 31; 4 Preludes, Op. 33; 3 Preludes, Op. 35; 4 Preludes, Op. 37; 4 Preludes, Op. 39; Op. 45/3; 4 Preludes, Op. 48; Preludes, Op. 49/2; Op. 51/2; Op. 56/1; Op. 59/2; 2 Preludes, Op. 67; 5 Preludes, Op. 74.

(N) *** Hyp. CDA 67057/8. Lane.

Piers Lane has the measure of Scriabin's idiom and seems completely attuned to his musical language and sensibility. These preludes range from his formative Chopinesque years, around 1889, through to 1914, and Lane traverses them with flair. They are generally more successful than his complete set of *Etudes*.

Piano Sonatas Nos. 1–10; Sonate-fantaisie in G sharp min.

*** Hyp. CDA 67131/2. Hamelin.

Piano Sonatas Nos. 1–10; Etude in C sharp min., Op. 2/1; Feuillet d'album, Op. 58; 2 Morceaux, Op. 57; 2 Poèmes, Op. 63; 4 Preludes, Op. 48; 5 Preludes, Op. 64; 2 Preludes, Op. 67; Vers la flamme, Op. 72.

(B) *** EMI double forte CZS5 72652-2 (2). Ogdon.

Piano Sonatas Nos. 1–10; 2 Danses, Op. 73; 4 Morceaux, Op. 51; 4 Morceaux, Op. 56; 2 Poèmes, Op. 32.

(B) *** Double Decca ADD/Dig. 452 961-2 (2). Ashkenazy.

Marc-André Hamelin commands the feverish intensity, the manic vision, wide dynamic range and fastidious pedalling that Scriabin must have. There are other fine Scriabin cycles and, of course, celebrated accounts of single sonatas from

Richter and others, but of newer cycles Hamelin's must now be a first recommendation.

Ogdon is nothing if not persuasive, and the only reservation one need feel about his playing is an occasional tendency to be less than scrupulous in observing dynamic indications and a certain lack of finish. His account of the *Tenth Sonata*, however, is particularly fine, and if in the *Ninth* (*The Black Mass*) he does not match the demonic fury and power of Horowitz (and who, for that matter, does?) his is still a thoroughly felt and vividly realized reading. The shorter pieces are particularly appealing (the richly coloured *Etude in C sharp minor* which opens the first disc should tempt anyone to explore further). The piano is very well recorded throughout (at Abbey Road in 1971).

Ashkenazy's Scriabin set was made over a decade between 1972 and 1984, but the sound is remarkably consistent. Ashkenazy is clearly attuned to this repertoire: he is as thoroughly at home in the miniatures as in the sonatas, readily finding their special atmosphere and colour. If he is at his very finest in the earlier sonatas, the last three are given with brilliance and vision, and there is no lack of awareness of the demonic side of Scriabin's personality.

Piano Sonatas Nos. 2 in G sharp min., Op. 19; 5 in F sharp, Op. 53; 6 in G, Op. 63; 7 in F sharp (White Mass), Op. 64; 9 in F (Black Mass), Op. 68; Fantaisie in B min., Op. 28.

(BB) ** Naxos 8.553158. Glemser.

This is announced as being the first volume of the complete Scriabin *Sonatas* and would make an eminently serviceable choice at its modest asking price. Bernd Glemser shows a natural sympathy for this repertoire. He commands a keen imagination, a wide range of keyboard colour and he possesses an impressive technical address. No one buying these sonatas will feel short-changed.

Piano Sonatas Nos. 3 in F sharp min., Op. 23; 10 in C, Op. 70; in E flat (1890); Poème nocturne, Op. 61; Vers la flamme, Op. 72.

(N)(BB) ** Naxos 8.555468. Glemser.

These performances are very good indeed. Bernd Glemser has an excellent feel for the Scriabin world. However, against the finest competition, this falls short – not least in the rather synthetic and unventilated recording.

Piano Sonata No. 3 in F sharp min., Op. 23; 2 Poèmes, Op. 32; Vers la flamme, Op. 72.

(*) Kingdom KCLCD 2001. Fergus-Thompson –
   BALAKIREV: *Piano Sonata.* **(*)**

Gordon Fergus-Thompson here gives a splendid account of Scriabin's overheated *F sharp minor Sonata* and sensitive, atmospheric performances of the other pieces here. A reverberant but good recording.

Piano Sonatas Nos. 4, Op. 30; 5, Op. 53; 9 (Black Mass); 10, Op. 70; Etude, Op. 2/1; 8 Etudes, Op. 42.

(*) ASV CDDCA 776. Fergus-Thompson.

Fergus-Thompson is thoroughly inside this idiom. At the same time it must be conceded that his performances are not as individual as those of Ashkenazy and in the cruelly competitive world of recorded music would not be a first choice. Nevertheless there is much musical nourishment here to satisfy the collector.

Piano Sonatas Nos. 8, Op. 66; 9, Op. 68; 10, Op. 70; 2 Danses, Op. 73; 2 Poèmes, Op. 69; 2 Poèmes, Op. 71; 2 Preludes, Op. 67; 5 Preludes, Op. 74; Vers la flamme, Op. 72.

*(**) Altarus AIR-CD 9020. Amato.

Donna Amato seems wholly attuned to Scriabin's sensibility and plays all his late music (Opp. 66–74), including the last three *Sonatas*, to the manner born. Scriabin's world is claustrophobic – but unfortunately so is the recording, which sounds as if it was made in a small acoustic environment but with some echo added. The sound-quality diminishes the pleasure this CD gives but not of course Amato's artistry.

SCULTHORPE, Peter (born 1929)

Piano Concerto.

(N) **(*) Australian ABC Eloquence 426 483-2. Fogg, Melbourne SO, Fredman – EDWARDS: Piano Concerto **(*); WILLIAMSON: *Concerto for 2 Pianos.* **(*)

In many ways, Sculthorpe's *Piano Concerto* is the most difficult of the three works to get to grips with on this Australian Eloquence CD. Written during a very sad time in the composer's life, its mood reflects that. It is not a virtuosic showpiece for the pianist, but stands as an interesting modern concerto, that repays listening. The performance here is excellent and the recording acceptable.

(i) *Nourlangie* (for solo guitar, strings and percussion). *From Kakadu; Into the Dreaming.*

*** Sony SK 53361. Williams; (i) Australian CO, Hickox – WESTLAKE: *Antarctica Suite.*

Peter Sculthorpe was born in Tasmania. *Nourlangie* is an extraordinarily imaginative and evocative piece, inspired by the composer's first sight of the enormous monolithic rock of that name in the Kakadu National Park. The music fuses evocation (the opening, with sounding gongs, is very compelling) and local dance song, which are effectively and naturally integrated into the texture to give a strong underlying melodic vein. The performance here is superb, with John Williams's guitar heard in a concertante role, admirably balanced within the overall sound-picture. The other two pieces are for solo guitar. *From Kakadu* is an intimate, improvisatory piece, somewhat minimalist in conception, in four changing sections. *Into the Dreaming* opens mystically but generates much energy in its central section before returning to the restrained mood of the opening. John Williams plays both pieces with total spontaneity and complete improvisational freedom. He is most naturally, if forwardly, recorded. Highly recommendable.

SEARLE, Humphrey (1915–82)

Symphonies Nos. 1, Op. 23; 4, Op. 38; Night Music, Op. 2; Overture to a Drama, Op. 17.

*** CPO CPO 999 541-2. BBC Scottish SO, Francis.

Although he was a pupil of Webern, Humphrey Searle could think in long paragraphs as these symphonies show. The *First*, composed in 1952–3 is the more. The basic 12-note series is drawn from Webern's Op. 28 *Quartet*, but the overall musical character is far from the doctrinaire serialism of the 1950s and 1960s. There is an impressive breadth and concentration, and a powerful sense of menace. The *Fourth Symphony* (1960–62) is stark and severe, again intensely concentrated, and far from easily assimilated – but then why should everything be 'accessible'. It is a tough nut to crack but one worth taking trouble with. Two earlier pieces – the *Night Music* (1943), a tribute to Webern on his 60th birthday, and the *Overture to a Drama* (1949) – complete a disc that makes a representative introduction to this fine composer. Excellent playing and recording.

SEGERSTAM, Leif (born 1944)

(i) *Symphonies Nos. 21 (September; Visions at Korpijärvi); (ii) 23 (Afterthoughts, Questioning Questionings).*

**(*) Ondine ODE 928-2. (i) Finnish RSO; (ii) Tampere PO (both without conductor).

There are some refined and sensitive touches in the course of these shapeless and sprawling pieces. They seem more like the improvisational sketches a composer makes prior to composition than the finished work of art. There is no feeling of a distinctive musical personality. The heavily scored and seemingly interminable tutti subdue and overpower the listener but the overall impact is underwhelming. Very good performances and excellent recording. If you try these pieces, you may like them more than we do.

SEIBER, Mátyás (1905–60)

Clarinet Concertino.

*** Hyp. CDA 66215. King, ECO, Litton – BLAKE: *Concerto;* LUTOSLAWSKI: *Dance Preludes.* ***

Mátyás Seiber's highly engaging *Concertino* was sketched during a train journey (in 1926, before the days of seamless rails) and certainly the opening *Toccata* has the jumpy, rhythmic feeling of railway line joints and points. Yet the haunting slow movement has a touch of the ethereal, while the Scherzo has a witty jazz element. Thea King has the measure of the piece; she is accompanied well by Andrew Litton, and very well recorded.

SEIXAS, Carlos de (1704–42)

Harpsichord Concerto in A; Sinfonia in B flat; Keyboard Sonatas Nos. 1, 16, 32–3, 42, 46–7, 57, 71 & 79.

*** Virgin VC5 45114-2. Haugsand, Norwegian Bar. O.

The Portuguese composer, Carlos de Seixas, is revealed here as having a distinct musical personality, and the jolly outer movements of his *A major Concerto* – separated by only a brief Adagio – are enjoyably spirited in the hands of Ketil Haugsand, who also conducts the excellent period orchestral group. The *Sinfonia* is essentially an Italian overture with a fast closing minuet, and the *Keyboard Sonatas* also show Italian influences. The earlier works are in a single movement, but the last three are more ambitious. This is not great music but always inventive and very personable, and it is effectively presented here and very well recorded.

Motets: *Adebat Vincentius; Tantum ergo.*

(M) *** DG (ADD) 453 182-2. Smith, Magali, Schwartz, Fernando Serafim, Gulbenkian Chamber Ch. & O, Corboz – ALMEIDA: *Beatus vir* etc.; CARVALHO: *Te Deum;* TEIXEIRA: *Gaudate, astra.* ***

Carlos de Seixas was a contemporary of Almeida and Teixeira, with whom he is joined in this stimulating collection of motets used to back up the Carvalho *Te Deum. Adebat Vincentius* brings a lively interplay within the double chorus, juxtaposed with a soprano/contralto duet, and thus makes a fine contrast with the serenely beautiful setting of *Tantum ergo.* Fine singing and first-class recording enhance the appeal of this eloquent music.

SEREBRIER, José (born 1938)

(i) Partita (Symphony No. 2); Fantasia; Winterreise; (ii) Sonata for Solo Violin.

*** Reference RR 90 CD. LPO, composer; (ii) Acosta.

The *Partita* (or *Symphony No. 2*) is attractive and its exuberant finale sparkles with Latin-American dance rhythms. The *Fantasia for Strings* convincingly combines energy with lyricism, while *Winterreise* titillates the listener's memory by ingeniously quoting, not from Schubert, but from seasonal inspirations of Haydn, Glazunov and Tchaikovsky's *Winter Daydreams Symphony*, using all three snippets together, plus the *Dies irae* at the climax. The *Solo Violin Sonata* is unashamedly romantic and very well played, as are the orchestral works under the composer. An enterprising and worthwhile issue.

SERLY, Tibor (1901–78)

Rhapsody for Viola & Orchestra.

(BB) *** Naxos 8.554183. Hong-Mei Xiao, Budapest PO, Kovacs – BARTOK: *Viola Concerto* (2 versions; ed. Bartok & ed. Serly); *Two Pictures.* ***

Tibor Serly, friend of Bartók and first editor of the unfinished *Viola Concerto*, here offers a closely related work, less individual than Bartók's own, but well worth hearing. Beautifully played by the Chinese viola-player, Hong-Mei Xiao, it provides a good makeweight for the disc containing both editions of the Bartók *Concerto.*

SESSIONS, Roger (1896–1985)

Concerto for Orchestra.

*** Hyp. CDA 66050. Boston SO, Ozawa – PANUFNIK: *Symphony No. 8.* ***

Sessions's *Concerto for Orchestra* finds him at his thorniest and most uncompromising, with lyricism limited to fleeting fragments of melody; but the playful opening leads one on finally to a valedictory close, sharply defined. Ozawa makes a powerful advocate, helped by superb playing from the Boston orchestra.

Symphony No. 4; Symphony No. 5; Rhapsody for Orchestra.

*** New World NW 345. Columbus SO, Badea.

Roger Sessions's musical language is dense and his logic is easier to sense than to follow. The performances by the Columbus Symphony Orchestra under Christian Badea appear well prepared, and there is no doubt as to their commitment and expertise. The sound ideally needs a larger acoustic, but every strand in the texture is well placed and there is no feeling of discomfort.

SÉVERAC, Déodat de (1872–1921)

Piano, 4 hands: L'Album pour les enfants petits et grands: Le Soldat de plomb (Histoire vraie en trois récits). Solo piano: Baigneuses au soleil (Souvenir de Banyuls-sur-mer); Cerdaña (5 Etudes pittoresques); Le Chant de la terre (poème géorgique); En Languedoc (suite); En vacances (petites pièces romantiques); Les Naïades et le faune indiscret; Pipperment-get (Valse brillante de concert); Premier Recueil (Au château et dans le parc); Deuxième Recueil (inachevé); Sous les lauriers roses ou Soir de Carnaval sur la Côte Catalane; Stances à Madame de Pompadour; Valse romantique.

(B) **(*) EMI (ADD) CZS5 72372-2 (3). Ciccolini.

Déodat de Séverac came from the Pays d'Oc and always retained his roots in the region. He first studied law at Toulouse before deciding on music and becoming a pupil of Magnard and then d'Indy. He was a friend of Ravel, to whom his musical language is much indebted. All the music on these CDs is civilized and has great charm. The recordings were made between 1968 and 1977 and are serviceable rather than distinguished. But the set will give much pleasure.

SGAMBATI, Giovanni (1841–1914)

Piano Concerto in G min., Op. 15; Overture Cola di Rienzo; Berceuse-rêverie, Op. 42/2 (orch. Massenet).

(N) *** ASV CDDCA 1097. Caramiello, Nuremberg PO, Ventura.

Giovanni Sgambati grew up in Rome as a musical prodigy. But from his earliest years he was not interested in Italian opera, his tastes turning instead to the music of the nineteenth-century German masters. He conducted the first

Italian performances of the *Eroica Symphony* and *Emperor Concerto*, and in 1886 premiered Liszt's *Dante Symphony*. All these influences can be found in his music, yet he was his own man and his *Piano Concerto* is a real find, genuinely inspired, with the solo part marvelously conceived to work in harness with the orchestra, both heroically and poetically.

The concerto opens not with a grand gesture, but evocatively and thoughtfully, and a little forlornly. The piano entry is bold and strong, but soon slips into the lyrical secondary material, which it decorates with brilliant roulades. The movement is on the largest scale and produces continuous rhapsodical mood changes, and a remarkable variety of invention, and orchestral re-colourings, always holding the listener by its flowing spontaneity and structural security.

Schumann and Brahms hover over the remaining two movements. The *Andante* is like an intermezzo, at first hesitant, but soloist and woodwind soon enter into a gentle romantic dialogue. The finale opens on the brass and soon galumphs away with a syncopated theme, but with underlying lyrical warmth to counter the coruscating brilliance of the solo writing. Altogether it is a splendid work and it could hardly be played with more confidence and understanding than it is here by Francesco Caramillo and his excellent Nuremberg orchestral partnership with Fabrizio Ventura.

It is they who then give a completely convincing account of the Lisztian symphonic poem, which is designated the *Cola di Rienzo Overture*. One of the composer's earliest works, written in 1866, it opens with appealingly romantic melodic evocation and proceeds to describe an undocumented narrative, often excitingly, sometimes melodramatically, but with lovely orchestral colouring and powerful expressive feeling. The closing section is quite haunting.

The delightful *Berceuse-Rêverie*, originally a piano piece, but lusciously scored by Massenet, makes a delightful closing lollipop. With first-class recording, this disc is really worth exploring; the concerto is as fine, if not finer than any in Hyperion's 'Romantic Concerto' series.

SHANKAR, Ravi (born 1920)

Sitar Concertos Nos. (i) *1*; (ii) *2 (A Garland of Ragas).* *Morning Love* (based on the *Raga Nata Bhairav*); *Raga Purlya Kalyan*; (iii) *Prahhati* (based on the *Raga Gunkali*); *Raga Piloo. Swara-Kākall.*

(B) **(*) EMI double forte (ADD/Dig) CZS5 76255-2 (2). Shankar; with (i) LSO, Previn; (ii) LPO, Mehta; (iii) Menuhin.

It would be easy to dismiss this pair of concertos, particularly as they are in four movements each and seem very long (the first runs for 40 minutes, the second for nearly 52 minutes!) and, except for *aficionados*, will undoubtedly outstay their welcome. Fairly evidently they are neither very good Western music nor good Indian music. The idiom is sweet – arguably too sweet and unproblematic – but at least they represent a 'crossover' in the real sense – a painless tour over the geographical layout of the raga. It also prompts brilliant and atmospheric music-making both from Previn and the LSO

and from Mehta (himself Indian-born) and the LPO. Not to mention the composer himself, who launches into solos which he makes sound spontaneous in the authentic manner, however prepared they may actually be. He opens the first CD with a very Westernized raga, which he calls *Morning Love*; and in the ragas *Piloo* and *Prabhati*, when he is joined by Menuhin (who is on very good form), the latter's contribution draws an obvious parallel with Eastern European folk music.

SHAPERO, Harold (born 1920)

Symphony for Classical Orchestra.

(M) (***) Sony mono SMK 60725. Columbia SO, Bernstein – DALLAPICCOLA: *Tartiniana for Violin & Orchestra;* LOPATNIKOFF: *Concertino.* (***)

Symphony for Classical Orchestra; Nine-minute Overture.

**(*) New World NW 373-2. LAPO, Previn.

Stravinsky and Copland are the major influences on Shapero's exhilarating and masterly *Symphony for Classical Orchestra*. Copland spoke of his 'wonderfully spontaneous musical gift' and the listener is held throughout by his powerful sense of momentum. Although he is perhaps almost too much in thrall to Stravinsky, this is a gripping and inspiriting score, which benefits greatly from Bernstein's advocacy. The performance is greatly superior to its only rival so far by Previn and the Los Angeles orchestra, which is less well held together. The 1953 mono recording comes up well in this well-transferred and intelligently planned compilation.

Previn gets good results from the Los Angeles orchestra but does not bring the sheer vitality that distinguished Bernstein's pioneering record.

SHCHEDRIN, Rodion (born 1933)

Carmen (ballet, arr. from Bizet; complete).

(M) *** RCA 09026 63308-2. Boston Pops O, Fiedler – GLAZUNOV: *Carnival Overture;* SHOSTAKOVICH: *Hamlet: Incidental Music.* ***

(i) *Carmen* (ballet; arr. from Bizet): *Suite;* (ii) *Anna Karenina* (ballet): *Suite.*

(N) (M) **(*) BMG/Melodiya 7432 36908-2. (i) Bolshoi Theatre O (members), Rozhdestvensky; (ii) USSR SO, Svetlanov.

(i) *Carmen* (ballet; arr. from Bizet): *Suite; Concerto for Orchestra (Naughty Limericks).*

(BB) **(*) Naxos 8.553038. Ukrainian State O, Theodor Kuchar.

(i) *Carmen* (ballet; arr. from Bizet): *Suite; Humoresque. In Imitation of Albéniz; Stalin Cocktail.*

*** Chan. 9288. I Musici de Montréal, Turovski; (i) with Ens. Répercussion – TURINA: *La oración del torero.* ***

Rodion Shchedrin's free adaptation of Bizet's *Carmen* music uses Bizet's tunes, complete with harmony, and reworks them into a new tapestry using only strings and percussion (including vibraphone). The whole thing is brilliantly done and wears surprisingly well.

Arthur Fiedler offers the complete score and the result is dazzling, with superb playing from the Boston strings, especially in the tender and passionate *Adagio* (Don José's *Flower Song*) and the equally vibrant sequence called *The Fortune Teller* which quotes from *Carmen's* passionate music in the Card scene. The finale whimsically opens in the manner of Saint-Saëns with a sparkling xylophone solo, then after various reprises, the ballet ends gently. With extremely vivid remastering of the excellent 1969 recording this is one of Fiedler's finest records, for the couplings are equally successful.

This Chandos version by I Musici de Montréal was recorded in the richly resonant acoustic of the Eglise de la Nativité de la Sainte-Vierge, La Prairie, Quebec. The sound is very much in the demonstration bracket, with glittering percussion effects (marimba and vibraphone particularly well caught) and dramatic use of side drum snares. Yuli Turovsky's performance opens evocatively and is highly dramatic, winningly expressive and subtle in its use of the wide range of string colour and dynamic. The pastiche, *In Imitation of Albéniz*, and the grotesque, Shostakovich-like *Humoresque* are offset by a malignant parody-evocation of Stalin, full of creepy special effects and with a shout of horror at the end. They are very well presented here, but one would not want to return to them very often.

Rozhdestvensky's pioneering 1967 stereo recording of Rodion Shchedrin's very free adaptation of Bizet's *Carmen* music still has the ability to make the listener sit up. The playing of the Bolshoi strings is truly electrifying and the Soviet stereo is amazingly good, with the percussion effects both crisp and atmospheric. Svetlanov's performance of the suite from *Anna Karenina* – which centres entirely on the heroine – is hardly less gripping, with virtuoso playing from the violins. They are often taken shriekingly up into their extreme upper register to portray Anna's (very visceral) passion, and later her nightmares. At the close her death is signalled by the tolling bell and the sound of the train, plus a desperate spoken passage from Anna herself. Frankly this music is not worthy of Tolstoy: it is melodramatic rather than conveying the range and psychological depth of Anna's emotions as portrayed in the novel.

Kuchar's version is also vividly played, with wit as well as high drama and atmosphere. The Naxos recording is excellent. The brief *Concerto for Orchestra* with its curious subtitle is a kaleidoscopic scherzando, a whirlwind presentation of Russian folk-motives over a minimalist ostinato. It is played with great verve but rather outstays its welcome.

Concerto Cantabile.

*** EMI CDC5 56966-2. Vengerov, LSO, Rostropovich – STRAVINSKY: *Violin Concerto;* TCHAIKOVSKY: *Sérénade mélancholique.* ***

Shchedrin has said that he understands the term *cantabile* to express 'firstly a certain tension in the "soul" of the notes, and also the manner in which they are produced. The term also refers to the juxtaposition, interweaving, conflict and resolution of the soloist's singing lines against the orchestra.' The serene opening is deceptive, for the composer's arch-like structure forms a complex and at times dissonant work, even if 'in the finale the sound of the solo violin should come to resemble that of a shepherd's pipe'. With the vibrant support of Rostropovich, Maxim Vengerov's performance combines a powerful lyricism with the composer's required 'tonal variety'. The dancing centrepiece brings splendid bite of bow on strings, combined with a genuine sense of fantasy, and the finale produces a burst of radiance in the orchestral strings which the soloist follows with a ruminative soliloquy. The Abbey Road recording is first class.

Stihira.

*** Erato 0630 17722-2. Nat. SO, Rostropovich – GLAZUNOV: *Violin Concerto in A min., Op. 82;* PROKOFIEV: *Violin Concerto No. 1 in D, Op. 19.* ***

Shchedrin here celebrates the millennium of the introduction of Christianity into Russia with a measured passacaglia-like piece based on Russian Orthodox chant, which builds up to a central climax of Mussorgskian splendour. The recording, made in the Kennedy Center, Washington, is more airy and spacious than many from this venue.

SHEBALIN, Vissarion (1902–63)

(i) *Concertino for Violin & Orchestra, Op. 14/1;*
(ii) *Concertino for Horn & Orchestra, Op. 14/2;*
(iii) *Sinfonietta on Russian Folk Themes, Op. 43;*
(iv) *Symphony No. 5, Op. 56.*

** Olympia stereo/mono OCD 599. (i) Shulgin, USSR Academic SO Ens., Provatorov; (ii) Afanasiev, USSR R. and TV SO, Anosov; (iii) USSR R. and TV SO, Gauk; (iv) USSR State SO, Svetlanov.

The most important work here is the well-structured and finely crafted *Fifth Symphony*, composed in the last year of Shebalin's life. It is well worth investigating, though Shebalin's is not a strongly individual voice, even if his music is cultured and thoughtful. Svetlanov's is a live performance from 1963 recorded in mono. The two Op. 14 *Concertinos* come from the turn of the 1920s and 1930s, and reflect the more outward-looking spirit of Soviet music at the time – there are reminders of Hindemith and contemporary French music. These are both stereo recordings, well played, though the solo horn has an obtrusive rubato. The horns produce a pretty blowsy sonority in the *Sinfonietta*, here heard in a 1954 mono recording. Composed in 1949–51, it is a perfunctory, second-rate piece. An interesting issue just the same.

Symphonies Nos. (i) *1 in F min., Op. 6;* (ii) *3 in C, Op. 17.*

**(*) Olympia (ADD) OCD 577. USSR RSO, (i) Ermler; (ii) Gergiev.

Shebalin's *First Symphony* is heavily indebted to his mentor, Miaskovsky. The orchestral writing is assured and the thematic invention is intelligent though not as memorable and characterful as in Shostakovich's No. 1. The *Third Symphony* comes from the 1930s, and for all its moments of eloquence and undoubted expertise, its substance does not quite sustain its length. But both symphonies are well worth investigating. Good performances and decent 1970s recordings.

String Quartets Nos. 6 in B min., Op. 34; 7 in A flat (Slavonic), Op. 41; 8 in C, Op. 53.

(N) *** Olympia OCD 665. Krasni Qt.

Shebalin was a pupil of Miaskovsky and became one of the most influential teachers of his generation. He taught at the Moscow Conservatory and became its director during the war, but was later dismissed during the upheavals that overtook Soviet music in 1948. It is said that Shostakovich had pictures of only three composers in his study: Mahler, Mussorgsky ... and Shebalin! Apart from Shebalin's five symphonies there are nine string quartets, all of which have been recorded by the Krasni Quartet of St. Petersburg. Nos. 6 (1943) and 7 (1948) are like most of Shebalin's music, finely wrought and fluent. No. 8 (1960) was composed for the Borodin Quartet (in which his son played viola) and is perhaps the best known, having been recorded on Melodiya in the days of LP. Ultimately it is music that inspires respect rather than enthusiasm: it is well fashioned but lacks that individual profile that distinguishes Shostakovich. Very good playing and a faithful recording.

SHEPPARD, John (c. 1515–c. 1559)

Aeterne rex altissime; Audivi vocem de coelo; Beata nobis gaudia; Dum transisset Sabbatum (1st & 2nd settings); *In manus tuas* (2nd & 3rd settings); *Gaude, gaude, gaude Maria; Hostis Herodes impie; Impetum fecerunt unanimes; In manus tuas* (3rd setting); *Libera nos, salva nos* (2nd setting); *Sacris solemniis; Sancte Dei pretiose; Spiritus sanctus procedens* (2nd setting). *Second Service: Magnificat; Nunc dimittis. Te Deum laudamus. Western Wynde Mass.*

(B) *** Hyp. Dyad CDD 22022 (2). The Sixteen, Christophers.

Ave maris stella. Cantate Mass. Motets: *Deus tuorum militum* (1st setting); *Filiae Hierusalem venite; Haec dies; In manus tuas Domine* (1st setting); *In pacem in idipsum; Jesu salvator saeculi, redemptis; Jesu salvator saeculi verbum; Justi in perpetuum vivent; Laudem dicite Deo; Libera nos, salva nos* (1st setting); *Paschal Kyrie; Regis Tharsis et insulae; Salvator mundi, Domine; Spiritus sanctus procedens* (1st setting); *Verbum caro factus est.*

❀ **(B)** *** Hyp. Dyad CDD 22021 (2). The Sixteen, Christophers.

The first collection listed (CD 22022) is especially attractive as it includes Sheppard's *Western Wynde Mass*. However, this is a less elaborate setting of this famous theme than some others, notably that of John Taverner, for until the closing *Agnus Dei* Sheppard consistently places the melodic line on top, whereas Taverner moves the tune about within the lower parts. Nevertheless Sheppard's setting has an appealingly simple beauty, while the extended *Te Deum laudamus* is even richer in its harmonic progressions. The soaring second version of *Dum transisset Sabbatum* and the third version of the sombre *In manus tuas* (with their

characteristic dissonances) are also memorable. The set includes ten more responsories, all of high quality and offering considerable variety, from the flowing antiphon, *Libera nos, salva nos* to the gently serene second setting (for Palm Sunday) of *In manus tuas Domine*.

However, we have given our Rosette to the companion set (CD 22021), for it includes Sheppard's glorious six-voiced *Cantate Mass*, much more complex than *Western Wynde* and, with its glowingly textured polyphony, surely among his most inspired works. There are also eleven responsories, all showing the composer at his most concentrated in inspiration. The Sixteen consistently convey the rapturous beauty of Sheppard's writing, above all in the ethereal passages in the highest register, very characteristic of him. Even there, the Sixteen's sopranos seem quite unstressed by the tessitura. There are not many more beautiful examples of Tudor polyphony than this.

Christe redemptor omnium; In manus tuas; Media vita; Reges Tharsis; Sacris solemniis; Verbum caro.

*** Gimell CDGIM 916. Tallis Scholars, Phillips.

All the music here is based on chant, and much of it is for the six-part choir, which produces a particularly striking sonority. The *Media vita* ('In the midst of life we are in death') is a piece of astonishing beauty, and it is sung with remarkable purity of tone by the Tallis Scholars under Peter Phillips. Glorious and little-known music: the recording could hardly be improved on.

Missa cantate; Respond: 'Spiritus Sanctus'.

(B) *** Cal. Approche CAL 6621. Clerkes of Oxenford, Wulstan – GIBBONS: *Hymns.* ***

John Sheppard's *Cantate Mass* appears in the Hyperion Dyad collection, above; but is sung here a third higher than the manuscript indicates and, involving the sopranos in formidable problems of tessitura, is among the most distinctive of Sheppard's works, presenting surprises in a way uncommon in civilized polyphonic writing. The textures here are refreshingly clear, helped by the superb performances of the Clerkes of Oxenford. The five-part *Spiritus sanctus* is less striking but makes an excellent bonus, equally well recorded.

Missa cantate; Verbum caro.

(N) **(*) DG 457 658-2. Salisbury Boy Choristers, Gabrieli Consort, McCreesh.

Like previous issues in Paul McCreesh's revelatory series with the Gabrieli Consort, this aims to re-create a full celebration of the Mass using as centrepiece John Sheppard's *Missa cantate*, the most elaborate of his five mass settings. The powerful motet *Verbum caro* is then used as a recessional. Sheppard's polyphonic writing in the Mass and the motet is masterly, complex and moving. But it makes up only 30 minutes out of a total of over 80 on the disc, with the rest devoted to monophonic chant, and this may restrict the appeal of the performance to those who are addicted to plainsong. The performance is well up to the high standard of this stimulating series, with the boy choristers as well as the singers of the Consort atmospherically recorded against the reverberant acoustic of Salisbury Cathedral.

Motets: *Gaude, gaude, gaude Maria; In manus tuas* (1st setting); *Laudem dicite Deo; In pace; Verbum caro.*

(B) **(*) CfP (ADD) CD-CFP 4638. Clerkes of Oxenford, Wulstan – TALLIS: *Motets.* **(*)

The performances by the Clerkes of Oxenford under Davis Wulstan are full of fervour, particularly in the inspired *Gaude, gaude, gaude Maria* and the closing *Verbum caro.* Wulstan presses on very strongly, and some might feel there is a lack of contrasting repose and not enough subtlety in the sheer thrust of his direction. But the commitment of the singing will surely convince anyone who buys this CD on impulse that this is great music and that its composer's name should be more familiar. The 1978 analogue recording has plenty of body and atmosphere.

SHIELD, William (1748–1829)

Rosina.

(N) *** ABC Classics (ADD) 461 922-2. Elkins, Harwood, Sinclair, Tear, Macdonald, Ambrosian Singers, LSO, Bonynge – ELGAR: *Sea Pictures* **(*)

Shield's rustic comedy *Rosina* is a delight from beginning to end. First heard at Covent Garden in 1782, it is crammed full of delights. Even the overture, with its witty interjections from the woodwind, threatens to upstage the main work, but the engaging and piquant arias which follow easily match it. The dialogue rings through with crystal clarity, the country-accents delivered with relish. The performance is lively and fun, with Bonynge allowing the singers to embellish their vocal lines while the orchestra provides a stylish and vivid accompaniment.

Margreta Elkins is superb as Rosina, and she is matched by the rest of the team; whether they be joyful rustic arias, or sentimental ballads, each is characterized beautifully. The full English text is provided in the lavishly illustrated booklet, and with vintage Decca sound (1966) this CD is a winner. The unexpected couplings are well worth having too.

SHOSTAKOVICH, Dmitri

(1906–75)

The Adventures of Korzinkina (film music): *Suite, Op. 59; Alone* (film music): *Suite, Op. 26; The Bug* (incidental music): *Suite, Op. 19; The Golden Hills* (film music): *Suite, Op. 30a;* (i) *Jazz Band Suite No. 1; Scherzos: in F sharp min., Op. 1; in E flat, Op. 7; The Tale of the Priest and his Servant, Balda (suite), Op. 36; Theme with Variations in B, Op. 7.* Orchestral Transcriptions: D. SCARLATTI: *Pastorale & Capriccio.* Johann STRAUSS Jnr *Vergnügungszug Polka.* YOUMANS: *Tahiti Trot (Tea for Two).* Vocal Transcriptions: BEETHOVEN: *Es war einmal ein König.* RIMSKY-KORSAKOV: *Ya dolgo zhdal Tebya (I Waited for You).* (ii) *2 Fables After Ivan Krylov, Op. 4;*

Romance on Pushkin's Poem, Spring, Op. 128. Big Lightning (comic opera): excerpts.

(B) *** BMG/Melodiya Twofer 74321 59058-2 (2). USSR MoC SO & Chamber Ch., or USSR SO; or Moscow PO or Leningrad PO, with Soloists, or (i) Soloists Ens. or (ii) Moscow Conservatory Chamber Ch., Rozhdestvensky.

None of the music included in this highly recommendable Melodiya 'Twofer' is familiar or without interest to admirers of this composer, and most of it – tuneful and colourfully scored – has a wide general appeal. The *Scherzo in F sharp minor* (1919) and *Theme and Variations* (1922) are uncharacteristic, although the *Variations* has a burst of Russian flamboyance towards the close. The companion *E flat major Scherzo* is more individual – it includes a prominent part for the piano and there is already evidence of Shostakovich's special kind of wit, which certainly resurfaces in the film scores, which are from the 1930s and, whilst uncovering no masterpieces, bring much to relish. The *Golden Hills Suite* includes an extraordinary extended organ *Fugue* to which the orchestra adds plangent dissonance at the climax. Perhaps the most engaging of these suites is the quixotic *Tale of the Priest and his Servant, Balda,* originally written for an animated children's cartoon. The two Krylov fables are also early (1922): the first (*The Dragonfly and the Ant*) most characterfully sung by Galina Borisova, the second is a more ambitious choral setting of *The Ass and the Nightingale.* Shostakovich's satirical talent comes well to the fore in *The Bug:* the orchestra includes a flexotone and *Scene on the Boulevard* is a bizarre highlight. But the most remarkable find here is the 1932 score for the comic opera, *The Big Lightning.* Vigorously sung, it is full of witty, even riotous pastiche. The little *Jazz Suite* makes a delightful interlude with its *Waltz, Polka* and *Foxtrot,* as do the two charming Scarlatti woodwind arrangements and the exuberant *Excursion Train Polka* of Johann Strauss. But among the transcriptions it is Beethoven's *Song of the Flea* which stands out (superbly sung by Nesterenko and sounding for all the world like a Russian folk song) alongside the irrepressible *Tahiti Trot,* Shostakovich's exhilarating version of Vincent Youmans's *Tea for Two.*

The Age of Gold (suite), Op. 22; Ballet Suites Nos. 1–3; Pirogov, Op. 76a (suite from the film); *Zoya, Op. 64* (suite from the film).

(B) *** BMG/Melodiya Twofer (ADD) 74321 66981-2 (2). Bolshoi Theatre Ch. and O, M. Shostakovich.

This is an enjoyable collection: the *Ballet Suites* show Shostakovich at his most entertaining and tuneful – tempered with irony – and full of imaginative orchestral colours. The music from *The Bolt* is more bitingly ironic and some of the best music from the complete ballet is recorded here. The audaciously witty *Age of Gold* suite is well known, but the music from the films *Zoya* and *Pirogov* is rare: these suites are a degree more serious but are no less enjoyable – they contain several attractive tunes wrapped in consistently imaginative orchestration, and though not great music are well worth having. The performances (under the direction of the composer's son) of the Bolshoi orchestra and chorus could hardly sound more authentic, and the 1966 recording is good for the period. With the rare fill-ups, this set is well worth exploring at bargain price. However, Järvi's mid-priced recording of all five *Ballet Suites* (plus other music) on Chandos offers spectacularly wide-ranging modern recording and remains in a class of its own.

'The Film Album': Alone, Op. 26 (extended excerpts). *The Counterplan, Op. 33 (excerpts). The Gadfly: Romance. The Great Citizen, Op. 55: Funeral March. Hamlet, Op. 116 (excerpts). Pirogov, Op. 76a: Scherzo & Finale. Sofia Perovskaya, Op. 132: Waltz. The Tale of the Silly Little Mouse, Op. 56* (arr. Andrew CORNHALL).

*** Decca 460 792-2. Concg. O, Chailly.

Shostakovich's ready find of melody, and exotic orchestral palette spiced with touches of wit, make here for a kaleidoscope of memorable vignettes. The delightful opening *Presto* of the music from *The Counterplan* leads to a wistful romantic concertante violin episode, not unlike the more famous *Romance* from *The Gadfly*, which is also included. The continuous sequence illustrating *The Tale of the Silly Little Mouse* (an animated cartoon) is full of delicate charm; the engaging *Valse* from *Pirogov* is rather more robust, and *Hamlet* brings music of more pungency and dramatic power. But the most substantial set of excerpts is taken from the composer's second film score, *Alone* (1930). It opens roisterously, follows up with a Kabalevsky-like *Galop*, and the other numbers, with avant-garde flair, bring a wide range of picaresque and touching evocations, describing a barrel organ, schoolchildren, a tempest, and ending with an eerie calm after the storm. First rate Concertgebouw playing and the most vivid Decca recording ensure the success of this entertaining collection.

Ballet Suites Nos. 1–5; Festive Overture, Op. 96; Katerina Ismailova: Suite.

*** Chan. 7000/1. RSNO, Järvi.

This highly entertaining set again represents Shostakovich in light-hearted, often ironic mood, throwing out *bonnes-bouches* like fireworks and with a sparkling vividness of orchestral colour. The *Ballet Suites* reuse material from earlier works: the *Fifth Suite* draws entirely on music from the 1931 ballet, *The Bolt* (see below). This is the most extended of the five suites, and typical of the young Shostakovich. The *Suite* from *Katerina Ismailova* (*Lady Macbeth of Mtsensk*) consists of entr'actes from between the scenes which effectively act as emotional links. Järvi is entirely at home in all this music and clearly relishes its dry humour. The recording is spectacular and resonantly wide-ranging in the Chandos manner.

The Bolt (ballet; complete recording).

*** Chan. 9343/4 (2). Stockholm PO, Stockholm Transport Band, Rozhdestvensky.

The Bolt dates from 1931 and in its original form sank without trace, largely thanks to the feeble, cumbersome propagandist libretto. Yet the dances are so sharp and colourful in their inspiration that over the years suites of movements have been heard, and now Rozhdestvensky in this vivid, full-blooded recording resurrects the complete score of 43 move-

ments, lasting two and a half hours. Even if it is no masterpiece it demonstrates how dazzlingly inventive the young Shostakovich was, even when faced with an indifferent subject. Rozhdestvensky plainly believes passionately in this score, and he draws an electrifying performance from the Swedish orchestra. Demonstration sound.

Chamber Symphony, Op. 110a; Symphony for Strings, Op. 118a (both arr. Barshai); (i) From Jewish folk poetry.

(N) (M) *** Chan. 6617. I Musici de Montreal, Turovsky;
   (i) with Pelle, Hart, Nolan.

A fine record. The transcriptions for strings of the *Eighth* and *Tenth Quartets* were made by Rudolf Barshai, and if the performances here do not quite match their arranger's own recording (now withdrawn), they have plenty of bite and intensity and top-quality Chandos sound. The eleven vignettes, which Shostakovich based on Jewish folk music, have the widest diversity of mood and are splendidly sung here, the dialogue songs especially idiomatic. They are surprisingly upbeat, with the final concerted number, *Happiness*, ending the cycle robustly. Turovsky's framing accompaniments, too, are colourful and vividly caught by the engineers.

'The Dance Album': The Bolt: Ballet Suite, Op. 27a (1934 version); The Gadfly (extended excerpts from the film score), Op. 97 (original orchestration); Moscow-Cheryomushki (suite from the operetta), Op. 105.

*** Decca 452 597-2. Phd. O, Chailly.

Chailly offers 13 items from *The Gadfly* and reveals it to be far finer music than hitherto suspected, partly by using the original scoring. For all his sophistication of detail and expressive expansiveness, Chailly does not miss out on the witty audacity. The opening number of *Moscow-Cheryomushki*, *A Spin through Moscow* (when the chauffeur borrows the boss's car), has great energy and élan, the *Polka* from *The Bolt* combines wit with narrowly avoided vulgarity, and the boisterous opening of the following *Variations* will disappoint nobody. But, apart from the tunefulness, what one remembers most here is the superb playing of the Philadelphia Orchestra: the sonorous brass and vivid woodwind, while the strings have not sounded like this in decades. It is a joy to hear the luscious violins in *The Tango* from *The Bolt*, or *Montanelli* from *The Gadfly*; while the full body of tone in melancholy response to *The Slap in the Face* and the soft-voiced cellos and violas in *Gemma's Room* recall the Stokowskian era.

Cello Concerto No. 1 in E flat, Op. 107.

*** Chan. 8322. Wallfisch, ECO, Simon – BARBER: *Cello Concerto.* ***

Wallfisch handles the first movement splendidly and he gives a sensitive account of the slow movement and has thoughtful and responsive support from the ECO. The Chandos recording is outstandingly fine.

Cello Concertos Nos. 1; 2 in G, Op. 126.

*** Ph. 412 526-2. Schiff, Bav. RSO, M. Shostakovich.

(BB) *** Naxos 8.550813. Kliegel, Polish Nat. RSO (Katowice), Wit.

*** BIS CD 626. Thedéen, Malmö SO, DePreist.

*** Virgin VC5 45145-2. Mørk, LPO, Jansons.

(BB) **(*) Arte Nova (ADD) 74321 49688-2. Rodin, Russian PO, Krimets.

Schiff's superbly recorded account of the *First* can hold its own with the finest. The *Second Concerto* is a haunting piece, essentially lyrical; it is gently discursive, sadly whimsical at times and tinged with a smiling melancholy that hides deeper troubles. The recording is enormously impressive.

Maria Kliegel and the Polish National Radio Orchestra at Katowice under Antoni Wit give a very good account of both concertos that can be confidently recommended at this price, and on all counts is well worth considering.

The fine Swedish cellist, Torleif Thedéen, has a lot going for him and his passionately committed performances would honour any collection. He has the advantage of excellent engineering, which gives a very alive sound, plus good orchestral support from the Malmö orchestra under James DePreist.

Truls Mørk is an eminently forthright Shostakovich interpreter, and his account of both concertos also ranks among the very best. He is not afraid of allowing the music to speak for itself, and the amazingly present and vivid recording weighs heavily in Virgin's favour.

Kyrill Rodin dispatches the *First Concerto* with effortless élan and no mean eloquence. The important solo horn part in the slow movement has a vibrato which may possibly trouble some listeners. The searching opening to the *Second Concerto* is beautifully characterized however, and the orchestral playing is spirited and sensitive, though the strings are perhaps not quite weighty enough. The recordings are a trifle bright at the treble end of the spectrum but are generally very well balanced.

(i) *Cello Concerto No. 1; Piano Concertos Nos.* (ii) *1, Op. 35;* (iii) *2, Op. 102.*

(BB) *** Navigator 74321 29254-2. USSR RSO, with (i) Khomitser, cond. Rozhdestvensky; (ii) List, cond. M. Shostakovitch.

Eugene List plays the *First Piano Concerto* with splendid dash and brilliance. He opens the *Second* with comparably crisp, rhythmic vigour and takes the finale very much up to speed; throughout there is plenty of character and spirit. Though the sound is vivid, the strings of the USSR Radio Symphony Orchestra are somewhat wanting in bloom. But both slow movements have plenty of atmosphere and List has the advantage of the authority of Maxim Shostakovich's direction. Mikhail Khomitser is a formidable soloist in the *Cello Concerto*. The forward balance means that he dominates the performance, yet Rozhdestvensky provides a strong, concentrated backing. The orchestral recording could ideally be more refined but there is no lack of atmosphere. A real bargain.

(i) *Cello Concerto No. 1;* (ii) *Violin Concerto No. 1 in A min., Op. 99.*

⊕ (M) *** Sony stereo/mono MHK 63327. (i) Rostropovich, Phd. O, Ormandy; (ii) D. Oistrakh, NYPO, Mitropoulos.

Rostropovich's recording première of the Shostakovich *First*

Cello Concerto was made in 1959 and has for long enjoyed legendary status. It has probably not been surpassed, even by Rostropovich himself in subsequent recordings. David Oistrakh's mono recording of the *Violin Concerto* with Mitropoulos conducting the New York Philharmonic still sounds stunning. The presentation brings alive memories of the original issues and induces much nostalgia. This reissue is comparatively expensive but well worth it.

Cello Concerto No. 2, Op. 126.

(B) *** DG Double (ADD) 437 952-2 (2). Rostropovich, Boston SO, Ozawa – BERNSTEIN: *3 Meditations* etc.; BOCCHERINI: *Cello Concerto No. 2;* GLAZUNOV: *Chant du Ménestrel;* TARTINI: *Cello Concerto;* TCHAIKOVSKY: *Andante Cantabile* etc.; VIVALDI: *Cello Concertos.* ***

(i) *Cello Concerto No. 2; Symphony No. 12 (The Year 1917), Op. 112.*

** Chan. 9585. (i) Helmerson; Russian State SO, Polyansky.

Rostropovich plays with beautifully controlled feeling, and Seiji Ozawa brings sympathy and fine discipline to the accompaniment, securing admirably expressive playing from the Boston orchestra. The analogue recording is first class. As can be seen, this is part of a remarkably generous DG Double anthology, showing Rostropovich's art over the widest range.

This fine Swedish cellist plays with eloquence and authority in the *Second Cello Concerto* but the response from the Russian State Symphony Orchestra, under Polyansky, is a little disappointing. Moreover, the *Twelfth Symphony* calls for the advocacy of an outsize personality if it is to make a really positive impression.

Piano Concerto No. 1 in C min., Op. 35.

*** EMI CDC5 56760-2. Andsnes, Hardenberger, CBSO, Järvi – BRITTEN: *Piano Concerto;* ENESCU: *Légende for Trumpet & Piano.* ***

(i) *Piano Concerto No. 1;* (ii) *Symphony No. 5 in D min., Op. 47.*

**(*) Australian Decca Eloquence (ADD) 466 664-2. (i) Ogdon, ASMF, Marriner; (ii) SRO, Kertész.

Andsnes's is the finest account of the *Concerto for Piano, Trumpet and Strings* to have appeared for some time. Recorded at a live concert, it has well-judged tempi and offers sensitive, incisive pianism from Andsnes and great sensitivity and elegance from Håkan Hardenberger. Very good sound. This is now a first choice.

John Ogdon's clean, stylish performance of the *First Piano Concerto* – which encompasses both the humour and romanticism of the score – was one of his best records. He keeps a little more detached than Marriner in the tender slow movement, but the trumpet playing of John Wilbraham is masterly in the finale. Though the balance gives the performance a chamber quality, the sound is full and vivid.

Making its CD debut, Kertész's *Fifth Symphony* was recorded in the early 1960s, though you would hardly guess it. It is a thoroughly musical reading but others find much more tension and colour in the climax of the *Largo*. The finale is taken steadily, but there is a splendid outburst of controlled exuberance for the coda, and the excellent recording – with some impressive timpani – projects the reading effectively. An enterprising coupling.

Piano Concertos Nos. 1–2; The Unforgettable Year 1919, Op. 89; The Assault on Beautiful Gorky (for piano and orchestra).

(B) *** CfP CD-CFP 4547. Alexeev, Jones, ECO, Maksymiuk.

Alexeev is a first choice among couplings of both *Concertos*, and his record would sweep the board even at full price. The digital recording is excellent in every way and scores over most rivals in clarity and presence. There is a fill-up in the form of a miniature one-movement *Concerto* from a film-score called *The Unforgettable Year 1919*.

(i) Piano Concertos Nos. 1–2. Piano Sonata No. 2 in B min., Op. 61.

(N) (BB) *** Warner Apex 8573 89092-2. Leonskaya; (i) Saint Paul CO, Wolf.

We know from her fine Tchaikovsky recordings that Elisabeth Leonskaya is thoroughly at home in Russian music and so it proves in her sparkling and wittily pointed accounts of these two concertos of Shostakovich. The Saint Paul Chamber Orchestra, too, provide admirable backing. The strings play with striking beauty in both slow movements, the *Andante* of No. 2 is ravishing, and the solo trumpeter, Gary Borden, brings a nice sense of humour to his solos in the finale of No. 1. What makes this disc doubly attractive is Leonskaya's distinctive account of the *B minor Piano Sonata*, with thoughtful playing not only in the slow movement but in the finale, which is in essence a set of variations. Vivid recording, with a touch of hardness on the piano tone, which does not come amiss in this repertoire.

Violin Concerto No. 1 in A min., Op. 99.

*** Teldec 4509 92256-2. Vengerov, LSO, Rostropovich – PROKOFIEV: *Violin Concerto No. 1*. ***
*** Sony SK 68338. Midori, BPO, Abbado – TCHAIKOVSKY: *Violin Concerto*. ***
*** EMI CDC7 49814-2. Perlman, Israel PO, Mehta – GLAZUNOV: *Violin Concerto*. ***
**(*) Simax PSC 1159. Tellefsen, RPO, Berglund – BACH: *Violin Concerto No. 2*. **(*)

Vengerov comes into direct competition with Perlman in Shostakovich's *A minor Concerto*, yet his playing can dazzle the ear equally tellingly; he also really gets under the skin of the concerto and finds an added depth of poetic feeling, while fully retaining all the music's thrust and spontaneity. Rostropovich and the LSO give splendid support, and this Teldec disc becomes a first recommendation, except for those wanting both Shostakovich concertos together on a single CD.

Having the Tchaikovsky concerto together with this twentieth-century Russian masterpiece brings out the parallels between the two, a point enhanced by Midori's readings, recorded live, with rhythm and phrasing freely expressive. At the start of the *Moderato* first movement of the Shostakovich her tone is so withdrawn that one has to prick the ears, and in the *Passacaglia* third movement

she also conveys an ethereal poignancy in her pianissimo playing. Abbado is a powerful and sympathetic, yet discreet accompanist, with recording that is both warm and well detailed.

There is no violinist in the world who in sheer bravura can quite match Perlman, particularly live, and the ovation which greets his dazzling performance of the finale is richly deserved. Yet some of the mystery and the fantasy which Russian interpreters have found – from David Oistrakh onwards – is missing, and the close balance of the solo instrument, characteristic of Perlman's concerto recordings, undermines hushed intensity.

Arve Tellefsen gives a fine account of the concerto and brings fine musicianship and no lack of passion to it. Berglund proves a supportive accompanist and the RPO play well for him. Moreover the sound is very well balanced. But this is not a first choice.

Violin Concertos Nos. 1; 2 in C sharp min., Op. 129.

(BB)*** Virgin 2 x 1 VBD5 61633-2. Sitkovetsky, BBC SO, Davis.
*** Chan. 8820. Mordkovitch, SNO, Järvi.
(BB) *** Naxos 8.550814. Kaler, Polish Nat. RSO (Katowice), Wit.
(N) **(*) BBC (ADD) BBCL 4060. D. Oistrakh, (i) Philh. O, Rozhdestvensky; (ii) USSR State O, Svetlanov – YSAYE: *Amitié*. **(*)

Virgin's coupling by Sitkovetsky and the BBC Symphony Orchestra under Andrew Davis is impressive and intense; there is no doubt as to its excellence, it has tremendous bite. It is also splendidly recorded, and takes its place at the top of the list.

Mordkovitch's concentrated reading of No. 2 is matched by Järvi and the orchestra in their total commitment. She even outshines the work's dedicatee and first interpreter, David Oistrakh, in the dark reflectiveness of her playing, even if she cannot quite match him in bravura passages. In the better-known concerto (No. 1) the meditative intensity is magnetic, with a fullness and warmth of tone that have not always marked her playing on record before.

Ilya Kaler's technique is flawless, with playing that is not only brilliant but consistently beautiful tonally. The *Second Violin Concerto* is particularly fine, the more wayward, more problematic work, in which Kaler relishes the key role given to the cadenzas. The haunting beauty of the performance may be measured by the gentle cadenza and final ghostly coda of the first movement, leading to a wonderfully rarefied account of the central *Adagio* and a mercurial, quicksilver one of the finale. If in the better-known *First Concerto* Kaler's performance does not quite have the same intensity, that is partly a question of the marginally less taut orchestral accompaniment and of the recording balance.

David Oistrakh's recording of the *First Violin Concerto* comes from the Edinburgh Festival of 1962 and the *Second* from a Prom in 1968. Both are performances to cherish alongside the commercial recordings that the great violinist (the dedicatee of both works) made in the 1950s. Although neither performance supersedes these, there is the electricity of a live occasion that gives something extra, and the first movement (*Nocturne*) of the *First* has an atmosphere that is as powerful as it was under Mitropoulos. The sound is very good.

The Gadfly (suite), Op. 97a; Hamlet (film incidental music), Op. 116: excerpts; King Lear (suite), Op. 58a.

**(*) Koch 3-7274-2. Korean Broadcasting SO, Jordania.

The Korean Radio forces offer *The Gadfly* and *King Lear* suites and the first, third and fourth movements of the *Hamlet* music. The Koch disc is to be recommended for the great intensity and discipline of the orchestral response, and the three movements from *Hamlet* are keenly felt.

The Golden Age (ballet; complete).

**(*) Chan. 9251/2. Stockholm PO, Rozhdestvensky.

This is the first complete recording of Shostakovich's first ballet, with its extraordinary plot of Soviet and capitalist sportsmen and women. The famous *Polka* is meant to satirize a disarmament meeting in Geneva. The music as a whole is remarkably potent and full of succulent ideas (even *Tea for Two* arrives during Act II) and with the big set-pieces expansively and sometimes darkly symphonic. The score is well played in Stockholm, but the warm orchestral style does not always readily bring out the music's plangent character and moments of barbed wit.

Hamlet (1932 production); incidental music, (suite).

(M) *** RCA 09026 63308-2. Boston Pops O, Fiedler –
 GLAZUNOV: *Carnival Overture*; SHCHEDRIN: *Carmen*
 (ballet). ***

Fiedler chooses a baker's dozen of items from Shostakovich's vivacious, inventive score and the music suits the Boston Pops' vibrant style admirably. If *Ophelia's Song* is piquantly light-hearted, the following *Lullaby* is most tenderly and delicately played by the Boston violins, while the *Requiem* quotes the *Dies irae*, first dolefully and then with more passion. But most of the music is irreverently high spirited and is presented here with appropriately infectious gusto. The vivid 1968 recording is brilliantly remastered.

Hamlet (1932 production; complete incidental music), Op. 32; (1954 production; incidental music); King Lear (1941 production; complete incidental music), Op. 58a.

(M) *** Cala CACD 1021. Winter, Wilson-Johnson, CBSO, Elder.

An enterprising release, which offers Shostakovich's music for Nikolai Akimov's 1932 production of *Hamlet*. Akimov altered and extended Shakespeare's conception, even interpolating bits of Erasmus. Shostakovich's score has many biting and sarcastic episodes, and listening to the 30 short numbers – some only a few seconds long – makes for unsettled listening. There are spoken interpolations from the player-king and queen. Also included here is a a Gigue and finale from a 1954 production of *Hamlet*, and the Fool's songs, brilliantly sung by David Wilson-Johnson, from a 1941 production of *King Lear*, full of inventive things. This is not top-drawer Shostakovich, but congratulations are in order for Cala's enterprise in recording all this and to the City of Birmingham Orchestra under Mark Elder for the

vital and alert performances. The recording too is expertly and tastefully balanced.

The Limpid Stream (complete ballet; revised Rozhdestvensky).

** Chan. 9423. Stockholm PO, Rozhdestvensky.

Shostakovich's ballet enjoyed much the same fate as *Lady Macbeth of the Mtsensk District* for, after a successful run of eight months, *The Limpid Stream* was denounced in *Pravda*. It is not vintage Shostakovich nor complete, for as presented here it is a revision by Rozhdestvensky. Some of the numbers are familiar from *The Bolt* but there is nothing that is as good as, say, the polka from *The Age of Gold*. Good recording and the playing is very good if a little wanting in abandon.

New Babylon (film score). (i) From Jewish Folk Poetry (song-cycle).

*** Chan. 9600. Russian State SO, Polyansky with (i) Sharova, Kuznetsova, Martynov.

It makes an unusual and revealing coupling having Shostakovich's long-buried music for the satirical silent film, *New Babylon*, paired with the moving sequence of Jewish songsettings. Polyansky and an excellent trio of soloists bring out the expressive depth of these deceptively simple, lyrical songs, regularly reflecting the composer's sympathy with the suffering of the Jews. *New Babylon* was the composer's very first film score, with sharp parodies, 1920s-style, of French models reflecting the Parisian background of the story. Colourful, atmospheric orchestration beautifully caught in full-bodied, well-balanced sound.

Symphonies Nos. 1–15; (i; ii) From Jewish Folk Poetry; (ii) 6 Poems of Marina Tsvetaeva.

(B) *** Decca Dig./ADD 444 430-2 (11). Varady,
 Fischer-Dieskau, Rintzler; (i) Söderström, Karczykowski;
 (ii) Wenkel; Ch. of LPO or Concg. O; LPO or Concg. O,
 Haitink.

No one artist or set of performances holds all the insights into this remarkable symphonic canon, but what can be said of Haitink's set is that the playing of both the London Philharmonic and the Concertgebouw orchestras is of the highest calibre and is very responsive; moreover the Decca recordings, whether analogue or digital, are consistently of this company's highest standard, outstandingly brilliant and full. If without the temperament of a Mravinsky, Haitink proves a reliable guide to this repertoire, often much more than that, and sometimes inspired. All in all, a considerable achievement. The eleven discs are now offered together at bargain price, but they also remain available separately at mid-price – see below.

Symphonies Nos. 1–15.

(M) *** BMG/Melodiya (ADD) 74321 19952-2 (10). Soloists, Russian Republic Ch., Moscow PO, Kondrashin.

Symphonies Nos. (i) 2 in B (October Revolution), Op. 14; (ii) 14 in G min., Op. 135.

(M) *** BMG/Melodiya (ADD) 74321 19844-2. (i) Russian

Republic Ch.; (ii) Tselovalnik, Nesterenko; Moscow PO, Kondrashin.

Symphony No. 4 in C min., Op. 43.

(M) *** BMG/Melodiya (ADD) 74321 19840-2. Moscow PO, Kondrashin.

Symphony No. 7 in C (Leningrad), Op. 60.

(M) ** BMG/Melodiya (ADD) 74321 19839-2. Moscow PO, Kondrashin.

Symphonies Nos. 9, Op. 70; 15 in A, Op. 103.

(M) **(*) BMG/Melodiya (ADD) 74321 19846-2. Moscow PO, Kondrashin.

Symphony No. 13 in B flat min. (Babi Yar), Op. 113.

(M) *** BMG/Melodiya (ADD) 74321 19842-2. Eisen, Russian Republic Ch., Moscow PO, Kondrashin.

Kirill Kondrashin's cycle was made over a long period of time: the *Fourth Symphony* dates from 1962, not long after its first performance, while the last to appear were in the mid-1970s (Nos. 7, 14 and 15). The set is of importance in that Shostakovich himself expressed confidence in this conductor, and it is clear that in many instances he comes closer than most to the spirit of this music. Not all the performances strike us as *sans pareil*. In none of them is the playing of the Moscow Philharmonic as distinguished or as finely disciplined as in many rival accounts. Nor, to be fair, are Kondrashin's insights deeper than those of Mravinsky or (in the case of Nos. 5, 6, 7 and 11) Stokowski. Nos. 4, 13 and 14 make the strongest impression in Kondrashin's hands. Despite the sonic limitations inevitable over the course of nearly 40 years, the *Fourth* is almost indispensable. It has that sense of discovery, raw intensity and sheer eloquence which silence criticism – or should do. And the 1967 account of the *Thirteenth* has an authentic feel to it that makes its claims on the collector strong. Both the *Fourteenth*, song-cycle-cum-symphony, and the enigmatic *Fifteenth Symphony* have much to recommend them.

Elsewhere the cycle is less even. The brisk tempi Kondrashin adopts for the first movement of both the *Sixth* and *Eighth* symphonies diminish their intensity of feeling and directness of effect and, though he makes out a stronger case for the *Third* than some rivals, he is no match for Rozhdestvensky in the *Twelfth*. The Moscow Philharmonic strings are by no means as sumptuous as those of the USSR State Academic Symphony (or the 'USSR Symphony' as it was known at one time); and they do not sound quite as warm or smooth as on the LP. It is difficult to generalize, but the bass is sometimes firmer and definition is keener. There are roughnesses on the originals that are not quite smoothed out. Only four of the ten discs are currently available separately.

Symphony No. 1; (i) Piano Concerto No. 1.

*** EMI CDC5 55361-2. (i) Rudy; BPO, Jansons.

Drawing superb playing from the Berlin Philharmonic, Jansons conducts a finely detailed reading of the *First Symphony* which is both precise and intense. So the second-movement scherzando, despite a very fast speed, is never breathless, and the oboe solo at the start of the slow movement could

not be more tender in its refinement, while even the hectic close is perfectly controlled, both exciting and sharply focused. Mikhail Rudy in the concerto brings out new poetry, and the *Lento* slow movement has rarely been so yearningly beautiful, with the Berlin strings radiant. If in the outer movements Rudy does not bite as sharply as some pianists, his sensitivity is heightened by Jansons's idiomatic conducting. However, this coupling has just been deleted.

(i) Symphony No. 1 in F min., Op. 10; (ii) Festive Overture. Collection: The Age of Gold: Polka. Ballet Suite No. 1: Galop; Music-box Waltz; Dance. Ballet Suite No. 2: Polka; Galop. The Gadfly: Introduction; Barrel Organ Waltz; Nocturne; Folk Festival; Galop. Moscow-Cheryomushki: Overture Waltz; Galop.

❀ (B) *** Sony (ADD) SBK 62642. (i) Phd. O, Ormandy; (ii) Columbia SO, Kostelanetz.

Ormandy and the Philadelphia Orchestra recorded this version of the *First Symphony* in the presence of the composer in 1959. It is a beautifully proportioned, tense and vivid account. The sound, too, is excellent. Still, after 40 years, a front-runner in spite of some excellent successors. The coupling could not have been better chosen: a suite of Shostakovichian orchestral lollipops selected by Kostelanetz, a dab hand at this kind of audacious light music. Readers who know the *Polka* from *The Age of Gold* will know what to expect. Kostelanetz opens with a fizzing account of the *Festive Overture*, Op. 96. Then comes the series of miniatures – mixed up to provide maximum contrast. Many of the pieces were virtually unknown when these performances first appeared in 1965, and even today few of them are familiar to the wider public. The fast numbers (like the Offenbachian *Galop* from *The Gadfly*) are redeemed from vulgarity by momentum and brilliant scoring, many of them suggesting the composer thumbing his nose at the Soviet authorities, and there is no better example than the *Moscow-Cheryomushki Overture Waltz* with its trombone glissandi accompanying a very Russian dance-accelerando, followed by the equally infectious potpourri called *Folk Festival*. But the gentler pieces are more memorable still: the hauntingly tender *Nocturne* from *The Gadfly* and the delicious *Barrel Organ Waltz* from the same source, matched by the *Music-box Waltz* from the *Ballet Suite No. 1*. Kostelanetz plays this music for all it is worth, and if again the recording is brash, this time it fits the music like a glove.

Symphonies Nos. 1; 3 (First of May), Op. 20.

(M) *** Decca 425 063-2. LPO Ch., LPO, Haitink.

In this coupling, Haitink still leads the field, when the Decca recording is outstandingly clear and brilliant. His account of No. 1 is strong and very well played. It may lack something in youthful high spirits but not in concentration. No. 3 is not one of Shostakovich's finest works but is worth having when played as committedly as here.

Symphonies Nos. 1; 5 in D min., Op. 47; (i) 7 (Leningrad); Prelude No. 14 in E flat min., Op. 34 (arr. Stokowski).

(***) Pearl GEMM CDS 9044. Phd. O; (i) NBC SO, Stokowski.

Stokowski's *First Symphony* was recorded in 1934, less than a decade after its première under Malko. The sound is dryish. But there is tremendous atmosphere and concentration, and the transfers are excellent. Stokowski's (1939) pioneering *Fifth* is an electrifying performance, impeccably played and splendidly transferred. The slow movement has a gripping intensity that is quite exceptional. The famous transcription of the *E flat minor Prelude*, Op. 34, has a brooding, Mussorgskian menace all its own, while Stokowski's *Leningrad Symphony* is hardly less gripping. This *Leningrad* for all its sonic defects makes for exciting listening.

Symphonies Nos. 1; 6 in B min., Op. 54.

*** Chan. 8411. SNO, Järvi.

Järvi's account of the *First Symphony* is more volatile than Haitink's in the outer movements – there is no lack of quirkiness in the finale, while the *Largo* is intense and passionate. The *Sixth* has comparable intensity, with an element of starkness in the austerity of the first movement. The Scherzo is skittish at first but, like the finale, has no lack of pungent force.

(i) Symphonies Nos. 2 (To October), Op. 14; 3 in E flat (The First of May), Op. 20; The Bolt: Suite, Op. 27a.

(N) *** DG 469 525-2. Gothenburg SO, Järvi; (i) Gothenburg Ch.

Apart from the radical and imaginative opening of the *Second*, neither of these symphonies show the composer at his most individual or inspired. The *Third* must rank alongside the *Twelfth* as Shostakovich's least compelling work. Similarly *The Bolt* is not the best vintage, but it is still well worth having! Neeme Järvi benefits in having the excellent Gothenburg acoustic (and very good sound engineering from the Gothenburg team), and he secures eminently satisfactory playing from his orchestra.

(i) Symphonies Nos. 2 (October Revolution); 3 (First of May), Op. 20; 4 in C min., Op. 43; (ii) Hamlet (suite); (iii) Overture Poor Columbus, Op. 23.

(B) **(*) BMG/Melodiya Dig./ADD Twofer 74321 63462-2.
(i) Russian State Academic Ch. Cappella, USSR MoC SO;
(ii) Moscow PO; (iii) Leningrad PO, Rozhdestvensky.

The *Second Symphony* is made to sound convincing in Rozhdestvensky's hands with its eerily sombre opening and the Russian chorus at the end launching into a brief but potently ardent choral peroration, rather fiercely recorded. Rozhdestvensky catches the chimerical, often aggressive mood changes of the *Third*, then finds a central core of serenity before the spiky, belligerent closing section leads to another dynamically exuberant chorus. The orchestra plays brilliantly and is vividly if coarsely recorded in the Soviet digital manner of the 1980s. In the equivocal *Fourth Symphony*, the ironic humour, as well as the concentrated power of the work, come over tellingly even if the playing is not ideally refined. The second movement is highly idiomatic, as is the slow Mahlerian funeral march of the finale. As a bonus come fifteen extremely diverse movements from the *Hamlet Incidental Music*, and a brief but characteristically quirky *Christopher Columbus Overture*. Again, strongly charac-

terized brilliant performances, projected in bold, brightly lit sound.

Symphonies Nos. 2 (October Revolution); 10 in E min., Op. 93.

(M) **(*) BMG Melodiya Dig./ADD 425 064-2. LPO Ch., LPO, Haitink.

Haitink's performance of No. 2 is admirable, and it is given excellently balanced sound with great presence and body. No. 10 is a masterpiece, and Haitink really has the measure of the first movement, whose climaxes he paces with an admirable sense of architecture. He secures sensitive and enthusiastic playing from the LPO, both here and in the malignant Scherzo. In the third movement he adopts a slower tempo than usual, which would be acceptable if there were greater tension or concentration of mood; but here and in the slow introduction to the finale the sense of concentration falters. The 1977 analogue recording (like the digital *Second*, made in the Kingsway Hall) is outstandingly realistic.

Symphony No. 4 in C min., Op. 43.

*** EMI CDC5 55476-2. CBSO, Rattle (with BRITTEN: *Russian Funeral*. ***
*** Chan. 8640. SNO, Järvi.
(M) **(*) Decca (ADD) 425 065-2. LPO, Haitink.

Rattle conducts his Birmingham orchestra in a revelatory performance of the elusive *Fourth Symphony*, sustaining the expansive movements masterfully, bringing out the biting irony and humour of much of the writing, presented with Russian swagger, while never forgetting the underlying darkness. Above all, the orchestra plays incandescently, with an unstoppable thrust to convey the impression of a live, tensely dramatic event, with the full-bodied sound (recorded in Birmingham's Symphony Hall) adding to the weight and impact. The rare Britten piece is a valuable and generous makeweight.

Järvi draws from the SNO playing which is both rugged and expressive, consistently conveying the emotional thrust of the piece and making the enigmatic ending, with its ticking rhythm, warmer than usual, as though bitterness is finally evaporating. He is helped by exceptionally rich, full recording.

Haitink brings out an unexpected refinement in the *Symphony*, a rare transparency of texture. He is helped by recording of Decca's finest quality, vividly remastered. Detail is caught superbly; yet the earthiness and power, the demonic quality which can make this work so compelling, are underplayed.

Symphonies Nos. 4; 5 in D min., Op. 47.

(B) ** EMI double forte (ADD) CZS5 72658-2 (2). Chicago SO, Previn – BRITTEN: *Sinfonia da requiem* etc. *** ◉

Previn's is an eminently straightforward, superlatively played and vividly recorded account of the *Fourth Symphony*. Orchestral playing is also of the highest quality in the *Fifth Symphony*, but here there is little sense of momentum, freshness and urgency. The recorded sound is extremely impressive.

Symphonies Nos. 4 in C min., Op. 43; 8 in C min., 65.

(N) (B) *** Teldec Ultima 8573 87799-2 (2). Nat. SO of Washington, Rostropovich.

Any listener daunted by the remarkable *Fourth Symphony*, with its two vast outer movements, should listen to Rostropovich's powerfully committed, and intense, often thrustful Russian reading. Written immediately after *Lady Macbeth of Mtsensk*, which was vilified by the Soviet authorities, the composer withdrew the score during rehearsal, realizing that its emotional ambiguity would not fall easily on official ears.

Yet to modern ears its extraordinary expressive range with its combination of powerful angst and sometimes bizarre irony go together to make it an immensely stimulating work. The haunting atmosphere of the opening of the finale with its dolorous little march contrasts totally with the closing section, where a blaze of ecstatic defiance in the brass projects vividly over hammering timpani. In Rostropovich's hands this then ebbs away into an enigmatic darkness.

In the composer's other C minor symphony, the *Eighth*, Rostropovich gives a gripping account that can rank alongside the best performances one has ever heard, on or off record, and here again his intensity and that of his players does not spill over into excess. Both recordings are very fine, and this must be regarded as a key coupling in the Shostakovich discography.

Symphonies Nos. 4, Op. 43; 10, Op. 93.

(B) *** Sony (ADD) SB2K 62409 (2). Phd. O, Ormandy.

Ormandy pioneered the *Fourth Symphony* in the West. His reading of this strange and powerful symphony is less subtle than Kondrashin's Russian account, less refined than Haitink, but it is thoroughly convincing and has the Philadelphia Orchestra playing both brilliantly (witness the frenzied string passage at the climax of the first movement) and with real depth of feeling. The combination of irony, anguish and plangent lyricism is remarkably well caught. The 1963 recording, made in Philadelphia Town Hall, is spaciously full and vivid; it sounds excellent in the current CD transfer.

Ormandy went on to record No. 10 with equal success in the same venue in 1968, and again he makes a case for treating the work with a passion that is apt for Tchaikovsky. The result is not as refined in its effect as Karajan's DG version, but it still makes a compelling, indeed massive, impact, notably in the long first and third movements. Ormandy's control of string phrasing is again immaculate and his great orchestra is never less than convincing and is often superbly brilliant in the precision of its virtuosity. This makes a thoroughly worthwhile bargain coupling.

Symphony No. 5 in D min., Op. 47 (see also under Cello Concerto No. 1).

*** EMI CDC7 49181-2. Oslo PO, Jansons.
**(*) Everest EVC 9030. NY Stadium SO, Stokowski.
(M) **(*) Mercury (IMS) 434 323-2. Minneapolis SO, Skrowaczewski – KHACHATURIAN: *Gayaneh Ballet Suite.* **(*)

(i) *Symphony No. 5;* (ii) *Hamlet* (film incidental music), *Suite, Op. 116.*

(BB) *** RCA Navigator 74321 24212-2. (i) LSO, Previn; (ii) Belgian RSO, Serebrier.

Jansons's EMI version with the Oslo orchestra on top form brings a tautly incisive, electrically intense reading, marked by speeds notably faster than usual that yet have the ring of authenticity. The development section in the first movement, for example, builds up bitingly into a thrilling climax, with the accelerando powerfully controlled.

Previn's RCA version, dating from early in his recording career (1965), remains at the top of the list of bargain recommendations. This is one of the most concentrated and intense readings ever, superbly played by the LSO at its peak. In the third movement he sustains a slower speed than anyone else, making it deeply meditative in its dark intensity, while his build-up in the central development section brings playing of white heat. Only in the hint of analogue tape-hiss and a slight lack of opulence in the violins does the sound fall short of the finest modern digital recordings – and it is more vividly immediate than most. The new coupling is appropriate. *Hamlet* obviously generated powerful resonances in Shostakovich's psyche and produced vivid incidental music. The playing of the Belgian Radio Orchestra under Serebrier is eminently serviceable without being really distinguished, but with atmospheric recording this 28-minute suite makes a considerable bonus.

The Stadium Symphony Orchestra of New York is neither as flexible nor as virtuosic an ensemble as the superb instrument Stokowski created in Philadelphia during the first decade of electric recording, but the Stokowski electricity is here as intensely as ever and it makes this performance an unforgettable experience. The sound itself is surprisingly good, though there is background hiss.

Skrowaczewski's Minneapolis account of Shostakovich's *Fifth* brings great concentration in the pianissimo string-playing in the *Largo* and a finale which, after an exhilarating *Allegro*, has a trenchant, ponderous coda, anticipating much later performances, after the composer had revealed that his closing section was not intended to be an ingenuous triumphant celebration. The first movement has a fast opening speed, but the conductor understands Shostakovich's melodic line and, although this is a wilful reading, it is also an exciting one. The recording was made in the Northrop Auditorium in 1961 and is full yet astonishingly clear, but the upper strings have that curious thinness which was characteristic of Mercury's Minneapolis ventures at that time. However, this performance is very compelling.

Symphonies Nos. 5 in D min.; 9 in E flat, Op. 70.

(BB) *** Naxos 8.550427. Belgian R. & TV O, Rahbari.
(M) *** Decca 425 066-2. (i) Concg. O; (ii) LPO, Haitink.
(M) **(*) Sony (ADD) SMK 47615-2. NYPO, Bernstein.

Both in the hushed intensity of the lyrical passages and in the vigour and bite of Shostakovich's violent allegros Rahbari's reading is most convincing, with dramatic tensions finely controlled in a spontaneous-sounding way. In No. 9 Rahbari opts for a controversially slow *Moderato* second movement but sustains it well, and the outer movements are deliciously witty in their pointing. The playing of all sections is first rate, and the sound is full and brilliant.

An outstandingly generous coupling makes this a most attractive issue, even with no allowance made for the very low price.

In No. 5 Haitink is eminently straightforward, there are no disruptive changes in tempo, and the playing of the Concertgebouw Orchestra and the contribution of the Decca engineers are beyond praise. There could perhaps be greater intensity of feeling in the slow movement but, whatever small reservations one might have, it is most impressive both artistically and sonically. The coupled No. 9 is superb. Without inflation Haitink gives it a serious purpose, both in the poignancy of the waltz-like second movement and in the equivocal emotions of the outer movements. The recording is outstanding in every way.

This was Bernstein's first recording of the *Fifth*, made in 1959; he re-recorded it later digitally. His view of the work was admired by the composer, perhaps because the finale opens so ferociously. Bernstein revels in the high spirits of the *Ninth*, and he also manages the alternation of moods very successfully. The sound has been greatly improved in both symphonies.

(i) *Symphonies Nos. 6; (ii) 9, Op. 70.*

**(*) DG 419 771-2. VPO, Bernstein.
**(*) EMI CDC7 54339-2. Oslo PO, Jansons.
**(*) Everest (ADD) EVC 9005. (i) LPO, Boult; (ii) LSO, Sargent.

Perversely slow as Bernstein is in most movements of both symphonies, with the first movement of No. 6 and the *Moderato* (more like *Adagio*) of No. 9 minutes longer than any rival, the performances, recorded live, are electrifying, rhythmically alert to counter any slowness, helped by superb playing and spectacular recording.

Jansons in No. 6 is purposeful and strong, if emotionally restrained in the first movement, lithe and resilient in the Scherzo and finale, consistently adopting speeds on the fast side. No. 9 is then light and resilient, again with speeds on the fast side and with brilliant playing from the Oslo orchestra. Full, well-balanced recording, not as forward as the sound for most other Jansons Shostakovich discs.

Boult secures very good playing from the LPO and the late-1950s Walthamstow recording is excellent. But he is wanting a little in intensity. Sargent's account of the *Ninth* is lyrical and attractive, with infectious vitality in the odd-numbered of the five movements. Again the recording is very good indeed. This is undoubtedly an enjoyable coupling.

Symphonies Nos. 6; 12 (The Year 1917).

(M) *** Decca 425 067-2. Concg. O, Haitink.

Haitink's structural control, coupled with his calm, taut manner, is particularly impressive in the slow movement of No. 6. As a work, No. 12 is more problematic. There is much of the composer's vision and grandeur here but also his crudeness. However, the sheer quality of the sound and the superb responsiveness and body of the Concertgebouw Orchestra might well seduce many listeners. As with the *Sixth* the slow movement has a marvellous sense of atmosphere; the Amsterdam orchestra play as if they believe every

crotchet, although not even their eloquence can rescue the finale.

Symphony No. 7 in C (Leningrad), Op. 60.

*** Chan. 8623. SNO, Järvi.
(M) **(*) Decca 425 068-2. LPO, Haitink.
(M) **(*) Sony (ADD) SMK 47616-2. NYPO, Bernstein.

Järvi's is a strong, intense reading, beautifully played and recorded, which brings out the full drama of this symphony in a performance that consistently gives the illusion of spontaneity in a live performance, as in the hushed tension of the slow, expansive passages. There have been more polished versions than this, but, with its spectacular Chandos sound, it makes an excellent choice as a single-disc version.

Haitink is here eminently straightforward. There could perhaps be greater intensity of feeling in the slow movement, and the long first-movement *ostinato* is not presented histrionically; but the deep seriousness which Haitink finds in the rest of the work challenges comparisons with the other wartime symphony, the epic *Eighth*. The playing of the Concertgebouw Orchestra is beyond praise.

Bernstein brings a certain panache and fervour to his reading, particularly in the inspired slow movement, so one looks indulgently at its occasional overstatements.

Symphonies Nos. 7 (Leningrad); 8 in C min.; King Lear: (i) Introduction & Cordelia's ballad; (ii) 10 Buffoon's Songs, Op. 58a.

(B) **(*) BMG/Melodiya Twofer 74321 53457-2 (2). USSR MoC SO, Rozhdestvensky; with (i) Burnasheva; (ii) Nesterenko.

Rozhdestvensky's view of the *Leningrad Symphony*'s controversial first movement is unusually broad. It is undeniably powerful but many will prefer a brisker and more polished reading. The other movements also bring warmly expressive, spontaneous-sounding performances which lack only the last degree of subtlety. Rozhdestvensky then follows with a thrustful and incisive reading of the *Eighth*, with electrically intense playing that holds the enormous structure together. In both symphonies the digital recording is full-bodied and wide-ranging with a full depth of string-tone, but it grows coarse in the biggest climaxes. The songs for Shakespeare's *King Lear* are an additional asset to the set. Natalia Burnasheva sings Cordelia's touching lyrical ballad eloquently and Nesterenko characterizes strongly the ten brief *Buffoon's Songs* (most less than a minute in length) with their typical Shostakovian amalgam of grotesquerie and irony. No translations are offered, but there are good notes.

Symphonies Nos. 7 (Leningrad); 11 (1905).

(B) **(*) EMI double forte (ADD) CZS5 73839-2 (2). Bournemouth SO, Berglund.

Berglund directs a strong, powerful performance of the *Seventh*. Though he is not always sensitive to finer points of expressiveness, it is still a reading that holds together convincingly, especially when the sound is so full as well as vivid. In the *Eleventh* too, Berglund lets the music speak for itself, keeping the long opening *Adagio* at a very steady, slow tread, made compelling by the high concentration of the

Bournemouth playing. Indeed, he is at his finest here, again helped by exceptionally vivid, full-bodied recording.

Symphony No. 8 in C min., Op. 65.

**(*) BBC (ADD) BBCL4002-2. Leningrad PO, Mravinsky – MOZART: *Symphony No. 33 in B flat*, K.319. **
(M) *** Decca 425 071-2. Concg. O, Haitink.
**(*) Ph. 446 062-2. Kirov O, Gergiev.
(B) ** DG 463 262-2. LSO, Previn.

Mravinsky's BBC recording comes from the Festival Hall Concert given on the Leningrad orchestra tour in 1960 at which Shostakovich himself was present. This transfer reproduces the occasion with great realism and a wide dynamic range. This reading has tremendous intensity and authenticity of feeling. It comes with a bonus – the first half of the concert, which was given over to an elegant performance of the Mozart *Symphony No. 33*. Even among modern recordings this more than holds its own and the sound is very good indeed. Mandatory listening.

Haitink characteristically presents a strongly architectural reading of this war-inspired symphony, at times direct to the point of severity. After the massive and sustained slow movement which opens the work, Haitink allows no lightness or relief in the Scherzo movements, and in his seriousness in the strangely lightweight finale (neither fast nor slow) he provides an unusually satisfying account of an equivocal, seemingly uncommitted movement.

Gergiev's reading is remarkable for its concentration, with the massive span of the first movement held firmly together, leading to towering climaxes. Though the third-movement Scherzo is warmer and less tough than it might be, it erupts thrillingly when the brilliant trumpet solo enters and then resolves after the climax at the end on to a very slow, sustained *Largo*. The culminating resolution is tenderly achieved on the seemingly inevitable transition into the relative ease of the last, hushed movement. The sound is full-bodied but slightly cloudy.

Previn's (second) 1992 recording of this symphony for DG was a disappointment. He gets some very fine playing from the orchestra, especially the pianissimo strings, and the DG recording is resonantly spectacular. But the reading lacks the concentration and thrust of his earlier HMV analogue version, the Scherzo movements lack bite and the *Largo* has not the intensity of that EMI version which awaits reissue.

Symphony No. 9 in E flat, Op. 70; Festive Overture, Op. 96; Katerina Ismailova (Lady Macbeth of Mtsensk): 5 Entr'actes. Tahiti Trot (arr. of Youmans's Tea for Two), Op. 16.

*** Chan. 8587. SNO, Järvi.

Järvi's version of the *Ninth* brings a warmly expressive, strongly characterized reading in superb, wide-ranging sound. The point and wit of the first movement go with bluff good humour, leading on to an account of the second-movement *Moderato* that is yearningly lyrical yet not at all sentimental, contrasted with the fun and jokiness of the final *Allegretto*. The mixed bag of fill-up items is both illuminating and characterful, ending with the jolly little chamber arrangement that Shostakovich did in the 1920s of Vincent Youmans's *Tea for Two*, the *Tahiti Trot*.

Symphonies Nos. (i) 9 in E flat; (ii) 10 in E min.

(M) (***) Sony mono MPK 45698. NYPO, (i) Kurtz;
   (ii) Mitropoulos.

Dmitri Mitropoulos's pioneering account of the *Tenth Symphony* with the New York Philharmonic penetrates more deeply into the heart of this score than any newcomer; only Karajan's mid-1960s version can be put alongside it. It comes with Efrem Kurtz's 1949 version of the *Ninth* with the same orchestra, playing with great virtuosity. The sound is remarkably good for its period. An edit has removed one note from the opening phrase of the Scherzo, but apart from that hiccup this is a stunning performance.

Symphony No. 10 in E min., Op. 93.

*** DG 439 036-2. BPO, Karajan.
*** EMI CDC5 55232-2. Phd. O, Jansons – MUSSORGSKY: *Songs and Dances of Death*. ***
(M) ** EMI CDM7 64870-2. Philh. O, Rattle – BRITTEN: *Sinfonia da Requiem*. ***

Symphony No. 10 in E min., Op. 93; Ballet Suite No. 4.

*** Chan. 8630. SNO, Järvi.

Already in his 1967 recording Karajan had shown that he had the measure of this symphony; this newer version is, if anything, even finer. In the first movement he distils an atmosphere as concentrated as before, bleak and unremitting, while in the *Allegro* the Berlin Philharmonic leave no doubts as to their peerless virtuosity. Everything is marvellously shaped and proportioned, and the early (1981) digital sound is made firmer by this 'original-image' bit reprocessing.

Mariss Jansons's account of the *Tenth Symphony* is the finest of his series and the best version of this work we have had for some time. He draws a splendid response from the Philadelphia Orchestra, and the playing has tremendous fervour. Karajan's interpretation remains pre-eminent, but the EMI sound is generally preferable and Jansons offers a substantial coupling. Alas, this is now deleted.

Järvi, too, conducts an outstandingly strong and purposeful reading in superb sound, full and atmospheric. In the great span of the long *Moderato* first movement he chooses an ideal speed, which allows for moments of hushed repose but still builds up relentlessly. The curious little *Ballet Suite No. 4*, with its sombre *Prelude* leading to a bouncy *Waltz* and a jolly *Scherzo Tarantella*, makes a delightful bonus.

Rattle's Philharmonia version is curiously wayward in the two big slow movements, first and third in the scheme. In the first, Rattle is exceptionally slow, and tension slips too readily. So too in the third movement. The Scherzo and energetic finale are much more successful. The recording does not help, with the strings sounding thin and lacking body.

(i) *Symphony No. 10 in E min., Op. 93* (arr. for piano duet); (ii) *4 Preludes from Op. 34* (arr. for violin & piano).

(M) (***) Revelation mono RV 70002. Composer, with
  (i) Vainberg; (ii) Kogan.

The recording may be primitive but this is of great documentary interest, capturing Shostakovich and his fellow-composer Moisei Vainberg playing the *Tenth Symphony* in a piano-duet arrangement only a few months after its completion and not long before Mravinsky made the première recording. They play with great fervour and strain the instrument to the limit. The performance is surprisingly brisk (47 minutes as opposed to the usual 50) and completely involving. The transcriptions of the *Preludes* are wonderfully played by Kogan and the composer, and there are also a few bars from *The Gadfly* too.

Symphonies Nos. 10; 11 (The Year 1905); (i) 4 Monologues on Poems by Pushkin, Op. 91 (orch. Rozhdestvensky); (ii) Poor Columbus: Finale, Op. 23.

(B) **(*) BMG/Melodiya Dig./ADD Twofer 74321 63461-2 (2). USSR MoC SO, Rozhdestvensky; with (i) Safiulio; (ii) MoC Chamber Ch.

Following the pattern of his Melodiya Shostakovich series, Rozhdestvensky conducts a strong and spontaneous-sounding reading of the *Tenth*, not as portentous or intense as some but with a vein of spikiness that is totally idiomatic. Though the digital sound is full and bright (appropriately fierce in the second movement), the bass seems to be boomy and rather vague in the opening movement, and internal textures are somewhat coarsened at climaxes. Rozhdestvensky takes an exceptionally spacious view of the opening *Adagio* movement of No. 11 (*The Palace Square*). But overall his reading is red-blooded, and if not as bitingly intense as some, he consistently draws warmly expressive phrasing from his young players. The *Four Pushkin Monologues* (1952) are heard here in an orchestration by the conductor. No texts or translations are included. The *Poor Columbus Finale* is the second of the two pieces Shostakovich wrote in 1929 to frame an opera by a German composer, Erwin Kessel. It is a bizarre epilogue written to accompany a cartoon film, a lampoon of the USA, which introduces the trumpet tune familiar in the finale of *First Piano Concerto*, while also interpolating a briefly passionate choral appeal for international peace.

Symphonies Nos. 10; (i) 13 (Babi-Yar).

(B) *** EMI double forte Dig./ADD CZS5 73368-2 (2). LSO, Previn; (i) with Petrov, LSO Ch.

Previn's is a strong and dramatic reading of No. 10, marked by a specially compelling account of the long first movement. At marginally slower speeds than usual, Previn's rhythmic lift both in the Scherzo and in the finale brings exhilarating results, sparkling and swaggering. The digital recording is early (1982), but strikingly firm and full. The *Thirteenth Symphony*, inspired by the often angry poems of Yevtushenko, is presented at its most stark and direct. Previn takes a relatively literal view of the sprung rhythms in the ironic second movement, *Humour*, and makes the picture of peasant women queueing for food in the snow less atmospheric than it sometimes is. The result is that the work becomes a genuine symphony, rather than an orchestral

song-cycle, but ending in wistfulness on a final Allegretto, *A Career*, with weaving flutes and gentle lolloping pizzicato rhythms. Playing and analogue recording are superb, among the very finest from this source, making this a very attractive pairing on all counts.

Symphony No. 11 (The Year 1905), Op. 103.

*** Testament STB 1099. French R. O, Cluytens.
*** Delos D/CD 3080. Helsinki PO, DePreist.
(M) *** Decca 425 072-2. Concg. O, Haitink.

1905 was the year of the first Russian uprising, which foreshadowed the revolution to come rather more than a decade later. The result is a programme symphony conceived on a fairly large scale and, as in the *Leningrad Symphony*, its style is sometimes repetitive. The DePreist version won golden opinions: it certainly has the benefit of magnificent recording. The Helsinki orchestra may lack the weight and richness of sonority of the greatest orchestras but it plays with great intensity and feeling. A performance that has striking atmosphere and expressive power.

Cluytens was recorded in Paris in the presence of the composer. It appears now in stereo for the very first time and sounds quite astonishing. Indeed it stands up to modern competition very well. Shostakovich called the *Eleventh* his 'most Mussorgskian work' and it was clear to Soviet audiences that its 'sub-text' was not so much the abortive February rebellion of the title as the events in Budapest, where the Soviet Union had just suppressed the Hungarian uprising.

Haitink's sense of architecture is as impressive as always, even if at times he seems almost detached, lacking the last degree of tension. However, the Concertgebouw Orchestra plays superbly, and the Decca sound is as brilliant and realistic as ever.

Symphonies Nos. 11 (1905); 12 (1917); Age of Gold (suite); Hamlet (suite); October (symphonic poem), Op. 131; Overture on Russian & Kirghiz Folk Themes, Op. 115.

(B) **(*) DG Double 459 415-2 (2). Gothenburg SO, Järvi.

This is a generous package and besides the appropriately paired symphonies this DG Double has four additional inducements which are all brought off impressively. Neeme Järvi's account of the *Eleventh Symphony*, too, has much to recommend it, including good orchestral playing and very fine recorded sound. However, good though it is, the performance misses the last ounce of intensity, and the same comments must apply to Järvi's performance of No. 12 (even though here the recording has rather less transparency and sharpness of focus). If this symphony is to come off it has to be played with 200 per cent conviction and panache, and Järvi's performance does not really challenge Mravinsky or Rozhdestvensky.

(i) Symphonies Nos. 12 (Year 1917); (i; ii) 13 (Babi-Yar); (iii) Cello Concerto No. 1; 8 Preludes from Op. 34 (orch. Kelemen).

(B) **(*) BMG/Melodiya Dig./ADD Twofer 74321 63460-2.
  (i) USSR MoC SO; (ii) with Safiulin, Russian State Academy Male Ch.; (iii) Khomitser, USSR Large SO; Rozhdestvensky.

Rozhdestvensky is most persuasive in the out-and-out pro-gramme symphony, No. 12, bringing out the atmosphere and drama in its picture of events of the 1917 Revolution. The rugged strength of the writing – not merely illustrative – comes over powerfully. The bright, sometimes coarse recording is typical of the series. *Babi-Yar* is dramatically impressive too, a performance of genuine eloquence. The bass soloist Anatoli Safiulin is responsive to the music's combination of anguish and irony, and the Russian State Academy Male Choir make a comparably impressive contri-bution. This is worthwhile in its own right and the recording is one of the best in the series. Mikhail Khomitser's fine version of the *First Cello Concerto* is a considerable bonus, as are the eight *Preludes*, felicitously orchestrated by Milko Kelemen. They act as a final encore, often featuring the piano in concertante style. Wry cheekiness alternates with dance rhythms and a gentle *Largo* (No. 17 in the piano original), while No. 14 brings a plangent central *Adagio* (here given to the trombones) which Stokowski also orchestrated. They are beautifully played and recorded.

Symphony No. 13 in B flat min. (Babi-Yar).

(M) *** Decca 425 073-2. Rintzler, Concg. Male Ch. & O., Haitink.

*** Sup. SU 0160-2 231. Mikuláš, Prague Philharmonic Ch., Prague SO, M. Shostakovich.

The often brutal directness of Haitink's way with Shostako-vich works well in the *Thirteenth Symphony*, particularly in the long *Adagio* first movement, whose title, *Babi-Yar*, gives its name to the whole work. That first of five Yevtushenko settings, boldly attacking anti-Semitism in Russia, sets the pattern for Haitink's severe view of the whole. Rintzler with his magnificent, resonant bass is musically superb but, matching Haitink, remains objective rather than dashingly characterful. The resolution of the final movement, with its pretty flutings surrounding a wry poem about Galileo and greatness, then works beautifully. Outstandingly brilliant and full sound, remarkable even for this series.

Maxim Shostakovich's Supraphon version, with sound so vivid you hear some alien noises, is menacingly atmospheric, one of the finest of his recordings of his father's symphonies. Helped by the immediate sound, he sustains each movement with fine concentration, with each movement heightened by characterful singing from the superb Czech bass, Peter Mikuláš. So in the second movement, '*Humour*', brutal and tense, he conveys a gleam of manic menace in the music and brings out the full chilling horror of the third movement with its picture of women queueing. The chorus with its Slavonic timbres sounds totally idiomatic too, not balanced too close, making this one of the most convincing versions of this moving and atmospheric song-cycle symphony.

Symphony No. 14 in G min., Op. 135.

(BB) *** Naxos 8.550631. Hajóssyová, Mikuláš, Slovak RSO (Bratislava), Slovák.

(M) **(*) BBC (ADD) BBCB 8013-2. Vishnevskaya, Rezhetin, ECO, Britten – BRITTEN: *Nocturne*. **(*)

(i) Symphony No. 14; (ii) 6 Poems of Marina Tsvetaeva, Op. 143a.

(M) *** Decca 425 074-2. (i) Varady, Fischer-Dieskau; (ii) Wenkel; Concg. O, Haitink.

The *Fourteenth* is Shostakovich's most sombre and dark score, a setting of poems by Lorca, Apollinaire, Rilke, Brentano and Küchelbecker, all on the theme of death; Haitink's version gives each poem in its original language. It is a most powerful performance, and the outstanding recording is well up to the standard of this fine Decca series. The song-cycle, splendidly sung by Ortrun Wenkel, makes a fine bonus.

Slovák's account of No. 14 is one of the finest in his Shostakovich series for Naxos, strongly characterized in each of the eleven contrasted movements with the help of two superb soloists. Mikuláš is just as strong and individual as in No. 13, and Hajóssyová with her firm, Slavonic mezzo is equally idiomatic. Regularly, Slovák and his performers bring out the menace behind the composer's inspiration on the theme of death, with the fourth song, 'The Suicide', particularly moving in its tenderness. The booklet gives a summary of each poem, but no texts or translations. Full, immediate sound.

This was the symphony which Shostakovich dedicated to Britten, and this Snape Maltings performance of 1970 with the ECO conducted by Britten was the very first outside Russia. Galina Vishnevskaya's sharply distinctive soprano has rarely sounded so rich or firmly focused on disc, and the bass, Mark Rezhetin, firm and dark, sings gloriously too. The tensions of a live performance add to the drama, poignantly so, when both Britten and Shostakovich were facing terminal illness. Sadly this mid-priced issue gives none of the important texts.

(i; ii) Symphonies Nos. 14; 15, Op. 141; (ii) 4 Romances After Pushkin (orch. Rozhdestvensky); (ii) 6 Romances to Texts by British Poets. (iii) 6 Romances to Texts by Japanese Poets; (iv) 8 English & American Folk Songs.

(B) *** BMG/Melodiya Dig./ADD Twofer 74321 59057-2 (2). USSR MoC SO, Rozhdestvensky; with (i) Kasrashvill, (ii) Saifulin; (iii) Maslennikov; (iv) Ivanova; Yakovenko.

In the *Fourteenth Symphony*, the Ministry of Culture Sym-phony Orchestra is magnetic in drawing Shostakovich's chosen sequence of poems together; sadly however, the booklet does not include texts, only a summary of each poem (and that applies to the other song-cycles included here). The full, bright digital sound is more atmospheric than some in the Melodiya series, and though the voices are balanced close, their characterful Slavonic timbre will delight rather than offend Russian ears. As an instinctive interpreter of Shostakovich, Rozhdestvensky is very good at tapping the vein of wry humour in all the symphonies, a quality which comes to the fore in the equivocal *Fifteenth*. Again with vividly full-bodied sound this is another of the most recom-mendable of his Melodiya series, particularly when the ad-ditional couplings are so generous.

On the first disc the darkly ambivalent passion of the Japanese love poems matches the lack of optimism in the Pushkin *Romances*, and on the second the Russian melan-choly and resignation to Fate again imbues the six British settings (drawing on both Robert Burns and Shakespeare), especially when both singers are so involved and so persuasive. If the clouds finally lift for many of the closing group of English and American folk songs, sadness still goes hand in hand with high spirits. They are all sung in Russian, opening with *The Sailor's Bride* (more familiar as *Blow the wind southerly*), and both this and *Coming through the rye* are very engaging in the Slavic tongue. The first seven are sung quite delightfully by Elena Ivanova, then Sergei Yakovenko's vibrant baritone gives a curious new slant to *Johnny will come marching home again*.

Symphony No. 15; (i) Cello Concerto No. 1.

*(*) Chan. 9550. (i) Helmerson; Russian State SO, Polyansky.

Symphony No. 15; October; Overture on Russian & Kirghiz Folk Themes, Op. 115.

(B) **(*) DG 469 029-2. Gothenburg SO, Järvi.

(i) Symphony No. 15; (ii) From Jewish Folk Poetry (song-cycle), **Op. 79.**

(M) *** Decca (ADD/DDD) 425 069-2. (i) LPO;
 (ii) Söderström, Wenkel, Karczykowski, Concg. O; Haitink.

Symphony No. 15 in A, Op. 141; (i) Piano Sonata No. 2 in B min., Op. 61.

☻ (M) *** RCA 09026 63587-2. Phd. O, Ormandy; (i) Gilels.

Ormandy gave the American première of the *Fifteenth Symphony* as well as a number of other Shostakovich works, including the *Fourth*, *Thirteenth* and *Fourteenth Symphonies* and the *First Cello Concerto* with Rostropovich. He was not so much underrated as taken for granted during the early 1970s when this recording was made, but there is no doubt as to his authority and mastery. The playing could hardly be surpassed and the recording originally appeared in RCA's brand of Quadrophony, when it sounded pretty spectacular. Even now it sounds superb and stands up well against subsequent versions – and its coupling, Gilels's incomparable account of the wartime *Second Sonata*, recorded at Carnegie Hall in January 1965, is one of the classics of the gramophone. An indispensable reissue.

Early readings of the composer's last symphony seemed to underline the quirky unpredictability of the work, with the collage of strange quotations – above all the *William Tell* galop, which keeps recurring in the first movement – seemingly joky rather than profound. Haitink by contrast makes the first movement sound genuinely symphonic, bitingly urgent. He underlines the purity of the bare lines of the second movement; after the Wagner quotations which open the finale, his slow tempo for the main lyrical theme gives it heartaching tenderness, not the usual easy triviality. The playing of the LPO is excellent, with refined tone and superb attack, and the recording is both analytical and atmospheric. The CD includes a splendidly sung version of *From Jewish Folk Poetry*, settings which cover a wide range of emotions including tenderness, humour and even happiness as in the final song. Ryszard Karczykowski brings vibrant Slavonic feeling to the work which, with its wide variety of mood and colour, has a scale to match the shorter symphonies.

Neeme Järvi has a good feeling for this composer and his account is competitive: it has personality and is played

charterfully by the Gothenburg orchestra. *October* is a powerful work, written for the fiftieth anniversary of the Revolution in 1967, while the *Overture*, written in 1963 to mark the centenary of Kirghiz's 'incorporation' into Tsarist Russia, begins rather severely, but builds up to a lively, tuneful conclusion. Good sound, and if there are greater accounts of the symphony, the excellent couplings and bargain price make this CD a good bargain choice.

Valery Polyansky and the Russian State Symphony give a straightforward but ultimately rather undistinguished account of the *Fifteenth Symphony*. The slow movement in particular is lacking in atmosphere. In the *First Cello Concerto*, the distinguished Swedish soloist plays well but ensemble is not impeccable.

CHAMBER AND INSTRUMENTAL MUSIC

Cello Sonata in D min., Op. 40.

*** Virgin VC5 45274-2. Mørk, Vogt – PROKOFIEV: *Cello Sonata in C, Op. 119;* STRAVINSKY: *Suite italienne.* ***

*** Chan. 8340. Turovsky, Edlina – PROKOFIEV: *Sonata.* ***

*** BIS CD 336. Thedéen, Pöntinen – SCHNITTKE: *Sonata;* STRAVINSKY: *Suite italienne.* ***

(BB) *** ASV CDQS 6218. Gregor-Smith, Wrigley – MARTINU: *Variations;* JANACEK: *Pohádka;* PROKOFIEV: *Cello Sonata.* ***

(BB) **(*) Arte Nova 74321 27805-2. Klein, Beldi – PROKOFIEV: *Cello Sonata.* **(*)

(i) Cello Sonata, Op. 40 (ii) 7 Blok Romances, Op. 127.

(N) (M) *** Decca (ADD) 466 823-2. (i) Rostropovich, Britten; (ii) Vishnevskaya, Hurwitz – JANACEK: *Pohádka.* BRIDGE: *Phantasie Qt.*

Cello Sonata in D min., Op. 40; Moderato in A min.

(*) Chant du Monde LDC 2781112. Hoffman, Philippe Bianconi – PROKOFIEV: *Adagio; Ballade; Cello Sonata, Op. 119, etc.* *

With Britten and Rostropovich in inspired partnership, the hushed intensity in the Shostakovich *Cello Sonata* takes the work on to a new plane, a performance of high contrasts, with the wayward, offbeat element adding to the improvisational quality. Shostakovich's *Blok Romances*, recorded in 1968, the year after they were written, are strongly characterized too by all four artists, not just Vishnevskaya as soloist but the violinist, Emanuel Hurwitz. With each song bringing a different instrumental grouping, the work was perfectly designed for Aldeburgh and its corporate music-making as inspired by Britten.

Truls Mørk and Lars Vogt can more than hold their own with the best. The performances are very vital and intelligent, and eminently well recorded. The booklet is carelessly edited: it twice speaks of this as the 'Cello Sonata No. 2'.

Yuli Turovsky and Luba Edlina play the *Cello Sonata* with great panache and eloquence, if in the finale they almost succumb at times to exaggeration in their handling of its humour – no understatement here.

The Swedish cellist, Torleif Thedéen, has a real feeling for its structure and the vein of bitter melancholy under its ironic surface. Roland Pöntinen gives him excellent support and the BIS recording does justice to this partnership.

Expert and elegantly fashioned playing from Gary Hoffman and Philippe Bianconi. There are some exaggerations and some listeners may find the inward, withdrawn tone of the cellist in the third movement a bit affected. Still, the playing has enormous finesse and accomplishment and gives great pleasure. The *Moderato* is a slight piece composed in the same year, disinterred only after the composer's death.

Both the alternative bargain performances are very serviceable and are unlikely to disappoint. Bernard Gregor-Smith and Yolande Wrigley have the benefit of a recording with greater bloom and a more lively acoustic, though the piano is sometimes more dominant in the aural picture than is ideal.

Emil Klein and Cristian Beldi, both Romanian born, give a very well-characterized account of the *Sonata*, tautly held together and vital in feeling, though the sound is a bit dryish. The balance between cello and piano is very well judged, even if the timbre of the latter is less realistic than ASV's.

Cello Sonata in D min., Op. 40; (i) Piano Trio No. 2 in E min., Op. 67.

**(*) Sony MK 44664. Ma, Ax; (i) with Stern.

The *Trio* receives a deeply felt performance, one which can hold its own with any issue, past or present. The *Sonata* is another matter; the playing is as beautiful as one would expect, but here Ma's self-communing propensity for reducing his tone is becoming a tiresome affectation. Ax plays splendidly and the CBS recording is very truthful.

Piano Quintet in G min., Op. 57.

(***) Testament mono SBT 1077. Aller, Hollywood Qt – FRANCK: *Piano Quintet.* (***)

(M) **(*) CRD (ADD) CRD 3351. Benson, Alberni Qt – BRITTEN: *Quartet No. 1.* ***

Piano Quintet, Op. 57; Piano Trio No. 2 in E min., Op. 67.

**(*) Chan. 8342. Borodin Trio, Zweig, Horner.

Piano Quintet in G min., Op. 57; Piano Trio No. 2 in E min., Op. 67; 4 Waltzes for Flute, Clarinet & Piano.

(BB) *** Virgin Classics 2 x 1 VBD5 61760-2 (2). Nash Ens. – SCHOENBERG: *Chamber Symphony, Op. 9, etc.* **(*)

The Nash Ensemble on Virgin offer the ideal coupling – plus an interesting makeweight – of two of Shostakovich's key chamber works, written before his quartet series developed, when he had completed only the first, relatively trivial work. The *Piano Trio* is a particularly painful and anguished work, dedicated to the memory of a close friend, Ivan Sollertinsky, who died in the year of its composition. The Nash players bring out the dedicated intensity in this very personal writing, with refined readings which can be warmly recommended, even if they are not quite as characterfully individual as the very finest, and the new pairing with Schoenberg makes for a highly intriguing collection, well worth its modest cost.

On Testament a magisterial account of the *Piano Quintet* if ever there was one, this belongs among the finest of

interpretations. Its praises were sung by the authors of *The Record Guide* in the mid-1950s when they spoke of it in their down-to-earth manner as 'a dazzling performance and their tone, though often extremely delicate, is never skinny'. Readers who care about Shostakovich should find it an indispensable issue and need make few allowances for the 1952 sound.

The Chandos version is bold in character and concentrated in feeling. Alternatively, there is a vigorous and finely conceived account from Clifford Benson and the Alberni Quartet, vividly recorded; if the Britten coupling is wanted, this will be found fully satisfactory.

(i) Piano Quintet; Piano Trio No. 2; String Quartets Nos. 1 in C, Op. 49; 15 in E flat, Op. 144.

⊙ (N) (B) *** Teldec Ultima 8573 87820-2 (2). (i) Leonskaja; Borodin Qt.

With Leonskaja leading, yet still very much a partner, these Ultima performances of the *Piano Quintet* and *Second Trio* are very fine indeed, with inspired playing from all concerned. The very wide range of dynamic and string timbre of the *Fugue*, with the music initially sustained on a thread of tone, moving to a climax and back has enormous concentration, and the spikier humour of the *Scherzo* is splendidly pointed. After the poignant *Intermezzo*, the close of the finale is most subtly managed. Similarly, the valedictory *E minor Piano Trio* opens with an exquisitely withdrawn pianissimo, and the robust *Scherzo* has vehement bite.

The characterization of first and last of the *String Quartets* is equally strong and perceptive, the 'springtime' mood of the *First* contrasting absolutely with the bleakness of the last, and the playing itself is again of outstanding quality. A superb set in every way, very well balanced and most realistically recorded. There is no better place to start exploring Shostakovich's chamber music than here, and inexpensively too.

Piano Trios Nos. 1, Op. 8; 2, Op. 67.

*** Smax PSC 1147. Grieg, Trio – BLOCH: *3 Nocturnes;* MARTIN: *Piano Trio on Irish Folktunes.* ***

*** Nim. NI 5572. V. Piano Trio – SCHNITTKE: *Trio.* ***

Piano Trios Nos. 1, Op. 8; 2 in E min., Op. 67; (i) 7 Romances to Poems by Alexander Blok, Op. 127.

(N) *(*) Orfeo C465 991A. Munich Piano Trio. (i) Ablaberdyeva.

The first of the Shostakovich *Piano Trios* remained in the obscurity of manuscript, until one of Shostakovich's students, the composer Boris Tischenko, put it into performable shape (twenty bars had gone missing). The Grieg Trio play it with vital feeling and sensitivity; its dreamy opening, a kind of impressionistic Schumann, sounds exceptionally convincing in their hands. Moreover they give as fine an account of the wartime *Piano Trio in E minor* as any now before the public. The couplings further enhance the value of this issue.

The Vienna Piano Trio on Nimbus also give cogently argued and finely paced accounts of both the Shostakovich *Trios*. The Vienna is among the best and are naturally and vividly recorded. If the 1985 Schnittke *Trio* appeals as a coupling, this is an eminently desirable recommendation.

Although obviously a highly accomplished ensemble, the Munich Piano Trio do not convey much of the atmosphere of the eerily enigmatic and powerful *E minor Trio, Op. 67*, and Alla Ablaberdyeva is not wholly successful in the *Romances to Poems by Alexander Blok*.

Piano Trio No. 2 in E min., Op. 67.

*** Erato 0630 17875-2. Repin, Berezovsky, Yablonsky —
TCHAIKOVSKY: *Piano Trio.* ***

*** Decca 452 899-2. Mustonen, Bell, Isserlis — MESSIAEN:
Quatuor pour le fin du temps. ***

Vadim Repin, Boris Berezovsky and Dmitri Yablonsky give an eminently satisfying account of the *E minor Trio*, though the finale has some idiosyncratic touches that diminish pleasure. All the same there is a great deal to admire here. It is superbly recorded and comes with an outstanding account of the Tchaikovsky *Trio*.

The Decca is is a marvellously telling and perceptive account of Shostakovich's masterpiece, and is very truthfully balanced. The only snag is the very wide dynamic range of the recording. The opening *pianopianissimo* has ethereal concentration, but registers so quietly that the listener is tempted to turn up the volume. If one does, the *fortissimos* are not quite comfortable, for the microphones are fairly close. But it is possible to get it right, and then the rewards of the playing are very considerable.

2 Pieces for String Octet, Op. 11.

*** Chan. 9131. ASMF Chamber Ens. — ENESCU: *Octet in C;*
R. STRAUSS: *Capriccio: Sextet.* ***

The Academy of St Martin-in-the-Fields Chamber Ensemble play splendidly and with conviction; they are beautifully recorded and also offer a fine Enescu *Octet*.

String Quartets

String Quartets Nos. 1–15; (i) Piano Quintet in G min.;
(ii) 2 Pieces for String Octet, Op. 11.

(M) *** BMG/Melodiya (ADD) 74321 40711-2 (6). Borodin Qt;
with (i) Richter; (ii) Prokofiev Qt.

String Quartets Nos. 1–15. 2 Pieces for String Quartet,
Op. 36; 4 in D, Op. 83.

(M) **(*) Olympia (ADD) OCD 5009(5). Shostakovich Qt.

String Quartets Nos. 1 in C, Op. 49; 3 in F, Op. 73; 4 in D,
Op. 83; 2 Pieces for String Quartet, Op. 36.

*** Olympia (ADD) OCD 531. Shostakovich Qt.

String Quartets Nos. 10 in A flat, Op. 118; 11 in F min.,
Op. 122; 15 in E flat min., Op. 144.

*** Olympia (ADD) OCD 534. Shostakovich Qt.

String Quartets Nos. 2 in A, Op. 68; 5 in B flat, Op. 92; 7 in
F sharp min., Op. 108.

*** Olympia (ADD) OCD 532. Shostakovich Qt.

String Quartets Nos. 6 in G, Op. 101; 8 in C min., Op. 110; 9
in E flat, Op. 117.

*** Olympia (ADD) OCD 533. Shostakovich Qt.

String Quartets Nos. 12 in D flat, Op. 133; 13 in B flat min.,
Op. 138; 14 in F sharp, Op. 142.

*** Olympia (ADD) OCD 535. Shostakovich Qt.

String Quartets Nos. 1; 2; 4.

(***) Koch/Consonance mono 81-3005. Beethoven Qt.

String Quartets Nos. 3, Op. 73; 6, Op. 101.

*** Koch/Consonance (ADD) 81-3007. Beethoven Qt.

String Quartets Nos. 7 & 15.

*** Koch/Consonance (ADD) 81-3006. Beethoven Qt.

String Quartets Nos. 9–11.

*** Koch/Consonance (ADD) 81-3009. Beethoven Qt.

String Quartets Nos. 12–14.

*** Koch/Consonance (ADD) 81-3008. Beethoven Qt.

String Quartets Nos. 1–15; Adagio (Elegy after Katerina's
Aria from Scene 3 of Lady Macbeth of the Mtsensk
District); Allegretto (after Polka from The Age of Gold
ballet, Op. 22).

**(*) DG 463 284-2 (5). Emerson Qt.

The Shostakovich *Quartets* thread through his creative life like some inner odyssey and inhabit terrain of increasing spiritual desolation.

Originally issued on EMI and now reappearing on BMG/Melodiya, the Borodin Quartet's second recording is an economical investment when purchased complete. The present recordings are made in a generally drier acoustic than their predecessors, and Nos. 3 and 5 suffer noticeably in this respect. However, the ears quickly adjust and the performances can only be described as masterly. The Borodins possess enormous refinement, an altogether sumptuous tone and a perfection of technical address that is almost in a class of its own – and what wonderful intonation! These and the Bartók six are the greatest quartet cycles produced in the present century and are mandatory listening. The *Piano Quintet* was recorded at a concert at the Moscow Conservatoire, and it goes without saying that with Richter at the helm the account is powerful, although the quality of the sound here is noticeably dry and forward. The *Two Pieces for String Octet* are now added to the second CD.

The eponymous Shostakovich Quartet recorded a cycle over the period 1978 to 1985 and bring a special intensity to this repertoire as well as effortless technical address, and a tonal blend that gives their readings a strong claim on the collector's allegiance. It is no longer possible to talk of an out-and-out first choice in this repertoire.

Right from the *First Quartet* of 1938 through to the last, finished not long before his death, the Beethoven Quartet were closely associated with the composer and gave the first performances of nearly all the quartets. Since they collaborated so closely with him, their view of this cycle carries special authority. Collectors who were lucky enough to get the old Melodiya LPs from the 1950s and 1960s and who still treasure them, will welcome their reappearance in this cleaned-up form. With a few exceptions (Nos. 8, 10 and 13), theirs were also first recordings – and no other group was closer to Shostakovich's mind. Nos. 9, 10 and 11, for example, were made in 1965 and 1969, when the works were fresh from the composer's pen. Even if you have the fine cycles by the Borodins and the Fitzwilliams, this set is an important documentary record. In some of the earlier recordings allowances must be made for the sound; No. 3 is a later performance (1960) than the old mono LP, which used to be coupled to the *Piano Quintet* on Parlophone.

If sheer brilliance and virtuosity were all that mattered, the Emerson Quartet would lead the field. They offer us all fifteen quartets in chronological order on five CDs, plus two attractive encores, thus scoring over their main rivals who all take six. (Of course both the Borodins enjoy a price advantage). In terms of recorded sound the Emersons are wonderfully realistic, if a trifle too closely balanced. Their playing is immaculate technically, with spot-on intonation, accuracy and unanimity of ensemble. But they bring an unrelieved intensity to everything they touch and offer little real repose, when that is called for.

Gleaming and dazzling then, but they don't get very far under the surface here. There is infinitely more of Shostakovich's inner spirit to be found in the Borodin set, not to mention the old Beethoven Quartet, who premiered nearly all these works. If it is an exaggeration to say that the Emersons see the cycle as a vehicle for their own virtuosity, they certainly set great store by superb execution. These are public rather than private communications and one is not left feeling close to the anguish of most of this music.

String Quartets Nos. 1; 8 & 9.

(BB) *** Naxos 8.550973. Eder Qt.

If the Naxos disc is not necessarily a first choice, no one investing in it need fear they are getting short-changed. The Eder Quartet is a very distinguished ensemble and have a very good feeling for this repertoire. They are better recorded than the Borodins, and those for whom economy is a primary concern should consider this.

String Quartets Nos. 2; 3; 7; 8; 12.

(BB) *** Virgin 2x1 Dig. VBD5 61630-2 (2). Borodin Qt.

The new Borodin accounts now on a Virgin Double have the benefit of far better recording than their earlier, Melodiya versions on RCA. The sound is richer, cleaner and has a pleasing bloom as one would expect from the Snape Maltings. As far as the performances are concerned, some things come off better than others so that on balance there is little to choose between the sets; those who have the former need not make a change. This is one of the greatest quartets now before the public and they are completely inside this music. Those coming new to these works will probably opt for the newer, Virgin, digital versions.

String Quartets Nos. 3; 7 & 8.

*** BIS CD 913. Yggdrasil Qt.

The Yggdrasil are a young Swedish group embarking on a Shostakovich cycle. This issue is an auspicious start with a bold and searching account of the *Eighth*, and intelligent and satisfying readings of its companions.

String Quartets Nos. 2 in A, Op. 68; 12 in D flat, Op. 133.

(BB) *** Naxos 8.550975. Eder Qt.

String Quartets Nos. 4; 6–7.

(BB) *** Naxos 8.550972. Eder Qt.

If anything, the Eder coupling of Nos. 2 and 12 is even more impressive than their first disc. The account of the third-movement *Adagio: Recitativo and Romance* of No. 2 with its intense, improvisatory feeling is particularly fine, and the closing *Theme and Variations* is strongly characterized. Similarly the extended *Allegretto* second movement of No. 12 is powerfully argued and these performances have compelling concentration throughout.

Quite apart from its cost, this series is emerging as one of the most competitive of the newer versions of this powerful music. The recorded sound is superior to the Borodins and offers a serious challenge to them.

String Quartets Nos. 2 –3.

**(*) Hyp. CDA 67153. St Petersburg Qt.

String Quartets Nos. 4; 6; & 8.

** Hyp. CDA 67154. St Petersburg Qt.

The St Petersburg Quartet's performances display appropriate intensity and enthusiasm even if *piano* and *pianissimo* markings are at times a little exaggerated. The leader plays with evident feeling in the *Recitative and Romance* movement of the wartime *Second Quartet*, though intonation is not always impeccable. Some will find the first movement a little rushed. A promising start but the playing in tutti can be rough and the recording lends a certain hardness and glassiness to the leader's tone.

In the *Fourth Quartet* the St Petersburg group would not be a first choice. The leader's rapid rubato will not be to all tastes and the performance throughout is far too self-conscious. These Russian players give a good account of the *Sixth* (1956), but the *Eighth* is too full of emotion and vehemence: the greater reticence of the Borodins is the more telling. The St Petersburg group are decently recorded, though there is just a touch of wiriness above the stave.

String quartets Nos. 5; 7 & 9.

(N) ** Hyp. CDA 67155. St Petersburg Qt.

The St Petersburg Quartet play with impressive virtuosity and intensity in all three works. They are not free from expressive exaggeration and the leader's rapid vibrato will not give universal pleasure.

String Quartets Nos. 4; 8 & 11.

*** ASV CDDCA 631. Coull Qt.

The *Fourth Quartet* is a work of exceptional beauty and lucidity, one of the most haunting of the cycle; the *Eleventh Quartet* is a puzzling, almost cryptic work in seven short movements. The Coull are among the most gifted of the younger British quartets and give eminently creditable accounts of all three pieces. Good if slightly overlit recording.

String Quartets Nos. 4 ; 11 & 14.

*** DG 445 864-2. Hagen Qt.

The Hagen Quartet is as impeccable an ensemble as any now before the public, and if the appearance of this disc heralds a complete cycle it is very good news. Generally speaking, these belong among the most beautifully played and thoughtful readings of these *Quartets*.

String Quartets Nos. 7, Op. 108; 8, Op. 110; 9, Op. 117.

(N) (BB) **(*) Warner Apex 8573 89093-2. Brodsky Qt.

The Brodskys are recorded in good, well-detailed digital sound with an attractive ambience. These are well-prepared and committed accounts, and if the playing is generally less searching than the Borodin Quartet, these three performances do not lack depth of feeling (witness the slow movement of No. 8). The characteristically ambivalent mood changes in No. 9 are also thoroughly absorbed to make the performance seemingly spontaneous.

String Quartet No. 8, Op. 110.

⬤ *** Koch 3-6436-2. Medici Qt – BRITTEN: *Quartet No. 3*; JANACEK: *Quartet No. 1*; RAVEL: *Quartet*; SMETANA: *Quartet No. 1*. *** ⬤

(M) *** Classic fM 75605 57027-2. Chilingirian Qt – BORODIN: *Quartet No. 2*; DVORAK: *Quartet in F, Op. 96*. ***

(M) **(*) Decca (ADD) 425 541-2. Borodin Qt – BORODIN; TCHAIKOVSKY: *Quartets*. **(*)

Immediately creating a powerful atmospheric spell at the opening, attacking the second movement with great ferocity and finding a bleak emptiness of constituents for the other-worldly closing obituary, the Medici Quartet give a performance of rapt dedication and concentration, given a recording which achieves a remarkably natural presence.

On Classic fM the Chilingirians also give a tautly controlled performance, not as flexible as some but with the power enhanced by the rich, immediate, digital recording.

The Borodins' Decca performance is outstanding and the recording real and vivid, although the balance means that in the CD transfer the effect is very forward, almost too boldly immediate.

String Quartets Nos. (i) 14; (ii) 15.

*** HM/Praga PR 254043. (i) Glinka String Qt; (ii) Beethoven Qt.

(BB) *** Naxos 8.550976. Eder Qt.

The Glinka Quartet is a first-rate ensemble and their intense account of the *Fourteenth Quartet*, recorded only a year after the composer's death, is deeply felt. The Beethoven Quartet's account of the *Fifteenth* (they also recorded it commercially for Melodiya) penetrates deeply into this death-haunted music.

Cultured and finely shaped performances of two of Shostakovich's bleakest works. Of course the Beethoven and Borodin Quartets have special claims and arguably dig deeper into the dark hollows of these scores, but for those who do not want to buy all fifteen *Quartets* at one go, these offer an excellent alternative. As quartet playing goes, the Eder are second to none, and they have the benefit of very good recording. Certainly worth the money.

Violin Sonata, Op. 134.

*** Chan. 8988. Mordkovitch, Benson – PROKOFIEV: *Sonatas*; SCHNITTKE: *In Memoriam*. ***

*** Chan. 8343. Dubinsky, Edlina – SCHNITTKE: *Sonata No. 1* etc. ***

*(*) Olympia OCD 625. Bashmet, Richter – BRITTEN: *Lachrymae*; HINDEMITH: *Viola Sonata, Op. 11/4*. *(*)

The *Violin Sonata* can seem a dry piece, but Mordkovitch's natural intensity, her ability to convey depth of feeling without sentimentality, transforms it. Clifford Benson is the understanding pianist. In first-rate sound it makes a fine central offering for Mordkovitch's well-planned disc of Soviet violin music.

Rostislav Dubinsky's account is also undoubtedly eloquent, and Luba Edlina makes a fine partner. The recording is excellent too, although it is balanced a shade closely.

A partnership between Bshmet and Richter that excites the highest expectations in this repertoire proves disappointing. Recorded live in Germany in 1985, the forward balance and unpleasant acoustic robs this record of much of its value. The sound is too close and hard.

PIANO MUSIC

24 Preludes, Op. 34.

*** Decca 433 055-2. Mustonen – ALKAN: *25 Preludes*. ***

24 Preludes, Op. 34; Prelude & Fugue in D min., Op. 87/24; Piano Sonatas Nos. 1, Op. 12; 2 in B min., Op. 61.

*** Athene ATH CD 18. Clarke.

24 Preludes; Piano Sonata No. 2, Op. 61

** Cyprès CYP 2622. Schmidt.

24 Preludes; Piano Sonata No. 2, Op. 61; 3 Fantastic Dances, Op. 5.

*** Hyp. CDA 66620. Nikolayeva.

Raymond Clarke generously couples the two sonatas with the aphoristic and witty *Preludes*, Op. 34, and these new performances are a viable first-choice for anyone coming to this repertoire afresh.

Tatiana Nikolayeva is very well recorded indeed. She is one of the authentic advocates of Shostakovich, and her CD will be a must for most collectors. Recommended alongside Clarke and Mustonen.

The Decca version by the young Finnish pianist, Olli Mustonen, is also a very strong contender both artistically and technically.

Johan Schmidt is a young Belgian pianist with good fingers and clean articulation. He is fluent and intelligent but is let down by the synthetic sounding recording which is very two-dimensional. The piano is too close and the acoustic dry.

24 Preludes & Fugues, Op. 87.

⬤ (M) *** BMG/Melodiya (ADD) 74321 19849-2 (3). Nikolayeva.

*** Hyp. CDA 66441/3. Nikolayeva.

**(*) Decca 466 066-2. Ashkenazy.

(N) (BB) **(*) Naxos 8.554745-46. Scherbakov.

In this repertoire, the first choice must inevitably be Tatiana Nikolayeva, 'the onlie begetter', as it were, of the *Preludes and Fugues*. Her reading has enormous concentration and a natural authority that is majestic. There is wisdom and humanity here, and she finds depths in this music that have eluded most other pianists who have offered samples. No grumbles about the Hyperion recording, which is very natural. However, her Melodiya set, made in 1987, is if anything cleaner and better focused (if a bit dry). In neither reading will readers be disappointed.

Ashkenazy's set has the advantage of good Decca sound; there is a pleasing ambience and great clarity and warmth. His playing is very fine – that goes almost without saying – though he traverses the cycle in 141 minutes as opposed to Nikolayeva's 168. In comparing individual pieces, Nikolayeva always seems to find so much more in this music. She has been inside it and it shows in the subtlety of her colouring and depth of tone, and the sense of space. On its own terms the Ashkenazy is recommendable but he does not perhaps tell the whole story.

Konstantin Scherbakov commands a formidable technical address and much refinement of colour. Of course there are some formidable rivals in this repertoire, notably Tatiana Nikolaeyva but none is anywhere near as competitively priced. Scherbakov is often insightful, although there is some want of *Innigkeit* and some of the contemplative numbers find him almost on auto-pilot. All the same there is a lot to admire, and readers will find much that is rewarding. Nikolayeva's set on RCA/Melodiya remains a first choice.

Preludes & Fugues, Op. 87, Nos. 1; 5 & 24.

(***) Testament mono STB 1089. Gilels – CHOPIN: *Sonata No. 2*; MOZART: *Piano Sonata No. 17*. (***)

These three *Preludes and Fugues* were recorded in New York in 1955. The sound is a little dry and close, but the playing is magisterial.

24 Preludes & Fugues, Op. 87, Nos. 2–4, 8–10, 14–16, 20–22.

*(*) RCA 74321 61446-2 (2). Mustonen – BACH: *Preludes & Fugues*. *(*)

Olli Mustonen has chosen a dozen of the Shostakovich Op. 87 set of *Preludes and Fugues* and juxtaposes them with half of *Book I* of the Bach *Well-Tempered Clavier*. The eccentricities – exaggerated staccatos picked from the keyboard – and his narcissistic attention-seeking detract from the half of Shostakovich he does give us.

VOCAL MUSIC

Song of the Forests, Op. 81.

*** RCA 09026 68877-2. Kisseliev, Bezzubenko, Glinka College Boys' Ch., St Petersburg Ch. & PO, Temirkanov – PROKOFIEV: *On Guard for Peace*. ***

The *Song of the Forests*, unashamedly written as a Soviet propaganda piece, has regularly been dismissed as a potboiler but this fine recording under Temirkanov demonstrates that though Shostakovich deliberately simplified his idiom, the ideas are consistently fresh and memorable, not at all platitudinous. Solo and choral singing is first-rate, helped by full, atmospheric sound. Aptly and imaginatively coupled with the comparable Prokofiev propaganda piece.

OPERA

(i) *The Gamblers* (complete); (ii) *The Nose* (complete).

(M) *** BMG/Melodiya (ADD) 74321 60319-2 (2).
    (i) Rybasenko, Tarkhov, Belykh, Leningrad PO; (ii) Akimov, Belykh, Sasulova, Lomonosov, Sapegina, Moscow Chamber Theatre Ch. & O, (i & ii) Rozhdestvensky.

These two works, both based on Gogol, make an ideal coupling, each of them drawing on the satirical vein in the composer's personality. *The Gamblers* is only a fragment, written at the height of the Second World War in the same year as the *Leningrad Symphony*. As an attack on those who cheat society, its theme could be taken as both national (against Hitler) and domestic (against bureaucracy), and it is sad that it was never completed. In very immediate sound, with voices very clear, this is a live recording of the world première in Leningrad Philharmonic Hall in 1978, very well played and sung. *The Nose* dates from 1930, an even sharper attack on bureaucracy, and represents a full flowering of the Soviet avant-garde movement of the 1920s, soon to be suppressed. The singers and players of the Moscow Chamber Theatre give it a brilliantly idiomatic performance, vividly recorded, with Rozhdestvensky again the vigorous and colourful advocate. No librettos are provided, but the synopses are nicely detailed and linked to the copious index points, very necessary if the humour is to come over.

Lady Macbeth of Mtsensk (complete).

⚫ *** EMI (ADD) CDS7 49955-2 (2). Vishnevskaya, Gedda, Petkov, Krenn, Tear, Amb. Op. Ch., LPO, Rostropovich.
*** DG 437 511-2 (2). Ewing, Haugland, Larin, Langridge, Ciesinski, Moll, Kotcherga, Zednik, Paris Bastille Op. Ch. & O, Chung.

Rostropovich, in his finest recording ever, proves with thrilling conviction that this first version of Shostakovich's greatest work for the stage is among the most original operas of the century. Vishnevskaya is inspired to give an outstanding performance and provides moments of great beauty alongside aptly coarser singing; and Gedda matches her well, totally idiomatic. As the sadistic father-in-law, Petkov is magnificent, particularly in his ghostly return, and there are fine contributions from Robert Tear, Werner Krenn, Birgit Finnilä and Alexander Malta.

If ever Rostropovich's classic EMI recording of this opera is unavailable, then Chung's provides an alternative not quite so violent or powerful, but even more moving. The biggest contrast comes in the portrayal of the heroine. Where Vishnevskaya makes her a ravening fire-eater, with the voice abrasive and aggressive, Maria Ewing's portrait is much more vulnerable, with moods and responses subtly varied, her feminine charms more vividly conveyed in singing far more sensuous, with the beauty of hushed pianissimos most tenderly affecting. Sergei Larin as Katerina's labourer-lover equally gains over his EMI rival, Nicolai Gedda, by sounding more aptly youthful, with his tenor both firm and clear yet Slavonic-sounding. His touch is lighter than Gedda's, with a nice vein of irony. Aage Haugland is magnificent as Boris, Katerina's father-in-law, and Philip Langridge sings sensitively as her husband, Zinovi, while Kurt Moll as the Old Convict provides an extra emotional focus in his important solo at the start of the last Act.

SIBELIUS, Jean (1865–1957)

Andante festivo; Finlandia, Op. 26; Karelia Suite, Op. 11; King Christian II (suite); (i) Luonnotar, Op. 70; The Oceanides, Op. 73.

*** DG 447 760-2. (i) Isokoski; Gothenburg SO, Järvi.

This magnificent, impeccably recorded Sibelius anthology brings one of the best accounts of *The Oceanides* we have had since the celebrated Beecham version, made at the composer's own request, and a first-class *Luonnotar* – again, one of the best ever made. The remaining pieces are hardly less satisfying. The engineering is by the usual Gothenburg team that serviced this orchestra's BIS recordings.

Autrefois (Scène pastorale), Op. 96b; The Bard, Op. 64; Presto in D for Strings; Spring Song, Op. 16; Suite caractéristique, Op. 100; Suite champêtre, Op. 98b; Suite mignonne, Op. 98a; Valse chevaleresque, Op. 96c; Valse lyrique, Op. 96a.

*** BIS CD 384. Gothenburg SO, Järvi.

A mixed bag. *The Bard* is Sibelius at his greatest and most powerful, and it finds Järvi at his best. The remaining pieces are all light: some of the movements of the *Suite mignonne* and *Suite champêtre* could come straight out of a Tchaikovsky ballet, and Järvi does them with great charm. The last thing that the *Suite, Op. 100*, can be called is *caractéristique*, while the three pieces, Op. 96, find Sibelius in Viennese waltz mood. The rarity is *Autrefois*, which has a beguiling charm and is by far the most haunting of these pastiches. Sibelius introduces two sopranos and their *vocalise* is altogether captivating. The *Presto in D major for Strings* is a transcription – and a highly effective one – of the third movement of the *B flat Quartet, Op. 4*. Excellent recording, as one has come to expect from BIS.

The Bard; En Saga; Excerpts from Kuolema (incidental music): Valse triste, Scene with Cranes, Canzonetta, Valse romantique; Spring Song, Op. 16; Tapiola, Op. 112.

(N) *** DG 457 654-2. Gothenburg SO, Järvi.

Neeme Järvi recorded all these pieces in the 1980s with the Gothenburg Orchestra in the superb acoustic of its *Konserthus* and with the fine recording team which DG have inherited. *The Bard* is brooding and mysterious, all wonderfully atmospheric. *Tapiola* is a success: Järvi produces a performance of commanding power and the unhurried (and all the more terrifying) storm is judged excellently. *En Saga* on the other hand fares less well and at times seems almost matter of fact, although the introspective quieter

section in the middle and the closing paragraphs are evocative. The *Spring Song* also borders on the routine but then so does the music, emphatically not top-drawer Sibelius. In the four pieces from the incidental music to *Kuolema*, Järvi is back on form. The *Canzonetta* for strings and *Valse triste* have great poetry, and the *Scenes with Cranes* is full of atmosphere. We are placed a bit further forward in the hall than is ideal but this lends both presence and impact to the DG sound.

The Bard; Four Legends, Op. 22; Pohjola's Daughter.

(N) *** RCA 74321 68945-2. LSO, C. Davis.

This comes as an important supplement to Sir Colin Davis's complete cycle of the symphonies and it is equally fine – conducting of stature bringing superbly played performances, both atmospheric and gripping. The RCA recording, too, is first class.

Belshazzar's Feast (suite), Op. 54; Dance Intermezzo, Op. 45/2; The Dryad, Op. 45/1; Pan and Echo, Op. 53; Swanwhite, Op. 54.

*** BIS CD 359. Gothenburg SO, Järvi.

Belshazzar's Feast, a beautifully atmospheric piece of orientalism, and the incidental music for Strindberg's *Swanwhite* may not be Sibelius at his most powerful but both include wonderful things. Neeme Järvi's collection with the Gothenburg orchestra is first class in every way.

The Breaking of the Ice on the Oulo River; Press Celebrations Music; Song of the Athenians.

(N) *** BIS CD 1115. Lahti SO, Osmo Vänskä.

A recording which will be of compelling interest for all Sibelians. It contains the music Sibelius composed for a pageant in 1899, the so-called *Press Celebrations Music*, from which he later fashioned the first set of *Historic Scenes* and *Finlandia*. In all there is some forty minutes of music. Here we have Sibelius's original thoughts, as well as a *Prelude for Wind Instruments* and two movements which he left in manuscript. Not all of it is top-drawer Sibelius but the fifth tableau is powerful and atmospheric, and it is surprising that he made no effort to re-shape it and include it with the other *Historic Scenes*. The third tableau is the original version of the *Boléro*, which Sibelius revised in 1900 and then again in 1911 as *Festivo*. There are other rarities from the same period, including *The Breaking of the Ice on the Oulo River*, all worth hearing and given an excellent performance by Osmo Vänskä and the Lahti Symphony Orchestra and first-rate recorded sound.

Cassazione, Op. 6; Preludio; The Tempest: Prelude & Suites 1–2, Op. 109; Tiera.

*** BIS CD 448. Gothenburg SO, Järvi.

Järvi's recording of Sibelius's incidental music to *The Tempest* is among the most atmospheric since Beecham and, though it does not surpass the latter in pieces like *The Oak-Tree* or the *Chorus of the Winds*, it is still very good. The *Cassazione* resembles the *King Christian II* music in character, but it is well worth having on disc. Neither *Tiera* nor the *Preludio*, both from the 1890s, is of great interest or particularly characteristic.

Violin Concerto in D min. (1903–4 version); *Violin Concerto in D min., Op. 47* (1905; published version).

*** BIS CD 500. Kavakos, Lahti SO, Vänskä.

The first performance of the *Violin Concerto* left Sibelius dissatisfied and he immediately withdrew it for revision. This CD presents Sibelius's initial thoughts so that for the first time we can see the familiar final version struggling to emerge from the chrysalis. Comparison of the two concertos makes a fascinating study: the middle movement is the least affected by change, but the outer movements are both longer in the original score, and the whole piece takes almost 40 minutes. The Greek violinist, Leonidis Kavakos, proves more than capable of handling the hair-raising difficulties of the 1904 version and is an idiomatic exponent of the definitive concerto. The Lahti orchestra under Osmo Vänskä give excellent support and the balance is natural and realistic. An issue of exceptional interest and value.

Violin Concerto in D min., Op. 47.

(N) ✪ (M) *** Sony SMK 89748. Cho-Liang Lin, Philh. O, Salonen – NIELSEN: *Violin Concerto*. *** ✪

(M) *** Decca (ADD) 425 080-2. Chung, LSO, Previn – TCHAIKOVSKY: *Violin Concerto*. ***

(M) *** RCA (ADD) 09026 61744-2. Heifetz, Chicago SO, Hendl – GLAZUNOV: *Concerto*; PROKOFIEV: *Concerto No. 2*. ***

*** EMI CDC5 56418-2. Sarah Chang, BPO, Jansons – MENDELSSOHN: *Violin Concerto in E min*. ***

(N)(M) *** Ph. 464 741-2. Mullova, Boston SO, Ozawa – TCHAIKOVSKY: *Violin Concerto*. **(*)

*** EMI (ADD) CDC5 56150-2. Perlman, Pittsburgh SO, Previn – TCHAIKOVSKY: *Violin Concerto*. ***

(M) *** Sony (ADD) SMK 66829. Stern, Phd. O, Ormandy – TCHAIKOVSKY: *Violin Concerto*. ***

(M) *** CFP 573 1142. Little, RLPO, Handley – BRAHMS: *Violin Concerto*. ***

*** EMI CDC7 54127-2. Kennedy, CBSO, Rattle – TCHAIKOVSKY: *Concerto*. **(*)

*** Erato 4509-98537-2. Repin, LSO, Krivine – TCHAIKOVSKY: *Violin Concerto*. ***

(M) (***) EMI mono CDH7 61011-2. Neveu, Philh. O, Susskind – BRAHMS: *Concerto*. (***)

(BB) *** Naxos 8.550329. Kang, Slovak (Bratislava) RSO, Leaper – HALVORSEN: *Air norvégien* etc.; SINDING: *Légende*; SVENDSEN: *Romance*. ***

(BB) *** Royal Long Players DCL 705742 (2). Verhey, Netherlands RPO, Hans Vonk – BRAHMS; DVORAK; TCHAIKOVSKY: *Violin Concertos*. ***

(M) *(*) RCA (ADD) 09026 63591-2. Perlman, Boston SO, Leinsdorf – DVORAK: *Romance* **; TCHAIKOVSKY: *Violin Concerto*. *(*)

(N) (BB) (**(*)) Naxos mono 8.110938. Heifetz, LPO, Beecham – TCHAIKOVSKY: *Violin Concerto*; WIENIAWSKI: *Violin Concerto No. 2 in D min*. (***)

(M) (**) EMI mono CDH7 64030-2. Heifetz, LPO, Beecham –

GLAZUNOV: *Violin Concerto* (***) ✪; TCHAIKOVSKY: *Violin Concerto*. (***)

(i) *Violin Concerto; Karelia Suite; Belshazzar's Feast (suite)*.

**(*) Ondine ODE 8782. (i) Suusisto; Helsinki PO, Segerstam.

Violin Concerto; 2 Serenades, Op. 69; Humoresque No. 1 in D min., Op. 87/1.

*** DG 447 895-2. Mutter, Dresden State O, Previn.

(i) *Violin Concerto. The Tempest: Prelude; Suites Nos. 1 & 2, Op. 109*.

(N) *** Hänssler 98353. (i) Sitkovetsky; ASMF, Marriner.

Cho-Liang Lin's playing is distinguished not only by flawless intonation and an apparently effortless virtuosity but also by great artistry. He produces a glorious sonority at the opening, which must have been exactly what Sibelius wanted, wonderfully clean and silvery, and the slow movement has tenderness, warmth and yet restraint with not a hint of over-heated emotions. Lin encompasses the extrovert brilliance of the finale and the bravura of the cadenza with real mastery. The Philharmonia Orchestra rise to the occasion under Esa-Pekka Salonen, and the recording is first class. Lin's estimable account of the *Violin Concerto* is also available at mid-price, less attractively coupled with four favourite orchestra pieces. The *Finlandia* is underpowered and *En Saga* generates real excitement only towards the end, and then it sounds slick. *The Swan of Tuonela* is a fine performance, gentle and poetic. Salonen's *Valse triste*, if wanting the panache of Karajan, is quite effective. No complaints about the recording.

Kyung-Wha Chung has inimitable style and an astonishing technique, and her feeling for the Sibelius *Concerto* is second to none. André Previn's accompanying cannot be praised too highly: it is poetic when required, restrained, full of controlled vitality and well-defined detail. The 1970 Kingsway Hall recording is superbly balanced and produces an unforced, truthful sound. This is a most beautiful account, poetic, brilliant and thoroughly idiomatic, and must be numbered among the finest versions of the work available.

Heifetz's stereo performance of the Sibelius *Concerto* with the Chicago Symphony Orchestra under Walter Hendl set the standard by which others have come to be judged. It is one of his finest recordings; in remastered form the sound is vivid, the Chicago ambience making an apt setting for the finely focused violin line.

In her live recording, made at a concert in the Philharmonie, Sarah Chang gives an astonishingly mature reading of the Sibelius. She may not be as passionate as her fellow-Korean, Kyung-Wha Chung, but with sweet, refined tone the thoughtfulness and spontaneous poetry of the playing make her comparably magnetic. Warm, atmospheric sound.

Viktoria Mullova made the headlines during the 1980s by winning the Sibelius competition and subsequently making a dramatic escape to the West. Not surprisingly her account of the concerto is very successful, capturing its magical element right from the very opening, while the slow movement has a cool dignity that is impressive. What this concerto needs above all else is finesse and a certain aristocratic feeling, as well as warmth which is free of the *Zigeuner* element, and Mullova meets these combined needs admirably. The recording is excellent.

Itzhak Perlman (on EMI) plays the work as a full-blooded virtuoso showpiece and the Pittsburgh orchestra under André Previn him excellent support. He makes light of all the fiendish difficulties in which the solo part abounds and takes a conventional view of the slow movement, underlining its passion, and he gives us an exhilarating finale. The sound is marvellously alive and thrilling, though the forward balance is very apparent. This has now been recoupled with the Tchaikovsky concerto, but still at full price.

Where most violinists treat the opening as a deep meditation, Mutter makes it tougher than usual, less beautiful, using momentarily a vibratoless slightly steely tone. Not that her reading lacks inner qualities for, despite the close balance, the opening of the slow movement finds Mutter playing in rapt meditation on a half-tone. In the finale, taken fast, power is again the keynote. Previn draws a committed performance from an orchestra not noted for playing Sibelius. In the two *Serenades*, Mutter at her most inspired beautifully captures the wayward, quasi-improvisatory quality of these pieces.

With the *Violin Concerto* again not coupled with another violin work, this Hännsler CD makes a unique and imaginative Sibelius issue, recorded in full, clear, spectacular sound. Sitkovetsky's is a fine reading, positive, powerful and direct, with no suspicion of self-indulgence. With Marriner and the Academy in fresh, clear partnership, this is a performance that, warmly expressive as it is, keeps tempi steadier and less volatile than most. In terms of length, the incidental music for *The Tempest*, with 18 brief movements, is the major item here.

Thanks to the vividness of the recording, the originality of this late Sibelius inspiration comes over even more strikingly than usual, with echoes of other late Sibelius works brought out, not just the obvious links with *Tapiola* in the storm movements. Marriner reveals the charm of the dance rhythms in such colourful genre movements as *Caliban's Songs* in the *Suite No. 1* and the *Dance of the Nymphs* in the *Suite No. 2*.

Stern's 1969 recording has real passion yet, as the very opening demonstrates, there is no lack of feeling for the work's special atmosphere. Poetry is never in short supply, especially towards the close of the first movement, Ormandy provides a splendid accompaniment and the Philadelphia Orchestra matches Stern's virtuosity and warmth. The violin is forwardly placed, but the balance is much more satisfactory than some recordings from this source, while the re-mastering has greatly improved the sound: it has plenty of body and resonance.

Tasmin Little's hushed and mysterious account of the opening theme leads to a performance that is both poised and purposeful, magnetic in her combination of power and poetry. Her virtuosity culminates in an account of the finale in which, as in the Brahms, she finds an element of wit in the pointing of insistent dance rhythms. Throughout she is splendidly matched by the colourful playing of the RLPO under Vernon Handley.

Throughout, Nigel Kennedy's intonation is true and he takes all the technical hurdles of this concerto in his stride. There is a touch of the *zigeuner* throb in the slow movement, but on the whole he plays with real spirit and panache. This can be confidently recommended if the coupling with the Tchaikovsky, a rather more indulgent performance, is suitable. The playing of the Birmingham orchestra is excellent throughout as, indeed, is the EMI recording.

The purity and refinement of Vadim Repin's playing are what strike one first. The withdrawn darkness at the very start quickly opens out thrillingly to reveal his total command, the tautness of his control, with tone sharply focused. Here is a young artist who, for all the brilliance of his virtuosity, regularly keeps a degree of emotion in reserve, his very restraint adding to the intensity. The speed in the finale is thrillingly fast, yet Repin with light attack brings out the scherzando element as well as the passion.

The magnetism of Neveu in this, her first concerto recording, is inescapable from her opening phrase onwards, warmly expressive and dedicated, yet with no hint of mannerism. The EMI transfer is not as impressive as Dutton's coupled with the Second Symphony (CDEA 5016).

Dong-Suk Kang chooses some popular Scandinavian repertoire pieces, such as the charming Svendsen *Romance in G*, as makeweights. His version of the concerto is very fine, though the slow movement could do with more tenderness as opposed to passion. There is splendid virtuosity and authoritative in the outer movements. The orchestral playing is very acceptable too. In the bargain basement, this enjoys a strong competitive advantage, but even if it were at full price it would feature quite high in the current lists.

Emma Verhey's unforgettably full-blooded account of the Sibelius concerto comes from Netherlands EMI and has not previously been issued on CD. The force of personality of the solo playing is matched by its ardour and technical security. Although the orchestra is well back within a spacious acoustic, and the soloist placed forwardly, tuttis have impact, even if detail is not always ideally clear. With any reservations it is impossible not to respond to a performance of such eloquence.

Helped by a close balance and a full, rich and immediate recording, the Finnish violinist Pekka Suusisto, barely twenty, gives a strong and passionate reading, very outward-going, lacking some of the meditative, inner qualities that others find but compensating in his volatile imagination. His speeds are on the broad side, but the urgency and concentration are never in doubt. With a Finnish conductor and orchestra too, the result is both powerful and idiomatic. The playing is equally positive in the two suites. The exotic colours of *Belshazzar's Feast* are vividly caught.

Heifetz made his first historic recording of the Sibelius *Violin Concerto* Beecham in 1935, a reading that set standards in virtuosity for generations to come. Next to many later recordings, it may be short on mystery, but the passion as well as the brilliance of the playing is very clear, with Beecham a challenging partner. The Naxos transfer is well balanced but with surface hiss intrusive at times.

But despite Sir Thomas's direction, Heifetz gave the more powerful account of it in his later, Chicago, recording with Walter Hendl in the early days of stereo. (The reverse was the case with the Glazunov.) A good transfer nevertheless from EMI with different coupling although this CD costs more than the Naxos alternative.

The fault of Perlman's RCA disc – a fault which runs throughout this CD – is the orchestral sound and Leinsdorf's conducting, both of which are below par. Perlman's artistry is never in doubt, of course, but this is hardly a competitive reissue in view of the strong competition.

(i; iii) *Violin Concerto in D minor, Op. 47;* (i) *Finlandia; Karelia Suite, Op. 11; Kuolema: valse triste, Op. 44/1; Legend: the Swan of Tuonela, Op. 22/2;* (i) *Symphonies Nos. 2 in D, Op. 43;* (ii) *5 in E flat, Op. 82.*

(N) **(*) DG Panorama (ADD) 469 201-2 (2). BPO; (i) Kamu;
(ii) Karajan; (iii) Ferras.

There are several performances of stature in this Panorama package, notably Karajan's celebrated account of the *Fifth Symphony* from 1965 and his hardly less masterly performances of *Swan of Tuonela, Finlandia* and *Valse triste* from the same time. Okko Kamu's account of the *Second Symphony* is a good performance, eminently recommendable though not particularly special. Christian Ferras is impressive in the *Violin Concerto*, but there is some wiriness of tone. Even so, many will prefer him to Mutter, also on DG, though not to Lin or Kyung-Wha Chung. All the same a useful introduction to some deservedly popular Sibelius.

(i) *Violin Concerto;* (ii) *Symphony No. 7; Tapiola.*

(***) Ondine mono ODE 809-2. (i) D. Oistrakh, Finnish RSO, Fougstedt; (ii) Helsinki PO, Beecham.

David Oistrakh's account of the *Violin Concerto* has a marvellous strength and nobility, as well as an effortless virtuosity that carries all before it. His artistry inspires a warm response from the Finnish Radio Orchestra under Nils-Eric Fougstedt, who give magnificent support. There was always a special sense of occasion, too, at any Beecham concert and the opening of the *Seventh Symphony* is more highly charged than his EMI commercial recording with the RPO. *Tapiola* also has great intensity, though the orchestral playing does not have the finesse, magic and tonal subtlety of the RPO recording. Subfusc recording, but a coupling well worth investigating all the same.

(i) *En Saga, Op. 9; Finlandia;* (ii) *Karelia Suite;* (i) *Legend: The Swan of Tuonela, Op. 22/2; Tapiola, Op. 112.*

(M) **(*) EMI ADD/Dig. EMI CDM7 64331-2. BPO, Karajan.
(BB) *** Belart 450 018-2 (without *Tapiola*). (i) SRO, Horst Stein; (ii) VPO, Maazel – GRIEG: *Peer Gynt.* ***

Karajan's *En Saga* is more concerned with narrative than with atmosphere to start with; the climax is very exciting and the *lento assai* section and the coda are quite magical. *Tapiola* is broader and more expansive than the first DG version; at the storm section, the more spacious tempo is vindicated and the climax is electrifying. *The Swan of Tuonela* is most persuasively done. These recordings date from 1977. The later, digital recording of *Karelia* has been added for the current reissue.

Horst Stein shows a gift for the special atmosphere of Sibelius, and these distinguished and poetic performances offer some of the finest playing we have had from the Suisse

Romande Orchestra. Moreover Decca's 1972 recording approaches the demonstration class, especially in *En Saga*. Maazel's *Karelia* is also first rate.

(i) *En saga; Finlandia; Karelia Suite;* (ii) *Four Legends, Op. 22;* (i; iii) *Luonnotar;* (ii) *Night Ride and Sunrise, Op. 55; Pohjola's Daughter, Op. 49;* (i) *Tapiola.*

(B) *** Double Decca (ADD) 452 576-2 (2) [(M) id. import].
(i) Philh. O, Ashkenazy; (ii) SRO, Stein; (iii) with Söderström.

This Double Decca combines Ashkenazy's mid-priced digital collection from the 1980s as listed below with more distinguished and finely calculated performances from Horst Stein. *Night Ride and Sunrise* and *Pohjola's Daughter* date from 1971. At the time, we thought they showed the Suisse Romande Orchestra in much better form than usual, and the *Legends*, too, are impressive, with a hell-for-leather account of *Lemminkäinen's Return*. The 1980 analogue sound is again first class, having fine weight and definition. Again the Suisse Romande Orchestra plays very well. Even if the body of string tone does not match that of the Philharmonia, the brooding atmosphere of *The Swan of Tuonela* is well caught, and both the first and third *Legends* are well shaped and exciting. All in all, excellent value.

En Saga; Scènes historiques, Opp. 25, 66.

*** BIS CD 295. Gothenburg SO, Järvi.

Järvi has the advantage of modern digital sound and the Gothenburg orchestra is fully inside the idiom of this music and plays very well indeed. Järvi's *En Saga* is exciting and well paced.

Finlandia; Karelia Suite; Kuolema: Valse triste; Legend: The Swan of Tuonela; Scènes historiques: Festivo; Tapiola.

(M) (***) DG mono 447 453-2. BPO, Rosbaud.

Karajan was not the only champion of Sibelius's music in post-war Germany: Hans Rosbaud, the high priest of the Second Viennese School and the 1950s avant-garde, also included it in his repertoire and indeed insisted on conducting the *Fourth Symphony* when he came to the BBC Symphony Orchestra some months before his death in 1962. These recordings come from the mid-1950s and, although some allowance must be made for the mono sound, the performances themselves have the ring of conviction. The *Tapiola* is something special, among the most terrifying evocations of that dark Nordic forest, and worthy to keep company with those of Beecham, Koussevitzky and Karajan. *The Swan of Tuonela* is a little brisk, but it is not wanting in atmosphere. The *Alla marcia* of the *Karelia Suite* is a bit sedate, heavy-footed even, but Sibelians will want this disc for Rosbaud's intensely cold *Tapiola*.

Finlandia; Karelia Suite; Kuolema: Valse triste; Nightride and Sunrise; The Oceanides; Tapiola.

*** RCA 09026 68770-2. LSO, C. Davis.

The two performances of special interest here are *Night Ride and Sunrise* and *The Oceanides*, neither of which Sir Colin has recorded before. *The Oceanides* holds up alongside the celebrated Beecham in atmosphere and poetic feeling and

Night Ride and Sunrise, with its difficult transition from the trochaic ride to the stillness and grandeur of sunrise, is splendidly realized. Sir Colin's account of *Tapiola* is even more impressive and terrifying than his earlier Boston version. Very good sound.

Finlandia; Kuolema: Valse triste; Legend: The Swan of Tuonela, Op. 22/2.

*** DG 439 010-2. BPO, Karajan – GRIEG: *Holberg Suite* etc. ***

Coupled with Grieg, this is Karajan at his very finest in the early 1980s, and the remastered digital recording is impressively real and present, particularly in the languorous *Valse triste* and in *The Swan*, Karajan's third and final account on record, powerful in its brooding atmosphere. There is a touch of brashness in the brass in *Finlandia*, but generally this Berlin/Karajan partnership has never been surpassed.

Finlandia; Legends: The Swan of Tuonela; Kuolema: Valse triste.

(M) ** Sony (ADD) SMK 63156. NYPO, Bernstein – GRIEG: *Peer Gynt: Suites Nos. 1 & 2; Norwegian Dance; March of the Trolls.* **

Bernstein's account of *Finlandia* is quite exciting, but the recording is rather harsh. *The Swan of Tuonela* is beautifully played, with finesse and a sense of brooding atmosphere, and there is some lovely relaxed string playing in *Valse triste*. The sound is acceptable but not exceptional.

Finlandia; Legends: The Swan of Tuonela; The Oceanides; Pohjola's Daughter, Op. 49; Tapiola.

(M) **(*) Chan. 6508. RSNO, Gibson.

The Oceanides is particularly successful and, if Karajan finds even greater intensity in *Tapiola*, Gibson's account certainly captures the icy desolation of the northern forests. He is at his most persuasive in an elusive piece like *The Dryad*, although *En Saga* is also evocative, showing an impressive overall grasp. The RSNO are on peak form.

(i) 6 Humoresques, Opp. 87 & 89; 2 Serenades, Op. 69; 2 Serious Melodies, Op. 79; Ballet Scene (1891); Overture in E (1891).

*** BIS CD 472. (i) Kang, Gothenburg SO, Järvi.

The *Humoresques* are among Sibelius's most inspired smaller pieces. They are poignant as well as virtuosic and have a lightness of touch, a freshness and a sparkle. The two *Serenades* have great poetic feeling and a keen Nordic melancholy. They are wonderfully played by this distinguished Korean artist, who is beautifully accompanied. The two orchestral works are juvenilia which predate the *Kullervo Symphony*. There are some characteristic touches, but Sibelius himself did not think well enough of them to permit their publication. All the violin pieces, however, are to be treasured, and the recording is top class.

Karelia Suite: Intermezzo; Alla marcia; Finlandia; The Oceanides; Scènes historiques: Suite No. 1; Tapiola; (i) Kullervo Symphony, Op. 7; (ii) Serenades Nos. 1–2, Op. 69a/b.

(N) (B) *** EMI double fforte (ADD) CDZ5 74200-2 (2). Bournemouth SO, Berglund; (i) Soloists, Helsinki University Male Voice Ch., (ii) Haendel.

This was the first recording of *Kullervo*, with which Sibelius made his breakthrough in Finland in 1892 and which was not heard again until 1958, the year after his death. Berglund's account, recorded in 1971, comes up surprisingly well. The orchestral playing is full of enthusiasm and is well disciplined, and this re-issue (its first CD transfer) comes with a well-filled and desirable programme. Both *Tapiola* and *The Oceanides* are eminently competitive, and the two *Serenades* have the benefit of Ida Haendel, whose playing has elegance and poetry. The *Serenades* were composed in 1913 and 1914, when Sibelius was toying with the idea of a second violin concerto. Good transfers with the chorus fractionally more forward than on the original LP; cellos and basses are cleaner and better focused but less weighty. But those wanting a bargain *Kullervo* need have no misgivings, particularly in view of the excellence of the rest of the programme.

King Christian II (suite); Pelléas et Mélisande (suite), Op. 46; Swanwhite (suite: excerpts), Op. 54.

*** Chan. 9158. Iceland SO, Sakari.

The *King Christian II* music is a winner and full of the most musical touches. It also includes a previously unrecorded *Minuet* and the *Fool's Song*, excellently sung by Sauli Tiilikainen. Although the *Pelléas et Mélisande* suite does not displace either Beecham or Karajan, it makes a useful alternative to either – and that is praise indeed! It has plenty of atmosphere and, though tempi are on the slow side, there is always plenty of inner life. The *Swanwhite* (five movements only) is attentive to refinements of phrasing and dynamics and at the same time free from the slightest trace of narcissism. Beautifully natural recording, warm and well balanced.

Four Legends from the Kalevela (Lemminkäinen suite), Op. 22. Lemminkäinen and the Maidens of Saari; Lemminkäinen's Homeward Journey (1896 versions); Second ending of Lemminkäinen's Homeward Journey (1897 version); Excerpt from Lemminkäinen in Tuonela (1896 version).

*** BIS Dig. CD 1015 [id.]. Lahti SO, Vänskä.

As is well known, the *Four Legends* that comprise the *Lemminkäinen suite* (1895/6) were revised twice – in 1897 and then in 1900 – and, in the case of *Lemminkäinen and the Maidens of Saari* and *Lemminkäinen in Tuonela*, retouched for publication in 1939. BIS continues in its exploration of the first version of Sibelius's orchestral scores by bringing us the 1896 version of the former and also the first, much longer score of *Lemminkäinen's Homeward Journey* This is very nearly twice as long as the definitive version and considerably less effective. The first *Legend* underwent a particularly fascinating transformation. The disc also offers the alternative 1897 ending of *Lemminkäinen Homeward Journey* and an excerpt from *Lemminkäinen in Tuonela* which Sibelius excised. The finished work is played in exemplary fashion by Osmo Vänskä and his Lahti Orchestra and superbly recorded. *The Swan of Tuonela* is highly evocative and way up there among the best.

Four Legends, Op. 22 (see also above, under *The Bard*).

*** BIS CD 294. Gothenburg SO, Järvi.

Four Legends; The Bard; (i) Luonnotar.

(M) *** Chan. (ADD) 6586. SNO, Gibson, (i) with Bryn-Johnson.

Four Legends, Op. 22; En Saga.

(N) *** Ondine 953-2. Swedish RSO, Franck.

Four Legends; Finlandia; Karelia Suite.

(BB) **(*) Naxos 8.554265. Iceland SO, Sakari.

Four Legends; Night Ride and Sunrise.

**(*) Finlandia 3984 27890-2. Toronto SO, Saraste.

Four Legends, Op. 22; Night Ride and Sunrise, Op. 55; (i) Luonnotar, Op. 70.

(N) **(*) (M) Virgin VM5 61847–2. (i) Kringelborn, R. Stockholm PO, Paavo Järvi.

Four Legends; Night Ride and Sunrise; Pohjola's Daughter.

**(*) DG 453 426-2. Gothenburg SO, Järvi.

Four Legends; Tapiola.

*** Ondine ODE 852-2. Helsinki PO, Segerstam.

Although Segerstam perversely ignores Sibelius's instructions about the order of the *Legends* (so, for that matter, did Salonen) this is of little moment, given the fact that collectors can easily reprogramme the disc. The performances of both the *Legends* and *Tapiola* are first class and are infinitely preferable to the symphony cycle Segerstam recorded in Copenhagen for Chandos. This is now a first recommendation for the *Legends*, while *Tapiola* is one of the best since Karajan.

On BIS, Järvi has the advantage of modern digital sound and a wonderfully truthful balance. He gives a passionate and atmospheric reading of the first *Legend* and his account of *The Swan of Tuonela* is altogether magical, one of the best in the catalogue. He takes a broader view of *Lemminkäinen in Tuonela* than many of his rivals and builds up an appropriately black and powerful atmosphere. The disappointment is *Lemminkäinen's Homeward Journey* which lacks the possessed, manic quality of Beecham's very first record, which sounded as if a thousand demons were in pursuit.

Mikko Franck is a thoughtful interpreter and is obviously steeped in the atmosphere of this score and fresh in his musical responses. He is expansive in the bigger movements, too much so in *Lemminkäinen in Tuonela*, which does not wholly sustain tension. He does not match Beecham's hell-for-leather account of *Lemminkäinen's Homeward Journey*, but he is impressive nonetheless. His account of *En Saga* has a strong narrative feel and plenty of atmosphere. The Swedish Radio Orchestra play well for him, and there is plenty of personality. Recommended.

Gibson comes at mid-price and offers sensitive performances of *The Bard*, and *Luonnotar*, where the soprano voice is made to seem like another orchestral instrument. The Scottish orchestra play freshly and with much commitment. *The Swan of Tuonela* has a darkly brooding primeval quality,

and there is an electric degree of tension in the third piece, *Lemminkäinen in Tuonela*. The two outer *Legends* have ardent rhythmic feeling, and altogether this is highly successful. The recorded sound is excellent.

Paavo Järvi, son of the Estonian-born Neeme Järvi, draws fine and responsive playing from the Royal Stockholm Philharmonic and his account of the *Four Legends* can hold its own alongside current rivals. *The Swan of Tuonela* is atmospheric with the cor anglais solo beautifully played and, although *Lemminkäinen in Tuonela* does not have the dark, brooding concentration of Jensen's pioneering disc, it comes off very well indeed. *Luonnotar* is even more spacious than Järvi *père*, though Solveig Kringelborn does not make as strong an impression as her Finnish colleague on the Gothenburg DG recording. A good *Night Ride and Sunrise*, though again not quite a first choice. The sound is well detailed and present but has less depth than the finest recordings from this source. However, those looking for a mid-priced version of the *Legends* should find this Virgin reissue eminently satisfying.

Petri Sakari's account of the *Legends* with the Iceland orchestra has a lot going for it and is very decently recorded. Why he reverses the order of the middle two is something of a mystery. The *Karelia Suite* and *Finlandia* are well played and most CD machines can reprogramme the order of the *Legends*. On the whole, good value for money but not a first choice; that lies with Segerstam, although he too perversely reverses the playing order (ODE 852-2).

Saraste has recorded the *Four Legends* with the Finnish Radio Symphony Orchestra for RCA but this Canadian account is better, both in the quality of the orchestral playing and the recorded sound. Like Sakari on Naxos, Saraste reverses the order of the two central *Legends*, and those who wish to follow Sibelius's wishes have to programme their machines accordingly (1, 3, 2, 4). No lack of atmosphere all the same, particularly in *Lemminkäinen in Tuonela*, and no want of passion.

Yet Saraste does not match the urgent momentum and level of excitement in *Lemminkäinen's Homeward Journey* that Beecham, Segerstam or Vänskä achieve, and in the *Night Ride* Saraste sounds pedestrian. This remains recommendable, but not in preference to Segerstam.

Järvi's DG recording again has the advantage of the glorious acoustics of the Gothenburg Concert Hall and the expertise of the same recording team. The DG version has slightly greater transparency and smoothness, though the BIS version has marginally more presence. In any event this newer account is, technically speaking, among the very best *Legends*. The orchestral playing is first class but this time round Neeme Järvi is inclined to be inattentive to atmosphere – so important in this music. He knocks about six minutes off his earlier tempo and seems too intent on keeping things moving. Yet though his *Lemminkäinen's Return* is faster than in 1985, it has lower voltage and less excitement. *Pohjola's Daughter* and *Night Ride and Sunrise* are far more successful. The recording is three star but the performances are not.

The Oceanides; Night Ride and Sunrise; The Tempest (Suites Nos. 1 & 2).

**(*) Ondine ODE 914-2. Helsinki PO, Segerstam.

This is Segerstam's second recording of the first suite from *The Tempest* music, his earlier version on Chandos came as a fill-up to the *Fourth Symphony*. The newcomer is very fine indeed, full of atmosphere and power, and free from expressive exaggeration. *The Oceanides* is another matter: a generally rushed and breathless main section preceded by an insufferably slow opening. *Night Ride and Sunrise* is much finer: it is difficult to bring off well, but Segerstam paces it convincingly. State-of-the-art recording.

(i) *Pelléas et Mélisande* (incidental music; complete);
(ii) *Legend: The Swan of Tuonela.*

(B) **(*) Ph. Double 462 309-2. (i) Rotterdam PO, Zinman; (ii) Boston SO, Sir Colin Davis *** – FAURE: *Pelléas et Mélisande; Pavane, Op. 50* ***; SCHOENBERG: *Pelleas und Melisande; Verklaerte Nacht.* **(*)

The complete score is offered here (including *At the Seashore*) and the orchestral playing is of high quality. Zinman is undoubtedly warmly sympathetic, but the music is just a shade undercharacterized. Nevertheless the recording is pleasingly warm and natural, and the couplings are pertinent (although not all lovers of Fauré and Sibelius are likely to respond to Schoenberg). A quite attractive package, just the same, for Sir Colin Davis's performance of *The Swan of Tuonela* is memorably atmospheric.

Rakastava (suite), *Op. 14; Scènes historiques, Opp. 25, 66; Valse lyrique, Op. 96/1.*

(M) *** Chan. 6591. RSNO, Gibson.

Derived from music for a patriotic pageant, the first set of *Scènes historiques* are vintage Sibelius. In the *Love Song* Gibson strikes the right blend of depth and reticence, while elsewhere he conveys a fine sense of controlled power. Convincing and eloquent performances that have a natural feeling for the music. Gibson's *Rakastava* is beautifully unforced and natural, save for the last movement which is a shade too slow. The *Valse lyrique* is not good Sibelius, but everything else certainly is. Gibson plays this repertoire with real commitment, and the recorded sound is excellent, with the orchestral layout, slightly distanced, most believable. At mid-price this is a specially desirable collection.

Scaramouche, Op. 71; The Language of the Birds: Wedding March.

*** BIS CD 502. Gothenburg SO, Järvi.

Scaramouche is Sibelius's only ballet and scored for relatively small forces, including piano (not unlike Strauss's music for *Le Bourgeois Gentilhomme*; at its best it reminds one of the luminous colourings of the *Humoresques* of five years later. A wistful, gentle and haunting score, often inspired though slightly let down by its uneventful second Act. Sibelius did not think highly enough of the *Wedding March* to Adolf Paul's play, *The Language of the Birds*, to give it an opus number but it is in fact quite an attractive miniature. The playing of the Gothenburg orchestra under Neeme Järvi is altogether excellent and so, too, is the BIS recording.

SYMPHONIES

Symphonies Nos. 1–7.

(M) **(*) Chan. 6559 (3). SNO, Gibson.
(M) (**) Finlandia mono 3984-22713-2 (3). Stockholm PO, Ehrling.
*(*) Finlandia 3984-23389-2 (4). COE, Berglund.

Symphonies Nos. 1 in E min., Op. 39; 2 in D, Op. 43; 4 in A min., Op. 63; 5 in E flat, Op. 82.

(B) *** Ph. Duo (ADD) 446 157-2 (2). Boston SO, Davis.

Symphonies Nos. 1, 2, 4 & 5.

(N) (B) *(*) Finlandia Ultima 0630 18962-2 (2). Finnish RSO, Saraste.

Symphonies Nos. 3 in C, Op. 52; 6 in D min., Op. 104; 7 in C, Op. 105; (i) Violin Concerto; Finlandia; Legend: The Swan of Tuonela; Tapiola.

(B) *** Ph. Duo (ADD) 446 160-2 (2). (i) Accardo; Boston SO, Davis.

Symphonies Nos. 1, 2 & 4; Finlandia; Karelia Suite.

(B) *** Double Decca 455 402-2 (2). Philh. O, Ashkenazy.

Symphonies Nos. 3, 5, 6 & 7; En Saga; Tapiola.

(B) ***Double Decca 455 405-2 (2) Philh. O, Ashkenazy.

Symphonies Nos. 3, 6 & 7; (i) Kullervo Symphony.

(N) (B) ** Finlandia Ultima 3984 21348-2 (2). Finnish RSO, Saraste; (i) with Groop, Hynninen, Polytech Ch.

Symphonies Nos. 1–7; Finlandia; Karelia Suite, Op. 11; Kuolema: Valse triste; Legends: The Swan of Tuonela; Lemminkäinen's Return; Pelléas et Mélisande: Suite; Pohjola's Daughter; Rakastava; Romance for Strings in C, Op. 42; Scènes historiques: All'overtura; The Hunt; Scena.

(M) **(*) EMI (ADD) CMS5 67299-2 (5). Hallé O, Barbirolli.

(i) *Symphonies Nos. 1–7; (ii) Night Ride and Sunrise; (i) The Oceanides; Scene with Cranes.*

(M) **(*) EMI (ADD) CMS7 64118-2 (4). (i) CBSO, (ii) Philh. O, Rattle.

Symphonies Nos. 1–7; Night Ride and Sunrise, Op. 55; Pelléas et Mélisande: Suite, Op. 46; Pohjola's Daughter, Op. 49.

(M) (***) Beulah mono 1–4PD 8 (4). LSO, Collins.

Ashkenazy's Sibelius cycle has now been issued on a pair of Double Deccas, with four tone-poems added for good measure. It takes precedence, partly because of the generally superior digital recording; but on performance grounds, too, these readings are very rewarding. A rich and strong, consistently enjoyable cycle which is a great favourite of I. M.'s. Ashkenazy by temperament brings out the expressive warmth, colour and drama of the composer rather than his Scandinavian chill, reflecting perhaps his Slavonic background. The recordings – made between 1979 and 1984, either at Walthamstow or in the Kingsway Hall – are full and rich as well as brilliant, most of them still of demonstration quality. For those wanting a complete set, they make a most attractive recommendation, although the newest cycle from

Sir Colin Davis and the LSO on RCA takes pride of place at premium price.

Sir Colin Davis's set of the symphonies, recorded during the second half of the 1970s, is undoubtedly among the finest of the collected editions, and now it is not only very economical but three tone-poems and an estimable account of the *Violin Concerto* are thrown in for good measure. Indeed Accardo's performance of the latter is very high on the recommended list. *Tapiola*, too, is atmospheric and superbly played. Nos. 1, 2, 5 and 7 were the first to be recorded in (1975/6). The idiomatic playing Davis secures from the Boston orchestra is immediately apparent. Tempi are well judged and there is a genuine sense of commitment and power though the recording is not quite as fine as Ashkenazy's on Decca. However, the remastering has undoubtedly improved its overall depth. Davis's accounts of the *Third*, *Fourth* and *Sixth Symphonies* are among the best on disc and they are excellently recorded. In the *Third* Davis judges the tempi in all three movements to perfection; no conductor has captured the elusive spirit of the slow movement or the power of the finale more effectively. The *Fourth* is arguably the finest of the cycle; there is a powerful sense of mystery, and the slow movement in particular conveys the feeling of communication with nature that lies at the heart of its inspiration. The *Fifth* is no match for Karajan, the *Seventh* not as fine as with Rattle. The *Sixth* is altogether more impressive and much more vivid as sound.

It is good also to have Barbirolli's characteristically vibrant Sibelius oeuvre (recorded between 1966 and 1970) now for the first time gathered together in a box. Barbirolli favoured spacious tempi, but almost always held the listener in his spell. This certainly applies to the present account of the *First Symphony* which has a freshness and ardour that are very appealing. It is undoubtedly gripping, even if, compared with his enthusiastic account of the *Second*, it is just a little lacking in panache. All seven symphonies were recorded in the Kingsway Hall. The first two date from 1966, but in No. 1 in the present remastering string fortissimos are made fierce. No. 2 is in every way more successful. The Hallé Orchestra play particularly well and give a warm-hearted account, romantic in approach, Barbirolli's reading stressing the Slav ancestry and Italianate warmth of the work. The recording is splendidly full blooded. In No. 3, tempi are well judged, but the inner tension is less well maintained than in No. 2. None the less, there is some very fine wind-playing in the *Andante* and the transition to the finale is very convincingly managed.

Barbirolli's account of No. 4 has great authenticity of feeling. Here the Hallé strings produce an admirably chilling quality, far removed from the well-nourished string sound in Karajan's Berlin Philharmonic versions. Unfortunately things come adrift in the development of the first movement where the wind and strings are out of step for quite a few bars. The *Fifth*, like the *Second*, is one of the finest of the series and has great breadth and nobility. Sir John draws playing of high quality from the orchestra, who are on top form throughout. The *Seventh* is also powerful. The finale is admirably broad and extremely imposing. The *Seventh* makes a fine culmination for the cycle, bringing a feeling of power and a sense of inevitability which increases as the work progresses. The build-up to its climax is well paced. The recording is very fine.

Barbirolli included the *Sixth Symphony* in the last concert he conducted in Manchester on 3 May 1970, and he recorded it three weeks later, only two months before he died. It is easy to sense an elegiac feeling in the performance, which remains most compelling, especially in the beautiful closing passage for the strings, given the benefit of radiant sound.

The shorter orchestral works were recorded at Abbey Road during the same period and the charismatic 1966 collection including *Finlandia*, the *Karelia Suite*, *Valse triste*, *Lemminkäinen's Return* and *Pohjola's Daughter* was for some years one of Barbirolli's most successful discs. The suite from *Pelléas et Mélisande* is powerfully atmospheric, as is *The Swan of Tuonela*, but here Sir John's rather endearing vocalizations are clearly audible. *Pohjola's Daughter* is very strongly characterized, as are the *Scènes historiques*. *Rakastava*, and especially the touching *Romance for Strings*, are much rarer, originally having a short catalogue life. They are very well played and recorded. Barbirolli had a special feeling for Sibelius's world and this shows through. All in all this is a cherishable box, attractively illustrated with some of the original LP sleeve pictures.

Simon Rattle's performances with the City of Birmingham Symphony Orchestra are available both as a four-CD boxed set and as individual discs. The best advice is probably to opt for the individual disc for the *Fourth* and *Sixth*, coupled together. They are both impressive, as is his *Seventh*, coupled with the *Fifth* and the highly atmospheric *Scene with Cranes*. As a set the box is worth considering, but it would not be first choice.

Sibelians should note that Collins's highly distinguished accounts of the symphonies (with the fill-ups) make a four-disc set in a slip-case at a saving on the price of the individual records.

Sir Alexander Gibson's Sibelius cycle is impressive, both musically and from an engineering point of view; there are no weak spots anywhere. (Indeed, one respected critic chose Gibson's version of No. 1 as his first choice on a BBC 'Record Review' some years ago.) At the same time it must be conceded that the peaks do not dwarf, say, the Maazel *Fourth* or *Seventh*. The performances are eminently sane, sound and reliable, and no one investing in the set is likely to be at all disappointed. Taken individually, none would be an absolute first choice.

The very first survey comes from 1952–3, conducted by Sixten Ehrling. Their handsome sleeves are reproduced here. (Incidentally, the original LPs speak of the 'Stockholm Radio Symphony Orchestra'.) Sibelius himself is said to have heard and liked them. Ehrling is an admirably sound interpreter. In the first two symphonies the playing has more temperament than polish. In the *Third*, Ehrling – giving the symphony its first recording since the pioneering Kajanus set – is more measured than Collins, who set very brisk tempi in both the first and second movements. The *Fourth* is impressively dark and in the *Fifth* the transition between the body of the first movement and its Scherzo section is well negotiated. Not a real challenge to Collins, but though it lacks finesse and has some vulnerable wind intonation, it provides an interesting insight into how these symphonies sounded at the time.

Berglund's survey is available not only as a complete set but also broken down into separate formats. Nos. 1–3 are offered together on two discs: 3984-23388-2; Nos. 4 and 6 on 0630 14951-2; and Nos. 5 and 7 on 0630 17278-2. They are the product of an enthusiastic collaboration with the Chamber Orchestra of Europe. Berglund knows this music as intimately as any one alive. He is offers the scores plain and unadorned. There are good things – namely, a sober and vigorous *Third* and a finely paced and sensitively moulded *Sixth* – as well as one or two ugly details such as the ungainly stress he gives to the rhetorical string passage in the first movement of the *Second* (1 hour 35 minutes, five bars before letter B). One has to decide whether these performances, good though they are, convey enough new insights to justify displacing his earlier cycles with the Bournemouth and Helsinki orchestras. Those earlier sets, though they have solid merits, fall short of the ideal in terms of poetic imagination. But the same goes for this new set. In some ways Berglund's very first, 1969 recording of the *Fourth Symphony*, issued in 1973, remains the freshest and most keenly felt of his Sibelius recordings!

The pair of Finlandia Ultima Doubles offers all seven symphonies in performances recorded while the Finnish Radio Symphony Orchestra was in St Petersburg during the summer of 1993. It was only three or four years earlier that Saraste recorded a complete cycle for RCA with the same orchestra. None of these performances seems to mark an advance on that studio set, though at times there is the excitement generated in the concert hall to spice up the music-making.

Although there are good things here, including a fine account of the *Fourth*, there is nothing really special and the *Third Symphony* is hopelessly rushed. However, the second of the two Ultima sets includes the *Kullervo Symphony*, which was the finest performance in the cycle. It has a more urgent sense of movement and a greater dramatic intensity than most of its major competitors, and it has excellent soloists. We hope this will become available separately later on Warner's bargain Apex label.

Symphonies Nos. 1–3; 5; Belshazzar's Feast (incidental music); Karelia Suite; Pohjola's Daughter; Tapiola.

(M) (***) Finlandia mono 4509 95882-2 (3). LSO, Kajanus.

When the Finnish government sponsored recordings of the first two symphonies in 1930, Sibelius insisted on having Kajanus as the most authentic interpreter. These performances were all made in 1930 and 1932 and sound amazingly good for the period. The celebrated storm in *Tapiola*, taken at a much slower and more effective tempo than is now usual, still has the power to terrify despite the inevitable sonic limitations, and no conductor has ever given a more spell-binding and atmospheric account of the suite from *Belshazzar's Feast*. The broader, more leisurely view Kajanus takes of the *Third Symphony* comes as a refreshing corrective to the later, more hurried accounts by Anthony Collins and Lorin Maazel. No performer, save Beecham and Karajan, came closer to Sibelius's intentions. Essential listening for all Sibelians.

Symphonies Nos. 1–4.

(B) *** EMI double fforte CZS5 68643-2 (2). Helsinki PO, Berglund.

This is a very impressive set and first-class value as an EMI Double fforte. Berglund's rugged, sober but powerful readings bring a good feeling for the architecture of the music and no want of atmosphere. Both the playing and the interpretation of the *First* are involving in their breadth and concentration (even if in the first movement the climactic timpani echo of the main theme does not come through). In the *Second*, Berglund is scrupulously faithful to the letter of the score as well as to its spirit, although the Scherzo and finale are of a lower voltage than in the finest versions. The Helsinki Philharmonic respond with no mean virtuosity and panache, but the last degree of intensity eludes them. In the *Third*, Berglund adopts sensible tempi throughout and shapes all three movements well; he evokes a haunting feeling of tranquillity in the withdrawn middle section of the slow movement, a passage where Sibelius seems to be listening to quiet voices from another planet. This was Berglund's third account of the *Fourth* and it is a performance of considerable stature: it has a stark grandeur that resonates in the mind. There is not a great deal of *vivace* in the second movement but Berglund's finale is superb, even if some may find the closing bars not sufficiently cold and bleak. The digital recording throughout the set is excellent.

Symphony No. 1; Finlandia; Karelia Suite.

⊛ *** EMI CDC7 542732. Oslo PO, Jansons.

Symphony No. 1 in E min.; The Oceanides.

(M) **(*) EMI CDM7 64119-2. CBSO, Rattle.

Mariss Jansons's account of the *First Symphony* is the finest to have appeared since Maazel's in the 1960s. The Oslo Philharmonic is on peak form, playing with thrilling virtuosity both in the *Symphony* and *Finlandia* and in the *Karelia Suite*. Tempi are well judged, the players are responsive to every dynamic nuance, phrasing is beautifully shaped and the overall architecture of the piece is splendidly realized. A very exciting performance, which has you on the edge of your seat, and very vividly recorded too.

If Simon Rattle's account of the whole symphony were as fine as that of the first movement, this would carry a strong recommendation. Rattle has a powerful grasp of both its structure and character. The slow movement is for the most part superb, but he makes too much of the commas at the end of the movement, which are so exaggerated as to be disruptive. The Scherzo has splendid character but is a good deal slower than the marking. *The Oceanides* has an atmosphere that is altogether ethereal. Simon Rattle has its measure and conveys all its mystery and poetry.

Symphonies Nos. 1 in E min.; 3 in C, Op. 52.

(***) Testament mono SBT 1049. Philh. O, Kletzki.

(BB) *** Naxos 8.554102. Iceland SO, Sakari.

Kletzki is tauter than the traditional Kajanus school yet far less headlong (or headstrong) than Collins. In both scores he and the Philharmonia Orchestra strike the right balance between the romantic legacy of the nineteenth century and the more severe climate of the twentieth. The recordings are beautifully balanced and have great warmth, and they come up splendidly in these transfers.

Petri Sakari proves a sound and straightforward interpreter. The playing of the Iceland orchestra in both symphonies is spirited and vital, even if they do not command the virtuosity and polish of the major international ensembles. The *Third Symphony* is very well paced indeed and the playing has conviction. The recording, too, is natural and vivid with a good balance between the various sections of the orchestra. In any event good value for money.

Symphonies Nos. 1; 4 in A min., Op. 63.

*** BIS BIS CD861. Lahti SO, Vänskä.

In the *First Symphony* the Finnish conductor, Vänskä, secures a marvellously controlled and splendidly executed performance from his dedicated players. There is that sense of inevitability and of an irresistible forward movement throughout, though never at the expense of incidental beauty. The Scherzo is among the most exciting on disc, very fast and full of controlled abandon. The *Fourth Symphony* receives a perceptive and deeply intelligent reading. The Lahti orchestra play with keen concentration and intensity and though tempi are very slow (perhaps too much so in the case of the slow movement), the performance is marvellously sustained. The recording is natural and eminently well balanced. A distinguished issue.

Symphonies Nos. 1; 5 in E flat, Op. 82.

(N) (BB) *** RCA 74321 68017-2. LSO, C. Davis.

Sir Colin Davis's coupling of Nos. 1 and 5 is an unbeatable bargain on RCA's new budget label. No. 1 has great intensity and virtuosity and the recording is first class. No. 5 is praised below.

(i) Symphonies Nos. 1 & 5; Pohjola's Daughter; (ii) En Saga; Finlandia; Karelia Suite; Legend: The Swan of Tuonela.

(N)(BB) **(*) Royal (ADD) DCL 706702 (2). (i) BBC SO;
(ii) VPO, Sargent.

On the whole, Sargent is here shown as a fine Sibelian. The two symphonies come from the late 1950s. The *First* is powerfully held together with a notably expressive slow movement. If there is more to the *Fifth Symphony* than Sargent finds, there is no doubt about the enjoyment to be had from his performance, especially in the *Andante mosso, quasi allegretto*, where the romantic warmth of the interpretation uncovers no mysteries but instils an attractive glow into the writing. The work's final climax has both nobility and dignity, but here, as in the first movement, one misses the underlying sense of conflict. The original coupling, *Pohjola's Daughter*, was one of the best things Sargent did for the gramophone. It is convincing in every way and, like the symphony, it is very well played by the BBC Orchestra. The stereo, too, is outstanding for its time, full bodied, with the brass resplendent.

The collection of shorter works is also very successful, and the original 1963 LP held its place in the catalogue for more than a decade. The Vienna Philharmonic Orchestra

brings a distinct freshness to the playing of music that must have been fairly unfamiliar to them, and Sir Malcolm imparts his usual confidence. The brass is splendidly full-blooded in *En Saga*, and *Finlandia* sounds unhackneyed. Tempi for *Karelia* are on the brisk side, but none the worse for that. The CD transfer is very good, and Sargent admirers will not want to be without this inexpensive set.

Symphonies Nos. 1 in E min.; 6 in D min..

(BB) *** Arte Nova 74321 49705-2. Gran Canaria PO, Leaper.

The orchestra of the Gran Canaria is fine in every department. The strings are opulent and the wind too are first class. Adrian Leaper is an *echt*-Sibelian with both a command of the overall architecture and a feeling for the atmosphere. The *Sixth Symphony* is gripping, not perhaps in the same league as the Karajan, Davis and Ashkenazy but not far off. Although the *First Symphony* is very good, it does not represent the same challenge to existing recommendations. All the same, the disc is worth having, for both performances are good and the *Sixth* is magnificent. Excellent recording quality.

Symphonies Nos. 1 in E min.; 7 in C, Op. 105.

🅒 (***) Beulah mono IPD 8. LSO, Collins.

There are those who (justly) count Anthony Collins's magnificent account of the *First Symphony* of 1952, with its haunting, other-worldly opening clarinet solo, as the finest ever put on disc, for the tension throughout the performance is held at the highest level. The closely integrated *Seventh* is also well understood by Collins, and once again the closing moments of the symphony are drawn together very impressively. The Decca recording remains remarkably vivid and, if the fortissimos are more one-dimensional than we expect today and the massed violins could ideally be fuller, the brass certainly makes a fine impact. The comparatively rare *Karelia Overture*, which was recorded later (1955), makes a brief bonus.

Symphony No. 2 in D, Op. 43.

(N) (M) *** Ph. (ADD) 464 682-2. Concg. O, Szell –
BEETHOVEN: *Symphony No. 5*. **(*).

(M) ** Mercury (ADD) [434 317-2]. Detroit SO, Paray –
DVORAK: *Symphony No. 9 (From the New World)*. ***

Symphony No. 2; Andante festivo; Kuolema: Valse triste; Legend: The Swan of Tuonela.

*** EMI CDC7 54804-2. Oslo PO, Jansons.

Symphony No. 2; Finlandia; Legends: Lemminkäinen's Return; The Swan of Tuonela; Pohjola's Daughter.

(BB) (**) Naxos 8.110810. NBC SO, Toscanini.

(i) Symphony No. 2; (ii) Karelia Suite.

(B) **(*) DG (ADD) 439 499-2. (i) BPO; (ii) Helsinki RSO;
Kamu.

Symphony No. 2; (i) Luonnotar; Pohjola's Daughter.

(M) ** Sony (ADD) SMK 61848. NYPO, Bernstein; with
(i) Curtin.

Symphony No. 2; Romance in C.

*** BIS CD 252. Gothenburg SO, Järvi.

Symphony No. 2 in D, Op. 43; The Tempest Suite No. 1, Op. 109/2.

(N) (BB) **(*) Naxos 8.554266. Iceland SO, Sakari.

If the Oslo Philharmonic account of the *Second Symphony* under Mariss Jansons lacks something of the high voltage that charged his reading of the *First Symphony*, it has no lack of excitement; it is superbly controlled and tautly held together, with no playing to the gallery in the finale. There is an aristocratic feel to it, and this extends to *The Swan* and the *Andante festivo*, which is distinguished by string playing of great intensity. Jansons whips *Valse triste* into something of a frenzy towards the climax, but elsewhere these performances are totally free from exaggeration. Excellent recording.

Järvi is very brisk in the opening *Allegretto*: this Gothenburg version has more sinew and fire than its rivals, and the orchestral playing is more responsive and disciplined than that of the SNO on Chandos (see below). Throughout, Järvi has an unerring sense of purpose and direction and the BIS performance is concentrated in feeling and thoroughly convincing. The *Romance for Strings* is attractively done.

Szell's reading is powerfully and classically conceived, tautly held together and superbly played. The 1964 recording has plenty of body and range. This deserves a place near the top of the list although the coupling, good though it is, is misconceived.

The Berlin Philharmonic give Kamu excellent support and rich sonority in his 1970 account of the *Second Symphony*. One or two minor exaggerations apart, he gives a straightforward and dedicated account of the work. The fill-up in the form of the *Karelia Suite* is expertly played by the Helsinki Radio Orchestra.

Petri Sakari's Sibelius is natural and unaffected in the *Second Symphony*. When Sibelius himself conducted it in 1916 we know he was brisker even than Kajanus, whose performance took a little over 39 minutes, six less than Sakari's. Sakari scores points with his fine musicianship and by not playing to the gallery, but his first movement really could have had a little more sense of thrust. Throughout the piece there is a certain want of the fire and the high voltage one needs in this most 'public' of the Sibelius symphonies. The recording is more recessed in the symphony than in the *The Tempest*, which has greater presence and a more forward balance. Sakari gets a splendidly concentrated atmosphere and has a special feeling for the other-worldly qualities of *The Oak Tree* and the *Berceuse*, which come off beautifully. This visionary score is brought to life most imaginatively, and Sakari's is as good an account as any among recent recordings.

In December 1940, at the time of the Russian invasion of Finland, Toscanini conducted these Sibelius performances, tautly controlled but emotional too, reflecting corporate feelings of the time. The first movement of the symphony is unusually fast, a true allegro, and speeds are never leisurely, yet more than was usual for him. Toscanini allows expressive freedom to his orchestral soloists, notably the cor anglais in the *Swan of Tuonela*. Dry, limited sound, transferred better than with some in this series.

Paray's account has plenty of tension – indeed one is immediately gripped by the excitement of the opening movement. The *Andante*, however, does not bring enough contrast and its histrionics seem episodic. The Scherzo has great energy and the finale develops a full head of steam, but overall, in spite of excellent early (1959) Mercury stereo, this reading with its impulsiveness fails to create the feeling of an organic whole.

There is no lack of spirit or warmth in Bernstein's version of the *Second Symphony*, which offers some exciting and committed playing from the NYPO. There are some mannered touches in the slow movement and finale, but on the whole this performance has a spontaneity and virtuosity that are impressive. *Luonnotar* is not as successful: it is rather insensitively played and sung and lacks mystery, though *Pohjola's Daughter* finds the conductor back on form in this strong, well-proportioned reading. The recordings, dating from the mid-1960s, are acceptable, but there are many more positive recommendations.

Symphonies Nos. 2; 3 in C, Op. 52.

(M) *** EMI (ADD) CDM7 64120-2. CBSO, Rattle.

**(*) BIS CD 862. Lahti SO, Vänskä.

In No. 2 the CBSO play with fervour and enthusiasm except, perhaps, in the first movement where the voltage is lower – particularly in the development, which is not easy to bring off; however, the transition to the finale is magnificent and Rattle finds the *tempo giusto* in this movement. The Birmingham strings produce a splendidly fervent unison both here and elsewhere. Rattle's account of the *Third* is vastly superior to his *First* and *Second* and the way in which he builds up the finale is masterly and sure of instinct. The recording, made in the Warwick Arts Centre, sounds very well balanced, natural in perspective and finely detailed.

Osmo Vänskä's accounts of the *Second* and *Third Symphonies* are as thought-provoking as his remarkable pairing of Nos. 1 and 4, though they are not quite deserving of the same star-rating. The dynamic markings are sometimes a little too extreme, the second theme of the slow movement marked pianopianissimo is almost whispered rather than played, and to readers playing the disc at less than full-room volume, it will be barely audible. It is just a shade self-conscious. Everything is carefully thought out, and the general effect is impressive. The *Third Symphony* is generally well paced and has the right atmosphere. Those following the series will not be disappointed. Very wide-ranging but expertly balanced sound.

Symphonies Nos. 2; 5 in E flat, Op. 82.

(M) *** Chan. (ADD) 6556. SNO, Gibson.

(N) (BB) * Warner Apex. 8573 88434-2. Finnish RSO, Saraste.

The *Second* is among the best of Gibson's cycle and scores highly, thanks to the impressive clarity, fullness and impact of the 1982 digital recording. Gibson's reading is honest and straightforward, free of bombast in the finale. Tempi are well judged: the first movement is neither too taut nor too relaxed: it is well shaped and feels right. Overall this is most satisfying, as is the *Fifth*, which has similar virtues: at no time is there any attempt to interpose the personality of the interpreter, and the finale has genuine weight and power.

Saraste's performances are well played and acceptably

recorded, but considering these were concert performances there is a remarkable absence of real grip and forward thrust here.

Symphonies Nos. 2; 6 in D min., Op. 104.

*** RCA 09026 68218-2. LSO, Davis.

(***) Beulah mono 2PD 8. LSO, Collins.

The *Sixth* is a work for which Colin Davis has always shown a special affinity and understanding. Sir Colin's earlier recording with the Boston orchestra (see above) was one of the best in that magisterial cycle, and this newcomer is if anything even finer. There is 'nothing of the circus' (to quote the composer's own words *à propos* the *Fourth Symphony*) in his reading of the *Second*, and no playing to the gallery. There is a grandeur and a natural distinction about the playing.

The Decca sound in Collins's 1953 recording of the *Second Symphony* is fuller than in the *First Symphony*. The performance is superb, held together with a tension that carries the listener through from the first bar to the last. The closing pages of the finale, with the timpani again making a telling contribution, are particularly satisfying. The *Sixth* was recorded in 1955, and again the ear notices a further improvement in the sound, particularly at the radiant pastoral opening. The LSO play with much sensitivity, and woodwind and string detail is ever luminous; the conductor's special feeling for Sibelian colour and atmosphere is especially apparent in this work, with the beautiful final coda sustained with moving simplicity. Altogether a lovely performance.

Symphonies Nos. 2; 7 in C, Op. 105.

(B) *** Sony (ADD) SBK 53509. Phd. O, Ormandy.

Ormandy was not so much underrated as taken for granted in an age which had the good fortune to have so many great conductors. The 1957 sound is far better than you might expect and the strings (and practically every other department) are much more sumptuous and responsive than they seem to be in Philadelphia nowadays. The *Second* gets a powerful (and, in the finale, rousing) performance, and the architecture is held together well throughout. The *Seventh*, recorded in 1960, is very impressive indeed: marvellously paced, intense and felt.

Symphony No. 3; King Kristian II (suite).

*** BIS CD 228. Gothenburg SO, Järvi.

Symphony No. 3; Night Ride and Sunrise; Pelléas et Mélisande: Suite; Pohjola's Daughter.

(***) Beulah mono 3PD8. LSO, Collins.

With the *Third Symphony* there is a sense of the epic in Järvi's hands and it can hold its own with any in the catalogue. In Gothenburg, the slow movement is first class and the leisurely tempo adopted here by the Estonian conductor is just right. Järvi's coupling is the incidental music to *King Khristian II*. This is very beautifully played and recorded.

More outstanding performances from Anthony Collins: only *Night Ride and Sunrise*, although dramatically effective, is slightly less memorable than the other works here. The other reservation concerns the tempo for the second move-

ment of the symphony. Some listeners find it too fast, but the playing has much delicacy of feeling and texture; Collins's approach matches the whole reading, which has a strong momentum overall, and the build-up of tension to the work's climax is satisfyingly controlled. The account of *Pohjola's Daughter* is imaginative and colourful, and the excerpts from the incidental music to *Pelléas et Mélisande* are beautifully played. All the recordings, except *Night Ride* (1955), were made in the Kingsway Hall in 1954 and absolutely no apologies need be made for the mono sound, which in this admirable CD transfer is remarkable for its vivid immediacy and fullness.

Symphonies Nos. 3; 5 in E flat, Op. 82.

*** RCA 09026 61963-2. LSO, Davis.

*** EMI CDC5 55533-2. Oslo PO, Jansons.

Sir Colin Davis's account of the *Third Symphony* has a majesty and power that have few rivals. His *Fifth*, too, has tremendous grandeur as well as a feeling for the natural symphonic current that flows in these wonderful works. The recording has a splendour worthy of the music and the players. Both performances (and especially the *Fifth*) offer a marked advance on Davis's earlier, Boston versions – see above.

Mariss Jansons and the Oslo Philharmonic challenge Colin Davis and the London Symphony Orchestra on exactly the same ground. The Oslo orchestra can certainly hold its own with the LSO in terms of beauty and weight of sonority. Their *Third* is wonderfully lithe and virile, though Sir Colin's broader tempo is perhaps better judged. But everything is marvellously alive and youthful. The *Fifth* is impressive, too, though the transition into the Scherzo section of the first movement may strike some listeners as a shade precipitate. However, this has been deleted just at the time of going to press.

Symphonies Nos. 3; 6 in D min.; 7 in C.

(M) *** Chan. (ADD) 6557. SNO, Gibson.

With three symphonies offered, some 74 minutes overall, this is a fine bargain and an excellent way to experience Gibson's special feeling for this composer. The SNO is in very good form. The first movement of the *Third* has real momentum. The *Andantino* is fast, faster than the composer's marking. Such a tempo, while it gives the music-making fine thrust, means that Gibson, like Collins before him, loses some of the fantasy of this enigmatic movement. But there is more here to admire than to cavil at. The *Sixth* is impressive too, with plenty of atmosphere and some radiant playing from the Scottish violin section; the *Seventh* has a rather relaxed feeling throughout, but it does not lack warmth and, as in No. 1, Gibson draws the threads together at the close with satisfying breadth.

Symphonies Nos. 4 in A min.; 5 in E flat.

(***) Beulah mono 4PD 8. LSO, Collins.

(BB) *** Naxos 8.554377. Iceland SO, Sakari.

Collins's opening to the *Fourth Symphony* with its desolate, Nordic atmosphere is remarkably restrained, yet the work as a whole has extraordinary underlying intensity. With

Collins, every phrase breathes naturally and the lightening of mood in the Scherzo, with wind and string playing of great delicacy, is merely an interlude, before the powerfully sombre feeling of the *Il tempo largo* gives birth to a climax of compulsive power. In the finale the flux of mood and feeling that comes with its surge of animation is handled with great subtlety. The performance of the *Fifth Symphony* carries all before it, with the reading moving forward in a single sweep. In both symphonies the LSO is marvellously responsive. The 1954/5 Kingsway Hall mono recordings were among the finest in terms of balance and truthfulness that Decca made throughout the mono LP era, and this CD reproduces superbly.

Had one heard either of Sakari's performances in the concert hall, one would have left feeling very satisfied. Both grip the listener. They are straightforward and unaffected, dedicated and selfless, and free from interpretative point-making. Tempi are for the most part uncommonly well judged, and you feel that Sakari really sees the works as a whole, rather than as a sequence of wonderful episodes. The first movement of the *Fifth* has splendid breadth, and the transition into the Scherzo section is expertly handled. The Iceland orchestra may not be in the luxury league but their responses are keen and alert, and the performances have much greater inner life than, say, Paavo Berglund's set on EMI. Moreover the sound is truthfully balanced and well detailed.

Symphonies Nos. 4–7; Legend: The Swan of Tuonela; Tapiola.

(M) *** DG (ADD) 457 748-2 (2). BPO, Karajan.

This set is a convenient way of collecting Karajan's splendid DG performances of Sibelius's last four symphonies, including his outstanding version of the *Fourth*. All but the *Sixth* are available separately in other formats (see below) and his glorious 1967 account of the latter remains almost unsurpassed by more recent accounts. So with a brooding *Swan of Tuonela* and a thrilling *Tapiola* thrown in for good measure, this can be strongly recommended.

Symphonies Nos. 4–5; Finlandia.

(M) (***) EMI mono CDM5 66600-2. Philh. O, Karajan

Symphonies Nos. 6–7; Tapiola.

(M) (***) EMI mono CDM5 66602-2. Philh. O, Karajan.

These mono performances with Karajan and the Philharmonia Orchestra are of special interest. Walter Legge showed Sibelius's tempo and other suggestions to Karajan before he made his 1954 recording of the *Fourth Symphony*. After hearing it, Sibelius drafted a telegram speaking of Karajan's 'deep insights and great artistic grip' and went so far as to tell Legge that 'Karajan is the only one who really understands my music.' Certainly these performances are of stature and carry the composer's imprimatur. The *Fourth* was always a favourite of Karajan's, and in some ways this is even finer than the subsequent Berlin accounts – the sound is leaner and more spare and conveys the sense of desolation at the core of its bleak, wintry terrain.

The *Fifth*, recorded in 1952, has not been issued on CD before, but its breadth and majesty are difficult to surpass.

It does not quite match the achievement of the third and greatest of his four recordings, but it is a superbly realized and impressive reading. The *Sixth* and *Seventh* are hardly less fine, even if the latter concentrates more on the seamlessness of the structure than its power. As with the *Fourth Symphony*, Karajan recorded *Tapiola* no fewer than four times – and this is a dark, chilling version to rank with the best.

Symphonies Nos. 4 in A min.; 6 in D min.

(M) *** EMI (ADD) CDM7 64121-2. CBSO, Rattle.

Simon Rattle's account of the *Fourth* invokes a powerful atmosphere in its opening pages: one is completely transported to its dark landscape with its seemingly limitless horizons. The string-tone is splendidly lean without being undernourished and achieves a sinisterly whispering pianissimo in the development. The slow movement is magical and the finale is hardly less masterly. Rattle's account of the *Sixth* is almost equally fine. It is still a *Sixth* to reckon with and its closing bars are memorably eloquent.

Symphonies Nos. (i) 4; (ii) 6; (i) The Bard; Lemminkäinen's Return; The Tempest: Prelude.

✹ (M) (***) EMI mono CDM7 64027-2. (i) LPO, (ii) RPO, Beecham.

In its colour Beecham's account of the *Fourth Symphony* reflects his feeling that, far from being an austere work, as is often claimed, it is ripely romantic. No performance brings one closer to the music, while the recording, made over fifty years ago, sounds astonishingly fresh and bleak in this excellent transfer, and there is a concentration, darkness and poetry that few rivalled. In the three shorter works on the disc Beecham's rhythmic sharpness and feeling for colour vividly convey the high voltage of Sibelius's strikingly original writing. *Lemminkäinen's Homeward Journey* is positively electrifying, while the *Prelude* to *The Tempest* is every bit as awesome an evocation of a storm as we had remembered. Unfortunately, this is another of EMI's current deletions.

Symphonies Nos. 4; 7; Kuolema: Valse triste.

✹ (M) *** DG (ADD) 39 527-2. BPO, Karajan.

Karajan's celebrated 1965 account of the *Fourth Symphony* wears well. For many it remains the finest version of the *Fourth* on record. The plush sonority of the Berlin Philharmonic at first deceives one into thinking that Karajan has beautified the symphony's landscape, but he comes closer to the spirit of the score than most others. It is a performance of great concentration, deep thought and feeling. Although the new DG transfer of the recording does not have quite the body of violin-tone of the finest digital recordings, the acoustics of the Jesus-Christus-Kirche give weight and depth and a fine resonance to the bass. The performance is undoubtedly a great one. The *Seventh Symphony* is perhaps less successful though it comes off better than in Karajan's Philharmonia version, and the *Valse triste* is seductive. An indispensable record.

**Symphonies Nos. 4; 7; Pelléas et Mélisande Suite;
Swanwhite; Tapiola; The Tempest (incidental music):
Dance of the Nymphs.**

(***) BBC mono BBCL 4041-2 (2). RPO, Beecham (with British
and Finnish National anthems, and speeches by Beecham
including Beecham on Sibelius).

Beecham never re-recorded the *Fourth Symphony* commercially after his 1938 recording but, judging from this 1955 performance, his basic approach remained little changed. He also never recorded the *Swanwhite* suite. Here he omits only *The Prince Alone*. He did make stereo versions of the *Pelléas et Mélisande* music (without the brief *By the Seashore* movement) and *Tapiola* a few days on either side of the birthday concert. He also recorded the *Seventh* commercially at the same time but this performance comes from a Royal Albert Hall concert of the previous year and is slightly higher in voltage than his Abbey Road recording. There is a tremendous sense of occasion here, which is supplemented by his famous talk describing his long friendship with Sibelius and recounting his hilarious visit to his home the previous year.

Symphonies Nos. 5–7; Finlandia; The Oceanides; Tapiola.

(B) **(*) EMI Double fforte CZS5 68646-2 (2). Helsinki PO,
Berglund.

This double fforte completes Berglund's Sibelius cycle. Nos. 1–4 are on a companion reissue (see above). Sober, straightforward, powerful readings which maintain the high standards of performance and recording that have consistently distinguished Berglund's EMI Sibelius records. There is a good feeling for the architecture of this music and no want of atmosphere. In the *Fifth Symphony*, the development section of the first movement has a mystery that eluded Berglund first time around, and there is splendid power in the closing pages of the finale. The *Sixth* is particularly fine, though the Scherzo may strike some listeners as too measured. The *Seventh* has real nobility and breadth, and Berglund has the full measure of all the shifting changes of mood and colour. Moreover the Helsinki orchestra play magnificently and seem to have a total rapport with him. Berglund's account of *The Oceanides* is splendidly atmospheric and can be put alongside Rattle's, which is praise indeed! The recording is well detailed and truthful, and the perspective natural. *Tapiola* is given its impact by a spacious ruggedness, and the very close of the work has a moving intensity. All the same, despite the very good recorded sound and the economical price and packaging, these cannot be recommended in preference to the earlier Colin Davis set with the Boston Symphony, which is similarly priced and packaged on a pair of Philips Duos (see above).

Symphony No. 5 (1915 version); En Saga (1892 version).

*** BIS CD 800. Lahti SO, Vänskä.

Symphony No. 5 (1915 version & definitive 1919 version).

*** BIS CD 863. Lahti SO, Vänskä.

Not long after Sibelius's death, the orchestral material for the first version of the *Fifth Symphony* was discovered in the attic at Ainola. To reconstruct the actual score was a simple matter. It offers an invaluable insight into the workings of the creative process and is testimony to Sibelius's refusal to rest content until he had fully realized his vision. The work is in four (not three) movements, the opening horn-call is yet to be discovered; and there are no final hammer-blow chords. But there is much else that is different, and to study these differences offers an endless source of fascination. The *En Saga* we know comes from 1901, when it was extensively revised for Busoni to conduct in Berlin. There are some Brucknerian touches in one or two places, and the orchestration is less expert. Totally dedicated performances. An essential disc for all Sibelians, and magnificently recorded into the bargain.

BIS have also recoupled the original 1915 four-movement version of the *Fifth Symphony* with the definitive 1919 version, as part of their ongoing cycle from Osmo Vänskä and the Lahti orchestra. Vänskä has a great feeling for the general architecture of the piece and paces it superbly. Our only reservation is his penchant for extreme pianissimos – the development section in the finale drops beyond a whisper to virtual inaudibility.

Symphony No. 5 in E flat, Op. 82.

(M) *** EMI (ADD) CDM7 64737-2. Philh. O, Rattle –
NIELSEN: *Symphony No. 4 etc.* ***

**Symphony No. 5; En Saga; Finlandia; Kuolema: Valse
triste. Pohjola's Daughter.**

(M) ** Sony (ADD) SMK 66234. Philh. O, Swedish RO, or
LAPO, Salonen.

**Symphony No. 5; Finlandia; Kuolema: Valse triste.
Tapiola, Op. 112.**

(B) *** DG (ADD) 439 418-2. BPO, Karajan.

Symphonies Nos. 5; 6; Legend: The Swan of Tuonela.

(M) *** DG 439 982-2. BPO, Karajan.

Such is the excellence of the classic Karajan DG *Fifth* that few listeners would guess its age. It is a great performance, and this 1964 version is indisputably the finest of the four he made. The fillers are familiar performances, also from the mid-1960s. *Tapiola* is a performance of great intensity and offers superlative playing; *Finlandia* is also one of the finest accounts available, but *Valse triste* is played very slowly and in a somewhat mannered fashion.

The new mid-priced reissue is obviously even more attractive, coupled with his glorious 1967 account of the *Sixth*, which remains almost unsurpassed by more recent accounts. The brooding *Swan of Tuonela* is placed between the two symphonies and is played just as admirably by the Berlin Philharmonic on their finest form.

Simon Rattle's account of the *Fifth Symphony* with the Philharmonia was to the 1980s what Karajan's Berlin account was to the 1960s. Everything about it feels right: the control of pace and texture and the balance of energy and repose. The development of the first movement has a compelling sense of mystery and the transition to the Scherzo section is beautifully judged. The Philharmonia Orchestra play splendidly and the EMI recording is very good indeed.

Salonen's is an exceptionally spacious account of the *Fifth Symphony* and although there is much beauty of detail, even grandeur, the tension needs to be held in a tighter grip if such a broad approach is to succeed. In spite of fine playing from the Philharmonia Orchestra, the transition to the Scherzo section is not very deftly managed. On the other hand, the breadth of the reading works really well in the finale, which has genuine nobility. The account of *Pohjola's Daughter* certainly does not lack excitement, and the other items (added for this reissue) are well enough done too. But overall, in spite of the fine recording, this cannot be placed among the most commanding versions of the symphony on CD.

Symphonies Nos. 5; 7 in C, Op. 105.

(N) (M) **(*) Ph. (ADD) 464 740-2. Boston SO, Davis.

Symphonies Nos. 5; 7; Kuolema: Scene with Cranes. Night Ride and Sunrise.

(M) *** EMI (ADD) CDM7 64122-2. CBSO, Rattle.

What is particularly impressive in Rattle's account of the *Fifth Symphony* is the control of the transition between the first section and the Scherzo element of the first movement. There is a splendid sense of atmosphere in the development and a power unmatched in recent versions, save for the Karajan. The playing is superb, with recording to match. The *Seventh* is hardly less powerful and impressive: its opening is slow to unfold and has real vision. With the addition of an imaginative and poetic account of the *Scene with Cranes* from the incidental music to *Kuolema*, this is the finest single disc in Rattle's Birmingham cycle.

This was a curious choice from Sir Colin Davis's earlier Boston cycle to be included among Philips's '50 Great Recordings'. The *Fifth* is a little lacking in atmosphere and is no match either as a performance or recording for Davis's later LSO version for RCA. The *Seventh* is idiomatic and unfussy, but not a 'great recording'. The remastered sound is good, but still seems rather two-dimensional.

Symphonies No. 6; 7; Tapiola.

*** BIS CD 864. Lahti SO, Vänskä.

Symphony Nos. 6–7; The Tempest: Suite No. 2, Op. 109/3.

(N) (BB) *** Naxos 8.554387. Iceland SO, Sakari.

Osmo Vänskä's account of the *Sixth* and *Seventh Symphonies* brings his cycle to a fitting climax. The *Sixth* is serene yet taut, and the *Seventh* particularly fine both in pacing and character. Vänskä's reading of *Tapiola* has a thrilling intensity and if it is not the equal of Karajan or Beecham, it is certainly among the very best of the others. The Lahti orchestra always plays with enthusiasm and fire, and the BIS recording is first class.

Petri Sakari's accounts of the *Sixth* and *Seventh* symphonies re-affirm his strong Sibelian credentials. Indeed this Icelandic Sibelius cycle is admirably straightforward and unaffected. The *Sixth Symphony* is the best we have had since Vänskä: it is thoughtful, well prepared and dedicated, and even if the Iceland Orchestra is not in the same league as the Vienna Philharmonic or the Concertgebouw, they are a very good ensemble. The *Seventh* is powerful and has breadth and majesty; not the equal of Maazel or Colin Davis, perhaps, but eminently satisfying all the same. The second

suite from *The Tempest* is magnificent (the *Chorus of the Winds* sounds quite magical) and full of mystery and atmosphere. This is Sakari's finest Sibelius disc yet, and the well-balanced sound does credit to all concerned.

Symphony No. 7 in C, Op. 150.

(N) **(*) BBC (ADD) BBCL 4039-2. PO, Boult – BIZET: *Jeux d'enfants;* RAVEL: *Daphnis et Chloé: Suite No. 2.* SCHUBERT: *Symphony No. 8 (Unfinished).* **(*)

Symphony No. 7 in C; Canzonetta, Op. 62a; Kuolema: Valse triste; Scene with Cranes; Night Ride and Sunrise; Valse romantique, Op. 62b.

*** BIS CD 311. Gothenburg SO, Järvi.

Neeme Järvi and the Gothenburg orchestra bring great energy and concentration to the *Seventh Symphony*. The only disappointment is the final climax, which is perhaps less intense than the best versions. However, it is a fine performance, and the music to *Kuolema* is splendidly atmospheric; *Night Ride* is strongly characterized. The recording exhibits the usual characteristics of the Gothenburg Concert Hall and has plenty of body and presence.

Anyone who remembers Sir Adrian's set of the Sibelius tone poems on Pye Records from the 1950s or his broadcasts from the 1940s and 1950s will have high expectations of his *Seventh Symphony* and will not be disappointed. It is finely shaped and superbly paced. A Festival Hall performance from 1963, it is well worth rescuing from oblivion. Good sound too.

The Wood Nymph (tone-poem), Op. 15; (i) The Wood Nymph (melodrama) (1895); A Lonely Ski-trail; Swanwhite, Op. 54.

*** BIS CD 815. (i) Pöysti; Lahti SO, Vänskä.

Sibelius composed *The Wood Nymph* in 1894–5 when the four *Lemminkäinen Legends* were taking shape in his mind. It is a reworking of the melodrama written for two horns, piano and strings to accompany the recitation of verses by the mainland Swedish poet, Viktor Rydberg. It is stirring stuff and begins with echoes of the *Karelia* music and in places comes close to both the first of the *Legends* and *Lemminkäinen's Homeward Journey*. It improves with every hearing: its main ideas haunt the listener and are difficult to dislodge from the brain! *A Lonely Ski-trail* is slight, but *The Wood Nymph* melodrama is imaginative and highly unusual. The original music to *Swanwhite* has some poetic ideas that did not find their way into the suite, though for the most part there is not a great deal that is unfamiliar. Superb playing from the Lahti orchestra under Osmo Vänskä, and spacious, impeccably balanced recording.

CHAMBER MUSIC

(i) *Adagio in D min.;* (ii, iii) *Duo in C for Violin & Viola;* (i) *Fugue for Martin Wegelius;* (iii, iv, v) *Piano Trio in C (Lovisa);* (vi, vii) *Suite in E for Violin & Piano;* (iii, iv) *Water Drops for Violin & Cello.*

*** Ondine ODE 850-2. (i) Sibelius Qt; (ii) Hirvikangas;

(iii) Kimangen; (iv) Arai; (v) Lagerspetz; (vi) Kuusisto; (vii) Kerppo.

These are all slight pieces from Sibelius's youth and student years: *Water Drops* was written when he was ten and is of no artistic interest. The *Fugue* for his teacher, *Martin Wegelius* of 1888 was originally intended as the finale for his *A minor Quartet*, just as the *Adagio in D minor* (1890) was probably to have formed part of the *B flat Quartet*, Op. 4. This is the most individual of the pieces on this well-played and well-recorded set. With the exception of the *Lovisa Trio* of 1888, these are all first recordings.

Music for violin and piano

Adagio in D min.; Allegretto in C; 2 Pieces; 3 Pieces; Sonata Exposition: Allegro in A min.; Grave (Fragment) in D min.; Largamente (Fragments) in E min.; in D min.; Sonata in F; Suite in E; Tempo di valse in A. Music for solo violin: Allegretto in A; Etude in D; A Happy Musician; Romance in G.

(N) *** BIS CD 1023. Kuusisto, Gräsbeck.

This is the companion disc to BIS's complete youthful production for violin and piano (see below) and covers the years 1885–9 when Sibelius was in his early 20s. Always sensitive about his early music, Sibelius (except for one occasion) forbade both the performance and publication of such works as the *String Quartet, Op. 4* and the *Kullervo Symphony*. All the material recorded here is completely new. None has been performed publicly or recorded until these artists played them in 1999. We have known about them solely from John Rosas's pioneering study from the early 1960s and the first volume of Erik Tawaststjerna's biography, but most of Sibelius's unpublished juvenilia is a closed book. The *A minor Sonata* has echoes of early Beethoven and comes from his school years; the *Suite in D minor* (1887–8) shows that his writing for the violin was naturally fluent and idiomatic even then. It seems that the composer was sufficiently taken with it to show it to his first biographer, Erik Furujhelm. The performances here are expert and accomplished in every way. Good, well-balanced recorded sound.

Andante grazioso in D major (1884–5); *5 Pieces* (1886–7); *Violin Sonata in A minor* (1884); *Sonata Movement* (1885); *Sonata Fragment in B minor* (1887); *Suite in D minor* (1887–8); *Various short movements and fragments.*

*** BIS CD 1022. Kuusisto, Gräsbeck.

This disc collects some of Sibelius's youthful output for violin and piano, and covers the years 1884–8, from his school years through to his time at Helsinki. The violin was his chosen instrument and his writing for it is totally idiomatic with a natural fluency. None of the music has been heard before. The *A minor Sonata* of 1884, from his school years, is redolent of the early Beethoven sonatas: it is highly accomplished but totally derivative. There are a number of short movements, some mere fragments, and not all of them are worth committing to disc. The *Suite in D minor* (1887–8) is another matter and shows just how good his writing for the instrument was. Very good playing from

Jaakko Kuusisto and Folke Gräsbeck, as well as good and scholarly sleeve notes from the latter. Excellent sound.

5 Danses champêtres, Op. 106; Novellette, Op. 102; 5 Pieces, Op. 81; 4 Pieces, Op. 115; 3 Pieces, Op. 116.

*** BIS CD 625. Sparf, Forsberg.

Many of the items here, such as the delightful *Rondino* from Op. 81, are little more than salon music, but some of the others are rewarding pieces. Indeed the first of the *Danses champêtres* almost suggests the music to *The Tempest*, written at much the same time. Both the Opp. 115 and 116 pieces contain music of quality. As in the companion disc, Nils-Erik Sparf and Bengt Forsberg prove as imaginative as they are accomplished.

2 Pieces, Op. 2 (2 versions); Scaramouche: Scène d'amour. 2 Serious melodies, Op. 77; 4 Pieces, Op. 78; 6 Pieces, Op. 79; Sonatina in E, Op. 80.

*** BIS CD 525. Sparf, Forsberg.

This CD offers the first recording of the 1888 versions of the *Grave* and the *Perpetuum mobile*, the two pieces which Sibelius assigned to Opus 2, together with the 1911 versions, in which the former was revised as *Romance in B minor* and the latter overhauled as *Epilogue*. The former bears a certain affinity to the slow movement of the *Violin Concerto* and the prevalence of the tritone in the latter acts as a reminder that it was reworked in the wake of the *Fourth Symphony*. Exemplary performances of the later pieces, including *Laetare anima mea* and the 1915 *Sonatina, Op. 80*.

(i) *Piano Quartet in C min.* (for piano, two violins and cello); (ii) *String Trio in G min.; Suite in A for String Trio;* (iii) *Violin Sonata in F.*

*** Ondine ODE 826-2. (i) Novikov, Quarta, Miori, Rousi; (ii) Söderblom, Angervo, Gustafsson; (iii) Kovacic, Lagerspetz.

These are all early and uncharacteristic works. The *Violin Sonata in F major* (1889) shows Sibelius still under the spell of Grieg. Only three movements of the *Suite in A major* for string trio (1888) survive (these artists give us what remains of the fourth movement, a *Gigue*); and its companion, the *String Trio in G minor*, is also unfinished. Only the *Lento* survives intact, though the disc also gives a realization of what remains of the sketches of two other movements. The *Quartet in C minor* for piano, two violins and cello is a set of variations from the composer's Vienna year, 1891. All this is largely uncharacteristic and, save for the opening of the *A major Suite*, offers few glimpses of the mature Sibelius. The performances are dedicated and beautifully recorded.

(i) *Piano Quintet in G min.; Piano Trio in C (Lovisa); String Quartet in E flat.*

*** Finlandia 4509 95858-2. Sibelius Ac. Qt, (i) with Tawaststjerna.

(i) *Piano Quintet in G min.; String Quartet in D min. (Voces intimae), Op. 56.*

*** Chan. 8742. (i) Goldstone; Gabrieli Qt.

The *Piano Quintet* is a long and far from characteristic piece in five movements. Anthony Goldstone and the Gabrielis reverse the order of the second and third movements so as to maximize contrast. The first movement is probably the finest and Anthony Goldstone, an impressive player by any standards, makes the most of Sibelius's piano writing to produce a very committed performance. The *Voces intimae Quartet* is given a reflective, intelligent reading, perhaps at times wanting in momentum but finely shaped. Good recording.

The early *Quartet in E flat* is Haydnesque and insignificant, and the *Lovisa Trio*, so called because it was written in that small town in the summer of 1888, offers only sporadic glimpses of things to come. The *Piano Quintet* is given a fine performance on Finlandia, and there is little to choose between it and the more expansive Goldstone/Gabrieli account on Chandos.

String Quartets: in E flat (1885); A min. (1889); B flat, Op. 4 (1890); D min. (Voces intimae), Op. 56.

(M) *** Finlandia Dig./ADD 4509 95851-2 (2). Sibelius Ac. Qt.

The *A minor Quartet* proves a delightful surprise with something of the freshness of Dvořák and Schubert. Sibelius obviously had ambivalent feelings towards the *B flat Quartet* and discouraged its performance. Its second movement bears a slight resemblance to a theme from *Rakastava*. Both are well worth resurrecting even if they do not, of course, match the mature *Voces intimae Quartet* in artistry. The playing of the Sibelius Academy Quartet is exemplary and the recordings good: three are digital; *Voces intimae* dates from 1980 and is analogue.

String Quartet in D min. (Voces intimae), Op. 56.

(BB) *** Finlandia 09027 40601-2. New Helsinki Qt – GRIEG: Quartet in G min., Op. 56. ***
(***) Biddulph mono LAB 098. Budapest Qt – GRIEG: Quartet; WOLF: *Italian Serenade*. (***)

The most recent recording comes from the New Helsinki Quartet who couple *Voces intimae* with the Grieg *Quartet in G minor*. The performance is finely shaped and vital, yet full of sensitivity. It would be a very satisfying first recommendation among modern recordings, assuming price is no consideration. Apart from the excellence of the playing, the recording is also very present and well detailed.

A welcome transfer – the first on CD – of the 1933 pioneering *Voces intimae*, still unbeaten. It briefly appeared on LP (on the World Record label) and is newly (and well) transferred here by Ward Marston. Sibelians will need no reminders of its excellence – and the same goes for the couplings.

PIANO MUSIC

Andante in E flat; Aubade in A flat; Au crépuscule; A Catalogue of Themes; 50 Short Pieces; Con moto, sempre una corda; 3 Pieces; Scherzo in E & Trio in E min.; 3 Short Pieces; 5 Short Pieces; Trio in E min. (arr. for piano); Trånaden (Yearning); 11 Variations on a Harmonic Formula.

(N) *** BIS CD 1067. Gräsbeck.

As part of its ambitious scheme to record every note that Sibelius ever wrote, BIS has turned its attention to the early piano pieces Sibelius composed in his study years. They re-affirm how great were the strides he had taken by the time of the *B flat Quartet, Op. 4* and the *Kullervo Symphony*. All these are unpublished and give no hint of what was to come. Perhaps the most imaginative is *Trånaden* to accompany a recitation of Stagnelius's poem. Folke Gräsbeck plays very well, and the recording is natural and lifelike.

Autrefois, Op. 96b; 5 Esquisses, Op. 114; Finlandia, Op. 26; 8 Pieces, Op. 99; 5 Pieces, Op. 101; 5 Pieces, Op. 103; Valse chevaleresque, Op. 96c; Valse lyrique, Op. 96a.

*** Olympia OCD 635. Servadei.

6 Bagatelles, Op. 97; Melody for the Bells of Berghäll Church, Op. 65b; 5 Pieces, Op. 75; 13 Pieces, Op. 76; 5 Pieces, Op. 85; 6 Pieces, Op. 94.

*** Olympia OCD 634. Servadei.

10 Bagatelles, Op. 34; 6 Impromptus, Op. 5; 10 Pieces, Op. 24.

*** Olympia OCD 631. Servadei.

6 Finnish Folksongs; Kavaljeren; Mandolinato; Morceau romantique; Pensées lyriques, Op. 40; 10 Pieces, Op. 58; Spagnuolo; Till trånaden; Valse triste, Op. 44/1.

*** Olympia OCD 632. Servadei.

Kyllikki, Op. 41; 4 Lyric Pieces, Op. 74; 2 Rondinos, Op. 68; Sonata in F, Op. 12; Sonatinas Nos. 1 in F sharp min.; 2 in E; 3 in B flat min., Op. 67/1–3.

*** Olympia OCD 633. Servadei.

By the exalted standards he set elsewhere, Sibelius's contribution to the keyboard seems limited in inventive resource. The *Melody* he wrote for the bells of Berghäll Church is slight but charming. There are some echoes of the *First Sonatina* in *Aquileja*, and pieces like *När rönnen blommar* ('When the Rowan Blossoms'), from the Op. 75 set, and *Berger et bergerette* have a certain charm. *Finlandia*, the *Valse lyrique, Autrefois* and *Valse chevaleresque* are all transcriptions of orchestral pieces. No pianist, however imaginative and sensitive, could possibly convey the charm of *Autrefois*. Annette Servadei is a sympathetic and sensitive guide to this repertoire, and on the whole she is well recorded. She produces a wide range of keyboard colour and a good dynamic range. At times she is rather too closely observed by the microphone with a result that *forte* or *fortissimo* passages are insufficiently transparent. But on the whole the Olympia set makes a clear first choice in this repertoire.

10 Bagatelles, Op. 34; Barcarole, Op. 24/10; Esquisses, Op. 114; Kyllikki, Op. 41; 5 Pieces, Op. 75; Piano transcriptions: Finlandia, Op. 26; Valse triste, Op. 44/1.

(***) Ondine ODE 847-2. Gothoni.

Gothoni makes the most of every expressive gesture and every gradation of keyboard colour, without indulging in any exaggeration. These performances make out a stronger case for Sibelius's piano music than almost any other. Unfortunately they are badly let down by the recording, which is reverberant and clangorous; the piano itself hardly sounds in ideal shape. A pity about the sound.

10 Bagatelles, Op. 34; The Cavalier; Dance Intermezzo; 6 Finnish Folk Songs; Kyllikki (3 Lyric Pieces), Op. 41; Mandolinato; Morceau romantique; Pensées lyriques, Op. 40; Spagnuolo; To Longing.

(N) (BB) *** Naxos 8.554808. Gimse.

The Norwegian pianist Håvard Gimse follows up his earlier Sibelius recital with *Kyllikki*, two important sets of the piano pieces, Opp. 34 and 40, and the *6 Finnish Folk Songs*, the fifth of which, *Fratricide*, is slightly Bartókian. Sibelius's contemporary and countryman Selim Palmgren put it perfectly when he wrote that "even in what for him were alien regions, [Sibelius] moves with an unfailing responsiveness to tone colour", and Gimse brings finesse and distinction to this repertoire. This and the companion discs are first recommendations.

5 Characteristic Pieces, Op. 103; 5 Esquisses, Op. 114; 5 Pieces (The Trees), Op. 75; 5 Pieces (The Flowers), Op. 85; 5 Romantic Pieces, Op. 101.

(N) *** Chan. 9833. Tabe.

By the exalted standards Sibelius set elsewhere his keyboard writing is limited both in range and resource, but when it is played as sensitively as by Kyoko Tabe, the effect can be quite persuasive. She makes the most of these miniatures without making too much of them. Opp. 75 and 85 come from the period 1914–15 and the remainder from the 1920s. She conveys some of their charm and individuality with expertise and is recorded with a lifelike and natural sound.

6 Impromptus, Op. 5; Sonata in F, Op. 12; 10 Pieces, Op. 24.

(BB) *** Naxos 8.553899. Gimse.

The *Sonata* and *Impromptus* are early and come from the year in which the first version of *En Saga* was composed. The *Sonata* has a genuine sense of forward movement and some of its ideas are appealing. The Op. 24 *Pieces* were written at various times between 1894 and 1903. The Norwegian pianist Håvard Gimse has consistent tonal beauty and unfailing musicianship. He is imaginative and has that kind of natural eloquence which allows the music to speak for itself yet still makes it sound fresh and unsentimental. This is distinguished playing and a strong recommendation at any price level.

Kyllikki, Op. 41; 2 Rondinos, Op. 68; 3 Sonatinas, Op. 67; Sonata in F, Op. 12; Piano transcription: Finlandia.

**(*) Finlandia 4509-98984-2. Viitasalo.

Good performances of *Kyllikki* and the Op. 67 *Sonatinas*, by general consent the finest of Sibelius's piano compositions. Marita Viitasalo is an idiomatic interpreter of this repertoire, and though the rival survey by Servadei is marginally better recorded, there is not much to choose between them.

3 Lyric Pieces, Op. 41; 5 Characteristic Impressions, Op. 103; 6 Impromptus, Op. 5; 5 Pieces, Op. 75; 5 Pieces, Op. 85; Finlandia (arr. composer).

(BB) *** Naxos 8.553661. Lauriala.

Perfectly good playing and decent recording make this a useful alternative to the complete survey by Annette Servadei. Its price advantage will incline some readers to give it preference, and it also enjoys the benefit of decent recorded sound.

10 Pieces, Op. 58; 2 Rondinos, Op. 68; 3 Sonatinas, Op. 67.

(N) (BB) *** Naxos 8.554814. Gimse.

The *Ten Pieces* of Op. 58 date from 1909, the year of the *String Quartet (Voces intimae)*. They are delightful, and by no means just trivial. Each has its own sobriquet and shows real keyboard character. The final rather solemn *Summer Song* is memorable, as is the wistful mood of the first of the *Two Rondinos*, written two years later; the second sparkles most pianistically.

The three *Sonatinas*, written together in the summer of 1912, are also full of charming ideas, giving the impression of a composer relaxing in holiday mood. Håvard Gimse plays all this music freshly, and finds its simple beauty. He is very well recorded and this second of his Naxos discs more than bears out the promise of the first.

ORGAN MUSIC

Intrada, Op. 111a; Masonic Music, Op. 113/1 & 10; Surusoitto, Op. 111b.

(N) *** BIS CD 1101. Ericsson – DVORAK: *Preludes & Fugues* **(*). GLAZUNOV: *Preludes & Fugues etc.* ***

After the death of Sibelius's old friend and drinking companion, the artist Akseli Gallen-Kalela, the composer was forced not only to break with custom by attending the funeral (which he usually refused to do), but after much arm-twisting to compose something at short notice for the ceremony. *Surusoitto* was the result. In the late 1960s the composer Joonas Kokkonen put forward the theory that given the pressure of time, Sibelius might have drawn on material from the *Eighth Symphony*, on which he was working throughout 1931. Aino Sibelius, the composer's widow, also thought this likely. Not that this short piece gives many clues as to how the symphony would have sounded, any more than would the string threnody of the *Seventh Symphony* if it were taken out of context and played on the piano. The *Intrada* (1925) is powerful, but the *Funeral March* from the *Masonic Music* (1927) betrays its proximity to the *Tempest* music. Superb playing from Hans-Ola Ericsson on a magnificently powerful instrument.

VOCAL MUSIC

Academic March (1919); Andante festivo (1922);
(i) Cantata for the Conferment Ceremony of 1894;
(ii) Coronation Cantata (1896); Finlandia, Op. 26/7.

**(*) Ondine ODE 936-2 [id]. (ii) Isokoski, Kortekangas; (i & ii) Finnish Ph. Ch.; Helsinki PO, Segerstam.

These two early cantatas are completely new to the repertoire. Only two sections of the *Academic Cantata* or *Cantata* for the Conferment Ceremony of 1894 survive. It is hardly top-drawer Sibelius though there are occasional flickers of individuality in the orchestral writing. The *Coronation Cantata*, written for the accession of Tsar Nicholas II, has not been heard since 1896 and its inspiration is thin and commonplace. Good solo singing from Soile Isokoski and Jaakko Kortekangas and decent performances from all concerned. Segerstam's *Finlandia* was recorded in 1994, five years before the rest of the programme. It is a particularly striking account and the whole programme is very well recorded.

Academic March; Finlandia (arr. composer); *Har du mod?, Op. 31/2; March of the Finnish Jaeger Battalion, Op. 91/1;* (i) *The Origin of Fire, Op. 32; Sandels, Op. 28; Song of the Athenians, Op. 31/3.*

** BIS CD 314. (i) Tiilikainen, Laulun Ystävät Male Ch.; Gothenburg SO, Järvi.

The Origin of Fire is by far the most important work on this record. Sauli Tiilikainen is very impressive indeed, and the playing of the Gothenburg Symphony Orchestra under Neeme Järvi has plenty of feeling and atmosphere. None of the other pieces is essential Sibelius. The singing of the Laulun Ystävät is good rather than outstanding, and the Gothenburg orchestra play with enthusiasm. Fine recording in the best BIS traditions.

(i) **Belshazzar's Feast** (complete score), *Op. 51; The Countess's Portrait (Grefvinnans konterfej);* (ii) *Jedermann (Everyman)* (incidental music), *Op. 83.*

*** BIS CD 737. (i) Passikivi; Lahti SO, Vänskä; (ii) with Lehto, Tiilikainen, Pietiläinen, Lahti Chamber Ch.

The incidental music to Hugo von Hofmannsthal's morality play, *Everyman*, comes from the autumn of 1916, when Sibelius was also working on the second version of his *Fifth Symphony*. The score runs to 16 numbers and takes 40 minutes. A lot of the music is fragmentary, wisps of sound; all of it is atmospheric and the best of it (the *Largo* section from track 12 onwards) finds Sibelius at his most inspired. The complete score for Hjalmar Procopé's *Belshazzar's Feast* brings us some seven minutes of extra music. The scoring is different from and less effective than the concert suite. There is, for example, no oboe in the original; the seductive descending oboe theme in *Khadra's Dance* is assigned to the clarinet. *Grefvinnans konterfej (The Countess's Portrait)* is a short, wistful piece for strings which comes from 1906 and was originally designed to accompany a recitation of *Porträtterna*, a poem by the mainland Swedish poet, Anna-Maria Lenngren. Dedicated, sensitive performances from the Lahti Symphony Orchestra and excellent recording. An indispensable disc for all Sibelians.

Finlandia (version for orchestra and mixed chorus); *Homeland (Oma maa), Op. 92; Impromptu, Op. 19;* (i) *Snöfrid, Op. 29; Song to the Earth (Maan virsi), Op. 95; Song to Lemminkäinen, Op. 31; Väinö's Song, Op. 110.*

** Ondine ODE 754-2. (i) Rautelin (reciter); Finnish Nat. Op. Ch. & O, Eri Klas.

While most of Sibelius's songs are to Swedish texts, the choral music is predominantly Finnish. *Oma maa* ('Home-

land') is a dignified and euphonious work and includes a magical evocation of the wintry nights with aurora borealis and the white nights of midsummer. *Väinö's Song* is an appealing piece which bears an opus number between those for *The Tempest* and *Tapiola* – though it is not really fit to keep them company. The performances are decent.

(i) **Karelia** (complete incidental music); (ii) *Kuolema, Op. 44; Valse triste* (1904 version).

*** BIS CD915. (i) Laitinen, Hoffgren; (i & ii) Laukka; (ii) Tiilhonen; Lahti SO, Vänskä.

Although the *Karelia Suite* is familiar enough, few readers will have heard the complete score. It has only recently been put into performable shape. However, a set of parts survived, albeit incomplete, and the composer, Kalevi Aho, has prepared an edition which Osmo Vänskä and his musicians use for this score. Some things are disconcerting: the familiar cor anglais melody in the *Ballade* is given to a tenor, and the movement is far too long. But there is much of interest here that makes this essential listening for Sibelians. The incidental music to *Kuolema* (Death), written ten years later, was revised the following year (1904) and re-scored. The original second section, *Paavali's Song*, is quite inspired, though Sibelius was quite right to add wind to represent the bird cries in the following scene (he conflated scenes 3 and 4 to form *Scene with Cranes*). The disc also affords an opportunity to contrast the 1903 and 1904 versions of *Valse triste*, the differences will bring you up with a start. Superb playing and recording.

(i) **Karelia Suite, Op. 11** (original scoring); (ii) *King Christian II, Op. 27* (complete original score); (iii) *Pelléas et Mélisande* (original scoring).

*** BIS CD 918. (i & ii) Laukka; (iii) Jakobsson; Lahti SO, Vänskä.

Sibelius re-scored them for larger forces when he made his concert suite the following year, his first orchestral work to be published. It is particularly good to hear the *Musette* in such a characterful form – just for wind. The changes in the score Sibelius composed for Bertel Gripenberg's Swedish translation of Maeterlinck's *Pelléas et Mélisande* are less extensive but we do have an additional section that has never been published. The *Karelia Suite* is drawn from BIS CD 915. A highly successful issue of great interest to all Sibelians.

Kullervo Symphony, Op. 7 (see also above, in orchestral music, under *Karelia Suite* etc.).

(N) *** BIS CD 1215. Paasikivi, Laukka, Helsinki University Ch., Lahti SO, Vänskä.

*** Sony SK 52563. Rørholm, Hynninen, Helsinki University Ch., LAPO, Salonen.

**(*) Chan. 9393. Isokoski, Laukka, Danish Nat. RSO, Segerstam.

**(*) Virgin VC5 45292-2. Stene, Mattei, Nat. Male Voice Ch., Royal Stockholm PO, Järvi.

(i) **Kullervo Symphony; Symphony No. 7; En Saga; Rakastava.**

*** RCA 09026 68312. (i) Martinpelto, Fredriksson, LSO Ch.; LSO, Davis.

Sir Colin Davis's account of the *Kullervo Symphony* is more spacious and commanding than any other. Although he takes over eighty minutes (and as a result runs to a second disc), it seems shorter than most of its rivals, though the work emerges as bigger. It is a superb performance and very well recorded too. The two soloists, both Swedish, are very good though they are not superior to such rivals as Groop, Isokoski and Hynninen. However this is a performance of real stature. As well as Sibelius's earliest symphonic venture, he gives us the last – and a very impressive reading it is too. The work unfolds with a natural authority and there is space, power and serenity when required. Sir Colin recorded *En Saga* in the early 1980s during his Boston years – very successfully – and this is hardly less fine. *Rakastava* for strings and percussion is a touching work, all the more affecting for its unforced eloquence. All in all, an outstanding set, which sets the seal on a triumphant and magisterial survey.

Having completed an impressive cycle of the symphonies Osmo Vänskä and the Lahti Orchestra give us a finely paced reading of Sibelius's groundbreaking work with plenty of dramatic intensity and a strong atmosphere. There is the same sense of grip and epic sweep that distinguished Sir Colin Davis's RCA recording. Apart from two fine soloists he has the advantage of a Finnish male choir. Incidentally, some small errors in the published score have been corrected. This is the best performance of this wonderful symphony since Davis's version, and it is a strong challenger, in that the LSO version spreads over on to a second disc, which accommodates the *Seventh Symphony* and *En saga*. For many this BIS CD will be a first choice.

Esa-Pekka Salonen's account of Sibelius's early *Kullervo Symphony* is gripping and held together tautly. It has a sweep and momentum that eluded Salonen's less-than-overwhelming Nielsen cycle. The Los Angeles orchestra, to whom this score must have been new, play with the enthusiasm of fresh discovery and Marianna Rørholm proves a worthy companion to the ubiquitous Hynninen. The first movement is taut, brisk and dramatic – very much as Sibelius's son-in-law took it at its first performance in recent times; the fifth is very imaginatively done, and only the fourth is perhaps a bit too fast, almost headlong.

Segerstam gives what is for him an uncharacteristically straightforward account of this remarkable work. There are none of the idiosyncrasies that have proved so disruptive elsewhere. His soloists are good and both the playing of the Danish Radio Orchestra and the skill of their engineers are admirable. But this is not a first choice.

There is a lot right about Paavo Järvi's fine reading with the Royal Stockholm Philharmonic and his Swedish choir. The first two movements are admirably paced and in the central movement the Norwegian mezzo-soprano Randi Stene and the Swedish baritone Peter Mattei make admirable soloists. No reservations about the excellent EMI/Virgin recording. The big snag is the finale, *Kullervo's Death*, which Järvi *fils* drags out to almost fifteen minutes while most others get through it in about ten. The result is to make it sound bombastic and overblown.

The Tempest (incidental music), Op. 109 (complete).

*** BIS CD 581. Tiihonen, Passikivi, Hirvonen, Kerola, Heinonen, Lahti Opera Ch. & SO, Vänskä.

**(*) Ondine ODE 813-2. Groop, Viljakainen, Hynninen, Silvasti, Tiilikainen, Op. Festival Ch., Finnish RSO, Saraste.

Sibelius's original score for the 1926 Copenhagen production of Shakespeare's play is extensive: it runs to some 34 numbers in all for soloists, mixed chorus, harmonium and orchestra, and takes about 65 minutes. There are some unfamiliar effects here: the muted strings with which we are familiar in the *Berceuse* were an afterthought. In the original, their music is allotted to the harmonium; and although this is at first startling, the effect is other-worldly in a completely unexpected way. There are other master-strokes that are missing (the insinuating bass clarinet in *The Oak-tree*) but much else that will be new. The *Chorus of the Winds* with a real chorus is also quite magical – in fact the vocal writing is often highly imaginative – and the singers on the BIS CD are all good. The atmosphere is very strong and puts one completely under its spell. The BIS recording, though good, needs to be reproduced at a higher than usual level setting.

If clarity and definition are a first priority, the Ondine version under Saraste is the one to go for. There is good singing here, too, from Monica Groop, Jorma Hynninen and the rest of the cast. The performance is given in Danish (as it would have been in the 1926 version, rather than the Finnish text used by BIS). However, Saraste is nowhere near as sensitive as Vänskä and does not have his sense of mystery or atmosphere. His *Prospero* is too fast, almost routine by comparison with Vänskä, who draws the listener more completely into Sibelius's and Shakespeare's world. Both accounts are recommendable and either is to be acquired rather than none. But the BIS makes a clear first choice.

Songs

7 Songs, Op. 13; 6 Songs, Op. 50; 6 Songs, Op. 90; Resemblance; A song; Serenade; The wood-nymph; The Jewish girl's song; (i) The Thought.

*** BIS CD 757. Von Otter, Forsberg, (i) with Groop.

The Opp. 13 and 90 songs are all settings of Runeberg, Sibelius's favourite poet, but there are rarities such as *Skogsrået* ('The wood-nymph') – totally unrelated, by the way, to the melodrama and tone-poem of the same name which he wrote in the early 1890s – and never before recorded. Also new are the duet, *Tanken* ('The thought'), *Resemblance* and *A song*. Von Otter and her partner, characterize each song with the consummate artistry one expects from them, and the only possible reservation concerns the balance, which in some of the early songs favours the piano.

6 Songs, Op. 36.

*** Virgin VC5 45273-2. Kringelborn, Martineau – GRIEG, NIELSEN, RANGSTROM: *Songs*. ***

Solveig Kringelborn's anthology takes its name, '*Black Roses*', from the famous Sibelius song in this set. In some ways her recordings of Sibelius are the least satisfactory of the items in this welcome recital. She produces a beautiful sound throughout but her characterization, particularly in the setting of Fröding's *Tennis vid Trianon*, is less searching. All the same there is much here that gives pleasure and her pianist Malcolm Martineau is superb throughout. Excellent recorded sound too.

Songs with orchestra: *Arioso; Autumn evening; Come away, Death!; The diamond on the March snow; The fool's song of the spider; Luonnotar, Op. 70; On a balcony by the sea; The rapids-rider's brides; Serenade; Since then I have questioned no further; Spring flies hastily; Sunrise.*

*** BIS CD 270. Hynninen, Häggander, Gothenburg SO, Panula.

Jorma Hynninen is a fine interpreter of this repertoire: his singing can only be called glorious. Mari-Anne Häggander manages the demanding tessitura of *Arioso* and *Luonnotar* with much artistry, and her *Luonnotar* is certainly to be preferred to Söderström's. Jorma Panula proves a sensitive accompanist and secures fine playing from the Gothenburg orchestra. In any event, this is indispensable.

Arioso, Op. 3; Narcissus; Pelléas et Mélisande: The Three Blind Sisters. 7 Songs, Op. 17; 6 Songs, Op. 36; 5 Songs, Op. 37; 6 Songs, Op. 88; Souda, souda, sinisorsa.

*** BIS CD 457. Von Otter, Forsberg.

Miss von Otter always makes a beautiful sound, but she has a highly developed sense of line and brings great interpretative insight to such songs as *My bird is long in homing* and *Tennis at Trianon*, which has even greater finesse than Söderström's. And what a good accompanist Bengt Forsberg is. The recording is good if a bit reverberant.

OPERA

The Maiden in the Tower* (opera); *Karelia Suite, Op. 11.

*** BIS CD 250. Häggander, Hynninen, Hagegård, Kruse, Gothenburg Ch. and SO, Järvi.

The Maiden in the Tower falls into eight short scenes. The orchestral interlude between the first two scenes brings us the real Sibelius, and the second scene is undoubtedly impressive; there are echoes of Wagner, such as we find in some of the great orchestral songs of the following decade. All the same, it lacks something we find in all his most characteristic music: quite simply, a sense of mastery. Yet there are telling performances here from Mari-Anne Häggander and Jorma Hynninen and the Gothenburg orchestra. Neeme Järvi's account of the *Karelia Suite* is certainly original, with its *Intermezzo* too broad to make an effective contrast with the ensuing *Ballade*.

SIGNORETTI, Aurelio (1597–1635)

***Missa Looquebantur variis linguis apostoli in die Pentecoster; Vesperitina Psalmodia in Festas B.V. Bariae* (Venice, 1639).**

*** Tactus TC 561901. La Stagione Armonica, Balestracci.

(with PORTA: *Sonata detta La Porta a 4.;* VIADANA: Sinfonia detta La Reggiana ***).

Signoretti's four-part parody mass is based on a motet by Palestrina. It has a pleasing simplicity and eloquence and is presented here as a missa brevis, together with the Propers appropriate for the Feast of Pentecost (with the chants particularly pleasingly sung). Signoretti's remarkable collection of 1629 includes eighteen psalm settings plus three of the *Magnificat*. They are given here in an order to form Vespers for the Virgin Mary, including the appropriate antiphons and hymns, and are sung with great freshness and spontaneity. Two instrumental pieces of the same period act as prelude and postlude (the latter scored for brass). Altogether this is a thoroughly worthwhile enterprise, admirably thought out and impressively carried through. The recording is excellent.

SIMPSON, Robert (1921–97)

Energy; Introduction & Allegro on a Theme by Max Reger; The Four Temperaments; Volcano; Vortex.

*** Hyp. CDA 66449. Desford Colliery Caterpillar Band, Watson.

The Four Temperaments is a four-movement, 22-minute symphony of great imaginative power, and ingeniously laid out for the band. Simpson played in brass bands as a boy and this is doubtless where he acquired some of his expertise in writing for them. *Energy* came in response to a commission from the World Brass Band Championships. The *Introduction and Allegro on a Theme by Max Reger* is awesome and impressive. Together with *Volcano* and his most recent piece, *Vortex*, it makes up his entire output in this medium. The Desford Colliery Caterpillar Band under James Watson play with all the expertise and virtuosity one expects, and the recording has admirable clarity and body, though the acoustic is on the dry side.

Symphonies Nos. 1; 8.

*** Hyp. CDA 66890. RPO, Handley.

Robert Simpson's *First Symphony* was a dissertation he submitted for his doctorate of music at Durham University, and his first work to reach the gramophone. Sir Adrian Boult recorded it with the LPO in 1956. It is a one-movement work, albeit in three sections, powerfully constructed and forcefully argued. It holds up to the test of time remarkably well and better than much other music of the 1950s. Vernon Handley gives a spacious and magisterial account of it, and the Hyperion recording illuminates so much of the detail which Boult's old mono recording left uncharted. Like the *First Symphony*, the *Eighth* received its première from a Danish orchestra (the former under Launy Grøndahl, the latter under Jerzy Semkow). One critic has pointed to the *Eighth* as seeming to embody some 'colossal inner rage' and, like the *Fifth*, it undoubtedly has a combative tumult that rarely passes into tranquillity. Handley makes out a strong case for both scores, and the sound is absolutely first class. An indispensable issue for anyone who cares about the post-war symphony in Britain.

Symphonies Nos. 2; 4.

*** Hyp. CDA 66505. Bournemouth SO, Handley.

The *Second*, composed in 1956 for Anthony Bernard's London Chamber Orchestra, is one of the very best; its opening is one of Simpson's most mysterious and inspired ideas, lean and sinuous but full of poetic vision. The variation slow movement is one of the most virtuosic and remarkable exercises in the palindrome, yet such is Simpson's artistry in concealing his ingenuity that no one coming to it innocently would be aware of this. The *Second* is a work of enduring quality, music that is both accessible yet of substance. The *Fourth Symphony* is the more extended piece. Powerful and inspiriting music in totally dedicated performances by Vernon Handley, and excellent recording quality.

Symphonies Nos. 3 (1961); 5 (1971).

*** Hyp. CDA 66728. RPO, Handley.

Vernon Handley's new disc brings us the première recording of the *Fifth Symphony*, a work of striking power and range. It is combative and intense and enjoys at times an almost unbridled ferocity that enhances the admittedly few moments of repose. No admirer of the composer – and no one who cares about twentieth-century music in general – should pass these performances by, for it is music of a vital and forceful eloquence. Fine playing by the RPO under Handley, and exemplary recording.

Symphonies Nos. 6; 7.

*** Hyp. CDA 66280. RLPO, Handley.

The *Sixth* is inspired by the idea of growth: the development of a musical structure from initial melodic cells in much the same way as life emerges from a single fertilized cell in nature. The *Seventh*, scored for chamber orchestral forces, is hardly less powerful in its imaginative vision and sense of purpose. Both scores are bracingly Nordic in their inner landscape and exhilarating in aural experience. The playing of the Liverpool orchestra under Vernon Handley could hardly be bettered, and the recording is altogether first class.

Symphony No. 9.

✪ *** Hyp. CDA 66299. Bournemouth SO, Handley (with talk by the composer).

What can one say about the *Ninth* of Robert Simpson, except that its gestures are confident, its control of pace and its material are masterly? It is a one-movement work, but at no time in its 45 minutes does it falter – nor does the attention of the listener. The CD also includes a spoken introduction to the piece that many listeners will probably find helpful. It is played superbly by the Bournemouth Symphony Orchestra under Vernon Handley, and is no less superbly recorded.

Symphony No. 10.

*** Hyp. CDA 66510. RLPO, Handley.

The *Tenth Symphony* (1988) will be a tough nut to crack for many collectors. Its musical argument is unfailingly concentrated. Like its predecessor, it has a Beethovenian strength and momentum. The symphony lasts almost an hour and is not the ideal starting place from which to explore this composer's world. But make no mistake: it is a work of stature, and it is very well played and recorded here.

(i) *Canzona for Brass;* (i & ii) *Media morte in vita sumus;* (ii) *Tempi;* (iii) *Eppur si muove.*

*** Hyp. CDA 67016. (i) Corydon Brass Ens.; (ii) Corydon Singers, Best; (iii) Quinn.

The *Canzona for Brass* from 1957 has never sounded more impressive on CD. It has the dignity and grandeur of Gabrieli. The *Media morte in vita sumus* ('In the midst of death we are in life') comes from 1975 between the *Fifth* and *Sixth Symphonies* and is for voices and brass. It has a depth and eloquence completely at variance with so much contemporary music. *Tempi* (1988) is a setting for *a cappella* choir of various Italian tempo indications, written for a choral competition in the composer's adopted Republic of Ireland. Such is its beauty that it makes one regret that it is Simpson's only contribution to the medium. *Eppur si muove* (1988) is an imposing 30-minute piece for organ, not dissimilar in scope and ambition to Nielsen's *Commotio*. It derives its title from Galileo's response when he was compelled by the Church to recant his view that the earth revolved round the sun: 'But it *does* move.' Iain Quinn plays it with consummate mastery on the organ of Winchester Cathedral. The brass playing is superb and the Corydon Singers cope with Simpson's demanding vocal writing admirably even if the sopranos are obviously taxed at times above the stave. State-of-the-art recording. Not to be missed.

(i) *Clarinet Quintet; String Quartet No. 13;* (ii) *String Quintet No. 2.*

*** Hyp. CDA 66905. (i) King; (ii) Van Kampen; Delmé Qt.

The *Clarinet Quintet* is arguably the most searching example of the genre to have appeared anywhere since the Second World War. Throughout, with Beethoven's *C sharp minor Quartet*, Op. 131, not far from view, this is a subtle, concentrated and profoundly original – and profound – work, which is more than the sum of its parts and which resonates long in the memory. The *Thirteenth Quartet* is a concentrated piece and the Delmé Quartet are ideal exponents. The *String Quintet No. 2* occupied the composer from 1991 to 1994, during the first period of the stroke that afflicted his last years. It is a powerful and severe work, whose bleak and unconsoling closing paragraphs stay long in the listener's mind.

Horn Quartet (for horn, violin, cello & piano); *Horn Trio* (for horn, violin & piano).

*** Hyp. CDA 66695. Watkins, Lowbury, Armytage, Dearnley.

The *Quartet for Horn, Violin, Cello and Piano* of 1976 is of unfailing quality and imagination, and its development magnificently sustained. The composer's command of large-scale musical thinking is much in evidence – but so, too, is his feeling for sonority. He draws some extraordinary sounds from these four instruments. In some ways this is one of his most deeply original and compelling works. The later *Horn Trio*, written for Anthony Halstead, Frank Lloyd and Carol Slater, immediately pre-dates the *Ninth Symphony*. These are most impressive pieces, and the performances are completely dedicated and highly imaginative. Excellent recording too.

String Quartets Nos. 1–3.

(**) Pearl mono GEM 0023. Element Qt.

These are off-air recordings from the composer's own collection of the première broadcast performances in the Third Programme in the 1950s. They have a certain gutsy quality, a total and impassioned commitment that more than compensates for the odd rough edges.

String Quartets Nos. 1; 4.

*** Hyp. CDA 66419. Delmé Qt.

The *First Quartet* opens in as innocent a fashion as the Haydn *Lark Quartet* or Nielsen's *E flat*, but the better one comes to know it the more it is obvious that Simpson is already his own man. The second movement is a palindrome (many modern composers do not know how to write forwards, let alone backwards as well) but its ingenuity is worn lightly. The *Fourth* is part of the trilogy which Simpson conceived as a kind of commentary on Beethoven's *Rasumovsky Quartets*. Yet they live in their own right. Excellent performances from the Delmé Quartet, and fine recording.

String Quartets Nos. 2; 5.

*** Hyp. CDA 66386. Delmé Qt.

The *Second Quartet* is thought-provoking and full of character. The *Fifth*, composed over 20 years later in 1974, is one of the three modelled on Beethoven's *Rasumovsky Quartets* – in this case, Op. 59, No. 2 – and even emulates the phrase structure of the Beethoven. It is a long and powerfully sustained piece, which receives expert advocacy from the Delmé Quartet and excellent Hyperion sound.

String Quartets Nos. 3 & 6; String Trio (prelude, adagio & fugue).

*** Hyp. CDA 66376. Delmé Qt.

The *Third Quartet* is a two-movement piece. Its finale is a veritable power-house with its unrelenting sense of onward movement which almost strains the medium. Its first movement is a deeply felt piece that has a powerful and haunting eloquence. The *Sixth* is further evidence of Simpson's remarkable musical mind. The *String Trio* is a marvellously stimulating and thoughtful piece. Dedicated performances and excellent recording.

String Quartets Nos. 7 & 8.

*** Hyp. CDA 66117. Delmé Qt.

The *Seventh Quartet* has a real sense of vision and something of the stillness of the remote worlds it evokes, 'quiet and mysterious yet pulsating with energy'. The *Eighth* turns from the vastness of space to the microcosmic world of insect-life, but, as with so much of Simpson's music, there is a concern for musical continuity rather than beauty of incident. Excellent playing from the Delmé Quartet, and very good recorded sound too.

String Quartet No. 9 (32 Variations & Fugue on a Theme of Haydn).

*** Hyp. CDA 66127. Delmé Qt.

The *Ninth Quartet* is a set of thirty-two variations and a fugue on the minuet of Haydn's *Symphony No. 47*. Like the minuet itself, all the variations are in the form of a palindrome. It is a mighty and serious work, argued with all the resource and ingenuity one expects from this composer. A formidable achievement in any age, and a rarity in ours. The Delmé Quartet cope with its difficulties splendidly, and the performance carries the imprimatur of the composer. The recording sounds very good in its CD format.

String Quartets Nos. 10 (For Peace); 11.

*** Hyp. CDA 66225. Coull Qt.

The subtitle, *For Peace*, of No. 10 refers to 'its generally pacific character' and aspires to define 'the condition of peace which excludes aggression but not strong feeling'. Listening to this *Quartet* is like hearing a quiet, cool voice of sanity that refreshes the troubled spirit after a long period in an alien, hostile world. The one-movement *Eleventh* draws on some of the inspiration of its predecessor. It is a work of enormous power and momentum. Excellent performances and recording.

String Quartet No. 12 (1987); (i) String Quintet (1987).

*** Hyp. CDA 66503. Coull Qt, (i) with Bigley.

Robert Simpson's *Twelfth Quartet* is a masterly and absorbing score. His *String Quintet* is another work of sustained inventive power. We are unlikely to get another recording, so this is self-recommending; but it must be noted that the heroic demands this score makes on the players keep them fully stretched. The intonation and tone of the leader is not always impeccable, but the playing has commitment and intelligence.

String Quartets Nos. 14 & 15; (i) Quintet for Clarinet, Bass Clarinet & Strings.

*** Hyp. CDA 66626. (i) Farrall, Cross; Vanbrugh Qt.

The *Fourteenth Quartet* comes from 1990, and the *Fifteenth*, written when Simpson was seventy (in 1991), was his last. This is surely the greatest quartet cycle produced in the last half of the twentieth century and in terms of contrapuntal ingenuity and musical depth belongs with Bartók, Shostakovich and Holmboe. The *Clarinet Quintet* is not to be confused with the 1968 work listed above; it is an arrangement for clarinet, bass clarinet and string trio of a 1983 quintet intriguingly scored for clarinet, bass clarinet and three double basses. These are powerful Beethovenian scores whose stature and musical processes are easier to recognize than describe. Dedicated performances, superbly recorded.

Piano Sonata; Michael Tippett, his Mystery; Variations & Finale on a Theme by Beethoven; Variations & Finale on a Theme by Haydn.

*** Hyp. CDA 66827. Clarke.

The *Piano Sonata* is a concentrated, craggy, powerfully argued piece, not obviously pianistic but bristling with challenges and difficulties. The *Variations and Finale on a Theme of Haydn* (1948) evince Simpson's lifelong interest in the palindrome. The slow movement of the *Second Symphony* is a palindrome, and the theme he uses here (that of the minuet of Haydn's *Symphony No. 47*) also forms the basis of the mighty variations which comprise the *Ninth String Quartet*. The short piece written for Tippett was a contribution to a birthday tribute. The *Variations and Finale on a Theme of Beethoven* are based on a little-known *Bagatelle*, WoO 61a, and were written for Charles Burney's granddaughter, and with the present pianist in mind. The performances are authoritative and, apart from a certain over-resonance, the recording satisfactory.

SINDING, Christian (1856–1941)

Légende, Op. 46.

(BB) *** Naxos 8.550329. Dong-Suk Kang, Slovak (Bratislava) RSO, Leaper – HALVORSEN: *Air norvégien* etc.; SIBELIUS: *Violin Concerto;* SVENDSEN: *Romance.* ***

Dong-Suk Kang plays Sinding's *Légende* with great conviction and an effortless, songful virtuosity. It is by no means as appealing as the Halvorsen and Svendsen pieces but makes a good makeweight for an excellent collection in the lowest price range.

Suite (for violin and orchestra), *Op. 10.*

(M) *** EMI (ADD) CDM5 66060-2. Perlman, Pittsburgh SO, Previn – BARTOK: *Violin Concerto No. 2;* CONUS: *Violin Concerto.* ***

Heifetz recorded this dazzling piece in the 1950s, and it need only be said that Perlman's version is not inferior. The velocity of Perlman's first movement is little short of amazing. Alas, this disc is now deleted.

Symphonies Nos. 1 in D min., Op. 21; 2 in D, Op. 83; 3 in F, Op. 121; 4 (Winter and Spring), Op. 129.

(N) *** Finlandia 8573-82357-2. Norwegian R. O, Ari Rasilainen.

Sinding belonged to the Grieg–Delius circle and along with Halvorsen was in his day regarded as the leading Norwegian composers after Grieg. Despite the keen advocacy of the fine Norwegian Radio Orchestra and its Finnish conductor Ari Rasilainen, these four symphonies are unlikely to make great inroads into the repertory. Although the music is at times not unappealing it is wanting in real memorability. The *Fourth* and last comes from Sinding's last years and was completed in time for his 80th birthday concert in 1936. The *First* and *Second* symphonies were recorded in the days of LP but the *Third*, a long work lasting three-quarters of an hour, and *Fourth* are new to the catalogue as far as we know. Although it fills a gap in our knowledge of the symphony in Norway, these are of relatively peripheral interest musically, and lack that vital spark that distinguishes Svendsen before him and Sverud nearer our own times.

SIRMEN, Maddalena Lombardini (1745–1818)

String Quartets Nos. 1–6.

*** Cala CACD 1019. Allegri Qt.

*** Tactus TC 731201. Accademia della Magnifica Comunita, Casazza.

Maddalena Lombardini was born in Venice. She proved so talented that she was sent to study with Tartini and it was primarily as a violinist, in his view 'absolutely without equal', that she first made her reputation, although she also trained as a singer. When her style of fiddling became outmoded (as speed came to be considered more desirable than polish and elegance), she turned to singing and secured a well-paid five-year appointment at the Dresden Opera, then moving on to St Petersburg.

Her *String Quartets* were published in Paris in 1769 by another enterprising woman, Madame Berault. The string quartet medium was at that time in its infancy (the present contribution is approximately contemporary with Haydn's Opus 9 set) and thus her easy skill in handling the medium is the more remarkable. There are two movements to each quartet, but the structure often subdivides into sections using different tempi. The Allegri Quartet obviously lived with this music for some time before this record was made, and they play it with much style and conviction, conveying their own pleasure in part-writing which is obviously enjoyable to play. With excellent recording, admirably present but naturally balanced, this is very much worth exploring.

Confusingly, the excellent Tactus alternative recording is documented under Maddalena's maiden name, Lombardini, which is reasonable enough as the *Quartets* were written while she was single. The six works are played simply, freshly and pleasingly. Even though a conductor is listed, they are given with one instrument to each part, and one is not aware of any 'interpretative' interference with the music's flow. The recording is excellent and the disc can be recommended alongside the Cala version: it is equally enjoyable, if not more so, and the players are given a strikingly natural presence.

String Quartets Nos. 2 in B flat; 3 in G min.

*** CPO 999 679-2. Basle Erato Qt – Emilie MAYER: *Quartet No. 14;* Fanny MENDELSSOHN: *String Quartet.* ***

Many collectors will be satisfied with just two of these enjoyable quartets, particularly as the couplings here are so enterprising. They are two-movement works and fit rather well together: the catchy finale of the *B flat major* nicely complements the elegant opening *Tempo giusto* of the *G minor*. The performances here are excellent and so is the recording.

SJÖGREN, Emil (1853–1915)

Violin Sonatas Nos. 1, Op. 19; 2 in E min., Op. 24; 2 Lyric Pieces; Poème, Op. 40.

(N) *** BIS CD 995. Enoksson, Stott.

Emil Sjögren belongs to the generation of Swedish

composers before Stenhammar, though he is not in the same league and his attainments are more modest. He never tried his hand at orchestral music or opera, though he wrote some fine songs. The two *Violin Sonatas* come from the 1880s and are finely crafted, and the *Second Sonata* is generally thought of as his masterpiece. It is certainly the work of a cultured and inventive composer with strong classical instincts and is served excellently by Per Enoksson and Kathryn Stott. The recording is in the best traditions of the house.

SKORYK, Myroslav (born 1938)

Carpathian Concerto; Hutsul Triptych.

** ASV CDDCA 963. Odessa PO, Earle – KOLESSA:
  Symphony No. 1. **

Myroslav Skoryk teaches composition at Lvov and has a considerable output to his credit, including two piano concertos, two violin concertos and a good deal of music for the theatre. The *Hutsul Triptych* (1965) derives from a score Skoryk composed for the film, *Shadows of Forgotten Ancestors*, by Sergei Paradhzhanov. It is colourful, often atmospheric and inventive, not unlike some Shchedrin. The *Carpathian Concerto* (1972) is an expertly scored orchestral piece with strong folkloric accents – and some cheap orientalism. Not a good piece nor strongly individual, but the centerpiece of the *Hutsul Triptych* is worth hearing.

SKROUP, František (1801–62)

The Tinker Overture.

(**) Sup. mono SU 1914 011. Czech PO, Sejna – DVORAK:
  The Cunning Peasant Overture (**); SMETANA: *Festive
  Symphony* etc. (***)

The author of the sleeve-note speaks of 'the stunning melodic spontaneity' of Skroup's *The Tinker Overture*, which is no small claim. It is not a bad piece, but its melodic invention, while pleasant, is far from stunning. Sejna's performance is marvellously spirited, but the recording was made in 1951 and is rather thin on top!

SMETANA, Bedřich (1824–84)

Má Vlast (complete).

*** Sup. 11 1208-2. Czech PO, Kubelik.
(BB) *** Naxos 8.550931. Polish Nat. RSO (Katowice), Wit.
*** Telarc CD 80265. Milwaukee SO, Macal.
*** Chan. 9366. Detroit SO, Järvi.
(M) *** Ph. 442 641-2. Concg. O, Dorati.
(N) *** Sup. SU 3465-2 031. Czech PO, Mackerras.
(BB) **(*) Virgin 2 x 1 VBD5 61739-2. Czech PO, Pešek –
  DVORAK: *Symphony No. 4; Czech Suite; My Home:
  Overture.* **(*)
**(*) DG 431 652-2. VPO, Levine.

Má Vlast; The Bartered Bride: Overture; 2 Dances.

(B) ** Teldec Ultima 3984 28174-2 (2). Frankfurt RSO, Inbal.

In 1990 Rafael Kubelik returned to his homeland after an enforced absence of 41 years to open the Prague Spring Festival with this vibrant performance of *Má Vlast*. He had recorded the work twice before in stereo, but this Czech version is special, imbued with passionate national feeling, yet never letting the emotions boil over. At the bold opening of *Vyšehrad*, with the harp strongly profiled, the intensity of the music-making is immediately projected, and the trickling streams which are the source of *Vltava* have a delicacy almost of fantasy. *Sárka*, with its bloodthirsty tale of revenge and slaughter, is immensely dramatic, contrasting with the pastoral evocations of the following piece; the Slavonic lilt of the music's lighter moments brings the necessary contrast and release. The recording is vivid and full but not sumptuous, yet this suits the powerful impulse of Kubelik's overall view, with the build-up to the exultant close of *Blaník* producing a dénouement of great majesty.

Antoni Wit and his excellent Polish National Radio Orchestra give us a superbly played and consistently imaginative account. The spacious opening of *Vyšehrad*, marginally slower than usual, glows with romantic evocation; equally the flutes, trickling down from the sources of the *Vltava*, captivate the ear and the famous string-tune is unusually gracious and relaxed. The opening of *Sárka* brings tingling melodrama, which subsides naturally for the jaunty theme which follows. *From Bohemia's Woods and Fields* opens with opulent expansiveness, and later the ethereal high string entry is exquisitely made. *Tábor* develops great weight and gravitas. The warm resonance of the Concert Hall of Polish Radio in Katowice seems right for this very individual reading, full of fantasy, which goes automatically to the top of the list alongside Kubelik's distinguished, and justly renowned, 1990 Czech Philharmonic version on Supraphon, which is rather special.

Macal's Telarc version offers the finest recording of all; indeed it approaches the demonstration bracket. He provides a highly spontaneous and enjoyable performance, imaginatively conceived and convincingly paced. Other accounts, notably Kubelik's, have greater Slavic fire and find a more red-bloodedly patriotic feeling, but the excellent orchestral playing is responsive to his less histrionic view. *Sárka* has a folksy flavour, the melodrama good-humoured, while in *From Bohemia's Woods and Fields*, after the radiant high string passage, the horns steal in magically with their chorale. Throughout the brass are full and sonorous, mitigating any rhetorical bombast in the last two symphonic poems; and Macal's Czech nationality ensures that the performance has idiomatic feeling.

Järvi's, too, is an enjoyably vivid performance, and he has the double advantage of first-class playing from the highly committed Detroit orchestra and the splendid acoustics of Symphony Hall. The romantic *Vyšehrad* is fresh and immediate, and the mountain streams of *Vltava* gleam brightly in the sunlight before the string-tune arrives and moves on with plenty of lyrical impetus. *Sárka* is very dramatic indeed, with great melodramatic gusto and a heartfelt response from the strings. The opening of *Tábor* is tellingly ominous, and the weight of the Detroit brass makes a powerful contribution to both of the final two sections of the score; the zest of the Detroit music-making is always compelling, and the culminating climax is thrilling rather than expansively grandiloquent.

Dorati's reading brings both vivid drama and orchestral playing of the finest quality. The music-making has a high adrenalin level throughout, yet points of detail are not missed. The accents of *Vyšehrad* may seem too highly stressed to ears used to a more mellow approach to this highly romantic opening piece, and *Vltava* similarly moves forward strongly. In the closing *Blaník*, Dorati finds dignity rather than bombast and the pastoral episode is delightfully relaxed, with a fine rhythmic bounce to the march theme. The Philips sound is splendid, with a wide amplitude and a thrilling concert-hall presence, and this reissue on the Philips Solo label makes an obvious recommendation in the mid-price range.

Mackerras's affinity with Czech music is well known, and although his version of *Má Vlast* does not displace existing recommendations it ranks high among them. The sound has presence and body, and the warm, reverberant acoustic is pleasing yet allows plenty of detail to register.

Pešek's reading does not miss the music's epic patriotic feeling, yet never becomes bombastic. There is plenty of evocation, from the richly romantic opening of *Vyšehrad* to the more mysterious scene-setting in *Tábor*, while the climax of *Sárka*, with its potent anticipatory horn-call, is a gripping piece of melodrama. The two main sections of the work, *Vltava* and *From Bohemia's Woods and Fields*, are especially enjoyable for their vivid characterization, while at the very end of *Blaník* Pešek draws together the two key themes – the *Vyšehrad* motif and the Hussite chorale – very satisfyingly. This now comes coupled with a somewhat less recommendable Dvořák programme, but is very competitively priced.

Levine is upstaged by Dorati on Philips, who has a considerable price advantage plus the glorious acoustic of the Concertgebouw. Levine's performance is full of momentum and thrust, with much imaginative detail and most beautifully played. In *Tábor* and *Blaník* the VPO play with great vigour and commitment, and these patriotic pieces have both fervour and plenty of colour. The sound is full-bodied, with a wide amplitude and range, but it is less sumptuous and slightly less atmospheric than the Philips version.

The Teldec digital recording is strikingly fine and this is music where the vividly coloured and well-balanced, clear sound can be especially telling. The orchestral playing is first class too, and Inbal's reading is dramatic. However, the overall playing-time of the performance, at around 78 minutes, means that it would have fitted on to a single CD, and the *Bartered Bride* bonus is hardly generous.

(i) *Má Vlast* (complete); (ii) *Hakon Jarl, Op. 16; Prague Carnival; Richard III, Op. 11; Wallenstein's Camp, Op. 14;* (iii) *The Bartered Bride: Overture & 3 Dances.*

(B) *** DG Double ADD/Dig. 459 418-2 (2). (i) Boston SO; (ii) Bav. RSO, both cond. Kubelik; (iii) VPO, Levine.

Kubelik's 1971 recording of *Má Vlast* with the Boston Symphony Orchestra has much in its favour, even if it is not as inspired as his later Supraphon version with the Czech Philharmonic. In the earlier set Kubelik was concerned to temper the bombast which so readily comes to the surface of the music in the later sections of the work, especially when played by non-Slavonic orchestras. Yet the adrenalin flows freely and his skill with the inner balance brings much felicitous detail. *Vltava* and *From Bohemia's Woods and Fields* are very successful as is the opening *Vyšehrad*, where the ear notices that the new transfer has filled out the lower range of the recording and restored the analogue ambience, although the cymbal clashes still sound a bit too metallic.

Smetana's four symphonic poems can also be recommended to those who are attracted to the *Má Vlast* cycle. The jolly *Carnival in Prague*, the composer's last work, was written in 1883; the others are more melodramatic, dating from around 1860. The music has a flavour of Dvořák, if without that master's melodic and imaginative flair. The most spectacular is *Wallenstein's Camp* with its opportunities for offstage brass fanfares – very like Liszt's *Mazeppa* – well managed here. This is very enjoyable in its ingenuous way; but perhaps the most distinguished piece here is *Håkon Jarl*, which has a strong vein of full-blooded romanticism. The playing is first class throughout, and the recording has good body and atmosphere.

Levine's *Bartered Bride Overture* and *Dances*, which are used as makeweight are marvellously played and highly infectious. They were recorded digitally in the Musikverein in 1987. Levine offers the usual numbers plus the *Skočná*.

Má Vlast: Vltava.

(M) *** Sony (ADD) SBK 48264. Cleveland O, Szell – BIZET: *Symphony;* MENDELSSOHN: *Midsummer Night's Dream.* ***

(N) (M) *** DG 463 650-2. BPO, Fricsay – DVORAK: *Symphony No. 9 (New World);* LISZT: *Les Préludes.* ***

**(*) DG 439 009-2. VPO, Karajan – DVORAK: *Symphony No. 9 (New World).* **(*)

Má Vlast: Vltava. The Bartered Bride: Overture & Dances.

(M) **(*) Sony (ADD) SMK 60561. NYPO, Bernstein – DVORAK: *Symphony No. 7.* **

Má Vlast: Vltava. The Bartered Bride: Overture; Polka; Furiant; Dance of the Comedians. The Kiss: Overture. Libuše: Overture. The Two Widows: Overture & Polka.

**(*) Decca (IMS) 444 867-2. Cleveland O, Dohnányi.

The Clevelanders play *Vltava* superbly, from the opening trickle, through the village wedding and the moonlight sequence, to the climax at St John's rapids. The effect is both vivid and dramatic and the dynamic range not too restricted to spoil the element of contrast.

With Fricsay the *Vltava* river is obviously in full flood, yet every episode is freshly and characterfully detailed, with the lake twinkling in the moonlight, contrasting with the spectacle of the St John's rapids. A splendid bonus for a memorably individual account of the *New World Symphony*.

Bernstein's *Bartered Bride* excerpts are vivaciously entertaining, with much attractive pointing of detail. His *Vltava* is similarly enjoyable, and the mid-1960s recordings are full and detailed. A pity that the coupling is not so recommendable, which reduces the attractions of this reissue.

A good Smetana anthology from the Cleveland Orchestra

under Christoph von Dohnányi in excellent Decca sound. Charm may not be Dohnányi's strong suit, but this music induces enchantment all by itself. The Cleveland Orchestra play with great brio and virtuosity and, even though there is not too much in the way of spontaneous joy, this anthology will still give pleasure. At 57 minutes and premium price, it is, however, perhaps short measure these days.

Karajan's VPO performance is characteristically well structured, and the recorded sound sounds quite expansive in this remastered format, even if the balance is not quite natural.

CHAMBER MUSIC

Duo for Violin & Piano (From the Homeland).

(N) *** Praga PRD 250 153. Remès, Kayahara – DVORAK: *Sonatina;* JANACEK; MARTINU; SMETANA: *Violin Sonatas.* ***

Smetana's two-movement *Duo* (*From the Homeland*) is, not surprisingly, full of endearing Czech folk influences, with the dumka-style hovering over the first movement. The lyrical second part at first has something of a domestic atmosphere, yet the infectious spirit of the *Skočná* soon asserts itself. It is marvellously played by these two fine artists, who are thoroughly immersed in its local atmosphere. The recording is vividly live and present.

Piano Trio in G min., Op. 15.

*** Chan. 8445; Borodin Trio – DVORAK: *Dumky Trio.* ***

*** Ara. Z6661. Golub–Kaplan–Carr Trio – TCHAIKOVSKY: *Piano Trio.* ***

**(*) MDG MDGL 3247. Trio Parnassus – ARENSKY: *Piano Trio in D min.* **(*)

Piano Trio in G min., Op. 15; (i) Fantasy on a Bohemian Song; From my Homeland.

(M) ** Sup. (ADD) SU 3449-2 131. (i) Klánsky, (i) Pavlík, Jerie.

Writing the *Trio* was a cathartic act, following the death of the composer's four-year-old daughter, so it is not surprising that it is a powerfully emotional work. The writing gives fine expressive opportunities for both the violin and cello, which are taken up eloquently by Rostislav Dubinsky and Yuli Turovsky, and the pianist, Luba Edlina, is also wonderfully sympathetic. In short, a superb account, given a most realistic recording balance. Highly recommended.

Although the balance may place the listener a bit too close to the players for some tastes, the Arabesque CD offers a perfectly pleasing sound and the performance is eminently musical and unaffected. This is the kind of chamber-music playing to inspire confidence in the future: nothing over-driven, mechanized or attention-seeking. While it does not necessarily displace the Borodin Trio, it can be ranked among the best and is the only recording to offer so substantial a partner as the Tchaikovsky Trio – completely uncut, too.

The Trio Parnassus play very much in the nineteenth-century manner and tend to underline and italicize, but they give a likeable and convincing performance, very alive and vivid. Their coupling, the Arensky *D minor Trio,* may well sway some readers in their favour.

Idiomatic performances on Supraphon of the *G minor Piano Trio* and of the *Fantasy on a Bohemian Song* and *From my Homeland,* both for violin and piano. Decent recording, too, but at only 47 minutes' playing time, it is hardly good value, even at mid-price.

String Quartet No. 1 in E min. (From My Life).

⊛ *** Koch 3-6436-2. Medici Qt – BRITTEN: *Quartet No. 3;* JANACEK: *Quartet No. 1;* RAVEL: *Quartet;* SHOSTAKOVICH: *Quartet No. 8.* *** ⊛

*** Decca 452 239-2. Takács Qt – BORODIN: *Quartet No. 2.* ***

(N) (BB) *** Arte Nova 74321 34036-2. Alexander Qt – JANACEK: *String Quartet No. 1;* SCHUBERT: *Quartetsatz.* ***

*** EMI CDC7 54215-2. Alban Berg Qt – DVORAK: *String Quartet No. 12.* ***

(***) Testament mono SBT 1072. Hollywood Qt – DVORAK; KODALY: *Quartets.* (***)

(M) **(*) DG (IMS) (ADD) 437 251-2. Amadeus Qt – DVORAK: *String Quartet No. 12.* **(*)

Smetana's masterly autobiographical *Quartet* brings a performance of dramatic intensity and spontaneous warmth from the Medici, who are in inspired form throughout all five works in this outstanding set. They capture the touch of irony as well as the high spirits in the Scherzo and move us greatly in their deeply felt response to the beautiful, valedictory *Largo sostenuto,* while the sudden, violent change of mood in the finale is profoundly affecting. The recording has remarkable presence and realism.

The Takács Quartet play Smetana's autobiographical work with great ardour; indeed it is impossible not to become caught up in the vibrant feeling of this playing. The Decca recording gives the players a very striking presence. However, one can not help reflecting that there was room for more music here.

The prize-winning Alexander Quartet also give an exceptionally powerful reading of Smetana's movingly autobiographical quartet, tough and incisive, technically flawless. Their full-toned, purposeful playing also brings out the rustic element in Smetana's writing, notably in the second movement and in the polka finale, which is horrifically interrupted to illustrate the onset of the composer's deafness on a high-pitched whistle of tinnitus. The recording is full and immediate.

By the side of the Takács account, the Alban Berg Quartet sound just a shade polished and professional. There is not quite enough spontaneity. All the same, there is much more to admire in the Alban Berg's reading than to cavil at: the first movement comes off well, and the EMI recording is very truthful and present. There is no cause to withhold a third star, particularly as their Dvořák is very successful.

This Hollywood Quartet recording was never issued in the UK in the 1950s when it was made. It is a performance of tremendous fire and passion, with an exhilarating rhythmic drive and a powerful sense of momentum. Yet everything sounds perfectly natural and not overdriven. Great quartet playing – and perfectly acceptable sound, given the mid-1950s date.

A strongly felt and purposeful account from the Amadeus who are on top form: their ensemble, matching of timbre and unanimity of attack, is peerless. At times one feels that Norbert Brainin wears his heart too openly on his sleeve; but there is no doubt that the performance overall is gripping, and the 1977 recording vividly realistic.

String Quartet No. 1 (From My Life) – orchestral version by George Szell; The Bartered Bride: Overture & Dances.

*** Chan. 8412. LSO, Simon.

The Czech feeling of Szell's scoring is especially noticeable in the *Polka*, but overall there is no doubt that the fuller textures add a dimension to the music, though inevitably there are losses as well as gains. The powerful advocacy of Geoffrey Simon and the excellent LSO playing, both here and in the sparkling excerpts from *The Bartered Bride*, provide a most rewarding coupling. The recording is well up to the usual high Chandos standards.

String Quartets Nos. 1 (From My Life); 2 in D min.

*** ASV CDDCA 777. Lindsay Qt (with DVORAK: *Romance; Waltzes Nos. 1–2* ***).

(M) **(*) Sup. SU 3450-2 131. Panocha Qt.

The Lindsay Quartet bring dramatic intensity to the *E minor Quartet* and play with great fire and vitality. Their (perhaps slightly forward) recording is very good indeed, and readers wanting both the Smetana *Quartets* together need look no further.

The two string quartets from the Panocha Quartet are short measure at 45 minutes! These are well-played and intelligently shaped performances but there are finer, more spirited versions in the catalogue.

Memories of Bohemia in the Form of Polkas, Op. 12; Op. 13; 3 Poetic Polkas, Op. 8; Polkas in F min.; A; E; G min.; 3 Salon Polkas, Op. 7.

** Teldec 3984 21261-2. Schiff.

This issue serves as a reminder of the excellence and freshness of Smetana's keyboard music. Two-thirds of his output is for the piano. András Schiff is as sympathetic an interpreter as one could wish for, but the attractions of the disc are somewhat diminished by the claustrophobic acoustic, which lends a brittle tone to the instrument.

OPERA

The Bartered Bride (complete, in Czech).

*** Sup. 10 3511-2 (3). Beňačková, Dvorský, Novák, Kopp, Jonášová, Czech Philharmonic Ch. and O, Košler.

The digital Supraphon set under Košler admirably supplies the need for a first-rate Czech version of this delightful comic opera. The performance sparkles from beginning to end, with folk rhythms crisply enunciated in an infectiously idiomatic way. The cast is strong, headed by the characterful Gabriela Beňačková as Mařenka and one of the finest of today's Czech tenors, Peter Dvorský, as Jeník. Miroslav Kopp

in the role of the ineffective Vašek sings powerfully too. As Kecal the marriage-broker, Richard Novák is not always steady, but his swaggering characterization is most persuasive. The CDs offer some of the best sound we have yet had from Supraphon, fresh and lively. The discs are fairly generously banded, but this could now be fitted on a pair of CDs, so the set is unnecessarily expensive. The libretto, however, has been improved and is clear and easy to use.

The Bartered Bride: highlights.

(M) **(*) Sup. 112251-2 (from above recording, with Beňačková, Dvorský; cond. Košler).

A well-made if not strikingly generous set of highlights from Košler's sparkling complete set. But the documentation includes only a list of excerpts unrelated to any synopsis, and there is no translation.

The Brandenburgers in Bohemia (complete).

**(*) Sup. (ADD) 11 1804-2 (2). Zídek, Otava, Subrtová, Kalaš, Joran, Vich, Prague Nat. Theatre soloists, Ch. & O, Jan Hus Tichý.

Though much of the drama centres on the fate of the heroine, Liduše, abducted by a Prague burgher with the mercenary Germanic name of Tausendmark, the love interest which must sustain any romantic opera is sketched in only cursorily. The main duet between Liduše and her beloved, Junoš, is charming and jolly rather than heartfelt, an opportunity missed. Nevertheless there is much to enjoy in a performance as lively as this, with stirring patriotic choruses sung with a will, even if their melodic invention is hardly distinguished. Milada Subrtová sings with appealingly sweet, firm tone as Liduše, and the young Ivo Zídek makes a fresh-voiced hero, strained only a little on top. Tausendmark is sung by a stalwart veteran, Zdeněk Otava, making up in bite what he lacks in vocal quality. A collector's item.

Dalibor (complete).

*** Sup. (ADD) 11 2185-2 (2). Přibyl, Kniplová, Jindrák, Svorc, Horáček, Prague Nat. Theatre Ch. & O, Krombholc.

In the development of the plot, when the imprisoned hero's lover is disguised as the gaoler's assistant, *Dalibor* readily evokes associations with *Fidelio* and the subject prompted Smetana to write some of his most inspired music. The confrontations between hero and heroine also inspire Smetana to some glorious writing, richly lyrical, most notably the love duet in the prison scene of Act II. This vintage set of 1967, sounding more vivid and full-blooded than many more recent recordings, features in those roles two of the most distinguished Czech singers of their time, both in their prime, the tenor Vílém Přibyl and the dramatic soprano, Nadezda Kniplová. The other principals are not so consistent, but Krombholc proves a most persuasive advocate, consistently bringing out the red-blooded fervour of the writing. Highly recommended to anyone who wants to investigate beyond *The Bartered Bride*. A full translation is provided.

Libuše.

(*) Sup. 11 1276-2 633 (3). Beňačková, Zítek, Svorc, Vodička, Děpoltová, Prague Nat. Theatre Ch. & O, Košler.

Recorded live, the cast here is even stronger than that of the previous recording under Krombholc, with Gabriela Beňačková-Cápová as Libuše memorable in her prophetic aria in Act III. Václav Zítek as Přemysl, her consort, provides an attractive lyrical interlude in Act II which, with its chorus of harvesters, has affinities with *The Bartered Bride*. In Act I there is some Slavonic wobbling, notably from Eva Děpoltová as Krasava, but generally the singing is as dramatic as the plot-line will allow. Košler directs committedly; with the stage perspectives well caught, an unintrusive audience and no disturbing stage-noises with such a static plot, the recording is very satisfactory. The cues still provide poor internal access for an opera playing for not far short of three hours. Twelve extra index points have been added to the 14 bands – not nearly enough for a work of this kind.

The Two Widows (complete).

** Sup. (ADD) 11 2122-2 (2). Sormová, Machotková, Zahradníček, Horáček, Prague Nat. Theatre Ch. & O, Jílek.
** Praga PR 250 022/3 (2). Jonášová, Machotková, Svejda, Jedlička, Prague RSO, Krombholc.

The Two Widows is a tale of country life in the big house rather than among the peasantry, with the plot centring on two cousins, both widows, and inconsequential confusions over which of them is going to marry the hero, Ladislav. That said, Smetana offers much delightful music and there are some charming numbers in between, not least an aria for the hero, 'When Maytime arrives', at the beginning of Act II. Jiří Zahradníček is at his best there, singing lustily, though in gentler moments Slavonic unsteadiness develops. Jaroslav Horáček is effective in the *buffo* bass role of Mumlal but, sadly, the casting of the two widows, both sopranos, involves the major role of Karolina going to the shrill and wobbly Nǎda Sormová, while Marcela Machotková, who is altogether sweeter and firmer, with a mezzo-ish quality, is consigned to the role of Anežka with far less to sing, even though it is she who gets the hero. Recorded in 1975, this lively performance under Frantisek Jílek is on the whole well transferred to CD, though in a dry-ish acoustic the Prague Theatre violins sound undernourished. The libretto includes a very necessary translation.

Recorded in 1974, only eighteen months earlier than the Supraphon version, the Praga set, as transferred to CD by Chant du Monde, offers a more genial performance, a degree more expansive but in sound that is rougher and edgier, with less sense of presence. In the role of Ladislav, Miroslav Svejda has a more pleasing lyric tenor than his opposite number and is far more headily beautiful in the hero's aria. Jana Jonášová as Karolina is steadier than Sormová but, if anything, even shriller, not so warmly expressive in her Act II monologue. Again Machotková is excellent as Anežka, and Dalibor Jedlička is a first-rate *buffo* bass. Two balancing points against the Praga set are that Act II starts on the first disc, where Supraphon has one disc per Act, and that Praga offers only an English translation with no Czech text.

SMYTH, Ethel (1858–1944)

(i) *Concerto for Violin, Horn & Orchestra. Serenade in D.*

*** Chan. 9449. (i) Langdon, Watkins; BBC PO, De la Martinez.

The *Concerto for Violin, Horn and Orchestra* is a highly successful piece in every respect. The first movement begins with an ambitious string melody, then the soloists enter alternately with the endearing secondary idea (one of the composer's very best tunes), which is imaginatively developed in a free fantasia of flowing and dancing melody and varying moods; only at the recapitulation do the soloists share the opening theme. The romantic central *Elegy* brings a touchingly beautiful and nostalgic exchange between the two soloists.

The *Serenade in D major* might well be Brahms's. Not only does the rich string writing of the first movement have a glorious sweep, but the harmonic thinking and progressions are *echt*-Brahms. Yet Smyth's invention is of high quality, for all its eclecticism. With superb performances and warm, sumptuous recording, both these colourful and tuneful works will give great pleasure. This is easily the most impressive Smyth offering yet to have appeared on CD, conducted with understanding and commitment.

The Wreckers: Overture.

(B) *** CfP (ADD) CD-CFP 4635. RSNO, Gibson – GERMAN: *Welsh Rhapsody;* HARTY: *With the Wild Geese;* MACCUNN: *Land of the Mountain and Flood.* ***

Ethel Smyth's *Overture* for her opera, *The Wreckers*, is a strong, meaty piece which shows the calibre of this remarkable woman's personality for, while the material itself is not memorable, it is put together most compellingly and orchestrated with real flair. The recording is full and the CD has refined detail.

String Quartet in E min.; (i) *String Quintet in E, Op. 4.*

*** CPO 999352-2. Mannheim Qt, with (i) Griesheimer.

The *Quintet* of 1884 may suggest Dvořák's *American Quartet* and *New World Symphony* in its first movement, but the Smyth *Quintet* was written before either of those works, a strongly built piece with substantial outer movements framing three interludes, including a brief, magical *Adagio* which breathes the air of late Beethoven. Even more delightful and refreshing is the *Quartet*, begun in 1902 but not completed until ten years later. Instead of an allegro first movement, Smyth opts for an easy-going *Allegretto*, while the beautiful, peacefully lyrical slow movement equally belies the composer's political image.

COMPLETE PIANO MUSIC

Piano Sonatas Nos. 1 in C; 2 in F sharp min.; 3 in D; 2 Canons; Aus der Jugendzeit! (To Youth!); 4 Four-Part Dances; Invention in D; Piece in E; Preludes & Fugues: in F sharp; in C. Suite in E; Variations in D flat on an Original Theme.

(BB) ** CPO 999 327-2 (2). Serbescu.

The *C major Sonata* was Dame Ethel's first composition when she arrived to study in Leipzig in July 1877. It is a promising work, opening agreeably and with a gentle funeral march for its *Adagio* slow movement, which Liana Serbescu plays touchingly. The *Second Sonata* also has a pleasing but less distinctive *Andante*, and the *Third* is notable for its lively closing Scherzo. However, it cannot be said that any of these works are very distinctive, although the neo-classical *Suite* is jolly, with an engagingly soft-centred Minuet. The extended *Variations*, 'of an exceedingly dismal nature' according to the composer, are indeed rather heavy-going, although the theme itself is agreeable enough. There are immediate reminders of Brahms in the third and fourth of the *Four-Part Dances* which open the collection, and the two very successful *Preludes and Fugues* which close the second CD successfully evoke the world of Mendelssohn. All this music is played sympathetically and is well recorded, but none of it is likely to re-enter the repertoire.

VOCAL MUSIC

Mass in D; March of the Women; Boatswain's Mate: Mrs Water's aria.

(N) (M) *** EMI CDM5 67426–2. Harrhy, Hardy, Dressen, Bohn, Ch. & O of Plymouth Music Series, Minnesota, Brunelle.

Ethel Smyth's *Mass in D* is one of her most ambitious works, a piece that boldly seeks to echo Beethoven's great *Missa solemnis* in its moods and idiom. Though Smyth's invention is less memorable than Beethoven's, the drive and the vehemence of her writing make this a warmly rewarding piece, with Brahms's *Requiem* another, if less marked, influence. The composer herself counted the *Gloria*, the longest and most energetic movement, as the finest and prescribed that it should be performed, not in the usual liturgical sequence, but last, as a happy ending, as is done here. Philip Brunelle draws fine playing and singing from the members of the Plymouth Music Series. Smyth's once-celebrated suffragette march is done with polish rather than feminist fervour, and Eiddwen Harrhy makes a characterful soloist in the extended aria from Smyth's best-known opera. The sound is first rate.

SOLER, Antonio (1729–83)

(i) *Concertos for 2 Organs Nos. 1–6;* (ii) *Fandango in D min.; Harpsichord Sonatas Nos. 12 in G; 15 in D min.; 49 in D min.; 54 in C; 56 in F; 69 in F; 76 in F; 84 in D; 90 in F sharp.*

(B) *** Erato Ultima 3984 27005-2 (2). (i) Mathot & Koopman (organ); (ii) Ross (harpsichord).

Soler is an individual composer who has a large quantity of keyboard music to his credit, much influenced by Domenico Scarlatti. He has less character than his illustrious model, and is in many respects more conventional, but he still has the capacity to offer surprising and original touches. This Ultima Double makes a useful and inexpensive entry into

his world. The concertos (written for the Infante Gabriel of the Spanish royal family) are not here played on a pair of organs but on a single instrument whose sounds emanate over a fairly wide spectrum, so that the ear often enjoys the effect of a stereo interplay. The instrument itself, in the Basilica della Misericordia, San Elpidio a Mare, Italy, has some piquant stops, one very like a crumhorn, and the two players here register imaginatively. The music itself is ingenuous, but appealingly so. The collection is framed by No. 3 *in G major* which has a striking opening *Andantino* and No. 1 *in C* which ends with a characterful Minuet. Scott Ross then follows with the celebrated *Fandango* (uncut, though it is very repetitive), and ten well-chosen and diverse *Sonatas*, which cover the entire compositional period of Soler's life. No. 4 *in D minor* is appealingly lyrical, No. 59, with its glissando flourishes, is most like Scarlatti. The two closing works, Nos. 84 and 90 also demand and receive sparkling bravura. Indeed these performances are full of life and character and are, like the organ works, very well recorded.

KEYBOARD WORKS

Harpsichord Sonatas Nos. 1; 15; 18; 19; 43; 54; 85; 90; 91; 101; 110.

(BB) ** Naxos 8.553462. Rowland (harpsichord).

Harpsichord Sonatas Nos. 16; 17; 35; 42; 46; 52; 83; 87; 92; 106; 116.

(BB) ** Naxos 8.553463. Rowland (harpsichord).

Harpsichord Sonatas Nos. 28; 29; 32; 33; 34; 50; 55; 57; 69; 93; 117.

(BB) ** Naxos 8.553463. Rowland (harpsichord).

A new series of the Soler keyboard sonatas from Naxos is played with sensibility and often real panache by Gilbert Rowland on a modern copy of a French two-manual harpsichord. The snag is that while he is truthfully and not too forwardly recorded, the acoustic of Epsom College Concert Hall (Surrey) is over-resonant and spreads the sound somewhat uncomfortably in the fast bravura passages. In the more reflective minor key works (*17 in D minor; 52 in E minor*, for instance) there are no grumbles, and often the brilliance of the playing (as in the romping *No. 43 in G*, the sparkling *No. 69 in F* and *106 in E minor*, with its crisp articulation) projects through the resonance. The discs have really excellent documentation, describing each individual work in detail.

Keyboard Sonatas Nos. 15, 21, 42, 84–7, 89.

(B) *** Double Decca (ADD) 433 920-2 (2). De Larrocha, Mateo – ALBENIZ: *Sonata;* GRANADOS: *Escenas románticas; Goyescas* etc. ***

As is also the case with the music of Domenico Scarlatti, with an advocate of the calibre of Alicia De Larrocha these works are quite as pleasing heard on the piano as they are on the harpsichord. The performances are characteristically vital and the 1981 recording is excellent.

Keyboard Sonatas Nos. 18; 19; 41; 72; 78; 84–8; 90; Fandango.

(M) *** Virgin VER5 61220-2. Cole (harpsichord or fortepiano).

Maggie Cole plays a dozen Soler pieces, eleven *Sonatas* and the celebrated *Fandango*, half of them on the harpsichord and the remainder on the fortepiano; she gives altogether dashing performances on both. Good pieces to sample are *No. 87 in G minor* (track 5) and, on the harpsichord, *No. 86 in D major* (track 9) or the *Fandango* itself. The playing is all very exhilarating and inspiriting. Played at a normal level-setting, both instruments sound a bit thunderous, but played at a lower level the results are very satisfactory.

SORABJI, Khaikhosru (1892–1988)

Fantaisie espagnole.

*** Altarus AIR-CD 9022. Amato.

Sorabji's *Fantaisie espagnole* comes from 1919 and shows his preoccupation with exotic, Szymanowskian keyboard textures and voluptuous Ravel-like harmonies. Donna Amato seems completely attuned to the idiom. It is a short work (just under eighteen minutes) and is brilliantly played and recorded on this Altarus single.

SOUSA, John Philip (1854–1932)

The Bride Elect (including ballet: People Who Live in Glass Houses); El Capitan; Our Flirtations.

(N) **(*) Marco 8.223872. Razumovsky SO, Brion.

John Philip Sousa's Band was the first great commercial success of American popular music. Sousa became its primary focus in the last decade of the nineteenth century. He toured the American continent every year, and took his Band across the Atlantic on four European tours in the first five years of the new century. His quick marches and two-steps (danced as well as marched to) had a unique transatlantic rhythmic vitality.

One tends to forget that Sousa wrote things other than marches, and here we have some music from his operettas. Though successful in their day, like so many other stage works of their kind, they did not have the staying power of Gilbert and Sullivan, but the dances and incidental music from then remains fresh. *The Bride Elect* was written in 1897, but Sousa's ballet *People Who Live in Glass Houses* was used in the 1923 revival and is included here. It seems like a ballet for alcoholics, with its dances entitled *The Champagnes, The Rhine Wines, The Whiskies ('Scotch, Irish, Bourbon and Rye!')*, and is highly entertaining.

The waltzes and marches from *El Capitan* and *Our Flirtations* are enjoyable too, and display imaginative touches of orchestration. Keith Brion, musicologist, Pops Director of the Harrisburg Symphony, also leads his own touring Sousa band, so it is not surprising that he is thoroughly at home in this repertoire. Under his direction the Razumovsky Orchestra plays this music brightly and idiomatically, and the recording is good.

Caprice: The Coquette; Circus Galop; The Gliding Girl (tango); The Irish Dragoon: Myrrha Gavotte; On Wings of Lightning; Peaches and Cream (foxtrot); Presidential Polonaise; 3 Quotations; Sandalphon Waltzes; Silver Spray Schottische. Marches: Belle of Chicago; Fairest of the Fair; Federal; Gladiator; Hail to the Spirit of Liberty; Venus.

(N) **(*) Marco 8.223874. Razumovsky SO, Brion.

The present Sousa survey provides a fair degree of variety by including an attractive *Gliding Girl* tango, a flimsy *Caprice* and a disarming *Gavotte*, plus a slightly grander Presidential Polonaise, as well as the usual marches and waltzes on which Sousa excelled. As usual on this label, helpful notes are included, and this CD should not disappoint those drawn to this repertoire.

Colonial Dames waltz; Humoresque on Gershwin's Swanee; Looking Upwards (suite). Marches: Daughters of Texas; Foshay Tower; Hail to the Spirit of Liberty; Hands across the Sea; Imperial Edward; Invincible Eagle; Kansas Wildcats; Manhattan Beach; Power and Glory.

(N) (BB) *** Naxos 8.559058. Royal Artillery Band, Brion.

Naxos provide here a superb new collection of Sousa's wind band music, presented with tremendous vigour and panache by the Royal Artillery Band, directed by Keith Brion, who knows just how to play this repertoire. The old favourites – as well as some of the rarer items – come up as fresh as paint. The recording is very good – perhaps a little lacking in opulence, but vivid enough.

Dwellers of the Western World (suite); Humoresque on Gershwin's Swanee; Humoresque on Kern's Look for the Silver Lining; The Irish Dragoon: Overture; Rêverie: Nymphalin; Semper fidelis; Songs from Grace and Songs for Glory. Marches: Bullets and Bayonets; The Daughters of Texas; Jack Tar; Invincible Eagle; Power and the Glory; Stars and Stripes Forever.

(N) ** Marco 8.223873. Slovak RSO (Bratislava), Brion.

Opening with the bright and breezy *Irish Dragoon Overture*, the ensuing programme is laced with bracing marches, but balanced out with more reflective music, such as the *Rêverie*, and fantasias on famous popular songs, plus arrangements of popular religious themes. The three movements of *The Dwellers of the Western World* are entitled *Red Man, White Man* and *Black Man*. This is agreeable enough with its dashes of folksy colour, though much of the writing is less than first rate. Keith Brion persuades his Slovak orchestra to play it all convincingly enough, while the famous *Stars and Stripes March* generates plenty of gusto. The sound is fully acceptable, but lack ultimate range and richness. The documentation is good.

MARCHES

The Complete 116 Known Published Marches.

✪ (N) *** Walking Frog Records (ADD) WFR 300 (5). Detroit Concert Band, Leonard B. Smith (available from PO Box 680, Oskaloosa, Iowa 52577, USA (www.walkingfrog.com).

We are greatly indebted to an American reader who not only pointed out the omission of this key set of recordings from our survey, but subsequently arranged for Walking Frog Records (wonderful name) to send us the CDs for review. Their excellence is almost beyond compare. The Detroit Band is a superb ensemble in all departments, and Leonard B. Smith (distinguished cornet soloist and ex-member of the Goldman Band and later the US Navy Band) proves to be a outstandingly persuasive exponent of Sousa marches.

In his hands they swing along without any feeling of being pressed too hard; indeed, their gait and their sheer bonhomie brings an instant smile of pleasure. The playing is not only crisp and polished, but it has a consistent zest and spontaneity.

The recordings too are consistently demonstration-worthy. We were not surprised to discover that they have analogue masters. They were made between 1973 and 1979 in the main auditorium of the Masonic Temple in Detroit, Michigan, using a classic stereo microphone coverage without gimmicks, and the recording team was led by none other than Jack Renner (of Telarc); his colleagues were Robert Woods and James Schulkey. Tony Schmitt's digital re-mastering for CD calls for equal praise: nothing has been lost. The percussion (wonderful snare drums) and the full clear bass line are equally real. As the documentation truly claims: the sound you hear is what the listener would hear having 'the best seat in the house'.

We have not space to list the entire contents, but each of these five CDs is led by one of the most famous marches: Volume 1, *The Thunderer*; Volume 2, *El Capitan*; Volume 3, *The Washington Post*; Volume 4, *Hands across the Sea*; while Volume 5 has a double whammy, opening with a riveting *Semper fidelis*, with a splendidly built climax, and ending with the greatest march of all, *The Stars and Stripes Forever*. This is music-making that cannot but help but cheer you up.

The Complete Commercial Recordings of 60 Marches by the Sousa Band (1897–1930).

(N) (**(*)**) Crystal CD 461-3 (3). Introductory speech by Sousa. Sousa Band, Sousa; Arthur Pryor; Henry Higgins; Walter B. Rodgers; Nathaniel Shillkret; Rosario Bourdon; Herbert L. Clarke; Edwin G. Clarke; Joseph Pasternack.

Sousa himself briefly introduces this anthology, in a recording taken from a 1929 NBC broadcast celebrating the composer's seventy-fifth birthday, and he follows, of course, by conducting *The Stars and Stripes Forever*. These recordings, made over a period of thirty-three years, are an integral part of the history of the gramophone, for before the coming of the electric process a woodwind and brass concert band was the only instrumental ensemble which could be captured with a reasonable degree of realism by the acoustic recording process.

If the recordings deriving from early 7" Berliner discs are often of very poor quality, with more background noise than music, a cheerful 1899 record of *The Mikado March* (well laced with Sullivan tunes), conducted by Arthur Pryor, is an honourable exception, and Sousa's own later RCA recordings are often of surprising fidelity. In his historical note, Keith Brion reminds us than the musicians used for these RCA Camden sessions comprised many members of the Philadelphia Orchestra, plus a smattering of Sousa Band players who lived in the Philadelphia area.

Arthur Pryor usually got good results, too, although not all the playing here is immaculate. The ensemble slips badly at the opening of *Jack Tar*, yet the performance is redeemed by the middle section, which briefly quotes the *Sailor's Hornpipe* and has almost hi-fi percussion effects. However, the recordings Sousa himself made in 1917–18 bring some particularly crisp ensemble, and tempi that in *Sabre and Spurs* and *Solid Men to the Front*, for instance, are surprisingly relaxed.

Joseph Pasternack, who conducted the band in the 1920s, also did not press forward so forcefully as some modern American performances do, but followed Sousa's style, with a swinging pacing that would have been ideal for marching. Rosario Bourdon, who followed in the late 1920s (and had the benefit of fuller, though not necessarily clearer electric recording) added a little more pressure, and Arthur Pryor, who has the last word here with a 1926 Camden recording of *The Stars and Stripes*, certainly doesn't look back: the piccolo solo is a joy. Excellent documentation, with photographs

Marches: *The Ancient and Honorable Artillery Company; The Black Horse Troop; Bullets and Bayonets; The Gallant Seventh; Golden Jubilee; The Glory of the Yankee Navy; The Gridiron Club; High School Cadets; The Invincible Eagle; The Kansas Wildcats; The Liberty Bell; Manhattan Beach; The National Game; New Mexico; Nobles of the Mystic Shrine; Our Flirtation; The Piccadore; The Pride of the Wolverines; Riders for the Flag; The Rifle Regiment; Sabre and Spurs; Sesqui-centennial Exposition; Solid Men to the Front; Sound Off.*

(M) *** Mercury (ADD) 434 300-2. Eastman Wind Ens., Fennell.

Fennell's collection of twenty-four Sousa marches (73 minutes) derives from vintage Mercury recordings of the early 1960s. The performances have characteristic American pep and natural exuberance; the zest of the playing always carries the day. This remains an outstanding single-disc collection.

SPERGER, Johannes (1750–1812)

Symphonies in B flat; C; F.

(N) (BB) ** Naxos 8. 554764. Musica Aeterna Bratislava, Zajíček.

Johannes Sperger was a famous double-bass player in his day, and apart from appearing as a soloist, found his main livelihood playing in various court orchestras including that of the Cardinal Primate of Hungary. His symphonies are stylized works in three movements, the center piece in one instance here being a simple *Andante*; in each of the other two it is a *Minuet* and *Trio*. The most striking movement is the first of the *F major*, relatively (only relatively) strong and turbulent. But these are in essence undemanding works, well crafted, but with nothing very individual to say, and they never reveal that their composer was a virtuoso of the double bass. They are very well played by this excellent period instrument chamber orchestra and the recording cannot be faulted. But, alas, Johannes Sperger deserves his obscurity.

SPOHR, Ludwig (1784–1859)

(i) *Clarinet Concertos Nos. 1 in C min., Op. 26; 3 in F min., WoO19; (ii) Potpourri for Clarinet & Orchestra in F, Op. 80.*

(N) (BB) * Naxos 8.550688. Ottsensamer; (i) Slovak State PO (Košice); (ii) Slovak RSO (Bratislava), Wildner.

Clarinet Concertos Nos. 2 in E flat, Op. 57; 4 in E min.; Fantasia & Variations on a Theme of Danzi, Op. 81.

(N) (BB) * Naxos 8.550688. Ottsensamer, Slovak RSO (Bratislava), Wildner.

Spohr's four concertos were written between 1908 and 1929 for the clarinettist Johann Simon Hermstedt. But although they are all in a traditional three-movement format, Spohr was not content to rest on his laurels and each work has a character of its own. The *First* opens with a delightful chorale-like theme on the woodwind which then becomes the basis for the first movement. The *Adagio* features memorably tranquil melody, its mood broken only by the arrival of the rollicking *Rondo* finale, full of inventive ideas and with plenty of contrast.

The *Second Concerto in E flat* brings a bustling first movement with an engagingly dotted marching theme, very like Hummel. The line of the *Adagio* is distinctly operatic and the jocular *Polacca* finale opens with timpani and horns, which are to be featured throughout.

The very dramatic opening tutti of the *Third Concerto* introduces a charmingly doleful lyrical melody in the violins over a pizzicato accompaniment, to balance a dramatic restlessness in the orchestra. The lovely *Adagio* is deeply expressive, all but worthy of Mozart, and the finale lollops along engagingly, with bursts of bravura for the soloist, but has a tender secondary strain.

The *Fourth E minor Concerto* is in many ways the finest of all, opening with a solemn minor-key exposition, and even the secondary theme is lyrically restrained, with the orchestral tuttis reflecting a more searching mood than in the earlier works. The *Larghetto* too, has a questing, improvisational air, ending gently and pensively to make way for the contrast of the lively *Rondo al espagnole*. Yet even here the lyrical interludes make it plain that Spohr is determined to avoid any suggestion of triviality.

The Danzi *Fantasia* opens very dramatically, but its basic theme is simple and ingenuous, its treatment histrionically operatic. The Potpourri draws on themes from Peter von Winter's now forgotten opera *Das unterbrochene Opferfest.* Horns introduce an engaging *Larghetto* which then leads to a closing *Allegro/Allegretto* featuring another attractive idea, which is subject to various diverting embellishments.

Ernst Ottensamer is a most sensitive artist and a superb player with an appealingly warm, liquid tone. Apart from sailing through all Spohr's decorative roulades and technical extravagances with aplomb, he plays over the widest range of dynamic, often fining down his tone to a pianissimo to echo a phrase with magical effect. Johann Wildner provides lively, polished accompaniments, and the recording is first rate. It is difficult to imagine these performances being surpassed, and this pair of discs would be highly recommendable if they cost far more.

Clarinet Concerto No. 1 in C min., Op. 26.

(M) * Classic FM 75605 57019-2. Lawson, Hanover Band, Goodman – WEBER: *Clarinet Concertos Nos. 1–2 etc.* ***

On Classic FM the first of Spohr's *Clarinet Concertos* provides a generous bonus on an outstanding disc. Colin Lawson, principal clarinet of the Hanover Band, plays most imaginatively with attractively reedy tone to match the period instruments of his colleagues. Full and vivid sound.

Concerto for String Quartet & Orchestra in A min., Op.131.

**** Ara. Z 6723. San Francisco Ballet O, Lark Qt, Le Roux – HANDEL: *Concerto grosso in B flat, Op. 6/7;* SCHOENBERG: *Concerto for String Quartet & Orchestra after Handel's Concerto grosso, Op. 4/7;* ELGAR: *Introduction & Allegro for Strings.* ***

This is a consistently engaging work (Spohr's very last concerto), inventive and tuneful – the slow movement is particularly fine – using the players in the solo quartet individually as well as in consort. It is very persuasively played, and with the proviso that the solo group are balanced rather forwardly, the recording is very good too. With imaginative couplings this is very much worth trying.

Violin Concertos Nos. 1 in A, Op. 1; 14 in A min., Op. 110; 15 in E min., Op. 128.

**(N) **(*) CPO 999 403-2. Hoelscher, Berlin RSO, Frölich.

Spohr's eighteen violin concertos (three of which he withdrew) span the period from 1799 to 1844. No. 1, written in 1802, was the first to be published and is much more than a beginner's piece. It has an athletic opening movement, a charming *Siciliano* (with variations) as its centrepiece and a lively if more conventional *Polacca* finale. The *A minor* work is subtitled: *Concertino: Sonst und Jetzt* ('Then and now') and its contrasts were meant to ridicule Paganinian pyrotechnics, which had at the time found such favour with the public. But the piece turned out to be brilliant in its own right, especially in the vivace closing section.

No. 15 in E minor was composed in 1844, when Mendelssohn was completing his own more famous concerto in the same key, and there are surprising similarities, and not only in layout. Of course Spohr's *Larghetto* is not as fine as Mendelssohn's *Andante*, but it is warmly beguiling, and has a comparable simplicity of mood, while the *Rondo grazioso*, not as sparkling as Mendelssohn's finale, has a distinct Mendelssohnian air. Hoelscher gives excellent performances of all three works and is well accompanied, but the recording places the violin rather forwardly and the treble focus is less than perfect, and at times his upper range sounds a little scratchy.

Violin Concertos Nos. 7 in E min., Op. 38; 9 on D min., Op. 55; 10 in A, Op. 63.

(N) **(*) CPO 999 232-2. Hoelscher, Berlin RSO, Frölich.

Here again the key of Spohr's *E minor Concerto* brings a certain Mendelssohnian affinity, especially in the passage work. Its lyrical ideas are attractive, especially the rather lovely *Adagio*, and the bouncing finale dances in a fast waltz tempo. No. 9 opens pontifically, but with the secondary theme the mood relents lyrically ready for the entry of the soloist. The Adagio is songful and although Spohr described the *Rondo-allegretto* as 'tempestuous', here it is good-humouredly so.

No. 10 opens with a spaciously conceived introduction, but the main theme then appears jauntily in a 6/8 rhythm. The serenely poetic slow movement is one of Spohr's finest, and the skipping finale is engagingly light-hearted. Again excellent performances and good recording, with the focus of the soloist's upper range captured more cleanly, although he is not flattered by the microphones.

Symphonies Nos. 1 in E flat, Op. 20; 5 in C min., Op. 102.

**(*) Marco 8.223363. Slovak State PO (Košice), Walter.

Spohr wrote ten symphonies in all: the *First* when he was in his mid-twenties and still in thrall to Mozart; the *Fifth* comes from the late 1830s and was much admired by Schumann. Although he is no great symphonist, Spohr is an eminently civilized composer, and the case for him is well put by Alfred Walter and the Košice orchestra, who are decently served by the engineers.

Symphonies Nos. 2 in D min., Op. 49; 9 in B min. (The Seasons), Op. 143.

** Marco 8.223454. Slovak State PO (Košice), Walter.

The *Second Symphony* (1820) has dramatic undertones, but emerges here an amiable, Mendelssohnian work with a neat Scherzo and much Schubertian charm in the finale. Walter's performance is warm and polished, but one feels the music could be given a stronger profile. At the opening of *The Seasons,*, the Schumanesque depiction of *Winter* entirely lacks icicles, but the *Transition to Spring* brings some delightful birdsong and leads to a charming Ländler which later becomes more animated. *Summer* is hazily somnolent with 'distant sounds of thunder', then simple horn-calls lead into the more exuberant hunting and drinking scene of autumn, with some colourful orchestral effects. In imaginative force this is not a patch on Haydn, but one feels a really strongly characterized performance could make more of it than does the rather literal-minded Alfred Walter.

Symphonies Nos. 3 in C minor, Op. 78; 6 in G (Historical Symphony in the Style and Taste of Four Different Periods), Op. 116.

*** Marco 8.223349. Slovak State PO (Košice), Walter.

This coupling, which so far is the best of the Walter–Spohr series, is well worth getting. The *Historical Symphony* is a fascinating pastiche, and the *C minor* is one of the finest of Spohr's early symphonies inspiring Walter to give one of his most vigorous and committed performances. The *Larghetto*

has genuine depth, but the most ambitious movement is the highly inventive finale, both life-enhancing and energetic, and with plenty of contrapuntal interest, including a full-scale central fugue. It is very well played indeed. The *Historical Symphony* is most endearing in its respect for the great masters. It opens with a solemn, full-orchestral treatment of the *C major fugue* from Book I of Bach's '48', and also introduces pastoral reminders of Handel's *Messiah*, including an allusion to 'He shall feed his flock'. The slow movement, richly scored, remembers both Mozart's *39th* and *Prague Symphonies*, and in the curiously lyrical Scherzo. The timpani (rather too muted here) recall the Beethoven of the *Seventh Symphony*. The inappropriately but agreeably frivolous finale, 'the latest of the new', then bursts with energy, drawing on the vivacious ideas of Adam and Auber, in particular the *Muette de Portici Overture*. Walter is a convincing exponent of this curiously balanced work and his orchestra respond with enthusiasm.

Symphonies Nos. 7 in C (The Earthly and Divine in Human Life), Op. 121; 8 in G, Op. 137.

** Marco 8.223432. Slovak State PO (Košice), Walter.

In contrasting his *Irdisches und Göttliches im Menschenleben*, Spohr uses the concerto grosso principal, with an eleven-piece concertino representing the 'divine', while the full orchestra are the 'earthly'; here both elements are fairly fully integrated. He charmingly and successfully depicts *The World of Childhood*, but the profounder sentiments of *The Age of Passion* defeat him, and the *Final Triumph of the Heavenly*, moves from melodrama to a serene but complacent sentimentality. The *Eighth Symphony*, although conservative, is an altogether better proposition. The work's kernel is a fine, sombre *Poco Adagio*, with the strings effectively underpinned by trombone sonorities. The Scherzo opens with a romantic horn-call and features an obbligato solo violin in the Trio. Together with the engagingly songful finale, it almost turns the symphony into a serenade. Alfred Walter is clearly at home here and the Slovak orchestra creates a Bohemian bonhomie in the two final movements. Good, smooth, warm sound.

CHAMBER MUSIC

Double Quartet No. 1 in D min., Op. 65.

(M) ** EMI CDM5 65995-2. De Peyer, Melos Ens. –
   BERWALD: *Septet* ***; WEBER: *Clarinet Quintet.* **(*)
(N) (BB) ** Warner Apex 8573 89089-2. Kreuzberger Qt &
   Eden Qt – MENDELSSOHN: *Octet; String Quartet No. 1 in E flat, Op. 12.* **

The Melos performance has plenty of character, but the recording, though clear and quite full, sounds a little edgy in the present transfer.

The Kreuzberger and Eden Quartets join together to give a well-integrated and felicitous performance of Spohr's *Double Quartet*, which is distinctly enjoyable, especially the vivacious *Allegro molto* finale. The snag is that the remastered recording from the early 1980s has just a touch of edge on the string sound.

Double Quartets Nos. 1 in D min., Op. 65; 2 in E flat, Op. 77; 3 in E min., Op. 87; 4 in G min., Op. 136.

*** Hyp. Dyad CDD 22014 (2). ASMF Chamber Ens.

The opening of the first *Double Quartet* is inviting (as again is the rather solemn introduction of the *Third*, which then lightens, yet retains its nostalgic feeling). While this is all essentially amiable music, the standard of Spohr's invention is quite high throughout all four works, and the scoring cleverly makes the most of the antiphony between the two groups. So does the recording here, with a natural interplay within a pleasingly warm acoustic. The playing is predictably fluent and spontaneous-sounding, well blended and polished.

Nonet in F, Op. 31; Octet in E, Op. 32.

*** Hyp. CDA 66699. Gaudier Ens.

(M) *** CRD (ADD) CRD 3354. Nash Ens.

The Gaudier Ensemble give us a performance of the *Octet* as imaginative as it is spontaneous, and the work's finale with its lolloping main theme is joyously spirited. The *Nonet* is also very attractive. Spohr's invention is again at its freshest and his propensity for chromaticism is held reasonably in check. The Hyperion recording is fresh and warm, clearly detailed against a resonant acoustic, although this means that the first violin is given a fractional hint of wiriness by the fairly close microphones.

The sound on the competing CRD disc is that bit more mellifluous, yet it remains natural and lifelike; some may prefer the greater suavity of the analogue tonal blend in this urbane music. The Nash Ensemble play both works with much elegance and style, and these performances are very civilized and hardly less spontaneous.

Octet in E, Op. 32.

(M) *** Decca (ADD) 466 580-2. Vienna Octet – SCHUBERT: *Octet in F, D.803.* ***

Spohr's Octet is a particularly charming work, and the variations on Handel's *Harmonious Blacksmith*, which forms one of the central movements, offer that kind of naïveté which, when so stylishly done as here, makes for delicious listening. The playing is expert throughout, with the five strings blending perfectly with the two horns and clarinet, and altogether this is a winning performance. The 1960 recording is fresh and open and leaves little to be desired.

Piano Quintet in D min., Op. 130; Septet, Op. 147.

(N) *** MDG 304 0534-2. Villa Musica Ensemble.

The *Piano Quintet* is a dashingly amiable work and its first movement has a primary theme which includes a bravura passage of hair-raising filigree which the pianist of the excellent Villa Musica Ensemble, Kalle Randalu, manages with a nimbleness that the first violin's comparable arabesques can only just match. The following *Scherzo*, too, is full of virtuoso bonhomie, and its middle section produces more glittering pianistic roulades. The *Adagio* at last brings a mood of serenity to provide a peaceful interlude before the rollicking finale. The spirited MDG performance is most enjoyable and the much better-known *Septet* for piano and wind is

played with comparable relish and warmth. Excellent, vividly present recording makes this a most enjoyable coupling.

Piano Trios Nos. 1 in E min., Op. 119; 2 in F, Op. 123; 3 in A min., Op. 124; 4 in B flat, Op. 133; 5 in G min., Op. 142.

(BB) *** CPO CPO 999 246-2 (3). Ravensburg Beethoven Trio.

Piano Trios Nos. 3 in A min., Op. 124; 4 in B flat, Op. 133.

**(*) Chan. 9372. Borodin Trio.

Piano Trios Nos. 1–5; (i) Piano Quintet in D, Op. 130.

(B) ** Naxos 8.553206 (No. 1 & Quintet); 8.553205 (Nos. 2 & 4); 8.553164 (Nos. 3 & 5). Hartley Piano Trio; (i) with M. Outram.

Spohr's five *Piano Trios* are among his freshest, most appealing chamber works, full of attractive ideas and fine craftsmanship. The Ravensburg Trio give fine performances, mellow, with slightly more gravitas than sparkle, although they too have an excellent pianist in Inge-Susann Römchild, whose touch is often pleasingly light. The CPO recording is warm and full to suit the playing. The five *Trios* are just too long to fit on a pair of CDs, and the third plays for only 31 minutes.

The Borodin Trio offers plenty of life and the Chandos recording is pleasingly open and vivid. But Luba Edlina's vibrant temperament and timbre do not so readily match Spohr's relatively suave writing, and this coupling is less enjoyable than either of the complete sets.

The Naxos acccounts (available separately) are well played and serviceable, and have the advantage of including the *Piano Quintet* which has a remarkable, sparkling Scherzo, changing mood in the Trio. Its pensive *Adagio* is one of the composer's most expressively telling, and the finale then trips along gaily. Caroline Clemmov generally rises to the occasion. The recording is fully acceptable and this first disc of the three is worth sampling, and after that the third (with Nos. 3 and 5) for these players, if not having a particularly strong collective personality, are thoroughly musical and at home in this composer's idiom.

Piano & Wind Quintet in C min., Op. 52; Septet in A min. for Flute, Clarinet, Horn, Bassoon, Violin, Cello & Piano, Op. 147.

(M) *** CRD (ADD) CRD 3399. Brown, Nash Ens.

These two pieces are among Spohr's most delightful, both the sparkling *Quintet* and the more substantial but still charmingly lighthearted *Septet*. Ian Brown at the piano leads the ensemble with flair and vigour, and the recording quality is outstandingly vivid.

String Quartets Nos. 1 in C; 2 in C min., Op. 4/1–2; 5 in D, Op. 15/2.

*** Marco 8.223253. New Budapest Qt.

If you enjoy the earlier and middle-period Haydn Quartets, you might well try Spohr. He seems also to have an almost inexhaustible fund of ideas and writes enjoyably smooth, well-crafted works, which every so often produce a movement which is quite memorable – like the gentle *Adagio* of his very first essay in the medium, strikingly fresh, written when the composer had just turned twenty. Op. 4/2 has an opening movement which is worthy of Haydn and the *Poco Adagio* is just as thoughtful as its predecessor. The Rondo finale, with its dotted main theme is very catchy. Op. 15/2 is without a slow movement. However the accomplished fugal finale has a brief *Adagio* introduction. The performances here are always persuasive and well recorded too: it is a pity this series does not appear on the Naxos label, when it would be even more recommendable. However praise is due for the excellent documentation.

String Quartets Nos. 7 in E flat; 8 in C, Op. 29/1–2.

**(*) Marco 8.22355. New Budapest Qt.

The Op. 29 *Quartets* are associated with Johann Tost (dedicatee of Haydn's Opp. 54/5 and 65). Both are written in Spohr's friendly, accomplished style; the first ingeniously bases its opening movement on a two-note motto theme and has an outstanding set of variations for its slow movement. The tender *Adagio* of the *C major* is even finer, daring in its expressive chromaticism. Both performances are spontaneous and this is vibrant, felt quartet-playing, without artifice, and the recording is lively and present.

String Quartets Nos. 11 in E (Quatuor brillant), Op. 43; 12 in C, Op. 45/1.

**(*) Marco 8.223257. New Budapest Qt.

String Quartets Nos. 13 in E min.; 14 in F min., Op. 45/2–3.

*** Marco 8.223258. New Budapest Qt.

The *Quatuor brillant* dates from 1817, and its subtitle is deceptive, for, as its engaging opening suggests, it is essentially a lyrical work, although the closing Minuet sparkles brightly enough. The Op. 45 quartets are more romantic in feeling, suaver in texture, moving further away from the classical Haydn idiom. The melancholy introduction to the *F minor Quartet* certainly catches the listener up, but the clouds lift with the key change to *A major* and the first movement is essentially amiable, although the hymn-like *Adagio* returns to the mood of the opening. The 'fantasy' Scherzo is then most welcome, and the brilliant finale soon produces a lollipop lyrical idea, which then dominates the movement. The Budapest players are at their very best in these two fine works.

String Quartets Nos. 15 in E flat; 16 in A, Op. 58/1–2.

*** Marco 8.23256. New Budapest Qt.

The two Op. 58 *Quartets* written in 1821 show a new maturity, especially the noble *Adagio* of the *E flat major*, which reminds one of Mozart, after a cheerful first movement laced with effective pizzicatos. The light-hearted Scherzo, with its Viennese, Ländler-influenced Trio has much charm, and the work is capped by a springy closing Rondo. A splendid disc in every way.

String Quartets Nos. 20 in A min.; 21 in B flat, Op. 74/1–2.

*** Marco 8.223259. New Budapest Qt.

The Op. 74 *Quartets*, dating from 1826, are further evidence of Spohr's increasingly deft integration of his ideas in finely argued first movements, essentially lyrical but not lacking dramatic elements. The players here again respond very

sympathetically to these attractive quartets and capture their spirit admirably. Fine, natural recording.

String Quartets Nos. 27 in D min.; 28 in A flat, Op. 84/1–2.

**(*) Marco 8.223251. New Budapest Qt.

These two works, written in 1831–2, exemplify Spohr's smooth, finely integrated quartet-writing at its most characteristic. The slow movement, sustaining a mood of serene simplicity, is the most memorable in each case, although the lyrical finale of the *A flat major Quartet* is also rather appealing. Good performances, lively enough, but capturing the suaveness of the idiom. The recording is truthful.

String Quartets Nos. 29 in B min., Op. 84/3; 30 in A, Op. 93.

**(*) Marco 8.223252. New Budapest Qt.

In many ways *No. 29 in B minor* is the finest of the Op. 84 set, with its touch of melancholy in the first movement, a lively minuet and a pensive slow movement. Op. 93, written in 1835, is more extrovert in atmosphere in the first movement (after a sombre introduction), but it offers another thoughtfully intense slow movement and a very jolly finale. It brings out the best in these players – and there is plenty of bravura for the first violin – and, again, good tonal matching plus a smooth, warm recording combine effectively for this slightly suave music.

String Quintets Nos. 1 in E flat; 2 in G, Op. 3/1–2.

**(*) Marco 8.223597. Augmented Danubius Qt.

String Quintets Nos. 3 in B min., Op. 69; 4 in A min., Op. 91.

**(*) Marco 8.223599. Augmented Danubius Qt.

Spohr's *String Quintets* feature a second viola, which gives them a characteristically full, slightly bland texture. The suave opening theme of the *E flat major* is deceptive, for it is strong enough to influence the two following movements including the near-melancholy *Larghetto*, and the attractive Minuet and trio. In the *G major* work, a similarly mild opening theme is to dominate. The two minor-key works which followed have even more of the wistful mood for which the composer is noted, especially the *Adagio* of the *B minor*, and its rather memorable, rocking barcarolle finale. The quality of Spohr's invention is well maintained throughout all four works, which are warmly and sympathetically played by the Danubius Quartet and smoothly and pleasingly recorded.

String Quintet No. 4, Op. 91; String Sextet in C, Op. 140; Pot-pourri on Themes of Mozart, Op. 22.

**(*) Chan. 9424. ASMF Chamber Ens.

To be candid, the *A minor String Quintet*, although as always with this composer well crafted, is rather bland, a characteristic the well-rehearsed ASMF performance does very little to counteract. The Mozartian pot-pourri is much more entertaining. The fine *String Sextet in C major*, one of the composer's last chamber works, from 1848, has a particularly endearing Brahmsian main theme in the first movement, a hymn-like slow movement and a brilliant finale. The ASMF

Chamber Ensemble give a fine, polished account of it, well recorded.

SPONTINI, Gasparo (1774–1851)

Olympie (opera): complete.

**(*) Orfeo C 137862H (3). Varady, Toczyska, Tagliavini, Fischer-Dieskau, Fortune, Berlin RIAS Chamber Ch., German Op. Male Ch., Berlin RSO, Albrecht.

In Spontini's *Olympie*, based on an historical play by Voltaire about the daughter of Alexander the Great, the writing is lively and committed and, despite flawed singing, so is this performance. Julia Varady is outstanding in the name-part, giving an almost ideal account of the role of heroine, but Stefania Toczyska is disappointingly unsteady as Statire and Franco Tagliavini is totally out of style as Cassandre. Even Dietrich Fischer-Dieskau is less consistent than usual, but his melodramatic presentation is nevertheless most effective. The text is slightly cut.

STAINER, John (1840–1901)

The Crucifixion.

(B) *** CFP (ADD) CD-CFP 4519. Hughes, Lawrenson, Guildford Cathedral Ch., Rose; Williams.

(i) The Crucifixion. Come Thou Long-expected Jesus (hymn); I saw the Lord (anthem).

(B) *** Decca (ADD) 436 146-2. (i) Lewis, Brannigan; St John's College, Cambridge, Ch., Guest.

All five hymns in which the congregation is invited to join are included on the Decca (originally Argo) record. Owen Brannigan is splendidly dramatic and his voice makes a good foil for Richard Lewis in the duets. The choral singing is first class and the 1961 recording is of Argo's best vintage, even finer than its CfP competitor. Moreover the Decca disc includes two bonuses: a hymn set to the words of Charles Wesley and a fine eight-part anthem, *I saw the Lord*, both of which are equally well sung.

The Classics for Pleasure version (from the late 1960s) is of high quality and, although one of the congregational hymns is omitted, in every other respect this can be recommended. John Lawrenson makes a movingly eloquent solo contribution and the choral singing is excellent. The remastered recording sounds first class, but the Decca version is finer still.

STAMITZ, Carl (1745–1801)

Cello Concertos Nos. 1 in G; 2 in A; 3 in C.

(N) (BB) *** Naxos 8.550865. Benda, Prague CO.

These three delightful concertos are admirably played by Christian Benda, who also directs his own accompaniments. He is a present member of a well-known family of Czech musicians, a dynasty which reaches back to the court of Frederick the Great. The *First G major Concerto* is particu-

larly winning, with the opening movement based on two elegantly contrasted themes, another heart-warming tune for the central *Romance* and a jaunty *Rondo* to complete the listener's pleasure.

The spirited allegros of the other two works are hardly less amiable and each has a slow movement with a yearning contour, with the closing *Rondo* of the *C major* work the most infectious of all. The recording is excellent and if you enjoy cello concertos this group is not to be missed. One's small only reservation is that the cadenzas, composed by another member of the Benda family, could with advantage have been more succinct.

Clarinet Concertos Nos. 3 in B flat; 10 in B flat; 11 in E flat.

*** EMI CDC7 54842-2. Meyer, ASMF, Brown – Johann
STAMITZ: *Concerto in B flat.* ***

Clarinet Concertos Nos. 7 in E flat; 8 in B flat (Darmstadt Nos. 1–2); 10 in B flat; 11 in E flat.

(BB) *** Naxos 8.554339. Berkes, Nicholas Esterházy Sinfonia.

Clarinet Concerto No. 10 in B flat.

*** EMI CDC5 55155-2. Meyer, ASMF, Brown – MOZART:
Clarinet Concerto etc.; WEBER: *Clarinet Concerto No. 1.* ***

Sabine Meyer's performances are highly musical and she is given characteristically polished and elegant accompaniments by Iona Brown and the Academy. However Kálmán Berkes on Naxos is by no means a lesser soloist. He finds a Bohemian sense of fun in the closing Rondos which is less obvious with Meyer, although she still plays them lightheartedly and her collection remains very enjoyable. The accompaniments on Naxos are also warm and stylish and the recording excellent.

In No. 10 the slow movement is plain beside that of its Mozart coupling, but Sabine Meyer presents it persuasively and makes much of the genial passage-work of the outer movements, and especially the roulades of the dancing finale. She is stylishly accompanied and excellently recorded.

Sinfonias concertantes: (i) in C for 2 Violins & Orchestra; (ii) in D for Violin, Viola & Orchestra.

(BB) **(*) ASV CDQS 6140. Friedman, L. Festival O, Pople; with (i) Smith; (ii) Best – HAYDN: *Sinfonia concertante.* **(*)

Sinfonia concertante in D for Violin, Viola & Orchestra.

(M) *** Sony (ADD) I SM2K 66472 (2). Stern, Zukerman, ECO, Barenboim – VIVALDI: *Concertos.* **(*)

Stamitz may not match Mozart but he is a personality in his own right and such a work as the *Sinfonia concertante in C for Two Violins*, here projected with fine spontaneity, brings a slow movement where one of the two soloists, playing alone, presents a 'singing' cantilena almost worthy of his greater contemporary. This *Andante* is also felicitously scored, with effective writing for the horns. The first movement has some good ideas too, and it is only the *Minuet* finale that lapses into conventionality; even so, like the first movement, the writing for the two soloists is inventively conceived. The companion *Sinfonia concertante for Violin and Viola*, if not quite so interesting in its material, has a historic link with Mozart's work for the same combination; as such, it makes fascinating listening. However, although the two soloists here play freshly and stylishly, they lack individuality of profile. Ross Pople directs the orchestra strongly, with tenderness in the central *Romance*, but the earlier CBS/Sony account of this work by Stern and Zukerman has far more personality.

That was originally recorded (in 1971) quadrophonically at the EMI Abbey Road No. 1 Studio and was more appropriately coupled with Mozart's much greater *Sinfonia concertante*, featuring the same solo instruments. Stamitz's work gives these vital artists a chance to strike sparks off each other. The recording has plenty of atmosphere but the soloists are balanced unnaturally forward.

Symphonies: in D (La Chasse); in C & G, Op. 13/16, No. 4 & 5; in F, Op. 24/3.

*** Chan. 9358. L. Mozart Players, Bamert.

Carl Stamitz wrote over fifty symphonies and the present examples are most attractive examples of his three-movement 'Italian overture' style. His slow movements are Haydnesque and quite gracious; his finales are witty: that for the *F major* work is particularly catchy. *La Chasse* is the earliest work here and the outer movements have plenty of energy and whooping horn calls, with a rather wistful *Andante* to separate them. Excellent performances, very well played and recorded.

STAMITZ, Johann (1717–57)

Clarinet Concerto No. 1 in F; (i) Double Clarinet Concerto in B flat; (ii) Double Concerto for Clarinet & Bassoon in B flat.

(BB) *** Naxos 8.553584. Berkes, with (i) Takashima; (ii) Okazaki; Nicholas Esterházy Sinfonia.

The *F major* solo *Concerto* is a delightful work with a vigorous first movement leading to a lyrical minor-key *Andante* and a jig finale. The double concerto was a favourite form with Stamitz, with long opening tuttis in the slow movements as well as the first. Both works are linked to the sinfonia concertante format as well as to the earlier form of concerto grosso with its strongly contrasted, lightly scored passages for the solo instruments. Both are built on attractive material, but the work for clarinet and bassoon is the more successful, with instruments sharply contrasted. As soloist as well as director, Berkes with his reedy clarinet tone is well matched by his Japanese partners, helped by full, open recording.

Clarinet Concerto in B flat.

*** EMI CDC7 54842-2. Meyer, ASMF, Brown – Carl STAMITZ: *Concertos.* ***

Johann Stamitz's *Concerto* has a rather fine slow movement and an elegantly good-natured closing rondo. It is most persuasively played here and excellently recorded.

Trumpet Concerto in D (arr. Boustead).

*** Ph. Duo 464 028-2. Hardenberger, ASMF, Marriner –

HAYDN; HUMMEL; HERTEL; Leopold MOZART: *Concertos.* *** ⊙

This concerto was written either by Stamitz or by a composer called J. G. Holzbogen. The writing lies consistently up in the instrument's stratosphere and includes some awkward leaps. It is quite inventive, however, notably the finale, which is exhilarating on the lips of Håkan Hardenberger. There is no lack of panache here and Marriner accompanies expertly. Good if reverberant recording, with the trumpet given great presence. This now comes as part of a Duo anthology of concertos which is unsurpassed in all respects.

Symphonies: in A; B flat; G (Mannheim); in D, Op. 3/2; in E flat, Op. 11/2; Orchestral Trio in E, Op. 5/3.

(N) (BB) *** Naxos 8.553194. New Zealand CO, Armstrong.

The bold opening chords and immediately following crescendo of the *D major Symphony*, Op.3/2 (from the early 1750s) immediately establish its Mannheim credentials, as do the elegantly sophisticated scoring of the *Andantino* and the effective use of horns in the *Minuet* and *Trio*. The *E flat Symphony*, one of the composer's last, follows a similar pattern, but the three earlier works (from the 1740s) which are actually designated as 'Mannheim' *Symphonies* are altogether simpler, each with only three movements.

The *E major Trio* is much more ambitious, with a searchingly expressive *Adagio*, all but worthy of Haydn. The excellent New Zealand Chamber Orchestra under Donald Armstrong, play with finesse and vitality and are persuasive advocates of music which so far proves not especially adventurous. But this disc is described as Volume I, so perhaps they will make even more interesting discoveries later in their Naxos series.

(Orchestral) Trios, Op. 1/1–4.

(N) (BB) **(*) Naxos 8.553213. New Zealand CO, Armstrong.

Although designated Op. 1 the six *Orchestral Trios* appear to be relatively late works (1755–6) and were intended by the composer to be performed optionally either as trios or by a fuller chamber orchestra, as here. They are each in four movements, elegant, simply constructed, with a divertimento-like character, but not trivial. The most striking is *No.4 in C minor*, which explores a wider range of expressive feeling than its companions, but the Siciliana-like *Larghetto* of the *F major* (No. 3), followed by a rather striking *Minuet* and robust finale, also sets that work apart. They are very well played here, polished in ensemble with musical phrasing and good use of light and shade. The recording is very natural. But one cannot pretend this is anything but pleasing wallpaper music, although it must have been rewarding for talented amateurs to play.

STANFORD, Charles (1852–1924)

(i) Concert Piece for Organ & Orchestra; (ii) Clarinet Concerto in A min., Op. 80; Irish Rhapsodies Nos. 1 in D min., Op. 78; 2 in F min. (Lament for the Son of Ossian), Op. 84; (iii) 3 for Cello & Orchestra, Op. 137; 4 in A min. (The Fisherman of Lough Neagh and What He Saw),

Op. 141; 5 in G min., Op. 147; (iv) 6 for Violin & Orchestra, Op. 191; Oedipus Rex Prelude, Op. 29.

*** Chan. 7002/3. (i) Weir; (ii) Hilton; (iii) Wallfisch; (iv) Mordkovitch; Ulster O, Handley.

Stanford's set of *Irish Rhapsodies* (two of them concertante pieces with highly responsive soloists) are the more impressive when heard as a set. They originally appeared coupled with the symphonies but sometimes seemed stronger and more concentrated than these more ambitious works. They are splendidly played and recorded. Gillian Weir makes a first-class soloist in the *Concert Piece for Organ and Orchestra* and Janet Hilton is hardly less appealing in the work for clarinet. An essential supplement for those who have already invested in the four-CD box of the symphonies.

Clarinet Concerto in A min., Op. 80.

(N) (B) *** Hyp. Helios CDH 55101. King, Philh. O, Francis – FINZI: *Concerto.* ***

(i) *Clarinet Concerto in A min.;* **(ii)** *3 Intermezzi* (for clarinet and piano).

*** ASV CDDCA 787. Johnson; (i) RPO, Groves; (ii) Martineau – FINZI: *Clarinet Concerto etc.* ***

The Stanford *Clarinet Concerto* finds Emma Johnson inspired, even freer and more fluent than Thea King on the rival Hyperion disc. It is a delight how Johnson can edge into a theme with extreme gentleness. So her first entry in the slow movement, taxingly high, seems to emerge ethereally from nowhere, while Thea King's firmer, sharper attack is less poetic. In the finale too King is strong and forthright, but Johnson is warmer and more personal with her cheekily witty treatment of the first solo. Sir Charles Groves and the RPO are warmly sympathetic accompanists, very well recorded, though the solo instrument is rather too close. However at bargain price the Helios reissue remains competitive.

Piano Concerto No. 1 in G, Op. 59.

*** Hyp. CDA 66820. Lane, BBC Scottish SO, Brabbins – PARRY: *Piano Concerto.* ***

Written in 1894, the first of Stanford's two piano concertos brings even clearer Brahmsian echoes than usual, but the finesse of the writing and the ravishing beauty of the slow movement make it almost as enjoyable as the second and better-known concerto, particularly in a performance by turns as brilliant and poetic as Piers Lane's. Full, warm sound.

Piano Concerto No. 2 in C min., Op. 126; Concert Variations on an English Theme: 'Down Among the Dead Men', Op. 21.

(M) *** Chan. 7099. Fingerhut, Ulster O, Handley.

(i) *Piano Concerto No. 2* ; **(ii)** *Becket, Op. 48: The Martyrdom (Funeral March);* **(iii)** *The Fisherman of Lough Neagh and What He Saw (Irish Rhapsody No. 4), Op. 141.*

*** Lyrita (ADD) SRCD 219. (i) Binns, LSO; (ii–iii) LPO; (i; iii) Braithwaite; (ii) Boult.

Stanford's *Second Piano Concerto*, although in three rather

than four movements, is a work on the largest scale, recalling the Brahms *B flat Concerto*. Yet Stanford asserts his own melodic individuality and provides a really memorable secondary theme for the second movement. Margaret Fingerhut is a first-rate soloist both here and in the apt and entertaining coupling, for Stanford was a dab hand at the variations format. Handley and his Ulster Orchestra are completely at home in this repertoire, and the Chandos recording is well up to the usual high standards of the house.

Malcolm Binns too plays with spontaneous freshness. The Lyrita recording is surely a demonstration of just how a piano concerto should be balanced. The *Funeral March* comes from incidental music commissioned at the request of Tennyson for Irving's production of his tragedy, *Becket*. It has an arresting opening but otherwise is a fairly straightforward piece, strongly melodic in a Stanfordian manner. Like the more familiar *Irish Rhapsody*, it is splendidly played and recorded.

Violin Concerto in D, Op. 74; Suite for Violin & Orchestra, Op. l32.

(N) *** Hyp. CDA 67208. Marwood, BBC Scottish SO, Brabbins.

Starting magically with the violin entering over an impressionistic twitter on woodwind, the Stanford *Violin Concerto* provides an important link between the Brahms concerto of 1878 and the Elgar of 1909–10. After that poetic start, Stanford builds his expansive structure in a strong Brahmsian manner, using clear, positive themes. He ends with an Irish jig finale, the nationalistic equivalent of Brahms's Hungarian finale. Anthony Marwood gives a warm, clean-cut reading, as he also does in the *Suite*, an attractive if heavyweight example of 19th-century neo-classicism. A splendid addition to Hyperion's 'Romantic Violin Concerto' series, following up their brilliantly successful set of romantic piano concertos.

Symphonies Nos. 1–7.

*** Chan. 9279/82 (4). Ulster O, Handley.

Now available in a box of four CDs, with the fill-ups which accompanied the original CDs now put aside for separate reissue, this is obviously the most attractive way to approach this generally impressive if uneven British symphonic canon. Handley and his Ulster Orchestra are completely at home in this repertoire, and the Chandos recording is consistently of this company's best quality.

Symphonies Nos. 1 in B flat, Op. 78; Irish Rhapsody No. 2: The Lament for the Son of Ossian, Op. 84.

*** Chan. 9049. Ulster O, Handley.

Stanford's mature musical studies had been in Berlin and Hamburg, and he came back to England profoundly influenced by the German symphonic style. Now we can discover for ourselves that, although he could assemble a convincing structure, his melodic invention was not yet strong enough to achieve real memorability. Handley and the Ulster Orchestra do their persuasive best for a piece which is certainly not a silk purse. The *Irish Rhapsody* has distinctly more melodramatic flair. Excellent recording.

Symphony No. 2 in D min. (Elegiac); (i) Clarinet Concerto.

*** Chan. 8991. Ulster O, Handley; (i) with Hilton.

In the *Second Symphony* the influences of German masters are still strong but the work still has its own individuality, for the most part in the scoring. The delightful *Clarinet Concerto* makes a splendid coupling, with Janet Hilton at her most seductive, both in timbre and in warmth, and articulating with nimble expertise. A delightful performance.

Symphony No. 3 in F min. (Irish), Op. 28.

(M) *** EMI (ADD) CDM5 65129-2. Bournemouth Sinf., Del Mar – ELGAR: *Scenes from the Bavarian Highlands.* ***

Symphony No. 3 (Irish), Op. 28; Irish Rhapsody No. 5, Op. 147.

*** Chan. 8545. Ulster O, Handley.

This *Third* and most celebrated of the seven symphonies of Stanford is a rich and attractive work, none the worse for its obvious debts to Brahms. The ideas are best when directly echoing Irish folk music, as in the middle two movements, a skippity jig of a Scherzo and a glowing slow movement framed by harp cadenzas. The *Irish Rhapsody No. 5* dates from 1917, reflecting perhaps in its martial vigour that wartime date. Even more characteristic are the warmly lyrical passages, performed passionately by Handley and his Ulster Orchestra, matching the thrust and commitment they bring also to the *Symphony*.

Norman Del Mar directs an equally ripe performance, noting that the finale gives an attractive forward glance to Stanford's pupils, Holst and Vaughan Williams. The EMI recording is warm and well defined.

Symphony No. 4 in F, Op. 31; Irish Rhapsody No. 6 for Violin & Orchestra, Op. 191; Oedipus Rex Prelude, Op. 29.

*** Chan. 8884. Ulster O, Handley, (i) with Mordkovitch.

The *Fourth Symphony*, like the *Third*, is a highly confident piece and an effective symphony, even if it runs out of steam before the close of the finale despite attractive invention. The *Irish* concertante *Rhapsody* is a much later work, its nostalgia nicely caught by the soloist here, Lydia Mordkovitch, who is obviously involved. Handley, as ever, takes the helm throughout with ardent commitment and makes the most of the many nice touches of orchestral colour. Excellent recording.

Symphony No. 5 in D (L'Allegro ed Il Penseroso), Op. 56; Irish Rhapsody No. 4 (The Fisherman of Lough Neagh and What He Saw).

*** Chan. 8581. Ulster O, Handley.

Stanford's *Fifth Symphony* is colourfully orchestrated and full of easy tunes, illustrating passages from Milton's *L'Allegro* and *Il Penseroso*. The last two movements readily live up to Stanford's reputation as a Brahmsian, representing the *Penseroso* half of the work, and the slow epilogue brings reminders of Brahms's *Third*. The *Irish Rhapsody* is more distinctive, bringing together sharply contrasted, colourful and atmospheric Irish ideas under the title *The Fisherman of Lough Neagh and What He Saw*. Excellent recording of the finest Chandos quality.

Symphony No. 6 in E flat (In Memoriam G. F. Watts), Op. 94; Irish Rhapsody No. 1 in D min., Op. 78.

*** Chan. 8627. Ulster O, Handley.

Stanford's *Sixth Symphony* is not the strongest of the set, but it has a rather lovely slow movement, with a pervading air of gentle melancholy. The first movement has some good ideas but the finale is too long, in the way finales of Glazunov symphonies tend to overuse their material. Nevertheless Vernon Handley makes quite a persuasive case for the work and an even better one for the enjoyable *Irish Rhapsody No. 1*, which features and makes rather effective use of one of the loveliest of all Irish tunes, the *Londonderry Air*. Excellent sound.

Symphony No. 7 in D min., Op. 124; (i) Concert Piece for Organ & Orchestra, Op. 181; (ii) Irish Rhapsody No. 3 for Cello & Orchestra, Op. 137.

*** Chan. 8861. Ulster O, Handley; with (i) Weir; (ii) Wallfisch.

The *Seventh Symphony* sums up its composer as a symphonist – structurally sound, yet not now so heavily indebted to Germany, and with the orchestration often ear-catching. It is not a masterpiece, but it could surely not be presented with more conviction than here by Handley and his excellent orchestra. The *Irish Rhapsody* is very Irish indeed and makes the use of several good tunes. It is most sensitively played by Wallfisch, and Gillian Weir makes a strong impression in the *Organ 'Concertino'*, where the composer uses only brass, strings and percussion in the accompaniment. The music has a touch of the epic about it.

Serenade (Nonet) in F, Op. 95.

(N) (B) *** Hyp. Helios CDM 55061. Capricorn – PARRY: *Nonet.* ***

Like the Parry *Nonet*, with which it is coupled, the *Serenade* is an inventive and delightful piece, its discourse civilized and the Scherzo full of charm. Capricorn play this piece with evident pleasure and convey this to the listener. The recording is very natural and truthfully balanced, and this disc is most reasonably priced.

Violin Sonatas Nos. 1 in D, Op. 11; 2 in A, Op. 70; Irish Fantasy No. 1 (Caoine), Op. 54 No. 1; 5 Characteristic Pieces, Op. 93.

*** Hyp. CDA 67024. Barritt, Edwards.

One expected these to be enjoyably well-crafted works but they are a great deal more than that, teeming with memorable ideas, to make consistently delightful listing. Paul Barritt and Catherine Edwards play all this music with a spring-like freshness, and obviously enjoy every bar. They are beautifully recorded.

PIANO MUSIC

24 Preludes, Set 1, Op. 163; 6 Characteristic Pieces, Op. 132.

*** Priory PRCD 449. Jacobs.

24 Preludes, Set 2, Op. 179; 3 Rhapsodies from Dante, Op. 92..

(N) *** Olympia OCD 638. Jacobs.

The 24 *Preludes* are not bravura works like those of Chopin and Rachmaninov. Written in 1918, their chromatic key-sequence would suggest that they are more readily associated with Bach's *Well-tempered Clavier*, and the composer's following set in 1920 (to make a total of 48) seems to emphasize that parallel. The variety of Stanford's invention brings a continuing freshness throughout the set, which can be enjoyed as a progression as well as by selecting individual items. The *Characteristic Pieces* were written six years earlier and are also of high quality, with the engaging *Rondel* (No. 4) dedicated to the Schumann of *Kinderszenen*

In the second set, *Preludes Nos. 41* and *42* combine to form a pair of baroque dances, gavotte and musette, with a reprise of the former, while the last of the whole series in B minor is marked *Addio* and has a valedictory character. The *Three Rhapsodies from Dante* are highly romantic, with the passion of *Francesca* depicted with Lisztian flamboyance, followed by a simpler more tender evocation of *Beatrice*. The closing portrayal of *Capaneo*, who defied Jove's thunderbolts, combines the spirit of bold heroism with pianistic bravura. Peter Jacobs almost never disappoints and his performances here are accomplished, stylish, spontaneous and thoroughly sympathetic, while the recording is first class.

VOCAL MUSIC

3 Motets, Op. 38: Beati quorum via; Coelos ascendit; Justorum animae. Anthems: *For lo, I raise up; Glorious and powerful God; How beautiful are their feet; If ye then be risen with Christ; The Lord is my Shepherd; Ye choirs of new Jerusalem; Ye holy angels bright.* (Organ) *Preludes & Fugues in B & C, Op. 193/2–3.*

(M) *** CRD CRD 3497. New College, Oxford, Ch., Higginbottom; Plummer or Smith (organ).

Edward Higginbottom and his splendid choir never made a finer record than this. All this music shows Stanford at his most confidently inspired, readily carrying the listener with him, when the performances are so secure and committed and superbly recorded in the Chapel of New College, Oxford.

3 Motets, Op. 38: Beati quorum via; Coelos ascendit; Justorum animae. Anthems: *For lo, I raise up, Op. 145; The Lord is my Shepherd. Bible Songs: A song of peace; A song of wisdom, Op. 113/4 & 6.* Hymns: *O for a closer walk with God; Pray that Jerusalem. Magnificat for Double Chorus, Op. 164; Morning, Communion & Evening Services in G, Op. 81: Magnificat & Nunc dimittis. Morning, Communion & Evening Services in C, Op. 115: Magnificat & Nunc dimittis.* (Organ) *Postlude in D min.*

(M) *** EMI CDC5 55535-2. Ainsley, King's College, Cambridge, Ch., Cleobury (organ); Vivian (organ accompaniments).

Framed by eloquently beautiful settings of the *Magnificat* and *Nunc dimittis* from 1902 and 1909 respectively (Alastair Hussain the radiantly secure treble soloist in the former), this 75-minute collection celebrates Stanford's remarkable achievement within the Anglican tradition over a quarter of

a century. James Vivian, the current organ scholar, impressively provides some of the accompaniments which are usually important in their own right and make bravura demands on the player. Highly recommended alongside the CRD collection above. Both CDs are well worth having, even though some duplication is involved.

(i) *Requiem, Op. 63;* **(ii)** *The Veiled Prophet of Khorassan* (excerpts).

*** Marco Polo 8.223580/1. (i) Lucy, McGahon, Kerr, Leeson-Williams, RTE Philharmonic Ch.; (ii) Kerr; Nat. SO of Ireland, cond. (i) Leaper; (ii) Pearce.

Stanford's magnificent *Requiem* (1897) was composed in honour of the painter, Lord Leighton, who died in 1896. It is a powerfully conceived and moving work, integrating the soloists as a team with the choir in a particularly satisfying way. The contrasts of the writing, from the ethereal opening of the *Kyrie* to the blazing fortissimo of the *Tuba mirum*, are superbly caught here, the best recording we have had from Marco Polo and surely in the demonstration bracket. With fine solo singing to match the fervour of the chorus, Adrian Leaper can be congratulated on the great success of the first recording of a work that should surely be in the general choral repertoire. The exotic suite from Stanford's first opera, *The Veiled Prophet of Khorassan*, makes an agreeable if not distinctive encore.

Songs of the Fleet, Op. 117; Songs of the Sea, Op. 91.

(M) **(*) EMI CDM5 65113-2. Luxon, Bournemouth SO & Ch., Del Mar – DELIUS: *Sea Drift.* **

The four *Songs of the Sea* are more immediately memorable in their boisterous way, with *The Old Superb* a real hit; but the *Songs of the Fleet* (also setting Newbolt poems, but with SATB chorus) make a pleasant sequel. Luxon's voice is quite well caught by the microphones, but the resonance takes some of the bite from the words of the chorus. Yet Del Mar's understanding of the idiom makes for lively and enjoyable results.

(i) *Stabat Mater, Op. 96; Te Deum* (from *Service in B flat, Op. 10*); **(ii)** *6 Bible Songs, Op. 113.*

*** Chan. 9548. (i) Attrot, Stephen, Robson; (i; ii) Varcoe; (ii) Watson; Leeds Philharmonic Ch., BBC PO, Hickox.

Stanford, Irish to the core, here offers a Protestant setting of the deeply Catholic text of the *Stabat Mater*. In its directness and vigour, this relates to Stanford's healthily Anglican church music on the one hand and to his symphonic writing on the other. Like his *Requiem*, this is a piece, long-neglected, that richly deserves revival, and Hickox with his excellent forces directs a performance, atmospherically recorded, that demands its return to the repertory. The six settings of Biblical texts for baritone and organ (warmly done by Stephen Varcoe and Ian Watson) are fresh and forthright, leading to the stirring *Te Deum in B flat*, one of the glories of English church music.

STANLEY, John (1712–86)

6 Organ Concertos, Op. 10.

(M) *** CRD (ADD) CRD 3365. Gifford, N. Sinfonia.

These bouncing, vigorous performances, well recorded as they are on the splendid organ of Hexham Abbey, present these *Concertos* most persuasively. No. 4, with its darkly energetic C minor, is particularly fine. The recording is natural in timbre and very well balanced.

Concertos for Strings, Op. 2/1–6.

*** Chan. 0638. Coll. Mus. 90, Standage.

These six highly engaging *Concertos for Strings* are concerti grossi in the style of Corelli and, most closely, Handel. For Stanley shares the latter's gift for a noble melodic contour. No. 3 is a fine example and also has a buoyant fugue of the kind Handel would have written. No. 2 is equally memorable and brings a solo cello contribution in the second movement. The period-instrument performances here are wonderfully spirited – vitality without abrasive edge – as well as bringing the right degree of expressive warmth. The recording is first class.

Organ Voluntaries, Op. 5/1, 5, 8 & 9; Op. 6/2, 4, 5 & 6; Op. 7/6–9.

(N) *** Chan. 0639. Marlow (organ of Trinity College Chapel, Cambridge).

John Stanley wrote three sets of ten *Organ Voluntaries*. Opp. 5–7 were published in the 1740s and 1750s. Most are in two or three movements, although Op. 5/1 and Op. 6/6 (two of the most attractively diverse) extend to four. Richard Marlow presents four from each set. No pedals are used, but Stanley's published registrations are colourful (often quite orchestral, as in the *Vivace* of Op. 7/6), and as they are French-influenced it is right than a fine English organ should be used, one which has a colourful palette, sometimes piquant, but which is not too plangent in timbre. Op. 7/9 closes with a lively fugue, but the invention throughout is engaging, sometimes using echo passages and alternating fast and slow passages. The recording is very real and vivid, but not overwhelming, which makes for enjoyably relaxed listening. Recommended.

STEINBERG, Maximilian (1883–1946)

Symphony No. 1 in D, Op. 3; Prélude symphonique, Op. 7; Fantaisie dramatique, Op. 9.

*** DG 457 607-2. Gothenburg SO, Järvi.

These days, Maximilian Steinberg is best remembered as the teacher of Shostakovich. The *First Symphony* (1905–6) is very much influenced by Glazunov and is in no way inferior: indeed, Steinberg's scoring is more transparent and less congested. The melodic invention is perhaps less distinguished but, without making excessive claims, the music is well worth reviving. The *Fantaisie dramatique* (1910) is inspired by Ibsen's *Brand* and like its companions on this enterprising disc bears witness to Steinberg's continuing

debt to his mentors and his feeling for the orchestra is little short of remarkable. Neeme Järvi proves an invigorating and refreshing guide in these genial and sympathetic pieces, and the fine Gothenburg Orchestra respond to his enthusiasm. The recording is absolutely state-of-the-art, beautifully defined and present, yet transparent in detail.

STENHAMMAR, Wilhelm (1871–1927)

(i) Piano Concerto No. 1 in B flat min., Op. 1; Symphony No. 3 (fragment).

*** Chan. 9074. (i) Widlund; Royal Stockholm PO, Rozhdestvensky.

(i) Piano Concerto No. 1; (ii) Florez och Blanzeflor, Op. 3; (iii) 2 Sentimental Romances, Op. 28.

*** BIS CD 550. (i) Derwinger; (ii) Mattei; (iii) Wallin, Malmö SO, P. Järvi.

Stenhammar's *First Piano Concerto* is full of beautiful ideas and the invention is fresh. Love Derwinger proves an impressive and sympathetic intepreter and gets good support from Järvi *fils*. The early *Florez och Blanzeflor* ('Flower and Whiteflower'), a ballad by Oscar Levertin, brings a certain Wagnerian flavour but has a charm that is sensitively sung by the young Swedish baritone Peter Mattei.

Chandos offer the less substantial coupling, a three-minute fragment from the *Third Symphony*, on which Stenhammar embarked in 1918–19. In itself it is too insignificant a makeweight to affect choice. But in the *Concerto* Mats Widlund proves the more imaginative soloist and brings just that little bit more finesse to the solo part. Rozhdestvensky gives excellent support and the Stockholm orchestra (and in particular their strings) have greater richness of sonority. The Chandos recording also has the edge on its BIS competitor in terms of depth and warmth.

2 Sentimental Romances, Op. 28.

(BB) **(*) Naxos 8.554287. Ringborg, Swedish CO, Willén – AULIN; BERWALD: *Violin Concertos.* **(*)

These two charming Stenhammar pieces and are played to excellent effect in Tobias Ringborg's hands. Decent and well-balanced recorded sound.

Serenade for Orchestra, Op. 31.

✿ *** Finlandia 3984-25327-2. Royal Stockholm PO, A. Davis – BRAHMS: *Serenade No. 1.* ***

The *Serenade for Orchestra* is Stenhammar's masterpiece, its richness of invention, effortless contrapuntal ingenuity and subtlety of harmony giving constant delight and refreshment. The scoring and colours are full of fantasy and imagination. Its *Notturno* perfectly encapsulates the magic of the late Swedish summer nights. Sir Andrew Davis has a natural sympathy with and much feeling for the score, and is meticulous in his care for dynamic shadings and refinement of texture. Neeme Järvi on BIS includes the *Reverenza* movement that Stenhammar eventually discarded – and rightly so – when he transposed the outer movements from E major to F. Davis's is a wonderfully convincing account, very well recorded too.

(i) *Serenade in F, Op. 23*; (ii) *Symphony No. 2, in G minor, Op. 34*.

(N) *** Swedish Soc. SCD1115. Stockholm PO; (i) Kubelik; (ii) Mann.

Rafael Kubelik's pioneering recording from 1964 of the *Serenade for Orchestra*, is an excellent account which had a short lease of life here on DG's bargain Heliodor label, after which it has only been available fleetingly. It wears its years lightly and is fresh and full of poetry. Kubelik obviously loved this marvellous score, though now the Neeme Järvi and Andrew Davis versions (and in particular the BIS account which includes the rejected *Reverenza* movement) constitute strong competition. However, this re-issue sounds astonishingly good, and the new transfer removes the slight boom at the bottom end of the register which disfigured its last appearance. A pity it is at full price, as this will diminish the competitive appeal of what is an historically important CD. Of the *Second Symphony* Stenhammar once said that he had tried to compose 'sober and honest music free from frills', and this is just what Tor Mann gives us. His was its first LP recording, though Stenhammar's old orchestra, the Gothenburg Symphony, to which Sibelius dedicated the score, recorded it on the Radiotjänst label just after the war. Mann's performance is refreshingly straightforward and is held together well and imaginative in its handling of detail. It sounds much better than it did in its last incarnation when it was presented on its own.

(i) *Symphonies Nos. 1 in F; 2 in G min., Op. 34; Serenade for Orchestra, Op. 31* (with *Reverenza* movement); *Excelsior Overture, Op. 13; The Song (Sången): Interlude, Op. 44; Lodolezzi Sings (Lodolezzi sjunger): suite*; (ii) *Piano Concertos Nos. 1*; (iii) *2 in D min., Op. 23*; (iv) *Ballad: Florez och Blanzeflor*; (v) *2 Sentimental Romances*; (vi) *Midwinter, Op. 24; Snöfrid, Op. 5*.

(M) *** BIS Dig./ADD CD 714/716. (i) Gothenburg SO, Järvi; (ii) Derwinger; (iii) Ortiz; (iv) Matthei; (v) Wallin; (vi) Gothenburg Ch.; (ii–v) Malmö SO, P. Järvi.

Järvi's performances are now repackaged at a distinctly advantageous price. The *First Piano Concerto* makes use of Stenhammar's own orchestration, which came to light only recently in America; and this is the most comprehensive compilation of Stenhammar's orchestral music now on the market. All the performances and recordings are of high quality, and the only serious criticism to make affects the first movement of the *Second Symphony*, which Järvi takes rather too briskly. In the *Second Piano Concerto* Cristina Ortiz a good soloist. All the recordings are digital save for that of the *First Symphony*, which comes from a 1982 concert performance and has great warmth and transparency.

Symphony No. 2 in G min., Op. 34.

*** Cap. (ADD)CAP 21151. Stockholm PO, Westerberg.
** Swedish Soc. (ADD) SCD 1014. Stockholm PO, Mann.

Symphony No. 2; Overture, Excelsior!, Op. 13.

(BB) **(*) Naxos 8.553888. RSNO, Sundkvist.

Symphony No. 2; Excelsior! Overture, Op. 13; Serenade, Op. 31: Reverenza; (i) 2 Songs, Op. 4.

** Virgin VC5 45244-2. Royal Stockholm PO, P. Järvi; (i) with Von Otter.

This is a marvellous symphony. It is direct in utterance; the melodic invention is fresh and abundant, and the generosity of spirit it radiates is heart-warming. The Stockholm Philharmonic under Stig Westerberg play with conviction and eloquence; the strings have warmth and body, and the wind are very fine too. The recording is vivid and full-bodied even by the digital standards of today: as sound, this record is absolutely first class.

Tor Mann's performance is also admirable, well held together and very sympathetic. All the same it is unrealistic to ask full price for a 1959 recording running to only 46 minutes.

Petter Sundkvist's account of Stenhammar's glorious *Second Symphony* is absolutely first class interpretatively, though it is rather let down by the quality of sound, which does not match that of his Gothenburg rivals. It is a meticulous, dedicated account which radiates an understanding of and love for this music. The Royal Scottish National Orchestra respond with enthusiasm.

Paavo Järvi gives a finely shaped and sensitive account of both the symphony and the *Excelsior! Overture*. Virgin too have added the *Reverenza* movement, which originally formed part of the *Serenade for Orchestra* but which Stenhammar subsequently excised, feeling it made the work too long. It is a charming piece and is beautifully played by the Stockholm Orchestra, as for that matter is the symphony. The two Runeberg settings, Op. 4, date from 1892 and so Stenhammar's setting of *Flickan kom ifrån sin älsklings nöte* ('The girl returned from meeting her lover') precedes Sibelius's by almost a decade – and in some ways is the more refined of the two. The orchestration, which has never been recorded before, is masterly. Anne Sofie von Otter sings both to the manner born. The recording is acceptable, but is two-dimensional, not having enough front-to-back perspective; there is also a slight coarseness on some climaxes.

CHAMBER MUSIC

(i) *Allegro brillante in E flat; Allegro ma non tanto*; (ii; iii) *Violin Sonata in A min., Op. 19*; (iii) *Piano Sonata in A flat, Op. 12*.

** BIS CD 764. (i) Tale Qt (members); (ii) Olsson; (iii) Negro.

All this music comes from the 1890s, before Stenhammar's personality was fully formed. The *A flat Sonata*, written in the same year (1895) as the better-known and somewhat Brahmsian *Three Fantasies*, Op. 11, though derivative has some pleasing invention and a good feeling for form. Lucia Negro plays it with great authority and sensitivity. The *Violin Sonata* comes from 1899 and was written for Stenhammar's chamber-music partner, the composer Tor Aulin. The *Allegro ma non tanto* is the first movement of a projected piano trio (1895); and little is known about the even earlier *Allegro brillante* fragment. The pianist, who is unfailingly responsive, rather swamps her partners here and in the *Violin Sonata*, thanks to a less than satisfactory balance.

String Quartets Nos. (i) *1 in C, Op. 2*; (ii) *2 in C min., Op. 14*; (iii) *3 in F, Op. 18*; *4 in A min., Op. 25*; (i) *5 in C (Serenade), Op. 29*; (ii) *6 in D min., Op. 35*.

(M) *** Cap. (ADD) CAP 21536 (3). (i) Fresk Qt;
(ii) Copenhagen Qt; (iii) Gotland Qt.

The *First Quartet* shows Stenhammar steeped in the chamber music of Beethoven and Brahms, though there is a brief reminder of Grieg; the *Second* is far more individual. By the *Third* and *Fourth*, arguably the greatest of the six, the influence of Brahms and Dvořák is fully assimilated, and the *Fourth* reflects that gentle melancholy which lies at the heart of Stenhammar's sensibility. The *Fifth* is the shortest; the *Sixth* comes from the war years when the composer was feeling worn out and depressed, though there is little evidence of this in the music. Performances are generally excellent, as indeed is the recording, and it is good to have this thoroughly worthwhile set at mid-price.

PIANO MUSIC

Allegro con moto ed appassionato; 3 Fantasies, Op. 11; Impromptu; Impromptu-Waltz; Late Summer Nights, Op. 33; 3 Small Piano Pieces.

*** BIS CD-554. Negro.

Although he was by all accounts a wonderful pianist, Stenhammar wrote relatively little piano music of real quality. Brahms is a dominant influence in the early *Allegro con moto ed appassionato* and in the Op. 11 *Fantasies*, but there is a strong individual personality at work too, and the *Sensommarnätter* ('Late summer nights'), which come from the period of the *Serenade for Orchestra*, are wonderfully thoughtful and atmospheric pieces that inhabit a wholly personal world. Lucia Negro is thoroughly at home in this repertoire and is very persuasive, and the BIS recording is altogether first rate.

3 Fantasies, Op. 11; Impromptu in G flat; Late Summer Nights, Op. 33; 3 Small Piano Pieces; Sonata in G min.

(BB) *** Naxos 8.553730. Sivelöv.

Niklas Sivelöv proves a thoroughly idiomatic interpreter and is as much at home in the quasi-impressionistic third movement of the *Late Summer Nights* and the delicate *Poco allegretto* as he is in the virtuosic, big-boned, penultimate movement. He is very well served by the recording engineers. Well worth the money.

Piano Sonatas Nos. 1 in C; 2 in C min.; 3 in A flat; 4 in G min.; Fantasie in A min.

**(*) BIS CD634. Negro.

The *Fantasie in A minor* and the *First Sonata* were written when Stenhammar was nine and were followed a year later by another sonata. The *A flat Sonata* comes from 1883 when he was twelve (not two years later as stated on the sleeve-note). All these juvenilia are in the style of Mozart, Weber and Mendelssohn – and it is puzzling why they should be

thought worth recording. The *Sonata No. 4 in G minor* is another matter, and in it one recognizes the profile of the real Stenhammar. It comes from 1890, when he was nineteen, and has the breadth and scale of the mature composer. The ideas are long-breathed and the piano writing far more virtuosic and big-boned. The performances could not be more beguiling. Lucia Negro brings great charm and intelligence to the smaller pieces and she gives the *G minor Sonata* with total conviction. Good recording too.

VOCAL MUSIC

30 Songs.

*** Caprice (ADD) MSCD 623. Von Otter, Hagegård, Forsberg, Schuback.

These songs cover the whole of Stenhammar's career: the earliest, *In the forest*, was composed when he was sixteen, while the last, *Minnesang*, was written three years before his death. The songs are unpretentious and charming, fresh and idyllic, and nearly all are strophic. Hagegård sings the majority of them with his usual intelligence and artistry, though there is an occasional hardening of timbre. Anne Sofie von Otter is in wonderful voice and sings with great sensitivity and charm. Bengt Forsberg and Thomas Schuback accompany with great taste, and the recording is of the highest quality.

7 Songs from Thoughts of Solitude, Op. 7; 5 Songs to Texts of Runeberg, Op. 8; 5 Swedish Songs, Op. 16; 5 Songs of Bo Bergman, Op. 20; Songs and Moods, Op. 26; Late Harvest.

**(*) BIS CD 654. Mattei, Lundin.

Only two of the three-dozen Stenhammar songs on this disc last longer than four minutes: *Jungfru Blond och Jungfru Brunett* ('Miss Blonde and Miss Brunette') and *Prins Aladin av Lampan* ('Prince Aladdin of the Lamp'), both of which are to be found on the set of thirty songs recorded by Anne Sofie von Otter and Håkan Hagegård. As a song composer Stenhammar was often inspired and his craftsmanship is always fastidious and in the posthumously published *Efterskörd* ('Late Harvest') and the *Thoughts of Solitude*, Op. 7, he brings to light some songs of great eloquence and beauty that are not readily available outside Sweden. Peter Mattei is an intelligent singer, well endowed vocally; the voice is beautiful, but he has a tendency to colour the voice on the flat side of the note, and on occasion (in *Prins Aladin*, for example) is flat. Bengt-Ake Lundin deserves special mention for the sensitivity and responsiveness of his accompanying, and the recording is excellent.

Lodolezzi Sings: suite, Op. 39; (i) Midwinter, Op. 24; (ii) Snöfrid, Op. 5; The Song (interlude).

*** BIS CD 438. (i; ii) Gothenburg Concert Hall Ch., (ii) with Ahlén, Nilsson, Zackrisson, Enoksson; Gothenburg SO, Järvi.

Snöfrid is an early cantata. The young composer was completely under the spell of Wagner at this time and it offers only occasional glimpses of the mature Stenhammar. *Midwinter* is a kind of folk-music fantasy or pot-pourri on the lines of Alfvén's *Midsummer Vigil*, though not quite so appealing. *Lodolezzi Sings* has much innocent charm. None of this is great Stenhammar but it is well worth hearing; the performances under Neeme Järvi are very sympathetic, and the recording is natural and present.

(i) The Song (Sången), Op. 44; (ii) 2 Sentimental Romances, Op. 28; (iii) Ithaca, Op. 21.

*** Cap. (ADD) CAP 21358. (i) Sörenson, Von Otter, Dahlberg, Wahlgren, State Ac. Ch., Adolf Fredrik Music School Children's Ch., (ii) Tellefsen, (iii) Hagegård, Swedish RSO; (i) Blomstedt; (ii) Westerberg; (iii) Ingelbretsen.

The first half of *The Song* has been described as 'a great fantasy' and is Stenhammar at his best and most individual: the choral writing is imaginatively laid out and the contrapuntal ingenuity is always at the service of poetic ends: the second half is less individual. The solo and choral singing is superb and the whole performance has the total commitment one might expect from these forces. The superbly engineered recording does them full justice. The *Two Sentimental Romances* have great charm and are very well played, and Hagegård is in fine voice in another rarity, *Ithaca*.

Tirfing (opera): excerpts.

*** Sterling CDO 1033-2. Tobiasson, Morling, Taube, Stockholm Royal Op. O, Segerstam.

Tirfing is a 'mystical saga-poem', based on the Hervarar Saga, and tells of the warrior Angantyr, his valkyrie daughter Hervor and Tirfing, a sword with the magical power to destroy everything. It is all terribly Wagnerian, but even so, the music has the power and sweep of Stenhammar. There are characteristic modulations (one is reminded of *Excelsior!* among other things). Above all, even at its most Wagnerian, the music grips the listener from start to finish. Leif Segerstam gets first-rate results from the Royal Opera Orchestra and the same from the three soloists, in particular Ingrid Tobiasson as Hervor. Good wide-ranging recording. The growing band of Stenhammar's admirers will want this.

STERNDALE BENNETT, William (1816–75)

Piano Concertos Nos. 1 in D min., Op. 1; 3 in C min., Op. 9.

✿ *** Lyrita SRCD 204. Binns, LPO, Braithwaite.

Perhaps it was hearing Mendelssohn play his *G minor Concerto* in 1832 that prompted the sixteen-year-old Sterndale Bennett to write his concerto in D minor and a work of extraordinary fluency and accomplishment. David Byers, who has edited the concertos, speaks of Bennett's 'gentle lyricism, the strength and energy of the orchestral tuttis'; and they are in ample evidence, both here and in the *Third Piano Concerto*, composed when he was eighteen. No praise can be too high for the playing of Malcolm Binns whose fleetness of finger and poetic sensibility are a constant source of delight, and for the admirable support he receives from Nicholas Braithwaite and the LPO. The engineers produce sound of the highest quality. A most enjoyable disc.

Piano Concertos Nos. 2 in E flat, Op. 4; 5 in F min.; Adagio.

*** Lyrita SRCD 205. Binns, Philh. O, Braithwaite.

The *Second Concerto* proves to be another work of great facility and charm. It takes as its model the concertos of Mozart and Mendelssohn, and the brilliance and delicacy of the keyboard writing make one understand why the composer was so highly regarded by his contemporaries. The *F minor Concerto* of 1836 is eminently civilized music with lots of charm; the *Adagio*, which completes the disc, is thought to be an alternative slow movement for Bennett's *Third Concerto* (1837). Malcolm Binns plays with great artistry, and the accompaniment by the Philharmonia Orchestra and Nicholas Braithwaite is equally sensitive. First-class recording.

(i) Piano Concerto No. 4 in F min.; Symphony in G. min.; (i) Fantasia in A, Op. 16.

(M) *** Unicorn UKCD 2032. (i) Binns; Milton Keynes CO, Davan Wetton.

William Sterndale Bennett's eclectic *Fourth Piano Concerto* reflects Chopin rather more than Mendelssohn and is agreeable and well structured. Its slow movement, an engaging *Barcarolle*, is a winner. The *Symphony* is amiable, not unlike the Mendelssohn string symphonies, slight but enjoyable. Malcolm Binns is a persuasive advocate of the *Concerto*, while Hilary Davon Wetton paces both works admirably and clearly has much sympathy for them. Excellent sound and a good balance.

STEVENS, Bernard (1916–83)

(i) Cello Concerto; Symphony of Liberation.

*** Mer. (ADD) CDE 84124. (i) Baillie, BBC PO, Downes.

Bernard Stevens came to wider notice at the end of the war when his *Symphony of Liberation* won a *Daily Express* competition. What a fine work it proves to be, though the somewhat later *Cello Concerto* is even stronger. Dedicated performances from Alexander Baillie and the BBC Philharmonic. Good recording.

(i) Violin Concerto; Symphony No. 2.

*** Mer. (ADD) CDE 84174. (i) Kovacic; BBC PO, Downes.

The *Violin Concerto* is a good piece and well worth investigating. Stevens is a composer of real substance, and the *Second Symphony* (1964) is impressive in its sustained power and resource. Ernst Kovacic is persuasive in the *Concerto* and Downes and the BBC Philharmonic play well. Good (but not spectacular) recording.

STILL, William Grant (1895–1978)

Symphony No. 2 (Song of a New Race) in G min.

*** Chan. 9226. Detroit SO, Järvi – DAWSON: *Negro Folk Symphony*; ELLINGTON: *Harlem*. ***

Stokowski conducted the première of this attractive piece in

1937, seven years after the composer's *First Symphony* had been the first work by an Afro-American composer to be played by a major orchestra (the NYPO). Still worked as an arranger, so he knew how to score, and he had a fund of tunes: the slow movement is haunting, the high-spirited Scherzo whistles along like someone out walking on a spring morning. The idiom is totally American and, if the score is more a suite than a symphony, it remains very personable. It is played most persuasively here and is given a richly expansive recording.

STOCKHAUSEN, Karlheinz

(born 1928)

(i) *Mikrophonie 1; Mikrophonie 2;* (ii) *Klavierstücke 1–11.*

(M) *** Sony (ADD) S2K 53346 (2). (i) Members of W. German R. Ch. & Studio Ch. for New Music, Cologne, Kontarsky, Alings, Fritsch, Bojé, cond. Schernus; supervised by composer; (ii) Kontarsky (piano).

This reissue combines two important Stockhausen recordings from the mid-1960s. *Mikrophonie 1* is electronic music proper; *Mikrophonie 2* attempts a synthesis of electronic music and choral sounds, and it is the vocal work that is the more immediately intriguing. It may be in dispute just how valid performances like these are when the composer's score allows many variables, but at least it is the composer himself who is supervising the production. Outstanding recording-quality for its time – as of course it should be with so many musician-engineers around in the Cologne studios.

The *Klavierstücke* provide a stimulating coupling. Aloys Kontarsky plays these eleven pieces – arguably the purest expression yet of Stockhausen's musical imagination – with a dedication that can readily convince even the unconverted listener. Seven of the pieces are very brief epigrammatic utterances, each sharply defined. The sixth and tenth pieces (the latter placed separately on the second disc) are more extended, each taking over 20 minutes. The effect at the begining of the ninth piece provides a clear indication of Stockhausen's aural imagination. The pianist repeats the same, not very interesting discord no fewer than 228 times, and one might dismiss that as merely pointless. What emerges from sympathetic listening is that the repetitions go nagging on so that the sound of the discord seems to vary, like a visual image shimmering in heat-haze. The other pieces, too, bring similar extensions of musical experience, and all this music is certainly communicative. Excellent if forward recording and extensive back-up notes. A good set on which to sharpen avant-garde teeth.

Stimmung (1968).

*** Hyp. CDA 66115. Singcircle, Rose.

Gregory Rose with his talented vocal group directs an intensely beautiful account of Stockhausen's 70-minute minimalist meditation on six notes. Though the unsympathetic listener might still find the result boring, this explains admirably how Stockhausen's musical personality can hypnotise, with his variety of effect and response, even with the simplest of formulae. Excellent recording.

STRADELLA, Alessandro (1644–82)

Christmas Cantatas: (i) *Ah, ah, troppo è ver;* (ii) *Si apra al riso* (both *per Il Santissimo natale*).

(BB) *** DHM 05472 77463 2. (i) Bach, Ziesak, Prégardien, (i–ii) Wessel, Schopper; (ii) Schlick; La Stagione Frankfurt, Schneider.

With a freshness and originality one expects from the composer of *San Giovanni Battista*, Stradella's Christmas cantata, *Ah, ah, troppo è ver*, is a great deal more than a serene pastorella. Lucifer (Michael Schopper) appears at the very opening, strenuously to interrupt the good-natured *Sinfonia*, to announce his determination to thwart the influence of the Christ child. Then come three scenas, in turn depicting the Annunciation, the Nativity and the Adoration of the Magi with the Angel and Mary (Mechthild Bach), followed by the Shepherd (Ruth Ziesak), each given beautiful narrative arias, all of which are sung ravishingly here. Joseph (Christoph Prégardien) then rounds off the story-telling, and the work closes with an engagingly happy madrigal in which all participate. *Si apra al riso* is less dramatic but musically just as inspired, with two duets and a madrigal trio interspersed among the solo numbers, here with Barbara Schlick standing out from her excellent colleagues. Michael Schneider paces the music admirably and the instrumental playing is first class. Vivid recording in a pleasing acoustic completes the listener's pleasure. A real bargain.

Motets: (i) *Benedictus Dominus Deo; Chare Jesu suavissime. Crocifissione e morte di N. S. Giesù Christo; Lamentatione per il Mercoledì Santo; O vos omnes qui transitis.*

(BB) **(*) Virgin 2 x 1 VBD5 61588-2 (2). Lesne, Il Seminario Musicale; (i) with Piau – CALDARA: *Sonatas; Cantatas.* **(*).

Alessandro Stradella wrote church music which combined drama with remarkable serenity and expressive beauty. *Benedictus Dominus Deo* is a particularly beautiful duet cantata in which God is thanked for sending his son to earth to redeem mankind. *O vos omnes*, a solo cantata, is shorter but no less potent. The text first expresses a languishing adoration of Jesus, with sensuous use of descending chromatics, and the work ends with lively *Alleluias*. Lesne is a master of this repertoire, and in the former cantata he is radiantly joined by Sandrine Piau, who then goes on to dominate the joyously lyrical *Chare Jesu suavissime*, sweetly praising Saint Philip Neri. These works are framed by the more austere *Crocifissione e morte di N. S. Giesù Christo* (which has a memorably eloquent instrumental introduction, after which the solo line is both grave and plaintive) and the closing *Lamentatione for Ash Wednesday*, which is also restrained but touchingly beautiful. The accompaniments, by a small, authentic-instrument group, are very sensitive indeed. This is perhaps specialist repertoire, but Gérard Lesne has made it his own and his artistry is unsurpassed. Now reissued very inexpensively indeed, aptly coupled to dramatic cantatas and sonatas of Caldara, this is very recommendable – with the very important proviso that now no texts are included.

San Giovanni Battista (oratorio).

⚙ *** Erato 2292 45739-2. Bott, Batty, Lesne, Edgar-Wilson, Huttenlocher, Musiciens du Louvre, Minkowski.

Stradella's oratorio on the Biblical subject of John the Baptist and Salome is an amazing masterpiece and offers un-ashamedly sensuous treatment of the story. Insinuatingly chromatic melodic lines for Salome (here described simply as Herodias' daughter) are set against plainer, more forth-right writing for the castrato role of the saint, showing the composer as a seventeenth-century equivalent of Richard Strauss. There is one amazing phrase for Salome, gloriously sung here by Catherine Bott, which starts well above the stave and ends after much twisting nearly two octaves below with a glorious chest-note, a hair-raising moment. Herod's anger arias bring reminders of both Purcell and Handel, and at the end Stradella ingeniously superimposes Salome's gloating music and Herod's expressions of regret, finally cutting off the duet in mid-air as Charles Ives might have done, bringing the whole work to an indeterminate close. Quite apart from Catherine Bott's magnificent performance, at once pure and sensuous in tone and astonishingly agile, the other singers are most impressive, with Gerard Lesne a firm-toned counter-tenor in the title-role and Philippe Huttenlocher a clear if sometimes gruff Herod. Marc Min-kowski reinforces his claims as an outstanding exponent of period performance, drawing electrifying playing from Les Musiciens du Louvre, heightening the drama. Excellent sound. Not to be missed!

STRAUS, Oscar (1870–1954)

Marches: *Einzugs; Bulgaren; Die Schlossparade. Menuett à la cour.* Polka: *G'stellte Mäd'ln. Rund um die Liebe* (Overture); Waltzes: (i) *L'Amour m'emporte. Alt-Wiener Reigen; Eine Ballnacht; Der Reigen; Didi;* (i) *Komm, komm, Held meiner Träume; Tragante; Valse lente; Walzerträume.*

*** Marco 8.223596. (i) Kincses; Budapest Strauss SO, Walter.

Although Oscar Straus is no relation to the famous Strauss family, his style of writing echoed theirs, also absorbing influences from Lehár. His great hit was the operetta, *A Waltz Dream* (1907), which had a first run in Vienna of 500 performances. His *Walzerträume* is deftly based on the main theme from the operetta, and the *Einzugs-Marsch* comes from the same source. But he could also manage a neat polka and score it very prettily, as is instanced by *G'stellte Mäd'ln*, while the *Alt-Wiener Reigen Waltz* is also full of charm and is played here very seductively. *Komm, komm, Held meiner Träume* is of course the famous 'Come, come, my hero', which comes from a parody operetta based on George Bernard Shaw's *Arms and the Man*. In 1908 it was a flop in Vienna, under its title *Der tapfere Soldat* ('The brave soldier') but was a resounding success in England and the USA later, when its title was changed to *The Chocolate Soldier* and its hit song took the world by storm. It is nicely sung

here in soubrette style by Veronika Kincses. After the Second World War, he wrote an engaging hit, sung first by Danielle Darrieux in a 1952 French film, *Madame de . . .*, and here by Veronika Kincses, and he capped his movie career with a Parisian-style waltz, *Der Reigen*, for the famous Max Ophüls film, *La Ronde*, the song eventually becoming better-known than the movie. The programme opens with a pot-pourri overture irresistibly full of sumptuous and light-hearted melody. It is infectiously played here, like the rest of the programme, by the first-class Budapest Strauss Symphony Orchestra, conducted with affection and great élan by Alfred Walter – easily the best CD he has made so far. The recording, too, is gorgeously sumptuous, and this is a mar-vellous disc to cheer you up on a dull day. Highly recom-mended.

STRAUSS, Franz (1822–1905)

Horn Concerto in C min., Op. 8.

(B) **(*) Double Decca (ADD) 460 296 (2). Tuckwell, LSO, Kertész – R. STRAUSS: *Concertos.* **(*)

This concerto by Franz Strauss, Richard's father, at times half-anticipates the lyrical style his son was to favour a generation later. But the quality of the musical material is undistinguished, and with its florid ornamentation the writing shows a tendency to fall into the manner of the cornet air with variations. Tuckwell's performance is respon-sive and secure, but fails to convince the listener that the work should not be put back in the attic where it rightly belongs.

THE STRAUSS FAMILY

Strauss, Johann Sr (1804–49)
Strauss, Johann Jr (1825–99)
Strauss, Josef (1827–70)
Strauss, Eduard (1835–1916)
(all music listed is by Johann Strauss Jr unless otherwise stated)

Johann Strauss Jr: The Complete Edition
All played by the CSSR State PO (Košice) unless indicated otherwise.

Vol. 1: Mazurka: *Veilchen, Mazur nach russischen motiven.* Polkas: *Fledermaus; Herzenslust; Zehner.* Quadrilles: *Debut; Nocturne.* Waltzes: *Bei uns z'Haus; Freuet euch des Lebens; Gunstwerber; Klangfiguren; Maskenzug française; Phönix-Schwingen.*

**(*) Marco 8.223201-2. A. Walter.

Vol. 2: *Kaiser Franz Josef 1, Rettungs-Jubel-Marsch.* Polkas: *Czechen; Neue Pizzicato; Satanella; Tik-Tak.* Polka-Mazurka: *Fantasieblümchen.* Quadrilles: *Cytheren; Indra.* Waltzes: *Die jungen Wiener; Solonsprüche; Vermälungs-Toaste; Wo die Zitronen blüh'n.*

** Marco 8.223202-2. A. Walter.

Vol. 3: Polkas: *Aesculap; Amazonen; Freuden-Gruss; Jux;*

Vergnügungszug . Quadrilles: *Dämonen; Satanella.*
Waltzes: *Berglieder; Liebeslieder; Lind-Gesänge; Die
Osterreicher; Wiener Punsch-Lieder.*

**(*) Marco 8.223203-2. A. Walter.

Vol. 4: Polkas: *Bürger-Ball; Hopser; Im Krapfenwald'l
(polka française); Knall-Kügerin; Veilchen.* Marches:
Austria; Verbrüderungs. Quadrille: *Motor.* Waltzes:
Dividenden; O schöner Mai!; Serail-Tänze.

**(*) Marco 8.223204-2. Edlinger.

Vol. 5: *Russischer Marsch Fantasie.* Polkas: *Elisen (polka
française); Heiligenstadt Rendezvous; Hesperus; Musen;
Pariser.* Quadrille: *Sur des airs français.* Waltzes:
*Italienischer; Kennst du mich?; Nachtfalter; Wiener
Chronik.*

*** Marco 8.223205-2. O. Dohnányi.

Vol. 6: *Caroussel Marsch.* Polkas: *Bluette (polka française);
Camelien; Warschauer.* Quadrilles: *Nach Themen
französischer Romanzen; Nordstern.* Waltzes:
Concurrenzen; Kuss; Myrthen-Kränze; Wellen und Wogen.

** Marco 8.223206-2. O. Dohnányi.

Vol. 7: *Deutscher Krieger-Marsch; Kron-Marsch.* Polkas:
Bacchus; Furioso; Neuhauser. Polka-Mazurka: *Kriegers
Liebchen.* Quadrille: *Odeon.* Waltzes: *Ballg'schichten;
Colonnen; Nordseebilder; Schnee-Glöckchen; Zeitgeister.*

**(*) Marco 8.223207-2. Polish State PO, O. Dohnányi.

Vol. 8: *Banditen-Galopp; Erzherzog Wilhelm Genesungs-
Marsch.* Polkas: *Leichtes Blut; Wiedersehen; Pepita.*
Quadrilles: *Nach Motiven aus Verdi's 'Un ballo in
maschera'; Saison.* Waltzes: *Cagliostro; Carnevals-
Botschafter; Lagunen; Die Sanguiniker; Schallwellen.*

**(*) Marco 8.223208-2. Polish State PO, O. Dohnányi.

This extraordinary Marco enterprise – to record the entire
output of the Strauss family – began in 1988. All these initial
volumes centre on the music of Johann Junior. Johann and
his orchestra were constantly on the move and, wherever
they travelled to play, he was expected to come up with
some new pieces. While obvious 'hits' and favourites stayed
in the repertoire, often the novelties were treated as ephem-
eral and in many instances only the short piano-score has
survived. It was necessary – for the purpose of the recording
– to hire professional arrangers to make suitable orchestrations; from these, new orchestral parts could be copied. Such
is the perversity of human experience that quite regularly
the original orchestral parts would suddenly appear for some
of the pieces – after the recording had been made! It is
therefore planned to have an appendix and to re-record
those items later, from the autographs. So far the recordings
have been made in Eastern Europe. Apart from cutting the
costs, the Slovak Bohemian tradition provides a relaxed
ambience, highly suitable for this repertoire. Much of the
music is here being put on disc for the first time and indeed
the excellent back-up documentation tells us that three items
on the first CD were part of the young Johann's first concert
programme: the *Gunstwerber* ('Wooer of favour') *Waltz,
Herzenslust* ('Heart's desire') polka and, even more appropriately, the *Debut-Quadrille,* so that makes Volume 1 of the
series something of a collector's item, while Volume 3 also

seems to have above-average interest in the selection of its
programme.

Evaluation of these recordings has not been easy. The first
three CDs were made by the Slovak State Philharmonic
under Alfred Walter. The mood is amiable and the playing
quite polished. With the arrival of Richard Edlinger and
Oliver Dohnányi on the scene, the tension seems to increase,
and there is much to relish. Of this second batch we would
pick out Volumes 5, 7 and 8, all representing the nice touch
of Oliver Dohnányi, with Volume 5 perhaps a primary
choice, although there are many good things included in
Volume 8.

Vol. 9: *Habsburg Hoch! Marsch; Indigo-Marsch.* Polkas:
Albion; Anen; Lucifer. Polka-Mazurka: *Nachtveilchen.*
Quadrille: *Festival Quadrille nach englischen Motiven.*
Waltzes: *Carnevalsbilder; Gedanken auf den Alpen; Kaiser.*

** Marco 8.223209-2. Polish State PO, Wildner.

Vol. 10: *Pesther csárdás.* Polkas: *Bauern; Blumenfest;
Diabolin; Juriston Ball.* Quadrille: *Nach beliebten Motiven.*
Waltzes: *Feuilleton; Morgenblätter; Myrthenblüthen;
Panacea-Klänge.*

** Marco 8.223210-2. Polish State PO (Katowice), Wildner.

Vol. 11: *Revolutions-Marsch.* Polkas: *Frisch heran!; Haute-
volée; Herrmann; Patrioten.* Polka-Mazurka: *Waldine.*
Quadrilles: *Die Afrikanerin; Handels-élite.* Waltzes: *Aus
den Bergen; Donauweibchen; Glossen; Klänge aus der
Walachei.*

**(*) Marco 8.223211-2. A. Walter.

Vol. 12: *Krönungs-Marsch.* Polkas: *Aurora; Ella;
Harmonie; Neues Leben (polka française); Souvenir;
Stürmisch in Lieb' und Tanz.* Quadrille: *Fest.* Waltzes: *Die
Gemüthlichen; Hofballtänze; Man lebt nur einmal!;
Wiener Frauen.*

** Marco 8.223212-2. A. Walter.

Vol. 13: *Egyptischer Marsch; Patrioten-Marsch.* Polkas:
*Demolirer; Fidelen; Nur fort!; Tanzi-bäri; Was sich liebt,
neckt sich (polka française).* Quadrilles: *Nach Motiven aus
der Oper 'Die Belagerung von Rochelle'; Neue Melodien.*
Waltzes: *Sirenen; Thermen; Die Zillerthaler.*

**(*) Marco 8.223213-2. A. Walter.

Vol. 14: *Romance No. 1 for Cello & Orchestra.* Polkas:
*Champagne; Geisselhiebe; Kinderspiele (polka française);
Vöslauer.* Quadrilles: *Bal champêtre; St Petersburg
(Quadrille nach russischen Motiven).* Waltzes: *Du und du;
Ernte-tänze; Frohsinns-spenden; Grillenbanner;
Phänomene.*

**(*) Marco 8.223214-2. A. Walter.

Vol. 15: *Jubelfest-Marsch.* Polkas: *Bijoux; Scherz.* Polka-
Mazurkas: *Lob der Frauen; La Viennoise.* Quadrilles:
Alexander; Bijouterie. Waltzes: *Die Jovialen; Kaiser-
Jubiläum; Libellen; Wahlstimmen.*

** Marco 8.223215-2. CSR SO (Bratislava), Wildner.

Vol. 16: *Fürst Bariatinsky-Marsch.* Polkas: *Brautschau (on
themes from Zigeunerbaron); Eljen a Magyar!; Ligourianer
Seufzer; Schnellpost; Studenten. La Berceuse Quadrille;*

Zigeuner-Quadrille (on themes from Balfe's *Bohemian Girl*). Waltzes: *Bürgerweisen; Freuden-Salven; Motoren; Sangerfährten.*

**(*) Marco 8.223216. A. Walter.

With Volume 9, we move to Poland and a new name, Johannes Wildner. He has his moments, but his approach seems fairly conventional. He does not make a great deal of the famous *Emperor Waltz* which closes Volume 9, although he does better with *Gedanken auf den Alpen*, another unknown but charming waltz. Alfred Walter – who began it all – then returns for Volumes 11–14. Of this batch, Volume 11 might be singled out, opening with the jolly *Herrmann-Polka*, while the *Klänge aus der Walachei, Aus den Bergen* ('From the Mountains') and *Donauweibchen* ('Nymph of the Danube') are three more winning waltzes; but the standard seems pretty reliable here, and these are all enjoyable discs. Volume 16 has another attractive batch of waltzes, at least two winning polkas and a quadrille vivaciously drawing on Balfe's *Bohemian Girl*. It also includes the extraordinary *Ligourian Seufzer-Polka*, in which the orchestra vocally mocks the Ligourians, a despised Jesuitical order led by Alfonso Maria di Ligouri. Another good disc.

Vol. 17: *Kaiser Franz Joseph-Marsch.* Polkas: *Armen-Ball; 'S gibt nur a Kaiserstadt! 'S gibt nur a Wien; Violetta (polka française).* Quadrille: *Melodien.* Waltzes: *Adelen; Bürgersinn; Freiheits-Lieder; Windsor-Klänge.*

*** Marco 8.223217-2. CSR SO (Bratislava), Eschwé.

Vol. 18: *Alliance-Marsche; Studenten-Marsch.* Polkas: *Edtweder-oder!; Invitation à la polka mazur; Leopoldstädter; Stadt und Land; Cagliostro-Quadrille.* Waltzes: *Grössfürstin Alexandra; Lava-Ströme; Patronessen; Die Pulizisten; Rathausball-Tänz.*

**(*) Marco 8.223218-2. A. Walter.

Vol. 19: *Hoch Osterreich! Marsch.* Polkas: *Burschenwanderung (polka française), Electro-magnetische; Episode (polka française).* Quadrilles: *Le Premier Jour de bonheur; Opéra de Auber; Seladon.* Waltzes: *Dorfgeschichten (im Ländlerstil); Novellen; Rosen aus dem Süden; Seid umschlungen, Millionen; Studentenlust.*

**(*) Marco 8-223219-2. A. Walter.

Vol. 20: *Dinorah-Quadrille nach Motiven der Oper, 'Die Wallfahrt' nach Meyerbeer. Kaiser-Jäger-Marsch. Slovianka-Quadrille, nach russischen Melodien.* Polkas: *Auf zum Tanze; Herzel.* Polka-Mazurkas: *Ein Herz, ein Sinn; Fata Morgana.* Waltzes: *Aurora-Ball-Tänze; Erhöhte Pulse; Flugschriften; Märchen aus dem Orient; Schwärmereien* (concert waltz).

** Marco 8.223220-2. A. Walter.

Vol. 21: *Ottinger Reiter-Marsch.* Polkas: *Figaro (polka française); Patronessen (polka française); Sans-souci.* Polka-Mazurka: *Tändelei.* Quadrilles: *Orpheus; Rotunde.* Waltzes: *Cycloiden; G'schichten aus dem Wienerwald; Johannis-Käferin.*

** Marco 8.223221-2. Wildner.

Vol. 22: *Klipp-Klapp Galopp. Persischer Marsch.* Polkas:

L'Inconnue (polka française); Nachtigall. Polka-Mazurka: *Aus der Heimat.* Quadrilles: *Carnevals-Spektakel; Der lustige Krieg.* Waltzes: *Controversen; Immer heiterer (im Ländlerstil); Maxing-tänze; Ninetta.*

** Marco 8.223222-2. Wildner.

Vol. 23: *Deutschmeister-Jubiläumsmarsch.* Polkas: *Maria Taglioni; Die Pariserin (polka française); Rasch in der Tat!.* Polka-Mazurka: *Glücklich ist, wer vergisst.* Quadrilles: *Le Beau Monde; Indigo.* Waltzes: *Gross-Wien; Rhadamantus-Klänge; Telegramme; Vibrationen; Wien, mein Sinn!*

** Marco 8.223223-2. Wildner.

Vol. 24: *Gavotte der Königin. Viribus unitis, Marsch.* Polkas: *Demi-fortune (polka française); Heski-Holki; Rokonhangok (Sympathieklänge); So ängstlich sind wir nicht!.* Polka-Mazurka: *Licht und Schatten.* Quadrille: *Streina-Terrassen.* Waltzes: *Idyllen; Jux-Brüder; Lockvögel; Sinnen und Minnen.*

** Marco 8.223224-2. A. Walter.

Volume 17 introduces another new name, Alfred Eschwé, and a particularly good collection, one of the highlights of the set, and it is beautifully played. Volume 18 brings back Alfred Walter and another very good mix of waltzes and polkas. Johannes Wildner then directs Volumes 21–23, and it must be said that the middle volume shows him in better light than the other two, and with a well-chosen programme.

Vol. 25: *Grossfürsten Marsch.* Polkas: *Bonbon (polka française); Explosions; Lustger Rath (polka française); Mutig voran!.* Polka-Mazurka: *Le Papillon.* Quadrilles: *Künstler; Promenade.* Waltzes: *Frauen-Käferin; Krönungslieder; Spiralen; Ins Zentrum!*

** Marco 8.223225-2. Wildner.

Vol. 26: *Es war so wunderschön Marsch.* Polkas: *Elektrophor; L'Enfantillage (polka française); Gut bürgerlich (polka française); Louischen (polka française); Pásmán.* Quadrilles: *Industrie; Sofien.* Waltzes: *Juristenball-Tänze; Künstlerleben; Pasman; Sinngedichte.*

*** Marco 8.223226-2. Austrian RSO, Vienna, Guth.

Vol. 27: *Spanischer Marsch.* Polkas: *Drollerie; Durch's Telephon; Express; Gruss an Wien (polka française).* Polka-Mazurka. *Annina.* Quadrilles: *Künstler; Sans-souci.* Waltzes: *Aeolstöne; Souvenir de Nizza; Wein, Weib und Gesang; Frühlingsstimmen.*

✹ *** Marco Dig 8.223227-2. Austrian RSO, Vienna, Guth.

Vol. 28: *Freiwillige vor! Marsch (1887). Frisch in's Feld! Marsch.* Polkas: *Unter Donner und Blitz; Pappacoda (polka française).* Polka-Mazurkas: *Concordia; Spleen.* Quadrille: *Tête-à-tête.* Waltzes: *Einheitsklänge: Illustrationen; Lebenswecker; Telegraphische Depeschen.*

** Marco 8.223228-2. Wildner.

Vol. 29: *Brünner-Nationalgarde-Marsch. Der lustige Krieg, Marsch.* Polkas: *Die Bajadere; Hellenen; Secunden (polka française).* Polka-Mazurka: *Une bagatelle.* Quadrille: *Waldmeister.* Waltzes: *Deutsche; Orakel-Sprüche; Schatz; Tausend und eine Nacht; Volkssänger.*

** Marco 8.223229-2. A. Walter.

Vol. 30: *Fest-Marsch. Perpetuum mobile.* Polkas: *Alexandrinen; Kammerball; Kriegsabenteuer; Par force!* Quadrille: *Attaque.* Waltzes: *Erinnerung an Covent Garden; Kluh Gretelein; Luisen-Sympathie-Klänge; Paroxysmen; Reiseabenteuer.*

** Marco 8.223230-2. A. Walter.

Vol. 31: *Napoleon-Marsch.* Polkas: *Husaren; Taubenpost (polka française); Vom Donaustrande.* Polka-Mazurka: *Nord und Süd.* Quadrilles: *Bonivant; Nocturne.* Waltzes: *Gambrinus-Tänze; Die ersten Curen; Hochzeitsreigen; Die Unzertrennlichen; Wiener Bonbons.*

** Marco 8.223231-2. A. Walter.

Vol. 32: *Wiener Jubel-Gruss-Marsch.* Polkas: *Auf der Jagd; Olge; Tritsch-Tratsch.* Polka-Mazurka: *An der Wolga.* Quadrilles: *Methusalem; Hofball.* Waltzes: *Fantasiebilder; Ich bin dir gut!; Promotionen. Wiener Blut.*

** Marco 8.223232-2. Wildner.

Volume 26 brings another fresh name, and fresh is the right word to describe this attractive programme. From the bright-eyed opening *Elektrophor Polka schnell* this is winningly vivacious music-making and the waltz that follows, *Sinngedichte*, makes one realizes that there is something special about Viennese string-playing, for this is the Orchestra of Austrian Radio. Volume 27 features the same orchestra and conductor and opens with the delectable *Künster-Quadrille*. After the aptly named *Drollerie* polka comes the *Aeolstöne* waltz with its portentous introduction, and the waltz itself is heart-warming. The *Souvenir de Nizza* waltz is hardly less beguiling and *Wine, Women and Song* and, to end the disc, *Frühlingsstimmen* – two top favourites – simply could not be better played. These two Peter Guth CDs are the finest of the series so far, and we award a token Rosette to the second of the two, although it could equally apply to its companion. After those two marvellous collections it is an anticlimax to return to the following volumes. There is much interesting music here, but the performances often have an element of routine.

Vol. 33: *Saschen-Kürassier-Marsch.* Polkas: *Etwas kleines (polka française); Freikugeln.* Polka-Mazurka: *Champêtre.* Quadrilles: *Bouquet; Opern-Maskenball.* Waltzes: *Abschieds-Rufe; Sträusschen; An der schönen blauen Donau; Trau, schau, wem!.*

** Marco 8.223233-2. Wildner.

Vol. 34: (i) *Dolci pianti* (Romance for cello and orchestra). *Im russischen Dorfe, Fantasie* (orch. Max Schönherr). *Russischer Marsch. Slaven-potpourri.* Polkas: *La Favorite (polka française); Niko.* Polka-Mazurka: *Der Kobold.* Quadrille: *Nikolai.* Waltzes: *Abschied von St Petersburg; Fünf Paragraphen.*

*** Marco 8.223234-2. Slovak RSO (Bratislava), Dittrich,
  (i) with Sikora.

Vol. 35: *Zivio! Marsch.* Polkas: *Jäger (polka française); Im Sturmschritt!; Die Zeitlose (polka française).* Polka-Mazurka: *Die Wahrsagerin.* Quadrilles: *Der Blits; Der*

Liebesbrunnen. Waltzes: *Accelerationen; Architecten-Ball-Tänze; Heut' ist heut' Königslieder.*

** Marco 8.223235-2. Wildner.

Vol. 36: *Matador-Marsch.* Polkas: *Bitte schön! (polka française); Diplomaten; Kreuzfidel (polka française); Process.* Polka-Mazurka: *Der Klügere gibt nach.* Quadrilles: *Elfen; Fledermaus.* Waltzes: *D'Woaldbuama (im Ländlerstil)* (orch. Ludwig Babinski); *Extravaganten; Mephistos Höllenrufe; Neu-Wien.*

** Marco 8.223236-2. A. Walter.

Among the following batch, the CD that stands out features another new name, Michael Dittrich; working with the Slovak Radio Symphony Orchestra, he produces a splendid collection to make up Volume 34. The flexible handling of the *Slav Potpourri* shows his persuasive sympathy for Strauss, while the *Fünf Paragraphen* waltz has an equally delectable lilt. There is great charm in the elegant *La Favorite* polka and the *Abschied von St Petersburg* waltz has a nicely beguiling opening theme.

Vol. 37: *Triumph-Marsch* (orch. Fischer). Polkas: *Das Comitat geht in die Höh!; Sonnnenblume; Tanz mit dem Besenstiel!* (all arr. Pollack); (i) *Romance No. 2 in G min. for Cello & Orchestra, Op. 35* (arr.Schönherr); Quadrilles: *Die Königin von Leon* (arr. Pollack); *Spitzentuch. Neue Steierische Tänze* (orch. Pollack); *Traumbild II;* Waltzes: *Jugend-Träume* (orch. Pollack); *Schwungräder.*

*** Marco 8.223237. Pollack; (i) with Jauslin.

Volume 37 is among the most interesting and worthwhile issues so far. It includes the waltz with which the nineteen-year-old Johann Junior created his first sensation at Zum Sperlbauer in Vienna. He had taken over the orchestra's direction in February 1845, and during a summer's night festival in August of that same year *Jugend-Träume* was introduced. It received five encores! The waltz is entirely characteristic, opening with a lilting theme on the strings and moving from one idea to another with the easy facility that distinguishes his more famous waltzes. Christian Pollack is a Strauss scholar, and in almost every case here he has worked from piano scores or incomplete scoring. Particularly delectable is the set of *New Styrian Dances*, seductively written in the Ländler style of Lanner's *Steyrische Tänze*. Here an almost complete piano version was available, while the orchestral parts end with the third dance; Pollack has therefore scored the fourth dance (very convincingly) in the style of the other three. While the *Romance for Cello and Orchestra* is agreeably slight, the other striking novelty here is *Traumbild II*, a late domestic work in two sections, the first of which is a gentle and charming 'dream-picture' of Strauss's wife, Adèle; the second shows the other side of her nature – more volatile and capricious. Both are in waltz time. Christian Pollack is not just a scholar but an excellent performing musician, and the playing here is polished, relaxed and spontaneous in an agreeably authentic way.

Vol. 38: *Wiener Garnison-Marsch* (orch. Babinsky); *Ninetta-Galopp;* Polkas: *Damenspende; Lagerlust; Maskenzug* (2nd version); *Nimm sie hinn!; Zehner* (2nd version); Quadrilles: *Eine Nacht in Venedig; Serben* (orch.

Babinski); Waltzes: *An der Elbe; Faschings-Lieder* (orch. Kulling); *Leitartikel.*

**(*) Marco 8.223238. A. Walter.

An der Elbe is a real find among the waltzes, a charming melodic sequence with a striking introduction. But the *Ninetta-Galopp* with its perky main theme and swirling wood-wind answer has the potential to become a Strauss lollipop, while the more sedate *Maskenzug-polka française* closes the programme engagingly. This is one of Alfred Walter's better programmes, nicely played and well recorded.

Vol. 39: *Ninetta-Marsch.* Polkas: *I Tipferl; Sylphen; Unparteiische Kritiken;* Quadrilles: *Jabuka; Slaven-Ball* (both orch. Pollack); Quodlibet: *Klänge aus der Raimundzeit;* Waltzes: *Abschied; Irenen* (orch. Babinski); *Hell und voll.*

**(*) Marco 8.223239. Pollack.

The two most interesting items here both date from Johann's last years, the *Abschieds* ('farewell') *Waltz* and the *Klänge aus der Raimundzeit* (1898), an affectionate *pot-pourri* including tunes by Johann Senior and Lanner. Johann originally called this good-humoured quodlibet *Reminiscenz. Aus der guter alten Zeit* ('from the good old days'). The score of the waltz is written in the composer's own handwriting; his widow, Adèle, offered it to be performed posthumously in 1900. The *I Tipferl-polka française* is based on a popular comic song from Strauss's *Prinz Methusalem*, and the couplet: 'The man forgot – the little dot, the dot upon the i!' is wittily pointed in the music. Christian Pollack directs excellent perform-ances of all the music here which, although of varying quality, is never dull.

Vol. 40: *Hochzeits-Praeludium;* Polkas: *Herzenskönigin; Liebe und Ehe; Wildfeuer;* Quadrilles: *Ninetta; Wilhelminen* (orch. Babinski); Waltzes: *Heimats-Kinder* (orch. Babinski); *The Herald* (orch. Schönherr); *Irrlichter; Jubilee* (orch. Cohen).

*(*) Marco 8.223240. Slovak RSO (Bratislava), Bauer-Theussl.

Vol. 41: March: *Wo uns're Fahne weht;* Polkas: *Newa; Shawl;* Quadrilles: *Martha; Vivat!;* Waltzes: *Burschen-Lieder; Gedankenflug; Lagunen. Traumbild* (symphonic poem). *Aschenbrödel (Cinderella): Prelude to Act III.*

** Marco 8.223241. Slovak RSO (Bratislava), Dittrich.

Vol. 42: *Hommage au public russe;* March: *Piccolo;* Polkas: *An der Moldau; Auroraball; Grüss aus Osterreich; Sängerlust; Soldatespiel;* Waltzes: *Gartenlaube; Hirtenspiele; Sentenzen.*

**(*) Marco 8.223242. Pollack.

For volumes 40 to 42 Christian Pollack returns, but we also meet a new conductor, Franz Bauer-Theussl. As it turns out, the music-making in Volume 40 under Bauer-Theussl immediately proves heavy-handed in the opening waltz, and the feeling throughout is that he is conducting for the commercial ballroom rather than the concert hall. As Pollack demonstrates in Volume 42, much more can be made of relatively strict tempo versions than Bauer-Theussl does with the *Irrlichter* and *Herald Waltzes.* The *Jubilee Waltz* was written for the Strausses' American visit in 1872, when in Boston he conducted its première, played by a 'Grand Orchestra' of 809 players, including 200 first violins! With this kind of spectacle it is not surprising that he chose to end a not particularly memorable piece by including a few bars of the American national anthem in the coda.

Without being exactly a live wire, Michael Dittrich makes a good deal more of Volume 41. He is able to relax and at the same time coax the orchestra into phrasing with less of a feeling of routine, as in the *Shawl-Polka,* which lilts rather nicely, and the comparatively sprightly *Vivat!* Dittrich fails to make a great deal of the one relatively well-known waltz here, *Lagunen,* but he manages the *Aschenbrödel Prelude* colourfully and does very well indeed by the *Traumbild I* ('Dream picture No. 1'), a warmly relaxed and lyrical evo-cation, quite beautifully scored. It was written towards the end of the composer's life, for his own pleasure.

But when we come to Volume 42, so striking is the added vivacity that it is difficult to believe that this is the same orchestra playing. The opening *Piccolo-Marsch* and the *Auroraball polka française* are rhythmically light-hearted, as are all the other polkas in the programme, and if the *Hirtenspiele* (or 'Pastoral play') *Waltz* is not a masterpiece, it is still freshly enjoyable in Pollack's hands, despite the demands of a ballroom tempo. The *Gartenlaube-Walzer* is a real find; it has a charming introduction with a neat little flute solo, then the opening tune, lightly scored, is very engaging indeed. It is a great pity that Marco did not hire the services of Christian Pollack much earlier in the series. Even the recording sounds better-focused here.

Vol. 43: *Auf dem Tanzboden* (arr. Pollack); *Reitermarsch.* Polkas: *Herrjemineh; Postillon d'amour; Die Tauben von San Marco.* Quadrilles: *Simplicius; Des Teufels Antheil* (arr. Pollack); Waltzes: *Trifolien; Walzer-Bouquet No. 1; Wilde Rosen* (arr. Babinski & Kulling).

**(*) Marco 8.223243. Pollack.

Vol. 44: Polkas: *Auf freiem Fusse; Nur nicht mucken* (arr. Peak); *Von der Börse.* Quadrilles: *Hinter den Coulissen; Monstre* (with J. STRAUSS). *Maskenfest; Schützen* (with J. and E. STRAUSS). Waltzes: *Altdeutscher* (arr. Pollack); *Aschenbrödel (Cinderella); Strauss' Autograph Waltzes* (arr. Cohen).

** Marco 8.223244. Pollack.

Vol. 45: Ballet music from *Der Carneval in Rom* (arr. Schönherr); *Ritter Pásmán. Fest-Marsch. Pásmán-Quadrille* (arr. Pollack); *Potpourri-Quadrille; Zigeunerbaron-Quadrille.* Waltzes: *Eva; Ischler.*

**(*) Marco 8.223245. A. Walter.

With Christian Pollack directing with his usual light touch, Volume 43 is one of the best of the more recent Marco issues, even if the *Walzer-Bouquet* is less winningly tuneful than its title suggests. *Wilde Rosen* is rather better, though not really memorable like *An dem Tanzboden* ('On the dance floor'), which was inspired by a painting. It is a real lollipop with a charming introduction (with clarinet solo) and matching postlude. The main waltz-tune is captivating and Pollack plays it exquisitely. Strauss originally intended to feature a zither in his scoring, but later indicated a pair of flutes instead, which sound delightful here. This is a prime candidate for a New Year concert. The polkas and *Simply Delicious Quadrille* are amiably diverting too, but the *Trifolien Waltz*, though lively enough, is a run-of-the-mill piece.

Volume 44 includes the brief (three-minute) but pleasant *Altdeutscher Waltz*, arranged by the conductor, and the relatively familiar *Aschenbrödel*, which is attractive but not one of Strauss's vintage waltzes. As usual with Pollack, the various quadrilles and polkas are agreeably relaxed but never dull, and the recording is up to standard.

Alfred Walter returns to conduct Volume 45, and he is at his finest in the lively and tuneful waltz which is the central movement of the *Ritter Pásmán Ballet*. The other ballet music, from *Der Carneval in Rom*, is scored by Schönherr – and very vividly too. The *Eva Waltz* is brief but delightfully graceful; *Ischler*, however, is more conventional. The quadrilles are nicely managed and the sound is very good.

Vol. 46: March: *Vaterländischer*. Polkas: *Pawlowsk; Pizzicato* (with Josef). *Probirmamsell*. Quadrilles: *Marien; Annika*. Romance: *Sehnsucht*. Waltzes: *Cagliostro; Engagement; Greeting to America*. (i) Gradual: *Tu qui regis totum orbem*. SCHUMANN, arr. JOHANN STRAUSS: *Widmung*.

*** Marco 8.223246. Slovak RSO (Bratislava), Dittrich; (i) with Slovak Philh. Ch. (members).

Michael Dittrich is on top form in Volume 46 of this ongoing series, opening vivaciously with a musical switch in march form, beginning with the *Radetzky* 'fanfare' and proceeding to quote intriguing snippets from all kinds of sources, including the Austrian national anthem. The *Greeting to America waltz* has a very appropriate and recognizable introduction and is as attractive as the delightfully scored *Engagement Waltz*, also written for America. The *Marien-Quadrille* is another charmer, and we learn from the excellent notes that the famous *Pizzicato polka*, a joint effort between Johann and Josef, was composed in Pavlosk on a Russian tour in 1869. The transcription of Schumann's love song, *Widmung*, was made by Johann in 1862 as a tribute to his new bride, Jetty, who was a singer, but the *Romance* (*Sehnsucht*) was written as a more robust cornet solo. The Gradual, *Tu qui regis totum orbem* ('Thou who rulest the whole world'), is a surprise inclusion from the eighteen-year-old composer – an offertory sung in conjunction with the performance of a Mass by his teacher, Professor Dreschler – and very pleasing it is. The concert ends with one of the deservedly better-known waltzes, taken from the operetta *Cagliostro in Wien* and played in an elegantly vivacious but nicely flexible style, like the rest of this very appealing programme, one of the very best of the Marco series. The recording is excellent.

Vol. 47: Ballet music from *Die Fledermaus*; from *Indigo und die vierzig Räuber* (arr. Schönherr). *Eine Nacht in Venedig: Processional March*. GOUNOD, arr. Johann Strauss: *Faust* (*Romance*). Quadrille on themes from *Faust*. Marches: *Kaiser Alexander Huldinungs; Kaiser Frans Joseph Jubiläums; Der Zigeunerbaron*. Waltzes: *Coliseum Waltzes; Farewell to America; Sounds from Boston*.

*** Marco 8.223247. Bratislava City Ch., Slovak RSO, Wildner.

This is another very attractive compilation with many beguiling novelties. After the brief but lively march from *Der Zigeunerbaron* comes *Farewell to America*, an agreeable pastiche waltz which waits until its coda to quote *The Starspangled Banner*. The following *Faust Romance* is a robust flugelhorn solo, based on an aria which was later to disappear from Gounod's revision of his score. The lively *Quadrille*, however, includes many favourite tunes from the opera and genially climaxes with the *Soldiers' Chorus*. Strauss's own ballet-music, written to be played during Orlofsky's supper party in *Die Fledermaus*, is today almost always replaced by something briefer. It includes a number of short national dances (not forgetting a *Schottische*), and the *Bohemian Dance* is in the form of a choral polka, actually sung here ('Marianka, come here and dance with me'), while the Hungarian finale reprises the music from Rosalinde's *Csárdás*. On the other hand, Schönherr's audaciously scored (some might say over-scored) 11-minute *mélange* of tunes from *Indigo and the Forty Thieves* is at times more like Offenbach than Strauss: it coalesces the good tunes and presents them in a glittering kaleidoscope of orchestral colour. The engaging *Coliseum Waltzes* which follow uncannily anticipate the *Blue Danube*, complete with an opening horn theme. *Sounds from Boston*, written for the composer's Boston visit in 1872, is another pastiche waltz of considerable charm, resulting as much from its delicacy of scoring as from its ready melodic flow: the orchestral parts were discovered, hidden away in the music library of the Boston Conservatory. The ideas come from earlier waltzes and almost none of them are familiar. All this music is liltingly and sparklingly presented by the Slovak Radio Orchestra, and no one could accuse the conductor, Johannes Wildner, of dullness.

Vol. 48: Complete Overtures, Vol. 1: *Concert Overture: Opéra comique* (arr. Pollack). *Intermezzo* from *Tausend und eine Nacht*. Overtures: *Blindekuh; Cagliostro in Wien; Der Carneval in Rom; Die Fledermaus; Indigo und die vierzig Räuber. Prince Methusalem; Das Spitzentuch der Königen*.

**(*) Marco 8.223249. A. Walter.

Collections of operetta overtures are almost always entertainingly tuneful, and this one is no exception. It begins with a curiosity that may or may not be authentic, an *Overture comique* written by the young Johann Jr for large harmonium (a kind of orchestrion) and piano, and afterwards arranged by the Strauss scholar, Fritz Lange, for violin and piano. None of the ideas it contains can be traced to the composer's notebooks, but the piece is attractive and is well put together in the form of a concert overture. It is heard here in a new arrangement (following the Lange manuscript) by Christopher Pollack. *Indigo und die vierzig Räuber* ('Indigo and the forty thieves') is also interesting in that Strauss omits the waltz rhythm altogether, which makes its lightly rhythmic progress seem rather Offenbachian. The *Intermezzo* from *Thousand and One Nights* is a just favourite, although Walter's languorous performance could use a little more lift, and *Die Fledermaus* is a fairly routine performance.

However, Walter conducts the other overtures very agreeably and makes the most of their pretty scoring. The waltzes are always coaxed nicely, particularly that in *Cagliostro in Wien*, and the playing has charm; yet one feels that some of the livelier ideas might have been given a bit more zip.

Vol. 49: Complete overtures, Vol. 2: *Aschenbrödel (Cinderella): Quadrille.* Overtures: *Die Göttin der Vernunft (The Goddess of Reason); Der lustige Krieg. Jabuka: Prelude to Act III. Eine Nacht in Venedig: Overture* and *Prelude to Act III.* Overtures: *Simplicius; Waldmeister; Der Zigeunerbaron.*

**(*) Marco 8.223275. A. Walter.

Alfred Walter's second collection of overtures has distinctly more sparkle than the first. He is always good with waltzes and there are quite a few here, if only in snippet form. The pair included in *A Night in Venice* are presented with appealing delicacy, while *The Goddess of Reason* brings a waltzing violin solo complete with cadenza and, at the close, another waltz which swings splendidly. *Zigeunerbaron* is the best-known piece here, and it is laid out elegantly and is beautifully played. But Walter is inclined to dally by the wayside: in the theatre a performance like this would not hold the attention of the audience. *Simplicius* is much more lively, with a march near the beginning, and *Waldmeister* has real verve, with the horns skipping along nicely towards the end. What one rediscovers on listening through this pair of discs is not only the fecundity of Johann's invention and the charm of his orchestration, but also the felicitous way he turns a pot-pourri into a naturally spontaneous sequence of ideas. The recording throughout both collections is first class, spacious and with a ballroom warmth.

Vol. 50: (i) *Am Donaustrand;* **(i)** *Erste Liebe (Romanze); Erster Gedanke;* **(i)** *Ein gstanzi von Tanzl; Die Fledermaus: Csárdás and New Csárdás. Frisch gewagt (Galop); Da nicken die Giebel (Polka-Mazurka); Die Göttin der Vernunft (Quadrille);* **(i)** *Dolci pianti;* Waltzes: **(i)** *Frühlingsstimmen;* **(i)** *King Gretelein; Nachgelassener; Odeon-Waltz;* **(i)** *Wo die Citronen blüh'n;* **(i)** *Wenn du ein herzig Liebchen hast.*

*** Marco 8.223276. (i) Hill Smith; Slovak RSO (Bratislava), Pollack.

Marilyn Hill Smith was on hand for this collection, so one wonders why the opening *Csárdás* from *Die Fledermaus* is the orchestral version (arranged by Hans Swarowsky); but the excellent Christian Pollack makes a good case for it, his ebb and flow of mood and tempo very engaging. Hill Smith sings a number of items, and her light soubrette is just right for this repertoire. She presents *Wo die Citronen blüh'n* with much vivacity and is hardly less sparkling in the famous *Voices of Spring*. Moreover she offers as a charming vignette *Dolci pianti* (a song which Strauss composed for his singer-wife, Jetty), for which she has also provided the accompanying translation. The rest of the programme is agreeable, but there are no lost masterpieces here. Pollack makes the most of the waltzes and is especially characterful in the polka-mazurka, *Da nicken die Giebel*, which sounds a bit like a slow waltz with extra accents. Again, first-rate recording.

Vol. 51: *Auf der Alm* (Idyll); *Fürstin Ninetta* (Entr'acte); Galop: *Liebesbotschaft;* **(i)** Choral polka: *Champêtre (Wo klingen die Lieder).* Polka-mazurka: *Promenade-Abenteuer.* **(ii)** *Romance No. 2 for Cello & Orchestra.* Choral waltz: **(i)** *An der schönen, blauen Donau.* Waltzes: *Centennial; Enchantment; Engagement; Farewell to America; Manhattan; Tauben.* Songs: **(iii)** *Bauersleut' im Künstlerhaus; D'Hauptsach* (both arr. Rott).

☸ *** Marco 8.223279. Slovak RSO (Bratislava), Cohen; with (i) Slovak Philharmonic Ch.; (ii) Tvrdik; (iii) Eröd.

It is rather appropriate that Volume 51 should be special, and so it is. It opens with the enchanting choral *Polka mazurka champêtre*, introduced by the horns and gloriously sung by a male chorus with a nicely managed diminuendo at the coda. And it ends with Strauss's masterpiece, the *Blue Danube*, also for male-voice choir and sung with an infectious lilt, to leave the listener in high spirits. All the other half-dozen waltzes here are virtually unknown, and every one is delightful. The opening strain of *Manhattan* is ear-catching and Cohen later (rarely in this series) indulges himself in some affectionate rubato which is most seductive. The *Centennial* and the (well-named) *Enchantment Waltzes* are again most affectionately presented, and their beguiling introductions are in each case followed by a string of good tunes. The *Engagement Waltz* opens more grandly, but then the atmosphere lightens, and there is plenty of sparkle. *Farewell to America* (a pot-pourri) brings the American National Anthem delicately and nostalgically into the coda. The *Romance No. 2 for Cello and Orchestra*, tastefully played by Ivan Tvrdik, is surprisingly dolorous at its opening, then produces a romantic flowering, before ending nostalgically. The *Liebesbotschaft Galop* then arrives to cheer us all up, and it is followed by yet another unknown waltz, *Tauben*, in which Cohen coaxes the opening quite ravishingly. Of the two brief baritone solos the second, *D'Hauptsach*, has a most pleasing melody. No other record in the series so far offers such a fine package of unexpected delights or more hidden treasure, and there could be no better advocate than the present conductor, Jerome Cohen. He has the advantage of spacious, naturally balanced recording. A Rosette then for the sheer enterprise of the first half-century of this series and also for the special excellence of this collection with its discovery of six remarkably fine waltzes.

Potpourris, Vol. 1: *Cagliostro in Wien; Indigo und die vierzig Räuber; Der lustige Krieg; Eine Nacht in Venedig; Prinz Methusalem; Das Spitzentuch der Königin.*

*(*) Marco 8.225074. Pollack.

Potpourris, Vol. 2: *Fürstin Ninetta; Die Göttin der Vernunft; Jabuka (Das Apfelfest); Ritter Pásmán; Simplicius.*

*(*) Marco 8.225075. Pollack.

Even today, selections from musical shows are the mainstay of the bandstand, and so it was in the days of the Strauss family. However, although they include a fair smattering of good tunes, some of the pot-pourris here outlast their welcome (*Indigo und die vierzig Räuber* runs for over 18 minutes) and the scoring of the vocal numbers is seldom very imaginative. Curiously even Christian Pollack, usually an inspired Straussian, is below his best form, and he fails to make a case for them. In the end this becomes nothing more than wallpaper music. So this pair of discs, although well enough played, is of documentary interest only.

Boskovsky Strauss Edition

Galops: *Aufs Korn; Banditen.* Marches: *Egyptischer; Franz Joseph I Rettungs-Jubel; Napoleon; Persischer; Russischer; Spanischer. Perpetuum mobile.* Polkas: *Annen; Auf der Jagd; Bitte schön!; Champagner; Demolirer; Eljen a Magyar; Explosionen; Freikugeln; Im Krapfenwaldl; Leichtes Blut; Lob der Frauen; Ohne Sorgen; Pizzicato* (with Josef); *Neue Pizzicato; So ängst sind wir nicht; 'S gibt nur a Kaiserstadt, 's gibt nur a Wien!; Stürmisch in Lieb' und Tanz; Tik-Tak; Tritsch-Tratsch; Unter Donner und Blitz (Thunder and Lightning); Vernügungszug.* Quadrilles: *Fledermaus; Orpheus; Schützen* (with Josef & Eduard). Waltzes: *Accelerationen; An der schönen blauen Donau (Blue Danube); Bei uns z'Haus; Carnavals-Botschafter; Du und du; Errinerung an Covent-Garden; Freuet euch des Lebens; Frühlingsstimmen (Voices of Spring); Geschichten aus dem Wienerwald (Tales from the Vienna Woods); Kaiser (Emperor); Künstlerleben (Artist's Life); Lagunen; Liebeslieder; Mephistos Höllenrufe; Morgenblätter (Morning Papers); Nordseebilder; Rosen aus dem Süden (Roses from the South); Seid umschlungen, Millionen!; Schneeglöckchen; Tausend and eine Nacht; Wein, Weib und Gesang (Wine, Women and Song); Wiener Blut (Vienna Blood); Wiener Bonbons; Wo die Citronen blüh'n!.* JOHANN STRAUSS SR: Galops: *Sperl; Wettrennen. Radetzky march.* Polka: *Piefke und Pufka.* Waltz: *Loreley-Rhein-Klänge.* JOSEF STRAUSS: Polkas: *Auf Ferienreisen; Brennende Liebe; Eingesendt; Die Emancipirte; Extempore; Feuerfest; Frauenherz; Heiterer Mut; Im Fluge; Jokey; Die Libelle; Moulinet; Rudolfsheimer; Die Schwätzerin.* Waltzes: *Aquarellen; Delirien; Dorfschwalben aus Osterreich (Village swallows); Dynamiden; Mein Liebenslauf ist Lieb und Lust; Sphärenklänge (Music of the spheres); Transactionen.* EDUARD STRAUSS: Polkas: *Bahn Frei!; Mit Extrapost.* Waltz: *Fesche Geister.*

(B) **(*) Decca (ADD) 455 254-2 (6). VPO, Boskovsky.

These six vintage CDs (offering 86 titles) span Willi Boskovsky's long (analogue) recording career for Decca, stretching over two decades from the late 1950s onwards, when his records dominated the LP discography in the Strauss family repertoire. In 1979 he directed the first of the now famous VPO New Year Concerts (see below) and that recording tradition has continued until the present day. It has now become an annual event shared by different record companies and various conductors, capped in 1987 by Karajan, after he had set aside a period of his musical life to re-evaluate his interpretations. Since then there have been a series of fine discs from Abbado, Kleiber, Lorin Maazel, Mehta and Riccardo Muti, all of whom have risen to the occasion and been given admirable support by the various recording teams.

Even so, Boskovsky's achievement in this repertoire remains unique, both in its range – the output of Josef, particularly his polkas, is notably well covered – and the almost unfailing sparkle of the performances. Following a sequence begun by Decca in the days of mono LPs with Clemens Kraus, he showed a unique feeling for the Straussian lilt in the waltzes and the fizzing élan and exuberance of the polkas and marches, while the playing he drew from the Vienna Philharmonic Orchestra was consistently persuasive. The Decca engineers rose to the occasion (notably so when special effects were required, as in the *Explosion* and *Thunder and Lightning Polkas*) and the Sofiensaal provided an ideal ambience, with plenty of warmth and bloom. The one snag is the thinness of violin-tone, especially on the earlier records – it is immediately noticeable here on *An der schönen blauen Donau*, which rightly opens the first disc. The present CD transfers are very vivid and immediate, and their brightness has also served to add a hint of coarseness to some of the lively music (for instance the engaging quadrilles on disc 6). The ear adjusts, however, when the music-making is so zestful and alive: in spite of such reservations, there is no finer or more all-embracing collection of the best of the output of the Strauss family than in this box. Appropriately, the Decca recording producer, John Parry, has provided a biographical essay, and the documentation includes Edward Hanslick's obituary, which records that Johann Jr was not only a great composer but 'an extremely charming, genuine and benevolent person'. This is surely reflected in the life-enhancing geniality of his music.

NEW YEAR CONCERTS

New Year's Day concert in Vienna (1979): Polkas: *Auf der Jagd* (with encore); *Bitte schön! Leichtes Blut; Pizzicato* (with Josef); *Tik-Tak.* Waltzes: *An der schönen blauen Donau; Bei uns zu Haus; Loreley-Rheine-Klänge; Wein, Weib und Gesang.* JOSEF STRAUSS: *Moulinet Polka; Die Emanzipierte Polka-Mazurka; Rudolfsheimer-Polka; Sphärenklänge Waltz.* JOHANN STRAUSS SR: *Radetzky March.* EDUARD STRAUSS: *Ohne Bremse Polka* (with ZIEHRER: *Herreinspaziert! Waltz;* SUPPE: *Die schöne Galathée Overture*).

(B) *** Decca (ADD) (IMS) 448 572-2 (2). VPO, Boskovsky.

Decca chose to record Boskovsky's 1979 New Year's Day concert in Vienna for their very first digital issue on LP. The clarity, immediacy and natural separation of detail are very striking throughout, and the strings of the Vienna Philharmonic are brightly lit. There is some loss of bloom and not quite the degree of sweetness one would expect now on a record made today in the Musikvereinsaal, but the ear soon adjusts. The music-making itself is another matter. It gains much from the spontaneity of the occasion, reaching its peak when the side-drum thunders out the introduction to the closing *Radetzky March*, a frisson-creating moment which, with the audience participation, is quite electrifying.

'1987 New Year Concert in Vienna': Overture: *Die Fledermaus.* Polkas: *Annen; Pizzicato* (with Josef); *Unter Donner und Blitz; Vergnügungszug.* Waltzes: *An der*

schönen blauen Donau; (i) Frühlingsstimmen. J. STRAUSS
SR: Beliebte Annen (polka); Radetzky March. JOSEF
STRAUSS: Ohne Sorgen Polka; Waltzes: Delirien;
Sphärenklänge.

*** DG 419 616-2. VPO, Karajan; (i) with Battle.

In preparation for this outstanding concert, which was both
recorded and televised, Karajan re-studied the scores of his
favourite Strauss pieces; the result, he said afterwards, was
to bring an overall renewal to his musical life beyond the
scope of this particular repertoire. The concert itself produced music-making of the utmost magic; familiar pieces
sounded almost as if they were being played for the first time.
Kathleen Battle's contribution to Voices of spring brought
wonderfully easy, smiling coloratura and much charm. The
Blue Danube was, of course, an encore, and what an encore!
Never before has it been played so seductively on record. In
the closing Radetzky March, wonderfully crisp yet relaxed,
Karajan kept the audience contribution completely in control merely by the slightest glance over his shoulder. This
indispensable collection makes an easy first choice among
Strauss compilations. Unfortunately the current presentation is without proper musical documentation, which is a
disgrace. We have consequently removed our Rossette.

'1998 New Year Concert': Wo uns're Fahne March.
Overture: Prinz Methusalem. Polka: Trisch-Tratsch. Polka
schnell: Nur fort!. Waltzes: An der schönen blauen Donau;
Nachtfalter; Nordseebilder; Rosen aus dem süden; Wiener
bonbons. JOSEF HELLMESBERGER: Kleiner galop. JOSEF
STRAUSS: Polkas Mazur: Die Schwebenda; In der Heimat!.
Polkas schnell: Jocas; Plappermäulchen. Quadrille: Neue
Melodien. JOHANN STRAUSS SR: Annen-Polka; Radetzky
March; Marianka-Polka. EDUARD STRAUSS: Polka
schnell: Bahn frei!.

(B) *** RCA Double 09026 63144-2 (2). V. Boys' Ch., VPO,
   Mehta.

Zubin Mehta, trained in Vienna, lives up to tradition in this
his third 'New Year's Concert', mixing novelties – no fewer
than eight items totally new to the event – with old favourites, all immaculately presented. It is a novelty too having the
Vienna Boys' Choir adding sparkle to two of the well-known
polkas. The two-disc format at no extra charge allows the
whole concert to be included, traditional encores and all.

'1999 New Year Concert': Banditen-Galopp; Perpetuum
mobile; Polkas: Hopser; (i) Scherz (for violin and
orchestra); Tritsch-Tratsch; Unter Donner und Blitz;
Waltzes: An der schönen blauen Donau; Donauweibchen;
Geschichten aus dem Wiener Wald; Künsterleben;
Sinngedichte. JOHANN STRAUSS SR: Furioso-Galopp
(after Liszt); Radetzky-Marsch; Walzer à la Paganini (for
violin and orchestra).

*** RCA 74321 61687-2. VPO, Maazel (i) violin; & cond.

Lorin Maazel in this, his tenth New Year's Concert in Vienna,
consistently captures the right atmosphere, boldly taking up
his solo violin in the Scherz-Polka and Walzer à la Paganini,
entering into the fun in a way to lighten his once severe
image. To mark the centenary of the death of the younger
Johann, the programme starts with the very first of his

hundreds of opuses, the 'Epigram Waltz', Sinngedichte, just
as winningly lyrical as many later favourites. Some New
Year's Concerts take you by storm with their bite and energy,
but this one makes its point above all by charming, whether
in the languorous introduction to Tales from the Vienna
Woods or such rarities as the late Donauweibchen ('little
woman of the Danube'), the waltz on themes from the
operetta, Simplicius, and the insinuating Hopser-Polka. The
uproarious Banditen-Polka with its police-whistles and gunshots then raises the temperature, before the final traditional
jamboree.

'2000 New Year concert': Csárdás from Ritter Pasman;
March: Persischer. Polkas: Albion; Eljen a Magyar;
Hellenen; Process; Vom Donaustrande. Waltzes: An der
schönen blauen Donau; Lagunen; Liebeslieder; Wein, Weib
und Gesang. EDUARD STRAUSS: Polkas: Mit Extrapost;
Gruss an Prag. JOSEF STRAUSS: Polkas: Die Libelle;
Künstler-Gruss; Waltz: Marien-Klänge. JOHANN STRAUSS
SR: Radetzky March.

(M) *** EMI CDC5 67323-2 (2). VPO, Riccardo Muti (with
   SUPPE: Overture: Morning, Noon and Night in Vienna).

Like Lorin Maazel before him, Riccardo Muti loses any
prickly qualities, concentrating on charm rather than bite,
as is obvious from the very opening number in the 2000
concert. The Lagunen Waltz of Johann Strauss II makes
the gentlest possible start, leading to a couple of sparkling
novelties, never heard at these concerts before, the brisk
Hellenen Polka and the feather-light Albion Polka, dedicated
to Prince Albert. That sets the pattern for the whole programme. For all the brilliance of the playing, it is the subtlety
of the Viennese lilt (as in Josef Strauss's Marien-Klänge,
another novelty) that one remembers, or the breathtaking
delicacy of the pianissimo which opens the first of the
encores, the Blue Danube, perfectly caught by the EMI engineers. For its Millennium concert the Vienna Philharmonic could not be more seductive. The two-disc format at
mid-price – with the first half shorter than the second –
allows the whole programme to be included without cuts.

OTHER COLLECTIONS

Banditen-Galopp; Quadrille nach Motiven der Operette.
Marches: Egyptischer; Kaiser Franz Josef. Polkas: Annen-
Polka; Auf der Jagd; Eljen a Magyar; Fata Morgana;
Furioso-Polka quasi Galopp; Tritsch-Tratsch; Unter
Donner und Blitz. Waltzes: An der schönen, blauen
Donau; Morgenblätter; Rosen aus dem Süden; Tausend
and eine Nacht; Wiener Blut; Wiener Bonbons. EDUARD
STRAUSS: Weyprecht-Payer (march); Saat und Ernte
(polka). Waltzes: Leuchtkäferlin; Schleir und Krone. JOSEF
STRAUSS: Polkas: Die Libelle; Farewell!; Moulinet; Ohne
Sorgen. Waltzes: Aquarellen; Perlen der Liebe. J. STRAUSS
SR: Cachucha-Galopp.

(M) **(*) Chan. (ADD) 7129 (2). Strauss O, Rothstein.

These are relaxed, enjoyable performances which are hard
to fault. If they lack the Viennese distinction of Boskovsky
or the individuality of Karajan, the varied programme with

plenty of novelties, makes up for it. There are several agreeable surprise items in this 2-CD set and the sound is very good.

Egyptischer March; Perpetuum mobile. Polkas: Auf der Jagd; Pizzicato. Waltzes: An der schönen, blauen Donau; Frühlingsstimmen; Geschichten aus dem Wienerwald; Rosen aus dem Süden; Tausend and eine Nacht; Wiener Blut.

(B) *** Decca Penguin (ADD) 460 648-2. VPO, Boskovsky.

These performances, which include six favourite waltzes, have the magical Viennese glow that marked all of Boskovsky's Strauss Decca recordings right through from 1958 to 1979, with sound ranging from good to excellent. It makes an admirable collection for those thinking the Decca/Boskovsky 6-CD box (see above) too much of a good thing. These works could not sound more authentic if Johann Strauss himself were conducting. The specialist essay is by Allan Massie.

Marches: Egyptischer; Persischer. Polkas: Auf der Jagd; Pizzicato (with Josef); Unter Donner und Blitz; Postillon d'amour; Leichtes Blut. Waltzes: G'schichten aus dem Wienerwald; Morgenblätter; Wiener Blut. JOSEF STRAUSS: Sphärenklänge.

(M) *** DG (ADD) 449 768-2. BPO, Karajan.

The present collection is based on an LP originally published in 1971. A few prize items have been added, notably the engaging Postillon d'amour polka, which is bounced in true dance rhythm, and Josef's Sphärenklänge, which Karajan shapes most affectionately, particularly the lovely opening. But the original disc is most notable for the central section of the Egyptian March when the Berlin orchestral players make a robust vocal contribution to the middle section. The piece is then charmingly pared down, like a patrol disappearing into the distance. Of the waltzes, Wiener Blut lilts attractively, and Tales from the Vienna woods is coaxed most seductively with a particularly delicate zither solo. The sound is excellent, and altogether this is the best Karajan Johann Strauss disc in the DG catalogue, apart from his famous 1987 New Year concert in Vienna, which is unsurpassable.

Napoleon-Marsch. Polkas: Annen; Explosionen; Tritsch-Tratsch. Waltzes: An der schönen blauen Donau; Morgenblätter; Thousand and One Nights; Wein, Weib und Gesang; Wiener Bonbons. JOSEF STRAUSS: Dorfschwalben aus Osterreich. JOHANN STRAUSS SR: Radetzky March.

(B) *** Decca (ADD) 433 609-2. VPO, Boskovsky.

A particularly enjoyable concert of Boskovsky repertoire, chosen and ordered with skill, opening with the Blue Danube and closing with the rousing Radetzky March. The VPO are on their toes throughout. The recording dates range from 1958 to 1976; some are spikier than others in the upper range, but the warm Sofiensaal ambience is always flattering.

(i) Overture: Die Fledermaus. Waltzes: (ii) An der schönen blauen Donau; Carnavals-Botschafter; Donauweibchen; Du und du; Feuilleton; Flugschriften; (i) Geschichten aus dem Wienerwald; Kaiser; (ii) Die Leitartikel; Morgenblätter; (i) Tausend and eine Nacht; (ii) Wein, Weib und Gesang; Wiener Frauen. Polkas: (i) Im Krapfenwald'l; Leichtes Blut. JOSEF STRAUSS: Waltzes: Dynamiden; Sphärenklänge. JOHANN STRAUSS SR: Radetzky March.

(BB) *** EMI CES 68535-2 (2). (i) VPO, Kempe; (ii) J. Strauss O of V., Boskovsky.

A fascinating juxtaposition of two quite different styles of Johann Strauss performance. Boskovsky's Johann Strauss Orchestra balances an evocative Viennese warmth with vigour and sparkle; he is at his very best exploring the novelties – Donauweibchen and Wiener Frauen are particularly winning. Wein, Weib und Gesang; incidentally, has an abbreviated introduction. The digital recording from the early 1980s is excellent. Kempe in the waltzes is unashamedly indulgent, especially in the introductions of the two Josef Strauss items, and Tausend and eine Nacht. With quite gorgeous playing from the VPO strings this is almost decadently voluptuous, moving to a sumptuous climax. Both polkas are infectious and Im Krapfenwald'l, with its cuckoo calls, brings an affectionate smile. The recordings, from 1958 and 1961, sound amazingly good.

Overture: Die Fledermaus; Emperor Waltz; Perpetuum mobile; Tritsch-Tratsch Polka.

(N) *** BBC (ADD) BBCL 4038. Hallé O, Barbirolli – HAYDN: Symphony No. 83 in G min. (La Poule); LEHAR: Gold and Silver; R. STRAUSS: Der Rosenkavalier Suite. ***

Barbirolli's performance exudes the full communicative atmosphere of this 1969 Prom, and one can hear Sir John himself vocalizing in the overture. The performance of the Emperor Waltz is ravishing and an outrageous fun performance of Tritsch-Tratsch follows, with sudden pauses to bring bursts of laughter from the promenaders.

Overtures: Die Fledermaus; Waldmeister; Perpetuum mobile. Polkas: Eljen a Magyar!; Pizzicato (with Josef); Tritsch-Tratsch; Unter Donner und Blitz; Vergnügungszug. Waltzes: Accelerationen; An der schönen, blauen Donau; G'schichten aus dem Wienerwald; Kaiser; Morgenblätter; Rosen aus dem Süden. JOSEF STRAUSS: Polkas: Frauenherz; Die Libelle; Ohne Sorgen; Die tanzende Muse. Waltzes: Aquarellen; Delirien; Sphärenklänge; Transaktionen. JOHANN STRAUSS SR: Radetzky March.

(B) **(*) DG Double 453 052-2 (2). VPO, Maazel.

The presence of a New Year's Day audience is most tangible in the Pizzicato Polka, where one can sense the intercommunication as Maazel manipulates the rubato with obvious flair. He also gives a splendid account of Transaktionen, which has striking freshness and charm. The Waldmeister Overture is a delightful piece and readily shows the conductor's affectionate response in its detail, while the opening of the Aquarellen Waltz brings an even greater delicacy of approach and the orchestra responds with telling pianissimo playing. For the rest, these are well-played performances of no great memorability. The digital sound is brilliant and clear, somewhat lacking in resonant warmth.

Overtures: *Die Fledermaus; Der Zigeunerbaron.* Waltzes: *An der schönen blauen Donau; Geschichten aus dem Wiener Wald; Kaiser; Wiener Blut.*

(M) (***) Sony mono SMK 64467. Columbia SO, B. Walter (with BRAHMS: *Hungarian Dances Nos. 1, 3, 10 & 17* (***); SMETANA: *Vltava* (**)).

It is good to have a reminder of Bruno Walter's way with Johann Strauss, full of vivacity, and with *Wiener Blut* obviously the conductor's favourite among the waltzes here, as he coaxes the opening beguilingly and then draws some ravishing playing from the violins. The two overtures are bright and volatile. No apologies whatsoever about the 1956 mono recording, which is warm and spacious and sounds almost like early stereo.

Perpetuum mobile. Polkas: *Annen; Auf der Jagd; Pizzicato* (with Josef); *Tritsch-Tratsch; Unter Donner und Blitz.* Waltzes: *An der schönen blauen Donau; G'schichten aus dem Wienerwald; Kaiser; Wiener Blut.* JOSEF STRAUSS: *Delirien Waltz.*

(M) **(*) DG (IMS) (ADD) 437 255-2. BPO, Karajan.

Here is a selection taken from two analogue LPs which Karajan made in 1966 and 1969 respectively. The performances have characteristic flair and the playing of the Berlin Philharmonic has much ardour as well as subtlety, with the four great waltzes of Johann II all finely done (the *Emperor* has a particularly engaging closing section) and the polkas wonderfully vivacious. The current remastering is satisfactory, brightly lit, but with the Jesus-Christus Kirche providing ambient fullness.

Polkas: *Czech; Pizzicato* (with Josef). Waltzes: *Kaiser; Rosen aus dem Süden; Sängerlust; Wiener Blut; Wiener Bonbons.* J. STRAUSS SR: *Radetzky March.* JOSEF STRAUSS: Polkas: *Feuerfest; Ohne Sorgen.*

(BB) **(*) ASV (ADD) CDQS 6020. LSO, leader Georgiadis (violin).

The LSO is on top form and the rhythmic feel of the playing combines lilt with polished liveliness. There is delicacy (the *Czech polka* is enchanting) and boisterousness, as in the irresistible anvil effects in the *Feuerfest polka.* The closing *Radetzky March* is as rousing as anyone could wish, while the waltzes combine vitality and charm. With good recording in a suitably resonant acoustic, which tends to emphasize the bass, this is recommendable, especially at budget price.

Pappacoda polka; Der lustige Kreig (quadrille); *Klug Gretelein* (waltz). JOSEF STRAUSS: *Defilir marsch;* Polkas: *Farewell; For ever.* EDUARD STRAUSS: *Weyprecht-Payer marsch;* Polkas: *Mädchenlaune; Saat und Ernte;* Waltzes: *Die Abonnenten; Blüthenkranz Johann Strauss'scher.* J. STRAUSS III (son of Eduard): *Schlau-Schlau polka.*

*** Chan. 8527. Johann Strauss O of V., Rothstein, with M. Hill-Smith.

This programme is admirably chosen to include unfamiliar music which deserves recording; indeed, both the *Klug Gretelein waltz,* which opens with some delectable scoring for woodwind and harp and has an idiomatic vocal contribution

from Marilyn Hill-Smith, and *Die Abonnenten* (by Eduard) are very attractive waltzes. *Blüthenkranz Johann Strauss'scher,* as its title suggests, makes a pot-pourri of some of Johann's most famous melodies. The polkas are a consistent delight, played wonderfully infectiously; indeed, above all this is a cheerful concert, designed to raise the spirits; the CD sound sparkles.

Waltzes: *Accelerationen; An der schönen blauen Donau (Blue Danube); Du und Du; Frühlingstimmen (Voices of Spring); Geschichten aus dem Wiener Wald (Tales from the Vienna Woods); Kaiser (Emperor); Künstlerleben (Artist's Life); Liebeslieder; Morgenblätter (Morning Papers); Rosen aus dem Süden (Roses from the South); Tausend und eine Nacht; Wein, Weib und Gesang (Wine, Women and Song); Wiener Blut (Vienna Blood); Wiener Bonbons; Wo die Zitronen blühn (Where the Lemon Trees Bloom).* JOSEF STRAUSS: *Dorfschwalben aus Osterreich; Sphären-Klange (Music of the Spheres).*

(B) *** Double Decca (ADD) 443 473-2 (2). VPO, Boskovsky.

These recordings span Willi Boskovsky's long recording career with the VPO for Decca. The first group to be recorded (*Liebeslieder,* ending disc 1, *Wiener Blut, Wiener Bonbons* and *Artist's Life,* which open disc 2) are particularly 'live' and fresh, dating from 1958; and the last, a charmingly lilting performance of Josef Strauss's *Village Swallows,* comes from 1976. One might think that such a succession of Strauss waltzes spread over two discs might produce a degree of listening fatigue, but that is never the case here, such is Johann's resource in the matter of melody and freshness of orchestration. The earliest recordings show their age a bit in the violin tone, but on CD it is remarkable just how well these vintage recordings sound. With 145 minutes of music offered this is excellent value.

Waltzes: *Accelerationen; An der schönen Donau; Donauweibchen; Du und Du; Flugschriften; Frühlingsstimmen; Gedankenflug; Geschichten aus dem Wienerwald; Kaiser; Künstlerleben; Lagunen; Leitartikel; Morgenblätter; Rosen aus dem Süden; Schatz; Wein, Weib und Gesang; Wiener Blut; Wiener Frauen.*

(N) (B) **(*) EMI Double forte CZS 5 74311-2 (2). Johann Strauss O of Vienna, Boskovsky.

These inexpensive performances, given modern digital recording, would be totally recommendable were it not for the fact the Boskovsky recorded many of them even more magically for Decca with the Vienna Philharmonic. However, this set is by no means to be dismissed. There are some novelties here which are not included in Boskovsky's Decca survey, notably *Donauweibchen, Flugschriften, Gedankenflug, Leitartikel* and *Wiener Frauen.* Some of the favourites are very successful here, notably the *Blue Danube,* which from the very opening balances an evocative Viennese warmth with vigour and sparkle. Indeed, some of the best-known items (including the *Emperor, Roses from the South, Tales from the Vienna Woods* and *Voices of Spring*) sound freshly minted, rhythmic nuances are flexibly stylish and the spontaneity is obvious. Those preferring digital sound (which here is full and resonant) should certainly consider this set.

'The Strauss family in London': J. STRAUSS SR: *Almack's Quadrille; March of the Royal Horse Guards* (orch. Georgiadis); *Huldigung der Königen Victoria Grossbritannien* (waltz). Polkas: *Alice; Exeter-Polka; Fredrika.* EDUARD STRAUSS: *Greeting Waltz, on English Airs; Old England for Ever* (polka, orch. Georgiadis). J. STRAUSS II: *Erinnerung an Covent-Garden* (waltz); *Potpourri-Quadrille* (orch. Peak). J. STRAUSS III: *Krönungs-Walzer.*

(M) *** Chan. (ADD) 7128. LSO, Georgiadis.

A waltz which starts with *Rule, Britannia* and ends with *God save the Queen* may seem unlikely, but that's exactly how *Huldigung der Königen Victoria Grossbritannien* goes. The music here is the result of visits made to England by the Strausses, the first one instigated by one of their greatest admirers: Queen Victoria. Like Jack Rothstein's companion set this disc is full of delightful surprises and with idiomatic playing from the LSO, fine Chandos sound, and excellent sleeve notes by Peter Kemp, it is surely an essential purchase for all Straussians. The most striking novelty is the inclusion of a waltz by the now virtually forgotten Johann Strauss III.

Waltzes: *Kaiser; Rosen aus dem Süden* (both trans. Schoenberg) ; *Schatz Waltz* (from *Der Zigeunerbaron*; trans. Webern); *Wein, Weib ind Gesang* (trans. Berg).

(N) **(*) Australian DG Eloquence (ADD) 463 202-2. Boston SO Chamber Players.

A fascinating curiosity. Schoenberg, Berg and Webern made these transcriptions for informal private performances. Schoenberg's arrangements of the *Emperor* and *Roses from the South* are the most striking, though Berg's *Wine, Women and Song* is sweetly appealing with its scoring for harmonium. As might be expected, Webern's *Schatz Waltz* is aptly refined. With the Boston Chamber Players taking rather too literal a view and missing some of the fun, the lumpishness of some of the writing is evident enough, but the very incongruity and the plain love of these three severe atonalists for music with which one does not associate them is endearing. Good, fresh recording.

VOCAL MUSIC
Vocal waltzes

(i) *Auf's Korn! Bundesschützen-Marsch.* (ii) *Hoch Osterreich! Marsch.* Polkas: (i) *Burschenwanderung (polka française); 's gibt nur a Kaiserstadt! 's gibt nur ein Wien!;* (ii) *Sängerslust.* Waltzes: *An der schönen blauen Donau;* (i) *Bei uns z'Haus;* (ii) *Gross-Wien;* (i) *Myrthenblüthen;* (ii) *Neu-Wien; Wein, weib und gesang!*

**(*) Marco 8.223250-2. V. Männergesangverein, Czecho-Slovak RSO (Bratislava), (i) Track; (ii) Wildner.

A most enjoyable collection. Wildner is occasionally a bit strong with the beat, but the *Blue Danube* with chorus is much more enjoyable than his performance with orchestra alone. The singers are Viennese, so they have a natural lilt, and the recording has an ideal ambience.

OPERA

Die Fledermaus (complete).

(B) *** Ph. Duo 464 031-2 (2). Te Kanawa, Gruberová, Leech, W. Brendel, Bär, Fassbaender, Göttling, Krause, Wendler, Schenk, V. State Op. Ch., VPO, Previn.

(B) *** EMI double forte (ADD) CZS5 73851-2 (2). Scheyrer, Lipp, Dermota, Berry, Ludwig, Terkal, Waechter, Kunz, Philh. Ch. & O, Ackermann.

(M) *** EMI (ADD) CMS 7 66223 (2). Rothenberger, Holm, Gedda, Dallapozza, Fischer-Dieskau, Fassbaender, Berry, V. State Op. Ch., VSO, Boskovsky.

(M) (***) EMI mono CMS5 67074-2 [567153] (2). Schwarzkopf, Streich, Gedda, Krebs, Kunz, Christ, Philh. Ch. & O, Karajan.

(M) (**) RCA mono 74321 61949-2. Gueden. Streich, Waechter, Zampieri, Berry, Stolze, Kunz, Klein, Ott, Meinrad, V. State Op. Ch. & O, Karajan.

(M) *(*) DG (ADD) 457 765-2 (2). Varady, Popp, Prey, Kollo, Weikl, Rebroff, Kusche, Bav. State Op. Ch. & O, C. Kleiber.

Dame Kiri Te Kanawa's portrait of Rosalinde brings not only gloriously firm, golden sound but also vocal acting with star quality. Brigitte Fassbaender is the most dominant Prince Orlofsky on disc. Singing with a tangy richness and firmness, she emerges as the genuine focus of the party scene. Edita Gruberová is a sparkling, characterful and full-voiced Adèle; Wolfgang Brendel as Eisenstein and Olaf Bär as Dr Falke both sing very well indeed, though their voices sound too alike. Richard Leech as Alfred provides heady tone and a hint of parody. Tom Krause makes a splendid Frank, the more characterful for no longer sounding young. Anton Wendler as Dr Blind and Otto Schenk as Frosch the jailer give vintage Viennese performances, with Frosch's cavortings well tailored and not too extended. Vivaciously directed, this now goes to the top of the list of latterday *Fledermaus* recordings, though with one serious reservation: the Philips production in Act II adds a layer of crowd noise as background throughout the Party scene, even during Orlofsky's solos and in the lovely chorus *Bruderlein und Schwesterlein,* yearningly done. Otherwise the recorded sound is superb. Like Kleiber on DG, Previn opts for the *Thunder and Lightning Polka* instead of the ballet. Its reissue at bargain price is welcome and retains all the qualities of the original (except texts and translations).

Like Gui's Glyndebourne *Nozze di Figaro,* Ackermann's vintage *Die Fledermaus* has been promoted from Classics for Pleasure to EMI's own double forte bargain label. It remains splendid value, for the singing sparkles, and the opera has an infectious sense of Viennese style. Wilma Lipp is a delicious Adèle and Christa Ludwig's Orlofsky is a real surprise, second only to Brigitte Fassbaender's assumption of a breechers role that is too often disappointing. Karl Terkall's Eisenstein and Anton Dermota's Alfred give much pleasure, and Erich Kunz's inebriated Frosch in the finale comes off even without a translation. The recording is excellent.

For those wanting a fairly modern, mid-priced version should consider EMI's mid-priced Boskovsky set. Though he sometimes fails to lean into the seductive rhythms as much as he might, his is a refreshing account of a magic score. Rothenberger is a sweet, domestic-sounding Rosalinde, relaxed and sparkling if edgy at times, while, among an excellent supporting cast, the Orlovsky of Brigitte Fassbaender must again be singled out as the finest on record, tough and firm. The entertainment has been excellently produced for records, with German dialogue inserted, though the ripe recording sometimes makes the voices jump between singing and speaking. The remastering is admirably vivid.

The mono recording of Karajan's 1955 version has great freshness and clarity, along with the polish which for many will make it a first favourite. Schwarzkopf makes an enchanting Rosalinde, not just in the imagination and sparkle of her singing but also in the snatches of spoken dialogue (never too long) which leaven the entertainment. As Adèle, Rita Streich produces her most dazzling coloratura; Gedda and Krebs are beautifully contrasted in their tenor tone, and Erich Kunz gives a vintage performance as Falke. The original recording, crisply focused, has been given a suitable facelift as one of EMI's 'Great Recordings of the Century'.

Recorded live by Austrian Radio at the Vienna State Opera on New Year's Eve, 1960, the RCA set gives a vivid picture of the event, warts and all. For the non-German speaker, the acres of dialogue will be a serious detterent, notably in Act III with only 15 minutes of music out of 40. This is still a cherishable issue for capturing the atmosphere and special flavour of a great Viennese occasion. Hilde Gueden is the complete charmer (as on her early Decca set, a very Viennese heroine), with Walter Berry as Falke, Giuseppe Zampieri as Alfred and Peter Klein as Dr Blind, also relishing the comedy all the more. The party junketings in Act II include not just Erich Kunz singing the *Fiakerlied* by Gustav Pick, but a special guest, Giuseppe di Stefano, singing *O sole mio* and Lehár's *Dein ist mein ganzes Herz* (Italy's tribute to Vienna prompting wild cheering). Also a 10-minute ballet, *Schottisch, Russisch, Hungarisch und Polka*.

The glory of the Kleiber set is the singing of the two principal women – Julia Varady and Lucia Popp, magnificently characterful and stylish as mistress and servant – but much of the set is controversial, to say the least. Kleiber is certainly exciting at times and rejects many older conventions in performing style, which some will find refreshing, but he is not at all easy going. Other conductors allow the music's intrinsic charm to bubble to the surface like champagne; with Kleiber, one feels the charm, if one can call it that, being rammed down one's throat. But that is nothing compared to the falsetto of Ivan Rebroff, which has to be heard to be believed – it sounds grotesque and is likely to put most listeners off this recording. Full texts and translations are included.

Die Fledermaus: highlights.

(B) *** [EMI Red Line CDR5 69839]. Popp, Baltsa, Lind, Domingo, Bav. R. Ch., Munich RSO, Domingo.

(M) *** EMI (ADD) CDM7 69598-2 (from above complete set, with Rothenberger, Holm, Gedda; cond. Boskovsky).

It was not originally intended that Plácido Domingo should sing the role of Alfred as well as conducting EMI's newest digital recording of *Fledermaus*, but the tenor who had originally been engaged cancelled at the last minute, and Domingo agreed to do the double job, singing over accompaniments that had already been recorded. The happiness of the occasion is reflected in a strong and amiable, rather than an idiomatically Viennese, performance. Lucia Popp makes a delectable and provocative Rosalinde and Seiffert a strong tenor Eisenstein, with Baltsa a superb, characterful Orlofsky. With ensembles vigorous and urgent, this is a consistently warm and sympathetic selection.

Most should be happy with the excerpts from the mid-priced Boskovsky set, which is well cast; but the complete Ackermann version on double forte costs little more and is obviously a better proposition.

A Night in Venice (Eine Nacht in Venedig): complete.

(M) (***) EMI mono CDH7 69530-2. Schwarzkopf, Gedda, Kunz, Klein, Loose, Dönch, Philh. Ch. & O, Ackermann.

A Night in Venice, in Erich Korngold's revision, is a superb example of Walter Legge's Philharmonia productions, honeyed and atmospheric. As a sampler, try the jaunty little waltz duet in Act I between Schwarzkopf as the heroine, Annina, and the baritone Erich Kunz as Caramello, normally a tenor role. Nicolai Gedda as the Duke then appropriates the most famous waltz song of all, the *Gondola Song* but, with such a frothy production, purism would be out of place. The digital remastering preserves the balance of the mono original admirably. However, this is now deleted.

Wiener Blut (complete).

(M) **(*) EMI (ADD) CMS7 69943-2 (2). Rothenberger, Gedda, Holm, Hirte, Putz, Cologne Op. Ch., Philh. Hungarica, Boskovsky.

(M) (***) EMI mono CDH7 69529-2. Schwarzkopf, Gedda, Köth, Kunz, Loose, Dönch, Philh. Ch. & O, Ackermann.

The EMI set conducted by Willi Boskovsky makes a delightful entertainment, the performance authentic and with a strong singing cast. The recording is atmospherically reverberant, but there is no lack of sparkle. However, for some there will be too much German dialogue, which also involves two CDs.

To have Schwarzkopf at her most ravishing, singing a waltz song based on the tune of *Morning Papers*, is enough enticement for this Philharmonia version of the mid-1950s, showing Walter Legge's flair as a producer at its most compelling. Schwarzkopf was matched by the regular team of Gedda and Kunz and with Emmy Loose and Erika Köth in the secondary soprano roles. The original mono recording was beautifully balanced, and the facelift given here is achieved most tactfully. But this is now deleted.

Der Zigeunerbaron (The Gipsy Baron): complete.

(M) (***) EMI mono CDH7 69526-2 (2). Schwarzkopf, Gedda, Prey, Kunz, Köth, Sinclair, Philh. Ch. & O, Ackermann.

This superb Philharmonia version of *The Gipsy Baron* from the mid-1950s, alas just recently deleted, has never been matched in its rich stylishness and polish. Schwarzkopf as the gipsy princess sings radiantly, not least in the heavenly Bullfinch duet (to the melody made famous by MGM as

One day when we were young). Gedda, still youthful, produces heady tone, and Erich Kunz as the rough pig-breeder gives a vintage *echt*-Viennese performance of the irresistible *Ja, das Schreiben und das Lesen*. The CD transcription from excellent mono originals gives fresh and truthful sound, particularly in the voices.

Der Zigeunerbaron (arr. Harnoncourt; Linke: complete).

*(**) Teldec 4509 94555-2 (2). Coburn, Lippert, Schasching, Hamari, Holzmair, Oelze, Von Magnus, Lazar, Arnold Schoenberg Ch., VSO, Harnoncourt.

When *Zigeunerbaron*, second only to *Fledermaus* among Strauss operettas, has been so neglected on disc, this new Teldec set, offering a more expanded text than ever before, fills an important gap. Harnoncourt, as a Viennese and with a Viennese orchestra, ensures that the Strauss lilt is winningly and authentically observed from the *pot-pourri* overture onwards, and Harnoncourt's concern (as a period specialist) for clarity of texture gives the whole performance a sparkling freshness. Sadly, the casting is seriously flawed, when the central character of the gypsy princess, Saffi, is taken by a soprano, Pamela Coburn, who, as recorded, sounds strained and unsteady. The others are better, with Rudolf Schasching catching the fun behind the comic role of the pig-breeder, Zsupán, authentically but without exaggeration, and the light tenor, Herbert Lippert, is charming as the hero, Barinkay. Among the rest, the mezzo, Elisabeth von Magnus, sings in cabaret style in the supporting role of Mirabella, given a major point-number here, often omitted. Christiane Oelze as Arsena, the girl who does not get the hero, sings far more sweetly than Coburn, and Julia Hamari as Saffi's foster-mother, Czipra, sounds younger than her daughter. The recording is full and vivid, but many will feel that there is too much German dialogue – largely accounting for the extended length of two and a half hours.

STRAUSS, Josef (1827–70)

Josef Strauss: The Complete Edition

Vol. 1: Polkas: *Angelica; Bauern; Eislauf; Etiquette; Moulinet; Thalia*. March: *Galenz. Kakadu-Quadrille*. Waltzes: *Fantasiebilder; Marien-Klänge; Wiegenlieder*.

** Marco 8.223561. Budapest Strauss SO, A. Walter.

Vol. 2: *Amazonen-Quadrille*. Polkas: *Arabella; Diana; Genien; Stiefmütterchen; Sturmlauf; Sympathie*. *Schottischer Tanz*. Waltzes: *Petitionen; Tranz-Prioriräten*: Arr. of SCHUMANN: *Träumerei*.

** Marco 8.223562. S S PO (Košice), A. Walter.

Vol. 3: *Avantgarde March*. Polkas: *Gnomen; Die Lachtaube; Die Naïve; Ohne Sorgen; Sport*. Quadrilles: *Caprice; Flick-Flock*. Waltzes: *Assoziationen; Ernst und Humor; Mai-Rosen*.

** Marco 8.223563. Slovak State PO (Košice), A. Walter.

It is good to see Marco now exploring the output of Josef Strauss, of which we know remarkably little. Indeed almost all the items in this first volume are completely unfamiliar.

Alfred Walter's easy-going style permeates the whole programme, and most of the polkas are left badly needing a more vital pacing. The waltzes are lilting in a lazy way: Walter shapes the evocative opening of *Fantasiebilder* rather beautifully, helped by polished and sympathetic playing from a group of Hungarian players. *Wiegenlieder* (*Cradle Songs*) is another waltz which opens very enticingly and ought to be better known: it has a charming main theme and is nicely scored. The closing *Eislauf polka*, so very like the writing of Johann Junior, ends the concert spiritedly, and this well-recorded disc has great documentary interest, while the back-up notes are equally praiseworthy.

In Volume 2, Walter introduces two more waltzes which are fully worthy of Johann Jr; *Petitionen* is particularly inventive. The polkas are amiable, with *Diana* aptly introduced by the horns. They are, as usual, played in a relaxed dance tempo: the most successful is the charming, Ländler-like *Stiefmütterchen*. The Schumann arrangement is very straightforward and adds little or nothing to the original piano piece: Walter presents it without any attempt at romantic subtlety.

Volume 3 opens with a sprightly march (not too heavily articulated), but the highlights are the *Assoziationen* and *Ernst und Humor* waltzes and the *Sport polka*, played here with with great spirit. Of the two waltzes the latter ('In a serious and light-hearted manner') has some interesting changes of mood, with modulations to match. It ought to be at least as well known as the closing (and justly renowned) *Ohne Sorgen polka*, which the Slovak players present with much enthusiasm, including the vocal interpolations. Excellent recording.

Vol. 4: March: *Osterreichscher Kronprinzen*; Polkas: *La Chevaleresque; Jockey; Schlarffen; Titi; Wiener Leben;* Quadrilles: *Genovefa; Turner. Ständchen;* Waltzes: *Freudengrüsse; Frohes Leben; Vereins-Lieder*.

**(*) Marco 8.223564. Slovak RSO (Bratislava), Dittrich.

Josef usually proves most reliable in his polkas, and *Schlarffen* is one of his finest, while the *Titi polka* is delicious, with the portrait of that pretty bird implied in the scoring rather than with any imitations. Both are very infectious as presented here by the excellent Michael Dittrich, and the better-known *Jockey* bursts with vivacity. The *Turner Quadrille* is also captivating in its swinging rhythm, with some whistling piccolo embroidery near the close. The waltzes *Vereins-Lieder* and *Freudengrüsse*, however, are light-hearted without being truly memorable. *Frohes Leben* has more striking ideas. The programme ends with a simple *Serenade* that might or might not have been intended as a tribute to Wagner.

Vol. 5: *Defilier* (March); Polkas: *Die Gazelle; Maiblümchen; Die Marketenderin; Mignon; Vorwärts;* Quadrilles: *Csikos; Die Grossherzogin von Gerolstein;* Waltzes: *Dynamiden (Geheime Anziehungskräfte); Flammen; Huldigungslieder*.

**(*) Marco 8.223565. Slovak State PO (Košice), Pollack.

The very fetching *Die Grossherzogin Quadrille* gets this programme off to a good start. In English, of course this comes out as *The Grand Duchess of Gerolstein* and the piece is an agreeable pot-pourri of the many excellent tunes from Offenbach's operetta, presented one after another with little or no attempt at tailoring and with brief pauses in between. Pollack (as elsewhere) chooses a dancing tempo and one wants to get up and join in. The polka, *Marketenderin* ('Camp follower' – in this case a vivacious lady, generous with her favours) is charming too, though it reminds the listener a little of a more famous piece by Johann. *Vorwärts* ('Forward') then goes with a swing and is delightfully scored – one of Josef's very best. *Mignon* is very catchy too, and *Die Gazelle* has something of the grace of its title. Of the three waltzes included here, there is one masterpiece: *Dynamiden*, with its ravishing cantabile is fully worthy of Johann, and it is beautifully played. *Huldigungslieder* also begins impressively and has rather a good opening waltz-tune, but it is slightly less memorable overall. *Flammen* surprises the listener by opening with a fast, polka-like introduction. The main strain is very agreeable and there are some engagingly fresh ideas later on. Pollack takes the polka-mazurkas at dance tempi with a strong accent on the first beat, which is obviously authentic; but for concert perfomance a slightly faster tempo might have been more effective, and this especially applies to *Maiblümchen*, which closes the concert. Nevertheless this is one of the most rewarding Josef Strauss collections so far in the series.

Vol. 6: March: *Victor.* **Polkas:** *Carrière; Causerie; Figaro; Joujou; Tanz-Regulator; Waldröslein. Musen Quadrille.* **Waltzes:** *Die Industriellen; Krönungslieder; Nilfluthen.*

**(*) Marco 8.223566. S S PO (Kosice),Georgiadis.

Of the three waltzes here, the first, *Die Industriellen*, is marginally the most beguiling, and Georgiadis has its measure, both at the lilting opening tune and in its engaging secondary scalic figure that rises and falls in a busy little group of notes. *Nilfluthen* ('Nile waters') was written for the Concordia Ball, held during the celebrations for the opening of the Suez Canal (Emperor Franz Josef was there). It, too, has a nifty main theme and there is nothing in the least Egyptian about its style. *Krönungslieder* opens with a regal fanfare (it celebrated a royal political settlement in 1867 between the Austrian Empire and Hungary, when the Emperor and Empress were crowned in Budapest); but after that it is a routine sequence. Of the polkas, the *Causerie* ('Chatting') is the most ingenuously charming, while *Carrière* is one of Josef's most infectious galops. John Georgiadis is thoroughly at home here, and this music is all stylishly presented and again very well recorded.

Vol. 7: March: *Erzherzog Karl;* **Polkas:** *Bouquet; Frohsinn; Irenen; Jucker;* **Polka mazurs:***Die Idylle; Minerva;* **Quadrille:** *Parade;* **Waltzes:** *Friedenspalmen; Hesperus-Bahnen; Streichmagnete.*

** Marco 8.223567. Slovak State PO (Košice), Eichenholz.

Volume 7 opens winningly with the *Jockey Polka*, and the hardly less engaging *Parade Quadrille*. Here Mika Eichenholz displays a light rhythmic touch and the Slovak State Philharmonic continue to be thoroughly at home. The *Streichmagnete Waltz* has a beguilingly delicate introduction and its

main theme does not disappoint, but the following ideas are more conventional. *Friedenspalmen* and the very agreeable *Hesperus-Bahnen* also open atmospherically and in the former a fine stream of melodies follow, and it ought to be much better known. Eichenholz, who adopts a lazy Viennese waltz style readily responds to it. If he is less impressive in the two Polka mazurs which tend to hang fire, the *Irenen Polka* which ends the programme is delightfully pert.

Vol. 8: Polkas: *Die Amazone; Arm in Arm; En passant; Mailust; Saus und Braus; Seraphinen; Sylphide;* **Quadrille:** *Debardeurs;* **Waltzes:** *Die Clienten; Expensnoten; Wiener Stimmen.*

** Marco 8.223568. Slovak State PO (Košice), Eichenholz.

This collection is mainly of documetary interest. The various Polkas proceed in leisurely fashion, and it is not until the waltzes, *Die Clienten* and *Expensnoten* that the music rises much above routine formulas. Eichendorf indulges them in his casual manner, and also the seductive *Arm in Arm* polka masur, which follows, while *Wiener Stimmen* lilts most engagingly of all, with the main theme nicely lifted. Any of these items could be very impressive in the hands of a great conductor.

Vol. 9: March: *Deutscher Union;* **Polkas:** *Adamira; Eingesendet; Lieb' und Wein; Masken; Die Spinnerin; Zephir;* **Quadrille:** *Bivouac;* **Waltzes:** *Deutsche Sympathien; Rudolphsklänge; Studentenräume.*

*** Marco 8.223569. Slovak State PO (Košice), Pollack.

Not surprisingly, with Christian Pollack in charge, this is one of the best if not *the* best of Marco's Josef Strauss series. The opening *Adamira Polka* sparkles with life and the following *Bivouac-Quadrille* bounces along infectiously. These performance are in a completely different class to those directed by Mika Eichenholz, and all three waltzes glow with rhythmic and melodic life. The introduction to *Studentenräume* is quite enchanting. Indeed this collection continually shows that at its best Josef's invention, craftsmanship and orchestration could readily match that of his brother, Johann. Splendid playing and first-class rcording makes this a disc to treasure.

Vol. 10: Polkas: *Abendstern; For Ever; Gruss an München; Harlekin; Heiterer Muth; Herzbleamerl; Nachtschatten;* **Quadrille:** *Touristen;* **Waltzes:** *Herztöne; Wiener Fresken; Wiener Kinder.*

*** Marco 8.223570. Slovak State PO (Košice), Pollack.

The performances on Volume 10 are just as vivacious as those in Volume 9, and though the opening of the *Wiener Kinder Waltz* is not helped by its rather fruity horn solo, Pollack is persuasive enough when the waltzes proper begin, even if the tunes are not top drawer. The following series of polkas all sail along gaily and the two remaining waltzes are rather more striking, especially *Wiener Fresken*. The other highlight is the bouncing *Touristen-Quadrille*. Everything is played with affection and strong rhythmic character.

Vol. 11: Polkas: *Bon-bon; Die Emancipirte; Lust-Lager; Schwalbenpost; Die Schwätzerin; Victoria;* **Quadrilles:**

Dioscuren; Les Géorgiennes; Waltzes: *Gedenkblätter; Hochzeits-Klänge; Maskengeheimnisse.*

**(*) Marco 8.223571. Razumovsky SO, Eschwé.

There is nothing that really stands out in Volume 11, although the *Schwalbendpost Polka* is jolly enough, and there are some nice touches of orchestral colour throughout (notably in the *Schwätzerin Polka Masur*). Eschwé is a more flexibly imaginative conductor than Eichenholz, but does not have the natural flair of Pollack. He makes the most of the *Maskengeheimnis* and *Hochzeits-Klänge Waltzes*, both pleasing, if not in the first flight, and is pleasingly elegant in the *Victoria-polka française*, while the closing *Lust-Lager* is engagingly vivacious.

Vol. 12: March: *Schützen;* Polkas: *Allerlei; Amaranth; Frisch auf!; Laxenburger; Une pensée; Schabernack;* Quadrille: *Herold;* Waltzes: *Helenen; Schwert und Leyer; Tanzadressen an die Preisgekrönten.*

*** Marco 8.223572. Slovak State PO (Košice), Pollack.

Christian Pollack returns for Volume 12, as is immediately obvious from the spirited and vivid opening, *Herold-Quadrille*, which is fully worthy of Johann and very elegantly scored. Pollack also again brings a lilting sweep to the string tunes in all three waltzes. *Schwert und Leyer* opens melodramatically, but then a very seductive melody steals in on the strings. *Tanzadressen an die Preisgekrönten* is another of Joseph's best, and *Helenen* with its chattering opening flutes is a real charmer. There is a high proportion of the slower polkas in the collection, of which the closing polka masur, *Une Pensée* has a string of tunes rather like a waltz. The playing has a pleasingly urbane finish.

Vol. 13: *Phönix-Marsch.* Polkas: *Extempore; Farewell; Matrosen; Wiener.* Polka-Mazurka: *Die Galante.* Quadrilles: *Toto; Turnier.* Waltzes: *Deutsche Grüsse; Herbstrosen; Wintermärchen.*

** Marco 8.223573. Slovak State PO (Košice), Dittrich.

Michael Dittrich brings zest to the opening march and sparkle to the polkas and he shapes the three waltzes affectionately. But he is just a little bit too relaxed to realize their full potential, even though they are beautifully played, and the recording is well up to the usual standard of this fine series. The closing *Turnier-Quadrille* is an infectious highlight.

Vol. 14: Polkas: *Auf Ferienreisen; Bellona; Künstler-Gruss; Neckerei; La Simplicité; Springinsfeld; Die Tänzerin;* Quadrille: *Blaubart;* Waltzes: *Disputationen; Die guten, alten Zeiten; Die Zeitgenossen.*

** Marco 8.223574. Slovak State PO (Košice), Dittrich.

Volume 14 opens with a vivacious account of the spirited *Auf Ferienreisen Polka* and is also notable for the Bluebeard-Quadrille, an engaging Offenbach pot-pourri, neatly scored, with plenty of familiar tunes, where Dittrich too, is at his best. But again he makes too little of the three waltzes, being content to play them through *a tempo*.

Vol. 15: *Hesperus-Ländler.* March: *Ungarischer Krönungsmarsch.* Polkas: *Amouretten; Gedenke mein!;*

Plappermäulchen; Winterlust. Polka-mazurkas: *Die Nasswalderin; Vielliebchen.* Quadrille: *Theater.* Waltzes: *Combinationen; Lustschwärmer.*

** Marco 8.223575. Slovak State PO (Košice), Kulling.

Two famous numbers stand out here: the *Plappermäulchen Polka*, played here with considerable gusto and the waltz, *Mein Lebenslauf ist Lieb' und Lust* which is given a routine performance. Indeed Arthur Kulling is another conductor, who is at his best in the bright work, than in coaxing the waltzes. The very agreeable Ländler is also rather heavily presented. The *Theatre Quadrille* includes melodies from operas and operettas by Verdi, Suppé and Meyerbeer, among others, and as usual is nicely orchestrated. But Kulling does not make a great deal of it.

Vol. 16: March: *Schwarzenberg-Monument.* Polkas: *Fashion; Freigeister; In der Heimat; Punsch; Die Schwebende; Wilde Rose;* Waltzes: *Ball-Silhouetten; Frauenwürde; Wiener Couplets.* Quadrilles: *Lancer; Schäfer.*

** Marco 8.223618. Slovak State PO (Košice), Kulling.

Kulling opens with a rhythmically buoyant account of the march, the polkas have life and charm, and the two Quadrilles are elegant enough. All three waltzes here are among Josef's most appealing (often with a strong whiff of Johann) and *Frauenwirde* has a most enticing opening. They are well played, have a relaxed rhythmic feeling, and lilt warmly, but Pollack would surely have given them even more personality. As always in this series the recording ambience is very pleasing.

Vol. 17: March: *Wallonen.* Polkas: *Edelweiss; Feurfest!; Jocus; Die Sirene; Tag und Nacht; Verliebte Augen.* Quadrille: *Polichinello.* Waltzes: *Dorfschwalben aus Osterreich (Village Swallows); Perlen der Liebe; Sphärenklange (Music of the spheres).*

** Marco 8.223619. Slovak State PO (Košice), Märzendorfer.

Ernst Märzendorfer presents all the polkas here pleasingly enough. The opening *Die Sirene* is charming, and the famous *Feuerfest!* has gusto. The *Policinello–Quadrille* (complete with a brief chorus near the end) is winningly sprightly, and he also finds a nice bouncy rhythm for the *Wallonen-Marsch*, which is really a lilting two-step. But although the two great waltzes, *Music of the Spheres* and the chirping *Village Swallows* are nicely introduced, once the music gets underway, routine sets in, and *Perlen der Liebe* is at times mannerd. Good playing and excellent recording.

Vol. 18: March: *Armee.* Polkas: *Brennende Liebe; Gurli; Im Fluge; Die Libelle; Rudolfsheimer;* Quadrilles: *Colosseum. Sturm;* Waltzes: *Aquarellen; Die Ersten nach den Letzten; Normen.*

*** Marco 8.223620. Slovak State PO (Košice), Geyer.

There is an engaging story about the composition of *Die Ersten nach den Letzten*, one of Josef's best waltzes, and a real find. in August 1853 'Pepi' Strauss, as he was affectionately known, found himself obliged to direct the orchestra for the first time, because his brother was recuperating after a serious illness. For the same reason he had also to provide a waltz for the occasion. Determined that his substitute musical directorship should not be permanent, he called the waltz *Die Ersten und Letzen* ('the first and the last'). But the piece, published as his Op. 1, enjoyed considerable success, and he was unable to maintain his resolve. Thus, with a hint of irony, but also with a twinkle, he called his Opus 12 (above), *The First after the Last. Normen* ('Standards') is also a very attractive piece, with a chirruping main theme and plenty of good ideas. Geyer is a much more persuasive advocate than many of his colleagues, and with some perky polkas (*Gurli*, the lilting *Rudolfsheimer*, and *Im Fluge* among the most characteristic), the justly celebrated *Aquarellen*, and a pair of attractive quadrilles, this is one of the best discs in the series.

Although the crispness of ensemble is very striking, in Karl Geyer's collection there is also a feeling of a rhythmic straitjacket. This applies particularly to the *Quadrilles*. Yet if you don't mind the articulated precision, Geyer presents the *Waltzes* with plenty of sparkle, and there are three good ones here, two quite unfamiliar. After the introduction *Normen* takes off very seductively. The opening *Armee-Marsch* suits Geyer very well, but his *pièce de résistance* is the closing polka, *Im Fluge*, which bursts into the room and has enormous energy and projection. The recording is excellent.

Vol. 19: *Benedek-Marsch.* Polkas: *Dornbacher; Eile mit Weile; Nymphen; Sehnsucht; Souvenir; Die tanzende Muse.* Quadrille: *Folichon.* Waltzes: *Consortien; Frauenblätter; Musen-Klänge.*

(N) **(*) Marco 8.223621. Slovak State PO (Košice), Hilgers.

Walter Hilgers is most welcome on the podium. If he does not quite match Christian Pollack (see below) he gets good ensemble and articulates crisply, yet relaxes more flexibly than Geyer, so that the polka-mazurkas and quadrilles have their full Viennese charm. All three waltzes are well worth having on disc. Hilgers coaxes the beguiling opening of *Musen-Klänge* ('music for the muses') bewitchingly, and there is a nice lift for the charming *Frauenblätter* ('women's magazines'). The opening of *Consortien* is again most pleasingly shaped and the waltz itself, written for a gathering of prominent industrialists in 1869, is unexpectedly light-hearted and full of good things. Incidentally, Hilgers takes all the repeats, so each of the three waltzes play for over ten minutes, without outlasting their welcome.

Vol. 20: *Liechtenstein-Marsch.* Polkas: *Cupido; Dithyrambe; Frauenherz; Künstler-Caprice; Pêle-mêle; Vélocipède.* Quadrille: *Pariser.* Waltzes: *Actionen; Delirien; Flattergeister; Wiener Bonmots.*

(N) *** Marco 8.223622. Slovak State PO (Košice), Pollack.

This is perhaps the most delightful of the Josef Strauss collections so far. Not only does it include a most winning account of his greatest waltz, *Delirien*, but the lighthearted *Flattergeister* ('social butterflies'), after a robust introduction, opens the main waltz sequence with a lilting tune on the violins (fully worthy of Johann) and brings a stream of attractive ideas. *Wiener Bonmots*, too, chirps wittily.

Christian Pollack again shows himself a master of Viennese rhythmic inflection and the slower polka-mazurkas are even more seductive than the sparkling *Pell-Mell* and the fizzingly brilliant *Vélocipède*. The Slovak Orchestra are clearly on their toes and enjoying the dance, and the bright recording has a pleasing ambience.

There is no doubt that Marco Polo's Josef Strauss series is proving even more illuminating than that of his brother. Little of his music has been recorded until now, yet its excellence over the 20 CDs is matched by its consistency. Clearly much of it deserves to re-enter the repertoire.

STRAUSS, Richard (1864–1949)

Symphonic poems: *An Alpine Symphony, Op. 64; Death and Transfiguration, Op. 24; Don Juan, Op. 20; Ein Heldenleben, Op. 40.*

(M) *** Chan. 7009/10. RSNO, Järvi.

Symphonic poems: *Also sprach Zarathustra, Op. 30;* (i) *Don Quixote, Op. 35. Macbeth, Op. 23; Symphonia domestica, Op. 53; Till Eulenspiegel, Op. 38.*

(M) *** Chan. 7011/12. RSNO, Järvi; (i) with Wallfisch.

Järvi's generally distinguished survey of the Strauss symphonic poems was recorded in the sumptuous acoustics of the Caird Hall, Dundee, between 1986 and 1989. If occasionally the resonance prevents the sharpest internal clarity, the skilled Chandos engineering ensures that the orchestral layout is very believable, heard within a natural perspective. The account of *An Alpine Symphony* is ripely enjoyable, with the reverberant acoustic here very helpful. Järvi seeks to present a general scenic view within a performance that is not as electrically taut or crisp of ensemble as, say, Karajan's but which is very effective in giving a genial description of the changing landscapes. *Death and Transfiguration* shows the orchestra at its finest and here detail is revealed well, within a reading which has impressive control. *Don Juan* is portrayed as a bluff philanderer and the reading seeks sentience and amplitude rather than searing brilliance. *Ein Heldenleben* is strongly characterized and warmly sympathetic from first to last, marked by powerful, thrustful playing, lacking only the last degree of refinement in ensemble.

Järvi's *Symphonia domestica* is particularly successful, as indeed is his joyful portrait of *Till. Macbeth*, less than a masterpiece, is also presented very persuasively; few if any recorded performances make a better case for it. *Don Quixote* then takes a rather leisurely journey, although an amiable one. Raphael Wallfisch, the solo cellist, plays splendidly but, like the excellent violist, John Harrington, is very forwardly balanced, while inner orchestral detail is less than ideally clear. *Also sprach Zarathustra*, which closes the programme, is the least successful of the series, with the reverberant acoustic rather muddying the sound, without bringing compensating richness; moreover the organ pedal at the opening is much too dominant. At mid-price they are undoubtedly competitive, particularly for collectors who enjoy Chandos's rich tapestries of sound.

An Alpine Symphony; Macbeth, (74321 57128–2). *Also sprach Zarathustra, Der Rosenkavalier* (orchestral suite); *Don Juan*, (09026 68225–2). *Death and Transfiguration; Symphonia domestica*, (09026 68221–2). *Ein Heldenleben* (09026 68775–2).

*** RCA 09026 63265-2 (4). Bav. RSO, Maazel.

We have observed before that Lorin Maazel's interpretative instinct is usually transformed when he records in Vienna, and here it proves equally true in Munich. Of course he has the advantage of the Bavarian Radio Symphony Orchestra – a magnificent body, who have a natural affinity with Richard Strauss. But one is also stuck by the conductor's own freshness of approach and his imaginative insights in all of these wonderful scores.

The opening of *Also sprach Zarathustra*, which is taken very spaciously, must now be the most spectacularly recorded version available, crystal clear over the sustained pedal with blazing brass. But then the slow tempo is maintained, and the very wide dynamic range of the recording underlined by the delicacy of his portrayal of the 'Dwellers in the world beyond'. There is explosive passion later, but the 'Science' evocation has great atmosphere and the 'Tanzlied' much delicacy.

Similarly in the *Rosenkavalier suite* which opens and closes with enormous verve, the music for the lovers and the 'Silver rose presentation' is exquisitely tender, with lovely oboe playing. Of Strauss' two great fictional heroes, *Don Juan* is portrayed with a throbbing virility and energy: the strings thrillingly ardent, particularly in their final reprise, after the superb horn re-entry. The closing moments of utter disillusionment are then the more telling. *Till* is equally strongly characterized, portrayed as a robustly dynamic figure, unrepentantly humorous, who comes to a really spectacular end, and then, endearingly floats off to the next world without any regrets.

Death and Transfiguration is better recorded than Maazel's 1983 DG version, and the orchestral playing is equal in every way to the emotional and virtuosic demands of the score. Maazel's approach to the underrated *Symphonie domestica* is both subtle and refined and attractively free of any overblown exaggeration. These same qualities inform *Ein Heldenleben*, which has plenty of impetus and intensity, yet is splendidly detailed. *Macbeth* is remarkably successful too, but the most vivid pictorialization comes in the eventful *Alpine Symphony*, with the offstage hunting horns perhaps more thrilling here than on any other record. In short, these are first-class performances, the interpretations as sound as they are resourceful.

Of course Karajan, Kempe and Haitink all have something very special to say in this repertoire, but anyone wanting spectacular modern digital sound will find much to admire in Munich, with the ambience of the Herkulessaal adding an allure to three out of the four discs. *Ein Heldenleben* and *Till* were made in studio, but certainly do not lack ambience. The one snag is that the microphones have given a degree of unnatural digital brightness to the fortissimo high violins, but this can be tempered with flexible controls. Two of the four discs (which come in a slipcase) are each available separately (74321 57128-2 and 09026 68225-2 are not) but,

ungenerously, RCA offer no saving if you buy the complete set.

An Alpine Symphony, Op. 64

*** DG 439 017–2. BPO, Karajan.
*** Ph. (IMS) (ADD) 416 156–2. Concg. O, Haitink.
*** Australian Decca Eloquence 466 670-2. LAPO, Mehta.

An Alpine Symphony, Op. 64; Don Juan, Op. 20.

(M) *** Decca 466 423-2. San Francisco SO, Blomstedt.

An Alpine Symphony; Don Juan; Salome: Salome's Dance of the Seven Veils.

(B) **(*) Decca 448 714-2. Cleveland O, Ashkenazy.

An Alpine Symphony; Der Rosenkavalier: Suite.

(N) ** DG 469 519-2. VPO, Thielemann.

Blomstedt has developed into a conductor of real stature who knows how to control and pace a work and relate climaxes to one another. His *Alpine Symphony* is superbly shaped and has that rare quality of relating part to whole in a way that is totally convincing. The reading of *Don Juan* is equally convincing. Throughout he gets scrupulously attentive playing from the San Francisco Orchestra and a rich, well-detailed Decca recording.

This DG reissue in the Karajan Gold series is one of the most remarkable in its improvement of the sound over the original CD issue. The acoustic boundaries of the sound seem to have expanded. Detail is not analytically clear, but the sumptuous body of tone created by the orchestra is glorious, with the violins glowing and soaring as they enter the forest. Undoubtedly this performance is very distinguished, wonderfully spacious and beautifully shaped – the closing *Night* sequence is very touching – and played with the utmost virtuosity.

Haitink's account on Philips is a splendid affair, a very natural-sounding recording and strongly characterized throughout. The perspective is excellent, and there is plenty of atmosphere, particularly in the episode of the calm before the storm. Above all, the architecture of the work as a whole is impressively laid out and the orchestral playing is magnificent. This can hold its own with the best.

Mehta's version of *An Alpine Symphony* is perhaps the best of his Decca Strauss recordings. It is a virtuoso performance and he is supported by a superb recording which is wide in range and rich in detail. It is not overlit, yet the Decca engineers allow every strand of the texture to 'tell' without ever losing sight of the overall perspective, and it has transferred strikingly well to CD.

The Cleveland Orchestra commands as rich a sonority and as much virtuosity as any of its illustrious rivals. Ashkenazy's well-controlled and intelligently shaped reading of the *Alpine Symphony* has much to recommend it, but is not quite as strong in personality as the very finest versions. That applies also to *Don Juan*, which brings comparable virtuosity from the Clevelanders. However, with recording of Decca's top quality, this is good value at bargain price.

Thielemann's are live recordings made in the Grosser Saal of the Musikverein in October 2000, offering brilliant VPO playing, and these performances certainly do not lack tension. However, in the *Alpine Symphony* the conductor's scrupulous concern for pictorial detail means that we receive a series of vividly colourful pictures of each segment of the ascent and descent, rather than an overall impression of a continuing journey, although the closing nocturnal sequence is movingly gentle.

The digital recording is very spectacular, immensely so in the *Thunderstorm* sequence, but the ear senses the presence of the close microphones, so a natural concert hall effect is less readily conveyed. The *Rosenkavalier Suite* is again superbly played, but its sensory romantic atmosphere, and the perception of a lilting masquerade, eludes Thielman. Moreover, the vivid recording lacks the necessary lusciousness of string texture.

(i) *An Alpine Symphony; (ii) Also sprach Zarathustra; (i) Death and Transfiguration, Don Juan, Ein Heldenleben; (ii) Festliches Praeludium, Op. 61; Der Rosenkavalier: waltzes from Act III; Salome: Dance of the Seven Veils; Till Eulenspiegel.*

(B) *(**) DG mono/stereo 463 190-2 (3). (i) Dresden State O, (ii) BPO; Boehm.

Boehm's Strauss is impressive and this bargain box, comprising some mono but mainly stereo recordings, is a fine tribute to his natural affinity with this composer. *An Alpine Symphony, Don Juan* and *Ein Heldenleben* are mono, but are excellent performances: it is Boehm's attention to detail which one most enjoys, though there is excitement too, even if this music ideally requires stereo to make its full impact. The rest of the performances are stereo. *Also sprach Zarathustra* dates from 1958 and the sound is good if a little thin; it is a spacious and satisfying account, with splendid playing to support the conductor's conception. The rustic portrayal of *Till*, and the *Waltzes* from *Der Rosenkavalier*, are both effective, as is the highly sensuous account of *Salome's Dance*. The *Prelude*, written in 1913 for the opening of the Konzerthaus in Vienna, is a fascinating bonus: it is a somewhat inflated work, for organ and a huge orchestra, where the composer piles sequence upon sequence to produce a climax of shattering sonority. Boehm manages to give the work a dignity not really inherent in the music. All these were recorded a few years after *Also sprach Zarathustra* and have fuller sound. For *Death and Transfiguration*, Boehm's 1972 live Salzburg Festival recording was used; it is a performance of excitement and strong tensions (despite a couple of irritating coughs at the beginning), even if the recording is slightly overweighted at the top. At bargain price, this set is worth considering, and an essential purchase for admirers of this distinguished conductor.

An Alpine Symphony; Aus Italien, Op. 16; Dance Suite from Pieces by François Couperin; (i) Don Quixote. Macbeth, Op. 23; Metamorphosen for 23 Solo Strings.

(M) *** EMI (ADD) CMS7 64350-2 (3). (i) Tortelier; Dresden State O, Kempe.

This is the third of the three boxes of Richard Strauss's orchestral and concertante music, recorded during the first half of the 1970s. The Dresden orchestra is a magnificent body and the strings produce gloriously sumptuous tone, which is strikingly in evidence in *Metamorphosen*. Rudolf

Kempe had recorded the *Alpine Symphony* before with the RPO, and there is little to choose between the two so far as interpretation is concerned: he brings a glowing warmth to this score. His *Aus Italien* is more convincing than any previous version: the sound with its finely judged perspective is again a decisive factor here. He gives a most musical account of the delightful *Dance Suite* based on Couperin keyboard pieces, although here some might wish for more transparent textures. Perhaps one could also quarrel with the balance in *Don Quixote*, which gives Tortelier exaggerated prominence and obscures some detail. The performance, however, is another matter and must rank with the best available. *Macbeth* also is convincing, and well paced.

(i) *An Alpine Symphony; (ii) Also sprach Zarathustra, Don Juan, (iii) Ein Heldenleben; (ii) Till Eulenspiegel.*

(B) *** Double Decca (ADD) 440 618-2 (2). (i) Bav. RSO; (ii) Chicago SO; (iii) VPO; Solti.

The Bavarian Radio Orchestra recorded in the Herculessal in Munich could hardly sound more opulent in the *Alpine Symphony* and the superb quality of the 1979 analogue recording tends to counterbalance Solti's generally fast tempi. The performances of *Also sprach Zarathustra, Don Juan* and *Till Eulenspiegel* come from analogue originals, made in Chicago a few years earlier. Solti is ripely expansive in *Zarathustra*, and throughout all three symphonic poems there is the most glorious playing from the Chicago orchestra in peak form. For *Ein Heldenleben* Solti went (in 1977–8) to Vienna, and this is another fast-moving performance, tense to the point of fierceness in the opening tutti and elsewhere. It underlines the urgency rather than the opulence of the writing but Solti is at his finest in the final coda after the fulfilment theme, where in touching simplicity he finds complete relaxation at last, helped by the exquisite playing of the Vienna Philharmonic concertmaster, Rainer Küchl. The Decca recording is formidably wide-ranging to match this high-powered performance and, as with the rest of the programme, the transfers to CD are full-bodied and vividly detailed.

An Alpine Symphony; Don Juan; Suite for 13 Wind Instruments, Op. 4; Symphonia domestica; Till Eulenspiegel.

(BB) **(*) Virgin 2x1 Double VBD5 61460-2 (2). Minnesota O, De Waart.

An excellent and inexpensive anthology, very well played and recorded, over which there are only minor reservations. There is no lack of spectacle in the *Alpine Symphony*, which ends with an impressive storm and a rich-hued sunset: only the echoing horns on the way up seem rather too far away; but nothing is inflated needlessly. Similarly, anyone who feels that Strauss's domestic revelations need tempering with a little discretion will enjoy this performance, which is also very well played by the excellent Minnesota Orchestra. The *Suite in B flat* is beautifully blended and comparably refined. In *Don Juan* the orchestra may not succeed in producing quite the same sophisticated opulence of texture as is achieved by such Straussians as Reiner in Chicago or Karajan in Berlin, but they still play very well indeed; and throughout, the sound has both depth and clarity. Good value.

Also sprach Zarathustra, Op. 30.

(N) (M) *** DG (ADD) 463 627-2. Boston SO, Steinberg –
HOLST: *The Planets.* ***

Steinberg's 1972 *Also sprach Zarathustra* now reappears as one of DG's Originals. It is sumptuously recorded with the orchestra slightly recessed within a warm Boston acoustic, which adds to the sentient feeling of what is essentially a lyrical account of considerable ardour, reaching a superb climax. It is very well transferred indeed and will satisfy Steinberg admirers attracted to his fine and individual account of *The Planets* (equally impressively remastered).

Also sprach Zarathustra, Le Bourgeois Gentilhomme (suite) (i) Violin Concerto in D min., Op. 8. Death and Transfiguration; Josephslegende, Op. 63; Schlagobers (waltz), Op. 70; Symphonia domestica; Der Rosenkavalier: Waltz Sequence; Salome: Dance of the Seven Veils.

(M) *** EMI (ADD) CMS7 64346-2 (3). (i) Hoelscher; Dresden
State O, Kempe.

Ulf Hoelscher's eloquent account of this attractive early *Violin Concerto* is more than welcome, as is the *Symphonia domestica*. Kempe's version of this work is no less desirable than Karajan's, a little more relaxed without being in any way less masterly. His *Also sprach Zarathustra* is completely free of the sensationalism that marks so many newer performances. The rest of the programme is well worth having, particularly *Le Bourgeois Gentilhomme*. Recording and CD transfers are well up to standard.

Also sprach Zarathustra; (i) Burleske for Piano & Orchestra. Don Juan.

*** EMI CDC5 56364-2. (i) Ax; Phd. O, Sawallisch.

The new Philadephia Orchestra recording of *Also sprach Zarathustra* is passionate yet nobly contoured, and the famous opening is extremely spectacular and expansive. The recording was made in the New Jersey Studios at Collingswood. It is good, too, to have a fine, modern version of the witty *Burleske*, with Ax giving a sparkling account of the solo piano part. Sawallisch's view of *Don Juan* is spacious rather than hard-driven, but the climax is thrilling. Alas, this fine CD has just been deleted.

(i) Also sprach Zarathustra; (i) Burleske for Piano & Orchestra. Der Rosenkavalier: 1st & 2nd Waltz Sequence. Die Liebe der Danae (symphonic fragment); Metamorphosen for 23 Solo Strings.

(B) *** Delos Double DE 3707 (2) (i) Rosenberger; Seatle
Symphony, Schwarz.

Throughout this programme the Seattle Orchestra plays splendidly, with warmth, passion and finish, and the concert hall acoustic is just right for this richly scored music. With no loss of definition, there is a degree of sumptuousness and bloom here missing in Lorin Maazel's otherwise technically impressive RCA Bavarian CDs (see above), Gerard Schwarz's earlier recordings have already proved him a dedicated and idiomatic Straussian. His version of *Metamorphosen* (see

below) is sustained at a very spacious tempo indeed, But it is unfailingly eloquent and holds the listener in its grip throughout. So does *Also sprach Zorathustra,*, which has a fine forwardsweep but plenty fo imaginative detail. The *Burleske* is an affectionately fanciful performance, rather loosely held together, but with Carol Rosenberger an endearingly nimble and romantic soloist. The two *Waltz Sequences* from *Der Rosenkavalier* are spirited enough , but add up to nearly 22 minutes and would outstay their welcome if not cued into two separate groups. However, the *symphonic fragment* from *Die liebe der Danae*, Strauss's penultimate opera, is somberly and movingly powerful and makes an excellent foil for the seductive *Salome's Dance*, as volumptuosly involving an account as any on record, closing with thrilling abandon. With such fine playing and superb sound this pair of discs, offered for the cost of one, is worthy of any collector's outlay.

Also sprach Zarathustra; Death and Transfiguration; Don Juan.

*** DG (IMS) 439 016-2. BPO, Karajan.
*** Telarc CD 80167. VPO, Previn.

As a performance the 1983 Karajan *Also sprach Zarathustra* (coupled with an exciting account of *Don Juan*) will be hard to beat and could very well be first choice. And the newly remastered CD has great dynamic range and presence, particularly at the extreme bass and treble, and the massed violins produce wonderfully radiant textures, as in the section marked *Von der grossen Sehnsucht* ('of the great longing'). The soaring main theme of *Don Juan* is hardly less sumptuous and the playing is electrifying in its energy.

Previn draws magnificent playing from the Vienna Philharmonic in powerful, red-blooded readings of the symphonic poems, and the recording is among Telarc's finest. Strongly recommended for anyone wanting this particular coupling, and enjoying spectacularly voluptuous soundquality.

(i) Also sprach Zarathustra; Death and Transfiguration; Don Juan; Ein Heldenleben; Till Eulenspiegel; (ii) Der Rosenkavalier: Waltz sequence.

(B) *** Ph. Duo Dig./ADD 442 281-2 (2). Concg. O,
(i) Haitink; (ii) Jochum.

(i; ii) Also sprach Zarathustra; (ii; iii) Death and Transfiguration; (iv) Don Juan; (i; ii) Ein Heldenleben; (iv) Till Eulenspiegel; Der Rosenkavalier: Waltz Sequence.

(N) (B) **(*) RCA 2-CD 74321 84608-2 (2) (i) Chicago SO;
(ii) Reiner; (iii) RCA Victor O; (iv) Bamberg SO, Jochum.

Haitink finds added nobility in *Death and Transfiguration*, while there is no lack of swagger in the accounts of both the *Don* and *Till*. The easy brilliance of the orchestral playing is complemented by the natural spontaneity of Haitink's readings, seamless in the transition between narrative events, without loss of the music's picaresque or robust qualities. Haitink's 1974 *Also sprach Zarathustra* has breadth and nobility. The 1970 *Ein Heldenleben* is also one of Haitink's finest records. He gives just the sort of performance, brilliant and swaggering but utterly without bombast, which will delight those who normally resist this rich and expansive wok. The Philips sound here is admirably faithful and skilfully remastered. For good measure Jochum's *Waltz Sequence* from *Rosenkavalier* has been added, though here the recording, though good for its age (the early 1960s), has not quite the opulence of the Haitink recordings.

Instead of Haitink, the RCA Double puts Reiner's and Jochum's Strauss interpretations side by side, achieving just about equal measure. But although the Bamberg Orchestra play very well and draw a genial if not very rascally portrait of *Till*, Jochum is not the right conductor for the passionate sexuality of the climax of *Don Juan*, and his *Rosenkavalier Waltzes* are elegant and little more (better recorded but not better played here than on Philips).

When one moves to the second disc the overwhelming power and richness of the opening few bars of Reiner's *Also sprach* or *Heldenleben*, completely dwarf what has gone before, both musically and technically; and even Reiner's 1950 mono *Death and Transfiguration* (which sounds remarkably good) has a Straussian charisma which Jochum lacks.

Also sprach Zarathustra; Death and Transfiguration; Till Eulenspiegel.

(B) *** Decca 448 224-2. Cleveland O, Ashkenazy.

Glorious Decca Cleveland sound in this triptych and marvellously reponsive playing from the orchestra. As sound, this is in the demonstration bracket; but other readings, notably those of Karajan, are just that bit more characterful.

Also sprach Zarathustra; Death and Transfiguration; Till Eulenspiegel; Salomé: Dance of the Seven Veils.

(N) (BB) *** EMI Encore (ADD) CDE5 74756-2 Dresden State O, Kempe.

Kempe's *Also sprach Zarathustra* is powerful in its emotional thrust, without going over the top. It is admirably paced, and while the Dresden orchestra may yield in virtuosity – though not much – to the Berlin Philharmonic under Karajan, whose analogue version was made in the same year, the HMV digital remastering retains the opulence of the Dresden acoustic. The rather mellow portrait of *Till* is particularly attractive and *Salomé's Dance* is also superbly played. Excellent value.

Also sprach Zarathustra; Don Juan; Till Eulenspiegel; Salome: Dance of the Seven Veils.

(M) *** Decca (ADD) 466 388-2. VPO, Karajan.

Karajan's Decca version of *Also sprach Zarathustra* was a famous early stereo demonstration disc in its day (1959), with its wide dynamic range and thrilling orchestral virtuosity; all its tonal opulence is restored in the CD transfer. The other works were recorded a year later and sound freshly minted, amazingly full and sharply detailed. *Till* is irrepressibly cheeky and full of wit, and *Salome's Dance* is decadently sensuous. *Don Juan* brings a similar, richly voluptuous response from the Vienna strings. Again the playing is superb, as beguiling in the love music as it is exhilarating in the chase.

Also sprach Zarathustra; (i) Don Quixote, Op. 35.

(B) **(*) Sony (ADD) SBK 47656. Phd. O, Ormandy; (i) with Munroe.

Ormandy's 1963 Sony *Also sprach Zarathustra*, if not as overwhelming as his later, EMI version, has much virtuoso orchestral playing to commend it and many felicities of characterization. His (1961) *Don Quixote* will also give considerable pleasure. There is some marvellous orchestral playing and the two soloists play splendidly with plenty of character but without the 'star soloist' approach favoured by so many record companies. A very competitive coupling.

Also sprach Zarathustra; Ein Heldenleben.

✿ (M) *** RCA 09026 61494-2. Chicago SO, Reiner.

These were the first stereo sessions the RCA engineers arranged with Fritz Reiner, after the company had taken over the Chicago orchestra's recording contract from Mercury. It must be said – to their enormous credit – that the RCA recording team 'got it right' from the very beginning, and the series of records they made with Reiner and his players in Orchestra Hall remain a technical peak in the history of stereo recording and the impressive feeling of space it conveyed. Later reissues have improved on its definition but none has done so with the stunning success of the present transfer. *Ein Heldenleben* shows Reiner in equally splendid form. There have been more incisive, more spectacular and more romantic performances, but Reiner achieves an admirable balance and whatever he does is convincing. If anything, the recording sounds even better than *Also sprach* and the warm acoustics of Orchestra Hall help convey Reiner's humanity in the closing pages of the work.

Also sprach Zarathustra; Don Juan; Till Eulenspiegel; Salome: Salome's Dance.

(M) *** DG (ADD) 447 441-2. BPO, Karajan.

Karajan's 1974 DG analogue version of *Also sprach Zarathustra* is coupled with his vividly characterized performance of *Till Eulenspiegel* and a thrillingly ebullient *Don Juan*, plus his powerfully voluptuous account of *Salome's Dance*. The Berlin Philharmonic plays with great fervour (the timpani strokes at the very opening are quite riveting) and creates characteristic body of tone in the strings, although the digital remastering has thrown a much brighter light on the violins.

Aus Italien; Die Liebe der Danae (symphonic fragment); *Der Rosenkavalier: waltz sequence No. 2.*

(BB) *** Naxos 8.550342. Slovak PO, Košler.

On Naxos, a very well-recorded and vividly detailed account of *Aus Italien* with an excellent sense of presence. The orchestra plays very well for Zdeněk Košler both here and in the ten-minute symphonic fragment Clemens Krauss made from *Die Liebe der Danae* and in the *Rosenkavalier* waltz sequence. The Slovak Philharmonic is a highly responsive body, with cultured strings and wind departments and, given the quality of the recorded sound, this represents a real bargain.

Aus Italien, Op.16; Metamorphosen for 23 Solo Strings.

(N)(M) *** Chan. 7133. RSNO, Järvi.

Järvi offers an apt coupling of early and late Strauss. *Aus Italien* is early and does not do the composer the fullest justice, but it does have marvellous moments, including the beautiful slow movement. The finale quotes a famous Neapolitan tarantella by Denza but does not make a great deal of it. Järvi takes a spacious view of the work, and the Chandos sound is full-bodied, with a natural perspective, and there is plenty of warmth. The orchestra seems at home in the score, giving the finale a certain Celtic lilt. *Metamorphosen* is a late masterpieces. Järvi's account is deeply felt and ardent, and the Scottish strings convey the underlying angst of the music with moving passion: they also play very well indeed. The recording is rich, expansive and natural. All in all, a great success and attractively priced.

Le Bourgeois Gentilhomme (suite); *Dance Suite after Couperin, Op. 60.*

*** Ph. (IMS) 446 696-2. ASMF, Marriner.

Marriner keeps a classical poise in these charming examples of eighteenth-century pastiche from an arch late-romantic. The *Le Bourgeois Gentilhomme* suite was salvaged from the incidental music Strauss wrote for the Molière play, when the first version of *Ariadne auf Naxos* – for which Molière provided the introduction – proved too cumbersome. Winningly stylish, Marriner is helped by clear, well-balanced recording The *Dance Suite* –based on harpsichord pieces –dates from 1920, with Strauss again writing happily in a style he described as being 'with his left hand'. Marriner keeps a perfect balance between romantic expressiveness and classical precision, with rhythms light and pointed, with crisp ensemble, generally at flowing speeds. There is lightness of touch and the requisite finesse and charm.

Le Bourgeois Gentilhomme (suite); *Symphonia domestica.*

(M) *** RCA (ADD) 09026 68637-2. Chicago SO, Reiner.

Reiner's account of *Le Bourgeois Gentilhomme* is superbly done – possibly the finest ever – and sounding marvellously fresh, considering its date (1956). The *Symphonia domestica* comes from two years later and is another wonderful performance, a reading of stature worthy to rank alongside the best; and the CD transfer brings splendidly vivid sound-quality.

(i; ii; iii) *Burleske for Piano & Orchestra;* (iv; v) *Duet Concertino for Clarinet & Bassoon;* (vi; ii; vii) *Horn Concertos Nos. 1 in E flat, Op. 11; 2 in E flat;* (viii; v) *Oboe Concerto;* (ix; v) *Violin Concerto in D min., Op. 8.*

(B) **(*) Double Decca mono/stereo ADD/Dig. 460 296-2 (2). (i) Gulda; (ii) LSO; (iii) Collins; (iv) D. Ashkenazy, Walker; (v) Berlin RSO, V. Ashkenazy; (vi) Tuckwell; (vii) Kertész; (viii) Hunt; (ix) Belkin – FRANZ STRAUSS: *Horn Concerto.* **(*)

(i) *Burleske in D min. for Piano & Orchestra.* (ii) *Duet-concertino for Clarinet, Bassoon & Strings.* (iii) *Horn Concertos Nos. 1–2.* (iv) *Oboe Concerto in D. Don Juan; Ein Heldenleben,.* (v) *Panathenäenzug for Piano (Left Hand) & Orchestra; Parergon to Symphonia domestica for Piano (Left Hand) & Orchestra. Till Eulenspiegel.*

(M) *** EMI (ADD) CMS7 64342-2 (3). (i) Frager; (ii) Weise, Liebscher; (iii) Damm; (iv) Clement; (v) Rösel; Dresden State O, Kempe.

Most collectors will already have a *Don Juan*, which is perhaps the least electrifying of Kempe's symphonic poems, and the same surely applies to *Till Eulenspiegel*, although it is an excellent performance. The *Burleske* is well worth having (it is beautifully recorded) and there are few satisfactory alternatives in the *Parergon* to the *Symphonia domestica* or the *Panathenäenzug*, both written for the one-armed pianist, Paul Wittgenstein, and played impressively here. Peter Damm's performances of the *Horn Concertos* are first class. Similarly, while Manfred Clement's *Oboe Concerto* is a sensitive reading, his creamily full timbre may not appeal to those brought up on Goossens. There can be no reservations whatsoever about the *Duet Concertino*, where the sounds from bassoon and clarinet are beguilingly succulent, while the intertwining of both wind soloists with the dancing orchestral violins of the finale has an irresistible, genial finesse. Throughout, the superb playing of the Dresden orchestra under Kempe adds an extra dimension to the music-making.

For the *Burleske*, Decca have turned back to a first-rate 1954 mono performance in which Gulda, on top form, is vivaciously partnered by Anthony Collins. They respond readily to its scherzando wit, while the muted ending is quite touching. The recording is very good for its period, although with Strauss one ideally needs more opulence in the orchestral violin tone. The *Duet Concertino* is an elusive work and here the timbres of the clarinet and bassoon soloists are rather too sharply individual to gel, and the conductor holds the orchestral reins rather slackly: the result is characterful but lacks an ongoing fluency and grip. Barry Tuckwell's essentially lyrical approach to the two horn concertos misses some of the music's character and the more florid *Second Concerto* also needs a stronger impulse, although the finale brings engaging light-hearted bravura. Boris Bekin's performance of the *Violin Concerto* isn't technically flawless, yet is distinctly enjoyable (see below). But the highlight of the set is Gordon Hunt's superb account of the *Oboe Concerto*. His creamy tone is ideally suited to Strauss's songful late masterpiece, and its technical hazards are surmounted with easy aplomb. There is no finer version.

Burleske for Piano & Orchestra.

*** RCA 9026 68028-2. Douglas, R. France PO, Janowski – REGER: *Piano Concerto.* ***

(BB) **(*) RCA Navigator (ADD) 74321 21286-2. Janis, Chicago SO, Reiner – MAHLER: *Symphony No. 4.* **(*)

(B) *(**) Sony (ADD) SBK 53262. Serkin, Phd. O, Ormandy – BRAHMS: *Piano Concerto No. 2.* **(*)

Burleske; Parergon, Op. 73; Stimmungsbilder, Op. 9.

**(*) Ara. Z 6567. Hobson, Philh. O, Del Mar.

Barry Douglas gives a very brilliant and persuasive account of the Strauss, of which Serkin – also a champion of the

Reger *Concerto* – was a keen exponent. This is arguably his best record to date.

The brilliance of the *Burleske* is also brought out well by Byron Janis, who does not miss the music's witty or lyrical side.

On the bargain-price Navigator version, the recording gives a brilliantly sparkling, somewhat dry piano-image, and the orchestra too is brought forward by the comparatively close microphones (although there is no lack of ambience).

Ian Hobson's account, on its own terms, is eminently satisfactory, and he is well supported by Norman Del Mar and the Philharmonia, and is well recorded. The *Parergon* for left hand is again very well played. The *Stimmungsbilder* are early, rather Schumannesque pieces, written in 1884: Hobson gives a rather touching account of *Träumerei*, and though one can imagine a performance of the *Intermezzo* with greater charm, there is still much to admire here. Decent recording.

Horn Concerto No. 1 in E flat, Op. 11

(M) *** EMI CDM7 64851–2. Vlatkovič, ECO, Tate –
  MOZART:*Horn Concertos Nos. 1–4 etc.* **

Radovan Vlatkovič gives a superb account of the *First Concerto* which, although ripely romantic, has so much in common with the spirit of the Mozart Concertos with which it is coupled. He is particularly good in the bold central episode of the *Andante* and caps his performance with an exhilaratingly nimble account of the finale. Tate accompanies admirably and the rich, natural, Abbey Road recording could hardly be better balanced.

Horn Concerto Nos. 1 in E flat, Op. 11: 2 in E flat.

☀ (***) EMI mono CDC7 47834-2. Brain, Philh. O, Sawallisch
  – HINDEMITH: *Horn Concerto.* (***)

**(*) EMI CDC5 56183-2. Neunecker, Bamberg SO,
  Metzmacher – BRITTEN: *Serenade.* **(*)

(i) *Horn Concertos;* (ii) *2;* (iii) *Oboe Concerto;* (iv) *Duet Concertino for Clarinet & Bassoon.*

*** DG 453 483-2. (i) Janezic, (ii) Stransky; (iii) Gabriel;
  (iv) Schmidl, Werba; VPO, Previn

(i) *Horn Concertos Nos. 1–2;* (ii) *Duet Concertino for Clarinet & Bassoon. Wind Serenade in E flat, Op. 11.*

(B) *** CfP 573 5132. (i) Pyatt; (ii) Farrall, Andrews; Britten
  Sinfonia, Cleobury.

Dennis Brain's performances are incomparable and almost certainly will never be surpassed. Sawallisch gives him admirable support, and fortunately the latest EMI CD transfer captures the full quality of the 1956 mono recording.

David Pyatt gives a ripely exuberant performance of the first of Strauss's two *Horn Concertos.* The more elusive first movement of the *Second Concerto* is shaped – often quite subtly – in an attractively rhapsodical style, while the finale brings heady, lightly tongued bravura. The outer movements of the gently rapturous *Duet Concertino* are presented with enticing delicacy of texture, and the slow movement again brings a most touchingly doleful opening solo, this time from the bassoonist, Julie Andrews. Cleobury and the Britten Sinfonia give sensitive support throughout, and the early

Serenade is always fresh, never congealing, helped by the naturally balanced recording, made in the Henry Wood Hall, Southwark.

On DG some glorious music-making, relaxed, unforced and full of expressive delights. The virtuosity is at no time self-regarding and everybody appears to be enjoying themselves. The sound, too, is as natural as the music-making. A most welcome addition to the catalogue.

Marie-Luise Neunecker is a young German musician who plays with extraordinary flair and agility, relishing the virtuoso demands of both of Strauss's horn concertos in playing of winning freedom and spontaneity. The Britten *Serenade* makes an unusual and attractive coupling, though in all three works the orchestra is recorded relatively thinly.

Oboe Concerto.

*** ASV CDCOE 808. Boyd, COE, Berglund – MOZART: *Oboe
  Concerto.* ***

(i) *Oboe Concerto. Metamorphosen for 23 Solo Strings.*

**(*) Ph. 446 105-2. Holliger, COE.

Douglas Boyd winningly brings out the happy glow of Strauss's inspiration of old age, and his warm oboe tone, less reedy than some, brings out the *Rosenkavalier* element in this lovely concerto. With warm, well-balanced recording, the gentle contrast of romantic and classical in this work is conveyed delectably.

Holliger is never less than masterly and the assurance of his playing is remarkable. But, as with his earlier, analogue recording, there is a hint of efficiency at the expense of ripeness, and in the slow movement he fails to convey a sheer love for the music in its most absolute sense. He is not helped by being balanced rather too closely and the effect is not flattering to his timbre. As an apt coupling he takes up the baton and directs a very well-controlled and thoughtfully shaped performance of the *Metamorphosen*, but once again there is an absence of ripeness, and the recording, while it reveals every strand of detail, brings a degree of excess digital definition to the climax.

(i; ii) *Oboe Concerto;* (ii) *Metamorphosen for 23 Solo Strings;* (iv) *Violin Sonata in E flat;* (ii; iii) *Orchestral Lieder: Befreit; Freundliche Vision; Die Heiligen drei Könige aus Morgenland; Meinem Kinde; Morgen!; Ruhe, meine Seele; Waldseligkeit; Wiegenlied; Winterweihe.*

(BB) **(*) Virgin 2 x 1 VBD5 61766-2 (2) (i) Still; (ii) Academy
  of L., Stamp; (iii) Janowitz; (iv) Sitkovetsky, Gililov.

Ray Still, the principal oboe of the Chicago Symphony Orchestra, is fully equal to the technical and lyrical demands of Strauss's florid concerto. His accompaniment is warmly supportive, but Richard Stamp could be subtler in controlling the work's complex detail. However, the Academy play the *Metamorphosen* confidently, and with refinement and ardour. They also provide a rich backcloth for Gundula Janowitz's creamily sensuous performances of nine of Strauss's most beautiful Lieder. There is a certain uniformity about her approach to all these songs, but she certainly feels the words, and her rich timbre and flowing lines are so beautiful that criticism is disarmed. Dimitry Sitkovetsky also makes a comparably ardent lyrical response to the *Violin*

Sonata. Pavel Gililov too is a perceptive artist, but his playing is not quite the equal of Krystian Zimerman (see below). Nevertheless the Virgin sound balance is praiseworthy throughout this disc and this anthology is excellent value at its modest asking price.

(i) *Oboe Concerto.* (ii) *Serenade for Wind; Sonatine No. 1 in F for Wind (From an Invalid's Workshop); Suite in B flat for 13 Wind Instruments, Op. 4; Symphony for Wind (The Happy Workshop).*

(B) *** Ph. Duo (ADD) 438 733-2 (2). (i) Holliger, New Philh. O; (ii) Netherlands Wind Ens.; De Waart.

The *Serenade* is beautifully played, warm and mellifluous, and so is the *Sonatina,* a late work, written while Strauss was recovering from an illness and appropriately subtitled. It is a richly scored piece, as thoroughly effective as one would expect from this master of wind writing. Both this and the *B flat Suite,* delightful pieces, are given beautifully characterized accounts here, while the performance of the *Symphony for Wind Instruments* is crisp and alert. Throughout this music-making, the ear is struck by the Netherlanders' beautifully homogeneous tone, and their phrasing is splendidly alive. The recordings made between 1970 and 1972 are full, well-detailed and truthful. As if this were not bounty enough, Holliger's earlier (1970) version of the *Oboe Concerto* is thrown in for good measure. The playing is masterly, an assured, styish account, and Edo de Waart accompanies persuasively. Again very good recording.

Violin Concerto in D min., Op. 8.

*** ASV CDDCA 780. Xue Wei, LPO, Glover – HEADINGTON: *Violin concerto.* *** ⬤

(B) **(*) Decca 448 988-2. Belkin, Berlin RSO, Ashkenazy – BRAHMS: *Violin Concerto.* ***

With Jane Glover and the LPO warmly sympathetic accompanists, Xue Wei makes a very persuasive case for this very early work of Strauss, with its echoes of Mendelssohn and Bruch.

Though not quite a match for Xue Wei, partly because just occasionally his intonation is not absolutely immaculate, Belkin finds much charm in the Mendelssohnian second group of the opening movement, and he plays the *Lento* with an appealing fragile tenderness, then following with fairy-light articulation in the dancing finale. Ashkenazy provides a gracefully supportive accompaniment and the Decca sound is excellent.

Violin Concerto; (ii) Violin Sonata in E flat, Op. 18.

*** EMI CDC5 56870-2. Chang; with (i) Bav. RSO, Sawallisch; (ii) Sawallisch (piano).

Sarah Chang enjoys the support of that most authoritative of Straussians, Wolfgang Sawallisch, and a great Strauss orchestra. She brings out a youthful freshness in the writing, both in the *Concerto* and in the *Sonata* of five years later. The Bavarian Radio engineers give Chang a lifelike balance. In both works, Chang and Sawallisch are at their most memorable in the slow movements, which in their hushed intensity sound winningly spontaneous. Sawallisch is just as impressive at the keyboard as he is conducting, always

matching Chang's characterful playing. The sound is warm and full, and brings out the violinist's subtlety of tonal shading.

Death and Transfiguration; Don Juan, Till Eulenspiegel, Salome: Dance of the Seven Veils.

(M) *** EMI (ADD) CDM5 66823-2. Philh. O, Klemperer.

Although it is a pity that the *Metamorphosen* could not have been included, this compilation, reissued as part of EMI's 'Klemperer Legacy', admirably reassembles the conductor's other key Richard Strauss recordings. In his hands it is *Death and Transfiguration* that excites the greatest admiration, invested with a nobility too rarely heard in this work. But not everyone will respond to his teatment of the other two symphonic poems. *Don Juan* is clearly seen as 'the idealist in search of perfect womanhood' (even if his primary test is made between the sheets). Yet both here and in *Till Eulenspiegel* the all-important feeling of spontaneity is not always present. The account of *Salome's Dance,* however, is splendidly sensuous and, with marvellous Philharmonia playing and a superb new transfer of a recording made in the Kingsway Hall in 1960–61, this collection is certainly not lacking in strength of characterization.

Death and Transfiguration; Don Juan; Ein Heldenleben.

(N) *(**) DG (ADD) 453 190-2. SWR Stuttgart RSO, Celibidache (with bonus disc of rehearsals) (with RESPIGHI: *The Pines of Rome* *(**)).

Celibidache's wonderful feeling for sound is much in evidence here. If you can accept this conductor's intrusive (and to our ears disruptive) mannerisms (the musical argument unfolds through highly idiosyncratic eyes) then you will want this. The SudWestfunk Orchestra is a fine instrument which undoubtedly benefitted from Celibidache's demanding rehearsal schedules.

Death and Transfiguration; Don Juan; (i) Four Last Songs (Vier letzte Lieder).

(N) **(*) Teldec 3984 25990-2. NYPO, Masur; (i) Voigt.

Good performances from all concerned on Teldec and impressive recording. Deborah Voigt sings with eloquent feeling in the *Vier letzte Lieder.* Recommendable, but hardly a first choice.

Death and Transfiguration; Ein Heldenleben .

(N)(M) *** Ph. (ADD) 464 743-2. Concg. O, Haitink.

Haitink's coupling is also available above as part of a Duo (see above). The 1970 analogue *Ein Heldenleben* is outstanding, brilliant and swaggering, but utterly without bombast. The sound is of Philips's very best and and superbly remastered. The digital *Death and Transfiguration* is gripping too, its dignity and warmth of humanity genuinely moving.

Death and Transfiguration; Metamorphosen for 23 Solo Strings.

⬤ *** DG 410 892-2. BPO, Karajan.

Death and Transfiguration; Metamorphosen for 23 Solo Strings; (i) Vier letzte Lieder (Four Last Songs).

(M) **(*) DG 447 422-2. BPO, Karajan, (i) with Janowitz.

Karajan's digital account of *Metamorphosen* has even greater emotional urgency than the 1971 record he made with the Berlin Philharmonic and there is a marginally quicker pulse. The sound is fractionally more forward and cleaner but still sounds sumptuous, and the account of *Death and Transfiguration* is quite electrifying. It would be difficult to improve on this coupling by the greatest Strauss conductor of his day.

The earlier versions are still powerful and convincing In the *Four last Songs*, Janowitz produces a beautiful flow of creamy tone while leaving the music's deeper and subtler emotions under-exposed. The transfers are very impressive, and *Death and Transfiguration* can still be regarded as a showpiece among Karajan's earlier Berlin recordings.

(i) *Death and Transfiguration; Symphonia domestica;*
(ii) *Salome's Dance of the Seven Veils.*

(B) *** Sony (ADD) SBK 53511. (i) Cleveland O, Szell; (ii) Phd. O, Ormandy.

Szell's *Death and Transfiguration* has the most compelling atmosphere and the triumphant closing pages are the more effective for Szell's complete lack of indulgence. The recording has been vastly improved in the present transfer, with Cleveland's Masonic Temple providing a richly expansive ambience. The *Symphonia Domestica*, recorded in 1964, is less naturally balanced but the performance brings such powerful orchestral playing, with glorious strings especially in the passionate *Adagio*, that criticism is disarmed: there is certainly no lack of body here. The programme ends with an extraordinarily voluptuous Philadelphia performance of *Salome's Dance*, which conjures up a whole frieze of naked female torsos. Ormandy directs with licentious abandon, and the orchestra responds with tremendous virtuosity and ardour, unashamedly going over the top at the climax.

Death and Transfiguration, Op. 24; Till Eulenspiegel, Op. 28.

(N) (M) **(*) Decca (ADD) 467 122-2. VPO, Reiner – BRAHMS: *Hungarian Dances.* DVORAK: *Slavonic Dances.* **(*)

Reiner's *Death and Transfiguration* is immensely characterful and exciting, though not so refined or clean in detail as Karajan's two DG recordings. *Till Eulenspiegel* is, likewise, a splendidly alive reading, and the VPO responds in both works to this great Straussian in the manner born. The sound is a bit dated and there is some tape hiss, but, considering it dates from 1956, it is amazingly full and vivid, and preferable to some over-reverberant digital recordings.

Don Juan, Op. 20.

(M) *** RCA 09026 63301-2. Chicago SO, Reiner – WAGNER: *Götterdämmerung & Meistersinger*: excerpts. **(*)

Don Juan; Ein Heldenleben .

(B) (***) Dutton Lab. mono CDEA 5025. Concg. O, Mengelberg.

(i) *Don Juan;* (ii) *Ein Heldenleben;* (iii) *Till Eulenspiegel.*

(M) *** Sony (ADD) SBK 48272. (iii) Cleveland O, Szell; (ii) Phd. O, Ormandy.

(M) (**) Telefunken 3984-28409-2. (iii) Concg. O, Mengelberg; (iii) VPO, Krauss.

Don Juan; Till Eulenspiegel; Salome: Dance of the Seven Veils.

*** Everest EVC 9004. NY Stadium SO, Stokowski – CANNING: *Fantasy on a Hymn Tune.* ***

Reiner's performance of this great Strauss showpiece is among the finest ever, with a superbly thrilling climax when the great horn theme leaps out unforgettably, to be followed by a closing atmosphere of sombre sentience and disillusion. The new transfer of the 1960 recording is impressive in catching the full amplitude and brilliance of the Chicago Symphony Orchestra.

Szell's *Don Juan* delights ear and senses by its forward surge of passionate lyricism, the whole interpretation founded on a bedrock of virtuosity from the remarkable Cleveland players. *Till* is irrepressibly cheeky and here the recording acoustic is almost perfect, with a warm glow on the tone of the players and every detail – and Szell makes sure one can hear every detail – crystal clear, without any loss of momentum or drama.

Ormandy's *Ein Heldenleben* is an engulfing performance, and the composite richness of tone and the fervour of the playing, from the Battle section onwards, bring the highest possible level of orchestral tension, finally relaxing most touchingly for the fulfilment sequence. The 1960 recording is more two-dimensional, less full, than the Cleveland recordings (which, surprisingly, were made as early as 1957) but is still appropriately spacious.

This justly famous Stokowski triptych from the late 1950s, with the spacious recording cleaned up, now sounds very well indeed. Not surprisingly with the old magician in charge, Salome is made to languish more voluptuously than ever before, and even *Till* in his posthumous epilogue has a languishing mood on him. *Don Juan* indulges himself with rich sensuality, yet leaps off into the fray with undiminished vitality, while the great unison horn-call is held back with a compellingly broadened thrust. As ever, Stokowski is nothing if not convincing, and those looking for really ripe versions of these pieces need not hesitate. The Canning coupling is also worth having.

Willem Mengelberg and the Concertgebouw Orchestra were jointly the dedicatees of Richard Strauss's most ambitious orchestral work, *Ein Heldenleben*. They give a heartfelt performance, freely spontaneous and expansive, with old-fashioned string portamento intensifying the warmth. The splendid Dutton transfer is clear on detail with plenty of body and fair bloom on top. The *Don Juan* recording of 1938 is even more cleanly focused.

Telefunken's own transfer is full and beefy but not nearly so cleanly focused as the splendid Dutton transfer. The *Don Juan* recording of 1938 brings an even sharper contrast in favour of Dutton. Though the Telefunken disc has a bonus in Krauss's *Till Eulenspiegel*, with the Vienna Philharmonic, the price is higher.

Don Quixote.

(M) *** EMI (ADD) CDM5 66913-2 [566965]. Rostropovich, BPO, Karajan – SCHUMANN: *Cello Concerto.* *(*)

☼ *** EMI (ADD) CDC5 55528-2. Du Pré, New Philh. O, Boult – LALO: *Cello Concerto in D min.* ***

(BB) *** Virgin VBD5 61490-2. Isserlis, Minnesota O, De Waart – BLOCH: *Schelomo.* ELGAR: *Cello Concerto;* KABALEVSKY: *Cello Concerto No. 2;* TCHAIKOVSKY: *Rococo variations* etc. ***

(i) *Don Quixote;* (ii) *Horn Concerto No. 2.*

(M) *** DG (ADD) 457 725-2. (i) Fournier; (ii) Norbert Hauptmann; BPO, Karajan.

(i) *Don Quixote, Op. 35; Romance in F;* (i) *Cello Sonata in F, Op. 6.*

(N) *** RCA 74321 75398-2. (i) Isserlis, Bavarian Radio SO, Maazel; (ii) Hough, Maazel (piano).

(i) *Don Quixote; Till Eulenspiegel.*

**(*) DG (IMS) 439 027-2. (i) Meneses; BPO, Karajan.

The Karajan/Rostropovich account of *Don Quixote* is predictably fine. The recorded sound (1975) is impressively remastered, spectacular in its realism, with well-defined detail, superb warmth and body, and fine perspective, its only failing a tendency for Rostropovich to dominate the aural picture. He dominates artistically, too. His Don is superbly characterized, and the expressiveness and richness of tone he commands are a joy in themselves. This superb account of *Don Quixote* comes re-coupled with Schumann's *Cello Concerto* as one of EMI's 'Great Recordings of the Century' series, which the latter performance (with Bernstein) certainly is not. A sad mismatching!

Fournier's partnership with Karajan is also outstanding and so is the 1966 recording. It is of DG's very finest quality, with remarkable transparency, yet plenty of warmth and a believable perspective. The great cellist brings infinite subtlety and (when required) repose to his part, and Karajan's handling of the orchestral detail is quite splendid. The finale and Don Quixote's death are very moving. Norbert Hauptmann's account of the more florid of Strauss's two horn concertos is ripely assured with a most eloquent and touching *Andante.*

Maazel's Strauss series with the glorious Bavarian Radio Orchestra has made leisurely progress and now reaches *Don Quixote.* Steven Isserlis is an ardent soloist and is even more impressive than he was in his earlier recording with Edo de Waart (Virgin). He makes a glorious sound and characterizes each variation with flair and is well partnered by an anonymous Sancho Panzo, presumably the first violist of the Bavarian Orchestra. It is among the best of the recent *Dons* though it does not displace the likes of Rostropovich or Fournier (both with Karajan). One of the other attractions of the disc is a vibrant account of the early *Cello Sonata* with Stephen Hough as a splendid partner. The sound is very good.

Jacqueline du Pré's *Don Quixote* comes in a studio recording, dating from 1968, which has been lovingly pieced together from long-buried tapes. No doubt du Pré with more time would have sharpened up some of the bravura passages, but in its tenderness and poignancy this reading is

unsurpassed. The lyrical dialogue between Sancho Panza and Quixote in the third variation has a heartfelt warmth, with Herbert Downes a fine partner on the viola. Above all, the final death scene is more yearningly tender than on any rival recording, a magical example of her art.

On Virgin Steven Isserlis again gives a firmly characterized account of the solo part, and although Edo de Waart and the Minnesota Orchestra may not succeed in producing the same refinement of texture as such Straussians as Kempe, Reiner and Karajan, the orchestral playing is generally very good indeed. The sound has both depth and clarity, and the couplings are both incredibly generous and finely played.

Karajan's digital recording with Antonio Meneses and Wolfram Christ has been given the 'original image bit reprocessing' treatment and there is some improvement in the sound. But the perspective remains far from natural and neither the performance nor the recording is a patch on his earlier versions with Rostropovich (EMI) or the late Pierre Fournier.

Ein Heldenleben, Op. 40.

(M) *** EMI (ADD) CDM5 66108. BPO, Karajan – WAGNER: *Der fliegende Holländer: Overture; Parsifal: Preludes.* ***

(M) *** DG (ADD). 449 725-2 BPO, Karajan – WAGNER: *Siegfried idyll.* ***

(B) *** EMI double forte (ADD) CZS5 69349-2 (2). LSO, Barbirolli – MAHLER: *Symphony No. 6.* **(*)

(N) (M) ** BBC (ADD) BBCL 4055-2. LSO, Barbirolli – MOZART: *Symphony No. 36 (Linz).* **

Ein Heldenleben; Death and Transfiguration, Op. 24.

**(*) DG 439 039-2. BPO, Karajan.

Ein Heldenleben; Feuersnot: Liebszene; Intermezzo: Träumerei am Kamin; Salome: Dance of the Seven Veils.

(***) Testament mono SBT 11147. RPO, Beecham.

The 1974 EMI Karajan *Heldenleben* is superlatively recorded. The performance shows a remarkable consistency of approach on Karajan's part and an equal virtuosity of technique and even greater sumptuousness of tone on the part of the Berlin Philharmonic than the earlier, DG performance; indeed the sound is remarkably vivid and there seems little difference between the two readings. Couplings might dictate a choice; both discs offer the music of Wagner; the EMI is the more generous: an electrifying *Flying Dutchman overture*, and glorious playing (and recording) in the two *Parsifal Preludes.*

Although Karajan's 1959 *Heldenleben* cannot quite match his later EMI version in sumptuousness it still sounds remarkably impressive. Playing of great power and distinction emanates from the Berlin Philharmonic and, in the closing section, an altogether becoming sensuousness and warmth. The remastering makes the most of the ambient atmosphere and, while not losing body, firms up the orchestral detail.

Barbirolli recorded *Ein Heldenleben* at Abbey Road in 1969, not long before his death, and here he sets the seal on his Indian summer in the recording studio. All the tempi are slow, even by his latter-day standards. He luxuriates in every moment of this opulent score (his occasional groans of pleasure sometimes punctuating the score) and the LSO, in superb form, follows him with warmth and ardour through every expressive rallentando. The result has the inescapable electricity of a great occasion. The CD transfer has lost some of the original opulence, but there was enough and to spare, and the sound now has greater focus and detail.

This BBC recording from 1969 documents one of Sir John's last concert appearances. Made in the Royal Festival Hall it shows considerable vitality and zest, although it is far from being an ideal testimony to his art and career. The sound is very good and not greatly inferior to that in the studio recording.

Karajan's digital *Heldenleben* has tremendous sweep and all the authority and mastery we have come to expect – and indeed to take for granted. Nor is the orchestral playing anything other than glorious – indeed, in terms of sheer virtuosity, the Berlin players have never surpassed this. However, in spite of the 'original-image bit re-processing' the early (1983) digital recording falls short of the highest present-day standards. Since Karajan's superb *Death and Transfiguration* (recorded only three years later) has been added to it, the ear is drawn to notice that *Ein Heldenleben*, although firmly focused, has less warmth and the strings by comparison lack bloom, while the violins have a certain glassiness in the high treble, characteristic of the early digital era.

Beecham's 1947 account remains a model of its kind: authoritative, marvellously paced and beautifully transparent in its textures. A glorious performance which long held sway until Karajan's 1959 account came along. The other Strauss excerpts were recorded in the late 1940s before the advent of the mono LP.

Josephslegende (ballet; complete).

(N) *** DG 463 493-2. Dresden St. O, Sinopoli.

Josephslegende (ballet suite): Suite; Symphonia domestica, Op. 53.

**(*) Delos DE 3082. Seattle SO, Schwarz.

Josephslegende, based on the Old Testament story, was written for Diaghilev's Ballet Russes, and first produced in Paris in May 1914, the worst possible timing on the eve of the First World War. It did not help that Nijinsky was not available as planned to take the title role. Despite that failure, the idea has much in its favour, neatly following up in ballet the spectacular success of Strauss's opera, *Salome*. Here too the forces of goodness (represented by Joseph), are pitted against the hysteria of a lascivious woman, Potiphar's wife.

The trouble was that unlike John the Baptist in Salome, gritty and uncompromising, Joseph as 'one who seeks God' was too bland a figure to interest the sceptical Strauss. The fault lay largely with the scenario, prepared from Hofmannsthal's initial idea by Count Harry Kessler, which presents Joseph as a total innocent, not even as cunning as the biblical character. Even so, with Potiphar's wife and Pharaoh's decadent court as part of the scheme, Strauss offers a sumptuous feast of sound in a score using an enormous orchestra, which is over twice as long as the *Symphonic Fragment* of 1947 in which Strauss salvaged some of the music. Sinopoli relishes the opulence, drawing warmly expressive playing from the superb Dresden orchestra in a ripe recording edited from live performances.

Gerard Schwarz gives us the suite from the ballet in addition to a very idiomatic account of the *Symphonia domestica*. There is very good playing from the Seattle orchestra: cultured, thoroughly idiomatic and with splendid sweep; the recording, too, is splendidly detailed, if perhaps just a bit too brightly lit to be ideal.

Metamorphosen for 23 Solo Strings.

*** Chan. 9708. Norwegian CO, I. Brown – TCHAIKOVSKY: *Souvenir de Florence.* ***

(M) *** EMI (ADD) CMS5 67036-2 (2). Philh. O, Klemperer – MAHLER: *Symphony No. 9;* WAGNER: *Siegfried idyll.* ***

*** EMI CDS5 56580-2. VPO, Rattle – MAHLER: *Symphony No. 9.* ***

*** Delos DE 3121. Seattle SO, Schwarz – HONEGGER: *Symphony No. 2;* WEBERN arr. SCHWARZ: *Langsamer satz.* ***

(B) **(*) EMI double forte (ADD) CZS7 67816-2 (2). New Philh. O, Barbirolli – MAHLER: *Symphony No. 6.* **(*)

Iona Brown's performance has a powerfully passionate impetus that is wholly spontaneous, with intense valedictory feeling in the shading down of the closing pages, which has wonderful concentration. The Chandos recording is outstandingly fine.

With Klemperer, *Metamorphosen* has a ripeness that exactly fits Strauss's last essay for orchestra, helped by the superb Philharmonia string-playing, rich in texture but with striking refinement of detail. The remastering of the 1961 Kingsway Hall recording for the 'Klemperer Legacy' is very impressive.

Rattle with the Vienna Philharmonic, producing string sounds of magical beauty, brings out the visionary intensity behind this late flowering of Strauss's genius, sustaining its long span masterfully. Warm, atmospheric sound. An excellent coupling for Mahler's *Ninth*.

Gerard Schwarz's account of Strauss's elegiac threnody is as deeply felt and dignified as it is unhurried, and it should be heard. The listener is completely drawn into its world and, although it does not supersede the Kempe or any of the the Karajan accounts except perhaps in terms of recorded realism, it deserves to be recommended alongside them. At 32 minutes it may be the slowest *Metamorphosen* on disc, but it is certainly one of the best.

Barbirolli's version of the *Metamorphosen* is a fine one, with a warm glow and an intense, valedictory feeling, and the playing of the NPO strings is most eloquent. The 1967 Abbey Road recording still sounds well; however, although it still has weight, the present CD transfer has lost some of its original bloom and opulence.

Serenade for Wind; Sonatine No. 1 in F for Wind (From an Invalid's Workshop); Suite in B flat for 13 Wind Instruments; Symphony for Wind (The Happy Workshop).

(B) *** Hyp. Dyad CDD 2015. London Winds, Collins.

The London Winds on Hyperion are fairly closely observed by the microphone-balance and the effect is clearly defined and dramatic. The playing has the strongest impulse, the autumnal feeling less apparent in the *Serenade*. But one cannot help being caught up by playing that is so vividly robust and vital, and by no means lacking in warmth and affection. Even if there is a touch of over-projection, inner detail is clear and many will like the extra bite on the sound.

Symphonia domestica, Death and Transfiguration.

(M) *** EMI (ADD) CDM5 66107-2. BPO, Karajan – WAGNER: *Lohengrin: Preludes; Tristan und Isolde: Prelude & Liebestod*. ***

*** RCA 09026 68221-2. Bav. RSO, Lorin Maazel.

Symphonia domestica; Festliches Praeludium; Till Eulenspiegel.

*** EMI CDC5 55185-2. Phd. O, Sawallisch.

Strauss's *Symphonia domestica* is quite admirably served by Karajan's mid-priced 1973 EMI reissue. The playing is stunningly good and the sumptuous Berlin strings produce tone of great magnificence. EMI provide a recording (made in the Salle Wagram, Paris, in 1973) of wide range, but this is another of their current deletions.

   Wolfgang Sawallisch's *Symphonia Domestica* is *echt*-Strauss, unexaggerated and civilized. He draws excellent playing from the Philadelphia Orchestra and gives a performance that reveals this score for what it is: one of the finest of Strauss's works. This is easily the best *Symphonia Domestica* since the Karajan version of the 1970s, and it is accorded refined and well-detailed sound.

Symphony in F min. Op.12; Symphony in D min.

**(*) Koch 3-6532-2. Berlin RSO or Bav. RSO, Rickenbacher.

Symphony in F min.; (i) 6 Lieder, Op. 68.

*** Chan. 9166. (i) Hulse; RSNO, Järvi.

Like Korngold a generation later, Strauss was a composing prodigy. These two early symphonies, the one written when he was barely 16, the other at 19, may give little idea of the mature composer's style, but the skill of the writing is astonishing, not least the instrumentation. The *D minor* has many Mendelssohnian echoes, strikingly so in the first movement, while Opus 12 brings an admixture of Brahms, with just occasional Wagnerian hints. Clean-cut performances and recording on Koch.

   However Järvi paces the score with real mastery and gets very good playing from the Royal Scottish National Orchestra. The glorious Brentano *Lieder*, Op. 68, date from 1918 and Strauss transcribed them for orchestra in 1941. Eileen Hulse produces some beautiful tone and is sensitively supported throughout. Not core repertory this, but a disc for Straussians.

Till Eulenspiegel.

(B) (***) Dutton Lab. mono CDEA 5013. Boston SO, Koussevitzky – BERLIOZ: *Harold in Italy*. (**(*))

Till Eulenspiegel, recorded in 1945, makes a spectacular fill-up to Koussevitzky's pioneering account of the Berlioz, another fizzing performance, both warm and brilliant, very well transferred in sound both full-bodied and airy.

CHAMBER MUSIC

Piano Quartet in C min., Op. 13.

(N) *** Black Box BBX 1048. Lyric Piano Qt – TURINA: *Piano Quartet in A min., Op. 67*. ***

By general consent the *Piano Quartet in C minor* is not great Strauss, but it is well played and recorded here and coupled with another rarity by Turina. A disc for those with a taste for offbeat repertoire.

String Quartet in A, Op. 2.

(B) **(*) Hyp. Helios CDH 55012. Delmé Qt – VERDI: *Quartet*.

The Strauss *Quartet* is early and derivative, as one might expect from a sixteen-year-old, but it is amazingly assured and fluent. The Delmé version is well played; however, although the basic acoustic is pleasing, the sound-balance remains a little on the dry side.

(i) Metamorphosen (arr. for string septet). Capriccio: Prelude.

*** Nim. NI 5614. Brandis Qt., with Küssner, Schwalke – SCHOENBERG: *Verklaerte Nacht*. ***

The first ideas for *Metamorphosen* came to Strauss as a string septet. In 1990, Strauss's pencil sketch came to light and, with the aid of that and the definitive score, Rudolf Leopold has carefully reconstructed the original. The Brandis Quartet and three Berlin colleagues play with magnificent artistry and eloquence, both here and in the opening sextet from *Capriccio*. The Nimbus sound is first class.

Violin Sonata in E flat, Op. 18.

(N) *** Erato 8573-85769-2 Repin, Berezovsky – BARTOK: *Roumanian folk dances;* STRAVINSKY: *Divertimento*. ***

(M) *** DG 457 907-2. Chung, Zimerman – RESPIGHI: *Sonata*. ***

The sheer sweep and intensity of the extraordinary Repin–Berezovsky partnership brings captivating reading which unlikely to soon be surpassed. It is arguably the best we have had since the days of Neveu and Heifetz.

   Among other versions Kyung Wha Chung is also outstanding and her version of the Strauss scores over most rivals as well in the power and sensitivity of Krystian Zimerman and the excellent DG recording. There is, however, a cut of 42 bars in the coda of the first movement (Universal Edition) which appears to be sanctioned.

Piano Sonata in B min., Op. 5; 5 Pieces, Op. 3; (i) Enoch Arden, Op. 38; (ii) Ophelia Lieder.

(M) ** Sony (ADD) SM2K 52657 (2). Gould; with (i) Rains; (ii) Schwarzkopf.

Neither the early Op. 3 *Pieces* nor the *Piano Sonata in B minor* are top-drawer Strauss, but Glenn Gould plays with such intensity that he almost convinces you that they are. Moreover the intensity is not overstated, and eccentricity surfaces only in his accompaniments of Elisabeth Schwarzkopf's *Ophelia Lieder*. Strauss's mélodrame to Tennyson's

Enoch Arden is hardly one of the composer's success stories, but it has a certain period fascination that makes this Sony disc worth collecting. Unfortunately, the sound is dry and the balance almost claustrophobic.

Enoch Arden, Op. 38 (Melodrama for narrator and piano).

***(*) VAI Audio (ADD) VAIA 1179-2 (2). Vickers, Hamelin.

Jon Vickers, the narrator on VAIA, recommends (in English) how so 'soul-satisfying' a piece gives a powerful reminder of 'the timeless truths of Love, Patience, Fidelity and Steadfastness'. In his powerful declamation he makes a persuasive case for the piece, but even Marc-André Hamelin, equally persuasive, cannot mask the fact that the piano-writing in its illustrative naivety has much in common with the accompaniments for silent films, which soon after became so popular. The live recording (with much applause beforehand) is aptly atmospheric.

CHORAL MUSIC

Der Abend; Hymne, Op. 34/1–2; Deutsche Motette, Op. 62.

(B) *** Double Decca (ADD) 455 035-2 (2). Cash, Temperley, Evans, Varcoe, Schütz Choir of L., Norrington –
BRUCKNER: *Mass No. 2 etc.* **

The *German Motet*, with 16 choral lines plus soloists, has the sopranos soaring to top D flat and staying there, while the basses at one point go down to bottom B, and the shifting harmonies make one's head reel. But what matters is that in superb performances like these the music is richly poetic, quite distinct within the whole choral repertoire, with glowing reminders of Strauss's loveliest music, from the *Rosenkavalier Trio* and *Ariadne* to the *Four Last Songs*. *Der Abend* might be a direct tribute to the heaven-vision of Strauss's friend, Mahler. The (originally Argo) recording is gloriously resonant and clear.

(i) *An den Baum Daphne*; (ii) *Der Abend; Hymne, Op. 34/ 1–2*; (iii) *Deutsche Motette, Op. 62*; (iv) *Die Göttin im Putzzimer.*

*** Chan. 9223. (i) Lund, Lisdorf, Copenhagen Boys' Ch.; (iii) Kiberg, Stene, Henning-Jensen, Cold; (i–iv) Danish Nat. R. Ch., Parkman.

This disc brings very good performances of some very beautiful and curiously little-known music. The engineers produce a realistic sound too.

Feierlicher Einzug; Festliches Preludium; Olympic Hymn; Taillefer; Wanderers Sturmlied.

(N) (BB) *** Arte Nova 74321 72107-2. Munich Motet Choir & SO, Siemens.

Strauss in occasional music like this often went wildly over the top. In such exuberant performances, recorded live, the results will delight any Straussian. The *Olympic Hymn*, written for the 1936 Berlin Games and designed for a huge open-air choir, sounds like teutonic Elgar. The tune may not be distinctive enough, but the orchestration is gorgeous, and that is so in the other works too, including the *Wanderers Sturmlied*, a Goethe setting. The finest piece, also the longest

and most opulent of all, is *Taillefer*, setting a poem by Uhland involving William the Conqueror. First given in Heidelberg in 1903 by 700 performers, it makes a wonderfully rich celebration, Strauss's thank you on receiving an honorary doctorate.

LIEDER

8 Lieder, Op. 10; 5 Lieder, Op. 15; 6 Lieder, Op. 17; 6 Lieder, Op. 19; Schlichte Weisen, Op. 21; Mädchenblumen, Op. 22; 2 Lieder, Op. 26; 4 Lieder, Op. 27; Lieder, Op. 29/1 & 3; 3 Lieder, Op. 31; Stiller Gang, Op. 31/4; 5 Lieder, Op. 32; Lieder, Op. 36/1–4; Lieder, Op. 37/1–3 & 5–6; 5 Lieder, Op. 39; Lieder, Op. 41/2–5; Gesänge älterer deutscher Dichter, Op. 43/1 & 3; 5 Gedichte, Op. 46; 5 Lieder, Op. 47; 5 Lieder, Op. 48; Lieder, Op. 49/1 & 2; 4–6; 6 Lieder, Op. 56; Krämerspiegel, Op. 66; Lieder, Op. 67/4–6; Lieder, Op. 68/1 & 4; 5 kleine Lieder, Op. 69; Gesänge des Orients, Op. 77; Lieder, Op. 88/1–2; Lieder ohne Opuszahl.

(M) *** EMI (ADD) CMS7 63995-2 (6). Fischer-Dieskau, Moore.

Fischer-Dieskau and Moore made these recordings of the 134 Strauss songs suitable for a man's voice between 1967 and 1970, tackling them in roughly chronological order. With both artists at their very peak, the results are endlessly imaginative, and the transfers are full and immediate, giving fine presence to the voice.

Lieder: Allerseelen; Ach Lieb ich muss nun Scheiden; Befreit; Du meines Herzens Krönelein; Einerlei; Heimliche Aufforderung; Ich trage meine Minne; Kling!; Lob des Leidens; Malven; Mit deinen blauen Augen; Die Nacht; Schlechtes Wetter; Seitdem dein Aug; Ständchen; Stiller Gang; Traume durch die Dämmerung; Wie sollten wir geheim; Wir beide wollen springen; Zeltlose.

*** Ph. 416 298-2. Norman, Parsons.

Jessye Norman's recital of Strauss brings heartfelt, deeply committed performances, at times larger than life, which satisfyingly exploit the unique glory of the voice. The magnetism of the singer generally silences any reservations, and Geoffrey Parsons is the most understanding of accompanists, brilliant too. Good, natural recording.

Lieder: Befreit; Hat gesagt, bleibt's nicht dabei; Ich trage meine Minne; Meinem Kinde; Der Rosenband; Die sieben Siegel; Wie sollten wir geheim sie halten.

*** DG 437 515-2. Von Otter, Forsberg – BERG: *Early Lieder.* KORNGOLD: *Lieder.* ***

Anne Sofie von Otter and Bengt Forsberg follow up their prize-winning disc of Grieg songs with another inspired set of performances. Though they are even more illuminating in Berg and Korngold, the imaginative selection of seven Strauss songs brings warm, intense singing and sensitive accompaniments.

Lieder: Des Dichters Abendgang; Freundliche Vision; Heimliche Aufforderung; Ich trage meine Minne; Liebeshymnus; Morgen!; Das Rosenband; Ständchen;

Traum durch die Dämmerung; Verführung; Waldseligkeit; Zueignung.

(B) **(*) Ph. 432 614-2. Jerusalem, Leipzig GO, Masur.

Starting with an account of *Heimliche Aufforderung* that is both heroic and glowingly beautiful, Siegfried Jerusalem's collection of Strauss Lieder in orchestral arrangements provides a male counterpart to Jessye Norman's magnificent disc, also recorded with Masur and the Leipzig Gewandhaus Orchestra. The shading of tone which Jerusalem commands is most sensitive, as in *Morgen* or a delicate rendering of *Ständchen*. Naturally balanced recording, warmly reverberant to bring out the ravishing beauty of Strauss's orchestrations. However, the reissue has no documentation whatsoever apart from a list of titles. How can a major company like Philips allow this to happen?

Four Last Songs – see also under *Death and Transfiguration*.

(N) (M) *** Ph. 464 742-2. Norman, Leipzig GO, Masur –
  WAGNER: *Wesendonck Lieder*. **(*)

(N) **(*) Sony SK 61720. Eaglen, LSO, Runnicles – WAGNER:
  Wesendonck-Lieder; BERG: *7 Early Songs*. ***

Strauss's publisher, Ernest Roth, says in the score of the *Four Last Songs* that this was a farewell of 'serene confidence', which is exactly the mood that Jessye Norman conveys. The start of the second stanza of the third song, *Beim Schlafengehen*, brings one of the most thrilling vocal crescendos on record, expanding from a half-tone to a gloriously rich and rounded forte. In concern for detail, Norman is outshone only by Schwarzkopf, but the stylistic as well as the vocal command is irresistible, and the radiance of the recording matches the interpretations. Unfortunately, for this reissue Philips have exchanged the six other orchestral songs on the original CD (which included a powerfully operatic account of *Cäcile*) for Norman's earlier (mid 1970s) recording of Wagner's *Wesendonck Lieder*, which were rather less successful.

As in the Wagner and Berg items Jane Eaglen produces warm, vibrant tone in the Four *Last Songs*, and in scale she matches Jessye Norman in her fine Philips version (see below). Yet sumptuous sounds are not enough in these subtle songs, with Runnicles and the LSO marginally less responsive than in Wagner and Berg. A good coupling none the less, ripely recorded with a wide dynamic range.

Four last Songs; Lieder: Allerseelen; Freundliche Vision; Geduld; Die Georgine; Meinem Kinde; Morgen!; Muttertändelei; Die Nacht; Nichts; Das Rosenband; Ruhe, meine Seele!; Die Verschwiegenen; Wiegenlied; Die Zeitlose; Zueignung.

**(*) Decca 460 812-2. Bonney, Martineau.

Barbara Bonney uses her creamy soprano with great sensitivity and concern for detail in this generous selection of Strauss Lieder, even if the tonal range could be wider. With a high proportion of favourite songs, the disc can be fairly warmly recommended, though the *Four Last Songs* are not entirely successful with piano instead of orchestral accompaniment. Even the keenly imaginative Malcolm Martineau cannot conceal the problems in the last two songs, which

cry out for a sustained legato beyond anything possible on the piano, notably in the long link between stanzas in *Beim schlafengehen*. Warm, well-balanced sound.

Four Last Songs; Lieder: Das Bächlein; Befreit; Cäcilie; Freundliche Vision; Die heiligen drei Könige aus Morgenland; Mein Auge; Meinem Kinde; Morgen; Muttertändelei; Ruhe, meine Seele!; Waldseligkeit; Wiegenlied.

**(*) Chan. 9054. Lott, SNO, Järvi.

Drei Hymnen, Op. 71. Orchestral songs: Des Dichters Abendgang; Frühlingsfeier; Gesang der Apollopriesterin; Liebeshymnus; Das Rosenband; Verführung; Winterliebe; Winterweihe; Zueignung.

*** Chan. 9159. Lott, SNO, Järvi.

Felicity Lott's two discs bring together a whole series of recordings of Strauss songs in their orchestral versions which originally appeared as couplings for Järvi's discs of the Strauss symphonic poems. She sings them beautifully, though the voice is not always caught at its most golden, notably in the *Four Last Songs* which yet are movingly done. The second CD includes the first recording of *Drei Hymnen*, Holderlin settings composed in 1921, pantheistic poems about love of nature which are full of ardour and are provided with the most opulent accompaniments. Lott's voice, for the most part well focused, rides over the rich orchestral textures impressively, and throughout both discs there is agreeably warm, full, orchestral sound.

Four Last Songs; Orchestral Lieder: Das Bächlein; Freundliche Vision; Die heiligen drei Könige; Meinem Kinde; Morgen; Muttertändelei; Das Rosenband; Ruhe, meine Seele; Waldseligkeit; Wiegenlied; Winterweihe; Zueignung.

⊕ (M) *** EMI (ADD) CDM5 66908-2 [566960]. Schwarzkopf,
  Berlin RSO or LSO, Szell.

(i) *Four Last Songs; Orchestral Lieder: Befreit; Cäcilie; Muttertändelei; Waldseligkeit; Wiegenlied. Der Rosenkavalier: suite.*

**(*) RCA 09026 68539-2. (i) Fleming; Houston SO,
  Eschenbach.

Four Last Songs; Orchestral Lieder: Cäcilie; Freundliche Vision; Frühlingsfeier; Gesang der Apollopriesterin; Verführung; Waldseligkeit.

*** DG 445 182-2. Mattila, BPO, Abbado.

(i) *Four Last Songs; (ii) Arabella (opera): excerpts.*
(i) *Capriccio (opera): Closing scene.*

(M) (***) EMI mono CDH5 67495-2. Schwarzkopf, (i) Philh. O,
  Ackermann; (ii) Metternich, Gedda, Philh. O, Von Matačcić.

Four Last Songs; (i) Arabella: excerpts. Ariadne auf Naxos: Ariadne's Lament. Capriccio: Closing scene.

(N) (M) (***) Decca mono 467 118-2. Lisa Della Casa; (i) with
  Gueden, Schoeffler Poell; VPO, Boehm, Moralt; Hollreiser.

Four Last Songs; Die heiligen drei Könige. Capriccio (opera): Moonlight Music & Monologue (closing scene); Metamorphosen for 23 Solo Strings.

(M) *** DG 445 599-2. Tomowa-Sintow, BPO, Karajan.

For the reissued CD version of Schwarzkopf's raptly beautiful recording of the *Four Last Songs*, EMI have added not just the old coupling of Strauss orchestral songs but also the extra seven which she recorded three years later in 1969, also with George Szell conducting, but with the LSO instead of the Berlin Radio Symphony Orchestra. There are few records in the catalogue which so magnetically capture the magic of a great performance, with the intensity of Schwarzkopf's singing in all its variety of tone and meaning perfectly matched by inspired playing. The current remastering seems to add even more lustre to voice and orchestra alike, and this CD is one of the highlights of EMI's 'Greatest Recordings of the Century'.

With Abbado and the Berlin Philharmonic providing sensuously beautiful support, Karita Mattila gives one of the most moving of all the many recordings of Strauss's *Four Last Songs*. She is at once youthfully ardent, yet poised and controlled, floating her loveliest, creamy tone in breathtaking pianissimos, as at the start of the final song, *Im Abendrot*. She touches the deeper emotions behind these valedictory pieces, using a wide tonal and dynamic range. Consistently she brings out their mystery, in singing the more intense for being recorded live. The fill-up offers very short measure (50 minutes in all), but the orchestral songs, recorded under studio conditions, bring performances just as commanding. Warm, full sound to match.

Schwarzkopf's 1953 mono version of the *Four Last Songs* comes with both its original coupling, the closing scene from *Capriccio*, also recorded in 1953, and the four major excerpts from *Arabella* which she recorded two years later. The *Four Last Songs* are here less reflective, less sensuous, than in Schwarzkopf's later version with Szell, but the more flowing speeds and the extra tautness and freshness of voice bring equally illuminating performances. Fascinatingly, this separate account of the *Capriccio* scene is even more ravishing than the one in the complete set, and the sound is even fuller, astonishing for its period.

Lisa della Casa with her creamily beautiful soprano was a radiant Straussian, as these precious excerpts demonstrate. Her account of the *Four Last Songs* (given in the original order, not that usually adopted) has a commanding nobility. *Ariadne's Lament* also receives a heartfelt performance, soaring to a thrilling climax, and the *Arabella* duets with Gueden, Schoeffler and Poell are hauntingly tender. For this superb reissue in Decca's Legends series, the transfer has been vastly improved; both voice and orchestra and the ambience of the Grosser Saal in the Musikverein are faithfully caught, with no lack of bloom. A treasurable disc.

Karajan's recording of the closing scene from *Capriccio* with Anna Tomowa-Sintow is a ravishing performance with one of his favourite sopranos responding warmly and sympathetically; if lacking the final touch of individual imagination that such inspired music cries out for, one senses the close rapport between conductor and singer. Similarly in the *Four Last Songs*, Tomowa-Sintow's lovely, creamy-toned singing tends to take second place in the attention, almost as if the voice was a solo instrument in the orchestra, and

the result is undoubtedly very touching. The orchestral version of Strauss's nativity-story song makes an attractive extra item. For this reissue Karajan's 1980 digital account of *Metamorphosen* has been added; it has even greater emotional urgency than his earlier, analogue version.

Renée Fleming with her rich, mature soprano gives warmly sympathetic readings of the *Four Last Songs*, thrilling in climaxes as the voice is allowed to expand, and full of fine detail, even if these readings lack the variety of a Schwarzkopf. The five separate orchestral Lieder also bring a wide expressive range, with *Waldseligkeit* beautifully poised and ending boldly on *Cäcilie*. The singer is not helped by the way that Eschenbach makes the accompaniments seem a little sluggish, polished though the playing is. Something of the same lack of thrust marks his account of Strauss's own arrangement of the *Rosenkavalier* excerpts, despite beautiful playing from the Houston orchestra. How much more welcome would it have been to have had extra items from the singer.

OPERA

Die Aegyptische Helena (complete).

(M) **(*) Decca (ADD) (IMS) 430 381-2 (2). Jones, Hendricks, Kastu, Detroit SO, Dorati.

Dorati, using the original Dresden version of the score, draws magnificent sounds from the Detroit orchestra, richly and forwardly recorded. The vocal sounds are less consistently pleasing. Gwyneth Jones has her squally moments as Helen, though it is a commanding performance. Matti Kastu manages as well as any Heldentenor today in the role of Menelaus, strained at times but with a pleasing and distinctive timbre.

Vienna State Opera: Vol. 5 (1933–43): (i) *Die Aegyptische Helena*: excerpts; (ii) *Daphne*: excerpts; (iii) *Die Frau ohne Schatten*: excerpts.

(M) (***) Koch Schwann mono 3-1455-2 (2). V. State Op. O; with (i) Viorica Ursuleac, Franz Völker, Margit Bokor, Alfred Jerger, Helge Roswaenge, cond. Clemens Krauss; (ii) Maria Reining, Alf Rauch, Anton Dermota, cond. Rudolf Moralt; (iii) Torsten Ralf, Hilde Konetzni, Elisabeth Höngen, Josef Herrmann, Else Schulz, Herbert Alsen, Emmy Loose, Wenko Wenkoff; cond. Karl Boehm.

These excerpts from *Die Aegyptische Helena* from 1933 are conducted by Clemens Krauss, with Franz Völker superb but with Viorica Ursuleac rather raw in the title-role. The *Daphne* excerpts under Rudolf Moralt date from 1942, with Maria Reining below her best but with two excellent tenors, Alf Rauch as Apollo and the lyrical Anton Dermota as Leukippos. Central to this volume is the selection from *Die Frau ohne Schatten* under Karl Boehm, almost an hour and a half of excerpts with Torsten Ralf as the Emperor and Hilde Konetzni as the Empress, though Boehm went on to make two complete recordings of this opera with infinitely better sound. A fascinating pair of discs, just the same, in spite of the very primitive sound.

Arabella (complete).

**(*) Decca (ADD) 460 232-2 (2). Della Casa, Gueden,
London, Edelmann, Dermota, V. State Op. Ch., VPO, Solti.

*** Decca (ADD) 417 623-2 (3). Te Kanawa, Fontana,
Grundheber, Seiffert, Dernesch, Guttstein, ROHCG Ch. &
O, Tate.

(M) (***) DG mono (IMS) 445 342-2 (3). Reining, Hotter,
Della Casa, Taubmann, VPO, Boehm.

Della Casa soars above the stave with the creamiest, most
beautiful sounds and constantly charms one with her swiftly
alternating moods of seriousness and gaiety. Perhaps Solti
does not linger as he might over the waltz rhythms, and it
may be Solti too who prevents Edelmann from making his
first scene with Mandryka as genuinely humorous as it can
be. Edelmann otherwise is superb, as fine a Count as he was
an Ochs in the Karajan *Rosenkavalier*. Gueden, too, is ideally
cast as Zdenka and, if anything, in Act I manages to steal
our sympathies from Arabella, as a good Zdenka can. George
London is on the ungainly side, but then Mandryka is a
boorish fellow anyway. Dermota is a fine Matteo, and Mimi
Coertse makes as much sense as anyone could of the ridiculously difficult part of Fiakermilli, the female yodeller. The
sound is brilliant. It has now been impressively remastered
onto two discs with the break coming just before Milli begins
her yodelling song. However, this set is no longer at mid
price.

Dame Kiri Te Kanawa, in the name-part, gives one of her
very finest opera performances on record. It is a radiant
portrait, languorously beautiful, and it is a pity that so
unsuited a soprano as Gabriele Fontana should have been
chosen as Zdenka next to her, sounding all the more shrill by
contrast. Franz Grundheber makes a firm, virile Mandryka,
Peter Seiffert a first-rate Matteo, while Helga Dernesch is
outstandingly characterful as Arabella's mother. Tate's conducting is richly sympathetic and the Decca recording is first
class.

Recorded live in August 1947 at the Salzburg Festival, the
Boehm recording is a radiant account with an outstanding
cast. Maria Reining is here in firm, true voice, conveying
not just the dignity of the heroine but the depth of feeling
behind her often imperious manner. Hans Hotter too in his
early maturity is in splendid voice, a superb Mandryka,
characterful and well focused. Lisa della Casa, destined to
make the role of Arabella a speciality, is here a charming
Zdenka, fresh and girlish; and the rest of the cast includes
many Viennese stalwarts of the period. Despite the limitations of the orchestral sound and some very rough playing,
it is a most cherishable set.

'Vienna State Opera Live': Vol. 15: (i) *Arabella*: excerpts; (ii) *Friedenstag*: complete; (iii) *Ariadne auf Naxos*: excerpts.

(M) (**) Koch Schwann mono 3-1465-2 (2). (i) Viorica
Ursuleac, Margit Bokor, Alfred Jerger, Adele Kern, Gertrude
Rünger, Richard Mayr; (ii) Hans Hotter, Ursuleac, Herbert
Alsen, Josef Wit, Hermann Wiederman, Mela Bugarinovic;
V. State Op. O; both cond. Clemens Krauss; (iii) Anny
Konetzni, Sev Svanholm, Kern, Else Schulz, Jerger,

Alexander Pichler, Alfred Muzzarelli; V. State Op. O, Rudolf
Moralt.

Strauss's one-Act opera *Friedenstag* was first heard in 1938,
barely a year before the outbreak of the Second World War.
It ends in a triumphalist final ensemble which plainly roused
the audience, and could well do the same in a modern
performance. This is one of only two complete operas in the
May Archive of Vienna State Opera recordings, and in one
brief patch of 30 seconds the sound is totally submerged
beneath the background noise, which remains heavy
throughout. Happily, the voices generally come over well.
Clemens Krauss, to whom the opera was dedicated, is a
warmly responsive interpreter, drawing out the rich lyricism
of this score, not least when his wife, the principal soprano,
Viorica Ursuleac, is singing. Her monologues, as well as the
duets with the heroine's husband, the Commandant of a
besieged fortress, are the high points of the score.

It is also fascinating to have, on the first disc, four extracts
from the first Vienna production of *Arabella*, given only
four months after the Dresden première, with the same
principals and conductor, Krauss again. In 1933 Ursuleac is
even warmer and firmer than in 1938, though the sound is
even more seriously obscured by background noise. The
Ariadne excerpts, recorded in 1941, are also valuable but even
more frustrating, with the extracts fading in and out of big
numbers at awkward moments. The casting too is flawed,
with Anny Konetzni a fruity and none too steady Ariadne,
Else Schulz shrill on top as the Composer, while the brilliant
contribution of the Zerbinetta, Adele Kern, is undermined
by suddenly distant recording.

Ariadne auf Naxos (complete).

⚫ (M) (***) EMI mono CMS5 67077-2 (2) [5 67156].
Schwarzkopf, Schock, Rita Streich, Dönch, Seefried,
Cuénod, Philh. O, Karajan.

*** Ph. 422 084-2 (2). Norman, Varady, Gruberová, Asmus,
Bär, Leipzig GO, Masur.

(M) **(*) Decca (ADD) 460 233-2 (2). Price, Troyanos,
Gruberová, Kollo, Berry, Kunz, LPO, Solti.

(B) **(*) DG Double 453 112-2 (2). Tomowa-Sintow, Battle,
Baltsa, Lakes, Rydl, Prey, Zednik, VPO, Levine.

(M) **(*) EMI (ADD) CMS7 64159-2 (2). Janowitz, Geszty,
Zylis-Gara, King, Schreier, Prey, Dresden State Op. O,
Kempe.

(M) (*(**)) DG (IMS) 445 332-2 (2). Della Casa, Gueden,
Seefried, Schock, Schöffler, VPO, Boehm.

Elisabeth Schwarzkopf makes a radiant, deeply moving
Ariadne, giving as bonus a delicious little portrait of the
Prima Donna in the Prologue. Rita Streich was at her most
dazzling in the coloratura of Zerbinetta's aria and, in partnership with the harlequinade characters, sparkles engagingly. But it is Irmgard Seefried who gives perhaps the
supreme performance of all as the Composer, exceptionally
beautiful of tone, conveying a depth and intensity rarely if
ever matched. Rudolf Schock is a fine Bacchus, strained less
than most, and the team of theatrical characters includes
such stars as Hugues Cuénod as the Dancing Master. The
fine pacing and delectably pointed ensemble add to the
impact of a uniquely perceptive Karajan interpretation.

Though in mono and with the orchestral sound a little dry, the voices come out superbly.

Jessye Norman's is a commanding, noble, deeply felt performance, ranging extraordinarily wide. Julia Varady as the Composer brings out the vulnerability of the character, as well as the ardour, in radiant singing. The Zerbinetta of Edita Gruberová is a thrilling performance and, even if the voice is not always ideally sweet, the range of emotions Gruberová conveys, as in her duet with the Composer, is enchanting. Paul Frey is the sweetest-sounding Bacchus on record yet, while Olaf Bär as Harlekin and Dietrich Fischer-Dieskau in the vignette role of the Music-Master are typical of the fine team of artists here in the smaller character parts. Masur proves a masterly Straussian and he is helped by the typically warm Leipzig recording.

Brilliance is the keynote of Solti's set of *Ariadne*. What the performance is short of is charm and warmth. Nevertheless, Leontyne Price makes a strong central figure, memorably characterful. Tatiana Troyanos is affecting as the composer, and Edita Gruberová establishes herself as the unrivalled Zerbinetta of her generation, though here she is less delicate than on stage. René Kollo similarly is an impressive Bacchus. The new Decca CD transfer is characteristically vivid, although it is not wanting in warmth and atmosphere.

As Ariadne, Tomowa-Sintow with her rich, dramatic soprano adds to the sense of grandeur and movingly brings out the vulnerability of the character. But ultimately she fails to create as fully rounded and detailed a character as her finest rivals, and the voice, as recorded, loses its bloom and creaminess under pressure, marring the big climaxes. Both Agnes Baltsa as the Composer and Kathleen Battle as Zerbinetta are excellent: the one tougher than most rivals with her mezzo-soprano ring, little troubled by the high tessitura, the other delectably vivacious, dazzling in coloratura, but equally finding the unexpected tenderness in the character. The *commedia dell'arte* characters and the attendant theatrical team are strongly taken by stalwarts of the Vienna State Opera, among them Kurt Rydl, Hermann Prey and Heinz Zednik, while the Heldentenor role of Bacchus, always hard to cast, is strongly taken by Gary Lakes, clear-toned and firm, at times pinched but never strained. The very reasonable cost of this set should tempt many collectors to sample this very rewarding opera, particularly when the recording is so warmly flattering to both singers and orchestra.

Kempe's relaxed, languishing performance of this most atmospheric of Strauss operas is matched by opulent recording, warmly transferred to CD. Gundula Janowitz sings with heavenly tone-colour (marred only when hard-pressed at the climax of the Lament), and Teresa Zylis-Gara makes an ardent and understanding Composer. Sylvia Geszty's voice is a little heavy for the fantastic coloratura of Zerbinetta's part, but she sings with charm and assurance. James King presents the part of Bacchus with forthright tone and more taste than do most tenors.

Boehm's affection for this elegant, touching score glows through the whole performance. Lisa della Casa is a poised, tender Ariadne, totally rapt in the final duet with Bacchus. Even though her later studio recordings of the *Lament* are more assured than this, the passion of the climax of that key solo is most involving. As in Karajan's studio recording,

Irmgard Seefried as the Composer and Rudolf Schock as Bacchus have few equals; but what crowns the whole performance is the charming Zerbinetta of Hilde Gueden, not just warmly characterful but fuller-toned than almost any. The snag is the recording, fizzy in the orchestral sound, with even the voices rather thinly recorded.

'Vienna State Opera live': Vol. 23: *Ariadne auf Naxos* (complete).

(M) (***) Koch 3-1473-2 (2). Reining, Seefried, Noni, Lorenz, Schoeffler, Vienna State Op. O, Boehm — WAGNER: *Meistersinger*: excerpts. (**)

Recorded live in June 1944, *Ariadne* is here presented in sound that is astonishingly full-bodied for the period. The sense of presence on the voices is most compelling, and it is fascinating to hear Seefried in the first of her three magnificent recorded performances, singing with, if anything, even more passion than later, in full, firm sound. Maria Reining makes a warm, touching Ariadne, and Max Lorenz as Bacchus has rarely been matched in subsequent recordings, sweeter and less strenuous than most Heldentenoren. Alda Noni makes a bright, mercurial Zerbinetta, not always note-perfect in her coloratura but with plenty of sparkle, and Paul Schoeffler is warm and wise as the Music-master. With 40 minutes of *Meistersinger* excerpts as filler, it is a historic set for non-specialists to consider.

(i) *Ariadne auf Naxos* (excerpts). Lieder: (ii) *Befreit; Einerlei; Hat gesagt; Morgen!; Schlechtes Wetter; Seit dem dein Aug'; Waldseligkeit.*

*** Testament SBT 1036. Della Casa, with (i) Schock, BPO, Erede; (ii) Peschko.

The 1959 stereo recording is full and immediate, bringing out the glories of Della Casa's creamy soprano but failing to convey the full, atmospheric beauty of the music, notably in the echo chorus of Naiads. Della Casa had earlier recorded *Ariadne's Lament* for Decca, but this is even more powerful. The first excerpt is of the opening of the entertainment from the overture through to Ariadne's first solo. There follow her second solo, *Ein Schönes war*, and the *Lament*, while the last extended excerpt has the whole of the final scene from the entry of Bacchus. Rudolf Schock, as in the Karajan version, sings nobly, and Erede brings out the lyrical warmth of the writing. Della Casa is less imaginative in the Strauss Lieder but still sings very beautifully and persuasively. The faithful and full Testament transfers bring out the wide range of the recording, tending to emphasize sibilants in the singing.

Ariadne auf Naxos: Prelude & Final Duet; Elektra: Recognition Scene & Finale.

(N) (M) (***) Preiser 90341. Cebotari, Friedrich; Schluter, Schoffler, Widdop, Welitsch, Ch. & RPO, Beecham.

These two historic opera recordings were made by RCA at the time of the Strauss festival that Beecham organized in London in October 1947. The *Elektra* excerpts, bitingly dramatic, were issued on 78 straight away, but the *Ariadne* excerpts have been kept in limbo, with the ill-fated Maria Cebotari in one of her very rare recordings joined by Karl

Friedrich, a stalwart tenor of the Vienna State Opera at the time, otherwise totally neglected on disc. It makes a generous package, with Beecham not only persuasive in his direction of Strauss but urgently dramatic, adopting speeds in *Elektra* faster than have become the norm, with electrifying results, not least in Elektra's moving recognition of her brother, Oreste. Erna Schluter, singing the title role, may not have had the most beautiful voice, but it is consistently fresh, incisive and accurate. The *Ariadne* excerpts generously offer the final scene from the first offstage entry of Bacchus to the end, though it is a pity that Cebotari was not recorded in Ariadne's Lament. Excellent, undistracting transfers.

Capriccio (complete).

(N) (M) ✿ (***) EMI mono CMS5 67394-2 (2) [567391-2]. Schwarzkopf, Waechter, Gedda, Fischer-Dieskau, Hotter, Ludwig, Moffo, Philh. O, Sawallisch.

(N) *** Forlane 268052 (2). Lott, Allen, Kunde, Genz, von Kannen, Vermillion, SWR Stuttgart Vocal Ens. & Radio SO, Prêtre.

(M) **(*) DG (ADD) 445 347-2 (2). Janowitz, Troyanos, Schreier, Fischer-Dieskau, Prey, Ridderbusch, Bav. RSO, Boehm.

**(*) Orfeo C 518 992 1 (2). Tomowa-Sintow, Schöne, Büchner, Grundheber, Jungwirth, Schmidt, Ridder, Scarabelli, Ballo, Minth, VPO, Stein.

In the role of the Countess in Strauss's last opera, Elisabeth Schwarzkopf has had no equals. This recording, made in 1957 and 1958, brings a peerless performance from her, full of magical detail both in the pointing of words and in the presentation of the character in all its variety. Not only are the other singers ideal choices in each instance, they form a wonderfully co-ordinated team, beautifully held together by Sawallisch's sensitive conducting. As a performance this is never likely to be superseded. This is truly one of EMI's 'Great Recording of the Century' and Andrew Walter's new transfer reveals the naturalness and beauty of the mono sound, both of the voices and the orchestra relatively backwardly balanced Excellent documentation and a full libretto.

Recorded at a series of concert performances in Mannheim in 1999, the Forlane set, with Prêtre an understanding Straussian, offers vivid, immediate sound, giving extra intensity to this inspired 'conversation-piece' on the subject of opera. Central to the set's success is the inspired portrayal of the Countess by Dame Felicity Lott in one of her great roles. Her feeling for the idiom is unerring, and though the closeness of the recording brings out the occasional unevenness under pressure, this will delight Dame Felicity's many admirers. Schwarzkopf may offer an even more thoughtful, more deeply reflective portrayal on the classic EMI set under Sawallisch, and Gundula Janowitz with Boehm on DG is even more radiantly beautiful, but there is a bite to Lott's reading that brings out how formidable the character is. With Thomas Allen ideally cast as the Count, with Gregory Kunde as the composer, Flamand, and Stephan Genz as the poet, Olivier, the supporting cast is first rate, with voices cleanly focused, and conversational exchanges beautifully timed. This team yields only to the even more sharply characterful one on EMI.

On DG, Gundula Janowitz is not as characterful and pointful a Countess as one really needs (and no match for Schwarzkopf), but Boehm lovingly directs a most beautiful performance of a radiant score, very consistently cast, beautifully sung and very well recorded for its period (1971). There is full documentation, including translation.

The Austrian Radio recording from Orfeo offers a warm, rich performance in satisfyingly full sound, made the more compelling for being taken live at a Salzburg Festival performance in August 1985. Tomowa-Sintow sings with poise and tenderness, with the rest of the cast making a strong team. Outstanding is Trudeliese Schmidt as the flamboyant actress Clairon, and Horst Stein is inspired by the beauty of the score to conduct with more passion than in studio recordings. Though the jewel-case promises German and English texts, no libretto is provided, only a detailed synopsis, a serious shortcoming in this of all operas with its complex interchanges.

Capriccio, Op. 85: String Sextet.

*** Hyp. CDA 66704. Ens. – BRUCKNER: *String quintet.* ***
*** Chan. 9131. ASMF Chamber Ens. – ENESCU: *Octet in C*; SHOSTAKOVICH: *2 Pieces for String Octet.* ***

The opening sextet from Strauss's last opera, *Capriccio*, makes an excellent fill-up to the Bruckner *String quintet*. Obviously readers are unlikely to buy the Bruckner for the sake of such a short work, even though it is of great beauty, but those who do will be rewarded by some fine music-making and recording.

The autumnal preface to *Capriccio* is also the expertly played fill-up to Enescu's remarkable *Octet*; very well recorded it is, too.

Capriccio: Prelude. Feuersnot: Love scene. Guntram: Prelude.

*** DG 449 571-2. German Opera, Berlin, O, Thielemann – PFITZNER: *Das Herz* etc. **(*)

These Strauss items, two of them rare, make an excellent coupling for the Pfitzner which Thielemann chose for his début recording with DG. Though in the *Feuersnot* Love scene the orchestra of the Deutsches Opera in Berlin is not quite as poised or refined as the Staatskapelle in Dresden for Sinopoli, the thrust and passion are even greater, with a freer expressiveness. Excellent sound.

Elektra (complete).

✿ *** DG 453 429-2 (2). Marc, Schwarz, Voigt, Jerusalem, Ramey, V. State Op. Konzertvereinigung, VPO, Sinopoli.

*** Decca (ADD) 417 345-2 (2). Nilsson, Collier, Resnik, Stolze, Krause, V. State Op. Ch., VPO, Solti.

(N) (B) ** Ph. Duo 464 985-2 (2). Behrens, Ludwig, Secunde, Ulfson, Hynninen, Matthews, Tanglewood Fest. Ch., Boston SO, Ozawa.

Sinopoli directs an incandescent performance of *Elektra*, at once powerful and sensuous, vividly recorded in full-bodied sound. Alessandra March is here aptly cast in the title-role, instantly establishing her command in the opening monologue, magnetically done. Where she scores even over

Nilsson is in the warmth and beauty of tone. Not only are the dramatic outbursts thrillingly projected with firmly focused tone, she is just as compelling in gentler moments, whether reflecting the creepily sinister side of Elektra's character or in her radiant ecstasy following her recognition of her brother, Orest. The glorious solo ending with the rapturous cry of 'Seliger' ('happier') has never been caught so seductively on disc as here, with Sinopoli drawing glowing playing from the Vienna Philharmonic. Deborah Voigt as Chrysothemis is clear and firm too, well contrasted, and Hanna Schwarz is a powerful Klytemnestra, with bitingly well-focused tone. Having such a fine, heroic tenor as Siegfried Jerusalem in the small role of Aegist is another tribute to the casting, crowned by the choice of Samuel Ramey as a warm and strong Orest, a perfect foil for Alessandra Marc. The performance is rounded off with a thrilling account of the final scene, capturing Elektra's hysterical joy with rare intensity.

Nilsson is almost incomparable in the name-part, with the hard side of Elektra's character brutally dominant. Only when – as in the Recognition scene with Orestes – she tries to soften the naturally bright tone does she let out a suspect flat note or two. As a rule she is searingly accurate in approaching even the most formidable exposed top notes. One might draw a parallel with Solti's direction – sharply focused and brilliant in the savage music which predominates, but lacking the languorous warmth one really needs in the Recognition scene, if only for contrast. The brilliance of the 1967 Decca recording is brought out the more in the newest digital transfer on CD, aptly so in this work. The fullness and clarity are amazing for the period.

Ozawa's version of Elektra was recorded at live performances of the opera in Boston in 1988, using stage cuts. Its great glory is the singing of Hildegard Behrens in the name part, who is perhaps finer here than she has ever been on record. Hers is a portrayal that movingly brings out the tenderness and vulnerability in this character, as well as the unbalanced ferocity. She it is – along with Christa Ludwig, a marvellous foil as Klytemnestra, searingly intense, and letting out a spine-chilling off-stage scream at her murder – who provides the performance's dramatic tension, rather than the conductor.

Though this is a live recording, it lacks the very quality which may justify the inevitable flaws in such a project: an underlying emotional thrust. The tension-building passage leading to Elektra's recognition of Orestes is plodding and prosaic and, against radiant singing from Behrens in the carol of joy which follows, the orchestra might as well be playing a Bruckner slow movement for they provide no emotional underpinning of this supreme moment of fulfilment after pain. The other soloists are disappointing, even Jorma Hynninen who is dry-toned and uningratiating as Orestes. Ragnar Ulfung as Aegistheus is also dry-toned, aptly if unpleasantly so, and Nadine Secunde is far too wobbly as Chrysothemis. Voices are well caught, but the orchestral sound is again too dry to bring out the glory of Strauss's orchestration.

(i) *Elektra: Soliloquy; Recognition Scene; Finale. Salome: Dance of the Seven Veils; Finale.*

(M) *** RCA (ADD) 09026 68636-2. Borkh, Chicago SO, Reiner; (i) with Schoeffler, Yeend, Chicago Lyric Theatre Ch.

With Borkh singing superbly in the title-role alongside Paul Schoeffler and Francis Yeend, this is a real collectors' piece. Reiner provides a superbly telling accompaniment; the performance of the Recognition scene and final duet are as ripely passionate as Beecham's old 78-r.p.m. excerpts and outstrip the complete versions. The orchestral sound is thrillingly rich, the brass superbly expansive. For the reissue, Reiner's full-blooded account of Salome's Dance has been added, and Borkh is comparably memorable in the finale scene. No Straussian should miss this disc.

Feuersnot (complete).

(B) *** Arts 47546-2 (2). Varady, Weikl, Bergere-Tuna, Tölz Boys' Ch., Bav. R. Ch., Munich RO, Fricke.

Feuersnot, Strauss's second opera, which was first given in 1901, is an allegory with an element of satire, set in medieval times. Like his first (*Guntram*) it is opulently scored, and in three compact Acts tells its story of Kunrad, a young sorcerer who, when rejected and ridiculed, puts a curse on the town, extinguishing all fire and light. This Bavarian Radio recording made in 1985 fills an important gap and is the more welcome on a bargain label. The performance is a fine one, with Bernd Weikl as Kunrad and Julia Varady as Dimut, his beloved, the Mayor's daughter – both outstanding. Heinz Fricke directs a warmly expressive performance in well-balanced digital radio sound. Recommended.

Die Frau ohne Schatten.

⊛ *** Decca 436 243-2 (3). Behrens, Varady, Domingo, Van Dam, Runkel, Jo, VPO, Solti.

(M) (**(*)) DG mono 457 678-2 (3). Rysanek, Hoffman, Ludwig, Thomas, Berry, Popp, Wunderlich, V. State Op. Ch. & O, Karajan.

In the Heldentenor role of the Emperor, Plácido Domingo, the superstar tenor, gives a performance that is not only beautiful to the ear beyond previous recordings but which has an extra feeling for expressive detail, deeper than that which was previously recorded. Hildegard Behrens as the Dyer's wife is also a huge success. Her very feminine vulnerability is here a positive strength, and the voice has rarely sounded so beautiful on record. Julia Varady as the Empress is equally imaginative, with a beautiful voice, and José van Dam with his clean, dark voice brings a warmth and depth of expression to the role of Barak, the Dyer, which goes with a satisfyingly firm focus. Reinhild Runkel in the key role of the Nurse is well in character, with her mature, fruity sound. Eva Lind is shrill in the tiny role of the Guardian of the Threshold, but there is compensation in having Sumi Jo as the Voice of the Falcon. With the Vienna Philharmonic surpassing themselves, and the big choral ensembles both well disciplined and warmly expressive, this superb recording is unlikely to be matched, let alone surpassed, for many years. Solti himself is inspired throughout.

The 1964 Karajan recording from Austrian Radio captures the intensity of the live occasion, with ecstatic applause for each of the Acts. With orchestral sound in mono thin and limited (a serious shortcoming in Strauss) the voices are paramount, with words made the clearer by the closeness. The cast is an outstanding one, with Leonie Rysanek powerful as the Empress and Jess Thomas exploiting his cleanly focused Heldentenor as the Emperor. The young Walter Berry is firmly commanding as Barak, the Dyer; and best of all is Christa Ludwig as the Dyer's Wife, here early in her career singing with a freshness and intensity that she retained in her later studio recording with Solti for Decca. The mono sound is limited, but with voices well caught. The usual stage-cuts are made in this epic score.

Friedenstag (complete).

*** EMI CDC5 56850-2. Weikl, Hass, Rhyhänen, Moll, Bav.
State Op. Ch. & RSO, Sawallisch.

Long neglected but full of the ripest inspiration, *Friedenstag*, dating from 1936, is the odd-one-out among Strauss operas in having no love interest. On a single disc, EMI offers a live recording of a superb performance conducted by Sawallisch in 1988. It was first given with Hans Hotter as the Commandant and Viorica Ursuleac as his wife Maria in 1938, and their partnership under Clemens Krauss survives from a recording made the following year – in Volume 15 of the Vienna State Opera Live Recordings (see above). This new EMI recording derives from a broadcast taken from the Staatsoper, Munich, with one of the greatest living Strauss conductors at the helm and a magnificent cast. Bernd Weikl, singing nobly, is a superbly authoritative Commandant and Sabine Hass, in radiant voice, sings powerfully as Maria, whose attempts to dissuade her husband from his inflexibility and dedication to duty are affectingly portrayed. She tackles the role's cruel demands with apparently effortless ease. Kurt Moll, the Hollsteiner, Commander of the besieging army, has impressive dignity and eloquence. *Friedenstag* is half-oratorio, half-opera, whose dramatic action is of the simplest. The chorus is in impressive form and Sawallisch gets a first-class response from the fine Munich orchestra.

Guntram (complete)

(BB) ** Arte Nova 74321 61339-2 (2). Woodrow, Wachutka,
Konsulov, Scheidegger, Marchigiana PO, Kuhn.

Strauss's very first opera, set in the age of chivalry, is an opulent piece, unashamed in its high romanticism. On the Arte Nova label Gustan Kuhn conducts a warm, thrustful performance, recorded live at Garmisch-Partenkirchen, with the rich orchestral tapestries beautifully caught in open, refined sound, only occasionally disturbed by audience noises. Alan Woodrow makes a strong Guntram, with his firm Heldentenor tone only occasionally strained. Elisabeth Wachutka with her fruity soprano sounds too mature for the heroine, Freihild, and none of the other singers quite matches those in the currently withdrawn rival version on Sony, but this makes an excellent super-bargain set for those wanting to sample this opera inexpensively, although we hope the preferable CBS/Sony set will soon return to the catalogue.

Intermezzo (complete).

*** EMI (ADD) CDS7 49337-2 (2). Popp, Brammer,
Fischer-Dieskau, Bav. RSO, Sawallisch.

The central role of *Intermezzo* was originally designed for the dominant and enchanting Lotte Lehmann; but it is doubtful whether even she can have outshone the radiant Lucia Popp, who brings out the charm of a character who, for all his incidental trials, must have consistently captivated Strauss and provoked this strange piece of self-revelation. The piece inevitably is very wordy, but with this scintillating and emotionally powerful performance under Sawallisch, with fine recording and an excellent supporting cast, this set is as near ideal as could be, a superb achievement. The CD transfer is well managed but – unforgivably in this of all Strauss operas – no translation is given with the libretto, a very serious omission.

Intermezzo: Symphonic Interludes.

*** Chan. 9357. Detroit SO, Järvi – SCHMIDT: *Symphony
No. 1*. ***

Neeme Järvi is an underrated Straussian and here he proves equal to the very best. He and his Detroit musicians give a thoroughly persuasive account of the interludes Strauss extracted from *Intermezzo*, and this comes as a generous fill-up to Schmidt's derivative but delightful *First Symphony*. Strongly recommended.

Die Liebe der Danae (complete).

(N) **(*) Telarc CD 80570 (3). Flanigan, Coleman-Wright,
Smith, Lewis, Saffer, NY Concert Chorale, American SO,
Botstein.

Strauss's penultimate opera has in many ways been the unluckiest of all. Written at the beginning of the Second World War, it was given only a private performance in the composer's lifetime – in Salzburg in 1944 – and was quickly dismissed when it finally reached the stage in Salzburg in 1952. It has never recovered, yet this stereo recording of a highly enjoyable concert performance given in New York, with Leon Botstein as conductor, amply demonstrates what riches the piece contains.

Die Liebe der Danae is an ingenious conflation – originally suggested by Hugo von Hofmannsthal – of two myths involving gold, the legend of Midas and the golden touch, and Jupiter's seduction of Danae in the guise of golden rain. Sadly, Joseph Gregor as librettist had little of the finesse of Hofmannsthal, but what emerges from this concert performance is that in defiance of the whimsy of the libretto the big emotional confrontations inspired Strauss to the most seductive writing, rich and lyrical, often anticipating *Capriccio*.

The scale is formidable, with a climactic final duet between Danae and Jupiter of Wagnerian grandeur, echoing the farewells of Wotan and Brünnhilde. The love duets too between Danae and Midas – true love more valuable than gold – are movingly tender, with the tenor for once in Strauss an equal partner. Their duet in Act II ends terrifyingly, when Midas, embracing Danae, unwittingly turns her into a golden statue.

Leon Botstein, a dedicated advocate of the piece, conducts a loving performance with his excellent cast. As Danae, Lauren Flanigan has ample richness and power, yet remains girlish, while Hugh Smith makes an engaging Midas, fresh and unstrained, with Peter Coleman-Wright in the difficult role of Jupiter repeating his formidable Garsington interpretation. The quartet of queens – all of them, like Leda and Semele, seduced by Jupiter in their time – and the quartet of kings are beautifully integrated, and Lisa Saffer is outstanding as Xanthe, Danae's maid, who has just one ravishing and very demanding duet with her mistress in Act I. First-rate chorus work. Though the clean if rather dry recording fails to do justice to the sumptuous scoring, with voices to the fore, the result is still magnetic, a fine stopgap until we get an all-star version.

Der Rosenkavalier (complete).

⦿ (M) *** EMI (ADD) CDM5 67605-2 (3). Schwarzkopf, Ludwig, Stich-Randall, Edelmann, Waechter, Philh. Ch. & O, Karajan.

*** EMI CDS7 54259-2 (3). Te Kanawa, Von Otter, Rydl, Grundheber, Hendricks, Dresden Op. Ch., Dresden Boys' Ch., Dresden State O, Haitink.

**(*) Decca (ADD) 417 493-2 (3). Crespin, Minton, Jungwirth, Donath, Wienr, V. State Op. Ch., VPO, Solti.

**(*) DG 423 850-2 (3). Tomowa-Sintow, Baltsa, Moll, Perry, Hornik, VPO Ch. & O, Karajan.

(N) (M) (**(*)) Decca mono 467 111-2 (3). Reining, Jurinac, Gueden, Weber, Poell, Dermota, V. State Op. Ch., VPO, Erich Kleiber.

(B) (**) Naxos mono 8.110034/36 (3). Lehmann, Stevens, Farrell, List, Schorr, Met. Op.Ch. & O, Bodanzky (with Lieder Recital of 5/8/1948): Lehmann with Phd. O, Ormandy: *Allerseelen; Morgen; Traum durch die Dämmerung; Zueignung.* (Commentary: Little) – SCHUBERT: *Ständchen.* BRAHMS: *Wiegenlied* (both with piano).

Karajan's 1956 version, one of the greatest of all opera recordings, is in a class of its own, with the patrician refinement of Karajan's spacious reading combining with an emotional intensity that he has rarely equalled, even in Strauss, of whose music he remains a supreme interpreter. Matching that achievement is the incomparable portrait of the Marschallin from Schwarzkopf, bringing out detail as no one else can, yet equally presenting the breadth and richness of the character, a woman still young and attractive. Christa Ludwig with her firm, clear mezzo tone makes an ideal, ardent Octavian and Teresa Stich-Randall a radiant Sophie, with Otto Edelmann a winningly characterful Ochs, who yet sings every note clearly. This has now rightly been reissued (at mid-price) as one of EMI's 'Great Recordings of the Century', with sound further enhanced.

Vocally the biggest triumph of Haitink's beautifully paced reading is the Octavian of Anne Sofie von Otter, not only beautifully sung but acted with a boyish animation to make most rivals sound very feminine by comparison. If the first great – and predictable – glory of Dame Kiri's assumption of the role of the Marschallin is the sheer beauty of the sound, the portrait she paints is an intense and individual one, totally convincing. The portrait of Sophie from Barbara Hendricks is a warm and moving one, but less completely satisfying, if only because her voice is not quite so pure as one needs for this young, innocent girl. Kurt Rydl with his warm and resonant bass makes a splendid Baron Ochs, not

always ideally steady, but giving the character a magnificent scale and breadth. Whatever the detailed reservations over the singing, it is mainly due to Bernard Haitink that this is the most totally convincing and heartwarming recording of *Rosenkavalier* since Karajan's 1956 set. This recording, unlike the Karajan, opens out the small stage cuts sanctioned by the composer.

The current remastering of the Solti *Der Rosenkavalier* from the late 1960s has brought the most striking improvement in the sound among all the Decca reissues of his Strauss opera series and there is now body and ambient warmth, so essential for this gloriously ripe score. The VPO strings have a lovely sheen, yet inner detail is glowingly clear. Crespin is here at her finest on record, with tone well focused; the slightly maternal maturity of her approach will appear for many ideal. Mandfred Jungwirth makes a firm and virile, if not always imaginative Ochs, Yvonne Minton a finely projected Octavian and Helen Donath a sweet-toned Sophie. Solti's direction is fittingly honeyed, with tempi even slower than Karajan in the climactic meoments. The one serious disappointment is that the great concluding Trio does not quite lift one to the tear-laden height one ideally wants. Even so this *Rosenkavalier* offers much to ravish the ear.

Karajan's digital set brings few positive advantages. For the principal role he chose Anna Tomowa-Sintow; the refinement and detail in her performance present an intimate view of the Marschallin, often very beautiful indeed, but both the darker and more sensuous sides of the character are muted. The Baron Ochs of Kurt Moll, firm, dark and incisive, is outstanding, and Agnes Baltsa as Octavian makes the lad tough and determined, if not always sympathetic. Janet Perry's Sophie, charming and pretty on stage, is too white and twittery of tone to give much pleasure.

Now reissued in the Legends series, Decca's set conducted by Eric Kleiber was the first ever complete recording of *Rosenkavalier*, and it has long enjoyed cult status. Sena Jurinac is a charming Octavian, strong and sympathetic, and Hilde Gueden a sweetly characterful Sophie, not just a wilting innocent. Ludwig Weber characterizes deliciously in a very Viennese way as Ochs; but the disappointment is the Marschallin of Maria Reining, very plain and lacking intensity. She is not helped by Kleiber's refusal to linger; with the singers recorded close, the effect of age on what was once a fine voice is very clear, even in the opening solo of the culminating trio. And ensemble is not good, with even the prelude to Act I a muddle. Even with the latest remastering, it is the prelude more than anywhere in which the CD transfer brings out a thinness in the strings and a lack of amplitude in the orchestral sound, although because of the warm ambience of the Grosser Saal of the Musikverein one adjusts fairly quickly, and the voices are well caught.

Here with a live performance, recorded at the Met. in 1939 on acetate discs, Naxos fill in many of the gaps in EMI's classic recording of Lehmann as the Marschallin, made earlier in Vienna. The orchestral sound is thin and variable, the swishing surface noise often intrusive, but the voices are surprisingly well caught, with Lehmann rich, firm and true, giving a commanding performance, cherishable in every detail. Risë Stevens at the beginning of her career makes a clear, positive Octavian, an excellent foil, characterizing well, and Marita Fareli as Sophie is bright and clear. The presentation of the silver rose scene is clean and accurate, with fine attack, but remains dry-eyed, lacking tenderness. Emanual List is a splendid Ochs, never letting the comedy undermine vocal lines, even if he is challenged at both top and bottom of the range. Friedrich Schorr is a commanding Faninal – luxury casting. Artur Bodzansky is an efficient conductor, opting for fastish speeds. In the manner of the day the score is savagely cut, with even the big ensemble reprise of the main waltz-theme omitted before the final scene. There is a brief Lieder recital from Lotte Lehmann as a bonus.

Der Rosenkavalier (complete; remastered under direction of Schwarzkopf).

(M) (**(*)) EMI mono CMS5 56113-2 (3). Schwarzkopf, Ludwig, Stich-Randall, Edelmann, Philh. Ch. & O, Karajan.

It was at the urgent request of Schwarzkopf herself that this original mono version of Karajan's classic set of *Rosenkavalier* was transferred to CD in a remastering she herself approved. The main contrast with the stereo version – itself subject to several remasterings over the years – is that the voices are more sharply focused and, as it seems, more forwardly placed. One can understand Schwarzkopf's preference, but the orchestral sound in the stereo version is warmer, fuller and richer, and will certainly be preferred by the majority of collectors.

(i) Der Rosenkavalier (abridged version); Lieder: (ii) All' mein Gedanken; Freundliche Vision; Die Heiligen drei Könige; Heimkehr; Ich schwebe; Des Knaben Wunderhorn: Hat gesagt . . .; Morgen; Muttertändelei; Schlechtes Wetter; Ständchen (2 versions); Traum durch die Dämmerung; (iii) Mit deinen blauen Augen; Morgen; Ständchen; Traum durch die Dämmerung.

(M) (***) EMI mono CHS7 64487-2 (2). (i) Lehmann, Schumann, Mayr, Olszewska, Madin, V. State Op. Ch., VPO, Heger; (ii) Schumann; (iii) Lehmann (with var. accompanists).

It is good to have a fresh CD transfer, immaculate in quality, of this classic, abridged, early recording of *Der Rosenkavalier*, containing some 100 minutes of music, made in 1933 in Vienna. Lotte Lehmann as the Marschallin and Elisabeth Schumann as Sophie remain uniquely characterful and, though 78-r.p.m. side-lengths brought some hastening from Heger, notably in the great trio of Act III, the passion of the performance still conveys a sense of new discovery, a rare Straussian magic. There is no libretto, but a synopsis is cued with each excerpt. As a bonus we are offered a glorious Lieder recital, featuring both the principal sopranos, and demonstrating Lehmann's darker timbre, the richness immediately noticeable at her first song, the lovely *Mit deinen blauen Augen*. Versions of *Traume durch die Dämmerung* and the soaring *Ständchen are* sung by both artists, and two different Schumann performances are included of the latter: one (from 1927) fresh and lilting, the other (from 1930) faster and with much clearer sound. *Heimkehr* (1938) is ravishing, and *Die Heiligen drei Könige*, from ten years earlier, with a

remarkably well-recorded orchestral accompaniment, is also memorable. No song translations are included, and this is among the sets currently deleted by EMI.

Der Rosenkavalier: highlights.

(M) *** EMI CDM5 65571-2. Schwarzkopf, Ludwig, Stich-Randall, Edelmann, Waechter, Philh. Ch. & O, Karajan.

On EMI we are offered the Marschallin's monologue to the end of Act I (25 minutes); the Presentation of the silver rose and finale from Act II; and the Duet and Closing scene, with the Trio from Act III, flawlessly and gloriously sung and transferred most beautifully to CD. A superb disc in every way.

Der Rosenkavalier: highlights (in English).

(M) **(*) Chan. 3022. Kenny, Montague, Joshua, Tomlinson, Shore, Mitchell Ch., Kay Children's Ch., LPO, Parry.

This generous 80-minute selection from *Der Rosenkavalier* sung in English, reflects the strength of English National Opera's highly successful stage production. David Parry paces the score most persuasively, and the orchestral sound is aptly sumptuous, if a little clouded on detail. The selection of items, concentrating on the beginnings and endings of Acts, cannot be faulted, except that John Tomlinson's strongly characterized Baron Ochs – with nobility part of the mixture – is represented only by the end of Act II, with its great Waltz theme. One snag is, that the recording tends to exaggerate the singers' vibratos, intrusively so only with Yvonne Kenny as the Marschallin. She is strong but not very warm with such a noticeable flutter in the voice. On the other hand, Diana Montague is a winningly expressive Octavian, and Rosemary Joshua a sweet-toned Sophie. The booklet includes full text in the English version of Alfred Kalisch.

Der Rosenkavalier Suite.

(N) *** BBC (ADD) BBCL 4038. Hallé O, Barbirolli – HAYDN: *Symphony No. 83 in G min. (La Poule)*; LEHAR: *Gold and Silver*; JOHANN STRAUSS JNR *Emperor Waltz* etc. ***

A glorious performance from Barbirolli with the kind of affectionate attention to detail which all but disguises the fact that this is a musical patchwork. The horns and strings of the Hallé Orchestra excel themselves in a performance that is full of uninhibited ardour, yet the *Presentation of the Rose* sequence is lovingly tender, and the final *Trio* full of bliss.

Salome (complete).

*** DG. 431 810-2 (2). Studer, Rysanek, Terfel, Hiestermann, German Opera, Berlin, Ch. & O, Sinopoli.

*** Chan. 9611 (2). Nielsen, Hale, Goldberg, Silja, Danish National RSO, Schonwandt.

*** Decca (ADD) 414 414-2 (2). Nilsson, Hoffman, Stolze, Kmentt, Waechter, VPO, Solti.

*** EMI CDS7 49358-8 (2). Behrens, Bohme, Baltsa, Van Dam, VPO, Karajan.

(M) *** RCA (ADD) GD 86644 (2). Caballé, Lewis, Resnik,
  Milnes, LSO, Leinsdorf.
*** Decca 444 178-2 (2). Malfitano, Terfel, Riegel, Schwarz,
  Begley, VPO, Dohnányi.
(M) **(*) DG (IMS) (ADD) 445 319-2 (2). Jones,
  Fischer-Dieskau, Dunn, Cassilly, Hamburg State Op. O,
  Boehm.

The glory of Sinopoli's DG version is the singing of Cheryl
Studer as Salome, producing glorious sounds throughout.
Her voice is both rich and finely controlled, with delicately
spun pianissimos that chill you the more for their beauty, not
least in Salome's attempted seduction of John the Baptist.
Sinopoli's reading is often unconventional in its speeds, but
it is always positive, thrusting and full of passion, the most
opulent account on disc, matched by full, forward recording.
As Jokanaan, Bryn Terfel makes a compelling recording
début, strong and noble, though the prophet's voice as heard
from the cistern sounds far too distant. Among modern sets
this makes a clear first choice, though Solti's vintage Decca
recording remains the most firmly focused, with the keenest
sense of presence, especially in the newly remastered version.

With an outstanding cast, the Chandos version, superbly
recorded in co-operation with the Danish Broadcasting Corporation, stands out among modern digital versions. Inga
Nielsen is a superb Salome, pingingly precise in her vocal
attack, with an apt hint of acid in the voice but always firm,
with no shrillness. The result is a portrayal with all the
strength needed, not least for the unrelenting malevolence
at the end, but leaving one with the impression of a character
still young. Robert Hale is a characterful and expressive,
if at times gruff, Jokanaan, and the Heldentenor, Reiner
Goldberg, and the veteran Anja Silja, make an exceptionally
strong, well-characterized duo as Herod and Herodias.
Smaller roles are also well cast.

Birgit Nilsson is splendid throughout; she is hard-edged
as usual but, on that account, more convincingly wicked:
the determination and depravity are latent in the girl's
character from the start. Of this score Solti is a master. He
has rarely sounded so abandoned in a recorded performance.
Waechter makes a clear, young-sounding Jokanaan. Gerhardt Stolze portrays the unbalance of Herod with frightening conviction, and Grace Hoffman does all she can in
the comparatively ungrateful part of Herodias. The vivid
CD projection makes the final scene, where Salome kisses
the head of John the Baptist in delighted horror (*I have
kissed thy mouth, Jokanaan!*), all the more spine-tingling,
with a close-up effect of the voice whispering almost in one's
ear.

Hildegard Behrens is also a triumphantly successful
Salome. The sensuous beauty of tone is conveyed ravishingly, but the recording is not always fair to her fine projection of sound, occasionally masking the voice. All the same,
the feeling of a live performance has been captured well, and
the rest of the cast is of the finest Salzburg standard. In
particular José van Dam makes a gloriously noble Jokanaan,
and in the early scenes his offstage voice from the cistern at
once commands attention. Karajan – as so often in Strauss
– is at his most commanding and sympathetic, with the
orchestra, more forward than some will like, playing raptur-

ously. This is a performance which, so far from making
one recoil from perverted horrors, has one revelling in
sensuousness.

Montserrat Caballé's formidable account of the role of
Salome was recorded in 1968, utterly different from that of
Birgit Nilsson on Decca and much closer to the personification of Behrens on the Karajan set on EMI. For some
listeners Caballé might seem too gentle, but in fact the range
of her emotions is even wider than that of Nilsson. There
are even one or two moments of fantasy, where for an instant
one has the girlish skittishness of Salome revealed like an
evil inverted picture of Sophie. As for the vocalization, it is
superb, with a glorious golden tone up to the highest register
and never the slightest hesitation in attack. Lewis, Resnik
and Milnes make a supporting team that matches the
achievement of the Decca rivals, while Leinsdorf is inspired
to some of his warmest and most sympathetic conducting
on record.

Dohnányi's is a clear, sharply focused reading, in full-
ranging sound more refined than any. With the orchestra
set further behind the voices than usual in Decca opera
recordings, the violence is to a degree underplayed and the
chamber quality of the score (intended by Strauss) enhanced. Catherine Malfitano brings out the girlish element
in Salome, while also bringing out her malevolence. The
beat in her voice can be distracting, occasionally turning
into a wobble, but she rises superbly to the final scene, with
full power and precision, a thrilling climax. As Jokanaan,
Bryn Terfel is even finer than he was for Sinopoli, rich and
firm, with the voice of the prophet from the cistern clearly
focused. Kenneth Riegel as a neurotic Herod, Hanna
Schwarz as a powerful, sharply dramatic Herodias and Kim
Begley as a ringing Narraboth are all outstanding.

In this violent opera Boehm conducts a powerful, purposeful performance which in its rhythmic drive and spontaneity is most compelling, not least in *Salome's Dance*, which
seems a necessary component rather than an inserted showpiece. Gwyneth Jones, though squally at times, is here at her
most incisive, and her account of the final scene is chilling,
above all when she drains her voice for the moment of
pianissimo triumph, having kissed the dead lips of Jokanaan.
Fischer-Dieskau characteristically gives a searchingly detailed, totally authoritative performance as John the Baptist:
one believes in him as a prophet possessed. With Richard
Cassilly as a powerful Herod, the rest of the cast is strong,
making this a fair contender among live recordings.

Die schweigsame Frau (complete).

(M) (***) DG (IMS) mono 445 335-2 (2). Gueden, Wunderlich,
  Prey, Hotter, VPO, Boehm.
**(*) Orfeo stereo C 516 992 (2). Böhme, Mödl, McDaniel,
  Kusche, Grobe, Grist, Schädle, Loulis, Peter, Proebstl,
  Bellgardt, Strauch, Horn, Schreiber, Bav. State Ch. and O,
  Sawallisch.
(M) **(*) EMI (SIS) CMS5 66033-2 (3). Adam, Scovotti,
  Burmeister, Trudeliese Schmidt, Dresden State Op. Ch. &
  State O, Janowski.

With a cast that could hardly be bettered, Boehm masterfully
relishes the high spirits as well as the classical elegance of

this late Strauss opera and, though the acoustic is dry and stage noises are often fearsomely intrusive, the sense of presence on the voices makes it consistently involving. Hans Hotter in his prime makes a wonderfully bluff curmudgeon, pointing every word characterfully. Hilde Gueden – greeted with wild applause on her first entry along with Fritz Wunderlich – is a deliciously minx-ish heroine, using her distinctive golden tone, while the young Wunderlich gives a glorious performance. As the barber who aids the conspiratorial young couple against the old man, Hermann Prey has rarely sounded stronger or more beautiful on disc.

Recorded live at the Bavarian State opera in July 1971, this performance consistently demonstrates the mastery of Sawallisch as a Strauss interpreter. The orchestral sound is atmospheric if rather thin, and stage noises are often intrusive, but one can still readily appreciate how perfectly Sawallisch paces this adaptation of Ben Jonson's *The Silent Woman* to bring out not just the humour and vigour but the beauty of the score. Reri Grist is a charming heroine, with the edge on her bright soprano making her the more compelling as a scold. Kurt Böhme right at the end of his long career sings most characterfully as the old man, Sir Morosus, with the supporting team consistently strong. An enjoyable alternative to Karl Boehm on DG and Marek Janowski on EMI, though only the latter (on three discs, not two) offers the score without cuts. Disappointingly, despite the promise of German, English and French texts, no libretto is provided, only a synopsis.

Janowski conducts an efficient rather than a magical performance, and Theo Adam's strongly characterized rendering of the central role of Dr Morosus is marred by his unsteadiness. Jeanette Scovotti is agile but shrill as the Silent Woman, Aminta. A valuable set of mixed success. The CD transfer brings the usual advantages but underlines the oddities of the recording. The reissue (unlike the previous full-priced set) includes a libretto/booklet with full English translation.

COLLECTIONS

'Famous Scenes' from: (i) *Arabella*; (ii) *Ariadne auf Naxos*; (iii) *Elektra*; (iv) *Die Frau ohne Schatten*; (iv) *Der Rosenkavalier*; (v) *Salome* (with (vi) *Dance of the Seven Veils*).

(N) (M) ** Decca (ADD) 458 250-2. (i) Della Casa, Gueden, VPO; (ii) Price, Gruberová, McDaniel, LPO; (iii) Nilsson; VPO, Solti; all cond. Solti; (iv) Crespin, Gueden, Söderström; Varviso; (iv) Rysanek, Hellwig; Boehm; (v) Silja; VPO, Dohnányi or (vi) Karajan (all with VPO).

This is a mixed collection of Strauss scenes: not exactly an easy composer for stringing together pop hits – as can be seen here from somewhat dramatic fades which, out of necessity, affect several times. They are rather disconcerting, but once you get into the 'groove' of each track, it is generally enjoyable, for Decca has a rich catalogue to draw upon. The great Trio from Act III of *Der Rosenkavalier* is with Crespin, Gueden and Söderström (Varviso conducting); Nilsson's incomparable *Elektra*; The *Dance of the Seven Veils* (VPO/

Karajan); Leontyne Price in *Ariadne auf Naxos* (though she has sung more beautifully), and Della Casa and Gueden in *Arabella*. The closing number is a disappointment: the finale of *Salome* with Anja Silja, recorded in 1973 and conducted by Dohnányi. Silja is certainly a vibrant singer with a strong personality, but the technical flaws in her singing tend to damp one's enthusiasm. Full texts and translations are included in this Opera Gala release.

Arias and scenes from: *Ariadne auf Naxos; Capriccio; Die Liebe der Danae; Salome.*

(N) *** Orfeo C 511991A. Varady, Bamberg SO, Fischer-Dieskau.

Recorded just before Julia Varady's retirement in 1999, still at the height of her powers, this wide-ranging collection of excerpts contains some of the most magnificent Strauss singing in years. The wonder is that any soprano can range so wide, while producing the most beautiful, full and even stream of sound, whether in the closing scene of *Salome*, in Ariadne's monologue and lament, in the heroine's big Act III solo from *Die Liebe der Danae* or as the Countess in the closing scene of *Capriccio*. Helped by the understanding conducting of her husband, Dietrich Fischer-Dieskau – who contributes a solitary line of singing as major domo at the end of *Capriccio*– she sings with consistent fervour. This *Salome* may not be as sinister as many in kissing the lips of John the Baptist – the sound is too beautiful for that – but the poise as well as the power and the detailed expressiveness are magnetic. Excellent sound to match.

'Strauss's Heroines': *Arabella*, Act I: *Duet. Capriccio: Moonlight Music* and closing scene. *Der Rosenkavalier*, Act I: closing scene, Act III, *Trio* and finale.

*** Decca 466 314-2. Fleming, Bonney, Graham, VPO, Eschenbach.

Under the title 'Strauss's heroines', this ravishing disc offers a generous collection of the most seductive scenes in the Strauss operas. In the end of Act I of *Rosenkavalier*, Renée Fleming and Susan Graham come near to matching the example of Elisabeth Schwarzkopf and Christa Ludwig as the Marschallin and Octavian. Then, sadly, the Act III Trio has Christoph Eschenbach opting for an absurdly sluggish speed, but the singing is superb, and so it is in the lovely duet between the sisters in *Arabella* and the magical closing scene of *Capriccio*, where Fleming is at her most moving. Opulent sound to match.

STRAVINSKY, Igor (1882–1971)

The Stravinsky Edition: Vol. 1, Ballets, etc.: (i) *The Firebird*; (i) *Fireworks*; (iii) *Histoire du soldat*; (i) *Petrushka*; (iv, iii) *Renard the Fox*; (i) *The Rite of Spring*; (i) *Scherzo à la russe*; (ii) *Scherzo fantastique*; (v) *The Wedding (Les Noces)* (SM3K 46291) (3).

Vol. 2, Ballets etc.: (vi) *Agon*; (i) *Apollo*; (i) *Le Baiser de la fée*; (i) *Bluebird (pas de deux)*; (vii) *Jeu de cartes*; (viii) *Orphée*; (ix, i) *Pulcinella*; (ii) *Scènes de ballet* (SM3K 46292) (3).

Vol. 3, Ballet suites: (i) *Firebird; Petrushka; Pulcinella* (SMK 45293).

Vol. 4, Symphonies: (i) *Symphony in E*; (ii) *Symphony in C*; (i) *Symphony in 3 movements*; (x, ii) *Symphony of Psalms*; (i) Stravinsky in rehearsal: *Apollo; Piano Concerto; Pulcinella; Sleeping Beauty; Symphony in C; 3 Souvenirs* (SM2K 46294).

Vol. 5, Concertos: (xi, i) *Capriccio for Piano & Orchestra* (with Robert Craft); *Concerto for Piano & Wind*; (xii; i) *Movements for Piano & Orchestra*; (xiii; i) *Violin Concerto in D* (SMK 46295).

Vol. 6, Miniatures: (i) *Circus Polka; Concerto in D for String Orchestra; Concerto for Chamber Orchestra, 'Dumbarton Oaks'*; (ii) *4 Etudes for Orchestra*; (i) *Greeting Prelude*; (ii) *8 Instrumental miniatures; 4 Norwegian moods; Suites Nos. 1–2 for Small Orchestra* (SMK 46296).

Vol. 7, Chamber music and historical recordings: (iii) *Concertino for 12 Instruments*; (xiv; xv) *Concerto for 2 solo Pianos*; (xv; xvi) *Duo concertante for Violin & Piano*; (xvii; xviii) *Ebony Concerto (for Clarinet & Big Band)*; (iii) *Octet for Wind*; (xix; iii) *Pastorale for Violin & Wind Quartet*; (xv) *Piano Rag Music*; (xviii) *Preludium*; (xx; iii) *Ragtime (for 11 instruments)*; (xv) *Serenade in A*; (iii) *Septet*; (xii) *Sonata for Piano*; (xxi) *Sonata for 2 Pianos*; (xviii) *Tango*; (xxii) *Wind Symphonies* (SM2K 46297).

Vol. 8, Operas and songs: (xxiii; iii) *Cat's cradle songs*; (xxiii; xxiv) *Elegy for J. F. K.*; (xxv; ii) *Faun and shepherdess*; (xxvi; iii) *In memoriam Dylan Thomas*; (xxvii; iii) *3 Japanese Lyrics* (with Robert Craft); (xxvii; xxix) *The owl and the pussycat*; (xxvii; iii) *2 poems by K. Bal'mont*; (xxx; i) *2 poems of Paul Verlaine*; (xxiii; i) *Pribaoutki (peasant songs)*; (xxiii; i) *Recollections of my childhood*; (xxviii; xxxi) *4 Russian songs*; (xxxvii) *4 Russian peasant songs*; (xxiii; iii) *3 songs from William Shakespeare*; (xxvii; i) *Tilim-Bom (3 stories for children)*; (xxxii) *Mavra*; (xxxiii) *The Nightingale* (SM2K 46298).

Vol. 9: (xxxiv) *The Rake's progress* (SM2K 46299).

Vol. 10, Oratorio and melodrama: (xxxv; i) *The Flood* (with Robert Craft); (i) *Monumentum pro Gesualdo di Venosa (3 madrigals recomposed for instruments)*; (vii) *Ode*; (xxxvi) *Oedipus Rex*; (xxxvii; xxxviii, i) *Perséphone* (SM2K 46300).

Vol. 11, Sacred works: (x) *Anthem (the dove descending breaks the air)*; (x) *Ave Maria*; (xxxix; x, i) *Babel*; (xxviii; xxvi; x, iii) *Cantata*; (xl) *Canticum sacrum*; (x; ii) *Credo*; (x, iii) *Introitus (T. S. Eliot in Memoriam)*; (xli) *Mass*; (x; i) *Pater noster*; (xlii; i) *A Sermon, a narrative & a prayer*; (xliii; i) *Threni*; (x, i) *Chorale: Variations on: Vom Himmel hoch, da komm ich her* (arr.); *Zvezdoliki* (SM2K 46301).

Vol. 12, Robert Craft conducts: (xliv, i) *Abraham and Isaac*; (iii) *Danses concertantes*; (xlv) *Double Canon: Raoul*

Dufy in memoriam; (xlvi) *Epitaphium*; (i) *Le Chant du rossignol* (symphonic poem); (i) *Orchestral Variations: Aldous Huxley in memoriam*; (xlvii) *Requiem Canticles*; (i) *Song of the Nightingale* (symphonic poem) (SM2K 46302).

Complete Stravinsky Edition.

(B) *** Sony SX22K 46290 (22). (i) Columbia SO; (ii) CBC SO; (iii) Columbia CO; (iv) Shirley, Driscoll, Gramm, Koves; (v) Allen, Sarfaty, Driscoll, Samuel Barber, Aaron Copland, Lukas Foss, Roger Sessions, American Chamber Ch., Hills, Columbia Percussion Ens.; (vi) Los Angeles Festival SO; (vii) Cleveland O; (viii) Chicago SO; (ix) Jordan, Shirley, Gramm; (x) Festival Singers of Toronto, Iseler; (xi) Philippe Entremont; (xii) Charles Rosen; (xiii) Isaac Stern; (xiv) Soulima Stravinsky; (xv) Igor Stravinsky; (xvi) Szigeti; (xvii) Benny Goodman; (xviii) Columbia Jazz Ens.; (xix) Israel Baker; (xx) Tony Koves; (xxi) Arthur Gold, Robert Fizdale; (xxii) N. W. German RSO; (xxiii) Cathy Berberian; (xxiv) Howland, Kreiselman, Russo; (xxv) Mary Simmons; (xxvi) Alexander Young; (xxvii) Evelyn Lear; (xxviii) Adrienne Albert; (xxix) Robert Craft; (xxx) Donald Gramm; (xxxi) Di Tullio, Remsen, Almeida; (xxxii) Belinck, Simmons, Rideout, Kolk; (xxxiii) Driscoll, Grist, Picassi, Smith, Beattie, Gramm, Kolk, Murphy, Kaiser, Bonazzi, Washington, D. C., Op. Society Ch. & O; (xxxiv) Young, Raskin, Reardon, Sarfaty, Miller, Manning, Garrard, Tracey, Colin Tilney, Sadler's Wells Op. Ch.; John Baker, RPO; (xxxv) Laurence Harvey, Sebastian Cabot, Elsa Lanchester, John Reardon, Robert Oliver, Paul Tripp, Richard Robinson, Columbia SO Ch., Gregg Smith; (xxxvi) Westbrook (nar.), Shirley, Verrett, Gramm, Reardon, Driscoll, Chester Watson Ch., Washington, D. C., Op. Society O; (xxxvii) Gregg Smith Singers, Gregg Smith; (xxxviii) Zorina, Molese, Ithaca College Concert Ch., Fort Worth Texas Boys' Ch.; (xxxix) John Calicos (nar.); (xl) Robinson, Chitjian, Los Angeles Festival Ch. & SO; (xli) Baxter, Albert, Gregg Smith Singers, Columbia Symphony Winds & Brass; (xlii) Verrett, Driscoll, Hornton (nar.); (xliii) Beardslee, Krebs, Lewis, Wainner, Morgan, Oliver, Schola Cantorum, Ross; all cond. composer. (xliv) Richard Frisch; (xlv) Baker, Igleman, Schonbach, Neikrug; (xlvi) Anderson, Bonazzi, Bressler, Gramm, Ithaca College Concert Ch., Gregg Smith; cond. Robert Craft.

On these 22 bargain-price discs (each volume also available separately at mid-price) you have the unique archive of recordings which Stravinsky left of his own music. Presented in a sturdy plastic display box that enhances the desirability of the set, almost all the performances are conducted by the composer, with a few at the very end of his career – like the magnificent *Requiem canticles* – left to Robert Craft to conduct, with the composer supervising. In addition there is a handful of recordings of works otherwise not covered, mainly chamber pieces. With some recordings of Stravinsky talking and in rehearsal (included in the box devoted to the symphonies) it makes a vivid portrait.

Of the major ballets, *Petrushka* and *The Firebird* are valuable, but *The Rite* is required listening: it has real savagery and astonishing electricity. (It is also available in a separate issue – see below) The link between *Jeu de cartes* from the mid-1930s and Stravinsky's post-war opera, *The Rake's Progress*, is striking, and Stravinsky's sharp-edged conducting style underlines it, while the *Scènes de ballet* certainly have their attractive moments. If *Orpheus* has a powerful atmosphere, *Apollo* is one of Stravinsky's most gravely beautiful scores, while *Agon* is one of the most stimulating of Stravinsky's later works, and here the orchestra respond with tremendous alertness and enthusiasm to Stravinsky's direction. The recording of *Le Baiser de la fée* is a typical CBS balance with forward woodwind. However the splendid performance overcomes such a technical drawback. Stravinsky's recording of *Pulcinella* includes the vocal numbers, while in the orchestra the clowning of the trombone and the humour generally is strikingly vivid and never too broad. Similarly with the chamber scoring of the suite from *The Soldier's Tale*, the crisp, clear reading brings out the underlying intense emotion of the music with its nagging, insistent little themes. There is a ruthlessness in the composer's own reading of *Les Noces* which exactly matches its primitive Russian feeling, and as the performance goes on so one senses the added alertness and enthusiasm of the performers. *Renard* is a curious work, a sophisticated fable which here receives too unrelenting a performance. The voices are very forward and tend to drown the instrumentalists.

In the early *Symphony in E flat*, Op. 1, the young Stravinsky's material may be comparatively conventional, but in this definitive performance the music springs to life. Each movement has its special delights to outweigh any shortcomings, while in the *Symphony in Three Movements* Stravinsky shows how, by vigorous, forthright treatment of the notes, the emotion implicit is made all the more compelling. The Columbia Symphony plays superbly and the recording is full and brilliant. Stravinsky never quite equalled the intensity of the pre-war 78-r.p.m. performance of the *Symphony of Psalms*, but the later, stereo version is still impressive. It is just that, with so vivid a work, it is a shade disappointing to find Stravinsky as interpreter at less than maximum voltage. Even so, the closing section of the work is very beautiful and compelling. The CD transfers of the American recordings are somewhat monochrome by modern standards but fully acceptable.

The iron-fingered touch of Philippe Entremont has something to be said for it in the *Capriccio for Piano and Wind*, but this performance conveys too little of the music's charm. The *Movements for Piano and Orchestra* with the composer conducting could hardly be more compelling. Stern's memorable account of the *Violin Concerto in D* adds a romantic perspective to the framework. But an expressive approach to Stravinsky works marvellously when the composer is there to provide the bedrock under the expressive cantilena.

The *Dumbarton Oaks Concerto* with its obvious echoes of Bach's *Brandenburgs* is one of the most warmly attractive of Stravinsky's neo-classical works, all beautifully played and acceptably recorded. The *Octet for Wind* of 1924 comes out with surprising freshness and if the *Ragtime* could be more lighthearted, Stravinsky gives the impression of knowing what he wants. The *Ebony Concerto*, in this version conducted by the composer, may have little of 'swung' rhythm,

but it is completely faithful to Stravinsky's deadpan approach to jazz.

In *Le Rossignol* the singing is not always on a par with the conducting, but it is always perfectly adequate and the recording is brilliant and immediate. *Mavra* is sung in Russian and, as usual, the soloists – who are good – are too closely balanced, but the performance has punch and authority and on the whole the CD quality is fully acceptable. The songs represent a fascinating collection of trifles, chips from the master's workbench dating from the earliest years. There are many incidental delights, not least those in which the magnetic Cathy Berberian is featured.

The Rake's Progress has never since been surpassed. Alexander Young's assumption of the title-role is a marvellous achievement, sweet-toned, accurate and well characterized. In the choice of other principals, too, it is noticeable what store Stravinsky set by vocal precision. Judith Raskin makes an appealing Anne Trulove, John Reardon is remarkable more for vocal accuracy than for striking characterization, but Regina Sarfaty's Baba is marvellous on both counts. The Sadler's Wells Chorus sings with great drive under the composer, and the Royal Philharmonic play with warmth and a fittingly Mozartian sense of style to match Stravinsky's surprisingly lyrical approach to his score. The CDs offer excellent sound.

The *Cantata* of 1952 is a transitional piece between Stravinsky's tonal and serial periods. However, of the two soloists, Alexander Young is much more impressive than Adrienne Albert, for her voice brings an unformed choirboy sound somehow married to wide vibrato. The *Canticum sacrum* includes music that some listeners might find tough (the strictly serial choral section). But the performance is a fine one and the tenor solo from Richard Robinson is very moving. The Bach *Chorale Variations* has a synthetic modernity that recalls the espresso bar, though one which still reveals underlying mastery. The *Epitaphium* and the *Double canon* are miniatures, dating from the composer's serial period, but the *Canon* is deliberately euphonious.

The *Mass* is a work of the greatest concentration, a quality that comes out strongly if one plays this performance immediately after *The Flood*, with its inevitably slack passages. As directed in the score, trebles are used here, and it is a pity that the engineers have not brought them further forward: their sweet, clear tone is sometimes lost among the lower strands. In *The Flood*, originally written for television, it is difficult to take the bald narrations seriously, particularly when Laurence Harvey sanctimoniously keeps talking of the will of 'Gud'. The performance of *Oedipus Rex*, too, is not one of the highlights of the set. *Perséphone*, however, is full of that cool lyricism that marks much of Stravinsky's music inspired by classical myths. As with many of these vocal recordings, the balance is too close, and various orchestral solos are highlighted.

Of the items recorded by Robert Craft, the *Requiem canticles* stands out, the one incontrovertible masterpiece among the composer's very last serial works and one of the most deeply moving works ever written in the serial idiom. Even more strikingly than in the *Mass* of 1948, Stravinsky conveys his religious feelings with a searing intensity. The *Aldous Huxley variations* are more difficult to comprehend but have similar intensity. Valuable, too, is the ballad *Abraham and Isaac*.

OTHER RECORDINGS

Agon (ballet; complete); *Petrushka* (ballet; 1911 score; complete); *Fireworks*.

(BB) **(*) Virgin 2 x 1 VBD5 61754-2 (2). Melbourne SO, Iwaki – BARTOK: *Concerto for Orchestra; Miraculous Mandarin* (complete). **(*)

Agon was written in the mid-1950s when Stravinsky was beginning to turn his attention to what had been anathema to him, serialism. There are already signs here of the developments in idiom which were to mark his last period. But, although on first hearing it is not easily cogent listening, it is worth persevering, for in every bar the bright focus of the argument with its distinctive orchestral colourings is immediately identifiable as the work of Stravinsky. This Melbourne performance is a very acceptable stopgap, atmospheric and very well played and recorded. As with the coupled Bartók, the reading lacks bite and dash, though remains aurally fascinating. *Petrushka* is crisply colourful, vividly dramatic and spontaneously enjoyable. Both ballets are generously cued and *Fireworks* acts as an effervescent encore.

Apollo (Apollon musagète); Le Baiser de la fée (complete ballet & *Divertimento*); (i) *Capriccio for Piano & Orchestra; Concerto for Piano & Wind Instruments. Le Chant du rossignol; Circus Polka; 4 Etudes; The Firebird* (complete ballet); *Petrushka* (1911 version; complete); *Pulcinella* (suite and (ii) complete ballet); *Rite of Spring; Scherzo à la russe; Soldier's Tale* (suite); *Suites Nos. 1 & 2; Symphony in C; Symphony in 3 Movements; Symphonies of Wind Instruments;* (iii) *Les Noces* (ballet-cantata); (iv) *Symphony of Psalms;* (v) *Mavra;* (vi) *Renard*.

(N) (B) **(*) Decca (ADD) 467 818-2 (8) SRO, Ansermet, with (i) Magaloff; (ii) Tyler, Franzini, Carmeli; (iii) Retchitzka, Devallier, Cuénod, Rehfuss, Diakoff, Geneva Motet Ch. (iv) Choeur des Jeunes & Ch. of R. Lausanne; (v) Carlyle, Watts, Sinclair, Macdonald; (vi) English, Mitchinson, Glossop, Rouleau.

Having begun his Stravinsky recordings for Decca during the days of ffrr 78s, Ansermet finally undertook his major survey with the coming of stereo. *Apollon Musagète*, the complete *Firebird* ballet and the two piano concertos – with Nikita Magaloff in fine form – date from as early as 1955, yet the recording still sounds remarkably well, and if in the concertante works Ansermet's direction lacks some of the bite and sharp wit that this neoclassical music needs, they follow an authentic tradition from Parisian music-making between the wars.

The Firebird was highly praised by us for its clarity of detail when it first appeared, although we commented on the lack of body to the upper strings. Undoubtedly Ansermet's later Philharmonia recording (not included here) is finer still, better played and with richer sound, but this remains impressive for its time.

Le Chant du rossignol and the *Pulcinella Ballet Suite* followed in 1956, both showing Ansermet at his interpretative best. The recordings, too, were considered demonstration-worthy in their day, with *The Song of the Nightingale* showing how clearly and beautifully Decca could cope with a big Stravinsky orchestra, while *Pulcinella* showed even more impressively how a small chamber group of instruments could be projected with vivid realism.

The 1957 *Petrushka* also set high standards of clarity and vividness, although the Swiss violins were not flattered by the close microphones and, fine as it was, Ansermet's performance did not quite match his earlier 78 version (available in a fine Dutton transfer – see below) in dramatic and emotional vividness. It was soon to be upstaged by Dorati's famous Mercury version. The *Rite of Spring* however, recorded in the same year, was a performance of great integrity. Ansermet's scrupulous insistence on maintaining the score's natural balance brought an awe-inspiring relentlessness and a wild primitive beauty.

In 1960 came the *Symphony in C*, strongly played, and often incisive, but the companion *Symphony in Three Movements* lacks a feeling of strong rhythmic vitality, and is without the fullest impetus. However, the clean stylish account of *The Soldier's Tale*, given (1961) sound of tingling immediacy, is matched by the fine performance of the haunting *Symphonies for Wind Instruments*, where Ansermet's warmth more than compensates for any lack of tautness.

The *Quatre Etudes* (from 1962) have considerable subtlety, and the *Suites* are enjoyable in a spontaneous, extrovert way. Both show the lighter side of Stravinsky, and Ansermet plays them with spirit and style. However, there is something curiously heavy and lethargic about his account of the *Symphony of Psalms*, even though this account is better than the earlier version on 78s (see Dutton reissue below). Fortunately the well-projected recording adds sharpness to a reading which might otherwise have sounded flat.

In *Les Noces*, recorded that same year, Ansermet fails to capture the essential bite in Stravinsky's sharply etched portrait of a peasant wedding. The hammered rhythms must sound ruthless and here they are merely tame. This was followed with complete versions of *Le Baiser de la fée* (in 1963), and *Pulcinella* (with vocal numbers) in 1965, neither of which was as successful as the earlier recordings of the *Fairy's Kiss Divertimento* and the *Pulcinella Ballet Suite*, primarily because of moments of slackness and under-par orchestral playing. However, yet again Ansermet's warmth, and the splendidly vivid recording help to project the music in spite of the inadequacies of the playing.

The series culminated in 1964 with *Mavra* and *Renard* (where one enjoys the clear English). Both were a great success, vividly performed and brilliantly recorded. Here more than usual Ansermet caught the sort of toughness one recognizes in the composer's own performances of his music, and the haunting yet light-hearted *Scherzo à la russe*, with its bouncing main theme, is a splendid bonus.

(i) *Apollo (Apollon musagète)* complete ballet.

(N) (M) *** DG 463640-2. (i) BPO, Karajan – BARTOK: *Music for String, Percussion and Celeste* **(*)

(i) *Apollo* (ballet): complete; *Circus Polka;* (ii) *Petrushka* (ballet: 1911 score): complete.

(B) *** DG (ADD) 439 463-2. (i) BPO, Karajan; LSO, Dutoit.

(i) *Apollo;* (ii) *The Firebird; Petrushka* (1911 score); *The Rite of Spring* (complete ballets).

⚙ (B) *** Ph. Duo (ADD) 438 350-2. (i) LSO, Markevitch; (ii) LPO, Haitink.

Apollo (complete ballet; revised, 1947 version); *Firebird* (ballet) *suite* (1945); *Scherzo fantastique.*

**(*) Decca 458 142-2. Concg.O, Chailly.

Apollo; Orpheus (ballets).

*** ASV CDDCA 618. O of St John's, Lubbock.

Apollo is a work in which Karajan's moulding of phrase and care for richness of string texture make for wonderful results, especially in the glorious *Pas de deux.* The 1972 recording is of DG's highest quality and in no way sounds its age. It now comes alternatively coupled either with Bartók's *Music for Strings, Percussion and Celeste* on one of DG's Originals at mid-price or, more attractively, on DG's bargain Classikon label with more Stravinsky. Here the *Circus Polka* is played with comparable panache. The coupling is Charles Dutoit's first recorded *Petrushka,* made for DG in the Henry Wood Hall in 1975/6. The result is triumphantly spontaneous in its own right, with rhythms that are incisive yet beautifully buoyant, and a degree of expressiveness in the orchestral playing that subtly underlines the dramatic atmosphere. Excellent value.

Markevitch's gravely beautiful reading of *Apollon musagète* here comes with Haitink's strikingly refined account of the other key ballets. In *The Firebird* the sheer savagery of *Katshchei's Dance* may be a little muted, but the sharpness of attack and clarity of detail make for a thrilling result, while the magic and poetry of the whole score are given a hypnotic beauty. In *Petrushka* the rhythmic feeling is strong, especially in the Second Tableau and the finale, where the fairground bustle is vivid. The natural, unforced quality of Haitink's *Rite* also brings real compulsion. Other versions may hammer the listener more powerfully, thrust him or her along more forcefully; but the bite and precision of the LPO playing here are most impressive, as hroughout the set, while the recording's firm definition and the well-proportioned and truthful aural perspective make it a joy to listen to. Outstanding value.

The ASV issue offers an ideal coupling, with refined performances and excellent recording. The delicacy of the rhythmic pointing in *Apollo* gives special pleasure, and there is a first-rate solo violin contribution from Richard Deakin.

With superb demonstration-worthy Decca recording, and wonderfully delicate orchestral textures, Chailly achieves glowingly diaphonous sounds in Stravinsky's early *Scherzo fantastique* and then he revels in the rich Rimskyan colours of the extended 1945 *Firebird Suite,* which includes the three delectable *Pantomimes.* Bold dramatic contrast comes with the explosive *Kachtchei's Danse infernale* and in the more expansive finale. A similar warm sensuousness pervades Chailly's somewhat indulgent reading of *Apollo,* where the score's refined neoclassicism is muted in favour of opulent warmth. Some of the ballet's rhythmic profile is lost, especi-

ally in the celebrated *Pas de deux,* which is far more voluptuous here than with Karajan. But with such gorgeous sound this is easy to enjoy.

(i–ii) *Le Baiser de la fée* (ballet; complete); (i; iii) *Ode;* (iv) *Symphonies of Wind Instruments;* (i; ii) *Symphony in E flat, Op. 1;* (i; iii) *Symphony in C; Symphony in 3 Movements.*

(B) *** Chan. 2-for-1 ADD/Dig. 241-8 (2). (i) RSNO; (ii) Järvi; (iii) Gibson; (iv) Nash Ens., Rattle.

(i) *Le Baiser de la fée (divertimento); Le Chant du rossignol;* (ii) *Dumbarton Oaks Concerto;* (iii) *Petrushka* (1911); *The Rite of Spring.*

(N) (B) **(*) RCA 2CD stereo/mono 74321 84609-2. (i) Chicago SO, Reiner; (ii) NDR SO, Wand; (iii) Boston SO, Monteux.

(i) *Le Baiser de la fée (Divertimento);* (ii) *Petrushka:* excerpts: *(Danse russe; Chez Petrushka; La Fête populaire);* (i) *Pulcinella* (suite); (ii) *The Rite of Spring* (complete ballet).

(B) (***) EMI mono CZS5 69674-2 (2). (i) French Nat. R. O; (ii) Philh. O, Markevitch – PROKOFIEV: *Love for 3 Oranges* etc. (**)

(i, v) *Le Baiser de la fée* (complete); *Pulcinella* (complete); *Symphony in C;* (ii, iii, v) *L'histoire du soldat: Suite;* (ii, iv, v) *Octet for Wind Instruments.*

(M) (***) Sony mono MH2K 63325 (2). (i) Cleveland O; (ii) Oppenheim, Glickman, Nagel, Price; (iii) Howard, Schneider, Levine; (iv) Baker, Deutscher, Weis, Hixson; (v) composer.

On Chandos Strauss's deft scoring of *Le Baiser de la fée* is a constant delight, much of it on a chamber-music scale; and its delicacy, wit and occasional pungency are fully appreciated by Järvi, who secures a wholly admirable response from his Scottish orchestra. The ambience seems exactly right, bringing out wind and brass colours vividly. As for the symphonies, even when compared with the composer's own versions, the performances by the Royal Scottish Orchestra – in excellent form under Sir Alexander Gibson – stand up well, with Järvi directing the early *E flat* work equally impressively. The vivid naturalness of the splendid 1982 digital recordings compensates for any slight lack of bite. The cool, almost whimsical beauty of the *Andante* of the *Symphony in Three Movements* is most subtly conveyed, and the inner movements of the *Symphony in C* are beautifully played. Moreover the Nash Ensemble's perceptive account of the *Symphonies of Wind Instruments* under Rattle does not let the side down. It is good to have also as a bonus the *Ode* in memory of Natalia Koussevitzky, which has an extrovert, rustic scherzo section framed by short elegies.

Reiner's Chicago recordings of *Le Baiser de la fée* and *Le Chant du rossignol* are legendary. The latter is praised below, where it is coupled with Rimsky's *Scheherazade;* the equally delightful *Fairy's Kiss Divertimento* has character and life as well as much charm, with the *Pas de deux* beautifully done. The overall performance has great atmosphere, with distinguished woodwind and brass contributions, helped by the astonishingly vivid 1958 Chicago recording.

Wand's hardly less engaging account of the *Dumbarton Oaks Concerto*, played with great geniality and finesse, is also most naturally recorded in an attractive acoustic.

For *Petrushka* and *The Rite of Spring* RCA have turned to Monteux, who conducted the première of the latter. But not to his Paris Conservatoire stereo performances. Instead they have chosen the alternative Boston versions, which are much better played. The *Rite* dates from 1951 and is mono, with a recording which harshens at climaxes. But the performance powerfully captures the wild intensity of the ballet's violent pagan ritual, and, just as tellingly, projects the hauntingly mysterious evocation of the opening of the second part.

The Boston recording of *Petrushka* is stereo and dates from 1959. There is still an edge to the sound at climaxes, but the Boston acoustic adds its ambient glow throughout, and the performance is extremely lively, with memorable solo contributions in the central tableaux and a particularly exciting and dramatic account of the final scene, all the bustle of the Shrovetide carnival brilliantly conveyed.

Markevitch's electrifying 1959 recording of *The Rite of Spring* has long been famous, even though the documentation suggests that it is mono. The Philharmonia playing is superbly exciting, and the conductor's rhythmic vitality and ruthless thrust are matched by an amazingly spectacular recording which hardly sounds dated even now. In the elegant *Divertimento*, which Stravinsky culled from his Tchaikovskian ballet *Le Baiser de la fée*, the French orchestral playing here has both finesse and flair. The three excerpts from *Petrushka* are similarly lively and colourful, and only *Pulcinella* is slightly disappointing: the trombones blow raspberries in their famous *Vivo* duet with the double basses, and elsewhere Markevitch dilutes the music's charm by his forcefulness. However this is certainly value for money.

The Cleveland Orchestra was apparently Stravinsky's favourite American orchestra and he made these recordings with them in the early 1950s. Generally speaking, the performances have a greater polish and style than the later versions Stravinsky made in stereo with the CBC (Toronto) or the Columbia Symphony. The *Symphony in C* and *Le Baiser de la fée* are particularly good. As always with their Heritage series, Sony gives us handsome presentation and documentation. But they are priced at the very top-end of the mid-range.

Le Chant du rossignol (Song of the Nightingale): symphonic poem.

☸ (M) *** DG (ADD) 449 769-2 (2). Berlin RSO, Maazel – RAVEL: *L'heure espagnole; L'enfant et les sortilèges;* RIMSKY-KORSAKOV: *Capriccio espagnol.* ***

(M) *** RCA (ADD) 09026 68168-2. Chicago SO, Reiner – RIMSKY-KORSAKOV: *Scheherazade* ***

Le Chant du rossignol; Feux d'artifice; Petrushka (original version).

*** RCA 74321 57127-2. VPO, Maazel.

Le Chant du rossignol, which Stravinsky made from the material of his opera, deserves a much more established place in the concert repertoire. Maazel's justly famous DG version dates from 1958, slightly later than Reiner's. Maazel

is nothing if not dramatic, but above all he revels in the glittering orchestral detail and the marvellous atmosphere this score commands. The Berlin Radio Orchestra produces a feast of chimerical glowing colours and the DG engineers of the time surpassed themselves. It is well coupled with Ravel's two delightful neo-classical operas and Maazel's superb Berlin Philharmonic version of Rimsky-Korsakov's *Capriccio espagnol* from the same period.

Le Chant du rossignol glows even more vividly in the Musikverein, with the players of the Vienna Philharmonic sounding unexpectedly at home in its exotic chinoiserie. The closing scene portraying the illness and death of the Emperor is marvellously evoked and very affecting. The VPO playing is hardly less brilliant in the other works, with *Petrushka* vividly dramatic yet affectionately detailed by Maazel. Once again it is the closing tableau which is the most memorable, taken fairly briskly and arrestingly involving at the appearance of Petrushka's ghost. The recording has a touch of fierceness in fortissimos (not out of place in Stravinsky), but otherwise is often of demonstration standard. This is one of Maazel's finest records for some time, and his brilliant account of *Feux d'artifice* brings a prophetic anticipation of the composer's later works.

Reiner's version of 1956 in its currently remastered form also brings astonishingly full and vivid sound, full of presence, an excellent coupling for his strong and dramatic reading of *Scheherazade*. Reiner's virile, sharply focused reading relates it more clearly than usual to the *Rite of Spring.* The virtuosity of the playing and the clarity of its direction are arresting, yet the refined but glittering detail of the orchestral palette is most evocative.

Le Chant du Rossignol; Complete ballets: *The Firebird; Petrushka* (1911 version); *The Rite of Spring.*

(N) (B) **(*) Delos Double DE 3702 (2). Seattle SO, Schwarz.

The Delos Schwarz performances are finely played, and the extremely vivid and well-focused internal detail heard against an attractively resonant acoustic will thrill audiophiles with equipment capable of making the most of the projection and clarity of these first-class digital recordings. *Le Chant du Rossignol* and *The Firebird* both glow luminously, but in *Petrushka* one would liked more bite in the articulation, and the picture of the Shrovetide Fair is a broad canvas rather than a sharply dramatic sequence of events. *The Rite of Spring* could not be more different from the Mehta version, except that the drums make a fine impact. But it is not ferocious, yet gathers tension as it proceeds, and the great horn entry in the *Ancestors' Ritual* is splendidly bold, leading to exciting concluding *Sacrifice.*

(i; ii) *Le Chant du rossignol;* (iv; v) *L'histoire du soldat (The Soldier's Tale);* (i; iii) *Pulcinella* (complete ballet); (iv; vi) *Renard* (burlesque).

(B) **(*) Erato Ultima 3984 24246-2 (2). (i) O Nat. de France, (ii) Boulez; (iii) Ens. InterContemporain, with Murray, Rolfe Johnson, Estes; (iv) Instrumental Ens., Dutoit; (v) with Simon, Berthet, Carrat; Huttenlocher, Bastin; (vi) Tappy, Blazer, Huttenlocher, Bastin.

The two discs included in this Ultima Double make a particularly apt pairing, as the four works assembled here date from a notable period in Stravinsky's development when, shortly after composing *The Rite of Spring*, he moved from his Russian style into neoclassical mode. The symphonic poem marks the crossover, while *Pulcinella* draws on the music of Pergolesi. Here Boulez secures suberb playing from the Ensemble Intercontemporain and his singers are first class in every way. His is a fine performance, but his pacing is more extreme than some versions with contrasts between movements almost over-characterized, helped with periodic added edge in the timbre.

The remaining two works are directed no less admirably by Dutoit, who brings out all their wit and irony and in *L'histoire du soldat*, the underlying melancholy. He is helped by splendid casts (Gérard Carrat a lively narrator and François Simon a cunning devil in the latter, with characterful violin solos from Nicolas Chumachenco, and Eric Tappy particularly impressive in the bizarre animal burlesque, *Renard)*. The ensemble playing, too is crisp and plangent. Excellent recording. The one snag, and it is serious, is that while the use of the French language is a stimulating choice, the complete absence of librettos with translations is not – and there is a great deal of spoken dialogue in *L'histoire du soldat*.

Concertino for 12 Instruments; Concerto in D for Strings; Praeludium for Jazz Ensemble; Ragtime for 11 Instruments; Scherzo à la Russe; Suites Nos. 1–2 for Small Orchestra; Tango; Duet for Bassoons; Fanfare for a New Theatre (for 2 trumpets); *Octet for Wind; 3 Pieces for String Quartet.*

(N) *** DG 453 458-2. Orpheus CO.

This is a delightful and sparkling programme, played with light, springy rhythms and zest. First class in every way, not least in the exemplary and vivid recording quality. Strongly recommended, a clear leader in this repertoire.

(i) *Concerto, Dumbarton Oaks;* **(ii)** *The Firebird* (suite; 1919); **(iii)** *Pétrouchka;* **(iv)** *Pulcinella* (suite); **(v)** *The Rite of Spring; Circus Polka;* **(vi)** *Symphony of Psalms.*

(N) (B) *** DG Panorama (ADD) 469 205-2 (2).
   (i) Intercontemporain Ens., Boulez; (ii) Berlin RSO, Maazel;
   (iii) LSO, Dutoit; (iv) ASMF, Marriner; (v) BPO, Karajan;
   (vi) Russian State Ch. & O, Markevitch.

This set begins with Maazel's glittering *Firebird Suite* – one of the finest versions ever – then goes on to Karajan's smoothly powerful *Rite*, and Markevitch's vibrant if somewhat rough and ready account of the *Symphony of Psalms* (with plenty of Russian wobble in the brass). Dutoit's *Pétrouchka* is splendidly alive and atmospheric, and Marriner's superbly etched *Pulcinella* suite (originally on Argo), sounds as fresh as paint. This is of the very best compilations in the not always well-chosen Panorama series.

Concerto for Chamber Orchestra, 'Dumbarton Oaks'; 8 Instrumental Miniatures; **(i)** *Ebony Concerto.*

(M) *** DG (ADD) 447 405-2. (i) Arrignon; Ens. InterContemporain, Boulez – BERG: *Chamber Concerto.* ***

The playing of the Ensemble InterContemporain is very

brilliant indeed. There is much to enjoy in these performances, which are spiced with the right kind of wit and keenness of edge, and even those who do not normally respond to Boulez's conducting will be pleasantly surprised with the results he obtains here.

Concerto for Strings in D.

(M) *** DG (ADD) 447 435-2. BPO, Karajan – HONEGGER: *Symphonies Nos. 2 & 3* *** ●

Karajan's version of the *Concerto in D for Strings* – written within a few months of the Honegger *Symphonie Liturgique*, with which it is coupled – may strike some listeners as not quite acerbic or biting enough, but the finesse and lightness of touch of the Berlin strings and their rhythmic legerdemain are a delight. The recording is first class.

(i) *Violin Concerto;* **(ii; iii)** *Ebony Concerto;* **(iv)** *Symphony in C; Symphony in 3 Movements;* **(iii)** *Symphonies for Wind Instruments;* **(v)** *Symphony of Psalms.*

(B) **(*) Ph. Duo (ADD) 442 583-2 (2). (i) Grumiaux, Concg. O, Bour; (ii) Pieterson; (iii) Netherlands Wind Ens., De Waart; (iv) LSO, C. Davis; (v) Russian State Ac. Ch. & SO, Markevitch.

A lithe, refined, yet vital account of the *Violin Concerto* from Grumiaux and the Concertgebouw Orchestra. The 1967 recording is just a little dated but well balanced. George Pieterson's version of the *Ebony Concerto* with the Netherlands Wind Ensemble is not as overtly jazzy as some but its dry, sardonic wit and the dark sonorities of the finale make it individual. The *Symphonies for Wind Instruments* also show the controlled blend of colour for which this Dutch wind group are famous. Sir Colin Davis's account of the *Symphony in C* is splendidly alert, well played and stimulating. The performance of the *Symphony in Three Movements* is also lively, but compared with Stravinsky's own it is over-tense. Markevitch's 1964 Russian performance of the *Symphony of Psalms* is as vibrantly Slavonic as one could wish, yet the closing 'Alleluias' still bring a frisson in their raptly gentle expressive feeling. The sound is brightly vivid but not harsh.

Violin Concerto in D.

(M)***Decca (ADD) 425 003-2. Chung, LSO, Previn – PROKOFIEV: *Concertos Nos. 1–2.* ***

*** Sony SK 53969. Lin, LAPO, Salonen – PROKOFIEV: *Violin Concertos Nos. 1 & 2.* *** ●

*** Teldec 4509 98255-2. Perlman, Chicago SO, Barenboim – PROKOFIEV: *Violin Concerto No. 2.* ***

*** EMI CDC5 56966-2. Vengerov, LSO, Rostropovich – SHCHEDRIN: *Concerto cantabile;* TCHAIKOVSKY: *Sérénade mélancholique.* ***

(M) *** DG (ADD) 447 445-2. Perlman, Boston SO, Ozawa – BERG: *Concerto;* RAVEL: *Tzigane.* ***

*** Ph. 456 542-2. Mullova, LAPO, Salonen – BARTOK: *Violin Concerto No. 2.* **

(M) (***) Sony mono SMK 64505. Stern, Columbia SO, composer (with ROCHBERG: *Violin Concerto) *(**).

Kyung Wha Chung is at her most incisive in the spicily swaggering outer movements which, with Precin's help, are presented here in all their distinctiveness; tough and witty at the same time. In the two movements labeled *Aria*, Chung brings fantasy as well as lyricism, less overtly expressive than Perlman but conveying instead an inner, brooding quality. Brilliant Decca recording, the soloist diamond-bright in presense but with plenty of orchestral atmosphere.

As in the two Prokofiev concertos, so in the Stravinsky Cho-Liang Lin plays with power and warmth, while Salonen terraces the accompaniment dramatically, with woodwind and brass bold and full. The Prokofiev coupling is outstanding.

Though Perlman's coupling of the Stravinsky *Concerto* and Prokofiev No. 2 on Teldec is most ungenerous, this performance, recorded live in 1994, is more compelling than his earlier studio recording, with Barenboim adding to the urgency and energy. Far more Stravinskian wit is conveyed in the outer movements, with rhythms more bouncy and with phrasing more seductively individual. In the two slow inner movements, Arias I and II, Perlman opts for speeds marginally more flowing, with Aria II more inward than before, more reflective even at a faster speed.

A brilliant, biting account of Stravinsky's concerto from the symbiotic Russian partnership of Vengerov and Rostropovich, which admirably catches the work's wide range of mood, rhythm and colour, with its genial opening *Toccata* giving way to touchingly spare Stravinskian lyricism in the central *Arias*, and the superbly spiky *Capriccio* capping a reading of remarkable imaginative range. The brightness of the recording gives plenty of edge to the solo projection, yet the balance ensures that the orchestral detail makes the strongest impression. A *tour de force*.

Perlman's precision, remarkable in both concertos on the DG disc, underlines the neo-classical element in the outer movements of the Stravinsky, while the two *Aria* movements are more deeply felt and expressive. The balance favours the soloist, but no one will miss the commitment of the Boston orchestra's playing, vividly recorded. The Ravel *Tzigane* has now been added for good measure.

The Stravinsky *Concerto* suits Viktoria Mullova and her brilliant partners in Los Angeles rather better than does the Bartók coupling, and this version can certainly be put in our recommended list The Philips recording is first rate in every respect.

Stern's 1951 mono recording with the composer has never been surpassed and seldom approached. The outer movements have an exhilarating combination of rhythmic bite and wit, and the two central arias bring a very special subtlety of colour and feeling. The sound is of the highest quality: no apologies whatsoever need be made for it. Listening to the record lifts the spirits, and we would have given it a Rosette were it not for the Rochberg coupling, which (as music) is very much of the second grade, even if Stern's performance is not.

(i) *Concerto for Piano & Wind. Danses concertantes;*
(ii) *Pulcinella* (ballet; complete); (iii) *3 Pieces for Clarinet Solo; Pour Pablo Picasso.*

*** Koch 3 7470-2. (i) Dichter, 20th Century Classics Ens.; (ii) Montague, Leggate, Beesley, Philh. O; (i; ii) Craft; (iii) Neidich.

This delightful collection of Stravinsky works written between 1917 and 1942 completely gives the lie to the idea that Robert Craft, the composer's amanuensis, is a chilly interpreter. This is a delectably pointed and witty account of the complete *Pulcinella ballet*, beautifully played by the Philharmonia. Excellent solo singing, though Robin Leggate's tenor is too dry. The other items were recorded in America, with sound less immediate, though the rhythmic spring of the *Danses concertantes* and of the *Concerto*, with Dichter a fine soloist, is comparably infectious. The unaccompanied clarinet works include a 23-second fragment never recorded before, written over dinner with Picasso, when the composer was drunk.

Danses concertantes; Orpheus (complete ballet).

*** DG 459 644-2. Orpheus CO.

One continues to marvel at the sophistication and the seeming spontaneity of the playing from this unique conductorless chamber orchestra. The refined colouring and feeling for atmosphere at the opening of *Orpheus* and the sharp rhythmic bite of the later *Pas d'action*, is matched by the wit of the *Pas de deux* of the *Danses concertantes*, and the delicacy distilled in the *Thème varié*, with the closing sections of both works particularly satisfying. These performances are unsurpassed, and the recording is of DG's finest, very much in the demonstration bracket for ambient warmth, clear detail and natural balance.

(i) *Ebony Concerto; L'histoire du soldat* (ballet suite); *Octet for Wind; Symphonies of Wind Instruments;*
(ii) *Piano Rag-Music;* (ii; iii) *Ragtime for 11 Instruments.*

(N) (M) ** Sup. SU 3168-2 911. (i) Prague Chamber Harmony, Pešek; (ii) Novotný, (iii) Zlatnikova.

These Prague performances from the 1960s are no match for the Orpheus Chamber Orchestra in their shared repertoire (the *Octet* and *Ragtime*) or the quality of the recorded sound. However, given the moderate price-tag they remain very serviceable.

Complete ballets: (i) *The Firebird;* (ii) *Orpheus;*
(i) *Petrushka* (1947 version); *The Rite of Spring.*

(N) (M) **(*) Ph. 464 744-2 (2) (i) Concg. O; (ii) LSO, C. Davis.

An outstanding set. Sir Colin Davis directs a magically evocative account of the complete *Firebird*, helped not just by the playing of the Concertgebouw Orchestra (the strings outstandingly fine) but by the ambience of the hall, which allows inner clarity yet gives a bloom to the sound, open and spacious, superbly co-ordinated. Similarly the Philips recording of *Petrushka* (although not so well balanced as *Firebird*) reveals details of the rich texture that are often obscured. Again Davis draws brilliant playing from the orchestra, rarely if ever forcing the pace, though always maintaining the necessary excitement. The piano starts a little cautiously in the *Russian Dance* but that is an exception in an unusually positive reading.

Davis also has his idiosyncrasies in *The Rite of Spring* (one of them his strange hold-up on the last chord), but generally he takes a direct view and the result is strong, forthright and powerful. *Orpheus* is much less frequently heard. It is a post-war ballet, written in 1974, and its mellow classical lines mark a return to the manner of *Orpheus*. But the material is never quite so memorable, or for that matter so varied, and even Davis's excellent account cannot create a richness of colour to match its companions. The recording is warm and very natural, if not so lustrous at those made in the Concertgebouw, but that is partly the effect of the composer's scoring.

The Firebird (ballet: complete).

*** Ph. 446 715-2. Kirov O, Gergiev – SCRIABIN: *Prometheus*. ***

(B) **(*) EMI double forte (ADD) CZS5 72664-2 (2). O de Paris, Ozawa – BARTOK: *Concerto for Orchestra* **(*); JANACEK: *Sinfonietta* ***; LUTOSLAWSKI: *Concerto for Orchestra*. **(*)

The Firebird (complete); Le Chant du rossignol; Fireworks; Scherzo à la russe.

✿ (M) *** Mercury (ADD) 432 012-2. LSO, Dorati.

The Firebird (ballet: complete); Symphonies of Wind Instruments.

(N) (M) *** Virgin VM5 61848-2. LSO, Nagano.

Kent Nagano's vividly detailed LSO recording of the original Stravinsky *Firebird* score was produced by Andrew Keener and recorded at Abbey Road in 1991/2. We missed it on its original appearance but the mid-priced reissue must go to the very top of the recommended list. From the very opening the brilliantly detailed kaleidoscope of orchestral colour reminds the listener of Dorati's famous Mercury record, but the new Virgin sound balance (engineered by Mark Vigars) is even more realistic, slightly softer-grained in its etching, warmer, more lustrous. At the opening the intensity of the LSO playing is slightly less tangible than with Dorati, but the concentration steadily increases and the orchestral colour glows. Katschei's venomous *Danse infernale* contrasts with the glowing *Princesses' Round Dance* and the *Berceuse*; all are superbly played. The final climax expands gloriously, yet has plenty of bite. The original 1920 score of the *Symphonies of Wind Instruments* makes a diverting coupling, with sonorities and textures keenly balanced.

The CD transfer of Dorati's electrifying, 1960 Mercury version of *The Firebird* with the LSO still makes the recording sound as fresh and vivid as the day it was made; the brilliantly transparent detail and enormous impact suggest a modern digital source rather than an analogue master made over 30 years ago. The performance sounds completely spontaneous and the LSO wind playing is especially sensitive. Only the sound of the massed upper strings reveals the age of the original master, although this does not spoil the ravishing final climax; the bite of the brass and the transient edge of the percussion are thrilling. The recording of Stravinsky's glittering symphonic poem, *The song of the nightingale*, is hardly less compelling. Dorati's reading is urgent and finely pointed, yet is strong, too, on atmosphere. The other, shorter pieces also come up vividly.

The complete *Firebird* (on Philips) played by Russian artists has, as one might expect, a strong sense both of atmosphere and theatre, and Valery Gergiev manages the transitions between sections, dramatic characterization and contrasts with consummate mastery. The orchestra play with effortless virtuosity and are recorded with remarkable realism and definition. Although it is difficult to speak of a first choice in so hotly contested a field, Gergiev's would be a viable contender. The coupling, Scriabin's *Prometheus*, can hold its own alongside most rivals.

Ozawa's first (1972) recording with the Orchestre de Paris is a *Firebird* of luxurious and exotic plumage. True, in one or two pianissimo string passages there could be greater mystery and more tenderness, but for the most part this is very well played indeed. In its CD transfer the upper range now has that added digital sharpness of focus that is not quite natural.

(i) The Firebird (complete); (ii) The Rite of Spring (complete).

✿ (M) *** Sony SMK 60011. Columbia SO, composer.

(B) *** Decca Penguin (ADD) 460 644-2. Detroit SO, Dorati.

(BB) *** ASV (ADD) CDQS 6031. (i) RPO, Dorati; (ii) Nat. Youth O of Great Britain, Rattle.

Stravinsky's own (1961) version of *Firebird* is of far more than documentary interest, when the composer so tellingly relates it to his later work, refusing to treat it as merely atmospheric. What he brings out more than others is the element of grotesque fantasy, the quality he was about to develop in *Petrushka*, while the tense violence with which he presents such a passage as *Kaschei's Dance* clearly looks forward to *The Rite of Spring*. That said, he encourages warmly expressive rubato to a surprising degree, with the line of the music always held firm. But the revelatory performance here is *The Rite of Spring*, for Stravinsky's own (1960) reading has never been surpassed as an interpretation of this seminal twentieth-century score. Over and over again, one finds passages which in the balancing and pacing (generally fast) give extra thrust and resilience, as well as extra light and shade. The digital transfer may be on the bright side, but brass and percussion have thrilling impact, sharply terraced and positioned in the stereo spectrum. This is a CD that should be in every basic collection.

Dorati's Detroit version of *The Firebird* has the benefit of spectacular digital recording. The clarity and definition of dark, hushed passages are amazing, with the contra-bassoon finely focused, never sounding woolly or obscure, while string tremolos down to the merest whisper are uncannily precise. The performance is very precise, too; though Dorati's reading has changed little from his previous versions with London orchestras, there is just a little more caution. Individual solos are not so characterful and *Katschei's Dance* lacks just a degree in excitement; but overall this is a strong and beautiful reading, even if the Mercury LP account is not entirely superseded.

Similarly, in terms of recorded sound, Dorati's *Rite* with the Detroit orchestra scores over almost all its rivals. This has stunning clarity and presence, exceptionally lifelike and vivid sound, and the denser textures emerge more cleanly than ever before. It is a very good performance too, almost but not quite in the same league as those of Karajan and

Muti, generating plenty of excitement. The only let-down is the final *Sacrificial Dance*, which needs greater abandon and higher voltage. Yet too much should not be made of this. The performance is so vivid that it belongs among the very best. Its release on Penguin Classics makes it an undoubted bargain. The personal essay is by Philip Hensher.

On ASV, Dorati's tempi in the *Firebird* are comparatively fast. But this matches his dramatic approach, as does a recording balance which is rather close, although there is no serious lack of atmosphere. Not surprisingly with Simon Rattle at the helm, the performance of the *Rite* by the National Youth Orchestra is not just 'good considering', but 'good absolute'; the youngsters under their young conductor (the recordings here date from 1976/7) produce warm and spontaneous playing, and the penalty of having a few imprecisions and errors is minimal. The sound here is slightly more atmospheric than in the coupling, but again there is plenty of bite and the timpani make a fine effect.

The Firebird: Suite (1919 version).

*** DG 437 818-2. O de l'Opéra Bastille, Chung –
   RIMSKY-KORSAKOV: *Scheherazade.* ***

Myung-Whun Chung gets very musical results from his players and there are many imaginative touches. The sound has great warmth and richness, but the perspective is absolutely right too.

Ballets: The Firebird (suite; 1919 version); *Jeu de cartes*; *Petrushka* (1911 version); (i) *Pulcinella* (1947 version); *The Rite of Spring*.

(B) *** DG Double (ADD) 453 085-2 (2). LSO, Abbado; (i) with
   Berganza, R. Davies, Shirley-Quirk.

(i) Pulcinella (ballet; complete); *The Rite of Spring*.

(B) *** DG 439 433-2. (i) Berganza, R. Davies, Shirley-Quirk;
   LSO, Abbado.

The highlight on this DG Double is *Petrushka*, while both the *Firebird Suite* and *Jeux de cartes* are given stunning performances. The LSO plays with superb virtuosity and spirit. The neo-classical score of *Pulcinella* is given a surprisingly high-powered reading, and not just the playing but the singers too are outstandingly fine. Abbado's feeling for atmosphere and colour is everywhere in evidence, heard against an excellently judged perspective. There is a degree of detachment in Abbado's reading of *The Rite of Spring*, although his observance of markings is meticulous and the orchestra obviously revels in the security given by the conductor's direction. As can be seen, *Pulcinella* and *The Rite of Spring* are also available separately on a bargain Classikon CD.

The Firebird (ballet suite; 1919 version) ; *Petrouchka* (ballet, 1911 version); (i) *Symphony of Psalms*.

(N) ✪ (B) *** Dutton mono (ADD) CDBP 9700. LPO,
   Ansermet, with (i) London Phil. Ch.

At long last, this famous 1946 recording of *Petrouchka*, the recording that really launched Decca's Full Frequency Range Recordings, has made it (officially) on to CD in a magnificent

transfer by Mike Dutton. In its day it caused a sensation with, in the words of John Culshaw, 'a clarity and depth of dynamic range without precedent in the history of recording'. It may not sonically amaze those who know only digital blockbusters, but by any standard, it is hard to believe that this vivid music making happened so long ago. The performance is superbly dramatic, tauter than Ansermet's two subsequent recordings, although they were in even more brilliant sound. *The Firebird*, as the March/April 1947 'EMG Monthly Letter' pointed out, is marginally even more impressive. (It also includes the scherzo, *Dance of the Princesses with the Apples*, not usual in the 1919 suite.) It was a score in which Ansermet always excelled, and with which he made his last recording. The *Symphony of Psalms* was recorded in 1947, and was always rather murky in sound quality; but Dutton has done his usual wonders in transforming it into something much more acceptable. Ansermet is not as electric here as in the ballets, and does not match the composer's own pre-war 78rpm recording; but Ansermet's interpretation does bear studying. He premiered the work and his performances rarely fail to offer fresh insights. This is an essential purchase for anyone who cares for the history of recorded music.

Firebird Suite (1919 version); *The Rite of Spring*.

(N) ** Delos DE 3278. Oregon SO, De Preist.

The Oregon Symphony under James De Preist give a sumptuously romantic account of the *Firebird Suite*, helped by the warm acoustics of the Baumann Auditorium, at the George Fox University in Newberg. But although the mystic atmosphere of the lyrical pages of the *Rite of Spring* is hauntingly conveyed, the score's inherent violence and sacrificial brutality is under-emphasized, and there is a lack of pungent rhythmic bite.

Jeu de cartes.

(M) (**) EMI mono CDM5 66601-2. Philh. O, Karajan –
   BRITTEN: *Variations on a Theme of Frank Bridge*;
   VAUGHAN WILLIAMS: *Fantasia on a Theme by Thomas Tallis.* (***) ✪

First-class Philharmonia playing, of course, but Karajan's approach to Stravinsky's ballet rhythms is too suave to give satisfaction. This is music which, above all, needs at least a degree of bite – and that is not forthcoming here. But the Britten and Vaughan Williams couplings are a different matter; indeed, they more than justify the cost of this CD. However, this superb disc is now deleted.

Orpheus (ballet suite); *Petrushka* (ballet suite); *Fireworks*; *Ode* (elegiac chant); *Song of the Volga Boatmen* (arr. for wind and percussion).

(M) ** Melodiya (ADD) 74321 33220-2. Moscow PO or USSR
   SO, composer (with speech of thanks).

An issue of special historic interest in that it recorded Stravinsky's return to his native country in his eightieth year for the first time after the Revolution. The performances have a sense of occasion. The *Petrushka* starts just before the *Russian Dance*, omits the whole of the Third Tableau and abruptly cuts short the Fourth, with the concert ending; it lasts eighteen and a half minutes. Stravinsky takes brisk (some might say headlong) tempi, and the impression is of the orchestra taking plenty of risks and playing to the very limits of their ability. Nor is the *Orpheus* with the USSR Symphony Orchestra among the most idiomatic of performances. The 1917 arrangement of the *Song of the Volga Boatmen* for wind and percussion is more effective. There is a short word of thanks from Stravinsky, and all devotees of the composer will want to have this memento of a historic occasion.

Petrushka (ballet): complete.

(***) Testament mono SBT 1139. Philh. O, Stokowski –
RIMSKY-KORSAKOV: *Scheherazade.* **

Petrushka (1911 original version)

(M) *** RCA mono 09026 63303-2. Boston SO, Monteux –
FRANCK: *Symphony in D min.**** 🌐

Petrushka (1911 version; complete). The Firebird: Suite (1919). Fireworks; Pastoral (arr. Stokowski).

🌐 (***) Dutton Lab. mono CDAX 8002. Phd. O, Stokowski
(with: SHOSTAKOVICH: *Prelude in E flat min., Op. 34/14,*
arr. Stokowski (***)).

Petrushka (1947 version); (i) Pulcinella (complete ballets).

*** Decca 443 774-2. Concg. O, Chailly; (i) with Antonacci,
Ballo; Shimell.

(i) Petrushka (1947 score); (ii) Pulcinella (suite)

**(*) Testament SBT 1156. (i) New Philh O; (ii) Philh. O;
Klemperer

A splendid digital *Petrushka* from Chailly, vividly characterized and with genuine pathos in Petrushka's cell scene. The orchestral playing is superb and the Decca engineers have pulled out all the stops, providing glittering detail, yet making full use of the warm Concertgebouw ambience. *Pulcinella* is equally winning, perhaps not as high-powered as the Abbado version, but with some splendidly incisive string-playing and plenty of rhythmic lift. Again the recording is in the demonstration bracket.

Stokowski's *Petrushka* with the Philharmonia Orchestra is superb. The orchestral playing is exciting and full of colour. It is almost as impressive as his famous pre-war set with the Philadelphia Orchestra – and that is saying something. It is coupled, however, with a somewhat idiosyncratic *Scheherazade*.

Stokowski's 1937 version of *Petrushka* is very special indeed, the sound tremendously present and amazingly detailed for its period – high fidelity even by today's standards – and the performance is marvellously characterized and full of atmosphere: indeed it is difficult to think of a portrayal of Petrushka himself that is more poignant, keenly felt or brilliantly coloured. The playing of the Philadelphia Orchestra is quite stunning, and the Dutton transfer gets far more detail on to CD than the RCA rival (now deleted); it is also smoother on top. The 1935 *Firebird Suite* (its ending cut, to fit on a 78-r.p.m. side) takes wing too – equally strongly characterized and full of atmosphere. The shorter pieces are rarities. A marvellous collection – indeed, a desert island disc.

As he conducted the ballet's première, it is good to have

Monteux's 1931 Boston recording at last satisfactorily remastered, with the sound now vivid and the Boston ambience more of an advantage than a drawback. The performance has undoubted flair and is very well played.

Following a concert performance in 1967, Klemperer insisted on recording *Petrushka*. EMI initially edited together a finished copy that was rejected. What Stewart Brown of Testament has done is to investigate the original tapes, and put together a recording drawn from the first day's sessions instead of the third – sharper and more intense. The result is a fascinating version, strong and symphonic rather than atmospheric, and magnetic from first to last. Vivid recording, full of presence. The *Pulcinella Suite* of four years earlier has already appeared on CD, an attractively fresh performance, not quite as biting as that of *Petrushka*.

(i) Petrushka (1947 version); (ii; iii; iv) Pulcinella; (i) The Rite of Spring; (ii; iii) Suites Nos. 1 & 2; (v; iii) Danses concertantes.

(N) (BB) **(*) EMI ADD/Dig. CZS5 74305-2 (2). (i) Phd. O,
Muti; (ii) ASMF; (iii) Marriner; (iv) with Kenny, Tear Lloyd;
(v) Los Angeles CO.

Muti's 1978 *Rite* is as red-blooded as you could wish for, with the fast tempi highlighting the brutal qualities of the score to the full. The orchestra relishes the virtuosity of the performance, which is certainly exciting. (This is also available separately on EMI's new Encore label, see below.) *Petrushka*, dating from 1981, is not quite so successful. Once again Muti achieves stunning playing from the Philadelphians, but if their response is breathtaking, his reading can be best described as breathless. There is an unremitting drive here with the *Danse russe* taken at break-neck speed and everything far too regimented. The recording has splendid impact and clarity, but there is too little tenderness and magic.

Marriner directs the rest of the programme and it is good to have these excellent ASMF recordings back in the catalogue. Their playing is very fine indeed. Some might feel that a more astringent bouquet is called for in *Pulcinella*, and here the voices are a bit forward, but the singing is good enough for that not to matter, and Marriner's approach brings out the geniality. The fine often witty response of the Academy is no less beguiling in the delectably scored orchestral *Suites*. They are no less successful in the *Dances concertantes*, one of Stravinsky's most light-hearted pieces, where the highly original scoring is a constant delight, particularly when recorded as vividly as here. The sound in all these recordings has a natural balance with plenty of air around the instruments and no want of depth.

(i) Petrushka (complete 1911 score); (ii) The Rite of Spring.

(M) **(*) Sony SMK 64109. (i) NYPO; (ii) Cleveland O;
Boulez.

Petrushka (ballet; complete 1947 version); The Rite of Spring; Circus Polka.

(B) ** Australian Decca Eloquence (ADD) 460 509-2. LAPO,
Mehta.

(i) *Petrushka* (1947 score); *The Rite of Spring;* (ii) *4 Etudes for Orchestra.*

(M) **(*) Mercury (ADD) 434 331-2. (i) Minneapolis SO;
  (ii) LSO; Dorati.

Petrushka (1947 score); *The Rite of Spring; Fireworks, Op. 4.* .

(M)** RCA (ADD) 09026 63311-2. (i) Boston SO; (ii) Chicago
  SO, Ozawa.

There is a controlled intensity about Boulez's 1971 New York performance of *Petrushka*, and it is a pity that the 1971 recording, made in the Avery Fisher Hall, becomes fierce at higher dynamic levels. In *The Rite of Spring*, recorded two years earlier in Severance Hall, Cleveland, Boulez is less lyrical than the composer but compensates with relentless rhythmic urgency. The massive vividness of sound matches the monolithic quality of the interpretation.

Dorati's (1959) Mercury recording of *Petrushka* is exceptionally clean and vivid, with the semi-clinical Minneapolis recording bringing stereoscopic detail in the two central tableaux. There is plenty of drama too, and the final scene is touchingly done. Inevitably the sound is dated: the bright upper range adds a sharp cutting edge and impact to Dorati's extremely violent performance of *The Rite of Spring*. His speeds are fast – sometimes considerably faster than is indicated in the score – but the LSO players carry complete conviction, the tautness of the work the more clearly revealed. The orchestral *Etudes* were recorded later (1964) in Watford, and have a fuller ambience.

Mehta's Los Angeles *Rite of Spring*, despite extreme tempi, some very fast, others slow, is an interesting and individual reading, very well recorded. *Petrushka* is superbly played, but lacks the character of the finest versions. What makes it compelling, in its way, is the astonishingly brilliant recording, which startlingly brings the Los Angeles orchestra into your sitting room. The *Circus Polka* makes a sparkling bonus, but this CD is primarily recommendable to audiophiles.

Recorded in 1968 and 1969 respectively, Ozawa's accounts of *Petruska* and the *Rite of Spring* are unequal in appeal. *Petruska* is a lightweight interpretation in the best sense, with Ozawa's feeling for the balletic quality of the music coming over, sometimes at the expense of dramatic emphasis. However, he is at times too dainty, and the underlying tension suggesting the strong feelings of the puppet characters is not always apparent. There are certainly more earthy accounts of the *Rite of Spring* available, even if the Chicago acoustic adds to the weight of the performance. Curiously, the early *Fireworks*, which one would have thought suited Ozawa's talents best of all, sounds rather aggressive.

(i) *Pulcinella* (complete); *Danses concertantes.*

(BB) *** Naxos 8.553181. (i) James, Bostridge, Herford;
  Bournemouth Sinf., Sanderling.

The Naxos complete *Pulcinella* ballet, is fresh and alert and with the impact of the crisp, clean ensemble reinforced by full and immediate sound on an apt chamber scale. This was one of the very first recordings made (in 1993) by the tenor, Ian Bostridge, and the heady beauty of his voice is superbly caught in such vocal numbers as the *Serenata*. The other soloists are also good. A full text and English translation are given, and it is good to have the far later *Danses concertantes* (1941–2) as a valuable makeweight, done with equal point and polish. Strongly recommended.

The Rite of Spring (complete ballet) (see also above, under *Petrushka*).

(BB) *** EMI Encore CDE5 74742-2. Phd. O, Muti –
  MUSSORGSKY: *Pictures*. ***

(M) **(*) DG (ADD) 463 613-2. BPO, Karajan – PROKOFIEV:
  Symphony No. 5. ***

(M) (**) Dutton Lab. mono CDK 1206. Concg. O, Van Beinum
  – BARTOK: *Concerto for Orchestra.* (***) ●

The Rite of Spring; Circus Polka; Fireworks, Op. 4; Greeting Prelude (Happy Birthday).

(BB) **(*) CfP 573 441-2. LPO, Mackerras.

The Rite of Spring; (i) *The Firebird* (suite; 1919 score).

(M) **(*) Sony (ADD) SMK 60694. LSO, or (i) NYPO;
  Bernstein.

The Rite of Spring; Symphony in 3 Movements.

(N) (BB) **(*) Teldec Apex 8573 89095-2. NYPO, Mehta.

Muti generally favours speeds a shade faster than usual, and arguably the opening bassoon solo is not quite flexible enough, for metrical precision is a key element all through, and the performance presence the violence with a red-blooded forcefulness that is very compelling. The recording, not always as analytically clear as some rivals, is strikingly bold and dramatic, with brass and percussion caught exceptionally vividly. At super-bargain price, coupled with an equally outstanding version of Mussorgsky's *Pictures*, this is very competitive indeed.

Mackerras's version brings a powerful, often spacious performance, recorded in opulent and finely textured, if slightly distanced sound. The weight of the recording adds powerfully to the dramatic impact, though it is a pity that timpani are backward and less sharply focused than they might be. Though short measure, the three little orchestral trifles are done by Mackerras with delectable point and wit.

Karajan's approach may have excitement but, next to other more extrovert accounts, it sounds a bit too smooth and civilized. His attention to detail is striking, but at the expense of sheer elemental strength, though it is interesting to hear such a sophisticated reading of this score. The recording is technically outstanding, with its vivid projection counteracting the high degree of reverberation. Not a top recommendation, but an interesting performance with integrity, which will not disappoint Karajan admirers, and those coming new to it will certainly see the work in a different light. The Prokofiev coupling is outstanding in every way.

The Decca version conducted by Edward van Beinum was the first *Rite of Spring* to appear in Europe after the war, when Stravinsky's own set on five 78s, and Stokowski's on four, still held sway. The sound is pretty remarkable for its period and shows how far ahead the Decca engineers were in 1946, but the overall impression is not as exciting as the astonishing Bartók with which it is coupled.

Bernstein's *Rite* (1972) was recorded with quadraphonic 'surround sound' in mind. Although it does not have the pinpoint precision of some other versions, the electric intensity is never in doubt. Bernstein is more consciously romantic in expressiveness than is common, but conveys the illusion of a live performance – it was this recording which convinced him of the advantages of recording live from then on. It still makes an impact on CD, but is not in the demonstration bracket. The *Firebird Suite* (1957) is in most ways better recorded: more open, better defined and with rather greater depth. It is an exciting performance but lacks atmosphere.

Although the effect is often rhythmically ferocious – some might say crude – no one could suggest that Mehta's New York *Rite of Spring* isn't exciting, partly because the NYPO play very well indeed, but are also obviously caught up in Mehta's impulsive forward thrust. It is also very brilliantly recorded, with spectacular use of the drums, and the acoustics of New York's Manhattan Center providing a spacious dimensional layout. If the bold horn entry in the penultimate movement echoes resonantly rather than having a biting forward projection, the final *Sacrificial dance* could not be more brutal. The *Symphony in Three Movements* also has forceful accents, and makes its progress very purposefully, yet the central *Andante* is neatly done, and has charm.

The Soldier's Tale (L'histoire du soldat; complete).

*** Chan. 9189. Haugland, SNO, Järvi.

(i) The Soldier's Tale (complete); (ii) Dumbarton Oaks Concerto in E flat.

(BB) *** Naxos 8.55366-2. D. Thomas, Soames, Keeble, & Instrumental Ens.; (ii) N. Ch. O; Ward.

With recording ideally balanced, intimate but not too dry, with fair bloom on voices and instruments, Nicholas Ward on Naxos offers a crisp and well-lifted account, with seven stylish players from the Northern Chamber Orchestra. Using the idiomatic English version of Michael Flanders and Kitty Black, the three actors characterize well without exaggeration. From the full chamber orchestra the *Dumbarton Oaks Concerto* makes a generous and apt coupling, similarly crisp and persuasive

Aage Haugland takes a forthright view, with the Devil given a crypto-French accent as a very oily character. Where the Chandos scores is in the sharp focus of the performance, generally brisk and taut at fast speeds, helped by a close recording which yet has plenty of air round the sound.

The Soldier's Tale (suite)

(M) *** Van. 08.8013.71. Instrumental Ens., Leopold Stokowski – THOMSON: *Film Scores.* ***

Stokowski works his magic upon this surprisingly neglected score, making the most of its lyrical warmth as well as the more abrasive Devil's music, which has plenty of rhythmic bite. The septet of expert instrumentalists is naturally recorded in a studio acoustic, but one which has plenty of ambience.

Symphony in 3 Movements.

(M) *** EMI (ADD) CDM5 67337-2. Philh. O, Klemperer – HINDEMITH: *Nobilissima visione;* WEILL: *Kleine Dreigroschenmusik* *** (with KLEMPERER: *Merry Waltz* **).

Symphony in 3 Movements; Symphonies of Wind Instruments; (i) Symphony of Psalms.

**(*) DG 457 616-2. BPO, Pierre Boulez; (i) with Berlin R. Ch.

With superb playing from the Philharmonia and a strong rhythmic pulse in the outer movements, Klemperer's is a highly stimulating performance, which does not miss the work's balletic associations, while the Stravinskian subtleties of mood, colour and balance in the central movement are astutely caught. The recording has fine bloom and excellent detail.

The *Symphony in Three Movements* brings a more violent approach from Boulez, with the Berliners relishing the jazzy outbursts of the outer movements and the warmth of the central slow movement. An unexpected but revelatory disc. Refined recording to match. The results are refined rather than biting in the *Symphony of Psalms* and *Wind Symphonies*, where Boulez's restraint combined with beautifully moulded ensemble gives way to dramatic power only at key climaxes. The poignancy of the *Wind symphonies* is reinforced, and the beauty of the *Symphony of Psalms* culminates in a glowing account of the final apotheosis, one of Stravinsky's most sublime inspirations.

CHAMBER AND INSTRUMENTAL MUSIC

Ballad; Chanson russe; Danse russe; Divertimento; Duo concertante; Pastorale; Suite italienne.

*** Chan. 9756. Mordkovitch, Milford.

Divertimento.

(N) *** Erato 8573–85769-2. Repin, Berezovsky – BARTOK: *Roumanian folk dances;* STRAUSS: *Violin Sonata.* ***

(i) Divertimento; Duo concertante; Suite italienne; (ii) Mavra: Chanson russe.

(M) *** EMI (ADD)/Dig. CDM5 66061-2. Perlman, with (i) Canino; (ii) Sanders (with RACHMANINOV: *Vocalise, Op. 34/14; Songs: It's peaceful here* (arr. Heifetz); *Daisies* (arr. Kreisler) ***; TCHAIKOVSKY: *Andante cantabile* from *Op. 11; Chanson sans paroles* (arr. Kreisler); *Souvenir d'un lieu cher: Mélodie, Op. 42/2* (arr. Flesch) **).

Lydia Mordkovich, truly Russian, defies the idea of Stravinsky as a cold composer, finding radiant intensity even in the neoclassical *Duo concertante*, notably in the lovely final *Dithyrambe*. This was a work Stravinsky wrote for himself to play with the violinist Samuel Dushkin, and the other pieces, all lighter, are arrangements he also made for their recitals, based on some of his most approachable works. So the ballets *Pulcinella* and *The Fairy's Kiss* prompted respectively the *Suite italienne* and the *Divertimento*, while the other shorter pieces culminate here in a fizzing account of the *Danse russe* from *Petrushka*.

Perlman plays all this music with warmth and understanding, and his achievement in the *Duo concertante* is particularly remarkable. Bruno Canino makes a sympathetic partner and the 1974 recording, originally excellent, has been clearly and cleanly transferred to CD, the sound more strongly etched than on LP. Perlman's seductively slinky account of the *Chanson russe* from *Mavra* was recorded four years later, and the two Rachmaninov songs, which are played with a delightful flowing lyricism, are digital; but in all these encores the sound is warmer and smoother. Samuel Sanders gives admirable support, although he is made to sound a little self-effacing by the recording balance.

On Erato Repin and Berezovsky give a performance of immense character and elegance, and ideally balanced.

Concertino; Double Canon; 3 Pieces. ***

(N) (M) *** EMI CDM5 67550-2 [567551]. Alban Berg Qt – DEBUSSY; RAVEL: *String Quartets.* **(*)

(N)(BB) *** Naxos 8.554315. Goldner Qt – SZYMANOWSKI: *String Quartets Nos. 1–2.* ***

Stravinsky's original titles for the *Three Pieces* were *Danse, Excentrique* and *Cantique*, with the second an etching of the contortions of the famous clown, Little Tich, and the third a Russian chant. The playing of the Alban Berg Quartet has tremendous bite and grip, and the music's spare lyricism and irony is indelibly caught, as is the rhythmic energy and bustle of the *Concertino*. The economic *Double Canon* is dedicated to the memory of the painter Raol Dufy, and this short valediction is touchingly realized. First class, vividly present recording certainly gives these performances the right to be considered as among the 'Great Recordings of the Century', although we are much less sure about the claims of the Debussy and Ravel couplings.

Stravinsky's bright and brittle miniatures for string quartet, with their compressed and cryptic arguments, make a striking contrast with the rich and exotic quartets of Szymanowski. The excellent Goldner quartet play them with dramatic bite, underlining that contrast. Excellent sound.

3 Pieces for String Quartet.

*** ASV CDDCA 930. Lindsay Qt – DEBUSSY; RAVEL: *Quartets.* **(*)

A vital, finely etched performance of these delightful pieces from the Lindsays. A good fill-up to thoughtful and vigorous account of the Debussy and Ravel *Quartets*. Good recordings.

Suite italienne for Cello & Piano.

*** Virgin VC5 45274-2. Mørk, Vogt – PROKOFIEV: *Cello Sonata in C, Op. 119.* SHOSTAKOVICH: *Cello Sonata.*

Suite italienne for Violin & Piano.

*** BIS CD 336. Thedéen, Pöntinen – SCHNITTKE: *Sonata;* SHOSTAKOVICH: *Sonata.* ***

Stravinsky made several transcriptions of movements from *Pulcinella*, including the *Suite italienne* for both cello and alternatively violin and piano. The performances by Torleif Thedéen and Roland Pöntinen, are felicitous and spon-

taneous, and they are afforded strikingly natural recording.

Truls Mørk and Lars Vogt also give a very lively account. It is a welcome makeweight for their eloquent accounts of the Shostakovich and Prokofiev sonatas.

PIANO MUSIC
Piano duet

Rite of Spring (arr. composer).

(BB) **(*) Arte Nova 74321 51638-2 (2). Tchernoussova, Romanovskaya – RACHMANINOV: *Suites Nos. 1–2* etc. **(*)

This splendid Russian duo plays Stravinsky's own piano-duet version of the *Rite of spring* with superb precision and clarity, aerating the complex textures. If the result is light and clear rather than barbaric, it certainly provides an illuminating view of this masterpiece, a generous and apt coupling for the Rachmaninov duets making up this two-disc issue.

Solo piano music

Circus Polka; 4 Etudes; Piano Rag Music; Ragtime; Scherzo; Serenade; Sonata; Sonata in F sharp min.; Tango; Valse pour les enfants. Piano transcriptions: Le Chant du rossignol (probably made by Arthur Lourié); 3 Movements from The Firebird (trans. Agosti); 3 Movements from Petrushka; Symphonies for Wind Instruments (arr. Arthur Lourié).

(N) (B) *** Nimbus NI 5519/20. Jones.

A fascinating and immensely valuable survey. The piano was Stravinsky's indispensable work-tool. He thought of it as 'a utility instrument which sounds right only as percussion', but Rubinstein convinced him otherwise, and it was for Rubinstein that he transcribed the *Three Movements from Petrushka*. Martin Jones plays them vividly, and is particularly evocative in the central *Chez Pétrouchka* (as he is in the *Firebird* finale). The other piano transcriptions, wanted for use at ballet rehearsals, were made by others. *Le Chant du rossignol* is very orchestral and prolix, but again Martin Jones finds atmospheric magic in the third and final tableau.

The earliest work here is the charming *Scherzo* with its rhythmic hoppity-jump, while Jones relishes the full-blooded Tchaikovskian romanticism of the *F sharp minor Sonata*, an entirely uncharacteristic but very enjoyable student work from 1903–4: its simple *Andante* is touching. The *Etudes* of 1908 move into the world of Scriabin and the *Valse pour les enfants* is rather like Poulenc, but the *Piano Rag Music* and the engaging *Ragtime* (1918–19) are harder-edged and more typical.

The *Sonata* (1924) with its cool, almost Ravelian *Adagietto* and the delightful *Serenade* (1925) are perhaps Stravinsky's two finest solo works, and ought to be much better known. The much later and beguiling *Tango* (1940) contrasts with the *Circus Polka* (1942), which, with its parody of Schubert's *Marche militaire*, brings an element of the bizarre. Martin Jones readily encompasses the wide range of these pieces, and even if his playing is less percussive than the composer's own drier approach, it remains fully authoritative, as well as giving much enjoyment when so well (if fairly resonantly) recorded.

3 Movements from Petrushka.

(M) *** DG (ADD) 447 431-2. Pollini – *Recital*. ***

Staggering, electrifying playing from Pollini, creating the highest degree of excitement. This is part of an outstandingly generous recital of twentieth-century piano music.

Piano Sonata; Piano-rag Music; Serenade in A.

*** Chan. 8962. Berman – SCHNITTKE: *Sonata*. ***

Boris Berman is an artist of powerful intelligence who gives vivid and alertly characterized accounts of all these pieces. Excellent piano sound, too, from the Chandos engineers. Strongly recommended.

VOCAL MUSIC

(i) Mass; (ii) Les Noces.

(M) *** DG (IMS) 423 251-2. (i) Trinity Boys' Ch.; E. Bach Festival O; (i, ii) E. Bach Festival Ch.; (ii) Mory, Parker, Mitchinson, Hudson; Argerich, Zimerman, Katsaris, Francesch (pianos), percussion; Bernstein.

In the *Mass* the style is overtly expressive, with the boys of Trinity Choir responding freshly, but it is in *Les Noces* that Bernstein conveys an electricity and a dramatic urgency which give the work its rightful stature as one of Stravinsky's supreme masterpieces, totally original and – even today – unexpected, not least in its black-and-white instrumentation for four pianos and percussion. The star pianists here make a superb, imaginative team.

(i) Perséphone. The Rite of spring.

(M) **(*) Virgin VMD5 61249-2 (2). (i) Fournet, Rolfe Johnson, Tiffin Boys' School Ch., LPO Ch.; LPO, Nagano.

Where Stravinsky himself – at speeds consistently more measured than Nagano's – takes a rugged, square-cut view of *Perséphone*, Nagano, much lighter as well as more fleet, makes the work a far more atmospheric evocation of spring. The narration of Anne Fournet brings out all the beauty of Gide's words, with Anthony Rolfe Johnson free-toned in the taxing tenor solos. Nagano's reading of *The Rite of Spring* has similar qualities. If it is less weightily barbaric than many, the springing of rhythm and the clarity and refinement of instrumental textures make it very compelling, with only the final *Danse sacrale* lacking something in dramatic bite.

Symphony of Psalms (1948 version).

(B) *** Sony (ADD) SBK 61703. E. Bath Festival Ch., LSO, Bernstein – ORFF: *Catulli Carmina*. **(*)

Bernstein's *Symphony of Psalms* ranks among the finest ever recorded, though his view of the work is not as austere and ascetic as the composer's own. Yet there is grandeur and a powerful sense of atmosphere as well as first-class singing and playing from the chorus and orchestra. The recording is distinguished by clarity and range, and with few alternatives available this is an essential purchase for all Stravinskians.

OPERA

Oedipus Rex (opera-oratorio).

*** Sony SK 48057. Cole, Von Otter, Estes, Sotin, Gedda, Chéreau, Eric Ericson Chamber Ch., Swedish RSO & Ch., Salonen.

Salonen with his Swedish forces and an outstanding cast offers an ideal combination of rugged power and warmth, delivered expressively but without sentimentality. The pin-point precision of ensemble of the choruses does more than anything else to punch home the impact of this so-called opera-oratorio, with its powerful commentary, Greek-style. The singing of the two principals, Vinson Cole as Oedipus and Anne Sofie von Otter as Jocasta, then conveys the full depth of emotion behind the piece. Simon Estes as Creon and Hans Sotin as Tiresias are both firm and resonant, with Nicolai Gedda still strong as the Shepherd. With recorded sound both dramatically immediate and warm, and with splendid narration in French from Patrice Chéreau, this displaces all rivals, even the composer's own American version.

Stravinsky Edition, Vol. 9: The Rake's Progress (complete).

(M) *** Sony (ADD) SM2K 46299 (2). Young, Raskin, Reardon, Sarfaty, Miller, Manning, Sadler's Wells Op. Ch., RPO, composer.

The Rake's Progress (complete).

***DG 459 648-2 (2). Bostridge, York, Terfel, Robson, Howells, Von Otter, Monteverdi Ch., Gardiner.

*** Erato 0630 12715-2 (2). Hadley, Upshaw, Lloyd, Ramey, Collins, Bumbry, Lyon Opéra Ch. & O, Nagano.

**(*) Decca 411 644-2 (2). Langridge, Pope, Walker, Ramey, Dean, Dobson, L. Sinf. Ch. & O, Chailly.

Stravinsky's own recording of *The Rake's progress* has many elements of the original Sadler's Wells production. The casting is uniformly excellent with the Rake of Alexander Young dominating but Judith Raskin an attractive heroine. Regina Sarfaty's Baba is superbly characterized and her anger at being spurned just before the 'squelching' makes a riveting moment. The composer conducts with warmth as well as precision, both chorus and orchestra respond persuasively, and the CD transfer is excellent.

Gardiner's incisive direction, with brilliant, polished playing from the LSO confirms this as the finest of modern versions. It all but outshines the composer's own vintage version, equally well cast, when Gardiner at speeds often faster than usual, brings extra sparkle to the rhythmic neo-classical writing and conveys a hushed intensity in the many tender moments of this moral tale. Bostridge's lyric tenor might seem light for the role of Tom but with fine pointing of words he underlines the Rake's vulnerability, the ease with which he gives way to temptation. Terfel makes a seductive Nick Shadow, strong and sardonic, singing su-perbly, and the young American, Deborah York, sings with golden tone and dazzling flexibility as Anne, untroubled by high tessitura. The rest of the team is equally strong, with Anne Sofie von Otter making Baba the Turk the most eloquent nagger. Well-balanced recording – the point on which other modern versions fall short – with well-defined sound staging.

Kent Nagano, with his Lyon Opera forces and an outstanding cast of soloists, directs a fresh and crisp account. In the title-role Jerry Hadley, with his fresh, clear tone, is aptly youthful-sounding and brings out the pathos of the final scenes when struck insane by Nick Shadow. Samuel Ramey is powerful and sinister in that devilish role, as he was in the earlier, Chailly version, and Dawn Upshaw makes a tenderly affecting Anne Trulove, bringing out the heroine's vulnerability. Robert Lloyd as Trulove and Anne Collins as Mother Goose are both very well cast, and the veteran, Grace Bumbry, makes a fruity Baba the Turk. Excellent ensemble from the Lyon Opera chorus, though the balance is a little backward. Otherwise first-rate sound.

Riccardo Chailly draws from the London Sinfonietta playing of a clarity and brightness to set the piece aptly on a chamber scale without reducing the power of this elaborately neo-classical work. Philip Langridge is excellent as the Rake himself, very moving when Tom is afflicted with madness. Samuel Ramey as Nick, Stafford Dean as Trulove and Sarah Walker as Baba the Turk are all first rate, but Cathryn Pope's soprano as recorded is too soft-grained for Anne. Charming as the idea is of getting the veteran Astrid Varnay to sing Mother Goose, the result is out of style. The recording is exceptionally full and vivid but the balances are sometimes odd: the orchestra recedes behind the singers and the chorus sounds congested, with little air round the sound.

(i) *Le Rossignol* (complete).

⚙ (***) Testament mono SBT 1135. Micheau, Moizan, Giraudeau, Lovano, Roux; French R. Ch. & O, Cluytens – DELAGE: *4 Poèmes hindous.* **

(i) *Le Rossignol* (complete); (ii) *Renard* (histoire burlesque).

*** EMI CDC5 56874-2. Paris Nat. Opéra Ch. & O, Conlon; (i) Dessay, McLaughlin, Urmana, Schagidullin; (i; ii) Grivnov, Naouri, Mikhailov; (ii) Caley. Naouri, Mikhailov.

Stravinsky's early opera, *Le Rossignol*, in three compact acts, is a problematic work, and Conlon here provides a near-ideal reading. Evocative and atmospheric in Act 1, the work is then transformed into something far more tautly dramatic, even while its Russian roots are still clear. Natalie Dessay with her bright soprano is very well suited to the role of the Nightingale, with the tenor Vsevolod Grivnov producing honeyed tones as the Fisherman who acts as commentator. Warm playing and singing from the whole company. The relatively brief burlesque *Renard* brings a performance just as committed, though it lacks the rustic bite and bluff humour that ideally are needed. Warm sound to match.

Apart from the powerful atmosphere that Cluytens evokes from his fine orchestra, the performance is unforgettable on account of the superlative singing of Janine Micheau in the title role and the general excellence of the other soloists. It has something of the same quality of sheer perfection that distinguished Ernest Bour's recording of Ravel's *L'enfant et les sortilèges*, which Testament restored to circulation some years ago.

STROZZI, Barbara (c. 1619–64)

Cantatas: *Op. 2* (1651): *Amor dormiglione; L'amante segreto; Begl'occhi bel seno; Costume de' grandi; L'Eraclito amoroso; La sol fa mir re do (La mia donna); La vendetta.* *Op. 3* (1654): *Cor che reprime alla lingua.* *Op. 7* (1659): *Sino alla morte mi protesto; Lamento: Lagrime mie.* *Op. 8:* *Serenata con violini: Hor che Apollo è a Teti in seno.*

(N) *** HM HMC 905249. Rydén, Musica Fiorita.

Born in about 1619, Barbara Strozzi was the adopted daughter of the poet Giulio Strozzi, librettist for Monteverdi and Cavalli, and she became a highly regarded pupil of the latter composer. She initially made her name both as a singer and as a woman of great beauty, and her writing combines purity of feeling and line with a sensuous spiritual ecstasy that is uniquely feminine.

Even more than earlier collections, this recital from Susanne Rydén shows the remarkable range of Strozzi's vocal music. The major cantatas alternate free recitativo and arioso, producing a rich variety of mood, while the laments carry her instantly recognizable chromatic style. The very touching lament of *Hereclitus* and *L'amante segreto* both use the telling device of a constantly repeated descending ground bass (very like a chaconne), though in the latter it is freely interrupted. The *Lamento* (for Lydia, whose father 'keeps her a prisoner') is extraordinarily chromatic, with swooning expressive sweeps and characteristic downward scales. The *Serenade* with two violins is another more florid lament of unrequited love ('*Apollo Rests upon Thetis's Bosom*'). Livelier numbers in popular style use operta texts by Giulio Strozzi which his daughter re-set for her own use. The light-hearted comments on inconstancy and cheating in love in *The Customs of the Great* is typical, while the pastoral portrait of the sleeping Cupid (*Amor dormiglione*) has much charm. *Begl'occhi* is an erotic song of praise for an unnamed lover, ('Beautiful eyes, gates to a paradise, beautiful breast, beautiful hair, beloved lips'). The cantata *Sino alla morte* ('Till Death do us Part'), brings an echoing cello, as ardent as the vocal line and *La sol fa mi re do* is a witty scalic accolade to a lover who prefers to sell her charms, refusing her swain 'unless she hears the clinking of gold coins'. The cheeky *La vendetta*, with lively instrumental accompaniment makes a sparkling end to a recital which is full of contrasts. The versatile Susanne Ryden is as fully at home in the dolorous espessivo as she is in the lighter numbers, and the slight flutter in her voice adds great character to her singing. She gets splendid support from members of Musica Fiorita.

Sacri musicali affetti, Libro I, Op. 5 (extracts): *Erat Petrus; Hodie oritur; Mater Anna; Nascente Maria; O, Maria; Parasti cor meum; Salve Regina; Salve sancta caro.*

⚙ *** HM ED 13048. Kiehr, Concerto Soave (with: GIANONCELLI: *Tastegiatas 1–2;* BIAGIO MARINI: *Sonate da chiesa e da camera; Sinfonia secondo tuono;* TARQUINIO MERULA: *Capriccio cromatico; Canzon* ***).

The opening *Salve Regina* with its sighing phrases and melancholy descending scale is wonderfully tender, yet the music has a life-celebrating vitality too. The motet *Erat*

Petrus (the Gospel story of Peter set free from prison) is virtually an operatic scena, set with great rhythmic variety and using a dialogue device between 'two' voices with aplomb. The melodic line of *Mater Anna* is simple but quite lovely, and here it is a rising scale which brings a ravishing frisson. Perhaps most remarkable of all is the ravishing F minor *Parasti cor meum*, bringing sliding chromatic glissandi – surely a perfect illustration of the Italian word, *affetti*. Maria Kiehr's singing here is unforgettable, as is her bravura decorative flair; indeed her ornamentation is a model of expressive understanding throughout. She is beautifully accompanied by the appropriately named Concerto Soave. To make the programme even more enjoyable, the vocal items are interspersed with admirably chosen intrumental pieces by Strozzi's contemporaries. The recording is admirably balanced and very natural. This is a treasurable collection and a musical revelation.

SUK, Josef (1874–1935)

Asrael Symphony, Op. 27.

✪ *** Chan. 9042. Czech PO, Bělohlávek.

(***) Sup. mono 11 1902-2 (2). Czech PO, Talich (with DVORAK: *Stabat Mater* (*)).

*** EMI CDM5 73480-2. RLPO, Pešek.

Jiří Bělohlávek, the principal conductor of the Czech Philharmonic, draws powerfully expressive playing from the orchestra in a work which in its five large-scale movements is predominantly slow. Next to Pešek's fine Liverpool performance, the speeds flow a degree faster and more persuasively, and the ensemble, notably of the woodwind, is even crisper, phenomenally so.

Václav Talich's pioneering mono account from the early 1950s has great intensity of utterance and poignancy and provides a link with the composer himself. Talich knew him well and conducted many Suk premières. The sound is very acceptable for the period, and it is a pity that it comes harnessed to a less successful Dvořák *Stabat Mater*.

Pešek's Liverpool version has sensitivity and imagination and the sympathy of the Liverpool players is very apparent, but there is no doubt that Bělohlávek's gutsier Czech performance has a greater sense of thrust and power, and for those coming new to this fine work it will be a revelation.

A Fairy-Tale Op. 16.

(**) Biddulph mono WHL 048. Czech PO, Talich – DVORAK: *Symphony No. 9 (New World); Polonaises.* (**)

A Fairy-Tale; Praga Op. 26.

*** Sup. 10 3389-2. Czech PO, Libor Pešek.

A Fairy-Tale; Serenade for Strings in E flat, Op. 6.

*** Chan. 9063. Czech PO, Bělohlávek.

A Fairy-Tale is full of charm and originality. Talich was a friend of Suk, and he conveys its character with great poignancy and warmth. The sound is very acceptable, given its period, and the disc is worth having for this piece alone.

It is also persuasively played under Pešek. It is coupled with *Praga*, a patriotic tone-poem reflecting a more public,

out-going figure than *Asrael*, which was to follow it. Libor Pešek secures an excellent response from the Czech Philharmonic; the recordings, which date from 1981–2, are reverberant but good.

On Chandros the Czech Philharmonic strings play with their customary warmth and eloquence. *A Fairy-Tale* (*Pohádka*) is beautifully played and the *Serenade* is captivating and certainly better recorded than in the earlier version Bělohlávek made with the Prague Symphony for Supraphon.

Fantasy in G min. (for violin and orchestra), *Op. 24.*

*** Decca 460 316-2. Frank, Czech PO, Mackerras – DVORAK: *Violin Concerto; Romance in F min.* **

(M) *** Sup. (ADD) SU 1928-2 011. Suk, Czech PO, Ančerl – DVORAK: *Violin Concerto* etc. ***

Pamela Frank's is a really exceptional performance of the rare Suk *Fantasy*, at 24 minutes longer than many romantic violin concertos. Under Sir Charles Mackerras the Czech Philharmonic launch into the opening with a bite and fire which prepares one well for the soloist's concentrated passion, using the widest range of expression, dynamic and tone. The sound is superb, markedly fuller than that given to the two Dvořák works, which are relatively disappointing.

Suk's playing is refreshing and the orchestral accompaniment under Ančerl is no less impressive. Good remastered 1960s sound.

Fantastic Scherzo, Op. 25.

*** Chan. 8897. Czech PO, Bělohlávek – MARTINU: *Symphony No. 6*; JANACEK: *Sinfonietta.* ***

This captivating piece brings playing from the Czech Philharmonic under Bělohlávek which is even finer than any of the earlier performances and it cannot be too strongly recommended, particularly in view of the excellence of the couplings.

Praga; (i) *Ripening, Op. 34*

*** Virgin VC7 59318-2. (i) RLPO Ch.; RLPO, Pešek.

Ripening came after the *Asrael Symphony* and *A Summer Tale* and there is no doubt as to its imaginative resource and richness of invention. Libor Pešek and his Liverpool forces give as dedicated an account of this as one could possibly wish. *Prague*, an earlier piece from 1904, is not quite in the same league but it is still an admirable makeweight and is played with exemplary commitment. Very good recorded sound too.

Serenade for Strings in E flat, Op. 6.

(BB) *** ASV (ADD) CDQS 6094. Polish R. CO, Duczmal – TCHAIKOVSKY: *Serenade* ***; GRIEG: *Holberg Suite.* **(*)

(BB) *** Virgin 2 x 1 VBD5 61763-2 (2). LCO, Warren-Green – DVORAK: *Serenade for Strings;* ELGAR: *Introduction & Allegro; Serenade;* TCHAIKOVSKY: *Serenade;* VAUGHAN WILLIAMS: *Fantasia on Greensleeves* etc. ***

(BB) *** Naxos 8.550419. Capella Istropolitana, Krěchek – DVORAK: *String Serenade.* **(*)

Serenade for Strings; Meditation on an Old Czech Hymn (St Wenceslas), Op. 35a.

(B) **(*) Discover DICD 920234. Virtuosi di Praga, Vlček –
JANACEK: *Suite.* ***

Suk's *Serenade* is a gorgeous work and it receives a lovely
performance from the Polish Radio Chamber Orchestra
under Agnieszka Duczmal. This is altogether first rate, and
the recording is full-textured and well balanced, bringing out
Duczmal's many fine shadings of colour. This inexpensive
version is second only to the full-priced Chandos account
above from Bělohlàvec coupled with *A Fairytale* (see above).

Warren-Green and his LCO also give a wonderfully persuasive account of Suk's *Serenade*, making obvious that its
inspiration is every bit as vivid as in the comparable work
of Dvořák. The recording, made in All Saints', Petersham,
is fresh, full and natural without blurring from the ecclesiastical acoustic. This now comes as part of an incredibly
generous Virgin Double, one of the most desirable bargain
collections of string music in the catalogue.

On Naxos another entirely delightful account of Suk's
Serenade. The innocent delicacy of the opening is perfectly
caught and the *Adagio* is played most beautifully and then,
with a burst of high spirits (and excellent ensemble), the
finale bustles to its conclusion with exhilarating zest. The
recording is first class, fresh yet full-textured, naturally balanced and transparent.

The Prague Virtuosi create a richly full-bodied sonority
here and play this music idiomatically and with ardent,
expressive feeling. Some might feel that the *Serenade* benefits
from a slightly more subtle and less extrovert approach, but
the passionately gripping account of the *Wenceslas Meditation* brings an entirely appropriate emotional intensity.
Splendidly vivid recording,

A Summer Tale, Op. 29; A Winter's Tale, Op. 9.

(BB) **(*) Naxos 8.553703. Slovak RSO, Mogrelia.

Good, very musical performances, with fine sound to boot.
The Slovak Orchestra are not the equal of the Czech Philharmonic but they produce eminently decent results. This is
lovely music and the performances are enjoyable and well
worth the modest outlay.

CHAMBER MUSIC

Piano Quartet in A min., Op. 1.

(N) (B) *** Virgin 2 X 1 VBD5 61904-2 (2). Domus –
MARTINU: *Piano Quartet No. 1* etc. DOHNANYI:
Serenade. DVORAK: *Bagatelles.* KODALY: *Intermezzo.* ***

Suk's early *Piano Quartet* shows this master below his inspired best, but it is still worth having in so sympathetic a
performance as Domus give us. It is a well-filled set and well
worth having in particular for the Martinů pieces which are
not generously represented on disc.

*String Quartets Nos. 1 in B flat, Op. 11; 2, Op. 31; Ballade;
Barcarolle; Meditation on the Czech Choral, St Wenceslas,
Op. 35a; Minuet.*

✪ (M) *** CRD 3472. Suk Qt.

The early *B flat Quartet* is essentially a sunny work, yet its
Adagio has a remarkable potency of elegiac feeling, which is

very affecting in a performance as ardently responsive as
that by the eponymous Suk Quartet on CRD. The *Second
Quartet* is far more concentrated than its predecessor, its
thematic material is curiously haunting and in some ways its
boldness and forward-looking writing suggest that Janáček's
quartets are just around the corner. The performance here
is not only deeply moving and seemingly spontaneous, it is
wonderfully full of observed detail. Of the other works here
the simple *Meditation* is played very touchingly, while the
Barcarolle is a charming piece of juvenilia, a real lollipop, to
show the composer's ready melodic facility. CRD have never
made a better record than this superb collection. The beauty
and internal transparency of string texture is matched by
the natural presence of the group itself.

PIANO MUSIC

*About Mother, Op. 28; Lullabies, Op. 33; 4 Piano Pieces,
Op. 7; Spring, Op. 22a; Summer, Op. 22b; Things Lived and
Dreamed, Op. 30.*

*** Chan. 9026/7. Fingerhut.

It is striking how the earliest works here have a carefree,
sweetly lyrical character, gentler than Dvořák but typically
Czech. Then, after the death in 1904 and 1905 of his mentor,
Dvořák, and his wife (Dvořák's daughter), even these fragmentary inspirations, like the massive *Asrael Symphony*,
become sharp, sometimes even abrasive. The second disc
brings the finest and most ambitious of the suites in which
Suk generally collected his genre pieces, *Things Lived and
Dreamed*. Margaret Fingerhut proves a devoted advocate,
playing with point and concentration, helped by full-ranging
Chandos sound.

(i) *Epilogue, Op. 37. A Fairy Tale, Op. 16.*

*** Virgin VC5 45245-2. (i) Orgonasova, Kusnjer, Mikulás;
RLPO & (i) Ch.; Pešek.

The *Epilogue*, for soprano, baritone, bass, large and small
mixed choruses and orchestra is a big piece, taking some 40
minutes. Suk spoke of it as the last part of a cycle, beginning
with *Asrael* and 'going through the whole of human life,
into reflection on death and the dread of it', before the
appearance of the song of earthly love – all this leading up
to the 'exhilarating song of liberated mankind'. It is a
powerful and eloquent summation of his work, and Pešek
gets very fine results from his Liverpool forces. There is a
fine account of *A Fairy Tale* as a generous makeweight.
Excellent recording and very good notes from John Tyrrell.

SULLIVAN, Arthur (1842–1900)

(i) *Henry VIII* (incidental music): *March; Graceful Dance.*
Overtures: (ii) *Di ballo;* (i) *Macbeth; Marmion.*
(iii) *Pineapple Poll* suite (arr. Mackerras; for band:
Duthoit); (i) *Victoria and Merry England suite No. 1.*
(iv) *The Lost Chord;* (v) *My dearest heart;* (vi) *Onward
Christian Soldiers* (arr. Rogers).

(M) ** Decca (ADD) 468 810-2. (i) RPO, Nash; (ii) Philh. O,

Mackerras; (iii) Eastman Wind Ens., Fennell; (iv) Burrows, Ambrosian Singers, Morris; (v) Palmer, Constable; (vi) Rogers Ch. & O., Rogers.

The highlight here is Mackerras's account of the delightful *Overture di ballo*, showing more delicacy of approach than usual, though certainly not lacking sparkle. The *Macbeth Overture* is dramatic and brightly coloured, but not inspired, worthier of another Savoy opera rather than Shakespeare. *Marmion* too is not really distinctive. The two excerpts from *Henry VIII* are agreeable enough and the selection from *Victoria and Merry England* also includes some pleasing ideas, but with only eleven minutes of music included collectors would do far better to investigate the complete ballet on Marco Polo. The selection from *Pineapple Poll*, however, makes an engaging novelty as it is heard in a military band arrangement and is superbly played by an American ensemble of the highest calibre directed with elan by Frederick Fennell. Of the vocal items Felicity Palmer sings the ballad *My dearest heart* with an appropriate degree of sentimentality, *The Lost Chord* is presented in an elaborate arrangement with luscious chorus, and *Onward Christian Soldiers* as a patrol. The sound throughout is variable, always good but only outstanding in *Di ballo* and the Mercury recording of *Pineaple Poll*.

L'Ile enchantée (complete ballet); *Thespis*: suite.

**(*) Marco 8.2234560. RTE Concert O, Dublin, Penny.

L'Ile enchantée, using lyrical brass solos as well as engaging woodwind, is quite lively, with a splendid final *Galop*. *Thespis* was an early Gilbert and Sullivan creation which did not survive, and the very introduction of the ballet suite unmistakably establishes the jolly rhythmic pattern we associate with the Savoy Operas, while its closing *Galop* has a character which draws on both influences. Andrew Penny secures bold, lively playing from the Dublin orchestra, and the resonant recording is very suitable, if without the lustrous glow we associate with Decca's ballet records.

King Arthur (incidental music): suite; *Macbeth* (incidental music): suite; *The Merry Wives of Windsor* (incidental music): suite.

*** Marco 8.223635. MacDonald, RTE Chamber Ch. & Concert O, Dublin, Penny.

The opening *Chorus of Lake Spirits* in *King Arthur* might well have come out of *Patience* (they sound very much like lovesick maidens). But the following, more confident *Unseen Spirits* would have fitted more readily into *Iolanthe*. The music for *Macbeth* brings a fine Overture with some striking brass writing, and the *Introduction to Act IV* has a rather good tune (though hardly with the flavour of Shakespearean tragedy). But easily the finest number is the deliciously fairy-like, Mendelssohnian *Chorus of the Spirits in the Air*. All the music for *The Merry Wives of Windsor* sounds as if it were part of an operetta, and the closing *Dance* with chorus rounds the whole programme off in exhilarating fashion. Sullivan's flow of attractive ideas makes for a most enjoyable 50 minutes, and all the performers rise to the occasion. The recording is excellent.

(i) *The Merchant of Venice (Masquerade); Henry VIII* (incidental music): suite. Overture: *The Sapphire Necklace; Overture in C (In Memoriam)*.

** Marco 8.223461. RTE Concert O, Dublin, Penny; (i) with Lawler.

Here is a more extended suite from *Merchant of Venice* which includes a solo tenor *Barcarolle* with a strong flavour of *The Gondoliers*. There are plenty of good ideas here, and nice orchestral touches, and a grand G&S-style finale to round things off spiritedly. The *Henry VIII* incidental music opens with regal trumpet fanfares and the scoring is well laced with brass (which made it popular on the bandstand) but it is also notable for a pleasing tenor contribution, *King Henry's song* (well sung here by Emmanuel Lawler). *The Sapphire Necklace overture* is a re-arrangement of the military band score. The piece is well constructed and has a rumbustious ending, but it would have been more effective had it been shorter. Andrew Penny secures lively, well-played performances throughout; but in the last resort this is a disc for curious Sullivan fans rather than for the general collector.

(i) *Overtures: Cox and Box; Princess Ida; The Sorcerer;* (ii) *Overture in C (In Memoriam)*.

(M) **(*) EMI CMS7 764409-2 (2). (i) Pro Arte O, Sargent; (ii) RLPO, Groves – *The Pirates of Penzance.* ***

This collects together the overtures from the operas not recorded by Sargent in his EMI series. The performances are characteristically bright and polished. *In Memoriam* is a somewhat inflated religious piece written for the 1866 Norwich Festival.

Pineapple Poll (ballet; arr. Mackerras).

(M) *** Decca 436 810-2 (2). Philh. O, Mackerras – *Princess Ida.* ***

(B) *** CfP (ADD) CD-CFP 4618. LPO, Mackerras – VERDI: *Lady and the Fool.* ***

(i) *Pineapple Poll* (ballet; arr. Mackerras); (ii) Overtures: *Iolanthe; The Mikado; Ruddigore; The Yeomen of the Guard.*

(M) *** EMI (ADD) CDM5 66538-2. (i) RPO; (ii) Philh. O; Mackerras.

On Decca Mackerras conducts with warmth as well as vivacity, and the elegantly polished playing of the Philharmonia Orchestra gives much pleasure. The record was made in the Kingsway Hall with its glowing ambience, and the CD transfer, though brightly vivid, has a pleasing bloom. Indeed the quality is in the demonstration bracket, with particularly natural string textures.

Mackerras's earlier (1960) Abbey Road recording is still striking for its sheer brio, while the playing has a real feeling of the ballet theatre, the recordings is now freshly remastered and sounds splendidly vivid. What makes the reissue a collector's item is the group of four overtures, recorded by the Philharmonia at their peak in 1956. They are played with marvellous vivacity and sparkle and a delightful lilting flow in the lyrical melodies. The recording is excellent and does not betray its age.

Mackerras's LPO version of the suite on CfP, made in the London Henry Wood Hall in 1977, is also striking for its affection and vivacity. With an apt Verdi coupling, this is excellent value, very well transferred to CD.

Symphony in E (Irish); Imperial march; Overture in C (In Memoriam); Victoria and Merrie England suite.

** CPO 999 171-2. BBC Concert O, Arwel Hughes.

Symphony in E (Irish); In memoriam Overture; The Tempest: Suite, Op. 1.

(N) *** Chan. 9859. BBC PO, Hickox.

Richard Hickox makes a strong and persuasive case for these Sullivan pieces, notably the attractive *Irish Symphony*, which at last receives a first-class recording. The BBC Philharmonic respond with alert and sensitive playing. Sullivan wrote the *In memoriam Overture* in the space of ten days following the sudden death of his father. *The Tempest* music, composed when he was only 18, is not otherwise available. The recording is in the best traditions of the house and serves to enhance this CD's appeal.

On CPO, with Hughes and the BBC Concert Orchestra, the first movement of the *Irish Symphony* obstinately refuses to take off and, as Hughes observes the exposition repeat, its 16 minutes' length seems like a lifetime. The other movements are rather more successful, but in almost every way this performance is inferior to the new Chandos version. The other items here pass muster, with the ballet suite easily the most enjoyable item, especially the finale, *May Day Festivities*, which might well have been an undiscovered interlude from *The Yeomen of the Guard*.

Victoria and Merrie England (complete ballet).

*** Marco 8.223677. RTE Sinf., Dublin, Penny.

Victoria and Merrie England was not a ballet as we understand it today, but a uniquely British combination of mime to music, written to celebrate Queen Victoria's Diamond Jubilee and so was also well laden with patriotism. Essentially a historical cavalcade, its six principal scenes dealt in turn with Ancient Britain, May Day in Queen Elizabeth's time, The Legend of Herne the Hunter, Christmas revels in the time of Charles II, the Coronation of Queen Victoria and, finally, a celebration of Britain's Glory, with a military parade and the entrance of Britannia. It's engaging stuff, with plenty of allusions to the Savoy Operas and plenty of jolly tunes and jaunty ideas. Whoever was responsible for the scoring, it works well. Sullivan used his *Imperial March* for the Coronation scene. But it is the final section, 'Britain's Glory', which is the most robustly enjoyable, with the entrance of English, Irish, Scottish and Colonial troops celebrated with a series of folk tunes, wittily climaxed with 'For he is an Englishman' borrowed from *HMS Pinafore* and sentimentally followed with *There's no place like home*, and finally a brassy version of the National Anthem. It's all very endearing, and Andrew Penny presents it with warm affection and much gusto.

OPERAS

Haddon Hall (complete without dialogue).

✿(N) *** Divine Art 21201 (2). Timmons, Griffin, Lawson,

Smart, Main, Borthwick, Boyd, Thomson, Edinburgh Prince Consort Ch. & O, Lyle.

In 1892 Sullivan was at the apex of his career. *The Gondoliers* had been a great success at the Savoy, and his grand opera *Ivanhoe* had been very well received at the Royal English Opera House. But its success was to be comparatively short-lived, and certainly it had not benefited him financially. He needed a new source of income, yet had fallen out with Gilbert. So he decided to collaborate with a different librettist, Sidney Grundy, with a considerable reputation in the field of light opera.

The result was *Haddon Hall*, based on a true story about the elopement of Lady Dorothy Vernon with her Royalist lover, John Manners, from her ancestral home. But Grundy resourcefully predated the action so that he could use period costumes, and bring in a chorus of Puritans who in the last act, in true topsy-turvy fashion, renounce 'being thoroughly miserable' and instead plan to 'merry-make the livelong day'.

At the beginning of Act II Grundy also introduces an unforgettable Scottish character, The McCrankie, from the Isle of Rum, and he appears to an extraordinarily convincing orchestral evocation of bagpipes. *My name is McCrankie* is followed by his duet with Rupert, *There's no one by*, a wittily dour exposition of their Puritan creed ('We'd supervise the plants and flowers, prescribe them early-closing hours'). Then follows *Hoity-toity*, a delightful trio with Dorcas, the heroine's maid (who sings most engagingly in her own solos), to make three of the most delightful numbers in the whole opera.

Sir John Manners's servant, Oswald (the excellent Alan Borthwick), arrives disguised as travelling salesman and introduces himself with the engagingly lively *Come simples and gentles*, full of musical quotations, and this leads to a heavenly duet with Dorcas, *The sun's in the sky*. But it is Rupert, the heroine's Roundhead cousin, splendidly sung by Ian Lawson, who is the key humorous figure. He only wants Lady Dorothy's hand as it comes with the Haddon Hall estates, and his very winning *I've heard it said* is an inimitable patter style we all recognize; he also has a fine number with chorus, *When I was but a little lad*.

Sydney Grundy tried to avoid the Gilbertian style, but fortunately for the most part he fails to do so: his libretto is certainly more fey than a Gilbertian scenario, but the lyrics are often charming, and there is plenty of felicitous rhyming, to bring one catchy number after another, to which Sullivan provides some of his most delightful music. The lyrical solos and ensembles for the principal characters are often fully operatic and the chorus is richly served. Sullivan also scored more imaginatively than usual, as in the shrieking clarinets in the central Storm sequence.

The performance by the semi-professional Prince Consort, from the Edinburgh Festival Fringe, but using a professional orchestra, may have its rough patches, but it is very well cast, with Mary Timmons a pleasing heroine, who blends appealingly with Steven Griffin as her lover, John Manners. He sings very strongly, especially when he dominates the opera's spectacular finale, when everything is happily resolved.

Davis Lyle's conducting is full of life and the many ensembles come off splendidly, notably the enchanting *Now step lightly, hold me tightly,* in Act II as the lovers elope. Indeed, the opera comes vividly to life in this excellent recording, well balanced and with a fine, full theatrical ambience.

The recording was financially sponsored, not just by the Sullivan Society, but also by individuals, Mike Leigh, of *Topsy-Turvy* fame, among them. It deserves support and in return will give much pleasure, for so much of its music brings fascinating reminders of other G.&S. operas from the Savoy canon. It certainly deserves professionally restaging, perhaps in London's Regent's Park Open Air Theatre, which has recently done so well for *HMS Pinafore.*

The major Decca and EMI sets

(i) *Cox and Box* (libretto by F. C. Burnand) complete;
(ii) *Ruddigore* (complete; without dialogue).

(M) *** Decca (ADD) 417 355-2 (2). (i) Styler, Riordan, Adams; New SO of L.; (ii) Reed, Round, Sandford, Riley, Adams, Hindmarsh, Knight, Sansom, Allister, D'Oyly Carte Op. Ch., ROHCG O, Godfrey.

The Gondoliers (complete; with dialogue).

(M) *** Decca (ADD) 425 177-2 (2). Reed, Skitch, Sandford, Round, Styler, Knight, Toye, Sansom, Wright, D'Oyly Carte Op. Ch., New SO of L., Godfrey.

The Gondoliers (complete; without dialogue).

(M) **(*) EMI (ADD) CMS7 64394-2 (2). Evans, Young, Brannigan, Lewis, Cameron, Milligan, Monica Sinclair, Graham, Morison, Thomas, Watts, Glyndebourne Festival Ch., Pro Arte O, Sargent.

(i; ii) The Grand Duke. (ii) Henry VIII: March & Graceful Dance. (iii) Overture Di Ballo.

*** Decca (ADD) 436 813-2 (2). (i) Reed, Reid, Sandford, Rayner, Ayldon, Ellison, Conroy-Ward, Lilley, Holland, Goss, Metcalfe, D'Oyly Carte Op. Ch.; (ii) RPO, Nash; (iii) Philh. O, Mackerras.

HMS Pinafore (complete; with dialogue).

☙ (M) *** Decca (ADD) 414 283-2. Reed, Skitch, Round, Adams, Hindmarsh, Wright, Knight, D'Oyly Carte Op. Ch., New SO of L., Godfrey.

HMS Pinafore (complete; without dialogue); Trial by Jury.

(M) *** EMI (ADD) CMS7 64397-2 (2). G. Baker, Cameron, Lewis, Brannigan, Milligan, Morison, Thomas, M. Sinclair, Glyndebourne Festival Ch., Pro Arte O, Sargent.

Iolanthe (complete; with dialogue).

(M) *** Decca (ADD) 414 145-2 (2). Sansom, Reed, Adams, Round, Sandford, Styler, Knight, Newman, D'Oyly Carte Op. Ch., Grenadier Guards Band, New SO, Godfrey.

Iolanthe (complete; without dialogue).

(M) *** EMI (ADD) CMS7 64400-2 (2). G. Baker, Wallace, Young, Brannigan, Cameron, M. Sinclair, Thomas, Cantelo, Harper, Morison, Glyndebourne Festival Ch., Pro Arte O, Sargent – Di Ballo Overture. **

The Mikado (complete; without dialogue).

(M) *** Decca (ADD) 425 190-2 (2). Ayldon, Wright, Reed, Sandford, Masterson, Holland, D'Oyly Carte Op. Ch., RPO, Nash.

(M) **(*) EMI (ADD) CMS7 64403-2 (2). Brannigan, Lewis, Evans, Wallace, Cameron, Morison, Thomas, J. Sinclair, M. Sinclair, Glyndebourne Festival Ch., Pro Arte O, Sargent.

Patience (complete; with dialogue).

(M) *** Decca (ADD) 425 193-2 (2). Sansom, Adams, Cartier, Potter, Reed, Sandford, Newman, Lloyd-Jones, Toye, Knight, D'Oyly Carte Op. Ch. & O, Godfrey.

The Pirates of Penzance (complete; with dialogue).

(M) *** Decca (ADD) 425 196-2. Reed, Adams, Potter, Masterson, Palmer, Brannigan, D'Oyly Carte Op. Ch., RPO, Godfrey.

The Pirates of Penzance (complete; without dialogue).

(M) *** EMI (ADD) CMS7 64409-2 (2). G. Baker, Milligan, Cameron, Lewis, Brannigan, Morison, Harper, Thomas, Sinclair, Glyndebourne Festival Ch., Pro Arte O, Sargent – Overtures. **(*)

(i) Princess Ida (complete; without dialogue);
(ii) Pineapple Poll (ballet; arr. Mackerras)

(M) *** Decca (ADD) 436 810-2 (2). (i) Sandford, Potter, Palmer, Skitch, Reed, Adams, Raffell, Cook, Harwood, Palmer, Hood, Masterson, D'Oyly Carte Op. Ch., RPO, Sargent; (ii) Philh. O, Mackerras.

(i) The Sorcerer (complete, without dialogue); (ii) The Zoo (libretto by Bolton Rowe).

*** Decca (ADD) 436 807-2 (2). (i) Adams, D. Palmer, Styler, Reed, C. Palmer, Masterson; (ii) Reid, Sandford, Ayldon, Goss, Metcalfe; nar. Shovelton; (i; ii) D'Oyly Carte Op. Ch., RPO; (i) Godfrey; (ii) Nash.

(i) Utopia Ltd (complete). Overtures: Macbeth; Marmion. Victoria and Merrie England.

**(*) Decca (ADD) 436 816-2 (2). (i) Sandford, Reed, Ayldon, Ellison, Buchan, Conroy-Ward, Reid, Broad, Rayner, Wright, Porter, Field, Goss, Merri, Holland, Griffiths, D'Oyly Carte Op. Ch.; RPO, Nash.

(i) The Yeomen of the Guard (complete; without dialogue); (ii) Trial by Jury.

(M) *** Decca (ADD) 417 358-2. Hood, Reed, Sandford, Adams, Raffell; (i) Harwood, Knight; (ii) Round; D'Oyly Carte Op. Ch.; (i) RPO, Sargent; (ii) ROHCG O, Godfrey.

As can be seen, the two basic sets of recordings of the major Savoy Operas, nearly all from Godfrey (on Decca) and Sargent (on EMI), are available at mid-price, although the EMI sets of *Patience, Ruddigore* and *The Yeomen of the Guard* have been withdrawn. The Decca series usually has the advantage (or disadvantage, according to taste) of including the dialogue. Certain of the operas are available only in D'Oyly Carte versions, and of these the most fascinating is *Cox and Box.* This pre-Gilbertian one-Acter was written in 1867 and thus pre-dates the first G&S success, *Trial by Jury,* by eight years. The D'Oyly Carte performance is splendid in every way. It is given a recording which, without sacrificing clarity, conveys with perfect balance the stage atmosphere.

The Grand Duke, on the other hand, was the fourteenth

and last of the Savoy operas. The present recording, the only complete version, came after a successful concert presentation in 1975, and the recorded performance has both polish and vigour, although the chorus does not display the crispness of articulation of ready familiarity. The recording is characteristically brilliant. The bonuses are well worth having, with Mackerras's account of the *Overture Di Ballo* showing more delicacy of approach than usual, though certainly not lacking sparkle.

Turning now to the major G&S successes, it seems sensible to consider the Decca and EMI alternatives together. EMI usually offer some orchestral bonuses and, in the case of *HMS Pinafore*, add *Trial by Jury* as well (as was the practice in the theatre in the heyday of the D'Oyly Carte Opera Company). Godfrey's Decca *Trial by Jury* is saved for inclusion with their outstanding *Yeomen of the Guard*. The Sargent version of *Trial by Jury* (with George Baker as the Judge) is by general consent the best there is, if only by a small margin, and the EMI version of *Pinafore* is wonderfully fresh too, beautifully sung throughout, while the whole of the final scene is musically quite ravishing.

But the 1960 Godfrey set of this opera is very special indeed, and *HMS Pinafore* is in our view the finest of all the D'Oyly Carte stereo recordings. While Owen Brannigan, on EMI, without the benefit of dialogue conveys the force of Dick Deadeye's personality remarkably strongly, Donald Adams's assumption of the role on Decca (which does have the dialogue) is little short of inspired, and his larger-than-life characterization underpins the whole piece. The rest of the cast make a splendid team: Jean Hindmarsh is a totally convincing Josephine – she sings with great charm – and John Reed's Sir Joseph Porter is a delight.

In D'Oyly Carte set of *The Gondoliers* the solo singing throughout is consistently good, the ensembles have plenty of spirit and the dialogue is for the most part well spoken. As a performance this is on the whole preferable to the Sargent account, if only because of the curiously slow tempo Sargent chooses for the *Cachucha*. However, on EMI there is still much to captivate the ear, and Owen Brannigan, a perfectly cast Don Alhambra, sings a masterly *No possible doubt whatever*. The age of the 1957 recording shows in the orchestra but the voices sound fresh and there is a pleasing overall bloom.

With *Iolanthe*, choice between the two alternatives is a case of swings and roundabouts. The 1960 Decca set was given added panache by the introduction of the Grenadier Guards Band into the *March of the Peers*. Mary Sansom is quite a convincing Phyllis, and if her singing has not the sense of style that Elsie Morison brings to the part, she is completely at home with the dialogue. Also Alan Styler makes a vivid and charming personal identification with the role of Strephon, an Arcadian shepherd, whereas John Cameron's dark timbre on EMI seems much less suitable for this role, even though he sings handsomely. However, on EMI the climax of Act I, the scene in which the Queen of the Fairies lays a curse on members of both Houses of Parliament, shows most excitingly what can be achieved with the 'full operatic treatment': this is a dramatic moment indeed. George Baker, too, is very good as the Lord Chancellor: the voice is fuller, more baritonal than John Reed's

dryly whimsical delivery, yet he provides an equally individual characterization. Godfrey's conducting is lighter and more infectious than Sargent's in the Act I finale, but both performances offer much to delight the ear in the famous Trio of Act II with the Lord Chancellor and the two Earls.

The 1973 stereo remake of *The Mikado* by the D'Oyly Carte Company directed by Royston Nash is a complete success in every way and shows the Savoy tradition at its most attractive. It is a pity no dialogue is included, but the choral singing is first rate, and the glees are refreshingly done, polished and refined, yet with plenty of vitality. John Reed is a splendid Ko-Ko, Kenneth Sandford a vintage Pooh-Bah and Valerie Masterson a charming Yum-Yum. John Ayldon as the Mikado provides a laugh of terrifying bravura, and Lyndsie Holland is a formidable and commanding Katisha. The Sargent set, with its grand operatic style, brings some fine moments, especially in the finales to both Acts. Owen Brannigan is an inimitable Mikado and Richard Lewis sings most engagingly throughout as Nanki-Poo, while Elsie Morison is freshly persuasive as his young bride-to-be. All in all, there is much to enjoy here, but this remains very much a second choice.

Owen Brannigan was surely born to play the Sergeant of Police in *The Pirates of Penzance*, and he does so unforgettably in both the Decca and EMI sets. On Decca there is a considerable advantage in the inclusion of the dialogue, and here theatrical spontaneity is well maintained. Donald Adams is a splendid Pirate King. John Reed's portrayal of the Major General is one of his strongest roles, while Valerie Masterson is an excellent Mabel. Godfrey's conducting is as affectionate as ever. Sargent's version is great fun, too. Its star is George Baker, giving a new and individual portrayal of the Major General. The opera takes a little while to warm up, but there is much to enjoy here. On balance, the Decca set is to be preferred, for Brannigan is especially vivid, and the dialogue undoubtedly adds an extra sense of the theatre.

Patience and *Ruddigore* were the two greatest successes of the Sargent series and it is sad that they have been deleted. However, the extra card in the D'Oyly Carte hand in *Patience* is the dialogue, so important in this opera above all, with its spoken poetry; if Mary Sansom does not give the strongest portrayal vocally, of the main role, both Bunthorne and Grosvenor are well played, while the military numbers, led by Donald Adams in glorious voice, have an unforgettable vigour and presence.

The D'Oyly Carte *Ruddigore* comes up surprisingly freshly, in fact better than we had remembered it, though it is a pity the dialogue was omitted. The performance includes *The battle's roar is over*, which is (for whatever reason) traditionally omitted. There is much to enjoy here (especially Gillian Knight and Donald Adams, whose *Ghosts' high noon* song is a marvellous highlight). Isidore Godfrey is his inimitable sprightly self and the chorus and orchestra are excellent. A fine traditional D'Oyly Carte set, then, brightly recorded.

Princess Ida is fake feminism with a vengeance. Elizabeth Harwood in the name-part sings splendidly, and John Reed's irritably gruff portrayal of the irascible King Gama is memorable; he certainly is a properly 'disagreeable man'. The rest of the cast is no less strong and, with excellent teamwork from the company as a whole and a splendid recording, spacious and immediate, this has much to offer, even if Sullivan's invention is somewhat variable in quality. The CD transfer is outstanding and the 1965 recording has splendid depth and presence. As a bonus we are offered Mackerras's vivacious and polished 1982 digital recording of his scintillating ballet score, *Pineapple Poll*.

The Sorcerer is the Gilbert and Sullivan equivalent of *L'elisir d'amore*, only here a whole English village is affected, with hilarious results. John Reed's portrayal of the sorcerer himself is one of the finest of all his characterizations. The plot drew from Sullivan a great deal of music in his fey, pastoral vein. By 1966, when the set was made, Decca had stretched the recording budget to embrace the RPO, and the orchestral playing is especially fine, as is the singing of the D'Oyly Carte chorus, at their peak. John Reed gives a truly virtuoso performance of his famous introductory song, while the spell-casting scene is equally compelling. The final sequence in Act II is also memorable. The sound is well up to Decca's usual high standard .

Both recordings of *The Yeomen of the Guard*, Decca's and EMI's deleted set, were conducted by Sir Malcolm Sargent. The later Decca account has marginally the finer recording and Sir Malcolm's breadth of approach is immediately apparent in the *Overture*. Both chorus and orchestra (the RPO) are superbly expansive and there is again consistently fine singing from all the principals (and especially from Elizabeth Harwood as Elsie). This Decca *Yeomen* is unreservedly a success, with its brilliant and atmospheric recording. In any case, the considerable bonus is the inclusion of Godfrey's immaculately stylish and affectionate *Trial by Jury* with John Reed as the Judge.

Utopia Ltd was revived for the D'Oyly Carte centenary London season in 1974, which led to this recording. Its complete neglect is unaccountable. Royston Nash shows plenty of skill in the matter of musical characterization, and the solo singing is consistently assured. When Meston Reid as Captain FitzBattleaxe sings 'You see I can't do myself justice' in *Oh, Zara*, he is far from speaking the truth – this is a performance of considerable bravura. The ensembles are not always as immaculately disciplined as one is used to from the D'Oyly Carte, and *Eagle high* is disappointingly focused: the intonation here is less than secure. However, the sparkle and spontaneity of the performance as a whole are irresistible. Of the fillers, the *Macbeth Overture* is dramatic and brightly coloured but not inspired, and the *Marmion Overture*, too, is not really memorable. The selection from *Victoria and Merry England* includes some pleasing ideas. All are vividly played and brightly recorded.

The Zoo (with a libretto by Bolton Rowe, a pseudonym of B. C. Stevenson) dates from June 1875, only three months after the success of *Trial by Jury* – which it obviously seeks to imitate, as the music more than once reminds us. Although the libretto lacks the finesse and whimsicality of Gilbert, it is not without humour, and many of the situations presented by the plot (and indeed the actual combinations of words and music) are typical of the later Savoy Operas. As the piece has no spoken dialogue it is provided here with a stylized narration, well enough presented by Geoffrey Shovelton. The performance is first class, splendidly sung,

fresh as paint and admirably recorded, and it fits very well alongside *The Sorcerer*. The opera has animal noises to set and close the scene.

Alas, as we go to press the EMI sets of *Iolanthe* and *The Gondoliers* have been deleted.

Telarc Mackerras Series

HMS Pinafore.

✪ *** Telarc CD 80774. Suart, Allen, Evans, Schade, Palmer, Adams, Ch. & O of Welsh Nat. Opera, Mackerras.

The Mikado.

✪ *** Telarc CD 80284. Adams, Rolfe Johnson, Suart, McLaughlin, Palmer, Van Allan, Folwell, Ch. & O of Welsh Nat. Opera, Mackerras.

The Pirates of Penzance.

*** Telarc CD80353. Mark Ainsley, Evans, Suart, Van Allan, Adams, Knight, Ch. & O of Welsh Nat. Opera, Mackerras.

(i) The Yeomen of the Guard; (ii) Trial by Jury.

*** Telarc 809404 (2). (i) Mellor, Archer, Palmer; (i; ii) Suart, Adams, Maxwell; (ii) Evans, Banks, Savidge; Ch. & O of Welsh Nat. Opera, Mackerras.

HMS Pinafore; The Mikado; The Pirates of Penzance; Trial by Jury; The Yeomen of the Guard.

(M) *** Telarc CD 80500 (5). Above five complete recordings cond. Mackerras.

As can be seen in the final listing above, the five Telarc operas (reviewed individually below) also come together in a slip-case, with five CDs offered for the cost of three – in every way a superb bargain.

Sir Charles Mackerras here gives an exuberant reading of the first operetta of the cycle, *HMS Pinafore*. The lyricism and transparency of Sullivan's inspiration shine out with winning freshness. The casting is not just starry but inspired. Even such a jaunty number as the 'encore' trio, *Never mind the why and wherefore*, gains in point when so well sung and played as here, with Allen joined by Rebecca Evans as an appealing Josephine and Richard Suart as a dry Sir Joseph Porter. Michael Schade is heady-toned as the hero, Ralph Rackstraw, while among character roles Felicity Palmer is a marvellously fruity Little Buttercup, with Richard van Allan as Bill Bobstay and the veteran, Donald Adams, a lugubrious Dick Deadeye. As with the previous CDs of *Mikado* and *Pirates of Penzance*, Telarc squeezes the whole score on to a single CD, vividly recorded.

With the overture again omitted (not Sullivan's work) and one of the stanzas in Ko-Ko's 'little list' song (with words unpalatable today), the whole fizzing Mackerras performance of *The Mikado* is fitted on to a single, very well-filled disc. The cast, has no weak link and Mackerras is electrically sharp at brisk speeds, sounding totally idiomatic and giving this most popular of the G&S operettas an irresistible freshness at high voltage. The tingling vigour of Sullivan's invention is constantly brought out, with performances from the WNO Chorus and Orchestra at once powerful and refined. With that sharpness of focus Sullivan's parodies of grand opera become more than just witty imitations. So Katisha's aria at the end of Act II, with Felicity Palmer the delectable soloist, has a Verdian depth of feeling. It is good too to hear the veteran Savoyard, Donald Adams, as firm and resonant as he was in his D'Oyly Carte recording made no less than 33 years earlier.

The Pirates of Penzance is characteristic of the rest of this splendid Telarc series. Mackerras's exuberant direction often brings fast tempi (as in How beautifully blue the sky) but the underlying lyricism is as ardently conveyed as ever, especially by John Mark Ainsley, who is a really passionate Frederic. Rebecca Evans makes him a good partner and sings with great charm as Mabel. Needless to say, Richard Suart is a memorable Major General (his patter song is thrown off at great speed) and Donald Adams has not lost his touch. His vintage portrayal of the Pirate King is well matched by Gillian Knight's Ruth in their engaging 'Paradox' duet of Act II. While memories of Owen Brannigan are far from banished, Richard van Allan is a suitably bumptious Sergeant of the Police, and the Welsh Opera Chorus are splendidly fervent in Hail poetry! The recording has fine depth and realism and as a single-disc modern digital version this will be hard to beat.

The Yeoman of the Guard, the fourth Telarc issue of G&S, is very involving as a performance, conveying most exuberantly the sparkle as well as the emotional weight of this most serious of the canon. Alwyn Mellor makes an appealing heroine. Among the others, Felicity Palmer makes a delectably fire-snorting Dame Carruthers, and the veteran, Donald Adams, an incomparable Sergeant Meryll. (His cries of 'Ghastly, ghastly' when cornered by the Dame are wonderful.) Richard Suart as Jack Point characterizes vividly in authentic style, and the only weak link is the Fairfax of Neil Archer, who too often sounds strained. Even so, the final bringing-together of Fairfax and Elsie could not be more touching. The absence of spoken dialogue allows Trial by Jury to be included as a fill-up, with Suart even more aptly cast and Adams again incomparable as the Usher, while the WNO Chorus again sings with ideal clarity. Otherwise it involves different singers, with Rebecca Evans golden-toned as the Plaintiff and Barry Banks firm if light as the Defendant.

Other complete recordings

Cox and Box (original, full-length, 1866 version).

*** Divine Arts 2-4104. Berger, Kennedy, Francke, Barclay.

This lively and enjoyable performance re-creates the original version of Cox and Box, first heard at a private gathering at the librettist Burnand's own house in May 1866, with Sullivan himself improvising the accompaniment at the piano. The orchestration came a year later for the work's prèmiere at the Adelphi Theatre, and the Overture and the duet Stay Bouncer stay, were also added subsequently.

The present account (based on a professional production for London Chamber Opera) is spirited and polished, and its considerable length (over an hour) serves to demonstrate the reasons for Sullivan's own shortened version in 1894. It was further truncated in 1921 to produce the concise version which remained in the D'Oyly Carte Company's repertoire

until the late 1970s. However, the performance on the present disc is most enjoyable and does not outstay its welcome. Donald Francke is a splendidly rumbustious Bouncer. The charming original compound-time version of the Bacon lullaby is considerably different from the song known in the revised score. Stay Bouncer stay is added in for good measure. Of course, one misses the orchestra, but the piano accompaniment, using a suitable period instrument, is well managed. The words are admirably clear, a consideration which would surely have been just as important to Burnand as to Gilbert. It is good to see that the production is dedicated to the memory of the late Arthur Jacobs, biographer of Sullivan, at whose insistence this recording (sponsored by the Sullivan Society) was issued commercially.

The Gondoliers (complete; without dialogue); *Overture Di Ballo.*

*** That's Entertainment CD-TER2 1187; (2). Suart, Rath, Fieldsend, Oke, Ross, Hanley, Woollett, Pert, Creasy, D'Oyly Carte Op. Ch. & O, Pryce-Jones.

The That's Entertainment set of The Gondoliers was recorded at Abbey Road studios in 1991, offers very good sound and speaks well for the standards of the resuscitated D'Oyly Carte company. The men are very good indeed. Richard Suart's Duke of Plaza-Toro is as dry as you could wish, while the voice itself is resonant, and his duet in Act II with the equally excellent Duchess (Jill Pert), in which they dispense honours to the undeserving, is in the best Gilbertian tradition. Perhaps Gianetta (Lesley Echo Ross) and Casilda (Elizabeth Woollett) are less individually distinctive and slightly less vocally secure than their counterparts on the Godfrey and Sargent versions, but they always sing with charm. The chorus is first class – the men are especially virile at the opening of Act II. The orchestral playing is polished, and the ensembles are good, too; John Pryce-Jones conducts with vigour and an impressive sense of theatrical pacing. The finale brings an exhilarating closing Cachucha to round the opera off nicely. The acoustic of the recording has both warmth and atmosphere.

(i) *HMS Pinafore*; (ii) *The Pirates of Penzance* (both complete, without dialogue).

(***) Romophone mono 89002-2 (2). (i) Lytton, G. Baker, Goulding, Griffin, Lewis, Fancourt, Ch. & LSO; (ii) Dawson, G. Baker, Oldham, Griffin, Sheffield, Gill, Ch. & Light Op. O; Sargent.

These were the first electrical recordings of the Pirates and Pinafore, recorded in 1929 and 1930 respectively. They are clearly and cleanly remastered and expertly transferred to CD by Mark Olbert-Thorn, with a minimum of background noise, and give considerable pleasure, for the words are very clear. But what is astonishing is the slackness of ensemble, not only with the pick-up chorus but more remarkably in the concerted numbers from the principals. Obviously in that early part of his career, Dr Sargent was not the stickler for polish that he was later to become.

The cast lists here include principals who were not established D'Oyly Carte singers, notably Peter Dawson as a stirring Pirate King and George Baker an excellent Major-

General. Derek Oldham portrays Frederic with rather dated, slightly 'posh' vowels, yet makes the climax of *Pirates*, with its Gilbertian paradox, more dramatically like grand opera than usual, and in this Elsie Griffin's touching Mabel gives him fine support. Leo Sheffield gives a curiously low-key portrayal of the Sergeant of the Police, even adding embellishments to his famous solo.

HMS Pinafore is dominated by a vintage performance from Sir Henry Lytton. Vocally acidulous, his gaunt portrayal of a sparsely timbred Sir Joseph Porter is very much that of an old man, less humorously sympathetic than usual. This makes the resolution of the plot the more telling, especially as Charles Goulding as Ralph and Elsie Griffin as Josephine, make a highly sympathetic pair of lovers. George Baker is again on form as the Captain, and that greatest of Savoyards, Darrell Fancourt, makes his sinister mark as Dick Deadeye. Bertha Lewis is a particularly pleasing Buttercup, singing freshly with *mezzo* colouring.

Iolanthe (complete; without dialogue). *Thespis* (orchestral suite).

**(*) That's Entertainment CD-TER2 1188 (2). Suart, Woollett, Blake Jones, Richard, Creasy, Pert, Rath, Hanley, D'Oyly Carte Opera Ch. & O, Pryce-Jones.

After the success of the new D'Oyly Carte *Gondoliers*, this fresh look at *Iolanthe* is something of a disappointment. John Pryce-Jones obviously sees it as a very dramatic opera indeed, and he ensures that the big scenes have plenty of impact (the *March of the Peers* is resplendent with brass). But his strong forward pressure means that the music feels almost always fast-paced, and the humour is completely upstaged by the drama, especially in the long Act I Finale, which is certainly zestful. The Lord Chancellor's two patter songs in Act I, *The law is the true embodiment* and *When I went to the bar*, are very brisk in feeling, and Richard Suart, an excellent Lord Chancellor, is robbed of the necessary relaxed delivery so that the words can be relished for themselves. Jill Pert is certainly a formidable Queen of the Fairies, but elsewhere the lack of charm is a distinct drawback.

(i) *Iolanthe*: highlights; (ii) *The Mikado* (complete, without dialogue).

(B) *** CfP (ADD) CD-CDPD 4730 (2). (i) Shilling, Harwood, Moyle, Dowling, Begg, Bevan, Greene, Kern; (ii) Holmes, Revill, Wakefield, Studholme, Dowling, Allister, John Heddle Nash; Sadler's Wells Op. Ch. & O, Faris.

The Sadler's Wells *Iolanthe* is stylistically superior to Sargent's earlier EMI recording and is often musically superior to the Decca/D'Oyly Carte versions. Alexander Faris often chooses untraditional tempi. *When I went to the bar* is very much faster than usual, with less dignity but with a compensating lightness of touch. Eric Shilling is excellent here, as he is also in the *Nightmare song*, which is really *sung*, much being made of the ham operatic recitative at the beginning. The lovers, Elizabeth Harwood as Phyllis and Julian Moyle as Strephon, make a charming duo, and the Peers are splendid. Their entry chorus is thrilling and their reaction to the Fairy Queen's curse is delightfully, emphatically horrified, while the whole Act I finale (the finest in any

of the operas) goes with infectious stylishness. All the solo singing is of a high standard and Leon Greene sings the Sentry song well. But one has to single out special praise for Patricia Kern's really lovely singing of Iolanthe's aria at the end of the opera. The recording has splendid presence and realism.

The Sadler's Wells *Mikado* is traditional in the best sense, bringing a humorous sparkle to the proceedings, which gives great delight. Clive Revill is a splendid Ko-Ko; John Heddle Nash is an outstanding Pish-Tush, and it is partly because of him that the *Chippy chopper* trio is so effective. Denis Dowling is a superb Pooh-Bah, and Marion Studholme a charming Yum-Yum. Jean Allister's Katisha is first rate in every way; listen to the venom she puts into the word '*bravado*' in the Act I finale. Even the chorus scores a new point by their stylized singing of *Mi-ya-sa-ma*, which sounds engagingly mock-Japanese. The one disappointment is John Holmes in the name-part. He sings well but conveys little of the mock-satanic quality. But this is a small point in an otherwise magnificent set, which has a vivacious new overture arranged by Charles Mackerras.

The Mikado (complete without dialogue).

(N) (BB) (***) Naxos mono 8.110176/7. Fancourt, Green, Mitchell, Osborn, Watson, Hallman, Styler, Gillingham, Wright, D'Oyly Carte Op. O, New Promenade O, Godfrey.

Decca's 1950 set of *The Mikado* appeared at the very beginning of the mono LP era, and did as much as any recording, apart from Ansermet's *Petrushka*, to establish the credentials of the new medium. The clarity of the sound, coupled with the convenience of having the whole opera complete on four sides, immediately made converts, including I.M., who revisited the set countless times.

The performance was to be preferred to both its later full-priced Decca/Godfrey and EMI stereo competitors (but not the 1973 D'Oyly Carte stereo remake under Royston Nash). Not only does it cast Martyn Green in his best part (his *Little List* and the charming *Tit willow* are unsurpassed), but it has Darrell Fancourt in splendid form singing his Mikado's song superbly, with that great gusty laugh between verses.

Leonard Osborn was perhaps just past his best, but *A wand'ring minstrel* shows what a fine singer he was, especially in the contrasting middle verses. Ella Halman's Katisha was incomparably magisterial, and if her intonation had become slightly suspect at the top, her lower register was still superb and her Act II lament, *Alone and yet alive*, is most affecting. Margaret Mitchell was a charmingly petite Yum-Yum and Richard Watson a splendid Pooh Bah and the glees *Brightly dawns* and *Here's a how-de-do* (in which on stage Martyn Green used to provide hilarious business for up to five encores) still sound as fresh as ever.

Over the whole proceedings presides the sparkling conducting of Isadore Godfrey. The vivid recording makes every word clear. It always had moments of excess sibilance, but the present transfer (like Decca's earlier Ace of Clubs LP set) loses some of the bloom and slightly exaggerates the upper range. Only Mike Dutton understands that Decca's early ffrr recording process requires a carefully managed treble roll-off when remastering for CD. But at Naxos price this is well worth having.

Ruddigore (complete recording of original score; without dialogue).

*** That's Entertainment CDTER2 1128. Hill Smith, Sandison, Davies, Ayldon, Hillman, Innocent, Hann, Ormiston, Lawlor, New Sadler's Wells Op. Ch. & O, Phipps.

What is exciting about the New Sadler's Wells production of *Ruddigore* is that it includes the original finale, created by the logic of Gilbert's plot which brought *all* the ghosts back to life, rather than just the key figure. The opera is strongly cast, with Marilyn Hill Smith and David Hillman in the principal roles and Joan Davies a splendid Dame Hannah, while Harold Innocent as Sir Despard and Linda Ormiston as Mad Margaret almost steal the show. Simon Phipps conducts brightly and keeps everything moving forward, even if his pacing is not always as assured as in the classic Sargent version. The recording is first class, with fine theatrical atmosphere.

The Yeomen of the Guard (complete; with dialogue).

(B) **(*) Ph. Duo (ADD) 462 508-2 (2). Allen, Streit, Dean, Terfel, Mackie, McNair, Collins, Rigby, ASMF and Ch., Marriner.

Sir Neville Marriner's version is cast from strength but fails to capture the exuberance and fun in the writing that Mackerras's WNO performance does. It is good to have Thomas Allen as Jack Point, singing beautifully and giving emotional weight to the rejected clown in love with the heroine. The excellent Mozart tenor, Kurt Streit, makes an impressive hero, and even the smallest roles are taken by singers of the calibre of Bryn Terfel, Neil Mackie and Judith Howarth. The big disappointment is the way Sylvia McNair's usually sweet soprano is caught in the role of Elsie: often sour with suspect intonation. Spoken dialogue is included, which for some will be a deciding factor.

Collections

'The Best of Gilbert and Sullivan': highlights from *The Gondoliers; HMS Pinafore; Iolanthe; The Mikado; Patience; The Pirates of Penzance; Ruddigore; Trial by Jury; The Yeomen of the Guard.*

(B) *** EMI (ADD) CZS5 73869-2 (3). Morison, M. Sinclair, Thomas, G. Baker, Lewis, Brannigan, Young, Wallace, Cameron, Evans, Milligan, Glyndebourne Festival Ch., Pro Arte O, Sargent.

This three-disc EMI set makes a good supplement for the comparable Double Decca collection (see below). The Sargent recordings are generally more grandly operatic in style and at times they are rather less fun. But, as might expect from the starry cast list, there is some outstandingly fine solo and concerted singing from the principals in the lyrical numbers. Obviously with the film *Topsy-Turvy* in mind, the major selection is from *The Mikado* (some twenty items), and Sargent's expansive manner has much in common with Carl Davis's approach (especially in the Finale). With Owen Brannigan as The Mikado, Monica Sin-

clair as Katisha, Richard Lewis as Nanki-Poo, Elsie Morison as Yum-Yum and Ian Wallace as Pooh Bah, the results will surely please those who enjoyed the movie.

Princess Ida and *The Sorcerer* are not represented, but the other key operas (apart from the single Learned Judge's number from *Trial by Jury*) have from between five to eight items each, including the substantial and treasurable finales from *Iolanthe* and (to conclude the programme) *The Yeomen of the Guard*. Besides taking the role of the Judge in *Trial*, George Baker is a stalwart of the series and he delivers the famous patter songs with aplomb.

No less than Sir Geraint Evans takes his place as the Duke of Plaza-Toro (*Gondoliers*), and Jack Point (*Yeomen*). Owen Brannigan is an unfogettable Sergeant of Police (*Pirates*), and is hardly less memorable as Private Willis (*Iolanthe*), and Sir Despard (*Ruddigore*). The choral contribution is first class, and Sir Malcolm Sargent conducts freshly throughout, although not always with the sparkle that Godfrey commanded, as is instanced by his curiously measured *Cachucha* in *The Gondoliers*. But the selections from *Patience* and *Ruddigore* show him and this talented company (Elsie Morison especially) at their very finest.

'The Best of Gilbert and Sullivan': excerpts from: *The Gondoliers; HMS Pinafore; Iolanthe; The Mikado; Patience; The Pirates of Penzance; The Yeomen of the Guard.*

(M) **(*) Sony SMK 89248. Soloists, D'Oyly Carte Opera Company Ch. & O, Owen Edwards or Pryce-Jones.

Intended as a companion selection to *Topsy-Turvy* below, these present-day D'Oyly Carte recordings have plenty of life and vigour. Indeed, both conductors favour very brisk tempi, and often there is a sense that the music is being driven very hard, with the *Tripping thither* chorus in *Iolanthe* rhythmically almost over-pointed. Simon Butteriss's *Am I alone and unobserved* is very dramatic indeed, but this certainly gives the number a fresh impetus. There is plenty of good singing, and among the other principals Richard Suart does not disappoint in the Lord Chancellor's patter songs in *Iolanthe* and in *From the sunny Spanish shore* from the *Gondoliers*. Eric Robertson takes over effectively as the Major-General, and Eric Rogers is an engaging Ko-Ko for *Tit-willow* in *The Mikado*. Marilyn Hill-Smith's *Poor wand'ring one* is pleasingly fresh and Donald Maxwell provides a military zest for his two numbers in *Patience*. The disc is generously full, but each selection is rather meagre. *The Yeomen of the Guard* only has two items, and the second, *Here's a man of jollity*, cuts off rather suddenly. Better to have omitted the two overtures (beautifully played as they are) and perhaps to have concentrated on fewer operas and offered more music from each. Still this is all enjoyable enough and vividly recorded.

Highlights from: *The Gondoliers; HMS Pinafore; Iolanthe; The Mikado; The Pirates of Penzance; The Yeomen of the Guard.*

(B) **(*) CfP (ADD) CD-CFP 4238. Soloists, Glyndebourne Festival Ch., Pro Arte O, Sargent.

An attractive selection of highlights offering samples of six of Sargent's vintage EMI recordings. There is some distinguished solo singing and, if the atmosphere is sometimes a little cosy, there is a great deal to enjoy. The recordings have transferred well.

'The Very Best of Gilbert and Sullivan': extracts from: (i; iv) *The Gondoliers; HMS Pinafore; Iolanthe.* (ii; v) *The Mikado.* (i; iv) *Patience.* (ii; iv) *The Pirates of Penzance.* (ii; vi) *Princess Ida; Ruddigore.* (ii; iv) *The Sorcerer.* (iii–iv) *Trial by Jury.* (ii; vi) *The Yeomen of the Guard.*

🅑 (B) *** Double Decca (ADD) 460 010-2 (2). Reed, Masterson, Knight, Round, Adams, Sandford, Wright, Brannigan, Toye, Styler and soloists, D'Oyly Carte Op. Ch., (i) New SO; (ii) RPO; (iii) ROHCG O; cond. (iv) Godfrey; (v) Nash; (vi) Sargent.

If you are looking for a CD to cheer you up on a dull day, either of the pair which make up this Double Decca will serve admirably. The overall selection earns full marks for perception and variety. *The Mikado* is (understandably) the most generously treated, including ten items, and the only real miscalculation was to end the second disc with the trio, *This helmet I suppose* from *Princess Ida*, which, following immediately after John Reed's delicious *Whene'er I spoke sarcastic joke*, comes as an anticlimax. The joyous trio, *If you go in, you're sure to win*, from *Iolanthe* (which comes earlier) would have been more effective or, better still, the Act I finale, which is omitted and for which there would have just about been room. Yet this is carping. The consistent wit of Gilbert's words, the delightful Sullivan melodies and the sparkle of Godfrey's conducting are a constant joy

Highlights from: (i; ii) *HMS Pinafore*; (iii; iv) *The Mikado*; (ii; iv; v) *The Pirates of Penzance*; (ii; vi) *Trial by Jury*; (vii) *The Yeomen of the Guard.*

*** Telarc CD 80431. Suart, with (i) Allen, Palmer; (ii) Evans; (iii) Rolfe Johnson, McLaughlin, Howells, Watson; (iv) Van Allan, Folwell; (v) Mark Ainsley, Gossage; (vi) Banks, Garrett, Savidge, Rhys Davies; (vii) Archer, Mellor, Stephen; Welsh Nat. Op. Ch. & O, Mackerras.

Even with 76 minutes' playing time, this can be no more than a sampler of Mackerras's effervescent G&S series for Telarc, dominated by the dry-timbred Richard Suart in the key patrician roles. As can be seen, most of the other soloists change with each opera, but the standard remains extraordinarily high. The choice of excerpts is inevitably arbitrary with about half-a-dozen items from each of the two-Act operas and three from *Trial by Jury*. If you buy this, you will inevitably be tempted to go on to one or other of the complete sets. Nevertheless it is a splendid collection in its own right. Characteristically first-class Telarc sound.

'Topsy-Turvy' (music from the film soundtrack, with interludes arr. Carl Davis): includes excerpts from: *The Grand Duke* (orchestral only); *The Mikado; Princess Ida; The Sorcerer; The Yeomen of the Guard; The Lost Chord; The long day closes* (arr. Davis).

**(*) Sony SK 61834. Soloists Ch. & O, Carl Davis.

Mike Leigh's film *Topsy-Turvy* was a personal indulgence.

The choice of music is also personal and arbitrary, and not all of it works especially effectively in the cinema. But the film centres on the conception, writing and première of *The Mikado*. The excerpts from this masterpiece are as splendidly sung as they are extravagantly costumed, although, considering its importance as the emotional climax of the plot, it is surprising that the Mikado's famous Act II solo is not heard complete. Carl Davis's arrangements used as interludes are pleasing if not charismatic, but for many the principal weakness of this collection will be Davis's often over-deliberate tempi. Yet the quality of the singing triumphs over this drawback, with Timothy Spall and Louise Gold splendid as the Mikado and Katisha respectively, while Martin Savage is in his element in the patter songs. But why, oh why, was *Tit-willow* omitted? The recording is outstanding, often approaching demonstration quality, and the accompanying booklet is handsomely colour-illustrated and includes full texts.

SUPPÉ, Franz von (1819–95) ˙

Complete overtures

Vol. 1: Overtures: *Carnival; Die Frau Meisterin; Die Irrfahrt um's Glück (Fortune's Labyrinth); The Jolly Robbers (Banditenstreiche); Pique Dame; Poet and Peasant; Des Wanderers Ziel (The Goal of the Wanderers). Boccaccio: Minuet & Tarantella. Donna Juanita: Juanita march.*

** Marco 8.223647. Slovak State PO (Košice), A. Walter.

Vol. 2: Overtures: *Beautiful Galatea (Die schöne Galatea); Boccaccio; Donna Juanita; Isabella; Der Krämer und sein Kommis (The Shopkeeper and His Assistant); Das Modell (The Model); Paragraph 3; Tantalusqualen. Fatinitza march.*

** Marco 8.223648. Slovak State PO (Košice), A. Walter.

Vol. 3: Overtures: *Fatinitza; Franz Schubert; Die Heimkehr von der Hochzeit (Homecoming from the wedding); Light Cavalry; Trioche and Cacolet; Triumph. Boccaccio: March. Herzenseintracht polka; Humorous variations on 'Was kommt dort von der Höhv'; Titania waltz.*

** Marco 8.223683. Slovak State PO (Košice), A. Walter.

Alfred Walter's performances here are unsubtle, but they have a rumbustious vigour that is endearing and, with enthusiastic playing from the Slovak Orchestra who are obviously enjoying themselves, the effect is never less than spirited. Many of the finest of the lesser-known pieces are already available in more imaginative versions from Marriner. But Walter has uncovered some attractive novelties, as well as some pleasing if inconsequential interludes and dances. On Volume 1 *Carnival* (nothing like Dvořák's piece), opens rather solemnly, then introduces a string of ideas, including a polka, a waltz and a galop. *Des Wanderers Ziel* begins very energetically and, after brief harp roulades, produces a rather solemn cello solo and brass choir; later there is an attractive lyrical melody, but there are plenty of histrionics too, and the dancing ending brings distinctly Rossinian influences.

In Volume 2 *Isabella* is introduced as a sprightly Spanish lady, but Viennese influences still keep popping up, while *Paragraph 3* summons the listener with a brief horn-call and then has another striking lyrical theme, before gaiety takes over. *Das Krämer und sein Kommis* proves to be an early version (the ear notices a slight difference at the dramatic opening) of an old friend, *Morning, Noon and Night in Vienna*. *Donna Juanita* brings a violin solo of some temperament; then, after some agreeably chattering woodwind, comes a grand march.

On the third CD, *Trioche and Cacolet* immediately introduces a skipping tune of great charm and, after another of Suppé's appealing lyrical themes, ends with much rhythmic vigour. The biographical operetta about *Schubert* opens with an atmospheric, half-sinister reference to the *Erlkönig* and follows with further quotations, prettily scored; however, the writing coarsens somewhat vulgarly at the end. But the prize item here is a set of extremely ingeniuous variations on a local folksong, which translates as *What comes there from on high?* It seems like a cross between 'A hunting we will go' and 'The Grand old Duke of York'.

Vol. 4: Overtures: *Dame Valentin oder Frauenräuber und Wanderbursche; Dolch und Rose oder Das Donaumädchen; Der Gascogner; Die G'frettbrüderln; Die Hammerschmidin aus Steiermark oder Folgen einer Landpartie; Kopf und Herz; Reise durch die Märchenwelt; Unterthänig und Unabhängig; Zwei Pistolen.*

(N) **(*)** Marco 8.223865. Slovak State PO (Košice), Pollack.

The intriguing titles here provide the entrée to music of much charm and inexhaustible melody – little of the music here is dull. The opening *Der Gascogner* ('The Man from Gascogne') begins with a rather haunting series of held notes on the horn, and the melodramatic opening of *Dolch und Rose* ('the dagger and the rose') is not quite what we expect from this composer. *Dame Valentin oder Frauenräuber* ('Dame Valentin or Lady Robber') has a piquant opening, complete with triangle, before melting into some delightful melodies, including, of course, some spirited waltzes and gallops. There is plenty to enjoy here, especially some of Suppé more ambitious writing – *Reise durch die Märchenwelt* ('journey through the world of fairies') has passages which sound almost Wagnerian. The performances here are sympathetic, although the recording lacks ideal richness.

Beautiful Galatea: Overture.

(M) ***** Sony (ADD) SMK 61830. NYPO, Bernstein – BIZET: *Symphony in C;* OFFENBACH: *Gaîté parisienne,* etc. **

An excellent performance of the *Beautiful Galatea* overture from Bernstein: frothy in the fast sections, but sensitive in the quiet passages – especially in the strings. The 1967 recording is warm and vivid, though the couplings are not quite so recommendable.

Overtures: *Beautiful Galatea; Boccaccio; Light Cavalry; Morning, Noon and Night in Vienna; Pique-dame; Poet and Peasant.*

(M) ***** Mercury 434 309-2. Detroit SO, Paray – AUBER: *Overtures.* ***** ●

Listening to Paray, one discovers a verve and exhilaration that are wholly Gallic in spirit. His chimerical approach to *Beautiful Galathea* (with a wonderfully luminous passage from the Detroit strings near the very opening) is captivating, and the bravura violin playing in *Light Cavalry* is remarkably deft. With its splendid Auber coupling this is one of Mercury's most desirable reissues.

Overtures: Disc 1: *Beautiful Galathea; Jolly robbers (Banditenstreiche); Light Cavalry; Morning, Noon and Night in Vienna; Pique-dame; Poet and Peasant.* **Disc 2:** *Fatinitza; Die Frau Meisterin; Der Gascogner; Die Irrfahrt um's Glück; Juanita; Das Modell; Wiener-Jubel.*

(B) ***** RCA Twofer 74321 34174-2. RPO, Kuhn.

By joining up Gustav Kuhn's two separate collections in a Twofer, RCA have created a comprehensive single grouping of key Suppé overtures. The first disc assembles the six best known, including the four popular favourites, among which *Beautiful Galathea* stands out; the second, equally distinctive, offers seven hardly less memorable novelties. Kuhn lavishes much care over detail. Tempi are spacious, generally slower than usual, but the effect is not to rob the music of vitality, rather to add to its stature. In the lyrical sections he conjures the most beautiful, expansive playing from the RPO, yet he can be racy in the galops while not rushing the music off its feet. The second programme is especially valuable in offering CD débuts for three items. Kuhn is in his element in the powerfully solemn opening of *Die Irrfahrt um's Glück* with its magical/mystical portents; yet the more volatile introduction to *Donna Juanita* is hardly less telling, and very beautifully played. Throughout, Kuhn seeks to remove any suggestion of cheapness from the music, and these are performances of real breadth. While they do not have the unbuttoned gusto of some versions, the added gravitas more than compensates. Full, resonant recording of very high quality adds to this impression.

Overtures: *Die Frau Meisterin; Die Irrfahrt um's Glück; Light cavalry; Morning, Noon and Night in Vienna; Pique-dame; Poet and Peasant; Tantalusqualen; Wiener-Jubel (Viennese Jubilee).*

● ***** EMI CDC7 54056-2. ASMF, Marriner.

Marriner's collection of Suppé *Overtures* goes straight to the top of the list. It is expansively recorded and it produces the most spectacular demonstration quality. The performances have tremendous exuberance and style: this is one of Marriner's very best records. The novelties are delightful. *Die Irrfahrt um's Glück* – concerned with magical goings-on – has a massively portentous opening, superbly realized here; *Die Frau Meisterin* produces a deliciously jiggy waltz tune, and *Wiener-Jubel*, after opening with resplendent fanfares, is as racy as you could wish. Not to be missed.

Die schöne Galathée.

(N) ***** CPO 999 726. Bogner, Rickenbacher, Heyn, Kupfer, Koblenz State Theatre Ch., Rhenish State Op. O, Eitler.

Starting with the famous galumphing overture, Suppé's

one-act operetta on a classical theme is a delight. Pygmalion may still fall in love with his statue of Galatea, when she comes to life – a marvelous moment for the bright, clear soprano, Andrea Bogner – but in this comic retelling she is just a provocative coquette, who much prefers the young Ganymed, taken here by another soprano, Juliane Heyn. First heard in Vienna in 1865, this starts like Offenbach in German, but turns into a precursor of Viennese operetta the moment that waltz-time is engaged. Based on a production in Koblenz on the Rhine, this is a sparkling, well-balanced recording, with the comic persona characterfully taken by Hans-Jurg Rickenbacher and Michael Kupfer. It might have been even more fun had a sprinkling of spoken dialogue been included. As it is, the single disc comes with libretto and translation in a cumbersome double-disc jewel-case.

SVENDSEN, Johan Severin

(1840–1911)

Romance in G, Op. 26.

(BB) *** Naxos 8.550329. Kang, Slovak (Bratislava) RSO, Leaper – HALVORSEN: *Air Norvégien* etc.; SIBELIUS: *Violin Concerto*; SINDING: *Légende*. ***

Dong-Suk Kang plays Svendsen's once-popular *Romance in G* without sentimentality but with full-hearted lyricism. The balance places him a little too forward, but the recording is very satisfactory.

Symphonies Nos. 1 in D, Op. 4; 2 in B flat, Op. 15.

(BB) *** Naxos 8.553898 [id.]. Bournemouth SO, Engeset.
(BB) **(*) Finlandia 0927 40621-2. Norwegian R. O, Rasilainen.

Symphonies Nos. 1–2; 2 Swedish Folk-Melodies, Op. 27.

*** BIS CD 347. Gothenburg SO, Järvi.

Svendsen excelled in the larger forms and, as befits a conductor, was a master of the orchestra. The *D major Symphony* is a student work of astonishing assurance and freshness, in some ways even more remarkable than the *B flat*. Neeme Järvi gives a first-class performances, sensitive and vital, and the excellent recordings earn them a strong recommendation.

Järvi's recording is strongly challenged by Bjarte Engeset and the Bournemouth Orchestra. These players are obviously encountering this music with enthusiasm and they are well served by both the acoustic and the engineering. At the Naxos price it is a real bargain.

There is nothing wrong with the Finlandia version from the Norwegian Radio Orchestra under Ari Rasilainen either, though the recording is not as good as BIS for Järvi and at full price does not displace it.

Symphony No. 2; Carnival in Paris, Op. 9; Norwegian Artists' Carnival, Op. 14; Norwegian Rhapsody No. 2, Op. 19; (i) Romance in G, for Violin & Orchestra, Op. 26.

** Chatsworth FCM 1002. Stavanger SO, Llewelyn; (i) with Thorsen.

Decent performances from Stavanger of the *Second Sym-*

phony and other popular Svendsen pieces under the Welsh conductor, Grant Llewelyn. The strings do not have the depth of sonority of their immediate rivals, but the orchestra plays with freshness and enthusiasm.

(i) Octet in A, Op. 3; (i) Romance in G for Violin & Strings, Op. 26.

*** Chan. 9258. ASMF Chamber Ens. (i) with Sillito – NIELSEN: *String Quintet in G*. ***

(i) Octet; String Quartet in A min., Op. 1.

*** BIS CD 753. Kontra Qt; with (i) Bjørnkjaer, Madsen, Rasmussen, Johansen.

Svendsen's youthful *Octet, Op. 3* is a product of his student years at Leipzig, and was obviously inspired by Mendelssohn. But, it has a strong personality of its own and is full of lively and attractive invention. The scherzo is particularly delightful. The Kontra Quartet and their colleagues give a spirited account of it, coupling it with another student work, the *A minor Quartet, Op. 1*. A good well-balanced sound.

However, those primarily wanting the *Octet* should turn to the Academy of St Martin-in-the-Fields Chamber Ensemble whose leader, Kenneth Silito plays the G major *Romance* as a fill-up. First-rate performances and recording.

SWEELINCK, Jan (1562–1621)

ORGAN MUSIC

Ballo del Granduca; Echo fantasia; Engelsche Fortuyn; Puer nobis nascitur.

*** Chan. 0514. Klee (organ of St Laurens Church, Alkmaar) – BUXTEHUDE: *Collection*. ***

Sweelinck lived during the Dutch Golden Age and was a contemporary of Rembrandt. His music is colourful and appealing, and it could hardly be better represented than in this engaging 'suite' of four contrasted pieces, three of which are based on melodies by others. Piet Klee is a very sympathetic advocate and he is given a recording of demonstration standard.

Ballo del Granduca; Chorale variations: Erbarm dich mein, O Herr Gott; Mein junges Leben hat ein End'. Echo fantasia in A min.; Malle Sijmen; Onder een linde groen; Poolsche dans; Ricercar; Toccatas: in A min. & C.

(N) (BB) *** Naxos 8.550904. Christie (C.B. Fisk organ, Houghton Chapel, Wellesley College, USA).

Those wanting a larger, more fully representative collection of Sweelinck's organ music can turn to Naxos, who do not usually let us down with their one-disc surveys. Certainly the Wellesley College organ sounds right, James David Christie is a persuasive exponent, and his pacing is convincing. The two *Toccatas* are the most commanding pieces here, the *C major* quite virtuosic. Sweelink's chorale variations repeat the cantus firmus clearly with embellishments of increasing complexity. The secular variations are simpler. Those based on a Dutch song are derived from an English ballad, *All in a garden green*, and the jolly *Malle Sijmen*

('Simple Simon') is based on an old English dance-tune, and is piquantly registered. *Poolsche dans* ('Polish dance') is much more elaborate. It is in the middle section of the *Echo Fantasia* that the cuckoo-like echoes finally appear and the piece concludes like a toccata. Excellent recording.

Cantiones sacrae (1619).

*** Hyp. CDA 67103 (Nos. 1–21); CDA 67104 (Nos. 22–37).Trinity College Chapel Ch., Cambridge, Marlow.

Sweelinck wrote a great deal of vocal music (though none in his own language), including French chansons and Psalm settings, and Italian madrigals. The 37 *Cantiones sacrae*, which date from 1691, are in Latin, for five-part choir, and surely represent him at a peak of inspiration. The range of texts is wide, but most pertain to major feasts of the liturgical year. This pair of Hyperion discs (each available separately) offers glorious music, gloriously sung. The simplicity and underlying vitality of the very first piece, *Non omnis qui dicit mihi, Domine* captures the listener's ear, and the opening sequence of some half-a-dozen fairly serene settings is then interrupted by three exuberant motets of praise, *Ecce nunc benedicte Dominum, Cantata Domino* and the exultant *Venite exultemus Domino*. But the sequence which opens the second disc, beginning with *In illo tempore*, celebrating the naming of Jesus, is hardly less fine. The resonant acoustic is right for the music, but brings some distinct blurring of the upper focus. Nevertheless this is an outstanding set.

SZYMANOWSKI, Karol (1882–1937)

(i) Violin Concertos Nos. 1; 2. Concert Overture, Op. 12.

*** Chan. 9496. (i) Mordkovitch; BBC PO, Sinaisky.

(i) Violin Concertos Nos. 1–2, Op. 61; (ii) Romance, Op. 23; 3 Paganini Caprices, Op. 40.

*** EMI CDC5 55607-2. Zehetmair, (i) CBSO, Rattle; (ii) Avenhaus.

Thomas Zehetmair's deeply felt versions with Rattle and the CBSO conjure up the Szymanowskian sound-world with real flair, and the soloist characterizes each phrase with impeccable instinct. The engineers deliver first-rate sound in both works and in the four violin and piano makeweights, in which Zehetmair is well supported by the young German pianist, Silke Avenhaus.

Lydia Mordkovitch is also admirably suited, full-toned and red-blooded, for these exotic concertos, helped by playing, richly recorded, from the BBC Philharmonic under Vassily Sinaisky, the orchestra's Principal Guest Conductor. Both works are strongly contrasted with the early and extrovert *Concert Overture*, an illuminating coupling.

(i) Violin Concerto No. 2; (ii) Symphonies Nos. 2, Op. 19; (iii) 3 (Song of the Night), Op. 7.

(B) **(*) Double Decca 448 258-2 (2). (i) Juillet, Montreal SO, Dutoit; (ii) Detroit SO, Dorati; (iii) with Karczykowski, Jewell Ch. – LUTOSLAWSKI: *Concerto for Orchestra* etc. **(*)

Chantal Juillet is a selfless and dedicated interpreter of the *Second Violin Concerto* and she is truthfully balanced, for her small tone does not always sing through Szymanowski's opulently coloured textures. But the orchestral detail emerges with great fidelity and Dutoit's conducting is unfailingly sympathetic. So is Dorati in the two symphonies, and the Decca recording is better detailed than the competing EMI version, with the richness of Szymanowski's textures fully revealed and the chorus clear and well balanced in No. 3. If the Polish performances are in some ways more penetrating, there is no doubting the superiority of the Decca sound.

(i) Harnasie (ballet pantomime), Op. 55; (ii) Mandragora (pantomime), Op. 43; Etude for Orchestra in B flat min., Op. 3 (orch. Fitelberg).

(BB) *** Naxos 8.553686. Polish State PO (Katowice), Stryja; (i) with Grychnik, Polish State PO Ch.; Meus.

Harnasie, like the Op. 50 *Mazurkas*, is the fruit of Szymanowski's encounter with the Polish folk music of the Góral mountains, and its heady exoticism is quite captivating. Stryja's recording is a good one and, though not quite as intoxicating as the full-price Satanowski on Koch, runs it pretty close. Like its rival, it is coupled with *Mandragora*, a harlequinade for chamber forces from 1920 – not Szymanowski at his most fully characteristic but a cultivated and intelligent score. Worth the money.

Symphonies Nos. 1 in F min., Op. 15; 2, Op. 19.

(BB) *** Naxos 8.553683. Polish State PO (Katowice), Stryja.

The two-movement *First Symphony* (1906–7) was first performed in 1909 and was received coolly. Alistair Wightman called it heavily overscored even by the standards of the period. The *Second* (1911) is heavily indebted to Reger, Scriabin and Strauss. It is overlong and overscored, but it contains original and memorable passages. Given the price asked, it justifies the modest expense involved.

Symphony No. 2 in B flat, Op. 19; Concert Overture, Op. 12; (i) Slopiewnie (Wordsong), Op. 46; Songs of the Infatuated Muezzin, Op. 42.

(N) *** Telarc CD 80567. LPO, Botstein (i) with Kilanowicz.

Neither of the orchestral pieces are quite *echt*-Szymanowski, the *Symphony* and *Overture* being still very much under the influence of Strauss and Reger. All the same, both are heard to best advantage in this finely detailed recording with highly persuasive performances. The two sets of songs are rarities; indeed, *Slopiewnie* is not otherwise available on disc in its orchestral form and the *Songs of the Infatuated Muezzin* – composed at the height of the composer's interest in the oriental and the exotic in 1918 (four of which he later scored in 1934) – are not generously represented on disc. Zofia Kilanowicz has just the right blend of purity and seductiveness and the orchestral playing under Leon Botstein is first class.

Symphonies Nos. 2; (i) 4 (Sinfonia concertante).

*** Chan. 9478. (i) Shelley; BBC PO, Sinaisky.

The *Second* and *Fourth* Symphonies are two decades apart. The soft-focus Chandos recording of No. 2 is less clearly defined than, say, Dorati's brightly lit, well-detailed account on Decca (see above), but it presents a more atmospheric aural picture. Vassily Sinaisky is a highly sympathetic interpreter of the piece, and this BBC version must be a prime recommendation. So, too, is the coupling, the *Sinfonia concertante* (1932). Howard Shelley produces a quality of sound that is luminous, refined and velvet-toned. The balance between piano and orchestra is particularly well managed, and the lush orchestral textures are more lucid than we have heard them elsewhere.

Symphonies Nos. (i) 3 (Song of the Night), Op. 27; (ii) 4, Concert Overture, Op. 12.

(BB) *** Naxos 8.553684. (i) Ochmann, Polish State Philharmonic Ch.; (ii) Zmudzinski; Polish State PO (Katowice), Stryja.

(i) Symphony No. 3 (Song of the Night), Op. 27; (ii) Litania do Marii Pany, Op. 59; (iii) Stabat Mater, Op. 53.

*** EMI CDC5 55121-2. (i) Garrison; (ii–iii) Szmytka; (iii) Quivar, Connell; CBSO Ch., CBSO, Rattle.

Szymanowski has that fastidious ear for texture and heightened sense of vision that distinguish mystics, and nowhere is atmosphere more potent than in the *Third Symphony*, the *Song of the Night*. Sir Simon is equally committed and persuasive in the *Stabat Mater*, these days a standard coupling, and one of the unequivocally great choral works of the century. These are very good performances and the sumptuous and finely detailed recording is absolutely state-of-the-art.

Stryja's set of the *Song of the Night* and the *Fourth Symphony* offers a well-filled disc that is worth its asking price. He uses a tenor in the *Third Symphony* and Taduesz Zmudzinski is an effective soloist in the *Fourth Symphony* or *Sinfonia concertante* for piano and orchestra. The performance of the Straussian and derivative *Concert Overture* is as persuasive as it can be. The sound in the *Third Symphony* is good, in the remaining pieces rather less impressive but still acceptable.

Symphony No. 4 (Sinfonia concertante).

** Koch 3-6414-2. Kupiec, Bamberg SO, Judd – LUTOSLAWSKI: *Piano Concerto.* ***

As she shows in her inspired account of the Lutoslawski concerto, with which this symphony is coupled, Ewa Kupiec is a pianist with a formidable technique, who conveys a feeling of spontaneous expressiveness even when taxed by bravura writing. Though this is not as purposeful a performance as that of the Lutoslawski coupling – largely a question of the orchestra not sounding so well attuned – this makes an unusual if rather ungenerous coupling of two concertante works for piano by Polish composers of successive generations. First-rate sound.

CHAMBER MUSIC

Mythes, Op. 30; Kurpian Folk Song; King Roger: Roxana's Aria (both arr. Kochanski).

⊙ (M) *** DG (IMS) (ADD) 431 469-2. Danczowska, Zimerman – FRANCK: *Violin Sonata.* ***

Kaja Danczowska brings vision and poetry to the ecstatic, soaring lines of the opening movement of *Mythes, The Fountains of Arethusa*. Her intonation is impeccable, and she has the measure of these other-worldly, intoxicating scores. There is a sense of rapture here that is totally persuasive, and Krystian Zimerman plays with a virtuosity and imagination that silence criticism. An indispensable reissue.

String Quartets Nos. 1–2.

(N) (BB) *** Naxos 8.554315. Goldner Qt – STRAVINSKY: *Concertino; 3 Pieces; Double Canon.* ***

Even within the comparatively limited medium of the string quartet, Szymanowski creates characteristically rich and exotic textures in these original and tautly constructed works. They were written ten years apart in 1917 and 1927, demonstrating the way his style was developing ever more personally over that period. Occasionally echoing Debussy and Ravel, they make a pointful contrast with Stravinsky's characteristically cryptic essays in the genre, sharp and often brittle. The Goldner Quartet prove understanding, refined interpreters of both composers, playing with rapt intensity in the hushed slow movements of the Szymanowski works. Excellent sound.

Violin Sonata in D min., Op. 9.

(B) *** EMI Début CZS5 72825-2. Zambrzycki-Payne, Presland – BRITTEN: *Suite for Violin & Piano, Op. 6;* GRIEG: *Violin Sonata No. 3.* ***

Violin Sonata; La Berceuse d'Aïtacho Enia, Op. 52; 3 Mythes; Nocturne & Tarantella; Romance in D, Op. 23. arr.: 3 Paganini caprices, Op. 40.

(BB) *** ASV CDQS 6215. Hahn, Fielding.

Violin Sonata; Mythes, Op. 30; Nocturne & Tarantella, Op. 28.

**(*) Chan. 8747. Mordkovitch, Gusk-Grin.

With Hahn producing consistently rich, full tone, the warmth of the writing is brought out most persuasively, and the chronological arrangement of the pieces lets one appreciate the stylistic development of the composer from the *Sonata*, Brahmsian with Slavonic tinges, through to the highly imaginative writing of the later years from 1915 onwards. That was the watershed year which produced both the *Notturno e tarantella* and the three *Mythes*. Both artists have a good feel for Szymanowski as can be heard in that evocative piece. The sound is basically full, but the upper range is rather bright and there is at times a hint of glare. This is not enough to inhibit a strong recommendation, for the artists respond to the music with great sympathy and their playing gives much pleasure.

Rafal Zambrzycki-Payne more than earns a place in the Szymanowski discography. He has a strong musical personality and intelligence, and gets splendid support from his pianist, Carole Presland. The Abbey Road recording is expertly balanced and sounds very natural.

Lydia Mordkovitch is ideally attuned to this sensibility and plays both the *Sonata* and the later works beautifully, and she is sensitively partnered by Marina Gusk-Grin. This can be recommended, though this account of the *Mythes* does not displace Danczowska and Zimerman, and the ASV CD above offers more music for less cost.

PIANO MUSIC
Complete piano music

Disc 1: *9 Preludes, Op. 1; Variations in B flat min., Op. 3; 4 Etudes, Op. 4; Sonata No. 1 in C min., Op. 8* (NI 5405).

Disc 2: *Variations on a Polish Theme in B min., Op. 10; Fantasia in C min., Op. 14; Prelude & Fugue in C sharp min., (1909); Sonata No. 2 in A, Op. 21* (NI 5406).

Disc 3: *Métopes (3 Poèmes), op. 29; 15 Etudes, Op. 34; Sonata No. 3, Op. 36* (NI 5435).

Disc 4: *20 Marzukas, Op. 50; 2 Mazurkas, op. 62; 4 Polish Pieces (1926); Romantic Waltz (1925)* (NI 5436)

*** Nim. NI 1750 (4). Jones.

This complete Nimbus survey invites enthusiasm, particularly as the music is presented in historical sequence. The *Nine Preludes* of Op. 1, although published in 1906, were composed much earlier and are simple, romantic miniatures, with at times a flavour of Chopin. The two sets of *Variations* of Op. 3 and Op. 10, although appealingly inventive, are in the received German tradition; but the *Four Etudes* of Op. 4 and the opening movement of the impressive *First Sonata* already suggest Scriabin. The *Second Sonata* (1910/11) is much more complex in both its structure and use of chromaticism. The later pieces, *Masques* and *Métopes*, written at about the time of the *First Violin Concerto*, show Szymanowski responding to French influences and early Stravinsky, and evolving a sophisticated exoticism all his own. The beautiful and always imaginative *Etudes* (1916) draw on a whole range of styles from Ravel and Debussy, and even Bartók, but they are well assimilated. The *Third Sonata* (1917) is wholly impressionistic and Martin Jones manages its quixotic changes of mood and atmosphere most compellingly. The *Mazurkas*, from the 1920s, find Szymanowski seeking to create an authentic Polish idiom in contemporary terms. The advantage of listening to this rewarding music in sequence means that one senses the composer gradually forging his own individuality, Martin Jones is a consistently persuasive advocate and he is naturally recorded. A most rewarding set, the most attractive for being inexpensive.

4 Etudes, Op. 4; Fantasy, Op. 14; Masques, Op. 34; Métopes, Op. 29.

(n) (B)*** Hyp. Helios CDH 55081. Lee.

Dennis Lee not only encompasses the technical hurdles of *Masques* and *Métopes* with dazzling virtuosity but also provides the keenest artistic insights. His Hyperion CD is quite simply the finest record of Szymanowski's piano music to have appeared to date; he conveys the exoticism and hothouse atmosphere of these pieces; moreover he handles the early Chopinesque *Etudes* and the *Fantasy* with much the same feeling for characterization and artistry. The Hyperion sound is very good indeed. An excellent bargain.

4 Etudes, Op. 4; Mazurkas, Op. 50/1–4; Metopes, Op. 29; Piano sonata No. 2 in A, Op. 21.

(BB) *** Naxos 8.553016-2. Roscoe.

Fantasia in C, Op. 14; Masques, Op. 34; Mazurkas, Op. 50/5–12; Variations on a Polish theme, Op. 10.

(BB) *** Naxos 8.553300. Roscoe.

Martin Roscoe proves a perceptive and sensitive interpreter of Szymanowski and the first two discs augur well for this ongoing series. In the four *Mazurkas*, Op. 50, that open the first CD he shows real feeling and insight. He is equally persuasive in the early Chopinesque *Etudes*, Op. 4, and the refined impressionism of *Metopes*. The *Second Sonata* is a problematic piece, full of virtuosic hurdles, romantic gestures and Regerian ingenuity. The second disc gives us the *C major Fantasy*, Op. 14, and the Op. 10 *Variations*, in which the debts to Scriabin and Chopin have yet to be fully discharged. A fine account of the *Masques*, too. This is playing of quality. As far as recording is concerned, Martin Roscoe is well served.

Piano Sonatas Nos. 1 in C min., Op. 8; 2 in A, Op. 21; 3, Op. 35; Prelude & Fugue in C sharp min. .

*** Athene ATHCD 19. Clark.

Readers who want to explore just the three piano sonatas should consider this excellently played offering. No less than Martin Jones, Raymond Clarke has an intuitive grasp of – and affinity with – Szymanowski's sound-world. He is second to none in terms of sensibility and keyboard command. His version of the *First Sonata* is particularly convincing. Good recording, though not in the demonstration class.

VOCAL MUSIC

(i) *Demeter, Op. 37b;* (ii) *Litany to the Virgin Mary;* (iii) *Penthesilea;* (iv) *Stabat Mater, Op. 53;* (v) *Veni Creator, Op. 57.*

(BB) *** Naxos 8.553687. Polish State PO (Katowice), Stryja, with (i) Malewicz-Madej; (iii) Owsinska; (iv) Gadulanka, Szostek-Radkowa, Hiolski; (v) Zogórzanka; (i–ii; iv–v) Polish State Ch., Katowice.

Szymanowski's *Stabat Mater* is not only one of his greatest achievements but one of the greatest choral works of the present century. This welcome account has the advantage of highly sensitive conducting and an excellent response from the orchestra, but some of the solo singing is less distinguished, and Jadwiga Gadulanka's intonation is less than perfect. The *Litany to the Virgin Mary* is another late work of great poignancy, but *Demeter* has exotic, almost hallucinatory textures. It is all heady and intoxicating stuff, and not to be missed by those with a taste for this wonderful composer.

(i) *3 Fragments of the Poems by Jan Kasprowicz, Op. 5;* (ii) *Love Songs of Hafiz, Op. 24;* (iii) *Songs of the Fairy-Tale Princess, Op. 31;* (iv) *Songs of the Infatuated Muezzin, Op. 42.*

*** Schwann CD 314 001. (i) Szostek-Radkova; (ii) Rorbach; (iii) Klosinska; (iv) Zagórzanka, Polish Nat. Op. O, Satanowski.

(i) *3 Fragments of the Poems by Jan Kasprowicz*; (ii) *Love Songs of Hafiz*; (iii) *Songs of the Fairy-Tale Princess*; (iv) *Songs of the Infatuated Muezzin*; (v) *King Roger: Roxana's Song.*

(BB) **(*) Naxos 8.553688. (i) Malewicz-Madej; (ii & iv) Ryszard Minkiewicz; (iii) Gadulanka; (v) Zagórzanka; Katowice Polish State PO, Stryja.

In the *Songs of the Fairy-Tale Princess*, one feels that Szymanowski must have known Stravinsky's *Le Rossignol* – Izabella Klosinska certainly sings like one. All the singing is very good, but Barbara Zagórzanka in the imaginative *Songs of the Infatuated Muezzin* deserves special mention. Satanowski achieves marvellously exotic and heady atmosphere throughout, and the recording is excellent.

On Naxos, both the *Songs of the Infatuated Muezzin* and the *Love Songs of Hafiz* are sung by a tenor (Ryszard Minkiewicz) with impressive insight, but the 1989 recording is more resonant and does not flatter him. Jadwiga Gadulanka is hardly less impressive than Klosinska in the extraordinary *Songs of the fairy-tale princess* and Barbara Zagórzanka sings the famous *Chant de Roxane* beautifully, and both she and Anna Malewicz-Madej in the Kasprowicz songs are very well balanced.

STAGE WORKS

(i) *Harnasie, Op. 55*; (ii) *Mandragora, Op. 43.*

*** Schwann Musica Mundi 311064. (i) Stępień; (ii) Raptus; (i) Polish Nat. Op. Ch.; Polish Nat. Op. O, Satanowski.

Robert Satanowski's version of Szymanowski's choral ballet, *Harnasie*, is the best so far. It is an opulent score and, like the Op. 50 *Mazurkas*, is the product of the composer's encounter with the folk music of the Gorá mountains. It is richly coloured and luxuriant in texture and has a powerfully heady atmosphere. Full justice is done to its opulence and character in this excellent performance. *Mandragora* is a harlequinade for chamber forces, and the performance is persuasive. Both works are very well served by the engineers. A most valuable addition to the catalogue.

(i) *King Roger* (complete); (ii) *Symphony No. 4* .

✪ *** EMI CDC5 56824/25-2 (2). (i) Hampson, Szmytka, Minkiewicz; CBSO Ch. & Youth Ch.; (i; ii) CBSO, Sir Simon Rattle; (ii) Andsnes.

King Roger stands on the borderline between opera and music drama. The opening in Palermo Cathedral is of awesome opulence, and given such sounds one hardly needs a stage representation. All the singers are first-rate: Thomas Hampson has what one can only call magisterial presence, and the Roksana is quite ethereal. Only Ryszard Minkiewicz's Shepherd is, perhaps, wanting in tonal bloom. Of course, the glorious orchestral tapestry is the centre-piece of attention: the opening of the Hellenic Third Act is inspired and atmospheric. Rattle shows great feeling for Szyman-

owski. He is accorded excellent recording. There have been three earlier recordings, all Polish: Mierzejewski's set from the 1960s has long disappeared, Robert Satanowski's 1988 Warsaw version (Koch) and Karol Stryja's 1990 Katowice account (MArco) were recently reissued on Naxos. But this sweeps the board and has much more refined sound. Incidentally, there is a bonus, for, at the end of the first CD, Roksana's famous aria is given with its concert ending. An even more important bonus comes in the shape of the *Fourth Symphony*, the *Sinfonia concertante for Piano and Orchestra*. This has greater lucidity of textures than any of its previous rivals and brings magical playing from the soloist.

TAILLEFERRE, Germaine

(1892–1983)

(i; iv) *Chansons populaires françaises*; (ii) *Forlane*; (iii) *Galliarde*; (iv) *Images*; (v) *Sonata for Harp*; (vi) *String Quartet*; (vii) *2 Valses.*

(N) **(*) Helicon HE 1008. (i) Maginnis, (ii) Miller, Herrmann; (iii) Baccaro, McGuishin; (iv) Ens., Paiement; (v) Cass; (vi) Porter Qt; (vii) Herrmann, McGuishin.

Germaine Tailleferre was born in the same year as Milhaud and Honegger, but outlived them both; indeed, she lived into her nineties and died in the same year as Georges Auric, the last remaning member of *Les Six*. Her music is slight but well wrought and civilized. The *Sonata for Harp* of 1957 is cool and elegant. The *String Quartet* was written 40 years earlier, when Satie proclaimed her his 'daughter in music' having heard *Jeux de plein air*. It is rather charming. Overall this is smiling music, but of no great substance. The performances are dedicated and well performed, and the recording is serviceable, though nowhere near the demonstration bracket.

TAKEMITSU, Toru (1930–96)

Fantasma/cantos.

*** EMI CDC5 56832-2. Meyer, BPO, Abbado – DEBUSSY: *Première rapsodie*; MOZART: *Clarinet Concerto*. ***

In this sequence of works designed to bring out the full artistry of Sabine Meyer, the hypnotic 16-minute span of this Takemitsu work seems to develop out of the evocative Debussy piece, similarly inhabiting a dream-like world of sound, with ravishing clarinet tones over the widest range. An unusual but revealing coupling.

To the Edge of Dream.

*** EMI CDC7 54661-2. Bream, CBSO, Rattle – RODRIGO: *Concierto de Aranjuez*; ARNOLD: *Guitar Concerto*. ***

A highly sympathetic account of Takemitsu's hypnotically evocative concertante work, using a large orchestra with great economy so as never to overwhelm the soloist. The music is very atmospheric, texturally beautiful but essentially static. It could hardly be better recorded.

TALLIS, Thomas (c. 1505–85)

Complete music, Vol. 1: The Early works: *Alleluia: Ora pro nobis; Ave Dei patris filia; Ave rosa sine spinis; Euge celi porta; Kyrie Deus creatore; Mass Salve intemerata; Salve intemerata.*

*** Signum SIG 001. Chapelle du Roi, Dixon.

The London-based Chapelle du Roi is undertaking the recording of all the music of Tallis (over a series of nine CDs). The choir is made up of of ten young singers, and was founded by Alistair Dixon in 1994. The first disc augurs extremely well for the project. The programme is framed by three Marian votive antiphons, the first two comparatively immature and rather similar: *Ave Dei patris filia* (in a reconstructed text), and *Ave rosa sine spinis*; the second is rather more purposeful than the first. *Salve intemerata*, however, is masterly in its concisely integrated part-writing (with some soaring treble solos, beautifully sung here). It can surely be compared with the famous *Spem in alium*, and becomes remarkably complex, and yet very succinct at the closing *Amen*. The mass sharing its name uses much of the same material: the *Gloria* and *Sanctus* are particularly fine. The *Alleluia* and *Eugi celi porta* are less ambitious, but still serenely beautiful, four-part plainchant settings used as part of the Ladymass. The standard of singing here is very high indeed, beautifully blended and secure, and Alistair Dixon's pacing is very convincing. The recording, made at St Augustine's Church, Kilburn, is admirable in every way.

Complete music, Vol. 2: Music at the Reformation: *Benedictus; Conditor kyrie; Hear the Voice and Prayer; If ye love me; Magnificat; Mass for Four Voices; A New Commandment; Nunc dimittis; Remember not O Lord God; Sancte deus; Te deum for meanes.*

*** Signum SIG 002. Chapelle du Roi, Dixon.

Most, and possibly all the music here dates from the 1540s and reflects the remarkable diversity of musical response that came directly from the profound change in reformed religious procedures which developed in England within a single decade. Much liturgical music was still sung in Latin, notably the splendid *Magnificat* and the deeply felt *Sancte deus*, but already there are settings in English, including three fine early anthems, an extended English *Benedictus* and a remarkable five-part *Te Deum*, all very different from the music on Volume 1 of this series. The surprisingly homophonic setting of the Latin *Mass* is forward-looking too, and very telling. The *Agnus Dei* is most beautiful. *If ye love me* resourcefully alternates chordal and imitative sections. The sheer variety of the music here is remarkable and makes a stimulating second volume in this distinguished series.

Complete music, Vol. 3: Music for Queen Mary: *Beati immaculati; Gaude gloriosa* (Votive antiphon); *Deus Creator* (Kyrie); *Mass Puer natus est nobis: Gloria. Sanctus, Benedictus & Agnus Dei* (with Introit): *Puer natus est nobis*; Alleluia: *Dies sanctificatus*; Sequence: *Celeste organum*; Gradual & Communion: *Viderunt omnes; Suscipe quaeso.*

**(*) Signum SIG 003. Chapelle du Roi, Dixon.

Volume 3 returns to the Latin rite and all the works here date from the reign of Mary Tudor (1553–8). The collection opens with the Psalm setting, *Beati immaculati*, and includes also the glorious, large-scale votive antiphon, *Gaude gloriosa*, magnificently sung. The key work, however, is the seven-part *Mass Puer natus est* which is incomplete. Here the *Gloria, Sanctus* and *Agnus Dei* are performed with the plainchant Propers for the third mass of Christmas. As usual the singing is splendid, but there is a good deal of monodic chant here, beautifully phrased certainly, but which will reduce the appeal of this volume for some collectors.

Complete music, Vol. 4: Music for the Divine Office: *Dum transisset sabbatum; In pace in idipsum; Jam Christus astra ascenderat; Jesu salvator saeculi; Hodie nobis caelorum; Loquebantur variis linguis; Magnificat; Quod chorus vatum; Salvator mundi; Sermone blando; Videte miraculum.*

*** Signum SIGCD 010. Chapelle du Roi, Dixon.

Volume 4 in this ever-rewarding series is the first to concentrate on music for the cycle of eight services, Matins, Lauds, Prime, Terce, Sext, None, Vespers and Compline, sung daily in Latin Christendom. The riches of the polyphony here are unending. *Dum transisset sabbatum* and the six-part *Videte miraculum* are particularly fine, while the seven-part *Loquebantur variis linguis* with its recurring *Alleluias* spins an even more complex contrapuntal web. Even the simplest of the settings here, *Quod chorus vatum*, is moving by its comparative austerity. The earlier four-part version of the *Magnificat* ends the programme, considered not to be one of the composer's most felicitous settings, but it still makes a resounding closing piece. Splendid singing, as ever from this group, and recording which could hardly be bettered in its clarity and vocal bloom.

Absterge Domine; Candidi facti sunt; Nazareri; Derelinquat impius; Dum transisset sabbatum; Gaude gloriosa Dei Mater; Magnificat & Nunc dimittis; Salvator mundi.

(M) *** CRD (ADD) 3429. New College, Oxford, Ch., Higginbottom.

The performances by the Choir of New College, Oxford – recorded in the splendid acoustic of the College Chapel – are very well prepared, with good internal balance, excellent intonation, ensemble and phrasing. The *Gaude gloriosa* is one of Tallis's most powerful and eloquent works.

Audivi vocem; Ave Dei patris filia; Magnificat (4 vv); *Mass Puer natus est nobis.*

*** Gimell CDGIM 934. Tallis Scholars, Phillips.

The performance by the Tallis Scholars of the reconstructed Tallis Christmas Mass has an appealing directness and simplicity and is well up to the standard of its competitors. The four-part *Magnificat* is an early work, but is again very impressively sung here and the programme is completed with two votive antiphons. *Ave Dei patris filia* is particularly appealing. It has a particularly striking soaring opening from the trebles emphasizing the word 'Ave' which illuminates the music throughout its seven stanzas. Excellent recording, but there would have been room for more music here.

(i) *Audivi vocem;* (ii–iii) *Derelinquat impius;* (ii; iv) *Dum transisset sabbatum;* (ii–iii) *Ecce tempus idoneum;* (ii; iv) *Honor, virtus et potestas;* (ii–iii) *In ieiunio et fletu; In manus tuas; Lamentations of Jeremiah I & II;* (ii; iv) *Loquebantur variis linguis;* (ii–iii) *O nata lux de lumine; Salvator mundi; Sancte Deus; Spem in alium* (40-part motet); *Te lucis ante terminum* (2 settings); *Veni Redemptor gentium; Videte miraculum;* (i) *Te Deum.* (Organ) (v) *Clarifica me, pater; Fantasy; Iam lucis;* (vi) *Lesson.*

(B) **(*) Double Decca ADD/Dig. 455 029-2 (2). (i) St John's College, Cambridge, Ch., Guest; (ii) King's College, Cambridge, Ch.; (iii) Willcocks; (iv) Cleobury; (v) White; (vi) A. Davis.

The King's College Choir are in their element in music mostly written for Waltham Abbey or the Chapel Royal, whether conducted by Willcocks or Cleobury. The highlight of their programme is the magnificent 40-part motet, *Spem in alium,* in which the Cambridge University Musical Society joins forces with King's. The *Lamentations* are performed authentically, using men's voices only. The motets, *Sancte Deus* and *Videte miraculum,* are for full choir, and here the balance gives slight over-prominence to the trebles. The choir of St John's College under George Guest sing well in the *Te Deum* but sound happier in their motet, *Audivi vocem.* Andrew Davis is an excellent advocate of the *Organ Lesson;* the other two organ pieces are musically less interesting but are well played by Peter White. The (originally Argo) recording is full and atmospheric throughout, although the choral focus is not always sharp.

Anthems: *Blessed are those that be undefiled; Christ, rising again; Hear the voice and prayer; If ye love me; A new commandment; O Lord, in Thee is all my trust; O Lord, give thy holy spirit; Out from the deep; Purge me; Remember not, O Lord God; Verily, verily I say: 9 Psalm Tunes for Archbishop Parker's Psalter.*

*** Gimell CDGIM 907. Tallis Scholars, Phillips.

This disc collects the complete English anthems of Tallis and is thus a valuable complement to the discs listed above. Here women's voices are used instead of boys', but the sound they produce has boyish purity, and the performances could hardly be more committed or idiomatic. Strongly recommended.

Motets: *Ecce tempus idoneum; Gaude gloriosa Dei Mater; Loquebantur variis linguis; O nata lux de lumine; Spem in alium.*

(B) **(*) CfP (ADD) CD-CFP 4638. Clerkes of Oxenford, Wulstan – SHEPPARD: *Motets.* **(*)

A useful issue, since it not only juxtaposes motets by Tallis against those of his great (but less familiar) contemporary, John Sheppard, but also gives us a strongly sung bargain version of the famous forty-part motet, *Spem in alium.* Here the resonance of Merton College Chapel means that definition could be more refined, and throughout the pro-

gramme David Wulstan's tempi are somewhat brisk, while at times there is also some sense of strain among the women. Reservations notwithstanding, there are fine things on this inexpensive CD, and it can be recommended.

Gaude gloriosa; Loquebantur variis linguis; Miserere nostri; Salvator mundi, salva nos, I & II; Sancte Deus; Spem in alium (40-part motet).

⦿ *** Gimell (ADD) CDGIM 906. Tallis Scholars, Phillips.

Within the ideal acoustics of Merton College Chapel, Oxford, the Tallis Scholars give a thrilling account of the famous 40-part motet, *Spem in alium,* in which the astonishingly complex polyphony is spaciously separated over a number of point sources, yet blending as a satisfying whole to reach a massive climax. The *Gaude gloriosa* is another much recorded piece, while the soaring *Sancte Deus* and the two very contrasted settings of the *Salvator mundi* are hardly less beautiful. The vocal line is beautifully shaped throughout, the singing combines ardour with serenity, and the breadth and depth of the sound are spectacular.

Lamentations of Jeremiah. Motets: *Absterge domine; Derelinquat impius; In jejunio et fletu; In manus tuas; Mihi autem nimis; O sacrum convivium; O nata lux de lumine; O salutaris hostia; Salve intemerata virgo.*

*** Gimell CDGIM 925. Tallis Scholars, Phillips.

This, the third of the Tallis Scholars' discs devoted to their eponymous composer, is centred on the two great settings of the *Lamentations.* They have often been recorded before, but never more beautifully than here, performances that give total security. As well as the eight fine motets, the collection also has a rare Marian antiphon, *Salve intemerata,* that is among Tallis's most sustained inspirations. Clear, atmospheric recording of striking tangibility.

Mass for 4 Voices; Motets: *Audivi vocem; In manus tuas Domine; Loquebantur variis linguis; O sacrum convivium; Salvator mundi; Sancte Deus; Te lucis ante terminum; Videte miraculum.*

(B) *** Naxos 8.550576. Oxford Camerata, Summerly.

The Oxford Camerata with their beautifully blended timbre have their own way with Tallis. Lines are firm, the singing has serenity but also a firm pulse. In the *Mass* (and particularly in the *Sanctus*) the expressive strength is quite strongly communicated, while the *Benedictus* moves on spontaneously at the close. The motets respond particularly well to Jeremy Summerly's degree of intensity. The opening *Loquebantur variis linguis* has much passionate feeling, and this (together with the *Audivi vocem,* and especially the lovely *Sante Deus*) shows this choir of a dozen singers at their most eloquent. The recording, made in the Chapel of Wellington College, is very fine indeed. Excellent value.

Mass: Puer natus est nobis (for seven voices).

(M) *** EMI CDM5 65211-2. King's College, Cambridge, Ch., Ledger – BYRD: *Mass for 5 Voices;* TYE: *Mass: Euge Bone.* ***

The magnificent seven-part writing in the *Mass* (a work assembled in recent years from a variety of sources – see below) contrasts well with the Byrd and Tye *Masses*, both masterpieces, with which it is coupled. The choir, at its finest, is beautifully recorded (digitally, in 1981, whereas the two couplings are analogue) against the ample acoustic of the King's Chapel.

Mass Puer natus est; Motets: *Salvatore mundi; Suscipe quaeso Dominus.*

⦿ (M) *** Cal. 6623. Clerkes of Oxenford, Wulstan – WHITE: *Motets*. ***

An outstanding reissue, made the more desirable by the inclusion of the four beautiful motets by the neglected Elizabethan contemporary of Tallis, Robert White. The Tallis *Mass* was reconstructed by David Wulstan and Sally Dunkley, prompted by the researches and speculations of Joseph Kerman and Jeremy Noble. The *Credo* exists only as a fragment, but the results are intensely beautiful. The *Mass* is among the finest Tallis, and it is performed with dedication and authority. The analogue recording could hardly be bettered.

TANEYEV, Sergei (1856–1915)

Suite de concert (for violin and orchestra), *Op. 28.*

(M) *** EMI (ADD) CDM5 65419-2. Oistrakh, Philh. O, Malko – MIASKOVSKY: *Cello Concerto*. *** ⦿

David Oistrakh's superb account of Taneyev's attractively diverse *Suite*, ranging from rhapsodic ardour in the first (of five movements) to sparkling virtuosity in the *Tarantella* finale, has been available only rarely, even on LP. The early (1956) stereo is of high quality and few would guess the age of the recording from the present CD transfer. However, this coupling is deleted as we go to press.

Symphonies Nos. (i) 2 in B flat (ed. Blok); (ii) 4.

** Russian Disc (ADD) RD CD11008. (i) USSR R. & TV Grand SO, Fedoseyev; (ii) Novosibirsk PO, Katz.

Symphony No. 4 in C min., *Op. 12; Overture The Oresteia, Op. 6.*

*** Chan. 8953. Philh. O, Järvi.

The *Fourth Symphony*, sometimes known as the *First* as it was the first to be published in Taneyev's lifetime, is a long piece of 42 minutes. Though some of its gestures are predictable, the best movement is the delightful scherzo which betrays his keenness of wit. Elsewhere neither his ideas nor their working out are quite as fresh or as individual as in such pieces as, say, the *Piano Quintet*. Neeme Järvi gets very good playing from the Philharmonia.

In the *Fourth Symphony* Arnold Katz and the Novosibirsk orchestra give a spirited, characterful reading which can hold its own against Järvi's excellent account. The recording is very good, though not quite in the three-star bracket. This version of the *Second Symphony in B flat* seems to be identical with Fedoseyev's 1969 LP; climaxes are a bit raw and raucous. The performance itself is satisfactory, and there is at present no alternative.

Piano Quartet in E, *Op. 20.*

**(*) Pro Arte CDD 301. Cantilena Chamber Players.

The *Piano Quartet* is a finely wrought and often subtle work. With a superbly sensitive contribution from Frank Glazer, the performance is altogether first rate, though the acoustic in which it is recorded is not quite big enough.

Piano Quintet in G min., *Op. 30.*

*** Ara. Z 6539. Lowenthal, Rosenthal, Kamei, Thompson, Kates.

Not only is the *Piano Quintet* well structured and its motivic organization subtle, its melodic ideas are strong and individual. It is arguably the greatest Russian chamber work between Tchaikovsky and Shostakovich. The recording is not in the demonstration bracket, but it is very good; and the playing, particularly of the pianist Jerome Lowenthal, is excellent. Strongly recommended.

Piano Trio in D, *Op. 22.*

*** Chan. 8592. Borodin Trio.

This *Trio* is a big, four-movement work. The invention is attractive – and so, too, is the excellent performance and recording. Strongly recommended.

String Quartets Nos. 1 in B flat Min., *Op. 4; 2 in C, Op. 5.*

(N) *** OCD 697. Krasni Qt.

This fine coupling offers yet more evidence that, in his chamber music especially, Taneyev was a more important figure in Russian music than has hitherto been suspected. The *First Quartet*, written in 1890 and dedicated to his former teacher, Tchaikovsky, is a distinctly individual piece in five movements, alternating slow and fast tempi. The beautiful Largo is searching, with an almost improvisatory feel, the Scherzo dances along spiritedly, and a delicately nostalgic Intermezzo intervenes before the light-hearted *Giocoso* finale, which has a charming secondary theme.

The *Second Quartet* (1895) has a pervading folksy quality, and is certainly Slavic in feeling, especially the melody that forms the centrepiece of the Scherzo. The *Adagio espressivo* is very intense, but also restless; the finale (*vigorosamente*) resolves matters cheerfully, and halfway through introduces a double fugue, gathering together the work's principal ideas. Then the tempo quickens, the texture lightens, and the movement ends jokingly, with a *moto perpetuo* over growling low scales from the cello. These performances are first class, and the recording is truthful (even if perhaps a little close). Recommended.

John of Damascus.

(N) *** DG 471 029-2. Mescheriakov, Larin, Chernov, Moscow State Ch.O, RNO, Mikhail Pletnev – RACHMANINOV: *The Bells*. ⦿ ***

Taneyev was the teacher of Glière, Scriabin, Medtner and Rachmaninov. His mastery of counterpoint was legendary and (as Calvocoressi and Gerald Abraham remind us in their *Masters of Russian Music* (Duckworth, London, 1936)) he would make countless drafts and preparatory exercises, fugues and canons and the like, so as to master every possibility and potential of his ideas before he embarked on a score. Taneyev's *John of Damascus* is his Opus 1 and a noble piece whose long neglect on the gramophone is at last remedied. An earlier version from Valéry Polyansky on Chandos made a strong impression but was encumbered with a perfectly adequate but unwanted performance of Tchaikovsky's *Fourth Symphony*. In any event this is vastly superior in every way.

TANSMAN, Alexandre (1897–1986)

Violin concerto; 4 Danses polonaises; Danse de la Sorcière; 5 Pièces; Rhapsodie polonaise.

(N) *** Olympia OCD 685. Halska, Polish RSO, Le Monnier.

Born in Lódz in Poland, Alexandre Tansman spent most of his adult life in Paris apart from the war years which he spent in Los Angeles. (His radio opera *Le Serment (The Solemn Oath)*, a French Radio commission, is little short of a masterpiece, full of atmosphere and often redolent of Szymanowski. It should be recorded and his cantata *Isaiah*, once available in the days of LP deserves revival.) The opening of the *Violin Concerto* (1937) is heady and intoxicating, and will strongly appeal to those who respond to Szymanowski. If it is a little diffuse, and not wholly consistent in inspiration, its beauties are sufficiently abundant to reward the listener. Beata Halska and the Polish Radio Symphony Orchestra under Bernard Le Monnier serve it well, as indeed they do the slighter accompanying pieces. The *Chanson et boîte à musique* from the *Cinq pièces* of 1930 is enchanting and Ms Halska dashes off the *Mouvement perpetuel* with great virtuosity and wit. Very well-balanced recording with plenty of space round the aural image.

Symphony No. 5 in D min.; 4 Movements for Orchestra; Stèle in memoriam d'Igor Stravinsky.

**(*) Marco 8.223379. Slovak PO (Košice), Minsky.

The Polish-born Alexandre Tansman was a prolific composer. Readers will recognize a certain affinity with his countryman Szymanowski; his craftsmanship is fastidious and his command of the orchestra impressive. His music is highly atmospheric, with shimmering textures enhanced by celeste, piano and vibraphones and sensitively spaced pianissimo string chords, plus poignant wind writing. The *Quatre mouvements pour orchestre* is impressive and resourceful. The *Fifth Symphony*, which dates from his Hollywood years, is less successful. The ideas are pleasing without being as memorable or as individual as the two companion works. The performances are very serviceable and the recordings decent.

TARP, Svend Eric (born 1908)

(i) *Piano Concerto in C, Op. 39*; (ii) *Symphony No. 7 in C min., Op. 81*; (iii) *The Battle of Jericho, Op. 51*; (iv) *Te Deum, Op. 33*.

**(*) dacapo DCCD 9005. Danish Nat. RSO, with (i) Per Solo;

(i; iii) Schønwandt; (ii) Schmidt; (iv) Danish Nat. R. Ch., Nelson.

The only familiar work here is the neo-classical, Françaix-like *Piano Concerto*, a light, attractive piece. There is a distinctively Danish feel to the *Te Deum*, though the piece is eclectic and owes a lot to Stravinsky and may even at times remind English listeners of Walton. The *Seventh Symphony* is neo-classical in feeling, very intelligent music, and only occasionally bombastic. The performances, which come from 1986–90, are enthusiastic and committed, and the recordings are serviceable without being top-drawer.

TARTINI, Giuseppe (1692–1770)

Concerti grossi Nos. 3 in C; 5 in E min. (trans. by Giulietto Menghini from *Sonatas, Op. 1/3 & 5*); (i) *Cello Concerto in D. Violin Concertos:* (ii) *in A min.;* (iii) *in G.*

(B) *** HM HMX 290853.55 (3). (i) Dieltiens; (ii) Gatti; (iii) Banchieri; Ens. 315 – CORELLI: *Trio Sonatas, Op. 5/1–6.* VIVALDI: *Chamber Sonatas.* ***

Here Banchieri's flexible Ensemble 315 expands to become a chamber orchestra (8;2;2;2) and in the *Cello Concerto* horns are added. All three works have eloquent slow movements and they are played admirably, using period instruments very persuasively. The concertos are framed by a pair of *Concerti grossi* effectively arranged from two of Tartini's *Trio Sonatas*. Warmly resonant sound ensures that orchestral textures are not wanting in body. The disc comes at bargain price in a slip case in harness with *Sonatas* of Corelli and Vivaldi.

Cello Concerto in A.

(B) *** DG Double (ADD) 437 952-2 (2). Rostropovich, Zurich Coll. Mus., Sacher – BERNSTEIN: *3 Meditations;* BOCCHERINI: *Cello Concerto No. 2;* GLAZUNOV: *Chant du Ménestrel;* SHOSTAKOVICH: *Cello Concerto No. 2;* TCHAIKOVSKY: *Andante cantabile* etc.; VIVALDI: *Cello Concertos.* ***

As with the other works in this fine 1978 collection, Rostropovich's view of Tartini's *A major Concerto* is larger than life; but the eloquence of the playing disarms criticism, even when the cellist plays cadenzas of his own that are not exactly in period. This is part of a first-class Double DG anthology which can be recommended almost without reservation.

(i; ii) *Cello Concerto in A;* (iii; ii) *Violin Concertos in D min., D.45;* (iv; ii) *in E min., D.56;* in G, D. 82; (iii; v) *Violin sonatas (for violin & continuo): in A; in G min.; in F, Op. 1/1, 10 & 12; in C, Op. 2/2; in G min. (Devil's Trill).*

(B) *** Erato Ultima 3984 25601-2 (2). (i) Toso; (ii) Sol. Ven.

Here is a collection to make the listener understand why Tartini was so admired in his day. Spanning both halves of the eighteenth century as he did, he possesses the lyrical purity of Corelli and Vivaldi with a forward-looking sensibility that is highly expressive. Indeed his invention is almost romantic at times and there are moments of vision which leave no doubt that he is underrated. The first work on the opening disc is the *Violin Concerto in D minor*, D.45 which opens with a richly winning orchestral ritornello and has a very beautiful central *Grave* which Piero Toso plays exquisitely. The other concertos also have memorable slow movements to which Amoyal and Zannerini both respond persuasively. The orchestral playing is committed and the fresh, warm analogue recording from the 1970s is pleasingly transferred. Tartini's sonatas take their virtuosity for granted; even the *Devil's Trill* does not flaunt its bravura until the finale with its extended trills – considered impossibly difficult in his day. Instead these works call for playing of the greatest technical finesse and musicianship. Pierre Amoyal plays them superbly; he makes no attempt to adapt his style to period-instrument practice. Instead his performances have a sweetness of tone and expressive eloquence to commend them, and though he is forwardly placed, the (unimportant) harpsichord continuo just comes through to give support. The violin is beautifully recorded. A most desirable pair of CDs.

Cello Concerto in D.

*** Teldec 9031 77311-2. Rostropovich, St Paul CO, Wolff –
   C. P. E. BACH; VIVALDI: *Concertos.* ***

A commanding performance by Rostropovich of the Tartini concerto, originally written for viola da gamba and transcribed for cello in the late 1920s by Rudolf Hindemith and revised here by Hugh Wolff. It is a mellifluous and beautiful work, played with great eloquence not only by the distinguished soloist, but also the fine Saint Paul orchestra. Excellent recorded sound.

Violin Concertos: in E min., D.56; in A, D.96; in A min., D.113.

(M) *** Erato 4509 92188-2. Ughi, Sol. Ven.

The three violin concertos on this record are all very rewarding. The *Concerto in A major*, which comes last on the disc, has an additional (probably) alternative slow movement, a *Largo Andante* which is particularly beautiful. Uto Ughi's performances are distinguished by excellent taste and refinement of tone, and I Solisti Veneti are hardly less polished. The harpsichord continuo is reticent, but otherwise the recording is exemplary. Highly recommended.

(Unaccompanied) Violin Sonatas: in A min., B:a3; in G min.; (Sonata de Diavolo), B:g5; L'arte del arco, B:f11; 14 Variations on the Gavotte from Corelli's Op. 5/10; Pastorale for violin in scordatura, B:a16.

⬤ HM HMU 907213. Manze.

Andrew Manze plays those genuinely fiendish trills in the finale of the *Devil's Trill Sonata* quite hair-raisingly. He re-creates here the electrifying effect Tartini's playing must have had on his own generation. Manze calls the opening *Largo* an 'infernal siciliana' (yet presents it with great poise and refined espressivo), and the central movement (hardly less remarkable) becomes a 'demonic moto perpetuo'. Yet Corelli's gavotte is played with engaging delicacy, the bravura left for the variations. The *A minor Sonata* also includes a set of variations which again offers an amazing range of musical and technical opportunities, as does the colourful hurdy-gurdy finale of the *Pastorale* which ends so haunt-

ingly. These works were left with a written bass line – omitted here because, according to Manze, this was the composer's stated 'true intention' and own practice. Manze's playing is totally compelling and certainly confirms that the music is 'complete' without a continuo. The recording is very real and immediate.

Violin sonata in G min. (Devil's trill), arr. Zandonai for violin and strings.

**(*) DG 463 259-2. Mutter; Trondheim Soloists – VIVALDI:
   The 4 Seasons. ***

Mutter, as in her previous recording of the sonata – one of the items on a virtuoso showpiece disc (*Carmen Fantasy*) – uses Zandonai's string arrangement, this time with harpsichord and cello rather than piano continuo. As in the Vivaldi, Mutter again takes an unashamedly romantic view of the piece, providing an unauthentic but interesting makeweight to a version of *The Four Seasons* which, whatever its controversial points, is magnetic from first to last.

TAVENER, John (born 1944)

(i) Eternal Memory for Cello & Strings; (ii) The Hidden Treasure (for string quartet); (iii) Svyati (O Holy One) for cello and chorus; (iv) Akhmatova Songs for soprano and cello. Chant for solo cello.

*** RCA 09026 68761-2. Isserlis; with (i) Moscow Virtuosi,
   Spivakov; (ii) Phillips, Feeney, Phillips; (iii) Kiev Chamber
   Ch., Gobdych; (iv) Rosario.

All this music is constructed simply (simplistically, some might say) and is based for the most part on a simple rising and falling scalic sequence, in the case of the *Svyati* and *Eternal Memory* linked thematically. Their atmosphere is magnetic. *Eternal Memory* moves on from *The Protecting Veil* and the composer describes its evocation as 'the remembrance of death; the remembrance of Paradise lost': its serene outer sections frame a more troubled centrepiece, 'grotesque, dance-like and rough'. *The Hidden Treasure* for string quartet still has a dominating cello role and might be described as a religious pilgrimage, closing with a mystical transformation. In the *Akhmatova Songs* the rising and falling sequence is floridly ornamented, and the singer is required to soar up ecstatically to the top of her range, which Patricia Rosario manages confidently. *Svyati* returns to a simple but radiant dialogue, alternating cello soliloquy with a mystical choral response. Steven Isserlis has never made a finer record than this, and he gives the feeling of quiet improvisation (especially in his solo *Chant*); throughout, the singing and playing capture the music's atmosphere superbly. The beautiful recording has a natural presence.

(i) The Protecting Veil; (ii) The Last Sleep of the Virgin (a Veneration for Strings & Handbells).

**(*) Telarc CD 80487. (i) Springuel; (ii) Willems; I
   Flamminghi, Werthen.

(i) The Protecting Veil; Thrinos.

(M) *** Virgin VM5 61849-2. Isserlis, (i) LSO, Rozhdestvensky
   – BRITTEN: *Cello Suite No. 3.* ***

(i) *The Protecting Veil;* (ii) *Wake up . . . and die.*

*** Sony SK 62821. Ma, with (i) Baltimore SO; (ii) cellos of
Baltimore SO; Zinman.

(i) *The Protecting Veil;* (ii) *In alium* (for soprano, tape
and orchestra).

(BB) *** Naxos 8.554388. (i) Kliegel; (ii) Hulse; Ulster O,
Yuasa.

In the inspired performance of Steven Isserlis, dedicatedly
accompanied by Rozhdestvensky and the LSO, *The Protecting Veil* has an instant magnetism, at once gentle and
compelling. The 'protecting veil' of the title refers to the
Orthodox Church's celebration of a tenth-century vision,
when in Constantinople the Virgin Mary appeared and
cast her protecting veil over the Christians who were being
attacked by the Saracen armies. Tavener, himself a Russian
Orthodox convert, echoes the cadences of Orthodox chant,
ending each section with passages of heightened lyricism for
the soloist. Each time that guides the ear persuasively on
into the next section, leading at the end to the work's one
sharply dramatic moment, when a sudden surge represents
Christ's Resurrection. Much is owed to the performance,
with Isserlis a commanding soloist. He is just as compelling
in the other two works on the disc, not just the Britten but
also the simple lyrical lament, *Thrinos*, which Tavener wrote
especially for him. Excellent recording.

Yo-Yo Ma, rather more withdrawn, is equally concentrated, daringly adopting an even slower tempo in the central
section, *Lament of the Mother of God.* He is helped by
the sympathetic accompaniment of David Zinman and the
Baltimore Orchestra, with recording a degree more transparent than the original RCA. The fill-up is a new work,
similarly visionary, commissioned from Tavener by Sony,
in which, using a palindromic motif, the spacious cello solo
is enhanced by cellos from the orchestra.

Using a warm, wide vibrato, Maria Kliegel gives a dedicated performance. With Yuasa drawing superb playing
from the Ulster Orchestra, this is an unusually spacious
reading that sustains its length well. What makes it specially
attractive is the coupling, *In Alium*, a piece for soprano, tape
and orchestra which is at once devotional and sensuous. The
layering of textures, with dramatic contasts, is vividly caught
in the excellent Naxos recording. Warmly recommended.

The cello soloist in the Telarc version is relatively reticent
emerging out of the orchestra, but the playing is beautiful
in its gentle way. *The Last Sleep of the Virgin*, written originally for string quartet in memory of Dame Margot Fonteyn,
makes an apt coupling in the conductor's enriched version
for string orchestra.

Diódia (String Quartet No. 3) – see below under
Akhmatova Songs.

String quartets: *The Hidden Treasure;* (i) *The Last Sleep of
the Virgin.*

*** Virgin VC5 45023-2. Chilingirian Qt, (i) with Simcock
(handbells) – PART: *Fratres; Summa.* ***

'Quiet and intensely fragile' is Tavener's guide to performances of *The Last Sleep of the Virgin*, a work which might be
described as an ethereal suggestion, using the simplest means

(string quartet and tolling bell) to convey both the reality
and the implications of the death and burial of 'the Mother
of God'. *The Hidden Treasure* in its seeking for Paradise
offers more violent contrasts (a brief cello cadenza-soliloquy
a key factor) interrupting the flow of the spiritual journey.
Tavener's world is all his own and the artists convey the
music's logic with hypnotic concentration, helped by a resonant acoustic. The mystical close of *The Hidden Treasure*
brings a shimmering *pianissimo-diminuendo* of remarkable
intensity.

VOCAL MUSIC

(i) *Akhmatova Songs; Many Years; The World* (all for
soprano and string quartet). *Diódia (String Quartet
No. 3).*

(N) *** Hyp. CDA 67217. (i) Rozario; Vanbrugh Qt.

Tavener's six *Akhmatova Songs* are among the most beautiful
and directly communicative of all his settings. Originally
written for soprano and cello, here they are rearranged even
more tellingly, using a string quartet but still relying a great
deal on a solo cello. Patricia Rozario is now completely
at home in the soaring melisma and surpasses her earlier
performance for RCA, with her account of the exotic melody
of *The Muse*, sounding like a celestial Russian folksong.
However, it is the hauntingly passionate closing evocation
of *Death* which gains most from the new instrumentation.
The World depends much on sustained high notes for the
voice over a gentle pedal and 'should be performed at
maximum intensity throughout', which it certainly is here.
The simply harmonized *Many Years* is a brief but melodious
prayer of supplication for the longevity of the Prince of
Wales, given as a present on his fiftieth birthday.

But the most ambitious work here is the *Third String
Quartet, Diódia*, which in a series of very similar episodes,
considers 'the posthumous states of being of the soul'. Tavener is directly concerned with the balance between heaven
and hell in music which is predominantly reflective and
serene, but with dramatic and sometimes savagely violent
interruptions. The performance has great concentration,
achieving a remarkable closing pianissimo over a beating
drum (perhaps a fading heartbeat). The recording is of
Hyperion's best quality.

The Akathist of Thanksgiving.

⬤ *** Sony SK 64446. Bowman, Wilson, Westminster Abbey
Ch., BBC SO & Singers, Neary.

The Akathist of Thanksgiving, the composer's personal response to the text by a monk in the Stalin era, inspires
striking atmospheric contrasts of motif and texture, with
the main choir set against a phalanx of 16 soloists, mainly
counter-tenors and basses, led by James Bowman and
Timothy Wilson. The recording, taken live from the performance given in January 1994 at Westminster Abbey, is
both warmly atmospheric and well defined, with high dynamic contrasts involving not just choral forces but strings,
heavy brass and percussion. Martin Neary proves an inspiring conductor, drawing incandescent tone from the

choirs, thrillingly reinforced by the underlying weight of instrumental sound.

Annunciation; 2 Hymns to the Mother of God; (i) Innocence; The Lamb; (ii) Little Requiem for Father Malachy Lynch; Song for Athene; The Tyger.

*** Sony SK 66613. Westminster Abbey Ch., Neary; with (i) Rozario, Titus, A. Nixon, M. Neary, Baker; (ii) ECO.

With Martin Neary drawing incandescent singing from the Westminster Abbey Choir, this CD offers a sequence of Tavener's best-known short works – such as the Blake settings, *The Lamb* and *The Tyger*, and the *Hymns to the Mother of God* – as well as longer pieces in which he movingly exploits spatial effects. *Innocence* encapsulates in its 25-minute ritual what many of his more expansive pieces have told us, with multi-layered elements atmospherically contrasted, near and far, starting with apocalyptic organ-sounds and ending with a surging climax. The elegiac *Song for Athene*, heard at the funeral of Princess Diana, is also among Tavener's most beautiful and touching inspirations, a ritual inspired by Orthodox chant over a drone bass. The Sony recording vividly captures the Abbey acoustic, with extreme dynamics used impressively to convey space and distance.

As one who has slept; Funeral Ikos; God is with us (Christmas Proclamation); 2 Hymns to the Mother of God; The Lamb; The Lord's Prayer; Love bade me welcome; Magnificat & Nunc dimittis; Song for Athene; (i) Svyati (O Holy One); The Tiger.

(N) (BB) *** Naxos 8.555256. Choir of St John's College, Cambridge, Christopher Robinson; (i) with Hugh.

The Christmas Proclamation, *God is with us*, is the striking first item in this collection of John Tavener's shorter choral pieces. It was inspired, like so many of Tavener's works, by Greek Orthodox liturgy, rising in thrilling crescendo and punctuated at the end by fortissimo organ chords. The *Song for Athene*, well remembered from the funeral of Princess Diana, is here presented as an anthem rather than a processional. The longest work, *Svyati*, with its cello solo magnetically played by Tim Hugh, echoes the example of Tavener's visionary cello work *The Protecting Veil*, while the shorter pieces include most of the favourite Tavener items. Superb singing throughout and vividly atmospheric sound.

(i; ii) Canticle of the Mother of God; (i; ii) Ikon of the Nativity; (iii) Out of the Night (Alleluia); (iv) Threnos.

*** Sony SK 61753. (i) Taverner Ch., Parrott; (ii) McFadden; (iii) Atkins, Nixon; (iv) Walsh – PART: *Fratres.* ***

Tavener's music is here effectively juxtaposed with works by his Estonian contemporary, Arvo Pärt, with the sustained but brief *Out of the Night* (for tenor voice and viola) acting as an evocative repeated refrain as it is heard (and performed) four times throughout this programme. The *Canticle of the Mother of God*, with its strange soprano melisma and choral dissonance, is ecstatically powerful and contrasts with the ruminative cello solo of *Threnos*, while the *Ikon of the Nativity* (which ends the concert ardently) is a set of three variations heard within a long melodic arch. The

performances are undoubtedly compelling, the resonant sound just right for the music.

(i) Eternity's Sunrise; (ii) Funeral Canticle; Petra; A Ritual Dream; (i; iv) Sappho: Lyrical Fragments;(i; v) Song of the Angel.

*** HM HMU 907231. (i) Rozario, (ii) Mosely, AAM Ch., (iv) Gooding, (v) Manze; with AAM, Goodwin.

Eternity's Sunrise is an elegiac setting of words by Blake in Tavener's rapt and intense style, with the soprano, Patricia Rozario, both pure and sensuous in singing the soaring cantilena. The final work on the disc *Funeral Canticles* for baritone and chorus, is related in being written in memory of the composer's father; 'calm and mesmeric' as Paul Goodwin says in his note, over an extended span, one of the finest, most intense examples of Tavener's religious minimalism. Of the rest *Sappho* represents Tavener at an earlier period, grittier in expression, while *Petra* and the *Song of the Angel* bring etereal violin solos from Andrew Manze set against the voices. Radiantly atmospheric sound to match.

Fall and Resurrection.

*** Chan. 9800. Rozario, Chance, Hill, Richardson, Peacock, BBC Singers, St Paul's Cathedral Ch., City of L. Sinf., Hickox.

Fall and Resurrection is the hour-long work which Tavener wrote for the Millennium celebrations in January 2000. Heard first in the echoing expanses of St Paul's Cathedral, it was simultaneously televised, and here comes in a sound recording of that premiere which in important ways brings advantages. Not only is there greater clarity, with clean directional stereo effects heightening the impact of the writing in massive blocks of sound, with chords endlessly sustained, but the inclusion of a full text in the booklet lets one follow the slow progress of the piece more closely.

Tavener's ambitious aim is to 'encompass in brief glimpses the events which have taken place since the beginning of time and before time'. Using broad brush-strokes in illustrative effects, both choral and instrumental, this becomes a physical experience rather than a musical argument. So, after the slow emergence of the prelude out of silence, darkness and the representation of Chaos (with massive banks of timpani), the voice of Adam is heard against a chill flute solo, a simple dedicated vision. The first of the three parts is then devoted to the fall of Adam and Eve, with the Serpent illustrated by a whining saxophone. The second section, representing prediction, leads from the fall to a quotation from Psalm 121, *I lift my eyes to the hills*, movingly sung by the countertenor, Michael Chance. The final part, *The Incarnation of the Logos*, in telegraphic brevity encompasses the birth of Jesus, the Crucifixion and finally the Resurrection in a Cosmic dance, when 'all is transfigured'. The final sustained chord fades away to reveal the sound of the bells of the cathedral outside, ringing out to the world, a theatrical coup underpinned by a heartfelt performance here under Richard Hickox with a superb team of choirs and soloists.

Funeral Ikos; (i) Ikon of Light. Carol: The Lamb.

*** Gimell CDGIM 905. Tallis Scholars, (i) Chilingirian Qt (members), Phillips.

Ikon of Light is a setting of Greek mystical texts, with chant-like phrases repeated hypnotically. The string trio provides the necessary textural variety. More concentrated is *Funeral Ikos*, an English setting of the Greek funeral sentences, often yearningly beautiful. Both in these and in the brief setting of Blake's *The Lamb*, the Tallis Scholars give immaculate performances, atmospherically recorded in the chapel of Merton College, Oxford.

We Shall See Him as He Is.

*** Chan. 9128. Rozario, Ainsley, Murgatroyd, Britten Singers, Chester Festival Ch., Hickox.

We Shall See Him as He Is is a sequence of what Tavener describes as musical ikons, setting brief, poetic texts based on the Epistle of St John, each inspired by a salient event in the life of Christ: His baptism, the Wedding Feast at Cana, the cleansing of the Temple, and on to the Last Supper, the Crucifixion and the Resurrection. Each ikon is punctuated by a choral Refrain, setting the words of the work's title in Greek. Though at first the inspiration may seem painfully thin, the simple ritual becomes magnetic, with its structured, highly atmospheric use of large-scale choral forces progressing towards rapt contemplation of the Resurrection, the ultimate ikon. The recording was made live at a dedicated Prom performance. The tenor, John Mark Ainsley, in the central solo role of St John sings with deep feeling, while Patricia Rozario makes her brief, wide-ranging solo a soaring climax.

Mary of Egypt (complete).

*** Regis RRC 2026 (2). Rozario, Varcoe, Goodchild, Ely Cathedral Ch., Britten – Pears Chamber Ch., Aldeburgh Festival Ens., Friend.

Mary of Egypt was recorded live at the Aldeburgh Festival first performances in June 1992 and, characteristically, Tavener compels you to accept his slow pacing and paring down of texture. In many ways the disc works better than the live staging, when with the help of the libretto the developments in the bald, stylized plot can be more readily followed. The musical landmarks are sharply defined in clear-cut, memorable motifs, with moments of violence set sharply against the predominant mood of meditation. What is disconcerting is the disembodied voice representing the Mother of God, Chloe Goodchild, using weird oriental techniques, sounding like a raw baritone. Under Lionel Friend the performance has a natural concentration, with Patricia Rozario as Mary and the baritone, Stephen Varcoe, as Zossima both outstanding. Their confrontation in Act III brings a radiant duet that acts as a climactic centrepiece to the whole work. A synopsis and libretto are provided, but instead of notes there is a 15-minute interview with the composer, informative but disconcertingly overamplified.

TAVERNER, John (c. 1495–1545)

Missa Corona spinea; Motets: Gaude plurium; In pace.

✲ (B) *** Hyp. Helios CDH 55051. The Sixteen, Christophers.

Missa Corona spinea; Motet: O Wilhelme, pastor bone.

**(*) ASV CDGAU 115. Christ Church Cathedral Ch., Grier.

As with the *Missa Mater Christi sanctissima* below, we are offered a choice of performance style for the inspired *Missa Corona spinea*, perhaps the most thrilling of all the Taverner Mass settings. In the Christ Church performance Francis Grier has transposed the music up, and his choir, although always eloquent, have to try very hard to cope with the highest tessitura. The Sixteen, using professional singers (and secure female trebles), have no such problems and they sing gloriously throughout. Taverner's inspiration is consistent and his flowing melismas are radiantly realized, with fine support from the lower voices; indeed, the balance and blend are nigh perfect. The two motets are no less beautifully sung, and the recording, made in St Jude's Church, Hampstead, is outstanding both in clarity and in its perfectly judged ambience. A superb disc and an astonishing bargain.

Missa Gloria tibi Trinitas; Audivi vocem (responsory); anon.: *Gloria tibi Trinitas.*

(B) *** Hyp. Helios CDH 50552. The Sixteen, Christophers.

Missa Gloria tibi Trinitas; Dum transisset sabbatum; Kyrie a 4 (Leroy).

*** Gimell CDGIM 995. Tallis Scholars, Phillips.

This six-voice setting of the Mass is richly varied in its invention (not least in rhythm) and expressive in a deeply personal way very rare for its period. Harry Christophers and The Sixteen underline the beauty with an exceptionally pure and clear account, superbly recorded and made the more brilliant by having the pitch a minor third higher than modern concert pitch.

Peter Phillips and the Tallis Scholars give an intensely involving performance of this glorious example of Tudor music. The recording may not be as clear as on the rival Hyperion version, but Phillips rejects all idea of reserve or cautiousness of expression; the result reflects the emotional basis of the inspiration the more compellingly. The motet, *Dum transisset sabbatum*, is then presented more reflectively, another rich inspiration.

(i) *Missa Mater Christi sanctissima; Hodie nobis coelorum rex; Magnificat a 4: Nesciene mater. Mater Christi sanctissima;* (ii) *In nomine a 4; Quemadmodum a 6.*

(B) *** Hyp. Helios CDH 55053. (i) The Sixteen, Harry Christophers; (ii) Fretwork.

Continuing their outstanding Taverner survey The Sixteen here offer the *Missa Mater Christi sanctissima* plus the votive anthem on which it is based. Christophers presents the Mass as it stands, and the music itself is all sung a tone up, which certainly makes it sound brighter. His pacing is rather restrained, and that adds a touch of breadth. The Helios disc includes extra music, including the Christmas responsory

Hodie nobis, a fine four-part *Magnificat* and, a surprise –
two rather grave pieces for viols from Fretwork to frame the
Mass itself. The recording is outstandingly fine, spacious yet
clear.

Mass, O Michael; Dum transisset sabbatum; Kyrie a 4 (Leroy).

(B) *** Hyp. Helios CDH 55054. The Sixteen, Harry
Christophers.

The *Missa O Michael* is an ambitious six-part Mass lasting
nearly 40 minutes which derives its name from the respond,
Archangeli Michaelis interventione, which prefaces the performance. The chant on which the Mass is built appears no
fewer than seven times during its course. The so-called Leroy
Kyrie (the name thought to be a reference to *le roi* Henry)
fittingly precedes it: the *Missa O Michael* has no Kyrie.
The Easter motet, *Dum transisset sabbatum*, completes an
impressive disc.

Missa Sancti Wilhelmi; Dum transisset Sabbatum; Ex eius tumba; O Wilhelme, pastor bone.

(B) *** Hyp. Helios CDH 55055. The Sixteen, Christophers.

The *Missa Sancti Wilhelmi* (known as 'Small Devotion' in
two sources and possibly a corruption of *S. Will devotio*) is
prefaced by the antiphon, *O Wilhelme, pastor bone*, written
in a largely syllabic, note-against-note texture, and the
second of his two five-part settings of the Easter respond,
Dum transisset Sabbatum, and washed down, as it were, by
the Matins responds for the Feast of St Nicholas, *Ex eius
tumba*, believed to be the only sixteenth-century setting of
this text. The singing of The Sixteen under Harry Christophers is expressive and ethereal, and the recording impressively truthful. Recommended with confidence.

Mass: The Western Wynde; Christe Jesu pastor bone; Dum transisset Sabbatum; Kyrie Le Roy; Mater Christie.

(B) *** Double Decca (ADD) 452 170-2 (2). King's College,
Cambridge, Ch., Willcocks – BYRD: *Masses for 3, 4 & 5
Voices* etc. ***

Mass: The Western Wind; Alleluia, Veni, electa mea; O splendor gloria; Te Deum.

(B) *** Hyp. Helios CDH 55056. The Sixteen, Christophers.

John Taverner's remarkable individuality is admirably
shown by this excellent King's concert. The *Western Wynde
Mass* (so called because of its use of this secular tune as a
constantly recurring ground) is a masterpiece. Its lines soar
to express rich expressive feeling, particularly in the *Sanctus*,
and overall it is hauntingly memorable. The other music
here also shows the composer's wide range of expressive
power: the motets, works of great beauty, match the Mass
in their inspiration. With first-class King's performances,
appropriately more extrovert in feeling than the coupled
music of Byrd, this makes an outstanding collection, with
the highly evocative 1961 (originally Argo) recording giving
the trebles an abundant body of tone.

Western Wynde Mass is also beautifully sung and recorded
by Harry Christophers' Sixteen in what must be regarded as
an ideally paced and proportioned performance. But what

makes this inexpensive Helios reissue doubly attractive is
the collection of other works included. *O splendor gloria*
carries the exulted mood inherent in its title (referring to
Christ and the Trinity) and the *Alleluia* is equally jubilant.
Most remarkable and individual of all is the masterly five-
part *Te Deum*, a profoundly poignant setting, harmonically
and polyphonically, even richer than the Mass, and using
those momentary shafts of dissonance that can make music
of this period sound so forward-looking. The recording is
superb and this CD is obviously the place to start for those
wanting to explore this excellent Helios series.

TCHAIKOVSKY, Peter (1840–93)

Andante cantabile for Cello & Orchestra, Op. posth; (i) Variations on a Rococo Theme, Op. 33.

(B) *** DG Double (ADD) 437 952-2 (2). Rostropovich, BPO;
(i) cond. Karajan – BERNSTEIN: *3 Meditations*;
BOCCHERINI: *Cello Concerto No. 2*; GLAZUNOV:
Chant du Ménestrel; SHOSTAKOVICH: *Cello Concerto
No. 2*; TARTINI: *Cello Concerto*; VIVALDI: *Cello
Concertos*. ***

Rostropovich indulges himself affectionately in the
composer's arrangement of the *Andante cantabile*, and the
balance – all cello with a discreet orchestral backing – reflects
his approach. Rostropovich's famous and much-praised account of the *Rococo Variations* with Karajan (see below) has
been added as part of a highly desirable anthology.

Andante cantabile, Op. 11; Nocturne, Op. 19/4; Pezzo capriccioso, Op. 62 (1887 version); 2 Songs: Legend; Was I not a little blade of grass; Variations on a Rococo Theme, Op. 33 (1876 version).

*** Chan. 8347. Wallfisch, ECO, Simon.

Andante cantabile; Nocturne (both arr. for cello & orchestra); Pezzo capriccioso; Variations on a rococo theme (original versions).

(BB) *** Virgin 2 x 1VBD5 61490-2 (2). Isserlis, COE, Gardiner
– BLOCH: *Schelomo*. ELGAR: *Cello Concerto*;
KABALEVSKY: *Cello Concerto No. 2*; R. STRAUSS: *Don
Quixote*. ***

Andante cantabile; Nocturne; Pezzo capriccioso; Variations on a Rococo Theme.

(M) **(*) BMG/Melodiya (ADD) 74321 40724-2. Feighin,
Estonian State SO, Järvi – HAYDN: *Cello Concerto*. **(*)

Andante cantabile; Nocturne; Souvenir de Florence, Op. 70; Variations on a Rococo Theme; Eugene Onegin: Lensky's aria.

*** DG 453 460-2. Maisky, Orpheus CO.

The delightful Chandos record gathers together all of Tchaikovsky's music for cello and orchestra – including his
arrangements of such items as the famous *Andante cantabile*
and two songs. The major item is the original version of the
Rococo Variations with an extra variation and the earlier
variations put in a more effective order, as Tchaikovsky
wanted. Geoffrey Simon draws lively and sympathetic

playing from the ECO, with Wallfisch a vital if not quite flawless soloist. Excellent recording, with the CD providing fine presence and an excellent perspective.

On this bargain Virgin Double, not only are all the performances of high quality, but Isserlis offers Tchaikovsky's original versions of both the *Pezzo capriccioso* and the *Rococo Variations*. The solo playing has at times a slight reserve, but also an elegant delicacy, most noticeable in the *Andante cantabile*. Throughout, Gardiner and the Chamber Orchestra of Europe provide gracefully lightweight accompaniments and the Virgin recording is faithfully balanced, fresh in texture and warm in ambience. Although there is some sparkling and flawless bravura in the variations, the performance here has less extrovert feeling than that of Rostropovich, but many will feel that its lightness of touch has a special appeal.

Understandably, with Mischa Maisky as star, the *Rococo Variations*, not the longest work, get top billing, and they receive a warmly persuasive reading, at once impulsive and freely expressive. Long versed in conductorless playing, the brilliant Orpheus Chamber Orchestra follow him loyally, as they do in the other concertante items, as arranged by the composer. In the celebrated *Andante cantabile* Maisky uses full tone for the opening melody and then most beautifully begins the middle section in a hushed pianissimo. Paradoxically, much the longest work, the *Souvenir de Florence*, is the one which gives Maisky the least to do as soloist. The original string sextet version is here adapted for full strings, with Maisky coming to the fore only in the second movement. The playing is just as rich and persuasive, with finely polished ensemble. Excellent recording, warm and well balanced.

Järvi's disc is one of a half-dozen devoted to his early recordings made in the USSR, issued by BMG/Melodiya to mark his sixtieth birthday. Most were made in the mid-1960s, but these are the last recordings he made in 1978 in Tallinn with the Estonian State Orchestra before he left for Sweden and the USA. It comprises Tchaikovsky's major output for cello and orchestra and features Valentin Feighin, a player of great naturalness and expressive eloquence, little known in the West. These are glorious performances, a worthy companion to Daniil Shafran's Haydn Concerto with which they are coupled.

Capriccio italien, op. 45.

❀ (M) *** RCA (ADD) 09026 63302-2. RCA Victor SO, Kondrashin – KABALEVSKY: *The Comedians Suite*; KHACHATURIAN: *Masquerade Suite*. RIMSKY-KORSAKOV: *Capriccio espagnol*. ***

Kondrashin's 1958 recording of Tchaikovsky's *Capriccio italien* has never been surpassed. The arresting opening still surprises by its impact, the brass fanfares – first trumpets, then horns, then the full tutti – sonically riveting. The music is alive in every bar and a model of careful preparation, with the composer's dynamic markings meticulously terraced. Kondrashin's pacing throughout is absolutely right and the closing section is highly exhilarating. This is a stereo demonstration disc if ever there was one. And the couplings are pretty good too.

Capriccio italien; (i) 1812 Overture.

(M) **(*) DG (ADD) 463 614-2. BPO, Karajan; (i) with Don Cossack Ch. – RIMSKY-KORSAKOV: *Scheherazade*. **(*)

Capriccio italien; (i) 1812. Festival Coronation March; Marche slave; Eugene Onegin: Polonaise; Waltz. Mazeppa: Cossack Dance.

(N) **(*) Telarc CD 80541. Cincinnati Pops O, Kunzel; (i) with Kiev Symphony Ch., Cincinnati Children's Ch., Cannon & Cleveland carillon.

Capriccio italien, Op. 45; 1812 Overture, Op. 49; Marche slave, Op. 31; Swan Lake (ballet): suite.

**(*) Teldec 4509 90201-2. Israel PO, Mehta.

Karajan's *1812* is very well presented and very exciting, with fine orchestral playing, and the Russian chorus used to open the piece certainly adds an extra dimension, sonorously recorded. If the closing pages have the cannon added in a calculated fashion rather than showing a touch of engineering flair, the result is still impressive. Although Karajan takes a while to get going, the *Capriccio italien* is also impressive, with the Berlin brass particularly telling. The recording is bright and vividly resonant, but there are more genuinely idiomatic accounts available.

The Telarc CD is aimed straight at audiophiles. But the snag is that the real cannon, spectacularly reproduced, the carillon and choruses singing the folktunes in *1812* very freshly cannot turn a good performance into a thrilling one, and here the adrenalin does not run as free as it should. *Marche slave*, however, is much more successful. The other works, too, are very well played, but there are more sparkling versions available elsewhere, and though the recording is sumptuous, the frequent presence of the bass drum thundering away eventually becomes too much of a good thing.

With the Israel brass sonorously robust, Mehta's concert opens with a lively and warmly conceived *Capriccio italien*, a Slavonically solemn yet exciting *Marche slave* and an exuberant *1812* with a spectacular fusillade at the end. The highlight is the suite from *Swan Lake*, played with style and affection and with good contributions from woodwind, violin and cello soloists.

Capriccio italien; 1812 Overture; Fatum, Op. 77; Festive Overture on the Danish National Anthem, Op. 15; Francesca da Rimini, Op. 32; Hamlet (fantasy overture), Op. 67a; Romeo and Juliet (fantasy overture); The Tempest (symphonic fantasy), Op. 18.

*** Olympia OCD 512 A/B. (2). SO of Russia, Dudarova.

(i) *Capriccio italien; 1812 Overture;* (ii) *Fatum; Francesca da Rimini; Hamlet* (i) *Marche slave;* (ii) *Romeo and Juliet* (fantasy overture); *The Tempest; The Voyevoda, Op. 78.*

(B) **(*) Double Decca 443 003-2 (2). (i) Nat. SO of Washington, DC; (ii) Detroit SO; Antal Dorati.

This exciting Olympia Tchaikovsky compilation includes one of the finest performances of *The Tempest* ever recorded, structurally convincing, full of atmosphere. Veronika Dudarova cannot do quite so much for *Fatum*, which remains an obstinately clumsy structure. *Romeo and Juliet* has passion, excitement and a certain Slavonic reserve at the presentation of the love theme, which make for a very satisfying whole; and a spacious gravity informs *1812*, although it does not lack impetus, with the climax (using drums rather than cannon) bringing a gloriously expansive treatment of the Russian hymn. *Capriccio italien* is very Russian too, especially the nostalgic treatment of the broad string melody, but there is plenty of energy and spectacle, and the end is almost alcoholically rumbustious, with a not quite convincing sudden accelerando at the coda. *Francesca da Rimini* and *Hamlet* here can almost be spoken of in the same breath as the famous Stokowski versions. The former has some glorious playing in the middle section, full of rich woodwind colouring, and a ferociously demonic portrayal of the inferno and the lovers' final, cataclysmic punishment; the latter has a uniquely touching portrayal of Ophelia's onset of madness (a poignant oboe solo) and a passionately sombre close. The Symphony Orchestra of Russia is apparently a permanent pick-up group, formed from members of other Russian orchestras, who play with great ardour and virtuosity. The 1992 digital recording is spectacular to suit the music-making, yet not blatant.

Dorati made his recordings of the symphonic poems in Washington in the early 1970s, while the triptych of *Capriccio italien*, *1812* and *Marche slave* dates from the beginning of 1979. The recording has the benefit of the splendid Detroit acoustics, although *1812*, rather endearingly, has a spectacular laminated eruption of American Civil War cannon and bells – including Philadelphia's Liberty Bell – at the end. The performance of the *Capriccio* is not without elegance, but *Marche slave* seems too sombre until the brisk coda. The symphonic poems are vividly done. *Fatum* is quite successful, but Dorati's accounts of *Francesca da Rimini* and *Hamlet* are rather underpowered compared with Stokowski, but they are spacious, individual readings. *Romeo and Juliet* after a cool start works up persuasively, and *The Tempest* is vividly done. *The Voyevoda* is not one of the composer's more inspired pieces, but Dorati makes the most of its melancholy and dark wind colouring, matching sombre lower strings.

(i) *Capriccio italien*; *1812 Overture*; *Romeo and Juliet*; (ii) Song: *None but the lonely heart*. *Eugene Onegin*: *Lensky's Aria*.

(B) *** [EMI Red Line CDR5 69844]. (i) Philh. O, Domingo; (ii) Domingo, Philh. O, Behr.

Here we have Domingo in his latter-day role as conductor giving heartfelt and individual readings of three popular orchestral favourites, with plenty of drama and with the passion worn on the sleeve. *1812* is ceremonially measured, with the organ adding breadth and spectacle at the close. The recording is appropriately spacious and resonant. Any lack of sharp co-ordination of ensemble is compensated for by the impact. The vocal items show that Domingo can still tug at the emotions in his more familiar role. The recording, made in All Saints', Tooting, is expansively resonant.

***Capriccio italien*; *1812 Overture*; *Marche slave*; *Romeo and Juliet* (fantasy overture).**

(BB) *** Naxos 8.550500. RPO, Leaper.

Adrian Leaper proves a natural Tchaikovskian: whether in the colourful extravagance of the composer's memento of his Italian holiday, the romantic ardour and passionate conflict of *Romeo and Juliet*, the sombre expansiveness of *Marche slave* with its surge of adrenalin at the close, or in the extrovert celebration of *1812*, he draws playing from the RPO that is spontaneously committed and exciting. The brilliantly spectacular recording, with plenty of weight for the brass, was made in Watford Town Hall, with realistic cannon and an impressively resonant imported carillon to add to the very exciting climax of *1812*.

***Capriccio italien*; *Manfred Symphony, Op. 58*; *Romeo and Juliet* (fantasy overture); *Serenade for strings in C, Op. 48*; *The Tempest*.**

(B) *** Melodiya Twofer 74321 34164-2 (2). USSR SO, Svetlanov.

Svetlanov's recordings of the major Tchaikovsky orchestral works, made in the late 1960s, still stand up well to current competition; the remastering for CD is highly successful, retaining the vividness and colour and minimizing any coarseness. The key work here is *Manfred*, and Svetlanov provides a superb account, strong and uninhibited, among the finest available: the orchestral playing has splendid colour and urgency, with plenty of passion from the strings. The full-blooded Russian recording is entirely appropriate and, while the work's weaker moments are not totally disguised, this is altogether most satisfying.

***Piano Concertos Nos. 1–3*; *Concert Fantasy, Op. 56*.**

(BB) **(*) Virgin 2 x 1 Double VBD5 61463-2 (2). Pletnev, Philh. O, Fedoseyev.

(N) (B) **(*) Teldec Ultima 8573 85196-2 (2). Leonskaya, NYPO, Masur.

Piano Concertos (i) *1 in B flat min.*; (ii) *2 in G*; (iii) *3 in E flat*; (iv) *Violin Concerto in D*; (v) *Variations on a Rococo Theme for Cello & Orchestra.***

(B) **(*) EMI ADD/Dig. CZS5 69695-2 (2). (i) Cziffra, Philh. O, Vandernoot; (ii) Kersenbaum, Fr. R. O, Martinon; (iii) Donohoe, Bournemouth SO, Barshai; (iv) Kogan, Paris Conservatoire O, Silvestri; (v) Fournier, Philh. O, Sargent.

Mikhail Pletnev's masterful account of the *First Concerto* has all the qualities we associate with his remarkable pianism. This high-voltage account, together with that of the *Concert Fantasy*, is among the very finest of modern recordings in the catalogue. Vladimir Fedoseyev and the Philharmonia Orchestra give excellent support and the recording is exemplary. The *Second Concerto* brings comparably commanding playing from Pletnev, but it also brings a small but unnecessary cut in the slow movement. It would be difficult to improve on the *Third Concerto*, which is characterized strongly and interestingly. The recording is very good, but not in the demonstration bracket. Admirers of this pianist will count this Virgin Double an outstanding bargain.

Leonskaya is a splendid Tchaikovskian and she finds a sympathetic partner in Kurt Masur. Their account of the *Concert fantasia* is particularly chimerical, catching its changes of mood spontaneously and not missing the ballet condiment in the orchestration. There is some dazzling solo playing and the orchestra are clearly enjoying themselves. The elusive *Second Piano Concerto* is even finer, weighty, expansive and compelling. The red-blooded orchestral tuttis are matched by Leonskaya's bold, forwardly balanced pianism, and if in the (uncut) slow movement she misses some of its delicacy, she is ardently lyrical. The finale, if not as charismatic as with Donohue on EMI, is forceful in its exuberance, powerful and exciting, and the rich Leipzig recording matches the style of the performance. The *Third Concerto* follows on with equal success, and offers brilliant playing with plenty of zest and ardour from soloist and orchestra alike. If only the *First Concerto* had matched the other performances, this would have been even more recommendable than its Pletnev competitor. But the account of the first movement, though full-blooded, is rather square and predictable, and although Leonskaya often plays brilliantly, and there are some impressive moments in the last two movements, there is an element of routine in the reading as a whole.

Although Cziffra's *B flat minor Piano Concerto* is disappointingly idiosyncratic, everything else on the EMI double is very valuable indeed, notably Leonid Kogan's splendid account of the *Violin Concerto* and Pierre Fournier's distinctive and stylish *Rococo Variations*. After Cziffra, brilliant but wilful in the *B flat minor Concerto*, Sylvia Kersenbaum's 1972 account of the *Second Piano Concerto* with Martinon is a different matter, absolutely complete in its text. The tempo for the opening movement is perfect, and Martinon's opening has a sweep to compare with that of the *B flat minor Concerto*. The violin and cello soloists in the slow movement play most sensitively, as does the pianist, and she is splendidly ebullient in the finale. One's only slight reservation concerns the recording, full but very resonant. Peter Donohoe provides a totally satisfying account of the *Third Concerto*, in an excellent, modern, digital recording. The compilation is crowned by Kogan's warm and spontaneous-sounding 1959 version of the *Violin Concerto*, and Fournier's aristocratic and elegant account of the *Rococo Variations*, dating from 1956, with sound still full and brilliant.

Piano Concerto No. 1 in B flat min., Op. 23; (ii) 2 in G, Op. 44 (arr. Siloti).

(N) (M)** DG mono 457 751-2. Cherkassky, BPO; (i) Ludwig; (ii) Kraus.

Cherkassky's were famous performances in their day. Some might find the opening of the *First Concerto* too slow and massive, but the performance soon settles down to offer plenty of thrills and, in the second subject (and later in the slow movement), sensitive playing from all concerned. There is also the kind of spontaneity one enjoys at a live performance. The DG sound is clear and well balanced, with excellent piano image. The upper strings, however , are less smooth than usual.

The *Second Concerto* was recorded before conductors had discovered that the first movement is split in common time, and meant to be taken at two-beats-in-a-bar. Richard Kraus plods along emphatically using four, and Tchaikovsky's opening is immediately bogged down. Cherkassky's playing

in superb throughout, but he uses the truncated Siloti edtion. Some will feel that his flair and poetry more than compensate – but not the present writer. This recording comes in excellent mono sound.

Piano Concerto No. 1 in B flat min., Op. 23.

*** Häns. CD 98.932. Ohlsson, ASMF, Marriner – RACHMANINOV: *Piano Concerto No. 2.* ***

*** Ph. 446 673-2. Argerich, Bav. RSO, Kondrashin – RACHMANINOV: *Piano Concerto No. 3.* ***

(BB) *** EMI CZS5 73765-2 (3). Rudy, St Petersburg PO, Jansons – RACHMANINOV: *Piano Concertos Nos. 1–3; Rhapsody on a Theme of Paganini.* ***

(M) **(*) Melodiya (ADD) 74321 40721-2. Sokolov, USSR SO, Järvi – SAINT-SAENS: *Piano Concerto No. 2.* **(*)

(B) **(*) Decca Penguin 460 653-2. Ashkenazy, LSO, Maazel – CHOPIN: *Piano Concerto No. 2.* ***

(M) (**) DG (ADD) 447 420-2. Richter, VSO, Karajan – RACHMANINOV: *Piano Concerto No. 2.* ***

(N) *(**) Chan. 9913. Judd, Moscow PO, Lazarev – PROKOFIEV: *Piano Concerto No. 3* *(**).

(i) Piano Concerto No. 1. (ii) Francesca da Rimini; Romeo and Juliet (fantasy overture).

(N) *(*) Dutton (ADD) CDSJB 1019. (i) Ogdon Philh. O; (ii) New Philh. O; Barbirolli.

(i) Piano Concerto No. 1; Nutcracker (ballet): excerpts.

(M) **(*) RCA (ADD) 09026 68530-2. (i) Gilels; Chicago SO, Reiner.

(i) Piano Concerto No. 1; (ii) Nutcracker suite, Op. 71a (arr. Economou, for 2 pianos).

(N) *** DG (ADD/DDD) 449 816-2. Argerich, (i) BPO, Abbado; (ii) with Economou.

(i) Piano Concerto No. 1. Theme & Variations, Op. 19/6.

(M) *** EMI (ADD) CDM7 64329-2. Gavrilov, (i) Philh. O, Muti – BALAKIREV: *Islamey*; PROKOFIEV: *Concerto No. 1.* ***

Argerich's 1994 live performance with the Berlin Philharmonic under Abbado is undoubtedly the finest of her three recordings. It has prodigious virtuosity, while in the first movement, after a richly commanding opening, conductor and pianist find a perfect balance between dynamism and magically gentle poetry. Even though Argerich's impetuosity is famous, on first hearing the listener will surely be astonished by her two tempestuous octave entries, where she carries all before her. And the cadenza, like the barnstorming closing pages of the finale, brings a thrilling all-out bravura of the kind one normally only associates with Horowitz. Yet, the *Andante semplice* has wonderful delicacy with the central *Prestissimo* glittering like a shower of meteorites. The first-class analogue recording is fully worthy of the music-making, and the audience is astonishingly silent. However, one wonders about the wisdom of DG's choice of coupling. Economou's arrangement of the *Nutcracker suite* for two pianos works well enough, though it does not banish memories of the dazzling transcription made by Pletnev (recorded by him for HMV and now deleted). However, if the present 1983 performance is not quite so breathtaking, it is still playing of a high order. The digital recording is good but rather dry. However, this CD, fine as it is, should have been reissued at mid-price.

It is good to have a really splendid, modern coupling of these two most popular romantic concertos from Ohlsson and Marriner that can measure up to the finest versions from the past, presented in naturally balanced, modern, digital recording of the very highest quality. The Tchaikovsky opens with a commanding melodic sweep, and the first-movement allegro is as full of poetic detail as it is exciting, leading on to the cadenza in the most spontaneous way. The *Andante semplice* is charmingly light-hearted and, after the scintillating centrepiece, is very tender at its reprise. The dancing finale brings all the bravura you could ask for, with weight and power as well as excitement.

Argerich's Philips issue comes from a live performance given in October 1980, full of animal excitement, with astonishingly fast speeds in the outer movements. The impetuous virtuosity is breathtaking, even if passage-work is not always cleanly articulated. The CD version clarifies and intensifies the already vivid sound, which is fuller than her DG version of nine years earlier (see below), and the new coupling with her even more sensational account of Rachmaninov's *Third Concerto* from earlier makes this a very desirable issue.

Like the Rachmaninov collection with which it is coupled, Mikhail Rudy's account of the Tchaikovsky *Concerto* treats it less as a warhorse than as a fresh, unhackneyed masterpiece, with poetry and refinement set alongside bravura display. As always, Rudy exhibits much artistry and taste in this eloquent St Petersburg account, partnered by Mariss Jansons. His playing is not short on virtuosity and command, but never at the expense of poetic feeling; the warmly idiomatic orchestral playing under Mariss Jansons has great character and personality. The recording balance too does justice to both soloist and orchestra. Altogether it makes a refreshing alternative version, here offered in a bargain package with equally illuminating accounts of the Rachmaninov concertos. Excellent sound, full and vivid.

Grigory Sokolov was only sixteen when he won the Tchaikovsky Piano Competition in 1966 with a dazzling account of the Saint-Saëns *G minor Concerto*, with which the Tchaikovsky *B flat minor Concerto* is coupled. The Tchaikovsky performance from the following year is no less remarkable, and not just for virtuosic display but also for poetic depth. Remarkable playing, not just from the young soloist but also from the USSR Symphony Orchestra and Neeme Järvi. The recording may be rough, but, given the excitement generated by this young performer, few will be worried.

Gilels's early (1955) RCA recording is over-reverberant, with the sound less refined than usual from this source. The *Nutcracker* ballet music, very well played if without much charm, is also rather inflated. The performance of the concerto, however, is very exciting and full-blooded, with Gilels giving a beautifully gentle account of the outer sections of the slow movement.

Gavrilov is stunning in the finale of the *Concerto*; however, the final statement of the big tune is too broadened to be convincing. In the main Allegro contrasts of dynamic and tempo are extreme, in a performance that often sounds self-conscious. The recording is full and sumptuous. In the *Variations*, Op. 19, Tchaikovsky is full of felicitous invention, Gavrilov's playing is stylishly sympathetic, and the Balakirev and Prokofiev couplings are dazzling.

Terence Judd contributed his powerful and urgent reading at the 1978 Tchaikovsky Piano Competition in Moscow, and though it has its moments of roughness, and the recording is limited and badly balanced, the compulsion and urgency of the playing are hard to resist. This is hardly a competitive version for general listening, especially at full price but with the equally magnetic Prokofiev, it is a splendid reminder of a fine pianist who died tragically young.

The element of struggle for which this work is famous is all too clear in the Richter/Karajan performance; not surprisingly, these two musical giants do not always agree: each chooses a different tempo for the second subject of the finale and maintains it, despite the other. In both the dramatic opening and the closing pages of the work the approach is mannered and self-conscious, not easy to enjoy. The recording is full-blooded, with a firm piano image.

John Ogdon's reading of the concerto also does not appear entirely consistent. In a work which represents an intense and consistent struggle between pianist and orchestra, under no circumstances must the soloist seem to give up that fight and go his own way. Where Barbirolli is at the helm, as in the broad-spanned, majestic opening and the vivacious full-blooded finale, the music has a strong forward emotional thrust, which Ogdon follows well; but as the solo piano part takes over the style of the performance alters, and in the quieter, lyrical music the tension sags. Fortunately in the *Andantino* both Ogdon and conductor see eye to eye and the result is an appealing simplicity. *Francesca da Rimini* shows Barbirolli at his very best, the inferno sequence intensely exciting, and the orchestral re-colouring of Francesca's lovely clarinet theme is magical. The polyphonic climax brings a tremendous sense of conflicting passions, and the actual moment when the lovers are slain is more dramatic here than on any other recording. The 1971 Abbey Road sound, too, is splendidly full and expansive. Alas, *Romeo and Juliet* stops short just before the coda, for the 1979 sessions were never completed. But in any case this recording does not show Barbirolli at his best. The reprise of the love theme, with the sighing horn solo, tends to sag, and it is certain that Barbirolli would not have passed this performance for issue, even if it had an ending.

(i) *Piano Concerto No. 1*; (ii) *Violin Concerto in D, Op. 35*.

(B) *** DG (ADD) 439 420-2. (i) Argerich, RPO, Dutoit;
(ii) Milstein, VPO, Abbado.

(N) (BB) **(*) Warner Apex 8573 89096-2. (i) Berezovsky,
(ii) Suwanai, Moscow PO, Kitaenko.

(N) (BB) ** EMI Encore (ADD) CDE5 74757-2. (i) Cziffra, Philh.
O, Vandernoot; (ii) Kogan, Paris Conservatoire O, Silvestri.

Martha Argerich's 1971 version of the *First Piano Concerto* with Dutoit has long been among the top recommendations. The sound is firm, with excellent presence. The weight of the opening immediately sets the mood for a big, broad performance, with the kind of music-making in which the personalities of both artists are complementary. Argerich's conception encompasses the widest range of tonal shading.

Milstein's 1973 performance of the *Violin Concerto* is equally impressive, undoubtedly one of the finest available, while Abbado secures playing of genuine sensitivity and scale from the Vienna Philharmonic, with a recording that is also well balanced.

The Berezovsky/Suwanai coupling was made at the prize-winner's concert after the 1990 Moscow Tchaikovsky Competition, and the recording balances (and occasional coughs) reflect that. Berezovsky's account of the *Piano Concerto* shows a dazzling ease of execution, but poetry too, especially in the *Andantino*. In the first movement, after the conductor's rather stolid opening, his skittish approach to the main allegro is engagingly like a Russian dance. Unfortunately Kitaenko provides him with a routine accompaniment which, in the heavily accented reprise of the big tune of the last movement, does not help to provide the final climax the concerto needs. Akiko Suwanai (only eighteen at the time) fares much better. Even though her approach to the first movement is relaxed, she responds to Tchaikovsky's lyricism with great warmth, and revels in the first movement cadenza which is marvellously detailed. There is spontaneity in every bar. The microphones are rather too near and do not flatter her upper tessitura but she has a glorious tone. The slow movement is again richly lyrical, with lovely touches of light and shade to which the woodwind respond, and in the sparkling finale she pulls back for each deeply felt entry of the very Russian secondary theme and makes it all her own. Kitaenko is obviously inspired by her playing, and gives her a totally supportive accompaniment and the orchestra, carried away in the sheer animation of the coda, drop a brick at the very end. Even so this is a very rewarding coupling and well worth its modest cost.

In the famous Tchaikovsky warhorse, Cziffra displays a prodigious technique, but during the first movement he and Vandernoot seem not wholly to agree on the amount of forward thrust the music needs and, in spite of the use of Kingsway Hall, the strings tend to shrillness. Kogan's performance of the *Violin Concerto* is a different matter. Enjoyment and spontaneity are written in every bar of his interpretation. His account of the finale is especially infectious with a lilt to the rhythm to really make it a Russian dance. In the first two movements, where he and Silvestri are more concerned with the architecture, he is steadier, but the build up of tension when the main theme is developed is most exciting through his very refusal to slacken the basic speed. His tone is gloriously rich and only occasionally does he mar a phrase with a soupy swerve. He rarely achieves a true pianissimo, but that may be the fault of the early stereo recording, which is very good, fuller and warmer than many Paris issues of this period.

(i) *Piano Concerto No. 1; Symphony No. 6 in B min. (Pathétique).*

(B) (**(*)) Naxos mono 8.110807. (i) Horowitz; NBC SO, Toscanini.

Horowitz's 1941 performance, given at Carnegie Hall, is even faster and more exciting than the better-known 1943 version, The playing is not always immaculate, but it is wonderfully incisive in articulation. This version of the *Pathétique* sym-

phony comes from the same concert, taut and urgently exciting rather than warmly emotional, marginally broader in the outer movements than his 1947 reading on RCA. Typically limited sound, not quite as dry as many from this source.

Piano Concerto No. 2 in G, Op. 44; Concert Fantasy, Op. 56.

(N) (BB) *** Naxos 8.550820. Glemser, Polish Nat. RSO, Wit.

This Naxos coupling can be strongly recommended on all counts, quite irrespective of cost. Bernd Glemser and the Polish National Radio Symphony Orchestra give an outstanding account of Tchaikovsky's underrated *G major Concerto*, flamboyant and poetic by turns. The unnamed orchestral principle cellist introduces the *Andante* gently and tenderly and his two string colleagues join him with equal sensitivity. The finale has plenty of sparkle and gusto and the whole account is very enjoyable indeed.

The *Concert Fantasy* too, is treated as a large-scale work. Both pianist and orchestra play it with total conviction, and much virtuosity (the cadenza very impressive). The *Contrasts* of the second movement are most tellingly made, with the lyrical minor key *cantabile* touching, and the Russian dance element as vigorous as one could wish. Excellent, well-balanced, full-bodied recording.

Piano Concertos Nos. 2 in G, Op. 44; 3 in E flat, Op. 75.

⊛ *** EMI CDC7 49940-2. Donohoe, Bournemouth SO, Barshai.

*** Ara. Z 6583. Lowenthal, LSO, Comissiona.

Donohoe's much-praised recording of Tchaikovsky's *Second Piano Concerto* is coupled with his excellent account of the *Third*. This superb recording of the full, original score of the *Second* in every way justifies the work's length and the unusual format of the slow movement, with its extended solos for violin and cello; these are played with beguiling warmth by Nigel Kennedy and Steven Isserlis. Barshai's pacing is perfectly calculated. The first movement goes with a splendid impetus, and the performance of the slow movement is a delight from beginning to end. Peter Donohoe plays marvellously and in the finale he is inspired to Horowitz-like bravura. The recording is spacious, but alas, this splendid disc has been deleted as we go to press.

In another attractive coupling of two unjustly neglected works, the energy and flair of Lowenthal and Comissiona combine to give highly spontaneous performances, well balanced and recorded. If the *G major Concerto* has not quite the distinction of the EMI version, it is still satisfyingly alive; the soloist brings an individual, poetic response as well as bravura. With very good sound, this is well worth investigating, as the account of the *Third Concerto* is comparably spontaneous.

Piano Concerto No. 3.

(*) Chan. 9130. Tozer, LPO, Järvi – *Symphony No. 7.* *

It was a good idea to record the *Third Piano Concerto* alongside the *Seventh Symphony*, on whose first movement it is based (see below). Geoffrey Tozer is an excellent soloist and, as in his Medtner performances for Chandos, plays with sympathy as well as powerful bravura. The playing of the London Philharmonic is not so consistent, with violin tone as recorded often thin, not opulent enough for big Tchaikovsky melodies.

Violin Concerto in D, Op. 35.

*** Teldec 4509 90881-2. Vengerov, BPO, Abbado – GLAZUNOV: *Violin Concerto.* ***

*** Erato 4509 98537-2. Repin, LSO, Krivine – SIBELIUS: *Violin Concerto.* ***

(M) *** Decca (ADD) 425 080-2. Chung, LSO, Previn – SIBELIUS: *Violin Concerto.* ***

*** Sony SK 68338. Midori, BPO, Abbado – SHOSTAKOVICH: *Violin Concerto No. 1.* ***

*** EMI CDC7 54753-2. Chang, LSO, C. Davis – BRAHMS: *Hungarian Dances.* ***

⊙ (M) (***) Dutton Lab. mono CDK 1204. Haendel, Nat. SO, Cameron – DVORAK: *Violin Concerto*; SAINT-SAENS: *Introduction & Rondo capriccioso.* (***)

*** EMI (ADD) CDC5 56150-2. Perlman, Phd. O, Ormandy – SIBELIUS: *Violin Concerto.* ***

(BB) *** Royal Long Players DCL 705742 (2). Spivakov, Philh. O, Ozawa – BRAHMS; DVORAK; SIBELIUS: *Violin Concertos.* ***

(BB) *** Naxos 8.550153. Nishizaki, Slovak PO, Jean – MENDELSSOHN: *Concerto.* ***

(B) *** DG Double (ADD) 453 142-2 (2). Milstein, VPO, Abbado – BEETHOVEN: *Concerto* ***; BRAHMS: *Concerto* **(*); MENDELSSOHN: *Concerto.* ***

(M) *** Penguin DG (ADD) 460 619-2. Milstein, VPO, Abbado – MENDELSSOHN: *Concerto.* ***

(M) *** Sony (ADD) SMK 66829. Stern, Phd. O, Ormandy – SIBELIUS: *Violin Concerto.* ***

(***) Testament mono SBT 1038. Haendel, RPO, Goossens – BRAHMS: *Violin Concerto.* (***)

(M) (***) EMI mono CDH7 64030-2. Heifetz, LPO, Barbirolli – GLAZUNOV: *Violin Concerto* (***) ⊙; SIBELIUS: *Violin Concerto.* (**)

(N) (BB) (***) Naxos 8.110938. Heifetz, LPO, Barbirolli – SIBELIUS: *Violin Concerto*; WIENIAWSKI: *Violin Concerto No. 2 in D min.* (***)

(N) (M) **(*) Ph. 464 741-2. Mullova, Boston SO, Ozawa – SIBELIUS: *Violin Concerto.* ***

**(*) Globe GLO 5174. Lubotsky, Estonian Nat. SO, Volmer – ARENSKY: *Violin Concerto;* RIMSKY-KORSAKOV: *Concert Fantasy.* **(*)

(M) ** Sony SMK 64127. Stern, Nat. SO of Washington, Rostropovich (with BEETHOVEN: *Romance No. 1 in G, Op. 40* *; MENDELSSOHN: *Violin Concerto* **).

(M) (**) DG mono 463 175-2 (2). Menuhin, Berlin RIAS SO, Fricsay – BEETHOVEN: *Violin sonatas Nos. 5, 7 & 9; Rondo in G.* ***

(i) *Violin Concerto in D, Op. 35; Méditation for Violin & Orchestra, Op. 42/1. Romeo and Juliet* (fantasy overture).

(N) **(*) Häns 98346. (i) Sitkovetsky; ASMF, Marriner.

Violin Concerto in D; Sérénade mélancolique, Op. 26; Souvenir d'un lieu cher, Op. 42/3: Mélodie. Valse-scherzo, Op. 34.

*** ASV CDDCA 713. Xue-Wei, Philh. O, Accardo.

Violin Concerto in D; Sérénade mélancolique. String Serenade: Waltz.

(M) **(*) RCA (ADD) 09026 61743-2. Heifetz, Chicago SO, Reiner – MENDELSSOHN: *Concerto.* ***

Vengerov gives an inspired performance, with magic inspiration breathing new life into well-known music. This Tchaikovsky reading immediately establishes itself as a big performance, both in the daring manner and in the range of dynamic of the playing. For all his power and his youthfully eager love of brilliance, Vengerov is never reluctant to play really softly. The central *Canzonetta* is full of Russian temperament, and the finale is sparklingly light, with articulation breathtakingly clean to match the transparency of the orchestral textures.

Repin's withdrawn tone in moments of meditation and his fondness for the gentlest pianissimos are as remarkable as his purity and sharpness of focus in bravura. He brings many moments of magic, such as the gentle lead-in to the second subject and the whispered statement of the main theme in the central *Canzonetta*, enhanced by the natural balance of the soloist in refined and well-detailed Erato recording, making this a highly recommendable alternative to Chung in this favourite coupling.

Kyung Wha Chung's earlier recording of the Tchaikovsky *Concerto* with Previn conducting has remained one of the strongest recommendations for a much-recorded work ever since it was made, right at the beginning of her career. Although she recorded it later with Dutoit, anyone should be well satisfied with Chung's 1970 version with its Sibelius coupling. With Previn a most sympathetic and responsive accompanist, this has warmth, spontaneity and discipline, every detail is beautifully shaped and turned without a trace of sentimentality. The recording is well balanced and detail is clean.

In her live recording, Midori, with the solo instrument naturally balanced, gives a reading which makes its impact as much in hushed poetry as in virtuoso display, with rhythms and phrasing freely expressive. Though the central *Canzonetta* is taken dangerously slowly, the rapt intensity is most compelling. As in the Shostakovich, Abbado and the Berlin Philharmonic give warm and powerful support, very well recorded. Midori adopts the tiny traditional cuts in the finale, arguably the preferable course.

Sarah Chang plays with exceptionally pure tone, avoiding heavy coloration, and her individual artistry does not demand the wayward pulling-about often found in this work. In that she is enormously helped by the fresh, bright and dramatic accompaniment provided by the LSO under Sir Colin Davis, always a sensitive and helpful concerto conductor, and here encouraging generally steady speeds. The snag is the ungenerous coupling, but Chang's performances of the four Brahms *Hungarian dances* are delectable.

The Dutton CD offers Ida Haendel's first orchestral recording for Decca, made in April 1945. She later re-recorded the work for EMI, but this first version has a very special magic and a natural warmth that is irresistible (in some ways comparable with Chung's first Decca account with Previn). The whole performance flows with a remarkably spontaneous freshness. Basil Cameron's accompaniment is professional and little more, but the orchestra obviously responded to their young soloist, and the wind playing in her ravishingly delicate *Canzonetta*, and in the secondary 'Russian-folk' material of the sparkling finale is richly hued. The admirably balanced recording is little short of amazing, as is the naturalness of the Dutton transfer. This surely ranks alongside the 78-r.p.m. Heifetz/Barbirolli version as one of the most memorable ever committed to disc.

Xue-Wei gives a warmly expressive reading of this lovely concerto, missing some of the fantasy and mystery. With rich, full tone, he brings out the sensuousness of the work, while displaying commanding virtuosity. The central *Canzonetta* is turned into a simple song without words, not over-romanticized. The coupling will be ideal for many, consisting of violin concertante pieces by Tchaikovsky, not just the *Sérénade mélancolique*, but the *Valse-scherzo* in a dazzling performance, and *Mélodie*, the third of the three pieces that Tchaikovsky grouped as *Souvenir d'un lieu cher*, freely and expressively done. The orchestral playing under another great violin virtuoso is warmly sympathetic but could be crisper, not helped for detail in tuttis by the lively acoustic.

There can be no real reservations about the sound of the present remastering of Heifetz's 1957 stereo recording, both full and brilliant. Heifetz is closely balanced, but the magic of his playing can be fully enjoyed. There is some gorgeous lyrical phrasing, and the slow movement marries deep feeling and tenderness in an ideal performance. The finale is dazzling but is never driven too hard. Reiner always accompanies understandingly, producing fierily positive tuttis. The Mendelssohn coupling is equally desirable, and the *Sérénade mélancolique* makes a splendid bonus.

Taken from an analogue original of the late 1970s, Perlman's Philadelphia version sounds all the fuller and more natural in its CD format, with the soloist balanced less aggressively forward than usual. His expressive warmth goes with a very bold orchestral texture from Ormandy and the Philadelphia Orchestra, and anyone who follows Perlman – in so many ways the supreme violin virtuoso of our time – is not likely to be disappointed. The old coupling of just the *Sérénade mélancolique* has now been more generously replaced with the Sibelius concerto, but this disc remains at full price.

Spivakov's reading, rich and warm, may be extrovert, but is easy to enjoy, helped by exceptionally full digital recording and a close balance of the violin. At the same time, with Ozawa directing a most persuasive accompaniment from the Philharmonia, this is also a reading which brings out the almost Mozartean elegance of much of the writing, not missing the gentle Russian melancholy of the central *Canzonetta*, but emphasizing the overall happiness of Tchaikovsky's inspiration. Coupled with three other outstanding performances, this two-disc set is an outstanding bargain.

Takako Nishizaki gives a warm and colourful reading, tender but purposeful and full of temperament. As in the Mendelssohn with which this is coupled, the central slow movement is on the measured side but flows sweetly, while the finale has all the necessary bravura, even at a speed that avoids breathlessness. Unlike many, Nishizaki opens out the little cuts which had become traditional. With excellent playing and recording, this makes a first-rate recommendation in the super-bargain bracket.

Milstein's fine (1973) version with Abbado remains among the more satisfying recordings. It now comes as part of a DG Double with three other concertos, although it is Zukermann rather than Milstein who plays the Beethoven (and very impressively too). However this same Milstein Tchaikovsky performance is also available on a single Penguin Classics CD, coupled with Mendelssohn, which some collectors may prefer. The author's note, by Jan Morris, concentrates on the Mendelssohn coupling.

Stern was on peak form when he made his first stereo recording with Ormandy. It is a powerfully lyrical reading, rich in timbre and technically immaculate. The playing is poetic, but it is not helped by the very close balance of the soloist, so that pianissimos consistently become *mezzo fortes*. The orchestral sound is vivid but lacks amplitude.

Made in Henry Wood Hall, this Hänssler recording of the Tchaikovsky concerto matches the qualities of the performance in beauty and refinement. Sitkovetsky gives an immaculate reading, with every note in place, crisply articulated in bravura passages, and with no hint of haste in the finale, lacking just a little in fire. Both in the slow movement and in the *Méditation* there is a purity in the approach, a hint of detachment, even though Sitkovetsky's tone is warm with vibrato, carefully controlled. This may not be a front-runner in a keenly competitive field for the concerto, but the disc is worth considering by those who want this unique triptych, with the overture as a welcome coupling, similarly fresh and direct.

Recorded in mono in 1953, Ida Haendel's red-bloodedly romantic account is such a distinctive, positive and powerful reading, one is grateful to Testament for bringing back so unjustly neglected a recording, and in such a vivid transfer. With speeds on the broad side in the first two movements, and generally kept steady, Haendel's warmly expressive style is the more compelling, leading to a fast and muscular account of the finale. It is generously and ideally coupled with Haendel's masterly reading of the Brahms, similarly neglected.

Heifetz's first (mono) recording of the Tchaikovsky *Violin Concerto*, made in 1937, has tremendous virtuosity and warmth. The sound is opaque by modern standards but the ear quickly adjusts, and the performance is special even by Heifetz's own standards. The transfer, too, is very good and, coming as it does with a classic account of the Glazunov and a fascinating Sibelius, this is a fine bargain.

Though the alternative Naxos transfer has rather high surface hiss, it captures the violin well, with the central *Canzonetta* sweet yet unsentimental, and the finale marked by dazzlingly clean articulation. A generous triptych.

This was Viktoria Mullova's first commercial recording and it is a resounding success. Her performance is immaculate and finely controlled – as is the coupling – but she does not always succeed in achieving the combination of warmth and nobility that this score above all requires. However, her playing has an undeniable splendour and an effortless virtuosity. Ozawa and the Boston Orchestra give excellent support and the recording is exemplary.

Mark Luybotsky is perhaps best known for his recording of the Britten *Concerto* with the composer conducting. His performance of the Tchaikovksy with Arvo Volmer and the fine Estonian National Orchestra is wonderfully musical and natural. Not perhaps as high-powered or flamboyant as many rivals, but everything unfolds naturally and effortlessly. It comes with enterprising couplings, including the endearing Arensky *Concerto*.

Stern's later (1977) version with Rostropovich is a good deal more impressive than its Mendelssohn coupling. Stern's technique is still impeccable and this too is a distinguished and often sensitive account. The orchestral response is more than adequate and often responsive, though Rostropovich is not free from the charge of over-emphatic accentuation in one or two places. The balance somewhat favours the soloist but is not as exaggeratedly forward as in the earlier, analogue version.

Menuhin's 1949 account of the Tchaikovsky *Violin Concerto* is his only recording of the piece. It first appeared in 1994 as part of the ten-CD set devoted to Ferenc Fricsay, when it was coupled with the *Pathétique Symphony*. There is no doubt that it is deeply felt and touches a vein of raw emotion, though there are one or two moments of dubious intonation to offset the undoubted insights Menuhin brings, and the great violinist is probably best remembered by other things.

(i) *Violin Concerto*; (ii) *Variations on a Rococo Theme*, Op. 33.

**(*) EMI CDC7 54890-2. (i) Kennedy, LPO, Kamu; (ii) P. Tortelier, N. Sinfonia, Y. P. Tortelier.

Nigel Kennedy gives a warmly romantic and very measured reading of the *Concerto*, full of temperament. For all his many *tenutos* and *rallentandos*, however, Kennedy is not sentimental, and his range of tone is exceptionally rich and wide, so that the big moments are powerfully sensual. Okku Kamu and the LPO do not always match their soloist, sometimes sounding a little stiff in tuttis. This performance is available coupled to an outstanding version of the Sibelius *Concerto* with Sir Simon Rattle (EMI CDC7 54559-2) as well as in this pairing with Paul Tortelier's finely wrought account of the *Rococo Variations*, with excellent analogue recording.

(i) *Violin Concerto*; (ii) *Symphony No. 5 in E min.*; (iii) *Capriccio italien*; *1812 Overture*; *Eugene Onegin: Polonaise & Waltz*; *Marche slave*; *Romeo and Juliet* (fantasy overture).

(B) **(*) Sony (ADD) SB2K 63281 (2). (i) Francescatti, NYPO, Schippers; (ii) Cleveland O, Szell; (iii) Phd. O, Ormandy.

Francescatti's 1965 account of the *Violin Concerto* does not disappoint: it has brilliance and flair, with sterling support from Schippers and his New York orchestra, and a particularly exciting finale. Szell's 1959 version of the *Fifth symphony* is also superb – almost matching his classic, thrilling account of the *Fourth* on Decca. Its sense of romantic urgency is finely judged, with a splendid surging momentum in the outer movements. The style of the horn soloist in the *Andante* may not suit every taste, but in all other respects, the orchestral playing is first rate. The Ormandy performances

of the popular orchestral works all offer polish and characteristic Philadelphia panache; the sound is good throughout the set, though the Philadelphia recordings are a touch glossy at times.

1812 Overture, Op. 49.

(N) (BB) **(*) EMI Encore CDE5 74751-2. Phd. O, Muti – RIMSKY-KORSAKOV: *Scheherazade*. **(*)

(i) *1812 Overture*; *Capriccio italien*.

⚫ (M) *** Mercury (ADD) 434 360-2. (i) Bronze French cannon, bells of Laura Spelman Rockefeller Memorial Carillon, Riverside Church, New York City; Minneapolis SO, Dorati (with separate descriptive commentary by Deems Taylor) – BEETHOVEN: *Wellington's Victory*. *** ⚫

Just as in our listing of this famous Mercury record we have placed *1812* first, so in the credits the cannon and the glorious sounds of the Laura Spelman Carillon take precedence, for in the riveting climax of Tchaikovsky's most famous work the effects completely upstage the orchestra. On this remastered CD the balance is managed spectacularly, with the 'shots' perfectly timed, while the Minneapolis orchestra clearly enjoy themselves both in *1812* and in the brilliant account of *Capriccio italien*. Deems Taylor provides an avuncular commentary on the technical background to the original recording.

An urgent, crisply articulated version of *1812* from Muti, concentrated in its excitement. The Philadelphia Orchestra takes the fast speed of the main allegro in its stride, with immaculate ensemble. Geniality is missing, but with a splendidly evocative sense of anticipation the coda produces a spectacular closing climax. The digital recording is a little fierce on top, but it gives the performance plenty of impact.

1812 Overture; *Hamlet* (fantasy overture); *The Tempest*.

*** Delos D/CD 3081. Oregon SO, DePreist.

The Oregon orchestra show their paces in this vividly colourful triptych, and James DePreist is a highly sympathetic Tchaikovskian. In *1812*, the cannon are perfectly placed and their spectacular entry is as precise as it is commanding. The performance overall is highly enjoyable, energetic but with the pacing unforced. The performances of both *Hamlet* and *The Tempest* are passionately dramatic, the latter generating comparable intensity to (but more melodrama than) Dorati's Decca version.

1812 Overture; *Marche slave*; *Romeo and Juliet* (fantasy overture); *The Tempest, Op. 18.*

**(*) DG 453 496-2. BPO, Abbado.

Abbado's *1812* is both exciting and satisfyingly held together, with some superbly placed 'cannon shots' during the spectacular closing section, which all but dwarf the orchestra. The *Slavonic March* opens rather slowly, but the very Russian melody evokes a profound sense of melancholy; the pacing then gathers momentum and excitement and the coda is thrilling. The performance of *The Tempest* is unsurpassed. After the evocative opening, with its flowing horn theme depicting Prospero's enchanted island and the sea, the storm sequence is vigorously exciting. The ecstatic lover's theme is introduced with touching delicacy of feeling and its climactic reappearance near the close explodes with passion. But Abbado's expansive approach to *Romeo and Juliet* is rather less successful. Here the introduction of the love theme is touchingly refined, but as the veiled moonlight sequence creeps in Abbado withdraws to a pianissimo, and the tension slips a little. The development is really exciting, capped by the thrilling return of the Friar Laurence theme on the trumpets and a passionate romantic apotheosis; but overall this is not an entirely convincing reading, in spite of the marvellous Berlin Philharmonic playing and brilliant, full-blooded recording.

(i) *1812 Overture;* (ii) *Romeo and Juliet* (fantasy overture); (iii) *Serenade for strings in C, Op. 48.*

(B) **(*) DG 439 468-2. (i) Gothenburg SO, Järvi; (ii) Philh. O, Sinopoli; (iii) Orpheus CO.

Järvi's *1812* is exciting – and not just for the added Gothenburg brass and artillery or for the fervour of the orchestra at the opening. He clearly knows how to structure the piece, and he obviously enjoys the histrionics, and so do we. Sinopoli's reading of *Romeo and Juliet* brings a hint of self-consciousness at the first entry of the big love theme, but there is plenty of uninhibited passion later. In the *Serenade for strings* no one could accuse the Orpheus Chamber Orchestra of lack of energy in the outer movements. Overall it is an impressive performance, even if the problems of rubato without a conductor are not always easily solved. The sound is first class.

(i) *1812 Overture* (arr. Buketoff). *Sleeping Beauty* (ballet), *Op. 66:* excerpts; *The Voyevoda* (symphonic ballad), *Op. 78;* (i; ii) *Moscow* (coronation cantata).

**(*) Delos DE 3196. Dallas SO, (i) and Ch.; (ii) with Furdui and Gerello; Litton.

Tchaikovsky's *Voyevoda* was underrated – even by the composer, who, soon after he had written it, destroyed the score. Fortunately the orchestral parts survived. Taken from Pushkin, it has a rather similar plotline to *Francesca da Rimini*. Its Tchaikovskian melancholy is most persuasively brought out by the excellent Dallas Symphony under Andrew Litton. He is equally impressive in a rather arbitrary set of excerpts from the *Sleeping Beauty* ballet. The programme opens with a choral *1812* in Ivor Buketoff's arrangement, which returns to the words of the original folksongs on which the music is based. At the close the Dallas chorus sings with an expansiveness that almost overwhelms cannon and carillon. Tchaikovsky's cantata *Moscow* was an 1883 commission for the coronation of Alexander III, a lyrical work, sung here with feeling by the chorus and two ardently Slavonic soloists. The recording is rich and spacious.

(i) *Fatum* (symphonic poem), *Op. 77;* (ii; iii) *Francesca da Rimini* (fantasy after Dante), *Op. 32;* (ii; iii) *Hamlet* (fantasy overture), *Op. 67a;* (iv; v) *Romeo and Juliet* (fantasy overture); (i) *The Storm, Op. 76; The Tempest, Op. 18; The Voyevoda, Op. 78* (symphonic poems); (iv; iii) *1812 Overture, Op. 49.*

(B) **(*) Ph. Duo (ADD) 442 586-2 (2). (i) Frankfurt RSO,

Inbal; (ii) New Philh. O; (iii) Markevitch; (iv) Concg. O; (v) Haitink.

Strongly committed performances of four of Tchaikovsky's little-known symphonic poems in excellent recordings from the mid-1970s. The most remarkable piece (which is superbly performed by Inbal and the Frankfurt orchestra) is *The Storm* of 1864, well-argued in sonata form, Tchaikovsky's first fully fledged orchestral composition. *The Voyevoda* is a very late work which is unconnected with the opera of the same name, but *Fatum*, written four years after *The Storm*, is less successful. *The Tempest* is here passionately performed and Markevitch's accounts of *Francesca da Rimini* and *Hamlet* have characteristic intensity and drive. Haitink's *Romeo and Juliet* is full of atmosphere and spaciously conceived. *1812*, distinctively paced, makes a lively bonus. The four novelties are what make this set worthwhile.

Festival Overture on the Danish National Anthem, Op. 15; (i) *Hamlet: Overture & Incidental Music, Op. 67a Mazeppa: Battle of Poltava & Cossack Dance; Romeo and Juliet* (fantasy overture; 1869 version); *Serenade for Nikolai Rubinstein's Saint's Day.*

*** Chan. 8310/11. LSO, Simon, (i) with Kelly, Hammond-Stroud.

Tchaikovsky himself thought his *Danish Festival Overture* superior to *1812*, and though one cannot agree with his judgement it is well worth hearing. The *Hamlet* incidental music, however, shows the composer's inspiration at its most memorable. The music from *Mazeppa* and the tribute to Rubinstein make engaging bonuses, but the highlight of the set is the 1869 version of *Romeo and Juliet*. It is fascinating to hear the composer's early thoughts before he finalized a piece which was to become one of the most successful of all his works. The performances here under Geoffrey Simon are excitingly committed and spontaneous.

Francesca da Rimini.

(M) *** DG (ADD) 453 988-2. Leningrad PO, Rozhdestvensky – SHOSTAKOVICH: *Symphony No. 5.* **(*)

(N) (M) ** Virgin VM5 61837-2. Houston SO, Eschenbach – DVORAK: *Symphony No. 9 (New World).* **

Francesca da Rimini; Hamlet (fantasy overture), *Op. 67a.*

⏀ *** Everest EVC 9037. NY Stadium O, Stokowski.

Francesca da Rimini; Romeo and Juliet (fantasy overture).

(M) ** BBC (ADD) BBCB 8012-2. ECO, Britten – FALLA: *El amor brujo.* **(*)

Stokowski's famous Everest coupling – one of his greatest records – is here remastered for CD with great success, with the sound cleaner and clearer, yet remarkably expansive in the bass in *Hamlet*. Stokowski's performance is inspired: he plays the central lyrical tune so convincingly that it conveys a sombre passion apt for a Shakespearean tragedy. *Francesca* is hardly less exciting: the opening whirlwinds have seldom roared at such tornado speeds before, the central section is played with beguiling care for detail and balance and, when the great polyphonic climax comes, the tension is extreme. The New York Stadium Orchestra drew on the New York Philharmonic for its players and their deep commitment more than makes up for any slight imperfections of ensemble. An indispensable record for all Tchaikovskians.

Rozhdestvensky's *Francesca da Rimini* is a *tour de force* and can almost be spoken of in the same breath as Beecham's electrifying pre-war recording with the LPO. As with Beecham, the inferno music is breathtakingly done and the music for the lovers' passion is conveyed with enormous intensity by the Leningrad orchestra. The 1959 recording, made in Wembley Town Hall, is reverberant, with the Russian brass rather blatant in climaxes, but the excitement and spontaneity of the performance are dominant.

Eschenbach's performance of Francesca da Rimini has similar qualities to those in the Dvořák symphony, with which it is coupled. With clean textures and ensemble, with rhythms crisply resilient and with the brass section gloriously ripe, it is a refreshing performance which yet lacks Tchaikovskian passion. It makes a generous and unusual fill-up for the *New World Symphony*.

Britten's love of the music of Tchaikovsky may seem strange when he was so vitriolic about other high romantics like Puccini. He conducted these live performances at the Aldeburgh Festival – *Romeo* in 1968 and *Francesca* in 1971. Although the lack of weight in the ECO strings (not helped by recording balances) and the overall lack of brilliance tells against these pieces being as dramatic as they might be, the warmth of feeling in spontaneous expressiveness is never in doubt. But this is for Britten's admirers rather than Tchaikovskians.

(i) Hamlet: Overture & Incidental Music, Op. 67a Romeo and Juliet (fantasy overture: original (1869) version).

*** Chan. 9191. (i) Kelly, Hammond-Stroud; LSO, Simon.

An admirable recoupling. The (1869) original version of *Romeo and Juliet*, a most enjoyable rarity, is very different from the 1880 revision we all know, with a completely different opening section. After a less well-organized development of the feud and love music, it ends sombrely but rather less tellingly than Tchaikovsky's final masterpiece. Geoffrey Simon is a committed advocate and the performances here are exciting and spontaneous. The *Hamlet Incidental Music* is hardly less valuable. The overture is a shortened version of the *Hamlet Fantasy Overture*, but much of the rest of the incidental music is unknown, and the engaging *Funeral March* and the two poignant string elegies show the composer at his finest. *Ophelia's Mad Scene* is partly sung and partly spoken, and Janis Kelly's performance is most sympathetic, while Derek Hammond-Stroud is suitably robust in the *Gravedigger's Song*. A translation of the vocal music is provided, here sung in French as in the original production of *Hamlet* at St Petersburg. The digital recording has spectacular resonance and depth.

Manfred Symphony, Op. 58.

💿 *** Chan. 8535. Oslo PO, Jansons.
(***) Testament mono SBT 1048. Philh. O, Kletzki –
BORODIN: *Symphony No. 2.* (***)
**(*) BBC (ADD) BBCL 1007-2. Bournemouth SO, Silvestri –
RESPIGHI: *Pines of Rome.* ***

*(*) Testament mono SBT 1129. Fr. Nat. R. O, Silvestri –
LISZT: *Tasso.* ***

Manfred Symphony; The Tempest, Op. 18.

*** DG 439 891-2. Russian Nat. O, Pletnev.

Except in a relatively relaxed view of the *vivace* second movement, Jansons favours speeds flowing faster than usual, bringing out the drama but subtly varying the tensions; his warmly expressive phrasing never sounds self-conscious when it is regularly given the freshness of folksong. The performance culminates in a thrilling account of the finale, leading up to the entry of the organ, gloriously resonant and supported by luxuriant string sound. The Chandos recording is among the finest in the Oslo series.

Pletnev identifies with the ongoing sweep of the work, yet he can relax glowingly in the pastoral evocation of the slow movement. In *The Tempest*, which is uneven in inspiration, Pletnev again carries the piece through on a wave of passionate romantic feeling. The recording is first class and this is one of his finest Tchaikovsky records.

Though Kletzki makes cuts and one or two amendments of orchestration, this is a reading which, far more than usual, carries you warmly and thrustfully through music which can seem unduly episodic. So the electricity which Kletzki generates in the central *Allegro con fuoco* section of the finale is remarkable, with the playing throughout marked by superfine clarity of articulation and subtle rubato. As to the mid 1950s recording and transfer, the brass and wind have thrilling immediacy, and the dynamic range is astonishing for the time.

Silvestri at Bournemouth does bring a highly charged emotional current to this score and much spontaneity of feeling, but the music is still pulled about in a way which will not enjoy universal acclaim. The recording is very good and the Respighi coupling outstanding.

In the earlier *Manfred* Symphony he recorded with the Orchestre National de France, Silvestri tarted up Tchaikovsky's orchestration , but it is not that as much as the moments of sour intonation and agogic distortion, that diminish the appeal of his recording. The Bournemouth broadcast is to be preferred but the Testament does have the benefit of a first-class fill-up in Liszt's *Tasso*.

The Nutcracker, Op. 71; The Sleeping Beauty, Op. 66; Swan Lake, Op. 20 (complete ballets).

(B) **(*) Decca (ADD) 460 411-2 (6). Nat. PO, Bonynge.
(B) **(*) EMI (ADD) CZS5 73624-2 (6). LSO, Previn.

Bonynge's Tchaikovsky performances are all recommendable. *Swan Lake* receives a red-blooded performance in which the forward impulse of the music-making is immediately striking. The 1975 recording is vivid and bright, though a little dry, producing a leonine string-tone sound rather than a feeling of sumptuousness. If the full romantic essence of this masterly score is not totally conveyed (partly as a result of the recording), the commitment of the orchestral playing is never in doubt. *The Sleeping Beauty* was recorded a year later with similarly vivid sound. Bonynge secures brilliant and often elegant playing from the National Philharmonic, and his rhythmic pointing is always characterful. He is especially good at the close of Act II when, after the magical *Panorama*, the Princess is awakened – there is a frisson of tension here and the atmosphere is most evocative. Bonynge's *Nutcracker* is finely done too, with plenty of colour in the characteristic dances. The recording from 1974 is rich and brilliant. All are packed in one of Decca's space-saving 'Collector Boxes' and this set is undoubtedly a bargain.

Previn's 1972 *Nutcracker* is superbly played by the LSO – it is a wonderfully warm account which gets more involving as it goes along. If *The Sleeping Beauty* is not as vital as it could be (though never slack), it makes up for it with the superb playing of the orchestra: the *Panorama* is beautifully done. The recording (1974) could sparkle a little more though. *Swan Lake* (1976) is given a similarly warm performance, though the overall effect is at times just that bit too 'cosy' for such dramatic writing. The music never drags though, and the excellence of the orchestral playing does much to enhance one's pleasure. The choice between these two bargain boxes is a matter of personal taste: Bonynge offers the more vivid performances (thanks also to the sound), while Previn has more opulence. Both are equally enjoyable and well packaged.

The Nutcracker (ballet), Op. 71 (complete).

*** Ph. 462 114-2. Kirov O & Ch., Gergiev.

*** Decca 433 000-2 (2). Finchley Children's Group, RPO, Ashkenazy – GLAZUNOV: *Seasons*.

*** Telarc CD 8137 (2). L. Symphony Ch., LSO, Mackerras.

(B) *** Melodiya Twofer (ADD) 74321 40067-2 (2).Bolshoi Theatre Children's Ch. & O, Rozhdestvensky.

(M) *** CfP CD-CFPD 4706 (2). Amb. S., LSO, Previn.

(B) *** Double Decca (ADD) 444 827-2 (2). Nat. PO, Bonynge – OFFENBACH: *Le Papillon*. ***

**(*) EMI CDS7 54600-2 (2). New L. Children's Ch., LPO, Jansons.

(i) The Nutcracker (complete); (ii) Serenade for Strings in C, Op. 48.

(M) **(*) Mercury (IMS) (ADD) 432 750-2 (2). (i) LSO; (ii) Philh. Hung., Dorati.

(i) The Nutcracker (ballet): complete; (ii) Sleeping Beauty (ballet): highlights.

(B) *** Ph. Duo (ADD) 444 562-2 (2). (i) Concg. O, with boys' Ch., Dorati; (ii) LSO, Fistoulari.

(i) The Nutcracker (complete); (ii) Orchestral Suites Nos. 3 in G; 4 (Mozartiana).

(N)(M) *** Ph. (ADD) 464 747-2 (2). (i) Concg. O, with boys' Ch; (ii) New Philh. O, Dorati.

The Nutcracker (complete); The Sleeping Beauty: Aurora's Wedding.

*** Decca (IMS) 440 477-2 (2). Face School Children's Ch., Montreal SO, Dutoit.

The Nutcracker (complete); Eugene Onegin: Introduction; Waltz; Polonaise.

*** Ph. (IMS) 420 237-2 (2). BPO, Bychkov.

Gergiev's new complete recording is on a single full-priced CD (over 81 minutes) and it is magnificently played and recorded. Tchaikovsky's inspired score emerges pristine and fresh as one of his most perfect masterpieces. The great *Adagio* for the two principal dancers has a passionate Russian ardour; the lively characteristic dances are simply bursting with Slavonic fervour. If, alongside Ashkenazy, there is a certain want of magic and charm, Gergiev everywhere displays a keen ear for Tchaikovsky's vivid orchestral detail. There are no pauses between numbers in the *Divertissement*, and this may well be dictated by the single-disc format. But it also increases the feeling that the score overall is a composite whole, and this is emphasized by the sense of apotheosis in the finale. Unless you are looking for a more relaxed spacious approach, this can be highly recommended.

Ashkenazy's digital *Nutcracker* also takes its place at the top of the list, ideally coupled with Glazunov's *Seasons*, in an equally enticing performance. It has the benefit of Walthamstow acoustics and state-of-the-art Decca digital sound, glowingly warm. The *Snowflakes* choral *waltz* has warmth as well as charm and the famous characteristic dances of the Act II *Divertissement* match elegance and character with a multi-hued palette of colour. Ideally the recording could be more generously cued, but for the music-making and recording there can only be the highest praise.

Dutoit's recording is beautifully played, with much sophisticated detail, and the Montreal acoustic provides brilliance, vivid colouring and striking transparency of detail. The party scene has great zest and character and the famous characteristic dances of the Act II *Divertissement* are made to sound wonderfully fresh, as is the *Waltz of the Snowflakes*, with its charming chorus of children. The sound is less sumptuous than with Ashkenazy, but both recordings are of Decca's finest quality and each of the two sets has its own felicities. For a coupling Dutoit offers *Aurora's Wedding*, a truncated version of *The Sleeping Beauty* which swiftly encapsulates the storyline, then moves on to the last-Act *Divertissement*, and the Decca recording is most successful.

The Telarc set was recorded in Watford Town Hall, which adds glamour to the violins and a glowing warmth in the middle and lower range. When the magic spell begins, the spectacularly wide dynamic range and the extra amplitude make for a physical frisson in the climaxes, while the glorious climbing melody, as Clara and the Prince travel through the pine forest, sounds richly expansive. Before that, the battle has some real cannon-shots interpolated but is done good-humouredly, for this is a toy battle. The great *Pas de deux* brings the most sumptuous climax, with superb sonority from the brass on the Telarc version. The Telarc presentation is ideal, with a detailed synopsis.

Semyon Bychkov has the services of the Berlin Philharmonic, and they offer superlative playing, of striking flair and character. Although a concert-hall ambience is favoured, the strings seem more forward. There is some superbly stylish playing in the *Divertissement*, and there are many moments when the extra vividness of the Berlin recording is especially compelling. As a modest bonus the *Eugene Onegin* excerpts are brilliantly done. The Philips notes are extensive but not well matched to the CD cues.

Dorati's 1975 complete *Nutcracker* with the Concertgebouw Orchestra makes a good first choice in the bargain category, very well coupled with Fistoulari's equally outstanding 1962 set of highlights from the *Sleeping Beauty*. In the former the playing of the Concertgebouw Orchestra is most refined as well as very dramatic. The CD transfer brings less sumptuous sound than on the old LPs, but the Concertgebouw ambience ensures body as well as vividness. Fistoulari's greatness as a ballet conductor is well celebrated by the *Sleeping Beauty* selection, which was extremely well recorded in its day and has transferred to CD with striking amplitude and brilliance.

The Dorati/Concertgebouw set has also been reissued, reasonably enough, as one of Philips's 'Great Recordings' re-coupled with what are perhaps the two most attractive *Orchestral Suites* (reviewed below). The remastering is excellently done and many collectors might well prefer this to the *Sleeping Beauty* ballet selection.

Rozhdestvensky's recording has a very strong Russian colouring, nowhere more strikingly different from a Western approach than in the *Waltz of the Snowflakes*, with the children's voices singing lustily. The timbres of woodwind and brass are robustly textured, the colouring bold. There is never the slightest hint of sentimentalizing the music, while the opening party scene conveys the rumbustious character of adults and children enjoying themselves. Every point of Tchaikovsky's music tells, and the vigour of the playing disarms any criticism. The excellent recording dates from 1960, given a lively projection on CD.

With Dorati's LSO *Nutcracker* the Mercury engineering has natural balance, warmly atmospheric with typically refined detail. Dorati relishes every detail, his characterization is strong, and the playing is full of life and elegance. In Act II the characteristic dances have much colour and vitality. The *Serenade for Strings* is less compelling. The slightly dry effect does not capture quite enough of the hall ambience, focusing closely on the Philharmonia Hungarica, who could at times be more polished. It is an affectionate performance, but not a very vital one.

Previn's earlier (1972) analogue set with the LSO has been freshly remastered. As in his later, digital version (only available combined with the other two ballets), the famous dances in Act II are given with refinement and point, and the orchestral playing throughout is of very high quality. With Act I sounding brighter and more dramatic than in its original LP format, this CfP reissue makes a fine bargain alternative to Dorati's mid-priced Mercury set, also with the LSO.

Bonynge's set is made the more attractive by its rare and substantial Offenbach coupling. His approach is sympathetic and the orchestral playing is polished, even if in the opening scene he misses some of the atmosphere. With the beginning of the magic, as the Christmas tree expands, the performance becomes more dramatically involving and Bonynge is at his best in the latter part of the ballet, with fine passion in the Act II *Pas de deux*. The Decca Kingsway Hall recording is brilliant on top, yet has a glowing ambient warmth.

Jansons's EMI version is highly dramatic, the histrionic effect emphasized by spectacular recording, especially of the brass which sounds almost Wagnerian at times. This is certainly lively and exciting, and it is stylishly played, but it has less warmth and magic than the Decca Ashkenazy digital recording, and there is no coupling. Moreover it has just been deleted.

The Nutcracker excerpts.

** Chan. 9799. Danish Nat. RSO, Temirkanov – RAVEL: *Ma Mère l'Oye (suite); La Valse* ** (with GADE: *Tango Jalousie).*

This CD offers only some of the *Nutcracker* and the Ravel coupling is hardly a rarity. The fine Danish Radio Orchestra plays excellently but Temirkanov is, as so often, all too idiosyncratic. No complaints about the sound.

Nutcracker Suite, Op. 71a.

(M) **(*) Sony SBK 46550. Phd. O, Ormandy – CHOPIN: *Les Sylphides;* DELIBES: *Coppélia; Sylvia: Suites.* ***

The Philadelphia Orchestra made this wonderful music universally famous in Walt Disney's *Fantasia* and they know how to play it just as well under Ormandy in 1963 as they did under Stokowski. Perhaps there is less individuality in the characteristic dances, but the music-making has suitable moments of reticence (as in the neat *Ouverture miniature*) as well as plenty of flair. In the *Waltz of the flowers* Ormandy, with no justification, takes the soaring violin tune an octave up on its second appearance.

Nutcracker Suite; Romeo and Juliet (fantasy overture).

**(*) DG 439 021-2. BPO, Karajan.

Originally designed to accompany a picture biography of Karajan, this not very generous Tchaikovsky coupling brings superbly played permorfances. The suite is delicate and detailed, yet perhaps lacks a little in charm, notably the *Arab Dance* which, taken fairly brisky , loses something of its gentile sentience. The performance of *Romeo and Juliet* is both polished and dramatic, but Karajan draws out the love theme with spacious moulding, and there is marginally less spontaneity here than in his earlier recordings.

The Nutcracker (highlights); Sleeping Beauty (highlights); Swan Lake (highlights).

(N) **(*) (B) EMI Double forte (ADD) CZS5 74308-2 (2). Phil. O, Kurtz.

Kurtz was a persuasive Tchaikovskian, and these excerpts from *Sleeping Beauty* and *Swan Lake* are nicely turned, fresh performances dating from the late 1950s, with the advantage of particularly beautiful Philharmonia wind playing. The recording is good, set in a natural, theatrical acoustic, and its early date only hinted at in the slight thinness of violin sound. *The Nutcracker*, though enjoyable, falls just below this fine quality, both as a performance and as a recording (it is not quite so open) and, inexplicably, the *Chinese Dance* is omitted from the otherwise complete 'suite'. With the bonus of a star violin soloist, Yehudi Menuhin – though he doesn't have a great deal to do until it comes to *Swan Lake*), this two-disc compilation remains good value.

(i) The Nutcracker. Sleeping Beauty; Swan Lake: excerpts.

(B) **(*) EMI (ADD) CZS7 62816-2 (2). LSO, Previn, (i) with Amb. S.

(N) (B) * Sony (ADD) SBK 89284. Philadelphia O, Ormandy.

The Nutcracker: Suite; The Sleeping Beauty (excerpts); Swan Lake (excerpts).

(B) ** Decca Penguin (ADD) 460 639-2. SRO, Ansermet.

By the use of two CDs, offering some 148 minutes of music, this EMI box covers a substantial proportion of the key numbers from all three ballets. *The Nutcracker* selection is particularly generous in including, besides virtually all the most famous characteristic dances, the 13-minute episode in Act I starting with the Battle sequence, continuing with the magical Pine forest journey and finishing with the delightful choral *Waltz of the Snowflakes*. Previn and the London Symphony Orchestra provide vivacious playing and the recording is full, bright and vivid. The remastering, however, loses some of the smoothness and refinement of focus of the original, analogue recordings. This remains very enjoyable and excellent value.

What we have from Ansermet is a pretty meagre selection of excerpts (60 minutes – similar to the previous LP) which fails to convey the full effect he achieved in the complete sets from which these are taken. The late-1950s recordings, despite some tape hiss, are excellent (especially in *The Nutcracker* and *The Sleeping Beauty*). The contributory essay is by Sir Roy Strong.

The Philadelphia Orchestra plays with marvellous assurance, of course, but this is not one of Ormandy's successes. Much of the fault is due to the variable recording quality which is very glassy indeed, and not at all pleasant to listen to after a while. It has the effect of smoothing out the colours and character of the music, though the conductor is also partly to blame.

Nutcracker Suite; Sleeping Beauty: Suite; Swan Lake: Suite.

✱ (M) *** DG (ADD) 449 726-2. BPO, Rostropovich.
(BB) *** EMI Encore (ADD) CDE5 74758-2. LSO, Previn.
(M) *** Decca (ADD) 466 379-2. VPO, Karajan.

Rostropovich's triptych of Tchaikovsky ballet suites is very special. His account of the *Nutcracker Suite* is enchanting: the *Sugar Plum Fairy* is introduced with ethereal gentleness, the *Russian Dance* has marvellous zest and the *Waltz of the Flowers* combines warmth and elegance with an exhilarating vigour. The *Sleeping Beauty* and *Swan Lake* selections are hardly less distinguished, and in the former the *Panorama* is gloriously played. The CD remastering now approaches demonstration standard, combining bloom with enhanced detail. Sixty-nine minutes of sheer joy and at mid-price.

The digital remastering has also been very successful on the EMI disc, freshening the sound of the excellent recordings, taken from Previn's analogue complete sets (which means that the *Dance of the Sugar Plum Fairy* in *The Nutcracker* has the longer coda rather than the ending Tchaikovsky devised for the *Suite*). The performances are at once vivid and elegant, warm and exciting. Previn's *Panorama* from *Sleeping Beauty* is hardly less beguiling than Rostropovich's and the recording has comparable warmth.

As reissued in Decca's Legend series, the Karajan recording is very impressive indeed; tuttis are well focused by the digital transfer, and the glowing ambience of the Sofiensaal flatters the strings and adds to the woodwind colourings, particularly in the *Nutcracker Suite*, which is less bland here than in Karajan's later re-recording with the BPO. Overall this disc offers very fine playing from the VPO

and, although the atmosphere is generally relaxed (especially in *Sleeping Beauty*), there is a persuasive warmth.

Romeo and Juliet (fantasy overture and excerpt).

(M) *** Classic fM 75605 57047. RPO, Gatti – PROKOFIEV: *Romeo and Juliet* (ballet): excerpts. ***

Daniele Gatti's performances could not be more highly charged romantically, and with a vividly passionate (if not always immaculate) response from the RPO, the climaxes are thrilling, with the horns and trumpets ringing out superbly at the climax of the duel sequence. The recording too is splendidly full and sumptuous, and the rare coupling with Prokofiev could not be more apt. This is one of Classic fM's finest issues so far.

Sérénade mélancholique (for violin and orchestra), Op. 26.

*** EMI CDC5 56966-2. Vengerov, LSO, Rostropovich – SHCHEDRIN: *Concerto cantabile*; STRAVINSKY: *Violin Concerto*. ***

The disarmingly simple lyricism of Tchaikovsky's gentle, yet ardent Serenade is well caught by Vengerov and Rostropovich in a refined reading that catches the composer's Russian melancholy to perfection. It makes a perfect encore for Vengerov's superb account of the spikier Stravinsky concerto.

(i) Sérénade mélancolique; (ii) Souvenir d'un lieu cher, Op. 42/1.

(M) *** Sony (ADD) SMK 66830. Stern, with (i) Columbia SO, Brieff; (ii) Nat. SO, Rostropovich – BRUCH: *Violin Concerto No. 1*; WIENIAWSKI: *Violin Concerto No. 2*. **(*)

Glorious playing from Stern. He is recorded too closely (as is the Columbia Symphony in the *Sérénade*) but his warm timbre is caught lusciously and he knows just how to catch the composer's nostalgic feeling. Both accompaniments are sympathetic.

Serenade for Strings in C, Op. 48.

(BB) *** Virgin 2 x 1 VBD5 61763-2 (2). LCO, Warren-Green – DVORAK: *Serenade for Strings in E, Op. 22*; ELGAR: *Introduction & allegro; Serenade*; SUK: *Serenade*; VAUGHAN WILLIAMS: *Fantasia on Greensleeves etc.* ***.
(BB) *** ASV (ADD) CDQS 6094. Polish R. CO, Duczmal – SUK: *Serenade* ***; GRIEG: *Holberg Suite* etc. **(*)

Serenade for Strings; Souvenir de Florence. Op. 70.

(BB) **(*) Naxos 8.550404. V. CO, Entremont.

Serenade for Strings; Suite No. 4 in G (Mozartiana), Op. 61; (i) Nocturne in C sharp min., Op. 19/4 (arr. for cello and orchestra); (ii) Legend: Christ in his Garden.

(M) ** BBC stereo/mono BBCB 8002-2. ECO, Britten; with (i) Rostropovich; (ii) Pears.

Not surprisingly, Christopher Warren-Green's reading of Tchaikovsky's *Serenade* with the excellent London Chamber Orchestra is full of individuality. The first movement's secondary idea has an appealing feathery lightness, and when the striding opening theme reappears at the end of the movement it brings a spontaneous-sounding burst of expressive intensity characteristic of this group. The *Waltz* lilts gently, with the tenutos nicely managed, the *Elégie* has delicacy as well as fervour, and the finale develops plenty of energy. Very well recorded, it is a performance to give pleasure for its freshness and natural impetus, and the couplings are amazingly generous and equally stimulating.

The Polish Radio Chamber Orchestra give a reading full of subtlety and grace, and this account often finds a rare quality of tenderness alongside its vigour and expansiveness. The Waltz is relaxed and gentle, and there is a wistful delicacy in the *Elégie*. The finale is exquisitely prepared, then the allegro is off with the wind, very fast, light and balletic, again with engagingly crisp articulation. This is a performance to make one appreciate this as among the composer's greatest works, with its Mozartian elegance and perfection of form. The recording is excellent, full, transparent, yet with a fine bloom.

Philip Entremont's performances of Tchaikovsky's two major string works communicate above all a feeling of passionate thrust and energy. After the ardour of the *Elégie*, the finale steals in persuasively, with dance-rhythms bracing and strong. The *Souvenir de Florence* has comparable momentum and eagerness. The dashing main theme of the first movement swings along infectiously, while the wistful secondary idea also takes wing. Entremont brings out the charm in writing inspired by Russian folksong. The VCO are committed, persuasive advocates to make one wonder why the *Souvenir* does not have a more central place in the string repertoire.

Britten's relaxed accounts of the *Serenade* and *Suite* are warmly persuasive but not distinctive. The solo contributions from Rostropovich and Pears add to the character of the programme, but there are more memorable recordings available of both the major works.

The Sleeping Beauty (ballet), *Op. 66* (complete).

✪ *** DG 457 634-2 (2). Russian Nat. O, Pletnev.
(BB) *** Naxos 8.550490/2. Slovak State PO (Košice), Mogrelia.
*** Ph. 434 922-2 (3). Kirov O (St Petersburg), Gergiev.
(M) **(*) EMI (ADD) CMS7 64840-2 (2). LSO, Previn.

Pletnev's is a performance of individuality and high quality. It is a strongly narrative and dramatic account that has tenderness (as in the opening of the *Pas de six* in the Prologue) and much the same virtuosity that Pletnev exhibits at the keyboard. The articulation is pretty dazzling throughout and the there is plenty of wit in the Act III *Divertissement*. Even though there are times when tempi seem too brisk for dancing, everything sounds fresh. The recording is very good, wide in dynamic range and well balanced, though not in the demonstration bracket (perhaps wanting a shade in amplitude). DG accommodate the set on two CDs (of 79 and 80 minutes respectively).

Andrew Mogrelia conducts Tchaikovsky's score with an ideal combination of warmth, grace and vitality. Moreover the Slovak State Philharmonic prove to be an excellent orchestra for this repertoire, with fine wind-players and equally impressive string principals for the important violin and cello solos. The Naxos digital recording is full and brilliant without being overlit, and the acoustics of the House of Arts in Košice bring a spacious ambience, with vivid orchestral colours.

The Kirov recording of Tchaikovsky's complete ballet is in every way satisfying. The playing – from an orchestra completely inside the music – is warmly sympathetic and vital, with no suggestion that familiarity has bred any sense of routine. Gergiev is a subtle interpreter, and his performance of the beautiful *Panorama* floats gently and radiantly over its rocking base. The Act III *Pas de Quatre* for all four fairies is a highlight of the sparkling Act III *Divertissement* The Philips recording is sumptuous without being cloudy and it expands magnificently for Tchaikovsky's rhetorically exciting climaxes without assaulting the ears.

With warm, polished orchestral playing and recording to match, Previn conveys his affection throughout; but too often – in the famous *Waltz*, for instance – there is a lack of vitality. On the other hand, the *Panorama* shows Previn and his orchestra at their very best, the tune floating over its rocking bass in the most magical way. With Previn's tempi sometimes indulgently relaxed, it has been impossible to get the complete recording on to a pair of CDs, and the *Pas berrichon* and *Sarabande* included in the original (three-disc) LP issue have been cut.

Sleeping Beauty: Aurora's Wedding (suite selected and edited by Diaghilev).

✪ (N) (M) *** Cala (ADD) CACD 0529. Nat. PO, Stokowski (with 'Encores', all arr. Stokowski: DEBUSSY: *Clair de lune; Soirée dans Grenade.* ALBENIZ: *Ibéria: Fête-Dieu à Seville.* NOVACEK: *Perpetuum mobile.* SHOSTAKOVICH: *Prelude in E flat min.* RIMSKY-KORSAKOV: *Flight of the Bumble-Bee.* TCHAIKOVSKY: *Humoresque in G, Op. 10/ 2.* CHOPIN: *Mazurka in B flat min.; Prélude in D min. Op.28/24.* ***).

Diaghilev staged the first performance of Tchaikovsky's *Sleeping Beauty* outside Russia in a London season in 1921. The result was a financial disaster. The public, used to the usual Diaghilev triptych of three different ballets, found the work too long and stayed away. The following year the great impresario devised a one-act version centering on the Act III *Divertissement*, framed by the Introduction and final *Apothéose*. It is a perceptively chosen selection, with *Panorama* the only obvious omission.

Stokowski was attracted to the score and recorded it twice. His stereo version, made when he was 94, dates from 1976, ye,t as with so many of the recordings he made during his 'Indian summer', the electricity crackles throughout, and his charisma is felt in every bar. The Sony recording is vividly brilliant, lacking sumptuousness in the violins, but otherwise very good.

It was an inspired idea of Edward Johnson of the Stokowski Society to link *Aurora* with his even more charismatic collection of encores, recorded three months later. Here the sound is even better, approaching demonstration quality, and there is no finer programme on record to show Stokowski's genius as an orchestral arranger (indeed 're-creator'), and his ability to rethink piano music in orchestral terms.

Even the lusciously seductive *Clair de lune* is surpassed by the spectacular excerpt from *Ibéria*, the sombre *E flat minor* Shostakovich *Prelude*, and the delightful Tchaikovsky *Humoresque*, which Stravinsky also scored, quite differently – using horns, in *Le Baiser de la fée*. Most astonishing of all are the two Chopin items, the *Mazurka* totally transformed, and the fiercely dramatic *Prélude* almost unrecognizable. The sparkling orchestral bravura in Nováček's *Perpetuum mobile* and Rimsky's *Bumble-bee* provide light relief and altogether this is a wonderfully entertaining concert, superbly played.

Souvenir de Florence, Op. 70 (String Orchestra Version).

*** Chan. 9708. Norwegian CO, I. Brown – R. STRAUSS: Metamorphosen. ***

Iona Brown and the Norwegian Chamber Orchestra give us a splendid account of the full orchestral version of Tchaikovsky's invigorating and captivating *Souvenir de Florence*, bouncingly rhythmic in the opening movement, and buoyantly exuberant in the swinging secondary theme of the finale. There is both warmth and subtlety in the inner movements; and it is given one of Chandos's most brilliant and full-bodied recordings. The result is irresistible.

Souvenir d'un lieu cher, Op. 42; Valse scherzo in C, Op. 34 (orch. Glazunov).

*** DG 457 064-2. Shaham, Russian Nat. O, Pletnev – GLAZUNOV; KABALEVSKY: *Concertos*. ***

Eloquent and dazzling playing of these Tchaikovsky pieces by Gil Shaham and the Russian National Orchestra under Pletnev are an additional inducement to get this fine disc of the Glazunov and Kabalevsky *Concertos*.

Suites Nos. 1 in D min., Op. 43; 2 in C; 3 in G, Op. 55; 4 in G, (Mozartiana), Op. 55.

*** Chan. 9676 (2). Detroit SO, Järvi.

(B) *** Melodiya Twofer 74321 59054-2 (2) USSR SO, Svetlanov.

(B) *** Ph. Duo (ADD) 454 253 (2). New Phil. O, Dorati.

(B) *** Naxos 8.550644 (Nos. 1–2); **(*) 8.550728 (Nos. 3–4). Nat. SO of Ireland, Sanderling.

Tchaikovsky's four *Orchestral Suites*, for which the composer had a great affection, are full of good things. Their extraordinary range of colour demands recording of the very highest quality and that is just what Chandos for the most part provides, which gives Järvi's set a place at the top of the list, even though Svetlanov's Melodiya 'Twofer' remains very competitive indeed, and also has excellent sound.

Järvi generally adopts somewhat brisk tempi, especially in No. 1, but the Detroit orchestral response in both the two earliest suites is consistently winning. The performance of the *Fourth Suite* also has an agreeable warmth, aptly Tchaikovskian even more than it is elegantly Mozartian. In No. 3, the most ambitious of the set, Järvi continues to draw warmly expressive playing from his Detroit musicians even if his treatment here is a little heavy-handed (as it is just occasionally in No. 2). The performance is well characterized – not least in the colourfully varied variations which make up the last and longest movement and which are given an ebullient finale – but lacks something in charm. In this the acoustic of the Detroit hall is not as helpful as it might be to high fortissimo violins.

Svetlanov and the players of the USSR Symphony Orchestra have something to teach Järvi here. After opening warmly with delicate lyrical phrasing from the violins, the music steadily gathers passion as the whole orchestra takes up Tchaikovsky's flowing melody. Svetlanov treats the whole suite very flexibly and freely, supported by the most eloquent response from one of the premier Russian orchestras. In the *Theme and Variations* some of his tempi are unexpected, and the final *Polacca* is less overwhelming than with Järvi, seeking to emphasize dance rhythms rather than be grandiose. Helped by some of the finest digital sound on the Melodiya label and a pleasingly warm acoustic, Svetlanov also gives the *First Suite* a strong Russian feeling; the account of the *Second* is truly inspirational, doubly distinctive for making the listener realize that this is a far more substantial work than was previously thought. In the *Fourth Suite* the *Preghiera* is more restrained than with Järvi and the closing variations (where Mozart used Gluck's '*Unser dummer Pöbel meint*') are a delight.

Dorati's sound has some lack of transparency and ultimate vividness alongside the Detroit and Russian recordings, but it is pleasingly naturally balanced. Dorati was a masterly ballet conductor and he brings out the balletic feeling in the first two suites especially, revelling in the infinitely inventive orchestral detail which shows the composer consistently seeking new orchestral colourings. *Mozartiana* is neatly and stylishly done. In the *Third Suite* Svetlanov demonstrates more Russian temperament, but Dorati is thoroughly at home in the *Theme and Variations*, capped by a splendid closing *Polacca*: the Philips recording expands impressively here and rises to the occasion.

On Naxos, Stefan Sanderling (son of Kurt) gives nicely turned performances of the first two suites, neatly characterized and with much charm and colour. The *Third* and *Fourth Suites* are slightly less successful. Sanderling shows much delicacy of feeling, both in the opening *Gigue* of *Mozartiana* and in the *Elégie*, the first movement of the *Third Suite* and it is a pity that one has reservations about the sets of variations which Tchaikovsky uses for his final movements. In *Mozartiana* Sanderling is very romantic. The masterly *Theme and Variations* which end the *Third Suite* are splendidly done until the finale, which refuses to take off: Sanderling is that bit too grandiose and measured.

Swan Lake (ballet), Op. 20 (complete).

*** Decca 436 212-2 (2). Montreal SO, Dutoit.

*** ROH 301/2. ROHCG O, Ermler.

(B) *** CfP CD-CFPD 4727 (2). Philh. O, Lanchbery.

(B) **(*) DG Double 453 055-2 (2). Boston SO, Ozawa.

**(*) EMI CDS5 55277-2 (2). Phd. O, Sawallisch.

(M) (**(*)) Mercury mono 462 950-2. Minneapolis SO, Dorati.

(B) ** Melodiya Twofer 74321 66978-2 (2). USSR R. & TV Grand SO, Rozhdestvensky.

Dutoit offers the original score virtually complete, as Tchaikovsky conceived it. The Montreal orchestra play it beautifully, rising to the plot's histrionic moments and while not lacking the final apotheosis. Dutoit's reading, while not lacking drama, emphasizes the warmth and grace of the music, its infinite variety.

Mark Ermler's deeply sympathetic direction has both refinement and red-blooded commitment, and one is constantly aware of the idiomatic feeling born of long acquaintance. The sound is exceptionally full and open, with the brass in particular giving satisfying weight to the ensemble without hazing over the detail. The set has now been reissued on a pair of CDs with the break coming in Act II after the *Dance of the Little Swans*. Ermler's broad speeds consistently convey, more than most rivals', the feeling of an accompaniment for dancing, as in the great andante of the Act I *Pas de deux*. This is a set to have you sitting back in new enjoyment.

Lanchbery's 1982 *Swan Lake* makes a superb bargain. The CfP reissue on a pair of CDs, which play for 79 minutes and 75 minutes respectively, accommodates Acts I and II on the first disc and Acts III and IV on the second. Though two numbers are cut, the set includes the extra music (a *Pas de deux*) which Tchaikovsky wrote to follow the *Pas de six* in Act III, when Siegfried dances with Odile, mistakenly believing her to be Odette. The EMI recording, made at Abbey Road, is very fine indeed: spacious, vividly coloured and full, with natural perspective and a wide dynamic range. The orchestral playing is first class. Lanchbery's rhythmic spring is a constant pleasure; everything is alert and there is plenty of excitement at climaxes.

Ozawa's version omits the Act III *Pas de deux* but otherwise plays the complete original score. His performance is alive and vigorous (as at the opening *Allegro giusto*), but it has not quite the verve of Lanchbery's CfP version; Ozawa's approach is more serious, less flexible. Yet with polished, sympathetic playing from the Boston orchestra there are many impressive and enjoyable things here, with wind (and violin) solos always giving pleasure. The end result is a little faceless, in spite of a spectacular, wide-ranging analogue recording, as vivid as it is powerful.

Sawallisch approaches Tchaikovsky's greatest ballet score with appealing freshness, as if it had been written yesterday, and the Philadelphia Orchestra play superbly. But, as so often, they are let down by the recording, with its unnaturally close microphone placing. There is no lack of atmosphere, as the very opening demonstrates, yet fortissimos are unrefined, with fierce cymbals, grainy violins. But there is also much to enjoy, and splendid vigour. The first and most famous *Waltz* (gorgeously played) lilts attractively, and the thrilling final climax (with gorgeously full horn-tone at the restatement of the famous *idée fixe*) makes an overwhelming apotheosis, even with shrill violins.

Rozhdestvensky's is a sympathetic and idiomatic performance that does not disappoint. The caveat is the 1969 recording, which does not offer the richness and depth this colourful music ideally demands. At bargain price, it might be worth considering, especially if you like the distinctive Russian brass, but bargain hunters will find that John Lanchbery's 1982 Philharmonia set on Classics for Pleasure is preferable on almost all counts.

Swan Lake (ballet), *Op. 20* (slightly abridged recording of the European score).

(B) **(*) Double Decca (ADD) 440 630-2 (2). SRO, Ansermet
 – PROKOFIEV: *Romeo and Juliet*. **

Returning to Ansermet's 1959 recording of *Swan Lake*, one is amazed by the vigour of the playing and the excellence of the recording. The Drigo version of the score, which Ansermet uses, dates from 1895; Drigo added orchestrations of his own, taken from Tchaikovsky's piano music (Op. 72), yet he left out some 1,600 bars of the original score. Ansermet offers the Act I introduction and Nos. 1–2, 4, 7 and 8; Act II, Nos. 10–13; Act III, Nos. 15, 17–18 and 20–23, with No. 5 (the *Pas de deux*) then interpolated before Nos. 28 and 29 from Act IV. Despite the obvious gaps, most of the familiar favourites are included here, and the music-making has such zest and colour that one revels in every bar. The solo wind playing is not always as sweet-timbred as in some other versions, but the violin and cello solos are well done. The transfer is well managed, full-blooded and bright. It was a happy idea to couple this on its Double Decca reissue with a selection of 15 items from the two suites from Prokofiev's *Romeo and Juliet* ballet, even if here the orchestral playing is less impressive.

SYMPHONIES

Symphonies Nos. 1–6.

(M) *** DG (ADD) 429 675-2 (4). BPO, Karajan.
**(*) DG 449 967-2 (5). Russian Nat. O, Pletnev.

Symphonies Nos. 1–3; Francesca da Rimini, Op. 32.

(B) **(*) Melodiya Twofer (ADD) 74321 34163-2 (2). USSR SO, Svetlanov.

Symphonies Nos. 4–6 (Pathétique); Andante cantabile in B flat, Op. 11; The Voyevoda, Op. 78.

(B) **(*) Melodiya Twofer (ADD) 74321 40066-2 (2). USSR SO, Svetlanov.

Symphonies Nos. 1–6; Capriccio italien; Manfred Symphony.

⬤ (M) *** Chan. 8672/8. Oslo PO, Jansons.

Jansons's Tchaikovsky series, which includes *Manfred*, is self-recommending. The full romantic power of the music is consistently conveyed and, above all, the music-making is urgently spontaneous throughout, with the Oslo Philharmonic Orchestra always committed and fresh, helped by the richly atmospheric Chandos sound. The seven separate CDs offered here are packaged in a box priced as for five premium discs.

Karajan offers the six symphonies fitted on to four mid-priced CDs, the only drawback being that Nos. 2 and 5 are split between discs. From both a performance and a technical point of view, the accounts of the last three symphonies are in every way preferable to his later, VPO digital versions; all offer peerless playing from the Berlin Philharmonic.

Pletnev's readings have all the innate aristocratic feeling Tchaikovsky could ask for, but at no time does Pletnev wear his heart on his sleeve. Some may feel that the emphasis in the *First Symphony* is too much on the *rêveries* of the title, and Tchaikovsky's rhetoric might be handled more convincingly; but, for the most part, Pletnev's approach throughout the cycle is the reverse of the overblown. Indeed the highly charged, high-voltage sound which we associate with Mravinsky surfaces in the *Pathétique,* but otherwise he sets greater store by classicism, carefully balanced proportions and a masterly sense of line. DG have accorded the cycle very fine and well-detailed sound.

Svetlanov's are performances of much temperament and fire, though the orchestral playing is a little variable. With fast tempi in the outer movements the *First Symphony* comes fully alive, with the atmosphere of the Russian winter felt in the *Adagio.* The *Little Russian* has plenty of character too. The *Polish Symphony* is a performance of strong contrasts between the inner and outer movements. The *Fourth,* bold and direct, stands out among the last three symphonies, very well held together. In the finale Svetlanov makes no pause each time the second subject appears. The *Fifth,* while it has a fine lyrical impulse, is surprisingly undramatic. The *Pathétique* is much more convincing, with a beautifully moulded second subject. The Scherzo-march is somewhat relaxed but the finale is powerfully controlled and eloquent. The extra items are well worth having, especially the rare *Voyevoda,* while the middle section of *Francesca da Rimini* has a unique lyrical fervour. The sound throughout is bright and full-blooded to match the performances.

Symphonies Nos. 1–6; (i) Piano Concerto No. 1; (ii) Violin Concerto; Capriccio italien; Eugene Onegin: Polonaise & Waltz; Marche slave; The Nutcracker Suite; 1812 Overture; Romeo and Juliet (fantasy overture); Sleeping Beauty: Suite; String Serenade; Swan Lake: Suite; (iii) Variations on a Rococo Theme.

(B) *(**) DG (ADD) 463 774-2 (8). (i) Richter, VSO; (ii) Ferras; (iii) Rostropovich; BPO; all cond. Karajan.

Having recorded the last three Tchaikovsky symphonies three times over in little more than a decade, Karajan then turned to the early symphonies, and brought to them the same superlative qualities. These Berlin performances are fine in every way; perhaps a bit of over-refinement creeps in from time to time, but by any standards they are a magnificent achievement. The *Violin Concerto* is superbly shaped by Karajan, though some will find Ferras's tone lacking charm – his close vibrato in lyrical passages tends to emphasize schmaltz on the G string. Richter and Karajan are, to say the least, controversial in the *Piano Concerto.* In the first movement, both artists play havoc with any sense of forward tempo (though there are occasional bursts of real excitement), and Richter's excessive rubato in the lyrical second subject sounds unspontaneous. Clearly two major artists at work, but the result is none too convincing. The *Rococo Variations* with Rostropovich is a breath of fresh air after all that – lovely glowing accounts – and the orchestral music is generally fine, but not outstanding, and a hint of glossiness creeps in from time to time (though the *Sleeping Beauty* and *Swan Lake* suites are quite superb). The sound throughout the set is of a generally high standard.

Symphonies Nos. 1–6; Manfred Symphony; Capriccio italien; Romeo and Juliet (fantasy overture); Serenade for Strings; The Tempest; Eugene Onegin: Polonaise.

(N) (BB) *** Virgin VB5 61893-2 (6). Bournemouth SO, Litton.

Andrew Litton's set of the Tchaikovsky symphonies, including *Manfred,* is in many ways his finest achievement on record, and this super-bargain Virgin box is very desirable indeed. The cycle gets off to a splendid start with the first two symphonies, which are very successful indeed. With warm and full recording, less distanced than many on this label, these urgently spontaneous performances rival any in the catalogue. Litton reveals himself as a volatile Tchaikovskian, free with accelerandos and slowings yet never sounding self-conscious or too free. The hushed pianissimos of the Bournemouth strings in the slow movement of No. 1 are ravishing and the *Second Symphony* too brings a beautifully sprung reading, allowing plenty of rhythmic elbowroom in the jaunty account of the syncopated second subject in the finale.

Again in the outer movements of No. 3 Litton challenges his players to the limit, setting fast speeds, but the clean purposeful manner is very satisfying, even if some other versions spring rhythms more infectiously. Litton's finesse comes out impressively in the *Andante elegiaco,* where he chooses a flowing tempo needing no modification for the broad melody that follows, which is then nobly moulded.

No. 4 is essentially spacious, both in choice of tempi and the rather backward balance of the orchestra. Ideally one needs a brighter focus in this symphony, yet Litton, with ensemble crisp, builds the structure of the first movement steadily and unerringly. The dotted clarinet theme of the second subject opens with an enticing tenuto, then the tension is carried through the development to make a strong climax before the recapitulation. The slow movement, warmly lyrical, is similarly purposeful with a delightfully decorated reprise, while the finale is weighty as well as athletic, with the secondary theme bringing another striking expressive contrast.

The first movement of the *Fifth* is surprisingly slow and steady, and here the reading lacks the high voltage of Litton's finest Tchaikovsky performances. But the slow movement brings a beautiful horn solo, and the Waltz is delightfully fresh and delicate. The finale is again on the broad side, warm rather than ominous, with very clean articulation in the playing.

The *Pathétique* caps the cycle impressively: an outstanding performance, full of temperament, not just fiery but tender too, arguably the finest of the whole cycle. The Bournemouth playing has never been more clearly articulated. The only idiosyncrasy is that in the big second-subject melodies of the outer movements Litton again prefers speeds broader than usual, but with no hint of self-indulgence in the finely moulded phrasing.

Manfred is both individual and satisfying. The Astarte theme in the first movement has rarely been moulded so affectionately and throughout Litton controls the tension to bring out the narrative sequence and heighten the dramatic cohesion. He points the chattering semi-quavers of the 'Alpine Fairy' *Scherzo* with engaging wit and fantasy, and the spacious treatment of the third-movement *Andante* allows the oboist to play his opening solo with a tender expressiveness to make most others seem prosaic. The sound is clean-cut and well balanced, with the organ entry at the end of the finale among the most dramatic on record.

The encores are substantial and add much to the attractions of the set. In the *Capriccio italien* both playing and recording display the dramatic contrasts of texture and dynamic to the full, while the *Eugene Onegin Polonaise* brings an even more infectiously rhythmic lift. On the other hand the *String Serenade* is warmly romantic, with the *Waltz élégant* and the *Elégie* expressively intense, and the finale bursts with energy.

The Tempest is given an outstanding performance, while *Romeo and Juliet* builds up powerfully from a restrained start to reach a splendid culmination. All in all, this is an astonishing bargain (to match Menuhin's equally generous Mozart collection from the same label) with – at the time of going to press – the six discs offered at under twenty pounds.

Symphonies Nos. 1 (Winter Daydreams); 2 (Little Russian); 3 (Polish).

(B) *** Mercury Double (ADD) 434 391-2 (2). LSO, Dorati – ARENSKY: *Variations on a Theme by Tchaikovsky.* *(*)

(i) Symphonies Nos. 1–3; (ii) Francesca da Rimini.

(B) *** Ph. Duo (ADD) 446 148-2 (2). (i) LSO; (ii) New Philh. O; Markevitch.

Symphonies Nos. 1–3; Romeo and Juliet (fantasy overture).

(N) (B) *** Double Decca (ADD) 467 264-2 (2). VPO, Maazel.
(N) (B) ** Teldec Ultima 8573 87807-2 (2). Leipzig Gewandhaus O, Masur.

Dorati had clearly thought deeply about each symphony, for each of his interpretations is individual and all three have a striking freshness. After its comparatively mellow beginning, the opening movement of the *First Symphony* generates great thrust and excitement, while the lovely, wistful *Adagio* expands romantically to its powerful climax on the horns, before the touchingly nostalgic closing section. The horn solo which introduces and closes the first movement of the *Little Russian Symphony* is not bold but hauntingly evocative, and the following allegro is crisp and energetic with a powerful recapitulation. Again in No. 3 Dorati catches the full character of the music's Russian melancholy which dominates the introduction, and he infuses the *Allegro vivo* with great thrust and rhythmic strength. The three central movements are the heart of the symphony and they are beautifully played, full of doleful colouring and nostalgia. The brilliant, spacious and full-blooded recording is just right for this music. There is a touch of fierceness at times, but it adds to the bite, and altogether these performances are remarkably satisfying. The Arensky coupling is apt, but in the event somewhat disappointing.

Markevitch is a good Tchaikovskian and his readings have fine momentum and plenty of ardour. In the *First Symphony* he finds the Mendelssohnian lightness in his fast pacing of the opening movement, while there is real evocation in the *Adagio* and a sense of desolation at the reprise of the *Andante lugubre*, before the final rousing peroration. In the *Little Russian Symphony* the opening horn solo is full of character and the allegro tautly rhythmic. The *marziale* marking of the *Andantino* is taken literally, but its precise rhythmic beat

is well lifted. The finale is striking for its bustling energy rather than its charm. The *Polish Symphony* has a comparably dynamic first movement, but the central movements are expansively warm, the ballet-music associations not missed. *Francesca da Rimini* is very exciting too, and there is some lovely wind playing from the New Philharmonia in the central section. Excellent sound, warmly resonant and full-bodied.

Maazel's performances, made with the VPO in the 1960s, clearly look forward to the emotional tautness of the mature symphonies from the *Fourth* onwards. But if the first movement of the *Winter Daydreams Symphony* is driven hard and the Mendelssohnian quality of the opening is not as evocative as in some versions, with the slow movement not as dreamy as one might ask, it is not without atmosphere and the strong, thrusting horns in the final statement of the tune are very telling. Maazel also gets some splendidly crisp and rhythmic playing from the VPO strings in the allegros of the *Little Russian* and *Polish Symphonies* to create an exciting brio, while the *Andantino marziale* of the former is nicely pointed (as are the *Scherzos* of all three symphonies). Much felicitous detail emerges throughout all three symphonies and Maazel is clearly at home in Tchaikovsky's rhetoric, especially in the finale of No. 3. In short, although charm is not Maazel's strong suit, the vitality of this music-making is compelling. The spectacularly resonant and brilliantly engineered recording suits the performances.

The *Winter Daydreams Symphony* is the least successful of Masur's triptych. Though there is much to be said for bringing out the symphonic weight of Tchaikovsky's writing, Masur and his superb Leipzig Orchestra with their smooth manner and rhythmically four-square approach, go too far in removing all hints of Slavonic temperament. Even in this lightest of the Tchaikovsky cycle, the result is heavy. Unexpectedly, such a squarely symphonic view works rather better in the first movement of the *Little Russian Symphony*, even if the *Andantino* is charmless. But then Masur begins to lift rhythms in a way generally missing earlier. The end of the finale – with the coda taken very fast, and with an extra accelerando – is as exciting as any, flouting good manners and skirting vulgarity. He is helped by the recording, clearer, more forward and less bass-heavy than usual from this source. *The Third Symphony* is a work that needs a little coaxing, which is not Masur's strong point: his reading is characteristically direct, crisply disciplined, with emotions underplayed. His preference for fast speeds leads him in the central slow *Andante elegiaco* to a tempo that comes near to being eccentric, undermining the elegiac quality. *Romeo and Juliet* however, is a most refreshing performance, passionate and direct, without a hint of vulgarity. Again excellent sound, but this is a set for Masur aficionados rather than the general collector.

Symphony No. 1 in G min. (Winter Daydreams).

*** Chan. 8402. Oslo PO, Jansons.
(M) **(*) DG (ADD) 463 615-2. Boston SO, Tilson Thomas – DEBUSSY: *Images.* **(*)

Symphony No. 1; Hamlet (fantasy overture).

(BB) *** Naxos 8.550517. Polish Nat. RSO, Leaper.

Refreshingly direct in style, Mariss Jansons with his brilliant orchestra gives an electrically compelling performance of this earliest of the symphonies. Structurally strong, the result tingles with excitement, most of all in the finale, faster than usual, with the challenge of the complex fugato passages taken superbly. The recording is highly successful.

Adrian Leaper conducts a taut and sympathetic reading of *Winter Daydreams*, with excellent playing from the Polish orchestra enhanced by vivid recording, fresh and clear, with plenty of body and with refined pianissimo playing from the strings in the slow movement. This is among the finest Tchaikovsky recordings on the Naxos list, with all four movements sharply characterized. The overture too comes in a tautly dramatic reading. An outstanding bargain.

Michael Tilson Thomas's is a good, affectionate account which captures well the spirit of the music. The slow movement is hauntingly atmospheric, with the Russian melancholy brought out to great effect. It is a pity that the recording is a bit over-reverberant: it tends to dull the conductor's pointing in the first movement and, especially, in the Scherzo. The finale too, although splendidly played, loses its full bite and impact. But this performance is easy to enjoy, and has never sounded better than on this remastered DG Originals CD.

Symphonies Nos. 1 (Winter Daydreams); 2 (Little Russian).

(N) *** Delos DE 3087. Seattle Symphony, Schwarz.

This Delos coupling has the sobriquet 'The Young Tchaikovky', but the effect of Schwarz's performances, both expansive and exciting, is to make each symphony sound more mature than usual. His brings a free rubato style to both readings, but he is a natural Tchaikovskian, and the result is very enjoyable indeed, particularly when the spacious Seattle acoustic and superbly wide-ranging Delos recording brings the finest sound yet given to these symphonies, with particularly rich strings, while one must mention especially the glorious horns at the end of the lovely *Adagio* of the *Winter Daydreams*. Every detail of Tchaikovsky's scoring is glowingly revealed and the ear revels in the charm of the *Andantino marziale* of the *Little Russian* and the kaleidoscopic variations at the beginning of the finale. Here the gutsy middle strings too are splendidly caught, as is the spectacular closing hyperbole of both finales. In short if you want a modern digital pairing of these two splendid symphonies, it is hard to better this.

Symphony No. 2 in C min. (Little Russian), Op. 17 (original (1872) score); Festive Overture on the Danish National Anthem, Op. 15; Serenade for Nikolai Rubinstein's Saint's Day; Mazeppa: Battle of Poltava; Cossack Dance.

*** Chan. 9190. LSO, Simon.

This is the first recording of Tchaikovsky's original score of the *Little Russian Symphony* and probably the first performance outside Russia. In 1879 Tchaikovsky retrieved the score and rewrote the first movement. He left the *Andante* virtually unaltered, touched up the scoring of the Scherzo, made minor excisions and added repeats, and made a huge cut of 150 bars (some two minutes of music) in the finale. He then destroyed the original. (The present performance has been possible because of the surviving orchestral parts.) Though this first attempt cannot match the reworked first movement, and the finale – delightful though it is – needs no extra bars, it is fascinating to hear the composer's first thoughts, and this is an indispensable recording for all Tchaikovskians. Geoffrey Simon secures a committed response from the LSO, and the recording is striking in its inner orchestral detail and freshness. The music from *Mazeppa*, the *Danish Festival Overture* and the tribute to Rubinstein make engaging bonuses.

Symphony No. 2 (Little Russian).

(BB) **(*) Finlandia 09027 40597-2. Norwegian R. O, Railainen – BORODIN: *Symphony No. 1*. **(*)

Symphony No. 2; Capriccio italien, Op. 45.

*** Chan. 8460. Oslo PO, Jansons.

Jansons prefers a fastish speed for the *Andantino* second movement, but what above all distinguishes this version is the joyful exuberance both of the bouncy Scherzo – fresh and folk-like in the Trio – and of the finale, and the final coda brings a surge of excitement, making most others seem stiff. The coupling is a fizzing performance of the *Capriccio italien*. With some edge on violin tone, this is not the finest of the Chandos Oslo recordings, but it is still fresh and atmospheric.

A very enjoyable and recommendable account of the *Little Russian Symphony* from the Norwegian Radio Orchestra and their Finnish conductor. Not necessarily a first choice but it is well enough played and recorded, and gives pleasure.

Symphonies Nos. (i) 2 (Little Russian); (ii) 4 in F min.

(B) *** DG (ADD) 429 527-2. (i) New Philh. O; (ii) VPO; Abbado.

Abbado's account of the *Little Russian Symphony* is very enjoyable, although the first movement concentrates on refinement of detail. The *Andantino* is nicely pointed, and the Scherzo is admirably crisp and sparkling. The finale is superb, with fine colour and thrust and a memorably spectacular stroke on the tam-tam before the exhilarating coda. The 1967 recording still sounds excellent. The account of the *Fourth Symphony*, is almost unsurpassed on record. Abbado's control of the structure of the first movement is masterly. The *Andantino*, with its gentle oboe solo, really takes wing in its central section, followed by a wittily crisp Scherzo, while the finale has sparkle as well as power. It was recorded in 1975 in the Musikverein and still sounds very good indeed.

Symphony No. 3 in D (Polish), Op. 29.

*** Chan. 8463. Oslo PO, Jansons.

Tchaikovsky's *Third* is given a clear, refreshingly direct reading by Jansons, but it is the irresistible sweep of urgency with which he builds the development section of the first movement that sets his performance apart, with the basic tempo varied less than usual. The second movement is beautifully relaxed, the *Andante elegiaco* heartwarmingly expressive, tender and refined, and the Scherzo has a Mendelssohnian elfin quality; but it is the swaggering reading of the finale which sets the seal on the whole performance. Though the recording does not convey a genuinely hushed pianissimo for the strings, it brings full, rich and brilliant sound.

Symphonies Nos. (i) 4; (ii) 5; 6 (Pathétique).

(B) *** DG Double (ADD) 453 088-2. BPO, Karajan.

(B) *** Double Decca (ADD) 443 844-2 (2). Philh. O, Ashkenazy.

(M) (***) DG mono 447 423-2 (2). Leningrad PO; (i) K. Sanderling; (ii) Mravinsky.

(B) **(*) Ph. Duo (ADD) 438 335-2 (2). LSO, Markevitch.

(N) (BB) *(**) Royal (ADD) DCL 706752 (2). Philh. O, Silvestri.

(i) Symphonies Nos. 4–6 (Pathétique); Andante cantabile for Strings; Marche slave; Romeo and Juliet (fantasy overture); (ii) Serenade for Strings.

(BB) *** Royal Classics HR 704032 (3). (i) Hallé O; (ii) LSO; Barbirolli.

Karajan's 1977 analogue version of No. 4 (the most atmospherically recorded of the three) is more compelling than his previous recordings and also is preferable to the newer, digital, Vienna version. Similarly the 1976 reading of the Fifth stands out from his other recordings. The Berlin Philharmonic string-playing is peerless. Karajan had a special affinity with Tchaikovsky's Pathétique Symphony, and of his five stereo versions this one from 1977 is the finest. The digital remastering of the analogue recordings is first rate.

Ashkenazy's set makes a fine alternative bargain on Double Decca. Apart from the emotional power and strong Russian feeling of the readings, the special quality which Ashkenazy conveys is spontaneity. The freshness of his approach, his natural feeling for lyricism on the one hand and drama on the other, is consistently compelling. The late-1970s Kingsway Hall recording quality is full and atmospheric.

Mravinsky re-recorded the three last symphonies of Tchaikovsky with his Leningrad orchestra for DG in stereo, but these legendary earlier, mono performances, without loss of concentration, were less exaggeratedly histrionic, and Sanderling's speeds for the finale of the Fourth Symphony particularly, but also Mravinsky's for the Fifth, were not as frenetic as in the latter's stereo versions. The opening of the Fifth again brings an added dimension of Russian melancholy, and Mravinsky sustains a lyrical intensity throughout the symphony characteristic of all his Tchaikovsky readings. The slow movement brings a performance of great dramatic extremes, the only drawback for Western ears being the solo horn sounding like a euphonium. The emotional power of Mravinsky's Pathétique has never been surpassed and the finale is deeply eloquent, genuinely touching rather than hysterical, with a characterful rasp from the Russian trombones.

Markevitch's Fourth is as exciting as almost any available. It has a superb thrusting first-movement Allegro, and Markevitch brings to the first movement of the Fifth a similarly forthright, highly charged approach. He makes no concessions to the second-subject group, which is presented with no let-up on the fast pace at which he takes the main Allegro. In the Pathétique Markevitch provides great intensity in his account of the first movement. The second movement has both warmth and elegance, and the march is treated broadly, providing suitable contrast before a deeply felt performance of the finale, where the second subject is introduced with great tenderness.

Barbirolli's very inexpensive Tchaikovsky set is self-recommending. The current EMI transfers have immeasurably improved the sound, mostly from the late 1950s, although the two string works come from the following decade. The power and drive of the outer movements of the Fourth Symphony is matched by the passionate romantic drama of the Fifth, while the Pathétique has the widest emotional range of all, opening rather gently but combining great ardour and sombre dignity in the finale. There is refinement of romantic feeling as well as excitement and passion in Romeo and Juliet. All these were originally Pye recordings, but the String Serenade was made with the LSO at Abbey Road. It has all the expressive warmth one might expect. The Andante Cantabile is also comparatively refined, balanced by a rumbustious Marche slave.

The finale to Silvestri's Fourth was included on the EMI's stereo demonstration LP. Curiously, neither the original LP nor this remastered CD capture the opulent richness of texture which made that excerpt so memorable in its day, and the CD has brought an added artificial brightness to the strings. The conductor puts his seal on the performance at the very commencement by a distorted rhythm for the brass fanfare, with a fractional pause after the triplet. This is repeated whenever the motto theme reappears. The ben sostenuo section of the first movement is very slow, indulged with obvious personal affection, and in the slow movement Silvestri is similarly mannered at the reprise of the main theme on the strings. This is again in its way a very affectionate piece of playing, with the little woodwind decorations deliciously managed, and even the idiosyncrasies of the first movement can be acceptable in a reading so compelling. The brilliance of the finale is notable, and the scherzo is even better. But this is hardly a general recommendation. The highly introspective Fifth suits Silvestri's temperament, and in spite of the usual touches of rubato (which are not always quite spontaneous) he builds up the climaxes in the first two movements with great excitement. The opening of the Andante cantabile, with its sombre introduction on the lower strings, is very effective, and the Waltz too is given its proper elegance. The finale opens with dignity, although perhaps is over-accented, and then the allegro vivace goes with the wind. There is brilliant virtuosity from the Philharmonia here, and the recording is fuller than the Fourth, although recorded in the same year (1957). However there is a degree of stridency in the brass. Silvestri's Pathétique is obviously deeply felt. The first movement takes some time to get under way, but the great second theme is shaped most affectionately and after the exciting climax the coda has a fine restrained nobility. The second movement is very slow but almost convincing when you get used to it, and in the third – more of a march than a scherzo – the excitement is pithily contained, leaves the symphony's real climax for the finale which is played in a very individual way, but deeply touching, and with the bursts of passion seemingly spontaneous. This is the finest recording of the three, dating from 1959, and it helps one's enjoyment, if one is willing to place oneself unreservedly in Silvestri's hands.

Symphony No. 4 in F min., Op. 36.

*** Chan. 8361. Oslo PO, Jansons.

**(*) DG (IMS) 439 018-2. VPO, Karajan.

Symphony No. 4; Capriccio italien.

(M) *** DG (ADD) 419 872-2. BPO, Karajan.

(i) Symphony No. 4; (ii) Romeo and Juliet (fantasy overture).

⚫ (B) *** Decca Penguin (ADD) 460 655-2. (i) LSO, Szell; (ii) VPO, Karajan.

All four movements of his superb performance of the *Fourth Symphony* show how Szell has rethought every detail of the score. The Scherzo has seldom sounded more kaleidoscopic in its colour contrasts, and the characterization of the slow movement is equally strong. The reading has great emotional power and a surging spontaneity underpinned by finely rehearsed orchestral playing and Szell's consistency. The finale is breathtaking: a searingly white-hot culmination. The actual sound is something of a marvel too: full-blooded, detailed, warm and clear. Karajan's even earlier *Romeo and Juliet* is hardly less distinguished, far finer than his later, DG version. The VPO bring a chilling beauty to the opening, subtly setting the scene for the ensuing drama. The great love theme has real passion, yet the delicate 'moonlight' sequence is played with ethereal beauty. The recording is rich and full (the timpani make a wonderful impact). This is a Penguin bargain not to be missed on any account. The specialist essay is by David Leavitt.

Jansons conducts a dazzling performance, unusually fresh and natural in its expressiveness, yet with countless subtleties of expression, as in the balletic account of the second-subject group of the first movement. The *Andantino* flows lightly and persuasively, the Scherzo is very fast and lightly sprung, while the finale reinforces the impact of the whole performance: fast and exciting, but with no synthetic whipping-up of tempo. That is so until the very end of the coda, which finds Jansons pressing ahead just fractionally as he would in a concert, a thrilling conclusion made the more so by the wide-ranging, brilliant and realistic recording.

Karajan's 1977 analogue version with the BPO is more compelling than any of his other versions. It is the vitality and drive of the performance as a whole that one remembers above all, but also the beauty of the wind playing at the opening and close of the slow movement. The CD transfer is extremely vivid. The *Capriccio italien* makes a good filler.

Although the playing of the VPO under Karajan does not match that of the Berlin Philharmonic in earlier versions, the performance itself has greater flexibility and more spontaneity. The freer control of tempo in the first movement brings a more relaxed second-subject group, while in the *Andantino* the phrasing is less calculated. The warmly resonant acoustic is attractive; even if detail is not absolutely clear, there is no lack of fullness.

Symphony No. 4; Capriccio italien; Romeo and Juliet (fantasy overture).

*** Lodia LO-CD 791. Moscow New Russian O, Païta.

Païta offers a highly compelling, at times interpretatively eccentric, Tchaikovsky collection, played with great ardour and conviction, if with not always precise ensemble by the Moscow New Russian Orchestra. The recording, made in the Great Hall of the Moscow Conservatoire in 1994, has all the necessary richness and amplitude, and plenty of brilliance; although orchestral textures are at times a little thick, the overall effect is full-bloodedly spectacular. *Romeo and Juliet*, which opens the concert, begins rather sombrely, but there is a riveting climax at the trumpet entry with the Friar Laurence theme and no lack of passion. Païta's *Capriccio italien* makes a superb encore after the symphony. It is exhilaratingly uninhibited, the opening fanfare matched by a sensational climax which almost defeats the engineers by its amplitude.

Symphony No. 5 in E min., Op. 64.

⚫ *** Ph. 462 905-2. VPO, Gergiev.

*** Chan. 8351. Oslo PO, Jansons.

(M) **(*) EMI CDM5 67032-2. Philh. O, Klemperer – HAYDN: *Symphony No. 98.* **

**(*) DG (IMS) 439 019-2. VPO, Karajan.

Symphony No. 5; Francesca da Rimini.

(B) **(*) [EMI Red Line CDR5 69842]. Phd. O, Muti.

Symphony No. 5; Marche slave.

(M) *** DG (ADD) 419 066-2. BPO, Karajan.

(i) Symphony No. 5; (ii) Nutcracker Suite, Op. 71a.

(B) *** DG (ADD) 439 434-2. (i) Leningrad PO, Mravinsky; (ii) BPO, Karajan.

Symphony No. 5; Serenade for Strings.

(B) *** Sony SBK 46538. Phd. O, Ormandy.

Symphony No. 5; (i) Eugene Onegin: Tatiana's letter scene.

(M) *** EMI CD-EMX 2187. LPO, Edwards; (i) with Hannan.

Valery Gergiev's account of the *Fifth Symphony* is really quite special. It is a performance of real stature, totally electrifying. No wonder the audience went wild at the end. It certainly belongs among the best *Fifths* on record. Some collectors will find full price a bit steep for 46 minutes, however marvellous the performance and excellent the recording; but if you can put economy to one side, you will be rewarded with out-of-the-ordinary music-making.

Sian Edwards also conducts an electrifying and warm-hearted reading of Tchaikovsky's *Fifth*, which matches almost any version in the catalogue, particularly when it comes with an unusual and exceptionally attractive fill-up, *Tatiana's letter scene* from *Eugene Onegin*. That is freshly and dramatically sung, in a convincingly girlish impersonation, by the Australian, Eilene Hannan. Sian Edwards's control of rubato is exceptionally persuasive, notably so in moulding the different sections of the first movement of the symphony, while the great horn solo of the slow movement is played with exquisite delicacy by Richard Bissell. The Waltz third movement is most tenderly done, while the finale brings a very fast and exciting allegro. However, this fine disc is deleted as we go to press.

In the first movement, Jansons's refusal to linger never sounds anything but warmly idiomatic, lacking only a little in charm. The slow movement again brings a steady tempo, with climaxes built strongly and patiently but with enormous power, the final culmination topping everything. In the finale, taken very fast, Jansons tightens the screw of the excitement without ever making it a scramble, following Tchaikovsky's notated slowings rather than allowing extra rallentandos. The sound is excellent, specific and well focused within a warmly reverberant acoustic, with digital recording on CD reinforcing any lightness of bass.

Mravinsky's earlier stereo version of the *Fifth* with the Leningrad Philharmonic on DG would occupy a distinguished place in any collection. The performance is full of Slavonic vitality and the reading is romantic as well as red-blooded. The solo horn has a faint wobble in the famous solo in the slow movement, and the trumpets in the final peroration of an exhilaratingly fast finale also have a vibrato, but these details are unimportant when the reading has such fire and individuality. The recording, made in Watford Town Hall in 1960, is resonant and full, if not always absolutely clean in focus. By comparison Karajan's 1966 *Nutcracker Suite* sounds a little cool, but it is marvellously polished and vivid, and the *Waltz of the Flowers* is most elegant.

Karajan's 1976 recording (419 066-2) stands out from his other recordings of the *Fifth*. The first movement is unerringly paced and has great romantic flair; in Karajan's hands the climax of the slow movement is grippingly intense, though with a touchingly elegiac preparation for the horn solo at the opening. The Waltz has character and charm too – the Berlin Philharmonic string playing is peerless – and in the finale Karajan drives hard, creating a riveting forward thrust. The remastered recording brings a remarkable improvement.

Ormandy's *Fifth*, splendidly recorded in the spacious acoustics of Philadelphia's Broadwood Hotel, is early (1959) stereo and is one of his very finest Tchaikovsky performances. There is not a suspicion of routine, and the Philadelphia strings play gloriously, particularly in the *Andante cantabile*, which generates great passion. Again the weight of string-tone at the opening of the *Serenade* (recorded the following year) establishes the full-blooded character of Ormandy's approach. The finale opens delicately but soon generates great bustle. Overall this coupling is a magnificent demonstration of the Ormandy regime in Philadelphia at its very peak.

Klemperer's performance is surprisingly successful in a way one would not perhaps expect. There is an expanding emotional warmth in the treatment of the opening movement with the second subject blossoming in a ripely romantic way. The slow movement too, if not completely uninhibited, is played richly with a fine horn solo from Alan Civil. The Waltz is perhaps marginally disappointing but the Finale has splendid dignity. Good recording and an excellent transfer, but the Haydn coupling is less recommendable.

The oddity of Muti's Philadelphia version is that, though

the first two movements have the disappointingly over-relaxed manners that marked his *Pathétique* earlier, often with surprisingly slack ensemble, the last two movements are played with the high voltage one expects of this conductor and orchestra at their finest. The fill-up is also played at white heat, a powerful performance. It makes a rare and worthwhile coupling. The sound, not as clear as it might be, has warmth and weight beyond most recent Philadelphia issues.

Karajan's last VPO version of the *Fifth* brings a characteristically strong and expressive performance; however, neither in the playing of the Vienna Philharmonic nor even in the recorded sound can it quite match his 1977 Berlin Philharmonic version for DG.

Symphony No. 5; (i) Piano Concerto No. 1.

(N)(***) Biddulph mono WHL 051. BPO, Mengelberg; (i) with Hansen.

This is not the famous Mengelberg *Fifth Symphony*, which we all knew in the 78s era, which was recorded with the Concertgebouw Orchestra (and issued by Columbia), but a later version with the Berlin Philharmonic from 1940, and first issued on Telefunken. Yet the interpretation is similar in every detail. It is an extraordinary performance; by its side the Silvestri version (see above) seems straightforward and relatively unmannered.

Mengelberg takes Tchaikovsky's marking for the slow movement, 'con alcuna licenza' to apply to the whole symphony (even the Waltz). For him every bar is open to constant twists of personal rubato and fluctuations of tempo. Also he feels able to adjust the harmony if needed, and make two major cuts in the finale.

Yet it is a great performance. For Mengelberg had both the will to impose his own personality on Tchaikovsky's music and the charisma to carry it off. His passionate response remains so compelling that the listener is taken along with him, even when, as in the last movement, he adopts a comparatively modest pacing for the main allegro. The recording has an element of harshness but is fully acceptable in this excellent Biddulph transfer.

The performance of the concerto is not in this league. Conrad Hanson, a pupil of Edwin Fischer, has his moments, but in the finale (rather like the Richter/Karajan version) he and Mengelberg tend to press the music along at different degree of forcefulness. A fascinating reissue nonetheless.

Symphony No. 6 in B min. (Pathétique), Op. 74.

*** Chan. 8446. Oslo PO, Jansons.

(B) **(*) Penguin DG (ADD) 460 609-2. BPO, Karajan.

(M) **(*) EMI (ADD) CDM5 67336-2. Philh. O, Klemperer – SCHUMANN: *Symphony No. 4.* ***

(**(*)) BBC mono BBCL 4023-2. Philh. O, Giulini – MUSSORGSKY: *Pictures at an Exhibition.* (**(*))

(***) Biddulph mono WHL 046. Phd. O, Ormandy – MUSSORGSKY: *Pictures at an Exhibition* (orch Cailliet). (***)

Symphony No. 6 (Pathétique); Capriccio italien; Eugene Onegin: Waltz & Polonaise.

(B) **(*) Sony (ADD) SBK 47657. Phd. O, Ormandy.

Symphony No. 6 (Pathétique); Marche slave.

⬤ (BB) *** Virgin 2 x 1 VBD5 61636-2(2). Russian Nat. O,
Pletnev – *The Seasons*, etc.

Symphony No. 6 (Pathétique); Romeo and Juliet (fantasy
overture).

(M) *** DG (IMS) 445 601-2. Philh. O, Sinopoli.

**(*) Ph. 456 580-2. Kirov O, Gergiev.

(M) **(*) [Mercury 434 352-2]. LSO, Dorati.

(i) *Symphony No. 6 (Pathétique);* (ii) *Swan Lake* (ballet):
suite.

(B) *** DG (ADD) 439 456-2. (i) Leningrad PO, Mravinsky;
(ii) BPO, Karajan.

(BB) **(*) ASV CDQS 6091. (i) LPO; (ii) RPO; Bátiz.

** Ph. 446 725-2. Saito Kinen O, Ozawa.

The way in which Pletnev launches us into the development
of the first movement still takes one aback, even when
one knows what to expect. His hand-picked orchestra is as
virtuosic as Pletnev himself can be on the keyboard, with a
challengingly fast tempo for the Scherzo. There is a stirring
account of *Marche slave* too, and a very fine recording,
perfectly balanced, although the effect is a little recessed.
This is now linked to Pletnev's *Seasons* on a Virgin Double
– an astonishing bargain.

Mariss Jansons and the Oslo Philharmonic crown their
magnetically compelling Tchaikovsky series with a superbly
concentrated account of the last and greatest of the symphonies. It is characteristic of Jansons that the great second-
subject melody is at once warm and passionate yet totally
unsentimental, with rubato barely noticeable. The very fast
speed for the third-movement *March* stretches the players
to the very limit, but the exhilaration is infectious, leading
to the simple dedication of the slow finale, unexaggerated
but deeply felt. Fine, warm recording as in the rest of the
series.

Sinopoli's reading of the opening movement is beautifully
shaped, with the second subject introduced very tenderly.
He adopts slow speeds for the middle two movements but
sustains them well, with a moving and eloquent account
of the finale. The big advantage that Sinopoli has in this
mid-priced reissue is that it is generously coupled with
Romeo and Juliet, which is also very exciting. In short this is
one of the finest digital versions of the *Pathétique*. Excellent
recording.

Mravinsky's very Russian (stereo) account of the *Pathétique* is justly renowned. It is deeply passionate, yet the
second subject of the first movement is introduced with
much tenderness. The last two movements are very fine
indeed; the Scherzo/March is brilliantly pointed, yet has
plenty of weight, and the finale is very moving without ever
letting the control slip. The present transfer of the 1960
recording (made in Wembley Town Hall) maintains the
agreeable ambience, even if at times the Russian brass comes
over raucously. Karajan's *Swan Lake Suite* is most exciting,
with polished and brilliant BPO playing, and the recording,
made a decade after the symphony, has rather less alluring
string sound.

Karajan had a very special affinity with Tchaikovsky's
Pathétique Symphony and recorded it five times in stereo. For

many, this 1977 version, now reissued on Penguin Classics, is
the finest, and it is a pity that the CD transfer is brightly lit
to the point of harshness in the loudest climaxes. Yet the
impact of Tchaikovsky's climaxes is tremendously powerful,
the articulation of the Berlin players precise and strong. The
climactic peaks generate tremendous tension and the effect
on the listener is almost overwhelming. The finale has great
passion and eloquence, with two gentle sforzandos at the
very end to emphasize the finality of the closing phrase. The
accompanying author's note is by Edmund White.

It was in 1936 that, having been music director of the
Minneapolis orchestra, Ormandy was appointed co-
conductor in Philadelphia alongside Leopold Stokowski.
This electrifying performance of the *Pathétique Symphony*
on Biddulph, one of the fastest ever on disc, was Ormandy's
first Philadelphia recording, begun in December of 1936 and
completed the following month. So in the first movement
Ormandy is more volatile than in his later recordings,
tending to press on faster after setting a tempo. The result is
very powerful and exciting, not at all sentimental. First-rate
transfer.

Ormandy's fine 1960 performance on Sony is a reading of
impressive breadth, dignity and power, with no suggestion
of routine in a single bar. The orchestra makes much of the
first-movement climax and plays with considerable passion
and impressive body of tone in both outer movements; yet
there is an element of restraint in the finale which prevents
any feeling of hysteria. In short, this is most satisfying, a
performance to live with; the CD transfer, while brightly lit,
avoids glare in the upper range. Ormandy's panache and
gusto give the *Capriccio italien* plenty of life without driving
too hard, and the dances are rhythmically infectious.

Valery Gergiev's *Pathétique* has much of the intensity and
dramatic power of his *Fifth* but less of its pathos. Some may
find it hard driven at times. There is no want of excitement
or firmness of grip, though Gergiev is by no means as subtle,
certainly in matters of dynamic nuance, as Pletnev, though
his Scherzo is nearly as headlong. The recording has impressive depth and impact, and must be ranked along with
the best. The performance will be a little more controversial
and will not appeal to everyone.

Klemperer's *Pathétique* was recorded in the Kingsway
Hall in 1960. Nobility rather than agonized intensity is the
keynote, and the climax of the first movement carries that
hallmark (with a superb contribution from the Philharmonia trombones). The Scherzo/March is much more of a
march than a scherzo but the neatly articulated playing
prevents heaviness, and the finale is given a spacious dignity,
even if the emotional thrust sounds consciously under control. But with such an impressive response from the Philharmonia strings the closing pages have great poignancy.

Giulini conducted this live performance at the 1961 Edinburgh Festival. As in the studio, Giulini preserves a degree
of restraint, finding nobility in Tchaikovsky's great melodies.
But here the adrenalin of a live occasion brings a slightly
more passionate treatment. Although this is not the most
overwhelming of recorded *Pathétiques* it still represents Giulini at his most impressive, but the snag, almost as much as
in the coupled Mussorgsky is the dryness of the mono
sound, recorded in the unhelpful acoustic of the Usher Hall,

Edinburgh. Alas the audience is never quite silent, and is especially noisy at the beginnings of movements.

Bátiz's (1982) reading of the *Pathétique* is attractively fresh and direct, with the great second-subject melody the more telling for being understated and with transitions a little perfunctory. The brass are set rather forward, but this makes for very exciting climaxes. Otherwise the balance is good and the sound excellent. It is even better in the *Swan Lake suite*, recorded five years later. The RPO playing is polished, warm and alert, with Barry Griffiths and Françoise Rive sensitive string soloists in the *Danse des cygnes*. An excellent super-bargain coupling.

Dorati's 1960 reading has plenty of dynamism in the first movement and the 5/4 movement, unusually brisk, is exhilarating. There are some minor eccentricities of tempi in the Scherzo/March but the climax is thrilling, and the finale is finely done, volatile, but grippingly so. *Romeo and Juliet* opens with dignity, is tender in the love music and brings plenty of excitement at the climax.

Characteristically, Seiji Ozawa brings out the balletic overtones in Tchaikovsky's symphonic masterpiece – a point emphasized by having the *Swan Lake* coupling. With him the start of the symphony is deceptively light, not ominous, and the sweet beauty of the Saito Kinen string playing adds to the feeling of poise and control. With exceptionally clean ensemble, even the central development section has no hint of hysteria. Taken very fast, the third movement march is so light it might almost be fairy music, opening out brilliantly as the march develops. The ballet suite, by contrast, comes in an understated performance, less alert than that of the symphony. The Japanese recording enhances the refinement and transparency of the playing.

Symphony No. 7 (arr. Bogatyryev).

*** Chan. 9130. LPO, Järvi – *Piano Concerto No. 3.* **(*)

This reconstructed symphony, abandoned not long before Tchaikovsky wrote his culminating masterpiece in the *Pathétique Symphony*, may be no match for the regular canon, but it brings many Tchaikovskian delights. Having symphony and concerto, on which the first movement was based, side by side makes it very easy to compare Bogatyryev's reconstruction of the original version, in structure identical except for the central solo cadenza. In the *Symphony* Järvi finds poetry and fantasy, and the modern digital recording allows far more light and shade over a much wider dynamic range. Apart from the thinness on the upper strings, the recorded sound is satisfyingly full and warm. Geoffrey Tozer – see above – gives a fine performance of the *Concerto*.

The Tempest, Op. 18.

(BB) *** Virgin Classics 2 x 1 VBD5 61751-2 (2). Bournemouth SO, Litton – BORODIN: *Prince Igor: Overture & Polovtsian dances;* MUSSORGSKY: *Night on the Bare Mountain;* etc. **; RIMSKY-KORSAKOV: *Scheherazade.* **(*)

The Shakespearean symphonic fantasy *The Tempest* – not to be confused with the much less ambitious overture of the same name, written for Ostrovsky's play – is given a glowing performance under Litton, passionately committed, yet refined, to suggest a forgotten masterpiece. It is a pity that the rest of the performances here do not measure up to this standard, although all are very well played and recorded.

Variations on a Rococo Theme for Cello & Orchestra, Op. 33.

⊛ *** EMI CDC5 56126-2. Chang, LSO, Rostropovich – BRUCH: *Kol Nidrei;* FAURE: *Elégie;* SAINT-SAENS: *Cello Concerto No. 1.* ***

(M) *** DG (ADD) 447 413-2. Rostropovich, BPO, Karajan – DVORAK: *Cello Concerto.* *** ⊛

(BB) *** CfP Double (ADD) CDCFPSD 4775 (2). Cohen, LPO, Macal – BEETHOVEN: *Triple Concerto;* DVORAK: *Cello Concerto;* ELGAR: *Cello Concerto.* ***

(B) *** Sony (ADD) SBK 48278. Rose, Phd. O, Ormandy – BLOCH: *Schelomo* ***; FAURE: *Élégie* ***; LALO: *Concerto.* **(*)

(N) (M) **(*) Virgin VM5 61838–2. Truls Mørk, Oslo PO, Jansons – DVORAK: *Cello Concerto.* **(*)

The phenomenally gifted 13-year-old Korean-born cellist, Han-Na Chang has the most ravishing tone and a wonderfully musical sense of line. Rostropovich as conductor sets the scene with an affectionate elegance, and then Chang introduces Tchaikovsky's theme with disarming simplicity. *Andante grazioso*, introduced very gently, is quite ethereal and the finale has the expected dash, and the crispest articulation. The LSO are inspired by Chang to give a wonderfully sensitive accompaniment, and the recording is in the demonstration class.

Like Chang, Rostropovich uses the published score rather than the original version which more accurately reflects the composer's intentions. But this account, with Karajan's glowing support, is so superbly structured in its control of emotional light and shade that one is readily convinced that this is the work Tchaikovsky conceived. The recording (made in the Jesus-Christus Kirche) is beautifully balanced and is surely one of the most perfect examples of DG's analogue techniques.

An excellent bargain version from Robert Cohen, warmly expressive as well as strong. First-class recording, but deleted as we go to press.

Leonard Rose's warm and elegant – at times ardent – account of these splendid variations is balm to the senses, and Ormandy provides admirable support. The recording is forwardly balanced but the dynamic range remains reasonably wide, and the cello is firmly and realistically focused.

A fine performance from Truls Mørk, with plenty of energy and finesse, and the *Andante* of Variation 11 played with an appealingly Slavonic, plaintive feeling. Very good recording too, but in sheer elegance and panache this is no match for Rostropovich.

CHAMBER AND INSTRUMENTAL MUSIC

Piano Trio in A min., Op. 50.

*** Erato 0630 17875-2. Repin, Berezovsky, Yablonsky – SHOSTAKOVICH: *Piano Trio, Op. 67.* ***

*** Ara. Z 6661. Golub–Kaplan–Carr Trio – SMETANA: *Piano Trio.* ***

**(*) EMI (ADD) CDC7 47988-2. Ashkenazy, Perlman, Harrell.

(B) *(**) EMI double forte (ADD) CZS5 73650-2 (2). Zukerman, Barenboim, Du Pré – BEETHOVEN: *Violin Sonatas.* **(*)

**(*) Sony SK 53269. Bronfman, Lin, Hoffman – ARENSKY: *Piano Trio No. 1.* **(*)

(N) * Classics Live LCL 194. Kagan, Gutman, S. Richter.

An outstanding and involving account of the Tchaikovsky from Vadim Repin, Boris Berezovsky and Dmitri Yablonsky, is superbly recorded by the Erato team. This now makes a clear first choice for a splendid and highly characteristic work that is still undervalued by many Tchaikovskians. Moreover, it has a fine version of the wartime Shostakovich *Trio* as coupling.

The Golub/Kaplan/Carr account of the Smetana *G minor Piano Trio* is well matched in the Tchaikovsky, which has the merit of being completely uncut. The balance places the listener rather too close to the players, but the sound is perfectly pleasing and the performance refreshingly unaffected. Nothing is overdriven, mechanized or attention-seeking. While it does not necessarily displace the Chung Trio or Ashkenazy, Perlman and Harrell, it can be ranked alongside them.

With the keyboard dominating, the first movement of Tchaikovsky's *Piano Trio* can so easily sound too rhetorical, and that is not entirely avoided by Ashkenazy, Perlman and Harrell. The *Variations* which form the second part of the work are very successful, with engaging characterization and a great deal of electricity in the closing pages. Generally this group carry all before them, with their sense of artistic purpose and through their warmth and ardour. The sound is on the dry side, with the digital remastering increasing the sharpness of focus, not ideally atmospheric. This is still at full price and comes without a coupling.

The Zukerman, Barenboim, Du Pré performance has great ardour and all the immediacy of a live concert, and that more than compensates for the odd inelegance that might have been corrected in the recording studio. There is nothing routine about Barenboim's playing: he takes plenty of risks and is unfailingly imaginative; it is a pity that the instrument itself is not worthy of him, for it sounds less than fresh. Zukerman also sustains a high level of intensity and at times is close to schmaltz. However, this is without doubt a high-voltage performance, though the sound quality is very average. Incidentally, the traditional cut sanctioned by the composer is observed here.

The Sony account from Yefim Bronfman, Cho-Liang Lin and Gary Hoffman is a keenly lyrical and expressive performance of this work, which suffers from a less than ideally balanced recording. Yefim Bronfman is allowed to swamp the texture when the dynamic level rises, even though, as in the Arensky with which it is coupled, it is obvious that he is playing with delicacy. Both Cho-Liang Lin and Gary Hoffman are marvellous players whose refinement and purity give unfailing delight.

The Classics Live disc is part of an ongoing series devoted to Oleg Kagan, here recorded with Richter and Natalia Gutman in the Pushkin Museum in 1982. Artistically there is not much to quarrel with the playing, although Richter bangs out the chords of the main theme with a quite uncharacteristic insensitivity. However, the shallow and clangorous sound poses problems and despite the eminence of the artists this does not challenge existing recommendations.

(i) Souvenir de Florence, (string sextet). Op. 70.

*** Hyp. CDA 66648. Raphael Ens. – ARENSKY: *String Quartet in A min..* ***

*** Chan. 9878. ASMF Chamber Ens. – GLAZUNOV: *String Quintet.* ***

** Mer. CDE 84211. Arienski Ens. – ARENSKY: *String Quartet No. 2* ***; BORODIN: *Sextet movements.* **

A first-rate performance from the Raphael Ensemble. They play with total unanimity of ensemble and richness of tone. Their coupling, the Arensky *Quartet with Two Cellos* is magnificently played. The recording may be a snag for some collectors – it is all a bit too forward and we are very much in the front row – but there is no reason to withhold a third star given its artistry and authority.

From the ASMF Chamber Ensemble, a very sympathetic and well-recorded account which deserves a warm recommendation as an alternative to either of the Borodin versions. Its coupling, which brings a Glazunov rarity, strengthens its claims.

A very good rather than a distinguished performance of Tchaikovsky's eloquent *Souvenir de Florence* on Meridian, very decently recorded. The strength of the issue lies in the interest of its coupling, an Arensky rarity, the *A minor Quartet*, from which the well-known *Variations on a Theme of Tchaikovsky* derive, and two Mendelssohnian movements from the Borodin *Sextet*.

String Quartet in B flat; String Quartets Nos. 1–3; (i) Souvenir de Florence.

(M) *** Melodiya (ADD) 74321 18290-2 (2). Borodin Qt, (i) with Rostropovich, Talalyan.

*** Teldec 4509 90422-2 (2). Borodin Qt, (i) with Yurov, Milman.

(N) (B) **(*) Erato Ultima 8573 84254-2 (2). Keller Qt; (i) with Kashkashian, Perénti.

In the mid-priced BMG/Melodiya set the *Souvenir de Florence* with Rostropovich and Talalyan comes from 1965, whereas the three *Quartets* plus the student *Quartet Movement* that Tchaikovsky wrote in 1865 were all recorded at roughly the same time (1979–80) in the Berlin Teldec studios, is digital and the sound is a shade drier: it also includes the early *B flat Movement*. Both sets are superb, unassailable recommendations.

Warmly sensitive performances of the three *Quartets* from the Kellers, and the same could be said of the delightful *Souvenir de Florence*, where they are joined by Kim Kashkashian and Miklos Perényi. They are well recorded too, and at Ultima price this is distinctly competitive. But either of the Borodin versions has more to offer in this music, with an added dimension of Russian feeling, subtlety of detail, and depth.

String Quartets Nos. 1 in D; 2 in F, Op. 22.

(N) (BB) **(*)** Naxos 8.550847. New Haydn Qt.

Very well-played accounts of both quartets from the New Haydn Quartet which, taken on their own merits, have much to recommend them – warmth, intelligence and some finesse. In the slow movement of the D major the group has real eloquence, and in the finale it scores by observing the exposition repeat. However, it is not in the same league as the Borodin which remains a strong first choice.

String Quartet No. 1 in D, Op. 11.

(M) *** Cal. 6202. Talich Qt – BORODIN: *Quartet No. 2.* **(*)**

(***) Testament mono SBT 1061. Hollywood Qt – GLAZUNOV: *5 Novelettes*; BORODIN: *String Quartet No. 2 in D.* (***)

(M) **(*)** Decca (ADD) 425 541-2. Gabrieli Qt – BORODIN; SHOSTAKOVICH: *Quartets.* **(*)**

A glorious account of Tchaikovsky's best-loved quartet from the Talich group. They play the opening movement with an unassertive, lyrical feeling that is quite disarming, while the famous *Andante cantabile* has never sounded more beautiful on record, shaped with a combination of delicacy of feeling and warmth that is wholly persuasive. The Scherzo has plenty of verve, and the finale winningly balances the music's joyful vigour and its underlying hint of melancholy with a typical lightness of touch. The 1987 digital recording is beautifully balanced. Highly recommended.

The Hollywood Quartet's LP first appeared in 1953 and their fervent account has a persuasive eloquence which still puts one under its spell. The sound has been improved, and the addition of the Glazunov, which is new to the catalogue, enhances its value. The disc runs to one second short of 80 minutes, and the sleeve warns that some older CD players may have difficulty in tracking it.

The Gabrielis give a finely conceived performance, producing well-blended tone-quality, and the 1977 recording is clean and alive; but ideally the upper range could be less forcefully projected.

PIANO MUSIC
Solo piano music

Album for the Young, Op. 39.

(N) (BB) *** Naxos 8.550885. Biret – DEBUSSY: *Children's Corner Suite*; SCHUMANN: *Kinderszenen.* ***

This is perhaps the highlight of Idil Biret's apt triptych of suites of piano music for children. She has the full measure of Tchaikovsky's two dozen vignettes and plays them all with affection and charm. They range from miniature portraits of *Maman*, *Dolly*, a *Lark*, and even a witch (*Baba-Yaga*) to a *Toy Soldier's March* and an *Organ-grinder's Song*, as well as folksy pieces from Italy, France, Germany and Russia's own *Kamarinskaya*. The recording cannot be faulted.

Album for the Young, Op. 39: (i) original piano version; (ii) trans. for string quartet by Dubinsky.

*** Chan. 8365. (i) Edlina; (ii) augmented Borodin Trio.

These 24 pieces are all miniatures, but they have great charm; their invention is often memorable, with quotations from Russian folksongs and one French, plus a reminder of *Swan Lake*. Here they are presented, in their original piano versions, sympathetically played by Luba Edlina, and in effective string quartet transcriptions arranged by her husband, Rostislav Dubinsky. The Borodin group play them with both affection and finesse. The CD has plenty of presence.

Capriccioso in B flat, Op. 19/5; Chanson triste, Op. 40/2; L'Espiègle, Op. 72/12; Humoresque in G, Op. 10/2; Méditation, Op. 72/5; Menuetto-scherzoso, Op. 51/3; Nocturne in F, Op. 10/1; Rêverie du soir, Op. 19/1; Romances: in F min., Op. 5; in F, Op. 51/5; The Seasons: May (White nights), June (Barcarolle), November (Troika); January (By the fireplace). Un poco di Chopin, Op. 72/15; Valse de salon, Op. 51/2; Waltz in A flat, Op. 40/8; Waltz-scherzo in A min., Op. 7.

*** Olympia OCD 334. S. Richter.

It is good to hear Richter (recorded in 1993 by Ariola-Eurodisc) given first-class, modern, digital sound and on top technical form, showing that he had lost none of his flair. These miniatures are invested with enormous character in playing of consistent poetry; there is never a whiff of the salon. The opening *Nocturne in F major*, the charming neo-pastiche *Un poco di Chopin* and the haunting *Rêverie du soir* readily demonstrate Richter's imaginative thoughtfulness, while the apparently simple *Capriccioso in B flat* produces a thrilling burst of bravura at its centrepiece. They are all captivating, and the bolder *Menuetto-scherzoso* also shows Tchaikovsky at his most attractively inventive. With its truthful sound-picture, this is a first recommendation for anyone wanting a single CD of Tchaikovsky's piano music.

The Seasons, Op. 37a.

(*) Chan. 8349. Artymiw.

The Seasons; Aveu passioné; Berceuse, Op. 72/2; Méditation, Op. 72/5; Polka peu dansante, Op. 51/2; Tendres reproches, Op. 72/3.

*** Decca 466 562-2. Ashkenazy.

The Seasons; 6 Pieces, Op. 21; Sleeping Beauty (excerpts) arr. Pletnev.

*** Virgin/EMI Dig. 2 x 1 VBD5 61636-2 (2) Pletnev – *Symphony No. 6.* *** ●

Tchaikovsky's twelve *Seasons* (they would better have been called 'months') were written to a regular deadline for publication in the St Petersburg music magazine, *Nuvellist*. Mikhail Pletnev has exceptional feeling for Tchaikovsky, revealing depths that are hidden to most interpreters. He grips one from first note to last, not only in *The Seasons* but also in the charming and touching *Six morceaux*, Op. 21. Fresh and natural recorded sound. This now comes together with the *Sleeping Beauty* excerpts and the *Pathétique Symphony* on a remarkably generous Virgin Double.

Vladimir Ashkenazy gives a poised and finely prepared

account of *The Seasons* which is very well recorded. At the same time it does not match Pletnev in terms of poetic insight or tenderness. The charming numbers from the *Eighteen Pieces*, Op. 72, are beautifully done too.

It is the gentler, lyrical pieces that are most effective in the hands of Lydia Artymiw, and she plays them thoughtfully and poetically. Elsewhere, she sometimes has a tendency marginally to over-characterize the music. The digital recording is truthful.

Piano Sonata No. 2 in G (Grand), Op. 37a; Capriccio in G flat, Op. 8; Children's Album, Op. 39; 12 Pieces, Op. 40; Romance in F min., Op. 5.

(B) *** Melodiya Twofer (ADD) 74321 66975-2 (2). Pletnev.

These performances all come from 1986–7 when Pletnev was in his late twenties and include a wholly convincing account of the *G major 'Grand' Sonata*, with its long and somewhat intractable first movement splendidly handled. Pletnev's virtuosity is dazzling, and the delicacy and range of keyboard colour, together with his depth of feeling, is ever in evidence. The 23 miniatures which make up the delightful *Children's Album* and the *12 Pieces*, Op. 40, 'of average difficulty' consistently show the composer's melodic gift at its most engaging, and Pletnev's playing is wonderfully sympathetic. He finds a Chopinesque influence in the two charming *Waltzes* of Op. 40. Yet always the Russian colouring brings a special flavour, particularly to the *Romance in F minor*. The Melodiya digital recording is unexpectedly good. There is a touch of hardness in the more forceful playing in the *Sonata*. Elsewhere, the piano timbre is for the most part quite full and, at lower dynamic levels, warmly coloured. Most enjoyable – music to return to for sheer pleasure.

VOCAL MUSIC

4 Duets: *Dawn; Evening; In the Garden by the River; Tears.*

BBC (ADD) BBCB 8001-2. Harper, Baker, Britten – BRAHMS: *Liebeslieder Waltzes, Op. 52.* ROSSINI: *Soirées musicales.* ***

Heather Harper and Janet Baker, recorded at the 1971 Aldeburgh Festival, make a dream partnership in these tenderly sentimental duets, sung in English. Britten's inspired accompaniment adds poetry to Tchaikovsky's distinctive piano writing. No texts are given, but James Bowman writes movingly of such 'family music-making' at Aldeburgh.

Liturgy of St John Chrysostom, Op. 41.

(BB) **(*) Naxos Dig 8.553854.2. Ovdiy, Mezhulin, Kiev Chamber Ch., Hobdych.

Liturgy of St John Chrysostom; (ii) 9 Sacred pieces (for unaccompanied chorus); (ii) An angel crying.

*** Hyp. CDA 66948. Corydon Singers, Best.

Liturgy of St John Chrysostum; 6 Sacred Pieces: Blessed are they whom Thou hast chosen; The hymn of the Cherubim; It is meet; Now the angels are with us; Our Father; To Thee we sing.

(B) *** EMI double forte (ADD) CZS5 68661-2 (2). Soloists, Bulgarian a Cappella Ch., Robev.

The a capella *Liturgy of St John Chrysostom*, which dates from 1878, was not commissioned but written simply to reflect Tchaikovsky's devotion to the Russian Orthodox Church. Best and the Corydon Singers in their refined, dedicated performances bring out the freshness and energy in this inspired music, with basses cleanly focused down to subterranean depths, echoing authentic Russian examples. The disc also contains the sequence of *9 Sacred choruses* which Tchaikovsky wrote five or six years after the *Liturgy*, even simpler in style, but showing his ready melodic gift, and a separate piece, a dramatic Easter Day anthem, *An angel crying*, which is a miniature masterpiece. Warm, clear sound.

The alternative Bulgarian performances (although the cost is about the same) stretch to a pair of CDs, and include only six of the nine choruses. Yet the Bulgarian singing has an added idiomatic Slavonic colouring and great intensity of feeling, and aided by the cathedral acoustic, the effect is wonderfully spacious. Indeed this music could hardly be performed more convinvingly and the recording is superb.

In contrast with rival versions of this masterpiece of Russian orthodox music, which offer substantial couplings, the Naxos issue presents a liturgical performance complete with the priests' solos, almost 70 minutes long. Not all collectors will want such a format for repeated listening, but for those who prefer such an authentic course, this Naxos disc can be warmly recommended, strongly and idiomatically performed with fine solos, and atmospherically recorded in a church in Kiev.

The Snow Maiden, Op. 12 (complete incidental music).

*** Chan. 9324 Mishura-Lekhman, Girshko, Michigan University Ch. Soc., Detroit SO, Järvi.

(M) *** Chant du Monde RUS 788090. Erasova, Arkipov, Vassiliev, Sveshnikov Russian State Ch., Bolshoi Theatre O, Chistiakov.

(BB) **(*) Naxos 8.553856. Okolysheva, Mishenkin, Moscow Capella, Moscow SO, Golovschin.

Ostrovsky's play, *The Snow Maiden*, based on a Russian folk-tale, prompted Tchaikovsky to compose incidental music, no fewer than 19 numbers, lasting 80 minutes, a cherishable rarity. Much of it is vintage material, very delightful, bringing reminders of *Eugene Onegin* in the peasant choruses and some of the folk-based songs, and of the later Tchaikovskian world of *The Nutcracker* in some of the dances. He himself thought so well of the music that he wanted to develop it into an opera, but was frustrated when Rimsky-Korsakov wrote one first.

The consistent freshness and charm of invention comes out in Järvi's reading of the 19 numbers, lasting just under 80 minutes. It makes a delightful, undemanding cantata, very well played and sung, and is a clear first choice.

Chistiakov's fine 1994 performance, now reissued on Chant du Monde's mid-priced Russian label, is in every way recommendable at mid-price. The three excellent soloists are characterfully Slavonic, rather too forwardly balanced but well caught by the recording, and the fine singing of the chorus is given both sonority and plenty of bite. The orchestral playing is highly persuasive in a pleasingly atmospheric acoustic.

Tchaikovsky's engaging score also inspires Golovschin and his Moscow forces to a warmly idiomatic performance on Naxos, richly and colourfully recorded, if without quite the same degree of vividness. This may not match the Chant du Monde version in vitality, which at generally faster speeds sparkles more and offers crisper ensemble, but it is similarly persuasive. The conductor's affection is obvious. There are only two soloists to share the vocal music, but they are convincingly Slavonic and they are balanced slightly less forwardly. This Naxos disc is well worth its more modest cost. Both recordings offer full translations. However, Järvi's Chandos version is even finer.

Songs

Songs: *Amid the noise of the ball; Behind the window; The canary; Cradle song; The cuckoo; Does the day reign?; Do not believe; The fearful minute; If only I had known; It was in the early spring; Last night; Lullaby in a storm; The nightingale; None but the lonely heart; Not a word, O my friend; Serenade; Spring; To forget so soon; Was I not a little blade of grass?; Why?; Why did I dream of you?*

*** Hyp. CDA 66617. Rodgers, Vignoles.

The warmly distinctive timbre of Joan Rodgers' lovely soprano has been heard mainly in opera but she is equally compelling in this glowing disc of songs. Her fluency with Russian texts as well as the golden colourings of her voice make this wide-ranging collection a delight from first to last. Though the voice is not quite at its richest in the most celebrated song of all, *None but the lonely heart*, the singer's subtle varying of mood and tone completely refutes the idea that Tchaikovsky as a song-composer was limited. One of the finest discs issued to mark the Tchaikovsky centenary in 1993.

OPERA

Eugene Onegin (complete).

*** Decca (ADD) 417 413-2 (2). Kubiak, Weikl, Burrows, Reynolds, Ghiaurov, Hamari, Sénéchal, Alldis Ch., ROHCG O, Solti.

**(*) DG 423 959-2 (2). Freni, Allen, Von Otter, Shicoff, Burchuladze, Sénéchal, Leipzig R. Ch., Dresden State O, Levine.

**(*) Ph. 438 235-2 (2). Hvorostovsky, Focile, Shicoff, Borodina, Anisimov, St Petersburg Chamber Ch., O de Paris, Bychkov.

Solti, characteristically crisp in attack, has plainly warmed to the score of Tchaikovsky's colourful opera, allowing his singers full rein in rallentando and rubato to a degree one might not have expected of him. The Tatiana of Teresa Kubiak is most moving – rather mature-sounding for the *ingénue* of Act I, but with her golden, vibrant voice rising most impressively to the final confrontation of Act III. The Onegin of Bernd Weikl may have too little variety of tone,

but again this is firm singing that yet has authentic Slavonic tinges. The rest of the cast is excellent, with Stuart Burrows as Lensky giving one of his finest performances on record yet. Here, for the first time, the full range of expression in this most atmospheric of operas is superbly caught, with the Decca CDs vividly capturing every subtlety – including the wonderful off-stage effects.

The DG version brings a magnificent Onegin in Thomas Allen, the most satisfying account of the title-role yet recorded. It is matched by the Tatiana of Mirella Freni, even at a late stage in her career readily conveying girlish freshness in her voice. The other parts are also strongly taken. The tautened-nerves quality in the character of Lensky comes out vividly in the portrayal by Neil Shicoff, and Anne Sofie von Otter with her firm, clear mezzo believably makes Olga a younger sister, not too mature a character. Paata Burchuladze is a satisfyingly resonant Gremin and Michel Sénéchal, as on the Solti set, is an incomparable Monsieur Triquet. What welds all these fine components into a rich and exciting whole is the conducting of James Levine. The Leipzig Radio Choir sings superbly as well. The snag is that the DG recording is dry and studio-bound, with sound close and congested enough to undermine the bloom on both voices and instruments. In every way the more spacious acoustic in the Solti set is preferable.

Dmitri Hvorostovsky makes a strong, heroic Onegin in the Philips set, though Bychkov's conducting does not always encourage him to be as animated as one wants, and the voice at times comes near to straining. Nuccia Focile also emerges at her most convincing only in the final scene of confrontation with Onegin. Earlier, her voice is too fluttery to convey the full pathos of the young Tatiana in the *Letter Scene*, edgy at the top. Neil Shicoff as Lensky also suffers, though he sings with passionate commitment, conveying the neurotic element in the poet's character. As Gremin, Alexander Anisimov also has a grainy voice. Olga Borodina sings impressively as Olga, but on balance the other characters are better cast in Solti's Decca set.

Eugene Onegin: highlights.

(N) (B) **(*) DG 469588-2 (from above complete set, with Allen, Freni, Von Otter, Shicoff, Burchuladze; cond. Levine).

Even though the Levine set is not a first choice for the complete opera, this 75-minute Classikon selection brings out the superb qualities of the singing. It includes the *Letter Scene* (with Freni a freshly charming Tatiana), the Waltz and Polonaise scenes (with the excellent Leipzig Radio Chorus), also the Act II Duel scene and other key arias, all strongly characterized, and the entire closing scene (11 minutes). The recording, made in the Dresden Lukaskirche, is too closely balanced and unatmospheric, but the disc is inexpensive and provides a succinct synopsis of each excerpt.

Mazeppa (complete).

*** DG 439 906-2 (3). Leiferkus, Gorchakova, Larin, Kotscherga, Dyadkova, Stockholm Royal Op. Ch., Gothenburg SO, Järvi.

Full of magnificent music, *Mazeppa* – dating from 1884, five years after *Eugene Onegin* – has been sadly neglected on disc.

Sergei Leiferkus sings the title-role superbly, with his very Russian-sounding tone a little grainy and tight in the throat, and entirely apt for the character. There is no flaw either among the other principals. Sergei Larin, in what might seem the token tenor part of Andrey, sings with such rich, heroic tone and keen intensity that the character springs to life. Equally, the magnificent, firm-toned bass, Anatoly Kotscherga, father of the heroine, Maria, confirms the high impressions he created in his Boris recording with Abbado. As Maria, Galina Gorchakova also emerges as one of the latter-day stars among Russian singers, with her rich mezzo gloriously caught, even if the final lullaby for her dead lover, Andrei, could be more poignant. Järvi draws electric playing from the Gothenburg orchestra, not least in the fierce battle music which opens Act III. The only disappointment is that the opportunity was not taken of also recording the conventional finale to the opera which Tchaikovsky originally wrote.

The Queen of Spades (Pique Dame) (complete).

*** Ph. 438 141-2 (3). Grigorian, Putilin, Chernov, Solodovnikov, Arkhipova, Gulegina, Borodina, Kirov Op. Ch. & O, Gergiev.

When each new recording of this opera for many years has been flawed, it is good that Gergiev and his talented team from the Kirov Opera in St Petersburg have produced a winner. The very opening, refined and purposeful, sets the pattern, with Gergiev controlling this episodic work with fine concern for atmosphere and dramatic impact, unafraid of extreme speeds and telling pauses. Though the engineers fail to give a supernatural aura to the voice of the Countess when she returns as a ghost, the recorded sound is consistently warm and clear. It is good to have the veteran Irina Arkhipova singing powerfully and bitingly in that key role, while the other international star, Olga Borodina, is unforgettable as Pauline, singing gloriously with keen temperament. Otherwise Gergiev's chosen team offers characterful Slavonic voices that are yet well focused and unstrained, specially important with the tenor hero, Herman, here dashingly sung by Gegam Grigorian. As the heroine, Lisa, Maria Gulegina sings with warm tone and well-controlled vibrato, slightly edgy under pressure.

Yolanta (complete).

*** Ph. 442 796-2 (2). Gorchakova, Alexashkin, Hvorostovsky, Grigorian, Kirov Op. Ch. & O, Gergiev.

(M) **(*) Erato 2292 45973-2 (2). Vishnevskaya, N. Gedda, Groenroos, Petkov, Krause, Cortez, T. Gedda, Anderson, Dumont, Groupe Vocale de France, O de Paris, Rostropovich.

Gergiev and his outstanding Kirov team give a warm, idiomatic reading of Tchaikovsky's charming fairy-tale opera of the blind princess. Bringing out the atmospheric beauty of the score, it completely outshines the Rostropovich version on Erato, Galina Gorchakova gives the most moving portrait of the heroine, tender and vulnerable, with words delicately touched in. As Vaudémont, the knight who falls in love with her, Gegam Grigorian sings with rather tight, very Russian tenor-tone, not always pleasing but with a fine feeling for

the idiom and a natural ease in high tessitura. Dmitri Hvorostovsky sings nobly and heroically as Robert, his more vigorous friend and rival, while Sergei Alexashkin sings with dark, grainy – again very Russian – tone as King René, Iolanta's father. Above all, the exchanges between characters consistently convey the feeling of stage-experience. The recording, not ideally clear but well balanced, was made in the theatre but under studio conditions.

Rostropovich's performance has a natural expressive warmth to make one tolerant of vocal shortcomings. Though Vishnevskaya is far too mature for the role of a sweet young princess, she does wonders in softening her hardness of tone, bringing fine detail of characterization. Gedda equally by nature sounds too old for his role, but again the artistry is compelling and ugly sounds are few. More questionable is the casting of Dimiter Petkov as the King, far too wobbly as recorded. Now reissued on a pair of mid-priced CDs, this is still well worth exploring.

Arias from: The Enchantress; Eugene Onegin; Iolantha; Mazeppa; The Queen of Spades.

*** Ph. (IMS) 426 740-2. Hvorostovsky, Rotterdam PO, Gergiev – VERDI: Arias. ***

Hvorostovsky presents an eager, volatile Onegin, a passionate Yeletski in Queen of Spades and an exuberant Robert in Iolantha. One can only hope that he will be guided well, to develop such a glorious instrument naturally, without strain.

TCHEREPNIN, Alexander

(1899–1977)

10 Bagatelles for Piano & Orchestra, Op. 5.

(M) *** DG (ADD) 463 085-2. Weber, RSO, Berlin, Fricsay – MARTINU: Fantasia concertante ***; WEBER: Konzertstück **(*); FALLA: Nights in the Gardens of Spain. ***

Tcherepnin's Ten Bagatelles, originally piano pieces, are full of imaginative touches. Essentially light in spirit, they are not without some haunting melancholy passages too. The performances, by Weber and the Berlin Radio Symphony Orchestra, conducted by Ferenc Fricsay, are ideal, and the 1960 recording is full and vivid.

(i) Piano Concerto No. 5, Op. 96. Symphonies Nos. 1 in E, Op. 42; 2 in E flat, Op. 77.

*** BIS CD 1017. Singapore SO, Shui (i) with Ogawa.

(i) Piano Concerto No. 6, Op. 99. Symphonies Nos. 3 in F sharp, Op. 83; 4 in E , Op. 91.

*** BIS CD 1018. Singapore SO, Shui (i) with Ogawa.

Alexander Tcherepnin was the son of the composer Nikolai, who conducted when the Diaghilev Ballet made its Paris début. The First Symphony of 1927 caused a stir, not so much on account of its radical musical language as the fact that its Scherzo was written for percussion only. It is inventive and stimulating, and full of personality. The Second Symphony did not follow until the end of the 1939–45 war, and two successors followed in the 1950s: the *Third* in 1952, and the *Fourth*, commissioned by Charles Munch and the Boston Symphony Orchestra, in 1958–59.

It is with the *Fourth* that the newcomer to Tcherepnin's music should start. Its invention is wonderfully alert and fresh, and the control of pace masterly. It is neoclassical in feeling with a great sense of wit and style. This well-recorded account displaces the Slovak orchestra's version on Marco Polo. The two piano concertos are from the 1960s and are elegantly played by Noriko Ogawa. The Singapore orchestra has greatly improved since its early Marco Polo records under Choo Hoey, and the Chinese conductor Lan Shui gets generally good results from them.

Symphony No. 4; Romantic Overture, Op. 67; Russian Dances, Op. 50; Suite for Orchestra, Op. 87.

**(*) Marco 8.223380. Czech-Slovak State PO (Košice), Yip.

The *Fourth Symphony* is among Tcherepnin's finest works. Written in the mid1950s, it is colourful and tautly compact, neo-classical in idiom, very well organized and full of lively and imaginative musical invention. The *Suite*, Op. 67, is less individual and in places recalls the Stravinsky of *Petrushka* and *Le Chant du rossignol*. Like the much earlier *Russian Dances*, it is uneven in quality but far from unattractive. The *Romantic Overture* was composed in wartime Paris. Generally good performances, decently recorded too under the young Chinese conductor, Wing-Sie Yip, who draws a lively response from her players.

TCHEREPNIN, Nikolai (1873–1945)

Narcisse et Echo, Op. 40.

*** Chan. 9670. Hague Chamber Ch., & Residentie O, Rozhdestvensky.

This endearing and atmospheric choral ballet, *Narcisse et Echo* for much of the time sounds more French than Russian, with fascinating anticipations of *Daphnis*, not least in obbligato choral passages. Other sections mirror what the young Stravinsky was writing, but toned down. There also is a lot of Rimsky-Korsakov in it, and if you respond to that Russian master as well as Scriabin and Ravel, you will like this. It is somewhat static and in the last part of the ballet Narcissus is simply absorbed in gazing at his own reflection. However, though it is emphatically not great music, there is much that enchants. Rozhdestvensky is the ideal advocate, helped by ripe Chandos sound.

Le Pavillon d'Armide (ballet; complete).

**(*) Marco 8.223779. Moscow SO, Shek.

Le Pavillon d'Armide was the ballet with which Diaghilev opened his first *Ballets russes* season introducing Nijinsky. Its invention is fluent, owing much to Tcherepnin's teacher, Rimsky-Korsakov, and to Glazunov and Tchaikovsky. It runs to well over an hour and the inspiration is uneven. At its best, though, it has real charm, and the scoring is always full of colour. It is very well recorded.

Le Pavillon d'Armide (ballet suite), Op. 32a; La Princesse lointaine: Prelude; Svat: Overture; Tàti-Tàti (paraphrases on a children's theme).

(N) *** Olympia OCD 693. Rheinland-Pfalz State PO, Blashkov.

It is good that Olympia have recorded the suite from Tcherepnin's *Le Pavillon d'Armide*, a ballet that scored a huge success in its day, for the selection includes virtually all the highlights from the score (35 minutes in all) and much to tickle the ear. The *Danse des heures* and *La Scène d'animation du goblin* are reminiscent of Glazunov at his most orchestrally felicitous and *La Plainte d'Armide* and the *Danse des gamins* are hardly less engaging. The *Svat Overture* is brief and very Russian, the *Prelude to La Princesse lointaine* measured and evocative. The variations on the onomatopoeic *Tàti-Tàti* are as ingenious as they are ingenuous, and clevely scored; the snag is that the basic idea although catchy is limited – you may decide that its possibilities are exhausted before the *Carillon* finale. But Tcherepnin's kaleidoscopic scoring is impressive in itself. The Rheinland-Pfalz State Philharmonic Orchestra under Igor Blashkov are pesuasive exponents and the ballet score sparkles. The recording too is excellent.

TEIXEIRA, António (1707– after 1759)

Motet: *Gaudate, astra.*

(M) *** DG 453 182-2. J. Smith, Serafim, Calabrese, Ferreira, De Macedo, Fernandes – ALMEIDA: *Beatus vir* etc.; CARVALHO: *Te Deum.* SEIXAS: *Adebat Vincentius* etc. ***

Teixeira's non-liturgical, Italianate motet, *Rejoice, stars, rejoice*, alternates tenor recitative with a pair of delightful soprano arias, gracefully and – in the case of the second – brilliantly sung by Jennifer Smith. The continuo support here is excellent, and the recording is fresh and pleasing. Most enjoyable.

TELEMANN, Georg Philipp
(1681–1767)

Concertos: for 2 Chalumeaux in D min.; for Flute in D; for 3 Oboes, 3 Violins in B flat; for Recorder & Flute in E min.; for Trumpet in D; for Trumpet & Violin in D.

*** DG (IMS) 419 633-2. Soloists, Col. Mus. Ant., Goebel.

As Reinhard Goebel points out, Telemann 'displayed immense audacity in the imaginative and ingenious mixing of the colours from the palette of the baroque orchestra', and these are heard to excellent effect here. Those who know the vital *B flat Concerto* for three oboes and violins, from earlier versions, will find the allegro very fast indeed and the slow movement quite thought-provoking. The chalumeau is the precursor of the clarinet, and the concerto for two chalumeaux recorded here is full of unexpected delights. Marvellously alive and accomplished playing, even if one occasionally tires of the bulges and nudges on the first beats of bars.

Concerto for 2 Chalumeaux in D min.; Sonata for 2 Chalumeaux in F; G; Viola Concerto in G; Overture des Nations anciens et modernes in G; Völker Overture (Suite in B flat).

*** Chan. 0593. Lawson, Harris, Standage, Coll. Mus. 90.

Colin Lawson and Michael Harris with their 'liquid' timbres find a delicate charm in the two works for chalumeax and the Sonata has a rather touching Grave, which is played very serenely. Standage himself takes the solo part with distinction and pleasingly full timbre in the famous Viola Concerto, and his characterization of the Ancient and Modern Overture, is alert and strong, finding dignity in Les Allemands and not overdoing the closing parody lament for Les Vieilles Femmes. He is equally positive in the so-called 'Folk' Overture, played vibrantly: Its last five movements each draw on a different culture – Turkish, Russian and so on – but with their rhythms given a Western overlay.

Flute Concertos: in B min.; C; D (2); E; E min.

*** VAI Audio VAIA 1166. Stallman, Phd. Concerto Soloists CO.

Every one of these fine concertos, galant and Italianate by turns, shows the composer's invention at its most fertile and imaginative. All but one is in four movements. The E minor, which is in five, is perhaps finest of all. The Vivaldian Dolce e staccato opening movement of the E major is also particularly striking. The D major's finale is a bouncing Minuet, with delicious bird trills in the Trio, while in the extended first movement of the B minor work Telemann heralds the return of the final tutti with a repeated 'posthorn' call from the soloist emerging distinctly from his running roulades. Robert Stallman is a stylish and elegant player and he is given crisply sympathetic modern instrument accompaniments from the Philadelphia Chamber Orchestra. Excellent recording too.

Concerto for Flute, Oboe d'amore & Viola d'amore in E; Concerto polonois; Double Concerto for Recorder & Flute in E min.; Triple Trumpet Concerto in D; Quadro in B flat.

*** O-L (IMS) 411 949-2. AAM with soloists, Hogwood.

'An attentive observer could gather from these folk musicians enough ideas in eight days to last a lifetime,' wrote Telemann after spending a summer in Pless in Upper Silesia. Polish ideas are to be found in three of the concertos recorded here – indeed, one of the pieces is called Concerto polonois. As always, Telemann has a refined ear for sonority, and the musical discourse with which he diverts us is unfailingly intelligent and delightful. The performances are excellent and readers will not find cause for disappointment in either the recording or presentation.

(i) Concerto for 2 Flutes, 2 Oboes & Strings in B flat; (ii) Triple Concerto for Flute, Oboe d'amore, Violin & Strings in E; Oboe d'amore Concerto in D; Trumpet Concerto in D; (iii) Concerto for Trumpet & 2 Oboes in D; (ii) Double Viola Concerto in G; (i) Concerto for 3 Trumpets, 2 Oboes, Timpani & Strings in D; (iv) Double Concerto for Violin, Trumpet & Strings in D; (i) Suite in G

(La Putain); Tafelmusik, Part I: Conclusion in E min. for 2 Flutes & Strings.

(M) *** Van. (ADD) 08.9138.72 (2). (i) Soloists, Esterházy O, Blum; (ii) Soloists, I Solisti di Zagreb, Janigro; (iii) Masseurs, Amsterdam Bach Soloists; (iv) Minchev, Chochev, Sofia Soloists, Kazandiev.

The diversity of Telemann's inexhaustible invention is well demonstrated. In the Concerto for Two Violas the soloists interweave with the orchestral texture, a device borrowed from Vivaldi, who named it 'violette all'inglese'. The solo Oboe d'amore Concerto and Trumpet Concerto are both fine, four-movement works, but it is the collective concertos that offer the greatest interest. The Concerto for Two Flutes, Two Oboes and Strings begins elegantly with richly mellifluous blending; then, after a busy Presto, the two oboes open the Cantabile unaccompanied in a gravely Handelian melody. The Triple Concerto for Flute, Oboe d'amore and Violin in E major opens with an imposingly spacious Andante, very like an introduction to an aria or a chorus from an oratorio; then, after a lively allegro, comes a particularly fine Siciliano. The Concerto for Three Trumpets, Two Oboes and Timpani brings a sprightly Handelian fugue, including trumpets and oboes within the part-writing. The oboes gently dominate the gravely expressive Largo arietta, followed by a rollicking finale. The result is irresistible. The suite La Putain ('The Prostitute') contains an invitation by way of a folksong, (Ich bin so lang nicht bei dir g'west), to 'Come up and see me sometime'. The Concerto for Trumpet and Two Oboes in D is added on to the end of the first CD, and the performance by the Amsterdam Bach Soloists (with Peter Masseurs a splendid trumpet soloist) appears to use original instruments. The second CD closes the programme with a brief contribution from Sofia, the Concerto for Violin, Trumpet and Strings in D, vividly played but rather thinly recorded. But overall this highly stimulating set must receive the warmest possible welcome.

Horn Concerto in D.

(N) *** Arabesque Z 6750. Rose, St Luke's Chamber Ens. – FORSTER; HAYDN; Leopold MOZART: Horn Concertos. ***

Telemann's D major Horn Concerto (designated for the corno di caccia or hunting horn) is one of his best, and indeed one of the most attractive of all concertos for the instrument, other than those of Mozart. It opens with a catchy, swiftly articulated moto perpetuo which puts any soloist on his metal; then follows a melancoly Largo which reaches up into the instrument's highest tessitura. The finale is a Minuet with plenty of decorative passages and trills again taking the horn up to its highest register (all excellently managed here). Stewart Rose's broad, open tone suits this robust music admirably and he plays with confident finesse; the crisply stylish accompaniment provides an excellent backcloth and the recording is excellent.

Triple Horn Concerto in D; Alster (Overture) Suite; La Bouffonne Suite; Grillen-Symphonie.

*** Chan. 0547. Coll. Mus. 90, Standage.

This collection offers some of Telemann's most colourful

and descriptive music, often quite bizarrely scored. The *Triple Horn Concerto* opens the programme with the hand-horns rasping boisterously. Then comes *La Bouffonne Suite*, with its elegant *Loure* and the extremely fetching *Rigaudon*, while the work ends with a touchingly delicate *Pastourelle*, beautifully played here. The *Grillen-Symphonie* ('cricket symphony') brings a piquant dialogue between upper wind and double-basses in the first movement, while the second has unexpected accents and lives up to its name *Tändelnd* ('flirtatious'). The horns (four of them) re-enter ambitiously at the colourful *Overture* of the *Alster Suite*, add to the fun in the *Echo* movement, and help to simulate the Hamburg glockenspiel which follows. The entry of the Alster Shepherds brings a piquant drone effect, but best of all is the wailing *Concerto of Frogs and Crows*, with drooping bleats from the oboe and then the principal horn. Standage and his group make the very most of Telemann's remarkable orchestral palette and play with great vitality as well as finesse.

Oboe Concertos: in C min.; D (Concerto grazioso); E; E flat; F; Oboe d'amore Concerto in G.

*** Unicorn DKPCD 9128. Francis, L. Harpsichord Ens.

Oboe Concertos in C min.; D min.; F min.; Oboe d'amore Concertos in E; E min.; (i) Triple Concerto for Oboe d'amore, Flute & Viola d'amore.

*** Unicorn DKPCD 9131. Francis; (i) Mayer, Watson; L. Harpsichord Ens.

Sarah Francis's survey of Telemann's *Oboe* and *Oboe d'amore Concertos* brings modern-instrument performances, which are a model of style. The *G major Oboe d'amore Concerto* on the first disc is most gracious (with colouring dark-timbred like a cor anglais in the *soave* first movement). The *Concerto gratioso*, too, is aptly named. The *C minor Oboe Concerto* begins with a *Grave*, then the main Allegro brings a witty dialogue between soloist and violins, with the theme tossed backwards and forwards like a shuttlecock. But it is the works for oboe d'amore that are again so striking. Most imaginative of all is the *Triple Concerto* with its sustained opening *Andante* (rather like a Handel aria) and *Siciliano* third movement with the melody alternating between oboe d'amore and viola d'amore, and nicely decorated by flute triplets. The performances are full of joy and sparkle as well as expressive. They are beautifully recorded and make a very good case for playing this repertoire on modern instruments.

Oboe Concertos in C min.; D; D min.; E min.; F min.

*** Ph. (IMS) 412 879-2. Holliger, ASMF, Brown.

The *C minor Concerto* with its astringent opening dissonance is the most familiar of the concertos on Holliger's record. Telemann was himself proficient on the oboe and wrote with particular imagination and poignancy for this instrument. The performances are all vital and sensitively shaped and a valuable addition to the Telemann discography. Well worth investigation.

Oboe Concertos: in C min.; D (Concerto grazioso); D min.; E min.; Oboe d'amore Concertos: in A; G.

(N) (M) *** Van./Passacaille 99701. Dombrecht, Il Fondamento.

The famous opening dissonance of the *C minor Oboe Concerto* sounds the more poignantly penetrating on period instruments, although Il Fondamento never seek to be abrasive. Their textures are transparent, their playing light and graceful. Paul Dombrecht's timbre on both the oboe and oboe d'amore could not be more appealing, as the engaging *Siciliano* of the *Oboe d'amore Concerto in A major* and the *Grazioso* of the *D major Oboe Concerto* readily demonstrate. A delightful disc, most naturally balanced and recorded.

(i) Oboe Concertos: in D min.; E min.; F min.; (ii) Sonatas: E min. (from Esercizi musici); in G (from Sonata metodiche, Op. 13/6); G min. (from Tafelmusik, Part III).

(N) (BB) *** Virgin 2 x 1 VBD5 61878-2 (2). De Vries; (i) Amsterdam Alma Musica, Van Asperen; (ii) Van Asperen, Möller – ALBINONI: *Concerti a cinque, Op. 9.* ***

Hans de Vries is a fine player and he produces an attractively full timbre on his baroque oboe. All three concertos are characteristically inventive, with alert and stylish accompaniments, but the three *Sonatas* are a delight, the work from the *Tafelmusik* particularly diverse. The slight snag is the very forward balance of the solo instrument, which reduces the overall range of dynamic, but apart from that the sound is vivid, and the harpsichord image in the *Sonatas* is pleasing. This comes as part of an inexpensive Double, but the present CD only plays for just over 40 minutes and one wonders what has happened to the fourth concerto in C minor which was on the original CD.

Double Concertos: for 2 Oboes d'amore in A; for Recorder and Flute in E min.; Violin Concerto in B flat; Overtures (Suites) in F sharp min. and D.

(N) *** Chan. 0661 Holtslag, Brown, Robson, Eastaway, Coll. Mus. 90, Standage

The title of this Chandos disc, '*Ouverture comique*', refers to the last of the five Telemann works included in this delightful programme. It is a weirdly surreal musical portrait – eighteenth-century style – of a hypochondriac afflicted with gout. Over seven movements he, in turn, finds remedies in dancing – cue for inserted dance-fragments – in a coach-ride, and even a visit to a brothel. Telemann wrote this sparkling piece in his eighties with his imagination still working over-time. The other works, more conventional but just as inventive, include another overture/suite and three refreshing concertos, all beautifully done.

Concerto in B flat for 3 Oboes & 3 Violins; Concerto in E for Flute, Oboe d'amore & Viola d'amore. Tafelmusik, Part I: Concerto in A for Flute, Violin & Cello; Part II: Concerto in F for 3 Violins.

*** Chan. 0580. Soloists, Coll. Mus. 90, Standage.

The Triple concertos here are all among the composer's most colourful works and the period wind-instruments here are piquant in their mixed colours, the strings lithe, yet not abrasive. The opening of the *E major Concerto* (which comes last in the programme) tickles the ear engagingly with its opening *Andante* and the third movement *Siciliano* is equally diverting. The lively opening movement of the *Tafelmusik triple violin Concerto* momentarily recalls Handel's *Queen of Sheba*, and it has a particularly eloquent *Largo*. First-class playing and recording throughout.

Concerto for 3 Oboes & 3 Violins in B flat, TWV 44:43; (i) Concerto for Recorder, Bassoon & Strings in F; Concerto for 4 Violins in G, TWV 40:201; Overture (Suite) in F for 2 Horns, Violins & Continuo, TWV 44:7.

(M) *** Teldec (ADD) 0630 12320-2. VCM, Harnoncourt,
   (i) with Brüggen, Fleischmann.

The five-movement Overture or Suite featuring a pair of horns shows the composer at his most characteristic (natural horns are used), and the performances are most persuasive. The oboes also sound splendidly in tune, not easy with the baroque instrument, and phrasing is alive and sensitive. Only the *Concerto for Recorder and Bassoon* lets the disc down a little; it is also not as well played as the others. The quality is good and the digital remastering has not tried to clarify artificially what is basically a resonant recording with inner detail mellowed by the ambience. One would not guess that it dates from 1966.

Recorder Concertos in C; in F; Suite in A min. for Recorder & Strings; (i) Sinfonia in F.

**(*) Hyp. CDA 66413. Holtslag, Parley of Instruments, Holman or (i) Goodman.

The three solo concertos here are a delight. Peter Holtslag's piping treble recorder is truthfully balanced, in proper scale with the authentic accompaniments, which are neat, polished, sympathetic and animated. The *Sinfonia* is curiously scored, for recorder, oboe, solo bass viol, strings, cornett, three trombones and an organ, with doubling of wind and string parts. Even with Roy Goodman balancing everything expertly the effect is slightly bizarre. About the great *Suite in A minor* there are some reservations: it is played with much nimble bravura and sympathy on the part of the soloist, but the orchestral texture sounds rather thin.

Recorder Concerto in C; (i) Double Concerto for Recorder & Bassoon.

*** BIS CD 271. Pehrsson, (i) McGraw; Drottningholm Bar. Ens. – VIVALDI: *Concertos.* ***

Clas Pehrsson and Michael McGraw are most expert players, as indeed are their colleagues of the Drottningholm Baroque Ensemble; the recordings are well balanced and fresh.

Double Concertos: for 2 Tenor Recorders in A min. & B flat; for Recorder & Bassoon in F; in E min. for Recorder & Flute; in A min. for Recorder, Gamba & Strings.

(N) **(*) BIS CD 617. Pehrsson, Laurin, McCraw, Evison, Larsson, Drottingholm Bar. Ens., Spark.

Among what is claimed are the 'complete double concertos with recorder' the most attractive work here is for recorder and flute, with its engaging drone finale, using a Polish folk dance. Here Telemann contrasts 'ancient and modern' baroque flute types effectively against each other. The com-

bination of recorder and bassoon is effective too, but the writing for recorder and gamba works less well. The performances here are expert, authentic and stylish, but not all the solo playing is strong in personality and this is an agreeable rather than an indispensable collection.

Double Concerto in F, for Recorder, Bassoon & Strings; Double Concerto in E min., for Recorder, Flute & Strings; Suite in A min., for Recorder & Strings.

*** Ph. (IMS) 410 041-2. Petri, Bennett, Thunemann, ASMF, I. Brown.

The *E minor Concerto* for recorder, flute and strings is a delightful piece and is beautifully managed, even though period-instrument addicts will doubtless find William Bennett's tone a little fruity. The playing throughout is most accomplished and the *Suite in A minor*, Telemann's only suite for treble recorder, comes off beautifully. The orchestral focus is not absolutely clean, though quite agreeable.

(i–iii) Double Concerto in E min. for Recorder & Transverse Flute; (iv) Viola Concerto in G; (i; v) Suite in A min. for Flute & Strings; (iii) Overture des Nations anciens et modernes in G.

(M) *** Teldec (ADD) 9031 77620-2. (i) Brüggen, (ii) Vester, (iii) Amsterdam CO, Rieu; (iv) Doctor, Concerto Amsterdam, Brüggen; (v) SW German CO, Friedrich.

All these works show Telemann as an original and often inspired craftsman. His use of contrasting timbres in the *Double Concerto* has considerable charm; the *Overture des Nations anciens et modernes* is slighter but is consistently and agreeably inventive, and the *Suite in A minor*, one of his best-known works, is worthy of Handel or Bach. Frans Brüggen and Franz Vester are expert soloists and Brüggen shows himself equally impressive on the conductor's podium accompanying Paul Doctor, the rich-timbred soloist in the engaging *Viola Concerto*. The 1960s sound, splendidly remastered, is still excellent, with fine body and presence.

Concerto in A min. for 3 Treble Recorders & Strings; Paris Quartet No. 6 in E min.; Quadro in G min.; Sonata in F (Corellisierende); Trio Sonata in B flat.

**(*) Channel Classics CCS 5093. Florilegium.

Instead of recording groups of categorized works, Florilegium often prefer to take a varied cross-section of a composer's output and create an ongoing concert. This works pleasingly here, with a fair amount of instrumental variety, and playing which is sensitive and vigorous by turns. If the well-known *Triple Concerto in A minor* sounds more effective with a larger ripieno, the *Quadro* with its whirlwind *allegros* and memorable central *Adagio* is very successful as is the opening Corellian pastiche. The group are very well recorded but this is not one of their more memorable collections.

Concertos for Strings: in B flat (Concerto polonaise); in G (Concerto polonaise; Divertimenio for Strings in A & B flat; Viola Concerto in G; Double Concerto in G for 2 Violas; Chamber Concerto in G for 2 Solo Violins, 2 Ripeno Violins & Viola.

(N) **(*) DG 463 074-2. Cologne Musica Antiqua, Goebel.

Both the string concertos with the sobriquet *polonaise* are through-composed, and each is based on a Polish folk dance, although the effect is very German, for here as in the *Double Viola Concerto* the ear is often aware of the heavy accenting that Goebel seems to favour. The *Divertimenti* are lighter, each consisting of a series of scherzi, although varying greatly in tempi. The B flat piece includes a *Tempi di minuetto tedesco* and a *Tempo di minuetto francese.*

Easily the finest work here is the *Viola Concerto*, given an impressive period-instrument performance by Florian Deuter, while the delicately textured *Chamber Concerto for Two Solo Violins, Two Ripeno Violins and Viola* is also very engaging, the textures beautifully transparent.

Trumpet Concerto in D; (i) Double Trumpet Concerto in E flat; (ii) 2 Concertos in D for Trumpet, 2 Oboes & Strings; (i; iii) Concerto in D for 3 Trumpets & strings.

*** Ph. 420 954-2. Hardenberger, with (i) Laird; (ii) Nicklin, Miller; (iii) Houghton; ASMF, I. Brown.

The effortless playing of Hardenberger in the highest register and his admirable sense of style dominate a concert where all the soloists are expert and well blended by the engineers. The concertos with oboes offer considerable variety of timbre and have fine slow movements; there is for instance an engaging *Poco andante* where the oboes are given an *Aria* to sing over a simple but effective continuo, given here to the bassoon (Graham Sheen). That same work is structured unusually in five movements, with two short *Grave* sections to provide pivots of repose. Telemann is always inventive and, with such excellent playing and recording, this can be recommended to anyone who enjoys regal trumpet timbre.

(i) Viola Concerto in G; (ii) Suite in A min. for Recorder & Strings; Tafelmusik, Part 2: (iii) Triple Violin Concerto in F; Part 3: (iv) Double Horn Concerto in E flat.

✪ (BB) *** Naxos 8.550156. (i) Kyselak; (ii) Stivín;
(iii) Hoelblingova, Hoelbling, Jablokov; (iv) Z. & B. Tylšar, Capella Istropolitana, Edlinger.

It is difficult to conceive of a better Telemann programme for anyone encountering this versatile composer for the first time and coming fresh to this repertoire, having bought the inexpensive Naxos CD on impulse. Ladislav Kyselak is a fine violist and is thoroughly at home in Telemann's splendid four-movement concerto; Jiři Stivín is an equally personable recorder soloist in the masterly *Suite in A minor*, his decoration is a special joy. The *Triple violin Concerto* with its memorable *Vivace* finale and the *Double horn Concerto* also show the finesse which these musicians readily display. Richard Edlinger provides polished and alert accompaniments throughout. The digital sound is first class.

Darmstadt Overtures (Suites), TWV 55/C6 (complete).

(M) *** Teldec (ADD) 4509 93772-2 (2). VCM, Harnoncourt.

Darmstadt Overtures (Suites): for 3 Oboes, Bassoon, & Strings: in C, TWV 55/C6; in D, TWV 55/D15; in G min., TWV 55/G4.

(BB) *** Naxos 8.554244. Cologne CO, Müller-Brühl.

These overtures or suites originate from Telemann's period in Frankfurt, and were almost certainly composed for the Darmstadt Court. They are in either seven or eight movements, for the most part dances, such as Loures and Gigues, but also include free instrumental diversions with titles such as *Harlequinade, Irrésoluts, Espagnole, Sommeille, Bourée en trompette* and *Réjouisance*, and it is here that the composer lets his hair down a little, with piquant instrumental effects. But the scoring throughout brings much variety of colour and plenty of tuneful invention.

What strikes one with renewed force while listening to these once again is the sheer fertility and quality of invention that these works exhibit. This is music of unfailing intelligence and wit and, although Telemann rarely touches the depths of Bach, there is no lack of expressive eloquence either. The Harnoncourt performances are light in touch and can be recommended with real enthusiasm. This would make an excellent start to any Telemann collection. The modern-instrument performances on Naxos are delightfully vivacious and elegant. This is a first-class chamber orchestra and Müller-Brühl's light rhythmic touch keeps the dance movements sparkling. The recording is excellent. A most entertaining collection.

Overtures (Suites) in F (Alster); in B flat (La Bourse); Burlesque on Don Quixote.

(N) *** Analekta Fleur de Lys FL2 3138. Tafelmusik, Lamon.

Not surprisingly the performance of the *Alster Suite* by the superb Tafelmusik under Jean Lamon upstages all the competition, with superbly exuberant horn-playing and especially imaginative echo effects. The pictorial characterization, too, is remarkably vivid, with the frogs leaping and shepherds enjoying their raucous dance music. The *Don Quixote Burlesque* is scored for strings without wind, but Telemann is as resourceful as ever and the portrayal of Sancho Panza is as striking as the gallop of Sancho's donkey. The lively *Windmills* sequence contrasts with the Don's gentle sighs for *Dulcinée*. The vivid performance of *La Bourse* is equally memorable. With outstanding recording, this is one of the most winning of all Telemann orchestral discs.

Overtures (Suites) in F (Alster); in F (La Chasse); in G min. (La Musette); in D (for the Jubilee of the Hamburg Admiralty); in D (Ouverture jointe d'une suite tragi-comique).

(N) *** HM HMC 901654. Berlin Akademie für Alte Musik.

The opening *Overture in D*, written for the Hamburg Admiralty's centenary celebration, is remarkably like Handel's *Fireworks Music* and makes a festive start to this very attractive Harmonia Mundi period-instrument collection. (The complete work for which it is the prelude is also available – see below.) We have had the *Alster Suite* before, with all its pictorial effects (from the Collegium Musicum 90 on Chandos and Tafelmusik) – see above. Sufficient to say that the bravura horn playing is exciting here too, in the *Overture* and *Echo* movement, and the bizarre characterization strong, especially the *Dorfmusik* ('shepherds' music') with its drone, and the balancing delicate evocation of Pan.

In the *Musette Suite* Telemann reuses a drone effect for his fifth movement (hence the sobriquet), but this is otherwise a collection of lively dance vignettes from various national sources, of which the most attractive are the Italian *Napolitaine* and *Harliquinade*.

La Chasse is scored for wind instruments alone, again featuring horns, who have plenty to do. But there is engaging writing for oboes too, and they echo the horns in the *Sarabande*. The *Minuet* closing movement, *Le Plaisir*, pictures the hunting party gathered for drinks when the chase is over.

The atmosphere of the witty *Tragi-comique suite* depicts human aches and pains, from the gout-stricken *Loure* to a hypochondriac, cured by being forced to dance in swiftly changing style and time-signature, while the brass dauntlessly depict the only general remedy available (apart from a suggested alternative visit to a brothel): 'souffrance héroïque'. Excellent, lively playing and vivid recording.

Overtures (Suites): in G (La Bizarre); in C (La Bouffone); in G min. (La Changeante).

(N) **(*) Koch Schwann 3-1214-2. Philh. Virtuosi, Kapp.

These are brighter rather more vivid and sharply characterized performances than those from the Northern Chamber Orchestra on Naxos (see below). The Philharmonia Virtuosi of New York provide crisply animated playing, with somewhat more edge and less depth to the string timbre. The conductor (a little self-consciously at times) indulges himself in echo-like dynamic contrasts. But the disc is well worth considering for *La Bizarre*. It does not sound very grotesque to modern ears, yet the *Overture* is restless, and the sixth movement *Fantaisie* is like a moto perpetuo. In between come a noble *Branle* and *Sarabande*, but the closing *Rossignole* abandons its usual vocal eloquence and pecks at an alarming rate. Good, clear recording.

Overture (Suite) in B flat (La Bourse); Suites in C & G.

(M) *** Van./Passacaille 99710. Il Fondamento, Dombrecht.

Paul Dombrecht and Il Fondamento follow up the success of their *Water music* coupling (see below) with characterful period-instrument performances of three more of Telemann's suites. The *C major Suite* (which comes last on this CD) is one of the most sprightly and its third number (*Les Etudiants galliards*) is something of a hit. There is also a fine *Sarabande*, while the penultimate *Canaries* and closing *Air Italien* also have much charm. The *Overture in B flat* is also a suite of dances, and every number is given a sobriquet, such as the charming *Le Repos interrompu*, *La Guerre en la paix* and, more remarkably, *L'Espérance de Mississippi*. Its overall title, *La Bourse*, is associated with the ground floor of the composer's mansion, where he lived between 1712 and 1721, which at that time housed the Hamburg Stock Exchange. Excellent recording.

Overtures (Suites): La Changeante; Les Nations anciens et modernes; in D.

(N) (BB) **(*) Naxos 8.553791. Northern CO, Ward.

These are agreeably mellow performances on modern instruments, which come into their own in the warmly Handelian lyrical melodies, like the *Avec douceur* from *La Changeante* and the *Plainte* from the *D major Suite for Strings and Horns*

(which is the highlight of the disc), and in neatly making the contrasts between the *Ancient and Modern* pairs of movements, the first slow, the second more animated.

Overtures (Suites): in B flat, TW 55/B 10; in C, TWV 55/C6; in D, TWV 55/D 19.

(B) *** DG 463 260-2. E. Concert, Pinnock.

There is some marvellous music here, and each suite has its own lollipops, the Hornpipe and charming Plainte in the *B flat major Suite*, the sensuous Someille in the *C major* work (although one can imagine this would sound even creamier on modern wind instruments) while the *D major* work has a most fetching Bourrée, fully worthy of Handel. It brings a feather-light moto perpetuo for strings at its centre, and the Ecossaise with its witty Scottish snap has a similar contrast, bringing the neatest possible articulation from the English Concert players. There is lots of vitality here and crisp, clean rhythms. Just occasionally one feels the need for more of a smile and greater textural warmth – the rasping, integrated hunting horns don't add a great deal to the *D major* Suite – but this is still a very worthwhile and generous collection (76 minutes), realistically recorded.

Tafelmusik (Productions Nos. 1–3) complete.

(M) *** Teldec 4509 95519-2 (4). Concerto Amsterdam, Brüggen.

*** DG (IMS) 427 619-2 (4). Col. Mus. Ant., Goebel.

(N) (M) *** Teldec (ADD) 3984 26798-2 (4). VCM, Harnoncourt.

(B) **(*) Naxos 8.553724/5 & 8.553731. O of the Golden Age.

**(*) MDG 311 0580-2 (3). Camerata of the 18th Century, Hünteler.

Brüggen's Teldec set was made in the mid-1960s. The playing is very good indeed, and the recorded quality, like so many of these Das Alte Werk reissues, is first rate, with the usual proviso that the balance is forward, reducing the range of dynamic. The solo playing is expert (Hermann Baumann and Adriaan van Woudenberg are the impressive horn players in the *Double Concerto* in the Third Book). The performances have vitality throughout, the sound is full yet has a spicing of astringency, and this mid-priced reissue compares very favourably with the premium-priced sets.

The playing of the Musiqua Antiqua is distinguished by dazzling virtuosity and unanimity of ensemble and musical thinking. They also have the advantage of very vivid and fresh recording quality; the balance is close and present without being too forward and there is a pleasing acoustic ambience. However, Brüggen's set has a price advantage.

Harnoncourt has a slightly more distant, less analytical balance, and his recording has the added poignancy of offering the last performances by the oboists Jürg Shaftlein and David Reichenberg. It also offers distinguished playing, always sensitive to Telemann's unfailingly inventive resource, and the breadth of the music-making tells in its favour. It is now reissued at mid-price, impressively remastered.

The Orchestra of the Golden Age is a new chamber group based in Manchester, playing with a good sense of style, plenty of life and a convincing linear manner in expressive music. They represent one of Naxos's first excusions into period-instrument music-making and are very well recorded. While Brüggen, Harnoncourt and Reinhard Goebel's versions have something special to offer in this music, this Naxos set is excellent value and will give considerable satisfaction.

The Camerata of the 18th Century are based in Amsterdam. They too give expert performances of this repertoire which show an appealing affectionate warmth. But they are recorded in a fairly resonant church acoustic and while this gives a pleasing added warmth, and makes the overall effect more orchestral, with less chamber intimacy, inner detail is less readily revealed. But the solo playing is felicitous and many will enjoy the fuller string textures here.

Tafelmusik, Production No. 3: *Overture in B flat; Quartet in E min.; Production No. 2: Concerto in F; Trio Sonata in E flat; Solo (Violin) Sonata in A; Conclusion in B flat.*

*** DG (IMS) 429 774-2 (from above set, directed Goebel).

For those not wanting a complete set, this arbitrary but well-chosen 75-minute selection may prove useful. The recording is faithful, though the edginess of Goebel's violin timbre will not suit all tastes.

Water Music (Hamburger Ebb' und Fluth).

(M) *** Van./Passacaille 99713. Il Fondamento, Dombrecht –
HANDEL: *Water Music.* ***

*** Hyp. CDA 66967. King's Cons., King – HANDEL: *Water Music.* ***

Telemann's *Water Music* is rightly one of his most popular works, and it is good to have a thoroughly recommendable period-instrument performance available at mid-price and aptly coupled with Handel. The playing is of a high standard and the reed instruments of Il Fondamento are characterful. Telemann's invention never fails him, not only in the lively numbers but also in the expressive writing: the Loure (*Der Verliebte Neptunes*) is most memorable. But most striking of all is the Gigue entitled *Ebbe und Fluth*, which ingeniously suggests the shifting currents of the Alster. The recording is excellent.

The King's Consort performance is comparably enjoyable. There is exhilarating playing from the oboes in the Overture and the following Sarabande (with recorders) is seductive, as is the later Minuet (*Der angeneheme Zephir*). In short this is excellent in every way and like the Vanguard disc, which we prefer by the smallest margin, similarly coupled with the *Water music* of Handel.

CHAMBER MUSIC

6 Concertos & 6 Suites (1734) for Flute, Violin, Viola da gamba, or Cello & Harpsichord (Lute, or Organ).

(N) *** CPO 999 690-2 (3). Camerata Köln.

This remarkable set of four-movement *Concertos* and seven- or eight-movement *Suites*, published by Telemann in Hamburg in 1734, was resourcefully written so that in each case the four parts could be played by a varying combination of instruments, which is what happens here, with sometimes only three instruments in use, sometimes four. This adds variety and freshness to music, which constantly shows the composer's astonishing musical fertility. Throughout, the ear is always entertained, when the period-instrument playing is so expert, with the musicians clearly enjoying themselves. As an example the four *Airs* which conclude Suite No. 1 (*Dolce, Allegro, Spiritoso*, the charming *Piacevole* and the closing *Allegro*) are all ear-tickling, and, throughout, the more expansive concerto slow movements always have memorable expressive content, as in the *Adagio* of *Concerto No. 3*, the engaging *Dolce* of *Concerto No. 4* or the delicate *Gratioso* of *Concerto No. 5*. The recording is excellent.

Music for oboe and continuo: Esercizi musici: Solo V in B flat; Solo XI in E min.; Trio No. 12 in E. No. XXI. Der getreue Music-Meister: Lesson No. 17, Sonata in A min. Harmonischer Gottes-Dienst: Nos. 26, Am Sonntage Jubilate in C min.; 31, Am ersten Pfingstfeiertage in G. Kleine Cammermusic: Partita No. 2.

(N) **(*) HM HMU 907152. Goodwin, North, Sheppard, Toll, Cranham.

Music for oboe and continuo: Esercizi musici: Trio Sonata in E flat. Der getreue Music-Meister: Lesson No. 17, Sonata in A min. Kleine Cammermusic: Partita No. 4 in G min. Tafelmusic: Trio Sonata in G min. Concerto in D for Trumpet, 2 Oboes & Continuo; Sonata in G min. for 2 Oboes & Continuo.

(N) **(*) Accent ACC 95110D. Ponseele, Kitazato, Lindeke, Jacobs, Richte Van Der Meer, Hantal.

After the success of *Kleine Cammermusic* (see below) in 1716, Telemann went on in 1725 to publish the *Harmonischer Gottes-Dienst*, twenty-seven sacred cantatas, accompanied by violin, oboe, flute or recorder with continuo. Here the vocal line is effectively allotted to a baroque cello. In 1728 he offered the first instalment of *Der getreue Music-Meister*, a kind of music magazine, including a varied anthology of solos, duets, trios, suites *et al*, which invited contributions from other composers, of which Bach was one.

The very ambitious *Esercizi musici* followed in 1739, and probably represents the peak of Telemann's output of solos and trio sonatas. Paul Goodwin's selection from these various publications has been well made, notably the *Esercizi musici*, while the excerpts from *Harmonischer Gottes-Dienst* (each of two movements) are especially characterful, and both the *Sonata in A minor* from *Der getreue Music-Meister* and the *Partita No. 2* from *Kleine Cammermusic* include memorable *Sicilianas*, which suit the baroque oboe so well. The performances are of high musical quality and are very well recorded. But is was a pity that other solo instruments could not have been included to provide more diversity.

The Accent collection offers a very similar repertoire, again very well played and recorded in authentic style, and the programme does mitigate the lack of variety of timbre by including a work featuring a baroque trumpet (with a timbre of the 'throttled' kind), and also a charming *Trio Sonata*, including a pair of oboes who converse animatedly together. Even so the Harmonia Mundi performances have rather more personality and are marginally to be preferred.

12 Fantasias for Unaccompanied Violin (complete).

(M) *** Maya MCD 9302. Homburger.

Telemann's *12 Fantasias* for solo violin are a decade later than Bach's *Partitas* and *Sonatas*, and they are less ambitious and less demanding. Each is in either three or four movements, usually opening with a *Largo* or *Grave*, alternating with *Allegros*. With striking invention, they make very enjoyable listening, especially when played with such life and style. Maya Homburger uses a baroque violin and has joined in recordings with the Academy of Ancient Music, English Baroque Soloists and the English Concert. This is cheerful music and it would be difficult to imagine these works being played more freshly or with a more sensitive espressivo. Homburger is recorded most naturally against a warm but not too resonant acoustic, and there is not a trace of vinegar in her timbre.

Kleine Cammermusic (*6 Partitas* for Violin, Flute or Oboe & Continuo).

(N) (BB) *** CPO 999 497-2. Camerata Köln.

The six *Partitas* of the *Kleine Cammermusik*, published in 1716, were written – as was the composer's policy – to be playable by three alternative solo instruments with harpsichord. Each consists of an opening slow introduction, followed by a group of six *Arias* (or airs), varying in style and tempo. As ever, Telemann never seems to run out of attractive ideas and here the works are allotted in turn to oboe (Nos. 1 and 3, both delightful, the latter with a lovely opening *Adagio*), flute (No. 2, which opens *dolce* with a charming *Siciliana*, and is worthy of comparison with Bach), viola da gamba (No. 4 and very well chosen), violin (No. 5) and recorder (No. 6, with organ continuo, and another of the most attractive). The performances here could hardly be bettered and they are beautifully balanced and recorded. The variety of instrumentation makes this one of the most enticing of all the Telemann chamber music CDs.

12 Paris (Flute) Quartets: Nos. 1–6 (Hamburg, 1730); 7–12 (Nouveaux quatuors en 6 suites) (1738) (complete).

*** Sony S3K 63115 (3). Barthold, S. and W. Kuijken, Leonhardt.

6 Nouveaux Paris (Flute) Quartets (1738).

(N) (B) *** Virgin 2 x 1 VBD5 61812–2 (2). Trio Sonnerie.

(i) *6 Nouveaux Paris Flute Quartets* (1738):
(ii) (Orchestral) *Suites: in E flat (La Lyra) for Strings;*
(iii) *in F for Solo Violin, 2 Flutes, 2 Oboes, 2 Horns, Strings & Timpani.*

(M) *** Teldec (ADD) 4509 92177-2 (2). (i) Quadro Amsterdam (Brüggen, Schröder, Bylsma, Leonhardt); (ii) Concerto Amsterdam, Brüggen; (iii) with Schröder.

In 1730 Telemann published in Hamburg a set of six quartets for violin, flauto traverso, viola da gamba and bass continuo, and these were sufficiently popular to be pirated by the French publishing house, Le Clerk, and reprinted in 1736 – without the composer's permission. Telemann learned by this experience: during a long and fruitful visit to Paris in 1737/8, by virtue of a Privilège du Roi, he was able himself to publish a new and even finer set, which he called *Nouveaux*

quatuors. Here the invention, felicitous enough in the earlier works, is even more diverting, with the six-movement format giving greater variety of style and expression. The complete set by the Kuijken group is thoroughly recommendable, the playing always sympathetic, consistently fresh, alert, and sunny: these period instruments all emerge with pleasing countenance. The digital recording is beautifully clear and immediate within a most agreeable ambience.

The performances on Teldec of the second set are of such virtuosity that they silence criticism, and Frans Brüggen in particular dazzles the listener. The recording too is first class, and the CD transfer is immaculate. To fill out the second CD, there are two orchestral suites. The *Suite in F* is the more ambitious and probably dates from the beginning of the 1730s; the autograph score was found in Dresden, and this was almost certainly one of the works '*per molti strumenti*' written (and not only by Telemann), for the local orchestra, so famous at the time. The *La Lyra Suite in E flat major* is much earlier, but its invention is hardly less resourceful and in the third movement, *La Vieille*, Telemann gives an imitation of a hurdy-gurdy.

The performances on Virgin are of a high calibre and are representative of modern practice, using original instruments and bringing lighter textures and greater delicacy of style. Thus, they have a different kind of charm. Tempi with this group are almost always brisker, with both losses and gains; for instance the *Tendrement* second movement of *First Quartet* is just that but more seductive with Frans Brüggen in Amsterdam, while in the *Gai* second movement of No. 5 Hazelzet probably wins on points. The Trio Sonnerie are led by the expert Monica Huggett, and their timbre is cleaner, more transparent, perhaps slightly less substantial than that of Quadro Amsterdam, but who can say which is the more authentic? Certainly, the results on Virgin Veritas are refreshingly different, while the sound is truthful and again very well balanced.

Paris Quartets (1730): Nos. 2, Concerto secondo in D; 3, Sonata prima in A; 4, Sonata seconda in G min.; 5, Première suite in E min. Fantasias: Nos. 5 in A for (solo) Violin; Nos. 7 in D for (solo) Flute; 8 in G min. for Harpsichord.

*** Channel Classics CCS 13598. Florilegium.

Instead of providing a set, Florilegium have chosen four of the earlier quartets and set them in the context of a concert, interspersed with solo *Fantasias*. They play with affectionate warmth, readily bringing out shades of melancholy in slow movements, to contrast with the busy allegros, played with real virtuosity, with the tone of Ashley Solomon's period flute particularly enticing. But the timbre and clean articulation of the two string players, Rachel Podger (violin) and Daniel Yeadon (viola da gamba), are hardly less appealing, and the overall blend of tone in a warm but intimate acoustic could not be more attractive. These players convey a deeper expressive feeling than the Kuijkens.

6 Flute Quartets or Trios (Hamburg, 1733). Der Getreu Musikmeister: Cello Sonata (for cello and continuo) in D.

**(*) Lyrichord LEMS 8028. Mélomanie.

Telemann himself published his *Six quatuors ou trios*, ensuring their success by making them available for performance on various alternative combinations of flutes, violins, bassoon and cello, with a flexible continuo. This is their first complete recording. The collection divides into two groups. The first three works are three- or four-movement sonatas in an elegant conversational style; the last three each open with a slow movement followed by three unpredictable 'Divertimenti', showing the composer imaginatively trying out different dance forms. The four-movement *Cello sonata* offered as bonus also shows the composer at his best. It is very well played, as are the Quartets (favouring two period flutes – not always absolutely immaculate in tuning – cello and harpsichord).

Paris Flute Quartets, Book 4 (c. 1752): Sonatas Nos. 1–6.

**(*) Globe GLO 5146. Hazelzet, Stuurop, Wim tem Have, Ogg, Scheifes.

Although they are listed in the *New Grove*, there is some doubt about the authenticity of these simple, four-movement works, which the composer designated as *Sonatas*. They are not trivial, but pleasingly inventive, with a charming simplicity. If they are Telemann's, he probably wrote them earlier than the published date. Wilbert Hazelzet uses a modern copy of a mid-eighteenth-century flute, and his nimble playing, with immaculate tuning, and decorative flourishes (never overdone) readily tweak the ear. His supporting group provide a somewhat insubstantial (though not edgy) backing, but the solo playing is so adept and full of personality that one accepts Hazelzet's ready domination of the proceedings.

Quadros (Quartets): in A min. for Recorder, Oboe, Violin & Continuo, TWV 43:a3; in G, for Recorder, Oboe, Violin & Continuo, TWV 43:g6; in G min. for Oboe, Violin, Viola da gamba & Continuo, TWV43:g92; in G min. for Recorder, Violin, Viola da gamba & Continuo, TWV43:g94. Esercizi musici: Trio Sonatas: in C min. for Recorder, Oboe & Continuo, TWV 42:c2; in F for Recorder, Viola da gamba & Continuo, TWV 42:f3. Trio Sonata in D min. for Recorder, Violin & Continuo, TWV 42:d10.

*** Globe GLO 5154. Ens. Senario.

These *Quadros* (or Quartets) are among Telemann's very finest chamber music, every bit as inventive and diverting as the more famous *Paris* quartets. Telemann writes parts of equal interest for all three of his solo instruments, and provides slow movements of considerabe expressive intensity, framed by winningly virtuosic allegros. Perhaps finest of all is the *G major Quartet*, with its solemn central *Grave*, but the *G minor Quartet* (TWV 43:g94) which opens the programme, is hardly less seductive. Telemann subtitles the *A minor* work 'Concerto', and indeed there is plenty of opportunity for virtuoso display here, and its four movements also include a pair of touching *Adagios*. The *Trio sonatas*, slighter in texture, are also very enjoyable when presented so freshly. Indeed the performances here could hardly be bettered. The brilliant recorder playing of Saskia Coolen, is well matched by the oboeist, Peter Frankenberg,

and the group overall integrates splendidly. The balance and recording could hardly be improved on.

Quartets (Concertos) for Flute, Bassoon, Viola da gamba & Continuo, in B min., TWV 43:b3; in C TWV 43:C2; Quartet in G for Flute, 2 Violas da gamba, TWV 43:G12; Trio Sonatas: in F for Violin, Viola da gamba & Continuo TWV 42:F10 in G min., for Flute, Viola da gamba & Continuo TWV42:G7 (from Darmstadt manuscripts).

(N) *** Astrée Audivis E 8632. Limoges Bar. Ens., Coin.

All these manuscripts come from the Darmstadt Library and the two most attractive quartets (which include a bassoon) bear the additional title *Concerto*. All five works here are in the four-movement Italian *sonata di chiesa* form (slow–fast–slow–fast), although the *Trio Sonata in G minor* has additionally a characteristic opening *Siciliana*. Although the allegros are lively enough, the pervading mood is often attractively dolorous and the intimacy of the excellent performances enhances that impression. Very good recording.

Sonatas Corellisante Nos.1–6; Canonic Duos Nos. 1–4.

** Chan. 0549. Standage, Comberti, Coe, Parle, Coll. Mus. 90.

The six (Trio) *Sonatas Corellisante* of 1735 are not transcriptions, as might be first expected, but original works 'in the Italian style', although it is essentially an overlay rather than intrinsic to Telemann's invention. Frankly this is too often routine, and fails to either sparkle or have the sunshine sonority of the real thing. Perhaps it might sound better on the fuller sound of modern instruments. These performances here are alert, but hardly beguiling, and the simpler *Canonic duos*, which are played with sprightly vivacity, completely upstage them.

Sonatas for 2 Flutes, TW 40: 130–35.

**(*) Lyrichord LEMS 8019. Reighley, Moore.

Telemann wrote four sets of sonatas for two flutes, all designed for amateurs to play and enjoy, for they do not make too many bravura demands. However, this fourth series (which remained unpublished but which probably dates from the end of the 1730s or the beginning of the 1740s) uses keys which were more difficult for the one-keyed flute of that time, so these works were clearly aimed at players with fair performance skills. They are each in four movements, and the slow movement is usually marked *Dolce* or *Amoroso*. They are well presented here on period instruments although, amiable as it is, this is music to take in small doses.

Recorder Sonatas: Esercizi musici: in C, TWV 41:C5; D min., TWV 41:d2. Der getreue Musicmeister: in A (Canonic Sonata), TWV 41:A3; in C, TWV 41:C2; in F, TWV 41F2; in F min., TWV 41:f1; Neue Sonatinen; in A min., TWV 41:a4; in C min., TWV 41:c2.

(N) **(*) Globe GLO 5151. Ehrlich, Egarr, Levy.

Once again comes the problem of an unvarying sameness of timbre, and Robert Ehrlich's authentic recorder image is small, which partly limits his range, both expressive and dynamic. The solo playing itself is nimble and highly musical: the *C major Sonata* from *Esercizi musici* is particularly charming, while in the *Canonic Sonata* the interplay with the viola da gamba is in perfect scale. The recording is well balanced and truthful, but if this is to be enjoyed it must be taken a sonata at a time.

Sonatas for 2 Recorders Nos. 1–6; Duetto in B flat.

*** BIS CD 334. Pehrsson, Laurin.

Canon Sonatas Nos. 1–6; Duettos Nos. 1–6.

*** BIS CD 335. Pehrsson, Laurin.

All the *Duet Sonatas* are in four movements, the second being a fugue; the *Canon Sonatas* are for two flutes, violins or bass viols. Needless to say, listening to two recorders for longer than one piece at a time imposes a strain on one's powers of endurance, however expert the playing – and expert it certainly is. The BIS versions can be recommended. However, although it is good to have the two treble recorders blending so well together, a clearer degree of separation would have helped in the imitative writing.

Sonata Metodiche Nos. 1–6 (1728); 7–12 (1732).

*** Accent ACC 94104/5D (2). B. and W. Kuijken, Kohnen.

Telemann's *Methodical Sonatas* were written in two sets of six, the first designated 'for violin or flute', the second 'for flute or violin', which is a curious alternation of emphases, the more so as the second set sometimes uses keys which are less comfortable for the baroque flute. Not that this is apparent in these expert performances, lively and expressive by turns, and there is plenty of variety in the music itself. One of the purposes of these sonatas was to instruct amateurs in the art of ornamentation, so Telemann wrote out ornaments in the French style for each first movement, while mixing French and Italian styles in the writing itself. A worthwhile addition to the catalogue, very well recorded.

6 Trio Sonatas in the Italian Style (Sonates en Trios dans le Goût Italien) TWV 42: g3; c1; a2; d2; e1; d4; Trio Sonata in G, TWV 42: g12.

*** Lyrichord LEMS 8035. Moore, Myford, Fournier, Palumbo.

Telemann had altogether greater success with his *Trio Sonatas in the Italian Style* than he did with his Corelli imitations. They are pleasingly lightweight, sunny works, played here with the second part authentically given to the violin rather than a flute. The *C minor* and *A major* works are particularly attractive, but the standard of invention is high, and particularly striking in the minor-key works. They are most felicitously played by this very musical period-instrument group, who know all about elegance, and very well balanced. Tom Moore's baroque flute has a most agreeably watery timbre that is wholly authentic.

COLLECTION

Esercizi Musici: Solo 2: Flute Sonata in D; Solo 4: Recorder Sonata in D min. Solo 5: Chalumeau Sonata in B flat; Solo 8: Flute Sonata in G. Der getreue Music-Meister: Bassoon Sonata in F min. Tafelmusik, Part III: Oboe Sonata in G min. Harpsichord Fantasias: in E min. & F Set 1/4–5; Harpsichord Overture in G min.

(N) *** Meridian CDE 84347 Bandinage.

This is an ideal way of assembling a concert of Telemann's chamber and instrumental music, not centering on a single instrument, but making a hand-picked selection of music (much of it from the *Solos* in the *Esercizi musici*) featuring a wide range of instrumental colour, from the dolorous bassoon and the piquantly watery timbre of the primitive chalumeaux to the brighter recorder and flute. All the soloists here are expert, and the fine harpsichordist provides interludes, lively and *dolce* at three strategic points in the programme. The recording is excellent.

KEYBOARD MUSIC

6 Overtures for Harpsichord, TWV 32:5/10.

(N) ** CPO 999 645-2. Hoeren (harpsichord).

Telemann's six *Overtures* were published between 1745 and 1749. Each is in three movements, beginning grandly in the French style (the rhythm dotted) and moving on to a toccata-like fugato. The central movement is usually marked *Largo e scherzando*, and each work ends with a lively presto. This layout was regarded as a feature of the 'Polish style', often incorporating local rhythmic influences; for Telemann said: 'A Polish song sets the whole world a-jumping.' Harald Hoeran plays boldly on a modern copy of a Flemish harpsichord from around 1750. He is suitably vigorous in allegros, yet inclined to be rhythmically metric elsewhere.

Music for harpsichord and chamber organ: (i) Overture in G min.; Fantasias II in C; VII in G min.; IX in B min.; X in D; XII in E flat; Suite in A; Esercizi musici: Solo in F. (ii) 6 Chorale Preludes; 3 Little Fugues.

(N) *** Meridian CDE 84333. Gifford (i) harpsichord; (ii) chamber organ.

Gerald Gifford has already given us an attractive compilation of the keyboard repertoire of Johann Krebs. The lion's share of the music here is for harpsichord, played on a modern copy (by Philip Smart of Oxford) of a Hemsch instrument dating from 1756. While Gifford cannot wholly be absolved from a metrical approach to the opening *Overture in G minor*, elsewhere his playing is attractively buoyant, helped by the vivid sound of the instrument itself.

The splendid *A major Suite* was admired by Bach, for it was found copied into the *Klavierbüchlein* for Wilhelm Friedman, while the *Solo* from the *Esercizi musici* is an even more generous collection of dances, prefaced by a *Cantabile* rather than a French overture. The three-movement *Fantasias* are each attractively inventive, and all this keyboard music is played spiritedly and in fine style.

The organ *Chorale Preludes* are much less elaborate than Bach's but they are piquantly registered, and the presentation of the three simple *Fugues* is similarly colourful. All-in-all, this makes an excellent survey, very well recorded, which can be highly recommended.

Organ music: 6 Chorale Preludes; Fantasia in D; Pasacaille in B min.; Sonata in D for 2 Manuals & Pedal. Concerto in

G min., (trans. Bach as *BWV 985*). *Concerto per la chiesa on G* (trans. J.G. Walther).

**(N) **(*) MDG 320 0078-2. Baumgratz (Bach organ, Bremer Dom).

This collection opens commandingly with the *Concerto in G minor*, attributed to Telemann, and transcribed by Bach. But it is such a magnificent tripartite piece that one is tempted to believe that there is more Bach in it than Telemann. The *Passacaglia* which follows, with its decoration increasingly florid, moves to a fair climax, and the four *Chorale Preludes* which come next (each in two sections) are agreeably managed, *Komm heiliger Geist* easily the most telling, especially the jaunty second part. However, the pair of chorales based on *Nun freut euch lieben Christen g'mein*, brief as they may be, show Telemann nearer to Bach in his manipulation of variations around a clear cantus firmus.

The *D major Sonata* sounds like an arrangement of a trio sonata and the three-part *Fantasia*, with its characteristic central *Dolce*, is much more impressive. Finally comes J. G. Walther's transcription of the *G major Concerto per la chiesa*, which has an effective opening fugato, but only springs fully to life, in organ terms, in the finale. Wolfgang Baumgratz makes the most of all this music by registering brightly and imaginatively, and he is very well recorded. But this collection serves to confirm that Telemann's talent lay not with the organ, but with the baroque orchestra and in the world of chamber music.

VOCAL MUSIC

Die Auferstehung (The Resurrection): Easter Oratorio; Cantata: De Danske, Norske og Tydske Undersaaters Glaede (The Joy of the Danish, Norwegian and German Citizens).

(N) *** CPO 999 634-2. Mields, Schwarz, Post, Mertens, Decker, Magdeburg Chamber Ch., Michaelstein Telemann CO, Rémy.

Telemann's *Easter Oratorio* of 1761 has an appealing simplicity. It opens without preamble with a solo lament from the soprano, and only then does the chorus enter, joyfully asserting 'The Lord Has Risen'. The bass then tells of the angel arriving 'fast as a flash of lightning' (illustrated by a brilliant violin obligato) and the narrative continues with the alto and chorus dramatically describing the despair of Hell, while the reappearance of the risen Christ is depicted in a lovely soprano aria (beautifully sung here by Dorothy Mields). The Resurrection is then further celebrated in fine expressive arias from tenor and bass, before the joyful closing chorus with trumpets.

The reconstructed cantata celebrating the birthday of the Danish King Frederick V, written four years earlier, was a curious choice of coupling, but it is a happy work. The text alternates verses in Danish, German and Latin with lyrical solos, pleasingly small-scale choruses and a rather engaging soprano–bass duet before the closing chorus. Both performances here are first class, with a sensitive team of soloists and excellent support from the fine chorus and orchestra. The recording is very well balanced, spacious and natural.

Betrachtung der 9 Stunde an dem Todstage Jesu (Passion Oratorio); Cantatas: Ein Mensch is in seinem Leben wie Gras, TWV 4:18; Herr, ich habe lieb die Stätte deines Hauses, TWV 2:2.

(N) *** CPO 999 500-2. Zádori, Jochens, Wessel, Cordier, Wimmer, Schreckenberger, Van der Kamp, Rheinisch Kantorei, Kleine Konzert, Maz.

Telemann's *Passion Cantata, Reflection of the Ninth Hour on the Day of Jesus's Death* (with a text by Joachim Zimmerman), is an unusual conception, in that the figure who is involved in these personal reflections is not a biblical character but a poetic creation, who provides a reflective meditation on the events surrounding the Crucifixion. Telemann added three chorales to create a binding structure and the vocal observations are not centred on a single soloist but four, with tenor alto and two basses together providing the introduction. The first bass aria, *Whither then in vain you impudent people*, boldly accompanied by horns, dramatically sets the scene, and each soloist continues the reflective commentary, the work ending with a philosophical bass aria of acceptance, and a reassuring closing chorale. If the musical result is less imaginative than the conception, the work is still well worth hearing, as are the pair of contrasted canatatas with which it is coupled, which show Telemann's invention at his freshest. All three pieces are very well sung and accompanied and the recording is well up to the high standard of this excellent CPO series.

Cantatas for the first Sunday of Advent: Saget den verzagten Herzen, TWV 1:1233; Saget der Tochter Zion, TWV 1: 1235. Cantatas for the first day of Christmas: Auf Zion! Und lass in geheilgten Hallen, TWV 1: 109; Kündlich gross ist das Gottselige Geheimnis, TWV 1: 1020.

*** CPO 999 515-2. Mields, Schwarz, Jochens, Schmidt, Magdeburg Chamber Ch., Michaelstein Telemann CO, Rémy.

This is marginally the finest of Ludger Rémy's series of Telemann's festive cantatas so far. The opening of *Saget den verzagten Herzen* brings a splendid interchange between soloists and chorus, and the following alto aria (marked *Affettuoso*) – *So komm den auch* – is touchingly eloquent, while the bass and tenor soloists both have lively arias to follow. The bravura bass aria, *Zerstreuet euch*, which opens *Saget de Tochter Zion*, has even more brilliant trumpet parts and the opening bass aria of *Auf, Zion*, decorated with flutes, is equally memorable. The Christmas story is then told in a series of brief recitatives and choruses, much more atmospheic and dramatic than the so-called 'Christmas oratorio' below. The second of the two Christmas Day cantatas, *Kündlich gross ist das Gottselige Geheimnis* is even more dramatic and has a remarkable soprano aria punctuated by trumpets and drums. The alto air *Göttlich Kind* is a Handelian alto and trumpet duet, and the trumpets stay for the bass aria. Rémy directs with flair, and with strikingly good male soloists, fine choral singing and first-rate playing from his period-instrument accompanying group, this is well worth seeking out. The documentation (as throughout the series) is impeccable, including full translations.

Christmas Oratorio: Die Hirten on der Krippe zu Bethlehem, TWV 1:797; Christmas Cantatas: Siehe, ich verkündige Euc (1761), TWV 1:1334; Der Herr hat offenbaret (1762): TWV 1: 262.

**(*) CPO 999 419-2. Backes, George, Post, Mertens, Michaelstein Chamber Ch. & Telemann CO, Rémy.

The so-called 'Christmas Oratorio' opens with the chorale we know as 'In dulci jubilo', fully scored with trumpets, to the words, O *Jesu parvule* – and is simply structured and comparatively unambitious, with the chorus interleaving the arias with chorales. Flutes and trumpets are used to decorate the pastoral scenes. There is a fine bass aria welcoming the shepherds. But the cantatas are much more ambitious. The 1761 work opens arrestingly with a brilliant soprano aria when the angel sings those famous words '*Behold I bring you glad tidings*' with trumpets blazing, and she is answered dramatically by the choral heavenly host who return to praise God after fine contributions from both the tenor and bass. The 1762 cantata opens and closes with a chorus, and the following arias for soprano and bass (again using trumpets and futes) are both rather fine. Fortunately the soloists here are again excellent and if the conductor of the small period-instrument ensemble is at times rhythmically a bit emphatic in the oratorio, he keeps the music alive and flowing. The recording is excellent.

Cornett Cantatas: Cantata for the 2nd Sunday after Epiphany: Sehet an die Exempel der Alten, TWV 1: 1259; Cantata for Exaudi Sunday Ich halte aber dafür, TWV 1: 840; Cantata for Rogation Sunday: Erhöre mich, wenn ich rufe, TWV 1: 459.

*** CPO 999 542-2. Spägele, Vass, Jochens, Mertens, Leipzig Bläser Collegium, Michaelstein Telemann CO, Rémy.

The rich textures Telemann creates are very much his own, not like Gabrieli, rather nearer to Schütz. In consequence he does not demand a chorus, and the chorales are sung by the soloists, never more effectively than at the end of *Epiphany cantata*, following a fine soprano aria. Telemann uses his colourful ripieno imaginatively throughout, and especially so in the *Rogation cantata* which is shared by tenor and bass. Wilfried Jochens and Klaus Mertens are in splendid form, and make the most of all their opportunities, especially their fine penultimate duet, richly embroidered by the brass and wind, *Herr, auf dein Wort verlass ich mich*, which is again followed by the closing chorale. The *cantata for Exaudi Sunday* opens with a spectacular polyphonic interplay, shared by singers and orchestra, and after an alto recitative the cornetti decorate the bass aria, while oboes are used later for the alto solo, and the work closes with a serene Martin Luther hymn. If the invention in these works is less dramatic than in the *Advent* and *Christmas cantatas*, many of the individual numbers are lyrically very persuasive, especially when they are so well sung, and so musically accompanied by this strikingly well-balanced period-instrument ensemble under the excellent Ludger Rémy.

Hamburg Admiralitätsmusik (1723); Water Music (Hamburger Ebb' und Fluth).

(N) (BB) *** CPO 999 373-2 (2). Mieke van der Sluis, Pushee, Müller, Mertens, Thomas, Schopper, Alsfeder Vokalensemble, Bremen Baroque O, Helbich.

CPO took advantage of a live performance in Bremen in 1995 to make this excellent recording of a work which otherwise would have been an unlikely choice for CD. Telemann's occasional piece, which he called a *Serenade*, was written for the Hamburg Admiralty's centenary celebration of the founding of the local Naval College in 1723. It was first performed at a gala concert, together with the composer's much-better known *Water Music*, hence the coupling.

As the main work is set to a poem by Michael Richey in praise of Hamburg, the allegorical characters represented by the soloists are all associated with the city. The soprano (as Hammonia) embodies Hamburg itself and the principal bass (as Neptunus) symbolizes the North Sea, and he has a memorable lyrical aria celebrating Hamburg's prosperity. More remarkably, the two tenors, as Themis and Mercurius respectively, represent the prospering economy, and the privileges and rights of the constitution.

One of the other two bases symbolizes Mars, and sings a dramatic aria of defiance of lightning and stormy blasts. The third bass as Albis (the Elbe) celebrates his flowing currents and then has a charming tête-à-tête with Hammonia. Not surprisingly, there is a chorus of Nymphs and Tritons and the finale, *Long live the Admiralty*, is almost worthy of Sullivan! The performance is full of life, and of high quality, with no weak link in the cast, and with excellent recording, overall this is a delightful surprise.

(i) *St Mark Passion;* (ii) *Magnificats in C & G.*

(B) **(*) Ph. Duo (ADD) 462 293-2 (2). Giebel, Malaniuk, Altmeyer, Rehfuss, Lausanne Youth Ch., Munich Pro Arte O, Redel; with (i) Günter; (ii) Reuter-Wolf.

Telemann's is an expressive piece, but only in places does the writing show real individuality. This performance, however, is an outstandingly good one, with fresh intelligent solo singing and thoroughly committed and understanding direction from Kurt Redel. The two settings of the *Magnificat* – one in Latin, one in German – then make a fascinating contrast, the German work altogether gentler than the Latin setting. Telemann may not match Bach in sublimity of inspiration, but the vigour of his choral writing is very refreshing here. Strong, well-tuned performances except for some unsteadiness from contralto and bass soloists. All three recordings come from the early 1960s and still sound well.

THOMAS, Ambroise (1811–96)

Mignon; Overture & Gavotte.

*** Chan. 9765. BBC PO, Y. P. Tortelier (with Concert: 'French bonbons' ***).

Overtures: Mignon; Raymond.

(M) *** [Mercury 434 321-2]. Detroit SO, Paray – BIZET: *L'Arlésienne; Carmen: Suites.* **(*)

Thomas's opera *Mignon* has one of the most delectable of all French overtures, with its opening woodwind and harp solos followed by a romantic horn tune. It is beautifully played and recorded on Chandos in this first-rate concert of French lollipops.

Raymond is perhaps more of a bandstand piece. The Detroit orchestra play both with wonderful finesse and Gallic spirit: this is repertoire which Paray directs incomparably, like his Auber overtures on the same label. The excellent (1960) recording was made in the Cass Technical High School Auditorium.

Hamlet (complete).

*** EMI CDS7 54820-2 (3). Hampson, Anderson, Ramey, Graves, Kunde, Garino, Le Roux, Trempont, Amb. S., LPO, Almeida.

(M) *** Decca (IMS) 433 857-2 (3). Milnes, Sutherland, Morris, Winbergh, Conrad, Tomlinson, WNO Ch. & O, Bonynge.

Thomas's *Hamlet* may be an unashamed travesty of Shakespeare, complete with happy ending (in its original form), but it remains a strong and enjoyable example of French opera of its period. So much was evident from Richard Bonynge's 1983 Decca set. If the EMI set is even more strikingly successful, it is not just that it provides an unusually full text – with the tragic, so-called Covent Garden ending and the ballet music in an appendix – but that Thomas Hampson gives such a commanding performance in the title-role. One no longer finds the aria, *Etre ou ne pas être*, sounding conventional or trivial, and consistently Hampson magnetizes the attention the moment he begins to sing. June Anderson is not so happily cast as Ophelia. The voice is inclined to sound too edgy, and she is hardly more successful at sounding girlish than Sutherland, but the singing is felt and expressive. Almeida is understanding, and the presentation of the full text, with a recently discovered duet for Claudius and Gertrude as a bonus, makes it invaluable.

On the Decca set, Ophélie (Sutherland) takes all the challenges commandingly. Ophelia's famous Mad scene was one of the finest of her early recordings, and here, 24 years later, she still gives a triumphant display, tender and gentle as well as brilliant in coloratura. The role of Hamlet is here taken strongly if with some roughness by Sherrill Milnes. Outstanding among the others is Gösta Winbergh as Laërte (in French without the final 's'), heady and clear in the only major tenor role. John Tomlinson as Le Spectre sings the necessary monotones resonantly, James Morris is a gruff Claudius and Barbara Conrad a fruity Gertrude. Bonynge's vigorous and sympathetic conducting of first-rate Welsh National Opera forces is brilliantly and atmospherically recorded.

Mignon (complete).

(M) *** Sony (ADD) SM3K 34590 (3). M. Horne, Vanzo, Welting, Zaccaria, Von Stade, Méloni, Battedou, Hudson, Ambrosian Op. Ch., Philh. O, Almeida.

Thomas's once-popular adaptation of Goethe has many vocal plums, and here a very full account of the score is given, with virtually all the alternatives which the composer devised for productions after the first – not least one at Drury Lane in London where recitatives were used (as here) instead of spoken dialogue; an extra aria was given to the soubrette Philine and other arias were expanded. The role of Frédéric was given to a mezzo-soprano instead of a tenor, and here the appropriately named Frederica von Stade is superb in that role, making one rather regret that she was not chosen as the heroine. However, Marilyn Horne is in fine voice and sings with great character and flair, even if she hardly sounds the frail figure of the ideal Mignon. Nonetheless, with Alain Vanzo a sensitive Wilhelm, Ruth Welting a charming Philine, and colourful conducting from Almeida, this is an essential set for lovers of French opera. The 1977 recording has a pleasingly warm ambience and the voices are naturally caught in the present transfer.

THOMPSON, Randall (1899–1984)

Symphony No. 2 in E min.

(BB) **(*) Sony (ADD) SMK 60594. NYPO, Bernstein – DIAMOND: *Symphony No. 4*; HARRIS: *Symphony No. 3*. **(*)

*** Chan. 9439. Detroit SO, Järvi – CHADWICK: *Tam O'Shanter* etc. ***

Randall Thompson's *Second Symphony* (1931) does not have the strongly distinctive personality of Harris or Piston. Leonard Bernstein's New York recording comes from 1968 and has great vitality and momentum to commend it. Despite its star rating, the performance rates higher than the Järvi – good though that is – for it has stronger character and drive. The sound is good, too, but not in the same street as the Chandos. Neeme Järvi and the Detroit orchestra give an eminently satisfying account, and have a finely detailed and luxurious recording. Those for whom sound is very important can safely invest in this, for the Chadwick coupling is well worth having.

THOMSON, Virgil (1896–1989)

Film music: *Louisiana Story: Arcadian Songs & Dances & Suite. The Plow that Broke the Plains: Suite. Power among Men: Fugues & Cantilenas.*

**(*) Hyp. CDA 66576. New L. O, Corp.

Apart from his opera *Four Saints in Three Acts* (available on two separate recordings in the USA), Virgil Thomson is best known for his film score to Flaherty's *Louisiana Story*. Here we are offered both the four-movement suite and a series of brief vignettes, called *Arcadian Songs and Dances*, of which the first (*Sadness*) and last (*The Squeeze Box*) are the most striking. The *Fugues and Cantilenas* from *Power among Men* are also not what one might expect from the titles, but are atmospheric and imaginatively scored. All this music is quite appealing, even if only very occasionally does one feel it is first rate. The performances by Ronald Corp and the New London Orchestra, are deft, evocatively played, and well recorded.

Film scores: *The Plow that Broke the Plains; The River* (suites).

(M) *** Van. 08.8013.71. Symphony of the Air, Stokowski –
   STRAVINSKY: *Soldier's Tale.* ***

Virgil Thomson's orchestral music may be sub-Copland (he
too uses cowboy tunes like *Old paint*), but in Stokowski's
charismatic hands these two film scores emerge with colours
glowing and their rhythmic, folksy geniality readily communicating. The recording is resonantly atmospheric, but
vivid too. Most enjoyable, and with a worthwhile coupling.
This is at upper mid-price in the USA.

TICHELI, Frank (born 1958)

Postcard; Radiant Voices.

*** Koch 3-7250-2. Pacific SO, St Clair – CORIGLIANO: *Piano
   Concerto.* ***

Frank Ticheli, composer-in-residence to this Pacific
orchestra largely made up of musicians from film studios,
here offers two warm, unproblematic works, ingeniously
and wittily argued, full of engaging echoes of composers
from Bartók and Copland to John Adams, with a flavouring
of Walton in the jazz rhythms. First-rate performances and
sound. An attractive coupling for the ambitious, similarly
communicative *Piano Concerto* of John Corigliano.

TIOMKIN, Dimitri (1894–1979)

Film music: *The Fall of the Roman Empire: Overture; Pax
Romana. The Guns of Navarone: Prologue-Prelude;
Epilogue. A President's Country. Rhapsody of Steel. Wild is
the Wind.*

(M) **(*) Unicorn UKCD 2079. Royal College of Music O,
   Willcocks; D. King (organ).

Dimitri Tiomkin contributed scores to some of the most
famous movies of all time, for Hitchcock and Frank Capra
among others. But it was Carl Foreman's *High Noon* that
produced his most memorable idea, and he quotes its
famous theme, among others, in *A President's Country*, a
well-crafted medley used as background music for a documentary about President Johnson's Texas. *Wild is the Wind* is
another familiar melody; Christopher Palmer's arrangement
makes a tastefully scored showcase. The latter has arranged
and orchestrated all the music here except *Rhapsody of Steel*,
a complex pseudo-symphonic score written for another
documentary, which lasts some 22 minutes. The music of
Pax Romana has the robust character of a typical Hollywood
epic costume spectacular, featuring a bold contribution from
the organ. All the music is played with obvious enjoyment
by the Orchestra of the Royal College of Music; no apologies
need be made for their technique, which is fully professional.
Sir David Willcocks conducts with understanding of the
idiom and great personal conviction. The recording is very
impressive too, if with brass and percussion rather too
prominent.

TIPPETT, Michael (1905–98)

Concerto for Orchestra; (i) Triple Concerto.

*** Chan. 93842. (i) Chilingirian, Rowland-Jones, De Groote;
   Bournemouth SO, Hickox.

Hickox's coupling of these two major orchestral works is a
fine supplement to his set of the four Tippett symphonies,
also with the Bournemouth orchestra, warmly recorded in
well-focused sound. Levon Chilingirian makes a powerful
leader for the trio of soloists, heightening the sharp contrasts
of the elliptical argument in Tippett's late return to lyricism.
The *Concerto for Orchestra*, written in very much the same
vein as the opera, *King Priam*, is presented with similar
concentration and concern for lyrical warmth.

(i) *Concerto for Double String Orchestra; (ii–iv) Piano
Concerto; (i) Fantasia concertante on a Theme of Corelli;
Little Music for Strings; (v; iv) Praeludium for Brass, Bells
& Percussion; Suite for the Birthday of Prince Charles; (vi;
iii–iv) Triple Concerto for Violin, Viola, Cello &
Orchestra; (vii) The Blue Guitar (sonata for solo guitar).*
Vocal music: *(viii–ix) Bonny at morn (Northumbrian
folksong for unison voices and 3 recorders); (viii) A Child
of Our Time: 5 Negro Spirituals. (viii; x) Crown of the Year
(cantata); (viii) Dance, Clarion Air (madrigal);
(xi) Evening Canticles; (viii) Music (unison song); Plebs
Angelica (motet for double choir); The Weeping Babe
(motet for soprano and choir). The Midsummer Marriage:
(v; iv) Ritual Dances; (xii) Sosostris's Aria.*

(BB) *** Nim. NI 1759 (4). (i) E. String O, Boughton;
   (ii) Tirimo; (iii) BBC PO; (iv) cond. composer; (v) E. N.
   Philh. O; (vi) Kovacic, Causé, Baillie; (vii) Ogden;
   (viii) Christ Church Cathedral Ch., Oxford (members),
   Darlington; (ix) Copley, Hodges, Nallen; (x) Medici Qt, with
   wind soloists, Jones (piano) and percussion; (xi) St John's
   College, Cambridge, Ch., Guest; (xii) Hodgson.

This bargain collection of Tippett, issued to commemorate
the composer's death in 1998, is specially valuable for containing two discs of recordings made by Tippett himself.
When he did them, he was already in his late eighties, and
the performance of the *Ritual Dances* from *A Midsummer
Marriage* is not as incisive as most other versions, but the
warmth of expressiveness and the sense of occasion conveyed
are most compelling, the more so in Alfreda Hodgson's rich
and resonant performance of Sorostris's aria from the same
opera, even though the voice is backwardly balanced. It is
good too to have Tippett offering a rare example of his
occasional music in the uncomplicated *Prince Charles suite*.
Even more valuable is the concerto disc, again more relaxed
at more spacious speeds than rival versions, but with outstanding soloists revealing Tippett at his most warmly magnetic. Martino Tirimo is particularly impressive in the
elaborate figuration of the *Piano Concerto* which can easily
sound empty. Broad speeds, well sustained, also mark William Boughton's readings of the string pieces on the fourth
disc; the *Guitar sonata*, tautly played by Craig Ogden, and
Evening canticles sung by the St John's College Choir under
George Guest (for whom they were written) make a splendid

supplement. The choral singing from Christ Church Cathedral Choir on the second disc is also excellent, with the school cantata, *The Crown of the Year*, revealing the composer at his most open and least enigmatic. Warm, atmospheric sound, characteristic of Nimbus.

Concerto for Double String Orchestra.

(N) *** BBC BBCL mono 4059-2. LSO, Stokowski –
GABRIELI: *Sonata pian e forte*. LISZT: *Mephisto Waltz No. 1*. NIELSEN: *Symphony No. 6*. ***

As far as we know Stokowski did not conduct any other Tippett and this eloquent account of the *Double Concerto* is a 'must', particularly as it comes with another rarity, a studio performance of Nielsen's *Sixth Symphony*. Commanding accounts, recorded in vivid and well-balanced mono sound.

Concerto for Double String Orchestra; Divertimento on 'Sellinger's round'; Little Music for Strings; (i) The Heart's Assurance (orch. Meirion Bowen).

**(*) Chan. 9409. City of L. Sinf., Hickox, (i) with Mark Ainsley.

Hickox draws warm and energetic performances from his chamber orchestra, opulently recorded with fine definition. The first movement of the *Concerto* may lack a little in bite, but the slow movement is ravishing and the finale fizzes with energy. The playing may not always be quite as polished as that of the Academy on the rival EMI disc, but the big bonus is the first recording of the song-cycle, *The Heart's Assurance*, in the orchestration prepared by Meirion Bowen with the composer's express approval. What with piano accompaniment can seem a gritty, uncompromising piece here emerges with warmth and beauty, thanks also to the fine singing of John Mark Ainsley.

Concerto for Double String Orchestra; Fantasia on a Theme of Corelli; (i) The Midsummer Marriage: Ritual Dances.

(N) ⬤ (BB) *** Warner Apex 8583 89098-2. BBC SO, A. Davis; (i) with BBC Symphony Chorus.

This outstanding bargain disc offers superb performances from Sir Andrew Davis and the BBC Symphony Orchestra of Tippett's two string masterpieces, both in the great tradition of English string-writing, coupled with an equally inspired account of the vividly atmospheric *Ritual Dances* from *A Midsummer Marriage*. The *Concerto* and *Fantasia* are warmly passionate, yet wonderfully detailed, helped by a spaciously resonant recording which is internally clear, yet has a wide dynamic range to match the dynamic contrasts of the playing. In the third of the *Ritual Dances*, *The air in spring*, the chimerical delicacy of the orchestral playing makes the bold entry of the BBC Chorus, near the close, the more arresting and thrilling. If you buy only one Tippett CD, this is the one to have; for apart from being ridiculously inexpensive, it makes an ideal introduction to his music and the sound could hardly be more vivid.

Little Music for String Orchestra.

(M) **(*) Chan. 6576. Soloists of Australia, Thomas – BLISS: *Checkmate*; RUBBRA: *Symphony No. 5*. ***

Tippett's *Little Music* was written in 1946 for the Jacques Orchestra. Its contrapuntal style is stimulating but the music is more inconsequential than the *Concerto for Double String Orchestra*. It receives a good if not distinctive performance here, truthfully recorded.

(i) The Rose Lake; (ii) The Vision of St Augustine.

⬤ *** Conifer 75605 51304-2. LSO; (i) C. Davis (ii) with Shirley Quirk, L. Ch., composer.

As Sir Colin Davis's superb recording with the LSO demonstrates from first to last, *The Rose Lake* is arguably the most beautiful of all Tippett's works. It was in 1990 on a visit to Senegal that the 85-year-old composer visited a lake, Le Lac Rose, where at midday the sun transformed its whitish-green colour to translucent pink. It led to this musical evocation of the lake from dawn to dusk, centred round the climactic mid-moment when the lake is in full song. The 12 sections, sharply delineated, form a musical arch, with the lake-song represented in five of them on soaring unison strings in free variation form.

That culminating masterpiece is well coupled with Tippett's own 1971 recording, never previously available on CD, of his cantata, *The Vision of St Augustine*. First heard in 1965, it is a work which can now be recognized as the beginning of his adventurous Indian Summer. His reading is expansively atmospheric rather than tautly drawn, bringing out the mystery of the piece.

Symphony No. 1; (i) Piano Concerto.

*** Chan. 9333. (i) Shelley; Bournemouth SO, Hickox.

Those who thought that Sir Colin Davis's pioneering recordings of the first three Tippett symphonies (which are currently withdrawn) were definitive will find fresh revelation in Richard Hickox's readings, not least in the *First Symphony*. Hickox gives an extra spring to the chattering motor rhythms at the start, and from then on the Bournemouth performance is regularly warmer and more expressive, as in the distinctive trumpet melody in the slow movement. In the last two movements too, Hickox finds more fun and jollity in Tippett's wild inspirations. The *Piano Concerto*, with Howard Shelley a superb soloist, brings another revelatory performance, warm and affectionate but purposeful too, rebutting any idea that with their fluttering piano figurations these are meandering arguments. Warm, full, atmospheric sound, with the piano balanced within the orchestra instead of in front of it. This must now be a first recommendation.

Symphony No. 2; New Year (opera): Suite.

*** Chan. 9299. Bournemouth SO, Hickox.

As in the *First Symphony*, Hickox brings out the joy behind Tippett's inspirations without ever losing a sense of purpose. This may be a less biting performance than Sir Colin Davis's was on Decca, but it is consistently warmer, with extra fun and wit in the third-movement Scherzo. The coupling is also valuable, when Tippett's own suite from his last opera, *New Year*, brings out the colour and wild energy of this inspiration of his mid-eighties. If anything, the music seems the more telling for being shorn of the composer's own problematic libretto. The obbligato instruments – saxophones, electric guitars and kit drums – are most evocatively balanced in the warm, atmospheric recording.

(i) Symphony No. 3. Praeludium for Brass, Bells & Percussion.

*** Chan. 9276. Bournemouth SO, Hickox; (i) with Robinson.

In two long movements, each lasting nearly half an hour, the *Third Symphony* is not easy to hold together and, though Richard Hickox and the Bournemouth orchestra cannot match the original performers, Sir Colin Davis and the LSO, in power, they find more light and shade. Hickox gives wit to the Stravinskian syncopations in the first section and then dedicatedly carries concentration through the pauses of the slow second half of the movement. Though Faye Robinson's voice in the blues sections of the second movement is not as warm or firm as Heather Harper's was, she is more closely in tune with the idiom, helping to build the sequence to a purposeful conclusion in the long final scena. The recording is full and warm to match. The *Praeludium for Brass, Bells & Percussion* was written in 1962 for the 40th anniversary of the BBC, a gruff, angular piece hardly suggesting celebration, but none the less welcome in a well-played performance.

Symphony No. 4; Fantasia concertante on a Theme of Corelli; (i) Fantasia on a Theme of Handel (for piano and orchestra).

*** Chan. 9233. (i) Shelley; Bournemouth SO, Hickox.

In the *Fourth Symphony* Richard Hickox and the Bournemouth Symphony are less weighty than the work's originators, but they are generally warmer and more atmospheric. In place of Solti's fiery brilliance, Hickox brings an element of wildness to the fast sections and he also finds a vein of tenderness in the meditative sections. The well-known *Corelli Variations* have never sounded quite as sumptuous and resonant as here, and the disc is generously rounded off with a welcome rarity: the early *Handel Fantasia for Piano & Orchestra*. Howard Shelley is most convincing in the weighty piano-writing, like his accompanists giving the music warmth. Full-blooded sound to match.

String Quartets Nos. 1–5.

*** ASV ADD/Dig. CDDCS 231 (2). Lindsay Qt.

String Quartet No. 4.

*** ASV CDDCA 608. Lindsay Qt – BRITTEN: *Quartet No. 3*. ***

String Quartet No. 5.

*** ASV CDDCA 879. Lindsay Qt (with BROWN: *Fanfare to Welcome Sir Michael Tippett*; MORRIS: *Canzoni ricertati*; PURCELL: *3 Fantasias*; WOOD: *String Quartet* ***).

This set neatly brings together the première recordings of Tippett's last two quartets with the recordings the same players made in the 1970s for L'Oiseau-Lyre of the first three quartets in the series, long unavailable. The notes include the composer's own commentary on the first three quartets, written for the original issue. He explains that he regards these works, written between 1935 and 1946, as a sequence, each developing out of the other. The Lindsays give performances as near definitive as could be, making one realize

why they inspired the composer so positively. The analogue sound for Nos. 1–3, as transferred, is brighter, with less body than the digital recordings for Nos. 4 and 5.

As can be seen, the *Fourth* and *Fifth Quartets* are also available separately, the *Fourth* well coupled with Britten's *Third*. The other varied items which come on CDDCA 879 with No. 5 are designed as a pendant to the Tippett, music by composers with whom he is associated, from Purcell, always a strong influence, to Christopher Brown from a young generation, paying tribute in a vigorous fanfare. R. O. Morris and Charles Wood were Tippett's teachers, both represented in beautifully crafted quartet pieces, the one a pair of contrasted fugal movements, the other a crisp, four-movement work with echoes of Irish folksong and dance-rhythms, a most attractive piece.

Piano Sonatas Nos. 1 (Fantasy-Sonata); 2–3.

*** Chan. 9468. Unwin.

Piano Sonatas Nos. 1 (Fantasy Sonata); 2–4.

(M) *** CRD 34301 (2). Crossley.

Paul Crossley has been strongly identified with the Tippett sonatas; he recorded the first three for Philips in the mid-1970s: indeed, No. 3 was written for him. The *Fourth* and last (1983–4) started life as a set of five bagatelles. Crossley contributes an informative and illuminating note on the sonata and its relationship with, among other things, Ravel's *Miroirs*; his performance has all the lucidity and subtlety one would expect from him. These masterly accounts are matched by truthful and immediate sound-quality.

Nicholas Unwin has an exceptionally wide range of colour, though at times Crossley has more subtlety and delicacy when Tippett's fantasy takes wing. The Chandos recording is superb. Crossley's set takes two CDs but, if you happen not to need or want the *Fourth*, this is a viable alternative.

VOCAL MUSIC

A Child of Our Time (oratorio).

*** Chan. 9123. Haymon, Clarey, Evans, White, L. Symphony Ch., LSO, Hickox.

Hickox's version of Tippett's oratorio, *A Child of Our Time*, establishes its place against severe competition largely through the exceptionally rich recording and its distinctive choice of soloists, a quartet of black singers. Not only do Cynthia Haymon, Cynthia Clarey, Damon Evans and Willard White make the transitions into the spirituals (used in the way Bach used chorales) seem all the more natural, their timbres all have a very sensuous quality. The London Symphony Chorus, though not at its most incisive, sings well, responding to Hickox's warmly expressive style, often even more expansive than the composer himself on his recent recording.

(i) A Child of Our Time (oratorio); (ii) The Knot Garden (opera; complete).

*** Ph. (ADD) 446 331-2 (2). (i) Norman, J. Baker, Cassily, Shirley-Quirk, BBC Singers, BBC Ch. Soc. & SO; (ii) Herinx,

Minton, Gomez, Barstow, Carey, Tear, Hemsley, ROHCG O; C. Davis.

Sir Colin Davis's superb recorded performance of *The Knot Garden* is here aptly coupled with Davis's 1975 recording of the oratorio, *A Child of Our Time*, on a pair of well-filled CDs at full price. *The Knot Garden* is a conversation-piece, set in a garden, to a libretto by the composer, very much in the style of a T. S. Eliot play. The brief central Act, called *Labyrinth*, has characters thrown together two at a time in a revolving maze, a stylized effect which contributes effectively to Tippett's process of psychiatric nerve-prodding. Recorded in vivid, if rather dry, sound, the message comes over if anything more effectively than on stage. The recording of *A Child of Our Time* is also cleanly defined, here suiting Davis's sharply focused performance. Speeds are on the fast side, both in the spirituals, which here take the place that Bach gave to chorales, and in the other numbers. Consistently Davis allows himself far less expressive freedom than the composer in his outstanding Collins version and he misses the tenderness which can make the setting of *Steal away* at the end of Part 1 so moving. He has a superb quartet of soloists; and their fine contribution, together with that of the chorus, matches this approach.

The Midsummer Marriage (complete).

⚫ *** Lyrita (ADD) SRCD 2217 (2). Remedios, Carlyle, Burrows, Herincx, Harwood, Watts, Ch. & O of ROHCG, C. Davis.

Originally on Philips, this 1970 recording of Tippett's first opera firmly establishes this as a warmly melodic, rich-textured work that should be in the standard repertoire, alongside Britten's *Peter Grimes*. That Tippett's visionary conception, created over a long period of self-searching, succeeds so triumphantly on record is a tribute above all to the exuberance of the composer's glowing inspiration, his determination to translate the beauty of his vision into musical and dramatic terms. There are few operas of any period which use the chorus to such effect, often in haunting offstage passages, and, with Sir Colin Davis a burningly committed advocate and with a cast that was inspired by live performances in the opera house, this is a set hard to resist, even for those not normally fond of modern opera. The so-called 'difficulties' of the libretto, with its mystical philosophical references, fade when the sounds are so honeyed in texture and so consistently lyrical, while the story – for all its complications – preserves a clear sense of emotional involvement throughout. The singing is glorious, the playing magnificent and the recording outstandingly atmospheric, and the Lyrita transfer intensifies the keen sense of realism, the feeling of sitting in the stalls inside an opera house with perfect acoustics.

King Priam (complete).

*** Chan. 9406/7. Bailey, Harper, Allen, Palmer, Langridge, Minton, Tear, Roberts, L. Symphony. Ch., LSO, Atherton.

'The future of any twentieth-century opera depends quite a lot on recording,' Sir Michael Tippett said on the appearance of this superb set, and it is no exaggeration that it set the seal on the acceptance of a masterly work which yet seemed disconcerting when it first appeared in 1962. The dry fragmentation of texture and choppy compression of the drama then seemed at odds with an epic subject, particularly after the lyrical, expansive warmth of Tippett's preceding opera, *The Midsummer Marriage*. With an outstanding cast of the finest British singers of the time, Atherton in this 1980 recording brings out the sharp cogency of the writing, the composer's single-mindedness in pursuing his own individual line. The Wagnerian, Norman Bailey, sounds agedly noble in the title-role, with Robert Tear a shiningly heroic Achilles and Thomas Allen a commanding Hector, illuminating every word. The digital recording, originally made by Decca, comes out brilliantly on CD, with each Act fitted conveniently on a single disc.

TJEKNAVORIAN, Loris (b. 1937)

Piano Concerto, Op. 4.

*** ASV CDDCA 984. Babakhanian, Armenian PO, composer
  – BABADZHANIAN: *Heroic Ballade; Nocturne*. ***

A highly coloured work, very much in the tradition of Khachaturian, but rather more dissonantly pungent, Tjeknavorian's *Fourth Concerto* certainly makes an immediate impact on the listener. There is a central pianistic soliloquy at the centre of the first movement, sinuously Armenian in flavour, which leads to a huge climax, ridden by the pianist's thundering bravura, before the wildly obstreperous orchestra returns to add to the melée. Introduced by a yearning horn theme, the *Andante* wears its romantic heart on its sleeve, even though the soloist ruminates; and the rumbustious, syncopated finale also has a sinuous lyrical interlude, before the orchestra returns for the riotous race to the winning post. Babakhanian is surely an ideal soloist, producing explosions of virtuosity whenever needed, yet persuasively sensitive to the work's lyrical side. With the composer conducting, and the orchestra on their toes, the result surely is definitive, for the recording is extremely vivid.

TOCH, Ernst (1887-1964)

5 Pieces for Wind & Percussion.

*** Virgin VC5 45056-2. Deutsche Kammerphilharmonie Wind
  – HINDEMITH: *Septet for Wind;* WEILL: *Violin Concerto*. ***

The Viennese-born Ernst Toch is better known as a teacher than as a composer. While he was an influential figure in Germany in the 1920s and early '30s, he never really recovered the ground lost when he was forced out of Germany by the Nazis. These *Five Pieces for Wind and Percussion* of 1959 are charming, lyrical and full of imagination – as well as (in the third, *Night Music*) humour (as in the second *Caprice*) and a gentle melancholy, as in the *Roundelay*. Beautiful playing and superbly life-like, well-balanced recording. Highly recommended.

Tanz-Suite, Op. 30.

** Edition Abseits EDA013-2. Kammersymphonie Berlin, Bruns
 – SCHREKER: *Der Geburtstag der Infantin.* **

Ernst Toch's *Dance Suite* comes from 1923. It is an expertly
crafted piece, inventive and resourceful. The playing of the
Kammersymphonie Berlin under Jürgen Bruns is first-rate
and the recording eminently serviceable.

TOMKINS, Thomas (1572–1656)

Music for viols: *Almain in F* (for 4 viols); *Fantasias 1, 12 &
14* (for 3 viols); *Fantasia* (for 6 viols); *Galliard: Thomas
Simpson* (5 viols & organ); *In Nomine II* (for 3 viols);
Pavane in A min. (for 5 viols & organ); *Pavane in F; Ut re
mi (Hexachord fantasia)* (both for 4 viols); (Keyboard)
(i) *Fancy for two to play. Pavan & Galliard: Earl Strafford.*
(Organ) *In nomine; Miserere; Voluntary;* Verse anthems:
*Above the stars; O Lord, let me know mine end; Thou art
my King.*

⏺ (BB) *** Naxos 8.550602. Rose Consort of Viols, Red Byrd;
 Roberts; (i) with Bryan.

This well-planned Naxos programme is carefully laid out in
two parts, each of viol music interspersed with harpsichord
and organ pieces and ending with an anthem. It gives collectors an admirable opportunity to sample, very inexpensively,
the wider output of Thomas Tomkins, an outstandingly fine
Elizabethan musician whose music is still too little known.
Though he is best known for his magnificent church music,
it is refreshing to discover what he could do with viols,
experimenting with different combinations of sizes of instrument, usually writing with the polyphony subservient to
expressive harmonic feeling, as in the splendid and touching
Fantasia for 6 voices. Perhaps the most remarkable piece here
is the *Hexachord fantasia,* where the scurrying part-writing
ornaments a rising and falling six-note scale (hexachord).
The two five-part verse anthems and *Above the stars,* which
is in six parts, are accompanied by five viols, with a fine
counter-tenor in *Above the stars* and a bass in *Thou art my
King.*

Music for harpsichord and virginals: *Barafostus Dreame; 2
Fancies; Fancy for Two to Play; Fortune my Foe; Galliard
of 3 Parts; Galliard Earl Stafford; 2 Grounds; In nomine;
Lady Folliott's Galliard; Miserere; Pavan; Pavan Earl
Strafford with its devision; Pavane of 3 parts; A Sad
Pavane for these Distracted Times; Toy made at Poole
Court; What if a Day; Worcester Brawls.*

(N) *** Metronome METCD 1049. Cerasi.

Carole Cerasi offers here the finest available collection of
the keyboard music of last of the great English virginalists,
Thomas Tomkins. Indeed it is the repertoire played on
the virginals which stands out, especially her exquisitely
spontaneous performance of *A Sad Pavane for these Distracted Times,* and her equally sensitive response to the
dolorous *Fortune my Foe* (the two most extended pieces
here). In contrast the charmingly good-humoured *Toy made
at Poole Court* is given the lightest rhythmic lift. She uses a
modern copy of an early seventeenth-century Ruckers and it

could hardly be more realistically recorded. The harpsichord
pieces (using a copy of an instrument by Bartolomeo
Stephanini) are more robust and often have exuberant decoration, as in the disc's title piece *'Barfostus' Dreame'. Earl
Strafford's Galliard* is another splendid example of her exciting bravura on the latter instrument and the closing
Ground with extended variations is a *tour de force.* The
recording venue has a pleasing ambience and the balance is
ideal if you set the volume level carefully.

The Great Service (No. 3); Anthems: *Know you not; Oh,
that the Salvation; O Lord, let me know mine end; Organ
Voluntaries: in A; in C; in G.*

(M)*** CRD 3467. New College, Oxford, Ch., Higginbottom;
 Burchell.

*The Great Service (No. 3); When David Heard; Then David
Mourned; Almighty God, the Fountain of All Wisdom;
Woe is Me; Be Strong and of a Good Courage; O Sing unto
the Lord a New Song; O God, the Proud are then Risen
Against Me.*

*** Gimell CDGIM 924-2. Tallis Scholars, Phillips.

The *Great Service,* in no fewer than ten parts, sets the four
canticles – *Te Deum, Jubilate, Magnificat* and *Nunc dimittis*
– with a grandeur rarely matched, using the most complex
polyphony. The following motets bring comparable examples of his mastery. These complex pieces bring the flawless matching and even tone for which the Tallis Scholars
are celebrated, and with recording to match.

  Many will prefer the more direct and throatier style of the
Choir of New College, Oxford; even if the choral sound
(recorded in the chapel of New College) is less sharply
defined, the effect is very satisfying and real. The service is
given added variety by the inclusion of three organ voluntaries, well played by David Burchell. What makes this record
especially attractive is the inclusion of three of Tomkins'
most beautiful anthems. The treble solos in *Know you not*
and *Oh, that the salvation* are ravishingly done, and the
alto soloist in *O Lord, let me know mine end* is hardly less
impressive.

TOMLINSON, Ernest (born 1924)

*Aladdin: 3 Dances (Birdcage Dance; Cushion Dance; Belly
Dance); Comedy overture; Cumberland Square; English
Folk-Dance Suite No. 1; Light Music Suite; Passepied;
(i) Rhapsody & Rondo for Horn & Orchestra. Brigadoon;
Shenandoah* (arrangement).

*** Marco 8.223513. (i) Watkins; Slovak RSO (Bratislava),
 composer.

The opening *Comedy Overture* is racily vivacious, and there
are many charming vignettes here, delectably tuneful and
neatly scored, and the pastiche dance movements are nicely
elegant. The *Pizzicato humoresque* (from the *Light Music
Suite*) is every bit as winning as other, more famous pizzicato
movements, and in the *Rhapsody and Rondo* for horn Tomlinson quotes wittily from both Mozart and Britten. The
composer finally lets his hair down in the rather vulgar *Belly
Dance,* but the concert ends well with the charming *Georgian*

Miniature. The playing is elegant and polished, its scale perfectly judged, and the recording is first class.

An English Overture; 3 Gaelic Sketches: Gaelic Lullaby. Kielder Water; Little Serenade; Lyrical Suite: Nocturne. Nautical Interlude; 3 Pastoral Dances: Hornpipe. Silverthorne Suite; 2nd Suite of English Folk Dances; Sweet and Dainty; arr. of Coates: The Fairy Coach; Cinderella Waltz.

*** Marco 8.223413. Slovak RSO (Bratislava), composer.

Ernest Tomlinson's orchestral pieces charm by the frothy lightness of the scoring. The winningly delicate *Little Serenade*, which opens the disc, is the most famous, but the gentle, evocative *Kielder Water*, the captivating *Canzonet* from the *Silverthorne Suite* and the *Nocturne* are hardly less appealing. *Love-in-a-mist* is as intangible as it sounds, with the most fragile of oboe solos, and it is not surprising that *Sweet and Dainty* has been used for a TV commercial. There is robust writing, too, in the *Folk Dance Suite* – but not too robust, although the jolly *English Overture* begins with *Here's a health unto His Majesty* and certainly does not lack vitality. The music is played with much grace and the lightest possible touch by the remarkably versatile Slovak Radio Orchestra under the composer, and the vivid recording has delightfully transparent textures, so vital in this repertoire.

TORCH, Sidney (1908–90)

All Strings and Fancy Free; Barbecue; Bicycle Belles; Comic Cuts; Concerto incognito; Cresta Run; Duel for Drummers; Going for a Ride; London Transport Suite; Mexican Fiesta; On a Spring Note; Petite Valse; Samba Sud; Shooting Star; Shortcake Walk; Slavonic Rhapsody; Trapeze Waltz.

*** Marco 8.223443. BBC Concert O, Wordsworth.

Sydney Torch worked frequently with the BBC Concert Orchestra – the orchestra on this CD – and for many he is remembered for his weekly broadcasts: 'Friday Night is Music Night'. The *London Transport Suite* was commissioned by the BBC for their Light Music festival of 1957, and was inspired by the withdrawal of 'The Brighton Belle' on the London to Brighton railway service. Each of its three movements represents a mode of transport: *The Hansom Cab, Rosie, the Red Omnibus* and *The 5:52 from Waterloo*. All the music here is tuneful, sometimes wistful and nostalgic, at others bright and breezy – *All Strings and Fancy Free* is both. *Barbecue* sounds like a Scottish snap, whilst the *Trapeze Waltz* is reminiscent of the circus music of Satie. The *Concerto incognito* is very much in the *Warsaw Concerto* mould, and the *Petite waltz* (also with piano), is more robust than its title suggests. The *Mexican fiesta* and *Samba Sud* produce some fine local colour and are very jolly, whilst the *Slavonic rhapsody* (with two pianos) is a fun work drawing on the music of Rimsky-Korsakov, Tchaikovsky, Knipper, Borodin and Khachaturian, to form an entertaining if outrageous pastiche. The longest work is the *Duel for drummers* which, as its title suggests, is a *tour de force* for the percussion department; it has some ideas which are reminiscent of Eric Coates and a few surprises, including a cockerel crowing,

and a desert-island storm in the central movement. It ends with a lively galop. Barry Wordsworth conducts with flair and the recording is excellent.

TORKE, Michael (born 1961)

(i) *Book of Proverbs*; (ii) *4 Proverbs.*

**(*) Decca 466 721-2. (i) Anderson, Ollman, Netherlands R. Ch. & PO, De Waart; (ii) Bott, Argo Band, composer.

Taking cryptic fragments from the Book of Proverbs in the Old Testament, Michael Torke uses the words to create musical patterns, both in the eight orchestral songs of *Book of Proverbs* and in the four chamber-scale settings of the second work. This is all warmly approachable music, often sounding suspiciously like Aaron Copland in full American mode, with syncopated rhythms and colourful instrumentation. Only two of the orchestral set involve soloists – both excellent – with the choir warmly expressive as the main protagonist, even if the backward balance is hardly a help. Catherine Bott, best known as an early music specialist, proves an outstanding soloist in the chamber-scale songs, singing with sensuous tone, though Torke as a conductor is less incisive than de Waart in the Dutch performances.

TOSTI, Francesco (1846–1916)

Songs: L'alba sepàra della luce l'ombra; Aprile; 'A vucchella; Chanson de l'adieu; Goodbye; Ideale; Malia; Marechiare; Non t'amo; Segreto; La serenata; Sogno; L'ultima canzone; Vorrei morire.

(M) *** Ph. (IMS) (ADD) 426 372-2. Carreras, ECO, Muller.

Tosti (knighted by Queen Victoria for his services to music) had a gently charming lyric gift in songs like these, and it is good to have a tenor with such musical intelligence – not to mention such a fine, pure voice – tackling once-popular trifles like *Marechiare* and *Goodbye*. The arrangements are sweetly done, and the recording is excellent.

TOVEY, Donald (1875–1940)

Piano Concerto in A, Op. 15.

*** Hyp. CDA 67023. Osborne, BBC Scottish SO, Brabbins – MACKENZIE: *Scottish Concerto.* ***

Hyperion in its imaginative series of Romantic piano concertos here offers two Scottish works. Sir Donald Tovey is best known for his analytical essays, and his *concerto*, if less distinctively Scottish, is the grander work, with weighty textures and a strongly controlled structure. The young Scottish pianist, Steven Osborne, is a brilliant advocate.

TOWER, Joan (born 1939)

Concerto for Orchestra; Duets for Orchestra; Fanfares for the Uncommon Woman Nos. 1–5.

*** Koch 3-7469-2. Colorado SO, Alsop.

Joan Tower studied and began composing as a serialist, but hearing Messiaen's *Quartet for the End of Time* was 'bowled over by the emotional directness of the music . . . I felt like an acrobat . . . it [serial music] was a sport, it wasn't like being a musician. So I pulled out'. Although the *First* makes an opening nod towards Copland, the style of the *Five Fanfares* is nearer to John Adams, although there are influences from Stravinsky too. The writing is complex and florid, rhythmically vibrant and vivid. In the ambitious *Concerto for Orchestra*, Bartók (not surprisingly) can be discerned too, but it is the atmospheric use of colour and the yearningly lyrical kernel of the work that one remembers, for all the dynamism and orchestral brilliance, and that applies equally to the *Duets*. Marin Alsop presents all this music with a Bernstein-like intensity and dedication, and the Colorado Symphony produce playing of great bravura and obvious depth of response, with an eloquent tuba among the lyrical solos at the centre of the *Concerto*. The recording, in the spacious acoustic of Denver's Boettcher Concert Hall, could hardly be bettered.

TRIMBLE, Joan (born 1915)

(i) *Phantasy Trio*; (ii; iii) *Music for 2 pianos: The Baird of Lisgoole; Buttermilk Point; The Green Bough; The Humours of Carrick (Hop-jig); Pastorale: Homage à Poulenc; Puck Fair; Sonatina. 3 Traditional songs: The cows are a-milking; Gartan Mother's lullaby; The heather glen;* (iv; iii) *County Mayo Song Cycle: The County Mayo; Peggy Mitchell; Inis Fail; In the poppy field;* (v; iii) *3 Songs: Girl's song; Green rain; My grief on the sea.*

**(*) Marco 8.225059. (i) Dublin Piano Trio; (ii) Hunt; (iii) Holmes; (iv) Corbett; (v) Bardon.

In the 1930s, at the suggestion of Arthur Benjamin, Joan and Valerie Trimble established a celebrated piano duo, and in turn he wrote for them the *Jamaican Rumba*, which they made world famous. But Joan proved a talented composer in her own right, drawing on the rich vein of Irish folk song and composing her own pieces in a similar style. Their simplicity and freshness of inspiration give much pleasure, as does the deft keyboard writing. There are other influences too, from the French school in the *Sonatina* and the *Pastorale* and from Vaughan Williams, who suggested the composition of the passionate, yearning *Piano Trio (Phantasy)*, which is very English in feeling. But it is for the winning Irish keyboard duo pieces that Joan Trimble will be remembered and they are played here with just the right lightness of touch. The songs are certainly worth preserving on disc, although their performances are less so. Joe Corbett is a sympathetic 'Irish' interpreter of the *County Mayo Cycle*, but his presentation is only really distinctive in the lively final song, *In the poppy field*, with the *Buttermilk Reel* piano duo making a sparkling postlude. The soprano songs, although eloquently sung, are let down by Patricia Bardon's intrusively wide vibrato.

TRUNK, Richard (1879–1968)

7 Christmas Lieder, Op. 71: Advent; Weihnachten; Maria; In der Krippe; Die heiligen drei Könige; Idyll; Christbaum.

⚙ *** EMI CDC5 56204-2. Bär, Deutsch (with Recital: 'Christmas Lieder' *** ⚙).

These delightful Christmas settings by Richard Trunk are the surprise at the centre of Olaf Bär's superb collection of German Christmas songs. Trunk, a pupil of Rheinberger, lived in America for a period, returning to Germany after the outbreak of the First World War, and he established himself as conductor and academic in Cologne. His remarkable feeling for words and easy melodic lyricism are very much in the mainstream of German Lieder and, even if the style of the music is more eclectic, its invention is engagingly individual and never flags. Olaf Bär gives inspired performances, relishing the subtleties in the marriage of text and vocal line. The highlight is the masterly *Idyll*, picturing Mary beneath a lime tree rocking her son to sleep with four angels on guard overhead. Unfortunately, at the time of going to press this issue has been deleted.

TRUSCOTT, Harold (1914–92)

Symphony in E; Elegy for String Orchestra; Suite in G.

*** Marco 8.223674. Nat. SO of Ireland, Brain.

Harold Truscott broadcast as a pianist for the BBC, specializing in Schubert, and this record suggests that his own music, for all its eclectic influences, has genuine individuality and power. The moving *Elegy* for strings, elliptical in structure, is a near-masterpiece, and the three-movement *Symphony*, which dates from the end of the 1940s, is a powerfully argued piece. The *Suite in G* has a *Molto Andante* which confirms the intensity of feeling the composer could create with string textures. Gary Brain has an instinctive feel for all these works and holds together the turbulent moods of the first movement of the *Symphony* coherently, while the Dublin orchestra rise to the occasion and play with much conviction throughout. The recording is full-bodied, with the resonance at the service of the music but without clouding textures.

(i; ii) *Cello Sonata in A min.;* (iii; ii) *Clarinet Sonata No. 1 in C;* (iv; v; vi) *Flute Trio (for flute, violin and viola) in A;* (i) *Meditation for Solo Cello on Themes from Emmanuel Moór's Suite for 4 Cellos;* (v) (Solo) *Violin Sonata in C.*

(N) *** Marco 8.223727. (i) Domonkos; (ii) Lugossy; (iii) Varga; (iv) Kovács; (v) Eckhart; (vi) Bársony.

This fine collection of Truscott's chamber music bears out the promise of the orchestral disc below. The *Flute Trio* (1950) is strikingly fresh, with a spirited, spikily colourful ostinato-like opening movement, followed by a charming *quasi allegretto*. But the heart of the work is the third movement, a simple Elegy. The finale is then a winning *Tempo di menuetto*, characteristically quirky.

The lyrical writing in the *Clarinet Sonata* of nine years later immediately makes full use of the instrument's *chalumeau* range and then contrasts an engaging repeated-note scherzo with a serene *Adagio*, maintaining the romantic, lyrical flow in the finale. Both the rather serious-minded single-movement *Solo Violin Sonata* and the darker *Cello Meditation* (1946) are short but memorable. The *Cello Sonata* dates from much later and the writing style is more concentrated, with a bravura finale. Yet the central *Allegretto scherzando* and searching *Adagio* have much in common with the earlier music. Fine, eloquent performances throughout, and truthful if reverberant recording, although the resonance is most troubling in the *Clarinet Sonata*.

TUBIN, Eduard (1905–82)

(i) *Balalaika Concerto; Music for Strings; Symphony No. 1.*

*** BIS CD 351. (i) Sheynkman; Swedish RSO, Järvi.

The opening of the *First Symphony* has a Sibelian breadth, but for the most part it is a symphony apart from its fellows. The quality of the musical substance is high; its presentation is astonishingly assured for a young man still in his twenties, and the scoring is masterly. Emanuil Sheynkman's account of the *Balalaika Concerto* with Neeme Järvi is first class, both taut and concentrated. Excellent recording.

(i) *Ballade for Violin & Orchestra;* (ii) *Double-bass Concerto;* (i) *Violin Concerto No. 2; Estonian Dance Suite; Valse triste.*

*** BIS CD 337. (i) Garcia; (ii) Ehren; Gothenburg SO, Järvi.

Tubin's highly imaginative *Double-bass Concerto* has an unflagging sense of momentum and is ideally proportioned; the ideas never outstay their welcome and one's attention is always held. The *Second Violin Concerto* has an appealing lyricism, is well proportioned and has a strong sense of forward movement. The *Ballade* is a work of gravity and eloquence. *Valse triste* is a short and rather charming piece, while the *Dance suite* is the Estonian equivalent of the *Dances of Galánta*. Splendid performances from both soloists in the *Concertos* and from the orchestra under Järvi throughout, and excellent recording.

Symphonies Nos. 2 *(The Legendary); 6.*

*** BIS CD 304. Swedish RSO, Järvi.

The opening of the *Second Symphony* is magical: there are soft, luminous string chords that evoke a strong atmosphere of wide vistas and white summer nights, but the music soon gathers power and reveals a genuine feeling for proportion and of organic growth. If there is a Sibelian strength in the *Second Symphony*, the *Sixth*, written after Tubin had settled in Sweden, has obvious resonances of Prokofiev – even down to instrumentation – and yet Tubin's rhythmic vitality and melodic invention are quietly distinctive. The Swedish Radio Symphony Orchestra play with great commitment under Neeme Järvi, and the recorded sound is magnificent.

Symphonies Nos. 3; 8.

*** BIS CD 342. Swedish RSO, Järvi.

The first two movements of the wartime *Third Symphony* are vintage Tubin, but the heroic finale approaches bombast.

The *Eighth* is his masterpiece; its opening movement has a sense of vision and mystery, and the atmosphere stays with you. This is the darkest of the symphonies and the most intense in feeling, music of great substance. Järvi and the Swedish orchestra play it marvellously and the recording is in the demonstration bracket.

Symphonies Nos. (i) 4 *(Sinfonia lirica);* (ii) 9 *(Sinfonia semplice); Toccata.*

⚫ *** BIS CD 227. (i) Bergen SO, (ii) Gothenburg SO, Järvi.

The *Fourth* is a highly attractive piece, immediately accessible, the music well argued and expertly crafted. The opening has a Sibelian feel to it but, the closer one comes to it, the more individual it seems. The recording comes from a concert performance with an exceptionally well-behaved audience. The *Ninth Symphony* is in two movements: its mood is elegiac and a restrained melancholy permeates the slower sections. Its musical language is direct, tonal and, once one gets to grips with it, quite personal. If its spiritual world is clearly Nordic, the textures are transparent and luminous, and its argument unfolds naturally and cogently. The playing of the Gothenburgers under Järvi is totally committed in all sections of the orchestra. The performances are authoritative and the recording altogether excellent.

Symphony No. 5 in B min.; *Kratt* (ballet suite).

*** BIS CD 306. Bamberg SO, Järvi.

The *Fifth* makes as good a starting point as any to investigate the Tubin canon. Written after he had settled in Sweden, it finds him at his most neo-classical; the music is finely paced and full of energy and invention. The ballet suite is a work of much character, tinged with folk-inspired ideas and some echoes of Prokofiev.

Symphony No. 7; (i) *Concertino for Piano & Orchestra; Sinfonietta on Estonian Motifs.*

*** BIS CD 401. (i) Pöntinen; Gothenburg SO, Järvi.

The *Seventh* is a marvellous work and it receives a concentrated and impressive reading. As always with Tubin, you are never in doubt that this is a real symphony which sets out purposefully and reaches its goal. The ideas could not be by anyone else and the music unfolds with a powerful logic and inevitability. Neeme Järvi inspires the Gothenburg orchestra with his own evident enthusiasm. The *Concertino for Piano and Orchestra* has some of the neo-classicism of the *Fifth Symphony*. Roland Pöntinen gives a dashing account of the solo part. The *Sinfonietta* is a fresh and resourceful piece, a Baltic equivalent of, say, Prokofiev's *Sinfonietta*, with much the same lightness of touch and inventive resource. Superb recording.

Symphony No. 10; (i) *Requiem for Fallen Soldiers.*

*** BIS CD 297. Gothenburg SO, Järvi; (i) with Lundin, Rydell, Hardenberger, Lund Students' Ch., Järvi.

Tubin's *Requiem*, austere in character, is for two soloists (a contralto and baritone) and male chorus. The instrumental forces are merely an organ, piano, drums, timpani and trumpet. The simplicity and directness of the language are affecting and the sense of melancholy is finely controlled.

The final movement is prefaced by a long trumpet solo, played here with stunning control and a masterly sense of line by the young Håkan Hardenberger. It is an impressive and dignified work, even if the choral singing is less than first rate. The *Tenth Symphony* is a one-movement piece that begins with a sombre string idea, which is soon interrupted by a periodically recurring horn call – and which resonates in the mind long afterwards. The recordings are absolutely first class.

(i; iii) *Ballade; Capricci Nos. 1 & 2; The Cock's Dance; Meditation; 3 Pieces; Prelude.* **(i)** *Sonata for Unaccompanied Violin.* **(i; iii)** *Violin Sonatas Nos. 1 & 2; Suite of Estonian Dance Tunes; Suite on Estonian Dances.* **(ii; iii)** *Viola Sonata; Viola Sonata (arr. of Alto Saxophone Sonata).*

*** BIS CD 541/542 (2). (i) Leibur; (ii) Vahle; (iii) Rumessen.

Although the smaller pieces are finely wrought, Tubin seems to come into his own on a larger canvas. Particularly impressive are the *Second Violin Sonata* (*In the Phrygian mode*), the visionary *Second Piano Sonata*, and the two sonatas for viola, one a transcription of the alto-saxophone sonata with its foretaste of the *Sixth Symphony* (1954) in which that instrument plays a prominent, almost soloistic role, and the later *Viola Sonata* (1965). As so often with Tubin's non-symphonic music, there is much of interest to reward the listener. Highly accomplished performances from Arvo Leibur and Petra Vahle, and exceptionally thorough documentation from the pianist Vardo Rumessen, with over 40 music-type examples. The recording is truthful, but the acoustic lends a shade too much resonance to the piano, which is often bottom-heavy.

Complete piano music: *Album leaf; Ballad on a Theme by Maat Saar; 3 Estonian folk-dances; 4 Folksongs from my Country; A Little March for Rana; Lullaby; 3 Pieces for Children; Prelude No. 1; 7 Preludes; Sonatas Nos. 1–2; Sonatina in D min.; Suite on Estonian Shepherd Melodies; Variations on an Estonian folk-tune.*

*** BIS CD 414/6. Rumessen.

Tubin's first works for piano inhabit a world in which Scriabin, Ravel and Eller were clearly dominant influences but in which an individual sensibility is also to be discerned. The resourceful *Variations on an Estonian folk-tune* is a lovely work that deserves a place in the repertoire, as does the *Sonatina in D minor*, where the ideas and sense of momentum are on a larger scale than one would expect in a sonatina. The *Second Sonata* is a key work in Tubin's development. It opens with a shimmering figure in free rhythm, inspired by the play of the aurora borealis, and is much more concentrated than his earlier piano works. Vardo Rumessen makes an excellent case for it and it is impressive stuff. The performances are consistently fine, full of understanding and flair, and the recording is very natural.

OPERA

Barbara von Tisenhusen.

*** Ondine ODE776-2 (2). Raamat, Sild, Kuusk, Puurabar, Kollo, Estonian Op. Company & O, Lilje.

Tubin's opera with its theme of illicit passion is not long, consisting of three Acts of roughly 30 minutes each. It has pace and variety of dramatic incident and musical textures, and the main roles in the action are vividly characterized. The musical substance of the opera is largely based on a chaconne-like figure of nine notes heard at the very outset, yet the theme changes subtly and skilfully to meet the constantly shifting dramatic environment so that the casual listener will probably not be consciously aware of the musical means Tubin is employing. All the singers are dedicated and serve the composer well and, though the orchestra is not first class, it too plays with spirit and enthusiasm under Peeter Lilje. The recording produces a sound comparable to that of a broadcast relay rather than the opulent sound one can expect from a commercial studio recording. A strong recommendation.

The Parson of Reigi; **(i)** *Requiem for Fallen Soldiers.*

*** Ondine ODE783-2 (2). Maiste, Eensalu, Tônuri, Kuusk, Estonian Op. Company & O, Mägi; (i) Tauts; Deksnis, Leiten; Tiido, Roos, Estonian Nat. Male Ch., Eri Klas.

After the success of *Barbara von Tisenhusen*, the Estonian Opera immediately commissioned Tubin to compose *The Parson of Reigi*, and it, too, concerns an illicit relationship. Tubin's music powerfully evokes the claustrophobic milieu of a small, closely knit fishing community and is particularly successful in conveying atmosphere. The dawn scene where the parson, Lampelius, blesses the departing fishermen is particularly imaginative, as is the evocation of the white summer nights in the Garden scene, where the heroine confesses her illicit passion. As in *Barbara von Tisenhusen*, Tubin's powers of characterization of both the major and supporting roles are striking, and there is a compelling sense of dramatic narrative as well as variety of pace. The performance of the three principal singers is very good – especially the parson, splendidly sung by the baritone, Teo Maiste – and the only let-down is in the quality of the orchestral playing, which is little more than passable.

The coupled *Requiem for Fallen Soldiers* is generally to be preferred to the rival account on BIS coupled with the *Tenth Symphony* (see above). The Estonian singers produce better focused and darker tone than their Swedish colleagues, though the BIS recording has some amazingly lyrical playing by Håkan Hardenberger. The Estonian player, Urmas Leiten, is very eloquent too. Strongly recommended.

TURINA, Joaquin (1882–1949)

(i) *Danzas fantásticas, Op. 22; La oracion del torero, Op. 34;* **(ii)** *Rapsodia sinfónica, Op. 66.*

(B) Double Decca 433 905-2 (2). (i) SRO, López-Cobos; (ii) de Larrocha, LPO, Frühbeck de Burgos – ALBENIZ: *Iberia;*

GRANADOS: *Andaluza etc.*; SARASATE: *Aires gitanos* ***.

López-Cobos secures sophisticated playing from the Suisse Romande Orchestra in *La oración del torero* and the three *Danzas fantásticas*, which are given an unexpected subtlety of detail. Of course the splendid Decca recording helps, colourful and brilliant, yet comparatively refined.

La oración del torero (version for string orchestra).

*** Chan. 9288. I Musici di Montréal, Turovsky – SHCHEDRIN: *Carmen ballet suite etc.* ***

The composer's string-orchestral version of the haunting *Oración del torero* is warmly and sensitively played and very well recorded here, and if the quartet version is even more subtle (see below) this makes an enjoyable foil for Shchedrin's brilliant arrangement of music from Bizet's *Carmen.*

Rapsodia sinfónica (arr. Halfter).

(B) *** Decca 448 243-2. De Larrocha, LPO, Frühbeck de Burgos – ALBENIZ: *Rapsodia española*; RODRIGO: *Concierto de Aranjuez etc.* ***

(N) (BB) *** Warner Apex 8573 89223-2 Heisser, Lausanne CO, López-Cobos – ALBENIZ: *Concierto fantástico; Rapsodia española*; FALLA: *Nights in the Gardens of Spain.* ***

Turina's *Rapsodia sinfónica* has been recorded by others, but in the hands of Alicia de Larrocha it is played with such éclat that it becomes memorable and thoroughly entertaining. Excellent, vivid sound.

The performance by Jean-François Heisser (with López-Cobos a brilliantly idiomatic partner) is also first class in every way, combining seductive poetic feeling, brilliant colouring and excitement. The digital recording is vividly balanced and the couplings are no less attractive.

CHAMBER MUSIC

La oración del torero.

(***) Testament mono SBT 1053. Hollywood Qt – CRESTON: *Quartet*; DEBUSSY: *Danses sacrées*; RAVEL: *Introduction & Allegro*; VILLA-LOBOS: *Quartet No. 6.* (***)

It is difficult to imagine Turina's famous piece being played with greater expressive eloquence or more perfect ensemble than by the incomparable Hollywood Quartet and it comes as part of a valuable and beautifully transferred anthology.

Piano Quartet in A min., Op. 67.

(N) *** Black Box BBX 1048. Lyric Piano Qt – STRAUSS: *Piano Quartet in C min., Op. 13.* ***

Turina's *Piano Quartet in A minor* comes from 1931, and though it is not great music it is far from negligible. It is well played and recorded here, and the coupling is equally rare.

GUITAR MUSIC

Fandanguillo, Op. 36; Homenaje a Tarréga; Ráfaga, Op. 53; Sevillana (Fantasia), Op. 29; Sonata, Op. 61.

(M) *** EMI CDM5 66574-2. Barrueco – ALBENIZ: *Suite española.* ***

It was Segovia who prompted Turina to write these vibrantly colourful pieces which are now central to any classical guitarist's repertoire. The *Fandanguillo* (its percussive thumping imitates the stamping feet of the zapateado) and *Sevillana* are vibrant with flamenco rhythms, while the spectacular and evocative *Ráfaga* translates as 'gust of wind'. They are played here with panache and glittering virtuosity. The *Sonata* requires a more subtle palette, and a sense of structure. Barrueco's account is masterly, seducing the ear in the gentle, seemingly improvisatory central *Andante* and then creating a flashing pulse for the chimerical finale. The recording is intimate, yet with a fine sense of presence.

TURNAGE, Mark-Anthony

(born 1960)

(i) *Blood on the Floor*; (ii) *Dispelling the Fears*; (iii) *Night Dances*; (iv) *Your Rockaby* (for saxophone and orchestra); (v) *Some Days.*

(N) (M) *** Decca 468 814-2 (2). (i) Ens. Modern, Rundel; (ii) Hardenberger, Wallace, Philh. O, Harding; (iii) Hulse, Tunstall, Constable, Wallace, L. Sinf., Knussen; (iv) Robertson, BBC SO, Andrew Davis; (v) Clarey, Chicago SO, Haitink.

Turnage is a natural communicator who can happily draw on the widest range of influences and produce music that, for all its modernity, is immediately enjoyable to more than the specialist. These five works offer an impressive survey of his progress from 1981, when he wrote *Night Dances*, to his most recent collaboration with the established jazz soloists of the Ensemble Modern, when he rescored a shortened version of *Dispelling the Fears* as the final movement of the ambitious nine-movement suite, *Blood on the Floor.*

Dispelling the Fears for two trumpets and orchestra is also included here in its longer original version, with the atmospheric passage, with its undoubled blues influence at the end providing a welcome resolution to what is otherwise a comparatively tough piece.

Throughout, jazz and popular music provide an underlying strand in Turnage's writing. *Night Dances* has a movement directly drawing on Miles Davis, and *Your Rockaby* is in effect a saxophone concerto, with a percussive background. Improvisatory, and powerfully expressive, kalaidoscopic in mood, it is based on a Beckett monologue centering on a woman in a rocking-chair hauntingly rethinking her life.

The poetry on which the mezzo-soprano song-cycle *Some Days* draws has a despondently black voice, reaching despair in its haunting closing 'I am absolutely alone forever'. It has an awkward vocal line which is powerfully sung by Cynthia Clarey, and there is a curiously ambivalent *Tango* as a central orchestral interlude, where Haitink, who directs the work confidently and fluently, seems slightly less rhythmically at home.

Throughout the collection there is no doubt about Turnage's genuine originality, but it is in the ambitious *Blood on the Floor* that his different sources of inspiration coalesce most readily into a satisfying whole, with the jazz influences made especially strong by the starry cast of players. The opening movement combines a kind of complex, vibrant minimalism with something approaching a jam session, and the following sections move from the melodic, bluesy *Junior Addict* through an extraordinary mélange of orchestral colours to a lively saxophone break, (*Needles*), an *Elegy for Andy* (the composer's brother) on the electric guitar, and a highly rhythmic interlude, (*Cut-up*), that draws boldly and unashamedly on Stravinsky's *Rite of Spring*.

A free-drumming sequence, ornamented instrumentally, then leads to the finale; but whether it was wise to use the earlier *concertante* trumpet piece here is open to question. Turnage obviously wanted to end with the remarkably atmospheric coda which resolves that work, where the two soloists ruminate freely and hauntingly together. But even in abbreviated form it takes the overall length of the suite to nearly 69 minutes. However, the quality of performance and recording is in no doubt.

Greek (opera; complete).

*** Argo 440 368-2. Hayes, Suart, Kimm, Helen Charnock, Greek Ens., Bernas.

Turnage's opera, *Greek*, is out to shock at all costs, beginning with a spoken introduction from the central character, Eddy, rich in vulgarities. This is the Oedipus myth freely adapted to the East End of London ('Eddy-pus' you might deduce). The colour and energy of Turnage's writing, violently dissonant with copious percussion, is brilliantly caught. The unprepared listener may resist at first, but Turnage with his echoes of popular music and his element of lyricism is a powerful communicator. What comes out less well than on stage is the humour, which seems heavy-handed, though the parody of a music-hall duet for Mum and Dad at the end of Act I has plenty of wit. Quentin Hayes has all the impact needed as the central rough diamond, with Richard Suart as Dad, Fiona Kimm as Wife and Helen Charnock as Mum all singing with bite and conviction, tackling not just those roles but incidentals too. On a single disc with libretto and notes, it can be strongly recommended to the adventurous.

CHAMBER MUSIC

An Invention on Solitude; Cortège for Chris; 2 Elegies Framing a Shout; 3 Farewells; 2 Memorials; Sleep On; True Life Stories: Tune for Toru.

(N) *** Black Box BBM 1065. Nash Ens. (members).

Anyone coming new to Turnage could not do better than start here, for all this music is intensely expressive and instantly communicative. Its overriding character is thoughtful and contemplative, although *An Invention of Solitude* is the exception, for while inspired by the Brahms *Clarinet Quintet*, the writing, for the same combination, 'fluctuates between stillness and violence'. The *Cortège for Chris* (Christopher Van Kempen, the Nash Ensemble's cellist who died in 1998) features both cello and clarinet, as well as a ruminative piano, while the *Two Memorials* are commemorated with haunting soliloquizing from the solo saxophone.

The *Three Farewells* are strangely obsessive: each has a hidden text, the second, *Music to Hear*, for viola and muted cello, a Shakespeare sonnet. The finale, *All will be well*, was written as a wedding piece, and the composer observes ironically 'the marriage didn't last'.

Not surprisingly some of the most peaceful and serene writing comes in *Sleep On*, for cello and piano, a triptych framed by a lovely *Berceuse*, and a restful *Lullaby*. The solo saxophone returns for the first of the *Two Elegies* and after being exuberantly interrupted by the *Shout* – a spiky and restlessly energetic boogie – the piano (with the saxophone) 'searches for and finds repose'.

The reflective closing *Tune for Tora* (a gentle piano piece) was written in response to the death of the Japanese composer Toru Takemitsu and readily finds the stillness the composer was searching for in his *Invention on Solitude*. Superbly responsive performances throughout and vividly real recording, within an attractively spacious acoustic.

TURNBULL, Percy (1902–76)

Piano music: Character Sketches Nos. 2–4 & 7; 3 Dances; Fantasy Suite; 3 Miniatures; Pasticcio on a Theme by Mozart; 2 Preludes; Sonatina; 3 Winter Pieces.

(N) *** Somm SOMMCD 1015. Jacobs.

Percy Turnbull, born in Newcastle-upon-Tyne, is yet another of the lost generation of English composers whose virtually forgotten music is now being rescued by the gramophone. His student contemporaries at the Royal College of Music included Tippett, Maconchy and Rubbra, yet at the time (the early 1920s) his talent shone out from among them.

He was a fine pianist and is a natural-born composer of piano music, his style a beguiling diffusion of many influences from Delius and John Ireland in England, to Fauré and Ravel among his French contemporaries. Yet his musical personality has its own individuality and his writing gives great refreshment and pleasure, his style notable for its gentle colouring, clarity and lightness of texture, without any hint of triviality.

The delightful *Pasticcio on a Theme of Mozart* displays his classical background, for each of the twelve variations absorbs the manner of another composer, from Bach to Brahms, Fauré and Ravel to Delius and Bartók. The *Sonatina* is entirely his own, moving from gentle English lyricism to a witty, syncopated finale. The other miniatures continually delight the ear and the *Three Winter Pieces* (1956), which were his last completed works for piano, are typical of his easy and innocent inventiveness at its most sophisticated and communicative. Throughout Peter Jacobs is an admirable and persuasive advocate and he is beautifully recorded. Well worth exploring.

TVEITT, Geirr (1908–81)

Piano Concertos Nos 1 in F, Op. 1; 5, Op. 156.

(N) (BB) *** Naxos 8.555077. Gimse, RSNO, Engeset.

Geirr Tveitt (pronounced with a soft 'G' and surname as in 'Tate') studied in Paris with Honegger, Florent Schmitt and Villa Lobos and was almost as prolific as the latter of those three. There are six piano concertos, thirty-two piano sonatas, and numerous orchestral suites. Much of his output, however, is lost and then the rest (almost 80 per cent) was destroyed in a fire which devastated his farmhouse, but thanks to the fact that he gave copies of various autographs to friends, works thought lost are still coming to light. He was obviously an accomplished pianist as, when he gave the first performance of the *Fifth Piano Concerto* in 1954 in Paris under Jean Martinon, he also played the *B flat minor Concerto* of Tchaikovsky and Brahms's *D minor Concerto*! Håvard Gimse takes account of some of the alternative readings Tveitt himself made in taped performances. The *First Piano Concerto* is a student work from his Leipzig days and far from negligible. The idiom is post-romantic with a strong element of the Hardanger folk music that inspired Grieg in his Op. 73 *Slåtter*. Håvard Gimse is an artist of quality and well supported by the Royal Scottish National Orchestra under Bjarte Engeset.

Prillar, Op. 8 (completed Jon Øivind Ness); *Solgud-Symfonien (The Sun God Symphony), Op. 81* (re-created by Kaare Dyvyk Husby).

(N) **(*) BIS CD 1027. Stavanger SO, Ole Kristian Ruud.

Both pieces come from the thirties and the *Sun God Symphony*, originally part of a ballet, *Baldur's Dreams*, has been restored thanks to the existence of a piano score and two recordings, one from 1938 and the other of a revision from 1958. It is much indebted to folksong and brilliantly scored. There are some attractive ideas even if the middle movement, *The Gods Forget the Mistletoe*, goes on too long.

Prillar refers to the Norwegian folk instrument, the *Prillarhorn*, and is very much in his post-Grieg nationalist vein. The second movement is distinctly Gallic and the piece was actually given in Paris in 1938 by the Orchestre National under Manuel Rosenthal. Decent performances though the Stavanger strings are a bit thin and a good (if not characteristically spectacular) BIS recording.

TYE, Christopher (c. 1505–c. 1572)

Complete instrumental music: *Amavit a 5; Christus Resurgens a 5; Dum Transisset a 5* (4 versions); *In Nomines a 4, a 5, a 6* (21 settings); *Lawdes Deo a 5; Sit fast a 3.*

(N) (M) **(*) Astrée ES 9939. Hespèrion XX, Savall.

Tye is associated as a vocal composer with Ely Cathedral and the Chapel Royal, but his consort music is unjustly neglected. The present collection includes all of his surviving instrumental pieces. Virtually all the music is slow and expressive; many of the *In nomine* pieces have biblical allusions in their simple titles. The performances here make a very strong impression; the viol timbre unexpectedly full-bodied. Indeed, the playing of Hespèrion XX has been criticized for being too rich in timbre for the period. We have no quarrel with the sound, but would have liked greater dynamic contrast in the playing. Excellent recording.

Mass: Euge bone (in 6 parts).

(M) ** EMI (ADD) CDM5 65211-2. King's College, Cambridge, Ch., Ledger – BYRD: *Mass for 5 voices*; TALLIS: *Mass: Puer natus est nobis*. ***

Euge bone; Kyrie: Orbis factor; Motets: *Miserere mei, Deus; Omnes gentes, plaudite minibus; Peccavimus cum patribus nostris; Quaesumus omnipotens Deus.*

(N) (B) ** Hyp. Helios CDH 55079. Winchester Cathedral Ch., Hill.

Masses *Euge bone; Peterhouse; Western Wind.*

(M) ** ASV CDGAU 190 (2). Ely Cathedral Ch., Trepte.

Christopher Tye spent most of his musical life in Cambridge and Ely and became master of the chorus and organist at Ely Cathedral in 1543; he retired to take holy orders in 1560 but remained living near Ely. So the soaring acoustics of Ely Cathedral and performances by its present-day choir could not be more apt for his three greatest masses, of which the large-scale *Euge bone* is the most splendid. The passionate singing on ASV is fully worthy, the choral sound glorious. With a playing time of 83 minutes, the three works would not fit onto a single CD, but the two discs are offered for the price of one.

Christopher Tye's *Mass for Six Voices* is one of the glories of early Tudor music, amazingly rich and complex. This fine (1980) EMI recording – attractively coupled with Byrd's masterpiece and the wonderfully reconstructed Tallis work – is well balanced between clarity and atmosphere, and the quality of the singing is a fine tribute to Ledger's work with this unique choir.

The performance from the splendid Winchester Cathedral Choir under David Hill is no less eloquent; the contrast between the *Gloria*, pressed on ardently, and the serene *Sanctus* is particularly telling. Moreover the four accompanying motets are also very fine, especially the exuberant *Omnes gentes* (a setting of Psalm 46 from the Vulgate), and the extended and very beautiful supplication, *Peccavimus cum patribus nostris*, which soars up to the heavens. Fine atmospheric recording makes this bargain reissue particularly tempting.

URBANNER, Erich (born 1936)

String Quartet No. 3.

(M) ** Teldec (ADD) 3984 21967-2. Alban Berg Qt – BERG: *Lyric Suite* etc.; WEBERN: *6 Bagatelles* etc. ***

Urbanner's avant-garde *Third Quartet* is expertly played, but its single-movement form, Schoenbergian in ancestry, does not yield music of real memorability. The Berg and Webern couplings are what make this finely recorded reissue a desirable acquisition.

USTVOLSKAYA, Galina (born 1919)

(i) *Piano Concerto* (for piano, string orchestra and timpani); (ii; iii) *Grand Duet* (for cello and piano); (iv) *Octet* (for 2 oboes, 4 violins, timpani and piano); (iii) *Piano Sonata No. 3.*

(M) ** BMG Melodiya (ADD) 74321 49956-2. (i) Serebryakov, Leningrad State Philharmonic Soc. CO; (ii) Stolpner; (iii) Malov; (iv) Kosoyan, Chinakov & Ens.

Galina Ustvolskaya was first a pupil of Shostakovich at the Leningrad Conservatoire and then became his assistant until the Zhdanov decree resulted in their dismissal along with Shebalin and others. The *Piano Concerto* comes from 1946, the period of her studies with Shostakovich, whose imprint it bears; and this 1970 performance by Pavel Serebryakov and the Leningrad Chamber Orchestra was its première. The *Octet*, a strong piece with some of the heiratic feeling of Stravinsky, was composed in 1949–50 but again not pre-mièred until the 1970s. There are six piano sonatas, composed between 1947 and 1988, and the *Third*, from 1952, has a spare, uncompromising angularity that is extraordinarily radical for the early 1950s, astonishingly so for the Soviet Union. The *Cello Duet* was composed in the 1960s for Rostropovich. For many it will be a tough nut to crack, but there is no doubt that, like so much of the music of this reclusive figure, it springs from a genuine vision. An interesting and worthwhile issue, though (with the exception of the *Cello Duet*) the recordings come from the 1970s and are not top-drawer.

VACHON, Pierre (1731–1803)

String Quartets, Op. 5/2; Op. 7/2.

*** ASV CDGAU 151. Rasumovsky Qt – JADIN: *Quartets.* ***

Although none of the works on this disc are masterpieces, the music provides us with an interesting and enjoyable sampler of the French school of quartet writing at the end of the eighteenth century. Vachon, born in Arles, was a frequent visitor to London, playing in his own concertos at the Haymarket Theatre. He wrote his quartets in a *galant* style which the French called the *quatuor concertant ou dialogué*. Op. 5 and Op. 7 were both published in London during the composer's first visit, at the beginning of the 1770s. The performances here are polished and well recorded. Enjoyable in an innocuous way.

VAINBERG, Moishei (1919–96)

Chamber Symphonies Nos. 1, Op. 145; 4, Op. 153

**(*) Olympia OCD 651. Umeå SO, Svedlund.

The chamber symphonies come from the last decade of Vainberg's life. The opening movement of the *First* is a pastoral in character, closer in feeling to a divertimento or sinfonietta than a real symphony. The *Fourth* is a dark, bleak score that is as unremitting as late Shostakovich, and strongly valedictory in feeling. A haunting piece, music of real sub-

stance and well worth investigating. The Swedish orchestra play well and are decently recorded.

(i; ii) *Violin Concerto in G min., Op. 67.* (iii) *Rhapsody on Moldavian Themes, Op. 47/1;* (ii) *Symphony No. 4 in A min., Op. 61.*

**(*) Olympia (ADD) OCD 622. (i) Kogan, (ii) Moscow PO, Kondrashin; (iii) USSR Ac. SO, Svetlanov.

The *Fourth Symphony* is an inventive and inspiring work with occasional reminders of Hindemith and Mahler. It is highly intelligent music, invigorating, with a powerful sense of inevitability and momentum – and touches of humour too. The *Violin Concerto* was championed by Kogan and much admired by Shostakovich, whose spiritual kinship the work seems to record. It is one of the finest Russian concertos of the 1960s, and Kogan plays it wonderfully. The two performances appeared on the HMV Melodiya label in the early 1970s. Vainberg's mother came from Kishinyov in Moldavia, which may account for his choice of the *Rhapsody on Moldavian Themes*, which is much a earlier piece (1949). In addition to the orchestral version, it exists in versions for violin and piano, and violin and orchestra, and was in David Oistrakh's repertoire. These performances are from the 1960s, save for the *Rhapsody* (1974), and make an ideal introduction to this interesting composer.

The Golden Key (ballet), *Op. 55: Suites Nos. 1–3; Suite 4:* excerpts.

*** Olympia (ADD) OCD 473. Bolshoi Theatre O, Ermler.

The Golden Key is a full-length ballet dating from 1955, based on a story by Alexis Tolstoy. The scenario concerns a troupe of puppets with a Petrushka or Pierrot-like figure at the centre. This generous selection (not far short of 80 minutes) gives a good idea of the quality of Vainberg's invention and his skill in making telling character-studies. There is some arresting music here and it is well performed by Bolshoi forces under Mark Ermler, and decently recorded.

Symphonies Nos. (i) *6 in A min.;* (ii) *10 in A min.*

** Olympia mono/stereo OCD 471. (i) Moscow Ch. School Boys' Ch., Moscow PO, Kondrashin; (ii) Moscow CO, Barshai.

The *Sixth Symphony* is a dark and powerful work, more satisfying than the *Tenth* for strings, in which the invention does not fully sustain its length. Both works are nevertheless worth exploring and, though the recordings are analogue (the *Sixth*, only in mono), they are very acceptable. The performances under Kirill Kondrashin and Rudolf Barshai are persuasive and authoritative.

Symphonies Nos. (i) *7, Op. 81;* (ii) *12, Op. 114 (In memory of Dmitri Shostakovich).*

**(*) Olympia (ADD) OCD 472. (i) Moscow CO, Barshai; (ii) USSR TV & R. SO, M. Shostakovich.

The present issue couples the *Seventh Symphony*, written for the unusual combination of strings and harpsichord and which comes from the early 1960s, and the *Twelfth*, which takes 52 minutes and was written in 1976 after Shostakovich's death. This inventive music is much indebted to, but never wholly overshadowed by, Shostakovich. Both the recordings are analogue and come from 1967 and 1979 respectively, but they reproduce well.

Piano Sonatas Nos. 1, Op. 5; 2, Op. 8; 3, Op. 31; 17 Easy Pieces, Op. 34.

** Olympia OCD 595. McLachlan.

Piano Sonatas Nos. 4, Op. 56; 5, Op. 58; 6, Op. 73.

** Olympia OCD 596. McLachlan.

Vainberg's output was extensive (22 symphonies and some 17 string quartets) but he wrote very little for the piano. He was a good pianist himself and a duet partner of Shostakovich on occasion. The first two sonatas come from the early 1940s and are close in idiom to Prokofiev and Shostakovich. The *Third Sonata* and the *17 Easy Pieces* are both post-war (1946). The impressive *Fourth Sonata* (1955) enjoyed the advocacy of Gilels, who recorded it two years after its composition (he had also given the earlier sonatas in recital programmes). Its two successors are strong, well-wrought pieces, and the *Fifth* has an imposing well-argued *Passacaglia*, but after the *Sixth* (1960), Vainberg seems to have abandoned the medium. The enterprising Murray McLachlan's commitment to and belief in the present repertoire is never in doubt. He is recorded in Gothenburg – not in the Concert Hall unfortunately but the university's hall, and although the sound is satisfactory it is not as open or fresh. All the same, those whose appetite has been aroused by the *Fourth Symphony* or the late *Chamber Symphonies* will want to explore these for themselves. The notes by Per Skans are very informative

VALEN, Fartein (1887–1952)

(i) *Violin Concerto;* (ii) *Symphony No. 1;* (iii) *Le Cimetière marin, Op. 20;* (iv) *Nachtstücke; Ode to Solitude, Op. 35; Pastorale, Op. 11; Song Without Words.*

(N) *** Runegrammofon RCD 2013. (i) Tellefsen, Trondheim SO, Ruud; (ii) Bergen PO, Ceccato; (iii) Oslo PO, Caridis; (iv) Torgersen.

The Norwegian composer Fartein Valen enjoyed cult status for a few years after the Second World War, but interest has waned since his death in the early 1950s. He grew up in Madagascar, where his father was a missionary, and studied philology and languages before turning to music: as early as the 1920s he developed a kind of 12-note technique, but for much of his life he was something of an outsider in Norwegian music. At times there is a strong sense of nature and refinement of texture, as if he were a mildly atonal Delius; at others there is a feeling of claustrophobia, as if the fjords are shutting out light. After a time the ear tires of the concentration of activity above the stave.

The *Violin Concerto* is Valen's masterpiece; it is short and intense and like the Berg concerto an outpouring of grief on the death of a young person. It ends like the Berg by quoting a Bach chorale. Incidentally Valen was adamant that he had never heard the Berg. (Music did not travel easily in 1940, and Valen lived in a particularly isolated part of Norway.)

His own concerto is played marvellously here by Arve Tellefsen.

The longest work here is the *First Symphony*, which began life as a piano sonata but reached its definitive orchestral form two years later in 1939. The textures are fairly dense though the opening of the second movement is an exception: the pale luminous colouring is distinctly northern.

Le Cimetière marin is one of the better known of Valen's works and is highly evocative. All are given well-prepared and dedicated performances and eminently serviceable recordings made between 1972 and 1997. The presentation is impossibly pretentious. The CD label contains no information of any kind and appears to come from the Tate Modern: the front cover reads 'fartein valen – the eternal' (all lower case) and the backing slip gives in absolutely microscopic print, the titles of the works – again lower case, black on a darkish red. You need to consult the booklet for track information, which is all in funereal black. That apart, this anthology serves as a useful introduction to this intriguing composer.

VAŇHAL, Jan (1739–1813)

Double-Bass Concerto in D.

(N) *** Hyp. CDA 67179. Nwanoku, Swedish CO, Goodwin – DITTERSDORF: *Double-Bass Concertos Nos. 1 & 2.*

Vaňhal, an exact contemporary of Dittersdorf, was equally prompted to write concertos for the virtuoso double-bass player, Johann Matthias Sperger, himself a composer. This charming work makes an idea supplement to the two fine Dittersdorf works, with Chi-Chi Nwanoku making light of the problems presented by such a cumbersome solo instrument. First-rate sound.

(i) *Double Bassoon Concerto in F; Sinfonias: in A min.; F.*

**(*) BIS CD 288. (i) Wallin, Nilsson; Umeå Sinf., Saraste.

The best work here is the *Concerto,* an arresting and inventive piece, with the slow movement touching a deeper vein of feeling than anything else on the disc. The two *Sinfonias* are less musically developed but very interesting: the minuet of the *F major* has a *Sturm und Drang* feel to it: Vaňhal's symphonies may well have paved the way for Haydn at this period; they were certainly given by Haydn while Kapellmeister at the Esterhazy palace. The recording is good, as one has come to expect from this source, even if the acoustic is on the dry side. Very good playing by the Umeå ensemble.

Violin Concerto in B.

(B) *** Discover DICD 920265. Zenaty, Virtuosi di Praga, Oldrich Vlček – MYSLIVECEK: *Violin Concerto.* ***

Vaňhal was born in Bohemia, almost a generation before Mozart; he similarly wrote inventive, lively music, of which this violin concerto is an appealing example, with the central slow movement a nostalgic intermezzo. On this well-recorded bargain issue Ivan Zenaty with his clean, full tone proves an outstanding advocate, with the Virtuosi di Praga providing lively support on modern instruments. Excellent recording.

Symphonies in A, Bryan:A9; in C, Bryan:C3; in C, Bryan:C11; in D, Bryan:D17.

(BB) *** Naxos 8.554341. Esterházy Sinfonia, Grodd.

Among the many new discs of forgotten music by Mozart's contemporaries this Naxos issue stands out. These four compact symphonies are all winningly colourful and inventive, often bringing surprises that defy the conventions of the time. The Esterházy Sinfonia under Uwe Grodd give attractively lively performances with some stylish solo work, vividly recorded.

Symphonies in B flat, Bryan B flat 3; in D min., Bryan d2; in G, Bryan G11.

(N) (BB) *** Naxos 8.554138. City of L. Sinfonia, Watkinson.

The second disc in the Naxos Vaňhal series is hardly less impressive than the first. The *B flat Symphony* (from the early 1760s) has a lovely, graceful *Andante arioso* for strings alone that reminds the listener of both Haydn and Mozart, and the vigorous finale uses woodwind and horns in an almost concertante fashion. The *D minor Symphony* in only three movements, written a decade later, is scored for five horns, yet the main string theme of the first movement is quite haunting, while the central *Cantabile* is dominated by a beautiful oboe solo over pizzicati; the horns are often to the fore in the finale. The *G major* work (1775) has an endearingly gracious first movement, although horns are still prominent in the scoring. A flute is used to give added colour to the violins in the elegant *Andante* and the *Minuet* and *Trio* are equally engaging, followed by a finale which begins meekly but soon develops a quite powerful head of steam, sustained through to the coda. Excellent, polished performances from the City of London Sinfonia under Andrew Watkinson and very good recording.

Symphonies in A min.; C (Sinfonia comista); D min.; E min.; G min.

**(*) Teldec 0630 13141-2. Concerto Köln.

These works were composed during the 1760s and 1770s. This was the period of the so-called *Sturm und Drang* symphonies in a minor key with a keen, driving intensity, of which Haydn's *La passione* is a good example. These are works of vivid and lively invention which also embrace a wide diversity of approach. The *C major (Sinfonia comista)*, one of his later symphonies, differs from its companions in its richness of scoring and programmatic inspiration. The Concerto Köln play with spirit, enthusiasm and style, but the recording is too forwardly balanced so that the tuttis are at times a little rough.

Symphonies: in C min., Bryan Cm2; in D, Bryan D4; in G min., Bryan Gm2.

*** Chan. 9607. L. Mozart Players, Bamert.

The *G minor Symphony*, the second of Vaňhal's symphonies in that key, is an absolute delight, full of good ideas and comparable with the *Sturm und Drang* of Haydn's No. 39 or Mozart's No. 25 in the same key. The *C minor Symphony* (1770) is also a work of originality with an occasional foreshadowing of Beethoven. Matthias Bamert and the London Mozart Players give an excellent account of themselves, and are recorded with great clarity and warmth.

Oboe Quartets, Op. 7

(N) (B) **(*) Hyp. Helios CDH 55033. Francis, Tagore String Trio.

These six *Oboe Quartets* bubble along with tuneful amiability, with little of the *Sturm und Drang* writing we know from Vaňhal's stormy minor-keyed symphonies. The performances are eminently enjoyable rather than distinctive, and the recording is bright and vivid.

Missa pastoralis in G; Missa solemnis in C.

(N) (BB) *** Naxos 8.555080. Haines, Ainsworth, Pitkanen, Tower Voices, New Zealand Arcadia Ens.,Grodd.

Vaňhal's *Pastoral Mass* has a delightfully lyrical *cantabile* feeling, which gives the music a warmth and Arcadian simplicity that is very beguiling. Not all the solo contributions are absolutely secure, especially when two female voices are combined, but the choral response is very persuasive and the result is most rewarding. The *Missa solemnis* is rather more conventional, but Vaňhal's setting is still richly enjoyable with the *Bendictus* and *Agnus Dei* particularly lovely. And he always makes the most of his 'Amens'. The spacious recording adds to one's enjoyment, and any minor reservations are swept aside when the disc is so inexpensive.

VARÈSE, Edgar (1883–1965)

Tuning Up; Amériques (original version); *Arcana; Dance for Burgesses* (i) *Density 21.5. Déserts;* (ii) *Ecuatorial;* (iii; iv) *Un grand sommeil noir* (original version). (iii) *Un grand sommeil noir* (orch. Beaumont). *Hyperprism; Intégrales; Ionisation;* (v; vi) *Nocturnal. Octandre;* (v) *Offrandes; Poème électronique.*

✿ *** Decca 460 208-2 (2). Concg. O or ASKO Ens., Chailly; with (i) Zoon, (ii) Deas; (iii; iv) Delunsch, (iv) Kardoncuff; (v) Leonard; (vi) Prague Philharmonic Male Ch.

Varèse first came to public notice in the 1930s when Percy Scholes chose him to represent the last word in zany modernity in his 'Columbia History of Music', but his mockery backfired. *Octandre* (one movement then recorded) sounds as quirkily original now as it did then (it is played marvellously here). The witty opening *Tuning Up* sets the mood for writing which is ever ready to take its own course regardless of tradition, and set new musical paths. *Amériques*, which follows, is heard in its original (1921) version, lavishly scored, with reminiscences of music by others, not least the Stravinsky of *The Rite of Spring*. It makes fascinating listening. *Ionisation*, less ear-catching, stands as a historic pointer towards developments in percussion writing. *Poème électronique* originated at the 1958 Brussels World Fair, where it was played through more than 400 loudspeakers inside the Philips pavilion. The montage of familiar and electronic sounds (machine noises, sonorous bells, etc.) comes from the composer's own original four-track tape. But all the works here are sharply distinctive and show the composer as a true revolutionary, usually decades ahead of his time.

The vocal pieces are among the most fascinating aurally, not least *Ecuatorial*, a setting in Spanish with bass soloist of a Maya prayer, brightly coloured and sharp with brass, percussion, organ, piano and ondes martenot. *Un grand sommeil noir* is a rare surviving early song, lyrically Ravelian in feeling, heard here in both the original version with piano, and in an orchestration by Antony Beaumont. *Nocturnal*, Varèse's haunting last piece, was left unfinished. Completed by Professor Chou, it is as extravagant and uninhibited as ever, featuring male chorus and a solo soprano voice, used melodically to evoke a mysterious dream-world. All the performances here are superbly definitive and this set will be hard to surpass. The recording acoustic, too, is open, yet everything is clear.

(i) *Amériques; Arcana.* (ii) **Density 21.5; Intégrales; Ionisation;** (ii) *Octandre;* (iii) *Offrandes.*

(M) *** Sony ADD/Dig. SK 45844. (i) NYPO; (ii) Ens. InterContemporain, (iii) with Yakar; Boulez.

Boulez brings out the purposefulness of Varèse's writing, not least in the two big works for full orchestra, the early *Amériques* and *Arcana*, written for an enormous orchestra in the late 1920s. Those two works, here played by the New York Philharmonic, are not digitally recorded. The selection recorded more recently in digital sound covers his smaller but equally striking works for chamber ensembles of various kinds, with Rachel Yakar the excellent soprano soloist in *Offrandes*.

Arcana.

(M) *** RCA (ADD) 09026 63315-2 [id]. Chicago SO, Martinon – BARTOK: *The Miraculous Mandarin;* HINDEMITH: *Nobilissima visione.* ***

Arcana is a splendidly high-spirited work; it requires an enormous orchestra and is a good introduction to this composer who was admired by such contrasting figures as Debussy and Stravinsky. Excellent recording – not quite as stunning as some recent versions, but this High Performance CD is well worth considering, especially as Martinon conducts with such dash and virtuosity.

VAUGHAN WILLIAMS, Ralph
(1872–1958)

'*Portrait of Vaughan Williams*': (i–iii) *Oboe Concerto;* (i; ii) *Fantasia on Greensleeves; Fantasia on a Theme by Thomas Tallis; 5 Variants of Dives and Lazarus;* (iv) *The Lark Ascending. The Wasps Overture.* (v; vi) *Phantasy Quintet;* (v) *String Quartets Nos. 1–2.* (vii; viii; i) *Flos campi;* (vii) *Mass in G min.;* (vii; i) *O, clap your hands; The Old Hundredth Psalm Tune;* (viii; i; ix) *An Oxford Elegy.* (vii) *3 Shakespeare Songs.* Sacred and secular songs: *Blessed Son of God; Lord, Thou hast been our refuge; No sad thought his soul affright; O taste and see; Valiant for truth;* (vii; i) *Te Deum.*

(BB) *** Nim. NI 1754 (4). (i) English String O, (ii) Boughton; (iii) with Bourge; (iv) with Bochman; (v) Medici Qt; (vi) with

S. Rowland-Jones; (vii) Christ Church Cathedral Ch., Oxford, Darlington; (viii) with Best; (ix) with May (narrator).

This splendid super-budget Nimbus boxed set offers a wonderfully illuminating cross-section of Vaughan Williams's music, showing its consistent inspiration, and both its diversity and its linkages. The orchestral and concertante music included here is all very familiar, but is most sympathetically played under William Boughton (with sensitive soloists) and presented amply and atmospherically, and with a rich amplitude of string tone. The chamber music shows a more intimate side of the composer: the special atmosphere of these works, with moments of haunting delicacy, is warmly and idiomatically caught, but with no lack of concentration and intensity. The Medici players were recorded in The Maltings, which means a sympathetic ambience, but also that the microphones are rather close. The glorious sonorities of the unaccompanied *Mass in G minor*, with its double choir and four soloists, draw an immediate vocal parallel with the *Tallis Fantasia*. The *Mass* opens with a *Kyrie* which looks back to the Elizabethan era and beyond, and then blossoms polyphonically in the *Gloria* and swaying *Sanctus* before the beautiful closing *Agnus Dei*. The *Oxford Elegy* brings more fine music, but the narrative, confidently and clearly delivered here by Jack May, remains as intrusive as ever (its inclusion was not one of the composer's best ideas). With Roger Best a fine viola soloist, *Flos campi* is particularly successful, as are the *Te Deum* and the shorter unaccompanied choral songs, especially the three imaginative Shakespeare settings. All in all this is a cornucopia of musical joys, worth getting, even if you already have recordings of the better-known orchestral pieces.

(i) *Concerto accademico. Fantasia on Greensleeves; 5 Variants of Dives and Lazarus; 2 Hymn tune Preludes;* (i) *The Lark Ascending; Oboe Concerto. Old King Cole (ballet); The Poisoned Kiss: Overture; 49th Parallel: Prelude; Prelude on an Old Carol Tune; 2 Preludes on Welsh Hymn Tunes; The Running Set; Sea Songs: Quick march. Serenade to Music* (orchestral version); (ii) *5 Mystical Songs.*

(B) *** EMI CZS5 73986-2 (2). (i) Creswick; (ii) Roberts; E. N. Sinfonia Hickox.

This disc comprises the bulk of three LPs Richard Hickox made in the mid-1980s. It includes some rarities and occasional pieces written for particular events or projects, such as the *Prelude* to the film, *49th Parallel*. The ballet music for *Old King Cole* is lively and full of charm, as is the tuneful overture to the sadly neglected opera, *The Poisoned Kiss*. Bradley Creswick's account of the *Concerto accademico* is one of the finest available, with the complex mood of the *Adagio*, both ethereal and ecstatic, caught on the wing, and he seems equally at home in *The Lark Ascending*. Roger Wingfield is hardly less engaging in the *Oboe Concerto*, his timbre full of pastoral colour, while he displays a deliciously light touch in the finale. *Greensleeves* is taken spaciously, but Hickox brings out the breadth as well as the lyrical beauty of the melody. *Dives and Lazarus*, rich in sonority, and the two *Hymn-Tune Preludes* have their elegiac mood judged perfectly. The *Five Mystical Songs* are sensitively done, though Stephen Roberts displays a rather gritty vibrato. All in all, an excellent bargain collection, very well recorded. The *Serenade to Music*, however, loses a dimension in its orchestral version.

Concerto grosso for Strings; (i) *Concerto accademico for Violin;* (ii) *Oboe Concerto;* (iii) *Piano Concerto in C;* (iv) *Tuba Concerto. 2 Hymn-Tune Preludes;* (v) *The Lark Ascending. Partita for Double String Orchestra;* (vi) *Towards the Unknown Region.*

*** Chan. 9262/3. (i) Sillito; (ii) Theodore; (iii) Shelley; (iv) Harrild; (v) M. Davis; (vi) L. Symphony Ch.; LSO, Thomson.

Chandos offer here as a separate compendium the series of mostly concertante works that were used as fillers for Bryden Thomson's set of the *Symphonies*, and with generous measure and characteristically fine recording this pair of CDs is very attractive. With immaculate LSO string ensemble, the *Concerto grosso* under Thomson's persuasive direction shows how in glowing sound its easy, unforced inspiration brings it close to the world of the *Tallis Fantasia*. While many performances of the *Concerto accademico* make the composer's neo-classical manner sound like Stravinsky with an English accent, Thomson and Sillito find a rustic jollity in the outer movements very characteristic of Vaughan Williams. David Theodore's plangent tones in the *Oboe Concerto* effectively bring out the equivocal character of this highly original work, making it far more than just another pastoral piece. Howard Shelley addresses the neglected *Piano Concerto* with flair and brilliance, making light of the disconcerting cragginess of the piano writing and consistently bringing out both the wit and the underlying emotional power. The bluff good humour of the *Tuba Concerto* is beautifully caught in Patrick Harrild's rumbustious account and this outstanding tuba soloist plays with wit and panache. Michael Davis makes a rich-toned soloist in *The Lark Ascending*, presenting it as more than a pastoral evocation. The *Hymn-Tune Preludes* are unashamedly pastoral in tone; then the *Partita* finds the composer in more abrasive mood, less easily sympathetic. *Towards the Unknown Region* is the only relative disappointment – a setting of Whitman that antedates the *Sea Symphony*. The choral sound is beautiful, but this early work really needs tauter treatment.

(i) *Concerto grosso for Strings;* (i–ii) *Oboe Concerto;* (i) *English Folksongs Suite* (trans. Gordon Jacob); *Fantasia on Greensleeves* (arr. GREAVES); (iii) *Fantasia on a Theme by Thomas Tallis;* (i; iv) *The Lark Ascending;* (iii) *5 Variants of Dives and Lazarus; In the Fen Country; Norfolk Rhapsody No. 1;* (v) *Partita for Double String Orchestra;* (i; vi) *Romance for Harmonica, Strings & Piano.*

(B) **(*) Double Decca ADD/Dig. 460 357-2 (2). (i) ASMF, Marriner; (ii) Nicklin; (iii) New Queen's Hall O, Wordsworth; (iv) I. Brown; (v) LPO, Boult; (vi) Reilly.

This Double Decca offers a fascinating comparison in that the first disc offers modern-instrument recordings (from Marriner and his Academy) and the second a special kind of period-instrument performance, although it is Boult and the LPO who give us the *Partita*. With the ASMF, Celia Nicklin gives a most persuasive account of the elusive *Oboe Concerto* while the *Concerto grosso* is lively and polished. The atmospheric *Romance*, although not one of the composer's most inspired works, is still worth having, and the *Folksongs* could hardly be presented more breezily; *The Lark Ascending* is superbly balanced and refined, with Iona Brown an inspirational soloist. The performances on the second disc are given by the re-formed New Queen's Hall Orchestra playing instruments in use at the turn of the century. *Portamento* is featured in the string style but here it is applied very judiciously, and for the most part the ear notices the fuller, warmer sonority of the violins, the treble less brilliant in attack. In works like the *Tallis Fantasia* and *Dives and Lazarus* one can readily wallow in the richly refined textures, but Wordsworth's performance of *Tallis* misses the final degree of intensity at the climax, and the opening of *Dives and Lazarus* is also rather relaxed, even indulgent in relishing the sheer breadth of sonority achieved, though the closing pages are ethereally lovely. The performers are at their finest in the evocative opening of the *Norfolk Rhapsody*, while *In the Fen Country* has a fine idyllic ardour, with some very sensitive playing from wind and brass in the coda. The Wordsworth recording, made in Walthamstow Assembly Hall, is splendidly expansive and natural.

(i; ii) *Oboe Concerto;* (i; iii) *Tuba Concerto.* (iv) *Fantasia on Greensleeves; 5 Variants of Dives and Lazarus; Sinfonia antartica (No. 7); The Wasps: Overture.*

(M) (***) EMI mono CMS5 66543-2 (2). (i) LSO; with (ii) Rothwell; (iii) Catelinet; (iv) Hallé O, Barbirolli – ELGAR: *Cockaigne; Introduction & Allegro; Serenade* (***).

Vividly transferred, this double-disc collection brings together Barbirolli's superb readings of Vaughan Williams and Elgar from the early 1950s. Strong and warmly expressive, these performances reflect the quality of the Hallé in the early 1950s, with the LSO equally responsive in the concertos. Central to the collection is the première recording of the *Sinfonia antartica*, made only five months after Barbirolli had conducted the first performance in January 1953. The thrust and power have never been surpassed, and the clear, immediate recording brings out the originality of the orchestration. Evelyn Rothwell, Lady Barbirolli, plays the *Oboe Concerto* with heartfelt warmth and understanding, while the *Tuba Concerto* is superbly characterized, bluff in the outer movements, tender in the slow movement. With the coupled Elgar items, an outstanding reissue.

(i) *Oboe Concerto. English Folksongs Suite; Fantasia on Greensleeves; Fantasia on a Theme by Thomas Tallis; Partita for Double String Orchestra.*

(B) **(*) EMI CD-EMX 2179. (i) Small; RLPO, Handley.

The charmingly lyrical *Oboe Concerto* is given a delectable performance here by Jonathan Small, the flowing pastoralism of its first movement perfectly caught and the more demanding finale impressively handled by conductor and soloist alike. The rarer *Partita for Double String Orchestra* is also very well played and sonorously recorded. It is chiefly remembered for the *Intermezzo* headed 'Homage to Henry Hall', a unique tribute to the leader of a 1940s dance-band. Handley gives a rhapsodic account of the *Tallis Fantasia*, relaxing in its central section and introducing an accelerando in the climax. Ideally the recording needs a little more resonance, although it is rich-textured and truthful.

(i) Oboe Concerto. Fantasia on Greensleeves; Fantasia on a Theme of Thomas Tallis; 5 Variants of Dives and Lazarus; (ii) The Lark Ascending. The Wasps: Overture.

(M) *** Nim. NI 7013. (i) Bourgue; (ii) Bochmann; E. String O or SO, Boughton.

Opening with an exuberant account of *The Wasps Overture*, this is a very attractive and generous 70-minute collection of favourite Vaughan Williams orchestral pieces, most sympathetically played under William Boughton and presented atmospherically. The spacious acoustic of the Great Hall of Birmingham University ensures that the lyrical string-tune in the overture is properly expansive without robbing the piece of bite, and that both the deeply felt *Tallis Fantasia*, with its passionate climax, and *Dives and Lazarus* have a rich amplitude of string-sound. Michael Bochmann, the sympathetic soloist in *The Lark Ascending*, playing simply yet with persuasive lyrical freedom, is nicely integrated with the warm orchestral backing. More questionable is the *Oboe Concerto*, with the superb French soloist Maurice Bourgue balanced too close. Bourgue's playing, sharply rhythmical and with a rich, pastoral timbre, is ideally suited to the piece.

(i) Oboe Concerto. Fantasia on Greensleeves; (ii) The Lark Ascending.

(M) *** DG (ADD) 439 529-2. (i) Black; (ii) Zukerman, ECO, Barenboim – DELIUS: *Aquarelles* etc.; WALTON: *Henry V.* ***

Neil Black's creamy tone is ideally suited to Vaughan Williams's *Oboe Concerto* and he gives a wholly persuasive performance. Zukerman's account of *The Lark Ascending* is full of pastoral rapture – not always quite idiomatic but totally ravishing. The recordings, from the late 1970s, are warmly atmospheric in the digital remastering.

Piano Concerto in C.

*** Lyrita (ADD) SRCD 211. Shelley, RPO, Handley – FOULDS: *Dynamic Triptych.* ***

(M) *** EMI CD-EMX 2239. Lane, RLPO, Handley – DELIUS: *Piano Concerto;* FINZI: *Eclogue.* ***

This Lyrita CD offers the first recording of the *Concerto* in solo form. The wonder is that, though the solo piano writing is hardly pianistic, the very challenge to as fine an exponent as Shelley brings out an extra intensity to a highly individual work, compared with VW's two-piano arrangement. Despite the thick textures, there is lightheartedness in much of the writing, whether the urgently chattering *Toccata* or the *Alla tedesca* which emerges out of the toughly chromatic fugue of the finale. Howard Shelley has re-recorded the piece digitally for Chandos (see below), but that is coupled with the *Ninth Symphony*, and many may find the stimulating Foulds coupling on Lyrita even more enticing. The 1984 recording is very impressive in its remastered form.

Piers Lane defies the old idea of this as a grittily unpianistic work, giving it a powerful, refreshing reading, helped by fine playing from the RLPO under Handley, always a sympathetic Vaughan Williams interpreter. Though this hardly outshines Howard Shelley's Lyrita version, the apt and unusual coupling can be warmly recommended.

(i) Piano Concerto; Symphony No. 9 in E min.

*** Chan. 8941. (i) Shelley, LPO, Thomson.

The most strikingly original of the three movements of the *Piano Concerto* is the imaginative and inward-looking *Romanza*, which has some of the angularity of line one finds in *Flos campi*, while the finale presages the *Fourth Symphony*. The piece abounds in difficulties, which Howard Shelley addresses with flair and brilliance. He makes light of the disconcerting cragginess of the piano writing and consistently brings out both the wit and the underlying emotional power. Bryden Thomson conducts a powerful performance of the last of Vaughan Williams's symphonies. Though the playing may not be ideally incisive, it brings out an extra warmth of expression. Both performances are greatly helped by the richness and weight of the Chandos sound, warmly atmospheric but with ample detail and fine presence.

(i) Double Piano Concerto in C; (ii) Job (A Masque for Dancing).

(M) *** EMI (ADD) CDM5 67220-2. (i) Vronsky, Babin, LPO; (ii) LSO, Boult.

Sir Adrian Boult is the dedicatee of *Job*, and this 1970 LSO performance was his fourth and probably most successful recording of the score. The LSO plays superbly throughout and the recording has exceptional range and truthfulness, which is the more impressive on CD. The *Double Concerto* was created when Vaughan Williams decided that his solo concerto would be more effective with two pianos, and this new arrangement was first performed in 1946. It remains one of VW's less tractable works, with its characteristic first movement *Toccata*, but Vronsky and Babin are very persuasive, with the authoritative help of Boult and the LPO. The 1969 recording is very good, with the thick textures well handled by the engineers.

English Folksongs Suite; Fantasia on Greensleeves; In the Fen Country; (i) The Lark Ascending; Norfolk Rhapsody No. 1; (ii) Serenade to Music.

(M) *** EMI (ADD) CDM7 64022-2. LPO, LSO or New Philh. O, Boult; (i) with Bean; (ii) 16 soloists.

All the music here is beautifully performed and recorded. Hugh Bean understands the spirit of *The Lark Ascending* perfectly and his performance is wonderfully serene. The transfers are fresh and pleasing; in the lovely *Serenade* (which Boult does in the original version for 16 soloists) the voices are given greater presence.

English Folksongs Suite; Flourish for Wind Band; Toccata marziale.

*** Chan. 9697. Royal N. College of Music Wind O, Reynish – HOLST: *Hammersmith* etc. ***

Vaughan Williams's music for wind band is less inspired

than that of Holst, but the jaunty *English Folksongs Suite* certainly sounds more vivid in its original scoring than it does in the orchestral version. It could hardly be played more breezily than it is here, and the other two pieces also come off splendidly. Demonstration sound.

English Folksongs Suite; Toccata marziale.

(BB) *** ASV (ADD) CDQS 6021. L. Wind O, Wick – HOLST: *Military Band Suites* etc. ***

As in the Holst suites, the pace of these performances of the original scores is attractively zestful, and if the slow movement of the *English Folksongs Suite* could have been played more reflectively, the bounce of *Seventeen Come Sunday* is irresistible.

Fantasia on Greensleeves; (i) Fantasia on a Theme of Thomas Tallis.

⚫ (M) *** EMI (ADD) CDM5 67240-2 [567264]. Sinfonia of L.; (i) with Allegri Qt; Barbirolli – ELGAR: *Introduction & Allegro for Strings*, etc. *** ⚫

Fantasia on Greensleeves; Fantasia on a Theme of Tallis; (i) The Lark Ascending.

(BB) *** Virgin 2 x 1 VBD5 61763-2 (2). LCO, Warren-Green; (i) with Warren-Green (violin) – DVORAK: *Serenade for Strings*; ELGAR: *Introduction & Allegro; Serenade;* SUK: *Serenade;* TCHAIKOVSKY: *Serenade.* ***

(B) *** Sony (ADD) SBK 62645. (i) Phd. O, Ormandy; (ii) Druian; Cleveland Sinf., Lane – DELIUS: *Brigg Fair,* etc. ***

Barbirolli's inspirational performance of the *Tallis Fantasia* now rightly takes its place among EMI's 'Great Recordings of the Century'. His ardour combined with the magically quiet playing of the second orchestra is unforgettable. The recording has magnificent definition and sonority, achieving dramatic contrasts between the main orchestra and the distanced solo group, which sounds wonderfully ethereal.

Christopher Warren-Green and his London Chamber Orchestra give a radiant account of *The Lark Ascending*, in which Warren-Green makes a charismatic solo contribution, very free and soaring in its flight and with beautifully sustained true pianissimo playing at the opening and close. For the *Tallis Fantasia*, the second orchestra (2.2.2.2.1) contrasts with the main group (5.4.2.2.1) and here, though the effect is beautifully serene, Warren-Green does not quite match the ethereal, other-worldly pianissimo that made Barbirolli's reading unforgettable. The performance overall has great ardour and breadth, almost to match the coupled *Introduction & Allegro* of Elgar in its intensity. The recording, made at All Saints' Church, Petersham, has resonant warmth and atmosphere yet sharp definition. This now comes as part of one of the most desirable of all the Virgin 2 x 1 Doubles, offering a remarkably generous programme of string music, all very well played and recorded.

The excellent performances from 1963 on Sony demonstrate the special feeling American musicians can find for English music. In the *Tallis Fantasia* Ormandy (like Barbirolli) characteristically underlines the drama of a work that is often regarded as delicate and atmospheric. The recording of *The Lark Ascending* was made during the period when

Louis Lane was a colleague of George Szell at Cleveland and the orchestra was at the peak of its form. Rafael Druian is the intensely poetic violin soloist, producing the most delicate sustained pianissimos, even though the balance is close. The orchestral playing is both polished and characterful. The CD transfers have expanded the original sound most strikingly. With expressive Delius performances as coupling, this is one of the most desirable of Sony's 'Essential Classics'.

Fantasia on Greensleeves; Fantasia on a Theme of Thomas Tallis; 5 Variants of Dives and Lazarus; (i) Flos campi.

(M) *** Van. (ADD) 08.4053.71. (i) Peck, Utah University Ch.; Utah SO, Abravanel.

(i) Fantasia on Greensleeves; (ii) Fantasia on a Theme by Thomas Tallis; 5 Variants on Dives and Lazarus; In the Fen Country; (i; iii) The Lark Ascending; (ii) Norfolk Rhapsody No. 1.

*** Chan. 9775. (i) LSO; (ii) LPO; Thomson; (iii) with M. Davis.

On Vanguard *Greensleeves* is slow and gracious, and there are more passionate versions of the *Tallis Fantasia* available, but the important point is the way Abravanel catches the inner feeling of the music. Both here and in *Dives and Lazarus* the full strings create a gloriously rich sonority. Sally Peck, the violist, is placed with her colleagues rather than as a soloist in *Flos campi* (following the composer's expressed intention), yet her personality still emerges well. Abravanel, always a warm, energetic conductor, displays keen understanding, allowing the music to relax as it should in this evocation of the Song of Solomon, but never letting it drag either. The CD transfer is excellent, retaining the naturalness of the original recording.

It is good to have *In the Fen Country* and the *First Norfolk Rhapsody* in such beautiful modern digital sound and played so sympathetically. Indeed, Bryden Thomson is a most persuasive guide in all this repertoire, although in the *Tallis Fantasia* he is rather more concerned with sonority, beauty and contrasts of texture than with subtlety. Michael Davis makes a rich-toned soloist in *The Lark Ascending*, presenting it as more than a gentle pastoral invocation. Although these recordings are now nearly a decade old, the generous measure (79 minutes) almost compensates for the continued premium price.

Fantasia on Greensleeves; (i) The Lark Ascending.

(B) *** DG (ADD) 439 464-2. (i) Zukerman; ECO, Barenboim – BRITTEN: *Serenade;* DELIUS: *On Hearing the First Cuckoo in Spring* etc. ***

This DG Classikon bargain CD makes a most attractive anthology. Zukerman's account of *The Lark Ascending* has a uniquely rapturous pastoralism and it is beautifully played and recorded.

(i–ii) *Fantasia on Greensleeves;* (iii–iv) *2 Hymn-Tune Preludes;* Overtures: *The Poisoned Kiss;* (v; ii) *The Wasps:* Overture. (vi) *Romance for Harmonica & Orchestra;* (iii; iv) *The Running Set;* (iii; iv) *Sea Songs* (march); (iii; vii; viii) *Suite for Viola & Orchestra;* (ix) *6 Studies in English Folksong;* (iii; vii; viii; x) *Flos campi;* (xi) *Linden Lea;*

(xii) *The House of Life: Love-sight; Silent noon; Heart's haven.* **(ii; v)** *Serenade to Music.*

(B) **(*) Chan. 2-for-1 ADD/Dig. 2419 (2). (i) BBC PO;
(ii) Handley; (iii) Bournemouth Sinf.; (iv) Hurst; (v) LPO;
(vi) Reilly, ASMF, Marriner; (vii) Riddle; (viii) Del Mar;
(ix) Hilton, Swallow; (x) Bournemouth Sinf. Ch.;
(xi) Huddersfield Ch., Kay; (xii) Varcoe, City of L. Sinfonia,
Hickox.

A generally attractive, if rather bitty, anthology, including a fair proportion of lesser-known Vaughan Williams. Exceptionally well recorded and vividly impressive, Vernon Handley's readings of the *Wasps Overture*, the *Greensleeves Fantasia* and the *Serenade to Music* in its orchestral version are most sympathetically done. The *Overture* to the opera *The Poisoned Kiss* is merely a pot-pourri, but it is presented most persuasively here. *The Running Set* is an exhilarating fantasy on jig rhythms. Fine performances under George Hurst, who also includes the two very characteristic *Hymn-Tune Preludes*. The evocation of the Song of Solomon contained in *Flos campi* shows Vaughan Williams at his most rarefied and imaginative, while the *Suite for Viola and Orchestra* is lightweight but engagingly unpretentious music with its charming *Carol* and quirky *Polka mélancolique*. Frederick Riddle is an eloquent soloist, even if the playing is not always technically immaculate, and Norman Del Mar directs sympathetically. Tommy Reilly, with Marriner, gives a haunting account of the *Romance for Harmonica and Orchestra*, while the attractive arrangements for clarinet and piano of the *Folksong Studies* are also played most sensitively by Janet Hilton and Keith Swallow. Roger Varcoe is the generally sympathetic soloist in three of the songs from the Rossetti cycle, *The House of Life* (orchestrated by Maurice Johnson), of which the most famous is *Silent noon*. His vibrato is occasionally intrusive, but the warmth of Hickox's accompaniment is a considerable plus point. *Linden Lea* is heard in its choral arrangement, pleasingly sung a cappella by the Huddersfield Choral Society under Brian Kay.

Fantasia on Sussex Folk Tunes for Cello & Orchestra.

(N) (M) *** RCA (ADD) 74321 84112-2 (2). Julian Lloyd Webber, LPO, López-Cobos – BRUCH: *Kol Nidrei*; DELIUS: *Concerto; Serenade*; HOLST: *Invocation*; LALO: *Concerto*; RODRIGO: *Concierto como un divertimento.* *** (with Recital 'Celebration' ***)

The *Fantasia on Sussex Folk Tunes* was composed for Casals and comes from the same period as *Job* and the *Piano Concerto*. The piece has lain neglected since its first performance in 1930 and it proves something of a discovery. It is a highly appealing work and is most persuasively played here, making a further attractive novelty within this splendid RCA collection reissued to celebrate Julian Lloyd Webber's fiftieth birthday.

Fantasia on a Theme by Thomas Tallis.

(M) *** EMI (ADD) CDM5 66760-2. RPO, Stokowski – DVORAK: *String Serenade*; PURCELL: *Dido and Aeneas: Dido's Lament.* ***

✿ **(M) (***)** EMI mono CDM5 66601-2. Philh. O, Karajan –

BRITTEN: *Variations on a Theme of Frank Bridge* (***) ✿; STRAVINSKY: *Jeu de cartes.* (**)

(M) **(*) EMI CDM5 66761-2. City of L. Sinf., Hickox – ELGAR: *Introduction & Allegro for Strings* **(*); WALTON: *Sonata for Strings.* ***

Stokowski's care with tonal balance brings radiant antiphonal effects as the various string-groups are contrasted. Surprisingly, the performance is unusually straightforward; there is less variation of speed than is common and there is little *stringendo* at the approach to the main climax. Stokowski is comparatively serene, yet his restraint does not in any way interfere with the music's forward momentum. He conjures the ripest string playing from the RPO and some lovely, refined instrumental solos. Alas, this CD has been withdrawn just as we go to press.

Karajan's version of the *Tallis Fantasia*, coupled with Britten's *Variations on a Theme of Frank Bridge*, is one of the outstanding records of the 1950s, sounding as fresh and sonorous today as it did then. Sonically it is little short of amazing, and artistically it is no less impressive. The playing of the Philharmonia strings is superlative, and the *Tallis Fantasia* sounds both idiomatic and vivid, like a newly cleaned painting. But this CD is also deleted.

Although recorded in a church (St Augustine's, Kilburn) the comparatively close microphones bring a sound-picture less than ideally atmospheric for Richard Hickox's 1993 version of the *Tallis Fantasia*. Fine playing and no lack of ardour, but the Barbirolli and Warren-Green versions are more evocative, to say nothing of Karajan and Stokowski.

Fantasia on a Theme of Thomas Tallis; 5 Variants of Dives and Lazarus; In the Fen Country; Norfolk Rhapsody.

*** Chan. 8502. LPO, Thomson.

(i) *Fantasia on a Theme by Thomas Tallis; 5 Variants of Dives and Lazarus; Norfolk Rhapsody No. 1;* **(ii)** *In Windsor Forest;* **(i; iii)** *Toward the Unknown Region.*

(M) *** EMI (ADD) CDM5 65131-2. (i) CBSO;
(ii) Bournemouth Symphony Ch. & Sinf.; (iii) with CBSO Ch.; Del Mar.

Fantasia on a Theme by Thomas Tallis; 5 Variants of Dives and Lazarus; In the Fen Country; Norfolk Rhapsody No. 1 in E min.; Variations for Orchestra (orch. Jacob); *The Wasps Overture.*

**(*) Ph. 442 427-2. ASMF, Marriner.

Norman Del Mar's strong and deeply felt account of the *Tallis Fantasia* is given a splendid digital recording, with the second orchestral group creating radiant textures. The direct approach, however, lacks something in mystery, and not all of the ethereal resonance of this haunting work is conveyed. The early (1907) cantata, *Toward the Unknown Region*, set to words of Walt Whitman, and *In Windsor Forest*, which the composer adapted from his Falstaff opera, *Sir John in Love*, make a perfect coupling. Norman Del Mar directs warmly sympathetic performances, given excellent sound.

Bryden Thomson is a most persuasive guide in all this repertoire and more than holds his own with most of the opposition.

Opening with a bright and brisk account of *The Wasps*

Overture, this Marriner is valuable in including the rare *Variations*, written as a brass band test-piece in 1957 and skilfully orchestrated by Gordon Jacob. Not a masterpiece, but worth having on disc. The other works are very well played; but *Tallis*, though beautiful, lacks the last degree of ethereal intensity. Marriner makes up with the climax of *Dives and Lazarus*, which is richly expansive, and he and the ASMF are at their finest in the gentle, evocative opening and closing sections of the *First Norfolk Rhapsody*. *In the Fen Country* brings more fine playing and overall this is an enjoyable programme, if not showing these artists at their very finest. The recording too, though spacious, is good rather than outstanding.

Film music: *Coastal Command* (suite); *Elizabeth of England: Three Portraits*. *49th Parallel: Prelude*. *The Story of a Flemish Farm* (suite).

**(*) Marco 8.223665. RTE Concert O, Dublin, Penny.

Vaughan Williams's wartime film music was of the highest quality. The Powell/Pressburger movie *49th Parallel* (1941), made in the early years of the war, inspires a *Prelude* with a nostalgic patriotic feeling. *Coastal Command* (1942) was a dramatized documentary which centred on the romantic profiles of the Catalina flying-boats, resulting in warmly evocative music, with echoes from the composer's symphonic writing. The even more imaginative (1943) score for *The Story of a Flemish Farm* (a true story about personal sacrifice which enabled a wartime escape to England) brings similar resonances. The masterly evocation of *Dawn in the Barn* clearly anticipates the *Sixth Symphony*, while the haunting sequence, *The Dead Man's Kit*, evokes the *Sinfonia antartica*. *Elizabeth in England* (1955–7), another documentary, narrated by Alec Clunes, has its Elizabethan hey-nonny flavour, but there is a haunting *Poet* sequence which introduces a magically gentle tune, also used in the *Sea Symphony*. Finally comes a celebration of *The Queen*, not just regal but thoughtful in restrained nobility. Andrew Penny is a splendid advocate in performances eloquent in their mood-painting. The recording is bright and full, if rather two-dimensional.

Job (A Masque for Dancing); (i) *The Lark Ascending.*

(BB) *** Naxos 8.553955. E. N. Philh., Lloyd-Jones, (i) with Greed.

Job (A Masque for Dancing); The Wasps Overture.

(BB) (***) Belart mono 461 122-2. LPO, Boult.
*(**) Everest EVC 9006. LPO, Boult (with ARNOLD: *4 Scottish Dances*: cond. composer **(*)).

David Lloyd-Jones – at super-budget price on Naxos – upstages all competition. He gives a performance tingling with drama, yet with great delicacy. The opening scene is particularly atmospheric and the *Saraband of the Sons of God* brings a noble dignity, especially when it returns expansively on the full brass. There is much fine orchestral playing. The big climaxes bring a superb brass contribution, almost submerging the organ at the vision of Satan. The dance rhythms are caught superbly – bitingly so in *Satan's Dance of Triumph*, genially Holstian in the *Galliard of the Sons of the Morning*. The Epilogue is touchingly ethereal. The

recording, made in Leeds Town Hall, has an ideal spaciousness, yet combines vivid detail with glowing textures. For an encore the orchestral leader, David Greed, provides an exquisitely delicate portrayal of *The Lark Ascending*, with a beautifully sustained closing *pianissimo*.

Of Boult's four LP recordings of *Job*, this Belart/Decca mono version has great warmth and freshness. The mono recording sounds fuller and more atmospheric than some early digital stereo discs, and the same comment might apply to the delightful incidental music for *The Wasps*, with the lovely string-tune in the *Overture* warm and spacious and the delicious *March past of the kitchen utensils* piquant.

The Everest performance of *Job* under the work's dedicatee was Boult's second LP of Vaughan Williams's ballet. It is sensitive and spontaneous but, unusually for this label, the recording is made aggressive at climaxes because of the close microphoning of the brass, which sound strident, while the massed strings are somewhat tight, reflecting the problems of recording in the Royal Albert Hall. *The Wasps Overture* was done at Walthamstow and sounds full and unconfined. This outstanding performance sparkles, and has a very broad tempo for the beautiful secondary theme. Malcolm Arnold conducts his own *Scottish Dances* with élan and is especially persuasive in the third with its glorious picture of the Highland scenery, which produced one of the loveliest tunes the composer ever wrote. The recording is expansive; otherwise the brightly vivid sound is not quite as smooth as the best Everest reissues.

The Lark Ascending.

*** EMI CDC5 56413-2. Kennedy, CBSO, Rattle – ELGAR: *Violin Concerto*. ***

Kennedy provides a valuable and welcome fill-up to his fine remake of the Elgar *Concerto* in this spacious and inspirational account of Vaughan Williams's evocative piece, beautifully recorded.

SYMPHONIES

Symphonies Nos. 1–8; Partita for Double String Orchestra.

(BB) (***) Belart mono 461 442-2 (5). Baillie, Cameron, Ritchie, Gielgud, LPO Ch., LPO, Boult.

In some ways Boult's mono set of the Vaughan Williams *Symphonies* (No. 8 is in stereo) is unsurpassed, and the recording still sounds amazingly realistic, especially in the *Sea Symphony*, a demonstration LP in its day. The composer was present at the recording sessions and the orchestral playing was notable for its inspirational intensity. The five discs are handsomely packaged in a strong cardboard box with an engaging portrait of the young composer on the front. A set which is as indispensable as it is inexpensive. The discs are all available separately. Boult's first recording of No. 9 is on Everest (EVC 9001).

Symphonies Nos. 1–9.

**(*) Chan. 9087/91. LSO, Thomson (with Kenny, Rayner Cook in *No. 1*; Kenny in *No. 3*; Bott in *No. 7*; L. Symphony Ch. in *Nos. 1 & 7*).

Symphonies Nos. 1–9 (complete); Fantasia on Greensleeves; Fantasia on a Theme of Tallis; Norfolk Rhapsody No. 1; 5 Variants of Dives and Lazarus.

(M) **(*) RCA 09026 61460-2 (6). Philh. O, Slatkin.

Symphonies Nos. 1–9; (i) Flos campi; Serenade to Music.

(M) *** EMI Dig./ADD CD-BOXVW 1 (6). Soloists, Liverpool Philharmonic Ch., RLPO, Handley; (i) with Balmer.

Handley's set consists of the six individual CDs in a handsome blue slipcase, and it will especially suit those needing both economy and modern, digital sound; only the *Sinfonia Antartica* is analogue – and that is still a fine modern recording, offering also the orchestral version of the *Serenade to Music* as a fill-up. In all his Vaughan Williams recordings Handley shows a natural feeling for expressive rubato and is totally sympathetic. Many of his performances are first or near-first choices and No. 5 is outstanding in every way. This disc also includes a very successful account of *Flos campi*.

Leonard Slatkin, following in the footsteps of André Previn in the earlier VW cycle for RCA (now withdrawn), shows consistent sympathy for the idiom. Like the composer himself in his surviving recordings, Slatkin prefers speeds faster than usual, and that makes the central symphonies of the cycle less warmly expressive and less atmospheric than some rivals, but the earliest and, notably, the last symphonies find Slatkin at his finest. His achievement in this cycle is above all to demonstrate that the last three symphonies make a worthy conclusion, unconventionally but tellingly symphonic. Fine playing and generally full, atmospheric recording. The six CDs are offered for the price of four.

By omitting the various fillers, Chandos have fitted the nine Vaughan Williams symphonies on to five CDs; each work is offered without a break. However, Bryden Thomson's achievement is somewhat uneven through the cycle. In the *Sea Symphony* the chorus lacks the sharpest focus and the microphone is not kind to Brian Rayner Cook, the baritone soloist. In the *Pastoral Symphony* the orchestral sound is almost too tangible, losing some of the more gentle atmospheric feeling, and this applies also to the *Sinfonia Antartica*. Generally there is no lack of power, and the readings have both individuality and warmth as well as wide-ranging digital recording.

A Sea Symphony (No. 1).

(B) **(*) EMI CD-EMX 2142. Rodgers, Shimell, Liverpool PO Ch., RLPO, Handley.

(BB) (***) Belart mono 450 144-2. Baillie, Cameron, LPO Ch. & O, Boult.

*** EMI CDC7 49911-2. Lott, Summers, LPO Ch., LPO, Haitink.

(M) *** EMI CDM7 64016-2. Armstrong, Carol Case, LPO Ch., LPO, Boult.

Vernon Handley conducts a warmly idiomatic performance, which sustains relatively slow speeds masterfully. The reading is crowned by Handley's rapt account of the slow movement, *On the Beach at Night Alone*, as well as by the long duet in the finale, leading on through the exciting final ensemble, *Sail Forth*, to a deeply satisfying culmination in *O*

my Brave Soul! Joan Rodgers makes an outstandingly beautiful soprano soloist, with William Shimell drier-toned but expressive. The recording, full and warm, has an extreme dynamic range, placing the two soloists rather distantly.

As a performance, Boult's (early 1952) Decca mono recording with outstanding soloists and incisive and sympathetic singing from the LPO Choir has never been surpassed. This conveys the urgency as of a live performance, with the dramatic opening astonishiingly vivid and real in the vintage sound. Boult was at his most inspired. This Belart CD makes the very most of the master tape, and only the lack of body of the massed upper strings betrays the age of the original. The choral sound is full and well focused and the Kingsway Hall acoustic spacious and warm; the closing section, *Away O soul*, is particularly beautiful.

As in the rest of his Vaughan Williams series, Bernard Haitink takes what to traditional English ears may seem a very literal view, not idiomatic but strong and forthright. Speeds are almost all unusually spacious, making this (at well over 70 minutes) the slowest version on record; but Haitink sustains that expansiveness superbly. It is the nobility of the writing, rather than its emotional warmth, that is paramount. The recording is the fullest and weightiest yet given to this work, with the orchestra well defined in front of the chorus. Felicity Lott and Jonathan Summers are both excellent.

Boult's stereo version demonstrates his affectionate style, drawing consistently expressive but never sentimental phrasing from his singers and players. John Carol Case's baritone does not sound well on disc with his rather plaintive tone-colour, but his style is right, and Sheila Armstrong sings most beautifully. The set has been remastered with outstanding success.

(i) A Sea Symphony (No. 1); Symphony No. 6 in E min.; Fantasia on a Theme of Thomas Tallis; (ii) The Lark Ascending.

(N) (B) ** Teldec Ultima 8573 84070-2 (2). BBC SO, A. Davis; with (i) Roocroft, Hampson, BBC Ch.; (ii) Little.

Helped by clear, finely focused sound, Sir Andrew Davis conducts a performance of the *Sea Symphony* that can hardly be faulted on any detail whatever, but which fails quite to add up to the sum of its parts: it is a degree too literal. So you have two of the finest international soloists available who yet convey too little of the mystery behind these settings of Walt Whitman, and even with the bright clean choral sound one is less involved than with the finest rival versions.

The reading of the *Sixth* is taut and urgent, but with emotions kept under firm control, and Teldec's wide-ranging sound, setting the orchestra at a slight distance, blunts the symphony's impact in the first three movements, but then works beautifully on the chill of the hushed pianissimo meditation of the finale.

The two shorter works which come as supplement are given more warmly expressive, indeed beautiful, performances, with Tasmin Little an immaculate soloist in *The Lark Ascending*. But overall this generous Ultima reissue is disappointing.

A London Symphony (No. 2) (original 1913 version).

(N) ✪ *** Chan. 9902. LSO, Hickox (with BUTTERWORTH: *The Banks of Green Willow.* (***)

A London Symphony was Vaughan Williams's own favourite among his symphonies (and I. M.'s too). It was the one he revised most often – first between 1918 and 1920, and later even more radically in the 1930s, with the definitive score finally published in 1936. What this revelatory recording demonstrates is that the 20 minutes or so of music which was excised includes many passages which represent the composer at his most magically poetic. There is even a case for saying that in an age which now thrives on expansive symphonies – the examples of Bruckner, Mahler and Shostakovich always before us – the original offers the richer experience. Vaughan Williams undoubtedly made the work structurally tauter, but discursiveness in a symphony is no longer regarded as a necessary fault.

No one could make the case for this 1913 version more persuasively than Hickox. He draws ravishing sounds throughout from the LSO, with an unerring feeling for idiomatic rubato and a powerful control of massive dynamic contrasts. In this first version the first movement is no different, but each of the other movements here includes substantial sections completely eliminated later, some of them echoing the Ravel of *Daphnis and Chloé*, including an extended one in the Scherzo. The sumptuous Chandos sound, with an extraordinarily wide dynamic range, adds to the impact of the performance, which comes with a short but valuable and beautifully played fill-up.

A London Symphony (No. 2) (1920 version).

(***) Biddulph mono WHL 016. Cincinnati SO, Goossens – WALTON: *Violin Concerto* (***) (with Concert (***)).

This is the only recording ever made of the 1920 version of Vaughan Williams's *London Symphony*. That involves three minutes of intensely poetic music, later excised in RVW's definitive 1936 edition. The sessions immediately followed the first recording of the Walton *Violin Concerto* with Heifetz in 1941 in which Eugene Goossens and the Cincinnati orchestra provided the accompaniment. The coupling (together with other British music) is among the most valuable of all the reissues in the Biddulph catalogue, with excellent CD transfers.

A London Symphony (No. 2).

(M) **(*) EMI (ADD) CDM5 65109-2. Hallé O, Barbirolli – IRELAND: *London Overture.* ***

A London Symphony; Fantasia on a Theme of Thomas Tallis.

(M) *** EMI (ADD) CDM7 64017-2. LPO, Boult.
*** EMI (ADD) CDC7 64017-2. LPO, Haitink.

A London Symphony (No. 2); Fantasia on a Theme of Thomas Tallis; (i) Serenade to Music.

(N)**(*) Decca 467 047-2. LPO, Norrington; (i) with Lott, Milne Mannion, Kenny, Murray, Montague, Della Jones, Wyn-Rogers, Rolfe-Johnson, Mark Ainsley, Spence, Robinson, Roberts, Maltman, George, Lloyd.

A London Symphony; Partita for Double String Orchestra.

(BB) *** Belart mono/stereo 461 008-2. LPO, Boult.

A London Symphony; The Wasps: Overture.

(BB) *** Naxos 8.550734. Bournemouth SO, Bakels.

The Naxos version of Vaughan Williams's *London Symphony*, coupled with the *Wasps Overture*, is powerful and dedicated. Kees Bakels draws ravishing sounds from the Bournemouth Symphony Orchestra, notably the strings, with the Scherzo cleanly pointed and the slow movement both warm-hearted and refined, and with pianissimos that have you catching the breath. The problem is the extreme range of dynamic in the recording. A thrilling experience none the less.

Norrington's new recording of the *London Symphony* is the finest for some years, helped by Decca's superbly wide-ranging recording. Indeed, the wide dynamic range might offer domestic problems. The opening *pianopianissimo* is superbly sustained, so that when the main theme of the allegro bursts in it makes an overwhelmingly forceful contrast. Norrington's reading of the score is most perceptively detailed, so that the composer's many picaresque touches of local colour emerge with exceptional vividness, from the errand boy's folksy secondary melody and the quotations of street cries, to the lively cockney 'accordion' dance sequence in the scherzo. The slow movement brings both a haunting atmosphere and a climax of great power, even if it is not as richly expansive as Barbirolli's famous version. After the powerful march sequence of the finale, the epilogue returns us to the misty Turneresque evocation of the opening, which is again most tellingly caught.

The famous *Tallis Fantasia*, however, is beautifully played but is surprisingly lacking in passion. Indeed, it is made to sound more like a concerto grosso based on an Elizabethan theme. The cast of the *Serenade to Music* is star-studded, and Lott leads confidently, but she does not erase memories of Isobel Baillie in that famous first recording.

The sound is spacious on Boult's splendid 1970 version and the orchestra produces lovely sounds in deeply committed playing. With Boult's noble, gravely intense account of the *Tallis Fantasia* offered as a coupling, this remains a very viable option. The CD transfer is very successful indeed.

In jaunty themes, Haitink's straight manner at times brings an unexpected Stravinskian quality, and his expansively serene handling of the lovely melodies of the slow movement brings elegiac nobility rather than romantic warmth. In the *Tallis Fantasia*, the straight rhythmic manners make the result sensitively unidiomatic too but very powerful in its monumental directness. The recording has spectacular range.

In his 1968 EMI recording of the *London Symphony*, Barbirolli did not quite achieve the intensity of his earlier, Pye version, choosing a more relaxed and spacious approach. In many places this brings a feeling of added authority, as at the end of the first movement where the threads are drawn together with striking breadth. The slow movement gains from the fuller recording but has less passion, while the Scherzo, taken slowly, is more controversial, though the finale is powerful, with the Epilogue finely graduated in its dynamics. An impressive account.

Boult's 1952 mono recording of the *London Symphony* has

great atmosphere and intensity. His later, EMI performance is warmer, but the voltage of this first LP version is very compelling, bringing the feeling of a live performance. The mono sound is spacious, but the violins sound very thin above the stave, and the remastering has not improved that. The *Partita* was recorded in the earliest days of stereo in 1956. It is not one of the composer's most striking works, but it is well played and the string sound is very agreeable.

(i) *A London Symphony (No. 2); Fantasia on Greensleeves; The Wasps Overture;* (ii) *Serenade to Music.*

(BB) (***) Dutton Lab. mono CDBP 9707. (i) Queen's Hall O;
(ii) Baillie, Allen, Suddaby, Turner, Balfour, Desmond, Brunskill, Jarred, Nash, Widdop, Jones, Titterton, Henderson, Easton, Williams, Allin, BBC SO; Wood.

The historic Decca recording of Vaughan Williams's *London Symphony*, with the specially assembled group of musicians designated as the 'Queen's Hall Orchestra', conducted by Sir Henry Wood, brings a most striking discrepancy of pace with modern performances. The first movement alone takes over three minutes less than in most latter-day recordings. The not-so-slow introduction may lack mystery but there has never been a more passionate account of the work than this on record, and even with limited dynamic range – no true pianissimo is caught – the hushed intensity of the slow movement is tellingly conveyed. The *Symphony* comes coupled with shorter Vaughan Williams works, *The Wasps Overture, Greensleeves* and, best of all, the original (1938) Columbia recording of the *Serenade to Music*, with the 16 soloists specified in the score, a stellar group. The gently soaring phrase 'of sweet harmony' has never sounded so sweetly angelic as when sung here by Isobel Baillie. The Dutton Laboratory transfers are outstandingly true to the originals.

(i) *A Pastoral Symphony (No. 3); Symphony No. 4 in F min.*

(M) *** EMI CD-EMX 2192. (i) Barlow; RLPO, Handley.

Although Vernon Handley's speeds are relatively fast – as those of his mentor, Boult, tended to be – he has the benefit of refined modern digital recording to help bring out the element of mystery in the *Pastoral Symphony*. Handley's approach to the *Fourth Symphony* is relatively light and not at all violent, but makes a good case for his alternative approach.

(i) *A Pastoral Symphony (No. 3);* (ii) *Symphony No. 5 in D.*

(M) *** EMI (ADD) CDM7 64018-2. (i) M. Price, New Philh. O; (ii) LPO; Boult.
(BB) (***) Belart mono 461 118-2. (i) Ritchie; LPO, Boult.
** Decca 458 357-2. LPO, Norrington.

On EMI, in the *Pastoral Symphony* Boult is not entirely successful in controlling the tension of the short but elusive first movement, although it is beautifully played. The opening of the *Lento moderato*, however, is very fine, and its close is sustained with a perfect blend of restraint and intensity. In a generous coupling Boult gives a loving and gentle performance of No. 5, easier and more flowing than

most rivals', and some may prefer it for that reason, but the emotional involvement is a degree less intense, particularly in the slow movement. Both recordings have been very successfully remastered.

It is good to have Boult's earlier, Kingsway Hall recordings back in the catalogue. They were made in 1952/3 with the composer present; although some allowances have to be made for the lack of amplitude in the upper string climaxes, the CD transfer is impressively full and the recording luminous. The translucent textures Boult creates in the *Pastoral Symphony*, with its ethereal opening, and his delicacy later are balanced by his intensity in the *Fifth*, where the climax of the first movement has wonderful breadth and passion. The LPO of the time play with great sympathy and warmth.

Norrington takes a cool view of these two symphonies. Textures are exceptionally clean, the playing of the LPO most refined, but Norrington's preference for a very steady beat, rarely allowing himself much rubato even at climaxes, prevents these performances from having full emotional impact, a degree of restraint that might be approved by those who prefer an objective view. But there is a dimension missing here, especially in No. 5. Refined Decca sound to match.

A Pastoral Symphony (No. 3); Symphony No. 6 in E min.

(BB) **(*) Naxos 8.550733. Bournemouth SO, Bakels.

Kees Bakels's serenely expressive account of the *Pastoral* has moments of drama to heighten its quiet, atmospheric intensity. There is much lovely orchestral playing, with the soloists in the Bournemouth Symphony Orchestra very sympathetic to the music's subtle, lyrical resonance. The account of the *Sixth* does not catch the degree of underlying menace in the *Lento* second movement, but the performance has plenty of life and vigour, and Bakels sustains the epilogue with an ethereal, glowing pianissimo. First-rate Naxos recording in both works.

Symphony No. 4 in F min..

(N) (***) Cala mono CACD 0528. NBC SO, Stokowski –
ANTHEIL: *Symphony No. 4* (***); BUTTERWORTH: *Shropshire Lad* (**).

(i–ii) *Symphony No. 4 in F min.;* (ii–iv) *Oboe Concerto;* (iii; v) *Fantasia on a Theme of Thomas Tallis; The Wasps: Overture.*

(M) **(*) EMI (ADD) CDM5 66539-2. (i) RPO; (ii) Berglund; (iii) Bournemouth SO; (iv) with Williams; (v) Silvestri.

Symphony No. 4; Fantasia on Greensleeves; Fantasia on a Theme by Thomas Tallis; (i) *Serenade to Music.*

(M) **(*) Sony (ADD) SMK 47638. NYPO, Bernstein, (i) with vocal soloists.

The only time that Stokowski ever conducted Vaughan Williams's provocative *Fourth Symphony* was in March 1943, when this high-powered red-blooded reading was recorded, the first to be made outside Britain. The violently dissonant opening is broad and emphatic, leading to a warm, passionate account of the lyrical second subject, and throughout the performance one marvels that Stokowski could draw sounds from the NBC Orchestra so different from those the same players produced under Toscanini. The chill and poignancy of the slow movement and the bluff humour of the *Scherzo*, each strongly characterized, lead to a comparably positive account of the finale, making one regret that Stokowski never returned to this work. The sound, limited in range, is yet satisfyingly full-bodied.

Bernstein's account of the *Fourth Symphony* is strangely impressive. His first movement is slower than usual but very well controlled; he captures the flavour and intensity of the score as well as the brooding quality of the slow movement. The New York orchestra plays extremely well and the 1965 recording is full and vivid. The *Serenade to Music* is less successful: the solo singers are too forwardly balanced and the sound in general is unimpressive, though the performance itself is not without interest. The two *Fantasias* are expansively done (American performances of *Greensleeves* are always slow), and the *Tallis* certainly has plenty of tension.

Berglund directs a rugged, purposeful account of the *Fourth Symphony*, one which refuses to relax even in the more lyrical passages. Berglund follows the composer himself in preferring an unusually fast speed in the first movement, while the second movement is superbly sustained at a very slow tempo. Any lack of polish in the playing of the RPO must be balanced against its extra bite. Silvestri's individual reading of the *Tallis Fantasia* is brilliant and not expansive, with keen tension in the opening and closing pages. His account of *The Wasps Overture* emphasizes the brio, with the great lyrical melody not allowed to interfere with the forward momentum. The vivacity of the playing is well projected in vivid recording. The *Oboe Concerto*, beautifully played by the Bournemouth orchestra's principal in the mid-1970s, makes a charming pastoral interlude between the two major works.

Symphonies Nos. 4; 5 in D; 9 in E min.; Job.

(N) (B) ** Teldec Ultima 8573 87798-2 (2). BBC SO, A. Davis.

Though Andrew Davis draws beautiful, refined playing from the BBC Orchestra in each of these symphonies, there is a lack of dramatic tension which – particularly in the violent No. 4 – prevents the performance from catching fire. In No. 9 the setting back of the orchestra again means that some of the impact is lost, especially in the nightmarish *Scherzo*, and overall as in the earlier symphonies, although the BBC Symphony Orchestra plays splendidly, the performance, though finely shaped, lacks the ultimate degree of concentration. Even allowing for the backward balance, *Job* is very successful, and no one could say that the spectacular organ entry (recorded earlier by Andrew Davies in Cambridge's King's College Chapel and effectively dubbed in) does not make a huge impact, while *Job*'s comforters are strongly characterized, and the serene closing music, including the lovely *Pavane of the Sons of the Morning*, is radiantly presented.

Symphonies Nos. 4 in F min.; 6 in E min.

(M) **(*) EMI (ADD) CDM7 64019-2. New Philh. O, Boult.
(BB) (**(*)) Belart mono 461 117-2. LPO, Boult (with speech by the composer).

Symphonies Nos. (i) 4 in F min.; (ii) 6 in E min.; (i) Fantasia on a Theme by Thomas Tallis.

(B) (***) Sony mono SBK 62754. NYPO, (i) Mitropoulos; (ii) Stokowski.

The recordings of Vaughan Williams's two apocalyptic symphonies made by the New York Philharmonic – No. 4 conducted in 1956 by Dmitri Mitropoulos (in a reading approved by the composer himself) and No. 6 in 1949 by Stokowski (directing with unsentimental thrust) – make a fascinating coupling. As transferred to CD they sound far better than they ever did on LP. Both demonstrate what idiomatic power and brilliance American players could bring to the composer's two most abrasive symphonies. Stokowski's reading is the more controversial, disconcertingly fast in the slow movement and unpointed in the slow, visionary finale. Mitropoulos in a generous fill-up shows equal understanding of the rarefied *Tallis Fantasia*.

In the *Fourth Symphony* Sir Adrian draws from the New Philharmonia playing of the highest quality, and the slow movement is particularly successful. The recording, too, is first class, enhancing the sharp attack in the powerful first movement of the *Sixth Symphony*. Though the rarefied finale is played beautifully, atmospheric and mysterious, tension is too low.

On Belart, Boult shows himself to be a master interpreter of Vaughan Williams, but in the tearingly dramatic *Fourth Symphony* the age of the recording and its relative lack of amplitude blunt the work's impact. By contrast, in the *Sixth* Boult drew from the LPO some of the very finest and most committed playing in the whole cycle, unmatched in his later EMI cycle. After the ebullience of the first movement comes the frightening warning of the slow movement. The complete desolation of the hushed finale is wonderfully sustained. A spoken eulogy is included from the composer, who was present at the sessions. Impressive Decca mono recording.

Symphony No. 5 in D; (i) Flos campi (suite).

⊛ (M) *** EMI CD-EMX 9512. RLPO, Handley; (i) with Balmer & Liverpool Philharmonic Ch.

Symphony No. 5 in D; Hymn-Tune Prelude; Prelude & Fugue in C min.; (i) The Pilgrim Pavement; Psalm 23; Valiant for Truth.

(N) *** Chan. 9666 (i) Hickox Singers; LSO, Hickox.

Symphony No. 5 in D; (i) The Lark Ascending. Norfolk Rhapsody.

*** EMI CDC5 55487-2. LPO, Haitink, (i) with Chang.

Hickox with the LSO captures a similar visionary fervour in this most characteristic of the series. Hickox's style is warmly expressive, moulding phrases and tempo affectionately, always sounding spontaneous, building climaxes with shattering power. The LSO respond with playing both rich and refined, helped by the wide-ranging Chandos sound. Equally, the rarities on the disc are most persuasively done, three of them première recordings. *The Pilgrim Pavement* is a touchingly direct devotional motet written for the church of St John the Divine in New York, and the setting of *Psalm 23* for soprano is adapted from his opera, *The Pilgrim's*

Progress, while the *Prelude and Fugue* is an amplification of an organ work of 1930, which anticipates the abrasive Vaughan Williams of *Job*.

Vernon Handley's disc is outstanding in every way, a spacious yet concentrated reading, superbly played and recorded, which masterfully holds the broad structure of this symphony together, building to massive climaxes. The warmth and poetry of the work are also beautifully caught. The rare and evocative *Flos campi*, inspired by the Song of Solomon, makes a generous and attractive coupling, equally well played if rather closely balanced. The sound is outstandingly full, giving fine clarity of texture.

Haitink's measured, dedicated view of VW, broad and steady in tempo, goes with beautiful playing from the LPO, notably in refined pianissimos from the string section. This may not be as passionate as some other versions in climaxes, but it compensates in monumental strength. After the measured speeds in earlier movements, the finale brings extra purposefulness in a flowing tempo. Haitink draws out comparable qualities in the rare *Norfolk Rhapsody*, while Sarah Chang proves an intensely poetic soloist in *The Lark Ascending*, volatile at the start in the bird-like fluttering motif and magnetically concentrated throughout. Full, atmospheric recording to match.

Symphonies Nos. 5 in D; 9 in E min.

(BB) *** Naxos 8.550738. Bournemouth SO, Bakels.

Kees Bakels and the Bournemouth Symphony follow up their earlier issues with a superb coupling of No. 5, arguably the peak of the series, and the very last symphony, long underestimated. Drawing the most refined playing from the Bournemouth orchestra, not least the strings, he finds in a relatively direct reading an extra purity and nobility, pointing the big emotional climaxes of the first and third movements most tellingly. Speeds are on the fast side, but the visionary beauty is perfectly caught. No. 9, with its original structure flouting convention, emerges strong and fresh, with the *Andante tranquillo* finale bringing echoes of the comparable movement of No. 6. Clear, refined recording to match.

Symphony No. 6 in E min.; Fantasia on a Theme of Thomas Tallis; (i) The Lark Ascending.

*** Teldec 9031 73127-2. (i) Little; BBC SO, A. Davis.

Symphony No. 6 in E min.; In the Fen Country; (i) On Wenlock Edge.

**(*) EMI CDC5 56762-2. LPO, Haitink; (i) with Bostridge.

Andrew Davis's reading of the *Sixth* is taut and urgent, with emotions kept under firm control. The two shorter works which come as supplement are given more warmly expressive, exceptionally beautiful performances, with Tasmin Little an immaculate soloist in *The Lark Ascending*. Teldec's wide-ranging sound, setting the orchestra at a slight distance, blunts the impact of the symphony in the first three movements, but then works beautifully in the chill of the hushed pianissimo meditation of the finale, as it does too in the fill-ups.

As in his other recordings of Vaughan Williams symphonies, Bernard Haitink takes a direct, literal view of No. 6,

bringing out the power and thrust of the argument at steady speeds. It may miss some of the mystery of the piece, as in the contrapuntal writing of the hushed epilogue, but the purposefulness is tellingly conveyed with superb playing from the LPO and firm, refined sound. With Ian Bostridge the sensitive, honey-toned soloist, the Housman song-cycle makes a welcome fill-up.

(i) Symphony No. 6 in E min.; (ii) The Lark Ascending; (iii) A Song of Thanksgiving.

(N) (B) (***) Dutton Lab. mono CDBP 9703. (i) LSO;
   (ii) Pougnet; (ii, iii) LPO; (iii) with Dolemore, Speight, Luton Choral Soc. & Girls' Ch., all cond. Boult.

Boult Conducts Vaughan Williams is the title of this valuable issue in Dutton's excellent bargain series of historic reissues. Boult's pioneer 1949 recording of the *Sixth Symphony* with the LSO, vividly transferred from 78s, has the original, heavily scored version of the *Scherzo* included as a supplement. It remains among the finest ever versions of this bitingly dramatic work. The total chill of the slow finale has never been more tellingly conveyed, even though the relatively close-up sound cannot convey an extreme pianissimo. Jean Pougnet, then leader of the LPO, proves a most understanding soloist in *The Lark Ascending*, with *A Song of Thanksgiving* providing an attractive makeweight, a piece with narrator, soprano soloist and chorus, written to celebrate victory in the Second World War.

Symphonies Nos. 6 in E min.; 9 in E min.

(M) *** EMI CD-EMX 2230. RLPO, Handley.

Handley, with rich, full recording, gives warm-hearted readings of Nos. 6 and 9, two works that in their layout – both ending on measured, visionary slow movements – can be seen as related, quite apart from sharing the same key. Next to Previn's now withdrawn recording in the same coupling, Handley lacks some of the darker, sharper qualities implied. Though his speeds are consistently faster, his is a more comfortable reading, and the recording adds to that impression. Handley's approach is a valid one, when the slow pianissimo finale, here presented as mysterious rather than desolate, was inspired not by a world laid waste by nuclear war as was once thought, but by Prospero's 'cloud-capp'd towers' in Shakespeare's *The Tempest*.

Sinfonia Antartica (No. 7).

*** EMI CDC7 47516-2. Armstrong, LPO Ch., LPO, Haitink.

(BB) *** RCA Navigator (ADD) 74321 29248-2. Harper, Richardson, L. Symphony Ch., LSO, Previn – WALTON: *Cello Concerto*. ***

(i) Sinfonia Antartica (No. 7); Serenade to Music.

(M) *** EMI CD-EMX 2173. (i) Hargan; RLPO and Ch., Handley.

(i) Sinfonia Antartica (No. 7); The Wasps (incidental music): Overture & Suite.

(M) **(*) EMI (ADD) CDM7 64020-2. (i) Armstrong; LPO, Boult.

With exceptionally full and realistic recording, Haitink directs a revelatory performance of what has long been thought of as merely a programmatic symphony. Based on material from VW's film music for *Scott of the Antarctic*, the symphony is in fact a work which, as Haitink demonstrates, stands powerfully as an original inspiration in absolute terms. Only in the second movement does the 'penguin' music seem heavier than it should be, but even that acquires new and positive qualities, thanks to Haitink.

Previn's interpretation concentrates on atmosphere rather than drama in a performance that is sensitive and literal. Because of the recessed effect of the sound, the portrayal of the ice-fall (represented by the sudden entry of the organ) has a good deal less impact than in Vernon Handley's version. Before each movement Sir Ralph Richardson speaks the superscript written by the composer on his score. As can be seen, Previn's *Sinfonia Antartica* is coupled with Walton's *Cello Concerto* – a real bargain on RCA's super-budget Navigator label.

Handley shows a natural feeling for expressive rubato and draws refined playing from the Liverpool orchestra. At the end of the epilogue Alison Hargan makes a notable first appearance on disc, a soprano with an exceptionally sweet and pure voice. In well-balanced digital sound it makes an outstanding bargain, particularly when it offers an excellent fill-up, the *Serenade to Music*, though in this lovely score a chorus never sounds as characterful as a group of well-chosen soloists. This can be recommended alongside Haitink but costs much less.

Sir Adrian gives a stirring account and is well served by the EMI engineers. The inclusion of Vaughan Williams's Aristophanic suite, *The Wasps*, with its endearing participation of the kitchen utensils plus its tuneful *Overture*, is a bonus, although in the *Overture* the upper strings sound a bit thin.

(i) *Sinfonia Antartica (No. 7); Symphony No. 8 in D min.*

(BB) *** Belart mono/stereo 461 116-2. LPO, Boult; (i) with Ritchie, LPO Ch.; superscriptions spoken by Gielgud.

(BB) *** Naxos 8.550737. Bournemouth SO, Bakels; (i) with Russell, Waynflete Singers (superscriptions read by Timson).

Boult's 1953 mono performance of the *Sinfonia Antartica* has never been surpassed; the atmospheric recording, with its translucent icy vistas and Margaret Ritchie's floating, wordless soprano voice sounding ethereal, remains a model of balancing. Boult and the LPO achieve keen concentration throughout, and the evocation of the frozen landscapes and the shifting ice-floes is as compelling as his control of the structure of a work that is never easy to hold together. Sir John Gielgud's superscriptions (from the score) act as moving preludes. The recording of the *Eighth Symphony* is early stereo (1956). The LPO plays beautifully, and the Decca engineers have relished the challenge of balancing the exotic sounds of glissando tubular bells, tuned gongs, vibraphone and xylophone. The string-tone sounds far fuller than it did when this recording last appeared, crowning this remarkably successful series of Belart super-bargain reissues.

Kees Bakels gives powerful, intense performances of two of the more problematic works, written towards the end of the composer's career, when he deliberately defied sym-

phonic convention. The *Antartica* is particularly impressive, helped by vividly atmospheric recording which, with superb separation, clarifies textures – not least the percussion and wind-machine – and beautifully captures the ethereal sound of Lynda Russell singing off-stage. Bakels's fast speed for the opening movement tautly draws together a structure which can seem dangerously episodic, and the thrust is maintained through the other movements. Sensibly the superscriptions are included on separate tracks at the end of the disc. No. 8 is excellently done too, with an element of wildness brought out in the sharp contrasts of the first movement, bouncing humour in the Scherzo and refinement in the slow movement and finale.

Symphonies Nos. 8 in D min.; 9 in E min.

(N) *** EMI CDC5 57086-2. LPO, Haitink.

(M) *** EMI (ADD) CDM7 64021-2. LPO, Boult.

Bernard Haitink in his cycle of the symphonies, thoughtfully built over a long period, has regularly demonstrated what rich rewards there are from his intense, soberly serious approach to the composer, never more so than in these last two symphonies of RVW's extreme old age. He may miss some of the fun in the woodwind *Scherzo* of No. 8 – taking it very fast, so that it is brilliant rather than well-sprung – but the dedication of the following slow movement for strings is ample compensation. Above all, he finds a new weight and gravity in the long opening movements of each symphony, which with their seemingly rhapsodic structures can easily fall apart.

The darkness of the E minor opening of No. 9 brings chilling echoes of the *Sinfonia antartica* (which marked the start of Haitink's exploration of Vaughan Williams), building on from there with rare power and concentration. Equally the slow finale brings echoes of the comparable movement in No. 6 (also in E minor). After hearing Haitink no one should try to dismiss these works as a disappointing coda to the cycle. Powerful, refined playing and full, warm recording. Highly recommended, even if you already have other versions of these works.

Boult's account of the *Eighth* may not be as sharply pointed as Bakels's version, but some will prefer the extra warmth and lyricism. The *Ninth* contains much noble and arresting invention, and Boult's performance is fully worthy of it. He draws most committed playing from the LPO, and the recording is splendidly firm in tone. The digital remastering is well up to the high standard EMI have set with these reissues of Boult's recordings.

Symphony No. 9 in E min.

**(*) Everest (ADD) EVC 9001. LPO, Boult – ARNOLD: *Symphony No. 3.* **(*)

Boult's first stereo record of the *Ninth* on Everest is prefaced on CD by a brief speech from the conductor, regretting the composer's death seven months before the recording sessions. The sound was very good for its day, with a wide dynamic range, and it sounds even better now, lacking only a little in warmth and lustre. Boult's interpretation changed very little over the years; this early version seems tauter than the later remake for EMI, but this may be partly the effect of the less expansive sound.

CHAMBER MUSIC

(i) *Phantasy Quintet (for 2 violins, 2 violas & cello); String Quartet No. 2 in A min. (For Jean on her birthday);* (ii; iii) *6 Studies in English Folk-Song for Cello & Piano;* (iii; iv) *Violin Sonata in A min.*

(M) *** EMI (ADD) CDM5 65100-2. (i) Music Group of L.; (ii) Croxford; (iii) Parkhouse; (iv) Bean.

This collection of relatively little-known chamber works, very well performed and recorded at Abbey Road in 1972/3, can be recommended strongly. The *Phantasy Quintet* dates from the composer's full maturity in 1912. The ethereal opening of this compressed one-movement work is Vaughan Williams at his most ecstatic. The *Six Studies in English Folk-Song* are highly characteristic too, while the *Violin Sonata* (1954) is a relatively gawky work but one which, like much later Vaughan Williams, has a tangily distinctive flavour, especially in a performance as fine as this. The *Second Quartet*, written between the *Fifth* and *Sixth Symphonies*, was offered as a birthday present to a viola player friend of the composer, Jean Stewart. It contains some strikingly original ideas, notably in the purposefully sombre but bleakly haunting *Largo*. The performances by the Music Group of London bring out the deeper qualities of both this and the richly scored *Quintet*.

6 Studies in English Folk-Song for Clarinet & Piano.

*** Chan. 8683. Hilton, Swallow – BAX: *Sonata* **(*); BLISS: *Quintet.* ***

These *Folk-Song Studies*, which Vaughan Williams published in arrangements for the viola and cello, come from the mid-1920s and are very beautiful, most sensitively played by Janet Hilton and Keith Swallow.

String Quartets Nos. 1 in G min.; No. 2 in A min.; (i) Phantasy Quintet.

(N) ✹ *** (BB) Naxos 8.555300. Maggini Qt, with (i) Jackson.

The Maggini Quartet, even more responsive than on their previous discs of British music, give revelatory performances of works that too often have been underestimated, regarded as mere diversions from the composer's regular path. The Magginis find a rare clarity and warmth in both quartets. The one was written soon after Vaughan Williams's studies with Ravel in Paris, with obvious echoes not just of Ravel but of the Debussy *Quartet*. The *Second Quartet* dates from 1942 to 1943, written in the crucial gap between the lyrical *Symphony No. 5* and the abrasive *No. 6*. Most revelatory of all is the Maggini performance of the *Phantasy Quintet* of 1912, a masterpiece long neglected, weighty and compressed. A slow prelude as intense as that of a Purcell Fantasy leads to three comparably strong and sharply characterized sections.

Violin Sonata in A min.

(M) **(*) EMI (ADD) CDM5 66122-2. Y. Menuhin, H. Menuhin – ELGAR: *Sonata* **(*); WALTON: *Sonata.* (**)

The late Vaughan Williams *Sonata* is an unexpected piece for the Menuhins to record and, though in the first movement (as in the Elgar) their tempo is controversially slow, giving the music unexpected weight, the whole performance makes a fine illumination of an elusive piece, not least from the pianist, who copes splendidly with the often awkward piano-writing. The recording is first rate.

VOCAL MUSIC

Benedicte; Let Us Now Praise Famous Men; O Clap Your Hands; Old Hundreth Psalm; O Taste and See; Toward the Unknown Region.

(N) **(*) Australian Decca Eloquence 467 613-2. Byram-Wigfield, Winchester Cathedral Ch., Waynefleet Singers, Bournemouth SO, Hill – WALTON: *Coronation March & Te Deum* etc. **(*)

Enthusiastic performances, set in a reverberant acoustic and well recorded. They may not be the most polished available but the infectious quality of the music-making is very involving. The *Bendedicte*, a strong sixteen-minute work, which is too often overlooked, is hugely enjoyable. Well worth considering.

Dona nobis pacem; 4 Hymns; Lord, Thou hast been our refuge (Psalm 90); O clap your hands (Psalm 47); Toward the Unknown Region.

*** Hyp. CDA 66655. Howarth, Mark Ainsley, Allen, Corydon Singers & O, Best.

Dona nobis pacem; 5 Mystical Songs.

*** Chan. 8590. Wiens, Rayner-Cook, LPO Ch., LPO, Thomson.

(i; ii) *Dona nobis pacem;* (ii; iii) *Sancta civitas.*

*** EMI CDC7 544788-2. (i) Kenny; (ii) Terfel; (iii) Langridge, St Paul's Cathedral Choristers; L. Symphony Ch., LSO, Hickox.

These two visionary masterpieces, both seriously neglected, both with Latin titles and both dating from the interwar period, make an ideal and generous coupling. Drawing passionate performances from his choir and soloists (notably from Bryn Terfel in both works), Hickox brings out not only the visionary intensity and atmospheric beauty – as in the offstage trumpets and 'Alleluias' near the start of *Sancta civitas* – but also the dramatic power. Both these works may be predominantly meditative, but they have moments of violence which relate directly to the dark side of VW, as expressed in the *Fourth Symphony*, such as the chorus, *Beat! Beat! Drums!*, the second section of *Sancta civitas*. In that same work it is fascinating to have the words 'Babylon the great is fallen' set as a hushed lament instead of as a shout of triumph, as in Walton's *Belshazzar's Feast*. Hickox is a degree broader in his speeds than previous interpreters on disc, but is all the warmer for it.

Using a relatively small choir and orchestra, Best takes an intimate view of *Dona nobis pacem* but one which as a result is even sharper in focus, capturing the dramatic contrasts as a big performance would, with words unusually clear. The sweet-toned Judith Howarth and the warmly expressive Thomas Allen are ideal soloists. *Toward the Unknown Region* was VW's first big choral work, not as distinctive as his later music but with many typical fingerprints. Best brings out the beauty of the choral writing, as he does in the even rarer *Four Hymns* for tenor, viola and strings, which the composer intended as a counterpart to the *Five Mystical Songs*. Ainsley is the clear tenor soloist, though strained a little at the top. The setting of *Psalm 90* is the more effective here for having, instead of a semi-chorus, the optional baritone soloist, with Allen again singing with deep dedication.

The *Dona nobis pacem* is also performed well on the Chandos disc, with Edith Wiens and Bryan Rayner-Cook as soloists. The latter gives an eloquent account of the much earlier *Five Mystical Songs*, with Bryden Thomson drawing committed playing from the LPO. The recording is warmly resonant, with clear orchestral detail.

(i) *Epithalamion;* (ii) *Merciless Beauty.*

(M) *** EMI Dig./ADD CDM7 64730-2. (i) Roberts, Shelley, Bach Ch., LPO, Willcocks; (ii) Langridge, Endellion Qt – *Riders to the Sea.* ***

Vaughan Williams's setting of *Epithalamion* began life as a masque in the late 1930s and, only a year before he died, he expanded it into the coolly lyrical cantata recorded here. Scored for baritone and small orchestra with piano (Howard Shelley superb) and solo parts for flute and viola, it is an eloquent and thoroughly characteristic piece. Stephen Roberts gives a beautiful account of it, and Philip Langridge is hardly less impressive in *Merciless Beauty*, three much earlier settings for voice and string trio. *Riders to the Sea* is also indispensable – see below. This reissue makes a most valuable addition to the Vaughan Williams discography. The first two works were recorded digitally; *Riders to the Sea* is analogue (1970) but sounds equally vivid and well focused. Splendid performances throughout.

(i) *Fantasia on Christmas Carols.* Arr. of carols: *And all in the morning; Wassail Song* (also includes: TRAD., arr. Warlock: *Adam lay y-bounden; Bethlehem down*).

(M) ** EMI (ADD) CDM7 64131-2. Guildford Cathedral Ch., Pro Arte O, Rose; (i) with Barrow – HELY-HUTCHINSON: *Carol Symphony;* QUILTER: *Children's Overture.* **

Vaughan Williams's joyful *Fantasia on Christmas Carols* is comparatively short. It was written for performance in 1912 in Hereford Cathedral, so the acoustic at Guildford Cathedral is apt. The performance here is suitably exuberant, and John Barrow is a good soloist, but not everyone will respond to his timbre and style, and the King's performance with Hervey Alan (currently unavailable) is marginally preferable. But the Christmas carol arrangements are delightful, beautifully sung and recorded. Valuable couplings too.

(i) *Fantasia on Christmas Carols;* (ii) *Flos campi;* (i) 5 *Mystical Songs;* (iii) *Serenade to Music.*

*** Hyp. CDA 66420. (i) Allen, (ii) Imai & Corydon Singers; (iii) 16 soloists; ECO, Best.

This radiant record centres round the *Serenade to Music* and, as in the original performance, sixteen star soloists are here lined up; though the team of women does not quite match the stars of 1938, the men are generally fresher and clearer. Above all, thanks largely to fuller, modern recording, the result is much more sensuous than the original, with ensemble better matched and with Matthew Best drawing glowing sounds from the English Chamber Orchestra. The other items are superbly done too, with Nobuko Imai a powerful viola soloist in the mystical cantata, *Flos campi*, another Vaughan Williams masterpiece. Thomas Allen is the characterful soloist in the five *Mystical Songs*. Warmly atmospheric sound to match the performances.

(i) *Flos campi. Household Music (3 Preludes on Welsh Hymn Tunes).*

*** Chan. 9392. (i) Dukes, N. Sinfonia, Hickox – *Riders to the Sea.* ***

Philip Dukes proves a rich and eloquent viola soloist in *Flos campi*, in which the Northern Sinfonia Chorus is balanced more forwardly and powerfully than usual, and this is a remarkably successful performance on all counts. The *Household Music*, never recorded before, offers three delightful miniatures, written in 1941 as a wartime exercise, intended for amateur musicians as well as professionals.

(i) *Hodie (Christmas Cantata);* (ii) *Fantasia on Christmas Carols.*

(N) (M) *** EMI (ADD) CDM5 67427-2. (i) J. Baker, Lewis, Shirley-Quirk, Bach Ch., Westminster Abbey Ch., LSO, Willcocks; (ii) Barrow, Guildford Cathedral Ch. & String O, Rose.

Hodie; Fantasia on Christmas Carols.

**(*) EMI CDC7 54128-2. Gale, Tear, Roberts, L. Symphony Ch., LSO, Hickox.

In sixteen separate numbers, lasting close on an hour, the Christmas cantata, *Hodie*, brings one of Vaughan Williams's late, characteristically rumbustious inspirations. It is, above all, bluff and jolly, not very subtle in its effects, but full of open-hearted humanity. Those qualities are splendidly realized in this fine performance, not just by the choir, but most of all by the excellent trio of soloists, with Dame Janet as ever giving heartfelt intensity to Vaughan Williams's broad melodic lines. The *Fantasia on Christmas Carols*, easy and approachable, makes a generous and apt coupling. The transfers of both recordings are newly done and give an excellent example of mid-1960s EMI sound.

Though the three soloists cannot match the original trio in Sir David Willcocks's pioneering version, Hickox directs a more urgent and more freely expressive reading of the big Christmas cantata, *Hodie*, helped by refined and incisive choral singing. As on the earlier disc, the *Christmas Carols Fantasia* proves an ideal coupling, also warmly done.

Lord Thou hast been our refuge; Prayer to the Father of Heaven; A Vision of Aeroplanes.

*** Chan. 9019. Finzi Singers, Spicer – HOWELLS: *Requiem* etc. ***

These three choral pieces make an apt coupling for the Howells choral works on the Finzi Singers' disc. *A Vision of*

Aeroplanes improbably but most imaginatively uses a text from Ezekiel.

Mass in G min.

(M) *** EMI (ADD) CDM5 65595-2. King's College, Cambridge, Ch., Willcocks – BAX; FINZI: *Choral Music.* ***

Here, with the finest band of trebles in the country, Sir David Willcocks captures the beauty of the Vaughan Williams *Mass* more completely than any rival, helped by the fine, atmospheric, analogue recording. This is a work which, on the one hand, can easily seem too tense and lose its magic or, on the other, fall apart in a meandering style; Willcocks admirably finds the middle course. Although recorded two decades before the Bax and Finzi couplings, the remastered analogue sound is still full and fresh.

5 Mystical Songs; O Clap Your Hands.

(M) *** EMI (ADD) CDM5 65588-2. Shirley-Quirk, King's College, Cambridge, Ch., ECO, Willcocks – FINZI: *Dies natalis;* HOLST: *Choral Fantasia; Psalm 86.* ***

In the *Five Mystical Songs* to words by George Herbert, John Shirley-Quirk sings admirably, and the motet, *O Clap Your Hands,* makes a fine bonus for a recommendable triptych of English vocal works.

(i) 5 Mystical Songs; (i; ii) 5 Tudor Portraits.

(B) **(*) Hyp. Helios CDH 55004. (i) Herford; (ii) Walker; Guildford Ch. Soc., Philh. O, Davan Wetton.

The contrast of the religious pastoralism of the *Five Mystical Songs* and the rumbustious vigour of the *Tudor Portraits* is well understood by Hilary Davan Wetton. Henry Herford is the rather restrained but sympathetic soloist in the former (an early work, concurrent with the *Sea Symphony*); his vocal style is less well suited to the portrait of *Pretty Bess* in the latter, written a quarter of a century later. Sarah Walker touchingly sings her *Lament* for her pet sparrow (the victim of her cat), and although she is a little strained at the climax, the chorus opens up powerfully and then paints a touching epitaph. She also paints a robust picture of *The Tunning of Elinor Running.* The chorus are boldly enthusiastic both here and in the burlesque *Epitaph on John Jayberd of Diss.* The Philharmonia play sensitively and enter fully into the spirit of the bawdy Elizabethan frolics, playing with colourful vigour in the brilliant closing scherzo, *Jolly Rutterkin,* with its lively cross-rhythms. Henry Herford, too, is more vociferous here. The recording is truthful, although the chorus could have been given more bite, for the words are not ideally clear. Otherwise an enjoyable and recommendable bargain coupling, which supplies full texts and even a brief glossary of unfamiliar Elizabethan terms.

On Wenlock Edge (song-cycle from A. E. Housman's *A Shropshire Lad*); (i) 10 Blake Songs for Voice & Oboe. 4 Hymns: (Lord, come away!; Who is this fair one?; Come love, come Lord; Evening hymn); Songs: Merciless beauty; (ii) The new ghost; The water mill.

(M) *** EMI (ADD) CDM5 65589-2. I. Partridge, (i) Craxton, Music Group of L.; (ii) J. Partridge.

This EMI mid-priced CD is an outstandingly beautiful record, with Ian Partridge's intense artistry and lovely individual tone-colour used with compelling success in Vaughan Williams songs both early and late. The Housman cycle has an accompaniment for piano and string quartet which can sound ungainly but which here, with playing from the Music Group of London, matches the soloist's sensitivity; the result is atmospheric and moving. The *Ten Blake Songs* come from just before the composer's death: bald, direct settings that with the artistry of Partridge and Craxton are darkly moving. The tenor's sister accompanies with fine understanding in two favourite songs as a welcome extra. The other rare items make an attractive bonus, with the *Four Hymns* distinctively accompanied by viola and piano.

(i) On Wenlock Edge; (ii) Songs of Travel (song-cycles).

(M) *** EMI CDM7 64731-2. (i) Tear; (ii) Allen, CBSO, Rattle – BUTTERWORTH; ELGAR: *Songs.* ***

Vaughan Williams's own orchestration of his Housman song-cycle, made in the early 1920s, has been curiously neglected. It lacks something of the apt, ghostly quality of the version for piano and string quartet, but some will prefer the bigger scale. The orchestral version brings home the aptness of treating the nine songs as a cycle, particularly when the soloist is as characterful and understanding a singer as Thomas Allen. The Housman settings in the other cycle are far better known, and Robert Tear, as in his earlier recording with Vernon Handley, proves a deeply perceptive soloist. Warm, understanding conducting and playing, and excellent sound.

(i; ii) An Oxford Elegy; (i; iii) Flos campi; (iv) Sancta civitas; (i) Whitsunday Hymn.

(M) *** EMI (ADD) CDM5 67227-2. King's College, Cambridge, Ch., Willcocks, with (i) Jacques O; (ii) Westbrook (speaker); (iii) Aronowitz; (iv) Partridge, Shirley-Quirk, Bach Ch., LSO.

An Oxford Elegy, written in 1949, is an example of a work that rises well above its original commission – its richly flowing inspiration characteristic of the composer's ripe Indian summer. The spoken quotations from Matthew Arnold are effectively presented by John Westbrook, while the Cambridge choir is admirable in its words of tribute to Oxford. *Flos campi,* with its inspiration in the Song of Solomon, is one of the composer's most sensuously beautiful works, with its deeply expressive solo for the viola, here beautifully played by Cecil Aronowitz. It needs a persuasive interpretation, and that it certainly receives. *Sancta civitas* ('The holy city') is a product of the composer's visionary years in the early 1920s. A masterpiece, elusive in its apparent meandering, but in fact as sharply focused as his *Pastoral Symphony* of the same period. The words are mostly from the Book of Revelation and are set to sublime, shifting choral textures (with the main chorus set against a semi-chorus and an off-stage boys' chorus) and the whole effect is evocatively captured on this CD. The *Whitsunday Hymn* is a short but beautiful piece composed for the Leith Hill Festival at Dorking in 1929, yet it somehow remained unpublished at the time; this performance provides its CD début and, like the rest of the programme, is a tribute to the conductor in his eightieth birthday year. A valuable and stimulating release.

The Pilgrim's Progress (incidental music, ed. Palmer).

*** Hyp. CDA 66511. Gielgud, Pasco, Howells, Corydon Singers, City of L. Sinfonia, Best.

Vaughan Williams had a lifelong devotion to Bunyan's great allegory, which fired his inspiration to write incidental music for a BBC radio adaptation of the complete Pilgrim's Progress. Much of the material, but not all, then found a place in the opera. Christopher Palmer has here devised a sequence of twelve movements, which – overlapping with the opera and the Fifth Symphony – throws up long-buried treasure. Matthew Best draws warmly sympathetic performances from his singers and players, in support of the masterly contributions of Sir John Gielgud, taking the role of Pilgrim as he did on radio in 1942, and Richard Pasco as the Evangelist.

The Shepherds of the Delectable Mountains; 3 Choral Hymns; Magnificat; A Song of Thanksgiving; Psalm 100.

*** Hyp. CDA 66569. Gielgud, Dawson, Kitchen, Wyn-Rogers, Mark Ainsley, Bowen, Thompson, Opie, Terfel, Best, Corydon Singers, L. Oratory Junior Ch., City of L. Sinfonia, Best.

With Sir John Gielgud as narrator and Lynne Dawson as the sweet-toned soprano soloist, Best gives A Song of Thanksgiving a tautness and sense of drama, bringing out the originality of the writing, simple and stirring in its grandeur, not for a moment pompous. The Magnificat brings more buried treasure, a massive setting designed not for liturgical but for concert use. With its haunting ostinatos it is closer to Holst's choral music than most Vaughan Williams. The Three Hymns and the setting of Psalm 100 are comparably distinctive in their contrasted ways, and it is good to have a recording of the Bunyan setting, The Shepherds of the Delectable Mountains. Most of the solo singing is excellent, and the chorus is superb, helped by warmly atmospheric recording.

Songs of Travel; The House of Life (6 sonnets); 4 Poems by Fredegond Shove; 4 Last Songs: No. 2, Tired; Songs: In the spring; Linden Lea.

**(*) Chan. 8475. Luxon, Williams.

Though Benjamin Luxon's vibrato is distractingly wide, the warmth and clarity of the recording help to make his well-chosen collection of Vaughan Williams songs very attractive, including as it does not only the well-known Stevenson travel cycle but the Rossetti cycle, The House of Life (including The water mill), as well as the most famous song of all, Linden Lea.

(i) 5 Tudor Portraits; (ii) Benedicite; (iii) 5 Variants of Dives and Lazarus.

(M) **(*) EMI (ADD) CDM7 64722-2. (i) Bainbridge, Carol Case, Bach Ch., New Philh. O; (ii) Harper, Bach Ch., LSO; (iii) Jacques O; Willcocks.

In the Five Tudor Portraits, the composer deliberately chose bawdy words by the early Tudor poet, John Skelton, and set them in his most rumbustious style. This is a good, strong

performance, but the soloists are not earthy enough for such music. The digital remastering has brought splendid bite and projection to the chorus without losing too much of the original ambience. The Benedicite is another strong work, compressed in its intensity, too brief to be accepted easily into the choral repertory, but a fine addition to the RVW discography. Five Variants of Dives and Lazarus is beautifully played and warmly recorded, bringing serenity after the vigour of the vocal works.

OPERA

A Cotswold Romance (adapted by Maurice Jacobson in collaboration with the composer from Hugh the Drover); Death of Tintagiles.

*** Chan. 9646. Mannion, Randle, Brook, LPO Ch., LSO, Hickox.

This makes a splendid supplement to Hickox's outstanding recording of Vaughan Williams's last opera, The Pilgrim's Progress. Saddened towards the end of his life that his tuneful ballad opera, Hugh the Drover, was seriously neglected, he adapted some of the most winning sequences to produce this cantata, A Cotswold Romance – never recorded before. Even though some striking items from the opera are omitted, it helps that the role of the chorus is expanded, with the colour and vigour of the original enhanced. The Death of Tintagiles, even more neglected, is drawn from Vaughan Williams's incidental music for a Maeterlinck play, six dark and spare fragments anticipating later Vaughan Williams works.

Hugh the Drover (complete).

*** Hyp. CDA 66901/2. Bottone, Evans, Walker, Van Allan, Opie, Corydon Singers & O, Best.

Described as a ballad opera, Hugh the Drover uses folk-themes with full-throated Puccinian warmth. The Hyperion version in atmospheric digital sound offers a fresh, light view, resilient and urgent in the first Act, hauntingly tender in the second. Rebecca Evans is superb as the heroine, Mary, with Bonaventura Bottone an amiable Hugh, only occasionally strained, well supported by a cast of generally fresh young singers.

The Pilgrim's Progress (complete).

🏵 (B) Chan. 9625 (2). Finley, and soloists, ROHCG Ch. & O, Hickox.

(M) *** EMI (ADD) CMS7 64212-2 (2). Noble, Burrowes, Armstrong, Herincx, Carol Case, Shirley-Quirk, Keyte, LPO Ch., LPO, Boult.

Richard Hickox not only brings out the visionary intensity of much of the writing – notably in the ideas drawn from the Fifth Symphony – but also the passion and urgency, pacing the music to bring out the underlying drama in heightened contrasts. As in his recording of that symphony, Hickox is masterly in moulding phrases to magnetize the ear, always a warm interpreter, reflected in the unfailing ardour of the Covent Garden Chorus and Orchestra. The big cast is a strong one, mainly of young singers, led by

Gerald Finley as a firm fresh-voiced Pilgrim, and with Peter Coleman-Wright introducing the opera strongly as John Bunyan. The Chandos recording is superb, spacious and atmospheric, with the many offstage effects beautifully balanced, yet with words always clear. It is one of the many delights of this opera to register the heightened moments when the libretto quotes a Psalm or other familiar sources. Vaughan Williams may not have been a practising Christian, but the depth of his humanitarian faith was never more powerfully demonstrated than here, supremely so in this overwhelming recording.

On EMI John Noble gives a dedicated performance in the central role of Pilgrim, and the large supporting cast is consistently strong. Vanity Fair may not sound evil here, but Vaughan Williams's own recoil is vividly expressed, and the jaunty passage of Mr and Mrs By-Ends brings the most delightful light relief. Boult underlines the virility of his performance with a fascinating and revealing half-hour collection of rehearsal excerpts, placed at the end of the second CD. The outstanding recording quality is confirmed by the CD transfer, which shows few signs of the passing of two decades.

Riders to the Sea (opera) complete.

*** Chan. 9392. Finnie, Daymond, Dawson, Attrot, Stephen, N. Sinfonia, Hickox – *Flos campi* etc. ***

(M) *** EMI (ADD) CDM7 64730-2. Burrowes, M. Price, Watts, Luxon, Amb. S., L. O Nova, M. Davies – *Epithalamion; Merciless Beauty.* ***

As in other Vaughan Williams works, Hickox takes a broad, warmly idiomatic view, less urgent than the previous, EMI recording, more timeless and mysterious, helped by opulently atmospheric recording. He is helped too by an excellent cast. Even if Linda Finnie as the old woman, Maurya, who loses all her sons to the sea, cannot quite match Helen Watts on the original recording, her final monologue of lament and resignation provides a moving, deeply expressive culmination. Among the others, Karl Daymond as Bartley, the last son to drown, is a newcomer to note, as impressive here as he was in Hickox's recording of Purcell's *Dido*. The generous coupling adds to the disc's attractions.

The earlier, EMI disc offers a strong, clean-cut performance with Helen Watts giving one of her finest performances as the old woman, Maurya. It is also beautifully recorded in wonderfully atmospheric sound, though the wind machine is too prominent. With its rare couplings, this can be strongly recommended alongside the Chandos version. All who care about this composer should investigate one or other of these records.

Sir John in Love (complete).

(N)*** Chan. 9928 (2). Maxwell, Gritton, Claycomb, Connolly, Owens, Padmore, Thompson, Best, Williams, Varcoe, Sinfonia Ch., Northern Sinf., Hickox.

(M) *** EMI (ADD) CMS5 66123 (2). Herincx, Bainbridge, Watts, English, Eathorne, Tear, John Alldis Ch., New Philh. O, M. Davies.

Richard Hickox follows up his long list of Vaughan Williams recordings, not least the original version of the *London Symphony*, with a warm, dramatic reading of the opera which Vaughan Williams, conscious of Verdi's example, based on *The Merry Wives of Windsor*. In his own relatively complex libretto he sticks much closer to Shakespeare than Verdi and Boito, and as Ursula Vaughan Williams has said, he wrote the piece 'just to please himself'.

While this is the opera which provided the material for the *Greensleeves Fantasia*, and uses other folk material, it has been wrongly dismissed as just a collection of folk-tunes. In fact, as Hickox's incisive account of the *Prelude* with its cross-rhythms instantly establishes, there are many links here with the sharper Vaughan Williams of *Flos campi* (written at the same period) and the later symphonies.

As an opera this may not match Verdi's *Falstaff* in polish or sophistication, but in its more relaxed, more lyrical way it offers a comparably individual slant on Shakespeare, with the title, *Sir John in Love*, clearly indicating a different emphasis on the character of Falstaff. With Vaughan Williams he is not just comic but a believable lover, more genial and expansive than in Boito's portrait.

The 1974 EMI set of the opera remains a formidable competitor, but quite apart from the extra fullness of the digital Chandos sound, Hickox's reading is a degree more warmly expressive, more sharply dramatic than Meredith Davies's on EMI.

In the casting the central strength of the Chandos set is the Falstaff of Donald Maxwell, with his full, dark bass fatter-sounding than that of Raimund Herincx. Susan Gritton is also outstanding as Anne, rich and golden, relishing the glorious duet she sings with Fenton in the very first scene, with Mark Padmore fresh and youthful too. Not all the others are as characterful as their predecessors, good as they are, as for example Laura Claycomb as Mistress Page. Yet the very large cast works together splendidly, with clear differentiation of the many extra characters that Vaughan Williams includes.

In the EMI set Meredith Davies relishes the colourfulness of the score. Raimund Herincx is a positive and sympathetic Falstaff, and Helen Watts as Mrs Quickly and Elizabeth Bainbridge as Mrs Ford rise ripely to the occasion. Wendy Eathorne as Anne Page and Robert Tear as Fenton make a delightful pair of lovers, and such singers as Gerald English as Dr Caius add to the stylishness. The 1974 Abbey Road recording is vivid and warmly atmospheric and beautifully balanced, and this is still very much worth considering at mid-price.

VEALE, John (born 1922)

Violin Concerto.

(N) *** Chan. 9910. Mordkovitch, BBC SO, Hickox – BRITTEN: *Violin Concerto.* ***

Surgingly lyrical in a melodic idiom echoing Mahler on the one hand, Walton on the other, John Veale's *Violin Concerto* of 1984 makes an unusual, highly enjoyable coupling for Lydia Mordkovitch's searching account of the Britten. Seriously neglected, with not a note of his music otherwise available on disc, John Veale, born in Kent in 1922, writes in a confident tonal idiom, which with its colourful orchestration reflects his work as a film composer in the post-war period. His development was strongly influenced by his consultations with Walton, and the vigorous finale of this concerto with its swinging Cuban rhythms directly echoes not only Walton but Lambert too. That prompts Mordkovitch to a dazzling performance, with Hickox drawing brilliant, vigorous playing from the BBC Orchestra.

Yet the first two movements, both more expansive, are the ones that bear the main emotional weight, with Mordkovitch's passionate intensity heightening the impact. The first movement sets yearning lyricism against sharply rhythmic writing, rather as Walton does, yet the specific echoes are more from Mahler, occasionally from Vaughan Williams, culminating in a long, brilliant cadenza before a tarantella coda. The central slow movement is entitled *Lament*, but the mood is sensuous rather than elegiac, with ecstatic outpouring of melody high above the stave from the soloist at the beginning and end, and with a passionate climax in the middle. On one plane one might regard this as a self-indulgent work, yet the heartfelt commitment is never in doubt. A most rewarding coupling for the Britten for anyone who enjoys post-romantic writing, superbly recorded in the richest Chandos sound.

VECCHI, Orazio (1550–1605)

L'amfiparnaso (commedia harmonica).

(BB) *** Naxos 8.553312. Cappella Musicale di Petronio di Bologna, Vartolo.

L'amfiparnaso (commedia harmonica); *Il convito musicale* (musical banquet: excerpts): *O Giardiniero; Lunghi danni; Bando del asino.*

(B) *** HM HMC 90856.58 (3). Ens. Clément Jannequin, Visse – BANCHIERO: *Barca di Venetia per Padova* ***; MARENZIO: *Madrigals* **(*); LASSUS: *Madrigal comedies.* ***

Unlike Lassus, Vecchi, although earning his living as a *maestro di capella* in the church, leaned in his own music towards the secular. Described as a 'madrigal comedy', *L'amfiparnaso*, first performed in 1594, fascinatingly points forward to the development of opera as a new genre in the following decade. The text in a Prologue and three brief Acts develops a comic plot stocked with *commedia dell'arte* characters, but, instead of solo voices representing different characters, here each scene is set as a madrigal for a small group of voices. Each madrigal, three in the first Act, five in both the other two, is preceded by a brief spoken summary, the whole making up a taut entertainment that still sounds fresh and charming after 400 years. Much is owed to the liveliness of the Naxos performance, using a first-rate ensemble from Bologna under Sergio Vartolo. With splendidly crisp ensemble the singers consistently bring out the sharply rhythmic quality of Vecchi's writing, with clear, well-balanced sound. Full texts and an English translation are provided.

It is also brought vividly to life by the solo and ensemble singing on Harmonica Mundi. *Il convito musicale* (of which we are given only excerpts) is an innocent pastoral sequence set in a garden. A touching lament, *Lunghi danni*, follows; but it is the closing section, with its engaging vocal imitations of instruments and animals croaking all together, which makes the piece memorable. The recording is first class and so is the documentation.

VELASQUEZ, Glauco (1884–1914)

Album-leaves Nos. 1–2; Brutto Sogno; Canzone Strana; Danse de silphes; Devaneio; Divertimento No. 2; Impromptu; Melancolia; Minuetto e Gavotte Moderni; Petite Suite; Prelúdios Nos. 1–2; Prelúdio e Scherzo; Rêverie; Valsa lenta; Valsa romântica.

*** Marco 8.223556. Sverner.

Glauco Velasquez was an illegitimate child, born in Naples to a Brazilian mother and fathered by a Portuguese singer. When their relationship collapsed, his mother took the boy to Brazil, where he was brought up in ignorance of his father's identity. He soon showed musical aptitude, and by his mid-twenties he had attracted some attention in musical circles with his piano miniatures, recorded here. Their heady melancholy, often in Scriabinesque chromatic writing, is most beguiling. Clara Sverner brings out the personality and charm, and they are very well recorded.

VERACINI, Francesco Maria (1690–1768)

Violin Concertos: a cinque in A & D; a otto stromenti in D. Aria schiavona in B flat for Orchestra (attrib.); *Overture No. 5 in B flat.*

(N)(BB) *** Naxos 8.553413. Accademia I Filarmonici (Verona), Martini.

Veracini's *Violin Concerto a otto stromenti* is endearingly ambitious in its scoring, and the brilliant opening with its two trumpets and oboes must have made quite an impression when first heard in Venice in 1712 at a concert to celebrate the visit of the Ambassador of the new Holy Roman Emperor.

Tartini's influence is apparent. The decorative figurations in the outer movements rise and fall in scalic sequence. Some solo passages are left to the soloist to fill in and the unusual minor-key slow movement is very improvisatory in feeling.

The two earlier *Concerti a cinque* are more modest, closer to Vivaldi, although Veracini's own presence is very apparent at times and especially in the finale of the A major work. The *Overture in B flat* is one of the finest of the complete set discussed below, and the *Aria schiavona* is an engaging minuet lollipop, very gallant in feeling, and almost certainly not by Veracini at all. First-class performances throughout with fine solo contributions presumably from Alberto Martini, the leader of the Accademia I Filarmonici, which claims to have no conductor. The recording is excellent.

Overtures (Suites) Nos. 1–6.

*** DG (IMS) 439 937-2. Col. Mus. Ant., Goebel.

(N) (BB) *** Naxos 8.553412. Accademia I Filarmonici (Verona), Martini.

These overtures were composed for the Dresden court orchestra, probably around 1716. Their character brings a curious amalgam of Italian volatility and German weight, and they have something in common with the orchestral suites of Telemann. Yet Telemann loved instrumental light and shade, whereas Veracini favoured tutti scoring. The music is strong in personality and there is no shortage of ideas, but energy is more important than expressive lyricism, with usually a single brief sarabande to provide contrast as the centrepiece of up to half-a-dozen dance movements. Musica Antiqua of Cologne, often abrasive, seem custom-made for this repertoire, playing with consistent vitality and obvious enjoyment. The recording is first class, within a spacious acoustic.

The Accademia I Filarmonici claim to use the original manuscripts, but they play on modern instruments, and their bright, gleaming sound is full of Italian sunshine. The performances too are (not surprisingly) more Italianate than those of the Cologne group, and they play the *Sarabandes* of Nos. 1 and 2 with an attractive air of relaxed graciousness, while the sparkling opening movement of No. 6 is made to seem almost a tarantella. So at Naxos price, unless period instruments are essential, this could well be a first choice.

12 Sonate accademiche, Op. 2.

*** Hyp. CDA 66871/3 (3). Locatelli Trio.

Alongside his fame as a composer, Veracini was renowned as a master of the violin: he boasted that there 'was but one God and one Veracini', so that even Tartini was initimidated by his prowess. The twelve *Sonate accademiche* date from 1744. They are much more Italianate than the overtures, though German influence remains strong. The writing has a rhapsodic exuberance and drive, and, as with the overtures, dance movements predominate. But there are touching lyrical interludes and some lovely slow movements. The last *Sonata* is masterly, opening with a descending minor scalic theme, which is first used for a *Passacaglia*, then for a *Capriccio cromatico*, and finally provides the basis for an ambitious closing *Ciaccona*. The Locatelli Trio, led by Elizabeth Wallfisch, are a first-class group and their authentic style, strongly etched, is full of joy in the music's vitality, while the composer's lyrical side is most persuasively revealed. Paul Nicholson's continuo is very much a part of the picture, especially in the works using an organ – which is very pleasingly balanced. The recording is vivid and immediate.

VERDI, Giuseppe (1813–1901)

(i) *Ballet Music from: Aida (including Triumphal March); Macbeth; Otello.* (ii) *Overtures: Aroldo; La forza del destino; Giovanna d'Arco; Luisa Miller; Nabucco; Oberto, conte di San Bonifacio; I vespri siciliani.*

(B) *** Decca 448 238-2. (i) Bologna Teatro Comunale O; (ii) Nat. PO; Chailly.

Chailly's version enjoys brilliant Decca recording. Besides the ballet music, which is presented with gusto and style, he offers the four most obviously desirable overtures plus three rarities, including the overture to Verdi's very first opera, *Oberto*, and the most substantial of the early ones, *Aroldo*. Crisp and incisive, Chailly draws vigorous and polished playing from the excellent National Philharmonic.

The Lady and the Fool (ballet suite; arr. Mackerras).

(B) *** CfP CD-CFP 4618. LPO, Mackerras – SULLIVAN: *Pineapple Poll.* ***

Mackerras's arrangement of Verdi has not caught the public fancy in quite the way of the coupled *Pineapple Poll*, but the scoring is witty and the music vivacious, and it is very well played and recorded here.

Complete Overtures, Preludes and Ballet Music

Vol. 1: Overtures and Preludes: *Alzira (Overture); Attila (Prelude); La battaglia di Legnano (Overture); Il corsaro; I due Foscari; Ernani (Preludes); Un giorno di regno (Il finto Stanislao); Giovanna d'Arco (Overtures); Macbeth (Prelude with ballet music); I Masnadieri (Prelude); Nabucco; Oberto (Overtures).*

*** Chan. 9510. BBC PO, Downes.

Vol. 2: *Jérusalem (Overture and ballet music); Luisa Miller (Overture); Rigoletto (Prelude); Il trovatore (ballet music).*

*** Chan. 9594. BBC PO, Downes.

Vol. 3: *Un ballo in maschera (Prelude); Simon Boccanegra (Prelude: 1st version, 1857); La traviata (Preludes to Acts I & III); Les Vêpres siciliennes: Ballet of the Four Seasons.*

*** Chan. 9696. BBC PO, Downes.

Vol. 4: *Aida (Prelude for Cairo première, 1871; Overture for Italian première, 1872; 2 Dances & Act II ballet music); Don Carlos (Prelude to Act III and ballet music: La peregrina); La forza del destino (Prelude, 1862); Otello (ballet music, Act III).*

*** Chan. 9788. BBC PO, Downes.

Preludes, Overtures and Ballet Music (as above).

*** Chan. 9787 (4). BBC PO, Downes.

Overtures and Preludes: *Aida (Prelude); Alzira; Aroldo (Overtures); Attila; Un ballo in maschera (Preludes); La battaglia di Legnano; Il corsaro (Sinfonias); Ernani (Prelude); La forza del destino (Overture); Un giorno di regno; Giovanna d'Arco (Sinfonias); Luisa Miller (Overture); Macbeth; I Masnadieri (Preludes); Nabucco (Overture); Oberto, Conte di San Bonifacio (Sinfonia); Rigoletto; La traviata (Preludes); I vespri siciliani (Overture).*

(B) *** DG Double (ADD) 453 058-2 (2). BPO, Karajan.

Overtures and Preludes: *Aida (Prelude); Alzira (Sinfonia); Aroldo (Sinfonia); Attila (Prelude); Un ballo in maschera (Prelude); Il corsaro (Prelude); Luisa Miller (Sinfonia); Oberto, Conte di San Bonifacio (Sinfonia); La traviata (Preludes to Acts I & III); I vespri siciliani (Sinfonia).*

(BB) **(*) Naxos 8.553018. Hungarian State Op. O, Morandi.

Overtures and Preludes: *La battaglia di Legnano*

(Sinfonia); *Don Carlos* (Prelude to Act III); *I due Foscari* (Prelude); *Ernani* (Prelude); *La forza del destino* (Sinfonia); *Un giorno di regno* (Sinfonia); *Giovanna d'Arco* (Sinfonia); *Macbeth* (Sinfonia); *I Masnadieri* (Prelude); *Nabucco* (Overture); *Rigoletto* (Prelude).

(BB) **(*) Naxos 8.553089. Hungarian State Op. O, Morandi.

Since we went to print with our last main volume, Edward Downes's Verdi survey has been extended to cover virtually all the overtures, preludes and ballet music, the latter full of charm when so elegantly played and beautifully recorded. Original versions are chosen where available, so we get the first 1857 score of the *Prelude* to *Simon Boccanegra* and the brief 1862 *Overture* to *La forza del destino*, rather than the familiar expanded 1869 version. (It is most successful here in its more succinct format, although one misses the tune made famous by the film *Manon des sources*.) The outstanding novelty is Verdi's extended 1872 overture written for the Italian première of *Aida*. The composer rehearsed it secretly, and then wisely decided that first thoughts were best, and the shorter Prelude heard at the opera's Cairo première was substituted at the last moment. The 1872 piece was never heard of again. The ballet music was of course an essential requirement if a work was to be performed at the Paris Opéra. (Legend has it that wealthy patrons insisted on its inclusion in order to choose their newest mistresses, after watching the dancers.) To fit the ballet into Act III of *Otello* the stage entry of the Venetian ambassador was announced and the dancers entertained him for a brief six minutes before the narrative continued. Verdi often rises to the occasion and produces charming, tuneful music, felicitously scored. In the suite from *Il trovatore* (an unlikely subject for a balletic diversion), the delightful third section, *La Bohémienne*, is worthy of Delibes in its use of the graceful violins and piquant woodwind. Not surprisingly Edward Downes has the full measure of this music. The finer overtures are played with bold characterization and dramatic fire, *Nabucco*, with its dignified sonority, and *Giovanna d'Arco* both show the BBC Philharmonic brass at their finest in quite different ways, and *Luisa Miller* is another very strong performance. The strings play most beautifully in the *Traviata Preludes*. With such richly expansive recording, showing Chandos engineering at its most spectacular, the effect is less bitingly leonine than in Karajan's electrifying two-disc survey. But even if not all of this music is top-class Verdi, the Chandos set offers much to enjoy, and the spontaneity and elegance of the music-making are never in doubt.

It is good also to have Karajan's complete set of Overtures and Preludes back in the catalogue. The 1975 recording was one of the very best made in the Philharmonie: the sound combines vividness with a natural balance and an attractive ambience. The performances have an electricity, refinement and authority that sweep all before them. The little-known overtures, *Alzira*, *Aroldo* and *La battaglia de Legnano*, are all given with tremendous panache and virtuosity. Try the splendid *Nabucco* or the surprisingly extended (8-minute) *Giovanna d'Arco* to discover the colour and spirit of this music-making, with every bar spontaneously alive, while there is not the faintest suggestion of routine in the more

familiar items. As a DG Double this is even more strongly recommendable.

Morandi has served his time conducting at La Scala and he gives ripely robust accounts of these colourful overtures and sinfonias, with excellent playing from his Hungarian musicians, notably from the strings in the *Traviata* and *Aida Preludes* and from the brass in *Nabucco*. *La forza del destino* ends the second disc strongly. Full-bloodedly resonant sound (with the second collection at times marginally sharper in definition) makes this an excellent bargain, even if the readings are not as individual as those of Chailly, Downes and Karajan.

String Quartet in E min.

(M) *** CRD CRD 3366. Alberni Qt – DONIZETTI: *Quartet No. 13;* PUCCINI: *Crisantemi.* ***

(B) **(*) Hyp. Helios CDH 55012. Delmé Qt – R. STRAUSS: *Quartet.*

The Alberni Quartet's performance is strong and compelling, and it is most imaginatively and attractively coupled with the Puccini and Donizetti pieces.

The Delmé are not a 'high-powered', jet-setting ensemble and they give a very natural performance of the Verdi which will give much pleasure: there is the sense of music-making in the home among intimate friends, refreshingly unforced, even if the sound is on the dry side.

String Quartet in E min. (arr. Toscanini for string orchestra).

(N) **(*) DG 463 579-2. VPO, Previn – BEETHOVEN: *String Quartet Op. 131.* **(*)

Toscanini's arrangement for full strings of the Verdi *Quartet* makes an apt and attractive coupling for the comparable string arrangement of the late Beethoven work. The result is to soften and sweeten Verdi's original conception, with generally charming results. Refined playing from the Vienna strings, reverbantly recorded.

CHORAL MUSIC

Ave Maria (2 versions); *Laudi alla Vergine Maria; Messa per Rossini: Libera me, Domine. Stabat Mater; Te Deum. Otello: Ave Maria.*

(N) *** DG 469 075-2. Santa Cecilia Ch. & O, Chung.

Myun-Whun Chung conducts dedicated performances of this nicely balanced group of Verdi's sacred works, by the Santa Cecilia Chorus and Orchestra, centring on the *Four Sacred Pieces*. Set in a warm acoustic, the choir is distantly balanced, not focused cleanly enough, though the two main pieces, the *Stabat Mater* and the *Te Deum*, bring powerful dramatic and dynamic contrasts, with fine singing from the chorus as well as the soprano soloist, Carmela Remigio. Verdi himself did not intend his *Ave Maria* of 1889 (fourth of the *Four Pieces*) to be grouped with the other three, his very last works dating from 1896–7, a point which Chung highlights by setting it alongside the *Ave Maria* of 1880, as well as Desdemona's *Ave Maria* from *Otello*, which developed from it. Similarly, the *Libera me* which Verdi wrote in 1869 for the composite *Messa per Rossini* developed into his own full *Requiem Mass*. In the outburst of *Dies irae* the washy acoustic blunts the edge of the drama, but it is a powerful reading, again with Carmela Remigio, who is an excellent soloist, sweet and tender. This is a stimulating and worthwhile collection.

Messa solenne (Messa di Gloria); Ave Maria; Laudate pueri; Libera me (Messa per Rossini 1869); Pater noster; Qui tollis; Tantum ergo in F; Tantum ergo in G.

(N) *** Decca 467 280-2. Scano, Gallardo-Domas, Diego, Florez, Tarver, Aliev, Pertusi, Milan Ch. & SO, Chailly.

It is quite a surprise on this Verdi disc to find the message 'Five world premières'. What Riccardo Chailly has done is to record a series of Verdi's student works, all of them sacred, which have been unearthed in recent years in his native Busseto. They provide a fascinating view of the young composer's development, led as he was towards operatic models, notably Rossini, by his teacher, an anti-clerical choirmaster. The major item is the *Messa solenne*, which after a weighty, almost Beethovenian opening, sadly lacking in distinctive ideas, has a vigorously rhythmic second *Kyrie* and chirpy woodwind writing. There are also echoes of Mozart and Bellini. If none of this offers insights in the manner of Berlioz's youthful inspirations, it is all enjoyable, and is warmly performed under Chailly by the Milan Choir and Symphony Orchestra and a fine line-up of soloists, fresh and clear. In addition to the student works there are three rarities from later on. The *Libera me*, part of a composite work commemorating Rossini, led directly to the great *Requiem* of 1874, where Verdi developed the same material even more effectively. More revelatory are the linked but contrasting settings of the *Pater noster* and *Ave Maria*, which were first performed at La Scala in 1880, and which deserve to be far better known, with their anticipations of the last scene of *Otello*.

Requiem Mass.

*** Chan. 9490. Crider, Hatziano, Sade, Lloyd, L. Symphony Ch., LSO, Hickox.

(B) *** EMI double forte (ADD) CZS5 68613-2 (2). Scotto, Baltsa, Luchetti, Nesterenko, Amb. Ch., Philh. O, Muti – CHERUBINI: *Requiem in C min.* ***

*** BBC (ADD) BBCL 4029-2 (2). Shuard, Reynolds, Lewis, Ward, Philh. Ch. & O, Giulini (with *Overture: La forza del destino* ***) – SCHUBERT: *Mass in E flat.* ***

⊛ (B) (***) DG Double mono 439 684-2 (2). Stader, Dominguez, Carelli, Sardi, St Hedwig's Cathedral Ch., Berlin RIAS SO, Fricsay – ROSSINI: *Stabat Mater.* (***)

(M) (***) DG mono 447 442-2. Stader, Radev, Krebs, Borg, St Hedwig's Cathedral Ch., Berlin RIAS O, Fricsay.

(N) **(*) Ph. 468 079-2 (2). Fleming, Borodina, Bocelli, d'Arcangelo, Kirov Ch. & O, Gergiev.

(M) (**(*)) EMI mono CMS5 65506-2 (2). Schwarzkopf, Dominguez, Di Stefano, Siepi, La Scala, Milan, Ch. & O, De Sabata (with VERDI: *La traviata*: Preludes to Acts I & III; *I vespri siciliani*: Overture; WOLF-FERRARI: *Susanna's Secret*: Overture and Intermezzo; RESPIGHI: *The Fountains of Rome*; ROSSINI: *William Tell Overture* **(*)).

**(*) Decca (ADD) 411 944-2 (2). Sutherland, Horne, Pavarotti, Talvela, V. State Op. Ch., VPO, Solti.

(M) **(*) RCA (ADD) 09026 61403-2 (2). L. Price, J. Baker, V. Luchetti, Van Dam, Chicago Symphony Ch. & SO, Solti.

(*)** DG (IMS) 439 033-2 (2). Tomowa-Sintow, Baltsa, Carreras, Van Dam, V. State Op. Konzertvereinigung, VPO, Karajan.

(M) **(*) Sony (ADD) SM2K 47639 (2). Arroyo, Veasey, Domingo, Raimondi, L. Symphony Ch., LSO, Bernstein.

(i) Requiem Mass; (ii) 4 Sacred Pieces.

*** Ph. 442 142-2 (2). (i) Orgonasova, Von Otter, Canonici, Miles; (ii) D. Brown; Monteverdi Ch., ORR, Gardiner.

*** DG 435 884-2 (2). Studer, Lipovšek, Carreras, Raimondi, V. State Op. Ch., VPO, Abbado.

(M) **(*) EMI CMS5 67560-2 [567563]. (i) Schwarzkopf, Ludwig, Gedda, Ghiaurov; (ii) J. Baker; Philh. Ch. & O, Giulini.

(BB) **(*) Naxos 8.550944/5 (2). Filipova, Scalchi, Hernández, Colombara, Hungarian State Op. Ch. & O, Morandi.

(N) (B) **(*) Decca (ADD) 467 118-2 (2). (i) L. Price, Elias, Björling, Tozzi, V. Musikverein, VPO, Reiner; (ii) Minton, Los Angeles Master Ch., LAPO, Mehta.

(i) Requiem Mass. Choruses from: Aida; Don Carlo; Macbeth; Nabucco; Otello.

*** Telarc CD 80152 (2). (i) Dunn, Curry, Hadley, Plishka; Atlanta Ch. & SO, Shaw.

It says much for Richard Hickox's recording for Chandos with the LSO and London Symphony Chorus that in important ways – not just practically as the only modern single-disc version – it marks the first of what could be a new generation of readings of Verdi's choral masterpiece. His pacing flows more freely than has become the rule in latterday performances, yet there is never a feeling of haste, simply of heightened intensity when his control of rubato and phrase is so warmly idiomatic. These are very much the speeds which made the vintage Serafin recording of 1939 so compelling, but with singing from the London Symphony Chorus infinitely finer than that of Serafin's Italian chorus. In their fire they rival Giulini's classic Philharmonia set, even outshining that in luminosity, thanks in part to the spacious and full recording which, in a reverberant church acoustic, yet reveals ample detail. The warm-toned soprano, Michele Crider, has a glorious chest register, and the mezzo, Markella Hatziano, is equally warm and characterful, while the tenor, Gabriel Sade, sings with clear, heady beauty, not least in a radiant *Ingemisco*, and Robert Lloyd gives one of his noblest, most commanding performances. A winning set in every way.

Gardiner, using period forces, is searingly dramatic and superbly recorded, with fine detail, combining transparent textures, weight and atmospheric bloom. It can still be recommended as a fine alternative among modern digital recordings even to collectors not drawn to period performance. The soloists make a characterful quartet, with the vibrant Orgonasova set against the rock-steady von Otter, and with Canonici bringing welcome Italianate colourings to the tenor role. The *Four Sacred Pieces* are equally revealing. The longest and most complex, the final *Te Deum*, is the most successful of all, marked by thrillingly dramatic contrasts, as in the fortissimo cries of '*Sanctus*'.

With spectacular analogue sound – not always perfectly balanced, but vividly wide in its tonal spectrum – Muti's 1979 Kingsway Hall performance makes a tremendous impact and is in almost all respects preferable to his later version, recorded live eight years later at La Scala. Characteristically he prefers fast speeds, and in the *Dies irae* he rushes the singers dangerously, making the music breathless in its excitement. Unashamedly, from first to last this is an operatic performance, with a passionately committed quartet of soloists, under-pinned by Nesterenko, in glorious voice, giving priestly authority to the *Confutatis*. Scotto is not always sweet on top, but Baltsa is superb, and Luchetti sings freshly. Now offered, very inexpensively, and aptly coupled with a splendid (digital) account of Cherubini's *C minor Requiem*, so admired by Berlioz, this makes an outstanding bargain.

Giulini's performances of the Verdi *Requiem* in the early 1960s have become legendary, electrifying occasions that led to a benchmark studio recording of 1964, still unsurpassed. Here the BBC Legends series puts an important gloss on that in offering a Prom recording of 1963, even more dramatically involving for the extra spontaneity of a live performance. The stereo sound is first-rate, and though the British soloists may not be such stars as their studio counterparts, they sing beautifully, with firm, clear tone. The Schubert *Mass*, recorded at the Edinburgh Festival of 1968, makes a welcome and generous coupling.

Fricsay's second recording, which DG have now reissued on a bargain Double coupled with Rossini, is of a live performance given in 1960, the very last he conducted before his untimely death. In biting drama it has never been surpassed, and even though speeds are often measured when compared with his fine studio recording (which DG have also currently reissued on a single disc as an 'Original'), such is the voltage of this later performance that it doesn't sound slower. Moreover, it is underpinned by a commanding gravity that plainly reflects the conductor's own emotions during his last illness. Like him, the two male soloists are Hungarian, and both are first rate, with the tenor, Gabor Carelli, pleasingly Italiante of tone (his *Ingemisco* is ravishing). Maria Stader, the soprano soloist as before, sings with clear, pure tone and Oralia Dominguez is the rich mezzo. The chorus is superbly disciplined, yet ardent: the *Dies irae* is electrifying, the *Sanctus* wonderfully light and joyfull and the closing *Lux aeterna* raptly beautiful. The CD transfer enhances the bite of the choral projection without losing the atmospheric warmth of a recording which, even today, can startle by its immediacy of sound.

Fricsay's superb mono studio recording of Verdi's *Requiem* caused a sensation when it first appeared on LP in 1954. Its tingling drama anticipated the later version, and though tempi are generally faster than in that live account there is marginal extra precision and polish. This makes a worthy reissue in DG's 'Legendary Recordings' series, with the full, spacious mono recording already showing that the DG engineers, using mono techniques, could achieve a combination of clarity and atmosphere. The solo team is first class with the contribution of Kim Borg standing out, as in the live performance.

Claudio Abbado's DG live recording was taken from performances at the Vienna Musikverein with the Vienna Philharmonic and Vienna choirs, as well as Cheryl Studer, Marjana Lipovšek, José Carreras and Ruggero Raimondi, all in superb voice and finely matched, even if Carreras has to husband his resources. In detail Abbado's reading is little different from his earlier, La Scala version, but the sense of presence, of the tension of a live occasion, makes the later account far more magnetic, from the hushed murmurings of the opening onwards. The Vienna forces are not only more expressive but more polished too. The *Four Sacred Pieces* are also superbly done in another live recording.

Robert Shaw, in the finest of his Atlanta recordings, may not have quite the same searing electricity as Toscanini's classic NBC recording (for which he trained the chorus), but it regularly echoes it in power and the well-calculated pacing. In the *Dies irae*, for example, like Toscanini he gains in thrust and power from a speed marginally slower than usual. With sound of spectacular quality, beautifully balanced and clear, the many felicities of the performance, not least the electricity of the choral singing and the consistency of the solo singing, add up to an exceptionally satisfying reading. The fill-up of five Verdi opera choruses is colourful, and again brings superb choral singing.

Recorded at a church in North London during the Kirov Company's visit to Covent Garden in 2000, Gergiev's reading is one of high contrasts. Though the chorus often sounds misty and distant in hushed passages, the fervour of the singing is never in doubt in the big dramatic moments, as in the opening of the *Dies irae*. Yet what above all makes a powerful impact is the orchestra recorded close, so that the instrumental fire of the *Dies irae* has rarely come over so vividly, complete with shattering bass drum.

Renée Fleming and Olga Borodina could hardly be bettered as the two women soloists, both characterful and well-contrasted, yet with a fine blend in their duets. Borodina's firm, tangy chest register is a special delight, and the involvement of Fleming in the soul-searching of the final *Libera me* is most moving, as on the words *Tremens factus*, 'I am seized with fear and trembling.' Andrea Bocelli produces a fine flow of sweet tenor-tone controlling the *Ingemisco* well, if at times with excessive portamento, but Ildebrando d'Arcangelo sounds rather underpowered in the bass role, with *Mors stupebit* intimate rather than commanding. Gergiev is wonderfully fiery in the big dramatic moments, but with phrasing elaborately moulded, he too often seems to make the music drag in slow numbers. Not a first choice but a characterful one.

What Giulini on EMI proved was that refinement added to power can provide an even more intense experience than the traditional Italian approach. In this concept a fine English chorus and orchestra prove exactly right. The array of soloists could hardly be bettered. Schwarzkopf caresses each phrase, and the exactness of her voice matches the firm mezzo of Christa Ludwig in their difficult octave passages. Gedda is at his most reliable, and Ghiaurov with his really dark bass actually manages to sing the almost impossible

Mors stupebit in tune without a suspicion of wobble. Giulini's set also finds space to include the *Four Sacred Pieces* in polished and dramatic performances which bring out the element of greatness in often uneven works. This has been carefully remastered as one of EMI's 'Great Recordings of the Century' but the otherwise excellent new transfer of the 1963/4 recording still reveals roughness in heavy climaxes of the *Dies irae* in the *Requiem*.

Well recorded, with first-rate Hungarian chorus and orchestra, the Naxos version offers an enjoyable account of Verdi's *Requiem* which may lack something in dramatic intensity but which consistently brings out the work's lyrical warmth. Though the tenor, César Hernández, is at times coarse, the other three soloists are very good, notably the Bulgarian soprano, Elena Filipova, with her opulent tone. This is a performance which gains in intensity as it progresses and, if anything, the *Four Sacred Pieces*, an apt fill-up, bring performances even more dedicated, with refined choral singing, with the chorus set slightly behind the orchestra. A good bargain version, though it is worth remembering that Richard Hickox's outstanding Chandos version of the *Requiem*, coming on a single full-priced disc, is also a bargain, with much more sharply detailed recording of the chorus.

Victor de Sabata's legendary 1954 recording unashamedly adopts the most spacious speeds and a deeply devotional manner, helped by a starry quartet of soloists. When it came out, it was not well received by many, who found the slow speeds self-indulgent, the very opposite of those adopted by Tullio Serafin, whose early recording made an obvious comparison, lasting a full 22 minutes less. Also, this de Sabata version, master-minded by Walter Legge, was superseded ten years later by Giulini's stereo version. It never reappeared on LP, making this CD transfer very welcome, limited in sound but with fine dynamic contrasts. Dedication is the keynote in a performance of extremes, totally concentrated but very personal in its new look. The four superb soloists respond with total commitment, Schwarzkopf most of all, in radiant voice. Oralia Dominguez excels herself, as cleanly focused as Schwarzkopf, with her rapid flicker-vibrato adding character to the firm mezzo timbre. Giuseppe di Stefano sings with headily fresh tone, while Siepi is splendid too. The chorus sing lustily but not always with discipline. The fill-ups are just as characterful: the *Traviata Preludes* rapt and finely shaded, the Respighi sensuously atmospheric, the *William Tell Overture* given surprising refinement. Best of all are the two little Wolf-Ferrari items, witty and sparkling, but this is now deleted.

Reiner's opening of the *Requiem* is very slow and atmospheric. He takes the music at something like half the speed of Toscanini and shapes everything very carefully. Yet as the work proceeds the performance soon sparks into life, and there is some superb and memorable singing from a distinguished team of soloists. The recording has a spectacularly wide dynamic range, enhanced by the CD format, and, with the chorus singing fervently, the *Dies irae* is overwhelming. Mehta's performance of the *Sacred Pieces* is enhanced by brilliant, sharply focused recording.

There is little or nothing reflective about Solti's Decca account, and those who criticize the work for being too operatic will find plenty of ammunition here. The team of soloists is a very strong one, though the matching of voices is not always ideal. It is a pity that the chorus is not nearly as incisive as the Philharmonia on the EMI Giulini set. But if you want an extrovert performance, the firmness of focus and precise placing of forces in the Decca engineering of 1967 make for exceptionally vivid results on CD.

On RCA, Solti's 1977 Chicago version, with an unusually sensitive and pure-toned quartet of soloists – Luchetti perhaps not as characterful as the others, Leontyne Price occasionally showing strain – and with superb choral singing and orchestral playing, has all the ingredients for success. The set is well worth having for Janet Baker's deeply sensitive singing, but the remastered recording – not well balanced – tends to be fierce on climaxes, and, in other ways too, Solti's earlier, Decca/Vienna set is preferable.

Though Karajan's smooth style altered relatively little after his earlier version, the overall impression in his later DG set is fresher, though as transferred the recording is inconsistent. Even with 'original image bit reprocessing' improving the focus and impact, the sound is not impressive. Though Tomowa-Sintow's un-Italian soprano sometimes brings a hint of flutter, she sings most beautifully in the final rapt account of *Libera me*.

Bernstein's 1970 *Requiem* was recorded in the Royal Albert Hall. By rights, the daring of that decision should have paid off; but with close balancing of microphones the result is not as full and free as one would have expected. Bernstein's interpretation remains most persuasive, with the drama exaggerated at times, red-blooded in a way that is hard to resist. The quartet of soloists is particularly strong, notably the young Plácido Domingo.

(i; ii) *Requiem Mass;* **(iii; iv)** *Inno delle nazione;* **(ii)** *Te Deum;* **(iii)** *Luisa Miller: Quando le sere al placido.* **(iv)** *Nabucco: Va pensiero.*

(M) (***) RCA mono 74321 72373-2 (2). (i) Nelli, Barbieri, Di Stefano, Siepi; (ii) Robert Shaw Ch.; (iii) Peerce; (iv) Westminster Ch.; NBC SO, Toscanini.

Toscanini's account of the *Requiem* brings a supreme performance, searingly intense. The opening of the *Dies irae* has never sounded more hair-raising, with the bass-drum thrillingly caught, despite the limitation of dry mono recording. And rarely has the chorus shone so brightly in this work on record, while the soloists are near-ideal, a vintage team. The other works make fascinating listening, too. The *Te Deum* was one of Toscanini's very last recordings, a performance more intense than usual with this work, and it is good to have the extraordinary wartime recording of the potboiling *Hymn of the Nations*. The *Internationale* is added to Verdi's original catalogue of national anthems, to represent the then ally, the USSR.

Te Deum (from *Quattro pezzi sacri*).

(N) (B) *** Warner Apex 8573 89128-2. Soloists, Bielefeld Musikvereins Ch., Philh. Hungarica, Stephani – BRUCKNER: *Te Deum.* ***

Although Verdi's *Te Deum* was published as the last of the *Four Sacred Pieces*, Verdi did not expect them to be performed as a group, and the *Te Deum* for double chorus makes a fine independent work. Supported by spectacular orchestration, Verdi's dramatic setting, from the pianissimo opening onwards, makes frequent use of bold dynamic contrasts, which are well realized here. The choral singing is first class, the brass resplendent and the conductor, Martin Stephani, keeps everyone on their toes. The recording has a warmly resonant acoustic against which the singing projects thrillingly. Aptly coupled with Bruckner's much more devotional setting, this can be strongly recommended, especially at such a modest cost. Text and translation are included.

OPERA

Aida (complete).

(M) *** EMI (ADD) CMS7 69300-2 (3). Freni, Carreras, Baltsa, Cappuccilli, Raimondi, Van Dam, V. State Op. Ch., VPO, Karajan.

(B) *** Double Decca (ADD) 460 765-2 (2). L. Price, Gorr, Vickers, Merrill, Tozzi, Rome Op. Ch. & O, Solti.

(M) *** Decca (ADD) 460 978-2 (3). Tebaldi, Simionato, Bergonzi, MacNeil, Van Mill, Corena, V. Singverein, VPO, Karajan.

(M) (***) RCA mono GD 86652 (3). Milanov, Björling, Barbieri, Warren, Christoff, Rome Op. Ch. & O, Perlea.

(N) (BB) (***) Naxos 8.110156/7. Caniglia, Gigli, Tajo, Stignani, Bechi, Pasero, Rome Op. Ch. & O, Serafin.

(N) (***) Romophone mono 89004-2 (2). Giannini, Pertile, Minghini-Cattaneo, Inghilleri, La Scala Ch. and O, Sabajno.

(**) EMI mono CDS5 56316-2 (3). Callas, Tucker, Barbieri, Gobbi, La Scala, Milan, Ch. & O, Serafin.

On EMI, Karajan's is a performance of Aida full of splendour and pageantry, which is yet fundamentally lyrical. On disc there is no feeling of Freni lacking power even in a role normally given to a larger voice, and there is ample gain in the tender beauty of her singing. Carreras makes a fresh, sensitive Radames, Raimondi a darkly intense Ramphis and Van Dam a cleanly focused King, his relative lightness no drawback. Cappuccilli gives a finely detailed performance as Amonasro, while Baltsa as Amneris crowns the whole performance with her fine, incisive singing. Despite some over-brightness on cymbals and trumpet, the Berlin sound for Karajan, as transferred to CD, is richly atmospheric, both in the intimate scenes and, most strikingly, in the scenes of pageant, reflecting the Salzburg Festival production which was linked to the recording. The set has been attractively re-packaged and remains a first choice, irrespective of price.

Leontyne Price is an outstandingly assured Aida on Decca, rich, accurate and imaginative, while Solti's direction is superbly dramatic, notably in the Nile Scene. Merrill is a richly secure Amonasro, Rita Gorr a characterful Amneris, and Jon Vickers is splendidly heroic as Radames. Though the digital transfer betrays the age of the recording (1962), making the result fierce at times to match the reading, Solti's version otherwise brings full, spacious sound, finer, more open and with greater sense of presence than most versions since. As a Double Decca reissue this is a formidable bargain

and the new-style cued synopsis with 'listening guide' is a fair substitute for a full libretto.

On Decca, as on EMI, Karajan was helped by having a Viennese orchestra and chorus; but most important of all is the musical teamwork of his soloists. Bergonzi in particular emerges here as a model among tenors, with a rare feeling for the shaping of phrases and attention to detail. Cornell MacNeil too is splendid. Tebaldi's creamy tone-colour rides beautifully over the phrases and she too acquires a new depth of imagination. Among the other soloists Arnold van Mill and Fernando Corena are both superb, and Simionato provides one of the finest portrayals of Amneris. The recording has long been famous for its technical bravura and flair. It has now been impressively remastered for Decca's current Legend series, and remains a remarkable technical achievement.

All four principals on the historic RCA set under Perlea are at their very finest, notably Milanov, whose poise and control in O patria mia are a marvel. Barbieri as Amneris is even finer here than in the Callas set, and it is good to hear the young Christoff resonant as Ramphis. A flamboyant performance.

Serafin's 78 rpm version was recorded in July 1948, the last of the complete opera sets from HMV that featured Beniamino Gigli as the hero. It is an electrifying performance, with Serafin at his most magnetic leading an outstanding cast of principals, all with voices firm and true. Heralded by trumpets that vividly leap out of the speakers, Gigli launches into Celeste Aida at the start with a clarity and bravura that mark his whole performance. Maria Caniglia in the title role is at her very finest, using the widest range of expression, a fire-eater who knows tenderness too, while Gino Bechi is a superbly sinister Amonasro with a natural snarl in the voice. The others characterize strongly too, with the close balance of the voices and relative dryness of acoustic vividly bringing out words and expression. The transfers by Ward Marston are outstanding, making this one of the very finest of the impressive Naxos historic opera series.

Recorded in 1928, Sabajno's pioneering version of Aida – the first after the introduction of electrical recording – demonstrates what a remarkable combination of beauty and technical security marked the Verdi stars of that time. Aureliano Pertile was the leading Radames of the period, and his singing here, always characterful, finely shaped if occasionally idiosyncratic, helps to explain his reputation as Toscanini's favourite tenor. Dusolina Giannini is in her way just as remarkable, bright and totally secure, attacking even the most exposed top-notes with precision, clarity and beauty. Irene Minghini-Cattaneo, less well known, makes a formidable Amneris, just as incisive, as is Giovanni Inghilleri as Amonasro. Ward Marston's transfers are excellent, vividly capturing the voices without damping them down.

The Nile Scene has never been performed more powerfully and characterfully on record than in this vintage La Scala set. Though Callas is not a sweet-toned Aida, her detailed imagination is irresistible, and she is matched by Tito Gobbi at the very height of his powers. Tucker gives one of his very finest performances on record, and Barbieri is a commanding Amneris. The mono sound is greatly improved in the latest transfer, but this remains at full price.

Aida: highlights.

(M) *** Decca (ADD) 458 206-2 (from above complete recording, with L. Price, Vickers, Gorr, Merrill, Tozzi; cond. Solti).

(B) **(*) DG 439 482-2 (from complete recording, with Ricciarelli, Obraztsova, Domingo, Nucci, Ghiaurov, La Scala, Milan, Ch. & O, cond. Abbado).

(BB) **(*) [EMI Encore CDE5 74759-2]. Caballé, Domingo, Cossotto, Ghiaurov, ROHCG Ch., New Philh. O, Muti.

(M) (***) EMI mono CDM5 66668-2 (from above complete recording, with Callas, Tucker, Barbieri, Gobbi; cond. Serafin).

The selection from Solti's full-price recording is generous (71 minutes) and makes an obvious first choice, for not only is it handsomely packaged in a slipcase in Decca's Opera Gala series but it comes with full translation.

In Abbado's 1981 La Scala *Aida*, it was the men who stood out: Domingo a superb Radames, Ghiaurov as Ramphis, Nucci a dramatic Amonasro, and Raimondi as the King. Ricciarelli is an appealing Aida, but her legato line is at times impure above the stave, and Elena Obraztsova produces too much curdled tone as Amneris. The recording is bright and fresh, but not ideally expansive in the ceremonial scenes. As is usual with DG's bargain Classikon series, the documentation is good, though without translations. The selection offers 64 minutes of music.

On Muti's set of highlights, Caballé's portrait of the heroine is superb, full of detailed insight into the character and with plenty of examples of superlative singing, while Cossotto makes a fine Amneris. Domingo produces a glorious sound, but this is not one of his most imaginative recordings. The sound is relatively small-scale, underlining the fierceness of Muti's reading.

The set of highlights from the Callas *Aida* includes the Nile scene and is slightly more generous, at 58 minutes, than many other reissues in this series. It certainly conveys the overall strength of the cast.

Alzira (complete).

(N) *** Ph. 464 628-2 (2). Mescheriakova, Vargas, Gavanelli, Ch. & SRO, Luisi.

(N) **(*) Orfeo (ADD) CO 57832 (2). Cotrubas, Araiza, Bruson, Rootering, Bav. R. Ch., Munich RO, Gardelli.

Alzira, dating from 1845, is at once the least cherished and the most compact of Verdi's operas, yet on disc, when brevity is often an asset, it emerges as far from perfunctory. A performance like this new one on Philips, well conducted and well sung with characterful soloists, makes clear that in musical quality it can stand comparison with any of the other operas Verdi wrote in his years 'in the galleys'.

This set, recorded in Geneva, fills in the gap created when the company abandoned its fine series of early Verdi operas conducted by Lamberto Gardelli. Gardelli recorded the piece for Orfeo instead, with an excellent cast, helped by warm and well-balanced recording supervised by Munich Radio engineers. But the soloists on Philips are a degree subtler in expression yet also more characterful.

The vibrant Marina Mescheriakova is weightier than Cotrubas on Orfeo yet just as flexible in coloratura, Ramon

Vargas as the Inca hero, Zamoro, more imaginative than his couterpart, Francisco Araiza, and Paolo Gavanelli more refined than Renato Bruson as Gusmano, Governor of Peru. Though the Orfeo recording is excellent, the Philips has the added advantage of modern digital sound.

Attila (complete).

(M) *** Ph. (ADD) 426 115-2 (2). Raimondi, Deutekom, Bergonzi, Milnes, Amb. S., Finchley Children's Music Group, RPO, Gardelli.

With its dramatic anticipations of *Macbeth* and musical ones of *Rigoletto*, and the compression which (on record if not on the stage) becomes a positive merit, *Attila*, in a fine performance under Gardelli on this Philips set, is an intensely enjoyable experience. Deutekom, not a sweet-toned soprano, has never sung better on record, and the rest of the cast is outstandingly good. The 1973 recording is well balanced and atmospheric.

Un ballo in maschera (complete).

*** Decca 410 210-2 (2). M. Price, Pavarotti, Bruson, Ludwig, Battle, L. Op. Ch., Royal College of Music Junior Dept Ch., Nat. PO, Solti.

(M) *** DG 449 588-2 (2). Domingo, Barstow, Nucci, Quivar, Jo, V. State Op. Konzertvereinigung, VPO, Karajan.

(B) *** DG Double 453 148-2 (2). Ricciarelli, Domingo, Bruson, Obraztsova, Gruberová, Raimondi, La Scala, Milan, Ch. & O, Abbado.

(M) *** EMI CMS5 66510-2 (2). Arroyo, Domingo, Cappuccilli, Grist, Cossotto, Howell, ROHCG Ch., New Philh. O, Muti.

(***) EMI mono CDS5 56320-2 (2). Callas, Di Stefano, Gobbi, Ratti, Barbieri, La Scala, Milan, Ch. & O, Votto.

(B) **(*) Double Decca (ADD) 460 762-2 (2). Tebaldi, Pavarotti, Milnes, Resnik, Donath, St Cecilia Academy, Rome, Ch. & O, Bartoletti.

Shining out from the cast of Solti's set of *Ballo* is the gloriously sung Amelia of Margaret Price in one of her richest and most commanding performances on record, ravishingly beautiful, flawlessly controlled and full of unforced emotion. The role of Riccardo, pushy and truculent, is well suited to the extrovert Pavarotti, who swaggers through the part, characteristically clear of diction, challenged periodically by Price to produce some of his subtlest tone-colours. Bruson makes a noble Renato, Christa Ludwig an unexpected but intense and perceptive Ulrica, while Kathleen Battle is an Oscar whose coloratura is not just brilliant but sweet too. Solti is far more relaxed than he often is on record, presenting a warm and understanding view of the score. The recording is very vivid within a reverberant acoustic.

Recorded in Vienna early in 1989, *Un ballo in maschera* was Karajan's last opera recording. It makes a fitting memorial, characteristically rich and spacious, with a cast – if not ideal – which still makes a fine team, responding to the conductor's single-minded vision. Standing out vocally is the Gustavo of Plácido Domingo, strong and imaginative, dominating the whole cast. He may not have the sparkle of Pavarotti in this role, but the singing is richer, more refined and more thoughtful. This Amelia is Josephine Barstow's finest achievement on record, dramatically most compelling.

Leo Nucci, though not as rough in tone as in some of his other recordings, is over-emphatic, with poor legato in his great solo, *Eri tu*. Sumi Jo, a Karajan discovery, gives a delicious performance as Oscar the page, coping splendidly with Karajan's slow speed for her Act I solo. Florence Quivar produces satisfyingly rich tone as Ulrica. Though the sound is not as cleanly focused as in the Decca recording for Solti, it is warm and full.

Abbado's powerful reading, admirably paced and with a splendid feeling for the sparkle of the comedy, remains highly recommendable at bargain price. The cast is very strong, with Ricciarelli at her very finest and Domingo sweeter of tone and more deft of characterization than on the Muti set of five years earlier. Bruson as the wronged husband Renato (a role he also takes for Solti) sings magnificently, and only Obraztsova as Ulrica and Gruberová as Oscar are less consistently convincing. The analogue recording clearly separates the voices and instruments in different acoustics, which, though distracting at first, brings the drama closer.

The quintet of principals on Muti's earlier set is unusually strong, but it is the conductor who takes first honours in a warmly dramatic reading. Muti's rhythmic resilience and consideration for the singers go with keen concentration, holding each Act together in a way he did not quite achieve in his earlier recording for EMI of *Aida*. Arroyo, rich of voice, is not always imaginative in her big solos, and Domingo rarely produces a half-tone, though the recording balance may be partly to blame. The sound is full and vivid, and for the present reissue a new booklet has been provided with full translation.

Votto's 1956 mono recording, with voices set close but with a fair amount of space round them, is among the best of the sets with Callas from La Scala, and CD focuses its qualities the more sharply. Cast from strength, with all the principals – notably Gobbi and Giuseppe di Stefano – on top form, this is indispensable for Callas's admirers.

The main interest in the earlier Decca set rests in the pairing of Tebaldi and Pavarotti. The latter was in young, vibrant voice but Tebaldi made her recording in the full maturity of her career. She gives a commanding performance, but there is no mistaking that her voice here is not as even as it once was. The supporting cast is strong, not only Milnes as Renato and Donath as Oscar, but Resnik a dark-voiced Ulrica. Bartoletti directs the proceedings dramatically, and the (1970) Decca recording remains strikingly vivid and atmospheric. Now re-issued as a Double Decca with new-style cued synopsis, this makes a good bargain recommendation.

La battaglia di Legnano (complete).

(M) *** Ph. (ADD) 422 435-2 (2). Ricciarelli, Carreras, Manuguerra, Ghiuselev, Austrian R. Ch. & O, Gardelli.

La battaglia di Legnano is a compact, sharply conceived piece, made the more intense by the subject's obvious relationship with the situation in Verdi's own time. One weakness is that the villainy is not effectively personalized, but the juxtaposition of the individual drama of supposed infidelity against a patriotic theme brings most effective musical contrasts.

Gardelli directs a fine performance, helped by a strong cast of principals, with Carreras, Ricciarelli and Manuguerra all at their finest. Excellent recording, with the depth of perspective enhanced on CD.

Il corsaro (complete).

(M) *** Ph. (ADD) 426 118-2 (2). Norman, Caballé, Carreras, Grant, Mastromei, Noble, Amb. S., New Philh. O, Gardelli.

In *Il corsaro*, though the characterization is rudimentary, the contrast between the two heroines is effective, with Gulnara, the Pasha's slave, carrying conviction in the *coup de foudre* which has her promptly worshipping the Corsair, an early example of the Rudolph Valentino figure. The rival heroines are taken splendidly here, with Jessye Norman as the faithful wife, Medora, actually upstaging Montserrat Caballé as Gulnara. Gardelli directs a vivid performance, with fine singing from the hero, portrayed by José Carreras. Gian-Piero Mastromei, not rich in tone, still rises to the challenge of the Pasha's music. Excellent, firmly focused and well-balanced Philips sound.

Don Carlos (complete).

*** EMI CDS5 56152-2 (3). Alagna, Van Dam, Hampson, Mattila, Meier, Ch. de Théâtre du Châtelet, O de Paris, Pappano.

*** Ph. 454 463-2 (3). Gorchakova, Borodina, Hvorostovsky, Margison, Scandiuzzi, ROHCG Ch. & O, Haitink.

(M) *** EMI (ADD) CMS7 69304-2 (3). Carreras, Freni, Ghiaurov, Baltsa, Cappuccilli, Raimondi, German Op. Ch., Berlin, BPO, Karajan.

(M)*** EMI CMS5 67401-2 (3) [567397]. Domingo, Caballé, Raimondi, Verrett, Milnes, Amb. Op. Ch., ROHCG O, Giulini.

(M) (**(*)) EMI mono CHS5 67439-2 (3). Christoff, Stella, Nicolai, Filippeschi, Gobbi, Neri, Rome Op. Ch. & O, Santini.

**(*) DG 415 316-2 (4). Ricciarelli, Domingo, Valentini Terrani, Nucci, Raimondi, Ghiaurov, La Scala, Milan, Ch. & O, Abbado.

Recorded live at the Châtelet Théâtre in Paris, the EMI set of the full five-Act version makes a clear first choice for anyone wanting this epic opera in the original French. In the five-act version Pappano may not include as much of the extra and optional material as Abbado has on his four-disc DG La Scala set (the only rival in French), but his judgement on the text is good, with one or two variants included. The whole performance sounds more idiomatic, helped by a cast more fluent in French than Abbado's. Regularly Pappano conveys the dramatic thrust more intensely. Naturally impetuous as well as expressive, he inspires his players as well as his singers, an exceptionally strong team. Roberto Alagna is both youthfully lyrical and heroic. Thomas Hampson as Posa and José van Dam as King Philip are both centrally strong and expressive, projecting firmly. Waltraud Meier is not caught at her best as Eboli, but relishes the drama of *O don fatale*. As the Grand Inquisitor, Eric Halfvarson is not quite steady enough, even if (thanks to Pappano) the confrontation with the King is thrilling. Crowning the whole performance is the Elisabeth of Karita

Mattila, giving her most commanding performance to date, culminating in a magnificent account of her big Act V aria, sure and true as well as deeply moving. The live recording brings some odd balances, with the sound transferred at a lowish level, but the opera-house atmosphere, vividly caught, amply compensates for any shortcoming.

The very opening of the Haitink set, based on the Covent Garden production, indicates a clear advantage over previous versions – the vividness of the sound, with off-stage choruses sharply focused left and right. If Haitink often takes a measured view, that matches the dramatic weight of this epic opera, with the pacing consistently reflecting experience in the opera-house. The three Slavonic singers heading the cast are all superb, with Galina Gorchakova a powerful Elisabetta, Olga Borodina a vibrant Eboli and Dmitri Hvorostovsky a moving and intense Posa. Though Richard Margison is too consistently loud in the title role, he has a good heroic timbre; Roberto Scandiuzzi as Philip II, rather light for the role, and Robert Lloyd as the Grand Inquisitor, not quite as steady as he once was, are well contrasted and dramatically intense.

Karajan opts for the four-Act version of the opera, merely opening out the cuts he adopted on stage. The *Auto da fé* scene is here superb, while Karajan's characteristic choice of singers for refinement of voice rather than sheer size consistently pays off. Both Carreras and Freni are most moving. Baltsa is a superlative Eboli and Cappuccilli an affecting Rodrigo. Raimondi and Ghiaurov as the Grand Inquisitor and Philip II provide the most powerful confrontation. The sound is both rich and atmospheric and is made to seem even firmer and more vivid in its current remastering, giving great power to Karajan's uniquely taut account, full of panache.

Yet it is Giulini's 1971 set that EMI have chosen as one of their 'Great Recordings of the Century'. He uses the full, five-Act text. Generally the cast is strong; the only vocal disappointment among the principals lies in Caballé's account of the big aria *Tu che le vanità* in the final Act. The CD transfer of the analogue recording brings astonishing vividness and realism, a tribute to the original engineering of Christopher Parker. Even in the big ensembles the focus is very precise, yet atmospheric too, not just analytic. Excellent documentation and a full libretto and translation.

The vintage EMI mono recording offers a seriously cut version of the four-Act score. Indifferently conducted by Gabriele Santini, it is still an indispensable set, with performances from Tito Gobbi as Rodrigo and Boris Christoff as Philip that remain unsurpassed. Gobbi's singing in the Death scene is arguably the finest recorded performance that even this glorious artist ever made, with a wonderful range of tone and feeling for words. The bitingly dark tone of Christoff as the King also goes with intense feeling for the dramatic situation, making his big monologue one of the peaks of the performance. Antonietta Stella, never a distinctive artist, gives one of her finest recorded performances as Elisabetta. As Eboli, Elena Nicolai controls her fruity mezzo well, even if the vibrato becomes obtrusive; and the most serious blot is the singing of the tenor, Mario Filippeschi, too often strained.

Abbado's set was the first recording to use the language which Verdi originally set, French, in the full five-Act text. The first disappointment lies in the variable quality of the sound, with odd balances, yet the cast is a strong one. Domingo easily outshines his earlier recording with Giulini (in Italian), while Katia Ricciarelli as the Queen gives a tenderly moving performance, if not quite commanding enough in the Act V aria. Ruggero Raimondi is a finely focused Philip II, nicely contrasted with Nicolai Ghiaurov as the Grand Inquisitor in the other black-toned bass role. Lucia Valentini Terrani as Eboli is warm-toned if not very charactered, and Leo Nucci makes a noble Posa.

Don Carlos: highlights.

(M) *** EMI CDM7 63089-2 (from above complete recording, with Domingo, Caballé; cond. Giulini).

Giulini's disc of highlights can be highly recommended. In selecting from such a long opera, serious omissions are inevitable, but the *Auto da fé* scene is included. Vivid sound; the only reservation concerns Caballé's *Tu che le vanità*, which ends the selection disappointingly.

I due Foscari (complete).

(M) *** Ph. (ADD) 422 426-2 (2). Ricciarelli, Carreras, Cappuccilli, Ramey, Austrian R. Ch. & SO, Gardelli.

I due Foscari brings Verdian high spirits in plenty, erupting in swinging cabalettas and much writing that anticipates operas as late as *Simon Boccanegra* and *La forza del destino*. The cast here is first rate, with Ricciarelli giving one of her finest performances in the recording studio to date and with Carreras singing tastefully as well as powerfully. Crisp discipline from the Austrian, though this is less atmospheric than the earlier, London-made recordings in the series.

Ernani (complete).

*** Decca 421 412-2 (2). Pavarotti, Sutherland, Nucci, Burchuladze, Welsh Nat. Op. Ch. & O, Bonynge.

(M) *** RCA (ADD) GD 86503 (2). L. Price, Bergonzi, Sereni, Flagello, RCA Italiana Op. Ch. & O, Schippers.

**(*) EMI CDS7 47083-2 (3). Domingo, Freni, Bruson, Ghiaurov, La Scala, Milan, Ch. & O, Muti.

(M) **(*) Ph. 446 669. Lamberti, Sass, Kovats, Miller, Takacs, Hungarian State Op. Ch. & O, Gardelli.

Made in May 1987, this was the final collaboration between Sutherland and Luciano Pavarotti, yet for over ten years it remained on the shelf. The hero is a nobleman who becomes a bandit after the death of his father, offering Verdi what William Weaver in his note describes as 'a kind of rough draft for Manrico in *Il trovatore*'. Yet it is the heroine, Elvira, with her challenging aria, *Ernani involami*, who captures first attention. Here Sutherland gives a commanding account of the role, and though the beat in the voice betrays her age, that showpiece aria brings not just power but all the old flexibility. Helped by the sympathetic conducting of her husband, Richard Bonynge, she endearingly throws caution to the wind. Pavarotti too, balanced rather close, gives a vividly characterful portrayal of Ernani himself, always ready to shade down his tone, characteristically bringing out word-meaning. Leo Nucci as Don Carlo, the King, his rival in love, is also firmer and more characterful than others on disc, and

Paata Burchuladze as the vengeful de Silva was caught here at the brief peak of his career with his dark, sinister bass well controlled. On sound the new set easily outshines its rivals.

At mid-price, Schippers' set, recorded in Rome in 1967, is an outstanding bargain. Leontyne Price may take the most celebrated aria, *Ernani involami*, rather cautiously, but the voice is gloriously firm and rich, and Bergonzi is comparably strong and vivid, though Mario Sereni, vocally reliable, is dull, and Ezio Flagello gritty-toned. With Schippers drawing the team powerfully together, it remains a highly enjoyable set, with the digital transfer making voices and orchestra sound full and vivid.

The great merit of Muti's set, recorded live at a series of performances at La Scala, is that the ensembles have an electricity rarely achieved in the studio, even if the results may not always be so precise and stage noises are often obtrusive. The singing, generally strong and characterful, is yet flawed. The strain of the role of Elvira for Mirella Freni is plain from the big opening aria, *Ernani involami*, onwards. Even in that aria there are cautious moments. Bruson is a superb Carlo and Ghiaurov a characterful Silva, but his voice now betrays signs of wear. As Ernani himself, Plácido Domingo gives a commanding performance, but under pressure there are hints of tight tone. The CD version gives greater immediacy and presence, but also brings out the inevitable flaws of live recording the more clearly.

Originally issued on Hungaraton, this early digital set returns to the catalogue on Philips at mid-price with full libretto and translation. Gardelli's conducting is most sympathetic and idiomatic in the Hungarian version and, like Muti's, it is strong on ensembles. Sylvia Sass is a sharply characterful Elvira, Callas-like in places, and Lamberti a bold Ernani, though both are vocally flawed. Capable rather than inspired or idiomatic singing from the rest. The digital recording is bright and well balanced, although the CD transfer brings out the resonant acoustic.

Ernani (complete; in English).

(N) (M) *** Chan. 3052 (2). Gavin, Patterson, Opie, Wedd, Rose, ENO Ch. & O, Parry.

Early Verdi in English can sound like an anticipation of Gilbert and Sullivan, particularly in the jolly choruses, but in a lively, vibrant performance like this, recorded soon after the ENO production in 2000, it is in some ways even more vital than a performance in Italian. The principals are first rate, with Susan Patterson a formidable Elvira, tackling her big aria in Act I firmly and confidently, at once rich-toned and agile with a perfect trill. The Australian tenor Julian Gavin is also well cast in the title role, with a cleanly focused voice and clear diction, while Alan Opie gives a vintage performance in the baritone role of the King. Full, vivid recording. A welcome if unexpected addition to the Peter Moore/Chandos Opera in English series.

Falstaff (complete).

*** DG 410 503-2 (2). Bruson, Ricciarelli, Nucci, Hendricks, Egerton, Valentini Terrani, Boozer, LA Master Ch., LAPO, Giulini.

*** EMI CDS5 67083-2 (2). Gobbi, Schwarzkopf, Zaccaria, Moffo, Panerai, Philh. Ch. & O, Karajan.

(N) *** Ph. 462 603-2 (2). Lafont, Martinpelto, Evans, Mingardo, James, Michaels-Moore, Palombi, Monteverdi Ch., ORR, Gardiner.

(M) **(*) Decca (ADD) 417 168-2 (2). Evans, Ligabue, Freni, Kraus, Elias, Simionato, RCA Italiana Op. Ch. & O, Solti.

(M) **(*) DG 447 686-2 (2). Taddei, Kabaivanska, Perry, Ludwig, Panerai, Araiza, De Palma, Zednik, V. State Op. Ch., VPO, Karajan.

(N) (M) ** RCA 09026 60705-2 (2). Panerai, Titus, Sweet, Kaufmann, Horne, Lopardo, Bav. R. Ch. & RSO, Davis.

Giulini's *Falstaff* brings a care for musical values which at times undermines the knockabout comic element, yet the clarity and beauty of the playing are caught superbly on CD. Bruson, hardly a comic actor, is impressive on record for his fine incisive singing, giving tragic implications to the monologue at the start of Act III after Falstaff's dunking. The Ford of Leo Nucci, impressive in the theatre, is thinly caught, whereas the heavyweight quality of Ricciarelli as Alice comes over well, if at times her singing lacks purity. Barbara Hendricks is a charmer as Nannetta, but she hardly sounds fairy-like in her Act III aria. The conviction of the performance puts it high among modern digitally recorded versions.

The earlier (1956) Karajan recording presents not only the most pointed account orchestrally of Verdi's comic masterpiece (the Philharmonia Orchestra at its very peak) but the most sharply characterful cast ever gathered for a recording. If you relish the idea of Tito Gobbi as Falstaff (his many-coloured voice, not quite fat-sounding in humour, presents a sharper character than usual), then this is clearly the best choice. The rest of the cast too is a delight, with Elisabeth Schwarzkopf a tinglingly masterful Mistress Ford, Anna Moffo sweet as Nannetta and Rolando Panerai a formidable Ford. On CD the digital transfer is sharply focused.

With the orchestra playing period instruments from around 1900, Gardiner's period performance of *Falstaff* is a revelation, letting one hear the elaborate texture of Verdi's writing with new transparency, revealing detail usually buried. Not that that concern for detail gets in the way of dramatic and comic thrust, for this Philips set was recorded after a long series of concert performances with the same singers and orchestra, and has clearly benefited from that.

Jean-Philippe Lafont makes a characterful Falstaff. His voice may not be as powerful as some, but on disc it is satisfyingly fat-sounding, with a wide tonal and expressive range, which Lafont exploits superbly to bring out detailed meaning, as in his Act 3 monologue, with self-pity convincingly turning into anger.

Anthony Michaels-Moore is compellingly thoughtful and self-searching as Ford, and the quartet of women is outstanding, with Hillevi Martinpelto fresh and bright as Alice, Sara Mingardo wonderfully resonant as Mistress Quickly, and Rebecca Evans singing ravishingly as Nannetta. As Fenton, Antonetto Palombi may not quite be quite so secure as Evans, but his voice is headily youthful to make a good match. A sparkling version quite distinct from others in a very strong field of contenders and well worth considering as a supplemental purchase if you already have either the Giulini or Karajan recordings.

Sir Geraint Evans's assumption of the role of Verdi's Falstaff, in partnership with Sir Georg Solti, was originally issued by RCA, and here it comes up as sparkling as ever on a pair of mid-priced CDs. There is an energy, a sense of fun, a sparkle that outshines rival versions, outstanding as they may be. Evans never sounded better on record, and the rest of the cast live up to his example admirably. Solti drives hard, but it is an exciting and well-pointed performance, and the rest of the cast well contrasted.

Karajan's second (1980) recording of Verdi's last opera, made over twenty years after his classic EMI Philharmonia version with Gobbi and Schwarzkopf, is far less precise in a relaxed and genial way. With the exception of Kabaivanska, whose voice is not steady enough for the role of Alice, it is a good cast, with Ludwig fascinating as Mistress Quickly. Most astonishing of all is Taddei's performance as Falstaff himself, full, characterful and vocally astonishing from a man in his sixties. The digital sound is faithful and wide-ranging, and the CD transfer vividly captures the bloom of the original reverberant recording.

While many will welcome the return to the catalogue of Sir Colin Davis's RCA set for the fine performance of Rolando Panerai, strong and resonant in the title role, the reverberant acoustic remains a problem in an opera where inner clarity is so important. Here the resonance, though flattering to the voices, confuses detail (with even the semiquaver figure of the opening barely identifiable), making it harder for the fun of the piece to come over. Davis, as he has shown many times at Covent Garden, is masterly in his Verdian timing, but the result here lacks sparkle: it is all too serious and Germanic. Alongside Panerai the cast is a good one, including another veteran, Marilyn Horne, producing stentorian tones as Mistress Quickly. Sharon Sweet is a forceful Alice, with Julie Kaufmann as Nanetta well matched against Frank Lopardo's Fenton, stylish in Verdi as he was in Rossini. Yet with such sound the recording has distinct limitations. A full libretto/translation is included.

La forza del destino (complete).

(M) *** RCA (ADD) 74321 39502-2 (3). L. Price, Domingo, Milnes, Cossotto, Giaiotti, Bacquier, Alldis Ch., LSO, Levine.

*** DG 419 203-2 (3). Plowright, Carreras, Bruson, Burchuladze, Baltsa, Amb. Op. Ch., Philh. O, Sinopoli.

(M) *** RCA (ADD) GD 87971 (3). L. Price, Tucker, Merrill, Tozzi, Verrett, Flagello, Foiani, RCA Italiana Op. Ch. & O, Schippers.

(M) **(*) EMI (ADD) CMS7 64646-2 (3). Arroyo, Bergonzi, Cappuccilli, Raimondi, Casoni, Evans, Amb. Op. Ch., RPO, Gardelli.

Leontyne Price recorded the role of Leonora in an earlier RCA version made in Rome in 1956, but the years hardly touched her voice. The roles of Don Alvaro and Don Carlo are ideally suited to the team of Plácido Domingo and Sherrill Milnes so that their confrontations are the corner-

stones of the dramatic structure. Fiorenza Cossotto makes a formidable rather than a jolly Preziosilla, while on the male side the line-up of Bonaldo Giaiotti, Gabriel Bacquier, Kurt Moll and Michel Sénéchal is far stronger than on rival sets. In a vivid transfer of the mid-1970s sound, this is a strong, well-paced version with an exceptionally good and consistent cast.

Sinopoli draws out phrases lovingly, sustaining pauses to the limit, putting extra strain on the singers. Happily, the whole cast thrives on the challenge, and the spaciousness of the recording acoustic not only makes the dramatic interchanges the more realistic, it brings out the bloom on all the voices, above all the creamy soprano of Rosalind Plowright. Though José Carreras is sometimes too conventionally histrionic, even strained, it is a strong, involved performance. Renato Bruson is a thoughtful Carlo, while some of the finest singing of all comes from Agnes Baltsa as Preziosilla and Paata Burchuladze as the Padre Guardiano, uniquely resonant.

On the earlier RCA set, under Thomas Schippers, Leontyne Price's voice was fresher and more open; on balance this is a more tender and delicate performance than the weightier one she recorded with Levine. Richard Tucker as Alvaro is here far less lachrymose and more stylish than he was earlier in the Callas set, producing ample, heroic tone, if not with the finesse of a Domingo. Robert Merrill as Carlo also sings with heroic strength, consistently firm and dark of tone; while Shirley Verrett, Giorgio Tozzi and Ezio Flagello stand up well against any rivalry. The sound is remarkably full and vivid.

Gardelli, normally a reliable recording conductor in Italian opera, here gives a disappointing account of a vividly dramatic score. The cast is vocally strong and each member of it lives up to expectations. Moreover the recording – made in 1969 in Watford Town Hall – is first rate, vivid, full and atmospheric. But it is vital in so long and episodic a work that overall dramatic control should be firm. Admirers of the individual artists will find much to enjoy when the sound is so flattering to the voices. The layout places Acts I and II on the first disc, while Acts III and IV are each allotted a CD apiece.

La forza del destino (slightly abridged).

(***) EMI mono CDS5 56323-2 (3). Callas, Tucker, Tagliabue, Nicolai, Rossi-Lemeni, Capecchi, La Scala, Milan, Ch. & O, Serafin.

Though there are classic examples of Callas's raw tone on top notes, they are insignificant next to the wealth of phrasing which sets a totally new and individual stamp on even the most familiar passages. Apart from his tendency to disturb his phrasing with sobs, Richard Tucker sings superbly; but not even he – and certainly none of the others (including the baritone Carlo Tagliabue, well past his prime) – begin to rival the dominance of Callas. Serafin's direction is crisp, dramatic and well paced, again drawing the threads together. The 1955 mono sound is less aggressive than many La Scala recordings of this vintage and has been freshened on CD.

La forza del destino: highlights.

(B) *** DG 463 261-2 (from above complete set, with
   Plowright, Carreras, Bruson, Baltsa; cond. Sinopoli).

A self-recommending set of highlights from a first-class
complete set. With a 65-minute selection and a cued synopsis
this is excellent value.

Un giorno di regno (complete).

(M) *** Ph. (ADD) 422 429-2 (2). Cossotto, Norman,
   Carreras, Wixell, Sardinero, Ganzarolli, Amb. S., RPO,
   Gardelli.

Un giorno di regno may not be the greatest comic opera of
the period, but this scintillating performance under Gardelli
clearly reveals the young Verdi as more than an imitator of
Rossini and Donizetti, and there are striking passages which
clearly give a foretaste of such numbers as the duet *Si
vendetta* from *Rigoletto*. Despite the absurd plot, this is as
light and frothy an entertainment as anyone could want.
Excellent singing from a fine team, with Jessye Norman and
José Carreras outstanding. The recorded sound is vivid.

Giovanna d'Arco (complete).

(M) **(*) EMI (ADD) CMS7 63226-2 (2). Caballé, Domingo,
   Milnes, Amb. Ch., LSO, Levine.

The seventh of Verdi's operas, based very loosely indeed on
Schiller's drama, is typical of the works which the master
was writing during his 'years in the galleys', exuberantly
melodic. James Levine, a youthful whirlwind in his very first
opera recording, presses on too hard in fast music, with the
rum-ti-tum hammered home, but is warmly sympathetic in
melodic writing, particularly when Caballé is singing. What
had become a standard trio of principals for the 1970s
here gives far more than a routine performance. With fine
recording there is much to enjoy, even when the plot –
involving merely Joan, her father (who betrays her) and the
King – is so naïve.

Jerusalem (complete).

(N) *** Ph. 462 613-2 (3). Mescheriakova, Giordani,
   Scandiuzzi, SRO Ch. & O, Luisi.

To have a long-buried Verdi opera dusted down and given
a brilliant first recording like this is a rare joy, particularly
when it confounds the adverse verdict trumpeted for 150
years. *Jerusalem* is the radical reworking of Verdi's second
big success, *I Lombardi*, which he made for the Paris Opéra
in 1847, his first essay in setting French.
   The general view, with one glowing exception, has been
that *Jerusalem* is a failure, even dottier in its plot than *I
Lombardi*. Yet Julian Budden, that most perceptive of Verdi
scholars, has voiced the opposite view in his comprehensive
survey of the operas, and it is here triumphantly justified.
Where in *I Lombardi* the tenor hero is excluded from Act 1
and dies before Act 4 – in which he is absurdly brought back
as a heavenly voice – the layout of *Jerusalem* is clearly
preferable.
   The big hit number, the trio for the three principals,
which in *I Lombardi* comes at the end of Act 3, is placed far
more effectively in *Jerusalem* at the end of Act 4, with only

a brief denouement to follow, and with its saccharine solo
violin removed. Other changes are also in favour of the later
work.
   This première recording offers brilliant sound and fine,
incisive playing from the Suisse Romande Orchestra, with
electrifying singing from the Geneva Chorus. The principals
are more variable. Roberto Scandiuzzi in the principal baritone role, Roger, sounds too old, but Marcello Giordani as
the hero, Gaston, is youthfully fresh and Marina Mescheriakova is a sweetly vibrant heroine, if rather taxed in coloratura.

I Lombardi (complete).

*** Decca 455 287-2 (2). Pavarotti, Anderson, Leech, Ramey,
   Met. Opera Ch. and O, Levine.

(M) *** Ph. (ADD) 422 420-2 (2). Deutekom, Domingo,
   Raimondi, Amb. S., RPO, Gardelli.

With the help of brilliant Decca recording, Levine consistently brings out this early work's adventurousness, its
striking anticipations of *La forza del destino*. Based on the
staging of the opera at the Met in New York, the chief glory
of the set is the casting of Pavarotti as the hero, Oronte. As
Oronte does not appear until Act II and dies at the end of
Act III (signal for the *Great Trio*, much the finest number in
the opera), it is not a role one would have expected Pavarotti
to take on at this stage of his career. He does it masterfully,
on the whole, with even more imagination than the young
Domingo on the rival Philips set under Gardelli. Unfortunately, the visionary appearance of the dead hero in Act IV
(*Benedetto del cielo*) has the singer placed far too close, a
very corporeal ghost. Samuel Ramey sings strongly in the
baritone role of the evil brother, Pagano (who appears later
as a Hermit), but vocally cannot quite match Ruggero Raimondi on Philips. On the other hand June Anderson as the
heroine, Giselda, is both sweeter and more sympathetic than
Cristina Deutekom on Philips.
   I Lombardi reaches its apotheosis in the famous *Trio*, well
known from the days of 78-r.p.m. recordings. By those
standards, Cristina Deutekom is not an ideal Verdi singer:
her tone is sometimes hard and her voice is not always
perfectly under control. Domingo as Oronte is in superb
voice, and the villain Pagano is well characterized by Raimondi. Impressive singing too from Stafford Dean and
Clifford Grant. Gardelli conducts dramatically, heightening
the impact of the plot.

Luisa Miller (complete).

*** Decca 417 420-2 (2). Caballé, Pavarotti, Milnes, Reynolds,
   L. Op. Ch., Nat. PO, Maag.

(B) *** DG Double (ADD) 459 481-2 (2). Ricciarelli,
   Obraztsova, Domingo, Bruson, Howell, ROHCG Ch. & O,
   Maazel.

(M) *** RCA GD 86646 (2). Moffo, Bergonzi, Verrett,
   MacNeil, Tozzi, Flagello, RCA Italiana Op. Ch. & O, Cleva.

On Decca, Caballé, not flawless vocally, yet gives a splendidly
dramatic portrait of the heroine and Pavarotti's performance
is full of creative, detailed imagination. As Federica, Anna
Reynolds underlines the light and shade, consistently

bringing out atmospheric qualities. Vividly transferred to CD.

Maazel's 1979 Covent Garden set returns to the catalogue as a DG Double and would have been very competitive indeed had it included a full libretto and translation instead of just a synopsis. Though taut in his control, Maazel uses his stage experience of working with these soloists to draw them out to their finest, most sympathetic form. Ricciarelli gives one of her tenderest and most beautiful performances on record, Domingo is in glorious voice and Bruson as Luisa's father sings with a velvet tone. Gwynne Howell is impressive as the Conte di Walter and Wladimiro Ganzarolli's vocal roughness is apt for the character of Wurm. The snag is the abrasive Countess Federica of Elena Obraztsova.

In many ways the Cleva RCA set provides a performance to compete with the Maazel version and is just as stylish, with Moffo at her very peak, singing superbly, Carlo Bergonzi unfailingly intelligent and stylish, and Verrett nothing less than magnificent in her role as a quasi-Amneris. MacNeil and Tozzi are also satisfyingly resonant, and Fausto Cleva tellingly reveals his experience directing the opera at the Met. Good recording.

Macbeth (complete).

*** Ph. 412 133-2 (3). Bruson, Zampieri, Shicoff, Lloyd, German Op. Ch. & O, Berlin, Sinopoli.

(M) *** DG (ADD) 449 732-2 (2). Cappuccilli, Verrett, Ghiaurov, Domingo, La Scala, Milan, Ch. & O, Abbado.

(M) *** EMI (ADD) CMS7 64339-2 (2). Milnes, Cossotto, Raimondi, Carreras, Amb. Op. Ch., New Philh. O, Muti.

(M) (*(**)) EMI mono CMS5 66447-2 (2). Callas, Mascherini, Tajo, Penno, Della Pergola, La Scala, Milan, Ch. & O, De Sabata.

Sinopoli presents *Macbeth* as a searing Shakespearean inspiration, scarcely more uneven than much of the work of the Bard himself. In the Banqueting scene, for example, Sinopoli creates extra dramatic intensity by his concern for detail and his preference for extreme dynamics, and Renato Bruson and Mara Zampieri respond vividly. Zampieri's voice may be biting rather than beautiful, but, with musical precision an asset, she matches exactly Verdi's request for the voice of a she-devil. Neil Shicoff as Macduff and Robert Lloyd as Banquo make up the excellent quartet of principals, while the high voltage of the whole performance clearly reflects Sinopoli's experience with the same chorus and orchestra at the Deutsche Oper in Berlin. CD adds vividly to the realism of a recording that is well balanced and focused but atmospheric.

At times Abbado's tempi are unconventional, but with slow speeds he springs the rhythm so infectiously that the results are most compelling. Together making a fine team, each of the principals is meticulous about observing Verdi's detailed markings, above all those for *pianissimo* and *sotto voce*. Verrett, powerful above the stave, yet makes a virtue out of necessity in floating glorious half-tones, and with so firm and characterful a voice she makes a highly individual Lady Macbeth. Cappuccilli has never sung with a finer range of tone or more imagination on record than here, and Plácido Domingo makes a real, sensitive character out of

the small role of Macduff. Excellent recording, splendidly remastered as one of the first operas to be included in DG's 'Legendary Recordings' series, and now at mid-price on two discs.

Muti's 1976 version of *Macbeth*, made at Abbey Road, appeared within weeks of Abbado's, confirming that, in this opera, new standards were being set on record. Though Muti and his team do not quite match the supreme distinction of Abbado and, later, Sinopoli, they provide a strong alternative. Both Milnes and Cossotto sing warmly and are richly convincing in their relatively conventional views of their roles, while the comfortable reverberation and warmth of the EMI recording conceal any slight shortcomings of ensemble. The reissue therefore provides a firm mid-priced recommendation for this opera, neatly fitted on two CDs, but without the supplementary items originally included as an appendix.

The role of Lady Macbeth could hardly have been more perfectly suited to Maria Callas, and though there are serious flaws in this live recording of 1952 – evidently taken off a radio relay – the commanding presence, the magnetic musical imagination and the abrasive tones make this a unique experience. In 1952 the vocal flaws that beset Callas were largely in the future, with thrilling sound in every register. Also Victor de Sabata, despite some odd misjudgements like his brisk tempo for the Sleepwalking scene, is comparably incisive. Sadly, nothing else in the performance matches such mastery, with Enzo Mascherini a dull, uncharacterful Macbeth and only the resonant Italo Tajo as Banquo otherwise commanding attention. Scrubby, limited sound which most ears will still accommodate for the sake of such a performance.

I Masnadieri (complete).

(M) *** Ph. (ADD) 422 423-2 (2). Caballé, Bergonzi, Raimondi, Cappuccilli, Amb. S., New Philh. O, Gardelli.

Few will seriously identify with the hero-turned-brigand of *I Masnadieri* who stabs his beloved rather than lead her into a life of shame; but, on record, flaws of motivation are of far less moment than on stage. The melodies may only fitfully be of Verdi's more memorable quality, but the musical structure and argument often look forward to a much later period with hints of *Forza*, *Don Carlo* and even *Otello*. With Gardelli as ever an urgently sympathetic Verdian, and a team of four excellent principals, splendidly recorded, the set can be warmly welcomed.

Nabucco (complete).

*** DG 410 512-2 (2). Cappuccilli, Dimitrova, Nesterenko, Domingo, Ch. & O of German Op., Berlin, Sinopoli.

*** Decca (ADD) 417 407-2 (2). Gobbi, Suliotis, Cava, Previdi, V. State Op. Ch. & O, Gardelli.

With Sinopoli one keeps hearing details normally obscured. Even the thrill of the great chorus *Va, pensiero* is the greater when the melody first emerges at a hushed pianissimo, as marked. Dimitrova is superb in Abigaille's big Act II aria, noble in her evil, as is Cappuccilli as Nabucco, less intense than Gobbi was on Gardelli's classic set for Decca, but stylistically pure. The rest of the cast is strong too, including Domingo in the unusually small tenor role and Nesterenko superb as the High Priest, Zaccaria. Bright and forward digital sound, less atmospheric than the 1965 Decca set with Gobbi and Suliotis, conducted by Gardelli.

On Decca, the Viennese chorus lacks bite in *Va, pensiero*; but in every other way this is a masterly performance, with dramatically intense and deeply imaginative contributions from Tito Gobbi as Nabucco and Elena Suliotis as the evil Abigaille. Suliotis made this the one totally satisfying performance of an all-too-brief recording career, wild in places but no more than is dramatically necessary. Though Carlo Cava as Zaccaria is not ideally rich of tone, it is a strong performance, and Gardelli, as in his later Verdi recordings for both Decca and Philips, showed what a Verdian master he is, whether in pointing individual phrases or whole scenes, simply and naturally. Vivid and atmospheric 1965 Decca recording.

Nabucco: highlights.

(M) *** Decca (ADD) 458 246-2 (from above recording, with Souliotis; Gobbi; cond. Gardelli).

Souliotis's impressive contribution is well represented on the Decca highlights disc, and there are fine contributions too from Gobbi. Needless to say the chorus *Va, pensiero* is given its place of honour and the reissued selection now runs for 69 minutes. As in other Opera Gala reissues, a full translation is now included.

Otello (complete).

*** DG 439 805-2 (2). Domingo, Studer, Leiferkus, Ch. & O of Bastille Opera, Chung.

(M) *** RCA (ADD) 74321 39501-2 (2). Domingo, Scotto, Milnes, Amb. Op. Ch., Nat. PO, Levine.

*** Decca 433 669-2 (2). Pavarotti, Te Kanawa, Nucci, Rolfe Johnson, Chicago SO & Ch., Solti.

(M) *** RCA (ADD) GD 81969 (2). Vickers, Rysanek, Gobbi, Rome Op. Ch. & O, Serafin.

(M) *** EMI CMS7 69308-2 (2). Vickers, Freni, Glossop, Ch. of German Op., Berlin, BPO, Karajan.

(B) **(*) Music & Arts CD 1043 (2). Domingo, Freni, Cappuccilli, Ciannella, Raffanti, La Scala, Milan, Ch. & O, C. Kleiber.

(M) (***) EMI mono CHS5 65751-2 (2). Vinay, Martinis, Schöffler, Dermota, V. State Op. Ch., VPO, Furtwängler.

(B) **(*) Double Decca 460 756-2 (2). Cossutta, M. Price, Bacquier, V. Boys' Ch., V. State Op. Ch., VPO, Solti.

(M) (**(*)) RCA mono GD 60302 (2). Vinay, Valdengo, Nelli, Merriman, Assandri, NBC Ch. & SO, Toscanini.

Plácido Domingo's third recording of *Otello* proves to be his finest yet, more freely expressive, even more involved than his previous ones; the baritonal quality of his tenor has here developed to bring extra darkness, with the final solo, *Niun mi tema*, poignantly tender. Cheryl Studer gives one of her finest performances as Desdemona, the tone both full and pure, while Sergei Leiferkus makes a chillingly evil Iago, the more so when his voice is the opposite of Italianate, verging on the gritty, which not everyone will like. With plenty of light and shade, Myung-Whun Chung is an urgent Verdian, adopting free-flowing speeds yet allowing Domingo full expansiveness in the death scene. The Chorus and

Orchestra of the Bastille Opera excel themselves, setting new standards for an opera recording from Paris, and the sound is first rate.

On RCA, Domingo as Otello combines glorious heroic tone with lyrical tenderness. Scotto is not always sweet-toned in the upper register, and the big ensemble at the end of Act III brings obvious strain; nevertheless, it is a deeply felt performance which culminates in a most affecting account of the all-important Act IV solos, the *Willow song* and *Ave Maria*. Milnes makes a powerful Iago, a handsome, virile creature beset by the biggest of chips on the shoulder. In the transfer of the 1977 analogue original the voices are caught vividly and immediately, and the orchestral sound too is fuller and cleaner than in many more recent versions.

In the Decca Chicago set the key element is the singing of Pavarotti, new to his role of Otello, as was Nucci as Iago. In obedience to Solti, Pavarotti often adopts faster speeds than usual. Whatever the detailed reservations, this is a memorable reading, heightened by Pavarotti's keen feeling for the words and consistently golden tone. With a close microphone-balance, like the others he is prevented from achieving genuine pianissimos; but above all he offers a vital, animated Otello, always individual. Dame Kiri Te Kanawa produces consistently sumptuous tone; the *Willow song* is glorious. The impact of the whole is greatly enhanced by the splendid singing of the Chicago Symphony Chorus, helped by digital sound that is fuller and more vivid than on any rival set.

No conductor is more understanding of Verdian pacing than Serafin and, with sound that hardly shows its age (1960), this alternative RCA set presents two of the finest solo performances on any *Otello* recording of whatever period: the Iago of Tito Gobbi has never been surpassed for vividness of characterization and tonal subtlety; while the young Jon Vickers, with a voice naturally suited to this role, was in his prime as the Moor. Leonie Rysanek is a warm and sympathetic Desdemona, not always ideally pure-toned but tender and touching in one of her very finest recorded performances. The sense of presence in the open, well-balanced recording is the more vivid on CD, thanks to a first-rate transfer.

Karajan directs a big, bold and brilliant account, for the most part splendidly sung and with all the dramatic contrasts strongly underlined. There are several tiny, but irritating, statutory cuts, but otherwise on two mid-price CDs this is well worth considering. Freni's Desdemona is delightful, delicate and beautiful, while Vickers and Glossop are both positive and characterful, only occasionally forcing their tone and losing focus. The recording is clarified on CD.

Music and Arts offers a live recording of the legendary performance in December 1976. If Carlos Kleiber can often sound cold or even uninvolved in his studio recordings, this demonstrates the high voltage electricity he can produce on a big occasion, here matching the seering intensity of Toscanini in this work. Placido Domingo, having just completed a series of performances in Hamburg and Paris, is in superb form, with the voice at its finest, and his personal magnetism as an actor heightened by the conductor's challenge. Mirella Freni as Desdemona is at her freshest, sweet and vulnerable, while Cappuccilli sings with keen incisiveness as Iago, not always sinister-sounding but musically superb. Stage noises are endlessly intrusive, but the atmosphere of a great occasion is vividly caught.

Furtwängler is incandescent, a performance of extremes. Set against rapt concentration and tender expressiveness in such passages as the Act I love duet and Desdemona's final scene, the fierily dramatic attack of the main drama is heightened all the more. So the oath duet of Otello and Iago in Act II is thrilling, and the clarity of both Ramon Vinay in the title-role and of Paul Schoeffler as a clean-cut, Germanic Iago adds to the bite. Vinay, who recorded the role with Toscanini four years earlier, has a focus and power ideally suited to the role, even if the voice is rarely beautiful. Sadly, the Austrian Radio recording of the stage production often balances him distantly. Dragica Martinis, whose career was sadly short, is here revealed as a tender and charming Desdemona, a match for her more celebrated colleagues. The orchestral sound is limited and dim, with intrusive stage-noises. However, this set is now deleted.

The warmth and tenderness of Solti's Vienna reading of *Otello* as well as its incisive sense of drama take one freshly by surprise. The recording is bright and atmospheric to match. As Desdemona Margaret Price gives a ravishing performance, with the most beautiful and varied tonal quality allied to deep imagination. Carlo Cossutta as Otello is not so characterful a singer but he sings sensitively with clear, incisive tone. Gabriel Bacquier gives a thoughtful, highly intelligent performance as Iago, but he is disappointingly weak in the upper register. The Decca recording is full and vivid, and in its new Double Decca format this can be counted excellent value. The libretto is replaced by Decca's new-style synopsis with 'listening guide'.

Toscanini's historic 1947 reading suffers more than usual from dry, limited sound but in magnetic intensity it is irresistible, bringing home the biting power of Verdi's score as few other recorded performances ever have. Ramon Vinay makes a commanding Otello, baritonal in vocal colouring but firm and clear, with a fine feeling for words. Giuseppe Valdengo had few rivals among baritones of the time in the role of Iago, strong, animated and clean in attack, though the vocal differentiation between hero and villain is less marked than usual. Herva Nelli is sweet and pure if a little colourless as Desdemona. The recording prevents her from achieving a really gentle pianissimo, and Toscanini, for all his flowing lines, fails to allow the full repose needed.

Rigoletto (complete).

(B) *** Ph. Duo 462 158-2 (2). Bruson, Gruberová, Shicoff, Fassbaender, Lloyd, St Cecilia Ac., Rome, Ch. & O, Sinopoli.

*** Decca (ADD) 414 269-2 (2). Milnes, Sutherland, Pavarotti, Talvela, Tourangeau, Amb. Op. Ch., LSO, Bonynge.

*** DG 447 064-2 (2). Chernov, Pavarotti, Studer, Scandiuzzi, Graves, Met. Op. Ch. & O, Levine.

(***) EMI mono CDS5 56327-2 (2). Gobbi, Callas, Di Stefano, La Scala, Milan, Ch. & O, Serafin.

(M) **(*) RCA GD 86506 (2). Merrill, Moffo, Kraus, Elias, Flagello, RCA Italiana Op. Ch. & O, Solti.

(M) **(*) DG (ADD) 457 753-2 (2). Cappuccilli, Cotrubas, Domingo, Obraztsova, Ghiaurov, Moll, Schwarz, V. State Op. Ch., VPO, Giulini.

Edita Gruberová might have been considered an unexpected choice for Gilda, remarkable for her brilliant coloratura rather than for deeper expression, yet here she makes the heroine a tender, feeling creature, emotionally vulnerable yet vocally immaculate. Similarly, Renato Bruson as Rigoletto does far more than produce a stream of velvety tone, detailed and intense, responding to the conductor and combining beauty with dramatic bite. Even more remarkable is the brilliant success of Neil Shicoff as the Duke, more than a match for his most distinguished rivals. Here the *Quartet* becomes a genuine climax. Brigitte Fassbaender as Maddalena is sharply unconventional but vocally most satisfying. Sinopoli's speeds, too, are unconventional at times, but the fresh look he provides is most exciting, helped by full and vivid recording, consistently well balanced.

Just over ten years after her first recording of this opera, Sutherland appeared in it again, this time with Pavarotti, who is an intensely characterful Duke: an unmistakable rogue but an unmistakable charmer, too. Thanks to him and to Bonynge above all, the *Quartet*, as on the Sinopoli set, becomes a genuine musical climax. Sutherland's voice has acquired a hint of a beat, but there is little of the mooning manner which disfigured her earlier assumption, and the result is glowingly beautiful as well as supremely assured technically. Milnes makes a strong Rigoletto, vocally masterful rather than strongly characterful. The digital transfer is exceptionally vivid and atmospheric.

With an excellent cast James Levine conducts a thrustful, exceptionally high-powered reading of *Rigoletto*, vividly dramatic. The sound is full and immediate, with the solo voices in sharp focus, enhancing the power. Vladimir Chernov is a firm, clear, virile Rigoletto, not as searchingly characterful as some, but maybe because he sings with no hint of strain, with the beauty and accuracy of the singing consistently satisfying. Cheryl Studer is a tenderly affecting Gilda, singing with a bright, girlish tone, at once youthful and mature, defying age. Pavarotti was fresher in his earlier recording with Bonynge, but heard in close-up his is a thrillingly involving performance still, and the rest of the cast are first-rate too. Not a first choice perhaps, but a strong and sound one.

There has never been a more compelling performance of the title-role in *Rigoletto* than that of Gobbi on his classic La Scala set of the 1950s. At every point, in almost every single phrase, Gobbi finds extra meaning in Verdi's vocal lines, with the widest range of tone-colour employed for expressive effect. Callas, though not naturally suited to the role of the wilting Gilda, is compellingly imaginative throughout, and Di Stefano gives one of his finest performances. The transfer of the original mono recording is astonishingly vivid in capturing the voices. This remains at full price.

Anna Moffo makes a charming Gilda in the Solti set of 1963. Solti at times presses too hard, but this is a strong and dramatic reading, with Robert Merrill producing a glorious flow of dark, firm tone in the name-part. Alfredo Kraus is as stylish as ever as the Duke, and this rare example of his voice at its freshest should not be missed. A good bargain, though there are statutory cuts in the text.

Unlike Solti, Giulini, ever thoughtful for detail, seems determined to get away from any conception of *Rigoletto* as melodrama; however, in doing that he misses the red-blooded theatricality of Verdi's concept, the basic essential. Although it may be consistent with Giulini's view, the dramatic impact is further reduced by the fact that Cappuccilli (with his unsinister voice) makes the hunchback a noble figure from first to last, while Domingo, ever intelligent, makes a reflective rather than an extrovert Duke. Cotrubas is a touching Gilda, but the close balance of her voice is not helpful, and the topmost register is not always comfortable. The recording, made in the Musikverein in Vienna, has the voices well to the fore, with much reverberation on the instruments behind, an effect emphasized by the CD transfer.

Rigoletto: excerpts.

(N) **(*) Claremont CDGSE 1567. Fourie, Goodwin, Gabriels, Andrews, EOAN Group, Cape Town Municipal O, Manca.

A historic recording with a difference, this offers generous excerpts from a live recording made in Cape Town in 1960, when for the first time in South Africa an Italian opera was performed complete by an all-coloured cast. Most of these singers were amateurs, with little or no formal vocal training, and despite the lively conducting of Joseph Manca, the mastermind behind the EOAN Group, ensembles and choruses are often ragged.

Yet the performance has a thrust and energy which reflect an occasion which plainly moved the audience in the City Hall as much as the cast. Its success rests to a great degree on the qualities of the three principals, all of them intelligent singers, not always polished, who use fresh clear voices with admirable technique. Joseph Gabriels, a tenor with an attractively Italianate quality, who sings the role of the Duke, went on to study in Milan and make a successful career in Europe, notably in Germany.

As Gilda, Ruth Goodwin uses her light, bright, flexible soprano most stylishly, with coloratura presenting no problems for her. The Rigoletto of Lionel Fourie is comparably secure, a firm, cleanly focused baritone, finely controlled. He may not be ideally characterful but delivers the big solos with fine attack and plenty of feeling. The three Gilda–Rigoletto duets are among the highlights of the whole performance. The sound is limited, with balances sometimes odd, but generally with voices well forward, so that words are clear. An unusual offering which provides a fascinating insight into music-making in South Africa during apartheid.

Rigoletto: highlights.

(M) *** Decca 458 243-2 (from above complete recording with Sutherland, Pavarotti, Milnes; cond. Bonynge).

(M) (***) EMI mono CDM5 66667-2 (from above complete recording, with Callas, Gobbi, di Stefano; cond. Serafin).

This new Decca highlights selection includes more music (70 minutes) than before, and Decca provide full texts and translations for their handsome Opera Gala reissue.

The 58-minute selection from the Gobbi/Callas Rigoletto is well chosen to represent an extremely compelling performance, and the synopsis is properly cued.

Rigoletto (complete; in English).

(M) *** Chan. 3030 (2). Rawnsley, Field, A. Davies, Tomlinson, ENO Ch. & O, Elder.

The flair of the original English National Opera production, setting Rigoletto in the Little Italy area of New York in the 1950s and making the Mafia boss the 'Duke', is superbly carried through to this originally EMI studio recording. The intensity and fine pacing of the stage performances are splendidly caught, thanks to Mark Elder's keenly rhythmic conducting, making this one of the most successful of the ENO's Verdi sets. Outstanding vocally is the heady-toned Duke of Arthur Davies, and though neither John Rawnsley as Rigoletto nor Helen Field as Gilda has a voice so naturally beautiful, they too sing both powerfully and stylishly. Excellent recording, clean and full, and the production of the opening scene includes an effective crowd ambience of the kind pioneered by Decca.

Simon Boccanegra (complete).

⊛ (M) *** DG (ADD) 449 752-2 (2). Freni, Cappuccilli, Ghiaurov, Van Dam, Carreras, La Scala, Milan, Ch. and O, Abbado.

(M) (***) EMI mono CHS5 67483-2 (2). Gobbi, Christoff, De los Angeles, Campora, Monachesi, Dari, Rome Op. Ch. & O, Santini.

(BB) **(*) Discover DICD 920225/6. Tumagian, Gauci, Aragall, Mikulas, Sardinero, BRTN Philharmonic Ch. and O, Rahbari.

Abbado's 1977 recording of Simon Boccanegra is one of the most beautiful Verdi sets ever made. The playing of the orchestra is brilliantly incisive as well as refined, so that the drama is underlined by extra sharpness of focus. The cursing of Paolo after the great Council Chamber scene makes the scalp prickle, with the chorus muttering in horror and the bass clarinet adding a sinister comment, here beautifully moulded. Cappuccilli, always intelligent, gives a far more intense and illuminating performance than the one he recorded for RCA earlier in his career. He may not match Gobbi in range of colour and detail, but he too gives focus to the performance; and Ghiaurov as Fiesco sings beautifully too. Freni as Maria Boccanegra sings with freshness and clarity, while Van Dam is an impressive Paolo. With electrically intense choral singing as well, this is a set to outshine even Abbado's superb Macbeth, and it is superbly transferred to CD. The set is now all the more desirable at mid-price.

Tito Gobbi's portrait of the tragic Doge of Genoa is one of his greatest on record, and it emerges all the more impressively when it is set against equally memorable performances by Boris Christoff as Fiesco and Victoria de los Angeles as Amelia. The Recognition scene between father and daughter has never been done more movingly on record; nor has the great ensemble, which crowns the Council Chamber scene, been so powerfully and movingly presented, and that without the help of stereo recording. The transfer is full and immediate, giving a vivid sense of presence to the voices.

On the Discover bargain label Alexander Rahbari's well-paced reading is newly recorded in good digital sound with strong casting. Excellent East European principals are joined by the long-established Spanish tenor, Giacomo Aragall, and the baritone, Vincente Sardinero. Miriam Gauci is a vibrant, sympathetic Amelia, and though Eduard Tumagian is not the most characterful Boccanegra and Peter Mikulas could be darker-toned in the bass role of Fiesco, their voices are clear and well focused, despite backward balance. Libretto in Italian only. Good value.

Stiffelio (complete).

(M) *** Ph. (ADD) 422 432-2 (2). Carreras, Sass, Manuguerra, Ganzarolli, Austrian R. Ch. & SO, Gardelli.

Coming just before the great trio of masterpieces, Rigoletto, Il trovatore and La traviata, Stiffelio is still a sharply telling work, largely because of the originality of the relationships and the superb final scene in which Stiffelio reads from the pulpit the parable of the woman taken in adultery. Gardelli directs a fresh performance, at times less lively than Queler's of Aroldo but with more consistent singing, notably from Carreras and Manuguerra. First-rate recording from Philips, typical of this fine series.

La traviata (complete).

🌑 *** Decca 448 119-2 (2). Gheorghiu, Lopardo, Nucci, ROHCG Ch. & O, Solti.

*** Decca 430 491-2 (2). Sutherland, Pavarotti, Manuguerra, L. Op. Ch., Nat. PO, Bonynge.

(M) **(*) EMI CDS7 47538-8 (2). Scotto, Kraus, Bruson, Amb. Op. Ch., Philh. O, Muti.

(B) **(*) EMI double forte (ADD) CZS5 73824-2 (2). De los Angeles, Del Monte, Sereni, Rome Op. Ch. & O, Serafin.

**(*) Teldec 9031 76348-2 (2). Gruberová, Shicoff, Zancanaro, Amb. S., LSO, Rizzi.

(B) **(*) Double Decca (ADD) 460 759-2 (2). Sutherland, Bergonzi, Merrill, Ch. & O of Maggio Musicale Fiorentino, Pritchard.

(N) (BB) (***) Naxos mono 8.110115/6 (2). Steber, Di Stefano, Merrill, Met Ch. & O, Antonicelli (with Steber Recital (***)).

(B) **(*) DG Double (ADD) 453 115-2 (2). Scotto, Raimondi, Bastianini, La Scala, Milan, Ch. & O, Votto.

(M) (**(*)) Fonit mono 3984 29354-2 (2). Callas, Albanese, Savarese, Turin R. Ch. & O, Santini.

(M) (*(**)) EMI mono CMS5 66450- (2). Callas, Di Stefano, Bastianini, La Scala Ch. & O, Giulini.

(B) **(*) Double Decca 443 002-2 (2). Lorengar, Aragall, Fischer-Dieskau, Ch. & O of German Op., Berlin, Maazel.

(B) **(*) Ph. Duo 464 982-2 (2). Te Kanawa, Kraus, Hvorostovsky, Maggio Musicale (Florence) Ch. & O, Mehta.

Defying the problems of recording opera live at Covent Garden, the Decca engineers here offer one of the most vivid and involving versions ever of La traviata. As on stage, Gheorghiu brings heartfelt revelations, using her rich and vibrant, finely shaded soprano with consistent subtlety. Youthfully vivacious in the first Act, dazzling in her coloratura, she already reveals the depths of feeling which compel her later self-sacrifice. In Act II she finds ample power for the great outburst of Amami, Alfredo, and in Act III almost uniquely uses the second stanza of Addio del passato (often omitted) to heighten the intensity of the heroine's emotions. Frank Lopardo emerges as a fresh, lyrical Alfredo with a

distinctive timbre, passionate and youthful-sounding too. Leo Nucci, a favourite baritone with Solti, provides a sharp contrast as a stolid but convincing Germont. A video version – taken from a single performance, not (like the CDs) an edited compendium of a series – is also offered (VHS 071 431-3; Laserdisc 071 428-1), letting one appreciate how Gheorghiu's physical beauty matches her voice, and how elegant and atmospheric Richard Eyre's Covent Garden production is, with sets by Bob Crowley.

Sutherland's second recording of the role of Violetta has a breadth and exuberance beyond her achievement in the earlier version of 1963, conducted by John Pritchard, and the richness and command of the singing put this among the very finest of her later recordings. Pavarotti too, though he overemphasizes Di miei bollenti spiriti, sings with splendid panache as Alfredo. Manuguerra as Germont lacks something in authority, but the firmness and clarity are splendid. Bonynge's conducting is finely sprung, the style direct, the speeds often spacious in lyrical music, generally undistracting. The digital recording is outstandingly vivid and beautifully balanced but the CD booklet is not ideal.

Muti has no concern for tradition; at the start of the Act I party music, he is even faster than Toscanini, but the result is dazzling; and when he needs to give sympathetic support to his soloists, above all in the great Act II duet between Violetta and Germont, there is no lack of tenderness. Overall, it is an intensely compelling account, using the complete text (like Bonynge), and it gains from having three Italy-based principals. Scotto and Kraus have long been among the most sensitive and perceptive interpreters of these roles, and so they are here; with bright digital recording, however, it is obvious that these voices are no longer young, with Scotto's soprano spreading above the stave and Kraus's tenor often sounding thin. Bruson makes a fine, forthright Germont, though it does not add to dramatic conviction that his is the youngest voice. Small parts are well taken, and the stage picture is projected clearly on CD in a pleasantly reverberant acoustic.

Even when Victoria de los Angeles made this EMI recording in the late 1950s, the role of Violetta lay rather high for her voice. Nevertheless it drew from her much beautiful singing, not least in the coloratura display at the end of Act I which, though it may lack easily ringing top notes, has delightful sparkle and flexibility. As to the characterization, De los Angeles is a most sympathetically tender heroine. Though neither the tenor nor the baritone can match her in artistry, their performances are both sympathetic and feeling, thanks in part to the masterly conducting of Serafin. All the traditional cuts are made, not just the second stanzas. The CD transfer is vivid and clear and at bargain price a fair recommendation, though only a synopsis is provided.

Carlo Rizzi draws subtle, refined playing from the LSO, which in turn brings refined singing from a well-matched cast. Giorgio Zancanaro is a characterful Germont, giving depth of feeling to the first scene of Act II up to Di Provenza il mar. Though Edita Gruberová's bright soprano acquires an unevenness under pressure, she is freshly expressive and, increasingly through the opera, up to the great challenge of the death scene, produces the most delicate pianissimos, with phrasing and tone exquisitely shaded. She may not match the finest Violettas of the past, and the tenor, Neil Shicoff, sings with less finesse than the other principals, but this stands high in the list of modern, digital versions.

In Sutherland's 1963 recording of *La traviata*, it is true that her diction is poor, but it is also true that she has rarely sung on record with such deep feeling as in the final scene. The *Addio del passato* (both stanzas included and sung with an unexpected lilt) merely provides a beginning, for the duet with Bergonzi is most winning, and the final death scene, *Se una pudica vergine*, is overwhelmingly beautiful. This is not a sparkling Violetta, but it is vocally close to perfection. Bergonzi is an attractive Alfredo and Merrill a clean-cut Germont. This is excellent value as a Double Decca, although now the libretto has been replaced with Decca's cued synopsis and 'listening guide'.

Few singers on disc can match Eleanor Steber as Violetta in the historic live recording of *La traviata*, made at the Met in New York on New Year's Day 1949, and now reissued on Naxos. The beauty and precision as well as the power of Steber's singing are phenomenal, with each note clearly defined down to ornamentation of diamond clarity.

With the eager and youthful Giuseppe di Stefano as Alfredo, and Robert Merrill as a rock-steady, intense Germont, the emotional thrust of the drama comes over at full force, with Giuseppe Antonicelli drawing playing and singing from his Met forces to match even a Toscanini. Limited radio sound clearly transferred. As a very welcome supplement come a series of Steber's commercial recordings of different arias, showing her versatility, from Verdi, Rossini and Puccini to Romberg and Richard Rodgers.

It is worth having the 1962 DG La Scala set for the moving and deeply considered singing of Renata Scotto as Violetta, fresher in voice than in her later, HMV set. In a role which has usually eluded the efforts of prima donnas on record, she gives one of the most complete portraits, with thrilling coloratura in Act I and with the closing scene unforgettably moving. It is sad that the rest of the cast is largely undistinguished. Gianni Raimondi as Alfredo is stirring if not refined, and Bastianini is a coarse Germont *père*. The conductor, Antonino Votto, gives routine direction but keeps the music alive. The usual stage cuts are observed. The recording is vividly atmospheric, a fair bargain on a DG Double. There are good notes and a well-cued synopsis.

Like the companion Cetra set of *La gioconda*, this Fonit set was made by Callas very early in her career (in 1952). She was to record it again three years later with Giulini and Di Stefano, and that is still available, showing her at her very peak, but the sound of the transfer deteriorates towards the end. The 1952 recording is more consistent, noticeably fierce at the opening (affecting both the orchestral strings and the vocal fortissimos), but it seems to settle down (with occasional peakiness) and in the present transfer the overall effect is quite open. Callas's characterization of Violetta had not fully reached maturity, but the fresh youthfulness of the voice more than compensates. All the singing is very characteristic (including an odd mistake in the vocal flurries before *Sempre libera* – otherwise an excitingly brilliant account). Francesco Albanese is a sympathetic Alfredo, especially in the closing Act, but Ugo Savarese as Germont *père* is

no more distinguished than Bastianini in the later La Scala set. However, Callas admirers will surely find this well-managed reissue worth having alone for Callas's very moving closing scene. The Italian libretto, though, is without a translation.

Callas's version with Giulini was recorded in 1955. There is no more vividly dramatic a performance on record than this, unmatchable in conveying Violetta's agony; sadly, the sound, always limited, grows crumbly towards the end. It is sad too that Bastianini sings so lumpishly as Germont *père*, even in the great duet of Act II, while di Stefano also fails to match his partner in the supreme test of the final scene. The transfer is fair.

With the 1968 Maazel set, much will depend on the listener's reaction to Lorengar's voice. Her interpretation is most affecting, deeply felt and expressive, but the vibrato is often intrusive. That will not worry all ears, and with Fischer-Dieskau a searchingly intense Germont (if hardly an elderly-sounding one) and Aragall making a ringingly impressive Alfredo, this is a strong cast. Maazel's conducting is characteristically forceful. The recording quality is excellent and the fine CD transfer belies the age of the recording.

Though both Alfredo Kraus as Alfredo and Dmitri Hvorostovsky as Germont sing well on Philips, they offer an unconvincing partnership. Kraus's musical imagination is masked by a dry tone and strain on top, with a very gusty entry for example in the duet *Parigi o cara*. Equally the rich-toned Hvorostovsky hardly sounds fatherly, though he does his best in a firm, spacious account of the aria *Di Provenza*. Dame Kiri Te Kanawa is tenderly beautiful as Violetta, finely poised in *Ah fors'è lui* and the Farewell, as well as in a hushed, intense account of the Act II duet with Germont.

La traviata: highlights.

(M) *** Decca (ADD) 458 211-2 (from above complete set, with Sutherland, Bergonzi, Merrill; cond. Pritchard).

**(*) Decca 458 274-2 (from above complete recording with Gheorghiu, Lopardo, Nucci; cond. Solti).

(M) *** EMI CDM5 65573-2 (from above complete recording with Scotto, Kraus, Bruson; cond. Muti).

(B) **(*) DG 439 421-2. Cotrubas, Domingo, Milnes, Bav. State Op. Ch. & State O, C. Kleiber.

Decca's highlights from Sutherland's first (1963) recording make a clear first choice. They come handsomely packaged in Decca's Opera Gala series, with a generous selection (73 minutes) and including a full translation. Sutherland is in ravishing voice, and Bergonzi is also in excellent form. The set is discussed more fully above.

The alternative Decca set of highlights (74 minutes) from the Gheorghiu/Solti set would seem to be highly recommendable, but it is a premium-priced disc and offers only a synopsis and no texts and translations. Musically and technically there are no grumbles. Curiously the *Prelude* to Act I is included, but not the *Prelude* to Act III.

Muti's complete set is hardly a first choice at full price, so many will be glad to have this 61-minute, mid-price disc of highlights, including both the Act I and Act III *Preludes* and a well-balanced selection from each of the three Acts, with most of the key numbers included.

For many, Cotrubas makes an ideal star in *Traviata*, but unfortunately the microphone-placing in Carlos Kleiber's complete set (DG 415 132-2) over-emphasizes technical flaws and the vibrato is exaggerated. The strong contributions of Domingo and Milnes make this bargain-priced Classikon highlights CD recommendable, with 71 minutes of music, including the two *Preludes*. The documentation is well thought out, except that it omits a track-by-track synopsis of the narrative.

La traviata (complete in English).

(M) *** Chan. 3023 (2). Masterson, Brecknock, Du Plessis, E. Nat. Op. Ch. & O, Mackerras.

Mackerras directs a vigorous, colourful reading which brings out the drama, and Valerie Masterson is given the chance on record she has so long deserved. The voice is caught beautifully, if not always very characterfully, and John Brecknock makes a fine Alfredo, most effective in the final scene. Christian Du Plessis's baritone is less suitable for recording. The conviction of the whole enterprise is infectious – but be warned, Verdi in English has a way of sounding rather like Gilbert and Sullivan on record.

Il trovatore (complete).

❀ (M) *** RCA (ADD) 74321 39504-2 (2). L. Price, Domingo, Milnes, Cossotto, Amb. Op. Ch., New Philh. O, Mehta.

*** DG 423 858-2 (2). Plowright, Domingo, Fassbaender, Zancanaro, Nesterenko, Ch. & O of St Cecilia Academy, Rome, Giulini.

*** Sony S2K 48070 (2). Millo, Domingo, Chernov, Zajick, Morris, Kelly, Met. Op. Ch. & O, Levine.

(***) EMI mono CDS5 56333-2 (2). Callas, Barbieri, Di Stefano, Panerai, La Scala, Milan, Ch. & O, Karajan.

(M) (***) RCA mono GD 86643 (2). Milanov, Björling, Warren, Barbieri, Robert Shaw Ch., RCA Victor O, Cellini.

(B) *** DG Double (ADD) 453 118-2 (2). Stella, Bergonzi, Cossotto, Bastianini, La Scala, Milan, Ch. & O, Serafin.

(M) **(*) EMI (ADD) CMS7 69311-2 (2). L. Price, Bonisolli, Cappuccilli, Obraztsova, Raimondi, German Op. Ch., Berlin, BPO, Karajan.

(BB) ** Arte Nova (ADD) 74321 72110-2 (2). Bogza, Svetanov, Alperyn, Morosow, Bratislava Nat. Op. Ch., Bratislava Slovak RSO, Anguelov.

(B) *(*) Double Decca 460 735-2 (2). Sutherland, Pavarotti, Wixell, Horne, Ghiaurov, L. Op. Ch., Nat. PO, Bonynge.

The soaring curve of Leontyne Price's rich vocal line is immediately thrilling in her famous Act I aria, and it sets the style of the RCA performance, full-bodied and with dramatic tension consistently high. The choral contribution is superb; the famous *Soldiers'* and *Anvil choruses* are marvellously fresh and dramatic. When *Di quella pira* comes, the orchestra opens with great gusto and Domingo sings with a ringing, heroic quality worthy of Caruso himself. There are many dramatic felicities, and Sherrill Milnes is in fine voice throughout; but perhaps the highlight of the set is the opening section of Act III, when Azucena finds her way to Conte di Luna's camp. The ensuing scene with Fiorenza Cossotto is vocally and dramatically electrifying.

Giulini flouts convention at every point. The opera's white-hot inspiration comes out in the intensity of the playing and singing, but the often slow tempi and refined textures present the whole work in new and deeper detail. Rosalind Plowright, sensuous yet ethereal in *Tacea la notte*, confidently brings together not just sweetness and purity but brilliant coloratura, flexibility and dramatic bite. Plácido Domingo sings Manrico as powerfully as he did in the richly satisfying Mehta set on RCA, but the voice is even more heroic in an Otello-like way, only very occasionally showing strain. Giorgio Zancanaro proves a firm and rounded Count di Luna and Evgeny Nesterenko a dark, powerful Ferrando, while Brigitte Fassbaender, singing her first Azucena, sings with detailed intensity, matching Giulini's freshness. The recording is warm and atmospheric with a pleasant bloom on the voices, naturally balanced and not spotlit.

James Levine conducts his Met. cast in a performance that with full, forward sound brings out the blood-and-thunder of the piece, not least in ensembles. Plácido Domingo as Manrico shows few if any signs of wear in the voice, even in relation to his singing on his two fine earlier sets – with both Mehta on RCA and Giulini on DG. Aprile Millo as Leonora has never been more impressive on record, disciplining a voice that can often sound unruly. Vladimir Chernov is a magnificent Count di Luna, with James Morris formidably cast as Ferrando. Dolora Zajick is aptly fruity-toned as Azucena, but heavy vibrato in the voice disturbs her legato singing. Strong as the performance is, it yields before both the vintage Mehta and the inspired Giulini.

The combination of Karajan and Callas is formidably impressive. There is toughness and dramatic determination in Callas's singing, whether in the coloratura or in the dramatic passages, and this gives the heroine an unsuspected depth of character which culminates in Callas's fine singing of an aria which used often to be cut entirely – *Tu vedrai che amore in terra*, here with its first stanza alone included. Barbieri is a magnificent Azucena, Panerai a strong, incisive Count, and Di Stefano at his finest as Manrico. On CD the 1956 mono sound, now greatly improved, is one of the more vivid from La Scala at that period.

Though dating from 1952, using a cut text as in the Met. production, the Cellini version brings a vivid reminder of that great opera house at a key period. Milanov, though at times a little raw in Leonora's coloratura, gives a glorious, commanding performance, with the voice at its fullest. Björling and Warren too are in ringing voice, and Barbieri is a superb Azucena, with Cellini – rarely heard on record – proving an outstanding Verdian.

There is room for a recommendable bargain set of *Il trovatore*, and Serafin's splendidly red-blooded La Scala version on a DG Double fits the bill well. For the present DG Double reissue, the documentation has been improved with the synopsis well cued, but with no libretto. The performance is most enjoyable, with the contributions of Cossotto as Azucena and Carlo Bergonzi, splendid as Manrico, matching almost any rival. Stella and Bastianini give flawed performances, but they have many impressive moments; as Leonora's opening aria readily demonstrates, Stella is in full voice and identifies strongly with the heroine. The conducting of Serafin is crisp and stylish, and the 1963 recording is vividly transferred to CD with plenty of atmosphere.

The later Karajan set with Leontyne Price promised much but proves disappointing, largely because of the thickness and strange balances of the recording, the product of multi-channel techniques exploited over-enthusiastically. So the introduction to Manrico's aria *Di quella pira* provides full-blooded orchestral sound, but then the orchestra fades down for the entry of the tenor, Bonisolli, who is in coarse voice. In other places he sings more sensitively, but at no point does this version match that of Mehta on RCA. CD clarifies the sound but makes the flaws in the original recording all the more evident.

The Arte Nova version, an enjoyable super-bargain issue, stems from a live concert performance, well-recorded, with a good team of young soloists and fresh, vigorous playing and singing from the Bratislava choir and orchestra under the conductor Ivan Anguelov. This may not be a subtle performance, but the dramatic bite of a live occasion, well-rehearsed, comes over very well. Anda-Louise Bogza makes a strong, vehement Leonora with plenty of temperament, and Boiko Svetanov as Manrico sings with clean, firm tone, if explosively from time to time. Shining out even from the others is Graciela Alperyn as Azucena with a firm, strong mezzo and a splendid chest register, well-controlled, attacking notes fearlessly. As the Conte di Luna, Igor Morosow is strong and clear except under strain on top. A full libretto in Italian is provided but no translation.

Bonynge in most of his opera sets has been unfailingly urgent and rhythmic, but his account of *Il trovatore* is at an altogether lower level of intensity. Nor does the role of Leonora prove very apt for Sutherland late in her career; the coloratura passages are splendid, but a hint of unsteadiness is present in too much of the rest. Pavarotti for the most part sings superbly, but he falls short in, for example, the semiquaver groups of *Di quella pira* and, like Sutherland, Marilyn Horne as Azucena does not produce a consistently firm tone. Wixell as the Count sings intelligently, but a richer tone is needed. The CD transfer cannot be faulted.

Il trovatore: highlights.

(M) ✶✶✶ DG (ADD) 457 908-2 (from above complete recording with Plowright, Domingo, Fassbaender, Zancanaro; cond. Giulini).

(M) (✶✶✶) EMI mono CDM5 66669-2 (from above complete recording with Callas, Di Stefano, Panerai, Barbieri; cond. Karajan).

(M) ✶✶(✶) Decca 458 227-2 (from above complete recording, with Sutherland, Pavarotti, Horne, Wixell; cond. Bonynge).

Many collectors who have opted for the Mehta RCA set will want a reminder of Giulini's masterly, individual and highly compelling alternative interpretation. This Galleria disc is a straight reissue taken from a 1984 LP, and the content (just over an hour) seems less generous than it did then. The synopsis is cued.

The Callas/Karajan set is also represented by an hour of music, and this highly dramatic partnership comes over as strongly in excerpts as it does in the complete recording.

The selection from Bonynge's 1976 Decca set offers a useful reminder of Sutherland's Leonora. The size of the voice and its flexibility are splendidly caught, though a latter-day beat afflicts the more sustained passages and Bonynge does not conduct with his usual urgency. A full translation is included.

I vespri siciliani (complete).

✶✶(✶) EMI (ADD) CDS7 54043-2 (3). Merritt, Studer, Zancanaro, Furlanetto, Ch. & O of La Scala, Milan, Muti.

This EMI set is among the most successful of the live recordings made by Muti at La Scala, Milan, plagued by a difficult acoustic. The atmosphere is well caught and, though Muti can be too tautly urgent a Verdian, his pacing here is well geared to bring out the high drama. Outstanding in the cast is Cheryl Studer as the heroine, Elena, singing radiantly; while the tenor Chris Merritt as Arrigo sounds less coarse and strained than he has in the past. Giorgio Zancanaro also responds to the role of Monforte – the governor of Sicily, discovered to be Arrigo's father – with new sensitivity, and though Ferruccio Furlanetto as Procida lacks the full weight to bring out the beauty of line in the great aria, *O tu Palermo*, his is a warm performance too.

COLLECTIONS

Arias, Vol. I: *Don Carlos: Tu che le vanità. Ernani: Surta è la notte . . . Ernani! Ernani, involami. Macbeth: Nel di della vittoria . . . Vieni!, t'affretta; La luce langue; Una machia è qui tuttora! (Sleepwalking scene). Nabucco: Ben io t'invenni . . . Anch'io dischiuso un giorno.*

(M) ✶✶✶ EMI (ADD) CDM5 66460-2. Callas, Philh. O, Rescigno.

Originally issued under the title 'Verdi heroines', this recital marked Callas's only visit to record at Abbey Road, in September 1958. Much of it shows the great diva at her very finest. Despite the top-note wobbles, the performances are enthralling in the vividness of characterization and the musical imagination, not least as Lady Macbeth in her Act I aria and the Sleepwalking scene, and as Elisabetta in *Don Carlos*, which are magnetic. Abigaille, Elvira and Elisabetta all come out as real figures, sharply individual. Finely balanced recording, with the CD transfer well up to the high standard of the Callas Edition. This is the disc to choose from these three collections of Verdi arias.

Arias, Vol. II: *Aroldo: Ciel ch'io respir! . . . Salvami, salvami tu gran Dio! O Cielo! Dove son io. Don Carlos: Non pianger, mia compagna; O don fatale. Otello: Mia madre aveva una povera ancella . . . Piangea cantando . . . Ave Maria piena di grazia.*

(M) ✶✶(✶) EMI (ADD) CDM5 66461-2. Callas, Paris Conservatoire O, Rescigno.

Arias, Vol. III: *Aida: Ritorna vincitor. Attila: Liberamente or piangi! . . . Oh! ne! fuggente nuvolo. Un ballo in maschera: Ecco l'orrido campo; Morrò, ma prima in grazia. Il corsaro: Egli non riede ancor . . . Non so le tetre immagini; Né sulla terra . . . Vola talor dal carcere . . . Verrò . . . Ah conforto è sol la speme. Il trovatore: Tacea la notte placida . . . Di tale amor. I vespri siciliani: Arrigo! ah parli a un core.*

(M) **(*) EMI (ADD) CDM5 66462-2. Callas, Paris Conservatoire O or Paris Opéra O, Rescigno.

For her second and third collections of Verdi arias, Callas went to Paris in December 1963 and February 1964 (Volume II); and then she began a third compilation in April 1964, returning in 1965 and 1969. She approved some of the tracks for release in 1972, and the rest first appeared in 1978. In the second volume, the Shakespearean challenge of the Desdemona sequence from *Otello* is commandingly taken, very distinctive, and all the singing is dramatic. Allowances have to be made, but there is much here to cherish. The third is much more uneven, with the later items coming from a period when the voice had detriorated, particularly in the items recorded as late as 1969. There are exceptions: Aida's *Ritorna vincitor*, vehemently done, is magnificent, and the two arias from *Il corsaro*, although among the last recordings she ever made, show the vocal technique at its most assured (particularly in the legato phrasing) and the artistry at its most commanding. This third disc is essential for Callas devotees only.

Arias: *Aida: Ritorna vincitor!; Qui Radamès verrà! O patria mia. Il trovatore: Che più t'arresti; Tacea la notte;* (i) *Di tale amor. Timor di me?; D'amor sull'ali rosee.*

(M) *** RCA (ADD) 09026 68883-2. L. Price, Rome Op. O, De Fabritiis or Basile; (i) with Londi – PUCCINI: *Arias.* **(*)

This recital, known as the 'blue album' (the colour of the original LP is reproduced on the CD), has justly become a collectors' item, for the glorious flow of tone makes one understand why, even if tension is lower than in Price's performances of the complete operas. CD brings added bloom to the excellent recording.

Arias from: *Aida; Un ballo in maschera; Don Carlos; Ernani; La forza del destino; Luisa Miller; Macbeth; Otello; Rigoletto; Simon Boccanegra; La traviata; Il trovatore.*

(N)(M) **(*) Ph. (ADD) 454 390-2. Bergonzi, Amb. Singers, New Philh. O, Santi.

These arias come from a three-LP survey, spanning the whole of Verdi's career, which Carlo Bergonzi made for Philips in 1974. The present selection centres on the popular favourites and it was a pity that Philips did not decide to issue the whole sequence as a Duo, for it is the less familiar and more valuable items from *Alzira, Aroldo, Attila, La battaglia di Legnano, Il corsaro, I due Foscari, Un giorno di regno, Giovanna d'Arco, I Lombardi, I Masnadieri, Oberto* and even *I vespri siciliani* which have been omitted.

Though Bergonzi fails to contrast the characters very distinctly, few tenors of his generation could have undertaken such an exacting project with such consistently satisfying musicianship. The recording is good and clear and generally the accompaniments are stylish, with good support from the Ambrosian Singers. However, unlike comparable Decca Opera Gala collections, there are no texts and translations.

Arias from: *Aida; Un ballo in maschera; I due Foscari; Luisa Miller; Macbeth; Rigoletto; La traviata; Il trovatore.*

(M) *** Decca ADD/Dig. 458 244-2. Pavarotti with various orchestras and conductors.

Taken partly from a recital which Pavarotti put on disc early in his career, conducted by Edward Downes in 1968 (*I due Foscari, Luisa Miller* and *Macbeth*), and from others in 1969 and 1971 (*Il trovatore*) and 1974 (*Aida*), this Verdi Opera Gala collection can be warmly recommended to anyone wanting a survey of the tenor's recording career, confirming that his vocal timbre was very consistent over the years. The *Rigoletto* and *Traviata* excerpts come from the complete sets directed by Bonynge in 1971 and 1979, respectively, and the *Un ballo* scenes from the Solti set, the last to be recorded (in 1982–3). Vivid transfers and full translations.

Arias: *Don Carlo: Son io, mio Carlo . . . Per me giunto . . . O Carlo, ascolta. Luisa Miller: Sacra la scelta. Macbeth: Perfidi! All'anglo contra me v'unite . . . Pietà, rispetto, amore. La traviata: Di Provenza il mar. Il trovatore: Tutto è deserto . . . Il balen.*

*** Ph. (IMS) 426 740-2. Hvorostovsky, Rotterdam PO, Gergiev – TCHAIKOVSKY: *Arias.* ***

With a glorious voice, dark and characterful, and with natural musical imagination, Dmitri Hvorostovsky on this disc made his recording début in the West not just in Tchaikovsky arias, but here in Verdi, stylishly sung. With a voice of such youthful virility, he hardly sounds like the father-figure of the *Traviata* and *Luisa Miller* items, but the legato in Macbeth's Act IV aria is most beautiful. He also brings the keenest intensity to Posa's death-scene aria from *Don Carlo.*

Arias: *Don Carlos: Tu che la vanità. La traviata: Ah fors è lui. Il trovatore: Timor di me.*

(M) *** Sony SMK 60975. Te Kanawa, LPO, Pritchard, or LSO, Maazel – PUCCINI: Arias *** (with MOZART: *Don Giovanni: Ah! Fuggi il traditor; In quali eccessi . . . Mi tradì;* HUMPERDINCK: *Der kleine Sandmann bin ich;* DURUFLE: *Requiem: Pie Jesu ***).

*** Sony CD 37298. Te Kanwa, LPO, Pritchard – PUCCINI: *Arias.* ***

The Verdi part of Kiri Te Kanawa's Verdi–Puccini recital brings three substantial items, less obviously apt for the singer, but in each the singing is felt as well as beautiful. The coloratura of the *Traviata* and *Trovatore* items is admirably clean, and it is a special joy to hear Elisabetta's big aria from *Don Carlos* sung with such truth and precision. Good recording, enhanced on CD. However these same excerpts are also available as part of a more generous mid-priced recital.

'Gala': *Aida:* (i) *Ritorna vincitor;* (ii) *Celeste Aida.* (iii) *Un ballo in maschera: Sapper vorreste. Don Carlo:* (iv) *Ella giammai m'amò!;* (v) *O don fatale.* (vi) *La forza del destino: Pace, pace mio Dio!.* (vii) *Luisa Miller: Quando le sere al placido.* (viii) *Otello: Willow song & Ave Maria. Rigoletto:* (ix) *La donna è mobile;* (x) *Caro nome. Il trovatore: Di quella pira.* (xi) *I vespri siciliani: Mercé dilette amiche.*

(M) *** Decca (ADD) 458 226-2. (i) L. Price; (ii) Vickers;

(iii) Battle; (iv) Ghiaurov; (v) Bumbry; (vi) Tebaldi;
(vii) Bergonzi; (viii) Te Kanawa; (ix) Pavarotti; (x) Anderson;
(xi) Chiara.

The Verdi 'Gala' is a companion to a similar Puccini programme and is also full of memorable performances. The programme opens and closes with Pavarotti, crisply stylish in *La donna è mobile*, uninhibited in *Di quella pira*. Among the highlights are excerpts from Solti's *Aida* (with Leontyne Price and Jon Vickers), Kiri te Kanawa's very beautiful *Willow Song* and *Ave Maria* from *Otello*, Grace Bumbry's commanding *O don fatale* from *Don Carlo* and, in a wholly different style, Kathleen Battle's engaging portrayal of Oscar in *Un ballo in maschera*. Maria Chiara offers a sparkling *Bolero* from *I vespri siciliani*; and another unexpected choice is June Anderson's *Caro nome*, taken from the 1988 Chailly *Rigoletto*. Full translations are included.

Scenes and duets from: *Aida; Don Carlos; I Lombardi; I masnadieri; Otello; Rigoletto; Simon Boccanegra; La traviata; Il trovatore; I vespri siciliani; etc.*

*** EMI CDC5 56656-2. Gheorghiu, Alagna, L. Voices, BPO, Abbado.

Whatever the hype surrounding this starry operatic couple, this is an imaginatively planned collection of relative rarities as well as favourites, which inspires some ravishing singing. It helps that the presentation is lavish, with the chorus contributing far more than is common on such a disc, setting each duet in context. Dramatically and musically, Gheorghiu is very much the dominant partner, using the widest range of dynamic and tone-colour, not just exploiting her voice in every register, but turning each phrase with memorable individuality. Though Alagna is not quite so inspired, and such a role as Otello is not quite his yet, there are few tenors today who could match him. The disc is crowned by the ripe and responsive playing of the Berlin Philharmonic Orchestra under Claudio Abbado, opulently recorded. An operatic feast!

Choruses: *Requiem* excerpts: *Dies irae; Tuba mirum; Sanctus.* Choruses from *Aida; Un ballo in maschera; Don Carlo; Ernani; I Lombardi; Macbeth; Nabucco; Otello; Simon Boccanegra; Il trovatore.*

(N) (M) *** DG (ADD) 463 655-2. Ch. & O of La Scala Milan, Abbado.

The basic collection here, of nine opera choruses, was welcomed by us with enthusiasm (and a 🌑), when it was first issued in 1975. The combination of precision and tension is riveting and the analogue recording is of DG's highest standard, offering a wide dynamic range, fine detail in the pianissimos, and splendid weight in the moments of spectacle. The diminuendo at the end of the *Anvil Chorus* is most subtly managed, while the fine rhythmic bounce of *Si, redesti* (from *Ernani*) is matched by the expansive brilliance of the excerpts from *Aida* (lovely fruity trumpets) and *Don Carlo*, and by the atmospheric power of *Patria oppressa* from *Macbeth*.

For the reissue, as one of their 'Originals', DG have expanded the contents to a more realistic 68 minutes, by adding some more items from Abbado's complete recordings, including *Un ballo in maschera* and *Simon Boccanegra*. The snag is that the collection ends with three excerpts from Abbado's 1980 set of the *Requiem*, where, compared with what has gone before, there is a degree of slackness and lack of bite. In the *Dies irae* the chorus sounds too small and there is little excitement. However, the recording is excellent and the rest of the programme none the less remains highly desirable.

Choruses from: *Aida; La battaglia di Legnano; Don Carlo; Ernani; La forza del destino; Macbeth; Nabucco; Otello; La traviata; Il trovatore.*

(BB) *** Naxos 8.550241. Slovak Philharmonic Ch. & RSO, Dohnányi.

Under Oliver Dohnányi's lively direction the chorus sings with fervour. The collection ends resplendently with the Triumphal scene from *Aida*, omitting the ballet but with the fanfare trumpets blazing out on either side most tellingly. With a playing time of 56 minutes this is an excellent bargain, with a naturally balanced recording from the Bratislava Radio Concert Hall.

Choruses: *Aida: Gloria all'Egitto. Don Carlos: Spuntato ecco il dì. I Lombardi: Gerusalem!; O Signore, dal tetto natio. Macbeth: Patria oppressa! Nabucco: Va pensiero; Gli arredi festivi. Otello: Fuoco di gioia! Il trovatore: Vedi! le fosche; Or co' dadi . . . Squilli, echeggi.*

(M) **(*) Ph. (ADD) 462 064-2. Dresden State Op. Ch. & O., Varviso.

Varviso's collection of choruses brings polished and full-bodied but at times soft-grained performances, beautifully supported by the magnificent Dresden orchestra. The gentler choruses are excellent, but the dramatic ones lack something in bite. One of the highlights is the *Fire chorus* from *Otello*, in which the choral and woodwind detail suggests the flickering flames of bonfires burning in Otello's honour. The recording is warmly atmospheric and natural, but the selection is short measure at barely 46 minutes.

'The World of Verdi': (i) *Aida: Celeste Aida;* (ii) *Grand March & Ballet.* (iii) *La forza del destino: Pace, pace, mio Dio.* (iv) *Luisa Miller: O! Fede negar potessi . . . Quando le sere al placido.* (v) *Nabucco: Va pensiero.* (vi) *Otello: Credo. Rigoletto:* (vii) *Caro nome;* (viii) *La donna è mobile;* (vii; viii; ix) *Quartet: Bella figlia dell'amore.* (x) *La traviata: Prelude, Act I;* (vii; xi) *Brindisi: Libiamo ne'lieti calici. Il trovatore:* (xii) *Anvil Chorus;* (xiii) *Strida la vampa;* (viii) *Di quella pira. I vespri siciliani:* (xiv) *Mercè, diletti amiche.*

(M) *** Decca (ADD) 433 221-1. (i) Vickers; (ii) Rome Op. Ch. & O, Solti; (iii) G. Jones; (iv) Bergonzi; (v) Amb. S., LSO, Abbado; (vi) Evans; (vii) Sutherland; (viii) Pavarotti; (ix) Tourangeau, Milnes; (x) Maggio Musicale O, Fiorentino, Pritchard; (xi) Bergonzi; (xii) L. Op. Ch., Bonynge; (xiii) Horne; (xiv) Chiara.

Opening with the *Chorus of the Hebrew Slaves* from *Nabucco* and closing with Pavarotti's *Di quella pira* from *Il trovatore*, this quite outstandingly red-blooded Verdi compilation should surely tempt any novice to explore further into Verdi's world, yet at the same time it provides a superbly arranged 74-minute concert in its own right. The choice of items and performances demonstrates a shrewd knowledge of both popular Verdi and the Decca catalogue, for not a single performance disappoints. Joan Sutherland's melting 1971 *Caro nome* with its exquisite trills is the first of three splendid excerpts from *Rigoletto*, ending with the famous *Quartet*, and other highlights include Dame Gwyneth Jones's glorious *Pace, pace, mio Dio* from *La forza del destino*, Sir Geraint Evans's superb account of Iago's evil *Credo* from *Otello* and Marilyn Horne's dark-timbred *Strida la vampa* from *Trovatore*. Solti, too, is at his most electric in the great March scene from *Aida*. The stereo throughout is splendidly vivid.

VERESS, Sándor (1907–92)

(i; ii) *Concerto for Piano, Strings & Percussion;* (i; ii; iii) *Hommage à Paul Klee;* (i) *6 Csárdás.*

*** Teldec 0630-19992-2. (i) Schiff; (ii) Budapest Festival O, Holliger; (iii) Várjon.

Sándor Veress studied with Bartók and Kodály and became assistant to László Lajtha at the Budapest Ethnological Museum. He taught at the Franz Liszt Academy for a time, where his pupils included Ligeti and Kurtág. In 1949 he left his native Hungary to settle in Switzerland where he first saw some of Klee's work. The *Hommage à Paul Klee* (1951) takes the form of seven fantasias for two pianos and strings (the pictures that inspired them are reproduced in the informative booklet). They are all inventive and diverting; the second, *Fire Wind*, in particular, is dazzling, as is the last, *Little Blue Devil*, which Gunther Schuller was later to include in his *Klee Studies*. The *Concerto for Piano, Strings and Percussion* (1952) was commissioned by Paul Sacher and is an appealing and finely fashioned score which springs from the world of Bartók and perhaps Hindemith but, as you come to know it, inhabits an individual place of its own. The exuberant Bartókian quasi-serial finale comes off brilliantly. András Schiff is the expert and authoritative soloist and he dispatches the *Six Csárdás* (1939) for solo piano with great spirit. They are dance paraphrases that conceal studies in strict counterpoint. Heinz Holliger, who studied with Veress at the Berne Conservatory, directs with great sympathy, and the engineers produce excellent sound. It would be good to have the *Quattro danze transilvane* and the *Violin Concerto* on CD.

VICTORIA, Tomás Luis de

(c. 1548–1611)

Ascendens Christus (motet); *Missa Ascendis Christus in altum; O Magnum mysterium* (motet); *Missa O Magnum mysterium.*

*** Hyp. CDA 66190. Westminster Cathedral Ch., Hill.

Ave Maria; Beati immaculati; Domine, non sum dignis; Duo seraphim clamabant; Ildephonse; Magnificat; O sacrum convvium (2 settings); *Quam pulchra sunt; Sancta Maria; Salve regina; Senex pierum portabat; Super flumina Babylonis.*

(N)(BB) **(*) Teldec (ADD) 8573 85560-2. Pro Cantione Antiqua, London Cornet and Sackbut Ens., Turner.

This was very much a pioneering compilation. When it was issued in 1978 the music of Victoria was interspersed (on several LPs) with music of his contemporaries, which afforded extra variety. Almost all these pieces (the *Magnificat* a more vigorous exception) are slow and serene, and today one would expect some of this music to be pressed on with rather more Latin temperament and momentum. Nevertheless the cast of the Pro Cantione Antiqua at that time featured many names which were to become famous, including James Bowman, Paul Esswood, Ian Partridge, Edgar Fleet and others. They blend together for the most part very impressively, even if occasionally the counter-tenors are perhaps a fraction over-prominent. But to sample the calibre of this singing try the lovely, serene *Domine, non sum dignus* with its effectively contrasting dynamics. Elsewhere the sonority is often filled out with brass, as in the closing *Ave Maria* (for double choir), which is most impressive. The recording has a pleasing warm resonance and the disc is well worth its modest price.

Ave Maria; Ave Maris stella (hymn). *Missa Vidi speciosam. Ne timeas, Maria; Sancta Maria, succurre miseris; Vidi speciosam* (motets).

*** Hyp. CDA 66129. Westminster Cathedral Ch., Hill.

An outstanding collection of some of Victoria's most beautiful music celebrating the Virgin Mary. The four-part *Ave Maria* may not be authentic, but the composer would surely not be reluctant to own it. The Westminster Choir again show their flexibly volatile response to this music with that special amalgam of fervour and serenity that Victoria's writing demands. The acoustics of Westminster Cathedral add the right degree of resonance to the sound without clouding.

Missa Ave maris stella; O quam gloriosum est regnum (motet); *Missa O quam gloriosum.*

⊛ *** Hyp. CDA 66114. Westminster Cathedral Ch., Hill.

The Latin fervour of the singing is very involving; some listeners may initially be surprised at the volatile way David Hill moves the music on, with the trebles eloquently soaring aloft on the line of the music. The spontaneous ebb and flow of the pacing is at the heart of David Hill's understanding of this superb music. The recording balance is perfectly judged, with the Westminster acoustic adding resonance (in both senses of the word) to singing of the highest calibre, combining a sense of timelessness and mystery with real expressive power.

Missa Gaudeamus; Missa Pro Victoria; Motets: Cum beatis Ignatius; Descendit Angelus Domini; Doctor bonus, amicus Dei Andreas; Ecce sacerdos magnus; Estote fortes in bello; Hic vir despiciens mundum; O decus apostolicum; Tu es Petrus; Vieni sponsa Christis.

⊛ *** ASV CDGAU 198. Cardinall's Musick, Carwood.

Happily the name of the opening *Missa Gaudeamus*, for six voices, celebrates the label on which it is issued. It is a relatively serene 'backward-looking' work, yet with the closing *Sanctus* and *Agnus Dei* richly memorable. The shorter *Missa Pro Victoria* is even finer, indeed one of Victoria's most powerful expressive utterances and unique in being based on a secular chanson, *La guerre, escoutez lous gentilz* by Janequin. Andrew Carwood's performance moves forward with true Latin passion and grips the listener from first to last. Among the nine very varied additional motets, *Tu es Petrus* and *O decus apostolicum* and the remarkable *Descendit Angelus Domini* stand out. The recording is of the very highest quality.

Mass and Motet: *O magnum mysterium*. Mass and Motet: *O quam gloriosum*. *Ardens est cor meum*; *Ave Maria*.

(BB) *** Naxos 8.550575. Oxford Camerata, Summerly (with Alonso LOBO: *Versa est in luctum* ***).

Like David Hill, Jeremy Summerly moves the music of each Mass on fairly briskly until the *Sanctus* and *Agnus Dei*, when the spacious *espressivo* of the singing makes a poignant contrast. The two motets on which the Masses are based are sung as postludes and very beautiful they are, especially the idyllic *O magnum mysterium*. Finally the short *Versa est in luctum* (a setting of a section of the Requiem Mass) by Alonso Lobo, a Spanish contemporary, ends the concert serenely. The recording is excellent and this is a fine bargain.

Mass and Motet: *O quam gloriosum*.

(BB) *** Belart (ADD) 461 018-2. Thomas, Allister, Fleet, Keyte, Carmelite Priory Ch., London, McCarthy — PALESTRINA: Masses: *Ecce ego Joannes; Sine nomine*. ***

Like the Palestrina couplings, this paired Mass and motet are exceptionally distinguished performances, and they are made the more attractive (in all three cases) by this ideal recorded presentation which couples the motet which is musically connected with each Mass, something which we expect these days as a matter of course but which happened less frequently in the early 1960s, when these recordings first appeared. The sound is remarkably fine, with the part-writing clearly defined.

Officium defunctorum.

*** Gimell CDGIM 912. Tallis Scholars, Phillips (with LOBO: Motet: *Versa est in luctum* ***).
*** Hyp. CDA 66250. Westminster Cathedral Ch., Hill.

The *Officium defunctorum* is a work of great serenity and beauty. Honours are fairly evenly divided between the Westminster Cathedral Choir on Hyperion and the Tallis Scholars under Peter Phillips. The Westminster Choir has the advantage of boys' voices and larger forces; they are recorded in a warmer, more spacious acoustic. By comparison with the Gimell recording, the sound seems a little less well focused, but on its own terms it is thoroughly convincing. They permit themselves greater expressiveness, too. Moreover the *Requiem* is set in the wider liturgical context by the use of some chants.

The Tallis Scholars achieve great clarity of texture; they

are twelve in number and, as a result, the polyphony is clearer, and so too are their words. They offer also a short and deeply felt motet by Alonso Lobo (*c.* 1555–1617). The recording has a warm, glowing sound which almost persuades you that you are in the imperial chapel.

Officium decorum (1592): *Libera me Domine; Peccantem me quotidie*. Officium decorum (1605): *Taedet animam meam*. *Libera me Domine* (with Plainchant taken from Graduale Romanum).

**(*) ECM 457 851-2. James, Covey-Crump, Potter, Jones — PALESTRINA: *Responsories*. **(*)

This CD combines music by Palestrina and Victoria for the Office and Matins for the Dead and the Burial service, including one text, *Libera me Domine*, set by both composers. The four singers blend their voices persuasively and are beautifully recorded, but the prevailing mood is of unremitting deep melancholy.

(i) Officium defunctorum (Requiem); (ii) Mass and Motet: *O quam gloriosum*; (iii) Responsories for Tenebrae; (i) Motets: *Ascendens Christus in altum; Ave Maria; Gaudent in coelis; Litaniae de Beata Virgine; Magnificat primi toni; O Magnum mysterium*.

(B) **(*) Double Decca ADD/Dig. 433 914-2 (2). (i) St John's College, Cambridge, Ch., Guest; (ii) King's College, Cambridge, Ch., Cleobury; (iii) Westminster Cathedral Ch., Malcolm.

The motets included here must be counted among the finest Victoria gave us and the *Requiem* is masterly too. On the whole the St John's performances are admirably done. The snag in the *Requiem* is the choirboys' lack of robustness in the plainchant and the men, too, sing with a big vibrato. But one has to accept that English choirs usually lack the harsh lines drawn by the firmer-toned Spanish bodies. The King's College Choir under Cleobury offer eloquent but slightly reserved accounts of the Mass and Motet *O quam gloriosum*, although the voices are finely blended to produce an impressive range of sonority. However, they sound very different from the Westminster Cathedral Choir. Their recording of the *Tenebrae responsories* dates from 1960, a period when the choir was at its peak under George Malcolm. The performance has great vigour and ardour, and the recording is excellent.

Responsories for Tenebrae.

*** Hyp. CDA 66304. Westminster Cathedral Ch., Hill.
** Gimell CDGIM 922. Tallis Scholars, Phillips.

The *Tenebrae responsories* are so called because of the tradition of performing them in the evening in increasing darkness as the candles were extinguished one by one. The Tallis Scholars are flawless in both blend and intonation but are curiously uninvolving. They are beautifully recorded and technically immaculate but lack intensity of feeling. The Westminster Cathedral Choir under David Hill on Hyperion find far more atmosphere in this music and bring a sense of spontaneous feeling to their performance. Of recent versions, this can be welcomed without reservation.

VIERNE, Louis (1870–1937)

Suite No. 3, Op. 54: Carillon de Westminster.

*** DG 413 438-2. Preston (organ of Westminster Abbey) –
WIDOR: *Symphony No. 5.* ***

The Vierne *Carillon de Westminster* is splendidly played by
Simon Preston and sounds appropriately atmospheric in
this spacious acoustic and well-judged recording. It makes
an attractive makeweight to the Widor *Fifth Symphony*.

ORGAN SYMPHONIES

*Symphonies Nos. 1 in D min., Op. 14; 2 in E min., Op. 20; 3
in F sharp min., Op. 28; 4 in G min., Op. 32; 5 in A min.,
Op. 47; 6 in B min., Op. 32.*

(N) ✿ *** MDG 316 0732-2 (4). Ben van Ooosten
  (Cavaillé-Coll organs in Saint-François-de-Sales, Lyon
  (*Symphonies 1 & 4*); St Ouen, Rouen (*Symphonies 2 & 6*);
  Basilica Saint-Sernin, Toulouse (*Symphonies 3 & 5*).

**(*) Meridian (ADD) CDE 84192 (1–2); CDE 84176 (3–4);
  CDE 84171 (5–6). Sanger (organ of La Chiesa Italiana di San
  Piedro, London) (available separately).

Symphonies Nos. 1 & 3.

(N) *** Telarc CD 80239. Murray (Calaillé-Coll organ of Saint
  Ouen, Rouen).

Symphonies Nos. 2–3.

(N) **(*) Priory PRCD 446. Walsh (organ of Lincoln
  Cathedral).

Symphonies Nos. 3 & 6.

(N) (BB) *** Naxos 8.553524. Mathieu (Dalstein-Haerpfer
  organ of Eglise Saint-Sébastien de Nancy).

Symphonies Nos. 4 & 6.

(N) **(*) Priory PRCD 425. Simcock (organ of Westminster
  Cathedral).

In the second half of the nineteenth century the organ-
builder Ariste Cavaillé-Coll (1811–99) created a special kind
of organ in France, with the richest diversity of colour,
underpinned by firm yet expansive pedals. These instruments proved as suitable for the earlier organ masses of
Couperin as for the semi-orchestral canvases of César
Franck, whose *Grande pièce symphonique* initiated a whole
new approach to organ-writing which was to find its peak
in the organ symphonies of Vierne and Widor.

Widor's symphonies certainly have their impressive moments, but Vierne's are far more consistent in quality, and
if you have not already explored them, this new survey
from Ben van Ooosten, superbly recorded on three different
Cavaillé-Coll organs provides an admirable opportunity to
do so.

Vierne's *First Symphony* dates from 1899 and was written
for the organ of Saint-Sulpice. It opens with a monumental
Prélude, which Ben Van Ooosten plays very commandingly
indeed, and he provides glowing registration for the *Pastorale* and *Andante* – although, in the clearly laid out *Fugue*
and more particularly the *Allegro vivace scherzo* (which is

very orchestral in conception), while the playing is certainly
lightly *vivace*, the Lyon resonance brings slight blurring to
the detail. But these are minor criticisms of performances
of outstanding quality. The magnificent finale, obviously
influenced by Widor (its main theme on the pedals with a
carillon effect above), makes an overwhelmingly spectacular
close.

The cyclic *Second Symphony* (admired by Debussy) came
three years later, with its marcato opening movement balanced by a lyrical secondary theme. The Franckian *Choral*
and engaging *Scherzo*, followed by a delicate, mellifluous
Cantabile, make a perfect foil for the powerful sonorities of
the finale.

The *Third* (1911) has been the most popular of the six,
until now, with its bold *maestoso* first movement ending
with great dynamism, the *Cantilène* featuring the *hautbois*
and reprised calmly on the *trompette harmonique*. The
piquant *Intermezzo* (like a *marche miniature* but in triple
time) is followed by a meditative but romantic *Adagio*
already full of chromatic influences from both Franck and
Wagner. The *Toccata* finale, which has a memorable chorale-
like secondary figure, builds to another overpowering final
climax.

The last three symphonies are all cyclical. The *Fourth*,
composed in 1914, took a long time to make its mark and
was not premiered until 1923. Until its finale, it is the least
flamboyant of the six. The dominating theme of the *Prélude*
is introduced dolefully on the pedals, and that mood is
maintained, even through a sequential apex. The sturdy
Allegro eventually expands to a big climax to make way for
a dainty *Minuet* and a freely lyrical *Romance*, enhanced
by an restrained underlying rapture. The finale, at last, unleashes the composer's more usual exuberance and the
closing section is most tumultuous, with a very affirmative
coda.

The *Fifth Symphony* (1924), the most ambitious of the six,
is one of Vierne's two final masterpieces. It is the most
Wagnerian, developing its two main themes almost like
leitmotifs, and opens gravely with a powerfully chromatic
and very orchestral 'Tristan-like' *Prelude*. The inner movements are then argued and contrasted like an orchestral
symphony, with the extended *Larghetto* passionately expansive, while the joyful finale opens like a peal of bells. But
the great culmination, with the principal tune thundering
forth, all stops open, is as thrilling a climax as in many more
famous nineteenth-century orchestral symphonies.

The Franckian chromaticism at the opening of the *Sixth
Symphony*, written in 1934 in sight of – and obviously inspired by – the Mediterranean, is immediately apparent,
and the agitated introduction brings a tremendous surge of
energy from which the symphonic argument develops a
momentum flowing ever forward. The *Aria* has a calming
effect, but the highly imaginative *Scherzo* swirls in, and a
pointed diabolic rhythm (not to be taken too seriously)
dances bizarrely (one inevitably thinks here of Saint-Saëns).
The mood darkens perceptibly as the *Larghetto* opens
sombrely over a sustained pedal to create a darker, other-
worldly atmosphere, its mysterious concentration steadily
increasing until the stygian mood is forcibly shattered by
the sheer joy of the fortissimo opening of the finale, with its

exuberant main theme bringing the waves sweeping over the listener, and the work storms to its tempestuous close.

Ben van Ooosten's performances cannot be too highly praised. He is deeply committed, has a wonderful ear for sonority and detail (witness his uniquely grotesque playing in the *Scherzo* of No. 6), and every performance creates the thrill and spontaneity of live music-making, while the recording of all three organs is magnificent.

Until now we have recommended David Sanger's recordings on Meridian, and many organ enthusiasts will enjoy the very appealing sound of the San Pietro organ. The quality throughout is of a very high standard: the resonance of the pedals is very telling without muddying the overall sound picture. But overall this set is now completely upstaged by the new one from MDG.

Among the individual CDs, Michael Murray's pairing of *Symphonies Nos. 1 and 6* can also be strongly recommended. He has the full measure of this music, and ensured the success of his coupling by also choosing the superb Rouen organ. Not surprisingly the Telarc recording is both very spectacular and naturally balanced – very much in the demonstration bracket.

The Naxos pairing is also more than worth its modest price. Bruno Mathieu is a pupil of Marie-Claire Alaine, and a splendid organist in his own right. Moreover, he chooses the 'historic' organ at Nancy, which still has mechanical traction, and provides a very characterful baroque palette of its own, richly displayed in the *Cantilène* of No. 3. But the pedals are very telling, too, and the finale of No. 6 is powerfully spectacular; yet overall, inner detail is remarkably clear. The only small disappointment is the *Scherzo* of No. 6, where the diabolic rhythmic figure is not as ironically piquant as with Von Oosten.

On Priory, both Colin Walsh at Lincoln Cathedral, and Ian Simcocks at Westminster (the more suitable organ of the two) show their metal and understanding of this repertoire, and Vierne's music is projected powerfully and colourfully. But the Vierne symphonies gain much from being recorded on Cavaillé-Coll instruments, so these discs must take second place to the others.

VIEUXTEMPS, Henri (1820–81)

(i) *Violin Concertos Nos. 1 in E, Op. 10;* (ii) *4 in D min., Op. 31.*

(BB) *** Naxos 8.554506. Keylin, (i) Janáček PO, Burkh;
(ii) Arnhem PO, Yuasa.

Misha Keylin couples the unfamiliar *First* with the much better-known *D minor Concerto*, which we are told he plays on a famous Stradivarius violin. Certainly its *Andante religioso* brings a generous-toned romanticism. But the solo timbre in the E major work is sweet and full, and he plays the dazzling lightweight finale with charm as well as sparkle. This is an excellent coupling, very well recorded, and both accompanying groups, Czech and Dutch respectively, are very supportive indeed.

Violin Concertos Nos. 2 in F sharp min., Op. 19; 3 in A, Op. 25.

(BB) *** Naxos 8.554114. Keylin, Janáček PO, Burkh.

Nos. 2 and 3 are by no means inferior to the better-known Nos. 4 and 5. They are full of good tunes, both slow movements are warmly touching and finales have lyrical as well as histrionic appeal. Misha Keylin gives highly persuasive performances that constantly tickle the ear in their subtlety of bowing and colour, easy rubato and imaginative dynamic shading. Dennis Burkh provides the strongest backing: his spirited introductions for both works (and especially the *Third*, with its throbbing drama) are arresting, and the orchestral playing, somewhat leonine in timbre, is excellent. So too is the recording, made in the Janáček Concert Hall, Ostrava.

Violin Concertos Nos. 4 in D, Op. 31; 5 in A min., Op. 37.

(M) *** EMI (ADD) CDM5 66058-2. Perlman, O de Paris, Barenboim – RAVEL: *Tzigane*; SAINT-SAENS: *Havanaise.* ***
(N) (BB) (***) Naxos mono 8.110943. Heifetz, (i) LPO, Barbirolli; (ii) LSO, Sargent (with SAINT-SAENS: *Introduction & Rondo capriccioso; Havanaise; SARASATE: *Zigeunerweisen* (with LPO or LSO, Barbirolli); WAXMAN: *'Carmen' Fantasy* (with RCA Victor SO, Voorhees) (***)).

Violin Concerto No. 4 in D min., Op. 31.

(M) (***) EMI mono CDH7 64251-2. Heifetz, LPO, Barbirolli – SAINT-SAENS: *Havanaise* etc.; SARASATE: *Zigeunerweisen*; WIENIAWSKI: *Concerto No. 2.* (***)

Violin Concerto No. 5 in A min., Op. 37.

(M) (***) EMI mono CDH5 65191-2. Heifetz, LSO, Sargent – MENDELSSOHN: *Concerto* (**(*)); MOZART: *Concerto No. 5.* (***)

Perlman is both aristocratically pure of tone and intonation and passionate of expression. In his accompaniments Barenboim draws warmly romantic playing from the Paris orchestra. The 1976–7 recording, as usual with Perlman, balancing the soloist well forward, now sounds a little dated, with a touch of shrillness on the upper range of the violin. However, this remains a three-star record, the more so for its inclusion of two of Perlman's very finest recordings as couplings.

Heifetz was the first leading violinist to revive the long-neglected concertos of the nineteenth-century Belgian violinist-composer, Henri Vieuxtemps, recording *No. 4* in 1935 and *No. 5* in 1947. Both are compact works, rhapsodic in structure, which brilliantly exploit violin technique, making an attractive centrepiece for this disc of showpieces. The two Saint-Saëns pieces inspire Heifetz to much witty pointing and seductive phrasing, as do the Sarasate firework piece and the *Fantasy on Themes from Bizet's Carmen*, written for the film, *Intermezzo*, by the Hollywood composer, Franz Waxman. Each has remarkably good recorded sound for the period, well transferred if with some surface hiss. On EMI two CDs are involved and the couplings are different, offering Wienlawski, Mendelssohn and Mozart instead of Waxman. Again, good transfers.

Violin Concerto No. 5 in A min., Op. 37.

*** EMI CDC5 55292-2. Chang, Philh. O, Dutoit – LALO: *Symphonie espagnole.* ***

(M) *** Sony SMK 89715. Lin, Minnesota O, Marriner – BRUCH; MENDELSSOHN: *Concertos.* ***

(M) *** DG 457 896-2. Mintz, Israel PO, Mehta – LALO: *Symphonie espagnole;* SAINT-SAENS: *Introduction & Rondo capriccioso.* ***

(M) *** RCA (ADD) 09026 61745-2. Heifetz, New SO of L, Sargent – BRUCH: *Violin Concerto No. 1* etc. ***

(M) *** Decca 460 007-2. Chung, LSO, Foster – LALO: *Symphonie espagnole;* RAVEL: *Tzigane.* ***

(M) **(*) Sony (ADD) SBK 48274. Zukerman, LSO, Mackerras – BRUCH: *Concerto No. 1;* LALO: *Symphonie espagnole.* **(*)

Sarah Chang's recording, coupling a scintillating account of the Lalo *Symphonie espagnole*, goes readily to the top of the list. It is beautifully recorded, with a perfect balance, in an agreeably warm acoustic. Chang's vitality is matched by Dutoit and her playing has a magically gentle tenderness in presenting the engaging lyrical themes of the first movement and the *Adagio*. The brief finale has splendid élan.

Cho-Liang Lin plays with flair and zest and is well supported by Sir Neville Marriner and the Minnesota Orchestra. The recording is first class, and the couplings of the more famous concertos of Bruch and Mendelssohn could not be more appropriate.

Mintz's performance has enormous dash and also real lyrical magic. Mehta, obviously caught up in the inspiration of the solo playing, provides an excellent accompaniment. This is another example of a memorable live performance 'recorded on the wing' and, if the acoustic is not very flattering, the sound is truthful and well balanced.

The quicksilver of Heifetz is well suited to the modest but attractive *Fifth Concerto* of Vieuxtemps, and Sir Malcolm again provides a musical and well-recorded accompaniment. The balance of the soloist is rather close but the digital remastering is successful, and the couplings are both attractive and generous.

Even more than the Lalo *Symphonie espagnole* which forms the major coupling, the Vieuxtemps No. 5 needs persuasive advocacy, and that is certainly what Kyung Wha Chung provides, not just in her passionate commitment in the bravura sections but also in the tender expressiveness of the slow movement, so much more compelling than the usual, more extrovert manner. The 1974 Kingsway Hall recording has perhaps lost a little of its original allure in the matter of the solo violin timbre but is otherwise very satisfactory.

Zukerman provides here an enjoyable bonus to his dazzling accounts of the Bruch and Lalo works. There is comparable dash for Vieuxtemps, yet he coaxes the *Adagio* tenderly. Again a very forward balance, but the ear adjusts.

Viola Sonata in B flat, Op. 36; Elégie, Op. 30; Morceaux, Op. 61.

*** Chan. 8873. Imai, Vignoles – FRANCK: *Viola Sonata in A.* ***

*** Simax PSC 1126. Tomter, Gimse – FRANCK: *Viola Sonata in A.* ***

The Vieuxtemps *Sonata* is expertly crafted and well laid out for the instruments but it is no masterpiece. Nobuko Imai and Roger Vignoles give an exemplary account of it and are given expert recording from the Chandos engineers.

The Norwegian, Lars Anders Tomter, is hardly less accomplished and every bit as eloquent a player as his celebrated rival, and his countryman, Håvard Gimse, is a first-rate pianist. There is absolutely nothing to choose between them, and both couple the Vieuxtemps with the Franck sonata arranged for viola.

VILLA-LOBOS, Heitor (1887–1959)

Alvorada na floresta tropical (Dawn in a tropical rainforest); Bachianas brasileiras No. 2 (for orchestra): includes The Little Train of the Caipira. Dança frenética; (i) Mômoprecóce (fantasy for piano & orchestra).

(BB) *** Arte Nova 73421 54465-2. (i) De Almeida; Jena PO, Montgomery.

Like Cristina Ortiz (below), Marco Antonio de Almeida is Brazilian born, and he and Montgomery give an invigorating account of the *Mômoprecóce* ('Carnival King'). If the Jena Philharmonic strings lack a little in body of tone, the often glittering detail is very effectively projected by the modern digital recording, and the notes with the disc give useful programmatic detail. The exotic sounds of the tropical rainforest are also vividly caught, and the energetic toccata rhythms have plenty of energy. The sultry, jazzy atmosphere of *The Song of the Vagabond*, the first movement of the *Bachianas brasileiras No. 2*, is seductive, and the catchy trombone tune of the fourth (*Song of the Desert*) is equally engaging, famous mainly for its charming portrayal of *The Little Train of the Caipira*.

Amazonas; Dawn in a Tropical Forest; Erosão; Gênesis.

*** Marco 8.223357. Czecho-Slovak RSO (Bratislava), Duarte.

These are imaginative scores with tropical colouring and exotic textures, all sounding rather similar in their luxuriance – but who cares! *Amazonas* is the earliest and most astonishing score, dating from the First World War, and in its vivid sonorities affirms Villa-Lobos's contention that his first harmony book was the map of Brazil. The Bratislava strings could be more opulent, but the performances under a Brazilian conductor are very good indeed, as is the recording.

Bachianas brasileiras Nos. 1–9; Chôros Nos. 2 (for flute & orchestra); 5 (for piano, Alma brasileira); 10 (for chorus & orchestra); (i) 11 (for piano & orchestra). 2 Chôros (bis) (for violin & cello); (i) Piano Concerto No. 5. Descobrimento do Brasil; Invocação em defesa da Patria; (i) Mômoprecóce (fantasy for piano & orchestra). Symphony No. 4. Qu'est-ce qu'un Chôros? (Villa-Lobos speaking).

(M) (**(*)) EMI mono CZS7 67229-2 (6). De los Angeles, Kareska, Basrentzen, Braune, Tagliaferro, Du Frene, Plessier, Cliquennois, Bronschwak, Neilz, Benedetti;

(i) Blumental; Chorale des Jeunesses Musicales de France, Fr. Nat. R. & TV Ch. & O, composer.

This six-CD box is a colourful, warm-hearted collection, not helped by dull mono recordings and ill-disciplined performances, but full of a passionate intensity that plainly reflects the personality of a composer of obvious charisma, if of limited ability as a conductor. Endearingly, there is a 10-minute track spoken in French by Villa-Lobos himself. All nine of the *Bachianas brasileiras* are recorded here, including the celebrated No. 5 for soprano and eight cellos, with Victoria de los Angeles a radiant soloist. That recording is already well known, but most of the others have had very limited circulation. Despite the dull sound, the warmth of the writing never fails to come over.

Bachianas brasileiras Nos. 1 for Cellos; 2 for Orchestra; (i) 5 for Soprano & 8 Cellos; 9 for String Orchestra.

(M) (**(*)) EMI mono CDM5 66912-2 [CDMS 66964]. Fr. Nat. R. & TV O, composer; (i) with De los Angeles.

Understandably, this EMI 'Great Recordings of the Century' reissue opens with No. 5, with its floating melodic line so delicately and ravishingly sustained by Victoria de los Angeles. Elsewhere the dry, lustreless orchestral recording will limit the appeal of this disc for the general, rather than the historically minded collector, for the composer's direction of the orchestra is of documentary rather than inspirational interest.

Bachianas brasileiras Nos. (iii) 1; (i; ii) 5; (i; ii) Suite for Voice & Violin. (iii) Arr. of BACH: The Well-Tempered Clavier: Prelude in D min., BWV 583; Fugue in B flat, BWV 846; Prelude in G min., BWV 867; Fugue in D, BWV 874.

*** Hyp. CDA 66257. (i) Gomez, (ii) Manning, (iii) Pleeth Cello Octet.

Jill Gomez is outstanding in the popular *Bachianas brasileiras No. 5* and with the violinist, Peter Manning, in the *Suite* (1923). Villa-Lobos's favourite 'orchestra of cellos' produce sumptuous sounds in both the *Bachianas brasileiras*, and an added point of interest is the effective transcriptions for cellos of unrelated Bach preludes and fugues. A most attractive introduction to this most colourful of composers.

Bachianas brasileiras No. 2: The Little Train of the Caipira.

(*) Everest (ADD) EVC 9007. LSO, Goossens – ANTILL: *Corroboree* **(*); GINASTERA: *Estancia; Panambi*. *

It is good to have a recommendable mid-priced version of Villa-Lobos's engaging tone-picture of a little country train in São Paulo, Brazil, with Brazilian percussion instruments suggesting train noises. The performance is excellent and the recording vivid, if slightly over-resonant, with a slight edge to the violins.

Bachianas brasileiras Nos. 2 (The Little Train of the Caipira); 4; (i) 5 for Soprano & 8 Cellos; (ii) Chôros No. 10: Rasga o Coração; (iii) Miniaturas Nos. 2 (Viola); 3, Cantilena; (iv) Mômoprecóce (fantasy for piano and orchestra).

(***) EMI stereo/mono CDC5 55224-2. (i) French Nat. R.O, composer; (i) with De los Angeles; (ii) Ch. des Jeunesses Musicales de France; (iii) Fuller; (iv) Tagliaferro.

No one has been more persuasive than the composer in *The Little Train of the Caipira*, and the recording certainly has plenty of local colour with its exotic percussive effects. Victoria de los Angeles's golden voice sounds ravishing in the famous *Bachianas brasileiras No. 5*, even if the recording is not entirely flattering; and the other, rarer works, notably the *Fantasy for Piano and Orchestra*, are welcome in this reissue in EMI's Composer in Person series, which now takes the two most familiar items into the premium-price bracket.

(i–ii) Bachianas brasileiras No. 3; Mômoprecóce; (iii) Guitar Concerto; (iv) Fantasia for Soprano Saxophone & Chamber Orchestra; (i) Piano music: A próle do bébé No. 1 (suite); A lenda de caboclo; Alma brasileira (Chorus No. 5); Ciclo brasileiro: Festa no sertão; Impressões seresteiras.

(B) *** EMI double forte CZS5 72670-2 (2). (i) Ortiz; (ii) New Philh. O, Ashkenazy; (iii) A. Romero, LPO, López-Cobos; (iv) Harle, ASMF, Marriner.

In many ways this is the finest Villa-Lobos collection in the catalogue, certainly the most varied. His rather melancholy piano piece, *A lenda de caboclo* ('Legend of a half-caste') gives a clue to the unique identity of this music, for the composer's mother was Hispanic, his father of Indian descent. No. 3 of the *Bachianas brasileiras*, which dates from 1938, is the only one of the series to involve the piano. The *Mômoprecóce* began life in 1920 (while the composer was living in Paris) as the set of piano pieces called *Carnaval das Crianças*, and it was reworked in its concertante form later. Like so much of Villa-Lobos's music, the score is rowdy and colourful. Cristina Ortiz, herself Brazilian, is a natural choice for this repertoire. She plays with appropriate vigour, reflective feeling and colour, and Ashkenazy gives splendid support. The late-1970s recording is excellent, with the CD transfer adding a little edge to high violins. Ortiz is equally impressive in the solo piano pieces (again very well recorded), which she plays with flair and at times with touching tenderness, as in Villa-Lobos's portraits of the *Clay* and *Rag Dolls*, the third and and sixth members of *A próle do bébé* ('baby's family'). Angel Romero makes the very most of the comparatively slight *Guitar Concerto*, bringing out its Latin feeling. The *Fantasia for Soprano Saxophone* is a more substantial piece with three well-defined movements, contrasted in invention. John Harle is a perceptive soloist with a most appealing timbre; one of the highlights of the set. The recordings in both these concertante works (made in 1984 and 1990 respectively) are well up to the best Abbey Road analogue standards.

Guitar Concerto.

(M) *** Sony SMK 60022. Williams, ECO, Barenboim – CASTELNUOVO-TEDESCO: *Guitar Concerto;* RODRIGO: *Concierto de Aranjuez.* ***

(BB) *** Naxos 8.550729. Kraft, N. CO, Ward –

CASTELNUOVO-TEDESCO: *Concerto* ***; RODRIGO: *Concierto de Aranjuez.* ***

*** Guild GMCD 7176. Jiménez, Bournemouth Sinf., Frazor — ANGULO: *Guitar Concerto No. 2 (El Alevín)*; RODRIGO: *Concierto de Aranjuez.* ***

(i) Guitar Concerto. 12 Etudes; 5 Preludes.

(M) *** RCA (ADD) 09026 61604-2. Bream, (i) LSO, Previn.

A highly distinguished account of the *Guitar Concerto* from Bream, magnetic and full of atmosphere in the slow movement and finale. Previn accompanies sympathetically and with spirit. The rest of the programme also shows Bream in inspirational form. He engages the listener's attention from the opening of the first study and holds it to the last. The recording has a nice intimacy in the concerto and the solo items have fine presence against an attractive ambience.

John Williams's compulsive performance makes the very most of the finer points of Villa-Lobos's comparatively slight concerto, and especially the rhapsodic quality of the *Andantino*. The recording is bright and fresh, the soloist characteristically close, but the effect is vividly present.

An excellent account from Norbert Kraft, spontaneous and catching well the music's colour and atmosphere. If it is not quite as individual as Bream's version, it has the advantage of vivid, well-balanced, modern, digital recording and excellent couplings. Another genuine Naxos bargain.

Rafael Jiménez also proves a natural soloist for Villa-Lobos's intimate concerto and Terence Frazor and the Bournemouth Sinfonietta make the very most of the orchestral colouring, which sounds more vivid than usual. Yet the balance integrates the soloist appealingly within the orchestral texture.

Piano Concertos Nos. 1–5.

(B) *** Double Decca 452 617-2 (2). Ortiz, RPO, Gómez-Martínez.

What emerges from the series of concertos, as played by Cristina Ortiz here, is that the first two are the most immediately identifiable as Brazilian in their warm colouring and sense of atmosphere, even though the eclectic borrowings are often more unashamed than later, with many passages suggesting Rachmaninov with a Brazilian accent. No. 3, the work Villa-Lobos found it hard to complete, tends to sound bitty in its changes of direction. No. 4, more crisply conceived, has one or two splendid tunes, but it is in No. 5 that Villa-Lobos becomes most warmly convincing again, returning unashamedly to more echoes of Rachmaninov. With Ortiz articulating crisply, there is much to enjoy from such colourful, undemanding music, brilliantly recorded and sympathetically performed.

Discovery of Brazil: Suites Nos. 1–3; (i) 4.

**(*) Marco 8.223551. Slovak RSO (Bratislava), Duarte; (i) with Blazo, Slovak Philharmonic Ch.

The *Discovery of Brazil* derives from an ambitious film project and Villa-Lobos fashioned three orchestral suites from it, plus a fourth which employs a soloist and choir. Though there are good things in this music and some exotic orchestral effects, the colours are not quite as vivid and dazzling as one would have expected from this prolific Brazilian master. Enjoyable performances.

Symphonies Nos. 4 (A Vitória); 12.

(N) *** CPO 999 525-2. SWR RSO, Stuttgart, St Clair.

The *Fourth Symphony* (1919) evokes the composer's feelings at the conclusion of the First World War and calls for extravagant musical forces, including a small internal group of E flat clarinet, saxophone quartet and percussion, and another brass fanfare group. Exuberant, rumbustious, larger than life – Gallic influences are strong but there are some lovely individual touches in parts of the second movement and the inspired elegiac third movement. The *Twelfth* (1957) was completed on the composer's seventieth birthday. Although its finale is overscored, there is a great deal of lively invention and luxuriant orchestration to enjoy. Very good performances by Carl St Clair and the Sudwestfunk Orchestra of Stuttgart and exemplary recording, well-detailed and vivid.

Symphonies Nos. 6 (Sobre a linha das montanhas do Brasil); 8; Suite for Strings.

(N) *** CPO 999 517-2. SWR RSO Stuttgart, St Clair.

The subtitle of the *Sixth Symphony* of 1944 (*On the Profiles of the Mountains of Brazil*) has a more than programmatic significance. Villa-Lobos supposedly used the contours of the mountain peaks in Rio de Janeiro (drawn on graph paper) to create some of his melodic lines. It is true that the energetic first movement does seem a little incoherent, but the touching *Lento-Adagio*, with its cor anglais and clarinet solos has expressive material that reaches above such mundane methodology. The robust *Scherzo*, with its lyrical underlay, also has popular themes from ground level, and the rhythmic drive of the closing *Toccata* suggests raw humanity rather than mountain peaks.

The *Eighth Symphony*, written six years later, is more concerned with symphonic purpose than local geography. It has striking themes and the first movement thrusts forward with infectious momentum, the *Lento assai* is profoundly searching, the *Scherzo* engagingly unpredictable but with a rather luscious string theme at its centre. The finale follows on as if there had been no break, and carries the piece to a boisterous toccata-like conclusion.

The *Suite for Strings* is an orchestral version of what was originally a work for double string quintet. Its three movements are entitled *Timide*, *Mysterious* and *Restless (Air de ballet)*, but the music has much more depth than such a description would suggest and the opening section is quite haunting. All three works are splendidly played and recorded, and this CD is well worth exploring, if you enjoy symphonies which are genuine, are garbed in unusual colours, and move in unexpected directions.

GUITAR MUSIC

Chôros No. 1 (Typico); 12 Etudes; 5 Préludes; Suite populaire brésilienne.

(N) (BB) *** Naxos 8.553987. Kraft.

Norbert Kraft show his absolute mastery of his instrument in his dazzling account of the *Twelve Etudes*, which have contrasting moments of reflection. He plays the *Five Préludes* beautifully, too, with a fine control of atmosphere and rubato. The *Chôros* and *Suite populaire brésilienne* are marginally less spontaneous-sounding, and the latter is not as colourfully idiomatic as in the hands of Julian Bream. But this inexpensive disc gathers together all the composer's important music for solo guitar, and by any standards this is fine playing. The recording is naturally balanced and has a vivid but not exaggerated presence.

5 Preludes for Guitar.

(B) *** Sony (ADD) SBK 62425. Williams (guitar) –
GIULIANI: *Variations on a Theme by Handel*;
PAGANINI: *Caprice No. 24; Grand Sonata*;
D. SCARLATTI: *Sonatas*. ***

Although John Williams is balanced a shade too closely, he is very well recorded; his playing, improvisationally spontaneous and full of magical evocation, is of the highest level of mastery. A lower-level setting compensates for the balance and enables this artist's playing to register effectively. These are as perfect and as finely turned as any performances in the catalogue.

CHAMBER MUSIC

Assobio a jato (for flute & cello); *Bachianas brasileiras No. 6* (for flute & bassoon); *Canço do amor* (for flute & guitar); *Chôros No. 2* (for flute & clarinet); *Modinha*; *Distribuição do flores* (both for flute & guitar); *Quinteto en forma e chôros* (for wind); *Trio for Oboe, Clarinet & Bassoon.*

(N) (B) *** Hyp. Helios CDH 55057. Bennett, Tunnell, O'Neill, Wynberg, King, Black, Knight.

Although it was originally published in 1999, we have not before encountered this winning collection of Villa-Lobos's chamber music for wind, superbly played and recorded, and now an inestimable bargain. Indeed, there are few more inviting introductions to the exotic colours and indelible invention that this Brazilian composer has made his own. With the superb flautist William Bennett at the centre of the group, the performances could hardly be more enticing, or indeed more polished. For the engaging Parisian *Quinteto en forma de chôros* of 1928, with its wild mood changes, there is equally expert playing from Thea King (clarinet), Neil Black (oboe), Robin O'Neill (bassoon) and Janice Knight (cor anglais). Among the various duos in the improvisatory duet style of Rio's street musicians (to which Charles Tunnell, guitar, also contributes) the romantic *Modinha*, the lovely *Distribution of Flowers*, the *Song of Love* and the chirping flute and fluid cello lines of the *Jet Whistle*, with its touching centrepiece, contrast with the witty *Chôros No. 2*. The most ambitious Brazilian piece is the unpredictable *Trio* with its raw jungle voicings, dextrous rhythms and syncopations and lyrical *Languisamente*. This slow central section and the *Vivo* finale are faintly Stravinskyan, but with

an added touch of witty geniality. First-class recording, present but not too close. Not to be missed.

String Quartets Nos. 2 (1915); 7 (1941).

** Marco 8.223394. Danubius Qt.

The *Seventh Quartet* comes from 1941 – a good vintage for Villa-Lobos – and is conceived on an ambitious scale, not far short of 40 minutes. Unlike Villa-Lobos's music from the 1930s, this is less exotic in feel, and his discovery of Bach in the *Bachianas brasileiras* also makes itself felt here. There is an abundance of melodic invention and contrapuntal vitality, even if his musical thinking remains essentially rhapsodic. The Danubius Quartet give a straightforward if rather languid account of the piece. The *Second Quartet* of 1915 is much shorter and of less interest.

String Quartets Nos. 4 (1917); 6 (Quarteto brasileiro) (1938); 14 (1953).

*** Marco 8.223391. Danubius Qt.

The three quartets recorded here are all well crafted and their ideas are of quality. The *Fourth* is perhaps the most Gallic; the *Sixth* (*Quarteto brasileiro*) is one of the most individual and rewarding. It makes intelligent use of Brazilian folk-material. The *Fourteenth*, like so much of Villa-Lobos, is not entirely free from note-spinning. The Danubius Quartet are an accomplished ensemble and play with evident commitment. The recording places them rather forward in the aural picture.

String Quartet No. 6 (Quarteto brasileiro).

(***) Testament mono SBT 1053. Hollywood Qt – CRESTON: *Quartet*; DEBUSSY: *Danses sacrées*; RAVEL: *Introduction & Allegro*; TURINA: *La oración*. (***)

The *Sixth Quartet* is a slight but amiable score, ultimately facile but pleasing and well crafted. It would be hard to imagine a finer performance than this.

PIANO MUSIC

Alma brasileira, Bachianas brasileiras No. 4; Ciclo brasileiro; Chôros No. 5; Valsa da dor (Waltz of sorrows).

*** ASV CDDCA 607. Petchersky.

Alma Petchersky's style is romantic, and some might find her thoughtful deliberation in the *Preludio* of the *Bachianas Brasileiras No. 4* overdone. Her very free rubato is immediately apparent in the *Valsa da dor*, which opens the recital. Yet she clearly feels all this music deeply, and the playing is strong in personality and her timbre is often richly coloured. She is at her finest in the *Brazilian Cycle*. The recording is excellent.

Cirandas; Rudepoêma.

*** ASV CDDCA 957. Petchersky.

Not only is the playing here first class, but the music itself is of much interest. *Rudepoêma* (1921–6) is a musical portrait of Artur Rubinstein and is full of temperament and virtuosity. Alma Petchersky rises to its innumerable challenges with great spirit and panache. The *Cirandas* (1926), which make formidable technical demands on the pianist, are despatched with great brilliance and poetic feeling. Alma Petchersky is very well recorded and, if the standards of this series are maintained, future issues will be self-recommending.

VOCAL MUSIC

Bachianas brasileiras No. 5 for Soprano & Cellos.

(B) *** Double Decca 444 995-2 (2). Te Kanawa, Harrell and instrumental ens. – CANTELOUBE: *Songs of the Auvergne.* ***

The Villa-Lobos piece makes an apt fill-up for the Canteloube songs, completing Kiri Te Kanawa's recording of all five books. It is, if anything, even more sensuously done, well sustained at a speed far slower than one would normally expect. Rich recording to match.

VIOTTI, Giovanni Battista (1755–1824)

Violin Concerto No. 13 in A.

*** Hyp. Helios CDH 55062. Oprean, European Community CO, Faerber – FIORILLO: *Violin Concerto No. 1.* ***

Viotti wrote a great many violin concertos in much the same mould, but this is one of his best. Adelina Oprean's quicksilver style and light lyrical touch give much pleasure – she has the exact measure of this repertoire and she is splendidly accompanied and well recorded. The measure, though, is short.

VISÉE, Robert de (1650?–1732)

Suites de danses: in A min.; B min.; C min.; D min.

(N) (M) *** Virgin VM5 61541-2. Monteilhet (theorbo).

Robert de Visée was among the last representatives of the French school of lute and theorbo playing, for the lute was soon to be replaced by the guitar in public favour in the way that the viola da gamba was to be superseded by the cello. In his day De Visée was both a celebrated lutenist and a respected composer, and at the height of his career he was summoned to the French court, where he gave guitar lessons to the Dauphin, and played for the King (Louis XIV) after supper in the evening.

It is significant that all the chosen suites here are in the minor key, for while each, after an introductory *Prélude*, includes a set of dances – allemande, courante, gavotte, sarabande and gigue – their atmosphere is not as light-hearted as you would expect. It is the sarabande in each case which finds the composer writing with a particularly haunting melancholy, whereas the style of the allemandes is consistently serious. That in the *A minor Suite* is dedicated to *La Royale*, and in the *C minor* it is in the form of a *Plainte* ('for the tomb of the composer's daughters'), a noble commemoration of a personal tragedy.

The theorbo could be supplemented by a set of very low-sounding strings which added support to the harmony with their rich tone and added resonance, as Pascal Monteilhet shows here in these remarkably evocative performances, warmly recorded, which transport the listener back to a different age.

VIVALDI, Antonio (1675–1741)

Philips Vivaldi Edition, Vol. 1: Concertos: (i) *L'estro armonico, Op. 3;* (ii) *La stravaganza, Op. 4;* (iii) *6 Violin Concertos, Op. 6.* Chamber music: (iv) *12 Sonatas for 2 Violins, Op. 1;* (v) *12 Violin Sonatas, Op. 2;* (vi) *6 Sonatas for 1 or 2 Violins, Op. 5.*

(B) *** Ph. (ADD) 456 185-2 (10). (i) Michelucci; (ii) Ayo; (iii) Carmirelli; (i–iii) I Musici; (iv–vi) Accardo, Canino, De Saram; (iv) Gulli; (vi) Gazeau.

Philips Vivaldi Edition, Vol. 2: Concertos: (i–ii) *12 Concertos for Oboe or Violin, Op. 7;* (iii) *Il cimento dell'armonia e dell'inventione (The Trial between Harmony and Invention, including The Four Seasons), Op. 8; La cetra, Op. 9;* (i) *6 Violin Concertos, Op. 11; 6 Violin Concertos, Op. 12.*

(B) *** Ph. (ADD) 456 186-2 (9). I Musici, with (i) Accardo (ii) Holliger; (iii) Ayo; (iv) Gazzelloni.

Philips's Vivaldi Edition is very competitively priced, and any reservations tend to be swept aside when the coverage is so uniquely comprehensive and the music-making so warmly enjoyable. These are refreshing and lively performances, and the current transfers offer gleaming tuttis, while the soloists are realistically placed and cleanly focused. The reissue of the chamber music is particularly welcome, as these sonatas are not otherwise readily obtainable. In any case it is unlikely that Accardo's performances, so ably supported by Franco Gulli (in Opus 1), Rohan de Saram (cello) and Bruno Canino (harpsichord) could be surpassed in terms of fluency, musicianship and sheer beauty of tone. The Opp. 11 and 12 *Violin Concertos* were recorded in 1974–5. The best of them are very rewarding indeed and, played by Salvatore Accardo, they are likely to beguile the most reluctant listener.

L'estro armonico (12 Concertos), Op. 3.

*** DG (IMS) 423 094-2 (2). Standage & soloists, E. Concert, Pinnock.
*** Virgin VMD5 45315-2 (2). Biondi, Longo, Casazza, Negri, Naddeo, Europa Galante.

L'estro armonico, Op. 3; (i) Bassoon Concerto in A min., RV 498; (ii) Flute Concerto in C min., RV 441; (iii) Oboe Concerto in F, RV 456; (i; iii; iv) Concerto in F for 2 Oboes, Bassoon, 2 Horns & Violin, RV 574.

(B) *** Double Decca (ADD) 443 476-2 (2). ASMF, Marriner; with (i) Gatt; (ii) Bennett; (iii) Black; (iv) Nicklin, T. Brown, Davis, I. Brown.

(i) L'estro armonico, Op. 3; (ii) 6 Flute Concertos, Op. 10.

(B) *** Double Decca 458 078-2 (2). (i) Holloway, Huggett, Mackintosh, Wilcock; (ii) Preston; AAM, Hogwood.

Vivaldi's *L'estro armonico* includes some of his finest music. The chamber version from Pinnock (with one instrument to a part) brings together the best features from past versions:

there is as much sparkle and liveliness as with Hogwood, for rhythms are consistently resilient, ensemble crisp and vigorous. Yet in slow movements there is that expressive radiance and sense of enjoyment of beauty without unstylish indulgence that one expects from the ASMF. The recording was made in EMI's Abbey Road studio, atmospheric and perfectly balanced.

There is no question about the sparkle of Christopher Hogwood's performance with the Academy of Ancient Music. The captivating lightness of the solo playing and the crispness of articulation of the accompanying group bring music-making that combines joyful vitality with the authority of scholarship. Hogwood's continuo is first class, varying between harpsichord and organ, the latter used to add colour as well as substance. The balance is excellent, and the whole effect is exhilarating. In Op. 10 Stephen Preston plays a period instrument, a Schuchart, and the Academy of Ancient Music likewise play old instruments. Their playing is eminently stylish, but also spirited and expressive, and they are admirably recorded, with the analogue sound enhanced further in the CD format. A first choice among period-instrument performances, this makes a more than generous coupling for Op. 3.

Fabio Biondi and Europe Galante start with No. 2, whose arresting opening *Adagio e spiccato* is very dramatic indeed. Indeed, these performances are tremendously alert, crisply rhythmic and marvellously played, with the lyrical writing always winningly expressive. Almost all of these works are for two or more soloists, and here the concertino work splendidly together. But when Biondi plays alone his contribution is very stylish indeed and the *Largo* of the solo concerto, RV 356 (No. 6), is exquisite. Equally Biondi and Isabella Longo make a captivating partnership in the *Double Violin Concerto*, RV 519 (No. 7). Period-instrument playing of Vivaldi has clearly matured and, with first-class modern recording, this offers a strong challenge to both Pinnock and Hogwood.

Those who have not been won over to the more abrasive sound of period instruments will find Marriner's set no less stylish. As so often, he directs the Academy in radiant and imaginative performances of baroque music and yet observes scholarly good manners. The delightful use of continuo – lute and organ as well as harpsichord – the sharing of solo honours and the consistently resilient string playing of the ensemble make for compelling listening. The 1972 recording, made in St John's, Smith Square, is immaculately transferred, and as a bonus come four of Vivaldi's most inventive concertos, each with its own special effects.

(i) *L'estro armonico*, Op. 3 (complete); (ii) *6 Flute Concertos*, Op. 10. Miscellaneous concertos:

CD 1: *Double Mandolin Concerto, RG 532; Oboe Concertos, RV 548 & 461; Concerto for Strings (alla rustica), RV 151; Con molti stromenti, RV 558; Double Violin Concerto, RV 516.*

CD 2: *Concertos for Bassoon, RV 484; for Flute, RV 436; for Oboe & Bassoon, RV 545; for Strings, RV 159; for Viola d'amore & Lute, RV 540; for Violin (L'amoroso), RV 271.*

(N)(B) *** DG 471 317-2 (5). (i) Standage, Wilcock, Golding, Comberti, Jaap ter Linden; (ii) Beznosiuk; & Soloists, E. Concert, Pinnock.

Pinnock's performances of *L'estro armonico* and the Op. 10 *Flute Concertos* with Lisa Beznosiuk are among our top recommendations, and the two separate single-CD collections, one entitled *Alla rustica* the other *L'amoroso*, offer lively, communicative performances, using period instruments in the most enticing way. The sheer variety of Vivaldi is constantly established, totally contradicting the old idea that he wrote one concerto hundreds of times over. The playing time of these two discs is not particularly generous (53 and 57 minutes respectively), but now they come within a bargain box in DG Archiv's Collectors Edition this seems less important than the consistently high quality of the performances and recordings. The documentation is excellent.

L'estro armonico, Op. 3/1, 2, 4, 7, 8 & 10–11.

(BB) *** Naxos 8.550160. Capella Istropolitana, Kopelman.

Jozef Kopelman and the Capella Istropolitana are robustly competitive with their bargain disc. The performances are lively, and the recording has warmth and presence. Good value for money.

La stravaganza (12 concertos), *Op. 4* (complete).

⚫ (B) *** Double Decca 444 821-2 (2). Soloists, ASMF, Marriner.
(BB) **(*) Naxos 8.55323 (Nos. 1–6); 8.55324 (Nos. 7–12). Watkinson, City of London Sinfonia, Kraemer.

Marriner's performances make the music irresistible. The solo playing of Carmel Kaine and Alan Loveday is superb and, when the Academy's rhythms have such splendid buoyancy and lift, it is easy enough to accept Marriner's preference for a relatively sweet style in the often heavenly slow movements. The contribution of an imaginatively varied continuo (which includes cello and bassoon, in addition to harpsichord, theorbo and organ) adds much to the colour of Vivaldi's score. The recording, made in St John's, Smith Square, in 1973/4, is of the highest quality, with CD transfers in the demonstration class.

Nicholas Kraemer has fully absorbed period-instrument manners, and these athletic performances, full of vitality, on modern instruments, certainly have an authentic feel and sound. However, Andrew Watkinson's solo personality is not strong in individuality and while this set, which is very well recorded, is excellent value, those looking for the very best in an inexpensive format should turn to Marriner.

Violin Concertos, Op. 6 – see under *Violin Concertos* below.

The Trial between Harmony and Invention (12 Concertos), *Op. 8.*

(N)(M) *** Virgin VMD5 61980-2 (2) Biondi, Europa Galante.
(B) **(*) Ph. Duo 438 344-2 (2). Ayo, I Musici.
(M) **(*) Teldec 0630 13572-2 (2). A. Harnoncourt, Schaeftlein, VCM, Harnoncourt.

The Trial between Harmony and Invention (12 Concertos),

Op. 8; (i) Double Concertos: for Violin, Cello & Strings in A, RV 546; for 2 Violins in G, RV 516.

(BB) *** Virgin 2 x 1 VBD5 61668-2 (2). Huggett, Raglan Bar. Players, Kraemer; (i) with E. Wallfisch and Mason (cello).

The Trial between Harmony and Invention, Op. 8: Concertos Nos. 5–12.

(B) *** Sony SBK 53513. Zukerman, Black, ECO, Ledger.

Fabio Biondi and Europa Galante have already recorded the *Four Seasons* and their period-instrument performance is highly praised below. The new version, within the complete Op. 8, is just as fresh and certainly as vibrant, with some dazzling solo playing full of dynamic subtlety. One notices a few small differences in these new performances. In *Spring* the viola can surely never have barked more commandingly, and in the finale the ripieno achieves a very striking drone effect. In *Autumn* (and elsewhere) the continuo comes through especially tellingly in the slow movement, while the pianissimo opening of *Winter* moves from mysterious evocation to a strong climax. Clearly this particular winter is going to be a hard one.

The recording claims to use 'original manuscripts', and after considerable research (following Standage and Pinnock's example, Biondi used the recently discovered set of parts of the *Four Seasons* held in Manchester's Henry Watson Music Library. But for the other eight concertos in the set he has consulted alternative manuscripts held in libraries in Dresden and Turin. The reasons for this are well documented in the notes, and certainly Europa Galante make a dramatic case for the Dresden score of No. 5, *La tempesta di mare*.

They begin the second CD with an arresting account of *Concerto No. 11*, which Biondi considers is 'the richest in material of the whole collection', and very fine it is. *La caccia* (No. 10) follows, for which Biondi has turned to Turin, and the rest of the set has involved a great deal of detective work to determine the full detail of Vivaldi's intentions.

All the remaining concertos are played with the same energy and imaginative vitality which make the *Four Seasons* so enjoyable, and this new look is very stimulating indeed, for the recording is first class, and Europa Galante avoid all those linear excesses that can sometimes spoil period-instrument performances.

Kraemer's complete Op. 8 concertos with Monica Huggett make a fine alternative bargain recommendation in its new Virgin 2 x 1 format. In the *Four Seasons*, a lovely spontaneous feeling emerges: the light textures and dancing tempo of the finale of *Spring* are matched by the sense of fantasy in the central movement of *Summer*, while the rumbustious energy of the latter's last movement is gloriously invigorating. The adagio of *Autumn* has a delicate, sensuous somnambulance, and only the opening of *Winter* is relatively conventional, though certainly not lacking character. The rest of the concertos are hardly less imaginative, with no exaggeration of phrasing, which used to haunt early-music performances, and the recording is excellent. With two other enjoyable concertos thrown in for good measure, this is very highly recommendable.

The Teldec complete set is original in approach and full of character; there is, however, an element of eccentricity in Nikolaus Harnoncourt's control of dynamics and tempi, with allegros often aggressively fast and sharp changes of mood not always convincing. Alice Harnoncourt's timbre with a baroque instrument is leonine and her tone production rather astringent. The dramatic style of the solo playing is certainly at one with the vivid pictorialism of Vivaldi's imagery. The shepherd's dog in *Spring* barks vociferously, and the dance rhythms at the finale of the same concerto are extremely invigorating. The interpretative approach throughout emphasizes this element of contrast. The sound is bright, vivid and clean, if dry-textured and sometimes fierce in the Telefunken manner. The two discs, originally issued separately, are now in a box together.

Felix Ayo recorded the first four concertos (*The Four Seasons*) in 1959 and his was one of the finest of the early versions, although the recording was rather resonant. The remaining concertos in the set – full of typically Vivaldian touches which stamp these works as among the best of their time – date from 1961/2 and the recording, though still full-bodied, is less reverberant. The solo playing is attractively fresh, although Maria Teresa Garatti's continuo fails to come through adequately. Good value.

Zukerman's solo playing is distinguished throughout, and the ECO provide unfailingly alert and resilient accompaniments. In *Concerto No. 9 in D min.* oboist Neil Black takes the solo position and provides a welcome contrast of timbre – Vivaldi designed this concerto as optionally for violin or oboe, but it probably sounds more effective on the wind instrument. The full recording is lively, with a close balance for the soloists. This 77-minute CD encapsulates all the concertos from Op. 8 except the first four and includes such favourites as *La tempesta di mare* (RV 253), *Il piacere* (RV 108) and *La caccia* (RV 362).

The Four Seasons, Op. 8/1–4.

(B) *** Decca Penguin (ADD) 460 613-2. Loveday, ASMF, Marriner.

*** DG 463 259-2. Mutter, Trondheim Soloists – TARTINI: *Devil's Trill Sonata.* **(*)

(N) **(*) EMI CDC5 57015-2. Chung, St Luke's Chamber Ens.

**(*) BIS CD 275. Sparf, Drottningholm Bar. Ens.

**(*) EMI CDC7 49557-2. Kennedy, ECO.

The Four Seasons, Op. 8/1–4 (with sonnets in Italian and English).

(B) *** Hyp. Helios CDH 88012. Bruni, Edwards (readers), Oprean, European Community CO, Faerber.

(i) The Four Seasons; (ii) Bassoon Concerto in A min., RV 498; (iii) Double Concerto for 2 Oboes in D min., RV 535; (iv) Piccolo Concerto in C, RV 443.

(M) *** Decca (ADD) 466 232-2. (i) Loveday; (ii) Gatt; (iii) Black, Nicklin; (iv) Bennett; ASMF, Marriner.

(i) The Four Seasons; (ii) Oboe Concertos in C, RV 447; in F, RV 457.

(B) **(*) Sony (ADD) SBK 60711. (i) S. Kuijken, La Petite Bande; (ii) Haynes, O of 18th Century, Brüggen.

The Four Seasons; Violin Concerto in D, RV 171; Concerto for Strings in B flat (Concha), RV 163.

*** Opus 111 OPS 912. Biondi, Europe Galante.

The Four Seasons; Violin Concertos: in E flat (La tempesta di mare), RV 253; in C (Il piacere), RV 108, Op. 8/5–6.

(N) *** Warner Apex 8573 89097-2. Blankestijn, COE.

*** Ph. (IMS) 446 699-2, Sirbu, I Musici.

(i; ii) The Four Seasons; (i; iii) Violin Concerto in E flat (La tempesta di mare), Op. 8/5, RV 253; (iv) Triple Concerto in F for Flute, Oboe & Bassoon, RV 570; Double Concerto in G min. for Flute & Bassoon (La notte), RV 104.

(BB) *** ASV CDQS 6148. (i) Garcia; (ii) ECO; (iii) Fort Worth CO, Giordano; (iv) Bennett, Black, O'Neill, ECO, Malcolm.

(i) The Four Seasons; (ii) Violin Concertos: L'estro armonico: in A min., Op. 3/6. La stravaganza: in A, Op. 4/5. Concerto in C min. (Il sospetto), RV 199.

(N) (BB) *** EMI Encore (ADD) CDE5 74761-2. Perlman, (i) LPO; (ii) Israel PO.

The Four Seasons; (i) L'estro armonico: Quadruple Violin Concerto in B min., RV 580, Op. 3/10.

(B) *** Discover DICD 920202. Vlček; (i) with Hessová, Kaudersová, Nováková; Virtuosi di Praga.

The Four Seasons; L'estro armonico: Quadruple Violin Concerto in B min., RV 580, Op. 3/10. Sinfonia in B min. (Al Santo Sepolcro), RV 169.

✪ *** Sony SK 48251. Lamon, Tafelmusik.

(i) The Four Seasons; Concerto for Strings in G (Alla rustica), RV 151; (ii) Violin Concerto in E (L'amoroso), RV 271; Sinfonia in B min. (Al Santo Sepolcro), RV 169.

(B) *** DG (ADD) 439 422-2. (i) Schwalbé; (ii) Brandis; BPO, Karajan.

The Four Seasons, Op. 8/1–4; Violin Concertos: in D, RV 211; in E flat, RV 257; in B flat, RV 276.

(N) *** Sony SK 51352. Carmignola, Venice Bar. O, Marcon.

(i) The Four Seasons; Quadruple Violin Concerto in B flat, RV 553. Concerto for Strings in G (Alla rustica), RV 151; Sinfonia in G, RV 146.

(M) *** Virgin VC5 45117-2. (i) Banchini, Bury, Holloway, Wallfisch; Taverner Players, Parrott.

The Four Seasons; Violin Concerto in E (L'amoroso), RV 271.

(N) (M) **(*) Ph. (ADD) 464 750-2. Ayo, I Musici.

If most versions offered without fill-ups in a crowded marketplace now seem uncompetitive, Marriner's 1970 Academy of St Martin-in-the-Fields version with Alan Loveday is an exception and still remains at the top of the list. The performance is as satisfying as any and will surely delight all but those who are ruled by the creed of authenticity. It has an element of fantasy that makes the music sound utterly new; it is full of imaginative touches, with Simon Preston subtly varying the continuo between harpsichord and organ. The opulence of string tone may have a romantic connotation, but there is no self-indulgence in the interpretation, no sentimentality, for the contrasts are made sharper and fresher, not smoothed over. This has now appeared as one of the Penguin Classics at bargain price. The author's note is a fascinating reminiscence by Seamus Deane. However, as we go to print, Decca have made a further reissue of the Marriner performance on the Legends label (466 232-2) including, as a bonus, concertos for bassoon, piccolo and two oboes.

Tafelmusik offer a superbly imaginative version of Vivaldi's *Four Seasons* on period instruments, which is for the 1990s what Marriner's famous ASMF version was for the seventies. The playing is at once full of fantasy and yet has a robust gusto that is irresistible. The opening of *Spring*, with its chirruping bird calls, sets the scene and the second movement brings a lovely cantilena from Jeanne Lamon, while the barking dog is as musical as he is gruff. The performances throughout are full of dramatic contrasts. After *Winter*'s boisterous finale comes the hauntingly austere texture of the opening of the highly original *Sinfonia al Santo Sepolcro*; and the famous *Concerto for Four Violins* makes a fitting finale. The Sony recording is first class, absolutely clean in focus, with plenty of body and the most refined detail.

For those still preferring the fuller texture of modern instruments, the Apex version with the COE provides the perfect alternative and at super-bargain price too. The chimerical solo playing of Marieke Blankestijn is a delight and her clean style shows that she has learned from authentic manners. There is more imaginative delicacy here, particularly in the improvisatory central movement of *Summer* and the gentle haze of *Autumn*, where the gutsy finale has splendid bite and energy. The opening of *Winter* mirrors the impressionism of the Tafelmusik version, but the cheerful COE approach to the *Largo* central movement is even more attractive than with Tafelmusik. With two extra concertos from Opus 8 also included, this is now also a top recommendation. The Teldec recording is superb.

Fabio Biondi and his similarly excellent period-instrument group, Europe Galante have already given us an outstanding set of *L'estro armonico*, and their account of *The Four Seasons* is equally fresh. There is not a hint of routine anywhere, the solo playing is often exquisite; and even if the soloist nearly gets blown away by the gusto of the summer winds, the central reverie in *Autumn* is hauntingly gentle and serene. *Winter* opens very dramatically indeed and the solo roulades have great bravura; the central movement makes a charmingly relaxed contrast. The bonuses are imaginative and include another of Vivaldi's most individual violin concertos and the *Concerto for Strings* given the nickname *Concha* because it is supposed to simulate a primitive instrument made from a seashell, notably in the central *Andante* with its echoing fifth (B flat and F). Again the performances are strongly characterized and very well recorded.

The Sony version, with Giuliano Carmignola the breathtakingly brilliant soloist, is another period performance with no holds barred. Incredibly fast tempi for allegros contrast with gently lyrical, highly atmospheric slow movements in which one is given the feeling almost of ruminative improvisation. Certainly the performances are full of imagination and there are many new touches (witness the *sotto voce* opening of *Winter*). It is impossible not be gripped by the magnetic concentration and visceral excitement of this playing. But one wonders if Vivaldi would not have been astonished by such bravura, from the orchestra as well as the soloist. Carmignola offers as his bonus similarly dazzling accounts of what are described as première recordings of three more violin concertos, all very attractive, the D major, RV 211 (which comes last), especially so, with its siciliana *Larghetto* and striking finale. The brilliant yet transparent recording matches the performances admirably. Both CDs offer texts and translations of the poems with which the works are associated.

Mutter on DG is above all deeply reflective, reacting emotionally to each movement, allowing herself a free expansiveness at generally broad speeds. Not surprisingly, this is a far more intimate reading than her previous version with Karajan and the Vienna Philharmonic, with sound bright and immediate so that dynamic contrasts are dramatically underlined, with Mutter less spotlit than most violin virtuosos tackling this work. With the Norwegian players consistently reacting as chamber-music partners, the result is a performance which repeatedly brings out mystery in these atmospheric sound-pictures. She takes a similarly romantic view of the Tartini, using Zandonai's string arrangement, as she did in her previous recording.

The Taverner Players on Virgin offer yet another authentic version which stimulates the ear without acerbity. They are not the first group to use a different soloist for each of Vivaldi's *Four Seasons*, and this works well, with plenty of tingling vitality overall and a good deal of imaginative freedom from each in turn, with Chiara Banchini setting the style in her duets with the leader in her volatile account of *Spring*. In the *Adagio* of *Summer*, Alison Bury's timbre is pure, with a minimum of vibrato, yet the playing is appealingly expressive. The four players join together for the *Concerto for Four Violins in B flat*, offered as the principal bonus; it is an interesting work, if not quite as memorable as its more familiar companion in B minor, but it demands and receives virtuosity from its soloists. The *Sinfonia* and *Concerto alla rustica* are played with energy and tonal bite, and the recording is suitably vivid throughout.

The ASV version of *The Four Seasons*, with José-Luis Garcia as soloist and musical director, is very pleasing, with the violins of the accompanying group sweetly fresh and the soloist nicely balanced. The overall pacing is beautifully judged, and each movement takes its place naturally and spontaneously in relation to its companions. The one drawback is that there is only one track for each of the *Four Seasons*. The new couplings add two versions of *La tempesta del mare*, both the one with solo violin (from Op. 8) and the even more engaging triple concerto arrangement for flute, oboe and bassoon. The equally attractive flute/bassoon version of *La notte* completes the collection. The wind soloists are all celebrated, and George Malcolm's accompaniments are a model of baroque style.

Mariana Sirbu has a beautiful tone and an admirable line, and she can be expressive and vigorous by turn, without putting the timbre under strain. I Musici are thoroughly at home and sound fresh in a work which they must have played countless times. All the points of programmatic detail are nicely observed, from the bold shepherd's dog onwards. This is a first-class modern-instrument performance, if not as characterful as some, with the lute and harpsichord continuo adding to the effect of slow movements. The two

bonus concertos are equally well played, and the recording is natural, with fine projection.

Perlman's imagination holds the sequence together superbly, and there are many passages of pure magic, as in the central *Adagio* of *Summer*. The digital remastering of the 1976 recording is managed admirably, the sound firm, clear and well balanced, with plenty of detail. Now this record has been made much more competitive by the addition of three extra violin concertos, all fine works. Although the acoustic is somewhat dryish, this does not prevent these extra works from sounding very good.

Karajan's 1972 recording of *The Four Seasons* was a popular success and remains very enjoyable. Its tonal beauty is not achieved at the expense of vitality and, although the harpsichord hardly ever comes through, the overall scale is acceptable. Michel Schwalbé is a memorable soloist; his playing is neat, precise and imaginative, with a touch of Italian sunshine in the tone. The remastering for DG's bargain label, Classikon, has restored the body and breadth of the original, and in the additional works (recorded in the St Moritz Französische Kirche in Switzerland two years earlier) the string-sound is glorious. The charismatic BPO playing, notably in the expressive *Sinfonia al Santo Sepolcro*, is difficult to resist, and the *Concerto alla rustica* sounds sumptuous.

Another excellent bargain version comes from the Virtuosi di Praga, fresh, bright and clean, with a strong, highly responsive soloist in Oldřich Vlček. *Spring* is immediately vivacious and the viola produces a nice little rasp for the shepherd's dog. *Autumn* is delicately somnambulant, and the opening of *Winter* is well below zero and is decorated with a clink from the continuo. The *Concerto for Four Violins* makes for a popular encore. Excellent sound and very good value.

The Four Seasons may be the most over-duplicated work in the CD catalogue, but EMI seem to think that they can still market a performance by a star name like Kyung-Wha Chung at premium price without any couplings. Undoubtedly this joyful performance stands out for its freshness and spontaneity, with the soloist, Kyung-Wha Chung, directing the St Luke's Chamber Ensemble. It is the more welcome in that Chung has become a rather reluctant recording artist, not always displaying the vibrant, magnetic qualities that distinguished her playing as a young virtuoso. Here she once again seems totally relaxed in the studio, springing rhythms infectiously, defying period practice in warmly expressive phrasing at speeds that avoid extremes. This is music-making among friends, made the more vivid by the richness and immediacy of the recorded sound. The absence of a coupling makes it poor value, but admirers of Chung may not mind.

The BIS recording by Nils-Erik Sparf and the Drottningholm Baroque Ensemble has astonishing clarity and presence, and the playing is remarkable in its imaginative vitality. These Swedish players make the most of all the pictorial characterizations without ever overdoing them: they achieve the feat of making one hear this eminently familiar repertoire as if for the very first time.

The novelty of the Helios issue is the inclusion of the sonnets which Vivaldi placed on his score to give his listeners a guide to the illustrative detail suggested by the music.

Before each of the four concertos, the appropriate poem is read, first in a romantically effusive Italian manner and then in BBC English (the contrast very striking). On CD one can conveniently programme out these introductions. The performances are first class. Adelina Oprean is an excellent soloist, her reading full of youthful energy and expressive freshness; her timbre is clean and pure, her technique assured. Faerber matches her vitality, and the score's pictorial effects are boldly characterized in a vividly projected sound-picture.

On Sony, La Petite Bande, with Kuijken as soloist and director, offers an authentic version of considerable appeal. Although the accompanying group can generate plenty of energy when Vivaldi's winds are blowing, this is essentially a small-scale reading, notable for its delicacy, and the result is refreshing. The new coupling is a pair of *Oboe Concertos* played on a characterfully squawky and not entirely tractable period instrument by Bruce Haynes. If the end result is less refined than the main work, the duck-like noises occasionally bring a smile.

Philips have returned Ayo's 1960 version with I Musici to the catalogue as one of their 'Great Recordings'. It is hardly that, and ought by rights to be restored to its previous bargain category. But the warm recording still sounds well and this will be enjoyed by those for whom sustained richness of string textures is paramount, even at the cost of vitality. Felix Ayo produces lovely tone, both here and in the bonus concerto, and he certainly plays stylishly. But at 57 minutes this CD seems expensive.

Kennedy's account is among the more spectacular in conveying the music's imagery, with *Autumn* involving controversially weird special effects, including glissando harmonics in the slow movement and percussive applications of the wooden part of the bow to add rhythmic pungency to the hunting finale. There is plenty of vivid detail elsewhere. The ECO's playing is always responsive, to match the often very exciting bravura of its soloist, and allegros have an agreeable vitality. However, at 41 minutes, with no fillers, this is not generous and it would not be our first choice for repeated listening.

(i) *The Four Seasons; Bassoon Concerto in E min., RV 484; Flute Concerto in G min. (La notte), RV 439; Double Mandolin Concerto in G, RV 575; Double Concerto for Oboe & Violin in B flat, RV 548; Concerto for Orchestra 'con molti instrumenti', RV 550; Concerto for Strings in G (Alla rustica), RV 151; Concerto for 4 Violins (from L'estro armonico), RV 549;* (ii) *Gloria in D, RV 589.*

(N) (B) *** DG Panorama 469 220-2 (2). (i) Standage;
(ii) Smith, Argenta, Wyn Rogers, E. Concert Ch.; E. Concert & Soloists, Pinnock.

Pinnock's Archiv performance of *The Four Seasons* was always among the top contenders for the period-instrument crown. It had the advantage of using a newly discovered set of parts found in Manchester's Henry Watson Music Library which additionally brought the correction of minor textual errors in the La Cène text in normal use. The English Concert players create a relatively intimate sound, though their approach is certainly not without drama, while Simon

Standage's solo contribution has impressive flair. The overall effect is essentially refined, treating the pictorial imagery with subtlety. The outcome is less voluptuous than with Marriner, but finds a natural balance between vivid projection and atmospheric feeling. Now it is joined by a collection of half a dozen favourite concertos in lively, refreshing performances with fine solo playing from wind and string players alike, again using period instruments in the most enticing way. The sheer variety of Vivaldi is what is immediately established here, totally contradicting the old idea that he wrote just one concerto hundreds of times over. As an added bonus we are offered a lively and vivid account of the favourite Vivaldi choral work, very well sung and played, with excellent soloists. An admirable introduction to the composer and thoroughly worthwhile for the experienced collector as well as the newcomer. Excellent recording too.

The Four Seasons, Op. 8/1–4 (arr. for flute and strings).

(M) *** RCA (ADD) GD 60748. Galway, Zagreb Soloists.

James Galway's sensitive transcription is so convincing that at times one is tempted to believe that the work was conceived in this form. The playing is marvellous, full of detail and imagination, and the recording is excellent, even if the flute is given a forward balance, the more striking on CD.

'The Seven Seasons': The Four Seasons, Op. 8/1–4 with Interludes by Jaako Kuusisto.

(N) **(*) Finlandia 8573 84714-2. Reka Szilvay, Helsinki Strings, Csaba Szilvay, Géza Szilvay – KUUSISTO: *Between Seasons, Op. 7.* ***

The Finlandia disc, entitled *The Seven Seasons*, offers a unique version of Vivaldi's much-recorded set of four concertos. Fresh, clear and direct as an interpretation, it brings interludes between each of the concertos, prompting that eye-catching title. The Finnish composer and violinist, Jaakko Kuusisto, born 1974, wrote the interludes so that they could be performed either in connection with the Vivaldi or on their own. The young violinist, Reka Szilvay, born in Helsinki into a Hungarian-Austrian family, is the bright-toned soloist, consistently pure, polished and refined, articulating with phenomenal precision. Though there is no lack of feeling in expressive slow movements, those who favour star soloists in this work might feel that this is a relatively undercharacterized version. The orchestra is of young players brought together by two older members of the Szilvay family, the conductors here. At fifty strong it is a very large group for Vivaldi, but the unanimity of ensemble is astonishing, with rhythms light and resilient. Vivid, immediate sound, very well balanced.

La cetra (12 Violin Concertos), Op. 9.

(BB) *** Virgin 2 x 1 VBD5 61594-2 (2). Huggett, Raglan Bar. Players, Kraemer.

(i) *La cetra;* (ii) *Double Oboe Concerto in D min., RV 535;* (iii) *Piccolo Concerto in C, RV 443.*

◉ (B) *** Double Decca 448 110-2 (2). (i) I. Brown, ASMF;
(ii) Black; (iii) Nicklin; both with ASMF, Marriner.

Iona Brown here acts as director in the place of Sir Neville

Marriner. So resilient and imaginative are the results that one detects no difference from the immaculate and stylish Vivaldi playing in earlier Academy Vivaldi sets. There is some wonderful music here; the later concertos are every bit the equal of anything in *The Trial between Harmony and Invention*, and they are played gloriously. The recording too is outstandingly rich and vivid, even by earlier Argo standards with this group, and the Decca transfer to CD retains the demonstration excellence of the original analogue LPs, with a yet greater sense of body and presence. For the Double Decca reissue, two of Vivaldi's most engaging wind concertos have been added, winningly played by two fine Academy soloists. The sound is just as fine as in the concertos for violin.

Monica Huggett and the Raglan Baroque Players offer performances so accomplished and in such good style that they are unlikely to be surpassed in authentic-instrument versions of *La cetra*. She is in excellent form and her virtuosity always appears effortless. The Raglan Baroque Players are of the same size as the Academy of Ancient Music and some players are common to both groups. First-class recording.

6 Flute Concertos, Op. 10; Flute Concertos: in A min., RV 108; in D, RV 429; in G, RV 438; in A min., RV 440; in C min., RV 441; (i) Double Flute Concerto in C, RV 533. Piccolo Concerto in A min., RV 445.

(B) *** Ph. Duo (ADD) 454 256-2 (2). Gazzelloni, I Musici;
(i) with Steinberg.

This Duo set purports to contain Vivaldi's 'complete flute concertos', but it is an unlikely claim: the works for sopranino recorder, RV 443 and 444, are not here, nor is the arrangement of *La notte* (RV 104) which includes also a bassoon. However, the solo flute version is (Op. 10/2) and, with its movements representing ghosts (*Fantasmi*) and sleep (*Il sonno*), is a masterpiece by any standards. A Duo collection entirely made up of concertante works for flute might be thought a rather daunting prospect, but Gazzelloni is an artist of such quality and poetry that such doubts are banished. And it must be added that these concertos all show Vivaldi in the best light, not only in the best-known, *La tempesta di mare* and *Il gardellino*, from Op. 10, but in many of the miscellaneous concertos, too: witness the delicate slow movement of the *A minor*, RV 440, the touching *Largo* of the *C minor*, RV 441, or the lively opening movements of the *D major*, RV 429, and *A minor*, RV 108. In these modern-instrument performances Gazzelloni's tone is admirably fresh and clean, with I Musici giving him splendid support. The analogue recordings (from the 1960s and 1970s) are first rate.

6 Flute Concertos, Op. 10.

*** DG (IMS) 437 839-2. Gallois, Orpheus CO.
*** DG (IMS) 423 702-2. Beznosiuk, E. Concert, Pinnock.
(M) **(*) RCA (ADD) 09026 61351-2. Galway, New Irish CO.
(N)(BB) **(*) Naxos 8.553101. Drahos, Nicolaus Esterházy Sinf.

The Patrick Gallois/Orpheus version on DG is the lightest and most spirited of any, be they on period instruments or not. Collectors who recall Gallois' dazzling account of the Nielsen *Concerto* will know what to expect: effortless virtuosity, refined musicianship, intelligence and taste. He has an excellent rapport with the splendid Orpheus Chamber Orchestra and is very well served too by the engineers. A most distinguished issue.

There is some expressive as well as brilliant playing on the DG Archiv CD, which should delight listeners. Try track 8 (the *Largo* movement of *Concerto No. 2 in G minor, La notte*) for an example of the beautifully refined and cool pianissimo tone that Liza Beznosiuk can produce – and almost any of the fast movements for an example of her virtuosity. Trevor Pinnock and the English Concert provide unfailingly vital and, above all, imaginative support. The DG recording is exemplary in its clarity. Recommended with enthusiasm.

James Galway most effectively directs the New Irish Chamber Orchestra from the flute. The playing is predictably brilliant and the goldfinch imitations in *Il gardellino* (which comes first on the disc) are charming. Slow movements demonstrate Galway's beauty of timbre and sense of line to consistently good effect, although some may find the sweet vibrato excessive for baroque repertoire. First-rate recording quality.

Béla Drahos is an excellent soloist on Naxos, and he phrases very musically: the *Siciliana* slow movement of *Il gardellino* is beautifully played. He gets lively support from the Nicolaus Esterházy Sinfonia, who are also suitably gentle and evocative in the dream world of *La notte*. However, although this set of Op. 10 is very enjoyable, some might feel that the string tuttis are rather too well-upholstered to satisfy current ideas of how this music should sound. But if you are firmly wedded to modern-instrument performances of baroque music, this should offer no problems, for the recording is excellent. The *C minor Concerto* makes a welcome bonus, for in the finale the Goldfinch of *Il gardellino* appears to have flown back in through the window.

(i; ii)Flute Concertos. Op. 10: Nos. 1 in F (La tempesta di mare), RV 433; 2 in G min. (La notte), RV 439; 3 in D (Il gardellino), RV 428; (i; iii) 5 in F, RV 434. Flute Concerto in A min., RV 108s; Sopranino Recorder (Piccolo) Concertos: in C, RV 553..

(BB) *** Naxos 8.554053. Soloists; (i) Capella Istropolitana,
(ii) Krechek; (i;iii) Dohnányi; (iv) City of L. Sinfonia,
Kraemer.

An attractive regrouping of Naxos recordings (78 minutes) brings a particularly generous clutch of modern-instrument performances which will especially suit those who want only the most famous named concertos from Op. 10. They are most persuasively played and the recording is excellent throughout.

Complete bassoon concertos

Bassoon Concertos: in C, RV 466; in C, RV 467; in C, RV 469; in C, RV 470; in C, RV 471; in C, RV 472; in C, RV 473; in C, RV 474; in C, RV 475; in C, RV 476; in C, RV 477; in C, RV 478; in C, RV 479; in C min., RV 480; in

D min., RV 481; in E flat, RV 483; in E min., RV 484; in F, RV 485; in F, RV 486; in F, RV 487; in F, RV 488; in F, RV 489; in F, RV 490; in F, RV 491; in G, RV 492; in G, RV 493; in G, RV 494; in G min., RV 495; in G min., RV 496; in A min., RV 497; in A min., RV 498; in A min., RV 499; in A min., RV 500; in B flat (La notte), RV 501; in B flat, RV 502; in B flat, RV 503; in B flat, RV 504.

(M) *** ASV CDDCX 625 (6). Smith, ECO, Ledger; Zagreb Soloists, Ninic.

The bassoon brought out a generous fund of inspiration in Vivaldi, for few of his 37 concertos for that instrument are in any way routine. Daniel Smith plays with constant freshness and enthusiasm. His woody tone is very attractive and he is very well caught by the engineers. This set can be welcomed almost without reservation and, dipped into, the various recordings will always give pleasure. Even if some of the more complicated roulades are not executed with exact precision, Smith's playing has undoubted flair. For the last three CDs of the series the Zagreb Soloists take over the accompaniments and offer alert, vivacious playing that adds to the pleasure of these warm, affectionate performances. Daniel Smith, too, responds with vigour and polish.

Bassoon Concertos: in C, RV 472; in D min., RV 482; in E min., RV 484; in F, RV 491; in G, RV 494; in G min., RV 495; in A min., RV 499.

*** Ph. 446 066-2. Thunemann, I Musici.

Bassoon Concertos: in C, RV 473; in E flat, RV 483; in F, RV 485; in G, RV 492; in A min., RV 497; in B flat, RV 503.

*** Ph. (IMS) 416 355-2. Thunemann, I Musici.

Klaus Thunemann makes every work seem a masterpiece. His virtuosity is remarkable, and it is always at the composer's service. Moreover the polish of the playing is matched by its character and warmth. I Musici are on their finest form, and all the slow movements here are touchingly expressive, with Thunemann's ease of execution adding to the enjoyment. The Philips recording, ideally balanced, is in the demonstration bracket.

Bassoon Concerto in F, RV 485; (i) Double Concerto in G min., for Recorder & Bassoon (La notte), RV 104.

*** BIS CD 271. McGraw, (i) Pehrsson; Drottningholm Bar. Ens. – TELEMANN: Concertos. ***

The concerto subtitled *La notte* exists in three versions: one for flute (the most familiar), RV 439; another for bassoon, RV 501; and the present version, RV 104. Clas Pehrsson, Michael McGraw and the Drottningholm Baroque Ensemble give a thoroughly splendid account of it, and the *Bassoon Concerto in F major* also fares well. Excellent recording.

Complete cello concertos

Vol. 1: Cello Concertos: in C, RV 398; in C, RV 399; in D, RV 404; in D min., RV 406; in F, RV 410; in F, RV 412; in A min., RV 419.

(BB) *** Naxos 8.550907. Wallfisch, City of L. Sinfonia, Kraemer.

Vol. 2: Cello Concertos: in C, RV 400; in C min., RV 401; in E flat, RV 408; in G, RV 413; in A min., RV 422; (i) Double Cello Concerto in G min., RV 531.

(BB) *** Naxos 8.550908. Wallfisch, (i) with Harvey; City of L. Sinfonia, Kraemer.

Vol. 3: Cello Concertos: in C min., RV 402; in D, RV 403; in D min., RV 407; (i) in E min., RV 409; in A min., RV 418; in B flat, RV 423; in B min., RV 424.

❀ (BB) *** Naxos 8.550909. Wallfisch, (i) with Graham; City of L. Sinfonia, Kraemer.

Vol. 4: Cello Concertos: in D min., RV 405; in F, RV 411; in G, RV 414; in G min., RV 416 & RV 417; in A min., RV 420 & RV 421.

(BB) *** Naxos 8. 550910. Wallfisch, City of L. Sinfonia, Kraemer.

Vivaldi liked to write for instruments playing in the middle to lower register, and he left 27 solo concertos for the cello, all of which are here. The choice of Raphael Wallfisch as soloist could hardly have been bettered. He forms an admirable partnership with the City of London Sinfonia, directed from the harpsichord or chamber organ by Nicholas Kraemer. The first concerto of Volume 1, the fine *F major*, RV 412, sets off with great energy and produces a characteristically atmospheric central *Larghetto*. Wallfisch plays with restrained use of vibrato and a nicely judged expressive feeling. In the *A minor* work which follows (RV 419), Kraemer effectively uses an organ continuo to enliven the opening tutti and underpin the singing cello line in the *Andante*. The alert, resilient orchestral string-playing in the allegros is a pleasure in itself.

Besides several very striking solo works, Volume 2 of the Naxos series includes Vivaldi's only *Double Cello Concerto*, with much bustling interchange in the outer movements and the soloists answering each other eloquently in the *Largo*. In the *G major* solo *Concerto*, RV 413, there is a brilliantly articulated *moto perpetuo* semiquaver theme which alternates between soloist and orchestra; then follows a thoughtful slow movement, improvisatory in feeling, in which Wallfisch is in his element, over Kraemer's gentle organ continuo.

Volume 3 is a particularly fine collection. The soloist's bravura staccato playing at the opening of the *B flat major*, RV 423, commands the listener's attention at the very beginning of the disc, and this work has a matching good-humoured finale. The *Concerto in D minor*, RV 407, is one of Vivaldi's very best, and its central *Largo e sempre piano* again brings a touching solo response. Vivaldi is never predictable, and perhaps the most striking work of all here is the *E minor Concerto*, RV 409, where the cello is joined by a subservient and somewhat doleful solo bassoon. In the *Adagio–Allegro molto* opening movement, the two soloists wind their way through a melancholy recitativo, regularly interrupted by bursts of energy from the string tutti, reminding one of *The Four Seasons*; then in the much briefer *Allegro–Adagio* slow movement the procedure is reversed.

Volume 4 brings a further batch of concertos notable for their vitality and the vigorous bravura demanded from the soloist. Throughout these four discs there is never a hint of routine. Wallfisch's playing has extraordinary precision, and both he and the accompanying group continually communicate their enthusiasm for this endlessly inventive music. The recording is vividly realistic and the balance seems very well judged indeed. A remarkable achievement, standing very high in the Vivaldi discography.

Cello Concertos: in C, RV 398; in G, RV 413.

(B) *** DG Double (ADD) 437 952-2 (2). Rostropovich, Zurich Coll. Mus., Sacher – BERNSTEIN: 3 *Meditations;* BOCCHERINI: *Cello Concerto No. 2;* GLAZUNOV: *Chant du Ménestrel;* SHOSTAKOVICH: *Cello Concerto No. 2;* TARTINI: *Cello Concerto;* TCHAIKOVSKY: *Andante cantabile* etc. ***

Performances of great vigour and projection from Rostropovich; every bar comes fully to life. Spendidly lively accompaniments and excellent CD transfers, bright and clean with no lack of depth. Rostropovich's performances come as part of a very generous Double DG compilation, with the two discs offered for the price of one.

Cello Concerto in D min., RV 406.

*** Teldec 9031 77311-2. Rostropovich, St Paul CO, Hugh Wolff – C. P. E. BACH; TARTINI: *Concertos.*

Who says that modern chamber orchestras cannot achieve the same transparency as period ensembles? Admittedly the Saint Paul Chamber Orchestra have had the advantage of Christopher Hogwood's presence, but the sound they produce blends transparency of texture with warmth and subtlety of colouring. Rostropovich is as masterly and eloquent as one could imagine, and he is accorded excellently balanced sound.

Cello Concertos: in G, RV 413; in G min., RV 417.

(M) **(*) EMI (ADD) CDM7 64326-2. Harrell, ECO, Zukerman – HAYDN: *Concertos.* **(*)

Though Lynn Harrell is hardly a classical stylist among cellists (as he shows in the Haydn coupling), he gives lively, imaginative performances of two fine Vivaldi concertos (the *G major* particularly attractive) and is well accompanied by Zukerman. The sound is lively and full, if not as smooth as on the Haydn concertos, which are interspersed with Vivaldi. However, this CD is now deleted.

Flute concertos, Vol. 1: Chamber Concertos: in C, for Flute, Oboe, Violin, Bassoon & Continuo, RV 88; in D, for Flute & 2 Violins, RV 89; in D, for Flute, Violin, Bassoon & Continuo (Il gardellino), RV 90; in D, RV 91; in D min., RV 96 (both for Flute, Violin, Bassoon & Continuo); in F, RV 99; in G min., RV 107 (both for Flute, Oboe, Violin, Bassoon & Continuo).

(BB) *** Naxos 8.553365. Drahos and soloists, Nicolaus Esterházy Sinf.

This Naxos disc collects multiple concertos, but with a continuo instead of an orchestra. Although not to be played at a single sitting, these works offer a great deal of pleasure stemming from their rich textural interplay with plenty of imitation among the soloists. The quality of invention is astonishingly high. *Il gardellino* (which opens the pro-

gramme) is justly famous, but the G minor work, RV 107, is also remarkable, with a touching *Siciliano* slow movement; it ends with a chaconne which maintains the minor key. RV 88 has a strikingly cheerful opening movement, then gives prominence to the flute both in its central *Largo cantabile* and in another chirping finale. RV 89 effectively brings a change of colour in the use of a pair of violins in juxtaposition to the flute. The performances here are admirable and the recording is most effectively balanced.

Flute Concertos: in A min., RV 108; in F, RV 434; Double Flute Concerto in C, RV 533; Sopranino Recorder Concertos: in C, RV 443 & RV 444; in A min., RV 445.

(BB) *** Naxos 8.550385. Jálek, Novotny, Stivin, Capella Istropolitana, Dohnányi.

The Capella Istropolitana, who are drawn from the excellent Slovak Philharmonic, play with vitality and sensitivity for Oliver Dohnányi and the soloists show appropriate virtuosity and flair. As always, there are rewards and surprises in this music. The sound is very good indeed, and so is the balance.

Flute Concertos in D, RV 427; in D (Il gardellino), RV 428; in D, RV 429; in G, RV 436; in G, RV 438; in A min., RV 440; (i) in C, for 2 Flutes, RV 533.

(M) *** HM HMT 905193. See, (i) S. Schultz; Philh. Bar. O, McGegan.

Janet See is not only a first-class player but also an artist whose phrasing is alive and imaginative. Moreover the Philharmonia Baroque Orchestra, a West Coast American group, give her excellent support. The diversity and range of these pieces is astonishing. Highly enjoyable.

Guitar Concertos in C, RV 82; in D, RV 93.

(M) *** DG (IMS) (ADD) 439 984-2. Behrend, I Musici – CARULLI: *Concerto in A;* GIULIANI: *Concerto in A, Op. 30.* ***

Both these concertos are transcriptions of chamber works intended for the lute. They work well on guitar and are most elegantly played here. Although – as the opening of the *D major* shows – there is no lack of life in these smooth, elegant performances, a more robust and sinewy approach can be more telling in this repertoire.

Guitar Concertos in D, RV 93; in B flat, RV 524; in G min., RV 531; in G, RV 532. Trios: in C, RV 82; in G min., RV 85.

*** DG (IMS) 415 487-2. Söllscher, Camerata Bern, Füri.

Göran Söllscher further enhances his reputation both as a master-guitarist and as an artist on this excellently recorded issue, in which he has first-class support from the Camerata Bern under Thomas Füri. In RV 532, Söllscher resorts to technology and plays both parts. The DG balance is admirably judged.

Guitar Concertos: in D, RV 93 (arr. Malipiero); in A (arr. Pujol from Trio Sonata in C, RV 82); (i) Double Concerto for Guitar & Viola d'amore in D min., RV 540 (arr. Malipiero).

(B) **(*) Decca 448 709-2. Fernández, ECO, Malcolm, (i) with Blume – GIULIANI: *Concerto*; PAGANINI: *Sonata*. **(*)

Eduardo Fernández is a musician's guitarist whose playing is consistently refined and sensitive, always responsive to the composer's needs, if at times perhaps a little too self-effacing. The performance of the *Double Concerto for Guitar and Viola d'amore* is winningly intimate, particularly in the very gentle central *Largo*, in which Fernández is perfectly balanced with Norbert Blume. The solo concertos are similarly refined, with bravura unexaggerated and Malcolm always providing the most understanding and polished accompaniments. The recording is first class and beautifully balanced.

Guitar Concertos: in C, RV 425; for 2 Guitars in G, RV 532; for 4 Guitars in D, RV 93; in B min., RV 580 (from L'estro armonico, Op. 3/10); for Guitar, Violin, Viola & Cello in A, RV 82.

(B) *** Ph. 426 076-2. Los Romeros, San Antonio SO, Alessandro.

Though their composer did not conceive these works with guitars in mind, they sound quite effective in their present formats. Vivaldi's concertos of this kind are often more enjoyable when grouped in a miscellaneous collection with varying solo timbres. However, guitar and mandolin enthusiasts should find this satisfactory, for the recording is truthful, if a little studio-ish in feeling.

Concertos for lute and mandolin: Lute Concerto in D, RV 93; Mandolin Concerto in C, RV 425; Double Mandolin Concerto in G, RV 532; Double Concerto in D min. for Viola d'amore, Lute & Strings, RV 540; Concerto in C for 2 Recorders, 2 Violins 'in tromba marina', 2 Mandolins, 2 Theorbos, 2 Salmoé, Cello & Strings, RV 558. Trios: in C, RV 82; in G min., RV 85, for Violin, Lute & Continuo.

**(*) Teldec 4509 91182-2. Il Giardino Armonico, Antonini.

In these period performances from the pioneering Italian group in this field the opening of the multiple-instrument concerto, with two long, single-string violins 'in tromba marina', is strikingly gutsy. The playing throughout has plenty of energy, and textures are fresh and transparent, with slow movements appealingly fragile. The *Largo* duet between lute and viola d'amore in RV 540 is delightful, as are the pair of *Trios*, which bring similar delicacy of texture. The one snag is the curious flowing dynamic surge in the allegros, which some listeners will find disconcerting. Otherwise, with the excellent recording we take for granted with Das Alte Werk, this can be recommended.

Mandolin Concerto in C, RV 425; Double Mandolin Concerto in G, RV 532; (Soprano) Lute Concerto in D, RV 93; Double Concerto in D min. for Viola d'amore & Lute, RV 540. Trios: in C, RV 82; in G min., RV 85.

*** Hyp. CDA 66160. Jeffrey, O'Dette, Parley of Instruments, Goodman and Holman.

These are chamber performances, with one instrument to each part, providing an ideal balance for the *Mandolin Concertos*. An organ continuo replaces the usual harpsichord, and very effective it is; in the *Trios* and the *Lute Concerto* (but not in the *Double Concerto*, RV 540) Paul

O'Dette uses a gut-strung soprano lute. The delightful sounds here, with all players using period instruments, are very convincing. The recording is realistically balanced within an attractively spacious acoustic.

Oboe Concertos: in C, RV 447 & RV 451; in F, RV 455 & RV 457; in A min., RV 461 & RV 463.

(BB) *** Naxos 8.550860. Schilli, Budapest Failoni CO, Nagy.

Oboe Concertos: in C, RV 450 & RV 452; in D, RV 453; in D min., RV 454; (i) Double Oboe Concertos: in C, RV 534; D min., RV 535; A min., RV 536.

(BB) *** Naxos 8.550859. Schilli; (i) with Jonas; Budapest Failoni CO, Nagy.

Excellent playing from these Budapest musicians. The second of these two discs offers the three *Double Concertos*, and the two CDs between them include half the solo works. They are often surprisingly florid, requiring considerable bravura from the soloist. A good example is the Minuet finale of RV 447, which is a cross between a Rondo and a theme and variations. Vivaldi is never entirely predictable, except that his invention never seems to flag, and many of the simple *Grave*, *Larghetto* and *Largo* slow movements are very pleasing indeed.

(i) *Oboe Concertos: in C, RV 450; in D min., RV 454; in F, RV 457;* (i–ii) *Double Oboe Concerto in D min., RV 535;* (i; iii) *Double Concerto for Oboe, Bassoon & Orchestra in G, RV 545;* (i–iii) *Concerto for 2 Oboes, 2 Violins, Bassoon & Orchestra, RV 557;* (i) *Recorder Concerto in F, RV 442.*

(B) *** HM HMA 1903018. (i) Wolf (oboe or recorder); (ii) Brandisz; (iii) Tognon; Capella Savaria, Németh.

While two of the solo oboe concertos here were conceived for bassoon, Marie Wolf with her warm phrasing and clean tonguing makes them all sound custom-made for her principal instrument. The tone of her baroque oboe is robust yet creamy, especially in the *Largo* of RV 454, while the chromatic 'slides' in the work's first movement are most seductively managed. In the double concertos the other wind soloists produce equally characterful timbres: the two oboes blend well together, yet have individuality, while the combination of oboe and the woody bassoon are specially felicitous. Then Marie Wolf turns to her recorder and charms us yet again. There are few more appealing bargain collections of Vivaldi wind concertos played on period instruments than this. The recording is beautifully balanced and truthful.

Oboe Concertos: in C, RV 451; in D min., RV 454; in F, RV 457; in G min., RV 460; in A min., RV 461 & RV 463.

(N)(M) **(*) Van Pasacaille 99723. Dombrecht, Il Fondamento.

No information is given about the baroque oboe the excellent Paul Dombrecht uses in his Vanguard collection. It has a uniquely creamy sound for a period instrument in slow movements, but in allegros at times one is forced to cover a smile, for when the soloist is vigorously playing his decorative roulades, as during the opening concerto here, RV 457, the result sounds like a very musical duck. However, he must be on dry land for he also directs Il Fondamento, and they provide polished and spirited accompaniments. The *Largo* of RV 463, with its gentle pizzicatos, very like rain, is nicely managed and Dombrech duly quacks his pleasurable response, while in the spiccato finale one can visualize him vigorously pecking.

The oboe's syncopated theme in the *D minor Concerto*, heard against chromatically swerving strings, is especially diverting and the following *Largo*, with its organ continuo, is quite lovely. The *Allegro molto* which opens RV 451 shows Dombrecht's virtuosity (and that of the orchestra) at its most sparkling, and the piquant finale is no less diverting . This CD, very well recorded, is a real collector's item.

Recorder Concertos: for Alto Recorder in D (Il gardellino), RV 428; in G, RV 425; for Flautino: in C, RV 443 & RV 444; in A min., RV 445. Chamber Concertos: in D for Alto Recorder, Violin & Continuo, RV 92; in A min., for Alto Recorder, 2 Violins & Continuo, RV 108.

(N) **(*) BIS CD 865. Laurin, Bach Collegium, Japan, Masaaki Suzuki.

The BIS Collection, with Dan Laurin as soloist, includes three concertos for flautino ('little flute'). This is not a piccolo, but a minor member of the recorder family, with a small piquant timbre which balances well with period strings, as the three quite engaging but very similar concertos here effectively demonstrate. The performance of *Il gardellino* (from Op. 10) is the highlight of the programme, very effectively using an organ continuo in the siciliana *Largo*, and the *G major Concerto*, RV 425, is hardly less impressive. Of the other two chamber works with continuo, the *Double Concerto* with violin is rather pale and lacking in profile, but the *A minor Concerto* with two violins is stronger with an attractive finale. Even so this well-recorded anthology is not nearly as vivid as the Hyperion collection of chamber concertos for recorder below.

Concertos for Strings & Continuo: in C, RV 114; in C min., RV 118; in C min., RV 120; in D min., RV 128; in E min., RV 133; in F min., RV 143; in G (Alla rustica), RV 151; in G min., RV 152; in G min., RV 157; in A, RV 158; in B flat (Conca), RV 163; in B flat, RV 167. Sinfonias for Strings & Continuo: in C, RV 116; in E, RV 132; in E min., RV 134; in F, RV 137; in F, RV 140; in G, RV 146; in B min., RV 168.

(N) (B) *** Erato Ultima ADD/Dig. 8573 88049-2 (2). Sol. Ven., Scimone.

For Vivaldi the terms 'sinfonia' and 'concerto for strings' seem to be interchangeable; indeed, RV 134, which has a fugal opening movement, was first called a concerto, and the composer added the description 'sinfonia' later to the manuscript. The finales of RV 120 and RV 152, both called concertos, are also contrapuntal and these fugues show an attractive, extrovert vitality. But Vivaldi is never predictable, and many of the individual movements here show his imagination at full stretch. The *Sinfonia in G*, RV 146, opens the first disc with typically arresting flourishes, followed by a wistful *Andante*, with the melody floating over gentle pizzicatos like a song with mandolin, while the *Concerto in C*, RV 114, has a highly inventive *Chaconne* for the finale. It

is a fast movement and so within its 3′ 25″ a great deal happens. We all know the *Alla rustica Concerto*, but RV 163 (curiously subtitled *Conca*) is another short but masterly piece, its three movements all springing from the opening phrase. The central *Andante* is for all the world like an operatic aria without the vocal line. Indeed, many of the slow movements here are very touching, not least the restless *Andante molto* of RV 152, the lyrical A minor cantilena of RV 158, the solemn *Largo* of RV 120 and, perhaps most strikingly of all, the *Sinfonia in F*, RV 137, where the 'singing' *Andante*, with its touch of chromatic melancholy, contrasts so well with the very positive outer movements. This makes a fine close to a fascinating programme, revealing a little-known side of a great composer. The performances (using modern instruments) are vital and expressively penetrating, and the recording, whether analogue or digital (as with RV 116, 118, 137 and 143), is fresh and naturally balanced.

Concertos for Strings, Vol. 1: Paris Concertos: Nos. 1 in G min. (with woodwind), RV 157; 2 in E min., RV.133; 3 in C min., RV 119; 4 in F, RV 136; 5 in C (with woodwind), RV 114; 6 in G min., RV 154; 7 in A, RV 160; 8 in D min., RV 127; 9 in B flat, RV 164; 10 in D, RV 121; 11 in G (with woodwind), RV 150; 12 in A, RV 159.

*** Chan. 0547. Col. Mus. 90, Standage.

Vivaldi wrote over forty *concerti a quattro* for strings alone, without a soloist, and the present group were gathered together in a single manuscript, written in the hand of Vivaldi's father, and have been preserved in the Paris Conservatoire Library ever since. They are each in three movements, with the central slow movement quite brief and acting as an expressive interlude linking the two vivacious framing allegros. The exception is RV 114, which is in two movements, the first moving from a sharply dotted allegro to adagio, with a jolly *Chaconne* to round things off. RV 133 has a striking *Rondeau* finale, and it is thought that these two works may have been composed separately from the others. They are all freshly inventive and played here with springing rhythms and plenty of vitality. In three concertos, though not specified by the composer, woodwind have been added to give extra colour. The touch of abrasiveness on the string sound is aurally bracing, and slow movements have a nicely ruminative improvisatory feel. The recording is first class.

Concertos for Strings: in C, RV 113 & RV 114; in D min., RV 127; in F, RV 138; in G (Alla rustica), RV 151; in G min., RV 153, RV 156 & RV 157; in A min., RV 161; in B flat, RV 167.

(BB) **(*) Naxos 8.553742. Accademia I Filarmonici, Martini.

The Accademia I Filarmonici is a conductorless chamber orchestra, to some extent led from the bow by Alberto Martini. They do not use period instruments, but their style, brisk and athletic, with comparatively lean textures, is well removed from that of I Musici. They make the most of this group of Vivaldi's string concertos – which might equally well have been called sinfonias. The only famous one is *Alla rustica*, which is vigorously done. Slow movements are delicate in texture with the harpsichord continuo coming through naturally. Not all this music is equally appealing, but the best movements are memorable, for instance the jogging opening allegro of RV 113 and its minor-key *Grave* slow movement. Excellent recording.

Viola d'amore Concertos: in D, RV 392; in D min., RV 393, RV 394 & RV 395; in A, RV 396; in D min., RV 397.

**(*) Hyp. CDA 66795. Mackintosh, OAE.

The viola d'amore was greatly admired in Vivaldi's time for its tone, apparently sweeter than that of the contemporary violin. Yet to today's ears its character is more plangent, and that especially applies to performance style on a baroque instrument. As can be seen, Vivaldi favoured the key of D minor above others for his concertos for that instrument, which are generally less striking than most of his violin concertos. Catherine Mackintosh gives expert performances with the Orchestra of the Age of Enlightenment, using rather astringent tone.

6 Violin Concertos, Op. 6; Concerto in A (The Cuckoo).

(N) *** O-L 455 653-2. Manze, AAM.

Vivaldi's *Opus 6* contains only six concertos instead of the usual dozen. They were printed in Amsterdam soon after *La stravaganza* and in his notes Michael Talbot tells us that the engraved parts included many errors which Ricordi's modern edition has perpetuated, but which have been corrected here. They are all fine works and seem to get better and better as the set proceeds, although every concerto has its own particular point of interest. No. 1 opens commandingly and has a memorable siciliano *Adagio*, scored for just the soloist and continuo, while in the *Largo* of No. 2 the soloist has a dialogue with the bass. No. 3 brings a particularly strong opening movement, while No. 4 begins with an ear-tickling *raddoppiate* stuttering effect, and the slow movement of No. 6 is quite haunting. The so-called *Cuckoo Concerto* was understandably very popular in its day, although the bird calls are surely wrongly identified, as no use is made of the interval of a third for which the cuckoo is famous. The performances here have superb élan and polish; the accompaniments are as vital as the solo playing. The continuo includes attractive use of a chamber organ, and the balance is first rate.

'Dresden Violin Concertos', Vol. 1: Violin Concertos: in C, RV 170; in G, RV 314a; in G min., RV 319; in A, RV 341; in B flat (Il carbonelli), RV 366; in B flat, RV 383.

(BB) *** Naxos 8.553792. Martini, with Accademia I Filarmonici.

This series concentrates on concertos which survive in manuscript in the Dresden Saxony Landesbibliothek, and which were used by the Court Orchestra. They do not derive from the composer's residence in the city, and the sleeve note suggests that their existence may be connected with Vivaldi's association with an influential group of Dresden musicians, and most notably the violinist, Johanne Pisendel, who visited and studied under the composer during the latter part of 1716, and to whom Vivaldi dedicated a number of his concertos. The quality of these works is often remarkably high, reflecting the calibre of the orchestra and indeed Pisendel's virtuosity and musicianship. They sound ex-

tremely well in these excellent modern-instrument performances. Volume 1 gets off to very good start indeed. Alberto Martini directs bright, resilient performances, aptly paced, and he also proves a splendid soloist. There is nothing routine about any of these six works, as is demonstrated by the haunting *Largo* of the A major, RV 341, where the soloist plays over a gentle quasi-tremolando; the result is exquisite.

'Dresden Violin Concertos', Vol. 2: Violin Concertos: in C, RV 184; in D min., RV 241; in E, RV 267; in F, RV 292; in G min., RV 329; in B flat (Posthorn), RV 363.

(BB) *** Naxos 8.553793. Baraldi, Accademia I Filarmonici, Martini.

The concertos on the second disc are full of surprises, and Roberto Baraldi gives them the strongest profile. He is a very positive soloist, with a bolder sound image than Martini, which is not to say he is in the least insensitive. He likes to echo phrases, followed by the orchestra. His strength of purpose is especially telling in the *Posthorn Concerto*, which features octave rhythmic figures on B flat, and also just right for the *D minor Concerto*, RV 241. But perhaps the most striking work here is the *F major*, RV 292, where the six-minute first movement interpolates a slow central section and is virtually a miniature concerto in itself. The *E major Concerto* goes one further with four tempo changes, *Allegro–Adagio–Largo–Allegro*, while the *C major*, not to be outdone, has its opening and closing ritornello interrupted by a two-bar *Adagio* from the soloist; it also has a very lively and highly inventive finale. Again excellent sound.

'Dresden Violin Concertos', Vol. 3: Violin Concertos: in D, RV 228; in D min., RV 245; in E flat, RV 262; in F, RV 285; in G min., RV 323; in B min., RV 384.

(BB) *** Naxos 8. 553860. Fornaciari, Accademia I Filarmonici, Martini.

One is struck by the vigour of the *allegros* in Volume 3, emphasized by Marco Fornaciari's extrovert style and very open timbre. Yet in slow movements he fines down his tone most beautifully. The *Largo* of the *B minor Concerto*, accompanied solely by the basso continuo, is particularly fine, while RV 262 brings a memorable central siciliana. The first movement of the F major, RV 285, introduces a second solo violin to echo the first, and the central melody of the slow movement is framed by a remarkable chromatic series of repeated descending chords.

'Dresden Violin Concertos' Vol. 4: Violin Concertos: in D, RV 213; in D, RV 219; in D, RV 224; in D min., RV 240; in E flat, RV 260; in A, RV 344; in B min., RV 388.

(BB) *** Naxos 8. 554310. Rossi, Accademia I Filarmonici, Martini.

The use of a different soloist for each of these Naxos Dresden collections adds to their variety and interest. Cristiano Rossi's style is more intimate than that of Marco Fornaciari, yet his playing is by no means without personality and rhythmic flair. *Allegros* bustle with life in the orchestra, and Vivaldi's slow movements never fail to bring textural interest, apart from their melodic appeal. The last three of the seven concertos on this disc are all in D major, yet there is no sense of monotony, and RV 213 brings a stimulating close. Excellent recording.

Violin Concertos 'for Anna Maria': in D, RV 229; in D min., RV 248; in E, RV 267a; in E flat, RV 260; in B flat (Posthorn), RV 363; in A, RV 349.

*** Ph. 454 459-2. Sirbu, I Musici.

Anna Maria, a foundling, was one of the star pupils of Vivaldi's Pietà and he wrote at least two dozen concertos specifically for her to play. She did not have a monopoly on them, for two of those included here are also found in the Dresden collection above. The *E major Concerto*, RV 267a, however, is fascinatingly different from the Dresden manuscript, RV 267. Not only does it have an alternative, more ambitious slow movement but the first movement has its tempo changes further extended. Mariana Sirbu takes on the mantle of her celebrated predecessor very persuasively. Her tone is enticingly beautiful, her bravura unostentatiously sparkling, and she brings memorable delicacy to slow movements, while in the *Largo* of the *Posthorn* she bounces the rhythmic main theme with engaging buoyancy. I Musici give her splendid support and the recording balance is particularly pleasing. So is the overall sound, with sunshine in the place of period-instrument acidity. Highly recommended.

Violin Concertos, Op. 8, Nos. 5 in E flat (La tempesta di mare), RV 253; 6 in C (Il piacere), RV 108; 10 in B flat (La caccia), RV 362; 11 in D, RV 210; in C min. (Il sospetto), RV 199.

(B) *** CfP CD-CFP 4522. Menuhin, Polish CO, Maksymiuk.

Menuhin's collection of five concertos – four of them with nicknames and particularly delightful – brings some of his freshest, most intense playing. Particularly in slow movements – notably that of *Il piacere* ('pleasure') – he shows afresh his unique insight in shaping a phrase. Fresh, alert accompaniment and full digital recording.

Miscellaneous concerto collections

(i) *The Trial between Harmony and Invention: Violin Concertos Nos. 5 in E flat (La tempesta di mare); 6 in C (Il piacere), Op. 8/5–6; (ii) Bassoon Concertos: in C, RV 472; in C min., RV 480; in A min., RV 498; in B flat, RV 504.*

(M) *** Chan. 6529. (i) Thomas, Bournemouth Sinf.;
(ii) Thompson, LMP, Ledger.

The two concertos included here from *The Trial between Harmony and Invention* were among the best of the complete set recorded by Ronald Thomas in 1980. The use of modern instruments does not preclude a keen sense of style, and the balance is convincing. The bassoonist Robert Thompson turns a genial eye on his four concertos. He is rather forwardly projected but the performances are, like the sound, agreeably fresh, among the most attractive accounts of Vivaldi's bassoon concertos available on CD.

Bassoon Concerto in E min., RV 484; Flute Concerto in G min. (La notte), Op. 10/2, RV 439; Double Mandolin Concerto in G, RV 532; Concerto con multi instrumenti in C, RV 558; Double Concerto for Oboe & Violin in B flat, RV 548; Concerto for Strings (alla rustica), RV 151; Concerto for 2 Violins & 2 Cellos in G, RV 575; L'estro armonico: Concerto for 4 Violins in D, Op. 3/1, RV 549.

(M) *** DG 447 301-2. Soloists, E. Concert, Pinnock.

This generous 72-minute collection of varied works is very enticing at mid-price, showing Pinnock and the English Concert at their liveliest and most refreshing, although not always so strong on charm. The *Concerto for Four Violins* is very lithe, and throughout the concert the solo playing is most expert. The orchestral concerto, RV 558, involves an astonishing array of instruments.

Bassoon Concertos in A min., RV 497; in B flat (La notte), RV 501; Double Mandolin Concerto in G, RV 532; Piccolo Concerto in C, RV 443; Viola d'amore Concerto in D min., RV 394; Double Violin Concerto for Violin & Violin per eco lontano in A, RV 552.

(M) *** Vernay PV 730052. Soloists, Paul Kuentz CO, Kuentz.

Although described as 'six rare concertos', this most enjoyable, 71-minute collection is made up entirely of favourites, all played with much character. The two mandolinists, Takashi and Sylvia Ochi, are as personable as the sprightly bassoonist, Fernand Corbillon, with his woody French timbre, while the *Echo Violin Concerto* (the echoes feature in the ripieno as well as the solo writing) comes off to great effect. Fine accompaniments from Kuentz and first-rate digital sound, naturally balanced.

Bassoon Concerto in A min., RV 498; Flute Concerto in C min., RV 108; Double Horn Concerto in F, RV 539; Oboe Concerto in F, RV 456; Double Oboe Concerto in D min., RV 535; 2 Concertos for 2 Oboes, Bassoon, 2 Horns & Violin in F, RV 569 & RV 574; Piccolo Concerto in C, RV 208.

(B) *** Double Decca (ADD) 452 943-2 (2). Soloists, ASMF, Marriner – BELLINI: *Oboe Concerto in E flat;* HANDEL: *Oboe Concertos etc.* ***

Marriner's modern-instrument performances of favourite Vivaldi wind concertos, made between 1965 and 1977, have long been praised. The soloists are all distinguished and the playing here is splendidly alive and alert, with crisp, clean articulation and well-pointed phrasing, full of imagination, yet free from over-emphasis. The *A minor Bassoon Concerto* has a delightful sense of humour. Although the musical substance may not be very weighty, Vivaldi was never more engaging than when writing for wind instruments, particularly if he had more than one in his team of soloists, as in the two attractive composite works included in the programme. The vintage recordings remain in the demonstration bracket.

Bassoon Concerto in A min., RV 498; Flute Concerto in C min., RV 441; Oboe Concerto in F, RV 456; Concerto for 2 Oboes in D min., RV 535; Concerto for 2 Oboes, Bassoon, 2 Horns & Violin in F, RV 574; Piccolo Concerto in C, RV 444.

(B) *** Decca Penguin (ADD) 460 745-2. ASMF, Marriner.

The recordings here are also included in the Double Decca set above. They were made in 1976/7 and have been transferred to CD with pleasing freshness; their bargain release on Penguin Classics (with contributory essay by Vikram Seth) makes this an excellent single-disc modern-instrument choice.

Cello Concerto in B min., RV 424; Oboe Concerto in A min., RV 461; Double Concerto for Oboe & Violin, RV app. 17; Violin Concerto in D (Il grosso Mogul), RV 208; Sinfonia in B min. & Sonata in E flat. (Al Santo Sepolcro), RV 169 & RV 130.

(N) (BB) ***(*)** Teldec 4509 97454-2. Möller, Piguet, Schröder, Concerto Amsterdam, Schröder.

The forward balance here seems to emphasize a somewhat stiff approach, although the allegros are alert and lively, and the opening *Adagio* of the *Sinfonia* achieves an impressive pianissimo. The 1978 analogue recording sounds quite modern: the digital remastering is clean without loss of ambience. The robust and somewhat plangent timbres are readily captured and those who favour Vivaldi played on baroque instruments will certainly find the effect characterful. The playing time, however, is only 48'30".

Concerti 'con molti istromenti': *Concerto funèbre in B flat for Oboe, Chalumeau, Violin, 3 Viole all'inglese, RV 579; Concerto in C for 2 Recorders, Oboe, Chalumeau, Violin, 2 Viole all'inglese; 2 Violins 'in tromba marina', 2 Harpsichords, RV 555; Concerto in D min. for 2 Oboes, Bassoon, 2 Violins, RV 566; Double Trumpet Concerto in D, RV 781; Concerto in F for viola d'amore, 2 Horns, 2 Oboes & Bassoon, RV 97; Concerto in F for Violin, 2 Oboes, Bassoon, 2 Horns, V 574; Concerto in D for Violin, 2 Oboes, 2 Horns, RV 562.*

*** Hyp. CDA 67073. Soloists, King's Consort, King.

This is one of the most attractive of all the CD groupings of Vivaldi's often extraordinarily scored multiple concertos, in which the period-instrument playing is not only expert, but constantly tweaks the ear. The braying horns often dominate, especially in the pair of concertos, RV 562 and RV 574, either rasping buoyantly or boldly sustaining long notes. The oboes are used to decorate the *Grave* of the latter, and elegantly open the finale of the former, before a bravura violin sends sparks flying. The horns again return spectacularly for the outer movements of RV 97, but the central *Largo* brings a delightul interplay between the languishing viola d'amore, and the oboes. The *Concerto funèbre*, not surprisingly, opens with a *Largo* and combines the remarkable solo combination of muted oboe, tenor chalumeau, a trio of viole all'inglese accompanied by muted strings. Then (in RV 555) comes the most remarkable array of all. Vivaldi even throws in a pair of harpsichords for good measure, and they are given some most attractive solo passages and used to provide a gentle rocking background for a most engaging violin soliloquy in the central *Largo*. Throughout the solo playing is wonderfully stylish and appealing, and Robert King maintains a fine vigour in allegros and an often gentle espressivo in slow movements. The recording is first class. Very highly recommended.

Double Cello Concerto in G min., RV 531; Flute Concerto in C min., RV 441; Concerto in G min. for Flute & Bassoon (La notte), RV 104; Concerto in F for Flute, Oboe & Bassoon (La tempesta di mare), RV 570; Guitar Concerto in D, RV 93; Concerto in F for 2 Horns, RV 539; Concerto in B flat for Violin & Cello, RV 547.

*** ASV CDDCA 645. Soloists, ECO, Malcolm.

With George Malcolm in charge it is not surprising that this 65-minute collection of seven diverse concertos is as entertaining as any in the catalogue. Perhaps most striking of all is the *Double Cello Concerto*, vigorously energetic in outer movements, but with a short, serene central *Largo*, with overlapping phrases at the beginning, to remind one of the slow movement of Bach's *Double Violin Concerto*. The concert ends with the duet version of *La notte*, which has much to charm the ear. Accompaniments are sympathetic and stylish, and the whole programme brims with vitality. The digital sound is vivid and realistic.

Double Cello Concerto in G min., RV 531; Concerto for Flute, Oboe, Bassoon & Violin in F (La tempesta di mare), RV 570; Concerto funèbre in B flat for Violin, Oboe, Salmoé & 3 viole all'inglese, RV 579; Flute Concerto in G min. (La notte), RV 439; Violin Concertos: in D (L'inquietudine), RV 234; in E (Il riposo – per il Natale), RV 270; in A (Per eco in lontano), RV 552.

*** Virgin VC5 45424-2. Europa Galante, Biondi.

This collection of some of Vivaldi's most imaginative concertos, played on period instruments, is just as attractive as its looks. All the special effects, from the ghost and sleep evocations in *La notte* to the echoing second violin in RV 552, are neatly managed, and the atmosphere of the *Concerto funèbre* is well sustained. This concerto features a theme taken from *Tito Manlio* where it was used as part of a procession to execution, and the scoring is very telling (see above). Fabio Biondi leads an excellent team of soloists and directs sparkling accompaniments, with a touch of vintage dryness to the bouquet of string timbre. Excellent recording.

Double Cello Concerto in G min., RV 531; Lute Concerto in G, RV 93; Double Mandolin Concerto in G, RV 532; Recorder Concertos: in C min., RV 441; in C, RV 443. Trio for Violin, Lute & Continuo in G min., RV 85.

(M) *** DG (IMS) 445 602-2. Demenga, Häusler, Söllscher, Copley, Camerata Bern, Füri.

An excellent mid-priced digital collection on original instruments. Söllscher's account of the *Duet Concerto* for mandolins (in which he takes both solo roles) is quite outstanding, and there is some breathtaking virtuosity from Michael Copley in the *Recorder Concertos*. Further variety is provided by the *Trio*, which is also an attractive work. The well-balanced recording has splendid presence and realism.

Double Cello Concerto in G min., RV 531; Lute (Guitar) Concerto in D, RV 93; Oboe Concerto in F, F.VII, No. 2 (R.455); Double Concerto for Oboe & Violin; Trumpet Concerto in D (trans. Jean Thilde); Violin Concerto in G min., Op. 12/1, RV 317..

*** Naxos 8.550384. Capella Istropolitana, Kreček.

This is a recommendable disc from which to set out to explore Vivaldi concertos, especially if you are beginning a collection. Gabriela Krcková makes a sensitive contribution to the delightful *Oboe Concerto in F major F.VII, No. 2 (R. 455)*, and the other soloists are pretty good too.

Double Concertos: for 2 Cellos in G min., RV 531; for Violin, Cello & Strings in F (Il Proteo ò sia il mondo rovescio), RV 544; for 2 Violins in A (per eco in lontano), RV 552. Triple Concertos: for 3 Violins in F, RV 551; for Violin & 2 Cellos in C, RV 561. Quadruple Concerto for 2 Violins & 2 Cellos: in C, RV 561; in D, RV 564..

*** Teldec 4509 94552-2. Coin and soloists, Il Giardina Armonico, Antonini.

An exceptionally rewarding collection of concertos for multiple, stringed instruments, made the more striking by the inclusion of RV 544 with its curious subtitle evoking Proteus and an upside-down world. Christophe Coin leads an excellent team of soloists and the imaginative continuo (organ, harpsichord and arch-lute) adds to the colour of performances which are full of life, yet which also reveal the music's more subtle touches and are remarkably free from the exaggerated stylistic devices often associated with period instruments. The recording is excellent.

Double Concertos: for 2 Cellos in G min., RV 531; for 2 Oboes in D min., RV 523; for 2 Violins in C, RV 505; in D, RV 511; Triple Concerto for Oboe & 2 Violins, RV 554.

*** Chan. 0528. Coe, Warkin, Robson, Latham, Standage, Comberti, Coll. Mus. 90, Standage.

Period-instrument performances are increasingly identified with the style of their performing groups, and that of Simon Standage's Collegium Musicum 90 is most invigorating, stylish with no lack of expressive feeling. The rhythmic crispness and buoyancy and the plangent string-sound make for characterful performances. The ripe sound of the baroque oboes and the crunchy cello timbre are particularly attractive, although the tingling astringency characteristic of the accompanying group is even more strongly focused in the solo playing for the concertos for two violins, and especially in the busy finale of RV 511. Outstanding Chandos sound.

Double Concertos: for 2 Flutes in C, RV 533; for 2 Horns in F, RV 538 & RV 539; for 2 Trumpets in C, RV 537; for Oboe & Bassoon in G, RV 545; Concerto (Sinfonia in D) for Strings, RV 122; Quadruple Concerto for 2 Oboes & 2 Clarinets, RV 560.

(BB) *** Naxos 8.553204. Soloists, City of L. Sinfonia, Kraemer.

A lively clutch of concertos, very well recorded in All Saints' Church, East Finchley. The opening double concertos for two horns, RV 539, two flutes, RV 533, and two trumpets, RV 537, all go well enough and offer expert solo contributions, but then at the arrival of the *Quadruple Concerto for Two Oboes and Two Clarinets* the playing suddenly sparks into extra exuberance, and one senses the musicians' enjoyment of one of Vivaldi's most imaginatively scored multiple works. The *Concerto for Two Horns* which follows (RV 538)

has a similar ebullience, and the concert is rounded off by a captivating account of RV 545, where both the oboe and bassoon clearly relish every bar of their engaging dialogue. Kraemer's accompaniments are polished and spirited.

Double Flute Concerto in C, RV 533; Double Horn Concerto in F, RV 539; Double Mandolin Concerto in G, RV 536; Double Oboe Concerto in A min., RV 536; Concerto for Oboe & Bassoon in G, RV 545; Double Trumpet Concerto in D, RV 563.

*** Ph. (IMS) 412 892-2. Soloists, ASMF, Marriner.

Apart from the work for two horns, where the focus of the soloists lacks a degree of sharpness, the recording often reaches demonstration standard. On CD, the concerto featuring a pair of mandolins is particularly vivid, with the balance near perfect, the solo instruments in proper scale yet registering admirable detail. The concertos for flutes and oboes are played with engaging finesse, conveying a sense of joy in the felicity of the writing. As ever, Marriner makes a very good case for the use of modern wind instruments in this repertoire.

Flute Concerto in G min. (La notte), Op. 10/2, RV 439; Concertos for Strings: in D min. (Madrigalesco), RV 129; in G (Alla rustica), RV 151. Violin Concertos: in D (L'inquietudine), RV 234; in E (L'amoroso), RV 523; Sinfonia in B min. (Al Santo Sepolcro).

(B) **(*) DG (ADD) 449 851-2. Soloists, BPO. Karajan.

This collection dates from 1971 (except for the *Flute Concerto*, which was recorded a decade later) and shows Karajan indulging himself in repertoire which he clearly loves but for which he does not have the stylistic credentials. Yet the charismatic playing and the glorious body of tone are irresistible. The orchestra dominates even the solo concertos and the soloists seem to float, concertante style, within the glowing acoustic.

Fourteen concertos: Disc 1: (i–ii)Lute Concerto in D, RV 93; Double Concerto for 2 Mandolins in G, RV 532;(i, iii)Recorder Concertos: in A min., RV 108; in G min. (La notte); (iv)Violin Concerto in D (Grosso Mogull), RV 208. Disc 2: Double concertos: (v) Double Concertos: for 2 Cellos in G min., RV 531; 2 Flutes in C, RV 533; 2 Trumpets in C, RV 443; Concertos for Strings: in D min. (Madrigalesco), RV 129; in G (alla rustica), RV 151; in G min., RV 153; Quadruple Concerto for 2 Violins & 2 Cellos in D, RV 564; L'estro armonico: Quadruple Violin Concerto in B min., Op. 3/10, RV 580.

(B) *** O-L Double Dig./ADD 455 703-2. (i) New London Cons., Pickett, with (ii) Finucane; (iii) Pickett; (iv) Ritchie, Bach Ens., Rifkin; (v) Soloists, AAM, Hogwood.

The 14 concertos on this Oiseau-Lyre Double readily demonstrate the extraordinary diversity of Vivaldi's musical ideas, and in many cases his originality too. None more so than the remarkable *Violin Concerto*, RV 208 (written about 1710), nicknamed – probably not by the composer – 'Grosso Mogull'. The outer movements with their *moto perpetuo* arpeggios demand great virtuosity from the soloist, and the slow movement is a long recitativo, more like an improvisation. The remarkable seven-minute finale, perhaps the longest in any Vivaldi concerto, has a central cadenza which demands and is given a performance of dazzling virtuosity by the soloist here, Stanley Ritchie. An unforgettable performance, very well recorded. The concertos for lute, mandolins and recorder are also expertly and pleasingly played by Philip Pickett and his group, whose brand of authenticity is rather less abrasive than Hogwood's. The digital sound is first class. The *Concerto for Two Flutes* has great charm and is dispatched with vigour and aplomb. Performances and recording alike are first rate. For the reissue, three extra works have been added, most notably the famous *Quadruple Violin Concerto* from *L'estro armonico*, taken from the Academy's splendid complete set, with John Holloway, Monica Huggett, Catherine Mackintosh and Elizabeth Wilcock the excellent soloists.

Double Mandolin Concerto in G, RV 532; Oboe Concertos: in A min., RV 461; in B flat, RV 548; Concertos for Strings: in G (alla rustica), RV 151; in C (Con molti istromenti), RV 558; Double Violin Concerto in G, RV 516.

(M) *** DG 457 897-2. E. Concert, Pinnock.

Taking its title, *Alla rustica*, from the charming little *G major Concerto*, RV 151, with its drone in the finale, this collection is a straight reissue of a 1986 CD, offering only six concertos and a playing time of barely 53 minutes. Nevertheless, it makes up in quality for what it lacks in quantity, finding Pinnock and English Concert at their liveliest and most refreshing. Outstanding in a nicely balanced programme is the *C minor Concerto*, RV 558, involving a remarkable array of concertino instruments including two violins (in 'tromba marina') and pairs of recorders, mandolins and theorbos, plus one cello. Excellent recording, giving a most realistic perspective.

Concerto per l'Orchestra di Dresda in G min. (for 2 Recorders, 2 Oboes & Bassoon), RV 577; Concerto per la Solennità di S. Lorenzo in C, RV 556; Chamber Concerto for Recorder, Oboe, Violin, Bassoon & Continuo in D (La pastorella), RV 95; Flute Concerto in G min. (La notte), Op. 10/2, RV 439; Concerto for Strings (Sinfonia) in C, RV 114; Quadruple Concerto for 2 Violins & 2 Cellos in G, RV 575.

(M) *** Virgin VER5 61275-2. Soloists, Taverner Players, Parrott.

This is a particularly winning collection – an hour of Vivaldi at his most creative. The opening Dresden concerto with its interplay between the wind groups, but including also solo violin obbligati, is particularly original; then comes the delightful pastoral chamber concerto, with its rustic woodwind charm. The two-movement 'Sinfonia', RV 114, is also notable for its inventive finale – in the form of a ciaconna. *La notte* is (by common consent) among Vivaldi's most imaginative works for flute. The following concerto, for a pair each of violins and echoing cellos, at times sounds more like a concerto grosso. The grand opening of the *Concerto for S. Lorenzo* is Handelian, but Vivaldi's own personality reasserts itself firmly in the following allegro. The work is richly scored and, apart from the main protagonists – a pair of

solo violins – features recorders, oboes and (a great novelty at that time) clarinets, with ear-catching results. This is its first recording in its original form; Vivaldi, for practical reasons, later dispensed with the clarinets. It makes a splendid conclusion to an outstanding concert, excellently recorded.

Concertos for Strings: in D min. (Concerto madrigalesco), RV 129; in G (Alla rustica), RV 151; in G min., RV 157. (i) Motet: In turbato mare irato, RV 627; Cantata: Lungi dal vago volto, RV 680. Magnificat, RV 610.

*** Hyp. CDA 66247. (i) Kirkby; Leblanc, Forget, Cunningham, Ingram, Tafelmusik Ch. & Bar. O, Lamon.

Mingling vocal and instrumental items, and works both well-known and unfamiliar, Jean Lamon provides a delightful collection, with Emma Kirkby a sparkling, pure-toned soloist in two items never recorded before: the motet, *In turbato mare irato*, and the chamber cantata, *Lungi dal vago volto*. The performance is lively, with fresh choral sound. The Tafelmusik performers come from Canada, and though the use of period instruments has some roughness, their vigour and alertness amply make up for that. Good, clear recorded sound.

CHAMBER MUSIC

Cello Sonatas Nos. 1–9, RV 39/47.

(M) *** CRD 3440 (*Nos. 1–4*); CRD 3441 (*Nos. 5–9*). L'Ecole d'Orphée.

All nine *Sonatas* are given highly musical performances on CRD; they do not set out to impress by grand gestures but succeed in doing so by their dedication and sensitivity. Susan Sheppard is a thoughtful player and is well supported by her continuo team, Lucy Carolan and Jane Coe. The CRD recording is well focused with fine presence.

Chamber Concertos: in D, RV 84; (Sonata) in A, RV 86; in D, RV 94; in D (La pastorella), RV 95; in F, RV 99; in G min., RV 103 & 105.

(N) (BB) *** HM HCX 3957046. Verbruggen, Goodwin, Holloway, Godburn, Toll, Comberti.

Vivaldi was at his most imaginatively inventive in his chamber concertos. The spicy, chirping opening of *La pastorella* (RV 95) is scored for recorder, oboe and bassoon to depict a shepherd piping. RV 94 opens with a simulated hurdy-gurdy effect, and RV 99 depicts a hunt (without horns!) and has a very rustic central *Largo*, while the slow movement of RV 105 is an almost bucolic duet for recorder and bassoon, with oboe added spiritedly in the finale. RV 84 was written for performance by the Dresden Orchestra and includes the composer's chromatic 'Sleep' motif in its finale, though it is not in the least somnambulent. The *Sonata* (for recorder and bassoon with continuo) provides a piquant further change of texture. The soloists group together for the tutti and the playing is vividly colourful and the recording excellent. Most delectable.

Chamber Concertos: in C for Recorder, Oboe, 2 Violins, Cello, Harpsichord & Lute, RV 87; in D for Flute, Violin, & Cello, RV 92; in G min. for Flute, Oboe, Bassoon, Cello, Organ & Lute, RV 107; in D min. for Solo Organ & Flute, 2 Violins, Viola, Cello, Violone & Lute, RV 541; in F for Organ & Violin solo, 2 Violins, Viola, Cello, Violone & Lute, RV 542. Trio Sonata in D min. (La folia), RV 65.

*** Channel Classics CCS 8495. Florilegium.

These concertos could hardly be played more persuasively (one instrument to each part) than they are by Florilegium, an oustanding period-instrument ensemble. The concertos which include a solo organ are enchanting in their piquant colouring, and are full of splendid ideas. The finale of RV 107, for instance, is a kaleidoscopic chaconne, in effect a chimerical set of variations. But every work here is inspired and aurally stimulating, and they could hardly be better played. The programme ends with Vivaldi's extensive variations on *La folia* in the form of a *Trio Sonata*, which is presented with bravura, a wide range of dynamic and a sense of fantasy. The group, led by Ashley Solomon (flute/recorder), are all masters of their instruments and play infectiously as a team. The recording is ideally balanced, within an acoustic with the right feeling of ambient space.

Chamber Concertos for Treble Recorder in A min., RV 108; in C min., RV 441; in F, RV 442; for Sopranino Recorder in C, RV 443 & RV 444; in A min., RV 445.

(N) (B) *** Hyp. Helios CDH 55016. Holstag, Parley of Instruments, Holman.

These are all treated as chamber concertos, with one instrument to each part, and by alternating treble and sopranino recorders Peter Holman provides variety, although this is not a CD to undertake all at one session. But the *C major Sopranino Concerto*, played with sparkling virtuosity, cannot fail to cheer you up. Even the *Largo* is perky, and the trilling finale is projected with superb aplomb. The same might be said for its two companions here.

The mellower sound of the treble recorder still gives pleasure too, of course, especially in the *A minor Concerto*, RV 445, while the *Rondo* finale of the *C major*, RV 443, is also very diverting. Excellent recording and good value.

4 Chamber Sonatas for 2 Violins: in F, RV 68 & RV 70; in G, RV 71; in E flat, RV 77; 2 Trio Sonatas for 2 Violins & Continuo in D min., Op. 1/8 & 12 (La folia), RV 63 & RV 64.

(B) *** HM HMX 290853.55 (3). Ens. 315 (Banchieri, Méjean, Gohl, Christensen) – CORELLI: *Trio Sonatas, Op. 5/1–6*; TARTINI: *Concerti grossi etc.* *******

The four *Chamber sonatas* were not published until after the composer's death. They are genuine duet sonatas, written in the three-movement format which Vivaldi favoured in his concertos, with the interplay between the two violins often demanding considerable bravura. Vivaldi indicated the bass line as optional, and it is omitted here. It is not missed and these works might be compared (if not quite in the same breath) with Bach's sonatas for a single, unaccompanied violin. Vivaldi's variations on *La folia* extend to 11 minutes and are highly inventive, while Op. 1/12 also includes an

extended set of variations, all in D minor, with the two violins sometimes in dialogue with each other. These expert musicians certainly convey their enjoyment of this rewarding music. The recording has striking presence and realism.

Trio Sonatas, Op. 1/1–12. Trio Sonatas in C, RV 60; in G min., RV 72; Cello Sonata in A min., RV 43; Double Violin Sonata in F, RV 70; Sonata for Violin & Cello in C min., RV 83.

(N) *** CPO 999 511-2 (2). Sonnerie.

Trio Sonatas Op. 1/1–12. Trio Sonatas in B flat; in G min., Op. 5/17–18; 2 Sonatas (Al Santo Sepolcro) in E flat, RV 130; in B min., RV 169; Violin Sonata in C, RV 114.

(N) *(**) BIS CD 1025/26. L. Bar., Medlam.

Vivaldi's Op. 1 *Trio Sonatas* were published during 1712–13, just after *L'estro armonico* had appeared and made its composer famous. It is unlikely that this dates their composition, and many of them could have been written up to a decade earlier. While Corelli was a major influence on these works, Vivaldi's own voice and originality come through again and again, and these sonatas are every bit as rewarding musically as his concertos of this period.

There is no problem here as to choice. Both performances are from expert period-instrument performers. But whereas the bright violin timbre of Monica Huggett of Sonnerie is smoothly caught within an attractively warm acoustic, and her colleagues too are naturally recorded and balanced. Ingrid Seifert, who leads London Baroque, has no such good fortune. The BIS engineers (perhaps because they were recording in a church) have put their microphones close, and the result is unattractively edgy and aurally tiring. So the CPO set is the one to go for, and if you acquire it you will especially enjoy the final sonata of the set, Vivaldi's brilliant set of nineteen ostinato variations on the famous *La folia*, which is brilliantly played. The various bonuses are enjoyable too.

12 Violin Sonatas, Op. 2.

**(*) Signum SIGCD 014 (2). Cordaria (Reiter, Ad-El, Sharman or Sayce).

Vivaldi's Op. 2 was first published in 1709. In 1712 the sonatas were republished, more elegantly printed in Amsterdam, so they must have been a success. They are early rather than mature Vivaldi, but pleasingly inventive all the same, with the bass line fairly free, sometimes detaching itself from the continuo and engaging in dialogue with the violin. The performances here are lively and musical, not distinctive, but Walter Reiter is certainly up to the bravura demanded of him in some of fizzing *Presto* finales. Good, clear recording.

'Manchester' Violin Sonatas (for violin and continuo) Nos. 1–12 (complete).

**(*) Arcana A 4/5. Biondi, Alessandri, Naddeo, Pandolfo, Lislevand.
** HM HMU 907089/90. Romanesca.

The so-called 'Manchester' *Sonatas* were discovered as recently as 1973 in Manchester's Henry Watson Music Library.

Within simple structures Vivaldi wrote fine music offering much refreshment. Neither disc is ideal. Romanesca are recorded fairly dryly, though they are very well balanced. Nigel North's archlute, theorbo or guitar makes a very pleasing contribution and John Toll's harpsichord is nicely in the picture, but the sound of Andrew Manze's baroque violin is rather raw. On the other hand, the Romanesca phrasing has marginally less of that curious accented lunging often favoured by period groups, which is at times more noticeable on the Arcana set. However, one adjusts to this when Fabio Biondi's tone is so much sweeter and his colleagues are afforded an altogether warmer sound by the more expansive Arcana recording. Tempi are generally faster with Romanesca, appreciably so in the Correntes, but overall the Arcana disc is the more persuasive.

VOCAL MUSIC

Sacred music, Vol. 1: *Credo in unum Deum, RV 591; Dixit Dominus, RV 594; Kyrie eleison, RV 587; Lauda Jerusalem, RV 608; Magnificat, RV 610.*

*** Hyp. CDA 66769. Gritton, Milne, Denley, Atkinson, Wilson-Johnson, Choristers and Ch., King's Consort, King.

Hyperion's series aims to cover all the key sacred choral works of Vivaldi, and this first volume could not be more promising. All the music here is for double choir except the simple *Credo*, which is without soloists but has great intensity of feeling expressed in the *Et incarnatus est* and *Crucifixus*. Apart from the splendidly grand and masterly *Dixit Dominus*, RV 594 (gloriously sung here), there are two fine, shorter works which also include double string orchestra: the *Kyrie eleison* and the *Lauda Jerusalem*. But most striking of all is Vivaldi's first setting of the *Magnificat* – in G minor, dating from around 1715 although revised in the 1720s – made memorable by its highly individual chromatic writing, but also adding to the poignancy of the *Et misericordia*. Robert King has gathered an excellent team of soloists for this collection (witness the following soprano duet, *Esurientes*, which is delightful), but it is the stirringly eloquent choral singing one remembers most, vividly directed by King and splendidly balanced and recorded.

Sacred music, Vol. 2: Motets: (i) *Canta in prato, ride in monte, RV 623;* (ii) *Clarae stellae, scintillate, RV 625; Filiae maestae Jerusalem, RV 638;* (i) *In furore iustissimae irae, RV 626;* (iii) *Longe mala, umbrae, terrores, RV 629;* (i) *Nulla in mundo pax sincera, RV 630.*

*** Hyp. CDA 66779. (i) York; (ii) Bowman; (iii) Denley; King's Consort, King.

All the appealing works here are very well sung indeed, with those for the soprano, the very agile Deborah York, the most memorable. The opening of *In furore iustissimae irae* ('In wrath and most just anger') is delivered with dramatic venom, but then the Largo, *Tunc meus fletus* ('Then shall my weeping'), follows exquisitely. The other highlight of the collection is James Bowman's *Filiae maestae Jerusalem*, which brings a touching Larghetto, *Silenti Zephyri* ('Let the winds be hushed'). The closing soprano cantata opens with

a gentle siciliana with a typically evocative string accompaniment. The nimble following aria depicts a hidden snake waiting for the unwary, and the closing, fast-flowing *Alleluia* requires virtuosity from the singer, sparklingly delivered here. A first-class collection, excellently recorded.

Sacred music, Vol. 3: *Beatus vir* (two versions), *RV 597 & RV 598; Crediti propter quod, RV 605; Dixit Dominus, RV 595; Domine ad adjuvandum, RV 593.*

*** Hyp. CDA 66789. Gritton, Wyn-Davies, Denley, Daniels, N. Davies, George, King's Consort and Ch., King.

Vivaldi's two settings of the *Beatus vir* are quite different. RV 597 is for double choir and is on an ambitious scale, with a refrain that reappears in various sections of the work. RV 598 is in a single movement and is written for soloists and a single choir, rather in the manner of a concerto grosso. The present setting of *Dixit Dominus* is for single chorus (but with sopranos sometimes divided). *Domine ad adjuvandum* is a superbly concentrated short work for double choir, based on Psalm 69. The performances here are well up to the standard of this excellent series, and the soloists sing with bravura, especially in duets. The Hyperion recording is of high quality, although ideally one would have welcomed more choral bite.

Sacred music, Vol. 4: *Juditha triumphans* (complete).

*** Hyp. CDA 67281/2. Murray, Bickley, Kiehr, Connolly, Rigby, Ch. & King's Consort, King.

Juditha triumphans, Vivaldi's only surviving oratorio, works well on disc, with its elaborate instrumental textures. Written for the Ospedale di Pietà in Venice, a home for foundlings, it involves only women's voices in the solo roles and here is exceptionally well cast. Anne Murray, in one of her most beautiful performances on disc, is seductive as Judith rather than sharply dramatic, and it is left to Susan Bickley as the tyrannical general, Holofernes, to steal first honours, strong and incisive. The others are excellent too, with the chorus (involving male voices as well as female) heightening the drama from the opening martial chorus onwards. Robert King relishes the rich instrumentation with its brilliant and original obbligato solos, beautifully caught in vivid, atmospheric recording.

Sacred music, Vol. 5: *Confitebor tibi, Domine; Deus tuorum militum; In turbato mare, RV 627; Non in pratis aut in hortis, RV 641; O qui coeli terraeque serenitas, RV 631; Stabat mater, RV 621.*

*** Hyp. CDA 66799. Gritton, Rigby, Blaze, Daniels, N. Davis, King's Consort, King.

Volume 5 of this excellent Hyperion series offers two solo motets, a simple Vesper hymn (*Deus tuorum militum*) sung as a contralto/tenor duet, and ends with a very fine three-voice setting of Psalm 110, *Confitebor tibi, Domine*, which in its final movement draws on a sparkling terzet from Vivaldi's opera *La fida ninfa*. It makes a satisfying close to a programme which has as its centrepiece the glorious *Stabat Mater* (1712), very beautifully sung here by the male alto, Robin Blaze. As an ideal prelude to this masterpiece Jean Rigby sings most movingly the 'Introduzione to the Miserere', *Non in pratis aut in hortis*, which has a beautiful lament as its solo aria. To open the concert Susan Gritton despatches *In turbato mare irato* with biting bravura, but is later able to show her lovely lyrical style in *O qui colei terraeque serenitas*.

Sacred music, Vol. 6: Beatus vir, RV 795; In exitu Israel, RV 604; Laudate Dominum, RV 606; Nisi Dominus, RV 608; Salve Regina, RV 617.

(N) **(*) Hyp. CDA 66809. Gritton, Stutzmann, Summers, Gibson, King's Ch. & Consort, King.

While the two motets *In exitu Israel* and *Laudate Dominum* are for choir alone, the ambitious setting of *Beatus vir* (only comparatively recently confirmed as authentic Vivaldi), which alternates extended solos with a brief repeated chorale, involves Susan Gritton immediately in spectacularly florid solo singing. Later she is joined by Hilary Summers and Alexandra Gibson in the seraphic trio *In memoria aeterna*, and both contraltos then make major solo contributions. Gritton is at her finest in the *Salve Regina*, where Simon Jones provides elaborate violin obbligatos. In *Nisi Dominus* further bravura is demanded from Nathalie Stutzmann and she nimbly rises to the occasion. The soaring *Gloria* brings more instrumental embroidery from Katherine McGillivray (viola d'amore) and the closing *Amen* is another virtuoso display. The microphones are kinder to Stutzmann's voice than Gritton's and for some reason the choral sound in the motets is edgy.

Cantatas: (i) All'ombra di sospetto, RV 678; (ii–iii) Amor hai vinto, RV 651; (i) Lungi dal vago volto, RV 680; Vengo a voi, luci adorate, RV 682. (iv) Gloria in D, RV 589; (v; iii) Nisi Dominus (Psalm 127), RV 608; (ii–iii) Nulla in mundo pax sincera, RV 630. (vi) Trio Sonata (La folia), RV 63.

(B) *** O-L Double ADD/Dig. 455 727-2 (2). (i) Bott, New London Cons., Pickett; (ii) Kirkby; (iii) AAM, Hogwood; (iv) Nelson, Kirkby, Watkinson, Christ Church Cathedral Ch., AAM, Preston; (v) Bowman; (vi) Standage, Mackintosh, Hogwood.

Vivaldi's secular cantatas are lightweight but have much charm. Combining recitative and a pair of arias, they usually express the dolours of unrequited love in an Arcadian setting. In each case the words are written from the male point of view, yet here they are treated as soprano solos – delightfully so, for, after Emma Kirkby has opened the programme with a characteristically fresh-voiced *Amor hai vento*, Catherine Bott takes over with her softer focus and more plaintive style. As a central instrumental interlude we are offered a lively and stylish account of the *Trio Sonata* which Vivaldi based on *La folia*. The first CD opens with the familiar *Gloria*. The choristers of Christ Church Cathedral excel themselves and the recording is remarkably fine. The solo motet, *Nulla in mundo pax sincera*, brings back Emma Kirkby, who copes splendidly with the bravura writing for soprano. James Bowman is also a persuasive soloist in the more extended, operatic-styled setting of Psalm 127. But since Vivaldi probably wrote *Nisi Dominus* for the Pietà, a

Venetian orphanage for girls, there is a case here for preferring a woman soloist.

Cantatas: (i) Amor hai vinto, RV 683; Cesssate, omai cessate, RV 684. La stravaganza: (ii) Violin Concerto in D min., Op. 4/8, RV 429. (iii) Cello Concerto in A min., RV. 422; Concertos for Strings in C & E min., RV 117 & RV 134; in G (Alla rustica), RV 151.

(N) *** Op. 111 OPS 30-181. (i) Mingardo; (ii) Vicari; (iii) Piovano; Concerto Italiano, Alessandrini.

Rinaldo Alessandrini opens this concert with an exhilaratingly crisp account of the bouncing allegro of *Concerto for Strings in C major* and sets the scene for *Amor hai vinto*, the first of the two pastoral cantatas sung with comparably bracing vocal virtuosity. The singer alternately languishes in unrequited love or looks back despairingly in 'immeasurable grief' and then in revengeful anger, after betrayal. There are plenty of dramatic and expressive opportunities, well taken here by the fine alto soloist, but also long passages of bravura runs when the lover obsessively repeats the indignant admonishments.

In effect these are concertos for voice, and Sarah Mingardo's virtuosity brings an instrumental ease of execution, the keenly honed articulation quite exhilarating. The two cantatas are framed and interleaved by the five instrumental concertos, all with excellent soloists, and the concert ends as invigoratingly as it began with the best-known work, ingenuously subtitled *Alla rustica*.

Beatus vir, RV 597; Credo, RV 592; Magnificat, RV 610.

(M) *** Ph. (IMS) (ADD) 420 651-2. Soloists, Alldis Ch., ECO, Negri.

Beatus vir, RV 598; Dixit Dominus in D, RV 594; Introduzione al Dixit: Canta in prato in G, RV 636 (ed. Geigling); Magnificat in G min., RV 611 (ed. Negri).

(M) *** Ph. (IMS) (ADD) 420 649-2. Lott, Burgess, Murray, Daniels, Finnie, Collins, Rolfe Johnson, Holl, Alldis Ch., ECO, Negri.

Crediti propter quod, RV 105; Credo, RV 591; Introduction to Gloria, RV 639; Gloria, RV 588; Kyrie, RV 587; Laetatus sum, RV 607.

(M) *** Ph. (IMS) (ADD) 420 650-2. M. Marshall, Lott, Finnie, Rolfe Johnson, Alldis Ch., ECO, Negri.

Dixit Dominus, RV 595; In exitu Israel, RV 604; Sacrum, RV 586.

(M) *** Ph. (IMS) (ADD) 420 652-2. Alldis Ch., ECO, Negri.

Introduction to Gloria, RV 642; Gloria in D, RV 589; Lauda Jerusalem in E min., RV 609; Laudate Dominum in D min., RV 606; Laudati pueri Dominum in A, RV 602.

(M) *** Ph. (IMS) (ADD) 420 648-2. Marshall, Lott, Collins, Finnilä, Alldis Ch., ECO, Negri.

These Philips recordings come from the late 1970s. Vittorio Negri does not make use of period instruments, but he penetrates as deeply into the spirit of this music as many who do, and they come up splendidly in their new format, digitally refurbished. Any lover of Vivaldi is likely to be astonished that not only the well-known works but the rarities show him writing with the keenest originality and intensity. There is nothing routine about any of this music, nor any of the performances either.

(i–v) Beatus vir in G, RV 597; (vi) Introduction to Gloria, RV 639; (i; iv; vi–vii) Gloria in D, RV 588; (i–ii; viii) Gloria in D, RV 589; (i; iii; vi–vii; ix) Magnificat in G min., RV 611; (x) Nulla in mundo pax sincera, RV 630; (xi) Stabat Mater, RV 621.

(B) *** Ph. Duo (ADD) 462 170-2 (2). (i) Marshall; (ii) Murray; (iii) Collins; (iv) Rolfe Johnson; (v) Holl; (vi) Finnie; (vii) Lott; (viii) Finnilä; (ix) Burgess; (x) Ameling; (xi) Kowalski; Alldis Ch., ECO, Negri.

This Philips Duo offers a splendid selection of Vivaldi's choral work taken from Negri's survey, above. It includes the two Glorias and the double-choir version of the Magnificat, while the Beatus vir, also for two choirs, is a similarly stirring piece. The collection opens with striking vocal bravura from Linda Finnie, who sings the Introduction to Gloria, RV 639, with spectacular virtuosity; later there is a comparable display from Elly Ameling in Nulla in mundo pax sincera, with the brilliant upper tessitura of the closing Alleluia testing her to the limit of her powers. Jochen Kowalski is the fine soloist in the touching Stabat Mater. The other soloists are also splendid, while the choir, vividly recorded, captures the dark, Bach-like intensity of many passages, contrasted with more typical Vivaldian brilliance. The analogue recordings are transferred to CD most impressively. A splendid introduction to Vivaldi's inspired writing for voices.

Beatus vir, RV 597; Canta in prato; Credo in E min., RV 591; Gloria in D, RV 589; In furore; Kyrie in G min., RV 587; Lauda Jerusalem, RV 609; Magnificat in G min., RV 610; Nulla in mundo pax sincera, RV 630.

(B) **(*) Erato Ultima (ADD) 0630 18969-2 (2). J. Smith, Staempfli, Schweizer, Sprecckelsen, Rossier, Schaer, Maurer, Huttenlocher, Lausanne Vocal Ens. & CO, Corboz.

About the time Negri was making his Vivaldi recordings for Philips, Michel Corboz, an equally fine choral conductor, was working in Lausanne. Modern instruments are used to produce a warm, well-focused sound; the acoustic is spacious and the performances vital and musical. The professional singers of the Lausanne Choir are admirable, and the soloists are sweet-toned. The programme opens with a lively performance of the more famous Gloria, and the first CD closes with the Magnificat, given in its simpler, first version on a relatively small scale, with the chorus singing the alto solo Fecit potentiam. The Kyrie in G minor with its double chorus, double string orchestra, plus four soloists makes a fine contrast in its magnificence. The Beatus vir is another stirring piece, used to open the second disc. Warmly recommendable, even if the Negri survey is stylistically the more satisfying.

Beatus vir, RV 597; Gloria in D, RV 589.

(BB) **(*) Naxos 8.550767. Crookes, Quitaker, Lane, Trevor, Oxford Schola Cantorum, N. CO, Ward.

This Naxos coupling of what are probably the two favourite Vivaldi choral works is beautifully recorded and well worth

its modest cost. Although some listeners will want greater attack in the famous opening and closing sections of the Gloria and in the Potens in terra in the companion work, these spacious performances, directed by Nicholas Ward, are still warmly enjoyable, partly because of the freshness of the solo contributions, but also because the choral singing has considerable intensity, especially in the continual return of the haunting Beatus vir chorale in RV 589. The Paratum cor eius, too, brings a surge of choral feeling, and the chorus rises to the occasion for the splendid closing Gloria Patri. Full translations are included.

Motets: Canto in prato, RV 623; In furore giustissimae irae, RV 626; Longa mala umbrae terrores, RV 640; Vos aurae per montes (per la solennita di S. Antonio), RV 634.

(M) *** Erato 4509 96966-2. Gasdia, Sol. Ven., Scimone.

Though the booklet for this collection of Vivaldi rarities fails to provide texts for these four solo motets, they make a delightful collection, also displaying the formidable talent of a rising star among Italian sopranos, Cecilia Gasdia. Vivaldi's solo motets might be described structurally as concertos for voice, but generally with a recitative between first movement and slow movement. Canto in prato is the exception, with three jolly, rustic allegros in succession. Lively performances and well-balanced recording.

(i) Motets: (i) Clarae stellae, scintillate, RV 625; Nisi Dominus, RV 608; Salve Regina, RV 616; Vespro principa divino, RV 633. Concertos for Strings: in C, RV 109; in F, RV 141.

(N) *** Decca 466 964-2. (i) A. Scholl; Australian Brandenburg O, Dyer.

This splendidly varied compilation of Vivaldi's sacred motets has claims to being Andreas Scholl's finest recital so far. Moreover, the Australian balance engineer, Allan Maclean, has caught his voice with the utmost naturalness.

Scholl's account of the Vesper psalm Nisi Dominus catches to the full the lyrical beauty of Vanum est vobis and the volatility of the following lively Surgite sagittae in manu potentis.

Cum dederit delectis suis somnum opens very mysteriously (Vivaldi asks his strings to play with piombi – lead mutes – instead of the normal wooden sordini) and Scholl sings his slowly rising chromatic scale with seraphic, sensuous beauty, a moment of sheer magic. The work's expressive climax, Gloria patri, with its viola da gamba obbligato, is transcendent, followed by the bravura release of Sidcut erat.

Not surprisingly Clarae stellae gleams and sparkles, but the other highlight here is Vivaldi's highly imaginative setting of the Salve Regina, with its antiphonal accompaniment for double orchestra, especially striking in the Ad te clamamus. But again it is the lyrical music which is so memorable, with the touching Ad te suspiramus poignantly accompanied by a 'sighing' flute, and the closing O clemens, op pia softly coloured by a pair of recorders: the final O dulcis virgo Maria is exquisite. The period-instrument Australian Brandenburg Orchestra contribute much to the success of this record, providing (as interludes) vibrantly infectious accounts of two of Vivaldi's String Concertos, of which the C major, with its lovely central *Adagio*, is particularly memorable. We shall surely hear more from this group and their impressive conductor, Paul Dyer.

Dixit Dominus, RV 595, with Introduzione, RV 635; Gloria, RV 588, with Introduzione, RV 639.

(N) **(*) Decca 458 837-2. Bott, Gooding, Christopher Robson, King, Grant, New L. Consort, Pickett.

Pickett provides not only the *Dixit Dominus* and the less familiar of the two *Glorias*, but also their cantata-styled *Introduzioni* for solo voice, which are especially well worth having on disc. They are very well sung by Catherine Bott and Christopher Robson -- even if not all ears take so readily to Robson's very individual timbre, which, as caught by the microphones here, sounds hooty; and this is even more striking in *Judicabit in nationibus*, announced by a dramatic call from the Judgement Day trumpet.

The two sopranos match their voices very successfully in their pair of duets, *Tecum principium* in *Dixit Dominus* and *Laudamus te* in the *Gloria*, and overall Pickett has an excellent team of soloists, who together with a splendid chorus give fine performances of the two main works, which are warmly spacious as well as alert, so combining most of the best features of modern- and period-instrument performances.

(i) Dixit Dominus in D, RV 594; (ii) Stabat Mater, RV 621.

(B) **(*) Sony (ADD) SBK 48282. (i) Hill Smith, Bernardin, Partridge, Caddy; (i–ii) Watts; E. Bach Festival ((i) Ch.) O, Malgoire – D. SCARLATTI: *Stabat Mater.* **(*)

Malgoire's overemphatic style of baroque playing, with first beats of bars heavily underlined, is inclined to be wearing, but these fine works make an excellent coupling, and the singing is first rate, from both the chorus and the soloists in the better-known setting of *Dixit Dominus*, and particularly from Helen Watts in the moving sequence of solo items that makes up the *Stabat Mater*. Reverberant, church-like acoustic.

(i) Gloria in D, RV 588; Gloria in D, RV 589; (ii) Concerto for Guitar & Viola d'amore, RV 540.

(B) *** Decca 448 223-2. (i) Russell, Kwella, Wilkens, St John's College, Cambridge, Ch., Wren O, Guest; (ii) Fernández, Blume, ECO, Malcolm.

(i) Gloria in D, RV 588; Gloria in D, RV 589; (ii; iii) Beatus vir in C, RV 597; Dixit Dominus in D, RV 594; (iv; iii) Magnificat in G min., RV 610.

(B) *** Double Decca Dig./ADD 443 455-2 (2). (i) Russell, Kwella, Wilkens, Bowen, St John's College, Cambridge, Ch., Wren O, Guest; (ii) J. Smith, Buchanan, Watts, Partridge, Shirley-Quirk, ECO, Cleobury; (iii) King's College, Cambridge, Ch.; (iv) Castle, Cockerham, King, ASMF, Ledger.

The two settings of the *Gloria* make an apt and illuminating pairing. Both in D major, they have many points in common, presenting fascinating comparisons, when RV 588 is as inspired as its better-known companion. Guest directs strong and well-paced readings, with RV 588 the more lively. Good,

warm recording to match the performances. *Dixit Dominus* cannot fail to attract those who have enjoyed the better-known *Gloria*. Both works are powerfully inspired and are here given vigorous and sparkling performances with King's College Choir in excellent form under Philip Ledger. The soloists are a fine team, fresh, stylish and nimble, nicely projected on CD. What caps this outstanding Vivaldi compilation is the earlier King's account of the inspired *Magnificat in G minor*. Ledger uses the small-scale setting and opts for boys' voices in the solos such as the beautiful duet (*Esurientes*), which is most winning. The performance overall is very compelling and moving, and the singing has all the accustomed beauty of King's. The transfer of an outstanding (1976) analogue recording to CD is admirable, even richer than its digital companions.

As can be seen, those seeking an inexpensive disc of the two *Glorias* will find the Eclipse CD a satisfactory alternative, and the *Concerto for Guitar & Viola d'amore* makes an attractively lightweight interlude between the two.

Gloria in D, RV 589.

*** EMI CDC7 54283-2. Hendricks, Murray, Rigby, Heilmann, Hynninen, ASMF Ch. & O, Marriner – BACH: *Magnificat.* ***

(M) *** Decca (ADD) 458 623-2. Vaughan, Baker, Partridge, Keyte, King's College, Cambridge, Ch., ASMF, Willcocks – HANDEL: *Coronation Anthem: Zadok the Priest;* HAYDN: *Nelson Mass.* ***

*** DG (IMS) 423 386-2. Argenta, Attrot, Denley, Ch. & E. Concert, Pinnock – A. SCARLATTI: *Dixit Dominus.* ***

(BB) *** Naxos 8.554056. Oxford Schola Cantorum, N. CO, Ward – BACH: *Magnificat.* ***

Gloria, RV 589; Magnificat, RV 611.

(M) EMI (ADD) CDM5 66987-2 [CMS5 760002]. Berganza, Valentini, Terrani, New Philh. Ch. & O, Muti.

(i) Gloria, RV 589; Magnificat, RV 611; Concerto for Strings in D min., RV 243; (ii) Double Concerto for Trumpet & Oboe, RV 563.

(N) *** Opus 111 OPS 1951. (i) York, Biccire, Mingardo, Champagne & Ardene Regional Vocal Ens., (ii) Soloists, Concerto Italiano, Alessandrini.

Gloria, RV 589; Ostro picta, armata spina, RV 642.

*** Chan. 0518. Kirkby, Bonner, Chance, Coll. Mus. 90, Hickox – BACH: *Magnificat.* ***

Hickox, Marriner and Alessandrini couple the more popular of the two *D major Glorias* with the Bach *Magnificat* and offer a clear choice between period and modern instruments. Honours are evenly divided between them: Hickox's purposeful account has the benefit of a fine team of soloists and good Chandos recording; Marriner's performance with the Academy on modern instruments is well paced, as is the Bach *Magnificat*. His soloists are also very fine, and the recording has warmth and immediacy. Both can be strongly recommended.

Rinaldi Alessandrini's dazzling speed for the opening of Vivaldi's more famous setting of the *Gloria* must be just about the fastest on record, and it is just as exciting in the reprise for the *Quoniam*. Yet ensemble remains remarkably crisp, and later the pair of sopranos revel in their virtuosity in the *Laudamus te*. Elsewhere, while there is plenty of vigour there is no feeling of the music being hurried. The *Domine Deus* and *Qui tollis* bring a contrasting element of calm, and the closing *Cum Sanctos Spiritu* makes a fittingly joyous conclusion.

The *Magnificat*, too, combines spaciousness with vitality. The mysteriously evocative *Et misericordia* contrasts dramatically with the dynamic *Deposuit potentes*; but, throughout, the essential Italianate warmth of Alessandrini's reading comes through, and the rich choral response is at its most embracing in the closing *Gloria Patri*.

The bonuses include a *Concerto for Strings* (which acts as a spirited intermezzo between the main works) and a lively *Double Trumpet Concerto* as an end-piece, arranged from a work for trumpet and oboe, with the oboe retained for just the slow movement.

At the time of going to press this CD comes in a slipcase with a full Op. 111 catalogue and a second (sampler) disc, offering nineteen excerpts from Op. 111 recordings of music from America, Germany, Italy, Russia and Scandinavia, including baroque and contemporary items.

Willcocks's version authentically uses comparatively small forces and has an excellent team of soloists. It is very stylish and very well recorded. Some might feel that consonants are too exaggerated but, in consequence, words are admirably clear.

Trevor Pinnock directs a bright, refreshing account, with excellent playing and singing from the members of the English Concert. Unusually but attractively coupled with the rare Scarlatti setting of *Dixit Dominus*, and very well recorded, it makes a first-rate alternative recommendation.

On Naxos it is most refreshing to have a performance of Vivaldi's most popular choral work that with modern instruments and a relatively small choir clarifies textures, revealing inner detail usually obscured. With Jeremy Summerly directing the choir and Nicholas Ward conducting the orchestra, the rhythmic point of the writing is reinforced, helped by superb sound, fresh, clear and immediate.

Muti offers the more expansive version of the *Magnificat*, including extended solo arias. His approach, both in that work and in the *Gloria*, is altogether blander than the authentic style adopted by Pinnock. Muti's expansiveness undoubtedly suits the larger-scaled *Magnificat* better than the *Gloria*, which lacks incisiveness. The 1977 analogue recording has been effectively remastered, but this is a curious choice for EMI's 'Great Recordings of the Century' series.

Laudate pueri Dominum, RV 601; Nisi Dominus, RV 608.

*** Mer. CDE 84129. Dawson, Robson, King's Consort, King.

The present setting of Psalm 113, RV 601, is a strong, consistently inspired work; Lynne Dawson sings with an excellent sense of style and is given splendid support. The coupling, the *Nisi Dominus*, a setting of Psalm 127, is much better known but makes an attractive makeweight. It is also given an excellent performance by Christopher Robson. Good recording.

Nisi Dominus (Psalm 127), RV 608; (ii) Nulla in mundo pax sincera, RV 630.

(M) *** O-L (ADD) 443 199-2. (i) Bowman; (ii) Kirkby; AAM, Preston – BACH: *Magnificat*; KUHNAU: *Der Gerechte kommt um*. ***

The solo motet, *Nulla in mundo pax sincera*, has Emma Kirkby as soloist coping splendidly with the bravura writing for soprano. James Bowman is also a persuasive soloist in the more extended, operatic-styled setting of Psalm 127. But since Vivaldi probably wrote *Nisi Dominus* for the Pietà, a Venetian orphanage for girls, readers might prefer a soprano voice.

(i) Stabat Mater in F min., RV 621; Cessate omai cessate, RV 684; Filiae mestae in C min., RV 638. Concerto for Strings in C, RV 114; Sonata al Santo Sepolcro in E flat, RV 130.

(M) *** HM HMX 29815171. (i) Scholl; Ens. 415, Banchini.

Chiara Banchini and Ensemble 415 have given us some fine period-instrument performances, but none is finer than this, thanks to the superb contribution of counter-tenor Andreas Scholl. His tenderly expressive account of the *Stabat Mater* is infinitely touching, while the pastoral cantata, *Cessate omai cessate*, is, dramatically and lyrically, no less involving. Here Vivaldi's imaginative accompaniments are relished by the instrumental ensemble, and they are equally on their toes in the similarly contrasted string works. Strongly communicative music-making, very well recorded, though the programme lasts less than an hour.

OPERA

Opera Overtures and Sinfonias: Bajazet: Sinfonia in F. La dorilla: Sinfonia in C. Il farnace: Sinfonia in C. Il giustino: Sinfonia in C. L'olimpiade: Sinfonia in C. Ottone in Villa: Sinfonia in C. La vertia' in cimento: Sinfonia in G.. Chamber Concerto in D min., RV 128; Concerto in F for Violin, 2 Oboes, 2 Horns & Bassoon, RV 571; Violin Concerto in C min. (Amato bene). Sinfonia in G, RV 149.

**(*) DHM 05472 77501-2. L'Arte Dell'Arco, Hogwood.

Although little of this music is top-drawer Vivaldi, all of it is of interest. Except for *L'olimpiade* (which includes a tempesta di mare and is in four sections), and *Ottone in Villa* (which is a concertante piece for violins and oboes and is in two), these are all typical three-movement Italian overtures. *Bajazet* (because of the plot) features hunting horns in the outer sections, but they are used even more spectacularly in the *Concerto in F*, RV 571 (which is associated with a Venetian performance of the opera *Arsilda, Regina di Ponto*, while its finale is based on the Storm aria from *Ottone in Villa*). The finale of the *Sinfonia* for *La dorilla* brings a surprise appearance of the introduction of *Spring* from *The Four Seasons*. The period performances here are highly energetic and certainly stylish, but a bit gruff. One might have thought Harnoncourt, rather than Hogwood, was in charge. Excellent documentation.

Opera Arias and Scenas: Bajazet (Il Tamerlano): Anch'il mar par che sommerga. Dorilla in Tempe: Dorilla'aura al sussurrar. Farnace: Gelido in ogni vena. La fida ninfa:

Alma opressa; Dite, oimè. Griselda: Dopo un'orrida procella. Giustino; Sorte, che m'invitasti . . . Ho nel petto un cor sì forte. L'olimpiade: Tra le follie . . . Siam navi all'onde algenti. L'Orlando finto pazzo: Qual favellar? . . . Anderò volerò griderò. Teuzzone: Di trombe guerrier. Arias with inidentified sources: Di due rai languir costante; Zeffiretti, che sussurrate.

*** Decca 466 569-2. Bartoli, Il Giardino Armonico (with Arnold Schoenberg Ch.).

This remarkable collection is valuable as much for its exploration of unknown Vivaldi operas as for coloratura singing of extraordinary bravura and technical security. It is a pity that the programme (understandably) opens with the excerpt from *Dorilla in Tempe*, with its echoes of *Spring* from *The Four Seasons*, as the chorus, although enthusiastic in praising those seasonal joys, is less than sharply focused. But the following aria from *Griselda*, with its stormy horns and fiendish leaps and runs, shows just how expertly Cecilia Bartoli can deliver the kind of thrilling virtuosity expected by Vivaldi's audiences of their famous castrato soloists. Farnace's tragic aria, *Gelido in ogni vena* (based on the *Winter* concerto) shows the other side of the coin with some exquisite lyrical singing of lovely descending chromatics. Similarly, while *Alma opressa* (from *La fida ninfa*) brings a remarkable display of melismatic runs with its almost unbroken line of semiquavers, the following *Dite, oimè*, very movingly sung, has an almost desperate melancholy. In short, this is dazzling singing of remarkable music, most stylishly and vividly accompanied. Indeed, the Storm aria from *Bajazet* brings a delivery of such speed and sharpness of articulation that the rapid fire of a musical machine-gun springs instantly to mind. Moreover, Decca have done their star mezzo proud with fine documentation, full translations and a presentation more like a handsomely bound hardback book than a CD.

L'incoronazione di Dario (complete).

(B) **(*) HM HMA 1901235/7. Elwes, Visse, Lesne, Ledroit, Verschaeve, Poulenard, Mellon, Nice Bar. Ens., Bezzina.

Set in the fifth century BC. at the Persian court, this Vivaldi opera involves the conflict which followed the death of King Cyrus and the succession of Darius. Written in 1717, it is one of Vivaldi's earlier operas, in places reflecting the great oratorio he had written the year before, *Juditha triumphans*, reworking three numbers. The opera here receives a lively performance, generally well sung. John Elwes as Darius himself, though stylish, does not sound as involved as some of the others, notably the male alto, Dominique Visse, who is superb both vocally and dramatically as the female confidante, Flora. Reliable singing from the whole cast, and first-rate recording. The full libretto is provided only in Italian, with translated summaries of the plot in English, French and German. A very welcome reissue on Harmonia Mundi's bargain Musique d'abord label.

Orlando furioso (complete).

*** Erato 2292 45147-2 (3). Horne, De los Angeles, Valentini Terrani, Gonzales, Kozma, Bruscantini, Zaccaria, Sol. Ven., Scimone.

Outstanding in a surprisingly star-studded cast is Marilyn Horne in the title-role, rich and firm of tone, articulating superbly in divisions, notably in the hero's two fiery arias. In the role of Angelica, Victoria de los Angeles has many sweetly lyrical moments, and though Lucia Valentini Terrani is less strong as Alcina, she gives an aptly clean, precise performance. The remastering has freshened a recording which was not outstanding in its analogue LP form.

Orlando furioso: Arias: Act I: *Nel profondo;* Act II: *Sorge l'irato nembo;* Act III: *Fonti di pianto.*

(M) *** Erato 0630 14069-2. Horne, I Solisti Veneti, Scimone – HANDEL: Arias. ***

These three key arias, the second fiery, the third very touching, come from Scimone's complete recording of Vivaldi's opera and show Horne in superb form. They make an apt bonus for a remarkable collection of Handel arias, recorded five years earlier and including an excerpt from Handel's own setting of the same narrative.

Ottone in Villa (complete).

*** Chan. 0614 (2). Groop, Gritton, Argenta, Padmore, Daneman, Coll. Mus. 90, Hickox.

Ottone in Villa was Vivaldi's very first opera, produced in 1713. It follows the conventions of the day in a sequence of da capo arias linked by recitatives, with no ensemble up until the final number for the characters in unison. With only five singers required, the scale of the piece is modest in treating the subject of the Emperor Ottone and the way he is fooled by the flirtatious Cleonilla. Vivaldi is here at his most tuneful and inventive, and Richard Hickox with an excellent cast of soloists and his fine period-instrument group, Collegium Musicum 90, presents the opera with a freshness and vigour that make one forget the work's formal limitations. Susan Gritton sings charmingly as the provocative Cleonilla, and Nancy Argenta brings flawless control to the castrato role of Caio Sillo, with the mezzo, Monica Groop, strong and firm in the title role of the Emperor. Fine production and sound add to the compulsion of the performance.

VOORMOLEN, Alexander

(1895–1980)

Baron Hop Suites 1–2; (i) Double Oboe Concerto; Eline (Nocturne for Orchestra).

*** Chan. 9815. Hague Residentie O, Bamert; (i) with Oostenrijk; Roerade.

Apart from Diepenbrock, late-nineteenth- and early-twentieth-century Dutch orchestral music still remains a virtually unexplored area. All the more reason to welcome this highly entertaining collection. Alexander Voormolen was born in Rotterdam, but his musical life centred on The Hague. His maternal grandmother was a Rameau (a descendant of Jean-Philippe's brother), which accounts for the French influences in his musical genes that were to attract the attention of Ravel, who became his sponsor, and whose personal recommendation ensured that the music was published.

Voormolen sought to create a truly Dutch style in his writing, but his genes thwarted him, and its charming eccentricity and unpredictability give a very un-Dutch impression. Indeed, one might think of him as a Netherlands equivalent of Lord Berners. His orchestral skill and witty humour are ideally suited to his musical evocations of the world of Baron Hop, a genial larger-than-life eighteenth-century Dutch diplomat and *bon viveur*, who so loved coffee that he had a famous sweetmeat made of it called 'Haagsche Hopjes'.

The two *Baron Hop Suites* (1924 and 1931) draw on material from an aborted *opéra comique*, and their spirited neo-classicism is well nourished by a richly coloured orchestral palette, and sprightly rhythms. There are Dutch popular tunes, and others too. In the first suite the witty opening overture (it has a false ending) quotes a snatch of the *Marseillaise*, and the closing *March of the Hereditary Prince-Stadtholder* even includes *The British Grenadiers*. In between come a slightly sensuous *Sarabande* and an engaging *Polka*.

The *Concerto for Two Oboes* is quaintly colourful with a unique 'quacking' closing Rondo. *Eline* (originally a piano work) is languorous and faintly Delian, but has other influences too. All this music is played very persuasively indeed by the composer's home orchestra, directed with complete understanding, the nicest touches of rubato and neat rhythmic pointing by Bamert. The Chandos recording is glowingly full and vivid. A real find.

VOŘÍŠEK, Jan Václav (1791–1825)

Symphony in D, Op. 24.

*** Hyp. CDA 66800. SCO, Mackerras – ARRIAGA: *Symphony in D min.* etc. ***

Voříšek is as close as the Czechs got to producing a Beethoven, and this remarkably powerful work has many fingerprints of the German master everywhere while displaying some individuality. The slow movement is impressive and, after an attractive Scherzo, the finale has something in common with that of Beethoven's *Fourth*. Mackerras offers the finest account this work has received on record so far. The Hyperion recording is warmly reverberant, but this serves to increase the feeling of Beethovenian weightiness, and the Scherzo is particularly imposing. The Arriaga coupling is indispensable.

Fantasia in C, Op. 12; Impromptus Nos. 1–6, Op. 7; Piano Sonata in B flat min., Op. 19; Variations in B flat, Op. 19.

*** Unicorn DKPCD 9145. Kvapil.
(N) *** Opus 111 OPS 30 241. Tverskaya.

Voříšek's *Sonata in B flat minor* (1820), like his *D major Symphony*, is one of his most representative and well-argued works and is the centrepiece of this beautifully played recital on Unicorn. Radoslav Kvapil is a sensitive and imaginative artist, deeply committed to this repertoire. The slightly later *B flat Variations* will be a welcome discovery for those who do not know them, and Kvapil's accounts of the *Impromptus*

are as good as, if not better than, any predecessor's. The recording, though not outstanding, serves him well.

The Russian-born but London-domiciled Olga Tverskaya is an eloquent advocate of this always interesting and often highly original music, and plays with great flair and conviction. Unlike Kvapil, she uses a period instrument, a copy of an 1823 Broadmann fortepiano by David Winston. The instrument comes from the exact period of the works included on this disc. The recording is altogether excellent and the disc in every respect, a success.

WAGNER, Richard (1813–83)

American Centennial March (Grosser Festmarsch); Kaisermarsch; Overtures: Polonia; Rule Brittania.

(N) (BB) ** Naxos 8.555386. Hong Kong PO, Kojian.

The *Polonia* overture (1836) is the best piece here. Although its basic style is Weberian, there is a hint of the Wagner of *Rienzi* in the slow introduction. The *Grosser Festmarsch (American Centennial march)* was commissioned from Philadelphia, and for this inflated piece Wagner received a cool five thousand dollars! The *Rule Britannia* overture is even more overblown and the famous tune, much repeated, outstays its welcome. The *Kaisermarsch* is also empty and loud. The Hong Kong orchestra play all this with great enthusiasm, if without much finesse. The recording is vividly bright, but on CD it is not a priority item, even for the most dedicated Wagnerian. However at the Naxos price it is more enticing for the curious collector than the original issue on Marco Polo.

Siegfried Idyll.

(M) *** DG (ADD) 449 725-2. BPO, Karajan – R. STRAUSS: *Ein Heldenleben.* ***
⊙ (M) *** Decca (ADD) 460 311-2. VPO, Solti – SCHUBERT: *Symphony No. 9.* *** ⊙
(M) *** EMI (ADD) CMS5 67036-2 (2). Philh. O, Klemperer – MAHLER: *Symphony No. 9; R. STRAUSS: Metamorphosen.* ***
(N) *(*) DG 469 008-2. Berlin Deutsche Oper O, Thielemann – SCHOENBERG: *Pelleas und Melisande.* *(*)

Karajan's account of Wagner's wonderful birthday present to Cosima is unsurpassed; it has never sounded better than in this transfer, aptly coupled with Strauss's *Ein Heldenleben*, Karajan's very first stereo recording for DG.

So rich is the sound that Decca provided for Solti (in 1965) that one can hardly believe that this is a chamber performance. The playing is similarly warm and committed and this coupling with Schubert's *Great C major Symphony*, is one of Solti's finest recordings.

Klemperer also favours the original chamber-orchestra scoring and the Philharmonia players are very persuasive, especially in the score's gentler moments. The balance is forward and, although the sound is warm, some ears may crave a greater breadth of string tone at the climax. However this triptych from the 'Klemperer Legacy' shows the conductor at his most compelling.

The playing of the Orchestra of the Deutsche Oper, Berlin,

is fine, but why does Thielemann not allow the music to unfold naturally? He is given to somewhat intrusive expressive exaggeration. Good, though not outstanding sound.

Siegfried Idyll; A Faust Overture; Gotterdämmerung: Siegfried's Rhine Journey. Lohengrin: Prelude to Act III. Overtures: Die Meistersinger; Rienzi.

(N) **(*) RCA 74321 68717–2. BPO, Maazel.

For the Berlin Philharmonic's Wagner programme directed by Lorin Maazel, RCA has returned to the Berlin Jesus-Christus-Kirche, where so many of the orchestra's most celebrated recordings were made. The *Siegfried Idyll* is beautifully played, the ebb and flow of tension admirably controlled, and the closing section is quite lovely. *Rienzi* and the *Lohengrin Third Act Prelude* are vivid and brilliant, and the *Faust* overture has plenty of character. But in the *Prelude to Die Meistersinger*, which Maazel paces most convincingly, the ear craves rather more amplitude in the recording itself, and a deeper, more resonant bass. The principal horn (who has also contributed impressively to the *Siegfried Idyll*, plays with panache (slightly distanced) in the closing *Siegfried's Rhine Journey*, which, after an atmospheric opening and a sudden impulsive accelerando, certainly makes a spectacular and gripping end to the concert. The digital sound picture is cleanly focused, fresh, clear and well balanced, but a little more reflection of the hall acoustics would have made the recording even finer.

Siegfried Idyll; A Faust Overture; Die Meistersinger: Prelude to Act I; Tannhäuser: Overture; Tristan und Isolde: Prelude & Liebestod.

(M) *(*) Sony (ADD) SMK 64108. NYPO, Boulez.

There is little or no mystery in Boulez's view of Wagner. The most successful item here is the *Meistersinger Prelude*, spacious and well-pointed, and the *Faust Overture*, after a matter-of-fact introduction, brings out the dark, biting quality in Boulez's conducting; but *Tannhäuser* sounds more like Meyerbeer, and *Tristan* lacks tension. The sound dating from 1970 is acceptable, but there are far better Wagner collections available

Siegfried Idyll; Der fliegende Holländer: Overture. Götterdämmerung: Siegfried's Funeral March. Lohengrin: Prelude to Act I; Hymn. Parsifal: Prelude to Act I. Rienzi: Overture. Tannhäuser: Overture & Bacchanale. Tristan und Isolde: Prelude to Act I..

(B) *** Double Decca Dig. 440 606-2 (2). VPO, Solti.

Solti's way with Wagner is certainly exciting: some may find the early 1960s performances of the Rienzi and *The Flying Dutchman* overtures a little hard-driven. But the *Siefried idyll*, played in its chamber version by members of the VPO, is most beautifully done, and the Lohengrin Prelude is similarly relaxed until its climax – two welcome moments of repose amid such drama.

Elsewhere one is easily caught up in the sheer force of Solti's music-making, and in the later recordings in the 1970s Solti has mellowed a little and the *Meistersinger Overture* has genuine grandeur and nobility. The VPO play splendidly, of course, and Decca has supplied brilliant sound to match.

An inexpensive way to explore Solti's special charisma in orchestral Wagner.

Siegfried Idyll (with rehearsal); Der fliegende Holländer: Overture; Die Meistersinger: Prelude to Act I; Lohengrin: Prelude to Act I; Parsifal: Prelude to Act I & Good Friday Music; Tannhäuser: (i) Overture & Venusberg Music.

(M) *** Sony (ADD) SMK 64456 (2). (i) Occidental College Ch.; Columbia SO, Walter.

Bruno Walter's is above all a gentle performance of the *Siegfried Idyll*. The 1963 recording seems fuller and more atmospheric than before, especially at the ardent climax, while the rapt closing ritenuto is magical. Before the performance comes an extended rehearsal sequence lasting three-quarters of an hour, which most listeners will find fascinating. The rest of the programme was recorded in 1959. Highlights include the glowing *Parsifal Prelude* and *Good Friday Music*, matching Jochum in its simple intensity, and the superb account of the *Tannhäuser Overture* and *Venusberg Music* with its thrillingly sensuous climax, and the closing pages – with the Occidental College Choir distantly balanced – bringing a radiant hush. Both here and in the *Flying Dutchman* and *Meistersinger* overtures the Columbia Symphony Orchestra has more body and weight, while the *Lohengrin Prelude*, which is relaxed but beautifully controlled, sounds radiant.

(i; ii) Siegfried Idyll. (iii; iv) Overture: Der fliegende Holländer. (i; v) Götterdämmerung: Siegfried's Rhine Journey. Lohengrin: (i; ii) Prelude to Act I; (vi; iv) Prelude to Act III. Die Meistersinger: (vi; iv) Overture; (vii; viii) Prelude to Act III. (ix; viii) Parsifal: Prelude & Good Friday Music. Overtures: (vi; iv) Rienzi; (vii; x) Tannhäuser. Tristan und Isolde: (iii; iv) Preludes to Acts I & III; (vi; iv) Death of Isolde. (i; v) Die Walküre: Ride of the Valkyries.

(B) *** DG Double (ADD) 439 687-2 (2) [id.]. (i) BPO; (ii) Kubelik; (iii) Bayreuth Festival O; (iv) Boehm; (v) Karajan; (vi) VPO; (vii) German Op., Berlin , O; (viii) Jochum; (ix) Bav. RSO; (x) Gerdes.

The *Siegfried Idyll* is beautifully shaped by Kubelik and equally beautifully played by the Berlin Philharmonic. He also conducts an impressive *Lohengrin Act I Prelude*, again with the BPO. Boehm not only provides a richly sustained opening for Rienzi but is exciting in *Der fliegenade Holländer* and at his finest in the *Tristan Preludes* – taken from his 1966 Bayreuth complete set– which glow with intensity. Karajan contributes only two items, but both surge with adrenalin. The highlight of the set comes last, Jochum's electrifying performance of the *Prelude* and *Good Friday* music from *Parsifal*. Recorded in the Munich Herculessaal, it is not only a demonstration record from the earliest days of stereo, but the playing has a spiritual intensity that has never been surpassed. The recordings, dating from the late 1950s to the early 1980s, have all been transferred vividly, mostly with fuller and more refined sound. The documentation is sadly inadequate.

Siegfried Idyll. Lohengrin: Preludes to Acts I & III. Die Meistersinger: Prelude to Act I. Parsifal: Prelude to Act I. Tristan und Isolde: Prelude & Liebestod.

(B) *** Ph. (ADD) 420 886-2. Concg. O, Haitink.

The addition of Haitink's simple, unaffected reading of the *Siegfried Idyll* to his 1975 collection of *Preludes* enhances the appeal of a particularly attractive concert. The rich acoustics of the Concertgebouw are ideal for *Die Meistersinger*, given a spacious performance, and Haitink's restraint adds to the noble dignity of *Parsifal*. The *Lohengrin* excerpts are splendidly played. The digital remastering is first-rate.

Siegfried Idyll. Lohengrin: Prelude to Acts I & III. Die Meistersinger: Overture. Die Walküre: Ride of the Valkyries; (i) *Wotan's Farewell & Magic Fire Music.*

*** ASV CDDCA 666. Philh. O, d'Avalos, (i) with Tomlinson.

The opening *Siegfried Idyll* has all the requisite serenity and atmosphere; here, as elsewhere, the Philharmonia play most beautifully. The sumptuous recording gives a thrilling resonance and amplitude to the brass, especially trombones and tuba, and in the expansive *Meistersinger Overture*, and again in *Wotan's Farewell* the brass entries bring a physical frisson. John Tomlinson's noble assumption of the role of Wotan, as he bids a loving farewell to his errant daughter, is very moving here, and the response of the Philharmonia strings matches his depth of feeling.

Siegfried Idyll. Tannhäuser: Overture. (i) *Tristan: Prelude & Liebestod.*

*** DG 423 613-2. (i) Norman; VPO, Karajan.

This superb Wagner record was taken live from a unique concert conducted by Karajan at the Salzburg Festival in August 1987. The *Tannhäuser Overture* has never sounded so noble, and the *Siegfried Idyll* has rarely seemed so intense and dedicated behind its sweet lyricism; while the *Prelude and Liebestod*, with Jessye Norman as soloist, bring the richest culmination, sensuous and passionate, remarkable as much for the hushed, inward moments as for the massive building of climaxes.

ORCHESTRAL EXCERPTS AND PRELUDES FROM THE OPERAS

(i) *A Faust Overture; Overtures: Der fliegende Holländer; Rienzi; Lohengrin: Prelude to Act I;* (ii) *Prelude to Act III. Tannhäuser: Overture & Grand March.*

(B) *** Sony (ADD) SBK 62403. (i) Cleveland O, Szell; (ii) Phd. O, Ormandy.

Szell's Wagner collection, recorded in Severance Hall in 1965, remains one of his most impressive. The inclusion of the still rarely heard *Faust Overture* is most welcome. Hearing this searingly dramatic and intense work, one again wonders why it has not become a repertory piece. To describe the playing of the Cleveland Orchestra as brilliant is inadequate, for the precision and beauty of tone clothe deeper understanding. The concert opens with Ormandy's physically thrilling account of the *Tannhäuser Overture*,

followed by the *Grand March* (sumptuous Philadelphia strings), and he also contributes an ebullient *Lohengrin* Act III *Prelude*. The Philadelphia recordings are less refined but the concert overall makes for a rich experience.

Der Fliegende Holländer: Overture. Lohengrin: Preludes to Acts I & III. Die Meistersinger: Overture; Dance of the Apprentices; Entry of the Masters. Rienzi: Overture; Tannhäuser: Overture.

(M) *** EMI (ADD) CDM5 66805-2. Philh. O, Klemperer.

Götterdämmerung: Siegfried's Funeral Music & Rhine Journey. Parsifal: Prelude. Das Rheingold: Entry of the Gods into Valhalla. Siegfried: Forest Murmurs. Tannhäuser: Prelude to Act III. Tristan und Isolde: Prelude & Liebestod. Die Walküre: Ride of the Valkyries.

(M) *** EMI (ADD) CDM5 66806-2. Philh. O, Klemperer.

It is good to have Klemperer's view of Wagner. Most of the performances reissued here as part of EMI's 'Klemperer legacy' have the kind of incandescent glow one associates with really great conductors, and the Philharmonia play immaculately. The *Tristan Prelude* and *Liebestod* do not have the sense of wonder that Toscanini and Furtwängler brought, but the noble passion at the climax communicates strongly. The characteristically spacious and superbly shaped *Parsifal* and *Lohengrin Preludes* are a highlight for similar reasons. Elsewhere, if the level of tension is more variable, Klemperer's readings are always solidly concentrated, even if this means that the plodding *Meistersingers* seem a bit too full of German pudding. Yet there is no lack of zest in the *Lohengrin: Prelude to Act III*. The remastering for CD has brought a gloriously full sound-picture, clearer than on the original LPs.

Der fliegende Holländer: Overture; Lohengrin: Preludes to Acts I & III; Die Meistersinger: Overture; Parsifal: Preludes to Acts I & III; Overtures: Rienzi; Tannhäuser.

(N) **(*) Chan. 9870. Danish Nat. RSO, Albrecht.

Splendidly full-blooded and expansive Chandos recording and first-class playing from the Danish Orchestra. They are at their finest in the beautifully shaped *Lohengrin: Prelude to Act I*, which has a superb cymbal-capped climax and an impressive closing diminuendo. But this is repertoire already available in outstanding performances from the likes of Karajan, Solti, Szell and Bruno Walter. Gerd Albrecht's very direct and well-detailed readings do not stand comparison with such exulted names. However, if you want straightforward accounts in top-quality sound, this disc may well be for you.

(i) *Der fliegende Holländer: Overture.* (ii) *Lohengrin: Prelude to Act I. Die Meistersinger: Overture.* (iii) *Parsifal: Prelude & Good Friday Music.* (iv) *Tannhäuser: Overture.*

(B) **(*) DG 439 445-2 (i) Bayreuth (1971) Festival O, Boehm; (ii) BPO, Kubelik; (iii) Bav. RSO, Jochum; (iv) German Op. O, Berlin, Gerdes.

Most of these performances are duplicated in the DG Double set of Wagner's orchestral excerpts, mentioned above, but this shorter, Classikon bargain collection includes Jochum's superb account of the *Parsifal* excerpts and is also well worthwhile.

(i) *Der Fliegende Höllander: Overture.* (ii) *Lohengrin: Prelude to Act I. Die Meistersinger: Overture.* (i) *Rienzi: Overture;* (ii) *Tannhäuser: Overture.* (i) *Tristan und Isolde: Prelude* (i) *Die Walküre: Ride of the Valkyries*

(M) **(*) Decca (ADD) 458 214-2. (i) VPO; (ii) Chicago SO: Solti.

Recorded between 1960 (*Rienzi*) and 1986 (*Lohengrin Prelude*) these performances were newly made in the studio, not taken from complete opera sets. So this is the self-contained *Tannhäuser Overture* from the Dresden version, and exciting it is with brilliant sound. The following *Meistersinger Prelude* is fuller and more expansive, but all the music-making here demonstrates Solti's characteristic Wagnerian flair and brings a high degree of tension. In *Der fliegende Höllander* the VPO are driven too hard and the effect is fierce, but *Rienzi* is mellower, with the big tune at the opening obviously relished. The CD transfers are vivid, if not always refined.

Overtures and Preludes: *Der Fliegende Höllander: Overture. Lohengrin: Preludes to Acts I & III; Parsifal: Prelude. Rienzi: Overture. Tannhäuser: Overture* (original version).

(M) *** DG (IMS) 453 989-2. VPO, Boehm.

Under Boehm, the Vienna Philharmonic Orchestra plays beautifully in a choice of overtures and preludes spanning Wagner's full career, from *Rienzi* to *Parsifal* – in which the performance of the *Prelude* is superbly eloquent. Above all, Boehm's approach is spacious with speeds broad rather than urgent, yet there is no lack of concentration, and the account of *Rienzi* has striking life and vigour. All the performances – and especially the *Lohengrin: Prelude to Act I* and the *Tannhäuser Overture* – show a compulsive inevitability in their forward flow. The recording is full and vivid, even if some balances do not seem quite natural.

Overtures: *Der fliegende Höllander; Die Meistersinger; Tannhäuser; Tristan: Prelude to Act I.*

(N) (M) *** Sup. (ADD) SU 3469–2 011. Czech PO, Konwitschny (with Richard STRAUSS: *Till Eulenspiegel* (***)).

Konwitschny's collection was highly regarded in its day (1960) for the excitement and spontaneity of the readings, with *Die Meistersinger* particularly well shaped and *Tannhäuser* bringing thrilling cascades from the Czech Philharmonic strings as well as fine brass playing. *Der fliegende Höllander* creates a vivid image of the storm-tossed ship. The analogue recording, made (like most of the other current Supraphon reissues) in the Dvořák Hall in Prague is impressively spacious. The transfer is bright and full, if not in the demonstration bracket. What makes the disc especially attractive is the 1952 mono coupling, a great credit to the sound engineer, František Burda. Konwitschny's performance takes off racily from the very opening bars. It has great zest, warmth and humour, plus spontaneous bursts of excitement. The closing section ends with a spectacular execution, before the touching little epilogue on the strings.

(However be warned: there are some curious ticking noises on the tape at the very opening of *Till*).

Der fliegende Höllander: Overture. Parsifal: Preludes to Acts I & III.

(M) *** EMI (ADD) CDM5 66108-2. BPO, Karajan – R. STRAUSS: *Ein Heldenleben.* ***

These recordings come from 1974 and are magnificently played and sumptuously recorded. There is urgency and edge in *The Flying Dutchman*, which is very exciting, and the string playing in the *Parsifal Preludes* is nobly shaped; if here perhaps the very last degree of tension is missing, the Berlin strings create a glorious sound.

Götterdämmerung: Dawn & Siegfried's Rhine Journey; Siegfried's Death & Funeral March; (i) *Brünnhilde's Immolation. Siegfried: Forest Murmurs. Die Walküre: Ride of the Valkyries.*

*** Erato 2292 45786-2. (i) Polaski; Chicago SO, Barenboim.

Here Barenboim dons his Furtwänglerian mantle in spacious performances. Even with tempi measured, he secures playing of great concentration and excitement from the Chicago orchestra, and the recording is one of the finest made in Chicago's Orchestra Hall. Deborah Polaski makes a bold, passionate Brünnhilde, and if her voice is not flattered by the microphones, and under pressure her vibrato widens, this is still histrionically thrilling, and Barenboim and the orchestra provide an overwhelming final apotheosis to the *Immolation Scene.*

Götterdämmerung: Siegfried's Funeral Music. Lohengrin, Act I: Prelude. Die Meistersinger, Act III: Prelude. Parsifal: Good Friday Music. Siegfried: Forest Murmurs. Tristan und Isolde: Prelude & Liebestod. Die Walküre: Ride of the Valkyries.

*** DG 447 764-2. NY Met. O, Levine.

Levine's performances are admirably paced, tingling with life, with climaxes finely graduated; and he secures sumptuously passionate playing from the Met strings. The richly full-bodied and atmospheric recording is just about the best yet to have come from the New York Manhattan Centre. The cymbals at the climax of the *Lohengrin Prelude* could ideally be more present, but otherwise the balance is realistically managed, and when the Valkyries ride in with splendid vigour, the sound avoids any sense of brashness. Jochum achieved a spiritual dimension in the *Good Friday music* from *Parsifal* which is missing here, but taken as a whole this 75-minute programme is a great success.

Götterdämmerung: Dawn & Siegfried's Rhine Journey; Siegfried's Death & Funeral Music. Das Rheingold: Entry of the Gods into Valhalla. Siegfried: Forest Murmurs. Tannhäuser: Overture. Die Walküre: Ride of the Valkyries; Wotan's Farewell & Magic Fire Music.

(N) (BB) *** EMI Encore CDE5 74762-2 BPO, Tennstedt.

This was EMI's first digital CD collection from the *Ring* and was recorded at the beginning of the 1980s with demonstrable brilliance. With steely metallic cymbal clashes in the *Ride of the Valkyries* and a splendid drum thwack at the opening of the *Entry of the Gods into Valhalla*, the sense of spectacle is in no doubt. There is weight too: the climax of *Siegfried's Funeral March* has massive penetration. There is also fine detail, especially in the atmospheric *Forest Murmurs*.

The playing itself is of the finest quality throughout and Tennstedt maintains a high level of tension. The opening and closing sections of the *Tannhäuser Overture* are given a restrained nobility of feeling without any loss of power and impact. But the early digital brass recording could be more expansive and at times the ear senses a lack of amplitude in the bass. However, the grip of the playing is well projected, the degree of fierceness at the top is tameable and this super-bargain reissue is good value.

Götterdämmerung: *Siegfried's Rhine Journey & Funeral Music; Die Meistersinger: Preludes to Acts I & III; Dance of the Apprentices; Procession of the Masters.*

(M) **(*) RCA (ADD) 09026 63301-2. Chicago SO, Reiner –
  R. STRAUSS: *Don Juan.* ***

The current remastering (by Hsi-Ling Chang) has greatly improved the balance. The *Götterdämmerung* excerpts are particularly impressive, the *Rhine Journey* buoyant and joyous, the *Funeral Music* powerful and sobre. Reiner choses spacious tempi in the *Meistersinger* excerpts with a further broadening at the (similar) climax of both the *Overture* and the *Procession of the Masters*: the result is very German in character. There is very fine playing from the horns in the *Prelude to Act III* from the same opera.

Götterdämmerung: *Dawn & Siegfried's Rhine Journey; Siegfried's Death & Funeral Music. Die Meistersinger: Prelude. Das Rheingold: Entry of the Gods into Valhalla. Siegfried: Forest Murmurs. Tristan und Isolde: Prelude & Liebestod. Die Walküre: Wotan's Farewell & Magic Fire Music.*

✪ (M) *** SBK (ADD) 48175. Cleveland O, Szell.

The orchestral playing here is breathtaking in its virtuosity. Szell generates the greatest tension, particularly in the two scenes from *Götterdämmerung*, while the *Liebestod* from *Tristan* has never been played on record with more passion and fire. The *Tristan* and *Meistersinger* excerpts (from 1962) have been added to the contents of the original LP, which contained the *Ring* sequences made later (in 1968), much improved on CD. This is well worthy of Szell's extraordinary achievement in Cleveland in the 1960s, even if the forward balance of the recording places a limit on the dynamic range. It is also available as a SuperAudio CD (SS 89035) which needs a special CD player.

Lohengrin: *Preludes to Acts I & III. Parsifal: Preludes to Acts I & III.*

(BB) *** EMI (ADD) CES5 69092 (2). BPO, Karajan –
  BRUCKNER: *Symphony No. 8.* ***

Lohengrin: *Preludes to Acts I & III. Tristan und Isolde: Prelude & Liebestod.*

(M) *** EMI (ADD) CDM5 66107-2. BPO, Karajan –
  R. STRAUSS: *Sinfonia domestica.* ***

Die Meistersinger: *Overture*. (i) *Tannhäuser: Overture & Venusberg music.*

(M) *** EMI (ADD) CDM5 66106-2. BPO, Karajan, (i) with German Op. Ch. – R. STRAUSS: *Don Quixote.* ***

These Karajan performances (again from 1974) are in a class of their own. The body of tone produced by the Berlin Philharmonic gives a breathtaking richness to the climaxes. That of the first *Lohengrin Prelude* is superbly graded, and in the *Tristan Liebestod* the orgasmic culmination is quite overwhelming, as is the thrilling brass playing in the famous *Lohengrin* Act III *Prelude*.

Karajan's Act I *Lohengrin Prelude* is graduated superbly; the *Parsifal* excerpts, too, are nobly shaped, yet here the tension is held at a marginally lower level. The *Parsifal* excerpts bring rapt serenity.

A superb sense of timing and spaciousness is applied to the *Tannhäuser* excerpts, and the *Die Meistersinger Prelude* has a similar imposing breadth. The sound is excellent. However, both CDM5 66106-2 and CDM5 66107-2 are now deleted.

Die Meistersinger: *Overture.*

(N) (M) (**) Beulah mono 3PD12. BBCSO, Boult –
  MENDELSSOHN: *Hebrides Overture* (**); SCHUBERT: *Symphony No. 9 in C (Great).* (**(*))

In this recording of 1933, constricted by the length of short-playing 78 discs, Boult takes an urgent and biting view of the *Meistersinger Overture*, fresh and dramatic. Surface hiss is high but even, with full-bodied sound set in a dry acoustic with no added reverberation. A good supplement to the Schubert.

Overtures and Preludes: *Die Meistersinger; Parsifal; Rienzi; Tannhäuser*

(N) (B) *** DG 469 538-2. BPO, Boehm.

This is a short (49 minutes) collection including a superbly expansive account of the *Die Meistersinger Overture*. This is Boehm at his finest: magnetic, marvellously played performances, creating an ideal balance between warmth and tension. The transfers are very good too.

Die Meistersinger: *Prelude to Act III. Tannhäuser: Overture & Venusberg Music. Tristan und Isolde: Prelude & Liebestod.*

**(*) DG (IMS) 439 022-2. BPO, Karajan.

In Karajan's digital concert the orchestral playing is superlative. But, in spite of the reprocessing, the upper strings lack space, and climaxes should be freer. The overall effect is rather clinical in its detail, instead of offering a resonant panoply of sound, but the playing is eloquent and powerful. The measure is not very generous for a reissued premium-price CD.

Parsifal, *Act III: Symphonic Synthesis. Tristan und Isolde: Symphonic Synthesis. Die Walküre: Wotan's Farewell & Magic Fire Music* (all arr. Stokowski).

*** Chan. 9686. BBC PO, Bamert.

Stokowski's recordings of Wagner excerpts always treated

the voices as a kind of adjunct to the orchestra, and he loved best to play the orchestral music without them So he made a series of symphonic syntheses, joining scenes together in a continuous sensuous and dramatic melodic flow, leaving the orchestra to convey the full narrative. *Parsifal* includes tolling bells and rich mysticism, and in *Tristan* Stokowski frames the *Liebesnacht* (including the distant hunting horns heralding the return of Tristan) with the passionate *Prelude* and *Liebestod*. Best of all he creates a symphonic poem out of Wotan's sad, loving farewell to his beloved Brünnhilde, making a great climax out of the *Fire Music*. Bamert is passionate and tender by turns and the BBC Philharmonic readily respond to the luscious orchestration. Perhaps the last degree of Stokowskian intensity is missing here, but with superbly spacious Chandos sound this is easy to enjoy.

VOCAL MUSIC

Lieder: *Les deux grenadiers; Lied des Mephistopheles (Es war einmal ein König; Was machst du mir); Mignonne; Der Tannenbaum; Tout n'est qu'images fugitives.*

⊕ *** EMI CDC5 55047-2. Hampson, Parsons – BERLIOZ: *Irlande;* LISZT: *Lieder.* *** ⊕

Starting with a charming French salon piece, *Mignonne*, to words by Ronsard, the Hampson collection presents an almost unknown side of the composer. As well as another French love-song, there is a setting in French of the Goethe poem about the two grenadiers, not as subtle as Schumann's version but building to a tremendous climax with a reference to the *Marseillaise*. Two of Mephistopheles' songs from *Faust* (in German) date from earlier, including a jaunty setting of the *Song of the Flea*. With Hampson in magnificent voice, powerfully accompanied by Geoffrey Parsons, this makes up a winning disc, very well recorded.

Wesendonck Lieder.

(N) *** Sony SK 61720. Eaglen, LSO, Runnicles – BERG: *7 Early Songs* ***; R. STRAUSS: *Four Last Songs* **(*).

(N) (M) **(*) Ph. (ADD) 464 742-2. Norman, LSO, Davis – R. STRAUSS: *Four Last Songs.* ***

(M) ** EMI (ADD) CDM5 67037-2. Christa Ludwig, Philh. O, Klemperer – BRUCKNER: *Symphony No. 6.* ***

The sumptuous vibrancy of Jane Eaglen's voice is at its most alluring in Wagner's cycle of songs setting poems by Mathilde Wesendonck. As Donald Runnicles, the conductor, says in his note, she has become a great Wagnerian, and the command and beauty of her performances confirm that not just in the scale but in the moulding of line. An imaginative coupling, too, with Runnicles drawing sumptuous playing from the LSO to match.

The poised phrases of the *Wesendonck Lieder* drew from Jessye Norman in this 1976 recording a glorious range of tone colour, though in detailed imagination this falls short of some of the finest rivals on record. Good, refined recording, made vivid on CD with an excellent transfer.

Christa Ludwig is less successful here in her partnership with Klemperer than in the Brahms *Alto Rhapsody* also dating from 1962. In Wagner she seems to be thinking in

operatic terms. She has a rich and beautiful vocal quality, but seems unable or unwilling to always reduce the tone sufficiently for the more intimate effect required in Lieder. The orchestral accompaniment is very well done.

Wesendonck Lieder: Der Engel; Stehe still; Im Treibhaus; Schmerzen; Träume. Götterdämmerung: Starke Scheite schichet mir dort. Siegfried: Ewig war ich. Tristan: Doch nun von Tristan?; Mild und leise.

(M) (***) EMI mono CDH7 63030-2. Kirsten Flagstad, Philh. O, Furtwängler, Dobrowen.

Recorded in the late 1940s and early 1950s, a year or so before Flagstad did *Tristan* complete with Furtwängler, these performances show her at her very peak, with the voice magnificent in power as well as beautiful and distinctive in every register. The *Liebestod* (with rather heavy surface noise) may be less rapt and intense in this version with Dobrowen than with Furtwängler but is just as expansive. For the *Wesendonck Lieder* she shades the voice down very beautifully, but this is still monumental and noble rather than intimate Lieder-singing.

OPERA

Der fliegende Holländer (complete).

*** DG 437 778-2 (2). Weikl, Studer, Sotin, Domingo, Seiffert, Ch. & O of German Op., Berlin, Sinopoli.

(M) *** Ph. 434 599-2 (2). Estes, Balslev, Salminen, Schunk, Bayreuth Festival (1985) Ch. & O, Nelsson.

(B) *** Naxos 8.660025/6. Muff, Haubold, Knodt, Seiffert, Budapest R. Ch., Vienna ORF SO, Steinberg.

(M) **(*) EMI 64650-2 (2). Van Dam, Vejzovic, Moll, Hofmann, Moser, Borris, V. State Op. Ch., BPO, Karajan.

**(*) Decca (ADD) 414 551-2 (3). Bailey, Martin, Talvela, Kollo, Krenn, Isola Jones, Chicago S & O Ch. O, Solti.

(N) (M) **(*) EMI (ADD) CMS5 67408-2 [567405-2] (2). Adam, Silja, Talvela, Kozub, Burmeister, Unger, BBC Ch., New Philh. O, Klemperer.

Sinopoli's is an intensely involving performance, volatile in the choice of often extreme speeds, slow as well as fast, but with fine playing from the orchestra of the Deutsche Oper, Berlin, it never sounds forced, with rhythms crisply sprung, making others seem dull or even pedestrian. The choral singing too is electrifying, and the line-up of principals is arguably finer than any. Cheryl Studer is a deeply moving Senta, not just immaculate vocally but conveying the intense vulnerability of the character in finely detailed singing. Bernd Weikl is a dark-toned, firmly focused Dutchman, strong and incisive. Hans Sotin is similarly firm and dark, nicely contrasted as Daland, and the luxury casting may be judged from the choice of Placido Domingo as an impressive, forthright Erik and Peter Seiffert (the fine *Lohengrin* in Barenboim's Teldec set) as a ringing Steersman. Full, vivid sound. A clear first choice.

Woldemar Nelsson conducts a performance glowingly and responsively. The cast is more consistent than almost any, with Lisbeth Balslev as Senta firm, sweet and secure, raw only occasionally, and Simon Estes a strong, ringing

Dutchman, clear and noble of tone. Matti Salminen is a dark and equally secure Daland and Robert Schunk an ardent, idiomatic Erik. The veteran, Anny Schlemm, as Mary, though vocally overstressed, adds pointful character, and the chorus is superb, wonderfully drilled and passionate with it. Though inevitably stage noises are obtrusive at times, the recording is exceptionally vivid and atmospheric. On two mid-priced discs only, it makes an admirable first choice.

Pinchas Steinberg here proves a warmly sympathetic Wagnerian. More than most rivals, he brings out the light and shade of this earliest of the regular Wagner canon, helped by the refined, well-balanced recording, and by brilliant, sharply dramatic playing from the orchestra. The chorus too sings with a bite and precision to match any rival. Alfred Muff as the Dutchman attacks the notes cleanly, with vibrato only occasionally intrusive. The vibrato of Ingrid Haubold is more of a problem but, except under pressure, it is well controlled, and she begins *Senta's Ballad* with a meditative pianissimo. Both tenors are excellent, Peter Seiffert as Erik and Joerg Hering as the Steersman, and though Erich Knodt, rather gritty in tone, is an uncharacterful Daland, his Act II aria is light and refreshing, thanks to Steinberg's fine rhythmic pointing. The recording is both atmospheric and clear, and the set comes with libretto, translation, notes and detailed synopsis, an outstanding bargain.

The extreme range of dynamics in EMI's recording for Karajan, not ideally clear but rich, matches the larger-than-life quality of the conductor's reading. He firmly and convincingly relates this early work to later Wagner, *Tristan* above all. His choice of José van Dam as the Dutchman, thoughtful, finely detailed and lyrical, strong but not at all blustering, goes well with this. Van Dam is superbly matched and contrasted with the finest Daland on record, Kurt Moll, gloriously biting and dark in tone, yet detailed in his characterization. Neither the Erik of Peter Hofmann, nor – more seriously – the Senta of Dunja Vejzovic matches this standard; nevertheless, for all her variability, Vejzovic is wonderfully intense in *Senta's Ballad* and she matches even Van Dam's fine legato in the Act II duet. The CD transfer underlines the heavyweight quality of the recording, with the *Sailors' Chorus* made massive, but effectively so, when Karajan conducts it with such fine spring.

What will disappoint some who admire Solti's earlier Wagner sets is that this most atmospheric of the Wagner operas is presented as a concert performance with no Culshaw-style production whatever. Characters halloo to one another when evidently standing elbow to elbow, and even the Dutchman's ghostly chorus sounds close and earthbound. But with Norman Bailey a deeply impressive Dutchman, Janis Martin a generally sweet-toned Senta, Martti Talvela a splendid Daland, and Kollo, for all his occasional coarseness, an illuminating Erik, it remains well worth hearing.

Klemperer's recording is perhaps a controversial candidate for inclusion as one of EMI's 'Great Recordings of the Century', but at least this means that it has returned to the catalogue at mid-price and on two well-filled CDs instead of three full-priced ones. Moreover, it is very well documented, with an essay by Richard Osborne, plenty of sessions photographs and a full libretto and translation. The reading is

predictably spacious in its tempi, and the drama hardly grips you by the throat. But Klemperer's symphonic approach is compelling, and the underlying intensity is irresistible. This could hardly be recommended as a first choice, but any committed admirer of the conductor should take the opportunity of hearing it. It is a pity that Anja Silja was chosen as Senta, even though she is not as squally in tone here as she can be. Otherwise, the vocal cast is strong, and there is much beautiful orchestral playing (particularly from the wind soloists), and the lively recording sounds much more full-bloodedly expansive and vivid in its newest CD transfer by Andrew Walter.

Der fliegende Holländer: highlights.

(M) **(*) Ph. (IMS) 446 618-2. Estes, Balslev, Salminen, Schunk, Bayreuth Festival (1985) Ch. & O, Nelsson.

**(*) Sony SK 61969. Morris, Voigt, Heppner, Rootering, Svendén, Groves, Met. Op. Ch. & O, Levine.

(M) **(*) EMI CDM5 66052-2. Van Dam, Vejzovic, Moll, Hofmann, Moser, Borris, V. State Op. Ch., BPO, Karajan.

A generous (76 minutes) and well-chosen selection from the outstanding Philips set is let down by the absence of any documentation, save a list of the twelve excerpts.

The highlights Sony CD is generously selected (76 minutes) and includes the Overture. But again there is no translation and the synopsis is not cued.

This EMI highlights disc is only slightly more generous than most of the rest of the series (67 minutes) but will be useful for those wanting to sample Karajan's 1983 recording, particularly as José Van Dam as the Dutchman and Kurt Moll as Daland are both so impressive, and *Senta's Ballad* (Dunja Vejzovic) is very movingly sung. The synopsis relates each excerpt to the narrative.

Götterdämmerung (complete).

*** Decca (ADD) 455 569-2 (4). Nilsson, Windgassen, Fischer-Dieskau, Frick, Neidlinger, Watson, Ludwig, V. State Op. Ch., VPO, Solti.

(M) *** DG (ADD) 457 795-2 (4). Dernesch, Janowitz, Brilioth, Stewart, Kelemen, Ludwig, Ridderbusch, German Op. Ch., BPO, Karajan.

*** Ph. (IMS) (ADD) 412 488-2 (4). Nilsson, Windgassen, Greindl, Mödl, Stewart, Neidlinger, Dvořáková, Bayreuth Festival (1967) Ch. & O, Boehm.

*** Teldec 4509 94194-2 (4). Jerusalem, Anne Evans, Kang, Von Kannen, Bundschuh, Meier, Turner, Bayreuth (1991) Festival Ch. & O, Barenboim.

*** EMI CD7 54485-2 (4). Marton, Jerusalem, Tomlinson, Adam, Hampson, Bundschuh, Lipovšek, Bav. R. Ch., RSO, Haitink.

(B) *** RCA 74321 45421-2 (4). Kollo, Altmeyer, Salminen, Wenkel, Nocker, Nimsgern, Sharp, Popp, Leipzig R. Ch., Berlin R. Ch., Dresden State Op. Ch., Dresden State O, Janowski.

(M) *** Ph. 434 424-2 (4). G. Jones, Jung, Hübner, Becht, Mazura, Altmeyer, Killebrew, (1979) Bayreuth Festival Ch. & O, Boulez.

(M) (***) Testament mono SBT 4175 (4). Varnay, Aldenhoff,

Uhde, Mödl, Weber, Bayreuth Fest. Ch. & O,
Knappertsbusch.
(B) (*(*)) Naxos mono 8.11041/3 (3). Melchior, Lawrence,
Hoffman, Habich, Schorr, Met. Op.Ch. & O, Bodanzky.

Solti's *Götterdämmerung* represented the peak of his achievement in recording the *Ring* cycle. There is not a single weak link in the cast. Nilsson surpasses herself in the magnificence of her singing: even Flagstad in her prime would not have been more masterful as Brünnhilde. As in *Siegfried*, Windgassen is in superb voice; Frick is a vivid Hagen, and Fischer-Dieskau achieves the near impossible in making Gunther an interesting and even sympathetic character. As for the recording quality, it surpasses even Decca's earlier achievement, and the current remastering has further improved the sound.

Karajan's singing cast is marginally even finer than Solti's, and his performance conveys the steady flow of recording sessions prepared in relation to live performances. Ultimately he falls short of Solti's achievement in the thrusting, orgasmic quality of the music. Dernesch's Brünnhilde is warmer than Nilsson's, with a glorious range of tone. Brilioth as Siegfried is fresh and young-sounding, while the Gutrune of Gundula Janowitz is far preferable to that of Claire Watson on Decca. The matching is otherwise very even. The new transfer has both freshened and filled out the sound.

Boehm's urgently involving reading of *Götterdämmerung*, very well cast, is crowned by an incandescent performance of the final *Immolation Scene* from Birgit Nilsson as Brünnhilde. It is an astonishing achievement that she could sing with such biting power and accuracy in a live performance, coming to it at the very end of a long evening. The excitement of that is matched by much else in the performance, so that incidental stage noises and the occasional inaccuracy, almost inevitable in live music-making, matter hardly at all. Josef Greindl is rather unpleasantly nasal in tone as Hagen, and Martha Mödl as Waltraute is unsteady; but both are dramatically involving. Thomas Stewart is a gruff but convincing Gunther and Dvořáková, as Gutrune, strong if not ideally pure-toned. Neidlinger as ever is a superb Alberich.

Barenboim's live recording is not quite the culmination one had hoped for in his cycle for Teldec. There is also the problem of stage noises, particularly at the end of the Immolation scene. Anne Evans sweetly and purely rises to the challenge of that radiant close of the tetralogy, compensating for any lack of power in the clarity of focus and expressive intensity of her singing, making Brünnhilde a very human figure to excite the deepest sympathy. The recording is satisfyingly weighty and has more presence than its direct digital rivals. On balance, it stands as the most recommendable of latterday versions of this final opera, thanks not only to the beauty as well as the imagination of Evans's singing, but also to the superb singing of Siegfried Jerusalem who outshines his already outstanding achievement in the same role in the Haitink version. Eva-Maria Bundschuh makes a fresh, bright Gutrune and Waltraud Meier a powerful Waltraute, giving an animated account of her Act I narration. Bodo Brinkmann is an old-sounding, rather uneven Gunther, Philip Kang a powerful but gritty Hagen and Gunter von Kannen an unsinister Alberich. As a

performance it may not outshine either Solti's pioneering version or Karl Boehm's live account from Bayreuth – both of which still sound splendid – but it satisfyingly completes the finest of modern *Ring* cycles on disc.

Haitink's reading is magnificent. In its strength, nobility and thrustfulness it crowns all his previous Wagner, culminating in a forceful and warmly expressive account of the final *Immolation Scene*. Siegfried Jerusalem clearly establishes himself as the finest latterday Siegfried, both heroic and sweet of tone. Thomas Hampson is a sensitive and virile Gunther, John Tomlinson a sinister but human Hagen, Marjana Lipovšek a warmly intense Waltraute and Eva-Maria Bundschuh a rich, rather fruity Gutrune. The obvious reservation to make is with the singing of Eva Marton as Brünnhilde, when the unevenness of the vocal production is exaggerated by the microphone in a way that at times comes close to pitchless yelping. That drawback is clearly outweighed by the set's positive qualities, and the scale of her singing is in no doubt, an archetypal Brünnhilde voice. However, this set has just been deleted.

With sharply focused yet warmly ambient sound, Janowski's *Götterdämmerung* hits refreshingly hard, at least as much so as in the earlier operas in the cycle. Speeds rarely linger but, with some excellent casting – consistent with the earlier operas – the result is rarely lightweight. Jeannine Altmeyer as Brünnhilde rises to the challenge, not so much in strength as in feeling, and here, as throughout the series, she consistently avoids the kind of squally and ill-focused – if powerful – tone-production that puts some listeners off Wagner altogether. Kollo is a fine Siegfried, only occasionally raw-toned, and Salminen a magnificent Hagen, with Nimsgern an incisive Alberich on his brief appearances. Despite an indifferent Günther and Gutrune and a wobbly if characterful Waltraute, the impression is of clean, strong vocalization matched by finely disciplined and dedicated playing, all recorded in faithful stereo, with very good detail. A remarkable achievement and a fine bargain.

Boulez's 1979 analogue recording is warm and urgent. The passion of the performance is established in the Dawn music before the second scene of the Prologue. Manfred Jung as Siegfried gives a fresh, clean-cut performance. Jeannine Altmeyer sings Gutrune, sweet but not always ideally clean of attack; Fritz Hübner a weighty Hagen, Franz Mazura a powerful Gunther and Gwendoline Killebrew a rich, firm Waltraute. Dame Gwyneth Jones as Brünnhilde, always very variable, has some splendid moments, notably at the close of the Immolation scene. The sound is aptly atmospheric but lacks something in weight in the brass, though there is no lack of excitement at the end of Act II.

The legendary Knappertsbusch recording made in 1951 during the first Bayreuth Festival after the war has produced for his Testament label a set astonishing in its vividness. This live recording was supervised by the Decca producer John Culshaw (later to mastermind Solti's complete *Ring* cycle) and the mono sound is even fuller and weightier than on the recording of *Parsifal* he also made at Bayreuth in 1951. Both operas were conducted by Hans Knappertsbusch, who in *Götterdämmerung* is even more electrifying than in *Parsifal*, defying his reputation as a relaxed, expansive Wagnerian. Vocally the star is Astrid Varnay, shiningly firm and incisive as Brünnhilde, rising magnificently to the final challenge of the Immolation scene. Siegfried is sung by the short-lived Bernd Aldenhoff, strained at times like most Heldentenoren, but generally lyrical and boyish. Hermann Uhde as Gunther and Ludwig Weber as Hagen are both outstanding too, with the immediacy and sense of presence carrying one on from first to last.

On Naxos, the 1936 radio transmission, roughly recorded, may often bring excruciating sound, with high surfaces and heavy interference, and Bodansky's conducting may often be perfunctory, but the thrill of a great Wagnerian occasion featuring some of the finest Wagner singers of the day certainly comes over. Bodansky, who sanctions substantial cuts, even gallops through Brünnhilde's final Immolation scene, but the glory of Marjorie Lawrence's singing at the beginning of her all-too-brief career has never been so vividly captured. Equally, to hear Melchior as Siegfried – even fuzzily – is not to be missed by any Wagnerian. The others make a strong team, with voices rather clearer than the muddy orchestra.

Götterdämmerung: highlights.

(M) Ph. (IMS) (ADD) 446 616-2 (from above (1979) Bayreuth set; cond. Boulez).

Many collectors will want to sample the Boulez set, and this CD offering 78 minutes of highlights should serve admirably, except for the lack of either translation or synopsis – or, indeed, any kind of documentation at all except for detailing the sixteen excerpts. They include *Siegfried's Rhine Journey* and *Funeral March* and the final *Immolation Scene*.

The Twilight of the Gods (Götterdämmerung; complete in English).

(N) (M) *** Chan. (ADD) 3060 (5). Hunter, Remedios, Welsby, Haugland, Hammond-Stroud, Curphey, Pring, ENO Ch. & O, Goodall.

Goodall's account of the culminating opera in Wagner's tetralogy may not be the most powerful ever recorded, and certainly it is not the most polished, but it is one which, paradoxically, by intensifying human as opposed to super-human emotions heightens the epic scale. The very opening may sound a little tentative (like the rest of the Goodall English *Ring*, this was recorded live at the London Coliseum), but it takes no more than a few seconds to register the body and richness of the sound. The few slight imprecisions and the occasional rawness of wind tone actually seem to enhance the earthiness of Goodall's view, with more of the primeval saga about it than the studio-made *Ring* cycles.

Both Rita Hunter and Alberto Remedios were more considerately recorded on the earlier Unicorn version (now Chandos – see below) of the final scenes, with more bloom on their voices, but their performances here are magnificent in every way. In particular the golden beauty of Remedios's tenor is consistently superb, with no *Heldentenor* barking at all, while Aage Haugland's Hagen is giant-sounding to focus the evil, with Gunther and Gutrune mere pawns. The voices on stage are in a different, drier acoustic from that for the orchestra, but considering the problems the sound is impressive. As for Goodall, with his consistently expansive tempi he carries total conviction – except, curiously, in the scene with the Rhinemaidens, whose music (as in Goodall's *Rheingold*) lumbers along heavily.

The Twilight of the Gods (Götterdämmerung): Act III: Excerpts (in English).

(M) *** Chan. (ADD) 6593. Hunter, Remedios, Bailey, Grant, Curphey, Sadler's Wells Opera Ch. & O, Goodall.

Originally recorded by Unicorn in the early 1970s, this single Chandos CD brings an invaluable reminder of Reginald Goodall's performance of the *Ring* cycle when it was in its first flush of success, covering the closing two scenes. It is good too to have this sample, however brief, of Clifford Grant's Hagen and Norman Bailey's Gunther, fine performances both. Fresh, clear recording, not as full as it might be. At mid-price this CD is well worth investigating.

Lohengrin (complete).

*** DG 437 808-2 (3). Jerusalem, Studer, Meier, Welker, Moll, Schmidt, V. State Op. Ch., VPO, Claudio Abbado.

*** Decca 421 053-2 (4). Domingo, Norman, Nimsgern, Randová, Sotin, Fischer-Dieskau, V. State Op. Concert Ch., VPO, Solti.

*** Teldec 3984 21484-2 (3). Seiffert, Magee, Struckmann, Polaski, Pape, Ch. & O of German Op.,Berlin, Barenboim.

(N) (M) *** EMI CMS5 67415-2 [56711-2] (3). Jess Thomas, Grümmer, Fischer-Dieskau, Ludwig, Frick, Wiener, V. State Op. Ch., VPO, Kempe.

(M) **(*) EMI (ADD) CMS5 66519-2 (3). Kollo, Tomowa-Sintow, Vejzovic, Nimsgern, Ridderbusch, German Op. Ch., Berlin, BPO, Karajan.

(M) **(*) Ph. (ADD) 446 337-2 (3). Thomas, Silja, Vinay, Varnay, Crass, Krause, Bayreuth Festival Ch. & O, Sawallisch.

Abbado keeps Wagner's square rhythms flowing freely, allowing himself a great measure of rubato. That Abbado's speeds are generally faster than Solti's (with the Act III *Prelude* a notable exception) means that the complete opera is squeezed on to three instead of four discs, giving it the clearest advantage. As Elsa, matching her earlier, Bayreuth performance on Philips, Cheryl Studer is at her sweetest and purest, bringing out the heroine's naïvety more touchingly than Jessye Norman, whose weighty, mezzo-ish tone is thrillingly rich but is more suited to portraying other Wagner heroines than this. Though there are signs that Siegfried Jerusalem's voice is not as fresh as it once was, he sings commandingly, conveying both beauty and a true Heldentenor quality. Where Plácido Domingo for Solti, producing even more beautiful tone, tends to use a full voice for such intimate solos as *In fernem Land* and *Mein lieber Schwann*, Jerusalem sings there with tender restraint and gentler tone. Among the others, Waltraud Meier as Ortrud and Kurt Moll as King Heinrich are both superb, as fine as any predecessor, and though in the role of Telramund Hartmut Welker's baritone is not ideally steady, that tends to underline the weakness of the character next to the positive Ortrud.

It is Plácido Domingo's achievement singing Lohengrin that the lyrical element blossoms so consistently, with no hint of Heldentenor barking; at whatever dynamic level, Domingo's voice is firm and unstrained. Jessye Norman, not naturally suited to the role of Elsa, yet gives a warm, commanding performance, always intense, full of detailed insights into words and character. Eva Randová's grainy mezzo does not take so readily to recording, but as Ortrud she provides a pointful contrast, even if she never matches the firm, biting malevolence of Christa Ludwig on the Kempe set. Siegmund Nimsgern, Telramund for Solti, equally falls short of Fischer-Dieskau, his rival on the Kempe set; but it is still a strong, cleanly focused performance. Fischer-Dieskau here sings the small but vital role of the Herald, while Hans Sotin makes a comparably distinctive King Henry. Radiant playing from the Vienna Philharmonic, and committed chorus work too. This is one of the crowning glories of Solti's long recording career.

The first glory of Barenboim's set is the sound, full and upfront, with the voices clearly focused and with plenty of bloom, set against a rich, incandescent orchestra. Having voices relatively close adds immediacy to the drama, and Barenboim's pacing adds warmth and often urgency, even if Elsa's dream sounds a little sluggish. Emily Magee's full, rich tone makes the heroine sound rather too mature, and the voice is not well contrasted with the Ortrud of Deborah Polaski, a soprano rather lacking the sinister chest-tones apt for this evil character, hardly conveying her full villainy. Peter Seiffert makes an outstanding Lohengrin, lyrical as well as heroic, with no hint of strain. One merit of the set is that the text is absolutely complete, including the extended solo after that Act III aria. The Telramund of Falk Strickmann is rather gritty, lacking weight, and Roman Trekel is a strained Herald, but René Pape is magnificent as the King, a fine successor to Kurt Moll.

Kempe directs a rapt account of *Lohengrin*, a fine monument to a great Wagnerian. The singers seem uplifted, Jess Thomas singing more clearly and richly than usual, Elisabeth Grümmer unrivalled as Elsa in her delicacy and sweetness, Gottlob Frick gloriously resonant as the king. But it is the partnership of Christa Ludwig and Fischer-Dieskau as Ortrud and Telramund that sets the seal on this superb performance, giving the darkest intensity to their machinations in Act II, their evil heightening the beauty and serenity of so much in this opera. This is a now awarded an honourable place among EMI's 'Great Recordings of the Century'. The new CD transfer has greatly improved the sound; ensembles are still rather close and airless, but not congested. Solo voices are naturally caught, and the glow and intensity of Kempe's reading come out all the more involvingly in the new format. The set is also very economically contained on three CDs instead of the four required by most of its rivals, though the first break between discs comes in the middle of Act II.

Karajan, whose DG recording of *Parsifal* is so naturally intense, fails in this earlier but related opera to capture comparable spiritual depth. So some of the big melodies sound a degree over-inflected and the result, though warm and expressive and dramatically powerful, with wide-ranging recording, misses an important dimension. Nor is much of the singing as pure-toned as it might be, with René Kollo too often straining and Tomowa-Sintow not always

able to scale down to the necessary purity her big, dramatic voice. Even so, with strong and beautiful playing from the Berlin Philharmonic, it remains a powerful performance, and it makes a fair mid-priced version on three CDs.

The Sawallisch recording was of a live performance at Bayreuth in 1962 and has a propulsive thrust over Wagner's expansive paragraphs, encouraged by the presence of an audience. For this dramatic tension one naturally has to pay in stage-noises, occasional slips and odd balances, but the recording captures the unique flavour of the Festspielhaus splendidly. What above all will dictate a listener's response is their reaction to the voices of Anja Silja as Elsa and of Astrid Varnay as Ortrud. Though Silja has been far less steady on record in other sets, this is often not a pretty sound, and Varnay was firmer in her earlier Bayreuth recording for Decca in mono. Jess Thomas is here not as reliable as he has been in other performances; but Sawallisch's direction is superb, fresh and direct, never intrusive. On CD the sound is marvellously refined as well as atmospheric. The opera fits neatly on three discs, with each Act complete and unbroken.

Lohengrin: Preludes to Acts I & III.

(N) *** Australian Decca Eloquence (ADD) 467 235-2. VPO, Mehta – MAHLER: *Symphony No. 4.* **

These beautifully and excitingly played and recorded preludes make a good bonus for Mehta's fresh account of Mahler's *Fourth Symphony*. There is something of an explosive thrill about the *Act III Prelude* which is really quite memorable.

Die Meistersinger von Nürnberg (complete).

*** Decca 452 606-2 (4). Van Dam, Heppner, Mattila, Opie, Lippert, Vermillion, Pape, Chicago SO Ch. & O, Solti.

*** DG (ADD) 415 278-2 (4). Fischer-Dieskau, Ligendza, Lagger, Hermann, Domingo, Laubenthal, Ludwig, German Op. Ch. & O, Berlin, Jochum.

*** Calig (ADD) CAL 50971-74 (4). Stewart, Crass, Hemsley, Konya, Unger, Janowitz, Fassbaender, Bav. R. Ch. & O, Kubelik.

*** EMI (ADD) CDS5 55142-2 (4). Weikl, Heppner, Studer, Moll, Lorenz, Van der Walt, Kallisch, Bav. State Op. Ch., Bav. State O, Sawallisch.

(M) (***) EMI mono CHS7 63500-2 (4). Schwarzkopf, Edelmann, Kunz, Hopf, Unger, Bayreuth Festival Ch. & O, Karajan.

(M) **(*) EMI (ADD) CMS5 67086-2 [567148]. Adam, Kollo, Donath, Ridderbusch, Evans, Schreier, Hesse, Leipzig R. Ch., Dresden State Op. Ch. & O, Karajan.

(M) (***) EMI mono CMS7 64154-2. Frantz, Schock, Grümmer, Frick, Kusche, Unger, Höffgen, St Hedwig's Cathedral Ch., German Op., Berlin, Ch., BPO, Kempe.

**(*) Decca (IMS) (ADD) 417 497-2 (4). Bailey, Bode, Moll, W. Kollo, Dallapozza, Hamari, Gumpoldskirchner Spatzen, V. State Op. Ch., VPO, Solti.

(N) ** Teldec 3984 29333-2 (4). Holl, Seiffert, Magee, Schmidt, Wottrich, Bayreuth Festival Ch. & O, Barenboim.

This is the only Wagner opera that Sir Georg Solti has recorded a second time. By comparison, his earlier, Vienna recording is stiff and metrical, often fierce, with bright, upfront recording, where this new live recording, made in Orchestra Hall, Chicago, is mellower, with plenty of air round the sound, enhancing the extra warmth, relaxation and subtlety of the performance. Central to the success of the later performance is the singing of Ben Heppner as Walther, not just heroic but clear and unstrained, ardently following Solti's urgency in the *Prize Song*, a performance more beautiful than any of recent years except his own for Sawallisch. Karita Mattila sings with comparable beauty as Eva. Though she is still young, her firm, clear voice is more mature, almost mezzo-ish at times, than one expects of an Eva, and she too naturally surges forward in the great solo of the *Quintet*. For some the controversial element will be the Sachs of José van Dam, clean and sharply focused rather than weighty, not quite the wise, old, genial Sachs in his duet with Eva in Act II. This is again unconventional casting which yet brings new beauty and new revelation, as in the hushed pianissimo at the end of the *Fliedermonolog* when he tells of the bird singing. With René Pape a powerful Pogner, Alan Opie a clean-cut, unexaggerated Beckmesser with plenty of projection, and Herbert Lippert and Iris Vermillion excellent as David and Magdalene, it is a cast to rival any on disc, making this a clear recommendation if you want a digital recording.

Above all, Jochum is unerring in building long Wagnerian climaxes and resolving them – more so than his recorded rivals. The cast is the most consistent yet assembled on record. Though Caterina Ligendza's big soprano is a little ungainly for Eva, it is an appealing performance, and the choice of Plácido Domingo to play Walther is inspired. The key to the set is the searching and highly individual Hans Sachs of Dietrich Fischer-Dieskau, and Horst Laubenthal's finely tuned David matches this Sachs in applying Lieder style. There is a lovely bloom on the whole sound and, with a recording which is basically wide-ranging and refined, the ambience brings an attractively natural projection of the singers.

The Calig issue, belatedly issued on commercial disc, is a radio recording, made in Munich in October 1967, and the vividness of the sound is astonishing, with more realism and presence than in almost any digital recording. Even the mêlée at the end of Act II emerges vividly. This is also one of Kubelik's most inspired recordings, incandescent in the way it builds up to the big emotional climaxes, just as in a live performance. When it comes to the casting, every single voice has been chosen not only for its firmness and clarity, with no wobbling or straining, but also for the central aptness of voice to character. It would be hard to think of a more radiant and girlish Eva than Gundula Janowitz, and the Hungarian tenor, Sandor Konya, too little heard on record, is a glowing Walther, beautiful in every register if not quite as subtle as the leading Walther today, Ben Heppner. Thomas Stewart as Hans Sachs is similarly unstrained, using his firm, dark baritone with warm expressiveness, while Thomas Hemsley has rarely been so impressive on disc, a sharp-focused Beckmesser who conveys the ironic humour but who never guys the role. Franz Crass is a fine, dark

Pogner, and it would be hard to find a match for Gerhard Unger as David or Brigitte Fassbaender as Magdalene, with the upfront sound heightening their subplot. A Wagner production as consistent as this is rare, the more surprising to find in a radio recording.

Sawallisch also paces the work in reflection of his long experience of performing it in the opera house with the same musicians. Add to that the most radiant and free-toned Walther on disc, the Canadian, Ben Heppner, and you have a superb set. In tonal beauty Heppner matches Plácido Domingo on Jochum's DG set, as he does in variety of expression and feeling. Cheryl Studer's contribution is hardly less remarkable than Heppner's, at once powerful and girlishly tender, with the voice kept pure. If she is less affecting than she might be in the poignant duet with Sachs in Act II and in the great *Quintet* of Act III, that has something to do with a limitation in Sawallisch's reading, fine as it is. It rarely finds the poetic magic that this of all Wagner's operas can convey. Bernd Weikl makes a splendid Sachs, firm and true of voice, but something of the nobility of the master-shoemaker is missing. Deon van der Walt is a strong David, clear-cut and fresh, with Cornelia Kallisch making a traditionally fruity yet firm Magdalene. Siegfried Lorenz is a well-focused Beckmesser who refuses to carica-ture the much-mocked Town Clerk, and Kurt Moll is a magnificent Pogner. The chorus (balanced a little back-wardly) and orchestra play with the warmth and radiance associated with recordings made in the Herkulessaal in Munich.

Recorded live at the 1951 Bayreuth Festival, Karajan's EMI mono version has never quite been matched since for its involving intensity. With clean CD transfers, the sense of being present at a great event is irresistible, with the big emotional moments – both between Eva and Walther and, even more strikingly, between Eva and Sachs – bringing a gulp in the throat. The young Elisabeth Schwarzkopf makes the most radiant Eva, singing her Act III solo *O Sachs, mein Freund!* with touching ardour before beginning the Quintet with flawless legato. Hans Hopf is here less gritty than in his other recordings, an attractive hero; while Otto Edelmann makes a superb Sachs, firm and virile, the more moving for not sounding old. There are inconsistencies among the others but, in a performance of such electricity generated by the conductor in his early prime, they are of minimal importance. The four mid-priced CDs are generously in-dexed and supplied with a libretto – however, unfortunately no translation has been included. EMI should have indicated the index points not just in the libretto, but in the English synopsis as well.

In setting up their later star-studded stereo version, EMI fell down badly in the choice of Sachs. Theo Adam, prom-ising in many ways, has quite the wrong voice for the part, in one way too young-sounding, in another too grating, not focused enough. However, after that keen disappointment there is much to enjoy, for in a modestly reverberant acoustic (a smallish church was used) Karajan draws from the Dresden players and chorus a rich performance which re-tains a degree of bourgeois intimacy. Donath is a touching, sweet-toned Eva, Kollo here is as true and ringing a Walther as one could find today. Sir Geraint Evans is an incomparably vivid Beckmesser, and Ridderbusch is a glorious-toned Pogner. Anyone wanting a widely expansive sound will be disappointed, but Karajan's thoughtful approach and the presence of perhaps the finest Eva on any current set makes this a good choice for those who are not upset by Adam's ungenial Sachs. However whether this is one of the 'Great Recordings of the Century' is much less sure. This description might much more readily have been applied to Karajan's earlier mono version.

Though Kempe's classic EMI set is in mono only, one misses stereo surprisingly little when, with closely balanced voices, there is such clarity and sharpness of focus. The orchestra to a degree loses out, sounding relatively thin; but with such an incandescent performance – not quite as intense as Karajan's live Bayreuth version of 1951 but consistently inspired – one quickly adjusts. The cast has no weak link. Elisabeth Grümmer is a meltingly beautiful Eva, pure and girlish, not least in the great Act III Quintet, and Rudolf Schock gives the finest of all his recorded performances as Walther, with his distinctive timbre between lyric and heroic well suited to the role. Ferdinand Frantz is a weighty, dark-toned Sachs, Gottlob Frick a commanding Pogner, Benno Kusche a clear-toned Beckmesser and Gerhard Unger an aptly light David.

The great glory of Solti's earlier set is the mature and involving portrayal of Sachs by Norman Bailey. Kurt Moll as Pogner, Bernd Weikl as Beckmesser and Julia Hamari as Magdalene are all excellent, but the shortcomings are comparably serious. Both Hannelore Bode and René Kollo fall short of their far-from-perfect contributions to earlier sets, and Solti for all his energy gives a surprisingly square reading of this most appealing of Wagner scores, pointing his expressive lines too heavily and failing to convey spontaneity. It remains an impressive achievement for Bailey's marvellous Sachs, and the Decca sound comes up vividly on CD.

Recorded live at the 1999 Bayreuth Festival, Barenboim's version starts well with a thrustful account of the Overture, helped by full, immediate sound, but problems develop rapidly from then on, with the orchestra close but the voices set in a far more spacious acoustic, with the chorus distant and ill-defined. Too often over the great span of the three acts, Barenboim's direction grows uncharacteristically stodgy and square, with jog-trot rhythms evenly stressed. Vocally the great glory of the set is the singing of Peter Seiffert as Walther, amply heroic in scale but clear toned and never strained. His feeling for words is always illuminating, and his performance is crowned by a superb account of the *Prize Song* in Act III. Emma Magee is an impressive Eva too, the voice warm, the manner fresh and girlish. Both of them are sharply contrasted with the pedestrian Hans Sachs of Robert Holl, lacking weight, with the voice no longer so cleanly focused and with little feeling for the character. This is a dull dog of a Sachs with little or no sense of humour. Andreas Schmidt sings well as Beckmesser in a clean-cut, unexaggerated reading, but that too minimizes the sparkle of the inspiration.

Die Meistersinger: highlights.

(M) *** DG 445 470-2 (from complete set; cond. Jochum).

(B) (***) CfP CD-CFP 6086 (from complete set; cond. Kempe).

(M) **(*) EMI CDM7 63455-2 (from complete set; cond. Karajan).

Jochum's DG excerpts are especially valuable for giving fair samples of the two most individual performances: Fischer-Dieskau as a sharply incisive Sachs, his every nuance of mood clearly interpreted, and Domingo a golden-toned if hardly idiomatic Walther. The 76-minute selection, opening with the *Overture*, includes the Act III *Quintet*, and also the opera's closing scene.

The 72-minute selection from Kempe's classic EMI mono set provides generous samples of Ferdinand Frantz's comparatively weighty, dark-toned Sachs. Rudolf Schock is ideally suited to the role of Walther, and Elisabeth Grümmer is a memorable Eva.

Many will prefer to have a sampler rather than investing in the complete Karajan stereo set, which is let down by the casting of Theo Adam as Sachs. The selection runs to nearly 68 minutes.

Parsifal (complete).

☀ *** DG 413 347-2 (4). Hofmann, Vejzovic, Moll, Van Dam, Nimsgern, Von Halem, German Op. Ch., BPO, Karajan.

*** Teldec 9031 74448-2 (4). Jerusalem, Van Dam, Hölle, Meier, Von Kannen, Tomlinson, Berlin State Op. Ch., BPO, Barenboim.

*** Decca (ADD) 417 143-2 (4). Kollo, Ludwig, Fischer-Dieskau, Hotter, Kelemen, Frick, V. Boys' Ch., V. State Op. Ch., VPO, Solti.

**(*) Koch-Schwann (ADD) 3-1348-2 (4). Kollo, Adam, Cold, Schröter, Bunger, Teschler, Leipzig and Berlin R. Choirs, Thomanenchor Leipzig, Leipzig RSO, Kegel.

**(*) DG 437 501-2 (4). Domingo, Norman, Moll, Morris, Wlaschiha, Rootering, Met. Op. Ch. & O, Levine.

(M) **(*) DG (ADD) 435 718-2 (3). King, Jones, Stewart, Ridderbusch, McIntyre, Crass, (1970) Bayreuth Festival Ch. & O, Boulez.

(M) (**(*)) RCA mono 74321 61950-2 (4). Uhl, Waechter, Höngen or Ludwig, Hotter, Berry, V. State Op. Ch. & O, Karajan.

(N) **(*) Ph. (ADD) 464 756-2 (4). Thomas, Dalis, London, Talvela, Neidlinger, Hotter, (1962) Bayreuth Festival Ch. & O, Knappertsbusch.

(M) (***) Teldec mono 9031 76047-2 (4). Windgassen, Mödl, Weber, London, Uhde, Van Mill, (1951) Bayreuth Festival Ch. & O, Knappertsbusch.

Communion, musical and spiritual, is what this intensely beautiful Karajan set provides. The playing of the Berlin orchestra is consistently beautiful, enhanced by the clarity and refinement of the recording. Kurt Moll as Gurnemanz is the singer who, more than any other, anchors the work vocally, projecting his voice with firmness and subtlety. José van Dam as Amfortas is also splendid. The Klingsor of Siegmund Nimsgern could be more sinister, but the singing is admirable. Dunja Vejzovic makes a vibrant, sensuous Kundry who rises superbly to the moment in Act II when she bemoans her laughter in the face of Christ. Only Peter Hofmann as Parsifal brings any disappointment; at times he develops a gritty edge on the voice, but his natural tone is admirably suited to the part and he is never less than dramatically effective. He is not helped by the relative closeness of the solo voices, but otherwise the recording is near the atmospheric ideal, a superb achievement.

With Siegfried Jerusalem a superb Parsifal, one of the finest ever, both characterful and mellifluous, Daniel Barenboim's is a dedicated version with an excellent cast. Like Karajan, Barenboim draws glorious sounds from the Berlin Philharmonic, even if he cannot quite match his predecessor in concentrated intensity, well sustained as his control of long paragraphs is. Waltraud Meier as in rival versions is an outstanding, darkly intense Kundry, and José van Dam is superb as Amfortas, clean of attack, as he was for Karajan. John Tomlinson is a resonant, if young-sounding Titurel, and Gunther von Kannen a clear and direct, if unvillainous, even noble Klingsor. The relatively weak link is the Gurnemanz of Matthias Hölle, warm-toned but slightly unsteady, not quite in character.

Solti's singing cast could hardly be stronger, every one of them pointing words with fine, illuminating care for detail; and the complex balances of sound, not least in the *Good Friday Music*, are beautifully caught; throughout, Solti shows his sustained intensity in Wagner. What is rather missing is a rapt, spiritual quality. The remastering for CD, as with Solti's other Wagner recordings, opens up the sound, and the choral climaxes are superb.

Recorded live at a concert performance in East Berlin in 1975, Kegel is a more passionate Wagnerian than Pierre Boulez, similarly brisk in this opera. Kegel draws incandescent singing from his massed choirs, with the spacious recording capturing the bloom on the vocal sound atmospherically, with choral antiphonies most beautiful. René Kollo as Parsifal and Theo Adam as Amfortas were then still in their prime and sing magnetically. The others, less celebrated, still comprise a fresh-sounding team, clean of attack, notably Ulric Cold as Gurnemanz. Gisela Schröter, lighter of tone than usual for Kundry and with a tight vibrato, also sings beautifully. Reid Bunger is a youngish-sounding Klingsor with a villainous snarl. The layout on four discs is not only inconvenient (with breaks in each Act) but extravagant, when it could easily have been accommodated on three.

James Levine's speeds outstrip almost anyone in slowness, with the New York studio performance at times hanging fire – as in the Transformation scene of Act I. Many will find it a small price to pay for a performance, vividly recorded, involving a cast as starry as any that could be assembled. Jessye Norman as Kundry and Plácido Domingo in the title-role give performances that in every way live up to their reputations, not just exploiting beauty of sound but backing it with keen characterization and concern for word-meaning. Kurt Moll as Gurnemanz and Ekkehard Wlaschiha as Klingsor are both magnificent, firm and characterful, while James Morris as Amfortas gives a powerful performance, with a slightly gritty tone adding to the character's

sense of pain. Jan-Henrik Rootering's bass as Titurel is atmospherically enhanced by an echo-chamber, pointing the relative lack of reverberation in the main, firmly focused recording, one of the most vivid yet made in the Manhattan Center.

By contrast, Boulez's speeds are so consistently fast that in the age of CD it has brought an obvious benefit in being fitted – easily – on three discs instead of four, yet Boulez's approach, with the line beautifully controlled, conveys a dramatic urgency rarely found in this opera, and never sounds breathless, with textures clarified in a way characteristic of Boulez. Even the flower-maidens sing like young apprentices in *Meistersinger* rather than seductive beauties. James King is a firm, strong, rather baritonal hero, Thomas Stewart a fine, tense Amfortas, and Gwyneth Jones as Kundry is in strong voice, only occasionally shrill, but Franz Crass is disappointingly unsteady as Gurnemanz.

The Karajan RCA recording from the Vienna State Opera was made live in 1961, almost twenty years before his incandescent studio recording for DG. In limited mono sound there is none of the glowing beauty of the later recording, but what matters is the thrusting intensity of the whole performance, magnetic throughout with a fine cast. The controversial point at the time – well described in the notes on the background to the recording – was that for the role of Kundry two singers were chosen, one for the haggard creature of Acts 1 and 3, Elisabeth Höngen, and another, Christa Ludwig, for the transformed seductress of Act 2, set in Klingsor's magic castle. In practice those are just the differences one wants, with the voices reflecting the visual contrast, for the young Ludwig sings with a more voluptuous tone, while Höngen, an older singer, giving weight to the drama. The others make a first-rate team, even if Fritz Uhl – later Tristan in the Solti recording – is on the light side. Hans Hotter at his peak makes a powerful Gurnemanz, with Eberhard Waechter a clear, incisive Amfortas and Walter Berry dark and sinister yet flexible as Klingsor. A fascinating document.

Knappertsbusch's expansive and dedicated 1962 reading is caught superbly in the Philips set, one of the finest live recordings ever made in the Festspielhaus at Bayreuth, with outstanding singing from Jess Thomas as Parsifal and Hans Hotter as Gurnemanz. Though Knappertsbusch chooses consistently slow tempi, there is no sense of excessive squareness or length, so intense is the concentration of the performance, its spiritual quality; and the sound has been further enhanced in the remastering for CD. The snag is that the stage noises and coughs are also emphasized, particularly disturbing in the *Prelude*.

The Teldec historic reissue is taken from the first season in 1951 and makes a striking contrast with the later Knappertsbusch recording, made in stereo for Philips eleven years later. The 1951 performance is no less than twenty minutes longer overall, with Knappertsbusch, always expansive, even more dedicated than in his later reading. The cast is even finer, with Wolfgang Windgassen making most other Heldentenors seem rough by comparison, singing with warmth as well as power. Ludwig Weber is magnificently dark-toned as Gurnemanz, much more an understanding human being than his successor, Hans Hotter, less of a conventionally noble figure. Martha Mödl is both wild and abrasive in her first scenes and sensuously seductive in the long Act II duet with Parsifal, and Hermann Uhde is bitingly firm as Klingsor. Though the limited mono sound is not nearly as immediate or atmospheric as the later stereo, with much thinner orchestral texture, the voices come over well, and the chorus is well caught.

Das Rheingold (complete).

*** Decca (ADD) 455 556-2 (2). London, Flagstad, Svanholm, Neidlinger, VPO, Solti.

*** Teldec 4509 91185-2 (2). Tomlinson, Brinkmann, Schreibmayer, Clark, Finnie, Johansson, Svendén, Von Kannen, Pampuch, Hölle, Kang, Liedland, Küttenbaum, Turner, (1991) Bayreuth Festival O, Barenboim.

(M) **(*) DG (ADD) 457 781-2 (2). Fischer-Dieskau, Veasey, Stolze, Kelemen, BPO, Karajan.

(M) **(*) Ph. (ADD) 412 475-2 (2). (from (1967) Bayreuth set; cond. Boehm).

(B) **(*) RCA 74321 45418-2 (2). Adam, Nimsgern, Stryczek, Schreier, Bracht, Salminen, Vogel, Büchner, Minton, Popp, Priew, Schwarz, Dresden State O & Ch., Janowski.

(N) (B) (***) Naxos mono 8.110047-48 (2). Schorr, Huehn, Clemens, Maison, Habich, Laufkötter, Cordon, List, Branzell, Manski, Doe, Andreva, Petina, Met. Op. O and Ch., Artur Bodanzky.

(BB) *(*) Arte Nova 74321 63650-2 (2) Dohmen, Michael, Martin, Zaladkiewicz, Bezuyen, San Carlo O, Naples, Kuhn.

The first of Solti's cycle was recorded in 1958. The immediacy and precise placing are thrilling, while the sound-effects of the final scenes, including Donner's hammer-blow and the Rainbow bridge, have never been matched since. Solti gives a magnificent reading of the score, crisp, dramatic and direct. Vocally, the set is held together by the unforgettable singing of Neidlinger as Alberich. He vocalizes with wonderful precision and makes the character of the dwarf develop from the comic creature of the opening scene to the demented monster of the last. Flagstad learned the part of Fricka specially for this recording, and her singing makes one regret that she never took the role on the stage. George London is sometimes a little rough, but this is a dramatic portrayal of the young Wotan. Svanholm could be more characterful as Loge, but again it is a relief to hear the part really sung. An outstanding achievement.

When Barenboim as Wagnerian has at times seemed lethargic, what is particularly surprising is the dramatic tension of the performance. Even with slow speeds, the sense of flow carries the ear on. Even with often-thunderous stage noises, the Barenboim performances magnetize you much more consistently, with the atmosphere of the Festspielhaus well caught by the engineers. It is very satisfying too to have on disc John Tomlinson's magnificent performance as Wotan, Graham Clark as an electrifying, dominant Loge and Linda Finnie a thoughtful, intense Fricka.

Karajan's reflectiveness of approach has its less welcome side, for the tension rarely varies. One finds such incidents as Alberich's stealing of the gold or Donner's hammer blow passing by without one's pulse quickening as it should. On the credit side however, the singing cast has hardly any

flaw at all, and Fischer-Dieskau's Wotan is a brilliant and memorable creation, virile and expressive. Among the others, Veasey is excellent, though obviously she cannot efface memories of Flagstad; Gerhard Stolze with his flickering almost *Sprechstimme* as Loge gives an immensely vivid, if (for some) controversial interpretation. The 1968 sound has been clarified and further opened up in the new transfer.

Boehm's performance is marred by the casting of Theo Adam as Wotan, keenly intelligent but rarely agreeable on the ear, at times here far too wobbly. On the other hand, Gustav Neidlinger as Alberich is superb, even more involving here than he is for Solti, with the curse made spine-chilling. It is also good to have Wolfgang Windgassen as Loge; among the others, Anja Silja makes an attractively urgent Freia.

Janowski's distinguished *Rheingold* is now the least expensive recommendable set on CD. The studio sound, nicely ambient, has the voices close and vivid, with the orchestra in the background. If the result lacks the atmospheric qualities which make the Solti *Rheingold* still the most compelling in sound, the effect still grips the listener, though Donner's hammer-blow brings only a very ordinary anvil stroke. Theo Adam, in spite of some grittiness of tone, makes a fine Wotan and the set is consistently well cast, including Peter Schreier, Matti Salminen, Yvonne Minton and Lucia Popp, as well as East German singers of high calibre. The current transfer is very impressive and the set is very well documented.

The briskness of Artur Bodanzky as a Wagnerian, often disturbing in other operas, works well in the narrative of *Rheingold*, with the dramatic bite of each scene strongly conveyed. The recording was made in April 1937 not at the Met itself but at the Boston Opera House with sound still limited but capturing the voices well. It is specially valuable to have the great Friedrich Schorr as Wotan, firm as a rock, strong and purposeful throughout, up to the magnificent final solo. Karin Branzell is a warm, clear Fricka, Eduard Habich an incisive Alberich and Emanuel List a magnificent Fafner, with the whole cast firm and clear if not always subtle. Even the neighing tone of Rene Maison as Loge can be regarded as characterful. A fascinating document, the more welcome at super-bargain price.

A recommendable super-bargain stereo version of *Rheingold* would be very welcome, but this live recording made at the Tirol festival, is very flawed. The playing of the Naples orchestra is limp at times, failing to create dramatic tension, and though the recording is full and immediate, it is too dry to convey much atmosphere or to put bloom on the voices. Albert Dohmen is a strong, virile Wotan, but his firm baritone grows gritty under pressure; Nadja Michael is a fruity-toned Fricka, Andrea Martin is a clear, incisive Alberich, and Arnold Bezuyen a characterful, snarling Loge. Otherwise a middling cast, reliable but with few beautiful voices. Libretto in German with synopsis in English. Janowski's bargain set on RCA is well worth the extra money.

The Rhinegold (Das Rheingold) (complete, in English).

(N) (M) **(*) Chan. (ADD) 3054 (3). Bailey, Hammond-Stroud, Pring, Belcourt, Attfield, Collins, McDonnall, Lloyd, Grant, ENO O, Goodall.

Goodall's slow tempi in *Rheingold* bring an opening section where the temperature is low, reflecting hardly at all the tensions of a live performance, even though this was taken from a series of Coliseum presentations. Nevertheless the momentum of Wagner gradually builds up so that, by the final scenes, both the overall teamwork and the individual contributions of such singers as Norman Bailey, Derek Hammond-Stroud and Clifford Grant come together impressively. Hammond-Stroud's powerful representation of Alberich culminates in a superb account of the curse. The spectacular orchestral effects (with the horns sounding glorious) are vividly caught by the engineers and impressively transferred to CD, even if balances (inevitably) are sometimes less than ideal.

Rienzi (complete).

(M) ** EMI (ADD) CMS7 63980-2 (3). Kollo, Wennberg, Martin, Adam, Hillebrand, Vogel, Schreier, Leipzig R. Ch., Dresden State Op. Ch., Dresden State O, Hollreiser.

It is sad that the flaws in this ambitious opera prevent the unwieldy piece from having its full dramatic impact. This recording is not quite complete, but the cuts are unimportant and most of the set numbers make plain the youthful exuberance of the ambitious composer. Except in the recitative, Heinrich Hollreiser's direction is strong and purposeful, but much of the singing is disappointing. René Kollo sounds heroic, but the two women principals are poor. Janis Martin in the breeches role of Adriano produces tone that does not record very sweetly, while Siv Wennberg as the heroine, Rienzi's sister, slides unpleasantly between notes in the florid passages. Despite good recording, this is only a stop-gap.

Der Ring des Nibelungen: an introduction to The Ring by Deryck Cooke, with 193 music examples.

(M) *** Decca (ADD) 443 581-2 (2). VPO, Solti.

The reissue of Deryck Cooke's fascinating and scholarly lecture is most welcome. Even though the CD reissue omits the printed text, the principal musical motives are all printed out in the accompanying booklet and they demonstrate just how the many leading ideas in *The Ring* develop from one another, springing from an original germ. The discourse is riveting, though even dedicated Wagnerians may not want to hear it many times over. The music examples, many of them specially prepared, are clumsily inserted, but this is still a thoroughly worthwhile acquisition for those who already have recordings of the operas.

Der Ring des Nibelungen (complete).

✪ (M) *** Decca (ADD) 455 555-2 (14). Nilsson, Windgassen, Flagstad, Fischer-Dieskau, Hotter, London, Ludwig, Neidlinger, Frick, Svanholm, Stolze, Böhme, Hoffgen, Sutherland, Crespin, King, Watson, Ch. & VPO, Solti.

(B) *** Ph. (ADD) 446 057-2 (14). Nilsson, Windgassen, Neidlinger, Adam, Rysanek, King, Nienstedt, Esser, Talvela, Böhme, Silja, Dernesch, Stewart, Hoeffgen, (1967) Bayreuth Festival Ch. & O, Boehm.

(B) *** EMI (ADD) CZS 72731-2 (14). Behrens, Varady,

Lipovšek, Schwarz, Hale, Kollo, Wlaschiha, Schunk, Tear, Rootering, Bav. State Opera Ch. & O, Sawallisch.

(B) *** RCA 74321 45417-2 (14). Altmeyer, Kollo, Adam, Schreier, Nimsgern, Vogel, Minton, Wenkel, Salminen, Popp, Jerusalem, Norman, Moll, Studer, Leipzig R. Ch., Dresden State Op. Ch. & O, Janowski.

(M) *** DG (ADD) 457 780-2 (14). Veasey, Fischer-Dieskau, Stolze, Kelemen, Dernesch, Dominguez, Jess Thomas, Stewart, Crespin, Janowitz, Vickers, Talvela, Brilioth, Ludwig, Ridderbusch, BPO, Karajan.

(M) **(*) EMI CMS7 64775-2 (14). Marton, Morris, Lipovšek, Sednik, Adam, Haage, Jerusalem, Te Kanawa, Rydl, Rappé, Studer, Goldberg, Meier, Salminen, Hampson, Tomlinson, Bundschuh, Bav. R. Ch. & SO, Haitink.

(M) (***) EMI mono CZS7 67123-2 (13). Suthaus, Mödl, Frantz, Patzak, Neidlinger, Windgassen, Konetzni, Streich, Jurinac, Frick, RAI Ch. & Rome SO, Furtwängler.

Solti's was the first recorded *Ring* cycle to be issued. Whether in performance or in vividness of sound, it remains the most electrifying account of the tetralogy on disc, sharply focused if not always as warmly expressive as some. Solti himself developed in the process of making the recording, and *Götterdämmerung* represents a peak of achievement for him, commanding and magnificent. Though CD occasionally reveals bumps and bangs which were inaudible on the original LPs, this is a historic set that remains as central today as when it was first released. The latest remastering is very impressive and the layout is improved, with the set now taking up 14 discs. The original artwork is used throughout on the boxes.

Recorded at the 1967 Bayreuth Festival, Boehm's fine set captures the unique atmosphere and acoustic of the Festspielhaus very vividly. Birgit Nilsson as Brünnhilde and Wolfgang Windgassen as Siegfried are both a degree more volatile and passionate than they were in the Solti cycle. Gustav Neidlinger as Alberich is also superb, as he was too in the Solti set; and the only major reservation concerns the Wotan of Theo Adam, in a performance searchingly intense and finely detailed but often unsteady of tone even at that period. The sound, only occasionally constricted, has been vividly transferred. In the UK Philips are offering this version of the *Ring* in a 14-disc limited edition (in effect for a limited time) at bargain price.

On 14 discs also at bargain price, the Sawallisch version of the *Ring* makes an excellent recommendation. This is the sound-track of the Bavarian State Opera production by Nikolaus Lehnhoff, as recorded in 1989 for television. The cast is as fine as any in rival versions of the digital age, the performances gain in dramatic momentum and expressive spontaneity from being recorded live, and – rather surprisingly – the sound is outstandingly rich, warm and spaciously atmospheric, in many ways outshining rival digital recordings. Sawallisch conducts with a thrust and energy not always present in his studio recordings, with speeds often faster than have become common. One minor quibble is that both *Walküre* and *Siegfried* could each have been fitted easily on to three CDs instead of four. As to the casting, Robert Hale proves a noble Wotan, virile and strong. The voice may not be beautiful, but the range of expression is great, so that in *Walküre* the final moment of his kissing Brünnhilde's godhead away could hardly be more tender.

Dedication and consistency are the hallmarks of the (originally Eurodisc) *Ring*, a series of studio recordings made between 1980 and 1983 with German thoroughness by the then East German record company, Eurodisc. It is now reissued by RCA on 14 budget-priced CDs, to make it a highly attractive bargain. Voices tend to be balanced well forward of the orchestra, but the digital sound is admirably full as well as clear. The clarity has one concentrating on the words, helped by Janowski's vividly direct approach to the score. Overall this is more rewarding than many of the individual sets that have been issued at full price over the years since it first appeared. The documentation is first class.

Karajan's DG recording originally followed close on the heels of Solti's for Decca, providing a good alternative studio version which equally stands the test of time, even if *Siegfried* has its disappointments. The manner is smoother, the speeds generally broader, yet the tension and concentration of the performances are maintained more consistently than in most modern studio recordings. Casting is not quite consistent between the operas, with Régine Crespin as Brünnhilde in *Walküre*, but Helga Dernesch at her very peak in the last two operas. The casting of Siegfried is changed between *Siegfried* and *Götterdämmerung*, from Jess Thomas to Helge Brilioth, just as strong but sweeter of tone.

Strong and purposeful, Haitink takes a thoughtful view which in each music-drama nevertheless builds up unerringly in tension and power, with the beauty of Wagner's orchestration consistently brought out. The recordings are warm and full, if not as sharply defined as they might be, and the principal snags lie in some of the casting, notably with Eva Marton as Brünnhilde, too often gusty and ill-focused. Theo Adam too is a disappointing Alberich, dramatically intense but unable any longer to sustain a steady line. James Morris as Wotan yields to other singers in the role. For the rest, a strong and compelling issue, still (arguably) technically the best studio recording of the *Ring* in digital sound. However, this set is now withdrawn.

In this digital transfer, the boxiness of the studio sound and the closeness of the voices still take away some of the unique Furtwängler glow in Wagner, but the sound is acceptable and benefits in some ways from extra clarity.

'The Best of The Ring': excerpts from *Das Rheingold; Die Walküre; Siegfried; Götterdämmerung*.

(B) *** Ph. Duo (ADD) 454 020-2 (2) (from (1967) Bayreuth Festival recordings; cond. Boehm).

The Ring: 'Great Scenes': *Das Rheingold: Prelude & Scene 1; Entry of the Gods into Valhalla. Die Walküre: Winterstürme; Ride of the Valkyries; Wotan's Farewell & Magic Fire Music. Siegfried: Forging Scene; Forest Murmurs. Götterdämmerung: Siegfried's Rhine Journey; Siegfried's Funeral March; Brünnhilde's Immolation Scene.*

(B) *** Double Decca (ADD) 448 933-2 (2). Nilsson, Windgassen, Kotter, Stolz, King, Crespin, VPO, Solti.

Although the Solti and Karajan selections have their appeal, as potted 'Rings' go, the Philips Duo is probably the best buy. Taken from Boehm's outstanding complete recording,

it can be warmly enjoyed as a summary of Wagner's intentions, with most of the key scenes included. The only snag is that Bernard Jacobson's very brief synopsis of the narrative fails to relate each track to the story.

With 144 minutes of music included on this Decca Double, the excerpts from Solti's *Ring* are quite extended. *Das Rheingold* begins with the Prelude and the sequence continues for 24 minutes, the *Entry of the Gods into Valhalla* opens spectacularly and offers some 10 minutes of music, while the excerpts from *Die Walküre* include the Sieglinde/Siegmund *Winterstürme* duet (15 minutes) and the whole of *Wotan's Farewell & Magic Fire Music*. *Götterdämmerung* leads with *Siegfried's Rhine Journey* and closes with the *Immolation Scene* – some 20 minutes for each excerpt, with the tailoring expertly done in between. The only snag is the absence of any narrative cues within the sparse documentation; but the music itself is thrillingly projected.

The Ring: highlights: *Das Rheingold: Lugt, Schwestern! Die Wenken lacht in den Grund; Zur Burg führt die Brücke. Die Walküre: Der Männer Sippe sass hier im Saal; Ride of the Valkyries; Wotan's Farewell & Magic Fire Music. Siegfried: Forest Murmurs; Aber, wie sah meine Mutter wohl aus?; Nun sing! Ich lausche dem Gesang; Heil dir, Sonne! Heil dir, Licht!. Götterdämmerung: Funeral Music; Fliegt heim, ihr Raben!*

(B) *** DG (ADD) 439 423-2 (from complete recording; cond. Karajan).

The task of selecting highlights to fit on a single disc, taken from the whole of the *Ring* cycle, is daunting. But the DG producer of this Classikon super-bargain issue has extended the previous selection to 77 minutes and managed to assemble many key items, either very well tailored or ending satisfactorily. The whole of Wotan's great *Farewell* scene with the *Magic Fire Music* is included, and much else besides. Moreover the *Funeral Music* from *Götterdämmerung* (where the previous CD ended) is now followed by *Brünnhilde's Immolation* and continues to the end of the opera. The transfers are extremely brilliant, making this a most attractive bargain reissue.

Siegfried (complete).

*** Decca 455 564-2 (4). Windgassen, Nilsson, Hotter, Stolze, Neidlinger, Böhme, Hoffgen, Sutherland, VPO, Solti.

*** Teldec 4509 94193-2 (4). Jerusalem, Anne Evans, Tomlinson, Clark, Von Kannen, Philip King, Svendén, Leidland, (1992) Bayreuth Festival Ch. & O, Barenboim.

*** Ph. (IMS) 412 483-2 (4). Windgassen, Nilsson, Adam, Neidlinger, Soukupová, Köth, Böhme, (1967) Bayreuth Festival Ch. & O, Boehm.

(M) *** Ph. 434 423-2 (3). Jung, G. Jones, McIntyre, Zednik, Becht, Wenkel, Hübner, Sharp, (1980) Bayreuth Festival O, Boulez.

(B) *** RCA 74321 45420-2 (4). Kollo, Altmeyer, Adam, Schreier, Nimsgern, Wenkel, Salminen, Sharp, Dresden State O, Janowski.

(N) (BB) *(**) Arte Nova 74321 72116-2 (4). Woodrow, Wachutka, Uusitalo, Harper, Singers of the Montegral Academy, Tyrol Fest. O, Kuhn.

(M) ** DG 457 790-2 (4). Dernesch, Dominguez, Jess Thomas, Stolze, Stewart, Kelemen, BPO, Karajan.

Siegfried has too long been thought of as the grimmest of the *Ring* cycle, but a performance as buoyant as Solti's reveals that, more than in most Wagner, the message is one of optimism. Each of the three Acts ends with a scene of triumphant joy. Solti's array of singers could hardly be bettered. Windgassen is at the very peak of his form, lyrical as well as heroic. Hotter has never been more impressive on record, his Wotan at last captured adequately. Stolze, Neidlinger and Böhme are all exemplary, and predictably Joan Sutherland makes the most seductive of woodbirds. With singing finer than any opera house could normally provide, with masterly playing from the Vienna Philharmonic and with Decca's most vivid recording, this is still unsurpassed. As with the rest of the series, the present newly remastered and enhanced CDs have cleaned up background noises.

Barenboim's live recording is the finest of latterday digitally recorded versions. There is no finer interpreter of the role of Mime today than Graham Clark. In the title-role Siegfried Jerusalem completely outshines his already fine performance on Haitink's studio recording for EMI. His voice has grown fuller and more powerful without losing any beauty, and the recording helps to give it more weight. Few Siegfrieds since Wolfgang Windgassen begin to match him, and John Tomlinson is the firmest, most darkly projected Wanderer among current rivals. Tomlinson's superb singing goes with keen musical imagination and concern for word-meaning. As for Anne Evans as Brünnhilde, she too brings out the beauty of Wagner's lines, focusing cleanly and purely, with some thrilling top notes and not a suspicion of a wobble. The fifth principal is the splendid Erda of Brigitta Svendén, with other roles cast well, if not outstandingly. But what confirms this, recorded last in the series, as the high point in Barenboim's Bayreuth cycle is the incandescence of his conducting, given extra impact by the vivid sound and consistently reflecting his experience of working with these musicians.

The natural-sounding quality of Boehm's live recording from Bayreuth, coupled with his determination not to let the music lag, makes his account of *Siegfried* as satisfying as the rest of his cycle, vividly capturing the atmosphere of the Festspielhaus, with voices well ahead of the orchestra. Windgassen is at his peak here, if anything more poetic in Acts II and III than he is in Solti's studio recording, and vocally just as fine. Nilsson, as in *Götterdämmerung*, gains over her studio recording from the extra flow of adrenalin in a live performance; and Gustav Neidlinger is unmatchable as Alberich. Erika Köth is disappointing as the woodbird, not sweet enough, and Soukupová is a positive, characterful Erda. Theo Adam is at his finest as the Wanderer, less wobbly than usual, clean and incisive.

Boulez's version takes a disc less than usual and comes at mid-price in the Philips Bayreuth series. Here the advantage is even greater when each Act is complete on a single disc. If anything, Boulez is even more warmly expressive than in *Rheingold* or *Walküre*, directing a most poetic account of the *Forest Murmurs* episode and leading in each Act to

thrillingly intense conclusions. Manfred Jung is an underrated Siegfried, forthright and, by latterday standards, unusually clean-focused, and Heinz Zednik is a characterful Mime. As in the rest of the cycle, Sir Donald McIntyre is a noble Wotan, though Hermann Becht's weighty Alberich is not as strongly contrasted as it might be. Norma Sharp as the Woodbird enunciates her words with exceptional clarity and, though Gwyneth Jones as Brünnhilde has a few squally moments, she sings with honeyed beauty when the Idyll theme emerges, towards the end of the love duet. The digital sound is full and atmospheric, though it is a pity that the brass is not caught more weightily.

Janowski's *Siegfried* is in almost every way impressive. The singing is generally first rate with Kollo fine in the name role, hardly ever strained, and Peter Schreier a superb Mime, using Lieder-like qualities in detailed characterization. Siegmund Nimsgern is a less characterful Alberich, but the voice is excellent, and Theo Adam concludes his portrayal of Wotan/Wanderer with his finest performance of the series. There are a few less effective moments (Act II rather scurries to a close with Siegfried in pursuit of a rather shrill woodbird in Norma Sharp), but this is a small blot on a performance that brings cumulative tension in the splendid final scene. The relative lightness of Jeannine Altmeyer's Brünnhilde comes out in this love duet, but this matters far less on record than it would in the theatre. The tenderness and femininity are most affecting, as at the entry of the idyll motif, where Janowski in his dedicated simplicity is also at his most compelling, so that the opera moves to a thrilling close, with both singers at their finest. Clear, beautifully balanced, digital sound with voices and orchestra firmly placed. At bargain price this is splendid value.

The super-budget issue from Arte Nova is taken live from performances in the Tyrol festival in Austria in July 1999. The excitement of a live performance comes over well, with each act leading to a thrilling conclusion. Gustav Kuhn directs a clean-cut, well-structured performance, set in a relatively dry acoustic, with ample orchestral detail caught. The result may not be as weighty as usual, but is certainly compelling, with Alan Woodrow an outstanding, energetic Siegfried, fresh and clear, unstrained, characterizing vividly. By contrast, though Juha Uusitalo sings well as the Wanderer (Wotan), similarly firm and clear, he is not commanding as a character. Thomas Harper is an incisive Mime, and Elisabeth-Maria Wachutka is fresh and bright as Brünnhilde in Act III. If at first she seems rather lightweight, her clarity of attack is ample compensation with the closing duet rising a fine, warm climax. The booklet provides notes and synopsis, and the full libretto in German only. But this remains a welcome bargain.

When Siegfried is outsung by Mime, it is time to complain, and though Karajan's DG set has many fine qualities – not least the Brünnhilde of Helga Dernesch – it hardly rivals the Solti or Boehm versions. Windgassen on Decca gave a classic performance, and any comparison highlights the serious shortcomings of Jess Thomas. Even when voices are balanced forward, the digital transfer helps little to make Thomas's singing as Siegfried any more acceptable. Otherwise, the vocal cast is strong, and Karajan provides the seamless playing which characterizes his cycle. Recommended only to those irrevocably committed to the Karajan cycle, even though the current remastering is very successful.

Love duets: *Siegfried*, Act III, Scene 3. *Tristan*, Act II, Scene 2.

✿ (N) *** EMI CDC5 57004-2. Voigt, Domingo, ROHCGO, Pappano.

The great novelty here is the concert version of the Tristan love duet. Before Tristan was ever staged, Wagner prepared this concert version of the love duet, but it was never performed. Only recently James Levine unearthed it in the Bayreuth archives, and here generously allowed Antonio Pappano to make this first recording. What is fascinating is that instead of the duet being cut off unceremoniously on the arrival of King Mark, the music merges seamlessly into the closing pages of the whole opera, the final minutes of the Liebestod, but with a part for Tristan included too. As performed by Placido Domingo as Tristan and Deborah Voigt as Isolde, with Pappano an exceptionally warm Wagnerian, the result is sensuously beautiful, radiantly played and recorded. The closing scene from Siegfried too makes one long to hear Pappano in complete Wagner performances, with Voigt and Domingo strong and full-toned.

Siegfried (complete, in English).

(N) (M) *** Chan. 3045 (4). Remedios, Hunter, Bailey, Dempsey, Hammond-Stroud, Grant, Collins, London, Sadler's Wells Op. O, Goodall.

More tellingly than in almost any other Wagner opera recording, Goodall's spacious direction here conveys the genuine dramatic crunch that gives the experience of hearing Wagner in the opera house its unique power, its overwhelming force; this is unmistakably a great interpretation caught on the wing. Remedios, more than any rival on record, conveys not only heroic strength but clear-ringing youthfulness, caressing the ear as well as exciting it. Norman Bailey makes a magnificently noble Wanderer, steady of tone, and Gregory Dempsey is a characterful Mime, even if his deliberate whining tone is not well caught on record. The sound is superbly realistic, even making no allowances for the conditions. Lovers of opera in English should grasp the opportunity of hearing this unique set. This original EMI recording has now been reissued by Chandos under the auspices of the Peter Moores Foundation.

Tannhäuser (Paris version; complete).

*** DG 427 625-2 (3). Domingo, Studer, Baltsa, Salminen, Schmidt, Ch. & Philh. O, Sinopoli.

*** Decca (ADD) 414 581-2 (3). Kollo, Dernesch, Ludwig, Sotin, Braun, Hollweg, V. State Op. Ch., VPO, Solti.

(M) (**(*)) DG mono 457 682-2 (3). Beirer, Wächter, Frick, Brouwenstijn, Kmentt, Ludwig, Janowitz, V. State Op. Ch. & O, Karajan.

Plácido Domingo as Tannhäuser for Sinopoli brings balm to ears, producing sounds of much power as well as beauty. Sinopoli here makes one of his most passionately committed opera recordings, warmer and more flexible than Solti's Decca version, always individual, with fine detail brought out, always persuasive, and never wilful. Agnes Baltsa is

not ideally opulent of tone as Venus, but she is the complete seductress. Cheryl Studer – who sang the role of Elisabeth for Sinopoli at Bayreuth – gives a most sensitive performance, not always ideally even of tone but creating a movingly intense portrait of the heroine, vulnerable and very feminine. Matti Salminen in one of his last recordings makes a superb Landgrave and Andreas Schmidt a noble Wolfram, even though the legato could be smoother in *O star of Eve*.

Solti, however, gives one of his very finest Wagner performances on record, helped by superb playing from the Vienna Philharmonic and an outstanding cast, superlatively recorded. Dernesch as Elisabeth and Ludwig as Venus outshine all rivals; and Kollo, though not ideal, makes as fine a Heldentenor as we are currently likely to hear. The compact disc transfer reinforces the brilliance and richness of the performance. The sound is outstanding for its period (1971), and Ray Minshull's production adds to the atmospheric intensity.

Tannhäuser was the one Wagner opera in the central canon which Karajan did not record for a regular record company. That makes this Austrian Radio recording in mono the more valuable, dry and limited in sound as it is, with voices well forward and with little bloom on either voices or instruments. Using the revised and expanded Paris version of the score, the recording dates from January 1963, revealing how Karajan varied his approach to each Act. With a hectic account of the *Venusberg Music* he is urgent and passionate in Act I, but that leads to a more measured manner in Act II, and an unusually spacious one in the tragedy of Act III. In the title-role the Heldentenor Hans Beirer is variable, with no bark in his powerful voice but with some juddery unevenness to spoil the focus, more happily cast in Acts II and III than in Act I. As in her later recording for Solti, Christa Ludwig is a magnificent Venus, and the Dutch soprano Gré Brouwenstijn, too little recorded, an impressive Elisabeth. Gottlob Frick is a powerful, dark-toned Hermann, and Eberhard Wächter a lyrical Wolfram, with fine legato in *O Star of Eve*.

Tannhäuser (Dresden version; complete).

(M) **(*) EMI (ADD) CMS7 63214-2 (3). Hopf, Grümmer, Fischer-Dieskau, Schech, Frick, German State Op., Berlin, Ch. & O, Konwitschny.

The Konwitschny set is a fine one, marred by one serious flaw: the coarse singing of Hans Hopf in the title role; he fails to convey the joyous lyricism of the part, straining much of the time and with plenty of intrusive aitches. The opening scene with Venus is particularly daunting since Marianne Schech is the other disappointing member of the cast and, when they wobble together, the result is not far from comic. Happily things improve rapidly. Elisabeth Grümmer, Fischer-Dieskau and Gottlob Frick are all magnificent, and Konwitschny draws enthusiastic playing and singing from everyone. The chorus, important in this opera, is especially good, and the atmospheric recording adds to the warmth of the performance.

Tannhäuser (Dresden version): highlights.

(M) *(**) Ph. (IMS) (ADD) 446 620-2 (from complete set, with Windgassen, Silja, Waechter, Bumbry, (1962) Bayreuth Festival Ch. & O, Sawallisch).

With a generally good cast, and with Bumbry's sensuous Venus getting the opera off to an impressive start, many collectors will be glad to have these extensive (78 minutes) excerpts from Sawallisch's dedicated performance of the Dresden version of *Tannhäuser*; the major drawback is the lack of a cued synopsis.

Tristan und Isolde (complete).

(M) *** EMI (ADD) CMS7 69319-2 (4). Vickers, Dernesch, Ludwig, Berry, Ridderbusch, German Op. Ch., Berlin, BPO, Karajan.

*** Teldec 4509 94568-2 (4). Meier, Jerusalem, Lipovšek, Salminen, Struckmann, Berlin State Op. Ch., BPO, Barenboim.

(M) *** DG (ADD) 449 772-2 (3). Windgassen, Nilsson, Ludwig, Talvela, Waechter, Bayreuth Festival (1966) Ch. & O, Boehm.

(M) *** Decca (IMS) (ADD) 430 234-2 (4). Uhl, Nilsson, Resnik, Van Mill, Krause, VPO, Solti.

(N) (M) (***) EMI mono CMS5 67621-2 (4). Suthaus, Flagstad, Thebom, Greindl, Fischer-Dieskau, ROHCG Ch., Philh. O, Furtwängler.

(M) **(*) Decca 443 682-2 (4). Mitchinson, Gray, Howell, Joll, Wilkens, Folwell, Welsh Nat. Op. Ch. & O, Goodall.

Karajan's is a sensual performance of Wagner's masterpiece, caressingly beautiful and with superbly refined playing from the Berlin Philharmonic. Dernesch as Isolde is seductively feminine, not as noble as Flagstad, not as tough and un-flinching as Nilsson; but the human quality makes this account if anything more moving still, helped by glorious tone-colour through every range. Jon Vickers matches her in what is arguably his finest performance on record, allowing himself true pianissimo shading. The rest of the cast is excellent too. The recording has been remastered again for the present reissue and the 1972 sound has plenty of body, making this an excellent first choice, with inspired con-ducting and the most satisfactory cast of all. The set has also been attractively repackaged.

As a Furtwängler devotee, Barenboim has learnt much from that master's classic recording, and Act I is comparably spacious. After that the urgency of the drama prompts speeds that move forward more readily than Furtwängler's. The cast is an exceptionally strong one, with Waltraud Meier as Isolde graduating from mezzo soprano to full soprano, breasting the top Cs easily, showing no sign of strain, and bringing a weight and intensity to the role that reflect her earlier experience. The vibrato sometimes grows obtrusive, and even in the final *Liebestod* there is a touch of rawness under pressure; but the feeling for line is masterly, always with words vividly expressed. Siegfried Jerusalem, with a more beautiful voice than most latterday Heldentenoren, makes a predictably fine Tristan, not quite as smooth of tone as he once was and conveying the poignancy of the hero's plight in Act III rather than his suffering. Marjana Lipovšek is among the most characterful of Brangänes, strong and vehement, while Matti Salminen is a resonant, moving King Mark. Only the gritty tones of Falk Struckmann

as Kurwenal fall short. With weighty, full-ranging and well-balanced sound, this is a first-rate recommendation for a modern digital set.

Boehm's Bayreuth performance offers one great benefit in presenting this without any breaks at all, with each Act uninterrupted. Boehm is on the urgent side in this opera and the orchestral ensemble is not always immaculate; but the performance glows with intensity from beginning to end, carried through in the longest spans. Birgit Nilsson sings the *Liebestod* at the end of the long evening as though she was starting out afresh, radiant and with not a hint of tiredness, rising to an orgasmic climax and bringing a heavenly pianissimo on the final rising octave to F sharp. Opposite Nilsson is Wolfgang Windgassen, the most mel-lifluous of Heldentenoren; though the microphone balance sometimes puts him at a disadvantage to his Isolde, the realism and sense of presence of the whole set bathes you in the authentic atmosphere of Bayreuth. Making up an almost unmatchable cast are Christa Ludwig as Brangaene, Eber-hard Waechter as Kurwenal, and Martti Talvela as King Mark, with the young Peter Schreier as the Young Sailor.

Solti's performance is less flexible and sensuous than Karajan's, but he shows himself ready to relax in Wagner's more expansive periods. On the other hand the end of Act I and the opening of the Love duet have a knife-edged dramatic tension. Nilsson is masterly in her conviction and she never attacks below the note, so that at the end of the Love duet the impossibly difficult top Cs come out and hit the listener crisply and cleanly, dead on the note; and the *Liebestod* is all the more moving for clean attack at the climax. Fritz Uhl is a sensitive Heldentenor, rather light-weight, but his long solo passages in Act III are superb. The Kurwenal of Tom Krause and the King Mark of Arnold van Mill are both excellent and it is only Regina Resnik as Brangäne who gives any disappointment. The production has the usual Decca/Culshaw imaginative touch, and the recording matches brilliance and clarity with satisfying co-ordination and richness.

Wilhelm Furtwängler's concept is spacious from the opening *Prelude* onwards, but equally the bite and colour of the drama are vividly conveyed, matching the nobility of Flagstad's portrait of Isolde. The richly commanding power of her singing and her always distinctive timbre make it a uniquely compelling performance. Suthaus is not of the same calibre as Heldentenor, but he avoids ugliness and strain. Among the others, the only remarkable performance comes from the young Fischer-Dieskau as Kurwenal, not ideally cast but keenly imaginative. One endearing oddity is that – on Flagstad's insistence – the top Cs at the opening of the Love duet were sung by Elisabeth Schwarzkopf. The Kingsway Hall recording was admirably balanced, catching the beauty of the Philharmonia Orchestra at its peak. The CDs have opened up the original mono sound and it is remarkable how little constriction there is in the biggest climaxes, and this now takes its place as one of EMI's 'Great Recordings of the Century'.

Goodall's recording of *Tristan* was made in 1980/81, not on stage but at Brangwyn Hall, Swansea, just when the cast was prepared for stage performances. Typically from Goodall, it is measured and steady, but the speeds are not all exceptionally slow and, with rhythms sharply defined and textures made transparent, he keeps the momentum going. The WNO orchestra is not sumptuous, but the playing is well-tuned and responsive. Neither Linda Esther Gray nor John Mitchinson is as sweet on the ear as the finest rivals, for the microphone exaggerates vibrato in both. But Mitchinson never barks, Heldentenor-style, and Gray provides a formidable combination of qualities: feminine vulnerability alongside commanding power. Gwynne Howell is outstandingly fine as King Mark, making his monologue at the end of Act II, so often an anti-climax, into one of the noblest passages of all. This may not have the smoothness of the best international sets but, with its vivid digital sound, it is certainly compelling, and a libretto in three languages is an additional bonus.

Tristan und Isolde (slightly abridged).

(B) (**) Naxos mono 8.110008/10. Melchior, Traubel, Thorborg, Huehn, Kipnis, Gurney, NY Met. Op. Ch. & O, Leinsdorf.

Recorded live at the Met. in New York in February 1943, the historic Naxos set offers a performance which vividly conveys the atmosphere of a big occasion on stage despite very limited and variable sound. Act I fares best, with the voices forward and well focused, working up to a thrilling, almost frenzied climax at the end of the Act. Lauritz Melchior gives a performance very similar to that in the EMI recording from Covent Garden in the 1930s (conducted partly by Beecham, partly by Reiner), establishing him as arguably the finest exponent of the role this century. Helen Traubel may not have the total security of Kirsten Flagstad, whether in that earlier historic recording or in Furtwängler's studio set, and in the love duet she misses out the difficult top Cs, but it is a rich, warmly expressive performance. Sadly, the glowing account of the *Liebestod* at the end is marred by some of the worst recording in the whole set. Acts II and III (both slightly cut, following the custom of the time) bring crumbly orchestral sound, and as a rule the voices are not as clear and fresh as in Act I, yet one can readily sense the stage atmosphere. The rest of the cast make a strong team, with Alexander Kipnis outstanding as King Mark, making his monologue into a magnetic experience.

Tristan und Isolde, Act II: Love Duet – See Siegfried: Love Duet (above).

Die Walküre (complete).

*** Ph. (ADD) 464 751-2 (4). King, Rysanek, Nienstedt, Nilsson, Adam, Burmeister, (1967) Bayreuth Festival Ch. & O, Boehm.

*** Decca (ADD) 455 559-2 (4). Nilsson, Crespin, Ludwig, King, Hotter, Frick, VPO, Solti.

*** Teldec 4509 91186-2 (4). Elming, Hölle, Tomlinson, Secunde, A. Evans, Finnie, Johansson, Floeren, Close, (1992) Bayreuth Festival O, Barenboim.

(M) (***) EMI mono CHS7 63045-2 (3) [Ang. CHS 63045]. Mödl, Rysanek, Frantz, Suthaus, Klose, Frick, VPO, Furtwängler.

(B) *** RCA 74321 45419-2 (4). Altmeyer, Norman, Minton, Jerusalem, Adam, Moll, Dresden State O, Janowski.

(N) (BB) (***) Naxos mono 8.110058/60 (3). Traubel, Melchior, Schorr, Kipnis, Varnay, Thorborg, Met Op. O, Leinsdorf.

**(*) EMI CDS7 49534-2 (4). Marton, Studer, Morris, Goldberg, Salminen, Meier, Bav. RSO, Haitink.

(M) **(*) DG (ADD) 457 785-2 (4). Crespin, Janowitz, Veasey, Vickers, Stewart, Talvela, BPO, Karajan.

(M) **(*) Ph. (ADD) 434 422-2 (3). Hofmann, Altmeyer, G. Jones, McIntyre, Schwarz, Salminen, (1980) Bayreuth Festival O, Boulez.

Rarely if ever does Boehm's preference for fast speeds undermine the music; on the contrary, it adds to the involvement of the performance, which never loses its concentration. Theo Adam is in firmer voice here as Wotan than he is in *Rheingold*, hardly sweet of tone but always singing with keen intelligence. As ever, Nilsson is in superb voice as Brünnhilde. Though the inevitable noises of a live performance occasionally intrude, this presents a more involving experience than any rival complete recording. The CD transfer transforms what on LP seemed a rough recording, even if passages of heavy orchestration still bring some constriction of sound.

Solti sees Act II as the kernel of the work, with the conflict of wills between Wotan and Fricka making for one of Wagner's most deeply searching scenes. That is the more apparent when the greatest of latterday Wotans, Hans Hotter, takes the role, and Christa Ludwig sings with searing dramatic sense as his wife. Before that, Act I seems a little underplayed. This is partly because of Solti's deliberate lyricism – apt enough when love and spring greetings are in the air – but also (on the debit side) because James King fails both to project the character of Siegmund and to delve into the word-meanings as all the other members of the cast consistently do. As Sieglinde Crespin has never sung more beautifully on record. As for Nilsson's Brünnhilde, it has grown mellower, the emotions are clearer. Newly remastered, the sound is more vivid than ever and the layout is admirable.

Barenboim's control of dramatic tension is masterly. Even with characteristically slow speeds, the results are magnetic. Consistently there is a natural sense of flow so that, despite intrusive stage noises, Barenboim compels attention from first to last. It could not be more welcome to have on disc John Tomlinson's magnificent performance as Wotan, even more demanding in *Walküre* than in *Rheingold*. The other British singer who stands out in this opera is Anne Evans, showing her paces on disc as a radiant Brünnhilde. Maybe she is not as powerful as such loud ladies as Eva Marton and Hildegard Behrens, but she is far truer and clearer in focusing notes, singing with more expressive variety. With Barenboim conveying the full emotional thrust, the final duet between Brünnhilde and Wotan has rarely been so moving on disc. Also outstanding is the Danish tenor, Poul Elming, as Siegmund. Again the Bayreuth atmosphere is very well caught.

Furtwängler, an excellent cast and the Vienna Philharmonic in radiant form match any of their successors. Ludwig Suthaus proves a satisfyingly clear-toned Heldentenor, never strained, with the lyricism of *Wintersturme* superbly sustained. Neither Léonie Rysanek as Sieglinde nor Martha

Mödl as Brünnhilde is ideally steady, but the intensity and involvement of each is irresistible, classic performances both. Similarly, the mezzo of Margarete Klose may not be very beautiful, but the projection of words and the fire-eating character match the conductor's intensity. Gottlob Frick is as near an ideal Hunding as one will find, sinister but with the right streak of arrogant sexuality; while the Wotan of Ferdinand Frantz may not be as deeply perceptive as some, but to hear the sweep of Wagner's melodic lines so gloriously sung is a rare joy. The 1954 sound is amazingly full and vivid, with voices cleanly balanced against the inspired orchestra. The only snag of the set is that, to fit the whole piece on to only three CDs, breaks between discs come in mid-Act.

Janowski's direct approach matches the clarity of the recording. Jessye Norman might not seem an obvious choice for Sieglinde, but the sound is glorious, the expression intense and detailed, making her a fine match for the good if less imaginative Siegmund of Siegfried Jerusalem. The one snag from so commanding a Sieglinde is that she dramatically overtops the Brünnhilde of Jeannine Altmeyer, who yet conveys a touching measure of feminine vulnerability in the leading Valkyrie, even in her godhead days. The beauty and the frequent sensuousness of her singing are the more telling against the strong, gritty Wotan of Theo Adam, and the illumination of the narrative is consistent and intense, well supported by Janowski with surges of orchestral tone. Kurt Moll is a gloriously firm Hunding, and Yvonne Minton a searingly effective Fricka. Very satisfyingly transferred to CD, this makes a splendid bargain.

Recorded live at the Met in New York in December 1941, the Naxos historical set offers an electrifying performance, starrily cast, with radio sound giving clear focus to the voices. With Astrid Varnay as Sieglinde making her debut at the Met and Helen Traubel too as Brünnhilde making her debut in that role, it was a great occasion, with Lauritz Melchior plainly intent on not being outshone. He is in heroic voice, the master Wagner tenor of his generation, daring to hold on to his cries of 'Walse, Walse' for extraordinary lengths.

Varnay is a warm Sieglinde, producing Flagstad-like overtones. Equally, Helen Traubel sings with a rock-like firmness that is all too rare in latter day Wagner sopranos, clear and incisive, never fluffing a note. Kirsten Thorborg is a magnificent Fricka, and Alexander Kipnis a thrilling Hunding, with his dark, incisive attack.

It is sad that next to these, the other great Wagnerian, Friedrich Schorr, as Wotan, reveals a sadly worn voice, strained and dry on top. It may be as well that his Act 2 monologue is severely cut. Yet the nobility of his portrayal still comes over powerfully, as in his final half-tone phrase, kissing away Brünnhilde's godhead. Leinsdorf draws incandescent playing from the Met Orchestra in a performance wilder than his RCA studio account but just as compelling.

Haitink's is a broad view, strong and thoughtful yet conveying monumental power. That goes with searching concentration and a consistent feeling for the detailed beauty of Wagner's writing, glowingly brought out in the warm and spacious recording, made in the Herkulessaal in Munich. The outstanding contribution comes from Cheryl Studer as Sieglinde, very convincingly cast, giving a tenderly affecting performance to bring out the character's vulnerability in a very human way. At *Du bist der Lenz* her radiant singing brings an eagerly personal revelation, the response of a lover. Despite some strained moments, Rainer Goldberg makes a heroic Siegmund, and Eva Marton is a noble, powerful Brünnhilde, less uneven of production than she has often been on record. Waltraud Meier makes a convincingly waspish and biting Fricka and Matti Salminen a resonant Hunding. James Morris is a fine, perceptive Wotan. However, this set has just been deleted.

The great merits of Karajan's version are the refinement of the orchestral playing and the heroic strength of Jon Vickers as Siegmund. With that underlined, one cannot help but note that the vocal shortcomings here are generally more marked, and the total result does not add up to quite so compelling a dramatic experience: one is less involved. Thomas Stewart may have a younger, firmer voice than Hotter, but the character of Wotan emerges only partially; it is not just that he misses some of the word-meaning, but that on occasion – as in the kissing away of Brünnhilde's godhead – he underlines too crudely. Josephine Veasey as Fricka conveys the biting intensity of the part. Gundula Janowitz's Sieglinde has its beautiful moments, but it is not a dynamic performance. Crespin's Brünnhilde is impressive, but nothing like as satisfying as her study of Sieglinde on the Decca set. The DG recording is very good, but not quite in the same class as the Decca.

The major advantage of the Boulez Bayreuth version of 1980 is that it comes at mid-price on only three discs, with atmospheric digital sound and a strong, if flawed, cast. Jeannine Altmeyer is a generally reliable Sieglinde, but Peter Hofmann's tenor had already grown rather gritty for Siegmund. Donald McIntyre makes a commanding Wotan, Hanna Schwarz a firm, biting Fricka and Gwyneth Jones is at her least abrasive, producing a beautiful, gentle tone in lyrical passages. Boulez's fervour will surprise many, even if he does not match Boehm's passionate urgency in this second instalment of the tetralogy.

Die Walküre: Act I (complete).

(M) (***) EMI mono CDH7 61020-2. Lehmann, Melchior, List, VPO, Walter.

**(*) Teldec 3984-23294-2. Domingo, Polaski, Tomlinson, Berlin Staatskapelle, Barenboim.

(N)(M) (**(*)) Orfeo mono C 019991 Z. Schech, Völker, Dalberg, Bav. State O, Solti.

(i) Die Walküre: Act I (complete). Götterdämmerung: Siegfried's Funeral March.

**(*) Australian Decca Eloquence 466 678-2. VPO, Knappertsbusch; (i) with Svanholm, Flagstad, Van Mill.

One is consistently gripped by the continuity and sustained lines of Walter's reading, and by the intensity and beauty of the playing of the Vienna Philharmonic. Lotte Lehmann's portrait of Sieglinde, arguably her finest role, has a depth and beauty never surpassed since, and Lauritz Melchior's heroic Siegmund brings singing of a scale and variety – not to mention beauty – that no Heldentenor today can match. Emanuel List as Hunding is less distinguished but reliable.

Barenboim's live recording of Act I is memorable for Plácido Domingo's magnificent portrayal of Siegmund, warm, heroic and unstrained, and he is well matched by John Tomlinson as a dark and incisive Hunding. Deborah Polaski is at her warmest in the opening scenes, but as the performance progresses the voice acquires an unwelcome shrillness on top. Conversely, the Berlin Staatskapelle sounds a little underpowered at the start, but grows ever more incisive up to the excitement of the closing duet, *Siegmund bin ich*. The sound is full and rich, and the relatively close balance of the voices gives extra immediacy to the drama.

All Solti devotees (and other Wagnerians) should hear his historic recording, made live at the Prinzregentem Theatre in Munich in 1947, when the young maestro was new to the post of principal conductor in Munich. Though at that time he had had remarkably little experience of conducting opera, this is already an electrifying example of his work as a Wagner conductor, culminating in a thrilling close to the act. The passionate build-up includes a cry of delight from Schech as Sieglinde when Siegmund retrieves the sword. The sound is close and unatmospheric, with stage noises obtrusive at times, but there is plenty of solid detail. Though the closeness does not help the singers, Marianne Schech is an impressive, vibrant Sieglinde, firmer than she later became, and Franz Völker as a veteran of the Vienna State Opera is a clear, heroic Siegmund, if strained at times at the top. Friedrich Dalberg makes an aptly sinister Hunding.

It was Kirsten Flagstad's wish that she should be able to record Sieglinde in Act I of *Walküre*, and she also wanted to work with the great Wagner conductor, Hans Knappertsbusch. If Flagstad is a bit too matronly for the role, it hardly matters, for there is an electric tension in this performance which makes it compellingly moving. The 1958 recording, though a bit tubby, is amazingly detailed, rich and full, and allows the inimitable Vienna glow to come through. With Siegfried's funeral march thrown in too, this Australian CD is well worth seeking out.

Die Walküre: Act III (complete).

(N) (M) *** Decca 467 124-2. Flagstad, Edelmann, Schech, VPO, Solti.

(M) (***) EMI mono CDH7 64704-2. Varnay, Rysanek, Bjoerling, (1951) Bayreuth Festival O, Karajan.

The Solti recording was made in 1957. Flagstad came out of retirement to make it, and Decca put us eternally in their debt for urging her to do so. She sings radiantly. The meticulousness needed in the recording studio obviously brought out all her finest qualities, and there is no more than a touch of hardness on some of the top notes to show that the voice was no longer as young as it had been. Edelmann is not the ideal Wotan, but he has a particularly well-focused voice and when he sings straight, without sliding up or sitting under the note, the result is superb, and he is never wobbly. But it is Solti's conducting that prevents any slight blemishes from mattering. Not surprisingly, the recording too is remarkably vivid, anticipating the excellence of the great *Ring* project which was to follow. This returns to the catalogue in Decca's Legend series, again remastered with an increase in the fullness of the sound as well as improved definition.

Recorded in 1951, the first season after the war, Karajan's Bayreuth version of Act III shows the still-young conductor

working at white heat. Speeds are far faster than in his DG studio recording. Ensemble inevitably is not as taut as it was in the studio performance, but the electricity is far keener, and his cast is a characterful one. Astrid Varnay is an abrasive Brünnhilde, presenting the Valkyrie as a forceful figure, even in penitence prepared to stand up against her father. Leonie Rysanek is a warm Sieglinde, powerful rather than pure, with a rather obtrusive vibrato even at that date. Sigurd Bjoerling by contrast, the least-known of the principals, proves a magnificently virile Wotan, steady as a rock in the *Farewell*, but colouring the voice with a near-shout at the command, '*Loge, hier!*' The mono sound is transferred with bright immediacy, with some harshness on top but plenty of weight in the bass.

Die Walküre: highlights.

(M) *** Ph. (IMS) 446 614-2 (from above (1980) Bayreuth Festival recording; cond. Boulez).

As with the others in this otherwise excellent Philips series of Wagnerian highlights, the documentation is totally inadequate, with the excerpts listed baldly and with no synopsis provided to relate each to the narrative. But as this is by no means a first choice among recordings of this opera, many collectors will be interested in such a generous sampler (78 minutes) rather than the complete recording.

The Valkyrie (Die Walküre) (complete, in English).

(N) (M) *** Chan. 3038 (4). Hunter, Remedios, Curphey, Bailey, Grant, Howard, ENO Ch. & O, Goodall.

Recorded by EMI at the London Coliseum in 1975 and now reissued by Chandos the glory of the ENO performance lies not just in Goodall's spacious direction but in the magnificent Wotan of Norman Bailey, noble in the broadest span but very human in his illumination of detail. Rita Hunter sings nobly too, and though she is not as commanding as Nilsson in the Solti cycle she is often more lyrically tender. Alberto Remedios as Siegmund is more taxed than he was as Siegfried in the later opera (lower tessituras are not quite so comfortable for him) but his sweetly ringing top register is superb. If others, such as Ann Howard as Fricka, are not always treated kindly by the microphone, the total dramatic compulsion is irresistible. The CD transfer increases the sense of presence and at the same time confirms the relative lack of sumptuousness.

VOCAL COLLECTIONS

'*Wagner Singing on Record*': Excerpts from: (i) *Der fliegende Holländer;* (ii) *Götterdämmerung;* (iii) *Lohengrin;* (iv) *Die Meistersinger von Nürnberg;* (v) *Parsifal;* (vi) *Das Rheingold;* (vii) *Siegfried;* (viii) *Tannhäuser;* (ix) *Tristan und Isolde;* (x) *Die Walküre.*

(M) (***) EMI mono/stereo (ADD) CMS7 640082 (4).
(i) Hermann, Nissen, Endrèze, Fuchs, Beckmann, Rethberg, Nilsson, Hotter; (ii) Austral, Widdop, List, Weber, Janssen, Lawrence; (iii) Rethberg, Pertil, Singher, Lawrence, Spani, Lehmann, Lemnitz, Klose, Wittrisch, Rosavaenge;

(iv) Schorr, Thill, Martinelli, Bockelmann, Parr, Williams, Ralf, Lemnitz; (v) Leider, Kipnitz, Wolff; (vi) Schorr; (vii) Nissen, Olszewska, Schipper, Leider, Laubenthal, Lubin; (viii) Müller, Lorenz, Janssen, Hüsch, Flagstad; (ix) Leider, Marherr, Larsen-Todsen, Helm, Melchior, Seinemeyer, Lorenz; (x) Lawrence, Journet, Bockelmann.

This collection, compiled in Paris as 'Les Introuvables du chant wagnerien', contains an amazing array of recordings made in the later years of 78-r.p.m. recording, mostly between 1927 and 1940. In 49 items, many of them substantial, the collection consistently demonstrates the reliability of the Wagner singing at that period, the ability of singers in every register to produce firm, well-focused tone of a kind too rare today. Some of the most interesting items are those in translation from French sources, with Germaine Lubin as Isolde and Brünnhilde and with Marcel Journet as Wotan, both lyrical and clean-cut. The ill-starred Marjorie Lawrence, a great favourite in France, is also represented by recordings in French, including Brünnhilde's Immolation scene from Götterdämmerung. Not only are such celebrated Wagnerians as Lauritz Melchior, Friedrich Schorr, Frida Leider, Lotte Lehmann and Max Lorenz very well represented, but also singers one might not expect, including the Lieder specialist, Gerhard Husch, as Wolfram in Tannhäuser and Aureliano Pertile singing in Italian as Lohengrin. Meta Seinemeyer, an enchanting soprano who died tragically young, here gives lyric sweetness to the dramatic roles of Brünnhilde and Isolde; and among the baritones and basses there is none of the roughness or ill-focus that marks so much latter-day Wagner singing. It is a pity that British-based singers are poorly represented, but the Prologue duet from Götterdämmerung brings one of the most impressive items, sung by Florence Austral and Walter Widdop. First-rate transfers and good documentation.

(i) *Der fliegende Holländer: Overture.*
(ii) *Götterdämmerung; Siegfried's Funeral Music;* (ii; iii; iv) *Immolation Scene.* (ii; v) *Lohengrin: Prelude to Act III; Bridal Chorus.* (i) *Die Meistersinger: Prelude to Act III.* (ii; vi) *Siegfried: Forest Murmurs.* (ii; vii) *Tannhäuser: Pilgrim's Chorus.* (ii; iii) *Tristan und Isolde: Liebestod.* (ii) *Die Walküre: Ride of the Valkyries.*

(B) *** Penguin Decca 460 610-2. (i) Chicago SO; (ii) VPO; (iii) Nilsson; (iv) Frick; (v) V. State. Op. Konzertvereinigung; (vi) Windgassen; (vii) V, State Op. Ch., Solti.

This well-organized, often very gripping, and (it hardly needs saying) very well-recorded collection, is essentially a sampler of Solti's Wagner – often showing him at his very best. The vocal excerpts come from his superb complete recordings, and this means they usually have to be judiciously faded at the end, although Birgit Nilsson's superb Liebestod from Tristan has a closing cadence, and of course the Immolation scene from Götterdämmerung is the masterful climax of The Ring. But never mind if these are 'bleeding chunks': the Ride of the Valkyries is so much more effective when heard with the voices of Wotan's formidable brood, and even Forest Murmurs from Siegfried (often played as an orchestral piece) here has a warmly lyrical contribution from Wolfgang Windgassen. The only snag, and it is a considerable one, is the inadequate documentation. The author's note (from Paul Johnson) concentrates on the sensuality and impact of Wagner's sound world.

Operatic scenes: *Götterdämmerung: Immolation Scene. Tristan und Isolde: Prelude & Liebestod. Die Walküre: Hojotoho!*

**(*) Sony SK 62032. Eaglen, ROHCG O, Elder – BELLINI: Scenes from *Bianca e Fernando*, etc. **(*)

Jane Eaglen with her rich, powerful voice copes splendidly with three of the most formidable passages which Wagner ever wrote for soprano: Isolde's Liebestod (preceded by the Tristan Prelude), Brünnhilde's Immolation Scene and her cries of 'Hojotoho!' in Walküre. The bright clarity of her top notes, fearlessly attacked with pinging precision, is thrilling, and she rounds off both the Tristan and Götterdämmerung solos with tenderness and great beauty, but with speeds so relentlessly steady that there is a static feeling, so that the music rather fails to carry you on, lacking the necessary thrust – partly the fault of Elder's conducting. Yet, in this coupling with Bellini scenes, this is an impressive demonstration of a young singer's potential.

Arias from: *Lohengrin; Die Meistersinger; Parsifal; Rienzi; Die Walküre.*

(N) (BB) *** Arte Nova 74321 82276-2. Dean Smith, Slovak RSO, Anguelov.

It is a coup for Arte Nova to have made this wide-ranging disc of tenor arias from the principal Wagner operas with Robert Dean Smith, the young American Heldentenor who has had such success at Bayreuth and other principal opera houses, notably in the role of Walther in Meistersinger. From first to last the disc explains just why, when Dean Smith has such a clear, fresh voice, which, incisive and unstrained, is both lyrical and heroic in these demanding solos. Walther's three solos, culminating in the Prize Song, have a rare freshness and clarity, while the three Lohengrin arias include the two solos from the last Act, In fernem Land and Mein lieber Schwann, and bring out the singer's gentle, velvety tone in fine legato. The tessitura for Siegmund's role in four main solos from Act I of Die Walküre is ideal for him, when the very top of the voice is not always so full-bodied as the rest, yet the heroic demands of Rienzi's big aria bring one of the most impressive performances of all. There are not many tenor recitals of Wagner as impressive as this at whatever price, let alone on a super-bargain label, with warmly sympathetic accompaniment from the Slovak Radio Symphony Orchestra, well recorded.

WAGNER, Siegfried (1869–1930)

Sternengebot (complete opera).

(N) *(*) Marco Polo 8.225150-51 (2). Kruzel, Roberts, Lukic, Horn, Kinzel, Wenhold, Sailer, Bav. Ch. & Youth O, Albert.

Tutored in composition by Humperdinck, Siegfried Wagner wrote no fewer than eighteen operas, some of them unfinished, which rather than echoing his father's music turn rather to the example of his tutor in easily romantic fairy-tale pieces. This one, *The Commandment of the Stars*, completed in 1906, draws on astrology in its story from the age of chivalry, dated around the time of King Henry the Fowler. The writing is easily lyrical, far less radical than that of his father, but with the occasional nod of acknowledgment to Richard's example in his own, very involved libretto, as for example in the tournament for the heroine's hand, when the hero, Helferich, is defeated.

Apart from a thinness on exposed violins the playing of the Bavarian Youth Orchestra is strong and expressive under the vigorous direction of Werner Andreas Albert, helped by full clear recording. The role of Helferich is well taken by the tenor, Volker Horn, if with some strain at times. Sadly, the other soloists are disappointing, notably Ksenija Lukic as the heroine, Agnes, whose shrill hooting tone in her opening scene is almost comical, even though she later improves slightly. In the principal baritone roles Karl-Heinz Kinzel as Adalbert and Andre Wenhold as Kurzbold are both very uneven. It is good to have on disc such a major score of Siegfried Wagner, but this set has to be approached with caution. A German libretto is provided, but no English translation, only a detailed synopsis.

WALDTEUFEL, Emile (1837–1915)

Polkas: *Les Bohémiens; Retour des champs; Tout ou rien.* Waltzes: *Ange d'amour; Dans des nuages; España; Fontaine lumineuse; Je t'aime; Tout-Paris.*

** Marco 8.223438. Slovak State PO (Košler), Walter.

Polkas: *Camarade; Dans les bois; Jeu d'esprit.* Waltzes: *Bien aimés; Chantilly; Dans tes yeux; Estudiantina; Hommage aux dames; Les Patineurs.*

** Marco 8.223433. Slovak State PO (Košice), Walter.

Polkas: *L'Esprit français; Par-ci, par-là; Zig-zag.* Waltzes: *Hébé; Les Fleurs; Fleurs et baisers; Solitude; Toujours ou jamais; Toujours fidèle.*

**(*) Marco 8.223450. Slovak State PO (Košice), Walter.

Invitation à la gavotte; Polkas: *Joyeux Paris; Ma Voisine.* Waltzes: *Pluie de diamants; Les Sirènes; Les Sourires; Soirée d'été; Très jolie; Tout en rose.*

** Marco 8.223441. Slovak State PO (Košice), Walter.

Béobile pizzicato. Polka-mazurka: *Bella.* Polka: *Château en Espagne.* Waltzes: *Acclamations; La Barcarolle; Brune ou blonde; Flots de joie; Gaîté; Tout à vous.*

**(*) Marco 8.223684. Slovak State PO (Košice), Walter.

Grand vitesse galop. Mazurka: *Souveraine.* Polka: *Les Folies.* Waltzes: *Amour et printemps; Dolorès; Mello; Mon rêve; Pomone; Sous la voûte étoilée.*

** Marco 8.223451. Slovak State PO (Košice), Walter.

Galop: *Prestissimo.* Polkas: *Bella bocca; Nuée d'oiseaux..* Waltzes: *Au revoir; Coquetterie; Jeunesse dorée; Un premier bouquet Rêverie; Trésor d'amour.*

** Marco 8.223 685. Slovak State PO (Košice), Walter.

Grand galop du chemin de fer; Polkas: *Désirée; Jou-jou* (all arr. Pollack). Waltzes: *La Berceuse: Entre nous; Illusion; Joie envolée; Mariana; Sur le plage.*

** Marco 8.223 686. Slovak State PO (Košice), Walter.

Waldteufel's music, if not matching that of the Strauss family in range and expressive depth, has grace and charm and is prettily scored in the way of French ballet music. Moreover its lilt is undeniably infectious. The most famous waltz, *Les Patineurs*, is mirrored in style here by many of the others (*Dans les nuages*, for instance), and there are plenty of good tunes. *Plus de diamants*, with lots of vitality, is among the more familiar items, as is the sparkling *Très jolie*, but many of the unknown pieces are equally engaging. Like Strauss, Waldteufel usually introduces his waltzes with a section not in waltz-time, and he is ever resourceful in his ideas and in his orchestration. The polkas are robust, but the scoring has plenty of character. The performances here are fully acceptable.

March: *Kamiesch* (arr. Pollack) Polkas: *Bagatelle; En garde!; Trictrac.* Waltzes: *Etincelles; Idyll; Naples; Nid d'amour; Roses de Noël; La Source.*

(N) **(*) Marco 8.223688. Slovak State PO (Košice), Walter.

For this latest in the ongoing Marco Polo series, Christian Pollack made the arrangement of the opening *Kamiesch March* and one could wish he had also conducted the disc, for Alfred Walter is often rather metrical. Yet he opens the charming *Bagatelle* and *Trictrac Polkas* flexibly enough and the closing polka militaire, *En garde!*, suits him admirably.

But the main attraction here is the inclusion of half a dozen waltzes, most of them unknown. Walter opens each affectionately enough (none actually begins in waltz tempo), is distinctly beguiling in both *Nid d'amour* and *Roses de Noël* and phrases the horn solo at the beginning of *Naples* very pleasingly. When each gets underway he is spirited, but a little more subtlety, a little less gusto, would have been welcome. Nevertheless the Slovak playing is full of spirit and the recording excellent.

Waltzes: *Acclamations; España; Estudiantina; Les Patineurs.*

(M) *** EMI (ADD) CDM7 63136-2. Monte Carlo Nat. Op. O, Boskovsky – OFFENBACH: *Gaîté parisienne.* **

Boskovsky's collection has the advantage of including, besides the three favourites, *Acclamations*, which he opens very invitingly. His manner is *echt*-Viennese, but *The Skaters* responds well to his warmth and there is no lack of sparkle here. The remastering of the mid-1970s recording is admirably fresh.

WALLACE, William (1860–1940)

Symphonic Poems Nos. 1, The Passing of Beatrice; 3, Sister Helen; 5, Sir William Wallace; 6, Villon.

*** Hyp. CDA 66848. BBC Scottish SO, Brabbins.

Like Hamish McCunn, William Wallace was born in Greenock, near Glasgow. The fifth of his symphonic poems was premièred at Sir Henry Wood's Queen's Hall Promenade Concerts in 1905. The composition's full title is *Sir William Wallace, Scottish Hero, Freedom-fighter, Beheaded and Dismembered by the English*. The music is not as melodramatic as it sounds. Its Scottish character is immediately obvious at the brooding opening; the main theme, 'Scots wha' hae', emerges only slowly but is celebrated more openly towards the end. *Villon*, an irreverent medieval poet, was a hero of a different kind, and Wallace's programme draws on the thoughts of his philosophical ballads (which are named in the synopsis) in music which is both reflective and vividly colourful. The very romantic *Passing of Beatrice* is a sensuous vision of Paradise, lusciously Wagnerian with an unashamedly Tristanesque close, reflecting the heroine's final transformation. The scoring is sensuously rich yet it retains also the spiritually ethereal quality of the narrative, rather as Wagner does in *Parsifal*. The final piece here is based on Rossetti and its full title is *Sister Helen, Villainess, Murdering by Sorcery; Insane with Jealous and Frustrated Love*. What is so remarkable is not only the quality of the musical material throughout these works, but also the composer's skill and confidence in handling it: they are musically every bit as well crafted as the symphonic poems of Liszt. Clearly the BBC Scottish Symphony Orchestra enjoy playing them, and Martyn Brabbins shapes the musical episodes skilfully to balance the warm lyricism and drama without becoming too histrionically melodramatic. The result is remarkably satisfying.

WALLACE, William Vincent

(1812–65)

Maritana (opera; complete).

**(*) Marco 8.223406-7. Cullagh, Lee, Clarke, Caddy, RTE Philharmonic Choir and Concert O, Ó Duinn.

Along with Balfe's *Bohemian Girl* and Benedict's *Lily of Killarney*, Wallace's *Maritana* marked a breakthrough in opera in Britain, and it held the stage for over 50 years. This lively recording, with Irish artists celebrating this nineteenth-century Irish composer, helps to explain the work's attractions, regularly reminding the modern listener of Gilbert and Sullivan. The big difference is that where G & S present a parody of grand opera, with tongue firmly in cheek, Wallace is intensely serious, with the big melodramatic moments quickly becoming unintentionally comic. To compound the similarity with G & S, the story, like that of the *Yeomen of the Guard*, depends on the heroine, by contract, marrying a man condemned to death who then escapes his punishment. What matters is that there are many more good tunes than that of the still-remembered aria for the heroine, *Scenes that are Brightest*, and the ensembles in this winning performance are always fresh and lively. The soloists too all have voices which focus cleanly, even if they are not specially distinctive. The recording is bright and forwardly balanced, with words crystal clear. Worth investigating as a period piece.

WALTON, William (1902–83)

(i) *Anniversary Fanfare; Coronation Marches: Crown Imperial; Orb and Sceptre;* (ii; v) *Cello Concerto;* (v) *Symphony No. 1 in B flat min.;* (iii–v) *Belshazzar's Feast;* (iv; v) *Coronation Te Deum.*

(B) ** Chan. 2-for-1 ADD/DDD. 241-10 (2). (i) Philh. O, Willcocks; (ii) Kirshbaum; (iii) Milnes; (iv) RSNO Ch.; (v) RSNO, Gibson.

The *Anniversary Fanfare* is designed to lead directly into *Orb and Sceptre*, which is what it does here. However the Kirshbaum/Gibson reading of the *Cello Concerto* is disappointing, lacking the warmth, weight and expressiveness that so ripe an example of late romanticism demands. And while Gibson's is a well-paced, convincingly idiomatic view of the *First Symphony*, ensemble is not always bitingly precise enough for this darkly intense music (malice prescribed for the Scherzo, melancholy for the slow movement). Recording first rate, but with less body than usual from Chandos and with timpani resonantly obtrusive. Gibson's view of Walton's brilliant oratorio *Belshazzar's Feast* tends towards brisk speeds, but is no less dramatic for that. It remains individually competitive, particularly with so magnificent a baritone as Sherrill Milnes as soloist, but overall this is not one of the more enticing issues in Chandos's 2-for-1 series.

Anniversary Fanfare; Crown Imperial; March for the History of the English-speaking Peoples; Orb and Sceptre; A Queen's Fanfare; (i) *Antiphon; 4 Christmas Carols: All this time; King Herod and his cock; Make we now this feast; What cheer?; In honour of the City of London; Jubilate Deo; Where does the uttered music go?.*

*** Chan. 8998. (i) Bach Ch.; Philh. O, Willcocks.

Sir David Willcocks conducts performances of the two *Coronation Marches* full of panache, with the brass superbly articulated and inner detail well caught. Also the *March for the History of the English-speaking Peoples*. The *a cappella* choral items are very well done too, if less intimately than on the Conifer disc of Walton choral music from Trinity College Choir. With the original organ parts orchestrated, the *Jubilate* and *Antiphon* gain greatly from having full instrumental accompaniment. The brief fanfares, never previously recorded, are a welcome makeweight, with the *Anniversary Fanfare*, designed to lead directly into *Orb and Sceptre*, which is what it does here.

Capriccio burlesco; Coronation Marches: Crown Imperial; Orb and Sceptre. Hamlet: Funeral March; Johannesburg Festival Overture; Richard III: Prelude & Suite; Scapino (comedy overture); Spitfire Prelude & Fugue.

(M) **(*) EMI (ADD) CDM5 67222-2. RLPO, Groves.

The 1969 collection of Walton's shorter orchestral pieces was made in Studio 2 (EMI's hi-fi-conscious equivalent of Decca's Phase 4) and now seems slightly over-bright with its digital remastering. The sound tends to polarize, with a lack of opulence in the middle range, so necessary in the *nobilmente* of the big tunes of the stirring *Spitfire Prelude and Fugue* and *Crown Imperial*. The Shakespearean film music was recorded much later (1984) and the quality is fuller, more warmly atmospheric. Although the two *Coronation Marches* could do with a little more exuberance, Groves is otherwise a highly sympathetic interpreter of this repertoire, and the playing of the Liverpool orchestra is excellent.

Capriccio burlesco; The First Shoot (orch. Palmer); *Granada* (prelude for orchestra); *Johannesburg Festival Overture; Music for Children. Galop Finale* (orch. Palmer); *Portsmouth Point: Overture; Prologo e fantasia; Scapino.*

*** Chan. 8968. LPO, Thomson.

The *Capriccio burlesco* is ravishingly orchestrated, with some apt echoes of Gershwin, and the *Prologo e fantasia* completes an American group. The *Granada* Prelude, written for the television company, taps Walton's patriotic march vein in a jaunty way. *The First Shoot* comes in Christopher Palmer's brilliant orchestration of the brass band suite. The opening *Giocoso* is a re-run of *Old Sir Faulk*, and the other movements bring more echoes of *Façade*. As for the other novelty, the ten brief movements of *Music for Children* are here supplemented by a *Galop Final*. Palmer has here orchestrated the piano score. Though the opulent Chandos recording tends to take some of the bite away from Walton's jazzily accented writing, the richness of the orchestral sound is consistently satisfying.

(i) *Capriccio burlesco;* (ii) *Music for Children; Portsmouth Point Overture;* (i) *The Quest* (ballet suite); *Scapino Overture;* (ii) *Siesta;* (i; iii) *Sinfonia concertante.*

*** Lyrita (ADD) SRCD 224. (i) LSO; (ii) LPO; composer; (iii) with Katin.

When Walton made these recordings, he was in his late sixties, and his speeds had grown a degree slower and safer. *Portsmouth Point* loses some of its fizz at so moderate a speed. By contrast *Scapino* suffers hardly at all from the slower speed, rather the opposite, with the opening if anything even jauntier and the big cello melody drawn out more expressively. *Siesta* too brings out the piece's romantically lyrical side, rather than making it a relatively cool intermezzo. The *Capriccio burlesco* and the ten little pieces of the *Music for Children* are delightful too, with the subtleties of the instrumentation beautifully brought out. Much the biggest work here is the *Sinfonia concertante*, and in the outer movements the performance lacks the thrust that Walton himself gave it in his very first wartime recording, in which Phyllis Sellick was a scintillating soloist (see below). Yet Peter Katin is a very responsive soloist too, and the central slow movement is much warmer and more passionate than on Conifer, with orchestral detail rather clearer. It is good too to have the first stereo recording of the suite from Walton's wartime ballet based on Spenser's 'Faerie Queene', *The Quest*, only a fraction of the whole but bright and colourful.

Cello Concerto.

*** Ph. 454 442-2. Lloyd Webber, ASMF, Marriner – BRITTEN: *Symphony for Cello & Orchestra, Op. 68.* ***

(N) (M) *** Ph. 464 760-2. J. Lloyd-Webber, ASMF, Marriner – ELGAR: *Concerto.* ***

(BB) *** RCA Navigator (ADD) 74321 29248-2. Piatigorsky, Boston SO, Munch – VAUGHAN WILLIAMS: *Sinfonia Antarctica.* ***

**(*) RCA 09026 61695-2. Starker, Philharmonia Orch, Slatkin – DELIUS: *Caprice & Elegy;* ELGAR: *Cello Concerto.* **(*)

(i; ii) *Cello Concerto;* (ii) *Improvisations on an Impromptu of Benjamin Britten; Partita for Orchestra;* (i) *Passacaglia for Solo Cello.*

*** Chan. 8959. (i) Wallfisch; (ii) LPO, Thomson.

Though Walton's *Cello Concerto*, written for Piatigorsky, and Britten's tough and gritty *Cello Symphony*, written for Rostropovich, are strongly contrasted in mood and style, Julian Lloyd Webber in a unique coupling, passionately performed, draws fascinating parallels. Helped by sumptuous recording, his reading of the Walton firmly establishes this as a worthy counterpart to Walton's two pre-war *concerto* masterpieces for viola and violin, bringing out the beauty as well as the romantic warmth, helped by fine playing from Marriner and the Academy. This performance also comes alternatively coupled at mid-price to an equally fine account of the Elgar concerto.

The *Cello Concerto* was written for Piatigorsky and he plays it with a gripping combination of full-blooded eloquence and subtlety of feeling, readily capturing the bittersweet melancholy of its flowing lyrical lines. The closing pages of the final variations are particularly haunting. Munch provides a totally understanding accompaniment, with the strings of the Boston Symphony finding the lyrical ecstasy which is such a distinctive part of this concerto. The 1957 recording is close, but the improvement of the CD over the old LP is enormous, and the ambience of Symphony Hall is much more apparent than before. This performance is coupled to Previn's fine account of Vaughan Williams's *Sinfonia Antarctica* on RCA's bargain Navigator label.

Janos Starker, not usually associated with British music, here takes a relatively tough, objective view of the romantic Walton work, superficially cooler but with emotion clearly implied. Playing with his characteristically firm, slightly wiry tone, he provides a clear alternative for those who resist a freely expressive approach. The Delius miniature makes a welcome bonus to the apt Walton/Elgar coupling.

With his rich, even tone, Wallfisch is just as warm and purposeful in the solo *Passacaglia* as in the *Concerto*, while Thomson relishes the vivid orchestral colours in both the *Improvisations*, here wider-ranging in expression than usual, and the brilliant *Partita*. Excellent Chandos sound.

(i) *Cello Concerto;* (ii) *Violin Concerto in B min.*

(BB) *** Naxos 8.554325. (i) Hugh; (ii) Kang; English Northern Philh. O, Daniel.

(i–iii) *Cello Concerto;* (iv; ii; iii) *Violin Concerto;* (v) *Overtures: Portsmouth Point; Scapino. Symphonies Nos.* (vi) 1 in B flat min.; (v) 2.

(B) ** EMI (ADD) Double fforte CZS5 73371-2 (2). (i) Paul Tortelier; (ii) Bournemouth SO; (iii) Berglund; (iv) Ida Haendel; (v) LSO, Previn; (vi) Philh. O, Haitink.

In many ways Tim Hugh's reading of the *Cello Concerto* is the most searching yet. He finds an intense thoughtfulness, a sense of mystery, of inner meditation in the great lyrical ideas of all three movements, daring to play with a more extreme pianissimo than any rival. The bravura writing finds him equally concentrated, always sounding strong and spontaneous in face of any technical challenge. As in their previous Walton recordings, Paul Daniel and the English Northern Philharmonia equally play with flair and sympathy, so that the all-important syncopations always sound idiomatic, even if the strings lack a little in weight. In the *Violin Concerto* Dong-Suk Kang here follows up the success of his Naxos recording of the Elgar *Violin Concerto*, playing immaculately with a fresh, clean-cut tone, pure and true above the stave. If this is a degree more objective than more overtly romantic readings, Kang makes a virtue of opting for speeds rather faster than usual, evidently aware of the example of the dedicatee, Jascha Heifetz.

Tortelier's account of the *Cello Concerto* is characteristically passionate. After the haunting melancholy of the first movement, the central Scherzo emerges as a far weightier piece than most such movements, while the final variations have seldom on record developed with such a sense of compulsion. Ida Haendel's version of the *Violin Concerto* is warmly appealing. Previn is at his finest in the *Second Symphony*, sparkling in the outer movements, warmly romantic in the central slow movement, while in the two overtures he finds more light and shade than usual. However, Haitink's reading of the *First Symphony* is more controversial. The malevolent demon which inhabits the first two movements is somewhat tamed, and in the opening movement some will feel that the lack of the relentless forward thrust demonstrated in the finest versions (including Previn's RCA reading) underplays the music's character. However, Haitink's directness leads to spacious and noble accounts of the slow movement and finale. The bright, digital recording is a little lacking in bass and not as impressive as the fine analogue sound that EMI provide for Previn in No. 1.

Viola Concerto.

*** RCA 09026 63292-2. Bashmet, LSO, Previn – BRUCH: *Concerto for Violin & Viola; Kol Nidrei; Romance.* ***

Yuri Bashmet with his opulent viola tone warmly relishes the ripe romanticism of the Walton concerto as well as the high-voltage electricity of its jazz-based writing. Like other latterday interpreters he opts for a daringly spacious speed for the haunting opening melody, but avoids any hint of sluggishness, relishing the bravura of the contrasting sections. The central Scherzo brings a dazzling display, with the fun of the scherzando passages winningly brought out, as it is too in the finale. Bashmet ends with another daringly slow speed for the wistful epilogue, again superbly sustained, thanks also to the ideal accompaniment of Previn and the LSO. First-rate sound. The coupling may seem odd, but all three Bruch works will delight anyone who enjoys romantic viola music.

Viola Concerto; Violin Concerto.

*** EMI CDC7 49628-2. Kennedy, RPO, Previn.

(i) *Viola Concerto;* (ii) *Violin Concerto;* (iii) *Partita for Orchestra.*

(M) **(*) EMI (ADD) CDM5 65005-2. (i) Menuhin, LSO; (ii) Menuhin, New Philh. O; (iii) Philh. O; composer.

(i) *Viola Concerto in A min.;* (ii) *Violin Concerto in B min.;* (iii) *Sinfonia concertante.*

(M) (**(*)) Avid mono AMSC 604. (i) Primrose; (ii) Heifetz; Cincinnati SO, Eugene Goosens; (iii) Sellick, CBSO, Composer.

Kennedy's achievement in giving equally rich and expressive performances of both works makes for an ideal coupling, helped by the unique insight of André Previn as Waltonian. Kennedy on the viola produces tone as rich and firm as on his usual violin. The Scherzo has never been recorded with more panache than here, and the finale brings a magic moment in the return of the main theme from the opening, hushed and intense. In the *Violin Concerto* too, Kennedy gives a warmly relaxed reading, in which he dashes off the bravura passages with great flair. He may miss some of the more searchingly introspective manner of Chung in her 1971 version, but there are few Walton records as richly rewarding as this, helped by warm, atmospheric sound.

The EMI disc couples Menuhin's late 1960s recordings of the two concertos with the 1959 one of the *Partita*. This transfer of the latter is fuller than in its pre-1994 incarnations, and reveals what fun the composer himself finds in his bouncing of the rhythms. Though Menuhin's account of the *Viola Concerto* is a little effortful, not always flowing as it should, his viola sound is gloriously rich and true, and when it comes to the *Violin Concerto*, this is a vintage Menuhin performance, marked by his very distinctive tone and poignantly tender phrasing.

In many ways, Heifetz's pioneering wartime version of the *Violin Concerto*, recorded in Cinncinati in 1941 at speeds far faster than we are used to now, has never been surpassed – even finer than his later remake with Walton and the Philharmonia, more fiery, with even more flair and spontaneity. This account of the *Viola Concerto* was the first of two which Primrose recorded, markedly cooler than the première recording on Decca, with the young Frederick Riddle accompanied by Walton and the LSO. The central Scherzo is taken at an astonishingly fast speed, on the verge of sounding breathless. By contrast, the première recording of the *Sinfonia concertante* with Phyllis Sellick is exceptionally warm and expressive, an interpretation never quite matched since. Despite the rough Avid transfers, such historic performances offered in a coupling on a bargain disc are self-recommending.

(i) *Viola Concerto. Johannesburg Festival Overture; Symphony No. 2.*

(BB) *** Naxos 8.553402. (i) Tomter; E. N. Philh. O, Paul Daniel.

(i) *Viola Concerto; Sonata for String Orchestra; Variations on a Theme of Hindemith.*

*** Chan. 9106. (i) Imai; LPO, Latham-Koenig.

Pride of place on Naxos goes to the thoughtful, deeply felt reading of the *Viola Concerto* with the Norwegian viola-player, Lars Anders Tomter. Though Tomter's tight vibrato is at times prominent, he brings out the tender poetry of this most elusive of Walton's string concertos, with its mixture of melancholy and wit. More than others, Tomter observes pianissimo markings, and rightly he adopts a flowing speed for the first movement while refusing to be rushed in the Scherzo and finale, which with delectable pointing acquire extra scherzando sparkle. The overture is given the most exuberant performance, rivalling the composer's own, with the orchestra's soloists playing brilliantly. In the *Symphony No. 2* Daniel gives extra transparency to the often heavy orchestration, making the work less weighty than usual but just as warmly expressive. A superb bargain.

Imai is satisfyingly firm and true in all her playing, keenly confident in the virtuoso passages, with the central Scherzo not at all breathless-sounding. Imai uses a very broad *Andante* to bring out the full lyrical warmth, but it means that the following bravura section enters with a jolt rather than developing naturally. The movement is not helped either by the forward balance of the soloist. Jan Latham-Koenig secures crisply rhythmic playing from the orchestra in all three movements. The main theme of the finale is even jauntier than usual, again at a speed fractionally slower than normal.

The warmth of the LPO string-tone comes over impressively in the *Sonata for Strings*, but the contrast between the passages for solo string quartet (echoing the original quartet version) and the full string ensemble is too extreme. Latham-Koenig is also warmly expressive in the *Hindemith Variations*, which is not as lightly pointed or cleanly detailed as it might be, partly a question of the recording. The three works on the disc not only make an exceptionally generous triptych, but one which reflects Walton's mastery throughout his long career.

Violin Concerto.

*** Decca 452 851-2. Bell; Baltimore SO, Zinman – BARBER: *Violin Concerto*; BLOCH: *Baal Shem*. ***

(M) *** Decca (ADD) 460 014-2. Chung, LSO, Previn – BEETHOVEN: *Violin Concerto*. **

(M) *** EMI (ADD) CDM7 64202-2. Haendel, Bournemouth SO, Berglund – BRITTEN: *Violin Concerto*. ***

(***) Biddulph mono WHL 016. Heifetz, Cincinnati SO, Goossens – VAUGHAN WILLIAMS: *A London Symphony (No. 2)* (***) (with Concert (***)).

(N) (BB) (***) Naxos (ADD) 8.110939. Heifetz, Cincinnati SO, Goossens – ELGAR: *Violin Concerto*. (***)

(*) Classico CLASSCD 233. Azizjan, Copenhagen PO, Bellincamp – BRITTEN: *Violin Concerto*. *

(i) *Violin Concerto. Capriccio burlesco; Henry V: Suite; Spitfire Prelude & Fugue.*

**(*) HM HMU 907070. (i) Rosand; Florida PO, Judd.

Violin Concerto; 2 Pieces for Violin & Orchestra; Sonata for Violin & Orchestra (both orch. Palmer).

*** Chan. 9073. Mordkovitch, LPO, Latham-Koenig.

From an American perspective, Walton's *Violin Concerto* can well be seen as a British counterpart of the Barber, similarly romantic, written at exactly the same period. This prizewinning Decca disc has Bell giving a commanding account of the solo part, even matching Heifetz himself in the ease of his virtuosity. Playing with rapt intensity, Bell treats the central cadenza of the first movement expansively, making it more deeply reflective than usual. Rich and brilliant sound, with the violin balanced forward, but not aggressively so.

In the brooding intensity of the opening, Kyung Wha Chung presents the first melody with a depth of expression, tender and hushed, that has never been matched on record. With Previn as guide and with the composer himself a sympathetic observer at the recording sessions, Chung then builds up a performance which remains a classic, showing the *Concerto* as one of the greatest of the century. Outstandingly fine recording, sounding the more vivid in its CD format. This now comes generously coupled with the Beethoven *Concerto*, not an ideal choice, when it is not among Chung's most successful recordings.

A sunny, glowing, Mediterranean-like view of the concerto from Ida Haendel, with brilliant playing from the soloist and eloquent orchestral support from the Bournemouth orchestra under Paavo Berglund. The CD transfer of the fine (1977) recording, made in the Guildhall, Southampton, brings a brilliant orchestral tapestry to provide the necessary contrast and, given the quality of the playing (as well as the interest of the equally successful Britten coupling), this is an eminently desirable reissue.

Lydia Mordkovitch gives the most expansive account of the Walton *Violin Concerto* on disc, sustaining spacious speeds warmly and persuasively. Latham-Koenig may not have quite the spark that Previn brings to the orchestral writing in both the Chung and Kennedy versions but he is keenly idiomatic, both in his feeling for sharply syncopated rhythms and in flexible rubato for Walton's romantic melodies. The characteristically warm Chandos recording is also a help. Christopher Palmer's scoring of the *Sonata* offers a sensuousness of sound comparable with that in the opera *Troilus and Cressida*. Though his use of the harp or pizzicato strings for arpeggio accompaniments is not always comfortable, Palmer is right in seeing much of the piano part as already implying orchestration. With Mordkovitch just as powerful and rich-toned as in the regular concerto, the work makes a far bigger impact than in its original chamber form, a valuable addition to the Walton repertory. The two shorter pieces make an agreeable supplement, with Palmer's lush orchestration removing them even further from their medieval source-material.

Jascha Heifetz made the very first recording in 1941 with Eugene Goossens and the Cincinnati orchestra, and it has never quite been matched since for its passionate urgency as well as its brilliance. Speeds are much faster than has latterly become the norm, but the romantic warmth of the work has never been more richly conveyed. On Biddulph in an excellent CD transfer it is coupled with the only existing recording of the original score of Vaughan Williams's *London Symphony*, plus other British music.

Heifetz's premier version of a work he himself commissioned is the only recording to use the original, unrevised orchestration. The Naxos transfer, less bright than RCA's original, is well balanced, making for comfortable listening. The generous Elgar coupling confirms this as in every way a winner.

Sergej Azizjan, the Leningrad-trained concertmaster of the Copenhagen Philharmonic, has a superb technique, marked by flawless intonation and a wide tonal range. His reading of the Walton is passionate in an aptly extrovert way, an excellent choice for anyone wanting this coupling, though the orchestra is a degree recessed, and such passages as the rhythmic opening of the Walton finale lack something in bite.

Judd draws warmly idiomatic playing from the Florida Philharmonic Orchestra in the colourful pieces based on wartime film music for *The First of the Few* and *Henry V*, with the oboe solo in the *Bailero* theme after the Agincourt music achingly beautiful, and with the brass consistently ripe and resonant. The *Capriccio burlesco* is aptly witty and spiky. It is good to have Aaron Rosand returning to the recording studio, and in this formidable concerto he shows that his virtuosity is as impressive as ever. The snag is that the recording balances the soloist so close that orchestral detail is dim, and tuttis lack the bite and thrust they need. Despite the dryness of sound in the concerto and a lightness in bass, Rosand's performance is most refreshing, while the *Henry V* and *Spitfire Music* are treated with great warmth.

Coronation Marches: Crown Imperial; Orb and Sceptre; Façade Suites Nos. 1 & 2; (i; ii) Gloria; (ii) Coronation Te Deum.

(M) *** EMI (ADD) CDM7 64201-2. (i) Robothom, Johnson, Cook, CBSO Ch.; (ii) Choristers of Worcester Cathedral; CBSO, Frémaux.

The three Walton works inspired by coronations are here splendidly coupled with the grand setting of the *Gloria*. Frémaux directs a highly enjoyable performance of this but it rather pales before the *Coronation Te Deum*, which may use some of the same formulas but has Walton electrically inspired, exploiting every tonal and atmospheric effect imaginable between double choirs and semi-choruses. The two splendid marches are marvellously done too. The rich, resonant recording is apt for the music. The *Façade Suites* have been added for the CD and here the remastering is even more telling, adding point to playing which is already affectionately witty. Frémaux's rhythmic control gives a fresh, new look to familiar music: his jaunty jazz inflexions in *Old Sir Faulk* are deliciously whimsical.

Coronation March: Orb and Sceptre; (i) Coronation Te Deum; Jubilate Deo; A Litany; Set me as a Seal upon thine heart.

(N) **(*) Australian Decca Eloquence 467 613-2. Bournemouth SO, Hill; (i) with Winchester Cathedral Ch., Waynefleet Singers – VAUGHAN WILLIAMS: *Benedicte* etc. **(*)

A swaggering vivacious *Orb and Sceptre* is marred by a rather over reverberant acoustic, though the effect is certainly exciting. The choral items are sympathetically sung, and the *Coronation Te Deum* is gusty, with the recording surprisingly well managed in the resonance.

Façade (an entertainment; complete).

(N) ● (M) *** Decca mono 468 801-2. Sitwell, Pears, English Op. Group Ens., Collins – BRITTEN: *Serenade for Tenor, Horn & Strings, Op. 31; Folksongs.* ***

(B) *** Discover DICD 920125. Hunter, Melologos Ens., Van den Broeck.

(N) *** Hyp. CDA 67239. Bron, Stilgoe, Nash Ens., Lloyd-Jones – LAMBERT: *Salome: suite.* ***

Façade (complete, including Façade 2).

**(*) ASV CDDCA 679. Scales, West, L. Mozart Players (members), Glover.

**(*) Chan. 8869. Walton, Baker, City of L. Sinfonia (members), Hickox.

Façade: Suites 1 & 2 & Other Edith Sitwell Poems.

*** Ara. Z 6699. Lynn Redgrave, Chamber Music Society of Lincoln Center, Shifrin

Anthony Collins's 1954 recording of *Façade* is a gramophone classic, sounding miraculously vivid and atmospheric in a CD transfer that seems like modern stereo. Dame Edith Sitwell has one of the richest and most characterful of speaking voices and here she recited her early poems to the masterly witty music of the youthful Walton with glorious relish. Peter Pears is splendid too in the fast poems, rattling off the lines like the *grande dame* herself, to demonstrate how near-nonsense can be pure poetry.

When the reciter, Pamela Hunter, has made a speciality of reciting these Edith Sitwell poems, not exactly imitating Dame Edith herself but observing the strictly stylized, rhythmically crisp manner originally laid down, it makes a welcome and delightful disc. Five items appear here for the first time, adding to those resurrected by Walton himself in *Façade 2*. What even registers here, even more than with *Façade 2* alone, is that the early settings are more experimental and less sharply parodistic than the later, well-known ones, though in the accompaniment to one of them, *Aubade* ('Jane, Jane, tall as a crane'), there is a clear tongue-in-cheek reference to Stravinsky's *Rite of Spring*. The recording is cleanly focused, balanced with the voice in front of the players yet obviously in the same acoustic, not superimposed; and the clarity and point of the solo playing, notably from the flute and clarinet, are splendid. Pamela Hunter is excellent too, happily characterizing with a minimum of 'funny voices'. At the price, a disc to recommend to all.

It is the first great merit of this excellent Hyperion version that not only has the conductor gathered together all the surviving *Façade* settings, written between 1922 and 1928, a dozen more than in the regular Entertainment, but provides a valuable commentary on when and how they were written. *Popular Song*, the best known of all *Façade* items, was one of the last two to be composed. Where Pamela Hunter on her Koch Discover disc supplies recitations of the poems for which the music is lost, the Hyperion issue provides the printed texts, leaving room for the newly discovered Lambert music for *Salome* as an attractive makeweight. Eleanor Bron and Richard Stilgoe make an excellent pair of reciters, and the recording in a natural acoustic balances them well – not too close, with no discrepancy between voices and instruments. They inflect the words more than Edith Sitwell and early interpreters did, but still keep a stylized manner, meticulously obeying the rhythms specified in the score, with Stilgoe phenomenally fluent, while Bron in slow poems adopts an effective trance-like manner. Under David Lloyd-Jones the brilliant sextet of players from the Nash Ensemble, including John Wallace on trumpet and Richard Hosford on clarinet, could not be more idiomatic, with rhythms delectably pointed. Pamela Hunter as a solitary reciter on her less expensive rival disc may lose on variety, but is crisply consistent and idiomatic.

With Lynn Redgrave an excellent reciter, characterful and sharply rhythmic, the ensemble from Lincoln Center under Joseph Silverstein give a virtuoso performance of the quirky score, both crisply disciplined and idiomatic. Far more than usual, the recording gets the balance right between voice and instruments, with words splendidly clear yet with no unnatural highlighting of the reciter. She also recites 11 *Façade* poems without music, a random choice, not those which Walton set, but for which the music is lost. Some may feel that Redgrave overdoes the characterizations, but she gets a very acceptable balance between expressive word-pointing and formality, characterizing precisely in different, stylized accents, as in the Noel Coward accent she adopts for the *Tango* and *Popular Song*.

Scales and West as a husband-and-wife team are inventive in their shared roles, and generally it works well. *Scotch Rhapsody* is hilariously done as a duet, with West intervening at appropriate moments, and with sharply precise Scots accents. Regional accents may defy Edith Sitwell's original prescription – and her own example – but here, with one exception, they add an appropriate flavour. The exception is *Popular Song*, where Prunella Scales's cockney accent is quite alien to the allusive words, with their 'cupolas, gables in the lakes, Georgian stables'. For fill-up the reciters have recorded more Sitwell poems, but unaccompanied.

Susana Walton, widow of the composer, makes a bitingly characterful reciter, matching with her distinctive accent – she was born in Argentina – the exoticry of many numbers. Richard Baker, phenomenally precise and agile in enunciating the Sitwell poems, makes the perfect foil, and Hickox secures colourful and lively playing from members of the City of London Sinfonia, who relish in particular the jazzy inflexions. *Façade 2* consists of a number of Sitwell settings beyond the definitive series of twenty-one. All of them are fun and make an apt if not very generous coupling for the regular sequence. Warm sound, a little too reverberant for so intimate a work.

(i) *Façade* (complete recording); (ii) *The Wise Virgins* (ballet suite); (iii) *The Bear* (extravaganza).

(N) (B) *** EMI (ADD) CZS5 73998-2 (2) (i) Fielding, Flanders, ASMF, Marriner; (ii) CBSO, Frémaux; (iii) Sinclair, Shaw, Lumsden, ECO, Lockart.

Walton's one-act piece *The Bear* was written for the 1967 Aldeburgh Festival and recorded almost at once with the original cast. It is one of his frothiest, most exuberant scores. He himself admitted what an important part parody plays in the piece, and it is fascinating to track down each thread – the echoes of Britten's 'snoring forest' music from *A Midsummer Night's Dream* at the very opening; the Weill-like aria, *I was a constant faithful wife*, for the widow, Popova; Smirnov's aria imitating Stravinsky's *Les Noces* and so on. When the word 'Salome' is mentioned, Walton even manages to put in a fleeting reference to Strauss, and his self-parody in a passage recalling the *Viola Concerto* is equally pointed.

On record the piece is, if anything, more effective than in the opera-house, for the humour is rather of the rib-tickling, smile-provoking kind and not a source for belly laughs. The timing is splendid, with fast and slow contrasted most assuredly, and the orchestration so skilful that it completely conceals the problems of writing for single woodwind. Monica Sinclair's highly individual tones suite the part wonderfully – lovely chest-register brought out – and John Shaw makes a splendidly gruff 'bear'. First-rate playing by the ECO under Lockart, and the documentation includes a full synopsis. In *Façade*, an apt coupling, Fenella Fielding and Michael Flanders make an equally characterful pair of reciters, the one relishing in echo the *grande dame* quality of the poetess, the other wonderfully fleet of tongue. The balance favours the reciters against Marriner's wittily pointed accompaniment, and with excellent early 1970s sound this is very enjoyable. So, too, is Frémaux's Birmingham performance of *The Wise Virgins*.

Façade: Suites Nos. 1–3; Overture Portsmouth Point (arr. LAMBERT); *Siesta;* (i) *Sinfonia concertante.* WALTON/ ARNOLD: *Popular Birthday.*

*** Chan. 9148. (i) Eric Parkin; LPO, Latham-Koenig or Thomson.

Adapted from a ballet score written for Diaghilev (but then rejected), the *Sinfonia concertante*, with its sharply memorable ideas in each movement and characteristically high voltage, has never had the attention it deserves. Eric Parkin as soloist is perfectly attuned to the idiom, warmly melodic as well as jazzily syncopated, making this a most sympathetic account, even if the *Maestoso* introduction is hardly grand enough. The recording sets the piano a little more backwardly, no doubt to reflect the idea that this is not a full concerto. Jan Latham-Koenig gives the witty *Façade* movements just the degree of jazzy freedom they need. The third suite, devised and arranged by Christopher Palmer, draws on three apt movements from the *Façade* entertainment, ending riotously with the rag-music of *Something Lies Beyond the Scene*. That is a first recording, and so is Constant Lambert's arrangement for small orchestra of the *Overture Portsmouth Point*, clearer than the original. *Siesta* is given an aptly cool performance under Bryden Thomson, and the *Popular Birthday* is Malcolm Arnold's fragmentary linking of 'Happy birthday to you' with the *Popular Song* from *Façade*, originally written for Walton's twentieth birthday.

Façade: Suites 1 & 2.

*** Hyp. CDA 66436. E. N. Philh. O, Lloyd-Jones – BLISS: *Checkmate* ***; LAMBERT: *Horoscope.* *** ●

Brilliantly witty and humorous performances of the two orchestral suites which Walton himself fashioned from his 'Entertainment'. This is music which, with its outrageous quotations, can make one chuckle out loud. Moreover it offers, to quote Constant Lambert, 'one good tune after another', all scored with wonderful felicity. The playing here could hardly be bettered, and the recording is in the demonstration bracket with its natural presence and bloom.

Film scores

As You Like It: Suite. The Battle of Britain: Suite. Henry V: Suite. History of the English-speaking Peoples: March. Troilus and Cressida (opera): *Interlude.*

(M) *** EMI CDM5 65585-2. LPO Ch. & O, Davis.

The Battle of Britain Suite presents the music that (for trumpery reasons) was rejected for the original film, including a Wagnerian send-up and a splendid final march. Another vintage Walton march here was written for a television series based on Churchill's history, but again was never used. It is a pity that the *Henry V Suite* does not include the Agincourt charge, but it is good to have the choral contributions to the opening and closing sequences. Most welcome is the long-buried music for the 1926 Paul Czinner film of *As You Like It*. Warm, opulent recording.

Film Music: As You Like It (poem for orchestra); *Hamlet* (Shakespeare scenario in 9 movements) (both arr. Christopher Palmer).

(BB) **(*) Naxos 8.553344. Sheen, Dublin RTE Concert O, Penny.

In adaptations of film music for concert performance by the late Christopher Palmer, both Penny and the RTE Concert Orchestra give warm, sympathetic performances. Michael Sheen recites the Hamlet soliloquies with the ardour of youth, and the unnamed soprano soloist in the *As You Like It* song, *Under the greenwood tree*, sings with fresh, girlish tone. With recording a little recessed, and with thinnish strings, this cannot match the Chandos issue of the same coupling at full-price, but it makes a good bargain.

Scenes from Shakespeare (compiled Christopher Palmer): *As You Like It; Hamlet; Henry V; Richard III.*

(M) **(*) Chan. 7041. Gielgud, Plummer, ASMF, Marriner.

This makes an apt and attractive compilation, putting together well-chosen selections from the recordings of Walton's Shakespeare film music, first issued in the complete Chandos edition, not just for the three masterly films directed by Laurence Olivier, but also for the pre-war *As You Like It*. Roughly two-thirds of the *Henry V* music is included here, and about half of each of the other three. However, many collectors will opt to have more music and will prefer to hear the Shakespearean text in the theatre or cinema.

The Battle of Britain (suite); *Escape Me Never* (suite); *The First of the Few: Spitfire Prelude & Fugue; Three Sisters; A Wartime Sketchbook.*

*** Chan. 8870. ASMF, Marriner.

The Spitfire Prelude and Fugue, from *The First of the Few*, was immediately turned into a highly successful concert-piece, but we owe it to Christopher Palmer that there is the

'Wartime Sketchbook', drawing material from three of the wartime films, plus scraps that Colin Matthews did not use in the suite from the much later *Battle of Britain* film music and not least in the stirring theme from the credits of the film, *Went the Day Well*. The brief suite from the music for Olivier's film of Chekhov's *The Three Sisters*, from much later, brings more than one setting of the *Tsar's Hymn* and a charming imitation of *Swan Lake*. Earliest on the disc is *Escape Me Never*, the first of Walton's film-scores, written in 1935 in a more popular idiom; but the war-inspired music is what this delightful disc is really about. Marriner and the Academy give richly idiomatic performances, full of panache. Aptly opulent recording.

Henry V: Suite (arr. Mathieson) and (i) *Scenes from the Film; Richard III: Prelude & Suite; Spitfire Prelude & Fugue.*

(M) *** EMI stereo/mono CDM5 65007-2. (i) Olivier (speaker); Philh. O, composer.

This reissue includes the 1963 recordings of the *Henry V Suite, Richard III Prelude and Suite* and the *Spitfire Prelude and Fugue*. The performances are vital and exciting, and with the sound vivid and full the result is hugely enjoyable. Also included is the complete 1946 *Henry V* sequence with Laurence Olivier, as recorded on four 78s, and originally issued on LP by RCA with seven minutes of cuts. This is the restored complete version, and it has been excellently transferred, though the mono sound lacks body. The recording has great atmosphere though, with Olivier at his magnificent best, and the orchestra responding with tremendous energy: the sound of the arrows at the climax of the Agincourt sequence has never seemed more chilling. A wonderful CD.

Henry V: A Shakespeare Scenario (arr. Christopher Palmer).

*** Chan. 8892. Plummer (nar.), Westminster Cathedral Ch., ASMF, Marriner.

Few film-scores can match Walton's for the Olivier film of *Henry V* in its range and imagination, the whole of the 'Scenario' devised by Christopher Palmer lasting just over an hour. The most controversial change is to 'borrow' the first section of the march which Walton wrote much later for a projected television series on Churchill's *History of the English-Speaking Peoples*; otherwise, the chorus's call to arms, *Now all the youth of England is on fire*, would have had no music to introduce it. As an appendix, three short pieces are included which Walton quoted in his score. Sir Neville Marriner caps even his previous recordings in this series, with the Academy and Westminster Choir producing heartfelt playing and singing in sumptuous sound. As narrator, Christopher Plummer makes an excellent substitute for Olivier, unselfconsciously adopting a comparably grand style.

Henry V: Passacaglia; The Death of Falstaff; Touch her Soft Lips and Part.

(M) *** DG (ADD) 439 529-2. ECO, Barenboim – DELIUS:

Aquarelles etc.; VAUGHAN WILLIAMS: *Oboe Concerto* etc. ***

These two fine Walton string pieces make an admirable complement to a sensuously beautiful collection of English music, with Barenboim at his most affectionately inspirational and the ECO very responsive, and with the 1975 recording retaining its warmth and bloom.

Macbeth: Fanfare & March; Major Barbara (suite); Richard III (Shakespeare scenario).

*** Chan. 8841. Gielgud (nar.), ASMF, Marriner.

Disappointingly, Sir John Gielgud underplays Richard III's great 'Now is the winter of our discontent' speech, but working to the underlying music – much of it eliminated in the film – may have cramped his style. The performance generally has all the panache one could wish for, leading up to the return of the grand Henry Tudor theme at the end. The six-minute piece based on Walton's music for Gielgud's wartime production of *Macbeth* is much rarer and very valuable too, anticipating in its Elizabethan dance-music the *Henry V* film-score. *Major Barbara* also brings vintage Walton material. Marriner and the Academy give performances just as ripely committed as in their previous discs in the series, helped by sonorous Chandos sound.

The Quest (ballet): Complete; *The Wise Virgins* (ballet): Suite.

*** Chan. 8871. LPO, Thomson.

Walton's two wartime ballet-scores make an attractive coupling. As that stage in his career Walton, even in a hurry, could not help creating memorable ideas and, with the help of Constant Lambert – not to mention Christopher Palmer, who has expanded the instrumentation in line with the suite – the orchestral writing is often dazzling. Quite apart from the dramatic power of the performance, the recording is superb, among the fullest and clearest from Chandos. The sound for *The Wise Virgins* is more reverberant and the performance has less electricity, though Walton's distinctive arrangements of Bach cantata movements – including *Sheep May Safely Graze* – remain as fresh as ever.

(i) *Sinfonia concertante. Spitfire Prelude & Fugue; Variations on a Theme of Hindemith; March: The History of the English-Speaking Peoples.*

(BB) *** Naxos 8.553869. (i) Donohoe, E. Northern Philh., Daniel.

Paul Daniel conducts the English Northern Philharmonia in electrifying performances of this varied group of orchestral works. As before he is splendid at interpreting Walton's jazzy syncopations with the right degree of freedom. Following the composer's own suggestion, the original version of the *Sinfonia concertante* is preferred to the revision, fuller and more brilliant. The performance is excellent, despite the placing of the soloist, Peter Donohoe, too far forward. Daniel draws playing both warm and scintillating from the orchestra in the *Hindemith Variations* – no finer version exists – while the *March* and the *Spitfire* music hit home all the harder through Daniel's refusal to dawdle.

Sonata for Strings.

(M) **(*) EMI CDM5 66761-2. City of L. Sinfonia, Hickox – ELGAR: *Introduction & Allegro for Strings;* VAUGHAN WILLIAMS: *Fantasia on a Theme by Thomas Tallis.* **(*)

Walton's *Sonata for Strings* (an arrangement of the 1947 *String Quartet*) is made to sound highly effective in this outstanding performance under Hickox. The passionate account of the third movement *Lento* is a highlight of a reading which is full of intensity, and Hickox's athletic style and the bright, clearly focused digital sound suit this work better than the Elgar or Vaughan Williams couplings.

Symphony No. 1 in B flat min.; (i) *Belshazzar's Feast.*

⚫ *** EMI CDC5 56592-2. CBSO, Rattle (i) with Hampson, CBSO Ch., Cleveland O Ch.

(M) (***) EMI mono/stereo CDM5 65004-2. (i) Bell; Philh. Ch. & O, composer.

Symphony No. 1; Overture Scapino; Siesta.

(BB) *** BMG Arte Nova 74321 39124-2. Gran Canaria PO, Leaper.

Symphony No. 1; Partita for Orchestra.

(BB) *** Naxos 8.553180. E. N. PO, Daniel.

Symphony No. 1; Varii Capricci.

*** Chan. 8862. LPO, Thomson.

It is Rattle's gift as a Walton interpreter that he can combine pinpoint precision of ensemble with expressive freedom, making Walton's jazzy syncopations sound idiomatic. this ideal coupling brings together two bitingly intense masterpieces of the 1930s. *Belshazzar's Feast*, dating from 1931, has never been given quite so spectacular a recording as here. With the Birmingham Symphony Chorus joined by the visiting Cleveland Orchestra Chorus, the recording clearly defines the many dramatic antiphonal effects. Interpretatively, where readings of this brilliant oratorio have tended to grow broader and slower than the composer's own, Rattle tautly echoes Walton's example, and the extra bite and urgency are thrilling – not that Rattle rushes at all in such beautiful choruses as *By the waters of Babylon*. Thomas Hampson is the resonant baritone soloist, not as chilling as some in his account of the writing on the wall, but firm and dramatic.

The composer's recording of the *First Symphony* (mono) dates from 1951 and always suffered from a poor transfer in its LP days. Its promotion to CD in 1994 was something of a revelation: the sound now has far more body and bite than its long-deleted LP incarnation, and reveals just what an exciting performance it really was. Walton treats the persistent syncopated rhythms with a jazzy freedom, while the passion behind the performance is intense, most of all in the slow movement, which gains from some superb playing from the Philharmonia soloists. Comparing Walton's 1959 stereo version of *Belshazzar* here with his earlier, 1943 account is fascinating, with speeds consistently more spacious, but with tensions just as keen, and ensemble crisper, though with less mystery conveyed. The one snag is the soloist, Donald Bell, clean of attack but uncharacterful. Never mind, this is a superb CD, and makes a generous 78-minute coupling of some wonderful music-making.

In the *First Symphony* Paul Daniel knows unerringly how to build up tension to breaking point before resolving it and then building again. He is also freer than many in his use of rubato, as well as in the degree of elbow-room he allows for jazzy syncopations, always idiomatic. The *Scherzo* is sparkily witty, not just full of malice. In the slow movement, after the poised opening, Daniel tends to press ahead slightly for the sections which follow, agonizingly intense. The finale with its brassy, more extrovert manner has plenty of panache, and the weight and bite of the sound are excellent. This is a version that vies with even the finest at whatever price, and it outshines most. Daniel's reading of the *Partita* brings out above all the work's joyfulness, with the outer movements relaxed in their brilliance and the central slow movement warmly expressive.

Leaper's disc of Walton's *First* competes very well with almost any version in the catalogue. With finely disciplined playing, the reading is fresh and alert, idiomatic in its rhythmic pointing and with intense poetry in such key moments as the distant trumpet-call in the final coda. Starting almost inaudibly at the very start, Leaper seems intent on making the music emerge from mists, then he quickly builds up tension and momentum, even if in the first movement his reading is not as weighty as many. The clarity of the recording compensates and there is no lack of weight in the heavy brass, which has impressive bite. The slow movement brings inspired wind solos, and the *Scherzo* and finale are crisp and resilient, with busy ensembles made unusually clear, even transparent, a point that also marks Leaper's witty and sparkling account of the *Scapino Overture*, in which the cello solo is most beautifully done. *Siesta* is aptly dreamy, not literal or chilly, making this a disc to recommend to Waltonians and newcomers alike.

Thomson's is a warmly committed, understandingly idiomatic account of the work, weighty and rhythmically persuasive, if not as biting as some. In the slow movement his tender expressiveness goes with a flowing speed, well judged to avoid exaggeration. If the *Scherzo* is a degree less demonic than it might be, at a speed fractionally slower than usual, it is infectiously sprung. The Chandos coupling brings the first recording of *Varii capricci*, the orchestral suite in five compact movements which Walton developed from his set of guitar *Bagatelles*, written for Julian Bream. With a brilliant performance and sumptuous sound, it makes a fine supplement.

Symphony No. 2; Partita for Orchestra; Variations on a Theme by Hindemith.

⊛ (B) *** Sony (ADD) SBK 62753. Cleveland O, Szell.

In a letter to the conductor, Walton expressed himself greatly pleased with Szell's performance of the *Second Symphony*: 'It is a quite fantastic and stupendous performance from every point of view. Firstly it is absolutely right musically speaking, and the virtuosity is quite staggering, especially the Fugato; but everything is phrased and balanced in an unbelievable way.' Listening to the splendidly remastered CD of this 1961 recording, one cannot but join the composer

in responding to the wonderfully luminous detail in the orchestra. Szell's performance of the *Hindemith Variations* is no less remarkable. Finally comes the *Partita*, which was commissioned by the Cleveland Orchestra and given its première a year before the recording was made. The recordings are bright, in the CBS manner, but the ambience of Severance Hall brings a backing warmth and depth, and these are technically among the finest of Szell's recordings in this venue.

The Wise Virgins (ballet suite arr. from Bach).

(M) *** EMI (ADD) CDM5 65911-2. Concert Arts O, Irving – GLAZUNOV: *The Seasons*; SCARLATTI/TOMMASINI: *Good Humoured Ladies.* ***

Walton's orchestral arrangements of Bach created a score for the Sadler's Wells ballet in 1940. All the music except the second piece, a chorale-prelude, is extracted from cantatas, and the delightful '*Sheep may safely graze*' (richly presented here) is a highlight, alongside the tranquil '*See what His love can do*' from Cantata No. 85. It could not be better presented than it is here, and the resonant recording emphasizes the ebullience of the uninhibited moments, especially the robust finale. Sadly, this disc has just been deleted.

CHAMBER MUSIC

(i) 5 Bagatelles for Solo Guitar; (ii; iii) Duets for Children; (iv; ii) 2 Pieces for Violin & Piano; Toccata for Violin & Piano; (ii) (Piano) Façade: Valse; (v; i) Anon in Love (for tenor & guitar); (v; ii) 2 Songs for Tenor: The Winds, The Tritons.

*** Chan. 9292. (i) Bonell; (ii) Milne; (iii) Dowdeswell; (iv) Sillito; (v) Ainsley.

The *Toccata for Violin and Piano* is a curious mixture of cadenza and rhapsody of 15 minutes in a disconcertingly un-Waltonian style. Two songs for tenor are fascinating too, with a rushing accompaniment for *The Winds*, while *The Tritons* is chaconne-like, with a melody quite untypical of Walton. Milne and Dowdeswell bring out what charming, sharply focused ideas are contained in the ten *Duets for Children*. The piano arrangement of the *Valse* from *Façade* is so thorny that even Hamish Milne has to go cautiously. The two violin pieces – using French troubadour songs – are spin-offs from the *Henry V* incidental music and, in the second, *Scherzetto*, reflect what their composer had learnt, writing for Heifetz. The two works with guitar are well known in Julian Bream's performances and recordings. Bonell is lighter and more delicate than Bream, both in the *Bagatelles* and in *Anon in Love*, but is no less persuasive. Similarly, John Mark Ainsley lacks some of the punch of Peter Pears, for whom the cycle was written, but in a gentler way taps the wit and point of these Elizabethan conceits. A delightful collection, full of revealing insights into the composer's complex character.

Passacaglia for Solo Cello.

*** Chan. 8499. Wallfisch – BAX: *Rhapsodic Ballad*; BRIDGE: *Cello Sonata*; DELIUS: *Cello Sonata.* ***

William Walton's *Passacaglia* for solo cello was composed in the last year of his life. It has restraint and eloquence, and Raphael Wallfisch gives a thoroughly sympathetic account of it. Excellent recording.

Piano Quartet; Violin Sonata.

*** Chan. 8999. Sillito, Smissen, Orton, Milne.

Piano Quartet; String Quartet in A min.

(BB) *** Naxos 8.554646.(i) Donohoe; Maggini Qt.

(i; ii) Piano Quartet; (i; iii) Violin Sonata; (iv) 5 Bagatelles (for guitar).

(B) *** EMI CZS 7243 573989-2 (2). (i) Graham;
(ii) Silverthorne, Welsh, Margalit; (iii) Alley; (iv) Kerstens –
BRITTEN: *Cello Sonata*, etc. ***

This performance of the *Piano Quartet* with Hamish Milne as pianist makes one marvel that such music could have been the inspiration of a 16-year-old. Admittedly Walton revised the piece, but here is music which instantly grabs the ear, with striking ideas attractively and dramatically presented in each movement. The two principal performers from the quartet make a warmly sympathetic rather than high-powered duo for the *Violin sonata* of 1949. Yet the combination of Sillito's ripely persuasive style and Milne's incisive power, clarifying textures and giving magic to the phrasing, keeps tensions sharp. The satisfyingly full sound helps too.

The young players of the Maggini Quartet – who earlier recorded Elgar for Naxos – give performances both refined and powerful of both works. The opening of the 1947 *String Quartet* is presented in hushed intimacy, making the contrast all the greater when Walton's richly lyrical writing emerges in full power. There is a tender, wistful quality here, which culminates in a rapt, intense account of the slow movement, with the world of late Beethoven much closer than most interpreters have appreciated. The poignancy of those two longer movements is then set against the clean bite of the second movement Scherzo and the brief hectic finale, with textures clear and transparent.

With Peter Donohoe a powerful, incisive pianist, the early *Piano Quartet* is also given a performance of high contrasts. The echoes of Stravinsky's *Petrushka* are colourfully brought out in the finale, a movement that looks forward more clearly than the rest to the mature Walton, even though the pentatonic writing in the earlier movements is here most persuasively presented. First-rate recording, even if the piano is a shade too forwardly balanced.

On EMI you get a worthwhile bonus in the Bagatelles for guitar, with Tom Kerstens even lighter and more volatile than Julian Bream, for whom they were written. With Israela Margalit injecting fire, the performance of the *Piano Quartet* is also lighter and more volatile than in the Chandos version, though the extra weight of that rival adds up increasingly in the last two movements. Janice Graham is also the soloist in the *Violin Sonata*, again fanciful and light, whilst bringing warmth and purposefulness to a work that can easily seem wayward. Though the three pieces were recorded in different venues, the sound is consistent, excellent in each. An excellent bargain set.

String Quartet in A min.

*** Hyp. CDA 66718. Coull Qt – BRIDGE: *3 Idylls*; ***
ELGAR: *Quartet.* **(*)

(N) *** Regis RRC 1015. Britten Qt – ELGAR: *Quartet.*

❀ *** Testament mono SBT 1052. Hollywood Qt –
HINDEMITH: *Quartet No. 3*; PROKOFIEV: *Quartet No. 2.* (***) ❀

String Quartet in A min; String Quartet No. 1.

*** Chan. 8944. Gabrieli Qt.
(N) *** Black Box BBM 1035. Emperor Qt.

Coupled ideally on Chandos with the mature *String Quartet in A minor*, completed in 1946, is the atonal *First Quartet*, long thought to be lost, which Walton wrote when an under-graduate at Oxford. The result, edited by Christopher Palmer, is hardly recognizable as Walton at all but is full of fire and imagination. The first movement is 'pastoral-atonal', lyrical in its counterpoint, but the Scherzo, built on vigorously rhythmic motifs and jagged ostinatos, has much more of Bartók in it than of Schoenberg, while the fugue of the finale seeks to emulate Beethoven's *Grosse Fuge* in its complexity and massive scale, alone lasting almost 16 minutes. The Gabrieli performance brings out all the latent power and lyrical warmth, often implying an underlying anger. It provides a fascinating contrast with the highly civilized *A minor* work of 25 years later. That comes in a red-blooded Gabrieli recording of 1986, earlier available in coupling with the Elgar *Quartet*. Both recordings were made in the warm, rich acoustic of The Maltings, Snape, with little discrepancy between them.

The young members of the Emperor Quartet give brilliant, incisive performances of both of Walton's string quartets, not just the one in A minor from his high maturity in 1947, but the very early work which after a handful of performances in the early 1920s Walton suppressed but did not destroy. For that earlier work, pointing forward to a very different atonal style from that which Walton quickly came to adopt, the Emperor Quartet have had access to extra material involving editing and cuts, observing those that were plainly the composer's own. The differences of text between this and the premiere recording by the Gabrieli Quartet are minimal.

More important is the difference of approach in both works, with the Emperor Quartet's speeds consistently faster than those of the Gabrielis, notably in the last of the three movements in the 1922 work, with the fugues even more clearly echoing Beethoven's *Grosse Fuge*. Helped by drier recording, the attack is more biting too, the approach more direct, less warmly expressive. A valid alternative, though in the 1947 work many Waltonians will miss the fuller romantic thrust of the Gabrielis and others.

The Elgar and Walton *Quartets* also makes an apt and attractive coupling, and here the Coulls, unlike their direct rivals, offer as bonus a fine example of Frank Bridge's quartet-writing. In the Walton, the reading captures movingly the spirit of Waltonian melancholy, bringing out the elegiac intensity of the extended *Lento* slow movement, taken at a very measured pace. The Coulls are splendid too in capturing the element of fun in Walton's scherzando ideas. The Brittens on Collins, also offering the Elgar, find less fantasy.

The Britten Quartet, bitingly powerful, bring out the emotional intensity, playing with refinement and sharp focus, finding a repose and poise in the slow movement that bring it close to late Beethoven. The contrasts of wistful lyricism and scherzando bite in the first movement make most other versions sound clumsy by comparison, and the incisiveness of Walton's jaggedly rhythmic writing is a delight.

In many ways the pioneering account by the Hollywood Quartet, made in 1950, has still not been surpassed. It first appeared on a Capitol LP in harness with the Villa-Lobos *Sixth Quartet*. The sound comes up very well, though it is not, of course, state of the art. Moreover it comes with equally strong couplings and cannot be too strongly recommended.

Violin Sonata.

(N) *** Nim. NI 5666. Hope, Mulligan – ELGAR: *Violin Sonata;* FINZI: *Elegy.* ***

(BB) *** ASV CDQS 6191. McAslan, Blakely – ELGAR: *Violin Sonata.* ***

(M) (**) EMI mono CDM5 66122-2. Menuhin, Kentner – ELGAR; WALTON: *Sonatas.* **(*)

As in the Elgar, Daniel Hope gives a big-scale, virtuoso reading of the Walton sonata, using the widest dynamic range. The warmth and thrust of Hope's performance brings out the purposefulness of the writing in a work that can seem wayward. So, with understanding support from his fellow Menuhin protégé, Simon Mulligan, Hope brings tautness to the wide-ranging variation movement that rounds off the two-movement structure. With Hope's sweet, finely focused violin tone beautifully caught in the Nimbus recording – full and warm but less reverberant than some – and well balanced against the piano, it makes an outstanding recommendation.

Lorraine McAslan gives a warmly committed performance of Walton's often wayward *Sonata*, coping well with the sharp and difficult changes of mood in both of the two long movements. The romantic melancholy of the piece suits her well and, though the recording does not make her tone as rounded as it should be, she produces some exquisite pianissimo playing, making this a very impressive début recording. John Blakely is a most sympathetic partner, particularly impressive in crisply articulated scherzando passages. At its modest cost this is very highly recommendable.

The Menuhins commissioned this sonata to be premièred by the present performers, and it was dedicated jointly to their wives. It was completed in 1940 but the composer withdrew it, and the present two-movement version was recorded in 1950. First recordings are always special, and this one is no exception; but it is a pity that the very forward recording tends to treble emphasis, which is unflattering to Menuhin's upper register in its CD transfer.

CHORAL MUSIC

(i) *Belshazzar's Feast. Coronation March: Crown Imperial; Henry V* (film incidental music): *Suite.*

*** Decca 448 134-2. (i) Terfel, Bournemouth Symphony Ch., Waynflete Singers, L'Inviti; Bournemouth SO, Litton.

(i) *Belshazzar's Feast. Improvisations on an Impromptu of Benjamin Britten; Overtures: Portsmouth Point; Scapino.*

(M) *** EMI (ADD) CDM7 64723-2. LSO, Previn, (i) with Shirley-Quirk, L. Symphony Ch.

Belshazzar's Feast; Coronation Te Deum; Gloria.

**(*) Chan. 8760. Howell, Gunson, Mackie, Roberts, Bach Ch., Philh. O, Willcocks.

On Decca *Belshazzar's Feast* was put into the grand setting of Winchester Cathedral. The reverberation time is formidably long, yet, thanks to brilliant balancing, there is ample detail and fine focus in exceptionally incisive choral and orchestral sound. The great benefit is that this emerges as a performance on a bigger scale than its rivals, with the contrasts between full chorus and semi-chorus the more sharply established. The vividly dramatic soloist is Bryn Terfel, pointing the words as no one else ever has, his expressive colourings even more individual here, both in 'Babylon was a great city' and in his spine-chilling narration describing the writing on the wall. The other items, the *Henry V Suite* and *Crown Imperial*, were recorded, like *Belshazzar*, in Winchester Cathedral, but sadly the opportunity was not taken for using a chorus in *Henry V*. The fanfares have never been more evocative, and the build-up of the Agincourt charge is thrilling. Despite the reverberation, *Crown Imperial* is also given a stirring performance.

Previn's EMI version of *Belshazzar's Feast* still remains among the most spectacular yet recorded. The digital remastering has not lost the body and atmosphere of the sound but has increased its impact. This fine performance was recorded with Walton present on his seventieth birthday and, though Previn's tempi are slower than those set by Walton himself in his two recordings, the authenticity is clear, with consistently sharp attack and with dynamic markings meticulously observed down to the tiniest hairpin markings. Chorus and orchestra are challenged to their finest standards, and John Shirley-Quirk proves a searching and imaginative soloist. The *Improvisations*, given a first recording, make a generous fill-up alongside the two overtures in which Previn, the shrewdest and most perceptive of Waltonians, finds more light and shade than usual. Again the remastered sound is excellent.

Willcocks scores over some rivals in his pacing. Speeds tend to be a degree faster, as in *By the Waters of Babylon* which flows evenly yet without haste. The soloist, Gwynne Howell, firm and dark of tone, is among the finest of all exponents but, with the Bach Choir placed rather more distantly than in most versions, this is not as incisive as its finest rivals. The *Coronation Te Deum* receives a richly idiomatic performance, and Willcocks also gives weight and thrust to the *Gloria*, with the tenor, Neil Mackie, outstanding among the soloists. The microphone unfortunately catches an unevenness in Ameral Gunson's mezzo. The recording is warmly reverberant, not ideally clear on choral detail but easy to listen to.

(i) *Christopher Columbus (suite of incidental music);* (ii) *Anon in Love;* (iii) *4 Songs After Edith Sitwell: Daphne; Through gilded trellises; Long Steel Grass; Old Sir Faulk. A Song for the Lord Mayor's Table; The Twelve (an anthem for the Feast of any Apostle).*

*** Chan. 8824. (i) Finnie, Davies; (ii) Hill; (iii) Gomez; Westminster Singers, City of L. Sinfonia, Hickox.

The composer's own orchestral versions of his song-cycles *Anon in Love* (for tenor) and *A Song for the Lord Mayor's Table* (for soprano) are so beautifully judged that they transcend the originals, and the strength and beauty of these strongly characterized songs is enormously enhanced, particularly in performances as positive as these by Martyn Hill and Jill Gomez. The anthem, *The Twelve*, also emerges far more powerfully with orchestral instead of organ accompaniment. The four Sitwell songs were orchestrated by Christopher Palmer, who also devised the suite from Walton's incidental music to Louis MacNeice's wartime radio play, *Christopher Columbus*, buried for half a century. It is a rich score which brings more happy anticipations of the *Henry V* film-music in the choral writing, and even of the opera *Troilus and Cressida*, as well as overtones of *Belshazzar's Feast*. Warmly committed performances, opulently recorded.

OPERA

The Bear (complete).

*** Chan. 9245. Jones, Opie, Shirley-Quirk, Northern Sinfonia, Hickox.

The one-Acter *The Bear*, based on Chekhov, matches in its point and flair Britten's own chamber operas also written for Aldeburgh, with Walton producing textures that are sumptuous rather than spare. It is a masterly score, with the farcical element reflected in dozens of parodies and tongue-in-cheek musical references, starting cheekily with echoes of Britten's own *Midsummer Night's Dream*. Richard Hickox with members of the Northern Sinfonia paces the music superbly, flexibly heightening the moments of mock-melodrama that punctuate this tale of a mourning widow who faces the demands of one of her dead husband's creditors. The casting of the three characters is ideal, with Della Jones commanding as the affronted widow, all her words crystal clear, Alan Opie clean-cut and incisive as the creditor or 'Bear' of the title, and with John Shirley-Quirk as the old retainer. In many ways this is a piece – with its climactic duel scene leading to an amorous *coup-de-foudre* – which comes off even better on disc than on stage.

Troilus and Cressida (complete).

⊕ ***** Chan. 9370/1** (2). Ar. Davies, Howarth, Howard, Robson, Opie, Bayley, Thornton, Owen-Lewis, Opera North Ch., English N. Philh. O, Hickox.

Few operas since Puccini have such a rich store of memorable tunes as *Troilus and Cressida*. As Chandos's magnificent recording shows, based on Opera North's 1995 production – using Walton's tautened score of 1976 but with the original soprano register restored for Cressida – this red-bloodedly romantic opera on a big classical subject deserves to enter the regular repertory. Judith Howarth portrays the heroine as girlishly vulnerable, rising superbly to the big challenges of the love duets and final death scene. Arthur Davies is an aptly Italianate Troilus, an ardent lover, and there is not a weak link in the rest of the characterful cast, with Nigel Robson a finely pointed Pandarus, comic but not camp, avoiding any echoes of Peter Pears, the originator. As Evadne, Cressida's maid, Yvonne Howard produces firm, rich mezzo tone, and the role of Calkas, Cressida's father, is magnificently sung by Clive Bayley. The role of Diomede, Cressida's Greek suitor, can seem one-dimensional but Alan Opie, in one of his finest performances on record, sharpens the focus, making him a genuine threat, a noble enemy. Richard Hickox draws magnetic performances from chorus and orchestra alike, bringing out the many parallels with the early Walton of *Belshazzar's Feast* and the *Symphony No. 1*. As for the recorded sound, the bloom of the Leeds Town Hall acoustic allows the fullest detail from the orchestra, enhancing the Mediterranean warmth of the score, helped by the wide dynamic range. The many atmospheric effects, often offstage, are clearly and precisely focused, and the placing of voices on the stereo stage is also unusually precise.

WARD, John (1571–1638)

Madrigals: *Come sable night; Cruel unkind; Die not, fond man; Hope of my heart; If heaven's just wrath; If the deep sighs; I have retreated; My breast I'll set; Oft have I tender'd; Out from the vale; Retire, my troubled soul; Sweet Philomel.*

*** Hyp. CDA 66256. Consort of Musicke, Rooley.

Ward's music speaks with a distinctive voice. He chooses poetry of high quality, his music is always finely proportioned, and such is the quality of this music and the accomplishment with which it is presented, these settings represent the madrigal tradition at its finest.

WARLAND, Bill (born 1921)

Amaro dolce; Bossa romantica; Brighton Belle; Dreaming Spires; Happy Hacienda; In the Shadows of Vesuvius; It's Spring Again; Latin Lover; Leeds Castle; Millennium: A Celebration March; Pepita; Rhapsodie Tristesse; Scottish Power; Shopping Spree; 3 Señoritas (suite); Sombrero; To Eleanor.

(N) *** Marco 8.225161. Dublin RTE Concert O, Sutherland.

An excellent addition to Marco Polo's 'British Light Music' series. The composer himself wrote the sleeve notes – making some interesting comments on 'the death of light music in popular culture'. Still, it thrives on CD, for which Marco-Polo, ASV and others have done splendid work. If none of the music here is momentous, it is thoroughly enjoyable and tuneful. There are nice splashes of local colour here and there (the rumbustious *Latin Lover* is especially enjoyable) and sentiment as well as humour are represented, and it's good to see that Bill Warland is still composing: his *Millennium March* was written for the January 2001 celebrations. In case you are thinking the Gaelic flavoured *Scottish Power* has something to do with the electricity supply, it was actually written, the composer tells us, 'as a dedication to a Scots lassie I know so well, with whom there was a magnetic attraction, and whose maiden name was Power'. Excellent performances and recording.

WARLOCK, Peter (1894–1930)

(i) *Capriol Suite; 6 English Tunes; 6 Italian Dance Tunes; Serenade for Strings;* (ii) *The Curlew (song-cycle).*

(BB) *** Arte Nova 74321 37868-2. (i) L. Festival O, Pople; (ii) Hill, Beckett, Alty, Gibbs, Smith, Stevens, Szucs.

Warlock's two most important works, the colourful *Capriol suite* and searchingly intense setting of Yeats's *The Curlew*, are here very well coupled with the *Six English Tunes* and the *Six Italian Dance Tunes*, both miniature suites on the lines of *Capriol*, but with movements barely a minute long unpretentiously making colourful points and moving on. The *Serenade* – lusciously echoes Delius in its string writing. Ross Pople directs clean-cut, consciously small-scale readings that rightly bring out the emotion of the writing. The tenor, Martyn Hill, placed well forward in *The Curlew*, similarly brings out the emotional thrust of the words with commendably clear diction. Warm recording to match.

Capriol Suite (orchestral version); *Serenade for Strings (for the sixtieth birthday of Delius).*

*** Chan. 8808. Ulster O, Handley – MOERAN: *Serenade* etc. ***

The effect of the present full orchestral score of the *Capriol Suite* is to rob the music of some of its astringency. A dryish wine is replaced with one with the fullest bouquet, for the wind instruments make the textures more rococo in feeling as well as increasing the colour. Handley's fine performance, is made to sound opulent by the acoustics of Ulster Hall, Belfast. The lovely *Serenade*, for strings alone, is also played and recorded very beautifully.

(i) *Capriol Suite;* (ii) *Serenade to Frederick Delius on his 60th Birthday.* Songs: (iii) *Adam lay ybounden;* (iv) *Autumn twilight;* (v) *Balulalow;* (vi) *Bethlehem Down;* (vii) *Captain Stratton's fancy;* (viii) *The Curlew (song-cycle);* (ix) *I saw a fair maiden;* (x) *The Lady's Birthday (arrangement);* (v) *Pretty ring time;* (x) *The shrouding of the Duchess of Malfi;* (xi) *Where riches is everlasting;* (xii) *Yarmouth Fair.*

(M) *** EMI (ADD) CDM5 65101-2. (i) E. Sinf., Dilkes; (ii) Bournemouth Sinf., Del Mar; (iii) Hammersley, Williams; (iv) Harvey, Moore; (v) Baker, Ledger; (vi) Guildford Cathedral Ch., Rose; (vii) Lloyd, Walker; (viii) Partridge, Music Group of London; (ix) Westminster Abbey Ch., Guest; (x) Baccholian Singers, Partridge;

(xi) King's College, Cambridge, Ch., Willcocks; (xii) Brannigan, Lush.

Opening with one of our favourite versions of the *Capriol Suite* from the English Sinfonia under Neville Dilkes, followed by Warlock's touchingly tender tribute to Delius, this selection ranges over a well-chosen selection of favourite songs, solo and choral. The other key item is *The Curlew*, Warlock's setting of a sequence of poems by Yeats which reflect the darker side of his complex personality. Ian Partridge, with the most sensitive response to word-meanings, gives an intensely poetic performance, beautifully recorded. Among other performances those of Dame Janet Baker stand out, but many of the songs here are persuasively beautiful. The transfers are consistently well managed.

(i) *Capriol Suite;* (ii) *The Curlew (song-cycle); 5 Nursery Jingles. The Birds; Chopcherry; Fairest May; Mourn No More; My gostly fader; Sleep; The Water Lilly.*

(BB) **(*) ASV CDQS 6143. (i) RPO, Barlow; (ii) Griffett, Haffner Qt; Murdoch, Ryan.

Though Griffett's performance of *The Curlew* is not so beautiful or so imaginative as Ian Partridge's, each one of these songs is a miniature of fine sensitivity, and James Griffett sings them with keen insight, pointing the words admirably. The instrumental playing is most sensitive, and the recording is warmly atmospheric yet clear. The performance of the *Capriol Suite* is also a very good one, and the digital recording is first rate. This CD is well worth its modest cost.

Adam lay ybounden; As dew in Aprylle; Benedicamus Domino; Bethlehem down; The Birds; Born is the babe; Balulalow; Carillon, Carilla; A Cornish Christmas carol; A Cornish carol; Corpus Christi; The first mercy; The five lesser joys of Mary; The frostbound wood; I saw a fair maiden; My little sweet darling; Out of the Orient crystal skies; The rich cavalcade; Song for Christmas Day; Sweet was the song the Virgin sang; The sycamore tree; Tyrley Tyrlow; What cheer? Good cheer!; Where riches is everlastingly.

*** Somm SOMMCD 011. Allegri Singers, Halsey; with Cable, Empett; Rosamunde Qt; M. Barnes; R. Barnes.

Most of these Christmas settings are little known, many are quite simple, but all are quite lovely. Among the more extended pieces the *Cornish Christmas carol* is strophic but the harmonic setting is constantly varied, while the ravishing *Corpus Christie* carol and simpler *Born is the babe* are set for solo voices and string quartet. *Out of the Orient crystal skies* and the gentle *Bethlehem down* are particularly haunting and the concert ends with the brief *Sycamore tree*, as joyful as an English carol can be. Fine, lively, dedicated performances throughout, with excellent accompaniments all round.

Songs: *As ever I saw; Autumn twilight; The bachelor; The bayly berith the bell away; Captain Stratton's fancy; First mercy; The fox; Hey, trolly, loly lo; Ha'nacker Mill; I held love's head; The jolly shepherd; Late summer; Lullaby; Milkmaids; Mourne no more; Mr Belloc's fancy; My gostly fader; My own country; The night; Passing by; Piggesnie;*

Play-acting; Rest, sweet nymphs; Sleep; Sweet content;
Take, o take those lips away; There is a lady sweet and fair;
Thou gav'st me leave to kiss; Walking the woods; When as
the rye; The wind from the west; Yarmouth Fair.

*** Chan. 8643. Luxon, Willison.

Songs like *Autumn twilight*, the powerfully expressive *Late summer* and *Captain Stratton's fancy* are appealing in utterly different ways, and there is not a single number in this programme that does not show the composer either in full imaginative flow or simply enjoying himself, as in *Yarmouth Fair*. Luxon's performances are first class and David Willison provides sensitive and sparkling accompaniments. The recording is first class.

WASSENAER, Unico Wilhelm
(1692–1766)

Concerti armonici Nos. 1–6.

*** Hyp. CDA 66670. Brandenburg Cons., Goodman.

Long been attributed to Pergolesi, these splendid concertos were in truth written by Unico Wilhelm, Graf von Wassenaer, a Dutch part-time composer of remarkable accomplishment. Their invention, vigorous and expressive, is sustained by a remarkably harmonic individuality: in short they are first-class works, almost on a par with the *concerti grossi* of Handel. These fine new performances are most presentable, and Hyperion's recording is very good indeed, to eclipse previous issues of this rewarding repertoire.

WAXMAN, Franz (1906–67)

The Song of Terezin (Das Lied von Terezin).
*** Decca 460 211-2. Jones, Berlin R. Ch., Children's Ch., &
SO, Lawrence Foster – ZEISL: *Requiem Ebraico.*

Dating from 1964, only three years before he died, Franz Waxman's *The Song of Terezin* is a moving setting of poems and other material left by children imprisoned in the notorious concentration camp of Terezin. Waxman's style, with its Schoenbergian echoes, is far more uncompromising than in his film music but still approachable, helped by superb performances and opulent sound. In such a context the settings of lighter poems are all the more poignant.

WEBER, Carl Maria von (1786–1826)

*Andante & Hungarian Rondo in E flat, Op. 35; Bassoon
Concerto in F, Op. 75.*

*** Chan. 9656. Popov, Russian State SO, Polyansky –
HUMMEL; MOZART: *Bassoon Concertos.* ***

Valeri Popov is in his element here. There is some astonishing spiccato bravura in the finale of the *Hungarian Rondo*, and both he and his accompanying orchestra under Polyansky capture the grand manner of the first movement of the concerto and are quite touching in the romantic cantabile of the *Andantino*. The finale then brings both a genial wit

and more solo fireworks. The recording is full-bodied and resonant, but clearly detailed in the Chandos manner.

(i) *Bassoon Concerto in F, Op. 75;* (ii) *Clarinet Concerto
No. 1 in F min., Op. 73;* (iii) *Horn concertino in E min.,
Op. 45.* Overtures: *Abu Hassan; Euryanthe; Der Freischütz;
Jubel; Oberon; Peter Schmoll.* (iv) *Piano Sonata No. 1:
Moto perpetuo* (arr. & orch. Leppard)

(N) (B) ** Erato Ultima (ADD) 3984 25602-2 (2). Bamberg SO,
Guschlbauer; with (i) Hongne; (ii) Lancelot; (iii) Barboteu;
(iv) SCO, Leppard.

The *Bassoon Concerto* sounds delightful here, and it is given a spirited and endearing performance by Paul Hongne, who has an attractively woody French bassoon timbre. Jacque Lancelot, too, is obviously French, and his clarinet tone is tangier, less mellow (some might say more nasal) than usual. His performance of the *F minor Clarinet Concerto* is admirably stylish but less succulent than his competitors, especially in the *Adagio*. Georges Barboteu, however, is as romantic as you could wish in the *Horn Concerto*, and finds all the necessary range and bravura for the theme and variations first movement, with its richly vocal main theme, and also in the lively polacca finale. Throughout, the accompaniments are warmly supportive, and the overtures, too, are well played, with impressive contributions from the horns in *Der Freischütz* and *Oberon* (one of the finest performances). The allegros in *Freischütz* and *Euryanthe* could do with more dramatic thrust, and it is the lighter *Abu Hassan* and *Peter Schmoll* which come off best. Raymond Leppard's sparkling, Mendelssohnian orchestration of the the *Rondo* from the *First Piano Sonata*, which he conducts himself, makes a winning encore. Good full analogue recording throughout, given a very natural transfer.

Clarinet Concertino in E flat, Op. 26.

*** ASV CDDCA 559. Johnson, ECO, Groves – CRUSELL:
Concerto No. 2 *** ❀; BAERMANN: *Adagio* ***;
ROSSINI: *Introduction, Theme & Variations.* ***

Emma Johnson is in her element here. Her phrasing is wonderfully beguiling and her use of light and shade agreeably subtle, while she finds a superb lilt in the final section, pacing the music to bring out its charm rather than achieve breathless bravura. Sir Charles Groves provides an admirable accompaniment, and the recording is eminently realistic and naturally balanced.

Clarinet Concerto No. 1 in F min., Op. 73.

*** EMI CDC 55155-2. Meyer, Dresden State O, Blomstedt –
MOZART; STAMITZ: *Concertos* ***.

Sabine Meyer gives a lusciously seductive account of the *F minor Concerto*, accompanying herself with aplomb. She is beautifully recorded

*Clarinet Concertos Nos. 1; 2 in E flat, Op. 74; Clarinet
Concertino.*

(N) *** DG (IMS) 435 875-2. Neidlich, Orpheus CO (with
ROSSINI: *Introduction, Theme & Variations in
E flat ***).

(M) *** Classic fM 75605 57019-2. Lawson, Hanover Band, Goodman – SPOHR: *Clarinet Concerto No. 1.* ***

(BB) *** Virgin 2 x 1 Double VBD5 61585-2 (2). Pay, OAE – CRUSELL: *Clarinet Concertos Nos. 1–3.* ***

(BB) *** Naxos 8.550378. Ottensamer, Slovak State PO (Košice), Wildner.

If you want these concertos on modern instruments, Charles Neidlich meets every need. His tone is beautiful, his phrasing warmly musical, he swings along most beguilingly in the *Andante* of the *Concertino* and the *Romanze* of the *F minor Concerto* is shaped with much delicacy. He lollops delightfully in the finales of all three works. He plays his own cadenzas and the Orpheus Chamber Orchestra, rather resonantly recorded, provide accompaniments of substance which are both polished and supportive.

The Rossini *Variations* make a witty and elegantly appealing bonus. However, the performances on the superbargain Warner Apex collection below are also first class in every way and every bit as well recorded, and this disc includes also the *Grand duo concertante*.

Stylish and imaginative period performances of all three works from Colin Lawson with the Hanover Band, vividly recorded, generously supplemented by the Spohr *First Concerto*. With his attractively reedy tone Lawson is a most persuasive soloist, moulding Weber's melodies seductively and pointing rhythms jauntily, with brilliant feats of tonguing in the light-hearted finales of each work.

Antony Pay uses a copy of a seven-keyed clarinet by Simiot of Lyons from 1800. The sonority is cleaner and less bland than can be the case in modern performances, and the solo playing is both expert and sensitive. A further gesture to authenticity is the absence of a conductor; however, the ensemble might have been even better and the texture more finely judged and balanced had there been one. The recordings are vivid and truthful and those attracted to the coupling with Crusell should be well satisfied.

Ernst Ottensamer is a highly sensitive clarinettist, who is a member of the Vienna Wind Ensemble. His account of the two *Clarinet Concertos* can hold its own against nearly all the competition, the Košice orchestra also responds well to Johannes Wildner's direction, and the recorded sound is very natural and well balanced. A real bargain.

(i; ii) *Clarinet Concertos No. 1 in F min.; 2 in E flat. Clarinet Concertino en E flat, Op. 26;* (iii) *Grand duo concertante for Clarinet & Piano, Op.48.*

⚙ *** ASV (ADD) CDDCA 747. (i) Johnson, (ii) ECO, cond. Tortelier, Schwarz or Groves; (iv) with Black.

(N) (BB) *** Warner Apex 8573 89246-2. (i) Boeykens; (ii) Rotterdam PO, Conlon; (iii) Meyer, Duchable.

(i) *Clarinet Concertos Nos. 1–2;* (ii) *Grand duo concertant for Clarinet & Piano.*

**(*) Teldec 0630 15428-2. Kam, (i) Leipzig Gewandhaus O, Masur.

Emma Johnson's scintillating accounts of these three Weberian showpieces were made at different times and with different conductors, all of whom prove to be highly sympathetic to their young soloist. Her subtlety of expression is remarkable, with pianissimos more daringly extreme and with distinctly persuasive phrasing in slow movements treated warmly and spaciously. In the sparkling finales she is wittier than almost any, plainly enjoying herself to the full. The *Concertino*, in some ways the most delightful work of the three, especially its delicious finale, is hardly less beguiling; and as a bonus we are offered a brilliant and individually expressive account of the *Grand duo concertante* for clarinet and piano. Here she finds an admirable partner in Gordon Black, who accompanies with equal flair.

However, if you are looking for a bargain alternative, Walter Boeykens will be hard to beat. He is a most sensitive player and phrases the expressive music meltingly, with a lovely tone, as the slow movement of the *F minor Concerto* readily demonstrates; and there are some subtle touches of rubato in the *Concertino*. James Conlon and the Rotterdam Orchestra provide firm, yet flexible accompaniments. Weber's chortling *Rondos* in all three works are delightfully presented, with the *Polacca* finale of the *E flat Concerto* very neatly pointed. Paul Meyer takes over in the romantic *Grand duo concertante*, quite perfectly balanced with Duchable, and they make a fine partnership. An excellent disc, given first-class recording.

As the opening movement of the *First Concerto* demonstrates, Sharon Kam has the gift of magicking a phrase, regularly holding tension over an exaggerated pause or tenuto. Most remarkable of all is the dark intensity of Kam's account of the slow, minor-key *Romanza* of the *Second Concerto*, taken at a measured tempo. She is similarly impressive in the *Grand Duo Concertant*, though there the piano tone of Itamar Golan is on the shallow side. The orchestral sound is warm, if rather opaque in tuttis. Emma Johnson's rival disc on ASV, with the *Clarinet Concertino* as an extra, remains marginally preferable.

(i) *Clarinet Concertos Nos. 1 in F min.; 2 in E flat;* (ii) *Konzertstück in F min. for Piano & Orchestra;* (iii) *Invitation to the Dance* (orch. BERLIOZ), *Op. 65; Overtures: Abu Hassan;* (iv) *Euryanthe; Der Freischütz; Oberon;* (v) *Symphony No. 1 in C., Op. 19;* (vi) *Clarinet Quintet.*

(B) ** Ph. Duo (ADD) 462 868-2 (2). (i) Michallik, Dresden State O, Sanderling; (ii) Magaloff, LSO, Sir Colin Davis; (iii) LSO, Mackerras; (iv) Concg. O, Dorati; (v) New Philh. O, Boettcher; (vi) Stahr, Berlin Philharmonic Octet (members).

The two *Clarinet Concertos* are well played by Oskar Michallik, with good support from Sanderling and the fine Dresden orchestra. But, as in Herbert Stahr's Berlin account of the *Quintet*, these artists are at their best in slow movements. Elsewhere, though thoroughly musical, the playing could do with more dash. However, Magaloff's poised and well-characterized account of the *Konzertstück* is most satisfying, well recorded and altogether one of the best versions on the market. The two performances under Mackerras are also a delight: *Abu Hassan* light and sparkling, and an elegant *Invitation to the Dance*. But in the other three overtures, the Concertgebouw string sound as recorded is brilliant to the point of fierceness and the effect is to emphasize Dorati's concentration on drama rather than atmosphere (though there is some beautiful horn playing). However the engaging *First Symphony* is well served both by the New Philharmonia and Boettcher, who favours a weighty approach but does not lack a lighter touch when needed. Overall this is fair value

(i) *Horn Concerto No. 1 in E. Invitation to the Dance* (orch. Berlioz), *Op. 65.* Overtures: *Abu Hassan; Der Beherrscher des Geister (The Ruler of the Spirits); Euryanthe; Der Freischütz; Oberon; Peter Schmoll. Symphonies Nos. 1–2.*

(N) (B) *** Nimbus Double NI 7062/3. (i) Halstead; Hanover Band, Goodman.

Not surprisingly, Anthony Halstead circumnavigates the fiendish bravura of Weber's *Horn Concerto* with consummate ease on his hand horn, and Goodman provides characteristically vital period performances of the two symphonies, even if they are not quite as beguiling as Georgiadis's outstanding modern-instrument versions on Naxos.

However what makes this Nimbus Double well worth considering is the persuasively delectable performances of the six overtures (plus *Invitation to the Dance* in Berlioz's arrangement), which are likely to convert anyone to authenticity in this repertoire. The rasp of trombones at the start of *Euryanthe* has a thrilling tang, and the warm acoustic ensures that the period string-players sound neither scrawny nor abrasive, yet present rapid passage-work with crystal clarity. Of feathery lightness, the scurrying violins in the *Abu Hassan* overture are a delight, and each item (including a rarity in *The Ruler of the Spirits*) brings its moments of magic, with Goodman both fresh and sympathetic, securing consistently lively and alert playing from his team.

Piano Concertos Nos. 1 in C, Op. 18; 2 in E flat, Op. 32; Konzertstück, Op. 79.

(B) **(*) Discovery DICD 920222. Protopopescu, Belgian R. & TV O, Rahbari.

Piano Concertos Nos. 1–2; Konzertstück; Polacca brillante (L'Hilarité), Op. 72 (orch. Liszt).

(BB) *** Naxos 8.550959. Frith, Dublin R. & TV Sinf., O'Duinn.

The young Hungarian pianist, Dana Protopopescu, plays all three works with striking freshness and an almost Chopinesque feeling in the lyrical music. Her sparkling passage-work and the chimerical changes of tempo and character of the *Konzertstück* are deftly managed. She is persuasively partnered by Alexander Rahbari, who enters fully into the spirit of her romantic style, convincing the listener that these works gain much from the added colour of a modern piano. Excellent recording.

However, Benjamin Frith's accounts are even finer and he receives splendid support from O'Duinn and the excellent Dublin Sinfonietta. In consequence, these performances all have more depth (the *Konzertstück* is particularly fine). Frith's playing has plenty of dash, yet its impetuosity is never inclined to run away with itself (as from time to time it almost does with Dana Protopopescu). The Naxos CD is not only better recorded and less expensive, it also includes the appropriately named *L'Hilarité – Polacca brillante*, which Frith plays with attractive panache.

Konzertstück.

(M) **(*) DG 463 085-2. Weber, RSO, Berlin, Fricsay – MARTINU: *Fantasia concertante;* FALLA: *Nights in the Gardens of Spain;* TCHEREPNIN: *10 Bagatelles.* ***

An excellent performance of the *Konzertstück* from Margrit Weber, let down a little by the 1960 sound, which while quite full and vivid is rather dry. But this should not deter anyone from trying this imaginatively programmed Galleria CD.

(i) *Konzertstücke for Piano & Orchestra; Invitation to the Dance; Overtures: Der Freischütz; Euryanthe; Oberon; The Ruler of the spirits; Die drei Pintos: Entr'acte*

*** DG 453 486-2. (i) Pletnev; Russian National Orchestra.

These are splendid performances, free from expressive exaggeration but excellently characterized in every way. Pletnev's account of the *Konzertstücke*, which he directs from the keyboard, is quite simply dazzling – and arguably the best ever! Very good recorded sound too.

Overtures: *Abu Hassan; Der Beherrscher der Geister (Ruler of the Spirits); Euryanthe; Der Freischütz; Jubel; Oberon; Peter Schmoll; Preciosa; Silvana; Turandot: Overture & March.*

(N) *(**) Chan. 9066. Philh. O, Järvi.

Overtures: *Abu Hassan; Der Beherrscher der Geister (Ruler of the Spirits); Euryanthe; Der Freischütz; Oberon; Peter Schmoll. Invitation to the Dance, Op. 65* (orch. Berlioz).

(N) (M) *** DG 419 070-2. BPO, Karajan.

Overtures: *Abu Hassan; Der Beherrscher der Geister (Ruler of the Spirits); Euryanthe; Der Freischütz; Jubel; Oberon; Preciosa.*

(N) (M) **(*) CDM7 69572-2. Philh., O, Sawallisch.

Chandos offer the most comprehensive collection of Weber overtures on CD and the performances certainly have more vitality than those in Bamberg above. But these recordings did not stem from one session, but three, and those made in the very resonant acoustic of St Jude's Church, in April 1989, suffer from thick orchestral textures, and unclear inner detail. They include *Der Beherrrscher, Euryanthe* and *Der Freischütz,* the two latter both fine performances, but with tuttis made to sound very heavy. *Turandot* is even more opaque, *Oberon* rather less so.

The others, using All Saints, Tooting, fare better, and throughout there is an impressive Philharmonia response, especially from the horns. But at times Järvi drives too hard, and by doing so loses much of the charm of *Abu Hassan.* In his efforts to keep the pot on the boil he also makes an unwritten accelerando at the end of *Oberon,* and presses on even more forcefully at the coda of *Peter Schmoll.* Fortunately the novelty, *Silvana,* is the finest performance on this disc, and has recording to match.

Sawallisch (in 1958) had the advantage of the Philharmonia at their peak. The orchestral playing is superb and the excitement of *Der Freischütz,* the Turkish colouring of *Abu Hassan* and the contrasts of *Euryanthe* (the timpanist notable) are presented with a strong sense of the individual character of each piece. There is real orchestral virtuosity in

The Ruler of the Spirits and the spectacular appearance of God save the Queen as the apotheosis of Jubel will cheer anyone up. The snag is the over-bright, sharply focused recording with a very light bass. However, this collection has just been deleted.

As it is, the less generous DG collection is the one to go for. Karajan's performances have great style and refinement and the Berlin Philharmonic playing in the two finest overtures, Oberon and Der Freischütz, is peerless (especially the horns). Both admirably epitomize the romantic spirit of the operas which they serve to introduce, while Karajan's elegant account of another Weberian innovation, the Invitation to the Dance (in Berlioz's brilliant orchestration), makes a valuable bonus. On CD the sound is brighter than the original LP, with some loss of weight in the bass, but it is still fuller than Sawallisch's EMI alternative.

Symphonies Nos. 1 in C; 2 in C.

**(*) ASV CDDCA 515. ASMF, Marriner.

Symphonies Nos. 1 in C; 2 in C, J.50/51. Die Drei Pintos: Entr'acte. Silvana: Dance of the Young Nobles; Torch Dance. Turandot: Overture; Act II: March; Act V: Funeral March.

⊛ (BB) *** Naxos 8.550928. Queensland PO, Georgiadis.

Weber wrote his two symphonies in the same year (1807) and, though both are in C major, each has its own individuality. The witty orchestration and operatic character of the writing are splendidly caught in these sparkling Queensland performances, while in the slow movements the orchestral soloists relish their solos, for all the world like vocal cantilenas. The Naxos recording is in the demonstration class, and the disc is made the more attractive for the inclusion of orchestral excerpts from two little-known operas and incidental music from Turandot. The Entr'acte from the incomplete Die Drei Pintos was put together by Mahler from Weber's sketches.

Sir Neville Marriner also has the full measure of Weber's two symphonies; these performances combine vigour and high spirits with the right degree of gravitas (not too much) in the slow movements. The recording is clear and full in the bass, but the bright upper range brings a touch of digital edge to the upper strings.

CHAMBER AND INSTRUMENTAL MUSIC

Cello Sonata in A; Adagio & Rondo.

(***) Testament mono SBT 2158. Piatigorsky, Newton –
BEETHOVEN: Cello Sonatas; (***) BRAHMS: Sonata No. 1. (***)

These records were made in 1934–5 and are arrangements by Piatigorsky of the Fifth of Weber's violin sonatas Op. 10. The playing has an impressive eloquence.

Clarinet Quintet in B Flat, Op. 34

*** ASV CDDCA 1079. Johnson, Takacs-Nagy, Hirsch, Boulton, Shulman – MOZART: Clarinet Quintet; Allegro in B flat, K.516c. **(*)

(i) Clarinet Quintet; Introduction, Theme & Variations for Clarinet & String Quartet, Op. posth.; (ii) Grand duo concertante in E flat, Op. 48; 7 Variations on a Theme from Silvana in B flat, Op. 33 (both for clarinet and piano).

(BB) *** Naxos Dig. 8.553122. Berkes, with (i) Auer Qt; (ii) Jandó.

(i) Clarinet quintet; Flute trio in G min., Op. 63 (for flute, cello and piano).

(M) *** CRD (ADD) CRD 3398. Nash Ens.

(i) Clarinet quintet; (ii) Grand Duo Concertant, Op. 48; 7 Variations on a Theme from Silvana, Op. 33.

**(*) Chan 8366. Hilton, (i) Lindsay Qt; (ii) Swallow.

Emma Johnson, always a characterful player with her distinctive reedy tone, gives a scintillating account of the Weber with brilliant support from her team of experienced chamber players. In this less well-known work she is more spontaneous-sounding than in the Mozart, full of sparkle and fun in the outer movements as well as the Scherzo, finding a rare depth of expression in the hushed writing of the second movement Fantasia, marked Adagio. The clarinet is forwardly balanced, but less obtrusively so than in the Mozart.

On the CRD version, Antony Pay (playing a modern instrument) makes the very most of the work's bravura, catching the exuberance of the Capriccio third movement and the breezy gaiety of the finale. The Nash players provide an admirable partnership and then adapt themselves readily to the different mood of the Trio, another highly engaging work with a picturesque slow movement, described as a Shepherd's Lament. The recording is first class, vivid yet well balanced.

However Naxos conveniently gather together expert and winning performances of all Weber's major chamber works featuring the clarinet, even if the amiable Introduction, Theme and Variations is now considered spurious. The Quintet is particularly successful with a lusciously appealing account af the Adagio and the finale chortles with great zest in its sparkling virtuosity. With Jandó an admirable partner, the Grand duo concertante is hardly less successful, and the two sets of variations are presented with both elegance and panache. The recording is realistic if too resonant, but the charisma and spontaneity of this Hungarian music-making carry the day in spite of this.

Janet Hilton plays with considerable authority and spirit though she is not always as mellifluous as her rivals. However, her account of the Grand duo concertante is a model of fine ensemble, as are the Variations on a Theme from Silvana of 1811, in both of which Keith Swallow is an equally expert partner.

7 Variations on a Theme from Silvana in B flat, Op. 33.

*** Chan. 8506. De Peyer, Pryor – SCHUBERT: Arpeggione Sonata; SCHUMANN: Fantasiestücke etc. ***

These engaging Weber Variations act as a kind of encore to Schubert's Arpeggione Sonata and with their innocent charm they follow on naturally. They are most winningly played by

Gervase de Peyer; Gwenneth Pryor accompanies admirably. The recording is first class.

PIANO MUSIC

Piano Sonatas Nos. 1–2; Rondo brillante in E flat (La Gaîté), Op. 52; Invitation to the Dance, Op. 65.

(M) *** CRD 3485. Milne.

Piano Sonata Nos. 3 in D min., Op. 49; 4 in E min., Op. 70; Polacca brillante in E (L'Hilarité) (with LISZT: Introduzione (Adagio)).

(M) *** CRD 3486. Milne.

These two Weber *Sonatas* are not easy to bring off, with their classical heritage and operatic freedom of line. Hamish Milne's performances have a lightness of touch that is most appealing, without ever being superficial, and his playing in the slow movements has attractive lyrical feeling. Moreover he also provides a sparkling account of the *Rondo brillante* and, as a final encore, a totally captivating account of the charming *Invitation to the Dance*. He makes a sterner approach to the opening *Allegro feroce* of *No. 3 in D minor*, cast in an almost Beethovenian mould, while the last sonata is more introspective in its colouring and feeling, and concludes with a ruthless Tarantella, driven on by its own restless energy. The *Polacca brillante* returns to the world of dazzling articulation and sparkling display. Hamish Milne's playing is thoroughly inside Weber's world and technically equal to the composer's prodigious demands. He is very well recorded.

OPERA

Abu Hassan (opera; complete).

(M) *** CPO/EMI (ADD) CPO 999 551-2. Forster, Gedda, Edda Moser, Moll, Bav. State Op. Ch. & O, Sawallisch.

(M) *** RCA (ADD) 74321 40577-2. Schreier, Hallstein, Adam, Dresden State Op. Ch., Dresden State O, Rogner.

Written in 1810, this frothy little farce reflects the then-current fashion for 'Turkish' themes. The overture is fizzingly brilliant, leading to a sequence of ten numbers, only three of them arias, including two for Abu Hassan's wife, Fatime. The plot involves the machinations of Abu Hassan to get himself out of debt, with the Caliph (one of three speaking roles) finally awarding him a thousand gold pieces. Sawallisch conducts a brilliant performance, with Nicolai Gedda in the title-role pointing his music lightly, with Edda Moser vibrantly expressive as his wife, and with Kurt Moll superb as the grasping money-lender, Omar. First-rate sound, engineered in 1975 by an EMI–Electrola team.

The alternative Eurodisc version, reissued on BMG/RCA, is not as starrily cast as its CPO/EMI competitor, but the singing of soloists and chorus is consistently pleasing. As with the reissued EMI set, the narrative and dialogue are often cued separately and can be omitted at will. The RCA libretto with translation omits this dialogue, assuming that the non-German listener will dispense with it. The 1971 recording is transferred smoothly and pleasingly.

Die drei Pintos (complete; adapted Mahler).

(M) *** RCA (ADD) 74321 32246-2 (2). Popp, Hollweg, Prey, Scovotti, Moll, Munich PO, Bertini.

Die drei Pintos was left unfinished by Weber; Mahler completed it in the 1880s, by adding rearrangements of other Weber. The performance here is recorded complete with the spoken dialogue separately cued so that one can bypass it if necessary. The soloists are excellent with Werner Hollweg a fresh-voiced Gaston, and the whole production is lively and dramatic, while the orchestral support under Gary Bertini is first rate. The sound is excellent, warmly atmospheric yet clear, but the libretto only includes a German text.

Der Freischütz (complete).

*** Teldec 4509 97758-2 (2). Orgonasova, Schäfer, Wottrich, Salminen, Berlin R. Ch., BPO, Harnoncourt.

(M) *** EMI (ADD) CMS7 69342-2 (2). Grümmer, Otto, Schock, Prey, Wiemann, Kohn, Frick, German Op. Ch., Berlin, BPO, Keilberth.

(M) *** DG (ADD) 457 736-2 (2). Janowitz, Mathis, Schreier, Adam, Vogel, Crass, Leipzig R Ch., Dresden State O, Kleiber.

(M) **(*) EMI (ADD) CMS5 65757-2 (2). Nilsson, Köth, Gedda, Berry, Ch. & O of Bav. State Op., Heger.

Harnoncourt's electrifying and refreshing version of this operatic warhorse was recorded live at concert performances in the Philharmonie in Berlin in 1995 and the engineers have done wonders in conveying the atmosphere of a stage performance rather than a concert one, not least in the Wolf's glen scene, helped by recording of a very wide dynamic range. Harnoncourt clarifies textures and paces the drama well, making it sound fresh and new. The cast is first rate, with Orgonasova singing radiantly as Agathe, not just pure but sensuous of tone, floating high pianissimos ravishingly. Christine Schäfer, sweet and expressive, makes Aennchen into far more than just a soubrette character, and Erich Wottrich as Max is aptly heroic and unstrained, if hardly beautiful. The line-up of baritones and basses is impressive too, all firm and clear, contrasting sharply with one another, a team unlikely to be bettered today. A clear first choice among modern, digital recordings.

Keilberth's is a warm, exciting account of Weber's masterpiece which makes all the dated conventions of the work seem fresh and new. In particular the Wolf's glen scene on CD acquires something of the genuine terror that must have struck the earliest audiences. The casting of the magic bullets with each one numbered in turn, at first in eerie quiet and then in crescendo amid the howling of demons, is superbly conveyed. Elisabeth Grümmer sings more sweetly and sensitively than one ever remembers before, with Agathe's prayer exquisitely done. Lisa Otto is really in character, with genuine coquettishness. Schock is not an ideal tenor, but he sings ably enough. The Kaspar of Karl Kohn is generally well focused, and the playing of the Berlin Philharmonic has plenty of polish. The overall effect is immensely atmospheric and enjoyable.

Kleiber's fine, incisive account of Weber's atmospheric and adventurous score fulfilled all expectations. With the help of an outstanding cast, excellent work by the recording producer, Eberhard Geller, and transparently clear recording, this is a most compelling version of an opera which transfers well to the gramophone. Only occasionally does Kleiber betray a fractional lack of warmth, but the full drama of the work is splendidly projected in the enhancement of the newly remastered sound.

Heger's EMI set, recorded in Munich in 1969, cannot match Keilberth's earlier EMI version of 1958 in atmospheric intensity, with the Wolf's glen scene markedly less chilling in its dramatic impact. Yet otherwise, with warm, open sound, there is a nice feeling for a stage performance, with an excellent team of soloists from the Bavarian State Opera. Nicolai Gedda as Max is stylish, even if he tends to bluster, while Birgit Nilsson masterfully scales her massive Wagnerian voice down, to produce a pure, sweet tone and smooth legato in Agathe's two sublime arias. Erika Köth is a light, bright, agile Aennchen, and the chorus sing splendidly. An enjoyable set, if not the finest version at mid-price. However, this has just been deleted.

Der Freischütz: highlights.

(B) *** DG (ADD) 439 440-2 (from above recording, cond. Kleiber).

Anyone looking for a set of highlights from *Der Freischütz* cannot better this bargain Classikon disc. The 73-minute selection includes the full Wolf's glen scene at the end of Act II, and the 1973 recording still sounds very well indeed.

WEBERN, Anton (1883–1945)

(i) *Concerto for 9 Instruments, Op. 24; 5 Movements for String Quartet* (orchestral version), *Op. 5; Passacaglia, Op. 1; 6 Pieces for Large Orchestra, Op. 6; 5 Pieces for Orchestra, Op. 10; Symphony, Op. 21; Variations for Orchestra, Op. 30*. Arrangements of: BACH: *Musical Offering: Fugue* (1935). (ii) SCHUBERT: *German Dances* (for small orchestra), *Op. posth.* Chamber Music: (iii) *6 Bagatelles for String Quartet, Op. 9; 5 Movements for String Quartet, Op. 5; (iv; v) 4 Pieces for Violin & Piano, Op. 7; (v; vi) 3 Small Pieces for Cello & Piano, Op. 11; (v; vii) Quartet, Op. 22* (for piano, violin, clarinet & saxophone); (iii) *String Quartet, Op. 28; String Trio, Op. 20; (v) Variations for Piano, Op. 27.* (Vocal) (viii; i) *Das Augenlicht, Op. 26; (ix; x) 5 Canons on Latin Texts, Op. 16; (viii; ix; i) Cantata No. 1, Op. 29; (viii; ix; xi; i) Cantata No. 2, Op. 31; (viii) Entflieht auf leichten Kähnen, Op. 2; (ix; x) 5 Sacred Songs, Op. 15; (xii; v) 5 Songs, Op. 3; 5 Songs, Op. 4; (xii; x) 2 Songs, Op. 8; (xii; v) 4 Songs, Op. 12; (xii; x) 4 Songs, Op. 13; 6 Songs, Op. 14; (ix; x; xiii) 3 Songs, Op. 18; (viii; i) 2 Songs, Op. 19; (xii; v) 3 Songs, Op. 23; (ix; v) 3 Songs, Op. 25; (ix; x) 3 Traditional Rhymes, Op. 17.*

(M) *** Sony SM3K 45845 (3). (i) LSO (or members), Boulez;
(ii) Frankfurt R. O, composer (recorded December 1932);
(iii) Juilliard Qt (or members); (iv) Stern; (v) Rosen;
(vi) Piatigorsky; (vii) Majeske, Marcellus, Weinstein;
(viii) John Alldis Ch.; (ix) Lukomska; (x) with Ens., Boulez;

(xi) McDaniel; (xii) Harper; (xiii) with John Williams. Overall musical direction: Boulez.

What Pierre Boulez above all demonstrates in the orchestral works (including those with chorus) is that, for all his seeming asceticism, Webern was working on human emotions. The Juilliard Quartet and the John Alldis Choir convey comparable commitment; though neither Heather Harper nor Halina Lukomska is ideally cast in the solo vocal music, Boulez brings out the best in both of them in the works with orchestra. A rare recording of Webern himself conducting his arrangement of Schubert dances is also included. There are excellent notes, every item is cued, and perhaps it is carping to regret that the *Passacaglia* and *Variations for Orchestra* were not indexed.

Collected works:

Disc 1: (i) *Im Sommerwind; 5 Movements for String Quartet* (orchestral version), *Op. 5; Passacaglia, Op. 1; 6 Pieces for Large Orchestra, Op. 6*. Arrangements of: BACH: *Musical Offering: Fugue;* SCHUBERT: *German Dances, D.820.*

Disc 2: (i) *5 Pieces for Orchestra* (1913); *Symphony, Op. 21; Variations for Orchestra, Op. 30; (iii; iv; v) Das Augenlicht, Op. 26; Cantatas Nos. 1, Op. 29; 2, Op. 31; 3 Orchesterlieder* (1913–24).

Disc 3: (ii; vi) *Concerto for 9 Instruments, Op. 24; (ii) 5 Pieces for Orchestra, Op. 10; (ii; vi) Piano Quintet; Quartet, Op. 22* (for piano, violin , clarinet & saxophone); (ii; iii; v; vii) *5 Canons on Latin Texts, Op. 15; Entflieht auf Leichten Kähnen, Op. 2; 2 Lieder, Op. 8; 4 Lieder, Op. 13; 6 Lieder, Op. 14; 5 Geistliche Lieder, Op. 15; 3 Lieder, Op. 18; 2 Lieder, Op. 19; 3 Volkstexte, Op. 17.*

Disc 4: (iii; viii) *3 Gedichte* (1899–1903); *8 frühe Lieder* (1901–4); *3 Avenarius Lieder* (1903–4); *5 Dehmel Lieder* (1906–8); *5 St George Lieder; 5, Op. 4; 4 St George Lieder* (1908–9); *4 Lieder, Op. 12; 3 Jone Gesänge, Op. 23; 3 Jone Lieder, Op. 25.*

Disc 5: (ix; x) *6 Bagatelles for String Quartet, Op. 5; (Langsamer) Slow Movement for String Quartet* (1905); *5 Movements for String Quartet, Op. 5; 3 Pieces for String Quartet* (1913); *Rondo for String Quartet* (1906); *String Quartet* (1905); *String Quartet, Op. 28; String Trio, Op. 20; Movement for String Trio, Op. posth.* (1925).

Disc 6: (xi; xii) *Cello Sonata* (1914); *2 Pieces for Cello & Piano* (1899); *3 Small Pieces for Cello & Piano, Op. 11; (xiii; xiv) 4 Pieces for Violin & Piano, Op. 7; (xv) Piano: Kinderstück* (1924 & 1925); *Piece* (1906); *Sonata Movement (Rondo)* (1906); (xiv) *Variations, Op. 27.*

(M) *** DG 457 637-2 (6). (i) Berlin PO, or (ii) Ens. Intercontemporain, Boulez; (iii) Oelz; (iv) Finley; (v) BBC Singers; (vi) Aimard; (vii) Pollet; (viii) Schneider; (ix) Emerson Qt; (x) McCormick; (xi) Hagen; (xii) Maisenberg; (xiii) Kremer; (xiv) Zimerman; (xv) Cascioli.

This monumental DG set goes far further than the earlier

Sony collection in its illumination of Webern as one of the great musical pioneers of the twentieth century. The first point is that where the earlier set limited itself to the numbered works, this one covers so much more (on six discs instead of three) with a far fuller portrait presented not only in the early works but also in such offerings as the incidental chamber works and his arrangements of Bach (the *Ricercar* from the *Musical Offering*) and Schubert (a collection of waltzes). Boulez's interpretations of the numbered works have developed too, with the Berlin Philharmonic exceptionally responsive, bringing out often unsuspected warmth and beauty. The point and purposefulness of these performances is particularly helpful in making such thorny late inspirations as the two *Cantatas* so much more readily approachable. The vocal soloists have been ideally chosen, with the fresh-toned Christiane Oelze taking on the majority of songs, but with Françoise Pollet and Gerald Finley equally assured. The starry list of instrumental contributors could not be bettered either, including as it does such luminaries of DG as the Emerson Quartet and Krystian Zimerman, and the recordings made over a period of years are uniformly excellent.

Concerto for 9 Instruments, Op. 24.

(M) *** Chan. 6534. Nash Ens., Rattle – SCHOENBERG: *Pierrot Lunaire.* ***

This late Webern piece, tough, spare and uncompromising, makes a valuable fill-up for Jane Manning's outstanding version of Schoenberg's *Pierrot Lunaire*, a 1977 recording originally made for the Open University. First-rate sound and a beautifully clean CD transfer.

Langsamer Satz (arr. Schwarz).

*** Delos DE 3121. Seattle SO, Schwarz – HONEGGER: *Symphony No. 2; R. STRAUSS: Metamorphosen.* ***

The slow movement Webern composed in 1905 for string quartet sounds even more Mahlerian in Gerard Schwarz's transcription for full strings, which is eloquently played and sumptuously recorded.

5 Movements, Op. 5; Passacaglia, Op. 1; 6 Pieces for Orchestra, Op. 6; Symphony, Op. 21.

(M) *** DG 427 424-2 (3). BPO, Karajan – BERG: *Lyric Suite; 3 Pieces;* SCHOENBERG: *Pelleas und Melisande; Variations; Verklärte Nacht.* ***

(M) *** DG (IMS) 423 254-2. BPO, Karajan.

Available either separately or within Karajan's three-CD compilation, this collection, devoted to four compact and chiselled Webern works, is in many ways the most remarkable of all. Karajan secures a highly sensitive response from the Berlin Philharmonic, who produce sonorities as seductive as Debussy. A strong recommendation, with excellent sound.

Passacaglia for Orchestra, Op. 1.

(M) *** DG (ADD) 457 760-2. BPO, Karajan – BERG: *Lyric Suite,* etc.; SCHOENBERG: *Variations.* ***

(BB) *** RCA Navigator (ADD) 74321 29243-2. Cologne RSO,

Wakasugi – BERG: *Violin Concerto;* SCHOENBERG: *Verklärte Nacht.* ***

This is a beautifully played and recorded version of Webern's *Passacaglia*, which will disappoint no one. It sounds especially haunting – even magical – in Karajan's hands, and has been superbly transferred.

The Cologne Radio Symphony Orchestra understand what this music is about and under Hiroshi Wakasugi give a powerfully committed and very well-played account of Webern's most spectacular orchestral work. The 1977 recording is full and atmospheric, but documentation is inadequate.

CHAMBER MUSIC

6 Bagatelles for String Quartet, Op. 9; Langsamer Satz; 5 Movements for String Quartet, Op. 5; Rondo for String Quartet (1906); String Quartet (1905); String Quartet, Op. 28; Movement for String Trio, Op. posth.; String Trio, Op. 20.

(N) *** Nim. NI 5668. Vienna Artis Qt.

With warm, purposeful performances recorded in full, close sound, the Artis Quartet present Webern's collected music for string quartet and string trio as a most persuasive survey of this problematic composer's creative career. The three works from 1905 and 1906 (those without opus number) represent his early post-romantic style at its ripest, while such works as the *Five Movements*, Op. 5, vividly illustrate the imaginative leap he made when adopting free atonality. Equally representative are the more astringent works of his later years, the *String Trio*, Op. 20 and the *String Quartet*, Op. 28, all presented with a purposefulness and commitment that readily helps to overcome any problems the listener may have. An excellent disc for anyone who wants to investigate a key twentieth-century figure.

6 Bagatelles, Op. 9; 5 Movements, Op. 5 for String Quartet.

(B) *** DG (ADD) 439 470-2. LaSalle Qt – SCHOENBERG: *Verklärte Nacht* etc. **(*)

Webern's six *Bagatelles*, written between 1911 and 1913, are characteristic of his brevity and density of expression; the earlier (1909) *Five Movements*, although succinct, are slightly more expansive. They are superbly played here and, while this is not easy music, it is certainly atmospheric and as arresting in impact as on the day it was written.

6 Bagatelles, Op. 9; 5 Movements, Op. 5; Quartet, Op. 28.

(M) *** Teldec (ADD) 3984 21967-2. Alban Berg Qt – BERG: *Lyric Suite* etc.; URBANNER: *String Quartet No. 3.* ***

Really outstanding playing of the Webern pieces by the Berg Quartet makes this a first choice in this repertoire as the recording is impeccable and the LaSalle CD also very well played, although it is less expensive omits the Op. 28 *Quartet*. The Berg couplings are hardly less fine, although the somewhat Schoenbergian quartet by the Austrian composer, Erich Urbanner, is less memorable.

Slow Movement for String Quartet (1905).

*** DG (IMS) 437 836-2. Hagen Qt – DEBUSSY; RAVEL: *Quartets.* ***

The single-movement Webern *Quartet* was composed in Carinthia in the summer of 1905 and was first heard in the 1960s. It has an intense and chromatic study, and is played with great refinement by the Hagen Quartet and beautifully recorded. An excellent *bonne bouche*, if that term is appropriate, for a superb Debussy and Ravel coupling.

Variations for Piano, Op. 27.

(N) *** Ph. 468 033-2. Uchida – BERG: *Piano Sonata;* SCHOENBERG: *Piano Concerto; Klavierstücke.* ***

(BB) *** Naxos 8.553870. Hill – BERG: *Piano Sonata;* SCHOENBERG: *Piano Pieces; Suite.* ***

The *Variations*, Op. 27, Webern's only mature piano piece, dates from the mid 1930s and calls for the most eloquent playing if it is to persuade the listener. Webern himself stressed that the music's structural intricacies must give rise to a 'profound expressiveness'. They have been recorded by Pollini, Glenn Gould and other celebrated pianists. Peter Hill can hold his own against any of the competition.

However, Uchida gives a highly imaginative and refined account, recorded with great clarity and presence in the Herkulessaal, Munich, and this *Gramophone* Award-winning performance is as fine as this piece has ever received. Moreover, the Philips couplings, too, are very highly recommendable.

WEILL, Kurt (1900–1950)

Violin Concerto (for violin, wind instruments and percussion), Op. 12. Kleine Dreigroschenmusik. (Vocal): (ii–iv) Berlin Requiem; (iii–vii) Happy End (concert version): (ii–vii) Mahagonny-Singspiel; (iii–vi) Der Protagonist (opera); Pantomime 1; (iv) Von Tod in Wald (Death in the Forest), Op. 23.

⏣ (M) *** DG (ADD) 459 442-2 (2). L. Sinfonietta, Atherton; with (1) Liddell; (ii) Langridge; (iii) Luxon; (iv) Rippon; (v) Thomas; (vi) Partridge; (vii) Dickinson.

This is a superb mid-priced Double, with full documentation, texts and translations, and in vividly real sound approaching demonstration quality. David Atherton and the London Sinfonietta recorded it all (on three LPs) immediately after returning from the Berlin Festival of 1975, and it will be a revelation for many to hear performances of such stylish incisiveness which put weight on purely musical as well as dramatic values. That remark covers all the clear-toned British soloists, who sound completely at home, while singing the notes with unusual precision. The real rarities here include the *Berlin Requiem*, rising intensely in tension, *Death in the Forest*, equally stark in the use of voices and wind, as well as the *Pantomime* from *Der Protagonist*. The early *Violin Concerto*, with Nona Liddell as a sensitive soloist, already underlines the compactness of Weill's writing, while the relatively well-known works all emerge with new freshness. *Happy End*, for example, is performed at original pitch, with the voices the composer intended, though sadly the hit number, the *Bilbao Song*, is left out. Excellent notes by David Drew who prepared the texts. Highly recommended.

Concerto for Violin & Winds, Op. 12.

*** Virgin/EMI VC5 45056-2. Tetzlaff, Deutsche Kammerphilharmonie Wind – HINDEMITH: *Septet;* TOCH: *5 Pieces for Wind & Percussion.* ***

Weill's *Concerto for Violin and Winds* has a seriousness of purpose and an originality that are persuasive, no doubt much helped by the highly sensitive and imaginative performance given by Christian Tetzlaff and the winds of the Deutsche Kammerphilharmonie; it is coupled with most interesting repertoire. It will surely convert any doubters about the quality of this work as it has us.

Kleine Dreigroschenmusik.

(M) EMI (ADD) CDM5 67337-2. Philh. O, Klemperer – HINDEMITH: *Nobilissima visione;* STRAVINSKY: *Symphony in 3 Movements;* *** (with KLEMPERER: *Merry Waltz* **).

Klemperer is thoroughly at home in the Kurt Weill suite, evoking perfectly the mood and style of the first performance in 1929 by the Prussian State Military Band and his stately and ironically Prussian version of *Mack the Knife* has a character all its own. Klemperer's own waltz is pleasant, modestly tuneful, chromatic, and with a strong flavour of Richard Strauss, although this disappears in the middle section which is more like a march.

STAGE WORKS

The Ballad of Magna Carta; Der Lindberghflug.

*** Cap. 60012-l. Henschel, Tyl, Calaminus, Clemens, Cologne Pro Musica Ch. & RSO, Latham-König; Wirl, Schmidt, Feckler, Minth, Scheeben, Berlin R. Ch. & O, Scherchen.

Der Lindberghflug ('The Lindbergh Flight') is a curiosity. Brecht wrote the text, but only later did Weill set the complete work, and that is how it is given in this excellent Cologne recording. A historic 1930 performance of the original Weill–Hindemith version, conducted by Hermann Scherchen, is given as an appendix, recorded with a heavy background roar but with astonishingly vivid voices. The fine, very German tenor who sang Lindbergh in 1930 was Erik Wirl and the tenor in the new recording is not nearly so sweet-toned, and the German narrator delivers his commentary in a casual, matter-of-fact way. Otherwise the performance under Jan Latham-König fully maintains the high standards of Capriccio's Weill series; and the other, shorter item, *The Ballad of Magna Carta* is most enjoyable too, a piece never recorded before. Clear, if rather dry, recording with voices vivid and immediate.

Die Bürgschaft (complete).

** EMI CDS5 56976-2 (2). Thompson, Burchinal, Travis, Sorenson, Panagulias, Westminster Ch., Spoleto Festival USA O, Rudel.

Die Bürgschaft, 'The Surety', is Kurt Weill's most ambitious theatre-piece, a full-scale opera in three acts first seen in

Berlin in 1932. Weill made substantial cuts when it was taken up by other opera-houses but the following year – like the rest of Weill's music – it was promptly banned by the Nazis, though it was not just them but others who deplored the heavy left-wing moralizing in a tale telling of how life in the ideal state of Urb is corrupted by greed. The disappointment of this première recording, taken from the first American production in 1998, is that the piece lacks the satirical bite of Weill's popular theatre-pieces of his German period. There are many characteristic sharp and colourful ideas, but too much is prettified Weill and even in its cut form, outstays its welcome. The performance, crisp and well-rehearsed, is well cast with fresh young voices, but the lack of bite in the orchestral sound – damped down in relation to the singers – seriously undermines any feeling of energy, with Julius Rudel less incisive than usual. None the less, devotees of Weill will find this an essential set.

Die Dreigroschenoper (The Threepenny Opera): complete.

*** Decca 430 075-2. Kollo, Lemper, Milva, Adorf, Dernesch, Berlin RIAS Chamber Ch. & Sinf., Mauceri.

*** Sony (ADD) MK 42637. Lenya, Neuss, Trenk-Trebisch, Hesterberg, Schellow, Koczian, Grunert, Ch. & Dance O of Radio Free Berlin, Brückner-Rüggeberg.

On Decca there are obvious discrepancies between the opera-singers, René Kollo and Helga Dernesch, and those in the cabaret tradition, notably the vibrant and provocative Ute Lemper (Polly Peachum) and the gloriously dark-voiced and characterful Milva (Jenny). That entails downward modulation in various numbers, as it did with Lotte Lenya, but the changes from the original are far less extreme. Kollo is good, but Dernesch is even more compelling. The co-ordination of music and presentation makes for a vividly enjoyable experience, even if committed Weill enthusiasts will inevitably disagree with some of the controversial textual and interpretative decisions.

The CBS alternative offers a vividly authentic abridged recording, darkly incisive and atmospheric, with Lotte Lenya giving an incomparable performance as Jenny. All the wrong associations, built up round the music from indifferent performances, melt away in the face of a reading as sharp and intense as this. Bright, immediate, real stereo recording, made the more vivid on CD.

Happy End (play by Brecht with songs); Die sieben Todsünden (The Seven Deadly Sins).

(M) *** Sony mono/stereo MPK 45886. Lenya, male quartet & O, Ch. & O, Brückner-Rüggeberg.

In the Sony/CBS performance of The Seven Deadly Sins, with the composer's widow as principal singer, the rhythmic verve is irresistible and, though Lenya had to have the music transposed down, her understanding of the idiom is unique. The recording is forward and slightly harsh, though Lenya's voice is not hardened, and the effect is undoubtedly vivid. Happy End was made in Hamburg-Harburg in 1960. Lenya turned the songs into a kind of cycle (following a hint from her husband), again transposing where necessary, and her renderings in her individual brand of vocalizing are so compelling they make the scalp tingle.

Der Silbersee (complete).

*** RCA 09026 63447 (2). Kruse, Gruber, Lascarro, Clark, Dernesch, Zednik, Wyn-Davies, Karnéus, Whelan, Saks, Alder, Weale, London Sinf. Ch. and O, Markus Stenz.

*** Cap. 60011-2 (2). Heichele, Tamassy, Holdorf, Schmidt, Mayer, Korte, Thomas, Cologne Pro Musica Ch., Cologne RSO, Latham-König.

This excellent RCA recording, recorded in the studio after a highly successful concert performance at a Prom in London, offers the complete musical score, including the passages of melodrama, speech over music, from Acts I and III. It is an angry piece, which inspired Weill to write strong, biting and positive music, here splendidly performed with the London Sinfonietta under Markus Stenz.

The casting is exceptionally strong, including in small roles such leading singers as the veterans Helga Dernesch and Heinz Zednik, tenor Graham Clark and rising star Katarina Karnéus. Both Heinz Kruse as the principal character, Severin, and H. K. Gruber as Olim, the policeman, are brightly idiomatic in German cabaret style, while Juanita Lascarro as the heroine, Fennimore, with her bright clear soprano provides the necessary contrast.

Led by Hildegard Heichele, bright and full-toned as the central character, Fennimore, the Capriccio cast is also an outstanding one, with each voice satisfyingly clean-focused, while the 1989 recording is rather better-balanced and kinder to the instrumental accompaniment than some from this source, with the voices exceptionally vivid.

(i) Die sieben Todsünden (The Seven Deadly Sins); Kleine Dreigroschenmusik.

(M) *** Sony SMK 44529. (i) Migenes, Tear, Kale, Opie, Kennedy; LSO, Tilson Thomas.

(i) Die sieben Todsünden (The Seven Deadly Sins); (ii) Mahagonny Singspiel.

*** Decca 430 168-2. Lemper, Wildhaber, Haage, Mohr, Jungwirth, Berlin RIAS Chamber Ens., Mauceri, (ii) with J. Cohen.

Using the lower-pitch version of The Seven Deadly Sins originally designed for Lotte Lenya, but with Weill's original instrumentation, the Decca issue presents Ute Lemper in one of her finest performances on record. Her sensuous, tough voice exactly suits the role of the first Anna, who does all the singing. Mauceri's speeds, consistently slower than those of Rattle or Tilson Thomas, also enhance the sensuous element while bringing out the strange poignancy of the Prologue and Epilogue. The chattering ensemble of four male singers is well cast, and John Mauceri equally brings out the tang of the instrumental writing. He is rather less successful in the Singspiel, perhaps reflecting the fact that Lemper's role – mainly in duet with a singer of similar timbre – is less distinctive. Yet with similar forces required, it makes the ideal coupling. Full, bright sound to bring out the bite of the music.

In Tilson Thomas's performance with the LSO, Julia Migenes also uses the lower version of the score, colouring the voice even more boldly than Ute Lemper, echoing, even imitating, Lenya closely. With voices and instruments forwardly focused in the same consistent acoustic, the bite of the writing and its tangy beauty are put over powerfully, with Tilson Thomas's relatively brisk speeds adding to the power rather than to the poignancy. This makes a formidable mid-priced alternative to the Rattle and Mauceri versions, in some ways more forceful than either, but with a coupling, apt as it is, rather less generous.

(i; ii) Die sieben Todsünden (The Seven Deadly Sins); (i) Songs: Berlin im Licht; Complainte de la Seine; Es regnet; Youkali; Nannas Lied (Meine Herren, mit Siebzehn); Wie lange noch?

**(*) HM HMC 90 1420. (i) Fassbaender; (ii) Brandt, Sojer, Komatsu, Urbas; Hanover R. PO, Garben.

This Harmonia Mundi version of *The Seven Deadly Sins* stars Brigitte Fassbaender who, using the original pitch, brings a Lieder-singer's feeling for word-detail and a comparable sense of style. Her account is obviously less streetwise than Lemper's (Decca 430 075-2) which remains first choice, but there is a plangent feeling that is highly appropriate. The songs are equally impressive, mostly connected in some way or another with the main piece but, especially alongside Rattle, the conductor, Cord Garben, at times seems on the leisurely side in his choice of tempi. Excellent, vivid recording.

Street Scene (opera): complete.

*** TER CDTER2 1185 (2). Ciesinski, Kelly, Bottone, Van Allan, ENO Ch. and O, Davis.

Street Scene was Kurt Weill's attempt, late in his Broadway career, to write an American opera as distinct from a musical. The TER set was made with the cast of the ENO production at the Coliseum, and the idiomatic feeling and sense of flow consistently reflect that. Some of the solo singing in the large cast is flawed, but never seriously, and the principals are all very well cast – Kristine Ciesinski as the much-put-upon Anna Maurrant, Richard van Allan as her sorehead husband, Janis Kelly sweet and tender as the vulnerable daughter, and Bonaventura Bottone as the diffident young Jewish neighbour who loves her. Those are only a few of the sharply drawn characters, and the performance on the discs, with dialogue briskly paced, reflects the speed of the original ENO production. Warm, slightly distanced sound.

The Threepenny Opera (complete).

*** RCA 74321 66133-2 (2). Raabe, Gruber, Hagen, Macdonald, Hellman, Böwe, Brauer, Holtz, Ens. Modern, H. K. Gruber.

** Decca 430 075-2. Kollo, Adorf, Dernesch, Lemper, Milva, Berlin RIAS Chamber Ch. & Sinfonietta, Mauceri.

Using the new Kurt Weill Edition, which includes extra stage music, H. K. Gruber conducts a bitingly dramatic, well-paced account of *The Threepenny Opera*, brightly recorded in full, immediate sound. Gruber himself sings the role of Peachum with flair, and he is matched by a strong cast, both characterful and stylish, with vocal qualities paramount, even if Nina Hagen as Mrs Peachum comes near to screaming. The performance reflects throughout the experience of live performance, with Sona Macdonald at once idiomatic, firm and often beautiful in vocal production. Max

Raabe as Macheath makes a believably youthful rogue, also firm and clear. Though the recording stretches to a second disc, it offers a more complete text than its single-disc rival, with reprises included.

The Decca version on a single disc may offer a temptingly starry cast, but all apart from Helga Dernesch as a rich, fruity Mrs Peachum are disappointing. René Kollo sounds far too old as Macheath, his voice a mere shadow of what it was, severely strained on top, while even Ute Lemper is disappointing, brilliantly characterful in fast music, but with the voice fluttery and unsteady in sustained lines. Mario Adorf as Peachum sings unsteadily, and none of the principals or the orchestra are helped by the slightly distanced recording balance, so that John Mauceri, normally an inspired conductor in this repertory, too often fails to make the music bite, often adopting relatively broad speeds. The RCA set is far preferable.

Der Zar lässt sich Photographieren (complete).

**(*) Cap. 60 007-1. McDaniel, Pohl, Napier, Cologne R. O, Latham-König.

This curious one-act *Opera Buffa* is a wry little parable about assassins planning to kill the Tsar when he has his photograph taken. Angèle, the photographer, is replaced by the False Angèle, but the Tsar proves to be a young man who simply wants friendship, and the would-be assassin, instead of killing him, plays a tango on the gramophone, before the Tsar's official duties summon him again. Jan Latham-König in this 1984 recording directs a strong performance, though the dryly recorded orchestra is consigned to the background. The voices fare better, though Barry McDaniel is not ideally steady as the Tsar.

'Kurt Weill on Broadway': excerpts from: The Firebrand of Florence; Johnny Johnson (Johnny's song); Knickerbocker Holiday; Love Life; One Touch of Venus (Westwind).

*** EMI CDC5 55563-2. Hampson, Futral, Hadley, Lehman, L. Sinf. Ch., L. Sinf., McGlinn.

Thomas Hampson's magical collection of Weill numbers reveals what richness there is even in the least-known of Weill's Broadway scores. So a full 40 minutes are devoted to Weill's biggest flop, *The Firebrand of Florence*, an offbeat biography of Benvenuto Cellini, and the selection here is a delight. The very start of the disc on *One touch of Venus* establishes instantly that poetry is the keynote of the American Weill. One of the numbers in the 20-minute selection from *Love Life* (lyrics by Alan Jay Lerner) is a duet, *I remember it well*. Only later did Lerner adapt it for Gingold and Chevalier in *Gigi*, for here it is a dreamy slow waltz. The only well-known number is *It never was you* from *Knickerbocker Holiday*, and even that comes as a duet, not a solo. Hampson sings superbly, and McGlinn draws deeply sympathetic performances from the London Sinfonietta and the other soloists. Scholarly and informative notes add greatly to enjoyment, as well as the texts. However, this collection has been deleted as we go to press.

WEINER, Leó (1885–1974)

Hungarian Folkdance Suite, Op. 18.

(N) (M) *** Chan. 6625. Philh. O, Järvi – BARTOK:
Hungarian Pictures. ENESCU: *Roumanian Rhapsodies 1–2*. ***

Weiner here remained orientated towards the German and French schools, and this lively and attractive suite represents a Hungarian folk style more Westernized than Bartók's; but with purposeful direction from Järvi, fine dramatic playing from the orchestra and ripely resonant recording, the full range of colour is brought out in these four movements, which last almost half an hour.

Serenade for Small Orchestra, Op. 3.

*** Decca 458 929-2. Budapest Festival O, Solti – BARTOK:
Cantata profana; KODALY: *Psalmus hungaricus, Op. 13.* ***

Solti's very last recording sessions in Budapest in June, 1997, resulted in inspired performances, designed as a tribute to his three teachers at his Liszt Academy, not just Bartók or Kodály but his favourite teacher, the far less known Leó Weiner. Weiner's *Serenade* proves a charmer, not so clearly Hungarian as Bartók or Kodály, but in its amiable way cleanly built on crisply conceived ideas.

Violin Sonatas Nos. 1 in D, Op. 9; 2 in F sharp min. Op. 11.

**(*) Biddulph LAW 015. Shumsky, Lipkin – DOHNANYI:
Violin Sonata in C sharp min., Op. 21; Andante. **(*)

The two violin sonatas of Léo Weiner were composed in 1911 and 1919 respectively, and they are heard here in good performances by Oscar Shumsky and Seymour Lipkin. They were recorded in New York in 1993 and if Shumsky's playing does not have the effortless mastery it possessed in the early 1980s, he still performs a service in restoring these enjoyable works to the wider musical public. A most worthwhile issue.

WEISSENBERG, Alexis (born 1929)

(i) 4 Improvisations on Songs from La Fugue; Le Regret; Sonata en état de jazz.

(N) *(**) Nim. NI 5688. Mulligan (with Walden).

As with other composer-pianists who have a wide repertoire, Weissenberg's own music does not project a strong individuality. *La Fugue* was a musical comedy for which he wrote the score in Paris in the 1960s. It was revived as a 'surrealistic musical' in Darmstadt in 1992, with the new name *Nostalgia*. The first of the *Four Improvisations* is a jazzy, jittery tarantella, brilliantly played here; the other three bear out the title admirably, with Frank Walden on saxophone joining the pianist to create the smoky, late-evening atmosphere in the second piece, *Mon destin*.

Le Regret is also written in a gentle improvisatory style, which seems to be the composer's forte, for it is the third movement of the *Jazz Sonata*, the rather haunting *Reflets d'un blues*, which is the most beguiling. The other three, which in turn supposedly embody the spirit of the tango,

charleston and samba, are somewhat intractable, and not very successful in their evocation, although the final *Provocation de samba* is the most rhythmically inventive. Weissenberg could not have a more committed advocate than Simon Mulligan, who plays with great flair and conviction, and is very well recorded. But this is not a disc for the general collector.

WELLESZ, Egon (1885–1974)

Prospero's Spell (Prosperos Beschwörungen), Op. 53; (i) Violin Concerto, Op. 84.

*** Orfeo C478 981A. Vienna Radio SO, Albrecht; (i) with Löwenstein.

Egon Wellesz pursued a dual career as a scholar and composer. *Prosperos Beschwörungen* (1935) is a highly imaginative score; Wellesz had toyed with the idea of writing an opera on *The Tempest* but these five orchestral pieces were the result. They are quite individual though they are closer to Hindemith than to the second Viennese school. The *Violin Concerto* (1961) is a made of sterner stuff and it provides a formidable challenge to the soloist to which Andrea Duka Löwenstein rises triumphantly. Good playing from the ORF (Oesterreiches Rundfunk) or Vienna Radio Orchestra under Gerd Albrecht. Good sound though perhaps a little studio bound.

WERT, Giaches de (1535–96)

Il settimo libro de madrigali.

(M) *** Virgin VER5 61177-2. Consort of Musicke, Rooley.

Giaches de Wert was Monteverdi's predecessor in Mantua at the court of Count Alfonso Gonzaga: this is the seventh of twelve books of madrigals, published in 1581. The opening madrigal is celebratory: *Sorgi e rischiara* ('Arise, light up the sky with thy approach, Holy Mother of love, lead in the day'), but many of the other varied settings are concerned with the trials and disappointments of love. De Wert certainly emerges here as a composer of expressive depth and personality and with a fine feeling for words. He is not another Monteverdi but his art is well worth knowing, and the singing here is persuasive, expressively responsive and beautifully blended, even if it does not always make the music project irresistibly. The recording is well up to the high standard of this stimulating Veritas series.

WESTLAKE, Nigel (born 1958)

Antarctica (suite for guitar and orchestra).

*** Sony SK 53361. Williams, LSO, Daniel – SCULTHORPE:
Nourlangie etc.

Antarctica is a film-score written to accompany an Imax large-screen documentary about the frozen continent. Westlake's music is highly imaginative and inventive and stands up memorably on its own. The guitar is used both with the orchestra and to play haunting, improvisatory-styled interludes. John Williams clearly relishes the considerable demands of the solo part, and Paul Daniel shapes the music spontaneously and skilfully. The recording is in the demonstration bracket, though the solo guitar is very forwardly balanced.

WEYSE, Christoph Ernst Friedrich
(1774–1842)

Symphonies Nos. 1 in G min., DF117; 2 in C, DF118; 3 in D, DF119.

**(*) dacapo 8.224012. Royal Danish O, Schønwandt.

The example of Haydn affected Weyse strongly, and the minor-key symphonies in particular are reminiscent of Haydn's *Sturm und Drang* symphonies. Michael Schönwandt gives vital yet sensitive accounts of all three symphonies and is well served by the engineers. This lively music is worth investigating.

Piano Sonatas Nos. 5 in E; 6 in B flat; 7 in A min.; 8 in G min

(N) ** dacapo 8.224140. Trondhjem.

The German-born Weyse played a key role in the development of song in Denmark, but he was also a fine pianist and among other things introduced some of the Mozart concertos to Copenhagen. These sonatas come from 1799, though the *Eighth in G minor* was not published until 1818. They are very much in the tradition of Clementi, Haydn and C. P. E. Bach, whose pupil Weyse nearly became. The *Eighth* even suggests the Beethoven of Op. 26. They employ a limited range of pianistic devices but have a certain grace. Thomas Trondhjem gives very acceptable performances and is decently recorded.

WHITE, Robert (*c.* 1538–74)

Motets: Christe qui lux es; Domine quis habitavit; Portio mea Domine; Regina coeli.

⊛ (M) *** Cal. CAL 6623. Clerkes of Oxenford, Wulstan – TALLIS: *Mass Puer natus est* etc. *** ⊛

Robert White's style of writing has a basic restraint and often shows a gentle, Dowland-like melancholy, so striking at the opening of *Domine quis habitavit*. But this is often offset by the soaring trebles, especially in the ravishing *Portio mea Domine*, while *Christe qui lux es*, the last motet on this record, is very touching indeed. Glorious performances by Wulstan and the Clerkes of Oxenford, who have the full measure of this repertoire. The analogue recording could hardly be bettered. Not to be missed.

WHITLOCK, Percy (1903–46)

Ballet of the Wood Creatures; Balloon Ballet; Come Along, Marnie; Dignity and Impudence March. The Feast of St Benedict: Concert Overture. Holiday Suite. Music for Orchestra: Suite. Susan, Doggie and Me; Wessex Suite.

(N) **(*) Marco 8.225162. Dublin RTE Concert O, Sutherland.

Percy Whitlock's style is attractive and easy-going with quite imaginative orchestration and nice touches everywhere. The marches are jolly and the waltzes nostalgic – *The Ballet of the Wood Creatures* is especially charming. Gavin Sutherland directs the RTE orchestra with his usual understanding. The sound is good, but occasionally the strings sound a little scrawny (the opening of *Waltz* in the *Holiday Suite*, for example).

WIDOR, Charles-Marie (1844–1937)

Symphony No. 3 for Organ & Orchestra, Op. 69.

*** Chan. 9785. Tracey (organ of Liverpool Cathedral), BBC PO, Tortelier – GUILMANT: *Symphony No. 2 for Organ & Orchestra, Op. 91*; FRANCK: *Choral No. 2*. ***

Widor's *Third Symphony* for organ and orchestra, although in two sections, moves in a series of episodes: *Adagio* – *Andante* (introducing a luscious string tune) – *Allegro* (end of first movement); *Vivace* – *Tranquillamente* – *Allegro* (which with its horn calls and galloping energy brings a curious reminder of Franck's *Chasseur maudit*); finally comes an overwhelmingly majestic *Largo* with the chorale melody shared by organ and orchestra, bursting at the seams in sheer amplitude. The decibels of the coda are worthy of the finest speakers. Ian Tracey makes the most of his opportunities, as does Tortelier. Certainly the huge Liverpool organ and the resonant cathedral acoustics seem custom made for such spectacle and the Chandos engineers capture it all with aplomb.

SOLO ORGAN MUSIC

Symphonies No. 2 in D, Op. 13/2; 8 in B, Op. 42/4.

*** BIS CD-1007. Fagius (organ of Kallio Church, Helsinki).

The Swedish organist Hans Fagius plays two Widor symphonies, the *Second in D major* and the *Eighth in B major*, on a new instrument made by the Swedish makers Akerman and Lund. The instrument itself is five years old and is modelled on the symphonic organs of Cavaillé-Coll tradition with which César Franck and Widor were so closely associated. Its disposition was the work of Kurt Lueders of Paris. Hans Fagius serves the music well and the engineers produce particularly impressive results. The opening *Allegro* of the *Eighth Symphony* gives a good idea of the impressive range this disc covers.

Symphony No. 3 in E minor, Op. 13/2: excerpts (Prélude; Adagio; Finale); Symphony No. 4 in F min., Op. 13/4; Symphony No.9 in C min.(Gothique), Op. 70.

(M) *** Erato 4509 98534-2. Marie-Claire Alain (Cavaillé-Coll organ of L'Eglise St-Germain, St-Germain-en-Laye).

In the hands of Marie-Claire Alain the St-Germain organ sounds very orchestral, and her colouring of the gentle *Adagio* (a perpetual canon) of the *Third Symphony* and the *Andante cantabile* of No. 4 is quite haunting. The spectacular Wagnerian finale of this *E minor Symphony* – played in the revised 1901 version – with its cascading sextuplets, is not musically as well focused as the more famous *Toccata* which closes its successor, but it sounds very exciting here, and as it ends gently, the opening *Toccata* of No. 4 makes a bold contrast. The *Gothic Symphony* has a notable third movement where a Christmas chant (*Puer natus est nobis*) is embroidered fugally. The finale section is a set of variations, and the Gregorian chant is reintroduced in the pedals. These are classic performances, given spacious analogue sound, with just a touch of harshness to add a little edge to *fortisssimos*.

Symphonies No. 3 in E min., Op.13/2; 6 in G min., Op. 42/2; 3 Nouvelles pièces, Op. 87.

(N) *** ASV CDDCA 1106. Patrick (Coventry Cathedral organ).

For the second issue in their spectacular Widor series, ASV have turned to David Patrick and the organ of Coventry Cathedral, of which he is obviously a master. If less obviously suited to this repertoire than a French organ, it still sounds very impressive. Unlike Marie-Claire Alain he plays the *Third Symphony* complete, but he and the organ are at their finest in the *Sixth*, with its grand opening and equally bold *Marcia* finale. They frame a gentle *Adagio* and a hushed *Cantabile*, with the most characteristic movement, a brilliant scherzando-like *Intermezzo*, as the work's centrepiece. Patrick plays this superbly, effectively exploiting his organ's wide range of dynamic.

Symphony No. 5 in F min., Op. 42/1.

*** Chan. 9271. Tracey (organ of Liverpool Cathedral), BBC PO, Tortelier – GUILMANT: *Symphony No. 1 for Organ & Orchestra* ***; POULENC: *Concerto.* **(*)

The long reverberation-period of Liverpool Cathedral gives a special character to Widor's *Fifth Symphony*, especially the mellow central movements. Ian Tracey makes the most of the colouristic possibilities of his fine instrument and also uses the widest possible range of dynamics, with the tone at times shaded down to a distant whisper. Yet the famous *Toccata* expands gloriously if without the plangent bite of a French instrument.

Symphonies Nos. 5 in F min.; 7 in A min., Op. 42/3.

*** ASV CDDCA 958. Parker-Smith (Van Den Heuvel organ), St Eustache, Paris.

Jane Parker-Smith is a complete master of this repertoire (and she shows that it does not always have to be played on a traditional Cavaillé-Coll instrument). The organ at St Eustache, Paris is new (1967), and is Netherlands-built. It is magnificent. Not only are the big tuttis, as in the finale of the *Seventh Symphony*, superbly expansive, but the organ has a ravishingly rich palette and a warm sonority to deal with Widor's gentler ideas, like the *Andante cantabile* and *Adagio* of the *Fifth* and the inner movements of No. 7, and particularly the *Allegro ma non troppo*, where the gently murmuring semiquavers flow along sensuously like a warm summer breeze. Because of this natural clarity of internal focus Jane Parker-Smith is able to use a very wide dynamic range and in the supreme test, the masterly *Toccata* which closes the *Fifth*, the calm at the centre of the storm does not lose contact with the listener, and the great reprise of the main theme, with thundering pedals, is unforgettable.

Symphony No. 8 in B, Op. 42/4.

(N) *** ASV CDDCA 1109. Fisell (organ of Liverpool Metropolitan Catholic Cathedral) (with COCHEREAU: *Variations sur un vieux Noël*).

It is good that the fine organ in Liverpool's Catholic Cathedral is at last receiving attention from the recording companies. Even if the circular building provides a very generous 8-second reverberation, even when the pedals get going, detail is not too muddied, and the reeds have a remarkably spicy French character. This is obvious at the powerful opening of the *B flat Symphony*, and even more so in the variations of the *Andante*. The pungent brilliance of the closing peroration is remarkable.

For his encore Jeremy Fisell has skilfully transcribed Pierre Cochereau's improvised variations on an old French carol, as played live by the composer and recorded on LP on Christmas Eve 1972. His own performance is thrillingly spontaneous, as if he were himself improvising. The animated first variation sets off exuberantly. Variation 4 is particularly ear-tickling, and the *Toccata* finale is a *tour de force*.

Symphony No. 10 in D (Romane), Op. 73; Suite Latine, Op. 86.

*** MDG 316 0406-2. Van Oosten (Cavaillé-Coll organ, at Sermin, Toulouse).

Ben van Oosten's gleaming registration at the opening of the *Symphony Romane* is quite dazzling, yet the central *Choral* and *Cantilène* (both based on plainchant from the Easter liturgy) are wonderfully serene. The cascading finale achieves a spectacular climax (still featuring the plainsong) then makes an extended diminuendo, culminating when the opening theme is reintroduced. The *Suite Latine*, one of Widor's last works and written when he was 83, again uses plainsong, but more introspectively. In Van Oosten's hands the central *Beatus vir*, *Lamento* and *Adagio* are gently withdrawn in colour and feeling, so that the exuberant finale is the more telling. These are undoubtedly distinguished performances, very well recorded on an impressively sonorous Cavaillé-Coll organ.

WIENIAWSKI, Henryk (1835–80)

(i) *Violin Concertos Nos. 1–2*; (ii) *Caprice in A min.* (arr. Kreisler); *Obertass-Mazurka, Op. 19/1; Polonaise de concert No. 1 in D, Op. 4; Polonaise brillante No. 2, Op. 21; Scherzo–tarantelle, Op. 16.*

(M) *** EMI (ADD) CDM5 66059-2. Perlman; (i) LPO, Ozawa; (ii) Sanders.

Violin Concertos Nos. 1–2; Fantaisie brillante on Themes from Gounod's Faust, Op. 20.

(BB) *** Naxos 8.553517. Bisengaliev, Polish Nat. RSO, Wit.

Violin Concertos Nos. 1–2; Légende, Op. 17.

*** DG 431 815-2. Shaham, LSO, Foster – SARASATE: *Zigeunerweisen.* ***

The Paganinian pyrotechnics in the first movement of Wien-iawski's *First Violin Concerto* , as Shaham readily demon-strates can be made to dazzle. Both soloist and orchestra are equally dashing, and lyrically persuasive in the better known *D minor Concerto*, while making an engaging encore out of the delightful *Légende*. With first-class DG recording this record is very recommendable.

Perlman also gives scintillating performances, full of flair, and is excellently accompanied. The recording, from 1973, is warm, vivid and well balanced. It is preferable to Perlman's digital re-make of the *Second Concerto*. The mid-priced reissue includes a mini-recital of shorter pieces, often dazz-ling, but losing some of their appeal from Perlman's insist-ence on a microphone spotlight. Samuel Sanders comes more into the picture in the introductions for the two *Polonaises*, although the violin still remains far too near the microphone.

Antoni Wit handles the long opening ritornello of the *F sharp minor Concerto* most impressively, and Marat Bisenga-liev proves a natural, understanding soloist in both con-certos, playing slow movements with warmly romantic feeling and sparkling with brilliance in the display passages and especially in the finales. The *Faust Variations* make a substantial (19-minute) and attractively tuneful bonus. Marat Bisengaliev has a fairly small, but sweet and beautifully focused tone; he is balanced naturally in relation to the orchestra, and both are very well recorded in the Polish Radio Concert Hall, which has an attractively warm acoustic.

Violin Concerto No. 2 in D min., Op. 22.

(M) (***) EMI mono CDH7 64251-2. Heifetz, LPO, Barbirolli – SAINT-SAENS: *Havanaise etc.*; SARASATE: *Zigeunerweisen*; VIEUXTEMPS: *Concerto No. 4.* (***)

(N) (BB) (***) Naxos mono 8.110938. Heifetz, LPO, Barbirolli – SIBELIUS: *Violin Concerto*; TCHAIKOVSKY: *Violin Concerto.* (***)

(N) **(*) CBC SMCD 5197. Kang, Vancouver SO, Comisiona – SCHUMANN: *Violin Concerto.* **(*)

(M) **(*) Sony (ADD) SMK 66830. Stern, Phd. O, Ormandy – BRUCH: *Violin Concerto No. 1* **(*); TCHAIKOVSKY: *Méditation; Sérénade mélancolique.* ***

Heifetz is in a class of his own. The concerto was recorded in 1935 with the young John Barbirolli, with whom Heifetz formed a strong rapport. It finds him at his most spon-taneously lyrical, revelling in the rhapsodic argument. The central *Romance* in particular is magnetic in its hushed, meditative intensity, with the finale swaggering confidently. The sound is perhaps less vivid than the best recordings of the day, but both transfers are very good.

The young Canadian violinist Juliette Kang, winner of the Menuhin International Competition, also plays with quicksilver brilliance. Dazzlingly clear as the playing is, this is a smaller-scale reading than most, largely a question of recording balance, with both violin and orchestra slightly distanced. What matters is that the performance, like that of the Schumann, is very persuasive. So Kang, light and volatile in the rapid passage-work, relaxes sweetly into the songful beauty of the motto theme, playing with a natural, unexaggerated lyricism. Both the slow movement and the

outer sections of the *Légende* have a similar songful flow, natural and unaffected, while the finale has Kang and Com-isiona choosing a speed that is fast and brilliant, allowing the dance rhythms to spring infectiously. A good recommen-dation for those who want this unique coupling.

Stern's recording comes from 1957, and the very close balance is not flattering to his upper range (although of course this playing can stand any kind of scrutiny). The songful slow movement is played simply and beautifully, and the finale is very *energico* indeed. Ormandy, as usual, provides fine support and the orchestra, though also bal-anced artificially, plays against a warm ambience.

Capriccio-waltz, Op. 7; Gigue in E min., Op. 27; Kujawiak in A min.; Légende, Op. 17; Mazurka in G min., Op. 12/2; 2 Mazurkas, Op. 19; Polonaise No. 1; Russian Carnival, Op. 11; Saltarello (arr. Lenehan); Scherzo-tarantelle; Souvenir de Moscou, Op. 6; Variations on an Original Theme, Op. 15.

(BB) **(*) Naxos 8.550744. Bisengaliev, Lenehan.

All the dazzling violin fireworks are ready to bow here, from left-hand pizzicatos in the *Russian Carnival* to multiple stopping (and some lovely, warm lyricism) in the *Variations on an Original Theme*, plus all the dash you could ask for in the closing *Scherzo-tarantelle*, while the beautiful *Légende* (which Wieniawski dedicated to his wife as a nuptial gift) is both touchingly gentle and passionately brilliant. Marat Bisengaliev is without the larger-than-life personality of a Perlman, but he is a remarkably fine player and a stylist. John Lenehan provides his partner with admirable support throughout. The snag is the very reverberant acoustic of the Rosslyn Hill Chapel, Hampstead – so obviously empty; otherwise the sound and balance are natural enough.

WIKMANSON, Johan (1753–1800)

String Quartet No. 2 in E min., Op. 1/2.

(M) *** CRD (ADD) CRD 3361. Chilingirian Qt – BERWALD: *Quartet.* ***

(M) *** CRD (ADD) CRD 33123 (2). Chilingirian Qt – ARRIAGA: *String Quartets Nos. 1–3.* ***

Wikmanson was a cultured musician, but little of his music survives and two of his five *Quartets* are lost. The overriding influence here is that of Haydn and the finale of the present quartet even makes a direct allusion to Haydn's *E flat Quartet*, Op. 33, No. 2. The Chilingirian make out a per-suasive case for this piece and are very well recorded. As can be seen, this work is available coupled with either Arriaga or Berwald.

WILBYE, John (1574–1658)

Madrigals (First Set, 1598): excerpts: *Adieu sweet Amaryllis; Alas what a wretched life; Cruel behold my ending; Die hapless man; Lady when I behold the roses* (2 versions); *Lady, your words do spite me; My throat is sore; Of joys and pleasing pains; Thus saith my Cloris bright;

Thou art but young; Weep O mine eyes; When shall my wretched life; Why dost thou shoot. (Second Set, 1609): excerpts: *Ah cannot sighs, nor tears; Draw on sweet night; O wretched man; Softly, of softly, drop my eyes; Stay, Corydon; Sweet honey suckling bee; Yes sweet, take heed; Ye that do live in pleasures.*

(B) ******* Double Decca (ADD) 458 093-2 (2) Consort of Musicke, Rooley – GIBBONS; WILBYE: *Madrigals.* *******

John Wilbye was one of the major figures in the English music of the period and this selection made from both his major sets of madrigals must be counted the best current available introduction to his art. The most famous madrigals such as *Draw on sweet night* and *Stay, Corydon* stay are matched by other sad settings like *O wretched man* and *Softly softly drop, mine eyes,* and while a lighter note is caught with *Adieu sweet Amaryllis* and *Sweet honey-sucking bees,* it is the melancholic nature of his finest works that give them their special character. The performances here are appealingly fresh rather than profound in their depth, but they are beautifully recorded and this anthology overall is a most important addition to the catalogue.

WILLAERT, Adrian (c. 1490–1562)

Ave Maria; Magnificat sexti toni; Missa Christus resurgens.

(B) ******* Naxos 8.553211. Oxford Camerata, Summerly – RICHAFORT: *Motet: Christus resurgens.* *******

Over the first half of the sixteenth century this Flemish composer was one of the key figures in Western music, instrumental in the development both of the madrigal and of church music for double chorus. From 1527 until his death he was Maestro di capella at St Mark's in Venice, but this music, dates mainly from his earlier years, when he achieved nine settings of the Mass. This splendid offering from Summerly and his Oxford camerata is the only one available, a magnificent 'parody mass', using as its base a motet by Jean Richafort, a piece included here as a prelude. Willaert's setting rises to a sublime conclusion in the extended *Agnus Dei,* in flowing polyphony. The *Magnificat* and *Ave Maria* offer inspired music too, performed with equal freshness and dedication. Vividly atmospheric sound. At Naxos price, not to be missed.

WILLAN, Healey (1880–1968)

Behold, the Tabernacle of God; Brightest and best of the Sons of the Morning; Gloria Deo per immensa saecula; Hail gladdening light; Hodie, Christus natus est; Immortal, invisible, God only wise (St Basil); Here we are in Bethlehem; How they so softly rest; Look down, O Lord; Lord enthroned in heavenly splendour; Missa brevis No. 4: Corde natus ex parentis (with Christmas Propers, motet, carol, and hymn); Missa brevis No. 11 (Sancti Johannis Baptiste); Motets in honour of Our Lady, the Blessed Virgin Mary: (I beheld her, beautiful as a dove; Fair in the face; Rise up my love;) O King, all glorious; O King to whom all things do live; O Saving Victim; O Trinity most blessed Light; Preserve us, O Lord; Very Bread, Good Shepherd tend us.

(N) ******* Virgin VC5 45109-2. St Mary Magdelene, Toronto Choirs. Hunter Bell.

Healey Willan was born in Balham, Surrey. His musical education and training were not at a cathedral choir school but at the modest St Saviour's Church School, Eastbourne. By 1910 he had joined the London Gregorian Association and was already organist at St John the Baptist, Holland Park, which celebrated the Anglo-Cathlic ritual, and these combined experiences were profoundly to shape his musical life. In 1913 he emigrated to Canada and by 1919 he had become organist, choirmaster, musical director and composer-in-residence of one of Canada's finest churches, St Mary Magdelene's in Toronto.

Here he developed the celebration of the full catholic ritual, teaching his choir of men and boys' choir to sing Plainsong and the Propers of the Mass in English. He then trained a second choir of men and women to sing unaccompanied, and soon this choir was moved to the rear gallery of the church – which has marvellous acoustics – and began to use the two choirs antiphonally. In 1931 the organ console was also moved to the gallery and everything was in place to create an ongoing musical tradition which became famous all over North America.

He continued as musical director for nearly fifty years and left behind him a choir of outstanding quality and an enormous amount of music. The present recording was made in 1995 to remember him tangibly on the twenty-fifth anniversary of his death. It includes the celebrated trio of 'Our Lady' motets, and some of his finest shorter works, but centres on a complete Christmas Midnight Mass with proper and a wonderfully vibrant setting of *Hodie, Christus natus est,* but also the lovely, simple *Kyrie, Sanctus, Benedictus* and *Agnus Dei* of the *Fourth Missa brevis.* The closing *Gloria Deo* is wonderfully exultant. Willan's music exists in a tradition of Anglican and Catholic church music which stretches back to Byrd, and the singing of the St Mary Magdalene choir reminds the listener of the great English Choirs at King's College, Cambridge, and other regional centres.

An Apostrophe to the Heavenly Hosts; Ave verum corpus; A Clear Midnight; 7 Great O Antiphons of Advent; I will lay me down in peace; I looked, and behold a white cloud; Lo, in the time appointed; Magnificat & Nunc dimittis; O how glorious; O Quanta Qualia; Sing to the Lord of Harvest; Tenebrae of Maundy Thursday.

✿ (N) ******* Virgin VC5 45183-2. Vancouver Chamber Ch., Washburn; Nixon.

The second collection of Willan's music is perhaps even finer than the first and includes his supreme masterpiece, *An Apostrophe to the Heavenly Hosts,* composed in 1921. Drawing on his experiences with the choral layout at St Mary Madgelene's it is written for eight-part double choir and two small 'mystic choirs' (reminding us of both Tallis and Elgar). It is magnificently compressed into just ten minutes, yet is in four sections, each ending with gentle echoing 'Amens' from the mystic chorus, which are especially magical in the pianissimo closing section. The *Magnificat* and *Nunc dimittis* of 1957 are also outstandingly fine, and the *Tenebrae of Maundy Thursday* achingly beautiful. Much simpler, but hardly less memorable, are the seven *Great O Antiphons*, which together only extend to just over eight minutes. The three final items in the programme, the lovely *Ave verum corpus*, the masterful *A clear midnight* and the most popular of his hymn anthems, *Sing to the Lord of Harvest*, cap the programme, which is all marvellously sung, with great dedication, and beautifully recorded.

WILLIAMS, Grace (1906–77)

(i) *Carillons for Oboe & Orchestra;* (ii) *Trumpet Concerto. Fantasia on Welsh Nursery Rhymes;* (iii) *Penillion;* (iv) *Sea Sketches* (for string orchestra).

*** Lyrita (ADD) SRCS 323. (i) Camden: (ii) H. Blake; both with LSO; (iii) RPO; all cond. Groves; (iv) ECO, D. Atherton.

It is good to have this attractive programme of works by a woman composer who (rarely among twentieth-century feminist musicians) glowingly shows that she believes in pleasing the listener's ear. No lack of imaginative resource either, particularly in the memorably individual *Sea Sketches,* a masterly suite of five contrasted movements which catch the sea's unpredictability as well as its formidable energy, while the two slow sections, the seductive *Channel Sirens* and the *Calm Sea in Summer,* are balmily, impressionistic and poetic. The other works here range attractively from the simple *Nursery-rhyme Fantasia* to *Penillion,* a set of four colourful, resourceful pieces, easy on the ear but full of individual touches retaining the idea of a central melodic line. The trumpet and oboe concertante pieces are superbly played by soloists from the LSO of the early 1970s – both show the affection and understanding of individual instrumental timbre which mark the composer's work. There are excellent performances throughout, and very good analogue sound.

(i) *Symphony No. 2; Ballads for Orchestra;* (ii) *Fairest of Stars* (for soprano and orchestra).

*** Lyrita (ADD) SRCS 327. (i) BBC Welsh SO, Handley; (ii) Janet Price, LSO, Groves.

In her *Second Symphony,* Grace Williams's most ambitious orchestral work, the writing is sharp and purposeful, relaxing more towards lyricism in the slow movement (which produces an endearing pastoral oboe theme) and the finale with its darkly Mahlerian overtones. The *Ballades* of 1968, characteristically based on Welsh ballad and 'penillion' forms, also reveal the darker side of Grace Williams's writing. The performances, originally recorded for radio, are expressive and convincing. *Fairest of Stars,* too, is a relatively tough setting of Milton, and is strongly sung by Janet Price. The recordings are all of good quality.

WILLIAMSON, Malcolm (born 1931)

Double Concerto for 2 Pianos & Strings.

(N) **(*) Australian ABC Eloquence 426 483-2. Williamson, Campion, Tasmanian SO, Tuckwell – EDWARDS: *Piano Concerto* **(*); SCULTHORPE: *Piano Concerto.* **(*)

Williamson's *Concerto for Two Pianos* has been recorded before (by EMI), but that is not currently available. This performance of this distinctive, but fairly tough – though by no means unapproachable – work is committed, well performed and reasonably well recorded, and is part of a valuable trilogy of rare concertos.

The Growing Castle.

(N) **(*) Universal ABC Classics, Australia (ADD) 461 922-2. Elkins, Bamberg SO, Gierster – SHIELD: *Rosina;* ELGAR: *Sea Pictures.*

This recording of *The Growing Castle* was part of a project, aborted owing to illness, to record a collection of arias, of which this was all that was completed. It was forgotten for thirty years but resurrected for this Australian Heritage release. A short work, it opens very dramatically before a rather beautiful lyricism takes over, and was specially re-orchestrated by the composer at the request of the singer, Margreta Elkins, for this recording. The performance is excellent, though the recording, while quite full and vivid, sounds a bit dated, with Margreta Elkins too closely miked. It makes an unexpected bonus for Shield's sparkling *Rosina* and a fine Elgar *Sea Pictures.*

WIRÉN, Dag (1905–86)

Serenade for Strings in G, Op. 11.

(BB) *** Naxos 8.553106. Bournemouth Sinf., Studt – (with Concert: *Scandinavian String Music.* ***)

The engaging *String Serenade* is Dag Wirén's one claim to international fame, and it is good to welcome an outstanding super-bargain version. The finale certainly earns its hit status, full of spontaneous, lilting energy. First-rate recording within an entirely recommendable concert of Scandinavian string music, not all of it familiar.

(i–ii) *Miniature Suite* (for cello & piano), *Op. 8b;* (ii) (Piano) *Improvisations; Little Suite; Sonatina, Op. 25; Theme & Variations, Op. 5;* (iii) *3 Sea Poems;* (iv; ii) *2 Songs from Hösthorn, Op. 13.*

*** BIS CD 797. (i) Thedéen; (ii) Bojsten; (iii) Jubilate Ch., Riska; (iv) Högman.

Dag Wirén was a miniaturist *Par Excellence* and few of the individual movements recorded here detain the listener for more than two or three minutes. The early (and inventive) *Theme and Variations,* Op. 5, is the longest work. Although it is slight, the *Sonatina for Piano* often touches a deeper vein of feeling than one might expect to encounter. Good performances from all concerned, and the usual truthful BIS recording.

Symphonies Nos. 2, Op. 14; 3 in C, Op. 20; Concert
Overtures Nos. 1 & 2.

(N) *** CPO 999 677-2. Norrköping SO, Dausgaard.

Apart from the celebrated *Serenade for Strings* (for years the
signature-tune of the BBC's *Monitor* TV programme) and
the *Sinfonietta Op. 7*, little of Dag Wirén's music is heard
nowadays. In some ways the most appealing and natural
Swedish composer of his generation, he lacks the breadth
and sense of scale of the born symphonist. The *Third* (1944)
was broadcast frequently during the 1940s, but even at the
time it seemed thin and short-breathed and the idiom in
thrall to Sibelius. The *Second Symphony* (1939) is the finer of
the two, though ultimately deficient in motivic vitality and
too reliant on ostinato figures. Good performances and
recordings of likeable but flawed works.

WITT, Friedrich (1770–1836)

Piano & Wind Quintet in E flat, Op. 5 .

(N) *** CBC MCVD 1137. Kuerti, Campbell, Mason,
   Sommerville, McKay – BEETHOVEN; MOZART:
   Quintets. ***

The German cellist Friedrich Witt modelled his *Quintet*
with uncanny closeness on those of Beethoven and Mozart,
though the *Adagio cantabile* – which opens with a bassoon
solo – also brings a dash of Hummel. Unlike his predecessors, Witt also includes a *Minuet* whose Ländler-like trio
is particularly engaging. Indeed, the quality of the invention
is by no means to be sniffed at, with the good-humoured
finale particularly successful in this vividly alive performance. The recording is first class – remarkably present and
realistic.

WOLF, Hugo (1860–1903)

Italian Serenade in G.

(N) *** Ph. 462 594-2. Saito Kinen O, Ozawa – BARTOK:
   Divertimento **(*); DVORAK: *Serenade for Strings*. *(*)

(***) Biddulph mono LAB 098. Budapest Qt – GRIEG;
   SIBELIUS: *Quartets*. ***

Wolf's *Italian Serenade*, under Ozawa, given in the
composer's own orchestral version, is delectably done,
making one regret the more that the performance of the
Dvořák is so flawed. The Wolf can be an elusive piece, but a
light, delicate performance like this brings out the infectious
wit, with lolloping dance rhythms given a delicious spring,
making one wonder why it is not far more often performed,
whether on disc or in the concert hall. Undistracting
recorded sound, warm rather than brilliant.

A welcome reissue on Biddulph – the first on CD – of the
1933 pioneering *Italian Serenade*. It has a spring in its step
and a lightness of touch that are almost unique, and it is
well transferred here by Ward Marston. The couplings also
show how special this ensemble was in the 1930s.

*String Quartet in D min.; Intermezzo in E flat; Italian
Serenade in G.*

*** CPO CPO 999 529-2. Auryn Qt.

Hugo Wolf's massive *String Quartet* may be a student work,
but in its concentration and complexity it harks back to
late Beethoven, as well as to Wagner. The formidable first
movement leads to a slow movement of heavenly length,
here interpreted with hushed intensity by the young Auryn
Quartet. Both in the *Quartet* and in the other two works,
including the winningly exuberant *Italian Serenade*, the
playing amply makes up in its warmth and spontaneity for
any slight lack of polish. Warm, full sound.

*Eichendorf Lieder: Nachtzauber; Die Zigeunerin. Mörike
Lieder: Elfenlied; Der Genesene an die Hoffnung;
Lebewohl; Storchenbotschaft. Lieder from Italienisches
Liederbuch: Du sagst mir; Ich esse nun mein Brot; Ich hab'
in Penna; Nein, junger Herr; Nur lass uns Frieden
schliessen; O wär' dein Haus durchsichtig; Schweig' einmal
still; Verschling' der Abgrund; Wer rief dich denn?. Lieder
from Spanisches Liederbuch: Bedeckt mich mit Blumen;
Geh', Geliebter, geh' jetzt; Herr, was trägt der Boden hier;
In dem Schatten meiner Locken; Klinge klinge mein
Pandero; Mögen alle bösen Zungen; Sie blasen zum
Abmrarsch. Encores: Trau' nicht der Liebe. Mörike Lieder:
Der Knabe und das Immelein; Nimmersatte Liebe;
Selbstgeständnis.*

(M) (***) EMI mono CDH5 65749-2. Schwarzkopf, Moore.

In many ways the extra degree of freedom in Schwarzkopf's
performances here, recorded live at Salfurg recitals in 1957
and 1963, adds to the intensity of the experience, both in
weighty songs and in lighter ones such as *Wer rief dich denn?*
(uniquely vehement) and *Ich hab' in Penna*. The recordings,
originally made by Austrian Radio, capture the voice beautifully, with words crystal clear. However, this CD has just
been deleted.

*Goethe Lieder: Anakreons Grab; Blumengruss; Erschaffen
und Beleben; Gleich und gleich; Harfenspieler I, II & III;
Ob der Koran von Ewigkeit sei?; Phänomen; Der
Rattenfänger; Sie haben wegen der Trunkenheit; So lang
man nüchtern ist; Spottlied; Trunken müssen wir alle sein!;
Was in der Schenke waren heute. Mörike Lieder: Abschied;
An die Geliebte; An eine Aolsharfe; Auf ein altes Bild; Bei
einer Trauung; Elfenlied; Er ist's; Fussreise; Der Gärtner;
Gebet; Gesang Weylas; Heimweh; Jägerlied; Nimmersatte
Liebe; Der Tambour; Verborgenheit.*

(BB) *** Virgin 2 x 1 Double VBD5 61418-2 (2). Allen, Parsons
   – BRAHMS: *Lieder*. ***

This is an exceptionally generous (74-minute) collection of
Wolf's Goethe and Mörike settings, which are much rarer,
both on disc and in the recital room. Thomas Allen enters
fully into the spirit of each song, and Geoffrey Parsons
accompanies with characteristic imagination. Whether the
words convey ardour (as in one of the best known, *An die
Geliebte*), are hauntingly evocative (as in the remarkable
Harfenspieler settings) or are exuberantly extrovert (*Der
Rattenfänger*), these artists unerringly project their mood.
Alas, this inexpensive reissue includes neither translations
nor song summaries, but the vocal treasure offered here and

the excellence both of performances and of Andrew Keener's recording balance at Abbey Road carries the day.

Goethe Lieder: *Anakreons Grab; 3 Harfenspieler Lieder.*

*** Decca 458 189-2. Goerne, Concg. O, Chailly – BRUCKNER: *Symphony No. 6 in A.* ***

The three *Harfenspieler* songs, setting verses from the novel, *Wilhelm Meister*, as well as *Anakreons Grab* make a valuable and generous fill-up for Chailly's superb, refined reading of the Bruckner symphony. Matthias Goerne with his headily lyrical baritone makes an ideal, thoughtful interpreter, well balanced in the warmly atmospheric recording.

Goethe Lieder: *Als ich auf dem Euphrat schiffte; Anakreons Grab; Die Bekehrte; Blumengruss; Dank des Paria; Epiphanias; Frühling über Jahr; Ganymed; Gleich und Gleich; Gretchen vor dem Andachtsbild der Mater dolorosa; Gutmann und Gutweib; Hoch beglückt in deiner Liebe; Kennst du dasLand; Mignon Lieder I–III; Nimmer will ich dich verlieren; Phänomen; Philine; St Nepomuks Vorabend; Der Schäfer; So lang man nüchtern ist; Die Spröde; Wandrers Nachtlied.*

(N) *** Hyp. CDA 67130. McGreevy, Johnson.

Geraldine McGreevy, winner of the 1996 Kathleen Ferrier Award, makes a fresh and pure-toned partner for Graham Johnson in a challenging selection of Wolf's settings of Goethe, with all but two of the twenty-four songs coming from the great Goethe songbook of his maturity in 1888–9. As ever, Johnson provides the most searching and illuminating notes on each song, enhancing enjoyment greatly with his words as well as his playing, but it is good to welcome so sensitive and responsive a young Lieder-singer as McGreevy, who here triumphs over even the most demanding of challenges. So it is good to have readings of the four *Mignon* songs (the three regular ones plus *Kennst du das Land*) which bring out the mystery of the writing with the benefit of girlish tone, apt for Goethe's heroine. *Kennst du das Land* is the more moving for that, with McGreevy providing a thrilling crescendo in the last stanza, perfectly controlled. Yet she responds to the lighter songs beautifully too, with a fine feeling for word-meaning. Excellent, well-balanced sound.

Goethe Lieder: *Die Bekehrte; Frühling übers Jahr; Ganymed; Mignon; Mignon 1–3; Philine; Die Spröde. Mörike-Lieder: Auf eine Christblume I & 2; Auf einer Wanderung; Begegnung; Er ist's; Der Gärtner; Der Knabe und das Immlein; In der Frühe; Lebe wohl; Nimmersatte Liebe; Nixe Binsefuss; Schlafendes Jesuskind; Verborgenheit; Das verlassene Mägdlein.*

(N) EMI ** CDC5 56988-2. Hendricks, Pöntinen.

With her warm, distinctive tone Barbara Hendricks, an animated singer, gives well-characterized readings of this carefully chosen selection of Wolf's settings of Mörike and Goethe. What is largely missing though is the thoughtfulness that should illuminate the more challenging songs. There is little sense of mystery, and when it comes to the supreme challenge of the four *Mignon Lieder* and the related Philine song, it is only the last, light and sparkling, that finds Hend-

ricks fully able to realize the composer's intentions. *Kennst du das Land* is capably sung, but without the emotional thrust that puts it among the greatest Lieder of all. Clean accompaniment from Pontinen and undistracting recording.

Italienisches Liederbuch (complete).

(M) *** EMI (ADD) CDM7 63732-2. Schwarzkopf, Fischer-Dieskau, Moore.

*** Hyp. CDA 66760. Lott, Schreier, Johnson.

On EMI all 46 songs of Wolf's *Italienisches Liederbuch* are sung by Schwarzkopf and Fischer-Dieskau on a CD playing for two seconds over 79 minutes, generous measure at mid-price! Few artists today can match the searching perception of these two great singers in this music, with Fischer-Dieskau using his sweetest tones and Schwarzkopf ranging through all the many emotions inspired by love. Gerald Moore is at his finest, and Walter Legge's translations will help bring the magic of these unique songs even to the newcomer. The 1969 recording has been admirably transferred. However, this recital has just been deleted.

Graham Johnson conjures up music-making full of magic, compelling from first to last. Yet, so far from being intrusive in his playing, he consistently heightens the experience, drawing out from Felicity Lott one of her most intense and detailed performances on record, totally individual. Peter Schreier, one of the supreme masters of Lieder today, also responds to this characterful accompanist; and having a tenor instead of the usual baritone brings many benefits in this sharply pointed sequence. The triumph of this issue is crowned by the substantial booklet provided in the package, containing Johnson's uniquely perceptive commentary on each song – alone worth the price of the disc. Excellent sound.

Mörike Lieder: *An eine Aeolsharfe; Bei einer Trauung; Denk' es, o Seele!; Heimweh; Im Frühling; Jägerlied; Lied eines Verliebten.*

(M) *** BBC (ADD) BBCB 8015-2. Pears, Britten – BRITTEN: *On his island,* etc.; SCHUBERT: *7 Lieder* *** (with ARNE: *Come away death; Under the greenwood tree;* QUILTER: *O mistress mine;* WARLOCK: *Take, o take those lips away;* TIPPETT: *Come unto these yellow sands* ***).

In the BBC's sensitive performances of seven of Wolf's Mörike settings – recorded at the Snape Maltings in 1972, not long before Britten was stricken by terminal illness – these unfailingly convey a sense of spontaneity, capturing the inspiration of the moment in a way that is rare on disc, thanks above all to Britten's accompaniments. Excellent radio sound.

Mörike Lieder: Michelangelo Lieder: *Alles endet, was entstehet; Fühlt meine Seele; Wohl denk' ich oft. Mörike Lieder: Abschied; An de Schlaf; An die Geliebte; Auf eine altes Bild; Auf eine Christblume I & II; Auf einer Wanderung; Auftrag; Begegnung; Bei einer Trauung; Denk' es, o Seele!; Der Feuerreiter; Füssreise; Der Gärtner; Gebet; Die Geister am Mummelsee; Der Genesene an die Hoffnung; Gesang Weyla's; Heimwek; Im Frühling; In der*

Fru'he; Der Jäger; Jägerlieg; Karwoche; Der König bei der Krönung; Lebe wohl; Lied eines Verliebten; Neue Liebe; Nimmersatte Liebe; Peregrina I & II; Schlafendes Jesuskind; Selbstgeständnis; Seufzer; Storchenbotschaft; Der Tambour; Um Mitternacht; Wo find' ich Trost; Verborgenheit; Zitronnenfalter im April; Zur Warnung.

(M) (***) EMI mono/stereo CMS7 63563-2 (2). Fischer-Dieskau, Moore.

This collection of Wolf's settings of Mörike, 44 songs, was recorded in 1957, with four songs completing the collection, added two years later. Those four are in stereo but, so compelling is Fischer-Dieskau's singing, one hardly worries that the others are all in mono only. The experience is the more vivid thanks to the close placing of the singer, as though face to face. However, this set has just been deleted.

Spanisches Liederbuch (complete).

(M) *** DG (ADD) 457 726-2 (2). Schwarzkopf, Fischer-Dieskau, Moore.
*** EMI CDS5 55325-2 (2). Von Otter, Bär, Parsons.

In this superb DG reissue, the sacred songs provide a dark, intense prelude, with Fischer-Dieskau at his very finest, sustaining slow tempi impeccably. Schwarzkopf's dedication comes out in the three songs suitable for a woman's voice; but it is in the secular songs, particularly those which contain laughter in the music, where she is at her most memorable. Gerald Moore is balanced rather too backwardly – something the transfer cannot correct – but gives superb support.

Completed barely six months before Geoffrey Parsons' untimely death, the EMI set of the *Spanish Songbook* makes a superb memorial to that great accompanist, here working with two of the most searching and stylish Lieder singers of the present generation. They opt for an order of the songs quite different from the original published order, seeking to find 'a dramatic shape that worked in the atmosphere of a concert'. Quite apart from Parsons' superb contribution, the performances of both soloists vie with those on the classic DG set with Schwarzkopf and Fischer-Dieskau. For the lighter songs von Otter uses a much brighter tonal range than elsewhere, though in such a song as *In dem Schatten meiner Locken* she remains more intimate than Schwarzkopf, pointing the words and phrases with comparable character. However, this has just been deleted.

(i) 3 Christmas Songs: *Auf ein altes Bild; Nun wandre, Maria; Schlafendes Jesuskind;* (ii) 3 Michelangelo Lieder: *Alles endet, was entstehet; Fühlt meine Seele; Wohl denk' ich oft.*

(M)*** BBC (ADD) BBCB 8011-2. (i) Pears; (ii) Shirley-Quirk, Britten – SCHUBERT: *11 Lieder.* ***

John Shirley-Quirk in his singing of three of Wolf's Michelangelo settings at the 1971 Aldeburgh Festival has never been more mellifluous on disc, just as sensitive in his treatment of Lieder as the others, and the whole programme is delightfully rounded off by Pears's charming performances of the three Wolf Christmas songs. Excellent sound.

Lieder: *Frage nicht; Frühling übers Jahr; Gesang Weylas; Kennst du das Land? (Mignon); Heiss mich nicht reden (Mignon I); Nur wer die Sehnsucht kennt (Mignon II); So lasst mich scheinen (Mignon III); Der Schäfer; Die Spröde.*

*** DG (IMS) 423 666-2. Von Otter, Gothoni – MAHLER: *Das Knaben Wunderhorn* etc. ***

Anne Sofie von Otter presents Wolf's *Mignon* songs with firm, persuasive lines. The gravity of *Kennst du das Land?* is then delightfully contrasted against the delicacy of *Frühling übers Jahr* or *Die Spröde*. The sensitivity and imagination of Rolf Gothoni's accompaniment add enormously to the performances in a genuine two-way partnership. Well-balanced recording.

WOLF-FERRARI, Ermanno

(1876–1948)

L'amore medico: Overture. Il campiello: Intermezzo; Ritornello. La dama bomba: Overture. I gioielli della Madonna (suite). I 4 rusteghi: Prelude & Intermezzo. Il segreto di Susanna: Overture.

*** ASV CDDCA 861. RPO, Serebrier.

Although this situation is currently changing, Wolf-Ferrari has long held a permanent place in the catalogue only with recordings of his operatic *intermezzi* – not surprising, perhaps, when they are so readily tuneful and charmingly scored. Serebrier conjures at times exquisite playing from the RPO (especially the strings) and, even though he takes Susanna's sparkling overture slightly slower than usual, it is hardly less successful. What is specially memorable is his delicate treatment of the gossamer string-pieces from *I quattro rusteghi* and the *Ritornello* from *Il Campiello* which almost have a Beecham touch. The ASV recording, made in the Henry Wood Hall, is slightly more open and indeed marginally more transparent and fresh.

Il Campiello: Prelude; Ritornello; Intermezzo. The Inquisitive Woman: Overture. Jewels of the Madonna: Neapolitan dance; The School for Fathers: Intermezzo. Susanna's secret: Overture. Serenade for strings.

(M) *** Berlin Classics 0091772BC. Berlin RSO, Rögner.

Rögner's collection comes from the late 1970s and has the advantage of natural, warmly resonant analogue sound which gives these attractive pieces a pleasing hall ambience. He offers an aptly paced, sparkling account of *Susanna's Secret*, while the sprightly *Inquisitive Woman Overture*, with its songful theme for the oboe, is hardly less winning, and a real find. The Berlin Orchestra play it with the lightest rhythmic touch, and are hardly less persuasive in the Neapolitan Dance, a brilliant show-piece of which they take full advantage. The charming *Intermezzo* from *The School for Fathers* is given with fragile delicacy and the music from *Il Campiello* is just as delectable; both the *Prelude* and *Ritornello* have a haunting atmosphere. The programme ends with a captivating account of the *String Serenade*, which charms and touches the listener by turns.

(i) *Cello Concerto in C (Invocazione), Op. 31. Symphonia Brevis in E flat, Op. 28.*

(BB) *** CPO CPO 999 278-2. (i) Rivinius; Frankfurt RSO, Francis.

Wolf-Ferrari's *Cello Concerto*, like the *Violin Concerto*, is a considerable work and its title *Invocazione* is well chosen. The opening movements are both marked *Tranquillo*, and even the use of a theme very like 'Three blind mice' does not rob the first of its serenity. The gay, dancing finale maintains the work's lightness of texture and feeling. The first movement of the *Sinfonia brevis* tries to sustain this tranquil mood, and finally does so at the close, after frequent interruptions, often quite boisterous. The jaunty *Capriccio* which follows acts as a colourful scherzo and might well be another of those intermezzi. The *Adagio* is both a barcarolle and a threnody, and again features a solo cello, pensive and darker-voiced than in the concerto. The finale dances away in a jiggy tarantella rhythm and ends in cheerful buoyancy. The performances here are full of life and feeling, and are given a vividly spacious recording.

(i) *Violin Concerto in D, Op. 26; Serenade for Strings.*

(BB) *** CPO CPO 999 271-2. (i) Hoelscher, Frankfurt RSO, Francis.

Wolf-Ferrari's warmly romantic *Violin Concerto* captures the listener's ear from the very opening, and Ulf Hoelscher is a superbly responsive soloist. The *Romanza* opens with ethereal delicacy, but passion soon comes to the surface and is always ready to burst into the *Improviso* third movement. The jolly, sparkling Rondo finale is in the best traditional mode of classical concerto finales. Again Hoelscher is on his mettle: he never made a better record than this, and his exquisite playing of the long cadenza–soliloquy towards the movement's close is especially fine. The *String Serenade* is an extraordinarily accomplished and individual four-movement student work, genuinely inspired, and it is most persuasively played here, with a more passionate less innocent performance than Heinz Rögner gives in his collection below. First-class recording.

CHAMBER MUSIC

Duo in G min., Op. 33b; Introduzione e balleto, Op. 35* (both for violin and cello); *String Trios: in B min.* (1894); *in A min., Op. 32.

(N) *** CPO 999 624-2. Deutsch String Trio (members).

The early *String Trio* of 1894 sounds not in the least immature, and has a nostalgic lyricism which reminds one a little of Schubert. Many years later, in 1947, Wolf-Ferrari wrote the *Duo in G minor* (originally intended for viola d'amore and viola da gamba). It is a delightfully inventive work, also in three movements, with a charming *Barcarole* as its centrepiece and a light-hearted finale, which suddenly darkens and becomes almost despondent, until the composer recovers his spirits.

The mature *A minor Trio* of 1945 is also ambivalent in mood, although it has a tranquil central *Pastorale*. Once again the finale opens wittily and energetically but has its moments of hesitancy, and a passage of strange bitter-sweet melancholy appears at its heart, which brings an uncertain close. The Deutsch String Trio are right inside this music and play it very persuasively indeed.

The *Introduzione* is much lighter in style and feeling, with a charming folksy element: the *Ballet* is a sentimental Viennese waltz, treated with great delicacy, yet expresses that underlying *fin de siècle* insecurity which characterizes all these remarkably rewarding works. It is marvellously played: the two instruments blend into a perfect partnership and their rubato sounds absolutely natural and spontaneous. First-class recording too.

Piano Trios Nos. 1 in D, Op. 5; 2 in F sharp, Op. 7.

*** ASV CDDCA 935. Raphael Trio.

Wolf-Ferrari wrote these two ambitious *Piano Trios* at the very beginning of his career. They may not be masterpieces, but the large-scale first movements show him as a fine craftsman, and more importantly, his themes already show the gift of easy memorability which marks his other major works. So the slow movement of No. 1 is like a Mascagni lament, and the chattering finale might be a sketch for an operatic interlude. No. 2 is even odder in its layout, with the first movement twice as long as the other two put together, but with well-disciplined performances from the Raphael Trio – an American group – the colour and charm of the writing is persuasively brought out.

OPERA

***Sly* (complete).**

(N) *** Koch 3-6449-2 (2). Carreras, Kabatu, Milnes, Barcelona Theatre Ch. & O, Giménez.

Though Giovacchino Forzano's libretto crudifies the Shakespearean source – the Timothy Sly episode from *The Taming of the Shrew* – Wolf-Ferrari's *Sly* is a striking, skillfully written piece that well deserves an airing on disc, particularly in a strong performance such as this. Act I – before the trick being played on Sly grows serious, and finally tragic – is a delight, a sparkling sequence of finely tailored ideas in not-too-distant echo of *Falstaff* and *Gianni Schicchi*. Later, with José Carreras giving what is probably his finest performance on disc since his debilitating leukaemia, the character of Sly acquires unexpected nobility, losing all absurdity.

Wolf-Ferrari's concentration remains impressive, even if the tragic close seems too conventionally operatic. As the heroine, Dolly, Isabelle Kabatu, Belgian, born in Zaire, sings warmly, bringing out the character's wilful, volatile nature, only occasionally raw on top. A veteran like Carreras, Sherill Milnes gives a powerful portrait of the Count who devises the trick of translating Sly, as though in a dream, to be master of his castle. The others make an excellent team in a live recording crisply conducted by David Gimenez, and vividly recorded.

WOLPE, Stefan (1902–72)

(i) *Symphony No. 1*; (ii) *Chamber Pieces Nos. 1–2*;
(iii) *Yigdal Cantata.*

(BB) *** Arte Nova 74321 46508-2. (i) NDR SO, Kalitzke;
  (ii) Instrumental Ens.; (iii) NDR Ch., H. Neumann.

Stefan Wolpe was one of Webern's most distinguished pupils. The *Yigdal Cantata* sets Hebrew texts in a way which brilliantly reconciles a serial technique with traditional Jewish music, warm and expressive. The purely instrumental works are far tougher, with the *Symphony* crisp and purposeful. The two *Chamber Pieces*, each for fourteen instruments, very much in the manner of Webern, are among Wolpe's last works, even more compressed, with each seeming to reflect his frustration and defiance over suffering from Parkinson's disease. At Arte Nova price, well worth investigating by the adventurous.

WOOD, Haydn (1882–1959)

Apollo Overture; *A Brown Bird Singing* (paraphrase for orchestra); *London Cameos* (suite) *Miniature Overture: The City*; *St James's Park in the Spring*; *A State Ball at Buckingham Palace. Mannin Veen* (Manx tone-poem); *Moods* (suite): *Joyousness* (concert waltz). *Mylecharane* (rhapsody); *The Seafarer* (*A nautical rhapsody*); *Serenade to Youth*; *Sketch of a Dandy.*

*** Marco 8.22340-2. Slovak RSO (Bratislava), Leaper.

Haydn Wood, an almost exact contemporary of Eric Coates and nearly as talented, spent his childhood on the Isle of Man, and much of his best music is permeated with Manx folk-themes (original or simulated). *Mannin Veen* ('Dear Isle of Man') is a splendid piece, based on four such folksongs. The companion rhapsody, *Mylecharane*, also uses folk material, if less memorably, and *The Seafarer* is a wittily scored selection of famous shanties, neatly stitched together. The only failure here is *Apollo*, which uses less interesting material and is over-ambitious and inflated. But the English waltzes are enchanting confections and *Sketch of a Dandy* is frothy and elegant. Adrian Leaper is clearly much in sympathy with this repertoire and knows just how to pace it; his Czech players obviously relish the easy tunefulness and the sheer craft of the writing. With excellent recording in what is surely an ideal acoustic, this is very highly recommendable.

A Day in Fairyland Suite: Dance of a Whimsical Elf; An Evening Song; Frescoes suite; London Landmarks: Horse Guards March; A Manx Rhapsody; May-Day Overture; Paris Suite; Roses of Picardy; Soliloquy; Variations on a Once Popular Humorous Song.

*** Marco 8.223605. Czech-Slovak RSO (Bratislava),
  Tomlinson.

The second CD opens with the charming *May-Day Overture*, with its dreamy sound-picture of dawn, giving way to the day's festivities. The *Variations* are effective, and the composer's *Paris Suite* introduces a distinct Gallic flavour: the *Montmartre March* is especially enjoyable. Wood's beloved Isle of Man inspired the *Manx Rhapsody*, which finds the composer again in his attractive folksy-mode, and the composer's most famous piece, *Roses of Picardy*, is a slightly dated highlight of this volume. The rest of the programme is equally enjoyable, and the performances, this time with Ernest Tomlinson, are excellent. The recording is a bit richer than in Volume I.

Piano Concerto in D min.

*** Hyp. CDA 67127. Milne, BBC Scottish SO, Brabbins –
  HOLBROOKE: *Piano Concerto No. 1.* ***

Haydn Wood writes fluently and attractively throughout both for the piano and the orchestra, and in its echoes of Grieg and Rachmaninov. With an English accent, it establishes itself as one of the more striking British piano concertos of the period. The orchestral introduction provides a grand fanfare for the entry of the piano with a strong main theme and, even when melodies enter which might have developed into drawing-room ballads, Wood ensures that they avoid banality. The slow movement is a tenderly beautiful interlude with muted strings, and the finale, built on a bold motif, leads to two grandiloquent climaxes based on the one theme which skirts banality. The result is exciting none the less, suggesting that this could become a viable repertory piece. Brilliant playing from Hamish Milne and warm, well-balanced recording.

WOOD, Hugh (born 1932)

Horn Trio.

(N) *** Erato 8523 80217-2. Pyatt, Levon Chilingirian, Donohoe
  – BERKELEY: *Horn Trio, Op. 44*; BRITTEN: *Canticle No. 3*; *Now sleeps the crimson petal.* ***

Hugh Wood's *Horn Trio* is a striking work, a splendid vehicle to show off the seductive playing of David Pyatt. Built on sharply drawn material, the first of the two movements presents brilliant flurries of energetic writing set against deeply reflective passages, with slow meditations finally predominating. The second movement, far shorter than the first, is a brilliant display piece, sharply rhythmic. In both movements Pyatt relishes the composer's almost Brahmsian love of the instrument, with Peter Donohoe and Levon Chilingirian as sympathetic partners.

WORDSWORTH, William (1908–88)

Symphonies Nos. 2 in D, Op. 34; 3 in C, Op. 48.

*** Lyrita SRCD 207. LPO, Braithwaite.

William Wordsworth (a direct descendant of the poet's brother, Christopher) was a real symphonist. The *Second*, dedicated to Tovey is distinctly Nordic in atmosphere and there is an unhurried sense of growth. It is serious, thoughtful music, both well crafted and well laid out for the orchestra, and the writing is both powerful and imaginative. The *Third* is less concentrated and less personal in utterance, but all the same this is music of integrity, and readers who enjoy, say, the symphonies of Edmund Rubbra should sample the *Second Symphony*. Nicholas Braithwaite gives a carefully prepared and dedicated account of it, and the recording is up to the usual high standard one expects from this label.

WRIGHT, Margot (1911–2000)

(i; ii) *Cello Sonata;* (iii) *Improvisation for Solo Clarinet;* (iv; ii) *3 Northumbrian Folksongs for Viola & Piano;* (ii; v) *Piano Quintet in D minor.* (vi; ii; iii) *Fear no more the heat o' the sun; 3 Songs with Clarinet Obbligato.*

(N) (M) *** Dutton CDLX 7109 (i) Phelps; (ii) Moll;
   (iii) Braithwaite; (iv) Wright; (v) Camilli Qt; (vi) Morgan.

The earliest piece here is the *Cello Sonata* (1930) and perhaps the finest the *Piano Quintet*. Margot Wright was much in demand as a pianist and was Kathleen Ferrier's partner. Eventually her role as a practising musician and a teacher displaced composition at the centre of her life. Her language is conservative and diatonic but she has a natural feeling for line and development, as the first movement of the *Quintet* shows. There are many imaginative things in her music, which makes one regret that recognition was never sufficient to encourage her to pursue her own creative path. The *Piano Quintet* is a work of quality and played with evident dedication: the violist, incidentally, is the daughter of the composer. Very natural recorded sound.

YSAŸE, Eugène (1858–1931)

Amitié, Op. 26.

(N) **(*) BBC mono BBCL4060-2. D. Oistrakh, I. Oistrakh, LPO, Sargent – SHOSTAKOVICH: *Violin Concertos Nos. 1 & 2.* **

Amitié, for two violins and orchestra, is the last of Ysaÿe's six tone-poems and is a piece steeped in the post-Wagnerian tradition which he had assimilated so completely by this time. David and Igor Oistrakh play with great eloquence and were recorded at the Royal Albert Hall in 1961 with very good sound for the period.

6 Sonatas for Solo Violin, Op. 27.

*** BIS CD 1046. Kavakos.

*** Chan. 8599. Mordkovich.

(B) *** Nim. 1735 (3). Shumsky – BACH; MOZART: *Violin Concertos.* ***

(BB) *** Arte Nova 74321 67511-2. Benjamin Schmid.

The technical and artistic challenges of the Ysaÿe *Solo Violin Sonatas* naturally fascinate violinists – more so than they do the wider musical public. Were they always played with as much character and artistry as they are by Leonid Kavakos, things might be different. This Greek violinist came to notice when he recorded the first version of the Sibelius concerto for BIS, and he impresses every bit as much here. Each sonata reflects the personality of the great violinists such as Szigeti, Thibaud, Kreisler and Enescu to whom they are dedicated. A very impressive recording, which displaces Mordkovich and Shumsky.

Lydia Mordkovich also plays with great character and variety of colour and she characterizes No. 4 (the one dedicated to Kreisler, with its references to Bach and the *Dies Irae*) superbly. These *Sonatas* can seem like mere exercises, but in her hands they sound really interesting. Natural, warm recorded sound. Recommended.

Oscar Shumsky is a player of the old school. His artistry is everywhere in evidence in this 1982 recording, in the authority and naturalness of his phrasing, the sweetness of his tone and the security of his technique. True, there are one or two moments of imperfect intonation, but there are very few performances (as opposed to recordings) where every note in these impossibly demanding pieces is in perfect place. It is all wonderfully musical and splendidly free as if Shumsky is improvising these pieces. These performances now come in a bargain box celebrating his supreme artistry which can be strongly recommended.

Benjamin Schmid is in every way an impressive player and very well recorded. No one investing in his recording (and the outlay is modest) will be disappointed, for this is satisfying in its own right. However, Kavakos makes one see these pieces in a fresher light.

ZANDONAI, Riccardo (1883–1944)

Francesca da Rimini: excerpts from Acts II, III & IV.

(M) **(*) Decca (ADD) 433 033-2 (2). Olivero, Del Monaco, Monte Carlo O, Rescigno – GIORDANO: *Fedora.* **(*)

Magda Olivero is a fine artist who has not been represented nearly enough on record, and this rare Zandonai selection, like the coupled set of Giordano's *Fedora*, does her some belated justice. Decca opted to have three substantial scenes recorded rather than snippets and, though Mario del Monaco as Paolo is predictably coarse in style, his tone is rich and strong and he does not detract from the achievement, unfailingly perceptive and musianly, of Olivero as Francesca herself. Excellent, vintage 1969, Decca sound.

ZEISL, Eric (1905–59)

Requiem Ebraico (92nd Psalm).

*** Decca 460 211-2. Della Jones, Berlin R. Ch., Children's Ch., & SO, Lawrence Foster – WAXMAN: *The Song of Terezin.* ***

Eric Zeisl, like Franz Waxman, had a successful career as a Hollywood composer, and in this *Hebrew Requiem* he translates his film style into a warm and lyrical work, written in memory of his father killed in a concentration camp, and using a Hebrew text from Psalm 92. It may not be as original as the Waxman work with which it is coupled, but with a similarly warm and committed performance, richly recorded, it s a welcome novelty.

ZELENKA, Jan (1679–1745)

Concerto a 8 concertanti in G, ZWV 186; Hipocondrie a 7 concertanti in A, ZWV 187; Ouverture a 7 concertanti in F, ZWV 188; Simphonia a 8 concertanti in A min.

(M) *** Vanguard 99724. Il Fondamento, Dombrecht.

Paul Dombrecht's period-instrument group play with a pleasing rhythmic buoyancy, the strings ever zestful. The oboe sounds are delightful, and the solo bassoon is engagingly lugubrious in the *Largo cantabile* of the *Concerto a 8*. This is a three-movement work in the form of a French overture, as in the *Hipocondrie*, and for that matter the attractive opening movement of the *Ouverture a 7*. Perhaps finest of all is the *Simphonia*, with its opening *Allegro* full of vitality and a crisply pointed central *Gavotte*. The eloquent following *Aria da Capriccio* opens as a concertante cello soliloquy, and after alternating slow and fast sections, ends with a spirited tutti. The work then closes with a pair of Minuets. Excellent recording.

Hippocondrie à 7 in A, ZWV 187; Overture à 7 concertanti in F, ZWV 188; Sonata No. 2 in G min. for 2 Oboes, Bassoon & Continuo, ZWV 181.

(M) **(*) Teldec (ADD) 0630 17386-2. VCM, Harnoncourt.

No one could accuse Harnoncourt of a lack of vitality in his performances of this lively, inventive and often unpredictable music by one of Bach's most remarkable contemporaries. There is some fine oboe-playing too, and the strings are brightly alert throughout. As usual with this conductor, accents are strong and rhythms bounce firmly, yet there is also some fine, expressive playing. The five-movement *Overture* (or suite), which shows well the diversity of Zelenka's invention, is particularly characterful. Recording (dating from 1980) is characteristically bright and forward, yet the range of dynamic is wide.

Trios Sonatas Nos. 1–6.

*** ECM 462 454-2 (2). Holliger, Bourgue, Zehetmair, Thuneman, Stoll, Rubin, Jaccotte.

With such a starry team it is not surprising that these performances of Zelenka's *Trio Sonatas* are so spirited and accomplished. They are scored for various colourful combinations of (almost always) two oboes and bassoon, with continuo, the violin taking the upper voice in No. 3. Zelenka's fast movements proceed with breathless polyphony of mounting intensity, granting neither players nor listeners any respite. So these works are better approached one at a time, stimulating as they are. Excellent if forward recording.

Trio Sonatas for 2 Oboes, Bassoon & Continuo Nos. 2, 5 & 6.

(N) *** Astrée E 8511. Ensemble Zefiro.

Here are three of the above sonatas which favour the scoring for a pair of oboes and bassoon and very piquant they are, although not to be taken all at one go. The playing of Ensemble Zefiro is lively, expressive and polished, and the recording is naturally balanced, with the continuo providing good support. A good choice if you want just a selection of these works.

Magnificats in C & D, ZWV 107–8.

*** BIS CD 1011. Persson, Nonoshita, Tachikawa, Türk, Urano, Bach Collegium, Japan, Masaaki Suzuki – BACH: *Magnificat in D*; KUHNAU: *Magnificat in C*. ***

These two *Magnificats* are quite delightful, very fresh and inventive. They are not otherwise available on CD. Masaaki Suzuki and his fine team of singers and players serve them with enthusiasm and affection, and the recorded sound is absolutely first class.

Missa dei Filii; Litaniae Laurentanae.

*** DHM/BMG RD 77922. Argenta, Chance, Prégardien, Jones, Stuttgart Chamber Ch., Tafelmusik, Bernius.

The *Missa dei Filii* (Mass for the Son of God), is a 'short' mass, consisting of *Kyrie* and *Gloria* only. It seems that Zelenka never heard that Mass, but his *Litany*, another refreshing piece, was specifically written when the Electress of Saxony was ill. Zelenka, like Bach, happily mixes fugal writing with newer-fangled concertato movements. Frieder Bernius is able to provide well-sprung support with his period-instrument group, Tafelmusik, and his excellent soloists and choir.

(i) *Missa in D: Missa gratias agimus tibi. 5 Responsoria pro Hebdomada Sancta; Antiphon: Su tuum praesidium.*

*** Sup. 11 0816-2. (i) Jonášová, Mrázová, Doležal, Mikuláš, Czech PO, (i; ii) Czech Philharmonic Ch., Bělohlávek.

This *Mass* (1730) is a splendid work; the *Responsoria* (for Maundy Thursday and Good Friday), were composed seven years earlier. The programme is completed with a movingly simple Marian antiphon, written after the Mass. These works could hardly be more authentically or persuasively presented than in these very fine Supraphon recordings from 1984. Remarkably individual music, distinctively performed and very well recorded.

ZEMLINSKY, Alexander von (1871–1942)

Sinfonietta, Op. 23; Symphony in B flat (1897); Prelude to 'Es war einmal . . .' (original version).

(N) *** Nim. NI 5682. Czech PO, Beaumont.

Zemlinsky's *Symphony in B flat* was written to compete for the Beethoven Prize of 1898, an award set up by Brahms. It tied for first place and then disappeared into oblivion. It's quite a find – a gorgeous work, rich textured and full of luscious ideas, the four movements linked by a haunting motto theme, with which the work begins and ends.

The *Adagio* is the setting-off point for the gentle march-theme which forms the *cantus firmus* for the passacaglia-like finale, which gives the work a clear link with Brahms. Elsewhere there are also Dvořákian touches (in which the Czech orchestral players revel). But Zemlinsky's invention here is still very much his own and the symphony ends triumphantly.

The *Sinfonietta*, a late work of 1934, was written just after the composer was forced to forced to leave Germany for Switzerland, after the Nazis had taken over. Again it has a linking motif and opens with a wild scherzo, a malevolent burlesque mixed with hope and despair. The central *Ballad* is both questing and ironic, rising more than once to a passionate entreaty but ending in resignation.

The *Rondo* finale returns to and amplifies the nightmare burlesque of the first movement, but at the last minute produces a positive closing flourish. Both these works are highly stimulating and played with great conviction.

In between comes a passionately sensuous Mahlerian prelude for the opera *Once upon a Time*, with a radiant close from the strings and oboe, which is balm to the senses.

Lyrische Symphonie, Op. 18.

(BB) *** Arte Nova 74321 27768-2. Vlatka Orsanic, Johnson, SWFSO, Gielen – BERG: *Lyric Suite: 3 Pieces* etc. ***

**(*) DG 449 179-2. Voigt, Terfel, VPO, Sinopoli.

At speeds markedly faster than usual, Michael Gielen conducts an exceptionally powerful and purposeful account of Zemlinsky's *Lyric Symphony*. Here the work emerges as very fresh and distinctive in its own right. The playing of the orchestra is outstanding and the two soloists are ideal, singing with clean attack and fresh tone. First-rate recording too. An outstanding bargain, well coupled with the Berg works. The only snag is that the booklet is totally inadequate, with poor notes and no texts or translations, and not even any identification of the seven Tagore poems used by Zemlinsky in the symphony.

Sinopoli's is a sensuous, expansive reading, bringing out its links with Mahler's *Lied von der Erde*. Bryn Terfel is excellent, even if the darkness of the voice is not always an advantage in bringing out the meaning of the text. The dramatic soprano, Deborah Voigt, rides easily over the richest textures, but she misses the beauty of the gentler moments, with the top of the voice spreading. No coupling is provided.

String Quartets Nos. 1 in A, Op. 4; 2, Op. 15.

*** Nim. 5563. Artis Qt.

String Quartets Nos. 3, Op. 19; 4, Op. 25.

*** Nim. 5604. Artis Qt.

String Quartets Nos. 1 in A, Op. 4; 4, Op. 25. 2 Movements.

(B)** Praga PRD 250107. Pražák Qt.

Of these two new sets (the Artis now offer fine performances of all four works) the Nimbus is the one to have. The *First Quartet* is very much in the received Brahmsian tradition and the Artis Quartet bring much warmth to it. The Pražák Quartet, however, seem less authoritative and their tone is both less rich and not as well blended. They make a good showing in the demanding *Fourth*, and include two movements from a quartet of 1927 which Zemlinsky put to one side and never completed.

VOCAL MUSIC

Complete Choral Works: *Aurikelchen; Frühlingsbegräbnis; Frühlingsglaube; Geheimnis; Hochzeitsgesang; Minnelied; Psalms 13, 23 & 83.*

*** EMI CDC5 56783-2. Voigt, Albert, Dusseldorf State Musikveriein Ch., Mülheimer Kantorei, Gürzenich O & Cologne PO, Conlon.

The major works here are Zemlinsky's passionate and intense settings of the three *Psalms*. If in a manner recognizable from his operas, the first two bring sensuous writing more apt for the Song of Solomon than the Psalms, the third, *Psalm 83*, brings dramatic martial music. Those three items as well as the cantata, *The Burial of Spring*, in seven compact movements, were recorded live in Cologne, and bring warm, committed performances under Conlon as a dedicated Zemlinsky interpreter. The other lighter items were recorded later in the studio. Opulent sound to match.

Gesänge Op. 5, Books 1–2; Gesänge (Waltz songs on Tuscan folk-lyrics), Op. 6; Gesänge, Opp. 7–8, 10 & 13; Lieder, Op. 2, Books 1–2; Op. 22 & Op. 27.

*** DG (IMS) 427 348-2 (2). Bonney, Von Otter, Blochwitz, Schmidt, Garben.

This two-disc DG collection of songs can be warmly recommended for the fresh tunefulness of dozens of miniatures. With Cord Garben accompanying four excellent soloists, the charm of these chips from the workbench comes over consistently. Best of all is Von Otter, more sharply imaginative than the others, making the one consistent cycle that Zemlinsky ever wrote, the six Maeterlinck Songs, Opus 13, the high-point of the set.

6 Maeterlinck Lieder, Op. 13.

(B) *** Double Decca (IMS) (ADD) 444 871-2 (2). Van Nes Concg. O, Chailly – MAHLER: *Symphony No. 6.* ***

Beautifully sung by Jard van Nes in her finest recording to date, these ripely romantic settings of Maeterlinck make an unusual but valuable fill-up for Chailly's rugged and purposeful reading of the Mahler *Symphony*. The rich, vivid recording captures van Nes's full-throated singing with new firmness.

Psalm 83.

*** Decca 460 213-2. Slovak Philharmonic Ch., VPO, Chailly – JANACEK: *Glagolitic Mass;* KORNGOLD: *Passover Psalm.* ***

Zemlinsky's aptly dramatic setting of *Psalm 83*, beautifully performed and richly recorded, makes an unusual and attractive coupling for the Janáček.

OPERA

Eine florentinische Tragödie (complete).

*** Schwann CD 11625. Soffel, Riegel, Sarabia, Berlin RSO, Albrecht.

A Florentine Tragedy presents a simple love triangle: a Florentine merchant returns home to find his sluttish wife with the local prince; but the musical syrup which flows over all the characters makes them repulsive, with motives only dimly defined. The score itself is most accomplished; it is compellingly performed here, more effective on disc than it is in the opera house. First-rate sound.

Der Traumgörge (complete opera).

(N) *** EMI CDC5 57087-2. Kuebler, Racette, Anthony, Martinez, Schmidt, Volle, Gürzenich O, Cologne Op. Ch. & Phil. O, Conlon.

Der Traumgörge, Zemlinsky's third opera, was never given in his lifetime, finally reaching the stage in 1980, and then in a seriously cut version. Mahler was due to present it at the Vienna State Opera in 1907, but resigned during rehearsals, and his successor promptly dropped it. The wonder is that even by Zemlinsky's standards this is an opulent, lusciously scored piece, which inspired James Conlon, for long a Zemlinsky specialist, to give a rich, red-blooded performance, with a fine cast superbly led by the fine tenor, David Kuebler as Gorge, the dreamy hero of the piece, a fantasist living in a world of fairy tales. He makes him into a touchingly innocent character, who forces on after his fiancée has left him, and who builds a moving relationship with Gertraud, finally recognizing her as his fantasy princess, bringing an ecstatic close.

In much of this Zemlinsky, with the help his librettist, Leo Feld, was trying to symbolize and to exorcise the effects of his brief affair with Alma Schindler, by this time married to Mahler. With ripe echoes not just of Wagner and Strauss but of Puccini too, the emotional thrust of the piece is most compelling, whatever the oddities of the story. This far outshines the only previous recording (on Capriccio), not just because of the performance but also because of the greatly expanded score, with substantial cuts made by Mahler and others restored.

Der Zwerg (Der Geburtstag der Infantin).

(M) *** EMI CDM5 66247-2 (2). Isokoski, Martinez, Kuebler, Collis, Cologne PO, Conlon.

*** Schwann CD 11626. Nielsen, Riegel, Haldas, Weller, Berlin RSO, Albrecht.

Der Zwerg, 'the dwarf', is the preferred title for the definitive edition of this most striking yet most disturbing of Zemlinsky's operas. The text here was prepared for Conlon from the autograph score, revised in detail by the composer. Deeply moving as Kenneth Riegel's performance is on the earlier recording below, David Kuebler here has the advantage of a more beautiful, younger-sounding voice, making the portrait more tenderly moving, bringing out the character's vulnerability. Nor is passion lacking, and Soile Isokoski makes an excellent Princess, with Iride Martinez also singing beautifully as her favourite maid. Live recording on the dry side, but still vivid and full.

Kenneth Riegel too gives a heart-rendingly passionate performance as the dwarf declaring his love. His genuine passion is intensified by being set against lightweight, courtly music to represent the Infanta and her attendants. With the conductor and others in the cast also experienced in the stage production, the result is a deeply involving performance, beautifully recorded.

ZIEHRER, Carl Michael (1843–1922)

Auersperg-Marsch; Landstreicher-Quadrille. **Polkas:** *Burgerlich und romantisch; Pfiffig; Die Tänzerin; Loslassen!* **Waltzes:** *Clubgeister; Diesen Kuss der ganzen Welt; Libesrezepte; Osterreich in Tönen; Wiener Bürger.*

**(*) Marco 8.223814. Razumovsky Sinfonia, Walter.

Fächer-polonaise; Mein Feld ist die Welt-Marsch. **Polkas:** *Endlich allein! Im Fluge; Lieber Bismarck, schaukle nicht; Matrosen.* **Waltzes:** *Heimatsgefühle; Herreinspaziert!; Sei brav; In der Sommerfrische; Tolles Mädel.*

**(*) Marco 8.223815. Razumovsky Sinfonia, Dittrich.

Ziehrer's style is very much in the Johann Strauss tradition but unlike many of Strauss's rivals, Ziehrer's music has a distinctive, robust quality, probably attributable to his career as a military band leader for many years. His music overflows with tunes, is thoroughly entertaining, and will disappoint no one who responds to the Viennese tradition.

Volume I opens with his most famous piece, *Wiener Bürger*, a delightful waltz that rivals the best of J. Strauss. The *Die Tänzerin* polka uses themes from the opera of the same name as its basis – to invigorating effect; the *Landstreicher-Quadrille* is composed in the same way, and contains some particularly jaunty numbers. Not surprisingly, Ziehrer was adept at writing marches, and the *Auersperg-Marsch* is one of his best – it had to be repeated several times at its premiere. The almost forgotten *Osterreich in Tönen waltz (Melodies of Austria)* is another highlight: all its melodies are in fact original, but it has an agreeably localized ethnic flavour.

Volume II offers more of the same: it begins with the fine *Herreinspaziert* waltz which soon lunges into a richly contoured theme to rival *Wiener Bürger*. The *Fächer* ('Fan') polonaise is memorable, and is still used to introduce the prestigious annual *Philharmonic Ball* in Vienna. The polkas are wittily crafted, and none of the waltzes here is without at least one memorable theme. The *Tolles Mädel* ('Crazy girl') waltz even begins to look forward to the American musical and is a winner in every way, as is the *Sei brav* ('Be good') waltz – a lively confection of music from Ziehrer's operetta *Fesche Geister* ('Lively spirits').

The performances from both conductors are lively and sympathetic, the recordings bright and vivid (the second disc a little less so), and the sleeve notes helpful and informative.

Marches: *Auf! in's XX; Freiherr von Schönfeld; Wen mann Geld hat, is man fein!* **Polkas:** *Ballfieber; Ein Blich nach Ihr!; Cavallerie; Wurf-Bouquet.* **Styrien Tänze:** *D'Kermad'ln;* **Waltzes:** *Auf hoher See!; Gebirgskinder; Ich lach'!; O, dies Husaren!; Zichrereien.*

(N) *** Marco 8.225172. Razumovsky Sinf., Pollack.

Volume III is easily the finest Ziehrer collection so far, and one laments again that Christian Pollack, who is a master of Viennese rhythmic inflection, did not direct the other two (and indeed all the Strauss family collections). The three marches have a light-hearted zest (*Wenn man Geld hat* almost sounds like Lehár). *Auf hoher See* opens with a trumpet/cornet solo, and not surprisingly the brass take the lead in the *Cavallerie Polka* while the *Ballfieber* polka français is also most beguiling, and Pollack's bold accents in *Wurf-Bouquet* add lift rather than heaviness.

The four charming Waltzes bounce along engagingly. *O, dies Hasaren!* has been rescued from its surviving piano score and orchestrated jointly by Martin Uhl and Pollack with idiomatic skill; and how beautifully Pollack opens the *Gebirgskinder*, with a zither solo reminiscent of Johann's *Tales from the Vienna Woods*. Indeed this is another of Ziehrer's waltzes with a string of melodies all but worthy of that master. The orchestra responds with lilt and sparkle throughout and the recording cannot be faulted.

ZWILICH, Ellen (born 1939)

Symphony No. 2.

** First Edition LCD 002. Louisville O, Leighton Smith —
  HINDEMITH: *Piano Concerto* **(*); (with LAWHEAD: *Aleost.* *(*)

Ellen Taaffe Zwilich was a pupil of Dohnányi. Her *First Symphony* (1982) won a Pulitzer Prize and prompted the San Francisco Orchestra to commission the *Second Symphony* in 1985. The work is called a 'cello symphony', since the cellos play a dominant role in the musical argument. The invention is solid and well argued, rather than inspired; it is music that commands respect though it is not easy to discern a voice of strong individuality. Good playing and decent recording.

DVDs

The following is a hand-picked selection of the finest currently available DVDs (digital versatile discs). We plan to provide a much fuller selection in our 2002/3 *Yearbook*. By this time, we believe, many more of our readers will have added a DVD player to their reproducing equipment. That DVD can add a new dimension to the experience of listening to music is very soon discovered, and obviously so in the field of ballet and opera. But orchestral, chamber and solo instrumental music, as well, can sometimes be profoundly enhanced by images, and certainly that applies to some of the recordings listed below. Remember you have complete control over the picture – it can be dispensed with at will and the music enjoyed without it.

BACH, Johann Sebastian (1685–1750)

(i) *Violin Concerto No. 2 in E, BWV 1042;* (ii) *Magnificat in D, BWV 243.*

(N) *** Sony DVD SVD 45983. BPO, Karajan; with (i) Mutter; (ii) Blegen, Mollinari, Araiza, Holl, Berlin RIAS Chamber Ch. (Director: Humphrey Burton.)

There are few better examples on DVD than this of a conductor's magnetism being almost tangible. It is apparent during Anne-Sophie Mutter's fine performance of the *Violin Concerto* although she is given the limelight, but in the *Magnificat* one can feel the whole orchestra, chorus and soloists responding to the conductor, while Karajan's actual movements are minimal, his face all but impassive. This is gloriously old-fashioned Bach, with a large orchestra, and when the camera dwells on the blazing trumpets, one feels almost able to reach out and touch them. It is a thrilling performance, richly and vividly recorded, and one feels right in the middle of it.

BEETHOVEN, Ludvig van

(1770–1827)

Symphonies Nos. 1 in C, Op. 21; 8 in F, Op. 93.

(N) **(*) Sony DVD SVD 46363. BPO, Karajan. (V/D: Ernst Wild.)

Symphonies Nos. 2 in D, Op. 36; 3 in E flat, Op. 55, (Eroica).

(N) **(*) Sony DVD SVD 46365. BPO, Karajan. (V/D: Ernst Wild.)

Symphonies No. 4 in B flat, Op. 60; 5 in C min., Op. 67.

(N) **(*) Sony DVD SVD 46366. BPO, Karajan. (V/D: Ernst Wild.)

Symphonies Nos. 6 in F, Op. 68, (Pastoral); 7 in A, Op. 92.

(N) **(*) Sony DVD SVD 46367. BPO, Karajan. (V/D: Ernst Wild.)

Karajan's Beethoven has been part of our staple diet since his 1947 account of the *Ninth Symphony*. His first complete cycle was made with the Philharmonia Orchestra in mono, and reigned supreme in the early LP era. Then came the classic 1963 cycle with the Berlin Philharmonic in stereo, which in some respects he never surpassed. His second Berlin set was issued in 1977, and offered some impressive readings (4, 5, 7 and 9) while later on came a third set in digital sound.

DG issued a number of recordings from the 1970s on video, and subsequently on Laserdisc, but the present Sony performances date from the early 1980s. The Laserdiscs were generously filled: Nos. 1, 2, 6 and 8 were all accommodated on one disc, though the *Pastoral*, a 1967 recording, suffers from rather pallid, hazy colours. The sound of the new Sony recordings is first class in every way, though the camerawork tends to be restricted to the same limited number of shots. (Hugo Niebeling's direction in the 1967 *Pastoral* was more imaginative.)

All the same, it is good to see as well as hear Karajan and the Berlin Philharmonic. It goes without saying that the orchestral playing is of the highest standard but at the same time it must be admitted that they do not have the same immediacy and spontaneity of the 1950s and 1960s performances. No. 1 is beautifully played yet curiously lifeless. No. 8 certainly does not match the post-War Vienna Philharmonic or the 1963 set in electricity.

The 1967 *Pastoral* had enormous grip (as did the 1963 LP) and held the listener in the palm of its hand, while this newcomer is much less fresh. So this Beethoven set is recommended but without the enthusiasm that Karajan so often inspired.

Overture, Coriolan, Op. 62; (i) *Piano concerto No. 1 in C, Op. 15; Symphony No. 7 in A, Op. 92.*

(N) *** Arthaus DVD 100 148. (i) Perahia; LSO, Solti. (V/D: Humphrey Burton.)

This is a straight recording directed by Humphrey Burton of a concert at London's Barbican Centre in 1987. The camerawork is discreet and unfussy and the sound impeccably balanced throughout. Nothing distracts the viewer or listener from Beethoven. In spite of some over-emphatic gestures, Solti's accounts of both the *Coriolan Overture* and the *Seventh Symphony* are very fine, and at no point do the LSO sound rough or rhythms overdriven. These are cultured and dedicated performances in every way and in the concerto Murray Perahia is unfailingly thoughtful, intelligent and imaginative. A memorable concert, and the first-rate recording will give much pleasure.

Violin Sonatas Nos. 1–10 (complete); *'A Life with Beethoven'* (documentary by Reiner Moritz).

(N) **(*) DG DVD 073 014-2. Mutter, Orkis.

Violin Sonatas Nos. 5 in F, Op. 24 (Spring); 9 in A, Op. 49 (Kreutzer). *'A Life with Beethoven'* (documentary by Reiner Moritz).

(N) ** DG DVD 073 004-9. Mutter, Orkis.

This hour-long documentary follows Anne-Sophie Mutter and Lambert Orkis during their year preparing and touring the Beethoven sonata cycle. The performances were recorded at the Théâtre des Champs Elysées in 1999. To follow them over an extended period yields useful insights, though the playing, particularly that of the distinguished violinist, will strike some as being at times just a bit self-regarding: there are some intrusive expressive exaggerations during these always highly accomplished and intelligent performances. However, the complete set yields considerable rewards and is probably a better investment than the single disc. Good straightforward camerawork and excellent sound. Subtitles for the English-language documentary are also available in German and French.

BELLINI, Vincenzo (1801–35)

Norma (opera; complete).

(N) *** Arthaus DVD 100 180. Sutherland, Elkins, Stevens, Grant, Opera Australia Ch., Sydney Elizabethan O, Bonynge. (V/D: Sandro Sequi.)

Recorded live at the Sydney Opera House in 1978 (not 1991 as the box seems to imply), this Australian Opera production by Sandro Sequi is chiefly valuable for presenting Dame Joan Sutherland in one of her most important roles when she was still at the peak of her powers. Her two audio recordings date from early and late in her career, where this provides an important bridge, with *Casta diva* finding Dame Joan in glorious voice, at once powerful, creamily beautiful and wonderfully secure.

With sets by Fiorella Mariani it is a traditional production, springing no surprises, encouraging the diva to relax in the role, never more so than in her big duet with Adalgisa, *Mira o Norma*, ending in a dazzling account of the cabaletta, where Margeta Elkins equally sparkles, and Richard Bonynge draws light, crisply sprung playing from the orchestra.

Less satisfying is the singing of Ronald Stevens as Pollione, powerful and heroic, but rather too coarse for Bellinian cantilena. Clifford Grant by contrast could hardly be more cleanly focused as Oroveso. The sound is a little dry, not as full-bodied as in the finest fully digital recordings, but the sharpness of attack heightens the dramatic thrust of Bonynge's conducting.

BIZET, Georges (1838–75)

Carmen (opera; complete).

(N) *** Columbia Tristar DVD CDR 10530. Migenes-Johnson, Domingo, Raimondi, Esham, French National RSO and Chorus, Maazel. (V/D: Franco Rossi.)

Filmed on location in the most atmospheric of sites, few operatic films add so vividly to the music as this version of *Carmen*, directed by Franco Rossi. It starts with a striking visual coup: the credits are shown with merely the murmur of a bullring crowd in the background, while a matador is seen playing with a bull. He finally brings his sword down for the kill, and Bizet's opening *Prélude* thunders out.

The film is set to a recording specially made in the studio, and issued on CD by Erato. An excellent performance, under Lorin Maazel, on DVD it projects as sharply dramatic, with Placido Domingo at his finest and Julia Migenes-Johnson the most vibrantly characterful of Carmens. Ruggero Raimondi makes a noble Ecamillo, and though Faith Esham's voice is not ideally sweet as Micaela, it is a tender, sensitive performance. The sound is first rate, and having the singers miming to the music is not too distracting. The DVD is markedly sharper in focus than the equivalent VHS. No booklet is provided, just a leaflet, with only sketchy details given, even of the cast.

BRITTEN, Benjamin (1913–76)

Death in Venice (opera; complete).

(N) ** Arthaus DVD 100 172. Tear, Opie, Chance, Glyndebourne Ch., L. Sinf., Jenkins. (S/D: Stephen Lawless, Martha Clarke. Producer: Dennis Marks.)

This Glyndebourne production of Britten's last opera, based on Thomas Mann's celebrated novella, offers a stark, even brutal view of a piece which originally, thanks both to Britten's score and John Piper's sets, highlighted the beauty of Venice. With Lawless and Clarke, using bare sets by Tobias Hoheise, predominantly black, blotting out the beauty of the city on water, the result seen in close-up is even more claustrophobic in presenting the dilemma of Aschenbach, the celebrated author, who to his horror finds himself passionately attracted to the young boy Tadzio.

Robert Tear's vividly detailed, totally compelling portrayal of Aschenbach is masterly, and his characterization may prompt many to consider the set, even though the voice itself is wanting in bloom, and very different from the moving but more relaxed approach of Peter Pears, for whom the role was written.

Similarly Alan Opie in the multiple baritone roles of characters dogging Aschenbach's path is far more sinister than John Shirley-Quirk, plainly representing evil, and even Tadzio is finally made to leer at Aschenbach, suggesting that he is after all the messenger of evil too, something quite different from Britten's original concept. In the counter-tenor role of Apollo, Michael Chance is also ideally cast, the opponent of evil and death, finally worsted.

The result is undeniably powerful, and musically the set

has a lot going for it – sensitive orchestral playing and Tear and Alan Opie thrillingly involving in a piece that can seem episodic, and with the conductor, Graeme Jenkins, also drawing the threads tautly together.

But the production is another matter: the action is confined within a distinctly cramped, small arena and there is no feeling of space or sense of atmosphere. This shoe-box dimension of the sets really lets the opera down badly. Nor is the recording as ample as one could wish and the piano sound is pretty uningratiating. Thus, vision adds little if anything to the musical experience and, such is its overwhelming claustrophobia, even detracts from it. Subtitles are provided in French, German and Spanish but there is no original English text, which at times would have been helpful.

However, readers will find the pioneering Decca CDs under Steuart Bedford, with Peter Pears as Aschenbach, James Bowman as the voice of Apollo and John Shirley-Quirk in multiple roles, a far more satisfying experience in every way.

The Turn of the Screw (opera; complete).

(N) *** Arthaus 100 198. Field, Davies, Greager, Obata, Stuttgart RSO, Bedford. (Director: Michael Hampe. V/D: Claus Viller.)

The hero of this production is Stuart Bedford, who gets vibrant singing and playing from all concerned. Helen Field is a thoroughly convincing governess and the cast is in every respect excellent, even if Machita Obata looks a little too mature for Flora. A good production, very atmospheric, and with generally unobtrusive video direction.

DEBUSSY, Claude (1862–1918)

Pelléas et Mélisande (opera; complete).

(N) ** Arthaus DVD 100 100. Le Roux, Alliot-Lugaz, Van Dam, Soyer, Taillon, Golfier, Schirrer, Lyon Op. Ch. & O., Gardiner. (S/D: Pierre Strosser. V/D: Jean-François Jung.)

The Lyon cast is strong: François Le Roux's Pelléas, familiar from Abbado's DG recording, has innocence and vulnerability, and the Mélisande of Colette Alliot-Lugaz is subtly drawn, more so than in her Decca recording with Dutoit. José van Dam, who also recorded the rôle with both Abbado and Karajan, conveys Golaud's torment of spirit to perfection, and it is difficult to fault any of the remaining characters.

Special interest lies in Gardiner's musical direction: he corrects various textual errors and removes the interludes Debussy wrote to cover scene changes in the original production, producing an altogether tauter dramatic experience. Gardiner also lays out the orchestra in the way Debussy had originally directed with a distinct gain in transparency.

The stage director shows no comparable respect for the original: the action is placed indoors in the large room of a château at the turn of the last century at the time when Debussy was composing the opera: so there are no tower, no sea-shore, no forest, no grotto, no sense of the sunless castle and no mystery.

A rather run-down Golaud is seen in a dressing-gown, turning over the past in his mind, and we lose the fountain, the impact of light when the lovers emerge from the vault – and so on. In any profession other than opera production this would be condemned as vandalism, although it is not quite as dire and impertinent as the 1997 Glyndebourne production which pictured Mélisande perched in a chandelier!! This performance comes from 1987.

Doubtless the 1992 Welsh National Opera production by Peter Stein, with Boulez conducting and Neil Archer and Alison Hagley in the title rôles, long available on video (DG 072 431-3) and Laserdisc (DG 072 431-1), will reach DVD during the lifetime of this volume. It shows a decent respect for Debussy's dramatic conception and is finer and more atmospheric than either of Boulez's CD accounts on Sony.

DELIBES, Léo (1836–91)

Coppélia (ballet; complete. Choreography: Ninette de Valois).

✿ (N) *** BBC DVD 1024. Benjamin, Acosta, Heydon, Royal Ballet, ROHCGO, Moldoveaunu. (Production: Ninette de Valois/Anthony Dowell. V/D: Bob Lockyer.)

With this production the Royal Ballet celebrated its return to Covent Garden after the Opera House's two-year closure. Ninette de Valois's choreography and production and Osbert Lancaster's colourful sets of *Coppélia* make a return after twenty years. It was televized in February 2000 and were you to compare a VTR of that broadcast with the present DVD, you would appreciate the greater sense of presence, cleaner focus and altogether firmer image that the new medium offers. In fact the colour is quite spectacular.

Leanne Benjamin's Swanhilda has much charm and the Cuban, Carlos Acosta, brings the appropriate ardour, grace and virtuosity to the role of Franz, while Luke Heydon's Dr Coppélius is exemplary. There is first-class dancing from the Corps and lively, well-paced orchestral playing under Nicolae Moldoveaunu. Moreover, the sound is well defined and musically balanced.

Deborah Bull introduces the ballet and the DVD includes a short feature about the Royal Ballet on the move after the closure of the Royal Opera House, and another on the work of Osbert Lancaster. An altogether delightful set which will give much pleasure.

DVOŘÁK, Antonín (1841–1904)

Symphony No. 9 in E min. (New World), Op. 95.

(N) *** Sony DVD SVD 48421. VPO, Karajan.

Karajan recorded this symphony four times with the Berlin Philharmonic (for Polydor in 1940, for Columbia, EMI, in 1958, for DG in 1964 and for EMI/HMV in 1977). This present account comes from February 1985 and appeared originally on both LP and CD on DG 415 509. At the time we thought the playing of the Vienna Philharmonic not quite as refined as the previous Berlin version (which at the time seemed unsurpassed in terms of sheer excitement).

Seeing as well as hearing this performance gives one pause. Does seeing the players and their conductor affect the listener's judgement? Whether or not it equals earlier versions or not, it is certainly a very fine account, its beauty of sonority is quite affecting, and the remaining movements are strikingly fresh.

The sound has an impressively wide dynamic range and the visual direction keeps the eye's attention where it would be in the concert hall. At 43:30 minutes it is perhaps short measure but artistically it is very satisfying and well worth the money.

GERSHWIN, George (1898–1937)

Porgy and Bess (complete).

⊕ *** EMI DVD 4 92496-9. White, Hayman, Blackwell, Baker, Clarey, Evans, Glyndebourne Ch., LPO, Rattle.

After the huge success of the Glyndebourne production of *Porgy and Bess*, EMI took the whole cast to the Shepperton Studios, where it was produced for video by Trevor Nunn and Yves Baignere, using the giant stage to move the actions around freely as in a film. The result is stunningly successful, with Willard White as Porgy, Cynthia Hayman as Bess, Gregg Baker as Crown, and Damon Evans as Sporting Life all singing superbly and bringing the story to life with extraordinary vividness. This is one of the most creative of all such productions so far, fully worthy of Gershwin's masterly score.

JANÁČEK, Leoš (1854–1928)

Jenufa (opera; complete).

(N) *** Arthaus DVD 100 208. Alexander, Silja, Langridge, Mark Baker, Glyndebourne Ch., LPO, Andrew Davis. (V/D: Nikolaus Lehnhoff).

The impact of Nikolaus Lehnhoff's production of *Jenufa* was always strong and positive, with the stark yet atmospheric designs of Tobias Hoheisel adding to the sharpness. On DVD, with close-ups in this television film of 1989 adding to the impact, the result is even more powerful. This visual treatment exactly matches the sharp originality of Janáček's score, with its often abrasive orchestration heightened by passages of surging beauty, superbly realized by Andrew Davis and the LPO.

Roberta Alexander makes a warm, slightly gawky Jenufa, with Philip Langridge as the frustrated lover, Laka, making this awkward character totally believable, an object for sympathy, finally fulfilled. Both sing superbly, and so do the rest of the cast, including Mark Baker as the wastrel, Steva, a tenor well contrasted with Langridge.

Yet dominating the cast is the Kostelnicka of Anja Silja. This was the production which brought this characterful soprano, veteran of many years of singing Wagner at Bayreuth, to Glyndebourne for the first time, where she has since added an Indian Summer to her long career singing this and other Janáček roles with enormous success.

The abrasiveness in her voice, which with Wagner heroines was often obtrusive, is here a positive asset, and her portrayal of this formidable character, positive and uncompromising yet ultimately an object of pity, is totally convincing in all its complexity. The way she delivers Kostelnicka's apprehensive cry at the end of Act 2 was 'as if death were peering into the house'. Full, vivid sound very well transferred, if with an edge that suits the music.

Káta Kabanová (opera; complete).

*** Arthaus DVD 100 158. Gustafson, Palmer, Davies, McCauley, Graham-Hall, Winter, Glyndebourne Ch., LPO, Andrew Davis. (V/D: Nikolaus Lehnhoff.)

First seen at Glyndebourne in 1988, this was the groundbreaking production by Nikolaus Lehnhoff with stark, striking designs by Tobias Hoheisel, which led to a whole sequence of memorable Janáček productions. It remains one of the most powerful, with Nancy Gustafson tenderly moving as the heroine starved of love, constantly frustrated by her implacable mother-in-law, the deeply unsympathetic Kabanicha, brilliantly portrayed and sung by Felicity Palmer, with a powerful cutting edge.

The production, too, is exactly suited to the distinctive idiom of Janáček, with its contrasts of abrasiveness and rich beauty. Strong contributions too from Ryland Davies as Tichon, Káta's husband, Barry McCauley as Boris, and John Graham-Hall as Kudrjas, with characterful contributions too from such a veteran as Donald Adams as Boris's father, Dikoj. Bright, forward sound adds to the impact.

MENDELSSOHN, Felix (1809–47)

A Midsummer Night's Dream (ballet; complete. Choreography by George Balanchine).

(N) *** BBC Opus Arte DVD OAo 108D. Pacific Northwest Ballet, BBC Concert O, Steven Kershaw. Producer: Francia Russell. (V/D: Nigel Shepherd.)

Balanchine's 1962 ballet was created for the New York City Ballet, and based not only on the inspired score to Shakespeare's play of Mendelssohn's *A Midsummer Night's Dream* but other Mendelssohn scores, including the overtures *Athalia*, *Die schöne Melusine* and *Son and Stranger*, plus two movements of the *Ninth* of his early symphonies for strings.

This performance was recorded in 1999 at the then newly reopened Sadler's Wells Theatre while the Pacific Northwest Ballet were on tour. It is a fine company with an enviable reputation and some altogether excellent principal dancers: Lisa Apple's Helena and Julie Tobiason's Hernia are particularly fine, and the scene between Titania and Bottom is quite touching. The fairy scenes are imaginatively handled and staged.

Mendelssohn's music is well served by the ever underrated BBC Concert Orchestra, who always excel when given a chance to play repertoire of quality – and Mendelssohn's score is always a source of wonder! The acoustic of the new Sadler's Wells does not have much warmth or space, but the engineers get a very good and well-defined sound. The camerawork and the quality of colour are very high. An enchanting ninety minutes.

MONTEVERDI, Claudio (1567–1643)

L'incoronazione di Poppea (opera; complete).

(N) *** Arthaus DVD 100 108. Schumann, Croft, Kuhlmann, Gall, Peeters, Brooks, Concerto Köln, Jacobs. (Director: Michael Hampe. V/D: José Montes-Baquer.)

The best *L'incoronazione di Poppea* so far on video/Laserdisc has been the Ponelle Zurich Opera production with Yakar as Poppea, and conducted by Harnoncourt from 1986 (Decca 071 406-1/3). (That occupied no fewer than four Laserdisc sides as opposed to the one DVD.) This newcomer from the 1993 Schwetzingen Festival is far more severe, both artistically and as a visual experience, and better conducted too.

It suffers from a less than ideal Poppea in Patricia Schumann but both Kuhlmann's Ottavia and Darla Brooks's Drusilla are expressive and intelligent singers, and the Seneca of Harry Peeters is exemplary. The performance as a whole is more compelling than the old Zurich alternative, which will presumably find its way on to DVD in the fullness of time. Subtitles are in English, French, German and Spanish.

MOZART, Wolfgang Amadeus (1756–91)

Don Giovanni (opera; complete).

**(*) Sony DVD SVD 46383. Ramey, Tomowa-Sintow, Varady, Battle, Winbergh, Furlanetto, Malta, Burchuladze; V. St. Op. Ch., VPO, Karajan. (Director: Michael Hampe. V/D: Claus Viller.)

This was one of Karajan's final productions at Salzburg and was recorded during a performance at the 1987 Festival. It first appeared on video and on Laserdisc, where it occupied three sides as opposed to a single double-sided DVD here. There are some impressive things. The Donna Anna of Anna Tomowa-Sintow and the Donna Elvira of Julia Varady are splendidly matched and both vocally and dramatically commanding: it is probably worth having solely for them. The Leporello of Ferruccio Furlanetto is vivacious, and has a dramatic flair that seems to elude Samuel Ramey's Don.

Kathleen Battle's Zerlina is better sung than acted but for the most part this is a satisfying performance, certainly superior to the *Don* that Karajan recorded in Berlin for DG two years earlier with an almost identical cast (save for the Elvira, who was Baltsa). Some have found Karajan a little stiff, but there is no question as to the tonal splendour of the Vienna Philharmonic or the dignity and spaciousness of his reading. The visual presentation is excellent, as indeed is the well-balanced sound. There are subtitles in English, German and French.

Le nozze di Figaro (opera; complete).

(N) (B) *** NVC DVD 0630-14013-2. Finley, Hagley, Fleming, Schmidt, LPO, Haitink. (Producer: Stephen Medcalf; V/D: Derek Bailey.)

This must be one of the great bargains of DVD. At the time of writing it retails at £19.99, and you would not find it easy to get a CD version of any distinction at the price. And this *is* a performance of distinction, wonderfully conducted by Bernard Haitink and with four first-class principals. Gerald Finley's Figaro is expertly characterized and beautifully sung, and the same goes for both Renée Fleming's Countess and Alison Hagley's Susanna. The sets and staging are admirable in every way. It was with this production that the Glyndebourne Opera House reopened in May 1994 after its successful renovation. The three hours nine minutes are accommodated on one double-sided DVD, which accommodates two acts per side. There are subtitles in English, French and German, together with cast and character screens. The quality of the colour and the sharpness of focus are in the demonstration bracket and so, too, is the vivid, well-balanced sound. A most musically satisfying set and one of the handful of DVDs that should be in every serious collection.

Die Zauberflöte (opera; complete).

(N) **(*) Arthaus DVD 100 188. Sonntag, Frei, Van der Walt, Mohr, Hauptmann, Connors (speaker), Ludwigsburg Festival Ch. & O, Gönnenwein. (Director: Axel Manthey. V/D: Ruth Kärch.)

(N) **(*) DG DVD 073 003-9. Battle, Serra, Araiza, Hemm, Moll, Schmidt (speaker), Met. Op. Ch. & O., Levine. (Producers: Guus Mostart/John Cox; (V/D: Brian Large).

The cast is less starry and the production less glamorous on the Arthaus DVD than the DG discssed below, but it has a good deal more style and gives more pleasure. None of the singers with the exception of Andrea Frei's Queen of the Night, who is inclined to be a little squally, falls seriously short of the highest standards and some are touched by considerable distinction – notably Ulrike Sonntag's Pamina and the Tamino of Deon van der Walt.

Musically there is not much wrong and a great deal right about this performance, which is well paced and sensitively conducted by Wolfgang Gönnenwein. It comes from the Ludwigsburger Festival of 1992. The staging has great simplicity and the sets and costumes are all in bright primary colours. And no production detail gets in the way of Mozart. Subtitles are in English, French and the original German.

The DG *Zauberflöte* is also pretty impressive. It derives from the Met's Mozart Bicentennial celebrations in 1991, and was issued on both video and Laserdisc but not on CD. It is not in the same league as the performances under Marriner, Gardiner, Boehm, Fricsay, Beecham and Karajan, under whom Araiza sang Tamino.

The best performances, however, are Kathleen Battle's Pamina, Manfred Hemm's Papageno and Kurt Moll's magisterial Sarastro. David Hockney's sets are an absolute delight, and though Levine does not always get a light or transparent texture from his players, there is still a lot of pleasure to be had.

Guus Mostart's adaptation of John Cox's production is pleasingly unobtrusive and Brian Large's visual direction up to his usual high standard. Though the quality of the picture does not match the definition and clarity of the BBC DVD of *Coppélia* or the Glyndebourne *Figaro*, it is still very impressive. Subtitles are in German, English, French and Mandarin.

OFFENBACH, Jacques (1819–80)

La Belle Hélène (opera; complete).

(N) **(*) Arthaus DVD 100 086. Kasarova, Van der Walt, Chausson, Vogel, Widmer, Zurich Op. Ch. & O, Harnoncourt. (Producer: Helmut Lohner. V/D: Hartmut Schottler.)

It is some fifteen years since EMI issued their fine set of *La Belle Hélène* with Jessye Norman as Hélène, John Aler as Paris, Charles Burles as Menelaus and Gabriel Bacquier as Agamemnon with the Toulouse Orchestra under the sparkling direction of Michel Plasson. Strange that such a masterpiece should have attracted so little attention in recent years. Not all the assumptions that Meilhac, Halévy and Offenbach made about their audience in 1864 can still apply, and modern audiences less familiar with classical legends are also not shocked by the irreverence of the operetta.

Musically *La Belle Hélène* offers special challenges and those who discovered it through René Leibowitz's pioneering Nixa mono recording with Janine Linda as Hélène will have found its pace, sense of style and sophistication hard to match let alone surpass in subsequent recordings.

However, the roster in this 1997 production at the Zurich Opera is a strong one and Kasarova makes a positive impression here, as for that matter do the remainder of the cast. Harnoncourt gets lively results from his players but crisper and more lightly accented rhythms would have been welcome. He is a touch heavy-handed. The production is inventive and flows smoothly and the evening is thoroughly enjoyable. The successful Paris production in early 2001 with Felicity Lott in the title role has been announced on CD as we go to press. Until it appears on DVD this can certainly be recommended, particularly for Vessalina Kasarova's Hélène. The French of the principals is wonderfully clear. Subtitles are in English and German.

POULENC, Francis (1899–1963)

Dialogues des Carmélites (opera; complete).

⚫ *** Arthaus DVD 100 004. Schmidt, Fassbender, Petibon, Henry, Dale, Choeurs de l'Opéra du Rhin, Strausbourg PO, Latham-Koenig.

Poulenc set great store by this opera and it was superbly served in the early days of LP by Pierre Dervaux with the incomparable Denise Duval as Blanche. (This is still available in the boxed set EMI issued to mark the Poulenc centenary year in 1999.) This DVD is a remarkably gripping and wholly convincing production which may well serve to persuade those who have not seen the light about this piece.

In Anne-Sophie Schmidt it has a Blanche who looks as good as she sounds, and a cast which has no weak member. The production conveys the period to striking effect and the claustrophobic atmosphere of the nunnery. The camerawork is imaginative without ever being intrusive and the

production so well managed that the *longueurs* that normally afflict the closing scene in the opera house pass unnoticed. Of the other roles Hedwig Fassbender (Mère Marie de l'Incarnation), Patricia Petibon (Soeur Constance), Didier Henry (Le Marquis de la Force) and Laurence Dale (as the Chevalier de la Force) are exemplary both as singers and as interpreters.

This production is excellent dramatically – and *looks* good. The stage director is Marthe Keller, who was the eponymous heroine of Honegger's *Jeanne d'Arc au bûcher* on DG. The Strasbourg Orchestra play well for Jan Latham-Koenig and, even apart from its compelling visual presence, it has the strongest musical claims as well. Subtitles are in English, German and Flemish.

PREVIN, André (born 1929)

A Streetcar Named Desire (opera; complete).

(N) *** Arthaus 100 138. Fleming, Futral, Forst, Gilfry, Griffey, San Franscisco Op. O, Composer. (V/D: Colin Graham.)

André Previn's ambitious project to turn Tennessee Williams's ground-breaking play into an opera has resulted in one of the richest, most moving American works in the repertory. The approach may be more conventional in operatic terms than the operas of leading American minimalists, and Colin Graham's richly evocative production with ingenious sets by Michael Yeargan follows that approach, yet the power of the result is undeniable.

Previn himself draws passionate playing from the orchestra of the San Francisco Opera, leading an exceptionally strong cast of soloists, each establishing a distinctive character as laid down in the play.

Central to the opera's success is the moving and powerful assumption of the central role of Blanche by Renée Fleming, relishing music that was specially tailored for her. The big melody of her solo '*I can smell the sea air*' inspires her to producing ravishing sounds, leading to the final scene, where she is led away to the asylum, which is made the more poignant by the sheer beauty of her singing.

Rodney Gilfry admirably copes with the problem of singing freshly and clearly, while making Stanley necessarily a slob. This DVD offers a video recording of the world premiere, a historic occasion, even more vivid when seen as well as heard.

'The Kindness of Strangers': A Portrait by Tony Palmer.

(N) *** Arthaus DVD 100 150.

Tony Palmer, second to none in portraying great musicians, made this film in 1988 to coincide with the world premiere of Previn's opera, *A Streetcar Named Desire*. Starting with that as a news item, together with a tempting sample of Renée Fleming in the central role of Blanche, the film offers a wide-ranging survey of Previn's achievements, covering his career since boyhood.

It is a measure of his breadth of achievement, not just as a classical conductor, composer and pianist but as a jazz performer and an Oscar-winning Hollywood film composer, that the 90 minutes is crammed with so much rich material.

That includes early and rare archive film, not just of Previn himself, but of clips of his early film-successes, *On an Island with You* and *The Sun Comes Out*.

Previn himself is the most engaging of musicians, full of sharp remarks, as when he turned down the idea of an opera as suggested by a German company: 'I can't write an opera where everyone's wearing a toga.' Or on gymnastic conducting: 'An orchestra does not play any louder if you jump, so why jump?' A film full of treasurable material about a fascinating and engaging musician.

PROKOFIEV, Serge (1891–1953).

Ivan the Terrible, Parts I and II (complete).

(N) (***) Eureka DVD EKA 40018 (2). Cherkassov, Tselikovskaya, Birman. (Film director: Sergei Eisenstein.)

When Sergei Eisenstein sought to follow up the brilliant success of his film *Alexander Nevsky* with an even more ambitious epic, *Ivan the Terrible*, he naturally turned again to Prokofiev to provide the music, whose score for *Nevsky* is uniquely memorable.

The subject of Ivan the Terrible equally inspired Prokofiev to write a powerful and distinctive score, which can stand on its own as a concert work. Yet over two films (94 and 85 minutes respectively) the result is necessarily more diffuse.

Eisenstein's astonishingly striking and beautiful images in black and white have remarkable impact on DVD, based on an excellent copy of the original film, but sadly, the soundtrack is depressingly crumbly and ill-focused. Though it makes it hard to enjoy Prokofiev's music, its power is still very clear, enhancing the heavyweight treatment of history.

Olivier's *Henry V* with Walton's music was made at exactly the same period, but offers infinitely finer sound than this. It is a pity that it was not possible to superimpose a modern recording of the music, as has been effectively done in live concert-showings of the film.

PUCCINI, Giacomo (1858–1924)

Turandot (opera; complete).

**(*) Arthaus DVD 100 088. Marton, Sylver, Mazzaria, Langan, San Francisco Op. Ch. & O, Runnicles. (Production/Design: David Hockney; Director: Peter McClintock, V/D: Brian Large).

This comes from a 1994 San Francisco production and has Eva Marton in the title role, which she has, of course, sung in Vienna under Maazel for Sony (1983), Roberto Abbado (RCA) and James Levine (DG). Thus the merits and shortcomings of her Turandot are well known: hers is a big, dramatic voice, but with far too little expressive variation in tone and she is content to sing loudly and leave it at that. However, there are other things in its favour: a decent Calaf in Michael Sylver, a good Ping (Theodore Baerg), Pang (Dennis Peterson) and Pong (Craig Estep). We have heard more moving accounts of Liù than Lucia Mazzaria's, but generally speaking the cast are more than acceptable. The orchestral and choral forces are very well harnessed by

Donald Runnicles, who fires on all cylinders and visually the designs by David Hockney are vivid and bold (some might think them garish, and they have had a dismissive press) but they will strike most readers as effective. The sound is rather forward and bright, and detail is very well captured by the engineers. Brian Large, as always, makes sure that the camera is where you would want it to be, and although there are more subtle Turandots to be found than Marton, the performance is thoroughly gripping. (There are sub-titles in English, French, Dutch and German.)

PURCELL, Henry (1659–95)

The Fairy Queen (complete).

(N) *** Arthaus DVD 100 200. Kenny, Randle, Rice, van Allan, ENO Ch. & O, Kok. (Director: David Pountney.)

Recorded live at the Coliseum in London in 1995, this ENO production of *The Fairy Queen*, conducted by Nicholas Kok, turns an entertainment which can, under modern conditions, seem cumbersome into a sparkling fantasy, thanks to the brilliant stage direction of David Pountney and choreography of Quinny Sacks. The sequence of masques are treated as a series of circus turns, and thanks also to the fantastic costumes of Dunya Ramicova the atmosphere of the circus is never far away, helping to hold together an episodic sequence of scenes, originally designed to back up a garbled version of Shakespeare's *A Midsummer Night's Dream*.

The result is as much a surreal ballet as an opera, with Nicholas Kok drawing stylish playing from the ENO Orchestra, echoing period practice, using a realization prepared by Clifford Bartlett. So the scene of the Drunken Poet proves genuinely funny, with Jonathan Best (identified only in the final credits on film) doing a jolly imitation of a 1950s poet with scruffy sports jacket and pullover.

By contrast Titania – Yvonne Kenny at her finest – and Oberon – the exotic Thomas Randle – stand out the more sharply as otherworldly figures thanks to their glamorous costumes. More equivocal is the presentation of Puck by Simon Rice, lively as he is. A fun entertainment, as unstuffy a presentation of Purcell's problematic masterpiece as could be, vividly filmed and recorded.

ROSSINI, Giacomo (1792–1868)

Il barbiere di Siviglia (opera, complete).

(N) **(*) Arthaus DVD 100 090. Bartoli, Quilico, Kuebler, Feller, Lloyd, Cologne City Op. Ch., Stuttgart RSO, Ferro. (Director: Michael Hampe.)

Recorded live at the Schwetzingen Festival in a very pretty theatre in 1988, this version of *Il barbiere* centres on the superb performances of the two principals, Cecilia Bartoli, already dominant, with voice and technique fully developed even before she became a superstar, and Gino Guilico as Figaro, wonderfully winning in his acting with voice magnificently firm.

David Kuebler with his rather gritty tenor is far from

winning as the Count, Robert Lloyd is an imposing Basolio and Carlos Feller a characterful Bartolo. Gabriele Ferro springs the rhythms persuasively, and Michael Hampe's production works well using realistic sets by Ezio Frigerio and costumes by Mauro Pagano. Excellent, cleanly separated sound.

La Cenerentola (opera; complete)

(N) *** Decca DVD 071 444-9. Bartoli, Dara, Giménez, Corbelli, Pertusi, Houston Grand Op. Ch. & Symphony, Campanella.(V/D Brian Large.)

(N) *** Arthaus DVD 100 214. Murray, Berry, Araiza, Quilico, Schöne, V. St. Op.Ch., VPO, Chailey. (Director: Michael Hampe. V/D: Claus Viller.)

Few Rossini operas have such fizz as Decca's Houston Opera production of *La Cenerentola*, a part Cecilia Bartoli was born to play. The rest of the cast is the same as the CD set, except that Raúl Giménez takes the part of Don Ramiro. Bruno Campanella conducts very spiritedly. Visually the production could not be more winning, and the camera placing is a great credit to Brian Large.

Riccardo Chailly (who directed the Decca CDs) conducts the alternative version, which comes from the 1982 Salzburg Festival, and had the Bartoli set not been available it would have been a very strong recommendation, for Ann Murray is delightful in the principal role and the rest of the cast is excellent. If in Act I Don Magnifico's castle looks run down and needing a coat of paint, the glamour of the Palace more than compensates. The recording is bright and sparking but has plenty of bloom and the camerawork is always well managed. Most enjoyable, with a dazzling *Non più mesta* and a particularly infectious finale. But Chailly is at his finest throughout and so are the chorus and orchestra.

L'Italiana in Algeri (opera; complete).

(N) ** Arthaus DVD 100 120. Soffel, Gambill, Von Kannen, Bulgarian Male Ch. Stuttgart Radio SO, Weikert.

This production from the 1987 Schwetzingen Festival was available in the early 1990s on a Pioneer Laserdisc and looks even better on this DVD with its sharper, steadier focus and good colour – and subtitles in English, French and German.

Doris Soffel is a vivacious Isabella and the Mustafà of Günter von Kannen is characterized with great zest. Michael Hampe's direction is witty and well paced, and the set design and costumes of Mauro Pagano colourful.

The stage is small (as is the theatre itself) and despite the merits of the singing and playing leaves the impression of being cramped and provincial with little sense of back-to-front perspective. But there is a lot to enjoy here, particularly the final ensemble of the first Act, and much that is of quality. The Südwestfunk Orchestra plays well for Ralf Weikert and the sound is well balanced and has good presence.

SAINT-SAENS, Camille (1835–1921)

Samson et Dalila (opera; complete).

(N) *** Arthaus DVD 100 202. Domingo, Verrett, Wolfgang Brendel, San Francisco Opera Ch. & O, Rudel. (Director: Nicolas Joel. V/D: Kirk Browning.)

Recorded in 1981 at the San Francisco Opera House, this DVD of Saint-Saens's biblical opera offers a heavily traditional production with realistic sets and costumes like those in a Hollywood epic. Sporting a vast bouffant wig like a tea-cosy (ripe for Dalila's shears in Act 2), Placido Domingo is in magnificent, heroic voice, with Shirley Verrett also at her peak as Dalila, at once seductive and sinister. Other principals are first-rate too, and the chorus, so vital in this opera, sings with incandescent tone in a riproaring performance under Julius Rudel, culminating in a spectacular presentation of the fall of the Temple of Dagon. Most enjoyable.

STRAUSS, Johann Jr (1825–99)

Die Fledermaus (opera; complete).

(N) DG **(*) 073 007-9. Coburn, Perry, Fassbaender, Waechter, Brendel, Hopferwieser, Bavarian St Op. Ch. & O, Kleiber. (Director: Otto Schenk.)

Recorded live at the Bavarian State Opera in 1987, Carlos Kleiber's film version of *Die Fledermaus* is preferable to his audio recording, also for DG, in fair measure because of the superb assumption of the role of Prince Orlofsky by Brigitte Fassbaender, a fire-eater who makes the most positive host in the party scene of Act 2, singing superbly, where the audio recording has a feeble falsettist. Though Janet Perry's soprano is shallow and bright, she has the agility and sparkle for the role of Adele, with Patricia Coburn as a warm, positive Rosalinde, whooping away persuasively in the waltz numbers, and entering into the spirit of the party, despite a violently unconvincing red wig. Eberhard Waechter sounds too old and unsteady as Eisenstein, and Josef Hopferwieser is also unconvincingly old as the philandering tenor, Alfred, both shown up by the dark firm Alfres Brendel as Falke. As on CD, Kleiber directs a taut performance, which yet has plenty of sparkle, helped by full-bodied sound.

Die Fledermaus (complete, in English).

(N) *** Arthaus 100 134 (2). Gustafson, Howarth, Kowalski, Otey, Michaels-Moore, Bottone, ROHCG Ch. & O, Bonynge. (Director: John Cox.)

Lasting well over three and a quarter hours, this version of *Die Fledermaus*, in an English version by John Mortimer, stretches to two DVDs, largely because in this gala performance at Covent Garden on New Year's Eve 1989/90 a half-hour of performances by the 'surprise guests' is included in the party scene: Luciano Pavarotti, Marilyn Horne and – making her farewell to the opera-stage – Dame Joan Sutherland. For Sutherland devotees it is an essential item, with the two duets specially cherishable, the *Semiramide* duet with Horne and *Parigi o cara* from *La Traviata* with Pavarotti.

Under Richard Bonynge's light, beautifully sprung direction, the gala fizzes splendidly with a first-rate cast, even though at the start of Act 2 Falke (Michaels-Moore) unwittingly loses his monocle. The countertenor, Jochen Kowalski, makes a characterful, distinctive Orlofsky with baritone speaking voice contrasted with his singing. Nancy Gustafson is a warm Rosalinde and Judith Howarth a sweet Adele, and the others all sing well, despite the pressure of the occasion.

STRAUSS, Richard (1864–1949)

Arabella (opera; complete).

(N) *** DG 073 005-9. Te Kanawa, Wolfgang Brendel, McLaughlin, Dessay, Kuebler, Dernesch, McIntyre, Met. Op. Ch.and O, Thielemann. (Producer: Otto Schenk. V/D: Brian Large.)

It would be hard to think of a starrier line-up of soloists for *Arabella* than in this live account, recorded at the Met in New York in November 1994. One of the great strengths of the production is the conducting of Christian Thielemann, who was then just emerging as a new star among Strauss conductors. He is at once thrustful and emotional, drawing ripe sounds from the orchestra.

Dame Kiri Te Kanawa gives a convincing dramatic account of the title role and is in glorious voice, producing ravishing sounds in her big numbers, even more charming when observed in close-up. She obviously relishes the sumptuous production, which is as traditional as could be, with grandly realistic sets by Gunther Schneider-Siemssen. The stage direction is by Otto Schenk, who shows appropriate respect for Hoffmansthal and Strauss's wishes, and the intelligence of the public.

The Mandryka of Wolfgang Brendel carries conviction even if he looks somewhat older than he should (mid-thirties). His voice is strong, firm and unstrained in a rather intimidating yet ultimately vulnerable characterization, and Marie McLaughlin is poignantly convincing as Zdenka, the younger sister forced to adopt the role of boy. Donald McIntyre and Helga Dernesch are vivldy characterful as Arabella's parents, and in the second act Natalie Dessay as the Fiakermilli is full of character, and she makes much of her brief appearance at the ball, bright and brilliant in her showpiece.

The balance favours the voices and not all the wealth of orchestral detail registers, but the recording is aptly rich and full-bodied. The visual side of the production is first rate (and a great improvement on the Laserdisc). As usual Brian Large's camera is pointing exactly where one wants it to point. On the videotape there were no subtitles at all, and on the Laserdisc there were English subtitles which could not be removed. Here not only are there subtitles in English, French and Mandarin, but the original Hofmannsthal text is also accessible. Strongly recommended.

Ariadne auf Naxos (opera; complete).

(N) (***) Arthaus DVD 100 170. Susan Anthony, Martinez, Koch, Villars. Junge, Adam, Semper Oper Ch., Dresden State O, C. Davis. (Producer: Marco Arturo Marelli. V/D: Felix Breisach.)

We are at odds about the Arthaus *Ariadne auf Naxos*, recorded live at the Semper Oper in Dresden. R.L. feels that for most collectors it will be a complete turn-off. The setting is in a present-day museum of modern art whose visitors wander in an out of the gallery throughout the whole opera to mightily distracting effect. It contributes nothing to an opera whose creators knew what they were doing. They were masters of their art and in no need of 'interpretation' from an attention-seeking director.

The performance is not particularly distinguished vocally either, save for Sophie Koch's Composer. The best of the others are John Villars's Bacchus and Theo Adam's Music Master, and the orchestra make a pretty sumptuous sound under Sir Colin Davis. The intrusive silliness of the production makes it difficult to sit through this performance once, let alone a second time!

E.G. on the other hand feels that Sir Colin Davis, at his most inspired, directs a glowing performance with a cast of young singers who respond superbly, both to the conducting and to the imaginative stage direction of Marco Arturo Marelli. The Prologue, updated to the twentieth century, takes you behind the scenes of an impromptu theatre, with a piano centre-stage and with a washroom half visible behind. The costumes, also designed by Marelli, add to the atmosphere of fantasy. The Composer, characterfully sung by Sophie Koch, heartfelt in the final solo, rightly provides the central focus, with his new passion for Zerbinetta well established. The main opera follows without an interval. The scene is neatly changed before our eyes to a picture gallery during a private view.

The composer (silent in this half) again provides a focus, with Ariadne and the others performing the opera as an impromptu charade. Central to the performance's success is the radiant singing of Susan Anthony as Ariadne with her firm, creamily beautiful voice. The sparky Zerbinetta of Iride Martinez, vivaciously Spanish-looking, unashamedly shows off in her big aria, both vocally in her dazzling coloratura and in her acting.

Jon Villars is a powerful, unstrained Bacchus in the final scene, with the commedia dell'arte characters all very well taken too. Though this is not as starry a cast as some, it is unusually satisfying, with no weak link. Clear, full-bodied sound, and, as in other Arthaus operas, a helpful booklet is provided.

Your Editor had not better enter the fray, as he hates almost all modern opera productions which make a time-change, and do not follow the original intentions of the composer and librettist. Readers can make up their own minds as to whose side they are on.

Elektra (opera; complete).

(N) *** Arthaus DVD 100 048. Marton, Fassbaender, Studer, King, Grundheber, V. St. Op. Ch. & O, Abbado.

Eva Marton recorded *Elektra* with Wolfgang Sawallisch in 1990 but the present account comes from a Vienna performance of the preceding year with Abbado conducting. It appeared on Laserdisc on the Pioneer label in 1993 and now makes a welcome appearance on DVD. A direct comparison between LD and DVD is definitely in the latter's favour: although the sound is equally good in both, the aural image is just that bit firmer and more finely focused even than on LD.

The performance has enormous intensity: both Marton's Elektra and Fassbaender's Klytämnestra stay long in the memory and all the remaining characters are triumphantly realized, not least Franz Grundheber's bloodthirsty Orest. Marton makes the most of the intent, obsessive, powerfully demonic Elektra and has enormous dramatic presence.

Harry Kupfer's production is gripping. The setting is dark though not quite so dismal as Götz Friedrich's 1981 production with Rysanek and Varnay under Boehm on a Decca LD). Musically this is an exciting and concentrated account, and the camera is musically handled by Brian Large. He has an unerring feel for directing our attention where it needs to be. Unlike the unsubtitled LD, the present issue offers subtitles in English and French and the original German.

Der Rosenkavalier (opera; complete).

⊕ *** DVD DG 073 008-9 (2). Lott, Von Otter, Bonney, Moll, Hornik, V. St. Op. Ch. & O, Carlos Kleiber. (Producer: Otto Schenck. V/D: Horant Hohlfeld.)

This celebrated production, recorded in Vienna in March 1994, appeared on videotape and Laserdisc the following year. Carlos Kleiber has spoken of Felicity Lott as his ideal Marschallin and she is probably currently as unrivalled in this role as was Schwarzkopf in the 1950s. She does not wear her heart on her sleeve and her reticence makes her all the more telling and memorable.

The other roles are hardly less distinguished, with Anne-Sofie von Otter's Octavian splendidly characterized and boyish, while Barbara Bonney's Sophie floats her top notes in the *Presentation of the Rose* scene with great poise and impressive accuracy. Kurt Moll's Ochs is one of the highlights of the performance, a splendidly three-dimensional and subtle reading.

Otto Schenck's production deserves the praises that have been lavished on it, and Rudolf Heinrich's sets are handsome. Carlos Kleiber gets some ravishing sounds from the Vienna Philharmonic and his reading of the score is as Straussian and as perfect as you are likely to encounter in this world. It is even finer than the version he did in Munich in 1979 with Dame Gwyneth Jones as the Marschallin, Fassbaender (Octavian) and Popp which was issued on video and Laserdisc, and which will presumably find its way onto DVD in the fullness of time.

The sound is very natural and lifelike, not too forward, and with a good perspective. On the video there were no subtitles though they were on LaserDisc. Things look up here as not only are subtitles given in English, French and Mandarin but Hofmannsthal's original is also available.

TCHAIKOVSKY, Peter (1840–93)

Piano Concerto No. 1 in B flat min., Op. 23.

** Sony SVD 45986. Kissin, BPO, Karajan (with PROKOFIEV: *Classical Symphony.* **(*))

Both works were recorded at a New Year's Eve concert at the end of 1988 and the concerto was issued on DG 427 485-2 as well as on video. Kissin was sixteen at the time of this performance, though he looks even younger, and the whole occasion must have been rather an awesome experience for him. His playing has great elegance and tremendous poise: his pianissimo tone is quite ravishing. But he tends not to let himself go, and there is just a slight feeling that he is playing safe, particularly in the finale. The performance as a whole, for all its finesse, lacks abandon.

The strings in the Prokofiev *Classical Symphony* have the characteristic Berlin sheen and the slow movement has great tonal sweetness. The *Scherzo* is a bit heavy-handed, but is offset by an altogether captivating finale, perfectly judged in pace and character. The camerawork is unobtrusive, and although the piano is rather forward the balance is well judged, though the overall sound is a shade dry.

Swan Lake (ballet; complete. Choreography: Patrice Bart).

(N) *** Arthaus DVD 100 001. Scherzer, Matz, Händler, Ballet of the Deutsche Oper, Berlin, Berlin State O, Barenboim.

This *Swan Lake* was recorded in performance at the Deutsche Staatsoper, Berlin, with the soloists and corps of the Lindenoper (it takes its name from Unter den Linden, where the Opera is based). Patrice Bart has been with the Paris Opéra since 1990, and his keenly inventive choreography brings fresh air into the Marius Petipa–Lev Ivanov original.

All the principals are fine dancers: Steffi Scherzer's Odette/Odile is strikingly characterized: she has been prima ballerina with the company since 1987, and Oliver Matz makes an elegant Prince Siegfried. Bart recasts the four acts as two, and his choreography gives much scope also to the part of Rotbart, danced brilliantly by Torsten Händler.

Apart from the excellence of the dancing, what a good ballet conductor Barenboim is! He has obviously thought long and deeply about this inexhaustible score, which emerges with eloquence and radiance in his hands. The camerawork is natural and unobtrusive, and the colour gloriously vivid. Watching the performance lifts the spirits, and makes one realize yet again what wonderful music this is.

Eugene Onegin (opera; complete).

** Arthaus DVD 100 126. Boylan, Gluschak, König, Burford, Michail Schelomianski, EU Opera Ch. & O, Rozhdestvensky. (Producer: Nikolaus Lehnhoff.)

This was staged at the 1998 Baden-Baden Festival and has the advantage of an excellent Onegin in Vladimir Glushchak but otherwise a not wholly convincing cast. (Ineke Vlogtman's Larina looks far too young to be a mother, let alone the mother of Orla Boylan, and Anna Burford!) There are good things, of course, among which the conducting of Gennady Rozhdestvensky ranks high.

But there is little sense of period, and the chorus certainly doesn't sound Russian despite the presence of a Russian conductor. Above all, there is little sense of atmosphere and the bright, overlit opening scene, with its abundance of kites, hardly induces confidence. Best to stick to a good CD set and the theatre of the imagination.

VERDI, Giuseppi (1813–1901)

Requiem.

(N) *** Arthaus DVD 100 146. Margaret Price, Norman, Carreras, Raimondi, Edinburgh Fest. Ch., LSO, Abbado.

As a performance this live recording, made for television at the Edinburgh Festival in 1982, outshines Claudio Abbado's regular audio recordings of the Verdi *Requiem*, not least thanks to the extraordinary line-up of soloists, with Jessye Norman taking the mezzo role against Margaret Price as the soprano.

All four are in superb voice, with Ruggiero Raimondi the more sinister in *Mors stupebit* when viewed in close-up with villainous expressions projected, quite apart from the power and precision of his singing. Similarly, José Carreras has never sounded more powerful, with such a big solo as *Ingemisco* flawlessly delivered. Jesye Norman sings gloriously too, in such big solos as the *Liber scriptus* and the *Recordare*, and makes a fine match with Margaret Price in their duetting, equally firm and secure, distinct yet blended.

Yet it is Margaret Price who crowns the whole performance in the final *Libera me*, deeply moving and keenly dramatic, the more so when seen in close-up. The Edinburgh Festival Chorus sing as though possessed, and Abbado draws passionate playing from the LSO, with none of the coolness that can mark this conductor's work in the studio. The sound cannot match the finest modern recordings, not helped by the dryness of the Usher Hall, where the performance was recorded, but as transferred to DVD the result is still full and vivid, with powerful impact.

La forza del destino (opera; complete 1862 version).

(N) *** Arthaus DVD 100 078. Gorchakova, Putilin, Grigorian, Tarasova, Kirov Ch. & O, Gergiev. (Producer: Elijah Moshinsky. V/D: Brian Large.)

This production of the 1862 version of *La forza* comes from St Petersburg, where the opera had its première. Philips have recorded it under Valéry Gergiev on 3 CDs with substantially the same cast. The major change is Marianna Tarasova (instead of Olga Borodina) as Preziola. In discussing the differences between the 1862 and 1869 versions of the opera itself Julian Budden says that there is 'not a change in the revision which is not an improvement', but all the same it is good to have Verdi's first thoughts together with some music that is unfamiliar.

In 1862 the overture was replaced by a short prelude, but otherwise the changes concern the final scenes of Act III, where the duo between Alvaro and Don Carlo follows rather than precedes the encampment scene. The finale is also different: the Alvaro–Carlo duel takes place on stage and Alvaro does not survive, but takes his own life. Of particular interest is the fact that the Kirov reproduce the original sets, which look quite handsome, even if the staging is at times a bit hyperactive.

The performance is much stronger than in the *Forza* that the Kirov brought to Covent Garden in the summer of 2001, and Gergiev here proves a more idiomatic Verdi conductor than he was during the London season. The cast is strong, with Gorchakova in good form as Lenora singing with great dramatic eloquence.

There are some differences between this cast and that of the Philips set (446 951-2). Mikhail Kit was the Padre Guardiano on the latter as opposed to Sergei Alexashin here and Borodina was Preziosilla as opposed to Marianna Tarasova. Otherwise the main characters are the same.

Gegam Grigorian is an impressively confident Alvaro and Nikolai Putilin's Don Carlo is every bit as good as on CD. Tarasova's Preziola does not disappoint and Sergei Alexashin's Guardiano is better focused than Mikhail Kit in the 1996 CD. The opera looks very good – and sounds very good: the audio balance first class. Brian Large's video direction is first class, too, and though Moshinsky's direction is busy, it is for the most part effective. Subtitles are in English, German, French and Dutch.

Macbeth (opera; complete).

(N) **(*) Arthaus DVD 100 140. Bruson, Zampieri, Morris, O'Neill, Deutsche Op. Ch. & O, Sinopoli. (Director: Luca Ronconi.)

In a recording made at the Deutsche Oper in Berlin in 1987, Giuseppe Sinopoli conducts a bitingly dramatic reading of *Macbeth*, dominated by the fine Macbeth of Reno Bruson, his self-searching the more compelling in close-up on DVD, and the powerful, if sometimes hooty, Lady Macbeth of Mara Zampieri, perfectly looking the part, young and handsome still.

She points the drinking-song well, and though she avoids the final top-note of the sleepwalking scene, it is still a magnetic performance. The rest of the cast is strong too, with Dennis O'Neill as Macduff and James Morris as Banquo. The chorus sings splendidly, with a line-up of dozens of witches in the opening scene, gathered behind the long table which dominates a fair proportion of scenes in Luca Ronconi's bare production, with sets and costumes by Luciano Damiani. Excellent, well-separated sound.

Otello (opera; complete).

(N) **(*) DG 073-006-9. Vickers, Freni, Glossop, Malagu, Bottion, Senechal, Van Dam, Deutsche Oper Ch., Berlin PO, Karajan.

As well as conducting, Karajan himself directed this glamorous film version of *Otello*, presenting it in spectacular settings, with effects going far beyond what is possible on stage, as in the opening storm scene. The singers mime their parts to an audio recording, with mouth-movements not always well-synchronized.

That is a small price to pay for a fine, bitingly dramatic performance, characterfully cast and beautifully sung. Jon Vickers was still at his peak when the recording was made in 1974, thrilling in the title role with not a hint of strain, backed up by powerful acting. Similarly, Peter Glossop has never been finer on disc, whether in his singing or his acting, a plausible yet uncompromising Iago, and Mirella Freni gives a radiant performance as Desdemona, rising superbly to the challenge of the final scene, both sweet and powerful.

The balance of the voices frequently follows the closeness or distancing of the camera-work, which can be distracting, but this is an involving presentation of the Verdi master-piece, intelligently rethought for the camera. The sound is good, though not as vivid as in the latest fully digital recordings.

La traviata (opera; complete).

🎵 (N) *** Decca 071 431-9. Gheorghiu, Lopardo, Nucci, ROHCG Ch. & O, Solti. (Director: Richard Eyre. V/D: Humphrey Burton & Peter Maniura.)

As the DVD rightly claims, this famous performance of *La Traviata* captures one of the most sensational debuts in recent operatic history. Singing Violetta for the first time Angela Gheorghiu made the part entirely her own. But the DVD can also claim a special plaudit for the magical opening, when the camera focuses closely on Solti while he conducts the *Prelude*, with every movement of his hands and the concentration in his eyes creating the music in front of us.

He holds the tension at the highest level throughout, with the strings playing marvellously, and recorded with absolute realism. Then the curtain goes up and Bob Crowley's superb stage spectacle spreads out in front of our eyes. The singing is glorious and this is one of the DVDs that should be a cornerstone in any collection.

VIVALDI, Antonio (1678–1741)

The Four Seasons, Op. 8/1–4.

(N) ** EMI DVD 4 92498-9. Kennedy, ECO.
(N) ** Sony DVD SVD 46380. Mutter, BPO, Karajan.

No one could say that Kennedy's *Four Seasons* is dull; the only snag on the DVD is that he talks a lot about it, not very illuminatingly, in his special kind of vernacular, and then introduces each movement as well. The performance itself is certainly spectacular in conveying the picturesque imagery (except for the viola's barking shepherd's dog, which is rather feeble).

Autumn brings a degree of controversy in that there are weird special effects, including glissando harmonics in the slow movement and percussive applications of the wooden part of the bow to add to the rhythmic pungency of the finale. Kennedy also likes to stomp about a bit. The ECO's playing is always responsive to match the brilliant bravura of its soloist. The total running time, including all the documentary bits, is still only 48 minutes.

Karajan sits and directs from the harpsichord for Mutter, and beautifully as she plays, the result is plushy and in the last resort rather bland.

'Viva Vivaldi': Arias:(i) *Agitata da due venti La Griselda, RV718. Gloria in D, RV589: Domine Deus. Opera arias: Bajazet (Il Tamerlano): Anch'il mar par che sommerga. Farnace: Gelido in ogni vedo. La fida Ninfa: Dite, Oimè. Giustino: Sventurata Navicelli. Juditha Triumphans: Armatae face et Angibus. L'Olimpiade, Tra la follie divers . . . Siam navi all'onde algenti. Ottone in villa, Gelosia, tu già rendi l'alma mia. Teuzzone: Di due rai languir costante; Zeffiretti che sussurrate. Tito Manlio: Non ti*

lusinghi la crudeltade. Concertos: in C for flautino, RV443; in D for lute, RV93.

(N) *** Arthaus DVD 100 128.(i) Bartoli; Il Giardino Armonico, Antonini. (V/D: Brian Large.)

Although Vivaldi is known to have composed ninety operas, only twenty have survived. For this programme Cecilia Bartoli has drawn on autograph material in the Turin Library and has come up with some valuable additions to the repertory. The recital was recorded in September 2000 at the Théâtre des Champs-Elysées and is presented very unobtrusively, albeit with a limited repertoire of shots.

In the two concertos, the Domine Deus and a couple of the arias, the score is available, though it must be said that its superimposition all but obliterates the visual image. As in her handsomely presented Decca set *The Vivaldi Album* (Decca 466 569-2), Bartoli sings effortlessly and magnificently – and she duplicates one or two arias here.

Il Giordano Armonico are full of virtuosity and delicacy, and the presence of Brian Large prevents the kind of ostentatious visual 'cleverness' that wrecked their recital listed below. The music is left to speak for itself, and the presence of Bartoli's Decca producer, Christopher Raeburn ensures an excellent and musical balance. It is a tribute to Vivaldi's spectacular fund of invention that there is so much of quality yet to be discovered. The CD is entitled *Viva Vivaldi* and that is what he does in this enjoyable and brilliant set. Sub-titles of the aria texts are in German, French, English and Spanish, and are also available in the original Italian.

WAGNER, Richard (1813–83)

Die Walküre (opera; complete).

(N) *** DG 073 011-9 (2). Behrens, Norman, Ludwig, Lakes, Morris, Moll, Metr Op. O, Levine. (Director: Otto Schenk.)

Recorded live at the Met in New York in April 1989, two years after the DG audio recording with the same personnel, this film offers an even more compelling experience, with James Levine even more thrustfully dramatic, drawing even more spontaneous-sounding performances from his team. To have the glorious voiced Jessye Norman as Sieglinde is luxury casting, totally secure and consistently intense. She is so commanding you feel that, far from being afraid, this Sieglinde could eat any of the Valkyries alive, including the Brünnhilde of Hildegard Behrens.

Powerfully projected and deeply expressive, Behrens's performance is none the less compelling. Gary Lakes makes a firm, secure Siegmund to match his Sieglinde, and the dark-voiced Kurt Moll is an ideal, sinister Hunding, with James Morris a noble Wotan, in his presence even more than his voice. Christa Ludwig as Fricka sounds hardly less fresh than she did in the famous Solti *Ring* on Decca.

Thanks to Levine this is above all a powerful reading, with the heavy brass superbly caught in the full-ranging recording. The traditonal production of Otto Schenk with heavily realistic sets by Gunther Schneider-Siemssen, enhanced by evocative back-projections, may have disappointed some critics, yet with well-planned close-ups it works splendidly on DVD. Nor do the production or the direction for the camera disappoint. The former is generally straightforward and refreshingly free from the kind of ego-centric attention-seeking 'creativity' that is so normal in the opera house these days. It is good to watch, and the only real reservation lies in the orchestral sonority (the opening storm and Hunding's entry sound pretty crude).

The Metropolitan is a fine orchestra and much that they do gives pleasure but ultimately one misses the nobility and eloquence one finds in so many of the sound-only versions from Boehm, Solti, Karajan and Furtwängler.

WALTON, William (1903–83)

Hamlet (film score).

(N) ** Carlton 37115 00183. Olivier, Herlie, Sydney, Simmons, Aylmer, Philh. O, Muir Mathieson. (Director Laurence Olivier.)

Though Laurence Olivier's film of *Hamlet* was made in 1948, four years after *Henry V*, the sound of Walton's evocative film-score, as transferred to DVD, is far inferior to that in the earlier film, with far less body and less sense of space. Though it is not nearly as crumbly as the soundtrack of Eisenstein's *Ivan the Terrible*, it is not even as full-bodied as the sound on the VHS equivalent, and like that offers only a truncated version of the most substantial section of the score, the final *Funeral March*. Muir Mathieson again conducted, but this time with the newly founded Philharmonia Orchestra. Needless to say, for all the lack of focus in the sound, the evocative camerawork in black and white, with swirling mists round the castle of Elsinore, is beautifully caught in sharp focus, and Olivier's truncated version of Shakespeare works very well as film.

Henry V (film score).

(N) ** Carlton 37115 00193. Olivier, Newton, Banks, Asherson, LSO, Muir Mathieson. (Director: Laurence Olivier.)

Walton's music for Laurence Olivier's film of *Henry V* has never been surpassed in the way it adds so vividly both to the dramatic impact and to the atmospheric beauty. The very opening, with a playbill fluttering to a flute figure, and a panoramic view of Elizabethan London to a haunting offstage chorus, sets the pattern even before the drama starts. Though the sound from a mono soundtrack is necessarily limited, it has been beautifully cleaned up for DVD, so that such effects are vividly atmospheric, giving a satisfying sense of space.

Much of Walton's music is well-known in concert-form, but the film brings it home how much more there is than that, and how it is even more effective in its original context. Even the Agincourt charge music, a uniquely effective set-piece, is more effective still when seen as well as heard.

Olivier's concept, with the film moving from the Globe Theatre at the start to an idealized setting in France, with medieval false perspectives, remains masterly. An extraordi-narily starry line up of leading British actors of the time brings a whole gallery of characterful portrayals, not least from Olivier himself, unforgettable in the title-role.

DOCUMENTARIES

The Art of Piano by Christian Labrande & Donald Sturrock.
With Arrau, Backhaus, Cortot, Cziffra, Annie Fischer, Edwin Fischer, Gilels, Gould, Myra Hess, Josef Hofmann, Horowitz, Michelangeli, Moiseiwitsch, Paderewski, Planté Rachmaninov, Richter, Rubinstein; and with commentaries by Pitor Andersewski, Daniel Barenboim, Sir Colin Davis, Evgeni Kissin, Zoltán Kocsis, Stephen Kovacevich, Paul Myers, Gennady Rozhdestvensky, György Sandor, Tamás Vásáry and others.

(N) *** Warner/NVC Arts DVD 3984-29199-2.

There is some valuable archival material here including a compilation of the *Appassionata* with a few bars each from Solomon, Arrau, Richter, Myra Hess, Richter and Rubin-stein. Some of the archival material is not as rare as in Bruno Monsaingeon's *Art of Violin* (let alone Richter) and the glimpses of Paderewski (taken from the 1936 film *Moonlight Sonata*) and Myra Hess playing the Mozart *G major concerto, K453*, are very familiar. But there is much else that is not, including Cziffra's dazzling *Grand galop chromatique* (which he included on his first HMV LP) and Moiseiwitsch playing the Rachmaninov *C minor Concerto* in 1944, which affords us a brief glimpse of Constant Lambert conducting.

The brief excerpts from the Brahms *B flat Concerto* and Beethoven's *C minor Sonata, Op. 111* from Arrau and Edwin Fischer's Bach are illuminating. The main commentary can be heard in English (John Tusa), French (Jean-Pierre Belissent) or German (Johannes Hitzelberger) and there are subtitles where required in all three languages. The production is limited to a greater or lesser extent by the availability of archive material and this is not quite as rich a yield as the companion issue and the commentaries (with some distinguished exceptions) not quite as illuminating. All the same, for obvious reasons it is still a 'must'.

The Art of Violin by Bruno Monsaingeon.
With Elman, Enescu, Ferras, Francescatti, Goldstein, Grumiaux, Heifetz, Kogan, Kreisler, Menuhin, Milstein, Neveu, Oistrakh, Rabin, Stern, Szeryng, Szigeti, Thibaud, Ysaÿe; and with commentaries by Itzhak Perlman, Ivry Gitlis, Ida Haendel, Hilary Hahn, Mstislav Rostropovich, Yehudi Menuhin.

(N) *** Warner/NVC Arts DVD 5 8573-85801-2.

Bruno Monsaingeon made a strong impression with his revealing studies of Sviatoslav Richter and David Oistrakh. As a glance at the list of artists here shows, he offers a glimpse of some of the great violinists of the last century and includes archival footage that will not only be new to many but, since some has only just come to light, new to all.

Virtuosity is common to all and transcendental in many, but it is the originality of their sound world which is at the centre of Monsaingeon's opening argument, which explores the expressive individuality and sonority of great violinists. No one listening to Szigeti or Kreisler, Oistrakh or Elman – and above all Heifetz – is ever in the slightest doubt as to who was playing. There are excellent commentaries by Itzhak

Perlman, Ida Haendel and the splendid Ivry Gitlis; only Hilary Hahn is completely out of her depth in their company.

There is rare footage of Thibaud and Ginette Neveu playing the closing bars of the Chausson *Poème* in Prague and an interesting montage of part of the Mendelssohn concerto in which the soloists (Oistrakh, Stern, Christian Ferras, Milstein, Menuhin, Grumiaux, Heifetz and Elman) change, thus bringing home their differences in tonal production and their rich diversity of approach.

Other rarities include a glimpse of Ysaÿe from 1912, looking like an emperor! A thoughtful and intelligent production that can be warmly recommended. Incidentally, on the credits nearly every European TV station is listed as supporting this venture but neither the BBC nor Channel 4 is among them – further evidence, perhaps, of the declining cultural ambition of British television in the last decade.

BRENDEL, ALFRED (piano)

Alfred Brendel: A Portrait. Documentary – Man and Mask. Produced by Emma Chrichton-Miller & Mark Kidel.

(N) *** BBC Opus Arte OA o811D (2).

The first DVD here is a straight recital recorded at the Snape Maltings Concert Hall, consisting of the Haydn *E flat Sonata, XVI:49*, the Mozart *C minor, K.457* and the Schubert *Impromptu in G flat, D.899/3*. The second gives a portrait of the great pianist in which he plays some Schubert and rehearses with Simon Rattle and the Vienna Philharmonic. He speaks of his parents, his early life in Zagreb, life in Vienna as a student, his love of art and the world of ideas. His geniality, culture and sophistication shine through, together with an engaging, self-deprecating humour ('I was not a good sight-reader, nor a virtuoso – in fact I don't know how I made it').

We hear him accompanying Matthias Goerne in Schubert, playing Schubert, talking about primitive art from New Guinea, rehearsing a Mozart piano quartet with his son Adrian and discussing the B flat and C minor Beethoven concertos with Rattle. He also reads some of his own poetry. The recital is impeccable, both visually and aurally: Brendel's finely poised and articulate playing is wonderfully thought out, but the Mozart is just a shade wanting in the charm and spontaneity he brought to that repertoire in earlier years. In short, an unobtrusively shot film which brings us closer to a notoriously (or should one not say, famously) private person, a joy to look at – and listen to!

Alfred Brendel in Portrait

BBC Opus Arte OAo811D (2DVDs). Profile, conversation with Sir Simon Rattle, poetry-reading and recital – HAYDN: *Piano Sonata in E flat, Hob XVI/49;* MOZART: *Piano Sonata in C min. K.457;* SCHUBERT: *Impromptu No. 3 in G flat, D.899.*

This seventy-minute portrait of Brendel, directed for television by Mark Kidel, takes the great pianist to many of the haunts of his early life, as well as showing him at home in Hampstead relaxing. As he wrily observes at the very start, he had none of the assets usually needed for a great musical career: he was not a child prodigy, he was not Jewish, he was not East European, his parents were unmusical and he is not a good sightreader. One of his earliest musical memories is of playing records of Jan Kiepura in operetta on a wind-up gramophone, to entertain the guests at the hotel his father managed. Later in Zagreb, where Alfred spent his years growing up between the ages of five and thirteen, his father was the manager of a cinema, which took him in other directions than music, towards painting among other things. His first recital came in Graz in 1948, and received glowing notices, when he concentrated on works with fugues, including a sonata of his own which boasted a double-fugue. Such revelations are amplified by the separate half-hour conversation Brendel has with Sir Simon Rattle on the subject of the Beethoven piano concertos, offering fascinating revelations from both pianist and conductor. Brendel's own poems in German then strike a rather grim note of humour, while on the second disc comes a recital recorded at the Snape Maltings, crowning this revealing issue with masterly performances of three of Brendel's favourite works.

Le Concours d'une Reine (A Queen's Competition) 1951–2001. (Documentary by Michel Stockhem and Benoît Vietinck.)

(B) *** Cypres DVD CYP1101 (12).

This absorbing and fascinating documentary brings some invaluable footage of Le Concours Reine Elizabeth, one of the major international competitions. There are glimpses of the 1937 performance in which David Oistrakh triumphed, and the commentary throughout is of unfailing interest. Marcel Poot, Arthur Grumiaux and other distinguished musicians have much to say about music competitions that is perceptive and humane. And we see something of the Belgian Queen herself, who studied with Ysaÿe, taking a keen interest in the young artists. In addition to the violin, there is of course a piano competition and, recently added, a vocal one. Some tantalizing glimpses of the final concerts engage the viewer almost as much as if they were going on now.

There is, incidentally, an accompanying twelve-CD set (Cypres CYP 9612): its material is too diverse and wide-ranging even to list! It includes Leonid Kogan playing the cadenza of the Paganini *Concerto No. 1 in D major* in 1951 (otherwise all the repertoire is complete) and some rarer material from the same decade: Jaime Laredo plays the Milhaud *Concert royal, Op. 373*, not otherwise available on CD, and Julian Sitkovetsky (father of Dmitry) the Ysaÿe *Sixth Sonata.*

When the competition broadened in 1952 to include the piano, Leon Fleischer was the winner with an impressive Brahms *D minor Concerto* (with Franz André conducting the Belgian Orchestre National). The Belgian composer Marcel Poot, for long the chairman of the competition, is represented by a *Piano Concerto*, heard in the late Malcolm Frager's 1960 performance, again with Franz André.

There are many mouth-watering opportunities to hear and see artists now famous at the early stages of their careers: Ashkenazy, the nineteen-year-old first-prize winner in 1956 in the Liszt *E flat Concerto*, the twenty-year-old Gidon Kremer (ranked third in 1967) playing Schumann, Mitsuko

Uchida, also twenty years of age, playing the Beethoven *C minor Concerto* – she was ranked tenth in 1968!

Some will feel that the twelve-CD set is too much of a good thing and too substantial an outlay, even at its competitive price. But the DVD is extraordinarily fascinating and involving – and often quite moving. Strongly recommended. The languages used are Dutch and French with subtitles in English, German and Spanish.

FONTEYN, MARGOT

Margot Fonteyn – A Portrait. Documentary produced and directed by Particia Foy (with Frederick Ashton, Ida Bromley, Robert Gottlieb, Nicola Kathak, Andrey King, Robert Helpmann, Rudolf Nureyev, Ninette de Valois).

(N) *** Arthaus DVD 100 92.

Margot Fonteyne dominated the ballet scene in Britain for more than forty years, which she was to cap in 1961 by creating her legendary partnership with Rudolph Nureyev. Here in 1989, only two years before her death, she tells her life story and is willing to talk about the tragic death of her huband. But she also tells us about the background to her long career, and there are contributions from most of those who played an important part in it. With plenty of clips, including legendary archive material, for anyone interested in ballet this will be an essential purchase.

RICHTER, SVIATOSLAV (piano)

Sviatoslav Richter (1913–97) – The Enigma. Documentary by Bruno Monsaingeon.

*** DVD Warner NVC Arts 3984 23029-2.

An altogether remarkable and revealing film in which Bruno Monsaingeon draws on rare archive material as well as the testimony of the great pianist himself. The result will be a revelation even to those well informed about this unique artist: Richter speaks of his early years and of his parents, the privations of the years leading up to the war and the war years themselves. His father, a pupil of Franz Schreker, disappeared during that period, and his relationship with his mother was obviously not untroubled after her remarriage.

Richter's own development was quite unique. He was self-taught and worked as a coach at the opera in Odessa, turning up in Moscow in 1937 (partly to avoid induction into the military), where he became a student of Heinrich Neuheus, who took him under his wing. In 1941 Prokofiev, about whom, incidentally, Richter is distinctly unflattering, asked him to play his *Fifth Piano Concerto*, which was an immediate success and launched him on his career. There is an astonishing clip of a 1958 Warsaw performance of it.

During the course of two-and-a-half hours, there are innumerable excerpts from his vast repertoire, ranging over Rachmaninov, Liszt and Debussy to Shostakovich, all of which are carefully indexed by chapter and time code and most of which are pretty breathtaking. There is archive material garnered from broadcast and private sources, which will be new to music-lovers.

There are some haunting images of wartime Russia and glimpses of him playing with others, including Rostropovich and Benjamin Britten. We also see his appearance at Stalin's funeral and his first tours abroad. Although he loved three things about America – its museums, its great orchestras and its cocktails – he disliked most other things and declined to revisit it after his fourth tour.

The portrait that emerges is indeed enigmatic and the frail expression as he says, 'I don't like myself', are painful and haunting. Moving, concentrated and frankly indispensable. A documentary which can be called great without fear of contradiction. This scores over its video not only in the sharper focus of the images but in the greater ease of access.

COLLECTIONS
Orchestral concerts

BERLIN PHILHARMONIC ORCHESTRA; CLAUDIO ABBADO

'New Year's Gala 1997'. BIZET: *Carmen:* excerpts (with Anne-Sofie von Otter, Roberto Alagna, Bryn Terfel); BRAHMS: *Hungarian Dance No. 5 in G min.;* FALLA: *El amor brujo: Ritual Fire Dance;* RACHMANINOV: *Rhapsody on a Theme of Paganini* (with Mikhail Pletnev); RAVEL: *Rhapsodie espagnole;* SARASATE: *Carmen Fantasy, Op. 25* (with Gil Shaham).

(N) *** Arthaus DVD 100 026.

A concert that takes Bizet's *Carmen* as a theme, or point of departure. The sound is very good indeed, very naturally balanced, and the camerawork discreet and unobtrusive. The excerpts from the opera come off very well but easily the best thing on the disc is the *Paganini Rhapsody*, played effortlessly by Mikhail Pletnev. Rachmaninov-playing does not come better than this. It is every bit as strongly characterized and brilliant in execution as his CD recording and indeed must be numbered among the very finest on disc. The individual variations do not have access points. Gil Shaham's performance of the Sarasate *Fantasy* is also played with virtuosity and panache. A rather strangely designed programme, but well worth having purely for the sake of Pletnev's dazzling Rachmaninov.

BERLIN PHILHARMONIC AND ISRAEL PHILHARMONIC ORCHESTRA; ZUBIN MEHTA

'Joint Concert, Tel Aviv (1990)': BEN-HAIM: *Symphony No. 1, 2nd Movement: Psalm;* SAINT-SAENS: *Introduction & Rondo capriccio, Op. 28* (with Vivian Hagner, violin); WEBER: *Clarinet Concertino in E flat, Op. 67* (with Sharon Kam, clarinet); RAVEL: *La Valse;* BEETHOVEN: *Symphony No. 5.*

(N) *(*) Arthaus DVD 100 068.

The visit of the Berlin Philharmonic had been keenly awaited in Tel Aviv, and this joint concert in the Mann Auditorium should have been an electrifying occasion. The two soloists are very good, and there is some splendid orchestral playing, with the two orchestras combined in the *Psalm* and the Beethoven, and sounding pretty splendid in the Ravel, in spite of the less than ideal acoustics. However, the account of the Beethoven *Fifth* simply fails to spark into life until the finale and even then it is hardly earth-shaking. Certainly the

DVD gives one a sense of being there, but the concert remains a disappointment.

BERLIN STATE OPERA ORCHESTRA; DANIEL BARENBOIM

'*Berliner Luft*' (Gala Concert from the State Opera, Unter den Linden): NICOLAI: *Overture: The Merry Wives of Windsor*; MOZART: *Don Giovanni: La ci darem di mano* (with René Pape, Dorothea Röschmann); SAINT-SAENS: *Introduction & Rondo capriccioso, Op. 28* (with Raphael Christ, violin); TCHAIKOVSKY: *Swan Lake: Dance of the Little Swans* (with Ballet); *Waltz*. SHOSTAKOVICH: *Tahiti Trot*; WEILL: *Berlin im Licht* (Heinz Gruber, Barenboim, piano); KOLLO: *Untern Linden* (Vocal Ens.); LINCKE: *Glow-Worm Idyll* (Simone Nold); *Berliner Luft*.
J. STRAUSS JNR: *Unter Donner und Blitz*.

(N) *** Arthaus DVD 100 094.

This is obviously the Berliners' equivalent of The Last Night of the Proms and this DVD has tremendous spirit and atmosphere. Clearly the well-dressed audience have a wonderful evening. Barenboim and the Orchestra, too, are obviously enjoying themselves and there are even magicians doing party tricks to add to the revels. Everyone joins in the closing popular numbers, and although it is not as uninhibited as at the Proms (the audience is much older for one thing) it is still very infectious and enjoyable. The recording obviously came from a broadcast, for it is compressed here and there, but it does not affect the sense of spectacle. One could criticize the cameras for being too volatile in moving around the orchestra, but it suits the occasion, especially in the delightful account of Shosta-

kovich's *Tahiti Trot* (based on Vincent Youmans's *Tea for Two*).

IL GIARDINO ARMONICO

CASTELLO: *Sonata concertante, Op. 2, Nos. 4 & 10*; MARINI: *Sonata, 'Sopra la Monica'*; MERULA: *Ciaconna*; SPADI: *Dominuziono*; SOPRA: *Anchor che co'l partire*; VIVALDI: *Lute Concertos in D, RV 93; in D, (Il giardellino), Op. 10/3. Recorder Concerto in G min., (La notte), RV 104.*

(N) * Arthaus DVD 100 010.

Il Giardino Armonico is a brilliant group who perform this repertoire with stunning virtuosity and imagination. Musically there are no quarrels here except, perhaps, for the over-bright sound. Moreover, the DVD facilities offer the scores, though when they are superimposed the visual image is masked – indeed, virtually disappears. The text in the Vivaldi is, of course, the Ricordi short score. Although the performances are expert enough, though very brightly recorded, the visual direction is irritatingly hyperactive. The musicians are superimposed on all sorts of Sicilian backdrops though never for more than a few seconds at a time. The empty 'cleverness' of the director, who cannot leave anything to speak for itself, is very tiresome to start with and insufferable after a few minutes. Two stars for the brilliant if exhibitionist music-making, but none for the distracting visual antics.